GUIDE TO
VENTURE CAPITAL & PRIVATE EQUITY FIRMS

DOMESTIC & INTERNATIONAL
WITH SEPARATE CANADIAN SECTION

GUIDE TO

VENTURE CAPITAL & PRIVATE EQUITY FIRMS

DOMESTIC & INTERNATIONAL
WITH SEPARATE CANADIAN SECTION

2023

GUIDE TO

VENTURE CAPITAL & PRIVATE EQUITY FIRMS

DOMESTIC & INTERNATIONAL
WITH SEPARATE CANADIAN SECTION

GREY HOUSE PUBLISHING

PUBLISHER: Leslie Mackenzie
EDITORIAL DIRECTOR: Stuart Paterson
MARKETING DIRECTOR: Jessica Moody
EDITORIAL ASSISTANT: Olivia Parsonson

Grey House Publishing, Inc.
4919 Route 22
Amenia, NY 12501
518.789.8700 • Fax 845.373.6390
www.greyhouse.com
books@greyhouse.com

While every effort has been made to ensure the reliability of the information presented in this publication, Grey House Publishing neither guarantees the accuracy of the data contained herein nor assumes any responsibility for errors, omissions or discrepancies. Grey House accepts no payment for listing; inclusions in the publication of any organization, agency, institution, publication, service or individual does not imply endorsement of the editors or publisher.

Errors brought to the attention of the publisher and verified to the satisfaction of the publisher will be corrected in future editions.

Except by express prior written permission of the Copyright Proprietor, no part of this work may be copied by any means of publication or communication now known or developed hereafter, including but not limited to use in any directory or compilation or other print publication, in any information storage and retrieval system, in any other electronic device, or in any visual or audio-visual device or product.

This publication is an original and creative work, copyrighted by Grey House Publishing, Inc. and is fully protected by all applicable copyright laws, as well as by laws covering misappropriation, trade secrets and unfair competition.

Grey House has added value to the underlying factual material through one or more of the following efforts: unique and original selection; expression; arrangement; coordination; and classification.

Grey House Publishing, Inc. will defend its rights in this publication.
Copyright © 2023 Grey House Publishing, Inc.

All rights reserved
First edition published 1996
Twenty-seventh edition published 2023
Printed in Canada

Publisher's Cataloging-In-Publication Data
(Prepared by The Donohue Group, Inc.)

Names: Grey House Publishing, Inc., publisher.
Title: Guide to venture capital & private equity firms : domestic & international with separate Canadian section.
Other Titles: Guide to venture capital and private equity firms
Description: Amenia, NY : Grey House Publishing, 2023- | Includes indexes.
Subjects: LCSH: Venture capital—Directories. | Venture capital—United States—Directories. | Private equity—Directories. | Private equity—United States—Directories.
Classification: LCC HG4751 .G85 | DDC 332/.04154—dc23

ISBN: 978-1-63700-522-4

Table of Contents

Introduction vii
User Guide & Key ix
KPMG Private Enterprise—Venture Pulse, Q3 2022,
    Global Analysis of Venture Funding xi
Moonfare—The Case for Venture Capital in 2022 and Beyond xxvii

DESCRIPTIVE LISTINGS

Domestic Firms 1
Canadian Firms 687
International Firms 757
National & State Associations 979

INDEXES

College & University Index 989
Executive Name Index 1051
Geographic Index 1077
Industry Preference Index 1109
Portfolio Companies Index 1217

Introduction

This twenty-seventh edition of the *Guide to Venture Capital & Private Equity Firms, Domestic & International* is a comprehensive database of more than 3,200 of the most active venture capital and private equity firms operating today, domestically and internationally. All company profiles include current contact information and specific industry data for a detailed picture of the firm and its investment parameters. Profiles include headquarters, other locations and branches, industry group preferences, average investment, portfolio companies, investment criteria and detailed lists of key executives.

As with previous editions, this 2023 edition includes a User Guide, followed by two industry reports that offer insight into the current state of this dynamic industry segment: *KPMG Enterprises—Venture Pulse Q3 2022, Global Analysis of Venture Funding;* and *Moonfare—The Case for Venture Capital in 2022 and Beyond.* Highlights include:

- VC investment in the U.S. declined in 2022, after its previous highs, due to a cloud of uncertainty on the world stage

- Resilient sectors include energy, business productivity, cybersecurity, and healthcare

- Interest in food and grocery delivery, consumer retail, and eCommerce falls

- M&A activity in the U.S. is expected to increase over the next quarter or two

The firm profiles in this edition present a most current, comprehensive picture of this dynamic industry. Hundreds of domestic and international firms have been updated, with a particular focus on firms based in Canada. More than 2,000 pieces of data have been updated, with a focus on key executives and company branches. In addition to the significant update effort put forth for this edition, we have added 10 brand new venture capital firms, and 56 new data points throughout the body of the work.

All domestic, Canadian and international profiles include, in addition to contact information, a mission statement, industry group preferences, portfolio companies, geographic preferences, average and minimum investments, and investment criteria. Each firm's partners are listed with extensive background information, such as education (degree and school), professional background (previous positions and companies) and directorships held. The specificity of both the firm and its partners add to the value of each firm's profile. Information for firms headquartered overseas include name, phone, fax, email and website.

Guide to Venture Capital & Private Equity Firms is organized into four major sections, Domestic Firms, Canadian Firms, Domestic Associations, and International Firms, each arranged alphabetically by company name. These sections are followed by five valuable indexes:

- **College/University Index** offers an alphabetical list of more than 1,000 educational institutions worldwide—and the venture capital executives who attended them. Each listing includes the reference number of the affiliated VC firm of the executive listed.

- **Executive Index** is an alphabetical list by last name of more than 10,000 key partners and the listing number of their affiliated firm.

- **Geographic Index** organizes all firms by state for domestic listings and by country for international listings.

- **Industry Preference Index** alphabetically lists more than 900 industry segments and the names of the firms that invest in them.

- **Portfolio Companies Index** alphabetically lists the more than 49,500 companies that received venture capital from a listed firm, and is referenced to that listing.

For even easier access to information, *Guide to Venture Capital & Private Equity Firms* is available in our online database platform, http://gold.greyhouse.com. Subscribers will have immediate access to all domestic and international venture capital and private equity firms to:

- Find firms that are specifically interested in their industry group. From agrifood to web infrastructure, this online database can be sorted into over 900 industry group categories.

- Search for firms that match the investment level they need. From $250,000 to $50 million, you'll be able to generate a list to match your requirements, within specific geographic areas.

- Find which venture capital firms have funded specific companies. Simply key in a company to generate a list of firms who funded them.

This online database platform offers a number of ways to search and sort data—Firm Name, Geographic Location, Geographic Preferences, Portfolio Companies, Industry Group Preferences, Average Investment, Fund Size, Investment Criteria, Managing Partners and much more. Visit www.greyhouse.com for a free search of this database and subscription details.

Praise for previous editions:

"...valuable reference...excellent indexes...recommended for business collections in large public, academic and business libraries..."
—*CHOICE*

"...excellent resource for public libraries supporting a business sector..."
—*ARBA*

"...extremely user-friendly..."
—*Library Journal*

"...only directory to list and index portfolio companies...a useful volume..."
—*Journal of Business & Finance Librarianship*

The 2023 edition of *Guide to Venture Capital & Private Equity Firms* is our strongest to date, and offers a valuable resource for those needing to research the investment community. Users are encouraged to bring new, unlisted, or changed firms to our attention.

User Guide

Descriptive listings in the *Guide to Venture Capital & Private Equity Firms* are organized into Domestic and International sections, with each arranged alphabetically by company name. The listings are supplemented by five indexes: College & University Index, Executive Index, Geographic Index, Industry Preference Index, and Portfolio Company Index. The record number, shown top left, rather than the page number, is how the listings are referenced.

Shown below is a fictitious listing illustrating the kind of information that is or might be included in an entry. Each numbered item is described on the following page.

    1234   1-   **GALIVANT VENTURE CAPITAL**
                  2-   14 State Boulevard
                        Suite 185
                        Millerton, NY 12546

        3-   060-555-4131

        4-   060-555-4132

              800-945-7411

        5-   info@gvaztx.com

        6-   www.gvaztx.com

7-   **Mission Statement:** To identify, support and counsel companies with strong management and proven growth in the communications industry.

8-   **Geographic Preference:** Eastern United States

9-   **Fund Size:** $20 million

10-   **Founded:** 1982

11-   **Average Investment:** $1.5 million

12-   **Minimum Investment:** $500,000

13-   **Investment Criteria:** Seed, Startup, First-Stage, Second-Stage, Mezzanine, LBO, MBO

14-   **Industry Group Preference:** Communications, Data Communications, Telecommunications, Internet Services, Television, Radio

15-   **Portfolio Companies:** HamStark Inc., Placid Internet, DuBois Inc., Berkshire Radio Co., Shir-Fire.com, Trail Communications, Holyoke Internet Services

16-   **Other Locations:**
       96 Club Road
       Suite 1982
       Milwaukee, WI 53212

17-   **Key Executives:**
       Gabriele O'Laughlin PhD, Managing Director
       019-931-6966
       Fax: 019-931-4967
       e-mail: glord@gvaztx.com
       Education: BA, Mount Holyoke College; MBA, PHD, Finance, Texas A&M University
       Background: CFO, Whitehouse Inc., IntelliCon Technologies
       Directorship: OverDrive Tech, BrynSore Group

User Key

1- **Company Name:** Formal name of the company.

2- **Address:** Location or permanent mailing address of the company.

3- **Phone Number:** The listed phone number is usually for the main office, but may also be for sales, marketing, or public relations as provided by the company.

4- **Fax Number:** This is listed when provided by the company.

5- **E-Mail:** This is listed when provided, and is usually the main office e-mail.

6- **Web Site:** Listed when provided by the company, and is also referred to as a URL address.

7- **Mission Statement:** This information is either provided directly by the company, or abridged from data on the company web site or in company literature.

8- **Geographic Preference:** This lists the geographic location the firm prefers to invest in.

9- **Fund Size:** This is the total amount of money a firm has to invest. International firms often calculate dollar amounts in their own currency.

10- **Founded:** The year in which the firm was established or founded. If the organization has changed its name, the founding date is usually for the earliest name under which it is known.

11- **Average Investment:** The average amount the firm generally invests in a company.

12- **Minimum Investment:** The smallest possible amount the firm would consider investing.

13- **Investment Criteria:** This indicates at what stage the firm is willing to invest in, i.e., Seed, Startup, First-Stage, Second-Stage, Mezzanine, LBO, MBO, etc.

14- **Industry Group Preference:** This indicates what industry the firm is most likely to invest in. Note that most of this information does not follow standard industry language; the Industry Group Preference Index is designed to help the reader summarize information, and should be reviewed carefully.

15- **Portfolio Companies:** This is a listing of the companies that the firm has invested in to date.

16- **Other Locations:** Divisions or subsidiaries of the main company. Also included may be the key executives of that location.

17- **Key Executives:** Names, titles, phone numbers, fax numbers and personal e-mail addresses of key executives—including Presidents, Partners, and Managing Directors. This section can also include educational data, including degree and school, and professional data, including previous positions and companies, backgrounds, as well as a list of directorships held.

Cloud of uncertainty drives VC investment in the US down for the third straight quarter

In Q3'22, VC investment in the US fell to $43 billion—the lowest amount since Q2'20—amidst ongoing concerns related to high inflation, rising interest rates, and a US recession—in addition to uncertainty related to the midterm elections scheduled for Q4'22. Despite the challenges permeating the US market, a number of companies raised large funding rounds during the quarter, including space exploration company SpaceX ($1.9 billion), electric vehicle infrastructure company TerraWatt Infrastructure ($1 billion), and nuclear innovation company TerraPower ($750 million).

Leverage shifting from startups to investors

Over the last few months, there has been a dramatic shift in the relationship between startups and investors given the challenging market conditions and the significant downward pressure on valuations. While there continues to be a robust amount of dry powder in the market, VC investors in the US have become a lot more cautious and selective in their deal-making activity, scrutinizing deal terms more rigorously than in recent years and asking for preferential treatment (e.g., liquidation preferences, preferred shares, allocation of board seats) from startups in exchange for funds.

AI and machine learning sectors reaching an inflection point

In recent years, a broad swath of companies focused on artificial intelligence and machine learning received a significant amount of attention from investors in the US. The space has now come to an inflection point, maturing enough that startups are now figuring out niche ways to use AI and machine learning to drive innovation in different industries, such as healthcare and financial services. Even in the current market, startups able to create real, sustainable value using AI and machine learning will likely be attractive to VC investors.

US exits practically dead in Q3'22 as companies try to wait out uncertainty

Exit activity in the US was incredibly soft in Q3'22, with just $14 billion in exit value — a level not seen since Q4'16 — as IPO activity continued to be non-existent in the wake of the volatility in the public markets and ongoing concerns related to valuations. M&A activity was also quite slow during Q3'22. While the depressed valuations environment has led to increasing interest from PE firms and corporates looking to make deals, startups that may have been ready for an exit earlier in the year are likely trying to wait out the uncertainty with the hope that valuations will bounce back.

As companies begin to run out of cash and potentially fail to attract new funding from investors, the US could see an uptick in M&A activity. Any deals will likely take longer to complete than in recent quarters, however, as buyers conduct significantly more due diligence on company financials and projections.

Growing number of SPACs calling it quits

Interest in SPACs has faded over the last twelve months, resulting in questions about whether the robust number of US-based SPACs initialized during 2020 and early 2021 would be able to find targets before their two-year deadlines. While a number of these SPACs are working to extend their identified deadlines, an increasing number are making the decision to refund their investors. During Q3'22, US-based VC firm Social Capital announced it would be winding up two of its SPACs — together worth $1.6 billion — because of the inability to find appropriate targets.[2]

Venture debt deals on the rise

During Q3'22, there was growing interest in venture debt in the US as a means to obtain capital without raising new funding rounds. The increase in interest came both from startups looking to avoid down rounds and from investors uninterested in providing new tranches of money to their portfolio companies but also wanting to avoid dilution of their cap tables. Some VC investors have also begun asking companies to obtain venture debt hand-in-hand with new funding rounds in order to provide some buffer from market uncertainties. During Q3'22, venture debt firms in the US were primarily interested in providing debt to companies already backed by top tier investors, recognizing them as relatively safer bets than others.

[2] https://www.nytimes.com/2022/09/20/business/chamath-palihapitiya-a-spac-king-will-wind-down-two-funds.html

Cloud of uncertainty drives VC investment in the US down for the third straight quarter, cont'd.

Trends to watch for in Q4'22

With the turbulent market conditions expected to continue in Q4'22 and into 2023, VC investors in the US will likely remain very cautious when making deals despite the availability of dry powder. Corporate valuations will likely remain depressed, while the number of companies holding down rounds will likely increase.

From a sector perspective, VC investment is expected to remain relatively resilient in areas like energy, business productivity, cybersecurity, and healthcare, while interest in food and grocery delivery, consumer retail, and eCommerce is expected to fall.

M&A activity in the US is well positioned to increase over the next quarter or two as companies fail to attract new funding and PE investors and corporates look for good deals. Should the IPO window remain firmly closed, some companies that may have been preparing to hold an IPO earlier in 2022 could decide to sell instead.

Q3 sees continued downturn

Venture financing in the US
2014–Q3'22

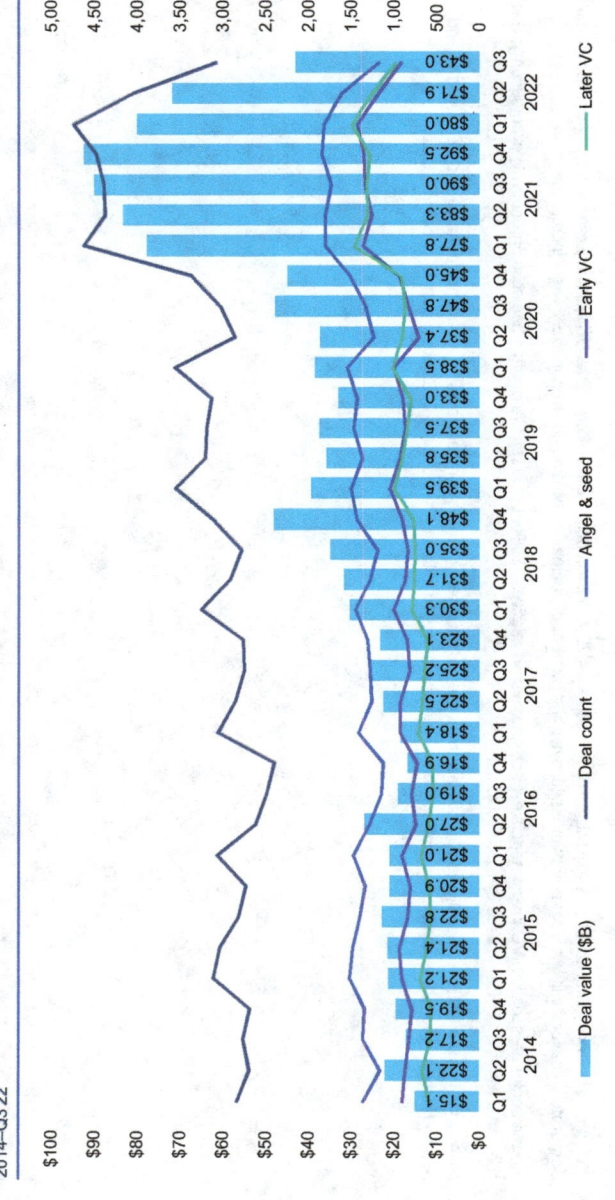

Once again it is important to stress that Q3 figures could tick upward somewhat in coming months as currently undisclosed deals come to light. That said, it is clear that there has been a softening in the pace of dealmaking in the US, with VC invested especially contracting after six straight quarters of massive capital outflows. Valuations and deal sizes are not yet normalizing much to historical averages, suggesting that investors and founders alike are still waiting to get a clearer picture of the currently murky macro environment.

Source: Venture Pulse, Q3'22, Global Analysis of Venture Funding, KPMG Private Enterprise. *As of September 30, 2022. Data provided by PitchBook, October 19, 2022.

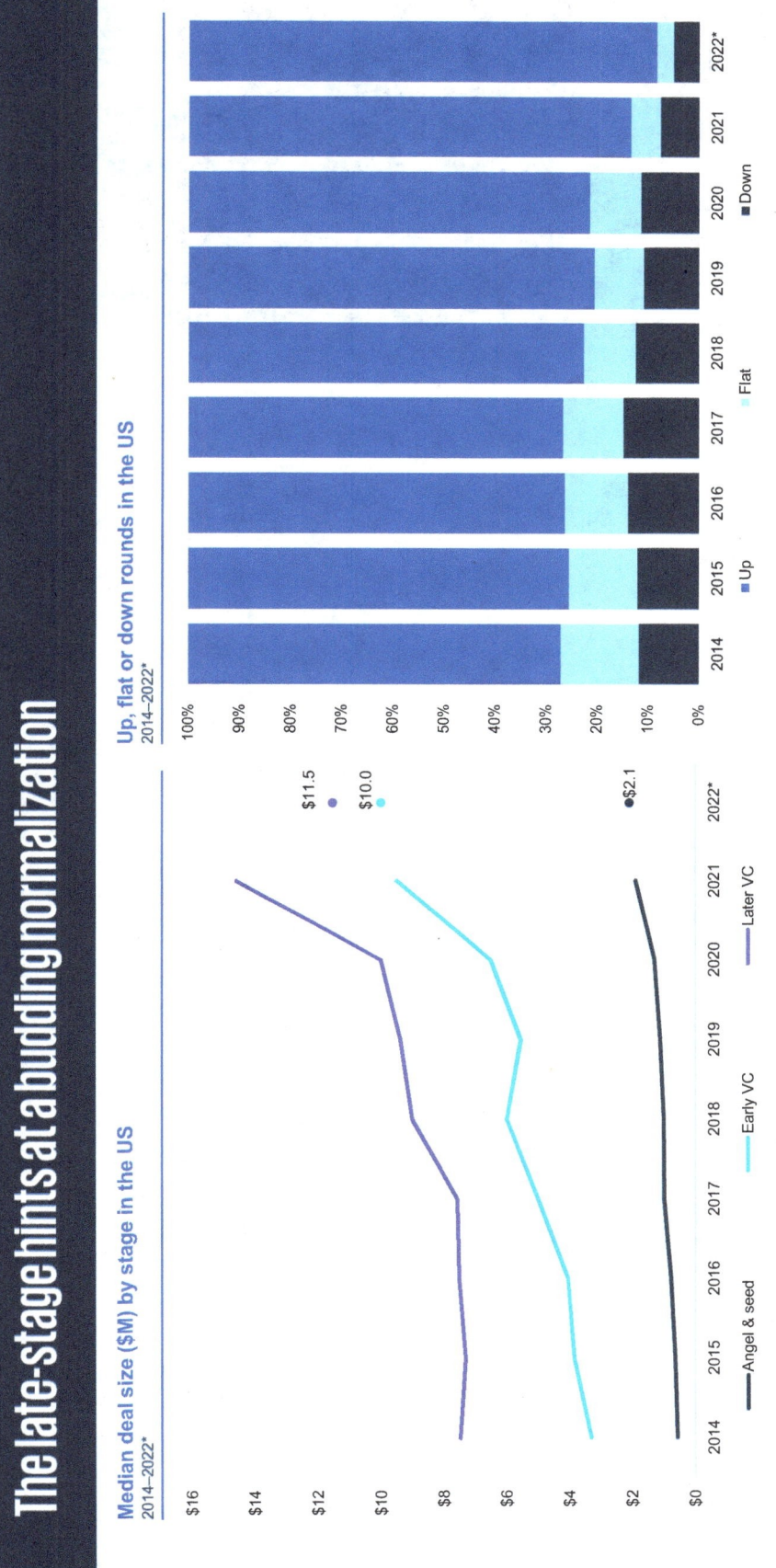

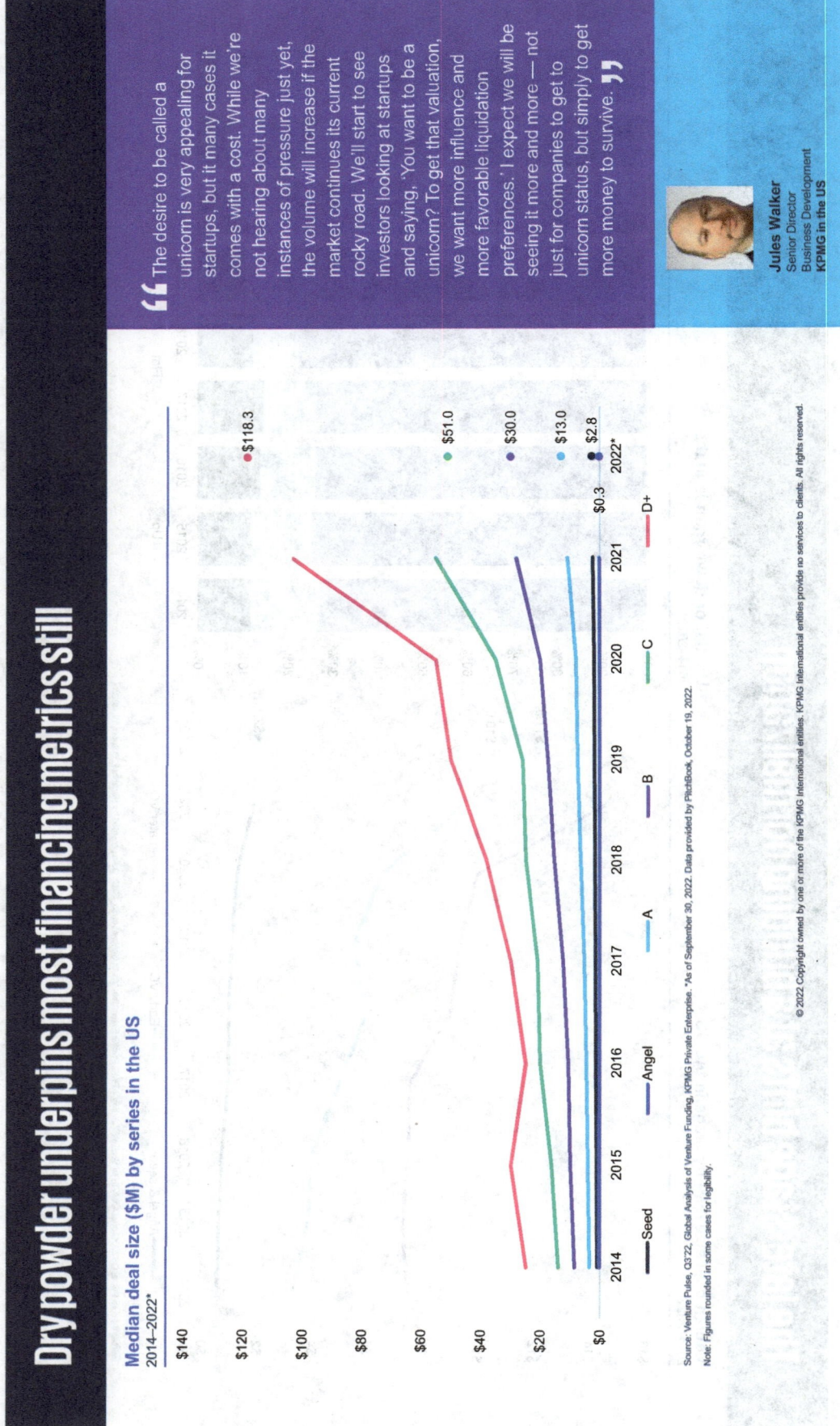

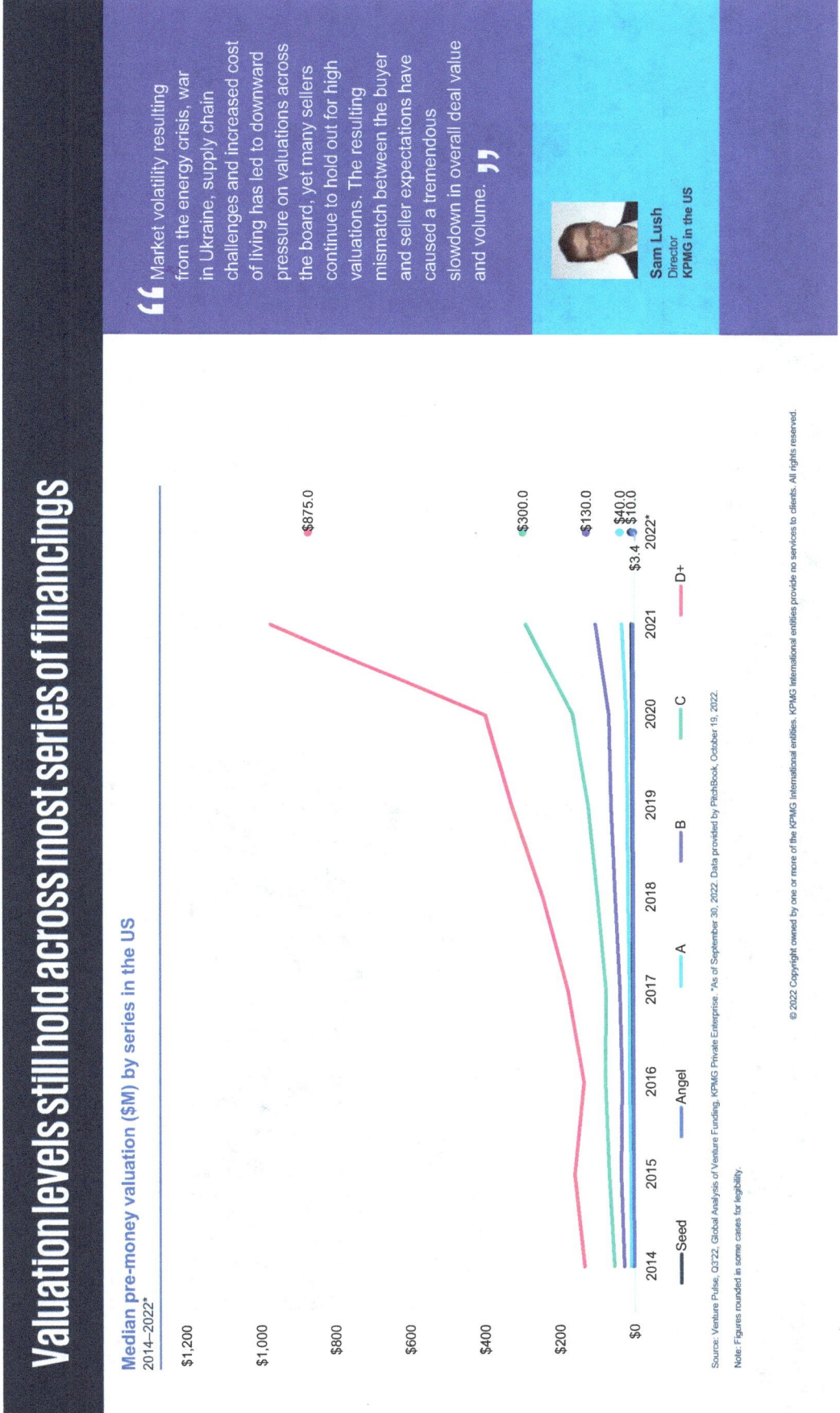

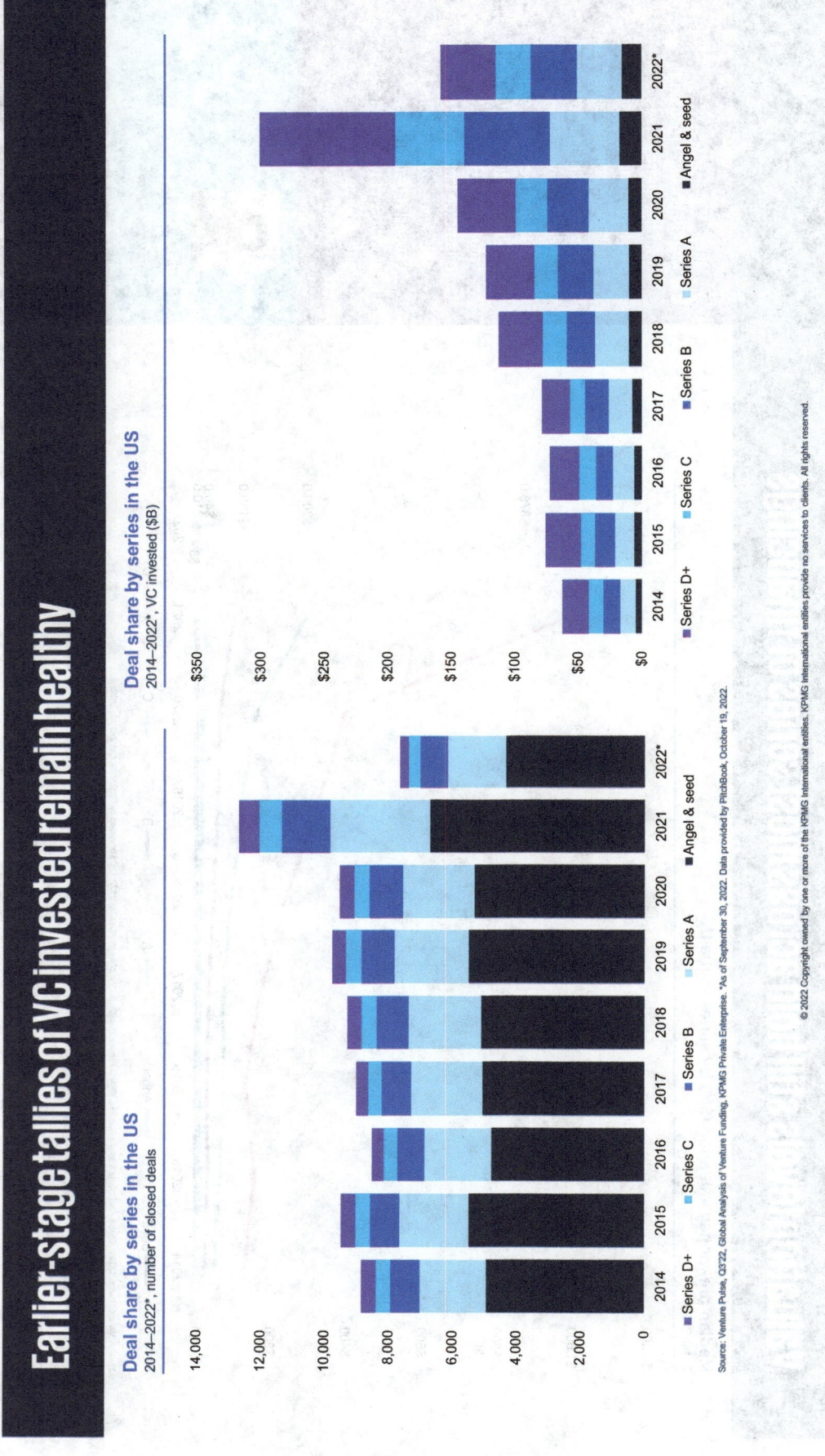

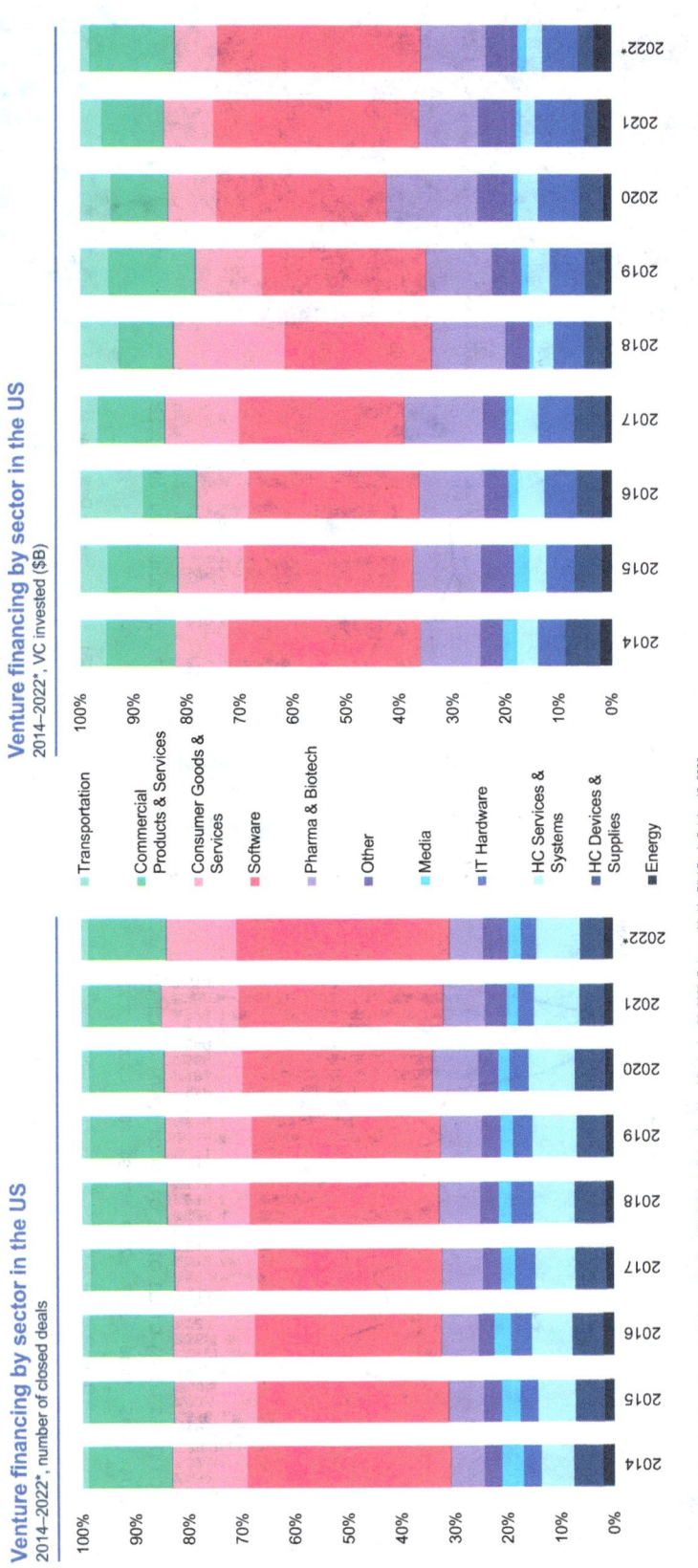

First-time financings still hold strong

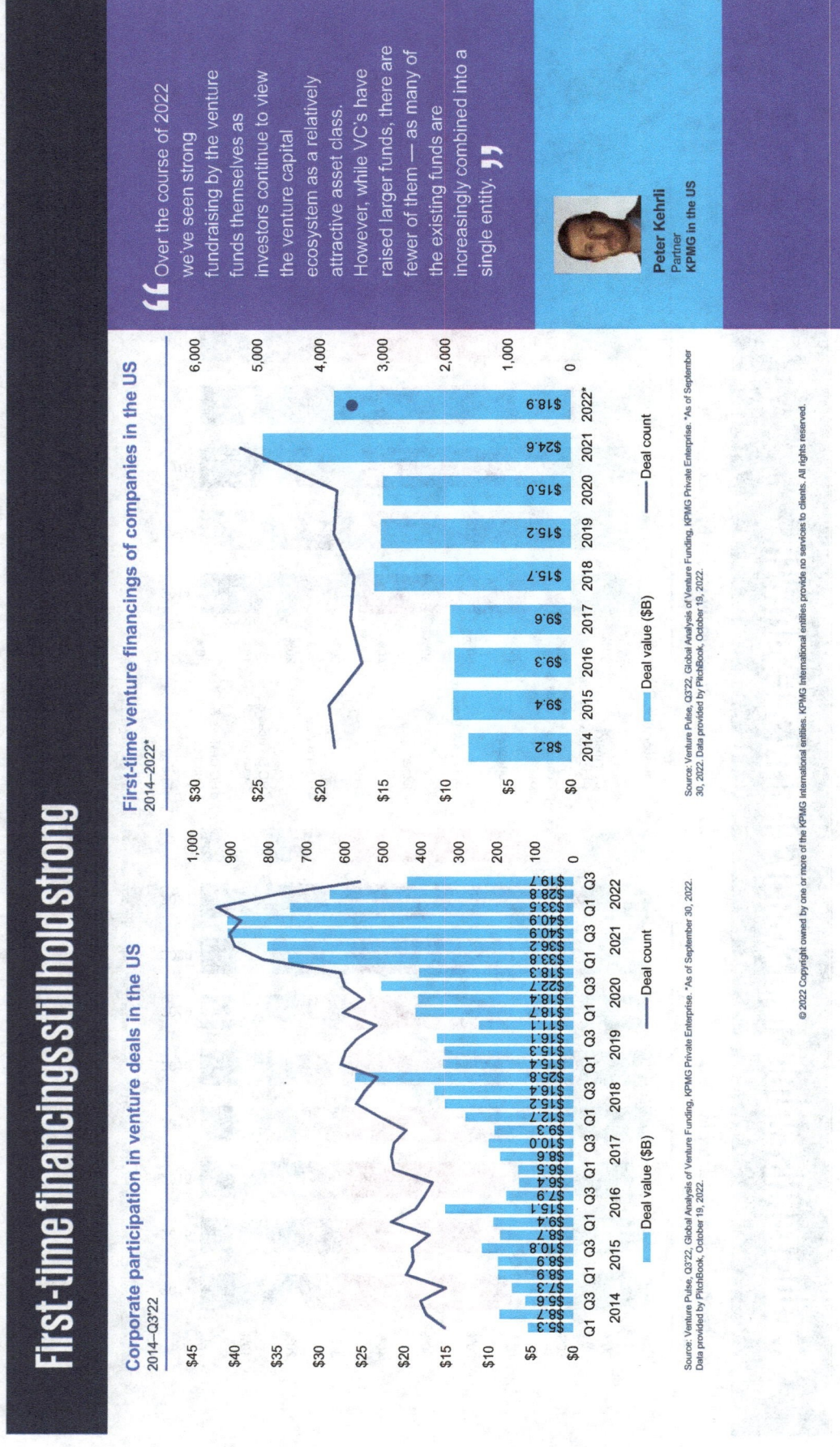

> Over the course of 2022 we've seen strong fundraising by the venture funds themselves as investors continue to view the venture capital ecosystem as a relatively attractive asset class. However, while VC's have raised larger funds, there are fewer of them — as many of the existing funds are increasingly combined into a single entity.

Peter Kehrli
Partner
KPMG in the US

Corporate participation in venture deals in the US
2014–Q3'22

First-time venture financings of companies in the US
2014–2022*

Source: Venture Pulse, Q3'22, Global Analysis of Venture Funding, KPMG Private Enterprise. *As of September 30, 2022. Data provided by PitchBook, October 19, 2022.

Exits continue to skid further downward

Venture-backed exit activity in the US
2014–Q3'22

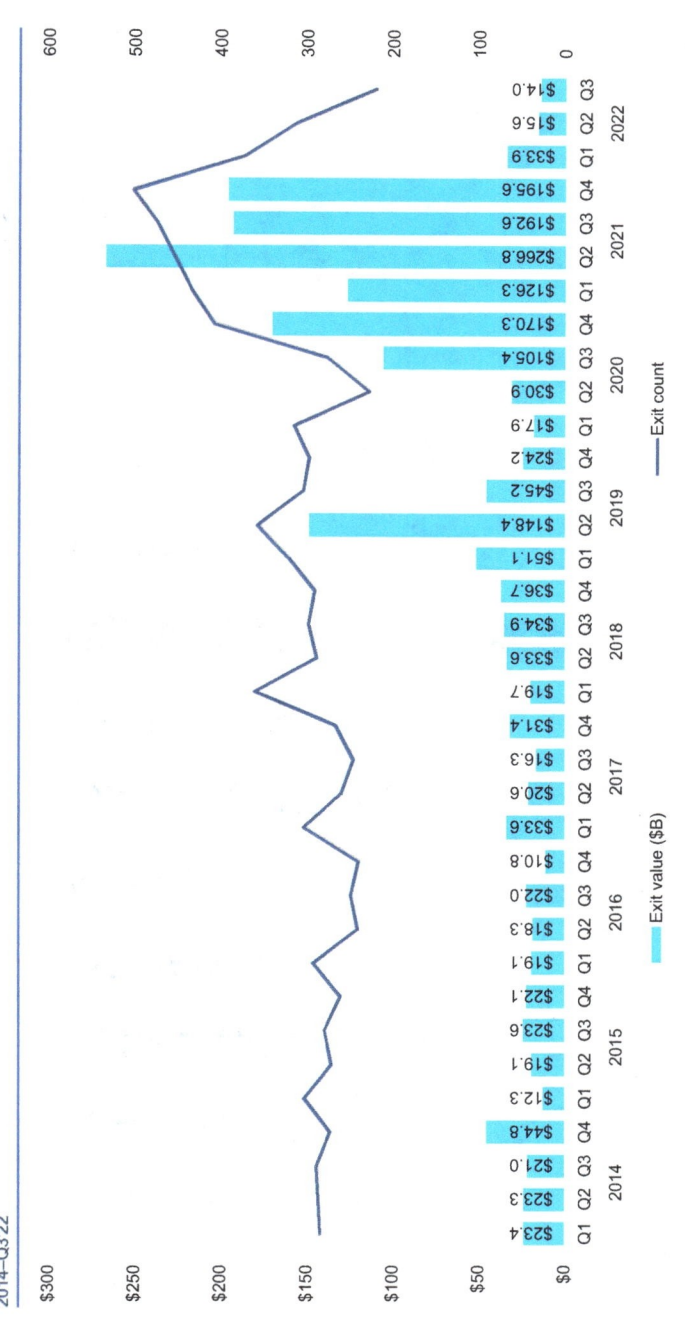

After the lofty heights of exits in 2020 and 2021, a potentially likely regression has now developed further into a skid, with exit volume falling precipitously alongside quarterly aggregate exit values. It is difficult to attribute such a decline to anything other than companies' and investors' response to market volatility and general caution amid a turbulent economic landscape. Players are essentially waiting to assess conditions further and also get clearer data on what the future holds for economic growth and geopolitical headwinds.

Source: Venture Pulse, Q3'22, Global Analysis of Venture Funding, KPMG Private Enterprise. *As of September 30, 2022. Data provided by PitchBook, October 19, 2022.

© 2022 Copyright owned by one or more of the KPMG International entities. KPMG International entities provide no services to clients. All rights reserved.

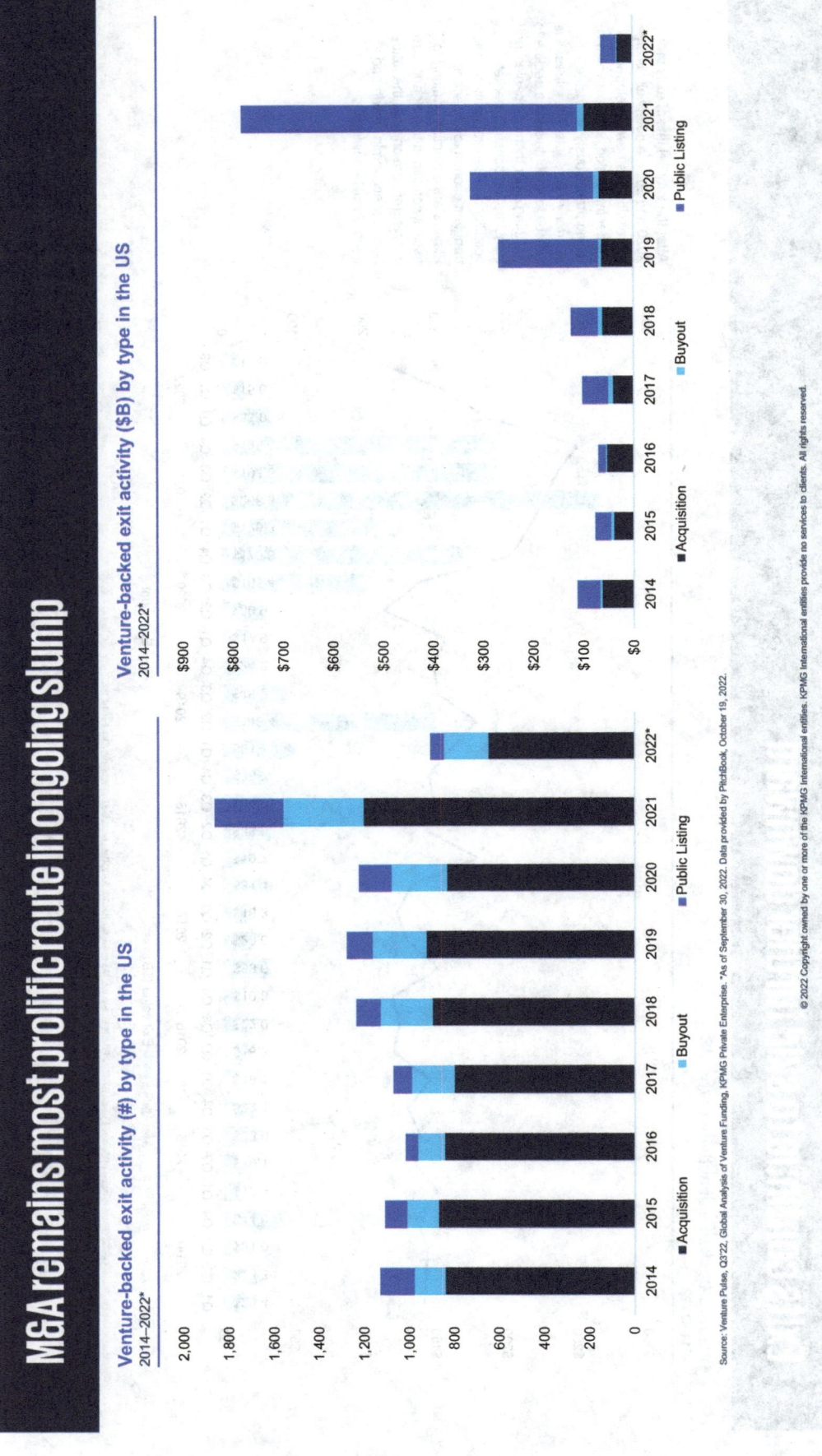

2022 hits new all-time high for capital commitments

US venture fundraising
2014–2022*

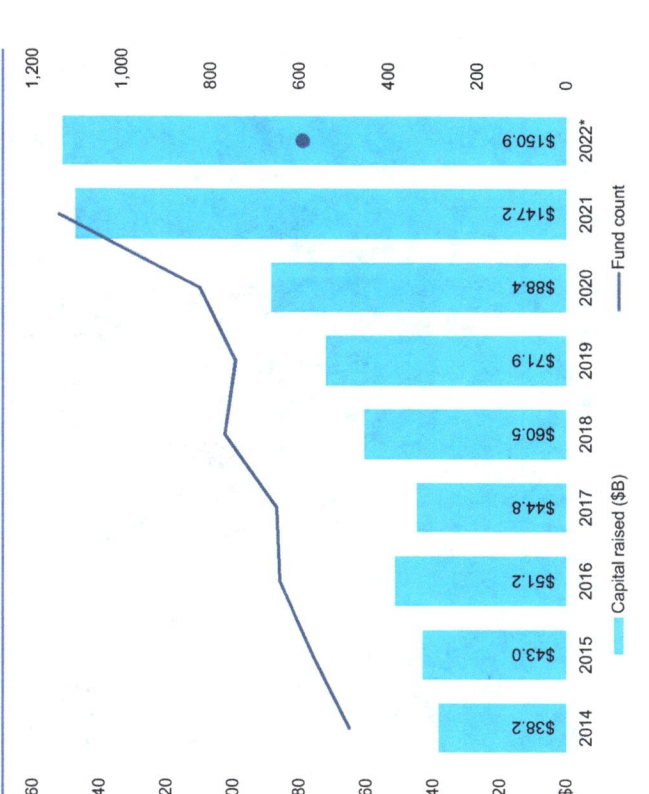

Regardless of budding concerns around the asset class's performance durability, capital allocators continue to pledge commitments to VC fund managers at such a clip that 2022 has already set a single-year record for funds raised. Given the slowdown in the number of funds closed, it is clear that larger, more experienced managers are attracting the bulk of dollars committed.

…even as fundraising volume has slowed somewhat, **2022 has already set a new high for capital committed, surpassing $150 billion.**

Source: Venture Pulse, Q3'22, Global Analysis of Venture Funding, KPMG Private Enterprise. *As of September 30, 2022. Data provided by PitchBook, October 19, 2022.

© 2022 Copyright owned by one or more of the KPMG International entities. KPMG International entities provide no services to clients. All rights reserved.

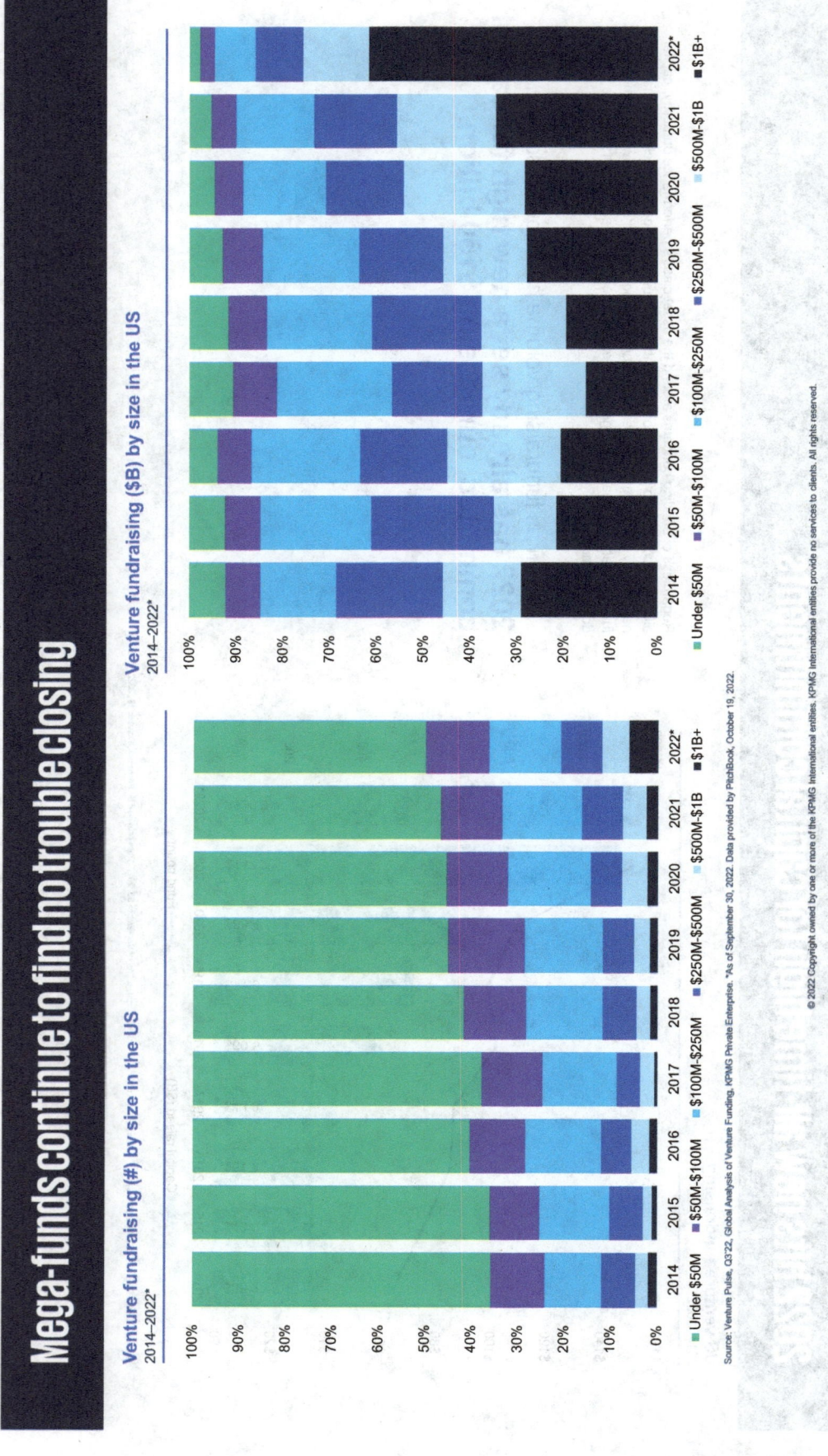

Venture Pulse, Q3 2022, Global Analysis of Venture Funding

Expertise is increasingly prized in the current market

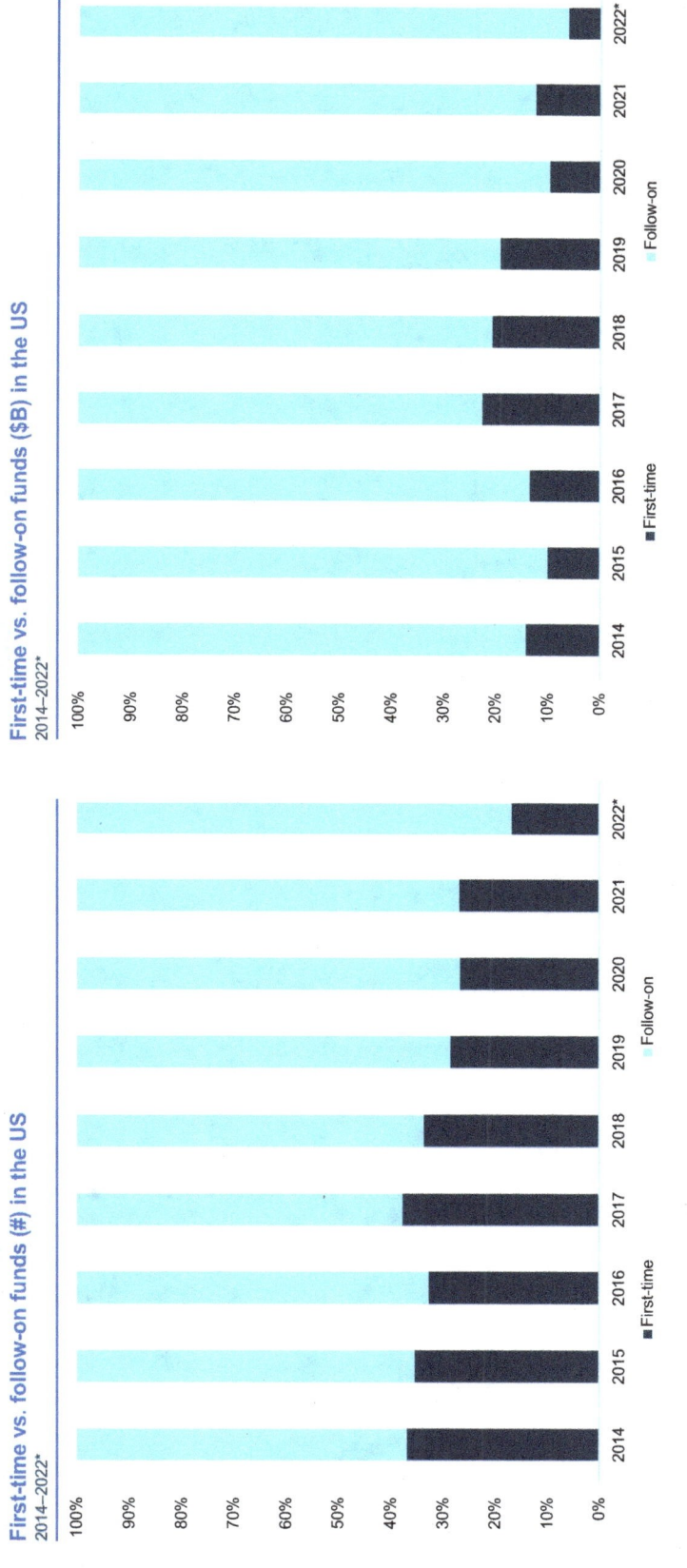

First-time vs. follow-on funds (#) in the US, 2014–2022*

First-time vs. follow-on funds ($B) in the US, 2014–2022*

Source: Venture Pulse, Q3 2022, Global Analysis of Venture Funding, KPMG Private Enterprise. As of 10/22/22. Data provided by PitchBook, 10/19/22.

White paper 2022

The Case for *Venture Capital* in 2022 and Beyond

Moonfare®

1. Venture Capital: *a brief explainer*

> "Venture capital is a game of home runs. It's about banking on high growth from a select few investments."

VC firms often look for rapidly growing, innovative, tech-focused startups, providing them with funding and mentorship in return for a minority equity stake. This is how many of today's most prominent tech companies first received major funding. For example, Airbnb raised $7.8 million in a 2010 series A round from VC investors including Greylock and Sequoia Capital.[5]

One common misconception about VC is that it's the first port of call for startups when it comes to investment. In reality, they have often raised funds from friends and family, or via crowdfunding. Later stage seed funding may even come from angel investors. Only once a startup is established will a VC enter the arena in the hope of an eventual exit via a high-value sale or IPO that provides a large return on its investment. Take Airbnb: at the time of its IPO in 2020, Sequoia Capital's stake on an initial $260 million investment was reportedly worth around $4.8 billion.[6]

Despite highly publicised success stories like Airbnb's, VC-backed companies still have a relatively low success rate. A 2018 study by CB insights tracked more than 1,100 VC-backed US startups that raised seed funding between 2008-2010 and found that fewer than half managed to raise a second round of funding. Just 15% went on to raise a fourth round of investment. Overall, roughly two-thirds of the companies ended up either failing or self-sustaining. And while the latter may prove good for the company, it isn't necessarily an ideal outcome for investors eyeing a big return.[7]

For a VC investment to be considered a genuine success, the fund needs to generate around three times the investment - and it's thought only 5% of venture-backed startups achieve that.[8] This is why VC is such a game of home runs. It's about banking on high growth from a select few investments that generate enough of a return to cover the losses from all the others. This is why a good manager is so important. Unlike angel investing, where investors must do time-intensive due diligence on even earlier-stage startups on their own, top VC managers know the market and how to build a portfolio that generates enough home runs to more than make up for the strike-outs.

---

5. https://assets.airbnb.com/press/press-releases/Airbnb_PressRelease_11112010.pdf
6. https://www.theinformation.com/articles/airbnbs-biggest-ipo-winners
7. https://www.cbinsights.com/research/venture-capital-funnel-2/
8. https://techcrunch.com/2017/06/01/the-meeting-that-showed-me-the-truth-about-vcs/

2. 2021: a *record breaking year* for VC

In almost every way, 2021 was an incredible year for VC. Global venture funding hit a record breaking $621 billion in 2021, per CB Insights, more than double 2020's figure of $294 billion. While the valuations of VC assets under management (AUM) were up three-fold from just five years ago, rising from $547 billion in 2016 to $1.68 trillion in March 2021.[9]

Last year, 517 startups became 'unicorns'; that is, VC-backed companies worth $1 billion or more. This was up 69% from 2020. These new unicorns include sustainable home marketplace GoodLeap (valued at $12 billion), bitcoin and blockchain supporters Digital Currency Group ($10 billion) and crypto-exchange Gemini ($7.1 billion). And for the first time ever, there were over a thousand $100 million-plus global mega-rounds. These included five funding rounds that topped $2 billion such as electric manufacturers Cruise and Rivian and stock trading app Robinhood.[10]

Fig. 01 Global venture funding reached record-breaking heights in 2021

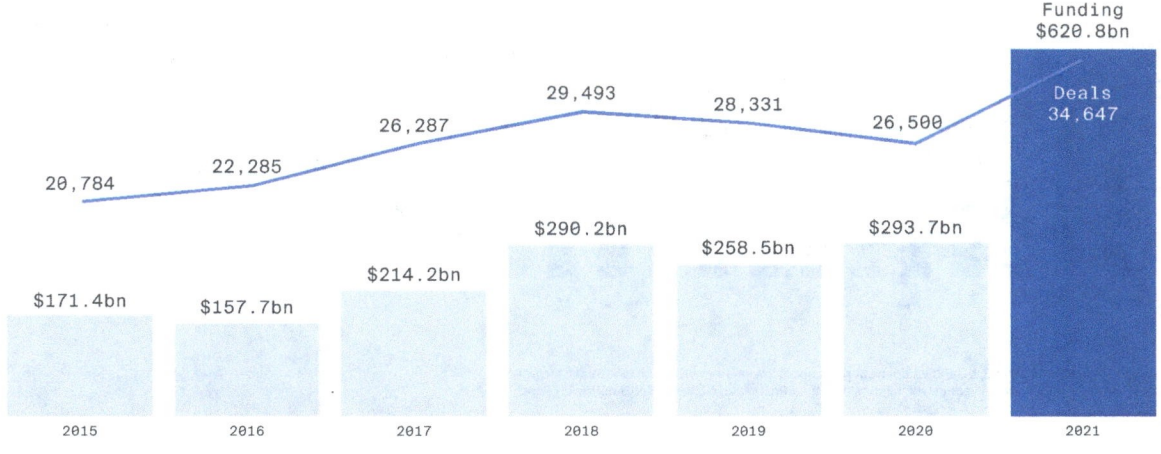

Source: CB Insights 2021

---

9. The State of Venture, Global 2021, CB Insights

Venture Capital 2021: a deeper look

There are a number of reasons why venture markets in general saw record-breaking levels of growth last year. Increased liquidity worldwide, boosted by trillions of central bank stimuli pumped into the economy as an antidote to global lockdowns, benefited private investors immensely. This liquidity has been also bolstered by the arrival of high net worth individuals (HNWIs) into private markets, while a quiet start to 2021 left investors with record levels of dry powder to invest over the second half of the year.[11]

Unmatched fundraising

VC was a huge part of record-breaking fundraising in private markets.[12] Along with growth and infrastructure, it grew faster relative to its five-year average and Q4 of 2021 closed the year with an all-time high of $176 billion in funding – the sixth straight quarter of growth.[13]

Fig. 02 **Private market investors flocked to venture capital funds in 2021**

Global private capital raised, by fund type ($bn)

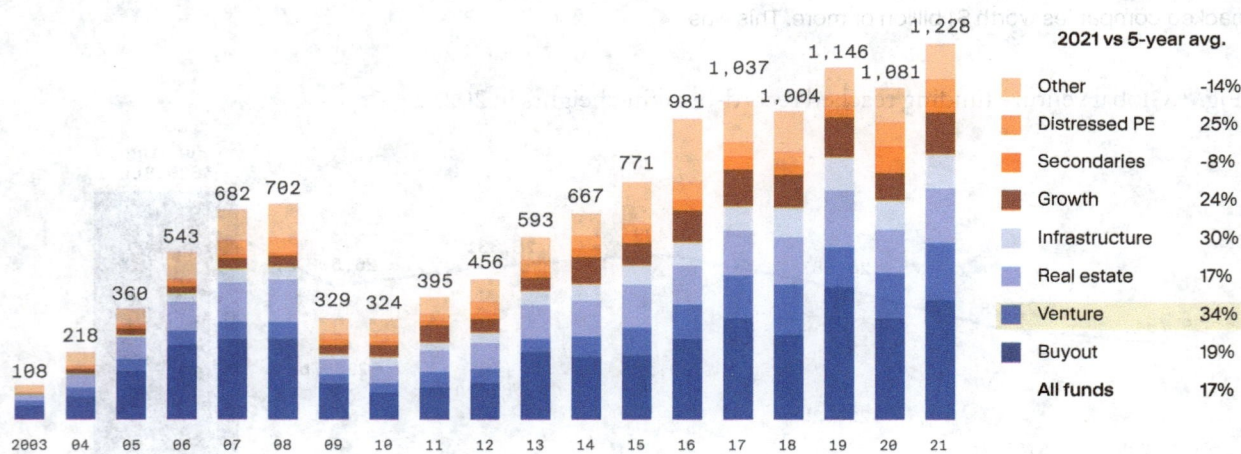

Notes: Buyout category includes buyout, balanced, coinvestment, and coinvestment multimanager funds; includes funds with final close and represents the year in which funds held their final close; excludes SoftBank Vision Fund

Source: Preqin 2022

---

10. https://news.crunchbase.com/startups/biggest-vc-startup-funding-deals-2021-cruise-rivian-robinhood/
11. https://www.pwc.com/us/en/industries/financial-services/library/private-equity-deals-outlook.html
12. https://www.bain.com/insights/private-equity-market-in-2021-global-private-equity-report-2022/
13. The State of Venture, Global 2021, CB Insights

Exits hit new heights

2021 was a strong year for VC exits too. The total value of VC-backed companies' exits reached a new high of $410 billion in the first three quarters of 2021. According to Preqin, 70% of exits were for financial services, healthcare, and information technology (IT) companies, mirroring the three sectors' fundraising success.[14]

IPOs are now the most prominent form of exit. In the first three quarters of 2021 alone, the proportion of start-ups that exited via IPO jumped to 28%, from just 14% in 2016[15]. This included six IPOs with valuations in the tens of billions of dollars, with number one being electric car manufacturer Rivian's November IPO. Valued at $66.5 billion, it launched at $78 a share, raising nearly $12 billion, with the company's VC backers including D1 Capital Partners and several corporate VC arms.[16] On the other hand, the largest trade sale of a VC-backed company in 2021 was for computer software company Nuance Communications, bought by Microsoft for $19.7 billion.[17]

Tech thrives among sectors

Global VC investment into technology startups hit a record level of $675 billion in 2021, double the previous all-time high of $340.6B in 2020.[18]

Although technology was already a focal point for many VC investors, the pandemic accelerated digitalisation even faster which encouraged even more funding to come in. This includes companies such as edtech startup Newsela, which provides online textbooks. The company opened up its services for free during the pandemic, giving it a huge boost. It became a unicorn in 2021 following a $100 million series D.[19]

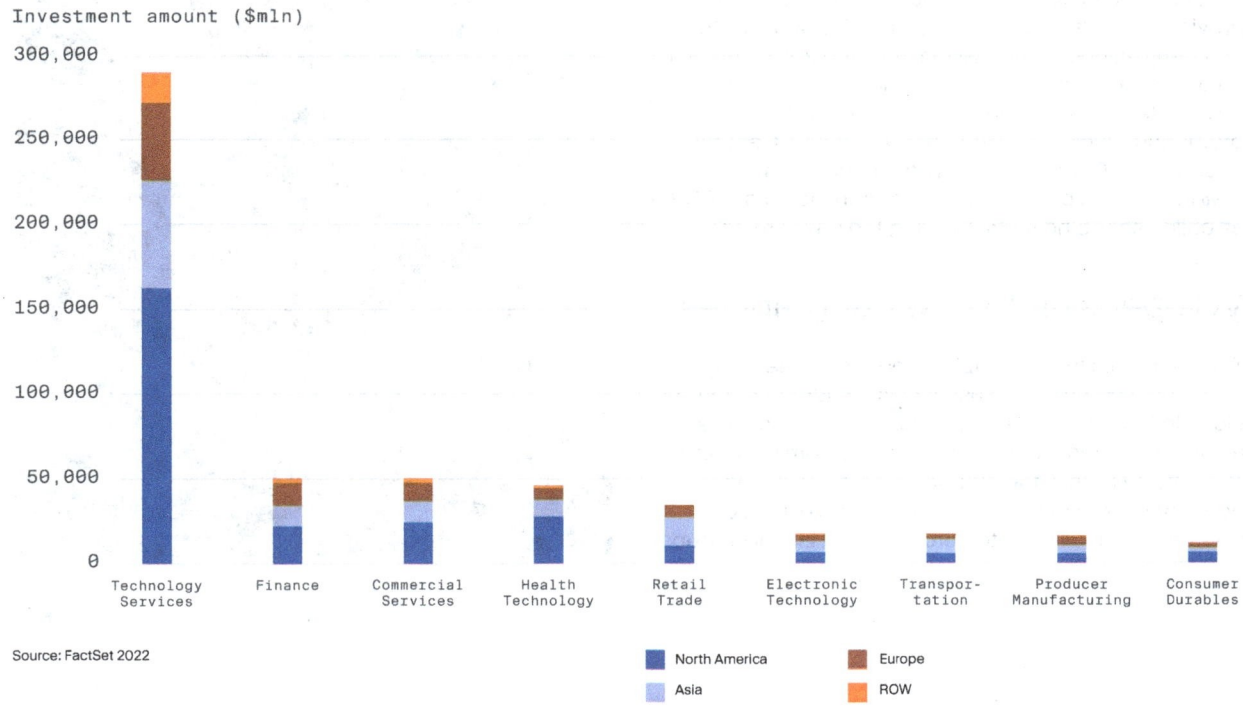

Fig. 03 Technology is a clear focal point for VC investors
Top venture capital sectors globally, in 2021

Source: FactSet 2022

---

14. 2022 Preqin Global Venture Capital Report, Preqin
15. 2022 Preqin Global Venture Capital Report, Preqin
16. https://www.investopedia.com/rivian-ipo-what-happened-and-why-it-matters-5209505
17. https://news.microsoft.com/2021/04/12/microsoft-accelerates-industry-cloud-strategy-for-healthcare-with-the-acquisition-of-nuance/
18. https://www.adgully.com/global-tech-vc-investment-in-startups-hits-record-high-of-675b-in-2021-113161.html
19. https://techcrunch.com/2021/02/25/newsela-the-replacement-for-textbooks-raises-100m-and-becomes-a-unicorn

Pandemic puts focus on healthcare investing

VC investments into healthcare in the US and Europe exceeded $80 billion, beating 2020's record by more than 30%. This follows a trend which has seen investment into healthcare companies double every two years since 2017, from $16 billion to $34 billion to over $80 billion last year.[20]

Biopharma firms were the biggest benefactor and were involved in three of 2021's top ten largest series A raises across all sectors. Neumora Therapeutics ($500 million), Odyssey Therapeutics ($218 million) and Avistone Pharmaceuticals ($200 million) focus on brain diseases, cancer and inflammatory diseases and oncology, respectively.[21]

Fintech funding continues to fly

The pandemic's ability to accelerate digital transformation across industries was certainly seen in financial services. In 2021, fintech firms raised $132 billion in funding, accounting for 21% of all venture dollars. In addition, one in every four unicorns is in fintech — the most by far of any industry.[22]

Notable funding rounds included Dutch payments provider Mollie's $800 million series C which saw the company valued at $6.5 billion. By June 2021, the company was on track to double its number of processed payments from $10 billion in 2020 to over $20 billion, prompting Blackstone Growth, EQT Growth, General Atlantic and TCV to invest.[23] The company also saw a 51% increase in buy now, pay later transactions[24] (BNPL) as online shopping surged during the pandemic.[25]

VC opens up to new geographies

The pandemic further emphasised the increasingly international nature of the asset class. Suddenly, startups close to traditional investment hubs possessed less of an advantage as meetings transferred from in-person to online. With this, the number of cross border VC deals increased dramatically. For example, US VCs invested $78.5 billion into European and Israeli startups

20. https://www.svb.com/trends-insights/reports/healthcare-investments-and-exits
21. https://www.svb.com/trends-insights/reports/healthcare-investments-and-exits
22. 2022 Preqin Global Venture Capital Report, Preqin
23. https://pitchbook.com/newsletter/fintech-company-mollie-worth-65b-with-series-c-tIE
24. https://www.mollie.com/en/news/post/mollies-black-friday-payment-data-reveals-51-increase-in-bnpl-usage
25. https://www.cnbc.com/2021/12/04/buy-now-pay-later-boom-shows-no-signs-of-slowing-this-holiday-season.html

(the two are often grouped together as one region), a 194% increase from 2020.[26]

US based startups continued to receive the most money per year, however, raising over $300 billion in 2021, around half the world's total of $621 billion. Elsewhere, Asian firms raised $174.4 billion from VCs, while European and Israeli startups collected €102.9 billion, an almost 120% increase from 2020.

Fig. 04 US continues to dominate global VC funding

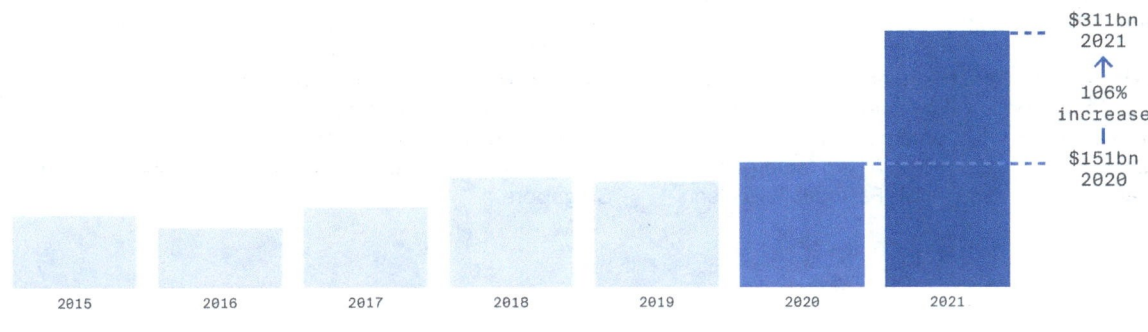

Source: CB Insights 2022

The dominance of the US was further enhanced by a huge increase in non-traditional investors (NTIs)—such as mutual funds and sovereign wealth funds (SWFs)—entering the VC space. A record number of NTIs were involved in over $200 billion worth of U.S. VC deals.[27] Meanwhile, global VC investments from SWFs surged by 81% to a record $18.2 billion and reached over 30 countries. Of those 328 investments, 120 still went to Silicon Valley.[28]

NTIs flocked to European VC as well, with VC deal value with NTI participation hitting a record €78.4 billion in 2021.

---

26. https://pitchbook.com/news/articles/2022-us-vcs-europe-deals
27. https://pitchbook.com/news/articles/2021-record-year-us-venture-capital-six-charts
28. https://globalswf.com/reports/2022annual

Fig. 05 Non-traditional investments in European VC surged in 2021

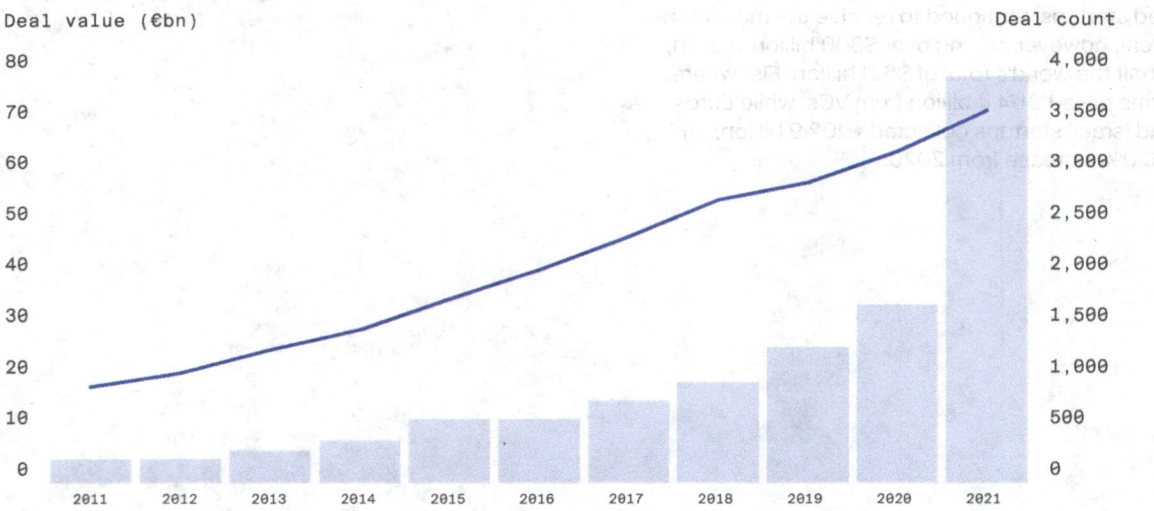

Note: Nontraditional investors are defined by PitchBook as including PE investors, mutual funds, sovereign wealth funds, hedge funds, corporations and family offices.

Source: PitchBook

Asia is also seeing an emergence of non-traditional investors in VC, led primarily by family offices. For example, Singapore's JL Family Office set up Odyssey Venture Holdings, a VC division, in September 2020, to invest in Singapore and US early-stage funds. While Shanghai-based Gopher Asset Management, the alternatives unit of family office Noah Holdings, backs series C and later rounds.[29]

This surge is likely down to the ever-longer venture cycles. The elongation of this process means many later-stage investments become out of reach for most traditional VC funds, leaving a gap for larger institutional investors, such as SWFs, to fill. This also provides NTIs access to VC-backed companies pre-exit, potentially allowing them to capitalise on a startup's faster pace of growth. Indeed, the average global IPO valuation rose from $500 million in 2015 to $3 billion in 2021. Non-traditional investors who wait for an IPO could miss out on billions in valuation growth.[30]

In terms of deal share, Asia was the 2021 VC leader with 36% of investments. Asia's 12,485 deals meant it surpassed the US's deal count for the first time in seven years. The region as a whole is increasingly attractive for VCs and has created a number of its own innovation hubs in cities such as Beijing, Bangalore, Shanghai and Singapore.[31]

---

29. https://www.businesstimes.com.sg/garage/asean-startups-shine-with-asia-pacific-vc-deals-set-to-surpass-us152b-record
30. https://investableuniverse.com/2021/04/15/non-traditional-investors-pitchbook-venture-capital-q1-nvca-mega-deals/
31. 2022 Preqin Global Venture Capital Report, Preqin

Fig. 06 Asia sees most VC deals of any region in 2021

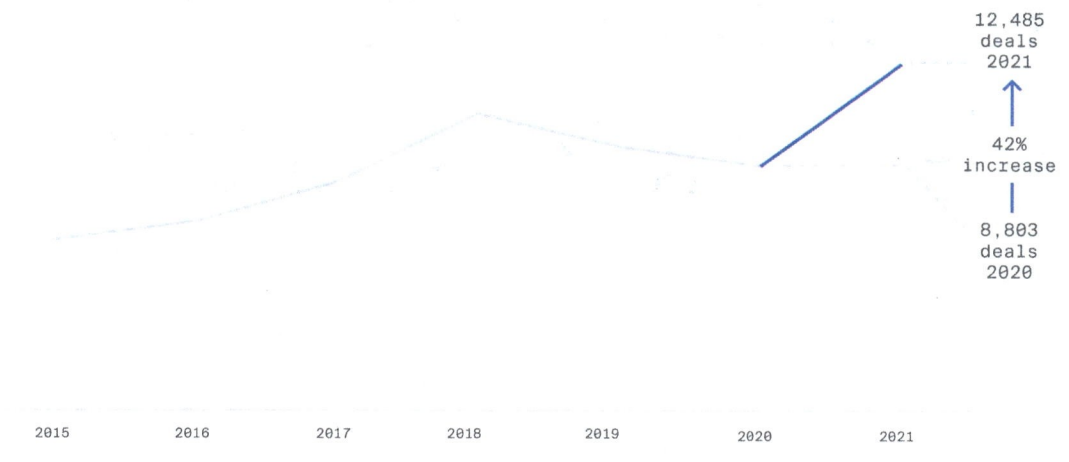

Source: CB insights 2022

A growing middle class—and thus, a growing consumer class—has boosted technological innovation and, as such, a number of the region's leading startups are consumer facing. This includes Neso Brands, a Singapore-based subsidiary of Indian eyewear e-commerce Lenskart, which completed a $100 million funding round in May 2022. As further evidence of the increasingly global nature of VC and non-traditional investors, backers of the raise included notable global firms including firms KKR and Alpha Wave Global and Singaporean SWF Temasek.[32]

---

32. https://www.techloy.com/indian-eyewear-company-neso-brands-raises-100-million/

3. The *lifecycle* of a VC-backed startup

Supporting companies in their formative stages grants VC investors access to a growing part of the economy that is not usually accessible through traditional markets. In addition, as equity investors, it gives them significant say in shaping the company's future from product development to future funding rounds, en route to hopefully a successful and profitable exit. It also provides VCs with networking opportunities to meet other founders and potentially find future investment opportunities.

These two case studies, WhatsApp and Samsara, demonstrate two examples of that lifecycle, ending with a trade sale and IPO.

Case study: WhatsApp

Looking back, the investment history of WhatsApp does not suggest the makings of a now-ubiquitous messaging service that would go on to be acquired in what is still history's biggest takeover of a VC-backed startup.

Other than initial angel backers, founders Brian Acton and Jan Koum received outside investment from just one VC firm, Sequoia Capital, from its founding in 2009 through to the 2014 $19 billion Facebook deal. In the end, Sequoia walked away with a reported $3 billion on the $60 million invested. Sequoia has previously invested in AirBnB, Instagram and most recently Stripe, highlighting the persistence of top tier managers.

The deal raised eyebrows when it was first announced. WhatsApp had recently made a net loss of $232.5 million. However, it was the rapid growth of the company - in 2014 it was bringing in over a million new users a day - and its high global usage in regions Facebook was struggling to reach that caused the social media giant to go all in on WhatsApp.[33]

WhatsApp timeline - from investment to exit[34]

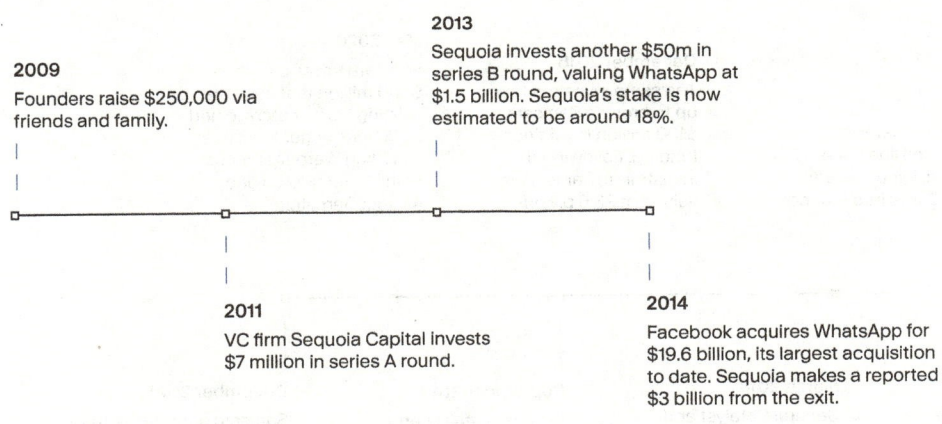

2009 Founders raise $250,000 via friends and family.

2011 VC firm Sequoia Capital invests $7 million in series A round.

2013 Sequoia invests another $50m in series B round, valuing WhatsApp at $1.5 billion. Sequoia's stake is now estimated to be around 18%.

2014 Facebook acquires WhatsApp for $19.6 billion, its largest acquisition to date. Sequoia makes a reported $3 billion from the exit.

---

33. https://www.investopedia.com/articles/investing/032515/whatsapp-best-facebook-purchase-ever
34. https://www.crunchbase.com/organization/whatsapp/company_financials

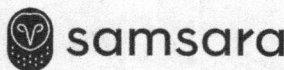

Case study: Samsara

Founded in 2015, Samsara offers businesses a cloud based platform for Internet-of-Things devices such as video cameras and data collection devices.

It was one of the VC success stories of 2021 when it went public after seven initial private funding rounds, picking up multiple investors along the way.

Prior to its IPO, Samsara reported annual recurring revenue (ARR) of $492.8m compared with $293.1 million in the year previous. ARR is a metric often used by software-as-a-service companies to show how much revenue the company can expect based on subscriptions.[35]

This level of potential saw some of the world's most prestigious VC firms invest including its primary investor Andreessen Horowitz (a16z). By the time Samsara went public in 2021, a16z owned almost 10% of the company.[36]

Samsara timeline - from investment to exit[37]

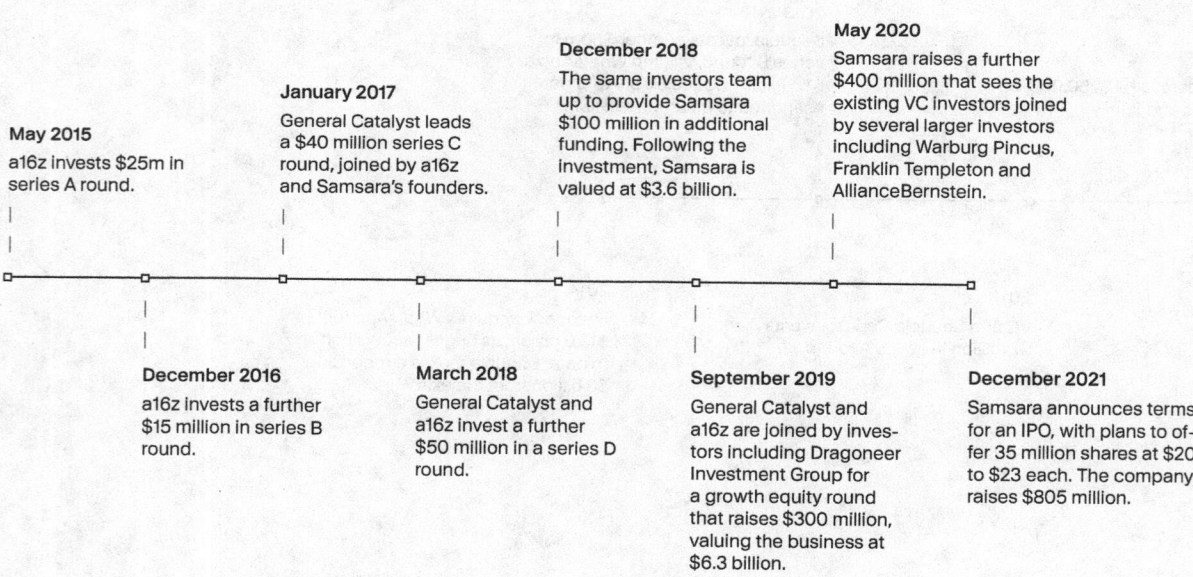

May 2015 — a16z invests $25m in series A round.

December 2016 — a16z invests a further $15 million in series B round.

January 2017 — General Catalyst leads a $40 million series C round, joined by a16z and Samsara's founders.

March 2018 — General Catalyst and a16z invest a further $50 million in a series D round.

December 2018 — The same investors team up to provide Samsara $100 million in additional funding. Following the investment, Samsara is valued at $3.6 billion.

September 2019 — General Catalyst and a16z are joined by investors including Dragoneer Investment Group for a growth equity round that raises $300 million, valuing the business at $6.3 billion.

May 2020 — Samsara raises a further $400 million that sees the existing VC investors joined by several larger investors including Warburg Pincus, Franklin Templeton and AllianceBernstein.

December 2021 — Samsara announces terms for an IPO, with plans to offer 35 million shares at $20 to $23 each. The company raises $805 million.

---

35. https://www.marketwatch.com/story/samsara-ipo-5-things-about-the-cloud-based-operations-company-11639435572
36. https://www.bloomberg.com/news/articles/2021-12-15/samsara-rises-in-trading-debut-after-ipo-fetches-805-million
37. https://www.crunchbase.com/organization/samsara-2/company_financials

4. Venture Capital in 2022 *and beyond*

Investing momentum to continue at a healthier pace

On almost every level, 2021 was a phenomenal 12 months for VC; and also quite clearly an outlier. Per PitchBook, if the pace of dealmaking for the final six months of 2021 was extrapolated for a full year, the total deal value would have outstripped the existing dry powder for all funds at the time.[38] This isn't sustainable and as we go through 2022, a drop off from last year has been inevitable.

Fig. 07 Venture capital funding slows down in 2022
Global funding by month through April 2022 ($bn)

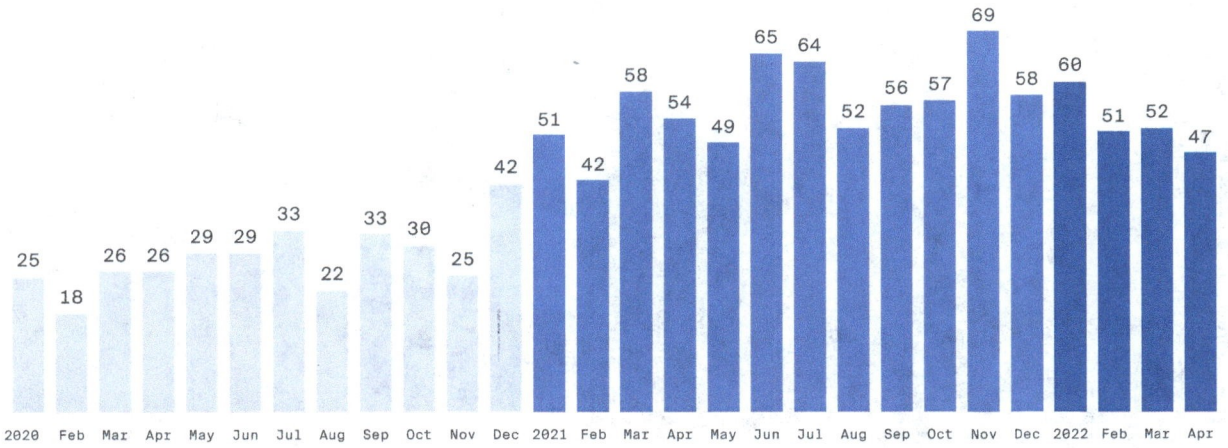

Note: Includes seed, venture and private equity for venture-backed companies
Source: Techcrunch 2022

---

38. https://pitchbook.com/news/articles/2021-pe-deals-tech-20-year-high

But there are wider reasons to be cautious. The war in Ukraine, rising inflation and interest rates, turbulence in the global capital markets, and ongoing supply chain challenges are all contributing to a slowdown in investment activity. In turn, this is causing VC investors to be increasingly wary.

Plus, this is all taking place against a backdrop of declining public market performance. This has naturally impacted venture capital deal sizes and valuations, especially for pre-IPO companies given the relatively muted exit environment and its proximity to public market valuations. As such, new unicorn births in Q2 of 2022 are on pace to reach 62, the lowest quarterly total since 2020.[39]

> "VC investing should maintain momentum as digital transformation continues at pace."

Despite this, we believe there are more reasons to be optimistic than pessimistic. Underlying secular trends around the importance of software and technology have remained incredibly strong. This is good news for VC investors on the search for new innovators. Although the world is hopefully entering the final days of the pandemic, our level of reliance on software and internet technology is bound to continue. Therefore VC investing should maintain momentum as the digital transformation continues at pace.

In addition, ongoing macroeconomic concerns could foster an environment that allows for large amounts of capital to be invested but in a potentially healthier valuation environment.

---

39. https://www.cbinsights.com/reports/CB-Insights_Venture-Report-Mid-Q2-2022.pdf

Key sectors to watch

Cybersecurity

The increasing importance of technology in most facets of our lives has, in turn, heightened focus on protecting people from being targeted by criminals for online theft or fraud, making cybersecurity more critical than ever. The aggregate deal value in the cybersecurity sector surged from $5.9 billion in 2016 to almost $13 billion in the first three quarters of 2021.[40]

With the global cost of cybercrime forecasted to reach $10.5 trillion by 2025, it's understandable why VCs are keen to back companies potentially offering solutions in this sector.[41] The first quarter of 2022 already saw $6 billion invested into cybersecurity startups, with 17 nine-figure rounds and three rounds of a quarter-billion dollars or more.[42] This included Texas start-up Securonix, a cloud-based security specialist, which raised over $1 billion from Vista Equity Partners in February.[43]

Web3

Web3 technology focuses primarily on blockchain technology and cryptocurrencies. It's deemed to be the third iteration of the internet. In our view, increased financial literacy and the continued adoption of blockchain infrastructure and cryptocurrencies will generate attractive opportunities for VC investors looking to inject capital into Web3 ventures.

In Q1 of 2022, $9.2 billion was invested in Web3 startups.[44] This included a number of mega rounds such as crypto infrastructure company Fireblock's $550 million series E. The round was led by D1 Capital Partners and Spark Capital.[45]

On top of this, Web3 startups have managed to avoid the valuation drops impacting consumer facing startups.[46] As of April 2022, late-stage post-money valuations for VC-backed cryptocurrency and blockchain companies had climbed 91% on average, to $3.95 billion. In contrast, average global late-stage VC valuations had fallen to $697.6 million—a drop of 14%.[47]

Enterprise Technology

The pandemic has accelerated technology adoption globally. This disruption has resulted in wider cloud adoption and the influence of AI. Indeed, research from Gartner forecasts that IT spending focused on enterprise software will grow by $672 billion this year, an uptick of around 11%.[48] We believe the Enterprise Technology sector will be highly attractive to VC investors, while the global shift to subscription-based revenue models speaks for more resilient revenue generation in the future.

In Q1 of 2022, we have seen a number of mega rounds, including a global logistics platform Project44. The supply chain specialist raised $420 million in its series F, in a round led by Thoma Bravo, TPG and Goldman Sachs Asset Management.[49] Specialist funds in the space also popped up, with Amazon launching its $1 billion Industrial Innovation Fund to invest in logistics startups.[50]

> "Enterprise technology will be highly attractive to VC investors as companies shift to more resilient subscription-based revenue models."

Artificial Intelligence (AI) and Machine Learning (ML)

In our view, with the ever-increasing computational power and the proliferation of structured data, AI and ML have the potential to generate outsized returns over the next few years. This is because almost all industries will be using it to enhance their products' capabilities.

---

40. 2022 Preqin Global Venture Capital Report, Preqin
41. https://cybersecurityventures.com/annual-cybercrime-report-2020/
42. https://news.crunchbase.com/cybersecurity/cyber-vc-funding-q1-2022-monthly-recap/
43. https://news.crunchbase.com/news/cyber-vc-funding-q1-2022-monthly-recap/
44. https://www.cbinsights.com/research/report/blockchain-trends-q1-2022/
45. https://www.blog.cointracking.info/top-crypto-vc-rounds-in-2022
46. https://medium.com/torre-capital/valuation-reset-who-are-the-gainers-and-losers-90957a5ec27
47. https://pitchbook.com/news/articles/crypto-blockchain-startups-venture-capital-valuations
48. https://www.networkworld.com/article/3648533/worldwide-it-spending-to-reach-45-trillion-in-2022-gartner-forecasts.html
49. https://www.prnewswire.com/news-releases/project44-receives-420-million-investment-led-by-thoma-bravo-tpg-and-goldman-sachs-valuing-business-at-2-2-billion-pre-money-301458551.html
50. https://www.geekwire.com/2022/amazon-launches-1-billion-industrial-innovation-fund-here-are-the-first-startups-to-land-cash/

For example, all of the top three cybersecurity funding rounds were for companies that used machine learning in some way.

In October 2021, Cloudera, an enterprise data cloud company with services that uses machine learning-enabled analytics, was sold to private equity firms Clayton, Dubilier & Rice, and KKR for $5.3 billion.[51]

It will even have an impact on the VC that powers these startups. Today less than 5% of VCs use AI algorithms to inform their investments. This is predicted to rise to 75% by 2025.[52]

Key trends to watch

Companies continuing to stay private for longer

VC-backed companies staying private for longer isn't new. The average age of companies going public over the last 10 years has been 12. Between 1997 and 2001, it was 5.5.[53] This important trend looks set to continue which is potentially good news for VC investors. Companies like Uber and Airbnb stayed private for over 10 years before filing for an IPO, with a large share of profits captured by private investors.

Valuations to come back down to earth

Valuations hit record highs in 2021. The year ended with 517 unicorn births, driven primarily by rapidly rising valuations at late-stage deals. As of January 2022, there were 44 decacorn startups - meaning they are valued at upwards of $10 billion - across the world.[54] In 2020, there were just 15.[55] However, many VC managers believe these valuations are overblown - inflated by the hope a start-up could be the next Uber or Airbnb.

A public market downturn in 2022 is having an impact on private market valuations and this is already being reflected in VC funding rounds. From the last two months of Q4 2021 to the first two of Q1 2022, the average Series A dropped by roughly $5m, series B by $13m and series C by $15m.[56]

This isn't great news for startups, but as already mentioned, could create a healthier investment environment for VCs as lower valuations at entry can mean favourably-priced deals, with the expectation that valuations will pick up again over the coming years and still result in solid exits for investors.

> "Lower valuations at entry can mean favourably priced deals, potentially resulting in solid exits for investors."

War in Ukraine to have an impact

While the pandemic created a headwind for VC investment, pulling in the other direction is Russia's invasion of Ukraine - especially for European investment and exits. After a blockbuster year for European IPOs, Russia's invasion of Ukraine depressed the potential for listing activity in the region.

We predict that new listings activity will stay muted until later in the year. However, broad secular trends such as digitalization and the energy transition will provide further impetus for new listings. As long as volatility eases, listings should return to European markets, just as they did following the pandemic's initial impact. The global IPO market dipped heavily during the first half of 2020, before picking up strongly in the second half of the year.

---

51. 2022 Preqin Global Venture Capital Report, Preqin
52. https://techcrunch.com/2022/04/24/deep-science-ai-simulates-economies-and-predicts-which-startups-receive-funding/
53. https://news.crunchbase.com/news/investing-early-late-startup-venture/
54. The State of Venture, Global 2021, CB Insights
55. https://news.crunchbase.com/news/decacorn-startups-2021-global-record-data-charts/
56. https://techcrunch.com/2022/03/16/new-data-shows-how-far-vcs-are-pulling-back-on-us-series-a-b-and-c-valuations/

Source: Ermoline, Pavel, Blazej Kupec, and Sean Lightbrown. "The Case for Venture Capital in 2022 and Beyond." Moonfare, July 1, 2022. https://www.moonfare.com/blog/case-for-venture-capital-in-2022. Reprinted with permission, 2023.

Domestic Firms

Venture Capital & Private Equity Firms / Domestic Firms

1 .406 VENTURES
470 Atlantic Avenue
12th Floor
Boston, MA 02210

Phone: 617-406-3300
e-mail: contact@406ventures.com
web: www.406ventures.com

Mission Statement: To provide capital, leadership and operational expertise for early stage companies in the technology industry.

Geographic Preference: New England
Fund Size: $1 billion
Founded: 2005
Investment Criteria: Early-Stage
Industry Group Preference: Technology, Digital Media & Marketing, Energy Technology, Fintech, Healthcare Information Technology, Information Services, Internet, Next Generation Software, Open Source, Real-Time Data, Web Infrastructure, Technology-Enabled Services, Cybersecurity, Data & Cloud
Portfolio Companies: Abacas Insights, AbleTo, Adtuitive, AristaMD, Ascellus, AuthAir, Bedrock Data, Bend, Better Life Partners, Business Intelligence Advisors, Carbon Black, CHAOSSEARCH, Chosen Security, ClosedLoop, CloudHealth Technologies, Compass, Connotate, CoPatient, Cortica, Corvus, Digitalsmiths, Edgewise Networks, Equip, Event Farm, Gamalon, GreatHorn, Health Dialog, Heartbeat, Hurdle, HYPR, Indico, Iora Health, Jisto, Kaltura, Laudio, Mashery, Memento, MineralTree, Nomad Health, Onapsis, Optaros, Promethium, Pwnie Express, Randori, Redox, Reltio, Retrain AI, Revmetrix, Sevco Security, Simon Data, Tausight, Terbium Labs, ThingMagic, Threat Grid, Threat Stack, ThreatX, Trilio, Vaultive, Veracode, Virtudent, Wayspring, WelbeHealth, WellAwareSystems, Wellist

Key Executives:
  Maria Cirino, Co-Founder/Managing Partner
  e-mail: mcirino@406ventures.com
  Education: BA, English Literature, Mount Holyoke College
  Background: SVP, VeriSign; CEO, Guardent; SVP, Sales & Marketing, Razorfish
  Directorships: Adtuitive, Attend, AuthAir, Carbon Black, Digitalsmiths, Edgewise Networks, Memento, MineralTree, Onapsis, Simon Data, Threat Grid, Threat Stack, Vaultive, Veracode
  Liam Donohue, Co-Founder/Managing Partner
  e-mail: ldonohue@406ventures.com
  Education: BS, Chemistry, Georgetown University; MBA, Tuck School of Business, Dartmouth College
  Background: Principal, Foster Management; Co-Founder, Arcadia Partners; CEO, Business Intelligence Advisors; Booz-Allen & Hamilton
  Directorships: AbilTo, Bedrock Data, Connotate, EnergyHub, Health Dialog, Redox, WellAWARE Systems
  Graham Brooks, Partner
  e-mail: gbrooks@406ventures.com
  Education: BSE, Computer Science, Princeton University; MBA, Tuck School of Business, Dartmouth College
  Background: Business Development Manager, Bose Corporation; Co-Founder, Accentus
  Directorships: AbilTO, Accentus, Attend, Bedrock Data, Connotate, MIT Enterprise Forum of Cambridge
  Greg Dracon, Partner
  e-mail: gdracon@406ventures.com
  Education: BS, Electrical Engineering, Pennsylvania State University; MBA, Entrepreneurial Management & Finance, Wharton School
  Background: VP, Core Capital Partners
  Directorships: Advanced Cyber Security Center, Ambient Devices, AuthAir, GreatHorn, HYPR, Jisto, Kaltura, Randori, Revmetrix, Sevco Security, Tausight, Terbium Labs, ThreatX, Trilio Data
  Payal Agrawal Divakaran, Partner
  e-mail: payal@406ventures.com
  Education: BS, Electrical Engineering, MIT; MBA, Harvard Business School
  Background: Co-Founder, SpotRocket; Corporate Development, Eventbrite; Associate, Spectrum Equity; J.P. Morgan

2 10X VENTURE PARTNERS
848 Elm Street
Suite 200
Manchester, NH 03104

Phone: 978-566-1230
e-mail: 10xventurepartners@gmail.com
web: www.10xvp.com

Mission Statement: 10X Venture Partners is a seed stage (and beyond) investment group.

Geographic Preference: New England
Founded: 2012
Average Investment: $50,000 - $500,000
Investment Criteria: Seed-Stage, Revenue between $5 to $10 Million
Industry Group Preference: Mobile, Internet, Wireless, Security, Social Media, SaaS, Cloud Computing, Green Technology, Medical Technology
Portfolio Companies: Addapptation, Applied Biomath, CoachUP, Datanomix, Eversound, Kantum Bio, Liquidware Labs, Lucky & Me, Meenta, Metrobi MyVBO (AirTank), NBD Nano, Nearpeer, Novolux, Paper Crane, Polymer, Simple Charters, Spiro Technologies, Splitwise, Thrvly, UConnect, Unruly Studios, UptimeHealth, Vetro FiberMap, XL Fleet

Key Executives:
  Jason Syversen, Managing Partner
  Education: BSCE, University of Maine; MSEE, Electrical Engineering, Worcester Polytechnic Institute
  Background: Founder, Siege Technologies; Program Manager, DARPA
  Directorships: NETSHIELD Corporation
  Matt Pierson, Partner
  e-mail: mpierson@10xvp.com
  Education: BBA, University of Rhode Island
  Background: Co-Founder, DTC Communications; Managing Director, Dunn Rush & Co.
  Directorships: Dunn Rush, Kincern, NanoComp Technologies, New Hampshire Charitable Foundation, New Hampshire Public Radio

3 11.2 CAPITAL
818 Mission Street
Suite 200
San Francisco, CA 94103

web: www.112capital.com

Mission Statement: 11.2 Capital invests in tech-based businesses focused on technologies such as AI, cyber security, robotics, new space, and date-driven healthcare.

Founded: 2013
Industry Group Preference: Artificial Intelligence, Cyber Security, Robotics, Space, Data Analytics, Healthcare
Portfolio Companies: Aeva, Anyscale, Auransa, Avaamo, ByteGain, Caption Health, Covariant AI, Cruise Automation, CryptoNumerics, Deep Genomics, Elucidate, Endear, Genturi, Forter, Ginkgo Bioworks, Hinge Health, JupiterOne, Kindred, Koko, Loop Genomics, Lucira Health, Mason, Mantle, Matchwell, Molecular Assemblies, Notable Labs, Orbital Sidekick, Outlier, Passage AI, Placenote, Sardine, Savioke, StrikeReady, Synthace, TigerGraph, uMed, White Ops

Key Executives:
  Shelley Zhuang, Founder/Managing Partner
  Education: BS, University of Missouri; PhD, University of California, Berkeley
  Background: Principal, Draper Fisher Jurvetson; EVP of

Venture Capital & Private Equity Firms / Domestic Firms

Business Development, Ecoplast Technologies
Directorships: Passage AI
Jacob Smith, Principal
Education: BS, Biochemistry and Cert. Global Health, University of Wisconsin-Madison; MBA, Corporate Finance, Investment Banking and Entrepreneurship, University of Wisconsin-Madison
Background: Principal & Venture Advisor, 30Ventures; Investor, uMed; Investor & Board Member, Matchwell
Pramod Gosavi, Principal
Education: Masters, Electrical Engineering, Purdue University; MBA, Venture Capital & Finance, The Wharton School
Background: Director, Corporate Venture Capital, Strategy and Corporate Development, VMware
Directorships: StrikeReady, VMware
David Dorsey, Principal
Education: BS, Computer Engineering, Drexel University; PhD, Electrical Engineering, Drexel University
Background: Principal, Osage University Partners (OUP); Lead Engineer, Lockheed Martin

4 1315 CAPITAL
2929 Walnut Street
Suite 1240
Philadelphia, PA 19104

Phone: 215-662-1315
web: www.1315capital.com

Mission Statement: 1315 Capital provides expansion and growth to commercial-stage healthcare services, medical technology and specialty therapeutics companies.
Fund Size: $500 million
Founded: 2014
Investment Criteria: Targets $10 to $30 million investments in commercial healthcare that have the potential to grow to $50 to $150 million of revenue
Portfolio Companies: Aktana, Biocoat, Centurion Service Group, CHC Solutions, Colorescience, Encore Dermatology, Genoptix, Greenbrook TMS, Homestead Smart Health Plans, Innovative Health, Interpace Biosciences, JDS Therapeutics, MiraDry, Misonix, Onkos Surgical, ProSciento, Reaction Biology, Restorative Therapies, Verogen
Key Executives:
Adele C. Oliva, Founding Partner
Education: BSc, St. Joseph's University; MBA, Cornell University
Background: Quaker Partners; Co-Head, US Healthcare, Apax Partners
Directorships: Colorescience
Michael Koby, Founding Partner
Education: BSc, Cornell University; MBA, The Wharton School
Background: Managing Director, Palm Ventures; Investor, Galen Partners; Analyst, Dillon, Read & Co.
Directorships: Palm Ventures

5 180 DEGREE CAPITAL
7 North Willow Street
Suite 4B
Montclair, NJ 07042

Phone: 973-746-4500 Fax: 973-746-4508
e-mail: ir@180degreecapital.com
web: www.180degreecapital.com

Mission Statement: An active investor committed to working side-by-side with the management of its portfolio companies to surmount the many challenges they confront. Formerly known as Harris & Harris Group.
Founded: 1983
Investment Criteria: Early stage, IPO, Acquisition, Tiny Technology
Industry Group Preference: Nanotechnology, Microelectronics
Portfolio Companies: ABS Materials, Adesto Technologies, Accelerator, AgBiome, D-Wave Systems, EchoPixel, Genome Profiling LLC, HALE.Life, HZO, Lodo Therapeutics, Mersana, Nanosys, NGX Bio, ORIG3N, Petra Pharma, Phylagen, ProSep, Synacor, TARA, TheStreet Inc., Xenio
Key Executives:
Kevin M. Rendino, Portfolio Manager, Chairman & CEO
Education: BS, Finance, Boston College
Background: Chairman/CEO, RGJ Capital
Directorships: Rentech Inc.
Daniel B. Wolfe, Ph.D, Portfolio Manager, President & CFO
Education: PhD, Chemistry, Harvard University; BA, Chemistry, Rice University
Background: Consultant, Nanosys; CW Group; Bioscale; Co-Founder/President, Scientific Venture Assessments

6 1843 CAPITAL
52 Mason St.
Greenwich, CT 06830

e-mail: info@1843capital.com
web: www.1843capital.com

Mission Statement: 1843 Capital is an early stage, technology venture firm advocating for gender equity to generate superior returns.
Founded: 2016
Investment Criteria: Early-Stage
Industry Group Preference: Technology, Consumer, Technology-Enabled Services
Portfolio Companies: Artemis, Avanti, Bishop Fox, Cariloop, Enveil, Finn AI, HopSkipDrive, Iotas, May Mobility, Recuro Health, Sagely Naturals
Key Executives:
Tracy Killoren Chadwell, Founding Partner
Education: JD, Loyola University of Chicago; BA, Trinity College
Background: Partner, Baker Capital; VP, Robertson Stephens
Gwen Weiss, Chief Financial Officer
Education: BS, Accounting & Finance, Fairfield University
Background: Controller, Bedford Funding; Manager, Oak Investment Partners; Sr. Associate, Deloitte & Touche

7 1ST COURSE CAPITAL
541 Jefferson Avenue
Suite 100
Redwood City, CA 94063

web: www.1cc.vc

Mission Statement: 1CC is an early stage venture capital firm investing in entrepreneurs and businesses looking to change how produce is grown, produced and distributed.
Industry Group Preference: Food Technology, Food Services, Agriculture, Environment, Nutrition, Food & Beverage
Portfolio Companies: AgriDigital, BlueCart, Bobbie, Dispatch Goods, Gooder Foods, Kosterina, Lumen, Maev, OpenCity, Over The Top Foods, Plant Based Co., Therma, Up To Good
Key Executives:
Peter Herz, General Partner
Education: BS, ECE, Carnegie Mellon University
Renske Lynde, General Partner
Education: BA, Boston University; MPP, University of California, Berkeley
Background: Board President, Food System 6 Accelerator; Associate Director of Policy & Advocacy, San Francisco Food Bank

Venture Capital & Private Equity Firms / Domestic Firms

8 **42 VENTURES**
6510 Millrock Dr.
#430
Salt Lake City, UT 84121

Phone: 801-893-2442
e-mail: info@42ventures.com
web: www.42ventures.com

Mission Statement: Partnering with entrepreneurs to grow software-driven businesses that deliver innovative products and services to highly defined markets.

Founded: 2006
Average Investment: $250,000 - $1.5 million
Investment Criteria: Early-Stage
Industry Group Preference: Software, SaaS, Mobile, Cloud Computing, Big Data, Artificial Intelligence
Portfolio Companies: Distribion, Fast, IdealEstate, Inside Real Estate, Insurance Technologies, New Media Gateway, Odin Enterprises, Sharp Analytics, Simpleview, Swipeclock Workforce Management, TouchPath, Vertical Nerve

Key Executives:
  Ned Stringham, Managing Director
  801-550-5024
  Education: BS, Philosophy & Political Science, University of Utah; MBA, Harvard Business School
  Background: Co-Founder, SBI Group; Co-Founder, Impact Group; McKinsey & Company
  Bob Howe, Executive Advisory Board
  Education: BBA, Southern Methodist University; MBA, Harvard Business School
  Background: Managing Partner, Highnote Ventures; Chairman, Montgomery Goodwin Investments; CEO/Chairman, Scient; Senior Vice President, Booz Allen Hamilton
  Tim Storer, Executive Advisory Board
  214-868-8484
  Education: BSc, Engineering and Mathematics, Vanderbilt University; MBA, Southern Methodist University
  Background: CEO, Distribion Inc.; Chairman, Vertical Nerve; Chairman, Marketingfx
  Blue VanDyke, Portfolio Partner
  Education: MS, International Management, Thunderbird
  Background: Co-Founder, Pride-Media Group; COO, Proxicom; Daimler-Benz; Ernst & Young
  Doug Folsom, Chief Financial Officer
  801-703-1625
  Education: BSc, University of Utah; CPA
  Background: CEO/Owner; FaxitFast; CEO/Owner, Phase 4 Financial

9 **4490 VENTURES**
111 North Fairchild Street
Suite 240
Madison, WI 53703

Phone: 608-501-0000
e-mail: info@4490ventures.com
web: 4490ventures.com

Mission Statement: 4490 Ventures rings capital, company-building experience and a network of resources to help entrepreneurs build their next great tech company.

Geographic Preference: Outside Silicon Valley
Founded: 2014
Average Investment: $6-10 Million
Investment Criteria: 4490 Ventures looks to invest early in a Company's lifecycle. They focus on Tech Company Start-Ups.
Industry Group Preference: Software, Technology-Enabled Services
Portfolio Companies: Abodo, Audience.Ai, Avid Ratings, Cortex, EatStreet, Fluree, HealthBridge, HealthMyne, Level Ex, Swerve Pay Health Services, Tiv, Trainual, UnderStory, Up Show

Key Executives:
  Greg Robinson, Managing Director
  Education: BSc, Arizona State University; MBA, Dartmouth College
  Background: Managing Director, Penninsula Ventures; Co-Founder, Cogent Technologies
  Directorships: Penninsula Ventures
  Dan Malven, Managing Director
  Education: BSc, Purdue University; MBA, Northwestern University, Kellogg School of Management
  Background: Principal, Flatiron Partners
  Directorships: HealthBridge, Tiv, Cortex, UPshow, Fluree, HealthMyne, SwervePay, Level Ex, physIQ, 1347 Ventures

10 **500 STARTUPS**
814 Mission Street
6th Floor
San Francisco, CA 94013

web: 500.co

Mission Statement: Based in Silicon Valley, 500 Startups has invested in more than 2,500 companies worldwide.

Geographic Preference: Global
Fund Size: $1.8 billion
Founded: 2010
Average Investment: $150,000
Investment Criteria: Seed, Series A
Industry Group Preference: Consumer Commercial, Family Tech and Education, Design, SMB Productivity & Cloud Services, International/Emerging Markets, Food Tech & Digital Healthcare, Mobile & Tablet, Payments & Financial Services, Online Video, Bitcoin, Ad Tech, Components & IoT
Portfolio Companies: 3TEN8, 42, 43Layers, 64 pixels, 82 Labs, AA Audience, Abbeypost, Abound, Accrue, ActivityHero, AdEspresso, Adraid, AdStage.io, Airpair, AirSeed, Albert, Alex & Von, Alfred X Camera, Algolia, AlgoPay, All Trails, Allay, AllDay, Alloy, AllVirtuous, AlphaFlow, Alpharank, Alumnify, Ambience Healthcare, Amixr.io, AMPAworks, Ample, Andromium, Anduin Transactions, Andy OS, AngelList, Anyroad, Apostrophe, App Onboard, AppBind, Applauze, AppRats, Appsamurai, AppZen, Apsalar, Arcturus BioCloud, Arka, ArrowPass, ArtCorgi, Assemble, Astroprint, Atrium, Attitude.ai, AuditFile, Aumet, AutoFi, Avanoo, AVATOUR, Avegant, Averon, Avision, Awayfind, Babelverse, BabyJunk, BabyList, Backtype, Bankons, Barn & Willow, Beam, Beeem, Beeline Bikes, Bellgram, BenRevo, Bento, BetterDoctor, BetterView Marketplace, Betterworks, BIGcontrols, Bigfinite, BillionToOne, BillTrim, Binpress, Biomarker.io, Bionic Panda Games, Bizeebee, BlackTies, Blavity, Blend Financial, Blissmo, BlockCypher, BlockVigil, Bloodhound, Blue Wire, Blueboard, Boatbound, Bondai, Book. Stay. Go., Bookmarq, Boomerang, BoomTrain, Boon, Boon + Gable, Boost Media, Boostable, Botoanalytics, BotSociety, BottlesTonight, Bottr, BrandBoards, Brave Credit, BridgeUS, BTCJam, Bucket, Built in Menlo, Bunndle, Burner, Butlr Technologies, Bytez, CakeHealth, Cambrian Genomics, Candyclub, Caplinked, Carbon Health, CardFlick, Cardmunch, Carelulu, Cashie Commerce, Causera, Celebrate, Chain, ChangeCoin, ChannelMeter, Chatfuel, Chewse, Chill, Chipper, Chirply, ChirpMe, Chorus, Chromatik, CircleCI, Cirrus Identity, Cityblis, Cloud Academy, Cloudpeeps, Cobalt, CoderBuddy, Cognuse, Coinding, Colingo, CollegeBacker, CommitChange, CompanyLine, Comparably, Connected, Console FM, Convoz, Copper Cow Coffee, Crave, Creative Market, CreditKarma, Crocodoc, Croma, Crowdfunder, Crowdplat, Crowdrally, Crowdz, Cube.js, Culture Kitchen, Curacubby, Curious Hat, Cushion AI, Daily Aisle, Datatron Technologies, DBA BuiltFirst, DCHQ, Dealflicks, Decisive Health Systems, Deep Fied Manna, DemandSphere, Department of Better Technology, DesignInc, Detexian, Digital Mortar, Disco, Dispatchr, Divshot, Dojo, Doughbies, Dr. Chrono, Dreamship, DriveMeCrazy, Drover AI, Drumbi, Drumpants, Easy as Pi, EatGeek, Eaze, EcoCart, EcoMom,

Venture Capital & Private Equity Firms / Domestic Firms

ELSA, Elva, Embark Labs, Embroker, Emburse, Enplug, Enter Health, EnvoyNow, Epic!, EquitySim, EST, Ethic, EverPix, Eversnap Photography, Evoz, ExitRound, FabFitFun, Fairbanc, Fan Stream, Fanbread, Feast, Fi.TT, FIGS, FileBoard

Key Executives:
Christine Tsai, Chief Executive Officer/Founding Partner
e-mail: christine@500.co
Education: BA, University of California, Berkeley
Background: Product Marketing Manager, Google; Product Marketing Manager, YouTube

11 5AM VENTURES
501 Second Street
Suite 350
San Fransisco, CA 94107

Phone: 415-933-8569
web: www.5amventures.com

Mission Statement: 5AM Ventures is focused on expanding early stage biotechnology and life science companies.
Fund Size: $350 million
Founded: 2002
Average Investment: $25 million
Minimum Investment: $4 million
Investment Criteria: Seed, Early Stage, Startups
Industry Group Preference: Life Sciences, Biotechnology, Biopharmaceutical, Drug Delivery Technology, Healthcare
Portfolio Companies: Achaogen, Akouos, Alexza, Ambrx, Aprea, Arvinas, Audentes, Bellerophon, Bird Rock Bio, BlueLight Therapeutics, Cabaletta Bio, Camp4, Cellular Research, Ceterix, Chrono, Cidara, CinCor, Cleave, Crinetics, CVS Sciences, Enliven Therapeutics, Ensoma, Entrada, Envoy, Epirus, Escient Pharmaceuticals, Expansion Therapeutics, Flexion, GlycoEra, Halio, Homology Medicines, Ideaya Biosciences, Igenica, Ikaria, Ilypsa, Impel Neuropharma, Incline, Inipharm, KalaBios, Kinaset Therapeutics, Magnetic Insight, Marcadia, Miikana, Millendo, Neurogastrx, NodThera, Nohla Therapeutics, Nouscom, Novira, Novome, Panomics, Pear Therapeutics, Pearl, PhaseRX, Portal, Precision NanoSystems, Pulmatrix, Purigen, Radionetics, Rallybio, RareCyte, Relypsa, Rennovia, Scientist.com, scPharmaceuticals, Semprus, Soteria, Spryx, Synosia, TMRW, VBI Vaccines, Viveve, Vor Biopharma, Wildcat Discovery Technologies

Other Locations:
200 Clarendon Street
45th Floor
Boston, MA 02116
Phone: 857-305-1825

Key Executives:
John D Diekman PhD, Founding Partner
Education: BA, Chemistry, Princeton University; PhD, Chemistry, Stanford University
Background: Founder/Managing Director, Bay City Capital; Chairman/CEO, Affymetrix; Chairman/Managing Director, Affymax
Directorships: Ambrx, Igenica, Wildcat, Chemdex, Envoy, Ingenuity, LJL BioSystems, Marcadia
Andrew J Schwab, Founding Partner
Education: BS, Genetics & Ethics, Davidson College
Background: Principal, Bay City Capital; VP, Business Development, Digital Gene Technologies; VP, Montgomery Securities
Directorships: Bellerophon, Biodesy, Cleave, DVS, Flexion, Ikaria, Ilypsa, Miikana, Pear Therapeutics, Precision NanoSystems, RuiYi, Synosia, Viveve
Scott M Rocklage PhD, Founding Partner
Education: BS, Chemistry, University of California, Berkeley; PhD, Chemistry, MIT
Background: Chairman/CEO, Cubist Pharmaceuticals; President/CEO, Nycomed; Salutar; Catalytica
Directorships: Achaogen, Cidara, Epirus, Kinestral, Novira, Pulmatrix, Rennovia
Kush M Parmar, MD, PhD, Managing Partner
Education: AB, Molecular Biology, Princeton University; PhD, Experimental Pathology, Harvard University; MD, Harvard Medical School
Background: VP, Strategy & Corporate Development, Novira
Directorships: Arvinas, Audentes, Novira, scPharmaceuticals
Rebecca Lucia, CFA, Chief Financial Officer/Chief Operating Officer
Education: MBA, JL Kellogg School Of Management; Chartered Financial Analyst; Canadian Chartered Accountant
Background: CFO, Prospect Venture Partners; CFO Asset Management Ventures
Paul A Stone JD, Chief Operating Officer/General Counsel
Education: University of Wisconsin
Background: SVP/General Counsel, Ethos Pharmaceuticals; SVP/General Counsel, Ilypsa; VP, Chief Patent Counsel, Symyx; Patent Attorney, Senniger, Powers, Leavitt & Roedel
Directorships: Save the Bay
Mason Freeman MD, Venture Partner
Education: BA, Harvard College; MD, University of California, San Francisco
Background: Chief, Lipid Metabolism Unit/Director, Translational Medicine, Massachusetts General Hospital
Directorships: Envoy
Richard J Ulevitch PhD, Venture Partner Emeritus
Education: AB, Washington & Jefferson College; PhD, Biochemistry, University of Pennsylvania
Background: Professor & Chairman, Department of Immunology, The Scripps Research Institute
James W Young PhD, Venture Partner Emeritus
Education: BS, Chemistry, Fordham University; PhD, Organic Chemistry, Cornell University
Background: CEO, Sunesis; SVP, ALZA Corporation; President, Pharmaceuticals Division, Affymax, N.V.; SVP/General Manager, Pharmaceuticals Division, Sepracor; VP, Research, Zoecon/Sandoz Crop Protection Corporation
Directorships: Chrono Therapeutics

12 645 VENTURES

e-mail: ideas@645ventures.com
web: 645ventures.com

Mission Statement: A tech-based venture capital firm interested in early-stage startups.
Founded: 2013
Investment Criteria: Early-Stage
Industry Group Preference: Technology, Artificial Intelligence, Retail, Consumer, Design, Entertainment, Industry, Health & Wellness, Infrastructure, Security
Portfolio Companies: AaDya, Abacus, Alice, Andrena, AptDeco, Beauty Bakerie, Bespoke Post, Betterview, Eden Health, Fat Llama, FiscalNote, Hire An Esquire, Iterable, League Apps, Negotiatus, Ovetime, Panther, Resident, Rifiniti, Rosie, Source3, Squire, Thinknum, Voodoo Manufacturing

Key Executives:
Nnamdi Okike, Co-Founder/Managing Partner
Education: BA, Harvard University; JD, Harvard Law School; MBA, Harvard Business School
Background: Principal, Insight Venture Partners; Business Development Officer, Verne Global
Aaron Holiday, Co-Founder/Managing Partner
Education: BS, Morehouse College; MBA, Cornell University
Background: Software Engineer, Goldman Sachs; Business Analyst, GFI Group; Associate, DFJ Gotham Ventures; Managing Entrepreneurial Officer, Cornell Tech

Venture Capital & Private Equity Firms / Domestic Firms

13 747 CAPITAL
880 Third Avenue
17th Floor
New York, NY 10022

Phone: 212-747-7474
e-mail: info@747capital.com
web: www.747capital.com

Mission Statement: Through the funding of funds and managed accounts, 747 Capital focuses exclusively on the smaller end of the private equity market in North America.

Geographic Preference: United States, Canada
Fund Size: $550 million
Founded: 2001
Minimum Investment: $50 million
Investment Criteria: Later-Stage
Industry Group Preference: Private Equity
Portfolio Companies: Crossplane Capital, Guardian Capital Partners, Hamilton Robinson Captial Partners, Periscope Equity, Tilia, Transom Capital Group

Key Executives:
  Gijs FJ Van Thiel, Managing Partner
  Education: BA, Webster University; MBA, Thunderbird School of Global Management, Arizona State University
  Background: Founder/General Partner, Triad Media Ventures; Director, Financial Services, Icon International; Assistant Area Director, Netherlands Foreign Investment Agency
  Marc der Kinderen, Managing Partner
  Education: BBA, European University, Belgium; MBA, Nijenrode School of Business
  Background: Executive VP, Greenfield Capital Partners; Noro Group of Companies; HomeBanc
  Directorships: CapCorp Investments
  Joshua Sobeck, Partner
  Education: BA, Molecular Biology & Biochemistry, Middlebury College; MBA, Finance, Columbia Business School
  Background: Product Marketing Manager, Citadon
  James Yang, Vice President
  Education: BAA, Finance, University Of Texas at Austin
  Background: University Of Texas Investment Management Company
  Greg Stupore, Associate
  Education: BA, Accounting, Boston College; CPA
  Background: Senior Auditor, Deloitte & Touche

14 A-GRADE INVESTMENTS
Los Angeles, CA

web: www.agradeinvestments.com

Geographic Preference: United States
Founded: 2011
Investment Criteria: Seed, Early Stage, Debt
Industry Group Preference: Consumer Internet, Technology
Portfolio Companies: Airtable, Amen, Getaround, GoButler, IfOnly, Kopari Beauty, Pair, ResearchGate, Sonic Notify, Tinychat, Willing

Key Executives:
  Guy Oseary, Founder
  Background: Principal, Untitled Entertainment; Executive Producer, NBC's Last Call
  Ron Burkle, Founder
  Background: Managing Partner, The Yucaipa Companies; Director, Yahoo; Director, Yucaipa Equity Partners, L.P.; Director, Occidental Petroleum Corp.; Director, KB Home Corporation
  Ashton Kutcher, Founder
  Background: General Partner, Sound Ventures; Co-Founder, Thorn: Digital Defenders of Children
  Chris Hollod, Managing Partner
  Education: BA, Economics, Finance, and Philosophy, Vanderbilt University
  Background: Founding Partner, Inevitable Ventures

15 AM VENTURES
65 Union Avenue
Suite 500
Memphis, TN 38103

Phone: 901-523-2000
web: www.archermalmo.com

Mission Statement: AM Ventures seeks to invest in early-stage companies by providing expertise and execution.

Geographic Preference: United States
Founded: 2010
Investment Criteria: Early-Stage
Industry Group Preference: Consumer Internet, Software
Portfolio Companies: Capital Farm Credit, Delaware North, Implus, Juice Plus, Massage Heights, Nations Hearing, Palm Beach Tan, Reynolds American, Smile Doctors Braces, Stoller, Valent, Zoetis

Key Executives:
  Russ Williams, Principal, Chief Executive Officer
  Education: MBA, Darden School Of Business, University of Virginia; BSc, Chemical Engineering, Christian Brothers University
  Background: Chemical Engineer, DuPont
  Directorships: Kraft Food Ingredients
  Gary Backaus, Principal, Chief Creative & Strategic Officer
  Education: BFA, Advertising Design, Memphis College of Art
  Wally Rose, SVP/Executive Creative Director
  Education: University of Memphis
  Background: Executive Creative Director, Sullivan Branding

16 AAVIN PRIVATE EQUITY
1245 First Avenue Southeast
Cedar Rapids, IA 52402

Phone: 319-247-1072
web: www.aavin.com

Mission Statement: Generates outstanding investment results by partnering with strong management groups to build companies into profitable acquisition candidates.

Geographic Preference: Mid-America Region
Fund Size: $87 million
Founded: 1999
Average Investment: $5 - $10 million
Minimum Investment: $5 million
Investment Criteria: Late Stage, Expansion Stage, High-Growth Opportunities, MBO, Recapitalization
Industry Group Preference: Medical Devices, Healthcare, Information Technology, Manufacturing, Distribution, Industrial Products, Retail, Consumer & Leisure, Software, Services
Portfolio Companies: American Industrial Machine, Brown Industries, CPI Luxury Group, Dream Giveaway, ECS Learning Systems, FedEx Ground, Graham Waste, Green Diamond Sand Products, Greenleaf Book Group, Happy Joe's, HH Ventures, Montana Silversmiths, Roanwell Corporation, Standard Precast, Transfer Tool Products, Verrex, Weeks Service Company

Key Executives:
  James Thorp, Managing Partner
  319-200-4354
  e-mail: jthorp@aavin.com
  Education: BS, Business Administration, Oklahoma State University; MBA, Finance, Wharton School, University of Pennsylvania
  Background: Principal, Allsop Venture Partners; Berthel Fisher & Company
  Eric Hender, Senior Partner
  319-200-4846
  e-mail: ehender@aavin.com
  Education: Colorado College; Banking Institute, University of Wisconsin; Securities Institute, Wharton

Venture Capital & Private Equity Firms / Domestic Firms

School, University of Pennsylvania
Background: Co-Founder/Managing Member, Marshall Venture Capital, LC; SCI Financial Group; President, Securities Corporation of Iowa
Directorships: Destinations Unlimited, Inter-Med
David Schroder, Senior Partner
319-247-1072
e-mail: dschroder@aavin.com
Education: BSFS, International Business, Georgetown University; MBA, University Of Wisconsin
Background: MorAmerica Capital Coproration, InvestAmerica
Directorships: NASBIC, Midwest RASBIC
Paul Rhines, Senior Partner
319-363-8971
e-mail: prhines@aavin.com
Education: BA, Accounting, University of Northern Iowa
Background: Founding General Partner, Allsop Venture Partners; Co-Founder/Managing Member/Executive VP, Marshall Venture Capital, LC; Regional VP, MorAmerica Capital Corporation
Directorships: GreatAmerica Financial Services, Stamats Communications Company, Schebler Company
Thies O Kolln, Partner
319-200-4355
Education: BA, Dartmouth College; JD, University of Chicago
Background: Boston Consulting Group; Orbitz; Kirkland & Ellis; Law Clerk, US Court of Appeals
Kevin Mullane, Partner
816-807-3817
e-mail: kmullane@aavin
Education: BSBA, MBA, Rockhurst Jesuit University
Background: MorAmerica Capital; Co-Founder, Invest America
Directorships: NASBIC, Midwest RASBIC

17 ABBOTT CAPITAL MANAGEMENT LLC
1290 Avenue of the Americas
New York, NY 10104

Phone: 212-757-2700
web: www.abbottcapital.com

Mission Statement: Abbott Capital Management, LLC is an investment management firm focused on building and managing private equity funds worldwide. Abbott Capital provides a number of solutions for institutional investors, and selects funds across venture capital, growth equity, buyouts, special situations and secondaries.

Geographic Preference: Worldwide
Founded: 1986

Key Executives:
Jonathan D Roth, Managing Director/President
Education: AB, Economics, Cornell University; MBA, The Fuqua School of Business, Duke University
Background: Associate, Elmrock Partners; Financial Analyst, Amoco Corporation; Corporate Lending Officer, Chemical Bank
Mary T Hornby, Managing Director/General Counsel
Education: BA, Boston College; JD, Boston College Law School
Background: Counsel, Private Equity Group, Testa Hurwitz & Thibeault LLP
Timothy W Maloney, Managing Director
Education: BS, Accounting, DePaul University; MBA, Finance, New York University; CPA
Background: Frye-Louis Capital Management; General American Transportation Corporation; Hewitt Associates
Lauren M Massey, Managing Director/Finance & Administration
Education: BS, Accounting, State University of New York at Binghamton; MBA, Finance & Marketing, New York University; CPA
Background: Audit Manager, Financial Services Division, Ernst & Young
Paolo Parziale, Managing Director/Chief Financial Officer
Education: BS, Accounting, St. John's University; MBA, Finance, New York University
Background: Audit Senior, Ernst & Young
Meredith L Rerisi, Managing Director
Education: BS, Applied Economics & Business Management, Cornell University; MBA, Duke University
Background: Equity Analyst, American High Growth Equities Corporation
Matthew M Smith, Managing Director
Education: AB, History, MBA, Finance, Georgetown University
Background: Federal Reserve Bank of New York; First Trust Washington; Bank of America
Kathryn J Stokel, Managing Director/Chief Operating Officer
Education: BS, Mathematics, University of Michigan; MBA, Finance, Wharton School, University of Pennsylvania; CFA
Background: Portfolio Manager, General Motors Investment Management Corporation
Charles H van Horne, Senior Advisor
Education: BA, Sociology, University of Pennsylvania
Background: AIG Capital Partners; Creditanstalt International Advisors; Bankers Trust; UBS Securities

18 ABELL FOUNDATION VENTURES
111 South Calvert Street
Suite 2300
Baltimore, MD 21202-6174

Phone: 410-547-1300 Fax: 410-539-6579
e-mail: abell@abell.org
web: www.abell.org

Mission Statement: The Abell Foundation is dedicated to supporting innovative initiatives that will enhance the quality of life in Maryland.

Geographic Preference: Baltimore, Nearby
Fund Size: $25 million
Founded: 1953
Average Investment: $150,000 - $500,000
Investment Criteria: Companies that create jobs in Baltimore and seek to challenge various social and environmental issues
Industry Group Preference: Telecommunications, Internet Technology, Software, Healthcare, Biotechnology, Medical Devices, Energy
Portfolio Companies: AMRM, Awarables, BioMarker Strategies, Breethe, Common Curriculum, CoolTech, CyberSpa, Dipole Materials, eNeura Therapeutics, Factory Four, Gemstone Biotherapeutics, Gliknik, GrayBug, Harpoon Medical, Lawrenceville Plasma Physics, Life Sprout, Longeviti, MF Fire, Network for Good, Next Step Robotics, NAWEC, Noxilizer, Oasis Marinas, OTEC International, PAICE, Perceptive Navigation, Personal Genome Diagnostics, Pixelligent, Propel Baltimore Fund, ReGelTec, Sisu Global Health, Sonavex, Sonify Biosciences, Sunrise, ThermoChem Recovery International, Vasoptic Medical, Vixiar Medical

Key Executives:
Robert C Embry Jr, President
Education: Williams College; Harvard Law School
Background: President, Board of School Commissioners, Baltimore City; Assistant Secretary, US Department of Housing and Urban Development
Directorships: Maryland State Board Of Education
Eileen O'Rourke, Chief Financial Officer
Education: Loyola College; CPA; Registered Securities Broker; Certified Financial and Operations Principal
Background: KPMG, VP, Legg Mason Inc
Directorships: eNeura, Pixelligent, Ceratech

Venture Capital & Private Equity Firms / Domestic Firms

19 ABERDARE VENTURES
235 Montgomery Street
Suite 1230
San Francisco, CA 94104
Phone: 415-392-7442 **Fax:** 415-392-4264
web: www.aberdare.com

Mission Statement: Experienced venture investors and operators of healthcare technology companies.
Geographic Preference: San Francisco area
Fund Size: $400 million
Founded: 1999
Average Investment: $1 - $15 million
Minimum Investment: $1 million
Investment Criteria: Early Stage
Industry Group Preference: Healthcare, Biopharmaceuticals, Medical Devices, Therapeutics
Portfolio Companies: Castlight, Clovis Oncology, ElationEMR, Gravie, Gritstone Oncology, Indigo Agriculture, Kaleido Biosciences, Kezar Life Sciences, MC10, Piper Bioscience, Vir

Key Executives:
  Paul Klingenstein, Founder/Managing Partner
  e-mail: pklingenstein@aberdare.com
  Education: AB, Harvard College; MBA, Stanford Graduate School of Business
  Background: Advisor, Rockefeller Foundation; Accel Partners; Warburg Pincus
  Directorships: Aviron, Isis Pharmaceuticals, Glycomed, Neurex, Xomed Surgica Products
  Sigrid Van Bladel, PhD, Venture Partner
  e-mail: svanbladel@aberdare.com
  Education: MA, Chemistry/Biology, University Of Ghent; PhD, Molecular Biology, University Of Ghent; MBA, Stanford Graduate School Of Business
  Background: Partner, New Enterprise Associates
  Directorships: Myogen, Kai Pharma, Novacept, SurgRx, Xcel Pharmaceuticals, Appriva Medical, Spiration Inc.
  Mohit Kaushal MD, Partner
  e-mail: mkaushal@aberdare.com
  Education: MBA, Stanford University; MD, Imperial College London
  Background: Director, Connected Health, Federal Communications Commission; Investment Professional, Polaris Venture Partners; Merrill Lynch; World Health Organization
  Directorships: goBalto, RxAnte
  Jake Odden, Partner/Chief Operating Officer
  e-mail: jodden@aberdare.com
  Education: AB, Bowdoin College; MBA, Tuck School of Business, Dartmouth College
  Background: Walt Disney Company; Goldman Sachs; Vanguard Group
  Directorships: Posit Science
  Sigrid Van Bladel, Venture Partner
  e-mail: svanbladel@aberdare.com
  Education: PhD, Molecular Biology, Ghent University; MBA, Stanford Graduate School of Business
  Background: Partner, New Enterprise Associates; Management Consultant, McKinsey and Company
  Directorships: Aviir, Conatus, Kai Pharmaceuticals

20 ABRY PARTNERS
888 Boylston Street
Suite 1600
Boston, MA 02199
Phone: 617-859-2959
e-mail: info@abry.com
web: www.abry.com

Mission Statement: ABRY Partners is a private equity investment firm focused on media, communications, business and information services companies based in North America. ABRY provides operational expertise, investment experience, capital and industry insight. The firm partners with superior management teams with the goal of helping to build stronger companies.
Fund Size: $1.7 billion
Founded: 1989
Average Investment: $25 million - $150 million
Minimum Investment: $10 million
Investment Criteria: Buyouts, Expansion Capital, Backing Platform Acquisitions, Mezzanine, Roll-ups/Consolidations, Recapitalization for partial liquidity
Industry Group Preference: Media, Communications, Business Products & Services, Education, Entertainment, Healthcare Services, Information Services, Digital Media & Marketing
Portfolio Companies: Accela, Access Information Management, Acrisure, AddSecure, AdSwerve, Aduro, Aegis Sciences Corporation, Aftermath, AFS Technologies Inc., Airband, Alliantgroup, American CyberSystems, Anju Software, ArchivesOne, Atlantic Broadband, Avalon Cable, Basefarm, B&H Education, Billing Services Group, Brash Entertainment, Broadcast Electronics, BSO, BTG, CafeMedia, CapRock Holdings, Casamba, Cast & Crew, Charleston Newspaper, CIBT, Citadel Communications, CitiXsys, Claranet, Commerce Connect Media, Commonwealth Business Media, Confie Seguros, Confirma Software, Conoisseur Communications, Consolitated Theatres, Consumer Media Network, Country Road Communications, CyrusOne, DataMentors, Datapipe, DF King World Wide, Direct Travel, Dolan Media Company, Donuts, Dr. Dental, Edgile, EduK Group, Emerging Markets Communications, Executive Health Resources, F+W Media, FanFare Media Works, FastMed Urgent Care, Finest City Broadcasting LLC, FLS Transportation, Franklin Energy, Frontline Performance Group, Gateway EDI, Gould & Lamb, Grande Communications, Hanley Wood, HealthPort, HealthSCOPE Benefits, HealthTrans, Hilb Group, Hispanic Yellow Pages, Home Town Cable, Hosted Solutions, Houghton Mifflin Harcourt, IMG, InfiLaw System, Integra, iTradeNetwork Inc., JAB Broadband, Kidz Bop, Kore Wireless Group, Legendary Pictures, Lighthouse Autism Center, Link Mobility, Masergy, Maya Cinemas, Media Rights Capital, Millennium Trust, Music Reports Inc., Muzak, North American Dental Group, Nuspire, One Source Networks, Orion HealthCorp, Penton Media, Pinnacle Towers, PowerFleet, Portfolio Group, PRO Unlimited, ProQuest, Prospect Park, Psychological Services Inc., Q9 Networks, Quo Vadis, Rackspace, RCN Cable, RIMES Technologies, Root Data Center, SambaSafety, Securus, Sentrum, Sermo, Sentry Data Systems, SiteLock, Smart Smart, SoftBrands Inc., Source Medical, Talent Partners, Trover Solutions, Unison, VerticalScope, Vocado, WideOpenWest, Writtle Holdings, Xand, York Risk Services Group

Key Executives:
  Royce G. Yudkoff, Co-Founder
  Education: Dartmouth College; Harvard Business School
  Background: Partner, Bain & Company; Founder, Information Partners
  Andrew Banks, Co-Founder
  Education: Harvard Law School; Oxford University; University of Florida
  Background: Partner, Bain & Co; TELCO Board, National Association of Broadcasters
  Peggy Koenig, Chair
  Education: Cornell University; MBA, Wharton School
  Background: Partner/Board Member, Sillerman Communications Management Corporation
  Jay Grossman, Managing Partner/Co-CEO
  Education: Dickinson College; MBA, Harvard Business School
  Background: Managing Director/Co-Head, Media and Entertainment Group, Prudential Securities; Corporate Finance, Kidder, Peabody & Company
  C.J. Brucato, Managing Partner/Co-CEO
  Education: Princeton University

Venture Capital & Private Equity Firms / Domestic Firms

Background: Media and Entertainment Group, Prudential Securities Inc.
John Hunt, Managing Partner
Education: University of Massachusetts Amherst
Background: General Partner, Boston Ventures Management
Brent Stone, Partner
Education: Cornell University
Background: Credit Suisse First Boston; Donaldson, Lufkin & Jenrette; Chase Securities
Robert MacInnis, Partner
Education: Merrimack College; MBA, Boston University; CPA
Background: CFO, Weather Services Corporation; Senior Manager, Mergers & Acquisition Group, PricewaterhouseCoopers
Anders Bjork, Partner
Education: BS, University of Denver; MSF, Daniels College of Business; MBA, Wharton School
Background: Fir Tree Partners; Guggenheim Partners; VSS; Former Professional Hockey Plaer in the American Hockey League, Represented the Swedish National team
Brian St. Jean, Partner
Education: University of Rhode Island; CPA
Background: Manager, Mergers & Acquisition Group, PricewaterhouseCoopers
John Connor, Partner
Education: Columbia University; MBA, Graduate School of Business, University of Chicago; CFA
Background: SVP, Hartford Investment Management Company
Michael Ashton, Partner
Education: BA, MBA, University of Rhode Island
Background: Senior Credit Analyst, Eaton Vance Management; Fortis Investments; Hartford Investment Management
Matt Lapides, Partner
Education: Colby College
Background: Senior Analyst, John Hancock Financial Services Inc.; VP, Finance, Diveo Broadband Networks; Chase Securities Inc.
Nicolas Massard, Partner
Education: HEC Paris
Background: Spectrum Equity Investors; Continuum Group; Morgan Stanley; Lehman Brothers
Directorships: Airband, JAB
Nicholas Scola, Partner
Education: Tufts University
Background: HIG Capital; Capital Resource Partners; Broadview International
Tomer Yosef-Or, Partner
Education: Rutgers Business School, Rutgers University
Background: Financial Instiution Group, Bear Stearns; Securitization Transaction Group, Deloitte & Touche
Tyler Wick, Partner
Education: Amherst College
Background: Ticonderoga Capital; Advest
Azra Kanji, Partner
Education: Duke University
Background: Communications, Media & Entertainment Group, Goldman Sachs
Debbie Johnson, Chief Financial Officer
Education: Boston University; CPA
Background: Senior Accountant, Audit Division, PricewaterhouseCoopers

21 ABS CAPITAL PARTNERS
400 East Pratt Street
Suite 910
Baltimore, MD 21202-3127

Phone: 410-246-5600
e-mail: abscapital@abscapital.com
web: www.abscapital.com

Mission Statement: To create significant, market-leading companies. Investment strategy focuses on companies in the healthcare, technology, business services, media and communications sectors.
Geographic Preference: United States
Fund Size: $500 million
Founded: 1990
Average Investment: $10 - $40 million
Investment Criteria: Later-Stage Growth, Expansion, Recapitalizations
Industry Group Preference: Business Products & Services, Information Technology, Communications, Healthcare, Media, Education
Portfolio Companies: Accurate Group Holdings, Alarm.com, Aldera, Bambeco, Bask, Bravo Wellness, ConnectYourCare, Defy Media, EXOS, FactorTrust, IgnitionOne, INTTRA, Invision, ISO Group, iZotope, Liquid Environmental Solutions, Modular Space Corporation, Pathology, PaySpan, Paystream, Power Reviews, Purch, Redzone Robotics, Scale Computing, Teachscape, Whitney International University System, Zoom Media Group

Other Locations:
3 Harbor Drive
Suite 108
Sausalito, CA 94965
Phone: 415-262-8100

Key Executives:
Donald B. Hebb, Jr., Chairman/Founding Partner
Education: Kenyon College; Harvard Law School; Harvard Business School
Background: President/CEO, Alex. Brown & Sons
Directorships: INTTRA, ISO Group, Modular Space Corporation, Zoom Media Group
Phil Clough, Managing General Partner
Education: United States Military Academy; Darden School of Business, University of Virginia
Background: CEO, SITEL Corporation; Investment Banking Group, Alex. Brown & Sons; Captain, United States Army
Directorships: Accurate Group Holdings, FactorTrust, Liquid Environmental Solutions, Liquidity Services, Teachscape, Whitney International University, System
John Stobo, Managing General Partner
Education: University of California, San Diego; Johnson Graduate School of Management, Cornell University
Background: Health Care Investment Banking Group, Alex. Brown & Sons
Directorships: Aldera, Bravo Wellness, EXOS, Pathology
Mike Avon, General Partner
Education: University of Virginia; University of Virgina School of Law
Background: Venture Capitalist, Millennial Media; Principal, Columbia Capital; Executive Chairman, ICX Media
Kimberly Kyle, General Partner
Education: Bloomsburg University; University of Baltimore
Ralph Terkowitz, General Partner
Education: Cornell University; University of California, Berkeley
Background: CIO/CTO, Washington Post Company; Founder/CEO, WashingtonPost.Newsweek Interactive
Directorships: Alarm.com, IgnitionOne, PowerReviews, Purch
Tim Weglicki, Founding Partner
Education: Johns Hopkins University; Wharton School
Background: Founder/Head, Capital Markets Group, Alex. Brown & Sons
Directorships: American Public Foundation, ConnectYourCare, PaySpan
Cal Wheaton, General Partner
Education: Colby College; Wharton School
Background: VP, Deutsche Bank, Alex. Brown & Sons; Kidder, Peabody & Co.

Directorships: Accurate Group Holdings, Bambeco, ConnectYourCare, PaySpan, PayStream
Paul Mariani, General Partner
Education: Stanford University
Background: Technology Investment Banking Division, Robertson Stephens; SoundView Technology Group
Directorships: Liquid Environmental Solutions, PowerReviews, Purch, Teachscape
James Stevenson, Chief Financial Officer
Education: University of North Carolina
Background: EVP/CFO, SITEL Corporation; Alex. Brown & Sons; KPMG

22 ABS VENTURES
950 Winter Street
Suite 2600
Waltham, MA 02451

e-mail: abs@absventures.com
web: www.absventures.com

Mission Statement: ABS Ventures is a venture capital firm that invests in mid-stage technology companies. Utilizing primary and secondary direct investing strategies, ABS Ventures works with management teams to help with the growth of portfolio companies.

Geographic Preference: United States
Fund Size: $320 million
Founded: 1983
Average Investment: $5 - $15 million
Minimum Investment: $5 million
Investment Criteria: Bridge, First Stage, Mezzanine, Second Stage, Mid-Stage
Industry Group Preference: Software, Communications, Healthcare, Technology-Enabled Services, Information Technology, Medical Technology
Portfolio Companies: Active Network, Adeptra, Alphablox, Certona Corp., Clearforest, Clicksquared Inc., Cognio, CVRx, End2End, Evalve Inc., Everbridge, Eyeonics, Farechase, Formation Systems, FoxHollow Technology, Gomez Inc., Highroads, Hotbar.com, I-Logix, Ilumin, Intact Medical Corps., Intralinks, Inxight Software, IQ Financial Systems, Lumend, Nuera, Overtone, Paratek, Powersdine, Qualys, Rib-X Pharmaceuticals, RiskMetrics, Synchronoss, Telogy, Theravance, Trema, Trivascular, Vesta GMS, Wimba, Workbrain

Key Executives:
Bill Burgess, Managing Partner
Education: BA, Dartmouth College; MBA, Harvard Business School
Background: Managing Director/Global Head/Vice Chairman, Deutsche Bank Venture Partners; Head of Technology Investment Banking, Alex. Brown & Sons
Directorships: Certona, ClickSquared, Highroads
Bruns Grayson, Managing Partner
Education: Harvard College; Univ. of Oxford; University of Virginia School of Law
Background: Adler & Company; Associate, McKinsey & Company; Manager, Venture Funds, Alex. Brown & Sons
Directorships: Active Network, Intact Medical, Rib-X Pharmaceuticals, Wimba
Susan Adams, Chief Financial Officer
Education: BS, Pennsylvania State University

23 ABSTRACT VENTURES
South Park
San Francisco, CA 94133

web: abstractvc.com

Mission Statement: A broad partnership of investors that funds the earliest stages of business formation.

Geographic Preference: California
Founded: 2016
Investment Criteria: Pre-Seed, Seed, Series A
Industry Group Preference: Insurance, Finance, Robotics, Healthcare, Software
Portfolio Companies: Ripple, Osaro, Neighborly, Brave Software, Starsky Robotics, Arrivo, Squadrun, Grabango, Contraline, Ccobox, Clara, Simple Health, ID By DNA, Simbi, RBC Signals, Drip, Catalia Health, Poncho, Polychain Capital, Cruncher, Clarity Money, Lunar, Petal, Prodigy, Hippo

Key Executives:
Ramtin Naimi, Founder/General Partner
Background: Founder/Senior Advisor, AutoHub; Partners, Flight Ventures; Core Innovation Capital
Directorships: AppOnboard, Arrivo, AutoHub, Bestow, Brave, BuildUp, Catalia Health, Ccobox, Clara, Clarity Money, Contraline, CUR, DeepCurrent Technologies, Dolo (Tea Time Labs), Drip, Hippo

24 ACACIA CAPITAL
101 S Ellsworth Avenue
Suite 300
San Mateo, CA 94401

Phone: 650-372-6400 Fax: 650-378-8977
web: www.acacia-capital.com

Mission Statement: A private investment banking firm which provides M&A and corporate finance advisory services to middle market businesses in support of client growth, refinance, and sale efforts.

Geographic Preference: United States
Fund Size: $100 million
Founded: 1999
Minimum Investment: $20 million
Investment Criteria: Existing Apartment Communities, 100+ Unites, Value Add & Core Opportunity
Industry Group Preference: Real Estate
Other Locations:
2398 E Camelback Road
Suite 200
Phoenix, AZ 85016
Phone: 602-253-5563 Fax: 602-253-0859

Key Executives:
Robert E. Larson, Founder/Co-CEO
Education: BA, MBA, Stanford University
Background: Morgan Stanley & Co.
Robert G. Leupold, Co-CEO
Education: BA, University of California, San Diego
Background: Asset Sales Group, Union Bank

25 ACADIA WOODS PARTNERS
New York, NY

Mission Statement: A New York based investment partnership with particular interest in early stage technology companies.

Investment Criteria: Early Stage
Industry Group Preference: Technology, Biotechnology
Portfolio Companies: Burlywood, Dispersol Technologies, Luminoso, SyncHR, VidMob

Key Executives:
Jeff Samberg, Managing Director
Education: BA, Economics, Princeton University; MBA, Stanford University Graduate School of Business
Background: Vice President of Corporate Strategy, PeopleSoft Inc.; Vice President of Business Development, Wily Technology; Entrepreneur in Residence, Greylock Partners

26 ACARIO INNOVATION
535 Middlefield Road
Menlo Park, CA 94025

web: www.acarioinnovation.com

Mission Statement: Acario Innovation was established by Tokyo Gas and is headquartered in Silicon Valley They aim to

Venture Capital & Private Equity Firms / Domestic Firms

bring sustainable energy solutions, collaboratinf with top labs and incubators to support their entrepreneurs and partners.

Key Executives:
Patrick Sagisi, Managing Partner
650-283-7026
e-mail: patrick@acarioinnovation.com

27 ACCEL
500 University Avenue
Palo Alto, CA 94301

Phone: 650-614-4800
web: www.accel.com

Mission Statement: A venture capital firm dedicated to helping outstanding entrepreneurs build category-defining technology companies.

Geographic Preference: U.S., Europe, India, Israel
Fund Size: $3 billion
Founded: 1983
Minimum Investment: $500K
Investment Criteria: Early-Stage, Growth Stage
Industry Group Preference: Consumer, Infrastructure, Media, Mobile, SaaS, Security
Portfolio Companies: 2Wire, 3LM, 99 Designs, Acalvio, Acko, Acopia, Actuate, Admob, AdRoll, Agile Networks, Agile Software, Agrostar, Airgo Networks, Airwatch, Alfresco, Algolia, Alphabox, Amino, Amitree, Amobee Media Systems, Anchor, ANSR, Aorato, Arcot, Arista, Arrowpoint, Ascend.io, Atlassian Software, Avici Systems, Avito, Away, Axio Biosolutions, BaubleBar, BBN Technologies, Bettercloud, Birch Box, Bird, Bizongo, BlaBlaCar, Blackbuck, Blameless, Blue Jeans Network, Bluestone, Bonobos, BookMyShow, Bounce, Braintree, Brightcove, Brightmail, Browserstack, Calastone, Callsign Inc, Campaignmonitor, Can Capital, Capricoast, Cardspring, Carestack, Carto, Carwow, Catawiki, Celions, Centrify, Chargebee, Check24, CheckR, Clevertap, Cloudera, Code42 Software, Cogoport, Cohesity, Complex Media, Comscore, Consure Medical, Corelight, Cormetrics, Cornershop, Couchbase, Coverfox, Crowdanalytix, CrowdStrike, Crownit, Curefit, Curejoy, Dashdash, Despegar, DocuSign, Dropbox, Dropcam, Educreations, Elo7, Ensatus, Etsy, Fiverr, Flaregames, Flipkart, ForeScout, ForgeRock, Forus Health, GameForge, GoCardless, Hailo, High Gear Media, HolidayIQ, HootSuite, HotelTonight, Hotelogix, HouseTrip, Invoca, Iron Planet, Joyus, Jut, KDS International, Kirusa, Knewton, Krux, KupiVIP, LearnVest, Legendary, LetsVenture, LightSpeed, Lookout, Lot18, Lynda.com, Lyst, Medio Systems, MemSQL, MetraTech, Mind Candy, Mind Lab, MindTickle, Mitra Biotech, MobStac, Model N, MyFitnessPal, Myntra, MySmartPrice, Nextbit, Nimble Storage, Noosh, Nor1, Olacabs, Omneon Video Networks, Onco, OnForce, Onsitego, Opal Labs, OpenGamma, OpenX, Opower, Origami Logic, Osmo, OzForex, Packlink, Pagerduty, Parature, Paxata, Payfit, P-Cube, Pearl Automation, Peopledoc, Peoplesupport, Perbit, Pharmaccx, Picture Tel, Pillpack, Pixate, Playfish, Plays.tv, Plex Systems, Podium, Polycom, Pond5, Poplicus, Portal Software, Portea, Power2SME, Prezi, Primaryio, Probe Information Services, Propeller Aero, Proptiger, Prosper, Qikpod, Qlik, QMC, Qriously, Qualtrics, Qubit, Quidsi, Quiklo, QwikCilver, Qwilt, Radar, Raise, Rapt, Reactivity, Realnetworks, RelatIQ, RGB Networks, Rovio, Scale, Seatgeek, Shopmium, Showroomprive, SilverRail, SimpliVity, Sonatype, Spotify, Spreadshirt, Squarespace, Sumo Logic, Sunrun, Supercell, SureWaves, Swiftkey, Taxi For Sure, Teabox, Tenable Network Security, Transcend, Trifacta, Trufa, TRUSTARC, Varonis Systems, Veritas, Vigilent Corp, Vinculum, Vox Media, Webroot, Wonga, WyzAnt, YapStone, Yodlee, YuMe, ZopNow

Other Locations:
2 Jack London Alley
San Francisco, CA 94107
Phone: 415-293-1100

1 New Burlington Place
6th Floor
London W1S 2HR
United Kingdom
Phone: 44 0 20 7170 1000

886/A Confident Electra
17th E. Main Road
6th Block, Koramangala
Bengaluru 560095
India
Phone: 91 80 4353 9800

Key Executives:
Andrew Braccia, Partner
Education: BS, Business Administration, University of Arizona
Background: Yahoo!
Directorships: 99designs, Anchor, Braintree, Cloudera, Cornershop, Etsy, Gametime, HotelTonight, Lynda.com, MyFitnessPal, PagerDuty, Prezi, Slack, Squarespace, UserTesting, Vox Media, Xero
Miles Clements, Partner
Education: University of Virginia; Harvard Business School
Background: lynda.com
Directorships: Atlassian, Bird, DJI, HudI, Lynda.com, MessageBird, Podium, SeatGeek, UiPath
Sameer Gandhi, Partner
Education: MSEE, BSEE, MIT; MBA, Stanford Graduate School of Business
Background: Partner, Sequoia Capital; Principal, Broadview
Directorships: Bonobos, CrowdStrike, DJI, Dropbox, Dropcam, Flipkart, Freshworks, Grovo, Jet, Plex Systems, Raise, Rylo, Spotify, Venmo, Yapstone
Amit Kumar, Partner
Education: University of California, Berkeley
Background: CardSpring; Twitter
Directorships: Amino, Cornershop, Deserve, Plays.tv, Skip, Smash.gg, Usertesting, Visor
Daniel Levine, Partner
Education: Yale University
Background: Dropbox; Chartio; TechCrunch
Directorships: Bird, Checkr, Heptio, MessageBird, Mux, Rylo, Scale, Sentry, Trifacta
Ping Li, Partner
Education: AB, Harvard University; MBA Stanford Graduate School of Business
Background: Senior Product Line Manager, Juniper Networks; Singapore Telecom; Goldman Sachs Asia
Directorships: Blue Jeans Network, Cloudera, Code42 Software, Demisto, Heptio, Lookout, Plays.tv, Split Software, Sysdig, Tenable Network Security, Trifacta
John Locke, Partner
Education: Woodrow Wilson School; Princeton University
Background: Senior Associate, Housitonic Partners
Directorships: Braintree, CrowdStrike, GoFundMe, Invoice2Go, Lightspeed, OzForex, Pond5, QMC, SeatGeek, Tenable Network Security, The Zebra, Venmo, WorldRemit, WyzAnt
Steve Loughlin, Partner
Education: Stanford University
Background: SalesforceIQ;
Directorships: Ascend.io, Ironclad, Split Software
Arun Mathew, Partner
Education: University of Pennsylvania; Stanford University
Background: Squarespace
Directorships: Avici Systems

Venture Capital & Private Equity Firms / Domestic Firms

Vas Natarajan, Partner
Education: University of Pennsylvania
Directorships: Blameless, DeepMap, Frame.io, InVision, Ironclad, Propeller Aero, Segment, Skydio, Spoke, Tune
Nate Niparko, Partner
Education: Dartmouth; Stanford Graduate School of Business
Background: Amazon Web Service; Invoice2Go
Directorships: Algolia, BrowserStack, CrowdStrike, Ethos, G2 Crowd, HootSuite, PagerDuty, RiskRecon, Tenable Network Security
Ryan Sweeney, Partner
Education: BBA, University of Notre Dame; MBA, Harvard Business School
Background: Summit Partners; North Bridge
Directorships: AirWatch, Atlassian, Braintree, BrowserStack, GOAT, HootSuite, Invoice2Go, Lightspeed, Narvar, Ozforex, PagerDuty, Qualtrics, Simility, Squarespace, Venmo, VSCO, Xero
Rich Wong, Partner
Education: BS, Materials Science & Engineering, MIT; MBA, MIT Sloane School of Management
Background: Senior Vice President, Openwave; Chief Marketing Officer, Covad Communications; Brand Manager, Proctor & Gamble; Brand Manager, McKinsey
Directorships: Atlassian, Checkr, Instabug, Osmo, Qwilt, ServiceChannel, Tune, UniPath

28 ACCEL-KKR LLC
2180 Sand Hill Road
Suite 300
Menlo Park, CA 94025

Phone: 650-289-2460 Fax: 650-289-2461
web: www.accel-kkr.com

Mission Statement: Accel-KKR seeks investment opportunities in lower middle market technology companies, primarily in the software and technology-enabled services industries, with strong growth potential.

Fund Size: $1.3 billion
Founded: 2000
Average Investment: $10 - $100 million
Minimum Investment: $10 million
Investment Criteria: Middle Market, Mid-Market Buyouts, Acquisitions, Recapitalizations, Going-Private Transactions
Industry Group Preference: Technology, Software, Hardware, Internet Technology, Enterprise Services, Infrastructure, IT Enabled Services, Data Storage, Storage Networking, Internet, Information Technology
Portfolio Companies: Abrigo, Agilence Inc., Cendyn, Cielo, ClickDimensions, Continuity, Datapipe, Delta Data Software, Duett AS, Efreightsolutions, Enverus, Envizi, Energy Services Group, ESO, FastSpring, FM:Systems, Green Mountain Technology, HighWire, Humanforce, InSight Mobile Data, IntegriChain, ISolved HCM, Insurance Technologies Corporation, Jaggaer, KCS, Kimble, Lemontech, Ministry Brands, OrthoFi, Patientco, Paymentus, Pegasus, Peppermint Technology, PointRight, PrismHR, Reapit, Safeguard Global, Salsa Labs, Sandata Technologies, Seequent, ShowingTime, Siigo, Smart Communications, SugarCRM, TEAM Software, TELCOR, ToolsGroup, TrueCommerce, US eDirect, Vistex, Vitu, Vobile

Other Locations:
3284 Northside Parkway Northwest
Suite 475
Atlanta, GA 30327
Phone: 678-809-5989 Fax: 678-905-6809

21 Queen Anne's Street
London SW1H 9BU
United Kingdom
Phone: 44-02077696736

Key Executives:
Tom Barnds, Co-Managing Partner
Education: AB, Princeton University; MBA, Stanford Graduate School of Business
Background: Managing Director, Nassau Capital; Business Development Manager, McGaw; Investment Banking Division, Alex. Brown & Sons
Directorships: Abila, Datapipe, EPiServer, Highjump, Kerridge Commercial Systems, Motor Vehicle Software Corporation, North Plains, Transzap
Rob Palumbo, Co-Managing Partner
Education: AB, Princeton University
Background: Co-Head, Software Investment Banking, Thomas Weisel Partners; Deutsche Bank; Information Technology Banking, Stephens, Inc.; Mergers & Acquisitions Analyst, Alex. Brown & Sons
Directorships: Cielo, EA Holdings, Infinisource, North Plains, On Center Software, Paymentus
Jason Klein, Senior Advisor
Education: BS, Finance & Accounting, Pennsylvania State University; MBA, Finance & Strategic Management, Wharton School
Background: Investment Banker, Goldman Sachs; PricewaterhouseCoopers; Financial Advisory Services, Cooper & Lybrand; Arthur Andersen
Directorships: EA Holdings, EPiServer, Highjump, Infinisource, Kerridge Commercial Systems, Motor Vehicle Software Corporation, Paymentus
Greg Williams, Managing Director
Education: AB, History, Harvard College; MBA, Darden School of Business, University of Virginia
Background: Managing Director, CapitalSoruce; Sturm Group; Mergers & Acquisitions Investment Banking, JP Morgan; Bond Corporation; Analyst, Fleet Financial Group
Directorships: Cielo, Clavis Insight, EPiServer, One.com, PageUp People, PrismHR
Patrick Fallon, Managing Director/COO/CCO
Education: AB, Economics, Harvard College; MBA, Amos Tuck School of Business Adminstration, Dartmouth College; CPA
Background: Partner & COO, Gryphon Investors; Investment Banker, Donaldson, Lufkin & Jenrette; Investment Banker, Credit Suisse; KPMG
Directorships: Banker's Toolbox, HighWire Press
Dean Jacobson, Managing Director
Education: AB, Harvard University; MBA, Stanford Graduate School of Business
Background: VP, Summit Partners; Director, Corporate Development, Vonage; Associate Director, 3i; Robertson Stephens
Directorships: Abila, Cielo, EPiServer, Infinisource, North Plains, Oildex
Park Durrett, Managing Director
Education: BS, Cornell University; MBA, Kellogg School of Management, Northwestern University
Background: Principal, The CapStreet Group; Associate, Technology Crossover Ventures; Associate, 3i Group; Robertson Stephens
Directorships: Abila, EA Holdings, HighWire Press, On Center Software

29 ACCELEPRISE
San Francisco, CA

web: acceleprise.vc

Mission Statement: Acceleprise focuses investments in SaaS accelerators.

Geographic Preference: US
Fund Size: $70 Million
Founded: 2012
Industry Group Preference: SaaS, Software, Technology
Portfolio Companies: Agreemint, Drishyam AI, ENVision Mobile, GroLens, PassRight, Piio, Sparkir, StoriiCare, TestRigor AI

Key Executives:
Michael Cardamone, Managing Director/General Partner
Education: BS, Syracuse University; MBA, Columbia

Venture Capital & Private Equity Firms / Domestic Firms

Business School
Background: Managing Partner, United States Federation of Small Business; VP of Partnerships, AcademixDirect Inc.; Venture Partner, SaaStr; Advisor, Mya Systems
Whitney Sales, General Partner
Education: BA, University of California, San Diego
Background: Inside Sales Manager, Meltwater Group; Director of Sales, SpringAhead; Director of Midwest Sales, Demandbase; VP of Sales, People Data Labs; Creator, The Sales Method
Nina Stepanov, Principal/Director of Partnerships
Education: BBA, Northeastern University
Background: Associate Marketing Manager, Inbound.org; Head of Marketing, ViewPoint Cloud; Associate, Techstars

30 ACCELERATOR LIFE SCIENCE PARTNERS
2815 Eastlake Avenue East
Suite 300
Seattle, WA 98102
Phone: 206-957-7300 **Fax:** 206-957-7399
e-mail: info@acceleratorlsp.com
web: www.acceleratorlsp.com

Mission Statement: Accelerator Corporation, founded in 2003, finances and manages companies in the biotechnology sector. The company has established and built a proprietary array of sources, as well as a key set of start-up resources. Accelerator aims to utilize these resources to help build emerging biotechnology companies and ensure their long-term success.

Fund Size: $305 million
Founded: 2003
Investment Criteria: Startup, Early Stage
Industry Group Preference: Biotechnology, Life Sciences, Healthcare
Portfolio Companies: ApoGen Biotechnologies, Lodo Therapeutics, Magnolia NeuroSciences, Petra Pharma, Proniras, Rodeo Therapeutics

Other Locations:
430 East 29th Street
Suite 840
New York, NY 10016
Phone: 646-282-5990 **Fax:** 646-828-5989

10996 Torreyana Road
Suite 270
San Diego, CA 92121
Phone: 206-957-7300 **Fax:** 206-957-7399

Key Executives:
Thong Q Le, Chief Executive Officer
Education: BA, Harvard University; Templeton College, Univ. of Oxford
Background: Managing Director, WRF Capital; President/CEO, MiniMeals Inc.; Consultant, Capital Management Consulting; Raymond James & Associates; Singer & Xenos Investment Management Company; Capital Management Group LLC
Directorships: Evergreen Venture Capital Association, Washington Biotechnology & Biomedical Association, Washington Global Health Fund
Ian A.W. Howes, Chief Financial Officer
Education: BS, Accounting and Finance, University Of Warwick; MBA, Kenan-Flagler Business School at the University Of North Carolina
Background: CFO, Heart Metabolics; CFO, Scioderm; CFO, Akebia Therapeutics; CFO, Senior VP, Coporate Development Of Serenex
Kendall Mohler, PhD, Chief Development Officer
Education: BS, University of Kansas; PhD, Immunology, University of Texas Health Science Center
Background: Senior Vice President, Chief Science Officer, Juno Therapeutics; Co-Founder, Trubion Pharmaceuticals; Vice President, Biological Sciences Of Imunex Corporation
Court R. Turner, J.D., Chief Business Officer
Education: BS, Psychology, San Diego State University; JD, San Diego School Of Law
Background: Operating Partner, ALSP; Venture Partner, Avalon Ventures; Executive Manager, Kalypsys; Director Of Business Development, Aurora Biosciences
Directorships: Synthorx, Cellular Approaches, RQx Pharmaceuticals
Alice Chen, PhD, Vice President
Education: BS, Chemical Engineering, University of California, Berkeley; PhD, Chemical Engineering, Stanford University
Background: Director Of Technologies, Quell Pharmaceuticals
Directorships: Evergreen Fund Advisory Committee, Fred Hutch Cancer Research Center, Life Science Washington

31 ACCELERATOR VENTURES
2020 Union Street
San Francisco, CA 94123
e-mail: info@acceleratorventures.com
web: www.acceleratorventures.com

Mission Statement: Accelerator Ventures is a San Francisco-based venture capital firm that invests in early stage technology companies. Accelerator Ventures brings to entrepreneurs its strong understanding of technology, capital, and venture markets. We actively help companies with financing strategy, business development, customer introductions and management team development. Our goal is to invest at the earliest stages of a company's fund raising efforts and to leverage our domain expertise in order to help companies get on the path toward profitability. We leverage our network of angel investors, early stage funds and venture capital firms in order to meet the funding needs of our portfolio companies.

Investment Criteria: Early Stage, Seed, Start-Up
Industry Group Preference: Technology
Portfolio Companies: Appboy, Data Pop, Cloudmark, Cornerstone On Demand, Double Dutch, FairLoan, FlashSoft, Freeform, Gigwalk, Grouply, Hivemapper, Indextank, Influitive, Insikt, iSocket, Lively, Locomobi, Longtail Video, Mytime, Nutanix, Oyster.com, Playnomics, Rinse, Rockbot, SALIDO, Siftery, SixUp, Smartling, Snapdocs, SocialWire, Sproutling, StudySoup, Talkable, Tapulous, Trigo, Trovix, Web Methods, Zappos.com, Zimbio, Zynga

Key Executives:
Alexander Lloyd, Managing Director
Education: BA, International Relations, University Of Pennsylvania; MBA, Entrepreneurial Management, The Wharton School
Background: Venture Partner, Rustic Canyon Partners; Business Development Manager, Microsoft; Product Manager, SGI; Marketing, Activision; Marketing, Apple Computer; Financial Analyst, Goldman Sachs
Directorships: SideLuck
Ben T. Smith, IV, Venture Partner
Education: BS, Mechanical Engineering, University Of California, Davis; MBA, Tepper School of Business
Background: President, Reply Media; Co-Founder & CEO, MerchantCircle; SVP Corporate Development, Bortlan; Co-Founder, Spoke
Directorships: Spoke, Giu Mobile
Tom Cervantez, Venture Partner
Education: BA, Business Administration, Loyola Marymount University; JD/MBA, Harvard
Background: Founder, Business Counsel Law Group LLP.
John Paul Milciunas, Entrepreneur In-Residence
Education: Georgia Institute of Technology
Background: Strategic Partnerships and Business Developmnet, Yahoo!; Product Strategy Consultant, Checkfree; CEO, SPI Dynamics; Business Strategy Consultant, Scient
Linda Jacobson, VR/AR Venture Partner
Education: BS, Journalism, Boston University College of Communication

Venture Capital & Private Equity Firms / Domestic Firms

32 ACCENT CAPITAL PARTNERS LLC
One Embarcadero Center
Suite 1540
San Francisco, CA 94111

Phone: 415-981-7238
web: www.accentcapitalpartners.com

Mission Statement: Accent Capital Partners is a private equity advisory firm based in San Francisco. The firm focuses on growing middle market companies and offers advice on a number of issues, including sources of growth capital and capital structure.
Geographic Preference: United States, California
Founded: 2002
Key Executives:
Milton K Reeder, Managing Partner
Education: BBA, University of Michigan
Background: President & COO, Meridian Industrial Trust; CPA, Deloitte Touche

33 ACCESS BRIDGE-GAP VENTURES
Cambridge, MA 02142

web: www.accessindustries.com

Mission Statement: Access BridgeGap Ventures is a life sciences venture investment initiative to fund early-stage companies in the therapeutics space. Leveraging its team's experience in startup creation, technology commercialization and venture investing, Access BridgeGap will fund early-stage startups and also create de-novo spinoffs around potential high-impact technologies, many of which are still in academic labs. Funding activities will focus on scientists, entrepreneurs, and companies that are developing novel and clinically relevant therapeutic approaches and platforms that can become must-have solutions for patients, physicians, and payers.
Fund Size: $75 million
Founded: 1986
Investment Criteria: Early-Stage
Industry Group Preference: Natural Resources & Chemicals, Media & Telecommunications, Real Estate
Portfolio Companies: 20 East End, Access Technology Ventures, Al Film, Amedia, Clal Industries Ltd., EP Energy, Faena Group, First Access Entertainment, Grand-Hotel du Cap-Ferrat, Grand Peaks, Ice Group, LyondellBesell, MBS Media Campus, One & Only Ocean Club, Perform, R.G.E. Group Ltd., Sunset Tower Hotel, UC RUSAL, Warner Music Group
Key Executives:
Len Blavatnik, Founder/Chairman
Education: MA, Computer Science, Columbia University; MBA, Harvard Business School

34 ACCESS CAPITAL
405 Park Avenue
New York, NY 10022

Phone: 212-644-9300 Fax: 212-644-5488
Toll-Free: 800-421-0034
e-mail: contactus@accesscapital.com
web: www.accesscapital.com

Mission Statement: Access Capital provide immediate capital to small and middle market companies, closely working with law firms and accounting firms.
Geographic Preference: United States
Founded: 1986
Investment Criteria: Early-Stage, Second-Stage
Industry Group Preference: Consumer Services, Distribution, Industrial Equipment, Medical & Health Related, Staffing, IT Consulting, Printing, Software, Transportation
Portfolio Companies: Avatar Alliance, Diagnostek, Inc., ETC, Inc., Inmark Services, Inc., National Tele-Communications (NTC), INC 500 Companies
Key Executives:
Angela Santi, Co-President
Education: BS, St. John's University
Paul Mehring, Co-President
Education: BS, Finance, Villanova University

35 ACCESS VENTURE PARTNERS LLC
8787 Turnpike Drive
Suite 260
Westminster, CO 80031

web: www.accessvp.com

Mission Statement: Access Venture Partners is an early stage venture capital fund. Together over the past 14 years, the partners at Access Venture Partners have invested in over fifty early stage companies and have served as founders and early executives of numerous companies. Through this experience Access Ventures Partners has built an understanding of how to navigate the challenges associated with building successful companies and drive them to success.
Geographic Preference: Mid Continent
Founded: 1999
Average Investment: $2 million
Minimum Investment: $250,000
Investment Criteria: Seed, Early Stage
Industry Group Preference: Computer Hardware & Software, Internet Technology, Telecommunications, Infrastructure, Semiconductors, E-Commerce & Manufacturing, Technology, Clean Technology, SaaS, Data & Analytics, New Media, Digital Media & Marketing, Cloud Computing, Consumer Internet, Data Security
Portfolio Companies: Alces Technology, AlchemyAPI, Accel Graphics, Alert Logic, Ascent 360, Bionumerik, Brightware, CCBN, Channel Technology, Cloud Elemts, Commercial Tribe, Convey, Craftsy, CVA, Dizzion, eSionic, Enterprise Link, ETI, Firehole Composites, Handel Information Technologies Inc., Hotrail, Innova, Inspirato, Kapost, Listen MD, LogRhythm, Nexgen Storage, Pawngo, Osteobiologics, Quickarrow, Rebit, Red Canary, RoundPegg, ShapeShift, Shotzr, Skydex, Slamdata, Spotlight, Tap Influence, Tenscorcomm, Thought Equity, Trividia, Taskeasy, Tendril, TopFan, TrackVia
Key Executives:
Kirk Holland, Managing Director
Education: BS, Electrical Engineering, University of Washington; MBA, Stanford University
Background: General Partner, Vista Ventures; Procter & Gamble; Jupiter Media
Directorships: RoundPegg, NexGen, Sympoz
Frank Mendicino III, Co-Founder/Managing Director
Education: BA, Political Science, University of California, Berkeley
Background: Analyst, Woodside Fund II; Senior Associate, Woodside Fund III
Directorships: LogRhythm, TrackVia, Thought Equity, Giveo, Inspirato
Brian D Wallace, Managing Director
Education: BS, Business Finance, University of Arizona
Background: Corporate Securities Attorney, Fairfield and Woods PC
Directorships: PitchEngine, Pawngo, Rebit, Firehole Composites, Alces, Spotlight
Frank Mendicino II, Venture Partner
Education: BS, Business Administration, Law Degree, University of Wyoming
Background: General Partner, Woodside Funds; Wyoming Attorney General; Board Director, University of Wyoming; Western Research Institute
Directorships: Skydex, TensorComm

Venture Capital & Private Equity Firms / Domestic Firms

36 ACCOLADE PARTNERS
2001 M Street North West
Suite 801
Washington, DC 20036

Phone: 202-775-5595
e-mail: info@accoladepartners.com
web: www.accoladepartners.com

Mission Statement: Accolade Partners' mission is to generate superior returns through a diversified portfolio of venture capital and growth equity investments focused on technology and healthcare.

Geographic Preference: United States
Investment Criteria: Early-Stage
Industry Group Preference: Technology, Healthcare
Portfolio Companies: Accel, Accel KKR, Andreessen Horowitz, Amplify Partners, Anthos, August Capital, Bolt, Clarus Ventures, Harrison Metal, IA Ventures, Ignition, JMI Equity, Leerink Transformation Partners, Level Equity, Mucker Capital, North Bridge Growth Equity, Notation Caption, OrbiMed Healthcare Fund Management, Pivot North Capital, Shore Capital Partners, Sverica, Radian Capital, Thoma Bravo, Water Street, Acquia, Avant Credit, Compuware, Hightail, Sun Basket, Tiger Text, Alloy, Centerpoint, Election, FFC, General Catalyst, Golden Gate, HLM, Impact, Sevin Rosen, Skyline, Sternhill, TCV, Telegraph Hill, Telesoft, Trident, Walden

Key Executives:
Joelle Kayden, Managing Member
Education: BA, Smith College; MBA, Stanford Graduate School of Business
Background: CFO, ABS Ventures, Alex Brown & Sons
Atul Rustgi, Partner
Education: BBA, University of Michigan; MBA, Harvard Business School
Background: Senior Management, McKinsey & Company; Robin Hood Foundation
Andrew Salenbier, Partner/Chief Operating Officer
Education: BA, University of Virginia; MBA, Georgetown University
Background: Georgetown Endowment; Cambridge Associates

37 ACCOMPLICE
56 Wareham Street
3rd Floor
Boston, MA 02118

Phone: 617-588-2600
web: www.accomplice.co

Mission Statement: Accomplice, formerly the technology side of Atlas Venture, is a venture capital firm that focuses on early stage technology investments.

Fund Size: $200 million
Founded: 2015
Investment Criteria: Early Stage
Industry Group Preference: Technology
Portfolio Companies: AngelList, Button, Captricity, Carbon Black, Clypd, Currency Cloud, DataRobot, DataXu, DraftKings, Earnest, Hopper, InsightSquared, Integral Ad Science, Joist, Keas, Kinvey, Lagoa, Maiden Lane Ventures, Mojo Motors, Moo, Nutonian, OwnerIQ, OYO Sportstoys, Patreon, PillPack, Plastiq, Quirky, Recorded Future, Reddo Mobility, SimpleReach, Skillz, Sqrrl, Threat Stack, Valore, Veracode

Key Executives:
Jeff Fagnan, Founding Partner
Education: BS, Management & Mathematics, University of Alaska; MBA, Finance & Operations, University of Rochester
Background: Partner, Seed Capital Partners; Booz Allen & Hamilton; Nortel Networks
Directorships: Bit9, InsightSquared, Objective Logistics, Snapguide, Whoop, Keas

Ryan Moore, Founding Partner
Education: AB, Princeton University
Background: General Partner, GrandBanks Capital; SOFTBANK Venture Capital
Directorships: Gocella, Plastiq, SimpleTuition, Flashnotes, Clypd, Moo

38 ACCRETIVE LLC
660 Madison Avenue
12th Floor
Suite 1215
New York, NY 10065

Phone: 646-282-3131 Fax: 646-282-3138
e-mail: info@accretivellc.com
web: www.accretivellc.com

Mission Statement: Accretive is a private equity firm focused on working with talented people to build world-class companies that deliver meaningful and unique value to their customers.

Geographic Preference: United States, Western Europe
Fund Size: $200 million
Founded: 1999
Investment Criteria: Startups
Industry Group Preference: Healthcare, Education
Portfolio Companies: Accolade, Accretive Commerce, Accretive Health, Accumen, AlphaStaff, Arise, Equitant, Everspring, Exult, Fandango, Insureon, Quantum Health, Xchanging

Key Executives:
J Michael Cline, Founding Partner
Education: BS, Cornell University; MBA, Harvard Business School
Background: General Partner, General Atlantic Partners; Co-Founder, Exult; Xchanging; Fandango; Accolade; Associate, McKinsey & Company
Directorships: Panthera, National Fish and Wildlife Foundation
Edgar Bronfman Jr, Managing Partner
Background: Chairman/CEO, Warner Music Group; Chairman/CEO, Lexa Partners LLC; Executive Vice Chairman, Vivendi Universal; President/CEO, The Seagram Company Ltd.
Directorships: Arise, Accolade, Accumen, Everspring, AlphaStaff
Anne-Marie Shelley, General Councel/Chief Compliance Officer
Education: BA, Yale University; JD, Villavona University School of Law
Background: Corporate Attorney, Chadbourne & Park, LLP; Associate, Fried, Frank, Harris, Shiriver & Jacobson
Tony Shum, Chief Financial Officer
Education: BA, Pace University; CPA
Background: Manager, Audit & Advisory Services, KPMG LLP
Mimi Wolfe Strouse, Senior Advisor
Education: BA, History & African Studies, Trinity College; University of Cape Town
Background: Managing Director & Partner, Warburg Pincus; Principal, General Atlantic Partners; Financial Analyst, Credit Suisse First Boston
Directorships: Everspring
Ben West, Advisor
Education: BBA, University of Oklahoma
Background: Consultant, Boston Consulting Group; Sevin Rosen Funds; RiskMetrics Group

39 ACCUITIVE MEDICAL VENTURES LLC
295 Premiere Parkway
Suite 100
Atlanta, GA 30097

Phone: 678-812-1101
e-mail: charlie@amvpartners.com
web: www.amvpartners.com

Mission Statement: Accuitive Medical Ventures LLC invests in and helps develop early stage and expansion stage medical device and technology companies.
Geographic Preference: United States
Fund Size: $230 million
Founded: 2003
Average Investment: $5 million
Minimum Investment: $1 million
Investment Criteria: Early Stage, Expansion Stage
Industry Group Preference: Health Related, Medical Technology, Information Technology, Medical Devices
Portfolio Companies: AcuFocus, AqueSys, AxoGen, CardioFocus, Inogen, Intuity Medical, LipoSonix, MyoScience, Neuronetics, Nevro, Respicardia, Sadra Medical, Sebacia, Softscope, Torax Medical, WaveTec Vision
Other Locations:
5542 First Coast Highway
Suite 301
Fernandina Beach, FL 32034
Phone: 904-261-9690
Key Executives:
Thomas D Weldon, Chairman/Managing Director
Education: BS, Industrial Engineering, Purdue University; MBA, Indiana University
Background: The Innovation Factory; Chairman/CEO, Novoste Corporation; Chairman, LipoSonix; Arthur Young & Company; Key Pharmaceuticals
Directorships: MyoScience, Respicardia, Sebacia
Charles E Larsen, Managing Director
Education: BS, Mechanical Engineering, New Jersey Institute of Technology
Background: Co-Founder/Vice Chairman, The Innovation Factory; Co-Founder, Novoste Corporation; Cordis Corporation; Key Pharmaceuticals; Parke-Davis/Warner Lambert
Directorships: Acufocus, CardioFocus, Inogen, Intuity
Gordon T Wyatt, Chief Financial Officer
Education: BS, Accounting & Finance, Lehigh University
Background: SVP, Finance, WebMD Corporation; General Electric Company
Cory S Anderson, Principal
Education: BS, MS, Biomedical Engineering, Tulane University; MBA, Emory University
Background: Program Manager, The Innovation Factory; Product Manager, Novoste Corporation
Directorships: AqueSys
Anthony V Lando, Partner
Education: BS, Physics, Manhattan College; Georgia Institute of Technology; University of California
Background: COO, BTG PLC; Senior Marketing & Product Development, Philips Medical Systems; Stone & Webster Engineering

40 ACERO CAPITAL
2440 Sand Hill Road
Suite 101
Menlo Park, CA 94025
Phone: 650-233-7100 **Fax:** 650-233-7112
web: www.acerovc.com

Mission Statement: Acero Capital is a venture capital firm that invests in technology enabled services, including enterprise mobility, IT infrastructure, enterprise cloud applications and data analytics. Acero actively pursues companies with resourceful management teams, capital-efficient business models, and innovative approaches to large and established markets.
Fund Size: $150 million
Industry Group Preference: Information Technology, Clean Technology, Energy, Technology-Enabled Services
Portfolio Companies: Argyle Data, Banyan Energy, Bitzer Mobile, Contrast Security, HyperGrid, Livehive, QuantPower, Swrve
Key Executives:
Rami Elkhatib, General Partner
e-mail: rami@acerovc.com
Education: BS, Computer & Electrical Engineering, Purdue University; MBA, Massachusetts Institute of Technology
Background: General Partner, Southeast Technology Funds; Co-Founder, Datacme Software; Oneworld Software Solutions; UBS Warburg
Directorships: Argyle Data, Banyan Energy, Contrast Security, Gridstore, LiveHive, Swrve Mobile
Elena Winefeld, Vice President
e-mail: jayme@acerovc.com
Education: BA, Economics and Management, Technion Israel Institute Of Technology
Background: Fund Controller, Financial Analysis Manager, Nokia Growth Parners
Elisa del Gaudio, Principal
e-mail: elisa@acerovc.com
Education: BA, Human Biology, Stanford University
Background: Deutsche Bank
Charles Ho, Venture Partner
e-mail: charles@acerovc.com
Education: BS, Chemical Engineering, University of Texas; MBA, Columbia University
Background: Standard Bank; COO/Director, Lithcon Group; Lehman Brothers; UBS Warburg; Deloitte Consulting

41 ACI CAPITAL
299 Park Avenue
34th Floor
New York, NY 10171
Phone: 212-634-3333 **Fax:** 212-634-3330
web: www.acicapital.com

Mission Statement: ACI Capital invests in middle-market companies across a variety of industries. The firm partners with exceptional management teams to help build valuable companies.
Geographic Preference: United States
Fund Size: $335 million
Founded: 1986
Average Investment: $20 - $50 million
Minimum Investment: $10 million
Investment Criteria: Middle Market, Lower-Middle Market
Industry Group Preference: Consumer Products, Manufacturing, Transportation, Infrastructure, Alternative Energy, Business Products & Services, Financial Services, Logistics, Media, Healthcare
Portfolio Companies: Accent Energy, Cornhusker Energy, Excel Polymers, Healthy Directions, Hollywood Tans, Sundance, United Logistics
Key Executives:
Kevin S Penn, Managing Director
e-mail: kspenn@acicapital.com
Education: BS, Economics, Wharton School, University of Pennsylvania; MBA, Harvard Business School
Background: EVP/Chief Investment Officer, First Spring Corporation; Principal, Adler & Shaykin; Founding Member, Leveraged Buyout Group, Morgan Stanley
Directorships: Accent Energy, Cornhusker Energy, Excel Polymers, Healthy Directions, SEMX, Sundance Catalog, Hollywood Tans, Mt. Sinai Hospital Department of Medicine
Matthew Bronfman, Managing Director
e-mail: mbronfman@acicapital.com
Education: BA, Williams College; MBA, Harvard Business School
Background: Chairman/CEO, Candle Acquisitions Company; Chairman/CEO, Sterling Cellular Holdings, LP; Goldman Sachs; Cadillac Fairview Corporation Limited
Directorships: Bronfman Fisher Real Estate Holdings, Earnest Partners, Palace Candles Inc.

Venture Capital & Private Equity Firms / Domestic Firms

Mitchell Quain, Managing Director
e-mail: mquain@acicapital.com
Education: University of Pennsylvania; Harvard Business School
Background: Schroder Wertheim; Industrial Manufacturing Group, Wall Street; President, Machinery Analysts Group
Directorships: Hardinge Inc., Titan International, Magnetek Inc.
Mira Muhtadie, Vice President
e-mail: mmuhtadie@acicapital.com
Education: BA, Economics, University of Pennsylvania; MBA, Wharton School, University of Pennsylvania
Background: Senior Associate, KPS Special Situations; Associate, Lightyear Capital; Analyst, Credit Suisse First Boston
Directorships: Hollywood Tans
Chad Ellis, Associate
e-mail: cellis@acicapital.com
Education: BA, Economics, University of Virginia
Background: Analyst, Mergers & Acquisitions Group, Rothschild Group

42 ACKERLEY PARTNERS LLC
1301 Second Avenue
Suite 1936
Seattle, WA 98101

Phone: 206-624-2888
e-mail: info@ackerley.com
web: ackerleypartners.com

Mission Statement: Ackerley Partners invests primarily in media and entertainment entities, including but not limited to: media content and programming, internet based media, digital broadcast and broadband, media metric/delivery technology and wireless marketing services.

Founded: 2002
Industry Group Preference: Media, Communications, Entertainment, New Media
Portfolio Companies: Cequint, CSTV, Elevation Partners, FastChannel, FlexPlay, Hidden City, Howcast, Jott, Judy's Book, Labrador Mobile, LicenseStream, Mobliss, Nascar Members Club, Plum, Screenlife, SpotTaxi.com, Twelvefold

Key Executives:
Christopher Ackerley, Co-Founder
Background: President, The Ackerley Group; Capital Markets Group, Bank of America
Ted Ackerley, Co-Founder
Background: Vice President, Ackerley Ventures
Directorships: LicenseStream, Hidden City Entertainment, Nascar Members Club
Kim Ackerley Cleworth, Co-Founder
Background: President, The Ginger & Barry Ackerley Foundation

43 ACKRELL CAPITAL
38 Keyes Avenue
South Lobby
Suite 200
San Francisco, CA 94129

Phone: 415-995-2000 Fax: 415-995-2002
e-mail: info@ackrell.com
web: www.ackrell.com

Mission Statement: A private investment bank interested in the following industries: Ag tech, cannabis, consumer goods, digital media, energy/alternative energy, entertainment, healthcare, real estate, semiconductors, software, and sports.

Founded: 2003
Investment Criteria: Middle-market
Industry Group Preference: Cannabis, Software, Technology, Healthcare, Consumer Goods, Digital Media, Entertainment, Sports, Semiconductors, Energy, Real Estate

Portfolio Companies: Vuber, Défoncé, PROHBTD, Purch, Street Light Data, Blinkx, BranchOut, Urbansitter, EnergyHub

Key Executives:
Mike Ackrell, Founder/Managing Partner
Education: BS, Economics, Wharton School, University of Pennsylvania
Background: Sr. Managing Director, ABN AMRO's US Technology Investment Banking Group; WR Hambrecht+Co.; SVP of Technology Investment Banking, Donaldson Lufkin & Jenrette; DLJ
Iian Bunimovitz, Partner
Education: BA, Psychology, Bar Iian University; Business Admin., Baruch College
Background: CEO/Founder, Mama's LLC; CEO, Private Media Group
Bryan Castillo, Managing Director
Education: BS, Economics, Pennsylvania State University
Background: Kema Partners

44 ACME CAPITAL
800 Market Street
8th Floor
San Francisco, CA 94102

Phone: 415-805-8500
e-mail: info@acme.vc
web: acme.vc

Mission Statement: ACME invests in companies that leverage technology and data to pursue massive opportunities that have the potential to reshape industies - or create completely new ones; companies led by founders who dream big and execute smartly. ACME invests in founders buulding disruptive models that can capitalize on current platforms, as well as founders building breakthrough technologies that will enable emerging platforms.

Geographic Preference: US, Europe
Fund Size: $181 million
Founded: 2018
Average Investment: $3-8 million
Investment Criteria: Series A & B
Industry Group Preference: Hardware, Infrastructure, Automation, Business Model Innovation
Portfolio Companies: Airbnb, Beyond Games, Brandless, Cue, Curology, Cymmetria, Didi, Doctor On Demand, Fair, Hired, Ipsy, Light Field Lab, Opengov, Owl, PillPack, Quip, Rent the Runway, Replika, Robinhood, Slack, Stance, Stealth Space Company, Uber, Virgin Hyperloop One, Wag, Zendrive

Key Executives:
Scott Stanford, Co-Founder/Partner
Education: AB, Harvard College; MBA, Harvard Business School
Background: Goldman Sachs; General Atlantic Partners
Kirby Bartlett, Chief Operating/Compliance Officer
Education: BA, University of California, Berkeley; MBA, University of San Francisco
Background: Bay City Capital; Burrill & Craves

45 ACON INVESTMENTS
1133 Connecticut Avenue Northwest
Suite 700
Washington, DC 20036

Phone: 202-454-1100 Fax: 202-454-1101
e-mail: contact@aconinvestments.com
web: www.aconinvestments.com

Mission Statement: ACON Investments is a private equity firm that targets middle-market companies based in the United States and Latin America.

Geographic Preference: United States, Latin America
Fund Size: $750 million
Founded: 1996
Average Investment: $20 - $150 million
Investment Criteria: Middle Market

Industry Group Preference: Energy, Financial Services, Healthcare Services, Industrial, Media, Telecommunications, Retail, Consumer & Leisure, Consumer

Portfolio Companies: Amfora Packaging, APR Energy, BetterWare de Mexico, BSM, Cabo Telecom, Cool Gear International, Credivalores, Fiesta Mart, Funko, Grupo Sala, Hidrotenecias, IDX, Igloo Products, Injured Workers Pharmacy, Milagro Exploration, ProEnergy Holdings, Refac Optical Group, Saga Resource Partners, Sequitur Energy Resources, Suzo-Happ Group, Vetra Energia, Videomar Rede Nordeste SA, Waldo's, White Oak Resources

Other Locations:
4640 Admiralty Way
Suite 500
Los Angeles, CA 90292
Phone: 310-788-5713 **Fax:** 310-277-7582

Carrera 7 No. 83-29
Oficina 604
Edificio la Cabrera
Bogota
Colombia
Phone: 57 1 616 1684

Bosque de Alisos 47-A, Piso 2
Bosques de las Lomas
Cuajimalpa
Mexico D.F. 05120
Mexico
Phone: 52 55 2167 0999

Rua Bandeira Paulista 726
Cj 191
Sao Paulo SP 04532-002
Brazil
Phone: 55 11 3017-7666

Key Executives:
Bernard Aronson, Founder/Managing Partner
e-mail: baronson@aconinvestments.com
Education: BA, Humanities, University of Chicago
Background: International Advisor, Goldman Sachs; US Assistant Secretary of State for Inter-American Affairs
Directorships: Sequitur Energy Resources, ACON Franchise Holdings, The Nature Conservancy
Kenneth Brotman, Founder/Managing Partner
e-mail: kbrotman@aconinvestments.com
Education: BSe, Wharton School, University of Pennsylvania; MBA, Harvard Business School
Background: Partner, Veritas Capital; Associate, Bain Capital; Principal, Wasserstein Perella Management Partners
Directorships: Credifinanciera, Fiesta Mart, Funko, Grupo Sala, IDX, Igloo Products, ProEnergy, Refac/US Vision, Suzo-Happ, NetUno
Jonathan Ginns, Founder/Managing Partner
e-mail: jginns@aconinvestments.com
Education: BA, History, Brandeis University; MBA, Harvard Business School
Background: Senior Investment Officer, GEF Funds; Management Consultant, Booz Allen Hamilton
Directorships: Sequitur Energy Resources
Jorge Dickens, Managing Partner
Education: Harvard Business School
Background: Darby Overseas Investments
Directorships: Grupo Vizion; Hidrotenencias

46 ACORN CAMPUS VENTURES
3235 Kifer Road
Suite 150
Canta Clara, CA 95051

Phone: 408-598-4239
web: www.acorncampus.com

Mission Statement: The Acorn Campus Ventures approach is anchored by innovative methods, differentiated competitive strategies, and key corporate alliances. With access to a vast network of professional and personal connections throughout the Pacific Rim region, Acorn Campus Ventures principals bring expertise, diversity of experience, and exceptional insight to the process of developing a new business.

Fund Size: $100 million
Founded: 2000
Average Investment: $5 million
Investment Criteria: Seed, Startup, First Stage
Industry Group Preference: Communications Equipment, Telecommunications, Networking, Wireless Technologies, Internet, Life Sciences, Semiconductors
Portfolio Companies: Agate Logic, Inc., Atoptech, Inc., Autekbio, Inc., Aviva Communications, Inc., Boly Media Communications, Inc., Crown Bioscience, Inc., Eureka Therapeutics, Nano Photonics, Inc., NStreams Technologies, Inc., Optovue Corporation, Rasilient Systems, Inc., Siargo, Inc., Toplogis, Inc., Waterstone Pharmaceuticals

Key Executives:
Wu-Fu Chen, Chairman
Education: BSEE, National Taiwan University; MSEE, University of Florida; Doctoral program, Computer Science, University of California, Berkeley
Background: Founder/VP Engineering, Cascade Communications; VP, Cisco Systems; Chairman/CEO, Ardent Communications; Arris Networks
Hsing Kung, Managing Partner
Education: BSEE, National Cheng Kung University; PhD EE, University of California at Berkeley; MBA, Santa Clara University
Background: President/CEO, Pine Photonics; Senior VP, Opnext Inc.; Chairman, Luxnet Cororation; Co-Founder/VP, SDL, Inc.; Chairman, Monte Jade
David Tsang, Managing Member/Co-Founder
Education: MSEE, Santa Clara University; honorary PhD, International Technical Universitry
Background: Founder/Chairman, Oak Technology; Founder, Data Technology Corporation; Founder, Xebec
T Chester Wang, Managing Partner
Education: Tsinghua University, Taiwan; PhD Physics, University of Oregon
Background: Founder, Pacific Rim Electronics; Co-Founder, CMC; Developer, Silicon Valley Science Park; Developer, first Chinese-American shopping/community center, Pacific Rim Plaza; College Professor of Computer Science

47 ACORN GROWTH COMPANIES
621 N. Robinson
Suite 550
Oklahoma City, OK 73102

Phone: 405-737-2676
web: www.acorngrowthcompanies.com

Mission Statement: Acorn Growth Companies is a private equity firm dedicated to creating value and assisting with the growth of companies. The firm exclusively invests in the aerospace and defense industries.

Fund Size: $100 million
Investment Criteria: Early Stage, Middle Market, Growth Capital
Industry Group Preference: Aerospace, Defense and Government
Portfolio Companies: Aerospares 2000, AGC AeroComposites, APSE, Berry Aviation, Black Sage, CIS, DIMO Corp., North Coast Composites, Paul Fabs, Raisbeck, Robbins-Gioia, SinglePoint, Tods Aerospace, TSS Solutions, Unitech Composites and Structures

Other Locations:
1015 15th Street NW
Suite 350
Washington, DC 20005

Unit 35
Barratt Way
Industrial Estate
Harrow HA3 5TJ

Venture Capital & Private Equity Firms / Domestic Firms

United Kingdom
Phone: +44 (0)20-8863-8578
Key Executives:
Jeff Davis, Founding Partner
Education: BS, Marketing, Walton College of Business, University of Arkansas; Institute for Organization Management, Southern Methodist University
Background: President, Oklahoma Venture Forum; Founder, Oklahoma Aerospace Alliance
Rick Nagel, Managing Partner
Education: BS, Environmental Science, University of Oklahoma College of Engineering
Background: Platinum Equity; President, DCA
Directorships: State Chamber of Oklahoma
Jeff Morton, Senior Partner
Education: BA, Finance, Baldwin-Wallace College
Background: Senior Manager, Ernst & Young; Deloitte & Touche; CFO, Eateries
Robert Hinaman, Senior Partner
Education: BA, Economics, Lafayette College
Background: Managing Director, Mergers & Acquisitions, Chase Manhattan Bank; Chemical Bank; JP Morgan Chase; Partner, Jefferies Quarterdeck
Directorships: Maden Consulting, Gryphon Emerging Markets, Hunsworth plc
Laura Siegal, Executive Vice President
Education: BA, Economics, University Of California, San Diego; CPA
Background: CFO, NEO Tech; Vice President, Corporate Controller, Kratos Defense & Security Solutions
Directorships: Iteris, Board Of Governors and Supply Chain Executive Committee of Aerospace Industries Association
Gregory Bloom, Chief Operations Officer
Education: BA Economics and Business, University of California, LA; MBA, UCLA Anderson School of Management; Certificate in Defense Technology, Georgia Institute of Technology
Background: President, Seal Science; President/CEO, MSM Industries; Operating General Manager/Financial Executive, KB Home; Founder/CEO, SAFC
Craig Woodruff, Vice President, Finance/Chief Compliance Officer
Education: BS Political Science And Philosophy, Oklahoma State University; MBA, Oklahoma City Univeristy's Meinders School of Business
Background: Finance Director, Chesapeake Energy
Directorships: OKC Metropolitan Library Trust
Matthew Ritchie, Managing Director
Education: BA Public Policy Analysis, University of North Carolina; MBA, McDonough School of Business at Georgetown University
Background: Senior Manager, Northrop Grumman; The Cohen Group; Renaissance Strategic Advisors
Directorships: Young Professionals Committe of USO Metropolitan Washington-Baltimore

48 ACREW CAPITAL
471 Emerson Street
Palo Alto, CA 94301

e-mail: info@acrewcapital.com
web: acrewcapital.com

Mission Statement: Acrew Capital is interested in long-term partnerships with its portfolio companies within the tech industry.

Founded: 2019
Investment Criteria: Early Stage
Industry Group Preference: Artificial Intelligence, Technology, Healthcare, Retail, Consumer
Portfolio Companies: Amino, Aqua, Augtera Networks, BaubleBar Inc., Cato Networks, Chime Banking, CipherTrace, Coinbase, Crew, Deserve Cards, Divvy, Eden Health, Evident, Exabeam, Finix, ForeScout, Future Family, Gusto, Hotel Tonight, Indegy, Integris Software, Klar, The Muse, Pie Insurance, Solv, Stem, Tara AI, The RealReal, Troops, TruStar Technology, Worklete

Other Locations:
3004 16th Street
San Francisco, CA 94103

Key Executives:
Lauren Kolodny, Founding Partner
Background: Partner, Aspect Ventures; Product Marketing, Google
Mark Kraynak, Founding Partner
Background: Investor, Aspect Ventures; General Manager, Imperva Enterprise Business; Product Marketing, Check Point Software Technologies Ltd.; Marketing, CacheFlow; Consutlant, Ernst & Young's Center for Technology Enablement
Theresia Gouw, Founding Partner
Background: Co-Founder/Partner, Aspect Ventures; Managing General Partner, Accel; VP of Business Development & Sales, Release Software; Product Manager, Silicon Graphics
Vishal Lugani, Founding Partner
Education: AB, Economics, Harvard University
Background: Aspect Ventures; Greycroft Partners; Bain & Company
Asad Khaliq, Founding Principal
Education: Stanford University
Background: Investor, Aspect Ventures; PricewaterhouseCooper
Directorships: NextGen Partners

49 ACT ONE VENTURES
662 N Sepulveda
Suite 300
Los Angeles, CA 95066

e-mail: info@actoneventures.com
web: www.actoneventures.com

Mission Statement: Act One Ventures is a venture capital firm investing in software companies. 70% of Act One's portfolio companies were founded by women or minorities.

Founded: 2016
Investment Criteria: Seed
Industry Group Preference: Software, Technology
Portfolio Companies: Aiva Health, AuditBoard, Battery Streak, BLAZE, Bloomlife, Blutag, Branch, Camera IQ, Dray Alliance, Finix Payments, Glitzi, Naked Biome, Narrativ, Ordermark, Polycera, PRZM, QLess, SilverSheet, Social Native, Storyblaster, Tapcart, Veryfi, Wizely Finance, WiZR

Key Executives:
Michael Silton, Managing Director
Background: Executive Director, UCLA Venture Capital Fund; Founder/CEO, Rainmaker Systems; Co-Founder/CEO, UniDirect Systems Inc.
Alejandro Guerrero, Principal
Education: BA, University of California, Los Angeles
Background: Associate, UCLA Venture Capital Fund; Founder/CEO, UniqApp; Co-Founder, Life Entertainment Network

50 ACTA CAPITAL
Washington, DC 20005

e-mail: info@actawireless.com
web: angel.co/company/acta-wireless

Mission Statement: Acta Capital incubates and invests in early stage companies that share their vision for wireless technology to improve the way people live, work, and play.

Founded: 2003
Investment Criteria: Early Stage
Industry Group Preference: Wireless Technologies
Portfolio Companies: Active Mind Technology, Bandsintown, CardStar, FounderFuel, Gimbal, Hook Mobile, Imagine K12, Launchbox Digital, Millenial Media, Moonlighting, Numerai, OZ Communications, Payzer,

Venture Capital & Private Equity Firms / Domestic Firms

PopUp, Real Ventures, Snaplytics, Sweet Relish, Task Force X Capital Management, WaveMetrix

Key Executives:
Alan MacIntosh, Managing Partner
Education: BSc, Offshore Engineering, Heriot-Watt University; MBA, INSEAD
Background: Co-Founder, GSM Capital; Schlumberger; Microcell
Directorships: WaveMetrix, Millennial Media, Cellfish Media
Mark McDowell, Executive Chairman
Education: BSEE, MSEE, MIT
Background: Founding Managment Team: Invertix, Telecorp PCS
Directorships: LaunchBox Digital, mphoria

51 ACTIVATE VENTURE PARTNERS
509 Madison Avenue
Suite 1006
New York, NY 10022

Phone: 212-223-7400
web: www.activatevp.com

Mission Statement: Formerly known as Milestone Venture Partners, Activate Venture Partners is a traditional venture capital partnership focusing on early stage, enterprising information technology companies in the New York metropolitan area. The fund targets companies that possess the nucleus of an exceptional management team, a compelling business model, a large market opportunity.

Geographic Preference: Primarily New York, New Jersey, Connecticut, Northeast, Mid-Atlantic
Fund Size: $70 million
Founded: 1999
Average Investment: $1 million
Minimum Investment: $250,000
Investment Criteria: Early
Industry Group Preference: Technology-Enabled Businesses
Portfolio Companies: Access Health, AnyTime Access, AppBus, BA Insight, Benefix, BTG, Canvs, CareGain, CEMA, ClickPay, Cloudnexa, Cosential, Cureatr, Diameter Health, Digital Pharmacist, eHealth Technologies, Elastomeric Technologies, Expert Plan, FSA Store, GQ Life Sciences, Grovo, Halfpenny Technologies, Healthify, High QA, ID Entropy, Innovative Solutions & Support, Integri Chain, IQE, Iris Plans, Katabat, Knovel, M5, Mapmy Fitness, Medidata, Medpage Today, Medtrex, MicroE Systems, Micro Interventional Devices, National Packaging Systems, Natural Insight, Octagon, Othot, Premise, Racemi, Ravisent Technologies, Rights Flow, Sequoia, Shyft Analytics, Skill Survey, Smartanalyst, Surefire Local, Tabula Rasa Healthcare, Turtle Beach, Ultracision, Visual Networks, Vitals

Other Locations:
116 Research Dr.
Bethlehem, PA 18015
Phone: 610-849-1990

Key Executives:
Glen R Bressner, Managing Partner
Education: BSBA, Boston University; MBA, Babson College
Background: NEPA Venture Funds; Originate Growth Fund I
Todd T Pietri, Managing Partner
Education: Duke University; MBA, Georgia State University
Background: VP, Legacy Services Corporation
Edwin A Goodman, Investment Partner
Education: BA, Yale University; MS, Columbia University
Background: Patricof & Company; Hambros Bank

52 ACTUA
555 East Lancaster Avenue
Suite 640
Radnor, PA 19087

Phone: 610-727-6900 Fax: 610-727-6901
e-mail: ir@actua.com
web: www.actua.com

Mission Statement: A venture capital firm that aquires and builds cloud companies. Formerly known as Internet Capital Group.

Geographic Preference: Worldwide
Founded: 1996
Industry Group Preference: Business to Business, E-Commerce & Manufacturing, SaaS, Marketing, Internet

Key Executives:
Walter W. Buckley III, Co-Founder/CEO
e-mail: buck@actua.com
Education: BA, Political Science, University of North Carolina
Background: Vice President, Safeguard Scientifics; President/Co-Founder, Centralized Management Systems; Commercial Loan Officer, CoreStates
Directorships: Internet Capital Group; ICG Commerce; Verticalnet; OneCoast Networks
John Loftus, Managing Director
e-mail: john@actua.com
Education: BEE, MSEE, MSCS, Villanova University; MSOD, University of Pennsylvania
Background: Founder, Swinford Group; Managing Director, Safeguard Scientifics; Co-Founder, Gestalt LLC; Senior Vice President, Breakaway Solutions
Directorships: GovDelivery
Vincent P. Menichelli, Managing Director
e-mail: vince@actua.com
Education: Lehigh University; MBA, Finance, Bloomsburg University; BS, Accounting
Background: Senior Manager, Arthur Andersen; Coopers & Lybrand LLP
Directorships: Freeboarders, GovDelivery, Metastorm, SeaPass, StarCite
Suzanne Niemeyer, Managing Director/General Counsel/Secretary
e-mail: suzanne@actua.com
Education: BA, Duke University; JD, Georgetown University Law Center
Background: Dechert LLP
Directorships: Investor Force
Kirk Morgan, Chief Financial Officer
e-mail: kirk@actua.com
Education: BS, Accounting, Pennsylvania State University; CPA
Background: Audit Manager, PriceWaterhouseCoopers LLP
Karen Greene, Managing Director/Investor Relations/Marketing Communications
e-mail: karen@actua.com
Education: BA, University of Rochester; MBA, Finance & Marketing, Temple University School of Business
Background: Investor Relations, Safeguard; Investor Relations, CIGNA
Scott Powers, Managing Director/Assistant General Counsel
e-mail: scott@actua.com
Education: BS, Fordham University; JD, James E Beasley School of Law, Temple University
Background: Dechert LLP

53 ACUITY VENTURES LLC
1960 The Alameda
Suite 200
San Jose, CA 95126-1493

Phone: 408-210-8394
web: www.acuityventures.com

Venture Capital & Private Equity Firms / Domestic Firms

Mission Statement: Based in Silicon Valley, Acuity Ventures offers investment capital and operational expertise to emerging growth companies. The fund provides capital through convertible preferred debit, direct equity investments and other investment participations.
Geographic Preference: United States
Founded: 2004
Investment Criteria: Early Stage, Emerging Growth Companies
Industry Group Preference: Internet, Software
Portfolio Companies: FlashFoto, GCommerce, Protocol Driven Healthcare Inc.
Other Locations:
  600 Hansen Way
  Palo Alto, CA 94304-1043
  Phone: 650-843-8766 Fax: 650-843-8768
Key Executives:
  Eric Hardgrave, Co-Founder
  Education: BA, Economics, Stanford University
  Background: Co-Founder, Sand Hill Capital
  Larry Hootnick, Managing Partner
  Education: BS Industrial Management, MIT; MBA, University of Maryland
  Background: SVP Finance/Administration, Intel Corporation; President/CEO, Maxtor Corporation; Consilium Corporation

54 ACUMEN
40 Worth Street
Suite 303
New York, NY 10013
Phone: 212-566-8821 Fax: 212-566-8817
web: www.acumen.org

Mission Statement: Acumen is dedicated to creating a world beyond poverty by investing in social enterprises in East Africa, India and Pakistan, with particular focus on the agriculture, education, healthcare and energy industries.
Geographic Preference: India, East Africa, Pakistan
Fund Size: $60 million
Founded: 2001
Average Investment: $250,000 - $3 million
Investment Criteria: Early Stage, Mid-Stage
Industry Group Preference: Healthcare, Energy, Agriculture, Water, Housing, Education
Portfolio Companies: Aarusha Homes, Aga Khan Rural Support Program, Ansaar Management Company, Asian Health Alliance, Avani Bio Energy, Azahar Coffee, Basix Krishi, Biolite, Broadreach, Burn Manufacturing, Cacao De Colombia, Circ Medtech, Consejosano, D.Light, Devergy, Drishtee, Earnup, Edubridge, Esoko, Ethiochicken, Everytable, Farmers Hope, First Access, Frontier Markets, Gigante Central Wet-Mill, Global Easy Water Products, Green Energy Biofuels, Greenway Grameen, Guardian, Gulu Agricultural Development Company, Healthify, Husk Power Systems, Ignis Careers, Jawabu Microhealth, Juhudi Kilimo, Kashf School Sarmaya, Labournet, Learners Guild, Lifespring, Listo, Micro Drip, Myvyllage, Nasra Public School, National Rural Support Program, Nizam Energy, Orb Energy, Our Family Clinic, Pagatech, Peg, Pharmagen Healthcare Ltd., PVRI, Shayog, Sanergy, Seed Education Corp., Sewa Grih Rin, Siembraviva, Solarnow, Sproxil, SRE Solutions, Uncommon Cacao, Under The Mango Tree, Vikalp, Viridis, Virtual City, Wasi Organics, Waterhealth International, Wellpass, Western Seed, Workamerica, Ziqitza Health Care Ltd.
Other Locations:
  203 Dheeraj Plaza
  Hill Road, Bandra West
  Mumbai 400 050
  India
  Phone: 91 (22) 6740-1500 Fax: 91 (22) 6740-1550

  3rd Floor, ABC Towers
  Waiyaki Way, Westlands
  Nairobi
  Kenya

  1st Commerical Lane
  Shahbaz Commercial Area
  Phase VI
  Karachi
  Pakistan
  Phone: 92 (21) 3584-6430-2 Fax: 92 (21) 3584-6490

  Somerset House, New Wing
  Strand
  London WC2R 1LA
  United Kingdom
  Phone: 44-20-3701-7382

  Carrera 7 No. 84A-29
  Oficina 502
  Bogota
  Colombia

Key Executives:
  Jacqueline Novogratz, Founder/Chief Executive Officer
  Education: BA, Economics/International Relations, University of Virginia; MBA, Stanford University
  Background: Chase Manhattan Bank, World Bank, UNICEF, Rockefeller Foundation
  Directorships: Sonen Capital
  Sasha Dichter, Chief Innovation Officer
  e-mail: sdichter@acumenfund.org
  Education: BA, Harvard College; MPA, International Development, Harvard Kennedy School, Harvard University; MBA, Harvard Business School
  Background: Global Manager, Corporate Citizenship, GE Money
  Andrew Tarazid-Tarawali, Portfolio Manager
  Education: MBA, IE Business School; BSc, Business Admin., Ashesi University
  Background: Senior Investment Professional, Injaro Investments
  Carlyle Singer, President
  Education: BA, History, Harvard College; MBA, Stanford University
  Background: President/CEO, Katun Corp.; Senior President of Operations, IKON Office Solutions

55 ADAMS CAPITAL MANAGEMENT
500 Blackburn Avenue
Sewickley, PA 15143
Phone: 412-749-9454 Fax: 412-749-9459
web: www.acm.com

Mission Statement: ACM deploys its discontinuity driven investment strategy to identify and invest in companies that have value propositions driven by economics and product roadmaps that have the potential to define and dominate product categories.
Geographic Preference: United States
Fund Size: $815 million
Founded: 1994
Investment Criteria: Startup, Series A, Early-Stage
Industry Group Preference: Information Technology, Telecommunications, Semiconductors, Network Infrastructure & Security, Technology
Portfolio Companies: Airnet Communications, AutoESL Design Technologies, Bluestone Software, CoManage, Context Media, CoreTek, Cytyc, DATAllegro, Dell, Dynamics, Factory Logic, First Insight, Flashline, InSoft, Innovative Solutions & Support, Intrinsity, Landslide Technologies, LibreDigital, Luminescent Technologies, Mirage Network, NetSolve, ON Technology, Optellios, Qspeed Semiconductor, ReturnCentral, Revenue Technologies, RoadRunner Recycling Inc., SmartOps,

Venture Capital & Private Equity Firms / Domestic Firms

SnapRetail, The Efficiency Network Inc., Touchdown Technologies, Uplogix, VBrick Systems

Key Executives:
Joel P. Adams, General Partner
412-749-9456
e-mail: jpa@acm.com
Education: MS, Industrial Administration, Carnegie Mellon University; BS, Nuclear Engineering, State University of New York at Buffalo
Background: VP/General Partner, Fostin Capital Corporation; Nuclear Test Engineer, General Dynamics
Directorships: Additech, First Insight, Intrinsity, Precision Therapeutics, SmartOps, TimeSys, Tiversa
Jennifer E. Parulo, Chief Financial Officer
Education: BS, Accounting, Grove City College; CPA
Background: Ernst & Young

56 ADAMS STREET PARTNERS, LLC
One North Wacker Drive
Suite 2700
Chicago, IL 60606-2823
Phone: 312-553-7890 Fax: 312-553-7891
web: www.adamsstreetpartners.com

Mission Statement: Private markets investment manager to institutional clients around the world.
Geographic Preference: United States, Western Europe, Israel, Asia
Fund Size: $27 billion
Founded: 1972
Average Investment: $5-$20 million
Minimum Investment: $5 million
Investment Criteria: First Stage, Second Stage
Industry Group Preference: Business to Business, Computer Hardware & Software, Healthcare, Technology, Life Sciences, Medical Devices, Biopharmaceuticals, Consumer Internet, Business Products & Services, Clean Technology, Communications, Components & IoT, SaaS, Fintech
Portfolio Companies: Actelis Networks, Adams Harris, Adesto, Alien Technology, American Wholesale, Amonix, Ancestry.com, APT, ArrowEye Solutions, AtHoc, Atlantis Computing, AVG Technologies, AWAS, Barracuda Networks, BrightRoll, CareCloud, cbanc Network, Cbeyond, Convio, CoreLab Partners, Couchbase, Criteo, Cybera, Damballa, Dolex, Enfora, FiftyOne, Glam Media, Global MailExpress, GlobeImmune, gWallet, INC Research, Integral Development, JasperSoft, Jazz Pharmaceuticals, KPG Ventures, Light Sciences Oncology, Luminous Medical, MachineryLink, Mintigo, Mpex, Neuraltus Pharmaceuticals, NewPath Ventures, NXP Semiconductor, OncoMed Pharmaceuticals, Paylocity, Peerless Networks, PneumRx, Proteus Biomedical, Q2ebanking, Retail Me Not, Revascular Therapeutics, Rimini Street, Sabre Holdings, Shermans Travel, Shred-it, SnagAJob.com, Solaria, SPS Commerce, Tavve Software, T3Media, TriReme Medical, Univision, USGI Medical, Visible World, Vocaltec, WhiteFence, YouSendIt, Ziggo

Adams Street Partners (Beijing) Co., Ltd.
China Central Place, No. 79 Jianguo Road
Chaoyang District
Beijing 100025
China
Phone: 86 10 8521 1499

501 Boylston Street
10th Floor
Boston, MA 02116
Phone: 312-553-8475 Fax: 312-553-8499

Adams Street Partners UK LLP
4th Floor
London W1K 5JN
United Kingdom
Phone: 44 20 7659 7700 Fax: 44 20 7659 7701

Adams Street Partners, Inc.
Suite 300
Menlo Park, CA 94025
Phone: 650-331-4860 Fax: 650-331-4861

Adams Street (Europe) GmbH
Munich 80539
Germany
Phone: 49 89 2620 7285 Fax: 312-553-7891

Adams Street Partners, Inc.
20th Floor
New York, NY 10020
Phone: 646-647-1000 Fax: 646-647-1001

Adams Street Partners, LLC (Korea Branch)
Eulji-ro
5-gil 19, Jung-gu
Seoul 04539
Republic of Korea

Adams Street Partners Singapore Pte. Ltd.
#12-01 Raffles City Tower 179101
Singapore
Phone: 65 6303 8730 Fax: 65 6303 8740

Adams Street Partners Japan G.K.
Otemachi 1-chome, Chiyoda-ku
Tokyo 100-0004
Japan
Phone: 081 3 6206 3545 Fax: 081 3 6206 3547

Key Executives:
T. Bondurant French, Chairman
e-mail: bfrench@adamsstreetpartners.com
Education: Northwestern University
Background: Brinson Partners; Connecticut General Insurance Company
Jeffrey Diehl, Managing Partner & Head of Investments
Education: Cornell University; Harvard University
Background: Brinson Partners; The Parthenon Group
Jim Walker, Partner & Chief Operating Officer
Education: Catholic University of America; MIT
Background: Credit Suisse Private Bank Americas; Morgan Stanley Global Wealth Management; Merrill Lynch
Quintin Kevin, Partner & Chief Financial Officer
Education: University of Illinois; University of Chicago
Background: KPMG
Kelly Meldrum, CFA, Partner & Head of Primary Investments
Education: Bentley College
Background: William and Flora Hewlett Foundation; Morgan Stanley
Jeff Akers, Partner & Head of Secondary Investments
Education: Indiana University; Northwestern University
Background: L.E.K. Consulting; William Blair & Company

57 ADOBE VENTURES LP
345 Park Avenue
San Jose, CA 95110-2704
Phone: 408-536-6000 Fax: 408-537-6000
e-mail: newventure@adobe.com
web: www.adobe.com/ventures.html

Mission Statement: The strength and experience of Adobe, partnered with the endorsement and investing experience of Granite Ventures, makes the Adobe Ventures funding model unique, and allows the entrepreneur access to additional resources within one program.
Fund Size: $100 million
Founded: 1982
Average Investment: $3-$5 million
Investment Criteria: Early Stage

Venture Capital & Private Equity Firms / Domestic Firms

Industry Group Preference: Infrastructure, Enterprise Services, Networking, Digital Media & Marketing, Media, Internet Technology, Communications, Publishing
Portfolio Companies: Acrodea, Arcot, AvantGo, BidClerk, Cell Co., Convio, DecisionView, Digimarc, Digital Fountain, DigitalThink, Demandbase, EFI, FiveAcross, Gigya, imeem, Indiagames, Kontiki, Netscape, Objectivity, Oversight Systems, PSS Systems, PlayJam, Scrybe, Sendmail, Siebel System, Skysoft, Shutterfly, Tumbleweed Communications, TuVox, Vignette, Virage, Virtual Ubiquity, 56.com

Key Executives:
John Leckrone, Managing Director
e-mail: jleckron@adobe.com
Education: MBA, Stephen M. Ross School of Business, University of Michigan
Background: Group Product Manager, Adobe; Business Development Manager, Netscape; Management Development Program, Ford Motor Compan

58 ADVANCED TECHNOLOGY VENTURES
500 Boylston Street
Suite 1380
Boston, MA 02116

e-mail: investorrelations@atvcapital.com
web: www.atvcapital.com

Mission Statement: A bio-coastal venture capital firm that takes an active role in their investments, offering a collaborative experience in regards to executive recruitment, market selection, business development, etc.

Geographic Preference: United States
Fund Size: $1.6 billion
Founded: 1979
Average Investment: $10 million
Minimum Investment: $250,000
Industry Group Preference: Information Technology, Healthcare, Clean Technology
Portfolio Companies: Accord Networks, Acme Packet, Actel, AppIQ, Application Networks, Adrian, Cepheid, Credence, CYTYC, DataSage, E-Security, Epigram, Healthshare Technology, Helixis, Hypnion, Microvention, Omneon Video Networks, Plexxikon, Proteolix, Qumu, RFMD, Redline Networks, Striva, Teradata, Tran Switch, Tripwire, Upshot.com, Verastem, Webline, [X+1], Zaperio Technologies, Aquion Energy, Accelero Pharma, Actifio, Alfalight, Alta Rock Energy, Altura Medical, Calithera Biosciences, Catabsis, Cedexis, Cenzic, Channel Advisor, Coskata, EndoGastric Solutions, Evergage, Five Prime, Gi Dynamics, Great Point Energy, Great Point Ventures, Gynesonics, Holaira, Host Analytics, Hydra Biosciences, Modria, Nominum, Oasys Water, Poly Remedy, Portola, Powervision, QuickPay, Rive Technology, Second Genome, Silicor Materials, Thinking Phone Networks, Therasos Therapeutics, Trans1, Valeritas, Wild Tangent

Other Locations:
2884 Sand Hill Road
Suite 121
Menlo Park, CA 94025

Key Executives:
Steven Baloff, General Partner
e-mail: sbaloff@atvcapital.com
Education: MBA, Stanford Graduate School of Business; BA, Harvard College
Background: CEO and Founder, Worldview Systems; Co-developer, Travelocity; Executive, Covalent Systems; Strategist, Booz Allen & Hamilton; Founder, Twin Lakes Ventures
Directorships: Covalent Systems
Mike Carusi, General Partner
Education: MBA, Amos Tuck School of Business Administration Dartmouth College; BS, Lehigh University
Background: Director of Business Development, Inhale Therapeutic Systems; Principal, The Wilkerson Group
Directorships: Acceleron Pharma; Emphasys Medical; EndoGastric Solutions; GI Dynamics; MicroVention; Plexxikon; TranS1; Xtent
Jean George, General Partner
Education: MBA, Simmons College Graduate School of Management; BS, University of Maine
Background: Various Operational Positions, Genzyme Corporation; Life Sciences Lead Investor, BancBoston Ventures
Directorships: Critical Therapeutics; Five Prime Therapeutics; Hydra Biosciences; Hypnion; Juniper Medical; Proteolix
Bob Hower, General Partner
Education: BA, Cum Laude, Harvard College; MBA, Amos Tuck School, Dartmouth College
Background: VP Sales, LHS Group; Sales/Marketing, Lotus Development; Sales/Marketing, General Mills; Director, BancNoston Ventures; Commercial Real Estate, Cabot, Cabot & Forbes
Directorships: Acme Packet; AppIQ; Application Networks; ChannelAdvisor; e-Security
Bill Wiberg, General Partner
Education: BS, Cornell University; MS, Stanford University; MBA, Columbia University
Background: Telecommunications, Lucent Technologies; President, Lucent's Cellular & PCS Wireless Networks; General Partner, Bowman Capital; General Partner, Orange Ventures; Board of Directors/ Executive Committee, Cellular Telecommunications and Internet Association
Directorships: CombineNet; Great Point Energy; HVVi

59 ADVANCIT CAPITAL
846 University Avenue
Norwood, MA 02062

e-mail: info@advancitcap.com
web: www.advancitcapital.com

Mission Statement: Advancit Capital is an early stage investment firm focused on media, entertainment and technology companies. The firm seeks the opportunity to form long-term partnerships with talented, focused and driven entrepreneurs. With its strategic and industry expertise, Advancit Capital provides value-added resources at the critical growth stages of companies.

Founded: 2011
Investment Criteria: Early-Stage
Industry Group Preference: Media, Entertainment, Technology
Portfolio Companies: 8I, MiTú, Maker Studios, HeadSpace, Unikrn, MasterClass, The Business of Fashion, Directr, Epoxy, Reserve, Brickwork, Molio, FitStar, Qualia, Lua, Draft, Wedgies, Victorious, Moat, NewsCred, Panna, MobCrush, Baobab, The Noun Project, Percolate, Skift, Speakaboos, Hyper, Amper, French Girls, Vistar Media, Mic Network, Push.io, BlitzESports, Msg.ai, Silver, Niche, CrowdTangle, SocialRank, Splash, The Outline, Thrive Global, Clique Media Group, Pop, Distractify, Women.com, Crypt TV, Block Six Analytics, REDEF, Base79, AllDefDigital, STRIVR, The Athletic, Mux, All Def Digital, Indigenous Media, Mux, JanusVR, Outpost Games, Woven Orthopedics

Other Locations:
99 University Place
3rd Floor
New York, NY 10003

Key Executives:
Jason Ostheimer, Co-Founder/Partner
Education: BS, Economics, Wharton School, University of Pennsylvania
Background: National Amusements Inc., Blackstone Group
Shari Redstone, Co-Founder/Managing Partner
Education: BS, Tufts University; JD, MA, Boston University

Background: President, National Amusements
Directorships: Vice Chair, Viacom Inc.; Vice Chair, Board of CBS Corp.; Co-Chair MovieTickets.com; Board of Directors & Executive Committee, National Theatre Owners Association
Jonathan Miller, Senior Advisor
Education: BA, Harvard College
Background: CEO/Chairman/Chief Digital Officer, Digital Media Group for News Corp.; CEO, AOL; CEO/President, USA Information and Services; VP, Programming, NBA Entertainment
Directorships: Nickelodeon International

---

60 ADVANTAGE CAPITAL PARTNERS
156 W 56th Street
Suite 801
New York, NY 10019

Phone: 646-685-8755
web: www.advantagecap.com

Mission Statement: Provides capital and value added services to well-managed companies with superior growth potential.

Geographic Preference: North, Southeast, Midwest
Fund Size: $700 million
Founded: 1992
Average Investment: $10 million
Minimum Investment: $1 million
Investment Criteria: Seed, Startup, Early Stage, Mezzanine, Special Situations
Industry Group Preference: Business Products & Services, Clean Technology, Communications, Energy, Financial Services, Information Technology, Life Sciences, Manufacturing
Portfolio Companies: 3DR Laboratories, Av Smoot, Able Planet, AgencyQ, AGIS, ARCMail Technology, Barton Nelson, BinOptics, Bizzuka, Butler's Pantry, Cardax Pharmaceuticals, CheckPoint Pumps & Systems, City Carting & Recycling, CodeRed, Computime, Contego Services Group, Crown Plastics, Digium|Asterik, Distech Systems, Elevate Digital, EmergingMed, Enersciences, Esperance Pharmaceuticals, FireRock, FleetCor, Game Equipment, Glori Energy, Greenleaf Biofuels, GridPoint, Group360 Worldwide, Hawaii Biotech, HRI, iCardiac Technologies, Illinois Neurospine Institute, ILMO Products, INDEECO, Inside Higher Ed, Jahabow, Lawrence Group, Lift for Life Academy, MannaPro, MarqueMedicos, Mason Manufacturing, Merill Industries, Mezmeriz, MicroGreen, Mid America Brick, Monarch Machine Tool, New England Linen Supply, NovaTract, Novelos, Owensboro Grain, Pasteuria Bioscience, Quality Wood Products, RepEquity, Rucker's, Selltis, Skyline Innovations, Soft Switching Technologies, Stout Industries, Summit Broadband, Sunburst Farms, Synacor, T&K Machine, TAS Environmental Services LP, TurboSquid, Veran Medical Technologies, Virent Energy, Willert Home Products, Worley Company, XIOLINK, Zadspace, Inc., Voxitas, Waste Remedies, Willert Home Products, Worley Catastrophe Response, Xiolink, Zadspace

Other Locations:
3 Lebanon Street
Hanover, NH 03755
Phone: 603-676-7160

909 Poydras Street
Suite 2230
New Orleans, LA 70112
Phone: 504-522-4850

7733 Forsyth Boulevard
Suite 1400
St. Louis, MO 63105
Phone: 314-725-0800

1028 33rd Street Northwest
Suite 200
Washington, DC 20007
Phone: 202-337-1661

900 South Capital of Texas Highway
Las Cimas Building 4
Suite 480
Austin, TX 78746
Phone: 512-380-1168

c/o Venture Investors
869 Lakeshore Boulevard
Incline Village, NV 89451
Phone: 775-298-1338

174 West Comstocl Avenue
Suite 209
Winter Park, FL 32789
Phone: 407-454-6184

207 East Side Square
Suite 200
Huntsville, AL 35801
Phone: 256-883-8711

6923 Silverado Trail
Napa, CA 94558
Phone: 707-944-2310

318 W Adams
16th Floor
Chicago, IL 60606
Phone: 312-767-2019

208 West Georgetown Street
Crystal Springs, MS 39059
Phone: 601-954-6636

c/o Ironwood Capital
45 Nod Road
Avon, CT 06001-3819
Phone: 860-409-2100

Key Executives:
Steven Stull, President
Education: BS, Finance/Economics & MBA, Washington University
Background: Investment Director, General American Life Insurance Company
Maurice Doyle, Managing Director
Education: BBA, University of Notre Dame; JD, Chicago-Kent College of Law
Background: Senior VP, UBS Securities; VP, Credit Suisse First Boston; VP, Winthrop Securities
Michael Johnson, Managing Director/COO
Education: Stanford School of Law; AB, Harvard College
Background: Jones, Walker, Waechter, Potevent, Carrere & Denegre
Damon Rawie, Managing Director
Education: BA, Wesleyan University; MBA, University of Chicago Graduate School of Business
Background: China International Capital Corporation; JP Morgan Securities
Louis Dubuque, Managing Director
Education: MBA, Washington University; Washington and Lee University
Background: US Bank
Scott Murphy, Managing Director/CIO
e-mail: smurphy@advantagecap.com
Education: AB, Harvard University; CFA
Background: United States Congress, New York
Thomas Keaveney, Advisor
Education: Fordham University
Background: Investment Banker, Credit Suisse First Boston
Jonathan Goldstein, Managing Director
Education: BA, Yale University; Washington University School of Law
Background: SVP, McCormack Baron Salazar; Founder, Taproot Ventures
Charles Booker, Principal
Education: BA, Vanderbilt University; JD, Tulane School

of Law
Background: Lawyer, Mayer Brown Platt; Lawyer, McGlinchey Stafford
Jeremy Degenhart, Principal
Education: BSBA, Finance, Economics & Accounting, Washington University, St. Louis
Background: Analyst, Wydown Capital
Directorships: Veran Medical Technologies, Quick Study Radiology, Waste Remedies, Carbolytic Materials Company, Sunflower Food & Spice
Jeffrey Craver, Principal
e-mail: jcraver@advantagecap.com
Education: Duke University; JD, University of Richmond; LLM, Taxation, Washington University, St. Louis
Background: Tax Counsel, Missouri Chamber of Commerce & Industry
W. Anthony Toups, Principal
e-mail: ttoups@advantagecap.com
Education: Louisiana State University; JD, Paul M Herbert Law Center, Louisiana State University
Background: Partner, Adams & Reese

61 ADVENT INTERNATIONAL CORPORATION
Prudential Tower
800 Boylston Street
Boston, MA 02199-8069

Phone: 617-951-9400
web: www.adventinternational.com

Mission Statement: Global private equity firm with $32 billion in investments.
Geographic Preference: Worldwide
Founded: 1984
Average Investment: $5 million
Investment Criteria: Buyouts, Growth Equity Investment
Industry Group Preference: Business & Financial Services, Healthcare, Industrial, Retail, Consumer & Leisure, Technology, Media & Telecommunications
Portfolio Companies: ABC Supply, AccentCare, Addiko Bank, Aimbridge Hospitality, BioDuro, Canvia, CCC Information Services Inc., Circet Groupe, Clearent/FieldEdge, Definitive Healthcare, Easynvest, First Watch, Laird Limited, Prisma Medios de Pagos S.A., Quala, QuEST Global Services, Roehm, Transcend Therapeutics, TransUnion, Zentiva

Other Locations:
12 East 49th Street
45th Floor
New York, NY 10017
Phone: 212-813-8300

8-10 rue Lamennais
Paris 75008
France
Phone: 33 0 1 55 37 29 00

Westhafenplatz 1
Frankfurt am Main 60327
Germany
Phone: 49 0 69 955 2700

Marqués de Villamagna 3 - 4 Dcha.
Madrid 28001
Spain
Phone: 34 91 745 48 60

160 Victoria Street
London SW1E 5LB
United Kingdom
Phone: 44 0 20 7333 0800

Av. Brig. Faria Lima 3400, Conj 41
Sao Paulo, SP 04538-132
Brazil
Phone: 55 11 3014 6800

Edificio Omega
Campos Eliseos 345 - 14th Floor
Col. Polanco
Mexico City 11560
Mexico
Phone: 52 55 5281 0303

Avenida Calle 82 #10-33
Oficina 702
Bogota 110221
Colombia
Phone: 57 1 254 4747

HKRI Centre One
Units 3305-3310
288 Shimen Road (No. 1)
Shanghai 200041
China
Phone: 86 21 6032 0788

Unit 1702, 17th Floor
One India Bulls Centre, Tower 2, Wing A
841, Senapati Bapat Marg
Mumbai 400 013
India
Phone: 91 (22) 4057 3000

5/F, Manulife Place
348 Kwun Tong Road
Kowloon
Hong Kong
China
Phone: 852 2278 3788

Key Executives:
Chris Egan, Managing Partner
Education: Dartmouth College
Background: Financial Sponsors Group, UBS Warburg
Directorships: Ansira Holdings; CCC Information Services Inc.; Clearent/FieldEdge; Definitive Healthcare, P2 Energy, Prisma Medios de Pagos S.A.; BondDesk; RedPrairie; TransUnion
John Maldonado, Managing Partner
Education: Dartmouth College; Harvard Business School
Background: Bain Capital; Parthenon Capital
Directorships: AccentCare; ATI Physical Therapy Holdings LLC; Definitive Healthcare; Health Care Private Equity Association; Syneos Health Inc.; American Radiology Services; Genoa Healthcare
Chris Pike, Special Partner
Education: Amherst College
Background: Coopers & Lybrand
Directorships: ATI Physical Therapy Holdings; CCC Information Services Inc.; Cotiviti; Genoa Healthcare; Americus Dental; Aspen Technology; BondDesk; GFI Group; Managed Healthcare Associates
Eileen Sivolella, Managing Director
Education: University of Delaware
Background: CFO, Bain Capital; Partner, Deloitte
Bryan Taylor, Managing Partner
Education: Stanford University; Stanford Graduate School of Business
Background: Co-Head, Technology Group, TPG Capital; Founder & Managing Director, Symphony Technology Group; Manager, Bain & Company
Directorships: Tanium; McAfee; CCC Information Services; Celerity; Decision Insight Information Group; Ellucian; Eze Software; Greensky; IQVIA; Intergraph; Sutherland Global Services
James Westra, Managing Partner & Chief Legal Officer
Education: Harvard College; Boston University
Background: Weil, Gotshal & Manges LLP

Venture Capital & Private Equity Firms / Domestic Firms

62 ADVENT-MORRO EQUITY PARTNERS
Banco Popular Building
Suite 903
206 Tetuan Street, Old San Juan
San Juan, PR 00902

Phone: 787-725-5285 **Fax:** 787-721-1735
web: www.adventmorro.com

Mission Statement: Advent-Morro Equity Partners is Puerto Rico's leading private equity investment firm with more than $120 million in equity capital under management. It has invested in over 50 companies, most of which are based or have operations in Puerto Rico. From 1997 to 2010, Advent-Morro was affiliated with Boston-based Advent International Corporation.

Geographic Preference: Puerto Rico, United States
Fund Size: $120 million
Founded: 1997
Average Investment: $2.5 - 10 million
Minimum Investment: $2.5 million
Investment Criteria: Later-Stage, Expansion Financing, MBO, Corporate Divestitures, Turnarounds, Re-Capitalizations, Industry Consolidations
Industry Group Preference: Diversified
Portfolio Companies: Abaco PR, AquaVentures Holdings LLC, Centennial Communications, Charlotte Russe Holdings Inc., Codigo Entertainment LLC, Datek Online, Dollar Express, FFI Holdings Inc., Hotel El Convento, ICPR Junior College, Infinity Laser Centers, Infopaginas Inc., Integration Technologies, International Meal Company Holdings SA, Islanet Communications, LendingPoint, Medical Card Systems, Next Level Learning Inc., Packers Provision, Pahteon Inc., Puerto Rico ASC Holdings Co. Inc., QMC Media, Quench USA Inc., QWS Holdings LLC, Trexel, Venture Steel, Vigilant Shipping Holding, Windstream

Key Executives:
   Cyril L. Meduna, Managing Partner/President
   Education: BS, Mechanical Engineering, Rensselaer Polytechnic Institute; MBA, George Washington University
   Background: President, Meduna & Co.; Regional Manager, Ehrlich Bober International
   Omar Mejias, Director
   Education: BS, Finance, Loyola University; MF, Tulane University
   Background: Senior Associate, BMO Capital Markets; Equity Research Associate, Bb&T Capital Markets

63 AEA INVESTORS
666 Fifth Avenue
36th Floor
New York, NY 10103

Phone: 212-644-5900 **Fax:** 212-888-1459
web: www.aeainvestors.com

Mission Statement: AEA's investment activities are primarily focused on the three market sectors in which AEA has developed considerable expertise: value added industrials, specialty chemicals and consumer products.

Geographic Preference: United States, Western Europe
Fund Size: $400 Million
Founded: 1968
Average Investment: $10 Million
Minimum Investment: $1 Million
Investment Criteria: Consolidations, Acquisitions, LBO, MBO, Recapitalization, Special Situations, Mezzanine
Industry Group Preference: Chemicals, Consumer Products, Business to Business, Manufacturing, Distribution
Portfolio Companies: Aramsco Holdings Inc., BOA Group, Brand Networks, Colony Hardware, CPG International, Dayton Parts LLC, Dematic, The Evans Network of Companies, Garden Ridge, Hospitalists Management Group LLC, Industrial Accoustics Company, Lone Star, NEW Global Talent, Phillips Pet Food & Supplies, PLZ Holding Corporation, PPC Industries Inc., Pregis Corporation, Reladyne Inc., SBP Holdings LP, Sextant Education Corporation, Shoes For Crews, Sparrows Group, Suhyang Networks, Swanson Industries Inc., Troxell Communication Inc.

Other Locations:
281 Tresser Boulevard
12th Floor
Stamford, CT 06901
Phone: 203-564-2660 **Fax:** 203-564-2661

78 Brook Street
London W1K 5EF
England
Phone: 44 (20) 7659-7800 **Fax:** 44 (20) 7491-2155

Widenmayerstr 3
Munich 80538
Germany
Phone: 49 (89) 244-173-0 **Fax:** 49 (89) 244-173-860

Suite 2903, 29F
Kerry Center, Tower 2
1539 Nanjing Road West
Jingan District 200040
Shanghai
Phone: 86-21-2308-7888 **Fax:** 86-21-2308-7880

Key Executives:
   John Garcia, Executive Chairman
   Education: SS, University of Kent, Canterbury England
   Background: KFedit Suisse First Boston: Global Head Chemicals Group, European Investment Banking Management Committee, Head European Acquisitions, Leveraged Finance, Financial Sponsors Group, Head European Natural Resources Group; Managing Director, Schroder Wertheim; Atlantic Richfield
   Directorships: Icetex Corp
   John Cozzi, Partner/Co-Head of Small Business Funds
   Education: BA, Union College; MBA, Wharton School
   Background: Managing Director, Arena Capital Partners; Managing Director, Leveraged Finance Group of Credit Suisse First Boston; Smith Barney; Harris Upham & Company; NYNEX Corp
   Joseph Carrabino, Jr., Partner/Executive Chairman
   Education: AB Economics, Harvard College
   Background: Co-Head Mezzanine Debt Group, Whitney & Co; Leveraged Finance/Financial Sponsor Coverage, Credit Suisse First Boston
   Shivanandan A. Dalvie, Consultant
   Education: MBA, Stanford University Graduate School of Business; BS, Yale University
   Background: Credit Suisse First Boston
   Directorships: Compresison Polymers, Telephia
   Brian Hoesterey, Chief Executive Officer
   Education: MBA, Harvard University; BBA, Accounting, Texas Christian University
   Background: BT Capital Partners; Bankers Trust; Morgan Stanley; McKinsey & Co.
   Thomas Pryma, Partner
   Education: Georgetown University
   Background: Merrill Lynch
   Directorships: Pro Mach, TricoBraun, Eviqua Water Technologies
   Martin Eltrich III, Partner
   Education: BS, Economics, Wharton School, University of Pennsylvania
   Background: Greenhill & Co.
   Directorships: Acosta, Burt's Bees, Cogen Healthcare, Henry Company, Li & Fung Distribution, Shoes for Crews, Tampico Beverage
   Alan Wilkinson, Partner/Co-Head of Small Business Funds
   Education: MBA, Columbia University; BS, Mathematics, King's College
   Background: Peter J Solomon Company; Lehman Brothers; Principal Investment Group
   Scott Zoellner, Partner/Head of Private Debt
   Education: BA, Economics and Political Science, Trinity

Venture Capital & Private Equity Firms / Domestic Firms

College; MBA, NYU Stern School of Business
Background: Principal, Allied Capital; Director, Callidus Capital Corp; Consultant, Carlyle Group; Credit Suisse First Boston; Leveraged Finance Group
Thomas Groves, Partner
Education: AB, Economics, Bowdoin College
Background: Credit Suisse First Boston
J. Louis Sharpe, Partner
Education: BA, Economics, Yale University
Background: Investment Banking Division, Morgan Stanley
Steven DeCillis II, Partner/Chief Financial Officer
Education: BS, Accounting, Villanova University; MBA, Columbia University; CPA
Background: CFO, Ripplewood Holdings LLC; Assurance & Business Advisory Services, PricewaterhouseCoopers LLP
Nannette McNally, Partner
Education: BS, Business Administration, University of North Carolina, Chapel Hill
Background: Investment Banking, Credit Suisse First Boston
Barbara Burns, Partner/General Counsel/Chief Compliance Officer
Education: BA, Economics and International Relations, and JD, University of Pennsylvania
Background: Morgan Stanley Real Estate
Baron Carlson, Partner
Education: BA, Government, Dartmouth College
Background: Arena Capital Partners
James Ho, Partner
Education: BA, Economics and Mathematical Methods in the Social Sciences, Northwestern University
Background: Bain & Co.

64 AEP CAPITAL LLC
366 Madison Avenue
8th Floor
New York, NY 10017

Phone: 212-641-5100 Fax: 212-641-5125
web: www.aepcapital.com

Mission Statement: An affiliate of Alpine Capital, principally involved in media, entertainment, communications and financial services.

Geographic Preference: North America
Founded: 1995
Average Investment: $10 - $75 million
Investment Criteria: Early Stage, Consolidations, Leveraged Buyout, Management Buyout, Recapitalization, Second Stage, Special Situations,
Industry Group Preference: Advertising, Broadcasting, Consumer Services, Internet Technology, Publishing, Telecommunications, Communications, Information Technology, Media, Entertainment, Business Products & Services
Portfolio Companies: Creme de la Creme, Uplifting Entertainment, Bonded Holdings LLC

Key Executives:
Richard Goldstein, Senior Managing Director
Education: Summa Cum Laude, Phi Beta Kappa, Queens College; Magna Cum Laude, Harvard Law School
Background: Partner, Paul, Weiss, Rifkind, Wharton & Garrison
Directorships: Alpine Capital Bank, American Community Newspapers, Creme de la Creme
Bruce Greenwald, Senior Managing Director
Education: BS, Business Economics & MBA, University of Rochester
Background: Arthur Young & Company
Directorships: American Community Newspapers, Creme de la Creme, Destina Theaters

65 AEROEQUITY
2500 N Military Trail
Suite 470
Boca Raton, FL 33431

Phone: 561-372-7820 Fax: 561-392-6908
e-mail: investorrelations@aeroequity.com
web: www.aeroequity.com

Mission Statement: To distinguish themselves from other private equity firms by bringing a unique set of capabilities, relationships and experiences to their portfolio companies in a way seldom seen in the middle market. In addition to providing substantial financial, human and intellectual capital to our platform investments, AE provides portfolio companies and management teams with unmatched access to critical decision makers within key OEMs and operators worldwide.

Founded: 1998
Industry Group Preference: Aerospace, Defense and Government
Portfolio Companies: AC&A, Belcan, BHI Energy, CDIm FMI, Global Jet Capital, Kellstrom Aerospace, Moeller Aerospace

Key Executives:
David H. Rowe, Co-Founder/Managing Partner
Education: BS, Tulane University
Background: EVP, Gulfstream Financial Services Corp.
Directorships: TurboCombustor Technology, Kellstrom Industries, AeroSat Corp
Thomas K Churbuck, Operating Partner
Education: John F Kennedy Special Warfare Center, Department of Defense Systems Management College
Background: Founder, Power Systems Manufacturing; Founder, Tropic Aviation
Michael Greene, Managing Partner
Education: BA, College of the Holy Cross; MBA, Harvard Business School
Background: Founding Partner, UBS Capital LLC
Thomas E. Brew Jr., Special Advisor
Education: BS, LLB, Boston University
Background: COO, Power Systems Manufacturing; CEO, Laclede Steel
Wayne P. Garrett, General Partner
Education: BS, MBA, Boston College
Background: CFO, Power Systems Manufacturing; CFO, Cambridge SoundWorks

66 AEROSTAR CAPITAL LLC
590 Sandhill Crane Road
PO Box 1270
Wilson, WY 83014-1270

Phone: 888-280-5566 Fax: 888-280-5566
web: www.aerostarcapital.com

Mission Statement: Private equity for aerospace, defense and telecom companies.

Geographic Preference: United States, Europe
Founded: 1997
Investment Criteria: Bridge, Consolidations, Leveraged Buyout, Management Buyout, Mezzanine, Middle Market, Recapitalization, Special Situations
Industry Group Preference: Aerospace, Defense and Government, Communications, Equipment, Telecommunications
Portfolio Companies: Firth Rixon, Ltd., Forged Metals, Inc., WESCO Aircraft, Inc.

Key Executives:
Robert Paulson, Founder/CEO
e-mail: bob4aerostar@gmail.com
Education: BA in Economics, University of California at Santa Barbara; MBA, Harvard
Background: Army Officer/Analyst, Assistant Secretary of Defense for Systems Analysis; Consultant, McKinsey & Company
Directorships: Director, Ducommum; Nationwide Health

Venture Capital & Private Equity Firms / Domestic Firms

Properties; Forgings International LP; Advisor, McKinsey & Company

67 AFFINITY CAPITAL MANAGEMENT
901 Marquette Avenue
Suite 2820
Minneapolis, MN 55402

Phone: 612-252-9900

Mission Statement: Affinity Capital Management works with innovative and visionary companies and entrepreneurs to create groundbreaking improvements in health care.

Geographic Preference: Upper Midwest US
Fund Size: $80 million
Founded: 1993
Average Investment: $5 million
Investment Criteria: Seed, Start-up, Early Stage, Mid Stage
Industry Group Preference: Healthcare, Medical Devices, Health Related
Portfolio Companies: Data Sciences International, LifeSync Corporation, National Dentex Corporation, Proteus Digital Health, Respicardia, Spineology, Uptake Medical, ValenTx

Key Executives:
  Edson W. Spencer Jr., Founder/Chairman
  e-mail: espencerjr@affinitycapital.net
  Education: BA, Williams College; MBA, Columbia University
  Background: Principal/Co-Founder, Peterson-Spencer-Fansler Company; Senior Officer, Dyco Petroleum
  B. Kristine Johnson, President
  e-mail: bkjohnson@affinitycapital.net
  Education: BA, St. Olaf College
  Background: Senior VP/CAO, Medtronic; Various Executive Positions, Cargill
  Robin Dowdle, Chief Financial Officer
  e-mail: rdowdle@affinitycapital.net
  Education: BS, University of Minnesota
  Background: Analyst/Operations Manager, USTrust

68 AGILITY CAPITAL LLC
10 E Figueroa Street
Suite 204
Santa Barbara, CA 93101

Phone: 805-568-0425
e-mail: info@agilitycap.com
web: www.agilitycap.com

Mission Statement: A private venture debt fund focused on providing senior debt solutions to venture capital-backed private companies and Small Cap public companies.

Geographic Preference: Western USA
Founded: 2000
Average Investment: $750,000
Minimum Investment: $250,000
Investment Criteria: Mezzanine Financing, Primary Bridge Loans, Lines of Credit, Factoring Lines of Credit, Non-Formula Lines of Credit, Restructuring Debt
Portfolio Companies: Alpha Innotech, Aurionpro, Inc., BlackFog, Blue Sky Research, Bravanta, Cake Marketing, CKL Design Automation, Computer Motion, Cyber Rain, DAX Solutions, DPS Inc., EdgeWave Software, Inc., Emmaus Life Science Inc., Everyone Counts, FastSoft, Flowplay, Fragmob, Fugoo, GCommerce, Gigoptix, GrabGreen, Haht Commerce, Harbinger, Home Chef, iBahn, INgrooves, iPass, Innovative Micro Technologies, Kana, Kanam Lifescript, Lucid, Lunera, MobileStorm, MiaSolé, MicroTech Systems Inc., Monet Software, Moving iMage Technologies, Nimble Commerce, NuvoSun, Oomba, Pathfire, PepperBall Technologies, Permlight, Petnet, Phizzle, Phoenix Energy Technologies, Predixion, Primaxx, Qubera Solutions, THE RESET, SimplyShe, StemCyte, Storactive, Inc., Superconductor Technologies, Inc., Supply Edge, Inc., Strasbaugh, Synapse Design, Tacit, Talenthouse, Triple Ring Technologies, TrueVision Systems Inc., Uniquify, Valant, Vantos, Vimana, Visto, Wordlock, Zhone

Key Executives:
  Jeff Carmody, Managing Director
  e-mail: jeff@agilitycap.com
  Education: University of California, Santa Barbara
  Background: Sand Hill Capital; Tech Coast Angels
  Daniel Corry, Managing Director
  e-mail: daniel@agilitycap.com
  Education: University of California, Santa Barbara
  Background: Co-Founder, Sand Hill Capital; Silicon Valley Bank; Bank of the West

69 AGMAN PARTNERS
12910 Pierce Street
Suite 210
Omaha, NE 68144

Phone: 402-882-0112
e-mail: ir@agmanpartners.com
web: www.agmanpartners.com

Mission Statement: Agman Partners is a multi-strategy investment fund attracted to areas of market inefficiency and fundamental value. Agnostic to industry and geography, the fund has flexibility to invest directly and through partnerships across asset classes and stages of development. Agman Partners emphasizes a long-term perspective to its investment approach.

Founded: 2005
Industry Group Preference: All Sectors Considered
Portfolio Companies: Accomplice, Agman Capital, Ampler, AngelList, Aparium Hotel Group, Atlas Venture, Brook Furniture Rental, Carbon Black, City Place, DataXu, DraftKings, FreshBooks, Malliouhana Resort, Metonic Real Estate Solutions, Nelson Cash, Omaha National, OMNE Partners, RA Capital, RedBird Capital Partners, Seldin Company, Senator Investment Group, Skillz, Stromedix, The Chicago Athletic Association, The Iron Horse Hotel, Tuscany Apartments, Universal Services, Veracode, Virtus, West Glen Town Center

Other Locations:
  10 East Ohio Street
  2nd Floor
  Chicago, IL 60611

Key Executives:
  Scott Silverman, Co-Founder/CEO
  Education: Dartmouth College, University of Oxford
  Background: Principal, Atlas Venture; Consultant, The Boston Consulting Group
  Jeff Silverman, Co-Founder
  Education: BS, Management, MIT
  Background: Vice-Chairman, National Securites Studies, Israel

70 AGRIBUSINESS MANAGEMENT COMPANY
One Burlington Place
1004 Farnam Street
Omaha, NE 68102

Phone: 402-444-1630 **Fax:** 402-930-3066
Toll-Free: 800-283-2357
web: burlingtoncapital.com

Mission Statement: The Burlington International Agribusiness Management Company is a global private equity fund focused on agribusiness and ancillary businesses.

Geographic Preference: Former Soviet Union, Eastern European
Fund Size: $100 million
Founded: 1995
Average Investment: $5 - 25 million
Minimum Investment: $5 million
Investment Criteria: Startup, First Stage, Consolidations, Privatizations

Venture Capital & Private Equity Firms / Domestic Firms

Industry Group Preference: Food Services, Food & Beverage, Distribution, Renewable Resources, Agriculture
Portfolio Companies: Rasko, FoodMaster, Bagrationi, Chicken Kingdom, Acodec, KLP, Polygraph, Saint Springs
Key Executives:
  Michael Yanney, Chairman Emeritus
  Education: Graduate, University of Nebraska; University of Wisconsin
  Background: Management, Valmont; EVP/Treasurer, Omaha National Bank; Omaha National Coarporation
  Directorships: Burlington Northern Santa Fe Corporation; Level 3 Communications
  Brad Muse, Vice President of Finance
  Education: BSc, Accounting, Indiana State University
  Background: Financial Planning and Analysis; ConAgra Foods; Coopers & Lybrand LLP
  Lisa Y. Roskens, Chief Executive Officer
  Education: Stanford Law School
  Background: Twin Compass, LLC; Business Development, Inacom Corporation; Finance Director, US Senate Campaign of Senator Chuck Hagel
  Directorships: Cantera Partners, LLC
  George Krauss, Managing Director
  Education: JD, MA, Business Admin., University of Nebraska
  Background: Partner, Kutak Rock
  Directorships: Chairman, MFA Mortgage Investment Inc.; Core Bank; Omaha State Bank; Gateway Inc.; West Corp.; First Apartment Investors Inc.; InfoGROUP Inc.

71 AHOY CAPITAL
530 Lytton Avenue
2nd Floor
Palo Alto, CA 94301

web: www.ahoycap.com

Mission Statement: Ahoy Capital is focused on investing in both early-stage venture capital and start-up companies. They seek opportunities in the application of disruptive technologies and ideas that will have profound effects on the ways in which people live and work.

Founded: 2018

Key Executives:
  Chris Douvos, Founder/Managing Director
  Education: BA, Yale College; MBA, Yale School of Management
  Background: Venture Investment Associates; Consultant, Monitor Company
  Cliff Gilman, Managing Director
  Education: AB, Duke University; MBA, Dartmouth College
  Background: Prime Buchholz & Associates; Associate VP/Founding Member, Merrill Lynch Private Equity Partners LP

72 AIRBUS VENTURES
Menlo Park, CA

Mission Statement: Airbus Ventures invests in early and growth-stage companies, acting as lead investors for new and fast-accelerating technologies that will reshape aerospace.

Key Executives:
  Thomas D'Halluin, Managing Partner
  Education: MS, McGill University
  Background: COO, Airbus Ventures; Chief of Staff, Airbus Vetures

73 AISLING CAPITAL
888 Seventh Avenue
12th Floor
New York, NY 10106

Phone: 212-651-6380 **Fax:** 212-651-6379
web: www.aislingcapital.com

Mission Statement: Aisling Capital is a leading investment firm that advises investment funds that invest in products, technologies and global businesses that advance health.
Average Investment: $20 - $50 million
Industry Group Preference: Healthcare, Life Sciences, Therapeutics, Biotechnology
Portfolio Companies: Aclaris Therapeutics, Adams Respiratory Therapeutics, Adma Biologics Inc., Advion, Agile Therapeutics, Aimune Therapeutics, Ajax Health, Allos Therapeutics, Admbit, Aragon Pharmaceuticals, Archimica, Arcus Biosciences, Armgo Pharma Inc., Ascendis Pharma, Aton Pharma, Audentes, Auxilum, Avanza Laboratories, Axcan Pharma, Barried Therapeutics Inc., Bioenvision, BioHaven Pharmaceuticals, Bridgebio, Cardiokine Biopharma, Catalent, Cempra, Chimerix, Cidara Therapeutics, Clovis Oncology, CollaGenex Pharmaceuticals, Colorescience, Cynapsus, Cytos, Dermira, Durata, Earlens, Esperion Therapeutics, F2G, Globalblood Therapeutics, GTx, Imbruvica, Infinity, Intercept, Intersent Ent., Lensar, Lombard Medical, Loxo Oncology, Map Pharmaceuticals, MEI Pharma, Menlo Therpeutics, Miramarlabs, Myogen, Next Wave, Novazyme Pharmaceuticals, Obseva, Oculex Pharmaceuticals, Paratek, Pernix Therapeutics, Pharmaron, Planet Biopharmaceuticals Inc., Powervision, Precision Dematology, Prolacta Bioscience, Promentis Pharmaceuticals Inc., Proragonist Therapeutics, Quintiles, Roka Bioscience, Seragon Pharmaceuticals, SIrion Therapeutics, SkinMedica, Sorrento, Spirox, Sunesis, Synergy, Syros, T2Biosystems, Topaz, TransEnterix, Tria, Verona Pharma, Versartis, ViewRay, Vivus, Zavante, Zeltiq
Key Executives:
  Dennis Purcell, Founder
  Education: BS, Accounting, University of Delaware; MBA, Harvard University
  Background: Managing Director, Life Sciences Investment Banking Group, Chase H&Q
  Directorships: Dynova Laboratories, Xanodyne Pharmaceuticals
  Steven A. Elms, Managing Partner
  Education: BA, Human Biology, Stanford University; MBA, Kellogg Graduate School of Management
  Background: Principal, Life Sciences Investment Banking Group, Hambrecht & Quist; Donaldson Lufkin & Jenrette
  Directorships: ADMA Biologics, Advion BioSciences, Ambit Biosciences Corporation, CeNeRx, BioPharma, LensAR, Next Wave Pharmaceuticals, Pernix Therapeutics, Scerene Healthcare
  Andrew Schiff, MD, Managing Partner
  Education: BS, Neuroscience, Brown University; MD, Cornell University Medical College; MBA, Columbia University
  Background: Internal Medicine, New York Presbyterian Hospital
  Directorships: ARMGO Pharma, Dynova Laboratories, Planet Technologies, SkinMedica, TransEnterix, Zeltiq Aestetics
  Robert J. Wenzel, Chief Financial Officer
  Education: BBA, Accounting, Baruch College
  Background: Controller, Aisling Capital; Vice President, Lazard Alternative Investments; Eisner & Lubin LLP
  JH Bilenker, MD, Operating Partner
  Education: BA, English, Princeton; MD, John Hopkins School of Medicine
  Background: President/CEO, Loxo Oncology; Medical Officer, Office of Oncology Drug Products, US Foods and Drug Administration
  Directorships: Loxo Oncology; LENSAR; Roka Biosciences; T2 Biosystems; ViewRay; Aragon Pharmaceuticals
  Eric Aguitar, MD, Partner
  Education: MD, Harvard Medical School; Cornell University
  Background: Partner, Thomas, Mcnerney and Partners; CEO, Genovo Inc.
  Directorships: HealthCare Ventures

Venture Capital & Private Equity Firms / Domestic Firms

Aftab R. Kherani, MD, Operating Partner
Education: BS, Biology, AB, Economics, MD, Duke University
Background: Engagement Manager, McKinsey & Company
Stacey D. Seltzer, Partner
Education: BS, MS, Yale University; MBA, The Wharton School
Background: Business Development, Schering-Plough
Directorships: Miramar Labs, Precision Dermatology

74 AKERS CAPITAL LLC
8436 Marina Vista
Fair Oaks, CA 95628

Phone: 916-966-2236
web: akerscapital.com

Mission Statement: The firm invests in underserved markets in California and the Northwestern US in technology based investment capital in IT, medical devices, and biotechnology.
Geographic Preference: California, Northwest
Founded: 1999
Average Investment: $3 million
Minimum Investment: $1 million
Investment Criteria: First Stage, Second Stage
Industry Group Preference: Computer Hardware & Software, Wireless Technologies, Electronic Components, Internet Technology, Chemicals, Telecommunications, Networking
Portfolio Companies: Telemetric Corporation, CustomerLink Systems Inc., IP Infusion, Inc.

Key Executives:
Roger Akers, Managing Partner
Education: CPA; MA, Business Admin
Background: Prodata Inc.
Directorships: Golden State Capital Network; Emerging Technology Institute; University of California Connect

75 ALABAMA FUTURES FUND
e-mail: info@alabamafuturesfund.com
web: alabamafuturesfund.com

Mission Statement: Fund seeks to be the first significant investment in an early-stage venture that can reach attainable milestones leading to series A financing within 12-24 months.
Geographic Preference: Alabama
Investment Criteria: Early-Stage
Industry Group Preference: Diversified
Portfolio Companies: Case Status, Condoit, Datacy, Doctor Wellington, HealNow, Joonko, Linq, MomentMD, Pinz, Prepaid2cash, SynsorMed, TeamingPro, True Load Time

76 ALACRITY VENTURES
Berkeley, CA 94707

Phone: 510-649-4030
e-mail: alacrity@alacrityventures.com
web: www.alacritymanagement.com

Mission Statement: Alacrity Ventures is an angel capital investment firm. Its main purpose is to fund and guide start-up companies through initial stages of development, offering seed financing and mentorship. Alacrity is primarily oriented toward working with Internet and technological companies with new and innovative ideas. Alacrity's goal is to identify people with a passion to create ground-breaking high-tech firms and to help them achieve success in building those businesses.
Investment Criteria: Seed-Stage, Startup
Industry Group Preference: Internet, High Technology
Key Executives:
Christopher Allen, Founder
Background: Chief Technology Officer, Certicom Corp; Founder, Concensus Development; Founder, Associated Computer Consultants

77 ALANTRA
75 State Street
Suite 1210
Boston, MA 02109

Phone: 617-482-6200
web: www.alantra.com

Mission Statement: To provide M&A services to mid-market family-ownded companies, mid-cap corporate and private equity investors.
Geographic Preference: Worldwide
Fund Size: $1 billion
Founded: 1975
Minimum Investment: $250,000
Investment Criteria: First stage, Second stage, Mezzanine, Corporate Acquisition, Divestiture, Capital Raising Services
Industry Group Preference: Aerospace, Defense and Government, Automotive, Business Products & Services, Consumer Products, Retail, Consumer & Leisure, Retailing, Food & Beverage, Healthcare, Material Handling, Logistics
Portfolio Companies: Adval Tech, Akta US LLC, Arneg SPA, Bruce Foods Corporation, C-4 Analytics, Centrax, conditorei Coppenrath & Wiese GmbH & Co., CHT Group, Crane & Co., Dearborn Mid-West Conveyor Company, Educational Holdings LLC, Equita GmbH & Co. Holdings, Flavor Infusion LLC, Fleetwood, FORTE Industrial Equipment Systems, Fortress, Freudenberg, Greencore Group Plc, Group Uriach, GSI Group Inc., HitecVision AS, HypothenkenZentrum AG, JacquelineBs Gourmet Cookies, Kaydon Corp., KRG Capital Partners, Landshire Inc., Leggett & Platt Incorporated, Lycored, Lydall Inc., Novozymes AS, Nutragenesis, PAS International Holdings, Pietro Rosa TBM, ProTec, Prudential Capital Group, RFE Investment Partners, Rogers Corporation, RTS Holdings Inc., Seabrook International, Smith Co., Superior Controls, TeraDiode, Trescal

Other Locations:
7 rue Jaques Bingen
Paris 75017
France
Phone: 33 (0) 1-70-91-35-70

WeWork Charlemont Exchange
Dublin 2
Ireland
Phone: 353-1-662-0175

77 Queen Victoria Street
2nd Floor
London EC4V 4AY
United Kingdom
Phone: 44 (0)20-7246-0500

Taunusanlage 15
Frankfurt 60325
Germany
Phone: 49 (0)69-977-886-0

Room 2008, Tower 1, Kerry Center
No. 1515 Nanjing West Road
Shanghai 200040
China
Phone: 86-21-62886218

Calle de José Ortega Y Gasset, 29
Madrid 28006
Spain
Phone: 34-91-745-84-84

Via Borgonuovo 16
Milan 20121
Italy
Phone: 39-02-6367-1601

Sophialaan 43
Amsterdam 1075 BM
Netherlands

Albertgasse 35
Vienna 1080

Venture Capital & Private Equity Firms / Domestic Firms

Austria
Phone: 43 717 28 990

Vasta Tradgardsgatan 15
Stockholm 111 53
Sweden
Phone: 46-705-086-725

Filellinon 1
Athens 105 57
Greece
Phone: 30 210 3278 900

Rua Alexandre Herculano
25-3rd Floor
Lisbon 1250-008
Portugal
Phone: 351-211522282

Av. Cervino 4407, 6b
1425
Buenos Aires
Argentina
Phone: 54 (11)5218-0030

Key Executives:
R. Wade Aust, Managing Partner
Education: BA, Finance & Mathematics, Salve Regina University; CFA

78 ALBION INVESTORS LLC
501 Madison Avenue
Suite 701
New York, NY 10022

Phone: 212-277-7520
e-mail: cgonzalez@albioninvestors.com
web: www.albioninvestors.com

Mission Statement: Seeks to provide mezzanine and private equity capital to attractive middle market companies to facilitate events such as leveraged acquisitions, refinancing/recapitalizations or growth capital requirements.
Geographic Preference: Northeastern, Mid-Atlantic & Southeastern United States
Fund Size: $170 million
Founded: 1996
Average Investment: $15 million
Minimum Investment: $2 million
Investment Criteria: Differentiated Products/Services, Solid Customer Base, Located in the Continental United States, Consistent Operating & Financial Performance
Industry Group Preference: Business Products & Services, Value-Added Distribution, Specialty Manufacturing, Consumer Products
Portfolio Companies: ARTONE Manufacturing, Addison McKee, Rimrock, S.I. Jacobson

Key Executives:
Mark Arnold, Managing Partner
212-277-7527
e-mail: marnold@albioninvestors.com
Education: London University; Fellow, Institute of Actuaries
Background: Partner/COO, BEA Associates; Co-Founder, Albion Asset Advisors
Directorships: Rimrock Corporation; North American Propane, Inc.
Alastair Tedford, Managing Partner
212-277-7525
e-mail: atedford@albioninvestors.com
Education: MBA, INSEAD; MA Law, University College
Background: Co-Founder, Albion Asset Advisors; Co-Head Emerging Market, Goldman Sachs
Directorships: Salomon Brothers
Charles Gonzalez, Managing Director
212-277-7537
e-mail: cgonzalez@albioninvestors.com
Education: BS Finance/Economics, University of Illinois; MBA, University of Chicago
Background: Management, Continental Bank; Management, Bank of America; Managing Director, Banc of America Securities
Directorships: Associated Packaging Technologies; Wood Resources; AddisonMckee; ShelterLogic
Basil Livanos, Managing Director
212-277-7524
e-mail: blivanos@albioninvestors.com
Education: BS Banking/Finance/International Business, MBA Finance, New York University
Background: Management, ACFG; Investments, Equitable
Christine Vogt, Vice President
212-277-7521
e-mail: cvogt@albioninvestors.com
Education: BS, Finance, Villanova University
Background: The Blackstone Group, LP
Edina Leiher, VP of Operations/Chief Compliance Officer
Education: BS/MPA, Policy Analysis, Marxe School of Public and International Affairs, Bernard M Baruch College

79 ALBUM VC
3451 N Trimpuh Boulevard
Suite 200
Lehi, UT 84043

e-mail: hello@album.vc
web: album.vc

Mission Statement: Formerly known as Peak Ventures, the firm focuses on investing in and growing innovative seed-stage companies in Utah and the West Coast through two funds, with a third in progress.
Geographic Preference: Utah, West Coast
Fund Size: $75 million
Founded: 2019
Investment Criteria: Seed Stage
Industry Group Preference: Technology, E-Commerce & Manufacturing, Mobile, Retail, Consumer & Leisure, SaaS, Real Estate Technology, Video Gaming
Portfolio Companies: Andela, BallerTV, Beynd, Bluestar.com, Cake, ClearVoice, ClientSuccess, Consensus, Converus, Degreed, Divvy, EquitySim, Filevine, GrassWire, Homie, Jolt, Lendio, Liingo Eyewear, MarketWare, Mighty, Molio, Mosyle, MX, Nav, Neighbor, ObservePoint, Omadi, Owlet, Pet IQ, PierianDx, Pillow, Podium, Prenda, Pronto, Qwick, Route, SalesRabbit, SaltStack, Spiff, Strala, Studio, TaxBit, Teem, Weave, Wooly, Zipbooks

Key Executives:
Sid Krommenhoek, Partner
Education: BS, Brigham Young University; University of Utah
Background: Managing Partner, Peak Ventures; Co-Founder, Zinch; Adjunct Professor of Entrepreneurship, Brigham Young University; Advisor, Braid Workshop; Partner, HKK Marketing; Director, Sales, Dealstreet; Founder, Soft Spot
Directorships: Podium, BallerTV, Jolt, Cake, ClientSuccess, EquitySim, SalesRabbit, Marketware, CampusLogic, Consensus
John Mayfield, Partner
Education: BS, MBA, Brigham Young University
Background: Partner, Peak Ventures; Sales, Instructure; Marketing, Qualtrics; Senior Associate, Duff & Phelps; Associate, Peterson Ventures; Operations, Innovasis
Directorships: Filevine, Route, Qwick, Neighbor, ZipBooks, Wooly, Consensus, ClearVoice
Diogo Myrrha, Partner
Education: BEcon, Brigham Young University
Background: Principal, Peak Ventures; Vice President, Stoneway Capital; Co-Founder, Finance, Operations, Luvaire; Special Projects, Braven
Directorships: Huckabuy, Beynd, TaxBit, Spiff, BlueStar Inspections, Mosyle, SalesRabbit

Venture Capital & Private Equity Firms / Domestic Firms

80 ALERION PARTNERS
23 Old Kings Highway South
Darien, CT 06820

Phone: 203-202-9900
e-mail: info@alerionpartners.com
web: www.alerionpartners.com

Mission Statement: Alerion's investment professional team offers financial and operating expertise to help accelerate the development of companies.

Founded: 2004
Average Investment: $3 - $10 million
Industry Group Preference: Consumer Products, Business Products & Services, Marketing, Media
Portfolio Companies: DeliverCareRx, EnviroScent, HydroMassage, InStadium, True Citrus
Key Executives:
   Bruce F Failing, Managing Partner
   e-mail: failing@alerionpartners.com
   Education: BA, Tufts University; MBA, Harvard Business School
   Background: Productivity Solutions Inc.; Actmedia; Lamaze Publishing Company; Newborn Channel; Tone Brothers; Spice Company; ERS International
   Directorships: EnviroScent, InStadium, HydroMassage, DeliverCareRx
   Michael B Persky, Managing Partner
   e-mail: persky@alerionpartners.com
   Education: BA, Economics and Organizational Behavior and Management, Brown University; MBA, Stanford Graduate School of Business
   Background: President & COO, Productivity Solutions; President & COO, ERS International; VP, Marketing, Executone Information Systems; VMX
   Directorships: EnviroScent, True Citrus, InStadium, HydroMassage, DeliverCareRx
   Robert Cioffi, Venture Partner
   e-mail: cioffi@alerionpartners.com
   Education: BA, Political Science & Economics, University of Vermont; MBA, Fuqua School of Business, Duke University
   Background: Senior VP, GE Equity; Evaluation Associates Capital Markets; Chase Manhattan; Staff, US Senator James M Jeffords
   Virginia Cargill, Venture Partner
   e-mail: cargill@alerionpartners.com
   Education: BA, Wellesley College; MBA, Kellogg School of Management, Northwestern University
   Background: President & CEO, CBS Outernet; Co-Founder, Caring Today; President, Lamaze Publishing; Actmedia; General Mills; Procter & Gamble
   Sayles Braga, Partner
   e-mail: braga@alerionpartners.com
   Education: BA, Economics, Harvard University
   Background: CEO, ABD3; Restructuring Group, Lazard
   Directorships: EnviroScent, True Citrus, InStadium, DeliverCareRx
   Nissa Bartalsky, Manager
   e-mail: bartalsky@alerionpartners.com
   Education: BA, Neuroscience, Mount Holyoke College; MBA, School of Business, University of Connecticut
   Rick Ruffolo, Venture Partner
   e-mail: rruffolo@enviroscent.com
   Education: BS, Business Administration, University Of Dayton; MBA From Olin School of Business at Washington University, St. Louis
   Background: CEO, Enviroscent; SC Johnson; Bath & Body Works; Yankee Candle; Crabtree & Evelyn

81 ALEUTIAN CAPITAL PARTNERS
100 Wall Street
Suite 900
New York, NY 10005

Phone: 212-652-4000 Fax: 212-652-4030
e-mail: info@aleutiancapital.com
web: www.aleutiancapital.com

Mission Statement: Aleutian Capital Partners is a private equity investment group that invests in and acquires privately-owned companies in North America and internationally.

Geographic Preference: North America
Industry Group Preference: Manufacturing, Distribution, Business Products & Services, Medical Devices, Aerospace, Defense and Government, Security, Consumer Products, Information Technology, Logistics, Transportation
Portfolio Companies: Rev H20, Global Sugar Art, Amtech Corporation
   Daniel Pfeffer, Managing Director
   Education: BA, University of Colorado, Boulder; MBA, University of Colorado, Denver
   Background: President/cEO, Lighting By Gregory; Senior Manager, Linkshare Corporation

82 ALEXANDER HUTTON
Raineier Towerue
Suite 3405
1301 Fifth Avenue
Seattle, WA 98101

Phone: 206-341-9800
e-mail: info@alexanderhutton.com
web: alexanderhutton.com

Mission Statement: Focuses on investments in technology companies in the areas of IT, Internet, telecommunications, medical services and healthcare infrastructure, particularly in business-to-business Internet space. Actively seeking new projects.

Geographic Preference: Northwest
Founded: 1999
Investment Criteria: All Stages, Seed, First Stage, Second Stage
Industry Group Preference: Business to Business, Communications Equipment, Computer Hardware & Software, Transportation, Electronic Components, Healthcare, Internet Technology, Manufacturing, Telecommunications, Networking, Online Content
Portfolio Companies: Madrona Solutions Group, Rite In The Rain, Damar Aerosystems, Olympic Physical Therapy
Key Executives:
   Scott Hardman, Managing Director
   Education: MBA, University of Washington
   Kent Johnson, Managing Director
   Education: BA, University of Washington; MBA, Seattle University

83 ALIGNED PARTNERS
2882 Sand Hill Rd.
Suite 100
Menlo Park, CA 94025

e-mail: info@alignedvc.com
web: www.alignedvc.com

Mission Statement: Aligned Partners believes in aligning the interests of founders and investors to generate high returns and sustainable growth.

Investment Criteria: Early-Stage, Series A
Industry Group Preference: Information Technology
Key Executives:
   Jodi Sherman Jahic, Managing Partner
   Education: Pomona College; MBA, Kellogg School of Management
   Background: Voyager Capital; SCG

Venture Capital & Private Equity Firms / Domestic Firms

Susan Mason, Managing Partner
Education: BS, University of Colorado; MBA, University of California, LA
Background: ONSET Ventures

84 ALLEGIS CYBER CAPITAL
200 Page Mill Road
Suite 100
Palo Alto, CA 94306

e-mail: businessplans@allegiscyber.com
web: www.allegiscyber.com

Mission Statement: Invests in early-stage startup companies developing enabling technology and infrastructure which serve emerging information technology markets. Allegis Cyber Capital is currently seeking new investments with the following criteria: visionary founders and winning managers, compelling products and technologies, ROI potential and realistic exit strategies.

Geographic Preference: West Coast, North America, Western Europe
Fund Size: $500 million
Founded: 1996
Average Investment: $3 - $5 million
Minimum Investment: $50,000
Investment Criteria: Seed, Early-Stage, Startup
Industry Group Preference: Enabling Technology, Infrastructure, Enterprise Services, Software, Broadband, Service Industries, Wireless Technologies, Internet Technology
Portfolio Companies: Area 1, Bracket Computing, Callsign, CyberGRX, Dragos Inc., E8 Security, eFileCabinet, Ironport, Lucidworks, Moki, Platfora, RedOwl Analytics, Shape Security, Signifyd, Solera Networks, Symplified, Synack, vArmour, SafeGuard Cyber, Source Defence, Prevailion

Other Locations:
8110 Maple Lawn Boulevard
Suite 200
Fulton, MD 20759

Key Executives:
Robert R. Ackerman, Jr., Founder/Managing Director
e-mail: ackerman@allegiscapital.com
Education: BS Computer Science, University of California
Background: Manager, Ackerman Group; CEO, UniSoft Corporation; Founder/Chairman, InfoGear Technology Corporation
Directorships: IronPort Systems, RFco
Spencer Tall, Managing Director
Education: BS Political Science/Japanese, Brigham Young University
Background: Co-Founder/General Partner, APV Technology Partners; Strategic Advsior: Motorola, Sony, Fujitsu, Samsung, Canon, TDK, Dacom; US Sales Operations, Marubeni Corporation; Sales Manager, GRE America
Directorships: IMVU; Allegiance; Solera Networks; Symplified
Peter Bodine, Managing Director
Education: MBA, University of Utah; BS, Brigham Young University
Background: Co-Founder, APV Technology Partners; Asia Pacific Ventures
Directorships: AdventureLink; Axcient, iBAHN, iPass
Steve Simonian, Chief Financial/Compliance Officer
Education: BA, Business Economics, University of California, Santa Barbara
Background: CFO, August Capital; CFO, Gabriel Venture Partners; CFO, Meritech Capital Partners

85 ALLIANCE OF ANGELS
719 Second Avenue
Suite 1403
Seattle, WA 98104

e-mail: aoa@allianceofangels.com
web: www.allianceofangels.com

Mission Statement: The Alliance of Angels is one of the largest and most active angel groups in the Pacific Northwest.

Geographic Preference: Pacific Northwest
Founded: 1997
Industry Group Preference: Clean Technology, Information Technology, Life Sciences, Consumer Products, Consumer Services
Portfolio Companies: 1000 Museums, Accium Biosciences, ADAPX, Airbiquity, Amnis, Ansyr, AppAttach, Apptentive, Array Health, Athleon, Balance, Banshee Bungee, Battlefly, Bidadoo Auctions, Blade, Buddy, BuddyTV, Cadence Biomedical, Cardiometrics, Celilo Group Media, Centri Technology, Chelsey Henry, Claim-Maps, Clairsonic, ClarityHealth, Cleverset, Clover, Conenza, Cordance, CourtLink, Crowd Compass, CultureMob, Daptiv, DashWire, Deep Domain, Delve Networks, Dendreon, Dentigenix, DigitalScirocco, DocuSign, Dry Soda Co., Earth Class Mail, Elemental, EnRoute, Entomo, Escapia.com, Esately, Estorian, Every Move, FluxDrive, Food.ee, Full Circle, GenPrime, GeoPage, Geospiza, Giftspot, Globesherpa, Healionics, HomeGrocer.com, iclick, Illumingen, ImageX, Impel Neuropharma, Infomove, Insitu, InSpa, Intelsoft Technologies, Intelligent ION, Julep, Lagotek, Limeade, LiquidPlanner, Livebid.com, Lumencor, Madfiber, MagicWheels, Mailchannels, Marketfish, Marketsync, Mercent, Meteor, Metron Systems, MicroGreen Polymers, Mirador Biomedical, MobiSante, Mobliss, Modumetal, Moprise, Movaya, Mporai, Neah, Nfluence, Novinium, Nuun, Onehub, OraHealth, Others Online, Overcast Media, PakSense, Pathable, PeopleMatter, Perlego, Pharmitas, Photobucket, Pier Systems, POW, PowerTech, Prepared Response, Protelus, Revel Body, Sash, ScaleOut Software, Scayl, Seattle Sensor Systems, Shelfari, Shiftboard, Signature Destinations, Skycast, Snapin, SnapNames, StressWave, Sunstream Boat Lifts, TalentSpring, Tatango, Teachtown, Tenfold Organic Textiles, Theo Chocolate, Trace Detect, Treema Labs, UpTap, Valant Medical Solutions, Venue Labs, Virticus, VoloMetrix, VueMed, Wavelink, Websync, Widemile, Wishpot, Wonderhorse, Zooppa

Key Executives:
Yi-Jian Ngo, Managing Director
Education: MBA, Johnson Graduate School of Management, Cornell University
Background: Founding Team Member, AT&T Corporate Venture Fund; Sierra Ventures

86 ALLOS VENTURES
6340 Westfield Boulevard
Indianapolis, IN 46220

Phone: 317-275-6800
web: www.allosventures.com

Mission Statement: Allos Ventures invests in early-stage companies, executing a hands-on approach with their clients.

Geographic Preference: Indiana, Michigan, Ohio
Founded: 2010
Investment Criteria: Early-Stage
Industry Group Preference: Software, Technology-Enabled Business, Specialty Healthcare, Medical Devices, Diagnostics, Advanced Manufacturing
Portfolio Companies: 7signal, Alung, Aprimo, Assure X Health, BidPal, Blue Pillar, Bolstra, Change Dynamix, Cordata, Dattus, Emplify, Enosix, Foxtrot Code, Fuzic, Healthcare Asset Network, Lessonly, Life Share Technologies, Lumavate, Octiv, Peach Works, Scale Computing, Vendor Registry, WebLink International

Venture Capital & Private Equity Firms / Domestic Firms

Other Locations:
2724 Erie Avenue
Suite 200
Cincinnati, OH 45280
Phone: 513-723-2309

Key Executives:
Dan Aquilano, Managing Director
317-275-6802
Education: BS, Arizona University; MBA, Harvard University
Background: Boston Consulting Group; Fox Group; Gazelle TechVentures

John McIlwraith, Managing Director
513-723-2311
Education: BA, Hillsdale College; JD, Case Western Reserve University
Background: Corporate Lawyer, Jones Day; Quantum Health Resources; Blue Chip Venture Company; Gazelle TechVentures

---

87 ALLOY VENTURES
1415 Hamilton Avenue
Palo Alto, CA 94301

web: www.alloyventures.com

Mission Statement: Seeks matches between emerging technologies with emerging market opportunities and looks for companies with the potential to achieve a large market capitalization and address a large and growing market. Each year Alloy invests in a small number of entrepreneurial ideas and young companies and strive to achieve long-term relationships.

Geographic Preference: Western United States
Fund Size: $370 million
Founded: 1977
Average Investment: $1 - $5 million
Minimum Investment: $50,000
Investment Criteria: Seed, Early-Stage, Later-Stage
Industry Group Preference: Information Technology, Life Sciences, Bioinformatics, Health Related, Energy, Clean Technology
Portfolio Companies: Aegea Medical, Agari, AnaptysBio, Apptera, Cambrios, CoAlign Innovations, Cortina, Ensenda, Genomatica, The GigaOM Network, Gradient, Hightail, KaloBios, KFx Medical, Labcyte Inc., Mavenir Systems, Molecular Imprints, Novasys Medical, NuGEN Technologies, Optimedica, Pacific Biosciences, RainDance Technologies, Restoration Robotics, Scifiniti, Siluria Technologies, SynergEyes, Teradici, Xactly

Key Executives:
Ammar H. Hanafi, General Partner
e-mail: ahanafi@alloyventures.com
Education: BS Applied/Engineering Physics, Cornell University; MBA, Stanford University
Background: VP New Business Ventures, Cisco Systems; PanAmSat Corporation; Morgan Stanley; Donaldson Lufkin & Jenrette
Directorships: YouSENDit, Retrevo, Mavenir Systems, Cortina Systems, GigaOM, Infineta Systems, Apptera

Michael Hunkapiller, General Partner
e-mail: mwhunk@alloyventures.com
Education: BS, Oklahoma Baptist University; PhD, California Institute of Technology
Background: President/General Manager, Applied Biosystems; Founder, Celera Genomics; Sr VP, Applera Corporation; Senior Research Fellow Biology, California Institute of Technology; Author of more than 100 scientific publications; Patentholder
Directorships: Pacific Biosciences, NuGEN, Verinata Health, RainDance Technologies

Doug Kelly MD, General Partner
e-mail: doug@alloyventures.com
Education: BA, Biochemistry/Molecular Biology, University of California, San Diego; MD, Albert Einstein College of Medicine; MBA, Stanford University
Background: Ligand Pharmaceuticals; Independent Consultant
Directorships: Aegea, Barrx, CoAlign Innovations, Crux Biomedical, Novasys, Restoration Robotics

Daniel I. Rubin, General Partner
e-mail: dan@alloyventures.com
Education: BA Physics, Pomona College
Background: Co-Founder, Artisan Components; Director Product Marketing/Managing Director, Ultratech Stepper
Directorships: CiraNova, Ensenda, Molecular Imprints, Gradient, Teradici, Integrated PhotoVoltaics

John F. Shoch, General Partner
e-mail: shoch@alloyventures.com
Education: BA Political Science, MS, PhD Computer Science, Stanford University
Background: President, Xerox Office Systems Division; CEO, Xerox; Founding Investor, Conductus and Remedy
Directorships: Knowledge Networks, Nitronex, ViVOtech, Xangati

Craig C. Taylor, General Partner
650-687-5000
Fax: 650-687-5010
e-mail: craig@alloyventures.com
Education: BS, MS Physics, Brown University; MBA, Stanford University
Background: Office of Technology Licensing, Stanford University
Directorships: ForteBio, Labcyte, Optimedica, Zyomyx, KFx Medical

Tony Di Bona, General Partner/CFO
e-mail: tony@alloyventures.com
Education: BS, Psychology & Biology, Rice University; MD, University of Texas Health Science Center
Background: Founder, Affymax NV; Founder, FluMist

David W. Pidwell, Venture Partner
e-mail: pidwell@alloyventures.com
Education: MS, Computer System Engineering, Ohio State University; 3 years on PhD in Engineering Economic Systems, Stanford University
Background: Founder/President/CEO, Rasna Corporation; ROLM
Directorships: Rainfinity, iPrint Systems, Informatica

J. Leighton Read, MD, Venture Partner
e-mail: leighton@alloyventures.com
Education: BS, Psychology & Biology, Rice University; MD, University of Texas Health Science Center
Background: Co-Founder, Affymax NV; Founder/Chairman/CEO, Aviron; Partner, Interhealth Limited; Peter Bent Brigham Hospital
Directorships: Avidia Research Institute

---

88 ALLSTATE INVESTMENTS LLC
3075 Sanders Road
Suite G5D
Northbrook, IL 60062

web: www.allstateinvestments.com

Mission Statement: Allstate Investment is a private equity, real estate, and mezzanine funds firm.

Geographic Preference: United States
Fund Size: $200 million
Founded: 2000
Average Investment: $50 million
Minimum Investment: $10 million
Investment Criteria: Mezzanine, Consolidations, Acquisition, LBO, MBO, Recapitalization, Privatizations
Industry Group Preference: Broadcasting, Cable, Radio, Communications Equipment, Diversified, Education, Electronic Components, Financial Services, Industrial Equipment, Manufacturing, Chemicals, Publishing, Wholesale, Advertising, Distribution

Venture Capital & Private Equity Firms / Domestic Firms

Other Locations:
444 W Lake Street
45th Floor
Chicago, IL 60606

36 Broadway
London SW1H 0BH
United Kingdom

Key Executives:
Peter Keehn, Managing Director, Private Equity
e-mail: pkeehn@allstate.com
Education: AB, Brown University; MBA, Northwestern University
Background: Pricinpal, Waud Capital Partners
Directorships: Northwestern Investment Management Company
John Dugenske, President, Investments & Financial Products
Education: BA, MA, Mechanical Engineering, MBA, University of Illinois
Background: UBS Asset Management; Neuberger Berman; Deutsche Asset Management; Portfolio Manager, NISA Investment Advisors
Russ Mayerfeld, Senior Managing Director, Alternative Investments
Education: BA, University of Illinois; MBA, Harvard University
Background: UBS LLC; Dean Witter Reynolds Inc.
Scott McConnell, Chief Information Officer
Education: BS, Business Admin., Miami University; MBA, University of Chicago Booth School of Business
Background: Technology & Operations, Alltstate; Accenture

89 ALMAZ CAPITAL
3274 Alpine Road
Portola Valley, CA 94028

Phone: 650-644-4530
e-mail: press@almazcapital.com
web: www.almazcapital.com

Mission Statement: Almaz Capital Partners is one of the leading venture capital firms serving entrepreneurs and companies with ties to Russia and the Commonwealth of Independent States (CIS).
Geographic Preference: United States, Russia
Fund Size: $170 million
Founded: 2008
Industry Group Preference: Technology, Digital Media & Marketing, Communications, Internet, Data Storage, Enterprise Software, E-Commerce & Manufacturing
Portfolio Companies: 2can, Acronis, Acumatica, Alawar Entertainment, AlterGeo, AppScotch, CarPrice, Cinarra Systems, Content Analytics, Dabbl, Fasten, FinalPrice, Flirtic, GoodData, GridGain, Hover, If You Can, Jelastic, MakeTime, Mobalytics, NFWare, Nival, nScaled, Odin, Parallels, Petcube, PIQ, Plesk, Qik, Sensity, StarWind Software, Vyatta, Yandex

Key Executives:
Alexander Galitsky, Co-Founder/Managing Partner
Education: PhD, Computer Science, Defense Research Institute, Moscow Institute of Physics
Background: Russian Technologies, Soviet Space Agency and Defense Industry
Charles E. Ryan, General Partner
Education: Harvard College
Background: Chairman, UFG Asset Management; Senior Advisor, Deutsche Bank AG; Associate/Principal Banker, European Bank for Reconstruction and Development; Co-Founder, United Financial Group; Chief Country Officer/CEO, Deutsche Bank Group
Pavel Bogdanov, General Partner
Education: BS, Moscow Institute of Physics; MBA, INSEAD; PhD, Stanford University
Background: Partner, Russian Technologies; Systems Design Engineer, KLA-Tencor
Directorships: Investment Director, Sistema Telecom
Geoffrey Baehr, General Partner
Education: BA, Biochemistry & Natural Sciences, Fordham University
Background: General Partner, US Venture Partners; Chief Network Officer, Sun Microsystems

90 ALPHA CAPITAL PARTNERS
Chicago, IL 60601

Phone: 312-322-9800
e-mail: info@alphacapital.com
web: www.alphacapital.com

Mission Statement: Actively seeking investments. Provides equity financing for promising growth businesses and for buyouts or recapitalizations of established companies; targets promising young companies with a commercially developed product needing financing primarily for marketing and business expansion.
Geographic Preference: Midwest United States
Fund Size: $90 million
Founded: 1984
Average Investment: $2 - 15 million
Minimum Investment: $500,000
Investment Criteria: Middle-market companies with current run rate revenues of at least $5 million; Buyouts, Recapitalizations, Acquisitions, Expansion, Late-Stage, Growth Stage
Industry Group Preference: Manufacturing, Industrial Distribution, Consumer Products, Consumer Services, Financial Services, Communications, Information Technology, Health Related
Portfolio Companies: America's PowerSports, Emerald BioAgricultre Corp., Factory Connection, NM Group Global LLC

Key Executives:
Andrew H Kalnow, President
e-mail: ahkalnow@alphacapital.com
Education: BA, Lawrence University; MBA, Babson College
Background: VP, First National Bank of Chicago; VP, First Chicago; CEO, National Machinery LLC; CEO, NM Group Global LLC

91 ALPHA VENTURE PARTNERS
1 Penn Plaza
Suite 3905
New York, NY 10119

Phone: 212-967-3332
web: alphavp.com

Mission Statement: Alpha Venture Partners is a growth-stage fund investing in the tech industry.
Geographic Preference: US
Average Investment: $20 million - $50 million
Minimum Investment: $500,000
Investment Criteria: Growth Stage, Series C, Revenue of $20 million
Industry Group Preference: Software, SaaS, Information Technology, E-Commerce, Mobile
Portfolio Companies: Careem, Cloud Technology Partners, Coupang, Doctor on Demand, Getaround, GoPuff, Lime, LiveIntent, Localytics, Rover, Socure, SportHero, Vroom, Wish.com

Key Executives:
Steve Brotman, Founder/Managing Partner
Education: BA, Duke University; JD/MBA, Washington University
Background: Strategic Advisor, Pritzker Group Venture Capital; Co-Founder/Managing Director, Greenhill SAVP
Brian Smiga, Co-Founding Partner
Education: BA, Swarthmore College; MA, Trinity College, Dublin

Venture Capital & Private Equity Firms / Domestic Firms

Background: Advisor, Priztker Group Venture Capital; Founder/CEO, Preclick; CEO, 3Path; SVP of Marketing, 1ClickCharge

92 ALPINE INVESTORS
One California Street
Suite 2900
San Francisco, CA 94111

Phone: 415-392-9100
web: www.alpineinvestors.com

Mission Statement: Alpine Investors believes in working with and learning from their portfolio companies.
Geographic Preference: United States, Canada
Fund Size: $1.4 Billion
Founded: 2001
Average Investment: $15 million
Minimum Investment: $10 million
Investment Criteria: Acquisition, LBO, MBO, Recapitalization, Special Situations, Minority Investments, EBITDA of $1-40 million, Enterprise Value of $5-400 million
Industry Group Preference: Software, Retail, Consumer & Leisure, Business Services
Portfolio Companies: AuthorityLabs, America's Thrift Stores, Apex Service Partners, ASG, Bill4Time, CarHop, Cleo, Comlinkdata, Cyfe, EcoInteractive, e-Courier Software, Evergreen Services Group, Exym, Foothold Technology, GatherUp, Grade Us, HealthComp Holdings, ImageQuix, Ingenio, Kaleidacare, Light Wave Dental Management, MidAmerica Administrative & Retirement Solutions LLC, Midwest Vision Partners, Minute Menu Systems, Photolynx, PracticePanther, Record 360, ReputationLoop, Reputology, Riverside Insights, Transcendent, Vendstar, Vionic, WebEquity, Windsor Fine Jewelers, YDesign Group, YouCaring

Key Executives:
Graham Weaver, Founding Partner
Education: BS, Engineering, Princeton University; MBA, Stanford Business School
Background: Vice President, Oak Hill Capital Management
Will Adams, Founding Partner
Education: BA, Colgate University; MBA, Kellogg Graduate School of Management
Background: Marketing, Clorox Company; CEO, Great Falls Marketing
Billy Maguy, Founding Partner
Education: BS, MS, Industrial Engineering, Stanford University; MBA, Stanford Graduate School of Business
Background: Director, Business Development, Telephia
Dan Sanner, Founding Partner
Education: BA, Economics, Dartmouth College
Background: Partner, Flowerdale Group
Directorships: YLighting
Mark Strauch, Founding Partner
Education: BSc, Lehigh University; MBA, Kellogg School Of Management
Background: Business Engine
Matt Moore, Managing Partner
Education: BS, Environmental Studies/Geography, University of California, Santa Barbara
Background: OpenDNS; Symantec; FireEye; SolidFire; Google; Virident

93 ALSOP LOUIE PARTNERS
943 Howard Street
San Francisco, CA 94103

Phone: 415-625-8752
web: www.alsop-louie.com

Mission Statement: Early-stage technology VC firm in San Francisco.

Founded: 2006
Investment Criteria: Early-Stage
Industry Group Preference: Information Technology
Portfolio Companies: Aerospike, Baton System, Device Authority, Digilens, drop, Gfycat, Hover, Intelyt, Jetlore, Karmic Labs, Keyssa, Looking Glass, Mixed Dimensions, Motive Medical Intelligence, New Matter, Niantic, Phase Four, Phizzle, Remedy, Sapho, The Cipher Brief, Ursa Major Tech, Wickr
Gilman Louie, Partner
Background: Founder & CEO, In-Q-Tel; Chief Creative Officer, Hasbro Interactive
Stewart Alsop, Partner
Background: General Partner, New Enterprise Associates; Editor in Chief, InfoWorld; Executive Editor, Inc. Magazine
Nancy Lee, CFO & Partner
Background: Walden International
Jim Whims, Partner
Background: Partner, Techfund Capital; Co-Founder, Worlds of Wonder
Directorships: Smith & Tinker
Joe Addiego, Partner
Background: Investment Partner, In-Q-Tel; EVP, Marketing & Sales, Talarian; Hewlett-Packard; AT&T
Bill Crowell, Partner
Background: Deputy Director, National Security Agency; CEO, Cylink
Directorships: Safenet Holdings, Fixmo, Airpatrol, DRS Technologies, Six3 Systems
Mark Fields, Partner
Education: BA, Rutgers Univ.; MBA, Pepperdine Univ.
Background: CME Ventures
Directorships: Advisory Council, Brennan School of Business; Lauren's Hope

94 ALTA PARTNERS
115 W Snow King Avenue
Suite 101B
Jackson, WY 83001

Phone: 415-362-4022
e-mail: alta@altapartners.com
web: www.altapartners.com

Mission Statement: Healthcare venture capital firm.
Fund Size: $2 Billion
Founded: 1996
Average Investment: $5-$12 million
Investment Criteria: Early-Stage, Later-Stage
Industry Group Preference: Technology, Life Sciences, Biotechnology, Biopharmaceuticals, Medical, Information Technology
Portfolio Companies: Ablynx, Adolor Corporation, Aerie Pharmaceuticals, Allakos, Angiosyn, Aspire Health, Astex Pharmaceuticals, ATS Medical, Augmedix, Avid, Bioventus, Calistoga Pharma, Cartiva, Cerenis Therapeutics, Chimerix, Clovis Oncology, Connetics Corporation, Cotherix, Cutera, Cytokinetics, DeCODE Genetics, Difinity Health, Dispatch Health, Encoded Genomics, Esperion Therapeutics, Esprit Pharma, ESP Pharma, Flamel Technologies FoldRx, Intarcia Therapeutics, InterMune, Immune Design, itriage, Kiadis Pharma, Kite Phrama, Kosan Biosciences, LJL Biosystems, MacroGenics Inc., Mako Surgical Corp., Maestro Health, NovaCardia, Oceana Therapeutics, Paladina Health, PatientKeeper, Plexxikon, PneumRx, Prolacta Bioscience, Proxima Therapeutics, U3 Pharama, US Acute Care Solutions, Sarcode Bioscience, Sienna Biopharmaceuticals, Sutro Biopharma, Tivity Health

Other Locations:
260 Josephine Street
Denver, CO 80206

Key Executives:
Dan Janney, Managing Director
Education: MBA, Anderson School, University of California, Los Angeles; BA History, Georgetown University

Background: Senior Investment Banker, Montgomery Securities; Leveraged Buyout/Private Equity Group, Bankers Trust Company
Directorships: Rebecca & John Moores Cancer Center; Corgentech; Dynavax Technologies
Bob More, Managing Director
Education: BA, Middlebury College; MBA, Darden School of Business
Background: Bill and Melinda Gates Foundation
Directorships: One Revolution; Foundation for Innovative New Diagnostics
Pete Hudson, Managing Director
Education: BA, Colorado College; MD, University of Colorado
Background: Aetna
Directorships: U.S. Acute Care Solutions; Maestro Health
Larry Randall, Chief Financial Officer
Education: BS, Accounting, Santa Clara University
Background: The Gap, Inc., Intel Corporation

95 ALTAIR VENTURES
18416 Chelmsford
Cupertino, CA 95014

Phone: 408-218-1920 Fax: 309-214-3195
web: www.altairventures.com

Mission Statement: An entry-level high-technology investment and consulting firm whose approach is to help with financial investments, human capital, and strategic consulting.

Founded: 2001
Minimum Investment: $250,000
Investment Criteria: Seed, Startup, Early-Stage
Industry Group Preference: Semiconductors, Consumer Products, Biometrics, Infrastructure, Networking, Security, Electronic Technology, Internet Technology
Portfolio Companies: Applied Wave Research, Path Scale, Syabas, Zenasis

Key Executives:
Sajid A. Sohail, General Partner
925-413-9286
Fax: 925-396-6032
Education: MS, Electrical Engineering, University of Illinois
Background: Founder/CEO, Dazzle Multimedia; Executive VP/General Manager, SCM Corporation; Director Engineering, C-Cube Microsystems; Tera Microsystems; Engineering/Design, Digital Equipment Corporation
Naeem Zafar, General Partner
408-218-1920
Fax: 309-214-3195
e-mail: naeem@altairventures.com
Education: BSEE, Brown University; MSEE, University of Minnesota
Background: President/CEO, Silicon Design Systems; President/CEO, Veridicom; VP Technology Strategy/VP Worldwide Marketing, Quickturn Design Systems ; VLSI Design Engineer/Research Scientist, Honeywell Research Labs; Lecturer

96 ALTAMONT CAPITAL PARTNERS
400 Hamilton Avenue
Suite 230
Palo Alto, CA 94301

Phone: 650-264-7750
e-mail: acp-info@altamontcapital.com
web: www.altamontcapital.com

Mission Statement: Private equity firm investing in middle market businesses, often ones in transition.

Fund Size: $2.5 Billion
Founded: 2010
Industry Group Preference: Business Products & Services, Financial Services, Industrial Services, Healthcare, Retail, Restaurants & Franchising, Consumer Products & Services
Portfolio Companies: Accelerant Holdings, Access Insurance, Alamo Drafthouse Cinema, Amplity Health, The Bayou Companies, Billabong, Byrider, Brixton, Cascade Windows, Che Behavioral Health Services, Celestite, Colorado Boxed Beef Company, Cotton Patch Cafe, Dakine, Embark General, Douglas Products, Excel Fitness, Fox Head, Hybrid Apparel, Intuitive Health, The Juice Plus Company, Kuvare, Maxi Canada, McLarens, Marvin Manufacturing, Meta Financial Group, ModernHealth, Omniplex, Renegade Brands, Robert Allen Duralee Group, Sequel Youth & Family Services, Tacala, Tall Tree Foods, Wunderlich

Jesse Rogers, Managing Director
Education: BA, Stanford University; MBA, Harvard Business School
Background: Co-Founder/Co-Principal Managing Director, Golden Gate Capital; Bain & Company
Directorships: Beringer Wine Estates, CCCS, Cydcor/2020, Employer's Direct Insurance
Randall Eason, Managing Director
Education: BA, Economics, MA, Sociology, Stanford University
Background: Principal, Golden Gate Capital; Consultant, Bain & Company
Keoni Schwartz, Managing Director
Education: BA, History, Princeton University
Background: Principal, Golden Gate Capital; Consultant, Bain & Company
Casey Lynch, Managing Director
Education: BA, Public Policy, Stanford University; MS, Management, Stanford Graduate School of Business
Background: Partner, SFW Capital Partners; Partner, Parthenon Capital
Steve Brownlie, Senior Director
Education: BSE, Electrical Engineering, Princeton University
Background: Vice President, Lazard Alternative Investments; Senior Associate, Golden Gate Capital
Kristin Johnson, Managing Director
Education: BA, Pomona College; MBA, Stanford Grad. School of Business
Background: Morgan Stanley
Carol Pereira, Chief Financial Officer
Education: MBA, Stanford Grad. School of Business
Background: Opus Capital Group

97 ALTARIS CAPITAL PARTNERS
10 East 53rd Street
31st Floor
New York, NY 10022

Phone: 212-931-0250
e-mail: info@altariscap.com
web: altariscap.com

Mission Statement: Altaris Capital Partners, LLC is an investment firm focused exclusively on the healthcare industry.

Fund Size: $2.3 Billion
Average Investment: $15-50 million
Industry Group Preference: Healthcare, Pharmaceuticals, Medical Devices, Healthcare Services, Healthcare Information Technology
Portfolio Companies: Acclara, Alterna LLC, AGS Health, Analogic, bk Medical, Brim, Chemical Computing Group, CI Medical Technologies, Clearwater, CMP Pharma, Creganna, CSafe Global, Endocare, Gaffey Healthcare, G&H Orthodontics, HealthTronics, HealthTronics IT Solutions, HSS, Healthcare Waste Solutions, Intralign, JDS Pharmaceuticals, Minnetronix, M2S, Oasis Outsourcing, OsoBio, Paragon Medical, Paramit, Penlon, Precyse, Quantum Health, Senior Helpers, Sparta Systems, SpecialtyCare, Tivity Health, Trean Corporation, US Health Works

Venture Capital & Private Equity Firms / Domestic Firms

George E. Aitken-Davies, Co-Founder & Managing Director
212-931-0230
Education: MS, Molecular & Cellular Biochemistry, University of Oxford
Background: Merrill Lynch Private Equity
Daniel G. Tully, Co-Founder & Managing Director
212-931-0234
Education: BS, Economics, University of Pennsylvania Wharton Undergraduate Program
Background: Merrill Lynch Private Equity
James D. O'Brien, Managing Director, Medical Devices
Education: BA, History, Princeton University
Background: Merrill Lynch

---

98 ALTIRA GROUP LLC
1675 Broadway
Suite 2400
Denver, CO 80202

Phone: 303-592-5500 Fax: 303-592-5519
e-mail: info@altiragroup.com
web: www.altiragroup.com

Mission Statement: Oil and gas investor.
Geographic Preference: North America
Founded: 1996
Average Investment: $5 million
Minimum Investment: $1 - $3 million
Investment Criteria: Seed, Early-Stage, Growth
Industry Group Preference: Energy, Oil & Gas, Information Technology, Power Technologies, Distribution, Renewable Energy, Electric Power, Technology-Enabled Services
Portfolio Companies: Seeq, Agile Upstream, FlexGen Power Systems, Infrastructure Networks

Dirk McDermott, Managing Partner
e-mail: dmcdermott@altiragroup.com
Education: MS Geophysics, MBA, Stanford University
Background: Geophysicist, Louisiana Land & Exploration Company; Co-Founder, Aspect Management; Brigham Oil & Gas; Energy Arrow; SouthTech Exploration; General Atlantic Resources
Directorships: Hyperion Evolutionary Genomics; DHI Services; Amended Silicates; MicroSeiomic; Beyond Compliance
Sean Ebert, Partner
Education: BS, Civil Engineering, MBA, University of Texas
Background: Principal, Booz Allen; CEO, Foresight Weather
Directorships: TransZap, Austin Geomodeling
J.P. Bauman, Principal
Education: BA, MBA, Univ. of Chicago
Background: Perseus LLC
Directorships: Seeq, Agile Upstream, FlexGen Power Systems

---

99 ALTITUDE INVESTMENT MANAGEMENT, LLC
205 East 42nd Street
20th Floor
New York, NY 10017

Phone: 212-381-9680
e-mail: info@altitudein.com
web: altitudein.com

Mission Statement: Invests in early-stage to growth companies in the cannabis industry.
Geographic Preference: US, Canada, Europe
Founded: 2016
Industry Group Preference: Cannabis
Portfolio Companies: BDS Analytics, C4 Distro, Canndescent, Enlighten, Flowhub, Front Range Biosciences, Grassroots, Grassroots Herbology, Grassroots Greenhouse, Green Flower, Liberty Cannabis, PathogenDx, Privateer Holdings, Segra, Springbig, Sunderstorm, The Green Organic Dutchman, Wurk

Key Executives:
John Brecker, Partner
Education: BS, Political Science, American University; JD, St. John's University School of Law
Background: VP, High Yield Department, The Bear Stearns Companies Inc.; Principal & Co-Founder, Longacre Fund Management; Founding Partner, Drivetrain Advisors
Michael Goldberg, Partner
Education: The London School of Economics and Political Science (LSE); BSM, Finance, A.B. Freeman School of Business, Tulane University; MBA, Finance & International Business, Columbia Business School
Background: Managing Director, Longacre Fund Management LLC; Owner/Portfolio Manager, Sonar Asset Management Group, Inc.; Managing Director, Banc of America Securities, LLC; Chase Securities, Inc.
Roderick Stephan, Partner
Education: BS, Biochemistry, University of Notre Dame; MA, Finance, Kellogg School of Management, Northwestern University
Background: Sr. Analyst, First Chicago Capital Corp.; Sr. Analyst, Bank of Montreal; Sr. Analyst, Citadel Investment Group LLC; Principal/Portfolio Manager/CEO, Longacre Fund Management (UK); Portfolio Manager, Cantibury Capital LLC
Jon Trauben, Partner
Education: BA, Political Science, Rutgers University; MSc, Real Estate, New York University
Background: Ernst & Young; VP, APC Realty Advisors; Managing Director, Credit Suisse; Managing Director, Cantor Fitzgerald; Managing Director, Barclays Capital; Sr. Managing Director, Hunt Mortgage Group; Principal, JAC Investments

---

100 ALTOS VENTURES
2882 Sand Hill Road
Suite 100
Menlo Park, CA 94025

e-mail: info@altos.vc
web: www.altos.vc

Mission Statement: Altos Ventures invests in growing North America and South Korea-based companies in the Internet, software and mobile sectors.
Geographic Preference: North America, South Korea
Fund Size: $300 million
Founded: 1996
Average Investment: $1 - $5 million
Investment Criteria: Early Stage, Growth Stage
Industry Group Preference: Technology, Mobile, Software, Internet
Portfolio Companies: Adop, Allocadia, April, Beat, Bench, Bluehole Studio, Book Jam, Bridea, Brightedge, Coupang, Demandbase, Digitalpath.net, Funizen, HireMojo, Hyperconnect, I-Um, Jobplanet, Joya, LendIt, Lohika, Memebox, My Real Trip, NetBase, One Up, Origin Games, Outbound Engine, PandaDoc, Pandora.TV, Piqora, Quizlet, Retrica, Roblox, Spicus, TrilibisMobile, TVU Networks, Upsight, Vesta, Viva Republica, Vonvon, WhiteHat Security, Xignite, Zigzag

Other Locations:
4th Floor
96-1 Cheongdam-dong
Gangnam-gu
Seoul 135-517
Korea

Key Executives:
Han Kim, Managing Director
Education: BS, United States Military Academy; MBA, Stanford University

Venture Capital & Private Equity Firms / Domestic Firms

Background: Booz Allen & Hamilton; Procter & Gamble; Captain, US Army Corps of Engineers
Anthony Lee, Managing Director
Education: BA, Politics & Economics, Princeton University; MBA, Stanford University
Background: Evolve Software; Strategy Consultant, McKinsey & Company; Chairman, TechSoup Global
Hodong Nam, Managing Director
Education: BS, Engineering, Harvey Mudd College; MBA, Stanford University
Background: Trinity Ventures; Bain & Company; Silicon Graphics; Octel Communications

101 ALTPOINT CAPITAL
600 Steamboat Road
Greenwich, CT 06830

Phone: 212-487-1100
e-mail: info@altpointcapital.com
web: altpointcapital.com

Mission Statement: Venture partner to growing companies in fintech, communications, cryptocurrencies and data-driven marketplaces.

Founded: 2009
Average Investment: $100K - $20MM
Minimum Investment: $100K
Industry Group Preference: Fintech, Communications, Data-driven marketplaces, Blockchain/cryptocurrencies
Portfolio Companies: Aces, Acorn, Brief, ByteGrid, Dreamlines, Edisun Microgrids, Enwoven, Factual, Ford Models, Honk, Just, lyft, Newbook, Redbooth, Saucey, Status, TLL, Vetter, VYTL, Zowdow

Key Executives:
Gerald T. Banks, Founder & Managing Partner
Education: Columbia Univ.; London Business School
Background: Merrill Lynch
Andrew Grapkowski, Managing Director & Partner
Education: Princeton; Univ. of Virginia
Directorships: ByteGrid Holdings; ANARAQ; Vazata

102 ALTRIA VENTURES
Richmond, VA

Mission Statement: Altria Group created Altria Ventures Inc. to invest in technology areas of interest to our core businesses. Our approach to investing is not limited to funding and may include the provision of other assistance, such as technical expertise.

Geographic Preference: Worldwide
Average Investment: $250,000 - $3 million
Investment Criteria: Growth Stage
Industry Group Preference: Safety, Biotechnology, Packaging, Clean Energy, Water, Sustainability, Recycling

103 ALTURA VENTURES LLC
9600 Blue Larkspur Lane
Suite 201
Monterey, CA 93940

Phone: 831-595-7501 Fax: 831-855-0206
e-mail: contactus@altura.com
web: www.altura.com

Mission Statement: Altura Ventures is an evangelist for the entrepreneurial approach to business. Altura believes that both the world's economy and everyone's quality of life will be best served when more motivated individuals (or small teams) tinkering in their garages and taking long brain-storming lunches away from their 9 to 5 jobs decide to take the plunge and start a company.

Founded: 2006
Portfolio Companies: CrossLoop, Living Gluten Free, UserBliss, JobCoin, KallOut

Key Executives:
Lee Lorenzen, President/CEO
e-mail: leel@altura.com
Education: BS, Computer Science, SMU
Background: Founder, SHOP.COM; Founder, Ventura Software; Xerox
Thomas E Mallett, Managing Director
e-mail: tomm@altura.com
Education: University of California, Davis
Background: Buck & Mallett

104 ALTUS CAPITAL PARTNERS
10 Westport Road
Suite C204
Wilton, CT 06897

Phone: 203-429-2000 Fax: 203-429-2010
web: www.altuscapitalpartners.com

Mission Statement: Focus on small and middle market domestic manufacturing companies.

Geographic Preference: Northeast, Mid-Atlantic, Southeast, Midwest, Rocky Mountains
Fund Size: $79.3 million
Founded: 2003
Average Investment: $12 million
Minimum Investment: $3 million
Investment Criteria: LBO, MBO, Recapitalization
Industry Group Preference: Military, Water Purification, Infrastructure, Building Materials & Services
Portfolio Companies: MGC Diagnostics, Max Environmental, Nichols Portland, GED Integrated Solutions, iimak, Thomson Plastics

Other Locations:
250 Parkway Drive
Suite 120
Lincolnshire, IL 60069
Phone: 847-229-0770 Fax: 847-229-9266

Key Executives:
Russell J. Greenberg, Founder & Managing Partner
e-mail: rgreenberg@altuscapitalpartners.com
Education: Graduate Economics with honors, Claremont McKenna College; MBA, Amos Tuck School, Dartmouth
Background: Head Investment Banking, Chatfield Dean and Company; Managing Director, Brean Murray, Foster Securities; Head Mergers/Acquisitions, Daiwa Securities America; Prudential Bache
Directorships: Duramax; Thomson Acquisition
Gregory L. Greenberg, Founder & Senior Partner
e-mail: ggreenberg@altuscapitalpartners.com
Education: Graduate Business Administration, Denver University
Background: SVP, JMB Realty Corporation
Heidi M. Goldstein, Partner
e-mail: hgoldstein@altuscapitalpartners.com
Education: Univ. of Connecticut
Background: GE Antares Capital
Directorships: Intl. Imaging Materials; Max Environmental Technologies; MGC Diagnostics; Nichols Portland
Thomas R. Groh, Partner, Business Development
e-mail: tgroh@altuscapitalpartners.com
Education: MBA, Booth School of Business
Background: KPMG
Peter Polimino, Partner, Chief Financial Officer and CCO
e-mail: ppolimino@altuscapitalpartners.com
Education: Iona College
Background: Fox Sports Net
Directorships: Nichols Portland; Thomson Plastics

Other Locations:
823 Congress Avenue
Suite 205

Austin, TX 78701
Phone: 512-532-2800

106 AMBERJACK CAPITAL PARTNERS
1021 Main Street
Suite 1100
Houston, TX 77002

Phone: 281-605-3900
e-mail: info@amberjackcapital.com
web: www.amberjackcapital.com

Mission Statement: Amberjack Capital is a specialized private equity firm that invests in and partners with entrepreneurs and business owners to build market leaders serving the industrial, infrastructure, and environmental end markets.

Founded: 2006
Average Investment: $20-$175 million
Industry Group Preference: Industry, Infrastructure, Environment
Portfolio Companies: Aegis Chemical Solutions, Best Trash, Enercorp, Entegra, Flex Energy Solutions, Innovex, Milestone Environmental Services, Rod And Tubing Services, Taurex Drill Bits, Tier 1 Energy Solutions, Transform Materials
Key Executives:
  Patrick Connelly, Co-Managing Partner
  Jason Turowsky, Co-Managing Partner
  Melissa Rocco, Chief Financial & Compliance Officer

107 AMD VENTURES
2485 Augustine Drive
Santa Clara, CA 94054

Phone: 408-749-4000
e-mail: amd.ventures@amd.com
web: www.amd.com

Mission Statement: Through AMD Ventures, AMD's investment program, AMD invests in strategic software and application ecosystem companies that serve large and growing markets.

Industry Group Preference: Software, Data Storage, Analytics, Security, Multimedia, Virtual Reality & Augmented Reality, Machine Learning
Portfolio Companies: BlueStacks, InContext Solutions, Matterport, Nitero, Personify, Raptr, Tango
Key Executives:
  Harry Wolin, Managing Director
  Background: SVP/General Counsel, AMD
  Shantnu Sharma, Managing Director
  Education: MIT
  Background: VP, Corporate Strategy/Business Development, AMD; Consultant, McKinsey & Co.

108 AME CLOUD VENTURES
Palo Alto, CA

e-mail: pr@amecloudventures.com
web: www.amecloudventures.com

Mission Statement: AME Cloud Ventures invests in seed to later stage companies that are involved in developing technology and data.

Investment Criteria: Seed to Later Stage
Industry Group Preference: Technology, Data & Analytics
Portfolio Companies: Accion, Amitree, Arterys, Astranis, AtScale, Atomwise, Berkeley Lights, Blast, BirdEye, Bitpay, Blast Motion, BlockCypher, Blockstream, Bowers & Wilkins, Boxed, Cala Health, Canvas Technology, Capella Space, Catalog, Citrine Informatics, Civil Maps, Clover Health, Cofactor Genomics, Coda, Cohere Technologies, Color Genomics, CrowdAI, Deepscale, DiDi, Docker, Edge Intelligence, Eero, Elementum, Embark, Enfore, Enso Relief, Everlance, Evernote, FiscalNote, Game Closure, Gusto, Holberton School, HyperScience, Illumio, Import.io, Impossible Foods, Inscopix, Interana, Inui Health, Joby, Just Inc., Katerra, Kindred.ai, Layer, Lighthouse, Litbit, Luminist, Lyft, Mammoth Biosciences, Matterport, Megabots, Minio, ModBot, Neurotrack, nStack, Openbucks, Osaro, PepperData, Planet Labs, PlotWatt, Primer, Qadium, QuantiFind, Radius, Recursion Pharma, Rigetti Computing, Ripple Labs, Sapho, Savioke, ShoCard, Siftery, Slack, Talech, Tekion, Tempo Auto, The Grid, TigerGraph, Tile, Transcriptic, Twist Bioscience, uBiome, VIDA, Vectra, Vicarious, Vicarious Surgical, Vium, Viz.AI, Voicera, Wevr, Wattpad, Whole Biome, Wish, Xapo, Zendrive, Zoom, Zume Pizza, Zymergen

Key Executives:
  Nick Adams, Managing Director
  Education: MEng, Imperial College
  Background: Cloud Valley
  Directorships: Zoom, Zume, Zymergen, Eero, Planet, Cruise
  Jeff Chung, Managing Director
  Education: BS, University of California, Berkeley; MBA, Harvard Business School
  Background: Silver Lake
  Directorships: Savioke, Nervana Systems, Freenome, Elementum, Synthego, Rigetti Quantum Computing

109 AMERICA FIRST INVESTMENT ADVISORS
Regency One Building
10050 Regency Circle
Suite 515
Omaha, NE 68114

Phone: 402-991-3388
web: www.am1st.com

Mission Statement: An employee-owned international investment management organization committed to successfully developing unique business opportunities for institutional, private and public fund investors, making investments in agribusiness and food processing companies in the former Soviet Union, and fully investing in companied located in Russia, Kazakhstan, Ukraine, Moldova and Georgia.

Geographic Preference: Former Soviet Union
Fund Size: $270 million
Founded: 1994
Average Investment: $8 million
Minimum Investment: $5 million
Investment Criteria: Agribusiness/Food processing companies that will benefit from capital and management expertise
Industry Group Preference: Agribusiness, Packaging, Food & Beverage
Key Executives:
  Eric M. Ball, Chief Executive Officer/Chief Compliance Officer
  Education: BS, Finance, University of Nebraska, Lincoln; CFA
  Background: VP/Portfolio Manager, Financial Institutions Investment Management; Investment Advisor, Wallace R. Weitz & Company; VP/Manager, FirsTier Westerchester Capital Management; Securities Analyst, Kirkpatrick, Pettis, Smith & Polian
  Barry Dunaway, Managing Director
  Education: BS, Economics, University of Nebraska, Omaha
  Background: Portfolio Manager, KPM Investment Management; Securities Analyst, Wallace R Weitz & Company
  David Guthrie, Vice President
  Education: BS, MBA, University of Nebraska, Lincoln
  Background: Vice President, Senior Private Banker, Wells Fargo Private Bank

Venture Capital & Private Equity Firms / Domestic Firms

110 AMERICAN INDUSTRIAL PARTNERS
450 Lexington Avenue
40th Floor
New York, NY 10017

web: www.americanindustrial.com

Mission Statement: A private equity firm that is dedicated to buying and improving manufacturing and industrial service companies based in North America.
Geographic Preference: United States, Canada, Mexico
Fund Size: $1.8 billion
Founded: 1989
Average Investment: $10 - $50 million
Minimum Investment: $10 million
Investment Criteria: MBO, Recapitalizations, Corporate Divestitures, Growth Capital investments to fund acquisitions or internal growth
Industry Group Preference: Manufacturing, Industrial Services
Portfolio Companies: ACPI, AHF Products, AIP Aerospace, Brock, Canam, The Carlstar Group, CQMS Razer, GE Current, Entrans International, Form Technologies, Gerber Technology, Manroland Goss, Molycop, Optimas, Rand Logistics, REV, Shape Technologies, Verico Technology, Vertex Aerospace, Brooks Instrument, Bucyrus, Consoltex, Great Lakes Carbon, Ichor Systems, JHT Holdings, Manac, Mark Andy, Mecs, Micro-Poise Measurement Systems, Northwest Hardwoods, Port Arthur Steam Energy, Stanadyne, Stolle Machinery Company, Williams Controls

Key Executives:
John Becker, Senior Managing Partner
Education: BS, Business, Oregon State University
Background: Founder, Newport Shrimp Company; COO, Clearwater Fine Foods, USA; Chairman, Newport Pacific Corporation
Kim Marvin, Senior Managing Partner
Education: BS, Ocean Engineering, Massachusetts Institute of Technology; MBA, Harvard Business School
Background: M&A, Goldman, Sachs & Co; COO, American Original Corporation
Dino Cusumano CFA, Senior Managing Partner
Education: BBA, University of Notre Dame; CFA
Background: Investment Banking, JP Morgan & Co. Inc.; Wedbush Morgan Securities
Eric Baroyan, Partner
Education: BS, Business Administration, University of Southern California
Background: Associate, Capital Z Financial Services Partners; Investment Banking Divison, Salomon Smith Barney
Ben DeRosa, Partner
Education: BS, Engineering, University of Pennsylvania; MBA, Stanford Graduate School of Business
Background: Managing Director, Liberty Partners; Principal, Donaldson, Lufkin & Jenrette/CSFB Private Equity; Associate, The Harlan Company; Senior Consultant, Coopers & Lybrand
Derek Leck, Partner
Education: BS, Mechanical Engineering, Massachusetts Institute of Technology; MBA, Finance & Statistics, University of Chicago Graduate School of Business
Background: Emerging Markets Product Manager, Caterpillar Inc.; VP, Corporate Planning, Fuji Heavy Industries (Subaru); General Motors
Jorge Amador, Partner
Education: BS, Industrial Engineering, University of Costa Rica; MS, Management & Engineering, MIT; MS, Manufacturing Systems Engineering, University of Texas
Background: Manager of Professional Services & Product Development, Factory DNA Inc.; Senior Consultant, Factory Logic Inc.; Project Manager, Applied Materials Inc.; Quality Manager, Central American Division of Unisys Corporation

111 AMERICAN SECURITIES LLC
590 Madison Avenue
38th Floor
New York, NY 10022

Phone: 212-476-8000
web: www.american-securities.com

Mission Statement: Private investment firm that makes equity investments into profitable companies in partnership with management teams.
Geographic Preference: Worldwide
Fund Size: $3 billion
Founded: 1947
Average Investment: $20 million
Minimum Investment: $5 million
Industry Group Preference: Consumer Products, Restaurants, Industrial, Aerospace, Defense and Government, Packaging, Agriculture, Environment, Paper, Power, Specialty Chemicals, Media
Portfolio Companies: Air Methods, American Axle & Manufacturing, Aspen Dental, Blount International, Blue Bird, Chromaflo Technologies, Emerald Performance Materials, Fairmount Santrol, Frontier Spinning Mills, Global Tel*Link, Henry Company, Learning Care Group, Milk Specialties Global, Mortgage Contracting Services, MW Industries, North American Partners in Anesthesia, SeaStar Solutions, Ulterra Drilling Technologies, Unifrax, United Distribution Group

Other Locations:
2 Grand Gateway
3 Hongqiao Road
Unit 4501-04
Shanghai 200030
China
Phone: 86 (21) 5419-1100

Key Executives:
Michael Fisch, Managing Director/CEO
212-476-8051
Education: BA, Dartmouth College; MBA, Stanford University
Background: Consultant, Bain & Company; Mergers & Aquisitions, Goldman Sachs
David Horing, Managing Director
212-476-8059
e-mail: dhoring@american-securities.com
Education: BS, Economics, Wharton School, University of Pennsylvania; BSc, Engineering, UUniversity of Pennslyvania; MBA, Harvard Business School
Background: Dyson-Kissner-Moran Corporation; Solomon Brothers; Boston Consulting Group
Kevin Penn, Managing Director
212-476-8020
e-mail: kpenn@american-securities.com
Education: BS, Economics, Wharton School; MBA, Harvard Business School
Background: Founder, ACI Capital; EVP & CIO, First Spring Corporation
Directorships: Healthy Directions, Presido
Will Manuel, Managing Director
212-476-8030
e-mail: wmanuel@american-securities.com
Education: BA, Government, Connecticut College
Background: Principal, Spectrum Equity Investors; Spire Capital Partners; CEA Capital Advisors; M&a, Chase Securities
Directorships: Senior Managing Director, Centerbridge Partners
Helen Chiang, Managing Director
212-476-8012
e-mail: hchiang@american-securities.com
Education: BA, Economics & International Studies, Yale University; MBA, Stanford Grad. School of Business
Background: VP, Morgan Stanley Capital Partners; Warburg Pincus; Weston Presidio

Directorships: Learning Care Group; Milk Specialities Global; United Planet Fitness
Loren Easton, Managing Director
212-476-8029
e-mail: leaston@american-securities.com
Education: BA, University of Pennsylvania; MBA, Wharton School
Background: Vice President, ACI Capital; Analyst, Lazard Freres
Directorships: Healthy Directions, NEP Broadcasting, Unifrax

---

112 AMERIMARK CAPITAL CORPORATION
320 Decker Drive
Suite 100
Irving, TX 75062

Phone: 214-638-7878
e-mail: admin@amcapital.com
web: www.amcapital.com

Mission Statement: Provides solutions to business owners who need additional capital for growth or personal liquidity. Seeking investment opportunities in a variety of industries. Established companies are preferred with a record of profitability and an opportunity for growth.

Fund Size: $50 million
Founded: 1988
Average Investment: $1 million
Minimum Investment: $500,000
Investment Criteria: Second-Stage, Mezzanine, LBO. Companies ranging in size from $5 - $300 million in annual sales.
Industry Group Preference: Communications, Consumer Services, Distribution, Industrial Equipment, Manufacturing, Service Industries
Portfolio Companies: Protel, Inc., City Mortgage Corporation, MSI Acquisition, Inc., Village Square Cabinet Supply, TTH Holdings, Superior Chaircraft Corporation, Texas B&B, Inc., Chartwell Healthcare, Inc., E.E. Stringer Funeral Homes, Lewis Electric Supply, Inc., Stohlquist Waterware, Inc., Fitting Valve and Control Corporation, Algas Industries, Inc., Commercial Financial Services, Full Vision, Inc., Service Strategies Interntional, Inc., Electronics, Inc.

Key Executives:
Charles R Martin, Managing Principal/CEO
e-mail: martin@amcapital.com
Education: BS Industrial Engineering, Auburn University; MBA, Southerm Methodist University; graduate studies in Marketing, Syracuse University
Background: VP/Principal, Capital Alliance Corporation; President, building supply distributor; VP Sales/Marketing, major home products manufacturer; Colonel, US Army Reserve
Directorships: Martin Industries, Amsouth Bank

---

113 AMGEN VENTURES
One Amgen Center Drive
Thousand Oaks, CA 91320-1799

Phone: 805-447-1000
e-mail: investor.relations@amgen.com
web: www.amgen.com

Mission Statement: Corporate venture capital fund designed to provide emerging biotechnology firms with resources to develop pioneering discoveries focused on human therapeutics. It can offer early stage companies access to Amgen's extensive capabilities while providing Amgen insight into external research paving the way for future collaborations.

Geographic Preference: North America, Asia, Europe
Fund Size: $100 million
Founded: 2004
Average Investment: $2-3 million
Minimum Investment: $1 million
Investment Criteria: Early-Stage, Equity, Venture Fund Investment
Industry Group Preference: Biotechnology, Therapeutics, Life Sciences, Pharmaceuticals
Portfolio Companies: Adheron Therapeutics, Ardelyx, Atara Bio, Avidia, Calistoga, Epizyme, Imago BioSciences, MiRagen, NexImmune, Ra pharma, Surface Oncology, Sutro Biopharma, TeraLogic Pharmaceuticals, Ziarco

Key Executives:
Janis Naeve, PhD, Managing Director
e-mail: amgenventures@amgen.com
Education: BS, Microbiology, Caltech, Pomona; PhD, Pathology, University of Southern California
Background: Director, Business Development, X-Ceptor Therapeutics; Aurora Biosciences

---

114 AMHERST FUND
401 East Stadium
Ann Arbor, MI 48104

Phone: 734-662-2102
e-mail: info@amherstfund.com
web: www.amherstfund.com

Mission Statement: To generate sound returns for portfolio companies, Amherst Fund makes venture capital investments (with focus on early stage companies) and private equity investments (with focus on later stage companies) across a broad range of industries.

Geographic Preference: Midwest
Fund Size: $30 million
Founded: 1998
Investment Criteria: Early Stage, Later Stage
Industry Group Preference: Manufacturing, Medical Devices, Advanced Materials, Mobile, Restaurants, Food & Beverage, Drug Development
Portfolio Companies: AdAdapted, BD Accuri, Fusion Coolant Systems, Michigan Ladder, Saline Lectronics Inc., SkySpecs

Key Executives:
Matt Turner, President/Chief Executive Officer
Education: BA, Economics, University of Michigan; MA, University of Monaco, Monte Carlo; Webster University, Vienna
Background: Professional Racecar Driver, Porsche Cars GB
Directorships: Saline Lectronics, Espresso Royale, FlockTAG, Fusion Coolant
Amherst Turner, Founder/Fund Advisor
Education: BA, University of Michigan
Background: Co-Founder, GT Products
Directorships: Saline Lectronics

---

115 AMICUS CAPITAL
1045 Sansome Street
Suite 306
San Francisco, CA 94111

Phone: 415-646-0120
e-mail: ideas@amicuscapital.com
web: www.amicuscapital.com

Mission Statement: Amicus Capital is a seed stage information technology investment fund, investing in entrepreneurs who are developing innovative information technology solutions to problems that affect large numbers of businesses or consumers.

Founded: 1998
Investment Criteria: Seed-Stage
Industry Group Preference: Information Technology
Portfolio Companies: ATMA Software, Adventa, Attributor, Automatic, BrightFunnel, Business Signatures, BuyersEdge, Closely, Corrigo, Food Genius, Greenling, GrubHub, IronPort, Kefta, Marin Software, Moseo, Octopus.com, Odeo, Oneforty, RethinkDB, Snocap, Soundflavor, Spotlife, Three Rings, TravelPotst.com, Visible Markets, Vividence, Vizu

Venture Capital & Private Equity Firms / Domestic Firms

Corp., VoxPop Network Corp., W&W Communications, WiredPlanet

Key Executives:
Bob Zipp, Co-Founder/Managing Director
Education: Duke University; Texas A&M University

116 AMIDZAD PARTNERS
370 Convention Way
Redwiid City, CA 94063

Phone: 650-216-2384
e-mail: marc@amidzad.com
web: www.amidzad.com

Mission Statement: Amidzad is a seed and early-stage investment firm focused on investing in emerging growth companies on the West Coast. They have over 50 years of combined entrepreneurial experience in building profitable, global enterprises from the ground up and over 25 years of combined investing experience in successful information technology and life science companies.

Geographic Preference: West Coast
Investment Criteria: Seed-Stage, Early-Stage
Industry Group Preference: Information Technology, Life Sciences
Portfolio Companies: Aquantia, Bix, Causes, Clear Spring, Clixtr, Course Hero, Danger, Dropbox, Ellie Mae, Equator, Extreme DA, Freewebs, Infoaxe, InMage, Integen, Jaxtr, LendingClub, LiteScape, Milo, Mywaves, Nextbio, OpTrip, ParAllele, Picoboo, Powerset, Preview System, Paypal, Quantenna, Sabio Labs, ScanScout, SGN, Sendori, SignmaQuest, Sonitus Medical, Songbird, SoundHound, Tau-Metrix, Techdirt, TokBox, VentureBeat, Zephyr, Zetta.net, Zoosk,

Rahim Amidi, Founding General Partner
e-mail: rahim@amidzad.com
Background: Co-Founder, Amidi Group
Saeed Amidi, Founding General Partner
e-mail: saeed@amidzad.com
Background: Co-Founder, Amidi Group

117 AMITI VENTURES
1603 Orrington Ave.
Suite 600
Evanston, IL 60201

e-mail: info@amitiventures.com
web: www.amiticapital.com

Mission Statement: Amiti Ventures is a venture capital firm based in Chicago and Tel Aviv that invests alongside leading Israeli venture capital firms in late stage Israeli high tech companies. We help fund Israeli entrepreneurs and partner with them to build great global companies.

Geographic Preference: Israel
Investment Criteria: Early Stage
Industry Group Preference: Mobile Technology, IT Infrastructure, Cloud Computing, Digital Media Delivery, Information Technology
Portfolio Companies: Amimon, Autotalks, Cycognito, Corephotonics, Innoviz, Flash Networks, Nextsilicon, Sckipio, Siklu, Valens Semiconductor, Vayyar

Key Executives:
Ben Rabinowitz, Managing Partner & Founder
Education: MBA, Georgetown University
Background: General Manager, Vice President, AudioCodes
Directorships: Valens Semiconductor
Shimrit Samuel, Venture Partner
Education: LLB, MBA, LLM, Tel Aviv University
Background: Board Member, Corephotonics Ltd.; Board Member, Cycognito; Teaching Professional, Tel Aviv University
Vered Digmy, Investor Relations
Education: BA, English Literature, Tel Aviv University
Background: Director of Investor Relations, Giza Venture Captial; Investor Relations Manager, Grove Venture Capital
Yafit Schwartz, Vice President, Finance
Education: BS, Accounting, Tel Aviv University
Background: Vice President, Finance, Perion; ERP Finance and Business Leader, Ceragon Networks

118 AMKEY VENTURES
44370 Old Warm Springs Boulevard
Fremont, CA 94538

Phone: 510-668-1816 Fax: 510-668-1017
e-mail: info@amkeyvc.com
web: www.amkeyvc.com

Mission Statement: Amkey Ventures is a California-based VC firm, whose mission is to identify investment opportunities by focusing on cutting-edge biomedical technologies.

Founded: 2001
Industry Group Preference: Biotechnology, Pharmaceuticals, Medical Devices
Portfolio Companies: Cardiva Medical, Inc., Renal Solutions, Inc., MedWaves Incorporated, U-Systems, Inc., Biokey, Inc., VM Discovery, Inc., GenePharm, Inc., Epitomics, Inc., Multispan, Inc. StemCyte, Inc.

Key Executives:
Woody Sing-Wood Yeh, Managing Director/Founder
Education: BS, Agricultural Chemistry, National Taiwan University; PhD, Food Science, University of Chicago, Champaign-Urbana
Background: CEO/Founder, Bioken Laboratories; CEO/Founder, BestLife; CEO/Founder, Soyeh Natural; Research Scientist, INTSOY
George J Lee, Managing Director/Founder
Education: BS, Agricultural Chemistry, National Taiwan University; PhD, Chemistry, SUNY Buffalo
Background: Co-Founder, Pharmout Labs

119 AMPERSAND CAPITAL PARTNERS
55 William Street
Suite 240
Wellesley, MA 02481

Phone: 781-239-0700
e-mail: info@ampersandcapital.com
web: ampersandcapital.com

Mission Statement: A middle market private equity firm focused on investments in two core sectors: Healthcare and Industrial.

Geographic Preference: United States, Canada
Fund Size: $1 Billion
Founded: 1988
Average Investment: $10-30 Million
Investment Criteria: Middle Market Growth Opportunities
Industry Group Preference: Biotechnology, Communications Equipment, Computer Hardware & Software, Electronic Components, Health Related, Medical, Information Technology, Industrial Equipment, Manufacturing, Chemicals, Medical Devices, Pharmaceuticals, Healthcare
Portfolio Companies: Accuratus Lab Services, Aclara, Agilux Labs, Alexis Biochemicals, Assay Designs, Avista Pharma, Bako, BioClinica, Bioventus, Brammer Bio, ChanTest, Confluent, CoreLab, Corpus Medical, CRI Worldwide, CutisPharma, Detector Technology, Dynex Technologies, Elite One Source, ETE Medical, Genewiz, Genoptix, Gyros Protein, Innovative Food Processors, LakePharma, Magellan, MedVenture, Invitrogen, Ortho Organizers, Panacos, Roadrunner Pharmacy, Sanova Dermatology, Signature Genomic, Stereotaxis, Talecris, TREK Diagnostic, TriPath Imaging, Viracor-IBT

Other Locations:
Gustav Mahlerplein 105-115
26th Floor
Amsterdam 1082 MS

Venture Capital & Private Equity Firms / Domestic Firms

Netherlands
Phone: 31-207671773
Key Executives:
Richard A. Charpie, Founder
Education: MS, Physics, PhD, Economics, Finance, MIT
Directorships: CoreLab Partners, NDC, RAND Worldwide
Herbert H. Hooper, Managing Partner
Education: BS Chemical Engineering, University of California; PhD, Chemical Engineering, University of California, Berkeley
Background: Chief Tech Officer/Executive VP, ACLARA BioSciences (Nasdaq: ACLA); Product/Business Development Manager, Air Products and Chemicals
Directorships: ATS Labs, Biomedical Structures, CoreLab Partners, Magellan Biosciences, ViraCor-IBT Laboratories
Stuart A. Auerbach, Advisory Partner
Education: BS Chemical Engineering, Columbia University; MBA, Harvard Business School
Background: Consulting, Bain; Manufacturing/Engineering, Lever Brothers; CFO ADFlex Solutions during the design implementation of its turnaround; Director, ADFlex, Smartflex
Directorships: Agilux Laboratories, MedVenture, Modified Polymer Components
David J. Parker, Partner
Education: BA, Government & Economics, Dartmouth; MBA, Wharton
Background: Consultant, Bain; Consultant, Mercer; Bank of Boston
Directorships: Blue Sky BioServices, Modified Polymer Components
David Q. Anderson, Partner
Education: BSc, Universty of Aberdeen; PhD, University of Sheffield; MBA, Olin Graduat School of Business, Babson College
Background: Director, Healthcare Group, Covington Associates; Consultant, Boston Healthcare Associates
Directorships: ATS Labs
Thomas de Jager, Vice President, Business Development
Education: BA, Economics, University of Pretoria; MBA, Pace University
Background: Founder, Savannah Acquisitions; Aleutian Capital Partners

120 AMPLIFIER VENTURE PARTNERS
1614 Brookside Road
McLean, VA 22101

Phone: 703-635-2655 **Fax:** 703-782-0222
web: www.amplifierventures.com

Mission Statement: Amplifier Ventures primary investment focus is emerging technology businesses located in the DC Region, a geographic region stretching from Maryland through Washington DC, and into Virginia. Amplifier Ventures' investment strategy is to capitalize on federal spending on technology research and development and consumption and invest in a balanced portfolio of entrepreneurial technology companies positioned to benefit from proximity to the federal government.
Geographic Preference: Maryland, Northern Virginia
Founded: 2004
Investment Criteria: Seed-Stage
Industry Group Preference: Software, New Media, Enterprise Software, Communication Technology, Materials Technology, Security, Clean Technology
Portfolio Companies: ArcheMedX, CardStar, College Factual, E-Chromic Technologies, Hook Mobile, Spyor Safe Mobile Security, Zenoss
Key Executives:
Jonathan Aberman, Founder/Managing Director
Education: BA, Political Science & Economics, George Washington University; MSc, International Economics, London School of Economics; MA, Downing College; LLM, New York University School of Law
Background: Partner, Fenwick & West; Fish and Richardson; Pillsbury Winthrop; Investment Banking, Daiwa Securities; Donadlson Lufkin & Jenrette; Goldman Sachs International

121 AMPLIFY
Venice, CA

web: amplify.la

Mission Statement: Amplify is a venture capital fund focused on technology, entertainment, and media in Los Angeles, California.
Geographic Preference: US
Investment Criteria: Seed, Early Stage
Industry Group Preference: Artificial Intelligence, SaaS, Software, Consumer, Commerce, Automation, Health & Wellness, Virtual Reality, Blockchain, e-Commerce
Portfolio Companies: Advekit, Alpha Draft, Alto, Battlefy, Bitium, Brighten, The Bouqs Company, Card, CarPay, Cheese, Clutter, Countertop Foods, DSTLD, Estify, Fama, FanBread, The Flex Company, FloQast, Gem, Goodfair, HelloTech, Honeybee Health, HyperVR, Iconery, Lantern, Ledge, Lensabl, Little Labs, Look.io, Mapsense, Manufactured, Markett, MedRepublic, Mover.io, Pete Health, ProGuides, Ready Set Food, Repost, SafeRide, Sensay, Ship Mate, Skylar Body, SmartLane, StackCommerce, Stop Breathe & Think, String AI, Tapcart, Thankful AI, The Kive Company, Trace, Trials AI, Vetted Petcare, Volley, WeeCare, Winc
Key Executives:
Paul Bricault, Managing Partner
Background: Venture Partner, Greycroft; EVP, William Morris; Founder, Mailroom Fund
Oded Noy, Managing Partner
Background: Co-Founder/CTO, TrueCare; CTO, Zefr; Founder/CTO, TargetClose; Founder/Chair, LA CTO Forum
Eric Pakravan, Vice President
Education: University of Southern California
Background: Founder, LavaLab
Amanda Schutzbank, Vice President
Education: BS, Wharton School
Background: Primary Venture Partners; Karma Mobility; Techstars; Merrill Lynch

122 ANALYTICS VENTURES
6450 Lusk Boulevard
Suite E208
San Diego, CA 92121

Phone: 619-866-4400
web: www.analytics-ventures.com

Mission Statement: Analytics Ventures is the premier early-stage venture capital firm for digital analytics startups in San Diego. They offer world-class entrepreneur experience to founders seeking initial capital. They help entrepreneurs with proven operation and go-to-market experience and bring a broad network of top industry professionals to help ensure their clients' success.
Geographic Preference: San Diego Area
Fund Size: $124 million
Investment Criteria: Early-Stage
Industry Group Preference: Artificial Intelligence, Machine Learning, Technology, Applications, Software, Medicine
Portfolio Companies: AdTheos, AV Lab, Cure Match, Cute Metrix, Kazuhm, Tinoro
Key Executives:
Blaise Barrelet, Managing Director
Background: Founder, WebSideStory

Venture Capital & Private Equity Firms / Domestic Firms

123 ANDERSON PACIFIC CORPORATION
Chicago, IL 60611

e-mail: kda@andersonpacific.com
web: www.andersonpacific.com

Mission Statement: Anderson Pacific Corporation leads investor groups in partnerships with strong management teams who acquire companies in various industries, predominantly in telecommunications, media and distribution.
Geographic Preference: Midwest
Founded: 1978
Average Investment: $5 million
Minimum Investment: $1 million
Investment Criteria: Early, Expansion, Turnaround, Buy-Out
Industry Group Preference: Telecommunications, Communications, Cable, Carriers, Cellular Service & Products, Internet Technology, Satellite Communications, Media
Portfolio Companies: Cityfront Partners LLC, ColoHub LLC, Cypress Cellular LP, Digital Capital Partners LLC, FBL Group LLC, iVelozity LLC, Neutral Path Communications LLC
Key Executives:
  Kenneth D. Anderson, Chief Executive Officer
  312-951-8500
  e-mail: kda@andersonpacific.com
  Education: University of Iowa
  Background: Combined Cable Corporation

124 ANDLINGER & COMPANY INC
520 White Plains Road
Suite 500
Tarrytown, NY 10591

Phone: 914-332-4900
e-mail: info@andlinger.com
web: www.andlinger.com

Mission Statement: Andlinger & Company look to acquire independent or family-owned companies and corporate divisions or subsidiaries and to grow them into stronger, profitable leaders in their industry.
Geographic Preference: United States, Canada, Western Europe, Eastern Europe
Fund Size: $100 million
Founded: 1976
Average Investment: $25 million
Minimum Investment: $1 million
Investment Criteria: Acquisition, LBO, MBO, Recapitalization, Special Situations, Privatizations
Industry Group Preference: Clean Technology, Biotechnology, Communications Equipment, Computer Hardware & Software, Aerospace, Defense and Government, Diversified, Electronic Components, Energy, Environmental Protection, Industrial Equipment, Manufacturing, Chemicals, Medical Devices, Pharmaceuticals, Telecommunications
Portfolio Companies: Alltec Global, CyberAlert, Clesse, CPI. Crown Van Gelder, ETI, Eska, Global Graphics, Magnum Materials, Seitz, Solvis, Spoolex, Suspa, Steward Advanced Materials, VP360

Other Locations:
  Sieveringer Strasse 36/9
  Vienna 1190
  Austria
  Phone: 43-1-328-7145

  Avenue Louise 326
  Box 12
  Brussels 1050
  Belgium
  Phone: 32-2-647-80-70

  660 Beachland Boulevard
  Suite 202
  Vero Beach, FL 32963
  Phone: 772-234-4998

Key Executives:
  Merrick Andlinger, President
  e-mail: mgandlinger@andlinger.net
  Education: AB, Princeton University; MBA, Stanford Grad. School of Business
  Background: Associate, Kroll Associates; VP Corporate Finance, Salomon Brothers; Managing Director, Smith Barney; President/CEO/Director, Pure Energy Corporation
  Charles E. Ball, Managing Director, FL
  Education: MBA, Suffolk University
  Background: Managing Director, Bank of Boston Ltd., London
  George Doomany, Managing Director, NY
  Education: BA, Mathematics and Music, University of Rochester; MBA, Columbia University
  Background: Finance and Accounting, Price Waterhouse & Co., New York; Managing Director, Bankers Trust Company; Managing Director, BT Capital Partners; Senior Managing Director, Mandarin Partners, LLC; Acting Chief Financial Officer, United States Manufacturing Co.
  Stephen A. Magida, Managing Director, NY
  Education: BS, Economics, Wharton School; University of Pennsylvania Columbia Law School, LLB
  Background: Assistant Professor of Business Law, Virginia Polytechnic Institute; Assistant Professor of Business Law, The Wharton School University of Pennsylvania; Partner, Olwine, Connelly, Chase, O'Donnell & Weyher; Partner, Dechert Price & Rhoads
  Ivar W. Mitchell, Managing Director, FL
  Education: BS, University of Bridgeport; LLB, Columbia Law School; LLM, School of Law, New York University
  Background: VP Taxes, ITT Levitt & Sons, Inc.; VP/Secretary, The Allen Group, Inc.; VP/CFO, Yusen Management Corp.

125 ANDREESSEN HOROWITZ
2865 Sand Hill Road
Suite 101
Menlo Park, CA 94025

e-mail: businessplans@a16z.com
web: a16z.com

Mission Statement: Aims to invest in seed to late-stage companies in the area of technology.
Fund Size: $7.1 Billion
Founded: 2009
Minimum Investment: $50,000
Investment Criteria: Start-Ups, Technology, Late-Stage
Industry Group Preference: Information Technology, Consumer Services, Enterprise Software
Portfolio Companies: Accolade, Actifio, AIQ, Affirm, Airbnb, Airware, Allset, Alluxio, Alt School, Ampersand, Anki, Apeel Science, Applied Intuition, Apptio, Asana, Asimov, Astranis, Atrium, Axoni, Barefoot Networks, Basis, Bebop, Benchling, Big, Bioage, Bitcoin, Blockspring, Boku, Bonfire, Box, Branch, Bromium, BuzzFeed, Cadre, Caffeine, Camp4, Capriza, Cardiogram, Cazena, Celo, Chia, Ciitizen, CipherCloud, Clear Story Data, CodeCombat, Coinbase, Comma, Compound, Cross River, Cumulus, CYNGN, CryptoKitties, Databricks, DEEPMAP, Descript, DFINITY, Dialpad, DigitalOcean, Dispatch, Dollar Shave Club, Doxel, Drishti, DWOLLA, dYdX, Earn.com, Earnin, Envoy, Ethereum, Everlaw, Facebook, Factual, Fanatics, Filecoin, Forward Networks, Foursquare, Freenome, Fusion.io, Genius, Gigster, GitHub, Glow, Gobble, GoodData, Granular, Groupon, Harbor, Hatch Loyalty, Health IQ, Honor, Human API, HVMN, iCracked, IFTTT, Illumio, Imgur, Imply, Improbable, Insitro, Instabase, Instacart, Instagram, Instart, Journera, Julep, Jungla, Keep, Keybase, Kong, Lime, Lookout, LTSE, Lyft, Lyrebird, Lytro, Magic Leap, Magnet, Maker, Maxta, Mayvenn, Medisas, Medium, Mesosphere, Meteor, Mixpanel, NationBuilder, Netlify, Micira, Oculus

Venture Capital & Private Equity Firms / Domestic Firms

VR, OfferUp, Okta, Omada, Onshape, OpenBazaar, Opengov, OpenInvest, Optimizely, Orchid, Overtime, Pagerduty, Patientping, PeerStreet, Pindrop, Pinterest, Point, Polychain Capital, Product Hunt, Propel, Proven., Q Bio, Rabbit, RapidAPI, Rappi, Reflektive, Rigetti, Samsara, Shapeways, Shield AI, Shift, Sigma, Signal fx, Sigopt, Sisu, Skydio, SkySafe, Slack, Smartcar, snapLogic, Soylent, Stack Overflow, Tanium, Teespring, Ten Fold, Tlon, Toka Cyber Builders, TradeBlock, TransferWise, TripActions, twoXAR, TXN Solutions, uBiome, Udacity, UnifyID, UnitedMasters, Usermind, Very Good Security, Walker and Company, Within, Wonderschool, Yubico, Zenefits, Zipline, Zulily, Zynga

Other Locations:
180 Townsend Street
San Francisco, CA 94107

Key Executives:
Marc Andreessen, Co-Founder & General Partner
Education: BS, Computer Science, University of Illinois at Urbana-Champaign
Background: Netscape; Loudcloud
Directorships: Anki; Bracket Computing; Dialpad; Honor; Lytro; Mori; OpenGov; Samsara; Facebook; Hewlett-Packard Enterprise
Ben Horowitz, Co-Founder & General Partner
Education: BA, Computer Science, Columbia University; MS, Computer Science, UCLA
Background: Lotus Development Corporation; Netscape; AOL; Opsware; Hewlett-Packard
Directorships: Caffeine, Capriza, Databricks, Foursquare, Genius, Lyft, Magnet Systems, Medium, NationBuilder, Okta, SignalFx, Sisu, Tanium, TripActions, United Masters, Usermind, CODE2040
Connie Chan, General Partner
Education: BA, Economics, MS, Management Science & Engineering, Stanford University
Background: HP; Private Equity Investor, Elevation Partners
Jeff Jordan, Managing Partner
Education: BA, Political Science & Psychology, Amherst College; MBA, Stanford University Graduate School of Business
Background: Senior VP/General Manager, eBay; President, PayPal; Chairman/CEO, OpenTable; Chief Financial Officer, Hollywood Entertainment; President, Reel.com; Senior VP of Finance, The Disney Stores
Directorships: Accolade, Airbnb, Hatch, Instacart, Lime, Lookout, OfferUp, Pinterest, Walter & Company, Wonderschool

126 ANGEL STREET CAPITAL
402 Angell Street
Providence, RI 02906

Phone: 401-854-1850
e-mail: rmaccini@angelstreetcapital.com
web: angelstreetcapital.wordpress.com

Mission Statement: Angel Street Capital assists companies in the early stages of their life cycle, providing both consulting services and capital. Principals have a long track record of successfully investing in digital media and related industries, and generating impressive returns.

Founded: 2010
Average Investment: $50,000 - $250,000
Investment Criteria: Early-Stage
Industry Group Preference: Digital Media & Marketing
Portfolio Companies: FlexReceipts, Closely

Key Executives:
Joseph V. Gallagher, Managing Director
401-841-9484
e-mail: jgallagher@angelstreetcapital.com
Education: BA, English & Classics, Georgetown University
Background: CEO, Aritaur Communications

Robert J. Maccini, Managing Director
401-854-1850
e-mail: rmaccini@angelstreetcapital.com
Education: BA, Economics, College of the Holy Cross; MBA, Finance, Babson College
Background: Founder/CEO, Ando Media
Stephan C. Sloan, Director
401-854-1850
e-mail: ssloan@angelstreetcapital.com
Education: Salve Regina University

127 ANGELENO GROUP
2029 Century Park East
Suite 2980
Los Angeles, CA 90067

Phone: 310-552-2790 Fax: 310-552-2727
e-mail: info@angelenogroup.com
web: www.angelenogroup.com

Mission Statement: Angeleno Group specializes in providing growth capital to next generation companies in the clean energy and natural resources sectors. Angeleno Group invests in a wide range of deal types and primarily seeks opportunities in the United States, Asia and Australia. Since its founding in 2001, AG has grown into one of the largest energy growth equity investment firms.

Geographic Preference: United States, Asia, Australia
Fund Size: $200 million
Founded: 2001
Average Investment: $5 - $25 million
Industry Group Preference: Energy, Alternative Energy, Clean Transportation, Emissions Control, Energy Efficiency, Power Infrastructure, Renewable Energy, Solar Energy, Waste & Recycling, Advanced Materials, Logistics
Portfolio Companies: ArzonSolar, Click Energy, Critigen, Crius Energy, eCullet, EdeniQ, Eka Systems, GT Advanced Technologies, INRIX, Kinematics, Konarka Technologies, Metriv, mPrest New Forests, newterra, ParkMe, Patriot Environmental Services, PowerGenix Systems, Renew Financial, Scodix, Soraa, Stem, Sunlink Corporation, Telogis, TPI Composites, Verdiem Corporation, Verengo Solar, Xicato, ZincFive

Key Executives:
Yaniv Tepper, Managing Partner/Co-Founder
Education: BS, Mechanical Engineering, University of California, Berkeley; MS, Civil & Environmental Engineering, MS, Management, Massachusetts Institute of Technology
Background: Aetna/ING Investment Management; Engineering R&D, Bechtel
Daniel Weiss, Managing Partner/Co-Founder
Education: BA, University of California, Berkeley; MA, Stanford University; JD, Stanford Law School
Background: Attorney, O'Melveny & Myers
Jeanne Li, Senior Analyst
Education: BA, Financial Economics, Columbia University; General Securites Representative
Background: Analyst, BNP Paribas; Analyst, Bank of America
William Miller, Chief Operating Officer
Education: BS, Accounting, California State University; CPA
Background: CFO, MuniMac Management Group; CFO, Themis Asset Strategies; COO, Transamerica Investment Management; CFO, Kanye Anderson; VP, Accounting & CCO, Pilgrim Group
Paula Robins, Chief Financial Officer
Education: Stanford University; MBA, Anderson Graduate School of Management, University of California, Los Angeles
Background: CFO, Smart Technology Ventures; Price Waterhouse; Treasury Department, Long Beach Bank; Tenet Healthcare
Danny Jaffe, Principal
Education: BS, Business Administration, Haas School of

Venture Capital & Private Equity Firms / Domestic Firms

Business, University of California, Berkeley
Background: Analyst, Leviticus Partners; Financial Analyst, Bay City Capital
Anil Tammineedi, Principal
Education: BE, Electrical Engineering, PSG College of Technology; MS, Electrical Engineering, Iowa State University; MBA, Anderson Graduate School of Management, UCLA
Background: Product Management, Broadcom; Applied Ventures; Clearstone Venture Partners
Michelle Kincanon, Vice President, Finance and Sustainability
Education: BS, Management Science, University of California, San Diego; MBA, University of California, Irvine
Background: Controller, Mayfield Fund; Bingham McCutchen
David Nguyen, Associate
Education: BS, Business Administration, Haas School of Business, University of California, Berkeley
Background: Analyst, Goldman, Sachs & Co.

128 ANGELO, GORDON & CO.
245 Park Avenue
New York, NY 10167
Phone: 212-692-2000 Fax: 212-867-9328
Toll-Free: 800-805-0024
e-mail: information@angelogordon.com
web: www.angelogordon.com

Mission Statement: Angelo, Gordon & Co. seek to generate absolute returns with low volatility by exploiting inefficiencies in selected markets and capitalizing on situations that qualify for alternative investments.

Fund Size: $10 million
Founded: 1988
Average Investment: $30 million
Minimum Investment: $10 million
Investment Criteria: Control Buyouts, Minority Investments, Management Buyouts, Private Company Recapitalizations, Corporate Lift-outs
Industry Group Preference: Financial Services, Retailing, Consumer Products, Healthcare, Business Products & Services
Portfolio Companies: Aveta, National Home Healthcare Corp., AG Semi, KEE Action Sports, Benihana, Firebirds Restaurants, Steve Nash Fitness Clubs, Crunch, Kings Foodmart, ClearBalance, Hamilton State Bank, Oak Street Funding

Other Locations:
2000 Avenue of the Stars
Suite 1020
Los Angeles, CA 90067
Phone: 310-777-5440 Fax: 310-246-0796

111 South Wacker Drive
36th Floor
Chicago, IL 60606
Phone: 312-763-5100

Angelo, Gordon Europe LLP
23 Savile Row
London W1S 2ET
United Kingdom
Phone: 44-207-758-5300 Fax: 44-207-207-758-5420

Angelo, Gordon Netherlands B.V.
Prinsengracht 919
Amsterdam 1017 KD
Netherlands
Phone: 31-020-262-0660 Fax: 31-020-262-0664

Angelo, Gordon Europe LLP
Milan, Galleria Vittorio Emanuele
Via Mengoni 4
Milan 20121
Italy
Phone: 39 02 3031 5120

Angelo, Gordon Asia Limited
Suite 1604, One Exchange Square
Central
Hong Kong
Phone: 852-3416-7300 Fax: 852-3416-7500

Angelo, Gordon Asia Limited
9F, A Tower, The-K Twin Towers
50 Jongno 1-Gil, Jongno-Gu
Seoul 03142
Korea
Phone: 822-721-5200 Fax: 822-721-5225

Angelo, Gordon International LLC
Roppongi Hills Mori Tower, 17th Floor
6-10-1, Roppongi, Minato-ku
Tokyo 106-6117
Japan
Phone: 81-3-5474-5610 Fax: 81-3-5474-5620

Key Executives:
Michael L. Gordon, Chief Executive Officer/Co-Chief Investment Officer
Education: BA, Colby College; JD, Boston Univ. School of Law
Background: Research Analyst, L.F. Rothschild
Directorships: Director, Research, L.F. Rothschild
Josh Baumgarten, Co-Chief Investment Officer
Education: BS, Economics, Wharton School, University of Pennsylvania
Background: Portfolio Manager, AG Super Fund; Portfolio Manager, Blackrock; Investment Banker, Jefferies
Directorships: Senior Managing Director, Blackstone
Kirk Whickman, President
Education: BA, Dartmouth College; JD, MBA, Brigham Young University
Background: General Cousel, Morgan Stanley's Global Wealth Management; Senior Vice President/General Counsel, Aetna Financial Services & Aetna Inc.
Adam Schwartz, Co-Chief Investment Officer
Education: BA, University of Pennsylvania
Background: M&A. Vornado Realty Trust

129 ANGELPAD
New York, NY
web: www.angelpad.org

Mission Statement: An intensive mentoship program to help startups build better products, raise the funding they need to succeed and ultimately grow more successful businesses

Fund Size: $200 million
Founded: 2010
Average Investment: $11 million
Minimum Investment: $ 120, 000
Investment Criteria: Startups,
Industry Group Preference: Marketing, API, Data, B2C, Advertising, Mobile, Healthcare, AI
Portfolio Companies: AgentDesks, Allay, Alltrails, Astronomer, Beamery, Buffer, Coverhound, Drone Deploy, Fieldwire, Hive, HumanAPI, Iterable, Kinnek, Loftsmart, Paintzen, Periscope Data, Pipedrive, Postmates, Rolepoint, Sensor Tower, Simplifeye, Tray.io, Truly Wireless, Upcounsel, Vungle, Wove, Zum

Key Executives:
Carine Magescas, Co-Founder
Education: M, Economics, Monetary International Relations, Unversité Paris Daupine; DESS (Post-Masters Degree), Logistics, Marketing and Merchandising, Université Paris Dauphine
Background: Founder, illico design; Moreover Technologies; Semio Corporation; Informatica
Thomas Korte, Co-Founder
Education: University of Mannheim; MBA, Freie

Venture Capital & Private Equity Firms / Domestic Firms

Universität Berlin; Stanford Graduate School of Business
Background: Google

130 ANGELS' FORUM LLC
2665 Marine Way
Suite 1150
Mountain View, CA 94043

Phone: 650-857-0700
web: www.angelsforum.com

Mission Statement: The Angels' Forum consists of a group of experienced investors who invest their own wealth in emerging companies. TAF reviews approximately 20 deals per week and makes 5-15 new investments per year.

Geographic Preference: Silicon Valley, Bay Area-based companies
Fund Size: $18 million
Founded: 1997
Average Investment: $1 - $3 million
Minimum Investment: $100,000
Investment Criteria: Seed, Startups, Early-Stage
Industry Group Preference: Consumer Products, Enterprise Services, Industrial Products, Internet Technology, Medical Devices, Networking, Software, E-Commerce & Manufacturing, Clean Technology
Portfolio Companies: Aravo Solutions, Bell Biosystems, Bouxtie, Cargo Chief, Chimera Bioengineering, DecisionNext, The Detection Group, Ensighten, FE3 Medical, Glue Networks, Intrapace, Kiana Analytics, Kinestral, Laughing Glass Cocktails, Mission Bio, OneMob, PanTerra Networks, RenovoRx, Revfluence, Sonos, Talent Sky, Taulia, Theron Pharmaceuticals, Tiatros, TranscribeMe, Vida, Vidlet

Key Executives:
Carol Sands Langensand, Managing Member/Founder
Education: BA, Political Marketing, University of Iowa
Background: Product Marketing Manager, Motorola; Marketing Officer, First Bank Systems; Director, Marketing, Arthur Young; Director, Marketing, Coopers & Lybrand Consulting; Founder & Owner, Sands MarketingPlus
Directorships: Silicon Valley Association of Startup Entrepreneurs
Leif Langensand, Chief Financial Officer
Education: BS, Forest Products, University of California, Berkeley
Background: Charles Schwab; Price Waterhouse; First Nationwide Bank; Decision Dynamics

131 ANNEX VENTURES
3031 Tisch Way
Suite 505
Jan Jose, CA 95128

web: www.annexventures.com

Mission Statement: Annex Ventures supports early-stage funding for entrepreneurs in the hi-tech, bio-tech and medical device markets.

Founded: 2005
Average Investment: $2 million
Minimum Investment: $100,000
Investment Criteria: Early-Stage
Industry Group Preference: High Technology, Biotechnology, Medical Devices
Portfolio Companies: Listo!, Lucid, Air Media, Im In, iWin.com, Alta Analog Inc., Blue 7 Communications, Jeda Technologies, iSeek, Loadstar Sensors, Nethra, Shimon Systems, PingPad

Key Executives:
Ven N. Reddy, General Partner
Education: BS, Information Systems & Electrical Engineering, San Jose State University
Background: Intel Corporation, Alliance Semiconductor

Mark E. Pearson, General Partner
Education: BS, University of San Francisco
Background: Founder, Catalyst Real Estate Group

132 ANTARES CAPITAL CORPORATION
PO Box 330309
Miami, FL 33233-0309

Phone: 305-894-2888 Fax: 305-894-3227
web: www.antarescapital.com

Mission Statement: A private venture capital firm investing equity capital in expansion stage companies and management buyout opportunities for firms headquartered in the Southeast and Texas.

Geographic Preference: Southeast, Texas
Fund Size: $2.4 billion
Founded: 1993
Average Investment: $500,000-$5 million
Minimum Investment: $250,000
Investment Criteria: Developmental, Expansion Stage
Industry Group Preference: Diversified
Portfolio Companies: AEMT, Inc., Alphatronix, Inc., AnyRiver, BancWest Bancorp, Inc., Bankrate, Inc., BML Pharmaceuticals, Inc., BRPH Architects-Engineers, Inc., Cellit, Inc., Clear-to-Send Electronics, Inc., Crystal Dynamics, Inc., Dispatch Management Services, DTx, Inc., Flood Data Services, Inc., ISO Group, JRL Systems, Inc., Masada Security, Inc., Micro Networks/Andersen Laboratories, National Product Services, Inc., Neotonus, Inc., Nueva Cocina Foods, Inc., Outback Steakhouse, Inc., Sano Corporation, SportsLine.com, Inc., StadiaNet Sports, Inc., Summit Financial Services Group, Triage Management Services

Other Locations:
PO Box 410730
Melbourne, FL 32941
Phone: 321-777-4884 Fax: 321-777-5884

Key Executives:
Randall E. Poliner, Founder/General Partner
e-mail: rpoliner@antarescapital.com
Education: BSEE, Georgia Institute of Technology; MSEE, Carnegie-Mellon; MBA, Harvard Business School
Background: Founder/COO, Macrodyne; President/CEO, Flood Data Services; VP Operations, Scientific Systems Services
Jonathan I. Kislak, General Partner
305-894-2888
Fax: 305-894-3227
e-mail: jkislak@antarescapital.com
Education: BA Economics, Harvard College
Background: Founder, Kislak Capital; Deputy Under Secretary, Small Community/Rural Development, US Department of Agriculture

133 ANTHEM VENTURE PARTNERS
225 Arizona Avenue
Suite 200
Santa Monica, CA 90401

Phone: 310-899-6225 Fax: 310-899-6234
e-mail: info@anthemvp.com
web: www.anthemvp.com

Mission Statement: Anthem Venture Partners seek to provide early-stage investments and operational guidance to distinctive entrepreneurs.

Geographic Preference: United States, Southern California
Fund Size: $100 million
Founded: 2001
Average Investment: $1 - 5 million
Minimum Investment: $1 million
Investment Criteria: Startup, Early Stage, First Stage, Second Stage, MBO
Industry Group Preference: Biotechnology, Communications Equipment, Telecommunications, Computer

Venture Capital & Private Equity Firms / Domestic Firms

Hardware & Software, Diversified, Education, Electronic Components, Health Related, Medical, Information Technology, Online Content, Networking, Pharmaceuticals, Internet, New Media
Portfolio Companies: Affinity Networks, Androit, Audyssey, Axiom Microdevices, Big Frame, Blurb, Card.com, Cognet, Corus Pharma, Cynvenio Biosystems, DemandMedia, Designers House, Dot Wireless, Entropic Communications, FileTrek, Glossi, Interset, Janrain User Management Platform, Layer, The Lucky Group, Matic, Meez, Madefire, Nevenvision, NewHound, Nextest System Corporation, Ocata Therapeutics, Panna, Planet A.T.E., Plixi, Pricelock, Prism Skylabs, RFmagic, Scopely, Siperian, SpinMedia, Solarflare, StackIQ, Surfair, Troika Networks, TrueCar, Video Amp, Viewdle, Vuvox, WaveStream

Key Executives:
William Woodward, Founder/Managing Director
Education: BS Business Administration, University of Southern California
Samit Varma, Partner
Education: BS, Mechanical Engineering, United States Naval Academy; MBA, Marshall School of Business, University of Southern California
Background: Audyssey Labs; United States Navy
Claudia L. Llanos, Partner/Chief Financial Officer
Education: BA, California State University at Northridge
Background: Ernst & Young, LlP

134 ANZU PARTNERS
44 Manning Road
2nd Floor
Billerica, MA 01821

Phone: 202-742-5870
e-mail: info@anzupartners.com
web: anzupartners.com

Mission Statement: Anzu Partners is an investment firm focusing on breakthrough life science technology companies.
Fund Size: $350 Million
Other Locations:
2223 Avenida De La Playa
Suite 204
La Jolla, CA 92037

12610 Race Track Road
Suite 250
Tampa, FL 33626

1399 New York Avenue NW
Suite 601
Washington, DC 20005

Key Executives:
Whitney Haring-Smith, Managing Partner
Education: Yale University; PhD, Oxford University
Background: Principal, Boston Consulting Group; Co-Founder, College Abacus
David Michael, Managing Partner
Education: BA, Harvard University; MBA, Stanford Business School
Background: Senior Partner, Boston Consulting Group
David Seldin, Managing Partner
Education: BS, University of Pennsylvania; MBA, University of Chicago
Background: President, Jacksonville Jaguars NFL Franchise; President, Catalyst Inc.
Directorships: Nice-Pak Products Inc.

135 AOL VENTURES
770 Broadway
4th, 5th, 6th & 9th Floors
New York, NY 10003-9562

e-mail: ventures@corp.aol.com
web: www.oath.com

Mission Statement: AOL Ventures is the venture capital arm of AOL, focused on early stage investing in technology-centric consumer Internet companies.
Geographic Preference: United States, Israel, India
Founded: 2010
Average Investment: $50,000 - $3 million
Investment Criteria: Seed-Stage, Series A, Early-Stage
Industry Group Preference: Consumer Internet
Other Locations:
13031 West Jefferson Boulevard
Building 900
Los Angeles, CA 90094

Key Executives:
Tim Armstrong, Chief Executive Officer
Education: BS, Economics/Sociology, Connecticut College
Background: Director, Integrated Sales & Marketing, Starwave; President, Operations/SVP, Google; The Walt Disney Company
Tim Lemmon, Chief Operating Officer
Education: University of Cambridge; Wharton School, University of Pennsylvania
Background: Vice President, American Express Business Travel

136 APAX PARTNERS
601 Lexington Avenue
53rd Floor
New York, NY 10022

Phone: 212-753-6300 Fax: 212-319-6155
web: www.apax.com

Mission Statement: Apax Partners has raised and advised 31 funds. The partnership was a venture investing pioneer in Europe and the U.S.
Geographic Preference: United States, Europe, Asia
Fund Size: $7 billion
Founded: 1969
Average Investment: $20 million
Minimum Investment: $3.5 million
Investment Criteria: All stages
Industry Group Preference: Technology & Telecommunications, Services, Healthcare, Consumer
Portfolio Companies: ADCO Group, Advantage Sales & Marketing, Answers Corporation, AssuredPartners, Attenti, Authority Brands, Auto Trader Group, Boats Group, Candela, Cengage Learning, Cole Haan, Duck Creek Technologies, ECi Software Solutions, Fractal Analytics, FULLBEAUTY Brands, GamaLife, General Healthcare Group Limited, Genius Sports, Global-e, Go Global Travel, Healthium MedTech, Huayue Education, Ideal Protein, Idealista, Inmarsat, Karl Lagerfeld, Kepro, Lexitas, Manappuram Finance Limited, Max, MetaMetrics, Moda Operandi, Neuraxpharm, Paycor Inc., Psagot, Quality Distribution, Ramet Trom, S.R. Accord, Safetykleen, Schulz Catering, Shriram City Union Finance, Signavio, Solita, Sophos, SoYoung, Takko, Ten10, ThoughtWorks, TIVIT, Tommy Hilfiger, Tosca Services, Trade Me, TRADER, Unilabs, Vyaire Medical, Wizeline, Zap Group, Zensar Technologies
Other Locations:
33 Jermyn Street
London SW1Y 6DN
United Kingdom
Phone: 44 20 7872 6300 Fax: 44 20 7666 3441

Apax Partners Betelingungsberatung GmbH
Theatinerstr. 3
Munich 80333
Germany
Phone: 49 89 99 89 09 0 Fax: 49 89 99 89 09 33

Apax Partners (Israel) Ltd.
Museum Tower
4 Berkowitz Street
Tel Aviv 64238

Venture Capital & Private Equity Firms / Domestic Firms

Israel
Phone: 972 3 777 4400 **Fax:** 972 3 777 4411

Apax Partners Hong Kong Ltd.
16/F Nexxus Building
41 Connaught Road Central
Hong Kong
China
Phone: 852 2200 5813 **Fax:** 852 2200 5820

Apax Partners India Advisers Private Limited
Peninsula Corporate Park, Ganpatrao Kadam Marg
Lower Parel (West)
Mumbai 400013
India
Phone: 91 22 4050 8400 **Fax:** 91 22 4050 8444

65th Floor, Shanghai World Financial Center
100 Century Avenue
Shanghai 200120
China
Phone: 86 21 5198 5600

Key Executives:
Mitch Truwit, Partner & Co-CEO
Education: Vassar College; Harvard Business School
Background: Orbitz Worldwide; priceline.com
Directorships: AssuredPartners, Inc.; Answers Corporation; Bankrate; Dominion Marine Media; Quality Distribution Inc.
Andrew Sillitoe, Partner & Co-CEO
Education: University of Oxford; INSEAD
Background: LEK
Directorships: Inmarsat; Intelsat; King; TDC; TIVIT; Unilabs
Simon Cresswell, Partner & General Counsel
Education: University of Melbourne; Edith Cowan University
Background: Goldman Sachs; Davis Polk & Wardwell; Mallesons
Ralf Gruss, Partner & Chief Operating Officer
Education: Technical University (Karlsruhe); University of Massachusetts; London School of Economics
Background: Arthur D. Little International Inc.
Directorships: LR Health; Beauty Systems GmbH

137 APERTURE VENTURE PARTNERS
645 Madison Avenue
20th Floor
New York, NY 10022
Phone: 212-758-7325 **Fax:** 212-319-8779
e-mail: info@aperturevp.com
web: www.aperturevp.com

Mission Statement: A venture capital group committed to working with exceptional entrepreneurs to tackle significant problems and create major new opportunities.

Geographic Preference: Northeast, West Coast
Founded: 1974
Average Investment: $1-4 million
Minimum Investment: $1 million
Investment Criteria: Second Stage or later, Healthcare Information Technology, Medical Devices, Healthcare, Biopharmaceuticals, Biotechnology
Portfolio Companies: Avedro, Aclaris Therapeutics, BioHaven Pharmaceuticals, Cameron Health, Cardiocore, Cardiomems, Cardiac Dimensions, Ceptaris Therapeutics, Ception Therapeutics, Channel Medsystems, College Pharmaceuticals, Concerro, Conor Medsystems, Endotronix, Entrigue Surgical, Interlace Medical, Inspire, Lyric Pharmaceuticals, Mako Surgical Corp., Neuros Medical, Therox, Tonomy, Trevi Therapeutics, Spirox, T2 Biosystems, Transmolecular, VenusConcept, Xlumena

Key Executives:
Paul E. Tierney Jr., General Partner
e-mail: paul@aperturevp.com
Education: BA, University of Notre Dame; MBA, Harvard Business School
Background: Co-Founder, Coniston Partners; Founder, Coniston Global Partners; Corporate Value Partners; Darwin Capital Partners
Directorships: Altea Therapeutics, TechnoServe
Thomas P. Cooper, MD, General Partner
e-mail: tom@aperturevp.com
Education: BA, DePauw University; MD, Indiana University
Background: Co-Founder, Spectrum Emergency Care; Co-Founder, Correctional Medical Services; Vericare; Mobilex USA
Directorships: Hanger Orthopedic, Kindred Healthcare
Eric H. Sillman, General Partner
e-mail: eric@aperturevp.com
Education: BA, Brown University; MBA, Harvard Business School
Background: UBS Warburg; Parthenon Group; TechnoServe
Directorships: TechnoServe

138 APEX VENTURE PARTNERS
225 West Washington Street
Suite 1500
Chicago, IL 60606
Phone: 312-857-2800 **Fax:** 312-857-1800
e-mail: apex@apexvc.com

Mission Statement: Apex Venture Partner's philosophy is to build significant value in their portfolio companies in close partnership with their management teams.

Geographic Preference: North America
Fund Size: $140 million
Founded: 1987
Average Investment: $10 million
Minimum Investment: $500,000
Investment Criteria: Seed to Growth Stage
Industry Group Preference: Consumer Services, Environment Products & Services, Information Technology, Software, Retailing, Telecommunications, Enterprise Services, Infrastructure, Applications Software & Services, Clean Technology, Business Products & Services
Portfolio Companies: Advanced Equities Financial Corp., Ali Solutions, Analyte Media, Appolicious, Bloom Energy, Combinenet, Current Analysis, Digitalwork, Dirtt Environmental Solutions, Enkata Technologies, Envestnet, Ifbyphone, Illumitex, IQS Inc., Sittercity, Solfocus, Suniva, Target Data, Timelines, Trunk Club

139 APHELION CAPITAL
100 Tiburon Boulevard
Suite 215
Mill Valley, CA 94941
Phone: 415-944-8123
e-mail: venture@aphelioncap.com
web: www.aphelioncapital.net

Mission Statement: Aphelion Capital is a venture capital firm focused on supporting the growth of innovative medical technology with an emphasis on fast to market, low capital intense products that reduce the cost of delivering quality healthcare.

Founded: 2005
Investment Criteria: Seed-Stage to Later-Stage
Industry Group Preference: Healthcare, Wellness
Portfolio Companies: ClearLab, ClearFlow, Cymedica Orthopedics, CytoPherx, Explorer Surgical, iHear, Mercator MedSystems, Neuroptics, Niveus Medical, Palo Alto Health Sciences, Providence Medical Technology, Siesta Medical, Vynca, Aurora SFC Systems, Catheter Connections, Corium, Insound Medical, Insulet Corp., OrthoScan, Surgicount Medical, Surgiquest, Tria Beauty, Vasonova

Venture Capital & Private Equity Firms / Domestic Firms

Key Executives:
Ned Scheetz, Managing Partner
Education: Colby College, Duke University Fuqua School of Business, Univ. of Oxford
Background: Partner, Piper Jaffray Ventures; Janus Capital
John Kim, MD, Principal
Education: Harvard University, Duke University School of Medicine, Fuqua School of Business
Background: Bear Stearns & Co.

140 APJOHN GROUP LLC
350 E Michigan Ave
Suite 500
Kalamazoo, MI 49007

Phone: 269-349-8999 Fax: 269-349-8993
web: www.apjohngroup.com

Mission Statement: Apjohn Group invests in early-stage life science opportunities, with a special focus on biopharmaceuticals.
Geographic Preference: Midwest
Investment Criteria: Early-Stage
Industry Group Preference: Biopharmaceuticals, Healthcare, Pharmaceuticals, Medical, Information Technology, Medical Devices
Portfolio Companies: Afmedica, Sierra Oncology, Armune BioScience, MuciMed, Tetra Discovery Partners

Key Executives:
Donald R. Parfet, Managing Director
e-mail: drparfet@ameritech.net
Education: BA Economics, University of Arizona; MBA Finance, University of Michigan
Background: SVP, Pharmacia; Trustee, WE Upjohn Institute for Employment Research; Trustee/Chairman, Bronson Healthcare Group; Chairman, Kalamazoo College
Directorships: Biocore International AB
Jack R. Luderer, MD, Founding Partner
Education: Masters Chemistry, Northwestern University
Background: ssociate VP Research, Western Michigan University; VP US Medical Affairs, Pharmacia; Board Certified in both Internal Medicine and Clinical Pharmacology
Peter R. Seaver, Founding Partner
Education: BA Biology, Bowdoin College
Background: President Healthcare Group, Kaleidoscope Television; Executive Director, Pharmacia and Upjohn; First Lieutenant, US Army Medical Service Corps
Directorships: University of Arizona Pharmacy School; National Association of Chain Drug Stores; Barr Laboratories; Nelson Information Systems; Fellows of the Harvard School of Dental
Joseph T. Sobota, MD, Founding Partner
e-mail: jts100@sbcglobal.net
Education: AB Chemistry, Drew University; MD, Georgetown University; Post MD residency, Tulane University
Background: CEO, Rubicon Genomics; President/COO, Biopure; EVP/COO, Chugai-Upjohn; Board Certifed in Anatomic and Clinical Pathology; Visiting Professor of Pathology, Dartmouth Medical School; Adjunct Professor of Medicine, Northwestern University School of Medicine
Eli L. Thomssen, Associate Director
Education: BS Animal Science, University of Nebraska; MBA, Western Michigan University
Background: Senior Consultant, Brakke Consulting; VP Business Development/Strategic Planning, Pharmacia Animal Health
Ronald J. Shebuski, PhD, General Partner
Education: BS, Microbiology, University of Wisconsin; PhD, Pharmacology, University of Minnesota Medical School
Background: Pharmacia & Upjohn; VP, Afmedica, Inc.; Senior Scientist, Merck Research Laboratories; Smith Kline & French

Charles M. Hall, PhD, General Partner
Education: University of the South in Sewanee, TN; PhD, Organic Chemistry, University of Minnesota
Phillip C. Carra, General Partner
e-mail: pccarra@sbcglobal.net
Background: VP, Public Affairs, Pfizer
M. Holly Folk, General Partner
Background: CFO, Afmedica; Peat Marwick & Mitchell

141 APOLLO GLOBAL MANAGEMENT
9 West 57th Street
43rd Floor
New York, NY 10019

Phone: 212-515-3200
web: www.apollo.com

Mission Statement: Apollo Global Management invests in private equity, credit and real estate. Dedicated to creating value, Apollo Global Management raises, manages and provides capital for investors and industry leading businesses.
Geographic Preference: North America, Europe, Asia
Fund Size: $17.5 billion
Founded: 1990
Average Investment: $200 million
Minimum Investment: $20 million
Investment Criteria: Traditional Buyouts, Distressed Buyouts, Debt Investments, Corporate Partner Buyouts
Industry Group Preference: Chemicals, Commodities, Consumer Products, Retail, Consumer & Leisure, Distribution, Transportation, Financial Services, Business Products & Services, Manufacturing, Industrial, Media, Packaging, Satellite Communications, Wireless, Leisure
Portfolio Companies: Berry Plastics, Caesars Entertainment, Claire's, Countrywide plc, CEVA Logistics, Hexion Specialty Chemicals, Jacuzzi Brands, LyondellBasell Industries, McGraw-Hill Education, Momentive Performance Materials, Novitex Enterprise Solutions, Realogy, Rexnord, Vantium Management, Verso Paper

Other Locations:
3 Bryant Park
New York, NY 10036
Phone: 212-515-3200

2000 Avenue of the Stars
Suite 510N
Los Angeles, CA 90067
Phone: 310-843-1900

1 Manhattanville Road
Suite 201
Purchase, NY 10577
Phone: 914-694-8000

7255 Woodmont Avenue
Bethesda, MD 20814
Phone: 240-630-2700

609 Main Street
Suite 2750
Houston, TX 77002
Phone: 832-708-2000

Apollo Management International LLP
25 St. George Street
London W1S 1FS
United Kingdom
Phone: 44-2070165000

Apollo Management Advisors GmbH
mainBuilding
Taunusanlage 16
Frankfurt 60325
Germany
Phone: 49-69789887000

Le Dome, 3rd Floor
2-8, Avenue Charles de Gaulle
Luxembourg L-1653

Luxembourg
Phone: 352-20881300

Apollo Management Asia Pacific Limited
36/F, One Exchange Square
8 Connaught Place
Central
Hong Kong
Phone: 852-35886300

Apollo Management Singapore Pte. Ltd.
8 Marina Boulevard, #07-02
Marina Bay Financial Centre Tower 1 018981
Singapore

AGM India Advisors Pte. Ltd.
The Grand Hyatt Complex
Suite F-11, Maharashtra
Mumbai 400 055
India
Phone: 91-2239571400

Key Executives:
Marc Rowan, Chief Executive Officer
Education: BS, MBA, Finance, Wharton School
Background: M&A Group, Drexel Burnham Lambert
Directorships: Athene Holding, Caesars Entertainment Corp., Caesars Acquisition Corp.
Scott Kleinman, Co-President
Education: BA, University of Pennsylvania; BS, Wharton School
Background: Investment Banking, Smith Barney
Directorships: Lyondell Basell Industries, Taminco Global Chemicals, Verso Paper, Realogy, Momentive Performance Materials
James Zelter, Co-President
Education: BS, Economics, Duke University
Background: CIO, Citigroup Alternative Investments; Trader, Goldman Sachs
Directorships: DUMAC

142 APPIAN EDUCATION VENTURES

e-mail: info@appianeducation.com
web: appianeducation.com

Mission Statement: A firm that invests in and operates high-growth, high-impact educational ventures. At the core of AppianBs vision is the idea that well-targeted, socially-conscious private investment in education can have a profound impact on the future.

Geographic Preference: Latin America
Founded: 2012
Industry Group Preference: Education, Vocational Training, Educational Technologies, Publishing
Key Executives:
Luis E Garcia Garcia de Brigard, Founder/Managing Partner
Education: LLB, Universidad Javeriana; MEd, Harvard University; MBA, MIT
Background: CEO, Americas, Inspired Education; Deputy Minister of Education, Government of Colombia
Directorships: Global Education Innovation Initiative; Varkey Foundation; SOS Children's Villages
Juan Uribe, Partner
Alejandro Maldonado, Partner

143 APPIAN VENTURES
4810 Prospect Street
Littleton, CO 80123

Phone: 303-830-2450
web: www.appianvc.com

Mission Statement: Appian's practice is to connect with entrepreneurs by treating them respectfully and their ideas thoughtfully. The firm's whole company investment method sharpens a company's business focus and connects industry resources to help accelerate success.

Geographic Preference: Western United States
Fund Size: $80 million
Founded: 2002
Average Investment: $5 million
Minimum Investment: $3 million
Investment Criteria: Seed, Startup, First Stage, Second Stage, Bridge
Industry Group Preference: Computer Hardware & Software
Portfolio Companies: AdPay, Auctionpay, Cadre, Carefx, Collective Intellect, ETI, IP Commerce, Lefthand Networks, mPay Gateway, OneRiot, OpenLogic, Oxlo, Ping Identity, Roving Planet, SkyeTek, Tendril, Thought Equity Motion, Univa, Valen Technologies
Key Executives:
Stacey McKittrick, Managing Director/Chief Financial Officer
e-mail: stacey@appianvc.com
Education: BA, College of William & Mary
Background: VP Operations, Centennial Ventures; Corporate Finance, Kirkland and Ellis; Hirschler, Fleischer; Founder/President, Timberlike-BEC Inc.
Don Parsons, Managing Director
Education: BS Electrical Engineering, Northwestern University; MBA, University of Michigan
Background: General Partner, Centennial Ventures; Associate Engineer, IBM's Personal Computer Division; Chairman/President, Colorado Venture Capital Association
Directorships: Roving Planet; Oxlo Systems; Univa; National Association for Corporate Directors; Valen Technologies; Collective Intellect
Mark Soane, Managing Director
Education: Graduated with highest distinction in History, Dartmouth College; MBA, Stanford Business School
Background: Managing Partner, Quest Capital Partnership; Senior Operating, Multum Information Services; Trade; Personics Corporation; Investment Associate, Bessemer Venture Partners; Current Chairman, Colorda Venture Capital Association
Directorships: Cadre Technologies, AdPay; OpenLogic; Carefx; Voyant Technologies; Datria Systems; Pixxures; Active Education

144 APPLE TREE PARTNERS
230 Park Avenue
Suite 2800
New York, NY 10169

Phone: 212-468-5800
e-mail: info@appletreepartners.com
web: www.appletreepartners.com

Mission Statement: Apple Tree Investments is a venture capital firm that invests in the healthcare, pharmaceuticals and biotechnology sectors. Apple Tree Investments is dedicated to providing capital and working with its portfolio company entrepreneurs to establish necessary corporate infrastructure.

Fund Size: $1.5 billion
Founded: 1999
Investment Criteria: All Stages
Industry Group Preference: Biotechnology, Genomics, Chemicals, Drug Development, Life Sciences, Pharmaceuticals, Healthcare
Portfolio Companies: Akero Therapeutics, Braeburn, Chinook Therapeutics, Corvidia Therapeutics, Elstar Therapeutics, Gala Therapeutics, Limelight Bio, Stoke Therapeutics, Stoke Therapeutics, Syntimmune, Tusker Therapeutics, VytronUS
Other Locations:
245 Main Street
12th Floor

Venture Capital & Private Equity Firms / Domestic Firms

Cambridge, MA 02142
Phone: 617-294-6790

The Gridiron Building, Suite 6.05
1 Pancras Square
London N1C 4AG
United Kingdom
Phone: 44 20 3897 6689

Key Executives:
Seth L. Harrison, M.D., Founder/Managing Partner
Education: AB, Princeton University; MD, MBA, Columbia University
Background: General Partner, Oak Investment Partners; Venture Partner, Sevin Rosen Funds
Directorships: International Partnership for Microbicides, ASOthera Pharmaceuticals, Cure Forward, Syntimmune, Braeburn Pharmaceuticals, Tokai Pharmaceuticals
Anna Batarina, Partner
Education: MA, Global Affairs, Yale University; MA, Clinical Psychology, Lomonosov Moscow State University; CFA
Background: SVP/Head of Capital Markets & Investor Relations, Uralkali; Associate, A1/Alfa Eco; Senior Consultant, Financial & International Tax Services, Ernst & Young
Andy Bayliffe, Venture Partner
Education: PhD, Molecular Biology, Leeds University
Background: GlaxoSmithKline
Michael Ehlers, Venture Partner/Chief Scientific Officer
Education: BS, Chemistry, Caltech; MD & PhD, Johns Hopkins University School of Medicine
Background: EVP of R&D, Biogen; Group SVP, BioTherapeutics; Chief Scientific Officer, Pfizer; George Barth Geller Professor & Investigator of the Howard Hughes Medical Institute, Duke University Medical Center
Paul Eisenberg, Venture Partner/Chief Medical Officer
Education: MD, New York Medical College
Background: Professor of Medicine, Washington University; Director of the Cardiac Intensive Care Unit, Barnes-Jewish Hospital; Cardiovascular Discovery; Translational Medicine; Amgen
Spiros Liras, Venture Partner
Education: PhD, Organic Chemistry, Iowa State University
Background: Biogen; Pfizer; Adjunct Professor, Dept. of Pharmaceutical Chemistry, University of California

145 APPLIED MATERIALS VENTURES
3050 Bowers Avenue
PO Box 58039
Santa Clara, CA 95054-3299

Phone: 408-727-5555
web: www.appliedventures.com

Mission Statement: Applied Ventures is the venture capital fund of Applied Materials, Inc. Applied Ventures invests in early-stage technology companies that promise to deliver high growth and exceptional returns. They seek to invest in companies that provide technologies that advance or complement Applied Materials' core business and stimulate the growth of applications for semiconductors, displays, solar PV, and related products and services.

Geographic Preference: United States, Israel
Fund Size: $50 million
Founded: 2001
Average Investment: $500,000 - $3 million
Minimum Investment: $500,000
Investment Criteria: Seed, Startup, First Stage, Second Stage
Industry Group Preference: Communications Equipment, Computer Hardware & Software, Semiconductors
Portfolio Companies: ActaCell, Adesto Technologies, Advanced Inquiry Systems, BT Imaging, ClearEdge Power, Devicescape, Enki Technology, Enphase Energy, Fat Spaniel Technologies, Glimmerglass, Grandis, Halation Photonics, Illumitex, Infinera, Infinite Power Solutions, Innolume, Kotak, Liquavista, Lumiode, Menara Networks, MTPV Power Corp., Nanomix, Nanosys Inc., Norsk Titanium, Oncoscope, Passport Systems Inc., Plextronics, Sage Electrochromics Inc., Semprius, Solaicx, SolidEnergy, SuNAM Co., SunEdison, Takumi Technology, Tera-Barrier Films, Tessolve, Twist Bioscience

Key Executives:
Omkaram Nalamasu, Ph.D., Senior Vice President/Chief Technology Officer
Education: PhD, University of British Columbia
Background: Professor, Rensselaer Polutechnic Institute; AT&T Bell Laboratories; Agere Systems Inc.
Directorships: Nanofabrication Research Laboratory, Bell Laboratories; MEMS; Waveguides Research

146 ARAGON VENTURES
1455 Adams Court
Menlo Park, CA 94025

Phone: 650-566-8000

Mission Statement: Aragon Ventures provides investment capital to high technology enterprises at early stages of their development from startup companies through and including expansion financing.

Investment Criteria: Early-Stage
Industry Group Preference: High Technology
Portfolio Companies: ScienceBased Health

Key Executives:
David Brewer, Managing Partner
Education: Business Degree, University of California, Berkeley; Law Degree, University of San Francisco
Background: Explore Technologies, eFax.Com, Monogram Software, Telebit, Packet Technologies
Directorships: HereUare, Notify Technology Corp, Cuica Technologies, FirstStone Incubators, PriaVision
Michael Ballard, Manager
Education: BFA, University of Utah
Background: President & CEO, eLingo; President & CEO, Telebit Corporation

147 ARAVAIPA VENTURES
Boulder, CO

e-mail: info@aravaipaventures.com
web: www.aravaipaventures.com

Mission Statement: Aravaipa Venture Fund LLC is the only fund investing exclusively in Impact Technology, low-capital-intensive, early-stage companies in Colorado.

Geographic Preference: Colorado
Founded: 2008
Investment Criteria: Early-Stage
Industry Group Preference: Technology, Renewable Energy, Energy Efficiency, Clean Technology
Portfolio Companies: aWhere, Bolder Industries, Clear Comfort, Lightning Systems, Raven Window, Silver Bullet, Steelhead Composite, Sundolier, Vision Chemical Systems

Key Executives:
Robert Fenwick-Smith, Founder/Senior Managing Director
Education: BA, Economics, HEC Lausanne; MBA, Harvard Business School
Background: Co-Founder/CEO, Robannic
Directorships: AXIT AG
Timothy Reeser, Managing Director
Education: BS, Mechanical Engineering, Colorado State University
Background: Co-Founder, Engineering Computer Consultants; Partner, 3t Systems

Venture Capital & Private Equity Firms / Domestic Firms

148 ARBOR INVESTMENTS
676 North Michigan Avenue
Suite 3400
Chicago, IL 60611

Phone: 312-981-3770
e-mail: arborinvestments@arborpic.com
web: www.arborpic.com

Mission Statement: Arbor Investments is a private equity firm focused on middle market companies in the food and beverage sector.

Geographic Preference: North America
Fund Size: $400 million
Founded: 1999
Investment Criteria: Middle Market
Industry Group Preference: Food & Beverage
Portfolio Companies: Best Maid Cookie Co., Columbus Manufacturing, Concord Foods, DPI Specialty Foods, Fieldbrook Foods Corporation, Hudson Baking Company, Keyes Packaging Group, Mister Cookie Face, New French Bakery, PBF Pita Bread Factory, Rice Garden, Trojan Lithograph Corporation

Other Locations:
410 Park Avenue
Suite 1620
New York, NY 10022

Key Executives:
Gregory J. Purcell, Chief Executive Officer
Education: BS, Marquette University; MBA, University of Chicago
Background: Senior VP, M&A, Reyes Holdings; American National Bank of Chicago
Directorships: Keyes Packaging, Trojan Lithograph Corporation, New French Bakery, Midland Packaging & Display, Chicago Public Library Foundation
Joseph P. Campolo, President
Education: BS, Villanova University; MBA, University of Pittsburgh
Background: VP, M&A, Reyes Holdings; American National Bank of Chicago
Directorships: Fieldbrook Foods Corporation
Timothy G. Fallon, Senior Operating Partner
Education: BS, St. Joseph's University; MBA, Fox School of Business, Temple University
Background: CEO, Columbus Foods; Operating Partner, Krave Jerky; Senior Exectuvie Positions at various companies, including: Procter & Gamble; Cadbury Schweppes; Pepsi; Vermont Pure; Annie's Homegrown; Kettle Foods
Ryan R. McKenzie, Chief Administrative Officer
Education: BA, University of Chicago; MM, Finance & Accounting, Northwestern University
Background: COO, Automatic Ice; Icemakers LLC; CIO & Head, Corporate Finance, American National Bank of Chicago; President & COO, Pullman Bank
Directorships: Rice Garden, Columbus Manufacturing, New French Bakery, Gold Standard Baking

149 ARBOR VENTURES
web: www.arborventures.com

Mission Statement: Arbor Ventures is a pioneer venture capital firm focused on technology investments in Hong Kong, Japan, Singapors and ASEAN.

Geographic Preference: Hong Kong, Japan, Singapore, ASEAN
Industry Group Preference: Technology
Portfolio Companies: Abra, Akulaku, A-Saas, BlockApps, Beam, Bob, C1X, Demyst Data, Ever Compliant, Forter, Fundbox, GlobaliD, Karmic, Lufax/Lu.com, NS8, Paidy, Planck Re, TrueAccord, Quancheng, Quottly, Skyline, Silot, Trumid, 2C2P

Key Executives:
Melissa Guzy, Co-Founder & Managing Partner
Education: Wellesley College; Master's degree in Finance, University of Florida
Background: Managing Director and Head of VantagePoint Asia
Directorships: InvestLab, Denyst.data
Wei Hopeman, Co-Founder & Managing Partner
Education: BA, International Relations, Pomona College; MBA, Stanford University Graduate School of Business
Background: Managing Director, Head of Asia, Citi Ventures
Directorships: Silot Pte Ltd.; GlobaliD; Akulaku; Karmic; Abra
Ari Fine, Senior Analyst
Education: Cornell University
Evelyn Sun, Senior Analyst
Education: BA, Economic Statistics, Xi'an Jiaotong University; MA, Management and Financial Engineering, Peking University & the National University of Singapore

150 ARBORETUM VENTURES
303 Detroit Street
Suite 301
Market Place Building
Ann Arbor, MI 48104

Phone: 734-998-3688
e-mail: info@arboretumvc.com
web: www.arboretumvc.com

Mission Statement: A private equity firm targeting investments in early stage life sciences companies.

Geographic Preference: United States
Fund Size: $220 million
Founded: 2002
Average Investment: $5 - 7 million
Investment Criteria: Seed, Startup, First Stage, Second Stage
Industry Group Preference: Biotechnology, Healthcare, Medical & Health Related, Information Technology, Medical Devices, Pharmaceuticals, Life Sciences, Healthcare Services
Portfolio Companies: Adavium Medical, Advance ICU Care, ArborMetrix, Aira, Cardio Dimensions, ConertoHealth, Delphinus Medical Technologies, Ebb Tehrapeutics, KFx Medical, Lucina Health, MyHealthDirect, NeuMoDx Molecular, nVision, NxThera, Pear Therapeutics, Rethink, SI-BONE, Strata Oncology, Swift Biosciences, Wellfount

Other Locations:
11000 Cedar Avenue
Cleveland, OH 44106
Phone: 216-658-3989 Fax: 216-658-3998

Key Executives:
Jan Garfinkle, Founder/Managing Director
e-mail: jgarfinkle@arboretumvc.com
Education: BS, University of California, Berkeley; MBA, University of Pennsylvania
Background: Management, Advanced Cardiovascular Systems; Devices for Vascular Intervention; President, Strategic Marketing Consultants; Manufacturing Engineer, Proctor and Gamble; President, Michigan Venture Capital Association
Directorships: HandyLab; Thermocure; Uptake Medical; NeoGuide
Timothy Petersen, Founder/Managing Partner
e-mail: tpetersen@arboretumvc.com
Education: BA, Williams College; MS, University of Wisconsin; MBA, University of Michigan
Background: Interium President, Thermocure; Managing Director, Zell Lurie Institute; Wolverine Venture Fund; Senior Management, Industrial Economics
Directorships: Asterand; HealthMedia; KFx Medical; Thermocure
Paul McCreadie, Partner/Chief Operating Officer
Education: BS, MS, Mechanical Engineering, University

Venture Capital & Private Equity Firms / Domestic Firms

of Michigan; MBA, Ross School of Business
Background: Ford Motor Company
Directorships: Frankel Commercilization Fund
Marcy Marshall, Chief Financial Officer
Education: BA, Economics, University of Michigan; MBA, Ross School of Business, University of Michigan
Background: Davenport Univesity; ITt Consumer Financial Corporation; 3M Corporation; May Department Stores Company
Tom Shehab, Managing Partner
Education: BS, Biology, Bowling Green State University; MD, Wayne State University, MA, Medical Management, Carnegie Mellon University
Background: Chief of Staff, St. Joseph Mercy Hospital, Ann Arbor; Chief of Medicine for Integrated Health Associates
Dan Kidle, Partner
Education: BBA, MBA, Ross School of Business, University of Michigan
Background: Analyst, Arboretum Ventures; Financial Analyst, Eli Lilly & Company

151 ARC ANGEL FUND
885 3rd Avenue
20th Floor
New York, NY 10022

e-mail: info@arcangelfund.com
web: www.arcangelfund.com

Mission Statement: ARC Angel Fund invests in seed and early-stage companies with high growth potential. ARC's primary focus is in software, digital media, internet services and other technology.
Geographic Preference: Northeast, Mid-Adlantic
Average Investment: $50,000 - $250,000
Investment Criteria: Seed-Stage, Early-Stage, Revenues of under $5 million
Industry Group Preference: Software, Information Technology, Internet, Technology-Enabled Services, Business Products & Services, Digital Media & Marketing, Mobile, Healthcare Information Technology
Portfolio Companies: Kanvas, Uptown Network, Human Demand, Nulabel, Statsocial, Offermobi, Prognos, Careerminds, Upnext, Sidecare, Yeildmo, BeneStream, Cirrusdata, Bow & Drape, Movie Pass, Partpic, Radius8, Crowded, Cuebiq, Lynq, Ollie
Key Executives:
Edward Reitler, Founding Partner
Education: Harvard Law School
Background: Senior Partner, Reitler Kailas & Rosebnlatt
Directorships: Business Financial Services
David Freschman, Founding Partner
Education: BS, Accounting, University of Delaware; MBA, Loyola College of Maryland
Background: Managing Principal, Innovation Capital Advisors
Michael Kelley, Founding Partner
Education: BA, History, University of Delaware
Background: Founder/Principal, Formation Capital
Joe Rubin, Founding Partner
Education: BS, Communications, Hofstra University
Background: Director/Co-Founder, FundingPost.com

152 ARCADIAN FUND
9663 Santa Monica Blvd.
Unit 1038
Beverly Hills, CA 90210

Phone: 424-279-8188
e-mail: info@arcadianfund.com
web: arcadianfund.com

Mission Statement: Invests in ancillary cannabis companies.
Founded: 2018
Investment Criteria: Late Stage
Industry Group Preference: Cannabis
Portfolio Companies: Baker Technologies, BDS Analytics, Flow Hub, High Times, Kush Bottles, Meadow, Quanta, Treez, Wurk
Key Executives:
Matthew J. Nordgren, Founder/Chief Executive Officer
Education: BA, Government/Business; Business Foundations Certifications, Red McCombs School of Business, University of Texas at Austin; MBA, University of Dallas
Background: CEO, Inspired Builders; Executive Director, Nordco Inc. Energy; Founder, Leadership Foundation; Executive/COO, St. Augustine Holdings; Managing Director, Camden Capital Partners; CEO, Nordco Consulting
Directorships: International Tower Group; Ballybunion Caplain Growth Fund
Krishnan Varier, Principal
Education: BA, Economics, University of Texas at Austin; MBA, Kenan-Flager Business School, University of North Carolina at Chapel Hill
Background: Associate, Morgan Keegan & Co.; Associate, Merrill Lynch; Sr. Investment Analyst, Health Care REIT; Health Care Investment Banking, Cowen & Co.; Principal Varier Venture Consulting
Lisa Riedmiller, Chief Financial Officer
Education: BA, California State University at San Jose
Background: OSCCO Ventures
Stacy Huynh, Director of Operations
Education: BA, Economics, San Francisco State University;
Background: Data Analyst, San Francisco's Hospitality House

153 ARCAPITA INC
1180 Peachtree Street NE
Suite 2280
Atlanta, GA 30309

Phone: 404-920-9000
web: www.arcapita.com

Mission Statement: Invests in established companies throughout the world, targeting growth-oriented private equity acquisitions with a total transaction value between $50 and $500 million.
Geographic Preference: North America, Europe, Russia, Middle East, India, China
Founded: 2005
Average Investment: $50 - $200 million
Industry Group Preference: Healthcare, Information Technology, Industrial Technology, Energy, Business Products & Services, Healthcare, Consumer Products
Portfolio Companies: Veolia, Arcapita Ventures I Limited, Meridian Surgical Partners, Saadiyat, Ascendas India Trust, Dubai Investment Park, MorningStar, The Arbor Company, Layetana Real Estate, Arcapita International Luxury Residential Developement I, Bainbridge, Bahrain Bay, Ampad, Arpatia India Growth Capital I, B.R. Lee Industries Inc., Bijoux Terner, Caribore Coffee, Church Street Health Management, Church's Chicken, Cirrus, Compagnie Européenne de Prestations Logistique, Computer Generation Inc., Cypress Communications, Falcon Gas Storage, DVT Corp., Freightliner, Loehmann's Medifax EDI, Pods, J. Jill, Profine, Roxar, Smart Document Solutions, South Staffordshire Place, Southland Log Homes, Varel International, Tensar, TLC Health Network, Transportation Safety Technologies Inc., Viridian, Watermark Inc, Al Rajhi Capital, Zephyr Investments Limited, Yakima, Mapletree, Gicram Groupe, Point Park Properties, Shurgard Self-Storage, CapitaLand, Arcapita Qatar Real Estate Investment I, Sunrise, Arcapita US Residential Development II, Arcapita US Residential Developmental III, Prescott Group, Archstone Smith, ProLogis, Riffa Views, Victory Heights, NAS, ARC UAE Logistics II

Venture Capital & Private Equity Firms / Domestic Firms

Other Locations:
Arcapita Investment Management B.S.C.
P.O. Box 1357
Manama
Bahrain
Phone: 973-17-218333

Arcapita Investment Advisors UK Limited
The Shard
32 London Bridge Street
London SE1 9SG
United Kingdom
Phone: 44-20-7824-5600

Arcapita Investment Management Singapore Pte.
24 Raffles Place
#16-03 Clifford Centre
Singapore 048621
Singapore
Phone: 65-6513-0395

Key Executives:
Atif Abdulmalik, Chief Executive Officer
Education: BBA, Saint Edward's University, Texas
Background: Investcorp
Hisham Al Raee, Deputy Chief Executive Officer
Education: MBA, University of Hull, UK; CSD, Business Admin., University of Behrain
Background: Senior Director, Business Development, Reuters Middle East; Finance, Citibank N.A.
Martin Tan, Chief Investment Officer
Education: BA, MBA, Washington State University
Background: CEO, CapitaLand Commericial & Integrated Development
Arthur Rogers, Managing Director/General Counsel
Education: BA, History, Hamilton College; JD, Emory University School of Law
Background: Managing Director, Falconvest; General Counsel, Gatehouse Bank; Director, Arcapita Bank; Corporate Attorney, Gibson, Dunn & Crutcher; Corporate Attorney, Testa, Hurwitz & Thibeault

154 ARCH VENTURE PARTNERS
8755 W Higgins Road
Suite 1025
Chicago, IL 60631
Phone: 773-380-6600 Fax: 773-380-6606
web: www.archventure.com

Mission Statement: One of the largest technology venture firms in the U.S.

Geographic Preference: Global
Fund Size: $2 billion
Founded: 1986
Average Investment: $5 million
Minimum Investment: $500,000
Investment Criteria: Seed- and Early-Stage
Industry Group Preference: Semiconductors, Advanced Materials, Clean Technology, Optics & Photonics, Electronic Components, Network Infrastructure & Security, High Performance Computing, Wireless, Pharmaceuticals, Genomics & Bioinformatics, Medical Devices, Diagnostic & Drug Discovery Platforms, Nano- and Microtechnologies
Portfolio Companies: Achaogen, Acylin Therapeutics, Adolor, Agios Pharmaceuticals, Allozyne, Alnylam Pharmaceuticals, Array BioPharma, Aviron, Bind Biosciences, Bluebird Bio, Caliper Life Sciences, Chiasma, Ensemble Therapeutics, Fate Therapeutics, Genvec, Groove Biopharma, Hua Medicine, Idun Pharmaceuticals, Ikaria, Illumina, ISB Accelerator, Kythera Biopharmaceuticals, Lycera, Neurogesx, Nura, Omeros, Oncofactor, Permeon Biologics, Phaserx, Pulmatrix, Receptos, Sorbent Therapeutics, Syros, Theraclone Sciences, Trubion Pharma, VBI Vaccines, VentiRx, VLST, Xcyte Therapies, Xenoport, Xori, deCODE Genetics, Fast Track Systems, Genomica, Medvantix, Nexcura, Ekos, R2 Technology, AgBiome, Cambrios Technology, NanoSys, Sapphire Energy, Twist Bioscience, Adesto Technologies, Artificial Muscle, CoolEdge Lighting, Crystal-IS, Eichrom Technologies, Innovalight, Nanophase Technologies, 908 Devices, Ahura Scientific, Alfalight, Alis, Isco International, Impinj, Intelligent Reasoning Systems, Kotura, Kilimanjaro Energy, Microoptical Devices, Nioptics, Nitronex, Xtera Communications, Semprius, Siluria Technologies, Caliper Life Sciences, Pixelexx Systems, Quanterix, Everyday Learning, Teach.com, Classmates Online, CelebrateExpress.com, Apropos Technology, Ciespace, Netbot, New Era of Networks, Univa UD

Other Locations:
188 E Blaine Street
Suite 125
Seattle, WA 98102
Phone: 206-806-8478

1700 Owens Street
Suite 535
San Francisco, CA 94158

Key Executives:
Clinton W. Bybee, Co-Founder & Managing Director, Emeritus
Education: MBA, University of Chicago; BS Engineering, Texas A&M University
Background: Associate, ARCH Development Corporation; Manager, Technology Venture Fund, Illinois Department of Commerce & Community Affairs; Production and Operations Engineer, Amoco Corporation
Directorships: Nanosys, Cambrios, AmberWave Systems, Aveso Displays, ePolicy Solutions
Keith L. Crandell, Co-Founder & Managing Director
Education: MBA, University of Chicago; MS Chemistry, University of Texas; BS Chemistry, Math, St. Lawrence University
Background: Senior Manager, ARCH Development Corporation; President, Eichrom Industries; Marketing, Hercules
Directorships: AlfaLight, Apropos, CelebrateExpress, ALIS, Crystal-IS
Robert T. Nelsen, Co-Founder & Managing Director
Education: MBA, University of Chicago; BS Biology, Economics, University of Puget Sound
Background: Senior Manager, ARCH Development Corporation
Directorships: Fred Hutchison Cancer Research Institute, Adolor Corporation, Accelerator, Xcyte Therapies, NeurogesX, Ikaria, Optobionics
Steven Gillis, Managing Director
Education: BA, Williams College; PhD, Dartmouth College
Background: Immunologist; pioneer in the field of cytokines; Founder/Director, Corixa Corp; Founder/Director, Immunex Corp; 300 publications
Kristina Burow, Managing Director
Education: BS, Chemistry, University of California, Berkeley; MA, Chemistry, Columbia University; MBA, University of Chicago
Background: Novartis BioVenture Fund; Business Development, Genomis Institute of The Novartis Research Foundation; Co-Founder, Sapphire Energy
Directorships: Sapphire Energy; Ensemble Discovery; Archaeogen; Kythera Biopharmaceuticals; Celula; Accelerator
Mark McDonnell, Managing Director, CFO & CAO
Education: BS, Marquette University; CPA
Background: CFO, Marquette Venture Partners

155 ARCHTOP VENTURES
Four International Drive
Suite 330
Rye Brook, NY 10570
e-mail: helloarchtop@archtopventures.com
web: www.archtopventures.com

Venture Capital & Private Equity Firms / Domestic Firms

Mission Statement: Archtop Ventures is focused on making investments in emerging growth and middle market companies in media, entertainment and new technology, positioning them for rapid growth and market leadership.

Average Investment: $20 - $75 million
Investment Criteria: Early-Stage
Industry Group Preference: Media, Entertainment, New Technology, Mobile, Social Media, Gaming, E-Commerce & Manufacturing, Publishing, Travel & Leisure, Health & Wellness, Advertising, Big Data, Education, Enterprise Software

Key Executives:

Jeff Demond, Chairman/CEO
Education: Business School Graduate, University of Alabama; CPA
Background: President & CEO, BCI Broadband; President & CEO, Bresnan Communications; Senior Manager, KPMG

Paul Gruenberg, Partner
Background: Founder, Video News International; Founder, Videovation; Founder, Plum Holdings; Rockefeller & Co.; Morgens Waterfall & Vintiadis

John Young, Partner
Background: Tribal DDB Worldwide, Moden Media/Poppe Tyson, Full Contact

---

156 ARCHYTAS VENTURES
1880 Century Park East
Suite 250
Los Angeles, CA 90067

Toll-Free: 866-822-2662
e-mail: info@archytasventures.com
web: archytasventures.com

Mission Statement: An investment holding firm offering flexible capital to emerging companies in the cannabis industry.

Founded: 2016
Investment Criteria: Early-Stage
Industry Group Preference: Cannabis
Portfolio Companies: Xtraction Services, Halo Labs, Grow Now

Key Executives:

David Kivitz, Co-Founder/Partner
Education: BBA, Finance, George Washington University
Background: Real Estate Analyst, CapitalSource; Fund Investment Analyst, Hamilton Lane; Co-Founder/Managing Principal, Alta Verde Group
Directorships: Xtraction Services

Tim Rotolo, Co-Founder/CIO
Education: BA, History, Tufts University
Background: Financial Analyst, Merrill Lynch; Analyst/VP, Sandalwood Securities; Founder/Managing Partner, Lloyd Harbor Capital Management
Directorships: Xtraction Services

Antony Radbod, Co-Founder/CSO
Background: Marketing Director, Georgetown Private Cliente; VP of Product Development, NuParadigm; Partner, StandAlone Consulting; Director of Marketing NearU Search; Director of Marketing, Creative Asylum; Advisor, Alta Verde Group; Founder/CEO, Pollen Partners; CMO, Xtraction Services
Directorships: Xtraction Services

Brooke Hayes, Partner/COO
Education: BS, Economics; MBA, Wharton School, University of Pennsylvania
Background: Associate, The Stratum Group; Associate, JPMorgan Chase H&Q; Partner, Milestone Partners; Private Equity Consultant, Meadowbrook Capital Advisors; CFO, Xtraction Services
Directorships: Agust Spark; Occasion Brands

---

157 ARCLIGHT CAPITAL PARTNERS
200 Clarendon Street
55th Floor
Boston, MA 02116

Phone: 617-531-6300
e-mail: info@arclightcapital.com
web: www.arclight.com

Mission Statement: Private equity firm focused on energy infrastructure investments.

Fund Size: $3.33 billion
Founded: 2001
Industry Group Preference: Power Technologies, Energy, Oil & Gas
Portfolio Companies: ACE Cogeneration, AL Gulf Coast Terminals, AL Shore, Anglo Suisse Offshore Partners, Arkoma Pipeline Partners, Atlantic Power Holdings, Bayonne Energy Center, Big Sandy Equipment Company, Black Point Petroleum, Black Bear Power, Blue Ridge Asphalt, Bridger Energy Funding, Bronco Midstream Holdings, Caithness Energy, Cardinal Power Funding, Charger Oil & Gas, Cherokee Partners, Colusa Power Development, CPV Wind Ventures, Crawfish Cogen, DG Power, Element Petroleum, Epsilon Power Holdings, Escalade Energy, Forst Point Power, G3 Global Energy, Galleon Oil & Gas, Grant Peaking Power, Great Point Power, Hurrikan Power, Juno Energy, Key Energy, KGen Power, Leeward Renewable Energy, Liberty Bell Power, Lightyear Holdings, Lincoln Peaking Power, Magellan Power Holdings, Matagorda Island Gas Ops, Mesquite Power, Michigan Power, Midland Cogeneration Venture, Mountaineer Gas Holdings, Navy Power, NET Midstream, North Sea Infrastructure Holdings, North Sea Midstream Partners, Petrotank, Pomifer Power Funding, ReNu Power, RepconStrickland, Republic Midstream, Ridgeline Midstream Holdings, Rockport Georgetown Partners, Scrubgrass, Southeast PowerGen, Southern Pines, Stamford Bridge Power, Terra-Gen Power, Waterside

Key Executives:

Daniel R. Revers, Founder & Managing Partner
Education: BA Economics, Lafayette College; MBA, Amos Tuck School of Business Administration, Dartmouth College
Background: Managing Director Corporate Finance, John Hancock; Wheelabrator Technologies

Mark A. Tarini, Partner
Education: BS, Accounting, Boston College
Background: CFO, EP Power Finance; CFO, Energy Investors Funds Group; Vice President, Finance, Legeis Resources; Manager, Utility & Real Estate, Arthur Anderson & Company

Carter A. Ward, Partner
Education: BS, Operations Research & Industrial Engineering, Cornell University
Background: VP, McManus & Miles

John F. Erhard, Partner
Education: BA, Arts in Economics, Princeton University; JD, Harvard Law School
Background: Associate, Blue Chip Venture Company

Lucius H. Taylor, Partner
Education: BA, Geology, Colorado College; MS, Hydrogeology, University of Nevada; MBA, Wharton School, University of Pennsylvania
Background: Vice President, Energy & Natural Resources, FBR Capital Markets; Geologist, CH2M HILL

---

158 ARCUS VENTURES
One Grant Central Place
60 East 42nd Street
Suite 1610
New York, NY 10165

Phone: 212-785-2236 **Fax:** 212-785-2237
e-mail: info@arcusventures.com
web: www.arcusventures.com

Venture Capital & Private Equity Firms / Domestic Firms

Mission Statement: Arcus Ventures (AV) consists of a team of professionals with experience in clinical and academic medicine, drug development, hospital management, healthcare industry consulting and private equity. AV is dedicated to investing in oncology focused companies with innovative biopharmaceuticals and or new drug delivery platforms in development, device companies with products that have pre-marketing approval, and service companies with positive revenue.

Industry Group Preference: Biopharmaceuticals, Healthcare, Drug Delivery

Portfolio Companies: Clear Vascular Inc., Marco Genics, Mi Bioresearch, Tracon Pharma, T2Biosystems, Epic Sciences, Exosome Diagnostics, Xtuit Pharmaceuticals, Cleave Biosciences, Genta, Oncoscope, Palyon Medical, Vascular Pathways

Key Executives:
   James B. Dougherty, MD, Co-Founder/General Partner
   e-mail: jd@arcusventures.com
   Education: BS, Biology, Georgetown University; MD, Pennsylvania State University, Hershey School of Medicine
   Background: Venture Partner, Cross Atlantic Partneres; Deputy Physician-in-Chief, Clinical Affairs, Memorial Sloan-Kettering Cancer Center
   Steven L. Soignet, MD, General Partner
   e-mail: ss@arcusventures.com
   Education: BS, University of New Orleans; MD, Louisiana State University
   Background: Co-Founder, The Arcus Group; Venture Partner, Cross Atlantic Partners; Faculty, Developmental Chemotherapy Service, Memorial Sloan-Kettering Cancer Center; Department of Medicine, Cornell University Medical Center

---

159 ARES CAPITAL CORPORATION
One Buckhead Plaza
3060 Peachtree Road NW
Suite 800
Atlanta, GA 30305

Toll-Free: 888-818-5298
e-mail: IRARCC@aresmgmt.com
web: www.arescapitalcorp.com

Mission Statement: Business development company serving private middle-market companies across diverse industries.

Fund Size: $12.3 billion
Investment Criteria: Revolver, first lien, second lien, stretch senior, unitranche, subordinated debt, private/public high yield, non-control equity
Industry Group Preference: All Sectors Considered
Portfolio Companies: 10th Street LLC, 1A Smart Start LLC, 42 North Dental LLC, Absolute Dental Management, ACAS Equity Holdings Corporation, ACAS Real Estate Holdings Corporation, Accomodations Plus Technologies, Acessa Health Inc., ADF Restaurant Group, Alteon Health LLC, Batanga Inc., Birch Permian LLC, Blue Wolf Capital Fund II, BluePay Processing Inc., Borchers Americas Inc., BRG Sports Inc., BW Landco LLC, Cadence Aerospace LLC, Care Hospice Inc., ChargePoint Inc., Chariot Acquisition LLC, Cority Software Inc., Cozzini Bros., CPV Maryland Holding Company II, Creation Holdings Inc., Directworks Inc., Dorner Holding Corp., Doxim Inc., Dynatrace Inc., First Insight Inc., Flow Control Solutions Inc., Foundation Risk Partners Corp., Liason Acquisition LLC, Masergy Holdings Inc., MB Aerospace Holdings II Corp., MB2 Dental Solutions LLC, McKenzie Creative Brands, Microstar Logistics, Moxie Patriot LLC, Nationwide Marketing Group LLC, NECCO Realty Investments, Nodality Inc., Nordco Inc., Southeast, nThrive Inc., Production Resource Group LLC, ProVation Medical Inc., Puerto Rico Waste Investment LLC, Pyramid Management Advisors, Pyramid Investors LLC, QC Supply LLC, QF Holdings, R2 Acquisition Corp., Radius Aerospace Inc., Raptor Technologies LLC, RecoveryDirect Acquisition, Reddy Ice Inc., Regent Education Inc., Respicardia Inc., Riverview Power LLC, RMP Group Inc., Synergy HomeCare Franchising LLC, Sundance Energy Inc., Teligent Inc., TimeClock Plus Inc., West Dermatology LLC

Key Executives:
   Kipp DeVeer, Director & CEO
   Education: BA, Yale University; MBA, Stanford University
   Background: Partner, RBC Capital Partners; VP, Indosuez Capital

---

160 ARES MANAGEMENT LLC
2000 Avenue of the Stars
Los Angeles, CA 90067

Phone: 310-201-4100
e-mail: IRARES@aresmgmt.com
web: www.aresmgmt.com

Mission Statement: Specializes in managing assets in both the private equity and leveraged finance markets.

Geographic Preference: United States
Fund Size: $4 million
Founded: 1997
Investment Criteria: LBO, Special Situations, Distressed Debt
Industry Group Preference: Business Products & Services, Consumer Products, Manufacturing, Aerospace, Defense and Government, Energy, Healthcare
Portfolio Companies: 99 Cents Only Stores, Air Lease Corporation, AmeriQual Group LLC, Aspen Dental Management, Inc., CHG Healthcare Services, City Ventures LLC, CPG International Inc., EXCO Resources, Inc., Floor & Decor Outlets of America, Insight Global, Jacuzzi Brands Corp., Marietta Corporation, National Bedding Company LLC, Neiman Marcus Group LTD Inc., Nortek, Inc., OB Hospitalist Group, Inc., Oro Negro, Plasco Energy Group, Inc., Sandridge Energy, Inc., Simmons Bedding Company, Smart & Final Stores LLC, Sotera Defense Solutions, Stram Global Services, Inc., True Oil Company LLC, Unified Physician Management LLC

Other Locations:
   245 Park Avenue
   44th Floor
   New York, NY 10167

   3344 Peachtree Road NE
   Suite 1950
   Atlanta, GA 30326
   Phone: 678-538-1900

   71 S Wacker Drive
   Suite 3500
   Chicago, IL 60606

   591 Redwood Highway
   Suite 3100
   Mill Valley, CA 94941
   Phone: 415-380-0520

   2 Bethesda Metro Center
   Mezzanine Level
   Suite 250
   Bethesda, MD 20814
   Phone: 301-951-6122

   10 New Burlington Street
   6th Floor
   London W1S 3BE
   United Kingdom
   Phone: 44 (0) 20-7434-6400

   25 Rue Blazac
   Paris F-75008
   France
   Phone: 33 (0) 17039-4150

   Taunusanlage 18
   Frankfurt 60325

Venture Capital & Private Equity Firms / Domestic Firms

Germany
Phone: 49 (0)69-97086-3400

Strandvagen 7A
4th Floor
Stockholm 114 56
Sweden
Phone: 46 (0) 8-450-39-69

14-16 Avenue Pasteur
Luxembourg L-2310
Luxembourg

1601 West Nan Jing Road
Unit 3701
Park Place Office Building
Shanghai 200040
China

Office 44 Gate, Building Level 15
Dubai International Financial Centre
P.O. Box 121208 UAE
Dubai
Phone: 971-4-401-9115

MLC Centre, Level 56
19-29 Martin Place
Sydney NSW 2000
Australia
Phone: 612-9238-2200

Key Executives:
Bennett Rosenthal, Founding Partner
Education: MBA, BS, Econmics, Wharton School, University of Pennsylvania
Background: Senior Advisor, Ares Capital Markets; Managing Director, Global Leveraged Finance Group; Senior Member, Merrill Lynch Leveraged Transaction Commitment Committee
Directorships: Douglas Dynamics; MF Acquisition Corporation; Marietta Corporation; National Bedding Company
David Kaplan, Founding Partner
Education: BBA, Finance, University of Michigan School of Business Administration
Background: Shelter Capital Partners, LLC; Apollo Management LP; Investment Banking, Donaldson, Lufkin & Jenrette Securities Corp
Anthony Ressler, Co-Founder/Executive Chairman
Education: BSFS, Georgetown University; MBA, Columbia Business School
Background: Senior Advisor, Ares Capital Markets Group; Co-Founder, Apollo Management; SVP, Drexel Burham Lambert; Founding Member, Painted Turtle's Camp
Directorships: Allied Waste Industries; Samsonite Corporation

161 ARETE CORPORATION
Arete Corporation
PO Box 1299
Center Harbor, NH 03226

Phone: 603-253-9797 Fax: 603-253-9799
e-mail: aretecorp@roadrunner.com
web: www.arete-microgen.com

Mission Statement: The Arete Corporation is a venture fund focused on alternative energy technologies.
Founded: 1983
Key Executives:
Robert Shaw, Jr., President
Education: BEP, MS, Cornell University; MPA, American University; PhD, Stanford University
Background: Managing Member, SC Green Tech Ventures; SVP, Booz, Allen & Hamilton Energy Division; Bell Laboratories

162 ARGENTUM GROUP
60 Madison Avenue
Suite 701
New York, NY 10010

Phone: 212-949-6262 Fax: 212-949-8294
e-mail: tag@argentumgroup.com
web: www.argentumgroup.com

Mission Statement: A private equity firm that provides expansion capital to rapidly growing small and mid-sized businesses with market leading potential. Argentum emphasizes the concept of partnership investing.
Geographic Preference: United States
Fund Size: $215 million
Founded: 1988
Average Investment: $3-10 million
Minimum Investment: $3 million
Investment Criteria: Later-Stage, Expansion Capital, Growth, MBO, Platform Acquisition Strategies, Recapitalizations
Industry Group Preference: Software Services, Outsourcing & Efficiency, Manufacturing, Technology, Healthcare
Portfolio Companies: Afs Technologies, Applieddata.net, Buyerquest, Chromeriver, CrossMedia Services, Cyclone Commerce, etouches, Expert Plan, Fleet Worth Solutions, Flightdocs, Hanweck, Image Cafe, Margin Point, Mediant Communications, Micro Focus, Netboa, NuOrder, Orion Labs, Paciolan, Parallaz Capital Partners LLC, Resonate, Structured Web, TCI, Trustwave, Tut Systems, VPNet, Wimba, Yello, Ytel
Key Executives:
Walter Barandiaran, Managing Partner
e-mail: walter@argentumgroup.com
Education: BBA, Baruch College (CUNY); attended New York University School of Business
Background: Senior VP, Steinberg & Lyman
Directorships: HorizonWimba, AFS Technologies, Conner Industries, LifeStar, M3 Technologies, Medsite.com, Metalico, StructuredWeb
Daniel Raynor, Managing Partner
e-mail: draynor@argentumgroup.com
Education: BS Economics, Wharton School, University of Pennsylvania
Background: Senior VP, Steinberg & Lyman
Directorships: Applied Data Systems, Community Education Centers, NuCo2, Paciolan, ReSearch Pharmaceutical Services, Transforce, ExpertPlan, FutureHealth, Bio-Kinetic Clinical Applications
Steve Berman, Partner/CFO
e-mail: sdberman@argentumgroup.com
Education: BS, Accounting, Temple University; MA, Taxation, Villanova University
Background: Assistant Controller/Tax Manager, Caxton Corporation; Tax Supervisor, Laventhol & Horwath; Certified Public Accountant
Directorships: Bio-Kinetic Clinical Applications
Chris Leong, Partner/Head of Business Development
e-mail: cleong@argentumgroup.com
Education: Wharton School
Background: VP, Sirit Inc.; Analyst, Lehman Brothers Merchant Banking Partners
Federica Norreri, Fund Administrator
e-mail: fregec@argentumgroup.com

163 ARGO GLOBAL CAPITAL
401 Edgewater Place
Suite 120
Wakefield, MA 01880

Phone: 781-213-9344 Fax: 781-213-9345
e-mail: info@argoglobal.com
web: www.argoglobal.com

Mission Statement: Venture capital firm focused on global investments in wireless communications companies.
Fund Size: $300 million

Venture Capital & Private Equity Firms / Domestic Firms

Founded: 1997
Average Investment: $4-$7 million
Investment Criteria: Initial Funding, Later-Stage, Startup, Through Buyout, Special Emphasis, Financings
Industry Group Preference: Wireless Technologies, Internet Technology, Communications
Portfolio Companies: 12snap AG, Amperion Cayman, ArgNor Wireless Ventures BV, Birdstep Technology ASA, Bytemobile Inc., Cambridge Positioning Systems, Ltd., Casero, Inc., Chinatron Group Holdings, Ltd., Digital Bridges, Ltd., Digital Route, Eftia OSS Solutions, Inc., Empower Interactive Group, Ltd., General Wireless, Handmark, Inc., Hotsip AB, inCode Telecom Group, Inc., IPeria, Inc., Kabira Technologies, Inc., LGC Wireless, Inc., Neural Technologies Ltd., Nuera Communications, Inc., OnMobile Systems, Inc., PhyFlex Networks, Inc., Q-go.com B.V., RV Technology, Ltd., SenseStream Ltd., SurfKitchen, Sylantro Systems Corporation, uReach Technologies, Inc., Vallent Corporation, VoluBill, Webraska Mobile Technologies SA, World Wide Packets

Other Locations:
40-44 Bonham Strand
28th Floor, EIB Center
Sheung Wan
Hong Kong
Phone: 852-22952209 **Fax:** 852-22953111

1250 Rene-Levesque Blvd West
38th Floor
Montreal, QC H3B 4W8
Canada
Phone: 514-397-8444 **Fax:** 514-397-8445

Key Executives:
H H Haight, President/CEO
781-592-5250 x18
e-mail: hhaight@argoglobal.com
Education: BS, University of California, Berkeley; MBA, Harvard Business School
Background: Founder/Managing Director, Advent International Corporation
Directorships: OnMobile, Neural Technologies Ltd., ArgNor, OnMobile Systems Global, Ltd., uReach, Surfkitchen, Nostix
Charles Sirois, Senior Partner
781-592-5250 x20
Education: Bachelors, Finance, Universite de Sherbrooke; Masters, Finance, Universite Laval; Honorary Doctorates, Universite du Quebec a Montreal, University of Ottawa, Concordia University, Laval University
Background: National Pagette; National Mobile Radio Communications Inc.; BCE Mobile Communications Inc.; Chairman/CEO, Teleglobe
Directorships: Chairman, Telesystem International Wireless; Microcell Telecommunications; Canadian Imperial Bank of Commerce; Chairman/CEO, Enablis Entrepreneurial Network
Amy Ssuto, Financial Controller
Education: BA, Commerce, Concordia University
Background: Chief Accountant, Ipex, Inc.

164 ARGONAUT VENTURES
180 Harbor Drive
Suite 101
Sausalito, CA 94965

Phone: 415-332-0707
web: www.argonautventures.com

Mission Statement: Argonaut Ventures provides funding, strategic consulting, and technical expertise to early-stage companies to build, manager on monetize new businesses. With 15 years of direct experience in building online businesses from the ground up, our goal is to create a portfolio of successful companies and share in the success of our clients.

Founded: 1995
Investment Criteria: Early-Stage
Industry Group Preference: Internet
Portfolio Companies: Malaria.com, MedNews, Heal.com, PhysiciansNet.com
Key Executives:
Matthew Naythons MD, Partner
Education: BS, Muhlenberg College; MS, Hahnemann University
Background: Founder, Epicenter Communications; PlanetRx; Co-Founder, EpiCom Media
Peter Goggin, Partner
Background: Vice President, NetHealth; Director of Project Management, PlanetRx; ISL Consulting

165 ARGOSY CAPITAL
950 West Valley Road
Suite 2900
Wayne, PA 19087

Phone: 610-971-9685 **Fax:** 610-964-9524
web: www.argosycapital.com

Mission Statement: Argosy Capital invests entrepreneurial capital in basic businesses in the lower middle market, focusing primarily on business services and manufacturing companies based in the United States.

Geographic Preference: Eastern, Midwestern United States
Fund Size: $600 million
Founded: 1990
Average Investment: $5 - $15 million
Minimum Investment: $3 million
Investment Criteria: Later Stage Expansion, Buyout, Recapitalization, Acquisitions, Growth Equity, revenues in the range of $15 - $100 million
Industry Group Preference: Manufacturing, Business to Business, Franchising, Distribution, Aviation Services, B2B Services, Engineered Materials, Industrial Electronics, Industrial Services
Portfolio Companies: AbelConn, American Huts, American Leather, Atlantic Diagnostic Laboratories, Capewell Aerial Systems, Casual Living and Trigon Plastics, CBT Technologies, Combined Public Communications, Component Sourcing International, CRS Reprocessing Services, Dan-Loc, ECS Environmental Solutions, Enefco International, Fairway Architectural Railing Solutions, Flow Dry Technology, GenServe, Great Western Leasing & Sale, Groome, HB&G Building Products, Joliet Holdings, KMCO, Library Systems & Services, Linkage, Linx Technologies, MFM, Nationwide Industries, Olympia Chimney Supply, Oneida Molded Plastics, Panhandle Oilfield, Paragon Energy Solution, Ranger Aerospace, Ranger AirShop, Reed City Tool, Revive Personal Products, Rita's, Roll Rite, SinterFire, SirsiDynix, Sound Lounge, Southerland, Vanguard Modular, Walpole

Key Executives:
Kirk B Griswold, Founding Partner
e-mail: kirk@argosycapital.com
Education: BS, Physics, University of Virginia; MBA, Wharton School, University of Pennsylvania
Background: Manager & Consultant, Mercer Management Consulting; Manager & Avionics Engineer, Integrated Logistics Support Division, Westinghouse Electric Corporation
Directorships: Managing Director, Odyssey Capital Group LP
John Paul Kirwin III, Founding Partner/CEO
e-mail: john@argosycapital.com
Education: BA, Dickinson College; JD, George Washington University
Background: Partner, McCausland, Keen & Buckman
Sarah G Roth, COO/CFO
e-mail: sroth@argosycapital.com
Education: BA, Political Science, William College; MBA, Kellogg School of Management at Northwestern University

Venture Capital & Private Equity Firms / Domestic Firms

Background: Partner, The Riverside Company; Merrill Lynch Ventures
Jason M Cunningham, Vice President, Business Development
e-mail: jcunningham@argosycprivateequity.com
Education: BS, Economics West Chester University
Background: Vice President, Ardenton Capital; Managing Director, Baker Tilly Captical; Senior Associate, Fleet M&A Advisors
Paul M Grassinger, Vice President, Finance and Accounting
e-mail: paul@argosycapital.com
Education: BS, Business Administration, Rowan University; CPA
Background: CFO, COO, Vice President, Corporate Controler, Ernst & Young
Steven J Morgenthal, Managing Director
e-mail: steven@argosycapital.com
Education: BS, Pace University; MS, Stevens Institute of Technology
Background: Venture Partner, SCP Private Equity Partners; COO, Unified Systems Solutioins
Melanie C Lyren, CCO/Vice President, Investor Reporting
e-mail: melanie@argosycapital.com
Education: BS, Economics, Wharton School, University Of Pennsylvania; CPA
Background: Senior Accountant, Enterprise Group Of Arthur Andersen
Lane W Wiggers, Managing Director
e-mail: lane@argosycapital.com
Education: Clemson University; MBA, Smith School of Business, University of Maryland
Background: Founder, Cordam Group; Partner, CS Capital Partners; Wachova Securities/Wells Fargo; Rockwell International

166 ARISTOS VENTURES
8300 Douglas Avenue
Suite 800
Dallas, TX 75225

Phone: 214-306-9554
e-mail: plans@aristosventures.com
web: www.aristosventures.com

Mission Statement: Aristos Ventures is a venture capital firm focusing on efficient technology companies primarily in Texas that need early capital in order to create their product.
Geographic Preference: Texas
Fund Size: $35 Million
Average Investment: $200,000 - $1,000,000
Investment Criteria: Aristos invests in companies that already have a product or service and need up to $1 million to get to profitability
Key Executives:
Felipe Mendoza, Managing Director
Education: BS, Texas Tech University; MBA, Southern Methodist University
Background: Engineer, Cisco Systems; CFO/Associate, Silver Creek Ventures; Co-Founder, TAC Portfolio Advisors

167 ARLINGTON CAPITAL PARTNERS
5425 Wisconsin Avenue
Suite 200
Chevy Chase, MD 20815

Phone: 202-337-7500 Fax: 202-337-7525
e-mail: requestinfo@arlingtoncap.com
web: www.arlingtoncap.com

Mission Statement: A middle market private equity firm focused on buyouts and recapitalizations in targeted growth industries in partnership with management. The firm leverages a combination of private equity and operating experience.
Geographic Preference: United States, Canada, Europe
Fund Size: $452 Million
Founded: 1999
Average Investment: $20-$75 Million
Minimum Investment: $20 Million
Investment Criteria: LBO, Recapitalization
Industry Group Preference: Business to Business, Aerospace, Defense and Government, Healthcare Services, Information Technology, Media, Education, Healthcare, Manufacturing, Outsourcing & Efficiency, Business Products & Services
Portfolio Companies: Ad Venture Interactive, Apogen Technologies, AHM, Avalign Technologies, Cambridge Major Laboratories, Chandler/May, Cadence Aerospace, Compusearch, Consolidated Precision Products Corp., Endeavor Robots, Grand River Aseptic Manufacturing, MB Aerospace, Micron Technologies, Micropact, Molecular, NLX, Novetta, Ontario Systems, Polaris Alpha, Quantum Spatial, Secor, Signal Tree Solutions, Textech Industries, TSI, United Flexible, Virgo, Xebec, Zemax
Key Executives:
Peter M. Manos, Managing Partner
Education: MBA, Harvard Business School; BA, Stanford University
Background: VP, Carlyle Group; Managing Partner, Capitol Partners; Fayez Sarofim & Co; Investment Banker, Donaldson Lufkin & Jenrette; Peers & Co; Founder/Manager, iFINANCE
Directorships: SECOR
Matthew L. Altman, Managing Partner
Education: BA, Economics, Duke University; MBA, Stanford Grad. School of Business
Background: Stonington Partners; Packard BioScience Corp.; Obagi Medical Products
Directorships: Advanced Health Media, Avalign Technologies, Endeavor Robotics. Grand River Aseptic Manufacturing, Molecular Products, Ontario Systems, Tex Tech Industries, United Flexible
Michael H. Lustbader, Managing Partner
Education: AB, Harvard College
Background: Lazard Freres & Co
Directorships: MicroPact, Polaris Alpha, Quantum Spatial, Zemax, Xebec
David C. Wodlinger, Partner
Education: AB, Economics, Georgetown University
Background: Deutsch Bank
Directorships: Polaris Alpha, Quantum Spatial, Xebec
C. Malcolm Little, Partner
Education: BS, University of Virginia; MBA, Harvard Business School
Background: Vice President, Avista Capital Partners; Associate, Oak Hill Capital Partners; Bear, Stearns & Co.
Directorships: Digital River; New Vision Group; Cherry Creek Radio
A. Bilal Noor, Vice President
Education: BS, Commerce, University of Virginia; MBA, Harvard Business School
Background: H.I.G. Capital; Leveraged Finance Group, Bank of American Merrill Lynch
Directorships: Cadence Aerospace, United Flexible, Zemax
Erica S. Son, Vice President
Education: BS, Finance/Accounting, Wharton School, University of Pennsylvania; MBA, Harvard Business School
Background: Associate, Thomas H. Lee Partners; Analyst, The Blackstone Group
Directorships: Tex Tech Industries
Benjamin J. Ramundo, Vice President
Education: BS, Finance, Georgetown University
Background: Jefferies' Aerospace, Defense, and

Venture Capital & Private Equity Firms / Domestic Firms

Government Services
Directorships: Xebec

168 ARMY VENTURE CAPITAL INITIATIVE

Mission Statement: The Army Venture Capital Initiative is a strategic private equity investor. They invest in companies that support all branches of the US army in defense and commercial markets. They invest at all stages of the investment lifecycle.

Average Investment: $500,000-$2,000,000

169 ARROWHEAD INNOVATION FUND
La Cruces, NM 88003

web: www.aifvc.com

Mission Statement: Arrowhead Innovation Fund is a venture capital fund focused on seed and early-stage investments to commercialize promising technologies developed and/or licensed by New Mexico start-up companies.

Geographic Preference: New Mexico
Founded: 2017
Average Investment: $50K-$150k
Investment Criteria: Pre-Seed; Seed; Series A
Industry Group Preference: Agriculture, Biotech, Healthcare Tech, IT, Engineering, Energy, Water Technology
Portfolio Companies: Circa, Electric Playhouse, Elroy SPAC, Enthentica, Evenus, Ganymede Games, GPER G-1 Development Group, MNT Smart Solutions, New Mexico Start-Up Factory, ORCTech, Osazda Energy, Parting Stone, TNeuroPharma, Vita

Key Executives:
  Beto Pallares, Managing Director, President & Chair
  Education: BA, Brandeis University; MBA & PhD, University of Texas-El Paso

170 ARROWHEAD INVESTMENT MANAGEMENT
33 Benedict Place
1st Floor
Greenwich, CT 06830

Phone: 203-485-0700 **Fax:** 203-295-3771
web: www.arrowheadmgt.com

Mission Statement: Formerly Arrowhead Mezzanine, Arrowhead Investment Management provides mezzanine capital to middle-market companies. Arrowhead provides capital in the form of subordinated debt, preferred stock and non-control common equity.

Fund Size: $479 million
Founded: 1996
Average Investment: $10 - 100 million
Investment Criteria: Acquisitions, Buyouts, Recapitalizations, Growth Capital
Industry Group Preference: Consumer Products, Industrial Manufacturing, Value-Added Distribution, Business Products & Services, Value-Added Distribution, Healthcare, Chemicals, Packaging
Portfolio Companies: Bare Escentuals, Berkshire, C.H.I. Overhead Doors, CPI, CMS, Driven Brands, Edwin Watts Golf, Express Oil Change and Service Center, Hoffmaster Group, ILP, Implus, Kurt Versen, Meineke, Multi Packaging Solutions, MW Industries, Otis Spunkmeyer, Polaris, PQ Corp., Quest, Ranpak Corp., Reef, Rough Country Suspension Systems, The Sheridan Group, SPI Polyols, Sram, Tempur World, Tidi Products, United Pet Group Inc.

Other Locations:
  10877 Wilshire Boulevard
  21st Floor
  Los Angeles, CA 90024
  Phone: 301-551-0101

Key Executives:
  Elliott Jones, Chief Investment Officer
  e-mail: ejones@arrowheadmgt.com
  Education: Colgate University; MBA, Columbia University
  Background: Subordinated Debt Group, The Chase Manhattan Bank; Gleacher NatWest; Lieutenant, US Navy
  Mary Gay, Managing Director
  e-mail: mgay@arrowheadmgt.com
  Education: BS, University of Richmond
  Background: Leveraged Finance Group, Gleacher NatWest; Consultant, Ernst & Young
  Craig Pisani, Managing Director
  e-mail: cpisani@arrowheadmgt.com
  Education: BA, Lafayette College; MBA, New York University
  Background: Leveraged Finance Group, Gleacher NatWest; Prudential Investment Corporation
  Jennifer Cerminaro, Chief Financial Officer
  e-mail: jcerminaro@arrowheadmgt.com
  Education: BS, Accounting, William Paterson University
  Background: Senior Associate, Goldman Sachs

171 ARROWPATH VENTURE PARTNERS
4477 Adams Drive
Houston, TX 77002

Phone: 979-475-2200
web: www.arrowpathvc.com

Mission Statement: Arrowpath Ventures seek companies in the storage, security, networking, infrastructure and other data center-related markets.

Geographic Preference: United States
Fund Size: $325 million
Founded: 1997
Average Investment: $3 - 10 million
Minimum Investment: $200,000
Investment Criteria: Seed, First Stage, Second Stage
Industry Group Preference: Computer Hardware & Software, Internet Technology, Telecommunications, Networking
  Teresa McDaniel, Chief Financial Officer
  Education: BS, Business Administration, Finance, San Jose State University
  Background: KPMG Peet Marwick LLP; Apple Computer

172 ARSENAL CAPITAL PARTNERS
100 Park Avenue
31st Floor
New York, NY 10017

Phone: 212-771-1717
e-mail: info@arsenalcapital.com
web: www.arsenalcapital.com

Mission Statement: A private equity firm that invests in middle market manufacturing, healthcare and business service companies. In particular, Arsenal invests where it believes it can add value by providing capital and resources to support management-led initiatives that accelerate growth, upgrade key business processes, and improve productivity.

Geographic Preference: United States
Fund Size: $3 billion
Founded: 2000
Average Investment: $300 million
Minimum Investment: $50 million
Investment Criteria: Buyouts, Recapitalizations, Growth Equity Investments
Industry Group Preference: Business to Business, Healthcare, Manufacturing, Retailing, Financial Services
Portfolio Companies: Accella, BIOIVT, Breen & Carolina Color, Certara, Charter Brokerage, Chromaflo Technologies, Cyalume, DG3, Elite Comfort Solutions, Flowchem, Genovique Specialties, IDQ, IGM Specialties, IMDS, Inhance Technologies, Kel-Tech, Novolyte Technologies, Polymer Solutions Group, Priority Solutions, Renaissance Mark, Royal Adhesives & Sealants, Scientific Protein Laboratories, Sermatech International, Solvaira Specialties, Sources Refrigeration & HVAC Inc., Spartech, TallyGenicom, TractManager, Vertellus Specialties, WCG

Venture Capital & Private Equity Firms / Domestic Firms

Key Executives:
Joelle Marquis, Senior Partner
e-mail: jmarquis@arsenalcapital.com
Education: BS, Business Admin., Western New England College; MS, Organizational Development, American International College; University of Michigan's Executive Leadership Certificates
Background: Chief Operating Officer, Baltimore Technologies; Senior Operating, National Grange Mutal Insurance; Senior Operating, Big Y Foods
Directorships: Renaissance Mark Holdings, TallyGenicom Holdings
Stephen McClean, Senior Partner
e-mail: smclean@arsenalcapital.com
Education: BS, Economics, MBA, Wharton School, University of Pennsylvania
Background: Managing Director, Courtagen Capital Group LLC; Founding Partner, Merrill Lynch Capital Partners Inc.
Directorships: BioIVT, TractManager Holdings, WIRB Copernicus Group, Certara
John Televantos, Senior Partner
e-mail: jtelevantos@arsenalcapital.com
Education: BS, Chemical Engineering, University of London; PhD, Chemical Engineering, University of London
Background: President, Hercules Inc.; President/Founder, Helios Chemical Co.; CEO, Foamex International; Vice President, Lyondell Chemical Co.; Vice President, Arco Chemical Co.; Director, R&D, Union Carbide Corp.
Timothy Zappala, Senior Partner
e-mail: tzappala@arsenalcapital.com
Education: BS, Chemical Engineering, Univerisity of New Hampshire; MBA, University of Houston
Background: President/CEO, Vertellus Specialties Inc.; Executive Vice President, Borden Chemical Inc.; The Dow Chemical Company; W.R. Grace & Co.
Terrence Mullen, Managing Partner & Co-CIO
e-mail: tmullen@arsenalcapital.com
Education: BBA, University of Notre Dame; MBA, Harvard Business School
Background: Morgan Stanley & Co.; Principal, Thomas H Lee Partners
Directorships: DG3 Holdings Inc.; KGS Holdings LP; Source Refridgeration & HVAC Inc.; IDQ Holdings Inc.; Renaissance Mark Holdings Corp.; Sermatech International Holdings Corp.
Jeffrey Kovach, Managing Partner & Co-CIO
e-mail: jkovach@arsenalcapital.com
Education: Dartmouth College; Tuck School of Business
Background: Thomas H Lee Partners; Leveraged Finance, Merrill Lynch
Directorships: Elit Comfort Solutions Inc.; Frontstream Payments Inc.; Breckenridge IS Inc.; Novolyte Technologies Corp.; Tempo Financial Corporation; DG3 Holdings Inc.; FirstAgain LLC

173 ARSENAL VENTURE PARTNERS
750 South Orlando Avenue
Suite 200
Winter Park, FL 32789

Phone: 407-838-1439
web: arsenalgrowth.com

Mission Statement: Arsenal Venture Partners invests in early-stage companies that target extremely large commercial markets, but can also leverage the defense industrial complex in a manner that is beneficial to both the company and the defense community. This focus enables AVP to source and identify high-quality opportunities, reduce the risk of each investment, and minimize the capital required to reach the market. This is accomplished by (1) activating defense resources to source opportunities or provide due diligence assessments, (2) obtaining synergistic funding for research, development and productization, or (3) attracting development partners, field trials or customers far in advance of the commercial market.

Geographic Preference: United States
Investment Criteria: Early-Stage
Portfolio Companies: Filter Easy, Blue Talon, Health Integrated, Thrive Market, Onapsis, Sharecare, Peach Works, Caremerge, Process Map, Highwinds, Protectwise, Le Tote, BoxC, CounterTack, UltraCell, Trust Digital, A123 Systems, Power Precise Solutions Inc., Varsity News Network, Root3, PowerGenix, Petra Systems, Byte Foods, The NanoSteal Company, MyUS.com, REG, InVisage, TravelTab, CrossFiber, 37.5, Blue Pillar, Sirrus, Arctic, MashNetworks

Other Locations:
385 Homer Avenue
Palo Alto, CA 94301
Phone: 650-838-9200

6701 Carnegie Avenue
Suite 100
Cleveland, OH 44103
Phone: 216-456-2678

303 Detroit Street
Suite 100
Ann Arbor, MI 48104
Phone: 734-436-1496

Key Executives:
Jason Rottenberg, General Partner
e-mail: jason@arsenalvp.com
Education: BS, Georgetown University; MBA, Harvard Business School
Background: Founder, Muse Ventures; IT Angel; Manager, Arthur Andersen
Directorships: PowerPrecise Solutions, Trust Digital, OnPoint Technologies, SpectrumBridge, PowerGenix, Ultracell, InVisage, Nanosteel, Teranex
Christopher Fountas, General Partner
Education: BS, Finance, Ohio State University; JD, University of Miami
Background: Partner, Baker & Hostetler
Directorships: PetraSolar, Atraverda, Akermin, Cocona, OnPoint Technologies, Z-Power, The Nanosteel Company
John Trbovich, General Partner
Education: School of Engineering, Columbia University; Harvard Business School
Background: Co-Founder/Principal, E*OFFERING; Senior Technology Banker, Robertson Stephens & Co.; Metzler Corp.
Directorships: A123 Systems, Nanosolar, Iosil Energy, SuperProtonics
Denny Behm, Strategic Advisor
e-mail: denny@arsenalvp.com
Background: Lockheed Martin Western Development Labs, McDonnell Douglas, US Navy
Jennifer Dunham, Partner
e-mail: jennifer@milcomvp.com
Education: BSBA, SUNY College of Technology; MBA, Rollins College
Henry Huey, Strategic Advisor
Education: PhD, Electrical Engineering, University of Southern California
Background: Director, Systems Engineering, Alidian Networks; Lockheed Martin Western Development Labs, TRW Electronic Systems Group, Hughes Aircraft Ground Systems, IBM Federal Systems

174 ARTHUR P GOULD & COMPANY
Scarsdale, NY 10583

Phone: 914-729-9116
e-mail: andrew@gouldco.com
web: www.gouldco.com

Venture Capital & Private Equity Firms / Domestic Firms

Mission Statement: To help clients conceptualize, identify, execute and finance acquisitions of new businesses, and license manufacture and distribution of new products worldwide.
Geographic Preference: Worldwide
Founded: 1967
Investment Criteria: Seed, Research and Development, Startup, Early Stage, First-Stage, Second-Stage, Mezzanine, LBO
Industry Group Preference: Technology, Seafood, Consumer Services, Distribution, Electronic Components, Medical & Health Related, Energy, Natural Resources, Genetic Engineering, Industrial Equipment
Key Executives:
  Arthur P. Gould, Chairman
  e-mail: arthur@gouldco.com
  Education: BA, New York University
  Background: Founder/President, Golden Shield Corp; Founder/General Manager, Bulova Radio Company; Manufacturer, transistor radios marketed worldwide
  Andrew G Gould, President
  e-mail: andrew@gouldco.com
  Education: BA, Yale University; MA, Finance/Economics, New York University
  Robert Frankel, Special Limited Partner/Senior Technology Analyst
  e-mail: rfrankel@gouldco.com
  Education: BS Electrical Engineering, State University of New York, Buffalo; PhD, Physiology, Buffalo Medical School State University of New York
  Background: R&D Management
  Harris Landgarten, Special Limited Partner
  Education: BS, Mathematics, Queens College of the City of New York
  Background: Co-Founder/Principal, SamsungCCTV; Co-Founder/President, Techland Systems; expert with Linux and embedded control systems
  Frank Simon, Operating Partner
  e-mail: fsimon@gouldco.com
  Education: BA, English Literature, University of Colorado
  Background: Founder, Rain Forest Aquaculture Products; Co-Founder, Great Eastern Mussel Farms, Inc.
  J. Russell Chapman, Operating Partner
  e-mail: rchapman@gouldco.com
  Education: BA, Earlham College; MBA, Harvard Business School
  Background: Managing Director, Atlantic Capital; CEO, Ecce Panis

175 ARTHUR VENTURES
210 Broadway North
Suite 301
Fargo, ND 58102

Phone: 701-232-3521 **Fax:** 701-232-3530
web: www.arthurventures.com

Mission Statement: Arthur Ventures began believes in the power of the growth cycle and the positive effect that well-managed businesses can have in society. Businesses that Arthur Ventures works with help solve crucial problems for customers while providing an opportunity for founders and team-members to create and impact powerful change in society.
Geographic Preference: Upper Midwest
Founded: 2008
Average Investment: $500,000 - $2 million
Investment Criteria: Early-Stage
Industry Group Preference: Information Technology, Enterprise Software, Web Applications & Services, Healthcare, Agriculture, Energy
Portfolio Companies: 250OK, Agronomic Technology, Ambassador, Avalara, Clariondoor, Cybrary, DataCamp, Datica, Everything Benefits, Flipgrid, Infusion Soft, Intelligent InSites, Invinsec, Ionic, Lead Pages, Linus Academy, Loyalty Builders, New Ocean Health Solutions, Preventice Solutions, Protenus, Rhiza, Stream, Talk Route, Terminus, Tiny Pulse, Total Expert, When I Work, Zipnosis
Other Locations:
IDS Center
80 South 8th Street
Suite 3760
Minneapolis, MN 55402
Key Executives:
  Doug Burgum, Founding Partner
  Education: North Dakota State University, Stanford Graduate School of Business
  Background: McKinsey & Co.; Founder, Great Plains Software; SVP, Microsoft Corporation
  Directorships: Atlassian, Intelligent InSites
  James Burgum, Co-Founder/Managing Partner
  Education: BSBA, North Dakota State University
  Background: President, Advenio Partners; Founding Team Member, North Dakota Trade Office
  Dave O'Hara, Venture Partner
  Education: BS, Economics, MBA, University of South Dakota
  Background: COO, Microsoft Advertising
  Lauris Molbert, Venture Partner
  Education: BSBA, JD, University of North Dakota
  Background: CEO, TMI Hospitality; EVP/COO, Otter Tail Corporation
  Patrick Meenan, Partner
  Education: BS, Business, Miami University
  Background: Corporate Development Group, Microsoft

176 ARTIMAN VENTURES
1731 Embaracadero Road
Suite 212
Palo Alto, CA 94303

Phone: 650-845-2020
e-mail: info@artiman.com
web: www.artiman.com

Mission Statement: Artiman typically supplies the first institutional capital, often at the concept phase. Artiman works are active partners with entrepreneurs, helping with all aspects of strategy, market definition, and execution.
Geographic Preference: United States
Fund Size: $1 billion
Founded: 2001
Average Investment: $2 - $6 million
Minimum Investment: $2 million
Investment Criteria: Seed, Startup, First Stage, Second Stage
Industry Group Preference: Business to Business, Communications Equipment, Computer Hardware & Software
Portfolio Companies: Aditazz, AppleBoard, Boxbot, Capella Space Inc., CellMax Life, Cellworks, Click Diagnostics, CORE Diagnostics, Crossbar, MedECUBE Healthcare, Niron Magnetics, OncoStem Diagnostics, Pavilion Data, Prysm, Silniva Inc., TeraPore, Tonbo Imaging, Virsec Systems Inc., Yanta Financial Technologies, zSpace Inc.

Key Executives:
  Amit Shah, Founding Partner
  e-mail: amit@artimancapital.com
  Education: BSEE, MS University Baroda; University of California, Irvine
  Background: General Partner, Anthelion; VP New Markets/Technology, Cisco Systems Business Development; Founded/CEO, PipeLinks; Founded, Zietnet; Taught coarses and seminars, University of California, Berkeley; InterOp
  Directorships: Auryn; Sierra Design Automation; NetDevices; InvenSense; SiOptical; Zyme
  Tom Dennedy, Partner
  e-mail: tom@artiman.com
  Education: BS, Electrical Engineering, US Air Force Academy; MS, Electrical Engineering, MIT; JD, Stanford

Venture Capital & Private Equity Firms / Domestic Firms

Law School
Background: Managing Director, Telesoft Partners, Inc.; Attorney, Brobeck Phleger & Harrison, LLP; Captain, US Air Force; Project Officer, Milstar Communication Satellite Joint Program Office
Yatin Mundkur, Partner
e-mail: yatin@artiman.com
Education: BSEE, MSU of Baroda, India, MSEE, University of Texas at Austin
Background: Managing Director, TeleSoft Partners; President, Equator Technologies; Vice President, Conexant; Chief Architect, Sun Microsystems; Ross Technology; Cypress Semiconductor
Ramesh Radhakrishnan, Partner
Education: BE, Indian Institute of Technology; ME, Systems Engineering, University of Virgina
Background: VP, Engineering, FireEye; Airgo Networks
Ajit Singh, Partner
Education: BS, Electrical Engineering, Banaras Hindu University; PhD, Computer Science, Columbia University; MS, Computer Engineering, Syracuse University
Background: President/CEO, BioImagene
Directorships: Aditazz, CardioDx, Oncostem
Tim Wilson, Partner, Emeritus
Education: BS, Physics, Bowdoin College; MBA, Fuqua School of Business
Background: General Partner, Paratech International; CMO, Digital Island

177 ARTIS VENTURES
809 Montgomery St.
San Francisco, CA 94133

Phone: 415-344-6200
e-mail: contact@artisventures.com
web: www.av.co

Mission Statement: Artis Ventures focuses on elegant solutions that are solving the world's greatest challenges, in turn creating tomorrow's extraordinary companies.
Industry Group Preference: Semiconductors, Advanced Energy, Energy, New Media, Internet, Healthcare, Telecommunications, Networking, Cloud Computing, Data Storage
Portfolio Companies: Aruba Networks, Chefsfeed, Cohesity, Eko, Excision Biotherapeutics, ID by DNA, Locus Biosciences, Modern Meadow, Nimble Storage, Quid, Stemcentrx, Tae Life Sciences, Versa Networks, YouTube, Zenrex
Key Executives:
  Stuart Peterson, Founding Partner
  e-mail: stuart@artisventures.com
  Education: BA, Economics, UCLA; MBA, Analytic Finance, University of Chicago Graduate School of Business
  Background: Managing Director, The Cypress Funds; Vice President & Co-Portfolio Manager, Portfolio Advisory Services
  Michael Harden, Founding Partner
  e-mail: mike@artisventures.com
  Education: BA, East Asian Studies, Washington & Lee University; MS, Finance, Olin Graduate School of Business, Babson College
  Background: Analyst, CSFB Technology Group
  Directorships: Chefs Feed, Practice Fusion
  Robert Riemer, Chief Operating Officer
  Education: BS, Accounting, Bradley University; JD, DePaul University College of Law
  Background: Controller, Blum Capital Partners; CFO & COO, Fort Point Capital Management

178 ASCENSION HEALTH VENTURES LLC
101 South Hanley Road
Suite 200
Clayton, MO 63105

e-mail: info@ascensionventures.org
web: www.ascensionventures.org

Mission Statement: Provides strategic funding to companies that offer healthcare-related products, services or technologies that represent potential service breakthroughs for Ascension Health's hospitals and health facilities.
Geographic Preference: United States
Fund Size: $800 million
Founded: 2001
Average Investment: $5 million
Minimum Investment: $2 million
Investment Criteria: Expansion- to Late-Stage
Industry Group Preference: Medical & Health Related, Information Technology, Medical Devices, Healthcare, Healthcare Information Technology
Portfolio Companies: Accretive Health, Advanced Practice Strategies, Aethon, Apama Medical, Augmenix, BardyDx, Body Media, Bio Imagene, Cheetah Medical, CHF Solutions, Cofactor Genomics, Comprehensive Pharmacyservices, Confluent Surgical, CSA Medical, EBR Systems, Ekos, Emageon, GetWellNetwork, Haven Behavioral Healthcare, Impulse Monitoring Inc., Ingenious Med, Instylla, IMO, Interventional Spine, ISTO Technologies, Ivantis, MedWentive, Millennium Pharmacy System Inc., MindFrame Inc., NaviHealth, NeuroLutions, NeuroStar, Novasys Medical, OB Hospitalist Group, Ocular Therapeutix, Omnicell, OptiScan, PathoGenetix, Phreesia, Quantros, Radianse, Reputation.com, SeQual, Servicys, Solstas Lab Partners, Sonoma, Stereotaxis, Steril Med, Syapse, TomoTherapy, TriMedx, Vascular Pathways, Visit Pay, Vivify Health, Voalte, Zipnosis, Zonare
Key Executives:
  Tara Butler, MD, Managing Director
  Education: MBA, Wharton School; MD, University of Pennsylvania School of Medicine
  Background: Honeywell; Laboratory Assistant, University of Pennsylvania School of Medicine
  Matthew Hermann, Senior Managing Director
  e-mail: mhermann@ascensionhealth.org
  Education: BS, Engineering, Tufts University; MBA, Finance, NYU Stern School of Business
  Background: VP, Atlantic Medical Management; Financial Management, Nutrition 21; Regeneron Pharmaceuticals; JP Morgan Chase and Company; PricewaterhouseCoopers
  Victor Kats, Managing Director
  Education: University of North Carolina, Chapel Hill; MBA, Wharton School
  Background: Allscripts-Misys; Vice President, Lehman Brothers Holdings
  John Kuelper, Managing Director
  Education: BA, Washington University; JD, Pritzker School of Law, Northwestern University; MBA, Kellogg School of Management
  Background: Founder/President, Qualia Holdings LLC
  Ryan Schuler, Managing Director
  Education: BS, Accounting, Christian Brothers University; MBA, Washington University
  Background: Investment Banking, AG Edwards & Sons; Associate, PricewaterhouseCoopers
  Jamie Wehrung, Senior Director, Finance & Administration
  Education: BA, Accountancy, Southern Illinois University, Carbondale
  Background: Accountant, Catholic Healthcare Systems; Deloitte & Touche LLP

Venture Capital & Private Equity Firms / Domestic Firms

179 ASCENT BIOMEDICAL VENTURES
142 West 57th Street
Suite 4A
New York, NY 10019

Phone: 212-303-1680 Fax: 212-752-3633
e-mail: info@abvlp.com
web: www.abvlp.com

Mission Statement: Ascent Biomedical Ventures (ABV) is a venture capital firm investing in seed and early-stage biomedical technology companies developing medical devices, biopharmaceuticals, healthcare services, and information technology. ABV's principals and advisors work closely with entrepreneurs to manage the risks associated with deploying capital in startup companies.

Investment Criteria: Seed-Stage, Early-Stage
Industry Group Preference: Medical Devices, Biopharmaceuticals, Healthcare Services, Healthcare Information Technology
Portfolio Companies: Arstasis, Ary Therapeutics, Azevan Pharmaceuticals, Biomerix, Cara Therapeutics, Cross Trees Medical, Curaseal, Guided Delivery Systems, InnerPulse, Metronome, Ouroboros Medical, SpinalKinetics, SpineView, Synecor, TargAnox, Vivasure Medical, Xlumena

Key Executives:
  Steve Hochberg, Managing Partner
  Education: BS, University of Michigan; MBA, Harvard Business School
  Background: Co-Founder: Biometrix Corporation, Eminent Research, Clinsights, Med-E-Systems, Physicians' Online
  Directorships: Biometrix Corporation, Synecor, Crosstrees Medical, Ouroboros, SpineView, Solar Capital, Solar Senior Capital
  Geoffrey W. Smith, Managing Partner
  Education: BA, Williams College; JD, University of Pennsylvania Law School
  Directorships: Azevan Pharmaceuticals, Anterios, BackBeat Medical, Biometrix, Caliber Therapeutics, TargAnox, Vivasure Medical
  Avi Kometz, MD, Partner
  Education: MD, University of the Witwatersrand Medical School
  Background: Healthcare Practice, McKinsey & Co.
  Lawrence S. Atinsky, Partner/General Counsel
  Education: BA, University of Wisconsin; JD, New York University School of Law
  Background: ABV; M&A Attorney, Skadden Arps Slate Meagher & Flom
  Jeffrey M. Sauerhoff, Partner/Chief Financial Officer
  Education: BS, Accountancy, CW Post Campus, Long Island University
  Background: CFO, Erisco
  Jon Edelson, MD, Venture Partner
  Education: BA, Yale University; MD, University of Chicago Pritzker School of Medicine
  Background: Co-Founder/CEO, Aureon Laboratories

180 ASCENT VENTURE PARTNERS
255 State Street
5th Floor
Boston, MA 02109

Phone: 617-720-9400
web: www.ascentvp.com

Mission Statement: Ascent is dedicated to financing and supporting innovative entrepreneurs striving to build emerging market leaders. Ascent is committed to backing companies with innovative and courageous ideas about how technology can transform business.

Geographic Preference: East Coast
Fund Size: $400 million
Founded: 1985
Average Investment: $2 - 5 million
Minimum Investment: $2 million
Investment Criteria: Early Stage, Investment Growth
Industry Group Preference: Technology, Networking, Communications, Information Technology, Enterprise Services, Software, SaaS
Portfolio Companies: BryterCX, Cloud Bees, CPX Security, Connected2fiber, Empow Networks, Exchange Solutions, Gr8 People, Invaluable, Knoa, Nova Scientific, Promo Boxx, Rapidminer, Revulytics, Sidecar, Splash, Startapp, Synovia Solutions, Timetrade, Vee24

Key Executives:
  Geoffrey S. Oblak, General Partner
  e-mail: goblak@ascentvp.com
  Education: BA Economics, Hamilton College; MBA, Boston University; Certified Public Accountant with a CFA Charter
  Background: Investment Analyst, Norwest Venture Partners; Audit/Business Advisory, Arthur Andersen LLP
  Directorships: Auction Holdings, ClickFox, Exchange Solutions, Fidelis Security, Forefield, VI Labs, WebLayers, Guardium, Network Intelligence
  Brian J. Girvan, General Partner
  Education: BBA, Accounting, Manhattan College
  Background: COO/CFO, Argo Global Capital; Various Positions, Fidelity Investments; Senior VP/CFO/Treasurer, Affiliated Managers Group; Senior VP/CFO, PIMCO Advisors
  Directorships: BlueSocket, Knoa Software, Placemark Investments, Pyxis Mobile, TimeTrade
  Christopher W. Lynch, Special General Partner
  e-mail: clynch@ascentvp.com
  Education: BS, Political Science, Colgate University; MBA, Harvard Business School
  Background: TA Associates, Investment Officer/VP, Massachusetts Capital Corporation; President, MCC Corp.
  Directorships: Everyday Wireless, Innoveer, The Corporate Marketplace, ZoomInfo
  Christopher W. Dick, General Partner
  Education: BS, Agricultural Economics, Cornell University; MBA, Babson College
  Background: President, Venture Capital & Corporate Finance Subsidiaries, UST Corp
  Directorships: BEZ Systems, Nova Holdings, Nova Scientific, Terascala, Whaleback Systems
  Matt Fates, General Partner
  Education: Double Major in Computer Science and Economics, Yale University; MBA, Tuck School of Business at Dartmouth College
  Background: Business Development, Gold Wire Technology; Management, Norwest Venture Partners; Technology Investment Banking, Alex Brown & Sons
  Directorships: The Corporate Marketplace, HubCast, StrikeIron, Terascala
  Luke Burns, General Partner
  Education: AB, Chemistry & Physics, Havard University; MBA, MIT Sloan School of Management
  Background: Management Consultant, Bain & Company; Co-Founder & CEO, Emercis Corporation

181 ASHBY POINT CAPITAL
1240 Ashby Court
Arnold, MD 21012

Phone: 410-544-6250 Fax: 410-544-3264
web: ashbypointcapital.com

Mission Statement: Ashby Point Capital is a private equity firm investing in the payment services and financial services industries.

Average Investment: $100K - $5MM
Minimum Investment: 100K
Investment Criteria: All Stages
Industry Group Preference: Payment Services, Financial Services
Portfolio Companies: PayKii, Card.com, HalCash North America, SVM Cards, Trade Harbor, Shanghai Harvest Network Technology, InstaMed

Venture Capital & Private Equity Firms / Domestic Firms

Key Executives:
  William J. Westervelt, Jr., Partner
  e-mail: bill@ashbypoint.com
  Education: BA, Economics, McDaniel College; MBA, University of Baltimore
  Background: Co-Founder, First Annapolis Consulting
  James D. Leroux, Partner
  e-mail: jim@ashbypoint.com
  Education: BA, Economics, Tufts University; JD, Boston College Law School
  Background: First Annapolis Consulting

182 ASPECT VENTURES
471 Emerson Street
Palo Alto, CA 94301

e-mail: info@aspectventures.com
web: www.aspectventures.com

Mission Statement: Aspect Ventures was launched with the goal of working with entrepreneurs in the emerging mobile industry. The firm invests in Seed and Series A companies that focus on the creation of multi-platform, multi-device technologies, with particular emphasis on the mobile, consumer Internet, healthcare IT, SaaS and enterprise software sectors.

Fund Size: $150 million
Founded: 2014
Average Investment: $500,000 - $2 million
Investment Criteria: Seed-Stage, Series A, Early-Stage
Industry Group Preference: Mobile, Consumer Internet, Enterprise Software, SaaS, Healthcare Information Technology
Portfolio Companies: Amino, Aqua, Astro, Athena Health, Balenda, Baublebar, Cato Networks, Chime, Cipher Trace, Crew, Deserve, Dfinity, Edgy Bees, Exabeam, Flurry, FollowAnalytics, ForeScout, Future Family, Grokker, Gusto, Hotel Tonight, Imperva, Indegy, Integris Software, Kosmix, Learn Vest, Mapper, Nano String Technologies, OHM Connect, People Support, PredictHQ, Qordoba, ShieldX, Solv, Stem, TalkIQ, Tari, The Muse, TheRealReal, Troops, Trulia, Tru Star Technology, UrbanSitter, Vida

Key Executives:
  Theresia Gouw, Co-Founder/Managing Partner
  Education: ScB, Engineering, Brown University; MBA, Stanford University
  Background: Partner, Accel; VP, Business Development & Sales, Release Software; Bain & Company; Product Manager, Silicon Graphics
  Jennifer Fonstad, Co-Founder
  Education: Georgetown University; MBA, Harvard Business School
  Background: Managing Director, Draper Fisher Jurvetson; Goto.com; Co-Founder, Broadway Angels; Bain & Company
  Directorships: Flurry, iCix, Intematic, Nantero
  Lauren Kolodny, Principal
  Education: BA, Brown University; MBA, Stanford University Graduate School of Business
  Background: Product Marketing, Google; Cowboy Ventures; Clinton Foundation
  Kamil Saeid, Associate
  Education: Stanford University
  Background: Associate Consultant, Bain & Company

183 ASSET MANAGEMENT VENTURES
2595 E Bayshore Road
Suite 240
Palo Alto, CA 94303

Phone: 650-621-8808
e-mail: plans@assetman.com
web: www.assetman.com

Mission Statement: Emphasizes involvement in seed or start-up companies in the information technology and life sciences sectors; often facilitates company formation, to take advantage of opportunities in markets and technologies.

Geographic Preference: Western, Northeastern Regions
Fund Size: $500 million
Founded: 1965
Average Investment: $4 million
Minimum Investment: $1 million
Investment Criteria: Seed, Early-Stage
Industry Group Preference: Telecommunications, Computer Hardware & Software, Environment Products & Services, Networking, Applications Software & Services, Information Technology, Database Services, Tools, Semiconductors, Nanotechnology, Energy, Healthcare
Portfolio Companies: Aegis, Amgen, Applied Biosystems, Applied Micro, Arterys, Audentes, Benefitter, Biogen Idec, BiPar Sciences, CardioDX, Cadiogen Sciences, Chmerix Inc., Coherent, CT Therapeutics, Evidation, Esperion Therapeutics, Freenome, Health, Icon, Huiseoul, InCarda Therapeutics Inc., Immune Cellular, Indi Molecular, KeepSafe, Kii, Lark, Liquid M, Maverix Biomics, Provade VMS, Mozio, Nuance, Ooma Pharmacyclics, Profusa, Properly, PMC, Proteus Digital Health, SenseOmics, Rally Point, Rapidscan, Reify, Stratavia, SignaVine, Skybox Imaging, Tandem Computers, Thunder, Twist Bioscience, Uni Key, Virtio, View Point Therapeutics, Welkin Health, WellDoc, Womply, 1 Doc Way, 3T Biosciences

Key Executives:
  Skip Fleshman, Partner
  Education: BS, Mechanical Engineering, University of California, Davis; MS, Management, Sloan Fellow, Stanford Grad. School of Business
  Background: Fighter Pilot, United States Air Force; Founder/Executive, BGI
  Lou Lange, MD, PhD, Partner
  Education: BA, University of Rochester; MD, PhD, Biological Chemisty, Harvard University
  Background: Founder, CV Therapeutics; Chief of Cardiology/Professor of Medicine, Jewish Hospital
  Richard Simoni, Partner
  Education: PhD, Electrical Engineering, Stanford University; BA/MA, Stanford University; and Rice University
  Background: Co-Founded Talkway Communications

184 ASTELLAS VENTURE MANAGEMENT
2882 Sand Hill Road
Suite 121
Menlo Park, CA 94025

web: www.astellasventure.com

Mission Statement: Astellas Venture Management LLC (AVM) is the corporate venture capital organization dedicated to helping Astellas Pharma Inc. to achieve its strategic goals. The venture capital activity of AVM can be traced back to the year 1999. Through its strategic investments in private early-stage companies, the funds aim to forge relationships with Astellas Pharma which may lead to larger collaborations in the future. AVM is able to provide portfolio companies with invaluable advice and assistance.

Founded: 1999
Investment Criteria: Early-Stage
Industry Group Preference: Therapeutics, Pharmaceuticals, Biotechnology
Portfolio Companies: Bicycle Therapeutics, Cleave Biosciences, Crescendo Biologics, DeImmune Therapeutics, eFFECTOR Therapeutics, Innocrin Pharmaceuticals, Oncorus Inc., PhaseBio Pharmaceuticals Inc., Raze Therapeutics Inc., Tacurion Pharma Inc., Tizona Therapeutics, Twentyeight-Seven, Viamet Pharmaceuticals

Key Executives:
  Shunichiro Matsumoto, PhD, President
  Education: MBA, McGill University; PhD, Medicine, University oF Tsukuba; MS, Agriculture, Kyoto University

Venture Capital & Private Equity Firms / Domestic Firms

Background: VP, Innovation Management, Astellas Pharma Inc.; Investment Director, AVM
Kazunori Maruyama, PhD, Executive Investment Director
Education: PhD, Agricultural Chemistry, University of Tokyo
Background: Director, Business Development, Astellas Pharma Inc.; Research Scientist, Yamanouchi
Ryosuke Munakata, PhD, Investment Director
Background: Associate Director, Innovation Management, Astellas Pharma Inc.

185 ATA VENTURES
4300 El Camino Real
Suite 205
Los Altos, CA 94022

Phone: 650-594-0189
e-mail: contact@ataventures.com
web: www.ataventures.com

Mission Statement: ATA Ventures offers seed and early-stage growth capital along with decades of proven operating experience to assist startups in their pursuit of building companies of tremendous value.

Fund Size: $400 million
Founded: 2003
Investment Criteria: Seed, Startup, First Stage
Industry Group Preference: Information Technology, Wireless Technologies, Consumer Internet, Enterprise Software
Portfolio Companies: Accelops, Argyle Data, Billeo, Cinova, Clustrix, FastScale, Givit, HarvestMark, Jobvite, Jolata, Lavante, Medagate, Milyoni, SalesPortal, Siaras, Sikka, Theranos, Trilibis Mobile, YottaMark, ZooskottaMark, Zoosk, Actelis, Adesto Technologies, Altierre, EdgeWave, NE Photonics, PureWave Networks, Revera, Shocking Technologies

Key Executives:
Michio Fujimura, Director Emeritus
e-mail: mfujimura@ataventures.com
Education: Bachelor Law, Chuo University
Background: Owned/Operated, Vanguard Systems Consulting; Founded, Aisys Corporation; Product Marketing, David Systems
Directorships: Aisys Corporation; IT-Farm Corporation; Vadem
Hatch Graham, Managing Director
e-mail: hgraham@ataventures.com
Education: BS Engineering, Idaho State University
Background: Co-Founded, Wave7; Optics in Georgia; Resonext; CEO, Zoran Corporation; Executive Officer, World Access; TCSI Corporation; Stanford Telecom
Directorships: College of Engineering Advisory Committee
Pete Thomas, Managing Director
e-mail: pthomas@ataventures.com
Education: BSEE magna cum laude, Utah State University; MS Computer Science, University of Santa Clara
Background: General Partner, Institutional Venture Partners; OEM Engineering Manager, Intel Corporation; Engineering, Fairchild Communications; Sylvania EDL
Michael Hodges, Managing Director
e-mail: mhodges@ataventures.com
Education: BSEE, MSEE, UC Berkeley
Background: Spectra-Physics
Nancy McCroskey, Chief Financial Officer
e-mail: nmccroskey@ataventures.com
Education: University of California, Berkeley; MBA, College of Notre Dame
Background: Redpoint Ventures
John Loiacono, Venture Partner/Market Strategist
e-mail: jloiacono@ataventures.com
Background: CMO, Sun Microsystems; SVP/General Manager, Adobe's Systems' Digital Media & Creative Solutions

186 ATEL CAPITAL GROUP
The Transamerica Pyramid
600 Montgomery Street
9th Floor
San Francisco, CA 94111

Phone: 415-989-8800 Fax: 415-989-3796
web: www.atel.com

Mission Statement: ATEL provides secured financing to emerging growth companies.

Founded: 1977
Portfolio Companies: Adenosine Therapeutics LLC, Adesto Technologies, ALBA Therapeutics, Altierre, AlveolUs, Amyris, Arbinet, Arsenal, ARYX Therapeutics, Asempra, Aspen Aerogels, Audience Science, Axial BioTech, AxoGen, Bloom Energy, Boingo Wireless, Cambrios, CedarPoint Communications, Chelsio Communications, Complete Genomics, Convio, CryoCor, Cymbet Corporation, Danger Inc, Deeya Energy Inc, DeliveryAgent, Doppelganger, Dorado, ecoATM, EcoLogic, EdeniQ, Enerkem Technologies, Enevate, Enphase Energy, Five9, Forma Therapeutics, GangaGen, Good, InfiniRoute Networks, Innovalight, InSite One, IntelePeer, Ioxus, Iperian, Kabam, Kaminario, Linden Lab, Lightship Telecom, Locus, LS9, Metabolon, Miasole, Microfabrica, Millennium Pharmacy Systems, MotoSport, ON24, NanoGram Corporation, NexPlanar, OpenPages, OpSource, Primet, QSr, Raydiance, Recyclebank, RenalSolutions, Reply.com, RewewData, Rubicon Technology, SilverPOP, Sixtron Advanced Materials, Sling Media, Solaria, SolFocus, Sorra, StarCite, Step Labs, Technorati, TelePacific Communications, Xlumena, Zeevo

Key Executives:
Steven Rea, President
e-mail: srea@atel.com
Education: BS, Finance, San Diego State University; EMBA, Business, Saint Mary's College of California
Background: Vice President, Imperial Bank; Vice President, LINC Capital Partner

188 ATHENAEUM FUND
3100 East Foothills Blvd
2nd Floor
Pasadena, CA 91101

Phone: 626-584-0913 Fax: 626-584-0953
web: www.athenaeumfund.com

Mission Statement: A venture capital limited partnership that provides seed funding to emerging technology companies based in Southern California. The Athenaeum Fund is committed to offering funding, management, and marketing skills to early stage companies in order to generate capital gains and help with the advancement of company products.

Geographic Preference: United States, Southwest, California, Northwest
Fund Size: $6 million
Founded: 1999
Average Investment: $250,000
Minimum Investment: $50,000
Investment Criteria: Seed, First Stage
Industry Group Preference: Biotechnology, Communications Equipment, Computer Hardware & Software, Chemicals, Pharmaceuticals, Telecommunications, Networking, Materials Technology
Portfolio Companies: Eidogen, Inc.

Key Executives:
Dr Philippe H Adam, Founder/General Partner
Education: Polytechnic University, Brooklyn; MS, PhD, Aeronautics, California Institute of Technology; MBA, Wharton School, University of Pennsylvania
Background: Jet Propulsion Lab, Caltech/NASA;

Venture Capital & Private Equity Firms / Domestic Firms

AlliedSignal/Honeywell; Houlihan Lokey; Avery Dennison; Beckman Coulter
Dr John Baldeschwieler, Founder/General Partner
Education: BS, Chemical Engineering, Cornell University; PhD, Physical Chemistry, University of California, Berkeley
Background: US Army; Teaching & Research, Harvard University; Professor, Chemistry, Stanford University; Deputy Director, Office of Science & Technology, White House; Professor, Chemistry, California Institute of Technology; Founder, Vestar; Founder & Director, Combion
Directorships: NeXstar
Malcolm Cloyd, Founder/General Partner
Background: Manager, Mergers & Acquisitions, Geosource Inc.; International Technology Corp.

189 ATHENIAN VENTURE PARTNERS
340 West State Street
Suite 137B
Athens, OH 45701

Phone: 614-360-1155 **Fax:** 740-593-9311
e-mail: info@athenianvp.com
web: www.athenianvp.com

Mission Statement: A venture capital firm that specializes in early stage information technology, digital health and healthcare investments.
Geographic Preference: United States
Fund Size: $100-$150 million
Founded: 1997
Average Investment: $1 - $5 million
Minimum Investment: $1 million
Investment Criteria: Early through Later Stage
Industry Group Preference: Information Technology, Life Sciences, Communications, Internet Technology
Portfolio Companies: Advanced Digital Internet Corp., Aerpio Therapeutics, Akebia Therapeutics, Alloptic, Analect Instruments, Archemix Corp., Asset Management Outsourcing, Baxano, Candera, Chaparral Network Storage, Comet Solutions, Cyber-Rain, DiAthegen, Manta Media, Integrated Energy Services, Intellispace, LigoCyte Pharmaceuticals, Micromet, PacketMotion, Pain Therapeutics, Phobos Corporation, Sendio, Servion Global Solutions, StorageApps, Verus Pharmaceuticals, Windy Hill Medical

Other Locations:
2400 Eat Commercial Boulevard
Suite 410
Ft. Lauderdale, FL 33308
Phone: 954-289-3000

Key Executives:
Daniel H. Kosoy, MD, Partner, Healthcare
614-360-1589
e-mail: kosoy@athenianvp.com
Education: BA, Philosophy/Biosciences, Yale University; MD, McGill University
Background: Management Consultant, Generics Group
Directorships: Windy Hill Medical; Akebia Therapeutics; LigoCyte Pharmaceuticals; Archemix; Verus Pharmaceuticals; CancerVax
David R. Scholl, Partner, Healthcare (Part-Time)
e-mail: scholl@athenianvp.com
Education: BS, Biology, Indiana University; PhD Microbiology, Ohio University
Background: President/CEO/Director of Research/VP of Research, Diagnostic Hybrids; Post-Doctoral Fellow, Roche Institute for Molecular Biology
Directorships: Pain Therapeutics; CancerVax; Ohio Governor's Technology Action Board; Trustee, BioOhio; The Ohio Business Development Corporation (OBDC); Ohio University ESP Advisory Council
Francois Helou, Senior Partner, Information Technology
e-mail: helou@athenianvp.com
Education: MS, Electrical Engineering, Federal Institute of Technology; MBA, INSEAD
Background: Strategic Consultant, Cambridge Positioning Systems; Logica; Operations, Brown Boveri; Compugraphic; Fujitsu-ICL
Directorships: Manta Media; Sendio; Chaparral Network Storage; StorageApps; Alloptic; Advanced Digital Internet Corp

190 ATHYRIUM CAPITAL MANAGEMENT
530 Fifth Avenue
25th Floor
New York, NY 10036

Phone: 212-402-6925
e-mail: info@athyrium.com
web: www.athyrium.com

Mission Statement: Athyrium invests in a wide range of financial instruments including royalties, structured credit, and equities as well as select special situations.
Founded: 2008
Average Investment: $25 - $75 million
Industry Group Preference: Healthcare, Biotechnology, Pharmaceuticals, Medical Devices, Diagnostics, Healthcare Services
Portfolio Companies: BioFire Diagnostics, Horizon Pharma, Ikaria, InnoPharma, Ironwood Pharmaceuticals, Lannett Company, MedPro Safety Products, Pernix Therapeutics Holdings, Progenity, Retrophin, Synarc-Biocore Holdings, SynCardia Systems, Tecomet, Tria Beauty, Universal Biosensors, Verenium, VIVUS, Zealand Pharma A/S

Key Executives:
Jeffrey A. Ferrell, Managing Partner
Education: AB, Biochemical Sciences, Harvard College
Background: Lehman Brothers; Principal, Schroder Ventures Life Sciences
Directorships: Lpath, Progenity
Laurent D. Hermouet, Partner
Education: BS, Economics, MS, Banking & Finance, University of Paris-Dauphine; CFA
Background: Vice President, Senior Credit Analyst, Tribeca Global Managment; Goldman Sachs
Jeremy D. Lack, Partner
Education: School of Industrial & Labor Relations, Cornell University; Doctorate, Biochemistry, University of Oxford
Background: Managing Director, Cortec Group; Principal, New Leaf Ventures; Associate, Oxford Bioscience Partners
Uttam Jain, Partner
Education: B.Tech, Chemical Engineering, Indian Institute of Technology; MS, Chemincal Engineering Practice, MIT; MBA, Healthcare Management, Wharton School at the University of Pennsylvania;
Background: Director, Thomas H. Lee Partners; Consultant, Boston Consulting Group
Hondo Sen, Partner
Education: A.B., Economics, Dartmouth College
Background: Sr. Associate, Littlejohn & Co.; Financial Analyst, J.P. Morgan Securities

191 ATLANTA VENTURES
Phone: 404-590-4660
web: www.atlantaventures.com

Mission Statement: Focused on serving entrepreneurs in earlier stages. Offers a unique community in partnership with the Atlanta Tech Village. Their platform is designed for entrepreneurs looking to launch at the ground floor of their business.

Average Investment: $250K - $1 million
Investment Criteria: Annual Recurring Revenue of less than $1 Million; Target for Current Capital Raise of less than $1 Million; Unaffiliated

Venture Capital & Private Equity Firms / Domestic Firms

Industry Group Preference: Technology, Sustainable Energy
Portfolio Companies: Actively Learn, Atlanta Tech Village, Calendly, Copient Health, Dragon Army, Gimme, GreenPrint, Greenzie, Hannon Hill, Intown Golf Club, LeaseQuery, Musical Overture, Sales Force Pardot, Rigor, SalesLoft, Sequr, SingleOps, Teamworks, Terminus

Key Executives:
David Cummings, Partner
Education: BS, Duke University
Background: Managing Director, Shotput Ventures; Founder/CEO, Pardot LLC; Founder/Chairman, Hannon Hill; Co-Founder, Rigor; SalesLoft; Dragon Army; Terminus Software
AT Gimble, Partner
Education: BS, Georgia Institute of Technology; MBA, Harvard Business School
Background: Manager, Bain & Company; Sr Director, LexisNexis Risk Solutions; Advisor, Atlanta Tech Village
Jon Birdsong, Partner
Education: University of Georgia
Background: Marketing Manager, OpenStudy; Head of Growth, SalesLoft; VP, AA-ISP; CEO, WideAngle
Karen Houghton, Venture Partner
Education: BS, Berry College; MA, Richmont Graduate University
Background: Retreats Director, YMCA; Consultant/Conselor, Hope Counseling Center/Family Conseling Associates; Business Consultant, Golden Coaching and Consulting; Founder/Director, Land of a Thousand Hills Coffee Co.; Marketing Manager, Pardot; VP, Atlanta Tech Villages
David Lightburn, Venture Partner
Education: BBA, Rhodes College
Background: Founder/CEO, Clickspace; Founder/Owner/Advisor, Village Realty - Atlanta; Co-Founder/President, Atlanta Tech Village

192 ATLANTIC CAPITAL GROUP
1 Olympic Place
Suite 1220
Towson, MD 21204

Phone: 410-602-6020
e-mail: info@atcapgroup.com
web: www.atcapgroup.com

Mission Statement: Atlantic Capital Group is a real estate and private equity investment firm.
Geographic Preference: United States
Industry Group Preference: Real Estate, Diversified
Portfolio Companies: Residence Inn by Marriott, Oil Purification Systems, 200-208 Sixth St. Jersey City NJ, Carchex, F.T. Silfies, Mariner Village, Lumiere Hotel, Noble Logistic Services, GigaTrust, Epic at Cub Run, Miami Green, 60 Erie St. Jersey City NJ, Castlefield, Ziggs.com, Honest Tea, Biometric Access Co.

Key Executives:
Steven B. Fader, Founder and Chairman
Education: BA, Western Maryland College; JD, University of Baltimore School of Law
Background: CEO, Atlantic Automotive Corp.
James M. Bannantine, Managing Partner
Education: Distinguished Graduate, West Point; MBA, Wharton School
Background: Founder, Acumen Capital; Dorsal Networks
Peter M. Rubin, Founder and Partner
Education: BA, Political Science, Duke University; JD, University of Baltimore Law School
Background: Litigator, Transactional Attorney
Directorships: Carchex, Affordable Hearing Networks
Howard Kra, Partner
Education: Political Science, Business Administration, University of Maryland
Background: Wealth Advisor, Lehman Brothers; SVP, Morgan Stanley; Streamline.com
Directorships: Carchex
Bruce Taub, Partner
Education: BA, University of Maryland; JD, California Western School of Law; LLM, Taxation, Georgetown University Law School
Background: Head of Acquisitions, Storage USA

193 ATLAS VENTURE
400 Technology Square
10t Floor
Cambridge, MA 02139

Phone: 857-201-2700
web: www.atlasventure.com

Mission Statement: Atlas Venture invests in the earliest stages of technology and life science innovation.
Geographic Preference: United States, Europe
Fund Size: $283 million
Founded: 1986
Average Investment: $500,000 - $5 million
Minimum Investment: $500,000
Investment Criteria: Seed, Startup, Early-Stage
Industry Group Preference: Information Technology, Life Sciences, Communications
Portfolio Companies: Acetelion, Adnexus Therapeutics, Alnylam Pharmaceuticals, Annovation Biopharma, ArQule, Arrow Therapeutics, Arteaus Therapeutics, Avila Therapeutics, Avrobio, Bicycle Therapeutics, Cadent Therapeutics, CoStim Pharmaceuticals, Crucell, deCODE Genetics, Delinia, Disarm Therapeutics, Egalet Corp., Exelis, F-Star Alpha Limited, Gemini Therapeutics, Harbour Antibodies, Horizon Pharma, IFM Therapeutics, Infacare, Intellia Therapeutics, JenaValve, Kymera Therapeutics, Kyn Therapeutics, Lysosomal Therapeutics Inc., Magenta Therapeutics, Micromet, MiRagen Therapeutics, Momenta Pharmaceuticals, MorphoSys, Navitor Pharmaceuticals, Nimbus Therapeutics, Novexel, Numerate, Obsidian Therapeutics, Padlock Therapeutics, Replimune, Robin Therapeutics, Spero Therapeutics, Stromedix, Surface Oncology, Synlogic, Translate Bio, U3 Pharma, Unum Therapeutics, Vitae Pharma, Zafgen

Key Executives:
Bruce Booth, Partner
Education: BS, Biochemistry, Pennsylvania State University; PhD, Molecular Medicine, University of Oxford
Background: Principal, Caxton Health Holdings LLC, Associate Principal, McKinsey & Company
Directorships: Zafgen; Lysosomal Therapeutics; Magenta Therapeutics; Unum Therapeutics
Peter Barrett, Partner, Legacy Funds
e-mail: pbarrett@atlasventure.com
Education: BS, Chemisty, Lowell Technological Institute; PhD, Analytical Chemistry, Northeastern University; Harvard Business School Management Development Program
Background: Co-Founder/Executive VP/Chief Business Officer, Celera Genomics; VP Corporate Planning/Business Development, Perkin-Elmer Corporation
Directorships: Alnylam Pharmaceuticals, Archemix Corporation, Aureon Biosciences, Momenta Pharmaceuticals
Kevin Bitterman, PhD, Partner
Education: BA, Rutgers University; PhD, Harvard Medical School
Background: Co-Founder, Genocea Biosciences; CEO, Editas Medicine; Partner, Polaris Partners
Directorships: InSeal Medical; Kala Pharmaceuticals; Neuronetics; Taris Biomedical
Jason Rhodes, Partner
Education: BA, Yale University; MBA, Wharton School
Background: Founder/CEO, Disarm Therapeutics; Founder/CEO, Torus Therapeutics; President, Epizyme;

Venture Capital & Private Equity Firms / Domestic Firms

Business Development, Alnylam; Founder, Fidelity Biosciences
Michael Gladstone, Principal
Education: AB, Biochemical Sciences, Harvard College
Background: Consultant, L.E.K. Consulting; Fellow, Eutropics; Viral Pathogenesis
David Grayzel, MD, Partner
Education: BA, Stanford University; MD, Harvard Medical School
Background: Infinity Pharmaceutical; Director, Coporate Development, Dyax Corp.; Curriculum Director, Stanford University Medical Center
Directorships: Acera
Jean-Francois Formela, MD, Partner
Education: MD, Paris University of Medicine; MBA, Columbia University
Background: Senior Director, Medical Marketing and Scientific Affairs, Schering-Plough; Practiced Emergency Medicine, Necker University Hospital in Paris; Involved in formation of companies such as ArQule; MorphoSys; Exelixis; deCODE Genetics; Nuvelo; Structural GenomiX; CellZome; Archemix; Aureon Biosciences

194 ATRIUM CAPITAL
3000 Sand Hill Road
Building 2
Suite 130
Menlo Park, CA 94025

Phone: 650-233-7878 Fax: 650-233-6944
web: www.atriumcapital.com

Mission Statement: Atrium has been co-managing strategic venture funds on an outsourced basis for Global 1000 corporations for 25 years.
Founded: 1991
Average Investment: $5 million
Minimum Investment: $1 million
Investment Criteria: Seed, Startup, First Stage, Second Stage
Industry Group Preference: Software, Natural Resources, Internet Technology, Chemicals, Publishing, Wireless Technologies, Energy, Materials Technology, Advertising
Portfolio Companies: Acal Energy, Adforce, Canto, Ciespace, ClassOwl, ClearGuage, CPC, Dataware Technologies, DigitalPersona, Fastsoft, FieldCentrix, Incentive Logic, InfoUSA, IPT, Landmark, Mapquest.com, Marketlive, Mediatel, MetaTV, ModViz, Multex.com, MyOffers, MyTango, NewsEdge, NxtGen Emission Controls, Pixim, RedEenvelope, ShowEvidence, Spectra, ThinkCERCA, Tumbleweed Communications, Virent, Vocabulary.com, Xeikon

Key Executives:
Russell Pyne, Founder & Managing Partner
e-mail: rpyne@atriumcapital.com
Education: AB, Princeton University; JD, MBA, Stanford University
Background: General Partner, Sprout Group
Bart Faber, Partner
Education: BA, Arizona State University; MBA, New York University
Background: CEO, Document Sciences Corporation
George Petracek, Partner
e-mail: gpetracek@atriumcapital.com
Education: MS Cybernetics, CVUT Institute of Technology; MBA, Stanford University
Background: Venture Investments, Hewlett-Packard; Investment Banker, UBS; Morgan Stanley; Computer Programmer, 3M
Jon Rattner, Chief Operating Officer
Education: BA, Economics & Business Administration, Vanderbilt University; JD, Columbia University School of Law
Background: General Counsel, SummerHill Homes; Partner, Gray Cary Ware & Freidenrich

Bob Shaw, Advisor
Education: BEP, MS, Cornell University; MPA, American University; PhD, Applied Physics, Stanford University
Background: President, Arete Corporation; Senior Vice President, Energy Division, Booz Allen & Hamilton; Bell Laboratories; Cavendish Laboratory
Directorships: Distributed Energy Systems Corporation, H2Gen Innovations
Chris Heivly, Advisor & Venture Partner
Education: BS, West Chester University; MA, University of South Carolina
Background: Executive Vice President, Ultimus Software; Chairman, Angular Systems; President, Rand McNally; Andersen Consulting; Founder, MapQuest
Directorships: Alphagraphics, MediaTel, Hands-On-Technology
Jim Hornthal, Venture Partner
Education: AB Economics, Princeton University; MBA, Harvard Business School
Background: Vice Chairman, Travelooty; Chairman/Founder, Preview Travel; General Partner, Oak Grove Ventures; Consultant, The Boston Consulting Group; Co-Founder, Healthcentral.Com
Directorships: University of California, Berkeley; Wingspring Companies

195 ATYPICAL VENTURES
New York, NY

e-mail: hello@atypical.vc
web: atypical.vc

Mission Statement: Atyoucal Ventures invests in engineers.
Investment Criteria: Early-Stage
Industry Group Preference: Engineering
Portfolio Companies: Buddy, Instnt, LogicInk, Nextmv, Oasis, Phosphorus, Pienso, Recycleye, Ribbon, Skopos Labs

196 AUA PRIVATE EQUITY PARTNERS
666 Fifth Ave
27th Floor
New York, NY 10103

Phone: 212-231-8600 Fax: 212-231-8601
e-mail: info@auaequity.com
web: auaequity.com

Mission Statement: AUA Private Equity Partners focuses on lower-middle market businesses that target the growing U.S. Hispanic population, or that take ethnic brands to the mainstream.
Geographic Preference: United States
Fund Size: $275MM
Industry Group Preference: Consumer Products, Consumer Services, Media, Business Products & Services
Portfolio Companies: Associated Foods, Cirque Dreams, Desi, Elegant Desserts, Gourmet Culinary Partners, Gourmet Foods, Gourmet Kitchen, Joey's Fine Foods, Kabobs, Love & Quiches, Indulge Desserts, Noga Dairy, Raymundos, Tijuana Flats, Trufood, Van-Lang Foods, Vistar Entertainment, Water Lilies

Key Executives:
Andy Unanue, Managing Partner
e-mail: andy.unanue@auallc.com
Education: BA, University of Miami; MBA, Thunderbird
Background: COO, Goya Foods
Directorships: KABR Real Estate Partners, Opt-Intelligence, TruFoods, eSchoolData
Steven Flyer, Partner
e-mail: steven.flyer@auaequity.com
Education: BA, Columbia University; JD, Cornell Law School
Background: Managing Director, Trimaran Capital Partners; CIBC World Markets
David Benyaminy, Partner
e-mail: david.benyaminy@auaequity.com

Education: BA, MBA, Hofstra University
Background: Investment Professional, CNPE Management; Executive Director, Trimaran Capital Partners
Kyce Chihi, Managing Director
e-mail: kyce.chihi@auaequity.com
Education: BS, Economics, Wharton School
Background: Investment Professional, CNPE Management
John Moore, Chief Financial/Compliance Officer
e-mail: john.moore@auaequity.com
Education: BA, Davidson College; MBA, University of Rochester
Background: ALPS Fund Services

197 AUDAX GROUP
101 Huntington Avenue
25th Floor
Boston, MA 02199

Phone: 617-859-1500
web: www.audaxgroup.com

Mission Statement: Audax Group is a premier investor in middle market companies. Audax manages over $5.0 billion of capital through its private equity, mezzanine debt, and senior secured debt funds. Audax focuses on building companies with leading market positions and superior management teams. Its mission is to partner with management to build long term value in its companies. Audux handles a variety of transactions, including leveraged buyouts and recapitalizations, corporate divestitures spin-offs and roll-outs.

Geographic Preference: United States
Fund Size: $5 billion
Founded: 1999
Investment Criteria: Small Cap, Lower-Middle Market
Industry Group Preference: Building Materials & Services, Business Products & Services, Distribution, Direct Marketing, Energy, Niche Manufacturing, Technology, Media, Consumer Products, Environment Products & Services, Education, Food & Beverage, Waste & Recycling, Water
Portfolio Companies: A & A Manufacturing Company, AAMP of America, A-D Technologies, Advanced Dermatology & Cosmetic Surgery, Affordable Interior Systems, API Heat Transfer, Arnold Magnetic Technologies, Artisan Entertainment, Astrodyne Corporation, ATG Rehab, Bridgeport Tank Trucks, Chart Industries, CIBT Global, Cinelease, Coast Crane, Colormatrix, Correct Care Solutions, Cozzini Bros, Denver Biomedical, Distribution International, Dynisco, Elgin Equipment Group, Elgin Fastener Group, Endurance International Group, Fibersense Technology, Flexstar Technology, Great Expressions Dental Centers, Help/Systems, Herald Media Holdings, In The Swim, Injured Workers Pharmacy, Koda Distribution Group, Kurt Versen, Laborie Medical Technologies, Lewis-Goetz and Company, Macgregor, Nash_Elmo, Neptune-Benson, Nivel Holdings, Northern Digital, Overton's, Phillips & Temro Industries, Phoenix Children's Academy, Quest Specialty Chemicals, Ready Mixed Concrete, Reed Group, Silent Preferred Partners, Silver State Materials, Thermon Industries, Trimark Usa, United Recovery Systems, Utex Industries, Winchester Electronics

Other Locations:
320 Park Avenue
19th Floor
New York, NY 10022
Phone: 212-703-2700

4 Embarcadero Center
37th Floor
San Francisco, CA 94111
Phone: 650-252-0600

Key Executives:
Geoffrey Rehnert, Co-Founder & Co-CEO
e-mail: grehnert@audaxgroup.com
Education: JD, Stanford Law School; AB, Duke University
Background: Managing Director, Bain Capital; Bain & Company; JP Morgan & Company
Marc Wolpow, Co-Founder & Co-CEO
e-mail: mwolpow@audaxgroup.com
Education: JD, Harvard Law School; MBA, Harvard Business School; BS, Wharton School, University of Pennsylvania
Background: Managing Director, Bain Capital; Founder, Sankaty Advisors; Drexel Burnham Lambert; Donaldson Lufkin & Jenrette
Richard Joseph, Managing Director & Chief Operating Officer
e-mail: rjoseph@Audaxgroup.com
Education: Boston College School of Management
Background: CFO, Streamline.com; CFO, Software Emancipation Technology; CFO, Planet Direct Corp.; CFO, ESSENSE Systems Inc.; Senior Manager, Ernst & Young
Daniel Weintraub, Managing Director, Chief Legal Officer & CAO
e-mail: dweintraub@audaxgroup.com
Education: Dartmouth College; Boston College Law School
Background: Ropes & Gray; Law Clerk to the Honorable Mark L. Wolf, United States District Judge for the District of Massachusetts

198 AUGMENT VENTURES
206 South 4th Avenue
Ann Arbor, MI 48104

e-mail: info@augmentventures.com
web: www.augmentventures.com

Mission Statement: To invest in innovative technology-based companies that can make an impact on quality of life and business efficiency around the world.

Fund Size: $20 million
Founded: 2010
Investment Criteria: Startups, Early-Stage
Industry Group Preference: Software, Cloud Computing, SaaS, Big Data, Analytics & Analytical Instruments, Energy
Portfolio Companies: Aperia Technologies, Cloud Agronomics, Crowdz, Fluid Screen, Flume, GeoTix, Iteros, LARQ, Llamasoft, Lumenetix, Mercatus, RayVio, Revolights, Slive

Key Executives:
Sonali Vijayavargiya, Founder/Managing Director
Education: BS, Statistics, Fergusson College; MBA, Symbiosis Institute of Business Management
Background: Founder, Augment Capital LLC; Industrial Development Bank of India; PricewaterhouseCoopers; Edelweiss Capital
Directorships: RayVio
David Armstrong, Partner/Chief Financial Officer
Education: BBA, Accounting, University of Michigan-Dearborn; MS, Taxation, Walsh College
Background: Partner, Edwards Ellis Armstrong & Company; Principal & CFO, Pinnacle Investment Advisors LLC; Treasurer, Riverside Arts Center

199 AUGURY CAPITAL PARTNERS
8025 Forsyth Blvd
2nd Floor
St. Louis, MO 63105

Phone: 314-448-1316 **Fax:** 314-335-7637
web: www.augurycapital.com

Mission Statement: Mid- and later-stage investors in the life sciences and financial services industries.

Investment Criteria: Mid-Stage, Later-Stage
Industry Group Preference: Life Sciences, Financial Services, Information Technology, Medical Devices, Biopharmaceuticals

Venture Capital & Private Equity Firms / Domestic Firms

Portfolio Companies: Force10 Networks, Clearent, Circle Medical, Texcel Medical, Paranet, PEX Card

Key Executives:
  David W. Truetzel
  Education: MBA, Wharton School
  Background: Founder/General Partner, Hela Capital Partners; CFO, Paymentech
  Directorships: Clearent
  Robert B. Wetzel
  Education: MBA, Carnegie Mellon Tepper School of Business
  Background: Founder, Alchemy Advisors
  Directorships: Circle Medical, Texcel Medical

200 AUGUST CAPITAL
San Francisco, CA 94107

web: www.augustcap.com

Mission Statement: Believes in the creative power of successful information technology entrepreneurs to envision sizable market opportunities, construct lasting technologies, and build enduring companies; prefers to act as a company's lead investor, moving swiftly on closing deals, helping management evaluate and complete their next financing stages, and providing counsel on how to create the most effective board of director teams.

Geographic Preference: Northwest, Southwest, Rocky Mountains, West Coast
Fund Size: $2 billion
Founded: 1995
Average Investment: $5 - $20 million
Minimum Investment: $2 million
Investment Criteria: Startup, Early-Stage, First Round, Special situations
Industry Group Preference: Communications, Computer Related, Distribution, Electronic Components, Information Technology, Business Products & Services
Portfolio Companies: Aardvark, Actional Corporation, Adara Media, Adchemy, Alibre, Alta Devices, Atheros Communications, Be, Bill.Com, Blippy, BroadLogic, Bubbli, Cobalt Networks, Compaq Computer, Crystal Decisions, Cygnus Solutions, Devicescape Software, DITTO, Done Right!, Dotnetnuke, Ebates, Encentuate, Enuvis, Evite, Flingo, Frame Technology, Genoa, Gigwalk, Grand Junction Networks, Gravity, Guru, Inrix, Intuit, Iridigm Display Corp, Jaxtr, Listen, Livemocha, LiveOps, Luminate, Luxtera, Magnum Semiconductor, Mainstreet Networks, Mavenir Systems, Memolane, Metrofi, Microdisplay Corporation, Microsoft, Mimosa Systems, MMC Networks, Neopath Networks, Netcell, Netopia, Netpulse, Nomis Solutions, Notiva, Ohai, Openlane, Packettrap, Paradise Electronics, Paycycle, Paynearme, Postini, Printpaks, Pubmatic, Pulsecore Semiconductor, Quantum, Radlan Computer Communications, Reconnex, Relayrides, Reputation.Com, Retailnext, Rocket Lawyer, SAY Media, Scintera, Seagate Technology, Sequence Design, Shopping.Com, Silicon Architects, Silicon Image, Six Apart, Skypilot, Snagajob, Splunk Technology, Stratus Computer, Stumbleupon, Summit Microelectronics, Sun Microsystems, SuVolta, Swoopo, Sybase, Symantec, Technorati, Tegile Systems, Telocity, Threatmetrix, Tickle, Topica, Trumba, Tumbleweed Communications, Tzero Technologies, Ubicom, Unity Semiconductor, Valicert, Virsto Software, Visio, WePay, Xilinx, Xirrus, Zulily

Key Executives:
  David Hornik, General Partner
  Education: Computer Music, Stanford University; MPhil, Criminology, Cambridge University; JD, Harvard Law School
  Background: Corporate Attorney, Venture Law Group; Cravath Swaine & Moore; Perkins Coie LLP
  Directorships: Nomis Solutions; Notiva; PayCycle; Six Apart; Splunk Technology; Actional Corporation

  John Johnston, Founding Partner
  Education: AB, English, Princeton University; MBA, Harvard University
  Background: General Partner, Technology Venture Investors; Hambrecht & Quist Venture Partners; Inter-Asia Management Company Ltd; Past Director, Western Association of Venture Capitalists
  David Marquardt, Founding Partner
  Education: BSME, Columbia University; MBA, Stanford University; MSEE, Stanford University
  Background: Co-Founder, Technology Venture Investors; Institutional Venture Associates; Design Engineer/Development Manager, Diablo Systems; President, Western Association of Venture Capitalists; Director, National Venture Capital Association; President, Western Assn of Venture Capitalists
  Howard Hartenbaum, General Partner
  e-mail: howard@augustcap.com
  Education: BS, Mechanical Engineering, MIT
  Background: General Partner, Draper Richards LP; Hughes Electronics; Honda Motor Company; Teledyne Relays
  Directorships: Livemocha, Pizazza, Soopo
  Eric Carlborg, General Partner
  e-mail: eric@augustcap.com
  Education: BA, Economics, University of Illinois; MBA, University of Chicago
  Background: Partner, Continental Investors; Investment Banking, Merrill Lynch & Co.
  Directorships: Blue Nile, CarHop, Dydacomp, PubMatic, SnagAJob, Zulily
  Vivek Mehra, Partner Emeritus
  Education: BS, Electronics, Punjab University; MS, Computer Engineering, Iowa State University
  Background: VP/General Manager, Cobalt Business Unit, Sun Microsystems; Co-Founder, Cobalt Networks; Apple; SGI; Digital Equipment
  Directorships: NeoPath Networks; Encentuate

201 AUGUSTUS VENTURES
1302 Colwell Ln.
Conshohocken, PA 19428

Mission Statement: Augustus Ventures is a leading venture capital advisory and consulting firm helping early-stage companies. We believe that building a business requires full-time attention of the management team. We help entrepreneurs stay focused on growing the business and assist them with the fundraising process and secure funding in the minimal time.

Investment Criteria: Early-Stage
Portfolio Companies: Legend3D, Legend Films, RiffTrax
Key Executives:
  Utkarsh Kanal, Founder
  Education: BS, Engineering, Regional Engineering College; MS, Mechanical Engineering, Oregon State University; MBA, University of Iowa
  Background: Blueprint Ventures, MCI Ventures

202 AURORA CAPITAL GROUP
11611 San Vincente Boulevard
Suite 800
Los Angeles, CA 90049

Phone: 310-551-0101
e-mail: info@auroracap.com
web: www.auroracap.com

Mission Statement: Using a discipline approach to selecting industries and cultivating high level contacts with senior executives, Aurora focuses on proactive and direct origination efforts.

Geographic Preference: United States, Canada
Fund Size: $2 billion
Founded: 1991
Average Investment: $200 million

Venture Capital & Private Equity Firms / Domestic Firms

Minimum Investment: $150 million
Investment Criteria: Middle Market, Consolidations, Acquisition, LBO, MBO, Recapitalization
Industry Group Preference: Aerospace, Defense and Government, Logistics, Energy, Healthcare, Industrial, Software, Technology-Enabled Services, Manufacturing, Distribution, Transportation
Portfolio Companies: ADCO Global, Aftermarket Technology, Ames Taping Tools, Anthony, Astor Corporation, Autocam, Coast Gas Industries, Cold Chain Technologies, Douglas Dynamics, DuBois Chemicals, FleetPride, Impaxx, Industrial Container Services, Inhance Technologies, Joerns, K&F Industries, Market Track, Mitchell, National Technical Systems, Newport Media, NuCO2, Pace Analytical, Petroleum Service Corporation, Porex Corporation, Randall-Reilly, RBC Bearings, Restaurant Technologies, SRP Companies, United Plastics Group, VLS Recovery Services, Western Nonwovens, Zywave

Key Executives:
John Mapes, Partner
Education: BA, University of California, LA; MBA, Harvard Business School
Background: Corporate Finance Group, Salomon Brothers
Directorships: National Technical Systems; Restaurant Technologies; The UCLA Foundation
Josh Klinefelter, Partner
Education: BA, Tulane University; MBA, Harvard Business School
Background: Bear Stearns
Directorships: Randall-Reilly; Zywave
Matthew Laycock, Partner
Education: BS, University of North Carolina; MBA, Harvard Business School
Background: Castle Harlan; JP Morgan
Directorships: Petroleum Service Corporation; VLS Recovery Services
Mark Rosenbaum, Partner
Education: BS, Wharton School, University of Pennsylvania; MBA, Anderson School of Management, University of California, LA
Background: Summit Partners; Montgomery Securities
Directorships: Restaurant Technologies; SRP Companies
Robert Fraser, Partner
Education: BA, Stanford University; MBA, Harvard Business School
Background: Senior Associate, BC Partners
Directorships: Randall-Reilly; SRP Companies; Zywave
Randy Moser, Partner
Education: BA, Claremont McKenna College; MBA, Wharton School
Background: Senior Associate, Bertram Capital Management; Investment Banker, Merrill Lynch
Directorships: Cold Chain Technologies; Inhance Technologies; National Technical Systems; Pace Analytical
Andrew Wilson, Partner
Education: BS, Princeton University; MBA, Harvard Business School
Background: Bank of America
Directorships: Petroleum Service Corporation; VLS Recovery Services
Michael Marino, Partner, Investor Relations
Education: BA, Boston College; MBA, Harvard Business School
Background: Banking Division at Goldman Sachs
Directorships: Inhance Technologies; National Technical Systems; Pace Analytical
Bob West, Chief Financial Officer
Education: BA, Miami University
Background: CFO, Northgate Capital; CFO, BGC Partners; CFO, Thomas Weisel Partners Group

204 AUSTIN CAPITAL PARTNERS LP
30799 Pinetree Road
#424
Perpper Pike, OH 44124

Phone: 216-574-2284 Fax: 216-574-4850
web: www.austincapitalpartners.com

Mission Statement: A private equity fund focusing on smaller private companies that are transitioning ownership to acquire growth capital or achieve liquidity. Austin Capital's objective is to partner with superior management teams to build a portfolio of profitable companies with competitive advantages.

Geographic Preference: Midwest, North Central United States
Founded: 2002
Average Investment: $5 - $20 million
Minimum Investment: $750,000
Investment Criteria: Acquisition, LBO, MBO, Recapitalization
Industry Group Preference: Industrial Equipment, Manufacturing, Chemicals, Medical Devices, Materials Technology, Wholesale Distribution
Portfolio Companies: Leather Resources of America Inc., Vanner Inc., Westny Building Products Company

Key Executives:
Darrell W Austin, Principal
Education: BA, Ohio Wesleyan University; MBA, Carroll School of Mangement, Boston College
Background: Vice President, Leveraged Capital Group; Vice President, Citicorp Investment Bank
Directorships: Westny Building Products Company, Vanner Inc., Omega Sea LLC, Leather Resources of America Inc.
Sam Hartwell, Principal
Education: BA, Yale University; MBA, Harvard University
Background: CEO, Southern Mill Creek Products; Founding Partner, Newmarket Partners; Sealy Inc.; McKinsey & Co.; Booz, Allen & Hamilton Inc.
Directorships: Vanner Inc.
William E Conway, General Partner
Education: BS, Yale University; Executive Program, University of California, Berkeley
Background: Executive Vice President, Pickands Mather & Co; Executive Vice President, Diamond Shamrock Corporation; Group Vice President, Capital Goods, Midland-Ross Corporation
Directorships: Fairmount Santrol Inc.

205 AUSTIN VENTURES
100 Congress Avenue
Suite 1600
Austin, TX 78701-2746

web: www.austinventures.com

Mission Statement: Austin Ventures is a venture capital firm invests in early stage and middle market companies, and form partnerships with their portfolio companies.

Geographic Preference: Texas
Fund Size: $3.9 billion
Founded: 1979
Average Investment: $20 million
Minimum Investment: $100,000
Investment Criteria: Seed-Stage, Growth Opportunities
Industry Group Preference: Business Products & Services, Enterprise Services, Computer Hardware & Software, Hardware, Applications Software & Services, Internet Technology, Semiconductors, Electronic Components, Financial Services, New Media, Internet
Portfolio Companies: 724 Solutions, Acorn Systems, Active Network, Active Power, Adometry, Agere, Alchemy Semiconductor, All Star Directories, AlterPoint, Ambiq Micro, AnswerSoft, Asset International, Augmentix, Bazaarvoice, Beecher Carlson, Benchmarq, BenefitMall, BetweenMarkets, Black Sand Technologies, Bloomfire, Boca,

Venture Capital & Private Equity Firms / Domestic Firms

Boundless Network, BreakingPoint Systems, BroadJump, BuildForge, Careline, Caringo, Celarix, Century Payments, Civitas Learning, ClearCommerce, ClearCube, ColdWatt, Complex Media, CompUSA, Conformative, Convio, Copan Systems, Credant Technologies, Credence Systems, CreditCards.com, CrimeReports, Crossroads Systems, CrunchFund, Crystal Semiconductor, Cygnal, D2 Audio, Dachis Group, Datical, Dazel, Delta Rigging & Tools, Donuts, Draker, Edgecase, Egenera, Emerus Hospital Partners LLC, Entact, Entorian Technologies, ESO Solutions, Explorys Inc., Exterprise, FiveRuns, Flash Valet, Floodgate, Food On The Table, Gazzang, Graduation Alliance, Grande Communications, Hire.com, HomeAway, Human Code, Idera, Ignite Technologies, iMark, Innography, Innovative Silicon, Intelliquest, ITinvolve, Jigsaw Data Corp., KD1, LDR Medical, LEAP Auto Loans, LifeSize Communications, Lincoln Clean Energy, Lion Street, Listen.com, Lombardi Software, Magnablend, Map My Fitness, Mass Relevance, Mavenir Systems, McData, Metasolv, MIQ Logistics, Mission Critical, Mobestream Media, MojoPages, Monitronics International, Motive, MyDocket, Naviant, Navini Networks, NetBotz, NetEffect, NetStream, New Hope Bariatric, Newgistics, Newisys, NileGuide, Nitero, Noesis Energy, Omni Water Solutions, Onit, OpenIncubate, Orion Marine Group, OutboundEngine, Paymetric, Pentasafe, Permeo Technologies, Pervasive Software, PetStuff, Pluck, Port Logistics Group, Powered, PreCash, Prenova, Proteon, Pyxis, Q Clubs, QuickArrow, Re:Trans, Reactivity, RetailMeNot, Revenue Cycle Solutions, RLX Technologies, RunTitle, SailPoint, SAM Inc., Santera Systems, Service Intelligence, SGN, Sheshunoff Information Services, SigmaTrak, Silicon Laboratories, Silicon Metrics, Silverback Enterprise Group, Silvercar, SMART Technologies, SolarWinds, Zilliant

Key Executives:
Chris Pacitti, General Partner
Education: BA, Economics, Johns Hopkins University
Background: Vice President, TL Ventures; Co-Founder/COO, Elsewhere Partners
Directorships: Microsoft Venture Capital Advisory Group; Entrepreneurs Foundation of Central Texas
John Thornton, General Partner
e-mail: johnt@ausven.com
Education: MBA, Stanford Graduate School of Business; BA, Trinity University
Background: McKinsey & Company
Joe Aragona, General Partner
Education: AB, Harvard University; MBA, Harvard Business School
Background: Bank of Boston
Directorships: National Venture Capital Association; Livestrong Foundation
Ken DeAngelis, General Partner
Education: BA, Harvard Uiversity; MBA, Wharton School, University of Pennsylvania
Background: Bank of Boston

206 AUSTRALIS CAPITAL
376 East Warm Springs Road
Suite 190
Las Vegas, NV 89119
Toll-Free: 800-898-0648
e-mail: ir@ausacap.com
web: www.ausacap.com

Mission Statement: Invests in the cannabis industry.
Geographic Preference: US, Canada
Founded: 2018
Investment Criteria: Early-Stage
Industry Group Preference: Cannabis
Portfolio Companies: Aurora Cannabis, Body and Mind, Quality Green, ShowGrow, Wagner Dimas Inc.
Key Executives:
Scott Dowty, Director/CEO
Education: National Sales Manager/Director, CIBC; SVP/General Manager, First Data Corp.; EVP Sales/CMO, Everi Holdings Inc.; Founder/Chairman, Passport Technology Inc.
Mike Carlotti, EVP/CFO
Education: BS, Finance, Boston College; MBA, Anderson School of Management, University of California, LA
Background: Investment Banking Analyst, Smith Barney; VP of M&A, Donaldson Lufkin & Jenrette; Partner, Palmyra Capital Advisors, SVP, Wachovia; VP of Treasury & Investor Relations, Bally Technologies; VP/Treasurer, Scientific Games; SVP/Treasure, MGM Resorts International
Daniel Norr, SVP/General Counsel
Education: JD, Chicago-Kent College of Law, Illinois Institute of Technology; MBA, Northern Illinois University
Cleve Tzung, SVP, Mergers & Acquisitions
Education: BS, Economics, University of Pennsylvania; Anderson School of Management, University of California, LA
Background: Strategist, PepsiCo; Product Manager, Airtouch; Associate, Deutsche Bank; VP, Berenson & Co.; Analyst, Lakeway Capital; Portfolio Manager, Ivory Capital; Head of Global Corp. Development/M&A, Mattel; Founder/CSO, Kidify
Casey Jones, Director, Business Development
Education: BS, Criminal Justice, Virginia Commonwealth University

207 AUTO TECH VENTURES
525 Middlefield Rd.
Menlo Park, CA 94025
e-mail: qg@autotechvc.com
web: www.autotechvc.com

Mission Statement: Auto Tech Ventures is a global independent transportation technology venture capital firm.
Founded: 2014
Investment Criteria: Early-Stage
Industry Group Preference: Transportation, Technology, Semiconductors, Energy Storage, Recycling
Portfolio Companies: Cogniac, Deepscale, Frontier Car Group, HDVI, Indie Semiconductor, Lyft, Metawave, Outdoorsy, Rollick, ShipHawk, Sport Hero, Volta, Work Truck Solutions, Xnor.Ai
Key Executives:
Quin Garcia, Managing Director
Education: BS, Applied Economics & Management, Cornell University; MSc, Management Science & Automotive Engineering, Stanford University
Background: Business Analyst, Management Consulting Strategic Management Solutinos; Founding Employee, Global Automotive AlliancesBetter Place; Advisor, Controlled Power Technologies
Directorships: Peloton Technology, Lyft
Alexei Andreev, Managing Director
Education: BS, Ph.D., Theoretical Physics, Moscow Institute of Steel and Alloys; MBA, Stanford Business School
Background: Managing Director, Harris & Harris Group
Maurice Gunderson, Managing Director
Education: BA, Mechanical Engineering, Oregon State; MS, Mechanical Engineering & Thermodynamics, Oregon State; MBA, Stanford University
Background: Control Systems Engineer, CH2M Hill; Systems Engineer, Garrett AiResearch; Director of Advanced Technologies, BOC; Founder & Managing Director, Nth Power; Co-Founder & Senior Advisor, Runway Capital Partners
Directorships: Gentherm, Contour Energy Systems, Scion-Sprays, Clean Air Power, Capstone Turbine
Daniel Hoffer, Managing Director
Education: BA, Philosophy, Harvard College; MBA, Columbia Business School
Background: Partner, Tandem Capital; Senior Director,

Concur; Co-Founder and CEO, CouchSurfing; Entrepreneur-In-Residence, Benchmark Capital

208 AUTOTECH VENTURES
525 Middlefield Rd.
Menlo Park, CA 94025

e-mail: info@autotechvc.com
web: autotechvc.com

Mission Statement: The firm aims to generate financial returns by helping passionate entrepreneurs to deploy revolutionary transportation technologies and business models.

Geographic Preference: Worldwide
Minimum Investment: $1 - 5 million
Investment Criteria: Early & Growth-Stage Startups
Industry Group Preference: Transportation, Ground Transportation
Portfolio Companies: Lyft, Realine, Outdoorsy, Volta, Deepscale, Work Truck Solutions, Spot Hero, Metawave, Rollick, Cogniac, Frontier Car Group

Key Executives:
Alexei Andreev, Managing Director
Education: MBA, Stanford University; PhD In Solid State Physics, Moscow Steel and Alloys Institute; MA, Liberal Sciences, Dartmouth College
Background: Managing Director, Harris & Harris Group; Draper Fisher Jurvetson.
Directorships: D-Wave Systems, Adesto Technologies, NeoPhotonics, Molecular Imprints
Quin Garcia, Managing Director
Education: BS, Applied Economics and Management, Cornell University; MS, Management Science and Automotive Engineering, Stanford University
Background: Co-Founder, Better Place; Management Consultant, Strategic Management Solutions; Stanford University's Dynamic Design Lab
Directorships: D-Wave Systems, Adesto Technologies, NeoPhotonics, Molecular Imprints
Maurice Gunderson, Managing Director
Education: BA, MS, Thermodynamics & Mechanical Engineering, Oregon State University; MBA, Stanford University
Background: Senior Partner, CMEA Ventures; Co-Founder, Nth Power
Directorships: Gentherm, Clean Air Power, Capstone Turbine, Pentadyne, NuScale Power, NeoPhotonics, Visyx

209 AVALON VENTURES
1134 Kline Street
La Jolla, CA 92037

Phone: 858-348-2180 Fax: 858-348-2183
e-mail: info@avalon-ventures.com
web: www.avalon-ventures.com

Mission Statement: Avalon Ventures is an early stage venture capital fund focused on information technology and life sciences. Avalon partners are passionate about backing talented entrepreneurs seeking to build market-leading companies.

Geographic Preference: United States, California
Fund Size: $200 million
Founded: 1983
Average Investment: $6 million
Minimum Investment: $250,000
Investment Criteria: Seed-Stage, Early-Stage
Industry Group Preference: Biotechnology, Communications Equipment, Computer Hardware & Software, Pharmaceuticals, Telecommunications, Networking, Wireless Technologies, Life Sciences, Information Technology
Portfolio Companies: Acceleron Pharma, AeroFS, Afraxis, Ambit Biosciences, Anaptys Biosciences, Ansa Software, Aratana Therapeutics, Ariad, Arista, MD, Attena Neurosciences, Aurora Biosciences Corp., Avelas Biosciences, Aware Point, Backupify, WeChi, BookBub, Byliner, Calliper, Cambrios, Cardeas Pharma, Carolus Therapeutics, Chart.io, Cheezburger, Cloudant, Cloudkick, Coi Pharmaceuticals, Conjur, E Band Communications, Edge Makers, FASTech Integration, Figure 8 Wireless, GenPharm, Good, Idun, Impath, Index, Inogen, Insight, Juliet Marine Systems Inc., Kaltura, Kinvey, Korrelated, Loop It, Memrise, Metra Biosystems, MPI, Mogi, Ningans, NeoRx, Network Switching Systems, Neurocrine, Node, Onyx, Orion, Ortiva Wireless, Otonomy, Panmira, Pharmacopeia, Pictela, Pingup, Pronoun, Proximal Data, Quippi International Gift Card Center, Redbooth, RethinkDB, River Medical, RQX Pharmaceuticals, Score Stream, Selectable Media, Sequana, Shelby.tv, Sidecar, Simulmedia, Skycatch, Smyte, Software Transformation Inc., Sova Pharmaceuticals, Spectra Biomedical Inc., StackIQ, Standingcloud, TechStars, Synaptics, Syndax, Synthorx, Talarian, Talla, Tapad, TheHappyCloud, Twinstrata, Uwanna?, Vertex, Vocera, Zacharon Pharmaceuticals, Zynga

Other Locations:
1770 Massachusetts Avenue
Suite 708
Cambridge, MA 02140
Phone: 617-299-2237

Key Executives:
Kevin J. Kinsella, Managing Director
e-mail: kkinsella@avalon-ventures.com
Education: BS, Management, MIT
Background: Solar Turbines International
Directorships: Amira, Anaptys, InCode
Steve Tomlin, Managing Director
e-mail: stomlin@avalon-ventures.com
Education: BA, American Studies, Yale University; MBA, Harvard Graduate School of Business
Background: Co-Founder, President & CEO, PersonaLogic; VP & General Manager, QVC Interactive; Director, New Business Development, Walt Disney Computer Software
Directorships: chumby industries, E-Band Communications Corporation
Jay Lichter, PhD, Managing Director
e-mail: jlichter@avalon-ventures.com
Education: BS/PhD, University of Illinois
Background: Co-Founder, Sequana Therapeutics
Rich Levandov, Managing Director
e-mail: rich@avalon-ventures.com
Education: BS, Binghamton University
Background: Co-Founder, Masthead Venture Partners; Affiliate Partner, Softbank Technology Ventures
Brady Bohrmann, Managing Director
e-mail: brady@avalon-ventures.com
Education: BS, Finance, Babson College
Background: General Partner, Masthead; President & COO, Watson Technologies
Directorships: Ad Summos, Afraxis, Backupify, Carolus, Cloudant, Cloudkick, Nabbr, Pictela, Twinstrata, Simulmedia
Tighe Reardon, Chief Financial Officer
Education: BS, Accounting, MS, Taxation, San Diego State University; CPA
Background: SVP, Tax & Treasury, DJO Global Inc.; Arthur Andersen LLP

210 AVANSIS VENTURES
Clifton, VA

web: www.avansis.com

Mission Statement: Avansis Ventures is a Mid-Atlantic, early-stage technology value fund that helps talented people build pioneering technology companies. As fellow entrepreneurs, the Avansis principals understand the difficulties of raising venture capital and the challenges of starting a new company.

Geographic Preference: Baltimore, Washington DC
Founded: 2000

Venture Capital & Private Equity Firms / Domestic Firms

Average Investment: $500,000-$1 million
Minimum Investment: $500,000
Investment Criteria: Early-Stage, Seed Stage
Industry Group Preference: Wireless Technologies, Software, Telecommunications, New Media, Enterprise Software, Internet Technology
Key Executives:
  Laura L. Lukaczyk, Founder/Managing General Partner
  Education: MBA, University of Virginia Darden School; BS, Chemical Engineering, University of Wisconsin-Madison
  Background: Consultant, New Enterprise Associates, Founding CFO, Denwa Communications; Director of Sales, International Communications Corporation; Multifinance Holding Corporation
  Brownell Chalstrom, Venture Partner
  Education: MIT; University of California Berkeley
  Background: General Manager, Lotus Notes; VP, BBN

211 AVENUE CAPITAL GROUP
11 West 42nd Street
9th Floor
New York, NY 10036

Phone: 212-850-7500
e-mail: investorrelations@avenuecapital.com
web: www.avenuecapital.com

Mission Statement: Headquartered in New York with offices in Europe and Asia, Avenue Capital specializes in distressed debt.
Geographic Preference: United States, Canada, Europe, Asia
Fund Size: $10.6 billion
Founded: 1995
Investment Criteria: Mezzanine, Bankruptcy, Recapitalization, Special Situations, Distressed Debt
Industry Group Preference: Diversified, Energy, Healthcare, Industrial Equipment, Manufacturing, Chemicals, Real Estate, Construction, Retailing, Telecommunications, Materials Technology, Transportation, Natural Resources
Key Executives:
  Marc Lasry, Chairman, Co-Founder & CEO
  Education: Clark University; New York Law School
  Background: Amroc Investments; Clerk for the Honorable Edward Ryan, former Chief Bankruptcy Judge of the Southern District of New York.
  Directorships: Bankruptcy and Corporate Reorganization Dept. at Cowen & Company; Private Debt Dept. at Smith Vasiliou Management Company
  Sonia Gardner, President, Managing Partner, Co-Founder
  Education: Clark University; Cardozo School of Law
  Background: Co-Founder, Amroc Investments
  Directorships: Mount Sinai Medical Center; Client Advisory Board of Citi Private Bank
  Jane Castle, Senior Portfolio Manager
  Education: Yale University; Stanford University
  Background: Managing Director & Head of U.S. Distressed Research, Lehman Brothers Inc.; High Grade Analyst, Citigroup Inc.
  Shawn Foley, Senior Portfolio Manager
  Education: University of Notre Dame
  Background: Merrill Lynch; Baker Nye Greenblatt
  Matthew Kimble, Senior Portfolio Manager
  Education: University of Illinois; NYU Stern School of Business
  Background: Bellport Capital Advisors LLC; Gordian Group LP; International Business Machines Corporation
  Randal Klein, Senior Portfolio Manager
  Education: University of Virginia; Wharton School, University of Pennsylvania
  Background: SVP, Lehman Brothers; Aerospace Engineer, The Boeing Company
  Craig Hart, Portfolio Manager
  Education: Colorado College; Yale School of Management; Yale School of Forestry & Environmental Studies
  Background: EVP & CFE, U.S. Power Generating Company; Managing Consultant, PA Consulting Group

212 AVISTA CAPITAL PARTNERS
65 East 55th Street
18th Floor
New York, NY 10022

Phone: 212-593-6900
e-mail: info@avistacap.com
web: avistacap.com

Mission Statement: Specializes in private equity investments in growth oriented energy, healthcare and media companies.
Geographic Preference: United States
Fund Size: $6 Billion
Founded: 2005
Industry Group Preference: Healthcare, Energy, Media, Communications, Consumer Products, Consumer Services, Industrial Services
Portfolio Companies: Accellent, Acino, AngioDynamics, BioReliance, Braeburn, Charles River, ConvaTec, Fisher Scientific, Focus Diagnostics, INC Research, Inform Diagnostics, IVAC, KCI, Lantheus Medical Imaging, MedServe, National Spine & Pain Centers, Nycomed, Optinose, Osmotica Pharmaceutical, Oxford Health Plans, Prometheus Therapeutics & Diagnostics, Shoppers Drug Mart, Strategic Partners, Trimb Healthcare, United BioSource, VWR Intl, Warner Chilcott, Zest Dental
Key Executives:
  Thompson Dean, Chairman & Co-Head, Investment Committee
  Education: BA, University of Virginia; MBA, Harvard Business School
  Background: DLJ Merchant Banking Partners
  Directorships: ConvaTec, IWCO, Nycomed, VWR
  David Burgstahler, Managing Partner & CEO
  Education: BS, Aerospace Engineering, University of Kansas; MBA, Harvard Business School
  Background: Partner, DLJ Merchant Banking Partners
  Directorships: BioReliance, Cidron, Lantheus Medical Imaging, Navilyst Medical, Visant, Warner Chilcott, WideOpenWest
  Sriram Venkataraman, Partner
  Education: MS, Electrical Engineering, University of Illinois; MBA, Wharton School
  Background: Vice President, Credit Suisses; GE Medical Systems
  Directorships: AngioDynamics, Lantheus Medical Imaging, OptiNose
  Robert Girardi, Partner
  Education: BS, Univ. of North Carolina; MBA, Wharton School
  Background: Quadrangle Group
  Directorships: ACP Mountain Holdings, Telular Corp., United BioSource

213 AWEIDA VENTURE PARTNERS
500 Discovery Parkway
Suite 300
Superior, CO 80027

Phone: 303-664-9520 **Fax:** 303-664-9530
e-mail: info@aweida.com
web: www.aweida.com

Mission Statement: Aweida Ventures invests in companies in data storage, software, and the life sciences, from seed through mezzanine rounds, encompassing the lifespan of a company. Industry specific skills are made available to partners with the intent of maximizing return for portfolio companies.
Fund Size: $100 million
Founded: 1988
Investment Criteria: Seed-Stage through Mezzanine
Industry Group Preference: Data Storage, Software, Life Sciences

Portfolio Companies: Atrato, Inc., Benchmark Storage Innovations, Channel Intelligence, Chaparral Network Storage, EStarCom, Illumitex, Info Trust, Permacharge Corp, RxKinetix, Storage Genetics, TerraXML, Turnleaf, Vertos Medical

Key Executives:
  Jesse Aweida, General Partner
  Background: Chairman & President, Storage Technology Corporation
  Dan Aweida, General Partner
  Education: BS, Business, University of Northern Colorado; MBA, Finance, Regis University
  Background: President, Aweida Properties

214 AXIA CAPITAL
84 State Street
Suite 320
Boston, MA 02109

Phone: 617-830-1117 Fax: 978-375-6784
e-mail: phunter@axia-partners.com
web: www.axia-partners.com

Mission Statement: Axia Capital is a private equity investment and advisory firm.

Investment Criteria: All Stages
Industry Group Preference: Automation, Robotics, Enterprise Software, Sensors, Instrumentation, Industrial Equipment
Portfolio Companies: Fiberoptic Components, Hydroid, Innovative Pressure Technologies, Network Vision, Segue Manufacturing Services

Key Executives:
  Peter A. Hunter, Managing Director
  e-mail: phunter@axia-partners.com
  Education: BS, Accounting, Suffolk University
  Background: CEO, Innovative Microplate; CEO, Inspectron Corporation
  James A. Pelusi, Managing Director
  e-mail: jpelusi@axia-partners.com
  Education: BS, Operations Research, Columbia University; MBA, Harvard Business School
  Background: SVP & General Manager, Factory Software Division, Brooks Automation

215 AXIOM VENTURE PARTNERS
185 Asylum Street
Suite 17
Hartford, CT 06103

Phone: 860-548-7799

Mission Statement: Serves investors, employees, and portfolio companies in a manner that generates superior returns for investors, fosters a challenging and collegial environment for employees, and engenders the respect of portfolio companies; provides capital and strategic assistance to rapidly growing high technology companies.

Geographic Preference: United States
Fund Size: $200 million
Founded: 1994
Average Investment: $5 million
Minimum Investment: $1 million
Investment Criteria: Early-Stage, Late-Stage
Industry Group Preference: High Technology, Communications, Software, Infrastructure, Information Technology, Biotechnology
Portfolio Companies: Aironet, Airwide Solutions, Alphion, Carrier Access Corporation, CiDRA, CenterPost, CipherOptics, LightSurf, Motia, Nufern, Sabre Communications, Tangoe, WellDog, WiDeFi, YDI Wireless, Albridge Solutions, DataTrak International, Shopping.com, Eprise Corporation, Evoke Software Corp., I-Film, Proximities, Inc., MetaStorm, Inc., MXLogic, Inc., Open Solutions, Inc., SilverStorm Technologies, Inc., SPS Commerce, Inc., Anika Therapeutics, Inc., Advancis Pharmaceutical Corp., Anesiva, Asprevea Pharmaceuticals, AVANT Immunotherapeutics, Inc., BioArray Solutions, Ltd., BioMimetic, Inc., Cellomics, Inc. Corixa Corp., Cyber-Care, Inc., Diversa Corp., Dynavax Corp., Exelixis Pharmaceuticals, Nextec Applications, Inc., PuriLens, Primera Biosystems, Rib-X Pharmaceuticals, Sagres Discovery, Small Bone Innovations

Key Executives:
  Alan Mendelson, Co-Founder/General Partner
  Background: Aetna Life & Casualty; Founding Investor/CEO, SyStemix; Founder, Thermoscan; President/CEO, Aetna, Jacobs & Ramo
  Directorships: ZipLink, Battery Ventures, Syncom II, Investment Committee of Connecticut Innovations
  Samuel McKay, Co-Founder/General Partner
  Background: Manager, CIGNA Insurance Company; Manager, Connecticut Seed Ventures; Manager, Ventech Partners; Founder/CEO, Targetech
  Directorships: Anika Therapeutics, Open Solutions, Aironet Wireless Communications, Sabre Communications

216 AZALEA CAPITAL
One Liberty Square
55 Beattie Place
Suite 1500
Greenville, SC 29601

Phone: 864-235-0201 Fax: 864-235-1155
web: www.azaleacapital.com

Mission Statement: A private equity firm that invests in lower middle-market firms in the Southeast region of the United States. Azalea specializes in management buyouts, business recapitalizations, and growth plans.

Geographic Preference: Southeast
Fund Size: $83 million
Founded: 1995
Average Investment: $1 - $10 million
Investment Criteria: Lower Middle-Market, Buyouts, Recapitalizations, Family-Owned
Industry Group Preference: Manufacturing, Distribution, Business Products & Services, Consumer Products, Healthcare, Energy, Aerospace, Defense and Government, Family-Owned
Portfolio Companies: ACL Airshop, Ark Naturals, InTech Aerospace, Jones Naturals, Modus, Muffin Mam, Power Services Group

Key Executives:
  Pat Duncan, Managing Partner
  Education: BA, MA, Economics, Clemson University
  Background: CFO & Director, Kent Manufacturing Company; First Union National Bank; Senior VP & Group Manager, Corporate Banking Group
  Directorships: Power Services Group, Orbital Tool Technologies, Star Packaging
  R Patrick Weston CFA, Managing Partner
  e-mail: patrick@azaleacapital.com
  Education: BS, Business Administration, University of South Carolina; MBA, Fiqua School of Business, Duke University
  Background: VP, Transamerica Mezzanine Financing; Liberty Capital Advisors; Merrill Lynch
  Directorships: MODUS, KLMK Group, Sunbelt Chemicals, ETAK Systems
  Marshall Cole, Chief Financial Officer/Managing Partner
  Education: BS, Business Administration, Middle Tennessee State University; CPA
  Background: CFO, National Electrical Carbon Corp.; CEO, Wright Metals
  Directorships: MODUS, KLMK, Star Packaging
  Meredith Pflug, Chief Compliance Officer/Controller
  Education: BS, Accounting, Bob Jones University
  Background: Senior Associate, KPMG

Venture Capital & Private Equity Firms / Domestic Firms

Ben Wallace, Partner
Education: BA, Davidson College; MBA, Vanderbilt University
Background: Product Manager & Business Analyst, ScanSource
Directorships: Power Services Group, Orbital Tool Technologies

217 AZCA
525 Middlefield Road
Suite 120
Menlo Park, CA 94025

Phone: 650-324-9100
e-mail: twilson@azcainc.com
web: www.azcainc.com/en

Mission Statement: AZCA Venture Partners is a corporate venture capital firm that assists corporations in developing new business. AZCA focuses on North American and Asian companies in IT, clean technology and life science industries.

Geographic Preference: North America, Asia
Founded: 1985
Industry Group Preference: Information Technology, Medical Devices, Diagnostics, Chemicals, Biotechnology, Life Sciences, Healthcare, Solar Energy, Telecommunication, Pharmaceuticals, Waste Water Treatment, Recycling Systems
Portfolio Companies: 360ip, Actel, ALCOM, Ballard, BigFix, Brookstone, Business Computer News, Ebara, Evergreen Solar, Exchange Resources, Fry's Electronics, Fulcrum Technologies, Gehl, Haas School of Business, iFire, Kaiser Permanente, KPMG, LecTec, Logitech, Marathon Products, Maxager, Micro Vision, Mitsubishi, Motorola, Nanogen, Nektar, Nikkiso, Nippon Steel, Oki, Panasonic, PARC, Quantum, Ricoh, Savvion, Shell, Shoshin, Sierra Ventures, Sony, SunPower, Sybase, Therma-Wave, Union Bank of California, Yamaha, Zaxel

Other Locations:
One Broadway
14th Floor
Cambridge, MA 02142
Phone: 650-73-71929

Ark Hills Executive Tower
Suite 601
1-15-5 Asaka, Minato-ku
Tokyo 107-0052
Japan
Phone: +81 (0)50-3567-9100

Key Executives:
Masazumi Ishii, Managing Director
e-mail: mishii@azcainc.com
Education: BE, Mathematical Engineering & Instrumentation Physics, University of Tokyo; MS, Computer Science, Stanford University
Background: Managing Director, Noventi; Senior Management Consultant, McKinsey & Company; Technical/Management, IBM, Japan
Directorships: Japan Society of Northern California, Japanese Chamber of Commerce
Wayne Doiguchi, Managing Director
e-mail: wdoiguchi@azcainc.com
Education: BA, Univesity of California, LA; MBA Santa Clara University
Background: Bank of Toyon; Union Bank of California; Park Plaza Investment Company; Strata Ventures
Directorships: Pan Pacific Bank
Leo Kim PhD, Managing Director
e-mail: lkim@azcavp.com
Education: BS, California State University; PhD, University of Kansas
Background: Founder & Managing Director, POSCO BioVentures; EVP, Research & CTO, Mycogen Corporation; Research Director, Shell Oil Company

218 AZURE CAPITAL PARTNERS
713 Santa Cruz Avenue
Suite 5
Menlso Park, CA 94025

web: www.azurecap.com

Mission Statement: Investor in early-stage technology companies.
Geographic Preference: United States, Canada
Fund Size: $750 million
Founded: 2000
Average Investment: $25 million
Minimum Investment: $1 million
Investment Criteria: Post-Seed, Series A
Industry Group Preference: Advertising, Applications Software & Services, Broadband, Cloud Computing, Digital Media & Marketing, Education, Networking, Financial Services, Gaming, Healthcare Information Technology, Mobile, Open Source, E-Commerce & Manufacturing, SaaS, Security
Portfolio Companies: BillMeLater, Broadlight, Calix, Cyan, Luminate, Native, NeoNova, phanfare, PSS Systems, Rooftop Media, Slide Rocket, Tripit, Top Tier Software, Vapps, VMWare, World Wide Packets, Zend

Other Locations:
2100 - 150 9th Avenue SW
Calgary, AB T2N 1Z6
Canada

Key Executives:
Paul Ferris, General Partner
Education: BA, Computer Science/English Literature, Amherst College
Background: Investment Banking, Credit Suisse First Boston; Morgan Stanley
Directorships: Calix, Personeta
Mike Kwatinetz, General Partner
Education: MA, PhD, University of California, Berkeley; MBA Accounting, New York University
Background: Global Head of Equity, Credit Suisse First Boston
Directorships: Education.com, I4 Commerce, Jacent, Knowledge Adventure, Medsphere OQO, ROME Corporation
Paul Weinstein, General Partner
Education: BS, Babson College
Background: Credit Suisse First Boston
Directorships: InterModal Data, K2 Software, Virtual Instruments, Switchfly, Unitas Global
Andrea Drager, Partner
Education: BComm, McGill University

219 B CAPITAL GROUP
1240 Rosecrans Avenue
Manhattan Beach, CA 90266

Phone: 310-698-1270
e-mail: info@bcapgroup.com
web: www.bcapgroup.com

Mission Statement: B Capital Group invests in B2B startups across four technology-enabled ategories: Enterprise technology and Consumer enablement, Healthcare Tech and Bio IT, Industrial and Transportation, and Fintech and Insurtech

Average Investment: $10 to 50 Million
Investment Criteria: Transformative Technology Start-Ups; Early Expansion Stage; Prepared for Rapid Growth and Acceleration

Other Locations:
2 Embarcadero Center
Suite 2400

Venture Capital & Private Equity Firms / Domestic Firms

San Francisco, CA 94111
Phone: 415-732-8052

10 Hudson Yards
New York, NY 10001

50 Raffles Place 048623
Singapore
Phone: 65 6429-2418

Key Executives:
  Howard Morgan, Co-Founder and Chair
  Raj Ganguly, Co-Founder and Managing Partner
  Eduardo Saverin, Co-Founder and Managing Partner

---

220 BABSON CAPITAL MANAGEMENT LLC
New York, NY

Mission Statement: Babson Capital Management LLC is an investment management firm that specializes in a variety of asset classes, including structured credit, private debt and high yield loans.

Geographic Preference: Worldwide
Fund Size: $182 billion
Founded: 1940

---

221 BACKSTAGE CAPITAL
Los Angeles, CA

web: backstagecapital.com

Mission Statement: Invests in seed and startup ventures whose founders identify as a woman, person of color, and/or LGBTQ+.

Geographic Preference: United States
Fund Size: $36 Million
Average Investment: $1,000,000
Investment Criteria: Seed, Startup, Women, People of Color, LGBTQ+
Industry Group Preference: All Sectors Considered
Portfolio Companies: Airfordable, Aquaai, Astral AR, Avisare, Bandwagon, BeVisible, Blendoor, CapWay, CareAcademy, Carrot, CEEK VR, Civic Eagle, CurlMix, Dibs, Drop, Filament, Flat Out of Heels, GoGrab, HabitAware, Haute Hijab, Healthy Roots, Hostfully, Houghton NYC, Ilerasoft, Jewelbots, Kairos, Laughly, Localeur, Mahmee, Mars Reel, NailSnaps, nedl, Nicolette, Nomiku, Novoron Bioscience, O.school, OmniSpeech, On Second Thought, Partake Foods, Pilotly, Please Assist Me, PopCom, Quarrio, Radial, Radiant RFID, Revry, Seeds, Seed&Spark, ShearShare, Siempo, Solstice Energy Solutions, Sunhouse, SUPA, Swivel Beauty, TextEngine, The Difference, The Door, The Mentor Method, Thesis Couture, Thurst, Tinsel, TresseNoire, Uncharted Power, Wedspire, Wildfang, Win-Win, Workfrom, XO, Zyrobotics

Key Executives:
  Arlan Hamilton, Founder/Managing Partner
  Background: Tour Manager, Atlantic Records
  Christie Pitts, General Partner
  Education: BA, San Jose State University; MBA, University of Phoenix
  Background: Venture Development Manager, Verizon Ventures
  Lisa Atia, Chief Revenue Officer
  Education: MA, Entrepreneurship & Strategy, Pepperdine University
  Background: Brand Strategist, Blavity

---

222 BAIDU VENTURES
463 Bryant Street
San Francisco, CA 94107

e-mail: hi@bv.ai
web: bv.ai/en/

Mission Statement: Baidu Ventures seeks to invest in the AI sector, from algorithms and sensors to computing paradigms and storage systems.

Geographic Preference: US, China
Investment Criteria: Seed, Series A & B
Industry Group Preference: Artificial Intelligence, Data Analysis
Portfolio Companies: 8i, Airmap, Alces, AMP Robotics, Catalog DNA, CiDi, Cytovale, Covariant, Engine Bio, Falcon Computing, Flow ++, Lightelligence, Magnetic Insight, MORE Health, OpenSpace, Pointcloud, RBC Signals, Ripcord, AutomationHero, Sensoro, Subtle Medical, Vesper Technologies, YI Tunnel, ZingFront, YunDing, Loock, Yunhan Financial Technology

Other Locations:
  China World Tower A, Suite 1601
  #1 Jianguomenwai Dajie
  Chaoyang District
  Beijing 100020
  China

Key Executives:
  Wei Liu, Chief Executive Officer
  Education: BS, University of Electronic Science and Technology of China; MS, Cambridge University
  Background: General Partner, Legend Star; Chairman, Comet Labs
  Saman Farid, Partner
  Education: BS, Control Systems Engineering, Cooper Union; MBA, MIT
  Background: Founder, Comet Labs; Honeywell; Verizon; Deloitte Consulting; Microsoft

---

223 BAIN CAPITAL PRIVATE EQUITY
John Hancock Tower
200 Clarendon Street
Boston, MA 02116

Phone: 617-516-2000 **Fax:** 617-516-2010
e-mail: privateequity@baincapital.com
web: www.baincapitalprivateequity.com

Mission Statement: Bain Capital Private Equity partners with management teams to help build and grow great companies.

Geographic Preference: Worldwide
Fund Size: $65 billion
Founded: 1984
Minimum Investment: $20 million
Investment Criteria: Seed, Late Growth, Buyout
Industry Group Preference: Consumer, Retail & Dining, Financial Services, Healthcare, Industrial, Technology, Media & Telecommunications, Energy
Portfolio Companies: Accellent, Air Medical Group Holdings, AMC Entertainment, Applied Systems, ASIMCO, Bellsystem24, Bloomin' Brands, Bombardier Recreational Products, Brakes Group, Bravida, Brenntaq, Bright Horizons, Broder Brothers Co., Burlington Coat Factory, Casda Biomaterials, Cerved, China Fire & Security Group, Clear Channel Communications, Consolidated Container Company, Contec, CRC Health Group, Cumulus Media, D&M Holdings, Denon & Marantz, Dollarama, Domino's Pizza Japan, Dunkin Brands, Edcon, Epoch, FCI, FleetCor, GA Pack, GOME Electrical Appliances, Guitar Center, Gymboree China, Gymboree Corporation, HCA, HD Supply, Hero Investments, Himadri, Ideal Standard, IMCD, International Market Centers, JinSheng International, Jupiter Shop Channel, Keystone Automotive Operations, Lilliput Kidswear, MEI Group, Michaels, MYOB, Novacap, NXP, Physio Control, QSI Restaurant Partners, Quintiles, Securitas Direct, Sensata Technologies, Sinomedia Holding Limited, SkillSoft, Skylark, Square Trade, Startronics, Styron, Sunac, SunGard, SunTelephone, Suzhou HiPro Polymers, TeamSystem, The Weather Channel, Toys 'R Us, Unisource, Uniview, Village Ventures, Warner Chilcott, Warner Music Group, WorldPay

Other Locations:
  535 Madison Avenue
  29th Floor

Venture Capital & Private Equity Firms / Domestic Firms

New York, NY 10022
Phone: 212-326-9420 Fax: 212-421-2225

50 Berkeley Steet
Mayfair
London W1J 8HD
United Kingdom
Phone: 44 20 7514 5252 Fax: 44 20 7514 5250

Maximilianstrasse 11
Munich 80539
Germany
Phone: 49-89244410700 Fax: 49-89244410731

One Pacific Place
Suite 2501, Level 25
88 Queensway, Admiralty
Hong Kong
China
Phone: 852-36566800 Fax: 852-36566801

Unit 2201, 22nd Floor Express Towers
Nariman Point
Mumbai 400 021
India
Phone: 91-2267528000 Fax: 91-2267528010

Room 3669, 36/F Two IFC
8 Century Boulevard
Shanghai 200120
China
Phone: 86-2160626120 Fax: 86-2160626121

Level 28
88 Phillip Street
Sydney NSW 2000
Australia
Phone: 61 2 9093 5500

1-1-1 Marunouchi, 5F
Chiyoda-ku
Tokyo 100-0005
Japan
Phone: 81-362127070 Fax: 81-362127071

Key Executives:
Stephen Pagliuca, Co-Chairman
Education: BA, Duke University; MBA, Harvard Business School
Background: VP, Bain & Company; Peat Marwick Mitchell & Company
Josh Bekenstein, Co-Chairman
Education: BA, Yale University; MBA, Harvard Business School
Background: Bain & Company
Blair Hendrix, Managing Director
Education: BA, Brown University
Background: EVP & COO, DigiTrace Care Services; Corporate Decisions
Ian Loring, Senior Advisor
Education: BA, Trinity College; MBA, Harvard Business School
Background: VP, Berkshire Partners; Corporate Finance, Drexel Burnham Lambert
Phil Loughlin, Managing Director
Education: AB, Dartmouth College; MBA, Harvard Business School
Background: Consultant, Bain & Company; Eagle Snacks; Norton Company
Robert Ehrhart, Managing Director
Education: BSBA, University of Missouri, Columbia
Background: Managing Director, Head of the Americas, Private Equity Group, Goldman Sachs & Co.
John Kilgallon, Managing Director
Education: BSE, Princeton University; MBA, Amos Tuck School of Business
Background: Leveraged Finance, Citadel
Luca Bassi, Managing Director
Education: Bocconi University; Columbia Business School
Background: Goldman Sachs
Nancy Lotane, Managing Director/Chief HR Officer
Education: BA, Tufts University; MBA, Amos Tuck School of Business
Background: Mercer Management Consulting
Amit Chandra, Managing Director
Education: Boston College
Background: DSP Merrill Lynch
Patrick Sullivan, Managing Director
Education: BS, ME, Rensselaer Polytechnic Institute; MBA, Columbia Business School
Background: Goldman Sachs Asset Management
Cécile Belaman, Managing Director
Education: Cornell University; London City University
Background: Morgan Stanley
Drew Chen, Managing Director
Education: Harvard Business School
Background: China Investment Corporation
John Connaughton, Co-Managing Partner
Education: BS, University of Virginia; MBA, Harvard Business School
Background: Consultant, Bain & Company
Ryan Cotton, Managing Director
Education: Princeton University; Stanford Grad. School of Business
Background: Bain & Company
Stuart Gent, Managing Director
Education: Bristol University
Background: Avis UK
Chris Gordon, Managing Director
Education: AB, Economics, Harvard College; MBA, Harvard Business School
Background: Consultant, Bain & Company
Steven Barnes, Senior Advisor
Education: BS, Syracuse University
Background: CEO, Dade Behring; President, Executone Business Systems; President, Holson Burnes Group; Senior Management, PriceWaterhouseCoopers
David Gross-Loh, Managing Director
Education: BS, Wharton School; MBA, Harvard Business School
Background: Consultant, Bain & Company

224 BAIN CAPITAL VENTURES
200 Clarendon Street
Boston, MA 02116

Phone: 617-516-2000
web: www.baincapitalventures.com

Mission Statement: Venture capital arm of Bain Capital.
Fund Size: $2 billion
Founded: 1984
Minimum Investment: $1 million
Investment Criteria: All Stages
Industry Group Preference: Infrastructure Software, SaaS & Data Services, Marketing Technology, Fintech, Healthcare
Portfolio Companies: 1-800-Dentist, Ability Network, Accelecare Wound Centers, Ameritox, AppNeta, Appriss, Aria Systems, Billtrust, Blip.TV, Bloomreach, Bluestem Brands, Booker Software, Boston Heart Diagnostics, BTI Systems, Captora, Celerion, CQuotient, Digital Compliance, Dynamics, Enservio, Evertrue, Experticity, GainSight, Garantia Data, Hazelcast, Hook Logic, InfoScout, INRIX, LiaZon, Linkable Networks, MedeAnalytics, Media Radar, MyEdu, National Cardiovascular Partners, Nomis Solutions, Novus, Nubisio, ObserveIt, Optimizely, Oyster.com, Persado, PGOA Media, Precision Therapeutics, Quanterix, Rapid7, Rave Mobile Safety, Regulatory Datacorp, Rent The Runway, ScaleBase, Scorebig, SevOne, Skyhook Wireless, Square Trade, Stack Driver, Symphony Commerce, Synapdx, Targetspot, Tellapart, Tennis Channel, The Receivables Exchange, Thefind, Travelclick, VMTurbo, Vonage, ZeroTurnaround, US Lec Corp., Vauto, Vmlogix, VMturbo, Vonage, Webputty, Wharton Economics, Work 'n Gear

Venture Capital & Private Equity Firms / Domestic Firms

Other Locations:
632 Broadway
New York, NY 10012
Phone: 212-822-2900

524 Hamilton Avenue
2nd Floor
Palo Alto, CA 94301

301 Howard Street
Suite 2200
San Francisco, CA 94105

Key Executives:
Ajay Agarwal, Partner
Education: BSEE, Stanford University; MBA, Harvard Business School
Background: Senior Executive, Trilogy Software; Consultant, McKinsey & Company; Patentholder
Directorships: AdReady, BloomReach, INRIX, Kiva Systems, m-Qube, Memento, Oyster.com, Rave Mobile Safety, Skyhook Wireless, Thumbplay, VMLogix
Scott Friend, Partner
e-mail: sfriend@baincapital.com
Education: BA, Electrical Engineering & Economics, Brown University; MBA, Harvard Business School
Background: Chairman, VP, Marketing, Oracle Retail; President & Co-Founder, ProfitLogic
Directorships: CQuotient, MagazineRadar, Norris Solutions, ProfitLogic, Rent The Runway, TheFind, TokBox
Matt Harris, Partner
e-mail: mharris@baincapitalventures.com
Education: Williams College
Background: Co-Founder, Village Ventures; Private Equity Group, Bain Capital
Mike Krupka, Partner
Education: BA, Chemistry, Dartmouth College
Background: Managing Director, Bain Private Equity Group; Principal, Information Partners
Directorships: Bluestem Brands, DataSynapse, Enservio, Invoke Solutions, iPay Technologies, Lala, Liberty Dialysis, MAXM Systems, MyEdu, The Learning Company, The Princeton Review
Enrique Salem, Partner
Education: BA, Computer Science, Dartmouth College
Background: CEO, Symantec; President & CEO, Brightmail
Directorships: DocuSign; FireEye; Atlassian; ForeScout
Sarah Smith, Partner
Education: BA, Music Education, University of Wisconsin-Madison; MBA, Stanford University
Background: VP of Advertising Sales/Operations & VP of HR/Recruiting, Quora; Director of Online Operations, Facebook
Yumin Choi, Partner
Education: BS, Entrepreneurship & Finance, Babson College
Directorships: AbleTo; Centivo; Datica; Iodine Software; Vetsource; ABILITY; MPulse Mobile; Oceans Healthcare; Payspan; Spinal Kinetics; Vets First Choice
John Connolly, Senior Advisor
e-mail: jconnolly@baincapital.com
Education: BA, St. Norbert College; Executive Education Program, INSEAD
Background: President, CEO & Chairman, M|C Communications; President & CEO, Institutional Shareholder Services
Directorships: EDGAR Online, Memento
Salil Deshpande, Senior Advisor
e-mail: salil@baincapital.com
Education: BS, Cornell University; MS, Stanford University
Background: Co-Founder/CEO, The Middleware Company
Ben Nye, Senior Advisor
e-mail: bnye@baincapital.com

Education: Harvard College, Harvard Business School
Background: SVP, Veritas Software; COO & CFO, Precise Software Solutions
Directorships: Apparent Networks, AppAssure Software, Archer Technologies, dynaTrace software, Network Intelligence, Rapid7, SolarWinds, VMTurbo

225 BAIRD CAPITAL PARTNERS
777 E Wisconsin Avenue
Milwaukee, WI 53233

Toll-Free: 800-792-2473
web: www.bairdcapital.com

Mission Statement: Seeks to provide financial advice and service to clients, helping them achieve their wealth management, investment banking and asset management goals.
Geographic Preference: United States, Europe, Asia
Fund Size: $512 million
Founded: 1919
Average Investment: $25 - $150 million
Minimum Investment: $5 million
Investment Criteria: Later Stage Growth, Change of Control, LBO
Industry Group Preference: Business to Business, Internet Technology, Telecommunications, Healthcare, Industrial Services, E-Commerce & Manufacturing, Life Sciences
Portfolio Companies: Accume Partners, American Auto Auction Group, AiCure, Alpha Source Inc., Amphora Medical, Apervita, Appcast, Arroweye, Autobooks, ADG, Bfinance, Car King, Ice Protection, Clear Water, Coal Fire, Datica, Eckler's, Elucent Medical, Emids, FullContact, Gabbro, Genome DX Biosciences, ChemDry, Hireology, Housecall Pro, Indi, Kason, Kedu Healthcare, Kindstar Global, Bioresearch, Montage, Muyingzhijia.com, Myelin Health, Neochord, NeuMoDx Molecular, New Vitality, Nigel Wright, NowSecire, ParkWhiz, Prescient Healthcare Group, R2I, Radius Global Growth Experts, RQI, SGX Sensortech, Signal, Sittercity.com, SloanLED, Snagajob, Startwire, Strata Oncology, Synap, Talent Academy, The SR Group, Veniti, Vitalyst, WordStream, Workforce Insight, Zaloni, Zurex Pharma Inc.

Other Locations:
227 West Monroe Street
Chicago, IL 60606

15 Finsbury Circus
London EC2M 7EB
United Kingdom

50 California Street
Suite 450
San Francisco 94111

Key Executives:
Paul Purcell, Chairman
Education: University of Notre Dame; MBA, Booth School of Business
Background: Managing Director, Kidder, Peabody & Co.
Directorships: RiverFront Investment Group LLC; Securities Industry and Financial Markets Association
C. Andrew Brickman, Partner
312-609-4702
Education: BA, Middlebury College
Background: M&a, Drexel Burnham Lambert; Private Equitym Wesray Capital; Heller Equity Capital
Directorships: Kason Corp., SloanLED, New Vitality, Harris Research Inc.
Martin Beck, Partner
49-172-852-71-24
Education: Business Administration, Catholic University of Eichstaett, Germany
Background: Senior Advisory Board, ZT Management Holding GmbH; CEO, MEC Holding GmbH
Gordon G. Pan, President
312-609-5498
Education: BA, Economics and Asian Studies, Colgate University; MBA, Kellogg School of Management,

83

Venture Capital & Private Equity Firms / Domestic Firms

Northwestern University
Background: Principal, One Equity Partners; Marquette Venture Partners; Founder, The Pangaea Group; Associate, Berkshire Partners

226 BAKER CAPITAL
575 Madison Avenue
8th Floor
New York, NY 10022

Phone: 212-848-2000 Fax: 212-646-0660
web: www.bakercapital.com

Mission Statement: A private equity fund that invests in digital communications at all stages.
Geographic Preference: Europe, North America
Fund Size: $1.5 billion
Founded: 1995
Average Investment: $30 million
Minimum Investment: $5 million
Investment Criteria: Early Stage, Later Stage
Industry Group Preference: Communications Equipment, Services, Applications Software & Services
Portfolio Companies: Adaptix, Akamai, Broadview Networks, Canal+, Cherry Road Technologies, Connected, CoreValue Software, Dotster, EM4, Immedia Semiconductor, Interxion, IQNavigator, Medianet, NTent, Offermatica, ParStream, PlusTV, QSC AG, SandVideo, Sequoia Software, Teem Photonics, Totality, Voltaire, Wine.com

Key Executives:
John Baker, Founding Partner
Education: Harvard College; Harvard Business School
Background: Patricof & Company Ventures
Directorships: Cherry Road Technologies, QSC AG
Henry G. Baker, Founding Partner
Education: BS/MS Electrical Engineering, PhD Computer Science, Massachusetts Institute of Technology
Background: Consultant, Privately
Directorships: Permabit, Sand Video
Joseph Saviano, CFO & COO
Education: BS, Finance, Lehigh University; MBA, Fordham University
Background: VP, Harvest Partners

227 BALLAST POINT VENTURES
401 E Jackson Street
Suite 2300
Tampa, FL 33602

Phone: 813-906-8500 Fax: 813-906-8514
e-mail: info@ballastpointventures.com
web: ballastpointventures.com

Mission Statement: Growth equity investors in companies in Florida, the Southeast and Texas.
Geographic Preference: Southeast, Texas
Fund Size: $164 Million
Founded: 2002
Average Investment: $6 Million
Minimum Investment: $4 Million
Investment Criteria: Late-stage expansion
Industry Group Preference: Healthcare, Software, Technology-Enabled Services, Communications, Consumer Products & Services
Portfolio Companies: Avoxi, Advanced Processing and Imaging, Blue Medical, Cbeyond Inc., Florida Bank, FSV Payment Systems, GHN Online, HotSchedules, InComm, Iconixx, Instawares, Innocutis, Intelligent Retinal Imaging Systems, KBI Biopharma, Knology, KSep Systems, Lifestyle Family Fitness, Matrix Medical Network, MeYou Health, MolecularMD, Optical Experts Manufacturing, PDQ South Texas, PDSHeart, PowerChord, PowerDMS, Prepaid Technologies, QOL Medical, SkuVault, SleepMed, Symphonic Distribution, TicketBiscuit, TissueTech, Theragen, Tower Cloud, Vazata, Wave7 Optics, YPrime, The Zebra

Key Executives:
Drew Graham, Partner
e-mail: dgraham@ballastpointventures.com
Education: BBA, Harvard Business School
Background: South Atlantic Venture Funds; Morgan Stanley & Co.
Paul Johan, Partner
Education: BA, Emory University; MBA, Darden School of Business
Background: Raymond James & Associates
Directorships: Prepaid Technologies, Instawares Holding Company, Vazata, InsuranceZebra
Matt Rice, Partner
Education: BComm, University of Virginia; MBA, Harvard Business School
Background: Raymond James
Directorships: MolecularMD, TissueTech, Y-Prime, MeYou Health, Theragen, Iconixx
Robert Faber, Partner
Education: BA, Princeton University; MBA, Tuck School of Business
Background: Wachovia Capital Partners

228 BALMORAL FUNDS
11150 Santa Monica Boulevard
Suite 825
Los Angeles, CA 90025

Phone: 310-473-3065 Fax: 310-479-1740
e-mail: thaynes@balmoralfunds.com
web: balmoralfunds.com

Mission Statement: Balmoral Funds LLC is a Los Angeles-based private equity firm which invests in recapitalization, special situations, and acquisitions of small and middle-market companies.
Geographic Preference: United States, Canada
Fund Size: $200 Million
Founded: 2005
Average Investment: $5-20 Million
Investment Criteria: Recapitalizations, Special Situations
Industry Group Preference: Manufacturing, Business Products & Services, Consumer Products, Retail, Consumer & Leisure, Value-Added Distribution
Portfolio Companies: Aero Interiors Company, Bennington Marine, Concurrent Manufacturing, Dispatch Transportation, Enesco LLC, GlobalOptions, IGPS Logistics LLC, Interstate Soutwest, KP Aviation, Mooyah, Silver Aero, tara Technologies, Things Remembered, VESTA Modular

Key Executives:
Jonathan Victor, Senior Managing Director
e-mail: jvictor@balmoralfunds.com
Education: AB, Economics, Princeton University; MBA, Stanford University; MA, Oxford University; JD, Stanford University
Background: Senior Advisor, Chanin Capital Partners; President/CEO, eBility Inc.; SVP of Finance, The Irvine Company' VP, Kaufman & Broad Inc.
Directorships: Bennington Marine; Dispatch Transportation; Concurrent Holdings; iGPS Holdings, Enesco Holdings; AgileX; Silver Aero; Mooyah
Skip Victor, Managing Director
e-mail: svictor@balmoralfunds.com
Robin Nourmand, Managing Director
e-mail: rnourmand@balmoralfunds.com
Education: BA/JD, University of California, Los Angeles; MBA, Anderson School of Management
Background: Sidley Austin LLP; Canyon Partners; Analysis Group Inc.
Directorships: Bennington Marine; Dispatch Transportation; Things Remembered; iGPS Logistics; KP Aviation; LifePort
Travis Haynes, Managing Director
e-mail: thaynes@balmoralfunds.com
Education: BA, University of California, Los Angeles

Venture Capital & Private Equity Firms / Domestic Firms

Background: VP, Platinum Equity
Directorships: Enesco LLC
David Shainberg, Principal
e-mail: dshainberg@balmoralfunds.com
Education: BA, New York University
Background: Brookfield Asset Management; JP Morgan
Luke Mau, Chief Financial Officer
e-mail: lmau@balmoralfunds.com
Education: BS, Finance & Accounting, University of Utah; MBA, ESADE, Spain
Background: JP Morgan; Citco Fund Services

---

229 BAND OF ANGELS LLC
750 Battery Street
7th Floor
San Francisco, CA 94111

Phone: 650-695-0400
e-mail: bandhq@bandangels.com
web: www.bandangels.com

Mission Statement: The Band of Angels is a seed funding organization based in Silicon Valley. The Band of Angels consists of over 150 high-tech executives dedicated to investing their money into startup companies.
Geographic Preference: California
Fund Size: $50 million
Founded: 1994
Average Investment: $300,000 - $1.5 million
Minimum Investment: $200,000
Investment Criteria: Seed, Startup, First Stage
Industry Group Preference: Semiconductors, Life Sciences, Biotechnology, Networking, Telecommunications, Software, Internet, Web Applications & Services
Portfolio Companies: Arovia, Basepaws, Car IQ, Cartogram, Cello Lighting, CNote, CoLabs, Combinati, Crater, Deep Blue Medical Advances, eyecandylab, Gravyty, HitCheck, Hupnos, HyperKey, IrisVision, IrriGreen, Kango, Mechanodontics, MisFit, Muzit, mxHero, Nwave Technologies, OneDome, OnScale, PlayFull, Purissima, RAM Medical Innovations, Raydiant Oximetry, Resonado, Rune Labs, Shyft, Snapwire, Strategikon Pharma, TrueData, U-Nest, Valfix, Visgenx, Your Fare
Other Locations:

Key Executives:
Ian Sobieski, PhD, Chairman
Education: BA, Philosophy, BS, Aerospace Engineering, Virginia Polytechnic Institute; MS, PhD, Aeronautics & Astronautics, Stanford University
Background: Evite.com; Enact Health Management; Kaman Aerospace
Directorships: Angel Capital Association, Venture Capital Network
Ed Canty, Chief Financial Officer
Background: General Partner, CFO, BayCom Partners; CFO, Teknowledge
Sonja Markova, MBA, Executive Director
Education: BS, Management, University Of St. Cyril and Methodius; MBA, Finance, California State University
Background: Vice President, Point Reyes Managment; Keiretsu Forum; Advisor, Camp BizSmart
Nicola Corzine, Partner/Deal Manager
Background: Founder & Executive Director, Financing Partners; Credit Suisse First Boston; Fundraising Forum

---

230 BANNEKER PARTNERS
600 Montgomery St
24th Floor
San Francisco, CA 94111

e-mail: khufford@bannekerpartners.com
web: www.bannekerpartners.com

Mission Statement: Banneker Partners is a private equity firm focused on investing in software/SaaS, Internet and business services companies.
Industry Group Preference: SaaS, Software, Internet, Business Products & Services
Portfolio Companies: Ancestry.com, Genesys, IQMS, Magento, Pepperjam
Key Executives:
Stephen Davis, Partner
Education: Carleton College; JD, MBA, Columbia University
Background: Co-Founder, Vista Equity Partners
Matthew McDonald, Partner
Education: BS, California Poly; MS, Santa Clara Univ.
Background: Square, Inc.; CVC Capital Partners
Adrian van Schie, Partner
Education: LLB, BComm, Univ. of Otago; Univ. of Chicago
Kyle Hufford, Vice President
Education: BS, W.P. Carey School of Business
Background: Serent Capital Partners

---

231 BARODA VENTURES
245 South Beverly Drive
Beverly Hills, CA 90212

web: www.barodaventures.com

Mission Statement: Baroda Ventures is a Los Angeles based venture capital firm who work side-by-side with scrappy entrepreneurs who are passionate about building lasting businesses.
Geographic Preference: Los Angeles
Founded: 1998
Investment Criteria: Seed-Stage, Series A
Industry Group Preference: Consumer Internet, E-Commerce & Manufacturing, Mobile, SaaS, Digital Media & Marketing
Portfolio Companies: Amplify, Blade, Bridg, Crexi, DSTLD Premium Denim Co., Embrace.io, Gem, HelloTech, Healthvana, ID90 Travel, Koh Founders, Launchpad LA, Local ID, Overnight, Pathmatics, Policy Genius, Retention Science, Revolution Credit, Science, Steelhouse, Surf Air, Thayer Ventures, Travo, Trebeca, Unglue, Chromatik, DogVacay, Gradient X, Lettuce, OVGuide, Shift
Key Executives:
David Bohnett, Founder
Education: BBA, University of Southern California; MBA, Finance, University of Michigan
Background: Founder, Geocities
Peter Lee, Managing Partner
Education: BS, MS, Engineering Product Development, MIT; MBA, Harvard Business School
Background: Investor, Clearstone Ventures; Investor, Prism Ventures; VP Operations & Product Development, Goldpocket; Manager, McKinsey

---

232 BASE VENTURES
Berkeley, CA

e-mail: hello@base.ventures
web: base.ventures

Mission Statement: Invests in seed-stage technology companies in various sectors including cannabis, health & wellness, information technology, real estate, and consumer goods.
Founded: 2012
Investment Criteria: Seed, Early-Stage
Industry Group Preference: Cannabis, Health & Wellness, Technology, Data Technology, Food & Beverage, Consumer Goods, Entertainment
Portfolio Companies: Olly, Luma, Dirty Lemon, Rapchat, inDinero, Style Seat, Netki, Genies, Cleanify, Ink, Armory, Rinse, PlanGlid, Mayvenn, Virool, 6 Sence, Travel Joy, Baker Technologies, Pigeonly, World View, Angellist, Pando Daily,

Venture Capital & Private Equity Firms / Domestic Firms

Modest, Balanced, Buffer, Rolltech, Naja, CultureIQ, BlackJet, SwapBox, Thinair, Revip, Glambot, Parade, GrowX

Key Executives:
Erik Moore, Founder/Managing Director
Education: AB, Dartmouth College; MA, International Relations; MBA, Wharton School, University of Pennsylvania
Background: VP, Gen Re; Director, Merill Lynch
Directorships: Surf Air; Pigeon.ly; Wildfang.com
Kirby Harris, Partner
Education: BA, Morehouse College; MBA, California State University Hayward
Background: VP/Consultant, Impact Capital Management; Principal, Monte Cresta Capital
Lisa Parks, Operations Partner
Education: BA, Political Science/Government, University of California, Berkeley
Background: Sr. Development Officer, Right to Play; Operations Partners, Three Bridges Venture
Directorships: PACE
Tami Flores, Director of Operations
Education: BA, English, University of California, Berkeley
Background: Production Associate, Clockdrive Productions; Finance Manager, Claremont Creek Ventures; Team Lead for Quality Control Operations, Googles; Technology Preferred Banker, First Republic Bank

233 BASECAMP VENTURES
1 Executive Drive
Suite 8
Moorestown, NJ 08057

Phone: 856-813-1100
e-mail: mel@basecampventures.com
web: www.basecampventures.com

Mission Statement: To invest in new technology companies with great potential and to offer support to management teams. BaseCamp's objective is to lead its portfolio companies to success.

Geographic Preference: Mid-Atlantic
Fund Size: $10 million
Founded: 2000
Average Investment: $250,000
Investment Criteria: Seed, Startup, First Stage, Mezzanine
Industry Group Preference: Technology, Internet Technology, Internet Infrastructure, Cloud Computing
Portfolio Companies: Coredial, IonField Systems

Key Executives:
Mel Baiada, Managing Partner
Education: BSEE, Computers, MA, Communications, Drexel University
Background: Founder, Bluestone
Directorships: Drexel University, New Jersey Technology Council, Bayada Home Health Care

234 BASELINE VENTURES
web: www.baselinev.com

Mission Statement: To help founders build and grow their early stage companies into change affecting enterprises.

Geographic Preference: United States
Founded: 2006
Investment Criteria: Seed-Stage
Industry Group Preference: Consumer Internet, Digital Media & Marketing
Portfolio Companies: Aardvark, Adara, Afresh, Alt School, Apiary, Appuri, Avocado, Backplane, Blekko, Bloc, BlueFox, BookFresh, Boombotix, Cake Financial, CarePort, CircleCI, Citrus Lane, Cluster, Copper, CoTweet, Crashlytics, Crayon, Datalot, Digit, Dishcraft Robotics, DocVerse, Dusty Robotics, ExactTarget, Expensify, Figure, Finxera, Flowtown, Freck, Formspring, Giftly, Gild, GoInstant, Good Eggs, Heartwork, Heroku, Homebase, Hunch, Indextank, Instagram, Instructables, Iron.io, J. Hilburn, LaunchKit, Librato, Liftoff, LoanSnap, Lucid, MachineZone, Mango Health, Metaresolver, MixerLabs, mLab, nWay, Okanjoya, OMGPop, OwnLocal, PacketZoom, Pagerduty, Pantheon, Parakey, Path, Peel, Pickwick & Weller, Piqora, Pocket, Projector, Pronoun, Reverb, Revere, Rivet & Sway, ROI DNA, Rupture, ScanScout, Seesaw, Sendori, Sendwithus, Shape, Smartbiz, Smyte., SoFi, Soma, Spruce, StackMob, Stax, Stitch Fix, StumbleUpon, Sun Basket, TaskRabbit, TastemakerX, TellApart, Threadflip, TINYpulse, Trazzler, TrialPay, TRUSTe, Twitter, Uservoice, Versly, Weebly, Xobni, Yardbarker

Key Executives:
Steve Anderson, Founder
Education: University of Washington, Stanford Graduate School of Business
Background: eBay, Microsoft, Kleiner Perkins, Starbucks, Digital Equipment Corporation

235 BASIS SET VENTURES
San Francisco, CA

web: www.basisset.ventures

Mission Statement: Mission is to invest in early stage startups in the area of artifical intelligence.

Fund Size: $140 Million
Investment Criteria: Seed/Series A Startups, Artificial Intelligence
Industry Group Preference: Artificial Intelligence
Portfolio Companies: Clara Labs, FarmWise, Falkonry, Foresight AI, Lime, Oasis Labs, Rasa, Rylo, Turing Video, Verge Genomics, Workstream

Key Executives:
Dr. Lan Xeuzhao, Founding/Managing Partner
Education: MA, Statistics, PhD, University of Michigan
Background: McKinsey; Dropbox
Andrew Kim, Operations Manager
Background: Meeno Babies; Project Gina

236 BATTELLE VENTURES
181 Rice Terrace Drive
Columbia, SC 29229

Phone: 843-535-2336

Mission Statement: The fund will principally, but not exclusively, focus on seed, startup, and first stage investments that will commercialize the technologies that emerge from Battelle and the laboratories that Battelle manages or co-manages for the US Department of Energy.

Geographic Preference: United States
Fund Size: $220 million
Founded: 2003
Investment Criteria: Seed, Startup, Early, First Stage
Industry Group Preference: Technology, Health Related, Life Sciences, Energy, Environment, Security
Portfolio Companies: 360ip Pte. Ltd., Aldis, BioNano Genomics, BioVigilant, Hepregen, Hi-G-Tek, Micro Interventional Devices, Proterro, Rajant, RemoteReality, SafeView, SmartSynch

237 BATTERSON VENTURE CAPITAL LLC
web: www.battersonvc.com

Mission Statement: Batterson Venture Capital provides venture capital to promising new or growing businesses. The firm's goal is to offer capital, operational expertise and strategic partnership to emerging entrepreneurs.

Geographic Preference: United States
Fund Size: $30 million
Founded: 1995
Average Investment: $100,000 - $12 million
Minimum Investment: $25, 000

Venture Capital & Private Equity Firms / Domestic Firms

Investment Criteria: Seed, Startup, First-Stage, Second-Stage
Industry Group Preference: Biotechnology, Communications, Computer Related, High Technology, Materials Technology, Medical & Health Related
Portfolio Companies: Cleversafe, NextGen Solar LLC, ThirdStream BioScience
Key Executives:
  Len Batterson, Chairman/CEO
  Education: BA, JD, Washington University, St. Louis; MBA, Harvard Business School
  Background: Managing General Partner, Batterson, Johnson & Wang; Director, Allstate Insurance Company; Control Video Corporation; Principal, Leonard Batterson Associates
  Directorships: Illinois Coalition
  James Vaughan, Managing Principal
  Education: San Francisco State University
  Background: CEO, JE Vaughan Financial Services; Founder & Manager, William Blair Select
  Annie Piotrowski, Vice President, Administration
  Education: BS, Legal Administration, Loyola University
  Background: Executive Assistant, Stein & Company; Environmental Paralegal, American National Can Company

238 BATTERY VENTURES
1 Marina Park Drive
Suite 1100
Boston, MA 02210

Phone: 617-948-3600
web: www.battery.com

Mission Statement: Focuses on investing in technology companies at all stages of growth, leveraging expertise and capital to actively guide companies to category dominance.
Geographic Preference: United States, Canada, Israel, India, China, Europe
Fund Size: $6.8 billion
Founded: 1983
Average Investment: $35 million
Minimum Investment: $5 million
Investment Criteria: Seed, Startup, Later Stage
Industry Group Preference: Communications, Infrastructure, Software, Technology, Media, Networking, Telecommunications, Online Content, Semiconductors, Digital Media & Marketing, Financial Services, Clean Technology, Industrial Technology
Portfolio Companies: 2nd Address, 6sense, AED-SICAD, Affirm, Agari, Alogent, Amplitude, Audio Precision, AuditBoard, BigPanda, Black Diamond IT Services, BloomReach, Blue Jeans Network, Boost Media, BounceX, BPSC, Braze, BrightEdge, Brookhaven Instruments, Catchpoint Systems, Champions Oncology, Chef, Cheq, ClearCare, Clip Industie, Clubessential, Clubhouse, ClubReady, Cohesity, Coinbase, Colibra, Concurrent Real-Time, Contrast Security, Cortera, Coupa, CrediFi, Cross River Bank, CrunchTime!, Cumulus Networks, Curve Dental, Dantec Dynamics, Data Physics, Databricks, Dataiku, Delphix, DGSI, Duetto, Dynament, EDR, Elastifile, Entelo, Enviance, Excelero, Expel, Fastly, FirstFuel, Forterro, Fungible, Gainsight, GetYourGuide, GoEuro, GuardiCore, Habana Labs, HotelTonight, Influxdata, Interana, InVision, Istra Research, J. Hilburn, James Heal, Jask, Jeeves, JFrog, JOOR, KeyMe, Kodiak Robotics, Lansmont, Latitude Geographics, LDetek, Leadspace, Learnosity, LiveIntent, Local Bushel, Lotame, Machinify, Mecmesin, Michell Instruments, Minute Media, N26, Narrative Science, Narvar, NDT Systems, Newforma, Niantic Inc., Nitro Software, Nova Instruments, Nova Metrix, NTRON, Nutanix, NVT Group, Optimizely, Outlyer, PageUp, Pendo, Performance IQ, Physical Property Testing, Plixer, PowerInbox, Precidian Investments, PrestoSports, Primerevenue, Process Sensing Technologies, Qognify, Quantum Machines, Quinyx, Reflektion, RelayFoods.com, RickIQ, Robotiq, Roctest, Rotronic, Scodix, SensorNet, Sensu, Serena & Lily, Service Titan, Sherborne Sensors, SigmaTEK Systems, Silog, Sisense, SmarterHQ, Sociable Labs, SolvAxis, SpotHero, Spredfast, Sprinklr, Status Scientific, StellaService, StockX, Stratoscale, StreamSets, Stretch Internet, Sylob, Tealium, Team Corporation, Thundra, TrendKite, TTP Labtech, UBQ Materials, UpKeep, Upsight, Vayyar Imaging, Vera, Vidyard, VividCortex, Wag!, WebPT, Workato, Woven, Xenex, Yesware, Zeitgold, Zerto

Other Locations:
2882 Sand Hill Road
Suite 280
Menlo Park, CA 94025
Phone: 650-372-3939

17 Arania Osvaldo Street
Tel Aviv
Israel
Phone: 972 (9) 972-4300

260 Townsend Street
7th Floor
San Francisco, CA 94107
Phone: 415-426-5900

3 Cavendish Square
4th and 5th Floors
London W1G 0LB
United Kingdom
Phone: 44 (0)20-7299-1480

636 - 6th Avenue
Suite 440
New York, NY 10011
Phone: 212-466-6340

Key Executives:
  Dharmesh Thakker, General Partner
  Education: BS, Electrical Engineering, University of Texas; MBA, Wharton School, University of Pennsylvania
  Background: Managing Director, Intel Capital; Advanced Technology Ventures; Keynote Systems; InterNetwork; Peakstone; Manhattan Associates
  Directorships: Agari, Collibra, Contrast Security, Databricks, Expel, Fungible, InfluxDatam JFrog, Machinify, Narvar, Reflektion, Sensu, StreamSets, UpKeep, Woven
  Dave Tabors, Private Equity Partner
  Education: Dartmouth College
  Background: Financial Consulting, Cambridge Associates
  Directorships: CrunchTime!, Enviance, Forterro,
  Scott Tobin, Senior Partner
  Education: BA, International Relations, Islamic and Middle Eastern Studies, Brandeis University
  Background: Investment Banking, First Albany Corporation; Director Corporate Development, Future Vision
  Roger Lee, General Partner
  Education: BA, Political Science, Yale University
  Background: Co-Founder, Corio; Manager Internet Products, Edify Corporation; Co-Founder/President, NetMarket
  Directorships: 6Sense, Blue Jeans Network, BrightEdge, Coinbase, Entelo, Gainsight, HotelTonight, Joya Communications, Live Intent, Lotame, Narrative Science, Narvar, Niantic Inc., etc.
  Neeraj Agrawal, General Partner
  Education: BS, Computer Science, Cornell University; MBA, Harvard Business School
  Background: Product Manager, Real Networks; Management Consultant, Booz-Allen; Operative Executive, SkyTV
  Michael Brown, General Partner
  Education: BS, Finance & International Business, Georgetown University
  Background: High Technology Group, Goldman, Sachs &

Co; Financial Anaylst, Goldman's Financial Institutions Group
Jesse Feldman, General Partner
Education: BA, Science in Society, Wesleyan University; MBA, Harvard Business School
Background: Ionian Management; GE Commercial Finance
Directorships: Healthvision, HighJump Software, Industrial Safey Technology, Nova Analytic, Nova Technologies, Rogue Wave Software
Itzik Parnafes, Advisor
Education: BSc, Computer Science & Mathematics, Technion Institute of Technology
Background: Co-Founder, Kagoor Networks; R&D, Class Data Systems
Directorships: 90min, Cheq, Elastifule, GoEuro, Insert, Kodiak Robotics, Quantum Machines, Sisense, Zeitgold
Alex Benik, Partner
Education: BA, Government, Wesleyan University
Background: Analyst, The Yankee Group
Directorships: Cask, Catchpoint, Cumulus Networks, Fungible, GuardiCore, Interana, Nutanix, Plixer, Stratoscale, Thundra, Vivid Cortex
Chelsea Stoner, General Partner
Education: BS, Chemical Engineering, Northwestern University; MBA, University of Chicago
Background: Associate, Key Principal Partners; Manager, Accenture; Principal, Battery Ventures; Merrill Lynch; Classified Ventures

239 BAXTER VENTURES
One Baxter Parkway
Deerfield, IL 60015-4625

e-mail: ventures@baxter.com
web: www.baxter.com

Mission Statement: Baxter Ventures identifies companies with promising, early-stage technologies, products and/or therapies, and provides them with the capital and expertise needed to drive successful innovation. Baxter Ventures was created by Baxter International Inc., which has an 80-year legacy of healthcare innovation and saving and sustaining lives worldwide.

Founded: 2011
Investment Criteria: Early-Stage
Industry Group Preference: Healthcare, Pharmaceuticals

240 BAY CITY CAPITAL LLC
1000 - 4th Street
Suite 500
San Rafael, CA 94901

Phone: 415-299-8196
web: www.baycitycapital.com

Mission Statement: To provide investment capital and strategic and transaction advisory review to publicly traded and privately held companies.

Geographic Preference: United States
Fund Size: $1.3 billion
Founded: 1997
Average Investment: $5 - $10 million
Minimum Investment: $100,000
Investment Criteria: All Stages
Industry Group Preference: Life Sciences, Pharmaceuticals, Biomedical, Diagnostics, Nutrition, Agribusiness, Biopharmaceuticals, Medical Devices
Portfolio Companies: Accriva Diagnostics, Aciex Therapeutics, Amerifit Nutrition, Antriabio, AquaBounty Technologies, Aragon Surgical, Ascendancy Healthcare, BioRen, BioSeek, Cadence Pharmaceuticals, Calupso Medical, Chemdex, Civitas Therapeutics, Conatus Pharmaceuticals, Cydan, CymaBay Therapeutics, Dermira, EnteroMedics, Eos, Epizyme, Epoch Biosciences, Epocrates, Fabric Genomics, GenturaDx, Gritstone Oncology, Hyperion Therapeutics, Idev, Imara, Ingenuity Systems, Intarcia Therapeutics, Interleukin Genetics, Ion Torrent, Itamar Medical, Iterum Therapeutics, Kezar Life Sciences, Lexicon, LJL BioSystems, Madrigal Pharmaceuticals, MAP Pharmaceuticals Inc., Maxia Pharmaceuticals Inc., Medarex, Menlo Therapeutics, Merus, Neorx, Nevro, Next Wave Pharmaceuticals, NuPathes, OcuLex, OmegaTech, Panomics, Pathway Diagnostics, Pharm Akea Therapeutics, Pharmanex, Pharmion, Presidio Pharmaceuticals Inc., Protez Pharmaceuticals, PTC Therapeutics, Radiant Medical, Reliant Pharmaceuticals Inc., Reset Therapeutics, Sembiosys, Senomyx. Sunesis, Symyx, SynGen, Syntonix, Syrrx, Tetraphase, Tria, Twist Bioscience, Vivaldi Biosciences, VNUS Medical Technologies Inc., Vtesse, Xeris Pharmaceuticals

Key Executives:
Fred Craves, PhD, Founder/Managing Director
Education: PhD Pharmacology/Toxicology, University of California San Francisco; BS Biology, Georgetown University
Background: Executive VP, Shering Beruin Inc; CEO and President, Berlex Buiosciences; Founding Chairman and CEO, Codon; Co-Founder of Creative BioMolecules/NeoRx
Directorships: Incyte Genomics, Medarex, Bioseek, Galileo Laboratories, Reliant Pharmaceuticals
Carl Goldfischer, MD, Advisor
Education: MD, Albert Einstein College; BA, Sarah Lawrence College
Background: CFO, ImClone Systems; Research Analyst, Reliance Insurance Company
Directorships: Diametrics Medical, Avera Pharmaceuticals, Etex, Metabolex, NeoRx, Oculex Pharmaceuticals, PTC Therapeutics, Syntonix Pharmaceuticals
Lionel Carnot, Advisor
Education: MS, Molecular Biology, University of Geneva; MBA, INSEAD
Background: KFitzker Organization; Principal, Oracle Partners; Product Manager for Prozac, Eli Lilly; Sales/Marketing, Booz Allen & Hamilton; Accenture Strategic Services
Directorships: Mervus BV
Manuel Lopez-Figueroa, Advisor
Education: MS, Molecular & Cell Biology, University of La Laguna; PhD, Medicine & Surgery, University of Las Palmas
Background: Scientific Liason, Pritzker Neuropsychiatric Disorders Research Consortium

241 BAY PARTNERS
2180 Sand Hill Road
Suite 345
Menlo Park, CA 94025

web: www.baypartners.com

Mission Statement: Bay Partners aim to build high value companies that provide exceptional returns to both the investors and entrepreneurs. Bay Partners works to create a strong alignment between the interests of the investors and those of the entrepreneur.

Geographic Preference: United States
Fund Size: $1 Billion
Founded: 1976
Average Investment: $7 - $10 million
Minimum Investment: $3 million
Investment Criteria: Seed and early-stage companies with validated concepts facing execution risk.
Industry Group Preference: Wireless Technologies, Semiconductors, Enterprise Software, SaaS, Equipment, Components & IoT, Consumer Services, Hardware, Energy Services
Portfolio Companies: AMEC, Apigee, BoardVantage, Code Green Networks, Covestor, DropCam, Engine Yard, Enphase Energy, Envia Systems, Eventful, Grand Junction, Interact Public Safety Systems, Lending Club, Mimoni, MuleSoft, OncoMed, RS LiveMedia, Sonatype, Xactly,

Venture Capital & Private Equity Firms / Domestic Firms

FinancialContent, Vaxart, Yapta, Junglee Games, Brocade Communications, Buddy Media, Cornerstone, Digital Island, Dynatrace, Eloqua, Excelan, Exodus Communications, G2One, Geoworks, Guidewire Software, Informatica, Like.com, Macromedia, Maxtor, NCM Services, Protocol Systems, Red Brick Systems, Shiva, SonicWALL, SpringSource, Tealeaf, WebLogic, Zenprise

Key Executives:
Stu Phillips, General Partner
e-mail: stu@baypartners.com
Education: BS, Electronics, University of Wales
Background: Founder, Ridgelift Ventures; General Partner, US Venture Partners; Cisco Systems
Neal Dempsey, General Partner
e-mail: neal@baypartners.com
Education: MBA, University of Washington
Background: CEO, Quibix Graphics Systems; CEO, Envision Technology; Senior Management, Sentec/Harris

242 BAYSIDE CAPITAL
1450 Brickell Avenue
31st Floor
Miami, FL 33131

Phone: 305-381-4100 Fax: 305-379-2013
e-mail: bayside@bayside.com
web: www.bayside.com

Mission Statement: Bayside Capital is an investment firm that provides debt and equity capital to middle market companies.
Geographic Preference: United States, Canada
Fund Size: $7 billion
Average Investment: $10 - $100 million
Investment Criteria: Recapitalizations, Debtor in Possession Financing
Industry Group Preference: Diversified
Other Locations:
151 N Franklin Street
21st Floor
Chicago, IL 60606
Phone: 312-214-1234 Fax: 312-345-5999

1271 Avenue of the Americas
22nd Floor
New York, NY 10020
Phone: 212-314-1000 Fax: 212-506-0559

H.I.G. European Capital Partners LLP
2nd Floor
London W1K 4QB
United Kingdom
Phone: 44 0 207 318 5700 Fax: 44 0 207 318 5749

H.I.G. European Capital Partners GmbH
Hamburg 20354
Germany
Phone: 49 40 41 33 06 100 Fax: 49 40 33 06 200

H.I.G. European Capital Partners Spain, S.L.U.
4th Floor
Madrid 28014
Spain
Phone: 34 91 737 50 50 Fax: 34 91 737 50 49

Ih.I.G. European Capital Partners Italy S.r.I.
Milan 20121
Italy
Phone: 39 02 45 37 5200 Fax: 39 02 45 37 5250

H.I.G. European Capital Partners SAS
5th Floor
Paris 75008
France
Phone: 33 0 1 53 57 50 60 Fax: 33 0 1 53 57 50 89

Key Executives:
John Bolduc, Executive Managing Director
Education: BS, Computer Science, Lehigh University; MBA, University of Virginia
Background: Bain & Company; Chemed Corporation

Jackson Craig, Managing Director
Education: BS, Business Administration, University of Vermont
Background: DDJ Capital Management; Morgan Stanley
Sean Britain, Managing Director
Education: BS, Business Administration, Wake Forest University
Background: Principal, Apax Partners; Saunders Karp & Megrue; First Union Securities
Duncan Priston, Managing Director
Education: Bristol University
Background: Strategic Value Partners; Houlihan Lokey; Morgan Stanley
Adam Schimel, Managing Director
Education: BS, Electrical Engineering & Economics, Duke University; MBA, Kellogg School of Management, Northwestern University
Background: Associate, Lindsay Goldberg; Goldman Sachs
Andrew Scotland, Managing Director
Education: Oxford University
Background: Special Situations Group, RBS; Equity Research, ABN AMRO; Citigroup; Credit Suisse

243 BBH CAPITAL PARTNERS
140 Broadway
New York, NY 10005-1101

Phone: 212-483-1818
web: www.bbh.com

Mission Statement: Provides highly customized, one-stop junior capital solutions to lower middle market companies.
Geographic Preference: United States
Fund Size: $2 billion
Founded: 1989
Average Investment: $20 to $50 million
Minimum Investment: $20 million
Investment Criteria: Leveraged Buyouts, Growth Initiatives, Recapitalizations, Balance Sheet Refinancings, Ownership Transactions, Generational Transfers, Buy & Build Strategies, Acquisitions
Industry Group Preference: Business Products & Services, Distribution, Healthcare, Niche Manufacturing, Communications, Consumer Products, Consumer Services
Portfolio Companies: Americam Physician Partners, Best Doctors, EdgeConneX, Haven Behavioral Healthcare, Heniff Transporation Systems, KabaFusion Holdings, Microban International, PrimeRevenue, Utility Pipeline, Vyve Broadband
Other Locations:
Brown Brothers Harriman Business Services Co.
Unit 2002-04, 20/F, Tower 2, China World Trade Center
No. 1 Jianguomenwai Avenue, Chaoyang District
Beijing 100004
China
Phone: 86-10-5783-2300

Brown Brothers Harriman Trust Company, N.A.
50 Post Office Square
Boston, MA 02110-1548
Phone: 617-772-1818

Brown Brothers Harriman Trust Company, N.A.
227 West Trade Street
Suite 2100
Charlotte, NC 28202-1675
Phone: 704-370-0500

Brown Brothers Harriman Trust Company, N.A.
77 W Wacker Drive
Suite 2700
Chicago, IL 60601
Phone: 312-781-7111

Fund Administration Services Limited
Trustee Services Limited
30 Herbert Street

Venture Capital & Private Equity Firms / Domestic Firms

Dublin 2
Ireland
Phone: 353-1-603-6200

Brown Brothers Harriman Trust Company Limited
18 Forum Lane
Camana Bay
Grand Cayman KY1-1106
Cayman Islands
Phone: 354-945-2719

Brown Brothers Harriman Limited
13/F Man Yee Building
68 Des Voeux Road Central
Hong Kong
China

185 Hudson Street
Suite 1150
Jersey City, NJ 07311-4003
Phone: 201-418-5600

Brown Brothers Harriman Sp. z o.o.
Orange Office Park
ul. Klimeckiego 1
Krakow 30-705
Poland
Phone: 48-12-340-6000

Brown Brothers Harriman Investor Services Ltd
Park House
16-18 Finsbury Circus
London EC2M 7EB
United Kingdom
Phone: 44-207-588-6166

Brown Brothers Harriman S.C.A.
80, Route D'Esch
Luxembourg L-1470
Luxembourg
Phone: 352-47-4066-1

3100 West End Avenue
Suite 450
Nashville, TN 37203
Phone: 615-279-8880

BBH Trust Company of Delaware, N.A.
1 Logan Square
14th Floor
Philadelphia, PA 19103-6908
Phone: 215-864-1818

Toranomon Kotohira Tower 15F
1-2-8- Toranomon
Minato-Ku
Tokyo 105-0001
Japan
Phone: 81-3-6361-6500

BBH Trust Company of Delaware, N.A.
Delle Donne Corporate Center
1013 Centre Rd, Suite 101
Wilmington, DE 19805
Phone: 302-552-4040

Brown Brothers Harriman Services AG
Talstresse 83
Zurich 8001
Switzerland
Phone: 41-44-227-1818

Key Executives:
Jeffrey A. Schoenfeld, Partner/Institutional Business Development & Relationship Mgmt
Education: BA, Economics, University of California, Berkeley; MBA, Wharton School
Daniel J. Greifenkamp, Managing Director/Head of Funds/CEO of BBH Investments
Education: BBA, Carroll University; MBA, University of Chicago
Background: Director of Business Development, Abbey Capital; Partner, Artisan Partners LP

Jean-Pierre Paquin, Partner/Head, Investment Management
212-493-8413
e-mail: jp.paquin@bbh.com
Education: Colgate University; MBA, Wharton School
Directorships: Tower Ventures, KabaFusion Holdings, Vyve Broadband
Anita K. Kerr, Managing Director/COO
Education: BA, Spanish, New York University
Background: Managing Director & Global Head of Regulatory Reform, Goldman Sachs Asset Management

244 BCM TECHNOLOGIES
2 Greenway Plaza
Suite 910
Houston, TX 77046
Phone: 713-795-0105 **Fax:** 713-795-4602

Mission Statement: An early stage venture capital firm formed by Baylor College of Medicine with a 20-year investment history in the Houston area.

Geographic Preference: Southwest
Fund Size: $20 million
Founded: 1983
Average Investment: $1 million
Minimum Investment: $500,000
Investment Criteria: Seed, Early Stage
Industry Group Preference: Biotechnology, Information Technology, Medical Devices, Life Sciences
Portfolio Companies: Diversigen, HGHI, Kardia Therapeutics, Kryptiq Corporation, Molecular Logix, Opexa Therapeutics, Progression Therapeutics, Relievant MedSystems, StepStoneMed, Synced Care

Key Executives:
Caroline Popper MD MPH, President
Education: MPH, Johns Hopkins University; MD, University of the Witwatersrand
Background: Becton Dickinson; Founding General Manager, BDGene; CBO, MDS Proteomics
Cynthia S Sheridan
Education: BBA, Economics, University of Memphis; MBA, Finance & Strategic Planning, University of Texas at Austin
Background: Division VP, GE Capital Consulting; CEO, IBT Technologies; Associate Professor, St. Edward's University
Stephanie Kreml MD
Education: BS, Electrical Engineering, University of Texas at Austin; MD, Baylor College of Medicine
Background: Product Engineer, Texas Instruments; Motorola Semiconductor; Medical Advisor, Televero Health

245 BEDFORD FUNDING
10 New King Street
Suite 104
White Plains, NY 10604
Phone: 914-287-4880
e-mail: info@bedfordfunding.com
web: www.bedfordfunding.com

Mission Statement: Bedford Funding is a private equity firm focused on software and IT services in the human capital management and healthcare IT sectors.

Geographic Preference: Worldwide
Founded: 2006
Industry Group Preference: IT Services, Healthcare IT
Portfolio Companies: MDLive, Voalte, KZO Innovations, Socialtext, Strategia, Aquire, Peopleclick, Authoria

Key Executives:
Charles S. Jones, Managing Partner and Founder
Background: President & CEO, Geac Computer Corporation

Larry Kaplan, Managing Director and Chief Financial Officer
Education: BS, Mathematics, SUNY Stony Brook; MBA, Carnegie Mellon University
Background: SVP, Geac; CFO, Healthology; Shandwick International

Jonathan D. Salon, Managing Director and General Counsel
Education: BA, Colgate University; JD, Boston University School of Law
Background: VP & General Counsel, Unica Corporation

246 BEE PARTNERS
50 Osgood Place
Suite 220A
San Francisco, CA 94133

e-mail: hello@beepartners.vc
web: www.beepartners.vc

Mission Statement: Bee Partners, a genesis-stage venture firm, pollinates visionary entrepreneurs with financial, human and social capital. The firm actively supports teams with customer development, marketing strategy, financing strategy and more.

Geographic Preference: United States
Founded: 2008
Average Investment: $200,000 - $400,000
Industry Group Preference: Business to Business
Portfolio Companies: TubeMogul, Indiegogo, Tradesy, Skycatch, Embroker, Magoosh, Parsec, LeadGenius, OrderGroove, Zipongo, BuildingConnected, StatMuse, Node.io, Vacatia, RBC Signals, Neighborly, Xola, AxleHire, SnapTravel, Identify3D, LocalWise, Voltaiq, Florence Healthcare, Capio, Iris Automation, VentureScanner, Airbanq, Sideqik, tbh, Zeus, Breezy, Preact, Modify Watches, Columbia Green, Pudget, FiveRun, Earbits, Bear Naked, Evol Foods, Phonio, Enliken, Pencil, Enthuse, Illumobile

Key Executives:
Michael Berolzheimer, Founder/Managing Partner
Education: BS, Economics & Computer Science, Vanderbilt University
Background: DLJ/Credit Suisse, Harvest Partners

247 BEECKEN PETTY O'KEEFE & COMPANY
131 S Dearborn Street
Suite 2800
Chicago, IL 60603

Phone: 312-435-0300 Fax: 312-435-0371
e-mail: partners@bpoc.com
web: www.bpoc.com

Mission Statement: Beecken Petty O'Keefe & Company (BPOC) is a private equity firm based in Chicago. The firm focuses exclusively on middle-market companies in the healthcare industry.

Geographic Preference: United States
Fund Size: Fund III: $400 million; Fund IV: $500 million
Founded: 1996
Average Investment: $7 million
Minimum Investment: $1.5 million
Investment Criteria: Middle-Market Buyout Transactions, Recapitalizations, Growth Platforms
Industry Group Preference: Healthcare, Medical Devices, Medical & Health Related
Portfolio Companies: Absolute Dental, ClareMedica Health Partners, Cranial Technologies, D4C Dental Brands, EMSI, Health-E Commerce, himagine Solutions, Maxor, Medicus Healthcare Solutions, MPE, Spectrum Professional Services, Zenith American Solutions

Key Executives:
David Beecken, Founder
Education: University of the South; MBA, Finance, University of Chicago; MS, Economics, London School of Economics
Background: Investment Banker, First National Bank of Chicago; Managing Director, Smith Barney
Directorships: AbilityOne, Corizon, D4C Dental Brands Holdings, DentalCare Partners, Heartland Information Systems, ISG Holdings, Paragon Medical, Sirona Dental Systems

Kenneth O'Keefe, Founder
Education: BA, Economics, Northwestern University; MBA, Finance, University of Chicago
Background: Managing Director, First National Bank Chicago; Corporate Finance, Smith Barney
Directorships: Corizon, Himagine Solutions, Jazz Pharmaceuticals, Origin Healthcare Solutions, PerfectServe, Same Day Surgery, Team Health

Gregory Moerschel, Managing Partner
Education: BA, Economics, Northwestern University; MBA, Finance & Health Services Administration, Kellogg Graduate School of Management
Background: VP/Sr Healthcare Analyst, ABN AMRO; Healthcare Investment Banking Group, The First National Bank of Chicago
Directorships: EMSI, Genezen Healthcare, Genoa Healthcare, Hospital Physician Partners, The Hygenic Corporation, Maxor, Medical Solutions, NetRegulus, NeuroSource, Preferred Homecare

David J Cooney, Managing Director
Education: BS, History, University of Illinois; MPP, International Finance, Georgetown University
Background: Corporate Finance, Smith Barney; Analyst, Overseas Private Investment Corporation
Directorships: ISG Holdings, Paragon Medical, Reichert, The MED Group

John Kneen, Partner, CFO/COO
Education: College of Wooster; MBA, Accounting & Finance, Kellogg Graduate School of Management
Background: Acquisitions & Corporate Development, Evergreen Healthcare; CFO, Alterra Healthcare; Healthcare Financial Consulting, Coopers & Lybrand

William Petty Jr, Founder
Education: BS, Business, University of Illinois
Background: Co-Founder, Omega Capital Ltd.; Evergreen Healthcare; Forum Group; Alterra Healthcare
Directorships: Sunrise Assisted Living, Omega Healthcare Investors, Forum Group, Axentis, Complient, DentalCare Partners, Genezen Healthcare, Take Care Health Systems

Thomas A Schlesinger, Managing Director
Education: BA, Economics, Rutgers University; MBA, Finance, University of Chicago
Background: Healthcare Investment Banker, ABN AMRO
Directorships: AbilityOne Corporation, DentalCare Partners Inc., Heartland Information Services, PerfectServe Inc., Scrip Holdings Corporation

Timothy D Sheehan, Managing Director
Education: BA, University of Virginia
Background: Director, Madison Dearborn Partners; Investment Banking Group, Solomon Brothers
Directorships: Hospital Physicians Partners, Path Lab Holdings, Sirona Dental Systems, Team Health Holdings, VWR International

Peter N Magas, Managing Director
Education: BS, Miami University (Ohio); MBA, Kellogg Graduate School of Management, Northwestern University
Background: Director, Healthcare Finance Group, CapitalSource Finance; GE Healthcare; Heller Healthcare Finance
Directorships: Hospital Physician Partners, Paragon Medical, Medical Solutions

Grant A Patrick, Managing Director
Education: BBA, Finance & Management, Emory University; MBA, Finance & Economics, University of Chicago Graduate School of Business
Background: Associate, BlueStar Ventures; Investment Banking, ABN AMRO

Venture Capital & Private Equity Firms / Domestic Firms

Directorships: Himagine Solutions, Origin Healthcare Solutions, Sunrise Assisted Living
M Troy Phillips, Managing Director
Education: BS, Finance & Computer Applications, University of Notre Dame; MBA, Harvard Business School; CFA
Background: Vice President, Edgewater Growth Capital Partners; Triple Tree Capital; Associate, Frontenac Company
Directorships: Corizon, EMSI, Genoa Healthcare, Maxor, Preferred Homecare, RSA Medical
Julian L Carr, Operating Partner
Education: BS, Economics, University of Tulsa; MBA, Indiana University
Background: Chairman & CEO, Valitas Health Services; Executive VP, Aramark Corporation
Directorships: Corizon, DentalCare Partners, Himagine Solutions, Living Centers of America, The MED Group, Medcor Holdings, Sanford-Brown, TIDI Products, VHA
Scott R Kabbes, Operating Partner
Background: Founder & CEO, EagleSoft; President, Professionals' Software Company
Directorships: Heartland Dental Care, Preferred Homecare, Scrip Product Corporation, TIDI Products

248 BEHRMAN CAPITAL
126 East 56th Street
27th Floor
New York, NY 10022

Phone: 212-980-6500 Fax: 212-980-7024
web: www.behrmancap.com

Mission Statement: Private equity investment firm invests in middle-market buyouts of growth companies.
Fund Size: $3 billion
Founded: 1991
Average Investment: $25 - $100 million
Minimum Investment: $2 million
Investment Criteria: All Stages, Management Buyouts, LBO, Recapitalizations
Industry Group Preference: Defense & Aerospace, Healthcare Services, Specialty Manufacturing & Distribution
Portfolio Companies: Ark Holding Company, Athena Diagnostics, Atherotech Diagnostics, Brooks Equipment Company, Condor Systems, Corfin Industries LLC, Emmes Corporation, Esoterix Inc., Executive Greetings Inc., Hunter Defence Technologies, ILC Dover, KSARIA, Nimbus CD International Inc., Peacock Engineering Company, Pelican Products, Plastics Industries Inc., Selig Sealing Products, Tandem Health Care, Tresys Technology, Waterline Renewal Technologies, WIL Research Laboratories

Key Executives:
Grant Behrman, Managing Partner
Education: MBA Marketing/General Management, Wharton School; University of Witwatersrand
Background: Fouding Member, Morgan Stanley Venture Capital Group; Consultant, Boston Consulting Group
Directorships: Esoterix, The Management Network Group, Brooks Equipment
Simon Lonergan, Managing Partner
Education: BA, University of Cambridge; MBA, Harvard Business School
Background: Partner & Senior Managing Director, The Blackstone Group
Directorships: Selig Sealing Products, Data Device Corppration
Mark Visser, Partner
Education: BS, Engineering, Physics, Rensselaer Polytechnic Institute
Background: Investment Banking Group, Merrill Lynch
Directorships: Ark Holding Company, Peacock Engineering Company

249 BEN FRANKLIN TECHNOLOGY PARTNERS
4801 S Broad Street
Suite 200
Building 100 Innovation Center
Philadelphia, PA 19112

Phone: 215-972-6700 Fax: 215-972-5588
e-mail: info@sep.benfranklin.org
web: www.sep.benfranklin.org

Mission Statement: Ben Franklin Technology Partners of Southeastern Pennsylvania provides technology entrepreneurs and established businesses with the capital, knowledge and networks they need to compete in the global marketplace.
Geographic Preference: Southeastern Pennsylvania
Founded: 1982
Average Investment: $200,000
Minimum Investment: $50,000
Investment Criteria: Seed, Early Stage, Growth Capital
Industry Group Preference: Technology
Portfolio Companies: Monetate, Health Market Science, Boomi, Brad's Raw Foods, Morphotek, Neat

Key Executives:
RoseAnn B. Rosenthal, CEO Emeritus
e-mail: roseann@sep.benfranklin.org
Education: BA, Temple University; Honorary PhD, Humane Letters, Philadelphia University
Background: Executive Director, Philadelphia Industrial Development Corp; Associate Director, Landing Corp; Executive Director, Children's Village
Directorships: Digital Delaware
Scott Nissenbaum, President/CEO
e-mail: scott@sep.benfranklin.org
Education: BS, Pennsylvania State University; MBA, Saint Joe's University
Anthony P. Green, PhD, Vice President, Science & Technology
215-972-6700
e-mail: anthony@sep.benfranklin.org
Education: BSc, Immunology, Brown University; PhD, Microbiology & Immunology, Temple University School of Medicine

250 BENAROYA COMPANIES
3600 136th Place SE
Suite 250
Bellevue, WA 98006

Phone: 425-440-6700 Fax: 425-440-6730
e-mail: larryb@benaroya.com

Mission Statement: Invest in high growth opportunities with strong management and developed technology.
Geographic Preference: Pacific North
Founded: 1995
Average Investment: $4 million
Minimum Investment: $500,000
Investment Criteria: Equity, Equity-Bridge Financings in Post Seed Stage Growth
Industry Group Preference: Telecommunications, Infrastructure, Manufacturing, Consumer Services, Data Communications
Portfolio Companies: Audiosocket, Avalara, Avail-TVN, Calico Energy Services, Capital Stream, Coinstar, CommQuest, DNA Response, Open Interface, Peapod, Prepared Response, Swype, Starbucks, Sparkbuy, Tegic

Key Executives:
Larry Benaroya, Manager
425-440-6704
e-mail: larryb@benaroya.com
Education: University of Pennsylvania

Venture Capital & Private Equity Firms / Domestic Firms

251 BENCHMARK
140 New Montgomery Street
San Francisco, CA 94105

web: www.benchmark.com

Mission Statement: Venture capital firm behind a number of successful startups. Noted for its compensation structure in which partners share profits equally.

Founded: 1995
Investment Criteria: Early-Stage
Industry Group Preference: Mobile, Cloud Computing, Social Media
Portfolio Companies: 1stdibs, Amplitude, Asana, Confluent, Couchsurfing, Docker, Dropbox, eBay, elastic, Glassdoor, Good Eggs, Grubhub, HackerOne, Hortonworks, Instagram, Lithium Technologies, Minted, New Relic, One Medical, OpenTable, Optimizely, Potbelly, Proofpoint, ResearchGate, Sailthru, Silver Peak, Snapchat, Software Integrity, Tinder, Twitter, Uber, Upwork, WeWork, Wix.com, Zendesk, ZipCar, Zuora

Other Locations:
2965 Woodside Road
Woodside, CA 94062

Key Executives:
Peter Fenton, General Partner
Education: BA, Philosophy, MBA, Stanford University
Background: Managing Partner, Accel Partners
Directorships: Buoyant, Docker, Cockroach Labs, Elasticsearch, Hortonworks, Minted, New Relic, Optimizely, Revinate, TimescaleDB, Yelp, Zuora
Matt Cohler, General Partner
Education: BA, Yale Universty
Background: VP & Special Advisor, Facebook; VP & General Manager, LinkedIn; Consultant, McKinsey & Company
Directorships: Tinder, Duo Security, Edmodo, 1stdibs, Domo, ResearchGate, Quora, Asana, Instagram
Mitch Lasky, General Partner
Education: Harvard College; University of Virginia
Background: Irell & Manella; Walt Disney Company; Serum Entertainment Software; Activision; JAMDAT
Directorships: Snapchat; Riot Games; Hammer & Chisel; Outpost Games; thatgamecompany; PlayFab; Manticore Games; Cyngn
Eric Vishria, General Partner
Education: Stanford University
Background: Rockmelt; Yahoo
Directorships: Benchling, Blue Hexagon, Contentful, Cerebras Systems, Bugsnag, Amplitude Analytics, Confluent

252 BENHAMOU GLOBAL VENTURES
540 Cowper Street
Suite 200
Palo Alto, CA 94301

Phone: 650-324-3680 Fax: 650-473-1347
web: www.benhamouglobalventures.com

Mission Statement: Early-stage venture capital firm focused on enterprise information technology with a particular emphasis on mobility, cloud architectures and technologies, and cyber security.

Geographic Preference: Silicon Valley
Investment Criteria: Early-Stage
Industry Group Preference: Cloud Infrastructure, Business Software, SaaS, Networking, Communications, Enterprise Mobility, Cyber Security
Portfolio Companies: 4IQ, 3com, 6d, Atricia, Ayehu, Bayshore, Blue Cedar, Carfit, Connected Signals, Contextream, Cyberinc, Dasient, DialOnce, Drishti, EcoPlant, Finjan, Flytrex, GoNetworks, Grid Dynamics, Identity Mind, IntelliVision, Kaptivo, Load Dynamix, Macrometa, MyTopia, NGD Systems, OneMob, Onymos, Palm, Platform.sh, Profitect, Qubell, Ripples, Scalefast, Secret Double Octopus, Spikes Security, SwanLabs, Tagnos, Tilera, Totango, Virtual Instruments, Voltaire, Webscale, Zentri

Key Executives:
Eric Benhamou, Founder/General Partner
e-mail: eric@benhamouglobalventures.com
Education: MS, Stanford University School of Engineering
Background: CEO, 3Com
Directorships: Swan Labs, Dasient, Voltaire, Finjan, Contextream, Load Dynamix, Grid Dynamics, Ayehu, Totango, Secret Double Octopus, 6d
Anik Bose, General Partner
e-mail: anik@benhamouglobalventures.com
Education: BA, Economics, University of Delhi; MBA, Boston College
Background: H3C; Partner, Deloitte Management Consulting
Directorships: Cyberinc, WebScale, Blue Cedar Networks
Eric Buatois, General Partner
e-mail: buatois@benhamouglobalventures.com
Education: MSc, Computer Science, Ecole Nationale Suprieure des Telecommunications; INSEAD
Background: General Partner, Sofinnova Ventures; Texas Instruments, Hewlett-Packard, Ericsson

253 BERGGRUEN HOLDINGS
304 S Broadway
Suite 550
Los Angeles, CA 90013

Phone: 213-430-2350
e-mail: pipeline@berggruenholdings.com
web: www.berggruenholdings.com

Mission Statement: Investment arm of the Nicholas Berggruen Charitable Trust.

Geographic Preference: Worldwide
Fund Size: $2 billion
Industry Group Preference: Real Estate, Alternative Energy, Financial Services
Portfolio Companies: Berggruen Car Rentals, Bonded Kayit Sistemleri AS, Equipwell, Gemini Equipment & Rents, Global Supply Chain Finance, International Education Corporation, NBP Capital LLC, Oreko Metal Mining, Transport Labor Holding Company, UEI Global

Key Executives:
Nicolas Berggruen, Investment Advisor
Education: BS, Finance, New York University
Background: Jacobson & Co.
Koonal Gandhi, Chief Investment Officer
Justin Topilow, Chief Financial Officer
Education: BA, Yale Univ.; MBA, NYU Stern School of Business
Samuel Czarny, Managing Director, Germany
e-mail: sc@berggruenholdings.com
Background: Hamburgische Immobilien Handlung GmbH
Mehmet Kosematoglu, Managing Director, Turkey
e-mail: mk@berggruenholdings.com
Education: BSc, Cornell University; MA, Public Administration, Harvard University
Background: CEO, AIG Blue Voyage Advisors
Kabir Kewalramani, Managing Director, India
e-mail: kk@berggruenholdings.com
Background: CEO, RDC Concrete India; Crosby Capital Partners; JP Morgan Partners

254 BERINGEA
32330 W 12 Mile Road
Farmington Hills, MI 48334

Phone: 248-489-9000
e-mail: info@beringea.com
web: www.beringea.com

Mission Statement: Beringea is a private equity firm that invests in and nurtures companies across a wide range of growth

Venture Capital & Private Equity Firms / Domestic Firms

industries, including life sciences, healthcare, Internet technology, manufacturing, clean technology and media. Beringea, which has offices in Detroit and London, offers capital, experience and expertise to entrepreneurs and utilizes these resources to create value for portfolio companies.

Geographic Preference: United States
Fund Size: $65 million
Founded: 1988
Average Investment: $2 - $10 million
Minimum Investment: $1 million
Investment Criteria: Expansion, Small Buyout, Later Stage
Industry Group Preference: Healthcare, Manufacturing, Media, Food Services, Retailing, Entertainment, Clean Technology, Information Technology
Portfolio Companies: Arrive, Avid Ratings, Blis, Brideside, Complion, D30, Delphinus, DIME, dscout, Fiber By-Products, Floyd, Freeosk, Gas Station TV, Hygenica, InContext Solutions, Intervention Insights, InTouch Health, Popular Pays, Sharecare, UICO, Xanitos

Other Locations:
39 Earlham Street
Covent Garden
London WC2H 9LT
United Kingdom
Phone: 44-02078457820

WeWork
1 St Peter's Square
Manchester M2 3DE
United Kingdom
Phone: 44-01615048500

Key Executives:
Charlie Rothstein, Founder/Senior Managing Director
Education: BBA, MBA, University of Michigan
Background: VP, Corporate Finance, JW Korth; European Gateway Acquisition Corp.
Directorships: Mophie, Detroit Institute of Music Education, Sakti3
Malcolm Moss, Founding Partner
Education: BA, MBA, Business Studies, Kingston Buiness School, Kingston University
Background: Planning Head, Baxter International/Uniroyal; Sr Strategist, Lloyds/TSB Group
Directorships: ProVen VCT, Income VCT
Michael Gross, Managing Director
Education: BA, Finance, Michigan State University; CFA
Background: VP, Investment Banking, P&M Corporate Finance; Stout Risius Ross
Directorships: Molecular Imaging, D3O, Delphinus Medical Technologies, InTouch Health, Intervention Insights, Xanitos, Freeosk, Rethink, Fiber By-Products
Harry Thomas, Principal
Education: MA, History, University of St Andrews
William Blake III, Vice President
Education: BA, Finance, Stephen M. Ross School of Business, University Of Michigan
Background: P&M Corporate Finance
Directorships: Brideside, Complion, Avid Ratings, Fiber By-Products
Stuart Veale, Managing Partner
Background: Senior Director, Lloyds Development Capital; 3i plc
Directorships: Contact Engine, DeepCrawl, Exonar, Firefly Learning, InSkin Media, ResponseTap

255 BERKELEY VC INTERNATIONAL LLC
PO Box 591748
San Francisco, CA 94159-1748

Phone: 415-249-0450
e-mail: info@berkeleyvc.com
web: www.berkeleyvc.com

Mission Statement: Berkeley VC International LLC is a venture capital firm that makes private placement investments into growing technology companies. The firm's investments typically serve as development capital for later-stage companies which are close to conducting alpha testing on their launch products.

Fund Size: $1 billion
Founded: 1977
Average Investment: $5 million - $50 million
Minimum Investment: $1 million
Investment Criteria: Second-stage, Late Stage
Industry Group Preference: Communications, Computer Related, Consumer Services, Distribution, Electronic Components, Industrial Equipment, Medical & Health Related
Portfolio Companies: Agility Communications Inc., Alacritech Inc., BeamReach Networks, BRECIS Communications Corporation, Catena Networks, Ceon Corporation, Fastchip Inc., KnowledgeNet Inc., LightChip Inc., LongBoard Inc., Mahi Networks Inc., Telera Inc., Triscend Corporation, Westwave Communications Inc., Xtera Communications

Key Executives:
Arthur Trueger, Founder/Chairman
Education: AB, MA, JD, University of California

256 BERKELEY VENTURES
727 Allston Way
Suite C
Berkeley, CA 94710

web: www.berkeleyventures.com

Mission Statement: Berkeley Ventures is an accelerator which helps serious entrepreneurs bring their innovations to the world. The firm is focused on helping startups in sectors including, but not limited to, internet, software, mobile, clean energy, and gaming. The firm offers access to mentors and advisors, introductions to investors, incubator space, connections to local talent/resources, and a year round program to help these companies grow.

Geographic Preference: California
Founded: 2009
Investment Criteria: All Stages
Industry Group Preference: Internet, Software, Mobile, Clean Energy, Gaming
Portfolio Companies: Blaze Mobile, BuySquare, CodeEval, FI Info Net, Power2Switch, Proxpur Labs, Virtual Labs, WAPIS

Key Executives:
Chris Doner, Founder/Executive Director
Background: Founder & CEO, Access Softek
Barak Berkowitz, Advisor
Background: Chairman/CEO, Six Apart; Apple; Logitech; Infoseek; Co-Founder, Omnisky
Jeff Braun, Advisor
Background: Founder & CEO, Maxis; SVP, North American Studios, Electronic Arts
Dean Frost, Advisor
Education: BA, University of California, Berkeley; MBA, Harvard Business School
Background: CEO, StockPower; Founder, Frost Capital Partners
Jonathan Morgan, Advisor
Background: Founder/Managing Partner, Rostrevor Partners; CEO, FirstVirtual Communications; Managing Director, Prudential Volpe Technology; Managing Director/Head of Investment Banking Operations, Sutro & Co.; M&A, Montgomery Securities
Rick Moss, Advisor
Education: Trinity College; MBA, Amos Tuck School, Dartmouth College
Background: Sun Microsystems; Oracle; Computer Sciences Corp.; Investment Banker, Salomon Brothers
Anthony Patek, Advisor
Education: BS, Philosophy & Biochemistry, University of Michigan; MS, Chemistry, Stanford University; JD, Boalt

School of Law
Background: Cooley Godward
Joel Serface, Advisor
Education: BS, Chemical & Environmental Engineering, University of Texas, Austin; MBA, MIT Sloan School of Management
Background: Entrepreneur in Residence, Kleiner Perkins

257 BERKSHIRE PARTNERS LLC
200 Clarendon Street
35th Floor
Boston, MA 02116

Phone: 617-227-0050
e-mail: investorrelations@berkshirepartners.com
web: www.berkshirepartners.com

Mission Statement: Private equity firm that strives to partner with management teams to increase the value of their businesses.
Geographic Preference: United States, Canada, Western Europe, Australia
Fund Size: $16 billion
Founded: 1986
Average Investment: $50 - $250 million
Minimum Investment: $20 million
Investment Criteria: LBO, Recapitalizations, Minority Investments, Privatizations Industry consolidations
Industry Group Preference: Consumer Products, Retailing, Business Products & Services, Transportation, Energy, Manufacturing, Communications
Portfolio Companies: Accela, Access, Advanced Drainage Systems, Affordable Care, Asurion, Consolidated Precision Products Corp., Curriculum Associations, Implus, Kendra Scott, Masergy, Parts Town, Portillo's, Precision Medicine Group, Protelindo, SRS Distribution, Teraco Data Environments, TransDigm, U.S. Anesthesia Partners, Vapor IO, Vi-Jon

Key Executives:

Samantha A. Adams, Managing Director
Education: AB, Harvard College; MBA, Harvard Business School
Background: SVP, Enterprise Brand Straegy, Bank of America; Hill Holliday Advertising; Discovery Health Channel; Bain & Co.

David C. Bordeau, Managing Director
Education: AB, Princeton University; MBA, Harvard Business School
Background: Ripplewood Holdings; Gleacher Partners
Directorships: Implus; SRS Distribution

Kenneth S. Bring, Managing Director & Chief Financial Officer
Education: BS, Duke University; M.Acc., University of North Carolina
Background: PrincewaterhouseCoopers

Kevin T. Callaghan, Managing Director
Education: BSE, Princeton University; MBA, Stanford Grad. School of Business
Background: Lehman Brothers
Directorships: Implus; Kendra Scott; Parts Town

Blake L. Gottesman, Managing Director
Education: MBA, Harvard Business School
Background: Deputy Chief of Staff at the White House; Special Assistant and Personal Aide to former U.S. President George W. Bush
Directorships: Consolidated Precision Products Corp.; Portillo's; Protelindo; Curriculum Associates; Vi-Jon

Christopher J. Hadley, Managing Director
Education: BS, University of Wisconsin; MBA, Wharton School, University of Pennsylvania
Background: Bain & Co.; Trustee, Dana-Farber Cancer Institute

Lawrence S. Hamelsky, Managing Director
Education: AB, Duke University; MBA, Harvard Business School
Background: Boston Consulting Group; Financial Analyst, Bowles, Hollowell, Conner & Co.
Directorships: Parts Town; Teraco Data Environment

Shar Heslam, Managing Director & General Counsel
Education: BA, Cornell University; JD, Harvard Law School
Background: Weil, Gotshal & Manges LLP
Directorships: Vi-Jon

Beth Hoffman, Managing Director
Education: BA, Macalester College; MBA, Kellogg School of Management, Northwestern University
Background: Sprout Group; Morgan Stanley
Directorships: Masergy; Protelindo; Vapor IO

Matthew A. Janchar, Managing Director
Education: BBA, University of Notre Dame
Background: Oak Hill Advisors; Goldman Sachs

Ross M. Jones, Managing Director
Education: BA, Dartmouth College; MBA, Stanford Grad. School of Business
Background: Bain & Co.
Directorships: Access; Advanced Drainage Systems; Asurion

Joshua A. Lutzker, Managing Director
Education: AB, Duke University; MBA, Harvard Business School
Background: Bain & Co.
Directorships: Portillo's; SRS Distribution

Greg J. Pappas, Managing Director
Education: BS, Lehigh University; MBA, Harvard Business School
Background: Senior Partner, The Parthenon Group; M&A Advisor, Deloitte
Directorships: Accela; U.S. Anesthesia Partners; Implus; SRS Distribution

Marni F. Payne, Managing Director
Education: BA, Dartmouth College; MBA, Harvard Business School
Background: McKinsey & Co.
Directorships: Kendra Scott

Raleigh A. Shoemaker, Jr., Managing Director
Education: AB, Duke University; MBA, Harvard Business School
Background: Sterling Capital Management; Audax Group; Bain & Co.; Bowels, Hollowellm Conner & Co.

Robert J. Small, Managing Director
Education: BA, Yale University; MBA, Harvard Business School
Background: Bain & Co.
Directorships: TransDigm; Active Aero Group; AmSafe; Citizens of Humanity; Cypress; Electro-Motive Diesel; Gordon Brothers; Hexcel; Party City; Skillsoft; Tranz Rail; WordWave

Samuel W. Spirn, Managing Director
Education: AB, Harvard College; MBA, Harvard Business School
Background: Summit Partners
Directorships: U.S. Anesthesia Partners; Parts Town; Farm Boy; Grocery Outlet; Mattress Firm; Tower Development Corporation

Edward J. Whelan, Managing Director
Education: BA, Dartmouth College; MBA, Harvard Business School
Background: Sterling Auto Boduy Centers; Bain & Co.
Directorships: Accela; Access; Curriculum Associations; AmSafe; Mattress Firm; Melissa & Doug; Party City; Skillsoft

Tim Heston, Partner
Education: BS, Finance, Boston College; MBA, HAAS School of Business
Background: Calera Capital; JP Morgan; Carl Marks & Co.
Directorships: Anord Mardix Group; Perennials and Sutherland

Venture Capital & Private Equity Firms / Domestic Firms

259 BERTELSMANN DIGITAL MEDIA INVESTMENTS
1745 Broadway
20th Floor
New York, NY 10019

e-mail: info@bdmifund.com
web: www.bdmifund.com

Mission Statement: Drawing upon the vast resources of Bertelsmann SE & Co. KGaA, BDMI is a strategic investor that brings a wealth of experience and opportunities to emerging companies. BDMI provides not only capital, but also a worldwide network of diverse businesses. The firm's goal is to partner with companies that can benefit from their innovative spirit and media leadership across the globe. BDMI is a wholly owned subsidiary of Bertelsmann SE & Co. KGaA.

Geographic Preference: Europe, North America, Israel
Fund Size: $180 million
Founded: 2006
Average Investment: $1 - $5 million
Minimum Investment: $500,000
Investment Criteria: Series A & B
Industry Group Preference: Digital Media & Marketing, Virtual Reality & Augmented Reality, Pub Tech, E-Commerce, Gaming, AD Tech
Portfolio Companies: 89, Adspert, Art19, The Athletic, Audible, Boostr, Fatherly, FloSports, Frank & Oak, Inked, Jukin Media, Marfeel, Nativo, Omaze, Pathmatics, Semasio, Skimlinks, Whisbi, Wibbitz, Wondery, ZergNet

Key Executives:

Urs Cete, Managing Partner
Education: Finance Degree, HHL Leipzig Graduate School of Management; MBA, Tulane University
Background: Chief of Staff, Bertelsmann

Keith Titan, Partner
Education: BA, English, University of Michigan; EdM, Harvard University; MBA, Rutgers University
Background: Random House Ventures; Simon & Schuster; Penguin Group; J. Walter Thompson
Directorships: Trion Worlds, Art19

Sim Blaustein, Partner
Education: MBA, MIT Sloan School of Management
Background: High Line Venture Partners; Gabriel Ventures

260 BERTRAM CAPITAL
950 Tower Lane
Suite 1000
Foster City, CA 94404

Phone: 650-358-5000 Fax: 650-358-5001
web: www.bertramcapital.com

Mission Statement: Private equity firm in Northern California targets lower middle market companies.

Fund Size: $1.3 billion
Average Investment: $25-100 million
Investment Criteria: MBO, Liquidity Events
Industry Group Preference: Business Products & Services, Consumer Products, Consumer Services, Industrial, Healthcare, Technology
Portfolio Companies: Anord Mardix, Bearcom, Best Version Media, Clarus Glassboards, CreativeDrive, ECS Tuning, Flow Control Group, Maxcress, PaulaBs Choice, Perennials and Sutherland LLC, Registrar Corp., Rowmark, Solo Stove, Spectrio, Spireon, Trademark Global, TydenBrooks, Author Solutions, Datavail, Extrusion Dies Industries, One Distribution, Power Distribution

Key Executives:

Jeff Drazan, Managing Partner
e-mail: jeff@bertramcapital.com
Education: New York University; MBA, Stern School of Business
Background: Co-Founder/Managing Director, Sierra Ventures
Directorships: Spireon, One Distribution, Sanare, Webex, Paula's Choice

Tom Beerle, Partner
Education: University of California, Berkeley; HAAS School of Business
Background: Opus Capital; Carl Zeiss Vision; Deloitte Consulting; Deloitte Audit
Directorships: ECS Tuning; Registrar; Trademark Global

Ryan Craig, Partner
e-mail: rcraig@bertramcapital.com
Education: BA, Stanford University; MBA, Stanford Graduate School of Business
Background: Health Net

David Hellier, Partner
e-mail: dhellier@bertramcapital.com
Education: BS, Business Administration, MA, Economics, University of Florida
Background: President & CEO, The Gemesis Corporation; Iomega

Jared Ruger, Partner
e-mail: jruger@bertramcapital.com
Education: BA, Princeton University; MBA, Stanford Graduate School of Business
Background: Oak Hill Capital Management; Investment Banking Group, DLJ

Brian Wheeler, Partner, Head of Bertram Labs
e-mail: bwheeler@bertramcapital.com
Education: BA, Chemistry, Pomona College

Kevin Yamashita, Partner
e-mail: kyamashita@bertramcapital.com
Education: BS, UCLA
Background: Calera Capital, Salomon Smith Barney

261 BERWIND CORPORATION
2929 Walnut Street
Suite 900
Philadelphia, PA 19104

Phone: 215-563-2800 Fax: 215-575-2314
e-mail: information@berwind.com
web: www.berwind.com

Mission Statement: Berwind Corporation is a family-owned investment management company that provides financial and operational support to manufacturing and service businesses.

Founded: 1886
Investment Criteria: Acquisitions
Portfolio Companies: Caplugs, Colorcon, CRC Industries Inc., Ecco Safety Group, Maxcess, Oliver Products, Tasi Group

Key Executives:

Charles Lewis, Vice President
e-mail: clewis@berwind.com
Education: BS, Electrical Engineering, MBA, Business, Drexel University
Background: VP, Corporate Development, Exelon

262 BERWIND PRIVATE EQUITY
200 Ayer Rd
Harvard, MA 01451

Phone: 978-391-1244 Fax: 978-391-1255
e-mail: info@berwindprivateequity.com
web: www.berwindprivateequity.com

Mission Statement: Berwind Private Equity is a multi-generational company that identifies investment opportunities for the Berwind family.

Portfolio Companies: Boston Color Graphics, Coolerado, Free Flow Power, MacDougalls' Cape Code Marine Service, PRE Resources, Southwest Nanotechnologies, Tantaline, ThermImage, MacuLogix

263 BESSEMER VENTURE PARTNERS
889 Winslow Street
Suite 500
Redwood City, CA 94063

Phone: 650-853-7000
e-mail: businessplans@bvp.com
web: www.bvp.com

Mission Statement: Invests in and helps build innovative, high-growth companies. Primary focus is investing in companies in the start-up or development phases. Plays an active role in partnering with entrepreneurs to build companies that dominate their sectors. Interested in working with exceptional people and experienced management teams who have a strong business model, growing market, defensible technology and industry leadership position.

Geographic Preference: United States, Israel, India, Brazil, Europe, Emerging Markets
Fund Size: $300 million
Founded: 1970
Average Investment: $4 - $10 million
Minimum Investment: $1 million
Investment Criteria: Seed, First-stage, Second-stage, Mezzanine, Late stage, MBI, MBO, LBO, Expansion
Industry Group Preference: Cloud Computing, Consumer, Cyber Security, Developer Platforms, Financial Services, Healthcare, Industry Software, Infrastructure, Marketplaces, Mobile, Space Technology
Portfolio Companies: 2U, 42 Floors, Abacus, Acceleron Pharma, AccuVein, ACTIV Financial Systems, Adap.Tv, ART, Affymax, Allena Pharmaceuticals, Allscripts, Alnara Pharmaceuticals, Altair Semiconductor, Altiga, American Federal Bank, American Superconductor, Anant Raj, Apperian, Applied Solar Technologies, Aptis, Arris Pharmaceutical, Avalanche Technology, AVEO Pharmaceuticals, Avnera, Axis Network Technology, Babycenter, Berkeley Design Automation, Betterment, BigBasket, BillGuard, Bizo, Bladelogic, Blue Nile, Box, Bright Horizons, Broadsoft, Businessland, BuyerZone, C-Port, Car Wash Partners, Castle Networks, Celcore, CellAccess, Celtel, Cerulean Pharma, ChinaEdu, Chrysalis, Ciena, Circadian, Clearslide, Community First, Compumotor, Convertro, Cornerstone OnDemand, Counterpane Internet Security, CPower, Criteo, CrowdFlower, Cyota, Dashlane, Diapers.com, Dick's Sporting Goods, DocuSign, DSP Group, Eagle, Echelon, eEye Digital Security, EKOS, Element14, Eloqua, Endeca, Enforta, Enzytech, Epic Therapeutics, Epix, eToys.com, Fiverr, Flarion, Flex Pharma, Flycast, FourPhase Systems, Fractyl, Ganesh Housing, Gartner, Gerson Lehrman Group, GetInsured.com, Glint, GMIS, Goal.com, Gracenote, GTS, Habana Labs, Harman International, Health Essentials, HFFC, Horizon Cellular Group, HotJobs.com, Hunch, IAG Research, Icot, IL&FS, Immulogic, Impact HQ, Ibpil, IEX, Individual.com, Insight Squared, Intacct, Intego, Intersil, Intucell, Involver, IPC, Iris, Fort James, K2, Kilkenny, Keynote, Kiran Energy, KnowMe, Kroll Bond Ratings, Kronos, KupiVip.ru, LBMS, Liazon, Life360, LifeLock, LightLogic, LinkedIn, Magnuson Computer Systems, Mainbancorp, Maker, Mashlogic, Maxim, MediAssist, Mellanox Technologies, Metalogix, Metapath, Micro Peripherals, Milo Local Shopping, Mind Body, MSI, Myco Pharma, Nephro Plus, NetAmbit, NetFrame, Netli, Netsmart, Netsys, NewPort Communications, Nominum, Numerax, Obsidian, Ocular Networks, OnLine Exchange, OMGPOP, Omnia, OMSignal, On Technology, OnMobile, OnX, Opta, OGP, OvaScience, Oxagen, Oximetrix, P-Com, Pa Semi, Palogix, Parallels, PTC, Periscope, PerSeptive Biosystems, Piazza, Pillar, Pinnacle Engines, Pinterest, Pirus, Playdom, Polaris Petroleum, Postini, Powertel, Proteon, PSINet, PureNetworks, Qualys, Quantopian, QED, Quidsi, Ravello, Register.com, Reputation.com, Resonext, Retail Solutions, Riddhi Siddhi, Sahara, Sarovar, SciQuest, Selectminds, SendGrid, Shopify, Sirtris, Siteadvisor, Skype, Staples, Twitch, UrbanClap, Verodin, Wandera, Yelp, Zoosk, Zylo

Other Locations:
196 Broadway
2nd Floor
Cambridge, MA 02139
Phone: 617-588-1700 **Fax:** 617-588-1701

285 Madison Avenue
Suite 1401
New York, NY 10017
Phone: 212-653-1900

1865 Palmer Avenue
Suite 104
Larchmont, NY 10538
Phone: 914-833-9100

539 Bryant Street
Suite 301
San Francisco, CA 94107
Phone: 415-800-8982

40 Vittal Mallya Road
3rd Floor
Bangalore 560 001
India
Phone: 91-80-3082-9000 **Fax:** 91-80-3082-9001

Key Executives:
Ed Colloton, Partner
Education: BA, Cornell University; JD, Harvard Law School
Background: COO, JP Morgan Capital; Mergers/Acquisitions Lawyer, Davis Polk & Wardwell; Officer, US Navy
Kent Bennett, Partner
Education: University of Virginia; Harvard Business School
Background: Bain & Co.
Charles Birnbaum, Partner
Education: BA, Northwestern University; MA, University of Pennsylvania; MBA, The Wharton School
Background: Foursquare
Directorships: 2U, August Home, Betterment, Bread Finance, BrightBytes, Eave, Fabric, Kroll Bond Ratings, Main Street Hub, Quantopian, Spruce, United Capital, Yodle, Zopa
David Cowan, Partner
Education: MBA, AB, Computer Science/Mathematics, Harvard University
Background: Co-Founder/Chairman/CFO, VeriSign
Directorships: Rocket Lab, Spire, GetInsured, Smule, Endgame, Claroty, Tile, Iris Automation, Auth0, Zapier
Byron Deeter, Partner
Education: Honors degree Political Economy, University of California, Berkeley
Background: Executive, IBM; Founding President/CEO, Trigo Technologies; TA Associates; McKinsey & Company
Brian Feinstein, Partner
Education: Harvard University
Background: Opera New Media; Blackstone
Alex Ferrara, Partner
Education: University of Pennsylvania; Columbia Business School
Background: Salomon Brothers; Goldman Sachs
Adam Fisher, Partner
Education: BSFS, International Economics, Georgetown University School of Foreign Service
Background: General Partner, Jerusalem Venture Partners
Directorships: Cloudinary, CTERA, Dynamic Yield, Fiverr, Habana Labs, HiBob, MyHeritage, Oryx, Prospera, ScyllaDB, Stratoscale, SiSense, Vayyer, Wandera, YotPo
Bob Goodman, Partner
Education: BA, Brown University; MBA, Columbia University
Background: Founder & CEO, Celcore; Founder & Celcore, Boatphone
Directorships: Affirmed Networks, Anaqua, Blue Apron,

Capsule8, Disco, Fuze, Light, MealPal, Qwilt, Sedona Systems, Sisense, Smashfly, Vayyar
Vishal Gupta, Managing Director, BVP India
Education: BA, Commerce, GS College; MBA, Indian Institute of Management
Background: Senior Manager, Reliance Group
Directorships: Anunta Technologies, Applied Solar Technologies, Bigbasket, Home First Finance, Hungama, Innoviti, LivSpace, MediAssist, NephroPlus, Perifos, Pharmeasy, Swiggy, Urbanclap
Felda Hardymon, Partner
Education: BS, Rose Polytechnic; MA and PhD, Duke University; MBA, Harvard
Background: Investor, Ungermann-Bass, Stratus Computer and Western Digital; Taught and served as Director Systems/Research, Duke University
Amit Karp, Partner
Education: BS, Technion; MBA, MIT Sloan School of Management
Background: Senior Associate, McKinsey & Company; Product Leader, Mercado
Directorships: Dynamic Yield, HiBob, Oryx Vision, otonomo, Prospera, ScyllaDB
Stephen Kraus, Partner
Education: BA, Yale University; MBA, Harvard Business School
Background: Director, Ironwood Equity Fund
Directorships: Alcresta, Bright Health, Collective Medical Technologies, Docent Health, Health Essentials, Groups, Qventus, Welltok
Rob Stavis, Partner
Education: Engineering School of University of Pennsylvania; Wharton School
Background: Co-Head, Global Arbitrage Trading, Salomon Smith Barney
Directorships: 2U, Betterment, BrightBytes, Knewton, Gerson Lehrman Group, Main Street Hubs, United Capital Financial Partners, Yodle
Ethan Kurzweil, Partner
Education: Stanford University; Harvard Business School
Background: Dow Jones & Co.
Jeremy Levine, Partner
Education: Duke University
Background: McKinsey & Co.; AEA Investors; Dash

264 BEVERAGE MARKETING CORPORATION
143 Canton Road
2nd Floor
Wintersville, OH 43953

Phone: 212-688-7640 Fax: 740-314-8639
e-mail: advisors@beveragemarketing.com
web: www.beveragemarketing.com

Mission Statement: BMC Advisors provides advisory services to middle-market beverage companies around the world. BMC Advisors specializes in a number of areas, including equity funding and asset sales and acquisitions.
Geographic Preference: United States, Latin America, Europe, Asia
Founded: 1972
Investment Criteria: Middle Market
Industry Group Preference: Beverages
Key Executives:
 Michael C Bellas, Chairman/Chief Executive Officer
 Education: Yale University; JD, University of Michigan; MBA, Columbia University
 Background: Co-Founder, The Beverage Forum; Staff Consultant & Project Manager, Cresap McCormick & Paget

265 BEZOS EXPEDITIONS
e-mail: info@bezosexpeditions.com
web: www.bezosexpeditions.com

Mission Statement: Manages Jeff Bezos' personal venture capital investments.
Investment Criteria: Seed, Early Stage, Late Stage
Industry Group Preference: Biotechnology, Clean Technology, Business Products & Services, Computers & Peripherals, Consumer Products, Education, Electronics, Financial Services, Food & Beverage, Gaming, Healthcare Services, Industrial, Internet/Web Services, IT Services, Lifestyle & Recreation
Portfolio Companies: 37 Signals, Airbnb, Aviary, Basecamp, Blue Origin, Business Insider, Chacha, Convoy, Denali Therapeutics, Domo, Doxo, D-Wave, Everfi, Fundbox, General Assembly, General Fusion, Glassybaby, Grail, Juno Therapeutics, Linden Lab, Makerbot, Mark43, MFG.com, Nextdoor, Plenty, Pioneer Square Labs, Qliance, Remitly, Rescale, Rethink Robotics, Sapphire Energy, Sonder, Stack Overflow, Twitter, Uber, Vicarious, Workday, ZocDoc

266 BIA DIGITAL PARTNERS LP
14150 Parkeast Circle
Suite 110
Chantilly, VA 20151

Phone: 703-227-9600
e-mail: contactdp@bia.com
web: www.biadigitalpartners.com

Mission Statement: A private equity firm providing flexible, cost-effective junior capital to growing middle market companies in the media, telecommunications, entertainment, and information services sectors.
Fund Size: $283 Million
Average Investment: $5-15 Million
Minimum Investment: $3-6 Million
Investment Criteria: Mezzanine
Industry Group Preference: Media, Telecommunications, Entertainment, Information Services, Business Products & Services, Education
Portfolio Companies: Ariston Global, Cash Cycle Solutions, Cooking.com, DigitalBridge Communications, Eli Research, EyeWonder, Global Telecom & Technology, Hibernia Atlantic, Hoffman Media, Manifest Digital, Market Tech Media Corporation, The Motley Food, Total Attorneys, Trio Video, United Metro Media, Vantage Media, Willamette Broadband
Key Executives:
 Thomas J. Buono, Principal
 e-mail: tbuono@bia.com
 Education: BS, Applied Mathematics, Clarkson University; MBA, Tuck School of Business, Darmouth College
 Background: BIA Financial Network; BIA Consulting; BIA Research; BIA Capital Corp.
 Gregg E. Johnson, Managing Principal
 e-mail: gjohnson@bia.com
 Education: BS, Commerce, University of Virginia; MBA, University of Rochester
 Background: Division Manager of Communications Lending, American Security Bank; Chase Lincoln First Bank
 Charles A. Wiebe, Principal
 e-mail: cwiebe@bia.com
 Education: BA, Comparative Literature and History, Cornell University
 Background: VP, Mellon Bank; VP, American Security Bank
 Scott E. Chappell, Principal
 e-mail: schappell@bia.com
 Education: BS, Business Administration, University of Georgia; MBA, Fuqua School of Business, Duke University
 Background: Media and Telecommunications Corporate Financial Team, Thomas Weisel Partners; Investment Banker, First Union Securities

Venture Capital & Private Equity Firms / Domestic Firms

Damien A. Dovi, Vice President
Education: BS, Ithaca College
Background: Banc of America Securities
Directorships: Cooking.com; Total Attorneys; Cross MediaWorks; Eyewonder; Hibernia Atlantic; Manifest Digital; The Motley Fool
Lloyd R. Sams, Managing Principal
e-mail: lsams@bia.com
Education: BS, Business Administration, Washington and Lee University; MBA, University of North Carolina
Background: First Union; First Chicago

267 BILTMORE VENTURES
1825 West Knudsen
Unit B-100
Phoenix, AZ 85027

Phone: 480-510-5550
web: www.biltmoreventures.com

Mission Statement: Biltmore Ventures works with talented entrepreneurs to build great companies. The firm invests during the early development stage with the following business goals: create rapid growth through access to capital, expertise, and relationships; build long-term sustainable value; provide substantial returns to entrepreneurs, employees and investors, most often through subsequent merger or acquisition; and lead investment rounds involving other firms, funds, or partners.

Average Investment: $10 million
Investment Criteria: Early-Stage
Industry Group Preference: Internet
Portfolio Companies: My Job Chart, GolfNow, Lifelock, American Legal Fund, Investar, Insymphony, Airpower Insurance, Mytrade, Adaptive Blue

Key Executives:
Adam Bruss, Managing Partner
Education: Art Center College of Design
Background: Founder/President, GD MAC

268 BINARY CAPITAL
1550 Bryant Street
Suite 700
San Francisco, CA 94103

e-mail: info@binarycap.com

Fund Size: $300 million
Founded: 2014
Investment Criteria: Early-Stage
Portfolio Companies: Twitter, Instagram, Snapchat

269 BIOADVANCE
3711 Market Street
8th Floor
Philadelphia, PA 19104

Phone: 610-230-0544
web: www.bioadvance.com

Mission Statement: Investing in emerging life sciences technologies with the most promising commercialization prospects.

Geographic Preference: Southeastern Pennsylvania
Fund Size: $20 million
Founded: 2002
Investment Criteria: Pre-Seed, Seed-Stage
Industry Group Preference: Therapeutics, Medical Devices, Research Tools, Diagnostics, Health IT
Portfolio Companies: Allevi, Bainbridge Health, BioDetego, CarePartners Plus, Cohero Health, Cytovas, Eagle Vision Pharmaceuticals, Enzium, GenPro Profiling, Group K Diagnostics, Halo Labs, Hsiri Therapeutics, Imiplex, Immunome, InfraScan, Innovative Supply Solutions, Intezyne, iView Therapeutics, Jenrin Discovery, Keriton, Mebias Discovery, Melior Discovery, Midway Pharmaceuticals, Olive Devices, Oncora Medical, The One Health Company, Opsidio, Ossianix, Palvella Therapeutics, PeriRx, Phoenix S&T, Pillo, QR Pharma, Relmada RiboNova, Ride Health, TalexMedical, TowerView Health, Treventis Corp., VenatoRx, WellSheet, WellTrackOne

Key Executives:
Barbara Schilberg, Managing Director and CEO
Education: JD, University of Virginia
Background: Incara Pharmaceuticals; VP/General Counsel, Locus Discovery, Inc.; Morgan, Lewis & Brockius
Shahram Hejazi, Partner
Education: PhD, Engineering, Stanford University
Background: President, Kodak Life Science Division; CEO, Zargis Medical Corporation
Gregory Harriman, Venture Partner
e-mail: gharriman@bioadvance.com
Education: University of California, Berkeley; MD, University of California, San Diego
Background: Founder, Main Line Ventures; Member, Robin Hood Ventures
Rick Jones, Partner
Education: BA, MD, MBA, Univ. of Pennsylvania
Background: Anchor Therapeutics

270 BIOGENERATOR
20 South Sarah St
St. Louis, MO 63108

Phone: 314-615-6355
e-mail: info@biogenerator.org
web: biogenerator.org

Mission Statement: BioGenerator's mission is to support bioscience in St. Louis.

Geographic Preference: St. Louis Region
Founded: 2003
Average Investment: Pre-Seed: $10K - $50K; Seed: $50K - $250K
Minimum Investment: $10,000
Investment Criteria: Seed-Stage, Early-Stage
Industry Group Preference: Therapeutics, Agriculture, Research Tools, Healthcare Services, Healthcare IT, Animal Health, Nutrition, Diagnostics, Research Services, Medical Devices
Portfolio Companies: Accuronix, Adarza, RNAgri, Arch Innotek, Arvegenix, Atomation, BacterioScan, Benson Hill Biosystems, Canopy Biosciences, Cardialen, Cofactor Genomics, Daya CNS, Edison Agrosciences, Electrochaea, Elira Therapeutics, EPharmix, Euclises, Galera Therapeutics, GeneriCo, Graematter, Immuno Photonics, Indalo Therapeutics, Katalyst Surgical, Kogent Surgical, Kypha, Medaware Solutions, MediBeacon, MedSocket, Mobius Therapeutics, Nanopore Diagnostics, NeuroLutions, Nitrogenics, Plastomics, PM Diagnostics, Pulse Therapeutics, S4 Agtech, Sentiar, Tioma Therapeutics, Unleash Immuno Oncolytics, YourBevCo

Key Executives:
Eric Gulve PhD, President
Education: BA, Chemistry, Occidental College; PhD, Physiology, Harvard University
Background: Cardiovascular Research, Pfizer; Associate Director, Cardiovascular & Metabolic Diseases, Pharmacia Corporation
Dan Broderick, Vice President
Education: BS, Biology, Iowa State University
Background: Prolog Ventures, Mason Wells Biomedical Fund
Edward Hamati, Director
Education: BS, Cellular Biology, University of California, Davis; MBA, California State University
Background: The Chi Rho Group, The Broadband Group
Charlie Bolten, Vice President
Education: University of Missouri, St. Louis
Background: Principal Scientist & Project Leader, Pfizer Exploratory Immunobiology
Directorships: Vasculox

Venture Capital & Private Equity Firms / Domestic Firms

271 BIOMATICS CAPITAL
188 E Blaine Street
Suite 126
Seattle, WA 98102

e-mail: info@biomaticscapital.com
web: www.biomaticscapital.com

Mission Statement: A for-profit venture firm investing in companies that focus on healthcare technology.
Geographic Preference: United States
Fund Size: $200 Million
Founded: 2016
Minimum Investment: $5-10 Million
Investment Criteria: Series A
Industry Group Preference: Healthcare Technology
Portfolio Companies: AiCure, Aledade, BlackThorn Therapeutics, BlueTalon, Compass Therapeutics, Cytrellis, Denali Therapeutics, eGenesis Bio, Encodia, GRAIL, Omniome, Twist Bioscience, Verana Health
Key Executives:
   Dr. Boris Nikolic, Managing Director
   Education: MD, University of Zagreb School of Medicine; PhD, Transplantation Immunology, Harvard Medical School
   Background: Assistant Professor of Medicine, Massachusetts General Hospital/Harvard Medical School; Chief Advisor For Science And Technology, Bill Gates
   Yeon Cramer, Business Operations Manager
   Background: bgC3; Research Assistant, Farallon Capital

272 BIOSTAR VENTURES
560 W Mitchell Street
Suite 500
Petoskey, MI 49770

Phone: 231-487-9186 Fax: 231-487-9183
e-mail: info@biostarventures.com
web: www.biostarventures.com

Mission Statement: BioStar Ventures invests in companies their key focus of cardiovascular, orthopedic and neuroscience areas.
Fund Size: $68.8 million
Founded: 2005
Average Investment: $2 - $6 million
Investment Criteria: Seed-Stage, Early-Stage
Industry Group Preference: Medical Devices, Medical Technology
Portfolio Companies: Ablative Solutions, Inc., Angioslide, Aria CV Inc., Autonomix Medical Inc., Avantis Medical Systems, CathWorks Ltd., Cibiem Inc., Conventus Orthopaedics Inc., Corindus Vascular Robotics Inc., Foldax Inc., Kona Medical Inc., MiCardia Corp., NewPace Ltd., OmniGuide Inc., Ortho-Space Ltd., SynergEyes Inc., TransMedic, Trice Medical Inc., TriVentures II Fund; V-Wave Ltd., VytronUS Inc., AorTx Inc., Atritech Inc., Bioabsorable Therapeutics Inc., Broncus Technologies, CD Diagnostics Inc., CV Ingenuity Corp., Devax Inc., Doman Surgical Inc., Ellipse Technologies Inc., Embrella Cardiovascular Inc., Hotspir Technologies Inc., Interventional Spine Inc., Nellix Endovascular Inc., Onset Medical Corp., ReVascular Therapeutics Inc., Reverse Medical Corp., Setagon Inc.
Key Executives:
   Louis Cannon, MD, Founder/Senior Managing Director
   Background: President, Cardiac & Vascular Research Center of Northern Michigan
   Directorships: Medtronic, Abbott, Boston Scientific, HotSpur, CardioVascular Ingenuity, TransLuminal Therapeutics, Nellix
   Renee Masi, Managing Director
   Education: BA, Stanford University; MBA, Wharton School
   Background: Partner, Windward Ventures; Advisor, Ventures Medical
   Directorships: SynergEyes, Axis Surgical, CardiacMD, Embrella Cardiovascular
   Steven L. Almany, MD, Managing Director
   Background: Director of Cardiac Cath Lab, William Beaumont Hospital; Partner, Michigan Heart Group
   Paul A. Scott, Managing Director/Chief Financial Officer
   Education: BA, Ithaca College; MBA, Loyola University of Chicago
   Background: CFO/Administrative Partner, Windward Ventures; President/CEO, VSI Enterprises Inc.
   Directorships: AdvancedMD
   William H. Kucheman, Director
   Education: BS, Virgina Polytechnic Institute; MBA, Virginia State University
   Background: Senior Advisor, Global Health Exchange; CEO, Boston Scientific

273 BIOVENTURES INVESTORS
70 Walnut Street
Suite 302
Wellesley, MA 02481

Phone: 617-252-3443 Fax: 617-621-7993
e-mail: info@bioventuresinvestors.com
web: www.bioventuresinvestors.com

Mission Statement: BioVentures invests in companies commercializing breakthrough life science and healthcare technology with clear application, a strong proprietary position and a well-understood development pathway. Seeks opportunities with a defined 'entrepreneurial advantage' that will enable a new venture to prevail in an extremely competitive environment.
Geographic Preference: Eastern Massachusetts
Fund Size: $133 million
Average Investment: $3 - $7 million
Investment Criteria: Life-Science Technology
Industry Group Preference: Life Sciences, Healthcare, Human Therapeutics, Medical Devices, Diagnostics, Healthcare Information Technology
Portfolio Companies: Cardiosolutions, CoNextions, Deep Vein Medical Inc., Endotronix, HydroCision, Locemia, POC Medical Systems Inc., Orachiotek, Verax BioMedical
Key Executives:
   Peter Feinstein, Co-Founder/Venture Partner
   Education: BA, English Literature, New York University
   Background: Feinstein Kean Healthcare; Co-Founder, Massachusetts Biotechnology Council; Financial Journalist, University Film Study Center, MIT
   Directorships: BioValve Technologies, Inc., HospitalCare Online, Inc.
   Walter Gilbert, PhD, Venture Partner
   Education: AB, Chemistry & Physics, Harvard College; MA, Physics, Harvard University; PhD, Mathematics, Cambridge University
   Background: Co-Founder, Biogen; Co-Founder, Myriad Genetics; Co-Founder, Paratek Pharmaceuticals; Co-Founder, Memory Pharmaceuticals; Co-Founder, Pintex Pharmaceuticals; Director, Transkaryotic Therapies
   Marc Goldberg, Co-Founder/Managing Partner
   Education: AB, Harvard College; MBA, Harvard Business School; JD, Harvard Law School
   Background: President/CEO, Massachusetts Biotechnology Research Institute; Safer, Inc.; Manager of Business Development, Genetics Institute, Inc.; Co-Founder, Massachusetts Biotechnology Council
   Jeffrey Barnes, Managing Director
   Education: BS, Physiology & Biophysics, MS, Biomedical Engineering, Duke University; MS, Management, Stanford University
   Background: Managing Partner, Oxford Bioscience Partners

Venture Capital & Private Equity Firms / Domestic Firms

274 BIP CAPITAL
Piedmont Center
3575 Piedmont Road
Building 15, 7th Floor, Suite 730
Atlanta, GA 30305

Phone: 404-495-5230 Fax: 404-495-5239
Toll-Free: 866-435-8877
web: bip-capital.com

Mission Statement: Atlanta-based investors in the Southeastern U.S.

Geographic Preference: Southeastern U.S.
Average Investment: $2-5 million
Investment Criteria: Growth Capital, Add On Acquisition, Partial Shareholder Liquidity
Industry Group Preference: Technology, SaaS, Business Products & Services, Franchising, Healthcare, Specialty Finance
Portfolio Companies: AchieveIt, Aspirion, Crescerance, Huddle, Ingenious Med, Inked, Ipreo, M Level, PlayOn! Sports, QASymphony, ReachHealth, Tin Drum Asian Kitchen, Tropical Smoothie Cafe

Key Executives:
Mark Buffington, Co-Founder and CEO
e-mail: mbuffington@bipfund.com
Education: Georgia Institute of Technology; MBA, Tulane University
Background: Founder, Buckhead Investment Partners; Peachtree Financial Management, Phoenix Capital
Scott Pressly, Co-Founder and Managing Director
e-mail: spressly@bipfund.com
Education: BS, Chemical Engineering, University of Florida; MBA, Harvard Business School
Background: Partner, Roark Capital Group; US Franchise Systems
Paul Iaffaldano, Managing Director

275 BIRCHMERE VENTURES
Pittsburgh, PA 15222

e-mail: info@birchmerevc.com
web: www.birchmerevc.com

Mission Statement: Focus on early-stage, IP-differentiated companies creating Engineering Driven Innovation. Specialize in being the first institutional investor in cleantech, medical and technology start-ups.

Geographic Preference: Mid-Atlantic Region
Fund Size: $250 million
Founded: 1996
Minimum Investment: $500,000
Investment Criteria: Start-Up, Early Stage
Industry Group Preference: Technology, Drug Development, Clean Technology, Medical Devices, Advanced Materials, Mobile, SaaS, Semiconductors, Social Media
Portfolio Companies: Admiral, BloomBoard, ContainerShip, Crystal, Cvent, Eargo, Earshot, Encentivenergy, Estimote, FreeMarkets, Gem, GradeSlam, Healthie, Idelic, Identified Technologies, Ikos, Jazz, Joany, Legal Sifter, Mapper, Modsy, Mom Trusted, Mona, Mosss, Neolinear, Nowait, One Kloud, Peloton, Presence Learning, Senic, Sleeperbot, Spidr Tech, SubCenter.io, Ten Marks, Treatspace, Umano, Yaypay, The Zebra

Key Executives:
Sean Sebastian, Partner
e-mail: sean@birchmerevc.com
Education: BS, Mechanical Engineering, Worcester Polytechnic Institute; MBA, Rensselaer Polytechnic Institute
Background: Assistant VP, Corporate Finance Group, PNC Bank; Founder/CEO, The Telford Group; International Systems Services; General Electric Information Services; American Management Systems; US Air Force; President, Pittsburgh Venture Capital Association
Directorships: CyOptics, Precision Therapeutics
Ned J Renzi, Partner
e-mail: ned@birchmerevc.com
Education: BS, Electrical Engineering, Pennsylvania State University; MBA, Katz Graduate School of Business at the University of Pittsburgh; MA, Engineering Management, George Washington University
Background: Manager, Information Transfer Technology, Concurrent Technologies Corporation; Sr Manager, US Department of Defense Special Projects Group
Directorships: Cvent, Plextronics, Solexant
Sean Ammirati, Partner
e-mail: sean@birchmerelabs.com
Education: BS, Computer Information Systems, Grove City College
Background: Partner, Birchmere Labs; Adjunct Professor of Entrepreneurship, Carnegie Mellon University's Tepper School

276 BIRD DOG EQUITY PARTNERS
221 South Phillips Avenue
#202
Sioux Falls, SD 57104

Phone: 605-310-2923 Fax: 605-357-5303

Mission Statement: As a private equity firm, we invest in companies with big dreams. We look for entrepreneurs throughout the Midwest with strong cash flow, experienced management, and an eye for growth. Formerly known as Nordic Venture Partners.

Geographic Preference: Midwest United States
Key Executives:
Chad Hatch, Managing Partner
Background: CFO, Destination Golf Ventures; Managing Partner, Sweet Deals; SVP, Strategic Capital, POET
Paul Schock, Managing Partner
Background: Founding Partner, Bluestem Capital Company; Chairman, Destination Golf Ventures

277 BISON CAPITAL ASSET MANAGEMENT LLC
233 Wilshire Boulevard
Suite 425
Santa Monica, CA 90401

Phone: 310-260-6573
web: www.bisoncapital.com

Mission Statement: A private equity firm which makes non-control investments in fundamentally strong middle-market companies, to finance their growth, balance sheet restructuring and/or recapitalization.

Average Investment: $10 million
Investment Criteria: Middle Market Companies with Revenues of $20 to $500 Million
Industry Group Preference: Business Services, Healthcare, Technology, Distribution, Logistics
Portfolio Companies: Advantmed, BC2Environmental Corp., Big Rock Sports LLC, Cartasite, Clinical Research Laboratories LLC, CutisCare, CVE Technology Group Inc., Ease Entertainment Services, EmpirecLS Worldwide Chauffeured Services, Fuel Systems Solutions Inc., Fyfe Group LLC, General Finance Corp., Global Benefits Group Inc., Helinet Aviation Services LLC, Indi Semiconductor, KeyTech Limited, Lime Energy Co., Metagenics Inc., Midwestern BioAg, Miva, MVConnect, Overland, Pacific & Cutler, Performance Team Freight Systems Inc., Royal Wolf Australia, Sentinel Offender Services LLC, Solarsilicon Recycling Services LLC, The Center for Wound Healing, Twin Med LLC, United Therapies Holding LLC

Other Locations:
780 Third Avenue
30th Floor

Venture Capital & Private Equity Firms / Domestic Firms

New York, NY 10017
Phone: 646-792-2080
Key Executives:
Douglas B. Trussler, Partner
310-260-6582
e-mail: dtrussler@bisoncapital.com
Education: MBA, Richard Ivey School of Business, University of Western Ontario
Background: Principal, Windward Capital Partners
Directorships: GTS Holdings, Inc., Performance Team Freight Systems, Inc.; Royal Wolf Australia, Ltd., Royal Wolf Trading New Zealand Limited, BC2 Environmental Corp, Big Rock Sports LLC
Yee-Ping Chu, Partner
310-260-6574
e-mail: pchu@bisoncapital.com
Education: BS, Economics, Wharton School, University of Pennsylvania
Background: VP, Lehman Brothers; Credit Suisse First Boston; Trust Company; Senior Analyst, TCW's International Private Equity; Public Accountant, Price Waterhouse
Directorships: Metagenics, Inc; Bc2 Environmental Corp; Performance Team Freight Systems, Inc
Lou Caballero, Partner
310-260-6573
e-mail: lcaballero@bisoncapital.com
Education: BA, Economics and Business, Westmont College; MBA, UCLA Anderson School of Management
Background: Senior Associate, Roth Capital Partners; Financial Analyst, Catellus Development Corporation
Directorships: BC2 Environmental Corp.
Peter Macdonald, Partner
646-792-2080
e-mail: pmacdonald@bisoncapital.com
Education: BS, Business Administration, University of Southern California; MBA, Wharton School, University of Pennsylvania
Background: Managing Director, BlackRock Kelso Corporation; Partner, Windward Capital Partners
Directorships: GTS Holdings, Inc.
Kurt Pilecki, Vice President
310-260-6578
e-mail: kpilecki@bisoncapital.com
Education: BS, Commerce with Concentrations in Finance & Accounting, University of Virginia
Background: Senior Analyst, CIBC World Markets / Oppenheimer & Co.; Associate, Bison Capital

278 BLACK DIAMOND VENTURES
450 North Brand Boulevard
Suite 600
Glendale, CA 91203

Phone: 818-245-6250 Fax: 818-245-6255
e-mail: info@bdventures.com
web: bdventures.com

Mission Statement: Black Diamond Ventures provides individual investors the opportunity to invest alongside institutional investors and first-tier venture capital firms in technology-leading companies.

Founded: 1998
Average Investment: $2 - $10 million
Industry Group Preference: Technology, Telecommunications, Biotechnology, Medical Devices, Semiconductors, Mobile Apps, Clean Technology
Portfolio Companies: Altwork, Berkeley Lights, Capella, Consumer Brands, Engage3, LiquidSpace, Mumo, NEI Treatment Systems, Obalon, Tela Innovations, Theranos

Other Locations:
475 Alberto Way
Los Gatos, CA 95032
Phone: 408-558-6300 Fax: 408-884-8840

19 Vista Tramonto
Newport Coast, CA 92657
Phone: 949-644-4288 Fax: 949-644-4628

Key Executives:
Christopher Lucas, Managing Director
e-mail: chris@bdventures.com
Education: BS, Mechanical Engineering, UCLA; MBA, University of Southern California
Background: Global One Distribution & Merchandising, Peripheral Systems
Rob Ukropina, Managing Partner
e-mail: rob@bdventures.com
Education: University of Southern California, Marshall School of Business
Background: Founder, Overnight Express
Directorships: Allyance Communications, Arenda Capital Management, C2 Reprographics, United Document Storage
Ana Quintana, Principal
e-mail: ana@bdventures.com
Education: BA, English Literature, California State University, Los Angeles
Background: Senior Editor, Goto.com; Corporate Finance, ING Barings

279 BLACKFORD CAPITAL LLC
190 Monroe Ave. NW
Suite 600
Grand Rapids, MI 49503

Phone: 616-233-3161 Fax: 616-828-5042
e-mail: info@blackfordcapital.com
web: www.blackfordcapital.com

Mission Statement: Acquires, manages, and builds middle-market manufacturing companies; provides attractive exit options for owners and operators of small to medium-sized privately held manufacturing enterprises, an provides divestiture opportunities for division of corporate parent companies that no longer reflect the company's strategic focus.

Geographic Preference: Midwest Region, Mid-Atlantic Region, New England
Founded: 2000
Average Investment: $50 million
Minimum Investment: $10 million
Investment Criteria: Small to medium-sized privately held manufacturing enterprises; Divestitures
Industry Group Preference: Distribution, Business Products & Services, Low-Tech Manufacturing
Portfolio Companies: Bond Street, Burgaflex, Custom Profile, Davalor, Dickinson, Ellison Bakery, Grand Equipment, Grand Power Systems, Hall Research, Industrial Piping, Key Health, McClarin Plastics, Mopec, Online Tech Stores, Quality Aluminium Products, Snowhite, Staging Concepts, Rhinotek Heavy Duty Computer Products

Other Locations:
150 West Second Street
Suite 400
Royal Oak, MI 48067

Key Executives:
Martin Stein, Founder & Managing Director
e-mail: mstein@blackfordcapital.com
Education: BA, University of Chicago; MBA, Harvard Business School
Background: Consultant, Mercer Management Consulting; Consultant, Council for Excellence in Government
Jeffrey Johnson, Managing Director
Education: MBA, Harvard Business School; BA, Claremont McKenna College
Background: Managing Director, Gilbert Global Equity Partners; Director, Alternative Investments, Russell

Investments
Directorships: Mopec, Quality Aluminium Products, Ellison Bakery
Carmen Evola, Managing Director
Education: BS, Electrical Engineering, University of Toledo
Background: President & CEO, Vari-Form Group (formerly Crowne Group)
Directorships: Grand Power Systems, Burgaflex, Grand Equipment, Davalor Mold

280 BLACKSTONE PRIVATE EQUITY GROUP
345 Park Avenue
New York, NY 10154

Phone: 212-583-5000 **Fax:** 212-583-5749
web: www.blackstone.com

Mission Statement: Blackstone Private Equity Group's approach to investing is guided by a set of proven principles: accountability, excellence, integrity, teamwork and entrepreneurship. The firm is committed to establishing corporate partnerships, focusing on opportunities in under-appreciated industries, and actively managing its portfolio companies.
Geographic Preference: North America, Western Europe, Latin America
Fund Size: $18 billion
Founded: 1987
Average Investment: $100 - $400 million
Minimum Investment: $100 million
Investment Criteria: Leveraged Buyouts, Middle Market, Growth Capital
Industry Group Preference: Business Products & Services, Consumer Products, Retail, Consumer & Leisure, Energy, Financial Services, Healthcare, Pharmaceuticals, Industrial, Media, Telecommunications, Travel & Leisure, Technology
Portfolio Companies: Allcargo, Bayview Financial, Bujagali Hydropower Project, Center Parcs, Cheniere, Crestwood Midstream Partners, Crocs, DJO, Emdeon, Gateway Rail Freight, Gokaldas Exports Limited, Intelenet, Jack Wolfskin, Leica, LLOG, Merlin Entertainments, Michaels Stores, MTAR, PBV Partners, Performance Food, Pinnacle Foods, Seaworld Parks and Entertainment, Steifel Laboratories, Summit Materials, Vivint

Other Locations:
100 Wilshire Boulevard
Suite 200
Santa Monica, CA 90401
Phone: 310-310-6949 **Fax:** 310-310-6998

40 Berkeley Square
London W1J 5AL
United Kingdom
Phone: 44-2074514000 **Fax:** 44-2074514001

Two International Finance Centre
Suite 901
8 Finance Street
Central
Hong Kong
Phone: 852-36568600 **Fax:** 852-26568601

Units 2 & 3, Level 61, China World Tower B
No. 1 Jianguomenwai Avenue
Chaoyang District
Beijing 100004
China
Phone: 86-1066497300 **Fax:** 86-1066497301

Abu Dhabi Global Market Square
Al Sila Tower, 24th Floor
PO Box 128666
Abu Dhabi
United Arab Emirates
Phone: 971-26948617

314 Main Street
15th Floor
Cambridge, MA 02142
Phone: 617-949-2200

Express Towers
Nariman Point
Mumbai 400 021
India
Phone: 91-2267528500 **Fax:** 91-2267528531

278 Boulevard Saint-Germain
Paris 75007
France
Phone: 33-0170982330 **Fax:** 33-0170982331

18F West Tower Mirae Asset Center 1 Building
26, Eulji-Ro 5-Gil
Jung-Gu
Seoul 04539
Korea
Phone: 82-262267110 **Fax:** 82-262267010

Unit 3901-3903, 39th Floor
HKRI Centre One HKRI
Taikoo Hei, 288 Shumen Yi Road
Shanghai 200041
China
Phone: 86-2161698188 **Fax:** 82-2161698189

Marina Bay Financial Centre Tower 2
Suite 13-01/02
10 Marina Blvd. 018983
Singapore
Phone: 65-68507500 **Fax:** 65-68507501

126 Philip Street
Sydney NSW L20
Australia
Phone: 61-280167200 **Fax:** 61-280167201

Marunouchi Building, 10th Floor
2-4-1 Marunouchi
Chiyoda-ku
Tokyo 100-6310
Japan
Phone: 81-0345778400 **Fax:** 81-0345778401

101 California Street
44th Floor
San Francisco, CA 94111
Phone: 212-583-5000

Key Executives:
Stephen A. Schwarzman, Chairman, Co-Founder & CEO
Education: BA, Yale University; MBA, Harvard Business School
Directorships: The Asia Society, New York-Presbyterian Hospital
Jonathan Gray, President & Chief Operating Officer
Education: BA, University of Pennsylvania; BS, Wharton School
Background: Chairman, Hilton Worldwide
Directorships: Harlem Village Academies
Joseph Baratta, Global Head, Private Equity
Education: Georgetown University
Background: Tinicum; McCown De Leeuw & Company; M&A, Morgan Stanley
Directorships: Seaworld Parks and Entertainment, Penn Engineering
Michael Chae, Chief Financial Officer
Education: AB, Harvard College; MPhil, Cambridge University; JD, Yale Law School
Background: The Carlyle Group LP; Dillon, Read & Co.
Prakash A. Melwani, Senior Managing Director/Chief Investment Officer
Education: Cambridge University; MBA, Harvard Business School
Background: Founding Partner, Vestar Capital Partners; The First Boston Corporation; NM Rothschild & Sons
Directorships: Crocs, Kosmos Energy, Performance Food Group, RGIS Inventory Specialists

Venture Capital & Private Equity Firms / Domestic Firms

David I. Foley, Senior Managing Director/Global Head, Blackstone Energy Partners
Education: BA, MA, Economics, Northwestern University; MBA, Harvard Business School
Background: AEA Investors; Monitor Company
Lionel Assant, Senior Managing Director
Education: Ecole Polytechnique
Background: M&A, Asset Management & Private Equity, Goldman Sachs
Directorships: Tangerine, Intertrust, Alliance Automotive Group
Gautam Banerjee, Senior Managing Director
Education: BS, LLD, University of Warwick
Background: Executive Chairman, PricewaterhouseCoopers Singapore
Directorships: Singapore Airlines, Piramal Enterprises, The Indian Hotels Company, GIC Private Limited
Martin Brand, Head, North America Private Equity
Education: BA, MA, Mathematics & Computation, Univ. of Oxford; MBA, Harvard Business School
Background: Goldman Sachs; McKinsey & Company
Thomas Iannarone, Managing Director
Education: BA, Siena College; JD, Villanova University
Background: Morrison & Foerster; Bingham McCutchen
Edward Huang, Senior Managing Director
Education: BA, Yale University; MBA, Harvard Business School
Background: Managing Director & Partner, Morgan Stanley; Merrill Lynch
Directorships: Pactera Technology International
Seth Meisel, Senior Managing Director
Education: BA, Economics, Princeton University; MBA, Harvard Business School
Background: Partner, Bain Capital; Mercer Management Consulting
Dwight Scott, Global Head, Credit
Education: University of North Carolina; McCombs School of Business, University of Texas
Background: EVP & CFO, El Paso Corporation; Managing Director, Donald Lufkin & Jenrette
Directorships: FourPoint Energy; GEP Haynesville
Michael Sotirhos, Senior Managing Director
Education: BA, JD, Georgetown University
Background: Partner, Atlantic Pacific Capital; Merrill Lynch
Peter Wallace, Senior Managing Director
Education: Harvard College
Directorships: Allied Barton Security Services, GCA Services, Michaels Stores, Outerstuff, SeaWorld Parks & Entertainment, Service King, Vivint, The Weather Channel Companies

281 BLADE VENTURES
27762 Antonio Parkway
Suite L1-426
Mission Viejo, CA 92694

Phone: 949-298-4595 Fax: 949-554-0181
e-mail: admin@bladeventures.com
web: www.bladeventures.com

Mission Statement: Blade Ventures' focus is on companies that drive the adoption of leading edge information, media, sensor and related systems technologies. Through select partners the firm also invests in life science opportunities such as medical devices, diagnostics, and operations-enhancing information technology. Blade Ventures' portfolio companies are capable of playing a disruptive role in emerging, high growth markets, and they are led by management teams that have a long term commitment to the success of their company.

Geographic Preference: United States
Average Investment: $250,000 - 1.5 million
Industry Group Preference: Media, Life Sciences, Medical Devices, Diagnostics
Portfolio Companies: 5iSciences, Apollo Enterprise Solutions, Clear Access, Good Technology, Infinera, LaserCure Sciences, Metric Stream, Motricity, Neilsoft, Vigilistics

Key Executives:
Craig Gunther, Managing Director
Education: BS, Engineering, UCLA; MS, Electrical Engineering, University of Southern California; JD, Loyola Law School
Background: President, Blade Capital Management
Directorships: ClearAccess, 5iScience, Lasercure, Vigilistics
Brian Flucht, Principal
Education: Northwestern University; MBA, University of Southern California
Background: Senior Analyst, Shepherd Ventures
Rajeev Varshneya, Venture Partner
Education: BSc, Electronics & Telecommunications Engineering, New Delhi, India; ME, Electronics, Eindhoven, The Netherlands
Directorships: Metric Stream, Vigilistics

282 BLAST FUNDING
900 Diamond Circle
Naples, FL 34119

Phone: 877-580-5754
e-mail: brian@blastfunding.com
web: www.blastfunding.com

Mission Statement: A private direct lender investing in various industries.

Fund Size: $500M
Minimum Investment: $200k
Investment Criteria: $3M Annual Revenue, Startups
Industry Group Preference: Cannabis, Oil & Gas, Aerospace Defense, Energy, Transportation, Gaming, Consumer Goods, Security, Technology, Software, HOA Financing

283 BLAZER VENTURES

e-mail: info@blazerventures.com
web: www.blazerventures.com

Mission Statement: Blazer Ventures is an early-stage investment firm primarily interested in consumer services.

Investment Criteria: Early-Stage
Industry Group Preference: Consumer Services, Business Products & Services
Portfolio Companies: Clothia, ClassPass, Combatant Gentlemen, Fondu, Keychain Logistics, Lovely, PlanGrid, Priceonomics, SpotOn, True & Co.

Key Executives:
Michael Wolf, Managing Partner
Education: Columbia University; Wharton School, University of Pennsylvania
Background: ClassPass

284 BLEU CAPITAL
110 E 25th Street
New York, NY 10010

web: www.bleucap.com

Mission Statement: Bleu Capital is a venture capital firm investing in supply chain optimization, data intelligence, AI voice intelligence, nd sustainable consumption.

Key Executives:
Jean Pierre Chesse, Founder

285 BLH VENTURE PARTNERS
75 5th Street NW
Suite 311
Atlanta, GA 30308

Phone: 404-941-8780
web: www.blhventures.com

Venture Capital & Private Equity Firms / Domestic Firms

Mission Statement: BLH Venture Partners invests in bright entrepreneurs tackling innovative opportunities and support them in any way possible. BLH understands entrepreneurs and the phases start-ups and young companies traverse on their path to success. BLH insights stem from hands-on experience operating companies and having faced many of the same challenges current and prospective partners face as well.

Investment Criteria: Early-Stage
Industry Group Preference: Technology-Enabled Services, Enterprise Software, Consumer Internet, E-Commerce & Manufacturing
Portfolio Companies: 3Birds, BetterCloud, Call Rail, Chrono.gg, Cypress.io, Evident, Forbes Travel Guide, Gro, Haste, KontrollFreek, Ionic Security, Mashburn, Salesfusion, Shinesty, StrataCloud, TripLingo, UserIQ, Vidyo, Acumen, Digital Assent, KidsLink, nCrowd, Overdog, SaveUp, Vocalocity

Key Executives:
Billy L. Harbert, Partner
Education: Auburn University; MBA, Goizueta Business School, Emory University
Background: President & CEO, BL Harbert International
Ashish H. Mistry, Partner
Education: Emory University
Background: Co-Founder, Virtex Networks; RCMS Group

286 BLOCKCHAIN CAPITAL
440 Pacific Avenue
San Francisco, CA 94133

Phone: 415-677-5340
e-mail: contact@blockchaincapital.com
web: blockchain.capital

Mission Statement: Blockchain Capital is a leading venture firm in blockchain technology.

Fund Size: $500 Million

Key Executives:
W Brad Stephens, Co-Founder and Managing Partner
Education: BA, Duke University
Background: Managing Partner, Stephens Investment Management LLC; Senior Analyst, CSFB Techonology Group; Research Analyst, Furman Selz
P Bart Stephens, Co-Founder and Managing Partner
Education: BA, Princeton University
Background: Co-Founder/Head, Business Development, Oncology.com; EVP, Ivanhoe Capital Corporation; Managing Partner, Stephens Investment Management

287 BLOOMBERG BETA
140 New Montgomery Street
22nd Floor
San Francisco, CA 94105

web: github.com/bloomberg-beta

Mission Statement: Venture firm backed by Bloomberg L.P.

Fund Size: $150 million
Investment Criteria: Early-Stage
Industry Group Preference: Data Services, Content, Media Distribution, Technology Platforms, Networks and Communities, Human-Computer Interaction, New Organizational Models

Other Locations:
731 Lexington Ave.
New York, NY 10022

Key Executives:
James Cham, Partner
Education: Harvard College; Massachusetts Institute of Technology - Sloan School of Management
Background: Principal, Trinity Ventures; Vice President, Bessemer Venture Partners; Consultant, Boston Consulting Group; Principal, Zefer; Senior Consultant, Accenture
Karin Klein, Founding Partner
Education: BA, University of Pennsylvania; BS/MBA, Wharton School
Background: VP, Softbank; Head of New Initiatives, Bloomberg
Directorships: Paramount Group; Regency Centers; Harvey Mudd College
Roy Bahat, Head
Education: Harvard University; University of Oxford; UC Berkeley
Background: President, IGN Entertainment; Vice President, News Corporation; Director of International Strategy, NYC2012; Senior Policy Director at Office of the Mayor, New York City; Associate, McKinsey & Co.
Shivon Zilis, Partner
Education: Yale University
Background: Chief Adventurer, Bloomberg Ventures; Senior Strategy Consultant, IBM; Strategy Consultant, IBM; Thought Leadership Analyst, IBM Institute for Business Value

288 BLU VENTURE INVESTORS
1577 Spring Hill Road
Suite 405
Vienna, VA 22182

web: www.bluventureinvestors.com

Mission Statement: Blu Venture Investors is a venture capital investment company that supports early stage entrepreneurs in the Mid-Atlantic Region. The firm's investors are experienced, successful operating executives with experience in a broad range of industries and business models. Each team member has successfully launched new companies, products or services.

Geographic Preference: Maryland, Virginia, Washington Dc, North Carolina
Average Investment: $250,000 - $1 million
Minimum Investment: $250,000
Investment Criteria: Early-Stage
Industry Group Preference: Technology, Business to Business, Software
Portfolio Companies: 3C Logic, Atomicorp, Avizia, Axon AI, Bandura Systems, Blue Triangle Technologies, Bright Greens, CyberSponse, Cybrary, Dark Cubed, Emu Solutions, Fischer Block, Graphus, GroupSense, Huntress Labs, ID.me, Immuta, Interfolio, Latista, Technologies, Link Labs, LKC Technologies, N5 Sensors, NewConnect, NS8, PacketSled, Pathsensors, PFP Cybersecurities, Pixspan, SenseWare, Sensics, Shevirah, SocialToaster, Solid Carbon Products, StreamLink Software, ThreatQuotient, Trip Tribe, Unveillance, Urgant, Vagabond Vending, VanGogh Imaging, Virgil Security

Key Executives:
J.S. Gamble, Co-Founder
Education: BS, McIntire School of Commerce; MBA, Wharton School, University of Pennsylvania
Background: CEO, Smart Imaging Systems; McKinsey & Company
Jim Hunt, Co-Founder
Education: BBA, University of Notre Dame
Background: Founder, BDS; System Integration Practice, Price Waterhouse
Bob Proctor, Co-Founder
Education: BS, MS, PhD, Applied Physics, Cornell University
Background: CEO, FlexEl; Co-Founder, Wiser Together

289 BLUE BRIGHT VENTURES
713 Greenwood Road
Chapel Hill, NC 27514-5924

Phone: 919-971-1377
e-mail: lee@bluebrightventures.com
web: bluebright.com

Venture Capital & Private Equity Firms / Domestic Firms

Mission Statement: Blue Bright Ventures invests in early-stage technology companies in the Southeast with a focus on the Raleigh-Durham area.
Geographic Preference: Southeast United States
Founded: 2009
Investment Criteria: Early-Stage
Industry Group Preference: Technology
Portfolio Companies: Adroit Digital, Aims, Bandsintown, Fabl, MarketBrief, Ocean Watch, Shoeboxed.com, Science Inc., Spring Metrics, Sweet Relish, Tethis, Windsor Circle, Womply, Wylan Energy, Zana

Key Executives:
  Lee Buck, Founder
  Education: BS, Systems Engineering, University of Virginia
  Background: Partner, LaunchBox Digital; Co-Founder, Near-Time

290 BLUE CHIP VENTURE COMPANY
1308 Race Street
Suite 200
Cincinnati, OH 45202

Phone: 513-723-2300
web: bcvc.com

Mission Statement: Helps entrepreneur partners build lasting enterprises, providing capital and business-building assistance to entrepreneurs seeking to build growth companies. Blue Chip provides 'last financing round' or 'pre-exit' capital for early stage investors and venture-backed companies.
Geographic Preference: United States, Canada
Fund Size: $600 million
Founded: 1990
Average Investment: $1 - $4 million
Minimum Investment: $1 million
Investment Criteria: Later Stage
Industry Group Preference: Information Technology, Enterprise Services, Media, Communications, Healthcare, Marketing, Internet, Healthcare Services
Portfolio Companies: Adelphic, Aprecia Pharmaceuticals, Bidtellect, Blue Chip Surgery Centers Partners, Endocyte, Genesis Media, Kinetic Social, Linkable, PCIX, Rocketfuel, Scale Computing, ShareThis, UberMedia, Verance, Vestmark, Wild Things, XOS Digital

Key Executives:
  Jack Wyant, Co-Founder/Managing Director
  e-mail: jack@bcvc.com
  Education: BA, Denison University; JD, Salmon P Chase College of Law
  Background: Brand Management; Proctor & Gamble Company; Taft Broadcasting Company
  Directorships: Blue Chip Broadcasting, Evergreen Assurance, Health Care Solutions, IntelliSeek/PlanetFeedback, Regent Communications, USinternetworking
  Richard Kiley, Advisor/Venture Partner
  e-mail: rlkiley@yahoo.com
  Education: BS, Rensselaer Polytechnic Institute
  Background: Procter & Gamble; CincyTech USA
  Mark Wright, Venture Partner
  e-mail: mark@bcvc.com
  Education: BA, Northwestern University; MBA, Vanderbilt University
  Background: Founder, Inforum; Founder, @plan
  Directorships: Atomic Dog Publishing, InternetWire, Space Holdings
  Christopher McCleary, Managing Director
  Education: BA, University of Kentucky
  Background: Founder/CEO, Evergreen Assurance; Co-Founder/Chairman/CEO, USinternetworking; Founded, USi; Chairman/CEO, DIGEX; Recipient, Ernst & Young Entrepreneur of the Year Award for software services

291 BLUE HERON CAPITAL
8730 Stony Point Parkway
Suite 280
Richmond, VA 23235

Phone: 804-212-3400 Fax: 804-212-3401
e-mail: info@blueheroncap.com
web: www.blueheroncap.com

Mission Statement: Invests in venture capital and management buyout opportunities in a broad range of industries. Blue Heron Capital's flexible and opportunistic investment philosophy allows them to creatively evaluate and structure investments to meet the individual needs of each situation.
Geographic Preference: Mid-Atlantic Region
Founded: 2006
Average Investment: $3 - $7 million
Minimum Investment: $3 million
Investment Criteria: Early-Stage, Growth Capital, Acquisitions, Direct Investments, Secondary Loans, Revenues between $5 to $25 million
Industry Group Preference: Healthcare, Tech-Enabled Business Services, Technology, Business Services
Portfolio Companies: Apogee IT Services, Avizia, Presence Learning, STARC Systems, Tricast, Verisma, Cartes Networks, CSA Medical, innRoad, Local Voice, WiserTogether

Key Executives:
  Tom Benedetti, Co-Founder/Managing Partner
  Education: BS, Government, College of William & Mary; MBA, Georgetown University
  Background: Co-Founder, Benedetti & Farris
  Andrew Tichenor, Co-Founder/Managing Partner
  Education: BS, Accounting, University of Richmond; MBA, Georgetown University
  Background: CPA, McGladrey & Pullen
  Sam Sezak, Partner
  Education: BS, Cornell University School of Hospitality Management; MBA, Georgetown University
  Background: Co-Founder & Managing Partner, Breo International
  Mike Marcantonio, Principal
  Education: BS, Finance & Accounting, James Madison University; MBA, Duke University
  Background: Harris Williams & Co.

292 BLUE OLIVE PARTNERS
web: www.linkedin.com/company/blue-olive-partners-llc

Mission Statement: Blue Olive Partners is a team of business operating executives devoted to identifying early-stage companies with tremendous growth potential. Blue Olive adheres to a comprehensive due diligence process prior to making equity investments. Blue Olive only invests in opportunities with a management team that embraces the Partners' hands-on involvement in the company's management, operations, finance and marketing strategies.
Founded: 2008
Investment Criteria: Preferred Equity

Key Executives:
  Ben Sheridan, Partner
  Education: BA, Duke University; MBA, Harvard University
  Background: General Manager, Progressive Insurance
  Larry Porcellato, Partner
  Education: BComm, University of Toronto
  Background: CEO, ICI Paints
  George L. Buzzy, Partner
  Education: BS, Business Administration, Lawrence University; CPA
  Background: CEO, Novagard Solutions
  Ed Weinfurtner, Partner
  Education: BA, Harvard University
  Background: EVP, Pella Window & Door Company

Venture Capital & Private Equity Firms / Domestic Firms

293 BLUE POINT CAPITAL PARTNERS
127 Public Square
Suite 5100
Cleveland, OH 44114-1312

Phone: 216-535-4700 Fax: 216-535-4701
web: www.bluepointcapital.com

Mission Statement: Blue Point Capital Partners is a private equity firm that invests in lower middle-market companies. Blue Point uses a range of operating resources to provide strategic support to its portfolio businesses.

Geographic Preference: United States, China
Fund Size: $1.5 billion
Founded: 1990
Average Investment: $10 - $50 million
Minimum Investment: $10 million
Investment Criteria: LBO, MBO, Middle Market, Recapitalizations
Industry Group Preference: Manufacturing, Distribution, Business Products & Services, Aerospace, Apparel & Footwear, Chemicals, E-Commerce, Environmental Services, Healthcare, Industrial Products, Transportation, Safety, Testing & Inspection
Portfolio Companies: Area Wide Protective, Consolidated Precision Products, Country Pure Foods, Fire & Life Safety America, FM Sylvan, Gesco Group of Companies, Italian Rose Gourmet Products, Kendall Vegetation Services, Mattco Forge, Next Level Apparel, Premier Needle Arts, Russell Hendrix, SASE Company, Spector & Co., TAS Environmental Services, Vetta, VRC Holdings

Other Locations:
 601 Union Street
 Suite 3022
 Seattle, WA 98101
 Phone: 206-332-9200 **Fax:** 206-332-9209

 201 S Tryon Street
 Suite 850
 Charlotte, NC 28202
 Phone: 704-347-1111 **Fax:** 704-347-1107

 Suite 4604B
 Wheelock Square
 1717 Nan Jing W Road
 Shanghai 200040
 China
 Phone: 86-2150474700

Key Executives:
Colleen Greenrod, CFO/CCO
216-353-4711
e-mail: cgreenrod@bluepointcapital.com
Education: BSBA, Accounting, Ohio State University; CPA
Background: J.P. Morgan; Citadel Investment; Arthur Andersen
Dennis Wu, Managing Director
86-2150474708
e-mail: dwu@bluepointcapital.com
Education: BE, Material Science, Shanghai University; MBA China Europe International Business School
Background: Purchasing Director Asia Pacific, Delphi Packard Electric Systems; Shanghai Printronics Circuit Board Co.
Directorships: Premier Needle Arts and Vetta
John LeMay, Partner
Education: BS, Economics & Finance, Miami University; MBA, Kellogg Graduate School of Management, Northwestern University
Background: Manager, Boston Consulting Group; Mergers & Acquisitions, Salomon Brothers
Directorships: Hilco Vision
Juli Marley, Partner
Education: BS, State University of New York, Oswego; CPA
Background: Mergers & Acquisitions, Ernst & Young
Directorships: The Lion Brewery, OrthoLite, Smith-Cooper International
Sean Ward, Partner
Education: BS, Economics, Allegheny College; MBA, John Carroll University
Background: Investment Banking & Credit Administration, KeyCorp
Directorships: Alco Manufacturing, AWP, Handi Quilter, LineStar Services, Shnier-Gesco, Trademark Global
Jim Marra, Director, Business Development
216-535-4703
e-mail: jmarra@bluepointcapital.com
Education: BS, Psychology, Pennsylvania State University; MBA, University of Pittsburgh
Background: Leveraged Capital, Investment Banking & Venture Capital Groups, Citicorp
Brian Castleberry, Partner
Education: BA, Economics & Mathematics, Washington and Lee University
Background: VP, Red Ventures; HOPE International; Harris Williams & Co.
Jonathan Pressnell, Partner
Education: BSBA, Accounting, University of Pittsburgh; MS, Accountancy, University of Notre Dame; MBA, Tuck School of Business, Dartmouth College
Background: Principal, Greenbriar Equity Group; Analyst, M&A, KeyBanc Capital Markets; Auditor, Ernst & Young

294 BLUE SAGE CAPITAL
2700 Via Fortuna
Suite 300
Austin, TX 78746

Phone: 512-536-1900 Fax: 512-236-9215
web: www.bluesage.com

Mission Statement: Blue Sage Capital is a private equity firm based in Austin, Texas. The firm invests across a wide range of sectors and specializes in growth financings, recapitalizations and buyouts of smaller middle-market businesses.

Geographic Preference: Texas, Southwest
Fund Size: $300 million
Founded: 2003
Average Investment: $20 - $40 million
Minimum Investment: $5 million
Investment Criteria: Small Middle-Market, Recapitalizations, Buyouts
Industry Group Preference: Industrial Equipment, Distribution, Service Industries, Healthcare, Manufacturing, Energy, Media
Portfolio Companies: All-State, Americo Manufacturing, BACOM, Frontier Waste Solutions, Ligchine International, Magnum System, Timber Automation

Key Executives:
Peter Huff, Founder/Managing Member
Education: Southern Methodist University; MBA, Stanford Graduate School of Business
Background: Partner, Austin Ventures; Managing Member, JH Whitney; McKinsey and Company
Directorships: Cobalt Environmental Solutions, Primus Sterilizer
Jim McBride, Founder/Managing Member
Education: BBA, Finance, MBA, University of Texas at Austin
Background: Senior Executive, The LBJ Holding Company
Directorships: C&M Conveyor, Marine Accessories, Baxley-LogPro, Cobalt Environmental Solutions
Jonathan Pearce, Partner
Education: BBA, MPA, Accounting, University of Texas; CPA
Background: Senior Associate, Avista Capital Partners; Analyst, Global Energy Group, Credit Suisse; Analyst, JP Morgan Chase
Eric Weiner, Partner
Education: BBA, Finance, BA, Government, University

Venture Capital & Private Equity Firms / Domestic Firms

of Texas; MBA, Stanford Graduate School of Business
Background: Associate, Berkshire Partners; Senior Associate Consultant, Bain & Company
Jonathan Kaskow, Vice President
Education: BA, Economics, Stanford University; MBA, University of Texas
Background: SunTx

295 BLUE SKY CAPITAL
3525 Del Mar Heights Rd
PO Box 862
San Diego, CA 92130

Phone: 877-424-7479 Fax: 877-424-7480
e-mail: info@blueskycapital.com
web: www.blueskycapital.com

Mission Statement: A private equity company that buys and sells distressed real estate.
Geographic Preference: Southern California
Founded: 2005
Industry Group Preference: Real Estate

296 BLUE TREE ALLIED ANGELS
PO Box 1323
Wexford, PA 15090

Phone: 724-475-4538 Fax: 888-550-3093
e-mail: info@bluetreecapital.com
web: www.bluetreealliedangels.com

Mission Statement: BlueTree Allied Angels is a network of private equity investors that invests in early stage companies. The organization seeks to leverage the experience and expertise of its members to mitigate investment risk and increase the probability of investment success.
Geographic Preference: Western Pennsylvania, Eastern Ohio, Northern West Virginia
Founded: 2003
Average Investment: $200,000 - $3 million
Investment Criteria: Early Stage, Exit Potential
Portfolio Companies: 101, 4moms, Aeronics, ALung Technologies, Angler Labs, ApartmentJet, Aspinity, Augment Therapy, Aurochs Brewing, Austin Coctails, Baebies, Bergen Medical Products, Bioptigen, BIOSAFE, BlastPoint, BoardBookit, C360, Carmell Therapeutics, ChromaTan, coeo, Cognition Therapeutics, Columbia Northwest, Complexa, Inc., Cryothermic Systems, CytoAgents, Edge Case Research, Figure8 Surgical, FlyCast, Holganix, INRange Management Systems, Iteros, JoyLux, Kold-Draft, LegalSifter, Lia Diagnostics, Lyndy Biosciences, Malcovery Security, Medrobotics, medSage, Neuros Medical, PECA Labs, Peptilogics, Physcient, Inc., PICKUP, PittMoss, RedPath Integrated Pathology, Rinovum, Shoefitr, StageMark, TalkShoe, Voci Technologies, Westmoreland Advanced Materials, Wombat Security, Wright Therapy Products, Zive, Zone2
Key Executives:
Catherine Mott, Founder
Education: BS, Education; Masters of Education; MBA, Finance
Sreekar Gadde, Executive Director
Education: BS, Cognitive Science, BS, MSc, Electrical and Computer Engineering, Carnegie Mellon Unveristy; JD, George Washington University Law School; MBA, Tepper School of Business, Carnegie Mellon University
Background: Ropes and Gray; Dynamics, Inc.; Intel

297 BLUEFISH VENTURES
San Francisco, CA

Phone: 415-614-1161

Mission Statement: Bluefish Ventures is a venture capital firm that invests in seed and early-stage Internet and technology companies. Bluefish targets markets with significant growth potential and specifically companies involved in, but not limited to, Internet infrastructure, enterprise software, wireless applications and power technology. Key criteria when making an investment decision include the strength of the company's management team, the potential size of the company's target market and the competitive advantages the company has versus other industry participants.
Investment Criteria: Seed-Stage, Early-Stage
Industry Group Preference: Internet, Technology, Internet Infrastructure, Enterprise Software, Wireless Applications, Power Technologies
Portfolio Companies: LiveVox, Powercell, Tangerine Technologies, Varro Technologies, Vivaro, vVault
Key Executives:
Alex Millar, Partner
e-mail: alex@bluefishventures.com
Education: School of Engineering & Applied Sciences, MBA, Wharton School, University of Pennsylvania
Background: Investment Banking Division, Donaldson Lufkin & Jenrette
Directorships: Epana Networks, LiveVox
David Istock, Partner
e-mail: distock@bluefishventures.com
Education: Wharton School, University of Pennsylvania
Background: Director/Head of Technology M&A, Cowen & Company; Executive Director, M&A, USB Investment Bank; VP, M&A, PaineWebber Inc.

298 BLUEPOINTE VENTURES
999 Baker Way
Suite 150
San Mateo, CA 94404

Phone: 650-293-4545
e-mail: info@bluepointeventures.com
web: www.bluepointeventures.com

Mission Statement: Seeks to invest in game-changing companies within the tech industry, including innovations in AI, Virtual Reality, and Big Data.
Founded: 2014
Investment Criteria: Early Stage
Industry Group Preference: Artificial Intelligence, Virtual Reality, Big Data, Cloud Data
Portfolio Companies: AngelPad, Avaamo, AdRise, Arkin, Boomtrain, Bullpen Capital, ClassPass, Compound, Cota Capital, Estate Assist, Fanduel, The Hive, Lemonade, Next Force Technology, Paintzen, Periscope Data, PipeDrive, Pogoseat, Postmates, Streamlined Ventures, Tadem Capital, Tekion Cloud, UpCounsel, Wanderu, Zodius
Key Executives:
Sandeep Sardana, Co-Founder/Managing Director
Education: BS, Rutgers University; MBA, Columbia Business School

299 BLUERUN VENTURES
545 Middlefield Road
Suite 250
Menlo Park, CA 94025

Phone: 650-462-7250
e-mail: ventures@brv.com
web: www.brv.com

Mission Statement: BlueRun operates globally as a single, ROI driven fund that invests in early stage mobile and information technology companies.
Founded: 1998
Average Investment: $1-6 million
Investment Criteria: Early-Stage
Industry Group Preference: Mobile Communications Devices, Information Technology, Internet, Media, Enterprise Software, Semiconductors, Components & IoT, Social Media, Digital Media & Marketing
Portfolio Companies: Airobotics, Apricot Forest, Availink, App Central, Banjo, BlueCart, BetterCompany, Changba, Chunyu, Channel Breeze, Coupa, Enpocket, FreedomPay, Foodspotting, Ganji, HumanAPI, Kitman Labs, Kabbage,

Venture Capital & Private Equity Firms / Domestic Firms

Location Labs, Meilishuo, Nom, PPTV, PayPal, Radius, SoundWall, Topsy, uMake, Verve, VisionScape, Varolii, Waze, ZeeMee, 140 Proof

Other Locations:
BlueRun Investment Consulting (Shanghai) Co.
Room 2361, 23/F, 5 Corperate Avenue
150 Hubin Road
Shanghai 200021
China
Phone: 86-21-8013-5016

BlueRun Investment Consulting (Shanghai) Co.
Suite 1308, Office Tower 1, China Central Place
No. 81 Jianguo Road, Chaoyang District
Beijing 100025
China
Phone: 86-10-5969-5680 **Fax:** 86-10-5969-5681

BRV Korea Advisors Co. Ltd.
4th Floor
Eonju-ro 168gil 6, Gangnam-gu
Seoul 06020
Korea
Phone: 82-2-2088-3900 **Fax:** 82-2-2088-3901

Key Executives:
John Malloy, Co-Founder/General Partner
Education: BA, Boston College; JD, George Mason School of Law
Background: Nokia; MCI; Co-Founder, Go Communications
Jonathan Ebinger, General Partner
Education: BS, Finance, Virginia Polytechnic Institute; MBA, Darden Grad. School of Business, University of Virginia
Background: VP Marketing, Qwest Communications; Bell Atlantic Internet Solutions; MCI Communications; Founder, Simply Savings
Directorships: ASIP; Enpocket; LightningCast; Qovia, SunRocket
Cheryl Cheng, General Partner
Education: BA, Stanford University; MBA, Kellogg School of Management, Northwestern University
Background: Clorox; The Sharper Image
Kwan Yoon, General Partner
Education: BA, Economics, MS, Management Science & Engineering, Stanford University
Jui Tan, General Partner
Education: BS, Electrical & Electronics Engineering, Nanyang Technological University; MBA, International Institute of Management Development
Background: Director Global Service Development, Singapore Telecom; Engineering Management, IBM
Jeff Tannenbaum, Venture Partner
Background: Founder, PhotoCrank; Co-Founder, DreamFront;

300 BLUESTEM CAPITAL COMPANY
101 S Phillips Avenue
Suite 501
Sioux Falls, SD 57104

Phone: 605-331-0091
e-mail: info@bluestemcapital.com
web: www.bluestemcapital.com

Mission Statement: Provides investors and portfolio companies with service and returns by creating an environment that fosters professional investing and stewardship of capital in accordance with proven strategies and beliefs.

Geographic Preference: Midwest United States
Fund Size: $66 million
Founded: 1989
Average Investment: $500,000 - $3 million
Minimum Investment: $500,000
Investment Criteria: Early Stage, Mid-to-Late Stage Companies
Industry Group Preference: Business Products & Services, Information Services, Agriculture, Retail, Consumer & Leisure, Healthcare, Real Estate, Energy, Manufacturing
Portfolio Companies: ACTV8me, Ambient Clinical Analytics, Clarify Medical, Conventus Orthopaedics, CRA Continental Realty Advisors, Dakotaland Manufacturing, EDCO, Equinox, eyeBrain Medical, ianTECH, Intelliflux, LENTECHS, MembranePRO, NoteSwift, Pivitol Health Solutions, POET, PolyCera Membranes, Regency Midwest, sight4all, SpringCM, Surface Pharmaceuticals, SYNQ3, Tear Film Innovations, TearClear, The Community Company, The Pairie Club, TherOptix, Virtual Incision, VIRUN

Key Executives:
Steve Kirby, Founding Partner
Education: BS, Political Science, Arizona State University; JD, University of South Dakota School of Law
Background: Western Surety Company; Lieutenant Governor, State of South Dakota
Tyler J Stowater, Partner/Vice President
Education: BS, Agriculture Economics, MS, Economics, South Dakota State University
Background: Budget Analyst, State Economist & Deputy Commissioner, Bureau of Finance & Management, State of South Dakota; Assistant Vice President, Citibank
Sandy Horst, Partner/CFO
Education: BS, Accounting, University of South Dakota
Background: Senior Manager, Tax Department, McGladrey & Pullen
Nikole Mulder, Partner/Vice President
Education: BS, Business Administration, Master of Professional Accountancy, University of South Dakota
Background: CPA, Eide Baily LLP

301 BLUETREE VENTURE FUND
PO Box 1323
Wexford, PA 15090

Phone: 724-475-4538
e-mail: info@bluetreeventurefund.com
web: www.bluetreeventurefund.com

Mission Statement: A venture capital firm based in Pittsburgh, the BlueTree Venture Fund invests in early stage companies across a variety of technology-based sectors.

Geographic Preference: Mid-Adlantic Region
Fund Size: $10 million
Investment Criteria: Early Stage
Industry Group Preference: Technology, Medical Technology, Information Technology, Software
Portfolio Companies: ALung Technologies, ApartmentJet, C360, ChromaTan, Encentiv Energy, Gemmus Pharma, HealthTell, Niche.com, Physcient, Rinovum Women's Health, SLED Mobile, Thread

Key Executives:
Catherine Mott, Managing Partner
Education: MBA, Finance
Background: Chairman, Angel Capital Education Foundation; Founder, Synergetic Sales Performance Group; Founder, Indigo Capital Development
David Motley, Managing Partner
Education: BS, Mechanical Engineering, University of Pittsburgh; MBA, Harvard Business School
Background: VP & General Manager, Covidien Inc. Surgical Devices; Respironics
Directorships: First National Bank, Optimal Strategix Group, Gemmus Pharma, ALung
Roger Byford, Managing Partner
Education: MA, Electrical Engineering, University of Cambridge
Background: President, Vocollect Healthcare Systems
Jon Pastor, Venture Partner
Education: BA, Chemistry & Economics, Case Western Reserve University; MBA, Harvard Business School
Background: Engagement Manager, McKinsey &

Venture Capital & Private Equity Firms / Domestic Firms

Company; President & Co-Founder, Rent Jungle; President & CTO, The Rainmaker Group

302 BLUFF POINT ASSOCIATES
274 Riverside Avenue
Westport, CT 06880

Phone: 203-557-9450
web: www.bluffpt.com

Mission Statement: Bluff Point Associates is a private equity firm based in Westport, Connecticut. Bluff Point actively invests in information services companies supporting the banking, trust, securities, retirement and wealth management sectors of the financial services industry, as well as the healthcare information services sector.

Investment Criteria: Growth Companies
Industry Group Preference: Fintech, Healthcare Technology
Portfolio Companies: fi360, FPS Group, HealthSavings Administrators, Innovest, PEX Card, TSA Consulting Group

Key Executives:
Thomas E. McInerney, CEO
Education: St. John's University
Background: General Partner, Welsh Carson Anderson & Stowe; Co-Founder/President, Dama Telecommunications
Paula G. McInerney, President
Education: BA, Manhattanville University; MBA, Stern School of Business
Background: COO, Oppenheimer Funds; Managing Director, Bankers Trust Company
Neil Q. Gabriele, Managing Director
Education: BA, Political Science, University of Richmond; MBA, Vanderbilt University
Background: Optech Systems
John L. McInerney, Managing Director
Education: BA, JD, St. John's University
Background: Cullen & Dykman; Counsel, New York City Police Department
John P. Gilliam, Managing Director
Education: BBA, Ohio University
Background: SVP, Finance, The BISYS Group
Kevin P. Fahey, Managing Director
Education: BBA, Accounting, Saint Bonaventure University
Background: SVP/CFO, Healthland
Jamie J. DeRubertis, Managing Director
Background: Matrix Settlement & Clearance Services

303 BLUM CAPITAL PARTNERS
909 Montgomery Street
San Francisco, CA 94133

Phone: 415-434-1111 Fax: 415-434-3130
web: www.blumcapital.com

Mission Statement: Blum Capital has established a record of generating superior risk-adjusted returns for its institutional and high net worth partners by adhering to a highly focused, distinctive investment strategy.

Fund Size: $3 Billion
Founded: 1975
Average Investment: $10 million
Industry Group Preference: Diversified
Portfolio Companies: Aimia Inc., American Reprographics Inc., Axipointe Inc., Athlon Holdings, The Bisys Group, BankThai, Ceridian Corp, Convergys Corp., CareFusion, CIMB Group Holding, CoreLogic, Career Education, Current Media, CBRE Group, Copart Inc., Dianon Systems Inc., Electronics for Imaging, Echostar Corp., Fairmont Hotels, Fair, Isaac & Company, First Health Group Corp., First American Financial, Glenrose Instruments, Haemonetics Corp., ITT Educational Services, JDA Software, John H. Harland Company, Janus Capital Group, Kinetic Concepts Inc., Korea First Bank, Laboratory Corp. of America, Lincoln Educational Services, Magellan Health Services Inc., MoneyGram International, Montpelier Re Holdings, Nu Skin Enterprises, NutriSystem Inc., National Data Corp., NCR Corp., Novell Inc., Nova Corp., Paxar Corp., Pegasus Solutions, PRGX Global, Pediatrix Medical Group Inc., Payless ShoeSource, Playtex Products Inc., Rovi Inc., Skillsoft PLC, Suntron Corp., Synopsys Inc., Ross Stores, Renal Care Group, Scott Technologies Inc., TCF Financial Corp., Thomson, Tiffany & Co., Timberland Corp., Western Wireless Corp., Tokeheim Corp., Waddell Reed Financial Inc., Washington Mutual, Williams Sonoma, Websense, Xtralis Group, Zebra Technologies

Key Executives:
Richard C. Blum, Chairman
Education: BA, MBA, University of California, Berkeley
Background: Co-Founder, Newbridge Capital
Directorships: PAG

304 BLUMBERG CAPITAL
501 Folsom St
Suite 400
San Francisco, CA 94105

Phone: 415-905-5000 Fax: 415-357-5027
e-mail: info@blumbergcapital.com
web: www.blumbergcapital.com

Mission Statement: Early-stage venture capital firm.

Fund Size: $40 million
Founded: 1991
Average Investment: $3 million
Minimum Investment: $500,000
Investment Criteria: Seed, Early Stage
Industry Group Preference: Networking, Enterprise Services, Wireless Technologies, Security, Technology, Infrastructure, Information Technology, Software, Digital Media & Marketing, Social Media, Mobile, Consumer Internet, SaaS
Portfolio Companies: Addepar, Any.do, Appboy, BrainRush, Carwoo, CaseStack, Chirpme, Cook Taste Eat, CoverHound, Credorax, Cyvera, Damballa, Dealsquare, Dekko, DoubleVerify, Elevator, Ellie, ePet World, Fanzila, FEEX, HootSuite, Isocket, Kreditech, Lenddo, LiteScape, mAdvertise, Mentad, Merchant Atlas, Mishor, Moment.Me, Mom Trusted, Mygola, Nutanix, Paid Piper, Parse.ly, Paymill, Revionics, Sonar, The One Page Company, Trulioo, Upfront Digital Media, Urbanara, VideoGenia, Wummel Kiste, Yap.tv, Zanbato, ZipZap

Other Locations:
39 Montefiore St
Tel Aviv 6520108
Israel
Phone: 972-3-7573107

Key Executives:
David J. Blumberg, Founder and Managing Partner
Education: AB, Government, Harvard College; MBA, Stanford Graduate School of Business
Background: Investment Manager, Claridge Investments; Investment Manager, Adler & Co; Investment Manager, Apax Partners; Investment Manager, T Rowe Price Associates
Directorships: CaseStack; Siperian; IP Infusion; Seclarity; Insightix; Board Member, Jewish Community Federation of San Francisco; Member, Pacific Council on International Policy
Bruce K. Taragin, Managing Director
Education: BA, Finance/Communications, Yeshiva University; MBA, JD, Fordham University
Background: Senior Management, Charles River Computers; Manager, Hambrecht & Quist; Manager, Mayer Brown & Platt; Manager, Bankers Trust Company
Directorships: CaseStack; Go Networks; Insightix; LiteScape; PureSight; Vista Research

Venture Capital & Private Equity Firms / Domestic Firms

305 BMW I VENTURES
2606 Bayshore Parkway
Mountain View, CA 94043

web: www.bmwiventures.com

Mission Statement: Seeks start-ups with the potential to create a lasting impact in the area of mobility services, primarily through cooperation with the BMW i brand. Additionally, these start-ups should have a strong focus on improving personal mobility in urban areas - automotive or otherwise. Whether it be intermodal travel, smart parking, recommendations, communication or other avenues, these services should deliver innovative and intelligent benefits to today's growing urban population.

Founded: 2011
Industry Group Preference: E-Mobility, Autonomous Driving, Digital Cars, Artificial Intelligence, Clean Energy
Portfolio Companies: Bus.com, Carbon, Caroobi, Charge Master, Charge Point, Desktop Metal, DSP Concepts, Embark, Fair, Gan Systems, Just Park, Life360, Moovit, Nauto, Proterra, Rever, RideCell, Shift, Skurt, Stratim, Strivr, Scoop, Xometry, ZenDrive

Key Executives:
 Uwe Higgen, Managing Director
 Background: Project Manager, BMW Group; Strategic Council, NAUTO
 Directorships: Gan Systems Inc.
 Ulrich Quay, Managing Director
 Zach Barasz, Partner
 Education: Stanford Graduate School of Business
 Background: Kleiner Perkins Caufield & Byers
 Michael Christoph Hammer, Chief Financial Officer

306 BNY MELLON CAPITAL MARKETS
240 Greenwich Street
New York, NY 10286

Phone: 212-495-1784
web: www.bnymellon.com

Mission Statement: BNY Mellon Capital Markets is dedicated to providing flexible and responsive financing solutions to private equity firms and middle market companies that seek junior capital solutions to finance growth, acquisitions or recapitalizations.

Geographic Preference: United States
Founded: 1991
Minimum Investment: $500,000
Investment Criteria: Prefer $3 - $20mm of subordinated debt or $2 - $10mm of private equity. Annual sales in excess of $25mm and operating cash flow of at least $3mm.

Key Executives:
 Thomas P (Todd) Gibbons, Chief Executive Officer
 Education: BS, Wake Forest University; MBA, Pace University
 Background: CEO, Clearing, Market & Client Management; CFO, BNY Mellon; CFO, Bank of New York; Assistant Treasurer, Handy & Harman
 Bridget E Engle, Chief Operating Officer/Chief Technology Officer
 Background: Executive/CIO, Bank of America; Managing Director, Depository Trust & Clearing Corporation; CIO, Lehman Brothers

307 BOLDCAP VENTURES LLC
750 Lexington Avenue
6th Floor
New York, NY 10022

Phone: 212-730-5498 **Fax:** 917-591-0880

Mission Statement: Boldcap Ventures LLC invests in early to mid-stage companies and focuses primarily on the healthcare and technology industries.

Average Investment: $5 - $15 million
Investment Criteria: Early-Stage, Mid-Stage
Industry Group Preference: Healthcare, Technology
Portfolio Companies: AgraQuest, Aquea Scientific, Cylex, Go Fish, The NewsMarket, Pivot Solutions, Proto Software, Precision Therapeutics

Key Executives:
 Amy Rosen Wildstein, Fund Manager
 Background: Blackstone Group; Principal, Solera Capital; Morgan Stanley

308 BOLDSTART VENTURES
3350 Virginia Street
Suite 262
Miami, FL 33133

web: www.boldstart.vc

Mission Statement: BoldStart Ventures is interested in IT infrastructure and software development.

Founded: 2010
Industry Group Preference: Information Technology, Data Analytics, Software, SaaS, Cyber Security, Virtual Reality, Artificial Intelligence, Mobility
Portfolio Companies: AskWonder, Auxon, BigID, Blaze Software, BlockDaemon, Catalytic, Clay, Coherent Path, Dark, Divide, Dropout Labs, Emissary, FortressIQ, Front, GoInstant, GoToMeeting, Greenplum, Handshake, HYPR, IOpipe, Init.ai, Jyve, Klipfolio, Kustomer, LivePerson, Manifold, MState, Pinpoint, Preact, Rapportive, Replicated, Robin, Security Scorecard, Sling, Smallstep, Snyk, SocialRank, Superhuman Labs, Rebel Mail, ThinkNear, Truly, Wallaroo Labs, WEVR, WorkRails, Yhat, Yipit Data

Key Executives:
 Ed Sim, Founder/General Partner
 Education: AB, Harvard University
 Background: Co-Founder, MState; Managing Director, Dawntreader Ventures; Investment Analyst, JP Morgan; Sr. Investment Analyst, Equitable Real Estate
 Charlotte Chapanoff, General Manager
 Education: BA, Long Island University
 Background: Assistant Account Manager, Under Armour
 Eliot Durbin, General Partner
 Education: BA, Georgetown University
 Background: Assistant VP, Permal Asset Management; Managing Director/Co-Founder, Penny Black Holdings LLC; Co-Founder, MState

309 BONFIRE VENTURES
725 Arizona Ave.
Suite 400
Santa Monica, CA 90401

web: www.bonfirevc.com

Mission Statement: Bonfire Ventures invests in companies that are designing software solutions that change the way business is conducted.

Investment Criteria: Early-Stage
Industry Group Preference: Business to Business, Software
Portfolio Companies: Adstage, Bitium, BlueCasa, Boulevard, Branch, Burstly, Cadforce, Campus Explorer, ChowNow, Clearwire, Clique, Comparably, Connexity, ConversionLogic, Credit Key, DataPop, Disqo, Divshot, Earnest, EdgeCast, Elephant Drive, Emailage, Embrace.io, EvConnect, Fama, FieldTest, Fuel 50, FutureVault, Gradient, Haawk, HiQ, HG Data, Honk, Inspire, InVia Robotics, Invoca, InvolveSoft, JazzHR, Kaleo, Keen IO, Kittyhawk, Launchpad LA, Lettuce, LiftIgniter, Local Market Launch, MessageLabs, Mobcrush, MomentFeed, mPulse, Niantic, Nord Sense, OpenDrives, OpenPath, Orbitera, Packet Island, Particle, Pathmatics, Pingg, PingThings, Pledgeling, Postie, Prevoty, Prompt.ly, Qordoba, Quietly, Rainforest, Raken, Ranker, Reaction Commerce, Remote.it, Rentlytics, RESC, Respondly, Rockbot, Saferide, Scopely, Sense360, Shift, Shippabo, Sideqik, Silversheet, SimpleLegal, SteelHouse, TallyGo!, TaxJar, theTradeDesk, ThinkIQ, Tradesy, Tray,

Venture Capital & Private Equity Firms / Domestic Firms

Trinity Mobile Networks, Tuition.io, Vintra, Windfall, Yello Mobile, Zingle

Other Locations:
803 Chapala St.
Santa Barbara, CA 93101

Key Executives:
Jim Andelman, Co-Founder/Managing Director
Education: BS, Economics, Wharton School; MBA, Tuck School of Business
Background: Managing Partner, Rincon Venture Partners; Broadview Capital Partners
Directorships: Campus Explorer, Conversion Logic, Keen IO, Qordoba, Rentlytics, Rainforst QA, Rockbot, SteelHouse, Tradesy
Mark Mullen, Co-Founder/Managing Director
Education: BSBA, University of Denver; MBA, Thunderbird School of Global Management
Background: Managing Partner, Double M Partners; Managing Partner, Mull Capital
Directorships: Fama, Trinity Mobile Networks, Altice USA

310 BOOST VC
55 East Third Avenue
San Mateo, CA 94401

e-mail: info@boost.vc
web: www.boost.vc

Mission Statement: Boost VC invests in innovative technology with a speciality in virtual realities and blockchain.
Geographic Preference: International
Founded: 2012
Average Investment: up to $50,000
Investment Criteria: Ownership of 7%
Industry Group Preference: Virtual Reality & Augmented Reality, Robotics, Space Technology, AI, Technology
Portfolio Companies: Mindshow, Kite & Lightingm, 89, Boom, Realities.io, TheWaveVR, SculptiVR, Fearless, JanusVR, Unimersiv, Vizor, Spaces, Casino VR Poker, VArchive, Aemass, Lingoland, BinaryVR, Beloola, Kokowa, Construct, Primitive, Jig Space, Twindom, Quark VR, Ease, Pixel Ripped, Jump, Ralph, Surreal, Bouncy, Imgnation, Virt, Orb, Spacesys, One Caring Team, Metaphysics VR, 3D-SensIR, Collect, Uraniom, Samo, Karobi, Beast, Dimension IO, Flipside, Galatea, Microtrip, Virtual Speech, Vrart, Xploadr, Wyre, Etherscan, Coinbase, Veem, Blockcypher, Ripio, T3, Abra, Aragon, Sfox, Unocoin, Polychain Capital, IPFS, Yours, Hijro, JoyStream, BitRefill, Filecoin, Volabit, Stampery, Coinut, Shake, BlinkTrade, Lawnmower, Hashrabbit, Leet, Coinprism, Celery, Bitquick, Simply Vital Health, The Sun Exchange, Pop Chest, Coinage, Atlas, Coin Jar, Factury, Loanbase, Mego, Coinhako, Blossom, Ownershipp, Rainvow, Rehive, Ubby, BitWall, Bitproof.io, Gliph, Surebits, Follow The Coin, Volt Markets, CleverCoin, Favor, Octane AI, 7 Shifts, & Ava, Blockscore, DeepGram, Pillow, Cobalt, Eagaveev, Mirror, Rebel Coast Winery, Swiftly, Trending, Kubos, CommitChange, Volley, Gravity, Feastly, Gun, GlycoProx, Listenloop, AuditFile.com, & Sunsama, Strengthportal, Eva, Unaptent, Globevestor, + GNEO, Appfuel, Perch, Checkbook, Swell Rewards, Seeds, Down, Scalpr, Ziibra, WorkingOn, Roam, AirBoard, Kriya, Launcher, LeadFlip, NearGroup, SenseiHub, Teamwork.ai, TensorFlight, Waylo

Key Executives:
Adam Draper, Founder/Managing Director
Education: University of California, LA
Background: Founder, Xpert Financial
Brayton Williams, Founder/Partner
Background: Morgan Stanley; Boost Bitcoin Fund, Xpert Financial; Northrop Grumman, Taylor Frigon Capital Management; Advisor at, Miffiel, 7 Shifts, Etherscan.io, Aragon, MyEtherWallet
Maddie Callander, Director of Operations
Education: BA, Art History & Spanish, Denison

University
Background: Private Aviation Department, Yellowstone Club; Event Coordination, Van Wyck & Van Wyck

311 BOREALIS VENTURES
10 Allen Street
Hanover, NH 03755

Phone: 603-643-1500
e-mail: team@borealisventures.com
web: www.borealisventures.com

Mission Statement: Borealis Ventures is a seed and early-stage venture capital firm uniquely focused on investing in companies in Northern New England and throughout the Dartmouth College network.
Average Investment: $2.5 million
Minimum Investment: $100,000
Investment Criteria: Seed, Early-Stage
Industry Group Preference: Applications Software & Services, Internet, Mobile Media, Technology
Portfolio Companies: Adimab, At Last Software, Avedro, Avitide, Blockable, Builtr Labs, Compass Therapeutics, CoUrbanize, Dandelion Energy, Dyn, Envista, Fieldlens, Foodbuzz, Flurry, Flux, GlyciFi, Handmark, Honest Buildings, Icovia, M2S, Makeover Solutions, Measurabl, Newforma, OmniEarth, Scribe Software, SketchFab, Smartvid.io, Spaceclaim, Tinkercad, Vets First Choice, VICO Software, Wingu

Other Locations:
31 St. James Avenue
6th Floor
Boston, MA 02116

Key Executives:
Jesse Devitte, Managing Director/Co-Founder
e-mail: jdevitte@borealisventures.com
Background: Softdesk; Autodesk; Handmark
Directorships: Envista, Handmark, Newforma, Vico
Phil Ferneau, Managing Director/Co-Founder
e-mail: phil@borealisventures.com
Education: BA, Dartmouth College; JD, University of Virginia School of Law; MBA, Tuck School of Business, Dartmouth College
Background: Executive Director, Center for Private Equity & Entrepreneurship, Tuck School of Business, Dartmouth College
Matt Rightmire, Managing Director
e-mail: matt@borealisventures.com
Education: MBA, Tuck School of Business at Dartmouth College; BS, Industrial Engineering, Stanford University
Background: COO, Efficient Frontier; Yahoo

312 BOSTON CAPITAL
One Boston Place
Boston, MA 02108

Phone: 617-624-8900
e-mail: bcinfo@bostoncapital.com
web: www.bostoncapital.com

Mission Statement: Boston Capital is the nation's leading provider of equity investments in multifamily real estate funds.
Geographic Preference: Nationwide
Fund Size: $250 million
Founded: 1974
Investment Criteria: Class A Apartments, Tax Credit Funds
Industry Group Preference: Real Estate, Property Development

Key Executives:
Jack Manning, President/Chief Executive Officer
617-624-8501
e-mail: jmanning@bostoncapital.com
Education: Boston College
Background: President's Export Council; President's Advisory Committee on the Arts

Venture Capital & Private Equity Firms / Domestic Firms

Directorships: Chairman, Distinguised Visitors Program; Liberty Mutual Group
Jeffrey H. Goldstein, Executive Vice President/Chief Operating Officer
617-624-8640
e-mail: jgoldstein@bostoncapital.com
Education: BA, University of Colorado; MBA, Northeastern University
Background: Manager of Finance, A.J. Lane & Co.; Manager, Homeowner Financial Services
Kevin P. Costello, Executive Vice President/Director, Institutional Investing
617-624-8550
e-mail: kcostello@bostoncapital.com
Education: Stonehill College; MBA, Finance, Rutgers Graduate School of Business Administration
Directorships: FamilyAid Boston

313 BOSTON CAPITAL VENTURES
Boston, MA 02109

e-mail: info@bcv.com
web: www.bcv.com

Mission Statement: Boston Capital Ventures is a private venture capital firm which invests in early-stage companies in the information technology and telecommunications services industries.

Geographic Preference: United States, Europe, Asia, Latin America
Fund Size: $150 million
Founded: 1982
Average Investment: $1 - $10 million
Minimum Investment: $1 million
Investment Criteria: Start-Up, Niche, Regional, Multinational, Fortune 100
Industry Group Preference: Technology, Software, Telecommunications, Enterprise Software, Infrastructure, Retailing, Transportation, Business to Business, Marketing
Portfolio Companies: Availant, Centric Software, Exa Corporation, FareChase, HubX, iBreva, ImpactXoft, Khimetrics, RealManage, Reflexion Network Solutions, Signiant, Thor Technologies, Veridiem, Wandrian, Yokel

Key Executives:
Johan von der Goltz, General Partner
e-mail: jgoltz@bcv.com
Education: Massachusettes Institute of Technology, Harvard Business School
Background: Otto Wolff AG; Trinkhaus Bank; Compania Argo Comercial SA; Cerveceria del Sur SA
Directorships: International Cornerstone Group, Fast Channel Networks, Conservative Tourism
Jack Shields, General Partner
e-mail: jshields@bcv.com
Education: Sorcester Polytechnic Institute's School of Industrial Management; Harvard Business School PMD; Honorary Doctorate of Engineering, WPI
Background: KFgital Equipment Corporation; President/CEOComputervision
Directorships: Iirector, Centric Software; Director, Exa; Director, ImpactXoft
Alex von der Goltz, Partner
e-mail: agoltz@bcv.com
Education: Brown University, MIT Sloan School of Management
Background: International Music Division, Bertelsmann Entertainment; Management Consultant, Roland Berger; Professional Services/Technical Sales, Oracle Corporation & Techgnosis
Directorships: Centric Software; Reflexion Network Solutions; Signiant; Thor Technologies

314 BOSTON GLOBAL VENTURES, LLC
One Broadway
14th Floor
Cambridge, MA 02142

Mission Statement: Boston Global Ventures is a Boston based venture capital firm supporting early-stage high-impact technology companies.

Investment Criteria: Early Stage
Industry Group Preference: Technology

315 BOSTON MILLENNIA PARTNERS
30 Rowes Wharf
Suite 400
Boston, MA 02110

Phone: 617-428-5150 **Fax:** 617-428-5160
web: www.bostonmillenniapartners.com

Mission Statement: Boston Millennia Partners is a private equity and venture capital firm active nationwide.

Geographic Preference: United States, Canada
Fund Size: $700 million
Founded: 1984
Average Investment: $10 - $15 million
Minimum Investment: $3 million
Investment Criteria: Early Stage, Later Stage, Expansion
Industry Group Preference: Healthcare, Business Services, Information Technology
Portfolio Companies: Arthrosurface, Athenix, CardioMEMS, Coapt Systems, Collegium, CombinatoRx, eMed Technologies, EpiGenesis Pharmaceuticals, EPIX Pharmaceuticals, Galt Associates, GlycoFi, Histogenics Corporation, ILEX, MedAptus, MedAptus, Medical Management of New England, MedSpan, Novalar, Parexel, PHT, Proteome, Sapphire Therapeutics, Tektagen

Key Executives:
Dana Callow, Managing General Partner
e-mail: dana@bmpvc.com
Education: MBA, Amos Tuck School, dartmouth college; tufts university
Background: General Partner, Co-Founder, Boston Capital Ventures; Sr Consultant, Braxton Associates
Directorships: Bright Horizons, Collegium, HotJobs, ILEX Oncology, Infotrieve, iVillage, Knowledge Impact, MedAptus, Medical Management of New England, PAREXEL International, PHT, Tektagen
Rob Sherman, Operating Partner
e-mail: robs@bmpvc.com
Education: MBA, Harvard Business School; Amherst College
Background: Boston Capital Ventures; General Partner, Hambro International Venture Fund
Directorships: Concentrix, MedSpan, Neoworld, NuVox Communications, TechSmart, UNIsite, V-Span
Marty Hernon, General Partner
e-mail: marty@bmpvc.com
Education: BA Economics, Boston College; MA Economics, University of Maryland; JD, Georgetown University
Background: President, Boston Capital Ventures; Asst General Counsel, Lifetime Corporation; Of Counsel Business Department, Warner & Stackpole/Kirkpartrick & Lockhart
Directorships: Dawntreader Funds, VIA Net.Works, WebCT, YankeeTek
Bruce Tiedemann, Partner/CFO
e-mail: bruce@bmpvc.com
Education: Graduate, Bentley College
Background: Founder, Tiedemann & Company; CFO/Controller, serveral startup venture funded companies; Certified Public Accountant

Venture Capital & Private Equity Firms / Domestic Firms

316 BOSTON SEED CAPITAL
37 Walnut Street
Suite 110
Wellesley, MA 02347

e-mail: info@bostonseed.com
web: www.bostonseed.com

Mission Statement: Boston Seed Capital provides seed state funding for internet-enabled businesses. The firm's approach is to identify and help extraordinary talent to create great new companies, and to contribute to the culture of invention, leadership and learning in Boston. Boston Seed's team is made up of operators who have founded companies, grown companies, raised capital, acquired companies, taken companies public, and exited companies.
Geographic Preference: United States
Founded: 2010
Industry Group Preference: Internet, Consumer Internet, Business to Business, SaaS
Portfolio Companies: Alignable, Altiscale, Blaze.io, BostInno, Careport Health, Clypd, Codeship, Contactually, Directr, Draft Kings, Evertrue, FamilyID.com, FlyWire, Gamersensei, GrapeviceLogic.com, Horse Network, Humanize, Indico.co, Jebbit, Kindara, Kinvey, Mylestoned, NBD Nano, OfferLogic, Openbay, Promoboxx, UberSense, RunKeeper, Shareaholic, Smackhigh, Sold.

Key Executives:
  Nicole M. Stata, Founder/Managing Director
  e-mail: nstata@bostonseed.com
  Background: Founder, Deploy Solutions; Restrac; Lotus Development Corporation
  Peter Blacklow, Senior Partner
  e-mail: pblacklow@bostonseed.com
  Education: Harvard University
  Background: President, Worldwinner; EVP, Digital, GSN; SVP, Marketing, Monster
  Directorships: eSkill.com, WGBH
  Dave Balter, Venture Partner
  e-mail: davebalter@gmail.com
  Background: CEO, BzzAgent; Co-Founder, Word of Mouth Marketing Association
  Directorships: Promoboxx, Relay Rides, eLaCarte, ProctorCam, HelpScout

317 BOSTON UNIVERSITY - TECHNOLOGY DEVELOPMENT
One Silber Way
8th Floor
Boston, MA 02215

web: www.bu.edu/researchsupport/project-lifecycle/bring-to-market

Mission Statement: Provides venture capital to early-stage companies. The Fund focuses on companies within the Information Technology and Life Sciences industries.
Geographic Preference: Northeast United States
Fund Size: $30 million
Founded: 1975
Average Investment: $500,000 to $1.5 million
Minimum Investment: $250,000
Investment Criteria: Early Stage
Industry Group Preference: Information Technology, Life Sciences
Portfolio Companies: Arradial, Artel Video, Boston Medical Technologies, C-Port Corporation, CardioFocus, Cellicon, Centagenetix, Cetaccean Networks, Commonwealth Network Technologies, Concord Communications, Continental Cablevision, Coriolis Networks, Crossbeam Systems, Cynosure, CytoLogix Corporation, Emperative, Evrest Broadband Networks, FASTech Integration, HPR, Holographix, InfoLibria, Invisable Hand Networks, Maple Tree Networks, MicroCHIPS, MicroE Systems, Nitro med, Nitronex, OutStart, Pharmadyne, Predictive Networks, Quanhtum Bridge Communications, Quarry Technologies, QuitNet, Sandburst Corporation, Scion, Seragen, SilverBack Technologies, StarGen, Synchrologic, Vibrant Technologies, Viewlogic Systems, Wave Systems

318 BOULDER VENTURES LTD
1941 Pearl Street
Suite 300
Boulder, CO 80302

Phone: 303-444-6950
e-mail: james@boulderventures.com
web: www.boulderventures.com

Mission Statement: Identifies exceptional entrepreneurs building market-leading technology companies and provides funding, contacts and experience needed to succeed in today's highly competitive environment.
Geographic Preference: Mid-Atlantic, Colorado, California
Fund Size: $300 million
Founded: 1995
Average Investment: $5-$10 million
Minimum Investment: $2-$4 million
Investment Criteria: Early-Stage
Industry Group Preference: Information Technology, Internet Technology, Retailing, Life Sciences, Biotechnology, Health Related, Nutrition, Food & Beverage, Data Storage, Communications
Portfolio Companies: ARCA Biopharma, Array BioPharma, Barofold, BiOptix, Bluesocket, BroadHop, Cadre Technologies, CenterStone Technologies, ClaraBridge, Cogent Communications, Compatible Systems, Datavail, Dharmacon, Entelos, Entevo Corp., Era, Estorian, Everest Software, Exactis.com, Federated Media Publishing, Finali Corporation, Genomica, Hiberna Corporation, iLumin Software, Interland, kSaria Corporation, LeftHand Networks, Lijit Networks, Market Force Information, Metron Aviation, Millennium Pharmacy Systems, MiRagen Therapeutics, ProStor Systems, Rally Software, SafeRent, TidalTV, Videology, Wall Street On Demand, XIFIN, Zenoss

Other Locations:
  5425 Wisconsin Avenue
  Suite 704
  Chevy Chase, MD 20815
  Phone: 301-913-0213

Key Executives:
  Kyle Lefkoff, General Partner
  e-mail: kyle@boulderventures.com
  Education: BA, Vassar College; MBA, University of Chicago
  Directorships: Metabolite Laboratories, Trust Company of America, Symetix, Vexcel Corporation, ArrayBioPharma, LeftHand Networks, Dharmacon
  Peter Roshko, General Partner
  e-mail: peter@boulderventures.com
  Education: MBA, Harvard Graduate School; BS, Industrial Engineering, Stanford University
  Background: General Partner, Mohr, Davidow Ventures
  Directorships: Trust Company of America, Finali, Xifin, BitBlitz, f4 Technologies
  Jonathan Perl, General Partner
  e-mail: jonathan@boulderventures.com
  Education: BA, Tufts University; MBA, Tuck School of Business, Dartmouth College
  Background: Kauffman Fellows

319 BOUNDS EQUITY PARTNERS
600 Central Avenue
Suite 230
Highland Park, IL 60035

Phone: 847-266-6300
e-mail: mab@boundsequity.com
web: www.boundsequity.com

Venture Capital & Private Equity Firms / Domestic Firms

Mission Statement: A private equity investment firm that invests in well-managed, entrepreneurial businesses.
Geographic Preference: United States, Canada
Fund Size: $100 million
Founded: 1998
Minimum Investment: $1 million
Investment Criteria: Companies With Minimum EBITDA of $1.5 Million
Industry Group Preference: Building Materials & Services, Business Products & Services, Distribution, Manufacturing, Healthcare Services
Portfolio Companies: Beacon Promotions, Clad-Rex, CrossCom, EastPoint Sports, Hollinee, L&S Mechanical, Norcraft Companies, Sportcraft, Thermo-Tech Windows

Key Executives:
  Mark Bounds, Managing Director
  e-mail: mab@boundsequity.com
  Education: BA, Marketing, University of Iowa; MBA, University of Chicago
  Background: Managing Director, Goense Bounds & Partners; Director, Allstate Private Equity; VP, Corporate Development, GAF Corporation; Co-Founder/Principal, Heller Equity Capital Corporation
  Stuart Skinner, Chief Financial Officer
  Education: BS, Accounting, Northeastern Illinois University
  Background: Controller, Goense Bounds & Partners; Controller, Allstate Private Equity
  Andy Reed, Operating Advisor
  Education: BA, History, Principia College; MBA, Indiana University
  Background: CEO, Shurline; CEO, US Builder Services, Goense Bounds; USBS

320 BOWERY CAPITAL
37 West 20th St.
New York, NY 10011

web: www.bowerycap.com

Mission Statement: We are a thesis-driven early-stage investor backing exceptional founders modernizing business through technology. From marketing and sales to analytics and infrastructure, our startups are changing the way business is done. We work hard on behalf of our founders and believe in a model of concentrated value-add with a central focus: building the base of flagship customers that startups need to achieve outsized early growth. We move fast, never waste an entrepreneur's time, always strive to be more resourceful than most, and focus our day-to-day on being the best possible partner to each and every founder we back, If you are a seed-stage entrepreneur and this is for you, let's talk.
Founded: 2010
Investment Criteria: Early-Stage
Industry Group Preference: Business Products & Services
Portfolio Companies: ActionIQ, Block Six Analytics, Carnival Mobile, ChannelEyes, Codeacademy, CredSimple, Drawbridge Networks, Electric AI, Elliot, Expedi, Fero Labs, Inpher, Leapfin, Metricly, Moat, Moment Snap, mParticle, msg.ai, Oncue, Oomnitza, Outlaw, Premise, Sailthru, Selfie Networks, StreetCred, SupplyShift, SwiftShift, TrackMaven, Transfix, VNDLY, Voxy, Wizeline, Zeus

Key Executives:
  Mike Brown Jr., Founder & Managing Partner
  Education: Columbia University
  Background: Co-Founder, AOL Ventures; Virgin Group; Morgan Stanley
  Nic Poulos, Partner
  Education: AB, History, Princeton University
  Background: Associate, AOL Ventures; Manager, Advertising.com; Technology Investment Banking Analyst, GCA Savvian Advisors

321 BOXGROUP
New York, NY

e-mail: hello@boxgroup.com
web: boxgroup.com

Mission Statement: Early stage investment fund in New York among the most active micro venture capital firms.
Geographic Preference: New York, Silicon Valley, Los Angeles
Average Investment: $50-250K
Investment Criteria: Pre-Seed, Seed
Industry Group Preference: Marketplaces, E-Commerce & Manufacturing, SaaS, Fintech
Portfolio Companies: 64x Bio, Aether Bio, Agora, Airtable, Amino, Amplitude, Apply, Arcadia, Artemys, Artsy, Astranis, Atom Computing, Baobab, Balsa, Binti, Blink Health, Boxed, Braavo, Brat TV, Bravo Sierra, The Browser Company of New york, By Humankind, Candidate Labs, Canopy Servicing, Capchase, Casetext, Celevity, Classpass, Clay, Cleancut, Codecov, Collective Retreats, Colu Technologies, CommandDot, Cricket Health, Crowd AI, Customer.io, Dataminr, David Energy, Dooly, Embrace.io, EnterMedicare, FairShake, Flexport, Giant Swarm, Goodcover, Good Dog, Harry's, Karuna Health, Kula Bio, Lotus Flare, Mantra Bio, memphis Meats, Modern Fertility, Modern Animal, Muze, Omni Labs, One Chronos, One Tap Away, OpenSpace, PaperSpace, Pickle Robot Co., Timebyping, PlanetScale, Prime Discovery, RankScience, Reverie Labs, Rockets Of Awesome, Scoot Science, Skillshare, Something Navy, Standard Bots, Terminal49, TrueAccord, Verto Education, Warby Parker, WayUp, WeRecover, Yoni Circle, OpenZeppelin, Zestful, Zipline, Zira.ai

Key Executives:
  David Tisch, Co-Founder & Managing Director
  Education: University of Pennsylvania; New York University
  Background: Vornado Realty Trust; LightsOver
  Adam Rothenberg, Co-Founder & Partner
  Education: University of Pennsylvania
  Background: Zimmer Lucas Partners; TechStars

322 BP ALTERNATIVE ENERGY VENTURES
501 Westlake Park Boulevard
Houston, TX 77079

Phone: 281-366-2000
e-mail: bpventures@bp.com
web: www.bp.com

Mission Statement: Invests in growth stage companies offering low carbon and secure energy solutions. Alternative Energy Ventures seeks to identify new technologies and business opportunities with the potential of making sound financial returns in the clean energy sector.
Fund Size: $150 million
Founded: 2006
Average Investment: $10 - $30 million
Investment Criteria: Early-Stage, Growth Stage
Industry Group Preference: Energy, Wind Power, Clean Technology, Alternative Energy, Renewable Energy, Carbon Management
Portfolio Companies: Advanced BioCatalytics, Beyond Limits, BiSN, Biosynthetic Technologies, Bright Source, Carbonfire, Chromatin, Drover, EOS, Fotech, Fulcrum, Helie Power, Lightning Hybrids, Modumetal, Peloton, Repair Pal, RocketRoute, Saltworks, Solidia Technologies, Synthetic Genomics, SMG, Tricoya, Verdezyne, Victor, Xact, Zubie

Key Executives:
  David Hayes, Chief Investment Officer/Managing Director
  Education: BA, Sheffield Hallam University
  Directorships: Chromatin, Lightning Systems, Xpansiv Data Systems, Mendal Biotechnology

Venture Capital & Private Equity Firms / Domestic Firms

323 BR VENTURE FUND
Johnson Graduate School of Management
Cornell University
106 Sage Avenue
Ithaca, NY 14853

Phone: 607-255-9395
e-mail: contact@brventurefund.com
web: www.brventurefund.com

Mission Statement: Early-stage venture capital fund operated by MBA students at Cornell University's Johnson Graduate School of Management.

Geographic Preference: Northeast United States
Average Investment: $50,000-$250,000
Investment Criteria: Seed-Stage
Portfolio Companies: Adenios, Appinions, e2e Materials, GNS Healthcare, Medical Care Corporation, NovaSterilis, Venga

324 BRADFORD EQUITIES MANAGEMENT LLC
360 Hamilton Avenue
7th Floor
White Plains, NY 10601

Phone: 914-922-7171 Fax: 914-922-7172
web: bradfordequities.com

Mission Statement: Investor in middle-market companies.

Geographic Preference: United States
Fund Size: $200 million
Founded: 1974
Average Investment: $15 - $75 million
Minimum Investment: $5 million
Investment Criteria: Middle-Market
Industry Group Preference: Distribution, Industrial Equipment, Retailing, Technology, Manufacturing
Portfolio Companies: Connecticut Color, Electron Beam Technologies, Metals Technology Corp., Sunbelt Modular, United Brass Works

Key Executives:
Robert J. Simon, Senior Managing Director
212-218-6917
Fax: 212-218-6901
Education: MBA, New York University Graduate School of Business Administration; BS in Finance, University of Minnesota School of Management
Background: Securities Analyst, Kidder, Peabody & Company; Acquisition Finance, Bancorp
Directorships: CR Gibson Company, Pamarco Technologies, Portugese Baking Company LP, VSC Corporation, Trimark USA, Wolverine Brass, Overseas Callander Fund Limited
David W. Jaffin, Senior Advisor
Education: BA, History, Harvard College; MBA, Finance/Accounting, New York University
Background: HoloPak Technologies Inc.; Poliwogg Holdings; B2B SFO; XShares Advisors LLC; Arthur Andersen & Co.
Neil J. Taylor, Principal/Chief Financial Officer
Education: BA, City of London University England; Graduate Enterprise Program, Cranfield School of Management England
Background: Senior Accountant, Dreyfus Corporation

325 BRAEMAR ENERGY VENTURES
350 Madison Avenue
New York, NY 10017

Phone: 212-697-0900
web: www.braemarenergy.com

Mission Statement: Braemar's mission is to partner with the most promising innovators to help unlock the enormous potential that exists in creating profitable solutions to the issues shaping the future of energy.

Founded: 2002
Average Investment: $1-10 million
Investment Criteria: Venture-Stage, Expansion-Stage, Early-Stage, Later-Stage
Industry Group Preference: Energy
Portfolio Companies: EnerNOC, BrightVolt, PowerGenix, Verenium, CoalTek, Utility, Stion, Afina, Fractal Systems, Cerion, CirisEnergy, Luminus, Climos, Enerkem, Laser Light Engines, Nuventix, Ioxus, Solazyme, Proterro, Opxbio, Fulham, Gridnet, Convey, General Fusion, Powervation, ViridityEnergy, LumEnergi, Amc10, Sirrus, Nexsteppe, Utilidata, Albeo, Sefaira, Chargepoint, Engine Efficiency, Aledia, Storiant, Flywheel, Next Step Living, Voxel8, Skyonic, Renew Financial, Getaround

Key Executives:
Neil S. Suslak, Managing Director
Education: BA, University of Rochester; MBA, Columbia Business School
Background: SG Warburg; Swiss Bank Corporation
Directorships: Venture Investors Association of New York; North American Advisory Board of The Cleantech Oganization
William D. Lese, Managing Director
Education: BA, Physics, MS, Energy Science; New York University
Dennis R. Costello, Partner
Education: BA, Economics, SUNY Fredonia; MA, Economics, Ohio State University; MS, Business, MIT
Background: Partner, Advent International; Managing Director, Rock Maple Ventures; General Partner, Zero Stage Capital; Executive Director, Colorado Advanced Technology Institute; Project Manager, Midwest Research Institute
Directorships: Nuventix, Climos, Fulham, Luminus, Laser Light Engines
Jiong Ma, Venture Partner
Education: PhD, Electrical Engineering, University of Colorado; MS, Electrical Engineering, Worcester Polytechnic Institute
Background: Lucent Technologies; Bell Labs

326 BRAIN TRUST ACCELERATOR FUND
800 Airport Boulevard
Suite 508
Burlingame, CA 94010

Phone: 650-375-0200 Fax: 650-375-0230
e-mail: john.reher@braintrustvc.com
web: www.braintrustvc.com

Mission Statement: Unique features of the fund include the focus and experience in brain related diseases, potential deal flow from philanthropies, operational as well as venture capital experience, and a focus on social as well as economic considerations.

Investment Criteria: Early-Stage
Industry Group Preference: Healthcare, Life Sciences, Therapeutics
Portfolio Companies: Anmestix, BrainScope Company, Chase Pharmaceuticals, NeuroFluidics, Satoris

Key Executives:
John M. Reher, Partner
Education: BS, Mathematics & Business Economics, Illinois Benedictine University; MS, Management, Northwestern University
Background: Co-Founder/General Partner, Medicus Venture Partners

Venture Capital & Private Equity Firms / Domestic Firms

327 BRAINSTORM VENTURES
4 Embarcadero Center
Suite 1400
San Francisco, CA 94111

e-mail: team@brainstorm.vc
web: brainstorm.vc

Mission Statement: BrainStorm Ventures was founded with a mission to fund emerging technology companies and actively assist them in their development.
Geographic Preference: Silicon Valley & San Francisco Bay Area
Founded: 1999
Investment Criteria: Seed-Stage, Early-Stage
Industry Group Preference: Enabling Technology, Enterprise Software, Broadband, E-Commerce & Manufacturing
Portfolio Companies: Adspace Networks, Aravo Solutions, Bid4assets, Cerego, Friend2friend, Kio Networks, Krush, Lightt, Lively, Me.com, OpenTable, Treatful, Uniscape, Vacatia, Yattos, Zappos.com

Key Executives:
Ariel Jaduszliwer, Managing Director
Education: BS, University of California Berkeley; MS, Georgia Institute of Technology; MBA, Wharton School
Background: Consultant, The Bridgespan Group; VP, Pacific Community Ventures; Fellow & Mentor, Kauffman Fellows
Directorships: ICU Eyewear Inc.; Bentek Corporation; New Leaf Paper; Freshology Inc.; Adina for Life
Eduardo Rallo, Co-Founder, Managing Director
Education: BA, Economics, University of California, San Diego; MBA, Harvard University
Background: Co-Founder, World Wrapps; Director of Special Projects, Cifra

328 BRAND FOUNDRY VENTURES
109 Nassau Street
New York, NY 10038

web: brandfoundryvc.com

Mission Statement: Brand Foundry Ventures is focused on consumer-based projects.
Industry Group Preference: Consumer, Retail
Portfolio Companies: Allbirds, Barnraiser, Birchbox, Bonobos, Brilliant Bicycles, Burrow, Clove, CoEdition, Cotopaxi, Crown Affair, Eden Health, Floravere, Floyd, Goby, Good Stock, Harry's, Haus, Henry The Dentist, Jinx, Judy, Keen Home, Kids On 45th, Kite, Kiwi Co., Koio, Leap, Lola, MixLab, Mosaic, NAJA, Nineteenth Amendment, Peachy, Peloton, Prefix, RMDY, Rockets of Awesome, Scratch Kitchen, Small Door, Smilo, Starface, Stay Tuned, The Still, The Wing, The Wonder, Warby Parker, Weller, Trace, Yumi

Other Locations:
119 Nueces Street
Austin, TX 78701

Key Executives:
Andrew Mitchell, Founder/General Partner
Education: BA, Lafayette College
Background: Co-Founder, Aspen Industries; Angel Investor
Wesley Gottesman, Principal
Education: BA, University of Virginia; MBA, Red McCombs School of Business, University of Texas
Background: Head of Product, PHLUR; Head of Product, Buzz Points Inc.; Special Projects Associate, The Idea Village
David Bell, Venture Partner
Education: BComm, University of Auckland; MA, University of Pennsylvania; MS, Stanford University; PhD, Stanford Grad. School of Business
Background: Co-Founder, Idea Farm Ventures; Associate Professor, Wharton School; Visiting Associate Professor, MIT Sloan School of Management
John Yang, Venture Partner
Education: BBA, Stephen M. Ross School of Business, University of Michigan; MBA, Wharton School
Background: Head of Strategy, Global Footwear, Nike; Director of Product Strategy & Marketing, Magic Leap; Director of Corporate Strategy & Development, NBCUniversal Media; Director of Customer Analytics, Comcast

329 BRANDON CAPITAL GROUP
459 Hamilton Avenue
Suite 205
Palo Alto, CA 94301

e-mail: info@mrcf.com.au
web: www.brandoncapital.com.au

Mission Statement: Seeks to invest in smaller middle-market business in the Northeastern US that have a defensible market position opportunity for growth, either internally or through acquisition.
Geographic Preference: Northeastern United States
Average Investment: $3 million
Minimum Investment: $1 million
Investment Criteria: Smaller Middle Market
Industry Group Preference: Manufacturing, Services, Distribution

Key Executives:
Leighton Read, Venture Partner
Education: BS, Rice University; MD, University of Texas Health Science Center
Background: Managing Director, Alloy Ventures; Managing Director/President, Pharma Division, Affymax NV; Chairman/CEO, Aviron

330 BRANFORD CASTLE
150 East 58th Street
37th Floor
New York, NY 10155

Phone: 202-317-2004 Fax: 212-317-2053
web: branfordcastle.com

Mission Statement: Branford Castle is a long-term investor in small- to medium-sized private companies.
Geographic Preference: North America
Fund Size: $200 million
Founded: 1986
Average Investment: $10 million equity
Minimum Investment: $1 million
Investment Criteria: Small to Medium Companies, Expansion
Industry Group Preference: Industrial, Oil and Gas, Marine, Chemicals, Consumer, Aerospace and Defence, Restaurants, Transportation and Infrastructure, Distribution, Media & Telecommunications, Energy, Healthcare Services, Business Services
Portfolio Companies: ABC Industries, Canada Metal Pacific, Drew Foam Companies Inc., EarthLite, Morton's The Steakhouse, PulseVet, Titan, TooJay's Restaurant & Deli, Vitrek, Washington Chain & Supply

Key Executives:
John S. Castle, President/CEO
212-317-2020
e-mail: jsc@branfordcastle.com
Background: Current Chariman/CEO, Castle Harlan, Former President/CEO, Donaldson, Lufkin & Jenrette
David Castle, Managing Partner
Education: Skidmore College; Cornell Law School
Background: Santa Fe Steakhouse; GE Capital
Eric R. Korsten, Senior Managing Director
212-317-2219
e-mail: ekorsten@branfordcastle.com
Education: BA, University of Pennsylvania; MBA, NYU

Venture Capital & Private Equity Firms / Domestic Firms

Stern School of Business
Background: VP, Jefferies & Co.; Senior Analyst, Dunbar Capital Management
Directorships: ABC Industries; Pulse Veterinary Technologies; TooJay's Restaurant & Deli; Surface Preparation Technologies
Laurence Lederer, Senior Managing Director
212-317-2037
e-mail: lbl@branfordcastle.com
Education: BA, Carleton College; MBA, Harvard Business School
Background: Founder, Rubicon Associates; Principal, ACG Capital; Associate, Morgan Stanley & Co.; Associate, Castle Harlan
Directorships: Earthlite Massage Tables; Vitrek; Drew Foam

331 BRAZOS PRIVATE EQUITY PARTNERS

Phone: 214-301-4225
web: www.brazosinv.com

Mission Statement: Specializes in leveraged acquisitions and recapitalizations of middle market companies that offer the potential for substantial capital appreciation.
Geographic Preference: Southwestern U.S., Texas
Fund Size: $1.4 billion
Founded: 1999
Average Investment: $25 - $100 million
Minimum Investment: $10 - $25 million
Investment Criteria: Buyouts, Recapitalizations, CEO-Backed Buy-and-Builds, Corporate Divestitures/Divisional Spin-Offs, Public-To-Privates
Industry Group Preference: Manufacturing, Consumer Products, Services, Healthcare, Media, Telecommunications, Business Products & Services, Financial Services, Distribution
Portfolio Companies: BlackHawk Industrial, Cheddar's Restaurants, Comark Building Systems, Eberly Design Inc., Ennis-Flint, European Wax Center, Fuel Systems, Healthcare Solutions, Impact Confections, Lone Star Overnight, Morton Industrial Group, National Surgical Care, ORS Nasco, Rennhack Marketing Services, Repulic Insurance, Sadler's Smokehouse, Shelter Distribution, Southern Tide, Strategic Equipment and Supply, TriNorthern Security Distribution, Vision Source, Walls Industries, Windebow Inc.

332 BREAKAWAY VENTURES

399 Boylston Street
5th Floor
Boston, MA 02116

Phone: 617-399-0635
web: www.breakawayventures.com

Mission Statement: Breakaway is a unique combination of strategic consultancy, creative agency and venture capital firm. Actively investing in early to growth stage businesses and trusted partners to established brands looking for agents of change.
Average Investment: $3 - $8 million
Investment Criteria: Early-Stage, Growth-Stage, Revenues greater than $2 million
Industry Group Preference: Consumer Products, E-Commerce & Manufacturing, Retail, Consumer & Leisure, Apparel, Accessories, Footwear, Entertainment, Sports
Portfolio Companies: Spartan Race, EverybodyFights, Oath, Rue Lala, Yasso, Mission, Sweetgreen, M.Gemi, Drizly, CoachUp, Idea Point, True Fit, Nic+Zoe, Draft, Convergent Dental
Key Executives:
  Dennis Baldwin, Founder/Managing Partner
  617-399-0635
  e-mail: dbaldwin@breakaway.com
  Education: Union College; MS, Industrial Relations, Cornell University
  Background: Chief Marketing Officer, Reebok International; Management Consultant, Ernst & Young
  John Burns, Managing Director
  617-399-0637
  e-mail: jburns@breakaway.com
  Education: Boston College; MBA, Babson College
  Directorships: Spartan Race, Oath Pizza, EverybodyFights
  Chaz Bertrand, Managing Director
  617-399-0635
  e-mail: cbertrand@breakaway.com
  Education: BS, Economics, US Naval Academy; MBA, Harvard Business School
  Background: CEO, RHG LLC; Investment Banker, Adams Harkness; Investment Banker, Roberston Stephens

333 BREAKWATER INVESTMENTS

1999 Avenue of the Stars
Suite 1150
Los Angeles, CA 90067

Phone: 424-777-4000
e-mail: info@breakwatermgmt.com
web: www.breakwatermgmt.com

Mission Statement: Breakwater Investment Management is a private investment firm that specializes in direct investments in small to lower middle market businesses ranging in annual sales of $10 million to $150 million. The firm serves as general partner of Breakwater Structured Growth Opportunities Fund, LP, a $100 million open-ended private investment partnership. The Fund's investment objective is to generate both current income and capital appreciation through secured debt investments, primarily in growth-oriented companies across a variety of industries.
Fund Size: $100 million
Founded: 2008
Average Investment: $2 - $20 million
Investment Criteria: Lower Middle Market: Growth Capital, Recapitalizations, Acquisitions, Bridge Financing, Liquidity-Based
Industry Group Preference: Healthcare, Medical Devices, Consumer Products, Retailing, Information Technology, Telecommunications, Business Products & Services, Financial Services, Energy, Alternative Energy, Manufacturing
Portfolio Companies: Alpha Media, Argo Tea, Bear Down Brands, Bleach Group, BMM Compliance, Consensus Orthopedics, Global Restoration Holdings, Hamilton Captive Management, Loot Crate, Open Road Entertainment, Planet Blue, Smarty Pants Vitamins, Split Rail Fence & Supply Co., The Madera Group, Veggie Grill
Key Executives:
  Eric Beckman, Managing Partner
  424-777-4024
  Fax: 424-777-4001
  e-mail: ebeckman@breakwatermgmt.com
  Education: BA, Cornell University; JD, Yale Law School
  Background: Senior Investment Professional, Ares Management; Golman Sachs

334 BREAKWATER MANAGEMENT

1999 Avenue of the Stars
Suite 3430
Los Angeles, CA 90067

Phone: 424-777-4000
e-mail: info@breakwatermgmt.com
web: www.breakwatermgmt.com

Mission Statement: Invests in various industries with a focus on companies within the lower-middle market size. Areas of interest include media & entertainment, retail, consumer products, health & wellness and cannabis.
Geographic Preference: US, Canada
Fund Size: 75M

Founded: 2008
Average Investment: 10-75M
Minimum Investment: 10M
Investment Criteria: Lower Middle Market
Industry Group Preference: Food & Beverage, Entertainment, Radio, Media, Health & Wellness, Consumer Products, Cannabis, Apparel
Portfolio Companies: Alpha Media, Argo Tea Inc., Bear Down Brands, Bleach Group Inc., BMM Compliance, Consensus Orthopedics, Hamilton Captive Management, Global Restoration Holdings, Loot Crate Inc., Open Road Entertainment, Planet Blue, SmartyPants Inc., U.S. Fence Solutions, Tocaya Organica, Toca Madera, Casa Madera, The Veggie Grill Inc., Isatori Inc, Optimus EMR Inc., Training Partners USA Limited, Yurbuds, Zealot Networks Inc.

Key Executives:
  Eric Beckman, Managing Partner
  424-777-4024
  Fax: 424-777-4001
  e-mail: ebeckman@breakwatermgmt.com
  Education: BA, Political Theory/Economics, Cornell University; JD, Yale Law School; Jawaharlal Nehru University
  Background: Associate, Investment Banking Division, Goldman Sachs; Sr. Partner, Ares Management; Investor/Advisor, Carmelina Capital Management
  Directorships: The Posse Foundation
  Saif Mansour, Managing Partner
  424-777-4010
  Fax: 424-777-4001
  e-mail: smansour@breakwatermgmt.com
  Education: BA, International Relations, Brown University
  Background: Strategy Counsultant to the Office of the President at Union Bank of California
  Darrick Geant, Management Director
  424-777-4020
  Fax: 424-777-4001
  e-mail: dgeant@breakwatermgmt.com
  Education: BA, Ivey Business School, Western University
  Background: Analyst, Donaldson Lufkin & Jenrette; VP, Credit Suisse; Managing Director, Goldman Sachs
  Directorships: Barclays Investment Bank
  Joe Kaczorowski, Managing Director/CFO
  424-777-4025
  Fax: 424-777-4001
  e-mail: joek@breakwatermgmt.com
  Education: BS, Accounting/Business Management, St. John's University
  Background: EVP/CFO, The Cannell Studios; EVP/CFO/President, House of Blues Entertainment; President, Grosvenor Park Media; Principal, Oakridge Partners
  Directorships: Napster; Roxio
  Walter Chung, Director
  424-777-4017
  Fax: 424-777-4001
  e-mail: wchung@breakwatermgmt.com
  Education: BA, Business Economics/Accounting, University of California, LA
  Background: Associate, FTI Consulting Inc.; Associate, Libra Securities
  Directorships: THL Credit
  Tammy Funasaki, Head of Investor Relations
  424-777-4028
  Fax: 424-777-4001
  e-mail: tfunasaki@breakwatermgmt.com
  Education: BA, International Business, University of Southern California; Pre-MBA, Anderson School of Management; MBA, NYU Stern School of Business
  Background: Marketing/Strategy Associate, Lexus; Private Wealth Advisor, Goldman Sachs; VP, Evolution Financial Group

335 BREGAL ENERGY
277 Park Avenue
29th Floor
New York, NY 10172

Phone: 212-704-3000 **Fax:** 212-704-3001
web: bregalenergy.com

Mission Statement: Bregal Energy, formerly known as Good Energies Capital is a private equity firm focused on the energy sector in North America, investing in companies in the growth stage of development.
Geographic Preference: North America
Founded: 2002
Average Investment: Up to $100 million
Industry Group Preference: Energy, Renewable Energy, Energy Services, Transmission, Midstream
Portfolio Companies: Atlantic Wind Connection, Champlin Wind, Fortune Greek Gas Gathering and Processing, IMG Midstream, Inflection Energy, SolarReserve

Key Executives:
  Raluca Florea, Senior Associate
  Education: BS, Interational Business, Academy of Economic Studies; MBA, Harvard Business School
  Background: McKinsey & Company; Procter & Gamble
  Sylvester Burley, Senior Associate
  Education: BA, Economics & Mathematics, Harvard University
  Background: Basalt Infrastructure Partners; Riverstone Holdings; JP Morgan

336 BREGAL SAGEMOUNT
200 Park Avenue
45th Floor
New York, NY 10166

e-mail: info@bregalsagemount.com
web: sagemount.com

Mission Statement: Bregal Sagemount is focused on investing in and acquiring high-growth companies.
Fund Size: $1.7 billion
Average Investment: $15-$75 million
Investment Criteria: Growth Stage
Industry Group Preference: Software, Enterprise Software, SaaS, Technology-Enabled Software, Business Products & Services, Cloud Computing, Internet, Healthcare, Healthcare Information Technology, Financial Services, Consumer Services, Direct Marketing, Education
Portfolio Companies: Accela, Adreima, Advanced Solutions, Align, Bite Squad, Buyers Edge Platform, CallTower, Connectria, Critical Start, DiscoverOrg, Discovery Data, Enprecis, Fluent Home, GPS Insight, Information Builders, Interface Security Systems, Irth Solutions, Keg Logistics, Key Health, LabVantage, Lux Research, MicroEdge, MOBI Wireless, Network Merchants, Open Lending, Options Technology, Procurement Advisors, Purchasing Power, RDX, Recondo Technology, Single Digits, STEELE Compliance Solutions, SurePrep, TradeGlobal, Trapp Technology, Truckstop.com, TrustArc, Vital Insights, Yapstone, ZeOmega

Key Executives:
  Cene Yoon, Managing Partner
  212-704-5375
  e-mail: gene.yoon@bregalsagemount.com
  Education: BS, Economics, MBA, Wharton School
  Background: Head of Private Equity, Goldman Sachs & Co.
  Phil Yates, Partner
  212-704-5377
  e-mail: phil.yates@bregalsagemount.com
  Education: BS, Business Administration, University of North Carolina, Chapel Hill
  Background: Great Hill Partners; Associate, Carousel Capital

Venture Capital & Private Equity Firms / Domestic Firms

Clayton Main, Partner, Head of Credit
212-704-5372
e-mail: clayton.main@sagemount.com
Education: BBA, Southern Methodist Univ.
Background: Goldman Sachs
Curt Witte, Partner, Head of Sagemount Growth Factors
212-704-5390
e-mail: curt.witte@sagemount.com
Background: Symphony Technology Group
Adam Fuller, Partner
Education: BA, Economics, Stanford University
Background: Goldman Sachs; Arbord Advisors
Blair Greenberg, Partner
Education: BBA, Kelley School of Business; MBA, Kellogg School of Management
Background: VP, Technology Crossover Ventures; UBS Investment Bank
Michael Kosty, Partner
212-704-5380
e-mail: michael.kosty@sagemount.com
Education: BSBA, Georgetown University
Background: Goldman Sachs
Pavan Tripathi, Partner
212-704-5383
e-mail: pavan.tripathi@safemount.com
Education: BEng, Electrical Engineering & Economics, University of California, LA; MBA, Stanford Grad. School of Business
Background: Goldman Sachs

337 BRENTWOOD ASSOCIATES
11150 Santa Monica Blvd.
Suite 1200
Los Angeles, CA 90025

Phone: 310-477-6611 Fax: 310-317-7200
e-mail: info@brentwood.com
web: www.brentwood.com

Mission Statement: Brentwood Associates is a leading consumer-focused private equity investment firm based in Los Angeles.
Geographic Preference: Midwest
Fund Size: $2.4 billion
Founded: 1972
Average Investment: $20 - $150 million
Minimum Investment: $1 million
Investment Criteria: Middle Market, Consumer Related Businesses
Industry Group Preference: Business to Business, Consumer Products, Consumer Services, Direct Marketing, Distribution, Education, Health Related, Marketing
Portfolio Companies: Allen Edmonds, Ariat, Array, Aspen Marketing Group, Bell Sports, Blaze Pizza, Boston Proper, Cardinal Business Media Inc., Chamilia, Chicken Salad Chick, Classroom Connect, ClassWallet, Credential Solutions, Excelligence Learning Corp., Exhale, Filson, FleetPride Inc., HIMS, J.Mclaughlin, Jefferson Dental Care, KFC, Marshall Retail Group, MD Now, Oriental Trading, Orange Theory Fitness, Pacific Catch, Pacific Island Restaurants Inc., Paper Source, Saxx, Soft Surroundings, Spectrum Athletic Clubs, Three Sixty Sourcing, Veggie Grill, Wiland, Z Gallerie, Zumiez

Key Executives:
William Barnum, Partner
Education: Stanford University; Stanford Law School; Stanford Graduate School of Business
Background: Investment Banking Division, Morgan Stanley & Comapny
Directorships: Filson Holdings; Oriental Trading Company; ThreeSixty Asia; Exhale Enterprises; FleetPride Corporation; Zumiez; Quicksilver; Stanford University; St Matthews Parish School
Roger Goddu, Senior Advisor
Education: Adrian College; University of Toledo; Completed, Executive Development Program, Harvard Business School
Background: Independent Director, Array Marketing Group; Chairman/CEO, Montgomery Ward; President, Toys R Us; Senior Management Positions, Target; RH Macy & Co; Federated Department Stores
Steven Moore, Partner
Education: BA, Mechanical Engineering, University of Michigan
Background: Merger/Acquisitions/Corporate Finance, Donaldson, Lufkin & Jenrette; Deloitte & Touche Consulting Group
Directorships: Filson Holdings; ThreeSixty Asia; Zumiez
Eric Reiter, Partner
Education: Dual Degree, in Finance/Operation/Information Management, magna cum laude, Wharton School University of Pennsylvania
Background: Merchant Banking Division, Donaldson, Lufkin & Jenrette
Directorships: Array Marketing; Oriental Trading Company; Monarch Designs
Rahul Aggarwal, Partner
Education: BS, Finance/International Relations, magna cum laude, University of Pennsylvania Wharton School of Business; BA International Relations, College of Arts and Sciences
Background: Financing, Donaldson, Lufkin & Jenrette
Directorships: Pacific Island Restaurants; Spectrum Clubs; Exhale Enterprises; FleetPride Corporation

338 BRERA CAPITAL PARTNERS
244 Fifth Avenue
Suite 2345
New York, NY 10001

web: www.brera.com

Mission Statement: Global private equity investment firm.
Geographic Preference: United States, Asia, Japan, Southern Europe, Italy
Fund Size: $680 million
Founded: 1997
Average Investment: $150 million
Investment Criteria: Management Buyouts, Recapitalizations, Restructurings
Industry Group Preference: Telecommunications, Healthcare, Financial Services, Outsourcing & Efficiency
Portfolio Companies: 2-10 Home Buyers Warranty, GAB Robins, Italtel, Western Industries

339 BREYER CAPITAL
2500 Sand Hill Road
Suite 300
Menlo Park, CA 94025

Phone: 650-681-3069 Fax: 650-433-4243
e-mail: info@breyercapital.com
web: breyercapital.com

Mission Statement: Breyer Capital is a global private equity and venture capital investor.
Geographic Preference: United States, China, India
Founded: 2006
Industry Group Preference: Social Media, Artificial Intelligence, Entertainment, Digital Health, Data Analytics, Fintech
Portfolio Companies: Facebook, Legendary, Kensho, IDG Capital Partners, Etsy, Circle, Marvel, C3 IoT

Key Executives:
Jim Breyer, Founder and CEO
Education: BS, Stanford University; MBA, Harvard University
Background: Partner, Accel; President, Accel Management Company; Management Consultant, McKinsey & Company

Venture Capital & Private Equity Firms / Domestic Firms

340 BRIDGE INVESTMENT FUND
Cleveland, OH

web: www.bridgefundllc.com

Mission Statement: Bridge Investment Fund is a venture capital fund focused on investing in Israeli medical device companies with strong synergies with the leading health care institutions and industries in Cleveland. Bridge is specifically focused on companies that have completed their initial clinical trials and are looking to the US market for further clinical validation and to establish a US sales marketing organization. Bridge's team brings excellent access to Israeli companies, deep regional networks and hands-on support to help their portfolio companies successfully enter the US market.

Geographic Preference: Israel
Average Investment: $250,000 - $1 million
Minimum Investment: $250,000
Industry Group Preference: Medical Devices
Portfolio Companies: EarlySense, IceCure Medical, Navotek, Medic Vision

Other Locations:
Tenram Investments
11 Tuval Street
Ramat Gan 52522
Israel

Key Executives:
Avshalom Horan, Managing Partner
Education: PhD, Engineering-Economic Systems, Stanford University
Background: Colonel, Israeli Defense Forces, Israeli Military Intelligence; VP, Bank Leumi Investment Group
Directorships: Simbionix

Michael Goldberg, Managing Partner
Education: BA, Woodrow Wilson School of Public and International Affairs, Princeton University; MA, International Relations, Johns Hopkins University
Background: Director, International Business Development, America Online

341 BRIDGE STREET CAPITAL
171 Monroe Avenue NW
Suite 410
Grand Rapids, MI 49503

Phone: 616-732-1050 Fax: 616-732-1055
web: www.bridgestreetcapital.com

Mission Statement: Bridge Street Capital Partners works with entrepreneurial companies throughout the Midwest and Great Lakes region and invests in a variety of industries, including healthcare, business services, manufacturing and consumer products. The firm provides the capital, operational expertise and practical experience necessary to meet the needs of portfolio companies.

Geographic Preference: Midwest & Great Lakes Region
Fund Size: $30 million
Average Investment: $2.5 - $7.5 million
Investment Criteria: Middle-Market Firms
Industry Group Preference: Industrial Manufacturing, Distribution, Logistics, Consumer Products, Healthcare, Business Products & Services
Portfolio Companies: Affy Tapple, Callpod, Jacob Ash, Performance Fabrics, Superior Fibers, V.I.O., Callpod, Zorch

Other Locations:
52 Village Place
Hinsdale, IL 60521
Phone: 630-323-9222 Fax: 630-323-9224

Key Executives:
Bill Kaczynski, Managing Director
Education: BS, Accounting, University of Illinois at Urbana-Champaign; MBA, Kellogg School of Management, Northwestern University
Background: Managing Director, Trivest Partners; Heller Financial; Fidelcor Business Credit; Price Waterhouse

John Meilner, Managing Director
Education: BS, Accounting, Drake University; Kellogg School of Management
Background: Managing Director, Investment Banking Group, McDonald Investments; Partner, Deloitte & Touche

342 BRIDGESCALE PARTNERS
Menlo Park, CA

Phone: 650-854-6100
web: www.bridgescale.com

Mission Statement: Bridgescale invests in technology companies that require equity to accelerate growth.

Geographic Preference: United States, Canada
Industry Group Preference: Information Technology, Consumer Internet, Digital Media & Marketing, Communications, Infrastructure, Business Products & Services, Mobile Technology
Portfolio Companies: Axonify, BlueCat Networks, Dayforce, Jasper Wireless, J. Hilburn, Plum Organics, Proofpoint, Rypple, Shutterfly, Xactly, Neonova, BitGo, IMVU, Vision Critical, Chronometriq

343 BRIGHTPATH CAPITAL PARTNERS
One Kaiser Plaza
Suite 650
Oakland, CA 94612

Phone: 510-488-4140
e-mail: info@bcplp.com
web: www.brightpathcapitalpartners.com

Mission Statement: Brightpath Capital Partners invests in talented management teams and high-growth businesses, creating jobs, wealth and sustainable environments in communities. BCP provides innovative investment solutions rooted in in-depth research and a disciplined investment process.

Geographic Preference: California, Western United States
Founded: 2010
Average Investment: $1-5 million
Investment Criteria: Late-Stage
Industry Group Preference: Clean Energy, Business Products & Services, Education, Food & Beverage, Manufacturing, Health & Wellness
Portfolio Companies: Blu Homes, Ecologic Brands, Sungevity

Key Executives:
Robert R. Davenport III, Managing Partner
510-488-4140
e-mail: rob@bcplp.com
Education: AB, MBA, Harvard University
Background: Chairman, Up Communication Services; President & CEO, Covad International
Directorships: MCI, Sungevity, One Pacific Coast Ank, FSB

Jonathan Mi, Principal
510-488-4143
e-mail: jonathan@bcplp.com
Education: BA, University of California, Berkeley
Background: Associate, Gryphon Investors

344 BRIGHTSTONE VENTURE CAPITAL
510 First Avenue North
Suite 200
Minneapolis, MN 55403

web: www.brightstonevc.com

Mission Statement: Brightstone Venture Capital Fund has a long history of helping build successful companies in the early-growth stage.

Fund Size: $100 million
Founded: 1985
Average Investment: $250,000 - $10 million

Venture Capital & Private Equity Firms / Domestic Firms

Minimum Investment: $250,000
Investment Criteria: Early Growth-Stage
Industry Group Preference: Technology, Digital Media & Marketing, Mobile, Virtual Reality, Cloud Computing, Data Storage, Enterprise Software, Consumer Internet, Energy, Life Sciences, Medical Devices, Healthcare Information Technology, Biotechnology, Clean Technology
Portfolio Companies: HomeSpotter, Bnocular, Celcuity, Fortus Medical Inc., Miromatrix, Flipgrid, TruBrain, Bite, Gravie, VR Chat, Real Vision, Stemonix, Atavium, Wasabi

Key Executives:
David Dalvey, Partner
e-mail: david@brightstonevc.com
Directorships: Homespotter, Definity Health, App Tec Laboratories, Navarre Corp, chf Solutions, Agiliti, Nature Vision, Celcuity, Bite Squad
Patrick O'Shaughnessy, Partner
e-mail: patrick@brightstonevc.com
Seth Degroot, Partner
e-mail: seth@brightstonevc.com

---

345 BRILLIANT VENTURES
520 Broadway
Suite 200
Santa Monica, CA 90401

web: www.brilliant.ventures

Mission Statement: Brilliant Ventures invests capital, experience, and a powerful network to build companies that are leveraging technology and data to accelerate growth and to shape the future of media, marketing, and commerce.
Industry Group Preference: Media, Marketing, Commerce, Technology, Data
Portfolio Companies: Beam Impact, CameraIQ, Cherrypick, Cognitiv, Happy Returns, Harper Wilde, Haute Hijab, Parachute, Postie, Relovv, RevCascade, Tamara Mellon, The Riveter, Skylar Body, Vela

Key Executives:
Kara Weber, Founder, Partner
Education: Williams College
Directorships: Happy Returns, CameraIQ, Cognitiv, RevCascade
Lizzie Francis, Founder, Partner
Education: BA, Cornell University
Directorships: Parachute Home, Tamara Mellon, Vow to be Chic

---

346 BROADHAVEN CAPITAL PARTNERS
521 Fifth Avenue
New York, NY 10175

Phone: 212-418-1240
e-mail: info@broadhaven.com
web: broadhaven.com

Mission Statement: Broadhaven Capital Partners is an independent investment bank and growth equity investor serving the financial technology sector.
Fund Size: $100 million
Founded: 2009
Average Investment: $5 - $15 million
Investment Criteria: Early-Stage, Growth Equity, Buyout
Industry Group Preference: Financial Services, Technology
Portfolio Companies: Binary Event Network, Mantara, UNX

Other Locations:
150 North Riverside Plaza
Chicago, IL 60606
Phone: 312-621-9800

2 Embarcadero Center
San Francisco, CA 94111
Phone: 415-295-4447

Key Executives:
Gerard von Dohlen, Co-Founder/Partner
Education: BS, Industrial Engineering, Columbia University; MBA, Columbia Business School
Background: Managing Director, Investment Banking, Goldman Sachs; UBS Investment Bank; Credit Suisse First Boston
Greg Phillips, Co-Founder/Partner
Education: BA, Economics, University of Chicago
Background: M&A Group, UBS Investment Bank; Wasserstein Perella & Co.
James T. Denton, Partner
Education: BA, Economics & Languages, Rutgers College; MBA, Columbia Business School
Background: Co-Head, Financial Institutions Group, Rothschild
Michael Deleray, Partner
Education: BA, History, University of California, Berkeley
Background: Founder, Bendigo; President, US Equity Services, Computershare
Todd G. Owens, Partner
Education: Williams College
Background: Fifth Street Finance Corp.
John H. Simpson, Partner
Education: Williams College; Harvard Law School
Background: Wasserstein Perella & Co.
Directorships: Lurie Children's Hospital
Christopher Spofford, Partner
Education: Amherst College
Background: Goldman Sachs
Kurt von Holzhausen, Partner
Education: Tufts University
Background: Goldman Sachs
Joseph J. Zabik, Partner
Education: Kent State University
Background: Sterne Agee
Esther Tian, Managing Director
Education: AB, Economics, Harvard University
Background: Davidson Kempner Capital Management, SAC Capital

---

347 BROADHORN CAPITAL
West Des Moines, IA

e-mail: info@broadhorn.com
web: www.broadhorn.com

Mission Statement: Broadhorn Capital is a venture development firm specializing in early and seed stage technology companies. Business services include: business plan advisment, board and management development, technology strategy and architecture, proof of concept, sales and marketing development and private placement services.
Investment Criteria: Seed-Stage, Early-Stage
Industry Group Preference: Technology
Portfolio Companies: AmericasOne, Appcore, ARC Center, Broadhorn Farm, Computility, Family Arc, GForce Group, Growth Ventures Group, Micoy, MinistryHub.com, MobileSmith, Palisade

Key Executives:
Brian Donaghy, Partner
e-mail: brian.donaghy@broadhorn.com
Background: Founder/CEO, Appcore; Partner/CTO, Growth Ventures Group

---

348 BROADMARK CAPITAL
1800 One Union Square
600 University Street
Seattle, WA 98101

Phone: 206-623-1200 **Fax:** 206-623-2213
web: www.broadmark.com

Mission Statement: Merchant bank that provides financing and management services and direct investment to help emerging companies grow and create shareholder value.
Founded: 1987
Average Investment: $5 - $75 million

Venture Capital & Private Equity Firms / Domestic Firms

Minimum Investment: $5 million
Investment Criteria: Early-Stage, First-Stage, Mid-Stage, Second-Stage, Mezzanine, LBO, Emerging Growth, Middle Market, Mergers & Acquisitions
Industry Group Preference: Information Technology, Life Sciences, Healthcare, Communications
Portfolio Companies: Pyatt, Vesiflo, NewsCrafted, FedTax
Key Executives:
   Joseph L. Schocken, President
   e-mail: jls@broadmark.com
   Education: Graduate, honors, University of Washington; MBA, Harvard University
   Background: Partner, New York Stock Exchange; Member, National Advisory Board of the Democratic National Committee
   Adam J. Fountain, Managing Director
   e-mail: afountain@broadmark.com
   Education: BA, International Relations, Stanford University
   Background: Associate, L.E.K. Consulting

350 BROADVIEW VENTURES
265 Franklin Street
Suite 1902
Boston, MA 02110

Phone: 617-459-4686
e-mail: ccolecchi@broadviewventures.org
web: www.broadviewventures.org

Mission Statement: Broadview's mission is to accelerate the development of promising technology in cardiovascular and neurovascular disease through targeted investments in and support of early stage ventures.

Geographic Preference: United States, Europe
Founded: 2008
Average Investment: $1 - 1.5 million
Investment Criteria: Early-Stage
Industry Group Preference: Healthcare, Life Sciences, Therapeutics, Medical Devices, Diagnostics
Portfolio Companies: 480 Biomedical, Acesion, Adient Medical, Aeromics, Aggamin, Allosteros, Apama, Aria CV, BioKier, Capricor, Cardero, CardiAQ Valve, CardiaLen, CellAegis, DecImmune, EP Sciences, FineHeart, GI Windows, Gila Therapeutic, InfoBionic, Intravascular Imaging Inc., Ischemia Care, Herantis, Mellitus, MiRagen, Nido Surgical, NuPulse, Provasculon, Pulmokine, Remedy, Vascular Graft Solutions, Vectorious, VentriNova, Zumbro Discover, ZZ Biotech
Key Executives:
   Christopher Colecchi, Managing Director
   Education: BA, Holy Cross College; MPH, University of Massachusetts School of Public Health
   Background: Vice President, Research Ventures & Licensing, Partners Healthcare; Director, Clinical Trials & Industrial Relations, Massachusetts General Hospital

351 BROCKWAY MORAN & PARTNERS
225 NE Mizner Boulevard
Suite 700
Boca Raton, FL 33432

Phone: 561-750-2000 Fax: 561-750-2001
e-mail: info@brockwaymoran.com
web: www.brockwaymoran.com

Mission Statement: Brockway Moran & Partners is a private equity firm with an unusual combination of financial resources, strategic expertise & operational know-how brought together to support management teams in maximizing opportunities for growth-oriented, middle-market companies.

Fund Size: $1.3 billion
Founded: 1998
Investment Criteria: $50-$300 Million in Value
Industry Group Preference: Consumer Products, Industrial Products, Services
Portfolio Companies: MD Now, Pennant Foods Corp., Turning Technologies, The Winebow Group
Key Executives:
   Peter C Brockway, Managing Partner
   e-mail: pbrockway@brockwaymoran.com
   Education: BBA, Stetson University; MBA, Harvard Business School
   Background: Senior Advisor, Blue Sea Capital;
   Directorships: Crisis Prevention Institute Inc., MD Now Medical Centers Inc., The Winebow Group, Turning Technologies, MW Industries Inc., Woodstream Corp., Gold's Gym, Norwesco, ElectroStar
   Michael E Moran, Managing Partner
   e-mail: mmoran@brockwaymoran.com
   Education: BS, Drake University; MBA, DePaul University
   Background: Founder, Moran Capital Partners
   Directorships: Pennant Foods Corp., Crisis Prevention Institute Inc., The Winebow Group, Turning Technologies, MD Now Medical Centers Inc., ElectroStar Inc.
   Peter W Klein, Partner/General Counsel
   e-mail: pklein@brockwaymoran.com
   Education: BA, Albion College; JD, Cleveland-Marshall College of Law; LLM, Taxation, New York University
   H Randall Litten, Partner
   e-mail: rlitten@brockwaymoran.com
   Education: BS, Ohio University; MBA, University of Toledo
   Background: General Manager, Owens-Illinois
   Directorships: Celeseste Industries Corp.; Norweso Inc.; Cosmetic Essense Inc.; Woodstream Corp.; MW Industries Inc; Penda Corp.
   Ari M. Zur, Partner
   e-mail: azur@brockwaymoran.com
   Education: BS, Economics, Wharton School; BA, University of Pennsylvania; MBA, Kellogg School of Management, Northwestern University
   Background: Associate, Cambridge Capital Partners; Investment Analyst, Frontenac Company; Financial Analyst, Bear, Stearns & Co.

352 BROOK VENTURE FUND
301 Edgewater Place
Suite 425
Wakefield, MA 01880

Phone: 781-295-4000 Fax: 781-295-4007
e-mail: rspencer@brookventure.com
web: www.brookventure.com

Mission Statement: To invest capital in high-growth, expansion-stage companies, within a focused set of industries, with the objective of realizing venture level returns for us, our investors, and for the other shareholders and managers of each portfolio company.

Geographic Preference: Northeastern, Mid-Atlantic States
Fund Size: $100 million
Founded: 1998
Average Investment: $2-15 million
Minimum Investment: $1 million
Investment Criteria: Expansion Stage
Industry Group Preference: Medical Devices, Information Technology, Chemicals, Optical Technology, Biotechnology, Publishing, Electronic Technology, Healthcare Information Technology
Portfolio Companies: Affordable Interior Systems, AHP Billing, Allegience Software, Anodyne, Apogee IT Services, Arigo G360, Atlas Water, BabyEarth, Certica, Cole Information, Coronis Health, D2 Hawkeye, Farm Market iD, HistoRX, IMN, Interwoven, itrac LLC, Laser Projection Technologies, LearnWell, Medicus IT, Mobile Medical International Corporation, OnBoard Security, Orbis Technologies Inc., PointCare, Relevate, Reveal, Robbinskertsten Direct, Security Innovation, SilverRail,

Venture Capital & Private Equity Firms / Domestic Firms

Software Unlimited, Spectral Dimensions, Texerity, Union Biometrica, Universal Software, V12 Data, Verge Health

Key Executives:
Frederic H. Morris, Partner
e-mail: morris@brookventure.com
Education: Economics, Yale University; MBA Finance, Harvard Business School
Background: Lieutenant, Navy's Reserve Officer Training; CFO Assistant, First National City Bank
Walter Beinecke, Partner
e-mail: wbeinecke@brookventure.com
Education: University of California
Background: President, RewardsNow; President/Co-Managing Partner, Affinity Marketing Group; CEO, S&H Partners; Founder/Executive VP, S&H Greenpoints; President/CEO, Biological Technologies International; Co-Founder/Managing Partner, MHB Partners; Founder/President/CEO, Silvan
Edward C. Williams, III, Partner
e-mail: ewilliams@brookventure.com
Education: University of Massachusetts; BS, Harvard University
Background: Private Equity, Winthrop Financial Associates; Equity Sales, Morgan Stanley; Investment Banking, Bank of Boston
Brennan Mulcahey, Partner
e-mail: bmulcahey@brookventure.com
Education: BA, University of Rochester; MBA, Simon School of Business
Directorships: Medicine-On-Time
Kyle Stanbro, Partner
e-mail: kstanbro@brookventure.com
Education: BS, St. John Fisher College; MBA, Simon School of Business
Background: Travelers; Kodak

353 BROOKE PRIVATE EQUITY ASSOCIATES
20 Custom House St
Suite 610
Boston, MA 02110

Phone: 617-227-3160 **Fax:** 617-227-4128
e-mail: info@brookepea.com
web: www.brookepea.com

Mission Statement: A private equity firm with a a diversified focus.
Founded: 2002
Industry Group Preference: Consumer, Retail, Healthcare, Industrial
Key Executives:
Peter Brooke, Co-Founder
Education: Harvard College, Harvard Business School
Background: Founder, TA Associates; Co-Founder, Sofinnova SA
John Brooke, Managing Director
Education: Harvard College, Harvard Business School
Background: Advent International, The Tucker Anthony Private Equity Group
Christopher Austen, Managing Director
Education: Duke University, Fuqua School of Business
Background: Partner, Southeast Interactive Technology Funds; BBDO, Foote Cone & Belding

354 BROOKLYN BRIDGE VENTURES
55-C 9th Street
Brooklyn, NY 11215

e-mail: charlie@brooklynbridge.vc
web: www.brooklynbridge.vc

Mission Statement: Brooklyn Bridge Ventures is a seed-stage investor. Brooklyn Bridge Ventures seeks to connect community leaders together, support new events, and encourage the creation of a thriving ecosystem.
Geographic Preference: New York City
Fund Size: $23 million
Average Investment: $500,000
Investment Criteria: Seed-Stage
Industry Group Preference: Technology
Portfolio Companies: Bravely, Wethos, Petal, Bazaar, Waggle, The Wing, Amper Music, Bizly, Radius, Talla, Agrilyst, C And Co., Seed, Ample Hills Creamery, Clubhouse, Homer, Drip, Wheelhouse, Hungry Root, Tinker Garten, Even Financial, Bezar, Plum Print, Vixxenn, LogCheck, ProofPilot, BioDigital, GoTenna, Ringly, Canary, Orchard, Makr, SocialSign.in, Tinybop, Floored, Windowfarms, Editorially, Superhuman, Versa
Key Executives:
Charlie O'Donnell, Founder
e-mail: charlie@brooklynbridge.vc
Background: Union Square Ventures, First Round Capital, General Motors Asset Management Private Equity Group

355 BROOKS HOUGHTON & COMPANY
1 Stamford Plaza
9th Floor
Stamford, NY 06901

Phone: 212-753-1991 **Fax:** 212-753-7730
web: www.brookshoughton.com

Mission Statement: Brooks, Houghton & Company provides investment banking services and direct investments to emerging growth companies as well as middle market companies. The firm has experience in a number of industries, including healthcare, media and entertainment.
Geographic Preference: United States
Founded: 1989
Average Investment: $15 million
Minimum Investment: $2 million
Investment Criteria: Middle Market, Public and Private Companies, Debt and Equity Private Placements, Mergers & Acquisitions, Growth and Expansion, Recapitalizations, Refinancings
Industry Group Preference: All Sectors Considered
Portfolio Companies: Competitive Technology, Happy Hour Creative, Mad Catz Interactive, Hennessy Capital Solutions
Key Executives:
Kevin Centofanti, President
e-mail: kcentofanti@brookshoughton.com
Education: BS, Pharmacy & Business, State University of New York at Buffalo; MBA, Finance & International Business, Columbia University; CFA
Background: Partner, The Nassau Group; Managing Director, WR Hambrecht & Co.; Daiwa Securities America
Anthony Moretti, Senior Managing Director/Head of Investment Banking
212-329-1667
e-mail: amoretti@brookshoughton.com
Education: BA, Business Economics, Brown University
Background: Director, BMO Capital Markets; Vice President, RBC Capital Markets
Domenico Pecorini, Senior Managing Director
e-mail: dpecorini@brookshoughton.com
Background: COO, Fondazione Parco Biomedico San Raffaele of Rome; Executive Director, Stilbon SA; President/CEO, Inveni Engineering
Directorships: Intensivecare SpA; Chairman, Life Episteme Group
David M Maher, Executive Director
212-329-1661
e-mail: maher@brookshoughton.com
Education: BA, Dartmouth College; MBA, Darden School of Business, University of Virginia
Background: Equity Capital Market Group member, Deutsche Bank Securities; Derivatives Trader, JP morgan Chase

Venture Capital & Private Equity Firms / Domestic Firms

356 BROOKSIDE EQUITY PARTNERS LLC
One Stamford Forum
201 Tresser Blvd
Suite 320
Stamford, CT 06901

Phone: 203-595-4520
e-mail: info@brooksideequity.com
web: www.brooksideequity.com

Mission Statement: Brookside Equity Partners, a part of The Brookside Group, focuses on private equity investments. The firm seeks to assist companies in creating long-term value.

Geographic Preference: United States
Founded: 1977
Average Investment: $3 - $8 million
Minimum Investment: $3 million
Investment Criteria: Leveraged Buyouts, Mezzanine, Growth Capital
Industry Group Preference: Food & Beverage, Plastics, Environment, Manufacturing, Distribution, Industrial, Financial Services, Specialty Chemicals
Portfolio Companies: Guardian Compliance, Hillsdale Furniture, Margaritaville Holdings, Meta Financial Group, New Energy, NSi, Operator of Full Service Restaurants, Performance Health & Wellness, SelectQuote, Superior Automotive, Tellermate Holdings, US Century Bank, Valterra Products

Key Executives:
Donald L Hawks III, Managing Director/President
Education: Georgetown University; MBA, Wharton School, University of Pennsylvania
Background: Strategy Consultant, Monitor Group
Raymond F Weldon, Managing Director
Education: La Salle University; Villanova University
Background: PricewaterhouseCoopers
Richard T Dell'Aquila, Managing Director
Education: BA, Economics, Hamilton College
Background: Managing Director, Parallel Investment Partners; Principal, Southfield Capital Advisors; Research Analyst, Sasco Capital

357 BRUCKMANN, ROSSER, SHERRILL & COMPANY
126 East 56th Street
29th Floor
New York, NY 10022

Phone: 212-521-3700 Fax: 212-521-3799
e-mail: info@brs.com
web: www.brs.com

Mission Statement: Private equity investment firm specializes in buyouts and recapitalization.

Fund Size: $1.2 billion
Founded: 1995
Investment Criteria: Management Buy-Outs, Recapitalizations of high quality, Middle Market Companies
Industry Group Preference: Consumer Services, Commercial Services, Healthcare, Consumer Products, Industrial Services, Industrial Equipment, Restaurants, Retailing
Portfolio Companies: 2nd Ave LLC, Airxcel Holdings Inc., Alliance Laundry Systems LLC, AmerisourceBergen Corporation, Anvil Holdings, Au Bon Pain Inc., B&C Foods Inc., Bally Engineering, Bravo Brio Restaurant Group Inc., California Pizza Kitchen Inc., Canada Pooch Ltd., Cort, Daisy Manufacturing Co., Davco Restaurants LLC, Del Monte Foods, Doane Pet Care Enterprises Inc., DTLR Inc., EOS Fitness Holdings LLC, Eurofresh Inc., Evolv Sports & Designs, Farm Fresh, Fox Photo, Galey & Lord, Gamo Outdoor SL, Gilbarco Veeder-Root, Golden Corral, H&E Equipment Services Inc., Hancor Inc., Healthplus Corporation, Heritage-Crystal Clean Inc., Inmotion Entertainment Group, J&L Specialty Steel, Logan's Roadhouse, Marshall Retail Group, McCormick & Schmick's Seafood Restaurants Inc., Milk Specialties Co., Morse Shoe Inc., MWI Veterinary Supply Inc., New Archery Products Corp., Not Your Average Joe's Inc., Organika Health Products, Penhall International Inc., Polyfibron Technologies Inc., Rax Restaurants Inc., Real Mex Restaurants Inc., Reliance Electric, Restaurant Associates Corporation, Royal Robbins Inc., Ruth's Hospitality Group, Reroyal Holdings LP, Simpson Performance Products, Steak & Ale Restaurant, Sheridan Group Inc., Things Remembered Inc., Totes Isotoner Corporation, Town Sports International Inc., Triumph Group Inc., Unwired Group Limited, Wilson Farms Inc., Zatarain's

Key Executives:
Bruce C. Bruckmann, Managing Partner & Founder
Education: AB, Harvard College; JD, Harvard Law School
Background: CVC Associate, Patterson, Belknap, Webb & Tyler
Directorships: Mohawk Industries, Town Sports International, Anvil Knitwear, MWI Veterinary Supply, HealthEssentials, Penhall International, Copelands' Enterprises, H&e Equipment Services
Stephen C. Sherrill, Managing Partner & Founder
Education: BA, Yale University; JD, Columbia Law School
Background: CVC, Paul, Weiss, Rifkind, Wharton & Garrison
Directorships: Galey & Lord, Doane Pet Care Enterprises, B&G Foods, HealthPlus Corporation, MWI Veterinary Supply, HealthEssentials, Alliance Laundry Systems, Eurofresh, Remington Arms
Thomas J. Baldwin, Managing Partner
Education: BBA, Siena College; MBA, Harvard Business School
Background: VP/Managing Director, INVUS Group; Boston Consulting Group
Directorships: B&G Foods, Eurofresh, The Sheridan Group
Rashad Rahman, Managing Director
Education: Economics, Wharton School, University of Pennsylvania
Background: DB Capital Partners; Investment Banking, Credit Suisse First Boston
Directorships: Seroyal Holdings
Tory Rooney, Managing Director
Education: BA, Goizueta Business School
Background: Wachovia Capital Markets
Directorships: Royal Robbins

358 BRUML CAPITAL CORPORATION
1801 East Ninth Street
Ohio Savings Plaza
Suite 1620
Cleveland, OH 44114

Phone: 216-771-6660 Fax: 216-771-6673
e-mail: info@brumlcapital.com
web: www.brumlcapital.com

Mission Statement: Independent investment banking firm in Cleveland.

Geographic Preference: Great Lakes
Fund Size: $15 million
Founded: 1986
Average Investment: $5 - $50 million
Minimum Investment: $1 million
Investment Criteria: Middle Market Companies, Management Buyouts, Acquisitions, Recapitalizations
Industry Group Preference: Manufacturing, Wholesale, Metals, Publishing, Chemicals, Retailing, Business to Business, Technology, Industrial Equipment, Distribution

Key Executives:
Robert W. Bruml, President
e-mail: bob@brumlcapital.com
Education: BA Economics, University of Rochester;

Venture Capital & Private Equity Firms / Domestic Firms

MBA, Wharton School
Background: KPMG Peat Marwick
Andrew S. Gelfand, Senior Vice President
e-mail: andy@brumlcapital.com
Education: BA Mathematics, Colgate University; MBA, Columbia University Graduate School of Business
Background: Investment Banking Officer, KeyCorp
James R. Deitzer, Asst. Vice President
e-mail: jim@brumlcapital.com
Education: BS, Univ. of Pittsburgh; MA, Columbia Univ.
Background: FTN Equity Capital Markets; RBC Capital Markets

359 BRYANT PARK VENTURES
web: bryantparkventures.com

Mission Statement: Bryant Park Ventures is a private investment fund and advisory services business.

Investment Criteria: Early-Stage
Industry Group Preference: Technology, Homeland Security, Law Enforcement, Healthcare

Key Executives:
  Michael G. Levine, Chairman & CEO
  e-mail: mgl@bryantparkventures.com
  Education: BS, SUNY Buffalo; MBA, Wharton School
  Background: President, Xact Technology; CFO, Maler Technologies

360 BRYNWOOD PARTNERS
8 Sound Shore Drive
Suite 265
Greenwich, CT 06830

Phone: 203-622-1790 Fax: 203-622-0559
e-mail: info@brynwoodpartners.com
web: www.brynwoodpartners.com

Mission Statement: Lower middle market buyout fund.

Fund Size: $725 million
Founded: 1984
Average Investment: Up to $80 million
Investment Criteria: Middle Market
Industry Group Preference: Manufacturing, Food & Beverage, Consumer Products, Business Products & Services
Portfolio Companies: Back To Nature, Balance Bar, Carolina Beverage Group LLP, DeMet's Candy Company, Harvest Hill Beverage Company, High Ridge Brands, Hometown Food Company, J.B. Williams Company, Joseph's Frozen Foods, Kretschmer, Lightlife Foods, Lincoln Snacks, Pearson's, Richelieu Foods Inc., Stella D'Oro

Key Executives:
  Hendrik J. Hartong III, Chairman/CEO
  e-mail: hhartong@brynwoodpartners.com
  Education: BA, History, Lafayette College; MBA, Harvard Business School
  Background: President/CEO, Lincoln Snacks Company; VP Marketing, Activision; Sales/Marketing: Baskin Robbins USA, Nestle USA
  Hendrik J. Hartong, Jr., Founder Partner Emeritus
  e-mail: huppsv@brynwoodpartners.com
  Education: BA, Economics, University of Cincinnati; MBA, Harvard Business School
  Background: President/CEO, Pittston Company; President/CEO, The Brink's Company; Group VP, North American Philips Corporation; Chairman/President/CEO, Simplex Wire & Cable Company; Consultant, McKinsey & Co
  Ian B. MacTaggart, President/COO/CFO
  e-mail: imactaggart@brynwoodpartners.com
  Education: BBA, Boston College; MBA, Fuqua School of Business, Duke University
  Background: M&A/Corporate Finance, Merrill Lynch & Co
  David A. Eagle, Managing Director
  Education: BS, Commerce, University of Virginia; MBA, Wharton School
  Background: Emigrant Capital, GC Andersen Partners, Stifel Nicolaus
  Vipul B. Soni, Managing Director
  Education: BS, Economics, University of Wisconsin-Madison; MBA, University of Chicago, Booth School of Business
  Background: Procter & Gamble

361 BULLPEN CAPITAL
215 2nd Street
3rd Floor
San Francisco, CA 94105

web: www.bullpencap.com

Mission Statement: Bullpen Capital is an early-stage venture fund which makes follow-on investments in start-ups funded by super-angels. Bullpen's market focus is on the social-mobile web sector (both enterprise and direct to consumer).

Fund Size: $85 million
Founded: 2010
Investment Criteria: Early-Stage
Industry Group Preference: Consumer Internet, Social Media, Enterprise Software
Portfolio Companies: About.me, Airmap, Aggregated Knowledge, Ayasdi, Bentobox, Betable, Beyond Pricing, Braze, Carbon, Chartio, Circulate, Citus Data, Classy, Cleanify, Confident Cannabis, CoverHound, Derby Jackpot, +Desk.com, Doubledutch, Drive Motors, Fanduel, Filament, FlashSoft, GameFlip, Grassroots Unwired, Grove Collaborative, Herb, HomeLight, Illumeo, Ipsy, Jump Ramp, Life360, LiveIntent, Lumoid, Mango Health, Marketo, Millennial Media, Namely, Navistone, Jackpocket, Paintzen, PayNearMe, Ranker, Reniac, Saucey, Sourceeasy, Splitwise, Spot Hero, Suiteness, Tanium, TubeMogul, Twenty20, Udemy, Urban Airship, Verbling, Wag, WedPics, Xumii, Zynga

Key Executives:
  Paul Martino, General Partner
  Education: BS, Mathematics, Lehigh University; MA, Computer Science, Princeton University
  Background: Founder, Ahpah Software; Founder, Tribe; Founder, Aggregated Knowledge
  Duncan Davidson, General Partner
  Education: BS, Physics/Mathematics, Brown University; JD, Michigan Law School
  Background: Founder, Covad Communications; Founder, Sky Pilot Networks; SVP, Business Development, InterTrust; Managing Director, VantagePoint Venture Partners
  Directorships: Drive Motors, Filament, Hologram, Illumeo, SpaceIQ
  Richard Melmon, Emeritus Partner
  Education: BA, Physics, University of California, Berkeley; MBA, Stanford University
  Background: Co-Founder, Electronic Arts; Co-Founder, Melmon Tawa & Partners; Co-Founder, Objective Software; Co-Founder, NetService Ventures Group
  James Conlon, Partner
  Education: BA, Bucknell University; JD, Washington College of Law, American University
  Background: Co-Founder, Venture Scanner

362 BUNKER HILL CAPITAL
16 Laurel Avenue
Suite 10
Wellesley Hills, MA 02481

Phone: 617-720-4030 Fax: 617-720-4037
web: www.bunkerhillcapital.com

Mission Statement: Bunker Hill Capital is a private equity firm with a singular focus on lower middle-market companies in four industry sectors: industrial products, business services, consumer products and specialty retail. Bunker Hill Capital invests in companies with exceptional management teams and the potential for significant growth.

Fund Size: $200 million
Average Investment: $30 - $50 million
Industry Group Preference: Industrial Products, Business Products & Services, Specialty Retail, Consumer Products
Portfolio Companies: Dyno Holdings, Hubbardton Forge, Medicinal Genomics, Taos

Other Locations:
12625 High Bluff Drive
Suite 320
San Diego, CA 92130
Phone: 858-793-4560 **Fax:** 858-793-4562

Key Executives:
Mark DeBlois, Co-Founder/Managing Partner
617-720-4035
Education: BA, Boston College
Background: Managing Director, BancBoston Capital; Bank of Boston
Directorships: ASPEQ Heating Group, Dyno Holdings, Hubbardton Forge, ImportLA, Rizing, Specialty Brands Holdings, Taos Mountain
Robert Clark Jr, Co-Founder/Managing Partner
617-720-4032
Education: BA, Harvard College
Background: Managing Director, BancBoston Capital; Bank of Boston
Directorships: ASPEQ Heating Group, California Family Fitness, Dyno Holdings, Hubbardton Forge, ImportLA, Rizing, Specialty Brands Holdings, Taos Mountain
Brian Kinsman, Co-Founder/Managing Partner
Education: BA, Yale University; MS, New York University
Background: Senior Managing Director, Pacific Corporate Group; Principal, Charterhouse Group International; Founding Partner, Milley & Company; Dyson-Kissner-Moran Corporation
Directorships: California Family Fitness, ImportLA
Jason Hurd, Co-Founder/Managing Partner
617-720-4034
Education: BA, Harvard College
Background: Director, BancBoston Capital
Directorships: Hubbardton Forge, Rizing, Specialty Brands Holdings
David L Gold, Partner
617-720-4033
e-mail: david.gold@bunkerhillcapital.com
Education: BA, Hobart College; MBA, Harvard Business School
Background: Procter & Gamble; Gerber; Aramark; CEO, Source4Teachers; Operating Partner, The Riverside Company
Directorships: ASPEQ Heating Group, Dyno Holdings
Robert Dreier, Principal/Director of Business Development
617-398-5517
e-mail: rob.dreier@bunkerhillcapital.com
Education: BS, University of Arizona; MBA, Kellogg School of Management, Northwestern University
Background: Managing Director & Co-Head, Financial Sponsors Group, BB&T Capital Markets; Vice President, M&A, RBC Capital Markets; Tucker Anthony
Jared B Paquette, Principal
617-398-5513
e-mail: jared.paquette@bunkerhillcapital.com
Education: AB, Bowdoin College; MBA, University of Chicago Booth School of Business
Background: Senior Associate, Nautic Partners; Associate, Weston Presidio; Associate, M&A, RBC Capital Markets; Tucker Anthony
Directorships: ASPEQ Heating Group, Dyno Holdings
Nathaniel P Bacon, Vice President
617-398-5518
e-mail: nat.bacon@bunkerhillcapital.com
Education: BA, Bucknell University
Background: Analyst, Morgan Stanley
Austin Wright, Vice President
617-398-5514
e-mail: austin.wright@bunkerhillcapital.com
Education: BBA, Stephen M. Ross School of Business, University of Michigan
Background: Analyst, Deutsche Bank
Anthony Giannobile, Associate
617-398-5524
e-mail: anthony.giannobile@bunkerhillcapital.com
Education: BS, Carroll School of Management, Boston College
Background: Analyst, Technology Services Group, Raymond James & Associates

363 BUSINESS CONSORTIUM FUND
39 West 37th Street
7th Floor
New York, NY 10018
Phone: 212-243-7360 **Fax:** 212-243-7647
web: www.bcfcapital.com

Mission Statement: A source of capital for certified minority-owned firms having difficulty obtaining financing from conventional sources on reasonable terms.

Geographic Preference: United States
Founded: 1994
Industry Group Preference: Diversified

Key Executives:
Serafin Mariel, President & COO
Background: New York National Bank, National Minority Supplier Development Council
Ruben Rodriguez, Sr. Vice President and Chief Lending Officer
Education: BA, Economics, Lehman College
Background: Relationship Manager, Seedco Financial Services
Thomas C. Fitzgerald, Advisor
Education: BA, Economics, Western Kentucky State University
Background: Vice President & Treasurer, Hershey Foods Corporation

364 BV INVESTMENT PARTNERS
125 High Street
17th Floor
Boston, MA 02110
Phone: 617-350-1500 **Fax:** 617-350-1509
e-mail: info@bvlp.com
web: www.bvlp.com

Mission Statement: Investment firm focused on the intersection of business and big data.

Geographic Preference: North America
Fund Size: $2.6 billion
Founded: 1983
Minimum Investment: $20 million
Investment Criteria: Middle Market Buyouts, Recapitalizations, Growth Equity, Industry Roll-Ups
Industry Group Preference: Business Services, Information Technology
Portfolio Companies: Albridge Solutions, Apps Associates, Butterfield Fulcrum Group, C-4 Analytics, CAMP Systems International, CF Stinson, CivicPlus, Consero Global, Decision Resources Inc., DTIQ, ECRM Holdings, EDCO, Edtech Holdings, Franco Signor, Geologic Systems LTD., Harron Communications LP, INetU Holdings, Intelliteach, Marshall & Swift Holdings, Medley Global Advisors, PetroSkills, Precision Nutrition, REAN Cloud, Reimagine Holdings Group, Right Networks, Risk International, RKD Group, SJI Holdings, SSI Holdings, TriCore Solutions, Vista III Media Holdings, Veracross LLC, WIRB Group Holdings

Venture Capital & Private Equity Firms / Domestic Firms

Key Executives:
Vikrant Raina, CEO & Managing Partner
Education: BS, Computer Science, Yale University; MBA, Harvard Graduate School of Business
Background: Executive Director, Communications, Media & Technology Group, Goldman Sachs (Asia); Project Leader, The Boston Consulting Group
Justin Harrison, Managing Director
Education: BA, Economics, Middlebury College
Background: Analyst & Associate, Chase Securities
Matt Kinsey, Managing Director
Education: BS, Finance, Ithaca College; MBA, Columbia Business School
Background: Analyst & Associate, Chase Securities
Jerry Hobbs, Operating Partner
Education: New York University, American Institute of Banking
Background: Chairman/CEO, VNU

365 BVM CAPITAL
820 Garrett Drive
Bossier City, LA 71111

Phone: 318-746-8430
web: www.bvmcap.com

Mission Statement: BVM Capital LLC is a Southeast-based venture capital firm that invests opportunistically. We provide equity capital to early and expansion stage companies with proprietary technology platforms or unique products addressing large markets.
Geographic Preference: Southeast United States
Founded: 2000
Portfolio Companies: Arcmail Technology, Cadforce, Cellfor, Embera Neurotherapeutics, Esperance Pharmaceuticals, LifeSync Corporation, NuPotential, SteriFx, Body Evolution, Jenrin Discovery, Calosyn Pharma, Chow Town, Fitness Interactive Experience

Key Executives:
Ross P. Barrett, Managing Partner
Background: Co-Founder, VC Experts; Capitol Hill, Legislative Aide to Senior US Senator, J Bennett Johnston

366 C&G CAPITAL PARTNERS
302 Merchants Walk
Suite 250
Tuscaloosa, AL 35406

web: www.candgcapitalpartners.com

Mission Statement: Christian values-oriented investment company in Tuscaloosa, Alabama.
Geographic Preference: Southeastern U.S.
Average Investment: $500,000 - $3 million
Investment Criteria: Early-Growth to Mature Stage
Industry Group Preference: Diversified

Key Executives:
John Gaffney, Principal
e-mail: jgaffney@candgcapitalpartners.com
Education: Vanderbilt University
Background: Management Committee Member, Commercial Banking Group Head, AmSouth Bank
Mike Chambers, Principal
e-mail: mchambers@candgcapitalpartners.com
Education: University of Texas
Background: Co-Founder/CEO/Chairman, River Gas Corporation

367 C3 CAPITAL PARTNERS LP
1511 Baltimore Avenue
Suite 500
Kansas City, MO 64108

Phone: 816-756-2225
web: www.c3cap.com

Mission Statement: To back successful and strong management teams and businesses with a vision for growth.
Geographic Preference: United States, Midwest, South
Fund Size: $500 million
Founded: 1994
Average Investment: $2 - $15 million
Minimum Investment: $2 million
Investment Criteria: Mezzanine, Later Stage, Strategic Acquisitions, Ownership Transitions, Recapitalizations
Industry Group Preference: Chemicals, Plastics, Energy, Business to Business, Distribution, Manufacturing
Portfolio Companies: A5, Air Waves, BP Express, Custom Steel Processing, Dynamatic, Equivalent Data, Flojos, GradLeaders, Green Compass, Grun Style, Hobbs Rental Corporation, iOR Partners, Lev, Market Fresh Produce, Monster XP, National Power, Nemaha Environmental, New World Natural Brands, Professional Environmental Engineers, Reynolds Plymer, Scrap Partners, SG360, Southern Spine Institute, SPOKE Custom Products, Steak 44, Stouse, SuccessEd, Sweet Additions, Transnational Foods, Warne, Wise Connect

Other Locations:
15169 North Scottsdale Road
Suite 320
Scottsdale, AZ 85254
Phone: 480-389-6955 Fax: 816-756-5552

Key Executives:
Andy Butler, Director
816-360-1808
e-mail: abutler@c3cap.com
Education: BS, Business, MAcc, University Of Missouri
Background: KPMG; BKD
Jared Poland, Managing Director
816-360-1827
e-mail: jpoland@c3cap.com
Education: BS, Accounting, Rockhurst University
Background: Senior Securities Analyst, Kansa City Life Insurance; Deloitte & Touche
Robert Smith, Partner
816-360-1805
e-mail: rsmith@c3cap.com
Education: BS, Engineering, University of Kansas; MBA, University of Chicago
Background: President, Koch Producer Services; EVP, Koch Oil; Koch Energy
Patrick Healy, Partner
816-360-1804
e-mail: phealy@c3cap.com
Education: BS, Accounting, University of Kansas
Background: Senior Tax Partner, Mayer Hoffman McCann
A Baron Cass III, Partner
214-292-2000
e-mail: bcass@c3cap.com
Education: BBA, Finance, Southern Methodist University; MBA, Wharton School, University of Pennsylvania
Background: Goldman Sachs & Company; Bear Stearns & Company
Steven Swartzman, Partner
816-360-1806
e-mail: sswartzman@c3cap.com
Education: AB, Harvard College; MBA, Columbia Business School
Background: President, Small Business Investment Alliance; KC Venture Group; VP, Citibank
D Patrick Curran, Partner
816-360-1802
e-mail: pcurran@c3cap.com
Education: BA, Economics, Stanford University; MBA, Kellogg School of Management, Northwestern University
Background: CEO, Cook Composites & Polymers; CEO, Cook Paint
Directorships: Applebee's International, Gold Banc,

Venture Capital & Private Equity Firms / Domestic Firms

Lockton Companies, Unitog, Sealright, JPS Packaging, American Safety Razor

368 CAI CAPITAL PARTNERS
300 Cadman Plaza W
One Pierrepont Plaza
12th Floor
New York, NY 11201

web: caifunds.com

Mission Statement: Founded in 1989, CAI is a private equity firm specializing in buyouts, restructurings, acquisitions, recapitalizations and other corporate growth initiatives. CAI offers financial expertise and access to capital, and aims to establish partnerships with capable management teams in order to ensure superior returns for investors.

Geographic Preference: Canada, United States
Founded: 1989
Average Investment: $20 - $75 million
Minimum Investment: $20 million
Investment Criteria: Lower Middle Market
Industry Group Preference: Consumer Products, Consumer Services, Business Products & Services, Infrastructure, Manufacturing, Aerospace, Defense and Government, Energy, Healthcare, Financial Services
Portfolio Companies: CustomAir, Javelin, Montigo, Sympli, CSAT Solutions, Feeney Brothers Utility Services

Other Locations:
510 Burrard Street
Suite 1000
Vancouver, BC V6C 3A8
Canada
Phone: 604-637-3411 **Fax:** 604-694-2524

Key Executives:
Peter Restler, Senior Advisor
212-319-3056
e-mail: prestler@caifunds.com
Education: BS, Wharton School, University of Pennsylvania
Background: Advisor, Island Natural Gas; Senior Vice President, Canada, Lehman Brothers; Vice President/Director, Wood Gundy
Directorships: Plastube, The Corix Group, Livingston International
Tracey McVicar, Managing Partner
e-mail: tmcvicar@caifunds.com
Education: BComm, Sauder School of Business, University of British Columbia; CFA Chartholder
Background: RBC Dominion Securities; Raymond James Ltd.; Goepel Shields & Partners
Directorships: Feeney Brothers Excavation, GeoStabilization International, White House Design, Tervita Corporation, Teck Resources
Curtis Johansson, Partner
604-694-2527
e-mail: cjohansson@caifunds.com
Education: BComm, Haskayne School of Business, University of Calgary
Background: RBC Capital Markets
Directorships: GeoStabilization International
Ashton Herriott, Director
604-637-1288
e-mail: aherriott@caifunds.com
Education: BComm, Finance, University of British Columbia; CFA
Background: Investment Banking Analyst, CIBC World Markets
Directorships: GeoStabilization International, Tervita Corporation, White House Design
Sherri Pittman, Managing Director

370 CALCEF CLEAN ENERGY FUND
5 Third Street
Suite 900
San Francisco, CA 94103

e-mail: info@calcef.org
web: calcef.org

Mission Statement: The Fund deploys deep industry networks and experience to support capital-efficient companies focusing on renewable energy, energy efficiency, energy storage and related products and services.

Fund Size: $24 million
Average Investment: $600,000
Investment Criteria: Seed-Stage, Early-Stage
Industry Group Preference: Clean Technology, Energy, Renewable Energy, Energy Efficiency

Key Executives:
Danny Kennedy, Managing Director
Christina Borsum, Chief Financial Officer

371 CALERA CAPITAL
580 California Street
Suite 2200
San Francisco, CA 94104

Phone: 415-632-5200
web: www.caleracapital.com

Mission Statement: Calera Capital invests in middle-market companies with proven management teams, sound business franchises and substantial unrealized potential. They accept public or private companies, family-controlled enterprises and corporate divestitures in virtually any sector.

Fund Size: $2.8 billion
Founded: 1991
Average Investment: $50 - $250 million
Investment Criteria: Leveraged Recapitalizations, Restructurings, Growth Investments, Corporate Spin-Offs, Take-Private Transactions
Industry Group Preference: Financial Services, Business Products & Services, Food Products & Services, Consumer Products, Healthcare, Building Materials & Services, Industrial Manufacturing
Portfolio Companies: Arnott, Bay State Physical Therapy, Carnegie Fabrics, Coldwell Banker, Crown Pacific, Direct General, Evans, First Republic Bank, Grandpoint, ImageFIRST, IPS Corporation, Ironshore, Juno Lighting, Kerr Group, Kinetic Concepts, LoopNet, Petro Shopping Centers, Transaction Services, RFIB, Rock-It Cargo, Sleepy's, Software Architects, Specialty Brands, SterlingBackcheck, Tapco International, United Dental Partners, United Site Services

Other Locations:
800 Boylston Street
Suite 1460
Boston, MA 02199
Phone: 617-578-0790

Key Executives:
Jim Farrell, Managing Partner
Education: AB, Princeton University; MBA, Harvard Business School
Background: Independent Investor; Associate, ESL Partners
Directorships: Modular Space Corporation, LoopNet, Rock-It Cargo
Mark N. Williamson, Managing Partner
Education: BA, Univ. of Oxford; MBA, Harvard Business School
Background: Managing Director, Harvard Private Capital Group; Associate, ESL Partners
Directorships: Direct General Corporation, IPS Corporation, Ironshore Corporation
Kevin Baker, Managing Director & General Counsel
Education: BA, Economics & Accounting, Claremont McKenna College; JD, Harvard Law School

Venture Capital & Private Equity Firms / Domestic Firms

Background: Partner, O'Melveny & Myers; Arthur Andersen & Co
Paul Walsh, Senior Managing Director
Education: BS, Engineering, Tufts University; MBA, Boston University
Background: Chairman & CEO, eFunds Corporation; CEO, Wright Express; CEO, BancOne Diversified Services; SVP, Norwest Capital Managment; CEO, Diners Club Germany
Ethan Thurow, Managing Director
Education: AB, Harvard University; MBA, Harvard Business School
Background: Associate, Audax Group; The Parthenon Group
Directorships: IPS Corporation
Brian Fearnow, Managing Director
Education: BS, Industrial Engineering, Stanford University; MBA, Stanford Graduate School of Business
Background: Investment Banking Group, Morgan Stanley; Franklin Templeton
James Halow, Managing Director
Education: BA, Stanford University
Background: Technology Investment Banking Group, Salomon Smith Barney
Directorships: Ironshore Corporation, Rock-It Cargo

372 CALGARY ENTERPRISES
Four Park Avenue
Suite 12G
New York, NY 10016

Phone: 212-683-0119 Fax: 212-683-3119
e-mail: insalaco@calgaryenterprises.com
web: www.calgaryenterprises.com

Mission Statement: Calgary Enterprises provides management consulting and advisory services to early stage and emerging middle market companies across a variety of industry sectors.
Geographic Preference: United States, Canada
Founded: 1988
Investment Criteria: Emerging, Early Stage, Growth, Middle Market, Management Buyouts, Acquisitions, Restructurings, Turnarounds
Industry Group Preference: All Sectors Considered
Key Executives:
  Steven Insalaco, President
  e-mail: insalaco@calgaryenterprises.com
  Education: BA, Social Science & Economics, St. John's University; MBA, Finance Management, Long Island University
  Background: Bank of America; Chemical Bank; Manufacturers Hanover Trust Corporation; Wood Gundy Corp; Merrill Lynch

373 CALIBRATE VENTURES
130 W Union Street
Pasedena, CA 91103

web: www.calibratevc.com

Mission Statement: Calibrate Ventures invests in early-revenue automation and AI technology companies.
Investment Criteria: Less than $5 million revenue; Recurring revenue business models and ambition to scale beyond $100 Million in sales
Key Executives:
  Kevin Dunlap, Co-Founder and General Partner
  Jason Schoettler, Co-Founder and General Partner

374 CALIFORNIA TECHNOLOGY VENTURES
670 N Rosemead Boulevard
Suite 201
Pasadena, CA 91107

e-mail: info@ctventures.com
web: www.ctventures.com

Mission Statement: California Technology Ventures (CTV) is a venture capital fund that makes direct investments in technology and life science companies. CTV has built a strong reputation for its entrepreneurial approach to investing and working with companies. CTV believes in guiding entrepreneurs through the strategic, operational, and management decisions critical to a company's success.
Average Investment: $250,000 - $2 million
Minimum Investment: $250,000
Investment Criteria: Seed-Stage/Startup, Early-Stage, First & Second Round, Later-Stage
Industry Group Preference: Life Sciences, Biopharmaceuticals, Medical Devices, Information Technology, Communications, Telecommunications, Electronics, Semiconductors, Software Systems, Multimedia, Internet
Portfolio Companies: Ablexis, Agile Materials & Technologies Inc., Akiva Inc., AngioScore, Aurora SFC Systems, Avita Biomedical, Blade Games World Inc., Ceregene Inc., China Genetics Holdings, Clear Flow Inc., Education.com, Dolphinsearch Inc., GoingOn Networks Inc., FanXChange, Health Hero Network, Gamevice, Insert Therapeutics, InSound Medical, MariaDB, MingPlan.com, Moss Software, Oerthalign Inc., Orthoscan Inc., Phothotera Inc., Surgrx Inc., Spine Wave Inc., SupplyEdge Inc., SurgiQuest Inc., Vasonova Inc., Thinglefin, Travelmuse Inc., Turbine Inc., Vivant Medical Inc.
Key Executives:
  Alex Suh, Managing Director/Founder
  e-mail: asuh@ctventures.com
  Education: BSBA, Management, University of Denver's School of Business
  Background: Jacobs Capital Group, LLC; JJ Jacobs Enterprises
  William A. Hanna, Managing Director
  e-mail: william@jacobscapitalgroup.com
  Education: MBA, Harvard University; BComm, McGill University
  Background: Jacobs Capital Group, LLC; Founding President/Director, Cedars Bank; Senior VP, Credit of Bank Audi USA; VP, Corporate Finance Department, Smith Barney & Company
  Andrea Devita, Director of Finance
  e-mail: andrea@ctventures.com
  Background: Controller, Main Line Equipment; Controller, CTL Environmental Services

375 CALLAIS CAPITAL MANAGEMENT
401 Focus Street
Thibodaux, LA 70301

Phone: 985-492-2323
web: callaiscapital.com

Mission Statement: Callais Capital leverages generations of entrepreneurship to pursue regional startup investment opportunities.
Geographic Preference: Louisiana and Regional
Key Executives:
  Harold Callais II, Managing Partner/Chief Investment Officer
  985-272-1324
  Education: BS, Nicholls University
  Corey Callais, Managing Partner/Chair
  985-492-2323
  e-mail: corey.callais@callaiscapital.com
  Education: BS, Nicholls State University
  Background: CEO, KLEB/KZZQ; CEO, Callais Cablevision; CEO Solid Waste Disposal Inc.
  Nicholas Callais, Managing Partner/CFO and Chief Compliance Officer
  985-492-2323
  e-mail: nicholas.callais@callaiscapital.com
  Education: BA, MBA, Tulane University

Background: VP, Terrebonne Parish Republican Party; Credit Analyst, United Community Bank

376 CALTIUS EQUITY PARTNERS
11766 Wilshire Blvd
Suite 850
Los Angeles, CA 90025

Phone: 310-996-9585
e-mail: info@caltius.com
web: www.caltius.com

Mission Statement: Makes equity investments in small and medium sized businesses throughout the United States.
Geographic Preference: United States
Founded: 1999
Average Investment: $10 - $30 million
Minimum Investment: $5 million
Investment Criteria: Late-Stage, Growth Capital, Leveraged Recapitalizations, Corporate Divestitures, Acquisitions, Buyouts
Industry Group Preference: Consumer Products, Consumer Services, Business Products & Services, IT & Managed Services, Industrial Services
Portfolio Companies: ACIS, Arrowhead Brass Products, CampGroup, Consolidated Fire Protection, CRC Health, DavexLabs, Diversified Human Resources, Electra Bicycle Company, Health Payment Systems, Impact Fire Services, La Dove, MC Sign Company, MCC Control Systems, MC Sign, Nicoat, Northwest Coatings, OrthoClassic, Polytex Environmental Inks, Scientech, SeniorBridge, SM&A, Starpoint Health, Talent Systems, Vision Holdings

Key Executives:
Jim Upchurch, President/CEO
e-mail: jupchurch@caltius.com
Education: BS, Accounting, Northern Arizona University
Background: President, Bancorp Libra; Libra Investments; Portfolio Manager, Columbia Savings & Loan Association; KPMG
Directorships: CampGroup, DavexLabs, Kiss My Face, OrthoClassic, SM&A, Starpoint Health
Garrick Ahn, Managing Director
e-mail: gahn@caltius.com
Education: BS, MS, Electrical & Computer Engineering, Johns Hopkins University; MBA, Harvard Business School
Background: Associate, Bastion Capital Corporation; Associate, McKinsey & Company; Financial Analyst, Morgan Stanley & Company
Directorships: Electra Bicycle Company, Health Payment Systems, Kiss My Face, Ortho Classic, Scientech
Jeffrey Holdsberg, Managing Director
Education: BS, Business, Eastern Illinois University
Background: CEO/President, Northwest Coatings; Advisor, Charlesbank Capital Partners; President, Alper Ink Group; Arthur Andersen
Directorships: Diversified Human Resources, Health Payment Systems, National Industrial Coatings, The Institute of Audio Research
Michael Morgan, Managing Director
e-mail: mmorgan@caltius.com
Education: BA, Economics, University of Pennsylvania; MBA, Anderson School of Management, University of California, Los Angeles
Background: Salomon Smith Barney; Kline Hawkes & Co.; Continental Illinois Venture Corporation
Directorships: Starpoint Health, MCC Control Systems, Diversified Human Resources, Kiss My Face
Justin Benshoof, Principal
e-mail: jbenshoof@caltius.com
Education: BA, Economics, Beloit College; MBA, University of Minnesota
Background: Analyst, Norwest Equity Partners
Directorships: Diversified Human Resources, Health Payment Systems, Impact Facility Services, MCC Control Systems, MC Sign

Greg Brackett, Chief Financial Officer
e-mail: gbrackett@caltius.com
Education: BA, Business Economics, University of California, Los Angeles
Background: Senior Accountant, Investment Management Services Assurance Group, KPMG

377 CALTIUS STRUCTURED CAPITAL
11766 Wilshire Blvd
Suite 850
Los Angeles, CA 90025

Phone: 310-996-9585
e-mail: info@caltius.com
web: www.caltius.com

Mission Statement: Makes investments in businesses with diverse customer bases, experienced management teams and strong market positions throughout the United States.
Geographic Preference: United States
Founded: 1999
Average Investment: $7 - $50 million
Minimum Investment: $7 million
Investment Criteria: Late-Stage, Growth Capital, Leveraged Recapitalizations, Acquisitions, Buyouts, Acquisition Financing, Management Buyouts, Refinancing, Shareholder Liquidity
Industry Group Preference: Consumer Products, Consumer Services, Business Products & Services, Healthcare, Specialty Manufacturing, Specialty Staffing, Tech Services
Portfolio Companies: Adrenaline, American Consolidated Media, Aspen Education Group, BrightHeart, Building Systems Design, Bulk Handling Systems, CampGroup, Closet world, CRC Health, Dickinson Frozen Foods, Diversified Human Resources, Divisions Maintenance Group, ETT, EXOS, ForeFront Education, Fullerton, GLM, Griplock Systems, Harris Research, HealthPlan, Healthy Pet, Hill Country Holdings, Homegrown Natural Foods, HSS, Imagenet, Insight Global, Integrated Healthcare Strategies, Intellectual Technology, J-B Weld, KCAEP, Kids Care Dental, Lucky Strike, Mercer Advisors, Meridian Surgical Partners, Monitor Group, MCRA, Nu Visions Manufacturing, Pacific Crest, Parking Company America, Pearl Meyer & Partners, PlanMember Financial, Plassein Packaging, Pritikin, QCI Marine Offshore, Quantic Industries, Radiant Logistics, Radiant Research, Scientech, Select Rehabilitation, SM&A, Soff-Cut, Spinnaker Support, Tri-Star Electronics, True Home Value, U.S. Pole Company, UHY Advisors, Unitech Aerospace, Universal Services Of America, Vantage Mobility International, Walker Edison, Wyle Laboratories, Zenith Adminstators

Key Executives:
Jim Upchurch, President/CEO
e-mail: jupchurch@caltius.com
Education: BS, Accounting, Northern Arizona University
Background: President, Bancorp Libra; Libra Investments; Portfolio Manager, Columbia Savings & Loan Association; KPMG
Directorships: CampGroup, DavexLabs, Kiss My Face, OrthoClassic, SM&A, Starpoint Health
Michael Kane, Managing Director
e-mail: mkane@caltius.com
Education: BA, Economics, MBA, Accounting, Rice University
Background: Building and Construction Capital Partners; General Electric Capital Corporation; Metropolitan Life Insurance
Directorships: Bulk Handling Systems, Fullerton Engineering, Perl Meyer & Partners, SM&A, Unitech Aerospace
Greg Howorth, Managing Director
e-mail: ghoworth@caltius.com
Education: BS, University of Southern California
Background: Senior Credit Officer, FINOVA Capital; Heller Financial

Venture Capital & Private Equity Firms / Domestic Firms

Directorships: Adrenaline, GLM Energy Services, Imagenet, J-B Weld
Alisa Frederick, Managing Director
e-mail: afrederick@caltius.com
Education: BA, Wellesley College
Background: Senior Vice President, Portfolio Manager, Fleet Capital Corporation; Chemical Bank
Directorships: MCRA, Pearl Meyer & Partners, SM&A, Spinnaker Support
Gavin Bates, Managing Director
e-mail: gbates@caltius.com
Education: BA, University of Nottingham; MBA, Haas School of Business at the University of California
Background: Director, CapitalSource; Compass Partners and Permira; HSBC Investment Bank
Directorships: Adrenaline, GLM Energy Services, J-B Weld, SM&A
Rick Shuart, Managing Director
e-mail: rshuart@caltius.com
Education: BA, Columbia University; MBA, UCLA Anderson School of Management
Background: Financial Analyst, Dillon, Read & Company; Donaldson, Lufkin & Jenrette
Directorships: Bulk Handling Systems, Fullerton, Imagenet, Select Rehabilitation, Unitech Aerospace
Don Jamieson, Vice President
e-mail: djamieson@caltius.com
Education: BA, Economics, Harvard University
Background: Financial Analyst, Salomon Smith Barney
Directorships: Adrenaline, Fullerton, GLM Energy Services, Imagenet, J-B Weld, MCRA, Pearl Meyer & Partners, Spinnaker Support
Alan Chen, Vice President
e-mail: achen@caltius.com
Education: BS, Finance and Business Economics, University of Southern California; MBA, Columbia Business School
Background: Associate, Endeavour Capital; Banking Analyst, Piper Jaffray & Co.

378 CALUMET VENTURE FUND
1245 E Washington Avenue
Suite 210
Madison, WI 53703
Phone: 308-310-3242 Fax: 888-310-3989

Mission Statement: Calumet Venture Fund was formed to invest in the next generation of high-growth technology companies in the Midwest.
Geographic Preference: Midwest United States
Founded: 2008
Investment Criteria: Early-Stage
Industry Group Preference: SaaS, Business Products & Services, Education, Healthcare, E-Commerce & Manufacturing, Mobile Technology, Wireless, Software, Networks, Bioinformatics
Portfolio Companies: CraftArtEdu, Craft Media Network, Montage Talent, OptiMine
Key Executives:
  Judy M. Owen, General Partner
  Education: BSEE, University of Wisconsin, Madison
  Background: Silicon Graphics, Chips & Technologies, Teknekron Communication Systems; CEO/Co-Founder, Wireless Access
  Directorships: Picazo Communication, SigmaQuest
  Toni F. Sikes, General Partner
  Education: BS, Mathematics, University of Alabama; MS, Market Research, University of Wisconsin, Madison
  Background: Investment Banking, Gruppo Levey & Co.

379 CALVERT INVESTMENT MANAGEMENT
1825 Connecticut Ave. NW
Suite 400
Washington, DC 20009-5727
Toll-Free: 800-368-2745
web: www.calvert.com

Mission Statement: Invests in high-risk, socially and environmentally responsible enterprises. Calvert is part of a larger financial services family, The AmeritasAcacia Companies.
Geographic Preference: United States
Fund Size: $9 billion
Founded: 1976
Average Investment: $100,000-$700,000
Minimum Investment: $1,000
Investment Criteria: Early-to-expansion stage; generally not a seed or start-up investor
Industry Group Preference: Environment, Education, Energy, Health Related
Portfolio Companies: Cylex, H2Gen Innovations
Key Executives:
  John Streur, President & Chief Executive Officer
  Education: BS, Agriculture & Life Sciences, University of Wisconsin
  Background: President & CEO, Managers Investment Group LLC
  Anthony Eames, Vice President, Director of Responsible Investment Strategy
  Education: BA, Wittenberg University
  Background: Vice President, Eaton Vance Management; Sr. Vice President and National Sales Manager, Calvert Investment Management.
  Hope Brown, Executive Directoe & Chief Compliance Officer
  Education: BA, English, University of Maryland
  Background: Vice President & Chief Compliance Officer, Wilmington Funds; Assistant Vice President, Risk Management & Compliance Lead Manager, T. Rowe Price Associates

380 CAMBER CREEK
5410 Edson Lane
Suite 220
Rockville, MD 20852
Phone: 240-621-3177
web: www.cambercreek.com

Mission Statement: Camber Creek is a venture capital firm providing strategic value and capital to operating technology companies focused on the real estate market. The investment team at Camber Creek has investing, operating, and technology experience and expertise across a range of real estate businesses, including construction, property management, development, and leasing.
Geographic Preference: United States
Investment Criteria: Seed-Stage, Early-Stage
Industry Group Preference: Real Estate, Software
Portfolio Companies: 42 Floors, Canvas, ClearEdge, Optii Solutions, Parkifi, Vedero Software, SalesWarp, Compstak, Fundrise, Motista, Latch, VTS, Revmetrix, BuildingEngines, Rachio, 3C Logic, Task Easy, Mobideo, Red IQ, Notion, Turbo Appeal, Latista, Bowery
Other Locations:
  450 West 17th Street
  Suite 1222
  New York, NY 10011
Key Executives:
  Jeffrey Berman, General Partner
  Directorships: LoftSmart, SalesWarp, AquaSeca
  Casey Berman, Managing Director
  Education: University of Michigan
  Background: NextGen Venture Partners; Founder, DATG Security Company; Advisor, Pervazive

Venture Capital & Private Equity Firms / Domestic Firms

381 CAMBRIA GROUP
Commonwealth Hall at Old Parkland
3899 Maple Avenue
Suite 150
Dallas, TX 75219

Phone: 469-513-2200 Fax: 469-513-2201
web: www.cambriagroup.com

Mission Statement: The Cambria Group is a private equity firm which invests in small and mid-sized businesses. The group targets control positions in stable, historically profitable entities with operating profits in excess of $1 million annually. the group does not invest in startups or turnarounds.

Geographic Preference: United States
Founded: 1996
Average Investment: $5 million
Minimum Investment: $500,000
Investment Criteria: Leveraged Buyouts, Management Buyouts, Recapitalizations, Industry Consolidations, Growth Equity, Transfers, Restructurings, Strategic Acquisitions
Industry Group Preference: Business Products & Services, Transportation, Consumer Products, Consumer Services, Manufacturing, Industrial Products, Retail, Consumer & Leisure, Education
Portfolio Companies: 8 Enterprises, Advanced Network Solutions, Allen Edmonds, Allrecipes.com, Ames Taping Tools, Ancient Mosaic Studios, Apartment Data Services, Bacrac Supply Company, Behavioral Health Group, Blue Dog Bakery, Boca Executive Beauty, Business Networking International, CalNet Technology Group, Care2.com, Classroom Connect, Cobblestone Golf Group, ConvenientMD, Crossbow Technology, Dakota Arms, Data Fusion Technologies, Dolce Hotels & Resorts, DSA/Phototech, DuBois Chemicals, Excelligence, Eyewitness Surveillance, FastSpring, Filson, FleetPride, Flexstar Technology, Funko, Gizmo Beverages, Globys, Gogotech, Griswold Home Care, Gwynnie Bee, Identified, iLight Technologies, iNet Interactive, InSight Eye Care, ISC Water Solutions, Ivize, KPI Consulting, Krueger-Gilbert Health Physics, Leader Technologies, Leocorpio, Liftoff Mobile, LM Foods, Lund Van Dyke, MarketTrack, Marshall Retail Group, Midwest Supplies, Mitchell, National Technical Systems, National Video Monitoring Corporation, NuCO2, O'Brien Veterinary Management, OOHA Wilkins, Ooyala, Opengov.com, Oriental Trading Company, Paragon Products, PEAK Broadcasting, Penn Warranty Corporation, Pet Loss Center, Planet DDS, Polaroid, Restaurant Technology, River Point Farms, Rock Ridge Stone, Rod and Tubing Services, Roman Decorating Products, Root Metrics, Scottish-American Insurance, Shoreline Solutions, SkyPipeline, Social Sentinel, Soft Surroundings, Sonoma Creamery, Sundance, Teaching Company, US Labs, Vector Disease Control, Veri Center, Warne Optics, WebEquity Solutions, Windley Ely, Windy Hill Spirits, YelloMobile, Yoforia, Z Gallerie, Zywave

Key Executives:
  Paul L Davies III, Founder/Managing Principal
  469-513-220 ext.870
  e-mail: davies@cambriagroup.com
  Education: BS, Industrial Engineering, Stanford University; MBA, Stanford Graduate School of Business
  Background: Principal, Brentwood Associates; The Fremont Group; Operating & Financing, Bechtel Group; Foreign Operations, Chevron Corporation
  Directorships: Hoover Institution, National Trustee of the Boys & Girls Clubs of America
  René Lajous, Principal
  469-513-200 ext. 878
  e-mail: lajous@cambriagroup.com
  Education: BAS, Industrial Engineering, University of Toronto; MBA, Wharton School, University of Pennsylvania
  Background: Consultant, Boston Consulting Group; Logistics & Operations, Procter & Gamble; Pillsbury

  Natalie D Cryer, Vice President
  469-513-220 ext. 861
  e-mail: cryer@cambriagroup.com
  Education: BS, Stanford University; MBA, Stanford Graduate School of Business
  Background: Senior Analyst, Accenture; Salt Creek Capital
  Natalie L Davies, Senior Associate
  e-mail: nld@cambriagroup.com
  Education: BS, Management Science & Engineering, Stanford University
  Background: Senior Analyst, Business & Systems Integration, Accenture

382 CAMBRIDGE ASSOCIATES
125 High Street
Boston, MA 02110

Phone: 617-457-7500
e-mail: contactca@cambridgeassociates.com
web: www.cambridgeassociates.com

Mission Statement: To deliver outperformance with a portfolio that is right for each entrepreneur.

Industry Group Preference: Diversified

Key Executives:
  David Druley, Chief Executive Officer
  Education: BBA/MBA, University of Texas
  Background: Founder, Druley Investment Management

383 CAMBRIDGE CAPITAL
525 S Flagler Drive
Suite 200
West Palm Beach, FL 33401

Phone: 561-932-1600 Fax: 561-655-6232
web: www.cambridgecapital.com

Mission Statement: Cambridge Capital provides private equity and supply chain knowledge to growth companies in the applied supply chain sector. The firm utilizes its resources and operational expertise to create value for portfolio companies. Cambridge Capital is an investment partner of BG Strategic Advisors.

Fund Size: $81 million
Founded: 2009
Average Investment: $10 - $50 million
Investment Criteria: Growth Capital, Leveraged Buyouts, Recapitalizations, Build Up Strategies
Industry Group Preference: Manufacturing, Packaging, Distribution, Recycling, Logistics, Supply Chain Technology, Transportation
Portfolio Companies: American Capital, DHL, Geologistics, Kuehne Nagel, Meritex, New Breed Logistics, Odyssey Logistics & Technology, Old Dominion Freight Line, Supervalu, Tibco, Translink, USCO Logistics

Key Executives:
  Benjamin Gordon, Managing Partner
  e-mail: ben@cambridgecapitcal.com
  Education: BA, Yale College, Yale University; MBA, Harvard Business School
  Background: Founder, 3Plex; Mercer Management Consulting; AMI
  Directorships: Palm Beach United Way, Palm Beach Federation, Pal Beach Youn Presidents' Organization
  Bill Conley, Operating Partner
  Education: BS, Aeronautics, St. Louis University
  Background: CEO, Sky-Trax; President, ATC Technologies Corporation; Vice President/General Manager, FedEx
  Herb Shear, Operating Partner
  Education: Southern Illinois University
  Background: CEO, GENCO Supply Chain Solutions
  Dave Stubbs, Operating Partner
  e-mail: dave@cambridgecapital.com
  Education: BA, Economics, Haverford College; MBA,

Venture Capital & Private Equity Firms / Domestic Firms

Finance, Wharton School, University of Pennsylvania
Background: Senior Vice President/General Manager, Kuehne + Nagel; Vice President, Supply Chain, Champion International
Rimas Kapeskas, Partner
e-mail: rimas@cambridgecapitcal.com
Education: BS, University of Connecticut; MBA, Goizueta Business School, Emory University; Stanford Business School
Background: VP Of Strategy, Managing Director, UPS
Directorships: National Venture Capital Association, Junior Achievement of Georgia
Shai Greenwald, Director Of Business Development
e-mail: shai@cambridgecapital.com
Education: MBA, Boston University
Background: FleetBoston Financial; EMC; Heidrick and Struggles
Matt Smalley, Vice President
e-mail: matt@cambridgecaptical.com
Education: Bachelor's, Leonard N. Stern School of Business, New York University
Background: Macquarie Capital; Insight Venture Partners

384 CAMBRIDGE CAPITAL CORPORATION
200 Madison Avenue
Convent Station, NJ 07960

Phone: 973-401-1414 Fax: 973-401-1417
e-mail: kjm@camcapcorp.com
web: www.camcapcorp.com

Mission Statement: Financial services including venture capital, capital sourcing, market planning, and consultation.
Geographic Preference: Middle Atlantic States
Founded: 1992
Average Investment: $2.5 million
Minimum Investment: $500,000
Investment Criteria: Early Stage, Well Capitalized, Institutional Investors, Affluent Individuals
Industry Group Preference: Assisted Living, Graphic Arts, Healthcare, Biotechnology, Manufacturing, Distribution, Computer Hardware & Software, Manufacturing, Financial Services, Banking

Key Executives:
Kenneth J Mathews, Managing Director
e-mail: kjm@camcapcorp.com
Education: BS, Economics, St. Peter's College
Background: Executive VP, First Fidelity Bancorporation

385 CAMBRIDGE VENTURES LP
4181 E 96th Street
Suite 200
Indianapolis, IN 46240

Phone: 317-843-9704 Fax: 317-844-9815
web: www.cambridgecapitalmgmt.com

Mission Statement: Invests in growth companies within a 200 mile radius of Indianapolis.
Geographic Preference: Mid-West
Fund Size: $20 million
Founded: 1991
Average Investment: $750,000
Minimum Investment: $100,000
Investment Criteria: Second-Stage, Mezzanine, LBO, Expansion, Acquisition
Industry Group Preference: Diversified

Key Executives:
Jean Wojtowicz, President
317-843-9704 ext. 126
e-mail: jwojtowicz@cambridgecapitalmgmt.com
Charles Kennedy, Portfolio Manager
317-843-9704 ext. 124
e-mail: ckennedy@cambridgecapitalmgmt.com

386 CAMDEN PARTNERS HOLDINGS LLC
500 East Pratt Street
Suite 1200
Baltimore, MD 21202

Phone: 410-878-6800 Fax: 410-878-6850
e-mail: info@camdenpartners.com
web: www.camdenpartners.com

Mission Statement: Capitalizes on the disconnect between business fundamentals and valuation in small and micro-cap markets.
Founded: 1995
Average Investment: $10 million
Minimum Investment: $3 million
Investment Criteria: Equity, Preferred Equity, Equity-Linked Debt Securities acquired directly from issuer in negotiated private placement
Industry Group Preference: Business Products & Services, Healthcare, Education, Financial Services
Portfolio Companies: Blisplay, Bluefin, Clavert Education Services LLC, CMC, eNeura, EGHC, Implantable Provider Group, InGo, Metabolon, Network For Good, New Horizons, Orpheris, OutMathc, Paragon Bioservices, Patient Safe Solutions, Pinnacle Automotive Hospitally, Planet Payment, PreScience Labs, Proposal Software.com, Ranir, Santa Rosa Consulting, Sisu Global Health, Tracx, Triumpth Higher Education Group, Viventium

Key Executives:
David L. Warnock, Founder/Partner
410-878-6810
e-mail: ssprigg@CamdenPartners.com
Education: BA, University of Delaware; MS, University of Wisconsin
Background: President/Consultant, T Rowe Price Strategic Partners; Co-Manager, T Rowe Price New Horizons Fund; Welch and Forbes
Directorships: Concorde Career Colleges, Environmental Safeguards, Touchstone Applied Science Associates, Blue Rhino Corporation, Nobel Learning Communities
Donald W. Hughes, Strategic Advisor
e-mail: ssprigg@camdenpartners.com
Education: BA, Lycoming College; MSF, Loyola University; CPA
Background: Executive VP/CFO, Broventure Company; Arthur Andersen LLP; CFO, Capstone Pharmacy Services
Directorships: Occupational Health + Rehabilitation, Touchstone Applied Science Associates, AqilQuest
Meghan M. McGee, Partner
e-mail: cbeal@camdenpartners.com
Education: BS, Family Studies, University of Maryland; MBA, Robert H. Smith School of Business, University of Maryland
Richelle P. Parham, Strategic Advisor
e-mail: richelle@camdenpartners.com
Education: BS, Business Admin. & Design Arts, Drexel University
Background: Visa Inc.; Digitas Inc.; Citibank; VP Chief Marketing Officer, eBay
Jason R. Tagler, Partner
e-mail: cbeal@camdenpartners.com
Education: BS, Applied Economics, MBA, Cornell University
Background: Alliant Partners
Directorships: Ranir, IncentOne

387 CAMP ONE VENTURES
101 California St.
Suite 2710
San Francisco, CA 94111

Phone: 415-856-7248 Fax: 415-856-7348
web: www.camponeventures.com

Mission Statement: Camp One Ventures seeks to combine the expertise, insights and relationships that the team possesses from their years of advising early stage companies with the core team's investment experience. The synergies among the team create unparalleled access into the realm of early stage technology investments, and bring to investors a unique opportunity to participate in exciting growth companies that would otherwise be reserved for Sand Hill Road insiders. Camp One Ventures will leverage the local team's client base, founder referral network, and proximity to Stanford and Silicon Valley to identify early stage companies. We want to keep a hands-on relationship with the company and help build out the team, as well as make introductions.

Geographic Preference: San Francisco, Silicon Valley
Investment Criteria: Early Stage
Industry Group Preference: Technology, Social Media, Mobility, Fintech, Cloud Computing, SaaS
Portfolio Companies: Aarki, Apple Pie Capital, Augmate, Balance, Booking Pal, Boomtown, CommerceSync, Credit Sesame, DoubleBeam, Earnin, Earn Up, Even, Fanbank, Fenway Summer, Float, Goodworld, InDinero, Karmic Labs, MetaBrite, Mobius, Momentum, One Inc., Otelic, Pulse.io, Rhiza, Ripple, Simple Disability Insurance, Stellar, Terabit Radios, Wade & Wendy, Xola, Zooz

Other Locations:
2501 20th Place South
Suite 275
Birmingham, AL 35223
Phone: 205-202-1083 **Fax:** 205-639-5678

Key Executives:
Robert Claassen
650-714-0538
e-mail: rob@camponeventures.com
Thomas P. Brown
415-856-7248
Fax: 415-856-7348
e-mail: tom@camponeventures.com
Madding King III
205-202-1083
Fax: 205-639-5678
e-mail: madding@camponeventures.com
J. Rainer Twiford
205-202-1083
Fax: 205-639-5678
e-mail: rainer@camponeventures.com

388 CAMP VENTURES
1216 Woodview Terrace
Los Altos, CA 94024-7046

Phone: 650-949-0804 **Fax:** 650-618-1719
e-mail: justin@campventures.com
web: www.campventures.com

Mission Statement: To engage with great companies in their earliest stage of development.

Founded: 1997
Average Investment: $500,000 - $1.5 million
Minimum Investment: $500,000
Investment Criteria: Seed-Stage
Industry Group Preference: Mobile Apps, Technology, Computer Software, Communications, Data, Semiconductors
Portfolio Companies: Abertis, AllTrails, Altera, Broadcom, Cepheid, deCarta, Dell, Qualcomm, GainSpan, GeoVector, LifeLock, Picaboo, Quantance, Riverbed, Seagate, Sierra Wireless, SiTime, Skype, SpreadTrum, YesVideo

Key Executives:
Justin Camp, Founder & Managing General Partner
e-mail: justin@campventures.com
Education: BA, Economics & Political Science, UCLA; JD, University of Pennsylvania Law School
Background: Corporate Attorney, Cravath Swaine & Moore; Author, Venture Capital Due Dilligenc
Jerome Camp, Founder & General Partner
Education: BS, Mechanical Engineering, University of Arkansas; BS, Electrical Engineering, University of Maryland; MS, Mechanical Engineering, Purdue University; PhD, Electrical Engineering, University of Arizona
Background: Founder, ComTier; Consultant, Lockheed-Martin
Kevin Negus, General Partner
e-mail: kevin@campventures.com
Education: BASc, MASc, Mechanical Engineering, University of Waterloo
Background: CTO, Proxim Corporation; VC Investments, Atheros Communications

389 CANAAN PARTNERS
2765 Sand Hill Road
Menlo Park, CA 94025

Phone: 650-854-8092
e-mail: hello@canaan.com
web: www.canaan.com

Mission Statement: Helps companies successfully grow over time by taking an active role in their development; investment capabilities range from $4 million to $20 million. The firm can invest in any stage of development from early through expansion stage; it has investments in over 100 companies, and has created a number of public companies.

Geographic Preference: United States, Israel
Fund Size: $2.0 billion
Founded: 1987
Average Investment: $4 - $20 million
Minimum Investment: $2 million
Investment Criteria: Seed- and Early-Stage
Industry Group Preference: Technology, Healthcare
Portfolio Companies: Abryx, AdNear, AdverCar, Aldea Pharmaceuticals, Artspace, Arvinas, Axial Exchange, Beckon, Bharat Matrimony, Blurb, Borro, Butterfly, Call My Name, Cardlytics, CarTrade, Chimerix, Inc., Civitas Therapeutics, CompStak, Cortina, Cuyana, CytomX Therapeutics, Data Sciences International, Dermira, Dicom Grid, Durata Therapeutics, ee4, Ebates, Echopass, Efficient Finance, EndoGastric Solutions, EnStorage, Envisia, Equitas, Gemvara, Groundwork, Happiest Minds, IndiaProperty.com, Instacart, ItBit, iYogi, Joor, Kabam, Koolbit, Labrys Biologics, Lancope, LendingClub, Liquidia Technologies, LiveU, Loyalty Rewardz, Marinus Pharmaceuticals, mCarbon, Metacloud, Minimally Invasive Devices, Inc., N-trig, Naaptol, Novira Therapeutics, On24, OneFineStay, OpenSky, Orchard, Prime Sense, Relievant, Revision Optics, Sample6, Semnur, ShopKeepPOS, SilverRail, Skybox Imaging, Soasta, Spine Wave, Stayful, Switchfly, Talena, The RealReal, Theraclone Sciences, Tobira Therapeutics, Transcend Medical, Tremor Video, UnitedLex, UrbanSitter, VaxInnate, Verance, Victorious, ViewBix, Vivox, Wibidata, Xirrus, Zoosk

Other Locations:
285 Riverside Avenue
Suite 250
Westport, CT 06880
Phone: 203-855-0400

821 Broadway
3rd Floor
Entrance at 51 East 12th
New York, NY
Phone: 646-374-4949

27 South Park
Suite 201
San Francisco, CA 94107
Phone: 415-405-4655

Key Executives:
John Balen, Partner
e-mail: jbalen@canaan.com
Education: MBA, BS, Electrical Engineering, Cornell University
Background: Managing Director, Horsley Bridge Partners; Sales Application Engineer, Codentoll Technology Corporation; Fiber Communications Start-Up/Engineer, Digital Equipment Corporation

Directorships: Blurb; Cardlytics; eStamp; ID Analytics; SilverRail; SOASTA; Switchfly; UberSitter
Guy M. Russo, General Partner
e-mail: grusso@canaan.com
Education: BS, Accounting, University of Connecticut; CPA & MBA, University of Connecticut
Background: Senior Accountant, Entrepreneurial Services Group of Ernst & Young
Deepak Kamra, General Partner
e-mail: dkamra@canaan.com
Education: BC, Carleton University; MBA, Harvard Business School
Background: Marketing, Aspect Communications; General Manager, TRW Datacomm International; ROLM Corporation
Directorships: Acme Packet; Capella Space; DoubleClick; Kickplay; Kustomer; Match.com; Matrimony; Node; ON24; Spark Networks; SuccessFactors; Turo; World View; Zoosk
Brent Ahrens, General Partner
e-mail: bahrens@canaan.com
Education: BS & MS Mechanical Engineering, University of Dayton; MBA, Tuck School of Business at Dartmouth College
Background: General Surgical Innovations; Ethicon Endo-Surgery; IAp Research
Directorships: Abyrx; Calixa Therapeutics; Cerexa; Data Sciences International; DexCom; EndoGastric Solutions; Grey Wolf Therapeutics; Patios Therapeutics; Unchained Labs
Maha Ibrahim, General Partner
e-mail: mibrahim@canaan.com
Education: BA Economics; MA Organizational Behavior, Stanford University; PhD Economics, MIT
Background: Numerous Roles; Qwest Communications; Management Consultant, Boston Consulting Group & Price Waterhouse
Directorships: Agile Stacks; Cuyana; Forte; Gen.G; Kabam; Komprise; ManiMe; The RealReal; Twenty20; Unifi
Brendan Dickinson, General Partner
e-mail: bdickinson@canaan.com
Education: BA, Political Science, Bowdoin College; MS, Computer Science, Brown University; MBA, NYU Stern School of Business
Background: Senior Quantitative Analyst, Lehman Brothers; Barclays Capital
Directorships: Embroker; Even Financial; Hugo; Journey Meditation; Ladder; Paxos; Quantum Circuits Inc.
Stephen Bloch, General Partner
e-mail: sbloch@canaan.com
Education: MA, History and Science, Harvard University; AB, History, Dartmouth College
Background: CEO, Radiology Management Sciences; Medical Director Omnisonics Medical Technologies
Directorships: Ambra Health; Amicus Therapeutics; Envisia; Genome Medical; Liquidia Technologies; Marinus Pharmaceuticals; Onkos Surgical; Truveris
Wende Hutton, General Partner
e-mail: whutton@canaan.com
Education: AB, Human Biology, Stanford University; MBA, Harvard Business School
Background: Mayfield Fund; Spring Ridge Ventures
Directorships: Alsius Corp; Apieron; Antiva Biosciences; BiPar Sciences Inc.; Calibra Medical; Chimerix; Dermira; Glooko; Hyalex Orthopaedics; OncoResponse; Theraclone Sciences
Tim Shannon, General Partner
e-mail: tshannon@canaan.com
Education: BA, Chemistry, Amherst College; MD, University of Connecticut
Background: President, CuraGen; Bayer's Pharmaceutical Business Group
Directorships: Arvinas; CytomX; IDEAYA Biosciences; NextCure; Rallybio; Vivace Therapeutics

390 CANAL PARTNERS
7114 E Stetson Dr
Suite 360
Scottsdale, AZ 85251

Phone: 480-264-0238
e-mail: info@canalpartners.com
web: canalpartners.com

Mission Statement: Canal Partners is a venture capital firm that provides professional investor services and capital to B2B software and internet technology companies.

Average Investment: $1 - $3 million
Industry Group Preference: Software, Internet Technology, SaaS
Portfolio Companies: PetDesk, Allbound, CallRail, Edaris Health, Iris PR Software, LightPost Digital, Firepoint, MobileLogix, Picmonic
Key Executives:
  Todd Belfer, Managing Partner
  Education: BS, Finance & Real Estate, University of Arizona
  Background: Co-Founder, Employee Solutions; Co-Founder, MD Labs
  Jim Armstrong, Managing Partner
  Background: CEO, JDA Software
  Directorships: JDA Software Group

391 CANNA ANGELS LLC
San Francisco, CA

Phone: 415-722-4849
e-mail: inquiries@cannaangelsllc.com
web: cannaangelsllc.com

Mission Statement: An angel investment firm focused on the cannabis industry. Areas of focus include genetics, plan & bio-science, real estate, data analytics, agriculture technology, business consulting & compliance, cultivation, and lab research.

Founded: 2016
Investment Criteria: Seed
Industry Group Preference: Cannabis, Agriculture, Business Consulting, Biotech, Research
Key Executives:
  Sherri Haskell, Founder/CEO
  Education: Washington University; Webster University
  Background: Sr. Partner/Marketing & Business Development, Bridgeway Capital; Investor Relations Specialist, National Financial Consultants; Investor Relations Dir., ZAP!; Praxis Capital; SVP of Marketing, Drever Capital Management; Marketing Communications, Granite Peak Partners; Principal, Capital Dynamics

392 CANNABIS CAPITAL
1 World Trade Centre
Long Beach, CA 90831

Toll-Free: 888-680-5548
web: www.cannabiscapitalinc.com

Mission Statement: An investment consulting and private equity firm focused on the cannabis industry.

Founded: 2013
Investment Criteria: Early-Stage
Industry Group Preference: Cannabis

393 CANNABIS CAPITAL GROWTH
1099 Main Avenue
Suite 215A
Durango, CO 81301

Phone: 970-403-4686
web: cannabiscapitalgrowth.com

Venture Capital & Private Equity Firms / Domestic Firms

Mission Statement: Managed by McMillan Capital Management, Cannabis Capital Growth focuses on investments within the cannabis industry.
Founded: 2007
Average Investment: $250,000
Minimum Investment: $5,000
Industry Group Preference: Cannabis
Portfolio Companies: Origin House, Aurora Cannabis, Green Thumb Industries, CannTrust Holdings, Aphria, Green Organic Dutchman, Acreage Holdings, Charlotte's Web Holdings, GW Pharmaceuticals, Ianthus, Kuschco Holdings, Emblem Corp.
Key Executives:
  Jaime McMillan, Founder, Managing Advisor
  Education: BA, Political Science, North Carolina State University; JD, Trinity Law School
  Background: Private Client Financial Advisor, Charles Schwab; Founder/Managing Advisor, McMillan Capital Management

394 CANNABIS STRATEGIC VENTURES
Beverly Hills, CA

web: cannabisstrategic.com

Mission Statement: To strive for evolution in the cannabis industry through people, products, and processes, as well as providing access to safe and high-performing cannabis products.
Geographic Preference: California and Canada
Founded: 2003
Investment Criteria: Leaders who are passionate about improving the cannabis industry.
Industry Group Preference: Cannabis
Portfolio Companies: Asher House Wellness, Budhire, Fitamins, Halo Filters, Lyxr, Pure Organix
Key Executives:
  Simon Yu, CEO
  Education: University of Southern California
  Arlene Guzman, Vice President of Communications & Operations
  Background: VantagePoint Capital Partners

395 CANOPY BOULDER
1002 Walnut Street
Boulder, CO 80302

Phone: 303-586-4745
e-mail: info@canopyboulder.com

Mission Statement: Dedicated to investing in and educating entrepreneurs in the cannabis industry.
Founded: 2014
Investment Criteria: Seed
Industry Group Preference: Cannabis, Data Analysis, Technology
Portfolio Companies: BDS Analytics, Leaf, PotGuide.com, Grownetics, Hemp Business Journal, Front Range Biosciences, W☐rk, The Beak Beyond, Andia, Sana Packaging, WeGrow, Estrohaze, Redfield Proctor, Adistry, Firesale, KNXit, GreenScreens, Miele Events, 420 Klean, BDTNDR, Vapor Slide, Cannabis Big Data, The Herbalista Set, Deepgreen, Treatment X, Canna Zoning, Who Is Happy, Grass-Pass, iDro, Virtugro, Spare, Croptimize Inc., Stashbox, Snapp Digital, Solutions Vending International, PenSimple, TwoCubes Inc., Serene Green, Elevate Accessories, MyStrain, Hello People Ops, Paragon, Dispensarly, Bloom Automation, Gram, Icatus RT, BudTender, DCN Media Inc., Event Hi, Apothecarry, Lodestone Data Technologies, Yobi, Cannactrl, MJ Hybrid Solutions, Ripe Metrics, Traffic Roots, VertiCann, Mycocann, Collectif, Urban Labs, Ganjaboxes, Ananas, Gupta Daniel, Acro Vape, Leaf Cart, Healthy Headie Lifestyle, Campfire, Blujays Brand, Trellis Research Group, Pot Scientist, Glasshouse, Tradiv, Highest Reward

Key Executives:
  Patrick Rea, Co-Founder/Chief Executive Officer
  Education: BA, Geology; BA, Organizational Behavior & Management, Brown University
  Background: Financial Analyst, Health Business Partners; Director of Research, Nutrition Business Journal; Director of eMedia, New Hope Natural Media/Penton Media; Market Leader, Penton; Managing Director, Health Business Partners; Executive Editor, The ArcView Group
  Directorships: GreenBroz, Pure Prescriptions, Co-Chair, The NBJ Summit
  Micah Tapman, Managing Director
  Education: MBA, George Washing University School of Business
  Background: Managing Partner, Aerstone; Founder/CEO, CBMT Creative; Founder/CEO, The Tapman Group; Advisor, FlapJacked; Advisor, Front Range Biosciences; Managing Director, Canopy Ventures
  Directorships: BDS Analytics, PotGuide.com, Tradiv
  Celia Daly, Marketing Manager
  Education: BS, Economics/International Relations, American University; MBA, Colorado State University
  Background: Research Associate, Geo Strategy Partners; Market Process Coordinator, Alexander Proudfoot; Co-Founder, Chaka Fibers; Market Strategy Design Consultant, Factor(E) Ventures; Freelance Counsultant; Marketing Coordinator, Surna Inc.
  Bob Goodman, Managing Director
  Education: BS, Engineering, United States Military Academy at West Point; MBA, St. Edward's University
  Background: CEO, Kentron Technologies; President/CEO, Phiar Corp.; President/CEO, Qs Semiconductor Corp.; Executive-in-Residence, Infield Capital; President/CEO, BASiC 3C; Founder/President/CEO, OpiSafe; Counsulting CEO, Blackbox AI
  Directorships: Partner/Board Member, Blackbox Foundation

396 CANROCK VENTURES
720 Northern Boulevard
Brookville, NY 11548

Phone: 516-828-2673

Mission Statement: Canrock Ventures is an early-stage technology venture capital fund focused on turning good technology ideas into great technology businesses.
Fund Size: $400 million
Average Investment: $500,000 - $1.5 million
Minimum Investment: $500,000
Investment Criteria: Early-Stage
Industry Group Preference: Technology, Software
Portfolio Companies: Crowdster, General Sentiment, ThriveMetrics, Sentiment Alpha, SEO Pledge

397 CANTOR VENTURES
499 Park Avenue
New York, NY 10022

web: www.cantorventures.com

Mission Statement: Cantor Ventures is the venture capital and enterprise development arm of Cantor Fitzgerald, which has over 65 years of expertise in providing capital raising and advisory services to growth oriented companies. Cantor Ventures invests in companies with business models focused on the development of innovative, technology-focused products, services and marketplaces. As an active partner, Cantor Ventures has guided and accelerated growth for numerous e-commerce businesses.
Founded: 2011
Investment Criteria: Early-Stage
Portfolio Companies: Delivery.com, Ritani, Topline Game Labs, AdFin

Venture Capital & Private Equity Firms / Domestic Firms

398 CANTOS VENTURES
San Francisco, CA

web: www.cantos.vc

Mission Statement: Cantos Ventures is an early-stage venture capital fund that invests in the newest technologies influencing industries like real estate, healthcare, and finance.

Founded: 2016
Average Investment: $25,000-$50,000
Investment Criteria: Pre-Seed, Seed-Stage
Industry Group Preference: Real Estate, Healtcare, Logistics, Parenting, Accessbility, Finance
Portfolio Companies: Alice, Advano, Aizon, Anagram, Arable, Astranis, Atom, Catalog, Chameleon, Circularis, Clara, Clover Tx, Concha, Curie Co., Debut Bio, Dhrama, Dusty, Earth AI, Eridan, Ethic, Helium, Humane, Knowde, Legit, Lively, Maxwell, Mission Barns, Opus 12, Phenomic, Pow Bio, Prellis, Public, Qwil, Shipamax, Skyryse, Solugen, Space Tango, Standard Cyborg, Super-Medium, Symbio, Vence, Visolis, X Genomes

Key Executives:
Ian Rountree, Founder/Managing Partner
Education: Vanderbilt University
Background: Invisible Technologies, Inc.

399 CANVAS VENTURES
3200 Alpine Road
Portola Valley, CA 94028

Phone: 650-388-7600 Fax: 650-388-7601
e-mail: press@canvas.vc
web: www.canvas.vc

Mission Statement: Silicon Valley firm focused on early-stage investments in fintech, marketplaces and digital health.

Geographic Preference: Silicon Valley
Founded: 2013
Average Investment: $5 - $15 million
Investment Criteria: Early-Stage
Industry Group Preference: Fintech, Digital Health, Marketplaces, New Enterprise
Portfolio Companies: CrowdFlower, Eden, Everwise, Folloze, FutureAdvisor, HealthLoop, Totango, Transfix, Vida, Viewics, Zola

Key Executives:
Gary Little, General Partner
e-mail: glittle@canvas.vc
Education: Harvard University; UCLA
Background: Morganthaler Ventures; Apple Computer; Sun Microsystems
Rebecca Lynn, General Partner
e-mail: rebecca@canvas.vc
Education: University of Missouri; University of California, Berkeley
Background: Procter & Gamble; NextCard; Morgenthaler Ventures
Paul Hsiao, General Partner
e-mail: paul@canvas.vc
Education: MIT, Harvard Business School
Background: Mazu Networks
Mike Ghaffary, General Partner
e-mail: mike@canvas.vc
Background: General Partner, Social Capital; CEO, Eat24; VP of Business & Corporate Development, Yelp; Director of Business Development, TrialPay; Co-Founder, Stitcher; Co-Founder, BarMax; Associate, Summit Partners

400 CANYON CREEK CAPITAL
Santa Monica, CA 90404

e-mail: buck.jordan@canyoncreekcapital.com
web: www.canyoncreekcapital.com

Mission Statement: Canyon Creek Capital strives to build game changing companies, investing in the "Bridge to A" stage of early development.

Geographic Preference: West Coast
Founded: 2010
Investment Criteria: Mature Seed, Series A
Industry Group Preference: Technology, Consumer Services, Media
Portfolio Companies: ChowNow, Jukin Media, Winc, HoneyBook, HelloTechm Gyft, ShipHawk, Amplify, Bridg, Relativity, Bringhub, Misco Robotics Kitchen Assistant, Vertical Mass, Figs, Blue Bottle Coffee Co., Pixalate, Harri, Social Annex, Study Soup, Verbling, Meadow, TrueChoice, Iconery, Wedgies, Native Tap, Lawn Guru, Final, Vydia, Matic, Tonx, Anymeeting, StrikeAd, ShopSavvy, Afinity, Pongolo

Key Executives:
Buck Jordan, Partner
e-mail: buck.jordan@canyoncreekcapital.com
Education: MBA, Anderson School of Management, University of California, LA

401 CAPITAL E
1054 31st Street NW
Suite 314
Washington, DC 20007

web: www.cap-e.com

Mission Statement: Capital-E invests in and works with leading corporations, cities, and technology firms to accelerate the transition to zero net carbon green buildings and cities.

Industry Group Preference: Renewable Energy, Green Building
Portfolio Companies: Bloom Energy, Skyline Innovations, Sunnovations, Calstar Products, BuildingIQ, MyEnergy, Green Wizard, Bright Frams, Better Workplace, Sage, GSI, Playa Viva, Scream Point, Sustainability Roundtable

Key Executives:
Greg Kats, President
e-mail: gkats@cap-e.com
Education: BA, University of North Carolina; MBA, Stanford University; MPA, Princeton University
Background: Managing Director, Good Energies

402 CAPITAL FOR BUSINESS, INC
11 South Meramec
Suite 1330
St. Louis, MO 63105

Phone: 314-746-7427 Fax: 314-746-8739
e-mail: info@cfb.com
web: cfb.com

Mission Statement: Capital For Business is a private investment firm that targets middle market companies with a potential for significant growth. The firm provides industry, operational and financial expertise to assist management teams with the growth of their businesses.

Geographic Preference: Central United States
Fund Size: $150 million
Founded: 1959
Average Investment: $3 - $5 million
Minimum Investment: $500,000
Investment Criteria: LBO, MBO, Recapitalizations, Corporate Divestitures, Growth Financings
Industry Group Preference: Plastics, Communications, Distribution, Electronic Components, Manufacturing, Industrial Equipment, Specialty Chemicals, Aerospace, Defense and Government, Education, Energy, Food & Beverage, Medical Devices, Diagnostics
Portfolio Companies: Arrow Material Handling Products, Bennett Tool & Die Company, Buse Industries, Central States Bus Sales, Custom Marketing, Domaille Engineering, Hi-Grade Welding & Manufacturing, Kieffer & Co., Lanair Holdings, Legacy Technologies, McNally Industries,

Venture Capital & Private Equity Firms / Domestic Firms

Perennial Energy, Polymer Technology, Presence From Innovation, Preston-Eastin, Sun Graphics, Vanguard Graphics International, Waples Manufacturing, Wayne Trademark Printing & Packaging, Whitworth Tool, Winco Mfg, Wisconsin Coil Spring

Key Executives:
Stephen Broun, Managing Partner
e-mail: steve.broun@capitalforbusiness.com
Education: BBA, St. Louis University; MBA, Olin Business School, Washington University
Background: Investment Analyst, AG Edwards; Senior Associate, Missouri Venture Partners
Directorships: Kansas Venture Capital, Missouri Venture Forum
Bill Witzofsky, Senior Vice President
e-mail: bill.witzofsky@capitalforbusiness.com
Education: BBA, Accounting, University of Missouri St. Louis
Background: Landmark Commercial Corporation; Norwest Business Credit; Boatmen's Bank of St. Louis; Deutsche Financial Services; Corporate Accountant, Save-A-Lot Foods
Brett A Parr, Vice President
Education: BS, Business Administration, University of Kansas; MBA, Olin School of Business, Washington University
Background: Banking Officer & Assistant VP, US Bank
Chris Redmond, Senior Vice President
e-mail: chris.redmond@cfb.com
Education: BBA, University of Notre Dame; MBA, Kellogg School of Management
Background: A.G. Edwards & Sons; Morgan Stanley & Co.; COO, Argent Capital Management
Matt Leinauer, Assistant Vice President
e-mail: matt.leinauer@cfb.com
Education: BS, Finance, DePaul University
Background: Analyst, JP Morgan Chase; Peabody Energy

403 CAPITAL MIDWEST FUND
10556 North Port Washington Road
Suite 201
Mequon, WI 53092
Phone: 414-453-4488 Fax: 414-453-4831
e-mail: seinhorn@capitalmidwest.com
web: www.capitalmidwest.com

Mission Statement: Capital Midwest Fund is a venture capital firm that invests primarily in areas where the Midwest spends most of its research dollars: life science and information technology. The fund concentrates on investments where companies have excellent management and technology, are performing an important function, and will address significant markets. The firm looks for management teams with successful previous experience; markets that are established and growing; defensible IP positions; and sustainable competitive advantages.

Geographic Preference: Midwest United States
Founded: 2010
Industry Group Preference: Life Sciences, Information Technology, Manufacturing, Business to Business, Healthcare Technology
Portfolio Companies: Adello Biologics, Always In Touch, Centron, CytoPherx, EpiCare, Gemphire Therapeutics, HarQen, Intellihot, LiquidCool Solutions, NanoStatics, NuCurrent, Ocularis Pharma, OPS Solutions, PegEx, Physician Software Systems, PreEmptive Meds, PrevaCept Infection Control, Rapid Diagnostek, ScholarCentric, Sierra Oncology

Key Executives:
Stephen Einhorn, Principal
Education: BA, Chemistry, Cornell University; MS, Chemical Engineering, Brooklyn Polytechnic Institute
Background: Founder, Einhorn Associates

Daniel Einhorn, Principal
Education: BS, Cornell University; MBA, Cox School, Southern Methodist University

404 CAPITAL PARTNERS
301 Merritt 7
Norwalk, CT 06851
Phone: 203-625-0770 Fax: 203-625-0423
e-mail: info@capitalpartners.com
web: www.capitalpartners.com

Mission Statement: Private equity investment firm that invests in and supports small and mid-sized companies.

Geographic Preference: North America
Founded: 1982
Industry Group Preference: Manufacturing, Distribution, Business to Business, Franchising, Education, Food & Beverage, Aftermarket Products
Portfolio Companies: American Leather, CMI Limited, M&Q Packaging Corp., Parkway Products, Premier Performance Products, Roll Rite

Key Executives:
Brian Fitzgerald, Founder & Chairman
Education: BA, History, Princeton University; MBA, Harvard Graduate School of Business
Background: Industrial Capital Group, General Electric Co., The Vencap Group
Mark Allsteadt, Managing Partner
e-mail: mallsteadt@capitalpartners.com
Education: BA, Bucknell University; MBA, Stanford Graduate School of Business
Background: Partner, Saugatuck Capital Company; SVP, Operations, Eye Care Centers of America
Robert Tucker, Managing Partner
e-mail: rtucker@capitalpartners.com
Education: BA, Physics & Economics, Middlebury College; MBA, Finance & Management, Columbia University Graduate School of Business
Background: Partner, Saugatuck Capital Company; Partner, Rutledge Capital
John Willert, Principal
Education: BA, Gettysburg College; MBA, Finance & Accounting, Ohio State University
Background: Principal, Family Capital Growth Partners; VP, de Visscher & Co.
Thorsten Suder, Principal
Education: BA, Economics, Manhattanville College; MBA, Cornell University
Background: Vice President, Hartford Investment Management Company
James Sidwa, Principal, CFO & COO
Education: BS, University of Connecticut; CPA
Background: Transaction Services Group, PricewaterhouseCoopers
Edwin Tan, Managing Director
Education: BSE, MSE, University of Pennsylvania; MBA, Booth School of Business
Background: Prospect Capital Corporation
Mark Langer, Principal
Education: BSBA, Management, Bucknell University; MBA, Columbia University Graduate School of Business
Background: The Compass Group

405 CAPITAL RESOURCE PARTNERS
83 Walnut Street
Unit 10
Wellesley, MA 02481
Phone: 617-478-9600 Fax: 617-478-9605
web: www.crp.com

Mission Statement: CRP invests in proven businesses, often in niche markets.

Geographic Preference: North America
Fund Size: $1 billion

Venture Capital & Private Equity Firms / Domestic Firms

Founded: 1987
Average Investment: $30 million
Minimum Investment: $5 million
Investment Criteria: Later Stage, Mezzanine, LBO, MBO, Special Situations, Management Quality, Security of Principal
Industry Group Preference: Business Services, Consumer Products & Services, Healthcare Services, Products & Technology, Proprietary Industrial Products & Services, Software & Information Services
Portfolio Companies: AllianceCare, Altra, Ardence, Aspen Dental Management, Athletes' Performance, Buckeye Nutrition, Commercialware, Context Integration, Coyne Textile Services, DynamicImaging, Ecollege, Enfield Logistics, ePartners, Epredix Campus Tele Video, Fantasy Entertainment, Fludrive, Gamma Medica-Ideas, Ganeden Biotech, Infotrieve, JDR Recovery Corporation, K2 Industrial Services, Kirkland's, Lamont Digital System, Lionbridge, L'Occitane, Lois Law Library, Loyaltyworks, MedMark Services, Monitronics, Odyssey Health Care, Paysys, Polar Beverages, PreVisor, Pro Group, Prometheus Laboratories, Revenue Cycle Solutions, The Richardson Group, RogersCasey, Rowland Coffee Roasters, Sam Seltzer's Steakhouse, SemperCare, Softbrands, Solis Women's Health, Specialty Filaments, Spirit Brands, Summit Global Partners, Supportkids.com, The Art of Shaving, Thrifty Lavanderia, Todd Combustion, Trintel, TVR Communications, United Country Real Estate, VMW Paducahbiltwpt, Women's Diagnostic of Texas, World Power Technologies

Key Executives:
Robert C. Ammerman, Managing Partner
e-mail: rammerman@crp.com
Education: BA, History/BS, Mathematics, Carnegie Mellon University; MS, Industrial Administration, Graduate School of Industrial Administration at Carnegie Mellon University
Background: General Partner, Advanced Technology Ventures II; VP, BT Capital; VP/Section Manager, Portfolio Investment Management Group, Bankers Trust Company
Andrew A. Silverman, Partner
617-478-9615
e-mail: asilverman@crp.com
Education: BA, Economics, Tufts University
Background: Consultant, Aitman Vilandrie & Co.; Senior Associate, Investor Group Services; Equity Division Sales Trader, Optiver Derivatives Trading

406 CAPITAL SOUTHWEST CORPORATION
5400 Lyndon B Johnson Freeway
Lincoln Center Tower 1
Suite 1300
Dallas, TX 75240

Phone: 214-238-5700 **Fax:** 214-238-5701
e-mail: request@capitalsouthwest.com
web: www.capitalsouthwest.com

Mission Statement: Capital Southwest is a public company making long-term investments.
Geographic Preference: United States
Fund Size: $628 million
Founded: 1961
Investment Criteria: Small and Medium Sized Businesses, MBO, Recapitalizations, Industry Consolidations, Early-Stage Financings, Expansion Financings
Industry Group Preference: Aerospace, Defense and Government, Energy, Specialty Chemicals, Industrial Technology
Portfolio Companies: AAC Holdings Inc., Ace Gathering Holdings LLC, Adams Publishing Group, AG Kings Holdings Inc., Alliance Sports Group, Amware Fulfillment LLC, American Nuts, Apollo MedFlight, Binswanger Glass, California Pizza Kitchen Inc., Capital Pawn, Chandler Signs, Clickbooth, Blaschak Coal Corp., Danforth Advisors LLC, Delphi Behavioral Health Group, Digital Media Agency, Digital River, Driven Inc., Dunn Paper Inc., Dynamic Communicaties, Environmental Pest Service, Envocore, Fast Sandwich LLC, GrammaTech Inc., IEnergizer Limited, LGM Pharma, OrthoBethesda, Precision Spine Care, Premier Global Services Inc., Relevant Rental Solutions, Research Now Group Inc., RJO Holdings Corp., Scrip Companies, STATinMed, Tax Advisors Group Inc., Trinity3 Technology, Vertex Business Services, Vistar Media Inc., Zenfolio Inc.

Key Executives:
Bowen S. Diehl, President/CEO
e-mail: bdiehl@capitalsouthwest.com
Education: Vanderbilt University; University of Texas
Background: American Capital
Michael S. Sarner, Chief Financial Officer
e-mail: msarner@capitalsouthwest.com
Education: James Madison University; George Washington University
Background: American Capital
Douglas M. Kelley, Managing Director
e-mail: dkelley@capitalsouthwest.com
Education: University of Texas
Background: American Capital
Joshua S. Weinstein, Managing Director
214-884-3835
e-mail: jweinstein@capitalsouthwest.com
Education: Columbia University; University of Southern California
Background: H.I.G. WhiteHorse

407 CAPITAL Z PARTNERS
142 West 57th Street
4th Floor
New York, NY 10019

Phone: 212-965-2400 **Fax:** 212-965-2301
web: www.capitalz.com

Mission Statement: Capital Z Partners identifies and selects financial services companies with the promise for growth. Through capital investments and ongoing support, Capital Z helps these companies to realize their full potential.
Geographic Preference: United States, Europe
Fund Size: $2.8 billion
Founded: 1990
Average Investment: $25 - $75 million
Industry Group Preference: Financial Services
Portfolio Companies: Aaccredited Home Lenders, Anchor BanCorp Wisconsin Inc., Argo Group, British Marine Holdings Ltd., Brookdale Senior Living Inc., Catlin Group Limited, Centrue Financial Corporation, Endurance Specialty Holdings Ltd., Hamilton Insurance Group Ltd., Jelf Group Plc., Kemper Corporation, Lancashire Holdings Limited, Minova Insurance Holdings Ltd., MountainView Capital, NACOLAH Holding Corporation, National Re Corporation, Opportunity Bancshares Inc., Pearl Capital, Permanent General Company Inc., Portfolio Group, Prestige Insurance Holdings Limited, Provident Companies Inc., SBJ Group Limited, Tarquin Plc., Transport Holdings Inc., Unionamerica Insurance Company Limited, Universal American Financial Corporation, UP&UP Inc., Health Extras Inc., USI Holdings Corporation

Key Executives:
Bradley E. Cooper, Partner
e-mail: brad.cooper@capitalz.com
Education: BBA, University of Michigan
Background: Financial Institutions Group, Salomon Brothers
Robert A. Spass, Partner
e-mail: bob.spass@capitalz.com
Education: BA, Business, State University of New York, Buffalo
Background: Director, Investment Banking Division, Salomon Brothers; Senior Manager, Peat Marwick Main & Co
Directorships: Lancashire Holdings

Jonathan D. Kelly, Partner
e-mail: jonathan.kelly@capitalz.com
Education: BS, Economics, Wharton School, University of Pennsylvania; BS, Electrical Engineering, School of Engineering & Applied Science
Background: Senior Vice President, Donaldson Lufkin & Jenrette
Roland V. Bernardon, Chief Financial Officer
e-mail: roland.bernardon@capitalz.com
Education: BBA & MBA, Accounting, Pace University
Background: Audit Director, Deloitte & Touche LLP

408 CAPITALA
4201 Congress Street
Suite 360
Charlotte, NC 28209

web: www.capitalagroup.com

Mission Statement: To provide private equity and mezzanine capital to lower middle-market companies.
Geographic Preference: Southern United States
Fund Size: $700 Million
Founded: 1998
Average Investment: $5-$25 million
Minimum Investment: $5 million
Investment Criteria: Lower Middle-Market
Industry Group Preference: Business Products & Services, Consumer Products, Energy, Healthcare
Portfolio Companies: Advantage Medical Electronics, Aerial Access Equipment, American Clinical Solutions, American Exteriors, AmeriMark, B&W Quality Growers, BigMouth, BlueStem Brands, BTM Company, Burgaflex Holdings, Burke America Parts Group, CableOrganizer, California Pizza Kitchen, Caregiver Services, Cedar Electronics, CIS Secure Computing, City Gear, Corporate Visions, CSM Bakery Solutions, Currency Capital, Eastport Holdings, Flavors Holdings, Fresh Dining Concepts, GA Communications, Hale and Hearty Soups, Immersive Media Tactical Solutions, Installs Inc., J&J Produce, Kelle's Transport Service, Long John Silver's, Micro Precision, MMI Holdings, myAgway, Nth Degree, On-Site Fuel Service, Portrait Innovations, Print Direction, Regent Education, Security Solutions of America, CarePoint Health, Sierra Hamilton, Staging Concepts, Stride Tool, Sur La Table, Taylor Precision Products, Tubular Textile, US Well Services, Velum Global Credit Mgmt., Vintage Stock, Vology, Western Windows Systems, Xirgo Technologies

Other Locations:
500 E Broward Blvd
Suite 1710
Fort Lauderdale, FL 33301
Phone: 954-848-2860

1450 Raleigh Rd
Suite 100
Chapel Hill, NC 27517
Phone: 704-376-5502 **Fax:** 704-376-5877

75 14th Street NW
Suite 2700
Atlanta, GA 30309
Phone: 678-666-3699 **Fax:** 678-999-8118

Key Executives:
Joseph B. Alala III, Chairman/CEO
Education: AB, Economics, Princeton University; MBA, Wake Forest University
Background: Director, Centura Bank; Principal, Halcyon Investments
M. Hunt Broyhill, Partner
e-mail: hbroyhill@capitalsouthpartners.com
Education: BA, Wake Forest University
Background: CEO, Broyhill Asset Management, LLC; President, Broyhill Investments
Jack McGlinn, Senior Managing Director
e-mail: jmcglinn@capitalsouthpartners.com
Education: BA, Accounting, University of Notre Dame
Background: President, Triangle Biomedical Sciences, Inc.; Senior Accountant, Price Waterhouse LLP
Michael S. Marr, Director of Portfolio Monitoring
704-936-4923
e-mail: mmarr@capitalsouthpartners.com
Education: BSBA, University of North Carolina; JD, Campbell University; Master of Laws in Taxation, Emory University
Background: Partner, Business Law Advisors
Christopher B. Norton, Director of Underwriting
e-mail: cnorton@capitalsouthpartners.com
Education: MBA, University of Virginia
Background: VP, Business Development, Waveguide Solutions; Associate, Bowles Hollowell Conner; First Union Securities; Summer Associate, Merrill Lynch-Mergers & Acquisitions; Senior Analyst, First Union Capital Markets

409 CAPITOL PARTNERS
7475 Wisconsin Avenue
Suite 750
Bethesda, MD 20814

Phone: 301-364-9020 **Fax:** 301-364-9022
e-mail: info@capitolpartners.com
web: www.capitolpartners.com

Mission Statement: Capitol Partners aims to achieve exceptional medium-term capital gains through investments in large, high growth industries, as well as partnerships with strong management teams.
Geographic Preference: Mid-Atlantic
Average Investment: $25 - $50 million
Investment Criteria: Recapitalizations, Management-Led Buyouts, Mergers and Acquisitions, Capital Investments
Industry Group Preference: Information Technology, Healthcare, Internet Technology, Infrastructure, Telecommunications, Energy
Portfolio Companies: Able Home Health, Advantage Home Health, Alliance Care, Amedisys Resource Management Division, Baylor Home Care, Baylor Home Infusion Therapy, Calvert Healthcare Partners, CareSouth Health System, Community Home Health, CS Indemnity, eCareOne.com, Family Care, Florida Pallative Homecare, Hand-In-Hand Home Health Care, HC360, Health at Home, Home Care of St. Francis, Integrity Services, Middle Tennessee Home Health Services, Paramount Healthcare, Rutherford Polk McDowell Home Health, Tenet Home Care, Total Home Health Care, US CareNet

Key Executives:
TJ Jubeir, Founder/Managing Partner
Education: BA, Quantitative Economics, MS, Engineering-Economic Systems, Stanford University; MBA, Harvard Business School
Background: Founder/Managing Partner, New Horizons Venture Capital; Investment Officer, International Finance Corporation; Strategy Consultant, Bain & Company; Strategy Consultant, Booz-Allen & Hamilton; Advisor, Office of the Saudi Arabian Minister of Petroleum and Mineral Resources
Directorships: CareSouth Health System, CarePartners@Home, CS Indemnity
Julie Jubeir, Senior Vice President
Education: BA, Economics & Environmental Studies, Bowdoin College; MBA, Marketing & Strategic Management, Kellogg Graduate School of Management, Northwestern University
Background: Management Consultant, Booz Allen & Hamilton Inc.; Marketing Consultant, Nestle USA Inc.
Alex Radcliffe, Associate
Education: BS, Systems Engineering & Financial Economics, University of Virginia; MBA, George Washington University School of Business
Background: Investment Director, The Legacy Foundation

Venture Capital & Private Equity Firms / Domestic Firms

410 CAPX PARTNERS
155 North Wacker Drive
Suite 1760
Chicago, IL 60606

web: www.capxpartners.com

Mission Statement: CapX Partners strives to be the premier capital provider to private equity and venture capital backed companies. The company invests in and supports small and medium sized growth stage businesses.
Geographic Preference: United States
Fund Size: $225 million
Founded: 1999
Average Investment: $7 million
Minimum Investment: $500,000
Investment Criteria: Private Equity & Venture Capital Backed Firms, High Growth, Turnaround, Rebuilding Companies, Recapitalization
Industry Group Preference: Consumer Products, Energy, Healthcare, Manufacturing, Technology
Portfolio Companies: Acumentrics Holding Corporation, All Around Roustabout, Aquion Energy, Arandell Corporation, Arro Corporation, Digital Ocean, Gro-Well Brands, Karmaloop, Lake County Press, Rupari Food Services, TGI Systems Corporation

Other Locations:
4370 La Jolla Village Drive
Suite 400
San Diego, CA 92122

1460 Broadway
New York, NY 10036

33 Arch Street
15th Floor
Boston, MA 02110

Key Executives:
Jeffry S. Pfeffer, Managing Partner
Education: BA, Economics, Brandeis University; MBA, Finance, Kellstadt Graduate School of Business, DePaul University
Background: VP/Regional Manager, Bac One Leasing Corporation; American National Bank & Trust Company of Chicago
James N. Hallene, Founding Partner
Education: BA, University of Illinois; MBA, Kellogg Graduate School of Management, Northwestern University
Background: Founder, Capital Concepts Holdings; Co-Founder, MaxMiles Inc.; American National Bank
Directorships: KeHE Distributors, HallStar Company, VSA Partners
Barrett D. Carlson, Partner
Education: University of Illinois
Background: Partner, Capital Concepts Holdings; Founder/Managing Partner, Nine Iron LLC; Co-Founder, Waterstone Consulting; Andersen Consulting
Directorships: VSA Partners, Illinois Venture Capital Association
Eric D. Starr, Partner
Education: Brandeis University; New York University Stern School of Business
Background: Risk Committee, Forest Investment Management; Owner, Starr Capital Management; Co-Founder, Aventine Investment Management; Refco; Union Bank of Switzerland

411 CARBON VENTURES
261 Madison Avenue
New York, NY 10016

e-mail: invest@carbonventures.com
web: www.carbonventures.com

Mission Statement: Carbon Ventures invests in technology serving a variety of industries, including education, agriculture, waste management, and transportation.
Founded: 2017
Average Investment: $500,000
Investment Criteria: Seed, Series A, Company Value of $5 million
Industry Group Preference: Technology, Education, Energy, Agriculture, Waste Management, Transportation, Manufacturing, Robotics, Artificial Intelligence, Machine Learning, Language Processing
Portfolio Companies: Andium, Fortify, Idelic, Mobius, Novel Effect, Sayspring, Smarter Sorting, Summit Sync, Transit Screen, Wasteplace

Key Executives:
Jason Cahill, Founder/Managing Partner
Education: MBA, Carnegie Mellon University
Background: Founder, Traansmission; Engineer, CSRA; Adjunct Professor, Columbia University; Veteran, Special Forces
Katherine Zamsky, Managing Partner
Education: MBA, Columbia University
Background: Fund Manager, Merrill Lynch; FinTech Builder, Bank of America
Gary Ragusa, Venture Partner
Education: MBA, Columbia University
Background: Consultant, PricewaterhouseCoopers; Head of Business Development, Outbrain; Co-Founder, StudioXchange; Co-Founder, Lustr Fasion App
Directorships: Savings United

412 CARDINAL EQUITY PARTNERS
8801 River Crossing Boulevard
Suite 320
Indianapolis, IN 46240

Phone: 317-663-0205 Fax: 317-663-0215
web: www.cardinalep.com

Mission Statement: To buy, build and operate a small number of middle-market businesses for long-term value creation.
Geographic Preference: Eastern United States
Founded: 1993
Minimum Investment: $250,000
Investment Criteria: Management Buyouts, Recapitalizations, Lower to Middle-Market
Industry Group Preference: Light Manufacturing, Distribution, Service Industries, Pharmaceuticals, Consumer Products, Industrial Equipment, Recreational Vehicles, Horticulture, Publishing, Healthcare, Financial Services, Home Improvement, Water Treatment
Portfolio Companies: Aqua Systems, Contour Industries, Eagle Battery, Guardian Pharmacy, MotionTech Automation, Poly-Wood, Wild Sports

Key Executives:
John F Ackerman, Co-Founder/Managing Director
e-mail: jackerman@cardinalep.com
Education: University of Michigan; Kellogg School of Management, Northwestern University
Background: Quaker Oats Company; National Bank of Detroit
Directorships: Eskenazi Health Foundation, Avondale Meadows Academy Charter School, Teach For America
James L Smeltzer, Managing Director
e-mail: jsmeltzer@cardinalep.com
Education: BS, Accounting, Ball State University
Background: CFO, Cardinal Communications; Senior Tax Advisor, KPMG Peat Marwick
Directorships: Contour Industries, Corporate Imaging Concepts, Essco, Guardian Pharmacy, New Aqua, Oak Security Group, Williams Sound
Peter Munson, Managing Director
e-mail: pmunson@cardinalep.com
Education: BA, Economics, DePauw University
Background: Senior Vice President, JPMorgan Chase

Directorships: Contour Industries, Motion Tech Automation, OrthoPediatrics, Williams Sound
Michael L Smith, Senior Advisor
Education: DePauw University
Background: EVP & CFO, Anthem; Chairman, President & CEO, Mayflower Group; Arthur Andersen & Co.
Directorships: HHGregg, Envision Healthcare Holdings, Vectren Corporation, Carestream Health Services, USI, Hulman & Company, Go Health
Darell E Zink Jr, Senior Advisor
Education: BA, Vanderbilt University; MBA, University of Hawaii; JD, Indiana University
Background: Duke Realty Corporation; Partner, Bose McKinney & Evans; Captain, United States Air Force

413 CARDINAL PARTNERS
230 Nassau Street
Princeton, NJ 08542

Phone: 609-924-6452 Fax: 609-683-0174
e-mail: info@cardinalpartners.com
web: www.cardinalpartners.com

Mission Statement: Venture capital partnership focused exclusively on healthcare.
Fund Size: $400 million
Founded: 1996
Average Investment: $6-12 Million
Investment Criteria: Early Stage
Industry Group Preference: Healthcare, Life Sciences, Medical Devices, Service Industries, Healthcare Information Technology, Biopharmaceuticals
Portfolio Companies: Abide Therapeutics, Alnylam Pharmaceuticals, aTyr Pharma, Cubist Pharmaceuticals, Momenta Pharmaceuticals, Rib-X Pharmaceuticals, Sirtris Pharmaceuticals, Verastem
Key Executives:
  John Clarke, General Partner
  e-mail: johnclarke@cardinalpartners.com
  Education: AB, Harvard University; MBA, Wharton School
  Background: General Partner, DSV; interim CEO, Alkermes/Arris/DNX Corporation/Cubist Pharmaceuticals; General Electric Company
  Directorships: Alnylam, Molecular Mining, Momenta Pharmaceuticals, Rib-X, TechRx, Visicu, Jackson Laboratory
  Thomas McKinley, General Partner
  Education: BS, Harvard University; MS, Accounting, New York University; MBA, Stanford Graduate School of Business
  Background: Co-Founder & Co-Managing Partner, Paratech International
  John Park, Partner/CFO
  e-mail: johnpark@cardinalpartners.com
  Education: BS, Villanova University; MBA, University of Michigan
  Background: CFO, DSV Partners; Financial Analyst/Corporate Tax Manager, Day & Zimmermann
  Directorships: Biotechnology and Life Sciences Advisory Committee for Ben Franklin Technology, Life Sciences Greenhouse of Central PA

414 CARDINAL VENTURE CAPITAL
325 Sharon Park Drive
Suite 107
Menlo Park, CA 94025-6805

Mission Statement: Cardinal Venture Capital is dedicated to investing in early-stage software companies in four specific focus areas: Digital Media, Financial Technology, Mobility and Software-as-a-Service. Cardinal takes a hands-on approach to partnering with their companies, dedicating significant time and resources into creating a successful company.
Founded: 2008
Investment Criteria: Early-Stage
Industry Group Preference: Software, Technology, Digital Media & Marketing, Financial Services, Mobility, SaaS
Portfolio Companies: Adaptive Insights, Chipcon, deCarta, DeliveryAgent, DIVX, GuardianEdge, ipinfusion, LiveCapital, PlayPhone, SuccessFactors, Wireless Security Corp., Zilliant
Key Executives:
  Derek Blazensky, General Partner
  e-mail: derek@cardinalvc.com
  Education: BA, Fairfield University; BS, Engineering & Computer Science, University of Connecticut
  Background: Adobe Ventures
  Directorships: GuardianEdge Technologies, Nimblefish Technologies, deCarta
  Christian Borcher, General Partner
  e-mail: christian@cardinalvc.com
  Education: Bachelor of Laws, Copenhagen University; MBA, Stanford Business School

415 CARE CAPITAL
Avon by the Sea, NJ 07717

Phone: 609-683-8300 Fax: 609-683-5787
e-mail: info@carecapital.com
web: www.carecapital.com

Mission Statement: Care Capital invests in companies developing pharmaceutical assets.
Geographic Preference: United States, Europe
Fund Size: $500 million
Founded: 2001
Average Investment: $5-20 million
Investment Criteria: Late Stage
Industry Group Preference: Life Sciences, Pharmaceuticals, Biotechnology
Portfolio Companies: Agile Therapeutics, NormOxys, Resolvyx Pharmaceuticals, Sentinella Pharmaceuticals, Vaxart
Key Executives:
  Jan Leschly, Partner
  Education: BBA, Copenhagen School of Economics and Business Administration; MS Pharmacy, Copenhagen College of Pharmacy
  Background: Chief Executive, SmithKline Beecham; President/COO, Squibb Corpoartion; Novo Nordisk
  Directorships: American Express, Viacom, Maersk Group, DaimlerChrysler, International Tennis Hall of Fame
  Argeris Karabelas, Partner
  Education: PhD Pharmacokinetics, Massachusetts College of Pharmacy
  Background: Head Healthcare/CEO Worldwide Pharmaceuticals, Novartis AG; Executive VP, SmithKline Beecham; Founder/Chairman, Novartis Bio Venture Fund
  Directorships: Massachusetts General Hospital, Visiting Committee for Health Sciences and Technology at MIT, SykePharma, Human Genome Sciences, Nitromed, Anadys
  David Ramsay, Partner
  Education: AB, Mathematics, Princeton University; MBA, Stanford Grad. School of Business
  Background: Managing Director, Rhone Group; Rhone Capital; Director, Primus International; Straightline Communications; Terphane; Nation One Mortgage; Investment Committee, Morgan Stanley Capital Partners

416 CARLYLE GROUP
1001 Pennsylvania Avenue Northwest
Washington, DC 20004-2505

Phone: 202-729-5626 Fax: 202-347-1818
web: www.carlyle.com

Mission Statement: Originates, structures and acts as lead equity investor in management-led buyouts, strategic minority

Venture Capital & Private Equity Firms / Domestic Firms

equity investments, equity private placements, consolidations and buildups and growth capital financings.
Geographic Preference: United States, Asia, Africa, Europe, South America
Founded: 1987
Investment Criteria: Buyouts, Privatizations, Strategic Minority Investments
Industry Group Preference: Aerospace, Defense and Government, Telecommunications, Automotive, Transportation, Consumer Products, Retail, Consumer & Leisure, Energy, Power, Financial Services, Healthcare, Industrial, Infrastructure, Technology, Business Products & Services
Portfolio Companies: 4Gas Holding BV, 7 Days Group Holdings, Accudyne Industries, Acosta, AcuFocus, Addison Lee Group, ADT CAPS Co., Al Nabil Food Industries, Alamar Foods, Alamosa Solar Generating Project, Alliance Boots plc, Allsec Technologies, Altice S.A., Apex Parks Group, Arabela Holding, ArtGo Holdings, ARUHI Corporation, Asia Satellite Telecom Holdings, Atlas Aerospace LLC, ATMU, Authentix, Avalon Advisors, AvanStrate, Axalta Coating Systems, AxieTech International Holdings, B&B Hotels, Bahcesehir Schools, Bank Of N.T. Butterfield & Son, Black Sea Oil & Gas SRL, Blyth, Bonotel, Booz Allen Hamilton, Bottle Rock Power, Brand Group Holdings, Brintons Carpets, BTI Studios, C.H.I. Overhead Doors, CalPeak Power, Cap Vert Finance SA, Carroll Cuisine, Catapult Learning, CDM MAX LLC, China Agritech, China Fishery Group, China Recycling Energy Group, Coalfire Systems, Coastal Carolina Clean Power LLC, Coates Hire, Cobalt International Energy, Cogentrix Power Management, Collingwood Ethanol, Combined Systems, CommScope, CommunityOne Bancorp, Companeo, Concord Medical Service Co., ConvaTec, Crystal Orange Hotel Holdings, Custom Sensors & Technologies, CVC Brasil Operadora e Agencia de Viagens S.A., CxS Corporation, Cyient, Dealogic, Dee Development Engineers, Diamond Bank, Discover Exploration, Document Technologies, Duff & Phelps, Dynamic Industries, Dynamic Precision Group, Eastern Broadcasting Company, ECi Software Solutions, Edelweiss Financial Services, Edgewood Partners Holdings, Ensus, Estok Comercio e Representacoes S.A., Etablissements Maurice Marie, ETC Group, Extreme Reach, Focus Media Holding, Foresight Energy, Fu Shou Yuan International Group, GDC Technology, General Secure Logistics Services, Getty Images, Global Health Private Limited, GOL Offshore, Greater China Intermodal Investments LLC, Green Earth Fuels LLC, Grupo Liderman, Guangxi Nanning Waterworks Co., H.C. Starck GmbH, Haier Bio-Medical and Laboratory Products Co., Hampton Roads Bankshares, HaoYue Education Group, HCR ManorCare, Hermes Transportes Blindados, HES International, Hitachi Metals Techno, Hoffmaster Group, Homair Group, Hopewell and Portsmouth, Hudson Product Holdings, Hyundai Communications & Network, HIS Global, Illinois Central School Bus, INC Research, Integrated Dental Holdings, Interlink Maritime, Itconic, ITRS Group, ITS Technologies & Logistics, J&J Africa, JIC Leasing, Landmark Aviation, Legend Natural Gas, Leyou, Lily O'Brien's, Malaga Power, Manna Pro Products, Marelli Motori Group

Other Locations:

Jachthavenweg 118
Amsterdam 1081
Netherlands
Phone: 31-205407575 **Fax:** 31-205407500

Pau Casals, 13
Barcelona 8021
Spain
Phone: 34-932000906 **Fax:** 34-932093510

China World Tower
No. 1 Jianguomenwai Avenue
Chaoyang District
Beijing 100004
China
Phone: 86-1057067000 **Fax:** 86-1057067003

201 North Illinois Street
Suite 1530
Indianapolis, IN 46204

One Vanderbilt Avenue
Suite 3400
New York, NY 10017
Phone: 212-813-4900 **Fax:** 212-813-4901

Dubai International Financial Centre
Gate Village, Building 5, Office 206
PO Box 506564
Dubai
United Arab Emirates
Phone: 971-44275600 **Fax:** 971-44275610

2 Pacific Place
88 Queensway
Hong Kong
China
Phone: 852-28787000 **Fax:** 852-28787007

Connaught House
1 Burlington Road
Floor 5
Dublin 4
Ireland
Phone: 353-16319738

15/F, One Pacific Place
Jl. Jnd. Sudirman No. 52-53
Jakarta 12190
Indonesia

1 st. James's Market
London SW1Y 4AH
United Kingdom
Phone: 44-2078941200 **Fax:** 44-2078941600

C Las Begonias 415
Torre Begonias, 16th Floor
San Isidro
Lima
Peru
Phone: 51-12066830

11100 Santa Monica Blvd
Los Angeles, CA 90025
Phone: 310-575-1700 **Fax:** 310-575-1740

2 Avenue Charles de Gaulle L-1653
Luxembourg
Phone: 35-226102747 **Fax:** 35-226862110

2710 Sand Hill Road
1st Floor
Menlo Park, CA 94025

Piazza Cavour 2
Milan 20121
Italy
Phone: 39-026200461 **Fax:** 39-0229013559

Quadrant A, The IL&FS Financial Centre
Bandra-Kurla Complex
Bandra East
Mumbai 400 051
India
Phone: 91-2266470800 **Fax:** 91-2266470803

Promenadeplatz 8
Munich D-80333
Germany
Phone: 49-892444600 **Fax:** 49-89244460460

299 Park Avenue
35th Floor
New York, NY 10171
Phone: 212-332-6240 **Fax:** 212-332-6241

112, avenue Kleber
Paris 75116

Venture Capital & Private Equity Firms / Domestic Firms

France
Phone: 33-153703520 **Fax:** 33-153703530

Av. Brigadeiro Faria Lima 3900
Sao Palo Sp 04538-132
Brazil
Phone: 55-1135687700 **Fax:** 55-1135687750

15F, Centropolis Tower A
26, Ujeongguk-Ro
Jongno-gu
Seoul 03161
Korea
Phone: 822-20048400 **Fax:** 822-20048440

Unit 4001, 40th Floor, Tower 2
Jing An Kerry Centre
1539 Nanjing Road West
Shanghai 200040
China
Phone: 86-2161033200 **Fax:** 86-2161033210

1 Temasek Avenue
Millenia Tower 039192
Singapore
Phone: 65-62129600 **Fax:** 65-62129620

Level 33
The Chifley Tower, 2 Chifley Square
Sydney NSW 2000
Australia
Phone: 61-292703500 **Fax:** 61-292703520

Shin-Marunouchi Building
1-5-1 Marunouchi Chiyoda-ku
Tokyo 100-6535
Japan
Phone: 81-352084350 **Fax:** 81-352084351

Key Executives:
William E Conway Jr, Founder/Co-Executive Chairman
Education: Dartmouth College; University of Chicago Graduate School of Business
Background: CFO, MCI Communications; The First National Bank of Chicago
Daniel A D'Aniello, Founder/Chairman Emeritus
Education: Syracuse University; Harvard Business School
Background: VP, Finance & Development, Marriott Corporation; Financial Officer, PepsiCo Inc.; Trans World Airlines
Directorships: AlpInvest
David M Rubenstein, Founder/Co-Executive Chairman
Education: Duke University; University of Chicago Law School
Background: Paul, Weiss, Rifkind, Wharton & Garrison; Shaw, Pittman, Potts & Trowbridge; Chief Counsel, Subcommittee on Constitutional Amendments, US Senate Judiciary Committee
Directorships: Lincoln Center for the Performing Arts, Memorial Sloan-Kettering Cancer Center, Johns Hopkins Medicine, Institute for Advanced Study
Glenn A Youngkin, President/Chief Operating Officer
Education: BS, Mechanical Engineering, BA, Managerial Studies, Rice University; MBA, Harvard Business School
Background: Management Consultant, McKinsey & Company
Directorships: Ri-Happy Brinquedos S.A., Rice Management Company
Curtis L Buser, Chief Financial Officer
Education: Georgetown University
Background: Ernst & Young LLP; Arthur Andersen
Jeffrey W Ferguson, General Counsel
Education: University of Virginia
Background: Associate, Latham & Watkins; Vinson & Elkins
Kewsong Lee, Chief Executive Officer
Education: AB, Harvard College; MBA, Harvard Business School
Background: Deputy Chief Investment Officer, Corporate Private Equity; Partner, Warburg Pincus

Brooke B Coburn, Managing Director/Partner
Education: BA, Princeton University
Background: Salomon Brothers
Directorships: ECi Software Solutions, PrimeSport, Coalfire, Catapult Learning, Worldstrides
Christopher Finn, Chief Operating Officer
Education: Harvard College
Background: Former Managing Director, Global Head of Operations, Carlyle

417 CAROLINA FINANCIAL GROUP
100 Elks Club Road
Brevard, NC 28712
Phone: 828-393-5401
e-mail: info@carofin.com
web: www.carofin.com

Mission Statement: An investment banking firm that specializes in raising debt and equity capital for privately-held middle market growth companies.

Founded: 1995

Key Executives:
Bruce Roberts, President/CEO
e-mail: bruceroberts@carofin.com
Education: BSE, Civil Engineering, Duke University
Background: Founder, Rehabilitation Support Services; Director, Investment Banking, Credit Suisse First Boston; Corporate Finance Specialist, Bank of America
Directorships: Accelerate Appalachia, North Carolina Aquarium
Craig Gilmore, Chief Operating Officer
e-mail: cgilmore@carofin.com
Education: BS, Bentley College
Background: Survey Center Manager & Database Specialist, REDA International Inc.
Bruce Smith, VP, Investor Development
e-mail: bsmith@carofin.com
Education: BA, American History, Princeton University
Background: Morgan Stanley; Merrill Lynch

418 CAROUSEL CAPITAL
201 N Tryon Street
Suite 2450
Charlotte, NC 28202
Phone: 704-372-2040
web: www.carouselcapital.com

Mission Statement: Carousel Capital is a private equity firm that invests in companies based in the Southeastern United States. The firm partners with management teams to build leading companies in the business services, consumer services and healthcare services sectors.

Geographic Preference: Southeastern United States
Fund Size: $265 million
Founded: 1996
Investment Criteria: Leveraged Buyouts, Recapitalizations
Industry Group Preference: Business Products & Services, Consumer Products, Consumer Services, Healthcare Services
Portfolio Companies: AG Data, Apex Analytix, Axium Healthcare Pharmacy, Brasseler USA, Caldwell & Gregory, Copac, Crescent, Crown Column, Driven Brands, Express Oil Change & Service Center, Hepaco, Jameson, Joe Hudson's Collision Center, Med Data, Meineke Car Care Center, Mergent, Nestor Sales, Pegasus TransTech, Southeastern Automotive Aftermarket Service Holdings, Simpson Performance Products, Sona

Key Executives:
Charles S. Grigg, Managing Partner
e-mail: cgrigg@carouselcapital.com
Education: BA, Economics, Yale University; MBA, Wharton School
Background: Orion Partners; Smith Barney
Directorships: Apex Analytix, Caldwell & Gregory, Mergent, Brasseler USA, Nestor Sales, HEPACO

Venture Capital & Private Equity Firms / Domestic Firms

Peter L. Clark, Jr., Partner
Education: BA, Economics, Davidson College
Background: Harris Williams & Co.
Directorships: Palmetto Infusion; Huseby; Consolidated Claims Group; Expedited Travel; Apex Analytix
Jason C. Schmidly, Managing Partner
e-mail: jschmidly@carouselcapital.com
Education: BBA, Finance & Organizational Behavior, Southern Methodist University
Background: M&A, Gregory & Hoenemeyer Inc.; M&A, Morgan Stanley
Directorships: Southeastern Automotive Aftermarket Service Holdings, Joe Hudson's Collision Center, Pegasus TransTech
Nelson Schwab III, Senior Advisor
e-mail: nschwab@carouselcapital.com
Education: BA, English, University of North Carolina at Chapel Hill; MBA, Wharton School, University of Pennsylvania
Background: Chairman & CEO, Paramount Parks; Chairman & CEO, Kings Entertainment Company; EVP, Attractions Group, Taft Broadcasting Company
Directorships: Herschend Family Entertainment, Messer Corporation

419 CARRICK CAPITAL PARTNERS
One California Street
Suite 1900
San Francisco, CA 94111

Phone: 415-432-4100
web: carrickcapitalpartners.com

Industry Group Preference: SaaS, Business Process Outsourcing, Transaction Processing
Portfolio Companies: Accolade, Axiom Law, Bay Dynamics, Complia Health, Everspring, Infinia ML, Infrascale, InstaMed, LaunchPoint, MavenLink, Perfect Sense, Saama, Seven Lakes Technologies

Key Executives:
Jim Madden, Co-Founder and Managing Director
Education: BBA, Finance, Southern Methodist University
Background: Founder/Chairman/CEO, Exult; Special Advisor, General Atlantic
Marc McMorris, Co-Founder and Managing Director
Education: BS, Economics, University of Pennsylvania; MBA, Wharton School
Background: Managing Director, General Atlantic; Vice President, Goldman Sachs
Alex Mason, Managing Director
Education: BS, Economics, University of Washington; Harvard Business School
Background: Vice President, Accel-KKR
Steve Unterberger, Managing Director, Operations
Directorships: Bay Dynamics, Infrascale, LaunchPoint, Mavenlink, Seven Lakes Technologies
Mike Salvino, Managing Director
Paul Zolfaghari, Managing Director, Operations
Mitchell Slodowitz, Managing Director & CFO

420 CASA VERDE CAPITAL
12530 Beatrice Street
Los Angeles, CA 90066

web: www.casaverdecapital.com

Mission Statement: Invests in companies focused on the ancillary cannabis industry, including health & wellness, financial services, technology, media, compliance, and laboratory technology.

Founded: 2015
Industry Group Preference: Cannabis
Portfolio Companies: Metrc, Dutchie, Oxford Cannabinoid Technologies, Green Tank Technologies, Weconnect, Vangst Talent Network, Green Bits, Cannalysis, Trellis, Leeflink, Eaze, Merry Jane

Key Executives:
Karan Wadhera, Managing Partner
Education: BA, Finance, Babson College
Background: Indian Equities, Goldman Sachs; VP of Equities, IIFL Capital; Head of India Sales Trading, Nomura Securities; Managing Director, Cashmere Asia; Advisor, MissMalini Publishing; Partner, Thursday Capital; Strategic Advisor, Stampede Management
Yoni Meyer, Partner
Education: BA, Economics, Tufts University
Background: Analyst, Herbert J. Sims & Co.; VP, Citigroup; Partner, TVP NYC

421 CASABONA VENTURES
2 Keil Avenue
Suite 244
Kinnelon, NJ 07405

e-mail: info@casabonaventures.com
web: www.casabonaventures.com

Mission Statement: Casabona Ventures provides management services, strategic planning, and early stage/Angel investment capital to technology driven start-up companies, with an emphasis on the Northeast region. By partnering with dynamic executive teams, the firm works to commercialize innovative, industry-impacting technologies, driving them from the laboratory to the marketplace.

Geographic Preference: Northeast United States
Investment Criteria: Early-Stage
Industry Group Preference: Technology, Renewable Energy, Environment, Communications, Electronics, Medical Technology, Information Technology
Portfolio Companies: AlgometR, NeuroFlow, Tech Launch, UBuildNet, Adaptive, Bluum, Fusar Technologies, Mobile Xoom, Mobile Arq, Outdoor Exchange, Retail Shopping Systems, Shielf Tech, Weldobot, BeautyStat.com, Inbox, Electro-Radiation Inc., StearClear, Nickle Bus, Powerhouse Dy Dynamics, Go-Now, SpeechTrans, Inc., Ray Sat, Skyworks Interactive, Fortress Technologies, Nuskool, MM Guardian, Untethered Labs

Key Executives:
Mario Casabona, Founder/Managing Director
Background: Founder/CEO, Electro-Radiation

422 CASDIN CAPITAL
1350 Avenue of the Americas
Suite 2600
New York, NY 10019

Phone: 212-897-5430
e-mail: info@casdincapital.com
web: www.casdincapital.com

Mission Statement: Casdin Capital, LLC is an investment firm focused on the life sciences and healthcare industry.

Industry Group Preference: Life Sciences, Healthcare
Key Executives:
Eli Casdin, Founder/Chief Investment Officer
Education: BS, Columbia University; MBA, Columbia Business School
Background: VP, Alliance Bernstein; Bear Stearns; Cooper Hill Partners
Brian Shim, Chief Financial Officer
Suzanne Angell, Director of Therapeutic Research
Education: BA, Yale University; MA, Johns Hopkins University
Background: COO/CFO, Jungell Inc.; Managing Director/Advisor, Alpine ESD; Research Analyst, Cooper Hill Partners

Venture Capital & Private Equity Firms / Domestic Firms

423 CASE TECHNOLOGY VENTURES Case Western Reserve University
10900 Euclid Avenue
Cleveland, OH 44106-7219

Phone: 216-368-2000
e-mail: techventures@cwru.edu
web: case.edu

Mission Statement: CWRU Technology Ventures (CTV) is Case Western Reserve University's pre-seed technology validation fund. CTV focuses on creating and supporting new companies for the Northeast Ohio region by providing capital to early stage companies based on intellectual property developed at CWRU and its affiliate institutions.

Geographic Preference: Northeast Ohio
Founded: 2002
Average Investment: $50,000 - $250,000
Investment Criteria: Seed-Stage, Early-Stage
Industry Group Preference: Life Sciences, Physical Sciences, Information Technology
Portfolio Companies: Neuros Medical Inc., CardioInsight Technologies Inc., Interventional Imaging Inc., Arteriocyte Inc., Synapse Biomedical Inc., Great Lakes Pharmaceuticals, Intwine Connect

424 CASTANEA PARTNERS
Three Executive Park Drive
Suite 304
Newton, MA 02462

Phone: 617-630-2400 Fax: 617-630-2424
e-mail: info@castaneapartners.com
web: www.castaneapartners.com

Mission Statement: Castanea is a middle-market consumer-focused private equity firm.
Geographic Preference: US, Canada
Fund Size: $600 million
Founded: 2001
Average Investment: $15-150 million
Investment Criteria: MBOs, Consolidations, Growth Equity, Acquisition Equity Capital Raises, Corporate Carve-Outs
Industry Group Preference: Publishing, Education, Training, Consumer Products, Specialty Retail, Marketing
Portfolio Companies: 4moms, Brew Dr. Kombucha, The Bruery, Drybar, Essentia, Jeni's, Mackenzie-Childs, Simms Fishing Products, Thymes, West Coast Fitness, Yasso

Key Executives:
  Steven T. Berg, Managing Partner
  617-630-2416
  e-mail: sberg@castaneapartners.com
  Education: MBA, The Wharton School of Business; BS, Engineering, magna cum laude, University of Michgian
  Background: Founder, Bain Outreach, Bain & Company
  Brian J. Knez, Managing Partner
  617-630-2401
  e-mail: bknez@castaneapartners.com
  Education: JD, cum laude, Boston College Law School; BS, Phi Beta Kappa, University of Arizona
  Background: Vice Chairman/Board of Directors, The Neiman Marcus Group Inc.; CEO, Harcourt General; General Cinema Beverages; Associate, Choate, Hall and Stewart
  Robert A. Smith, Managing Partner
  617-630-2410
  e-mail: rsmith@castaneapartners.com
  Education: AB, Harvard College; MBA, Harvard University
  Background: Vice Chairman/Board of Director, The Neiman Marcus Group Inc.; CEO, Harcourt General; President, General Cinema Corporation; Associate, Bain & Company
  Directorships: Children's Hospital, Facing History & Ourselves, Pan-Mass Challenge, Jumpstart, Harvard Committee on University Resources

425 CASTLE HARLAN
150 East 58th Street
New York, NY 10155

Phone: 212-644-8600 Fax: 212-207-8042
e-mail: info@castleharlan.com
web: www.castleharlan.com

Mission Statement: Invests in companies with the potential to grow and accrue successful returns with the help of capital and management expertise.

Fund Size: $900 million
Founded: 1987
Average Investment: $30 - $200 million
Minimum Investment: $5 million
Investment Criteria: Established
Industry Group Preference: Consumer Products, Consumer Services, Energy, Manufacturing, Distribution
Portfolio Companies: Baker & Taylor, Caribbean Restaurants, Gold Star Foods, Shelf Drilling, Tensar Corporation

Key Executives:
  John K. Castle, Chairman/CEO
  Education: Massachusetts Institute of Technology; MBA, Harvard Business School
  Background: Chairman/CEO, Branford Castle; President/CEO, Donaldson, Lufkin & Jenrette
  Directorships: Baker & Taylor, Equitable Life Assurance Society
  Leonard M. Harlan, Chairman, Castle Harlan Executive Committee
  Education: BS, Mechanical Engineering, Cornell University; MBA, Harvard Business School
  Background: Chairman/CEO, Harlan Company; VP/Stockholder, Donaldson, Lufkin & Jenrette
  Directorships: IDQ Holdings, The America for Bulgaria Foundation, Harvard Business School Club
  Marcel Fournier, Senior Managing Director
  Education: MBA, University of Chicago; Ecole Speciale des Travaux Publics; Paris-Sorbonne University
  Background: Managing Director, Investment Banking, Lepercq, de Neuflize & Co.; Assistant Director, US Office of the Agency of the French Prime Minister
  David B. Pittaway, Senior Managing Director
  e-mail: dpittaway@castleharlan.com
  Education: BA, University of Kansas; MBA, JD, Harvard University
  Background: VP, Strategic Planning, Lufkin & Jenrette; Management Consultant, Strategic Planning, Bain & Company; Attorney, Morgan, Lewis & Bockius
  Directorships: Gold Star Foods, Caribbean Restaurants
  Eric Schwartz, Vice President
  Education: BSE, Biomedical & Electrical Engineering, Duke University; MBA, Stanford Graduate School of Business
  Background: Citigroup
  Directorships: Baker & Taylor, Caribbean Restaurants, Shelf Drilling
  Sylvia F. Rosen, Vice President/Controller
  Education: BA, Accounting, Queens College; MBA, Taxation, St. John's University
  Background: Corporate Accounting Manager, Tishman Realty & Construction; Senior Auditor, Ernst & Young

426 CASTLELAKE
90 S Seventh Street
4600 Wells Fargo Center
Minneapolis, MN 55402

web: www.castlelake.com

Mission Statement: Castlelake strives to unlock value and generate risk-adjusted returns.
Founded: 2005

Venture Capital & Private Equity Firms / Domestic Firms

Other Locations:
510 Madison Avenue
24th Floor
New York, NY 10022

100 Crescent Court
Suite 825
Dallas, TX 75201

15 Sackville Street
London W1S 3DJ
United Kingdom

5 Rue De Strasbourg
Luxembourg L-2561
Luxembourg

Key Executives:
Dax Atkinson, Managing Director

---

427 CATALYST GROUP
1375 Enclave Parkway
Houston, TX 77077

e-mail: inquiries@tcgfunds.com
web: www.tcgfunds.com

Mission Statement: The Catalyst Group provides middle-market business owners access to capital and operational expertise, with the objective of achieving growth and exceptional returns for its partners.

Geographic Preference: United States, Southwest
Founded: 1990
Average Investment: $2 - $20 million
Minimum Investment: $1 million
Investment Criteria: Acquisitions, Buyouts, Expansion, Recapitalization, Middle-Market
Industry Group Preference: Manufacturing, Distribution, Services, Consumer Products, Media, Telecommunications, Energy
Portfolio Companies: Allocation Specialists, Auberge Resorts Collection, Axio, CellerateRX, Rochal Industries, Superior Plant Rentals, Triad Life Sciences, Trillian Surgical, YPS Anesthesia Services

Other Locations:
7500rialto Boulevard
Building II
Suite 220
Austin, TX 78735

Key Executives:
Ron Nixon, Founder/Managing Member
713-580-5231
e-mail: rnixon@tcgfunds.com
Education: BS, Mechanical Engineering, University of Texas
Background: TGC; LHC Group
Directorships: LHC Group, Ascent Automotive Group
David McWhorter, Principal
713-580-5254
e-mail: dmcwhorter@tcgfunds.com
Education: BS, Mechanical Engineering, University of Texas; MBA, Texas A&M University
Background: VP & General Manager, Control Business Unit, Cameron International; Director, Engineering, Texas Oil Tools
Brad Gurasich, Vice President/Principal
512-320-8600
e-mail: bgurasich@tcgfunds.com
Education: BBA, Finance, University of Notre Dame; MBA, University of Texas, Austin; CFA
Background: CFO/Investment Analyst, Goshawk Global Investments; Senior Finance Manager, Alta Colleges; Investment Banking Analyst, Credit Suisse First Boston
Directorships: Rochal Industries
Robert Norris, Principal
Education: BA, Economics, MBA, University of Texas, Austin
Background: VP, Corporate Development & Strategy, Civeo Corporation; VP, Corporate Development, Oil States

---

428 CATALYST HEALTH VENTURES
50 Braintree Hill Office Park
Suite 301
Braintree, MA 02184

Phone: 781-228-5228
e-mail: info@catalysthealthventures.com
web: www.catalysthealthventures.com

Mission Statement: Catalyst Health Ventures is an early-stage venture capital firm targeting technology solutions applied within the health care and life science industries. At the core of this strategy is a committed, hands-on approach to working with management and syndicate partners to build successful companies. This investment process leverages both intellectual and financial capital to originate deals, cultivate opportunities, and realize the full potential of emerging ventures in the health care and life science marketplace.

Geographic Preference: Northeast United States
Founded: 1998
Investment Criteria: Early-Stage
Industry Group Preference: Healthcare, Life Sciences, Medical Devices, Diagnostics
Portfolio Companies: Allegro Diagnostics, Aria CV, Augmenix, Biocius Life Sciences, Bio Trove, Cruzar Medical, Endo Via, G1 Dynamics, Hansen Medical, Kaleidoscope Medical, Lantos Technologies, Maxwell Health, Nova Zyme Pharmaceuticals, nVision, Pavilion Medical Innovations, Saphena Medical, Sera Prognostics, Seven Oaks Biosystems, Vortex Medical

Key Executives:
Joshua S. Phillips, Managing Partner
e-mail: jphillips@catalysthealthventures.com
Education: BE, Electrical Engineering, Vanderbilt University; MBA, Harvard Business School
Background: Manager, Lucas Group
Kevin M. McCafferty, Founder/Special Partner
e-mail: kmccafferty@catalysthealthventures.com
Education: BA, Harvard College; MBA, University of Chicago
Background: First Chicago Venture Capital, Madison Dearborn Partners
Robert A. Vigoda, Founder/Special Partner
e-mail: rvigoad@catalysthealthventures.com
Education: BA, University of Rochester; JD, University of Miami
Background: Partner, Rubin & Rudman LLP
Darshana Zaveri, Partner
e-mail: dzaveri@catalysthealthventures.com
Education: BS, Biochemistry, Bombay University; MS, Cell & Molecular Biology, Boston University; MPA, Harvard University
Background: Genome Therapeutics Corporation
Directorships: Lantos

---

429 CATALYST INVESTORS
711 Fifth Avenue
Suite 600
New York, NY 10022

Phone: 212-863-4848 Fax: 212-319-5771
e-mail: businessplans@catalyst.com
web: catalyst.com

Mission Statement: Catalyst Investors invests in technology-enabled businesses.

Geographic Preference: North America
Average Investment: $10 - $40 million
Investment Criteria: All Stages, Growth Buyouts, Expansion Capital, Roll-Ups
Industry Group Preference: Cloud Computing, Internet, SaaS, E-Commerce & Manufacturing, Internet-Enabled Hardware, Digital Media & Marketing, Healthcare

Venture Capital & Private Equity Firms / Domestic Firms

Information Technology, Education, Business Products & Services, Consumer Services, Wireless, Mobile
Portfolio Companies: BrightFarms, ChowNow, Clinicient, Conductor, Datavail, Envoy, Fusion Risk Management, Insite Wireless Group, Jobvite, MediaMath, PresenceLearning, Reputation Institute, Videology, Weave, WeddingWire, Xplornet

Key Executives:
Brian Rich, Managing Partner & Co-Founder
e-mail: brian@catalystinvestors.com
Education: BS, Industrial Engineering, SUNY Buffalo; MBA, Columbia University
Background: Founder, TD Capital
Ryan McNally, Partner & Co-Founder
e-mail: ryan@catalystinvestors.com
Education: AB, Harvard College
Background: Vice President, Daniels & Associates; Bear Stearns & Co.
Chris Shipman, Partner & Co-Founder
e-mail: chris@catalystinvestors.com
Education: BA, MA, Boston University; MBA, Anderson School of Management, UCLA
Background: Vice President, TD Capital
Todd Clapp, Partner
e-mail: todd@catalystinvestors.com
Education: BA, McGill University; MBA, Columbia University
Background: Lightyear Capital
Tyler Newton, Partner
e-mail: tyler@catalystinvestors.com
Education: BA, Middlebury College; CFA
Background: Vice President, TD Capital
Gene Wolfson, Partner, Investor Relations & Business Development
e-mail: gene@catalystinvestors.com
Education: BS, Marketing & Management, Montclair State University; MBA, Finance, Pace University
Background: Managing Director, Citigroup

---

430 CATAMOUNT VENTURES LP
400 Pacific Avenue
3rd Floor
San Francisco, CA 94133

Phone: 415-277-0300
e-mail: info@catamountventures.com
web: www.catamountventures.com

Mission Statement: Catamount Ventures is a venture capital firm investing in mission-driven companies, bringing with them connecttions and coaching to help grow leaders with a strong mission at their core.

Fund Size: $200 million
Founded: 2000
Investment Criteria: Early-Stage
Industry Group Preference: Information Technology, Environment, Consumer Internet, Enterprise Applications
Portfolio Companies: Amourvert, Banyan Water, Carezone, EdSurge, eSilicon, GridNet, Linden Lab, LuxResearch, MasteryConnect, ModuMetal, Numi Organic Tea, Plum Organics, Presence Learning, Quri, Revolution Foods, Seventh Generation, Ten Marks, Upworthy

Other Locations:
3000 Sand Hill Road
1-100
Menlo Park, CA 94025

Key Executives:
Jed Smith, Partner
Education: BA, Middlebury College; MBA, Harvard Business School
Background: Founder, drugstore.com; Co-Founder, Cybersmith; VP, Sales, Tribe Computer Works; Oracle Corporation
Directorships: Linden Lab, Numi Organic Tea, Banyan Water, Plum Organics, Revolution Foods

Mark Silverman, Partner
Education: JD, University of California, Los Angeles; BA, History, University of California, Berkeley
Background: President/CEO, Bocada; VP, Business Development, drugstore.com; Partner, Venture Law Group
Tory Patterson, Partner
Education: BA, Economics, Williams College; MBA, Stanford Graduate School of Business
Background: Investment Banking, GCA Sawian, Wells Fargo Securities
Directorships: MasteryConnect, Presence Learning, Ecologic Brands
Kate Chhabra, CFO/Partner
Education: BA, George Washington University
Background: Human Resources/Operations, ATEL Capital; Human Resources, CriticalArc Technologies Inc.

---

431 CATAPULT VENTURES
Los Altos, CA

e-mail: admin@catapultventures.vc
web: catapultventures.vc

Mission Statement: A tech-based venture capital firm seeking to work with entrepreneurs with an interdisciplinary perspective.

Founded: 2018
Investment Criteria: Seed
Industry Group Preference: Artificial Intelligence, Automation, Robots, Industrial Manufacturing, Aerospace, Construction, Smart Buildings, Consumer Electronics, Healthcare
Portfolio Companies: Advanced Farm Technologies, Anello Photonics, Aulera Autentication, Elroy Air, Engine ML, FlightWave Aero, Left Hand Robotics, Resonado, SpinLaunch, Starsky Robotics, Xnor.ai

Key Executives:
Darren Liccardo, Co-Founder/Managing Director
Education: BS/MS, Electrical Engineering & Computer Science, University of California, Berkeley
Background: Crossbow Technology Inc.; BMW Group; Tesla Motors; DJI
Rouz Jazayeri, Co-Founder/Managing Director
Education: BS/MS, Electrical Engineering, Purdue University
Background: Account Manager, Intel Corporation; Partner/Head of Business Development, Kleiner Perkins Caufield & Buyers

---

432 CATO BIOVENTURES
4364 South Alston Avenue
Durham, NC 27713

Phone: 919-361-2286 **Fax:** 919-361-2290
e-mail: cbvinfo@cato.com
web: www.catobioventures.com

Mission Statement: Cato BioVentures is the venture capital affiliate of Cato Research. Cato BioVentures primarily invests in biotechnology and pharmaceutical companies, and focuses on the successful development and commercialization of products.

Geographic Preference: United States, Canada
Founded: 1990
Investment Criteria: Early Stage, Mid Stage, Late Stage, Mezzanine
Industry Group Preference: Life Sciences, Biotechnology, Pharmaceuticals
Portfolio Companies: Avicin Therapeutics Ltd., Cancer Advances Inc., Hemodynamic Therapeutics Inc.

Other Locations:
1100 Winter Street
Bay Colony Corporate Center

Venture Capital & Private Equity Firms / Domestic Firms

Waltham, MA 02451-1427
Phone: 781-890-4477 **Fax:** 781-890-8118

9605 Medical Center Drive
Suite 390
Rockville, MD 20850
Phone: 301-309-8242 **Fax:** 301-308-8470

6480 Weathers Place
San Diego, CA 92121
Phone: 858-452-7271 **Fax:** 919-361-2290

9900 Cavendish Blvd
Suite 400
Saint-Laurent, QC H4M 2V2
Canada
Phone: 514-856-2286 **Fax:** 514-856-0100

Key Executives:
Allen Cato MD PhD, Co-Founder/Principal
Education: MD; PhD
Directorships: Advanced Pain Remedies, Cancer Advances, Hemodynamic Therapeutics, Nutritional Restart Pharmaceuticals
Lynda Sutton, Co-Founder/Principal
Education: BS
Directorships: Advanced Pain Remedies, Cancer Advances, Hemodynamic Therapeutics, Nutritional Restart Pharmaceuticals
Daniel Pharand, Principal
Education: CPA, CA
Background: CFO, Pharmacia Canada; Pharmacia KK; Innovatech Grand Montreal
Jo Cato, Vice President
Education: BS, Pharmacy, University of North Carolina at Chapel Hill; PhD, Biopharmaceutics, University of North Carolina at Chapel Hill
Background: Pharmacokineticist, Abbott Laboratories; Pharmacokineticist, Ligand Pharmaceuticals
Directorships: Cato Research
Daniel Pharand, Principal
Education: BCom, Concordia University
Background: CFO, Pharmacia Canada; CFO, Pharmacia KK; Portfolio Manager, Innovatech Grand Montreal

433 CAVA CAPITAL
132 B Water Street
Norwalk, CT 06854

Phone: 203-210-7477
e-mail: info@cavacapital.com
web: www.cavacapital.com

Mission Statement: Cava Capital is an innovative, early-growth stage investor, actively supporting talented entrepreneurs as they build their companies through various stages of expansion. Cava Capital's team members are experts in scaling revenue growth and are focused on enlisting the resources and connections to do so.
Founded: 2008
Average Investment: $1 - $5 million
Investment Criteria: Early Growth Stage
Industry Group Preference: Marketing, Mobile, Technology, Information Services, E-Commerce & Manufacturing, Social Media, Digital Media, Healthy Active Lifestyle
Portfolio Companies: Confirm.io, Drizly, Dstillery, Etouches, Freeletics, Gwynnie Bee., MVMNT, NeueHouse, Ocean's Halo, PageScience

Key Executives:
Geoff Schneider, Founder/Managing Partner
Education: BS, Business & Economics, Lehigh University; MBA, George Washington University
Background: Iconoculture, Gartner Groupscient, PointCast
Bob Geiman, Managing Partner
Education: BA, Dartmouth College; MBA, Harvard Business School
Background: Founder/President/CEO, EveryScreen

Media; General Partner, Polaris Venture Partners; Envoy Networks
Kevin Lynch, CFO & Fund Administrator
Education: BS, Fordham University; CPA
Background: AlpInvest Partners; Wall Street Technology Partners; Annex Capital; Equinox Capital; PJSC-JOSS Real Estate Partners; Atlantic Medical Capital; Kleinwort Benson Holdings; Credit Suisse First Boston; KPMG

434 CAYUGA VENTURE FUND
15 Thornwood Drive
Ithaca, NY 14850

Phone: 607-266-9266 **Fax:** 607-266-9267
e-mail: info@cayugaventures.com
web: cayugaventures.com

Mission Statement: Cayuga Venture Fund is a venture capital firm working to create and establish a thriving community of leading edge, high tech start-up companies in Ithaca and upstate New York by providing the necessary capital and other resources they need to grow and prosper.
Geographic Preference: New York
Founded: 1994
Investment Criteria: Seed to Growth Stage
Industry Group Preference: All Sectors
Portfolio Companies: Advion BioSciences, Adapt-N, Allworx, BinOptics, Calient Technologies, Cheribundi, e2E Materials, Ecovation, EkoStinger, GiveGab, Incomeda3D, Instinctiv, Intrinsiq Materials, Ioxus, iTellio, Kionix, Mezmeriz, Outmatch, Pathlight, Pom-Co, Primet, Rheonix, Silicon Video Inc., SocialFlow, SoundCloud, True Gault, VenueBook

Key Executives:
Zachary Shulman, Managing Partner
Education: BS, Industrial & Labor Relations, JD, Cornell University
Background: Corporate Law, Ropes & Gray
Phil Proujansky, Managing Partner
Education: BS, Engineering Physics, Cornell University
Background: Founder, IAD
Jennifer Tegan, Partner/VP Finance & Administration
Education: BA, MS, Geology, Smith College; MBA, Cornell University
Background: Consultant, Gemini Ernst & Young; Business Manager, EMF Corporation
Cliff Lardin, Venture Partner
Education: BA, English, MBA, Cornell University
Background: CEO, Cyan Data Systems; Founder, VP Systems, MiniGram

435 CCMP CAPITAL
1 Rockekeller Plaza
16th Floor
New York, NY 10020

Phone: 212-600-9600
e-mail: ContactIR@ccmpcapital.com
web: www.ccmpcapital.com

Mission Statement: Private equity firm focused on buyouts and growth equity investments.
Geographic Preference: North America, Europe
Fund Size: $12 Billion
Founded: 1984
Average Investment: $100-500 million
Investment Criteria: Buyouts, Growth Equity
Industry Group Preference: Consumer Products, Industrial, Healthcare
Portfolio Companies: Aramark, BGIS, Cabela's, CareMore Health, Chaparral Energy, Chromalox, Crosstown Traders Inc., Eating Recovery Center, Edwards Group, Founder Sport Group, Francesca's Collection, Generac Power Systems, Infogroup, Hayward, The Hillman Group, Jamieson Wellness, Jetro Cash & Carry, LHP Hospital Group, Medpace, Milacron, Newark Energy, Ollie's Bargain Outlet, PQ

Venture Capital & Private Equity Firms / Domestic Firms

Corporation, Pure Gym, Shoes for Crews, Truck Hero, Volotea

Other Locations:
24 Waterway Avenue
Suite 750
The Woodlands, TX 77380
Phone: 281-363-2013

Key Executives:
Greg Brenneman, Executive Chairman
Education: BA, Accounting/Finance, Washburn University; MBA, Harvard Business School
Background: Chairman & CEO, Burger King Corporation; President & CEO, PwC Consulting
Timothy Walsh, President & CEO
Education: BS, Trinity College; MBA, University of Chicago Graduate School of Business
Background: The Chase Manhattan Corporation
Directorships: Generac Power Systems, MetoKote
Mark McFadden, Co-Managing Partner
Education: BA & BBA, College of William and Mary
Background: CSFB; Bowles Hollowell Conner
Directorships: Hayward; PQ Corporation; BGIS
Joseph Scharfenberger, Co-Managing Partner
Education: BA, University of Vermont
Background: Bear Stearns Merchant Banking; Toronto Dominion Securities
Directorships: Founder Sport Group; The Hillman Group; Shoes for Crews; Truck Hero
Richard Zannino, Managing Director
Education: BS, Finance & Economics, Bentley College; MBA, Finance, Pace University
Background: CEO, Dow Jones & Company; EVP, Liz Claiborne; EVP/CFO, General Signal
Directorships: Francesca's Collections, Infogroup, IAC, Estee Lauder

436 CCP EQUITY PARTNERS
100 Pearl Street
14th Floor
Hartford, CT 06103

Phone: 860-249-7104 **Fax:** 860-249-7001
web: www.ccpequitypartners.com

Mission Statement: CCP Equity Partners is a private equity firm focused on financing innovative companies with exceptional growth potential, placing particular emphasis on the financial services and healthcare services sectors. CCP combines operating expertise, industry experience and the talents of proven executives to help build profitable companies.

Fund Size: $150 million
Founded: 1985
Average Investment: $5 - $20 million
Minimum Investment: $5 million
Investment Criteria: Growth Equity, Middle-Market, Later Stage
Industry Group Preference: Financial Services, Insurance, Healthcare, Business to Business
Portfolio Companies: Evolution Markets, GlobalView, Kinloch Holdings, Mezz Cap, MMV Financial, Prism Education Group, Vantage Oncology

Key Executives:
Michael E. Aspinwall, Managing Partner
203-904-3832
e-mail: maspinwall@ccpequitypartners.com
Education: BS, Worcester Polytechnic Institute; MBA, University of Chicago Graduate School of Business
Background: Managing Partner, Bear Stearns Health Innoventures; Senior VP, GE Equity; Chase Manhattan Bank; Pitney Bowes; FMC Corporation
Directorships: Vantage Oncology
Steven F. Piaker, Managing Partner
860-233-8959
e-mail: spiaker@ccpequitypartners.com
Education: BA Economics, University of Rochester; MBA, Duke University; CFA
Background: Senior VP, Conseco; VP, Financial Institutions Group, GE Capital; Chase Manhattan
Directorships: Mezz Cap, MMV Financial
David W. Young, Managing Partner
860-415-0834
e-mail: dyoung@ccpequitypartners.com
Education: BA, Rutgers University
Background: Chief Investment Officer, Progressive Corporation; Brown Brothers Harriman & Company; Salomon Brothers
Directorships: Evolution Markets, GlobalView
Diane M. Daych, Partner
203-314-5580
e-mail: ddaych@ccpequitypartners.com
Education: BA, Economics, Lehigh University; MBA, Tuck School of Business, Dartmouth College
Background: GE Capital; Signal Capital; President, Connecticut Venture Group
Directorships: Prism Education Group

Key Executives:
Hai Yang, Director
Background: Founder/CEO, Beijing SEL System; Chief Representative, Vantone Investment Group

438 CEDAR FUND
1050 Winter Street
Suite 2700
Waltham, MA 02451

Fax: 781-895-9099
Toll-Free: 800-844-3469
e-mail: info@cedarfund.com
web: www.cedarfund.com

Mission Statement: A venture capital firm investing in early stage, Israel-related high technology companies.

Geographic Preference: Israel
Fund Size: $225 million
Investment Criteria: Pre-Seed, Early Stage, First Round
Industry Group Preference: Telecommunications, Networking, Enterprise Services, Infrastructure, Internet Technology, Communications, Enterprise Software, Wireless Technologies, SaaS, Clean Technology
Portfolio Companies: 365Scores.com, Amimon, Appilog, BigBand Networks, ClickFox, CloudLock, Datorama, e-Glue, Guardium, HIRO, Iamba, Intigua, IPlight, iSonar, Kenesto, Netotiate, NewACT, Nolio, Octalica, Onaro, Orsus, PeerApp, Pentalum, Pixie, Personali, Primary Data, Red-C, StartApp, WebCollage, WiNetworks, Wochit

Key Executives:
Amnon Shoham, Co-Founder
Background: Managing Partner, Star Ventures Israel; Board of Directors, Accord Networks, BreezeCOM, Fourth Dimension Software, Fundtech, Jacada, NICEcom, Paradigm Geophysical, ViraNet; Attorney, Skadden, Arps, Slate, Meagher & Flom
Directorships: Intigua, ClickFox, PeersApp, Jsonar, Appilog, CloudLock, Guardium, Orsus, Onaro
Gal Israely, Co-Founder
Background: Managing Director, High Tech Investment Banking Group, Bear Stearns
Directorships: Wochit, StartApp, Pixie, Pentalum, Amimon, BigBand Networks, Celtro, NewAct, Octalica, WiNetworks, Red-C
Motti Vaknin, Partner
Background: CEO, BeInSync; CEO & Co-Founder, WebLayers; CEO, Bridges for Islands; VP, Sales & Marketing, Shiron Satellite Communications
Directorships: 365Scores, Datorama, Primary Data, Personali, Curiyo
Hila Leibovitz, Inhouse Counsel
Education: LLB, LLM, Bar Ilan University
Background: Herzog Fox & Neeman

Venture Capital & Private Equity Firms / Domestic Firms

Shlomi Shiloni Shem Tov, VP of Finance
Education: BA, Economics/Business, Bar Ilan University; MBA, Tel Aviv University; CPA
Background: Financial Controller/Analyst, Fortissimo Capital; Senior Auditor, EY

439 CEDAR VENTURES LLC
2870 Peachtree Road
Suite 450
Atlanta, GA 30305

Phone: 404-239-8416 Fax: 404-239-8417
web: www.cedarventures.com

Mission Statement: Cedar Ventures is an investment banking and financial advisory services firm that specializes in raising debt and equity capital for a variety of companies.
Geographic Preference: Louisiana, Texas, Alabama, Gulf Coast, North & South Carolina
Industry Group Preference: Medical Devices, Consumer Products, Food & Beverage, Energy, Technology, Life Sciences, Healthcare Information Technology
Key Executives:
  Karen Kassouf, Founder/Managing Member
  e-mail: kassouf@cedarventures.com
  Education: BA, Economics & Political Science, Bucknell University; JD, Villanova University School of Law
  Background: Cedar Equities, Western Indemnity Insurance Company; Healthcare Investment Banking Unit, Chemical Banking Corporation; Texas Commerce Bank

440 CEI VENTURES
30 Federal Street
Suite 100
Brunswick, ME 04011

Phone: 207-504-5900
Toll-Free: 877-340-2649
e-mail: info@ceimaine.org
web: www.ceiventures.com

Mission Statement: To create jobs and ownership opportunities for people with low income, to create socially beneficial products and services, and to promote progressive management practices while striving toward a competitive rate of return.
Geographic Preference: Northeast
Fund Size: $25.54 million
Founded: 1994
Average Investment: $750,000
Minimum Investment: $500,000
Investment Criteria: Job creation, socially responsible, good management, practical exit plan
Industry Group Preference: Industrial Services, Energy, Biotechnology, Financial Services, Consumer Products, Information Technology, Software, Healthcare, Business to Business, Networking, Media, Entertainment
Portfolio Companies: A&B Electronics, Avia Boisystems, Beacon Analytical Systems, BlueTarp Financial, BroadcastAmerica.com, Bush Equities dba Cuddledown, Certify Inc., Chemogen, Chomp, CitySoft, Clickshare Service, Coast of Maine Organic Products, Cormier Textile Products, CV Finer Foods, Definition6, eCopy, Ektron Inc., EnvisionNet Computer Services, Foreside Company, FreeBorders, Genicon Inc., HCI Systems, HomeBistro Foods, Hyperlite Mountain Gear, Innov-X Systems, Intellicare America, Juno Rising, Look's Gourmet Food, Maine Craft Distilling, Maine Trailer, Metrobility Optical Systems, Mingle Analytics, Native Energy, Navigator Publishing, NBT Solutions, New England 800 dba Taction, New England Audio Resource, NextMark, Ogee Inc., PenBay Solutions, Pika Energy Inc., RecruiterNet, RedZone Wireless, Research Enhanced Design + Development Inc., Rustic Crust, SciAps Inc., SmartPak Equine, Soleras, Stillwater Scientific Instruments, Sun & Earth, The Gelato Fiasco, Tilson Technology Management, Wentworth Technology Inc.

Key Executives:
  Betsy Biemann, Chief Executive Director
  e-mail: betsy.biemann@ceimaine.org
  Education: BA, Harvard University; MPA, Princeton University
  Background: President, Maine Technology Institute; Associate Director, The Rockefeller Foundation
  Keith Bisson, President
  e-mail: keith.bisson@ceimaine.org
  Education: BA, McGill University; MA, Yale School of Forestry & Environmental Studies

441 CELERITY PARTNERS
12121 Wilshire Boulevard
Suite 512
Los Angeles, CA 90025

Phone: 310-268-1710
web: www.celeritypartners.com

Mission Statement: Manages private equity and is dedicated to building businesses in partnership with management to achieve preeminence in their respective markets.
Geographic Preference: United States
Fund Size: $200 million
Founded: 1995
Minimum Investment: $1 million
Investment Criteria: Growth Equity, De-Leveraging Investments, MBO, Corporate Divestitures, Recapitalizations
Industry Group Preference: Manufacturing, Security, Outsourcing & Efficiency, Database Services, Niche Manufacturing, Marketing, Information Technology, Aerospace, Defense and Government, Military, Consumer Products, Life Sciences, Healthcare
Portfolio Companies: 360 PT Management, ABC Industries, ABC Laboratories, Advanced Accessory Systems, All Aboard America!, Ascension Insurance, Dynamic Details, estudy Site, Meridien Research, National Research Institute, OnCore Manufacturing Services, O Premium Waters, Ortho Organizers, PC Helps, Peer 1, Pinnacle Treatment Centers, Project Leadership Associates, Rincon Industries, SMTC Corporation, Streamline Circuits, SynteractHCR, Total Care RX, Tru Fit Athletic Clubs, Verari Systems, Vince & Associates Clinical Research, Well-Foam, Western Jet Aviation
Other Locations:
  3000 Sand Hill Rd
  Building 3
  Suite 100
  Menlo Park, CA 94025
  Phone: 650-646-3624
Key Executives:
  Mark Benham, Managing Director
  e-mail: mbenham@celeritypartners.com
  Education: BA English, University of California, Berkeley; MA, MBA, University of Chicago both with honors
  Background: Senior Investment Officer, Citicorp Venture Capital; Principal, Merchant Banking Group, Crocker/Montague
  Directorships: SMTC Corporation, several private companies
  Matt Kraus, Managing Director
  e-mail: mkraus@celeritypartners.com
  Education: BA Political Science, Bucknell University
  Background: Founder/Managing Director, Harvey & Company; Analyst, W.E. Myers & Company
  Directorships: AdB Industries; The New Release

442 CENTANA GROWTH PARTNERS
855 El Camino Real
Building 4, Suite 240
Palo Alto, CA 94301

web: www.centanagrowth.com

Venture Capital & Private Equity Firms / Domestic Firms

Mission Statement: Centana invests in rapidly growing companies in order to sustain or accelerate growth.
Founded: 2015
Other Locations:
1412 Broadway
Suite 1504
New York, NY 10018
Key Executives:
Steven Swain, Co-Founder/Partner
212-256-8452
e-mail: sswain@centanagrowth.com
Education: BA, Clark University; JD, Villanova University; MBA, George Washington University
Background: President, Global X Management; COO, Lyster Watson & Co.
Ben Cukier, Co-Founder/Partner
212-256-8451
e-mail: bcukier@centanagrowth.com
Education: BA, University of Pennsylvania; MBA, Stanford University
Background: Partner, FTV Capital; Consultant, McKinsey & Co.

443 CENTENNIAL VENTURES
10901 West Toller Drive
Suite 206
Littleton, CO 80127
Phone: 303-405-7500 **Fax:** 303-405-7575

Mission Statement: Centennial Ventures is a venture capital firm investing in network, software and technology companies with the potential to be market leaders.
Fund Size: $341 million
Founded: 1982
Average Investment: $4 - $10 million
Minimum Investment: $500,000
Investment Criteria: Early Stage, Later-Stage
Industry Group Preference: Global Industries, Media, Broadband, Infrastructure, Software, Internet Technology
Portfolio Companies: Accellos, Alereon, Extenet, FDN Communications, Grande, Hoak Media Corporation, InnerWireless, MarketForce Information, Masergy, Panasas, Siterra, Slackers, TriStar, Zayo
Key Executives:
Duncan Butler, Managing Director
Education: BBA, MBA, University of Texas; Doctor of Jurisprudence, University of Texas School of Law
Background: Principal, Prime New Ventures; VP, Corporate Development, Prime Cable
Steve Halstedt, Managing Director
Education: BS, Management Engineering, Worcester Polytechnic Institute; MBA, Tuck School of Business, Dartmouth College
Background: EVP/Director, Daniels & Associates; US Army; US Army Engineer School; Dartmouth College
Directorships: National Venture Capital Association
David Hull, Managing Director
Education: BS, Chemical Engineering, MBA, University of Texas, Austin
Background: Managing General Partner, Criterion Venture Partners, TransAmerica; SVP, Finance/Treasure/Director, General Leisure Corporation
Rand Lewis, Managing Director
Education: BS, Electrical & Computer Engineering, Brigham Young University; MS, Computer Science, University of Colorado; MBA, Kellogg School of Management, Northwestern University
Background: Management Consultant, McKinsey & Company; Software Engineer, US WEST
Neel Sarkar, Managing Director
Education: BS, Electrical Engineering, Massachusetts Institute of Technology; MBA, Kellogg School of Management, Northwestern University
Background: Director, Strategy & Business Development, Dell; Management Consultant, McKinsey & Company; Operations Manager, GE & Excelon
Jeffrey Schutz, Managing Director
Education: BA, Economics, Middlebury College; MBA, Colgate Darden Graduate School of Business Administration, University of Virginia
Background: VP/Director, PNC Venture Capital Group
Directorships: Small Business Administration

444 CENTERBRIDGE PARTNERS
375 Park Avenue
New York, NY 10152
Phone: 212-672-5000
web: www.centerbridge.com

Mission Statement: A private equity firm focusing on leveraged buyouts and distressed securities.
Fund Size: $5.5 billion
Founded: 2005
Investment Criteria: Leveraged Buyouts
Portfolio Companies: Aktua, American Renal, Banca FarmaFactoring, Bank United, Carefree, Dana, Extended Stay America, Great Wolf Lodge, Green Tree, GSI, Hearland, HydroChem, IPC, Kenan Advantage Group Inc., KIK Custom Products, Ligado Networks, Santander Consumer USA, Satmex, Senvion, Superior Vision
Key Executives:
Jeffrey Aronson, Co-Founder and Managing Partner
Education: BA, Johns Hopkins University; JD, New York University School of Law
Background: Partner, Angelo, Gordon & Co.; Senior Corporate Counsel, L.F. Rothschild & Co.; Securities Attorney, Stroock & Stroock & Lavan

445 CENTERFIELD CAPITAL PARTNERS
3000 Market Tower
10 W Market Street
Indianapolis, IN 46204
Phone: 317-237-2323 **Fax:** 317-237-2325
web: www.centerfieldcapital.com

Mission Statement: Provides growth and expansion capital to privately held companies in the Midwest.
Geographic Preference: Midwest
Fund Size: $150 million
Founded: 1985
Average Investment: $2 - $15 million
Minimum Investment: $2 million
Investment Criteria: Most interested in companies with annual revenues between $15 and $75 million and at a stage where they have a positive cash flow and proven products and customers.
Industry Group Preference: Healthcare, Business to Business, Information Technology, Telecommunications, Financial Services, Manufacturing, Distribution, Consumer Products, Specialty Chemicals, Food & Beverage, Education, Healthcare Services
Portfolio Companies: A&D Environmental Services, Advanced Physical Therapy, Aero Systems Engineering, Aerostar Global Logistics, Alpha Imaging, Automated Systems Design, Backyard Products, Banner Service Corp., Battery Solutions, Beacon Communications, Bell Automotive Products, Bil-Jax, California Medical Evaluators, Cargo Airport Services, CE Rental, Coast Composites, D.S. Brown, DCL Medical Laboratories, Dedicated Transport, Digital Medica Services, Direct Marketing Solutions, Diversified Graphics, eGix, Evriholder Products, First Source, Fresh Food Concepts, Gabriel Performance Products, Heartland Steel Products, Hunter's Specialties, IF&P Foods, Imaginetics, Indo-European Foods, Matilda Jane Clothing, MicroMass, Midland Container, Millennium Custom Foods, Pipp Mobile Storage Solutions, PowerWay, PRISM Plastics, Rice's Honey, RIO Brands, Roehm Marine, Rose America Corp., SCT, Shred All, Silbond Corp., Standard Locknut,

Venture Capital & Private Equity Firms / Domestic Firms

Swiff-Train Co., TCI, Thermafiber, Transolutions, Venture Technology Groups, Wild Sports, Woodmarc, Y-T Holdco

Key Executives:
  Scott Lutzke, Founding Partner
  e-mail: scott@centerfieldcapital.com
  Education: Physcics, Purdue University; MBA, Finance, Indiana University
  Background: First VP/Manager, Indiana Public Banking; 11 Years Experience in Private Equity; 20 Years in Corporate Banking
  Directorships: Venture Club of Indiana
  Farraz Abassi, Senior Partner
  e-mail: faraz@centerfieldcapital.com
  Education: MBA Finance, Indiana University; BS Chemical Engineering, University of Texas
  Background: Senior Product Engineer, Praxair; Sales Engineering, Rodel; Vice President, Young Professionals, 10 Years Experience in Private Equity
  Mark Hollis, Partner
  e-mail: mark@centerfieldcapital.com
  Education: BBA, University of Southern Indiana; MBA, Kelley School of Business, Indiana University
  Background: Vice President, National City Bank
  Michael Miller, Partner
  e-mail: michael@centerfieldcapital.com
  Education: BBA, Economics, Hanover College; MBA, Fuqua School of Business, Duke University
  Background: Eli Lilly & Company, Hatteras Venture Partners
  Jill Margetts, Partner
  e-mail: jill@centerfieldcapital.com
  Education: MBA, Kelley School of Business, Indiana University; BS, Chemical Engineering, MIT
  Background: Business Analyst, Midwest Independent Transmission System Operator; Process Engineer, ETEX Corporation

446 CENTERPOINT VENTURE PARTNERS
Two Galleria Tower
13455 Noel Road
16th Floor
Dallas, TX 75240

Phone: 972-702-1101 **Fax:** 972-702-1103
web: www.cpventures.com

Mission Statement: Leverages expertise and resources to help entrepreneurs in building productive management teams, implementing business models and developing strategic technologies that can revolutionize major market areas; constantly scans the horizon for inspired entrepreneurs with innovative business concepts to help them build successful ventures.

Geographic Preference: Texas, Southwest United States
Fund Size: $450 million
Founded: 1996
Average Investment: $5 - $15 million
Minimum Investment: $5 million
Investment Criteria: Early, Expansion, Seed
Industry Group Preference: Communications, Software Services, Semiconductors, Industrial Services, Infrastructure
Portfolio Companies: Active Power, Applied Science Fiction, Covaro Networks, D2Audio, Neoworld, NetBotz, Silicon Labs, Voyence

Other Locations:
  One Bridgepoint
  6300 Birdge Point Parkway
  Building 1, Suite 500
  Austin, TX 78730
  Phone: 512-795-5800 **Fax:** 512-795-5849

Key Executives:
  Bob Paluck, Managing Director
  Education: BS, Electrical Engineering, University of Illinois
  Background: Co-Founder/Chairman/CEO, Convex Computer Corporation; VP Product Development/Marketing, Mostek
  Cam McMartin, Managing Director/Chief Financial Officer
  Education: MBA, University of Michigan; BA, Trinity University
  Background: Senior VP Operations, Dazel Corporation; Senior Vice President/CFO, DataCard Corporation; CFO, Convex Computer Corporation
  Terry Rock, Managing Director
  Education: BS, Mechanical Engineering, South Dakota School of Mines & Technology
  Background: President, Convex; Operating Management, Texas Instruments; Co-Founded, STARTech Technology Incubator; Managing General Partner, STARTech Seed Fund

447 CENTRAL TEXAS ANGEL NETWORK
PO Box 5435
Austin, TX 78763-5435

Phone: 512-518-6054
e-mail: director@ctan.com
web: ctan.com

Mission Statement: The Central Texas Angel Network is a Texas-based angel organization dedicated to providing strong investment opportunities for angel investors as well as financial and educational resources for early stage growth businesses and entrepreneurs.

Geographic Preference: Central Texas
Founded: 2006
Investment Criteria: Startups, Early Stage
Industry Group Preference: Consumer Products, Consumer Services, Food & Beverage, Healthcare, Industrial, Internet, Mobile, Telecommunications, Software
Portfolio Companies: AccuWater, AdBm Technologies, Admittance Technologies, Agile Planet, Alzeca Biosciences, Apptive, Atonometrics, Autowraptec, Beauty Box 5, Better Voicemail, Bing Outdoor Media, Boomerang's, Bouldin Creek Distillery, Boxer, Cache IQ, CelAccess, City Bebe, ClearBlade, CSID, Curb, Cutting Edge Gamer, Daily Juice, DealerHQ, Deep Eddy, DiFusion Technologies, DisplayPoints, Dulce Vida, Edioma, EDHC, Enlyton, ENTvantage Diagnostics, ESO Solutions, FantasySalesTeam, Firefly LED Lighting, FlowBelow, Friends & Allies Brewing, Frontier Bank of Texas, Global Material Exchange, Goodybag, Greenling, GreenWorld Restoration, GRIDbot, Guidepath Medical, Guns & Oil Brewing, HeatGenie, HUVRData, Hyperwear, Infinite, JamHub, Job Cannon, Karmaback.com, KENGURU, KIMBIA, Localeur, Loku, MacuCLEAR, Mahana, ManagerComplete, Meals to Live, Meshify, MicroTransponder, Mixbook, MommyMixer, NanoMedical Systems, NanoRacks, Netsurion, NeuroChaos Solutions, Nexersys iPower Trainer, NuHabitat, NurturMe, Nuve, OneSpot, Order Corner, Ordoro, Ortho Kinematics, ParLevel, Perception Software, Phunware, Pioneer Bank, Quarri, Querium, Recursion, Rhythm Superfoods, Salient Pharmaceuticals, Savara, Senscient, Smart Picture Solution, SmarteSoft, SonarMed, Sports Tradex, StreamVine, Structured Polymers, Student Loan Genius, Suvola, TalentGuard, TEKVOX, Televero, TextureMedia, The Corner Vet, The Good Promise, Traitwise, Traumatec, Upspring Baby, Verb, VolunteerSpot, Wenzel, Wisegate, Wonder, Xeris, Zilker Brewing

Key Executives:
  Victoria Dominguez-Edington, Program Director
  Education: BA, Southwestern University; MA, University of Texas

Venture Capital & Private Equity Firms / Domestic Firms

448 CENTRE LANE PARTNERS
One Grand Central Place
60 East 42nd Street
Suite 1250
New York, NY 10165

Phone: 646-843-0710
e-mail: info@centrelanepartners.com
web: centrelanepartners.com

Mission Statement: Centre Lane is a private investment firm focused on making equity and debt, control and non-control, investments in North American middle market companies.

Geographic Preference: North America
Average Investment: $5 - $250 million
Minimum Investment: $5 million
Industry Group Preference: Diversified
Portfolio Companies: Alternative Biomedical Solutions, Clickbooth, Crown Brands, Infobase, Jobe's, Luminex Home Decor & Fragrance, MDC Vacuum Products, The Merit Group, Oracle Packaging, Saladworks, Sure Fit Home Decor, Vexos, WIS Intl., Zenfolio Inc.

Key Executives:
Quinn Morgan, Managing Director
Education: London School of Economics
Background: D.B. Zwirn & Co.
Kenneth Lau, Managing Director
Education: MIT
Background: D.B. Zwirn & Co.
Luke Gosselin, Managing Director
Education: Syracuse Univ.; Fordham Univ.
Background: Fort Hill Investment Partners
Mayank Singh, Managing Director
Education: Colgate Univ.; Stern School
Background: Monomoy Capital Partners

449 CENTRE PARTNERS MANAGEMENT LLC
601 Lexington Avenue
55th Floor
New York, NY 10022-4611

Phone: 212-332-5800 Fax: 212-758-1830
e-mail: info@centrepartners.com
web: www.centrepartners.com

Mission Statement: Private equity firm specializing in middle market businesses in the consumer and healthcare markets.

Geographic Preference: North America
Fund Size: $850 million
Founded: 1986
Average Investment: $20 - $60 million
Minimum Investment: $20 million
Investment Criteria: Buyouts, Spin-Outs, Growth Investments, Leveraged Build-Ups, Going Private Transactions
Industry Group Preference: Consumer Products, Industrial Products, Financial Services, Healthcare, Media, Retailing, Food & Beverage, Business Products & Services
Portfolio Companies: American Seafoods LP, Autoland Inc., Bellisio Food LLC, Bradford Health Services, Bravo Sports, Bumble Bee Foods LP, Catlin Westgen Group, Centre Pacific Holdings LLC, Covenant Care, Dan Howard Industries, Distant Lands Trading Co., Filament Brands Inc., Firearms Training Systems Inc., Garden Fresh Holdings, Gray Energy Services, Golding Farms Foods Inc., Guy & O'Neill Inc., Group Dekko Holdings Inc., Hyco International Inc., Jeepers! Inc., K2 Pure Solutions LP, Kaz Inc., Kinburn Corp, Laundry Mart Inc., MacNeill Pride Group, Manor House Retirement Centers Inc., Maverick Media LLC, Monte Nido Holdings LLC, Muzak Limited Partnership, Nationwide Credit Inc., Nearly Natural Inc., Nexus Gas Parttners, One World Fitness PFF, Orion ICG, Patient Education Media Inc., Q2 Publishing Inc., Quickie Manufacturing Corp, Rembrandt Photo Services, Rocky Mountain Financial Corporation, Ross Aviation, Salton Inc., Scientific Games Holdings Corp, Seaview Petroleum Co. LP, Sphere Drake Holdings Limited, Stonewall Kitchen LLC, Sun Orchard Inc., The Johnny Rockets Group, The Learning Company Inc., The Golden Financial Group Inc., United New Mexico Financial Corporation, United Retail Grop Inc., Uno Restaurant Holdings Corp, Vinters International Inc., Vision Innovation Partners, Wind River Environmental LLC, Wisconsin Cheese Group Holding LLC

Other Locations:
11726 San Vicente Blvd
Suite 450
Los Angeles, CA 90049
Phone: 310-207-9170 Fax: 310-207-9180

Key Executives:
Bruce Pollack, Managing Partner
e-mail: bruce.pollack@centrepartners.com
Education: Brandeis University
Background: TSG Holdings; RSG Partners; Becker; Merrill Lynch Capital Markets
Directorships: Salton, Bravo Sports, BumbleBee Seafoods, Maverick Media, Johnny Rockets Group, KIK Corporation Holdings, OSF, The Tiffen Company, Centre Palisades Ventures
David Jaffe, Managing Partner
e-mail: david.jaffe@centrepartners.com
Education: AB, Harvard University; MBA, Wharton School
Background: Managing Director, Merchant Banking Partners; DLJ Securities Corporation
Directorships: Catlin Westgen Group, Kaz, International Imaging Materials, Hyco International, Autoland, Target Media Partners
Jeffrey Bartoli, Partner
e-mail: jeffrey.bartoli@centrepartners.com
Education: BS, Georgetown University
Background: M&A, Smith Barney
Directorships: Environmental Logistics Services, K2 Pure Solutions, Maverick Media, Ross Aviation, US Retirement Partners
Michael Schnabel, Partner
e-mail: michael.schnabel@centrepartners.com
Education: BS, Duke University
Background: Director of Finance, OmniSky Corporation; Donaldson Lufkin & Jenrette Securities Corp.
Directorships: Centre Environmental Partners, Covenant Care, DSI Holding Company, Uno Restaurant Holdings
William Tomai, COO & CFO
e-mail: bill.tomai@centrepartners.com
Education: MBA, Wharton School; Vanderbuilt University
Background: Donaldson, Lufkin & Jenrette; Bank of New York; AspenTree Capital

450 CENTRIPETAL CAPITAL PARTNERS
Six Landmark Square
3rd Floor
Stamford, CT 06901

Phone: 203-326-7600
e-mail: info@centricap.com
web: www.centricap.com

Mission Statement: Centripetal Capital Partners, LLC. is an innovative venture capital firm with a distinctive investing and membership structure that provides greater flexibility and opportunity for limited partners than a traditional fund. We have an opportunistic growth capital investment approach, and seek investments in revenue generating companies with proprietary advantages, proven business models, and relevantly experienced management teams.

Founded: 2004
Average Investment: $2 - $7 million
Investment Criteria: Early-Stage, Growth Stage
Portfolio Companies: APJeT, Choice Pet, Cytogel, Dashbid, Earth Animal, IMCS Group, Meelo, Zing

Venture Capital & Private Equity Firms / Domestic Firms

Key Executives:
Steven Chrust, Senior Partner & Managing Director
Education: BA, Baruch College
Background: Founder, SGC Advisory Services; Sanford C Bernstein & Co.
Stephen Rossetter, Partner
Education: BA, Hartwick College; MBA, Pace University
Background: CFO/Partner, L&L Capital Advisors
Jeff Brodlieb, Partner
Education: BA, Brown University; MBA, Harvard Business School
Background: VP, Strategic Transactions, GE Capital

451 CENTURY PARK CAPITAL PARTNERS
2101 Rosencrans Avenue
Suite 4275
El Segundo, CA 90245

Phone: 310-867-2210 Fax: 310-867-2212
web: www.centuryparkcapital.com

Mission Statement: A private equity firm that partners with owners/managers to build successful companies.
Geographic Preference: North America
Average Investment: $10 - $40 million
Investment Criteria: Companies with a revenue of $20-100 million, historical and projected growth, manageable cyclicality, and diversified customer base
Industry Group Preference: Chemicals, Medical Products & Services, Business Services, Engineered Products, Consumer Products
Portfolio Companies: The Mochi Ice Cream Company, Better Life Technology LLC, Covercraft Industries LLC, ICM Products Inc., Cirtec Medical LLC, Hi-Tech Rubber Inc., Dickinson Frozen Foods Inc., Becker Underwood Inc., Eckler's Enterprises Inc., Kidsline Inc., Lynx Grills Inc., Specialty Manufacturing Inc., ROM Corp., Moss Inc., Packaging Plus LLC, Ryan's Express Transportation Services Inc., Aqua-Flo LLC

Other Locations:
750 Menlo Avenue
Suite 200
Menlo Park, CA 94025
Phone: 650-324-1956 Fax: 650-325-7757

Key Executives:
Martin A. Sarafa, Managing Partner
e-mail: msarafa@cpclp.com
Education: BS, Economics & Computer Science, University of Michigan; MBA, Wharton School, University of Pennsylvania
Background: Managing Director, Houlihan Lokey Howard & Zulkin
Directorships: Ryan's Express Transportation Services, Lynx Grills, Moss, Speciality Manufacturing Group, Cirtec Medical Systems, ICM Products
Charles W. Roellig, Managing Partner
e-mail: croellig@cpclp.com
Education: BA, Economics, Stanford University; MBA, Anderson Graduate School of Management, University of California, LA
Background: Principal, BT Capital Partners
Directorships: ROM Corporation, Lynx Grills, Eckler's Enterprises
Guy Zaczepinski, Managing Partner
e-mail: gzaczepinski@cpclp.com
Education: BS, Wharton School, University of Pennsylvania, MBA, Harvard Business School
Background: ACI Capital, DCMI
Directorships: Eckler's Enterprixes, Moss, Lynx Grills, ICM Products
Adam Zacuto, Vice President
e-mail: azacuto@cpclp.com
Education: BS, Finance, University of Southern California
Background: Analyst, Wells Fargo Securities

452 CEO VENTURES
600 Northpark Building
1200 Abernathy Road
17th Floor
Atlanta, GA 30328

Phone: 770-998-9999
e-mail: info@ceoventures.com
web: www.ceoventures.com

Mission Statement: CEO Ventures manages an angel fund that focuses on Software as a Service (Saas) seed stage companies and startups. CEO Ventures seeks to help entrepreneurs with the development and growth of new technology companies.
Investment Criteria: Seed-Stage, Startups
Industry Group Preference: Business to Business, Technology, SaaS
Portfolio Companies: CriticalFit, FindMatic, GoPresent, TeamEx

Other Locations:
Market Acceleration Center
Atlantic Station
201 17th Street, 12th Floor
Atlanta, GA 30363

228 Hamilton Avenue
3rd Floor
Palo Alto, CA 94301

Key Executives:
Michael Price, General Partner
e-mail: mprice@ceoventures.com
Education: Ohio State University, University of Akron
Background: IBM/Deibold

453 CERBERUS CAPITAL MANAGEMENT
875 Third Avenue
New York, NY 10022

Phone: 212-891-2100
e-mail: info@cerberus.com
web: www.cerberus.com

Mission Statement: Cerberus specializes in providing both financial resources and operational expertise to help transform undervalued companies into industry leaders for long-term success and value creation. Cerberus has numerous branches acorss the US, Europe and Asia.
Geographic Preference: United States, Europe, Asia
Fund Size: $20 billion
Founded: 1994
Industry Group Preference: Aerospace, Defense and Government, Transportation, Apparel, Automotive, Building Materials & Services, Commercial Services, Consumer Products, Financial Services, Healthcare, Manufacturing, Distribution, Paper, Real Estate, Technology

Key Executives:
John W. Snow, Chairman
Education: University of Toledo, George Washington University Law School, MS, Johns Hopkins University; PhD, Economics, University of Virginia
Background: United States Secretary of the Treasury
Stephen A. Feinberg, Co-Founder & Co-CEO
Education: Princeton University
Background: Gruntal & Co.
Frank W. Bruno, Co-CEO & Senior Managing Director
Education: Cornell University; MBA, Wharton School, University of Pennsylvania
William L. Richter, Co-Founder
Education: Harvard College; MBA, Harvard Business School
Background: President, Richter Investment Corp.

Venture Capital & Private Equity Firms / Domestic Firms

454 CERES VENTURE FUND
1750 Harding Road
Northfield, IL 60093

e-mail: contact@ceresventurefund.com
web: www.ceresventurefund.com

Mission Statement: Ceres Venture Fund is an established Chicago-based venture capital fund dedicated to funding high growth companies located in the Midwest in their early stages of growth. As growth-oriented investors, the fund seeks to partner with entrepreneurs of proven ability and provide them with the resources needed to achieve extraordinary success.

Geographic Preference: Midwest United States
Industry Group Preference: Healthcare, Information Technology, Business Products & Services
Portfolio Companies: Brill Street + Company, Coverity, Eved, INRange Systems, SynCardia Systems, SynTherix, TrafficCast International, Vormetric, Zorch International

Key Executives:
Sona Wang, Managing Partner
Education: BS, Industrial Engineering, Stanford University; MBA, Kellogg School of Management
Background: Investment Manager, Allstate Insurance; Co-Founder, Batterson Johnson & Wang; Co-Founder, Inroads Capital Partners
Donna Williamson, Managing Director
Education: ScB, Applied Mathematics, Brown University; Graduate Degree, MIT Sloan School of Business
Background: Managing Director, ABN Amro; Founding Officer & SVP, Caremark International
Laura Pearl, Managing Director
Education: BS, Accountancy, University of Illinois, Urbana-Champaign; MBA, University of Chicago
Background: Ernst & Young; Partner, Frontenac

455 CERRACAP VENTURES
650 Town Center Drive
Suite 1870
Costa Mesa, CA 92626

Phone: 949-309-8598
e-mail: info@cerracap.com
web: www.cerracap.com

Mission Statement: Cerracap Ventures is focused on investing globally in early stage B2B companies. Their sectors include healthcare, enterprise AI and cybersecurity.

Key Executives:
Saurabh Suri, Managing Partner
Education: MS, University of Reading

456 CERVIN VENTURES
705 Forest Avenue
Palo Alto, CA 94301

e-mail: info@cervinventures.com
web: www.cervinventures.com

Mission Statement: The Cervin Ventures team consists of entrepreneurs who have a deep understanding of what it takes to start, build and grow a business. The firm brings an extensive network of technology, venture capital, and business professionals to advise and help early stage companies through their life cycle. The partners work closely with their portfolio companies to help them realize their full potential.

Investment Criteria: Early-Stage
Industry Group Preference: Software, Business to Business
Portfolio Companies: Ampool, ArmorText, Bedrock Analytics, BetterCompany, Bright Pattern, Claritics, EdCast, Folloze, Involver, Software, Nexient, Reveel, PayStand, Punchh, QuanticMind, SnapLogic, Soha Systems, Spotzot, Tynker, Zephyr, Zycada Networks

Key Executives:
Preetish Nijhawan, Managing Director
Education: BSEE, Birla Institute of Technology & Science; MS, Computer Engineering, University of Southern California; MBA, MIT Sloan School of Management
Background: CFO, Neon Enterprise Software; McKinsey & Company
Neeraj Gupta, Managing Director
Education: BSEE, Punjab University; MSEE, University of Alabama
Background: Patni; Founder, Cymbal Corporation

457 CHARLES RIVER VENTURES
52 Zoe Street
San Francisco, CA 94107

Phone: 415-960-3000
web: www.crv.com

Mission Statement: To contribute to the creation of significant new enterprises by working in constructive partnership with driven, talented entrepreneurs. To invest in early-stage, high potential companies with the objective of building rigorous, high-growth businesses, which produce substantial capital gains.

Geographic Preference: Northeast United States
Fund Size: $1.5 billion
Founded: 1970
Average Investment: $10-$25 million
Minimum Investment: $25, 000
Investment Criteria: Early Stage, Series A
Industry Group Preference: Communications, Software, Information Technology, E-Commerce & Manufacturing, Consumer Internet, Infrastructure, SaaS, Cloud Computing
Portfolio Companies: 24M, Affirmed, Ark, Aveksa, Capriza, CarrierIQ, Cloudshare, Crossbeam Systems, Crushpath, DailyBreak, DataGravity, EnterpriseDB, Fiksu, Geni, Glyde, GrabCad, Greatcall, HubSpot, iControl Networks, Intellectual Ventures, InVisage, LearnBoost, Live Gamer, Magnetic, Maxthon, Millennial Media, Nantero, Neologin, Optaros, Progresso Financiero, Public Mobile, Qubole, Rethink Robotics, Rive Technology, RPX, Samplify, Scribd, SessionM, Simplivity, Sincerely, SpiderCloud Wireless, TalenBin, TerraPower, Tonian, ToyTalk, Twitter, Udacity, Vanu, Verenium, Viki, Wangyou.com, Wave Accounting, Xamarin, Yammer, Zendesk, CoTap, Dropbox, Gupshup, Pebble, Refresh, TopHatter, Usermind

Other Locations:
300 Hamilton Avenue
3rd Floor
Palo Alto, CA 94301
Phone: 650-687-5600

Virtual Office
Boston, MA
Phone: 781-768-6000

Key Executives:
Izhar Armony, Partner
e-mail: izhar@crv.com
Education: MBA, Wharton School of Business, University of Pennsylvania; MA, Cognitive Psychology, University of Tel Aviv; MA, International Studies, University of Pennsylvania
Background: Enterprise Software, General Atlantic Partners; Software Designer, Director, Buisiness Development, Onyx Interactive; Officer, Israeli Army
Jon Auerbach, Partner
781-768-6000
Education: BA, University of Pennsylvania
Background: General Partner, Highland Capital Partners; Technology Reporter & Editor, The Wall Street Journal
Saar Gur, Partner
Education: BS, Biochemistry, University of Wisconsin, Madison; MBA, Stanford University
Background: Co-Founder, Brightroll; Co-Founder, Carebadges.com; VP, Customer Acquisition, Adteractive; Founder, FounderDating
Bruce Sachs, Partner
Education: Master in Electrical Engineering, Cornell

Venture Capital & Private Equity Firms / Domestic Firms

University; MBA, Northeastern University
Background: AT&t Bell Laboratories; Memotec/Infinet; Xylogics; Bay Networks;
Devdutt Yellurkar, Partner
Education: BS, Fergusson College, India
Background: Venture Partner, Rho Ventures; Co-Founder & CEO, Yantra Corporation; Senior Vice President, Infosys Technologies
George Zachary, Partner
Education: BS, MIT Sloan School of Management
Background: General Partner, Mohr Davidow Ventures; Development, Nintendo/Silicon Graphics; Marketing Manager, VPL Research; CATS Software
Max Gazor, Partner
e-mail: max@crv.com
Education: BS, EECS, UC Berkeley; MS, EECS, MIT, MBA, Harvard Business School
Background: Corporate Development, Cisco
Richard Burnes, Partner Emeritus
e-mail: rick@crv.com
Education: MBA, Boston University; BA, Harvard University
Background: Co-Founder, Charles River Ventures; Chairman of the Board, The Middlesex School
Directorships: Concord Communications, Passport Corporation, SpeechWorks, Boston Science Museum, Sea Education Association
Ted Dintersmith, Partner Emeritus
e-mail: ted@crv.com
Education: PhD, Stanford University; BA, William and Mary College
Background: General Manager, Digital Signal Processing Division, Analog Devices; Congressional Staff Assistant

458 CHARLESBANK CAPITAL PARTNERS
200 Clarendon Street
54th Floor
Boston, MA 02116

Phone: 617-619-5400
web: www.charlesbank.com

Mission Statement: Charlesbank Capital Partners is a private equity firm committed to providing flexible capital and valuable collaboration to middle-market companies across a variety of sectors. The firm seeks to build companies with exceptional growth prospects.
Fund Size: $1.75 billion
Founded: 1991
Average Investment: $50 - $150 million
Investment Criteria: Growth Through Acquisition, Leveraged Acquisition, Middle Market, Small & Mid-Capitalization Public Companies, Later Stage
Industry Group Preference: Consumer Products, Distribution, Energy, Financial Services, Food & Beverage, Healthcare, Manufacturing, Media, Communications, Education
Portfolio Companies: American Residential Services, American Tire Distributors, Animal Health International, Aurora Organic Dairy, Bankruptcy Management Solutions, Blacksmith Brands, Blueknight Energy Partners, Catlin, Cedar Creek, CIFC, Citadel Plastics, CSI Leasing, DEI Holdings, Del Taco, Doit International, Ensono, Fullbeauty Brands, Galls, Gray Wolf Industrial, HDT Global, Hearthside Food Solutions, Helpsystems, Montpelier RE, Myeyedr., National Surgical Hospitals, Neo Tech, Park Place, Papa Murphy's, Peacock Foods, Plaskolite, Polyconcept, The Princeton Review, QC Supply, Regency Gas Services, RGL Reservoir Management, Rockport, Shoppers Drug Mart, Sightpath Medical, Six Degrees, Southcross Energy, StoneCastle, Tecomet, Technisource, Trojan Battery, United Road Services, Universal Technical Institute, Varsity Brands, Vestcom, Vision Group Holdings, Wolfpak Software, WorldStrides, Zayo Group, Zenith Products Corp.

Other Locations:
575 - 5th Avenue
36th Floor
New York, NY 10017
Phone: 212-903-1880
Key Executives:
Kim G. Davis, Managing Director/Founding Partner
Education: BA, MBA, Harvard University
Background: Managing Director, Harvard Private Capital Group; General Partner, Kohlberg & Co.; Partner, Weiss, Peck & Greer
Directorships: Cedar Creek, HDT Global, Horn Industrial Services, Southcross Energy, Varsity Brands
Michael R. Eisenson, Managing Director/Founding Partner
Education: BA, Economics, Williams College; MBA, JD, Yale University
Background: President, Harvard Private Capital Group; Managing Director, Harvard Management Company; Boston Consulting Group
Directorships: Blueknight Energy, DEI Holdings, Penske Auto Group, StoneCastle Partners, United Road Services
Michael Choe, Managing Director/CEO
Education: BA, Biology, Harvard University
Background: Harvard Private Capital Group; McKinsey & Company
Directorships: Acxiom ITO, DEI Holdings, Horn Industrial Services, Six Degrees, United Road Services, Zayo
Samuel Bartlett, Managing Director
Education: BA, History, Amherst College
Background: Bain & Company
Directorships: American Residential Services, HDT Global, Horn Industrial Services
J. Ryan Carroll, Managing Director
Education: BA, Economics, Harvard University
Background: LEK Consulting
Directorships: Acxiom ITO, DEI Holdings, Peacock Engineering, Six Degrees, Trojan Battery
Andrew S. Janower, Managing Director
Education: BS, Economics, Wharton School, University of Pennsylvania; MBA, Harvard University; CPA
Background: Harvard Private Capital Group; Research Associate, Harvard Business School; Consultant, Bain & Company
Directorships: American Residential Services, FULLBEAUTY Brands, WorldStrides, Varsity Brands
Joshua A. Klevens, Managing Director/COO
Education: BA, Woodrow Wilson School of Public Policy & International Affairs, Princeton University; MBA, Stanford University
Background: Bain Capital; Business Analyst, McKinsey & Company
Directorships: FULLBEAUTY Brands, HDT Global
Brandon C. White, Managing Director
Education: BA, Economics, Brigham Young University
Background: Harvard Private Capital Group; Business Analyst, McKinsey & Company
Directorships: Sightpath Medical, StoneCastle Partners, Trojan Battery, Varsity Brands, Vision Group Holdings
Mark Rosen, Co-Founder/Senior Advisor
Education: BA, Amherst College; JD, Yale University
Background: Managing Director, Harvard Private Capital Group; Principal, The Conifer Group; President, Morningside/North America Limited; Senior Partner, Hale and Dorr
Tim R. Palmer, Co-Founder/Senior Advisor
Education: BA, Purdue University; JD, University of Virginia; MBA, University of Chicago
Background: Managing Director, Harvard Private Capital Group; The Field Corporation; Sidley & Austin
Michael G. Thonis, Co-Founder/Senior Advisor
Education: BS, Geology, Syracuse University; MS, Geology, MIT; MBA, Harvard Business School
Background: Director of Research/Portfolio Management,

Venture Capital & Private Equity Firms / Domestic Firms

Harvard Management Company; Managing Director, Harvard Private Capital Group

459 CHART VENTURE PARTNERS
555 Fifth Avenue
19th Floor
New York, NY 10017

Phone: 212-350-8200
web: www.chartventure.com

Mission Statement: Chart Venture Partners invests in security related technologies with government and commercial applications. The firm invests in highly differentiated opportunities with large markets where value can be added through their industry experience, network of relationships and technology insight.

Fund Size: $100 million
Founded: 1994
Industry Group Preference: Homeland Security, Security, Aerospace, Defense and Government
Portfolio Companies: CoolIT, DisperSol, Flyby Media, GeoiQ, IntegriCo Composites, Nextreme Thermal Solutions, Ogmento, PacStar, PureEnergy Solutions, RemoteReality, Twisted Pair Solutions, WiSpry

Key Executives:
Christopher D. Brady, Founding Managing Partner
Education: BA, Middlebury College; MBA, Columbia University Graduate School of Business
Background: Lehman Brothers; Dillon Read
Chris Brady, Jr., Managing Partner
Education: BA, Yale University
Background: InSitech; Flyby Media
Directorships: CoolIT Systems, IntegriCo Composites, Flyby Media, Pacific Star Communications, RemoteReality

460 CHARTER LIFE SCIENCES
325 East Middlefield Road
Mountain View, CA 94043

Phone: 650-318-5411 Fax: 650-318-3425
web: www.clsvc.com

Mission Statement: Early-stage life sciences investor.

Fund Size: $300 million
Founded: 1982
Average Investment: $500,000-$5 million
Minimum Investment: $100,000
Investment Criteria: Early stage
Industry Group Preference: Life Sciences
Portfolio Companies: Amaranth Medical, MEI Pharma, CoMentis, EnteroMedics, Great Lakes Pharmaceuticals, Health Fidelity, Inviragen, Kereos, KFx Medical, Minimally Invasive Devices, Mirabilis Medica, Revascular Therapeutics, Visioneering Technologies, Xlumena

Other Locations:
3130 Highland Avenue
Suite 3A
Cincinnati, OH 45219
Phone: 513-475-6626

Key Executives:
A. Barr Dolan, Managing Partner
Education: BA, Chemistry, MS, Engineering, Cornell University; MBA, Stanford University; MA, Applied Science, Harvard University
Background: Arthur Andersen; CM Capital Corporation
Directorships: Heska Corporation, Integrated Biosystems, Metabolex, ShieldIP, UMD
Donald C. Harrison, Managing Partner
Education: BA, Birmingham Southern College; MD, University of Alabama School of Medicine; Honorary Doctor of Law Degree, Birmingham Southern College
Background: Senior VP/Provost Health Affairs, University of Cincinnati Medical Center; Chief of Department of Cardiology, Stanford University School of Medicine; Chief of Cardiology, Stanford University Hospital; Co-Director, Falk Cardiovascualr Research Center; President, AHA
Directorships: Co-Founder, EP Technologies; Co-Founder, Vesta; Founder, BIO/START; Kendle International; SciMed
Nelson Teng, Managing Partner
Education: Graduate of Postgraduate Program at the Stanford University Graduate School of Business; MD, University of Miami; PhD Biophysics, University of California Berkeley
Background: Chief Gynecologic Oncology, Stanford University School of Medicine; Research Scientist, MIT; President, Western Association Gynecological Oncology; Chairman, National Comprehensive Cancer Network

461 CHATTANOOGA RENAISSANCE FUND
201 W. Main Street
Suite 205
Chattanooga, TN 37408

e-mail: info@chattanoogarenaissancefund.com
web: chattanoogarenaissancefund.com

Mission Statement: To invest in seed and early-stage campnaies that display great habits and solid growth potential.

Geographic Preference: Chattanooga, Knoxville, Nashville, North Atlanta
Founded: 2010
Industry Group Preference: Diversified
Portfolio Companies: Collider, Vendor Registry, Branch Technology, Felt, TN Stillhouse, Aegle Gear, GreenPrint, Alumnify, Everly, BattleBin, Ambition Solutions, Blue Light, Rapid RMS, DataFlyte, XOEye Technologies, ReadyCart, PriceWaiter, Interntional Coffee Group, Iron Gaming, The Convenience Network, RecruitTalk, RentStuff, Tensor Surgical, Inova Payroll, Glenveigh Medical, RootsRated, Variable, Quickcue, Advanced Catheter Therapies, AudiencePoint, SupplyHog

Key Executives:
Miller Welborn, General Partner
Education: BA, Political Science & Government, University of Alabama
Background: Chairman, Cornerstone Community Bank; Chairman, SmartFinancial; President, Welborn Transport, Boyd Bros. Transportation; Co-Founder, Lamp Post Group; Chairman, Big Oak Ranch
Directorships: Federal Reserve Board of Atlanta

462 CHAZEN CAPITAL PARTNERS
150 East 58th Street
27th Floor
New York, NY 10155

Phone: 212-888-7800 Fax: 212-888-4580
e-mail: info@chazen.com
web: www.chazen.com

Mission Statement: Established in 1997, Chazen Capital Partners offers support and equity capital to economy businesses across a variety of sectors.

Founded: 1997
Industry Group Preference: Consumer Products, Consumer Services, Technology, Software
Portfolio Companies: 7thOnline, Black Book Magazine, eChalk.com, Kalisaya, LivePerson, Naked, Nerve, Nina McLemore, Return Path, Verterra

Key Executives:
Jerome A Chazen, Founder/Chairman
Education: University of Wisconsin; MBA, Columbia Business School
Background: Chairman, Liz Claiborne Inc.
Directorships: Taubman Centers Inc.
David F Chazen, Managing Director
Education: BS, Wharton School, University of Pennsylvania; MBA, Columbia Business School

Venture Capital & Private Equity Firms / Domestic Firms

Background: President, The Good Stuff Company; Principal, JLB Capital Partners; Manager, Strategic Government Partners; Goldman Sachs
Directorships: Jazz Aspen
Sid Banon, Managing Director
Education: BS, Accounting, State University of New York at Albany
Background: Co-Founder, The Good Stuff Company; Co-Founder, Win Stuff; Sony Corporation of America; Gulf & Western; Citicorp

463 CHB CAPITAL PARTNERS
299 Milwaukee Street
Suite 450
Denver, CO 80206

Phone: 303-571-0100 Fax: 303-571-0114
web: www.chbcapital.com

Mission Statement: Provide closely held and family-owned businesses with the equity capital and expertise for smooth ownership transition and sustained growth.
Geographic Preference: United States
Fund Size: $75 million
Founded: 1995
Average Investment: $5 - $15 million
Minimum Investment: $5 million
Investment Criteria: Leveraged Recapitalizations, Management-Led Buyouts, Growth Equity Investments
Industry Group Preference: Niche Manufacturing, Distribution
Portfolio Companies: Blu Dot, CanGen, Logic PD, Sorrento Networks, Alternative Technology Inc., Brandbase Holdings Inc., Champion Technologies Inc., HiRel Systems LLC, MACTEC, Newline Products Inc., Shoe Corp. of America, Spyder Active Sports, Trussway Holdings Inc., USA Capital Holdings Inc., Valent Aerostructures

Key Executives:
John W. Flanigan, Managing Partner
e-mail: jwflanigan@chbcapital.com
Education: BA, English & Economics, Amherst College; MBA, Harvad Business School
Background: Bain & Company; Cannon Associates
Thomas L. Kelly II, Managing Partner
e-mail: tlkelly@chbcapital.com
Education: BA, Economics, BS, Administrative Sciences, Yale University; MBA, Harvard Business School
Background: Bass Brothers; Richard Rainwater
David J. Anderson, Chief Financial Officer
e-mail: djanderson@chbcapital.com
Education: BA, Accounting, University of Wisconsin
Background: Independent Consultant; Financial Management, Capital Associates and Systems Marketing; Management Consultant, Ernst Whinney; Internal Auditing/Systems Development, Los Alamos National Laboratory; CPA

464 CHEROKEE & WALKER
6440 South Wasatch Blvd
Suite 200
Salt Lake City, UT 84121

Phone: 801-278-7800 Fax: 801-278-7818
web: cherokeeandwalker.com

Portfolio Companies: Green Light Auto Solutions, TopNoggin, Rimrock Construction, Red Bridge Capital, inthinc, Gold's Gym, Rockworth Companies, Vital Signs Staffing, Visible Equity, Campus Book Rentals, Financial Guard, Fortius Financial, Cornerstone Concrete, SYMBII, Wentworth Senior Living Services, Cottonwood Capital

Key Executives:
Shane R. Peery, Partner
e-mail: shane@cherokeeandwalker.com
Education: BS, MS, Accounting, Brigham Young University
Background: Ernst & Young
Paul K. Erickson, Partner
e-mail: paul@cherokeeandwalker.com
Education: BS, Accounting, Brigham Young University
Background: SunGard, IBM
J. Blair Jenkins, Partner
e-mail: blair@cherokeeandwalker.com
Education: BS, University of Utah; MS, Real Estate Development, Columbia University
Brent Wilson, Partner
e-mail: brent@cherokeeandwalker.com
Background: Progressive Finance LLC

465 CHEROKEE INVESTMENT PARTNERS
310 South West Street
Suite 200
Raleigh, NC 27603

Phone: 919-743-2500 Fax: 919-743-2501
web: www.cherokeefund.com

Mission Statement: To acquire environmentally impaired assets and protect sellers from the associated risks and liabilities. Cherokee invests through both private equity and venture capital.
Geographic Preference: North America, Europe
Fund Size: $2 billion
Founded: 1984
Average Investment: $130 million
Minimum Investment: $10 million
Investment Criteria: Primary and Secondary Markets
Industry Group Preference: Industrial Services, Manufacturing, Research & Development, Property Management, Real Estate, Commercial Services

Key Executives:
Bret Batchelder, Managing Director
e-mail: bbatchelder@cherokeefund.com
Education: BA, Morehead Scholar, University of North Carolina; MBA, JL Kellogg Graduate School of Management, Northwestern University; CPA; CFA; NC Real Estate License
Background: VP Mergers/Acquisitions, First Union Securities; Associate, Goldman, Sachs & Company; Portfolio Manager, Bank South N.A.
Tom Darden, Founder & CEO
919-743-2500
e-mail: tdarden@cherokeefund.com
Education: BA, Morehead Scholar, MRP, University of North Carolina; JD, Yale Law School
Background: Cherokee Sanford Group; Consultant, Bain & Company; Research Triangle Transit Authority; NC Board of Transportation
Directorships: Woodberry Forest School; Shaw University; University of North Carolina Environmental Department; REIT, Winston Hotels; Research Triangle Institute
John Mazzarino, Founder & Managing Principal
e-mail: jmazzarino@cherokeefund.com
Education: BA, Phi Beta Kappa, Colgate University; MS, Sloan School of Management, MIT
Background: Cherokee Sanford Group; President, Hackney Holdings; Carolina Ceramics; Manager, Bain & Company; Peat, Marwick, Mitchell & Company
Directorships: Center for Sustainable Enterprise, Kenan-Flagler School of Business; Oak Ranch Children's Home; Hometown America
Steven Hartanto, Senior Associate
Education: BA, Economics & Chinese Studies, Occidental College
Elizabeth Merritt, Managing Director
Education: BA, Economics & English, University of North Carolina, Chapel Hill
Background: Associate, Leveraged Finance Group, Goldman, Sachs & Co

Venture Capital & Private Equity Firms / Domestic Firms

466 CHERRY TREE COMPANIES
301 Carlson Parkway
Suite 103
Minnetonka, MN 55305

Phone: 952-893-9012
e-mail: info@cherrytree.com
web: www.cherrytree.com

Mission Statement: Cherry Tree provides investment banking services to middle market businesses and raises capital for growth companies through private placements.

Founded: 1980
Investment Criteria: Middle Market, Recapitalizations, Acquisitions, Growth Capital

Key Executives:
  Tony Christianson, Managing General Partner
  e-mail: tchristianson@cherrytree.com
  Education: BS, St. John's University; MBA, Harvard Business School
  Background: VP, Norwest Venture Capital; Consultant, Arthur Andersen
  Directorships: AmeriPride Services, Arctic Cat, Capella Education Company, Computer Petroleum Corporation, The Dolan Company, J3 Learning, Titan Machinery
  Gordon Stofer, Managing General Partner
  e-mail: gstofer@cherrytree.com
  Education: BS, Industrial Engineering, Cornell University; MBA, Harvard Business School
  Background: VP, Norwest Venture Capital; Marketing Manager, Honeywell; Westinghouse; Maine National Bank
  Directorships: VEE Corporation, Bright Start, Buffets, DataMyte Corporation, FilmTec, Harmony Brook, Insignia Systems, MakeMusic, National Information Systems
  Chuck Gorman, Senior Executive Director
  e-mail: cgorman@cherrytree.com
  Education: BA, Business, University of St. Thomas
  Background: President & CEO, Kobixx Systems; President, KnowledgeSoft; President & CEO, J3 Learning; Executive Vice President, Wilson Learning
  Chad Johnson, Managing Director
  e-mail: cjohnson@cherrytree.com
  Education: BA, MBA, University of Minnesota
  Background: VP, The M&A Group; General Manager, Ultralingua; Manager, Business Development, PLATO Learning; Venture Capital Analyst, Sherpa Partners
  Dave Latzke, Managing Director
  e-mail: dlatzke@cherrytree.com
  Education: BA, Accounting, University of Northern Iowa
  Background: SVP & CFO, SoftBrands; EVP & CFO, Fourth Shift Corporation; Manager, Arthur Andersen & Co.
  Elmer Baldwin, Senior Executive Director
  e-mail: ebaldwin@cherrytree.com
  Education: BBA, Finance, Loyola Marymount University
  Background: President & CEO, Internet Broadcasting Systems; SVP, Fujitsu Consulting; President & CEO, BORN Information Services; President & CEO, Nuvolution
  Directorships: Lifesprk, EA Sween Company, FileControl International
  Jane Bortnem, Chief Financial Officer
  e-mail: jbortnem@cherrytree.com
  Education: BS, Accounting, Minnesota State University
  Background: Consultant & Audit Manager, Boulay Heutmaker Zibell & Company; Accountant, Pepin Heights
  Mik Gusenius, Director
  e-mail: mgusenius@cherrytree.com
  Education: BA, Economics & Scandinavian Studies, Gustavus Adolphus College; MBA, Carlson School of Management, University of Minnesota
  Background: Analyst, Bayview Capital Group; Managing Director, Carlson Fixed-Income Fund; Assistant Director, The Gustavus Fund, Gustavus Adolphus College
  Mike Buttry, Senior Executive Director
  e-mail: mbuttry@cherrytree.com
  Education: BS, Creighton University
  Background: VP of Public Affairs and Strategy, Capella Education Company; Entrepreneur-In-Residence, Whiteboard Advisors; Managing Director, Chlopak Leonard & Schecter
  Directorships: Capella University; Angel Foundation; Shank Institute for Innovation in Education

467 CHESTNUT HILL PARTNERS
520 Madison Avenue
3rd Floor
New York, NY 10022

Phone: 212-687-3123 Fax: 212-972-2921
e-mail: info@chestnuthillpartners.com
web: www.chestnuthillpartners.com

Mission Statement: Chestnut Hill Partners is an investment banking boutique specializing in merger and acquisition originations for private equity investors.

Portfolio Companies: ERC Wiping Products Inc., Ecoscape Solutions, Caring People, Krauss Craft, Spill Magic Inc., Construction Labor Contractors, Sprayglo, Superior Contract Cleaners, Natural Balance Pet Foods Inc., Greg C. Rigamer & Associates, Contessa Premium Foods Inc., Berry Family Nurseries, DCS Sanitation Management, Uno Restaurant Holdings Corp., Granny's Kitchen Ltd., Crompco Corp., American Furniture Manufacturing, Compression Polymers Group, Andrews International Inc., Polar Plastics Ltd., Beckett Corp., Saisha Tehnology, Action Labs Inc., Contract Services Limited, ADS Technologies Inc., Advance Technology Services, Hickery Farms, Roscoe Manufacturing, AD-Tech Plastic Systems, K.G. Box Inc., Spacetec IMC Corp., Remco Maintenance Corp., Hooven Heat Treating, Michigan Induction Inc., Meer Corp., Buckner Equipment Rental, Chemseco, Merlin 200,000 Mile, American Stencil, Brentax Inc., Four Star Lighting Co., American Products Co., Compressor Controls Corp., Chamberlain Gard

Key Executives:
  Paul L. Schaye, Managing Director
  Education: BA, PhD, Business, University of Massachusetts
  Background: Consultant, A.T. Kearney and Booz Allen & Hamilton
  Jeff Davidson, Managing Director
  Education: University of Delaware
  Background: Managed Accounts Advisor, SEI; Co-Founder, Cathedral Partners; Director, Head of Americas, Palico
  David Rowley, Managing Director
  Education: University of Delaware
  Background: Co-Founder & Partner, Cathedral Partners; Vice President, SRS Capital
  Daniel Terpak, Director
  Education: BS, Villanova University

468 CHEVRON TECHNOLOGY VENTURES
1500 Lousiana
39th Floor
Houston, TX 77002

e-mail: techventures@chevron.com
web: www.chevron.com/technology/technology-ventures

Mission Statement: Identifies new technologies and business opportunities that can create value for Chevron. Then, using disciplined venture capital practices, Chevron invests in those opportunities that promise clear competitive advantages and superior financial returns.

Fund Size: $250 million
Founded: 1999
Investment Criteria: Early Stage, Mid Stage
Industry Group Preference: Technology, Energy, Power Technologies, Information Technology, Biotechnology,

Venture Capital & Private Equity Firms / Domestic Firms

Networking, Oil & Gas, Alternative Energy, Advanced Materials, Communications, Networking
Portfolio Companies: Acumentrics, Amphora, Apprion, Arisdyne, BlueArc, BrightSource Energy, Codexis, Cubility, DeepFlex, DynaPump, Ember Resources, Five Star Technologies, Frictionless Commerce, Foro Energy, Inficomm, Ironport Systems, Konarka Technologies, MetaCarta, Microfabrica, MicroSeismic, Moblize, Network International, Nimbus, OsComp Systems, Oxane, PanGeo Subsea, Panzura, PathScale, Production Science, Radiance Technologies, Reality Mobile, Sample6 Technologies, SchemaLogic, Silixa, Soane Energy, SpectraSensors, Spotfire, Southwest Windpower, Stingray Digital, Sub-One Technology, Tacit Technologies, Teros, TradeCapture, Tubel Technologies, Xenogen, Zi-Lift

Key Executives:
  Richard Pardoe, Venture Executive
  Education: BS, Chemical Engineering, University of California, Davis
  Background: Process Engineer, Chevron; Principal, Chevron Technology Ventures

469 CHEYENNE CAPITAL
1430 Wynkoop Street
Suite 200
Denver, CO 80202

Phone: 303-454-5453
e-mail: contact@cheyennefund.com
web: www.cheyennefund.com

Mission Statement: Private equity firm in Denver, Colorado.
Geographic Preference: United States
Investment Criteria: LBO, Recapitalizations, Expansion or Growth Equity
Industry Group Preference: Manufacturing, Financial Services, Business Products & Services, Consumer Products, Consumer Services, Media, Energy

Key Executives:
  John Fitzgerald, Managing Director & Co-Founder
  Education: BS, SUNY Oneonta; JD, New England School of Law
  Background: Partner, Kirkland & Ellis
  Brian Knitt, Managing Director
  Education: BS, Mathematics, Colorado State University; MS, Systems Management, University of Southern California; MBA, UCLA Anderson School of Management
  Background: Meritage Funds; Officer, U.S. Air Force
  Mike West, Chief Financial Officer
  Education: BS, Accounting, MBA, University of Denver; CPA
  Background: Arthur Andersen LLP
  Phil Parrott, Co-Founder
  Education: BA, Colorado State University; JD, University of Colorado
  Background: Chief Deputy District Attorney, Denver District Attorney's Office; Partner, Kirkland & Ellis

470 CHICAGO GROWTH PARTNERS
Attn: Parker Gale Suite 2.02
222 Merchandise Mart
12th Floor
Chicago, IL 60654

Phone: 312-698-6300 Fax: 312-201-0703
e-mail: info@cgp.com
web: www.cgp.com

Mission Statement: Helps companies achieve their goals by providing expansion and buyout capital, to create success for companies, their managers and investors.
Average Investment: $5 - $25 million
Investment Criteria: Middle-Market, Expansion Capital, Buyout Capital
Industry Group Preference: Education, Business Products & Services, Consumer Services, Healthcare, Healthcare Services, Industrial Services, Technology-Enabled Services, Industrial Technology
Portfolio Companies: 2Checkout, AC Lordi, Advanced Pain Management, Airpax, AnaJet, Benetech, Caprion Proteomics, CLP Resources, Compete, Comtempo Ceramic Tile, CryoCor, Daisytek International, DJ Pharma, eInstruction, Encore Paper, EndoGastric Solutions, FineLine Technologies, Footprint Retail Services, Genoptix, HouseValues, Jonathan Engineered Services, Lanx, Marathon Data Systems, Morton Grove Pharmaceuticals, NuVasive, Paramount Services, PharmaResearch, Point Biomedical, PRIMIS Marketing Group, Royall & Company, SchoolMessenger, Scribe America, Specialized Education Services, TargeGen, Teaching Strategies, The Tie Bar, U.S. Education Corporation, World 50, Workwave, Zogenix

Key Executives:
  David G Chandler, Managing Partner
  e-mail: dchandler@cgp.com
  Education: BA, Princeton University; MBA, Amos Tuck School, Dartmouth
  Background: Managing Director, William Blair Capital Partners; Investment Banking, Morgan Stanley
  Robert P Healy, Managing Partner
  e-mail: rhealy@cgp.com
  Education: United States Military Academy, West Point; MBA, Harvard Business School
  Background: Managing Director, William Blair Capital Partners; General Partner, ClearLight Partners; Principal, William E Simon & Sons
  Directorships: ABC Window Company, Advanced Pain Management, Aimnet Solutions, Apripax Corporation, AnaJet, Benetech, Contempo Ceramic Tile, eInstruction Corp., Footprint Retail Services
  Arda M Minocherhomjee, Managing Partner
  e-mail: arda@cgp.com
  Education: MS, Pharmacology, University of Toronto; PhD, MBA, University of British Columbia
  Background: Managing Director, William Blair Captial Partners; Senior Healthcare Analyst, William Blair & Company
  Directorships: Advanced Pain Management, DJ Pharma, EndoGastric Solutions, Genoptix, Lanx, Morton Grove Pharmaceuticals, NuVasive, PharmaResearch Corporation, Proteon, TargeGen, Zogenix
  Devin Mathews, Managing Partner
  e-mail: dmathews@cgp.com
  Education: BA, State University of New York, Binghamton; MBA, Tuck School of Business, Dartmouth
  Background: Baird Venture Partners, Great Hill Partners, William Blair Capital Partners
  Directorships: World 50, Vigo Remittance Corporation, Fellon-Mccord & Associates, Arroweye Solutions, LatinVest, TrueAdvantage, Encover, Payroll Associates
  Robert D Blank, Partner
  e-mail: rblank@cgp.com
  Education: BA, Economics, Miami University; MBA, Kellogg School of Management, Northwestern University
  Background: Managing Director, William Blair Capital Partnes; Partner, Private Market Group, Brinson Partners; Investment Manager, Wind Point Partners
  Directorships: AC Lordi Financial Services, Alternative Resources Corporation, Contractors Labor Pool, Cypress Medical Products, DJ Pharma, Jefferson-Wells, PRIMIS Marketing Group
  Timothy M Murray, Partner
  e-mail: tmurray@cgp.com
  Education: BA, Duke University; MBA, University of Chicago
  Background: Managing Director, William Blair Capital Partners
  Directorships: Airpax Holdings, CES, Compete, Daisytek Corp., Engineered Materials Corp., Extended Care Info.

Venture Capital & Private Equity Firms / Domestic Firms

Network, Paramount Services, Sanford Corp., TimePlus Payroll, Towne Holdings
James F Milbery, Operating Partner
e-mail: jmilbery@cgp.com
Education: BS, Management, Babson College
Background: Director, Competitive Intelligence, Oracle Corporation; Compuware; Computer Associates; Elevon; Digital Equipment Corporation
Jeff Farrero, Principal
e-mail: jfarrero@cgp.com
Education: BS, University of Illinois; MBA, Kellogg School of Management, Northwestern University
Background: Associate, Credit Suisse First Boston
Directorships: Airpax, AnaJet, Benetech, eInstruction, FineLine Technologies, Footprint Retail Services, Royall & Company, Specialized Education Services, Teaching Strategies
Kristina Heinze, Principal
e-mail: kheinze@cgp.com
Education: BS, Finance, University of Illinois
Background: Analsyt, Credit Suisse First Boston
Directorships: 2Checkout, Paramount Services, Contempo Ceramic Tile, Specialized Education Services, The Plastics Group, Union Corrugating
Sean Barrette, Principal
e-mail: sbarrette@cgp.com
Education: BS, SUNY Binghamton; MBA, Booth School of Business
Background: Associate & Analyst, Credit Suisse; Staff Accountant, Ernst & Young
Directorships: Advanced Pain Management, Caprion Proteomics
Ryan Milligan, Principal
e-mail: rmilligan@cgp.com
Education: BS, Management, Boston College; MBA, Kellogg School of Management
Background: Investment Banking, Analyst, Robert W Baird
Directorships: 2Checkout, Jonathan Engineered Solutions, Marathon Data Systems, SchoolMessenger, World50

471 CHICAGO PACIFIC FOUNDERS
980 North Michigan Ave.
Suite 1998
Chicago, IL 60611

Phone: 312-273-4750
e-mail: info@cpfounders.com
web: www.cpfounders.com

Mission Statement: Chicago Pacific Founders manages private funds with an exclusive interest in healthcare services. Chicago Pacific Founders is actively seeking to partner with companies that are dedicated to providing high quality healthcare services to patients, providers, and payers.

Industry Group Preference: Healthcare
Portfolio Companies: CPF Living Communities; Florida Elite Medical Group; It's Never 2 Late; Marquee Dental Partners; P3 Health Partners; Pinnacle Dermatology; Recovery Ways, Sage, SightMD

Other Locations:
135 Main St.
Suite 1350
San Francisco, CA 94111
Phone: 415-539-0630

Key Executives:
Mary Tolan, Founder/Managing Partner
Education: BBA, Loyola University; MBA, University of Chicago
Background: Founder, Accretive Health; Group Chief Executive, Accenture
Vance Vanier, Founder/Managing Partner
Education: MD, Johns Hopkins School of Medicine; MBA, Stanford University

Background: President, Verinata Health; CEO, Navigenics; Partner, Mohr Davidow Ventures

472 CHICAGO VENTURE PARTNERS LP
303 E Wacker Drive
Suite 1040
Chicago, IL 60601

Phone: 312-297-7000 Fax: 312-819-9701
web: www.chicagoventure.com

Mission Statement: Chicago Venture Partners helps entrepreneurs build successful technology companies. The firm seeks companies that have the potential to achieve leading positions in their industry. In addition to providing capital, Chicago Venture Partners works with its portfolio companies to provide advice on competitive positioning, establish strategic alliances, recruit key management and forge other key relationships.

Geographic Preference: United States
Fund Size: $45 million
Founded: 1998
Average Investment: $500,000 - $10 million
Investment Criteria: Emerging, Growth Stage, Small Cap
Industry Group Preference: Internet Technology, E-Commerce & Manufacturing, Software, Information Technology, Telecommunications, Consumer Products, Applications Software & Services, Networking, Equipment, Computer Related, Media, Energy
Portfolio Companies: Emergent Trading, Miller Fabrication, Pulse Systems, Typenex Medical,

Key Executives:
John Fife, Managing Partner
Education: BS, Statistics & Computer Science, Brigham Young University; MBA, Harvard Business School
Background: President, CEO & Chairman, Utah Resources International; Assistant VP, Continental Illinois Venture Corporation; Consultant, Oracle Corporation
Directorships: Edwards Trucking, Typenex Medical, Pulse Systems
Colin Robinson, Senior Associate
Education: BS, Management, Brigham Young University
Background: Consultant, Accenture
Tina Saxton, Project Manager
Education: University of Denver
Background: Assistant VP, Private Equity Fund Services, JPMorgan Chase; KPMG
Christopher R Stalcup, Associate
Education: BA, Finance & Economics, University of Illinois at Urbana-Champaign; CFA
Background: VP, Northern Trust Hedge Fund Services; Associate, Omnium

473 CHICAGO VENTURES
222 West Merchandise Mart Plaza
Suite 1212
Chicago, IL 60654

e-mail: info@chicagoventures.com
web: chicagoventures.com

Mission Statement: Chicago Ventures invests in well-managed seed-stage technology companies in Chicago and the Greater Midwest that have demonstrated a value proposition in a given market for their product or services.

Geographic Preference: Midwest
Founded: 2011
Average Investment: $750K - $1 million
Investment Criteria: Seed
Industry Group Preference: Analytics & Analytical Instruments, Business to Business, Sales & Marketing SaaS, Payments & Financial Services, Healthcare Information Technology, Marketplace/On-Demand Services, Loyalty
Portfolio Companies: Donde, Rocketmiles, Spring, Catalyze.io, MdotLabs, BloomNation, TempoDB, FindIt, Zipments, Blitsy, Pangea, Picturelife, Betterfly, Cartavi,

Venture Capital & Private Equity Firms / Domestic Firms

Shiftgig, Kapow Events, UpCity, SimpleRelevance, Retrofit, HealthFinch, Food Genius, Power2Switch

Key Executives:
Rob Chesney, Partner
Education: BA, McGill University; MBA, Kellogg School of Management, Northwestern University
Background: Associate, Lehman Brothers; VP of Buyer Experience & Verticals, eBay; COO, Trunk Club
Directorships: CoPilot; Cameo; LandscapeHub; TaskRabbit
Stuart Larkins, Partner
Education: BS, Southern Methodist University
Background: Branch Manager, Penske Logistics; Founder/Managing Director, Twin Capital;
Directorships: Ureeka; Forager; Veryable; Sunbit; Meritize; Project44; PerformLine Inc.; G2 Crowd; itemMaster; Shedd Aquarium; Spring Marketplace; Shiftgig; Trunk Club; Netconcepts

474 CHINAROCK CAPITAL MANAGEMENT VENTURES
475 Sansome St.
Suite 730
San Francisco, CA 94111

Phone: 415-578-5700
e-mail: vc@crcm.com
web: www.crcmvc.com

Mission Statement: Invests in startup companies in the areas of artificial intelligence, machine learning, augmented reality, virtual reality, emerging media, financial technology, blockchain, and smart cities. Has additional offices in Palo Alto, CA, and in China.
Geographic Preference: Global
Fund Size: $158 Million
Founded: 2006
Investment Criteria: Early Stage, Startup, Tech
Industry Group Preference: Artificial Intelligence, Machine Learning, Emerging Media, Financial Technology, Blockchain, Smart Cities
Portfolio Companies: Agentiq, Airy:3D, Arraiy, Baobab Studios, Cargo, Chariot, Civil Maps, Deep Motion, Drone Racing League, Fan AI, Felix & Paul, Gamer Sensei, Ming Yi Zhu Dao, Musical.ly, Orbeus, Ripple, Roam, Senyi, Sonavex, Vreal, Youku

Key Executives:
Chun Ding, Managing Partner
Education: BA, Economics, Middlebury College; MBA, Harvard Business School
Background: Farallon Capital Management; The Goldman Sachs Group, Inc.
Toby Zhang, Partner
Education: BA, MA, University of Michigan; MBA, The Wharton School, University of Pennsylvania
Background: Tradeversity Inc.; NBC Universal; Microsoft; Edison Partners
Matt Lee, Partner
Education: BE, MA, University of New South Wales; MBA, New York University; MBA, London Business School
Background: MacQuarie Group; Capco; authentiQ; Pobble; Pereg Ventures
Jessica Ngo, Partner/CFO
Education: BA, Economics, University of California, Berkeley
Background: Primarius Capital

475 CHINAVEST
P.O. Box 170985
San Francisco, CA 94147

e-mail: info@chinavest.com.cn
web: www.chinavest.com

Mission Statement: To provide long-term investment capital and management expertise to growing companies doing business in or with the economies of Greater China: China, Hong Kong and Taiwan.
Geographic Preference: Greater China
Founded: 1981
Average Investment: $5 million
Minimum Investment: $3 million
Investment Criteria: Early-Stage, Expansion Stage, Acquisitions, Buyouts
Industry Group Preference: Logistics, Healthcare, Media, Manufacturing, Telecommunications, Information Technology, Consumer Services
Portfolio Companies: AGI, Arima Communications, AsiaInfo, Brinks Home Security, Chubb, Clearwater, Coca-Cola, Danone, Domino's Pizza, evian, First Quality, Fosun, Heineken, Heinz, HNA Group, Hodo, Honeywell, IBM, ITW, John Deere, Kellogg Company, McDonald's, PrimeCredit Limited, Rockwekll Automation, Santa Fe Relocation, Suning.com, TGI Fridays, Valeo, Wendy's, XCMG

Other Locations:
19-27 Wyndham Street
Room 1103
Wilson House
Central
Hong Kong
Phone: 852-28101638 Fax: 852-28683788

Beijing China Resources Building
5th Floor, No. 8 Jian Guo Men Bei Avenue
Suite 508B
Beijing 100005
China
Phone: 8610-85191535 Fax: 8610-85191530

2801 Huaihai International Plaza
1045 Huaihai Middle Road
Xuhui Distric
Shanghai 200031
China
Phone: 8621-63232255 Fax: 8621-63293951

Key Executives:
Robert A Theleen, Chairman/CEO
Education: BA, Duquesne University; MBA, Thunderbird School of Global Management
Directorships: Beijing Enterprises
Jenny Hsui, President
Education: University of Singapore
André Dallaire, Senior Managing Director & COO
Education: BS, Business Adminstration and Management, Université Laval
Background: CEO, Chubb; Senior Vice President, Asia Pacific; AIG;
Kenneth Petrilla, Managing Director
Education: BA, Business Administration and Management, Bowling Green State University; MA, Golden Gate University
Background: U.S. Representative, American Chamber of Commerce in Shanghai; Executive Director, California-China Office of Trade and Investment; Executive Vice President, Wells Fargo
Steve Nelson, Vice President
e-mail: snelson@chinavest.com.cn
Education: BS, Business, Chapman University
Background: Halter Financial Services; Sterne Agee; The Seidler Companies

476 CHL MEDICAL PARTNERS
2507 Post Road
Southport, CT 06890

Phone: 203-324-7700 Fax: 203-724-1999
e-mail: info@chlmedical.com
web: www.chlmedical.com

Venture Capital & Private Equity Firms / Domestic Firms

Mission Statement: Create opportunities for entrepreneurs who have the skills necessary to build leading companies. We invest at the seed, start-up phases of companies, frequently as the lead investor. As portfolio companies grow, we continue our active support at the board level and through follow-on financings.

Geographic Preference: United States
Fund Size: $250 million
Founded: 1990
Average Investment: $4 million
Minimum Investment: $250,000
Investment Criteria: Startup, Early Stage
Industry Group Preference: Biotechnology, Pharmaceuticals, Genomics, Healthcare, Drug Development, Diagnostics, Medical Devices, Health Related, Instrumentation
Portfolio Companies: Ambra Health, Care Management Technologies, Inc., CareWell Urgent Care, Comprehensive Clinical Development, DICOM Grid, Ella Health, Fidelis Seniorcare, MedMark Services, Millenium Pharmacy Systems

Key Executives:
  Jeffrey J Collinson, Partner
  e-mail: jcollinson@chlmedical.com
  Education: Degree in Economics, Yale University; MBA Harvard Business School
  Background: Baxter International, Inc.
  Timothy F Howe, Partner
  203-324-7700 x223
  e-mail: thowe@chlmedical.com
  Education: BA, MBA, Columbia University
  Background: Schroder Ventures, Collinson Howe Venture Partners, Biotechnology Investment Group
  Gregory M Weinhoff MD, Partner
  e-mail: gweinhoff@chlmedical.com
  Education: Harvard College, Harvard Medical School, Harvard Business School
  Background: Whitney & Company, Fidelity Select Biotechnology, Healthcare Corporate Finance Group at Morgan Stanley & Company
  Myles D Greenberg, Partner
  e-mail: mgreenberg@chlmedical.com
  Education: BAS, University of Pennsylvania, MD, Yale University, MBA, Harvard Business School
  Background: A.M. Pappas & Associates, Assistant Professor At University Of North Carolina School Of Medicine, Assistant Clincial Director, Beth Israel Deaconess Medical Center
  Directorships: CareWell Urgent Care Centers

477 CHRYSALIS VENTURES
101 S Fifth Street
Suite 1650
Louisville, KY 40202-3122

Phone: 502-583-7644
e-mail: info@chrysalisventures.com
web: www.chrysalisventures.com

Mission Statement: Chrysalis Ventures is a leading source of equity capital for young, growing companies in Mid-America. Chrysalis invests primarily in early-and growth-stage Healthcare and Technology companies.

Geographic Preference: Midwest, South
Fund Size: $400 million
Founded: 1993
Average Investment: $3 - $5 million
Minimum Investment: $2 million
Investment Criteria: Early-Stage, Expansion-Stage
Industry Group Preference: Healthcare, Technology
Portfolio Companies: AfterBOT, Connecture, Edj Analytics, Foundation Radiology Group, GoNoodle, Health Information Designs, Intervention Insights, ITC Compounding Pharmacy, Lucina Health, MeQuilibrium, MyHealthDIRECT, Regent Education, StraighterLine, Xlerant

Key Executives:
  David Jones, Jr., Chairman/Managing Director
  Education: BA, Yale University; JD, Yale University Law School
  Background: Chairman, Humana, Inc.; US Department of State Legal Adviser; Commercial Banker, Bank of Boston
  Wright Steenrod, Partner
  Education: BA, Princeton University
  Background: Ygnition; Genscape; Appriss; VP, Business Development, Darwin Networks; SunTrust Bank; US Marine Corps
  Directorships: bCatalyst, Inc., Cybera Inc., Information Outfitters
  Charlie Crawford, Vice President
  Education: BA, Williams College
  Background: Innova Memphis

478 CI CAPITAL PARTNERS
500 Park Avenue
8th Floor
New York, NY 10022

Phone: 212-752-1850 **Fax:** 212-832-9450
e-mail: info@cicapllc.com
web: www.cicapllc.com

Mission Statement: CI Capital Partners, formerly Caxton-Iseman Capital, is a leading private equity investment firm specializing in leveraged buyouts of middle market companies located primarily in North America.

Geographic Preference: North America
Founded: 1993
Average Investment: $50 - 100 million
Investment Criteria: Leveraged Buyouts
Industry Group Preference: Consumer Services, Business Products & Services, Distribution, Government, Aerospace, Defense and Government, Light Manufacturing
Portfolio Companies: AlliedPRA, Epiphany Dermatology, Galls, Hero Digital, Impact Group, Maroon Group, Pivot Physical Therapy, Ply Gem Industries, SavATree, Simplified Logistics, Summit Companies, Tech Air

Key Executives:
  Frederick J Iseman, Chairman & Chief Executive Officer
  Education: BA, English Literature, Yale University
  Background: Chairman, Anteon International Corporation; Hambro International Equity Partners
  Directorships: Conney Safety Products, KIK Custom Products, CoVant Technologies, American Residential Services, Ply Gem Industries
  Jordan S. Bernstein, General Counsel
  Education: BA, History, University of Pennsylvania; JD, Havard Law School
  Background: General Counsel, AGM Partners; Associate General Counsel, Wasserstein Perello & Co.; M&A, Paul, Weiss, Rifkind, Wharton & Garrison
  Timothy T. Hall, Managing Director
  Education: BS, Lehigh University; MBA, Columbia Business School
  Background: Vice President, Frontline Capital; Assistant Vice President, GE Equity
  Directorships: KIK Custom Products, Prodigy Health Group, Ply Gem Industries
  Joost F. Thesseling, Managing Director
  Education: BA, Economics, MBA, Erasmus University School of Economics, Rotterdam
  Background: Director, Transplace; Director, Valley National Gases

Venture Capital & Private Equity Firms / Domestic Firms

479 CIC PARTNERS
3879 Maple Ave.
Suite 400
Dallas, TX 75219

Phone: 214-871-6812 Fax: 214-880-4491
e-mail: info@cicpartners.com
web: www.cicpartners.com

Mission Statement: As a mid-market private equity firm, Dallas-based CIC Partners has invested in more than 40 companies with revenues of $10 million to $1 billion in industries including energy exploration, food, healthcare services, restaurants and retail.

Average Investment: $5 - $100 million
Investment Criteria: Growth Capital, Recapitalizations, Buyouts
Industry Group Preference: Energy, Food & Beverage, Healthcare Services, Restaurants, Retail, Consumer & Leisure
Portfolio Companies: Activa Resources, Castex Energy, CIC Minerals, Continental Structural Plastics, Cornerstone Automation Systems, CraftMark Bakery, Dale Gas Partners, DynaGrid Construction Group, East Hampton Sandwich Co., Granite City Food & Brewery, L&L Foods, Magnolia Petroleum Co., OmniSYS, Pogo Resources, Red Mango, River Point Farms, RMX Resources, Schuepbach Energy, Select Product Group, Taco Mac, Tiff's Treats, Willie's Grill & Icehouse

Key Executives:
Fouad Bashour, Founding Partner
214-871-6825
Education: BA, Duke University
Background: The Boston Consulting Group
Directorships: Granite City Food & Brewery, Schuepbach Energy, Willie's Grill & Icehouse
Marshall Payne, Founding Partner
214-871-6807
Education: BS, Stanford University; MBA, Harvard Business School
Background: Cardinal Investment Company
Directorships: Activa Resources, CraftMark Bakery, Pogo Resources, RMX Resources, Schuepbach Energy
Michael Rawlings, Founding Partner
214-871-6864
Education: BA, Boston College
Background: President, Pizza Hut; CEO, DDB Needham Dallas Group; CEO, Legends Hospitality Management
Directorships: Willie's Grill & Icehouse

480 CID CAPITAL
10201 N. Illinois St.
Suite 200
Indianapolis, IN 46290

Phone: 317-818-5030 Fax: 317-644-2914
web: www.cidcap.com

Mission Statement: CID Capital's Private Equity Group makes majority investments in lower-middle-market companies with a strong history of consistent performance. Our focus is on companies that have the potential to grow significantly but have been constrained by lack of capital, operating systems, or management experience. CID provides the resources and capital to overcome these critical constraints.

Geographic Preference: United States
Fund Size: $75 million
Founded: 1981
Average Investment: $2-$10 million
Investment Criteria: Control Buyouts, Recapitalizations
Industry Group Preference: Consumer Products, Industrial, Distribution, Food & Beverage, Security, Medical & Health Related, Manufacturing, Medical Devices, Healthcare Services, Education, Value-Added Distribution
Portfolio Companies: ABC Industries, BigMouth, Chef'n, Classic Accessories, Fit & Fresh, Grandview Gallery, Matilda Jane, ProSource, Strahman Valves, Team Drive-Away

Key Executives:
John C Aplin, Managing Director
317-708-4852
e-mail: john@cidcap.com
Education: BA, Drake University; MBA, PhD, University of Iowa
Background: President/CEO, Fuller Brush Company; Consultant, Marathon Oil Company; Eli Lilly and Company; Borg-Warner; Faculty Member, Graduate School of Business, Indiana University; Chairperson, Master of Business Administration Program, Indiana University
Steve A Cobb, Managing Director
317-708-4853
e-mail: steve@cidcap.com
Education: BA, Economics, DePauw; MBA, Harvard Business School
Background: Director and Founding Member, Indiana Chapter of Association for Corporate Growth; Finance Manager, Proctor & Gamble; Business Valuation Group; Deloitte & Touche
Eric J Bruun, Managing Director
317-708-4857
e-mail: eric@cidcap.com
Education: BS, MBA, Purdue University
Background: Conseco Companies
Scot E Swenberg, Managing Director
317-708-4856
e-mail: scot@cidcap.com
Education: BEE, Purdue University; MCS, Arizona State University; MBA, University of Chicago
Background: Software Engineer/Financial Analyst, Bull Worldwide Information Systems; Irwin Financial Corporation

481 CINCYTECH
1311 Vine St.
Suite 300
Cincinnati, OH 45202-3559

Phone: 513-263-2720 Fax: 513-381-5093
e-mail: contactus@cincytech.com
web: www.cincytechusa.com

Mission Statement: CincyTech is a public-private seed-stage investor whose mission is to strengthen the regional economy by driving talent and capital into scalable, investable technology companies in Southwest Ohio.

Geographic Preference: Southwest Ohio
Fund Size: $10.4 million
Investment Criteria: Seed-Stage, Startup
Industry Group Preference: Enterprise Software, Technology-Enabled Services, Marketing, Digital Media & Marketing, Biosciences, Healthcare Information Technology
Portfolio Companies: Abre. Action Streamer, Aerpio Therapeutics, Aha!ogy, Airway Therapeutics, Akebia Therapeutics, AssureRx, Astronomer, Batterii, Blue Ash Therapeutics, Clarigent Health, ConnXus, Cordata, Data Inventions, Data Role, Eccrine Systems, Enable Injections, Family Tech, Genetesis, Ilesfay, Include Fitness, Invirsa, Jersey Watch, Lisnr, Losant, Myonexus, Nano Detection Technology, Navistone, Ready Set Surgical, Road Trippers, Sirrus, Stack, Standard Bariatrics, StoreLynkm StreamSpot, Talmetrix, Think Vine, Workflex Solutions, Xact Medical, ZipScene

Key Executives:
Mike Venerable, Chief Executive Officer
513-263-2727
e-mail: mvenerable@cincytechusa.com
Education: University of Dayton
Background: Co-Founder/CEO, Talus; Co-Author, Data Warehouse Design Solutions; Managing Director, Scius Capital
Doug Groh, Director
Education: University of Notre Dame
Background: Director of Sales & Marketing, Verifi;

Investor and VP of Sales & Marketing, RS Solutions; Investor and VP of Sales & Marketing, Ohmart/VEGA Corp.
John M. Rice, Director of Life Sciences
Education: BS, MS, PhD, Microbiology & Virology, Ohio State University
Background: Co-Founder & Managing Partner, Triathalon Medical Ventures; Managing Director, Senmed Medical Ventures; Research & Business Development, Battelle Memorial Institute

482 CINTRIFUSE
1311 Vine Street
Cincinnati, OH 45202

Phone: 513-246-2700
e-mail: info@cintrifuse.com
web: www.cintrifuse.com

Mission Statement: Cintrifuse is a community of talented people. We connect, we teach, we learn. We strive to foster inspiration. We support our city, and the people within it.

Founded: 2012
Investment Criteria: Startup
Industry Group Preference: Technology

Key Executives:
Pete Blackshaw, Chief Executive Officer
Education: BA, Politics, University of California; MBA, Harvard Business School
Background: Global Head of Digital Marketing & Social Media, Nestle; EVP, Digital Strategic Services, Nielsen Online

483 CIRCLE PEAK CAPITAL
New York, NY 10019

Phone: 917-992-6400 **Fax:** 646-349-2743
web: circlepeakcapital.com

Mission Statement: Circle Peak Capital invests in private companies based in the United States, focusing primarily on businesses with established or emerging brands that also demonstrate high growth potential.

Geographic Preference: United States
Founded: 2002
Average Investment: $10 - 100 million
Investment Criteria: Management Buyouts, Recapitalizations, Acquisition Platforms
Industry Group Preference: Consumer Products, Financial Services
Portfolio Companies: Hill & Valley, Luxury Optical Holdings, Rocket Dog, Shari's Management Corporation

Key Executives:
R Adam Smith, Founder/CEO
Education: BA, International Relations & Economics, Boston University; MBA, Columbia University
Background: Financial Sponsors Group, Lehman Brothers; Caxton-Iseman Capital; Castle Harlan; Columbus Advisors
Directorships: Rocket Dog Holdings, Fischbein, WealthTrust, Luxury Optical Holdings, Shari's Mangement Corp, Hill & Valley, Stride Capital

484 CIRCLEUP
San Francisco, CA 94108

e-mail: partners@circleup.com
web: circleup.com

Mission Statement: CircleUp focuses on the small American businesses in the early-stage of development.

Fund Size: $125 million
Founded: 2017
Industry Group Preference: Consumer Products
Portfolio Companies: Kettle & Fire, Nut Pods, Rhythm Superfoods, Smarty Pants, Winky Lux

Key Executives:
Ryan Caldbeck, Co-Founder/Chief Executive Officer
Rory Eakin, Co-Founder
Education: Princeton University
Background: Humanity United, The Boston Consulting Group

485 CISCO INVESTMENTS
300 East Tasman Drive
San Jose, CA 95134

web: www.ciscoinvestments.com

Mission Statement: The venture capital arm of Cisco Systems, Cisco Investments invests in innovative technology companies around the world, focussing on big data and analytics, internet of things, data centre, SaaS, security, semiconductor, and more.

Geographic Preference: United States, Canada, Europe, China, India, Israel
Fund Size: $220 million
Founded: 1993
Investment Criteria: Start-Ups, Early Stage, Late Stage, Pre-IPO
Industry Group Preference: Information Technology, Big Data & Analytics, IoT, Data Centre, SaaS, Infrastructure, Security, Semiconductor, Connected Mobility
Portfolio Companies: 3TS Capital Partners, 6WIND, Aavishkaar, Actility, AIMotive, Alchemist Accelerator, Algebra Ventures, Almaz Capital, Altiostar Networks, Ambiq Micro, AnDAPT, Apptio, Aravo, Archetype Ventures Fund, Ascendify, Aspect Ventures, Avi Networks, Ayla Networks, BehavioSec, Belly, Blackbird Ventures, BNI Video, Bolt, Bull City Venture Partners, CafeX Communications, Capnamic Ventures, Celeno, Cinarra, City Cloud International, CloudCherry, CloudFX, CNEX Labs, Cohda Wireless, Cohesity, Corvil, Covacsis, CRCM Ventures, CTERA, DataRobot, Deskera, Dremio, Dynamic Signal, Elastifile, eSilicon, Evolution Equity, Evrythng, Exabeam, Exent, Flashpoint, FuturePlay, Gainsight, Georgian Partners, Global Talent Track, Gobi Partners, Gong, Grid Net, GuardiCore, Helpshift, HyTrust, IDG Ventures India, Idinvest Partners, ILFS Technologies, illusive networks, Ineda Systems, Innovid, Inspur-Cisco Networking Technology, Intersec, Invitalia Ventures, Involvio, ItsOn, Kaszek Ventures, Kespry, KeyTone Cloud, Kii, Kumu Networks, Kustomer, Kyligence, LiveAction, Mapr, McRock Capital iNFund, Mist Systems, MobStac, Monashees, Moogsoft, Moxtra, mozaiq operations, N3N, Nantero, Near Pte Ltd, Netronome, Nexpa, Nimbus, Notion Capital, OMERS Ventures Fund II, One Mobikwik Systems Private Ltd., Ozon, Panaseer, Paris Saclay Fund, Partech, Paxata, Phunware, Pixvana, Plexo Capital, Prospera, PubNub, Puppet, Quantcast, Qwilt, Qyuki, Real Image, Redpoint eventures, RiverMeadow, SecurView, Sensity Systems, Servion, Silicon Badia, Sky-Tech Holdings Ltd, smart-FOA, Startupbootcamp, Stellaris Venture Partners, Stratoscale, Tagnos, Team8 Ventures, Teradici, ThreatQ, Turbonomic, u.Life Solutions, Upskill, VCE, Veniam, Verodin, Videonetics, VMware, Voicea, Walden International, Walden Riverwood Ventures II, Worldsensing, WSO2, ZillionSource

Other Locations:
126 Post Street
5th Floor
San Francisco, CA 94108

101 Collins Street
Levels 11, 14
Melbourne
Victoria 3000
Australia

Great Eagle Centre
23 Harbour Road
Wan Chai

Venture Capital & Private Equity Firms / Domestic Firms

Hong Kong
China

Dawning Centre West Tower
No. 500 Hongbaeshi Road
Changning District
Shanghai 201103
China

10 Finsbury Square
London, England EC2A 1AF
United Kingdom

Brigade South Parade
No. 10 Mahatma Gandhi Road
Bangalore, Karnataka 560001
India

Rothschild Boulevard 3
Tel Aviv-Yafo
Tel Aviv 6688106
Israel

UE BizHub East
8 Changi Business Park Avenue 1
Singapore 486018
Asia

Key Executives:
Derek Idemoto, Senior Vice President
Education: BS, Finance & Marketing, University of California, Berkeley; MBA, Anderson School of Management, UCLA
Background: Managing Director, ITOCHU Technology; VP, Corporate Development, Overture Services
Janey Hoe, Vice President
Education: BS, University of California, Berkeley; MS, Massachusetts Institute of Technology
Background: Management Consultant, McKinsey & Company; MIT LCS Laboratory; AT&T Laboratories; HP Laboratories

486 CIT GROUP
11 W 42nd Street
New York, NY 10036

e-mail: contact@cit.com
web: www.cit.com

Mission Statement: Financing solutions for small and middle market businesses and the transportation sector.
Geographic Preference: United States, Canada, Worldwide
Fund Size: $28 billion
Founded: 1908
Average Investment: $3.5 million
Minimum Investment: $1 million
Industry Group Preference: Aerospace, Defense and Government, Business Aircraft, Commercial & Industrial, Commercial Air, Communications, Consumer Goods, Energy, Entertainment, Healthcare, Maritime, Office Imaging & Technology, Rail, Restaurants, Retail, Consumer & Leisure

487 CITARETX INVESTMENT PARTNERS
1120 NASA Parkway
Suite 600
Houston, TX 77058

Phone: 281-984-7331 Fax: 281-984-7374
e-mail: jsheldon@citaretx.com
web: www.citaretx.com

Mission Statement: CitareTx Investment Partners is a venture development, investment, and start-up management company concentrated on promising new medical devices, technology, and business opportunities throughout the State of Texas and beyond.
Geographic Preference: Texas
Founded: 2008
Average Investment: $500,000 - $7 million
Investment Criteria: Seed-Stage and Series A
Industry Group Preference: Medical Devices
Portfolio Companies: EMIT Corporation, Houston Medical Robotics Inc., Coagulex Inc.
Key Executives:
Jeffrey Sheldon, General Partner
Education: BS, Aerospace Engineering, University of Minnesota; MBA, University of Houston, Clear Lake
Background: Founder, iDev Technologies; Nittany Polymedics

488 CITI VENTURES
260 Homer Avenue
Suite 101
Palo Alto, CA 94301

Phone: 650-798-8140
e-mail: citiventures@citi.com
web: www.citi.com/ventures

Mission Statement: Citi Ventures is Citi's global corporate venturing arm, chartered to collaborate with internal and external partners to conceive, partner, launch, and scale new ventures that have the potential to disrupt and transform the financial services industry, drive client success, and generate new value for Citi.
Geographic Preference: Worldwide
Founded: 2010
Industry Group Preference: Marketing, Security, Financial Services, Enterprise IT, Commerce, Data Analytics, Machine Learning
Portfolio Companies: Appboy, Ayasdi, Betterment, BlueVine, C2FO, Chain, Chef, Claritymoney, Cylance, Datameer, DB Networks, DocuSign, Dyadic, FastPay, Feedzai, HomeLight, Illusive Networks, Jet, Joist, Kinetica, Linkable Networks, LiveNinja, M-DAQ, Optimizely, Pepperdata Networks, Persado, Pindrop Security, Plaid, Platfora, SilverTrail Systems, Shopkick, Square, Tanium, Tealium, Trade It

Other Locations:
Citi Canary Wharf Office
33 Canada Square
10th Floor
London E14 5LB
United Kingdom

1 Court Square
18th Floor
Long Island City, NY 11101

1 Market Street
Steuart Tower
Suite 1550
San Francisco, CA 94105

Key Executives:
Vanessa Colella, Chief Innovation Officer
Education: MA, Columbia University; MA, MIT; PhD, MIT Media Lab
Background: Entrepreneur in Residence, US Ventures Partners; Head of NA Marketing/SVP of Insights, Yahoo; Partner, McKinsey & Co.
Emily Turner, Director/Head of Strategic Growth Initiatives
Education: BA, Sociology, Dartmouth College; MBA, Columbia Business School
Background: Management Consultant, McKinsey & Co.; Merrill Lynch; ABN Amro; UBS
Ramneek Gupta, Managing Director
Education: B-Tech, Mechanical Engineering, Indian Institute of Technology; MS, Mechanical Engineering, Stanford University
Background: Partner, Battery Ventures
Maja Lapcevic, Director/Co-Head of Strategic Growth Initiatives
Education: BA, Economics/Internation Affairs, Georgetown University
Background: Founder, SML Strategic Media

Venture Capital & Private Equity Firms / Domestic Firms

Arvind Purushotham, Managing Director
Education: B-Tech, Electrical Engineering, Indian Institute of Technology; MSEE, Case Western Reserve University; MBA, Harvard Business School
Background: Managing Director, Menlo Ventures

489 CITY HILL VENTURES
4653 Carmel Mountain Road
Suite 501
San Diego, CA 92130

web: www.cityhillventures.com

Mission Statement: City Hill Ventures is a healthcare focused investment firm whose mission is to restore human health through innovation, by building or helping other health care entrepreneurs build great companies that collectively have a transformative impact on patients, the healthcare industry, and society.

Founded: 2010
Industry Group Preference: Healthcare
Portfolio Companies: Bonti Inc., Eclipse Therapeutics Inc., Flex Pharma Inc., Independa Inc., Ignyta Inc., Inhibrx LLC, Medenovo LLC, Patara Pharma LLC

Key Executives:
Jonathan E. Lim, MD, Founder/Managing Partner
Education: BS, MS, Stanford University; MD, McGill University; MPH, Harvard College
Background: President, Halozyme Therapeutics
Directorships: Eclipse Therapeutics
Karen Gilmore, Controller
Education: BS, CalTech, Pomona; CPA
Background: CFO/VP, Finance, HRE Performance Wheels; CFO/Controller, QLogic Corp.; PacifiCare; FutureKids; Madge Networks; Auditor, PricewaterhouseCoopers
Zachary Hornby, Operating Partner
Education: BS, MS, Biology, Stanford University; MBA, Harvard Business School
Background: Vice President, Corporate Development, Ignyta; Halozyme Therapeutics; LEK Consulting

490 CITY LIGHT CAPITAL
335 Madison Ave
16th Floor
New York, NY 10017

Phone: 212-403-9514
e-mail: info@citylightcap.com
web: www.citylightcap.com

Mission Statement: We look for the most dynamic and experienced entrepreneurs passionate about leveraging the power of technology and markets to create substantial economic, social and environmental value.

Geographic Preference: United States
Founded: 2004
Investment Criteria: Early-Stage
Industry Group Preference: Security, Environment, Education, Information Services, Energy
Portfolio Companies: 2U, Arcadia Power, Envoy, Glacier Bay Technology, HeroX, iBeat, Identilock, Kinetic, Koru, Loris.ai, Legends of Learning, LiveSafe, Meritize, OhmConnect, Omnidian, Open Energy Efficiency, Practice, RapidSOS, Ready Responders, SafeTraces, Senet, ShotSpotter, SkyRyse, Square Roots, Straighterline, SVAcademy, Tinkergarten, Topcoder, Trilogy Education Services, Xage

Key Executives:
Josh Cohen, Managing Partner
Education: Angell Scholar, University of Michigan
Background: SV Group; Director, Business Development, Mobility Electronics
Directorships: 2U, HeroX, Straighterline, Practice, OhmConnect, Koru, Trilogy

Tom Groos, Partner
Education: Cornell University; MBA, Columbia Business School
Background: President, Viking Group
Directorships: Minimax-Viking
Bill Lyons, Environmental Expert
Education: BS, Operations Analysis, United States Naval Academy
Background: President, Climate Solutions Group, AES; Co-Founder, Seneca Creek Energy
Greg Gunn, Education Expert
Education: BS, University of Chicago; MS, MBA, MIT
Background: Founder, Wireless Generation; Product Manager, InterDimensions
Directorships: StraighterLine

491 CIVC PARTNERS
191 N Wacker Drive
Suite 1100
Chicago, IL 60606

Phone: 312-873-7300 Fax: 312-873-7301
e-mail: civc_partners@civc.com
web: www.civc.com

Mission Statement: To develop partnerships with exceptional business leaders and management teams.

Geographic Preference: United States, Canada
Fund Size: $650 million
Founded: 1970
Average Investment: $15 to $85 million
Minimum Investment: $15 million
Investment Criteria: Middle Market, Growth Capital, Acquisition Capital, Management Buyouts, Leveraged Acquisitions, Recapitalizations, Shareholder Liquidity Events
Industry Group Preference: Communications, Consumer Services, Business Products & Services, Financial Services, Media, Industrial Services, Education, Insurance, Telecommunications
Portfolio Companies: Computer Aided Technology, KPA, LendCare, Magna Legal Services, Magnate Worldwide, Right Pointe, Specialized Elevator Services, StoneRidge Insurance Brokers

Key Executives:
Chris Perry, Partner
e-mail: cperry@civc.com
Education: MBA, Pepperdine University; BS, Accountancy, University of Illinois; CPA
Background: Continental Bank's Mezzanine Investments & Structured Finance Groups; VP Corporate Finance, Northern Trust Company; Public Accounting, Coopers & Lybrand
Directorships: Brickman Group Ltd., RAM Reinsurance Company, TransWestern Publishing, Wastequip, LA Fitness International, Kellermeyer Building Services
Chris Geneser, Partner & CFO
e-mail: cgeneser@civc.com
Education: BBA, Accounting, University of Notre Dame; CPA
Background: Senior Manager, Ernst & Young; Managing of Financial Planning, US Robotics Inc.
John Compall, Partner
e-mail: jcompall@civc.com
Education: BS, Computer Science, University of Illinois; MBA, University of Chicago
Background: Ameritech Corporation; McKinsey & Company
Scott Schwartz, Partner
e-mail: sschwartz@civc.com
Education: BS, Economics, MBA, Wharton School, University of Pennsylvania
Background: VP, American Industrial Partners; Engagement Manager, McKinsey & Company
Marc McManus, Partner
e-mail: mmcmanus@civc.com
Education: BS, Economics & Computer Science,

Venture Capital & Private Equity Firms / Domestic Firms

Vanderbilt University; MBA, Harvard Business School
Background: Director, HSBC North America; Strategy Consultant, Accenture; Associate, Lehman Brothers
J.D. Wright, Partner
e-mail: jwright@civc.com
Education: BA, Economics, Vanderbilt University
Background: Investment Banking Analyst, Harris Williams & Co.
Alex Lieberman, Vice President
e-mail: alieberman@civc.com
Education: BBA, Finance/Accounting, Kellogg School of Management
Background: Senior Associate, RoundTable Healthcare Partners; Analyst, Deutsche Bank
Andrew Roche, Vice President
e-mail: aroche@civc.com
Education: BEng, Chemical Engineering/Mathematics, Vanderbilt University
Background: Raymond James
Directorships: CATI
Brian James, Vice President
e-mail: bjames@civc.com
Education: BBA, Finance, University of Notre Dame; MBA, Kellogg School of Management, Northwestern University
Background: Vice President, H.I.G. Capital; Associate, CIVC; Analyst, JPMorgan

492 CJV CAPITAL

web: www.cjvcapital.com

Mission Statement: Invests in companies within the cannabis industry that focus on consumer products and agro-breeding solutions for research and medical use.

Founded: 2016
Investment Criteria: Seed, Early-Stage
Industry Group Preference: Cannabis
Portfolio Companies: Corsica Innovations Inc.

493 CLAREMONT CREEK VENTURES
300 Frank H. Ogawa Plaza
Suite 350
Oakland, CA 94612

Phone: 510-740-5001
web: www.claremontcreek.com

Mission Statement: A venture capital firm investing in early stage information technology companies. Claremont maintains an expertise in the IT sector, with an interest in energy efficiency, sensor based systems, and securities markets.

Geographic Preference: California
Fund Size: $130 million
Average Investment: $500,000 - $3 million
Investment Criteria: Early Stage
Industry Group Preference: Information Technology, Healthcare, Energy Efficiency, Security, Mobility
Portfolio Companies: Alphabet Energy Inc., Alter G, Assurerx Health, Billeo, Blue Pillar, CellScope, Clean Power Finance Inc., Comfy, Cureus, DNAnexus, EcoATM, EcoFactor, Element Energy, Energy Cache, Fluxion Biosciences, Genalyte, GeneWEAVE Inc., GigaGen, Lefora, Natera, Numedii Inc., Project Frog, PropertyBridge, Renewable Funding, RidePal, Root3, Sentilla, ShotSpotter, SmartZip Analytics, Yerdle, ZipLine Medical

Key Executives:
Nat Goldhaber, Managing Director
Education: MA, Education, University of California, Berkeley
Background: CEO, Cybergold; Founder, Centram Systems West; Founding CEO, Kaleida Labs; Vice President, Sun Microsystems
Randy Hawks, Managing Director
Education: BSEE, University of Arkansas; Stanford University Exective Management Program
Background: General Partner, Novus Ventures; Venture Partner, Horizon Ventures
Harsh Patel, Director
Education: BS, Engineering, University of Illinois; MBA, Stanford Grad. School of Business
Background: General Partner, PRE Ventures; In-Q-Tel; President, Bina Technologies; Co-Founder, Orbit Commerce; R&D, Accenture
Ted Driscoll, PhD, Venture Partner
Education: BA, University of Pennsylvania; MA, Computer Graphics & Remote Sensing, Harvard University; PhD, Digital Imaging, Stanford University
Background: Founder, Be Here Technologies; Division President, Diasonics; Vice President, Engineering, Identix
Brad Webb, PhD, Venture Partner
Education: PhD, Biochemistry & Molecular Biology, University of California, Santa Barbara
Background: Founder, Vision Biology; R&D, 3M Company
Paul Straub, Director
Education: BS, Commerce, University of Virginia McIntire School of Commerce; MBA, Duke University Fuqua School of Business
Background: Product Management, VERITAS Sofware; Consultant, Red Hat Software
Directorships: TargetCast Networks, Adura Technologies
Gianna Conci Orozco, Finance Manager
Education: BS, Economics, Santa Clara University
Background: Virgin Green Fund; Sierra Ventures; Silver Lake Partners

494 CLARION CAPITAL PARTNERS LLC
527 Madison Avenue
10th Floor
New York, NY 10022

Phone: 212-821-0111 Fax: 212-371-7597
web: www.clarion-capital.com

Mission Statement: A private equity firm which seeks to make primarily control private equity investments in a diversified portfolio of middle-market companies.

Fund Size: $50 million
Founded: 1999
Average Investment: $15-50 million
Investment Criteria: Leverage Buyouts, Growth Equity, Recapitalizations, Revenue greater than $7.5 million
Industry Group Preference: Business Products & Services, Healthcare Services, Specialty Finance, Consumer Products, Specialty Retail, Media & Entertainment
Portfolio Companies: All-Clad Holdings Inc., AML RightSource, Ametros Financial Corp., Cascade Entertainment Group, Cross, Cross Mediaworks, Crowe Paradis Servicing Corp., Encore Capital Group Inc., Great Northwest Insurance Co., Hartmann, HROI, IMAX Corp., Lenox, Madison Logic, Moravia, Reliant Healthcare Professionals, Strategic Outsourcing Inc., SQAD, The Oceanaire Inc.

Key Executives:
Marc A Utay, Managing Partner
e-mail: mutay@clarion-capital.com
Education: BS, Wharton School, University of Pennsyvlania
Background: Managing Director, Wasserstein Perella & Company; Managing Director, BT Securities; Managing Partner, Kent Capital Partners; Partner, Drexel Burnham Labert Inc.; Financial Associate, Beverage Division, General Foods Corporation
Eric D Kogan, Partner
e-mail: ekogan@clarion-capital.com
Education: MBA, University of Chicago; BA, BSE, Wharton School, University of Pennsylvania
Background: Triarc Companies, Inc.; Associate, Mergers/Acquisitions, Farley Inc.; Analyst, Oppenheimer Inc.

Venture Capital & Private Equity Firms / Domestic Firms

Jonathan M Haas, Managing Director
e-mail: jhaas@clarion-capital.com
Education: MBA, Northwestern University Kellogg School of Management; BA, Dartmouth College
Background: Investment Banking Division, Credit Suisse First Boston; Associate, Industrials Group; Associate, A.T. Kearney Inc.
David B Ragins, Managing Director
e-mail: dragins@clarion-capital.com
Education: MBA, Wharton School, University of Pennsylvania; BS, Finance, Babson College
Background: Seaport Capital Partners; Merrill Lynch & Co.; NationasBanc Capital Markets, Inc.
Doug K. Mellinger, Managing Director/Head of Marketing
e-mail: dmellinger@clarion-capital.com
Education: Entrepreneurship, Syracuse University
Background: Managing Director, Palm Ventures; Founder, Foundation Source; Founder, Young Entrepreneurs Organization
Matthew S. Feldman, Managing Director
e-mail: mfeldman@clarion-capital.com
Education: BBA, University of Michigan
Background: Investment Banking Division, Bear Stearns & Co; Principal, Clarion Capital
Brandon M. Katz, Principal
e-mail: bkatz@clarion-capital.com
Education: BS, Business Admin., Boston University
Background: PioneerPath Capital; Investment Banking Division, Bear, Stearns & Co.
Edward W Martin, Principal
e-mail: emartin@clarion-capital.com
Education: BS, Systems Engineering, University of Pennsylvania; MBA, Columbia Business School
Background: Investment Banking, Merrill Lynch & Co.

495 CLARITAS CAPITAL
30 Burton Hills Blvd
Suite 100
Nashville, TN 37215

Phone: 615-690-7179
web: www.claritascapital.com

Mission Statement: Our overall approach is to be partners with our entrepreneurs, to provide value to them, to assist in their growth and success, and to drive the investment return targets we have for each investment through those efforts. These returns are achieved by sourcing, underwriting, post-investment portfolio management, network building, assessing market trends, and a combination of other operational tasks and processes we currently have and are continually enhancing. As a firm, we focus on sourcing the highest quality investment opportunities, and following our investment providing those companies and management teams with value creation services from building out management teams, accessing new customers, and assisting with acquisitions.

Founded: 2002
Investment Criteria: Early-Stage, Growth Equity
Industry Group Preference: Healthcare, Technology, Real Estate
Portfolio Companies: A Head For Profits, Apcela, Blue Chip Partners Surgery Centers, BuyHappy, Continuum, Counsel On Call, Cybera, Dobie Media, Employment Staffinf, Empyrean, Entrada, Expensable, Forbes Travel Guide, Genomind, Hospital Corporation of America, HCCA International, HCTec Partners, Innovatel, I-Payment, LearnVest, Nsight, Oasis Marinas, Pace, Pear, Rubicon, ShareCare, Snag A Slip, StudioNow, Tristar License Group, Tristar 600, TwelveStone Health Partners

Key Executives:
John H Chadwick, Partner
615-665-8250
e-mail: jhchadwick@claritascapital.com
Education: BA, University of Virginia; MBA, Wharton School
Background: Principal, Richland Ventures
Directorships: Empyrean Benefit Solutions, Forbes Travel Guide, Genomind, Sharecare, StudioNow, TwelveStone Health Partners
Theresa Sexton, Partner
615-690-7182
e-mail: tsexton@claritascapital.com
Education: BBA, Belmont University; MBA, MACC, Belmont University Massey Graduate School of Business
Background: Director, Investor Services, CAO, Massey Burch Capital Corp.
Directorships: Apcela, Forbes Travel, Genomind, nSight for Travel, Oasis Holdings, TwelveStone Health Partners
Bob Fisher, Partner
615-665-8419
e-mail: bfisher@claritascapital.com
Background: Founder/CEO, Jet Finance Group; Partner, Massey Burch Capital Corp.
Don McLemore, Partner
615-665-8419
e-mail: dmclemore@claritascapital.com
Background: Partner, Massey Burch Capital Corp.
Directorships: StudioNow, nSight, A Head for Profits, Apcela, Dobie Media, HCTec

496 CLARITY PARTNERS
11601 Wilshire Boulevard
Suite 1600
Los Angeles, CA 90025-0317

web: www.claritypartners.net

Mission Statement: Private equity firm focused on investment in communications, media and related services. More recently, Clarity Partners has broadened their interest to include energy and natural resources.

Geographic Preference: United States, China
Fund Size: $1 billion
Founded: 2000
Average Investment: $15 to $100 million
Minimum Investment: $15 million
Investment Criteria: Growth Equity, Leveraged Buyouts, Divisional Divestitures, Recapitalizations
Industry Group Preference: Broadband, Wireless Technologies, Business Products & Services, Communications, Media, Information Technology
Portfolio Companies: BASE Entertainment, Buytime Media, CaseStack, Crescent Entertainment, Comstellar, Critical Media, ImpreMedia, International Silver, IP Wireless, Liberation Entertainment, MetroPCS, Modern Luxury, Naylor, OpenReach, Opnext, Oxygen Media, PrimeCo, Skye Mineral Partners, TPx, Vaca Energy, Vue Entertainment, Westec Interactive, Woosh Wireless

Other Locations:
15260 Ventura Boulevard
Suite 1550
Sherman Oaks, CA 91403-5335

Key Executives:
Dr. David Lee, Co-Founder/Managing General Partner
Education: McGill University; PhD, California Institute of Technology
Background: Arthur Andersen & Company; Comsat; TRW Information Systems Group; Pacific Capital Group; Global Crossing
Directorships: Opnext, Impremedia, University of Southern California Keck School of Medicine
Barry Porter, Co-Founder/Managing General Partner
Education: BS, Wharton School; JD, MBA, University of California, Berkeley
Background: Wyman, Bautzer, Rothman, Kuchel & Silbert; Bear, Stearns & Company, Pacific Capital Group, Global Crossing
Directorships: PrimeCo Personal Communications, Vue Entertainment, eMind, MetroPCS, Board of Public Counsel

Venture Capital & Private Equity Firms / Domestic Firms

Stephen P. Rader, Co-Founder/Managing General Partner
Education: BS, University of Southern California School of Business; JD, University of Southern California School of Law
Background: Rader, Reinfrank & Company; Chartwell Partners; Bear, Stearns & Company; CPA
Directorships: Vue Entertainment, Impremedia, TelePacific Communications, eMind, Oxygen Media
Joshua L. Gutfreund, General Partner
Education: BA, Columbia University; MBA, New York University Business School
Background: Rader, Reinfrank & Company; Chartwell Partners; EM Warburg, Pincus & Company
Directorships: Oxygen Media, eMind, xSides Corporation
Clinton W. Walker, General Partner
Education: BBA, Pacific Union College; CPA
Background: VP, Global Crossing; VP, Pacific Capital Group; Price Waterhouse
Directorships: Woosh Wireless
W. Jack Kessler Jr., General Partner/CFO
Education: MBA, JD, University of Southern California Graduate Schools of Business and Law; Business Administration; Theology, Ambassador College; CPA; California State Bar
Background: CFO, Rader, Reinfrank & Company; Executive Director, Alschuler Grossman & Pines; Rader and Kessler; CFO, Lamborghini of North America
Mark Swaine, Managing Director
Education: BA, Economics, Emory University; JD, Pepperdine University School of Law; California State Bar
Background: The Wonderful Company
Andrea Caoile, Controller
Education: BS, Business Admin., University of California, Riverside; CPA
Background: Senior Accountant, Clarity Partners; Senior Accountant, Maryanov Madsen Gorden & Campbell

497 CLAYTON ASSOCIATES
5314 Maryland Way
Suite 100
Brentwood, TN 37027

Phone: 615-320-3070
web: www.claytonassociates.com

Mission Statement: Clayton Associates is an investment firm that is passionate about building businesses. We make seed, angel, and venture stage investments in helathcare and technology companies.
Founded: 1996
Investment Criteria: Seed Stage, Angel, Venture Stage
Industry Group Preference: Healthcare, Technology
Portfolio Companies: Catavolt, ChartWise Medical Systems, Clinical Ink, Haven Behavioral, KeraFAST, LogoGarden, MediQuire, Pathfinder Health Innovations, One Medical Passport, StudioNow

Key Executives:
Stuart McWhorter, Founder and President
Education: Masters in Health Administration, The University of Alabama-Birmingham; BS, Management, Clemson University
Background: CEO and Chairman, Medical Reimbursements of America; Vice President, Managed Care and Acquisitions, OrthoLink Physicians Corporation
Directorships: FirstBank of Tennessee, LaunchTN, Tennessee Business Roundtable, Belmont Unviersity
R. Clayton McWhorter, Founder and Chairman Emeritus
Education: BS, Pharmacy, Samford University
Background: Founder, Chairman and CEO, HealthTrust; Chairman, Hospital Corporation of America
John R. Burch, Managing Partner
Background: Co-Founder, MyOfficeProducts; Exec. Vice-President, Motorent
Directorships: Entrada, LogoGarden, KeraFAST, ProviderTrust, ChartWise, Armor Concepts, Thalerus Group, Gemino Healthcare Finance, Pathfinder Therapeutics, PharmMD
Matthew King, Managing Partner
Background: Vice President, Third National Bank; CEO, Radar Business Systems; Regional Vice President, U.S. Office Products; CEO, MyOfficeProducts
Directorships: NuScript Rx, edo Interactive, Entrada, onFocus Healthcare, Silvercare Solutions, LogoGarden, KeraFAST, ProCharging, HCCA International

498 CLEAN ENERGY VENTURE GROUP
Brookline, MA

Phone: 877-531-9017
web: cevg.com

Mission Statement: Clean Energy Venture Group is an investment group that provides seed capital and management expertise to early stage clean energy companies. The group is comprised of seasoned operating executives with strong capabilities in the energy and environmental sectors. The fund's primary focus is New England, but will occasionally consider investments located in other areas.
Geographic Preference: New England
Founded: 2005
Investment Criteria: Seed-Stage
Industry Group Preference: Clean Technology, Energy
Portfolio Companies: 7AC Technologies, Acumentrics, Autonomous Marine Systems Inc., Bevi, CIMCON Lighting, Energetic Insurance, EnergySage, eQuilibrium, FINsix Corp., MTPV, Multisensor Scientific, MyEnergyn, NG Advantage LLC, Pika Energy, Powerhouse Dynamics, PurposeEnergy, Quidnet Energy, REsurety, Solantro Semiconductor Corp., Ultracell, VCharge, Voltserver, WeSpire, Zagster

Key Executives:
David S. Miller, Founder/Executive Managing Director
Education: BS, MS, Computer Science & Engineering, MIT
Background: Founder, Quantum Telecom Solutions; Lucent
Directorships: Azima DLI, Next Step Living, MyEnergy, Cambrian Innovation

499 CLEAN PACIFIC VENTURES
425 California Street
Suite 2400
San Francisco, CA 94104

Mission Statement: Clean Pacific Ventures is a venture capital fund that invests in promising early stage clean technology companies. Clean Pacific focuses primarily on clean technologies related to energy, water, agriculture and materials.
Average Investment: $2 to $4 million
Investment Criteria: Early-Stage
Industry Group Preference: Clean Technology, Energy, Water, Agriculture, Energy Storage, Energy Efficiency, Advanced Materials, Renewable Energy
Portfolio Companies: American Efficient, Aquacue, Clean Power Finance, HydroNovation, LumiGrow, Marrone Bio Innovations, SunLink, Wireless Glue

Key Executives:
Sean Schickedanz, General Partner
Education: BA, English, Brigham Young University; JD, MBA, Duke University
Background: Managing Partner, Sunflower Capital Partners; Managing Director, Montgomery Securities; Investment Banking, Merrill Lynch
Directorships: The Renewables Exchange Inc.
Dave Herron, General Partner
Education: BA, English, University of California, Berkeley; MBA, University of Michigan
Background: Vice President, Robertson Stephen's Energy Technology Investment Banking; Senior Vice President, Van Kasper & Co

Venture Capital & Private Equity Firms / Domestic Firms

Directorships: SunLink; Wireless Glue Networks; The Renewables Exchange Inc.

500 CLEANPATH VENTURES
448 Pennsylvania Avenue
San Francisco, CA 94107

Phone: 415-244-6787
e-mail: info@cleanpath.com
web: www.cleanpath.com

Mission Statement: CleanPath is a premier solar project investment firm with deep development and engineering roots. CleanPath invests in, develops, builds and delivers high quality renewable energy assets to external long-term owners, or to their own portfolio. CleanPath was formed by pioneers of the U.S. clean energy industry, with deep industry and capital markets experience, execution capability and exceptional relationships. The fund's solutions provide significant capital resources coupled with proven project finance, development, engineering, and asset construction and management capabilities.

Fund Size: $300 million
Founded: 2001
Industry Group Preference: Renewable Energy
Key Executives:
Matt Cheney, Chief Executive Officer
Education: BS, American University; MS, Johns Hopkins University School of Advanced International Studies
Background: CEO, Fotowatio Renewable Ventures; MMA Renewable Energy

501 CLEAR SKY CAPITAL
2398 East Camelback Road
Suite 615
Phoenix, AZ 85016

e-mail: info@clearskycap.com
web: clearskycap.com

Mission Statement: Clear Sky emphasizes a team approach and looks for new investment opportunities where there is synergy with existing skills and disciplines. Clear Sky targets to invest in properties that, upon stabilization, (i) will continue to appreciate in value and generate attractive yields and (ii) will be well positioned with exit options to institutional real estate investors.

Industry Group Preference: Real Estate
Key Executives:
Marcus Kurshat, Founder & CEO
Matthew Collins, Chief Financial Officer
Christopher Herthel, Chief Operating Officer

502 CLEARLAKE CAPITAL
233 Wilshire Boulevard
Suite 800
Santa Monica, CA 90401

Phone: 310-400-8800
e-mail: info@clearlakecapital.com
web: www.clearlakecapital.com

Mission Statement: A leading investment firm focused on private equity and special situations transactions.

Geographic Preference: United States
Fund Size: $3.5 billion
Founded: 2006
Investment Criteria: Buyouts, Acquisitions, Carve-Outs, Growth Capital, Platform Investments, Special Situations
Industry Group Preference: Business Products & Services, Consumer Products, Consumer Services, Energy, Industrial Services, Technology, Communications, Aerospace, Defense and Government, Healthcare, Media
Portfolio Companies: 3alioty Technica, American Construction Source, AmQuip, Appriss, Ashley Stewart, Bluefly, Buy.com, Calero, Chef's Cut Real Jerky, CompuDyne Corporation, ConvergeOne, Diligent, Dude Solutions, Eagleview, From the Ground Up, Futuris, Gravity Oilfield Services Inc., International Textile Group, Inventus, Ivanti, Jacuzzi, Janus, JetSmarter, Knight Oil Tools, Lytx, MetricStream, Mformation, MYCOM OSI, NetDocuments, OnShift, OWYN, Perforce Software, Platinum Energy Solutions, Pomeroy, PrimeSport, Provation, Purple Communications, Sage Automotive Interiors, Sensible Problems, Smart Sand, Solutionary, Sunbelt Supply, Symplr, Team Technologies Inc., Syncsort, Thinsters, Unifrax, Vision Solutions, Wheel Pros

503 CLEARLIGHT PARTNERS
100 Bayview Circle
Suite 5000
Newport Beach, CA 92660

Phone: 949-725-6610 Fax: 949-725-6611
web: www.clearlightpartners.com

Mission Statement: ClearLight Partners is a private equity firm that invests in profitable middle-market companies across a variety of sectors, including education, healthcare, business services, consumer products and services, and specialty manufacturing. ClearLight Partners offers financial and operating expertise, and seeks to establish partnerships with management teams to help with the growth of companies.

Geographic Preference: United States, Canada
Fund Size: $300 million
Founded: 2000
Average Investment: $10 - $50 million
Investment Criteria: Middle-Market, Growth Capital
Industry Group Preference: Manufacturing, Distribution, Business Products & Services, Education, Healthcare Services, Financial Services, Consumer Products, Consumer Services
Portfolio Companies: Austin Fitness Group, Handel's Ice Cream, Katzkin Leather Interiors Inc., Moore Landscapes, Paul Fredrick, United Tactical Systems, Walker Advertising
Key Executives:
Michael S Kaye, Founder/Managing Partner
952-725-6628
e-mail: msk@clearlightpartners.com
Education: BA, Stanford University; JD, Harvard Law School
Background: President & CEO, Westec Security Group; Corporate Law, Gibson, Dunn and Crutcher
Joshua Mack, Partner
949-725-6625
e-mail: jmack@clearlightpartners.com
Education: BS, Finance, Pepperdine University
Andrew Brennan, Partner
949-725-6642
e-mail: ajb@clearlightpartners.com
Education: BA, Economics, Williams College
Background: EVP & COO, ValleyCrest Companies; Senior Associate, ClearLight; McKinsey & Company

504 CLEARSTONE VENTURE PARTNERS
1351 4th Street
4th Floor
Santa Monica, CA 90401

web: www.clearstone.com

Mission Statement: Clearstone embraces a longtime and active role in the business community as an incubator and financier of early-stage startups.

Geographic Preference: Southern California
Fund Size: $650 million
Founded: 1997
Investment Criteria: Early Stage
Industry Group Preference: Computer Related, Internet, Infrastructure, E-Commerce & Manufacturing, Social Media, Mobile
Portfolio Companies: AOptix, Apture, BillDesk, Clearfly Communications, Comet Systems, Composite Systems, Cooking.com, DiVitas, Games2Win.com, Geodelic Systems, Good Technology, HealthAllies, Idealab, Integrien,

Venture Capital & Private Equity Firms / Domestic Firms

Intersperse, Kazeon, Leisurelink, Meru Networks, Mimosa Systems, MP3.com, Nokeena, Novariant, Overture Services, PayPal, PeopleSupport, Phasebridge, Presto, Rubicon Project, Six Degrees Games, Soonr, Spock, SupplyFrame, ThisNext, United Online, UserTesting, Vast

Other Locations:
720 University Avenue
Suite 200
Palo Alto, CA 94301
Phone: 650-234-0400 **Fax:** 650-234-0401

Key Executives:
Bill Elkus, Founder & Managing Director
Education: BS, Mathematics, MS, Management, MIT; JD, Harvard Law School
Background: Boston Consulting Group; President, Nathan Todd & Company
Directorships: United Online, Overture, PayPal.com, Chronicle Publishing Company, Presto Services, Cooking.com, WeddingChannel.com
Jim Armstrong, Managing Director
Education: BA, Economics, University of California, Los Angeles; MBA, McCombs School, University of Texas at Austin
Background: Austin Ventures
Directorships: SupplyFrame, Internet Brands, Vast, Six Degrees Games, LeisureLink, Inegrien, Composite
William Quigley, Managing Director
Education: BS, Accounting, University of Southern California; MBA, Harvard Business School; CPA
Background: Mid-Atlantic Venture Funds; The Walt Disney Company; Senior Consultant, Arthur Andersen Financial Services Group
Directorships: AOptix, SoonR, Meru Networks, Novariant, Communicado, Spock Networks, Spock.com
Anil Patel, Venture Partner
Education: AB, Economics & Philosophy, Stanford University; MBA, Columbia Business School; JD, Columbia University School of Law
Background: Azure Capital Partners; Bessemer Venture Partners; Attorney, Wilson Sonsini Goodrich & Rosati; Software Developer, Information Management Consultants
Dana Moraly, Chief Financial Officer
Education: BA, Economics, UCLA; MBA, Anderson School of Management, University of California, LA
Background: Trust Company of the West; Senior Manager, Coopers & Lybrand; Senior Auditor, Deloitte & Touche
Vish Mishra, Venture Director
Education: BS, Electrical Engineering, Institute of Technology at Benares Hindu University; MS, Electrical Engineering, North Dakota State University; MBA, University of Minnesota
Background: Founder, Telera; Co-Founder, Excelan; VP, Operations, Excelan; VP, Novell; EVP, iPlanet; CEO, Info-Objects; CEO, Mindworks; CEO, InteliMatch; CEO, Ace Software
Directorships: Abeama, Cofix, Onjibe, PostMedia Group, Quantros, Ramp Networks, SloMedia, Verano, Xalted IP Networks
Prabakar Sundarrajan, Venture Advisor
Education: MS, Computer Science, University of Massachusetts, Amherst
Background: CTO, EVP Strategic Planning & Corporate Development, NetScaler, Inc.; Senior Vice President of Technology, Exodus Communications
David Stern, Venture Partner
Education: Cornell University; San Diego School of Law
Background: President, M Networks
Directorships: Apture, Geodelic Systems, The Rubicon Project, SoonR
Rajan Mehra, Venture Partner
Education: Sydenham College, Mumbai; MBA, Darden School, University of Virginia
Background: Country Manager, eBay India; eBay Asia Pacific Leadership Team; Baazee.com

505 CLEARVIEW CAPITAL
1010 Washington Blvd.
11th Floor
Stamford, CT 06901
Phone: 203-698-2777 **Fax:** 203-698-9194
e-mail: info@clearviewcap.com
web: www.clearviewcap.com

Mission Statement: A private investment firm specializing in the acquisition and recapitalization of North American companies with operating profit of $4 - $20 million. The firm's principals have a long track record of completing transactions and of working collaboratively with management to create and realize value.

Geographic Preference: North America
Investment Criteria: Recapitalizations
Industry Group Preference: Manufacturing, Specialized Services, Branded Goods
Portfolio Companies: Advanced Medical Personnel Services, Apothecare, Community Medicla Services, Controlled Products, Elevation Labs, Mudlick Mail, Nielsen-Kellerman, Wilson, Novik, Pediatric Health Choice, Pyramid Healthcare

Other Locations:
12100 Wilshire Blvd.
Suite 800
Los Angeles, CA 90025
Phone: 310-806-9555 **Fax:** 310-806-9556

Key Executives:
James G Andersen, Founder/Managing Partner
203-698-2777
Fax: 203-698-9194
e-mail: janderson@clearviewcap.com
Education: BSE, Civil Engineering, Princeton University; MBA, Wharton School
Background: Managing Director, Capital Partners; Management Consultant, Mars & Company
Calvin A Neider, Founder/Managing Partner
203-698-2777
Fax: 203-698-9194
e-mail: cneider@clearviewcap.com
Education: BA, Business Administration, SUNY Oneonta; MBA, University of Connecticut
Background: Managing Director, Capital Partners; SVP, LaSalle Business Credit
William F Case Jr, Partner
e-mail: wcase@clearviewcap.com
Education: BA, Union College; MBA, Wharton School
Background: Huntington Holdings
Paul Caliento, Partner
203-698-2777
Fax: 203-698-9194
e-mail: pcaliento@clearviewcap.com
Education: BA, Accounting & Marketing, University of Rhode Island
Background: Flackman Goodman & Potter
Lawrence R Simon, Partner
310-806-9555
Fax: 310-806-9556
e-mail: lsimon@clearviewcap.com
Education: Wharton School; MBA, Columbia Business School
Background: Principal, Triton Pacific Capital Partners
Anthony J Veith, Partner
203-698-2777
Fax: 203-698-9194
e-mail: aveith@clearviewcap.com
Education: BS, Finance, University of Arizona; MBA, City University of New York
Background: Senior Vice President, LaSalle Business Credit
Mathias Rumilly, Partner
203-698-2777
Fax: 203-698-9194

e-mail: mrummily@clearviewcap.com
Education: BS, Finance, University of Connecticut
Matthew Blevins, Partner
203-698-2777
Fax: 203-698-9194
e-mail: mblevins@clearviewcap.com
Education: BS, Business Administration, Accounting & Finance, Cental Michigan University
Background: Senior Consultant, Deloitte & Touche USA

506 CLEARWATER CAPITAL PARTNERS
15 River Rd.
Suite 15B
Wilton, CT 06897

Phone: 212-201-8544
e-mail: information@clearwatercp.com
web: www.clearwatercapitalpartners.com

Mission Statement: Clearwater Capital Partners provides investors with access to a full spectrum of special-situation investments in public and private debt or equity of local, Asia-region issuers. In doing so, Clearwater also assists owners and management, particularly of the region's often capital-constrained small-to-medium-sized enterprises (SMEs), to create financial and operating restructurings that will allow their companies to succeed. In addition, by facilitating these successful restructurings, the firm has become a valuable and trusted resource to the region's banks, brokers and other business intermediaries.

Geographic Preference: Asia, United States
Founded: 2001
Investment Criteria: Restructurings, Turn-Arounds

Other Locations:
Suite 3205
No. 9 Queen's Road
Central
Hong Kong
Phone: 852-3713-4800

Key Executives:
Robert Petty, Co-Founder/Managing Partner
Education: BA, Political Science, Brown University
Background: Amroc Investments, Peregrine Fixed Income, Lehman Brothers Holdings
Amit Gupta, Co-Founder/Partner
Education: B.Eng, Electronics & Communications, Indian Institute of Technology; Post Graduate Diploma, Management, Indian Institute of Management
Background: Goldman Sachs Asia, Peregrine Fixed Income, ICICI

507 CLOQUET CAPITAL PARTNERS
285 Hawks Hill Rd.
New Cannan, CT 06840

Phone: 203-286-6818
e-mail: contact@cloquetcapital.com
web: www.cloquetcapital.com

Mission Statement: Cloquet Capital Partners is a private equity firm that, along with its operating partners and affiliates, manages in excess of $50 million of available or invested capital. Its mission is to acquire and build a portfolio of exceptional businesses in niche markets. Cloquet invests in venture-stage communication software companies, management buyouts, growth equity investments and special situations. Cloquet seeks to enter into close operating partnerships with the managers of its portfolio companies, with Cloquet's resources providing support to help them achieve their strategic objectives and growth. Cloquet invests its own private capital, not that of third parties, with an investment approach based on trust, integrity and honesty.

Fund Size: $50 million
Founded: 2002
Investment Criteria: Management Buyouts, Growth Equity Investments, Special Situations

Industry Group Preference: Communications, Software
Portfolio Companies: Aeris, BitMinutes, FarmLogix, InSight Management, Micromatic, Qv21 Technologies, Side by Side, Tespo

Key Executives:
Burton McGillivray, Partner
Education: AB, Economics, Harvard College; MBA, Harvard Business School
Background: Continental Illinois Venture Corp., Carlisle Enterprises, First Chicago Equity Capital
Directorships: FarmLogix, Qv21 Technologies, Micromatic, Insight Management Group
Jim Zucco, Partner
Education: BA, Western Maryland College; MBA, Loyola College
Background: SVP, MCI Corp.; VP & General Manager, Business Communications Group; VP & General Manager, Lucent Technologies; CEO, Shiva Corp.
Krishnamurty Kambhampati, Partner
Education: MS, Computer Science, Cornell University; MS, Mathematics, Indian Institute of Technology
Background: Founder & CEO, monitor-io; Co-Founder, uReach Technologies

508 CLYDESDALE VENTURES
201 Spear Street
Suite 1150
San Francisco, CA 94105

Phone: 415-391-4085 Fax: 415-243-3000
web: www.clydesdaleventures.com

Mission Statement: Clydesdale Ventures is a seed and early-stage venture investment firm who partner with and invest in passionate entrepreneurs with big ideas for capital efficient and highly scalable businesses.

Average Investment: $25, 000 - $1.5 million
Investment Criteria: Seed-Stage, Early-Stage
Industry Group Preference: Consumer Products, Food & Beverage, Consumer Internet, Enterprise Technology, SaaS, Financial Services, Leisure, Health & Wellness, Restaurants
Portfolio Companies: HealthFusion, Inc., Bishop Rock Software, LLC, RemoteMDx, Inc., New Momentum LLC, UBmatrix LLC, Cleantech America, Inc., California Bank of Commerce, Chime Entertainment LLC, Mixonic, Inc., Airtreks, Inc., Java Detour, Inc., Duncan Media Group, Dream Dinners, Novint Technologies, Inc., Organic Style, Inc., NowMedia, Pangea World Corporation, QOOP, Inc., Hooja, Inc., The Concery Network, Inc., PayEase, Inc

Key Executives:
Paul Klapper, Partner
Background: PFK Acquisition Company, Creative World Travel; Chairman, A&W Restaurants
Brad Klapper, Partner
Background: Siebel Systems, Freepoint Telecom
Directorships: Bishop Rock Software, NowMedia Corp., The Concert Network Inc.

509 CM EQUITY PARTNERS
900 Third Avenue
33rd Floor
New York, NY 10022

Phone: 212-909-8400 Fax: 212-829-0553
e-mail: dcolon@cmequity.com
web: www.cmequity.com

Mission Statement: Specializes in investing in government contract service businesses. Since 1995, CMEP has purchased multiple platform companies that primarily serve the US federal government. CMEP is affiliated with Carl Marks & Co., LP.

Geographic Preference: United States
Fund Size: $200 million
Founded: 1995
Average Investment: $5 - 40 million
Minimum Investment: $500,000

Venture Capital & Private Equity Firms / Domestic Firms

Investment Criteria: Middle Market
Industry Group Preference: Federal Services, Aerospace, Defense
Portfolio Companies: A-TEK, Bogart Associates, Citizant, GracoRoberts, JANUS Research Group Inc., The Level Playing Field Corporation, Preferred System Solutions, Systems Planning and Analysis
Other Locations:
  1430 K Street NW
  12th Floor
  Washington, DC 20005
Key Executives:
  Joel R. Jacks, Co-Founder, Managing Partner
  Education: BComm, University of Cape Town; MBA, Wharton School; Chartered Accountant
  Background: Founding Manager, Carl Marks Consulting Group; Private Consultant; CFO/CEO, USSCO; Director Financial Planning, Penn Central Corporation; Deloitte Haskins & Sells
  Directorships: Echo Bridge Entertainment, ICF International, Falcon Communications, RGS Associates, Laguna Ventures, Preferred Systems Solutions, ATS Corporation
  Peter M. Schulte, Co-Founder, Managing Partner
  Education: BA, Harvard College; MPPM, Yale School of Management
  Background: Arnhold & S Bleichroeder; VP, Salomon Brothers; IBM
  Directorships: ICF International, ATS Corporation, Falcon Communications, Xebec Global Corporation, RGS Associates, Laguna Ventures, Preferred Systems Solutions
  Jeffrey Mark, Partner
  Education: BBA, Isenberg School of Management, University of Massachusetts
  Background: Director, Risk Arbitrage Group, Royal Bank of Canada; Managing Director, Bear Stearns & Co.
  Wesley H.R. Gaus, Managing Partner
  Education: BS, Economics, Wharton School; BS, Systems Engineering, University of Pennsylvania
  Background: ING Baring Furman Selz
  Directorships: Martin Designs
  Daniel Colon, Jr., Partner
  212-909-8445
  Fax: 212-371-7254
  e-mail: dcolon@cmequity.com
  Education: BA, University of Miami; MBA, Zicklin School of Business, Baruch College
  Background: Carl Marks & Co

510 CNF INVESTMENTS Clark Enterprises, Inc.
7500 Old Georgetown Road
15th Floor
Bethesda, MD 20814
Phone: 301-657-7100 Fax: 301-657-7263
e-mail: info@clarkenterprises.com
web: www.clarkenterprises.com

Mission Statement: CNF focuses on early and growth stage companies, but will consider investments in later stages and selective public investments as well. CNF looks to partner with other venture capital and private equity firms and is an active investor providing strategic advice to its management teams.

Fund Size: $225 million
Founded: 1972
Investment Criteria: Early-Stage, Growth-Stage
Industry Group Preference: Life Sciences, Oil & Gas, Technology, Telecommunications, Alternative Energy
Portfolio Companies: American Honors, Blitsy, Brown Advisory, Calvert Education Serices, Carbon 38, Ceros, Circle Back, Eagle Oil & Gas Co., Echo 360, Enven Energy Corporation, EU Networks, Gigya, Hubub, In Go Money, Kareo, Media Math, MonoSol RX PharmFilm Technology, Neotract, NUO Therapeutics, Placecast, Print Syndicate, Regent Education, Shared Spectrum Company, Sonatype, Surf Watch, Svelte Medical Systems, Sweet Green, TerraGo, Trov, Up Skill, Vascular Therapies, Verax Biomedical, View Lift

Key Executives:
  Robert J Flanagan, Chief Executive Officer
  Education: BBA, Georgetown University; MS, Taxation, American University School of Business
  Directorships: Brown Advisory, Eagle Oil & Gas, Svelte Medical Systems, Vascular Therapies
  Joe Del Guercio, President
  Education: BS, Boston College; MBA, Harvard Business School
  Background: Director, LPL Financial Services; Robertson Stephens; Goldman Sachs
  Directorships: American Honors College, Placecast, Terrago Technologies, Verax Biomedical

511 COATUE MANAGEMENT
9 West 57th Street
25th Floor
New York, NY 10019
web: www.coatue.com

Mission Statement: Hedge fund investor focused on the technology sector in both public and private equity markets.

Fund Size: $700 million
Founded: 1999
Investment Criteria: Early Stage
Industry Group Preference: Artificial Intelligence, Technology, Information Technology, Software, Applications
Portfolio Companies: Anaplan, Box, Careem, HONKON, Jet, Lending Club, Lyft, Meituan-Dianping, SnapChat, Uber

Other Locations:
  2885 Sand Hill Road
  2nd Floor
  Menlo Park, CA 94025

  21 South Park Street
  2nd Floor
  San Francisco, CA 94107

  2 International Finance Centre
  F8 Finance Street 6701
  Hong Kong

Key Executives:
  Philippe Laffont, Founder
  Education: MS, Computer Science, MIT
  Kris Fredrickson, Managing Partner
  Education: BS, Universith of Southern California; JD, University of California, LA; MBA, Harvard Business School
  Background: VP, Goldman Sachs; SVP of Operations & Strategy, Munchery; Principal, Benchmark; Co-Founder, Curology
  Andy Chen, Partner
  Education: BS/MS, Mechanical Engineering, University of California, San Diego
  Background: Mechanical Engineer, Los Alamos National Laboratory; Mechanical Engineer, Sensor Metrix; Manager, Engineer Recruiting, Riviera Partners; Analyst, Central Intelligence Agency; Partner, Kleiner Perkins
  Directorships: Challenge Success

512 COFOUNDERS CAPITAL
e-mail: tim@cofounderscapital.com
web: cofounderscapital.com

Mission Statement: Cofounders is an early-stage seed fund focused on B2B software ventures predominately in North Carolina.

Geographic Preference: North Carolina
Fund Size: $31 million
Founded: 2015
Industry Group Preference: Diversified

Portfolio Companies: Automation Intellect, Canopy, CareNexis, Certificial, Contractor Quotes, CureMint, EmployUs, EasyVote Solutions, Ecobot, Element451, Factivate, Feedtrail, ImpathIQ, Looma, MapMyCustomers, MarGo, Myxx, ParkMyCloud, RelayOne, Pattern Health, Revibe Technologies, RewardStock, Savii Care, Second Nature, ServusConnect, Slope, Tesser Health, Testive, Urban Offsets, ViewStub, WAAM

Key Executives:
 David Gardner, General Partner
 Tim McLoughlin, Partner
 Tobi Walter, Principal

---

513 COHEN PRIVATE VENTURES
Stamford, CT

Mission Statement: Invests long term capital in direct private investments in the areas of direct private equity, venture and growth equity financing, concentrated public markets positions, and real estate.

Geographic Preference: United States
Founded: 2010
Investment Criteria: Direct Private Equity, Growth Equity & Venture Capital, Structured Securities, Specialized Credit Investments, Real Estate
Industry Group Preference: Private Equity, Real Estate
Portfolio Companies: Autonomous Partners

Key Executives:
 Andrew B. Cohen, Co-Founder/Chief Investment Officer
 Education: BA, University of Pennsylvania; MBA, Wharton School, University of Pennsylvania
 Background: Dune Capital Management LP; Morgan Stanley; Point 72
 Directorships: The New York Mets Baseball Club; Laureate Education Inc.; Republic First Bancorp Inc.; Advisory Board of Metro Bank PLC

---

514 COLLABORATIVE FUND
web: www.collaborativefund.com

Mission Statement: Collaborative Fund uses capital to merge projects that are motivated by both self interest and by broader interest. The company looks to invest in successful businesses that are making the world a better place in the broader categories of cities, finances, consumer products, and children's needs.

Fund Size: $300 million
Founded: 2010
Industry Group Preference: Transportation, Technology, Banking, Sustainable Products, Children, Healthcare, Pharmaceuticals
Portfolio Companies: Beyond Meat, Blue Bottle Coffee, Dandelion Energy, Impossible, Kickstarter, LTSE, Lyft, Outdoor Voices, Quora, Reddit, SOCAR, sweetgreen, Tala, The Farmer's Dog, Upstart

Key Executives:
 Craig Shapiro, Founder/Managing Partner
 Background: Investment Committee, Goldhirsh Foundation
 Sophie Bakalar, Venture Partner
 Education: BS, Math, Public Health, Tufts University
 Background: III Captical Management; President & Co-Founder, di8it charts; Co-Founder, fable
 Tehinder Gill, Principal
 Education: BS, Evolutionary Biology, Harvard University
 Background: Insight Venture Partners; Social Capital LP; Delivery Hero; Altman Vilandrie & Company

---

515 COLOMA VENTURES
10795 West Twain Avenue
Suite 100
Las Vegas, NV 89135

Mission Statement: Coloma Ventures is a venture capital group with a focus on Internet based start-ups, representing a consortium of accredited investors including many of Las Vegas' most influential and preeminent business luminaries. Coloma seeks to invest in talented entrepreneurial teams and provide founders and developers access to capital for vetted and viable Internet start-ups in web, software, mobile, digital media, social, and gaming sectors.

Geographic Preference: Las Vegas
Founded: 2010
Investment Criteria: Early-Stage
Industry Group Preference: Internet, Software, Mobile, Digital Media & Marketing, Social Media, Gaming
Portfolio Companies: Break-Up Alert, Design Genie, Kemistry, Las Vegas Film Festival, Momentous, Progressive REI, Promise Pictures, Salon Share, Thought Division, Zip The Strip

Key Executives:
 Monty Lapica, Founder/Managing Partner
 Education: Loyola Marymount University
 Background: Founder, Recognition Networks
 Directorships: Thought Division
 Thomas Bell, Partner
 Education: University of Nevada, Las Vegas
 Background: Founder, Salon Share; Founder, Rakeless Room; Founder, KemistryHair.com
 Joey Paulos, Partner
 Background: Manager, Hotel Administration, MGM Grand Hotel & Casino; Financial Analyst/Hotel Operations Manager, New York, New York Hotel & Casino

---

516 COLORADO MILE HIGH FUND
e-mail: comilehighfund@gcmlp.com

Mission Statement: The Colorado Mile High Fund is a $50 million co-investment program designed to invest in a diversified, high-quality portfolio of companies with a nexus to Colorado. Investments will generally be in the form of co-investments alongside financial sponsors, with ultimately 12 to 15 investments targeted for the portfolio. With established industries, strong growth opportunities, a dedicated research community, and an active private equity market, the state is ripe for investment. The fund is managed by GCM Grosvenor.

Geographic Preference: Colorado
Fund Size: $50 million
Investment Criteria: Mezzanine, Buyout, Growth Capital, Infrastructure/Energy
Industry Group Preference: Business Products & Services, Clean Technology, Renewable Resources, Information Technology, Communications, Aerospace, Defense and Government, Aerospace, Defense and Government, Manufacturing, Infrastructure, Energy

---

517 COLT VENTURES
2101 Cedar Springs Road
Suite 1230
Dallas, TX 75201

Phone: 214-397-0176
web: www.coltventures.com

Mission Statement: Colt Ventures is a privately-held opportunistic investment firm primarily focused on the following investment activities: Private Equity, Venture Capital, Proprietary Trading, Oil and Gas, Hedge Funds and Real Estate. Colt engages in a broad range of investment activities and has the flexibility to invest in a wide variety of asset classes.

Industry Group Preference: Oil & Gas, Infrastructure, Biotechnology, Financial Services, Technology
Portfolio Companies: Rocket Pharma, Bonti, La Jolla Pharmaceutical, Ignyta, Intrexon, NeoStem, Maple, Colt WTX Resources, Colt CTX Resources, Acapella, Alamito Minerals, Colt Mineral Interests, The Realtime Group, VizSense, High Brow Cat, Waggoner Ranch, Euroseas, Waste Corporation of America, Barilla Draw, Colt Unconventional Resources, Credo West, Smith Pipe, Anterios, CardioSpectra,

Halozyme Therapeutics, Highlands Bank, Paetec International, ServiceNow Inc., Eloqua, Trulogica, Motive, OpsTechnology, Oscar Mike Games, Craft International

Key Executives:
Darren Blanton, Founder/Managing Director
Background: Perry E. Espin; Able Investments
J.D. McCulloch, Managing Director
Education: BS, Mechanical Engineering; MBA, University of Texas, Austin; CFA
Background: VP, Investments, TRT Holdings; Industrial/Consumer Investment Banking Group, JPMorgan

518 COLUMBIA CAPITAL
204 South Union Street
Alexandria, VA 22314

Phone: 703-519-2000
e-mail: info@colcap.com
web: colcap.com

Mission Statement: Columbia Capital is a premier venture capital franchise in wireless, broadband, media, and enterprise information technology investing. Since its formation, Columbia Capital has taken a sector-focused approach to investing, and has funded over 130 global companies. This sector focus enables the fund to regularly identify disruptive emerging companies and to recognize and build value throughout a company's lifecycle - from early-stage investments, to large growth stage financings and any singular situations.

Fund Size: $441 million
Founded: 1989
Average Investment: $15 - $40 million
Minimum Investment: $1 million
Investment Criteria: Early Stage, Late Stage
Industry Group Preference: Communications, Communication Technology, Information Technology, Enterprise Technology, Software, Wireless, Broadband, Media, Cyber Security, Internet Infrastructure
Portfolio Companies: 2nd Watch, Access Sports Media, Altamira, BillingPlatform, Canara, Cologix, Contino, Daz 3D, Devas Multimedia, Endgame, euNetworks, Fuse, Landways, Lemongrass, Local Media, Mandalay Sports Media, Mobile Posse, NewSignature, Nextnav, Omnispace, OPAQ Networks, Open Media, RockYou, Slacker Radio, SoundHouse LLC, SummitIG, TerraPact, Verato, VuBiquity

Other Locations:
Reservoir Place
1601 Trapelo Road
Suite 154
Waltham, MA 02451
Phone: 781-290-2240

Key Executives:
Jim Fleming, Partner
Education: BA, Stanford University
Background: President, Prime Cellular; Price Waterhouse
Directorships: Nuvox Communications, Tennis Channel, WCS Wireless
Arun Gupta, Venture Partner
Education: BS, Electrical Engineering, MS, Engineering Economics, Stanford University; MBA, Harvard Business School
Background: Carlyle Venture Partners; Arthur D Little
Directorships: Approva, Avail Media, Brickstream, Devas Multimedia, Envysion, FreeWebs, Gizmoz, InnerWireless, Intelliworks, Millenial Media, Netuitive
Patrick Hendy, Partner
Education: BA, Economics, Vanderbilt University
Background: Financial Analyst, Global Telecommunications and Media Investment Banking Group of J.P. Morgan; Financial Analyst, Debt Capital Markets Group
Jennifer Krusius, Venture Partner
Education: BS, Applied Economics & Management, Cornell University; MBA, Harvard Business School
Background: General Manager, Uber Technologies; Investor, IFC Asset Management Company; Investor, Emerging Capital Partners; Investment Banker, Credit Suisse Group
John Leibovitz, Venture Partner
Education: BA, University of Pennsylvania; M.Phil, Cambridge University; JD, Yale Law School
Background: Deputy Chief, Wireless Bureau/Special Advisor, Spectrum Policy, FCC; McKinsey & Co.
Evan DeCorte, Principal
Education: BS, Economics/Political Science, George Washington University
Background: Head of Marketing, Roshan TDCA; Analyst, JPMorgan Chase
Directorships: Landways, TerraPact
Jeff Patterson, Venture Partner
Education: BA, Bowdoin College; MBA, Kellogg School of Management
Background: First National Bank of Boston; European Cable & Telephony, London
Directorships: Rapid Communications, Si TV
John Siegel, Partner
Education: BA, Princeton University; MBA, Harvard Bsuiness School
Background: Morgan Stanley Private Equity Group; Fidelity Ventures; Alex Brown & Sons
Directorships: mindSHIFT Technologies, FDN Communications, Netifice Communications, ICG Communications, Integrated Solutions
Jason Booma, Partner
Education: BS, Computer Engineering, Northwestern University; MBA, Kellogg School of Management
Background: Centennial Ventures
Directorships: Cloud Sherpas, Envysion
Monish Kundra, Partner
Education: BS, Wharton School; BS, Chemical Engineering, University of Pennsylvania
Background: Senior VP, Corporate Development, Mobile Satellite Ventures
Directorships: NexNav, Local Media Partners

519 COLUMN GROUP
1700 Owens Street
Suite 500
San Francisco, CA 94158

Phone: 415-865-2050 Fax: 415-255-2048
e-mail: info@thecolumngroup.com
web: www.thecolumngroup.com

Mission Statement: The Column Group is a venture capital firm that provides capital and operational support to life sciences and biotechnology companies. The Column Group focuses on early stage drug discovery companies and is dedicated to the development of breakthrough therapies.

Fund Size: $176 million
Average Investment: $15 - $30 million
Investment Criteria: Seed, Early Stage
Industry Group Preference: Biotechnology, Pharmaceuticals, Life Sciences
Portfolio Companies: Carmot Therapeutics, Constellation Pharmaceuticals, eFFECTOR Therapeutics, FLX Bio, Gritstone Oncology, Igenica Biotherapeutics, Immune Design, Kallyope, Neurona Therapeutics, NGM Biopharmaceuticals, Nurix, Oric Pharmaceuticals, Peloton Therapeutics

Key Executives:
Peter Svennilson, Founder/Managing Partner
Background: Founder & Managing Partner, Three Crowns Capital; Associate Managing Director, Nomura Securities
Directorships: Immune Design, NGM Biopharmaceuticals, ORIC Pharmaceuticals, Gritstone Oncology
David V. Goeddel PhD, PhD, Managing Partner
Education: BA, Chemistry, University of California, San

Diego; PhD, Biochemistry, University of Colorado
Background: Co-Founder, Tularik; Senior Scientific Vice President, Amgen
Directorships: Constellation Pharmaceuticals, FLX Bio, Igenica Biotherapeutics, NGM Biopharmaceuticals, Nurix, Peloton Therapeutics
Tim Kutzkey, PhD, Managing Partner
Education: Stanford University; PhD, University of California, Berkeley
Background: Scientist, KAI Pharmaceuticals
Directorships: Carmot Therapeutics, Nurix, Peloton Therapeutics
Larry Lasky, PhD, Partner
Education: BA, PhD, University of California, Los Angeles
Background: Founding Scientist, Genetics Institute; Scientist, Genentech; General Partner, Latterell Venture Partners; Partner, USVP
Directorships: Carmot Therapeutics, eFFECTOR Pharmaceuticals
JJ Kang, PhD, Partner
Education: Harvard University; PhD, California Institute of Technology
Background: FibroGen
Directorships: Escient Pharmaceuticals; Tenaya Therapeutics
Leon Chen, PhD, Partner
Education: BA, Biochemistry, University of California, Berkeley; PhD, Molecular Pharmacology, Stanford School of Business; MBA, Stanford Grad. School of Business
Background: Founder, KAI Pharmaceuticals; Venture Partner, OrbiMed; Partner, Skyline Ventures
Directorships: E-Scape Bio; TranscripTx; Adicet

520 COMCAST VENTURES
One Kearny Building
23 Geary Street
10th Floor
San Francisco, CA 94108

web: www.comcastventures.com

Mission Statement: To turn startups into profitable businesses through innovation and business resources.
Geographic Preference: United States, Europe, Israel
Fund Size: $600 million
Founded: 1999
Investment Criteria: Seed-Late Stage; dedicated management team with clearly defined target market combined with strategic opportunities
Industry Group Preference: Media, Broadband, E-Commerce & Manufacturing, Data Communications, Communications, Applications Software & Services, Networking, Infrastructure, Advertising, Consumer Products, Enterprise Software
Portfolio Companies: Accolade, Atscale, Automat, Autonomic, Away, Axial, B8ta, Baobab, Baublebar, Bay Dynamics, Bento, Benu Networks, BigID, Birchbox, BitSight, Blink, Blockdaemon, Brightside, Bunker, Cheddar, Cloud Passage, College Ave Student Loans, Color, Comparably, Creative Live, Cross Mediaworks, CTI Towers, Cut, Data Plus Math, Datastax, Docu Sign, Dray Now, Earny, Eden, Edge Connex, Enigma, Fan Duel, Felix & Paul Studios, Flipboard, Fortress, Grokker, Heleo, Hippo, Hired, Hollar, Houseparty, Houzz, Instacart, Integrate, Interactions, Italic, Jornaya, K Health, KeyMe, KiwiCo, KodaCloud, Lendio, Life House, Lyft, Lytics, Madison Reed, MealPal, Meta, Modsy, Nextdoor, NextVR, Ninth Decimal, OfferUp, Osaro, Pony.ai, PrecisionHawk, Quantifind, Ramp, Retina AI, SevenR Rooms, SheKnows, Shine, Slack, SnagFilms, Spaces, Stella Service, SundaySky, Taboola, Talix, Tastemade, The Athletic, Trion, TuneIn, UberMedia, Uptycs, Videology, Vox Media, Windsor Circle, YouNow, Zenefits, Zola, ZoomData

Other Locations:
480 Cowper Street
Suite 200
Palo Alto, CA 94301

One Comcast Center
55th Floor
1701 John F. Kennedy Boulevard
Philadelphia, PA 19103

588 Broadway
Suite 202
New York, NY 10012

1335 - 4th Street
4th Floor
Santa Monica, CA 90401

Key Executives:
Andrew Cleland, Managing Director
Education: BS, Edinburgh University; MBA, INSEAD
Background: Managing Director, Time Warner Investments; Booz Allen & Hamilton; COO, TrustTheDJ
Sheena Jindal, Partner
Education: BS, MIT; MBA, Tuck School of Business
Background: Strategy & Operations Lead, Symphony Commerce; Corporate Strategy Group, Hudson Bay Company
Adam Spivack, Partner
Education: BA, Duke University
Background: Advertising Trading Group Lead, FreeWheel Media; Management Consultant, Deloitte Consulting

521 COMET LABS
703 Market Street
19th Floor
San Francisco, CA 94103

e-mail: hi@cometlabs.io
web: cometlabs.io

Mission Statement: Comet Labs is a venture capital firm and startup platform with an exclusive focus on AI and robotics technology.
Founded: 2015
Industry Group Preference: Artificial Intelligence, Robotics, Deep Technology, Industry Applications, Machine Learning
Portfolio Companies: 3scan, Abundant Robotics, Airmap, Akin, Alces Technology, AMP Robotics, Arch, Cobalt, Creator, Deep Vision, Doc AI, DotDashPay, Esperanto Technologies, Grabango, IAM Robotics, InsightRX, Iron Ox, Lightform, Maidbot, Matternet, Oculii, OtoSense, Percolata, Plutoshift, Point One Navigation, PRENAV, RBC Signals, Ripcord, Roost, SalesHero, Shaper, Simbe, SunTouch, Transcend Robotics, WiBotics

Key Executives:
Mingyao Wang, Chairman
Education: IMBA, Tsinghua University
Background: Manager, Dacheng Fund Management Co.; SVP, Zeo2IPO Group; Partner, Ninesail Capital; Executive Director, Legend Holdings
Lucas Wang, Managing Partner
Education: BA, Finance, National Taiwan University; MBA, National Sun Yat-Sen University
Background: Market Manager, Microelectronics Technology Inc.; Partner, WI Harper Group; Execution Partner/Founder, TMI Holding Corp.; CEO/Found, HWTrek; US Operations Partner, Legend Star;

522 COMMONS CAPITAL
320 Washington Street
4th Floor
Brookline, MA 02445

Phone: 617-739-3500 Fax: 617-739-3550
web: www.commonscapital.com

Mission Statement: Invests in early stage businesses whose products and services address significant social and environmental issues in the areas of healthcare, environment, energy and education.

Investment Criteria: Early-Stage
Industry Group Preference: Healthcare, Energy, Environment, Education
Portfolio Companies: Apex Learning, Claros Diagnostics, CodeRyte, Combinent BioMedical Systems, CTP Hydrogen, H2Gen Innovations, HistoRx, Medical Metrix Solutions, Niman Ranch, OutStart, Passport Systems, Pelamis Wave Power, Protonex, Solstice Capital, Sun & Earth, Teladoc

Key Executives:
  William Osborn, Investment Manager
  e-mail: wosborn@commonscapital.com
  Education: BA, Princeton University; JD, George Washington University Law School
  Background: Partner, Arete Corporation; Principal, Venture Investment Management Company, LLC; Management Consultant, Arthur D Little
  Directorships: Evergreen Solar, World Power Technologies, Evolutionary Technologies, Surgical Sealants, Fingerlakes Aquaculture, Conservation Services Group

523 COMMONWEALTH CAPITAL VENTURES LP
400 West Cummings Park
Suite 1725-134
Woburn, MA 01801

Phone: 781-890-5554
web: www.commonwealthvc.com

Mission Statement: Commonwealth Capital Ventures' experienced team works closely with entrepreneurial management teams to help them build outstanding growth companies and deliver superior returns to investors.

Geographic Preference: Northeast United States
Fund Size: $580 million
Founded: 1995
Average Investment: $2-6 million
Minimum Investment: $1 million
Investment Criteria: Early Stage, Venture Growth Stage
Industry Group Preference: Software Services, Internet Technology, Communication Technology, Instrumentation, Internet, Digital Media & Marketing, Communications, Wireless
Portfolio Companies: Aberdeen Group, Acacia, Accurev, Akibia, Altiga Networks, American Internet Corp, Antenna Software, Auction Holdings, BBN Technologies, BitSight, Brooks24x7, BuyerZone, ByAllAccounts, Carbon Design Systems, CardScan, Centra Software, Cerulean Technology, CloudSwitch, Compete, Constant Contact, Crossbeam Systems, Direct Hit Technologies, e-Dialog, Echo Nest, Envoy Networks, Expressor Software, Extrapraise, HubCast, i-Logix, Inframetrics, Innoveer Solutions, JAZD Markets, MacGregor Group, NBX Corp., Net2Net Corp., NeuroMetrix, Nova Analytics Corp., OneRiot, Oneshape Inc., Ounce Labs, Pactolus Communications, Qiave Technologies, Qvidian, RAMP, Reval, Sand 9, Seahorse Bioscience, SeniorLink, SoundBite Communications, Tally Systems, TIM Group, Vela Systems, Verivo, Visible Assets, Wavesmith Networks, Zinio Systems, Zoom Information

Key Executives:
  Michael T. Fitzgerald, General Partner/Founder
  Education: Amherst College; Harvard Business School
  Background: General Partner, Palmer Partners
  Jeffrey M. Hurst, General Partner/Founder
  Education: MBA, Tulane University; BA History & Economics, Duke University
  Background: GE Capital's Corporate Finance Group; Cox Partners; Bamkers Trust Company
  Stephen McCormack, General Partner/Founder
  Education: MBA, University of Michigan; Graduate, Psychology, Dartmouth College
  Background: 3i Corporation, Merrill Lynch Venture Capital, Massachusetts Technology Development Corporation, Bank of New York, Interactive Data Corporation
  Justin J. Perreault, General Partner
  Education: MBA, Harvard Business School; BS Mechanical Engineering, Rensselaer Polytechnic Institute
  Background: CEO, Object Deisgn; Harvard Management Company; McKinsey & Company
  Elliot M. Katzman, General Partner
  Education: BSBA, Salem State College
  Background: General Partner, Kodiak Venture Partners; Founder, Myteam.com
  Directorships: CloudSwitch, OneRiot, My Perfect Gig, Vela Systems, The Echo Nest

524 COMPASS GROUP
135 Eest 57th Street
30th Floor
New York, NY 10022

Phone: 212-355-7630 **Fax:** 212-355-2015
web: cgcompass.com

Mission Statement: A registered investment adviser servicing institutional and private clients specializing in Latin American investments. Compass Group aims to provide consistently better returns than competitors and the highest level of service and the best range of products to serve their clients' investment needs.

Geographic Preference: Latin America
Founded: 1995
Other Locations:
  Carlos Pellegrini 1023
  14th Floor
  Buenos Aires
  Argentina
  Phone: 54-11 4878 8000 **Fax:** 54-11 4878 8008

  Av. Rosario Norte 555
  Piso 14
  Las Condes
  Santiago 1001
  Chile
  Phone: 562-364-4660

  Av. La Paz 1049
  Piso 3
  Miraflores
  Lima
  Peru
  Phone: 511-611-5350 **Fax:** 511-611-5351

  Paseo de los Tamarindos No. 90
  Torre 1
  Piso 21
  Mexico DF 05120
  Mexico
  Phone: 5255-5010-2150 **Fax:** 5255-5570-9583

  Carrera 7 No. 113-43
  Suite 1508
  Bogota
  Columbia
  Phone: 57-1748-6096 **Fax:** 57-1214-3101

Key Executives:
  Manuel Jose Balbontin, Founder & Managing Partner
  Education: BS, Catholic University; MBA, Harvard University
  Background: Managing Director, Banco Santander; Citibank/Citicorp
  Jorge Aguilo, Partner/CEO
  Education: Civil Engineering, Catholic University, Chile; MBA, Instituto de Empresa Business School, Madrid

Venture Capital & Private Equity Firms / Domestic Firms

525 COMPASS GROUP MANAGEMENT LLC
301 Riverside Avenue
2nd Floor
Westport, CT 06880

Phone: 203-221-1703 **Fax:** 203-221-8253
web: www.compassequity.com

Mission Statement: Private investing in small to middle market companies for growth, ownership change and recapitalization.
Geographic Preference: United States, Canada
Fund Size: $300 million
Founded: 1998
Average Investment: $15-150 million
Minimum Investment: $4 million
Investment Criteria: Middle-Market, Acquisitions, MBO
Industry Group Preference: Manufacturing, Distribution, Services, Retailing, Diversified
Portfolio Companies: 55.1 Tactical, Advanced Circuits, Aeroglide Corporation, American Furniture Manufacturing, Arnold Magnetic Technologies, Camelbak, Clean Earth, Ergobaby, Foam Fabrications, Fox Racing Shox, Halo Branded Solutions, Liberty Safe, Manitoba Harvest, Silvue, Staffmark, Sterno Group, Tridien Medical, Velocity Outdoor Corporation

Other Locations:
2010 Main Street
Suite 1220
Irvine, CA 92614
Phone: 949-333-5033 **Fax:** 949-333-5043

Key Executives:
Ryan J. Faulkingham, Executive Vice President/CFO
Education: Lehigh University; Fordham University
Background: Merrill Lynch; WebMD Corp.; Arthur Andersen
Elias J. Sabo, Partner/CFO
Education: Rensselaer Polytechnic Institute
Background: Investment Banker, CIBC Oppenheimer; President/Chief Investment Officer, Boundary Partners; Acquisition Department, Colony Capital
Directorships: TransMarine Navigation, Venturi Partners, KBell Holdings, CBS Personnel Holdings
Patrick A. Maciariello, Partner/COO
Education: BBA, University of Notre Dame; MBA, Columbia University
Background: Management Consultant, Bain & Company; Deutsche Banc Alex. Brown

526 COMPASS TECHNOLOGY PARTNERS LP
1155 Broadway Street
Suite 210
Redwood City, CA 94063

Phone: 650-366-7595
e-mail: darscott@compasstechpartners.com
web: www.compasstechpartners.com

Mission Statement: Focused on investments in emerging companies with innovative products or services addressing high-growth markets.
Geographic Preference: San Francisco
Fund Size: $10 million
Founded: 1988
Average Investment: $500,000
Minimum Investment: $500,000
Investment Criteria: Seed/First Round
Industry Group Preference: Information Technology, Communications, Medical Devices, Computer Related, Silicon-Related Technologies
Portfolio Companies: Atherotech, Oculex Pharmaceuticals, Radio Therapeutics Corporation, NanoNexus, Photodigm, SoftBook Press, Dragnet Solutions, Torrex Equipment Corporation, Boxer Cross, DataCycles, Metara, Ripfire, Yield Dynamics, Tesla Motors, Toolwire, Percutaneous Systems, Sentinel Vision, Applied MicroStructures

Key Executives:
David G. Arscott, General Partner
e-mail: darscott@compasstechpartners.com
Education: BA, College of Wooster; MBA, University of Michigan
Background: Citicorp Venture Capital; Arscott, Norton & Associates
Directorships: Lam Research, Toolwire, Star Vox
Martha P.E. Arscott, General Partner/CFO
e-mail: marscott@compasstechpartners.com
Education: BA Economics, Hollins College; MBA, Darden School, University of Virginia
Background: Crocker National Bank

527 COMPOUND
156 Fifth Ave.
Suite 600
New York, NY 10010

Phone: 646-794-1330
e-mail: info@compound.vc
web: www.compound.vc

Mission Statement: Compound, formerly Metamorphic Ventures, is a New York City based venture capital fund that invests in start-up and early stage technology businesses focused on the digital media and digital commerce sectors. Compound believes that vast new waves of innovation and business opportunity are on their way leveraging the build out of the fixed and mobile broadband internet network. In fact, many are already here. Compound funds those early stage businesses in the digital media and digital commerce sectors. While it may appear that these are two distinct sectors, it is our view that they are in fact in the process of converging and that Compound is one of a few venture firms with the expertise in both domains.

Investment Criteria: Early-Stage
Industry Group Preference: Technology, Digital Media & Marketing, E-Commerce & Manufacturing
Portfolio Companies: Agrilyst, Allset, Alreverie, Ample, Away, BetterView, Boost Biomes, Blockstack, Braze, Buzz Points, Casa, Catalyst, Chango, Clear Genetics, Compound, Computable, Counselytics, CrowdAI, CryptoKitties, Deepgram, Digital Genius, Easecentral, Fetch Back, Finova Financial, Gem, Genies, Indiegogo, Indio, Kadena, Lenddo, Livepeer, Lotus Flare, Lune, Mass Relevance, Matteream, Mode, Modsy, Movable Ink, Nearbuy, Nectar, Noteworth, Nucypher, Ono, Orch1d, Osaro, Payjoy, Pluot, Rayv, Rebag, Remote.it, Sayspring, Sense360, Songza, Stamped, Stanza, StowAway, Symphony Commerce, Switch, Talkspace, Tap Commerce, Tapad, Thinknear, Thrive Market, Tia, Transactis, Trusted, TV Time, Upcounsel, Vitae, Wanderu, Wayve, Xperiel, Zipdrug, Zodiac

Key Executives:
David Hirsch, Managing Director
Education: BA, University of Maryland
Background: Google; Co-Founder, Google Vertical Markets Group; Snowball; AdSmart
Marc Michel, Managing Director
Education: BA, Emory University; MBA, Wharton School
Background: Group Head, TD Capital; Managing Partner, EOS Partners; Co-Founder, Precyse Solutions
Michael Dempsey, Partner
Education: BA, New York University
Background: Rothenberg Ventures; CB Insights; Crane Partners
Joshua Nussbaum, Partner
Education: BS, New York University
Background: Business Development, JustDecide; Digital Marketing, Bayard Advertising

528 COMSPACE
web: www.comspacedev.com

Mission Statement: Offers interim executive management, advisory, and early stage private equity investment to firms in

Venture Capital & Private Equity Firms / Domestic Firms

the aerospace/defense, wireless telecom, and information technology fields.
Geographic Preference: Worldwide
Founded: 1997
Average Investment: $500,000
Minimum Investment: $50,000
Investment Criteria: Early Stage
Industry Group Preference: Aerospace, Defense and Government, Information Technology, Telecommunications, Wireless Technologies
Portfolio Companies: CEL Polska, eLink Communications, Fiberight, Give More Media, Global Radio, Knight-Hub Computing, Peracon, Technikom Polska, Tracer Net, Tucana Technologies, Wall Street Sports

Key Executives:
   Michael W. Miller, President/Managing Director
   Education: MBA Finance, University of Chicago; Aeronautical/Astronautical Engineering/Electrical Engineering, University of Illinois
   Background: Fourtune 500; CEO, TracerNet; Arc Second; Sr Executive, Rockwell International/Orbital Science/Center for Innovative Technology
   Thien-Ly Ngo, Managing Director
   Education: BS, Electrical Engineering, General Motors Institute; MA, Telecommunications, George Mason University

529 COMSTOCK CAPITAL PARTNERS LLC
9430 Readcrest Drive
Beverly Hills, CA 90210

    Phone: 310-278-6444 **Fax:** 310-861-5010
    e-mail: info@comstockpartners.com
    web: www.comstockpartners.com

Mission Statement: A private capital firm that provides growth and buy-out capital, from senior debt to equity, and actively works with management to transform public and private companies from good to great. With extensive operating experience, they have created over $12 billion of value across a range of companies focused on consumer-facing and customer relationship business. The firm will consider deals across the nation, but focuses on the West Coast.
Geographic Preference: West Coast
Founded: 1992
Average Investment: $10 million - $500 million
Investment Criteria: Middle-market, minimum of $5 million EBIT, $50 million to $750 million in revenue
Industry Group Preference: Financial Services, Media, Entertainment, Distribution, Consumer Products, Outsourcing & Efficiency

Key Executives:
   Jeffrey L Balash, Partner
   Education: Summa cum laude, Princeton University; Baker Scholar, Harvard Business School; Cum laude, Harvard Law School
   Background: Managing Director, Lehman Brothers; Managing Director, Drexel Burnham; Co-Founder, Anthem Partners; Co-Founder, JL Furnishings; CFO/Chief Strategic Officer, Telephony@Work; Director Export Operations, Avon Products; CEO, Louis Dreyfus & Cie

530 COMVEST PARTNERS
525 Okeechobee Blvd
Suite 1050
West Palm Beach, FL 33401

    Phone: 561-727-2000
    web: www.comvest.com

Mission Statement: Comvest Partners provides equity capital to middle-market companies based in the United States.
Geographic Preference: United States
Fund Size: $893 million
Founded: 2000
Average Investment: $25 - $100 million

Investment Criteria: Divestitures, Management Buyouts, Restructurings, Industry Consolidations, Public-to-Private Transactions, Turnaround
Industry Group Preference: Software, Information Technology, Transportation, Healthcare, Industrial Manufacturing, Consumer Products, Fintech, Financial Services, Education
Portfolio Companies: AxisPoint Health, BEL USA, Cartera Commerce, Convey Health Solutions, D&S Community Services, EVCI Career Colleges, GroundLink, Haggen, Innovative Health Products, Old Time Pottery, Priority Holdings, Red Hawk Fire & Security, Robbins Brothers, Sunteck, US Pipe
Other Locations:
   181 West Madison Street
   Suite 3815
   Chicago, IL 60602
   Phone: 312-637-8455

Key Executives:
   Michael Falk, CEO & Managing Partner
   Education: BA, Economics, Queens College
   Background: Founder & CEO, Commonwealth Associates
   Roger Marrero, Managing Partner
   Education: BA, BBA, University of Texas at Austin; MBA, Harvard Business School
   Background: Principal, ABRY Partners; Apax Partners; Hicks, Muse, Tate & Furst; Goldman Sachs
   Tom Clark, Partner
   Education: BA, International Relations, Johns Hopkins University; MBA, Harvard Business School
   Background: Principal, Retail & Consumer, Apax Partners; Principal, Private Equity, Bain Capital; Analyst, M&A Group, Goldman Sachs
   Lee Bryan, Partner
   Education: BA, Georgia Institute of Technology; MBA, Harvard Business School
   Background: Director, Private Equity Group, Harbert Management Corporation; Bain & Company; Procter & Gamble; Delta Airlines
   Marshall Griffin, Principal
   Education: BS, Finance, Boston College; MBA, Duke University
   Background: Senior Associate, Crossbow Ventures; Analyst, TD Capital

531 CONCENTRIC EQUITY PARTNERS
Financial Investments Corporation
50 East Washington Street
Suite 400
Chicago, IL 60602

    Phone: 312-494-4513
    web: www.ficcep.com

Mission Statement: Concentric Equity Partners provides financial and operating expertise to profitable growth companies. The firm seeks opportunities in the service industry, including business, consumer, financial, and technology-enabled services.
Fund Size: $650 million
Average Investment: $10 - $30 million
Investment Criteria: Management Buyouts, Leveraged Buyouts, Growth Equity Investments, Majority & Minority Investment Structures
Industry Group Preference: Business Products & Services, Consumer Services, Financial Services, Healthcare Services, Technology-Enabled Services
Portfolio Companies: Airway Services, Aperture, Catastrophe Solutions International, Chicago Deferred Exchange Company, Coastal Waste & Recycling, Cole Taylor Bank, Colonial Claims, Consulting Solutions, Ellison Bakery, Energy Distribution Partners, Environmental Pest Services, Lario Oil & Gas Company, Liberty Oilfield Services, Marathon Data Systems, Market Express, MB Financial Bank, Mortgage Contracting Services, Microsystems,

Mountain Waste & Recycling, Nine Four Ventures, NSC Technologies, Online Tech Stores, Puttman Infrastructure, SaaS Capital, Southpaw Live, Stay Alfred, Tricoci University, UsAmeriBank, Vision, World Energy Partners

Key Executives:
  Ken Hooten, Partner
  Education: BS, University of Illinois; MBA, Kellogg School of Management
  Background: Founder, ServiceMaster Ventures; President & Founder, ServiceMaster Home Services Center
  Jennifer Steans, Partner
  Education: BA, Davidson College; MBA, Kellogg School of Management, Northwestern University
  Background: Consultant, Deloitte & Touche; Treasurer, Prime Graphics; Founder, Financial Investments Corporation
  Directorships: Chicago Deferred Exchange Corp., Prime Graphics
  Frank Reppenhagen, Partner
  Education: BS, Industrial Engineering, University at Buffalo; MBA, University of Chicago Booth School of Business
  Ian Ross, Partner
  Education: BA, Finance, Michigan State University; MBA, University of Chicago Booth School of Business
  Background: Edgewater Funds; Lincoln International; GE Capital Corporation
  David Gervase, Chief Financial Officer
  Education: BS, Accounting, University of Illinois; CPA
  Background: Director of Finance, Arena Football League

532 CONNECTICUT INNOVATIONS
470 James Street
Suite 8
New Haven, CT 06513

Phone: 860-258-7858 **Fax:** 860-563-5851
e-mail: info@ctinnovations.com
web: www.ctinnovations.com

Mission Statement: State of Connecticut's leading investor in high technology, making risk capital investments in high tech companies throughout the state. They offer a wide range of support from research assistance to financing for product development and marketing.

Geographic Preference: Connecticut
Founded: 1989
Average Investment: $1 million
Minimum Investment: $500,000
Investment Criteria: Seed, Start-up, First Stage, Second Stage. Applicants must be located in Connecticut, have a management team in place, provide a business plan and demonstrate sustainable competitive advantage.
Industry Group Preference: Advanced Marine Applications, Aerospace, Defense and Government, Energy, Photonics, Advanced Materials, Biotechnology, Information Technology, Renewable Energy, Applications Software & Services, Environment Products & Services, High Technology, Clean Technology, Medical Devices
Portfolio Companies: Achillion, Affomix Corp., Alexion, ATMI, Axiomx, Biohaven, Bioplexus, Bristol Technology, Cara Therapeutics, Cardium, CGI, Curagen, Cyberian Outpost, Cyvek, Cyvera, DEOS, Digital Graphics, Discover Video, EDR, Genaissance Pharmaceuticals, Hadapt, Idevices, Imstem Biotechnology, International Telecommunication Data Systems, Ipsogen Cancer Profiler, Job Direct, Keisense, Lexibridge, Lifecodes, Linksoft, Memry, Meta Server, Netkey, Neuvis, Nufern, NXT-ID, Online Tech, Open Solutions, Paragon, PCC Technology, Perosphere Inc., Photonics Applications, PolyVision, Post-N-Track, Preferred Systems, Premise, Proton, Silversky, Standing Stone

Key Executives:
  Peter Longo, Senior Managing Director, Investments
  860-258-7858
  e-mail: peter.longo@ctinnovations.com
  Education: BBA, University of Connecticut; MBA, University of Hartford; CPA; CFA
  Background: Senior Accountant, Ernst & Young
  Kevin Crowley, Managing Director, Investments
  860-258-7858
  e-mail: kevin.crowley@ctinnovations.com
  Education: MBA, Quinnipiac University
  Background: Director, Office of BioScience, Connecticut Department of Economic & Community Development
  Directorships: frevvo, Oil Purification Systems, RemoTV, Retail Optimization
  Pauline Murphy, Senior Managing Director, Investments
  e-mail: pauline.murphy@ctinnovations.com
  Education: BS Accounting, University of Connecticut; CPA
  Background: Controller, early stage software development company; Ernst & Young
  Matthew McCooe, Chief Executive Officer, Connecticut Innovations
  Education: BA, Boston College; MBA, Columbia University
  Background: Chart Venture Partners; Director, Columbia University Science and Technology Ventures; Co-Founder, Eureka Networks; Fortune 500; Becton Dickinson; MCI
  Philip Siuta, COO/CFO
  Education: BS, Accounting, Villanova University
  Background: Project Manager, Jackson Laboratory; Project Manager, Connecticut Ecosystem
  David Wurzer, Executive Vice President/Chief Investment Officer
  e-mail: david.wurzer@ctinnovations.com
  Education: BBA, Accountancy, University of Notre Dame
  Background: Executive Vice President, CuraGen Corporation; Senior Vice President, Value Health
  Daniel Wagner, Managing Director, Investments
  e-mail: daniel.wagner@ctinnovations.com
  Education: BS, Biology, University of Dayton; MBA, MS, Health Sciences, Quinnipiac University
  Background: CuraGen Corporation
  Directorships: Innovatient Solutions, RemoteReality Corp., FMP Products

533 CONSOR CAPITAL
Sausalito, CA

web: www.consorcapital.com

Mission Statement: Consor Capital LLC was formed by Josh and Jay Huffard to manage venture capital investments. Consor Capital focuses on early-stage companies serving consumers and small businesses. We seek to partner with companies run by strong leaders, focused on rapidly changing markets and leveraging technology as a key aspect of their business model.

Investment Criteria: Early-Stage
Portfolio Companies: Coveroo, NewCross Technologies, vSocial, Wallop

Key Executives:
  Jay Huffard, Manager
  Education: BA, Yale University; MBA, Stanford Graduate School of Business
  Background: Managing Director, Huffard & Co.; Managing Director & Principal, Prima Managment Corp.

534 CONSTELLATION TECHNOLOGY VENTURES

web: technologyventures.constellation.com

Mission Statement: The mission of Constellation Technology Ventures is to drive innovation through Exelon by investing in venture stage energy technology companies that can provide new solutions to Exelon and its customers.

Fund Size: $650 million
Founded: 1998
Average Investment: $15 million
Minimum Investment: $5 million

Venture Capital & Private Equity Firms / Domestic Firms

Investment Criteria: Early to mid-stage companies with emerging digital networks
Industry Group Preference: Digital Media & Marketing, Communications, Enterprise Services, Media, Information Technology
Portfolio Companies: Bidgely, C3 Energy, ChargePoint, Cool Planet Energy Systems, DemandQ, LevelTen Energy, Measurabl, Ouster, Owl Analytics, PosiGen, PrecisionHawk, Proterra, Qnovo, Sparkfund, Stem, V-Grid Energy Systems, XL Hybrids

Key Executives:
  Scott Dupcak, Managing Director
  e-mail: scott.dupcak@constellation.com
  Education: BS, Accounting, Fairfield University; MBA, Robert H. Smith School of Business, University of Maryland
  Background: Strategic Systems/Business Operations, Exelon Corp.
  Curtis Schickner, Principal, Investments
  e-mail: curtis.schickner@constellation.com
  Education: BA, Economics, University of Maryland
  Background: Exelon Generation Finance
  Megan Sparks, Director, Commercialization
  e-mail: megan.sparks@constellation.com
  Education: BS, Finance/Logistics, University of Maryland College Park; MA, Applied Economics, Johns Hopkins University
  Background: Constellation Retail & Wholesale
  Shounok Sinha, Principal, Investments
  e-mail: Shounok.Sinha@constellation.com
  Education: BS, Instrumentation Engineering, BMS College Of Engineering, India; MBA, University of Maryland

535 CONTOUR VENTURE PARTNERS
475 Park Avenue South
6th Floor
New York, NY 10016

Phone: 212-644-5482
e-mail: businessplan@contourventures.com
web: www.contourventures.com

Mission Statement: Contour Venture Partners is a venture capital firm based in New York. The firm invests in early stage companies that provide technology solutions to established sectors, including financial services, business services, software, and digital media. Contour Venture Partners seeks to help entrepreneurs and management teams to build companies that will transform their industries.
Geographic Preference: Northeast United States
Average Investment: $250,000 - $1.5 million
Investment Criteria: Seed-Stage, Early-Stage
Industry Group Preference: Financial Services, Digital Media & Marketing, Internet, Business Products & Services, Software, Technology, Information Technology
Portfolio Companies: Bench, BounceExchange, Clothes Horse, Contently, Datadog, Dstillery, EachScape, Edgecase, Ellevest, Estimize, EveryScreen Media, FieldLens, FinTech Innovation Lab, LeagueApps, Movable Ink, Octane Lending, Oggifinogi, OnDeck, OwnEnergy, Pathgather, Pendo, Punchbowl Software, Qwiki, Routehappy, Scratch Music Group, ShopKeep, Simpli.fi, Source3, SwapDrive, Ticketfly, TiqIQ, True Office, Ufora, Voxy, YellowJacket, Yhat, YouBeauty, Zipmark

Key Executives:
  Bob Greene, Managing Partner
  Education: BS, Wharton School, University of Pennsylvania; MBA, MIT Sloan School of Management
  Background: Managing Partner, Flatiron Partners; General Partner, Chase Capital Partners; Chemical Venture Partners
  Directorships: New York Venture Capital Association
  Matt Gorin, Managing Partner
  Education: BA, Economics & American Studies, Brandeis University; MBA, Harvard Business School
  Background: Promotory Financial Group; Strategic Planning & Corporate Development Group, Red Hat; Morgan Stanley; PricewaterhouseCoopers; Founder, StreetWise Partners

536 CONVERGE VENTURE PARTNERS
101 Main Street
Cambridge, MA 02142

web: converge.vc

Mission Statement: Converge Venture Partners provides capital to early stage technology companies in the software, cloud, mobile, digital media, Internet and SaaS sectors.
Geographic Preference: Boston, New England, New York City
Fund Size: $27 million
Founded: 1998
Average Investment: $100,000 - $1 million
Investment Criteria: Seed, Early Stage, Early Series A
Industry Group Preference: Information Technology, Software, Internet, Digital Media & Marketing, Mobile, SaaS, Cloud Computing
Portfolio Companies: Apperian, Coherent Path, Curoverse, Disruptor Beam, DocTracker, HapYak, HNW, Influitive, InsightSquared, InStream, Linkable Networks, N-of-One, Offerpop, ownCloud, OwnerIQ, ParElastic, Powerhouse Dynamics, Practically Green, Prime Student Loan, Promoboxx, Scratch Wireless, Skyhook Wireless, TimeTrade, TripleShot, TrueLens, Xconomy, YieldBot, wymsee

Key Executives:
  Maia Heymann, Senior Managing Director
  e-mail: maia@convergevp.com
  Education: BA, Wellesley College
  Background: Managing Director, Shott Capital Management; BancBoston Ventures; Bank of Boston
  Nilanana Bhowmik, Founder/General Partner
  Education: BEng, Computer Science, Indian Institute of Technology; MS, Computer Science, University of South Carolina; MBA, INSEAD
  Background: Managing Director, Longworth Venture Partners

537 CONVERSION CAPITAL
902 Broadway
Suite 1611
New York, NY 10010

e-mail: info@conversioncapital.com
web: www.conversioncapital.com

Mission Statement: Provides financial services venture capital.
Investment Criteria: Early Stage, Growth Stage
Industry Group Preference: Financial Services, Technology
Portfolio Companies: Blend, Booster, Dataminr, Fauna, Figure, FiscalNote, Frame.ai, Immuta, Improbable, LearnVest, Orchard, Osper, Paribus, Perpetua, Planetary Resources, Predata, Redowl, Sperical Defence

Key Executives:
  Christian Lawless, Founder & Managing Partner
  Education: BA, Economics, Wesleyan University
  Background: Managing Director, Capital Markets, Lehman Brothers
  Directorships: Booster Fuels, Immuta, Improbable, Blend Labs, Dataminr, WillCall, Paribus, Orchard Platform, LearnVest, Redowl Analytics

538 CORAL GROUP

Phone: 612-335-8682
web: www.coralgrp.com

Mission Statement: Coral Group has partnered with entrepreneurs and management teams to bring a new approach to solving problems and transforming companies. The group uses three strategies in parallel to achieve this goal. Those

strategic values are venture capital, holistic solutions and transformations.
Fund Size: $300 million
Founded: 1990
Average Investment: $2 million - $12 million
Minimum Investment: $100,000
Investment Criteria: Enterprises that exploit major industry trends, focus on substantial markets, grow through execution or effort as opposed to being research or equipment intensive and develop a global scope
Industry Group Preference: Communications, Information Technology, Media, Software, Healthcare, Life Sciences, Medical
Portfolio Companies: Advanced Fibre, AeroScout, Alfy, Baystone Software, BroadRiver Communications, Calix, Call Connect, Cerus, Computer Aided Services, Damark International, Delivery Agent, Digital Generation Systems, E/O Networks, ebix.com, Elity Systems, Entone, Exanet, FaxSav, Firetide, FlexLight Networks, Fon, Force10 Networks, Freeborders, Gearworks, Gift Certificate Center, GoDigital Networks, GoToCall.com, Iconoculture, Infinera, InfoGin, Integral Access, Macromedia, Magnet Communications, Movius, Myocor, NewCity Communications, NextNet Wireless, Optical Solutions, Picolight, Prodea, Racotek, Red Bend Software, RichFX, Systems & Networks, Teltech Resource Network, Tricord Systems, Veracicom, Vertical Communications, Vicarious, Vizrt, Zoran

Key Executives:
  Yuval Almog, Chairman
  e-mail: yuval.almog@coralgrp.com
  Education: BA, BS, University of Alabama; Massachusetts Institute of Technology
  Background: Co-Founder, Zoran Corporation; Raychem Corporation; Systems Officer/Fighter Pilot, Israeli Air Force
  Mark Headrick, Managing Director/General Counsel
  e-mail: mark@coralgrp.com
  Education: BA, Economics, Lake Forest College; JD, William Mitchell College of Law
  Robert Goldberg, Managing Director
  e-mail: robert@coralgrp.com
  Education: BS, Engineering & Applied Science, Columbia University
  Background: SVP, Busines Operations & Corporate Development, Zynga; Managing Director, Idealab
  Eyal Shaked, Managing Director
  e-mail: eyal@coralgrp.com
  Education: BA, Electrical Engineering, Technion Institute of Technology; MSc, Electrical Engineering & Computer Science, Tel Aviv University
  Background: COO, Playtika; EVP & General Manager, Network Solutions Division, ECI Telecom
  Miki Granski, Managing Director
  e-mail: miki@coralgrp.com
  Education: BSc, MSc, Electrical Engineering & Computer Science, Technion Institute of Technology; MBA, Kellogg School of Management, Northwestern University
  Background: Zoran; NeoMagic; LSI Logic
  Linda Watchmaker, Managing Director/Chief Financial Officer
  e-mail: lindawatchmaker@coralgrp.com
  Education: BBA, MBA, Finance & Marketing, University of Wisconsin, Madison; CPA
  Background: Consulting Manager, Ernst & Young; Financial Analyst & Manager, Kimberly-Clark Corporation

539 CORDOVA VENTURES
4080 McGinnis Ferry Road
Suite 1201
Alpharetta, GA 30005
Phone: 678-942-0300 Fax: 678-942-0301

Mission Statement: Experienced venture capital company managing a range of venture funds that provide both capital and value-added resources for growing companies.
Geographic Preference: Southeast
Fund Size: $130 million
Founded: 1989
Average Investment: $1 - $5 million
Minimum Investment: $250,000
Investment Criteria: Privately held, Seed, Start-Up, Early Stage, Later Stage
Industry Group Preference: Information Technology, Industrial Equipment, Real Estate, Life Sciences, Biotechnology, Communications, Healthcare, Financial Services, Telecommunications
Portfolio Companies: EcoSMART Technologies, Nexidia

Key Executives:
  Gerald F Schmidt, Co-Founder/Managing Partner
  e-mail: js@cordovaventures.com
  Education: BS, North Dakota State University; University of Minnesota
  Background: Jostens; Manderson & Associates
  Directorships: National Executive Committee for the Council of Growing Companies
  Charles E Adair, Partner
  e-mail: ea@cordovaventures.com
  Education: Vanderbilt University; BS, Accounting, University of Alabama; Advanced Management Program, Harvard Business School
  Background: Accountant, Haskins & Sells; Controller, Durr-Fillauer Medical
  Directorships: Tech Data Corporation, Performance Food Group Company, Torchmark Corporation, PSS World Medical, Sterling Bank, Jenkins Brick Company, UAB Health System
  Paul R DiBella, Partner
  e-mail: pd@cordovaventures.com
  Education: State University of New York at Albany; University of Miami School of Law
  Background: Founder, Industrial Technology Ventures
  Directorships: ASPEX, Ecovation, Axonn, Five Star Technologies, SkyBitz, EcoSmart Technologies, DemandPoint Systems
  Frank X Dalton, Partner
  e-mail: fxd@cordovaventures.com
  Education: BS, Accounting, University of South Carolina; UGA Board of Directors College; KPMG Audit Committee Institute
  Background: Partner, BDO Seidman; Ernst & Ernst
  Directorships: Technology Executives Roundtable, Atlanta Venture Forum, Moore School of Business, Xpanxion
  L Edward Wilson PE, Partner
  e-mail: lewdux@aol.com
  Education: BCE, Tennessee Technological University
  Background: President, L Edward Wilson & Associates; Founder, EDGe Group; CEO, OSCO Environmental Management; Sirrom Capital Corporation
  Directorships: Tennessee Tech

540 CORE CAPITAL PARTNERS
1717 K Street NW
Suite 920
Washington, DC 20006
Phone: 202-589-0090 Fax: 202-589-0091
e-mail: info@core-capital.com
web: www.core-capital.com

Mission Statement: Backed by sophisticated and experienced institutional and individual investors who are often actively involved in investment work. Each year thousands of potential transactions are reviewed. They have access to an extensive network of investors, bankers, service providers and entrepreneurs.
Geographic Preference: East Coast

Venture Capital & Private Equity Firms / Domestic Firms

Fund Size: $350 million
Founded: 1999
Average Investment: $6 million
Minimum Investment: $2 million
Investment Criteria: Early-Stage, Small to Mid-Sized Growth companies with disruptive technologies
Industry Group Preference: Communications, Information Technology, Internet Technology, Microelectronics, Nanotechnology, Networking, Optical Technology, Semiconductors, Enabling Technology, Infrastructure, Digital Media & Marketing, Technology-Enabled Services
Portfolio Companies: Aptology, BridgeWave Communications, buySAFE, DivvyCloud, Foresight, FreedomPay, Fugue, Genband, Infinite Power Solutions, Inlet Technologies, InPhonic, IXI, JackBe, KnowledgeTree, Load Dynamix, MedVentive, Mobile System7, NewEdge, OLO, Pendo.io, Radius Networks, Rally Software, Revulytics, Rollstream, Roundbox, RulesPower, Silver Storm Technologies, Soft Module, Solstice Software, Source Fire, Staq, Stardog, SwapDrive, Triumfant, Trust Digital, Twisted Pair, Univa, Update Logic, Valen Analytics, Vizbee, Vocal Data, ZeroFOX

Key Executives:
  William Dunbar, Managing Director
  e-mail: wdunbar@core-capital.com
  Education: MBA, Harvard University; BA, Davidson College
  Background: CEO/Founder, Pebble Hill Capital; Portfolio Manager, Allied Capital; President, Allied Capital Corporation II; LBO Lending, Chase Manhattan Bank; Technology Operations, NationsBank; Venture America
  Directorships: Young Presidents Organization; Venture Philanthropy Partners; Meyer Foundation; Madeira School
  Mark Levine, Managing Director
  e-mail: mlevine@core-capital.com
  Education: MBA Finance, George Washington University
  Background: GCI Venture Partners; GEO-CENTERS; Subcommittee Staff Director, Small Business Committee, US House of Representatives
  Directorships: ZeroFOX, Staq, Medventive, BuySAFE, New Edge, Revulytics, Valen, Univa, UpdateLogic, FreedomPay, Roundbox, InPhonic, Vizbee, VocalData
  Randy Klueger, Chief Financial Officer
  e-mail: rklueger@core-capital.com
  Education: BS, Business Administration, George Washington University
  Background: President, Klueger & Associates LLC; CFO, Global Material Technologies; President & CFO, Millennium Laser Eye Centers

541 CORIOLIS VENTURES
160 Mercer Street
3rd Floor
New York, NY 10012

web: coriolisventures.com

Mission Statement: Coriolis Ventures is a New York based early stage Venture and incubation fund specializing in new media and infrastructure technology related to Internet advertising. Coriolis provides its portfolio companies with both capital (and in many cases) incubation assistance to help nascent early stage companies accelerate their growth and development. Coriolis Ventures is associated with Coriolis Labs, a New York based marketing information research laboratory.

Investment Criteria: Early-stage
Industry Group Preference: Infrastructure Technology, Internet Advertising, New Media
Portfolio Companies: AppNexus, Crisp Media, Devpost, Dstillery, Every Screen Media, Integral Ad Science, Magnetic, NeueHouse, Triton Web Properties

Key Executives:
  Joshua Abram, Founding Partner
  Directorships: TMRW Life Sciences, Dstillery, Integral Ad Science, NeueHouse
  Alan Murray, Founding Partner
  Directorships: Dstillery, Integral Ad Science, NeueHouse

542 CORNERSTONE CAPITAL HOLDINGS
315 S Beverly Drive
Suite 320
Los Angeles, CA 90212

Phone: 310-499-5670 Fax: 312-275-7855
web: www.cstonecapital.com

Mission Statement: Cornerstone Capital Holdings is a private equity firm that invests in companies in the lower end of the middle market, with particular emphasis in aerospace, space, defense and industrial services sectors.

Geographic Preference: United States
Founded: 2000
Investment Criteria: Middle Market, Buyouts, Recapitalizations
Industry Group Preference: Industrial Services, Machinery, Manufacturing, Aerospace, Space, Defense
Portfolio Companies: AeroGen-TEK, Essner Manufacturing, N2 Imaging Systems, NuSpace, Powers Equipment Company, RSA Engineered Products, UST-Aldetec Group, Walbar Engine Components

Other Locations:
  650 Sentry Parkway
  Suite One
  Blue Bell, PA 19422
  Phone: 215-628-4486 Fax: 215-647-7473

Key Executives:
  Jonathan H Alt, Founder/Principal
  e-mail: jalt@cstonecapital.com
  Education: BA, Finance, College of Commerce and Business Administration, University of Illinois
  Background: BGL Capital Partners; Associate, Banque Paribas
  Andrew M Bushell, Founder/Principal
  e-mail: abushell@cstonecapital.com
  Education: BA, Economics, Cornell University; JD, Rutgers Law School; MBA, Kellogg School of Management; CPA
  Background: BGL Capital Partners; President, Sentry Fire Protection Systems
  Lili Zhou, Chief Financial Officer
  e-mail: lzhou@cstonecapital.com
  Education: BSBA, Accounting, Northeastern University, China; CPA
  Background: CFO, RSA Engineered Products; Corporate Finance Executive, Klune Industries
  Tim Martin, Executive Advisor/Board Member
  e-mail: tmartin@cstonecapital.com
  Education: BA, Business Administration
  Background: Chief Commercial Officer, President, Doncasters; VP Supply Chain and Strategic Initiatives, UTC Aerospace Systems

543 CORNERSTONE HOLDINGS
385 Interlocken Crescent
Suite 250
Broomfield, CO 80021

Phone: 303-410-2510
e-mail: info@bvcv.com
web: www.bvcv.com

Mission Statement: Cornerstone Holdings is a private equity and real estate development company. Privately owned, the company focuses on opportunistic investments in profitable middle market companies via direct investments. Cornerstone partners with strong management teams to actively add value and grow businesses. The team at Cornerstone has substantial private company investment experience which spans from startup ventures to traditional leverage buyouts to distressed

Venture Capital & Private Equity Firms / Domestic Firms

turnarounds. The real estate development division acquires land in resort markets and takes it through the development process.

Geographic Preference: United States
Average Investment: $4-$15 million
Investment Criteria: Recapitalizations, LBO, MBO, Growth Capital
Portfolio Companies: Apex Towers, B Media, Flat Iron Energy Partners, Gracon, Horizon Organic, Magna Energy Services, PetroCloud, Trispan
Other Locations:
1746 Union St.
San Francisco, CA 94123

Key Executives:
Tom McCloskey, Chairman/CEO
Education: BA, University of Notre Dame; MBA, Wharton School
Background: Chairman, Horizon Organic Holdings; Palmer Communications
Directorships: Magna Energy Services, Petro Cloud, B Media
Neville Vere Nicoll, President
Education: European Business School, Paris
Background: President & CEO, Kryptonics; CEO, Magna Energy Services
Clark Lipscomb, President, Real Estate
e-mail: clipscomb@cstoneholdings.com
Education: BBA, University of Texas, Austin
John Ord, Chief Financial Officer
e-mail: jord@cstoneholdings.com
Education: BS, Economics & Business Administration, Colorado State University; MoTM, University of Denver; CPA
Background: Co-Founder/CFO, BV-Cornerstone Ventures; CFO, Kryptonics; VP, Finance, Rustco Products
Ryan Williams, Principal
e-mail: rwilliams@cstoneholdings.com
Education: BS, Business Administration, Colorado State University; MS, Finance, University of Colorado, Denver; CFA
Background: Senior Consultant, Corporate Finance Group, FTI Consulting

544 CORNERSTONE VENTURE PARTNERS
120 East 23rd Street
New York, NY 10010

Phone: 646-942-0019
e-mail: contact@cornerstonevp.com
web: cornerstonevp.com

Mission Statement: Cornerstone Venture Partners is a tech-based fund interested in the Business-to-Business sector.

Geographic Preference: US, Israel
Average Investment: $1.5 million
Industry Group Preference: IoT, Big Data, FinTech, Cloud
Portfolio Companies: Axonize, DBSH, Dealhub, DeskForce, OptimalQ, Sixdof Space, Texel, User 1st, Youtiligent

Key Executives:
Michael Ozechov, Partner
Education: BS, University of Michigan
Background: Emerging Ventures Limited; Pall Mall Capital; EXP Federal; Jerusalem Venture Partners
Hanan Brand, Partner
Education: BA, Hebrew University; MBA, Israel Institute of Technology
Background: Jerusalem Venture Partners; Ofer Brothers Group; Made in Jerusalem

545 CORRELATION VENTURES
9255 Towne Centre Drive
Suite 350
San Diego, CA 92121

Phone: 858-412-8500
e-mail: dec@correlationvc.com
web: www.correlationvc.com

Mission Statement: Correlation Ventures is a new breed of venture capital firm, leveraging world-class analytics to offer entrepreneurs and other venture capitalists a dramatically better option when they are seeking additional capital to complete a financing round.

Geographic Preference: United States
Fund Size: $165 million
Investment Criteria: All Stages
Industry Group Preference: Life Sciences, Clean Technology, Information Technology, Consumer Services, Business Products & Services, Fintech, Healthcare, Enterprise Software
Portfolio Companies: 10% Happier, Able Lending, Admittedly, AirPR, AirXpanders, AlienVault, Alloy, Ando, Ankasa, Annexon Biosciences, Appthority, Apsalar, Arista MD, Betterworks, Bloomz, BlueVine Capital, Brandcast, Bravely, Care Well Urgent Care, Casper, Cloud Passage, Codefights, Contactually, Cotopaxi, Crossbar, Crowdpac, Descartes Labs, Distil Networks, Dizzion, Dolls Kill, Dropoff, Earnest, Earnup, Employee Channel, Empyr, Enlibrium, Entelo, FlexPharma, Fluid, Framehawk, FreeRange Games, Galera Therapeutics, Getaround, Gethuman, Goby, Good Eggs, Grokker, Gynesonics, Hello Tech, iBeat, Imperfect Produce, InstaEDU, Intervene, IOpipe, Ioxus, Karmic, Knock, Kwik, Labdoor, LeanData, Lemonade Health, Lever, Litbit, Lytro, Madefire, Manticore Games, Mirna Therapeutics, Mirror, MNectar, Nexlas, NumberFire, Ollie, Optimizely, Overtime, Pepo, Personal Capital, Pley, Inbox, Powervision, Prattle, Project Cohort, Prose, Reelgood, RQX Pharmaceuticals, Scale Arc, Scribble Live, SEE Forge, ShoCard, SigniFAI, Source3, Spirox, Splice Machine, Sun Basket, Sundar, SynthoRX, Talent Sonar, TBH, Trefoil Therapeutics, Trumaker & Co., Upstart, Urjanet, VigLink, Virsto Software, Wonderschool, Yumi, Zebit

Other Locations:
650 California Street
7th Floor
San Francisco, CA 94108
Phone: 415-890-5425

79 Madison Avenue
7th Floor
New York, NY 10016
Phone: 917-297-6295

Key Executives:
David Coats, Managing Director
858-412-8500 x115
e-mail: dec@correlationvc.com
Education: BS, Biology, Princeton University; MBA, Harvard Business School
Background: Managing Director, Hamilton BioVentures; Venture Partner, Windamere Venture Partners; President, Forge Medical Ventures; Founder, Spine Wave
Trevor Kienzle, Managing Director
650-843-3210 x10
e-mail: trevor.kienzle@correlationvc.com
Education: BA, University of Virginia; MBA, Harvard Business School
Background: Managing Director, Newbury Ventures; Vice President, GE Equity; Management Consultant, Deloitte & Touche
Grace Chui-Miller, Chief Financial Officer
858-412-8500 x123
e-mail: gcm@correlationvc.com
Education: BA, Quantitative Economics & Decision Sciences, University of California, San Diego; MBA, Anderson School, University of California, LA

Venture Capital & Private Equity Firms / Domestic Firms

Background: Audit Manager, KPMG; Chief Financial Officer, DCM
Anu Pathria, Partner, Analytics
858-412-8500 x117
e-mail: akp@correlationvc.com
Education: BS, Mathematics & Computer Science, University of Waterloo; MS, Computer Science, PhD, Operations Research, University of California, Berkeley
Background: HNC Software
Moiz Saifee, Principal, Analytics
858-412-8500 x127
e-mail: mas@correlationvc.com
Education: BS, Computer Science, IIT Kharagpur
Background: Info Edge

546 CORSA VENTURES
103 E 5th Street
Suite 208
Austin, TX 78701

web: www.corsaventures.com

Mission Statement: The Corsa philosophy is to actively help build businesses and not just monitor investments. The Fund's Managing Partners are patient investors with a long term view and are actively involved across all functional areas including financial strategy, talent acquisition, technology and product roadmap planning, sales and marketing, business development and company operations.

Geographic Preference: Texas, Southwest
Investment Criteria: Early-Stage
Industry Group Preference: Information Technology, Cloud Computing, Big Data, Mobile, Social Media
Portfolio Companies: Ad Mass, Bold Metrics, Clear Blade, Convey, Eye Q, Favor, Good Shepherd Entertainment, Gravitant, Help Social, Ideal Spot, Key Concierge, Local Libations, Optimizely, Real Savvy, Revival, Social Matterz, Tasting Room, Toopher, Violin Memory, Yellow Bird Sauce

Key Executives:
Brian Grigsby, Managing Partner
e-mail: brian@corsaventures.com
Education: BS, Mechanical Engineering & Physics, MS, Optical Electronics, University of Oklahoma
Background: Founder/General Partner, Raven Venture Partners & Venio Capital Partners
Directorships: Open Lending, Perception Software
Alex Gruzen, Partner
e-mail: alex@corsaventures.com
Education: BS, MS, Aeronautical & Astronautical Engineering, MIT; MBA, Harvard Business School
Background: Senior Vice President, Dell; Hewlett Packard
Directorships: Gravitant, Toopher
Kevin Green, Partner
Education: LLM, London School of Economics; JD, Baylor Law School; BA, Southern Methodist University
Background: U.S. Department of State; Patton Boggs

547 CORTEC GROUP
140 East 45th Street
43rd Floor
New York, NY 10017

Phone: 212-370-5600
e-mail: info@cortecgroup.com
web: www.cortecgroup.com

Mission Statement: Cortec Group is a private equity investment firm which uses the extensive operating experience of our principals to help management teams grow companies and meaningfully add value to their businesses.

Geographic Preference: United States
Fund Size: $2.6 billion
Founded: 2000
Average Investment: $25 million
Minimum Investment: $10 million
Investment Criteria: Equity Investments
Industry Group Preference: Manufacturing, Business to Business, Distribution
Portfolio Companies: 101 Mobility, Aspen Medical Products, Barcodes Inc., Center for Vein Restoration, Chauvet, Community Veterinary Partners, EVP EyeCare, Groome Transportation, Harmar, Rotating Machinery Services Inc., Urnex, Viradis, Weiman, Window Nation, Yeti

Key Executives:
R. Scott Schafler, Founding Partner
Education: BA, Johns Hopkins University; MBA, Harvard Graduate School of Business Administration
Background: VP Operations/Director, Condec Corporation; Founder/Chairman, UC Industries; Director, Fidelity Bank; Director, Unimation; Chock-ful-o-Nuts
Directorships: Sequa Corporation
David L. Schnadig, Co-President
212-370-5600
Fax: 212-682-4195
e-mail: dschnadig@cortecgroup.com
Education: BS, Economics, Trinity College; MM, Kellogg School of Management, Northwestern University
Background: Assistant Chairman, SunAmerica; Investment Banker, Lehman Brothers; Management Consultant, Cresap, McCormick & Paget
Jeffrey A. Lipsitz, Co-President
e-mail: jlipsitz@cortecgroup.com
Education: BA, Union College; MBA, Columbia University Graduate School of Business
Background: VP Corporate Development, PLY GEM Industries
Michael E. Najjar, Managing Partner
e-mail: mnajjar@cortecgroup.com
Education: BA, Cornell University; MBA, Wharton School, University of Pennsylvania
Background: Managing Director, Cornerstone Equity Investors; Investment Banker, Donaldson Lufkin & Jenrette
Jonathan A. Stein, Managing Partner
e-mail: jstein@cortecgroup.com
Education: BA, Harvard College
Background: Principal, Three Cities Research
Jeffrey R. Shannon, Managing Partner
e-mail: jshannon@cortecgroup.com
Education: US Naval Academy, BS, Ocean Engineering, Texas A&M University; MS, Civil Engineering, University of Illinois
Background: Analyst, Saloman Smith Barney
James W. Tucker, Partner
e-mail: btucker@cortecgroup.com
Education: BBA, Accounting, College of William & Mary; MBA, Columbia Business School
Background: Analyst, M&A Group, Wachovia Capital Markets

548 COSTANOA VENTURE CAPITAL
160 Forest Avenue
Palo Alto, CA 94301

Phone: 650-388-9310
e-mail: info@costanoavc.com
web: www.costanoavc.com

Mission Statement: Costanoa Venture Capital is an early stage investor in cloud-based services leveraging data and analytics to solve real problems for businesses and consumers. We aren't afraid of sectors before they are high profile and don't shy away from hard work. We've been there before and enjoy the journey. Our insight, network and business development skills can help change the trajectory of a company's business. We understand the challenges of leading young companies. We provide hands-on guidance while allowing entrepreneurs and CEOs the room to operate, improve and ultimately succeed.

Investment Criteria: Early Stage
Industry Group Preference: Cloud-Based IT Services
Portfolio Companies: 3scale, 6sense, Acme Technologies, Alation, Amplify.ai, AppOrbit, Apptimize, Aquabyte,

Venture Capital & Private Equity Firms / Domestic Firms

Auterion, Bugcrowd, Datalogix, Demandbase, Directly, Elevate Security, Fauna, Focal Systems, GameChanger, Grovo, Guardian Analytics, Inflection, Intacct, Isocket, Kahuna, Kenna Security, Kepler, Krypton, Landit, Leap, Lex Machina, Lively, NovoED, Parallel Domain, PayNearMe, PepperData, Propeller, Quizlet, Rayfay, Return Path, Roadster, Skedulo, Springboard, Stitch Labs, Upcounsel, VictorOps

Other Locations:
251 Rhode Island St.
Suite 107
San Francisco, CA 94103

Key Executives:
Greg Sands, Founder & Managing Partner
Education: BA, Harvard; MBA, Stanford Graduate School of Business
Background: Sutter Hill Ventures; Netscape Communications; Cisco; Corporate Decision, Inc (now Mercer Consulting)
Directorships: Alation, Directly, Focal Systems, Guardian Analytics, Inflection, Kepler Communications, Return Path, Roadster, Stitch Labs, VictorOps
Mark Selcow, Partner
Education: BA, English, Brown University; MBA, Stanford Graduate School of Business
Background: President, BabyCenter; President, Merced Systems
Directorships: Lively, Quizlet, Skedulo, Springboard

549 COSTELLA KIRSCH
3500 Alameda de las Pulgas
Suite 150
Menlo Park, CA 94025

Phone: 650-462-1890
e-mail: info@costellakirsch.com
web: www.costellakirsch.com

Mission Statement: Costella Kirsch is a venture lending firm that offers capital support to emerging technology companies.

Founded: 1986
Investment Criteria: Start-Up, Emerging
Industry Group Preference: Technology
Portfolio Companies: Accolo, AdBrite, AdvancePath, Aeris Communications, Athersys, Boombotix, BridgeLux, Centerbeam, Coyuchi, Discera, Doctor Evidence, Domain Surgical, Echo, Enkata, ID Watchdog, InfraScale, Invivodata, Kontera, Mantara, Maxwell Health, OnPharma, PaySimple, Remedy Interactive, RiseSmart, Silver Tail Systems, SnapLogic, Solaria, SpectraSensors, SpeedInfo, Toktumi, Twelvefold Media, U-Systems, Vast, Verimatrix, Zep Solar, Zolo Technologies, Zoosk

Key Executives:
Richard Ginn, Managing Director/Chief Financial Officer
650-462-1890
e-mail: rich@costellakirsch.com
Education: Stanford University; MBA, Anderson School, University of California, Los Angeles
Background: Program Manager, Philips Electronics
Bill Kirsch, Managing Director
650-462-5790
e-mail: bill@costellakirsch.com
Education: BS, Accounting & Economics, Lehigh University; MBA, Anderson School, University of California, Los Angeles
Background: Rolm Credit Corporation; GATX Capital Corporation
Beth Kelsey, Portfolio Manager
650-462-5792
e-mail: beth@costellakirsch.com
Background: Senior Administrator, Borland Software; Harmony Foods; Plantronics; Sprint Communications

550 COTTONWOOD TECHNOLOGY FUND
422 Old Santa Fe Trail
Santa Fe, NM 87501

Phone: 505-412-8537
e-mail: info@cottonwood.vc
web: www.cottonwoodtechnologyfund.com

Mission Statement: Cottonwood Technology Fund offers venture services and capital to seed-stage technology companies with significant commercial potential.

Geographic Preference: Paso del Norte Region from Los Alamos, NM to El Paso, TX
Investment Criteria: Seed-Stage, Early-Stage
Industry Group Preference: Technology, Biosciences, New Energy, Nanotechnology, Information Technology, Clean Technology, Aerospace, Defense and Government
Portfolio Companies: Clear Flight Solutions, Eurekite, Exagen Diagnostics, FibeRio Technology Corporation, Respira Therapeutics, Skorpios Technologies, xF Technologies

Other Locations:
Hengelosestraat 541
Enschede 7521 AG
Netherlands

Key Executives:
Dave Blivin, Managing Director
505-412-8537
e-mail: dave@cottonwoodtechnologyfund.com
Education: MBA, Fuqua School of Business, Duke University
Background: Managing Director, Southeast Interactive
Alain le Loux, General Partner
Education: University of Twente
Background: Getronics PinkRoccade; CEO, Virobuster Technologies

551 COUNCIL CAPITAL
30 Burton Hills Blvd.
Suite 576
Nashville, TN 37215

Phone: 615-255-3707
e-mail: pfulner@councilcapital.com
web: www.councilcapital.com

Mission Statement: Council Capital has approximately $150 million of capital under management and is actively investing out of its second fund, which was raised in 2008. The success of the initial fund, which is ranked in the top quartile in its vintage year by Private Equity Intelligence, is a credit to the deep expertise and extensive capabilities the partners and CEO Council members possess as healthcare investors and operators.

Fund Size: $150 million
Founded: 2000
Investment Criteria: Growth-Stage, Early Growth-Stage
Industry Group Preference: Healthcare, Healthcare Services, Healthcare Information Technology
Portfolio Companies: Adva-Net, Benefit Informatics, Caregiver Inc., CNNH NeuroHealth, Emids Experience Partnership, EndoChoice, EspriGas, EVault, EWC, Ingenious Med, Lancope, Medseek, NotifyMD, REACH Health, Senior Whole Health, Triad Behavioral Health

Key Executives:
Dennis C Bottorff, Co-Founder/Managing General Partner
615-255-3707 x326
e-mail: dbottorff@councilcapital.com
Education: BE, Electrical Engineering, Vanderbilt University; MBA, Northwestern University
Background: President/Chairman, Commerce Union; Vice Chairman/COO, Sovran Bank; President/COO, C&S Sovran; President/CEO, First American National Bank
Directorships: NuScriptRX, CapStar Bank, Ingram Industries

Venture Capital & Private Equity Firms / Domestic Firms

Katie H Gambill, Co-Founder/Managing General Partner
615-255-3707 x314
e-mail: kgambill@councilcapital.com
Education: BA, Economics, Vanderbilt University; CFA
Background: President, Equitable Securities; President, SunTrust Equitable Securities
Directorships: Reach Health
Grant A Jackson, Managing General Partner
e-mail: gjackson@councilcapital.com
Education: Florida State University; MBA, Kellogg Graduate School of Management
Background: Accenture, Compaq
Directorships: eMids, EspriGas, Experience Wellness Centers
Eric Keen, General Partner
e-mail: ekeen@councilcapital.com
Education: BA, Finance and Political Science, University of Illinois
Background: DW Healthcare Partners; Riverside Company; Northwest Equity Partners; Credit Suisse First Boston; Marakon Associates
Directorships: AdvaNet, Caregiver, Triad Learning Systems

552 COURT SQUARE VENTURES
455 Second Street Southeast
Suite 401
Charlottesville, VA 22902

Phone: 434-817-3300

Mission Statement: A venture capital firm that invests in early-stage communications, information technology, and media companies, with a particular interest in points of convergence between these industries.
Geographic Preference: United States
Fund Size: $118 million
Founded: 1945
Investment Criteria: Early Stage
Industry Group Preference: Communications, Information Technology, Media
Portfolio Companies: Automated Insights, Bug Labs, Continuum, Echo 360, Great Call, Mobile Posse, Seakeeper, Verance
Key Executives:
  James B Murray Jr, General Partner
  Education: BA, University of Virginia; JD, Marshall-Wythe School of Law, College of William and Mary
  Background: Founding Partner, Columbia Capital
  Directorships: Imagine Communications, GreatCall, Seakeeper, Continuum 700, Technology Crossover Ventures Internet Advisory Committee
  Randy Castleman, General Partner
  Education: BA, Princeton University; MBA, Darden School of Business, University of Virginia
  Background: Founder/Manager, Media & Technology Strategy Group, ASCAP; RheoGene; Egg Pictures; Interscope Communications; Ogilvy & Mather; BellSouth
  Directorships: Automated Insights, Bug Labs, TRAFFIQ, SNOCAP, Labrador Mobile, Grand Central, Optinel Systems
  Chris Holden, General Partner
  Education: Davidson College
  Background: Senior Executive, Rupert Murdoch's News Corporation; CEO, Kesmai Corporation; Vice President, News Technology Group; HarperCollins Publishers
  Directorships: Emerging Media Group, Grab Networks, Echo360, Mobile Posse
  Douglas Burns, Principal/Chief Financial Officer
  Education: BS, Accounting & Business Administration, Washington & Lee University; MBA, Darden School of Business, University of Virginia
  Background: Senior Auditor, Arthur Andersen's Enterprise Group
  Directorships: GreatCall, Imagine Communications, Seakeeper, Continuum 700

553 COWBOY VENTURES
Palo Alto, CA

e-mail: hello@cowboy.vc
web: www.cowboy.vc

Mission Statement: Cowboy Ventures is a seed-stage focused fund. We seek to back exceptional founders who are building products that 're-imagine' work and personal life in large and growing markets - we call it 'Life 2.0'.
Geographic Preference: United States
Founded: 2012
Investment Criteria: Seed-Stage
Industry Group Preference: Technology
Portfolio Companies: Abstract, Accompany, After School, Area 1, August, Aura, Aviso, Branch, Brandless, Brava, Brickwork, Brit+Co., Chime, Crunchvase, DocSend, Dollar Shave Club, Fullcast.io, Gixo, Guild, Guildery, HeartWork, Homebase, Hooked, Joyride, LendingHome, Librato, LightStep, LumaTax, Manifest, Massdrop, Memebox, Mighty Networks, Mutiny, NuOrder, nWay, Pantry, Philz Coffee, Polar, Product Hunt, Rise, Seneca Systems, Soma, Spruce, StyleSeat, Tally, Tenor, Textio, True, Vic.ai, Vorstella
Key Executives:
  Aileen Lee, Founder & Partner
  Education: MIT, Harvard Business School
  Background: Partner, Kleiner Perkins Caufield & Byers; Founding CEO, RMG Networks
  Ted Wang, Partner
  Education: AB, History & Latin, Duke University; JD, University of Virginia
  Background: Partner, Fenwick & West
  Samantha Kaminsky, Partner
  Education: Harvard Business School; Middlebury College
  Background: Operator, Eventbrite; Investor, J.P. Morgan; Co-Founder, vcgc

554 CRAWLEY VENTURES
600 S Cherry Street
Suite 1125
Denver, CO 80246

Phone: 303-592-1135
e-mail: info@crawleyventures.com
web: www.crawleyventures.com

Mission Statement: Crawley Ventures is the Denver-based private equity subsidiary of Crawley Petroleum Corporation. Crawley Ventures pursues investment opportunities in early stage companies with the potential for growth. The firm invests in a number of industries, including software, manufacturing, financial services, and wireless technologies.
Average Investment: $250,000 - $1.5 million
Investment Criteria: Seed-Stage, Early-Stage, Expansion-Stage
Industry Group Preference: Optics, Financial Services, Software, Manufacturing, Wireless Technologies
Portfolio Companies: CCELP Holding, CenterStone Technologies, Cequint, CertiPath, Collective Intellect, CSP Holdings, DNA Response, Energy Financial and Physical, Enertia Software, First Western Financial, Jetta Corp, NHW Holding, Perlego, REALD, Skydex Technologies, Taaz, TerraLUX, UsingMiles Inc., VarVee
Key Executives:
  Jason Garner, President
  Education: BEng & MS, Petroleum Engineering, West Virginia University
  Background: VP/COO, HighMount Exploration & Production
  S Kim Hatfield, Chief Executive Officer
  Education: BS, Petroleum Engineering, MS, Petroleum Finance, University of Oklahoma

Venture Capital & Private Equity Firms / Domestic Firms

Directorships: Crawley Petroleum, Enertia Software, CSP Holdings, Oklahoma Independent Producers Association
Martha Tracey, Vice President
Education: Williams College; MBA, Yale University
Directorships: Crawley Petroleum, CenterStone Technologies, First Western Financial, Collective Intellect, Opera Colorado

555 CREDIT SUISSE PRIVATE EQUITY Credit Suisse Group
11 Madison Avenue
New York, NY 10010

Phone: 212-325-5527
web: www.credit-suisse.com

Mission Statement: Comprised of investment funds that focus on domestic and international leverage buyouts, structured equity investments, mezzanine investments, real estate investments, venture capital and growth investments, and investments in other private equity funds.

Geographic Preference: Worldwide
Fund Size: $3 billion
Founded: 1856
Minimum Investment: $20 million
Investment Criteria: Leverage buyouts, Mezzanine, Private/Structured Equity
Industry Group Preference: Real Estate
   Helman Sitohang, CEO, Asia Pacific
   Education: BS, Engineering, Bandung Institute of Technology
   Background: Derivatives Group, Bankers Trust
   Romeo Cerutti, General Counsel
   Education: MA, JD, University of Fribourg; MA, Law, University of California, LA
   Background: Attorney, Latham & Watkins; Attorney, Homburger Rechtsanwälte, Zurich; Partner, Lombard Odier Darier Hentsch & Cie
   James B. Walker, Chief Operating Officer
   Education: BS, Mathematics, University of Glasgow; Postgraduate Diploma Finance, University of Stirling
   Background: Morgan Stanley; Merrill Lynch; Barclays Capital; Various Management Positions at Credit Suisse

556 CRESCENDO VENTURES
405 El Camino Real
Suite 126
Menlo Park, CA 94025

Phone: 650-470-1200 **Fax:** 650-470-1201
e-mail: investorservices@crescendoventures.com
web: www.crescendoventures.com

Mission Statement: Focuses exclusively on early-stage investments in the communications and enterprise infrastructure sectors.

Fund Size: $400 million
Founded: 1993
Investment Criteria: Early-Stage
Industry Group Preference: Communications, Enterprise Software, Infrastructure, Software, Components & IoT
Portfolio Companies: Airband Communications Holdings, Algety Telecom, Arteris, BDNA, Broadsoft, CREDANT Technologies, Compellent Technologies, CoreOptics, Cybrant, Cygent, Dash Navigation, Dust Networks, Ejasent, Ensemble Communications, Entera, Envivio, Fultec Semiconductor, Jasper @ Cisco, Metaplace, Morphics Technology, Netcentrex, Pure Digital Technologies, Quorum Systems, RHK. Salient Surgical Technologies, ShoZu, Sistina Software, StoneFly Inc., Transitive, Tropic Networks, WhereNet

Key Executives:
   David Spreng, Managing General Partner
   Education: BS, Accounting, University of Minnesota
   Background: President, IAI Ventures; Mutual Fund Manager, Investment Advisers; Investment Banker, Salomon Brothers; Investment Banker, Dain Bosworth
   Directorships: Ciena, CoSine, Digital Island, Lightspeed, Novalux, OneSecure, Oplink, Tut Systems
   John Borchers, General Partner
   Education: BS, University of Richmond; MBA, Harvard Business School
   Directorships: BDNA Corporation; Credant Technologies; Dust Networks; SealedMedia; Worksoft Inc; Transitive Corporation
   Wayne Cantwell, General Partner
   Education: BSEE, DeVry Institute of Technology
   Background: President/CEO, inSilicon Corporation; Worldwide Field Operations, Phoenix Technologies; Sales/Engineering, Intel Corporation; NEC Corporation
   Peter Van Cuylenburg, General Partner
   Education: Electrical Engineering diploma, Bristol Polytechnic
   Background: SealedMedia; Transitive; President, Quantum Corporation/S DSS Group; Executive VP, Xerox Corp; President, NeXT Computer; CEO, Mercury Communications; Marketing/General Manager, Texas Instruments
   Directorships: SealedMedia; Transitive Corp; QAD Inc; Elixent Ltd

557 CRESCENT CAPITAL GROUP LP
11100 Santa Monica Blvd
Suite 2000
Los Angeles, CA 90025

Phone: 310-235-5900
web: www.crescentcap.com

Mission Statement: A source of capital for private equity-backed companies in the United States. Crescent Capital Group invests in mezzanine debt and offers private capital to middle market companies in Europe.

Geographic Preference: United States, Europe
Fund Size: $3.4 billion
Founded: 1991
Average Investment: $50 - $150 million
Minimum Investment: $15 million
Investment Criteria: Mezzanine, Buyouts, Acquisitions, Recapitalizations, Refinancings
Industry Group Preference: All markets Considered
Portfolio Companies: Connect-Air International, The Copernicus Group IRB, Double E Company, Fairchild Industrial Products Company, Insource Contract Services, Lazer Spot, Mallet & Company, MooreCo, National Display Systems LLC, The Outsource Group, Precision Manufacturing Group LLC, Solidscape, Thorne Research Inc. & Diversified Natural Products, Tital Fitness LLC, Utrecht Art Supplies, Wearwell, Winchester Electronics

Other Locations:
   299 Park Avenue
   33rd Floor
   New York, NY 10171
   Phone: 212-364-0200

   100 High Street
   18th Floor
   Boston, MA 02110
   Phone: 617-854-1500

Key Executives:
   Jean-Marc Chapus, Managing Partner
   e-mail: jm.chapus@crescentcap.com
   Education: AB, MBA, Harvard University
   Background: Group Managing Director, TCW; Managing Director, Cresent Capital Corporation; Drexel Bumham Lamert
   Mark Attanasio, Managing Partner
   e-mail: mark.attanasio@crescentcap.com
   Education: AB, Brown University; JD, Columbia University School of Law
   Background: Group Managing Director, TCW; Co-Chief

Venture Capital & Private Equity Firms / Domestic Firms

Executive Officer, Crescent Capital Corporation; Drexel Burnham Lambert; Attorney, Debevoise & Plimpton
Christopher G. Wright, Managing Director & Head, Private Markets
e-mail: chris.wright@crescentcap.com
Education: BA, Michigan State University; MBA, Harvard Business School
Background: Managing Director, TCW; General Electric Company; GE Industrial Systems

558 CRESCO CAPITAL PARTNERS
8214 Westchester Drive
Dallas, TX 75225

web: www.crescocapitalpartners.com

Mission Statement: Invests in the cannabis industry.

Founded: 2014
Industry Group Preference: Cannabis
Portfolio Companies: FLRish, Alternative Solutions, Acres Cultivation & Cannabis, Libertas, Grow Healthy, Aurora Flower Co., Ebbu, Koan Agroscience, Vanguard Scientific, Pot Pots, Sakti, Faces Human Capital Management, High Street Capital Partners, National CC, Green Thumb Industries, Gesundheit Foods, Casimir Partners, Planted Supply Co., Harvest Cannabis Co.

Key Executives:
Matt Hawkins, Managing Partner
Education: University of Texas at Austin
Background: Principal, San Jacinto Partners; Managing Principal, Adjacent Capital Advisors
Todd Boren, Managing Partner
Education: University of Miami
Background: President/COO, International Assets Advisory; Partner, Arizona Rattlers; Team President/Managing Member, Tampa Bay Storm; President/CEO, Pinnacle Financial Group; VP, Bernstein Global Wealth Management; Partner, Orlando Predators Football Team; Managing Partner, MacArthur Capital
Andrew Sturner, Managing Partner
Education: BS, Washington University; JD, Bankruptcy, Brooklyn Law School
Background: Co-Founder/Director, Miami Angels; Co-Founder, Boatsetter; Founder, Orange Island Ventures; Manager, MacArthur Capital; Founder/Chairman, Aqua Marine Partners
Directorships: Snap-A-Slip; Boatyard; Oasis Marinas
Dov Szapiro, Managing Partner
Education: The Wharton School, University of Pennsylvania
Background: Co-Founder/CEO, AFS Acceptance; Director of Business Development, GovWorks Inc.
Matthew Bryant, Vice President
Education: BS, Finance/Accounting, University of Texas at Austin
Background: Hunt Realty Investments; Advisor, JPMorgan; Co-Founder/CFO, Drive Casa

559 CRESSEY & COMPANY LP
155 N Wacker Drive
Suite 4500
Chicago, IL 60606

Phone: 312-945-5700 Fax: 312-945-5701
web: www.cresseyco.com

Mission Statement: Cressey & Company invests in high-potential companies in the US healthcare market. The firm seeks to provide its capital and expertise to accelerate the growth of its portfolio companies and help build leading healthcare businesses.

Geographic Preference: United States
Fund Size: $615 million
Founded: 2008
Average Investment: $10 - $100 million

Investment Criteria: Middle Market, Later Stage, Growth Equity
Industry Group Preference: Healthcare, Healthcare Services, Information Technology
Portfolio Companies: Concentra, Dental Services Group, Haven Behavioral Healthcare, InnerChange, QualDerm Partners, RestorixHealth, Spine Wave, Unitek Information Systems, US Renal Care, VetCor, Wound Care Specialists

Other Locations:
2525 West End Avenue
Suite 1250
Nashville, TN 37203
Phone: 615-369-8400 Fax: 615-369-8444

Key Executives:
Bryan Cressey, Partner
312-945-5710
Education: BS, Economics, University of Washington; MBA, Harvard Business School; JD, Harvard Law School
Background: Co-Founder, Golder, Thoma, Cressey, Rauner; First Chicago Equity Group
Merrick Axel, Partner
312-945-5717
Education: BA, Economics & Political Science, Duke University; MBA, Harvard Business School
Background: Harvest Partners; JW Childs Associates; Morgan Stanley
Directorships: Academy for Urban School Leadership
Paul Diaz, Partner
Education: BS, Finance/Accounting, Kogod School of Business, American University; JD, Georgetown University Law Center
Background: President/CFO, Kindred Healthcare Inc.
Directorships: DaVita; PharMerica Corporation
Peter Ehrich, Partner
312-945-5724
Education: BS, Economics, Wharton School, University of Pennsylvania; MBA, Stanford University Graduate School of Business
Background: Principal, Black Diamond Capital Partners; Associate, Aurora Capital Partners
Sen. William H. Frist, MD, Partner
615-369-8400
Education: BA, Princeton University; MD, Harvard Medical School
Background: United States Senator, State of Tennessee; Majority Leader, United States Senate; Founder, Vanderbilt Multi-Organ Transplant Center
Directorships: Robert Wood Johnson Foundation, Kaiser Family Foundation
Bary Bailey, Operating Partner
312-945-5737
Education: BS, Finance, California State University, Long Beach
Background: CFO, AMN Healthcare Services Inc.; PacifiCare Health Systems Inc.; Premier Inc.; Tenet Healthcare; American Medical Holdings Inc.; Arthur Andersen & Co.

560 CRESTVIEW PARTNERS
590 Madison Avenue
42nd Floor
New York, NY 10022

Phone: 212-906-0700
web: www.crestview.com

Mission Statement: Crestview Partners is a private equity firm seeking opportunities with healthcare, media, energy, industrials and financial services companies.

Geographic Preference: United States
Fund Size: $3 billion
Founded: 2004
Average Investment: $100 - $250 million
Industry Group Preference: Financial Services, Media, Healthcare, Energy, Industrial

Portfolio Companies: Accuride Corporation, Arxis Capital Group, ATC Drivetrain, Camping World Holdings, Capital Bank Financial, Charter Communications, Concours Mold, Congruex Holdings, CP Energy, Cumulus Media, DARAG Group, DS Services, Elo Touch Solutions, Endurance Lift Holdings, FBR & Co., Fidelis Insurance Holdings Limited, H2Oil Energy, Hornblower Holdings, ICM Partners, Industrial Media, Insight Communications, Interoute Communications, JR Automation, Key Safety Systems, Lancashire Holdings, Martin Currie, Munder Capital Management, NEP Group, NYDJ Apparel, OneLink Communications, Oxbow Carbon, PartnerRe, Protect My Car, Samson Resources, Select Energy Services, Silver Creek Oil & Gas, Silver Creek Permian, Stackpole International, Symbion, US Well Services, ValueOptions, Venerable Holdings, Victory Capital, W Energy Partners, WOW!

Key Executives:
  Tom Murphy, Co-Founder & Partner
  Education: AB, Princeton University; MBA, Harvard Business School
  Background: Head, Financial Sponsors Group, Goldman Sachs
  Directorships: JR Automation
  Barry Volpert, Co-Founder & CEO
  Education: AB, Amherst College; MBA, Harvard Business School; JD, Harvard Law School
  Background: Partner, Goldman Sachs
  Directorships: Key Safety Systems, Oxbow Carbon
  Bob Hurst, Vice Chairman
  Education: AB, Clark University; MBA, Wharton School, University of Pennsylvania
  Background: Vice Chairman, Goldman Sachs
  Directorships: Oxbow Carbon, VF Corporation
  Jeff Marcus, Vice Chairman
  Education: BA, Economics, University of California, Berkeley
  Background: President & CEO, AMFM; Founder & CEO, Marcus Cable; CEO, WestMarc Communications
  Directorships: Camping World/Good Sam Enterprises, NEP Group
  Brian Cassidy, Co-President & Partner
  Education: AB, Physics, Harvard College; MBA, Stanford Graduate School of Business
  Background: Boston Ventures; Investment Banking Analyst, Alex Brown & Sons
  Directorships: Camping World/Good Sam Enterprises, NEP Group, Cumulus Media, Interoute Communications, WOW!
  Bob Delaney, Partner
  Education: AB, Hamilton College; MS, Accounting, New York University Stern School of Business; MBA, Harvard Business School
  Background: Goldman Sachs
  Directorships: Samson Resources, Select Energy Services, Silver Creek Oil & Gas, Synergy Energy, CP Energy
  Rich DeMartini, Vice Chairman
  Education: BA, San Diego State University
  Background: President, Asset Management Group, Bank of America; Morgan Stanley
  Directorships: Capital Bank Financial, Arxis Capital Group, Fidelis Insurance Holdings, Victory Capital Management
  Adam Klein, Partner & Chair, ESG Committee
  Education: AB, Harvard College; MBA, Harvard Business School
  Background: Analyst, Centennial Ventures; Analyst, Compass Partners; Financial Analyst, Donaldson Lufkin & Jenrette
  Directorships: Select Energy Services, Silver Creek Oil & Gas, Synergy Energy, CP Energy
  Alex Rose, Co-President & Partner
  Education: AB, Government, Harvard College; MBA, Wharton School, University of Pennsylvania
  Background: Business Development Associate, General Electric Company; Investment Banking Analyst, Goldman Sachs
  Directorships: JR Automation, Key Safety Systems

561 CROSS CREEK ADVISORS
505 Wakara Way
Suite 215
Salt Lake City, UT 84108

        Phone: 801-214-0010 **Fax:** 801-214-0020
        e-mail: info@crosscreekadvisors.com
        web: www.crosscreekadvisors.com

Mission Statement: Cross Creek Capital seeks to invest in late-stage private companies with significant return potential. Our late-stage venture investments mean shorter time to liquidity and lower risk relative to early stage venture investments.

Investment Criteria: Late Stage
Industry Group Preference: Internet, IT Services, Life Sciences
Portfolio Companies: Accolade, Alta Devices, Anaplan, Angie's List, AppDynamics, Assurex Health, BlueArc Corporation, Bounce Exchange, Bravo Health, Braze, Bright Health, Cardica, Care.com, CENX, Coupang, Cryocor, Data Science International, Dataminr, Datastax, Docker, DocuSign, Drillinginfo, e2Open, Earnest, ExactTarget, Extreme Reach, Fluidigm, ForeScout, FrameMax, Genvault, Gigya, Gusto, Hubspot, Icertis, IntegenX, Integral Ad Science, IronPlanet, Kollective, Legalzoom, Lifelock, Looker, Mavenir, MedManage, mFormation, Miramar Labs, MyHeritage, Netuitive, Neurogesx, Neutral Tandem, newScale, NxStage Medical, Ocera Therapeutics, OpGen, Ophthonix, OREXIGEN Therapeutics, ORQIS Medical, PCH International, Pendo.io, Pindrop, Pluralsight, Poshmark, RealtyShares, Responsys, Rocket Fuel, Rover, Rules Based Medicine, Scopely, ServiceMax, Shiftgig Silver Spring Networks, Simplus, Slice, Solera Networks, Sourcefire, Sumo Logic, Tegile, Telogis, Tethys Bioscience, TherOx, Thumbplay, Ticketfly, True Fit, TubeMogul, Vapotherm, Veracode

Key Executives:
  Karey Barker, CFA, Founding Managing Director
  Background: Portfolio Manager, Wasatch Small Cap Ultra Growth
  Peter Jarman, MBA, Managing Director
  Education: MBA, Northwestern Kellogg Graduate School of Management
  Background: Senior Investment Manager, Fort Washington Capital Partners Group; Ancestry.com; Campus Pipeline; Icon Health and Fitness
  Tyler Christianson, MBA, Managing Director
  Background: President, American Investment Financial
  Barbara Reininger, Director, Finance & Operations
  Background: Operations Manager, Duty Free Americas; Assistant Vice President, Moody's; Product Manager, InterSearch; Founder, BainbridgeBusinessWomen.com; Founder, MyKidsCookies.com

562 CROSSCUT VENTURES
373 Rose Avenue
Venice, CA 90291

        web: www.crosscutventures.com

Mission Statement: Seeking dedicated entrepreneurs who have the foresight and personal fortitude to take their ideas and make them happen in a big way.

Geographic Preference: Southern California
Founded: 2008
Portfolio Companies: Arsenic, Blitz, Boom, Boon & Gable, Branch Messenger, CandyClub, Comparably, ConversionLogic, DataScience, FanBank, FieldDay, Foray, GumGum, Hijro, HelloTech, Iconery, Immortals, Inspire, Jyve, Ledger, LittleLabs, Measurabl, MobCrush, Narvar, Omaze, Overnight, ProspectWise, Purple Squirrel, Reaction Commerce, Science, StreamLabs, StyleSaint, Super Evil

Megacorp, TechStyle, The Black Tux, Trace, Unmute, Verve Mobile, WeDo, Winc, Zingle

Key Executives:
  Rick Smith, Co-Founder/Managing Director
  Education: BS, Finance, University of Illinois; JD, Harvard Law School
  Background: Founder, SunAmerica Ventures; Partner, Palomar Ventures
  Directorships: DocStoc, Zadspace, Postcard on the Run, Pulpo Media, GraphEffect
  Brian Garrett, Co-Founder/Operating Partner
  Education: BS, Industrial Engineering, MBA, Stanford University
  Background: Partner, Palomar Ventures
  Directorships: StyleSaint, GraphEffect, GumGum, Verve Wireless, MyGlam, Lettuce Apps
  Brett Brewer, Co-Founder/Operating Partner
  Education: BA, Business/Economics, University of California, Los Angeles
  Background: Co-Founder, Intermix Media; President & Chairman, Adknowledge.com; CEO, Sensa
  Directorships: Sensa, Eventup
  Adam Goldenberg, Venture Advisor
  Background: Founder, Gamer's Alliance; COO, Intermix Media; Founder, Intelligen Beauty
  Clinton Foy, Managing Director
  Education: BA, University of Notre Dame; JD, University of Washington School of Law; MA, Stanford University
  Background: COO, Square Enix; Attorney, Heller Ehrman Venture Law Group

563 CROSSHILL FINANCIAL GROUP
201 North Union Street
Suite 300
Alexandria, VA 22314

Phone: 703-717-6420 Fax: 703-518-6122
e-mail: info@crosshill.com
web: www.crosshill.com

Mission Statement: CrossHill Financial Group provides private equity funding, bridge financing and advisory services to companies.

Investment Criteria: Growth Financing, Acquisitions, Restructurings, Crisis Management

Key Executives:
  Stephen X Graham, Principal
  Education: Georgetown University; MBA, University of Chicago
  Background: Principal, Kidder Peabody & Co.; Merill Lynch & Co.; Ernst & Young; Founder, Prestwick Companies; Founder, ACell Inc.

564 CROSSLINK CAPITAL
San Francisco, CA

Phone: 415-617-1800
web: www.crosslinkcapital.com

Mission Statement: Seeks to identify sectors of the economy where the rate of business change is greatest and investment opportunities are most profound; focuses efforts exclusively on the sectors that the firm believes offer outstanding opportunity in order to identify companies, add value, and help them achieve greater success.

Fund Size: $800 million
Founded: 1999
Average Investment: $7-15 million
Minimum Investment: $250,000
Investment Criteria: Any stage from seed to pre-IPO to PIPES
Industry Group Preference: Alternative Energy, Data & Analytics, Cloud Infrastructure, Consumer Internet, Software, Digital Health, Digital Marketing, Fintech, IP Services, Lighting, Semis/Coretech, Wireless Systems

Portfolio Companies: 365 Data Centers, 500friends, Adept, Alpha, UX, AmberPoint, Ancestry.com, Armory, Autofi, Ayla, BetterUp, Bigfinite, Bityota, Bizo, Bleacher Report, BlueArc, Bonfire, Brightfunnel, Brightwheel, Broderbound, Building Connected, Carbonite, Case Text, Casper, Cendura, Centerrun, Chart.io, Chime, Cirrus Logic, Comparably, Comprehend, Coupa, Cypress Semiconductor, Datastax, Descartes Labs, Devonway, Digital Cognition Technologies, Eargo, Educents, Enigma, Enview, Equinix, Espresa, Fairclaims, Fatherly, Filament, Flurry, Force10, Fountain, Global Analytics, Good, Great Jones, Haven, Hired, Homelight, Hotel Booking Solutions, Huckleberry, Hungry Root, ICurrent, IMlogic, Infinicon, Inpher, Insight Engines, Intematix, Inverse, Jack Erwin, Kinetic, Kinnek, Koan, Like.com, Livescribe, Madefire, Magma, Marble Security, Marin Software, Marketdial, Marketworks, Mavrx, Mirador Financial, Molekule, Nav, Newscale, Nodesource, Nucore, NWP Services, Omniture, On Display, Op Source, Pandora, Personal Capital, Phil, Phonespots, Pica, Postmates, Power To Fly, Prenav, Primer, Prosper, Protect Wise, Radiumone, Rainforst QA, Rebag, Red Swoosh, Reltio, Rentlytics, Revera, Richrelence, SABA, Schoolmint, Science Exchange, Seamicro, Servicemax, Set Media, Silicon Blue, Silk Road, Sionyx, Sonia, Stratalight, Surgient, Swift Shift, Synapsense, Take Lessons, TIVO, True & Co., Truspan, Validity, Verodin, Vertrue, Virage Logic, Visual.Ly, Vitalstream, Vitesse, Vungle, Weave, Werecover, Xilinx, Xsigo, Yipes,

Other Locations:
2180 Sand Hill Road
Suite 200
Menlo Park, CA 94025
Phone: 415-617-1800

Key Executives:
  Michael Stark, Co-Founder/Portfolio Manager
  e-mail: mjs@crosslinkcapital.com
  Education: BS, Engineering, Northwestern University; MBA, University of Michigan
  Background: Director Research/Equity Analyst, Robertson Stephens; Intel Corporation
  Directorships: Espresa, Apttus
  McLain Southworth, Venture Partner/Head, Strategic Relations
  Education: BSBA, Georgetown University; MBA, Stanford Graduate School of Business
  Background: Currenex; State Street; SV Angel; Apparent; CircleUp
  David Silverman, Partner
  e-mail: dsilverman@crosslinkcapital.com
  Education: BA, Dartmouth College; JD, Stanford University
  Background: Partner, 3i Ventures; Senior Officer, Robertson Stephens; Senior Officer, Piper Jaffray
  Directorships: BuildingConnected, Vungle, Weave, Casper, Enigma, AutoFi, BetterUp, BrightFunnel, Reltio
  Eric Chin, Partner
  Education: BA, Dartmouth College; MBA, Harvard Business School
  Background: Partner, Artiman Ventures; Partner, Bay Partners; IBM; MILCOM
  Directorships: Datastax, Hired, Postmates, Casper, Protectwise, TakeLessons, Vungle, Comparably, Descartes Labs, Nodesource, Flo, Molekule, Verodin, Enigma, JackErwin, Yotascale, Reltio
  Jim Feuille, Venture Partner
  e-mail: jmpf@crosslinkcapital.com
  Education: BA, Chemistry, Dartmouth College; JD, MBA, Stanford University
  Background: Global Head Technology Investment Banking, UBS Warburg; COO, Volpe Brown Whelan & Company; Robertson Stephens
  Directorships: Pandora, Coupa, Personal Capital, Reltio, Global Analytics, Zebit, Chime, Parkifi, Devon Way, Zoosk, SilkRoad
  Matt Bigge, Partner
  Education: BSFS, Georgetown University; MBA, Harvard

Venture Capital & Private Equity Firms / Domestic Firms

Business School
Background: Venture Partner, Paladin Capital; Co-Founder/CEO, Strategic Social Holdings; Co-Founder/President, MILCOM Technologies; U.S. Army
Directorships: Protectwise, Verodin, Descartes Labs, Nodesources, Enview, Inpher

565 CRUNCHFUND
410 Townsend Street
San Francisco, CA 94107

e-mail: partners@crunchfund.com
web: www.crunchfund.com

Mission Statement: Crunchfund invests in and works with information technology companies at any stage, but is primarily focused on seed and early stage investments.

Fund Size: $20 million
Founded: 2011
Investment Criteria: Seed Stage, Early Stage
Industry Group Preference: Technology
Portfolio Companies: Knowhere, Manticore Games, Marble, nTopology, Nylas, One Concern, Overclock Labs, Prodigy, Truework, Wonolo

Key Executives:
Michael Arrington, General Partner
Education: Claremont McKenna College, Stanford Law School
Background: Founder/Board of Directors, Edgeio, Co-Founder of Achex, Founder of TechCrunch
Patrick Gallagher, General Partner
Education: BA, Economics & Literature, Claremont McKenna College
Background: Partner, VantagePoint Capital Partners, Board of Directors, Core Security Technologies/Constant Contact/TouchTunes Interactive Networks/Grocery Shopping Network, Air2Web, YouMail, Board Observer, IntelePeer

566 CRYSTAL RIDGE PARTNERS
111 Dunnell Road
Suite 102
Maplewood, NJ 07040

Phone: 973-275-1100 Fax: 973-275-1120
e-mail: don@crystalridgepartners.com
web: www.crystalridgepartners.com

Mission Statement: Crystal Ridge Partners is a New Jersey based private equity firm with $70 million of committed capital that invests in smaller middle-market companies in partnership with management. CRP focuses primarily on the manufacturing, distribution, consumer products, and business services sectors. CRP invests in management buyouts, recapitalizations and growth equity transactions, it and has the flexibility to take control of minority positions.

Geographic Preference: United States, Northeast, Southeast, Mid-Atlantic, North Central Regio
Fund Size: $70 million
Founded: 2004
Average Investment: $3 - $10 million
Minimum Investment: $3 million
Investment Criteria: $10 to $50 million in sales, Management Buyouts, Recapitalizations, Growth Equity Transactions, Middle-Market Companies
Industry Group Preference: Manufacturing, Distribution, Consumer Products, Business to Business, Healthcare
Portfolio Companies: A.R.E. Accessories, Bronco Manufacturing

Key Executives:
Jack Baron, Managing Principal
e-mail: jack@crystalridgepartners.com
Education: BS, Lehigh University; MBA, Fordham University
Background: Partner, JP Morgan Partners
Directorships: Executive in Residence, MBA Program, Lehigh University
Don Hofmann, Managing Principal
e-mail: don@crystalridgepartners.com
Education: BA, Hofstra University; MBA, Harvard Business School
Background: Senior Partner, JP Morgan Partners; Founder, MH Equity, Manufacturers Hanover Trust Company
Mark G Solow, Senior Advisor
Background: Co-Founder, GarMark Partners; Senior Executive Vice President/Global Head, Investment & Corporate Banking, Chemical Banking Corporation; Manufacturers Hanover Trust Co.
Andrew Tananbaum, Senior Advisor
Education: BA, University of Michigan; JD, Fordham University Law School
Background: President & CEO, Capital Factors; President & CEO, Century Business Credit Corporation

567 CSA PARTNERS
333 N Plankinton Ave.
Suite 205
Milwaukee, WI 53203

web: www.csapartners.com

Mission Statement: CSA Partners, LLC is a venture fund investing in early stage, high growth, companies in the Midwest, with particular focus in Wisconsin. We partner with entrepreneurs to help them build and grow great innovative companies in our community.

Geographic Preference: Midwest
Investment Criteria: Early-Stage
Industry Group Preference: Software, Business Products & Services
Portfolio Companies: Bright Cellars, Carson Life, Dattus, Docalytics, Ease, EatStreet, Eventup, Gener8tor, Music Dealers, Openhomes, Prettylitter, Review Trackers, Scanalytics, Spiritshop, Understory, Yachtlife

Key Executives:
Chris Abele, Managing Director
Steve Mech, Managing Director
Education: BA, Lawrence University; Certificate in Real Estate, University of Wisconsin-Madison

568 CUE BALL GROUP
1 Faneuil Hall Square
7th Floor
Boston, MA 02109

Phone: 617-542-0100 Fax: 617-542-0033
e-mail: ping@cueball.com
web: www.cueball.com

Mission Statement: Cue Ball Group is a venture capital firm focused on companies in the consumer services, enterprise Internet and digital media sectors. The firm helps to build businesses by pursuing innovative ideas and creating close partnerships with management teams. Cue Ball Group is committed to adding value to its portfolio companies.

Founded: 2008
Average Investment: Startup: $500K - $1.5MM; Scaleup: $2 - $5MM
Investment Criteria: Start-Up, Scale-Up
Industry Group Preference: Digital Media & Marketing, Business Products & Services, Specialty Consumer Brands
Portfolio Companies: Argent, Athena Club, Banyan Water, Bread, Cambridge Blockchain, Centrl, ChatGrid, CMG, Codeverse, Ditto, Dubset, Eave, Epic Burger, Funding Gates, Futuredontics, Halo Neuroscience, Haute Hijab, Helpr, Ianacare, Ideeli, Inventables, Jopwell, JW Player, Kapost, Knovel, Landt, Leaders, Lex Machina, Livefyre, Miniluxe, Pex, PlanetTran, ProofPilot, Redline Trading Solutions, Rentlytics, Roti, ScrollMotion, Shade Up, SmartZip Analytics Inc., Sopris Health, StyleSight, TB12, Tea Drops,

195

TeachBoost, True Botanicals, Virgin Pulse, Wahed Invest, Wait What, Wynd, Yapp

Key Executives:
  Richard J Harrington, Chairman Emeritus
  Education: BS, Honorary Doctorate of Laws, University of Rhode Island
  Background: President & CEO, Thomson Reuters Corporation
  Directorships: Xerox Corporation, Aetna, MiniLuxe, PlanetTran, Knovel, StyleSight
  Tony Tjan, Managing Partner
  Education: AB, Harvard College; MBA, Harvard Business School
  Background: Senior Partner, The Parthenon Group; Chief Strategic Counselor, Thomson Reuters; Founder & CEO, ZEFER
  Directorships: Cyberplex, Knovel, Shape Up, Epic Burger, MiniLuxe
  John Hamel, Partner
  Education: AB, Harvard College
  Background: Director, Business Intelligence, Answerthink; Technology Advisor, ZEFER
  Directorships: MiniLuxe, Epic Burger, PlanetTran, Shape Up
  Mats Lederhausen, Operating Partner
  Education: Business Administration, Bromma Gymnasium; MS, Stockholm School of Economics
  Background: Managing Director, McDonald's Ventures; The Boston Consulting Group
  Ali Rahimtula, Partner
  Education: BA, Memorial University; MBA, Harvard Business School
  Background: Principal, Aquiline Capital Partners; VP, Financial Institutions Group, Goldman Sachs

569 CULTIVATE CAPITAL
17 West 76th Street
Suite 2D
New York, NY 10023

Toll-Free: 800-420-0634
e-mail: hello@cultivatecapital.com
web: www.cultivatecapital.com

Mission Statement: Offers capital loans, startup funding, bridge & inventory loans, real estate financing, and cannabis equipment financing.
Geographic Preference: US, Canada
Founded: 2018
Industry Group Preference: Cannabis, Finance

570 CULTIVATION CAPITAL
911 Washington Avenue
Suite 801
St. Louis, MO 63101

Phone: 314-216-2051
e-mail: info@cultivationcapital.com
web: www.cultivationcapital.com

Mission Statement: Cultivation Capital is an early-stage venture capital firm managed by experienced entrepreneurs seeking to partner with the next generation of great founders. All portfolio companies get the benefit of Cultivation Capital's General Partners and Entrepreneurs in Residence. These business-savvy entrepreneurs have built successful companies and thrive at getting great start-ups through the challenging early stages of business development.

Geographic Preference: Missouri
Average Investment: $250,000 - $1.5 million
Minimum Investment: $250,000
Investment Criteria: Post-Seed/Pre-Series A
Industry Group Preference: Technology, Life Sciences
Portfolio Companies: Adarza BioSystems, Aisle411, Arvegenix, Assembly, Benson Hill Biosystems, BlueStrata Her, Cardialen, Cheddar, CloudBeds, DealCloud, Emplify, Euclises Pharmaceuticals Inc., Gainsight, Galera Therapeutics, Gremlin Social, Hatchbuck, Host Analytics, Immune Photonics, Label Insight, Lockerdome, Mobius Therapeutics, Molecular Sensing, NarrativeDx, Pulse Therapeutics, Rentalutions, S4, SafeTrek, Salesvue, Sequoia Vaccines, Sfara FinLocker, TrackBill, Tioma Therapeutics, TopOPPS, Tunespeak, Upside, Veniti, WealthAccess, Yurbuds

Other Locations:
101 North Main Street
Suite 306
Greenville, SC 29601

1100 Corporate Square Drive
Suite 212
St. Louis, MO 63132

Key Executives:
  Brian Matthews, Co-Founder/Managing Partner
  Education: BS, Mechanical Engineering, Missouri University of Science & Technology
  Background: Mentor, Capital Innovators; Founder, River City Internet Group
  Cliff Holekamp, Co-Founder/General Partner
  Education: BA, Washington & Lee University; MBA, Washington University, St. Louis
  Background: Founder, Foot Healers, Back Experts & Pacheco Capital
  Directorships: LockerDome, Yurbuds, SoMoLend, Schoology, The Danube Fund, City Academy
  Kyle Welborn, Co-Founder/General Partner
  Education: Political Science, Loyola University Chicago
  Background: Founder, FinServe Tech Angels; Chicagoland Entrepreneurial Center; Analyst, I2A Fund

571 CULTIVIAN SANDBOX VENTURES
1000 West Fulton Market
Suite 213
Chicago, IL 60607

e-mail: contactus@cultiviansbx.com
web: www.cultiviansbx.com

Mission Statement: Cultivian Sandbox Ventures is a venture capital firm focused on cultivating the next generation of leading food and agriculture technology companies. The firm is a partnership between Cultivian Ventures and Sandbox Industries.

Geographic Preference: North America
Fund Size: $115 million
Average Investment: $5 - $15 million
Investment Criteria: Seed through Late Stage
Industry Group Preference: Food & Beverage, Agriculture, Water, Animal Health, Environment, Food Safety, Sustainability, Technology
Portfolio Companies: AbCelex Technologies, Advanced Adnimal Diagnostics, Agrivida, Allylix, AquaSpy, Aratana Therapeutics, Conservis, Corvium, Descartes Labs, Divergence, EnEvolv, Full Harvest, Geltor, Harvest Automation, HarvestPort, Novihum Technologies, Novogy, Nuritas, Phylagen, Proterro, Rivertop Renewables, Sound Agriculture, Vestaron, Virgin Plants

Key Executives:
  Ron Meeusen, PhD, Managing Director
  Education: PhD, Plant Cell Biology, University of California, Berkeley
  Background: Global Leader of Biotechnology, Dow AgroSciences; Founder, Immuneworks
  Directorships: AbCelex, Agrivida, Asilomar Bio, EnEvolv, Proterro, Rivertop Renewables, Vestaron, Virgin Plants
  Andy Ziolkowski, Managing Director
  Education: BS, Engineering, University of Pennsylvania; MBA, Wharton School
  Background: Managing Director, SAE Ventures; Forest Street Capital; Director, Venture Capital, Credit Suisse First Boston

Directorships: AquaSpy, Descartes Labs, EOSi, Harvest Automation, Novihum Technologies, Sample6
Bob Shapiro, Managing Director
Education: AB, Harvard College; JD, Columbia University School of Law
Background: Chairman & CEO, Monsanto Agriculture Group; CEO, The NutraSweet Company; VP & General Counsel, GD Searle & Co.
Directorships: Chromatin, Elevance Renewable Sciences, Intrexon Corporation, Conservis Corp., Advanced Animal Diagnostics
Nick Rosa, Managing Director
Education: BS, Political Science, Northern Illinois University; MBA, DePaul University
Background: CEO, NutraSweet Company; Senior Executive, Monsanto

---

572 CUSTER CAPITAL
14 Sout High Street
New Albany, OH 43054

Phone: 614-855-9980

Mission Statement: Established to make investments in a diversified portfolio of growth and expansion companies.

Geographic Preference: Midwest United States
Fund Size: $5 million
Founded: 1985
Average Investment: $200,000
Minimum Investment: $50,000
Investment Criteria: Debt Expansion, Spinoffs, Management Buyouts, Recapitalizations, Leveraged Acquisitions
Industry Group Preference: Healthcare, Manufacturing, Distribution, Business Products & Services, Technology

Key Executives:
William M. Custer, President/CEO
Education: BS, Corporate Finance, University of Southern California, NASD Series 7 and Series 63 License
Donald O'Shea, Managing Director
Education: MBA, Vrunel University; DMS, University of the West of England; BSc, University of London
Background: Managing Director, Leather Agencies; President/CEO, Minit Canada; Founder, BDF Group Ltd.

---

573 CUTLASS CAPITAL LLC
229 Marlborough Street
Boston, MA 02116

web: www.cutlasscapital.com

Mission Statement: Cutlass Capital is a private venture capital firm that exclusively pursues opportunities in the healthcare industry, with particular emphasis on the specialty healthcare services and medical device sectors. Cutlass Capital's objective is to provide its expertise to create value for its portfolio companies and to help cultivate the next generation of leading healthcare businesses.

Fund Size: $57 million
Founded: 2001
Industry Group Preference: Healthcare, Healthcare Services, Medical Devices
Portfolio Companies: Alere Medical Inc., Apneon Inc., Byram Holdings Inc., CardioKinetix Inc., Evalve Inc., GI Dynamics Inc., Hemosphere Inc., IntelliCare america Inc., Titan Health Corporation, TranS1 Inc., Xoft Inc.

Other Locations:
1750 Montgomery Street
San Francisco, CA 94111

Key Executives:
Jonathan W Osgood CFA, Co-Founder/Managing Member
617-867-0820
e-mail: jonosgood@cutlasscapital.com
Education: BA, Dartmouth College; MBA, Amos Tuck School of Business Administration, Dartmouth College
Background: Research Analyst, Deutsche Banc Alex Brown; Global Head, Health Care Research
Directorships: CardioKinetix, GI Dynamics, Hemosphere, TranS1, Xoft
E David Hetz, Co-Founder/Managing Member
415-806-4611
e-mail: hetz@cutlasscapital.com
Education: BA, Claremont McKenna College; MBA, Harvard Business School
Background: Investment Banker, Robertson Stephens & Co
Directorships: Titan Health Corporation, Xoft
Raymond Larkin, Venture Partner
e-mail: raylarkin@cutlasscapital.com
Education: BS, La Salle University
Background: CEO, Eunoe; CEO, Nellcor Puritan Bennett; National Sales Manager, Bentley Laboratories; Captain, United States Marine Corps.
Stephen B Solomon MD, Venture Partner
410-303-6901
e-mail: ssolomon@cutlasscapital.com
Education: AB, Biochemistry & Molecular Biology, Harvard College; MD, Yale School of Medicine
Background: Faculty Member, Johns Hopkins School of Medicine

---

574 CVF CAPITAL PARTNERS
1590 Drew Avenue
Suite 110
Davis, CA 95618

Phone: 530-757-7004 **Fax:** 530-757-1316
e-mail: info@cvfcapitalpartners.com
web: cvfcapitalpartners.com

Mission Statement: CVF Capital Partners grew out of California's Central Valley to become a lower middle market investor in the Western U.S. with special knowledge of the Hispanic market.

Geographic Preference: Western U.S.
Founded: 2005
Average Investment: $2 - $5 million
Investment Criteria: Later-Stage, Expansion, Strategic Acquisitions, Ownership Transitions, Recapitalizations
Industry Group Preference: Business Services, Distribution and Logistics, Manufacturing, Healthcare, Telecommunications
Portfolio Companies: Utility Telecom, ComAv, Pioneer Recycling, LightRiver Technologies, Signature Coast

Key Executives:
José Blanco, Managing Partner
Education: Saint Michael's College; MS, Economics, University of Utah; MBA, Claremont Graduate University; PhD, Economics, Utah State University
Background: Regional Vice President, CIO, AIG Investment Corporation
Edward McNulty, Managing Partner
Education: BA, Colgate University; MIA, Finance, Columbia University
Background: Founding Partner, ACI Capital America Fund
Brad Triebsch, Managing Partner
Education: Saint Mary's College
Background: Westhoff Cone & Holmstedt

---

575 CXO FUND
3031 Tisch Way
Suite 704
San Jose, CA 95128

web: thecxofund.com

Mission Statement: To create long-term value by helping entrepreneurs build companies and provide attractive returns to

Venture Capital & Private Equity Firms / Domestic Firms

our investors. CXO is a venture capital firm that works hands on with management to build innovative companies.

Geographic Preference: California
Investment Criteria: Early Stage, Seed/Pre-Series A
Industry Group Preference: Fintech, Health Care, Technology, Deep Tech, Software, Internet, Food Technology
Portfolio Companies: Avocado Systems, Breinify, Censia, Coddle, Cogni, CogX, Modjoul, TruU, Uniphore, Zapata

Key Executives:
   Gary Gauba, Founder/Managing Director
   Education: BEng, Gujarat University; MS, Chemical Engineering, West Virginia University
   Background: CEO/Founder, Softline; Systech Integrators; Cognilytics Inc.; TruU; Sr Partner, KPMG; President, ACS Systech Integrators; President, CenturyLink

576 CYPRESS GROUP

Mission Statement: Invests equity capital in privately negotiated transactions and builds value for investors. Investments are made in promising established companies, which are then helped to grow dynamically and profit as their plans are realized.

Fund Size: $2.5 billion
Founded: 1989
Minimum Investment: $500,000
Industry Group Preference: Manufacturing, Consumer Products, Media
Portfolio Companies: Affinia Group Inc., American Marketing Industries Holdings Inc., Anglian Group Plc., Atlanta Cable Systems, Brand Connections LLC, Catlin, Cinemark USA Inc., ClubCorp Inc., Communications & Power Industries Inc., Cooper-Standard Automotive Inc., Dank Business Systems Plc., Evergreen Media Corporation, Financial Guaranty Insurance Company, Illinois Central Corporation, Infinity Broadcasting Corporation, K&F Industries Inc., Lear Corporation, Loral Aerospace Holdings Inc., McBride Plc., MedPointe Inc., Meow Mix Company, Montpelier Re Holdings Ltd., Parisian Inc., Republic National Cabinet Corporation, RP Scherer Corporation, Scottish Re Group Limited, Stone Canyon Entertainment Corporation, WESCO International Inc., Williams Scotsman Inc.

Key Executives:
   James A. Stern, Chairman/CEO
   Education: BS, Tufts University; MBA, Harvard Business School
   Background: Head Merchant Banking, Lehman Brothers
   Directorships: Lear Corporation; AMTROL; Affinia Group; MedPointe; WESCO International

577 CYPRESS GROWTH CAPITAL
3899 Maple Ave.
Suite 100
Dallas, TX 75219

Phone: 214-304-7645
e-mail: inquiries@cypressgrowthcapital.com
web: www.cypressgrowthcapital.com

Mission Statement: An alternative to traditional debt and equity instruments, royalty financing offers entrepreneurs access to significant capital while preserving ownership and control. As one of the first and largest royalty financing firms in the United States, Cypress Growth Capital is actively investing in technology-enabled business services companies in the Southwest.

Geographic Preference: Southwest
Average Investment: $1 - $8 million
Investment Criteria: Growth Capital
Industry Group Preference: Technology-Enabled Services, SaaS, Software, Business Products & Services

Key Executives:
   Ed Mello, Co-Founder/Managing Director
   Education: University of Notre Dame
   Background: COO/Managing Partner, Computer Sciences Corporation Consulting Group; Co-Founder, Cypress Point Partners; President, Global Sales & Operations, nGenera; EDS
   Barton Goodwin, Co-Founder/Managing Partner
   Education: Economics & Managerial Studies, Rice University
   Background: Co-Founder, Cypress Point Partners; Information Technology, Accenture
   Vik Thapar, Venture Partner
   Education: BS, University of Texas, Dallas; MBA, Southern Methodist University
   Background: Director, Texas Regional Center for Innovation & Commercialization
   Directorships: TeXchange, TiE Dallas

578 CYPRIUM PARTNERS
200 Public Square
Suite 2020
Cleveland, OH 44114

Phone: 216-453-4500
web: www.cyprium.com

Mission Statement: A private investment firm that provides mezzanine and equity capital to profitable, middle-market companies. Cyprium strives to be a value-added investor that supports the growth, acquisition, refinancing or liquidity needs of private company owners and their management teams.

Geographic Preference: United States, Canada
Founded: 1998
Average Investment: $10 - $60 million
Investment Criteria: Mezzanine, Equity
Industry Group Preference: Manufacturing, Distribution
Portfolio Companies: ACT Lighting Inc., Backyard Products LLC, Bensussen Deutsch & Associates, Hobbico Inc., Irvin Automotive Products Inc., MC Assembly, M-D Building Products, MGS Mfg. Group Inc., Paper Machinery Corp., Phantom Fireworks, Weaber Inc.

Other Locations:
   461 Fifth Avenue
   26th Floor
   New York, NY 10017
   Phone: 616-571-1620

   77 West Wacker Drive
   Suite 4500
   Chicago, IL 60601
   Phone: 312-283-8800

Key Executives:
   John Sinnerberg, Partner
   Education: BA Economics, Bucknell University; MBA, Wharton School, University of Pennsylvania
   Background: CEO & Managing Partner, Key Principal Partners; Co-Founder, Key Mezzanine Capital Fund; Founder, Regis Capital Partners; Investment Banking, Barclays Group
   Cindy Babbit, Managing Partner
   Education: BS Biology, University of Miami; MBA, Case Western Reserve University
   Background: Partner, Key Principal Partners; Investment Banking, Carleton, McCreary, Holmes and Company; Laboratory Technical, Siebert Powder Coatings; Statistician, University Hospitals of Cleveland
   Drew Molinari, Principal
   Education: BBA, Finance, Kent State University; MBA, Booth School of Business, University oF Chicago
   Background: Associate, Corporate Development, Agilysys Inc.; Analyst, Croft & Bender; Analyst, Brown, Gibbons Lang & Co.
   Daniel Kessler, Partner
   Education: BS, Accounting, Indiana University; MBA, University of Chicago; CPA
   Background: Key Principal Partners; GlobalStreams
   Beth Haas, Partner
   Education: BA, Government, Dartmouth College; MBA, Wharton School, University of Pennsylvania

Venture Capital & Private Equity Firms / Domestic Firms

Background: Key Principal Partners; KeyBanc Capital Markets

579 CapitalG
web: capitalg.com

Mission Statement: Formerly known as Google Capital, CapitalG is a growth equity fund that invests in companies that harness long-term technology trends to drive market disruption. Our connection to Google is our key asset.

Geographic Preference: Global
Industry Group Preference: Technology
Portfolio Companies: Airbnb, Applied, Aye, Care.com, Car Dekho, Cloudflare, Commonfloor.com, Convoy, Credit Karma, Crowd Strike, Cuemath, Duolingo, Fanduel, Freshworks, Glassdoor, Gusto, Inno Light, Lending Club, Looker, Lyft, Mapr, MultiPlan, Oscar, Practo, Renaissance, Robinhood, Snap, Stripe, Survery Monkey, Ten-X, Thumbtack, UiPath, Zscaler

Key Executives:
Gene Frantz, Partner
Education: BS, University of California, Berkeley; MBA, Stanford Graduate School of Business
Background: Partner, TPG Capital
David Lawee, Partner
Education: McGill University; University of Western Ontario; MBA, University of Chicago
Background: VP, Corporate Development, Google; VP, Marketing, Google; Founder, Mosaic Venture Partners
Laela Sturdy, Partner
Education: AB, Harvard College; MSc, Trinity College Dublin; MBA, Stanford Graduate School of Business
Background: Director, Sales & Business Operations, Google; Consultant, Bain & Company

580 D.E. SHAW & CO. LP The D.E. Shaw Group
1166 Avenue of the Americas
9th Floor
New York, NY 10036

Phone: 212-478-0000 Fax: 212-478-0100
e-mail: inquiries@deshaw.com
web: www.deshaw.com

Mission Statement: The D.E. Shaw Group is a global investment firm that invests in a wide array of companies in both public and private markets across the world.

Geographic Preference: Worldwide
Fund Size: $39 billion
Founded: 1988
Investment Criteria: Early-Stage, Later-Stage
Industry Group Preference: All markets considered

Other Locations:
180 Linden Street
2nd Floor
Wellesley, MA 02482

7300 College Boulevard
Suite 620
Overland Park, KS 66210
Phone: 212-478-0050 Fax: 212-478-0060

821 Alexander Road
Suite 202
Princeton, NJ 08540

2735 Sand Hill Road
Suite 105
Menlo Park, CA 94025
Phone: 650-526-4300 Fax: 650-526-4301

3 Bermudiana Road
Third Floor
Hamilton HM 08
Bermuda
Phone: 441-278-4850 Fax: 441-278-4860

D.E. Shaw & Co. London LLP
55 Baker Street
7th Floor
London W1U 8EW
United Kingdom
Phone: 44-2074094300 Fax: 44-2074094350

D.E. Shaw & Co. Asia Pacific Limited
19th Floor, York House
The Landmark, 15 Queens Road
Central
Hong Kong
Phone: 852-35212500 Fax: 852-35212600

D.E. Shaw Investment Management Co., Ltd.
Level 12, Unit 1207, International Finance Center Tower 2
8 Century Avenue, Pudong
Shanghai 200120
China

Key Executives:
David E. Shaw, Founder
Education: PhD, Stanford University
Background: Chief Scientist, D.E. Shaw Research LLC; Senior Research Fellow, Center for Computational Biology & Bioinformatics, Columbia University; Adjunct Professor, Biochemistry & Molecular Biophysics, Columbia Medical School

581 DACE VENTURES
405 Waltham Street
Suite 140
Lexington, MA 02421

Phone: 781-250-0600 Fax: 781-250-0611
e-mail: info@daceventures.com
web: www.daceventures.com

Mission Statement: Dace Ventures actively invests in innovative businesses in the Internet industry, with particular focus on the mobile services, digital media and consumer marketing sectors. The firm seeks to work with passionate entrepreneurs and innovative companies with advantages in high-potential markets.

Fund Size: $70 million
Average Investment: $250,000 - $3 million
Investment Criteria: Early-Stage
Industry Group Preference: Digital Media & Marketing, Consumer Marketing, Mobile Services, Marketing
Portfolio Companies: Apptient, Cartera Commerce, Cityvoter, EveryScape, Healthguru, Howcast, Ticket Evolution, YieldMo

Key Executives:
Dave Andonian, Managing Partner
e-mail: dave@daceventures.com
Education: BA, Business, University of Massachusetts, Amherst
Background: Entrepreneur-in-Residence, Flagship Ventures; Chairman & CEO, Affinnova; President & COO, CMGI; PictureTel; IBM
Directorships: CityVoter, EveryScape, Ticket Evolution
Jon Chait, General Partner
e-mail: jon@daceventures.com
Background: Principal, Pod Holding; Managing Director, Garage Technology Ventures; CEO & Founder, Reality Bytes
Directorships: Cartera Commerce, Marlin Mobile
Doug Chertok, Venture Partner
Background: Founder, Vast Ventures; Founder, StreetEasy
Directorships: Daylife, StreetEasy, Hashable

582 DAG VENTURES
251 Lytton Avenue
Suite 200
Palo Alto, CA 94301

Phone: 650-543-8180 Fax: 650-328-2921
e-mail: info@dagventures.com
web: www.dagventures.com

Venture Capital & Private Equity Firms / Domestic Firms

Mission Statement: DAG Ventures is a venture capital partnership that helps promising entrepreneurs to build leading companies across a range of technology sectors.
Fund Size: $500 million
Investment Criteria: Early Stage, Mid-Stage
Industry Group Preference: Information Technology, Energy, Life Sciences, Software
Portfolio Companies: 3VR, Adamas Pharmaceuticals, Admob, Aerohive Networks, Aggregate Knowledge, Agrivida, Alta Devices, Altor Networks, Ambarella, Amyris Biotechnologies, Aoptix, Atara Biotherapeutics, Avnera, Avvo, Axiom Global, Birst, BitTorrent, Bloom Energy, Boku, CardioDx, Chegg, Clarizen, ClearStory Data, Cleartrip, Clickatell, Cloudera, D2S, DisplayLink, Engine Yard, Eventbrite, FireEye, Fortify Software, Funny or Die, Gigya, Glam Media, Glassdoor, GrubHub, Harvest Power, High Gear Media, Inspirato, Jasper Wireless, Kovio, LearnVest, Lithium Technologies, LiveOps, Loopt, Marin Software, Mcube, NEOS, New Relic, Newport Media, Nextdoor, Ninian Solutions, One Medical Group, OpenDNS, OpenX Software, Oportun, Origami Logic, Pacific Biosciences of California, Pentaho, Picarro, Pinger, Proofpoint, Quantenna Communications, Raptr, RightScale, Ring Central, Seeking Alpha, Silver Peak Systems, SilverSpring Networks, Solexel, StrongView Systems, SunRun, Taulia, TrialPay, True Ultimate Standards Everywhere, Upwork, uShip, Vectra Networks, Visible Measures, Wealthfront, Wetpaint, WeWork, Wixpress, Xoom, Yelp, YuMe, Zlango, Zuora, Zynga

Key Executives:
  John Caddedu, Managing Director
  Education: BA, Harvard College; MBA, Stanford Graduate School of Business
  Background: Managing Director, Amsterdam Pacific; Octel Communications; Tandem Computers; JP Morgan
  Young Chung, Managing Director
  Education: BA, Harvard College; MBA, Harvard Business School
  Background: Investment Banking Analyst, Goldman Sachs; Entrisphere
  Tom Goodrich, Managing Director
  Education: AB, Dartmouth College; MBA, Stanford Graduate School of Business
  Background: Principal, Bechtel Investments; Co-Founder & Vice President, Dimensional Corporate Finance
  Nick Pianim, Managing Director
  Education: BSc, Electrical Engineering, Tufts University; MBA, Stanford Graduate School of Business
  Background: Vice President, Corporate Development, Juniper Networks; CEO, iAsiaWorks
  Greg Williams, Managing Director
  Education: BSc, McGill University
  Background: Portfolio Manager, Teachers' Private Capital; Summerhill Ventures
  Joseph Zanone, Chief Financial Officer
  Education: BS, Pennsylvania State University; MBA, Santa Clara University; CPA
  Background: Finance Director, Siemens Venture Capital; Audit Manager, PricewaterhouseCoopers

583 DALLAS VENTURE PARTNERS
2801 Woodside St.
Dallas, TX 75204

e-mail: info@dallasventurepartners.com
web: www.dallasventurepartners.com

Mission Statement: Our mission at Dallas Venture Partners is to become the financial partner of choice for technology entrepreneurs seeking to build a world-class business. At DVP, we believe in creating and sustaining long term relationships within our own local venture community as well as within the larger venture industry. That means, if we think we can help you, we will - even if we are not able to invest in your business. It also means that if we choose to invest in your company, you can expect us to use every resource at our disposal to ensure that you will succeed.

Geographic Preference: Texas, Midwest
Investment Criteria: Early-Stage
Industry Group Preference: Software, Clean Technology, Networking, Mobile Apps, Gaming, Web Applications & Services
Portfolio Companies: AgSolver, Averify, Data Vision Resources, Device Fidelity, Eyelation, Parrable, PHYND, SmartyPig, Yvolver, Zest Health

Key Executives:
  Michael Coppola, Managing Partner
  Education: BBA, Southern Methodist University
  Background: President, Coppola Enterprises; Co-Founder, DataVision; Co-Founder, Businessolver.com; Co-Founder, Workcomp.net
  Directorships: Datavision, Businessolver, Social Money
  Jim Duda, Managing Partner
  Education: BA, Northwestern University; MBA, Fuqua School
  Background: Executive Vice President, Genus Holdings

584 DANEVEST TECH FUND ADVISORS
8215 Greenway Blvd.
Suite 560
Midleton, WI 53562

Phone: 608-830-2990

Mission Statement: DaneVest Tech Fund Advisors, LLC invests in privately held, early stage growth businesses with special technology and other advantages in the information technology, life science and consumer goods/service industries.

Geographic Preference: Midwest
Investment Criteria: Early-Stage
Industry Group Preference: Technology, Information Technology, Life Sciences, Consumer Products, Consumer Services
Portfolio Companies: Alice.com, Compact Particle Acceleration Corporation, Eso-Technologies, Sologear, Stemia Biomarker Discovery, TrafficCast China, TrafficCast International

Key Executives:
  Terrence R Wall, General Partner
  Education: Graaskamp Real Estage Program, University of Wisconsin-Madison
  Background: Founder, President & General Partner, T. Wall Properties Master Limited Partnership
  Joseph P Hildebrandt, General Partner
  Background: CEO/Manager, H Venture Management; Managing Director, Penomenelle Angels Fund I; Partner Emeritus, Foley & Lardner LLP
  Leon R Wilkosz, President
  Education: Univeristy of Wisonson, Madison
  Background: President/Owner, Resource Consulting LLC

585 DARBY OVERSEAS INVESTMENTS LTD
1133 Connecticut Avenue Northwest
Suite 400
Washington, DC 20036

Phone: 202-872-0500 **Fax:** 202-872-1816
web: www.darbyoverseas.com

Mission Statement: Darby Overseas Investments, Ltd. is the private equity arm of Franklin Templeton Investments. Experienced in the field of infrastructure, Darby pursues investments in sectors such as energy, transportation, waste management, water treatment and telecommunications, and specifically targets markets in Asia, Central and Eastern Europe and Latin America.

Geographic Preference: Latin America, Asian, Central Europe, Eastern Europe
Fund Size: $250 million
Founded: 1994
Average Investment: $10 - $15 million

Venture Capital & Private Equity Firms / Domestic Firms

Investment Criteria: Late Stage Venture Capital, Minority, Shared Control Stakes, Acquisitions, Mezzanine, Restructuring, Buyouts, Growth Capital, Middle-Market, Consolidation
Industry Group Preference: Financial Services, Energy, Consumer Products, Telecommunications, Information Technology, Healthcare, Industrial
Portfolio Companies: Amalgamated Bean Coffee Trading Company, ART Group, AUPU Group Holding Company, Bioerix SRL, Bhoruka Power, Brightex Industries, Bugukgangbyung Co., Career Point Infosystems, Daechun Greenwater, Daesan Energy, Datapoint, Electrosteel Steels, Empresa Generadora de Electricidad Haina, Energy Network, Enzen Global Solutions, ERG Services, Escorts Construction Equipment, Gangwon Wind Power, GKC Projects, Golden Harvest, Gramex 2000, Gyeonggi Expressway, Heemang Dream Haksa Co., Hisarlar, Hyosung Wind Power Holdings, Injae Tongil Village Co., Intertug, Junggwan Library Operation Co., Kerrera Company, Kimaya Fashions, Koza Gida, Leadcorp, Machang Bridge, Myungsung Environment, Nara-Sarang Co., Newgen Knowledge Works, OCI Solar, OCENSA, OCENSA Transportation Rights, Orion Holding, Paju Yangju Tongil Village Co., PECH, PSM Investments, Seoul Beltway Corporation, SFO Technologies, Shayne International Holdings, Storent Holding, Sun-Jin Boramae Co., Symbiotec Pharmalab, Tabacarcen, Top Image, Ver Se Innovation, Vital Renewable Energy Company, Walnut Investment Holding, Water Oasis Group, Yeongcheon Daegu Tongil Madang Co., Yuchai

Other Locations:
Fiduciary Trust International of the South
2 Alhambra Plaza
Penthouse 1
Coral Gables, FL 33134
Phone: 305-372-1260 **Fax:** 305-982-1593

Franklin Templeton Investments Svcs Mexico
Darby Private Equity, Paseo de la Reforma No. 342, piso 8
Col. Juárez
Delegacion Cuauhtémoc 06600
Mexico
Phone: 52-5550020696 **Fax:** 52-5526232643

Darby Colpatria Capital SAS
Cra. 7 80-49
Suite 201
Bogota
Colombia
Phone: 57-13131188

Franklin Templeton Investimentos Ltda
Avenida Brigadeiro Faria Lima
331 - 5o andar
Sao Paulo SP 04538-133
Brazil
Phone: 55-1132060080 **Fax:** 55-1130713775

Darby Asia Investors Limited
17th Floor Charter House
8 Connaught Road
Central
Hong Kong
Phone: 852-29109200 **Fax:** 852-25219815

Darby-Hana Infrastructure Fund Management Co.
10th Floor, CCMM Building
12 Youido-Dong, Youngdungpo-Gu
Seoul 150-968
Korea
Phone: 822-37740605 **Fax:** 822-37740667

Darby Asia Investors Private Limited
Indiabulls Finance Center, Tower 2, 13th Floor
Senapati Bapat Marg, Elphinstone (W)
Mumbai 400013
India
Phone: 91-02267519100 **Fax:** 91-02266391277

Franklin Templeton Austria GmbH
Dr. Karl Lueger-Ring 10
Vienna A-1010
Austria
Phone: 43-1532265500 **Fax:** 43-1532265550

Franklin Templeton Slovakia cro
Aupark Tower
Einsteinova 24
Bratislava 851 0
Slovakia
Phone: 421-232113720 **Fax:** 421-232113730

Franklin Templeton Magyarország Kft
Granit Tower, Sixth Floor
Szabadsag ter 7
Budapest 1054
Hungary
Phone: 36-13543700 **Fax:** 36-13543710

Darby Overseas Investments
Buyukdere Caddesi No. 191
Apa Giz Plaza Kat 12
Levent / Istanbul 34330
Turkey
Phone: 90-2123679204 **Fax:** 90-2123679202

Franklin Templeton Investments Poland sp Z.O.O., Rondo 1, 29th Floor
Rondo ONZ 1
Warsaw 00-124
Poland
Phone: 48-223371380 **Fax:** 48-223371373

Key Executives:
Richard H. Frank, President/CEO
Education: BS, Mechanical Engineering, South Dakota School of Mines and Technology; MS, Sloan School of Management, Massachusetts Institute of Technology
Background: World Bank; CFO, International Finance Corporation

586 DATA COLLECTIVE
500 2nd Street
Suite 200
San Francisco, CA 94107

e-mail: press@dcvc.com
web: www.dcvc.com

Mission Statement: Data Collective invests in entrepreneurs building Big Data companies. Big Data companies capture, store, secure, transmit, transform, and analyze data for economic advantage, either with huge volumes (terabytes to exabytes), or at tremendous speed (microseconds to seconds), or both. Big Data companies can come to market solving hard infrastructure problems, taking leadership in vertical B2B markets, or as truly data-driven consumer products. The common thread is that the founding team has the experience and discipline to solve data problems at novel scale, speed, or level of insight, and ideally all three.

Investment Criteria: Seed, Series A, Growth
Industry Group Preference: Data Storage, Cloud Computing, Internet, Software
Portfolio Companies: Amiato, Apcera, Appurify, Authy, BackOps, BitDeli, CardSpring, Carsabi, CircleCI, CitusData, Cloudability, Continuity, Cube, Elasticsearch, Feedzai, Firebase, FlipTop, FloType, FreshPlum, GetGOing, HeavyBit Industries, Ink, Kaggle, Keen IO, LevdUp, MatterMark, Memsql, Meteor, MindSumo, MixRank, Moleculo, MongoHQ, Morta Security, Parse, ParStream, Piston Cloud Computing, Planet Labs, Platfora, Priceonomics, PrimaTable, Prism Skylabs, Qumulo, Ranker, Rescale, RolePoint, Sentinel, ShopLogic, Signifyd, Simpler, SinoLending, SolidStage, Space Monkey, Srch2, Swiftype, Teambox, Tempo, Trifacta, TrustedInsight, Virool, Vurb, Weotta, Womply, ZenPayroll

Venture Capital & Private Equity Firms / Domestic Firms

Other Locations:
270 University Avenue
Palo Alto, CA 94301

Key Executives:
Zachary Bogue, Co-Managing Partner
Education: BS, Environmental Science, Harvard University; JD, Georgetown Law School
Background: Co-Founder, Founders Den; Co-Founder, Montara Capital Partners; Associate, Wilson Sonsini Goodrich & Rosati; Law Partner, Virtual Law Partners
Matt Ocko, Co-Managing Partner
Education: Physics, Yale University
James Hardiman, Partner
Education: University of California, Berkeley; University of Chicago
Background: ZS Associates; Blackstone Group

587 DATA POINT CAPITAL
One Marina Park Drive
10th Floor
Boston, MA 02210

Phone: 617-874-5152
e-mail: info@datapointcapital.com
web: www.datapointcapital.com

Mission Statement: Data Point Capital focuses on companies that can be leveraged and scaled on the Internet and touch the consumer. Categories of interest include mobile, gaming, social networks, payments, comparison shopping, e-commerce and emerging technologies. The fund is stage-agnostic, allowing for investments in all business stages or controlling interest deals and is made up of business executives and internet leaders who have created tremendous value through building a number of very successful companies.

Founded: 2012
Investment Criteria: All Stages
Industry Group Preference: Mobile, Gaming, Social Media, E-Commerce & Manufacturing, Internet
Portfolio Companies: Aperio, Blitsy, Clypd, CouchUp, Jebbit, Luxury Garage Sale, Paintzen, Print Syndicate, Smart Lunches, Vee24, Yieldify, YourMechanic

Key Executives:
Scott Savitz, Founder/Managing Partner
Education: BA, English, University of Colorado
Background: CEO, Shoebuy.com
Directorships: Olejo Stores, On The Spot Systems, Bluestem Brands
Mike Majors, Managing Partner
Education: BSE, Machine Learning/Robotics, Cambridge University
Background: Managing Partner, Siemens Venture Capital; CFO, Visible World; CFO, Indeed; Brand Equity Ventures
Mary Shannon, Principal of Finance
Education: MBA, Boston College
Background: Director, Planning & Analysis, Zefer; Director, Special Projects, Libery Mutual Group; Analyst, Burr Egan Deleage & Co.

588 DAUPHIN CAPITAL PARTNERS
108 Forest Avenue
Locust Valley, NY 11560

Phone: 516-759-3339 **Fax:** 516-759-3322
web: www.dauphincapital.com

Mission Statement: Dauphin Capital Partners is a venture capital firm that focuses primarily on the medical and healthcare industries.

Geographic Preference: Eastern Half of United States
Fund Size: $30 million
Founded: 1998
Average Investment: $2 - $3 million
Minimum Investment: $2 million
Investment Criteria: Early Stage
Industry Group Preference: Healthcare, Healthcare Services
Portfolio Companies: Supplemental Health Care Services

Key Executives:
James B Hoover, Founder/Managing Member
e-mail: jhoover@dauphincapital.com
Education: BS, Elizabethtown College; MBA, Finance, Indiana University
Background: General Partner, Welsh, Carson, Anderson & Stowe; General Partner, Robertson, Stephens & Company; VP, Investment Management Group, Citibank NA
Directorships: Quovadx, US Physical Therapy

589 DAVENPORT RESOURCES LLC
7 Seir Hill Road
Unit 21
Norwalk, CT 06850

Phone: 203-276-1600
e-mail: hebingham@davenportresources.com
web: www.davenportresources.com

Mission Statement: Direct investments and fund sponsorship for high growth in valuation.

Geographic Preference: United States, Europe
Fund Size: $2.5 million to $100 million
Founded: 1995
Minimum Investment: $50,000
Investment Criteria: Seed, Start-up, Early Rounds, Buy-Ins
Industry Group Preference: Clean Technology, Infrastructure, Renewable Energy, Technology, Energy
Portfolio Companies: Halite Energy Group, Castion Corp., CyGene Inc., Mensch & Natur AG, Mycotech Corp., Room Temperature Superconductors Inc. (ROOTS), Interative Retail Management Inc., Demegen Inc, I/SCRIBES Corp.

Key Executives:
Hiram A. Bingham, Managing Director
Education: BA, Yale, Columbia LLB
Background: President, Caithness Energy, Associate, Shearman & Sterling
Douglas S. Perry, Managing Director
Education: Law Degree, Emory University & Georgetown University; MBA, Duke University
Background: President, Constellation Holdings; Special Counsel/Attorney, SEC's Divisions of Corporation Finance and Enforcement

590 DAVID N DEUTSCH & COMPANY LLC
Westchester Financial Center
50 Main Street
10th Floor
New York, NY 10606

Phone: 212-980-7800
e-mail: office@dndco.com
web: www.dndco.com

Mission Statement: David N. Deutsch & Company is an investment banking firm and independent advisor based in New York. The firm provides financial services to closely-held private and public companies, including advisory services and merger, acquisition, divestiture and financing transactions.

Geographic Preference: US, Canada, Mexico, Western Europe, Israel, Asia, Pacific Rim
Founded: 1993
Industry Group Preference: Business to Business, Communications, Computer Related, Retailing, Real Estate, Consumer Services, Diversified, Financial Services, Food & Beverage, Industrial Equipment, Manufacturing, Chemicals, Publishing, Construction, Technology

Key Executives:
David N Deutsch, Founder/President
212-980-7800 x1
e-mail: dndeutsch@dndco.com
Education: AB, Economics, Middlebury College; MBA, Columbia University

Venture Capital & Private Equity Firms / Domestic Firms

Background: Managing Partner, The Presidents Council; Managing Director, Congress Financial; VP, Bear Stearns & Company; Lehman Brothers

591 DAVID SHEN VENTURES
e-mail: info@davidshenventures.com
web: www.davidshenventures.com

Mission Statement: David Shen Ventures focuses mainly on early-stage Internet and Internet-related businesses. The goal is to quickly bring a product to market in an inexpensive way, employ innovation to differentiate from competitors and delight consumers, and test its viability live in the marketplace. Once a product's viability has been validated, David Shen Ventures helps its businesses strategize on growth to the future.

Investment Criteria: Early-Stage
Industry Group Preference: Internet
Portfolio Companies: 5mina, Aerin Medical, Betaworks, Bit.ly, BombFell, Dekko, ElaCarte, Evoz, Ideeli, Knack, Liquor.Com, Micello, Miso Music, Nutrivise, Outspark, Proven, Quincy, Supplyhog, Tie Society, Tripping, User Voices

Key Executives:
David Shen, President
Education: BS, Computer Engineering, Renssalaer Polytechnic Insitute; MS, Computer Science, Stanford University
Background: Vice President, User Experience & Design, Yahoo!; Product Designer, Frog Design

592 DAVIS, TUTTLE VENTURE PARTNERS LP
110 West 7th Street
Suite 1000
Tulsa, OK 74103-3703
Phone: 918-584-7272 Fax: 918-582-3404
web: www.davistuttle.com

Mission Statement: Davis, Tuttle Venture Partners is a private investment partnership dedicated to providing long-term development capital and operating expertise to emerging companies.

Fund Size: $100 million
Average Investment: $5 million - $20 million
Minimum Investment: $500,000
Investment Criteria: Seed, Early Stage, Acquisitions, Expansion, LBO, Mezzanine
Industry Group Preference: Corporate Services, Financial Services, Asset Management
Portfolio Companies: AmPro Mortgage Corporation, EnLink Geoenergy Services, Hydrade, Outlast, Nationwide Graphics, Web Tpa

Other Locations:
8 Greenway Plaza
Suite 1320
Houston, TX 77046
Phone: 713-993-0440 Fax: 713-621-2297

Key Executives:
Barry M Davis, Managing General Partner
Education: BBA, Finance, University of Oklahoma
Background: Alliance Business Investment Company; Davis Venture Partners; Board Chairman, NASBIC; Director, NVCA; Founder, Venture Capital Institute; Chairman, Oklahoma Innovation Institute
Philip A Tuttle, General Partner
Education: BS, Rice University; MBA, Northwestern University; CPA
Background: Allied Bancshares Capital; Davis Venture Partners; Founder, Houston Venture Capital Association
W Michael Partain, Partner
Education: BS, Business Management, BS, Accounting, Oklahoma Christian University; CPA
Background: Deloitte, Haskins and Sells; Price Waterhouse; Gerrity Oil and Gas Corp.; Capital Management Company

H Lee Frost, Chief Financial Officer
Education: BS, Accounting, Northwestern Oklahoma State University; CPA
Background: Arthur Young & Company; Williams Companies; Mabee Petroleum Corporation; Capital Management Company

593 DAWNTREADER VENTURES
P.O. Box 571
Southport, CT 06890
Phone: 203-659-0346 Fax: 203-842-4098

Mission Statement: An early-stage venture capital firm collaborating with entrepreneurs to build the next generation of software, internet and digital media companies.

Fund Size: $270 million
Founded: 1998
Investment Criteria: Early-Stage
Industry Group Preference: Software, Internet, Digital Media & Marketing, Infrastructure, Technology-Enabled Services
Portfolio Companies: Answers.com, Colloquis, DeepNines Technologies, FlashBase, Gizmo5, GoToMyPC, Greenplum, HNW, Intersan, iPrint.com, Liverperson, Moreover, MortgageIT, NetForensics, Peer39, Perfect Commerce, ProactiveNet, Tutor.com, Visible World, Xora

594 DAY ONE VENTURES
e-mail: pitch@dayoneventures.co
web: dayoneventures.co

Mission Statement: Technology investor and marketing and communications partner.

Founded: 2018
Average Investment: $100K - $1 million
Investment Criteria: Early-Stage, Startups
Industry Group Preference: AI, Virtual Reality & Augmented Reality, Quantum, Fintech, Education, Healthcare, Self-Driving Cars
Portfolio Companies: DigitalGenius, Piper Inc., Domuso, lvl5, Feastly, Home61, Monscierge, Truebill, Unity Influence

Key Executives:
Masha Drokova, Founding Partner
Background: Houzz, HotelTonight, Gett, Toptal
Directorships: Oceanic
Natalie Issa, Head of Communications
Background: D-Wave Systems, Drive.ai, EchoPixel, Woopra

595 DAYLIGHT PARTNERS
e-mail: info@daylightpartners.com
web: www.daylightpartners.com

Mission Statement: Daylight Partners is a unique venture capital firm which seeks out entrepreneurs who value our operational experience and functional expertise as much as our capital commitment to their venture. Eleven former executives with expertise in marketing, operations, manufacturing, finance, information technology, technological innovation, accounting, real estate, oil and gas, as well as overall corporate management, are driven to have Daylight Partners take an active role in helping mid-stage companies turbo-charge their growth initiatives. While having made investments nationally, Daylight Partners has a particular affinity for Texas-based companies.

Geographic Preference: Texas
Minimum Investment: $250,000 - $750,000
Investment Criteria: Mid-Stage
Industry Group Preference: Technology
Portfolio Companies: CS Identity, DadLabs, Digby, DIYSEO, Edioma, Energetic Solutions, Fantrail, FGA Media, KLD Energy, FISOC, Pawngo, PlanetHS, SmarteSoft, Uplogix, YMAX

Venture Capital & Private Equity Firms / Domestic Firms

Key Executives:
William J. Amelio, Partner
Education: BS, Chemical Engineering, Lehigh University; Honorary Doctorate in Engineering, Lehigh University; MS, Management, Stanford Graduate School of Business
Background: President and CEO, Lenovo Group Limited; Senior Vice President, Asia-Pacific and Japan, Dell Inc; Executive Vice President and COO, NCR Corp's Retail and Financial Group; President and CEO, Honeywell International Inc's Transportation and Power-Systems Division; Senior Management Positions, IBM
Gil Burciaga, Partner
Education: BS, Engineering, Texas A&M University
Background: Senior Vice President, DYNEGY; President, NGC Energy Resources; Senior Vice President, Natural Gas Supply/Trading; Co-Founder, Asset Risk Management
Scott C. Helbing, Partner
Background: President, Scott Helbing Inc; Senior Officer and Executive Vice President, AT&T; Dell; YUM; Reebok; Whittle Communications
Dick Hunter, Partner
Education: Mechanical Engineering, Georgia Institute of Technology
Background: Vice President, Dell Americas Operations, Dell; General Electric; Texas Instruments; Ericcson
Directorships: Massachusetts Institute of Technology China Leaders for Manufacturing Governing Board
Terry Klein, Partner
Background: Vice President of the Advanced Systems Group, Dell;
Rod MacDonald, Partner
Education: BA, University of Missouri, St. Louis
Background: Vice President of Finance, Dell Inc; CFO, iChat/Acuity; CFO, GaSonics; CFO, GRiD; Emerson Electric; Monsanto
Rocky Mountain, Partner
Education: University of Texas at Austin; State University of New York, Albany
Background: Vice President and General Manager of Dell's US Consumer Business; Vice President and General Manager of Dell's Americas Transactional Group; Principle, The Galt Group
Directorships: FGA Media, Frontier Renewal
Scott O'Hare, Partner
Education: BA, Political Science, Stanford University; MS, Geophysics, Stanford University; MBA, Tuck School at Dartmouth College
Background: Vice President and General Manager of Dell's Software and Peripheral Group; Management Consultant, McKinsey and Company; Exploration Geophysicist, Chevron
Ro Parra, Partner
Background: SVP and General Manager, Dell Americas; Vice President and General Manager, Federal Division, GRiD; Radio Shack
Susan Sheskey, Partner
Education: Miami University
Background: Senior Vice President and Chief Information Officer, Dell; Ameritech; Ohio Bell
Directorships: StoredIQ, Digby
Elias "Lee" Urbina, Partner
Education: BBA, Accounting, University of Texas at Austin
Background: Co-Founder and CFO, US Infrastructure

596 DBL PARTNERS
One Montgomery Street
Suite 2375
San Francisco, CA 94104

Phone: 415-568-2901 Fax: 415-956-2561
web: www.dblpartners.vc

Mission Statement: DBL Partners employs a 'Double Bottom Line' investment strategy, which entails investing in businesses that can generate superior returns and working with portfolio companies to help enact positive social, environmental and economic change. DBL focuses on companies in the clean technology, information technology, healthcare and sustainable products and services sectors.

Geographic Preference: Western United States
Fund Size: $400 million
Founded: 2015
Industry Group Preference: Clean Technology, Healthcare Services, Information Technology, Sustainability
Portfolio Companies: Advanced Microgrid Solutions, Akros, Bentek, BrightSource Energy, Ecologic Brands, EcoScraps, eLoan, eMeter, Farmers Business Network, Five Prime Therapeutics, If You Can, Imergy, InSpa, Kaiam, Kateeva, Labcyte, Livescribe, Maiyet, Mapbox, The Muse, NEXTracker, Off Grid Electric, Ogin Energy, OPX Biotechnologies, Pandora, Peninsula Pharmaceuticals, Planet Labs, PowerGenix, PowerLight Corporation, Primus Power, RallyPoint, The RealReal, Revolution Foods, Ruby Ribbon, Siva Power, SolarCity, Solexel, SpaceX, Tesla, UrbanSitter, View Dynamic Glass, Wholeshare, XDx, Yerdle

Key Executives:
Nancy Pfund, Managing Partner
e-mail: nancy@dblpartners.vc
Education: BA, MA, Anthropology, Stanford University; MBA, Yale School of Management
Background: Managing Director, JPMorgan; Intel Corporation; Stanford University; State of California; Sierra Club
Directorships: SolarCity, Brightsource Energy, Primus Power, Farmers Business Network
Ira Ehrenpreis, Managing Partner
e-mail: ira@dblpartners.com
Education: BA, University of California, Los Angeles; JD, Stanford Law School; MBA, Stanford Grad. School of Business
Background: President, Western Association of Venture Capitalists; Chairman, VCNetwork; Founder/Chairman, World Energy Innovation Forum
Cynthia Ringo, Senior Partner
e-mail: cynthia@dblpartners.vc
Education: BS, Legal Systems, Georgia State University; JD, Emory University School of Law
Background: Managing Director, VantagePoint Venture Partners; CEO, Coppercom; SVP, Corporate Development, Madge Networks; VP, Marketing, Red Brick Systems
Mark Perutz, Partner
e-mail: mark@dblpartners.vc
Education: BS, MS, Mechanical Engineering, MIT; MBA, Sloan School of Management, MIT
Background: Investment Professional, JPMorgan; Equity Research Analyst, Robertson Stephens
Directorships: Revolution Foods, RallyPoint
Lisa Hagerman, Director, Programs
e-mail: lisa@dblpartners.vc
Education: BA, Bucknell University; MA, Political Science, University of North Carolina at Chapel Hill
Background: Director, More for Mission, Harvard Kennedy School; VP, Economic Innovation International
Carol Wong, Chief Administrative Officer
e-mail: carol@dblpartners.vc
Education: BS, Business Administration, California Polytechnic State University
Background: Fund Manager, Bay Area Equity Fund, JPMorgan

597 DCM
2420 Sand Hill Road
Suite 200
Menlo Park, CA 94025

Phone: 650-233-1400 Fax: 650-854-9159
web: www.dcm.com

Mission Statement: To build high-impact, global technology companies that maximize the success of our entrepreneurs.

Founded: 1996

Investment Criteria: Seed Stage, Early Stage, Mid Stage

Industry Group Preference: Mobile, Consumer Internet, Software & Services

Portfolio Companies: 1Mainsteam, 2Wire, 51job, 51Talk, 58.com, 99Bill.com, @Motion, About.com, Adspace Networks, Adways, AHAlife, AllAbout, Amalfi Semiconductor, Analogix, Appia, Apsalar, Arrayent, Arroyo, Auto Radio, Baike.com, Basis, Bill.com, BitAuto, BitTorrent, Bridgelux, Caring.com, Celsys, Cenx, Clearwire, Cmune, Coffee Meets Bagel, Cognitive Networks, Coradiant, Cortina, Crowdtilt, Dangdang.com, Digital Media Professionals, DXY.com, eDreams, Embark, Enovix, Etouch, Exablox, Fivestars, FocusEdu.cn, Force10, Fortinet, Foundry Networks, FreedomPop, Freee, Green Box, HaoDF.com, Happy Elements, Hi Corp., HireRight, Huodongxing, IMS, Internap, IPivot, Jaspersoft, Jawbone, Japan Communications, Kabu.com, Kakao, Kanbox, Keep Holdings, KNTV, LASO, Learn Zillion, Life360, Loki Studios, Lumi, Mbaobao.com, Mobix, MediaShare, Miox, MobilePeak Systems, Mobileum, Neopath Networks, Neutral Tandem, Nok Nok Labs, nQuire Software, NxEdge, OneChip Photonics, Oriental Standard, Pandora.TV, Papaya, PayCycle, PayPerks, Pedestal Networks, PGP, Pharmaron, PlayFirst, Playstudios, Pokelabo, Pose, RayVio, RealScout, Recourse Technologies, Renren, Revel Systems, Rockyou, SandForce, SavingStar, Scigineer, Ivxinevotech, SigFig, Sigmatel, Sihe Wood, Slice, Sling Media, SMIC, SoFi, Starflyer, SwanLabs, Tab, TransLattice, Trion, Trusper, Tuniu.com, UCloud, UStream, VanceInfo, Vendavo, ViMicro, Vindicia, Vip.com, Wandoujia, Wanxue, WePow, Whistle, Xishiwang, Yesmywine.com, Yongche.com, Youxinpai, Zenverge

Other Locations:
No. 1 East Chang An Avenue
Tower W2, Unit 1, Level 10
Oriental Plaza
Beijing 100738
China
Phone: 011-8610-6511-1700 **Fax:** 011-8610-6511-1799

The ARGYLE Aoyama 15F
2-14-4 Kita-Aoyama, Minato-Ku
Tokyo 107-0061
Japan
Phone: 011-81-3-4520-2310 **Fax:** 011-81-3-4520-2311

Key Executives:
David Chao, Co-Founder & General Partner
e-mail: dchao@dcm.com
Education: B.A. Brown University; MBA Stanford University
Background: Co-Founder/CTO, Japan Communications; Management Consultant, McKinsey & Company; Apple Computer; Account Executive, Recruit
Directorships: 51job, 99Bill, All About Japan, Careem, Eaze, eDreams, Fortinet, Kabu.com, Musical.ly, Resource Technologies, Sling Media, SMIC, SoFi, StarFlyer, UCloud

Dixon Doll, Co-Founder & Partner Emeritus
Education: B.S. Electrical Engineering, Kansas State University; M.S./PhD Electrical Engineering, University of Michigan
Background: IBM Systems Research Institute
Directorships: @Motion, About.com, Clearwire, Coradiant, Force10 Networks, Foundry Networks, IMS, Internap, IPivot, Neutral Tandem, nQuire, Vimicro

Osuke Honda, General Partner
e-mail: ohonda@dcm.com
Education: BA, MA, Law, Hitotsubashi University; MBA, Keio University Grad. School of Business Administration; Wharton School, University of Pennsylvania
Background: Principal, Globis Capital Partners; Mitsubishi Corporation; Machinery Group
Directorships: atama plus, Blind, CADDi, Coffee Meets Bagel, Coubic, DMP, every.tv, Folio, Fond, Freee, Happy Elements, Kakao, LASO, Loki Studios, Pandora.TV, PECO, PicsArt, RealScout

Jason Krikorian, General Partner
e-mail: jkrikorian@dcm.com
Education: BA, Psychology, University of CA, Berkeley; JD, MBA, University of Virginia
Background: Co-Founder, Sling Media; Partner, id8 Group
Directorships: 1 Mainstream, ART19, Basis, Brigit, Caavo, Cognitive Networks, Emprove, FiveStars, FloSports, fubo TV, Galore, Jackpocket, Kespry, Life360, Matterport, Mendel Health

598 DDJ CAPITAL MANAGEMENT
130 Turner Street
Building 3
Suite 600
Waltham, MA 02453

Phone: 781-283-8500 **Fax:** 781-419-9180
e-mail: inforequest@ddjcap.com
web: www.ddjcap.com

Mission Statement: DDJ Capital Management is an investment management firm focused on generating outstanding investment returns for its client base.

Founded: 1996
Minimum Investment: $5 million
Investment Criteria: High Yield Bonds, Bank Loans, Contol Distressed, Non-Control Distressed, Special Situations

Key Executives:
David J Breazzano, President/Chief Investment Officer
Education: BA, Union College; MBA, Johnson School, Cornell University
Background: VP & Portfolio Manager, High Income Group, Fidelity Investments; VP & Portfolio Manager, T Rowe Price Associates; VP & High Yield Analyst, First Investors Asset Management
Directorships: Bush Industries, Key Energy Services, Wornick Holding Company

Benjamin Santonelli, Portfolio Manager
Education: BA, Amherst University

John W Sherman, Portfolio Manager
Education: BBA, University of Notre Dame
Background: Associate, Healthcare Group, Thoma Cressey Equity Partners; Analyst, Global Healthcare Group, Citigroup

Michael S Weissenburger, Head of Origination
Education: BA, University of Connecticut; MBA, Northeastern University
Background: Director, Direct Loan Origination, Wells Fargo Capital Finance; Sonus Networks; Cognos; Converge

599 DE NOVO VENTURES
PO Box 2160
Saratoga, CA 95070

web: www.denovovc.com

Mission Statement: To provide financial capital to assist entrepreneurs in building leading healthcare companies.

Geographic Preference: California
Fund Size: $650 million
Founded: 2000
Average Investment: $8 - $15 million
Minimum Investment: $8 million
Investment Criteria: All Stages
Industry Group Preference: Medical & Health Related, Life Sciences, Technology, Healthcare, Medical Devices
Portfolio Companies: Asante Solutions, Astute Medical, Avedro, Axogen, Benvenue, BioParadox, C2 Therapeutics, Hansen Medical, MyoScience, OncoMed Pharmaceuticals, ProMed, Pulmonx, Simpirica, Spinal Kinetics, Spinal

Venture Capital & Private Equity Firms / Domestic Firms

Modulation, Spiracur, Synergeyes, TearScience, TRIA Beauty, WaveTec Vision

Key Executives:

Frederick J Dotzler, Managing Director
e-mail: fred@denovovc.com
Education: BS, Iowa State University; University of Louvain, Belgium; MBA, University of Chicago
Background: Managing General Partner, Medicus Venture Partners; General Partner, Crosspoint Venture Partners; Searle; Merrimack; Millipore; IBM
Directorships: Bayhill Therapeutics, Microvention, Point Biomedical, Senorx, Talima

Richard M. Ferrari, Managing Director
e-mail: rich@denovovc.com
Education: BS, Ashland University; MBA, University of South Florida
Background: CEO, Cardiovascular Imaging Systems; CardioThoracic Systems; Co-Founder, CTS; Co-Founder, Medical Technology Group; EVP & GM, ADAC Laboratories; Founder, Saratoga Ventures
Directorships: Bacchus Vascular, Sinus Rhythm Technologies

Joe Mandato, Managing Director
e-mail: joe@denovovc.com
Education: BS, Nasson College; MA, Long Island University; Advanced Executive Program, Northwestern University; Doctorate, Management, Case Western Reserve University
Background: Chairman, Confer Software; President & CEO, Origin Medsystems; Co-Founder & CEO, Gynecare; Entrepreneur-in-Residence, Mayfield Fund; CEO, Ioptex Research; Captain, US Army Medical Service Corps
Directorships: Axogen, Endogastric Solutions, Facet Solutions, Hansen Medical, InSound Medical, M2 Medical, Tear Science, WaveTec Vision Systems

600 DECIENS CAPITAL

267 Dorland St.
San Francisco, CA 94105

e-mail: partners@deciens.com
web: www.deciens.com

Mission Statement: Deciens Capital is a venture capital firm that focuses on making angel and seed investments. We invest time and money in founders who are seeking to reduce inefficiencies in large industries with demonstrable disruptive information technology or to create disruptive offerings in de novo industries. We are particularly interested in online-to-offline offerings, marketplaces, financial technology, and civic and education tech.

Investment Criteria: Angel Investments, Seed Investments
Industry Group Preference: Online To Offline Offerings, Marketplaces, Fintech, Civic Technology, Education, Financial Services
Portfolio Companies: 7 Cups of Tea, EarnUp, Funding University, TenderTree, Fuze Network, Keychain Logistics, Simple Legal, Sponsorhub, Subledger, True Link Financial, Wevorce, Work Hands

Key Executives:

Daniel Kimerling, Co-Founder & General Partner
Education: BA, MA, University of Chicago
Background: Policy Analyst, Hudson Institute and Center for Strategic and International Studies; COO, Giftly

601 DEEP FORK CAPITAL

580 Howard Street
Suite 404
San Francisco, CA 94105

web: www.deepforkcapital.com

Mission Statement: Deep Fork Capital (DFC) is a venture capital firm focused on consumer innovations through online, software, mobile or other advances. Whether a company is pre-product, pre-revenue or growth-focused, we look for inspired, creative teams with great ideas.

Investment Criteria: All Stages
Industry Group Preference: Consumer Internet, Digital Media & Marketing, E-Commerce & Manufacturing
Portfolio Companies: Algorithmia, Amplify, Artivest, Battlefy, Bkstg, Bowery, Boxed Wholesale, Canopy, Dash, Dataminr, Delectable, Digital Artists, Ease Central, Educents, Genius, MaestroIQ, Oodle, Paracosm, Playdeck, Radpad, Rebelmail, Robin, Songza, Transfix, Trulia, Vsporto, Wevr, Zebra

Key Executives:

Tim Komada, Co-Founder/Managing Director
e-mail: tim@deepforkcapital.com
Education: BS, BA, The Citadel; JD, MPP, William & Marry; MBA, Wharton School
Background: Co-Founder, Vintrust
Directorships: Songza, Spling, Playdek, Cloudy, weplay, Digital Artists Entertainment

602 DEERFIELD MANAGEMENT

345 Park Avenue S
New York, NY 10010

Phone: 212-551-1600 Fax: 212-599-3075
web: deerfield.com

Mission Statement: Deerfield Management is an investment firm dedicated to advancing healthcare for the sake of curing disease, improving the quality of life and reducing the cost of healthcare.

Fund Size: $13 billion
Founded: 1994
Industry Group Preference: Healthcare
Other Locations:
K Wah Center 3906
Middle Huaihai Road 1010
Shanghai 200031
China
Phone: 86 21-6079-3988

Key Executives:

James Flynn, Managing Partner
Education: BS, University of Michigan; MS, Johns Hopkins University
Background: Analyst, Furman Selz; Vice President of Corporate Development, Alpharma Inc.; Senior Analyst, Kidder, Peabody & Co.

603 DEFTA PARTNERS

111 Pine Street
Suite 1410
San Francisco, CA 94111

Phone: 415-433-2262
e-mail: information@deftapartners.com
web: www.deftapartners.com

Mission Statement: DEFTA Partners pursues opportunities in core technology sectors, with a focus on innovative healthcare and information technology businesses. A global venture capital firm, DEFTA Partners has invested in companies based in the United States, United Kingdom, Bangladesh, Japan and Israel.

Geographic Preference: Worldwide
Fund Size: $50 million
Founded: 1985
Average Investment: $500,000 - $3 million
Investment Criteria: Seed, Early Stage, Expansion
Industry Group Preference: Communications, Electronic Components, Information Technology, Medical, Medical Devices, Optical Technology, Software, Technology, Healthcare Information Technology
Portfolio Companies: 1World Online, Allocade, BracNet, Cloudfiling, Fortinet, Oplus, Oren Semiconductor, Orig3n, Tmsuk

Key Executives:
George Hara, Group Chairman/CEO
Education: LLB, Keio University; MS, Stanford University
Background: Partner, Accel Partners
Directorships: Pixera, Actuate Co. Ltd, Chemtrix
Masa Isono, Principal
Education: BA, Waseda University; MA, Economics, MBA, Boston University
Background: Director, Joint Venture Company, Hong Kong; The Security Analysts Association of Japan

604 DELL VENTURES

e-mail: DTCapital@dell.com
web: www.delltechnologies.com

Mission Statement: Dell Technologies Capital is the venture capital arm of Dell Inc. The fund invests in early-stage companies with a focus in areas such as software storage, security, machine learning, big data and analytics, cloud, and other internet ventures.

Founded: 2012
Average Investment: $2 - $5 million
Investment Criteria: Early-Stage
Industry Group Preference: Data Storage, Networking, Cloud Computing, Mobility, Software, Machine Learning, Security, Data Analytics
Portfolio Companies: Agari, Appdome, Aria, Barefoot Networks, Big Switch Networks, Binaris, Bluedata, Cloud66, CloudEndure, CNEXLabs, Cylance, Datometry, DocuSign, Druva, Edico Genome, Elatifile, FogHorn, Graphcore, GuardiCore, Iguazio, Jask, JFrog, Lastline, Minio, Mirantis, Moogsoft, Nantero, Nasuni, Netskope, Nexenta, OpsMx, Otonomo, Packet, Primary Data, Quali, Redislabs, Rich Relevance, Risk Lens, Risk Recon, Striim, Twistlock, ZingBox, Zscaler

Key Executives:
Scott Darling, President
Education: BS, Economics/Computer Science, University of California, Santa Cruz; MBA, Stanford Grad. School of Business
Background: President, EMC Corporate Developement and Ventures; General Partner, Frazier Technology Ventures; VP/Managing Director, Intel Capital; Product Marketing, Apple Computer
Raman Khanna, Managing Director
Education: Electrical/Electronics Engineering, Delhi College of Engineering; MS, Computer Science, Virginia Tech; MBA, Golden Gate University
Background: CIO, Stanford University IT; Co-Founder, Diamondhead Ventures; Managing Director, ONSET Ventures
Daniel Docter, Managing Director
Education: BS, Electrical Engineering, University of Minnesota; PhD, University of Bradford
Background: Director, Intel Capital; Advisor, Merrill Lynch; AT&T Bell Labs; Hughes Research Labs

605 DELPHI VENTURES

Phone: 650-854-9650
web: www.delphiventures.com

Mission Statement: Focused in early-stage healthcare investing, including medical devices and diagnostics, biotechnology, and healthcare services companies.

Fund Size: $1.1 billion
Founded: 1988
Average Investment: $500,000 - $12 million
Investment Criteria: Seed, Start-Up, Early Stage, First-Stage, Second-Stage
Industry Group Preference: Biotechnology, Medical & Health Related, Medical Devices, Healthcare Services
Portfolio Companies: Aegea Medical, Alder Biopharmaceuticals, Calithera Biosciences, Cardeas Pharma, EBR Systems Inc., Ivantis, Karyopharm Therapeutics, Labcyte Inc., Onco Med Pharmaceuticals, Relypsa Inc., Senseonics, Sequent Medical, SynergEyes, Tandem Diabetes Care, Trivascular

Key Executives:
James J. Bochnowski, Partner Emeritis
Education: MBA, Harvard University; BS Massachusetts Institue of Technology
Background: President, Shugart Associates; General Partner, Donaldson Lufkin & Jenrette's; Sprout Capital Group
David Douglass, Partner Emeritis
Education: MBA, MA, Stanford University; BA Amherst College
Background: Matrix Partners; Paladin Software Corporation; Collagen Corporation; McKinsey & Company
Matthew T. Potter, Parner/CFO
Education: BS, California Polytechnic State University
Background: Controller, Bluecurve Inc.; Public Accountant, Arthur Andersen
Deepa Pakianathan, PhD, Managing Partner
Education: BS, MS, University of Bombay; MS, PhD, Wake Forest University
Background: VP, Healthcare Group, JPMorgan; Biotechnology Research Analyst, Genesis Merchant Group
Doug Roeder, Managing Partner
Education: AB, Dartmouth College
Background: Associate, Healthcare Investments Group, Alex.Brown; Consultant, Putnam Associates

606 DENALI VENTURE PARTNERS

web: www.denalivp.com

Mission Statement: A partnership that invests capability and capital in entrepreneurial ventures, in order to build sustainable, high performance environments where people love what they do.

Founded: 1999
Investment Criteria: Early-Stage
Industry Group Preference: Cloud Computing, Data Infrastructure, Analytics, Enterprise Services, Consumer Products, Retail, Consumer & Leisure
Portfolio Companies: Aconex, FanPlayr, Heffron Consulting, Redbubble

Key Executives:
Richard Cawsey, Founder/Executive Chairman
Education: Australian National University
Background: St. George Bank; NatWest Financial Products; ANZ Banking Group; Managing Director, Morgan Stanley

607 DESCO CAPITAL
7795 Walton Parkway
Suite 175
New Albany, OH 43054

e-mail: info@descocapital.com
web: www.descocapital.com

Mission Statement: The investment arm of Desco Corporation, Desco Capital is a privately held company that focuses on working closely with management in the developing growth of businesses. Desco offers capital and management expertise with the objective of creating long-term value for its portfolio companies.

Fund Size: $75 million
Founded: 1992
Average Investment: $1 - $5 million
Minimum Investment: $500,000
Investment Criteria: Growth Businesses, Underperforming Businesses, Controlling or Minority Equity Positions
Industry Group Preference: Industrial Products, Manufacturing, Distribution, Building Materials & Services,

Venture Capital & Private Equity Firms / Domestic Firms

Energy Products, Rubber, Plastics, Process Controls, Consumer Products
Portfolio Companies: ARPAC, Blackeagle Energy Services, Crown Group, Marsh Bellofram Corporation, MDT Software, Medical Indicators, Mueller Electric Company, Republic Doors & Frames, Tek-Air Systems

Key Executives:
   Arnold B Siemer, Chief Executive Officer
   Education: BA, Banking & Finance, John Carroll University; Foreign Trade, American Graduate School; JD, Cleveland Marshall College of Law
   Background: Sprayon Products Inc.; Air-O-Matic Power Steering
   Paul D Kestler, Operating Director
   972-869-9099
   e-mail: pkestler@descocapital.com
   Education: BS, Marketing, Arizona State University
   Background: Senior Manager, Marsh Instrument-Juarez; Thermo-Couple Products; Tek-Air; Medical Indicators
   Roger D Bailey, Director/Chief Financial Officer
   614-888-8855 x101
   e-mail: rbailey@descocapital.com
   Education: BBA, Business Management, Texas Christian University; MBA, Marketing & Finance, Indiana University; MS, Chemical Engineering, Carnegie Mellon University Graduate School
   Background: PPG Industries; Treasurer & Chief Financial Officer, Asten Group

608 DETROIT VENTURE PARTNERS
Detroit, MI

web: www.detroitventurepartners.com

Mission Statement: To help rebuild the Detroit area by assisting entrepreneurs in growing meaningful businesses in the digital media, marketing technology, social media, e-commerce, software, and sports and entertainment sectors.

Geographic Preference: Detroit, Michigan
Fund Size: $28 million
Founded: 2010
Investment Criteria: Seed-Stage, Early-Stage
Industry Group Preference: E-Commerce & Manufacturing, Digital Media & Marketing, Social Media, Internet, Software, Sports, Entertainment, Marketing Technology
Portfolio Companies: 100 Thieves, Airspace Link, Are You A Human, Autobooks, Benzinga, Bloomscape, Branch, Breadless, Cargo, Dering Hall, detroit Labs, Digital Onboarding, Dwolla, Ethos, FarmLogs, Finicity, floyd, Genius, Grand Circus, Guardhat, Homie, Instore, IRule, Crossover, LevelEleven, MagicBus, Marxent, May Mobility, Opsmatic, PriorAuthNow, Quickly, Reach Influence, Rockbot, Sift, Skillo, Stylecaster, StockX, Sweet, Velos, Vroom, Waymark WSC Sports

Key Executives:
   Dan Gilbert, Founding Partner
   Background: Founder & Chairman, Quicken Loans
   Jake Cohen, Partner
   Education: BA, MBA, JD, University of Michigan
   Background: Co-Founder, eatBlue.com; Ugrub.com; Ubars.com
   Gabe Karp, Operating Partner
   Education: University of Michigan; Wayne State University
   Background: Executive Team, ePrize
   Jared Stasik, Partner
   Education: BBA, Ross School of Business, University of Michigan; MBA, University of California, Berkeley
   Background: Consultant, ZS Associates

609 DFJ GOTHAM VENTURES
44 South Broadway
Suite 100
White Plains, NY 10601

Phone: 212-279-3980
web: www.gothamvc.com

Mission Statement: DFJ Gotham is a generalist information technology investor, meaning that the firm will invest in all sub-sectors of the IT space. These sub-sectors include, but are not limited to: digital media, e-commerce, financial technology, mobile and network infrastructure.

Geographic Preference: East Coast
Average Investment: $100,000 - $500,000
Investment Criteria: Seed Stage, Series A Round
Industry Group Preference: Information Technology, Digital Media & Marketing, E-Commerce & Manufacturing, Fintech, Mobile, Infrastructure
Portfolio Companies: ADstruc, Altruik, DailyWorth, Drop.io, Gen.Video, Ingenio, JIBE, Lendkey, Local Response, Magnolia Broadband, Massive, Medialets, Mimeo.com, Nano Opto, Pantero, Panvideo, Philo, Pickie, Pivot, Pulse Point, Q Link Technologies, Quantiva, Sailthru, Seamless Receipts, Searchandise Commerce, Single Platform, Stella Service, Techstar, Totsy, Verterra, Vivo Tech, Widetronix, XO Soft, Yipit

Key Executives:
   Ross Goldstein, Co-Founder & Managing Director
   Education: BS, Applied Mathematics-Economics, Brown University; MBA, Stanford University Graduate School of Business
   Background: EVP & CFO, Interactive Imaginzations; Morgan Stanley
   Directorships: Mimeo.com, Lumeta, ContextWeb, Searchandise Commerce, Drop.io, Medialets, Altruik
   Daniel Schultz, Co-Founder & Managing Director
   Education: BA, Economics, Columbia University
   Background: Senior Banker, Lehman Brothers
   Directorships: Pivot Solutions, Magnolia Broadband

610 DFJ VENTURE CAPITAL
2882 Sand Hill Road
Suite 150
Menlo Park, CA 94025

Phone: 650-233-9000
e-mail: plans@dfj.com
web: www.dfj.com

Mission Statement: To support entrepreneurs who want to change the world. We focus on companies specializing in consumer and enterprise IT, commerce, cloud, enterprise, big data, and bold new technologies.

Investment Criteria: Early Stage, Growth Stage
Industry Group Preference: Technology, Software
Portfolio Companies: AngelList, Athena Health, Azuqua, Baidu, Balena, BetterUp, Box, BrightSource, Chartbeat, Chef Code Can, CircleCI, Diamanti, Doximity, DWave, Edeniq, Elation Health, Enernoc, Epocrates, FeedBurner, Flurry, Forward Networks, Front, Genomatica, Good Technology, Helix, Highlight, Hotmail, Human Longevity Inc., Insight Squared, Intematix, Kaiima, iYogi, Launch Darkly, Lendkey, Livongo, Location Labs, Loftium, Lumity, Memphis Meats, Mindshow, Mobile 365, Mythic, Nervana, Newsle, Ooda Health, Path, Periscope Data, Ping Identity, Planet Labs, Polaris Wireless, Pro.com, Raydiance, Redfin, Remity, Retrofit, Rich Relevance, Seamicro, Selligy, ShareThis, Shift, Skype, SolarCity, SpaceX, Spiral Genetrics, SugarCRM, SugarSync, Swell, Synthetic Genomics, Talk Desk, Tango, Tesla Motors, Tremor Video, Twilio, Verge Genomics, Vineti, Wellframe, Xtime, Yammer, Yellowbrick, Yodle, Z2Live, Zillabyte, Zoox, Zymergen

Key Executives:
   John Fisher, Managing Director
   Education: Harvard College; Harvard Business School

Venture Capital & Private Equity Firms / Domestic Firms

Background: ABS Ventures; Alex, Brown & Sons; Bank of America
Directorships: Katerra, Pulsepoint, Renovate America
Timothy Draper, Managing Director
Education: BS Electrical Engineering, Stanford University; MBA Harvard Business School
Josh Stein, Partner
Education: BA Dartmouth College; MBA Stanford University
Background: Vice President, Telephia; Co-Founder/Director/Chief Strategy Officer, ViaFone; Product Management, Microsoft/NetObjects
Directorships: Box, Chartbeat, LaunchDarkly, LendKey, Loftium, Lumity, Periscope, Talkdesk
Randy Glein, Partner - DJF Growth
Education: BSEE University of Florida; MSEE University of Southern California; MBA Anderson School of Management
Background: CFO, FeedBurner; DIRECTV; Screenz; Tribune Ventures; GM Hughes Electronics; Martin Marietta

---

611 DFW CAPITAL PARTNERS
300 Frank W. Burr Boulevard
Glenpointe Centre East
7th Floor
Teaneck, NJ 07666

Phone: 201-836-6000 Fax: 201-836-5666
web: www.dfwcapital.com

Mission Statement: DFW Capital Partners is a private equity investment firm that focuses on lower middle-market companies. DFW works with entrepreneurs and management teams and provides them with the support necessary for significant growth.
Geographic Preference: United States
Fund Size: $162 million
Founded: 1983
Average Investment: $5 - $20 million
Minimum Investment: $5 million
Investment Criteria: High-Growth, Lower Middle-Market Companies
Industry Group Preference: Business to Business, Industrial Services, Healthcare Services
Portfolio Companies: Children's Dental Health Associates, Envocore, Insight2Profit, Lotus Clinical Research, Regulatory and Quality Solutions, ReSource Pro, Restoration + Recovery, Saol Therapeutics, Sebela Pharmaceuticals, Sev1Tech, Theraplay, VertexOne

Other Locations:
4445 Willard Avenue
11th Floor
Chevy Chase, MD
Phone: 202-827-0722 Fax: 202-204-0724

Key Executives:
Donald F. DeMuth, Founder
Education: BA, BSEE, Rutgers University; MBA, Harvard University
Background: Systems Engineer, IBM; Investment Banker, Kidder, Peabody & Co.
Directorships: Tech Pharmacy Services, Garden State Dental, Copernicus Group, SoftWriters, Meta, Nurses 24/7
Keith W. Pennell, Managing Partner
Education: BA, Economics & Art History, Middlebury College
Background: Dean Witter; First Atlantic
Directorships: Versatech, Venio, Copernicus Group, SoftWriters
Brett L. Prager, Partner
Education: BA, Wharton School; BAS, Moore School of Engineering, University of Pennsylvania; MBA, Columbia Business School
Background: Founder & Partner, Theo Capital Partners; JP Morgan
Directorships: Venio, Garden State Dental
Douglas H. Gilbert, Partner
Education: BA, Political Economy, Williams College; MBA, Harvard University
Background: Managing Director, MCG Capital Corporation; Partner, Winston Partners; Thayer Capital Partners
Brian C. Tilley, Partner
Education: BS, Finance, Ohio University; MBA, Kellogg School of Management, Northwestern University
Background: Founder & Managing Member, Wenzi Capital Partners; United HealthGroup
Directorships: Garden State Dental

---

612 DIAMOND STATE VENTURES LP
200 River Market Avenue
Suite 400
Little Rock, AR 72201

Phone: 501-374-9247 Fax: 501-374-9425
Toll-Free: 800-216-7234
web: new.diamondstateventures.com

Mission Statement: Diamond State Ventures invests in growing companies and established industry leaders. The firm seeks to work with experienced management teams across a range of industry segments.
Geographic Preference: South, Southeast, Midwest
Fund Size: $100 million
Founded: 1999
Average Investment: $3 - $7 million
Investment Criteria: Growth Expansion, Buyouts, Acquisitions, Recapitalizations, Lower Middle-Market, Established Companies
Industry Group Preference: Manufacturing, Business Products & Services, Consumer Products, Consumer Services, Healthcare Services
Portfolio Companies: Evergreen Holdings, Integrated Aerospace Manufacturing, Jahabow, Mob Scene, NewKota Energy Group, Rio Ranch Markets, Sure Shot Drilling, Transfer Tool Products, Waples Manufacturing, Whitworth Tool

Key Executives:
Joe T. Hays, Co-Founder/Managing Director
e-mail: jhays@dsvlp.com
Education: University of Arkansas; MBA, Wharton School, University of Pennsylvania
Background: President, Southern Regional Association of Small Business Investment Companies
Directorships: UAMS Biotechnology Center
Larry B. Carter, Managing Director
e-mail: lcarter@dsvlp.com
Education: BS, Business Administration, University of Arkansas
Background: Investment Banking, PaineWebber; Equity Syndications, First Chicago Corp.; Deal Originations, Bank of America
Tyler A. Bozynski, Vice President
e-mail: tbozynski@dsvlp.com
Education: BS, Business Administration, University of Arkansas
Background: Associate, Diamond State Ventures; Stephens Inc.

---

613 DIAMOND TECHVENTURES
350 Oakmead Pkwy
Suite 200
Sunnyvale, CA 94085

web: www.diamondtechventures.com

Mission Statement: Diamond TechVentures is a venture capital firm focused on investing in technology companies based in China.

Geographic Preference: China

Venture Capital & Private Equity Firms / Domestic Firms

Investment Criteria: Start-Ups, Early-Stage
Industry Group Preference: Technology, Wireless
Portfolio Companies: Broadsoft, ClearAccess IP, IWatt, LGC Wireless, Packet Island, percolata, STEPLabs

Key Executives:
Henry Wong, Managing Partner
Education: BSc, Finance, University of Utah; MBA, Telecom Management, Golden Gate University
Background: Venture Partner, Crystal Ventures; Founder, Chairman & CEO, SS8 Networks; President, CNet Technology
Dr. Robert P Lee, Senior Venture Partner
Education: BA, University of California Berkeley; MS/PhD, University of California Los Angeles
Background: CEO, Accela; Achievo; Insignia; Inxight Software; EVP, Symantec
Directorships: chairman, AAMA (Asia America Multi-Technology Association)

614 DIAMONDHEAD VENTURES
1350 Bayshore Highway
Suite 920
Bulringame, CA 94010

Phone: 650-687-7550 Fax: 650-529-0777
web: www.dhven.com

Mission Statement: Invests in early stage technology companies. Affiliated with Diamondhead Ecosystem, a pool of venture capital advisors.
Geographic Preference: California, Bay Area
Fund Size: $140 million
Founded: 2000
Average Investment: $1 - $5 million, total of $8 - $10 million
Investment Criteria: Primarily Seed, Start-Up, Early Stage, First Stage, Limited Second Stage
Industry Group Preference: Internet Technology, Business to Business, IT Infrastructure
Portfolio Companies: Cavium Networks, Danger, Entercept Security Technologies, Orative, Passmark Security, Reactivity, Serus, Truviso, UPEK

Key Executives:
David Lane, Founding Managing Director
Education: MBA, Harvard University; BSEE, University of Southern California
Background: Hughes Aircraft; IBM; Harvard Management Company

615 DIFFERENTIAL VENTURES
40 Exchange Place
Suite 1110
New York, NY 10005

Phone: 212-300-2879
e-mail: info@differential.vc
web: www.differential.vc

Mission Statement: Differential Ventures focuses on early stage capital, looking to invest in companies that have advantages in data or machine intelligence. They especially look for Enterprise Tech, FinTech and Cybersecurity.
Investment Criteria: Pre-Seed or Seed stage ($250,000-$1 million); B2B or a Unique advantage in Data/Machine Intelligence

Key Executives:
David Magerman, Co-Founder/Managing Partner
Education: BA, BS, University of Pennsylvania; PhD, Stanford University
Background: Renaissance Technologies
Nick Adams, Co-Founder/Managing Partner
Education: BA, Brandeis University; MBA, Northeastern University
Background: Venture Partner, Supernode; Senior Sales Manager, Opower

Mitchell Kleinhandler, Managing Partner
Background: Venture Partner, Scout Ventures; Entrepreneur

Key Executives:
Yuri Milner, CEO/Founding Partner
Education: Moscow State University; MBA, Wharton School of Business
Background: Lebedex Physical Institute

617 DIMELING SCHREIBER & PARK
1629 Locust Street
Philadelphia, PA 19103

Phone: 215-546-8585 Fax: 215-546-5398
web: www.dsppartners.com

Mission Statement: An investment partnership that offers capital and strategic support to middle market companies. The firm pursues opportunities with superior management teams and specializes in leveraged acquisitions, management buyouts and assisting in generational ownership changes.
Fund Size: $1 billion
Founded: 1982
Average Investment: $5 - $30 million
Minimum Investment: $5 million
Investment Criteria: Middle Market, Acquisitions, Recapitalizations, LBO
Industry Group Preference: Manufacturing, Services
Portfolio Companies: Boston Ship Repair, Martin Color-Fi, Orchids Paper Products Company, Piper Aircraft, Rocky Mountain Helicopters, Wiser Oil Company

Key Executives:
Richard R Schreiber, Principal
e-mail: rschreiber@dsppartners.com
Education: BS, Wharton School, University of Pennsylvania
Background: Strouse, Greenberg & Company; Coldwell Banker
Steven G Park, Principal
e-mail: spark@dsppartners.com
Education: BS, Pennsylvania State University
Background: VP, Strouse, Greenberg & Company; Senior VP, Reading Company
Peter D. Schreiber, Principal
e-mail: pschreiber@dsppartners.com
Education: BS, Finance, Pennsylvania State University
Background: Corporate Banking Representative, Fidelity Bank

618 DISRUPTOR CAPITAL
315A Cameron St.
Alexandria, VA 22314

Phone: 703-659-1100
e-mail: info@disruptor.com

Mission Statement: Disruptor Capital is a Virginia-based seed and angel capital investment company focused on funding and growing disruptive technologies, ideas and entrepreneurs.
Investment Criteria: Seed, Angel Capital
Industry Group Preference: Technology
Portfolio Companies: Data Analytics Media, Echelon Insights, IJReview, Imge, Ledbury, Liftbump, Media Group of America, Pascal Metrics, Potomac Research Group

Key Executives:
Pete Snyder, CEO
Background: Founder & CEO, New Media Strategies; President of Emerging Markets Group, Meredith Xcelerated Marketing, Meredith Corporation

619 DIVERGENT VENTURES
1652 20th Avenue
Seattle, WA 98122

e-mail: ober@divergent.com
web: www.divergentvc.com

Venture Capital & Private Equity Firms / Domestic Firms

Mission Statement: An early-stage venture capital investment firm headquartered in Seattle Washington. The Managing Directors are Kevin Ober and Rob Shurtleff, both highly experienced and successful early-stage investors. The firm invests in early-stage companies, with an emphasis on big data, mobile data, virtualization/cloud and storage.

Geographic Preference: Northwest, West Coast United States
Investment Criteria: First Round
Industry Group Preference: Data Storage, Cloud Computing
Portfolio Companies: SpaceCurve, TempoDB, Shippable, Proximal Data, Piston Enterprise OpenStack, Iron.MQ
Key Executives:
   Kevin Ober, Managing Director
   e-mail: ober@divergent.com
   Education: BS, Business Administration, St. John's University; MBA, Santa Clara University
   Background: Vulcan Ventures, Conner Peripherals
   Rob Shurtleff, Managing Director
   e-mail: shurtleff@divergent.com
   Education: BA, Computer Science, University of California, Berkeley
   Background: Founder, Sightline Partners
   Directorships: Flashsoft, Piston, Asta Networks
   Todd Warren, Managing Partner
   e-mail: warren@divergent.com
   Education: BA, Northwestern University
   Background: Corporate Vice President, Microsoft; Adjunct Professor, Northwestern University

620 DN PARTNERS LLC
180 N LaSalle Street
Suite 3001
Chicago, IL 60601

Phone: 312-332-7960
web: www.dnpartnersllc.com

Mission Statement: DN Partners is a Chicago-based private equity firm that invests in lower middle-market companies. The firm generally focuses on businesses based in the Midwestern region of the United States and specializes in recapitalizations, management buyouts, buy and build strategies, and corporate spin-offs.

Geographic Preference: Midwest United States
Founded: 1995
Average Investment: $3 - $15 million
Investment Criteria: Lower Middle Market, Strong Market Position, Growth Potential, High Revenues $20 to $100 Million
Industry Group Preference: Distribution, Manufacturing, Services
Portfolio Companies: Central Can Company, Country Pure Foods, Crysteel Manufacturing, FCL Graphics, M&M Pump & Supply, Primary Packaging, PrimeCo Wireless Communications
Key Executives:
   John E Dancewicz, Managing Partner/Founder
   Education: BA, Economics, Yale University; MBA, Finance, Harvard Business School
   Background: Senior Managing Director, Bear Stearns; Manager, Midwest Corporate Finance; US Investment Banking Department, Continental Illinois National Bank
   Directorships: Central Can Company, Country Pure Foods, FCL Graphics
   Maurey J Bell, Managing Partner
   Education: BA, Economics, Northwestern University
   Background: M&A Group, EVEREN Securities; Managing Director, Midwest Corporate Finance Department, Bear, Stearns & Co.
   Directorships: FCL Graphics
   Christopher J Blum, Chief Financial Officer
   Education: BBA, Finance & Accounting, University of Notre Dame
   Background: CFO & Director of Corporate Development, Clayton Holdings; Principal, Diamond Management and Technology Consultants; CFO, MindBuilder Group
   Directorships: M&M Pump & Supply, Chinada Holdings

621 DOCOMO INNOVATIONS
3301 Hillview Avenue
Palo Alto, CA 94304

web: www.docomoinnovations.com

Mission Statement: A corporate venture arm of NTT DOCOMO of Japan. DOCOMO invests in companies introducing leading-edge mobile services based on innovative technologies.

Fund Size: $100 million
Founded: 2005
Industry Group Preference: Telecommunications, Communications, Wireless Technologies
Portfolio Companies: Elemtnal, Coinbase, Netpulse, Centrify, Nanosys, Beceem, GCT, Kyte, GestureTek, Daz3D, WiSpry, Verient, InvenSense, Arteris, Forté Media, Quantance, Tensilica, Evernote, Swyper, Tune Wiki, SkyCross, Couchbase, Cooliris, Fab, Anfacto, Cyphort
Key Executives:
   Neil Sadraranganey, Managing Director
   Education: BEng, University of Waterloo; MBA, Stanford University
   Background: Former VP of Business Development; General Partner, Bay Partners; Investor

622 DOMAIN ASSOCIATES LLC
202 Carnegie Center
Suite 104
Princeton, NJ 08540

Phone: 609-683-5656 Fax: 609-683-9789
web: www.domainvc.com

Mission Statement: Manages venture capital and provides early-stage financing and support to technology-based companies in the life sciences industry, with primary focus on the pharmaceuticals, diagnostics and medical devices sectors. Domain Associates offers experience in technology asssessment, operations, finance, and strategic planning, and pursues opportunities with high growth potential businesses with superior management teams and outstanding breakthrough technologies.

Fund Size: $500 million
Founded: 1985
Average Investment: $1 - $20 million
Minimum Investment: $500,000 (except seed financing)
Investment Criteria: Seed, First-Stage, Second-Stage
Industry Group Preference: Biopharmaceuticals, Life Sciences, Medical Devices, Instrumentation, Diagnostics, Advanced Materials, Healthcare Information Technology, Information Technology, Pharmaceuticals
Portfolio Companies: Achaogen, Achillion Pharmaceuticals, Adynxx, Afferent Pharmaceuticals, Aldeyra Therapeutics, Alimera Sciences, Applied Proteomics, Ascenta Therapeutics, Astute Medical, Atara Biotherapeutics, aTyr Pharma, Benvenue Medical, BioNano Genomics, Cantex Pharmaceuticals, Carticept Medical, Cartiva, Celator Pharmaceuticals, Celtaxsys, Clovis Oncology, CoDa Therapeutics, Colorescience, CoLucid Pharmaceuticals, Cotera, Dicerna Pharmaceuticals, Domain Elite Holdings, DRI Holdings Limited, Eddingpharm International Holdings Limited, Epic Sciences, Esperion Therapeutics, Evoke Pharma, Five Prime Therapeutics, Fractyl Laboratories, GI Dynamics, Glaukos Corporation, IntegenX, Kona Medical, Marinus Pharmaceuticals, Medico (Hong Kong) Limited, Milestone Pharmaceuticals, Miramar Labs, Neothetics, NeuroPace, Novadigm Therapeutics, Obalon Therapeutics, Ocera Therapeutics, Oraya Therapeutics, Orexigen Therapeutics, Otonomy, REVA Medical, ReVision Optics, RightCare Solutions, ROX Medical, Sebacia, Sequent

Venture Capital & Private Equity Firms / Domestic Firms

Medical, Sera Prognostics, Smart Medical Systems, Syndax Pharmaceuticals, Tandem Diabetes Care, Tragara Pharmaceuticals, VentiRx, Veracyte, Xagenic, Zyga Technology

Other Locations:
12481 High Bluff Drive
Suite 150
San Diego, CA 92130
Phone: 858-480-2400 Fax: 858-480-2401

Key Executives:
Jim Blair, PhD, Partner
Education: BSE, Princeton University; MSE, PhD, Electrical Engineering, University of Pennsylvania
Background: Managing Director, Rothschild Inc.; FS Smithers & Co.; White, Weld & Co.; Engineering Manager, RCA Corporation
Directorships: Prostate Cancer Foundation, Sanford-Burnham Medical Research Institute
Brian Dovey, Partner
Education: BA, Mathematics, Colgate University; MBA, Harvard Business School
Background: President, Rorer Group; President, Survival Technology; Howmedica; Howmet Corporation; New York Telephone
Directorships: Orexigen Therapeutics, REVA Medical, Center for Venture Education, La Jolla Playhouse
Brian K. Halak, PhD, Partner
Education: BSE, Bioengineering, University of Pennsylvania; PhD, Immunology, Thomas Jefferson University
Background: Associate, Advanced Technology Ventures; Consultant, Wilkerson Group
Directorships: Alimera Sciences, BioNano Genomics, Carticept Medical, Dicerna Pharmaceuticals, Kona Medical, Oraya Therapeutics
Kim Kamdar, PhD, Partner
Education: BA, Northwestern University; PhD, Biochemistry & Genetics, Emory University
Background: Kauffman Fellow, MPM Capital; Research Director, Novartis; Founder, Aryzun Pharmaceuticals
Directorships: Epic Sciences, Neothetics, Obalon Therapeutics, ROX Medical, Sera Prognostics, Syndax Pharmaceuticals, Tragara Pharmaceuticals, CONNECT Foundation, Hastings Center
Dennis Podlesak, Advisory Partner
Education: BA, Western Illinois University; MBA, Pepperdine University; Wharton School
Background: Senior VP & Head, North American Business Unit, Novartis AG; VP & Head, CEC Division, Allergan; SmithKline Beecham
Directorships: Adynxx, Syndax Pharmaceuticals, Tobira Therapeutics, RightCare Solutions, DRI Holdings
Kathleen Schoemaker, Partner/Chief Financial Officer
Education: BA, Wheaton College; MA, Middlebury College; MBA, New York University
Background: Auditor & Tax Specialist, KPMG
Jesse Treu, PhD, Partner Emeritus
Education: BS, Rensselaer Polytechnic Institute; MA, PhD, Princeton University
Background: VP, Wilkerson Group; CW Ventures; President & CEO, Microsonics; Technicon Instruments Corporation
Directorships: Afferent Pharmaceuticals, Aldeyra Pharmaceuticals, CoLucid Pharmaceuticals, RightCare Solutions, Sebacia, Tandem Diabetes Care, Veracyte, Xagenic
Nicole Vitullo, Partner
Education: BA, Mathematics, MBA, Finance, University of Rochester
Background: Senior VP, Rothschild Asset Management; Director, Corporate Communications & Investor Relations, Cephalon; Eastman Kodak
Directorships: Achillion Pharmaceuticals, Celator Pharmaceuticals, Celtaxsys, Esperion Therapeutics, Marinus Pharmaceuticals, VentiRx Pharmaceuticals

Eckard Weber, MD, Advisory Partner
Education: BS, Kolping College, Germany; MD, University of Ulm Medical School, Germany; Stanford University Medical School
Background: Professor of Pharmacology, University of California, Irvine
Directorships: Ocera Therapeutics, Orexigen Therapeutics, Adynxx, Tobira Therapeutics

623 DORM ROOM FUND

e-mail: info@dormroomfund.com
web: www.dormroomfund.com

Mission Statement: A student-run venture firm that invests in student-run companies.

Average Investment: $15,000 - $20,000
Portfolio Companies: 101, 3DFortify, A&B American Style, Acculis, Acention Digital, AdsNative, Aegis AI, Airbud, Airmada, Analytical Space, Athelas, AutismSees, Ava, Bevi, BevSpot, BioCollection, Blockstack, Blueprint Income, Boom Fantasy, Booya Fitness, BottleRocket, BrainSpec, Brooklinen, Bruzd Foods, Bungalow, C. Light Technologies, Capella, Cathbuddy, Clara, Cognitive Toybox, Colibri, CommonCents, Concierge Stat, Cookin, Cresilon, Curative Orthopaedics, Dagne Dover, Dash, Databetes, DegreeChamp, DribbleUp, Droice Labs, EagerPanda, Eat Makhana, EmCasa, Farther Farms, FeastFox, Finfox, FireHUD, Firefly, FiscalNote, Five, Five to Nine, Flare Technologies, Floating Point Group, Flourish, Flowtune, Forest Device, Forge, FreeWill, Gainful, Gauge Insights, Geneoscopy, Greo, Grove Labs, Harper Wilde, Harvest Labs, HealthWiz, Healthie, Homesuite, Humon, Hydrant, Immudicon, Infinite Uptime, InnaMed, Intelligent Flying Machines, Inventory Connections, Keriton, KitSplit, Laws of Motion, LeapYear Technologies, LearnLux, LightUp, LogRocket, Lovepop, MaestroQA, Markit Medical, Mati, Miramix, MoveButter, NERv, NEU, NeuroMesh, NextWave Hire, Nimble, Noken, OliLux Biosciences, Oncora Medical, Onfleet, PageVamp, PandaPay, Parable Health, Parsegon, Pavlov, Pison Technology, Pixorize, Plan, Plasticity, Players' Lounge, Podium, Polymorph, ProducePay, Project Applecart, Pundit, Py, Quithelp, Radiator Labs, RapidSOS, Reach Labs, Resonado, Reveal Media, RocketBolt, Rorus, Scholly, SheFly, ShieldAI, Solisite, Solstice, SolutionLoft, Soteria, Splash Technologies, Sprayable Energy, Spyce, Stash, Symbiont Health, TABu, TEQ Charging, Tardisk, TaskUnite, Teachley, Tetrascience, Theatre Galleria, Traveling Spoon, Trinity Mobile Network, TwentyEight Health, Twine, User Interviews, Veho Technologies, Verb Energy Inc., Vidrovr, WeTravel, WorkerSense, XStream Trucking, Yard Club, Young Alfred, Zenflow, Zinc, Zippity, Zodiac, rmdy

Key Executives:
Molly Fowler, CEO
Education: BA, Political Science, Yale University
Chauncey Hamilton, COO
Education: BA, History, Trinity College, Hartford
Background: Partner Operations Manager, First Round Capital; WIRED

624 DOT EDU VENTURES
514 Bryant Street
Suite 110
Palo Alto, CA 94301

e-mail: contact@doteduventures.com
web: www.doteduventures.com

Mission Statement: The firm provides seed funding along with strong technical and strategic support for early stage technology businesses.

Founded: 2000
Average Investment: $10,000 - $250,000
Investment Criteria: Seed-Stage
Industry Group Preference: Enterprise Software, Database Services, Data & Analytics, Communications Software, Wireless Communications

Venture Capital & Private Equity Firms / Domestic Firms

Portfolio Companies: 23 and Me, Accel Growth Fund, Accel IX Strategic Partners, Acromedia Inc., Adchemy, AH Parallel Fund III-Q, Andreessen Horowitz Fund II-A, Aster Data, Audiencescience Inc., August Capital Management V, Baynote, Belwater Capital Fund, Braigo Labs, ByteMobile, Coast Access, Concept 10 Inc., Composite Software, Criteria Investment Partners LLC, CSP II Destressed Opportunities Trust, Digmine, DilMil, Eatime Inc., FlexLogics, Fin Robotics, Fireweed Fund, Fraudwall/Anchor Intelligence, Funny or Die (Sabse Technologies Inc.), Gigya, GReply, Greylock XII Limted, Gridants Inc., Gwynnie Bee, Hive II, Inventus Capital Management, Ixoraa Media Inc., Jaxtr, Kawi Safi Ventures, Kluttr, Korra, Loomia, Mashery, Mayfield Associates Fund, MC Pelican Fund LP, Mechanical Zoo, Medio Systems, Menlo Entrepreneurs Fund X, Meraki Networks Inc., Meru Networks, Metamachinix, Mimosa Systems, Mixer Labs Inc., ML-CSP II Trust, Nanonet, NextForce, Nokeena Networks, Northgate Capital LLC, NthOrbit, PeerNova, Pinterest, Plusmo, ReckOne Inc., Renkoo, Revenue Science, RocketFuel, Rupture, Scintera Networks, Score Data, Seligman Spectrum Focus Fund, Sequoia Tech Partners, Simplyhired Inc., Snaptell, Stumbleupon Inc., Sunflower New Co., Supyo, SV Angel III, Tapulous/GoGoApps, Teapot Inc., Technology IQ US LLC, Teracent Corp., Threads, TiE LaunchPad, Tizor, TokBok Inc., Genie, Urban Engines, UTV LLC, Vdopia, Wifidabba, WowkKast, Xambala, Xinlab, Zazzle.com

Key Executives:
Asha Jadeja, Founder
Education: Stanford University
Background: CEO, iScale, Inc.

625 DOUBLE M PARTNERS
725 Arizona Ave.
Suite 400
Santa Monica, CA 90401

web: www.doublempartners.com

Mission Statement: Double M Partners is a $7.2MM early stage venture fund based in Los Angeles and formed in August 2012. The Fund invests in Internet, Media and Communications companies who primarily are either business to business infrastructure, software, management platform and/or technology focused companies. The Fund is managed by Mark Mullen who has more than 20 years of investing and investment banking experience across the IMC sector. The Fund's current portfolio is comprised of 21 companies primarily in Southern California, but also including companies in San Francisco, Oregon and Canada. The Fund is supported by a premier group of investors, as well as fund advisors who are all successful entrepreneurs, investors, and business leaders.

Geographic Preference: Southern California, Oregon, Canada
Fund Size: $7.2 million
Founded: 2012
Investment Criteria: Early Stage
Industry Group Preference: Internet, Media, Communications
Portfolio Companies: Adomic, AdStage, Bitium, ChowNow, Clique Media, EV Connect, Gradient, HiQ, Idealists, Kaleo Software, Lettuce, MediaPass, MindClick, MomentFeed, Mover, Postcard on the Run, Prevoty, Quiet.ly, Retention Science, Scopely, Seismic Games, Sense360, Shift, Solfo, The Trade Desk, Tradesy

Key Executives:
Mark Mullen, Managing Partner
Education: BA, University of Denver; International MBA, Thunderbird School of Global Management; University of Michigan
Background: Senior Advisor, McCafferty & Co; Managing Director, International M&A, RBC Capital Markets; Senior Partner, Daniels & Associates; Senior Advisor to Los Angeles Mayor Antonio Villaraigosa; Chief Operating Officer, Office of Economic and Business Policy, City of Los Angeles

626 DOUBLEROCK VENTURE CAPITAL
1 Sansome Street
Suite 3500
San Francisco, CA 94104

Phone: 415-910-0943
e-mail: admin@doublerock.com
web: www.doublerock.com

Mission Statement: DoubleRock invests primarily in early and growth stage technology companies.

Founded: 2012
Average Investment: Early: $2-5 million; Growth: $10-15 million
Investment Criteria: Early-Stage, Growth-Stage
Industry Group Preference: Consumer Internet, Cloud Computing, Mobile, Wireless, Software, Consumer Services
Portfolio Companies: Addvocate, Aromyx, Buzzstarter, Circa, Instawork, Jawbone, Oomnitza, Optim.al, Peer, Real5D, Silk Labs, SolveBio, Switch.co, TrustedInsight, Vurb, Wealthminder

Key Executives:
Suraj Rajwani, Co-Founder/Managing Partner
e-mail: suraj@doublerock.com
Background: Managing Director, Global Entrepreneurs Network Organization
Nick Dani, General Partner

627 DRAPER ATHENA
55 East Third Avenue
San Mateo, CA 94401

e-mail: info@draperathena.com
web: www.dfjathena.com

Mission Statement: Uses a team-oriented approach, making available the complete mix of talents and resources of all partners and affiliates to the investment companies; maintains interest in building companies for the long-term and in helping the companies fulfill their complete vision.

Geographic Preference: Worldwide, West Coast
Fund Size: $100 million
Founded: 1997
Average Investment: $1 - $3 million
Minimum Investment: $500,000
Investment Criteria: Seed, Early-Stage
Industry Group Preference: Big Data, Software, Semiconductors, Robotics, Clean Technology, Security, Fintech, Machine Learning
Portfolio Companies: CallGate, Coinplug, Idea, Minigate, MXD3D, Nexia Device, OG Planet, Ramsway (JSC), Relay2, Creative Design Systems, Demandtec, Imparto Software, Impli, Pivot, Khancera, Mobeam, Persist Technologies, Profitlogic, Vivd Semiconductor, Zantaz

Other Locations:
7th Floor
#712 Seocho-gu Heolleung-no 7
Seoul 137-749
South Korea
Phone: 82 (2)554-3131 Fax: 82 (2)553-2201

Key Executives:
Tim Draper, Chairman, USA
e-mail: tim@dfj.com
Education: BS, Electrical Engineering, Stanford University; MBA, Harvard Business School
Background: Founding Partner, Draper Fisher Jurvetson; DFJ Global Network
Perry Ha, Managing Director
e-mail: perry@draperathena.com
Education: BS, MS, MIT; MBA, Harvard Business School
Background: Product Development/Technology

Venture Capital & Private Equity Firms / Domestic Firms

Management, Gemini Consulting; Amicon
Directorships: FirstIP, Impli, ProfitLogic, Zantaz.com
Henry Chung, Managing Director, Korea
e-mail: henry@draperathena.com
Education: BA, English Literature, MBA, Seoul National University
Background: Arthur D Little; SK Group
Directorships: CEO, eCommunity
Steven Tang, Managing Director, Hong Kong
e-mail: steven@draperathenagp.com
Education: BS, Electiral Engineering, Nottingham University; MBA, Bradford University
Background: National Semiconductor, Honeywell, Coolsand Semiconductor, RDA Microelectronics, Mills & Partners; Warburg Pincus
Charles Rim, Venture Partner
e-mail: chasrim@gmail.com
Education: BA, University of Pennsylvania; JD, Emory University
Background: Corporate Development, Google; Director, Yahoo! Korea; Investment Banking, Credit Agricole

628 DRAPER RICHARDS KAPLAN FOUNDATION
1600 El Camino Real
Suite 155
Menlo Park, CA 94025

Phone: 650-319-7808 **Fax:** 650-323-4060
web: www.drkfoundation.org

Mission Statement: Draper Richards is a venture capital firm dedicated to helping entrepreneurs and early-stage technology-based companies achieve maximum growth. The firm provides its portfolio companies support in the areas of raising capital and strategy development.

Geographic Preference: United States
Fund Size: $35 million
Founded: 1996
Average Investment: $1 million
Minimum Investment: $75,000 - $250,000
Investment Criteria: Early, Expansion, Seed
Industry Group Preference: Communications, Software, Internet Technology, Electronic Components, Information Technology, Telecommunications
Portfolio Companies: Axiom Legal, Blue Vector Systems, Brilliant Telecommunications, EoPlex Technologies, Flurry, Kyte, Lohika, LucidPort Technologies, Nusym Technologies, ObjectVideo, Ooma, Polaris Wireless, Prolacta Bioscience, Tsumobi, Ultriva

Key Executives:
William H Draper III, Co-Chair
e-mail: bill@draperrichards.com
Education: BA, Yale University; MBA, Harvard Graduate School of Business
Background: Founder, Sutter Hill Ventures; President & Chairman, Export-Import Bank of the US; Head, United Nations Development Program
Robin Richards Donohoe, Co-Chair
e-mail: robin@draperrichards.com
Education: Stanford Graduate School of Business; University of North Carolina
Background: Managing Director, Seaboard Management Corporation

629 DRAPER TRIANGLE VENTURES
2 Gateway Center
Suite 2000
Pittsburgh, PA 15222

Phone: 412-288-9800 **Fax:** 412-288-9799
web: www.drapertriangle.com

Mission Statement: Draper Triangle Ventures is a venture capital firm that partners with high-technology companies based in Pennsylvania and the Midwest.

Geographic Preference: Pennsylvania, Ohio, Midwest
Fund Size: $68 million
Founded: 1999
Average Investment: $250,000 - $2 million
Investment Criteria: Seed-Stage, Early-Stage
Industry Group Preference: Technology
Portfolio Companies: Acrobatiq, Aethon, Amplifinity, Bjond, Commuter Advertising, Directworks, OnShift, Pixel Velocity, RE2, Rhiza, ThinkVine, Thread

Other Locations:
21 East State Street
Suite 2200
Columbus, OH 43215
Phone: 614-450-2888

303 Detroit Street
Suite 100
Ann Arbor, MI 48104
Phone: 734-215-7577

Key Executives:
Jay Katarincic, Founder/Managing Director
e-mail: jay@dtvc.com
Education: BA, Economics, College of the Holy Cross; JD/MSIA, University of Pittsburgh School of Law & Carnegie Mellon University Graduate School of Industrial Administration
Background: Associate, M&A Group, Skadden Arps Slate Meagher & Flom
Directorships: Amplifinity, DirectWorks, Thread, Acrobatiq, Pittsburgh Technology Council, 3RiversConnect
Mike Stubler, Founder/Managing Director
e-mail: mike@dtvc.com
Education: BBA, University of Notre Dame
Background: Co-Founder & VP, Finance, IndustryNet; VP & CFO, International Cybernetics Corp.; Touche Ross & Company
Directorships: Unitask, OnShift, Aethon, Rhiza, Ohio Venture Association, Innovation Works
Tom Jones, Managing Director
e-mail: tom@dtvc.com
Education: BS, College of Wooster
Background: VP, Marketing, IndustryNet; VP, Marketing, Exonic Systems
Directorships: Commuter Advertising, Thinkvine, RE2, Directworks, Bjond, Pittsburgh DataWorks
Jonathan Murray, Venture Partner
e-mail: jonathan@dtvc.com
Background: Spectra Laboratories; President, Volk Optical; Co-Founder, Early Stage Partners
Zach Malone, Principal
e-mail: zach@dtvc.com
Education: BS, Finance, Virginia Polytechnic Institute
Background: Analyst, UPMC; Gateway Financial
Directorships: Pittsburgh Venture Capital Association Emerging Leaders

630 DRESNER COMPANIES
10 S LaSalle Street
Suite 2170
Chicago, IL 60603

Phone: 312-726-3600 **Fax:** 312-726-7448
web: www.dresnerpartners.com

Mission Statement: Dresner Partners is an investment bank focusing on middle market companies in a variety of industries, including technology, business services, consumer products, healthcare and industrials. The firm specializes in mergers and acquisition advisory, private institutional financing and finance restructuring.

Geographic Preference: Worldwide
Founded: 1991

Investment Criteria: Corporate Divestitures, Acquisitions, Management Buyouts
Industry Group Preference: Communications, Computer Related, Consumer Products, Distribution, Electronic Components, Industrial Equipment, Medical & Health Related, Technology
Other Locations:
200 Park Avenue
Suite 1700
New York, NY 10166
Phone: 212-203-8449

401 E Las Olas Boulevard
Suite 1400
Fort Lauderdale, FL 33301
Phone: 954-951-0272
Key Executives:
Steven M Dresner, President
312-780-7206
e-mail: sdresner@dresnerco.com
Education: BS, Economics, Wharton School, University of Pennsylvania; MBA, Finance, University of Chicago
Background: First Chicago Corporation; Arthur Andersen; Heller Financial; GE Capital Corporation
Kevin W McMurchy, Senior Managing Director, Financial Institutions
212-444-8029
Education: AB, Harvard University; MBA, Wharton School, University of Pennsylvania
Background: Merrill Lynch Capital Markets; Deutsche Morgan Grenfell, Keefe, Bruyette & Woods; Houlihan Lokey
Omar Diaz, Managing Director, Industrials
312-780-7221
Education: BS, Mechanical Engineering, Cornell University; MBA, Finance, Kelley School of Business, Indiana University
Background: Managing Director, Allegiance Capital; SVP, Industrial Group, Houlihan Lokey; VP, Acquest Advisors; Associate, M&A Group, JP Morgan; Bank of America; Deloitte & Touche
W Robert Friedman Jr, Managing Director, Healthcare
212-390-0503
Education: BA, MBA, Wharton School, University of Pennsylvania
Background: Managing Director, Deutsche Morgan Grenfell; Managing Director, Prudential Bache Capital Funding; General Partner, Montgomery Securities; LF Rothschild Unterberg Towbin
Directorships: MaxiCare Health Plans, Health Plan of California
Brian Graves, Managing Director
312-780-7237
Education: BS, Industrial Engineering, Purdue University; MBA, Finance, University of Chicago Graduate School of Business
Background: Ernst & Young; Credit Suisse; Mesirow Financial; Motorola
Michelle Moreno, Managing Director
312-780-7207
Education: BA, Economics & French, University of Illinois at Urbana-Champaign; MBA, California State University, Fullerton
Background: First Analysis; CIBC World Markets
Directorships: Chicago Finance Exchange
Stephen P Mullin, Director, Marketing & Business Development
312-780-7213
Education: BS, Finance, Drake University
Background: Dun & Bradstreet Information Services; American National Bank
Paul E Hoffman, Director
312-780-7229
Education: BA, Economics, University of Chicago
Background: Bank of America Securities

631 DRIVE CAPITAL
629 North High Steet
Columbus, OH 43215
e-mail: info@drivecapital.com
web: www.drivecapital.com
Mission Statement: Drive Capital invests in innovative technology, healthcare, and consumer companies in the Midwest. Actively seeking innovative entrepreneurs addressing big market opportunities. Drive Capital partners with entrepreneurs that have audacious goals and strive to build large sustainable companies.
Geographic Preference: Midwest
Industry Group Preference: Technology, Technology-Enabled Services, Healthcare, Consumer Services, Consumer Products
Portfolio Companies: Aver Inc., Beam, Channel IQ, Civis Analytics, Clinc, Comply 365, CrossCHX, Duolingo, FarmLogs, Hologram, Immuta, Kapow, LeadPages, Muve, Nowait, Roadtrippers, Root, TriggrHealth, Trove, Udacity, When I Work
Key Executives:
Mark D. Kvamme, Co-Founder
Education: University of California, Berkeley
Background: Partner, Sequoia Capital; Chief Investment Officer/President, JobsOhio
Chris Olsen, Co-Founder
Background: Partner, Sequoia Capital; Technology Crossover Ventures

632 DUBILIER & COMPANY
Stamford, CT 06902
web: www.dubilier.com
Mission Statement: A private investment firm focused on buying and building companies in partnership with management.
Investment Criteria: Middle Market
Industry Group Preference: Consumer Products, Media, Publishing, Information Technology, E-Commerce & Manufacturing, Marketing
Portfolio Companies: Acrow Bridge, Amplified Technology Holdings, Bluegrass Dairy And Food Inc., Bulletin Intelligence, Cleareon Fiber Networks, Cavario, DC Safety, FourQ, MDT, ODC Nimbus, Old london, Ooska News, Phoenix, Rio SEO, Systech International, Zim's Crack Creme
Key Executives:
Michael M Cone, Director
Education: BA, Princeton University; PhD, Organic Chemistry, Yale University
Background: Partner, Crossway Ventures; Chemical Research, DuPont Company; Venture Manager, Somos
Dana Donovan, Director
Education: BA, Duke University; MBA, Amos Tuck School, Dartmouth College
Background: President, Clarion Capital; Managing Director, John Hancock Financial
Michael J Dubilier, Managing Partner
Education: Connecticut College; MBA, Garvin School of International Management; New York University Graduate School of Business Administration
Background: Partner, Clayton Dubilier & Ric; Drexel Burhham Lambert
Directorships: Phoenix Packaging Company, Magnetic Data Technologies, HEM Pharmaceuticals, APS, Old London Foods
Peter D Goodson, Director
Education: Stanford University; Harvard Business School
Background: Partner, CD&R; Managing Director, Kidder Peabody & Co

Venture Capital & Private Equity Firms / Domestic Firms

633 DUBIN CLARK & COMPANY
323 Newbury Street
Boston, MA 02115

Phone: 203-629-2030 Fax: 203-547-7444
web: www.dubinclark.com

Mission Statement: Dubin Clark & Company seeks to partner with management teams and help build businesses by providing capital and assisting with the development of new strategies.
Geographic Preference: North America
Founded: 1984
Investment Criteria: Platform company sales of $10-$100+ million and adjusted EBITDA of $2-$20 million (smaller for add-ons); businesses in transition; strong growth trajectory
Industry Group Preference: Construction, Building Materials & Services, Transportation, Manufacturing, Infrastructure, Aerospace, Defense and Government, Healthcare Services, Energy
Portfolio Companies: Action Target, Johnny on the Spot, Merex Group, Peterson Party Center, Reel Power International, Restoration Parts Unlimited, Sentient Medical Systems, SGA Production Services, USSC
Other Locations:
1030 2nd Street S
Suite 301
Jacksonville Beach, FL 32250
Phone: 203-629-2030 Fax: 203-547-7444
Key Executives:
  Thomas J Caracciolo, Managing Partner
  203-629-2030 x225
  e-mail: caracciolo@dubinclark.com
  Education: BS, Northeastern University; MBA, Harvard Business School
  Background: Partner, TCW Capital; Corporate Finance Group, GE Capital
  Directorships: Driven Performance Brands, Action Target, Reel Power International, Sentient Medical Systems, Merex Group
  Brent L Paris, Managing Partner
  203-629-2030 x228
  e-mail: paris@dubinclark.com
  Education: BS, Accounting, Indiana University School of Business; MBA, Finance & Entrepreneurship, University of Chicago Graduate School of Business
  Background: Associate, Latek Capital Corp.; Analyst, Waveland Capital Management; Brinson Partners
  Directorships: Driven Performance Brands, Restoration Parts Unlimited, Peterson Party Center, Association for Corporate Growth
  Michael P Hompesch, Partner
  203-629-2030 x223
  e-mail: hompesch@dubinclark.com
  Education: BS, Business Administration, American University; MBA, Finance, Wharton Graduate School of Business; CFA
  Background: General Electric Financial Management Program, Commercial Finance
  Directorships: Action Target, Reel Power International, Merex Group, Johnny on the Spot
  Frank J Pados Jr, Senior Advisor
  203-629-2030 x229
  e-mail: pados@dubinclark.com
  Education: BA, Economics, Boston College; MBA, Finance, University of Pennsylvania
  Background: EVP & Head, Private Equity, Desai Capital Management; Managing Director & Co-Founding Partner, TCW Capital
  Directorships: Sentient Medical Systems, Reel Power International, Merex Group, Johnny on the Spot

634 DUCHOSSOIS CAPITAL MANAGEMENT
444 W Lake Street
Suite 2000
Chicago, IL 60606

Phone: 312-586-2080
e-mail: info@dcmllc.com
web: www.dcmllc.com

Mission Statement: Duchossois Capital Management is a privately held investment company that seeks to create long term value by providing capital and operational expertise.
Geographic Preference: Midwest United States
Average Investment: $2 - $7 million
Investment Criteria: Growth Stage, Later Stage
Industry Group Preference: Networking, Semiconductors, Software, Technology, Information Technology, Communications
Portfolio Companies: Critical Signal Technologies, Echo Active Learning, GetWellNetwork, Infoblox, Milestone AV Technologies
Key Executives:
  Michael E Flannery, Chief Executive Officer
  Education: BS, Finance, University of Illinois; Indiana University School of Law
  Background: CEO, Trinity Rail Group; Vice Chairman, Thrall Car; Corporate Counsel, Cummins Engine Company
  Directorships: The Chamberlain Group, Milestone AV Technologies
  Eric A Reeves, Managing Director/Head, Private Capital Investments
  Education: BA, University of Michigan; JD, Ohio State University
  Background: EVP & General Counsel, The Chamberlain Group; Partner, Corporate Department, McDermott Will & Emery
  Directorships: Seaway Bank and Trust Company, Milestone AV Technologies
  Lauren K Bugay, Managing Director
  Education: BBA, University of Notre Dame; MBA, Booth School of Business, University of Chicago; CFA
  Background: Director of Business Development, The Duchossois Group; Corporate Finance, William Blair & Company
  Jason B Moskowitz, Managing Director
  Education: BBA, University of Notre Dame; MBA, Finance, Kellogg School of Management, Northwestern University
  Background: VP, Merit Capital Partners; Associate, Pfingsten Partners
  Michelle A Waldusky, Manager, Investment Operations
  Education: BS, Accounting, University of Illinois; CPA
  Background: Deloitte & Touche

635 DUNDEE VENTURE CAPITAL
3717 Harney Street
2nd Floor
Omaha, NE 68131

web: www.dundeeventurecapital.com

Mission Statement: Dundee Venture Capital is a venture capital firm that invests in early stage technology companies with high growth potential.
Fund Size: $20 million
Founded: 2010
Average Investment: $50,000 - $750,000
Investment Criteria: Startups, Early Stage
Industry Group Preference: E-Commerce & Manufacturing, SaaS, Consumer Networks, Technology
Portfolio Companies: ABODO, ABPathFinder, AgLocal, Briefcase, Built In Chicago, BuluBox, Business Exchange, Cosmic Cart, DivvyHQ, DonorPath, HuntForce, Inventables, Leap.It, Lockr, MindMixer, Phone2Action, RoundPegg, Techstars Ventures, TripleSeat, Viirt, Vine Street Ventures, Wide Open Spaces

Venture Capital & Private Equity Firms / Domestic Firms

Key Executives:
Mark Hasebroock, Founder
Education: BS, Business Administration, University of Nebraska-Lincoln; MBA, Finance, Creighton University
Background: Co-Owner, Tranquility Bay Resort; Co-Founder, Hayneedle; COO, GiftCertificates.com
Beth Engel, Advisor
Education: BS, Biochemistry, University of Notre Dame; MBA, Georgetown University
Background: Hayneedle; Co-Founder, Interface: The Web School; Straight Shot

---

636 DUNRATH CAPITAL
641 Courtland Circle
Western Springs, IL 60558

Phone: 312-546-4700
web: www.dunrath.com

Mission Statement: Dunrath Capital is a private equity and strategic advisory firm that invests in early and growth stage infrastructure surety companies.

Geographic Preference: United States
Fund Size: $100 million
Investment Criteria: Early-Stage, Growth-Stage
Industry Group Preference: Infrastructure, Aerospace, Defense and Government, Security
Portfolio Companies: Critical Signal Technologies, Exadigm, Keri Systems, Quantum Secure, RedSky Technologies

Key Executives:
John I Abernethy, Founder/Managing Director
312-546-4782
Fax: 866-255-7299
e-mail: john@dunrath.com
Education: BS, Accounting, Northern Illinois University
Background: CFO, Revere Group; CFO, APAC Customer Services; EVP & CFO, Commerce Clearing House; Audit Partner, Deloitte & Touche
Stephen S Beitler, Founder/Managing Director
847-847-4414
Fax: 847-432-4420
e-mail: steve@dunrath.com
Education: School of International Service, American University; University of Chicago; Defense Intelligence College
Background: Managing Director, Trident Capital; Sears Roebuck & Co.; Helene Curtis
Richard P Earley, Founder/Managing Director
630-871-8940
e-mail: rich@dunrath.com
Education: BA, University of Notre Dame; MBA, Benedictine University
Background: CEO & Chairman, Arxan Technologies; Arxan Defense Systems; President, Synergy Software Inc.

---

637 DUPONT CAPITAL
Chestnut Run Plaza
Building C735-1
974 Centre Road
Wilmington, DE 19805

Phone: 302-477-6167
e-mail: kimberly.a.fetterman@usa.dupont.com
web: www.dupontcapital.com

Mission Statement: DCM offers a diversified private equity program that was designed with the objective of providing superior, risk-adjusted, long-term private equity returns for investors. Fundamentally, the Private Markets Group (PMG) are value investors and believe the inherent inefficiency of the private market provides opportunities to acquire assets at prices below their intrinsic values. The PMG has diligently applied value investment principles to the private equity market since 1989.

Fund Size: $3.7 billion
Founded: 1989
Investment Criteria: Buyouts, Co-Investments, Mezzanine, Special Situations
Industry Group Preference: Diversified

Key Executives:
Lode J Devlaminck, Managing Director, Equities
Education: MA, Applied Economics, University of Antwerp
Background: CIO, Global Equities, Hermes North America; Portfolio Manager, Global Equities and Sector Specialist, Fortis Investments; Global Sector Manager, Fimagest
Krzysztof A. Kowal, CFA, Managing Director, Fixed Income Investments
Education: MS, Physics, Jagiellonian University; PhD, Materials Science and Engineering, University of Pennsylvania
Antonis Mistras, CFA, Managing Director, Alternative Investments
Education: BS, Forestry, Aristotellian University; MS, Wood Science and Technology, University of California, Berkeley; MBA, University of California, Berkeley
Background: Manager of Production, BARRA
Daryl B Brown, Director/Portfolio Manager
Education: BS, Mathematics, University of Texas; MBA, University of Delaware; CFA
Background: Associate Actuary, DuPont
Valerie J Sill, President & CEO
Education: BA, Wellesley College; MBA, Harvard University
Background: EVP, The Boston Company

---

638 DUTCHESS CAPITAL
50 Commonwealth Avenue
Suite 2
Boston, MA 02116

Phone: 617-301-4701
e-mail: dleighton@dutchesscapital.com
web: www.dutchesscapital.com

Mission Statement: Invests in several types of industries, including technology, ecommerce, and consumer products.

Geographic Preference: 7S, Canada, UK, Europe, Australia, Asia, Latin America
Founded: 1996
Average Investment: Up to $25M
Investment Criteria: Seed, Early-Stage, Late-Stage
Industry Group Preference: Technology, Ecommerce, Consumer Goods, Cannabis
Portfolio Companies: American Cannabis Company, Baobab Resources, Big Night Entertainment Group, CampusTap, Continental Coal Ltd., Dixie Elixirs, Foria, Independent Bank, Kandy Pens, Mannatech, Mass Roots, Nanigans, ProPhase Labs, Range Resources Ltd., Safety Quick Light, SMTP

Other Locations:
1110 Route 55
Suite 206
LaGrangeville, NY 12540
Phone: 845-575-6770 x202

New Broad Street House
35 New Broad Street
London EC2M 1NH
United Kingdom

Room 11A1, Block A, Han Wei Plaza
7 Guang Hua Road
Chaoyang District

Beijing 100004
China

Rua Itapeva, 378 - 120 Andar
Sao Paulo, SP 01332-000
Brasil

Key Executives:
Douglas H. Leighton, Founder/Managing Partner
e-mail: dleighton@dutchesscapital.com
Education: BS, Economics, University of Hartford
Michael A. Novielli, Founder/Managing Partner
845-575-6770 ext. 202
e-mail: mnovielli@dutchesscapital.com
Education: BS, Business, University of South Florida
Theodore J. Smith, Managing Director/COO
617-301-4702
e-mail: tsmith@dutchesscapital.com
Education: BS, Finance, Boston College
Jessica Geran, Head of Corporate Finance
617-301-4703
e-mail: jgeran@dutchesscapital.com
Education: BA, Economics, University of Colorado
Background: Financial Representative, Northwestern Mutual

639 DW HEALTHCARE PARTNERS
1413 Center Drive
Suite 220
Park City, UT 84098

Phone: 435-645-4050
web: www.dwhp.com

Mission Statement: DW Healthcare Partners invests exclusively in healthcare businesses across North America.
Geographic Preference: North America
Fund Size: $265 million
Founded: 2002
Average Investment: $15 - $40 million
Minimum Investment: $5 million
Investment Criteria: Middle-Market, Growth Capital, Management Buyouts
Industry Group Preference: Healthcare
Portfolio Companies: ABC Home Medical Supply, Arteriocyte Medical Systems, Med-Pharmex, Reliant Rehabilitation, Reliant Renal Care, Z-Medica

Other Locations:
1 Toronto Street
Suite 401
Toronto, ON M5C 2V6
Canada
Phone: 416-583-2420

Key Executives:
Andrew Carragher, Founder/Managing Director
416-583-2421
e-mail: acarragher@dwhp.com
Education: BS, University of Western Ontario; MBA, Harvard Business School
Background: VP, Business Development, Ventro Corporation; Total Renal Care; Divisional Manager, Weston Foods; Bain & Company
Directorships: Genesis Technology Partners, Verathon, Tandem Labs, Reliant Renal Care, Reliant Rehabilitation, Pentec Health, Career Step, Z-Medica Corporation, Health & Safety Institute
Jay Benear, Founder/Managing Director
435-645-4052
e-mail: jay@dwhp.com
Education: BA, Psychology, Rice University; MD, Oklahoma University
Background: President, Cancer Care Associates
Directorships: Arteriocyte Medical Systems, BGS Pharmacy Partners, Emphusion, Genesis Technology Partners, Global Physics Solutions, Hill Top Research, The Radlinx Group
Doug Schillinger, Managing Director
435-645-4056
e-mail: doug@dwhp.com
Education: BS, Cornell University; MBA, Harvard Business School
Background: Bain & Company; Manager, Accenture Consulting
Directorships: Tandem Labs, Pentec Health, Hill Top Research, Global Physics Solutions, ClinOps, BGS Pharmacy, Arteriocyte Medical
Lance Ruud, Managing Director/Chief Financial Officer
435-645-4054
e-mail: lance@dwhp.com
Education: BS, Accounting, University of Utah
Background: Senior VP & CFO, HTD Corporation; CFO & Director, TransAmerican Waste Industries; CFO, Republic Waste Industries
Directorships: Arteriocyte Medical Systems, Z-Medica Corporation

640 DYNAMO VC
800 Market Street
Suite 200
Chattanooga, TN 37402

e-mail: hello@dynamo.vc
web: www.dynamo.vc

Mission Statement: A venture capital fund investing in technology businesses that have the potential to transform commerce and trade.
Founded: 2016
Industry Group Preference: Commerce and Trade, Clean Technology, Energy, Software, Robotics, Entertainment, Travel, Network Infrastructure & Security, Data & Analytics
Portfolio Companies: Steam Logistics, Starksky Robotics, Skupos, Slope, Skydrop, Armada.ai, Numadic, Sennder, Zeelo, Autit, Wise, SynapseMX, Locatible, Shipamax, Work Hound, Stord, Sirenum

Key Executives:
Barry Large, Founder/Managing Director
Background: Founder, Lamp Post Group; Advisor, Bellhops; Advisor, FanJam
Ted Alling, Founder/Managing Director
Education: Samford University
Background: Founder/CEO, Access America Transport; Advisor, Skupos; Advisor, PriceWaiter; Advisor, Tripr; Advisor, Breeze; Advisor, Bellhops; Founder, Lamp Post Group
Directorships: Skupos
Allan Davis, Founder/Managing Director
Background: Founder, Lamp Post Group; Access America Transport; Advisor, Bellhops; Advisor, FanJam
Directorships: Bellhops
Santosh Sankar, Founder/Managing Director
Education: BS, Finance, Pennsylvania State University
Background: Citigroup; Wells Fargo Securities

641 E.VENTURES
600 Montgomery Street
43rd Floor
San Francisco, CA 94111

Phone: 415-869-5200 Fax: 415-869-5201
e-mail: info@eventures.vc
web: www.eventures.vc

Mission Statement: Focuses on emerging opportunities in new media, information technology and communications. With a team in each of our five regions, we have access to teams, markets, and investors in all the important places. And because we work together closely, we can offer significant synergies and benefits for entrepreneurs. These include global insights, recognition of emerging trends, and a strategic advantage for startups with global goals. In essence, we can bring you global virtually overnight.

Geographic Preference: United States, Europe
Investment Criteria: Early Stage, Growth Stage
Industry Group Preference: Media, Information Technology, Communications
Portfolio Companies: 36Kr, 9flats.com, Acorns, Add, Angie's List, Amplify, App Annie, Appfolio, Aptoide, Asana Rebel, Asap54, Axios, Azimo, BackOps, BankFacil, BetaWorks, BetterCloud, Bird, Blinkist, Bluekai, Braavo, Bright Health, Candid Co., CarPrice, Class Box, Clicksign, Clique Media Group, Code Fights, Copa90, Cornerjob, Cortex, Coya, Daily Secret, Del.Icio.Us, Delta Method, Deposit Solutions, Eucalyptus, Everything but the House, Experteer.dE, Exporo, FanTV, FarFetch, Flux, Fotolog, Freee, Friendsurance, Futrli, GamersFirst, Global Savings Group, GoPuff, GoToMeeting, Goyoo, Graylog, Groupon, Gympass, Hashgo, Hi-Media, Honeycomb.io, HouseCall, Huckleberry, Icertis, JMTY, Jow, JW Player, Karma, Kauf.da, LastLine, Layer, Made, Maker Studios, Medicinia, Memed, Merchantry, Mightybell, Minuto Seguros, Minutrade, MoyoGame, Munchery, Muse & Co., Nativo, Natural Cycles, nCircle, Nibo, Nginx, Nomnomnom, Online Tours, Order With Me, Ozon.ru, PasseiDireto, PayKey, Peanut Labs, Pink.oi, Plain Vanilla, Plated, PlayHaven, PSafe, Pulse, Recurly, Reelio, Rekoo, Resultados Digitais, Saatchi Art, Sapato, Savoteur, Scopely, Segment, Semrush, Shipt, Shopping.com, Shutl, Smartfrog, Soldsie, Sonim Technologies, Sonos, SpotHero, Stackshare, Staffbase, Streamlabs, Strikingly, StyleSaint, Tandem, Teamo.ru, TechTemple, Test.ai, The Real Real, The Young Turks, The Family, ThisClicks, Thrive Market, Trippy, TVSmiles, Upsight, Verse, ViajaNet, Vicampo, Waptx, WealthNavi, When I Work, Wine In Black, Wonderschool, YuMe

Other Locations:
Hohe Bleichen 21
Hamburg 20354
Germany
Phone: 49-4082225550 **Fax:** 49-408222555999

Friedrichstr. 206
Berlin 10969
Germany
Phone: 49-30467249770

Rua Joaquim Floriano, 1120 A, cj. 92
Itaim Bibi
Sao Paulo SP 04534-004
Brazil
Phone: 55-1140636061

Taikouen Bld.3F, 1-3-8
Shibakoen Minato-ku
Tokyo 105-0011
Japan
Phone: 81-9014672730

Tianhai Business Building B
Suite 107
Dongsi Bei St, Dongcheng District
Beijing
China

Key Executives:
Mathias Schilling, Co-Founder/Managing Partner
Education: Masters Finance, University of St. Gallen
Background: Consultant, Bertelsmann AG; Bertelsmann's Book Group, New York; Roland Berger & Partner
Thomas Gieselmann, Co-Founder/General Partner
Education: BA Economics/Business Administration, Rhodes College
Background: Chief Technology Officer, AOL Europe
Directorships: NGINX, Playhaven, Pulse News, Gamersfirst
Andreas Haug, Co-Founder/General Partner, Hamburg
Background: Co-Founder, InfoMedia Group, Co-Founder, Diligenz Management Consulting; Bertelsmann AG

Christin Leybold, Co-Founder/Managing Partner, Hamburg & Berlin
Education: Masters Degree, Electrical Engineering, University of Illinois at Urbana
Background: Detecon International; Daimler Chrysler Research
Akio Tanaka, Partner, Tokyo & Beijing
Education: MS, University of British Columbia
Background: Head of Venture Investment Program, Adobe
Anderson Thees, Partner, Sao Paulo
Education: BS, Computer Engineering, University of Campinas; MBA, Yale School of Management
Background: CEO, Apontador; Investment Principal, Naspers/MIH
Charles Yim, Venture Partner
Education: BA, Philosophy, Carleton College
Background: Head of Mobile Application Partnerships, Google; AdMob

642 EARLY STAGE PARTNERS
1801 East Ninth Street
Suite 1700
Cleveland, OH 44114

Phone: 216-781-4600
web: www.esplp.com

Mission Statement: Early Stage Partners is a venture capital firm dedicated to investing in Midwest-based early stage companies across a range of technology sectors.

Geographic Preference: Ohio, Michigan, Midwest
Fund Size: $55 million
Founded: 2001
Investment Criteria: Early Stage
Industry Group Preference: Information Technology, Clean Technology, Manufacturing, Healthcare, Industrial Technology
Portfolio Companies: Amplifinity, Arisdyne, AxioMed Spine, Ayalogic, Blue Spark Technologies, Cardiox, Cleveland Medical Polymers, CytoPherx, EcoSmart, Gensyn Technologies, Great Lakes Pharmaceuticals, HealthSpot, HistoSonics, Intelligent Clearing Network, Imalux, Juventas Therapeutics, LineStream, MAR Systems, NineSigma, OnShift, OPTEM, Reverse Medical Corp., Simbionix, SironRX, TOA Technologies, UniTask

Key Executives:
Jim Petras, Managing Director
Education: BA, Oberlin College; MA, MBA, University of Michigan
Background: President & Managing Director, Capital One Partners; Founder, Wolfensohn Ventures; Citicorp
Directorships: Blue Spark, EcoSmart, Simbionix, Arisdyne, OPTEM, Linestream, ICN
Jonathan Murray, Co-Founder
Education: BA, Biology & English Literature, George Washington University; MBA, University of Michigan
Background: President, Incubation Services; President, Volk Optical; Spectra Laboratories
Directorships: TOA Technologies, OnShift, ICN, Imalux, Ayalogic, Unitask, Amplifinity
Charlie MacMillan, Chief Financial Officer
Education: Ohio Wesleyan University
Background: CFO, Capital One Partners; VP, Administration, Manco; Manager, Entrepreneurial Services Group, Ernst & Young

643 EARTHRISE CAPITAL
80 Broad Street
5th Floor
New York, NY 10004

Phone: 212-757-1007
web: www.earthrisecapital.com

Mission Statement: Earthrise Capital Fund is a venture fund investing in emerging technologies for energy, power and water,

Venture Capital & Private Equity Firms / Domestic Firms

primarily in North America. Areas of interest include lower-carbon energy sources; energy and materials efficiency improvement, cost-effective energy storage; and environmental technologies and services. The Earthrise team has decades of collective experience in energy and environmental technology investing.

Geographic Preference: North America
Investment Criteria: Early-Stage, Later-Stage
Industry Group Preference: Energy, Water, Energy Efficiency, Energy Storage, Environment, Renewable Energy, Clean Energy, Green Technology
Portfolio Companies: Axion Power International, CoolChip Technologies, Forest2Market, NanoMas Technologies, Powerhouse Dynamics, TSO Logic Inc.

Key Executives:
  Ann Partlow, Co-Founder/General Partner
  e-mail: apartlow@earthrisecapital.com
  Background: Portfolio Manager, Rockefeller & Co
  James LoGerfo, Co-Founder/General Partner
  e-mail: jlogerfo@earthrisecapital.com
  Education: BA, International Studies, University of Washington; PhD, Political Science, Columbia University; CFA
  Background: Energy Technology Energy Research, Bank of America; General Motors Pension Fund; BOVARO Partners; Vortex Energy

644 EASTON CAPITAL INVESTMENT GROUP
767 Third Avenue
7th Floor
New York, NY 10017
Phone: 212-702-0950 Fax: 212-702-0952
web: www.eastoncapital.com

Mission Statement: Easton Capital Investment Group is a venture capital firm focusing on the healthcare and life sciences sectors. The firm invests in companies with capital efficient business models and seeks to generate superior returns while minimizing risks.
Geographic Preference: Eastern Seaboard, United States
Fund Size: $20 - $100 million
Founded: 1999
Average Investment: $10 - $20 million
Minimum Investment: $500,000
Investment Criteria: Early Stage, Mid-Stage, Late Stage, Growth Capital, PIPEs
Industry Group Preference: Life Sciences, Healthcare, Healthcare Services, Diagnostics, Medical Devices, Therapeutics, Healthcare Information Technology
Portfolio Companies: Bluebird Bio, Cardiomems, Claret Medical, Comprehend, Conor Medsystems, ElectroCore, EM Kinetics, Expanding Orthopedics, Kitcheck, Medikly, PerceptiMed, Precise Light Surgical, Promedior, Resolve Therapeutics, Shimojani, SOLX, TigerText, Trellis Bioscience, WellTrackOne, Wildflower, Within3

Key Executives:
  John H Friedman, Founding Partner/Managing Partner
  e-mail: friedman@eastoncapital.com
  Education: BA, Yale College, Yale University; JD, Yale Law School
  Background: Founder & Managing General Partner, Security Pacific Capital Investors; Manging Director & Partner, EM Warburg Pincus & Company
  Directorships: Promedior, Trellis Bioscience, MedCPU, PerceptiMed, TigerText, Within3, Precise Light
  Francisco Garcia, Managing Director
  e-mail: garcia@eastoncapital.com
  Education: AB, Harvard College, Harvard University; JD, Harvard Law School
  Background: Head, Corporate Finance, Cramer Rosenthal McGlynn; Neptune Management Company; VP, Corporate Finance, Kidder Peabody & Company; Attorney, Sullivan & Cromwell

  Directorships: Archibald, Autonet, Gentis, TransMolecular
  Charles B Hughes III, Managing Director/General Counsel
  e-mail: hughes@eastoncapital.com
  Education: AB, Princeton University; LLM, New York University School of Law; JD, University of Virginia School of Law
  Background: Partner, Torys LLP
  Kresimir Letinic MD PhD, Managing Director
  e-mail: kletinic@eastoncapital.com
  Education: MBA, PhD, Neuroscience, Yale University; MD, University of Zagreb
  Background: Fletcher Spaght Ventures; The Channel Group; Lesanne Life Sciences
  Directorships: Medikly, Wildflower Health
  Richard Lipkin, Managing Director
  e-mail: rlipkin@eastoncapital.com
  Education: Princeton University; MBA, Columbia University
  Background: Partner, Commerce Health Ventures; Laird & Co.; Goldman Sachs; Executive Director, Strang Cancer Prevention Center
  Ting-Pau Oei, Executive Partner
  e-mail: toei@eastoncapital.com
  Education: BA, Union College; MBA, Columbia University Graduate School of Business
  Background: Johnson & Johnson; Ortho Pharmaceutical International; Abbott Laboratories; Merck

645 EASTVEN VENTURE PARTNERS
17 Old Kings Highway South
Suite 140
Darien, CT 06820

Mission Statement: Seeks investments in companies with exceptional management teams, that have unique and proprietary technology, and that seek to capitalize on sizeable market opportunities.
Geographic Preference: North America
Fund Size: $50 million
Founded: 2001
Investment Criteria: Primary Focus Early Stage, Will Except All Stages Including Spin-Outs
Industry Group Preference: Software, Technology, Infrastructure, Communications, Semiconductors, Networking, Information Technology, Enabling Technology
Portfolio Companies: ByteMobile, Kirusa, Photobucket, RadioFrame Networks, Atrua, ReefEdge, Vallent

Key Executives:
  Mark Maybell, Founder/Partner
  Education: MBA, Taxation and Accounting, Indiana University; AB, Finance, University of Illinois
  Background: Merrill Lynch, Bear, Stearns and Company
  Directorships: WatchMark Corporation, RadioFrame Networks
  Mark McAndrews, Partner
  Education: BA, Economics, Yale University; MA, Accounting and Finance, New York University
  Background: Merrill Lynch
  Directorships: Bytemobile Corporation
  Jeff Low, Partner
  Education: Business Management degree, Harvard University; BA, MA, comparative literature, University of California, Unibersity of Massachusetts
  Background: Ericsson's Data Networking Division
  Directorships: I-Controls

646 EASTWARD CAPITAL PARTNERS
432 Cherry Street
West Newton, MA 02465

Phone: 617-969-6700 Fax: 617-969-7900
e-mail: contacts@eastwardcp.com
web: www.eastwardcp.com

Mission Statement: To work with venture capital firms to provide venture debt and equity financing to their portfolio companies.
Fund Size: $300 million
Founded: 1994
Industry Group Preference: Information Technology, Communications, Alternative Energy, Clean Technology, Healthcare
Portfolio Companies: Aurion Pro Solutions, Best Doctors, Blue Cod Technologies, Booker Software, Brickstream, Clearent, Conductor, Digital Ocean, Dormeo, eChalk, Ecosense Lighting, Edgewater Networks, Everbridge, FirstBest Systems, Gilt, Hillcrest, Host Analytics, Invaluable, Lifescript, Linkwell Health, Management Health Solutions, Menara, MinuteKey, Mutual Mobile, myThings, Neat, NetBio, The New Orleans Exchange, Next Step Living, Nomis Solutions, NutraClick, Persado, Plated, PlumChoice, Qualtre, Quantenna, Resilient Systems, Rocksbox, ScaleMP, Simplivity, SnagaJob, Solarflare Communications, Tabula Rasa, Tracx, Trade Desk, TraderTools, Travora, Triad Semiconductor, UStream, Vanu, View, Wealth Engine, Xactly, Xiotech, xMatters, Xtalic, Zest Finance

Key Executives:
Dennis P Cameron, Founding Partner
e-mail: dennis@eastwardcp.com
Education: BS, Marketing & Finance, Northeastern University
Background: Founder, CommVest; John Hancock Leasing; CIT; MeesPierson
Edward I Dresner, Investment Partner
e-mail: edward@eastwardcp.com
Education: BA, Economics, Hamilton College
Background: Managing Director, MeesPierson; Credit Analyst, Chemical Bank
Nick Bologna, Investment Partner
e-mail: nick@eastwardcp.com
Education: BS, Finance, University of Connecticut
Background: Applied Telecommunications Technologies; VP, Marketing, Stratus Computer; VP, Sales, Marketing & Service, Sequoia Systems; Senior Advisor, Needham & Company; IBM
Tim O'Loughlin, Investment Partner
e-mail: tim@eastwardcp.com
Education: BA, Economics, Boston College
Background: Vencore Capital; Silicon Valley Bank
Chris Bodnar, Investment Partner
e-mail: chris@eastwardcp.com
Education: Boston University; MBA, Cornell University
Background: Advisor, Metabolix; Bear Stearns; Great Hill Partners; Ladenburg Thalmann

647 ECHELON VENTURES
300 Fifth Ave.
3rd Floor
Waltham, MA 02451

Phone: 781-419-9850 Fax: 781-419-9851

Mission Statement: Seeks investments in companies with a proprietary enabling technology in IT, communications, and life sciences.
Geographic Preference: New England
Fund Size: $1-5 million
Investment Criteria: Early Stage
Industry Group Preference: Software, Hardware, Communications, Drug Discovery, Medical Devices, Semiconductor Manufacturing, Alternative Power
Portfolio Companies: BioTrove, LumeRx, Inc., Avedro, Inc., SiteScape, Inc.

Key Executives:
Alfred S Woodworth Jr, Managing Director
Education: AB, Harvard College; MBA, Amos Tuck School at Dartmouth
Background: State Street Bank; Director, Strategic Development, Commercial Banking Group
A Leigh Fulmer, Director Investor Relations
Education: cum laude, Finance, Boston University
Background: Manager, Investor Relations, Brodeur Worldwide

648 ECLIPSE VENTURES
514 High Street
Suite 4
Palo Alto, CA 94301

Phone: 650-720-4667
e-mail: admin@eclipse.vc
web: eclipse.vc

Mission Statement: Eclipse Ventures partners with companies who wish to transform and redefine industries.
Founded: 2015
Investment Criteria: Early Stage
Industry Group Preference: Artificial Intelligence, Automotive, Semiconductor, Manufacturing, Networking, Communications
Portfolio Companies: 6 River Systems, Angury, AxleHire, Bright Machines, BrightInsights, Cerebras Systems, Cheetah, ClearMetal, Clearpath Robotics, Common Networks, Flex Logix Technologies, InsidePacket, Impossible Aerospace, Instrumental, Invicta Medical, June Life, Kindred, Kinema Systems, Light, Lucira Health, Owlet Baby Care, Oxide, Reliable Robotics, Skyryse, Spell, Swift Navigation, SwipeSense, Symbio Robotics, Tenstorrent, Third Wave Automation, Tortuga Logic, Veev, VulcanForms, Wayve

Key Executives:
Lior Susan, Founding Partner
e-mail: lior@eclipse.vc
Background: Advisor, Intucell; Founder, Flextronics; General Partner, Formation 8; Co-Founder, Farm2050; Co-Founder, Bright Machines; Angel Investor
Pierre Lamond, Partner
e-mail: pierre@eclipse.vc
Education: MS, Physics, University of Toulouse, France
Background: Co-Founder/CTO/GM, National Semiconductor; General Partner, Sequoia Capital; General Partner, Khosla Ventures; Senior Advisor, Formation 8
Greg Reichow, Partner
e-mail: greg.reichow@eclipse.vc
Education: BS, Mechanical & Industrial Engineering, University of Minnesota
Background: Cypress Semiconductor; SVP of Operations, SunPower; VP of Operations/Production, Tesla Motors
Seth Winterroth, Partner
e-mail: seth@eclipse.vc
Directorships: Invicta Medical; Third Wave Automation; Wayve
Adam Bryant, Partner
e-mail: adam@eclipse.vc
Education: BS, Mechanical Engineering, Worcester Polytechnic Institute; MS, Mechanical Engineering, Northeastern University; MBA, Harvard Business School
Background: Lead Design Engineer, GE Aviation; Director of Product Control, Tesla Motors, Director of Customer Programs, Proterra Inc.
Justin Butler, Partner
e-mail: justin@eclipse.vc
Education: BS, Chemical Engineering, University of California, Santa Barbara; MBA, MIT Sloan School of Management
Background: Process Engineer, DuPont; Director of Business Development, Synthetic Genomics; VP of Commercial Development, Misfit Wearables
Directorships: Lucira Health; Tenstorrent Inc.; Common Networks; Tortuga Logic Inc.; Dragonfly Group; Spell; BrightInsight
Greg Lyon, Operating Partner/CFO
e-mail: greg@eclipse.vc
Education: BS, Accounting, Sonoma State University
Background: Manager, Financial Services,

Venture Capital & Private Equity Firms / Domestic Firms

PricewaterCooper; Financial Manager, Sequoia Capital; Controller, Formation 8

649 ECOAST ANGEL NETWORK
Portsmouth, NH

e-mail: ecoastangels@gmail.com
web: www.ecoastangels.com

Mission Statement: The eCoast Angel Network was formed in July 2000 by a group of like-minded investors from the Portsmouth NH area. Our members come from diverse backgrounds but have a unified purpose: to support economic development, principally in the Coast region, to foster entrepreneurial spirit and to identify investment opportunities.

Geographic Preference: New Hampshire Coastal Region
Average Investment: $250,000 - $2 million
Investment Criteria: Early-Stage
Industry Group Preference: Technology, E-Commerce & Manufacturing, Healthcare, Industrial Products
Portfolio Companies: Aras, AtlasWatersystems, Bortech, CitySquares, Content Raven, Environments@Work LLC, Groove Mobile, IAM Registry, In Addition, FastAsset, Parcxmart, Punchbowl, SemiNex, SingleToken Security, SmartPackets, SourceIQ, StatSocial, Thebizmo, V-Kernel, Vaward Communications, ZipRealty

650 ECOSYSTEM VENTURES
P.O. Box 3347
Saratoga, CA 95070

Phone: 408-426-8040 Fax: 408-867-1441
e-mail: info@ecosystemventures.com
web: www.ecosystemventures.com

Mission Statement: A venture capital investment and strategic consulting firm that is dedicated to building sustainable companies around significant technologies and innovative business ideas. We focus primarily, but not exclusively on companies that are based in Europe or have strong European ties.

Investment Criteria: Startup/Seed, Early Stage
Industry Group Preference: Clean Technology, Industrial, Technology, Energy
Portfolio Companies: AngelList, Appstores Inc., Attolight AG, Autonet Mobile, Bartab, Checkbook, Cleanify, cloudGuide SA, Collanos AG, Dekko, Draft, Facebook, Gladiator Entertainment, GolfNet, Graphic.ly, Illumenix, I Need MD, Investiere.ch, Lagotek, LESS, MamaMancini's, Microventures LLC, MixRank Inc., Mobile Mantra Inc., MothersClick, MXD3D Inc., Nanotion AG, NexTier Networks, NoiseToys, Oasis Media Corporation, OpenPeak, Philz Coffee, PlaySpanTM, Pooch, PowerInbox, Pure Swiss Water AG, Rainforest, rVita, SchooLa Inc., SDK Biotechnologies, shopobot Inc., Simplibuy, SpaceX, Spectralus Corporation, Squirro AG, StarStreet Inc., Storefront Inc., SVOX AG, TimeSight Systems, Twitter, VEENOME Inc., visual.ly, VoiceBase, Zikon, Zubio

Other Locations:
60 Weingartenstrasse
Zurich 8708 Mannedorf
Switzerland
Phone: +41 (44) 586-7108 Fax: +41 (44) 790-2187

Key Executives:
Alexander Fries, General Partner
Education: BA Finance/MBA Telecommunications, University of San Francisco; Swiss Banking Diploma, UBS
Background: Telecommunications Analyst, Credit Suisse; Executive Vice President of Sales & Marketing, Advance Visual Communications; Senior Market Manager, Lucent Technologies Wireless Broadband Division

651 EDELSON TECHNOLOGY PARTNERS
180 Summit Avenue
Suite 205
Montvale, NJ 07645

Phone: 201-930-9898 Fax: 201-930-8899
web: www.edelsontech.com

Mission Statement: Edelson Technology Partners is a venture capital firm focused on providing support to multinational technology corporations in the areas of venture capital, consulting, and mergers and acquisitions.

Geographic Preference: Mostly United States, Europe, Asia, Canada
Fund Size: $150 million
Founded: 1984
Average Investment: $1 - $3 million
Investment Criteria: Seed, Startups, First-Stage, Second-Stage, Later Stage, Mezzanine
Industry Group Preference: Technology, Telecommunications, Life Sciences, Software, Environment, Consumer, Internet
Portfolio Companies: EXA, GIGA, Lifelines Technology, Lithium Technology, Portable Energy Products, Satcom, Savoy Entertainment Group, Vehicular Technologies, xSides

Key Executives:
Harry Edelson, Founder/Managing Director
e-mail: harry@edelsontech.com
Education: BS, Physics, Brooklyn College; MBA, Management, New York University
Background: Computer Engineer, Unisys; Transmission Engineer, AT&T; CEO, Special Purpose Acquisition Company; Founder & President, China Investment Group

652 EDF VENTURES
425 North Main Street
Ann Arbor, MI 48104-1147

Phone: 734-663-3213 Fax: 734-663-7358

Mission Statement: EDF Ventures invests in growing companies that are early in their development, with a focus on untapped markets.

Geographic Preference: Midwest
Fund Size: $170 million
Founded: 1987
Average Investment: $1.5 - $5 million
Minimum Investment: $500,000
Investment Criteria: Early-Stage
Industry Group Preference: Healthcare, Information Technology
Portfolio Companies: AlfaLight, Alure, Arbor Networks, Arxan, BioSet, Cerensis Therapeutics, DirectFlow Medical, Eleme Medical, GenVec, Greenplum, HandyLab, HealthCareSolutions, IntelePeer, IntraLase, Lycera, Pixelworks, QuadraSpec, Sircon, Sonoma Orthopedic Products, TransCorp, ValenTx, Vontoo, Xtera, Zyray Wireless

Key Executives:
Mary Lincoln Campbell, Founder/Managing Director
Education: BA, English, MBA, University of Michigan; MA, Special Education, Fairfield University
Directorships: IntelePeer, ValenTx
Mike DeVries, Managing Director
Education: BA, Calvin College; MBA, Grand Valley State University
Background: President & CEO, A-Med Systems; Medtronic; DLP
Directorships: CardioMetrix, Direct Flow Medical
Linda Fingerle, Chief Financial Officer/Principal
Education: Michigan State University; MBA, Ross School of Business, University of Michigan; CPA
Background: Group Operating President, MascoTech; Senior Audit Manager, Arthur Andersen & Co.

653 EDGEWATER CAPITAL PARTNERS
5005 Rockside Road
Suite 840
Independence, OH 44131

Phone: 216-292-3838
e-mail: info@edgewatercapital.com
web: www.edgewatercapital.com

Mission Statement: Private equity investment firm focused on investing in lower middle market specialty performance material companies.

Geographic Preference: North America
Fund Size: $85 million
Founded: 1980
Average Investment: $10 - $50 million
Minimum Investment: $2 million
Investment Criteria: Corporate Divestitures, Family Businesses, Management Buyouts
Industry Group Preference: Technology, Chemicals, Distribution, Manufacturing, Pharmaceuticals
Portfolio Companies: Callery, ChemQuest chemicals, DanChem, Far Chemical Inc., FMI, Gabriel Performance Products, H&S, Haematologic Technologies, Lycus Ltd., Naprotek, Particle Dynamics, PChem, PolyAd Services, Preferred Rubber, Pure Wafer, Royal Adhesives & Sealands, Syrgis Performance Initiators, Tractech Inc., Tritec Performance Solutions, Turbonetics

Key Executives:
  Christopher Childres, Founder/Managing Partner
  Education: BA, English & American Literature, Northwestern University; JD, Fordham University School of Law
  Background: Attorney, M&A Department, Winthrop, Stimson, Putnam & Roberts
  Directorships: Lycus Chemical, Hahn Elastomer, Royal Adhesives and Sealants
  Ryan Meany, Managing Partner
  Education: BS, Business Administration, Miami University; MBA, Case Western Reserve University
  Background: Investment Analyst, NatCity Investments
  Richard Schwarz, Partner
  Education: BS, Chemical Engineering, Ohio State University; MBA, Case Western Reserve University
  Background: Founder, Sycamore Partners LLC; Director & President, Laurel Industries; Management Consultant, AT Kearney
  Directorships: Syrgis
  Brian Leonard, Chief Financial Officer/Chief Compliance Officer
  Education: BS, Accounting, Miami University
  Background: Director, Transaction Advisory Services, Grant Thornton LLP; VP, Finance, Workflow.com
  Directorships: Cleveland Chapter of the Association for Corporate Growth

654 EDGEWATER FUNDS
900 North Michigan Avenue
Suite 1800
Chicago, IL 60611

Phone: 312-649-5666
e-mail: info@edgewaterfunds.com
web: www.edgewaterfunds.com

Mission Statement: Based in Chicago, The Edgewater Funds is a private equity firm focused on providing lower middle market companies with resources to help drive their growth.

Fund Size: $1.4 billion
Minimum Investment: $10 - $20 million
Investment Criteria: Lower Middle Market, Buyouts, Growth Equity
Industry Group Preference: Business to Business, Information Technology, Software, Consumer Services, Service Industries, Services, Biotechnology
Portfolio Companies: Accutest Laboratories, American Piping Products, AMF, Apex Parks Group, Avante Health Solutions, BarrirerSafe Solutions International, Beverage House, Bolder Healthcare Solutions, Brilliance Financial Technology, Confluent Health, Dantom Systems Inc., DataBank, DBS Communications Inc., Deflecto, Dental Services Group, ETX, Extended Care Information Network, ExteNet Systems, Family Home Health Services, FishNet Security, Genesis Financial Solutions, G&H Orthodontics, Harrington Holdings Inc., Helicon Re, Horseburgh & Scott Co., Industrial Service Solutions, ITSolutions, Med America Recycling, Teddy Bear Portraits, NetCentrics, Nielsen-Kellerman, Orizon, PGI International, PowerQuest, Priority Express, Private Bancorp Inc., Rensa Filtration, Salter Labs, Sechrist Industries Inc., Sensor Solutions Holdings, Skyware Global, Testing Services Holdings, Southern Petroleum Laboratories Inc., State National Companies, Steel & OBbrien Manufacturing, TAL International, Technical Solutions Holdings Inc., Trausch Industries, Triwater Holdings, Unitech Aerospace, Vertical Bridge, Westar Aerospace & Defense Group, Would Care Solutions Inc., WRSCompass

Key Executives:
  James Gordon, Founder/Managing Partner
  e-mail: jim@edgewaterfunds.com
  Education: BA, Northwestern University
  Background: President, Gordon Foods; Gordon's Wholesale
  Gregory Jones, Senior Partner
  e-mail: greg@edgewaterfunds.com
  Education: BS, Miami University; MBA, Kellogg Graduate School of Management, Northwestern University
  Background: President & COO, Reliable Corporation; Senior VP, APAC Teleservices; Chairman & CEO, uBid.com
  David Tolmie, Senior Partner
  e-mail: dave@edgewaterfunds.com
  Education: BA, University of Virginia; MBA, Harvard Business School
  Background: CEO & President, Yesmail; Senior VP, Operations, Bally Total Fitness; Consultant, McKinsey & Company; Product Manager, General Mills
  Directorships: Field Museum of Natural History, Opportunity International, Illinois Venture Capital Association, Chicagoland Entrepreneurial Center
  Scott Brown, Senior Partner
  e-mail: scottbedgewaterfunds.com
  Education: BA, Economics, Colgate University; MBA, Booth School of Business
  Background: Baird Capital Partners; JP Morgan
  Brian Peiser, Partner
  e-mail: brianp@edgewaterfunds.com
  Education: BS, Electrical Engineering, Cornell University; MBA, University of Michigan Business School; CFA
  Background: Senior Associate, Deloitte & Touche Corporate Finance; Senior Analyst, Lehman Brothers
  Gerald Saltarelli, Partner
  e-mail: gerald@edgewaterfunds.com
  Education: BA, Bucknell University; MBA, University of Michigan Business School
  Background: Director, Conway MacKenzie & Dunleavy; Associate, One Equity Partners; Analyst, M&A Group, William Blair & Company
  Stephen Natali, Partner
  e-mail: stephen@edgewaterfunds.com
  Education: BA, Economics, Northwestern University
  Background: Associate, Investment Banking Division, JP Morgan Securities
  Scott Meadow, Associate Partner
  e-mail: scott.meadow@chicagobooth.edu
  Education: AB, Harvard College; MBA, Harvard Business School
  Background: Clinical Professor of Entrepreneurship, University of Chicago; General Partner, The Sprout Group

Venture Capital & Private Equity Firms / Domestic Firms

655 EDISON PARTNERS
281 Witherspoon Street
Princeton, NJ 08540

Phone: 609-896-1900
web: www.edisonpartners.com

Mission Statement: Edison Partners provides financing and guidance to growth companies. They are a leading investor focused on information technology companies located in the Mid-Atlantic region of the United States.

Geographic Preference: Boston to DC Corridor
Fund Size: $550 million
Founded: 1986
Average Investment: $6 - 10 million
Minimum Investment: $5 - 8 million
Investment Criteria: Venture Capital, Expansion, Acquisition, Consolidation, Secondary Stock, MBO, Corporate Spinout, Recapitalization
Industry Group Preference: Information Technology, Software, Communications, Internet Technology, Electronic Technology, Financial Services, Pharmaceuticals, Fintech, Healthcare Information Technology, Marketing, E-Commerce & Manufacturing, Enterprise Applications
Portfolio Companies: Act!, All Traffic Solutions, Andera, Archive Systems, Arkadium, Axent, Axial, Best!, BFS Capital, Bill Trust, Blue Cod Technologies, Bricata, Cadient Group, CambridgeSoft, Check Point HR, Clearpool, ClearPoint, Clinverse, ComplySci, Dendrite, DPM, Diagnosis One, Edge Trade, Esentire, EVO, Fiberlink, Fishbowl, FolioDynamix, Gain Capital, GAN Integrity, Giant Realm, Health Market Science, High Branch Software, IContracts, Itemmaster, IQ Media, Incurrent, Jornaya, Kemp Technologies, Kds, Liberty Tax Service, Lincor, Logfire, LookBookHQ, M5, Magnetic, Mathsoft, MDY, MoneyLion, Motionsoft, Neat, Netprospex, NFR Security, Notable Solutions, Octagon Research Soltuions Inc., Operative, Options City, PHX, Pixability, Plum Choice, Portico, Predata, Presidium, Princeton Financial Systems, Realmatch, Receptiv, Red Vision, Rewards Now, Salsa, Scivantage, Sentori, Signet Accel, Smartanalyst, Softgate Systems, Solovis, Sonicbids, Tangoe, Tartec, Telarix, Terminus, TetraData, Tracx, TraderTools, TrialScope, TripleLift, Truecommerce, Uptivity, Verilogue, VFA, VirtualEdge, Virutal Health, Visual Networks, Vocus, VoxMobile, Wyng, Zagster, Zelis

Key Executives:
Ryan Ziegler, General Partner
609-873-9225
e-mail: ryan@edisonpartners.com
Education: BS, Business Administration, BA, Biology, Bucknell University
Background: Associates Program, SEI
Directorships: Jornaya, Magnetic, Receptiv, Offerpop, Tracx, Terminus, TripleLift
Chris Sugden, Managing Partner
e-mail: csugden@edisonpartners.com
Education: BA, Accounting, Michigan State University
Background: EVP, Princeton eCom; Supervisor, PricewaterhouseCoopers
Tom Vander Schaaff, General Partner
e-mail: tvanderschaaff@edisonpartners.com
Education: BEng., Engineering/Management Systems, Princeton University
Background: Senior Associate, MMC Capital; Associate, CIBC Capital Partners; Financial Analyst, CIB Oppenheimer's Technology Investment Banking Group
Michael Kopelman, General Partner
e-mail: mkopelman@edisonpartners.com
Education: BA, Economics, University of Pennsylvania; MBA, Wharton School
Background: Investment Banker, Credit Suisse First Boston; Founder, E*OFFERING; Co-President, Wharton Private Equity Partners
Lenard Marcus, General Partner
e-mail: lmarcus@edisonpartners.com
Education: BA, Industrial Engineering, Stanford University; MBA, Columbia Business School
Background: Financial Analyst, IBM Global Services; Manager, Princeton eCom; Investment Banker, Wachovia Securities
Kelly Ford Buckley, General Partner
e-mail: kford@edisonpartners.com
Education: BA, Michigan State University
Background: SundaySky; LivePerson; Lotus; Groove Network

656 EGL HOLDINGS
3017 Bolling Way NE
No 18 Buckhead
Atlanta, GA 30305

Phone: 404-949-8300
e-mail: salmassaro@eglholdings.com
web: www.eglholdings.com

Mission Statement: Venture capital and corporate finance advisory services to companies in a wide variety of industries and geographical markets.

Geographic Preference: Southwestern United States
Fund Size: $70 million
Founded: 1988
Average Investment: $100,000 - $500,000
Investment Criteria: Mergers & Acquisitions, Divestiture, Expansion, Later Stage
Industry Group Preference: Medical Devices, Enterprise Software, Communications, Information Technology, Healthcare, Technology
Portfolio Companies: Echo11, Intellinet, MET-TEST, The Pedowitz Group, Purple Cows, SimCraft, SpeedTracs

Key Executives:
Richard V Lawry, Co-Founder/Chairman/Managing Partner
404-949-8306
e-mail: rlawry@eglholdings.com
Background: Co-Founder & President, British American Business Group; Divisional Accountant, BICC plc; Glynwed International; Atlanta Arrangements
Directorships: Airo Wireless, Alliance Theater
David O Ellis, Managing Partner
404-949-8310
e-mail: doellis@eglholdings.com
Education: BS, Chemistry, PhD, Biophysics, St. Andrews University; Senior Executive Program, MIT
Background: COO & CEO, BH Blackwell; CFO, Software Sciences International; Oxford Instruments plc
Salvatore A Massaro, Managing Director
404-949-8303
e-mail: samassaro@eglholdings.com
Education: BS, Business Administration, Georgetown University; MBA, Harvard University
Background: Prudential-Bache Venture Capital; Telesphere International; Price Waterhouse
Charles Elliott, Senior Vice President
704-300-8650
e-mail: celliott@eglholdings.com
Education: MBA, University of North Carolina, Charlotte
Tom McDermott, Managing Director
e-mail: tmcdermott@eglholdings.com
Education: MBA, University of North Carolina at Chapel Hill

657 ELAB VENTURES
635 Mariners Island
Suite 204
San Mateo, CA 94404

Phone: 650-551-5000
web: elabvc.com

Venture Capital & Private Equity Firms / Domestic Firms

Mission Statement: eLab Ventures is an early stage venture capital fund investing in disruptive technology that will fuel the rise of autonomous and connected vehicles.

Geographic Preference: Silicon Vallet and Michigan

Other Locations:
505 E Liberty Street
Suite LL500
Ann Arbor, MI 48104
Phone: 734-926-5221

Key Executives:
Rick Bolander, Managing Director
e-mail: rick@elabvc.com
Education: BS, MS, University of Michigan; MBA, Harvard Business School
Background: Founder, Blue Sky Ventures; General Partner, Apex Venture Partners; Co-Founder, Gabriel Venture Partners

Paul Brown, Managing Director
e-mail: paul@elabvc.com
Education: Ba, MBA, University of Michigan
Background: VP, Capital Markets, Michigan Economic Development Corp.; Co-Founder, Front Foor Insights

Scott Chou, Managing Director
e-mail: scott@elabvc.com
Education: Harvard University; Stanford University
Background: Gabriel Venture Partners

Doug Neal, Managing Director
e-mail: doug@elabvc.com
Education: Central Michigan University
Background: Co-Founder, Mobile Automation; Managing Director, University of Michigan Center for Entrepreneurship

Bob Stefanski, Managing Director
Education: University of Michigan
Background: EVP, TIBCO Software

658 ELEMENT PARTNERS
565 E Swedesford Road
Suite 207
Wayne, PA 19087

Phone: 610-964-8004 **Fax:** 610-964-8005
e-mail: patti@elementpartners.com
web: www.elementpartners.com

Mission Statement: Element Partners is a private equity firm focused on growth equity investments in companies that offer innovative products and services to the industrial, energy and environment industries.

Fund Size: $800 million
Founded: 1995
Average Investment: $10 - $50 million
Investment Criteria: Greater than $20 million in revenue, enterprise values between $20 to $200 million, Acquisitions, MBO, LBO, Corporate Divestitures, Industry Consolidations, Minority Investments
Industry Group Preference: Energy, Clean Technology, Manufacturing, Water, Environmental Controls, Chemicals, Advanced Materials
Portfolio Companies: 212 Resources, Agility Fuel Systems, Amp Electrical Distribution Services, AquaVenture Holdings, Detechtion Technologies, Ecore, Energex, Hayward Gordon, LumaSense Technologies, Petra Systems, Quench USA, Seven Seas Water, Soleras Advanced Coatings, TAS Energy, TPI Composites

Key Executives:
David Lincoln, Founder & General Partner
e-mail: david@elementpartners.com
Education: BA, Geology, Colgate University; MS, Energy Management & Policy, University of Pennsylvania
Background: Co-Founder & Managing Director, EnerTech Capital Partners; President & CEO, Deven Resources; Partners, CMS Companies; UGI Corporation
Directorships: 212 Resources, Amp, Detechtion, Electro-Petroleum, Environmental Drilling Solutions, Petra Solar, Wasatch Wind

Michael DeRosa, General Partner
e-mail: mderosa@elementpartners.com
Education: BS, Electrical Engineering, Georgia Tech; MBA, Wharton School, University of Pennsylvania
Background: Partner, Industrial Technology Fund, Cordova Ventures; Principal, EnerTech Capital Partners; Senior Associate, Safeguard International Fund
Directorships: Agility Fuel Systems, AMP Electrical Distribution Services, Detechtion Technologies, Ecore International, TPI Composites, TAS Energy

Michael Bevan, General Partner
e-mail: michael@elementpartners.com
Education: BA, English, Denison University; MBA, Wharton School
Background: Partner, Advent International; Principal, EnerTech Capital Partners; SEI Investments

659 ELEVATE VENTURES
50 East 91st Street
Suite 213
Indianapolis, IN 46240

Phone: 317-975-1901
web: www.elevateventures.com

Mission Statement: Elevate Ventures nurtures and develops emerging and existing high-potential businesses into high-performing, Indiana-based companies.

Geographic Preference: Indiana
Founded: 2011
Industry Group Preference: Life Sciences, Information Technology, Advanced Manufacturing
Portfolio Companies: 3BG Supply Co., Apl Next Ed, AgenDx Biosciences, AIT Bioscience, Animated Dynamics Inc., Apexian Pharmaceuticals, App Press, AquaSpy, Atlas 3D, Baby Plus, Blue Pillar, Bolstra, Clear Object, Clear Scholar, Compendium, Confuence Pharmaceuticals, Costello, Curvo, Diagnotes, Emerging Threats, Fast BioMedical, FNEX, Go Electric, Hc1.com, Healthcare Anywhere, Immune Works, Inscope, Jada Beauty, Kinney Group, Lumavate, Market Wagon, MyCoi, Oak Financial, Owl Manor Veterinary, PactSafe, PartTec, PayK12, PDS Biotechnology, Edwin, PolicyStat, Prosolia, RedPost, Salesvue, Sharpen, Sigstr, Smarter HQ, Smartfile, Solstice Medical, SonarMed, Spensa, Springbuk, SproutBox, SteadyServ Technologies, Stray Light, Sword Diagnostics, Targamite, The Bee Corp, Theratome Bio, Trek10, Ultra Angkle, Upper Hand Managed Sports, Vennli, Verve Health, VoCare, Wellfount, Wolfe Diversified, Wolfpack, Wordsentry, Xtreme Alternative Defense Systems, Zio

Key Executives:
Chris LaMothe, Chief Executive Officer
Education: Kelley School of Business, University of Indiana
Ting Gootee, Chief Investments Officer
Education: BA, Beijing University; MA, Purdue University; MBA, Finance, Indiana University
Background: Deputy Director, 21 Fund

660 ELEVATION PARTNERS
352 Sharon Park Drive
Suite 522
Menlo Park, CA 94025

Phone: 650-687-6700 **Fax:** 650-687-6710
e-mail: info@elevation.com
web: www.elevation.com

Mission Statement: A leading private equity firm focused on large-scale investments in media, entertainment and technology businesses.

Industry Group Preference: Media, Entertainment, Digital Media & Marketing, Software

Venture Capital & Private Equity Firms / Domestic Firms

Portfolio Companies: BioWare/Pandemic Studios, Facebook, Forbes, MarketShare, Move, Palm, Yelp

Key Executives:
Fred Anderson, Managing Director & Co-Founder
Education: BA, Whittier College; MBA, University of California, LA
Background: Executive Vice President, Apple Computer
Directorships: Apple, Crystal Decisions, 3COM
Roger McNamee, Managing Director & Co-Founder
Education: BA, Yale College; MBA, Amos Tuck School of Business Administration, Dartmouth College
Background: Co-Founder, Silver Lake Partners; Co-Founder, Integral Capital Partners
Bret Pearlman, Managing Director & Co-Founder
Education: BS, Economics, Wharton School, University of Pennsylvania; BS, Engineering, Moore School of Electrical Engineering
Background: Analyst, Blackstone Group
Directorships: BioWare/Pandemic Studios, SDI Media, Forbes Media
Avie Tevanian, Managing Director
Education: BA, Mathematics, University of Rochester; MS & PhD, Computer Science, Carnegie Mellon University
Background: Senior Executive Team, Apple, Inc.; Vice President, Software Engineering, NeXT Computer
Directorships: Dolby Laboratories, Tellme Networks
Adam Hopkins, Managing Director & Founding Member
Education: AB, Economics, Princeton University; MBA, Stanford University Graduate School of Business
Background: Associate, Silver Lake Partners; Morgan Stanley Capital Partners

661 ELM STREET VENTURES
33 Whitney Avenue
New Haven, CT 06510

Phone: 203-401-4201
e-mail: venture@elmvc.com
web: www.elmvc.com

Mission Statement: Elm Street Ventures offers experience and venture capital to seed and early stage businesses and is dedicated to helping entrepreneurs, scientists and engineers build significant technology and life sciences companies.

Fund Size: $22 million
Average Investment: $100,000 - $2.5 million
Minimum Investment: $100,000
Investment Criteria: Seed-Stage, Early-Stage
Industry Group Preference: Life Sciences, Diagnostics, Medical Devices, Therapeutics, Healthcare Information Technology, Healthcare Services
Portfolio Companies: Accelerated Orthopedic Technologies, Affomix Corporation, Ancera Corporation, Arvinas Corporation, AxioMx, BioRelix, Desmos, Iconic Therapeutics, Kolltan Pharmaceuticals, Occam Sciences, P2 Science, Retail Optimization, Samara Innovations, ScrollMotion, ShareGrove

Key Executives:
Rob Bettigole, Managing Partner
Education: BS, Engineering & Applied Science, Yale University; MPPM, Yale School of Management
Background: Partner, Rothschild Inc.; Partner, Investor AB; Founder, Surety Technologies
Directorships: AxioMx, Samara Innovations, Affomix Corporation, Metagenomix
Chris McLeod, Managing Partner
Education: BS, Yale University; MS, Sloan School of Management, MIT
Background: CEO, AxioMx; President/CEO, 454 Life Sciences; EVP, CuraGen; CEO, Havas Interative
Brian Dixon, Venture Partner
Education: BS, University of Michigan; PhD, Organic Chemistry, MIT
Background: VP, Bayer HealthCare; Presient/CEO, BioRelix Inc.
Rick Stahl, Venture Partner
Education: BS, Physics, Emory University; MD, Vanderbilt University; MBA, University of New Haven
Background: Limited Partner, Sachem Ventures; Senior Associate Dean for Strategic Relationships, Frank H. Netter MD School of Medicine, Quinnipiac University; VP, Yale New Haven Health System

662 ELYSIUM VENTURE CAPITAL
440 N Wolfe Road
Sunnyvale, CA 94085

Phone: 408-524-1600
e-mail: contact@elysium.vc
web: ely.vc

Mission Statement: Elysium's experienced team offers guidance in Business Development, International Markets, Deal Structuring, Strategy, Recruiting, and Product Marketing.

Geographic Preference: US, Europe, China
Investment Criteria: Early Stage, Growth Stage
Industry Group Preference: Consumer Tech, Blockchain, Fintech, Artificial Intelligence
Portfolio Companies: Acquired.io, Alpaca, Anchorage, Capture.io, Flo, Knack, LooNa, Node, Prisma, Telegram

Key Executives:
Peter Xu, Managing Partner
Background: Head of Alternative Investments, Galaxy Group
Nikolai Roeshkin, Managing Partner
Eric Ly, Venture Partner
Background: Co-Founder/CTO, LinkedIn
William O'Brien, Venture Partner

663 EMBARK HEALTHCARE

web: www.embarkhc.com

Mission Statement: Embark Healthcare invests in repurposing drugs. The company works with pharmaceutical companies in the later stage of their business to license and increase the potential benefit of both investors and patients in need.

Founded: 2001
Average Investment: $250,000 - $1 million
Investment Criteria: Later Stage
Industry Group Preference: Healthcare, Pharmaceutical
Portfolio Companies: Learmont Pharmaceuticals, Martin Pharmaceuticals, Remedy Pharmaceuticals, Woolsey Pharmaceuticals

Key Executives:
David M Geliebter, Managing Partner
e-mail: david@embarkhc.com
Background: Founder, Carson Group; Founding Principal/President, Evolution Capital; Founder, Harvard Capital
Directorships: Chairman/CEO, Critical Diagnostics; Executive Chairman, Remedy Pharmaceuticals
Sven M Jacobson, Partner
e-mail: sven@embarkhc.com
Education: BSc, Electrical Engineering, MBA, Business Administration & Management, University of the Witwatersrand
Background: Vice President, Leisureplanet; Board Member, Rennies Travel and Financial Services Group
Directorships: Critical Diagnostics, Remedy Pharmaceuticals

664 EMBARK VENTURES
610 Santa Monica Boulevard
Suite 226
Santa Monica, CA 90401

web: www.embark.com

Mission Statement: Embark Ventures invests in "deep tech" companies, within sectors such as life sciences, material science, robotics, automation, semiconductors, software computing and manufacturing.

Founded: 2017
Investment Criteria: Pre-Seed, Seed
Industry Group Preference: Security, Life Science, Manufacturing, Robotics, Material Science, Semiconductors
Portfolio Companies: Avro Life Sciences, CellFE, InVia Robotics, Jiko, K2 Cyber Security, Kebotix, Kula Bio, SafeAI, SeqOnce, Syntiant, Truvian Health, Via Separations

Key Executives:
Yipeng Zhao, Managing Partner
Education: BS, Michigan State University; MS, University of California, San Diego
Background: Managing Partner, ArcheMatrix Investment Group
Directorships: ZMXY Global Investment Inc.
Peter Lee, Managing Partner
Education: BS/MS, MIT; MBA, Harvard Business School
Background: Product Manager/Senior Engineer, Virtual Ink; Junior Engagement Manager, McKinsey & Company; Managing Director, Fortis Partners; Associate, Clearstone Venture Partners; Investor, Prism Venture; Managing Partner, Baroda Ventures

665 EMERALD OCEAN CAPITAL
1300 Dove Street
Suite 210
Newport Beach, CA 92660

Phone: 949-468-7474

Mission Statement: Invests in companies focused on technology, life sciences and media within the cannabis industry.

Founded: 2013
Industry Group Preference: Cannabis, Life Sciences, Technology

Key Executives:
Doug Francis, Managing Partner
Education: BS, George L. Argyros School of Business Economics, Chapman University
Background: Co-Founder/COO, Canna-Centers; CEO, Weedmaps
Justin Hartfield, Managing Partner
Education: BS, Computer & Information Sciences, University of California Irvine; MBA, Paul Merage School of Business
Background: CEO/Chairman, Weedmaps; SearchCore
Jerry Lotter, Managing Partner
Education: BA, International Relations; BS, International Business, Marshall School of Business, University of Southern California
Background: Co-Founder/Managing Member, Bonfire.com; COO, SearchCore

666 EMERGENCE CAPITAL PARTNERS
160 Bovet Road
Suite 300
San Mateo, CA 94402

Phone: 650-573-3100
e-mail: hello@emcap.com
web: www.emcap.com

Mission Statement: Venture capital firm focused on investing in early and growth-stage enterprise technology companies.

Geographic Preference: United States
Fund Size: $335 million
Founded: 2003
Average Investment: $1 - $10 million
Investment Criteria: Early-Stage, Growth-Stage
Industry Group Preference: Technology-Enabled Services, SaaS, Consumer Services, Digital Media & Marketing, Social Media, Information Services, Cloud Computing
Portfolio Companies: Augmedix, Bill.com, Box, Civitas Learning, Cotap, Crunchbase, Digital Air Strike, Donuts, Doximity, Drivewyze, DroneDeploy, EchoSign, Eversight, Gusto, Handshake, High Alpha, Hightail, InsideView, Insightly, Intacct, Janrain, Lithium, Lotame, Medeanalytics, Navera, Quasar Ventures, Replicon, Restorando, Salesforce.com, SalesLoft, ServiceMax, SteelBrick, SuccessFactors, Textio, Top Hat, TouchCommerce, Veeva Systems, VigLink, Welltok, Xad, Xapo, Yammer, Zoom

Key Executives:
Jason Green, Founder/General Partner
e-mail: jgreen@emcap.com
Education: BA, Economics, Dartmouth College; MBA, Harvard University
Background: General Partner, US Venture Partners; Bain & Company; Carson, Anderson & Stowe
Directorships: CoTap, Lotame, Replicon, ServiceMax, SteelBrick, SalesLoft, xAd
Gordon Ritter, General Partner
e-mail: gritter@emcap.com
Education: BA, Economics, Princeton University
Background: Co-Founder & CEO, Software As Service; Co-Founder & President, Whistle; Co-Founder, Tribe Communications; VP, Capital Markets, Credit Suisse First Boston
Directorships: Ketera Technologies, MarketingGenius
Brian Jacobs, General Partner
e-mail: bjacobs@emcap.com
Education: BS, MS, Mechanical Engineering, Massachusetts Institute of Technology; MBA, Stanford University
Background: General Partner, St. Paul Venture Capital; Security Pacific Venture Capital; Raychem Corporation
Directorships: Visage Mobile, Krugle, Intacct, DVDPlay
Kevin Spain, General Partner
e-mail: kspain@emcap.com
Education: BBA, University of Texas, Austin; MBA, Wharton School, University of Pennsylvania
Background: Corporate Development, Microsoft; Electronic Arts; Co-Founder & CEO, atMadison.com
Santi Subotovsky, Partner
e-mail: ssubotovsky@emcap.com
Education: BS, Economics, St. Andrew's University, Argentina; MBA, Harvard Business School
Background: Advisor, Aqua Capital Partners; Associate, Storm Ventures; Founder, AXG Tecnonexo
Everett Cox, Venture Partner
e-mail: ecox@emcap.com
Education: BS, MS, Stanford University; MBA, University of Southern California
Background: General Partner, St. Paul Venture Capital; Senior VP, Security Pacific Capital
Joe Floyd, General Partner
e-mail: jfloyd@emcap.com
Education: BA, Economics, BS, Business Administration, University of California, Berkeley; MBA, Wharton School, University of Pennsylvania
Background: Senior Associate, Technology Group, American Capital

667 EMERGENT MEDICAL PARTNERS
1735 North First Street
Suite 290
San Jose, CA 95112

Phone: 650-851-0091 **Fax:** 650-851-0095
e-mail: eassist@empllp.com
web: www.emvllp.com

Mission Statement: A life sciences investment firm experienced in the medical field, Emergent Medical Partners focuses on early stage healthcare and medical devices companies.

Fund Size: $37 million
Investment Criteria: Early-Stage

Venture Capital & Private Equity Firms / Domestic Firms

Industry Group Preference: Life Sciences, Medical Devices, Healthcare, Medicine
Portfolio Companies: Biomimedica, Cianna Medical, Crux Biomedical, CyberHeart, CytoPherx, Figure 8, Focal Therapeutics, HeartFlow, Hemosphere, ImaCor, Incline Therapeutics, InSite Medical Technologies, Intuity Medical, Nanostim, Niveus Medical, Novare, NovaSom, OncoHealth, Orlucent, Relievant Medsystems, Reverse Medical, Satiety, Sonoma Orthopedic Products, SP Surgical, Stimwave Technologies, TransCorp Spine, Venous Health Systems

Key Executives:
   Thomas J Fogarty MD, Managing Director
   e-mail: info@emvllp.com
   Education: Xavier University; MD, University of Cincinnati
   Background: Clinical Professor of Surgery, Stanford University; President, Medical Staff, Stanford University Medical Center; Director, Cardiovascular Surgery, Sequoia Medical Center; Founder & General Partner, Three Arch Partners
   Kirt Kirtland, Managing Director
   e-mail: jkirtland@empllp.com
   Education: BS, Biology, Stanford University; MBA, Stanford University School of Business
   Bob Brownell, Managing Director
   e-mail: rbrownell@emvllp.com
   Education: BA, University of California, Berkeley; JD, UCLA Law School
   Background: Partner, MedVenture Associates; VP & General Counsel, TheraSense

668 EMIGRANT CAPITAL
6 East 43rd Street
8th Floor
New York, NY 10017

Phone: 917-262-5245
web: www.emigrantcapital.com

Mission Statement: The private equity division of Emigrant Bank, Emigrant Capital provides financial, operational and strategic experience and resources to middle-market companies.
Geographic Preference: United States
Fund Size: $150 million
Founded: 1999
Average Investment: $5 - $20 million
Minimum Investment: $2 million
Investment Criteria: Middle Market, Growth Equity, Recapitalizations, Turnarounds, Buyouts
Industry Group Preference: Branded Goods, Chemicals, Distribution, Financial Services, Healthcare, Manufacturing, Business to Business, Technology, Education, Consumer Products, Consumer Services, Plastics
Portfolio Companies: AC Label, Cascade Drilling LP, CSA Service Solutions, East West Manufacturing, Fire Door Solutions, Intechra, M Cubed

Key Executives:
   William Staudt, Partner
   e-mail: staudtw@emigrant.com
   Education: BA, Economics, Yale University; JD, University of Michigan Law School
   Background: Founding Managing Partner, Environmental Capital Partners; Managing Partner, Hamilton Capital Partners; President & CEO, Sirit
   Robert Nardelli, Partner
   e-mail: nardellir@emigrant.com
   Education: Western Illinois University; MBA, University of Louisville
   Background: Senior Advisor & CEO, Cerberus Operations & Advisory Company; Chairman, President & CEO, The Home Depot; CEO, GE Transportation Systems; GE Power Systems
   Directorships: Pep Boys, Wounded Warrior Project, BWXT Technologies
   Christopher Staudt, Partner
   e-mail: staudtc@emigrant.com
   Education: BA, Physics, Pomona College; MBA, Harvard Business School
   Background: Co-Founder & Principal, Environmental Capital Partners; CIBC World Markets
   Rafael Romero, Principal
   e-mail: romeror@emigrant.com
   Education: BA, Business Administration, Augustana College; MBA, Harvard Business School
   Background: Invesment Professional, Prospect Capital Management; Analyst, Rockwood Equity Partners

669 EMIL CAPITAL PARTNERS
67 Mason Street
Greenwich, CT 06830

Phone: 203-900-1301
web: www.emilcapitalpartners.com

Mission Statement: Emil Capital is an entrepreneurial, private investment company based in Greenwich, Connecticut, and managed by the fifth generation of one of the world's most successful and venerable family business concerns. We select a small number of investments each year enabling us to complement strong, dedicated management teams with our skills, experience and relationships.
Geographic Preference: United States, Canada, Europe
Industry Group Preference: Consumer Products, Distribution, E-Commerce & Manufacturing
Portfolio Companies: 2|Beans, Aloha, American Giant, Amour Vert, Balance Water, Base Culture, Bare Snacks, Bright Farms, Chef's Plate, Cheribundi, Consumer Physics, Data Council, Goodbelly, Green & Tonic, Kidfresh, Kin Community, Klarna, Milk & Honey, NibMor, Ollie, Pasta Chips, Peach, Persona, Sipp, TCHO, Uber, United by Blue, VariBlend Dual Dispensing Systems, Volition Beauty, Whistle Sports, Wish, YouDinner, Zeel

Key Executives:
   Christian W.E. Haub, Co-Founder & President
   Education: University of Economics & Business Administration, Vienna
   Background: Co-CEO, Tengelmann Group; Chairman/President/CEO, The Great Atlantic & Pacific Tea Company; Investment Banking, Dillon Read
   Andreas Guldin, Founding Partner & Chief Executive Officer
   Education: MS, Psychology, MBA, PhD
   Background: EVP/Co-CFO, Tengelmann Group; CSC Index; PA Consulting

670 EMINENT CAPITAL PARTNERS
245 Park Avenue
39th Floor
New York, NY 10167

Phone: 212-372-8950 Fax: 212-419-9499
web: www.eminentcp.com

Mission Statement: Eminent Capital Partners is a private equity investment firm providing operating expertise to ensure the growth of companies.
Geographic Preference: United States
Fund Size: $100 million
Founded: 1999
Average Investment: $5 - $25 million
Minimum Investment: $5 million
Investment Criteria: Revenues of $10 to $100 million, operating margins of at least 10%
Industry Group Preference: Consumer Products, Light Manufacturing, Distribution, Imports/Exports, Business Products & Services, Industrial Products, Luxury Goods
Portfolio Companies: Bi Coastal Media, Card Personalization Solutions, CP Media LLC, Echolab, Jill-e Designs LLC

Venture Capital & Private Equity Firms / Domestic Firms

Key Executives:
Edward Anchel, Partner
Education: Pennsylvania State University
Background: Founder, President & CEO, Sparkomatic Corporation; Altec Lansing
Directorships: Three Springs Bottling Company
Chuck Parente, Partner
Education: King's College; CPA
Background: Haskins & Sells; Founder & CEO, Parente Randolph PC; President & CEO, C-Tec Corporation
Directorships: Bertels Can Co., Circle Bolt & Nut Co., WP Carey & Co., Community Bank Systems
Hagai Barlev, Venture Partner/Board Member
Education: BA, Economics, Hebrew University of Jerusalem; MBA, Kellogg School of Management
Background: Corporate Finance, Deloitte Consulting; Co-Founder, Addwise

671 EMP GLOBAL
1901 Pennsylvania Avenue NW
Suite 300
Washington, DC 20006

Mission Statement: A worldwide private equity firm with the resources and expertise to source, evaluate and manage private investments globally in both developed and developing markets and across many industrial and commercial sectors.
Geographic Preference: Latin America, Africa, Central and Eastern Europe
Founded: 1994
Investment Criteria: Strategic Partner, Local Partner, minimum rate of return criteria, must be infrastructure project
Industry Group Preference: Telecommunications, Water, Power Technologies, Natural Resources, Infrastructure, Transportation, Agriculture, Retailing
Key Executives:
Donald C. Roth, Managing Partner
Education: BA, Politics, Princeton University; MBA, International Finance, University of Chicago; MSc, The London School of Economics in International Monetary Economics
Background: VP/Treasurer, World Bank

672 ENCAP FLATROCK MIDSTREAM
1826 North Loop 1604 West
Suite 200
San Antonio, TX 78248

Phone: 210-494-6777 Fax: 210-494-6762
web: www.efmidstream.com

Mission Statement: Focuses on providing growth capital to proven midstream management teams in North America.
Geographic Preference: North America
Fund Size: $3 billion
Founded: 2008
Average Investment: $25 - $100 million
Investment Criteria: Growth Stage
Industry Group Preference: Energy, Natural Gas, Oil & Gas, Energy Infrastructure
Portfolio Companies: Aspen Midstream, Caiman Energy II, Candor Midstream, Cardinal Midstream III, Clear Creek Midstream, Cogent Midstream, Edgwater Midstream, Evolution Midstream, Greenfield Midstream, Ironwood Midstream Energy Partners II, Lotus Midstream, Moda Midstream, Nuevo Midstream Dos, Rangeland Energy III, Stakeholder Midstream, Tall Oak Midstream
Other Locations:
3856 South Boulevard
Suite 210
Edmond, OK 73013
Phone: 405-341-9993

1100 Louisiana Street
Suite 5025
Houston, TX 77002
Phone: 281-829-4901 Fax: 281-829-4902

Key Executives:
William D. Waldrip, Founder/Managing Partner
Education: BS, Civil Engineering, Louisiana Tech University; Executive Management Program, Indiana University Graduate School of Business
Background: COO, Lewis Energy Group; VP, Delhi Gas Pipeline
Dennis F. Jaggi, Founder
Education: BS, Mechanical Engineering, Missouri University of Science & Technology
Background: VP & COO, Enogex; VP & Regional Manager, Delhi Pipeline Corporation
William R. Lemmons, Jr., Founder/Managing Partner
Education: BS, Petroleum Engineering, Texas A&M University; MBA, Mays Graduate School of Business, Texas A&M University
Background: VP, Enron Corporation; Texas Oil & Gas Corporation

673 ENCAP INVESTMENTS LP
1100 Louisiana Street
Suite 5025
Houston, TX 77002

Phone: 713-659-6100 Fax: 281-829-4902
web: www.encapinvestments.com

Mission Statement: Provider of private equity to independent oil and gas companies.
Geographic Preference: United States
Fund Size: $6.5 billion
Founded: 1988
Industry Group Preference: Oil & Gas
Portfolio Companies: Advance Energy Partners, American Resource Development, Bold Energy III, Brigadier Oil & Gas, Broad Oak Energy II, Cinco Oil & Gas, Common Resources III, Cornerstone Natural Resources, Council Oak Resources, Dorado E&P, Eclipse Resources, ER Energy Group, EV Energy Partners, Excalibur Resources, Felix Energy, FireWheel Energy, Forge Energy, Fossil Creek Resources, Fuse Energy, Grenadier Energy Partners II, Halcon Resouces, Laramie Energy, Limestone II Holding Company, Lone Star Land & Energy II, Manti Exploration, Marlin Resources, Modern Resources, Oak Valley Resources, OGX Holding II, Paloma Partners IV, PayRock Energy, PennEnergy Resources, Phillips Energy Partners III, Piedra Resources III, Plantation Petroleum Holdings V, Protege Energy III, QStar, Sabalo Energy, Scala Energy, Sierra Oil & Gas, Silver Oak Energy, Silverback Exploration, Southland Royalty Company, Staghorn Petroleum, Talon Oil & Gas II, Tracker Resources Development III, Travis Peak Resources, Unconventional Resources, Venado Oil & Gas

Other Locations:
9651 Katy Freeway
6th Floor
Houston, TX 77024
Phone: 713-659-6100 Fax: 713-659-6130

Key Executives:
David B. Miller, Founder & Managing Partner
Education: BBA, MBA, Southern Methodist University
Background: President, PMC Reserve Acquisition Company; Co-CEO, MAZE Exploration; Republic National Bank of Dallas
Gary R. Petersen, Founder & Managing Partner
Education: BBA, MBA, Texas Tech University
Background: SVP, Corporate Finance, Energy Banking Group, Republic Bank; EVP, Nicklos Oil & Gas Company; US Army
D. Martin Phillips, Founder & Managing Partner
Education: BS, MBA, Louisiana State University
Background: SVP, Energy Banking Group, NationsBank; Republic Bank

Venture Capital & Private Equity Firms / Domestic Firms

Robert L. Zorich, Founder & Managing Partner
Education: BA, Economics, University of California, Santa Barbara; MS, International Management, American Graduate School of International Management
Background: SVP, Trust Company of the West; Co-Founder & Co-CEO, MAZE Exploration
Jason M. DeLorenzo, Managing Partner
Education: BBA, University of Texas
Background: Corporate Finance, ING Barings; Associate, Energy Group, Wells Fargo Bank
Douglas E. Swanson Jr., Managing Partner
Education: BA & MBA, University of Texas
Background: Frost National Bank; Amegy Bank
Directorships: Houston Producers' Forum

674 ENDEAVOUR CAPITAL
920 Southwest 9th Avenue
Suite 2300
Portland, OR 97205

Phone: 503-223-2721
web: www.endeavourcapital.com

Mission Statement: Partners with companies based in the Western United States region.
Geographic Preference: Western United States
Fund Size: $675 million
Founded: 1991
Average Investment: $25 - $100 million
Minimum Investment: $5 million
Investment Criteria: Growth Equity, Industry Consolidation, Management Acquisitions, Recapitalizations, Ownership Transfers
Industry Group Preference: Business Products & Services, Manufacturing, Food & Beverage, Consumer Products, Transportation, Logistics, Education
Portfolio Companies: The Aladdin Group, Alpha Media, Arizona Nutritional Supplements, Bristol Farms, DTC Logistics, ESCO Corporation, Genesis Financial Solutions, GlobalWide Media, Grant Victor, Johnny Was, K2 Insurance Services, Metropolitan Market, New Seasons Market, Nor-Cal Products, Port Logistics Group, ProKarma, Providien Medical, Tall Oak Learning, USNR, Vigor Industrial, Zoom+

Other Locations:
1001 Fourth Avenue
Suite 4301
Seattle, WA 98154
Phone: 206-621-7060

444 S Flower Street
Suite 4300
Los Angeles, CA 90071
Phone: 213-891-0115

1860 Blake Street
Suite 200
Denver, CO 80202
Phone: 303-355-3553

Key Executives:
Stephen E. Babson, Managing Director
e-mail: seb@endeavourcapital.com
Education: BA, Stanford University; JD, Stanford Law School; MBA, Stanford Graduate School of Business
Background: Chairman, Stoel Rives LLP; Member, Stanford University Committee for Undergraduate Education
Directorships: ESCO Corporation, Zoom+, USNR, New Seasons Market, Bristol Farms, Vigor Industrial, Genesis Financial Solutions, Johnny Was, Columbia Sportswear Company
Rocky Dixon, Managing Director
e-mail: jwd@endeavourcapital.com
Education: BS, University of Oregon
Background: West Coast Director, Earl Kinship Capital Corporation; Marketing & Sales Management, Stanley Tools; Co-Founder, Support Technologies
Directorships: Bi-Mart Corporation, El Aero Services, Adventure Funds, Beef Northwest
Mark Dorman, Managing Director
e-mail: dmd@endeavourcapital.com
Education: BS, Lewis & Clark College; MBA, Harvard Business School
Background: Partner, Green Manning & Bunch; Boettcher & Company; Morgan Stanley; President, Lake Oswego Schools Foundation
Directorships: Alpha Media, Arizona Nutritional Supplements, Grant Victor, Providien Medical, Nor-Cal Products
John Von Schlegell, Managing Director
e-mail: jevs@endeavourcapital.com
Education: BA, MBA, Stanford University
Background: Golder, Thoma, Cressey & Rauser Partner; Undersecretary, Health and Human Services, Massachusetts; Caterpillar Tractor
Directorships: K2 Insurance Services, GlobalWide Media, The Aladdin Group, ProKarma, Port Logistics Group, DTC Logistics, National Fish and Wildlife Foundation, Nature Conservancy
Chad Heath, Managing Director
e-mail: cnh@endeavourcapital.com
Education: BS, Business Administration, Georgetown University
Background: Charterhouse Group International; Merrill Lynch
Directorships: GlobalWide Media, Tall Oak Learning, Johnny Was
Leland Jones, Managing Director
e-mail: lmj@endeavourcapital.com
Education: BA, University of California, Davis; MBA, Stanford Graduate School of Business
Background: Coopers & Lybrand
Directorships: Bristol Farms, K2 Insurance Services, DTC Logistics, The Aladdin Group, Genesis Financial Solutions, Port Logistics Group
Aaron Richmond, Managing Director
e-mail: asr@endeavourcapital.com
Education: AB, Harvard College; MBA, Stanford Graduate School of Business
Background: Consultant, McKinsey & Company
Directorships: USNR, Vigor Industrial, Nor-Cal Products, ProKarma
Dietz Fry, Managing Director
e-mail: jdf@endeavourcapital.com
Education: University of Colorado Boulder
Background: Green Manning & Bunch
Directorships: Grant Victor, Providien Medical, Tall Oak Learning
Bradaigh Wagner, Managing Director
e-mail: bow@endeavourcapital.com
Education: AB, Princeton University; MBA, Wharton School, University of Pennsylvania
Background: Fenway Partners; The Beacon Group
Directorships: Arizona Nutritional Supplements, New Seasons Market
Derek Eve, Principal
e-mail: dae@endeavourcapital.com
Education: BABA, University of Washington; MBA, Columbia Business School
Background: Associate, Diamond Castle; Analyst, Financial Sponsors Group, Credit Suisse
Directorships: The Aladdin Group, Arizona Nutritional Supplements, USNR, Vigor Industrial

675 ENERGIA VENTURES
346 Queen Street
Fredericton, NB E3B 1B2
Canada

Phone: 506-261-0871
e-mail: unbenergiaventures@gmail.com

Mission Statement: Energia Ventures provides funding, mentoring and programming to take enertrepreneurs in the energy, smart grid, artificial intelligence, cleantech, and cybersecurity sectors to the next stage.

Joe Allen, Managing Director
Education: BBA, University of New Brunswick
Background: Director, Investments, New Brunswick Innovation Foundation; Chief Financial Officer, HJ Crabbe & Sons Ltd.

676 ENERGY CAPITAL PARTNERS
51 John F. Kennedy Parkway
Suite 200
Short Hills, NJ 07078

Phone: 973-671-6100 Fax: 973-671-6101
e-mail: info@ecpartners.com
web: www.ecpartners.com

Mission Statement: Energy Capital Partners is a private equity firm focused on investing in North America's energy infrastructure.

Geographic Preference: North America
Founded: 2005
Industry Group Preference: Power Generation, Midstream Oil & Gas, Electric Transmission, Energy Equipment & Services, Environmental Infrastructure, Other Energy Related Assets
Portfolio Companies: ADA Carbon Solutions, Brayton Point Power, Broad River Power, Calpine Corporation, Cardinal Gas Storage Partners, CE2 Carbon Capital, Chieftain Sand and Proppant, CIG Logistics, CM Energy, Cormetech, Dynegy, Empire Generating, EnergySolutions, EquiPower Resources Corp., FirstLight Power Enterprises, Furie Operating Alaska, Gopher Resource, NCSG Crane & Heavy Haul, NESCO, Next Wave Energy, NextLight Renewable Power, Odessa Power Holdings, PLH Group, ProPetro Services, Ramaco Resources, Red Oak Power, Rimrock Midstream, Sendero Midstream Partners, Southcross, Summit Midstream Partners, Sungevity, Sunnova, SunZia Southwest Transmission Project, Targa Resources, Terra-Gen, Triton Power Partners, US Development Group, Wheelabrator Technologies

Other Locations:
12680 High Bluff Drive
Suite 400
San Diego, CA 92130
Phone: 858-703-4400 **Fax:** 858-703-4401

One World Trade Center
Suite 48D
New York City, NY 10006
Phone: 212-266-2900 **Fax:** 212-266-2901

1000 Louisiana Street
52nd Floor
Houston, TX 77002
Phone: 713-496-3100 **Fax:** 713-496-3101

450 East Las Olas Blvd.
Suite 1400
Fort Lauderdale, FL 33301

Key Executives:
Doug Kimmelman, Senior Partner
Education: BA, Economics, Stanford University; MBA, Wharton School
Background: General Partner, Goldman Sachs
Directorships: Calpine Corporation, NESCO, Summit Midstream Partners, Sunnova, US Development Group
Pete Labbat, Managing Partner
Education: BA, Economics, Georgetown University; MBA, Wharton School
Background: Managing Director, Goldman Sachs
Directorships: NCSG Crane & Heavy Haul, Next Wave Energy, Sundero Midstream Partners, Summit Midstream Partners, Triton Power Partners
Tom Lane, Vice Chairman
Education: BA, Economics, Wheaton College; MBA, University of Chicago
Background: Managing Director, Goldman Sachs
Directorships: Sendero Midstream Partners, Summit Midstream Partners, US Development Group
Tyler Reeder, Managing Partner
Education: BA, Economics, Colgate University
Background: Vice President of Power and Fuel Markets, Texas Genco; Director for Energy Markets and Finance Manager, Orion Power Holdings; Goldman Sachs
Directorships: Calpine Corporation, EnergySolutions, Gopher Resource, Ramaco Resources, Terra-Gen, Wheelabrator Technologies
Andrew Singer, Partner & General Counsel
Education: BS, Electrical Engineering, Cornell University; JD, Harvard University
Background: Partner, Latham & Watkins LLP
Directorships: Calpine Corporation; Cormetech Inc.; Terra-Gen LLC; Furie Operating Alaska LLC
Schuyler Coppedge, Partner
Education: BA, Middlebury College; MBA, Wharton School
Background: Energy Investment Banking Division, JP Morgan
Directorships: CIG Logistics; Cormetech; Terra-Gen LLC; U.S. Development Group
Rahman D'Argenio, Partner
Education: BA, Mathematics and Economics, University of Pennsylvania
Background: First Reserve Corporation; Deutsche Bank Securities; Sempra Energy Trading
Directorships: CM Energy; NESCO; PLH Group; Sunnova; Triton Power Partners
Scott Rogan, Partner
Education: BBA and MPA, University of Texas at Austin; MBA, University of Chicago
Background: Managing Director and Co-Head of Barclay's Houston office
Directorships: Next Wave Energy; Sendero Midstream Partners; Summit Midstream Partners
Trent Kososki, Partner
Education: BS, Electrical Engineering, Duke University
Background: Financial Sponsors Investment Banking Group, Credit Suisse First Boston
Directorships: Furie Operating Alaska; Ramaco Resources
Kevin Clayton, Partner
Education: BA, Government, Lehigh University; MBA, St. Joseph's University
Background: Marketing and Client Relations, Oaktree Capital Management
Directorships: Aquicore
Matt DeNichilo, Partner
Education: BSE, Operations Research and Financial Engineering, Princeton University
Background: Energy Investment Banking Group, JP Morgan
Directorships: Sunnova; Terra-Gen
Murray Karp, CPA, Partner, CFO, COO
Education: BS, Accounting, Rutgers University School of Business
Background: CFO, AEA Investors LLC; Controller, Accordia; Assistant Controller, Caxton Corporation

677 ENERTECH CAPITAL
One Tower Bridge
100 Front Street
Suite 1225
West Conshohocken, PA 19428

Phone: 416-515-2759
e-mail: mmiles@enertechcapital.com
web: www.enertechcapital.com

Venture Capital & Private Equity Firms / Domestic Firms

Mission Statement: EnerTech Capital, a pioneer in energy and clean energy, is a firm focused on funding energy ventures and micro-infrastructure projects that address the global opportunity for cleaner, cheaper and more efficient energy usage.
Geographic Preference: North America
Fund Size: $500 million
Founded: 1996
Average Investment: $5 - $6 million
Minimum Investment: $1 million
Investment Criteria: Early to Mid Stage; Energy Tech
Industry Group Preference: Digital Networks, Clean Energy, Technology, Transportation, Waste & Resources, Solar Energy, Automation, Cyber Security, AI
Portfolio Companies: Blue Pillar, Enbala, Encycle, GeoDigital, N-Dimension, NanoSteel, Power Survey, Sofdesk, Tangent Energy Solutions, Vertex Downhole, Western Oilfield Equipment Ltd.

Other Locations:
333 7th Avenue SW
Suite 970
Calgary, AB T2P 2Z1
Canada

5 Place Ville Marie
Suite 1400
Montreal, QC H3B 2G2
Canada
Phone: 514-864-5500

1235 Bay Street
Suite 801
Toronto, ON M5R 3K4
Canada

2000 PGA Boulevard
Suite 4440
Palm Beach Gardens, FL 33408

755 Sansome Street
Suite 450
San Francisco, CA 94111

Key Executives:
Scott Ungerer, Founder/Managing Director
e-mail: sungerer@enertechcapital.com
Education: BS, Mechanical Engineering, Princeton University
Background: President/COO, Atlantic Energy Enterprises
Directorships: Enbala Power Networks, GeoDigital, NanoSteel, N-Dimension Solutions, Tangent Energy Solutions
Wally Hunter, Managing Director
e-mail: whunter@enertechcapital.com
Education: BA, University of Western Ontario
Background: Managing Director, RBC Capital Partners
Directorships: FilterBoxx, HPC Energy Services, N-Dimension Solutions, Western Oilfield Equipment Ltd.
Dean Sciorillo, Managing Director
e-mail: dsciorillo@enertechcapital.com
Education: BS, Finance, LaSalle University; MBA, Fox School of Business, Temple University
Background: Exelon Corporation; Business Planning Manager, Enterprise
Jarett Carson, Managing Director
e-mail: jcarson@enertechcapital.com
Education: BSc, Chemical Engineering, Louisiana Tech University; MBA, A.B. Freeman School, Tulane University
Background: Sound Energy Partners; Director, Energy Technology Research, Royal Bank of Canada .
Dean Sciorillo, Director
e-mail: dsciorillo@enertechcapital.com
Education: BS, Finance, La Salle University; MBA, Fox School, Temple University
Background: Exelon Corporation
Directorships: EnergySavvy
Anne-Marie Bourgeois, Vice President
e-mail: ambourgeois@enertechcapital.com
Education: BS, Geology, BA, Management, BA, Political Science, University of Ottawa; MA, International Management, University of Quebec
Background: Regional Director, Partnerships, Sustainable Technology Canada; Business Development Specialist, International Services for Sustainable Development
Eric Schmadtke, Vice President, Investments
e-mail: eschmadtke@enertechcapital.com
Education: BBA, Finance, Bishop's University; MBA, University of Ottawa; MBA, Haskayne School of Business, University of Calgary
Background: Director, Business Development, Suncor Energy

678 ENGAGE VENTURES
75 5th Street NW
Suite 2100
Atlanta, GA 30308

e-mail: info@engage.vc
web: engage.vc

Mission Statement: An independent venture fund collaborating with entrepreneurs emerging in the tech industry.
Founded: 2017
Average Investment: $500,000 - $25 million
Minimum Investment: $500,000
Investment Criteria: Early Stage
Industry Group Preference: Diversified

Key Executives:
Blake Patton, Managing Partner
Education: BS, Georgia Tech College
Background: Managing Partner, Tech Square Ventures; General Manager, Advanced Technology Development Center; President/COO, Interactive Advisory Software; Associate, SEI Corporation
Daley Ervin, Managing Director
Education: BS, Arizona State University
Background: VP of Business Development & Strategy, Nucleus; GM/Head of North American Operations for Students.com
Thiago Olson, Managing Director
Education: BEE, Vanderbilt University
Background: Venture Partner, Tech Square Ventures; CEO, Stratos Technologies
Scott Lopano, Principal
Education: Wharton School
Background: Associate, Tech Square Ventures; Associate Director/Lead Coverage Officer, Insurance Debt Capital Markets Group
Joelle Fox, Operating Partner/CFO
Education: BS, Accounting, University of Tennessee
Background: CFO/Operating Partner, Tech Square Ventures; Velocity Medical Solutions; Varian Medical Systems; iXL Inc.; PricewaterhouseCoopers

679 ENHANCED CAPITAL
601 Lexington Avenue
Suite 1401
New York, NY 10022

Phone: 212-207-3385 **Fax:** 212-207-9031
web: www.enhancedcapital.com

Mission Statement: Enhanced Capital is a small business investment firm focused on established lower middle market companies. We invest in growing businesses often overlooked by traditional sources of capital due to location or size.
Average Investment: $500,000 - $3 million
Investment Criteria: Lower Middle Market
Industry Group Preference: Renewable Energy, Real Estate Rehabilitation, Affordable Housing
Portfolio Companies: Accelerated Orthopedic Technologies, Advanced Network Solutions, Affinity Lab, Alereon, American Log Handlers, Aquasana, Autotether, BroadStar Energy, CK Mechanical Plumbing & Heating, CloudX, CMD

Venture Capital & Private Equity Firms / Domestic Firms

Bioscience, Community Cars, Dreyfus-Corney, Elm City Food Cooperative, Emme E2MS, Energy Source Partners, EnteGreat, Envirelation, FSI, Fire Rock, Fireside Glamping, Floop, FlowTech Feuling, Greenleaf Biofuels, GreyWall Software, Hadapt, Heliovolt, Invinia, Innovatient Solutions, Knoa Software, Lapolla Industries, Knoa Software, Lapolla Industries, Local Yokel Media, MedAdherence, Motion Computing, New Haven Pharmaceuticals, NovaTract Surgical, NuScriptRX, Optimal IMX, Optiwind, Oxford Performance Materials, PART Point, Payment America Systems, Peak Builders, Pinkgirls, Precipio Diagnostics, Queralt, RepEquity, SciApps, Session Title Services, Shareholder InSite, Sierra Industries, Solar Change, Southern Theaters, Sustainable Real Estate, Taurus, Teton Gravity Research, Townsend, Two Roads Brewing Company, Vacuum Technologies Corporation, Vault, WC Leasing, WRJ Design Associates, WhiteGlove Health, Wyoming Authentic Products, YouRenew.com

Other Locations:
201 St. Charles Ave.
Suite 3400
New Orleans, LA 70170
Phone: 504-569-7900

Key Executives:
Michael A.G. Korengold, President/CEO
e-mail: mkorengold@enhancedcapital.com
Education: Vassar College, University of Minnesota Law School
Background: Lawyer
Paul S. Kasper, Managing Director, New York City
e-mail: pkasper@enhancedcapital.com
Education: BS, Accounting, MS, Business Adminstration, Penn State University; MBA, Stanford Graduate School of Business
Background: Principal, American Securities Capital Partners; Hicks Muse Tate & Furst; Merrill Lynch
Shane McCarthy, CPA, Managing Partner/CFO, New Orleans
e-mail: smccarthy@enhancedcapital.com
Education: BS, MS, Accounting, University of Southern Mississippi
Background: Audit Manager, Ernst & Young

680 ENIAC VENTURES
San Francisco, CA

web: eniac.vc

Mission Statement: Seed-stage firm named after the world's first computer, developed at the University of Pennsylvania.

Founded: 1996
Investment Criteria: Seed
Industry Group Preference: Mobile, Financial Services
Portfolio Companies: 1upHealth, Airbnb, Alloy, Anchor, AutoFi, B8ta, Basket Savings, BioBeats, Bleximo, Boxed, Breezy, Brightwheel, Briq, Cameo, Chatgrid, CMRA, DemandSage, Dubsmash, Eden, Elevate, Embrace, Esports One, Fitocracy, Fleksy, Fondu, FortressIQ, Fritz AI, Fuzz Pet Health, Ginger, Grouparoo, Hinge, Imagine, IMRSV, Instinctive, Iovation, Iron Ox, isee, Jobr, Jump Ramp Games, Kanvas Labs, KitchenMate, LaunchKey, Lawmatics, Legit, LevelOps, Localytics, Luxe, MaestroQA, Medallia, MedCrypt, Meta Resolver, Mighty Meeting, Mio, MirrorMe, mParticle, N3twork, Neumob, Nextpeer, Onswipe, Owlet, Passbase, Pienso, ProdPerfect, Qualia, Quilt, Raken, Ready Robotics, Recharge, Sea Machines, Shaper, Shine, ShowMe, Simperium, Snips, SoundCloud, Spansive, Statsbot, SugarCRM, Superpeer, TalentShare, Tap to Learn, TapCommerce, Tempo AI, Vence, Virgin Hyperloop One, Vistar Media, Visual Vocal, Vungle, Workflow, Xwing, Zero

Key Executives:
Hadley Harris, Founding General Partner
Education: University of Pennsylvania; Wharton School
Background: Vlingo; Thumb
Nihal Mehta, Founding General Partner
Education: University of Pennsylvania
Background: LocalResponse
Vic Singh, Founding General Partner
Education: University of Pennsylvania; Columbia Business School
Background: RRE Ventures; NearVerse; Tracks; Kanvas
Tim Young, Founding General Partner
Education: University of Pennsylvania
Background: WebYes; Bridge; Quoteship

681 ENLIGHTENMENT CAPITAL
4445 Willard Avenue
Suite 1120
Chevy Chase, MD 20815

e-mail: info@enlightenment-cap.com
web: www.enlightenment-cap.com

Mission Statement: Enlightenment Capital is a private investment firm that provides flexible capital solutions to businesses in the Aerospace, Defense & Government sector.

Investment Criteria: Senior Debt, Mezzanine Debt, Minority Equity
Industry Group Preference: Aerospace, Defense and Government, Security, Government
Portfolio Companies: 1901 Group, Aurora Flight Sciences, Byte Cubed, Cadmus, CyberCore Technologies, The Diplomat Group, Emagine IT, EverWatch, Gleason Research Associates, MicroPact, North American Rescue, Opera Solutions, Phase One Consulting Group, PIXIA, REI, SolAero Technologies, Telos Corporation, Vanguard Space Technologies, Vistronix

Key Executives:
Devin Talbott, Co-Founder/Managing Partner
Education: BA, Law & Spanish, Amherst College; JD, MBA, Georgetown University
Background: Vice President, D.E. Shaw; TCG Financial Partners; M&A Group, Lazard
Pierre Chao, Co-Founder/Operating Partner
Education: Dual Degrees, MIT; CFA
Background: Co-Founder, Renaissance Strategic Advisors; Institutional Investor, Smith Barney; Morgan Stanley Dean Witter; Credit Suisse First Boston

682 ENTER VENTURES
350 Cambridge Avenue
Suite 225
Palo Alto, CA 94306

Phone: 650-323-5088 **Fax:** 650-323-5084
e-mail: info@enterventures.com
web: www.enterventures.com

Mission Statement: A business accelerator that works closely with early stage high-growth emerging technology companies towards the successful launch of and execution of their business models by providing guidance and support.

Geographic Preference: Worldwide
Fund Size: $100 million
Investment Criteria: Seed, Early Stage
Industry Group Preference: Financial Services, Ancillary Services, Management, Business to Business, Corporate Services

Other Locations:
601 California Street
Suite 2000
San Francisco, CA 94108
Phone: 415-505-5003

19-31 Pitt Street
Level 6

Venture Capital & Private Equity Firms / Domestic Firms

Sydney NSW 2000
Australia

Key Executives:
Rob Allan, Co-Founder/CEO/General Partner
e-mail: rob.allan@enterventures.com
Education: MBA, LLM, BSC
Background: Managing General Partner/CEO, PoleStar Business Development; Partner, The Anvil Group; Management Consultant, McKinsey & Company; Consultant, Egon Zehnder International
Directorships: VCMentors; Avelin Capital
Diana Saca, Co-Founder/COO
415-505-5003
e-mail: diana.saca@enterventures.com
Education: Political Science and Administration of Justice degrees; JD, Santa Clara University School of Law; Certification, Hong Kong International & Comparative Law Institute
Background: Partner, Hagan, Saca & Hagan Law Corporation; Outside General Counsel; Associate Editor, Santa Clara Law Review
John Chaisson, Co-Founder/Partner
e-mail: john.chaisson@enterventures.com
Education: Law degree, Stanford University
Background: Vice President Business/Corporate Development, DataMain; President, Interbiznet Group; General Counsel, several Bay Area technology companies; Vice President Business Development, Resumix; Wilson, Sonsini, Goodrich & Rosati
Bill Kelsall, Co-Founder/Partner
(0419) 811-988
e-mail: bill.kelsall@enterventures.com
Education: MBA, Cranfield School; Curtin University, Australia
Background: Strategy Practice, Arthur Andersen Melbourne; Strategy Consultant, McKinsey & Company/Mckinsey Global Innovation; Founder/CEO, Fresh Cosmetics; Physical Therapist (opened eight successful practices)

683 ENTREPIA VENTURES
101 Eisenhower Parkway
Suite 300
Roseland, NJ 07068

Phone: 973-467-0880
e-mail: info@entrepia.com
web: www.entrepia.com

Mission Statement: Entrepia Ventures manages venture capital funds that invest in private technology companies in the United States and Canada. The company further funds the business development initiatives of these companies in Asian markets.
Geographic Preference: United States, Japan, Canada
Founded: 1999
Investment Criteria: Early-Stage, Expansion-Stage, Private Companies, Japanese Startups, Japanese Seed Businesses
Industry Group Preference: Technology, Information Technology, Multimedia, Mobility, Web Applications & Services, Next Generation Computing, IT Infrastructure
Portfolio Companies: Achronix Semiconductor Corp., Bluestreak Technology Inc., Business Search Technologies Corp., FreeLinc, MagSil Corp., Vantrix

Other Locations:
1200 McGill College Avenue
Suite 1100
Montreal, QC H3B 4G7
Canada
Phone: 866-305-9610 Fax: 866-305-9610

2-5-7, Hirakawacho
Chiyada-ku
Tokyo 102-0093
Japan

Key Executives:
Amit Srivastava, Managing Partner
Education: BSc, Electrical Engineering, Indian Institute of Technology; MSc, Electrical Engineering, Rensselaer Polytechnic Institute; MBA, Wharton School, University of Pennsylvania
Background: JP Morgan Chase; Mercer Management Consulting
Directorships: Achronix, Bluestreak, Freelinc, Vantrix

684 ENTREPRENEUR PARTNERS
123 South Broad Street
Suite 1843
Philadelphia, PA 19109

Phone: 267-322-7000
e-mail: info@epfunds.com
web: www.epfunds.com

Mission Statement: Entrepreneur Partners brings operating insight to the assessment and ownership of direct marketing companies in the middle-market.
Geographic Preference: United States
Average Investment: $3 to $10 million
Minimum Investment: $3 million
Investment Criteria: Company Revenue of $10 to $150 million
Industry Group Preference: Business to Business, Direct Marketing, Retailing, Compliance/Traning/Certification, Publishers
Portfolio Companies: AmeriFile, Competitor Group, Future Publishing, Intelsat, Medical Arts Press, NEP Broadcasting, Northern Brewer, Peachtree Business Products

Key Executives:
Salem Shuchman, Managing Partner
e-mail: sshuchman@epfunds.com
Background: Senior Partner, Apax Partners; Principal, Odyssey Partners
Bruce Newman, Partner
e-mail: bnewman@epfunds.com
Background: Operating Partner, Graham Partners; President, Franklin Mint Company; President, Paramount Citrus
Lori Lombardo, Principal
Education: BA, Bates College; MS, University of Pennsylvania
Background: AVP, Lending Services & Operations, Merrill Lynch

685 ENTREPRENEURS ROUNDTABLE ACCELERATOR
415 Madison Avenue
4th Floor
New York, NY 10017

e-mail: pr@eranyc.com
web: www.eranyc.com

Mission Statement: Helps startup companies acclerate their visibility, access, and credibility with customers, mentors and investors.
Average Investment: $100,000
Investment Criteria: Seed Stage, Early Stage, Middle Stage
Industry Group Preference: Media, Business to Business, B2B, Business to Consumer, B2C, Marketing, Real Estate, Logistics, Fintech, E-Commerce
Portfolio Companies: ArtistOnGo, Coinapoly, FieldCLIX, Hailify, Hazel, Mouth Off Health, Nayya, Parento, RillaVoice, Salusion, Spotter, Top Corp, Undock

Key Executives:
Murat Aktihanoglu, Managing Director
Education: BSc, Electrics and Electronics, MSc, Computer Science, Bilkent University in Turkey

Venture Capital & Private Equity Firms / Domestic Firms

Background: Founder, Centrl; Founder, Entrepreneurs Roundtable; Co-Author, Location-Aware Applications; AT&T; Sony; Panasonic; Logitech; Pioneer
Directorships: Belgian American Chamber Of Commerce, MIT Enterprise Forum
Jonathan Axelrod, Managing Director
Education: AB, Social Studies, Harvard University
Background: Co-Founder, Co-CEo, MusicGremlin; Co-Founder, President, Music123
Directorships: Beth Israel Medical Center

686 EONCAPITAL

Phone: 303-850-9300
e-mail: inquiry@eoncapital.com
web: www.eoncapital.com

Mission Statement: Our experience working with and in start-up businesses, prompted us to establish our own private venture funds. eonCapital Venture Fund I and II invest in seed and early-stage Software as a Service (SaaS) and mobile application businesses. Like the creative entrepreneur, we saw a problem and desired a solution. Our goal is to help fill the funding gap for entrepreneurs of seed and early-stage companies. As entrepreneurs, we understood what it takes to build a company from the ground up and the challenges presented from concept through development and into the growth phase.

Investment Criteria: Start-Up, Seed-Stage, Early-Stage
Industry Group Preference: SaaS, Mobile Apps
Portfolio Companies: AllAboardToys, BirdBox, Circa, Closely, CollectiveIP, CrowdTwist, DailyBurn, eonMedia, FlexTrip, FlixMaster, Forkly, FullContact, GameChanger, GoChime, GoSpotCheck, Go Toast, Highlighter, LgDb, MadKast, Nextly, MobileStorm, Mocapay, Mocavo, Nimble, ReTel Technologies, Remitly, Roximity, Rubicon Project, Socialthing, Sycara, TeamSnap, TechStars, Vanilla, VerbalizeIt, Vizify

Key Executives:
Dave Carlson, Managing Director
Education: BA, Communications, Bethany College; MS, International Business Management, Thunderbird School of Global Management
Background: Founder, Go Toast; Founder, eonMedia
Directorships: MobileStorm

687 EOS PARTNERS LP
437 Madison Avenue
14th Floor
New York, NY 10022

Phone: 212-832-5800 Fax: 212-832-5815
web: www.eospartners.com

Mission Statement: To work with stellar management teams and provide strategic and financial expertise and knowledge in order to grow businesses into industry leading companies.

Geographic Preference: National
Fund Size: $1.5 billion
Founded: 1994
Average Investment: $20 - $100 million
Minimum Investment: $1 million
Investment Criteria: Lower Middle Market, Growth Equity, Recapitalizations, Buyouts, Acquisitions, Shareholder Liquidity, Corporate Divestitures
Industry Group Preference: Consumer Products, Consumer Services, Energy, Healthcare Services, Business to Business, Transportation, Logistics, Media
Portfolio Companies: Addus Healthcare, Arbonne, BeavEx, Country Fresh, CRS Proppants, KeyImpact Sales & Systems, MC2, Mercury Media, ProEnergy Services, RCG Global Services, Residential Mortgage Services, ShelterPoint Life, Summit Business Media, True Science

Key Executives:
Steven M. Friedman, Founding Partner
e-mail: sfriedman@eospartners.com
Education: AB, MBA, University of Chicago; JD, Brooklyn Law School
Background: VP, Citibank, NA; General Partner, Odyssey Partners
Brian D. Young, Founding Partner
e-mail: byoung@eospartners.com
Education: AB, Harvard University
Background: General Partner, Odyssey Partners; Managing Director, First Boston Corporation
Mark L. First, Parnter
e-mail: mfirst@eospartners.com
Education: BS, Wharton School; MBA, Harvard Business School
Background: Morgan Stanley
Brendan M. Moore, Managing Director
e-mail: bmoore@eospartners.com
Education: AB, Dartmouth College; BEng, Thayer School of Engineering, Dartmouth College
Background: Harbourton Enterprises; First Dominion Capital; Schroder & Co.
Adam S. Gruber, Managing Director
e-mail: agruber@eospartners.com
Education: BBA, University of Wisconsin, Madison
Background: Windward Capital Partners; Cred Suisse First Boston
Matthew Young, Vice President
e-mail: myoung@eospartners.com
Education: BA, Franklin & Marshall College
Background: Analyst, Kayne Anderson Mezzanine Partners
Beth L. Bernstein, Chief Financial/Compliance Officer
e-mail: bbernstein@eospartners.com
Education: BS, Fairleigh Dickenson University; CPA
Background: Senior Accountant, Coopers & Lybrand

688 EPIC PARTNERS
116 W 23rd Street
5th Floor
New York, NY 10011

web: www.epicpartnersllc.com

Mission Statement: A merchant banking firm focused exclusively on investing in the education and training sector.

Geographic Preference: United States, Canada
Founded: 2000
Investment Criteria: Minimum $2 Million in EBITDA; Company Revenue of $10 to $150 million; Experienced Management Teams
Industry Group Preference: Training, Education, Healthcare Services, Business Services
Portfolio Companies: EDUSS, Oasis Children's Services, Provant, St. Matthew's University, University of Sint Eustatius School of Medicine

Key Executives:
Robert Puopolo, Partner
646-375-2123
e-mail: rtpuopolo@epicpartnersllc.com
Education: AB Economics, Harvard University; MBA, Harvard Business School
Background: Partner, Leeds Equity Partners; Oppenheimer & Co; Bear Stearns & Co; Kidder, Peabody & Co
Directorships: Helma Institute; Oasis Children Services

689 EPIC VENTURES
15 West South Temple
Suite 500
Salt Lake City, UT 84101

Phone: 801-524-8939
e-mail: info@epicvc.com
web: www.epicvc.com

Venture Capital & Private Equity Firms / Domestic Firms

Mission Statement: To invest in companies positioned to become leaders in the technology industry.
Geographic Preference: Mountain & Western States
Fund Size: $60 million
Investment Criteria: Early-Stage
Industry Group Preference: High Technology, Clean Technology, Communications, Consumer Services, Business Products & Services, Enterprise Software, Internet Technology, Life Sciences
Portfolio Companies: Adaptive Computing, Alliance Health, Canopy, Clinkle, Cloud Lending, The Clymb, Dotgo, eSionic, Everspin, Exagen Diagnostics, Health Catalyst, HG Data, HyTrust, Insidesales.com, Instructure, Iovation, Janrain, Joyent, Knod, Lavu, Le Tote, Medsphere, Moki, NetDocuments, Nuvi, Primary Data, Q Therapeutics, Signal, SolutionReach, SpinGo

Key Executives:
  Nick Efstratis, Managing Director
  Education: BS, Entrepreneurship, Brigham Young University; MBA, Marriott School, Brigham Young University
  Background: Business Development Group, Excite; Founder, Management Team, NetDocuments; Founder, Ranchlife Adventures
  Kent Madsen, Managing Director
  Education: BS, Mechanical Engineering & Applied Mechanics, MA, International Studies, University of Pennsylvania; MSE, University of Michigan; MBA, Wharton School
  Background: Managing Director, Wasatch Venture Fund; Advanced Technology Group, Ford Motor Company
  Directorships: Pivot Solutions, Q Therapeutics, Zettacore, Everspin, S5 Wireless
  Ryan Hemingway, Managing Director
  Education: BS, Psychology, MSS, Economics, Utah State University; MBA, University of Oxford
  Background: Zions Bank Capital Markets Group; Nevada State Bank
  Katie Szczepaniak Rice, Venture Associate
  Education: BS, Engineering, Massachusetts Institute of Technology; MBA, University of Chicago
  Background: Strategic Market Analyst, Cabot Corporation; Consultant, Kline & Co.
  Directorships: Lavu, DOTGO, Figaro

690 EPIDAREX CAPITAL
7910 Woodmont Avenue
Suite 1210
Bethesda, MD 20814

Phone: 301-298-5455 Fax: 301-357-8517
e-mail: info@epidarex.com
web: www.epidarex.com

Mission Statement: Epidarex Capital is a venture capital fund that invests in early-stage, high-growth life science companies in the Unites Stages and United Kingdom. Their focus is on providing start-up and growth equity capital to young companies currently developing commercial applications of novel research.
Geographic Preference: United States, United Kingdom
Investment Criteria: Early-Stage
Industry Group Preference: Life Sciences
Portfolio Companies: AdoRx Therapeutics, Apellis Pharmaceuticals, Caldan Therapeutics, Clyde Biosciences, Confluences Life Sciences, Edinburgh Molecular Imaging, Enterprise Therapeutics, Eternygen, IGEM Therapeutics, Harpoon Medical, Mironid, NodThera, SIRAKOSS, Topas Therapeutics

Other Locations:
  4F Le Gratte-Ciel Building 3
  5-22-3 Shimbashi, Minatoku
  Tokyo 105-0004
  Japan
  Phone: 81-3-6459-0258

  137a George St.
  Edinburgh EH2 4JY
  United Kingdom
  Phone: 44-131-243-3700

Key Executives:
  A. Sinclair Dunlop, Managing Partner
  Education: MA, International Relations, Syracuse University; MA, Political Economy, Glasgow University; MBA, Columbia Business School
  Background: MASA Life Science Ventures
  Directorships: Apellis Pharmaceuticals; Clyde Biosciences; EM Imaging; Mironid; Sirakoss
  Kyparissia Sirinakis, CPA, Managing Partner
  Education: Boston College School of Management
  Background: Founder & Managing Director, WomenAngels.net; MLSV
  Directorships: Confluence Life Science; Harpoon Medical; Nodthera; Sirakoss

691 EPLANET CAPITAL
99 Almaden Blvd
Suite 600
San Jose, CA 95113

Phone: 408-236-6500
e-mail: siliconvalley@eplanetcapital.com
web: www.eplanetcapital.com

Mission Statement: ePlanet Capital seeks to partner with management teams and offer the contacts, resources, and expertise necessary to help portfolio companies achieve growth and success.
Geographic Preference: United States, Asia, Europe
Founded: 1999
Investment Criteria: Growth Capital, Expansion Stage
Industry Group Preference: Internet, E-Commerce & Manufacturing, Semiconductors, Electronics, Wireless, Telecommunications, Healthcare, Medical Technology, Green Energy, Energy Efficiency, Gaming
Portfolio Companies: Baidu, End2End, Focus Media, Friendi, High Power Lithium, HiSoft Technology International, iKang, Moreens, Naseeb Networks, Newgen, OrderDynamics, Palringo, Silicon Mitus, Skype, Tribe Mobile, Virgin Mobile

Other Locations:
  71-75 Uxbridge Road
  Ealing W5 5SL
  United Kingdom
  Phone: 44-20-3859-0140

  ePlanet Ventures Investment Group (HK) Ltd.
  RM152515F China World Tower A No 1
  Jianguomenwai Avenue, Chaoyang District
  Beijing 100004
  China
  Phone: 86-10-5737-2520

Key Executives:
  Asad Jamal, Founder/Chairman/Managing Partner
  Education: BSc, London School of Economics
  Background: Peregrine Investment Holdings
  Dennis Atkinson, Managing Partner, London
  Education: BS, Physics, Exeter University; MBA, Harvard Business School
  Background: Principal, Softbank Europe Ventures; Global Product Manager, Reuters Business Information
  Jerry Ilhuyn Cho, Managing Partner, Beijing
  Education: BEng, Dongguk University, Seoul; MS, Electrical Engineering, University of Southern California
  Background: Samsung Electronics
  Amira Atallah, Chief Financial Officer
  Education: BA, Economics, University of California, Davis; CPA
  Background: Deloitte Tax LLP; Arthur Andersen

Venture Capital & Private Equity Firms / Domestic Firms

Hemant Khatwani, Vice President, Bangalore
Education: BMS College of Engineering; MBA, Indian Institute of Management
Background: AMP Capital Investors; Project Finance & Principal Investments, Infrastructure Development Finance Company

692 EQUINOX CAPITAL
41 W Putnam Avenue
Greenwich, CT 06830

Phone: 203-622-1605 Fax: 203-622-4684
web: www.equinox-capital.com

Mission Statement: Equinox Capital makes equity investments in small- to medium-sized companies facing constraints and provides the corporate environment necessary to help build emerging market leaders.

Founded: 1996
Investment Criteria: Owner Recapitalizations, Add-On Acquisitions, Growth Capital, Management Buyouts, Turnarounds
Industry Group Preference: Healthcare, Communications
Portfolio Companies: Care Management Technologies, Comprehensive NeuroScience, Cushcraft Corporation, Medical University of the Americas, Saba University, St. Matthew's University

Key Executives:
Steven C Rodger, Founder
Education: BA, University of Virginia; MBA, Harvard Business School
Background: Principal, Bessemer Securities; Mergers & Acquisitions, Bear Stearns & Co.; Donaldson Lufkin & Jenrette
Gregory S Czuba, Managing Director
Education: BS, MS, Electrical Engineering & Computer Science, Massachusetts Institute of Technology
Background: CEO, Cushcraft Corporation; VP, Celient Corporation; President, Remec Wireless; Senior Director, Hughes Network Systems
Donald J Donahue Jr, Managing Director
Education: BA, Georgetown University; MBA, NYC Stern School of Business
Background: President, 1st Worldwide Financial Partners; Managing Director, Banc One Capital Markets
Patrick J Donnellan, Managing Director
Education: BS, Bates College; MBA, Carnegie Mellon University
Background: Principal, Booz Allen Hamilton

693 EQUITEK CAPITAL
3659 Green Road
Suite 101
Beachwood, OH 44122

Phone: 216-360-0151 Fax: 216-373-9399
web: www.Equitekcapital.com

Mission Statement: Equitek Capital is a venture capital firm that focuses on growth-stage deals. The firm invests in companies in the technology sector.
Investment Criteria: Growth Stage
Industry Group Preference: Technology
Portfolio Companies: Alien Technology, Chorum Technologies, DFT Microsystems, Eclipse Aviation, Embedded Planet, Flarion Technologies, Fsona Communications, Quicksilver Technology, Viztec

Key Executives:
Ken Ehrhart, Founding Managing Director
Education: BA, University of California, Berkeley
Background: Director of Research, Gilder Technology Report
Greg Somer, Founding Managing Director
Education: BSEE, MIT; MSEE, Stanford University
Background: Manager, New Products Planning Group, Cypress Semiconductor; Foreign Exchange Derivative Specialist, J.P. Morgan; BNP
Paul Grim, Founding Managing Director
Education: BSME, MIT; MBA, MIT Sloan School of Management
Background: Strategy Managing Consultant, Telecoms and Media Group, Gemini Consulting; Coopers & Lybrand France; IT Specialist, IBM France/CGI
John Gannon, Founding Managing Director
Education: BSAE, Pennsylvania State University; MBA, University of Chicago
Background: Orbit Specialist, General Electric Astro-Space Division; Risk Manager, Merrill Lynch; Barclays Capital

694 EQUITY SOUTH
2855 Marconi Drive
Suite 370
Alpharetta, GA 30005

Phone: 678-612-9876
e-mail: dld@equity-south.com
web: www.equity-south.com

Mission Statement: Pursues acquisitions or substantial equity investments in businesses with revenues from $10 million to $50 million and who have growth potential from internal efforts or through acquisitions.

Geographic Preference: Northeast, Southeast, Southwest
Fund Size: $42 million
Founded: 1987
Average Investment: $3 million - $5 million
Minimum Investment: $1 million
Investment Criteria: Mezzanine, LBO, Recapitalizations, Controlblock Purchases
Industry Group Preference: Services, Software, Manufacturing, Distribution
Portfolio Companies: American Screen Art, Carstar, F.B. Leopold Company, Loyaltyworks, Octane5 International LLC, PaySys International Inc., PolyVision Inc., Saunders Inc., Sherman & Reilly Inc., Sports & Recreation Inc., VCG Inc., VisAer Inc.

Key Executives:
Douglas Diamond, Managing Director
Education: BS, Commerce, University of Virginia
Background: CPA, Arthur Anderson and Co.; Director, Grubb and Williams, Ltd.; CEO, Octane5 International
Directorships: VisAER, Carstar, American Screen Art, LoyaltyWorks Inc.
Michael Dunn, Managing Director
Education: Liberal Arts, Pierce College
Background: Chairman, Octane5 International; CEO, PolyVision Corp.; CEO, Alliance International Group;

695 EQUUS TOTAL RETURN
700 Louisiana Street
48th Floor
Houston, TX 77002

Fax: 212-671-1534
Toll-Free: 888-323-4533
e-mail: info@equuscap.com
web: www.equuscap.com

Mission Statement: Focuses on the potential for long-term capital gains or a combination of capital gains with some level of current income.

Geographic Preference: United States
Fund Size: $70 million
Founded: 1983
Average Investment: $15 million
Minimum Investment: $1 million
Investment Criteria: Recapitalizations, Acquisitions
Industry Group Preference: Consumer Products, Distribution, Industrial Equipment, Medical & Health Related

Venture Capital & Private Equity Firms / Domestic Firms

Portfolio Companies: 5th Element Tracking, Biogenic Reagents, Equus Energy, Equus Media Development Company, MVC Capital, PalletOne Inc.

Other Locations:
2800 Park Place
666 Burrard Street
Vancouver, BC V6C 2Z7
Canada

Key Executives:
Robert Knauss, Chairman
Background: CEO, Baltic International USA; Chairman, Philip Services Corp.; Dean/Professor, University of Houston Law School; Dean, Vanderbilt Law School
John A. Hardy, Chief Executive Officer
Background: Chairman/CEO, Versatile Systems; Professor, University of British Columbia
Kenneth I. Denos, Director/Secretary/Chief Compliance Officer
Background: Chairman/CEO/President, London Pacific & Partners Inc.; CEO, MCC Global NV
Directorships: Start Scientific Inc.
Henry W. Hankinson, Director
Background: Co-Founder/Managing Partner, Global Business Associates; Senior Regional Executive, Haliburton/Brown & Root
L'Sheryl D Hudson, Senior Vice President, CFO & CCO
Bertrand Des Pallieres, Director
Background: Global Head of Structured Credit, JP Morgan
Directorships: Orco Property Group, SPQR Capital Holdings, Cadogan Petroleum, Attali Investment Partners, Versatile Systems, Euromax Capital Grlobal Finance
Richard F. Bergner, Director
Background: Attorney
Fraser Atkinson, Director
Background: Chairman, Green Power Motor Company Inc.; CFO, Versatile Systems Inc.; Partner, KPMG

696 ESCALATE CAPITAL PARTNERS
6300 Bridgepoint Parkway
Building 1
Suite 480
Austin, TX 78701

Phone: 512-651-2100
web: www.escalatecapital.com

Mission Statement: A mezzanine firm that invests in later stage companies experiencing growth. Escalate Capital focuses on the technology industry, particularly the tech-enabled services, healthcare and Internet sectors.

Investment Criteria: Mezzanine, Growth Capital, Permanent Working Capital, Acqusitin Financing, Recapitalizations, Later Stage
Industry Group Preference: Software, Mobile, Wireless, Technology-Enabled Services, Healthcare, Medical Devices
Portfolio Companies: Accolade, Adaptly, Allconnect, Arcadia, Arteriocyte, BlackDuck, Certona, ControlScan, Donuts, Dstillery, eFolder, Entrada, FireApps, Fishbowl, Glowpoint, HealthX, HotChalk, J.Hilburn, Kareo, LiveIntent, MarketForce, MoPro, Motionsoft, Needle, OneCommand, OwnerIQ, PaySimple, Peerless Network, Phreesia, Revionics, Signiant, SportVision, Viverae, WorkFront

Key Executives:
Tony Schell, Managing Director
Education: BBA, MBA, University of Texas
Background: Managing Director, Comerica Bank; Imperial Bank; The Sabre Group; Coopers & Lybrand; MBank Dallas; First Gibraltar Bank
Ross Cockrell, Managing Director
Education: BA, Harvard University; MBA, University of Texas
Background: General Partner, Austin Ventures; Lomas Financial
Simon James, Chief Financial Officer
Education: BBA, University of Washington

Background: Chief Administrative Officer, Technology & Life Sciences Division, Comerica; VP, Semiconductor Industry, Silicon Valley Bank
Larry Bradshaw, Principal
Education: BS, Duke University; MBA, University of Texas
Background: Associate, Healthcare Corporate Finance Group, JP Morgan; Research Analyst, Joel Mogy Investment Counsel
Chris Julich, Principal
Education: BA, Wake Forest University
Background: Senior Market Manager, RBC Centura Bank; VP, Technology & Life Sciences Group, Comerica Bank; Associate, Capital Investment Partners

697 ESCHELON ENERGY PARTNERS
712 Main Street
Suite 2200
Houston, TX 77002-3290

Phone: 713-546-2621 Fax: 713-546-2620
e-mail: tsg@eschelonadvisors.com
web: www.eschelonadvisors.com

Mission Statement: Eschelon Energy Advisors provides private equity capital to companies in the energy sector with the objective of giving its partners the chance to become involved in the growth of the North American energy industry.

Geographic Preference: North America
Average Investment: $5 million
Minimum Investment: $500,000
Investment Criteria: Management, Business Plan, Co-Investors, Valuation
Industry Group Preference: Energy, Oil & Gas
Portfolio Companies: Itron, Strand Energy

Key Executives:
Tom Glanville, Managing Partner
Education: BS, Economics, University of Virginia; MS, Mineral Economics, Colorado School of Mines
Background: Reliant; Enron Corp.; Bankers Trust Company
Directorships: Itron, Chroma Exploration & Production, Strand Energy

698 ESSEX WOODLANDS HEALTH VENTURES LLC
21 Waterway Avenue
Suite 225
The Woodlands, TX 77380

Phone: 281-364-1555 Fax: 281-364-9755
e-mail: houston@ewhealthcare.com
web: www.ewhealthcare.com

Mission Statement: Essex Woodlans Healthcare Ventures make growth equity investments in proven healthcare companies. The fund seeks opportunities with rapidly growing revenues and earnings, low to no risk of capital loss, and that are well positioned for a predictable exit.

Geographic Preference: United States, Europe, China, Latin America
Fund Size: $2.5 billion
Founded: 1985
Average Investment: $20 - $80 million
Minimum Investment: $20 million
Investment Criteria: Seed-Stage, Early Stage, Growth Stage, Private Equity, Later Stage PIPE
Industry Group Preference: Pharmaceuticals, Medical Devices, Healthcare, Life Sciences, Biotechnology, Medical Technology, Healthcare Services, Information Technology
Portfolio Companies: AxoGen, Biotoscana, Bioventus, BreatheAmerica Inc., Breg, Cognate Bioservices, Cota, Encore Dermatology, Endologix, EUSA Pharma, EyePoint Pharmaceuticals Inc., Healthgrades, Metabolon, Prolacta Bioscience, Suneva Medical, TissueTech, Venus Concept, Xenex Disinfection Services Inc., Yantai Beacon

Venture Capital & Private Equity Firms / Domestic Firms

Other Locations:
75 Rockerfeller Plaza
Suite 1700A
New York, NY 10019
Phone: 646-429-1251 **Fax:** 212-922-0551

Berkeley Square House
Berkeley Square
London W1J 6BR
United Kingdom
Phone: 44 (0)20 7529-2500 **Fax:** 44 (0)20 7529-2501

Key Executives:
Martin Sutter, Managing Director
e-mail: houston@ewhealthcare.com
Education: BS, Louisiana State University; MBA, University of Houston
Background: President, Woodlands Venture Capital Co.; various operations, marketing and finance positions in the health care industry
Directorships: Aronex Pharmaceuticals, Cell Therapeutics, EluSys, eNos, Sontra, NotifyMD, Zonagen, Rinat Neuroscience, Confluent Surgical
Petri Vainno, MD, PhD, Managing Director
e-mail: london@ewhealthcare.com
Education: MD, PhD Biochemistry with highest academic honors, Helsinki University of Technology; MBA, Stanford University
Background: General Partner, Sierra Ventures
Directorships: Chroma Theupeutics, Molecular Partners, Elisa Pharma, Prism
Ron Eastman, Managing Director
e-mail: paloalto@ewhealthcare.com
Education: BA, Williams College; MBA, Columbia University
Background: American Cyanamid Company; Pfizer
Directorships: OMT, Cerium, RaduSys, Cell Biosciences
Guido Neels, Operating Partner
e-mail: paloalto@ewhealthcare.com
Education: MBA, Stanford University; Business Degree, Engineering, University of Leuven, Belgium
Background: COO, Guidant
Directorships: LeMaitre Vascular, WMR Biomedical, EndGenitor Technologies, Radiant Medical
Scott Barry, Managing Director
e-mail: newyork@ewhealthcare.com
Education: BA, Wesleyan University; MBA, New York University
Background: Novartis Pharma AG
Directorships: Victory Pharma, Orthovita, United Orthotic Group, Ziopharm Oncology
Evis Hursever, Managing Director
e-mail: london@ewhealthcare.com
Education: BA, Macalester College; PhD, University of Pennsylvania
Background: LEK Consulting, Merrill Lynch

699 EUREKA GROWTH CAPITAL
1717 Arch Street
34th Floor
Philadelphia, PA 19103

Phone: 267-238-4200 **Fax:** 267-363-3109
web: www.eurekaequity.com

Mission Statement: Makes private capital investments in lower middle market growth companies.

Geographic Preference: Mid-Atlantic, Eastern United States
Fund Size: $175 million
Founded: 1999
Average Investment: $8 - $15 million
Minimum Investment: $4 million
Investment Criteria: Acquisitions, Corporate Divestitures, Minority-Interest Growth Equity
Industry Group Preference: Healthcare Services, Manufacturing, Business Products & Services, Consumer Products, Consumer Services

Portfolio Companies: CCA Floors & Interiors, Everite Machine Products, Jansy Packaging, NetBoss Technologies, Project Leadership Associates, Toxicology Holdings, UTC Retail, West Academic Publishing

Key Executives:
Christopher G Hanssens, Managing Partner
267-238-4218
e-mail: chanssens@eurekagrowth.com
Education: BS, Accounting, Villanova University; MBA, Wharton School, University of Pennsylvania
Background: VP, Murray, Devine & Co.; Management Consultant, Accenture
Directorships: CCA Floors & Interiors, Project Leadership Associates, West Academic Publishing
Jonathan Y Chou, Partner
267-238-4203
e-mail: jchou@eurekagrowth.com
Education: BA, Economics, Columbia University; MBA, Wharton School, University of Pennsylvania
Background: Engagement Manager, LEK Consulting; Associate, Value Asset Management; Financial Analyst, Alex. Brown
Directorships: Everite Machine Products, Project Leadership Associates
Christian T Miller, Partner
267-238-4204
e-mail: cmiller@eurekagrowth.com
Education: AB, Economics, Princeton University; MBA, Wharton School, University of Pennsylvania
Background: Consultant, LEK Consulting; Investment Banking Associate, Berwind Financial Group; Accenture
Directorships: CCA Floors & Interiors, Jansy Packaging, NetBoss Technologies, Toxicology Holdings, UTC Retail, West Academic Publishing

700 EVERCORE CAPITAL PARTNERS
55 East 52nd Street
New York, NY 10055

Phone: 212-857-3100 **Fax:** 212-857-3101
web: www.evercore.com

Mission Statement: Evercore is an advisory and investment banking firm offering advisory and management services on corporate transactions and institutional asset, wealth, and private equity funds management.

Founded: 1996
Average Investment: $10 - $90 million
Investment Criteria: LBO, MBO, Early Stage, Mergers & Acquisitions, Divestitures
Industry Group Preference: Communications, Storage, Enterprise Services, Technology, Internet Technology, Data Services, Software

Other Locations:
666 Fifth Avenue
11th Floor
New York, NY 10103
Phone: 212-446-5600

One International Place
Boston, MA 02110
Phone: 617-449-3502

One North Wacker Drive
Suite 4010
Chicago, IL 60606
Phone: 312-619-4260

2 Houston Center at 909 Fannin
Suite 1750
Houston, TX 77010
Phone: 713-403-2440 **Fax:** 713-403-2444

515 South Figueroa Street
Suite 1000

Venture Capital & Private Equity Firms / Domestic Firms

Los Angeles, CA 90071
Phone: 213-443-2620 **Fax:** 313-443-2630

11111 Santa Monica Blvd
Suite 1480
Los Angeles, CA 90025
Phone: 310-473-0362

2494 Sand Hill Road
Suite 200
Menlo Park, CA 94025
Phone: 650-561-0100 **Fax:** 650-561-0101

150 South Fifth Street
Suite 1330
Minneapolis, MN 55402
Phone: 612-656-2820 **Fax:** 612-656-2830

Three Embarcadero Center
Suite 1450
San Francisco, CA 94111
Phone: 415-989-8900 **Fax:** 415-989-8929

425 California Street
Suite 1500
San Francisco, CA 94104
Phone: 415-288-3000

5359 Highway North
Suite 103
St Charles, MO 63304
Phone: 636-447-7422

4030 Boy Scout Blvd
Suite 475
Tampa, FL 33607
Phone: 813-313-1190 **Fax:** 813-434-2462

1000 Winter Street
Suite 4400
Waltham, MA 02451
Phone: 781-370-4700 **Fax:** 781-370-4747

1130 Connecticut Avenue Northwest
Suite 625
Washington, DC 20036
Phone: 202-530-5626

15 Stanhope Gate
London W1K 1LN
United Kingdom
Phone: 44-2076536000 **Fax:** 44-2076536001

50 St Mary Axe
4th Floor
London EC3A 8FR
United Kingdom
Phone: 44-2078473500

7 Queens Gardens
Aberdeen AB15 4YD
United Kingdom
Phone: 44-1224619214 **Fax:** 44-1224218510

Torre Virreyes
Pedregal 24, Piso 15
Col Molino del Rey, Miguel Hidalgo
Mexico City, Distrito Federal 11040
Mexico
Phone: 52-5552494300 **Fax:** 52-5552494317

Batalion de San Patricio 111, Piso 29
Torre Comercial America
Col. Valle Oriente
San Pedro Garza Garcia 66269
Mexico
Phone: 52-8181335550 **Fax:** 52-8181335526

Two Exchange Square
Suite 1405-1407
Central
Hong Kong
Phone: 852-39832600 **Fax:** 852-28690319

12 Marina Blvd
33-01 Marina Bay Financial Centre
Tower 3 018982
Singapore
Phone: 65-62907000 **Fax:** 65-62907001

Av Brigadeiro Faria Lima 3311
10th Floor
Sao Paulo 04538-133
Brazil
Phone: 55-1130146868 **Fax:** 55-1130146869

Av Borges de Medeiros
633 Sala 206
Rio de Janeiro 22430 042
Brazil
Phone: 55-2132059180 **Fax:** 55-2132059181

181 Bay Street
Suite 3630
Toronto, ON M5J 2T3
Canada
Phone: 416-304-8100 **Fax:** 416-352-5897

Paseo de la Castellana 36-38
Pl 10
Madrid 28046
Spain
Phone: 34-911190584

Ulmenstr 37-39
Frankfurt am Main 60325
Germany
Phone: 49-697079990 **Fax:** 49-6970799910

Key Executives:
Ralph Schlosstein, Co-Chair/Co-CEO
Education: BA, Economics, Denison University; MPP, University of Pittsburgh
Background: CEO, HighView Investment Group; Co-Founder & President, BlackRock; Managing Director, Investment Banking, Lehman Brothers
Directorships: Pulte Corporation
John Weinberg, Co-Chair/Co-CEO
Education: BA, Princeton University; MBA, Harvard Business School
Background: Vice Chair, Goldman Sachs; Co-Head, Global Investment Banking
Roger Altman, Founder/Senior Chair
Education: AB, Georgetown University; MBA, University of Chicago
Background: General Partner, Lehman Brothers; Vice Chair, The Blackstone Group
Robert Walsh, Senior Managing Director/Chief Financial Officer
Education: BS, Villanova University
Background: Senior Partner, Deloitte & Touche LLP
Directorships: New York Cares, IFA Insurance Company

701 EVEREST GROUP
PO Box 27395
Omaha, NE 68127

Phone: 402-548-5600
web: www.everestusa.net

Mission Statement: Everest Group focuses specificlaly on Service-based businesses such as marketing, financial and business outsourcing services.

Key Executives:
Vinod Gupta, Managing General Partner
Education: MBA, University of Nebraska
Background: Founder, Business Research Services; Founder, American Business Lists

Venture Capital & Private Equity Firms / Domestic Firms

702 EVERGREEN ADVISORS
9256 Bendix Road
Suite 300
Columbia, MD 21045

Phone: 410-997-6000
e-mail: info@evergreenadvisorsllc.com
web: www.evergreenadvisorsllc.com

Mission Statement: Provides investment banking services to emerging growth businesses and middle market companies throughout the Mid-Atlantic region.

Geographic Preference: Mid-Atlantic
Founded: 2001
Investment Criteria: Emerging Growth, Corporate Finance, Exit Strategies, Middle Market, Mezzanine, Debt Financing, Divestitures
Industry Group Preference: Consumer Services, Financial Services, Database Services, Marketing, Business to Business, Information Technology, Healthcare Services, Medical Devices, Internet, Digital Media & Marketing

Other Locations:
2010 Corporate Ridge
Suite 320
McLean, VA 22102
Phone: 571-406-5230

Key Executives:
Rick Kohr, Founding Member/Chief Executive Officer
Education: BA, Accounting, MBA, Finance & Marketing, Loyola University
Background: Managing Member, Chesapeake Emerging Opportunities Club
Directorships: LifeJourney, Pathsensors, Economic Alliance of Greater Baltimore, Howard County Economic Development Authority, Healthcare Interactive, BWTech
Joseph Statter, Managing Director
Education: BS, Accounting, University of Maryland
Background: CFO, CTB Group; CFO, Capitol Acquisition Corp.; Managing Director, Friedman Billings & Ramsey & Co.; Senior Manager, Arthur Andersen
Directorships: iCore Networks
Greg Huff, Partner
Education: Harvard College; JD, University of Maryland School of Law
Background: Director, M&A, CoreStates Securities Corp.; VP, Corporate Finance Department, Mercantile-Safe Deposit & Trust Company

703 EVOLVE CAPITAL
P.O. Box 181569
Dallas, TX 75218

Phone: 214-220-4800
e-mail: jeff@evolvecapital.com
web: www.evolvecapital.com

Mission Statement: A private equity firm focused exclusively on leveraged capitalizations of entrepreneurial businesses.

Founded: 2005
Investment Criteria: $2 to $5 million EBITDA
Industry Group Preference: Healthcare, Industrial Services, Life Sciences
Portfolio Companies: Aspire Home Care, Biologos, Controlled Contamination Services, Doctor's Choice Home Care, Indigo Biosystems, Power Design Services

Key Executives:
Jeff Baker, Partner
e-mail: jeff@evolvecapital.com
Education: BA, Government, JD, University of Texas, Austin
Background: Attorney, Locke Lord Billell & Liddell; DLA Piper
Mike Crothers, Founder
e-mail: mike@evolvecapital.com
Education: BA, International Relations, University of Virginia
Background: Founder, Transition Capital Partners; Best Associates
Heidi Hargrove, Partner
e-mail: heidi@evolvecapital.com
Education: Texas A&M University, Commerce
Background: General Accounting, Transition Capital Partners; Accounting, Renshaw Davis & Ferguson
Matt Becker, Partner
e-mail: matt@evolvecapital.com
Education: BS, Physics, University of North Carolina; Siemens AG Executive Business Leadership Program
Background: CEO, Data Division, Volex Plc.; CEO, KVT Koenig; Operations, Siemens VDO
Ryan Shulz, Partner
e-mail: ryan@evolvecapital.com
Education: BBA, Master of Professional Accounting, McCombs School of Business, University of Texas, Austin
Background: CFO, Glass & Associates

704 EXCEL VENTURE MANAGEMENT
200 Clarendon Street
17th Floor
Boston, MA 02116

Phone: 617-450-9800 Fax: 617-450-9749
web: www.excelvm.com

Mission Statement: Excel Venture Management builds companies that are devoted to developing innovative and transformative life science technologies.

Fund Size: $125 million
Average Investment: $1 - $5 million
Investment Criteria: Early- to Late-Stage
Industry Group Preference: Life Sciences, Healthcare, Information Technology, Diagnostics, Medical Devices, Agriculture, Energy
Portfolio Companies: Activate Networks, Aileron Therapeutics, Aventura, Ayogo, Biocius Life Sciences, BioTrove, Catch, ClearDATA, Cleveland HeartLab, Gemphire Therapeutics, IlluminOss, InfoBionic, Lantos Technologies, MedVentive, Molecular Templates, NanoMR, Neosensory, N-of-One, Oculus Health, Openwater, Orionis Biosciences, Qstream, Saladax, ShapeUp, Synthetic Genomics, Tetraphase Pharmaceuticals, Virgin Pulse, WellDoc, Zipongo

Key Executives:
Rick Blume, Managing Director
Education: University of the Pacific; MBA, Stanford University
Background: Genentech; Co-Founder, CB Health Ventures
Directorships: Saladax Biomedical, Cytyc, EdenTec, Lantos Technologies, AbT, Zonare
Juan Enriquez, Managing Director
Education: BA, Harvard University; MBA, Harvard Business School
Background: Founding Director, Life Sciences Project, Harvard Business School; Founder, Biotechonomy Ventures
Directorships: Cabot Corporation, Genetics Advisory Council of Harvard Medical School, Visiting Committee of Harvard's David Rockefeller Center
Steve Gullans PhD, Managing Director
Education: BS, Union College; PhD, Duke University
Background: Co-Founder, RxGen; Senior Executive, US Genomics; CellActPharma GmbH; Senior Advisor, CB Health Ventures
Directorships: Molecular Templates, Cleveland HeartLab
Caleb Winder, Managing Director
Education: BA, Biology, Colby College; MBA, Babson College
Background: Principal, Biotechonomy; Synthetic Genomics; BioTrove; Biocius; Xcellerex
Directorships: Aileron, Aventura, Ayogo, ClearData,

Venture Capital & Private Equity Firms / Domestic Firms

InfoBionic, Molecular Templates, ShapeUp, Saladax Biomedical, MedVentive
Gaye Bok, Venture Partner
Education: BA, Harvard College; MBA, Finance & International Management, MIT Sloan School of Management
Background: Microbia; Senior Director, Business Development, Synthetic Genomics; Business Development Manager, Cabot Corporation
Directorships: QStream
Chris Seitz, Venture Fellow
Education: BA, Williams College
Background: Consultant, Health Advances; Partner, Dorm Room Fund; ZocDoc
Kathryn Taylor, Associate
Education: BA, Quantitative Economics & International Relations, Tufts University
Background: Project Manager, New Product Development, The Advisory Board Company; Consultant, Putnam Associates

705 EXCELL PARTNERS, INC.
343 State St.
Rochester, NY 14650

Phone: 585-458-7333
e-mail: info@excellny.com
web: www.excellny.com

Mission Statement: Excell is a VC fund that invests in Seed and Early Stage high-tech startups in New York State focused on Upstate NY. Excell has the dual mission of generating returns through its funds' that rank in the top-quartile of its benchmarks, and supporting regional economic development by providing entrepreneurs with hands-on support as well as investment capital.

Geographic Preference: Finger Lakes Region of Upstate New York
Founded: 2005
Industry Group Preference: High Technology
Portfolio Companies: Adarza, Advantage Home Telehealth, American Fuel Cell, Augmate, Cerebral Assessment Systems, Cerion Energy, Conamix, CypherWorX, Diffinity Genomics, Diligence Labs, Efferent Labs, EkoStinger, First Crush, Full Circle Feed, GiveGab, Glauconix, Graphenix Development, GRYT, IMSWorkX, Kinvolved, Koning, Mezmeriz, MicrOrganic Tech., Molecular Glasses, OSM Environmental, PharmAdva, Rialto, SanaBit, Sensor Films, Splyce, StrongArm Tech., TenCar, Tetragenetics, Traverse Biosciences, Viggi Corp., VitaScan, WexEnergy

Key Executives:
Theresa B Mazzullo, Chief Executive Officer
Rami Katz, Chief Operating Officer

706 EXIUM PARTNERS
144 Village Landing
#276
Fairport, NY 14450

Phone: 888-983-9486
e-mail: info@exiumpartners.com
web: www.exiumpartners.com

Mission Statement: We invest in healthy businesses with strong growth potential. In doing so, we bring liquidity to owners looking to sell majority ownership to a partner that will respect what they've built, care for their employees, and continue to grow the business in the future.

Geographic Preference: Upstate New York, Southeast, Midwest
Investment Criteria: Change of Control, Recapitalization, Corporate Spin-Outs, Public-to-Private
Key Executives:
Jeff Valentine, Co-Founder/Partner
Education: Materials Science & Engineering, Cornell University
Background: CEO, Callfinity
Josh Bouk, Partner
Education: BS, Computer Science and Mathematics, State University of New York, College at Brockport
Background: VP, Sales and Marketing, Expense Management Division, Cass Information Systems; Veramark Technologies; COO, Connected Energy Corp.

707 EXPANSION CAPITAL PARTNERS
58 Andrews Drive
Darien, CT 06820

Phone: 203-202-2109
e-mail: info@expansioncapital.com

Mission Statement: To partner with entrepreneurs to grow clean technology companies that become respected industry leaders. We invest in companies that offer improvements in resource efficiency and productivity, while creating more economic value with less energy and materials, or less waste and toxicity.

Founded: 2002
Average Investment: $2 - $7 million
Investment Criteria: Growth Stage; Revenues of $5-30 Million
Industry Group Preference: Clean Technology, Energy, Water, Manufacturing, Advanced Materials, Transportation
Portfolio Companies: Agile Systems, Biorem, CPower, Dirtt, ElementLabs, Orion, Powerit Solutions, Sensortran, TigerOptics

Key Executives:
Bernardo H. Llovera, General Partner
e-mail: bernardo@expansioncapital.com
Education: BA, Engineering Sciences, Dartmouth College; Diploma Accounting & Finance, London School of Economics; MBA, Kellogg Graduate School of Business Administration, Northwestern University
Background: Senior Vice President, GE Equity; Senior Manager, Sara Lee Corporation
Directorships: Biorem, Powerit Holdings, Tiger Optics
Diana Propper de Callejon, General Partner
e-mail: diana@expansioncapital.com
Education: BA, Duke University; MBA, Harvard Business School
Background: Founder & Managing Director, EA Capital
Directorships: Echoing Green
John A. (Tony) Mayer, Board Memeber/Advisor
Education: BA, Princeton University; MBA, Harvard Business School
Background: Managing Director/CEO, JP Morgan

708 EXPANSION VENTURE CAPITAL
250 West 57th Street
RM 1301
New York, NY 10107

Phone: 212-265-1220 Fax: 516-882-5307
e-mail: info@expansionvc.com
web: www.expansionvc.com

Mission Statement: Expansion VC is an angel/VC firm that provides capital investments to early-stage companies focused on the Internet, e-commerce, education, biotechnology, and energy markets.

Founded: 2011
Investment Criteria: Early-Stage
Industry Group Preference: Internet, E-Commerce & Manufacturing, Education, Biotechnology, Energy
Portfolio Companies: Able, Agentero, Alchemy 43, Allbirds, AngelList, Apptopia, Ark, Astro, Aurora Labs, Bear Flag Robotics, Beyond Games, Bizly, Boatbound, Boomtown!, Booster, Bowery, Bulletin, Caarbon, Capsalus, Carrot Fertility, Chalkable, Compstak, Crius Energy, Dataminr, Decartes Labs, Emergent One, Engrade, Enigma, eShares, Esquire Bank, FanAI, Firebase, Fitmob, Fitocracy,

HelloTech, Honk, Instamotor, InVenture, Latch, LegitParents, Lemonade, Life360, LoftSmart, Lola, Lunar, Maker's Row, May Mobility, Maz, Mino Monsters, Naadam, NewHound, Nexar, OrderUp, Outbox, Paintzen, Peek, Periscope, Pillow, PopExpert, Postmates, Pricing Engine, Recharge, Red Tricycle, Redcap, RelayRides, Rinse, See Me, Shuddle, Skurt, Slide, Socratic Labs, Sols, Stream, Student Loan Hero, Super, Tender Tree, TheFutureFM, The RealReal, Transfix, Turo, Unbound Concepts, Verificient Technologies, Via, VidIQ, Viridian, Viridis, Vive, YieldStreet, ZenDrive

Key Executives:
Joseph Melohn, Founder/CEO
Background: Owner, Platinum Brokerage Group LLC
Ryan Melohn, Co-Founder/COO
Education: BS, Business Management
Background: President, Expansion Group

709 EXPERIMENT FUND
67 Mt. Auburn St.
Cambridge, MA 02138

Phone: 650-204-1636
e-mail: start@xfund.com
web: xfund.com

Mission Statement: The Experiment Fund, anchored in Cambridge, invests in world-changing startups. We catalyze bold ideas and build transformative companies. XFund offers experimenters seed capital, expert guidance, and unparalleled access to America's top-tier universities and venture capital firms.

Geographic Preference: East Coast
Investment Criteria: Seed-Stage
Industry Group Preference: Information Technology, Healthcare, Energy, Technology
Portfolio Companies: 23andMe, Curebase, Fort Awesome, Guideline, Halo Neuro, Kensho, Kiite, Landit, Nebula Genomics, NewtonX, Parts Market, Philo, Ravel, Rest Devices, Service, Synapse, Tonic.ai, Zumper

Other Locations:
390 Lytton Ave.
Palo Alto, CA 94301

Key Executives:
Patrick Chung, Partner
e-mail: patrick@xfund.com
Education: JD, Harvard Law School; MBA, Harvard Business School; MS, Oxford University; AB, Harvard College
Background: Co-Head, NEA Seed
Directorships: 23andMe; Philo; Ravel Law
Brandon Farwell, Partner
e-mail: brandon@xfund.com
Education: BA, Economics and International Relations, Stanford University; MBA, Harvard Business School
Background: Investment Professional, DFJ; Rothenberg Ventures

710 EcoR1 CAPITAL
409 Illinois St.
San Francisco, CA 94158

Phone: 415-754-3517
e-mail: info@ecor1cap.com
web: ecor1.wpengine.com

Mission Statement: EcoR1 Capital invests in companies that seek to move medical research and biotechnology forward to advance an improve drug development.

Industry Group Preference: Biotechnology, Drug Development, Therapeutics
Portfolio Companies: Aldila Therapeutics, Accent Therapeutics, Anagin, Arcus Biosciences, Atara Bio, Atreca, aTyr Pharma, Avidity NanoMedicines, Clementia, Codiak, Collegium Pharmaceutical, Denali Therapeutics, Editas Medicine, FlexPharma, GossamerBio, Intellia Therapeutics, Kezar Life Sciences, Kindred Bio, Kura Oncology, Magenta Therapeutics, Metacrine, Morphic Therapeutic, Nabriva Therapeutics, Naurex, OmniOx, Oric Pharmaceuticals, Pellepharm, Prevail Therapeutics, Relay Therapeutics, Rubius Therapeutics, Sage Therapeutics, Scholar Rock, Syndax, Unity Biotechnology

Key Executives:
Oleg Nodelman, Founder/Managing Director
Education: BS, Georgetown University
Background: Portfolio Manager, BVF Partners; Mercer Management Consulting
Scott Platshon, Principal
Education: BS, Stanford University
Background: Aquilo Partners
Caroline Stout, Principal
Education: BA, Georgetown University
Background: Investment Banking Analyst, Credit Suisse

711 F-PRIME CAPITAL PARTNERS
1 Main Street
13th Floor
Cambridge, MA 02142

Phone: 617-231-2400
e-mail: info@fprimecapital.com
web: www.fprimecapital.com

Mission Statement: F-Prime Capital Partners combines two former venture funds, Fidelity Biosciences and Devonshire Investors. A global venture capital firm, F-Prime Capital invests in healthcare and technology companies in all stages of development.

Geographic Preference: Global
Investment Criteria: All Stages
Industry Group Preference: Biopharmaceuticals, Medical Technology, Therapeutics, Medical Devices, Healthcare Information Technology, Enterprise Software, Fintech
Portfolio Companies: AcaciaPharma, Aclaris Therapeutics, Adagene, Adaptimmune, Amphora Medical, AppsFlyer, Avidity Nanomedicines, Bang Er Medical, Better Life Medical, BioConnect Systems, BioRegen, Caribou Biosciences, Codeship, Cygnus Hospitals, Cytoville, Denali Therapeutics, Dimension Therapeutics, Eris Exchange, EVEN Financial, Eyebright Medical, Flywire, Forum Pharmaceuticals, Good Data, Gu Sheng Tang, HQ Medical Technology, Hua Medicine, Ikano Therapeutics, Innovent Biologics, Iora Health, Ivenix, Kensho Technologies, Kyruus, Laurus Labs, Madaket Health, MDDF, Medwell, Mersana Therapeutics, Neo4j, Novaerus, Orient Speech Therapy, OwnCloud, PatientPing, Ping Identity, Precision Biosciences, Procured Health, Prosper, Proteostasis, Pulmocide, Quartet Health, ReadMe, Receivables Exchange, Recurly, ReGenX Biosciences, Semma Therapeutics, Stride Health, Surface Oncology, Symbiomix, TraceLink, TradeBlock, Tradier, Trivitron Healthcare, Unum Therapeutics, US HealthVest

Other Locations:
33 Foley Street
London W1W 7TL
United Kingdom

Key Executives:
Stephen Knight MD, President/Managing Partner
Education: BS, Biology, Columbia University; MD, Yale University School of Medicine; MBA, Yale School of Organization & Management
Background: Researcher, AT&T Bell Laboratories; Consultant, Arthur D. Little; President & COO, EPIX Pharmaceuticals
Directorships: Innovent Biologics, Proteostasis Therapeutics, Iora Health, Pulmocide, Semma Therapeutics, Denali Therapeutics
Robert Weisskoff PhD, Partner
Education: AB, Physics, Harvard University; MBA, Columbia University; PhD, Physics, Massachusetts Institute of Technology
Background: Associate Professor, Radiology, Harvard Medical School; Faculty, Harvard-MIT Health Sciences

Venture Capital & Private Equity Firms / Domestic Firms

Technology Program; Associate Director, MGH-NMR Center, Massachusetts General Hospital
Directorships: Bioconnect Systems, Caribou Biosciences, FORUM Pharmaceuticals, Laurus Labs, Surface Oncology, Trivitron Healthcare, ViewRay
David Jegen, Managing Partner
e-mail: david@fprimecapital.com
Education: Indiana University; Harvard Law School
Background: Senior Executive, Cisco Systems; JP Morgan & Company; The Boston Consulting Group
John Raguin, Venture Partner
Education: BS, Electrical Engineering, Cornell University; MBA, New York University Stern School of Business
Background: Co-Founder & CEO, Guidewire Software; VP, Sourcing Solutions Group, Ariba; MRO Software; Work Technology Corporation

712 FA TECHNOLOGY VENTURES
1000 Winter Street
Waltham, MA 02451

Phone: 781-786-8780
web: www.fatechventures.com

Mission Statement: FA Technology Ventures seeks opportunities with innovative businesses founded on the development of breakthrough technologies. The firm places particular emphasis on early and expansion stage companies in the technology and enterprise software sectors.

Geographic Preference: Northeast NY
Fund Size: $125 million
Founded: 2000
Average Investment: $3 - $8 million
Minimum Investment: $3 million
Investment Criteria: Early Stage, Expansion Stage, Growth Capital
Industry Group Preference: Technology, Energy Technology, Enterprise Software, Robotics
Portfolio Companies: Auterra, CreditSights, Knoa Software, OnePIN
Key Executives:
  Gregory Hulecki, Founder/General Partner
  Education: BSEE, Kettering University; MBA, Harvard Business School
  Background: Founder & Managing Director, Seacoast Capital; Principal, Capital Growth Partners
  Directorships: Auterra
  Kenneth Mabbs, Founder/General Partner
  Education: BA, Denison University; MBA, Wharton School, University of Pennsylvania; PhD, Harvard University
  Background: Director, Investment & Merchant Banking, Gleacher and Company; Bear Stearns and Company
  Directorships: Knoa Software, OnePIN

713 FAIRHAVEN CAPITAL
1 Hampshire Street
Suite 3
Cambridge, MA 02139

Phone: 617-452-0800 Fax: 617-452-0801
e-mail: info@fairhavencapital.com
web: www.fairhavencapital.com

Mission Statement: Fairhaven Capital invests in and helps to build early stage technology companies that are positioned for growth.

Fund Size: $250 million
Founded: 2001
Investment Criteria: Early-Stage
Industry Group Preference: Technology, Consumer Products, Digital Media & Marketing, Financial Services, Materials Technology, Security, Mobile, SaaS, Data Storage, Semiconductors, Network Infrastructure, Advertising
Portfolio Companies: Celtra, Cloakware, Cocona, Contour Semiconductor, CounterTack, CrowdTwist, Cylance, Digital Guardian, Drizly, EqualLogic, Exoprise Systems, HelloSoft, Icera, InnoPad, Ionic Materials, iPhrase, Jibo, NanoSteel, Prelert, Pwnie Express, Ramp, Resilient, ShopWell, SiGe Semiconductor, SocialFlow, Softricity, Statisfy, Third Screen Media, TrackVia, Trust Digital, VeloBit, YottaMark
Key Executives:
  Paul Ciriello, Partner
  Education: BA, Political Science, State University of New York at Buffalo; MPA, Northeastern University
  Background: Founder, TD Capital Ventures; President, Fidelity Interactive, Fidelity Investments
  Directorships: Cloakware, Fortisphere, iPhrase, SiGe Semiconductor, Softricity, Spring Partners, Surge Trading, Third Screen Media
  Jim Goldinger, Partner
  Education: BS, MS, Electrical Engineering, Massachusetts Institute of Technology; MBA, MIT Sloan School of Management
  Background: Co-Founder, TD Capital Ventures; Chief Technical Architect, Adero
  Directorships: Cocona, Contour Semiconductor, HelloSoft, InnoPad, Lilliputian Systems, NanoSteel, SiRiFIC Wireless
  Rick Grinnell, Partner
  Education: BS, MS, Electrical Engineering, Massachusetts Institute of Technology; MBA, Harvard Business School
  Background: Co-Founder, TD Capital Ventures; Marketing, Content Bridge Division, Adero; ClearOne Communications
  Directorships: Brabeion, Bridgeport Networks, Dataupia, Everypoint, EqualLogic
  Rudina Seseri, Partner
  Education: BA, Economics & International Relations, Wellesley College; MBA, Harvard Business School
  Background: Senior Manager, Corporate Development, Microsoft Corporation; Investment Banking, Technology Group, Credit Suisse
  Directorships: Fashion Playtes
  Wan Li Zhu, Partner
  Education: Massachusetts Institute of Technology; MBA, Harvard Business School
  Background: Global Product Manager, Microsoft Dynamics CRM; General Manager, Online Sales & Operations in Asia Pacific, Google; Technology Investment Banking, Morgan Stanley

714 FAIRMONT CAPITAL
18340 Yorba Linda Blvd
Suite 107
Yorba Linda, CA 92286

Phone: 714-524-4770
web: www.fairmontcapital.com

Mission Statement: Fairmont Capital is a private equity firm that invests in middle-market businesses in the consumer-related sector.

Fund Size: $300 million
Founded: 1986
Average Investment: $10 - $20 million
Minimum Investment: $1 million
Investment Criteria: Leveraged Acquisitions, MBO, LBO, Private Restructurings, Recapitalization
Industry Group Preference: Manufacturing, Retailing, Restaurants, Distribution, Services
Portfolio Companies: Expressions Furniture, Garden Fresh Restaurant, Insurance Auto Auctions, Krause's Sofa Factory, Shari's Management Corporation, Stampede Meat, VICORP Restaurants, White Pine Company
Key Executives:
  Michael W Gibbons, President
  Education: BA, Harvard University; MBA, Stanford

Venture Capital & Private Equity Firms / Domestic Firms

University
Background: Co-Founder & EVP, Equivest Partners; VP, Crocker Bank; Senior Associate, ICF International; Consultant, Booz Allen Hamilton
Mark J Gill, Managing Director
Education: BA, Economics, University of California, Davis; MBA, Finance, Golden Gate University
Background: VP Controller, John Breuner Company; Weinstocks

715 FAIRVIEW CAPITAL PARTNERS
75 Isham Road
Suite 200
West Hartford, CT 06107

Phone: 860-674-8066
web: www.fairviewcapital.com

Mission Statement: Fairview Capital Partners is a venture capital and private equity investment management firm that offers fund of funds as well as investment strategies and services to investors.

Geographic Preference: United States
Fund Size: $3.7 billion
Founded: 1994
Investment Criteria: Growth Equity, Buyouts, Expansion
Industry Group Preference: All markets considered

Other Locations:
1 Ferry Building
Suite 201
San Francisco, CA 94111

Key Executives:
JoAnn H. Price, Co-Founder/Managing Partner
e-mail: jprice@fairviewcapital.com
Education: Howard University
Background: President, National Association of Investment Companies
Directorships: YMCA of Greater Hartford
Laurence C. Morse PhD, Co-Founder/Managing Partner
e-mail: lcmorse@fairviewcapital.com
Education: Howard University; MA, PhD, Princeton University
Background: TSG Ventures; Equico Capital Corporation; UNC Ventures
Directorships: Webster Financial Corporation, Institute of International Education
Kola Olofinboba, Managing Partner
e-mail: kolofinboba@fairviewcapital.com
Education: University of Ibadan, Nigeria; MBA, Financial Management, Massachusetts Institute of Technology Sloan School of Management
Background: Engagement Manager, McKinsey & Company; Assistant Professor, University of Connecticut Health Center
Directorships: National Association of Investment Companies, Connecticut Children's Medical Center
Alan Mattamana, Partner
e-mail: alanm@fairviewcapital.com
Education: BSE, Chemical Engineering, Princeton University; MBA, Harvard Business School
Background: Principal, Polaris Venture Partners; Strategy Consultant, McKinsey & Co.
Directorships: West Hartford YMCA
Edwin Shirley, Senior Advisor
e-mail: eshirley@fairviewcapital.com
Education: BA, Hampton University; MPA, Woodrow Wilson School of Public and International Affairs, Princeton University
Background: Equitable Capital Management Corporation
Directorships: Milestone Growth Fund, The Amistad Center for Art & Culture, Bushnell Performing Arts Center, Hartford Symphony Orchestra

716 FALCON FUND
100 N Barranca Street
Suite 920
West Covina, CA 91791

Phone: 626-966-6235 Fax: 626-966-0193

Mission Statement: We invest both in companies we alone have conceived, and in companies based on concepts that are brought to us by their founders. We do not invest in ideas, but in people who are willing to commit five or more years of their lives to making a company, and who have good knowledge of the markets they intend to serve. We can and do invest in ventures without complete management teams, and with very rudimentary business plans.

Geographic Preference: Southern California
Fund Size: $30 million
Founded: 1982
Investment Criteria: Seed, Very Early Stage
Industry Group Preference: Telecommunications, Software, Aerospace, Defense and Government
Portfolio Companies: Constellation Services International, IQinvision, NanoRacks, Napo Pharmaceuticals, Pascal's Pocket Corporation; Social Fabric Corporation, Touchdown Technologies, Vivature

717 FALCONHEAD CAPITAL
75 Rockerfeller Plaza
Suite 1600B
New York, NY 10019

Phone: 212-634-3304
e-mail: info@falconheadcapital.com
web: www.falconheadcapital.com

Mission Statement: Falconhead Capital is a private equity firm that invests in companies in the consumer services, media, sports, lifestyle and food and beverage sectors. Falconhead Capital seeks to establish partnerships with stellar management teams and to create long-term value for its portfolio companies.

Fund Size: $500 million
Founded: 1998
Average Investment: $10 - $100 million
Minimum Investment: $5 million
Investment Criteria: MBO, LBO, Expansion, Middle Market
Industry Group Preference: Leisure, Sports, Media, Entertainment, Wellness, Food & Beverage, Consumer Services
Portfolio Companies: GPSI Holdings, Javo Beverage Company, Multi-Flow Industries, Rita's Water Ice Franchise Company

Key Executives:
David Moross, Founder/Chairman/CEO
Education: BA, Economics, University of Texas at Austin
Background: Vice Chairman, Whitehall Financial Group; Chairman, Insco; President, Kalvin-Miller International
Directorships: ESPN Classic Sports Europe, Maritime Telecommunications Network, National Power Sport Auctions, NYDJ Apparel Company, ESCORT Holdings
David Gubbay, General Partner
Background: Chairman & CEO, Whitehall Insurance Holdings, Whitehall Financial Group; Chairman, NHP Holdings; Head, Operations, Norwegian Cruise Lines; Digital Seas International; Conseco; Fellow, Institute of Chartered Accountants, England
Directorships: EXL Service, Whitehall Financial Group
Robert J Fioretti, Managing Director
Education: BSc, MBA, Wharton School, University of Pennsylvania
Background: Managing Director, Mistral Equity Partners; Trimaran Capital Partners; CIBC World Markets Corp.
Directorships: Worldlynx Wireless, Worldwise, Abe's Market

Venture Capital & Private Equity Firms / Domestic Firms

718 FCA VENTURE PARTNERS
110 Winners Circle
Suite 100
Brentwood, TN 37027

Phone: 615-326-4848 Fax: 615-963-3847
web: www.fcavp.com

Mission Statement: FCA Venture Partners believes that by focusing on healthcare services and healthcare technology as well as information technologies opportunities, particularly in early and growth stage companies in the Southeastern region of the United States, it can take advantage of excellent investment opportunities. With its location in Nashville, Tennessee, as well as FCA Venture Partners deep involvement in the growth of the Nashville healthcare community, the Fund is poised to take advantage of the multiple opportunities provided by the current disruptions in the economy and efforts by the healthcare industry to reduce costs and become more efficient in this changing marketplace.

Geographic Preference: Southeast United States
Fund Size: $75 million
Founded: 1996
Average Investment: $2 million
Minimum Investment: $500,000
Investment Criteria: Start-Up, First Round, Second Round
Industry Group Preference: Healthcare, Information Technology, Wireless Technologies, Technology
Portfolio Companies: Catavolt, Clinical Ink, ChartWise Medical Systems, Entrada Health, Health iPass, IdentalSoft, KeraFAST, LogoGarden, Lumere, MediQuire, MRA Medical Reimbursements of America, One Medical Passport, Pathfinder Health Innovations, ProviderTrust, Remedly, Silvercare Solutions, Spiras Health, StudioNow, Vericred, Vivante Health

Key Executives:
  Matthew A King, Managing Partner
  Background: VP, Third National Bank; Chairman, President, and CEO, Radar Business Systems; Founder, MyOfficeProducts, Inc.
  Directorships: Clinical Inc.; KeraFAST; MediQuire; StudioNow; Vericred
  John Burch, Partner
  Background: Clayton Associates; Co-Founder, MyOfficeProducts
  Directorships: Armor Concepts; ChartWise; Lumere; One Medical Passport; Pathfinder Health Innovations; ProviderTrust; Thalerus Group
  Nancy S Allen, Partner & Chief Financial Officer
  Background: Partner, Heathcott & Mullaly & Hill

719 FCF PARTNERS LP
250 West Coventry Court
Suite 201
Milwaukee, WI 53217

Phone: 414-213-7091
web: www.fcffunds.com

Mission Statement: Wisconsin based private equity fund, established as an SBIC and investing in established companies located in the upper Midwest.

Geographic Preference: Upper Midwest
Fund Size: $62 million
Founded: 1999
Average Investment: $2 - $15 million
Minimum Investment: $2 million
Investment Criteria: Management Buyout, Corporate Spinout, Leveraged Buyout, Growth Investment
Industry Group Preference: Manufacturing, Distribution, Food Services, Food & Beverage, Medical Devices, Specialty Chemicals, Paper, Capital Equipment, Niche Manufacturing, Financial Services, Outsourcing & Efficiency, Packaging
Portfolio Companies: Alkar-RapidPak, CERAC, Kolpin Outdoors, Kolpin Powersports, Oshkosh Floor Designs, Riverside Engineering, Riverside Products, Rondele Specialty Foods, Sani-Matic, Seattle Systems, Sivyer Steel Corporation, Thiel Cheese & Ingredients, Waukesha Kramer

Key Executives:
  Gus Taylor, Senior Managing Director
  414-807-4204
  e-mail: taylor@facilitatorfunds.com
  Education: Middlebury College; Stanford Business School
  Background: Operations, Firststar Bank; Partner, Lubar & Company
  Scott D. Roeper, Managing Director
  414-881-2760
  e-mail: roeper@facilitatorfunds.com
  Education: Lawrence University
  Background: Prudential Capital; Firstar Bank; Harris Bank
  Paul J. Raab, Managing Director
  414-807-4178
  e-mail: raab@facilitatorfunds.com
  Education: Marquette University; University of Chicago; CFA
  Background: Firstar Bank
  G. Woodrow Adkins, Managing Director
  414-861-0168
  Education: University of Maryland
  Background: President, ConAgra's Deli Company; Armour Food Service; Wis-Pak Foods; Swift & Co.; Turnaround Capital Partners; New Glarus Foods Inc.; Acme Machell Rubber Products Company

720 FELICIS VENTURES
2460 Sand Hill Road
Suite 100
Menlo Park, CA 94025

web: www.felicis.com

Mission Statement: Felicis Ventures targets innovative companies in five principal areas of focus: mobile, e-commerce, enterprise, education and health. Felicis Ventures strives to provide quality support to its portfolio companies.

Geographic Preference: United States, International
Fund Size: $270 Million
Founded: 2006
Average Investment: $100,000 - $1,000,000
Investment Criteria: All Stages
Industry Group Preference: Consumer Internet, Mobile, SaaS, E-Commerce & Manufacturing, Education, Enterprise Applications, Financial Services, Gaming, Healthcare, Media
Portfolio Companies: aira.io, Alma, Aloha, Any.do, Ascend.io, Astranis, AvidBots, Azumio, Bioage Labs, bitpay, Bluecore, Breezy, Bright, Canva, CarDash, Chloe & Isabel, Civitas Learning, Class Dojo, Clear Labs, Cleo, Codesignal, Creative Live, Credit Karma, CrunchBase, Culture Amp, Cymmetria, Cyphy Works, Dedrone, Dialpad, Diffbot, dinda, DNAnexus, Dots, Drivetime, Earnin, EduK, Elevate, Emailage, ERPLY, Everalbum, Factual Beta, Figure Eight, First Opinion, Flexport, Fluxx, FundersClub, Gamalon, Gigster, Ginkgo Bioworks, Gobble, Granular, Greenhouse.io, Grove, Guideline, Guild, Happiest Baby, Hearsay Systems, Hippo, HireArt, HyperScience, Juniper Square, Kahuna, KISSmetrics, KiwiCo, Komodohealth, LeanData, Lighthouse, Matterport, Metromile, MightyHive, Mobile Action, Muse, Octave, Okera, Opendoor, Optimizely, PeerStreet, PetaSense, Philo, Piazza, Pindrop, Plaid, Planet., plotwatt, Practicefusion, Predict Spring, Recursion Pharmeceuticals, Rich Relevance, Rigetti, Roadmunk, Sano Intelligence, Sapho, Savioke, Scaled Inference, Scopely, Simplifeye, Smartling, SoundHound Inc., Spoke, Spring, Survios, Swift Navigation, Thirdlove, Top Hat, Trackvia, TripleByte, Troops, TrueAccord, Tynker, Vicarious, Warby Parker, Wild Earth, Wish, Zaarly, Zefr, Zipline

Key Executives:
  Aydin Senkut, Founder/Managing Partner
  Education: BS, Business Administration, Boston

Venture Capital & Private Equity Firms / Domestic Firms

University; MBA, Marketing, Wharton School; MA, International Studies, School of Arts, University of Pennsylvania
Background: Senior Manager, Google; Product Manager, MineSet, SGI
Sundeep Peechu, General Partner
Education: BS, Computer Science, Indian Institute of Technology, Madras; MS, Computer Science, University of Illinois, Urbana-Champaign; MBA, Stanford Graduate School of Business
Background: Product Manager, Intel; NEA; Simbol Mining
Victoria Treyger, General Partner
Education: Business/International Studies, University of Washington; MBA, Harvard Business School
Background: Chief Revenue Officer, Kabbage; Amazon; American Express; Travelocity; RingCentral
Directorships: Hippo Analytics; Deluxe Holdings
Wesley Chan, General Partner
Education: BS/MS, Computer Science, Electrical Engineering, Massachusetts Institute of Technology
Background: General Partner, Google Ventures; Founder, Google Analytics & Google Voice, Google; HP Labs; Microsoft

721 FENOX VENTURE CAPITAL
2680 North First Street
Suite 250
San Jose, CA 95134

Phone: 408-645-5532
e-mail: contact@fenoxvc.com
web: www.fenoxvc.com

Mission Statement: Fenox Venture Capital is a Silicon Valley-based venture capital firm founded by an exceptional team of seasoned entrepreneurs and proven international business leaders. Fenox VC works with emerging technology companies worldwide and specializes in assisting entrepreneurs in North America achieve global expansion in Asian and European markets. Fenox VC seeks to work with world-class management and technical teams that are targeting disruptive opportunities in the consumer internet, retail, and software sectors.

Geographic Preference: North America, Asia, Middle East, Europe
Founded: 2011
Industry Group Preference: Consumer Internet, Retailing, Software
Portfolio Companies: Jibo, Genius, Affectiva, Meta, Afero, Color Genomics, Blockstream, X.ai, ShareThis, MindMeld, Terra Motors, Money Forward, TechninAsia, Metaps, Ossia, Lark, Scanadu, Evolable Asia, Gobble, Bluesmart, Zuu, Edyn, Jetlore, Sense.ly, Block Cypher, QVentus, Osaro, Sano, FiNC, Ahlijasa, Darmiyan, Sidecar, Medikly, True Vault, Kii, Money Design, Bop.fm, Dream Link Entertainment, I and C-Cruise.Co, NextCaller, Memebox, Pomelo, 500V, Moshimo, AloDoketer, Bride Story, Circa, HijUp, Third Love, IMoney, Regalii, MNectar, 99.co, Socialize, Rigetti, Roximity, Deepgram, 3Sourcing, Priyo.com, Talenta, Nova, Jurnal, Mailtime, Optilly, Wevorce, AirHelp, Panda Whale, GTar, BellaBeat, Women.com, Schematic Labs, Code Combat, Joyful Frog Digital Incubator, Belazee, Geniee, Crossfader, Xwork, KlikDaily, Jojonomic, Ajker Deal, Moka, 4doctor, Exvivo, Local, Multiply Labs, TeleCTG, Pesanlab, Bulletin, PopLegal, Sinovia Technologies, Paprika, Millibatt, Digicon Technologies, Monstar Lab, BagDoom.com

Key Executives:
Bill Reichert, Partner
Education: BA, Harvard College; MBA, Stanford University
Background: Chief Evangelist, Startup World Cup; Managing Director, Garage Technology Ventures; McKinsey & Co.; Brown Brothers Harriman & Co.; World Bank
Anis Uzzaman, General Partner
Education: BEng, Tokyo Institute of Technology; MS, Engineering, Oklahoma State University; PhD, Computer Engineering, Tokyo Metropolitan University
Background: Business Development, IBM
Brent Traidman, Advisor
Education: BA, Psychology & Economics, University of Michigan
Directorships: Edyn
Chris Abshire, Venture Partner
Education: BS, Petroleum Engineering, University of Kansas
Background: Evangelist, Startup World Cup

722 FENWAY PARTNERS
108 Airport Road
Suite 103
Westerly, RI 02891

Phone: 212-698-9400 Fax: 212-581-1205
e-mail: info@fenwaypartners.com
web: www.fenwaypartners.com

Mission Statement: Fenway Partners is a middle-market private equity firm that focuses primarily on the consumer products and transportation, logistics, and distribution sectors. Fenway Partners works with management teams to help build valuable companies.

Fund Size: $2.1 billion
Founded: 1994
Average Investment: $50 - $75 million
Minimum Investment: $25 million
Investment Criteria: LBO, Middle Market of $100 - $600 million
Industry Group Preference: Consumer Products, Transportation, Logistics, Distribution
Portfolio Companies: 1-800 Contacts, American Achievement, Aurora Foods, Blue Capital, BRG Sports, Coach America, DCI Holdings, Delimex, Fastfrate, Elogex, Greatwide Logistics, Harry Winston, Iron Age, M2, MW Windows, North American Archery, Panther Expedited, Preferred Freezer Services, Quality Farm & Country, RoadLink, Refrigerated Holdings, Simmons, SunTek, Sleep Country, Targus, Transport Industries, Valley-Dynamo, VB&P

Key Executives:
Peter Lamm, Co-Founder/Managing Director
e-mail: plamm@fenwaypartners.com
Education: BA, English Literature, Boston University; MBA, Columbia University
Background: Managing Director, Butler Capital Corporation; Co-Founder, Photoquick of America
Directorships: Easton-Bell Sports, Fastfrate, Preferred Freezer
Gregg Smart, Managing Director
e-mail: gsmart@fenwaypartners.com
Education: BA, Davidson College; MBA, Wharton School, University of Pennsylvania
Background: Managing Director, Merrill Lynch & Company; First Union National Bank
Directorships: American Achievement, SunTek, Preferred Freezer, RoadLink Workforce Solutions
Walter Wiacek, Vice President/Chief Financial Officer
e-mail: wwiacek@fenwaypartners.com
Education: BS, Business Administration, Bryant College
Background: CFO, Jupiter Partners

723 FERRER FREEMAN & COMPANY LLC
10 Glenville Street
Greenwich, CT 06831

Phone: 203-532-8011 Fax: 203-532-8016

Mission Statement: Invests exclusively in healthcare and healthcare related companies. Ferrer Freeman & Company aims

Venture Capital & Private Equity Firms / Domestic Firms

to build leading healthcare businesses by helping to drive the growth of its portfolio companies.

Fund Size: $900 million
Founded: 1995
Average Investment: $10 - $40 million
Investment Criteria: Mezzanine, LBO, MBO, Later Stage
Industry Group Preference: Medical & Health Related, Healthcare
Portfolio Companies: AeroCare Holdings, AgaMatrix, Ancillary Advantage, Arcadia Healthcare Solutions, Ardent Health Services, Biotix, IC Axon, K2M, Medical Depot, Reliant Renal Care

724 FF VENTURE CAPITAL
989 Avenue of the Americas
3rd Floor
New York, NY 10018

Mission Statement: FF Venture Capital is one of the oldest early-stage venture capital firms in New York, with over 160 investments in over 50 companies. FFVC's strategy is to be the institutional-quality investor in the Seed/Series A space by identifying and helping to build startups that can be the low cost, disruptive player in their industry. FFVC has a dozen employees and extensive resources dedicated to portfolio acceleration, including strategy consulting, an experienced mentor network, recruiting assistance, pre-negotiated discounts with preferred service providers, an executive portfolio community, and in-house accounting.

Geographic Preference: United States, Canada, Isreal
Founded: 2008
Average Investment: $500,000 - $750,000
Minimum Investment: $500,000
Investment Criteria: Early-Stage, Series A
Industry Group Preference: Internet, Software
Portfolio Companies: 500px, Addepar, Alarts.com, Alpha Vertex, Appy Couple, Authorea, The Better Software Company, Bitesnap, Bloomz, Bowtie, Cambrian Intelligence, CardFlight, Cielo24, Clarity Money, Contently, Conerstone, CyberX, Dashbot, Deem, Distil Networks, Doc Authority, .tv, Drop, Earnest, Elicit, Estify, Founder Suite, Four Mine, GameSalad, GlucoVista, Gooten, GreatHorn, Hello Vera, Hijro, HowAboutWe.com, Identified, Indiegogo, InfoChimp, Ionic, Jazz, Klout, Klustera, Lithium, Livefyre, Mainframe, Movable Ink, Mount Cleverest, Muse, OfferIQ, Omaze, Omek, OpenCare, Owlet, Parse.ly, Parents.com, Pear, Pebblepost, Phone.com, Plated, Playdek, Qualia, Quigo, Rescale, Rhino, Rinse, SecondMind, SignUp.com, Skip, Skycatch, Socure, Software.com, Stae, Sure, Surfair, Tackk, Theatermania, ThinkNear, Top Flight Technologies, Track.com, Transactis, UniKey, Voxy, Wade & Wendy, Whisk, Wonder, YieldMo

Key Executives:
John Frankel, Founder/Partner
Education: BA, New College, Oxford
Background: Goldman, Sachs & Co.
Directorships: 500px, Apparel Media Group, Alerts.com, BlueDomains, Centzy, ClearPath, Immigration, Infochimps, Interaxon, Media Gobbler, Klout, Patents.com, Parse.ly, Phone.Com, Quigo, Voxy
Alex Katz, Managing Partner
Education: BSBA, Drexel University; JD, Temple University School of Law
Background: Mesirov Gelman; Founding Partner, Katz & Miele, LLP; CEO, Fastener Distribution & Marketing Company
David Teten, Venture Partner
Education: BA, Yale University; MBA, Harvard Business School
Background: Founder & Chairman, Navon Partners; CEO, Vertical Key; Bear Stearns

725 FGA PARTNERS
99 Wall Street
Suite 1770
New York, NY 10005

Phone: 646-397-0588
e-mail: info@fgapartners.com
web: www.fgapartners.com

Mission Statement: A private equity firm that has a focus on disruptive software and technology in the areas of Artificial Intelligence, Machine Learning, Augmented Reality, Virtual Reality, Smart Technology and Advanced Blockchain Technology. Looks to invest and build with partners that are looking to change the world in some way for the better. During Mid 2021 an accelerator program initiative will commence in which FGA will partner with various small companies globally to spark rapid growth and innovation in a number of industries.

Geographic Preference: United States, Europe
Fund Size: $1 Billion
Founded: 1998
Average Investment: $100K to $50 million
Minimum Investment: $500K
Investment Criteria: Startups & Turnaround situations in Tech
Industry Group Preference: Technology, Blockchain, Business to Business, Real Estate, Enterprise Software, Cybersecurity
Portfolio Companies: Megahoot LLC, Spartan MTech

Key Executives:
Louis Velazquez, Managing Partner
Background: CS First Boston; Smith Barney; Morgan Stanley; Bear Stearns; Lehman Brothers; Paine Webber
Directorships: Chariman, Spartan Modular Technologies; CEO, Megahoot.
Jenner Bendele, EVP of Acquisitions
Background: Clark Thomas & Winters; Assoc. Dir. of Development, University of Texas
Kenneth J. Kulaga, Executive Vice President
Education: MBA, Seton Hall University
Background: Consulting CFO/CAO for Start Ups; VP of Finance/Chief of Staff, CFO Global Foundries; Finance Director, ABM Industries; CFO, Consumer Electronics Division, Sirius Satellite Radio

726 FIELDSTONE PRIVATE CAPITAL GROUP
120 West 45th Street
Suite 1400
New York, NY 10036

Phone: 212-626-1400
web: www.fpcg.com

Mission Statement: Fieldstone Private Capital Group is an investment banking firm providing advisory services on leveraged buyouts, mergers and acquisitions, and private capital raises. Fieldstone specializes in global energy and infrastructure finance.

Geographic Preference: United States
Founded: 1990
Investment Criteria: Mergers & Acquisitions, Restructurings, Debt Financings, Equity, Divestitures, Leveraged Buyouts
Industry Group Preference: Natural Resources, Financial Services, Telecommunications, Transportation, Infrastructure, Energy

Other Locations:
11 Bolton Street
London W1J 8BB
United Kingdom
Phone: 44-2078081500

Kronenstr 3
Berlin 10117

Germany
Phone: 49-302123370 **Fax:** 49-3021233720

2nd Floor, Katherine and West
114 West Street, Sandown
PO Box 781589
Sandton 2146
South Africa
Phone: 27-117752000 **Fax:** 27-117752009

4B, Suryodaya, 1-10-60/3
Begumpet
Hyderabad, A.P. 500 016
India
Phone: 91-4066331960 **Fax:** 91-4066331965

Unit E-2-1
Plaza Damas
60 Jalan Sri Hartamas
Kuala Lumpur 50480
Malaysia
Phone: 6-0362017111 **Fax:** 6-0362019299

Key Executives:
  Andrew Smith-Maxwell, Chairman
  Jason Harlan, Chief Executive Officer

727 FIERA CAPITAL
375 Park Avenue
8th Floor
New York, NY 10152
Phone: 212-300-1600 **Fax:** 212-600-1650
e-mail: OfficeMgmtUS@fieracapital.com
web: www.fieracapital.com

Mission Statement: An independent asset management firm with a growing global presence
Fund Size: over $5 billion
Industry Group Preference: Diversified
Key Executives:
  Jean-Philippe Lemay, Global President & CEO
  Education: BSc, Laval University; MSc, Stanford University
  Background: Vice President, Natcan

728 FIFTH WALL
13160 Mindanao Way
Suite 100B
Marina Del Rey, CA 90292
e-mail: lpinquiry@fifthwall.com
web: fifthwall.com

Mission Statement: Fifth Wall is a venture capital firm that takes an advisory-based approach when partnering with companies.
Founded: 2016
Industry Group Preference: Artificial Intelligence, Information Technology, Software, Applications, Building Sciences, Real Estate, Consumer, Retail
Portfolio Companies: Appear Here, Aquicore, Aurora Solar, b8ta, Blend, Blueprint Power, BUILT Robotics, Built Technologies, ClassPass, Clutter, Cobalt Robotics, Cobli, Convene, Cotopaxi, Eden, Enertiv, Foxtrot, Harbor, Heyday, Hippo, Honest Networks, Hydra Studios, Industrious, Interior Define, Lime, Loft, Loggi, Lyric, Madison Reed, Notarize, Opendoor, PollyEx, Shipwell, States Title, Taft, UNTICKit, Urbint, VTS, WiredScore
Key Executives:
  Andriy Mykhaylovskyy, Managing Partner
  Education: BS, Princeton University; MBA, Stanford Grad. School of Business
  Background: Principal, Evergreen Coast Capital; VP, The Gores Group; CFO, Identified; Investment Banker, Morgan Stanley; Associate, Francisco Partners
  Brad Greiwe, Managing Partner
  Education: BA, Economics, Harvard University
  Background: Co-Founder, Invitation Homes; Investment Banker, UBS; Tishman Speyer; Starwood Capital
  Brendan Wallace, Managing Partner
  Education: BA, Political Science & Economics, Princeton University; MBA, Stanford Grad. School of Business
  Background: Co-Founder, Identified; Co-Founder, Cabify; Goldman Sachs

729 FIKA VENTURES
1950 Sawtelle Blvd.
Suite 183
Los Angeles, CA 90025
web: www.fika.vc

Mission Statement: Fika Ventures is a boutique seed fund that invests in founders engaged in problem solving through the use of data, artificial intelligence, and automation.
Geographic Preference: Los Angeles, Bay Area, Seattle, New York
Investment Criteria: Seed-Stage
Industry Group Preference: Data, Artificial Intelligence, Technology, Automation
Portfolio Companies: Atticus, Bowery, Chatdesk, FairClaims, Fullcast.io, Noyo, Openpath, Papaya, PathSpot, Policy Genius, Pull Request, Sierra Labs, Specright, Tolemi, Visor, WeeCare
Key Executives:
  Eva Ho, General Partner
  Education: BA, Harvard University; MBA, Cornell University
  Background: General Partner, Susa Ventures; Google; YouTube
  TX Zhuo, General Partner
  Education: BA, Wesleyan University; MBA, Stanford University
  Background: McKinsey & Co.; Co-Founder, Karlin Ventures

730 FINAVENTURES
541 Jefferson Avenue
Suite 100
Redwood City, CA 94063
Phone: 650-799-7725
e-mail: contact@finaventures.com
web: www.finaventures.com

Mission Statement: Finaventures focuses on early-stage to mid-stage growth equity technology companies. The firm seeks businesses with stellar management teams and a clear value proposition to its targeted market segment.
Geographic Preference: United States, Europe
Fund Size: Fund I: $20 million; Fund II: $80 million; Fund III: $120 million
Founded: 1999
Average Investment: $5 million
Minimum Investment: $3 million
Investment Criteria: Early-Stage, Mid-Stage, Growth Equity
Industry Group Preference: Software, Applications Software & Services, Mobile, Fintech, Components & IoT, Virtual Reality & Augmented Reality, Semiconductors
Portfolio Companies: Chartboost, DocuSign, Entropic Communications, General Photonics, Global Communications, Jawbone, Jumio, Kabam, Koinify, OEwaves, RockYou, Semiconductors
Other Locations:
  20715 N. Pima Rd.
  Scottsdale, AZ 85255
Key Executives:
  Rachid Sefrioui, Managing Director
  Education: BS, Operations Research & Management Science, Case Western Reserve University
  Background: Managing Director, Credit Agricole

Venture Capital & Private Equity Firms / Domestic Firms

Indosuez (Wafabank/Wafatrust); Managing Director, Bowco Investment Management
Sam Lee, Senior Advisor
Education: BS, Electrophysics, National Chiao Tong University; MS, PhD, Electrical Engineering, Ohio State University
Background: President, Raytheon Semiconductor Division; AMCC; Motorola; NCR
David Espitallier, Principal
Education: Reims Management School, France
Background: Manager, Transaction Services, KPMG; Founder, DealFlowFinder

731 FIRELAKE CAPITAL
350 Rhode Island St.
Suite 228
San Francisco, CA 94301-1648
Phone: 650-321-0880 Fax: 650-321-0882
e-mail: fkittler@firelakecapital.com

Mission Statement: While other firms look to invest in the tried-and-true, we seek out the disruptive. The ideas everyone else writes off as outrageous or impossible. The ones most venture capitalists would consider weird. We take the so-called wild and crazy ideas and develop them into intelligent, scalable solutions. We are early-stage investors with a long-term investment horizon. We aim to solve our world's most pressing problems through transformational, rather than incremental, change. That's why we invest in areas where we believe new technologies or even an early-stage idea can significantly change the economics of current markets: areas like energy, water, material sciences, and global supply chains.

Investment Criteria: Early-Stage
Industry Group Preference: Energy, Water, Materials Technology, Global Supply Chains
Portfolio Companies: Airware, Array Power, BluWrap, C2F, EnerG2, EOS Climate, HydroPoint Data Systems, Kurion, Liquidia Technologies, Nano-Tex, NovaTorque, Plextronics, QBotix, Ruckus Wireless, Scifiniti, Simbol Materials, Siva Power, Solicore, Sungevity, ZeaChem, ZT3 Technologies

Key Executives:
Fred Kittler, Managing Director
e-mail: fkittler@firelakecapital.com
Education: BA, Architecture, Princeton University; MA, Economics, Columbia University
Background: Co-President, Velocity Capital Management; JP Morgan Investment Management
Directorships: Kurion

732 FIRESTARTER FUND
e-mail: proposals@firestarterfund.com
web: www.firestarterfund.com

Mission Statement: We are not a traditional venture fund - we are 42 successful entrepreneurs who have come together to help fund the next generation of leading companies.

Geographic Preference: United States, Illinois, Midwest
Fund Size: $5.7 million
Minimum Investment: $25, 000
Investment Criteria: Any Stage
Industry Group Preference: Digital Media & Marketing, SaaS, E-Commerce & Manufacturing
Portfolio Companies: Retrofit, Kapow Events, Hireology, GiveForward, ShiftGig, UpCity, Pangea, Blitsy, Cartavi, Mighty Nest, Food Genius

Key Executives:
Shradha Aharwal, Member
Background: Current: Co-Founder & Chief Strategy Officer, ContextMedia
Stopher Bartol, Member
Background: Current: Founder & CEO of Legacy.Com
Alex Campbell, Member
Background: Current: Co-Founder of Vibes Media
Cary Chessick, Member
Background: Current: Founder & CEO of Restaurant.com
Jamie Crouthamel, Member
Background: Current: Founder of Old Town Capital; Past: Founder & CEO of Performics
Brandon Cruz, Member
Background: Current: Co-Founder & President of Norvax
George Deeb, Member
Background: Current: Managing Director, Red Rocket Venture Partners; Past: Founder & Former CEO iExplore and Former CEO of Media Recall
Steve Farsht, Member
Background: Current: COO of Tap.me; Past: Partner of Norwest Equity Partners
Michael Fassnacht, Member
Background: President of DraftFCB Chicago; Founder & CEO of Loyalty Matrix
Gian Fulgoni, Member
Background: Current: Executive Chairman and Co-Founder of comScore; President and CEO of Information Resources

733 FIRST ANALYSIS
One South Wacker Drive
Suite 3900
Chicago, IL 60606
Phone: 312-258-1400
web: www.firstanalysis.com

Mission Statement: First Analysis is a private growth equity investor that focuses on emerging growth companies in the healthcare, technology, software, clean technology and chemicals sectors. The firm seeks to help established businesses grow into market leaders. First Analysis also provides equity research and investment banking services.

Geographic Preference: United States
Fund Size: $700 million
Founded: 1981
Average Investment: $3 - $10 million
Minimum Investment: $1 million
Investment Criteria: Emerging, Growth Equity, Expansion
Industry Group Preference: Healthcare, Information Technology, Clean Technology, Broadband, Infrastructure, Medical Devices, Clinical Research, Pharmaceuticals, Behavioral Management, Diagnostics, Network Infrastructure & Security, Wireless, Outsourcing & Efficiency, Chemicals, Energy
Portfolio Companies: ANI Pharmaceuticals, BuyerQuest, Checkpoint Surgical, Chrome River, Courtagen, CSA Medical, DataSphere Technologies, Freeosk, GAPbuster Worldwide, Gyrodata, ITS Compliance, Learning.com, Mediant, QPS Pharmaceutical Services LLC, Scale Computing, Sonoma Orthopedic, SquareTwo Financial, UniversityNow, VisiQuate, Yello

Key Executives:
Matthew Nicklin, Managing Director
Education: BS, Biology, Lehigh University; MBA, University of Chicago
Background: William Blair & Co.
Michael Siemplenski, Managing Director Emeritus
Education: BA, Policial Science, Northern Illinois University; MBA, Marketing/Information Systems, University of Illinois
Background: Burroughs; ITT Courier; Sanders Associates
Richard Conklin, Managing Director, Investment Banking
Education: BA, Economics, University of Notre Dame; MBA, Finance, Wharton School
Background: Managing Director, Robert W. Baird & Co.; Principal, William Blair & Co.; Managing Director of Investment Management, ProLogis; SVP/Head of Equity Capital Markets, Jones Lang LaSalle
Tracy Marshbanks, Managing Director
Education: BS, Chemical Engineering, Colorado State University; PhD, Chemical Engineering, Purdue

Venture Capital & Private Equity Firms / Domestic Firms

University; MBA, University of Chicago
Background: Amoco Corp.
Eric Terhorst, Vice President
Education: BS, Chemistry/Environmental Engineering, California Polytechnic State University; MS, Industrial Administration, Purdue University; MS, Chemical Engineering, Stanford University
Background: Former Management Consultant

734 FIRST ATLANTIC CAPITAL LTD.
477 Madison Avenue
Suite 330
New York, NY 10022

Phone: 212-207-0300 **Fax:** 212-207-8842
web: www.firstatlanticcapital.com

Mission Statement: Investment firm that targets middle market companies.

Geographic Preference: United States
Fund Size: $500 million
Founded: 1989
Average Investment: $75 - $300 million
Minimum Investment: $5 million
Investment Criteria: LBO, MBO, Add-on-Acquisitions
Industry Group Preference: Consumer Products, Food & Beverage, Plastics, Aerospace, Defense and Government
Portfolio Companies: C-P Flexible Packaging, Resource Label Group, Sprint Industrial Holdings, TestEquity

Key Executives:
  Roberto Buaron, Chairman/CEO
  e-mail: rbuaron@first-atlantic.com
  Education: Politechnco of Milan; MBA, INSEAD; MBA, Harvard Graduate School of Business
  Background: Senior Partner, Overseas Partners; General Partner, First Century Partnership; Partner, McKinsey & Company
  Thomas A Berglund, Managing Director
  e-mail: tberglund@first-atlantic.com
  Education: BS, Lehigh University; MS, Purdue University; MBA, Wharton School, University of Pennsylvania
  Background: Partner, Jupiter Partners; Principal, Invus Group; Manager, Boston Consulting Group; Researcher, Bell Laboratories
  Emilio S Pedroni, Managing Director
  e-mail: epedroni@first-atlantic.com
  Education: Bocconi University, Italy
  Background: Engagement Manager, Corporate Finance & Strategy, McKinsey & Company; Executive Director, CIBC World Markets

Other Locations:
  12400 Coit Road
  Suite 910
  Dallas, TX 75251
  Phone: 214-382-1916 **Fax:** 214-382-1915

736 FIRST CAPITAL VENTURE
50 South Steele Street
Suite 500
Denver, CO 80209

Phone: 303-955-4394
web: www.firstcapitalventures.com

Mission Statement: Invests in various innovative technology companies serving emerging industries. Their Viridis Fund focuses on cannabis.

Founded: 2005
Investment Criteria: Early-Stage, Production-Ready, Serves a Niche Market, Foreseeable exit in 24 to 36 months.
Industry Group Preference: Technology, Cannabis, Healthcare, eSports, Biotech
Portfolio Companies: BuildingDNA, CereScan, Coda Signature, DigyScores, Esports Entertainment Group, Kaonetics Technologies, KromaTiD

Key Executives:
  Gary Graham, Executive Managing Director
  Education: BS, Business Management, Meyers College
  Background: President, First Capital Investments Inc.
  Scott Morris, CPA, Chief Financial Officer
  Education: BS, Accounting, University of Colorado; MBA, Finance/Accounting, Regis University
  Background: Controller, Bay4 Capital/Convergent Capital; CFO, Fortress Investment Group
  Paul Spieker, VP, Operations
  Education: BS-EE, Electircal Engineering, Iowa State University; MIT Sloan School of Management
  Background: VP, Voltelcon; VP of Network Services, Webb Interactive Services; SVP of Network Operations, Webb Interative; President, Spieker Consulting

738 FIRST FLIGHT VENTURE CENTER
2 Davis Drive
P.O. Box 13169
Research Triangle Park, NC 27709

Phone: 919-473-9420
e-mail: info@ffvcnc.org
web: www.ffvcnc.org

Mission Statement: The corporate mission of the First Flight Venture Center is to increase the number of successful technology-based small companies originating in or relocating to the Research Triangle Park region.

Geographic Preference: North Carolina
Fund Size: $140 million
Founded: 1991
Average Investment: $500,000
Minimum Investment: $50,000
Investment Criteria: Seed, Startup
Industry Group Preference: Information Technology, Life Sciences, Technology
Portfolio Companies: MAA Laboratories Inc., Iprobelabs Inc., Zenomics, InnoVision Imagine Laboratory, Microgrid Labs, Jericho Sciences, Techverse Inc., Hi Fidelity Genetics, Clairvoyant Networks, Ascent Bio-Nano Technologies, Learning Machines, CleanVolt Energy, Cell Microsystems, Indexus Biomedical, SonoVol, Gift Boogle, Clinical Sensors, ViraTree, 21st Century Creations, ElectroChemical Systems Inc., Excelerate Health Ventures, Verinetics, SciKon Innovation, Sirga Advanced BioPharma, Vindrauga Holdings; Inanovate, NIRvana Sciences Inc., Dignify Therapeutics, Trio Labs Inc., Camras Vision, Network Development Group

Key Executives:
  Krista Covey, President
  Education: BS, Southeastern University; MBA, Saint Leo University

739 FIRST GREEN PARTNERS
221 East Myrtle Street
Stillwater, MN 55082

Phone: 952-288-2760

Mission Statement: To invest in innovative early stage companies that intersect agriculture and technology.

Founded: 2011
Investment Criteria: Startups, Early Stage
Industry Group Preference: Agricultural Technologies
Portfolio Companies: Digital H2O, Monolith Materials, Rivertop Renewables, Trelys

Key Executives:
  Doug Cameron, Managing Director
  Education: BS, Biomedical Engineering, Duke University; PhD, Biochemical Engineering, Massachusetts Institute of Technology
  Background: Chief Scientist & Research Director, Cargill; Investor & Advisor, Cargill Ventures; Khosla Ventures; Piper Jaffray; Professor, University of Wisconsin-Madison
  Directorships: Trelys, Renmatix, Sirrus Chemistry

Venture Capital & Private Equity Firms / Domestic Firms

Thomas Erickson, Managing Director
Education: BA, Mathematics, St. Olaf College; MBA, Kellogg School of Management, Northwestern University; CFA
Background: Co-Founder & General Partner, BlueStream Ventures; Managing Director, Dain Rauscher Wessels
Directorships: Monolith Materials, Rivertop Renewables, Trelys

Constance Paiement, Chief Financial Officer/General Counsel
Education: BA, Accounting, University of St. Thomas; JD, University of Minnesota; CPA
Background: CFO & General Counsel, BlueStream Ventures; Co-Founder, Paiement Law Office; Gray Plant Mooty; Coopers & Lybrand

Matthew Strongin
Education: BA, Carleton College
Background: Piper Jaffray; Co-Founder, MS Consulting; Co-Founder, WaterQuant
Directorships: International Education Center

740 FIRST NEW ENGLAND CAPITAL LP
998 Farmington Avenue
Suite 216
West Hartford, CT 06107
        Phone: 860-293-3334 **Fax:** 860-293-3338

Mission Statement: First New England Capital specializes in providing debt and equity financing to small and medium sized later stage companies in the United States. FNEC assists portfolio companies with capital raising, strategic planning, financing decisions, and personnel recruiting.

Geographic Preference: Northeast, Southeast
Fund Size: $50 million
Founded: 1988
Average Investment: $2 - $5 million
Minimum Investment: $1 million
Investment Criteria: Later Stage, Equity Capital, Mezzanine
Industry Group Preference: Aerospace, Defense and Government, Healthcare, Business Products & Services, Consumer Services, Manufacturing, Distribution, Technology
Portfolio Companies: Awareness Technologies, Cecilware, Ranger International Services Group, VaultLogix

Other Locations:
285 Riverside Avenue
Suite 200
Westport, CT 06880

Key Executives:
Richard C Klaffky, Co-Founder/Managing Principal
860-293-3333
e-mail: rklaffky@fnec.com
Education: Brown University; MBA, Columbia University Graduate School of Business
Background: VP & Manager, Intermediate Term Lending Division, Barclays Business Credit; Securities Analyst, Travelers Corporation
Directorships: National Association of Small Business Investment Companies

John L Ritter, Co-Founder
860-293-3333
e-mail: jritter@fnec.com
Education: BA, Macalester College; MA, Religion, Yale University; JD, University of Connecticut School of Law
Background: Attorney, Blume & Elbaum; General Counsel, Independent Energy Corporation; Legislator, Connecticut State House of Representatives
Directorships: West Hartford Town Council

Seth W Alvord, Partner
203-341-9257
e-mail: salvord@fnec.com
Education: BA, Connecticut College; MBA, Cornell University
Background: Founder & Managing Partner, Balance Point Capital Partners; VP, Investment Banking Division, CRT Capital Group LLC; Morgan Stanley

741 FIRST RESERVE
262 Harbor Drive
3rd Floor
Stamford, CT 06902
        Phone: 203-661-6601 **Fax:** 203-661-6729
        web: www.firstreserve.com

Mission Statement: First Reserve Corporation is a private equity firm focused exclusively on investment opportunities in the energy industry.

Geographic Preference: United States, Canada
Fund Size: $3.4 billion
Founded: 1981
Average Investment: $200 million
Minimum Investment: $50 million
Investment Criteria: Add-On Acquisitions, Buyouts, Growth Capital
Industry Group Preference: Industrial Equipment, Energy, Oil & Gas, Alternative Energy, Renewable Energy
Portfolio Companies: 9Ren Group, Abengoa, AF Global Corporation, American Energy Permian Basin, Amromco Energy, Ascent Resources, Barra Energia, Century Midstream, CHC Helicopter Corporation, Cobalt International Energy, Connect Resource Services, Deep Gulf Energy, Diamond S, Dixie Electric, DOF Subsea, Energy Credit Partners, FR Midstream Holdings, Hoover Group, KrisEnergy Holdings, Midstates Petroleum, Mountaineer Keystone, NewWoods Petroleum, PrimeLine Utility Services, Sabine Oil & Gas, Templar Energy, TNT Crane & Rigging, TPC Group

Other Locations:
5847 San Felipe Street
Suite 3100
Houston, TX 77057
Phone: 713-227-7890 **Fax:** 203 661-6729

Gary D. Reaves, Managing Director
Education: BBA, University of Texas
Background: Analyst, UBS Investment Bank; Analyst, Howard Frazier Barker Elliott Inc.

Alex T. Krueger, President/CEO
Education: BS, Chemical Engineering, BS, Finance & Statistics, Wharton School
Background: Energy Group, Donaldson Lufkin & Jenrette

Will Honeybourne, Managing Director
Education: BSc, Oil Technology, Imperial College, London
Background: Senior Vice President, Western Atlas International; President & CEO, Computalog; Baker Hughes
Directorships: CNOOC

Jeffrey K. Quake, Managing Director
Education: BA, Economics, Williams College; MBA, Harvard Business School
Background: JP Morgan; Lehman Brothers

Joshua R. Weiner, Managing Director
Education: BA, Bowdoin College
Background: Associate, Warburg Pincus LLC; Associate, Morgan Stanley

Neil A. Wizel, Managing Director
Education: BA, Emery University
Background: Greenbriar Equity Group; Financial Analyst, Credit Suisse

742 FIRST ROUND CAPITAL
151 10th Street
San Francisco, CA 94103
        web: www.firstround.com

Mission Statement: Collectively, First Round partners have more than 100 years of experience working with founding teams.
Geographic Preference: San Francisco, New York, Los Angeles
Average Investment: $500-750K
Investment Criteria: Seed
Industry Group Preference: Enterprise, Consumer, Hardware, Fintech, Healthcare
Portfolio Companies: 33across, 64-x, 9GAG, Abl, Abra, Abstract, Against Gravity, Agari, Alma, Aloha, AltSchool, Amino, AppNexus, Area 1, Aster Data Systems, Atrium, Augury, Aviso, Axial, Bazaarvoice, Beautiful AI, Binti, Birchbox, Blue Apron, Boom.tV, Boulder, Bowery, Boxed, Bright, Caredox, Caspida, Castle, Civitas Learning, Clare, Clearbit, Clover Health, Collective Retreats, Confide, Continuity Control, Court Buddy, Cricket Health, Crossbeam, CrowdJustice, Curalate, Discourse, Dishcraft Robotics, DNAnexus, DoubleVerify, Drift, Dynasty, EAT Club, Eero, Engagio, Evie, Flatiron Health, Flexport, Flurry, Forward, Fundera, FundersClub, Gauntlet, Gem, Gigya, Gnip, Goat, Good Uncle, Gregor Diagnostics, Grokker, GroupMe, Grove, GumGum, Gumroad, Haven, Health IQ, HotelTonight, Human DX, Influitive, Inspirato, Instrumental, Intrinsic, June, Karuna Health, Keeps, Kentik, Kindred, KiwiCo, Knewton, Koru, Legion, LendingHome, Liftopia, LiveIntent, Lob, Looker, Lygos, Mango Health, Mashery, Massdrop, MemSQL, Metric Insights, Metromile, Mighty Networks, Mint, Mirror, Moat, Mobcrush, Modern Fertility, Monetate, Nimble Pharmacy, Nomad Health, North, Notable Labs, Notion, Nova Credit, Numerai, On Deck Capital, OpenX, Ossium Health, Outlier, Pantheon, Parsable, PatientPing, Perceptive Automata, Percolate, PerformLine, Ping, Pique Tea, Planet Labs, Poppin, Promise, PullString, RaiseMe, Rare Bits, RebelMouse, Refinery29, Relay Network, Remind, Righthook, Ring, Roblox, Rover, Sano, SavingStar, Shipwell, Sift Science, Simplifeye, SinglePlatform, SmartBiz, Smartling, SmartThings, Snackpass, Spark Thermionics, Splice, Spring Discovery, Square, Stensul, Stockwell, Suki, Superhuman, Swift Capital, Swift Navigation, Tesorio, TetraScience, The Black Tux, The Climate Corporation, Troops, Truveris, Twenty20, Uber, Ubiquity6, Upserve, Upstart, UrbanSitter, Velano Vascular, Verkada, Vinli, Wanelo, Warby Parker, Wikia, Wonder, Wonderschool, ZEFR, Zendrive

Other Locations:
37 E 28th St.
Suite 900
New York, NY 10016

2400 Market Street
Suite 237
Philadelphia, PA 19103

Key Executives:
Phin Barnes, Partner
Education: BA, Economics & Sociology, Haverford College; MBA, Wharton School, University of Pennsylvania
Background: Founder, ResponDesign; Creative Director, Footwear, AND1 Basketball
Chris Fralic, Partner
Education: BS, Finance, Villanova University; MBA, St. Joseph's University
Background: VP, Business Development, del.icio.us; Ad Sales & Business Development, eBay; VP, Business Development, Nextron; Director, Business Development, America Online
Rob Hayes, Partner
Education: BA, University of California, Berkeley; MBA, Columbia University
Background: Venture Investor, Omidyar Network; Palm
Josh Kopelman, Partner
Education: BS, Entrepreneurial Management & Marketing, Wharton School, University of Pennsylvania
Background: Co-Founder, Infonautics Corporation; Founder, Half.com; Founder, TurnTide
Bill Trenchard, Partner
Education: BA, Science & Technology Studies, Cornell University
Background: LiveOps; Founder, Jump Networks; Founder Partner, Founder Collective
Directorships: Readyforce, LiveOps, Looker, Samasource
Hayley Barna, Partner
Education: Harvard Business School
Background: Bain & Company; Birchbox
Brett Berson, Partner
Education: New York University

---

743 FIRST STEP FUND
600 Reniassance Center
Suite 1710
Detroit, MI 48243-1802

Phone: 313-259-6368 Fax: 313-259-6393
e-mail: info@investdetroit.vc
web: www.investdetroit.com/managed-funds/first-step-fund

Mission Statement: The First Step Fund is an early stage investment fund in partnership with the Invest Detroit Foundation, TechTown, Bizdom, Ann Arbor SPARK and Automation Alley serving emerging and newly-formed high growth, businesses in Southeast Michigan.
Geographic Preference: Southeast Michigan
Average Investment: $10,000 - $50,000
Investment Criteria: Early-Stage
Industry Group Preference: High Technology, Clean Technology, Life Sciences, Advanced Manufacturing, Consumer Products
Portfolio Companies: Accio Energy, Air Movement Systems, Algal Scientific, Are You A Human, Bandals, Clean Emission Fluids, Coliant Corporation, Current Motor Company, Delphinus, ERT Systems, FamilyMint, Fusion Coolant, GradeCheck, Heart Graffiti, IC Data Com, InfoReady Corporation, Ix Innovations, Launch Learning, Local Orbit, Myine Elecronics, NextCat, OWN POS, Reveal Design Automation, Wedit, UniTask, Apolife, SideCar, Estrakon, ArdentCause, Relume, Envy Modular Systems, Epsilon, Denovo Sciences, Larky, New Eagle, Molecular Imaging Research, Llamasoft, Stik.com, Ann Williams Group, FarmLogs

Key Executives:
David Blaszkiewicz, President
Background: President, Detroit Investment Fund

---

744 FIRSTMARK CAPITAL
100 Fifth Avenue
New York, NY 10011

Phone: 212-792-2200 Fax: 212-391-5700
e-mail: info@firstmarkcap.com
web: www.firstmarkcap.com

Mission Statement: Committed to investing in leading technology innovators who share our passion for making an impact by building exceptional, world-changing businesses.
Founded: 2008
Investment Criteria: All Stages
Industry Group Preference: Fintech, Gaming, Entertainment, Communications, Healthcare, Hardware, Mobile, Applications Software & Services, Infrastructure, Data & Analytics, Commerce, Education
Portfolio Companies: ActionIQ, Aereo, Airbnb, AppFirst, Aveksa, BioDigital, Blispay, Bluecore, Body & Labs, Bonusly, Boomi, Brooklinen, Cockroach Labs, Conductor, Dashlane, Data Iku, Digital Currency Group, Disconnect, Dovetail, Draft Kings, Eagle Eye Analytics, Emergent Payments, Engagio, Fame and Partners, Frame.ai, Frame.io, Gravie, Greenphire, Guru, HealthPlanOne, Helium, HopSkipDrive, HowGood, Hubble, HyperScience, IMImobile, Insikt, Invision, Jirafe, Kinsa, Knewton, Lolly

Venture Capital & Private Equity Firms / Domestic Firms

Wolly Doodle, Lot18, Lumosity, MarketFactory, Medico, Methodology, Mission U, NewsCred, Omaze, OpenGamma, Optimus Ride, Payoff, Phosphorus, Pinterest, Playnomics, Proletariat, Public Stuff, Recombine, Riot Games, Robin, Roli, Schoology, Secondmarket, Selfmade, Sence360, Shopify, Sketchfab, Spadac, Sproutling, Starry, Straighterline, Symphony Commerce, Tapad, TestFire, Tommy John, TraceLink, Tubular, Upgrade, Upwork, Virgin Mega, Welcome, X., Zipments

Key Executives:
Matt Turck, Managing Director
Education: LLM, Yale Law School
Background: Managing Director, Bloomberg Ventures; Co-Founder, TripleHop Technologies
Catherine Ulrich, Managing Director
Education: AB, Engineering, Harvard College
Background: Chief Product Officer, Shutterstock; Chief Product Officer, Weight Watchers
Beth Ferreira, Managing Director
Education: BA, University of Pennsylvania; MBA, Wharton School
Background: Managing Partner, WME Ventures; COO, Fab; Flatiron Partners; BCG; UBS
Rick Heitzmann, Managing Director
Education: BS, Georgetown University; MBA, Harvard Business School
Background: Partner, Pequot Ventures; Founding Member, First Advantage; Nationsbanc Montgomery Securities; Booz Allen Hamilton; Houlihan Lokey Howard & Zukin
Amish Jani, Managing Director
Education: BS, MBA, Wharton School, University of Pennsylvania
Background: Partner, Pequot Ventures
Greg Raiten, General Counsel
Education: BS, Computer Science, John Hopkins University; JD, New York University School of Law
Background: General Counsel, 500 Startups; Corporate Attorney, Gunderson Dettmer; Securities Attorney, Latham & Watkins

---

745 FISHER LYNCH CAPITAL
2929 Campus Drive
Suite 420
San Mateo, CA 94403

Phone: 650-287-2700 Fax: 650-287-2701
web: www.fisherlynch.com

Mission Statement: Fisher Lynch Capital is a boutique investment firm that focuses exclusively on private equity sectors around the world. FLC offers investors private equity solutions in the form of co-investments, fund-of-funds, and customized investment strategies.

Geographic Preference: Worldwide
Fund Size: $2 billion
Founded: 2003
Average Investment: $10 - $100 million
Investment Criteria: Buyouts, Growth Equity, Distressed, Mezzanine
Industry Group Preference: Financial Services, Business Services, Media, Communications, Software, Technology, Healthcare, Energy
Portfolio Companies: ADT Security, Aernnova, Allegro, Atlice, Coty Inc., CPA Global, Edward Don & Company, Endeavor, Finastra, Flexential, Biotoscana, HD Vest Financial Services, IQVIA, Ista International GmbH, Lifetime Fitness, McAfee, MultiPlan, NXP Semiconductors, Performance Food Group, Picard, Quest, SonicWall, Securus Technologies, Solera Holdings Inc., Vivint Smart Home, Woodstream, Zayo, Ziggo

Other Locations:
200 Clarendon Street
25th Floor
Boston, MA 02116
Phone: 617-406-3120 Fax: 617-406-3121

12 Hay Hill
Mayfair
London W1J 8NR
United Kingdom
Phone: 44-2071180603

Key Executives:
Marshall Bartlett, Managing Director
e-mail: marshall@fisherlynch.com
Education: BA, History, Yale University; MBA, Tuck School of Business, Dartmouth College
Background: Partner, Parthenon Capital; The Parthenon Group; Saugatuck Capital; Brown Brothers Harriman & Co.
Brett Fisher, Founder/Managing Director
e-mail: brett@fisherlynch.com
Education: BA, Economics & Mathematics, Yale University; MBA, Stanford Graduate School of Business
Background: SVP, GIC Special Investments; Director, Corporate Development, AirTouch Communications; VP, Genstar Investment Corporation; Marakon Associates
Leon Kuan, Managing Director
e-mail: leon@fisherlynch.com
Education: BS, Engineering & Business, Jerome Fisher Program in Management & Technology, MBA, Wharton School, University of Pennsylvania
Background: SVP, GIC Special Investments

---

746 FIVE ELMS CAPITAL
4801 Main St.
Suite 700
Kansas City, MO 64112

Phone: 913-953-8960
e-mail: ws@fiveelms.com
web: www.fiveelms.com

Mission Statement: Five Elms Capital is a global growth equity firm that invests in fast-growing B2B software businesses that users love. Five Elms provides capital and resources to help companies accelerate growth and further cement their role as industry leaders. Since firm inception in 2007, Five Elms has focused exclusively on software investing, building an unmatched network and deep domain expertise. Today with $700+ million AUM and a global team of over 50 investment professionals, Five Elms has invested in more than 40 software platforms globally.

Fund Size: $557 million
Founded: 2007
Average Investment: $5 -$50 million
Investment Criteria: Expansion Stage
Industry Group Preference: Business Products & Services, Consumer Services, Information Technology, Internet, Financial Services, SaaS, Advertising, Outsourcing & Efficiency, E-Commerce & Manufacturing
Portfolio Companies: ActiveProspect, Apptegy, Crelate Talent, Dark Owl, DeepCrawl, Field Agent, Go React, Hubb, LaborChart, MemberClicks, Outfit, Panopta, Passageways, PlayVox, Powwr, ProxyClick, Reachdesk, RFP360, Saylent, Sherpa, SimpliField, SingleOps, Skynamo, Smart Warehousing, Spring Venture Group, Userlane

Key Executives:
Fred Coulson, Founder/Managing Partner
e-mail: fred@fiveelms.com
Education: BS, Business Administration, University of Kansas
Background: TH Lee Putnam Ventures; Investment Banking, Morgan Stanley
Thomas Kershisnik, Partner
Joe Onofrio, Partner
Ryan Mandl, Partner
Stephanie Schneider, Partner
Austin Gideon, Partner

Venture Capital & Private Equity Firms / Domestic Firms

747 FIVE POINTS CAPITAL
101 N Cherry Street
Suite 700
Winston-Salem, NC 27101

Phone: 336-733-0350
e-mail: bkulman@fivepointscapital.com
web: www.fivepointscapital.com

Mission Statement: Makes control investments in privately-held companies in the lower-middle market.

Geographic Preference: United States
Fund Size: $230 million
Founded: 1998
Minimum Investment: $10 million
Investment Criteria: Buyouts, Acquisitions, Growth Capital, Recapitalizations
Industry Group Preference: Business & Commercial Services, Healthcare Services, Industrial Services, Value-Added Distribution, Niche Manufacturing
Portfolio Companies: Aaron Industries, Advanced Disposal Services, Alzheimers Research & Treatment Center, BrandFX, CareerStep, Cavalier Telephone, Cline Driving Solutions, ECP/CH Industries, Fire & Life Safety America, Five Star Foods, GrammaTech, Flint Trading Inc., Glassock Company, JML Optical Industries, Jones & Frank, Outsolve, PHC, Quick Med Claims, Safety Infrastructure Solutions, Smith-Cooper International, Specialty Applicances, Synoptek, The Lion Brewery, Thompson Industrial Services, TransGo, Triangle Ice, Unishippers Global Logistics, Universal Solutions International, Village Tavern, Women's Marketing, Young Innovations

Key Executives:

David G Townsend, Managing Partner
336-733-0355
e-mail: dtownsend@fivepointscapital.com
Education: BA, History, University of North Carolina, Chapel Hill; MBA, Finance & Accounting, University of North Carolina, Chapel Hill
Background: Investment Banking, Stephens Inc.; Ernst & Young
Directorships: BrandFX Holdings, JML Optical, Thompson Industrial Services

Martin P. Gilmore, Managing Partner
336-733-0361
e-mail: mgilmore@fivepointscapital.com
Education: BA, Finance, University of South Carolina
Background: Partner, Ernst & Young Corporate Finance Group; Vice President, Green Capital Investors; Wells Fargo
Directorships: Fire & Life Safety America, Five Star Food Services, TransGo, U.S. Drinks

Christopher N. Jones, Managing Partner
336-733-0360
e-mail: cjones@fivepointscapital.com
Education: BS, Mathematics, Davidson College; MBA, Wharton School, University of Pennsylvania
Background: CFO, Mega Force; Ernst & Young Corporate Finance Group; Kidder Peabody & Company
Directorships: JML Optical, Quick Med Claims, Thompson Industrial Services

Thomas H. Westbrook, Managing Partner
336-733-0359
e-mail: twestbrook@fivepointscapital.com
Education: BA, Economics, Wofford College; MBA, Finance, Kenan-Flagler School of Business, University of North Carolina
Background: Managing Director, Allied Capital Corporation; Associate, North Carolina Enterprise Fund
Directorships: Linkage, Outsolve, Quick Med Claims

Jonathan B. Blanco, Partner
336-733-0358
e-mail: jblanco@fivepointscapital.com
Education: BA, Economics, University of North Carolina, Chapel Hill; MBA, Darden School of Business Administration, University of Virginia
Background: Carousel Capital, Bowles Hollowel Conner & Co., Chase Securities

S. Whitfield Edwards, Partner
336-733-0353
e-mail: wedwards@fivepointscapital.com
Education: BA, Economics, University of North Carolina, Chapel Hill; MBA, Darden School of Business Administration, University of Virginia
Background: Gilbarco Veeder-Root; Vice President, Corporate Development, FairPoint Communications; Bowles Hollowel Conner & Co.

Scott L. Snow, Partner
336-733-0357
e-mail: ssnow@fivepointscapital.com
Education: BS, Business Management, Brigham Young University; MBA, Harvard Business School
Background: Investment Banking, Wachovia Securities; GE Capital; GE Plastics

Marshall C. White, Partner
336-733-0351
e-mail: mwhite@fivepointscapital.com
Education: BS, Finance and Accounting, Georgetown University
Background: American Capital, JP Morgan
Directorships: Thompson Industrial Services, TransGo

W. Brent Kulman, Director of Business Development
e-mail: bkulman@fivepointscapital.com
Education: BA, English, University of North Carolina, Chapel Hill; MBA, Wharton School, University of Pennsylvania
Background: Fund Executive, Charlotte Angel Partners; Investment Banking, Raymond James & Associates; Bank of Boston

748 FLAGSHIP PIONEERING
55 Cambridge Parkway
Suite 800E
Cambridge, MA 02142

Phone: 617-868-1888 **Fax:** 617-868-1115
web: flagshippioneering.com

Mission Statement: A venture capital firm investing in entrepreneurial scientists and their life sciences companies.

Fund Size: $1 billion
Founded: 2000
Industry Group Preference: Life Sciences, Therapeutics, Healthcare, Technology, Sustainability, Pharmaceuticals
Portfolio Companies: Acceleron Pharma, Accuri, Adnexus, Advanced Electron Beams, Affinnova, Agios, Alinea, Alvine Pharmaceuticals, Anvil, Avedro, Aveo, Avidimer Therapeutics, Axcella, Be Power Tech, BGMedicine, Bind Biosciences, BlackDuck, Cadena Bio, Celera, Celexion, CGI, CiBo, Codiak, Codon Devices, Concert Pharmaceuticals, Denali Therapeutics, Ecosense, Editas Medicine, Eleven Biotherapeutics, Emsemble Therapeutics, Epitome Biosystems, Evelo Biosciences, Everyday Solutions, Foghorn Therapeutics, Genomics Collaborative, Helicos BioSciences Corp., Hypnion, Idexx Laboratories, Inari, Incredible Foods, Indigo, Interactive Supercomputing, Intio, Joule, Kaleido, KSQ, LS9, Mascoma, MeddaMetrics, Midori Health, Moderna, Morphotek Inc., Nanostream, Novomer, Oasys, Permeon Biologies, Pervasis, Quanterix, Receptos, Red Rock Biofuels, Renovis, Resolvyx, Rubio Therapeutics, Seahorse Biosciences, Selecta Biosciences, Selventa, Seres Therapeutics, SeventhSense Biosystems, Sigilon Therapeutics, Syros, T2 Biosystems, Taris, Tarveda, Tetraphase, Torque, Transmedics, Visen, Visterra, Zalicus

Key Executives:

Noubar Afeyan, Founder/CEO
Education: PhD, Biochemical Engineering, MIT
Background: Founder/CEO, PerSeptive Biosystems; SVP/Chief Business Officer, Applera;
Directorships: Chemgenics Pharmaceuticals; Color Kinetics; Adnexus Therapeutics; Affinnova

Venture Capital & Private Equity Firms / Domestic Firms

Stephen Berenson, Managing Partner
Education: BS, Mathematics, MIT
Background: Investment Banker, JP Morgan
Directorships: Moderna Therapeutics, CiBO Technologies
David Berry, General Partner
Education: PhD, Biological Engineering, MIT; MD, Harvard Medical School, Harvard-MIT Health Sciences and Technology Program
Background: Co-Founder, Seres Therapeutics; Joule Unlimited; Evelo Biosciences; Eleven Biotherapeutics; LS9; Axcella Health; Indigo Agriculture
Doug Cole, Managing Partner
Education: AB, English, Darmouth College; MD, University of Pennsylvania School of Medicine
Background: Instructor, Harvard Medical School; Assistant in Neurology, Massachusetts General Hospital; Medical Director, Cytotherapeutics; Program Executive, Vertex Pharmaceuticals Inc; Co-Founder, Ensemble Therapeutics; Permeon Biologics; Moderna Therapeuticsl Syros Pharmaceuticals; Sigilon Therapeutics
Directorships: Denali, Editas, Fogorn, Quanterix, Sigilon, Taris, Torque
Jim Gilbert, Senior Partner
Education: BS, Industrial Engineering, Cornell University; MBA, Harvard Business School
Background: Managing Director, Bain & Co.; VP, Corporate Strategy, Boston Scientific; Senior Advisor, General Atlantic; Senior Operating Executive, Welsh Carson Anderson & Stowe
Directorships: Nestle Health Science, TransMedics, Rubius Therapeutics, Sigilon
Avak Kahvejian, General Partner
Education: PhD, McGill University
Background: Founding President/CEO, Cygnal Therapeutics; Co-Founder, Rubius Therapeutics; VP, Business Development, Helicos BioSciences
Ignacio Martinez, General Partner
Education: BS, Economics/Business Admin., Deusto University (Spain); MBA, Instituto de Empresa
Background: Managing Director, Syngenta Ventures; CFO, Progenika Group; Najeti Ventures Fund
Directorships: Indigo Agriculture, Novomer, Agtech Accelerator, CiBO Technologies
Stacie Rader, Senior Partner
Education: BS, Business, Babson College
Background: SVP/Executive Operations/Human Resources, BG Medicine; Corporate Director, Applera Corp.; Human Resources, PerSeptive; Interim VP/Human Resources, Celera Genomics
Leda Trivinos, Senior Partner, Intellectual Property
Education: Law Degree, University of California, Berkeley; PhD, Cell & Molecular Biology, Northwestern University Medical School
Background: Chief Patent Counsel, Momenta Pharmaceuticals Inc.; Assistant General Counsel for Intellectual Property, Biogen Idec.; Associate, Fish & Richardson PC
Geoffrey von Maltzahn, General Partner
Education: BS, Chemical Engineering, MIT; MS, Bioengineering, University of California, San Diego; PhD, Biomedical Engineering/Medical Physics, MIT
Background: Co-Founder, Sienna Biopharmaceuticals; Chief Innovation Officer/Director, Kaleido Biosciences; Chief Innovation Officer, Indigo Agriculture; VP of Discovery, Axcella
Harry Wilcox, Special Partner
Background: CFO/General Partner, Highland Capital Partners; CFO, Charles River Ventures; CFO/SVP, EXACT Sciences; Interim CEO, Thrasos Therapeutics; Interim CEO, Biostratym; President/CEO, Cambridge NeuroScience Inc.; SVP/CFO, Cellcor
Directorships: Seventh Sense Biosystems; Incredible Foods; MidoriUSA; BG Medicine; Be Power Tech

749 FLARE CAPITAL PARTNERS
800 Boylston Street
Suite 2310
Boston, MA 02199

Phone: 617-607-5060
web: www.flarecapital.com

Mission Statement: To provide support, strategic resources and industry insight to innovative healthcare technology companies.
Fund Size: $200 million
Founded: 2001
Investment Criteria: Early-Stage, Growth Equity
Industry Group Preference: Medical Devices, Biopharmaceuticals, Predictive Medicine Technology, Diagnostics, Healthcare Services
Portfolio Companies: CardioMEMS, CardioNet, Clear Data, Direct Flow Medical, Explorys, Functional Neuromodulation, Iora Health, Rise Health, SetPoint Medical, SynapDx, Valence Health, Welltok
Key Executives:
Michael Greeley, General Partner/Co-Founder
Education: BA, Chemistry, Williams College; MBA, Harvard Business School
Background: Founding General Partner, Flybridge Capital Partners; Polaris Venture Partners; SVP & Founding Partner, GCC Investments; Wasserstein Perella & Company; Morgan Stanley; Credit Suisse First Boston
Directorships: BlueTarp Financial, Explorys, Functional Neuromodulation, Iora Health, MicroCHIPS, Nuvesse, PolyRemedy, Predictive Biosciences, Predilytics, T2 Biosystems, TARIS Biomedical
Bill Geary, General Partner/CoFounder
Education: Carroll School of Management, Boston College
Background: Partner, North Bridge Venture Partners; Partner, Hambro International Equity Partners; CFO, MathSoft; CPA, Arthur Andersen & Company
Chris Kryder, Executive Partner
Education: BA, University at Buffalo; MD, Georgetown University; MBA, Massachusetts Institute of Technology
Background: Founder, D2Hawkeye; Co-Founder, Generation Health
Tom Mac Mahon, Executive Partner
Education: BS, Marketing, St. Peter's College; MBA, Fairleigh Dickinson University
Background: Chairman & CEO, LabCorp; CEO, Laboratory Group, America Holdings; SVP, Hoffman-La Roche; President, Roche Diagnostics Group

750 FLETCHER SPAGHT VENTURES
75 State Street
Suite 100
Boston, MA 02109

Phone: 617-247-6700
e-mail: info@fletcherspaght.com
web: www.fletcherspaght.com

Mission Statement: Fletcher Spaght Ventures is a venture capital firm focused on providing expertise and capital to high growth healthcare, life sciences and information technology companies.
Geographic Preference: United States
Fund Size: $100 million
Founded: 1983
Average Investment: $4 - $6 million
Investment Criteria: All Stages
Industry Group Preference: Healthcare, Life Sciences, Biotechnology, Diagnostics, Healthcare Information Technology, Medical Devices
Portfolio Companies: CardioFocus, Cayenne Medical, HistoSonics, Metabolon, Proteus Digital Health, Soleo Communications, Swift Biosciences

Venture Capital & Private Equity Firms / Domestic Firms

Key Executives:

John Fletcher, Managing Partner Emeritus
Education: BBA, Marketing, George Washington University; MBA, Southern Illinois University; PhD Candidate, The Wharton School, University of Pennsylvania
Background: CEO, Fletcher Spaght; Senior Manager, The Boston Consulting Group; Captain & Jet Pilot, U.S. Air Force
Directorships: Axcelis, Metabolon

Pearson Spaght, General Partner
Education: BS, Mechanical Engineering, MS, Aeronautical/Astronautical Engineering, MBA, Stanford University
Background: VP, Corporate Strategy & International, Raymark Corporation; Senior Manager, The Boston Consulting Group; Engineer, NASA
Directorships: Soleo Communications, Battery Resourcers

---

751 FLEXPOINT FORD LLC
676 North Michigan Avenue
33rd Floor
Chicago, IL 60611

Phone: 312-327-4520 Fax: 312-327-4525
web: www.flexpointford.com

Mission Statement: Flexpoint Ford is a private equity investment firm focused on providing operational and financial expertise, industry contacts, and development strategies to assist with the building of portfolio companies.

Geographic Preference: United States
Fund Size: $950 million
Founded: 2005
Average Investment: $200 million
Industry Group Preference: Healthcare, Financial Services
Portfolio Companies: AMD Holdings, CFGI, Credibly, GeoVera, Great Ajax, Jefferson Capital International, JetPay, Kastle Therapeutics, KingStar, Pelican AutoFinance, Service Finance Company, Summit Behavioral Healthcare, Top Rx, Vericlaim, WisdomTree Investments

Other Locations:
717 Fifth Avenue
20th Floor
New York, NY 10022
Phone: 646-217-7555 Fax: 646-217-7855

Key Executives:

Christopher J. Ackerman, Managing Director
312-327-4540
e-mail: cackerman@flexpointford.com
Education: BA, Mathematical Economics, Colgate University; MBA, Kellogg School of Management
Background: Executive Director, Investment Banking Division, Morgan Stanley

Perry O. Ballard, Managing Director
312-327-4539
e-mail: pballard@flexpointford.com
Education: BA, Economics, University of Michigan; MBA, Harvard Business School
Background: VP, Healthcare Group, GTCR; Analyst, Credit Suisse First Boston

Steven L. Begleiter, Managing Director
646-217-7572
e-mail: sbegleiter@flexpointford.com
Education: BA, Economics, Haverford College
Background: Director, MarketAxess Holdings; Senior Managing Director, Bear Stearns & Co.

Ethan A. Budin, Managing Director
312-327-4535
e-mail: ebudin@flexpointford.com
Education: AB, Mathematics, Harvard University
Background: Principal, GTCR; Principal, Leeds Group; Associate, The Boston Consulting Group; M&A Analyst, Lazard Freres & Co.

Charles E. Glew, Jr., Managing Director
312-327-4533
e-mail: cglew@flexpointford.com
Education: AB, Harvard University; MBA, Stanford University Graduate School of Business
Background: Principal, GTCR; Summit Partners; Analyst, Corporate Finance Group, Citicorp

Jonathan T. Oka, Managing Director
312-327-4547
e-mail: joka@flexpointford.com
Education: BA, Yale University; MBA, Harvard Business School
Background: Associate, GTCR; McKesson Corporation; M&A Analyst, Lazard Freres & Co.

Donald J. Edwards, Chief Executive Officer
312-327-4530
e-mail: dedwards@flexpointford.com
Education: BS, Finance, University of Illinois, Urbana-Champaign; MBA, Harvard Business School
Background: Principal, GTCR; Lazard Ltd.

---

752 FLOODGATE FUND
820 Ramona Street
Suite 200
Palo Alto, CA 94301

Phone: 650-204-7990
e-mail: mediarequests@floodgate.com
web: floodgate.com

Mission Statement: Floodgate helps today's most ambitious entrepreneurs develop tomorrow's great business success stories.

Geographic Preference: California, Texas
Founded: 2010
Average Investment: $150,000 - $1 million
Industry Group Preference: Enterprise Software, Business to Business, Consumer Internet, Software, Hardware
Portfolio Companies: 6D.AI, Aceable, Aconite, Adroll, Angellist, Applied Intuition, Atlas Obscura, Ayasdi, Bazaarvoice, Bigcommerce, Bolt Financial, Bot MD, Business Connect China, Camio, Chairman Mom, Cheetah Technology, Chegg, Civitas Learning, Clever, Clover Health, Consecutive Capital, Data.World, Demandforce, Dispatchr, Doubledutch, Egnyte, Enhatch, Finxera, Giftly, Goformz, Greatist, Greo, Handle Financial, Hodinkee, Hopscotch, IFTTT, Illumeo, Inscopix, IRL, Jodel, Joyrun, Kanler, Kapost, Keepsafe, Kindly Care, Labdoor, Liquidspace, LOB, Ligistics Exchange, Loris.AI, Lyft, Maker Media, Mango Health, Mighty Networks, Mixmax, Mobilize, Monetate, Myra Labs, N3twork, Newscred, NGMOCO, Nirvana, OHMConnect, OKTA, Openmind, Origin, OutboundDengine, Outreach, Pantheon, Parallel Wireless, Piccollage, Pingpad, Pley, Praxis, Rafay Systems, Rappi, Recharge, Refinery29, Reputation.Com, Rev Worldwide, Robin Systems, Sano, SBR Health, Sharethrough, Skale Labs, Smule, Snaplogic, Solarwinds, Sonos, Sparefoot, Spiceworks, Starkware, Swivel, Tango Card, Tapatalk, Taskrabbit, Tesorio, TetraScience, TextIQ, Thankx, The Zebra, Thinkful, Touch Of Modern, Townsquared, Try.Com, TTYL, Twitch, Twitter, Unitive, Virtual Instruments, Wanleo, Weebly, Whipclip, Workboard, Xamarin, Yup Technologies, Zeplin, Zeus

Key Executives:

Mike Maples Jr., Managing Partner
Education: BS, Engineering, Stanford University; MBA, Harvard Business School
Background: Co-Founder, Motive; Product Marketing, Tivoli
Directorships: Dasient, Swiftest, ModCloth

Ann Miura-Ko, Partner
Education: BS, Electrical Engineering, Yale University; PhD, Mathematical Modeling of Computer Security, Stanford University
Background: Lecturer, School of Engineering, Stanford University; Charles River Ventures; McKinsey & Company

Venture Capital & Private Equity Firms / Domestic Firms

Iris Choi, Partner
Education: BA, Harvard University; MBA, Wharton School, University of Pennsylvania
Background: M&A, Goldman Sachs

Arjun Chopra, Partner
Education: BS, University of Texas, Austin; MBA, Harvard Business School
Background: CTO, Cambridge Technology Enterprises; Microsoft; Motive; IBCC

Ryan Walsh, Partner
Education: BS, Computer Science, MS, Telecommunications, University of Pittsburgh
Background: Product Management, Apple; VP of Products, Beats by Dre

753 FLORIDA CAPITAL PARTNERS
500 N Westshore Blvd
Suite 605
Tampa, FL 33609
        Phone: 813-222-8000 Fax: 813-222-8001
        e-mail: newdeals@fcpinvestors.com
        web: www.fcpinvestors.com

Mission Statement: To help build private, middle-market companies into successful businesses.
Geographic Preference: United States
Fund Size: $350 million
Founded: 1988
Minimum Investment: $3 million
Investment Criteria: Recapitalizations, MBO, MBI, Family Successions, Corporate Divestiture, Industry Consolidation
Industry Group Preference: Consumer Products, Industrial Equipment, Services, Distribution, Manufacturing, Business to Business
Portfolio Companies: Bell'O International, Custom Molded Products, E-Z Shipper Racks, Levin HomeCare, Precision Aviation Group, United States Environmental Services

Key Executives:
Peter B Franz, Partner
e-mail: franz@fcpinvestors.com
Education: BS, Economics, Wharton School, University of Pennsylvania; MBA, JL Kellogg Graduate School of Management, Northwestern University
Background: VP, NationsCredit Commercial Corporation

Felix J Wong, Partner
e-mail: fjw@fcpinvestors.com
Education: BS, Business Administration, Wake Forest University
Background: Corporate Finance, Stephens

754 FLORIDA FUNDERS
        web: www.floridafunders.com

Mission Statement: Dedicated to partnering with the next generation of tech companies.
Geographic Preference: Florida
Industry Group Preference: Technology, Fintech, Software, Electronics, SaaS, AI, IoT
Portfolio Companies: 2ULaundry, Aerosens, Artie, Bambino, Bridge, Cast.AI, ChalkTalk, Chattr, Clientbook, Elevated, eMerge Americas, FlexEngage, Gentreo, Gigantor, Grow Credit, Harness, HealthSnap, Intecrowd, Itopia, Jassby, Kliken, Lula, Marco Financial, Mile Auto, NOCAP Sports, MyPorter, OTHRSource, OX Fulfilment Solutions, Presence, Professional Credentials Exchange, QuantHub, Rewst, RoboTire, Satisfy Labs, Secberus, Theoris Software, SegAna, Simplebet, Simplenight, Stratos Technologies, Stylust, Supply Wisdom, TempMee, TOP Inc., Vigtec, Vizetto, Vugo, WiTricity, XGen AI, Yac

Key Executives:
Tom Wallace, Managing Partner
Education: MS, Indiana University of Pennsylvania
Background: CEO, Waldec Group

Marc Blumenthal, General Partner
Education: BS, University of South Florida
Background: CEO, Progressive Business Solutions; Partner, Great Plains; CEO, Intelladon Inc.; Business Development Director, Tribridge

Kevin Adamek, General Partner
Education: BEng, Penn State University
Background: Co-Founder/COO, Monterey Waldec; Co-Founder/COO, The Waldec Group; CFO, Technology Services Division, IKON Office Solutions; Founder/President, Waldec & Associates

Marc Sokol, General Partner/Chairman of Investment Committee
Education: Illinois Institute of Technology
Background: Co-Founder/EVP, Realia Inc.; SVP of Worldwide Marketing, Computer Associates; Partner, JK&B Capital; Co-Founder/President, Commack Solutions

755 FLUKE VENTURE PARTNERS
520 Kirkland Way
Suite 300
Kirkland, WA 98033
        Phone: 425-896-4322 Fax: 425-827-4683
        e-mail: weston@flukeventures.com
        web: www.flukeventures.com

Mission Statement: Fluke invests in early-stage companies located in the Pacific Northwest.
Geographic Preference: Pacific Northwest United States
Fund Size: $65 million
Founded: 1982
Average Investment: $2.5 - $4 million
Minimum Investment: $500,000
Investment Criteria: Seed, Startup, First-Stage, Second-Stage, Mezzanine
Industry Group Preference: Technology, Consumer Services, Consumer Products, Healthcare
Portfolio Companies: AcryMed, Aldus, Calidora, Carena, Chatham Technologies, Coinstar, Concordia Coffee Company, Coinstar, Confirma, Creative Multimedia, Dantz Development Corporation, Drug Emporium, Eagle Hardware & Garden, Fios, Genoa Healthcare, Innova, Innovation, Integrex, Interlinq Software, Ioline Corporation, Klir Technologies, Luxar, MedManage Systems, MidStream Technologies, NetMotion Wireless, Pacific Edge Software, Pacific Star Communications, Panlabs International, Payscale, Pet's Choice, Phoseon Technology, RedHook Ale Brewery, Sightward, Starbucks, Sur La Table, Tegic Communications, Vantos, Viathan, Xcyte Therapies

Key Executives:
Denny Weston, Senior Managing Director
e-mail: weston@flukeventures.com
Education: BA, Central Washington University; MBA, University of Washington
Background: Certified Public Accountant; Founder, Evergreen Venture Capital Association
Directorships: PayScale Inc., Pacific Star Communications Inc., Carena Inc., Sur La Table, Confirma, Redhook Brewery

Kevin Gabelein, Managing Director
e-mail: gabelein@flukeventures.com
Education: BA, Business Admin., University of Washington; JD, Souther Methodist Univerity School of Law
Background: Attorney, Corporate Finance Group of Ridedell Williams PS; Certified Public Accountant, PricewaterhouseCoopers LLP
Directorships: Concordia Coffee Company; Phoseon Technology; Vantos Inc.; Genoa Healthcare; MedManage Systems; Fios

Venture Capital & Private Equity Firms / Domestic Firms

756 FLYBRIDGE CAPITAL PARTNERS
PO Box 369
Norwell, MA 02061

e-mail: hello@flybridge.com
web: www.flybridge.com

Mission Statement: Our goal is to find talented entrepreneurs and then partner with them to build exceptional and valuable companies. We focus on providing guidance and perspective in a complimentary way to the entrepreneurs we invest in and help them build connections to soar to the next level.

Geographic Preference: United States
Fund Size: $560 million
Founded: 2001
Investment Criteria: Seed-Stage, Early-Stage
Industry Group Preference: Consumer Technology, Energy Technology, Healthcare Information Technology, Information Technology
Portfolio Companies: 33Across, Aiera, Analytical Space, BetterCloud, BitSight, Bloxroute Labs, BlueTarp Financial, Bowery, Bulletin, Chief, Codecademy, Datalogue, DataXu, Eager, Enigma, Feature Labs, Hyr, I4CP, Imperfect, Infracommerce, Jibo, Kebotix, Lorem, Madeira Madeira, Minim, MongoDB, Narrator AI, Nasuni, NS1, Omni, Open English, Parachute, Philo, Pitzi, Plastiq, Precognitive, Proscia, Redox, Remote Year, Restorando, Saving Star, Sentenai, Shine, Skillist, Splice, Tracx, Valimail, Vidsys, Wanderset, Welltok, Wethos, Zest Finance

Other Locations:
16 W 23rd St.
5th Floor
New York, NY 10010

Key Executives:
David Aronoff, General Partner
Education: BS, Computer Science, University of Vermont; MS, Computer Engineering, University of Southern California; MBA, Harvard Business School
Background: Grelock Partneres, Chipcom
Directorships: BetterCloud, Bitsight, Minim, NS1, Valimail
Jeffrey Bussgang, General Partner
Education: BA, Computer Science, Harvard University; MBA, Harvard Business School
Background: Co-Founder, Upromise; Executive, Open Market
Directorships: 33Across, Analytical Space, BloXroute, BlueTarp Financial, Bowery Farming, Codecademy, DataXu, Enigma, Open English, Plastiq, Precognitive, Wanderset, ZestFinance
Jesse Middleton, General Partner
Education: Drexel University
Background: WeWork; CEO, Backstory
Directorships: Bulletin, Chief, Hyr, Imperfect Produce, Narrator, Omni, Remote Year, Skillist, Splice, Wethos
Chip Hazard, General Partner
Education: BA, Stanford University; MBA, Harvard Business School
Background: General Partner, Greylock Partners; Company Assitance Limited
Directorships: Datalogue, Feature Labs, Lorem, MongoDB, Nasuni, Parachute Home, Redox, VidSys, Welltok

757 FLYING FISH
Seattle, WA

e-mail: info@flyingfish.vc
web: www.flyingfish.vc

Mission Statement: Mission is to fund startups in the areas of cloud computing, artificial intelligence, speech and natural language, machine learning and internet and technology.

Geographic Preference: United States
Fund Size: $85 Million
Average Investment: $500,000 - $5,000,000
Minimum Investment: $500,000
Investment Criteria: Early Stage Startups, Cloud Computing, AI, Speech & Natural Language, Machine Learning, Info & Tech
Industry Group Preference: Artificial Intelligence, Cloud Computing, Speech and Natural Language, Machine Learning, Information and Technology
Portfolio Companies: Ad Lightning, Element Data, Finn.ai, Gradient, Joe, Message Yes, Streem, Tomorrow, Vivi

Key Executives:
Geoff Harris, Partner
Education: BA, Political Science, Brown University
Background: Microsoft
Directorships: Board Member, Seattle Angel Board of Directors
Heather Redman, Partner
Education: BA, Reed College; JD, Stanford University
Background: AtomShockwave, Inc.; Getty Images, Inc.; PhotoDisc, Inc.; Indix Corporation; Summit Power Group
Directorships: Washington Technology Industry Association; Greater Seattle Chamber; Hawthown Club; Global EIR Coalition & Beneficial State Bank
Frank Chang, Partner
Education: BA, Computer Science, Princeton University
Background: Reef Technologies; Amazon; Microsoft

758 FLYWHEEL VENTURES
341 East Alamada Street
Santa Fe, NM 87501-2229

Phone: 505-225-1618 Fax: 505-672-7053
web: www.flywheelventures.com

Mission Statement: Flywheel Ventures invests in seed-stage and early-stage companies with the potential to provide solutions to global challenges in digital services, as well as energy, water and infrastructure technology.

Fund Size: $35 million
Average Investment: $100,000 - $1 million
Investment Criteria: Seed-Stage, Early-Stage
Industry Group Preference: Digital Services, Infrastructure Software, Energy Technology, Water, Software, Clean Technology
Portfolio Companies: AfterCollege, Angaza Design, AppCityLife, Aravo Solutions, Bitsbox, Bytelight, Cinnafilm, Comet Solutions, Digabit, Jana, Jive Software, Lingotek, Lotus Leaf Coatings, MicroProbe, MIOX Corporation, RentPayment, SalmData, ShowEvidence, SkyFuel, Submittable, TempoDB, TheRetailPlanet.com, Tiatros, TrackVia, Tribogenics, TruTouch Technologies

Other Locations:
9204 San Mateo Northeast
Albuquerque, NM 87113

Key Executives:
Trevor R Loy, General Partner
e-mail: trevor@flywheelventures.com
Education: BS, MS, Electrical Engineering, MS, Management Science & Engineering, Stanford University
Background: Gigabeat; Brooktree; ParkingNet; Teradyne; Intel Corporation
Directorships: Astria Semiconductor Holdings, TrackVia, Tuscany Design Automation
David Jargiello, Venture Partner
e-mail: david@flywheelventures.com
Education: BA, Case Western Reserve University; MS, Stanford University; JD, University of California, Berkeley
Background: Co-Founder, Venture Law Group; Heller Ehrman White & McAuliffe; Virtual Law Partners
Chris Traylor, Venture Partner
e-mail: chris@flywheelventures.com
Education: BS/BA, Management, Kansas State University; MBA, University of New Mexico
Background: CEO, PureColor; Global Director,

Venture Capital & Private Equity Firms / Domestic Firms

Commercial & Institutional Markets, MIOX Corporation; Pumping Solutions

759 FOCUS VENTURES
525 University Avenue
Suite 225
Palo Alto, CA 94301
Phone: 650-325-7400 Fax: 650-325-8400

Mission Statement: Seeking companies that have completed initial development of their product or service. These leading technology companies have demonstrated clear market acceptance and are seeking additional capital to expand their sales and marketing efforts or to execute strategic acquisitions.

Fund Size: $830 million
Founded: 1997
Average Investment: $3 - $8 million
Minimum Investment: $500,000
Investment Criteria: Expansion-Stage
Industry Group Preference: Communications, Software, Technology, Semiconductors, Consumer Services, Internet
Portfolio Companies: 3VR, Acta Technology, Active Software, Agile Software, Alteon WebSystems, Aruba Networks, Apigee, Atmosphere Networks, Aventail, Barracuda Networks, Black Duck Software, Brand.net, Broadbase Software, BuzzMedia, Cedar Point Communications, CenterBeam, Centrality Communications, Choridiant Software, ClearCube, Com 21, Commerce One, Copper Mountain, Corio, CoSine Communications, Crossbeam Systems, Cyan Optics, DATAllegro, Delivery Agent, Digital Fuel, Drobo, DSL.Net, Ecast, edocs, Elance, Ensim, Entropic, EqualLogic, Exigen, Extricity Software, Fanfare, Financial Engines, FrontBridge, G-Log, Hara Software, inCode Telecom, Infoblox, Interwoven, Isilon Systems, Kace, Kazeon, LogLigic, MarkMonitor, Marin Software, Mimosa, Miradia, MuDynamics, Netmoshere, NetScaler, Niku, Oblix, Opsware, Orchestria, Outer Bay, PA Semi, Panasas, PCH International, Picarro, Pivot3, Pixelworks, Pure Digital, QuinStreet, Rafter, Ramp Networks, Repeater Technology, Reputation.com, RGB Networks, Ruckus Wireless, SAY Media, Sequence Design, Sepaton, ShoreTel, Silicon Optix, Six Apart, Sojern, Starent Networks, Stoke, Teknovus, Telera, Turn, Verisity, Vina Technologies, Virtusa, WebVisible, Wily Technology

760 FOG CITY CAPITAL
San Francisco, CA 94105
e-mail: deals@fogcitycapital.com
web: www.fogcitycapital.com

Mission Statement: A private equity firm that invests in lower middle-market software and business services companies and assists with growing them into leading businesses.

Average Investment: $2 - $10 million
Investment Criteria: Middle Market, Growth Capital Funding, Recapitalizations, Management Buyouts
Industry Group Preference: Business Products & Services, Technology, Media, Marketing, Software

Key Executives:
Adit Abhyankar
e-mail: adit@fogcitycapital.com
Education: BS, Electrical Engineering & Economics, MS, Engineering, Tulane University
Background: Co-Founder & VP, Gadgetworks; Xigo; BARRA
Ravi Bhaskaran
e-mail: ravi@fogcitycapital.com
Education: BS, Unversity of California, Berkeley; MBA, University of Chicago; London Business School
Background: Co-Founder & CEO, Pyramid Consulting; Management Consultant, Booz Allen & Hamilton

761 FOGEL INTERNATIONAL
5110 North 32nd Street
Suite 206
Phoenix, AZ 85018
Phone: 602-508-0728 Fax: 602-840-4970
e-mail: lfogel@fogelinternational.com
web: www.fogelinternational.com

Mission Statement: An investment/merchant banking firm dedicated to assisting companies throughout the United States in the fulfillment of their business and personal strategies and goals.

Geographic Preference: United States
Founded: 1969
Average Investment: $75 million
Minimum Investment: $10 million
Investment Criteria: Merger & Acquisition, Private Placements for Mature Companies
Industry Group Preference: All Sectors Considered

Key Executives:
Lawrence M Fogel, Senior Managing Principal
e-mail: lfogel@fogelinternational.com
Background: Account Executive, Walston & Company; HO Peet & Company
Ahim Kandler, Managing Director, Israeli & European Investments
Education: Graduate Degree, Business Administration, LMU University, Munich
Background: Founder & Managing Partner, AHIM Business Development; PricewaterhouseCoopers; Daimler Benz Aerospace
P Frank Limbaugh, Consultant, Specialty Finance
Education: MA, Management, Peter Drucker School of Management, Claremont University
Background: President, Technology Division, Deutsche Financial Services; Division Vice President, Borg Warner Acceptance Corporation
Bryan J. Toth, Senior Financial Analyst/Consultant
Education: BBA, University of Toledo; Obtained Series 7 and Series 66 licensing
Background: Management, Merrill Lynch; Deutsche Financial Services; Security Pacific; Bank One; Pacific Century Bank.

762 FONTINALIS PARTNERS
One Woodward Avenue
Suite 1600
Detroit, MI 48226
e-mail: info@fontinalis.com
web: www.fontinalis.com

Mission Statement: To find innovative companies in the transportation technology sector; bring its resources to bear and help companies grow and expand across markets on a global scale.

Industry Group Preference: Transportation, Communications
Portfolio Companies: Life 360, Masabi, Nano-C, ParkMe, Parkmobile, QuickPay, RelayRides, SQLstream, Streetline, Synovia Solutions, Zagster

Key Executives:
Ralph Booth, Founder/Managing Partner
Education: BA, Harvard University
Background: CEO/Chairman, Booth American Company
Directorships: Diveo Broadband Networks
Bill Ford, Founder/Partner
Education: BA, Princeton University; MS, Management, MIT
Background: Executive Chairman, Ford Motor Company
Chris Cheever, Founder/Managing Director
Education: BA, Harvard University; MBA, Yale School of Management
Background: Launch Capital; Wealth Management & Business Banking, UBS

Venture Capital & Private Equity Firms / Domestic Firms

Laura Petterle, Partner/CFO
Education: BA, University of Michigan
Background: EVP/CFO, Booth American Company

763 FORERUNNER VENTURES
1161 Mission St.
Suite 300
San Francisco, CA 94103

e-mail: info@forerunnerventures.com
web: forerunnerventures.com

Mission Statement: Forerunner Ventures invests in early-stage ventures by ambitious entrepreneurs who seek to challenge industry norms.

Investment Criteria: Early-Stage
Portfolio Companies: 11 Honoré, Alchemy 43, Away, Birchbox, Birdies, Bloomthat, Bonobos, Brickwork, Chime, Choosy, Cleo, Cotopaxi, Curology, Darby Smart, Dollar Shave Club, Draper James, Faire, Flow, Glossier, Hims, Hollar, Homebase, Hotel Tonight, Inturn, Jet, KiwiCo, Lolli, Lumi, M.Gemi, MoveWith, Nécessaire, Neighborhood Goods, Outdoor Voices, Packagd, Phil, Prose, Reformation, Rep, ReSci, Ritual, Rockets of Awesome, Serena & Lily, ShopShops, Sproutling, Stadium Goods, Stockwell, The Farmer's Dog, The Inside, Warby Parker, Zesty, Zola, Zyper

Key Executives:
Kirsten Green, Founder/Managing Director
Education: BA, Business Economics, UCLA; CPA; CFA
Directorships: Glossier, Outdoor Voices, Ritual, Inturn, Indigo Fair, Dollar Shave Club, Bonobos
Eurie Kim, Partner
Education: BS, Business Administrations, UC Berkeley; MBA, Wharton School
Background: Management Consultant, Bain & Co.; Investor, Castanea Partners
Directorships: Away, Alchemy 43, Curology, MoveWith, ShopShops, The Farmer's Dog
Brian O'Malley, Partner
Education: BS, Economics, Wharton School
Background: Accel; General Partner, Battery Ventures

764 FORESITE CAPITAL
600 Montgomery St.
Suite 4500
San Francisco, CA 94111

Phone: 415-877-4887
web: www.foresitecapital.com

Mission Statement: Foresite Capital invests at all stages in companies across all areas of healthcare including diagnostics, medical devices, therapeutics, and services.

Investment Criteria: All Stages
Industry Group Preference: Healthcare, Diagnostics, Healthcare Services, Medical Devices, Therapeutics
Portfolio Companies: 10x Genomics, Acceleron Pharma, Achaogen, Aclaris Therapeutics, Adaptimmune, Adaptive Biotechnologies, Aerie Pharmaceuticals, Aimmune Therapeutics, Akari Therapeutics, Alder Biopharmaceuticals, Alector, Ambit, Anacor, Arbutus Biopharma, Arcus Biosciences, Ardelyx, Argenx, Ascendis Pharma, Audentes, Auspex, Avanir, Avexis, Bellicum, Biodelivery Sciences, Biohaven Pharmaceuticals, Biotie Therapies, Blueprint Medicines, Bracket, Color, ConnectiveRx, CymaBay Therapeutics, Jenali, Dermira, DNAnexus, Dyax, Editas Medicine, Eidos, Epizyme, FibroGen, Fount Therapeutics, Fulcrum Therapeutics, Generation Bio, Genomics PLC, Global Blood Therapeutics, Grail, Immunomedics, Inscripta, Insitro, Insmed, Intarcia, Intellio Therapeutics, iRhythm, Iventis, Jounce, Juno, Juvenescence, LifeMine, Lipocine, Loxo Oncology, Mindstrong, Momenta, MyoKardia, NanoString, Natera, NeuroDerm, Nexvet, Optinose, OrexiGen, Oric Pharmaceuticals, PacBio, Pact Pharma, Peloton, Protagonist, RegenxBio, Replimune, Rhythm, RxSight, Sage, Sangamo, Scynexis, Solid Biosciences, Solta Medical Tocagen, Tricida, UniQure, Universal American, VenatoRx, Verona Pharma, Vitae Pharmaceuticals, Wave Life Sciences, WaveTec Vision, Zafgen

Other Locations:
1345 Ave. of the Americas
3rd Floor
New York, NY 10105
Phone: 212-804-6303

Key Executives:
Jim Tananbaum, CEO & Managing Director
Education: BS, BSEE, Yale University; MS, MIT; MD, MBA, Harvard University
Background: Co-Founder, GelTex; Co-Founder, Theravance
Dennis D Ryan, CFO & Managing Director
Education: BA, University of California, Berkeley; MBA, University of Santa Clara; CPA
Background: KPMG; Western Properties Trust; Lighthouse Capital Partners; Berkeley Advisors Group
Vikram Bajaj, Managing Director
Education: PhD, MIT
Background: Chief Scientific Officer, GRAIL; Co-Founder, Verily; Associate Professor, Stanford School of Medicine; Advisor, Department of Defense
Matthew Buten, Managing Director
Background: Healthcare Portfolio Manager, Catapult/Millennium Partners; Co-Founder, Sapphire Capital
Dorothy Margolskee, Managing Director
Education: BS, Harvard University; MD, Johns Hopkins Medical School
Background: Managing Director, Prospect Ventures; SVP, Marck Research Labs
Brett Zbar, Managing Director
Education: Yale University; MD, Harvard Medical School
Background: Partner, Aisling Capital

765 FORGEPOINT CAPITAL
400 S El Camino Real
Suite 1050
San Mateo, CA 94402

Phone: 650-289-4455
web: forgepointcap.com

Mission Statement: ForgePoint Capital is a venture investor for early stage cybersecurity companies.

Fund Size: $750 Million
Founded: 2015

Key Executives:
Will Lin, Co-Founder/Managing Director
Education: University of California
Donald Dixon, Co-Founder/Managing Director
Education: BSE, Princeton University; MBA, Stanford University
Background: Co-President, Partech International; Managing Director, Alex, Brown & Sons; VP, Morgan Stanley & Co.
Sean Cunningham, Managing Director
Education: MBA, Gonzaga University
Background: Intel Capital
Alberto Lopez, Managing Director
Background: Apple; Oracle; CEO, enCommerce, Entrust and Thor Technologies

766 FORMATIVE VENTURES
2905 Stender Way
Suite 2
Santa Clara, CA 95054

Phone: 650-245-7088
web: www.formative.com

Mission Statement: Works with early-stage entrepreneurial teams that are seeking a value-added partner for institutional financing.

Founded: 2000

Venture Capital & Private Equity Firms / Domestic Firms

Average Investment: $2 - $5 million
Investment Criteria: Early-Stage
Industry Group Preference: Communications, Wireless, Internet, Semiconductors, Infrastructure
Portfolio Companies: Capella, InboundWriter, InnoCOMM Wireless, IP Infusion, Marketocracy, Mashery, Pyxis Technology, Samplify Systems, Silicon Clocks, Smalltown, SOASTA, Veebeam, Zyray Wireless

Key Executives:
  Brian Connors, Managing Director
  e-mail: brian@formative.com
  Education: BS, Egineering, Northern Arizona University
  Background: Institutional Venture Partners; C-Cube; VP, North American Sales, Synopsys
  Directorships: IP Infusion, Pyxis Technology, Samplify Systems
  Clint Chao, Managing Director
  e-mail: clint@formative.com
  Education: BS, Electrical Engineering/Computer Science, University of California, Berkeley
  Background: VP Marketing, SkyStream; Senior Director Marketing, C-Cube Microsystems; Sales Management, Motorola's Semiconductor Products Sector
  Dino Vendetti, Managing Director
  e-mail: dino@formative.com
  Education: MSEE, MBA, University of Washington; BSEE, San Diego State University
  Background: Co-Founder, FoundersPad; General Partner, Bay Partners; Vulcan Ventures

767 FORREST BINKLEY & BROWN
19900 MacArthur Boulevard
Suite 69
Irvine, CA 92612

Phone: 949-566-9121

Mission Statement: Focuses on investing in middle-market buyouts and providing growth capital to companies that offer potential for a substantial increase in shareholder value and exceptional rates of return to investors.

Geographic Preference: Southern California
Fund Size: $215 million
Founded: 1993
Average Investment: $4 million
Minimum Investment: $2 million
Investment Criteria: First Stage, Second Stage, MBO, Middle Stage, Later Stage
Industry Group Preference: Technology, Communications, Computer Related, Consumer Services, Consumer Products
Portfolio Companies: AD PathLabs, AirClic, American Asphalt & Grading, American Lighting Supply, Artifact Entertainment, Ascendent Telecommunications, CallConnect Communications, Comcore Semiconductor, Cooking.com, Crosman Acquisition Corporation, Cytovia, DispenseSource, FieldCentrix, Golden State Vintners, HFSC Holdings, InnoTech, IPNet Solutions, Maxima Corporation, NextCard, OfficeSource, OnPrem Networks Corporation, Pearl Izumi, SpectraSensors, Stamps.com, Tekni-Plex, Teradiant Networks, Trikon Technologies, Tunable Photonics Corporations, UltraLink, Vativ Technologies, Vendavo, Vista Medical Technologies

Key Executives:
  Gregory J Forrest, Co-Founder\Partner
  e-mail: greg@fbbvc.com
  Education: BS, Chemical Engineering, Arizona State University; MBA, University of Southern California Graduate School of Business
  Background: President/CEO, Security Pacific Corporation; Chairman/President, BankAmerica Venture Capital
  Nicholas B Binkley, Co-Founder\Partner
  e-mail: nick@fbbvc.com
  Education: BA, Political Science, Colorado College; MA, International Studies, Johns Hopkins School of Advanced International Studies
  Background: Assistant VP, Security Pacific National Bank; Deputy Administrator, Security Pacific Financial Systems; Vice Chairman, Security Pacific Corporation
  Jeffrey J. Brown, Co-Founder/Partner
  Joseph Galligan, Chief Financial Officer
  Education: BA, Accounting, University of Northern Iowa; CPA
  Background: Controller, Automotive Safety Components International

768 FORT WASHINGTON CAPITAL PARTNERS GROUP
303 Broadway
Suite 1200
Cincinnati, OH 45202

Phone: 513-361-7600 **Fax:** 513-361-7605
Toll-Free: 888-244-8167
web: www.fortwashington.com

Mission Statement: Fort Washington Capital Partners Group is a private equity fund-of-funds manager and serves as the private equity division of Fort Washington Investment Advisors.

Fund Size: $450 million
Average Investment: $250,000 - $2 million
Investment Criteria: Growth Equity, Buyouts, Special Situations, Mezzanine
Industry Group Preference: Diversified
Other Locations:
  The Huntington Center
  Suite 1670
  41 South High Street
  Columbus, OH 43215
  Phone: 614-222-6500 **Fax:** 614-222-6535

  25800 Science Park Drive
  Suite 100
  Cleveland, OH 44122
  Phone: 216-378-2235 **Fax:** 513-357-4010

Key Executives:
  Maribeth Rahe, President and CEO
  Education: BS, Bowling Green State University; MBA, Thunderbird School of Global Management
  Background: JP Morgan; US Trust Company of NY
  Stephen A Baker, Managing Director/Co-Head, Private Equity
  Education: BA, History, University of Cincinnati; MBA, Finance, New York University Stern School of Business
  Background: Principal, Seaport Capital Partners; Providence Journal Company
  Robert Maeder, Managing Director/Co-Head, Private Equity
  Education: BA, MBA, Northwestern University
  Background: LEK Consulting; CIVC Partners; Merrill Lynch & Co.

769 FORTRESS INVESTMENT GROUP LLC
1345 Avenue of the Americas
46th Floor
New York, NY 10105

Phone: 212-798-6100
e-mail: grunte@fortress.com
web: www.fortress.com

Mission Statement: Fortress has one of the largest private equity businesses focused on acquiring undervalued assets and companies that can be improved through intensive asset management.

Geographic Preference: International
Fund Size: $36 billion
Founded: 1998
Industry Group Preference: Financial Services, Transportation, Energy, Infrastructure, Healthcare

Venture Capital & Private Equity Firms / Domestic Firms

Portfolio Companies: Air Castle, Brookdale Senior Living, CW Financial Services, Florida East Coast Industries, Florida East Coast Railway, Global Signal, Holiday Retirement, NationStar, New Fortress Energy, OneMain

Other Locations:
3290 Northside Parkwat NW
Suite 350
Atlanta, GA 30327
Phone: 404-264-4779

5221 North O'Connor Boulevard
Suite 700
Irving, TX 75039
Phone: 972-532-4300

GmbH FPM Deutschland GmbH
Fortress Germany Asset Management GmbH
An Der Welle 4
Frankfurt 60322
Germany
Phone: 49-69-2549-6700

Fortress Real Estate (HK) Limited
No. 8 Queen's Road Central
28th Floor
Central, Hong Kong
China
Phone: 852-5803-6500

FCF UK (A) III Limited
7 Clarges Street
London W1J 8AE
United Kingdom
Phone: 44-20-7290-5600

10250 Constellation Boulevard
Suite 1600
Los Angeles, CA 90067
Phone: 310-228-3030

220 Elm Street
Suite 201
New Canaan, CT 06840
Phone: 203-442-2442

Fortress Investment Consulting (Shanghai) Co.
Bldg 5, 858 Huanzhen Road South
Baoshan District
Shanghai 200436
China
Phone: 86-21-5650-8989

Fortress Investment Group (Australia) PTY
Level 19 Getaway
1 McQuarie Place
Sydney NSW 2000
Australia
Phone: 61-2-8239-1900

Fortress Investment Group (Japan) GK
Roppongi Hills Mori Tower 2gF
6-10-1 Roppongi, Minato-Ku
Tokyo 106-6129
Japan
Phone: 81-3-6438-4400

Key Executives:
Wesley R. Edens, Co-Founder/Co-CEO/Principal
Education: BS, Finance, Oregon State University
Background: Managing Director, BlackRock Financial Management Inc.; Partner/Managing Director, Lehman Brothers
Peter L. Briger Jr., Principal/Co-CEO
Education: BA, Princeton University; MBA, Wharton School
Background: Partner, Goldman Sachs
Directorships: Tipping Point, Caliber School
Randal A. Nardone, Co-Founder/Principal
Education: BA, English & Biology, University of Connecticut; JD, Boston University School of Law
Background: Managing Director, UBS; Principal, BlackRock Financial Management; Partner, Thacher Proffitt & Wood

770 **FORTÉ VENTURES**
Atlanta Technology Village
3423 Piedmont Road, NE
Suite 520 (225A)
Atlanta, GA 30303

Phone: 404-480-3090 **Fax:** 404-855-2840
web: www.forteventures.com

Mission Statement: Forté Ventures launched in January 2012 with a clear mission to deliver exceptional financial returns on a risk-reduced basis to limited partner investors by providing national visibility and privileged access to investment opportunities that are validated by a global network of strategic partners and corporate co-investors. We actively collaborate with a large cadre of corporate strategic partners to identify the most innovative and promising technology companies to invest in throughout North America. We invest across a diversified set of industry sectors including Information Technology, Mobility, Digital Media, Financial Technology and Industrial Technology.

Geographic Preference: North America
Founded: 2012
Minimum Investment: $100,000
Industry Group Preference: Information Technology, Digital Media & Marketing, Mobility, Internet, E-Commerce & Manufacturing, Fintech, Industrial Technology
Portfolio Companies: Adstage, AppBus, Aspen Aerogels, Ecosmart, Fision, Integrate, Liaison, News Distribution Network, RapidSOS, Remedy Informatics, SpringBot Commerce, Stella Service, Stockpile, TaDa Innovations, TidalScale, Urgent.ly, Ushr, Zeuss

Other Locations:
310 De Guigne Dr.
Sunnyvale, CA 94085

Key Executives:
Tom Hawkins, Managing Partner
Education: BA, Duke University; MBA, Kellogg School of Management
Background: Arcapita; Siemens Venture Capital; Cordova Ventures; Radiant Systems
Directorships: AppBus, Urgent.ly, Springbot, RapidSOS, StellaService
Louis Rajczi, Partner
Education: BS, Computer Engineering, University of Michigan; MBA, Southern Methodist University
Background: Siemens Venture Capital; Nortel Networks; TaDa Innovations
Directorships: AdStage, Integrate, IntelliVision, StellaService, Ushr, Urgent.ly
Paul Dibella, Partner
Education: University of Miami School of Law; SUNY Albany
David Nagel, PhD, Partner
Education: Bachelors and Masters, Engineering, UCLA; PhD, Perception and Mathematical Psychology, UCLA
Background: PalmSource; AT&T; Apple Computer; NASA's Ames Research Center
Melanie Martin, Director
Education: BS, Education, University of Georgia
Background: Cordova Ventures

771 **FORUM VENTURES**
149 Natoma Street
2nd Floor
San Francisco, CA 94105

web: www.forumvc.com

Mission Statement: Forum was started from a place of helpfulness, with the mission to make the B2B SaaS journey easier, more accessible and successful for early-stage founders.

Investment Criteria: Seed, Early Stage

Venture Capital & Private Equity Firms / Domestic Firms

Industry Group Preference: SaaS
Portfolio Companies: Coprocure, Courier, Firstbase, Fireflies.Ai, Indio, Inscribe, Oncue, People Data Labs, Roots Automation, Silq, Sote, Vendorpm

Key Executives:
  Mike Cardamone, CEO & General Partner
  Education: BSc, Syracuse University; MBA, Columbia Business School
  Background: AcademixDirect

772 FORWARD VENTURES
9255 Towne Centre Drive
Suite 350
San Diego, CA 92121

Phone: 858-677-6077
e-mail: info@forwardventures.com
web: www.forwardventures.com

Mission Statement: Seeks both to accelerate the development of innovative and effective treatments for serious diseases and produce significant returns for its investors in three to five years.
Geographic Preference: United States, Europe
Fund Size: $500 million
Founded: 1990
Average Investment: $3 - 5 million
Minimum Investment: $500,000
Investment Criteria: Seed, Startup, First Round, Later Stage;
Industry Group Preference: Pharmaceuticals, Healthcare, Life Sciences, Medical Devices, Biopharmaceuticals
Portfolio Companies: Acorda Therapeutics, Adiana, Affinium Pharmaceuticals, Ambit Biosciences, Applied Molecular Evolution, Ariad, Cabrellis Pharmaceuticals, Collective Therapeutics, Combichem, Conforma Therapeutics, Corixa, Dynavax, Essentialis Therapeutics, Hypnion, LigoCyte Pharmaceuticals, Micromet, Morphotek, Nereus, NovaCardia, Onyx Pharmaceuticals, Predix Pharmaceuticals, Proprius Pharmaceuticals, Sequana, Somatix, Syndax, TargeGen, Tioga Pharmaceuticals, Triangle Pharmaceuticals, Viracta

Key Executives:
  Standish Fleming, Founding Managing Partner
  Education: BA, Amherst College; MBA, University of California, LA
  Background: President, Biotechnology Venture Investors' Group
  Directorships: Ambit, Aventa Biosciences Corporation, Coverge Medical, Kemia, MitoKor, Sanarus Medical, Arizeke Pharmaceuticals, Nereus Pharmaceuticals
  Stuart Collinson, Partner
  Education: MBA, Harvard Business School; PhD, Physical Chemistry, University of Oxford
  Background: Chairman, CEO & President, Aurora Biosciences Corporation; CEO, Andaris Limited; GlaxoWellcome PLC; Baxter International, Consultant, The Boston Consulting Group
  Directorships: Affinium Pharmaceuticals, Asteres, Essentialis, Sequel Pharmaceuticals, Tioga Pharmaceuticals, Vertex Pharmaceuticals

773 FOUNDATION CAPITAL
250 Middlefield Road
Menlo Park, CA 94025

Phone: 650-614-0500
web: www.foundationcapital.com

Mission Statement: To build great companies, organizations that make a difference, not only in the lives of their constituents, but in the impact they have on their markets.
Geographic Preference: West Coast
Fund Size: $80 million
Founded: 1995
Average Investment: $10 million
Minimum Investment: $1 million
Investment Criteria: Early-Stage, Small-Seed
Industry Group Preference: Consumer Services, Internet Technology, Telecommunications, Data Communications, Software, Information Technology, Networking, Semiconductors, Clean Technology, Consumer Products, Data Storage, Cloud Computing
Portfolio Companies: 2nd Address, Acco, AdRoll, Aggregate Knowledge, Aquion Energy, Arthena, AutoGrid, Aux Money, Azure Power, Block Cypher, Board Vantage, Bold Threads, Calix, Cantaloip, Catalytic, Chegg, CliQr, CloudOn, Cohesity, Confer, Control4, Conviva, Converity, CoverWallet, Custora, Cyphort, DogVacey, Ebates, EMeter. Enernoc, Entropix, Envestnet, Everyday Health, Fastback Networks, Financial Engines, Finxera, ForgeRock, For Us All, Free Wheel, Funds India, Genies, Graphcore, Guardian Analutics, Health IQ, HomeBay, Hustle, Immersv, InsideView, Kik, League, LendingClub, LendingHome, Localytics, Luxe, MaestrolQ, MarkMonitor, Mesosphere, MobileIron, Mode, Motif Investing, Moxie, Mya, Netflix, OnDeck, Openspace, Pachyderm, Paribus, Peespace, Peribit, PhantomCyber, Plate Joy, Pocket, Prevedere, Private Core, QuanticMind, Quilt, Rappi, Refresj, Oracle Responsys, Lollicam, Sentient Energy, Shopular, ShoreTel, SilkRoad, Silver Spring Networks, SimplyHired, Skycure, Spotzot, Spring CM, SunRun, Tea Leaf, Triple, Trufa, TubeMogul, Tubi, Uber, Venafi, Visier, Wevorce, Xmos, Yozio, Zero Stack, Zetta.net

Key Executives:
  Bill Elmore, General Partner
  e-mail: belmore@foundationcapital.com
  Education: MBA, Stanford Graduate School of Business; BSEE & MSEE, Purdue University
  Background: President, Visual Engineering; General Partner, Inman & Bowman; Marketing Management, Hewlett-Packard; President, Western Association for Venture Capitalist
  Directorships: Onyx Software, Wind River Systems, Atheros Communications, Markmonitor, Packet Design, TeaLeaf Technology, Vernier Networks, Wherenet, Biz360, Uxcomm, Adexs
  Mike Schuh, General Partner Emeritus
  e-mail: mschuh@foundationcapital.com
  Education: BSEE, University of Maryland
  Background: CFO/Co-Founder/Chairman, Intrinsa Corporation; VP Sales, Clarify; VP Sales, Cadence Design Systems; VP Sales, Computervision
  Directorships: Netflix, Responsys, Barcelona, BoardVantage, CoWare, OnStor, Jasper Design Automation
  Ashu Garg, General Partner
  e-mail: agarg@foundationcap.com
  Education: BA, Indian Institute of Technology, New Dehli; MA, Indian Institute of Management, Bangladore
  Background: General Manager, Microsoft On-Line Service; McKinsey & Company
  Directorships: Vienova
  Paul Holland, General Partner
  e-mail: pholland@foundationcapital.com
  Education: MBA, University of California, Berkeley; MA, Foreign Affairs, University of Virginia; BS, James Madison University
  Background: Senior VP, Kana Communications; Pure Software; SRI International
  Directorships: Talking Blocks, manageStar, Ketera, RouteScience, TuVoxo Video Solutions, Silver Spring Networks
  Paul Koontz, General Partner Emeritus
  e-mail: pkoontz@foundationcapital.com
  Education: MA, Engineering Management, Stanford University; BS, Mechanical Engineering, Princeton University
  Background: VP Marketing, Netscape Communications; Sr Management, Silicon Graphics; Hewlett-Packard
  Directorships: United Online, Financial Engines, Apexon, Oberon Financial Technology, Pacific Edge, Vivecon, CloudShield

Skip Glass, Operating Partner
e-mail: sglass@foundationcapital.com
Education: BS, Sacramento State University; MBA, University of Arizona
Background: Canaan Partners; Sygate; SleepyCat Software; eHealth Insurance; Retention Education
Directorships: Voyence; Groundwork Open Solutions
Joanne Chen, Partner
e-mail: kbasco@foundationcap.com
Education: BS, University of California, Berkeley; MBA, Booth School of Business, University of Chicago
Background: Engineer, Cisco Systems; Jefferies & Company; Probitas Partners; Hyde Park Angels
Charles Moldow, General Partner
e-mail: cmoldow@foundationcapital.com
Education: BS, The Wharton School; MBA, Harvard University
Background: Tellme Networks; @Home Network; Co-Founder, OnTime Guide
Zach Noorani, Partner
e-mail: ecavanaugh@foundationcapital.com
Education: BS, Economics, Stanford University; MBA, Sloan School of Management, MIT
Background: Sherpa Ventures; Capital One Financial; North Hill Ventures
Dave Armstrong, Administrative Partner
e-mail: jslimmer@foundationcapital.com
Education: BS, Finance, Virginia Tech; JD, George Mason University School of Law
Background: Gunderson Dettmer
Steve Vassallo, General Partner
e-mail: svassallo@foundationcapital.com
Education: BS, Mechanical Engineering, Worcester Polytechnic Institute; MS, Mechanical Engineering, Stanford University; MBA, Stanford Graduate School of Business
Background: Ning; Director of Mechanical Engineering, Immersion; Project Leader, IDEO
Warren Weiss, General Partner
e-mail: wweiss@foundationcapital.com
Education: BS, Western Illinois University
Background: President & CEO, Asera; President, Prism Solutions
Directorships: eMeter.com; Guardian Analytics; InterAct; MarkMonitor; nGenera; Purfresh; Quantivo; Rearden Commerce; SilkRoad Technologies; Silver Spring Networks
Angela Nuttman, Operating Coordinator
e-mail: anuttman@foundationcap.com
Education: Santa Clara University
Background: Director of Operations, Olive Grove Consulting

774 FOUNDER COLLECTIVE
81 Greene Street
2nd Floor
New York, NY 10012

web: www.foundercollective.com

Mission Statement: Founder Collective is a venture capital fund investing in seed-stage companies around the world.
Geographic Preference: San Francisco, New York
Fund Size: $70 million
Investment Criteria: Seed
Industry Group Preference: Advertising Technology, Business to Business, Consumer, E-Commerce & Manufacturing, Health Related, Mobile
Portfolio Companies: BuzzFeed, Coupang, Cruise, Dia & Co., Hotel Tonight, Kuvee, Periscope, PillPack, SeatGeek, theTradeDesk, Uber
Key Executives:
David Frankel, Managing Partner
Education: Harvard Business School; University of the Witwatersrand
Background: Internet Solutions

Eric Paley, Partner
Education: Harvard Business School
Background: Brontes Technologies
Micah Rosenbloom, Partner
Education: Cornell University; Harvard Business School
Background: Brontes Technologies; Handshake; Sample6

775 FOUNDER PARTNERS
San Francisco, CA

web: www.founderpartners.co

Mission Statement: Seeking to partner with and invest in technical founders focused on mobile, internet and software products.
Founded: 2013
Industry Group Preference: Mobile, Internet, IoT, Software, Applications, Technology
Portfolio Companies: AddEvent, Admovate, Check Point Software Technologies LTD., Chairish, Cobalt, Dealix, Meltwater, Mixbook, Pinkoi, Relevad, Roblox, Wheelhouse, Yahoo!
Key Executives:
Brian Flynn, Co-Founder/Partner
e-mail: brian@founderpartners.co
Education: BA, University of Notre Dame; MBA, Harvard Business School
Background: Principal, Robertson Stephens & Co.; Partner, Investment Group of Santa Barbara; Co-Founder, IMsecure; Head of Corporate Development, Macromedia Inc.; Co-Founder, AdMovate Inc.; Co-Founder, Relevad Corporation; Founder, Esplanade Partners; Co-Founder, Braintrust Network
Greg Baszucki, Co-Founder/Partner
e-mail: greg@founderpartners.co
Education: BSEE, University of Minnesota
Background: Co-Founder/Executive, Knowledge Revolution; Co-Founder/President, Dealix; Divisional General Manager, The Cobalt Group; Co-Founder, AdMovate Inc.; Founder/CEO, Wheelhouse Enterprises
Directorships: Roblox; Mixbook; iDentalSoft; Band of Angels
Adam Jackson, Partner
e-mail: adam@founderpartners.co
Education: BS, Vanderbilt University
Background: Co-Founder/CEO, Doctor On Demand; Founder, Dopamine Labs; Co-Founder/Managing Partner, Cambrian Asset Management LLC
Directorships: Cleanshelf
Ted West, Partner
e-mail: ted@founderpartners.co
Education: BA, Princeton University; MBA, Harvard Business School
Background: Partner, Sage Partners LLC; Executive Director, Giving Assistant Inc.; Executive Director, CFO Plans; Strategic Advisor, Fresh Victor; Founding Chair, BOHH Labs; Co-Founder/CEO, Strateq Health Inc.
Directorships: BlueSpace Software; Colarity; RealNames
Dimitri Steinberg, Partner
Education: BA, Princeton University; MBA, Harvard University
Background: Morgan Stanley; Lazard; Merrill Lynch; HSBC
Steve McKay, Partner
e-mail: steve@founderpartners.co
Education: BSEE, University of Notre Dame; MBA, Kellogg School of Management
Background: Associate Partner/Management Consultant, Accenture; CEO, Entone Inc.; Mentor, Founder Institute; President of Global Sales & Business Development, Amino Communications; Founder/CEO, Ignite
Xavier Casanova, Partner
e-mail: xavier@founderpartners.com
Education: MS, Stanford University
Background: Founder, Fireclock; General Manager,

Venture Capital & Private Equity Firms / Domestic Firms

Digital River; Founder/CEO, Wambo; Founder/CEO, Liveclicker

776 FOUNDER'S CO-OP
1100 NE Campus Parkway
2nd Floor
Seattle, WA 9810G

web: www.founderscoop.com

Mission Statement: Founders Co-op is a seed-stage investment fund dedicated to working with talented entrepreneurs in the Pacific Northwest region.

Geographic Preference: Pacific Northwest
Investment Criteria: Seed-Stage, Early-Stage
Industry Group Preference: Mobile, Internet
Portfolio Companies: Amperity, Appature, AppFog, Apptentive, Apsalar, Array Health, Auth0, BigDoor, BloomAPI, Boomz, Bluecore, Bonanza, Boundless, Brand AI, C-sATS, Clipboard, Cody, Innervate, Instagift, Jobalign, KITT.ai, Komiko, Level Ten Energy, LiveStories, LendUp, Lighter Capital, Loftium, Meldium, MobileDevHQ, Moment, Onewed, Outreach, Reflect, Remitly, The Riveter, Shelf Engine, Shippable Simply Measured, SkyWard, Smore, Stackery, TalentWorks, Tavour, Thinkfuse, Tindie, Tred, TrueFacet, Tune, Unbounce, Urban Airship, Zappli

Key Executives:
   Chris DeVore, General Partner
   Education: BA, American Studies, Yale University
   Background: Co-Founder, Judy's Book; Vice President, Sapient Corporation; Senior Product Management, McCaw Cellular
   Andy Sack, General Partner
   Education: Brown University; MBA, Sloan School of Management, MIT
   Background: Co-Founder/CEO, Judy's Book; Co-Founder, Kefta; Co-Founder, Abuzz; Co-Founder, Firefly Network
   Directorships: Zango, Cooler Planet, Orange Line Media

777 FOUNDERS EQUITY
545 Fifth Avenue
Suite 401
New York, NY 10017

Phone: 212-829-0900 Fax: 212-829-0901
e-mail: info@fequity.com
web: www.fequity.com

Mission Statement: Committed to long-term value creation that generates above average returns.

Geographic Preference: East of the Rockies
Fund Size: $160 million
Founded: 1969
Average Investment: $10 million
Minimum Investment: $3 million
Investment Criteria: Small Buyout, Later Stage, Accelerating Stage, MBO, Recapitalizations, Special Situations/Turnarounds, Corporate Divestitures
Industry Group Preference: Business to Business, Marketing, Outsourcing & Efficiency, Logistics, Healthcare, Environment Products & Services, Security, Consumer Products, Food & Beverage, Food Services, Franchising, Manufacturing, Consumer Services
Portfolio Companies: Advantedge Healthcare Solutions, Core Business Technology Solutions, Glass America, In The Swim Inc., Pay-O-Matic Corporation, Richardson Foods, Stone Source

Key Executives:
   Warren H. Haber, Founding Partner
   212-829-0900 x201
   Fax: 212-829-0901
   e-mail: whaber@fequity.com
   Education: BBA Finance, Baruch College
   Background: Equity Research/Investment Banking, Merrill Lynch; Bear Stearns
   Directorships: CoStar Group; Warnex;
   John L. Teeger, Founding Partner
   Education: BS, University of Witwatersrand; MBA, Columbia University
   Background: VP, Bear Stearns & Company
   Directorships: American LifeCare, Bevglen Medical Systems of Delaware, Ensure Technologies
   John D. White, Founding Partner
   Education: BS, Finance and Accounting, Babson College; MS, Business Admin., Wharton School, University of Pennsylvania
   Background: Executive VP/CFO 3-D Geophysical; Senior VP, Laidlaw Holdings; Paine Webber; Digital Equipment Corporation
   Directorships: ForeAmerica
   J. Ryan Kelly, Partner
   e-mail: rkelly@fequity.com
   Education: BS, Finance & Accounting, Fairfield University
   Background: JH Whitney & Co.; RFE Investment Partners; Arthur Andersen Worldwide

778 FOUNDERS FUND
One Letterman Drive
Building C, Suite 420
San Francisco, CA 94129

e-mail: info@foundersfund.com
web: www.foundersfund.com

Mission Statement: Founders Fund is a venture capital firm that finances companies developing innovative and revolutionary technologies. The firm invests across a wide range of industries and seeks to help build great companies from the ground up.

Fund Size: $625 million
Founded: 2005
Average Investment: $500,000 - $150 million
Investment Criteria: Seed, Early Stage, Later Stage
Industry Group Preference: Aerospace, Defense and Government, Energy, Healthcare, Software, Biotechnology, Internet
Portfolio Companies: Airbnb, AltSchool, Asana, Bolt Threads, Collective Health, Counsyl, Emerald Therapeutics, Facebook, Flexport, Knewton, Lyft, Misfit, Nanotronics Imaging, Oscar, Palantir, Quantcast, Radius, ResearchGate, SpaceX, Spotify, Stemcentrx, Stripe, Wish, ZocDoc

Key Executives:
   Peter Thiel, Partner
   Education: BA, Philosophy, Stanford University; JD, Stanford Law School
   Background: Co-Founder, Chairman & CEO, PayPal; Founder, Clarium Capital Management; Palantir Technologies
   Napoleon Ta, Partner
   Education: BS, University of Colorado; MBA, Stanford University
   Directorships: RigUp; The Athletic; Zenreach
   Brian Singerman, Partner
   Education: BS, Computer Science, Stanford University
   Background: Executive, Google
   Lauren Gross, Partner/Chief Operating Officer
   Education: Stanford University
   Background: Clarium Capital Management; Citigroup Investment Bank
   Keith Rabois, Partner
   Education: BA, Policial Science, Stanford University; JD, Harvard University
   Background: Senior Executive, PayPal; COO, Square
   Directorships: Yelp; Xoom; YouTube; Palantir; Lyft; Airbnb; Eventbrite; Wish; Quora
   Scott Nolan, Partner
   Education: BS, MEng, Mechanical & Aerospace Engineering, Cornell University; MBA, Stanford University
   Background: SpaceX; Bain & Company
   Directorships: CollectiveHealth, Tachyus, Tribogenics

Venture Capital & Private Equity Firms / Domestic Firms

Neil Ruthven, Chief Financial Officer
Education: University of Johannesburg
Background: Controller, VantagePoint Capital Partners; Controller, 3i; Accounting Manager, Merriman Curhan Ford; Audit Manager, Ernst & Young

779 FOUNDRY GROUP
1050 Walnut Street
Suite 210
Boulder, CO 80302

web: www.foundrygroup.com

Mission Statement: Focused on making investments in early-stage information technology, internet and software startups.

Geographic Preference: North America
Fund Size: $225 million
Founded: 2007
Minimum Investment: $250,000 - $500,000
Investment Criteria: Early Stage
Industry Group Preference: Information Technology, Internet, Software
Portfolio Companies: 3D Robotics, About.me, Amper, AppDirect, Authentic8, Avidxchange, Beeswax, Betabrand, Boundless, Brightleaf, Broadly, Chewse, Chorus Fitness, Chowbotics, Chute, Cloudability, Crowdtap, Data Nerds, Distil Networks, Dwolla, Ello, FormLabs, FullContact, GlowForge, Harmonix, Havenly, Hellosign, Help Scout, Integrate, Joany, Jump Cloud, June, Leadpages, littleBits Electronics, Looking Glass, Maketime, Mapbox, Mattermark, Mighty Ai, Misty Robotics, Mlab, Modular Robotics, Moz, Nima, Nix Hydra, Oblong Industries Inc, Occipital, Pantheon, Pi Charging, Pilot, Pioneer Square Labs, Return Path, Roli, Rover.com, Sensu, Sourcepoint, Sovrn, Sphero, StockTwits, Taunt, Team Snap, Tech Stars, The Pros Closet, Tidelift, TrackR, Two Bit Circus, Urban Airship, VictorOps, VigLink, Wootmath, Work Market, Yesware

Key Executives:
Brad Feld, Partner
e-mail: brad@feld.com
Education: BS, MS, MIT
Background: Co-Founder, Mobius Venture Capital
Directorships: Gnip, Oblong, Zynga
Seth Levine, Partner
Education: Macalester College
Background: Mobius Venture Capital; FirstWorld Communications; ICG Communications
Ryan McIntyre, Partner
e-mail: ryan@foundrygroup.com
Education: BS, Symbolic Systems, Stanford University
Background: Co-Founder, Excite; Oracle Corporation; Software Engineer, Canon Research of America
Jason Mendelson, Partner Emeritus
e-mail: jason@foundrygroup.com
Education: BA, University of Michigan
Background: Managing Director, Mobius Venture Capital; Attorney, Cooley Godward Kronish LLP
Directorships: Accelergy, eCast, Stratify

780 FOUR RIVERS GROUP
156 2nd Street
San Francisco, CA 94105

web: www.fourriversgroup.com

Mission Statement: Four Rivers Group is an expansion stage venture capital firm that invests in high-growth, market leading technology companies globally. The fund provides custom, flexible financing and have no minimum threshold for investment size or ownership percentage.

Founded: 2008
Investment Criteria: Expansion-Stage
Portfolio Companies: Aerohive, Availink, Carbonite, Clutter, Corrigo, FireEye, GameFly, Kahuna, Namely, Numerify, PowerReviews, Return Path, ResearchGate, Sabrix, Satmetrix, ThousandEyes, Vidyo, New Relic. AssureRx Health, Nexenta, Talari Networks, Check, Agilone, Simply Measured, Tintri, Brightspace, Instart Logic, Dtex Systems, Outreach, Everwise, CloudPassage

Key Executives:
Farouk Ladha, Founder/Managing Partner
Education: BA, Economics, Dartmouth College; MBA, Harvard Business School
Background: Managing Director, SVB Capital; Broadview; PricewaterhouseCoopers
Aamir Virani, Strategic Limited Partner
Education: BS, Electrical Engineering; Rice University
Background: Co-Founder/COO/SVP, Product, Dropcam Inc.

781 FOX PAINE & COMPANY LLC
2105 Woodside Road
Suite D
Woodside, CA 94062-1153

Phone: 650-235-2075 Fax: 650-295-4045
e-mail: info@foxpaine.com
web: www.foxpaine.com

Mission Statement: Fox Paine specializes in providing solutions and capital for management buyouts, public-to-private transactions and growth capital investments.

Fund Size: $1.2 billion
Founded: 1996
Average Investment: $50 million
Investment Criteria: Management Buyouts, Public-To-Private Trasactions, Growth Capital
Industry Group Preference: Financial Services, Insurance, Industrial, Consumer Products, Energy, Oil & Gas, Agriculture
Portfolio Companies: ACMI, Alaska Communications Systems, Advanta, Byram Healthcare, Erno Laszlo, Global Indemnity Limited, L'Artisan Parfumeur, Maxxim Medical, Paradigm B.V., Penhaigon's, Seminis, United American Energy Corp., VCST, WJ Communications

Key Executives:
Saul A. Fox, Chief Executive Officer
Education: BS, Temple University; JD, University of Pennsylvania Law School
Background: General Partner, Kohlberg Kravis Roberts & Co.
Directorships: American Cytoscope Manufacturers, American Reinsurance, Canadian General, Global Indemnity, L'Artisan Parfumeur, Motel 6, Paradigm, Penhaligon's, Res-Fuel, Union Texas Petrol

782 FRANCISCO PARTNERS
One Letterman Drive
Building C, Suite 410
San Francisco, CA 94129

Phone: 415-418-2900 Fax: 415-418-2999
e-mail: info@franciscopartners.com
web: www.franciscopartners.com

Mission Statement: Working in close concert with management teams, we seek to reposition, rejuvenate, and grow businesses. With an intense focus on corporate strategy, operational excellence, and financial performance, we leverage our network, resources and experience to help build value for customers, employees, and shareholders.

Industry Group Preference: Software, Business Products & Services, Security, Internet, Healthcare Information Technology, Hardware, Industrial, Communications, Semiconductors, Components & IoT
Portfolio Companies: 2Checkout, Aconex, Aderant, Advanced M, Aesynt, Akqa, Allston Trading, AMI Semiconductor, API Healthcare, Attachmate, Attenti, Availity, Avalon, Barracuda Networks, Betterment, Blue Coat, Blu Jay, Bomgar, ByBox, C MAC Microtechnology, Capsilon, CityIndex, Click, Connecture, Corsair,

267

Venture Capital & Private Equity Firms / Domestic Firms

CoverMyMeds, Crossmatch, Dextrys, Discovery Education, Dynamo, EFJohnson, EFront, eSolutions, ExLibris, Foundation9, Frontrange, GoodRx, Grass Valley, GXS, HealthcareSource, Healthland, Hypercom, Ichor Systems, Iconectiv, K2, Landmark, LegalZoom, Legerity, Lumata, Lynx Medical Systems, Masternaut, Metaswitch, Metrologic, Mincom, Mitel, MyOn, Nextech, NexTraq, NMI, Np Text, Numonyx, OfficeTiger, Operative, Optanix, PayLease, Paymetric, Paysafe, Petcircle.com.au, Plex, Primavera, Prometheus Group, Prosper, QGenda, QuadraMed, Quantros, Quest, R2Net, RedPrairie, Renaissance, Sandvine, Sectigo, ShoreGroup, Smart Modular Technologies, SmartBear, Smart Focus, SonicWall, Source Photonics, Specific Media, The T System, Therapeutic Research Center, Trellis, Ultra Clean Technology, Vendavo, Verifone, WatchGuard, Webtrends, Xcellenet

Other Locations:
207 Sloane Street
Second Floor
London SW1W 9QX
United Kingdom
Phone: 44-020-7907-8600 **Fax:** 44-0-20-7907-8650

Key Executives:
Dipanjan (DJ) Deb, Founding Partner & CEO
e-mail: deb@franciscopartners.com
Education: BS, Electrical Engineering & Computer Science, UC Berkeley; MBA, Stanford Graduate School of Business
Background: Principal, Texas Pacific Group; Director of Semiconductor Banking, Robertson Stephens & Company; Managmement Consultant, McKinsey & Company
Directorships: Bomgar, Cross Match Technologies, GoodRx, K2, LegalZoom, Plex, Quest, Sectigo, Sonicwall, Verifone
Ben Ball, Founding Partner
e-mail: ball@franciscopartners.com
Education: AB, Harvard College; MBA, Stanford Graduate School of Business
Background: TA Associates, Genstar Capital
Directorships: Cross Match Technologies, MetaSwitch Networks, WatchGuard
Neil Garfinkel, Founding Partner
e-mail: garfinkel@franciscopartners.com
Education: AB, Harvard College; JD, Columbia Law School
Background: Managing Director, Friedman Fleischer & Lowe
Directorships: Quantros
Keith Geeslin, Partner
e-mail: geeslin@franciscopartners.com
Education: BS, Electrical Engineering, Stanford University; MS, Philosophy, Politics & Economics, Univ. of Oxford; MS, Engineering-Economic Systems, Stanford University
Background: Sprout Group
David Golob, Chief Investment Officer
e-mail: golob@franciscopartners.com
Education: AB, Harvard College; MBA, Stanford Graduate School of Business
Background: Managing Director, Tiger Management; General Atlantic Partners; McKinsey & Company
Directorships: Betterment, Bomgar, K2, Optaniz, Prosper, Quest, Sectigo, SmartBear, Sonicwall
Ezra Perlman, Co-President
e-mail: perlman@franciscopartners.com
Education: BA, Applied Mathematics, Harvard University; MBA, Stanford Graduate School of Business
Background: Battery Ventures, Advanta
Directorships: Availity, Avalon Healthcare, Cennecture, eSolutions, HealthcareSource, Landmark, Nextech, QGenda, Quantros, Renaissance
Deep Shah, Co-President
e-mail: shah@franciscopartners.com
Education: MA, Economics, University of Cambridge
Background: Morgan Stanley

Directorships: BluJay Solutions, ByBox, MetaSwitch Networks, Operative, Prometheus Group
Sanford Robertson, Co-Founder/Partner Emeritus
e-mail: robertson@franciscopartners.com
Education: BA, University of Michigan; MBA, University of Michigan
Background: Chairman, Robertson Stephens & Company; Founder, Robertson Coleman Siebel & Weisel

783 FRANKLIN STREET EQUITY PARTNERS
1450 Raleigh Road
Suite 300
Chapel Hill, NC 27517

Phone: 919-489-2600 **Fax:** 919-489-1666
Toll-Free: 877-489-2600
e-mail: franklin@franklin-street.com
web: www.franklin-street.com

Mission Statement: To provide independent, trusted and personalized advice, complementing in-house expertise with carefully selected external resources.
Geographic Preference: Southeastern United States
Fund Size: $2 billion
Founded: 1990
Minimum Investment: $500,000
Investment Criteria: Companies with rational business model and strong management team
Industry Group Preference: Technology, Business to Business
Key Executives:
Robert C. Eubanks Jr., Founder/Chairman Emeritus
Education: University of North Carolina, Chapel Hill
Background: Co-Founder/President, McMillion Eubanks Capital Management
Directorships: All Kinds of Minds Foundation, Kenan-Flagler Business School Foundation
William B. Thompson, Managing Director
Education: MBA, Darden Graduate School of Business; BS Chemical Engineering, North Carolina State University
Background: President/Co-Founder, Peacock-Thompson Investment Management; Management, Carolina Securities Corporation

784 FRASER MCCOMBS CAPITAL
1035 Pearl Street
Suite 401
Boulder, CO 80302

Phone: 210-382-6822
e-mail: chase@fmcap.com
web: www.fmcap.com

Mission Statement: Fraser McCombs Capital is a venture firm focused on early-stage technology companies within the automotive space. Fraser McCombs is the first and only venture fund that has managed by automotive entrepreneurs and dealers. The team has long standing relationships with Tier 1, 2, and 3 vendors, and connections with leading OEM executives and principals of the largest dealer groups. This allows the fund to provide key introductions for their portfolio companies.
Investment Criteria: Early-Stage
Industry Group Preference: Automotive, Transportation
Portfolio Companies: Autoniq, Confident Financial Solutions, Dataium, Dealer HQ, ESupply Systems, Gazillion, Kapost, Phunware, Relevant Solutions, Roximity, Scout, Showroom Logic, Smart Picture, Smule UParts, Verve, Autopay, Autotalks, Frontier Car Group, Keeps, Optimus Ride

Other Locations:
755 Mulberry Avenue
Suite 600
San Antonio, TX 78212

220 North Green Street
Chicago, IL 60607

Key Executives:
Chase Fraser, Managing Partner
210-382-6822
e-mail: chase@fmcap.com
Education: University of Texas, Austin
Background: Managing Partner, Circle P Capital; Founder, MarketQuiz; Vice President, IFCO Containers
Tony Rimas, Managing Partner
e-mail: tony@fmcap.com
Background: Director of Operations, McCombs Automotive Group

---

785 FRAZIER HEALTHCARE VENTURES
601 Union Street
Two Union Square
Suite 3200
Seattle, WA 98101

Phone: 206-621-7200
web: www.frazierhealthcare.com

Mission Statement: Makes partnerships with entrepreneurs who benefit from the company's network of technical, industry, academic, research and financial contacts; considers each opportunity on an individual basis, knowing that emerging companies are dynamic by nature, and looks for visionaries in emerging healthcare who have promising concepts.

Geographic Preference: United States
Fund Size: $3.4 billion
Founded: 1991
Average Investment: $2 million
Minimum Investment: $250,000
Investment Criteria: Seed, Series A, Series B, Early-Stage, Growth Equity, Later Stage
Industry Group Preference: Medical Devices, Healthcare, Life Sciences, Biopharmaceuticals
Portfolio Companies: Abode Healthcare, Acerta Pharma, Acheogen, Alcresta Therapeutic, Allena Pharmaceuticals, Alnara Pharmaceuticals, Alpine Immune Sciences, Alteon Health, Amicus, Anaptys Bio, Aptinyx, Array BioPharma, Ascension Orthopedics, Barrx Medical, Bravo Health, Cadence Pharmaceuticals, Calibra Medical, Calibrium, Calistoga, Calixa Therapeutics, Cerexa, CHG Healthcare Services, Chimerix Inc., Cidara Therapeutics, Cirius Therapeutics, Clovis Oncology, Collegium Pharmaceutical, Corixa, Cotherics, CVT Therapeutics, DSI Renal, Elements Behavioral Health, Entasis Therapeutics, FlowCadia Inc., Glaukos, Gritstone Oncology, Ignyta, Imago BioSciences, Incline Therapeutics, Iovance Biotherapeutics, Iterum Therapeutics, Labsco, Leiter's, Marcadia Biotech, Matrix Medical Network, Mavu Pharma, MedPointe, Millendo Therapeutics, Northfield, Oceana Therapeutics, OraPharma Inc., Ohi, Outpost Medicine, PCI Pharma Services, Pentec Health, Portola Pharmaceuticals, Powervision, Precision Dermatology, Priority Solutions, Quatrx, Rempex Pharmaceuticals, Rigel, Semnur Pharmaceuticals, Sierra Oncology, Silvergate Pharmaceuticals Inc., Sojournix, Solis Mammography, South Side, Stromedix, Sutrovax, TCG RX, The Core Institute, Threshold Pharmaceuticals, Tobira Therapeutics, Trident USA Health Services, Trubion Pharmaceuticals, Tularik, United Dermpartners, US Renal Care, VentiRx, ViroPharma, Vivus, XenoPort, Zavante, Zeltic, Zymo Genetics

Other Locations:
70 Willow Road
Suite 200
Menlo Park, CA 94025
Phone: 650-325-5156

Key Executives:
Alan D. Frazier, Founder/Chairman
e-mail: alan@frazierco.com
Education: BA, University of Washington
Background: EVP/CFO, Immunex Corporation; Senior Financial Advisor/CFO, Affymax; Co-Head of Technology Practice, Arthur Young & Company (Ernst & Young)
Directorships: UW Medicine Board, UW Medicine Strategic Initiatives Committee, University of Washington School of Medicine
James N. Topper, MD, PhD, Managing Partner
650-325-5156
e-mail: james@frazierhealthcare.com
Education: BS, University of Michigan; MD, PhD, Stanford University
Background: Director Cardiovascular R&D, Millennium Pharmaceuticals; Director, Millennium San Franciso; VP Biology, COR
Directorships: Amicus Therapeutics; Arete Therapeutics; MacuSight; Zelos Therapeutrics; Point Biomedical; Portola Pharmaceuticals; Harvard-Partners Center for Genetics and Genomics
Patrick Heron, Managing Partner
650-325-5156
e-mail: patrick@frazierco.com
Education: BA, University of North Carolina, Chapel Hill; MBA, Harvard Business School
Background: McKinsey & Company
Directorships: Tobira Therapeutics, Marcadia, Calixa, Cerexa, PreCision Dermatology, MedPointe, Collegium, Imago BioSciences, Iterum Therapeutics, Silvergate Pharmaceuticals, SutroVax
Nathan R. Every, MD, MPH, General Partner, Seattle
e-mail: nathan@frazierhealthcare.com
Education: BA, University of Pennsylvania; MD, Emory University School of Medicine; MPH, University of Washington School of Public Health
Background: Associate Professor of Medicine/Director, Cardiovascular Outcomes Research Center; Management, Merck & Company; Johnson & Johnson
Directorships: Apneon; BaroSense; BARRx; FlowCardia; MacuSight; SyneCor; Interventional Rhythm Management; PowerVision; Xoft Microtube; Alexza Pharmaceuticals; FoviOptics
Daniel Estes, PhD, General Partner
e-mail: dan.estes@frazierhealthcare.com
Education: BS, Electrical Engineering, Stanford University; PhD, Biomedical Engineering, University of Michigan
Background: Management Consultant, McKinsey & Company
Directorships: Semnur Pharmaceuticals, Outpost Medicine, Sierra Oncology, Cirius Therapeutics
Philip Zaorski, Principal
e-mail: philip.zaorski@frazierhealthcare.com
Education: BS, Wharton School, University of Pennsylvania
Background: Analyst, RBC Capital Markets
Kent Berkley, Principal
e-mail: kent.berkley@frazierhealthcare.com
Education: BS, Northwestern University; MBA, Kellogg School of Management, Northwestern University
Background: The Edgewater Funds; Associate, CIVC Partners, Dresner Partners; Lehman Brothers
Nader Naini, Managing Partner, Seattle
e-mail: nader@frazierco.com
Education: MBA, New York University; BA, University of Pennsylvania
Background: Aspen Education Group; Goldman, Sachs & Company; Chairman, CHG Healthcare
Directorships: Elements Behavioral Health, Northfield, Solis Mammography, Alteon Health

Venture Capital & Private Equity Firms / Domestic Firms

Carol Eckert, Director, Investor Relations, Seattle
e-mail: carol.eckert@frazierhealthcare.com
Education: BS, Accounting, University of Idaho
Background: Westin Hotels; Deloitte Touche
Directorships: Immunex Corporation
Elizabeth Park, Vice President, Investor Relations
e-mail: liz.park@frazierhealthcare.com
Education: BA, Mass Communications, University of California, Berkeley
Background: Product Project Manager, Amgen; Associate Project Manager, MacuSight
Brian Morfitt, General Partner, Seattle
206-621-7200
e-mail: brian@frazierhealthcare.com
Education: BS, MS, Management Science & Engineering, Stanford University
Background: Associate, Summit Partners
Directorships: Health Care Private Equity Association
James W. Brush, MD, Partner
Education: BA, Middlebury College; MD, University of Southern California
Background: Boston Consulting Group
Steve Bailey, Chief Financial Officer/Partner
e-mail: steveb@frazierhealthcare.com
Education: BS, Accounting, Central Washington University; MS, Tax, Portland State University
Background: Vice President, Finance, LapLink; Finance & Corporate Development, Elixis Corporations; Data Critical Corporation; Senior Manager, Tax Department, Ernst & Young LLP
Ben Magnano, Managing Partner, Seattle
e-mail: ben@frazierhealthcare.com
Education: BBA, University of Notre Dame; MBA, Tuck School of Business, Dartmouth College
Background: Associate, Morgan Stanley Venture Partners; Arthur Andersen
Directorships: Woodland Park Zoo; Matrix Medical Network, Northfield, TCGRx, United Derm Partners, US Renal Care
Ryan Lucero, Principal
e-mail: ryan.lucero@frazierhealthcare.com
Education: BS, Marriott School of Management, Brigham Young University
Background: JPMorgan Chase & Co.; TARP, US Department of the Treasury; Kohlberg & Co.
Anna H. Chen, PhD, Senior Associate
e-mail: anna.chen@frazierhealthcare.com
Education: AB, Biochemical Sciences, Harvard College; PhD, Systems Biology, Harvard University
Background: L.E.K.; Entrepreneurial Fellow, Flagship Pioneering; Business Mentor, National Science Foundation Innovation Corps program
Jeremy Janson, Senior Associate
e-mail: jeremy.janson@frazierhealthcare.com
Education: BA, Economics, Middlebury College
Background: Robert W. Baird

786 FREEMAN SPOGLI & CO.
11100 Santa Monica Boulevard
Suite 1900
Los Angeles, CA 90025

Phone: 310-444-1822
e-mail: IR@freemanspogli.com
web: www.freemanspogli.com

Mission Statement: Private equity firm focused on middle market companies in the consumer and distribution sectors.

Fund Size: $13 billion
Founded: 1983
Minimum Investment: $25 million
Investment Criteria: Exclusively middle-market
Industry Group Preference: Retailing, Direct Marketing, Distribution, Restaurants
Portfolio Companies: Arhaus, Batteries Plus Bulbs, Cafe Rio, City Barbeque, CRH Healthcare, El Pollo Loco, FASTSIGNS, Five Star Food Service, Floor & Decor, ISN, MicroStar, Osprey, PF Baseline Fitness, Plantation Products, Regent Holding, Sur La Table

Other Locations:
299 Park Avenue
20th Floor
New York, NY 10171
Phone: 212-758-2555

Key Executives:
Bradford M. Freeman, Co-Chairman
Education: BA, Stanford University; MA Business Administration, Harvard University
Background: Managing Director, Dean Witter Reynolds
Ronald P. Spogli, Co-Chairman
Education: Stanford University; MA Business Administration, Harvard University
Background: Managing Director Investment Banking, Dean Witter Reynolds
John M. Roth, Chief Executive Officer
Education: BA Accounting/MA Business Administration/Finance, Wharton School
Background: VP Mergers/Acquisitions, Kidder Peabody; Management Consultant, McKinsey & Co; Investment Banking, Dean Witter Reynolds
Jon D. Ralph, President & Chief Operating Officer
Education: BA History, Amherst College
Background: Analyst Investment Banking, Morgan Stanley
Brad J. Brutocao, Partner
Education: BS, Economics, University of California, Los Angeles
Background: Analyst, M&A, Morgan Stanley & Co.
Benjamin D. Geiger, Partner
Education: BS, Economics, Cornell University
Background: Analyst, M&A, Merrill Lynch & Co.
Todd W. Halloran, Senior Advisory Partner
Education: Economics Graduate, Colby College; MA Business Administration
Background: VP Mergers/Acquisitions, Soldman Sachs & Co; Financial Analyst, Amerian Brands/Manufacturers Hanover
John S. Hwang, Partner
Education: BS, Business Economics, University of California, LA
Background: Analyst, Citigroup Global Markets
Christian B. Johnson, Partner
Education: History, Colgate University
Background: Analyst, Leveraged Finance Group, Wachovia Securities
J. Frederick Simmons, Senior Advisory Partner
Education: Bachelor's, Williams College, Masters, New York University
Background: Vice President, Los Angeles Office Of Bankers Trust Company

787 FREESTYLE
e-mail: info@freestyle.vc
web: www.freestyle.vc

Mission Statement: Freestyle Capital is a seed stage investor and mentor for Internet software startups. Freestyle's community of veteran entrepreneurs offers real-world experience and business finesse without stuffy investor baggage or hidden agendas.

Fund Size: $216 million
Founded: 2009
Investment Criteria: Seed-Stage
Industry Group Preference: IoT, Software, Technology, Electronics
Portfolio Companies: 9gag, About.me, Adstage, Agentology, Airtable, Alpha Draft, Applie Pie Capital, Aviate, Backtype, BetterUp, Boomtown, BuildingConnected, Byliner, Camiocam, Cardpool, Chartbeat, Chute, Clarity, Clypd, CREXi, CrowdFlower, Easecentral, Embark, French Girls, Giftbit, Golnstant, Gradescope, Heart This,

Venture Capital & Private Equity Firms / Domestic Firms

Impermium, Indextank, Joyfride, Juvo, Kite, LaunchKit, Leo, Memoir, Mongolab, Nestio, New Co., Opsmatic, Payable, PicCollage, Range Me, Recurly, Riffsy, Rixty, SimpleGeo, Singly, Snapdocs, SnappyTV, Stitch, Swift Shift, Text Now, Trizic, TrueFacet, Typekit, UXPin, Webshots, Yobongo

Key Executives:
  Josh Felser, Founder/Board Partner
  Education: Duke University, Fuqua Business School
  Background: Co-Founder, FYI Living; Founder, Spinner; Founder, Grouper
  Dave Samuel, Founder/Partner
  Education: MIT
  Background: Founder, Thriller Designs; Oracle; Founder, Spinner; Founder, Brondell; Founder, Grouper

788 FRESH VC
San Francisco, CA

web: www.freshvc.com

Mission Statement: A venture capital and angel firm investing in the cannabis industry.

Founded: 2014
Industry Group Preference: Consumer Products, Cannabis, Healthcare, Technology, Hospitality
Portfolio Companies: Aptible, Bannerman, Crunchbutton, Eaze, Eight Sleep, FiscalNote, Gyroscope, Pijon, The Sails Company, Shyp, Unwind Me, Vessel

Key Executives:
  Shri Ganeshram, Founder/Managing Partner
  Education: BS, Mathematics/Computer Science, Massachusetts Institute of Technology
  Background: Founder/CTO, FlightCar; Software Consultant, Credit Suisse; VP of Growth, Analytics & Strategy, Eaze
  Brian Sheng, Co-Founder/Managing Partner
  Education: Princeton University
  Background: Founder, IvyBound; Analyst, Shenzhen Capital Group Co.; Partner, DreamTech Ventures; Foreign Investment Advisor, URI Investment Fund; General Partner, The Arcview Group
  Directorships: Eaze

789 FRESHTRACKS CAPITAL
29 Harbor Road, Suite 200
PO Box 849
Shelburne, VT 05482

Phone: 802-923-1500 **Fax:** 802-923-1506
web: www.freshtrackscap.com

Mission Statement: FreshTracks combines $25 million in venture capital with the strategic resources needed by entrepreneurs to build thriving companies throughout Vermont and beyond. Our Fund Managers have deep backgrounds in business finance and strategy, as well as direct operating experience with numerous growth companies. FreshTracks' resources, capital and networks support innovative businesses through multiple rounds of financing and stages of growth.

Geographic Preference: Vermont, New York, Massachusetts, New Hampshire
Fund Size: $25 million
Founded: 2000
Investment Criteria: Early-Stage
Industry Group Preference: Technology
Portfolio Companies: Auterra, Bridj, Budnitz Bicycles, Caledonia Spirits, CPS, Draker, DRINKmaple, Ello, Faraday, Horse Network, IrisVR, ISIS, Kohort, Lincoln Peak Partners, Mamava, Morphie, Native Energy, NEHP, Ogee, Patient Engagement Systems, Quirky, Redd, Reilly's Hempvet, Social Sentinal, Solais, SolarOne, SunCommon, THINKmd, Vermont Teddy Bear, Virtual Peaker, Vocate, Wuu

Key Executives:
  Cairn G Cross, Co-Founder/Managing Director
  Education: BS, Montana State University; MBA, New Hampshire College; Stonier Graduate School of Banking
  Background: Owner, Cross Vermont Financial; Assistant General Manager, Green Mountain Capital; Co-Chair, Vermont Investors Forum
  Directorships: Budnitz Bicycles, Faraday, Mamava, NativeEnergy, Vermont Teddy Bear
  Charles F Kireker, Co-Founder/Senior Advisor
  Education: Princeton University; MPP, Harvard University
  Background: Co-Founder, Green Mountain Capital; Co-Founder, North Country Angels
  Directorships: EatingWell Media Group, Vermont Teddy Bear, VEMAS, Autumn Harp
  Timothy C Davis, Managing Director
  Education: University of Vermont; MBA, Harvard Business School
  Background: Management, Advanced Materials Companies
  Directorships: Auterra, Moscow Mills, Solais, SolarOne
  Lee E Bouyea, Managing Director
  Education: Colgate University; MBA, Tuck School of Business
  Background: eBay, Nextel Communications, Ebates
  Directorships: Auterra, Ello, Horse Network, IrisVR, Mamava, Social Sentinal
  T.J. Whalen, Managing Director
  Education: BA, Economics and Education, Dartmouth College
  Background: Chief Strategy Officer & Chief Sustainability Officer, Keurig Green Mountain
  Directorships: Budnitz Bicycles, NativeEnergu, Ogee, Reilly's HempVet, SunCommon

790 FRIEDMAN, FLEISCHER & LOWE LLC
One Maritime Plaza
Suite 2200
San Francisco, CA 94111

Phone: 415-402-2100 **Fax:** 415-402-2111
e-mail: contact@fflpartners.com
web: www.fflpartners.com

Mission Statement: Actively seeking investment opportunities and encourage owners, managers, legal, financial and accounting professionals, and intermediaries to reach out with any questions, investment opportunities or ideas.

Geographic Preference: United States, Canada
Fund Size: $2 billion
Founded: 1997
Average Investment: $50 - $300 million
Minimum Investment: $15 million
Investment Criteria: Middle Market Companies: Ownership Restructuring, Going-Private Transactions, Growth Equity Funding, Recapitalizations, Management Buyouts (Public and Private)
Industry Group Preference: Education, Business to Business, Media, Marketing, Healthcare, Consumer Products, Financial Services
Portfolio Companies: Advanced Career Technologies, American Advisors Group, Bacharach, Banner Bank, BearingPoint, Benevis, CapitalSource, CHI, Church's Chicken, CPI, Curo, DataOnline, Discovery Foods, Enjoy Beer, Eyecare Partners, Eyemart Expressa, GeoVera Holdings Inc., Green Bank, Guardian, Icynene, Interactive Health, Iracore International Inc., JonesTrading, Korn Ferry, Midwest Dental, Milstone AV Technologies Inc., Monpelier RE, ProService Hawaii, Snap Financial Group, SteelPoint, Strategic Investment Group, Summit BHC, Tempur-Pedic, Transtar, Tritech, Well Street Urgent Care, Wilton Re

Key Executives:
  Tully M. Friedman, Managing Partner
  e-mail: tfriedman@fflpartners.com
  Education: AB, Stanford University; JD, Harvard Law School
  Background: Hellman & Friedman; Co-Chairman, American Enterprise Institute; Vice Chairman, Telluride

Venture Capital & Private Equity Firms / Domestic Firms

Foundation
Directorships: George Lucas Museum of Narrative Art
Spencer Fleischer, Managing Partner
e-mail: sfleischer@fflpartners.com
Education: MS, Univ. of Oxford; BA, University of Witwatersrand
Background: Morgan Stanley
Directorships: Eyemart Express; Korn Ferry International; Milestone AV Technologies; BearingPoint Inc.; Jones Trading Institutional Services LLC; Transtar Holdings; Wilton Re Holdings Ltd.
Christopher Masto, Co-Founder/Senior Advisor
e-mail: cmasto@fflpartners.com
Education: MBA, Harvard Business School; ScB, Brown University
Background: Bain & Company; Morgan Stanley & Company
Directorships: Curo Financial Technologies; Enjoy Beer LLC; TriTech Holdings; Tempur Sealy International
Rajat Duggal, Partner
Education: BS, Indiana University; JD, Yale Law School
Background: Bain Capital; Kirkland & Ellis; Deloitte & Touche
Directorships: Church's Chicken; Summit Behavioral Healthcare LLC; Benevis LLC; GeoVera Insurance Group; Jones Trading; Transtar Holdings; Guardian Home Care; Discovery Foods
Aaron Money, Partner
Education: AB, Economics, Duke University
Background: Assiciate, DB Capital; Investment Banking Analyst, Chase Securities
Directorships: Guardian Home Care Holdings, Speedy Cash Holdings Corp
Cas Schneller, Partner
Education: BBA, Finance & Business Economics, University of Notre Dame; MBA, Harvard Business School
Background: GTCR Golder Rauner; Analyst, William Blair & Company
Directorships: JonesTrading Institutional Services
Chris Harris, Partner
Education: BS, Management Science & Engineering, Stanford University; MBA, Stanford Graduate School of Business
Background: Associate, Berkshire Partners; Associate Consultant, Bain & Company
Directorships: EyeMart Express; Eye Care Partners; Summit Behavioral Healthcare; Strategic Investment Group; TriTech Software Systems
David Crussel, Operating Partner
Background: COO, SumTotal Systems; ADAC Laboratories; GE Medical Systems
Greg Long, Partner
Education: BS, Mechanical Engineering, Stanford University
Background: Senior Associate, The Parthenon Group
Directorships: American Advisor Group; CHI Overhead Doors; Big Brothers Big Sisters; Icynene

791 FRIEND SKOLER & COMPANY LLC
160 Pehle Avenue, Suite 303
Saddle Brook, NJ 07663

Phone: 201-712-0075 Fax: 201-712-1525
web: www.friendskoler.com

Mission Statement: Invests in leading middle market companies across a range of industries in partnership with skilled management teams who want to invest in and grow the businesses they operate.

Geographic Preference: United States
Fund Size: $231 million
Founded: 1998
Average Investment: $20 million - $200 million
Minimum Investment: $5 million
Investment Criteria: Minimum EBITDA of $5 million; Strong management; Good growth prospects, Middle Market
Industry Group Preference: Manufacturing, Distribution, Retailing, Services, Consumer Products, Industrial Services, E-Commerce & Manufacturing, Business Products & Services
Portfolio Companies: Hex Performance, Iconic Group, Slon Lofts Group, Banza, Madan Plastics Inc., Petmatrics LLC, Hopkins Manufacturing, Accessories Marketing Inc., Woodstream Corp., United Pet Group Inc., Ballet Jewels, Box, CNC Global, AllHeart, Fashion Cents, Kenlin Pet Supply,

Key Executives:
  Alexander A. Friend, Managing Director
  201-712-0075
  Fax: 201-712-1525
  e-mail: alex@friendskoler.com
  Education: BA, Harvard University; MBA, Stanford Graduate School of Business
  Background: Venture Partners Inc; Merrill Lynch; Mercer Consulting
  Directorships: CNC Global Limited, United Pet Group, HAS Holding Corp, Madan Plastics, Kenlin Pet Supply, Woodstream Corporation
  Steven F. Skoler, Managing Director
  e-mail: steve@friendskoler.com
  Education: BA, Harvard; MBA, Stanford
  Background: Venture Partners; Morgan Stanley; Braxton Associates
  Directorships: CNC Global, NAS Holdings, Madan Plastics, Kenlin Pet Supply, Woodstream
  Cheryl Moss, Director
  e-mail: cmoss@friendskoler.com
  Education: BS, Business Admin., McDonough School of Business, Georgetown University
  Background: Senior Analyst, Prudential Capital Group

792 FRONTENAC COMPANY
One South Wacker
Suite 2980
Chicago, IL 60606

Phone: 312-368-0044 Fax: 312-368-9520
e-mail: reception@frontenac.com
web: www.frontenac.com

Mission Statement: Frontenac Company provides resources and capital to help portfolio companies achieve long-term growth and success.

Geographic Preference: United States, Europe
Fund Size: $250 million
Founded: 1971
Average Investment: $15 - $50 million
Investment Criteria: Lower Middle Market, Recapitalizations, Buyouts, Growth Capital
Industry Group Preference: Business Products & Services, Technology, Commercial Services, Healthcare, Food & Beverage, Consumer Products
Portfolio Companies: AH Harris, Behavioral Health Group, Diversified Maintenance Systems, e+ CancerCare, GNAP, H-E Parts International, La Tavola Fine Linen Rental, Mercer Foods, Portfolio Group, Salient CRGT, SIGMA, Spice Chain Corporation, Wenner Bread Products, Whitebridge Pet Brands

Key Executives:
  Paul D Carbery, Managing Partner
  312-759-7315
  e-mail: pcarbery@frontenac.com
  Education: BA, Yale University; MBA, Stanford University Graduate School of Business
  Background: Strategic Planning Associates
  Directorships: GNAP, H-E Parts, La Tavola, Portfolio Group
  Walter C Florence, Managing Partner
  312-629-3152
  e-mail: wflorence@frontenac.com

Venture Capital & Private Equity Firms / Domestic Firms

Education: Dartmouth College; MBA, Kellogg School of Management, Northwestern University
Background: Analyst, Bear Stearns & Company
Directorships: Mercer Foods, Salient CRGT, Sigma, Spice Chain Corporation, Wenner Bread Products, Whitebridge Pet Products

Ronald W Kuehl, Managing Director
312-759-7330
e-mail: rkuehl@frontenac.com
Education: University of Notre Dame; MBA, Kellogg School of Management, Northwestern University
Background: Churchill Capital; H.I.G. Capital; Analyst, Morgan Stanley
Directorships: AH Harris, Diversified Maintenance Systems, Portfolio Group, Sigma, Wenner Bread Products

Michael S Langdon, Managing Director
312-759-7348
e-mail: mlangdon@frontenac.com
Education: University of Michigan; MBA, Harvard Business School
Background: Senior Associate, Genstar Capital; Analyst, DLJ Merchant Banking
Directorships: AH Harris, Behavioral Health Group, H-E Parts, Salient CRGT

Elizabeth C Williamson, Managing Director
e-mail: ewilliamson@frontenac.com
Education: Dartmouth College; MBA, Harvard Business School
Background: Associate, Thomas H. Lee Partners; Lehman Brothers; Director, Schlotterbeck & Foss; Director, Spice Chain Corporation

Julie A Bender, Vice President/Chief Financial Officer/Chief Compliance Officer
312-759-7345
e-mail: jbender@frontenac.com
Education: Indiana University; MBA, Kellogg School of Management, Northwestern University
Background: Associate, Heller Financial; NES Rentals; Chicago Corporation; Auditor, Arthur Andersen & Co.

Joseph R Rondinelli, Principal
312-759-7319
e-mail: jrondinelli@frontenac.com
Education: Northwestern University; MBA, University of Chicago Booth School of Business
Background: Analyst, Citigroup Global Markets
Directorships: GNAP, La Tavola, Whitebridge Pet Brands

Neal G Sahney, Principal
312-759-7335
e-mail: nsahney@frontenac.com
Education: University of Michigan; MBA, Wharton School, University of Pennsylvania
Background: Engagement Manager, McKinsey & Company; Senior Analyst, Corporate Strategy & Business Development, The Walt Disney Company
Directorships: AH Harris

793 FRONTIER CAPITAL
525 N Tyron St.
Suite 1900
Charlotte, NC 28202

Phone: 704-414-2880 Fax: 704-414-2881
e-mail: info@frontiercapital.com
web: www.frontiercapital.com

Mission Statement: Frontier Capital was founded in 1999 to provide capital and support to high growth business services companies. At the time, many of these companies were being overlooked by both investors and lenders. Many investors felt business services did not have the allure of high-tech venture investments and lenders were more interested in asset intensive, traditional businesses. We recognized an opportunity to help fill this void by focusing our investments on a sector that we believed would benefit from the rise of the service economy and a growing trend toward outsourcing.

Founded: 1999

Industry Group Preference: Business Products & Services
Portfolio Companies: AccessOne, Agreement Express, Aviacode, Dinova, Igloo, InteliSecure, Listen First, MediaPro, MediaRadar, Planet Risk, PowerDMS, Price Spider, Talent Reef, Tango, Vibe HCM, Viverae

Key Executives:

Richard Maclean, Managing Partner
e-mail: richard@frontiercapital.com
Education: College of Charleston; MBA, Darden School of Business
Background: Investment Banking Group, NationsBank; General Partner, Blue Ridge Capital
Directorships: Agreement Express, Anodyne Health, Celergo, Healthx, Peak 10, PMG Research, SecureWorks, VibeHCM, WilsonHCG, Zephyr

Andrew Lindner, Managing Partner
e-mail: andrew@frontiercapital.com
Background: Stephens, Inc., Bank of America, Weiss, Peck & Greer
Directorships: AccessOne, Azaleos, Conclusive Analytics, Daxko, Digital Envoy, Gazelle, Healthiest You, Igloo, Lanyon, Planet Risk, Quickparts, Ryla, Social Solutions, Tango, Teladoc, Vivera

Michael Ramich, Partner
e-mail: michael@frontiercapital.com
Education: Duke University; MBA, Harvard Business School
Background: General Electric
Directorships: Anodyne Health, Aviacode, Celergo, Daxko, Dinova, Healthx, Lanyon, ListenFirst, MediaRadar, MultiLing, Netdocuments, PowerDMS, Simpli.fi, Social Solutions, TalentReef, Viverae

Joel Lanik, Partner
e-mail: joel@frontiercapital.com
Education: Duke University; MBA, Darden School of Business
Background: VP, Finance & Strategy, LURHQ
Directorships: Anodyne Health, Azaleos, ConnectSolutions, InteliSecure, LurHQ, Peak10, PMG Research, WilsonhCG, Zephyr

Seth Harward, Partner
Education: BA, University of North Carolina
Background: Research Triangle's Council for Entrepreneurial Development
Directorships: Aviacode, Celergo, Dinova, HealthiestYou, InteliSecure, Lanyon, MediaPro, MultiLing, Netdocument, Simpl.fi, Tango, Wilson HCG, Zephyr

Scott Hoch, Partner
e-mail: scott@frontiercapital.com
Education: Furman University
Background: Edgeview Partners
Directorships: Aviacode, Celergo, Daxko, eVerifile, HealthiestYou, Healthx, InteliSecure, Lanyon, MediaPro, PMG Research, Simpl.fi, Social Solutions, TalentReef, Viverae, Wilson HCG, Zephyr

794 FRONTIER VENTURE CAPITAL
100 Wilshire Blvd
4th Floor
Santa Monica, CA 90401

Phone: 424-354-2244
e-mail: info@frontiervc.com
web: www.draperfrontier.com

Mission Statement: Frontier invests in start-up businesses with the potential to make significant changes in the world. Frontier aims to help entrepreneurs to create value and transform their ideas into self-sustaining businesses.

Geographic Preference: Western United States
Fund Size: $55 million
Average Investment: $100,000 - $1 million
Investment Criteria: Startups, Seed Stage
Industry Group Preference: Software, Information Services, Biotechnology, Nanotechnology, Alternative Energy

Venture Capital & Private Equity Firms / Domestic Firms

Portfolio Companies: Appletree.com, BigFrame, BondMart, Boom Studios, Chimeros, D.Light Design, Dragnet Solutions, Dx Biosciences, Game Salad, Graph Effect, HydraDx, Iconix, Instantly, Intematix, JanRain, Lottay, Marval Bioscience, Mogreet, MomentFeed, Netpulse, Neurovigil, NinthDecimal, OnTech, Planitax, Predixion Software, Prolacta Bioscience, Seismic Games, SkyGrid, SmartRG, Super Heat Games, Swink.tv, SynapSense, Synthetic Games, Tethys Bioscience, Tioga Energy, Zadspace

Key Executives:
    David Cremin, Founder/Managing Director, Los Angeles
    Education: BS, Industrial Engineering, Stanford University
    Background: Founding Partner, Zone Ventures; Founder & CEO, Vis-a-Vis Entertainment
    Directorships: Instantly, Janrain, MomentFeed, OnTech, UCode
    Scott Lenet, Founder/Managing Director, Los Angeles
    Education: AB, Comparative Literature, Princeton University; MBA, Entrepreneurial Management, Wharton School, University of Pennsylvania
    Background: CEO, SmartFrog.com; Product Marketing, Trilogy Software
    Directorships: Boom Studios, NinthDecimal, Seismic Games, Sacramento Philharmonic
    Frank Foster, Managing Director, Santa Barbara
    Education: BA, Harvard University; MBA, Harvard Business School
    Background: Investment Manager, Gideon Hixon Fund; General Partner, Allen & Buckeridge Pty Ltd
    Directorships: Dx Biosciences, HydraDx, Marval Biosciences, Predixion Software, Prolacta Bioscience, Swink.tv, Zadspace
    Eric Rosenfeld, Venture Partner, Portland
    e-mail: eric@frontiervc.com
    Education: Stanford University; MBA, Institute for Management Development, Lausanne, Switzerland
    Background: Founding Partner, Oregon Angel Fund; Capybara Ventures; Director, Corporate Business Development, Mentor Graphics
    Directorships: Catlin Gabel School
    Jim Schraith, Venture Partner, Sacramento
    Background: Quantum; ShareWave; Compaq; President & COO, AST Research; Co-Founder, QTV Capital
    Directorships: Achievo, Semtech, VisualCalc

795 FRONTIER VENTURES
19925 Stevens Creek Boulevard
Suite 100
Cupertino, CA 95014-2358

Phone: 650-250-1224
e-mail: media@frontier.ventures
web: frontier.ventures

Mission Statement: Frontier Ventures is a venture fund investing in early stage technology companies with network effects in the United States and globally.

Geographic Preference: North America, Asia, Europe
Founded: 2012
Industry Group Preference: Virtual Reality & Augmented Reality, Machine Intelligence, Robotics, Drones & 3D, Space Technology, Enterprise & Consumer
Portfolio Companies: 8i, AltspaceVR, Emergent, Fove, Immersv, Jaunt, matterport, Meta, River Studios, Wevr, booshaka, eBrevia, Gridspace, Tissue Analytics, Wade & Wendy, Auro Robotics, Boosted, maidbot, Scanse, Vicarious Surgical, Drone Base, HiveUAV, Kespry, Sols, Vantage Robotics, boom, Planet Labs, SpaceX, Ursa, World View, 1-Page, AngelList, Board Vitals, CarePort, Gusto, Hello Giggles, Luxe, Propeller, Revel Systems, Robinhood

Key Executives:
    Dmitry Alimov, Founder/Managing Partner
    Education: BS, Samara State Aerospace University; BSBA, University of Missouri; MBA, Harvard Business School
    Background: VP, Sputnik Group; First Deputy CEO, TNT Broadcasting Network; COO/Manging Director, Amedia; Managing Partner, RTP Global; Investor

796 FTV CAPITAL
555 California Street
Suite 2850
San Francisco, CA 94104

Phone: 415-229-3000 **Fax:** 415-229-3005
e-mail: businessplans@ftvcapital.com
web: www.ftvcapital.com

Mission Statement: FTV Capital invests in companies with innovative ideas, established business models and proven management teams that value a collaborative approach to building great companies.

Geographic Preference: United States
Fund Size: $1 billion
Founded: 1998
Average Investment: $10 to $75 million
Minimum Investment: $10 million
Investment Criteria: Any Stage, Middle Stage, Later Stage, Consolidations, Spinouts
Industry Group Preference: Software, Business Products & Services, Financial Services, Technology
Portfolio Companies: Actimize, Apex Fund Services, Aspire Financial Services, Aveksa, BlueGill Technologies, Cardconnect, CashStar, Castle Pines Capital, Catalyst, Cedar Capital, Centro, Clearent, Cloudmark, Company.com, Coremetrics, Covario, Credorax, Daylight Forensic & Advisory, Eloan, eBaoTech, Edgewater Markets, Empyrean, Enfusion, ETF Securities, EXL Service, Finanical Engines, Fleet One, Giga Spaces, Globant, GMI, Health Credit Services, ID.me, Index IQ, Intrepid Learning, Invest Cloud, KVS, LiveIntent, Markets and Markets, MarketShare, MedSynergies, Mu Sigma, NewsCred, Open Span, Perfecto, Powershares by Invesco, Presidio, Reliaquest, Rio Seo, Risk Alyze, Site Hands, Source Code, Predfast, Swan Global Investments, Symbio, True Potentional LLP, Trustwave, Varicent, VelocityShares, Verus, Vindicia, Vpay, WePay, Worldfirst, Xign

Other Locations:
535 Madison Avenue
32nd Floor
New York, NY 10022
Phone: 212-682-4800 **Fax:** 212-682-4480

Key Executives:
    Richard Garman, Managing Partner
    Education: BS, Southwest Missouri State University; MBA, Oklahoma State University
    Background: President/CEO, Electronic Payment Services
    Robert Anderson, Partner
    Education: AB, Economics, Princeton University
    Background: Merrill Lynch
    Brad Bernstein, Managing Partner
    Education: BA, Tufts University
    Background: Partner, Oak Hill Capital Management; Patricof & Company Ventures; Merrill Lynch
    Karen Derr Gilbert, Partner
    Education: BA, Economics, University of California, LA; MBA, Johnson Grad. School oF Management, Cornell University
    Background: Marketing, Wells Fargo; Merrill Lynch Capital Markets; Shearson Lehman Brothers
    Liron Gitig, Partner
    Education: BS, Wharton School, University of Pennsylvania; JD, Columbia Law School; MBA, Columbia Business School
    Background: Lazard Technology Partners; Giza GE Venture Fund; BRM Capital; Fundtech Corp.; Lehman Brothers
    Chris Winship, Partner
    Education: BA Government, Dartmouth College

Venture Capital & Private Equity Firms / Domestic Firms

Background: Investment Banker, Salomon Smith Barney's Media & Telecommunications Group; Sales/Marketing, Putnam Investments
Directorships: CapitalStream; Freeborders; MedSynergies; Verus Financial Management
David Haynes, Partner & COO
Education: BS, Mechanical Engineering, MBA, JD, University of California, Berkeley
Background: Executive Vice President & General Counsel, OffRoad; Executive Vice President & General Counsel, Examen; Montgomery Securities
Kyle Griswold, Partner
Education: BA, Economics & Mathematics, Trinity College
Background: Investment Banking Associate, Berkshire Capital Securities

797 FULCRUM EQUITY PARTNERS
Glenridge Highlands One
5555 Glenridge Connector
Suite 930
Atlanta, GA 30342

Phone: 770-551-6300 **Fax:** 770-551-6330
web: www.fulcrumep.com

Mission Statement: Fulcrum Equity Partners is a private equity firm that provides financing to high growth companies.

Fund Size: $93 million
Average Investment: $1 - $5 million
Investment Criteria: High Growth
Industry Group Preference: Technology, Information Technology, Healthcare
Portfolio Companies: Addiction Campuses of America, ALS Resolvion, Bright Light Systems, Logfire, m2M Strategies, Mobile Health Engagement Strategies, Path-Tec, PhishLabs, Prevalent, Red Bag Solutions, Regenesis Biomedical, Rival Health

Other Locations:
Tampa Bay Innovation Centre
501 First Avenue N
Suite 901
St Petersbourg, FL 33701

Key Executives:
Jeffrey S Muir, Partner
Education: BA, JD, University of Georgia
Background: COO, OnTarget; Executive VP, T2 Medical; VP, Information Systems of America; Managing Director, Corporate Finance, KPMG
Directorships: Red Bag Solutions, Bright Light Systems, Enduracare Acute Care Services, Partners Healthcare Group, Bruder Healthcare, Southern Capital Forum
Thomas L Greer, Partner
Education: BS, Finance, Clemson University; MBA, Wake Forest University
Background: Founder, President & CEO, Regency Healthcare; VP, Healthcare Investment Banking, Robinson Humphrey; Eli Lilly & Company; Director, Corporate Finance, KPMG
Directorships: Enduracare Acute Care Services, Regenesis Biomedical, Five Points Healthcare, Medical Direct Club, Addiction Campuses, Special Olympics Georgia
Frank X Dalton, Partner
Education: BS, Accounting, University of South Carolina
Background: General Partner, Cordova Ventures; CEO, Market Velocity; Chairman & CEO, Axonn; CFO, Caetec Systems; Director, Operations, Microsouth
Directorships: ContactatOnce, Mfg.com, Preparis, Path-Tec, Bruder Healthcare, Xpanxion
James S Douglass, Partner
Education: BBA, Finance & Accounting, Georgia State University
Background: CEO, Vesdia; CEO, Visionary Systems; Executive VP, Corporate Development & CFO, CheckFree Corporation; VP & Corporate Controller, Medaphis Corporation
Directorships: Cartera Commerce, FactorTrust, GetOne Rewards, Thumb-Friendly
Alston Gardner, Founder/Venture Partner
Education: BA, University of North Carolina
Background: CEO, OnTarget; Dun & Bradstreet Computing Services; ADP; Wallace Computer Services
Directorships: Human Rights First, Chatham Capital
Philip Lewis, Partner
Education: BS, Business Administration, Washington University, St. Louis
Background: Investment Banking Analyst, AG Edwards & Sons; Michelson Organization
Directorships: RivalHealth, MFG.com, ALS Resolvion, Venture Atlanta

798 FUNDERS CLUB
237 Kearny Street
Suite 424
San Francisco, CA 94108

Toll-Free: 888-405-9335
e-mail: contact@fundersclub.com
web: www.fundersclub.com

Mission Statement: The Funders Club builds around a unique online marketplace that allows accredited investors to become equity holders in managed venture funds, which then fund pre-screened, private companies.

Investment Criteria: Seed Stage, Startups, Series A Stage
Portfolio Companies: Actiondesk, Anyplace, Arpeggio Biosciences, AXDRAFT, Biorender, Caper, CognitionIP, CoLab, Convictional, Demodesk, Embrace, Envkey, Golinks, Grin, Habit Analytics, HRI, InsideSherpa, Intersect Labs, JetLenses, JITx, Kyte, Leena AI, Negotiatus, Obie, Patch, PopSQL, Precious, Pronto, Qulture.Rocks, Rain Neuromorphics, RevenueCat, Runa HR, Shogun, Substack, The Podcast App, Together, Treble.ai, Vathys, Worklytics, Xgenomes, YoGov, zeroheight

799 FUNG CAPITAL USA
Four Embarcadero Center
Suite 3400
San Francisco, CA 94111

Phone: 415-315-7440
e-mail: contact@fungcap.com
web: www.fungcapitalusa.com

Mission Statement: Core business is to help entrepreneurial companies achieve success by providing equity capital, Asian sourcing expertise, and operational support during their critical growth stage.

Geographic Preference: United States
Fund Size: $100 million
Founded: 1982
Average Investment: $1 - $10 million
Minimum Investment: $5 million
Investment Criteria: Early-Stage; Later Stage Expansion Rounds, Refinancings, MBOs, Turnaround Situations
Industry Group Preference: E-Commerce & Manufacturing, Internet, Enabling Technology, Consumer Products, Retailing
Portfolio Companies: 500friends, BodyFX, Celect, Centric Software, CYRK, Danskin, ecVision, Flow, Galoob, GT Nexus, Hook Logic, The Lodge, Millworks, Narvar, Onestop, Order Groove, Proclivity, Studio Direct, Third Channel, Tulip Retail, Wilke-Rodriguez, Wood Associates

Other Locations:
11812 San Vicente Boulevard
Suite 610
Los Angeles, CA 90049
Phone: 415-315-7440

Key Executives:
Michael Hsieh, President
Education: BA, Harvard College; MBA, Harvard

Venture Capital & Private Equity Firms / Domestic Firms

Business School
Background: RH Chappell Company; Merrill Lynch's Corporate Finance Division; Sun Hung Kai Securities (Hong Kong)
John Seung, Partner
Education: BSE, University of Pennsylvania
Background: Chief Information Officer, Li & Fung Group; Co-Founder, Castling; Advanced Technology Group, Andersen Consulting/Accenture
Janie Yu, Partner
e-mail: janie@fungcap.com
Education: MA, Havard University
Background: Burt's Bees; Journalist, BBC & PRI

800 FUNK VENTURES
15332 Antioch Street
Suite 119
Pacific Palisades, CA 90272

web: www.funkventures.com

Mission Statement: Provides business development, resources, expertise and management to companies generally too young to receive venture funding.
Industry Group Preference: Health & Wellness, Medical Devices, Lifestyle & Recreation, Clean Technology
Portfolio Companies: Alter G, Cyber Rain, Encore Fitness, Fuji Food Products, Game Ready, Organic To Go, Own, Prolacta Bioscience, UsedCardboardBoxes.com, Virgin Charter
Key Executives:
  Andy J. Funk, President
  Background: Founder/CEO, Microdyme; Founder/CEO, Helping.org; Co-Founder, Daily F1
  Directorships: Fuji Food Products, UsedCardboardBoxes, Strata Development Group

801 FUSE CAPITAL
P.O. Box 1251
Menlo Park, CA 94026-1251

Phone: 650-325-9600
web: www.fusecapital.com

Mission Statement: Invests in early stage communications and infrastructure companies, building them into market leading enterprises.
Geographic Preference: United States, India, China
Fund Size: $1.5 billion
Founded: 1974
Average Investment: $15 million
Minimum Investment: $12 million
Investment Criteria: Seed and Early Stage companies that are creating new markets, developing new technologies and addressing emerging business needs
Industry Group Preference: Communications, Digital Media & Marketing
Portfolio Companies: Vyatta, SpectraLinear, Radar Networks, PacketHop, ONStor, Next New Networks, NetDevices, MonoSphere, KOTURA, Hatteras Networks, Generate, Fultec Semiconductor, CloudShield Technologies, Caymas Systems, BBE, Ambric, Ahura Scientific, 5to1

802 FUSION FUND
550 Lytton Avenue
Palo Alto, CA 94301

e-mail: info@fusionfund.com
web: www.fusionfund.com

Mission Statement: A venture capital fund seeking to partner with entrepreneurs making waves in the tech industries, particularly AI.
Investment Criteria: Seed, Series A, Early Stage
Industry Group Preference: Artificial Intelligence, Healthcare, Network Technology, Industry, Applications, Software
Portfolio Companies: Assembly, Bluefox, Bluespace, Bodo, Catalia Health, Chat Sports, CodeSpark, Constructor.io, Cuseum, DreameGGs, Edge Compute, GrubMarket, Huma.ai, IAMRobotics, Locomation, Loop Genomics, Looptify, Lyft, Macrometa, MissionBio, Mojo Vision, NeuVector, Nucypher, NView, OTO.ai, Paperspace, Paradromics, Plexuss, PopularPays, Proscia, Quantapore, Safehub, Savonix, Scansite 3D, SpaceX, Sonavex, Stratifyd, Strongsalt, Stryde, Subtle Medical, This Is l, TVision Insights, Whoknows
Key Executives:
  Lu Zang, Founder/Managing Partner
  Education: MS, Materials Sciences & Engineering, Stanford University
  Background: World Economic Forum - Young Global Leader
  Homan Yuen, Partner
  Education: BA, University of California, Berkeley; MS/PhD, Stanford University
  Background: Co-Founder/CTO, Solar Junction
  Carol Mao, Principal
  Education: BS, Peking University; MS, HKUST; MBA, Columbia Business School
  Background: Senior Investment Banking Associate, Deutsche Bank

803 FUTURE VENTURES
San Francisco, CA

e-mail: kate@pluckpr.com
web: future.ventures

Mission Statement: A venture capital firm seeking to invest in trailblazing entrepreneurs focused on the AI industry.
Fund Size: $1 Billion
Investment Criteria: Seed, Early Stage
Industry Group Preference: Artificial Intelligence, Information Technology, Robotics, Blockchain, Sustainable Transportation, Quantum Computing
Portfolio Companies: Atai Life Sciences, The Boring Company, BrdgAI, Cambrian BioPharma, Capital, Commonwealth Fusion Systems, Deep Genomics, Latent AI, Medcorder, Memphis Meats, Mythic, Neuralink, Ockam, Skype, SpaceX, Sutro Biopharma, Synthetic Genomics, Tesla, Tradex Technologies, Zoox
Key Executives:
  Steve Jurvetson, Co-Founder
  Education: BS/MS, Electrical Engineering, Stanford University; MBA, Stanford Grad. School of Business
  Background: R&D Engineer, Hewlett-Packard; Management Consultant, Bain & Company
  Maryanna Saenko, Co-Founder
  Education: BS, BioMedical Engineering/MS, Materials Science & Engineering, Carnegie Mellon University
  Background: Khosla Ventures; Partner, Airbus Ventures; Consultant, Lux Research; Research Engineer, Cabot Corporation

804 FdG ASSOCIATES LP
499 Park Avenue
26th Floor
New York, NY 10022

Phone: 212-940-6260
e-mail: info@fdgassociates.com
web: www.fdgassociates.com

Mission Statement: To maximize the potential of its portfolio companies.
Geographic Preference: United States
Fund Size: $500 million
Founded: 1993
Average Investment: $15 - $50 million
Minimum Investment: $8 million
Investment Criteria: Recapitalizations, Management Buyouts, Growth Investments, Industry Consolidations

Venture Capital & Private Equity Firms / Domestic Firms

Industry Group Preference: Business to Business, Consumer Products, Consumer Services, Distribution, Manufacturing, Retailing, Financial Services, Construction, Transportation, Logistics
Portfolio Companies: Hercules, Infrastructure and Industrial Constructors USA, Limbach Facility Services, Proficio Bank, Seabrook International, USA Bouquet
Key Executives:
David S. Gellman, Managing Director
Education: AB, Cornell University; MM, Kellogg School of Management
Background: Managing Director, AEA Investors; Trump Group
Directorships: Hercules Tires, Seabrook International, ReTrans

805 G SQUARED
205 North Michigan Avenue
Suite 3770
Chicago, IL 60601

web: gsquared.com

Mission Statement: G Squared is a venture capital firm whose mission is to invest in companies challenging the status quo and shaking up industries. G Squared partners with world-class entrepreneurs tackling big problems by investing in businesses throughout their life cycle as performance is strong-a fundamentally different approach than the classical early-, mid-, or late-stage venture capital firms. Formerly known as Gentry Venture Partners.

Founded: 2006
Industry Group Preference: Cloud Computing, Big Data, Mobility, Social Media, New Age Media
Portfolio Companies: 23andMe, Agrivida, Alibaba Group, Bloom Energy, Coursera, Dropbox, Enjoy, Fair, Instacart, JAMF Software, Kik, Lyft, Palantir, Pinterest, Postmates, Snapchat, Spacex, Spotify, Twitter, Uber
Key Executives:
Larry L. Aschebrook, Managing Partner
Education: MBA, Arizona State University
Background: CEO, Gentry Financial Corporation
Thomas R. Raterman, Managing Partner
Education: MS, Management, Kellogg School of Management
Background: President, Building Street Capital; CFO, LKQ Corporation

806 G-51 CAPITAL LLC
3939 Bee Caves Road
C-100
Austin, TX 78746

Phone: 512-929-5151

Mission Statement: To identify, nurture and grow great people, technology, and business. G51 provides value-added resources to assist companies bridge the numerous support and financing gaps that companies encounter on the road to success.

Geographic Preference: United States
Fund Size: $9 million
Founded: 1996
Average Investment: $500,000
Minimum Investment: $200,000
Investment Criteria: Seed, Start-up, First Stage, Second Stage, Mezzanine
Industry Group Preference: Hardware, Software, Business to Business
Portfolio Companies: E5 Systems Inc., Motion Computing, Pilot Software Inc., Socialware
Key Executives:
Rudy Garza, Founder/Managing General Partner
e-mail: rudy@g51.com
Education: MBA, University of Texas; BBA, Saint Edwards University

Bill Kennedy, Founding Partner
Education: BA, History Education, MA, Mathematics & Physics, University of Texas, Austin
Background: Founder, Beacon Professional Services; Co-Founder, Waveset Technologies
Directorships: SailPoint; Bomgar

808 GABRIEL VENTURE PARTNERS
635 Mariners Island
Suite 204
San Mateo, CA 94404

Phone: 650-551-5000 **Fax:** 650-551-5001
e-mail: info@gabrielvp.com
web: www.gabrielvp.com

Mission Statement: Gabriel invests in early-stage startups run by passionate entrepreneurs that are taking advantage of changing markets with next-generation technologies and innovative business models.

Geographic Preference: United States
Fund Size: $260 million
Founded: 1999
Average Investment: $3-6 million
Minimum Investment: $500,000
Investment Criteria: Start-Up, Early Stage
Industry Group Preference: Software, Technology, Wireless Technologies, Infrastructure, Mobile, Communications, Consumer Products, Enterprise Applications, Systems & Hardware, Clean Technology
Portfolio Companies: AccessLine, Allsec Technologies, Arula Systems, Aurora Algae, Boston-Power, Chegg, Concord Communications, Connetbeam, CrossMedia Services, Encentuate, Exodus, iForem, IL & FS Investment Limited, IPWireless, Iridigm, Jacked, Kajeet, Level 7 Systems, MakeMyTrip.com, NeoPath Networks, NetScaler, NetG Networks, Persistent Systems, PlaceWare, PlantSense, Provogue, SkyCross, STEP Labs, Tejas Networks, YLX Corp.
Key Executives:
Scott Chou, Managing Director
Education: MS, Engineering, Stanford University; MS, Computer Science, Harvard University; BS, Electrical Engineering, California Institute of Technology
Background: Poqet Computers, ICE, Bellcore, IBM, Onset Ventures
Rick Bolander, Managing Director/Co-Founder
Education: MBA, Harvard Business School; BS/MS Electrical Engineering, University of Michigan
Background: Apex Investment Partners; Founder, Blue Sky Venture; AT&T; Engineer, Chevron Oil
Directorships: Jacked, iForem, Chegg, Kajeet, Persistent Systems
Phil Samper, Co-Founder/Partner Emeritus
Education: BS, Business Administration, UC Berkeley; BFT, International Management, American Graduate School of International Management; MSM, Management, MIT
Background: Vice-Chairman/Executive Officer, Eastman Kodak Company; President, Sun Microsystems Computer Corp.; CEO/Chairman, Cray Research;

809 GALEN PARTNERS
680 Washington Blvd
10th Floor
Stamford, CT 06901

Phone: 203-653-6400
e-mail: info@galen.com
web: www.galen.com

Mission Statement: Invests in emerging healthcare companies, with focus on the healthcare information technology, specialty pharmaceuticals, and medical devices sectors. Galen Partners is

Venture Capital & Private Equity Firms / Domestic Firms

committed to working collaboratively with entrepreneurs and management teams.

Geographic Preference: United States
Fund Size: $250 million
Founded: 1990
Average Investment: $10 - $30 million
Minimum Investment: $10 million
Investment Criteria: Mid-to-Late Stage, Growth Equity
Industry Group Preference: Healthcare Information Technology, Healthcare, Medical Devices, Pharmaceuticals
Portfolio Companies: Acura Pharmaceuticals Inc., Cambrooke Therapeutics, Cardiva, Consensys Imaging Services, Dakim, Derma Sciences, Integrated Diagnostic Centers, InTouch Health, LifeIMAGE, PeriGen, Quotient Biodiagnostics Holdings, Sharecare, SonaCare Medical, Tactile Systems Technology, Tech Pharmacy Services

Key Executives:

David W Jahns, Managing Partner
203-653-6440
e-mail: djahns@galen.com
Education: BA, Political Science & Economics, Colgate University; MBA, Health Services Management, Kellogg School of Management, Northwestern University
Background: Financial Analyst, Corporate Finance Division, Smith Barney
Directorships: Stamford Health System

Zubeen Shroff, Managing Partner
203-653-6430
e-mail: zshroff@galen.com
Education: BA, Biological Science, Boston University; MBA, Wharton School
Background: Principal, Wilkerson Group; Schering-Plough Pharmaceuticals

Philip Borden, Managing Director
e-mail: pborden@galen.com
Education: BS, Duke University; MBA, Harvard Business School
Background: Healthcare Analyst, Dain Rauscher Wessels; Sr Analyst, Frazier Healthcare Partners; Associate, Oxford Bioscience Partners; General Partner, Riverside Partners

Bruce Wesson, Founding Partner Emeritus/Senior Advisor
203-653-6420
e-mail: bwesson@galen.com
Education: BA, Colgate University; MBA, Columbia University Graduate School of Business
Background: Managing Director, Corporate Finance Division, Smith Barney
Directorships: MedAssets, Derma Sciences, Acura Pharmaceuticals, TPS

L John Wilkerson, Founder/Senior Advisor
203-653-6450
e-mail: wilker@galen.com
Education: Biological Sciences, Utah State University; PhD, Cornell University
Background: Group Product Director, Ortho Diagnostics; VP, Medical Analysis & Research, Smith Barney; Channing, Weinberg & Co.
Directorships: Cardiva, Quotient BioDiagnostics Holdings, TPS

Stacey Bauer, Chief Financial Officer
203-653-6473
e-mail: sbauer@galen.com
Education: BA, Business Administration, University of Massachusetts at Amherst
Background: Controller & CFO, Bedrock Capital Partners; Tax Manager, Financial Services, PriceWaterhouseCoopers

810 GARAGE TECHNOLOGY VENTURES
1059-1069 East Meadow Circle
Palo Alto, CA 94303

Phone: 650-397-1359
e-mail: info@garage.com
web: www.garage.com

Mission Statement: A seed-stage and early-stage venture capital fund looking to invest in entrepreneurial teams with big ideas and a need for seed capital to turn their ideas into great companies.

Geographic Preference: California, West Coast
Fund Size: $10 million
Founded: 1997
Average Investment: $2 million, up to $3 millin
Minimum Investment: $500,000
Investment Criteria: High Technology Startups, Seed Stage, Early Stage
Industry Group Preference: Software, Materials Technology, Technology, Clean Technology
Portfolio Companies: Business Layers, CastStack, CFares, Claria, ClearFuels Technology, ClearAccessIP, ClearFuels Technology, Digital Envoy, Digital Fountain, D.light Design, FilmLoop, FutureTrade, GuruNet Corp., Hoku Scientific, Immunix, iNest, Innovative Robotics, IP3 Networks, Kaboodle, Knightscope, LeftHand Networks, Miasole, The Motley Fool, NetConversions, NovaCentrix, Packet Island, Pandora, People, ai, PhatNoise, Price.com, Psionic, PureSight Inc., Qumu, Razz, Sapias, SignaCert, Simply Hired, Sixense, STEP Labs, Synacor, Thermo Ceramix, Tripwire, U-Nav Microelectronics, Vigilistics, Virtualis, VISANOW, VOKE, WebOrder, WhiteHat Security, Xora, Yoics

Key Executives:

Guy Kawasaki, Managing Director
e-mail: kawasaki@garage.com
Education: BA, Stanford University; MBA, University of California, Los Angeles
Background: Apple Computer
Directorships: BitPass, FilmLoop, SimplyHired

Bill Reichert, Managing Director
e-mail: reichert@garage.com
Education: BA, Harvard College; MBA, Stanford University
Background: Co-Founder/VP, Academic Systems Corporation; McKinsey & Company; Brown Brothers Harriman & Company
Directorships: CaseStack, IP3 Networks, Miasole, WhiteHat Security, ClearFuels Technology, SimplyHired, D.light Design, ThermoCeramix, VisaNow

Joyce Chung, Managing Director
e-mail: joyce@garage.com
Education: SB, Chemical Engineering, MIT; MBA, Stanford Graduate School of Business
Background: Founding Partner, Cardinal Venture Capital; Adobe Ventures

Henry Wong, Managing Director
e-mail: henry@garage.com
Education: BS, Business, University of Utah; MBA, Telecom Management, Golden Gate University
Background: Founder, Diamond TechVentures; Venture Partner, Crystal Ventures

811 GE CAPITAL
901 Main Avenue
Norwalk, CT 06851

web: www.gecapital.com

Mission Statement: To build a premier global investing business that creates value by leveraging GE Systems.

Geographic Preference: Worldwide
Fund Size: $28 billion
Founded: 1992
Average Investment: $20 million
Minimum Investment: $5 million

Venture Capital & Private Equity Firms / Domestic Firms

Industry Group Preference: Financial Services, Transportation, Logistics, Information Technology, Telecommunications, Healthcare, Insurance, Retailing, Consumer Products, Media, Industrial Equipment, Real Estate, Mining, Aviation, Energy

Key Executives:
Jennifer VanBelle, SVP & CEO
Education: BA, Bates College; MS, London Business School
Background: Chief Risk Officer - Capital Management, GE Capital

812 GE VENTURES
2882 Sand Hill Rd.
Suite 240
Menlo Park, CA 94025

Phone: 650-233-3900
web: www.ge.com/ventures

Mission Statement: GE Ventures assists entrepreneurs and start-ups by providing access to GE's technical expertise, capital, and network.

Industry Group Preference: Software, Analytics & Analytical Instruments, Advanced Manufacturing, Energy, Healthcare

Portfolio Companies: 1366 Technologies, Acutus Medical, Advanced Microgrid Solutions, Alchemist Accelerator, Ambyint, Apervita, Aras Corp., Arcadia, Arterys, Ascendify, Aver, Avitas Systems, Ayasdi, Balena, BiSN, Carbon, Caremerge, Catalant, China Materialia, Chrono, Clear Path Robotics, Cooledge, Desktop Metal, Drawbridge Health, Element Analytics, Elementum, Enbala, Equalum, Evidation, eVolution Networks, FlexGen Power Systems, FogHorn, Foro Energy, Freightos, Genome Medical, Gravie, Grid Net, Headsense, Health Reveal, Hyperloop One, i3 Equity Partners, Igenu, Iora Health, IoTium, Labcyte, LM, Maana, MedAware, Menlomicro, Mocana, Morphisec, mPrest, Nexar, Nuvolo, Nyshex, Oblong, Omada, Omni-ID, Optomec, Ornim, PingThings, Portworx, Rig Up, Sarcos, Sentient, Sight Machine, Sonnen, Stem, Syapse, Tamr, TTTech, Tendril, The Hive, Thetaray, Trilliant, Up Skill, Veran, Varana Health, View Dynamic Glass, Vineti, Volta, Xage Security, Xometry, Zinc, Zola Electric

Other Locations:
33-41 Farnsworth St.
Boston, MA 02210

Key Executives:
Leslie Bottorff, Managing Director
Education: BS, Biomedical Engineering, Purdue University; MBA, Harvard Business School
Background: General Partner, ONSET Ventures
Lisa Coca, Managing Director
Education: Wharton School; MBA, Stanford Graduate School of Business
Background: GE Capital; Bankers Trust; Deutsche Bank
Alex De Winter, Managing Director
Education: Amherst College; PhD, Stanford University; MBA, University of California, Berkeley
Background: Partner, Mohr Davidow Ventures; Senior Scientist, Pacific Biosciences
Michael Dolbac, Senior Managing Director
Education: BS, MS, Stanford University; MBA, Wharton School
Background: LG Electronics
Daniel Hullah, Managing Director
Education: BS, PhD, University of Oxford; MBA, INSEAD
Background: Director of Ventures, National Grid
Karen Kerr, Executive Managing Director
Education: AB, Bryn Mawr College; PhD, University of Chicago
Background: Managing Director, ARCH Venture Partners
Jonathan Pulitzer, Managing Director
Education: New York University

Ralph Taylor-Smith, Managing Director
Education: BA, MA, MIT; MA, PhD, Princeton University
Background: Cofounfer/General Partner/Managing Director, Battelle Venture Partners; Investment Banker, Goldman Sachs; Investment Banker, JP Morgan
Victor Westerlind, Managing Director
Education: BA, Cornell University; MA, Stanford University; MBA, Harvard Business School
Background: Intel Capital; General Partner, RockPort Capital; InterWest Partners

813 GEFINOR CAPITAL
2700 Westchester Avenue
Suite 303
Purchase, NY 10577

Phone: 212-308-1111 **Fax:** 212-308-1182
web: www.gefinorcapital.com

Mission Statement: Provides the reach, and power of presence of a large organization, with a focused entrepreneurial approach that enables devoted time and resources to companies from their inception.

Geographic Preference: United States
Fund Size: $10 million
Founded: 2002
Average Investment: $2 - 5 million
Investment Criteria: Early-Stage, Mid-Stage, Late-Stage
Industry Group Preference: Financial Services, Telecommunications, Semiconductors, Software, Services, Medical & Health Related, Manufacturing, Consumer Products

Portfolio Companies: Advion Inc., Anokiwave Inc., Beenz, BinOptics, BlueSpace Software Corp., Calient Technologies Inc., Carmichael Training Systems, Genesant Technologies Inc., GridApp Systems Inc., GoNoodle Inc., Kionix Inc., Knoa Software Inc., Metros Corp., Mimix Broadband Inc., ModbiTV Inc., Myriad Development, NetSpend Corp., Nextivity, Patton Surgical Corp., PeerNova Inc., RemitDATA Inc., Rheonix Inc., SciAps Inc., Scuf Gaming LLC, SocialFlow Inc., SiVerio Inc., Silicon Navigator Corp., Unwired Nation, Volaris Advisors, Wimba Inc., XAware Inc., ZeeWaves Systems Inc.

Key Executives:
Mimo Ousseimi, Managing Director
Education: MBA, John E Anderson School of Management, University of California, LA; BA Political Economy, University of California, Berkeley
Background: Merrill Lynch; State Street Research and Management Company
Directorships: Knoa Software
William Beckett, Partner
Education: MBA, Stanford Graduate School of Business
Background: Investment Banking, Merrill Lynch
Robert Porell, Chief Financial Officer
Education: BA, Economics, Harvard College; MS, Accounting, New York University
Background: CFO/CEO, Alexander Doll Company Inc.; Manager, Coopers & Lybrand; CPA
Chris Davis, Principal
Education: BComm, Information Systems, Queen's University; MBA, Financial Engineering, Sloan School of Management, MIT
Background: Systems Analyst, Credit Suisse First Boston; High Yield Origination Group, TD Securities

814 GELT VC
Ann Arbor, MI

e-mail: turner@gelt.vc
web: www.gelt.vc

Mission Statement: Gelt Venture Capital has networks in Los Angeles, San Francisco, New York City, and Ann Arbor.
Founded: 2019

Venture Capital & Private Equity Firms / Domestic Firms

Average Investment: $25,000 - $250,000
Minimum Investment: $25,000
Investment Criteria: Pre-Seed, Seed, Series A
Industry Group Preference: Diversified
Portfolio Companies: Alpha Foods, Babyscript, Domuso Inc., FlightWave Aero, Forelinx, Hykso, Jobs For Vets, Lambda, Marble Robot, May Mobility, Natilus Inc., OpenSponsorship, Phase Four, Sixa, Standard Cyborg, Starsky Robotics, Streamloan, SuperPhone

Key Executives:
  Turner Novak, General Partner
  Education: BBA, Grand Valley State University
  Background: Credit Analyst, Mercantile Bank of Michigan; Investment Analyst, Van Andel Institute; Founder, TDN Capital
  Keith Wasserman, General Partner
  Education: BBA, Marshall School of Business, University of Southern California
  Background: Co-Founder, Resident Relief Foundation; Co-Founder, Happy Home Communities; Co-Founder, Domuso Inc.; Co-Founder, Gelt Inc.
  Damian Langere, General Partner
  Education: University of California, Santa Barbara
  Background: Co-Founder, Domuso Inc.

815 GEMINI INVESTORS
20 William Street
Suite 250
Wellesley, MA 02481

Phone: 781-237-7001 **Fax:** 781-237-7233
web: www.gemini-investors.com

Mission Statement: Based in Massachusetts, Gemini Investors is a private equity firm that makes investments in lower middle-market companies in a wide range of industries. Gemini Investors targets established companies with significant growth potential.

Geographic Preference: United States
Fund Size: $64 million
Founded: 1993
Average Investment: $3 - $8 million
Investment Criteria: Established companies with at least three years operating history, Lower Middle Market, Growth Capital, Recapitalizations, MBO
Industry Group Preference: Technology, Business to Business, Consumer Services, Manufacturing, Distribution, Consumer Products, Healthcare, Education, Waste & Recycling
Portfolio Companies: 360 PT Management, Action Target, Advanced AV, All Aboard America, American Signcrafters, Bag Balm, Beryllium, Bonded Filter, Brady Enterprises, Center Rock, Conditioned Air, Coventor, Datacom Systems, Disaster Kleenup International, Dorsey Schools, DTT Surveillance, Express Window Films, FabEnCo/BlueWater, Garbanzo Mediterranean Grill, Geronimo Alloys, Hilco Technologies, Jan Pro, Jersey Precast, Just Brakes, KP Corporation, Marinello, Newpro, Phillips Screw Company, Phoenix Aromas and Essential Oils, Pinnacle Treatment Centers, PI Worldwide, Primestream, Quality Powder Coating, Scotia Technology, SGA, SolmeteX, Star Career Academy, TGaS Advisors, TJ Hale, Trois Petits Cochons, Ultracor, Valence Surface Technologies, Vanderveer Plastics, Vision Government Solutions, Wake Research Associates, Well-Foam, Workplace

Key Executives:
  James J Goodman, President
  e-mail: jgoodman@gemini-investors.com
  Education: AB, MBA, JD, Harvard University
  Background: Berkshire Partners; Bain & Company
  Jeffrey T Newton, Managing Director
  e-mail: jnewton@gemini-investors.com
  Education: BS, University of Vermont; MBA, Tuck School of Business, Dartmouth College
  Background: President, Concord Partners; Senior VP & Treasurer, Lifetime Corporation; VP, Investment Banking, Prudential Securities
  David F Millet, Managing Director
  e-mail: dmillet@gemini-investors.com
  Education: BA, Physical Sciences, Harvard University
  Background: President, Chatham Venture Corporation; Group Executive, NEC Corporation; Senior Consultant, Arthur D Little
  James T Rich, Managing Director
  e-mail: jrich@gemini-investors.com
  Education: AB, Dartmouth College
  Background: Senior Associate, Citizens Energy; Analyst, JP Morgan
  Matthew E Keis, Managing Director
  e-mail: mkeis@gemini-investors.com
  Education: BS, Boston College
  Background: Senior Associate, Arthur Andersen

816 GEN Y CAPITAL PARTNERS Young Entrepreneur Council
745 Atlantic Ave.
Boston, MA 02110

Phone: 484-403-0736
e-mail: info@yec.co
web: yec.co

Mission Statement: We invest in early stage companies that will benefit from the leverage provided by a network of many of the world's top young entrepreneurs through our partnership with the YEC (the Young Entrepreneur Council). We work with early stage, consumer facing mobile and internet companies where a network of highly connected young entrepreneurs from around the world can increase the likelihood that they become the leaders in their space.

Average Investment: $250,000 - $500,000
Investment Criteria: Early-Stage
Portfolio Companies: Classic Specs, Levo League, Flow, Virool, Sellercrowd

Key Executives:
  Scott Gerber, Co-Founder/Director of Communications
  Background: Founder, Young Entrepreneurs Council
  Carissa Reiniger, Founding Partner & Fundraising Chair
  Background: Founder, Silver Lining Ltd.

817 GEN7 INVESTMENTS
101 - 5th Street N
Fargo, ND 58102

e-mail: info@www.gen7investments.com
web: gen7investments.com

Mission Statement: Based in Fargo, N.D., Gen7 is built on over a century of experience in creating value for businesses and investors.

Industry Group Preference: Diversified
Portfolio Companies: Bushel, CoSchedule, Legacy Seed Companies, Levridge, Myriad Mobile, The Stable, Stoneridge, Whistle Sports

Key Executives:
  Bill Marcil, Jr., President & CEO
  Education: University of North Dakota
  Background: Publisher, The Forum of Fargo Moorhead; COO, Forum Communications Company

818 GENACAST VENTURES
One Comcast Center
55th Floor
Philadelphia, PA 19103

e-mail: hello@genacast.com
web: www.genacast.com

Mission Statement: A seed fund that invests in technology-centric Internet startups.

Geographic Preference: Northeastern United States, Boston to Washington DC corridor

Venture Capital & Private Equity Firms / Domestic Firms

Average Investment: Up to $1 million
Investment Criteria: Seed or Early-Stage
Industry Group Preference: Technology, Consumer Internet, Digital Media & Marketing, E-Commerce & Manufacturing, Gaming, Mobile, Online Advertising, Software, SaaS, Cybersecurity, Business to Business, B2B
Portfolio Companies: BigID, Blockdaemon, Confetti, Datadog, Demdex, Divide, DoubleVerify, DrayNow, Invited Media, Jornaya, Mortar Data, Overlap, PackLate, Revmetrix, Rocketrip, Staq, Uptycs, YieldMo, ZeroFox

Other Locations:
588 Broadway Street
Suite 202
New York, NY 10012

Key Executives:
Gil Beyda, Founder/Managing Partner
Education: BS, Computer Science, MBA, California State University, Northridge
Background: Founder, Mind Games; Founder, Real Media; CTO, TACODA; Managing Director, Comcast Ventures
Directorships: Neural Magic, Confetti, goTenna, Zapata Computing, Blockdaemon, DrayNow, BigID, STAQ
Morgan Polotan, Principal
Education: BS, Northeastern University
Background: Bloomberg Beta; Tapad; Charles Koch Institute

---

819 GENERAL ATLANTIC PARTNERS
Park Avenue Plaza
55 East 52nd Street
33rd Floor
New York, NY 10055

Phone: 212-715-4000 **Fax:** 212-759-5708
web: www.generalatlantic.com

Mission Statement: General Atlantic is a growth equity firm that offers capital and expertise to growth companies worldwide.

Geographic Preference: Globally
Fund Size: $900 million
Founded: 1980
Average Investment: $250 million
Minimum Investment: $25 million
Investment Criteria: Private and Public Companies
Industry Group Preference: Information Technology, Business Products & Services, Consumer Products, Financial Services, Healthcare
Portfolio Companies: Acumen Brands, Adyen, Affinion Group, Aimbridge, Airbnb, Alignment Healthcare, Amherst Pierpont Securities, AppDynamics, Appirio, Asian Genco, Avant, Axel Springer Digital Classifieds, Barteca, Bazaarvoice, Box, BuzzFeed, C&J Energy Services, Citco, CitiusTech, CLEAResult, Decolar.com, EN Engineering, EviCore Healthcare, Exp, Flixbus, FNZ, Garena, Gilt Groupe, House of Anita Dongre, Hyperion Insurance Group, IBS Software Services, Indusind Bank, KCG, Klarna, Markit, Meituan, MeteoGroup, Mu Sigma, National Stock Exchange, Network International, Oak Hill Advisors, OptionsHouse, Ourofino Saude Animal, Pague Menos, Privalia, QTS, Red Ventures, Sanfer, Santander Asset Management, SAS Sistema de Ensino, Saxo Bank, SnapAV, Squarespace, Studio Moderna, Sun Art Retail Group, Sura Asset Management, Tenfu, Too Faced Cosmetics, Tory Burch, TriNet, Uber, Vox Media, Xiabu Xiabu, XP Investimentos, Zhongsheng Group

Other Locations:
600 Steamboat Road
Suite 105
Greenwich, CT 06830
Phone: 203-629-8600 **Fax:** 203-622-8818

228 Hamilton Avenue
Palo Alto, CA 94301
Phone: 650-251-7800 **Fax:** 650-251-9672

23 Savile Row
London W1S 2ET
United Kingdom
Phone: 44-2074843200 **Fax:** 44-2074843290

Luitpoldblock
Amiraplatz 3
Munich 80333
Germany
Phone: 49-089558932710 **Fax:** 49-089558932730

5901-5903 & 5912, 59F China World Office Tower B
1 Jianguomenwai Avenue
Beijing 100004
China
Phone: 86-1059652500 **Fax:** 86-1058669533

Suite 5704-5706, 57F
Two IFC
8 Finance Street
Central
Hong Kong
Phone: 852-36022600 **Fax:** 852-22196600

Level 19, Birla Aurora
Dr. Annie Besant Road
Worli
Mumbai 400 030
India
Phone: 91-2266561400 **Fax:** 91-2266317893

Av Brigadeiro Faria Lima, 3477
7th Floor
Tower A, Itaim Bibi
Sao Paulo 04538-133
Brazil
Phone: 55-1132966100

Raamplein 1
Amsterdam 1016 XK
Netherlands
Phone: 31-206090301

Asia Square Tower 1
8 Marina View, 41-04 018960
Singapore
Phone: 65-66616700

Pedregal No. 24 Piso 4
Colonia Molino del Rey
Delegacion Miguel Hidalgo
Mexico 11600
Mexico
Phone: 52-5541646500

Key Executives:
Steven Denning, Chairman
Education: BS, Georgia Institute of Technology; MS, Naval Postgraduate School; MBA, Stanford Graduate School of Business
Background: Consultant, McKinsey & Company
Directorships: The Nature Conservancy, Council on Foreign Relations, Next Generation
William E. Ford, Chief Executive Officer
Education: BA, Amherst College; MBA, Stanford Graduate School of Business
Background: Investment Banking, Morgan Stanley & Co
Directorships: Tory Burch, Oak Hill Advisors, Markit
Frank Brown, Managing Director/Chief Risk Officer
Education: BSBA, Bucknell University
Background: Dean, INSEAD; PricewaterhouseCoopers
Directorships: The Home Depot
Thomas Murphy, Advisory Director
Education: BA, Economics, Colgate University; MBA,

Venture Capital & Private Equity Firms / Domestic Firms

Stern School of Business, New York University
Background: Senior Accountant, Deloitte & Touche
Gabriel Caillaux, Managing Director, Europe
Education: MBA, Finance, ESCP-EAP European School of Management
Background: Analyst & Associate, Merrill Lynch
Directorships: Santander Asset Management, Axel Springer Digital Classifieds, Citco, Network International, Privalia
Andrew Crawford, Managing Director, United States
Education: BS, Washington and Lee University; MBA, Harvard Business School
Background: Advent International
Directorships: Too Faced Cosmetics, Barteca
Cory Eaves, Operating Partner
Education: BSEE, University of Iowa; MBA, Babson College; Advanced Management Program, Harvard Business School
Background: EVP, CTO & CIO, Misys plc
Directorships: CitiusTech, EviCore, The Marfan Foundation, NetHope
Martin Escobari, Managing Director, Latin America
Education: BS, Harvard College; MBA, Harvard Business School
Background: Managing Director, Advent International; Co-Founder & CFO, Submarino.com; Associate, Boston Consulting Group
Directorships: Ourofino, Pague Menos, Sanfer, Sura Asset Management, XP Investimentos
David Hodgson, Vice Chairman
Education: AB, Mathematics & Social Sciences, Dartmouth College; MBA, Stanford University Graduate School of Business
Background: President, New England Software
Directorships: Alignment Healthcare, Hyperion Insurance Group, Amherst Pierpont Securities, TriNet
Rene Kern, Advisory Directpr
Education: BS, University of California, Berkeley; MBA, Wharton School, MA, School of Arts and Sciences, University of Pennsylvania
Background: VP, Morgan Stanley; Management Consultant, Bain & Company
Directorships: OptionsHouse, KCG
Chris Lanning, Managing Director/General Counsel
Education: BA, History, JD, University of Virginia
Background: Senior Associate, Corporate Finance, Hunton & Williams; Associate, Paul, Weiss, Rifkind, Wharton & Garrison
Directorships: Dice Holdings, Webloyalty
Anton Levy, Managing Director/Global Head of Technology
Education: BS in Commerce, Finance & Computer Science, University of Virginia; MBA, Columbia University
Background: Investment Banker, Morgan Stanley
Directorships: Squarespace, Acumen Brands, Klarna, Red Ventures, Gilt Groupe
Sandeep Naik, Managing Director, India
Education: BTech, Instrumentation Engineering, University of Mumbai; MS, Biomedical Engineering, Medical College of Virginia; MBA, Wharton School, University of Pennsylvania
Background: Partner, Apax; Global Marketing Manager, Medtronic; Consultant, McKinsey & Company; Co-Founder, InfraScan
Joern Nikolay, Managing Director, Munich
Education: WHU Otto Beisheim Graduate School of Management; Institut d'Etudes Politiques
Background: TA Associates; Case Team Leader, Bain & Company; Analyst, Morgan Stanley
Directorships: Axel Springer Digital Classifieds, Klarna, Flixbus
David Rosenstein, Managing Director/General Counsel
Education: BA, University of North Carolina; JD, New York University School of Law
Background: Associate, Paul, Weiss, Rifkind, Wharton & Garrison
Graves Tompkins, Managing Director/Head of Capital Partnering
Education: AB, Princeton University; MBA, Harvard Business School, MPA, Harvard Kennedy School of Government, Harvard University
Background: Merchant Banking Division, Goldman Sachs; McKinsey & Company
Directorships: Oak Hill Advisors
Robbert Vorhoff, Managing Director/Global Head of Healthcare
Education: BS, Commerce, McIntire School of Commerce, University of Virginia
Background: Greenhill Capital Partners; M&A Advisory Group, Greenhill & Co.
Directorships: Alignment Healthcare, EviCore Healthcare, Echoing Green

820 GENERAL CATALYST PARTNERS
20 University Road
4th Floor
Cambridge, MA 02138

Phone: 617-234-7000
e-mail: gcinfo@generalcatalyst.com
web: generalcatalyst.com

Mission Statement: General Catalyst Partners is a venture capital firm that seeks to help entrepreneurs build market leading companies. The firm targets innovative technology businesses that can transform industries. General Catalyst Partners focuses on making early stage and growth equity investments.

Fund Size: $1.4 billion
Founded: 2000
Investment Criteria: Early Stage, Growth Equity
Industry Group Preference: Infrastructure, Applications Software & Services, Industrial Equipment, Software, Clean Energy, Consumer, New Media, Internet, Fintech
Portfolio Companies: 6D.AI, Airbnb, AirMap, All Turtles, Allego, Anaconda, Anduril, Angle, Anomali, Atrium, Audius, B12, BigCommerce, Blade, Bowery, Brainly, Bustle, Cadre, Catalant, Circle, Clarabridge, ClassDojo, ClassPass, ClearSky, CoachUp, Color, Common Networks, Contentful, Contrast Security, Corelight, Corevia Medical, CouchSurfing, Cozy, Curai, Custora, CyPhy, Deliveroo, Digit, Drift, Elysium, Envoy, Espressive, Evolv Technology, Fancy, Feedvisor, Fractyl, Freebird, Fundbox, Giphy, GoodData, Grammarly, Gusto, Highfive, Hive, Hometap, HubHaus, Illumio, Ionic, Julia Computing, Kin Community, Kuvee, Lemonade, Livongo, Lola, Loom, Lose It!, M.Gemi, Major League Hacking, Mark43, Menlo Security, Merlin, Mindstrong, Monzo, Naturebox, Newstore, Nova, Oceans Healthcare, OM1, Oscar, Outdoor Voices, PathAI, Photoshelter, Preempt, Pumpup, Rebag, Remesh, Riskrecon, Ro, Rockets of Awesome, R Studio, Sabre, Samsara, Shift Technology, SignalFX, Singular, Spring Discovery, Strip, Super Evil Megacorp, Superpedestrian, Swirl, Teamworks, The Honest Company, ThoughtSpot, Tidelift, TrueMotion, Tunein, VerneGlobal, Viajanet, Vroom, Wag!, Warby Parker, WayUp, Yottaa

Other Locations:
434 Broadway
6th Floor

Venture Capital & Private Equity Firms / Domestic Firms

New York, NY 10013
Phone: 212-775-4000

564 University Avenue
Palo Alto, CA 94301
Phone: 650-618-5900

2 South Park Street
Suite 100
San Francisco, CA 94107

Key Executives:

Adam Valkin, Managing Director
Education: AB, Economics, Harvard University
Background: Venture Partner, Accel Partners; Global Head, Digital Media & New Business, Endemol; Partner, Arts Alliance; Co-Founder & Interim CEO, LOVEFiLM; Co-Founder, Propertyfinder; Marketing Manager, Firefly Network; Market Manager, BarnsandNoble.com
Directorships: Brainly, Bustle, ClassPass, Fundbox, Giphy, Super Evil Megacorp, Vroom, WayUp

Bill Fitzgerald, Strategic Advisor
Education: BA, College of the Holy Cross; JD, Suffolk University Law School
Background: Interim CFO, Miami Cruise Holdings; Manager, KPMG; Adjunct Professor, Boston College
Directorships: Private Equity CFO Association

David Orfao, Venture Partner
Education: BS, Business & Accounting, Norwich University
Background: President & CEO, Allaire Corporation; Senior VP, Sales Operations & Marketing, Frame Technology Corporation; Claris Corporation; SQA Corporation
Directorships: Circle Financial, Clearsky, Imprivata, RStudio

Dr. Steve Herrod, Managing Director
Education: BA, University of Texas, Austin; MS, Computer Science, PhD, Stanford University
Background: CTO & SVP, VMware; Transmeta Corporation; SGI
Directorships: Anomaly, Curai, Illumio, Menlo Security, Preempt Security, Contrast Security, SignalFX, Espressive, RiskRecon

Hemant Taneja, Managing Director
e-mail: htaneja@generalcatalyst.com
Education: BS, MS, Electrical Engineering & Computer Science, BS, Biology & Biomedical Engineering, BS, Mathematics, MS, Operations Research, Massachusetts Institute of Technology
Background: Founder, Advanced Energy Economy; Founder & CEO, Isovia; SVP, Operations, JP Mobile; Founder & Co-Chairman, New England Clean Energy Council
Directorships: ARC Energy, ClassDojo, Corvia Medical, CyPhy Works, Digit, FlightCar, Fractyl Laboratories, Fundbox, Gridco Systems, Gusto, Hey, Highfive, JuiceBox Games, Khan Academy

Joel Cutler, Co-Founder & Managing Director
e-mail: jcutler@generalcatalyst.com
Education: Colby College; Boston College Law School
Background: National Leisure Group; Retail Growth ATM Systems
Directorships: Airbnb, Cadre, Chloe + Isabel, Freedbird, Handy, Lemonade, Lola, M.Gemi, Oscar Insurance, Rockets of Awesome, Warby Parker

Larry Bohn, Managing Director
e-mail: lbohn@generalcatalyst.com
Education: BA, English, University of Massachusetts, Amherst; MA, English Linguistics, Clark University
Background: Chairman, President & CEO, NetGenesis; President, PC DOCS; SVP, Marketing & Business Development, Interleaf; Data General
Directorships: B12, Bigcommerce, Clarabridge, Drift, Feedvisor, GoodData, Mark43, Yottaa

David Fialkow, Co-Founder & Managing Director
e-mail: dfialkow@generalcatalyst.com
Education: Film, Colgate University; Boston College
Background: Co-Founder, National Leisure Group; Co-Founder, Alliance Development Group; Retail Growth ATM Systems; Starboard Cruise Services
Directorships: Facing History and Ourselves, Debate Mate, The Pan-Mass Challenge

Niko Bonatsos, Managing Director
e-mail: nbonatsos@generalcatalyst.com
Education: Dipl.-Ing, Electrical Engineering & Computer Science, Natl. Tech. University of Athens; MPhil, Manufacturing Engineering & Management, University of Cambridge; MS, Management Science & Engineering, Stanford University
Background: Yokogawa Electric Corporation
Directorships: 6d.ai, All Turtles, Atrium, Audius, Hive, HubHaus, ClassDojo, Cover, Livongo Health, Wag!

821 GENERAL MOTORS VENTURES
30470 Harley Earl Blvd
Warren, MI 48092

web: www.gmventures.com

Mission Statement: General Motors Ventures LLC, the venture capital arm of General Motors, was established in 2010 to build relationships with innovative businesses and other venture capital firms. GM Ventures invests in growth stage automotive-related technology companies with the objective of making the best technology available to GM's customers.

Geographic Preference: United States
Fund Size: $100 million
Founded: 2010
Investment Criteria: Early Stage, Growth Stage
Industry Group Preference: Automotive, Clean Technology, Transportation, Advanced Materials
Portfolio Companies: Algolux, Empower Energies, Envisics, Geodigital, Nanosteel, Nauto, Powermat, Proterra, Savari, Seaurat Technologies, Solid Energy, Springcoin, Tula, Weizuche, Yoshi

Key Executives:

Matt Tsien, President
Education: BS, Kettering University; MS, Stanford University; MS, MIT
Background: VP of Planning and Program Management, GM China; EVP, SAIC-GM-Wuling; Executive Director of Vehicle Systems; Electrical Engineer, Delco Electronics

Wade Sheffer, Managing Director
Education: BS, Michigan Technology University; MS, Rensselaer Polytechnic Institute
Background: Test Engineer, Milford Proving Ground; Global Commodity Manager for Vehicle Infotainment; Deputy Executive Director, Shanghai General Motors; Executive Director, Chassis Purchasing

Rohit Makharia, Investment Manager
Education: MS, Chemical Engineering, University of Rochester
Background: Tech Specialist & Program Manager, Global Battery Systems, General Motors

822 GENERATION PARTNERS
Two Lafayette Court
Greenwich, CT 06830

Phone: 203-422-8200 **Fax:** 203-422-8250
web: www.generation.com

Mission Statement: To invest in technology-enabled services businesses that can make a positive impact on society, and to create value for these companies.

Geographic Preference: United States
Fund Size: $350 million
Founded: 1996
Average Investment: $10 - $40 million
Minimum Investment: $6 million
Investment Criteria: Early Stage, Mid-Stage, Late Stage

Industry Group Preference: Business to Business, Media, Information Technology, Outsourcing & Efficiency, Communications, Healthcare Services, Healthcare Information Technology, Business Products & Services
Portfolio Companies: 3seventy, American Cellular Corporation, Captivate Network, Demand Media, DiscoverMusic, Donuts, High End Systems, Hotjobs.com, iCrossing, LVI Services, MedVance Institute, MethodCare, Muzak, New Wave Broadcasting, Office Media Network, Post University, Promatory Communications, ReCept Pharmacy, Rightside, Scientific Games, ShopWiki, Sterling InfoSystems, thePlatform, Virtual Radiologic Corporation, Zirmed

Other Locations:
Los Angeles, CA
Phone: 424-204-9683

Austin, TX 78759
Phone: 203-422-8200

Key Executives:
Mark Jennings, Managing Partner
512-459-7100
e-mail: jennings@generation.com
Education: BS, Mechanical Engineering, University of Texas at Austin; MBA, Harvard Graduate School of Business
Background: General Partner, Centre Partners; Corporate Finance Department, Goldman Sachs & Company
Directorships: Captivate Network, Virtual Radiologic Corporation, inVentiv Health, MedVance Institute, Agility Recovery Solutions, Sterling Infosystems, Post University
John Hawkins, Managing Partner
415-385-9575
e-mail: hawkins@generation.com
Education: BA, English, Harvard College; MBA, Harvard Graduate School of Business
Background: General Partner, Burr, Egan, Deleage & Company; Corporate Finance Department, Alex. Brown & Sons; Woodman, Kirkpatrick & Gilbreath; Salomon Brothers
Directorships: Captivate Network, P-Com, HotJobs, Demand Media, ShopWiki, ZirMed, iCrossing
Andrew Hertzmark, Managing Partner
203-422-8215
e-mail: hertzmark@generation.com
Education: BA, Economics & Political Science, MBA, Wharton School, University of Pennsylvania
Background: Associate, Galen Partners; Analyst, UBS; Analyst, Dillon Read & Co.; Business Development Group, Pfizer; National Economic Council
Directorships: Captivate Network, Post Education, ReCept Pharmacy, ShopWiki, Virtual Radiologic Corporation
Louis Marino, Senior Vice President/Chief Financial Officer
203-422-8212
e-mail: marino@generation.com
Education: BS, Accounting, Boston College; CPA
Background: Senior Associate, PricewaterhouseCoopers
Directorships: Agility Recovery Solutions, Captivate Network, MedVance Institute, Post Education, ReCept Pharmacy, ShopWiki

---

823 **GENSTAR CAPITAL LP**
4 Embarcadero Center
Suite 1900
San Francisco, CA 94111-4191

Phone: 415-834-2350 **Fax:** 415-834-2383
e-mail: ir@gencap.com
web: www.gencap.com

Mission Statement: Seeks opportunities to invest in unique businesses that can benefit from the productive relationship between proactive shareholders and a motivated management team.
Geographic Preference: United States, Canada
Fund Size: $2 billion
Founded: 1988
Average Investment: $15-75 million
Minimum Investment: $15 million
Investment Criteria: Companies with minimum revenues of $50 million, strong management, prospects for long-term growth and profitability, competitive advantages
Industry Group Preference: Life Sciences, Industrial Technology, Healthcare Services, Software, Financial Services
Portfolio Companies: Accruent, Acrisure, AleraGroup, AWL, Altegris, Apex, Ascensus, Association Member Benefits Advisors, Blue Star Sports, Boyd Corp., Blacket, Bullhorn, ConnectiveRx, Infinite Electronics Inc., Innovative Aftermarket Systems, Institutional Shareholder Services, Insurity, Mercer Advisors, Ministry Brands, Palomar Specialty, PDI, Power Products LLC, Pretium Packaging, Sphera, Stratetic Insight, Tekniplex, Telestream

Key Executives:
Jean-Pierre L. Conte, Chairman/Managing Director
415-834-2350
Fax: 415-834-2383
e-mail: jpconte@gencap.com
Education: MBA, Harvard Graduate School of Business; BA Colgate University
Background: NTC Group, Drexel Burnham Lambert, Chase Manhattan Bank
Directorships: BioSource International, PRA International
Ryan Clark, President/Managing Director
Education: AB, Environmental Science & Public Policy, Harvard College; MBA, Harvard Business School
Background: Associate, Hellman & Friedman
Katie Solomon, Managing Director/Talent Management
Education: BA, American Studies, MA, English, Stanford University; MBA, Stanford Grad. School of Business
Background: Vice President, Vector Capital; Executive Research, Russell Reynolds Associates; Marketing, Harvard Business School Career Services; Consultant, Bain & Company
Directorships: Global Investment Banking Recruitment Department, Robertson Stephen
Anthony Salewski, Managing Director
Education: Harvard College; MBA, Harvard Business School
Background: Chief of Staff, Operations, Barclays Global Investors; Associate, Hellman & Friedman
Directorships: MidCap Financial, TravelCLICK, International Aluminum Corporation
Rob Rutledge, Managing Director
Education: BComm, Queen's University; MBA, Stanford University
Background: Associate, Investment Banking, Salomon Smith Barney
Directorships: Woods Equipment Corporation, Confie Seguros, Voice Construction
Eli Weiss, Managing Director
Education: Yale University; MBA, Stanford Graduate School of Business
Background: Associate, Hellman & Friedman LLC; Greenhill & Co.
Directorships: Evolution1, Insurity, IAS

---

824 **GEODESIC CAPITAL**
950 Tower Lane
Suite 1100
Foster City, CA 94404

Phone: 650-781-0400
e-mail: info@geodesiccap.com
web: www.geodesiccap.com

Mission Statement: A venture capital firm investing in technologies. Geodesic Capital is dedicated to maintaining a strong connection between Sillicon Valley and Japan.

Geographic Preference: California, Japan
Founded: 2015
Investment Criteria: Early-Stage
Industry Group Preference: Technology, Applications, Hospitality, Media, Entertainment
Portfolio Companies: Airbnb, Tanium, Looker, Uber, Databricks, Duo, Netskope, Orbital Insight, Invision, Pindrop, Snapchat, Thoughtspot, Instartlogic

Key Executives:
  John Roos, Partner/Co-Founder
  Education: AB, Political Science, Stanford University; JD, Stanford Law School
  Background: Senior Advisor, Centerview Partners; CEO, Wilson, Sonsini, Goodrich & Rosati
  Directorships: Salesforce.com; Sony
  Ashvin Bachireddy, Partner/Co-Founder
  Education: BS, Management Science, University of California, San Diego
  Background: Head of Growth Stage Investing, Andreessen Horowitz; VC Invester, Lightspeed Venture Partners; VC Investor, 3i Group; VC Investor, JMI Equity; Investment Banker, Montgomery & Co.; Investment Banker, Salomon Smith Barney
  Nate Mitchell, Partner
  Education: Dartmouth College
  Background: Vulcan Capital; Index Ventures; Draper Fisher Jurvetson; Summit Partners
  Charlie Friedland, Partner
  Education: BA, Economics, Dartmouth College
  Background: Ipsy; Summit Partners; Morgan Stanley
  Jon Rezneck, Partner/Chief Operating Officer
  Education: MBA, Finance, Wharton School, University of Pennsylvanial; AB, Economics & East Asian Studies, Harvard College
  Background: Investment Banker, Greenhill & Co.; Investment Banker, JP Morgan & Co.
  Directorships: Business Development, Crowley Technologies
  Matt Fuller, Partner
  Education: MA, LBJ School of Public Affairs, University of Texas; Pepperdine University
  Background: National Security Council; Coalition Provisional Authority Administrator L. Paul Bremer's Special Assistant
  Morgan Livermore, Partner
  Education: BA, Government, Dartmouth College
  Background: Investor, Accel; Investment Banket, Vista Point Advisors
  Susie Roos, Partner/Chief Administrative Officer
  Education: AB, Stanford University; JD, University of Southern California
  Background: Co-Founder, The TOMODACHI Initiative
  James Kondo, Senior Advisor
  Education: BA, Keio University; Visiting Student, Brown University; MBA, Harvard Business School; World Fellow, Yale University
  Background: Co-Chairman, Silicon Valley Japan Platform; President, Rebuild Japan Initiative Foundation; Visiting Scientist, MIT Media Lab; VP, Twitter Inc.

---

825 GEORGIA OAK PARTNERS
The Office Tower at the Four Seasons
75 14th St. NE
Suite 2150
Atlanta, GA 30309

Phone: 404-961-7201
web: www.georgiaoakpartners.com

Mission Statement: Georgia Oak Partners is a highly differentiated investment platform focused on growth private equity investments in the Southeast US. Our model uniquely combines operational and financial expertise throughout the investing process: from deal sourcing, to strategic appraisal, to post-acquisition value creation. We believe our strategic approach and operational philosophy can generate long-term stakeholder value through the spectrum of business lifecycles, from turnaround situations to acquisition growth strategies.

Geographic Preference: Southeast
Average Investment: $5 - $20 million
Investment Criteria: Control Buyouts, Co-Investments, Minority Equity, Debt-for-Equity
Industry Group Preference: Business Products & Services, Transportation, Logistics, Consumer Services, Consumer Products, Restaurants, Manufacturing, Niche Manufacturing, Packaging, Building Materials & Services
Portfolio Companies: Farm Burger, Sailfish Boats, Spectrum Staffing, TeamOne Logistics, Your Pie

Key Executives:
  Michael A. Lonergan, Managing Partner
  Education: BBA, Finance & Management, Terry College of Business, University of Georgia
  Background: Vice President, Strategic Value Partners; Sun European Partners; Houlihan Lokey; Wells Fargo
  Doug Fisher, Partner
  Education: MBA, Emory University Goizueta Business School; MA, Terry College of Business, University of Georgia
  Background: Director of Finance
  David Barr, Director
  e-mail: dbarr@georgiaoakpartners.com
  Background: Chairman, Samuels Jewelers; Price Waterhouse
  Directorships: Your Pie, Del Frisco's Restaurant Group, BrightStar Care, The Spice & Tea Exchange, Capriotti's Sandwich Shops, Bistro Group, PMTD Restaurants

---

826 GERKEN CAPITAL ASSOCIATES
110 Tiburon Boulevard
Suite 5
Mill Valley, CA 94941

Phone: 415-383-1464 Fax: 415-383-1253
web: www.gerkencapital.com

Mission Statement: Investment firm and alternative asset fund manager specializing in private equity investment products.

Geographic Preference: Europe
Fund Size: $1.5 billion
Founded: 1989
Investment Criteria: LBO, MBO
Industry Group Preference: Data & Analytics, Financial
Portfolio Companies: Datalink, Infinite English, Sapiens Data Science, Zympay

Key Executives:
  Lou Gerken, Founder/Chief Executive Officer
  e-mail: lou@gerkencapital.com
  Education: University of Redlands; American Graduate School; MBA, Southern Methodist University Graduate School of Business
  Background: Managing Director & Group Head, Prudential Securities Technology; Montgomery Securities; Wells Fargo Capital Markets; Founder, TCG International; Senior Research Analyst, GT Capital Management
  Anthony J. Moore, Managing Director
  e-mail: anthony@gerkencapital.com
  Education: MA, Cambridge University; MBA, Finance & Accounting, Kellogg School of Management, Northwestern University
  Background: Wells Fargo Institutional Investments; Bankers Trust Company; Ziegler Securities; Northern Trust Company

Venture Capital & Private Equity Firms / Domestic Firms

827 GGV CAPITAL
3000 Sand Hill Road
Building 4
Suite 230
Menlo Park, CA 94025

Phone: 650-475-2150 Fax: 650-475-2151
web: www.ggvc.com

Mission Statement: GGV Capital leads venture capital investments across the United States and China.

Geographic Preference: United States, China
Fund Size: $2.6 billion
Founded: 2000
Average Investment: $5 - $25 million
Investment Criteria: All Stages
Industry Group Preference: Software, Internet, Digital Media & Marketing, Gaming, Marketing, Mobile, Cloud Computing
Portfolio Companies: 1More Design, 21Vianet, 7k7k, AAC Technologies, Aero, Affirm, Airbnb, Agora.io, Alibaba, AlientVault, Allume, Appirio, athenahealth, AvidBots, Baobao, BigCommerce, BingoBox, BitSight Technologies, BlackLake Technology, BlueKai, Brightwheel, Bowery Farming, Boxed, Buddy Media, Bustle Digital Group, CashShield, CDG, Chaoli, China Talent Group, Chukong Technologies, Chushou TV, Citrus Lane, Citybox, CityShop, Clobotics, Conviva, Curse, Diandian Yangche, Didi Chuxing, DOMO, Douguo, DraftKings, Drive.ai, EHANG, Electric, Endeca, Evolv, Farmland Keeper, FlightCar, Flipboard, Function of Beauty, Giphy, Giska, Gladly Software, Global Scanner, Glow Concept, Glu Mobile, Grab, GrubMarket, Haitunjia, HaoHaoZhu, HashiCorp, Hello ChuXing, Heptagon/AMS, HotelTonight, Houzz, Ibotta, Immotor, Iris Nova, Isilon, IWJW, Keep, Kingsoft WPS, Kintana, Ku6, Kuaidian, Kujiale, LAIX, Lambda School, Light Chaser, Lively, MediaV, Meicai, Meihua, Meili/Mogu, Misfit, Moka, Musical.ly, Namely, Netli, Netscaler, New Knowledge, Nimble Storage, NIU, Nozomi, NS1, OfferUp, OpenDoor, Pactera, Pandora, P-Cube, Peloton, Percolate, Petkit, Philm, Phoenix Labs, Phononic, PlushCare, Poshmark, Qpass, QuinStreet, Quixey, Qunar, Reebonz, Shiftgig, Shoppo, SinoSun Technology, Slice, SkyStream Networks, Slack, SmartMI, Social Touch, SoundCloud, Square, Structo, SuccessFactors, Synack, Tangdou, The Mighty, ThinCI, Tile, Tujia, Turbine, u51.com, UCWeb, Unravel Data, Vincross, Vocera, Wish, XCharge, Xfire, Xiangwushuo, Xiaohongshu, Xiaomi, Xiaozhan, Xinshang, Xpeng Motors, Yamibuy, Yellow, Yingying, Yodo1, Youku Tudou, Yummt Life, Yunmanman, YY, Zendesk, Zepp, Zhaoyou, Zimi, Zuiyou, Zuoyebang

Other Locations:
70 South Park St.
San Francisco, CA 94107
Phone: 650-475-2150 Fax: 650-475-2151

Unit 1806, Tower West, Genesis Beijing
No. 8 Xinyuan South Road
Chaoyang District
Beijing 100027
China
Phone: 86-1059897988

Unit 3501, Two IFC
8 Century Avenue, Pudong District
Shanghai 200120
China
Phone: 86-2161611720 Fax: 86-2154035580

Key Executives:
Jixun Foo, Managing Partner, Shanghai
Education: MSc, National University of Singapore
Background: Director, Draper Fisher Jurvetson ePlanet Ventures; Hewlett Packard
Jenny Lee, Managing Partner, Shanghai
Education: BSc, MS, Engineering, Cornell University; MBA, Kellogg School of Management, Northwestern University
Background: Singapore Technologies Aerospace; Morgan Stanley; JAFCO Asia
Directorships: eHang Technology, Yingying Finance, 51zhangdan, Xiaozhan
Eric Xu, Managing Partner, Shanghai
Education: Shanghai University; Master of Finance, University of Manchester School of Business
Background: Managing Director, SIG Investment Asia; Investment Professional, CITIC Capital; TDF Capital
Directorships: Zhaoyou, Cityshop, BingoBox, Citybox, Xinshang
Jeff Richards, Managing Partner, Silicon Valley
Education: BA, Government, Dartmouth College
Background: VP, Digital Content Services, VeriSign; Founder & CEO, R4 Global Solutions, Founder, QuantumShift
Directorships: Appirio, Boxed, Percolate, Reebonz, Tile
Glenn Solomon, Managing Partner, Silicon Valley
Education: BA, MBA, Stanford University
Background: General Partner, Partech International; Goldman Sachs; SPO Partners
Hans Tung, Managing Partner, Silicon Valley
Education: BS, Industrial Engineering, Stanford University
Background: Qiming Venture Partners; Bessemer Venture Partners; HelloAsia; Asia2B
Directorships: Wish, Xiaohongshu, GrubMarket, Totspot, FlightCar, Curse
Stephen Hyndman, Partner/CFO, Shanghai
Education: BS, Commerce, JD, Santa Clara University
Background: CFO, Prospero Ventures; CFO, ASCII Corporation
Erica Yu, Principal, Beijing
Education: Zhejiang University
Background: Senior Associate, China Renaissance Partners

828 GI PARTNERS
188 The Embarcadero
Suite 700
San Francisco, CA 94105

Phone: 415-688-4800 Fax: 415-688-4801
e-mail: info@gipartners.com
web: www.gipartners.com

Mission Statement: GI Partners' private equity and real estate groups work closely with portfolio investments to help them realize their full potential.

Portfolio Companies: Access, AdvoServ, Consilio & Advanced Discovery, California Cryobank Life Sciences, Daxko, Digital Reality, Doxim, Duckhorn, Far Niente, First Republic Bank, Flexential, Kellermeyer Bergensons Services, Ladder Capital, The Linc Group, Logibec, MRI Software, Netsmart, Plum, Softlayer, Telx, Together Work, Viawest, Wave, Waypoint Homes

Key Executives:
Rick Magnuson, Executive Managing Director
Education: BA, Dartmouth College; MBA, Stanford Graduate School of Business
Background: Director of Investment Banking, Merrill Lynch & Co.; Founder of Interactive Software
Directorships: Flexential, Far Niente Wine Estates, CenterPoint Properties Trust
David Smolen, Managing Director, General Counsel, Chief Compliance Oficer
Education: BA, International Relations, MA, Political Science, Stanford University; JD, Stanford Law School
Background: Senior Counsel & Chief Compliance Officer, Silver Lake; General Counsel, CFO & COO, Fort Mason Capital
Dave Kreter, Managing Director
Education: BA, Economics, Princeton University; MBA, Harvard Business School
Directorships: Logibec, Netsmart Technologies, California Cryobank Life Sciences

Venture Capital & Private Equity Firms / Domestic Firms

David Mace, Managing Director
Education: BA, Economics, Dartmouth College; MBA, Harvard School of Business
Directorships: Flexential, Far Niente Wine Estates
Howard Park, Managing Director
Education: BA, Rice University; MBA, Tuck School of Business, Dartmouth College
Directorships: Logibec, Netsmart Technologies, California Cryobank Life Sciences
Travis Pearson, Managing Director
Education: BA, MA, Duke University; JD, Harvard Law School
Background: Bain & Company
Directorships: Togetherwork, Doxim, Flexential, Logibec, MRI Software, Daxko
John K. Saer Jr., Managing Director
Education: AB, Economics, Dartmouth College; MBA, Stanford Graduate School of Business
Background: CFO, KSL Recreation Corporation
Directorships: CalEast Global Logistics, CenterPoint Properties
Philip Yau, Managing Director
Education: BA, Princeton University; MBA, Northwestern University
Background: UBS Private Funds Group
Hoon Cho, Managing Director
Education: BA, Princeton University; MBA, Harvard Business School
Directorships: Kellermeyer Bergensons Services, Access, Consilio

829 GIC GROUP
4328 Montgomery Ave.
Bethesda, MD 20814

Phone: 301-799-0840
e-mail: info@gicgroup.com
web: www.gicgroup.com

Mission Statement: Provides clients in agrobusiness and biotech with resources to reach their potential.
Investment Criteria: Later Stage, Expansion, Early Stage, Startup/Seed
Industry Group Preference: Biotechnology, Financial Services, Agribusiness
Key Executives:
Richard Gilmore, President/CEO
Education: MA, International and Development Economics, Johns Hopkins University; PhD, International Economics/Trade, Graduate Institute of International Studies

830 GIDEON HIXON FUND
2476 Lillie Ave.
Summerland, CA 93067

Phone: 805-962-2277 x11 Fax: 805-565-0929
web: www.gideonhixon.com

Mission Statement: The Gideon Hixon Fund is a venture capital investment fund representing the interests of the extended Hixon family. We take a long-term traditional approach to venture capital investing by supporting passionately committed entrepreneurs with visions of revolutionizing industries and by building strong lasting businesses. Our investment philosophy perpetuates the principals of Gideon Cooley Hixon-principles honored for six generations. The Gideon Hixon Fund believes that investors and entrepreneurs must align to build great companies, which ultimately will make the world a better place.
Geographic Preference: United States
Average Investment: $500,000 - $1.5 million
Investment Criteria: All Stages
Industry Group Preference: Biosciences, Biotechnology
Portfolio Companies: Boom Entertainment, Capella, Edufii, Genbad, Blycos Biotechnologies, Hansen Engine, Boka Sciences, Igrok, Illumitex, Instructure, Prolacta Bioscience, Shotspotter, Percona, Zadspace
Other Locations:
315 East Commerce Street
Suite 300
San Antonio, TX 78205
Phone: 210-225-3053 Fax: 210-225-5910
Key Executives:
Frank H Foster, Managing Partner
Education: BS, Harvard University; MBA, Harvard Business School
Background: Managing Director, DFJ Frontier; Venture Partner, Southern Cross Venture Partners; General Partner, Allen & Buckeridge
Directorships: Hixon Properties, Boka Sciences, Edufii, Prolacta Biosciences, Buyology, Predixion Software, Onsert Media
Dylan Hixon, Managing Partner
Education: BS, Yale University; MS, Mechanical Engineering, California Institute of Technology
Background: President, Arden Road Investments; PCI; Reel EFX
Debra P Geiger, General Partner
Education: BS, University of Colorado; JD, Santa Barbara College of Law
Background: Consultant, Santa Barbara District Attorney's Office
Eric Hixon, General Partner
Education: BS, , MS, Computer Science, New York University
Background: Founder, WebCal; Yahoo Mail; Torque Systems
Bryan Simpson Jr., General Partner
Education: BS, University of North Carolina; JD, University of Florida
Background: CEO/Chairman, Medcom Services; Chairman, Hixon Properties Inc.
Directorships: Compass Bank

831 GILBERT GLOBAL EQUITY PARTNERS
767 Fifth Avenue
15th Floor
New York, NY 10153-0028

Phone: 212-584-6200 Fax: 212-584-6211

Mission Statement: Makes private equity and equity-related investments in both public and private companies around the world, seeking attractive opportunities across global markets and industries.
Geographic Preference: United States, Europe, Latin America, Asia-Pacific
Fund Size: $1.2 billion
Founded: 1997
Average Investment: $20 to $150 million
Minimum Investment: $20 million
Investment Criteria: Mezzanine, LBO, MBO
Industry Group Preference: Telecommunications, Infrastructure, Optical Technology, Industrial Services, Consumer Services, Internet Technology, Business to Business, Networking
Portfolio Companies: Amkor Technology, CPM Holdings, Montpelier Re Holdings, Olympus Re Holdings, True Temper
Other Locations:
P.O. Box 984
New Canaan, CT 06840
Phone: 203-966-6022 Fax: 203-972-0250
Key Executives:
Steven J. Gilbert, Chairman
e-mail: sgilbert@gilbertglobal.com
Education: Wharton School; Harvard Law School; Harvard Business School
Background: Founder, Soros Capital; Founder, Commonwealth Capital Partners; Founder, Chemical

Venture Capital & Private Equity Firms / Domestic Firms

Venture Partners; EF Hutton International; Wertheim & Company; Morgan Stanley & Co.
Richard W. Gaenzle Jr., Partner
e-mail: rgaenzle@gilbertglobal.com
Education: Hartwick College; Fordham Graduate School of Business
Background: Soros Capital; PaineWebber
Jeffrey W. Johnson, Partner
e-mail: jjohnson@gilbertglobal.com
Education: Claremont McKenna College; Harvard Business School
Background: Soros Capital; Frank Russell Company; Goldman, Sachs & Company; Hallmark Cards
Steven Kotler, Partner
e-mail: skotler@gilbertglobal.com
Education: City College of New York
Background: President/CEO, Schroder & Company; Co-Head, Investment and Merchant Banking Activities Worldwide

832 GLADSTONE CAPITAL
1521 Westbranch Drive
Suite 100
McLean, VA 22102
Phone: 703-287-5800
e-mail: information@gladstonecompanies.com
web: www.gladstonecompanies.com

Mission Statement: The Gladstone Companies invests in small to middle-market companies based in the United States. The firm provides capital and traditional debt financing to businesses in a broad range of sectors, including industrial products, specialty manufacturing, transportation, specialty chemicals, media and communications, and business, healthcare and energy services.

Geographic Preference: United States
Fund Size: $280 million
Founded: 2001
Average Investment: $5 - $30 million
Minimum Investment: $5 million
Investment Criteria: Second Lien, Subordinated, Mezzanine
Industry Group Preference: Service Industries, Manufacturing, Distribution, Specialty Manufacturing, Media, Communications, Business Products & Services, Government Services, Consumer Products, Healthcare Services, Transportation, Specialty Chemicals, Energy Services
Portfolio Companies: ACME Cryogenics, Ag Trucking, Allison Publications, Alloy Die Casting, BAS Broadcasting, B-Dry, Behrens Manufacturing, Brunswick Bowling Products, B+T Group, Cambridge Sound Management, Circuitronics, Channel Technologies Group, Counsel Press, Country Club Enterprises, Danco Machine, Defiance Stamping Company, Drew Foam Companies, Edge Adhesives Holdings, Flight Trampoline Parks, Francis Drilling Fluids, Frontier Packaging, Galaxy Tool Corporation, GFRC Cladding Systems, GI Plastek, Ginsey Holdings, Head Country, Heartland Communications Group, JackRabbit, J.America, Legend Communications of Wyoming, Lignetics, LogoSportswear, Mathey Dearman, Meridian Rack & Pinion, Mikawaya, Mitchell Rubber Products, NDLI Logistics, Nth Degree, Old World Christmas, Precision, Precision Southeast, Profit Systems, Quench USA, Reliable Biopharmaceutical Corporation, Saunders & Associates, SBS Industries, Schylling, SOG Specialty Knives & Tools, Southern Petroleum Laboratories, Star Seed, Stellar Outdoor Media, StrataTech Education Group, Sunburst Media-Louisiana, Sunshine Media Holdings, Tread Corporation, United Flexible, Vision Government Solutions, WadeCo Specialties, Westland Technologies

Other Locations:
245 Park Avenue
39th Floor
New York, NY 10167
Phone: 203-661-1397
200 South Wacker Drive
Suite 3100
Chicago, IL 60606
17 E Gabilan Street
Salinas, CA 93901
Phone: 831-225-0883

Key Executives:
David Gladstone, Founder/Chairman/CEO
Education: BA, Government & Economics, University of Virginia; MA, American University; MBA, Harvard Business School
Background: Chairman, American Capital Strategies; Chairman & CEO, Allied Capital Corporation; Allied Capital Lending Corporation; Allied Capital Commercial Corporation; Allied Capital Advisors; President, CEO & Director, Business Mortgage Investors
Directorships: Capital Automotive REIT
Terry Brubaker, Vice Chairman/COO
703-287-5820
e-mail: terry.brubaker@gladstonecapital.com
Education: BSE, Aerospace & Mechanical Sciences, Princeton University; MBA, Harvard Business School
Background: Chairman & Founder, Heads Up Systems; VP, Paper Group, American Forest & Paper Association; President, Interstate Resources; President, IRI; James River Corporation; Strategic Planning & Marketing Manager, Boise Cascade; Senior Engagement Manager, McKinsey & Company
David Dullum, Director/President/Executive Managing Director, Private Equity
703-287-5891
e-mail: david.dullum@gladstonecompanies.com
Education: BME, Georgia Institute of Technology; MBA, Stanford Graduate School of Business
Background: Partner, New England Partners; Managing General Partner, Frontenac Company
Laura Gladstone, Managing Director, Gladstone Capital
212-792-4187
e-mail: laura.gladstone@gladstonecompanies.com
Education: BBA, George Washington University
Background: Associate, Equity Research, ING Barings; Assistant Analyst, Salomon Smith Barney
Erika Highland, Managing Director, Gladstone Investment
703-287-5840
e-mail: erika.highland@gladstonecompanies.com
Education: BS, Business Administration, Boston College
Background: Account Executive, Wells Fargo Retail Finance; Financial Analyst, AG Edwards
Kyle Largent, Senior Managing Director, Gladstone Investment
703-287-5880
e-mail: kyle.largent@gladstonecompanies.com
Education: BSBA, University of Tulsa; MBA, Georgetown University
Background: VP, National Capital; Associate Analyst, Research, Friedman Billings Ramsey
Christopher Lee, Managing Director, Gladstone Investment
703-287-5887
e-mail: christopher.lee@gladstonecompanies.com
Education: BA, MBA, Georgetown University
Background: VP, MCG Capital; Consultant, KPMG Consulting

833 GLASSWING VENTURES
275 Newbury St.
Boston, MS 02116
e-mail: info@glasswing.vc
web: glasswing.vc

Venture Capital & Private Equity Firms / Domestic Firms

Mission Statement: Glasswing Ventures in an early stage venture capital firm that invests in artificial intelligence and technology startups.
Geographic Preference: East Coast
Investment Criteria: Early-Stage
Industry Group Preference: Artificial Intelligence, SaaS, Technology, Cybersecurity
Portfolio Companies: Allure Security Technology, Armored Things, Autit, Base Operations, BotChain, ChaosSearch, Devcon Detect, Elsy, Terbium Labs, Zylotech
Key Executives:
  Rudina Seseri, Founder/Managing Partner
  e-mail: rudina@glasswing.vc
  Education: BA, Wellesley College; MBA, Harvard Business School
  Directorships: AUTIT, Celtra, ChaosSearch, CrowdTwist, Inrupt, Plannuh, SocialFlow, Talla, Zylotech
  Rick Grinnell, Founder/Managing Partner
  e-mail: rick@glasswing.vc
  Education: BS, MS, MIT; MBA, Harvard Business School
  Background: Managing Director, Fairhaven Capital
  Directorships: Allure Security, Armored Things, Terbium Labs
  Sarah Fay, Managing Partner
  e-mail: sarah@glasswing.vc
  Education: BA, University of Vermont

834 GLENCOE CAPITAL
444 N Michigan Avenue
Suite 2970
Chicago, IL 60611

Phone: 312-795-6300 **Fax:** 312-795-6301
web: www.glencap.com

Mission Statement: Targets control investments in lower middle-market companies.
Geographic Preference: United States, Canada
Fund Size: $789 million
Founded: 1993
Minimum Investment: $7 million
Investment Criteria: Lower Middle Market, Lead-Sponsored Acquisitions, Growth Equity
Industry Group Preference: Consumer Products, Industrial Equipment, Food & Beverage, Chemicals, Financial Services, Business to Business, Media
Portfolio Companies: Allegra Direct Communications, Budco, Campbell Grinder Company, Child Development Schools, Dialogue Marketing, Dixie Chemical Company, Fortis Energy Services, NOVO 1, Polyair Inter Pack
Other Locations:
  36700 Woodward Avenue
  Suite 107
  Bloomfield Hills, MI 48304
Key Executives:
  David S. Evans, Chairman/CEO/CIO
  Education: BGS, University of Michigan; MBA, University of Chicago Graduate School of Business
  Background: M&A Specialist, Donaldson, Lufkin & Jenrette; Associate Director, Growth Capital Foundation, University of Michigan
  Paul Smith, Managing Director
  Education: BS, Miami University; MBA, Kellogg School of Management
  Background: W.W. Grainger Inc.; General Electric
  Scott Mygind, Vice President, Finance/IT
  Education: BA, Finance/Economics, University of Illinois
  Background: Director of Financial Planning/Analyst, LKQ Corporation; Orbitz Worldwide; Whitehall Jewelers; Electronic Data Systems
  Nicholas Iovino, CCO/Vice President, Accounting
  Education: BA, Wesleyan University; CPA
  Background: Portfolio Accountant, Aurora Investment Management LLC; Senior Fund Accountant, Woodfield Fund Administration; Financial Services Tax Associate, McGladrey

835 GLENGARY LLC
25200 Chagrin Boulevard
Suite 300
Beachwood, OH 44122

Phone: 216-378-9200
e-mail: shaynes@glengaryllc.com

Mission Statement: Glengary combines an unparalleled network of support services with investment capital. The initial investment in an early-stage company is typically made after its product or service has been validated in the market. The firm then works with its leadership to achieve mutually-defined milestones before participating in follow-on rounds of financing.
Average Investment: $100,000 - $1.5 million
Minimum Investment: $100,000
Investment Criteria: Early-Stage
Industry Group Preference: Healthcare, Information Technology, Applied Technology, Business Products & Services
Portfolio Companies: Cardinal Commerce, Cleveland HeartLab, Connected Living Inc., Guardian Technologies, Germguardian, Juventas Therapeutics, Monarch Teching Technologies Inc., Neuros Medical Inc., On Shift, Predictive Service, Procuri, SupplierInsight, ToolingU
Key Executives:
  Stephen R Haynes, Founder/Chairman/Managing Partner
  Education: BS, Accountancy, Miami University; CPA
  Background: General Partner, Key Equity Capital; Kirtland Capital; Corporate Finance, McDonald & Company Securities
  Directorships: Cleveland HeartLab

836 GLENTHORNE CAPITAL
200 West Lancaster Avenue
Suite 206
Wayne, PA 19087

Phone: 610-688-6313 **Fax:** 610-688-3410
e-mail: dkollock@glenthornecapital.com
web: www.glenthornecapital.com

Mission Statement: Assists company owners and senior management groups to successfully meet the important strategic challenges of today's changing markets by providing financial advisory and investment banking services.
Geographic Preference: North America, Europe, South America
Founded: 1984
Average Investment: $1 million
Minimum Investment: $250,000
Investment Criteria: Mezzanine, LBO, MBO
Industry Group Preference: Chemicals, Life Sciences, Transportation, Packaging, Financial Services, Manufacturing, Medical
Portfolio Companies: Adco Technologies, Adco Products Inc, American Mirrex, Asplundh Tree Expert Co., Colorcraft Packaging, Crane Company, Heritage Inks International, Houghton International Inc, IMI Express, Inco Limited, Industrial Valley Title, Island Chemical, Lavino Shipping Company, Michael Huber Gmbh, Pecora Corporation, Philadelphia Financial Group, Public Financial Management, Quality Coach Inc., Resco Products Inc., Stixi Ag, Tasty Banking Company, Teleflex Inc., Thatcher Tubes, Valquip Corporation
Key Executives:
  David P Kollock, Founder/Managing Director
  e-mail: dkollock@glenthornecapital.com
  Education: BS, MBA, Wharton School of the University of Pennsylvania
  Background: American Mirrex Corporation; JM Huber

Venture Capital & Private Equity Firms / Domestic Firms

Company; CoreStates Financial; Towers Perrin Forester; Selby Battersby & Company
Roy C. Carriker, PhD, Director
e-mail: roy@global-advisors.net
Education: BS, MS, PhD, Physics, Washington State University
Background: Vice Chairman, Teleflex Inc.; Founder & Chairman, Global Advisors LLC
Directorships: Indivers BV
Craig N. Johnson, Advisory Director
Education: BS, Engineering, University of Pennsylvania; MBA, Wharton School
Background: President & CEO, Lavino Shipping Company
Directorships: Blair Corporation

837 GLOBAL CATALYST PARTNERS
530 Lytton Ave.
2nd Floor
Palo Alto, CA 94301

Phone: 650-486-2420 Fax: 650-560-6218
e-mail: plans@gc-partners.com
web: www.gc-partners.com

Mission Statement: Global Catalyst Partners is an international, multistage, technology-oriented venture capital firm. Our partners have significant operating experience serving in large public companies as well as building entrepreneurial ventures into major public companies.
Geographic Preference: United States, China, Israel, Japan
Investment Criteria: All Stages
Industry Group Preference: Technology
Portfolio Companies: Actelis Networks, Advanced Micro-Fabrication Equipment, Beceem Communications, Greenfield Networks, KargoCard, SoundHound, Newport Media, P-Cube, Teranetics, Velio, Verient

Other Locations:
1-1-1 Minami-Aoyama Minato-Ku
West Wing 7F
Tokyo 107-0062
Japan
Phone: 81-3-6455-5950 Fax: 81-3-6455-5950

Key Executives:
Kamran Elahian, Chairman/Co-Founder
Education: BS, Computer Science, BS, Mathematics, MS, Engineering, Computer Graphics, University of Utah
Background: Co-Chair, UNDESA-gAID
Directorships: SoundHound
Koji Osawa, Managing Principal/Co-Founder
Education: BS, Electronics, Keio University; PhD, Engineering, Tohoku University
Background: Mitsubishi Corporation
Directorships: Verient, KargoCard, Advanced Micro-Fabrication Equipment, SoundHound
Vijay C Parikh, Managing Principal
Education: BSEE, Birla Institute of Technology & Science; MBA, University of Michigan
Background: President, StratumOne Communications
Directorships: KargoCard, Verient
Arthur Schneiderman, Principal & Co-Founder
Education: Beloit College; JD, University of Wisconsin Law School
Background: Partner, Wilson Sonsini Goodrich & Rosati

838 GLOBAL ENVIRONMENT FUND
2 Bethesda Center
Suite 440
Bethesda, MD 20814

Phone: 240-482-8900 Fax: 301-656-1612
web: gefcapital.com

Mission Statement: To be the premier alternative asset management firm in the domain of energy and environment by delivering favorable risk-adjusted invested returns to our limited partners over multiple vintage years and through varied macroeconomic climates.
Geographic Preference: United States, China, India, Brazil, Turkey, Mexico, South Africa
Founded: 1990
Industry Group Preference: Renewable Energy, Energy Efficiency, Environment Products & Services, Forestry, Food & Agriculture
Portfolio Companies: Afram Plantation Limited, AGV Logistica, America Latina Logistica, athena Controls, Aurora Flight Sciences, Blue Ridge ESOP Associates, Blue Ridge Numerics, Cantaloupe Systems, Cape Pine Investment Holdings, CHAINalytics, ComRent, Concord Enviro, Dentistanbul, Dequingyuan, Derive Systems, Duoyuan, Empresas Verdes Argentina, Essex, Euromedic, Geodex Communications, Global Forest Products, Global Woods, Greenergy, Greenko, Gro-Well Brands, Haverfield, Hijauan Bengkoka, Imvelo Forests, indian Energy Exchange, IClean, IHC, Kalkitech, KEYW, Kilombero Valley, Knight & Carver Wind Group, Luminae, MAEH, Monte Alto Forestall, Mozwood, Neogas, Niko Resources Ltd., Peak Timbers, Pemba Sun and Mozwood, Product Software Development, Ramanas Farms, Red Ambiental, Renew Power, Reva, Rishabh Instruments, Rocklands, Saisudhir, Sanepar, Sensicast, Shakti, Signature Control Systems Inc., SPG Solar, Tecverde, Terszol, Unirac, UPC Renewable, Xymetrex

Other Locations:
WeWork, C20 - G Block
Bandra Kurla Complex
Bandra East
Mumbai 400051
India
Phone: 91-22-4445-1139

Rua Pais de Araujo, 29
14th Floor
Sao Paulo, SP 04531-090
Brazil
Phone: 55-11-3073-0444

Key Executives:
H Jeffrey Leonard, President/Founding Partner/CEO
Education: BA, Harvard University; MS, London School of Economics; PhD, Princeton University
Background: VP, World Wildlife Fund; VP, Conservation Foundation; Chairman, International Pepsi-Cola Bottlers Investments
Directorships: Global Forest Products
John Earhart, Chairman/Founding Partner
Education: BS, California State University; MA, Forestry, Yale School of Forestry and Environmental Studies
Background: Senior Fellow, World Wildlife Fund; Sr Fellow, Conservation Foundation; Associate Director, Peace Corporation
Alexandre Alvim, Managing Director, Sao Paulo
Education: BS, Electrical Engineering, Universidade Estadual de Campinas; MBA, Kellogg School of Management, Northwestern University
Background: Co-Founder/Managing Partner, Greentech Capital
Directorships: Energy & Business Development, Estre Ambiental
Scott MacLeod, Managing Partner
Education: BA, Yale University; MBA, Columbia University Graduate School of Business
Background: Division Manager, Finance Corporation
Stuart Barkoff, Managing Director/COO
Education: AB, Vassar College; JD & MBA, Emory University
Background: Attorney, Arnold & Porter LLP
Sridhar Narayan, Managing Director, GEF Advisors India
Education: Post Graduate Diploma, Management, Indian Institute of Management; Bachelor of Technology, Mechanical Engineering, Indian Institute of Technology

Venture Capital & Private Equity Firms / Domestic Firms

Background: JRE Partners; American International Group; Zurich Asset Management India
Daniel Prawda, Managing Director
Education: BA, Economics & International Relations, Tufts University
Background: ACON Investments; Latin America Corporate Finance Group, JP Morgan
Directorships: Gro-Well Brands Inc.
Anibal Wadih, Managing Director
Education: BS, Electrical Engineering, Universidad Simon Bolivar; MA, Finance, IESA; MBA, NYU Stern School of Business
Background: Managing Director, MacQuarie Capital; M&A, Deutsche Bank
Steve Guffey, Chief Financial Officer
Education: BBA, Accounting, James Madison University; CPA
Background: Assistant Controller, The Carlyle Group
Marta De La Cruz, Executive Services Associate
Education: BA, Marketing, Bernard Baruch College, Zicklin School of Business
Nupur Jalan, Vice President, GEF Advisors India
Education: BS, Computer Applications, University of Bangalore; MBA, Narsee Monjee Institute of Management Studies
Background: GE Capital
Raj Pai, Managing Director
Education: BS, Computer Engineering, University of Bombay; MA, Computer Science, Arizona State University; MBA, University of Chicago
Background: Managing Director, CID Capital
Katie Vasilescu, Chief Compliance Officer
Education: BA, Anthropology, University of Maryland
Background: Office Manager, GEF
Aditya Arora, Principal
Education: BComm, University of Calcutta; MBA, Indian School of Business
Background: Investment Manager, Navis Capital; JM Financial
Lisa Schule, Managing Director
Education: BA, Amherst College; JD, Georgetown University School of Law
Background: Vice President, Perseus LLC; PECO Energy
Derek Beaty, Principal
Education: BS, Accounting, University of Illinois; MBA, Kellogg School of Management, Northwestern University; CPA
Background: CIVC Partners; M&A, BMO Capital; M&A, Arthur Andersen
Nick Morriss, Senior Investment Partner, Managed Accounts
Education: BA, Economics, University of York
Background: Co-Founder & Managing Partner, EMAlternatives; Coopers & Lybrand
Justin Heyman, Principal
Education: BS, Economics, Wharton School, University of Pennsylvania; MBA, Columbia Business School
Background: Senior Associate, Oliver Wyman; Investor Growth Capital
Alipt Sharma, Principal
Education: BA, Economics, Shri Ram College of Commerce, Dehli University; MBA, Indian School of Business
Background: AMP Capital Investors; Ambit Corporate Finance; Arthur Andersen; Ernst & Young

839 GLOBESPAN CAPITAL PARTNERS
One Boston Place
Suite 2810
Boston, MA 02108

Phone: 617-305-2300
web: www.globespancapital.com

Mission Statement: Invests in Internet, mobile, IT infrastructure and SaaS businesses. Globespan Capital Partners is dedicated to establishing partnerships with entrepreneurs and helping companies to realize their potential.

Geographic Preference: Worldwide
Average Investment: $250,000 - $15 million
Investment Criteria: Early-Stage, Middle-Stage, Late-Stage
Industry Group Preference: Information Technology, Internet, Mobile Technology, Clean Technology, Communications, Software, Systems & Peripherals
Portfolio Companies: Analogix, BitSight, Coskata, Credit Sesame, Gild, Kaminario, Linden Lab, MarketLive, Nantero, Nominum, OpenSpan, Overture Networks, Pelican Imaging, Perfecto Mobile, Redfin, Rev, Roku, Silicor Materials, SMS GupShup, Solar Silicon Technology, Sonics, SundaySky, Upwork, VMTurbo, ZeaChem

Other Locations:
300 Hamilton Avenue
Palo Alto, CA 94301

Key Executives:
Andy Goldfarb, Co-Founder/Executive Managing Director
Education: AB, East Asian Studies & Economics, Harvard College; MBA, Harvard Business School
Background: Senior Managing Director, JAFCO Ventures; Founder & Director, TN Ventures; Corporate Development, Kikkoman Corporation
Directorships: Gild, Nominum, Overture Networks, Pelican Imaging, Redfin, Rev, SundaySky
Dave Fachetti, Managing Director
Education: BBA, University of Massachusetts, Amherst; MBA, Boston University, CPA
Background: Principal, JAFCO Ventures; SVP, Sales & Marketing, Family Education Network; SVP, Business Marketing, Trans National Group
Directorships: BitSight, Credit Sesame, Kaminario, Nantero, OpenSpan, Perfecto Mobile
Steve Wood, Chief Financial Officer
Education: BS, University of Vermont; MBA, Carroll School of Management, Boston College

840 GLYNN CAPITAL MANAGEMENT
3000 Sand Hill Road
Building 3, Suite 230
Menlo Park, CA 94025

Phone: 650-854-2215
web: www.glynncapital.com

Mission Statement: An investment management firm that focuses on generating substantial long-term capital gains for a small number of individual high-net-worth clients.

Fund Size: $50 million
Founded: 1970
Average Investment: $500,000
Minimum Investment: $250,000
Investment Criteria: Companies that can grow 20% of revenue and profits annually
Industry Group Preference: Business Products & Services, Medical & Health Related, Electronic Technology, Software, Digital Media & Marketing, Internet
Portfolio Companies: Intel, Electronic Arts, Sun Microsystems, Facebook, Linkedin, Palantir, Pure Storage, Cloudera, Dropbox, Etsy, Oscar, Domo, VS, Nimble Storage, Bonobos, Birchbox, Responsys, Suumologic, DocuSign, Redfin, Radius, OpenDNS, Financial Engines, SalesforceIQ, Xoom, Zappos.com, Okta, Evernote, Dataminr, The Climate Corporation, Giphy, Bigpanda, Rhumbix, Science37, Kalo, SeatGeek, Couchbase

Key Executives:
John W. Glynn, Founder & Managing Director
Education: BS, University of Notre Dame; JD, University of Virginia; MBA, Stanford University
Background: General Partner, Lamoreaux, Glynn Associates; Special Partner, New Enterprise Associates
Directorships: Molecular Design, The Learning Company

Venture Capital & Private Equity Firms / Domestic Firms

Steven J Rosston, Managing Director
Education: Harvard University; MBA & JD, Stanford University
Background: Product Manager, ROLM
Carl T Anderson, Managing Director
Education: BA, Economics, Princeton University; MBA, Stanford University Graduate School of Business
Background: Partner, Stonebrook Fund Management; AllAdvantage.com
Jacqueline Glynn, Managing Director
Education: Davidson College; MBA, Darden Graduate School of Business, University of Virginia
Background: Analyst, Alex Brown & Sons; Roberton Stephens
Sarah Rogers, Chief Operaring & Compliance Officer
Education: BA, Philosophy, Princeton University; MFA, University of Iowa; MBA, Stanford Graduate School of Business
Background: Lecturer, College of Business, University of Iowa; Director, Hawkinson Institute of Business Finance; Co-Founder, West Lake Partners
Scott Jordon, Managing Director
Education: University of California, Berkeley; MBA, Stanford University Graduate School of Business
Background: Associate, Westbrook Partners; Senior Analyst, Morgan Stanley, Hong Kong
David Glynn, President/Managing Director
Education: University of Notre Dame; MBA, Stanford Graduate School of Business
Background: Eric Gotland Management
Vivian Loh Nahmias, Chief Financial Officer
Education: MBA, Santa Clara University
Background: Consultant, RMC Group
John Fogelsong, Managing Director
Education: BS, Computer Science, Stanford University; MBA, Stanford University Graduate School of Business
Background: Co-Founder & CEO, Wearit; Zazzle.com

841 GOAHEAD VENTURES
Menlo Park, CA

web: www.goaheadvc.com

Mission Statement: GoAhead Ventures strives to work with entrepreneurs in the earliest stages of their company. They enjoy working with students and recent graduates, believing that young entrpreneurs possess a transformative ability when building a company.

Key Executives:
Clancey Stahr, Managing Partner
Education: BS, Stanford University
Background: ZenShin Capital
Phil Brady, Managing Partner
Education: BS, Stanford University
Background: Founder, Copernican Solutions; Andreessen Horowitz
Takeshi Mori, Managing Partner
Education: BS, University of Tokyo; MS, Stanford University
Background: Co-Founder/Managing Director, ZenShin Capital; VP, OnFiber Communications Inc.

842 GOENSE & COMPANY LLC
850 West Adams Street
Chicago, IL 60607

Phone: 312-870-9511
web: www.goense.com

Mission Statement: Goense & Company is an entrepreneurial, Chicago-based private equity firm which seeks to partner with dynamic management teams to make control investments in and help grow smaller middle market businesses & services companies.

Geographic Preference: United States, Canada
Founded: 2008
Average Investment: $5 - $30 million
Investment Criteria: Industry Cosolidations, Family-Owned Business Transactions, Shareholder Liquidity, Leveraged or Mangement Buyouts, Growth Equity
Industry Group Preference: Business Products & Services
Portfolio Companies: Bayview Financial, BKA Restoration, Capital Drywall, Crosscom National, ER Experts, Imagine Technology Group, Kirby Lester Group, Melco Electric, Response Team 1, US Builder Services, Latite Roofing & Sheetmetal Company

Key Executives:
John M. Goense, Partner
312-543-2721
e-mail: jmg@goense.com
Education: MBA, University of Chicago; BS, Accounting/Business Administration, Aquinas College
Background: Managing Partner, Goense Bounds & Partners; Founder/President, Heller Equity Capital Corporation; Managing Director, Allstate Insurance Company; Harris Bank; Co-Founder/Manager, American Paging; Kidder Peabody & Company
Directorships: Indian Head Industries, Imagine Technology Group, Bayview Financial, BSI Holdings
Erik W. Bloom, Partner
312-870-9511
e-mail: ewb@goense.com
Education: BA, Economics/Business Administration, Vanderbilt University; MBA, Wharton School, University of Pennsylvania
Background: Managing Parnter, Goense Bounds & Partners; Allstate Private Equity; Management Consultant, Bain & Company; Continental Illinois Venture Corporation
Directorships: Barjan Products, L&S Plumbing, Norcraft Industries, Sportcraft, USA Media

843 GOLDEN GATE CAPITAL
One Embarcadero Center
39th Floor
San Francisco, CA 94111

Phone: 415-983-2700 Fax: 415-983-2701
web: www.goldengatecap.com

Mission Statement: A leading private equity firm that generates superior returns for our investors through buyout and growth equity investments across a wide variety of industries.

Fund Size: $12 billion
Investment Criteria: Buyouts, Growth Equity
Industry Group Preference: Software, Information Technology, Semiconductors, Electronics, Retailing, Restaurants, Consumer Products, Financial Services, Media, Industrial Services
Portfolio Companies: Aeroflex, Apogee, Appleseed's, Aspect Software, Atrium, Attachmate Group, Blair, B-Line, California Check Cashing Stores, California Pizza Kitchen, Cedarcrestone, Celetronix, Clover, Coldwater Creek, Conexant, Critigen, Crosstown Traders, Cydcor, Data Direct, Devcon, Draper's & Damon's, Eddie Bauer, Employer's Direct Insurance Company, Endurance Specialty Insurance, Ep Minerals, Escalate, Ex Libris, Express, Eye Care Centers Of America, Inc., Gxs, Haband, Hansen, Herbalife, Infor, Interstate, Itronix, J. Jill, Jazz Pharmaceuticals, Lantiq, Lawson, Lexicon, Macaroni Grill, Massif, Max Media, Micro Focus, National Warranty Corporation, Neways, Next Model Management, Norm Thompson, On The Border, Oncore Manufacturing Services, Orchard Brands, Pacific Sunwear, Payless, Pinnacle Security, Plantcml, Rocket Dog, Sierra Systems, Signstorey, Symon, Teridian Semiconductor, Tollgrade, U.S. Silica, Vistec Semiconductor Systems, Wellco, Zale

Key Executives:
David Dominik, Managing Director
Education: AB, Harvard College; JD, Harvard Law School

Venture Capital & Private Equity Firms / Domestic Firms

Background: Manging Director, Bain Capital; Investment Committee, Brookside
Robert Kirby, Managing Director
Education: BS, Chemical Engineering, University of New Hampshire
Background: CEO, Atrium; CEO, Vi-Jon; CEO, Accellent
Felix Lo, Managing Director
Education: AB, Public Policy, Brown University
Background: Bain Capital
Steve Oetgen, Managing Director
Education: BS, Accountancy, University of Illinois; JD, Georgetown University Law Center
Background: Senior Partner, Kirkland & Ellis LLP
Dave Thomas, Managing Director
Education: BBA, Finance, University of Notre Dame
Background: Senior Associate Consultant, Bain & Company

844 GOLDEN PINE VENTURES
201 West Main Street
Suite 300
Durham, NC 27701

Phone: 919-473-9296
e-mail: information@goldenpineventures.com
web: www.goldenpineventures.com

Mission Statement: Golden Pine Ventures is a venture capital firm that targets companies in the biotechnology and biomedical fields. The firm identifies companies developing revolutionary technologies and helps to create value for these businesses.

Geographic Preference: North Carolina, Southeast United States
Founded: 2004
Industry Group Preference: Life Sciences, Biotechnology, Biomedical
Portfolio Companies: Arcato Laboratories, Kylin Therapeutics, Pique Therapeutics
Key Executives:
   Christopher S Meldrum, Managing Director
   Education: BA, Chemistry, University of Utah; MBA, Carlson School of Management, University of Minnesota
   Background: Director, Corporate Alliances, Paradigm Genetics; Licensing Associate, Purdue University
   John E Hamer PhD, Director
   Education: PhD, Microbiology, University of California, Davis
   Background: Burrill & Company; CSO & CEO, Paradigm Genetics; Professor, Biological Sciences, Purdue University
   James A Severson PhD, Director
   Education: BS, Zoology, PhD, Physiology, Iowa State University
   Background: VP, Global Networks for Veratect Corporation; President, Cornell Research Foundation; Amersham Corporation; President, Association of University Technology Managers

845 GOLDEN SEEDS
FDR Station
Box 642
New York, NY 10150

Phone: 888-629-6774
e-mail: info@goldenseeds.com
web: www.goldenseeds.com

Mission Statement: Golden Seeds is an investment group dedicated to supporting women entrepreneurs. Golden Seeds consists of an angel investing network as well as venture funds that focus on early stage growth companies.

Geographic Preference: United States
Founded: 2005
Average Investment: $250,000 - $2 million
Investment Criteria: Early Stage
Industry Group Preference: Consumer Products, E-Commerce & Manufacturing, Financial Services, Life Sciences, Social Media, Technology
Portfolio Companies: AboutOne, Amplyx Pharmaceuticals, Avaxia Biologics, Bergen Medical Products, Bespoke Global, Cabinet M, Chromis Fiberoptics, Cisse Cocoa, Cognition Therapeutics, Consensus Point, Crimson Hexagon, Dancing Deer Baking, Day One Response, Dry Soda, DxUpClose, Eachwin Capital, EpiEP, Gracious Eloise, Groupize, Gummicube, HarQen, Hatsize, HitFix, Kalion, Lark, Little Passports, Little Pim, Lovesac, Microenergy Credits, ModuMetal, NovaTract Surgical, nVision Medical, Open Road Media, OtoNexus, Paradigm4, Playrific, Plum Perfect, Poshly, ProSeeder, Rapt Media, RenovoRx, RuMe, Saladax, Shareablee, Source4Style, Sweetriot, Sylvatex, Tempo Automation, The Alberleen Group, TowerCare Technologies, United Catalyst, Wisegate, Work Truck Solutions, Zenflow
Key Executives:
   Ao Ann Corkran, Managing Partner
   Education: BS, Mathematics, New York University
   Background: Global Head, Cash & Short Duration, Credit Suisse; Consulting Actuary, Econometric Modeling Area, Buck Consultants
   Directorships: Crimson Hexagon
   Loretta McCarthy, Managing Partner
   Education: BA, University of Arizona; MBA, University of Colorado
   Background: Executive VP & CMO, Oppenheimer Funds; VP, Marketing, American Express
   Peggy Wallace, Managing Partner
   Education: BA, George Washington University
   Background: JP Morgan Chase

846 GOLDMAN SACHS INVESTMENT PARTNERS
200 West Street
New York, NY 10282

Phone: 212-902-1000
web: www.gsipventures.com

Mission Statement: Goldman Sachs targets late stage and growth equity companies with a focus on consumer and business technologies.

Geographic Preference: United States
Fund Size: $4 billion
Investment Criteria: Late Stage, Growth Equity
Industry Group Preference: Consumer, Business, Technology
Portfolio Companies: Baozen, Boqii, BOSS, Cadre, Care/of, CompareAsia, Compass, Doctor on Demand, FabHotels, Facebook, Fluid, foodpanda, GoEuro, Hubba, M-Service, Meican, Networks Insights, NextNav, Outcome Health, Pinterest, Plaid, Ring, ResearchGate, Shift, SMS Assist, Spotify, Tarena, thredUp, Uber, Zola

847 GOLDNER HAWN
3700 Wells Fargo Center
90 S 7th Street
Minneapolis, MN 55402

Phone: 612-338-5912
e-mail: reporting@goldnerhawn.com
web: goldnerhawn.com

Mission Statement: Investment philosophy is based on flexibility, patience, and the desire to deliver those resources that will make each portfolio company successful.

Geographic Preference: Mid-West
Fund Size: $200 million
Founded: 1989
Minimum Investment: $25 million
Investment Criteria: Middle-market companies that have sound performance records, high growth potential and distinct market advantages

Venture Capital & Private Equity Firms / Domestic Firms

Industry Group Preference: Business Products & Services, Consumer Services, Industrial Products, Distribution, Consumer Products, Food & Beverage, Manufacturing, Transportation, Niche Manufacturing
Portfolio Companies: Allen Edmonds Shoe Corp., American Engineered Components, American Lock, Animart LLC, Applied Adhesives, Bankers Systems, Byerly's, Cameron's Coffee & Distribution Co., Claire-Sprayway, Control Devices LLC, Crescent Sleep Products, CTM Group Inc., Deltak, Hartzell Manufacturing, Havco Wood Products, Houlihan's Restaurants Inc., Imperial Plastics Inc., Jacobson Machine Works, Knutson Mortgage, Lancaster Laboratories, Mark VII Equipment, Michael Foods, Mid-America Entertainment, Mid Valley Industries LLC, North America Central School Bus LLC, Petermann Bus Co., Quest Events LLC, Samuel Lawrence Furniture Co., Specialty Commodities Inc., Stellar Materials LLC, Stouse LLC, Transport Corp. of America Inc., Union Metal, Universal Turbine Parts LLC, VICORP Restaurants, Vitality Foodservice, Western Reserve Products, Westlake Hardware Inc., Wilson Leather, Woodcrafts Industries

Key Executives:
Timothy D. Johnson, Partner
612-347-0161
e-mail: johnson@goldnerhawn.com
Education: Denison University; Kellogg School of Management, Northwestern University
Background: Group VP, First Bank System; Corporate Finance, JP Morgan
Directorships: American Engineered Components, Woodstuff Manufacturing
Chad M. Cornell, Partner
612-347-1070
e-mail: cornell@goldnerhawn.com
Education: Marquette University; University of Pennsylvania Law School; CPA; CFA
Background: Corporate Development Group, Medtronic Inc.; Corporate Lawyer, Sidley Austin
Jason T. Brass, Partner
612-347-0172
e-mail: brass@goldnerhawn.com
Education: University of St. Thomas, University of Notre Dame Mendozza College of Business
Background: Norwest Equity Partners; Arthur Andersen
Directorships: Specialty Commodities, Westlake Hardware
Joseph H Heinen, Partner
612-347-0171
e-mail: heinen@goldnerhawn.com
Education: Knox College
Background: Corporate Development Group, Arthur Andersen
Directorships: Transport America, Remmele Engineering

848 GOLUB CAPITAL
200 Park Avenue
25th Floor
New York, NY 10166

Phone: 212-750-6060 Fax: 212-750-3756
web: www.golubcapital.com

Mission Statement: Invests in both privately and publicly held businesses, opportunistically selecting industries and geographic locations in which to invest; provides subordinated debt and equity capital to middle-market companies.
Geographic Preference: United States
Fund Size: $20 billion
Founded: 1994
Average Investment: $40 million
Minimum Investment: $10 million
Investment Criteria: Revenues in excess of $20 million, EBITDA margins greater than 10%, experienced management team, proprietary market positions, products with strong growth potential

Industry Group Preference: Consumer Products, Consumer Services, Manufacturing, Distribution, Media, Retailing, Healthcare, Food Services, Aerospace, Defense and Government, Healthcare Services, Restaurants
Other Locations:
4 Embarcadero
Suite 1400
San Francisco, CA 94111
Phone: 415-766-3549

150 S Wacker Drive
5th Floor
Chicago, IL 60606
Phone: 312-205-5050 **Fax:** 312-201-9167

130 Harbour Place
Suite 340
Davidson, NC 28036
Phone: 980-231-5657
Key Executives:
Lawrence E. Golub, Founder & Chief Executive Director
e-mail: lgolub@golubcapital.com
Education: AB, Economics, Harvard University; MBA, Harvard Business School; JD, Harvard Law School
Background: Editor, Harvard Law Review; Managing Director, Bankers Trust Company; Managing Director, Wasserstein Perella & Co; Officer, Allen & Company; Chairman, Mosholu Preservation Corporation; Treasurer, White House Fellows Foundation; President, Harvard JD-MBA Alumni Association
David B. Golub, President
e-mail: dgolub@golubcapital.com
Education: AB, Government, Harvard College; MPhil, International Relations, Univ. of Oxford; MBA, Stanford Graduate School of Business
Background: Managing Director, Centre Partners Management LLC
Gregory W. Cashman, Head of Direct Lending
e-mail: gcashman@golubcapital.com
Education: BS, Commerce, University of Virginia; MBA, Darden School of Business
Background: Manager Business Development, Bristol-Myers Squibb Consumer Products Division; Sr. Accountant, Arthur Andersen & Company
Andrew H. Steuerman, Vice Chair, Direct Lending & Golub Growth
e-mail: asteuerman@golubcapital.com
Education: BBA, Finance, Pace University; MBA, Finance, St. John's University
Background: Managing Director, Albion Alliance; Vice President, Bankers Trust Alex Brown
Gregory A. Robbins, Vice Chair
Education: BS, Economics, Wharton School, University of Pennsylvania
Background: Officer, Golub Capital BDC Inc.; VP, Merchant Banking Group, Indosuez Capital; Associate, Saw Mill Capital
Alissa Grad, Vice Chair & Chief Client Officer
Education: BS, American Labor History, Cornell University
Background: Head of Marketing & Investory Relations, Jemmco Capital
Directorships: Marketing & Investor Relations, D.B. Zwirn & Co.; Business Development, TAG Associates
Pierre-Olivier Lamoureux, CFO, GC Advisors LLC
Education: BBA, Accounting, HEC; MBA, Finance, NYU Stern School of Business; CPA; CFA
Background: VP, Merchant Banking Group, National Bank of Canada; Associate, Putnam Lovell NBF Securities; Associate, Arthur Andersen
Joshua M. Levinson, Co-General Counsel/Chief Compliance Officer
Education: BS, Political Science, Vanderbilt University; JD, Georgetown University Law Center
Background: Counsel, Magnetar Capital; Associate, King & Spalding; Corporate Associate, Wilson Sonsini

Venture Capital & Private Equity Firms / Domestic Firms

Goodrich & Rosati; Associate Editor, Georgetown Law Journal

849 GOOD GROWTH CAPITAL
997 Morrison Drive
Charleston, SC 29403

web: www.goodgrowthvc.com

Mission Statement: Seeks to invest in early-stage technology accelerators.

Geographic Preference: Southeast US, New England
Industry Group Preference: Artificial Intelligence, Clean Tech, Fintech, Cloud Computing, Consumer, Data Science, Electronics, Energy, Green Tech, Health Tech, IoT, Manufacturing, Software, Space Tech, Machine Learning
Portfolio Companies: Aluna, Angiocrine, Ateios, Base Operations, Blue Clean Gear, Bone Health Technologies, Coagulo, Databento, Dynepic, Eden Geotech, EncoraTherapeutics, Fermata, Fisherman, Fluree, Impact Biosystems, Interloop, IRYS, Leuko, Lindy Biosciences, LuminDX, Nala Systems, Obsidio, Orbit Fab, Pienso, Pryon, Questis, Radia, Radical Plastics, Republic, ReviveMed, Rheos, skyhawk Therapeutics, SwiftSolar, The New Primal, Trillbit, Unison, X-COR Therapeutics

Other Locations:
182 Beacon Street
Unit 14
Boston, MA 02116

Key Executives:
Maureen Stancik Boyce, Founder & Managing Partner
Background: Co-Founder/COO, Ignition Ventures; Consultant, Bain & Co.; Associate Partner, IMB
Amy Salzhauer McMarlin, Founder & Managing Partner
Education: MPhil, Cambridge University; AB, Harvard University
Background: CEO, Ignition Ventures
Carolyne Lasala, Managing Partner
Background: Various Roles, Apple
David Mendez, Managing Partner
Background: Co-Founder/Managing Partner, Capital A Partners; Managing Director, Katalyst Venture Partners
John Osborne, Managing Partner
Background: Executive Administrator, Charleston Angel Partners; Co-Founder The Harbor Entrepreneur Center; Founder/CEO, Fundingcharleston.com
Sophie Hagerty, Principal
Education: BA, Harvard University

850 GOTHAM GREEN PARTNERS
489 5th Avenue
Suite 29A
New York, NY 10017

e-mail: info@gothamgreenpartners.com
web: gothamgreenpartners.com

Mission Statement: Invests in companies serving the cannabis industry.

Industry Group Preference: Cannabis
Portfolio Companies: The High Note, Flow Kana, Grow Generation, iAnthus

Key Executives:
Jason Adler, Managing Partner
Background: CEO, Saiers Capital; Managing Partner, Alphabet Ventures
Directorships: Cronos Group
Devin Quarles, Operating Partner
Education: BS, Integrative Biology; MS, Plant Biology, University of Illinois at Urbana-Champaign
Background: Cultivator/IPM Specialist, PureGreens; Operations Manager, MJardin
Michael Henderson-Cohen, Principal
Education: BA, Economics, Colby College; MBA, Columbia Business School
Background: Analyst/Associate, Bear Stearns; VP, JPMorgan; Analyst, Andalusian Capital Partners; Principal, 838 Partners
Daniel Finkelstein, Principal
Education: BSM, A.B. Freeman School of Business, Tulane University
Background: Founder/Owner/Manager, Storyville Spirits Co.; Founder/Owner/Manager, HenryScott Ventures; Sales Consultant, Pacific Solar; Consultant, FTRE; Owner/Principal, Timber Ridge Stable
Directorships: CID Stables

851 GRAHAM PARTNERS
3811 West Chester Pike
Building 2
Suite 200
Newtown Square, PA 19073

Phone: 610-408-0500 Fax: 610-408-0600
web: www.grahampartners.net

Mission Statement: Seeking to invest in privately held middle market industrial companies.

Geographic Preference: United States, Canada, Western Europe
Fund Size: $1.5 billion
Founded: 1988
Average Investment: $50 million
Minimum Investment: $10 million
Investment Criteria: Domestic industrial businesses with revenues between $20-$250 million
Industry Group Preference: Plastics, Business Products & Services, Manufacturing, Industrial Equipment, Building Materials & Services, Transportation, Packaging
Portfolio Companies: Abrisa Technologies, Acme Cryogenics, Anaheim, Asahi Tec/Trimas, The Atlas Group, B+B SmartWorx, Berry, BrightPet Nutrition Group, Chelsea, Comar, Creative Mines, Desser Tire, Dynojet, EasyPak, Eberle, Eldorado Stone, Exteria, HB&G Building Products Inc., HemaSource, Henry, ICG Commerce, Infiltrator Systems, Line-X, The Masonry Group, Mercer Foods, Mitten, NDS, OptConnect, Schneller, SP Industries, Strata, Supreme Corq, Tidel, Transaxle, Universal Pure, Western Industries

Key Executives:
Steven C. Graham, Chief Executive Officer
Education: BA, Philosophy/English, Williams College; MBA, Amos Tuck School of Business, Dartmouth College
Background: Senior Group VP, Graham Packaging Company; Investment Banking Division, Goldman, Sachs & Company; Acquisition Officer, RAF Group
Directorships: Western Industries, National Diversified Sales, Eldorado Stone, HB&G Building Products, Nailite International, ICG Commerce
Bill McKee Jr., Chief Operating Officer
e-mail: bmckee@grahampartners.net
Education: BS, Economics, Wharton School, University of Pennsylvania
Background: Investment Banking Division, Bear Stearns
Directorships: National Diversified Sales, HB&G Building Products, Eldorado Stone
Christopher Lawler, Managing Principal
e-mail: clawler@grahampartners.net
Education: BS, Business Administration, University of Richmond; MBA, Wharton School, University of Pennsylvania
Background: Vice President, Financial Sponsors Gropu, NationsBanc Montgomery Securities; Vice President, NationsBank's Corporate Finance Group
Directorships: Dynojet, Schneller, Supreme Corq, Western Industries
Christina Morin, Managing Principal/Investor Relations
e-mail: cmorin@grahampartners.net
Education: BA, Economics, University of Virginia; MBA, Wharton School, University of Pennsylvania
Background: Investment Banking, Goldman Sachs & Co.;

Venture Capital & Private Equity Firms / Domestic Firms

Borders, Inc.
Directorships: Abrisa, Eldorado, HB&g
Robert Newbold, Managing Principal
e-mail: rnewbold@grahampartners.net
Education: BA, Business Administration, MA, Accounting, University of Texas; MBA, Wharton School, University of Pennsylvania
Background: Private Equity Group, Investcorp; Goldman Sachs & Co.
Directorships: B&B, Dynojet, Eldorado, HB&G, Infiltrator, National Diversified Sales, StormTech, TransAxle
Adam Piatkowski, Managing Principal
e-mail: apiatkowski@grahampartners.net
Education: BA, Economics, Williams College; CFA
Background: Equity Analyst, Monitor Asset Management; Mangement Consultant, Monitor Group
Directorships: Schneller
Andrew Snyder, Managing Principal
e-mail: asnyder@grahampartners.net
Education: BA, Political Science, Amherst College; MBA, Wharton School, University of Pennsylvania
Background: Concert Capital Partners; Adams Harkness Inc.
Directorships: Abrisa, B&B, TransAxle
Joshua Wilson, Managing Principal
e-mail: jwilson@grahampartners.net
Education: BA, Finance, James Madison University
Background: Global Investment Banking Division, Chase Securities
Directorships: Dynojet, Exteria Building Products, HB&G, Infiltrator, Line-X, Supreme Corq, TransAxle
Joseph Heinmiller, Managing Principal
e-mail: jheinmiller@grahampartners.com
Education: BS, Accountancy, Villanova University
Background: Investment Banking Analyst, Banc of America Securities
Directorships: Exteria Building Products, Infiltrator
William Timmerman III, Managing Principal
e-mail: wtimmerman@grahampartners.net
Education: BA, Economics, Vanderbilt University
Background: Director, M&A Group, UBS Securities

852 GRAND CENTRAL HOLDINGS
475 Park Avenue South
4th Floor
New York, NY 10016

Phone: 212-625-9710
web: www.grandcentralholdings.com

Mission Statement: Invests in technology-related businesses, with a fund consisting of ten holdings in the healthcare information, financial service technology and transportation industries.

Geographic Preference: Northeast
Founded: 1999
Average Investment: $1-$3 million
Minimum Investment: $250,000
Industry Group Preference: Healthcare Information Technology, Financial Services, Transportation
Portfolio Companies: Castle Connolly, Ez-Ways.Com, Free Decision, Japan Internet Ventures, MedEViewing, Online Benefits, Peanutpress.Com, Performance Logic
Key Executives:
   Gregory C. Belmont, Managing Partner
   Education: MIT; Harvard University
   Background: Arthur D Little; Mercer Management Consulting; The Wilkerson Group

853 GRANDBANKS CAPITAL
75 Second Avenue
Suite 360
Needham, MA 02494

Phone: 781-997-4300 Fax: 781-997-4301
e-mail: info@grandbankscapital.com
web: www.grandbankscapital.com

Mission Statement: To offer operating expertise and industry experience, build successful companies, and secure long-term capital gains. GrandBanks Capital seeks opportunities with early stage companies in the software, security, mobile media, financial technology, wireless technology and Internet technology sectors. The firm primarily invests in businesses based in the eastern region of the United States.

Geographic Preference: East Coast
Fund Size: $125 million
Founded: 2000
Average Investment: $1 - $5 million
Minimum Investment: $1 million
Investment Criteria: Early Stage
Industry Group Preference: Infrastructure, Software Services, Security, Media, Financial Services, Wireless Technologies, Internet Technology, Storage, Software, Mobile Media, Wireless Services, Fintech
Portfolio Companies: Achievers, Celtra Technologies, Clearfit, Coherent Path, Defense Mobile, Dispatch, EachScape, Knowledge Vision, SilverRail Technologies, TIM Group
Key Executives:
   Charles R Lax, Co-Founder/Managing General Partner
   Education: BS, Boston University
   Background: Founding General Partner, SOFTBANK Venture Capital; VP, SOFTBANK Holdings; Venture Partner, VIMAC Ventures; Co-Founder, Flatiron Partners; Phoenix Technologies
   Directorships: Defense Mobile, GlassHouse Technologies, KnowledgeVision, SilverRail Technologies, TIM Group
   Tim Wright, General Partner
   Education: BS, City University, London
   Background: CEO, International Operations, Geac Computer Corporation; Senior VP, CTO & CIO, Terra Lycos SA; Senior VP & CIO, The Learning Company
   Directorships: Celtra, Achievers, EachScape, Nexage, Coherent Path, Bison, TechStars Boston, ClearFit
   Jeffrey P Parker, Venture Partner
   Education: Bachelor & Master of Engineering, MBA, Cornell University
   Background: Founder, Technical Data Corporation; Founder, First Call Corporation; Chairman & CEO, Thomson Financial; Co-Founder, 38 Newbury Ventures; Co-Founder, Chairman & CEO, CCBN.com
   Directorships: KnowledgeVision, First Coverage
   JJ Healy, Venture Partner
   Education: BS, Chemistry, Saint Anselm College; MBA, International Finance, American Graduate School of International Management
   Background: VP, Corporate Development, Yahoo!; Principal, Von Gehr International; VP, Credit Suisse First Boston; EMC Corporation

854 GRANITE BRIDGE PARTNERS
420 Lexington Avenue
Suite 920
New York, NY 10170

Phone: 646-599-9900
e-mail: info@granitebridge.com

Mission Statement: Private equity firm that seeks to invest in and build successful middle-market companies.

Founded: 1991
Average Investment: $10-$30 million
Minimum Investment: $8 million

Venture Capital & Private Equity Firms / Domestic Firms

Investment Criteria: Expansion, Consolidation, Recapitalizations
Industry Group Preference: Services, Consumer Products, Manufacturing
Portfolio Companies: All Island Media, American Higher Educaion Development, Best Lighting Products, Century Fire Protection, Custom Wood Products, Freedom Scientific, Integrated Cable Assembly Holdings, MariTEL, Microdynamics Group, Mitchell Gold + Bob Williams, Phelps Industries, Smiles Services, Teraco
Key Executives:
   Peter Petrillo, Managing Partner
   Education: MBA, New York University; BS, Accounting, State University of New York Albany
   Background: Partner, Claymore Partners, Vice President, Lambert Brussels Capital Corporation; CPA
   Michael D Goodman, Partner
   Education: MBA, New York University; BS, Economics, Cornell University
   Background: Principal, Equinox Investment Partners, Vice President, Chase Manhattan Bank
   Ryan Wierck, Partner
   Education: MBA, Columbia Business School; BS Economics, Wharton School, University of Pennsylvania
   Background: Oppenheimer & Co - M&A and Corporate Finance Departments
   Jeffrey P Gerson, Partner
   Education: BA, History, University of Pennsylvania; MBA, MIT Sloan School of Management
   Background: Associate, Lane, Berry & Co.; Associate, Rhone Capital LLC; Analyst, Salomon Smith Barney

855 GRANITE EQUITY PARTNERS
122 12th Avenue North
Suite 201
St. Cloud, MN 56303
   Phone: 320-251-1800 **Fax:** 320-251-1804
   e-mail: rick@graniteequity.com
   web: www.graniteequity.com

Mission Statement: Private equity firm seeking co-ownership for portfolio companies in industrial companies focused on energy and manufacturing.
Geographic Preference: Minnesota, Wisconsin, Iowa, North Dakota, South Dakota
Founded: 2002
Investment Criteria: Companies with at least $5 million of revenue, Buyouts, Recapitalizations, Business Expansions and managers who have proven track records
Industry Group Preference: Manufacturing, Service Industries, Media, Distribution, Agriculture, Communications
Portfolio Companies: Aeration Industries, All Flex, Altimate Medical, Dezurik, GeoComm, Geotek, Massman Automation, Microbiologics, Vector
Other Locations:
   Calhoun Beach Club
   2925 Dean Parkway
   Suite 300
   Minneapolis, MN 55416
   Phone: 612-925-8350 **Fax:** 612-925-8320
Key Executives:
   Richard Bauerly, Managing Partner/CEO
   e-mail: rick@graniteequity.com
   Education: MA, Business Administration, Harvard Business School; MA, Public Administration, Harvard University; BA, Economics, Saint John's University
   Background: Founder, Venture Allies; Bauerly Brothers Incorporated; Deloitte & Touche Consulting Group
   Directorships: DeZurik Water Controls; UniqueScreen Media; Anderson Entrepreneurial Center; CentraCare Health System
   Patrick Edeburn, Partner
   Education: MA, Business Administration, Harvard Business School; BA, Carleton College
   Background: Medtronic; Deloitte & Touche Consulting Group
   Directorships: Vinylite Windows; Heartland Communications; Anderson Entrepreneurial Center
   Arthur Monaghan, Senior Advisor
   e-mail: art@graniteequity.com
   Education: BA, University of Notre Dame
   Background: Principal, Norwest Equity Partners; Arthur Andersen's Management Consulting Group
   Directorships: Heartland Communications; UniqueScreen Media; Vinylite Windows

856 GRANITE HILL CAPITAL PARTNERS, LLC
750 Battery St.
Suite 400
San Francisco, CA 94111
   Phone: 415-903-1457
   web: www.granitehill.net

Mission Statement: Granite Hill India Opportunities Fund is a venture and growth equity fund focused on India-related as well as selected High Tech investment opportunities. The fund is distinguished by the deep operating experience, investment track record, and the strong business network of the Partners. The three investment professionals have over 40 years of total investment and operating experience in Silicon Valley and India. India's economic growth, along with the wide range of private business which need to scale to meet robust demand, provides a unique opportunity for investment returns. In particular, we believe Financial Services, High Tech, Sustainability and Education are among the most promising verticals.
Geographic Preference: India, United States,
Industry Group Preference: Technology, Financial Services, Retail, Consumer & Leisure, Sustainability, Life Sciences
Portfolio Companies: Airspace, Aptus, Arceo Analytics, Attero Recycling, The Beer Café, CL Educate, Craxel, Efflux Systems, Imubit, Manappura, NAFA, nCrypted Cloud, Netcitadel, Orange Retail Finance India, Palantir, Seed Infotech, SentinelOne, Tamr, Treatful
Key Executives:
   Shailesh Mehta, General Partner
   e-mail: shailesh@granitehill.net
   Education: BS, Mechanical Engineering, IIT-Bombay; PhD, Operations Research, Case Western Reserve
   Background: Chairman and CEO, Providian Financial; Executive VP, AmeriTrust (now KeyCorp); Operating General Partner, WestBridge Capital
   Sameet Mehta, Managing General Partner
   e-mail: sameet@granitehill.net
   Education: BS, Electrical Engineering, Princeton; MBA, Stanford University
   Background: Cisco; Lehman Brothers
   Kamil Hassan, General Partner
   e-mail: kamil@granitehill.net
   Education: MS, Engineering, MIT; PhD, Engineering, UC Berkeley
   Directorships: America India Foundation

857 GRANITE VENTURES
300 Montgomery Street
Suite 638
San Francisco, CA 94104
   Phone: 415-591-7700 **Fax:** 415-591-7720
   web: www.granitevc.com

Mission Statement: Partners with promising and successful entrepreneurs to create businesses that have a competitive edge and achieve category leadership.
Geographic Preference: United States
Fund Size: $1 billion
Founded: 1998
Average Investment: $500,000 - $4 million

Venture Capital & Private Equity Firms / Domestic Firms

Investment Criteria: Seed, Series A & B, Early-Stage
Industry Group Preference: Technology, Application Software
Portfolio Companies: Agilence, Airbnb, AirPair, Anaplan, Aspen Avionics, Blockcypher, Fastback Networks, HireVue, Hobo Labs, HyTrust, Kindly, Kity, Lucideworks, Marqeta, Mojo Networks, Motiv, SellPoints, Smule, Survios, Telltale Games, Workboard, Arcot Systems, Auditude, AvantGo, Bidclerk, Bunchball, Cardiff Software, Connected, Convio, Digimarc, DigitalThink, Direct Medical Knowledge, Empowered Careers, Entropic Communications, Episodic, Five Across, Fractal Design, Fulcrum Microsystems, GigaNet, InfoGear Technology, Internap, Kontiki, Liquent, LSSi Data, Managing Editor, Mixamo, Navini Networks, NetBoost, Nexabit Networks, Oversight Systems, Ozmo, Percello, Plumtree, PSS Systems, Purisma, Quantance, Salon.com, Sense, Shutterly, Siebel Systems, Sierra Wireless, Skytide, SnapTrack, Speakeasy, StepUp Commerce, Symplified, Trovix, Tumbleweed Communications, Vignette, Virage

Key Executives:
Chris McKay, Managing Director
e-mail: cmckay@granitevc.com
Education: BA, University of Virginia
Background: Hambrecht & Quist
Directorships: HireVue, Lucidworks, Marqeta, Arcot Systems, Purisma, Sendmail, Symplified
Standish O'Grady, Managing Director
e-mail: sogrady@granitevc.com
Education: BSE, Chemical Engineering, Princeton University; MBA, Dartmouth College Tuck School of Business Administration
Background: Hambrecht & Quist
Directorships: Anaplan, Telltale Games, HyTrust, SellPoint
Jackie Berterretche, Managing Director/CFO
e-mail: jackieb@granitevc.com
Education: BS, Accounting, University of San Francisco; CPA
Background: CFO, Hambrecht & Quist Venture Capital; Audit Manager, Ernst & Young

858 GRANTHAM CAPITAL
5335 Wisconsin Ave. NW
Suite 400
Washington, DC 20015

Phone: 202-495-5939
web: www.granthamllc.com

Mission Statement: Grantham Capital makes select investments in US-based small businesses where we can provide significant value.
Geographic Preference: United States
Investment Criteria: Small Businesses
Industry Group Preference: Healthcare Services, Medical Devices, Infrastructure, Logistics, Business Services, Distribution, Transportation, Light Manufacturing
Portfolio Companies: Capstone Logistics, EDI, Energy Source, Fisk, Image Ware Systems, Intra Links, Iridian Technologies, NDS, Pharma Logic, Quantum Medical Imaging, Raleigh, Superior Recreational Products, Tegra Medical, Wave

Key Executives:
William Ford, Managing Partner
e-mail: bford@granthamllc.com
Education: BS, St. Lawrence University; MBA, Tuck School of Business, Dartmouth College
Background: SVP & Managing Director, MCG Capital; Managing Director, Perseus LLC; VP, Butler Capital Corp.; Price Waterhouse; General Electric
Michael Van Vleck, Managing Partner
202-247-0673
e-mail: mvanvleck@granthamllc.com
Education: BS, University of New Hampshire; MA, University of Pennsylvania; MBA, Wharton School
Background: Co-Founder & President, GeoGlobal Energy; Founder, Integra Partners

859 GRAPHENE VENTURES
530 Lytton Avenue
2nd Floor
Palo Alto, CA 94301

web: www.graphenevc.com

Mission Statement: Graphene bring strength, tranparency, and flexibility to their projects. They propel tech startups towards growth and maximize their returns.

Key Executives:
Nabil Borhanu, President and Managing Member
Education: MBA
Background: Guest Speaker; Entrepreneur

860 GRAY GHOST VENTURES
2200 Century Parkway
Suite 100
Atlanta, GA 30345

Phone: 678-365-4700 Fax: 678-365-4752
e-mail: info@grayghostventures.com
web: www.grayghostventures.com

Mission Statement: Gray Ghost Ventures is dedicated to investing in early-stage businesses who seek to serve low-income communities in developing nations.
Geographic Preference: India, South Asia, Sub-Saharan Africa
Fund Size: $100 million
Founded: 2005
Average Investment: $5 million
Investment Criteria: Start-Ups, Early-Stage
Industry Group Preference: Microfinance, Clean Technology, Information Technology
Portfolio Companies: Babajob, Beam, bKash, CellBazaar, d.light, Emergence BioEnergy, iSend, mDhil, M-Kopa, Movirtu, ParaLife, PharmaSecure, Range Networks, RentBureau, SourceTrace Systems, United Villages

Other Locations:
8/16, Seethammal Extension
2nd Cross Street
Chennai 600 018
India

Key Executives:
Arun Gore, President/Chief Executive Officer
Education: BSc, Sciences, BS, Accounting, MBA, Finance
Background: CFO, T-Mobile USA
Ashwini Sahasrabudhe, Chief Financial Officer
Education: BComm, University of Mumbai; CPA; CA
Background: Larsen & Toubro; Western Union; Marico Industries; Mattel & Ashok Piramal Group
Brian Cayce, Vice President, Investments
Education: BA, University of Georgia; MBA, Finance, Georgia State University
Background: Benevolink; Deputy Director, CARE International; Consultant, KPMG
Brenda Bracken, Treasurer
Education: Virginia Commonwealth University
Background: Controller, Robert Pattillo Properties; AP DW Industrial Portfolio; American Resurgens Management Corporation; Fleitz Construction Company; Weyman & Kruse; Graphic Ads
Bahniman Hazarika, Director of Investments
Education: BComm, Accounting, Shriram College of Commerce, University of Delhi; MBA, Finance and Accounting, Emory University
Background: Viscogliosi Brothers; Navigation Capital Partners; Ernst & Young

Venture Capital & Private Equity Firms / Domestic Firms

861 GRAYHAWK CAPITAL
4250 N Drinkwater Blvd
Suite 300
Scottsdale, AZ 85251

Phone: 602-956-8700
web: www.grayhawkcapital.us

Mission Statement: Invests in early stage and growth stage companies based in the southwestern region of the United States. Grayhawk Capital seeks companies with outstanding management teams and innovative product offerings in quickly growing technology markets.

Geographic Preference: Southwestern United States
Fund Size: $70 million
Founded: 2000
Average Investment: $1 - $15 million
Minimum Investment: $1 million
Investment Criteria: Early Stage, Growth Stage
Industry Group Preference: Financial Services, Consumer Products, Software, Internet Technology, Telecommunications, Healthcare Information Technology, Semiconductors, Business to Business, Cloud Computing, Mobile, Security
Portfolio Companies: Account Now, Alianza, AppsFreedom, Apptentive, BlueCedar, BroadHop, Camstar, CareFx, CellzDirect, Coinstar, Communispace, Efficient Networks, Environmental Support Solutions, eVisit, Folloze, Golfnow, Horizon Organic Dairy, Health Outcomes Sciences, Innovasic, Intesource, Itax Group, Lucid Software, MarketTools, MX Logic, Myriad Genetics, New Century Financial Corporation, P-Com, Plastc, PowerQuest, Profitect, Quality Care Solutions, Response Analytics Inc., Ribbit, Ryver, Siverion, Small Box Energy, SOCi, StackIQ, SyncHR, Totango

Key Executives:
  Sherman I Chu, Co-Founder/Managing Partner
  Education: BS, Marketing, University of Arizona; MBA, Texas A&M University
  Background: Partner, Cornerstone Equity Partners; Assistant VP, Banc One Capital Partners
  Directorships: AccountNow, Intesource, TM International
  Brian N Burns, Co-Founder/Managing Partner
  Education: BS, Accounting, Arizona State University; CPA
  Background: VP, SunVen Capital; Anderson & Wells; VP & CFO, Pinnacle West Capital Corp.; Senior Manager, Audit Division, Arthur Andersen & Co.
  Directorships: AppsFreedom, Innovasic, TM International
  Brian S Smith, Managing Partner
  Education: BS, Brigham Young University; MBA, Kelley School of Business, Indiana University
  Background: Managing Director, Peninsula Ventures; Dominion Ventures; Emerging Business Services Consultant, Deloitte Haskins & Sells
  Directorships: Contatta, Integrated Photovoltaics, Intesource, Response Analytics

862 GREAT HILL PARTNERS LLC
200 Clarendon Street
29th Floor
Boston, MA 02116

Phone: 617-790-9400 Fax: 617-790-9401
web: www.greathillpartners.com

Mission Statement: Great Hill Partners is a private equity firm that invests in growing middle market businesses in the software, media, communications, financial technology, business services, consumer services and healthcare industries.

Fund Size: $1.1 billion
Founded: 1998
Average Investment: $25 - $150 million
Investment Criteria: All investment stages beyond early stage, Acquisitions, Recapitalizations, Consolidations, Growth Equity
Industry Group Preference: Business to Business, Consumer Services, Fintech, Healthcare, Information Technology, Media, Communications, Software
Portfolio Companies: AffiniPay, BlueSnap, Bombas, CliqStudios, Custom Ink, Evolve IP, Examity, G/O Media, Ikon Science, Intapp, Mineral Tree, NMI, Pareto Health, PartsSource, Paytronix Systems Inc., Quantum Health, Reflexis, Reward Gateway, RxBenefits, The RealReal, TodayTix, Vanco, Vatica Health, YogaWorks

Key Executives:
  Christopher S. Gaffney, Managing Partner
  617-790-9420
  e-mail: cgaffney@greathillpartners.com
  Education: BS, Economics & Accounting, Boston College
  Background: Associate, Principal & General Partner, M/C Partners; Commercial Lending Officer, First National Bank of Boston
  Directorships: IntApp, Recruiting.com
  John G. Hayes, Senior Advisor
  617-790-9418
  e-mail: hayes@greathillpartners.com
  Education: BA, Economics, Williams College; MBA, Harvard Business School
  Background: Senior Associate, M/C Partners; Loan Officer, Bank of Boston
  Directorships: Ascenty, Symmetry Holdings
  Michael A. Kumin, Managing Partner
  e-mail: mkumin@greathillpartners.com
  Education: BA, Woodrow Wilson School of Public & International Affairs, Princeton University
  Background: Co-Founder & Executive VP, Creative Planet Incorporated; Associate, Apollo Advisors; Analyst, Goldman Sachs
  Directorships: Momondo Group, YogaWorks, The Shade Store, Legacy.com, Wayfair, SheKnows Media, Educaedu, Recruiting.com
  Mark D. Taber, Managing Partner
  617-790-9448
  e-mail: taber@greathillpartners.com
  Education: BA, Public Policy Studies, Duke University; JL Kellogg Graduate School of Management
  Background: Boston Consulting Group; Westlake Capital Group
  Directorships: RxBenefits, Qualifacts, DealerRater
  Matthew T. Vettel, Managing Partner
  617-790-9432
  e-mail: mvettel@greathillpartners.com
  Education: BS, Industrial Engineering & Management, North Dakota State University; MBA, Harvard Business School
  Background: Associate, GTCR Golder Rauner; Senior Associate, Accenture; Founding Member, PureSpeech
  Directorships: AffiniPay, Chrome River Technologies, Network Merchants, PlanSource, Reward Gateway, Vanco Payment Solutions, BlueSnap
  Christopher M. Busby, Partner
  e-mail: busby@greathillpartners.com
  Education: BA, Political Science & History, University of North Carolina at Chapel Hill; MBA, Harvard Business School
  Background: Analyst, JP Morgan; Associate, GCC Investments
  Directorships: Reward Gateway, PlanSource, Vanco Payment Solutions, BlueSnap

863 GREAT OAKS VENTURE CAPITAL
660 Madison Avenue
Suite 1600
New York, NY 10065

Phone: 212-821-1800
e-mail: info@greatoaksvc.com
web: www.greatoaksvc.com

Mission Statement: Great Oaks Venture Capital is a seed-stage investment firm committed to identifying, financing and

Venture Capital & Private Equity Firms / Domestic Firms

developing early-stage growth businesses led by promising entrepreneurs.

Average Investment: $50,000 - $500,000
Investment Criteria: Seed-Stage, Early-Stage
Industry Group Preference: E-Commerce & Manufacturing, Consumer Products, Advertising, Education, SaaS, Cloud Computing, Mobile, Social Media, Gaming
Portfolio Companies: 1 Doc Way, 33 Across, 500friends, Able Health, Acorns, Adcade, Affinity, Akido, Allbirds, Aloha, AptDeco, Arbor, Atomic, AugMedix, Away, Beaconhome, Bellhops, Despoke Post, Bluecrew, Blueshift, Boatsetter, Bolt, Bomfell, Bonobos, Breakthrough, Brewster, Built Robotics, Call9, Cameo, Canopy, Captain401, CardFlight, Cardpool, Chartio, Choozle, Circulate, Classkick, Cleanify, ClearGraph, Collective Health, Conduit, Conselytics, Counsyl, Course Hero, CoVenture, Cover, Crimson Hexagon, Directr, Discover.ly, Down, Dramafever, Drunc, Eat Club, Eat Street, Eaze, Eero, EquipmentShare, Expii, Fatherly, Fathom, Fetch, Flatiron, FlightCar, Future Advisor, Genies, GrubMarket, Health AP, Helix Sleep, Herb, Hinge, Hired, Homer, Houzz, HowGood, Huckleberry, Hullabalu, Hungry Root, Ibotta, Icon, ImageBrief, Interior Define, Interviewed, Invite Media, Joor, Jumpcut, Kickback, Kinnek, Kip, Knock, Knotch, Knowsy, Le Souk, Levo League, Locket, Lofty, Loom, Loverly, Love With Food, Mettermark, Maven, MemSQL, MightyBell, Minibar, Mino Games, ModCloth, Mojilala, Momentum Machines, Mortar, Move Loot, Notable Labs, Nylas, Okcupid, Olapic, Oportun, OrderAhead, Parcel, Pay Off, Peek, Permutation, Petal, Picasso Labs, PicnicHealth, Plastiq, Plated, Pluto, PocketGems, Popular Pays, Porter Road, Priori Legal, Propeller, Pure Wow, ReadMe, RecoverX, Replenish, Rep The Squad, RigUp, Rinse, Rise, Rise Art, Rock Health, Roostock, Roomi, Rumble, Sapho, Schoology, Scoutible, Seed Invest, Shift, SkyVu, SmithRx, SnappyTV, Soludos, SolveBio, Splash, Splitwise, Spreecast, Sprig, Stitcher Smart Radio, Storefront, Storify, Storyhunter, Streamable, StubHub, Studyblue, Studypool, Sugarfina, Sunshine, Supr, Sweeten, Symphony Commerce, Tentrr, The Muse, Think Cerca, Tidal, Touch Modern, Tred, Troops, Truebill, True & Co., Trulia, Truly, Trusted, Tula, Twice, Urbanstems, Verb, Verge Genomics, Very Apt, Viagogo, Virta, Vistar Media, VivaReal, Warby Parker, Welkin Health, Wim, Wonderschool, Wyre, Your Mechanic, Zady, Zesty, Zipongo

Key Executives:
  Andy Boszhardt, Founder/Managing Partner
  Education: BS, Accounting, MBA, University of Wisconsin-Madison
  Background: Managing Director & Portfolio Manager, Neuberger Berman; Goldman Sachs
  Ben Lin, Venture Partner
  Education: BS, Economics, Wharton School, University of Pennsylvania
  Background: Global Investment Research, Goldman Sachs & Co.
  John Philosophos, Partner, Business Development
  Education: BS, Finance & Marketing, University of Wisconsin-Madison
  Background: Co-Founder, Managing Partner, Wellspring Capital Advisors
  Celine Kwok, Chief Financial Officer
  Education: BA, Economics, Columbia University
  Background: Analyst, Morgan Stanley

---

864 **GREAT POINT PARTNERS**
165 Mason Street
Third Floor
Greenwich, CT 06830

Phone: 203-971-3300
web: www.gppfunds.com

Mission Statement: The principals of Great Point Partners have a long history of helping executives build successful healthcare companies.

Geographic Preference: United States
Fund Size: $156 million
Founded: 2003
Average Investment: $7 million - $25 million
Minimum Investment: $7 million
Investment Criteria: Recapitalizations, Growth Capital, Acquisitions, Management Buyouts, Corporate Spin-Offs
Industry Group Preference: Healthcare, Life Sciences, Healthcare Services, Healthcare Information Technology, Medical Devices, Pharmaceuticals
Portfolio Companies: American Surgical Professionals, Aris Teleradiology, Autism Learning Partners, Biotronic NeuroNetwork, Caprion Proteomics, Citra Health Solutions, Clinical Supplies Management, Connecture, Corrona, Cytovance Biologics, Equian, Mediatech Inc., Pro PT, Softbox Systems, United Claim Solutions, VitaLink Research

Key Executives:
  Jeffrey R. Jay, MD, Managing Director
  e-mail: jjay@gppfunds.com
  Education: BA, MD, Boston University; MBA, Harvard Business School
  Background: JH Whitney & Co., Canaan Partners, Salomon Brothers
  Adam B. Dolder, Managing Director
  e-mail: adolder@gppfunds.com
  Education: BS, Wake Forest University; MBA, Harvard Business School
  Background: JP Morgan Partners; JP Morgan Securities
  Joseph Pesce, CEO Advisory Board Member
  e-mail: jpesce@gppfunds.com
  Education: AB, Boston College; MBA, Wharton School, University of Pennsylvania
  Background: Thomas H Lee Partners, Renaissance Worldwide, Concentra Managed Care
  Noah F. Rhodes III, CEO Advisory Board Member
  e-mail: nrhodes@gppfunds.com
  Education: BS, Washington & Lee University
  Background: Wachovia Securities, Forest Hill Capital
  Rohan Saikia, Managing Director
  e-mail: rsaikia@gppfunds.com
  Education: BA, Columbia University
  Background: Cowen & Company

---

865 **GREEN LION PARTNERS**
2209 Larimer Street
Denver, CO 80205

e-mail: contact@greenlionpartners.com
web: www.greenlionpartners.com

Mission Statement: Invests in various consumer product companies within the cannabis industry. Green Lion is dedicated to elevating the public perception of cannabis through responsible and respectable business practices and partnerships.

Founded: 2015
Investment Criteria: Early-Stage
Industry Group Preference: Cannabis
Portfolio Companies: LeafList, Natural Order Supply, Dip Devices, America Isreal Cannabis Association, Two Bridges Design

Key Executives:
  Jeffrey M. Zucker, President
  Education: BS, Business Admin./Management, Questrom School of Business, Boston University
  Background: Co-Founder, Raining Combos; Director of Business Development, The InterTech Group; President/Co-Founder, Leaflist; President, America Isreal Cannabis Association; President, Devices; Co-Founder, Big Smits Entertainment; President, Two Bridges Design; Founder/President/CEOm, Saltshaker Holdings
  Directorships: Marijuana Policy Project

Venture Capital & Private Equity Firms / Domestic Firms

Mike Bologna, Chief Executive Officer
Education: BS, Marketing/Operations, School of Management, Boston University
Background: Supply Chain Buyer, General Dynamics C4 Systems; Subcontracts Manager, UTC Aerospace Systems; Trade & Logistics Consultant, Edgewater Fullscope

866 GREEN TOWER CAPITAL
20595 Arrow Creek Drive
Leesburg, VA 20175

Mission Statement: A hedge fund investing in companies serving the cannabis industry.

Founded: 2017
Industry Group Preference: Cannabis, Big Data, Info Technology, Machine Learning
Key Executives:
Ryan Gehringer, Chief Executive Officer
Background: CEO, Ripplechrome; Co-Founder, FindaFixr
Dan Chiriaev, Managing Director
Education: BA, Economics/Applied Math; Undergraduate Certificate in Conflict Management, Pepperdine University
Background: Chief Marketing Officer, CoArt; Co-Founder/CEO, Aarde.io

867 GREENBRIAR EQUITY GROUP LLC
555 Theodore Fremd Avenue
Suite A-201
Rye, NY 10580

Phone: 914-925-9600
e-mail: info@greenbriarequity.com
web: www.greenbriarequity.com

Mission Statement: Private equity firm focused exclusively on making investments in the global transportation industry, an area to which it brings distinct expertise and substantial resources.

Fund Size: $1.1 billion
Founded: 1999
Average Investment: $75 to $150 million
Minimum Investment: $50 million
Investment Criteria: LBO, Recapitalization, Growth Capital, Joint Ventures
Industry Group Preference: Global Industries, Transportation, Aerospace, Defense and Government, Logistics, Distribution
Portfolio Companies: Active Aero Group Holdings Inc., AerGen Leasing, Align Aerospace Holdings Inc., American Tire Distributors Inc., AmSafe Partners Inc., Ardmore Shipholding Ltd., Argo-Tech Corporation, Arotech, BDP International, DART Aerospace, EDAC Technologies, Electrical Source Holdings, Electro-Motive Diesel Inc., Frauscher Sensor Technology, GB Auto Service Inc., GENCO Distribution System Inc., Grakon International Inc., Hexcel Corporation, LaserShip, Lazer Spot Inc., Morgan Auto Group, Muth Mirror Systems, Nordco Holdings LLC, PetroChoice Holdings Inc., Ryan Herco Flow Solutions, SEKO Logistics, Stag-Parkway Inc., Spireon Inc., STS Aviation Group, Tinnerman Palnut Engineered Products Inc., Transplace Holdings, Western Peterbilt Inc., Whitcraft Group, World Freight Company International

Key Executives:
Gerald Greenwald, Chair
Education: BA, Princeton University; MA, Wayne State University
Background: Chairman/CEO, UAL Corporation; Vice Chairman/CFO, Chrysler Corporation
Reginald L. Jones III, Co-Founder/Managing Partner
Education: BA, Williams College; MBA, Harvard Business School
Background: Investment Banker, Goldman Sachs

John Daileader, Managing Director
Education: BS, Management, Rensselaer Polytechnic Institute; MBA, Stern School of Business, New York University
Background: Principal, JP Morgan Partners; Chemical Bank; Manufacturers Hanover Trust Company; National Westminster Bank
Jill C. Raker, Managing Director
Education: BS, Boston College Carroll School of Management; MBA, Harvard Business School
Background: Principal, Compass Partners International; Associate, The Blackston Group
Noah Roy, Managing Director
Education: BS, Georgetown University
Background: Managing Director, Goldman Sachs & Co.; Rothschild Inc.
Niall McComiskey, Managing Director
Education: BA, Economics, Yale University
Background: M&A Group, Deutsche Bank AG
Michael Weiss, Managing Director
Education: BA, Duke University
Background: Financial Sponsor & Leveraged Finance Group, Merrill Lynch & Co.

868 GREENHAVEN PARTNERS
9 W Broad Street
Suite 430
Stamford, CT 06902

Phone: 203-930-2702
web: www.greenhavenpartners.com

Mission Statement: Greenhaven Partners invests in and builds emerging businesses focused on developing information products and software.

Investment Criteria: Startups, Acquisitions
Industry Group Preference: Media, Publishing, Software
Portfolio Companies: Affirmify, Bongarde Holdings, Chief Executive Group, Dashboard Director, Institute of Finance & Management, Kennedy Information, LA 411, Pyramid Research, RecruitingTrends, Vizeum

Key Executives:
Wayne Cooper, Managing Partner
Education: BA, Stanford University; MBA, Harvard Business School
Background: CEO, Kennedy Information; Chairman & CEO, Visium; Consultant, Bain & Company; Monitor Company
Directorships: Bongarde Media, Chief Executive Group, Institute of Finance & Management
Marshall Cooper, Managing Partner
Education: BA, History & Political Science, University of Michigan; MBA, Tuck School of Business, Dartmouth College
Background: M&A, K-III Communications; The New York Times Company; Editor, Daily White House News Summary; President, Kennedy Information
Directorships: Bongarde, Chief Executive Group, Institute of Finance & Management, AIPAC
Giles Goodhead, Partner
Education: Cambridge University; MBA, Stanford University
Background: Stategy Consultant, Monitor Company; CEO, LA411/Media Publishing International
Directorships: Bongarde, Pyramid Research, TGI

869 GREENHILL SAVP
1271 Avenue of the Americas
New York, NY 10020

Phone: 212-389-1500 **Fax:** 212-389-1700
web: www.greenhill.com

Mission Statement: Specializes in small, worthy companies, providing them with money and high-quality advice and when the companies are ready, bringing them to the attention of later-stage funds for additional funding. Provides a vehicle for

Venture Capital & Private Equity Firms / Domestic Firms

angel investors, founders and entrepreneurs, as well as top-tier investment banks and VCs, institutional investors and other limited partners to participate in a diversified pool of top-line, early-stage Internet investments.

Geographic Preference: Greater Tri-State Area
Fund Size: $102 million
Founded: 2006
Average Investment: $1 - $8 million
Investment Criteria: Early-Stage
Industry Group Preference: Software, Information Technology, Internet Technology, Telecommunications
Other Locations:
Landsdowne House
57 Berkeley Square
London W1J 6ER
United Kingdom
Phone: +44 20 7198 7400 **Fax:** +44 20 7198 7500

Neue Mainzer Strasse 52
Frankfurt am Main D-60311
Germany
Phone: +49 69 272 272 00 **Fax:** +49 69 272 272 33

Biblioteksgatan 8
Stockholm SE-111 46
Sweden
Phone: +46 (8) 402 1370

Level 43, Governor Phillip Tower
1 Farrer Place
Sydney NSW 2000
Australia
Phone: +61 2 9299 1410 **Fax:** +61 2 9229 1490

79 Wellington Street West
Suite 3403
P.O. Box 333
Toronto, ON M5K 1K7
Canada
Phone: 416-601-2576

155 North Wacker Drive
Suite 4550
Chicago, IL 60606
Phone: 312-846-5000 **Fax:** 312-846-5001

1301 McKinney Street
Suite 2850
Houston, TX 77010
Phone: 713-739-2000 **Fax:** 713-739-2001

Suite 1201 York House, The Landmark
15 Queen's Road Central
Hong Kong S.A.R.
China
Phone: 852-3896-6400 **Fax:** 852-3896-6401

Level 30
101 Collins Street
Melbourne VIC 3000
Australia
Phone: +61 3 9935 6800 **Fax:** +61 3 9935 6850

600 Montgomery Street
33rd Floor
San Francisco, CA 94111
Phone: 415-216-4100 **Fax:** 415-216-4101

Marunouchi Building
2-4-1, Marunouchi
Chiyoga-ku
Toyko 100-6333
Japan
Phone: +81 3 4520 5100 **Fax:** +81 3 4520 5101

Key Executives:
Robert F. Greenhill, Founder/Chairman Emeritus
212-389-1500
Fax: 212-389-1700
e-mail: rfg@greenhill.com
Background: Chairman/CEO, Smith Barney Inc.; Chairman/President, Morgan Stanley Group
Directorships: Travelers Corp.
Scott L. Bok, Chairman/CEO
212-389-1520
Fax: 212-389-1720
e-mail: sbok@greenhill.com
Background: M&A, Wachtell, Lipton, Rosen & Katz
Directorships: M&A, Morgan Stanley & Co.
Kevin Costantino, President/Co-Head of US M&A
212-389-1528
Fax: 212-389-1728
e-mail: kevin.costantino@greenhill.com
Education: BBA, University of Michigan; JD, University of Michigan Law School
Background: Wachtell, Lipton, Rosen & Katz
Harold J. Rodriguez Jr., Managing Director/COO/CFO
212-389-1516
Fax: 212-389-1716
e-mail: hrodriguez@greenhill.com
Background: VP, Finance/Controller, Silgan Holdings; Ernst & Young

---

870 **GREENHILLS VENTURES, LLC**
The Chrysler Landmark Building
405 Lexington Avenue
26th Floor
New York, NY 10174

Phone: 917-368-8390
web: www.greenhillsventures.com

Investment Criteria: Early-Stage
Industry Group Preference: Healthcare Technology, Medical Devices, Mobile Software, Wireless Software, Cloud Software
Portfolio Companies: ACE*COMM, Acta Vascular Systems, Cyberis Group, Digital Angel, Extra Space Storage, Facet Pricing, Global Wireless Unified Messaging, I/OMagic Corporation, Infocrossing, Medarex, Netease.com, Nfocus Neuromedical, Photronics, Sigouria Groupe, Sysview Technology, True Share Vault, Viisage Technology, Vital Images, Wasabi Life
Other Locations:
The Hemsley Building
230 Park Ave.
10th Floor
New York, NY 10169

Key Executives:
Emanuel Martinez, General Managing Director
Education: M.B.A. Finance, B.A. Accouting, St. John's University
Background: Managing Director for Mergers & Acquisition, Citibank; Vice President of Finance, American Express Corporation
Patrick Tan, Managing Director
Education: B.A. Mathematics & Computer Science, SUNY Buffalo
Background: CIO Azerty Inc.

---

871 **GREENHOUSE VENTURES**
2401 Walnut Street
Suite 102
Philadelphia, PA 19103

e-mail: info@greenhouse.ventures
web: greenhouse.ventures

Founded: 2014
Average Investment: $2-5M
Minimum Investment: $250K
Investment Criteria: Seed, Startup
Industry Group Preference: Cannabis
Key Executives:
Kevin Provost, Co-Founder/CEO
Education: BA, Business Management, La Salle University

Venture Capital & Private Equity Firms / Domestic Firms

Background: Franchise Manager, College Pro; Founder, Crowdcampuses; Founder/CEO, CoFund360 LLC
Tyler Dautrich, Co-Founder/Operations Manager
Education: BBA, West Chester University of Pennsylvania; BBA, Fox School of Business, Temple University
Background: Community Manager, coPhilly; Director of Business Development, MoreBetter Ltd.

872 GREENSPRING ASSOCIATES
100 Painters Mill Road
Suite 700
Owings Mills, MD 21117

Phone: 410-363-2725 **Fax:** 410-363-9075
e-mail: info@gspring.com
web: www.greenspringassociates.com

Mission Statement: Greenspring Associates is a global venture investment firm that offers investment expertise and a number of investment solutions, including fund-of-funds, direct investment funds and secondary funds. The firm was founded in 2000 and has clients in North America, Europe, Asia and Australia. Greenspring Associates invests primarily in the healthcare and technology-enabled sectors.

Geographic Preference: United States, China, India, Israel, Europe
Fund Size: $430 million
Founded: 2000
Average Investment: $15 million
Minimum Investment: $5 million
Investment Criteria: Seed, Early-Stage, Growth Equity VC Funds, Late-Stage & Growth Equity Co-Investments
Industry Group Preference: Technology, Life Sciences, Technology-Enabled Services, Information Technology, Communications, Healthcare
Portfolio Companies: Chewy.com, CloudFlare, Cologix, Cyara, Demandbase, Entellus Medical, Everything But The House, Exinda, FanDuel, G5, Gigya, IL&FS Transportation, Intarcia Therapeutics, Intrinsic Therapeutics, JW Player, Kareo, Lithium Technologies, MapR Technologies, Namely, NeoTract, Nutanix, Ocera Therapeutics, Packaging Coordinators, PhotoBox, SolidFire, Sonos, Spredfest, TeamViewer, Teladoc, Ticket Monster, TriVascular, Turn, WalkMe, Woowa Brothers, WorkFront, Zayo Group

Other Locations:
228 Hamilton Avenue
3rd Floor
Palo Alto, CA 94301
Phone: 650-798-5392 **Fax:** 650-798-5001

Key Executives:
Ashton Newhall, Co-Founder/Managing General Partner
e-mail: ashton@gspring.com
Education: Elon College
Background: T. Rowe Price Associates
Directorships: National Venture Capital Association, Domain Associates, Pelion Venture Partners, QuestMark Partners
Jim Lim, Managing General Partner
e-mail: jlim@gspring.com
Education: Washington University; MBA, Finance, Indiana University
Background: Director, Commonfund Capital; Pfizer
Directorships: Bullpen Capital, Columbia Capital, Foundry Group, High Alpha Ventures, Lightspeed China, Meritech Capital Partners, Cloud Sherpas, Kareo
John Avirett, General Partner
e-mail: john@gspring.com
Education: BA, Political Science, Johns Hopkins University
Background: Associate, Zurich Financial Services
Directorships: Workfront, Volition Capital, Shasta Ventures
Deric Emry, Venture Partner
e-mail: deric@gspring.com
Background: General Partner, ABS Capital Partners; Deutsche Bank Alex Brown
Eric Thompson, Chief Operating Officer
e-mail: ethompson@gspring.com
Education: BBA, Accounting, MBA, Finance, Sellinger School of Business & Management, Loyola University
Background: Manager, Assurance & Business Advisory Services Practice, PricewaterhouseCoopers
Nathan Campbell, Partner
Education: BComm, Australian National University; MA, Applied Finance & Invetsment, Financial Services Institute of Australasia
Background: Associate Director, Macquarie Capital; Deutsche Bank AG
Directorships: Agile Energy, Atlantic Wind Connection, Nexamp

874 GREIF & COMPANY
633 West Fifth Street
65th Floor
Los Angeles, CA 90071

Phone: 213-346-9250 **Fax:** 213-346-9260
e-mail: owl@greifco.com
web: www.greifco.com

Mission Statement: Provides financial advisory services and execution to meet the specialized corporate finance needs of middle market growth companies.

Geographic Preference: United States, Canada, Latin America
Fund Size: $100 million
Founded: 1992
Average Investment: $1-$5 million
Minimum Investment: $1 million
Investment Criteria: Second-stage, Mezzanine, LBO, Control-block purchases
Industry Group Preference: Food and Beverage, Healthcare, Technology, Financial Services, Manufacturing, Media, Retailing, Aerospace and Defence, Consumer Products, Entertainment, Real Estate
Portfolio Companies: ABM Industris Inc., Advent International, Aerosol Servives Holdings Corp., Aerosol Services Company Inc., Outsourcing Services Group, Air Lease Corp., Allen Foods Inc., Allied Waste, American Apparel, AGS, AMF, Aquaria Inc., ASA Events, Back9 Network, Bebe, Blue Ribbon Baking Inc., Boone, Bossa Nova, Bristol Farms, Lazy Acres Merket, BF Acquisitions Company LLC, Buenavision Cable TV, Bumble Bee Seafoods, Uni Group Inc., Caesars Entertainment, California Manufacturing Enterprises, Center For Discover & Adolescent Change, Chromium Graphics Inc., City Center, Cole Real Estate Investments, Commericial Advance, Compel, Continental North Penn Technology, Contour Aerospace, Costco Wholesale, Century 21. CRL, Dacor, DTN, Del Amo Diagnostic Center, Dogswell, Dynamic Medical Systems Inc., E.B. Bradey Co., Evergreen, Express Energy Services, EZ Lube, Fantastic, First American Title Company of Marin, Fontainebleau, Ford Wholesale Co. Inc., Fred Sands, Fresh Express, Gaiam, Gary's Tux Shops, Gold Star Foods, Empire CLS, Hilton Worldwide, Inland American Real Estate Trust Inc., Interior Specialists Inc., Ixia, Kidsline, Kidsmart, Label-Aire, Landry's, Leisure Concepts, Levlad Inc., Lindora, LoopNet, Luciz, Lucky Brand, Malibu Grand Prix, Malone Mortgage Co., Marshall & Swift, Meico Crown Entertainment, MGM Resorts, MSA, Modnique, Mollie Stone's Markets, Morhterhood Maternity, Mrs. Gooch's, Nordstrom, Orange Plastics, Rose Hills, Skechers, UnitedHealth Group, WestwoodOne, Wynn Resorts

Key Executives:
Lloyd Greif, President/CEO
e-mail: greif@greifco.com
Education: BA, Economics, University of California, Los Angeles; MBA, Entrepreneurship, University of Southern California; JD, Loyola Law School

303

Venture Capital & Private Equity Firms / Domestic Firms

Background: Investment Banker, Sutro & Company; Management Consultant, Touche, Ross & Company
David S. Felman, Advisor
213-346-9225
e-mail: felman@greifco.com
Education: BA, Economics & Political Science, Stanford University; MBA, Finance & Entrepreneurship, University of California, Los Angeles
Background: Co-Founder, Cardinal Advisors; M&A, Moelis & Co.; Investment Banker, Morgan Stanley; UBS; Stanford Management Company; White House Concil of Economic Advisers; Goldman Sachs
Brad Money, Managing Director
213-346-9268
e-mail: money@greifco.com
Education: BS, Finance & Economics, David Eccles School of Business, University of Utah
Background: Financial Analyst, RSM EquiCo; Financial Analyst, Ameriprise Financial
Brian R. Nelson, Vice President
213-346-9267
e-mail: nelson@greifco.com
Education: BA, Business Economics, Brown University; MBA, Anderson School of Management, University of California, Los Angeles
Background: Vice President, Guggenheim Securities; Investment Banker, Citigroup Global Markets; Investment Banker, Focalpoint Partners; Trading Assistant, JP Morgan; Bear Stearns

875 GREY SKY VENTURE PARTNERS
10400 Northeast 4th St.
Suite 700
Bellevue, WA 98004

e-mail: info@gsvp.com
web: gsvp.com

Mission Statement: Grey Sky Venture Partners makes early-stage investments in healthcare and medical technology companies with the aim of improving clinical outcomes, enhancing quality of life, and reducing system costs.
Investment Criteria: Early-Stage
Industry Group Preference: Healthcare, Medical Technology
Portfolio Companies: Biolinq, Care Wave, Immunovalent Therapeutics, MatriSys Bioscience, Modulated Imaging, Nodexus, Persephone Biome, Quantum Diamond Technologies, Sonavex, Soundstim Therapeutics, WestFace Medical, Winterlight
Other Locations:
2710 Sand Hill Rd.
Menlo Park, CA 94025
Key Executives:
Michael Banks, Founder/Partner
Education: BA, MA, Stanford University; MBA, Anderson School
Background: Intel Capital; Steamboat Ventures; Palisades Ventures; DE Shaw Ventures; Windy Hill Capital
Todd McIntyre, Founder/Partner
Education: BA, Hendrix College; MBA, Stanford University
Background: Invention Science Fund; Microvision; Lumera Corp.
Paul Wu, Partner
Education: MBA, MIT Sloan School; PhD, Northwestern University
Background: Invention Science Fund; KLA-Tencor

876 GREYCROFT PARTNERS
292 Madison Avenue
8th Floor
New York, NY 10017

Phone: 212-756-3508 Fax: 212-832-0117
e-mail: media@greycroft.com
web: greycroft.com

Mission Statement: Greycroft Partners is a venture capital partnership, formed to invest in promising digital media companies.
Geographic Preference: New York, Los Angeles
Fund Size: $800 million
Founded: 2009
Average Investment: $2 million
Minimum Investment: $100K
Investment Criteria: Seed, Series A
Industry Group Preference: Digital Media & Marketing, Advertising, Marketing, SaaS, E-Commerce & Manufacturing, Mobility, Infrastructure, Gaming
Portfolio Companies: 33across, 9flats.com, 9gag, Ad.ly, AppAnnie, BalconyTV, Bauble Bar, BetterCloud, Boxed, Buzz Points, Ceros, Collective, Combatant Gentlemen, CrowdComputing Systems, Daily Secret, Elicit, Epoxy, ETouches, ExtremeReach, Fanhattan, Fight My Monster, Floored, Fortumo, FriendBuy, Game Salad, Glam Media, Hashgo, HealthPlanOne, Highlight, HIP Digital, HipSwap, Joyent, JWPlayer, GamersFirt, Kaleo, Klout, Knozen, Koding, Layer, Livefyre, Local Response, Maker, Media Armor, Merchantry, MightyBell, Moonfrye, Nativo, Netsertive, NewsCred, Nifty Thrifty, NimbleTV, Nomi, NuOrder, OpenBucks, ParentMedia, PeopleLinx, Phg, Plain Vanilla, Playdek, PrecisionDemand, ProdThink, Radiate Media, Resonate, Scopely, Skimlinks, SteelHouse, Sulia, TagMan, The Dodo, The RealReal, ThisClicks, Trunk Club, Trustev, uSamp, Viddy, Vitals, Who What Wear, WideOrbit, WochIt
Other Locations:
1375 East 6th Street
Suite 1
Los Angeles, CA 90021
Phone: 213-896-7126 Fax: 213-402-2859
Key Executives:
Alan Patricof, Co-Founder & Chair Emeritus
Background: Founder, Patricof & Co. Ventures
Dana Settle, Co-Founder & Managing Partner
Education: BA, Finance & International Studies, University of Washignton; MBA, Harvard Business School
Background: Business Development, Truveo; Investment Banking, Lehman Brothers; International Business Development, McCaw Cellular Communications
Directorships: Fanhattan, Gamersfirst, GameSalad, Joyent, Lucid Commerce, Maker Studios, Pulse, Sometrics, TrunkClub, uSamp, WideOrbit
Ian Sigalow, Co-Founder & Managing Partner
Education: BS, Economics, MIT; MBA, Columbia University Graduate School of Business
Background: Founder, StrongData Corporation; Boston Millenia Partners
Directorships: Buddy Media, Buzzd, Collective, CrowdFusion, Extreme Reach, Oggifinogi, Tynt, Vizu

877 GREYLOCK PARTNERS
2550 Sand Hill Road
Suite 200
Menlo Park, CA 94025

Phone: 650-493-5525 Fax: 650-493-5575
web: www.greylock.com

Mission Statement: Greylock Partners supports entrepreneurs who are building software companies that define new markets.
Investment Criteria: All Stages
Industry Group Preference: Software

Venture Capital & Private Equity Firms / Domestic Firms

Portfolio Companies: AI Fund, Airbnb, Angle Technologies, Apollo Fusion, Apptio, Aurora, Avi Networks, Awake Security, Blend, BountyJobs, Caavo, Caffeine, Cato Networks, Censys, Cleo, Coda, Coinbase, Convoy, CreativeLive, Crew, Delphix, Demisto, Discord, Docker, Domo, Entrepreneur First, Figma, Gixo, Gladly, GoFundMe, Grand Rounds, HealthHiway, Houseparty, Innovium, Instabase, Lightbend, Lyra Health, Mammoth Media, Matrixx Software, Medium, Nauto, Nextdoor, Notable Health, Nuro, Obsidian Security, Operator, Oportun, PullString, Rhumbix, Ribbon, richrelevance, Ritual, Roblox, Rockset, Rubrik, Silver Peak Systems, Solv, Sonder, Spoke, Sumologic, TechProcess Solutions, Trifacta, Trove, Upserve, Wealthfront, WildTangent, Wrapp, Xapo

Other Locations:
1600 District Avenue
Suite 104
Burlington, MA 01803

457 Bryant Street
San Francisco, CA 94107

Key Executives:

Reid Hoffman, Partner
Education: Bachelor's Stanford University; Master's Univ. of Oxford
Background: Co-Founder, LinkedIn; Executive Vice President, PayPal
Directorships: Airbnb, Apollo Fusion, Aurora, Coda, Convor, Entrepreneur First, Gixo, Nauto, Xapo

Jerry Chen, Partner
e-mail: jerry.chen@greylock.com
Education: BS, Industrial Engineering, Stanford University; MBA, Harvard Business School
Background: VP, Cloud and Application Services, VMware
Directorships: Blend, Cato Networks, Cloudera, Docker, Gladly, Isntabase, Notable Health, Rhumbix, Rockset, Spoke

Sarah Guo, Partner
e-mail: sguo@greylock.com
Education: Wharton School; University of Pennsylvania
Background: Casa Systems; Goldman Sachs
Directorships: AI Fund, Awake Security, Clea, Demisto, Obsidian Security

Josh McFarland, Partner
e-mail: jmcfarland@greylock.com
Education: BA, Economics, Stanford University
Background: VP of Product, Twitter; Product Manager, Google
Directorships: Coinbase, Ribbon

David Sze, Partner
e-mail: dsze@greylock.com
Education: BA Yale University; MBA Stanford University
Background: SVP Product Strategy, Exite; Product Marketing & Development, Electronic Arts/Crystal Dynamics; Management Consultant, Marakon Associates/Boston Consulting Group
Directorships: Caavo, Medium, Nextdoor, PullString, Roblox

Asheem Chandna, Partner
e-mail: achandna@greylock.com
Education: B.S./M.S. Electrical and Computer Engineering, Case Western Reserve University
Background: Vice President of Business Development, Check Point Software; Vice President of Marketing, CoroNet Systems; Strategic Marketing, SynOptics/Bay; AT&T Bell
Directorships: Avi Netowrks, Awake Security, Censys, Delphix, Innovium, Obsidian Security, Palo Alto Networks, Rubrik

878 GRIDIRON CAPITAL
220 Elm Street
New Canaan, CT 06840

Phone: 203-972-1100 Fax: 203-801-0602
web: www.gridironcapital.com

Mission Statement: A private equity firm focused on creating value by acquiring and building middle-market manufacturing, service and specialty consumer companies.

Geographic Preference: United States, Canada
Investment Criteria: Contol Equity Investments, $8-50 Million in EBITDA
Industry Group Preference: Manufacturing, Services, Specialty Consumer Products
Portfolio Companies: Consel On Call, Dent Wizard, Electronic Systems Protection, Engage2Excel, Essential Cabinetry Group, H.M. Dunn AeroSystems Inc., McKenzie Sports Products, Motion Recruitment Partners, PAS Technologies, Performance Health, Ramsey Industries, Rough Country, Schutt Sports, Tokyo Joe's, Travel Nurse Across America

Key Executives:

Thomas A. Burger Jr., Managing Partner & Co-Founder
e-mail: tburger@gridironcapital.com
Education: Mechanical Engineering Degree, Duke University; MBA, Wharton School, University of Pennsylvania
Background: Managing Director, RFE Investment Partners; Managing Director, Butler Capital Corporation

Eugene P. Conese Jr., Managing Partner & Co-Founder
e-mail: gconese@gridironcapital.com
Education: BA, Economics, Denison University
Background: President, Greenwich Air Services; President, Haskon Corporation
Directorships: Audit Committee

Kevin M. Jackson, Senior Managing Partner
e-mail: kjackson@gridironcapital.com
Education: BA, Economics & Latin American Studies, Oberlin College; MBA, Columbia Business Schoool
Background: Senior Associate, CCMP Capital; Analyst, Credit Suisse

Kallie Hapgood, Managing Director
e-mail: khapgood@gridironcapital.com
Education: BA, Dartmouth College
Background: Principal, NovaFund Advisors; Vice President, Knight Capital Partner; State Street Global Advisors; Merrill Lynch

Joseph A. Saldutti Jr., Managing Director
e-mail: jsaldutti@gridironcapital.com
Education: MBA, Harvard Business School
Background: President, TDA Capital Partners; Engineer, General Electric

Geoffrey D. Spillane, Managing Director
e-mail: gspillane@gridironcapital.com
Education: BA, Economics, Boston College
Background: Principal, Brookside International Inc; Creditanstalt Corporate Finance; Fleet Financial Group

Owen G. Tharrington, Managing Director
e-mail: otharrington@gridironcapital.com
Education: BS, Accounting, Fairfield University; MBA, Columbia Business School
Background: Vice President, Saugatuck Capital Company; KPMG LLP

Christopher M. King, Vice President
e-mail: cking@gridironcapital.com
Education: BSBA, Finance & International Business, Georgetown University; Wharton School, University of Pennsylvania
Background: Analyst, Lehman Brothers; M&A, Barclays Capital

Douglas J. Rosenstein, Vice President
e-mail: drosenstein@gridironcapital.com
Education: BS, Business, Indiana University; MBA, Booth School of Business, University of Chicago
Background: Analyst, Merrill Lynch

Venture Capital & Private Equity Firms / Domestic Firms

Sean M. Kelley, Principal/Director of Business Development
e-mail: skelley@gridironcapital.com
Education: BA, Economics, Wake Forest University; MBA, Darden School of Business, University of Virginia
Background: Vice President, Investment Banking Division, BB&T Capital Markets; Associate, Equity Research Division, Credit Suisse; Analyst, Investment Banking Division, Deutsche Bank

879 GRISHIN ROBOTICS
2735 Sand Hill Road
Suite 220
Menlo Park, CA 94025

web: www.grishinrobotics.com

Mission Statement: Grishin Robotics is a global investment company that is dedicated to supporting personal robotics around the world. Grishin Robotics is focused on raising the profile of the robotics industry and helping robotics entrepreneurs advance their products and ideas.
Fund Size: $100 million
Founded: 2012
Investment Criteria: Early-Stage
Industry Group Preference: Robotics, IoT, Technology, Software
Portfolio Companies: Bolt, Double Robotics, Eero, Embodied, Gobee.Bike, littleBits Electronics, OBike, Occipital, Petnet, Planetary Resources, Ring, Sphero, Spin, Spire, Starship, Swivi, Ring, Robots Lab, Wonder
Key Executives:
Dmitry Grishin, Founding Partner
Education: Faculty of Robotics & Complex Automation, Moscow State Technical University
Background: CEO, Mail.Ru

880 GROSVENOR FUNDS
888 17th Street NW
Suite 214
Washington, DC 20006

Phone: 202-861-5650 Fax: 202-861-5653

Mission Statement: Strives to invest in small businesses that stimulate the economic development and create new jobs in local communities.
Geographic Preference: Washington DC
Fund Size: $90 million
Founded: 1994
Average Investment: $1.5 million
Minimum Investment: $1 million
Investment Criteria: Early, Expansion
Industry Group Preference: Healthcare, Information Technology, Wireless Technologies
Key Executives:
Bruce B. Dunnan, Managing Partner
Education: Washington & Lee University; University of North Carolina School of Business
Background: President, Dunnan Securities Advisors; Alex Brown & Sons; Dean Witter Reynolds; First National Bank Atlanta
Douglas M. Dunnan, Managing Partner
Education: Cornell University, Harvard Law School, University of Chicago School of Business
Background: Attorney, Kirkland & Ellis; Investment Banking, Salomon Brothers; Founder, Grosvenor Fund
C. Bowdoin Train, Managing Partner
Education: Trinity College; JD, Georgetown University
Background: Counsel, Clean Air Capital Markets; Corporate Finance Law, Shaw Pittman Potts & Trowbridge; Environmental Protection Agency-George Bush Administration
Directorships: SnappCloud, Three Stage Media, iMove Inc., Inside Higher Ed

Oak Strawbridge, Partner
Education: George Washington University
Background: New Product Development Gropu, Concert Communications; Marketing Consultant, IGOR Communications
Directorships: DoublePOSITIVE, Appfluent, Generic Medical Devices, Inside Higher Ed, Omeros

881 GROTECH VENTURES
3033 Wilson Boulevard
Suite 200
Arlington, VA 22201

Phone: 703-637-9555
web: www.grotech.com

Mission Statement: Private equity investment firm investing in both emerging technology and traditional industry companies.
Geographic Preference: United States
Fund Size: $1 billion
Founded: 1984
Average Investment: $500,000 - $5 million
Minimum Investment: $500,000
Investment Criteria: All Stages, Recapitalization, Management Buy-Outs, Early, Emerging and Later Stages
Industry Group Preference: Enterprise Services, Business to Business, Communications, Healthcare, Consumer Products, Technology, Software, Infrastructure, Information Technology, Internet, Digital Media & Marketing
Portfolio Companies: Advertising.com, Adwerx, Airside, Anypresence, Atavium, Aztek Networks, Booker, Broadsoft, BuySafe, CDNow, Ceroc, Ceterus, Churnzero, CircleBack, Clarabridge, Closely, Cloud Elements, Collective Intellect, Commericial Tribe, Contactually, DB Networks, Digex, Direct Scale, Dizzion, Fieldglass, Fluid, Fusient Media Ventures, GutCheck, Healthcare Interactive, HealthScribe, HellaWaller, Hillcrest Labs, HiveLive, iBiquity, ICX Media, Intellinote, Invincea, Livingsocial, Login Analytics, LogRhythm, MedAssets, Medecision, Micro Prose, My Alerts, Nexgen Storage, Omnilink, OpenQ, Optoro, Overture, ParkiFi, Parsely, Passport, Payzer, Promoboxx, Rebit, RedPoint, RollStream, Secure, Social Radar, Spotlight, Stardog Union, Synchrologic, TapInfluence, Taskeasy, Tethr, Royalty Exchange, ThreatConnect, TwoSix Labs, UrbanBound, Urbanstems, Urjanet, USI, Verity, WebScal, WhiteOps, Wiser Together, Yet Analytics, Zenoss
Other Locations:
230 Schilling Circle
Suite 362
Hunt Valley, MD 21031
Phone: 703-637-9555

1685 South Colorado Boulevard
Unit S-251
Denver, CO 80222
Phone: 720-399-4952

Key Executives:
Frank A. Adams, Founder/Chaiman
703-637-9555
e-mail: fadams@grotech.com
Education: BS/JD, University of Baltimore; Management Programs in Finance & Information Technology, Stanford University; Harvard University
Background: Co-Founder, Mid-Atlantic Venture Association
Directorships: DIGEX; Global Software; Healthscribe; iBiquity Digital Radio; Interspec; Lloyds Foods; MasterPower; SimonDelivers.com; Thunderbird Technologies; USinternetworking
Chuck Cullen, General Partner/CFO/COO
703-637-9555
e-mail: ccullen@grotech.com
Education: BBA, Accounting, Loyola University; JD, University of Notre Dame Law School; MBA, Kellogg School of Management
Background: CFO/CAO, Avatech Solutions; AT Kearney

Venture Capital & Private Equity Firms / Domestic Firms

Directorships: buySAFE, Pelican Life Sciences, OpenQ, Sagittarius Brands
Steve Fredrick, General Partner
703-462-1343
e-mail: sfredrick@grotech.com
Education: BS, MS, Electrical Engineering, Virginia Tech
Background: General Partner, Novak Biddle Venture Partners; Research & Develpment, IBM
Directorships: LogiXML, Omnilink Systems, RollStream, Secure Command, TRAFFIQ
Don Rainey, General Partner
703-462-1348
e-mail: drainey@grotech.com
Education: BBA, James Madison University; MS, Bioscience Management, George Mason University
Background: Emerging Technology Consultant, US Department of Defense, DeVenCI Program; President, Attitude Network; IBM
Directorships: ARPU, Clarabridge, LivingSocial, Zenoss
Joseph Zell, Venture Partner
703-399-4952
e-mail: jzell@grotech.com
Education: BS, Marketing, Southwest Missouri State University
Background: US West Communications; CEO, Convergent Communications; Management, WilTel, LDXNet, United Technologies Communications, MCI Communications, Xerox
Lawson DeVries, Managing General Partner
703-637-9555
e-mail: ldevries@grotech.com
Education: BA, English Literature, Harvard University
Background: Associate, Institutional Equity Sales, The Buckingham Research Group

882 GROUND UP VENTURES

web: www.groundup.vc

Mission Statement: A seed and early stage venture capital firm investing in innovative companies from the group up.

Geographic Preference: US, Israel
Founded: 2017
Average Investment: $250,000 - $500,000
Minimum Investment: $250,000
Investment Criteria: Pre-Seed, Seed
Industry Group Preference: Artificial Intelligence, Automation, Consumer, Data Management, Finance, Retail, Cyber Insurance, Software
Portfolio Companies: build Ops, Catch, Dandelion, Frank., Jones, MeetElise, Neighborhood Goods, Paladin Cyber, Shapeshift, Wardrobe

Key Executives:
David Stark, Founding Partner
e-mail: david@groundup.vc
Education: BS, University of Pennsylvania
Background: Analyst, The Blackstone Group; General Partner, OurCrowd
Cory Moelis, Founding Partner
e-mail: cory@groundup.vc
Education: MBA, Wharton School
Background: Analyst, Moelis & Company; Research & Analytics Manager, AEG; Product Manager, Derby Games
Jordan Odinsky, Investor, Head of Platform
e-mail: jordan@groundup.vc
Education: BS, Queens College
Background: Business Development Manager, OurCrowd; Co-Chair, VC Platform Global Community; Global Mentor, WeWork Labs; Angel Investor

883 GROVE GROUP MANAGEMENT
New York, NY

Phone: 212-671-1951
e-mail: contact@grovegroupmanagement.com
web: grovegroupmanagement.com

Mission Statement: Grove's team is compiled of finance, markting, and operational experts with vast knowledge of the cannabis industry.
Geographic Preference: US, Canada
Founded: 2018
Industry Group Preference: Cannabis
Key Executives:
Kevin Shin, Co-Founder/CEO
Education: University of Michigan
Background: Financial Consultant, AXA; Founder, Craving; Founder, Paedea Inc.; Limited Partner/Senior Advisor, NewOak Capital; Co-Founder, iFood Korea
James Frischling, President
Education: BA, Government, Wesleyan University; MBA, Finance, Columbia Business School
Background: VP, UBS Securities; Managing Director/Head of US Structured Credit, Fortis Securities; Partner/Finance Director, Branded Restaurants; Principal, MuniRisk; Co-Founder/Strategic Advisor, NewOak Capital; Principal, Oak Branch Advisors; Co-Founder/Principal, Branded Strategic Hospitality
Directorships: Oak Branch Advisors
Tiki Barber, Co-Founder/Chief Business Development Officer
Education: BComm, Management Information Systems, University of Virginia
Background: Running Back, New York Football Giants; Co-Founder, Thuzio; Co-Host, Tiki & Tierney Show
Directorships: Chairman, Thuzio
Chris Chung, Chief Investment Officer
Education: BA, Economics, Northwestern University; University of Pennsylvania; NYU Stern School of Business
Background: SVP, RBC Dain Rauscher; SVP/Head of Fixed Income, Janney Montgomery Scott; Founder/CEO, Clubstest.com; SVP, UBS Investment Bank; SVP, Bank of America; President/CEO, AGI LLC; Head of Business Development, The PreTesting Company; President/CEO, Altibase; EVP-Cyber Security Analytics, Antuit
Bob DeSena, Chief Marketing & Communications Officer
Education: BS, Quantitative Analysis, Manhattan College; MBA, Saint John's University
Background: CEO, Engagement Marketing Group; CMO, TouchVision; Director of Relationship Marketing, Masterfoods USA; VP of Digital Media, Time Inc.; Adjunct Professor, NYU Graduate Program of Integrated Marketing' EVP/General Manager, Draft (now FCB)

884 GROVE STREET ADVISORS LLC
2221 Washington Street
Building 1
Suite 201
Newton, MA 02462

Phone: 781-263-6100
web: www.grovestreet.com

Mission Statement: Established with the objective of reengineering the traditional relationships between gatekeeper, fund manager and the major institutional investors in private equity.

Geographic Preference: North America, Western Europe, Isreal, China
Fund Size: $9 billion
Founded: 1998
Investment Criteria: Buy-outs, Mezzanine, Growth Equity
Industry Group Preference: Energy, Technology, Cloud Computing, Life Sciences, Healthcare, Agriculture
Portfolio Companies: Bedrock Capital, Flagship Pioneering, Hyperplane, M33 Grwoth, Quantum Energy Partners, Trive Capital

Key Executives:
Frank Angella, Managing Partner
Education: BA, Interdisciplinary Studies, University of

Virginia; MBA, Harvard Business School
Background: Co-Founder/VP, Biocode; Analyst, Advent Venture Partners; Associate, Innotage Management
Catherine Crockett, Co-Founder & Managing Partner
Education: BA, Business Admin./Government, University of Notre Damn; MPA, Kennedy School of Government, Harvard University
Background: 14 years of experience designin and building private equity programs
Christopher Quinn, CPA, Managing Partner & Chief Financial Officer
Education: BS, Bryant University; MT, Taxation, University of Denver
Background: CFO, Regiment Capital Advisors; Director of Tax, Bain Capital; Tax Manager, Highfields Capital; Senior Tax Consultant, Deloitte
Bruce Ou, Managing Partner
Education: BA, Williams College; MBA, Tuck School of Business, Dartmouth College
Background: Monitor Group

885 GROWTH FUND PRIVATE EQUITY
14929 Highway 172
Suite 302
P.O. Box 367
Ignacio, CO 81137

Phone: 970-563-5000 Fax: 970-764-6301
web: www.gfprivateequity.com

Mission Statement: The principal mission of GF Private Equity Group, LLC is to invest capital provided to it by the Southern Ute Growth Fund on behalf of the Southern Ute Indian Tribe in a variety of private equity funds and direct investments in companies for three primary reasons: pursue above-average investment returns, contribute to asset diversification of the Southern Ute Growth Fund, and provide long-term economic benefits to the Southern Ute Indian Tribe.

Founded: 2003
Portfolio Companies: Ahura Scientific, Applied Wave Research, Impinj, Kotura, Pixtronix, Redline Communications, Teknovus, Venda

Key Executives:
James Thompson PhD, President/COO
Jonathan Abshagen, Portfolio Manager

886 GRYPHON INVESTORS
One Maritime Plaza
Suite 2300
San Francisco, CA 94111

Phone: 415-217-7400 Fax: 415-217-7447
e-mail: info@gryphoninvestors.com
web: www.gryphon-inv.com

Mission Statement: Gryphon actively seeks companies where strong results can be achieved when the right management team is combined with Gryphon's focused industry approach and operational expertise.

Geographic Preference: United States
Fund Size: $900 million
Founded: 1995
Average Investment: $50 - $150 million
Minimum Investment: $25 million
Investment Criteria: Traditional Buyouts, Leveraged Build-Ups, Growth Equity Investments, Revunue of $25 to $250 million
Industry Group Preference: Education, Specialty Retail, Business Products & Services, Healthcare, Manufacturing, Consumer Products, Consumer Services
Portfolio Companies: Accelerated Rehabilitation Centers, Alliedbarton Security, Bright Now! Dental, C.B. Fleet Laboratories, Consolidated Fire Protection, Cora Health Services, Delta Career Education Corp., ECG Management Consultants, Eight O'Clock Coffee, Envision, Flagstone Foods, Hepaco, Intelligrated, Jen Sen Hughes, K&N Engineering Inc., Medfinders, Miller Heiman, MSD Ignition, OB Hospitalist Group, Orchid Underwriters, PHNS, Sheplers, Smile Brands, Synteratchr, TASQ Technology, The Original Cakerie, Trinity Consultants, Trusthouse Services Group, Update Legal, Washing Systems LLC, Wind River Environmental

Key Executives:
R. David Andrews, CEO/Managing General Partner
415-217-7410
e-mail: andrews@gryphoninvestors.com
Education: BA, Economics, Stanford University; JD, Stanford University; MBA, Stanford University
Background: Managing Director, Oak Hill Partners; Investor, Adler & Shaykin; Salomon Brothers; Shearson Lehman Brothers
Directorships: Delta Career Education, Envision, HEPACO, Jen Sen Hughes, Wind River Environmental
Alex Earls, Partner
415-217-7405
e-mail: earls@gryphoninvestors.com
Education: BA, Government, Harvard College
Background: Associate, Castle Harlan; Analyst, Princes Gate; Morgan Stanley
Directorships: DLC, HEPACO, Jen Sen Hughes, Orchid Underwriters, Wind River Environmental
Kevin Blank, Partner/General Manager, Healthcare
415-217-7449
e-mail: blank@gryphoninvestors.com
Education: BA, Medical Sociology, Boston University; MPH, Health Systems, Boston University School of Medicine
Background: CEO, FastMed Urgant Care; EVP, Evolution Benefits; President/COO, Benefit Point; nson
Directorships: OB Hospitalist Group
Will Lynn, Partner
415-217-7409
e-mail: lynn@gryphoninvestors.com
Education: Case Western Reserve University; Baldwin Wallace College
Background: President, LaChoy/Rosarita Foods Division, ConAgra; Group Vice President, Clorox Company; Private Equity Consultant, Oak Hill
Directorships: CORA Health Services, Delta Career Education, Envision, Smile Brands
Dennis O'Brien, Partner/General Manager, Consumer Products & Services
415-217-7414
e-mail: obrien@gryphoninvestors.com
Education: BS, Marketing, University of Connecticut
Background: President/COO, ConAgra; Armstrong Industries; Campbell's Soup; Nestle Foods; Procter and Gamble
Directorships: DLC, The Original Cakerie
Nick Orum, President
415-217-7440
e-mail: orum@gryphoninvestors.com
Education: BA, Quantitative Economics, Stanford University
Background: Principal Investor, Oak Hill Partners; High Yield Finance Group, Merrill Lynch
Directorships: Delta Career Education, CORA Health Services. DLC, ECG Management Consultants, OB Hospitalist Group, Orchid Underwriters, Smile Brands
Dorian Faust, Partner
415-217-7424
e-mail: faust@gryphoninvestors.com
Education: BA, University at Buffalo; MBA, Columbia Business School
Background: Principal, Norwest Equity Partners; Vice President, Thomas Weisel Capital Partners; Associate, JP Morgan Partners
Dell Larcen, Partner
415-217-7441
e-mail: larcen@gryphoninvestors.com
Education: BA, Sociology, Carson Newman College; MS,

Psycology/Psychiatric Social Work, University of Tennessee
Background: CEO, Larcen Consulting Group; Founder/CEO, Overlook Center; Founding Member, Mental Health Risk Rention Group; Adjunct Faculty Professor, University of Tennessee
Directorships: ECG Management Consultants, Jen Sen Hughes, Washing Systems LLC
Keith Stimson, Partner
415-217-7430
e-mail: stimson@gryphoninvestors.com
Education: BS, Economics, MBA, Wharton School, University of Pennsylvania
Background: Principal, Saunders Karp & Megrue; Big Flower Press Holdings; Bankers Trust
Directorships: The Original Cakerie; Lawler's Foods

887 GRYPHON MANAGEMENT COMPANY
101 Federal Street
Suite 1900
Boston, MA 02108

Phone: 617-619-3800 Fax: 617-619-3801
e-mail: wfa@gryphoninc.com
web: www.gryphoninc.com

Mission Statement: A diversified financial services firm which is actively seeking new investments. Focusing on the capital needs of technology-based companies in New England.

Geographic Preference: United States
Fund Size: $56 million
Founded: 1984
Average Investment: $3 million
Minimum Investment: $1 million
Investment Criteria: Early, Start Up
Industry Group Preference: Energy, Environment Products & Services, Industrial Services, Petrochemicals, Specialty Chemicals, Biotechnology

Key Executives:
William F Aikman, President/CEO
Education: Brown University; University of Pennsylvania; Harvard University
Background: President, Gryphon Management Company, Inc.; President and Chief Executive Officer, Massachusetts Technology Development Corporation
Directorships: Massachusetts Certified Development Corporation, Geltech, Optex

888 GSV VENTURES
171 2nd Street
San Francisco, CA 94105

Phone: 415-757-5634
e-mail: info@gsvaccelerate.com
web: gsvaccelerate.com

Mission Statement: Partners with entrepreneurs in the learning and talent technology sector.

Investment Criteria: Early-Stage
Industry Group Preference: Technology, Education, Human Resources
Portfolio Companies: Amira Learning, Andela, Ansaro, Begin, Campuslogic, ClassDojo, Clever, CLI Studios, Course Hero, Coursera, Create&Learn, Creativelive, Degreed, Educents, Fairygodboss, Glimpse, Goodtime, Gradescope, Handshake, HotChalk, Hustle, Intellispark, Lightneer, Masterclass, Mastery Connect, Mighty, Motimatic, Nearpod, NoRedInk, PeopleGrove, Pluralsight, RaiseMe, Remind, ScholarMe, Stride, Tara, Think Through Math, Toucan, Turnitin, Tynker, Verto Education, Voxy

Key Executives:
Michael Cohn, Co-Founder and Partner
Education: MBA, Kellogg School of Management, Northwestern University; BBA, University of Michigan
Directorships: GSV Advisors

Michael Moe, Co-Founder and Partner, GSV Asset Management
Education: BA, University of Minnesota; Chartered Financial Analyst
Background: Co-Founder, Chair And CEO, ThickEquity Partners; Head of Global Growth Research, Merrill Lynch; Head of Growth Research and Strategy, Montgomery Securities
Directorships: Coursera, Curious, GSVlabs, Course Hero, Class Dojo, Parchment, SharesPost, StormWind, OZY Media
Deborah Quazzo, Managing Partner and Co-Founder, ASU GSV Summit
Education: BA, History, Princeton University; MBA, Harvard University
Directorships: Aakash Educational Services Ltd., Ascend Learning, Degreed, Educational Testing Service, Intellispark, Mighty, Remind, Turnitin

889 GTCR
300 North LaSalle Street
Suite 5600
Chicago, IL 60654

Phone: 312-382-2200
e-mail: info@gtcr.com
web: www.gtcr.com

Mission Statement: GTCR is a private equity firm that seeks to partner with outstanding management leaders; leverage its expertise within the financial technology, healthcare, media, telecommunications, and technology industries; and acquire and build companies with the potential to become market leaders.

Fund Size: $3.85 billion
Founded: 1980
Average Investment: $30 - $250 million
Minimum Investment: $20 million
Investment Criteria: Operating profits $5-$150 million, Mezzanine, Growth Capital, Buyouts, PIPES Financing, Acquisitions
Industry Group Preference: Business to Business, Communications, Distribution, Financial Services, Health Related, Information Technology, Media, Telecommunications
Portfolio Companies: Avention, Callcredit Information Group, CAMP Systems, Cedar Gate Technologies, Cision, Cole-Parmer Instrument Company, Convergex, Correct Care Solutions, Crealta Pharmaceuticals, Fairway Outdoor, Global Traffic Network, IQNavigator, Maravai LifeSciences, Mondee, Opus Global Holdings, Rural Broadband Investments, Rx30, Sterigenics, The Townsend Group, XIFIN, Zayo Group

Key Executives:
Mark M. Anderson, Managing Director
312-382-2239
Education: BS, McIntire School of Commerce, University of Virginia; MBA, Harvard Business School
Background: Gracie Capital; Bowles Hollowell Conner & Company
Directorships: CAMP Systems, Cision, Global Traffic Network, IQNavigator, Mondee, Rural Broadband Investments, XIFIN
Craig A. Bondy, Managing Director
312-382-2224
Education: BBA, Finance, MBA, University of Texas
Background: Credit Suisse First Boston
Directorships: Avention, CAMP Systems, Fairway Outdoor, Mondee
Philip A. Canfield, Managing Director
312-382-2234
Education: BBA, University of Texas; MBA, University of Chicago
Background: Corporate Finance Group, Kidder Peabody and Company

Venture Capital & Private Equity Firms / Domestic Firms

Directorships: Avention, Global Traffic Network, IQNavigator, Rural Broadband Investments, Zayo Group
Aaron D. Cohen, Managing Director
312-382-2169
Education: BS, Accountancy, University of Illinois at Urbana-Champaign
Background: Hicks, Muse, Tate & Furst; M&A Group, Salomon Smith Barney
Directorships: Callcredit Information Group, Opus Global/Hiperos
Sean L. Cunningham, Managing Director
312-382-2260
Education: AB, BE, Dartmouth College; MBA, Wharton School
Background: Consultant, The Boston Consulting Group
Directorships: Cedar Gate Technologies, Cole-Parmer, Correct Care Solutions, Maravai LifeSciences, Rx30, Sterigenics
David A. Donnini, Managing Director
312-382-2240
Education: BA, Economics, Yale University; MBA, Stanford University
Background: Associate Consultant, Bain and Company
Directorships: Fairway Outdoor, Sterigenics, AssuredPartners, Classic Media, Coinmach, Gensar, HSM Electronic Protection Services
Constantine S. Mihas, Managing Director
312-382-2204
Education: BS, Finance & Economics, University of Illinois; MBA, Harvard Business School
Background: CEO & Co-Founder, Delray Farms; McKinsey & Company
Directorships: Cedar Gate Technologies, Cole-Parmer, ConvergEx, Crealta Pharmaceuticals, Maravai LifeSciences, Rx30, Sterigenics, XIFIN
Collin E. Roche, Managing Director
312-382-2214
Education: BA, Political Economy, Williams College; MBA, Harvard Business School
Background: Associate, EVEREN Securities; Analyst, Goldman Sachs & Company
Directorships: Callcredit Information Group, ConvergEx, Opus Global/Hiperos, Aligned Asset Managers
Anna May L Trala, Chief Financial Officer/Managing Director
312-382-2215
Education: BS, Accounting, Goldey Beacom College
Background: Partner, Transaction Advisory Services Group, Ernst & Young

890 GUGGENHEIM PARTNERS
330 Madison Avenue
New York, NY 10017

Phone: 212-739-0700
web: www.guggenheimpartners.com

Mission Statement: Guggenheim Partners is a privately held, diversified financial services firm characterized by a deep commitment to creating exceptional value for our clients throughout the world.
Fund Size: $210 billion
Investment Criteria: Early-Stage Venture Capital, Growth Capital, Distressed Venture Capital
Industry Group Preference: Technology, Semiconductors, Communications, Software, Digital Media & Marketing, Wireless

Other Locations:
227 West Monroe Street
Chicago, IL 60606
Phone: 312-827-0100

3060 Peachtree Road, NW
One Buckhead Plaza
Atlanta, GA 30305

222 Berkeley Street
Boston, MA 02116

3000 Internet Blvd.
Frisco, TX 75034

1301 McKinney
Houston, TX 77010

100 Wilshire Boulevard
Santa Monica, CA 90401
Phone: 310-576-1270

702 King Farm Boulevard
Rockville, MD 20850

50 California St.
San Francisco, CA 94111

231 South Bemiston Avenue
St. Louis, MO 63105

Office 602
Burj Daman Office Tower 6th Floor
Dubai International Financial Centre
Dubai
United Arab Emirates
Phone: +971 (4) 425-0605

South Dock House
Hanover Quay
Dublin 2
Ireland
Phone: +353 1616-8400

5th Floor, The Peak
5 Wilton Road
London SW1V 1AN
United Kingdom
Phone: +44 20 3059 6600

Otemachi First Square
West Tower 13F
1-5-1, Otemachi Chiyoda-Ku
Tokyo 100-0004
Japan

Key Executives:
Mark R. Walter, Chief Executive Officer
Background: Co-Founder, Liberty Hampshire
Thomas J. Irvin, Managing Partner
Alan D. Schwartz, Managing Partner
Background: CEO, The Bear Stearns Companies
B. Scott Minerd, Managing Partner
Background: Managing Director, Morgan Stanley & Credit Suisse
Peter O. Lawson-Johnston II, Managing Partner
Andrew M, Rosenfield, Managing Partner

891 GUIDE MEDICAL VENTURES
2 Oliver Street
Suite 616
Boston, MA 02109

web: www.guidemedicalventures.com

Mission Statement: Guide Medical Ventures was founded in 2011 to develop innovative medical devices that improve patient outcomes and reduce costs. GMV focuses on technology improvements for existing medical procedures and applications. Our team members have proven track records at both large companies and start-ups in the medical device industry, including experience leading companies from formation through acquisition. GMV guides its projects and start-ups from inception through acquisition, creating value for our shareholders and strategic partners in the most capital efficient manner.

Founded: 2011
Investment Criteria: Early-Stage
Industry Group Preference: Medical Devices
Portfolio Companies: CardioSolv Ablation Technologies, CSA Medical, Enspire DBS Therapy, NeuroAccess Technologies, Qr8 Health

Key Executives:
    Vince Owens, Founder/Managing General Partner
    Education: BS, Mechanical Engineering, Carnegie Mellon University; MBA, Ashland University
    Background: Co-Founder/CEO, Intelect Medical
    Scott Kokones, Founder/General Partner
    Education: BS, Mechanical Engineering, University of Michigan; MBA, Boston University
    Background: Co-Founder/SVP, Intelect Medical; Medtronic, Enpath Medical
    Keith Carlton, Founder/General Partner
    Education: BS, Biomedical Engineering and Engineering Mechanics, Johns Hopkins University; MBA, Boston University
    Background: CEO, HUINNO; Director of New Therapy Development, Boston Scientific
    Greg Schulte, Partner
    Education: BS, Mechanical Engineering, University of Michigan
    Background: 525 Medical; Mechanical Engineering, Intelect Medical; EnteroMedical, Enpath Medical; Medtronic

---

892 GUIDE VENTURES
12509 Bel-Red Road
Suite 201
Bellevue, WA 98005-2535

Fax: 425-688-7980
web: www.guideventures.com

Mission Statement: Actively work with each portfolio firm and their team to create the highest value possible through building a strong company culture, solid financial models, and leading-edge intellectual property.

Geographic Preference: West Coast, Western Canada
Fund Size: $21 million
Founded: 1999
Average Investment: $1.5 million
Minimum Investment: $500,000
Investment Criteria: Seed, Early
Industry Group Preference: Life Sciences, Infrastructure, Wireless Technologies
Portfolio Companies: AdRelevance, BOCADA, nCircle, Sharebuilder, Virtual Relocation

Key Executives:
    Russ Aldrich, Managing Director
    Education: Long Beach City College
    Background: VP/Co-Founder, Simba Technologies; Hal (Fujitsu) Computer Systems; Silicon Graphics; Altos Computer Systems; Convergent Technologies; SoftTech, Xerox Corporation; McDonnell-Douglas Aircraft
    Directorships: Flatrock, Netstock
    Jim Thornton, Managing Director
    Education: MBA, Rutgers University
    Background: Newsweek Magazine; VP of Finance & Operations, Aldus Corporation; CEO, Lifespex Corporation
    Directorships: Bocada
    Dave Kowalick, Senior Associate
    Education: Graduate Degree, MIT
    Background: Naval Officer, United States Naval Academy; Fund Manager, CKW LLC; Advanced Marine Technology; Tidemark Solutions
    Directorships: Detto
    Mike Templeman, Managing Director
    Education: BS, Zoology, University of Washington; MSE, Seattle University
    Background: Graphics & Systems Programmer, Boeing; Co-Founder, Aldus Corporation; Co-Founder, MetaBridge Corporation; Co-Founder, Netpodium
    Directorships: nCirle Network Security

---

893 GULFSTAR GROUP
700 Louisiana Street
Suite 3800
Houston, TX 77002-2731

Phone: 713-300-2020 **Fax:** 713-300-2021
e-mail: info@gulfstargroup.com
web: www.gulfstargroup.com

Mission Statement: Gulfstar provides investment and merchant banking services to a variety of industries, to both public and private middle market companies. Gulfstar is one of the South West's largest and most active investment banking firms serving the middle market, having completed over 225 assignments in over 15 industries.

Founded: 1990
Average Investment: $20 million
Minimum Investment: $5 million
Investment Criteria: Company with revenues between $10-$150 million
Industry Group Preference: Business Products & Services, Technology, Software, Energy, Manufacturing, Wholesale, Health Related, Consumer Products, Security, Consumer Services, Infrastructure, Financial Services, Information Technology, Transportation, Logistics

Key Executives:
    Cliff Atherton Jr., Managing Director
    713-300-2060
    e-mail: catherton@gulfstargroup.com
    Education: BA, Rice University; PhD, MBA, University of Texas; CFA
    Background: Managing Director, McKenna & Company; President, Emprise Consulting Group; Rice University 's Jesse H Jones School of Administration; Adjunct Professor of Finance, University of Houston.
    Directorships: Teas Nursery Company Inc
    Alan J. Blackburn, Managing Director
    713-300-2048
    e-mail: ablackburn@gulfstargroup.com
    Education: BBA, Accounting & Finance, University of Texas, Austin; MBA, Wharton School, University of Pennsylvania
    Background: Managing Director, Growth Capital Partners; Investment Banking Group, Merrill Lynch
    Chip Cureton, Advisory Director
    713-300-2033
    e-mail: ccureton@gulfstargroup.com
    Education: AB, History, Stanford University; MBA, Harvard Business School
    Background: Cureton & Company; VP, Rotam Mosle; United States Navy
    Directorships: Hankey Oil Company, Mobley Environmental Services, Modular Environmental Technologies, Midway Importing
    Bryan C. Frederickson, Managing Director
    713-300-2030
    e-mail: bfrederickson@gulfstargroup.com
    Education: BS, Economics, MBA, Finance, Vanderbilt University
    Background: Navigant Capital Advisors; Wachovia Securities
    Thomas M. Hargrove, Managing Director/Co-Founder
    713-300-2050
    e-mail: thargrove@gulfstargroup.com
    Education: BA, Economics, University of Texas
    Background: Senior VP, Rotan Mosle Inc.; First VP, Underwood, Neuhaus & Company; Assisitant VP, Corporate Finance, First City National Bank
    Directorships: Entrix, Stellar Event & Presentation Resources, Rimco Production Company

G. Kent Kahle, Managing Director/Co-Founder
713-300-2025
e-mail: kkahle@gulfstargroup.com
Education: MBA, Wharton School, University of Pennsylvania; AB, Brown University
Background: Senior VP, Investment Banking; Director, Rotan Mosle; Manager of Investor Relations, Geosource; Special Assistant to the Secretary of Commerce and Secretary of Interior, Ford Administration.
Directorships: US Legal Support; Total Safety
Stephen A. Lasher, Managing Director
713-300-2010
e-mail: slasher@gulfstargroup.com
Education: BA, Vanderbilt University
Background: Executive Vice President, Rotan Mosle Inc.
Directorships: Weingarten Realty
Colt Leudde, Managing Director
713-300-2015
e-mail: cluedde@gulfstargroup.com
Education: BBA, Finance, University of Texas, Austin
Background: Corporate Banking Group, NationsBank Corporation
Eric Swanson, Managing Director
713-300-2008
e-mail: eswanson@gulfstargroup.com
Education: BA, Biochemistry/Molecular Biology, MS, Evaluative Clinical Sciences, Dartmouth College; MBA, Kellogg School of Management, Northwestern University
Background: Investment Banker, Morgan Stanley; Deutsche; JP Morgan; ExxonMobil Corp.
Pamela L. Reiland, Senior Vice President
713-300-2003
e-mail: preiland@gulfstargroup.com
Education: BA, Spanish, Duke University; MBA & MPA, Rice University
Background: Director of Alumni Engagement, Rice University; Willbros USA; Galveston-Houston Company
Brian J. Lobo, Managing Director
713-300-2047
e-mail: blobo@gulfstargroup.com
Education: BBA, Finance, University of Texas, Austin
Background: Lazard Middle Market; Analyst, Advanced Micro Devices Inc.
Rupert Gerard, Vice President
713-300-2051
e-mail: rgerard@gulfstargroup.com
Education: BA, Government, Georgetown University; MBA, INSEAD
Background: Castleton Commodities International; Taylor Woods Capital
Scott D. Winship, Managing Director
713-300-2011
e-mail: swinship@gulstargroup.com
Education: BA, Political Science & Business Communcations, University of California, Davis
Background: Managing Director, 6Pacific Partners; BMO Capital Markets; JPMorgan Chase & Co.; Cowen & Co.
Ben Stanton, Vice President
713-300-2040
e-mail: bstanton@gulfstargroup.com
Education: BA, Business Admin., MS, Finance, Mays Business School, Texas A&M University; CPA
Background: Senior Associate, PricewaterhouseCoopers

---

894 GV
Mountain View, CA 94043

web: www.gv.com

Mission Statement: GV, formerly Google Ventures, provides venture capital funding to innovative new companies across a range of industries, including healthcare, life sciences, consumer Internet, robotics, and artificial intelligence.
Geographic Preference: United States
Fund Size: $2.4 billion
Founded: 2009
Investment Criteria: All Stages
Industry Group Preference: Consumer Internet, Software, Mobile Technology, Robotics, Life Sciences, Healthcare, Artificial Intelligence, Enterprise Software, Transportation, Cybersecurity
Portfolio Companies: 23andMe, 2nd Address, Abacus, About.me, Abundant Robotics, Acalvia, Agent, Airtime, Airwave, Alector, Aledade, Ambition, Amino, Anchor, Andela, AngelList, Anomali, Apptentive, Apptimize, Aspire Health, Basis, Benson Hill Biosystems, BlackThorn Therapeutics, Blavity, Blockchain, Bowery, Brandless, Breather, Bugsnag, Cambly, Cambridge Epigenetix, Carbon, Carmera, Carrick Therapeutics, Celsius Therapeutics, Censys, Checkr, CircleUp, CircuitHub, Clarifai, ClassPass, Clear Labs, ClearStory Data, Clever, Clover Health, Clutter, Cockroach Labs, Cohesity, Collective Health, Compass Therapeutics, Confide, Cool Planet Energy Systems, Copper, Corduro, Cozy, creativeLIVE, Creator, CTRL-Labs, Currencycloud, CyberGRX, DaileyCred, DataFox, Datanyze, Decibel Therapeutics, Delighted, Desktop Metal, Desmos, Dialpad, Digit, Disruptor Beam, DNAnexus, Doctor On Demand, Duo, Easy Post, Egnyte, Emergent, Emissary, English Central, Ethos, Evelo Bioscience, Evox Therapeutics, Farmers Business Network, Fauna, Flexport, Flux, FLX Bio, FogPharma, Freenome, FullStory, Gametime, Genomics Medicine Ireland, Giphy, GitLab, Grail, Gritstone Oncology, Gusto, Happiest Babby, HeadSpin, Helium, HelloSign, High Fidelity, Highfive, HomeLight, HOVER, Hustle, Ideaya Bioscience, Impossible Foods, Incorta, insitro, Intercom, IonQ, Ionic Security, Jaunt, JumpCam, KeepTruckin, Kitched United, Kindred, Kobalt, Lambada School, Le Tote, LedgerX, Lemonade, LendUp, LevelUp, LifeMine Therapeutics, Light, Lime, Lola, LostMyName, Lotus Flare, Luminate Wireless, mabl, Machinify, Managed by Q, MapD, Medium, MemSQL, Metabiota, Mighty AI, MindSumo, Mist, MixBit, Mode, Modsy, mParticle, N3twork, NewHound, Nextdoor, Nimble, NoRedInk, Obsidian Therapeutics, One Medical Group, Openbay, Opendoor, Optimizely, Orbital Insight, Oscar, Osito, Outdoor Voices, OWKIN, Oxford Science Innovation, Packagd, PACT Pharma, Panorama Education, PatientPing, Payrange, Percolata, Periscope Data, Peerspace, Pindrop, Plaid, PlanGrid, Plexxi, Podium, Poynt, Permise, Puppet Labs, Quartet, Rabbit, Rani Therapeutics, Reaction Commerce, Recorded Future, Relay Therapeutics, Reserve, Resolution Games, RightHandRobotics, Ripple Foods, Ripple Labs, Ripcord, Robinhood, Rockbot, RocketLawyer, Rocketrip, Rodin Therapeutics, SambaNova Systems, Savioke, Segment, Scalus, Scalyr, Scandit, Science 37, ScoutRFP, Secret Escapes, SecurityScorecard, Seddling, Sense, Shape Security, Shelf, Signpost, Skycatch, Clack, Snyk, Soylent, SpinLaunch, Spring, etc.

Other Locations:
San Francisco, CA 94105

Cambridge, MA 02142

New York, NY 10011

Key Executives:
David Krane, CEO & Managing Partner
Education: BA, Journalism, Indiana University, Bloomington
Background: Director, Global Communications & Public Affairs, Google; Apple Computer; QUALCOMM; Four11
Karim Faris, General Partner
Education: BS, Computer Engineering, Brown University; MS, Electrical Engineering, University of Michigan; MBA, Harvard Business School
Background: Corporate Development, Google; Atlas Venture; Director, New Ventures, Level 3 Communications; Intel; Siemens
Tom Hulme, General Partner
Education: BS, Physics, University of Bristol; MBA, Harvard Business School
Background: Design Director, IDEO Europe; Managing Director, Marcos; Founder, Magnom

Dave Munichiello, General Partner
Education: BS, Mathematics & Computer Science, Emory University; MBA, Harvard Business School
Background: Senior Executive, Kiva Systems; Management Consultant, The Boston Consulting Group; Captain, United States Military
M.G. Siegler, General Partner
Education: University of Michigan
Background: 500ish; Founding Partner, CrunchFund; Writer, TechCrunch; Writer, VentureBeat
Andy Wheeler, General Partner
Education: BS, MEng, Electrical Engineering & Computer Science, Massachusetts Institute of Technology
Background: CTO, Adura; CTO, Tendril Networks; Co-Founder, Ember Corporation; Zipcar; MIT Media Lab
Krishna Yeshwant, General Partner
Education: BS, Computer Science, Stanford University; MD, Harvard Medical School; MBA, Harvard Business School
Background: New Business Development Team, Google
Directorships: Editas Medicine, Flatiron, One Medical Group
John Lyman, Partner
Education: Georgetown University; MA, Public Policy, University of California, Berkeley
Background: Clinton Global Initiative; Center for American Progress; Google

895 GVA CAPITAL
906 Broadway
San Francisco, CA 94133

web: gva.capital

Mission Statement: The US investment arm of the Global Venture Alliance funds early-stage companies with a focus on education.
Geographic Preference: North America
Fund Size: $120 million
Founded: 2011
Investment Criteria: Early-Stage, Late-Stage, Secondary Market, Seed
Industry Group Preference: Fintech, Artificial Intelligence, Neural Networks, Big Data, Data Mining, Cloud Technologies
Portfolio Companies: Acquired.io, Cherry Labs, Establishment Labs, Opus12, WISeKey, Storj.iO, Diamond Factory, AstroDigital, Mlvch, Nopassword, People.ai, Qwil, I.AM+, Virool, Luminar, PolyUp, Omniscience, Pixlee, Mubert, SoLoMoTo, COUB, Kiana, Fiscal Note, RoboCV

Other Locations:
Plug and Play Tech Center
440 N Wolfe Road
Sunnyvale, CA 94085
US

Key Executives:
Pavel Cherkashin, Managing Partner
Roman Sobachevskiy, Managing Partner
Education: MBA, Stephen M. Ross School of Business, University of Michigan
Daria Gonzalez, Chief Executive Officer
Education: MBA, Stanford University

896 H KATZ CAPITAL GROUP
Southampton Office Park
928 Jaymor Road
Suite A-100
Southampton, PA 18966-3823

Phone: 215-364-0400 Fax: 215-364-5025
web: www.katzgroup.com

Mission Statement: H. Katz Capital Group is a private equity firm seeking to provide funding to companies with experienced management teams, unique products or services, and the ability to generate financial returns.
Investment Criteria: Management Buyouts, Recapitalizations, Early Stage, Expansion Stage, Growth Stage
Industry Group Preference: Consumer Services, Food & Beverage, Media, Healthcare, Financial Services, Franchising, Real Estate
Key Executives:
Harold Katz, Chairman
Background: Nutri/System Center; Owner, Philadelphia 76ers
Directorships: United Valley Bank, Hero Scholarship Fund of Philadelphia, Police Athletic League
Brian J Siegel, Managing Director
e-mail: bsiegel@katzgroup.com
Education: BS, Accounting & Finance, La Salle University; LLM, Taxation, Georgetown University; JD, University of Pennsylvania Law School
Background: Partner, Duane Morris & Heckscher; Lecturer, Accounting, University of Pennsylvania Wharton School of Finance & Commerce; Attorney Advisor, Arnold Raum, United States Tax Court; Coopers and Lybrand
David A Katz, Executive Vice President/Secretary
e-mail: davidkatz@katzgroup.com
Background: Co-Owner & Founder, Camp Big Pocono; D&S Camps; Sixer's Camp; Owner & President, Innovative Staffing Services; Analyst, Finance Department, Nutri System; Executive Investment Advisors; VP & Director, Marketing, Philadelphia 76ers Basketball Club

897 H&Q ASIA PACIFIC
228 Hamilton Avenue
3rd Floor
Palo Alto, CA 94301

Phone: 650-838-8025 Fax: 650-618-1699
web: www.hqap.com

Mission Statement: H&Q Asia Pacific is a private equity firm based in Asia.
Geographic Preference: Asia Pacific
Fund Size: $1.8 billion
Founded: 1986
Investment Criteria: Early Stage, Later Stage, Emerging, Buyout, Middle Market, Growth Capital
Industry Group Preference: All Sectors Considered
Portfolio Companies: Access, Acer, Advanced Analog Technology, Advanced Systems Automation, Amperex Technology, Aplix, Array Networks, Atop Holdings, Aztech Systems, Biosensors International, Bluebird, CareNet, Chimei Innolux, Dalipal Pipe Company, Darfon Electronics, D-Link, Esquire, Fabrinet, Falmac, Foxlink, Gonzo, Good Morning Securities, Grace THW Holdings, Groundhog Technologies, Hainan Airline, HANA Micron, Headstrong, Headway Technologies, Hi-mart, Hyunjin Materials and Yonghyun Base Materials, Korea Petrochemical, KSNet, The LeadCorp, Macronix International, MAG Technology, Mando, Megastudy, MTV Japan, Music Semiconductors, Mustek, Nan Ya PCB, Nitgen Technologies, O2Micro, One, Opto Tech, Optovue, Penta Securities Systems, PhiSkin, Primax Electronics, Ralink Technology, RITEK, Roly International Holdings, Semiconductor Manufacturing International, Shandong Winery, SiGen, Siliconware Precision Industries, SinoGen International, Sky Vision, Starbucks Beijing, SVI Public, Taiwan Semiconductor Manufacturing Company, Taiwan Sumida Electronics, Thai Cane Paper Public, TICON Industrial Connection Public, VIBE, Viscovery, Weltrend Semiconductor, Winbond Electronics, Wintek, You Yi Shopping City, Yuchai Engineering

Other Locations:
1650B, 16th Floor
The Hong Kong Club, Building 3A

Venture Capital & Private Equity Firms / Domestic Firms

Chater Road
Central
Hong Kong
Phone: 852-28684800 **Fax:** 852-28104883

3F Wonseo Building
171 Wonseo-Dong
Jongno-Gu
Seoul 110-280
Korea
Phone: 82-27872288 **Fax:** 82-237754589

32F-1, International Trade Building
333 Keelung Road
Sec. 1
Taipei 110
Taiwan
Phone: 8862-27209855 **Fax:** 8862-27222106

Suite 708, 7/FL Citigroup Tower
33 Hua Yuan Shi Qiao Road
Shanghai 200120
China
Phone: 86-2168878080 **Fax:** 86-2168878011

Key Executives:
Ta-Lin Hsu, Chairman/Founder
Education: BS, Physics, National Taiwan University; MS, Electrophysics, Polytechnic Institute of Brooklyn; PhD, Electrical Engineering, University of California, Berkeley
Background: Research, IBM; General Partner, Hambrecht & Quist
Directorships: ASE, Sinogen International, One
Benson He, Managing Director
Education: BEng, Electrical Engineering, Shanghai Jiao Tong University; CFA
Background: PwC Business Modelling and Valuation; JP Morgan; KPMG Corporate Finance
Mark Hsu, Managing Director
Education: BA, University of California, Los Angeles; JD, Columbia University
Background: Director, Business Development, Sina.com; Attorney, Simpson Thacher & Bartlett
Directorships: AAMA, East West Players, The Churchill Club, Vision New America
William Chung, Managing Director
Education: BS/MS, Agriculture, National Taiwan University
Background: VP, CIDC Consultants Ltd.; Deputy Manager, Industrial Bank of Taiwan Group
Robert Shen, Managing Director
Education: BS, National Cheng Kung University; MS, Marquette University; PhD, Southern Methodist University
Background: Chief Technical Officer & General Manager, Lucent Microelectronics; Founder, Enable Semiconductor; President, 8x8 Inc.; General Manager, VLSI Technology

898 HADDINGTON VENTURES LLC
2603 Augusta
Suite 900
Houston, TX 77057

Phone: 713-532-7992 **Fax:** 713-532-9922
web: www.hvllc.com

Mission Statement: Providing superior returns to its investors by focusing on the midstream energy sector.
Geographic Preference: United States
Fund Size: $850 million
Founded: 1998
Average Investment: $20 to $50 million
Minimum Investment: $20 million
Industry Group Preference: Energy, Natural Gas, Power Storage, Underground Hydrocarbon Storage, Midstream Growth
Portfolio Companies: Apax CAES, Bear Paw Energy, Bobcat Gas Storage, CAES Development Company, Endicott Biofuels, Eureka Resources, Fairway Energy, Gulf Coast LNG, IACX Energy, Lodi Gas Storage, Magnum NGLS, Magnum Energy, Nations Energy, Proton Energy Systems, Sago Energy, Silicon Energy, Tristream Energy, Zechstein Energy Storage

Key Executives:
J. Chris Jones, Managing Director
Education: BBA, Accounting, University of Texas, Austin
Background: SVP/CFO/COO, Tejas Power Corp.; Secretary/Treasurer/CFO, The Fisk Group Inc.
Directorships: Market Hub Partners, Dayton Power & Light, New Jersey Resources, NIPSCO, Public Service Electric and Gas
John A. Strom, Managing Director
Education: BS, Finance, University of Illinois
Background: Fish Engineering; Union Carbide; Co-Founder/President, TPC
Jim P. Wise, Advisory Board
Education: University of Houston, Bauer College of Business
Background: Managing Director, Haddington Ventures; CEO/Vice Chairman, Integrated Electrical Services; VP, Finance/CFO, Sterling Chemicals; EVP/CFO, Transco Energy Company
M. Scott Jones, Managing Director
Education: BA, Pomona College; JD, University of Texas School of Law
Background: VP/General Counsel, TPC; Dickerson, Carmouch & Jones
James K. Lam, Managing Director
Education: BBA, Finance, University of Houston
Background: Jefferies & Company; Merrill Lynch
Sam H. Pyne, Managing Director
Education: BA, Quantitative Economics, BS, Chemical Engineering, Tufts University; MBA, Rice University
Background: Equity Analyst, Howard Weil; Process Engineer, Lyondell
Directorships: Endicott Biofuels, Eureka, Apex CAES

899 HALIFAX GROUP LLC
1133 Connecticut Avenue NW
Suite 300
Washington, DC 20036

Phone: 202-530-8300
e-mail: inquiry@thehalifaxgroup.com
web: www.thehalifaxgroup.com

Mission Statement: Seeks to create substantial equity value for management teams and its investment partners. Halifax's goal is to form partnerships with proven management teams, bringing not only capital to the middle market but also a wealth of strategic, financial, and operating experience.
Geographic Preference: United States
Fund Size: $1.5 billion
Founded: 1999
Average Investment: $20 million
Minimum Investment: $10 million
Investment Criteria: The last twelve months EBITDA is between $5-$15 million.
Industry Group Preference: Consumer Products, Distribution, Financial Services, Health Related, Information Technology, Manufacturing, Telecommunications, Transportation, Logistics, Consumer Services
Portfolio Companies: Animal Supply Company, Aptiv Solutions, BCI Burke, Caring Brands International, Delphi Behavioral Health Group, Envision Pharma Group, Familia Dental, Golden State Overnight, IASIS Healthcare, InSight Health Services Corp. Inc., K2 Industrial Services, Maverick Healthcare, Meineke Car Care Centers, MTW Corp., North American Video, Nutrition Physiology Company LLC, NPSG, Papa Johns, Pirtek, PolyPipe, The PromptCare Companies, Service Champ, SoilSafe, Taylor Logistics LLC, Universal Hospital Services, U.S. Environmental Services, XLA

Venture Capital & Private Equity Firms / Domestic Firms

Other Locations:
200 Crescent Court
Suite 1030
Dallas, TX 75201
Phone: 214-855-8700

3605 Glenwood Avenue
Suite 490
Raleigh, NC 27612
Phone: 919-786-4420

Key Executives:
David Dupree, Founder/Senior Partner
202-530-8300
e-mail: ddupree@thehalifaxgroup.com
Education: BS, University of North Carolina-Chapel Hill; MBA, Graduate School of Management, Wake Forest University
Background: The Carlyle Group; Montgomery Securities; Alex.Brown & Sons
Directorships: K2 Industrial Services Inc., XLA, Aptiv Solutions, Envision Pharma Group, IASIS Healthcare Corp, InSight Health Services Corp., Meineke Car Care Centers, Soil Safe Inc.
Kenneth M. Doyle, Senior Partner
202-530-8300
e-mail: kdoyle@thehalifaxgroup.com
Education: BS, Boston College; MBA, Duke University
Background: GE Equity; Telecommunications Corporate Finance Group-Merrill Lynch; Chase Manhattan Bank-Media Telecommunications Group; Ernst & Young
Directorships: Famalia Dental, Pirtek Europe, XLA Inc., Caring Brands International, Sinsight Holdings, Maverick Healthcare, Meineke Car Care Centers Inc, North American Video, PJ United
Brent Williams, Senior Partner
214-855-8700
e-mail: bwilliams@thehalifaxgroup.com
Education: BA, University of Texas; MBA, Rice University
Background: Painewebber; Smith Barney; Sumitomo Bank
Directorships: Animal Supply Company, BCI Burke, GSO Delivery, Maverick Healthcare, MTW Corp., PolyPipe Holdings Inc., Taylor Logistics, Universal Hospital Services Inc.
Michael Marshall, Senior Partner/CFO/COO
919-786-4420
e-mail: mmarshall@thehalifaxgroup.com
Education: BA, Accounting, North Carolina State University
Background: KPMG; PricewaterhouseCoopers
Chris Cathcart, Managing Partner
202-530-8300
e-mail: ccathcart@thehalifaxgroup.com
Education: BA, Wake Forest University; MBA, Kellogg School of Management, Northwestern University
Scott Plumridge, Managing Partner
202-530-8300
e-mail: splumridge@thehalifaxgroup.com
Education: BS, Business, Wake Forest University; MBA, Stanford Grad. School of Business
Background: Chartwell Investments; JP Morgan & Co.
Davis Hostetter, Vice President
214-855-8705
e-mail: dhostetter@thehalifaxgroup.com
Education: BS, Economics & Political Science, Duke University; MBA, Wharton School, University of Pennsylvania
Background: Investment Analyst, Hayman Capital; Associate, Diamond Castle Holdings; M&A, Deutsche Bank

900 HALLEY VENTURE PARTNERS
876 Revere Road
Lafayette, CA 94549

Phone: 925-451-3310
web: www.halleyvp.com

Mission Statement: Invests in companies across the various sectors of the cannabis industry.
Founded: 2017
Industry Group Preference: Cannabis, Agriculture, Biosciences, Technology
Portfolio Companies: Front Range Biosciences, SpringBig
Key Executives:
Steve Schuman, Founder/Managing Director
Education: BS, Chemical Engineering, University of Dayton; BS, Ohio State University; MBA, Haas School of Business, University of California, Berkeley
Background: Coordinator/Process Engineer, The Dow Chemical Company; Marketing Manager, Bandwidth9; Sr. Equity Analyst, Prudential Equity Group; Sr. Equity Analyst, New Vernon Associates; Owner/Sr. Equity Analyst, Lafayette Research; Sr. Analyst/PM, Agriculture & Chemicals, Passport Capital

901 HALOGEN VENTURES
e-mail: hello@halogenvc.com

Mission Statement: Halogen Ventures is an early stage venture capital fund focused on female founded consumer technology companies.

Industry Group Preference: Consumer, Technology
Portfolio Companies: Armoire, Barn & Willow, BeautyCon, Block Cypher, Blue Fever, Broadway Roulette, Bulletin, Carbon38, Clover Letter, Dog Parker, Eloquii, Finery, Goodr, Handwriting.io, HopSkipDrive, Inked Brands, L., Laurel & Wolf Interior Design, Levo League, Molly, Naja, Naya, One Potato, PartySlate, Peek, Preemadonna, Seedling, Senreve, Shipsi, Silvernest, Sugarfina, Tea Drops, Tentrr, The Flex Company, The Relish, The Sill, The Skimm, Tinted, Trust & Will, Vida, Werk

Key Executives:
Jesse Draper, Founding Partner
Education: University of California, LA
Background: Creator/Host, The Valley Girl Show
Directorships: The Skimm, Laurel & Wolf, Carbon38, HopSkipDrive, The Flex Company, Sugarfina

902 HALYARD CAPITAL
140 E 45th Street
Floor 37
New York, NY 10017

Phone: 212-554-2121
e-mail: info@halyard.com
web: www.halyard.com

Mission Statement: Halyard Capital is a middle market private equity firm focused on creating value within the Information and Knowledge economies through thesis-driven investments. The firm invests in technology-enabled Information, Data Analytics, Communications and Business Services companies.

Geographic Preference: North America, Europe
Fund Size: $300 million
Average Investment: $10 - $40 million
Investment Criteria: Growth Equity, Acquisition Capital, Leverage Buyouts, Consolidations, Platform Builds, Turnarounds, Structured Equity, Going-Private Transactions
Industry Group Preference: Information Technology, Marketing, Communications, Business Products & Services, Healthcare, IT Cyber Risk, Data Analytics, Outsourced Solutions
Portfolio Companies: Aberdeen Group, Datamyx, Digital Fortress, Education Dynamics, Engauge, Focal Point Data Risk, Greeley Company, Hanley-Wood, Herld Media, impreMedia, Inflow Group, Inner City Media Corporation,

Venture Capital & Private Equity Firms / Domestic Firms

Jun Group, NETGEAR, North Dakota Holdings, NuLink, OneSource Virtual, Pfingsten Publishing, Practice Insight, Presidion Inc., Smith Broadcasting Group, StratEx, Tama Broadcasting, TCP Communications, TI Health, TRANZACT, WMI

Key Executives:
Robert B Nolan Jr, Founding Partner
212-554-2144
e-mail: rnolan@halyard.com
Education: BS, BA, Georgetown University; JD, Fordham University School of Law
Background: CEO, BMO Private Equity Group; Managing Director, CIBC World Markets; Telecommunications Group Head, UBS Securities; Goldman, Sachs & Co.
Directorships: Digital Fortress, Education Dynamics, Jun Group, Practice Insight

Bruce A Eatroff, Managing Partner
212-554-2145
e-mail: beatroff@halyard.com
Education: BA, Lafayette College; MBA, Wharton School
Background: Goldman Sachs; UBS Securities; CIBC World Markets
Directorships: Cyber Risk Management, Education Dynamics, Jun Group, NuLink, OneSource Vital

Jonathan P Barnes, Partner
212-554-2122
e-mail: jbarnes@halyard.com
Education: AB, Harvard University; MBA, Columbia Business School
Background: Morgan Stanley; Consolidated Press Holdings
Directorships: Aberdeen Group, OneSource Virtual, Stratex

Jonathan Grad, Managing Director
212-554-2194
e-mail: skim@halyard.com
Education: BA, Economics & Political Science, Colgate University
Background: Managing Director, Media, Communications & Technology, BMO Capital Markets
Directorships: Digital Fortress, Engauge Marketing, Women's Marketing Inc.

Brendyn T Grimaldi, Principal
212-554-2131
e-mail: bgrimaldi@halyard.com
Education: BS, Finance, Boston College
Background: Analyst, Credit Suisse
Directorships: Aberdeen Group, Stratex, TI Health

Kyle Grace, Associate
212-554-2143
e-mail: kgrace@halyard.com
Education: BA, Economics & Finance, University of Richmond
Background: Investment Banking Analyst, Jefferies & Company

903 HAMILTON ROBINSON CAPITAL PARTNERS
301 Tresser Boulevard
3 Stamford Plaza
Suite 1333
Stamford, CT 06901

Phone: 203-602-0011 Fax: 203-602-2206
e-mail: cld@hrco.com
web: www.hrco.com

Mission Statement: A private equity firm that specializes in serving small to medium size companies seeking equity capital for management buyouts, corporate growth, and recapitalizations for shareholder equity.

Geographic Preference: United States
Founded: 1984
Average Investment: $2-$20 million
Minimum Investment: $2 million
Investment Criteria: LBO, MBO, Recapitalization, Revenue of $25-$200 Million
Industry Group Preference: Industrial Equipment, Outsourcing & Efficiency, Energy, Business to Business, Manufacturing, Distribution, Business Products & Services
Portfolio Companies: Automatan LLC, Custom Engineered Wheels Inc., GrayMatter LLC, Horizon Food Equipment Inc., Sound Seal Inc., Systec Corp., Unifiller Systems Inc., W-Technology Inc.

Key Executives:
Scott I. Oakford, Managing Partner
203-602-0566
e-mail: sio@hrco.com
Education: BS, Economics, Claremont McKenna College
Background: CFO, AGCO; President, Maloney Industries; Goldome Strategic Investments; Chemical Bank
Directorships: W-Technology Holdings, Sound Seal Holdings, Inspire Automation, MEGTEC Holdings

Steve Crihfield, Senior Advisor
203-602-0085
e-mail: osc@hrco.com
Education: BA, Government, Pomona College; MBA, Harvard Business School
Background: General Partner, Saugatuck Capital Company; Merrill Lynch
Directorships: Horizon Bradco, Dexter Magnetic Technologies, Lifestyle Media, The Fitzpatrick Company, Custom Engineered Wheels

Phil Cagnassola, Partner/CFO
203-602-0514
e-mail: pjc@hrco.com
Education: BS, Accounting, Fairfield University
Background: VP, Walker Digital; CFO, PC Flowers and Gifts; Ernst & Young; GE Capital
Directorships: Black Clawson Converting Machinery

Chris Lund, Partner
203-602-0012
e-mail: cel@hrco.com
Education: BA, St. Lawrence University; MBA, Tuck School of Business, Dartmouth College
Background: GE Equity; Chase Manhattan Bank; Chemical Bank
Directorships: Sound Seal Holdings Inc, Inspire Automation, Unifiller Systems, Magnatech International, All Island Media

Stephen B. Connor, Director, Business Development
203-602-3309
e-mail: sbc@hrco.com
Education: BS, Wharton School; University of Pennsylvania; MBA, Columbia Business School; CPA; CFA
Background: SVP, Business Development, GE Capital; Smith Barney Venture Capital Group; Prudential Bache Corporate Finance Group; PricewaterhouseCoopers

904 HAMMOND, KENNEDY, WHITNEY & COMPANY
420 Lexington Avenue
Suite 2633
New York, NY 10170

Phone: 212-867-1010 Fax: 212-867-1312
e-mail: info@hkwinc.com
web: www.hkwinc.com

Mission Statement: Concentrates investments on private and public, small middle market manufacturing companies with low risk of technological obsolescence, providing transaction experience, investing in people and companies with solid fundamentals and creating shareholder value.

Geographic Preference: North America
Fund Size: $255 million
Founded: 1903
Average Investment: $20 - $150 million

Minimum Investment: $5 million
Investment Criteria: MBO, recaps, Revenues of $20 - $200 Million
Industry Group Preference: Manufacturing, Industrial Services, Distribution, Automotive, Medical Devices, Aerospace, Infrastructure, Energy, Cosumer Products
Portfolio Companies: Allied Vision Group Inc., Brant Instore Corp., Gatekeeper Systems Inc., GCR Inc., PANOS Brands LLC, Partners in Leadership Inc., ProAct Services Corp., Protect Plus Air Holdings, Royal Camp Services, Specialized Desanders, Xirgo Technologies

Other Locations:
8888 Keystone Crossing
Suite 600
Indianapolis, IN 46240
Phone: 317-574-6900 **Fax:** 317-574-7515

Key Executives:
Ted H. Kramer, President/CEO
317-705-8824
e-mail: tk@hkwinc.com
Education: BS, University of Michigan; MBA, Kelley School of Business, Indiana University
Background: Investment Manager, White River Venture Partners; Arthur Andersen

James C. Snyder, Partner
317-705-8815
e-mail: jcs@hkwinc.com
Education: BA, Wabash College; JD, Indiana University School of Law
Background: Vice President, Browing Investments

Luke A. Phenicie, Lead Transaction Partner
317-705-8826
e-mail: lap@hkwinc.com
Education: BS, Indiana University Kelley School of Business; MBA, University of Chicago Graduate School of Business
Background: Financial Analyst, Prospect Partners; M&A, A.G. Edwards & Sons

Caroline L. Young, Director of ESG
317-705-8823
e-mail: cly@hkwinc.com
Education: BA, University of Vermont; JD, University of Virginia School of Law
Background: Wooden & McLaughlin, LLP

John M. Carsello, Partner
317-705-8735
e-mail: jmc@hkwinc.com
Education: BS, Indiana University Kelley School of Business; MBA, Kellogg School of Management, Northwestern University
Background: Analyst, Norwest Equity Partners; Investment Banking, Credit Suisse

Michael A. Foisy, Lead Operations Partner
207-807-8695
e-mail: maf@hkwinc.com
Education: BS, University of Maine; MBA, University of New Hampshire Whittemore School of Business
Background: Business Unit Manager, First Technology Unit, Sensata Technlogy/Bain Capital Partners

Christopher M. Eline, Principal
317-705-8827
e-mail: cme@hkwinc.com
Education: BA, Indiana University
Background: Analyst, Sagent Advisors

905 HANCOCK PARK ASSOCIATES
10350 Santa Monica Boulevard
Suite 295
Los Angeles, CA 90025

Phone: 310-228-6900 **Fax:** 310-228-6939
e-mail: info@hpcap.com
web: www.hpcap.com

Mission Statement: A private equity firm with an investment approach distinguished by its strong orientation towards operations. Each of the firm's principals has significant operating experience which allows HPA to seek out investments in businesses where present management needs to be supplemented.

Geographic Preference: California, Western Region
Fund Size: $30 million
Founded: 1986
Average Investment: $10 million
Minimum Investment: $5 million
Investment Criteria: Controlling Investements in Small to Medium-Sized Companies; Revenues of $25 - $200 million
Industry Group Preference: Manufacturing, Retailing, Aerospace
Portfolio Companies: American Home/American Furniture Company, ASC Specialty Vehicle, Advent Aerospace Inc., Barcalounger, Charming Charlie, Crimson Well Services Inc., Priject Time & Cost, The Marktets LLC, Synchronous Aerospace Group

Other Locations:
1980 Post Oak Boulevard
Suite 2150
Houston, TX 77056
Phone: 713-940-8100 **Fax:** 713-986-8410

Key Executives:
Michael J. Fourticq Sr., Managing Partner
e-mail: mjfourticq@hpcap.com
Education: BA, LLB, Texas University, MBA Harvard Business School
Background: General Partner, Brentwood Associates
Directorships: Member, State Bar of Texas

Michael J. Fourticq Jr., Partner
Education: BA, Economics, University of Texas, Austin; CPA
Background: Corporate Finance, KPMG

Kevin L. Listen, Partner
e-mail: klisten@hpcap.com
Education: BBA, Finance & Real Estate, Southern Methodist University; MBA, University of California, Los Angeles
Background: The TCW Group Inc.

Kenton S. Van Harten, Partner
e-mail: kvanharten@hpcap.com
Education: BS, Accounting, Brigham Young University; CPA
Background: CEO, Fitness Holdings International; Interim CEO, American Furniture Corp.

Kenneth G. Walter Jr., Partner
e-mail: kwatler@hpcap.com
Education: BA, University of Texas, Austin

Martin Irani, Vice President
e-mail: mirani@hpcap.com
Education: BA, Economics, MBA, Finance, University of Southern California

Ted Fourticq, Principal
e-mail: tfourticq@hpcap.com
Education: BA, Vanderbilt University; JD & MBA, Loyola Marymount University
Directorships: Borga, American Furniture Corp, Project Time & Cost

Michael F. Gooch, Vice President, Finance
e-mail: mgooch@hpcap.com
Education: BS, Business Administration, University of Southern California; CPA

906 HANOVER PARTNERS
425 California Street
Suite 2000
San Francisco, CA 94104

Phone: 415-788-8680
e-mail: aaron@hanoverpartners.com
web: www.hanoverpartners.com

Mission Statement: Change of control acquisitions only. Hanover Partners acquires privately owned middle market

Venture Capital & Private Equity Firms / Domestic Firms

companies with a minimum of $2 million of operating cash flow annually.
Geographic Preference: United States, Canada
Founded: 1994
Average Investment: $8 million
Minimum Investment: $5 million
Investment Criteria: LBO, MBO, Middle market companies with earnings of at last #8 million
Industry Group Preference: Service Industries, Manufacturing
Portfolio Companies: Audio Precision, Bri-Mar Manufacturing LLC, Consolidated Equipment Group, Freedom Communication Technologies, Hamer LLC, Handi Quilter, Pyramid Technologies Inc., Rugby Manufacturing Company, Solidscape, Wohler Technologies Inc.

Other Locations:
201 B Avenue
Suite 270
Lake Oswego, OR 97034
Phone: 503-699-6410

Key Executives:
Andrew N. Ford, Co-Founder/Principal
503-699-6410
e-mail: andyf@hanoverpartners.com
Education: BA, Government, Dartmouth College; MBA, Kellogg School, Northwestern University
Background: Chairman, Freedom Communication Technologies; Consilidated Equipment Group; Pyramid Technologies; Solidscape; Bri-Mar Manufacturing; Product & Marketing Manager, Atlast Telecom; Management Consultant, Gemini Consulting
Directorships: Hamer LLC, Wohler Technologies, Handi-Quilter, Rugby Manufacturing
John E. Palmer, Co-Founder/Principal
415-788-8222
e-mail: johnp@hanoverpartners.com
Education: BA, Dartmouth College; MBA, Kellogg School of Business; Northwestern University; CFA
Background: VP, Wells Fargo; Management Consultant, Mercer Management Consulting; Chairman, Wohler Technologies; Hamer LLC
Directorships: Pyramid Technologies, Consolidated Equipment Group, Solidscape Inc., Bri-Mar Manufacturing
Aaron C. Aiken, Principal
415-788-8680
e-mail: aaron@hanoverpartners.com
Education: BA, History & Political Science, Northwestern University
Background: Analyst, Baird Capital Partners; LaSalle Capital Group
Directorships: Freedom Communication Technologies, Wohler Technologies

907 HARBERT MANAGEMENT CORPORATION
2100 Third Avenue North
Suite 600
Birmingham, AL 35203

Phone: 205-987-5500
web: www.harbert.net

Mission Statement: To partner with successful business leaders to build viable, dynamic companies. Harbert invests in a variety of asset classes to build a portfolio with the diversification that can balance risk and return.
Geographic Preference: Mid-Atlantic, Southeastern US
Fund Size: $150 million
Founded: 1995
Average Investment: $3 - $7 million
Minimum Investment: $500,000
Investment Criteria: Early Stage, Experienced Management Teams, Scalable Operating Platforms
Industry Group Preference: Communication Technology, Software, Communications Equipment, Semiconductors, Healthcare, Information Technology, Services, Technology
Portfolio Companies: Agility, Anutra Medical, Axial Exchange, Caresync, Clarabridge, Clinipace Worldwide, Cloud Elements, ControlScan, Envera, Healthcare Interative, Iconixx, Invincea, Jack Be, Kaleo, Ledbury, MapAnything, Mobile Posse, MaxCyte, Netsertive, nContact, NovaMin, Racemi Inc., Sidecar, Snagajob, Social SafeGuard, Springbot, Shipt, UniTrends, Wellcentive, Wiser Together, Yap

Other Locations:
5702 Grove Avenue
Suite 200
Richmond, VA 23226
Phone: 804-782-3800

555 Madison Avenue
25th Floor
New York, NY 10022
Phone: 212-521-6970

333 - 11th Avenue S
Suite 410
Nashville, TN 37203
Phone: 615-301-6400

Brookfield House
5th Floor
44 Davies Street
London W1K 5JA
United Kingdom
Phone: 44 (0) 207 408 4120

3715 Northside Parkway
Building 400, Suite 350
Atlanta, GA 30327
Phone: 404-760-8340

575 Market Street
Suite 2925
San Francisco, CA 94105
Phone: 415-442-8380

Suite 204
2nd Floor
Pinar, 5
Madrid 28006
Spain
Phone: 34-91-745-6859

200 Cresent Court
Suite 440
Dallas, TX 75201
Phone: 214-756-6590

29 rue de Bassano
Paris 75008
France
Phone: 33-17-673-2800

Key Executives:
Raymond J. Harbert, Chairman & Chief Executive Officer
Education: BS, Business, Auburn University
Background: Vice President, Harbert Properties Corp.
Directorships: Birmingham Business Alliance
Charles D. Miller, EVP, Global Head oF Distribution
Education: BS, Civival Engineering, Auburn University; Wharton Executive Program, Financial Management, University of Pennsylvania
Background: Operations, Harbert Corp.
John W. McCullough, EVP, General Counsel
Education: BA, Economics, Washington and Lee University; JD, Cumberland School of Law, Samford University
Background: Partner, Balch & Bingham LLP
J. Travis Prichett, President/Chief Operating Officer
Education: BS, Biology, Davidson College; MA, Environmental Management, Duke University; MBA, Kenan-Flagler Business School, University of North Carolina

Venture Capital & Private Equity Firms / Domestic Firms

908 HARBINGER VENTURE MANAGEMENT
3 Results Way
Cupertino, CA 95014

Phone: 408-861-3983
e-mail: uscontact@harbingervc.com

Mission Statement: Harbinger's mission is to be a value-added venture investor in the core technologies that will enhance the productivity and experience at the workplace or at home. Leveraging the MiTAC-SYNNEX Group's strong financial backing and web of networks, we strive to create synergy and forge strategic relationships among our investee companies and the Group's affiliated companies at every opportunity. Welcoming challenge, Harbinger will continue to be a forerunner in the technologies that will change the communications and computing networks of tomorrow while generating tangible results and real value for both its investees and investors.

Geographic Preference: North America, Asia
Average Investment: $1 - $5 million
Investment Criteria: Early-Stage to Late-Stage
Industry Group Preference: Communications, Networking, Wireless Technologies, Semiconductors, Internet, Software, Infrastructure, Computer Hardware & Software
Portfolio Companies: A10 Networks, ACTi, Alpha & Omega Semiconductor, Applied Optoelectronics, BroadSound, Cardiva Medical, Centrality Communications, CGCG, Continuous Computing Corp, CP Secure, EpiStar, Envivo, GemTek, HEP Tech, LighTuning, MedSphere International, Plaxo, Tsang Yow, Tyan, VeriSilicon, vvlogger, YeePay

Other Locations:
 7th Floor, No. 187
 Tiding Blvd, Sec 2
 Neihu
 Taipei 114
 Taiwan
 Phone: 886-22657-9368

Key Executives:
 C.K. Cheng, General Partner
 Education: BS, Physics, Tsing-Hua University; MBA, Chiao-Tung University
 Background: Senior Vice President, Product Marketing, SYNNEX
 M.R. Lin, Venture Partner
 Education: BSEE, National Taiwan University; MBA, National Chiao Tung University
 Background: Managing Director, H&Q Taiwan Co.; President, Hantech Venture Capital
 Matthew Miau, Chairman
 Education: University of California, Berkeley; MBA, Santa Clara University
 Background: Chairman, MiTAC-SYNNEX Group
 T.C. Chou, President, Harbinger Taiwan
 Education: BS, National Taiwan University; MBA, Wharton Business School; PhD, Rutgers University
 Background: Special Assistant to Chairman, MiTAC-SYNNEX Group; Director, Corporate Development, Roll International
 John Tzeng, Vice President, Harbinger Taiwan
 Education: BS, Business Administration, National Taiwan University; MBA, Purdue University
 Background: Senior Manager, O'Melvery & Myers; President, CT Tainjn Datian-Rel Estate
 Tzyy-Po Wang, Senior Vice President, Harbinger Taiwan
 Education: BSEE, MSEE, National Taiwan University
 Background: MIC/III
 Ronald Han, Vice President, Harbinger Taiwan
 Education: BS, Fu-Jen Catholic University, Taiwan; MBA, George Washington University
 Background: MITAC-SYNNEX Group; Union Petrochemical Corporation; Westpac Banking Corporation
 Ru-Guang Bal, Vice President, Harbinger China
 Education: BS, Physics, Beijing Normal University
 Background: Senior Investment Manager, RuYing Investment Management Co.
 Ronald Han, Vice President, Harbinger Taiwan
 Education: BS, Fu-Jen Catholic University; MBA, Finance, George Washington University
 Background: MiTAC-SYNNEX Group, Union Petrochemical Corporation

910 HARBOR LIGHT CAPITAL PARTNERS
91 Court St.
Keene, NH 03431

Phone: 603-355-9954 Fax: 603-355-1158
e-mail: info@hlcp.com
web: www.hlcp.com

Mission Statement: Harbor Light Capital Partners is a private investment firm seeking to invest in early and growth stage companies located in the Northeast. Our unique approach combines flexible capital and collaborative support to build successful, sustainable operating companies. Harbor Light's legacy, values, and experience provide the guiding light for superior results.

Geographic Preference: Northeast United States
Average Investment: $1 - $5 million
Investment Criteria: Early-Stage, Growth Stage
Industry Group Preference: Technology, Clean Technology, Healthcare
Portfolio Companies: Alcyone Lifesciences, Carmell Therapeutics, Courtagen Life Sciences, Direct Vet Marketing, Micronotes, Senet

Key Executives:
 Todd Warden, Managing Partner
 Education: BS, Mathematics, University of Vermont; MBa, Boston University
 Background: Vice President, Marketing & Business Development, MARKEM Corporation
 Directorships: Tauck, Senet
 Richard Upton, General Partner
 Education: BA, Economics & English, Amherst College; MBA, Darden School, University of Virginia
 Background: Founder & President, Upton Advisors
 Directorships: Alcyone, Courtagen Life Sciences, Castlewood Surgical, Carmell Therapeutics, Home Diagnostics
 Darby Kopp, General Partner
 Education: BA, Swarthmore College; MBA, Tuck School of Business, Dartmouth College
 Background: Business Development, MARKEM Corporation; Strategy Consultant, Pembroke Consulting
 Directorships: EBSCO Information Services

911 HARBOUR GROUP
7733 Forsyth Boulevard
23rd Floor
St. Louis, MO 63105

Phone: 314-727-5550
web: www.harbourgroup.com

Mission Statement: A privately owned operating company with a demonstrated record of success in acquiring and developing market leading companies for long term investment.

Geographic Preference: North America
Fund Size: $400 million
Founded: 1976
Investment Criteria: Companies with revenues between $30-$500 million
Industry Group Preference: Manufacturing, Distribution, Business Products & Services, Digital Media & Marketing, Logistics, Industrial Products
Portfolio Companies: LLP Holding Corporation, Green Creative LLC, Marshall Excelsior Company, Koch & Associates Inc., BASE Engineering Inc., SP Industries Inc., PennTech Machinery Corporation, Phillips & Temro Industries Inc., Wolverine Heaters, ONICON Incorporated,

Greyline Instruments Inc., Air Monitor Corporation, Fox Thermal Instruments Inc., Seattle Metrics Inc., Cleaver-Brooks Inc., Holman Boiler Works, Affiliated Power Services, Camus Hydronics Ltd., CPS Products Inc., Uview Ultraviolet Systems Inc., AAB Smart Tools LLC, STAR EnviroTech Inc., Lindsstrom LLC, Bossard Metrics Inc., Titan Fastener Products Inc., Anda Tool and Fasterner Ltd., Fleetgistics Enterprises Inc., Top Knobs USA Inc., Hardware Resources, Atlast Homewares Inc., SloanLED, Watchfire, Haydon Enterprises Inc., Kerk Motion Products Inc., Pearlman Industries Inc., Dimensional Tools Inc., Stone Tool Supply Inc., GranQuartz Holdings LLC, Somaca, Granite City Tool Company Inc., Lincoln International Corporation, Alemite LLC, Reelcraft Industries, Lincoln Helios Ltd., Tech Lighting LLC, LBL Lighting Inc., Merit Industries Inc., Rowe International Inc., Games Warehouse Ltd., View Interative, Tap.tv, Rock-Ola, NSM Music Group, Auto Meter Products Inc., STACK Ltd., Dedenbear Products, SIMCO Ltd., ProParts, Eckler Industries, Classic Chevy International, Late Great Chevy, Copperfield Chimney Supply, California Comfort Corp., Hancock's Wholesale Supply, Tubular Textile, Ashby Industries, RFG Enterprises, Marshall & Williams Co.

Key Executives:
Jeff Fox, Chairman & CEO
Education: BS, Universith of Southern California; MBA, Washington University
Directorships: Lincoln Industrial Corp.; JLG OmniQuip Inc.

912 HARBOURVEST PARTNERS LLC
One Financial Center
Boston, MA 02111
Phone: 617-348-3707 **Fax:** 617-350-0305
web: www.harbourvest.com

Mission Statement: A global private equity investment firm seeking investments in all types of private equity funds, and also directly in operating companies.
Geographic Preference: United States, Europe, Asia, Australia, South America
Fund Size: $4.4 billion
Founded: 1973
Average Investment: $12 million
Minimum Investment: $5 million
Investment Criteria: Late-Stage, Leveraged buyouts, Recapitalization, Mezzanine, Growth Equity
Industry Group Preference: Software, Hardware, Data Communications, Telecommunications, Financial Services, Asset Management, Technology, Media, Advertising, Consumer Products, Healthcare, Biotechnology
Portfolio Companies: Ability, ACG, Acrisure, Advance Health, Advanced Instruments Inc., Allegro, Alliant, Amri, Appriss, Advidxchange, BenefitMall, Benestra, Capsugel, CareCentrix, Catalina, Clix, Colisee, Consol, Cortefiel, EatonTowers, Exxcelia, Finanzcheck.De, Finjan Vital Security, Five Star Food Service, Flash Networks, Flinn Scientific Inc., GB Foods, Get Back, GCS, Gotha Cosmetics, Harbor Community Bank, Healthgrades, Heritage Foodservice Group, Hub International, Love'em Ingham, Intelex, Ista, Lionbridge Capital, Lucid, MedOptions, Mimeo.com, Ministry Brands, Moeller Aerospace, MultiPlan, Nero, OTG, Outbrain, Peloton, Pinnacle, Planview, Polyconcept, Polynt, Press Ganey, Preston Hollow Capital, Profi, Project Arriendo, Q4, RCN, Re Commmunity Recycling, Risk Strategies Company, Riverbed, Roland, Roompot, Saba, Safe, Salad Signature, Samba Safety, Schenck Process, SeaSwift, Sebia, Secure-24, Securus Technologies, ServOne, Sign-Zone Inc., Sirius Computer Solutions, Solace Systems, Solarwinds, Staples, Super Max, Team Viewer, Third Bridge, ThoughtSpot, Towne Park, Tritech Software Systems, Triton, Tyntec, United Surgical Partners International, Veriato, Vestcom, Videology, Vironclinics Biosciences, Vix, Wave Accounting, Wayfair, Xpressdocs, Zayo

Other Locations:
Champion Tower
3 Garden Road
Suite 1207
Central
Hong Kong
Phone: 852-2525-2214 **Fax:** 852-2525-2241

3rd Floor
33 Jermyn Street
London SW1Y 6DN
United Kingdom
Phone: 44 (0)20 7399 9820

Suite 5608 56/F China World Tower A
1 Jianguomenwai Avenue
Chaoyang District
Beijing 100004
China
Phone: 86 10 5706 8600 **Fax:** 86 10 5706 8601

Marunouchi Building, 34th Floor
2-4-1 Marunouchi
Chiyoda-ku
Tokyo 100-6326
Japan
Phone: 81 3 3284 4320 **Fax:** 81 3 3217 1077

Carrera 7 #113 - 43
Oficina 904
Edificio Samsung
Bogota
Colombia
Phone: 57 1 552 1400

Gran Seoul Tower 1 18th Floor
33 Jongro
Jongno-gu
Seoul 03159
South Korea
Phone: 82 2 6410 8020 **Fax:** 82 2 6937 1012

3 HaNechoshet Street
Building B
Tel Aviv 6971068
Isreal
Phone: 972 3 3720001 **Fax:** 972 3 7618120

Bay Adelaide Centre
333 Bay Street
Suite 2720
Toronto, ON M5H 2R2
Canada
Phone: 647-484-3022 **Fax:** 647-498-1448

Key Executives:
Frederick Maynard, Senior Advisor
617-348-3723
e-mail: fmaynard@harbourvest.com
Education: BA, Wesleyan University; MBA, Amos Tuck School of Busines Administration, Dartmouth College
Background: Loan Officer, Manufacturers Hanover Trust
Directorships: Apax Partners, First Capital-Oklahoma, Genesis Holdings International Management-London
Robert Wadsworth, Senior Advisor
617-348-3715
e-mail: rwadsworth@harbourvest.com
Education: MBA, Harvard University; BS Systems Engineering/Computer Science, University of Virginia
Background: Booz Allen and Hamilton
Directorships: Concord Communications, ePresence, Network Engines, Trintech Group PLC, Switchboard and several international companies
George Anson, Senior Advisor
44 (0)20 7399 9822
e-mail: ganson@harbourvest.com
Education: BA, Finance, University of Iowa
Background: Pantheon Ventures
William Johnston, Senior Advisor
Education: BA, Colgate University; MBA, Syracuse University

Venture Capital & Private Equity Firms / Domestic Firms

Background: Corporate Finance, John Hancock; State Street Bank
Directorships: Boston Communications Group, Masada Security, Transit Communications
Brett Gordon, Managing Director
617-348-3764
e-mail: bgordon@harbourvest.com
Education: MBA, Babson College; BS/BA Management, Boston University
Background: VP, Princeton Review of Boston
John Morris, Managing Director
617-348-3732
e-mail: jmorris@harbourvest.com
Education: BA Economics, Clark University; MBA, Columbia University
Background: Abbott Capital Management; VP Corporate Finance, CIBC; Canadian Imperial Bank of Commerce; Board of Directors, Applied Molecular Evolution
Directorships: Blackstone Communications, Bruckmann Rosser Sherrill & Co II, Concord Israel Ventures II, Cypress Merchant Banking Partners II, Domain Partners II-V, Draper Fisher Jurveston
John Fiato, Principal
617-348-3540
e-mail: jfiato@harbourvest.com
Education: BSBA, Accounting, Minor in Economics, Salem State College
Amanda Outerbridge, Managing Director
617-348-3518
e-mail: aouterbridge@harbourvest.com
Education: BS, Business Administration from Babson College
Background: XL Capital; Bank of Bermuda
Kathleen Bacon, Senior Advisor
44 (0)20 7399 9823
e-mail: kbacon@harbourvest.com
Education: BA, Russian, Dartmouth College; MBA, Tuck School of Business, Dartmouth College
Background: First National Bank of Boston
Gregory Stento, Managing Director
617-348-3588
e-mail: gstento@harbourvest.com
Education: BS, Cornell University; MBA, Harvard Business School
Background: Comdisco Ventures; Bridge Partners; NCR Corporation
Peter Lipson, Managing Director
617-348-3595
e-mail: plipson@harbourvest.com
Education: BA, Economics, Univesity of California San Diego; MS, Information Ssytems, University of Virginia; MBA, Harvard Business School
Background: Financial Analyst, M&A Group, Salomon Brothers
Julie Ocko, Managing Director
617-348-3532
e-mail: jocko@harbourvest.com
Education: BS, Business Administration, University of North Carolina; MBA, Darden School of Business Administration, University of Virginia
Background: AEW Capital Management; Narragansett Capital
Alex Rogers, Managing Director
647-348-3555
e-mail: arogers@harbourvest.com
Education: BA, Economics, Duke University; MBA, Harvard Business School
Background: McKinsey & Company
Michael Taylor, Managing Director
617-348-3721
e-mail: mtaylor@harbourvest.com
Education: BS, United States Naval Academy; MBA, Finance, The Wharton School, University of Pennsylvania
Background: Morgan Stanley; Lieutenant Commander, United States Navy; Naval Aviator

John Toomey Jr., Managing Director
617-348-3525
e-mail: jtoomey@harbourvest.com
Education: BS, Chemistry & Physics, Harvard University; MBA, Harvard Business School
Background: Analyst, Smith Barney
Martha DiMatteo Vorlicek, Senior Advisor
617-348-3709
e-mail: mvorlicek@harbourvest.com
Education: BS, Business Administration, Babson College
Background: Senior Audit Manager, Ernst & Young
Mary Traer CPA, Managing Director & Chief Administrative Officer
617-348-3778
e-mail: mtraer@harbourvest.com
Education: BS, Economics, MS, Accounting, University of Virginia
Background: Ernst & Young; University of Virginia's Treasurer's Office
Peter Wilson, Managing Director
44-20-7399-9824
e-mail: pwilson@harbourvest.com
Education: BA, McGill University; MBA, Harvard Business School
Background: European Bank for Reconstruction & Development; The Monitor Company
David Atterbury, Managing Director
44-20-7399-9836
e-mail: datterbury@harbourvest.com
Education: BSc, International Management & France, University of Bath
Background: Director of Private Equity, Abbey National Treasury Services; PricewaterhouseCoopers
Julie Eiermann, Managing Director/Chief Data Officer
617-348-3727
e-mail: jeiermann@harbourvest.com
Education: BA, University of New Hampshire
Background: Advent International Corporation
Jeffrey Keay, Managing Director
617-348-3536
e-mail: jkeay@harbourvest.com
Education: BA, Economics & Accounting, College of the Holy Cross
Background: Ernst & Young
Karin Lagerlund, Managing Director/CFO
617-348-3752
e-mail: klagerlund@harbourvest.com
Education: BA, Business Administration, Washington State University
Background: AEW Capital Management; Audit Manager, EY Kenneth Leventhal
Edward W Kane, Senior Advisor
Education: BA, University of Pennsylvania; MBA, Harvard Business School
Background: Co-Founder, HarbourVest Partners; New England Merchants National Bank; Board Member of Xylogics, Al Corp, Mutual Risk Management
Directorships: Advisory Committee Member to: Battery Ventures, Canadover (UK), Transpac Equity Investment, Latin American Enterprise Fund
Tatsuya Kubo, Managing Director
81 3 3284 4321
e-mail: tkubo@harbourvest.com
Education: BA, Economics, Waseda University; MBA, Duke University
Background: Managing Director, Fortress Investment Group Japan; Senior Manager, Norinchukin Bank
Scott Voss, Managing Director
852-2878-5630
e-mail: svoss@harbourvest.com
Education: BS, Marketing, Bryant College; MBA, Babson College
Background: Cannondale Corporation
McComma Grayson III, Principal
e-mail: mgrayson@harbourvest.com

Venture Capital & Private Equity Firms / Domestic Firms

Education: BA, Government, Harvard College; MBA, Harvard Business School
Background: Financial Analyst, Morgan Stanley's Global Energy Group

913 HARREN EQUITY PARTNERS
200 Garrett Street
Suite F
Charlottesville, VA 22902

Phone: 434-245-5800 Fax: 434-245-5802
e-mail: info@harrenequity.com
web: www.harrenequity.com

Mission Statement: Harren Equity Partners seeks to create long-term value for companies by forming strong partnerships with stellar management teams and assisting with operational improvement and strategic planning.

Geographic Preference: North America
Fund Size: $275 million
Founded: 2001
Average Investment: $10 million
Minimum Investment: $7 million
Investment Criteria: Lower Middle Market, Management Buyouts, Recapitalizations, Industry Consolidations
Industry Group Preference: Manufacturing, Distribution, Business Products & Services, Consumer Products, Industrial, Healthcare Services, Aerospace, Defense and Government, Restaurants, Energy Services, Transportation
Portfolio Companies: ARKLATEX Energy Services, Circa Corporation of America, Energy Fishing & Rental Services, Marianna Industries, Med-Legal, Persante Health Care, SimplyShe, Spartan Energy Services, Virginia Tile Company

Key Executives:
Thomas A. Carver, Co-Founder & Managing Partner
Education: BS, McIntire School of Commerce, MBA, Darden School of Business, University of Virginia
Background: Partner, HIG Capital; Interim President, Plastic Fabricating Company; Interim President, Virginia Explosives & Drilling Company
Directorships: Professional Directional Holdings, Keystone Air & Drill Supply
Lee J. Monahan, Partner
e-mail: leem@harrenequity.com
Education: BS, Finance, DePaul University; MBA, Harvard Business School
Background: Associate, HIG Capital; Lazard Freres & Co
Directorships: Keystone Air & Drill Supply, Med-Legal, Energy Fishing & Rental Services
C Taylor Cole Jr, Partner
e-mail: tcole@harrenequity.com
Education: University of Virginia; Darden School of Business
Background: Morgan Stanley; Kirkland Investment Corp.; Lehman Brothers; Charterhouse Group
Directorships: MedPro Healthcare Staffing
George McCabe, Partner
e-mail: gmccabe@harrenequity.com
Education: University of Virginia
Background: Freidman Billings Ramsey; Pine Creek Partners
Directorships: Shrimp Basket, Inc.

914 HARRISON METAL
2430 3rd St.
San Francisco, CA 94107

e-mail: info@harrisonmetal.com
web: www.harrisonmetal.com

Mission Statement: Harrison Metal invests in early stage technology companies leg by exceptional founders. We help founders build products that improve the daily lives of users, successfully take those products to market, and create a thriving business. If we do that right, we return many times our investors capital and help perpetuate the work of great institutions.

Founded: 2008
Investment Criteria: Early Stage
Industry Group Preference: Technology

Key Executives:
Michael Dearing, Founder
Education: AB, Economics, Brown University; MBA, Harvard Business School
Background: Senior Vice President & General Merchandise Manager, eBay.com; Bain & Company; Filene's Basement; The Walt Disney Company; Industrial Shoe Warehouse
Andrew Humphries, Head of School
Education: BS, Biology, Duke University; MA, Education, Stanford University
Background: Performer, Second City; Teacher, Francis W. Parker School; Teacher, Chicago Public School

915 HARTFORD VENTURES
690 Asylum Avenue
Hartford, CT 06155

Phone: 860-547-5000
e-mail: hartfordventures@thehartford.com
web: www.thehartford.com

Mission Statement: Hartford Ventures, partners with and invests in people with big ideas to spawn a new generation of possibilities to transform the insurance and wealth management industry.

Geographic Preference: Hartford, CT
Average Investment: $1 - $3 million
Investment Criteria: Early-Stage, Expansion-Stage
Portfolio Companies: DriverSide, Coulomb Technologies, GreenRoad, Insurance.com, Buysafe, Intelleflex, Co3Systems

Key Executives:
Tom Whiteaker, Managing Director
e-mail: thomas.whiteaker@thehartford.com
Education: MBA, International Management, Thunderbird School of Global Management
Background: Corporate Ventures, Visa

916 HARVARD CAPITAL GROUP
1800 Century Park East
6th Floor
Los Angeles, CA 90067

Phone: 213-290-0048
e-mail: corporate@harvardcapital.com
web: www.harvardcapital.com

Mission Statement: The Harvard Capital Group is an investment bank focused on providing advisory services and capital raising solutions to startups and middle-market private companies.

Average Investment: $1 - $20 million
Investment Criteria: Startups to Mezzanine Financing

Key Executives:
Ailliam Knoke, President/Managing Director
e-mail: bill.knoke@harvardcapital.com
Education: BA, Economics, Stanford University; MBA, Harvard Business School
Background: Founder, Badjao Foundation; VP, M&A, VI Capital
Rashid Alvi, Managing Director
e-mail: rashid.alvi@harvardcapital.com
Education: Columbia Law School
Background: Acro Healthcare; Davis Polk & Wardwell; Lehman Brothers; Goldman Sachs
Louie Ucciferri, Managing Director
e-mail: louie.ucciferri@harvardcapital.com
Education: Stanford University
Background: CCO & Financial Principal, EdgeLine

Venture Capital & Private Equity Firms / Domestic Firms

Capital; CEO, Regent Capital Group; VP, Operations, Commonwealth Financial Network

917 HARVEST PARTNERS
280 Park Avenue
26th Floor
New York, NY 10017

Phone: 212-599-6300
e-mail: info@harvestpartners.com
web: www.harvestpartners.com

Mission Statement: To pursue a risk-return approach that will generate stable, consistent and superior returns, as well as ensure the preservation of capital.

Geographic Preference: North America
Fund Size: $1.125 billion
Founded: 1981
Average Investment: $50 - $250 million
Investment Criteria: High free cash flow, revenue driven business model, control investment
Industry Group Preference: Manufacturing, Distribution, Industrial Services, Business Products & Services, Consumer Products, Specialty Retail, Healthcare Services
Portfolio Companies: Advanced Dermatology & Cosmetic Surgery, APC Automotive Technologies, Aquilex Corporation, Associated Materials Inc., Athletico, AxelaCare Holdings Inc., Bartlett Holdings Inc., Communications Supply Corporation, Continuum Energy, Coveright Surfaces Holding GmbH, Cycle Gear Inc., Dental Care Alliance, Driven Brands Inc., DTI Inc., Encanto Restaurants Inc., Epiq, Evenflo Company Inc., EyeCare Services Partners, FCX Performance Inc., Garretson Resolution Group, Green Bancorp Inc., Insight Global Inc., Integrity Marketing Group, Lazer Spot Inc., Natural Products Group Inc., Neighborly, New Flyer Industries Ltd., OnPoint Group, Packers Holdings LLC, PRO Unlimited, Regency Energy Partners LP, Service Express, TruckPro LLC, US Silica Company, Valet Living, VetCor, Yellowstone Landscape

Key Executives:
Thomas W. Arenz, Partner
Education: BS, Mechanical Engineering, United States Naval Academy; MBA, Harvard Business School
Background: Principal, Joseph Littlejohn & Levy; Kidder Peabody; Drexel Burnham Lambert
Directorships: Truck Pro, Cycle Gear, Coveright
Michael B. DeFlorio, Chief Executive Officer
Education: BS, Economics, Wharton School, University of Pennsylvania; MBA, Harvard Business School
Background: Partner, JH Whitney & Co.; American Industrial Partners; Donaldson, Lufkin & Jenrette
Directorships: FCX, Bartlett Holdings, Continuum Energy, Valet Waste
Stephen Eisenstein, Partner
Education: BA, Economics, Tufts University; MBA, Wharton School, University of Pennsylvania
Background: Founding Partner, Paribas Principal Partners; Corporate Finance, Chase Manhattan Bank; Equity Research, Paine Webber Inc.
Directorships: Packers Holdings, Green Bancorp, Encanto Restaurants
Ira D. Kleinman, Partner
Education: BS, Accounting, State University of New York, Binghamton; MBA, St. John's University
Background: Regional Controller, American International Group; Financial Analyst, Bank of New York; National Benefit Life Insurance Co.
Directorships: Athletico, Dental Care Alliance, Garretson Resolution Group, Insight Global, VetCor
Jay Wilkins, President
Education: BS, Vanderbilt University
Background: Principal, DLJ Merchant Banking Partners; North Castle Partners; Analyst, Leveraged Finance Group, Donaldson, Lufkin & Jenrette
Directorships: Athletico, Dental Care Alliance, Insight Global, Packers Holdings, VetCor

918 HATTERAS VENTURE PARTNERS
280 S Mangum Street
Suite 350
Durham, NC 27701

Phone: 919-484-0730 **Fax:** 919-484-0364
web: www.hatterasvp.com

Mission Statement: Hatteras Venture Partners is a venture capital firm that invests in early stage companies based in North Carolina and the Southeastern United States. The firm focuses primarily on human medicine-related sectors, including healthcare informational technology, biopharmaceuticals, diagnostics, and medical devices. Hatteras Venture Partners seeks innovative businesses with the potential to transform the practice of medicine and is dedicated to creating value for these companies.

Geographic Preference: North Carolina, Southeast United States
Fund Size: $125 million
Founded: 2000
Investment Criteria: Early-Stage
Industry Group Preference: Biopharmaceuticals, Medical Devices, Diagnostics, Life Sciences, Healthcare Information Technology
Portfolio Companies: Artus Labs, Clearside Biomedical, Clinipace Worldwide, Clinverse, Coferon, Contego Medical, Curoverse, Device Innovation Group, Embrella, G1 Therapeutics, GeneCentric, Graybug, Histosonics, Lysosomal Therapeutics, Medfusion, Medikidz, NeuroTronik, Nu Sirt Sciences, Orig3n, Pathfinder Technologies, PhaseBio, Qvella, Sideris Pharmaceuticals, SpineAlign, Spyryx Biosciences, TetraLogic, Viamet, Wildflower Health

Key Executives:
John Crumpler, General Partner
Education: AB, Harvard University
Background: Founder & CEO, E-Comm; XcelleNet
Directorships: Clinipace Worldwide
Robert A Ingram, General Partner
Education: BS, Business Administration, Eastern Illinois University
Background: Chairman & CEO, GlaxoWellcome; VP Chairman, Pharmaceuticals, GlaxoSmithKline
Directorships: Cree, Valeant Pharmaceuticals International, BioCryst Pharmaceuticals
Kenneth B Lee, General Partner
Education: BA, Lenoir-Rhyne College; MBA, University of North Carolina at Chapel Hill
Background: Co-Head, International Life Sciences, Ernst & Young; Genentech
Directorships: Clinverse, Clinipace
Douglas Reed MD, General Partner
Education: BA, Biology, MD, University of Missouri, Kansas City; MBA, Wharton School, University of Pennsylvania
Background: Vector Fund Management; SR One; VP, Business Development, NPS Pharmaceuticals; GelTex Pharmaceuticals
Directorships: Coferon, SpineAlign Medical, TetraLogic Pharmaceuticals
Christy Shaffer PhD, General Partner
Education: PhD, Pharmacology, University of Tennessee
Background: Associate Director, Pulmonary & Critical Care Medicine, Burroughs Wellcome; President & CEO, Inspire Pharmaceuticals
Directorships: G1 Therapeutics, Spyryx, Clearside, KinoDyn, GrayBug
Clay B Thorp, General Partner
Education: BA, Mathematics & Art History, University of North Carolina at Chapel Hill; MPP, Harvard University
Background: Co-Founder, Chairman & CEO, Synthematix; Co-Founder & Head, Corporate Development, Novalon Pharmaceutical Corporation; Co-Founder & President, Xanthon
Directorships: Clearside Biomedical, Curoverse, Lysosomal Therapeutics, Orig3n

Venture Capital & Private Equity Firms / Domestic Firms

919 HAWTHORN EQUITY PARTNERS
200 W Madison
Suite 2100
Chicago, IL 60606

Phone: 312-277-4010
e-mail: investors@hawthornep.com
web: www.hawthornep.com

Mission Statement: Formerly known as Genuity Capital Partners, Hawthorn invests in growth-oriented, knowledge-based middle market companies.
Geographic Preference: North America
Founded: 2005
Average Investment: $10 million - $45 million
Investment Criteria: Middle Market
Industry Group Preference: Specialty Consumer, Business Services, Infrastructure Services, Technology, Media
Portfolio Companies: Front Porch Digital, Green For Life, Ice Mobility, J Brand, Natural Food Holdings, Navantis, NGrain, One Floral Group, Railroad Controls Limited, Rx Label Technology, Solace Systems, Waterworks

Key Executives:
Christopher Payne, CEO & Managing Partner
416-687-5299
e-mail: christopher.payne@hawthornep.com
Education: BComm, Queen's University; MBA, The Wharton School
Background: CIBC; BMO Nesbitt Burns; Merrill Lynch; The Blackstone Group
John Tomes, Senior Partner
847-736-3844
e-mail: tomes@hawthornep.com
Education: BA, Kenyon College; Masters, University of Chicago
Background: Hilco Equity Partners; Wynnchurch Capital; Continental Bank; GE Capital
Eric Ceresnie, Partner
734-276-5632
e-mail: ceresnie@hawthornep.com
Education: BSc, MSc, Industrial & Operations Engineering, University of Michigan
Background: Monomoy Capital Partners; Ernst & Young LLP; Sleep Innovations; A.T. Kearney

920 HCI EQUITY PARTNERS
1730 Pennsylvania Avenue, NW
Suite 525
Washington, DC 20006

Phone: 202-371-0150 Fax: 202-312-5313
Toll-Free: 844-386-1764
web: www.hciequity.com

Mission Statement: Deliver superior risk adjusted returns to our limited partners through long duration investments in middle-market businesses based in the United States.
Geographic Preference: United States
Fund Size: $1.5 billion
Founded: 1993
Average Investment: $25 - $100 million
Minimum Investment: $5 million
Investment Criteria: MBO, LBO, Consolidations, Growth
Industry Group Preference: Industrial Equipment, Industrial Services, Aerospace, Defense and Government, Logistics, Automotive, Distribution, Industrial Distribution, Power Generation, Test & Measurement, Transportation
Portfolio Companies: Adept Plastic Finishing, AmerCareRoyal, Amtex, Certified Safety, Commercial Steel Trating Corporation, The Delaney Hardware Company, Dynamic Systems, Express Packaging, Go To Logistics, Group Transportation Services, HVH Transportation, JGB Enterprises, Milan Supply Chain Solutions, Naumann/Hobbs Material Handling, Power & Composite Technologies, Quadel Consulting Corporation, Regent Cabinetry, Roadrunner Transportation Systems, Southern Ag Carriers, Summit Interconnect, TDS, Tribar Manufacturing, TSM Corporation, Wellborn Forest

Other Locations:
1033 Skokie Boulevard
Suite 260
Northbrook, IL 60062
Phone: 59

Key Executives:
Daniel Dickinson, Managing Partner & Co-Founder
e-mail: dand@hciequity.com
Education: JD, MBA, University of Chicago, BS, Duke University
Background: Merrill Lynch
Douglas McCormick, Managing Partner & Co-Founder
e-mail: dmccormick@hciequity.com
Education: MBA, Harvard Business School, BS, U.S. Military Academy
Background: Morgan Stanley & Company, Captain, U.S. Army's 25th Infantry
Scott Gibaratz, Managing Director
e-mail: sgibaratz@hciequity.com
Education: MBA, Kellogg School of Management, BA, University of Michigan
Background: Merrill Lynch
Dan Moorse, Managing Director
e-mail: dmoorse@hciequity.com
Education: BS, Accounting, St. John's University
Background: CFO, Famous Daves
Carl Nelson, Managing Director
e-mail: cnelson@hciequity.com
Education: BS, Accounting, Winona State University
Background: Accounting & Advisory Group, Arther Andersen & Co

921 HEALTH ENTERPRISE PARTNERS
565 Fifth Avenue
26th Floor
New York, NY 10017

Phone: 212-981-6901 Fax: 212-981-9378
e-mail: info@hepfund.com
web: www.hepfund.com

Mission Statement: Health Enterprise Partners is a New York based private equity firm that invests in healthcare services and technology businesses.
Fund Size: $134 million
Founded: 2006
Average Investment: $5 - $15 million
Investment Criteria: Later Stage
Industry Group Preference: Healthcare, Biotechnology, Administrative Automation, Behavioral Health, Data Security, Genomics, Patient Safety, Pharma Data, Social Determinants
Portfolio Companies: Access Physicians, AllyAlign Health, AxiaMed, Bardy Diagnostics, Catapult Health, CenterPointe Behavioral Health, ContinuumRx, Evariant, HealthQx, InDemand Interpreting, Intraprise Health, Jet Health, Jvion, Nordic Consulting, Payer Compass, Sapphire Digital, Twistle, Wildflower Health

Key Executives:
Bob Schulz, Managing Partner
Education: BS, MS, Chemical Engineering, Massachusetts Institute of Technology; MBA, Columbia Business School, Columbia University
Background: Managing Member & Co-Founder, CB Health Ventures; President & COO, Harris & Harris Group; Credit Suisse First Boston
Directorships: ContinuumRx, SCIOinspire, AllyAlign Health, Skylight Healthcare Systems
Rick Stowe, Managing Partner
Education: BSEE, Rensselaer Polytechnic Institute; MBA, Harvard Business School
Background: Senior Advisor, CB Health Ventures; Senior Advisor, Capital Counsel; Principal, New Court

Venture Capital & Private Equity Firms / Domestic Firms

Securitites Corporation; General Partner, Welsh, Carson, Anderson & Stowe
Directorships: InDemand Interpreting, HMS Holdings Corp., HT-GAF Holdings

Dave Tamburri, Managing Partner
Education: United States Military Academy; MBA, Harvard Business School
Background: VP, Susquehanna Growth Equity; President/COO, Onward Healthcare; EVP, Pinnacor
Directorships: Bardy Diagnostics, Catapult Health, eVariant, Intraprise Health, Jet Health, Paer Compass, Access Physicians

Ezra Mehlman, Managing Partner
Education: BA, Wasthington University, St. Louis; MBA, Columbia Business School
Background: Senior Analyst, Advisory Board Company; Senior Consultant, Booz Allen Hamilton
Directorships: AxialMed, CenterPointe Behavioral Health System, Jvion, Twistle, Wildflower Health

Pete Tedesco, Principal
Education: AB, Princeton University; MBA, Kellogg School of Management, Northwestern University
Background: VP, Olympus Partners; Waud Capital Partners; Becton Dickinson & Co.; UBS Investment Bank

Elizabeth Colonna, Vice President
Education: BA, University of Virginia; MBA, Columbia Business School
Background: Senior Consultant, FTI Consulting; UCLA Health
Directorships: Wildflower Health, AxiaMed, Access Physicians

922 HEALTHCARE VENTURES LLC
47 Thorndike Street
Suite B1-1
Cambridge, MA 02141

Phone: 617-252-4343
e-mail: info@hcven.com
web: www.hcven.com

Mission Statement: Creates, finances and manages high science health care companies with significant growth potential, making investments in early-stage and emerging growth companies.

Geographic Preference: United States
Fund Size: $1.6 billion
Founded: 1985
Average Investment: $10 million
Investment Criteria: Early-Stage, Emerging Growth; Late-Preclinical & Early Clinical-Stage
Industry Group Preference: Biopharmaceuticals, Healthcare, Life Sciences
Portfolio Companies: Anchor Therapeutics, Apellis, Asterand Bioscience, Catalyst Biosciences, Cleveland HeartLab, Colore Science, DecImmune Therapeutics, InfaCare Pharmaceutical, Leap Therapeutics, Mosaic Biosciences, Promedior, Radius, Theraclone Sciences, Trevena, Vaxxas

Key Executives:
James H. Cavanaugh, PhD, Senior Advisor
Education: PhD, Health Economics, University of Iowa
Background: President, SmithKline & French Laboratories US; President, Allergen International; Deputy Assistant to the President, Domestic Affairs; Deputy Chief of White House Staff; Special Assistant to the Surgeon General; Director, Office of Comprehensive Health Planning; Founding Director, Marine Nat'l Bank

Augustine Lawlor, Managing Director
Education: BA, University of New Hampshire; MM, Yale University
Background: COO, LeukoSite; CFO/VP Corporate Development, Alpha-Beta Technology; CFO/VP Business Development, BioSurface Technology
Directorships: Slater Center

John W. Littlechild, Managing Director
Education: BS, University of Manchester; MBA, Manchester Business School
Background: Founder, Advent International Corporation; Citicorp Venture Capital; Rank Xerox; ICI

Douglas E. Onsi, Venture Partner
Education: BS, Biology, Cornell University; JD, University of Michigan Law School
Background: Vice President, Campath Product Operations & Oncology Portfolio Management; Vice President, Business Development, Genzyme Corporation; CFO, TolerRx

Harold R. Werner, Co-Founder/Senior Advisor
Education: BS, MS, Princeton University; MBA, Harvard Graduate School
Background: Director New Ventures, Johnson & Johnson Development Corporation; Sr VP, Robert S First

923 HEALTHINVEST EQUITY PARTNERS
2507 Post Road
Southport, CT 06890

Phone: 203-324-7700
web: healthinvestequity.com

Mission Statement: HealthInvest Equity Partners aim to invest in early stage healthcare services companies.

Key Executives:
Timothy Howe, Managing Partner
Education: Columbia College
Background: Co-Founder, CHL Medical Partners; Co-Manager

Wilfred Jaeger, Managing Partner
Education: BS, MD, University of British Columbia; MBA, Stanford University
Background: Co-Founder, Three Arch Partners; General Partner, Schroder Ventures

924 HEALTHQUEST CAPITAL
1301 Shoreway Rd.
Suite 350
Belmont, CA 94002

web: www.healthquestcapital.com

Mission Statement: HealthQuest Capital invests in healthcare innovation companies that are at or approaching the growth stage.

Average Investment: $7-25 million
Investment Criteria: Growth Stage
Industry Group Preference: Medical Devices, Diagnostics, Digital Health, Consumer Medicine, Technology-Enabled Services
Portfolio Companies: Ajax Health. Alcresta Therapeutics, Avedro, Avizia, BioIQ, Bio Theranostics, Castle Biosciences, CleanSlate, HealthChannels, inMediata, Lineagen, Magnolia Medical Technologies, Spirox, Springbuk, Trice Medical, Venus Concept, Vestagen, VirMedica

Key Executives:
Garheng Kong, Managing Partner
Education: BS, Stanford University; MD, PhD, MBA, Duke University
Background: Intersouth Partners; Sofinnova Ventures
Directorships: Ajax, Alcresta, Avedro, Avizia, Castle Biosciences, CleanSlate, Health Channels, Magnolia Medical, Spirox, Trice Medical, Venus, VirMedica

Randy Scott, Partner
Education: BS, Management, Georgia Institute of Technology
Directorships: Vestagen, VirMedica, Springbuk, Magnolia Medical, Avizia, Trice Medical

Todd Creech, Partner
Education: BA, Finance and Accounting, Miami University; MBA, Duke University
Background: CFO, Femasys; CFO, ZS Pharma; CFO, Sarcode; CFO, Sirion Therapeutics; Quintiles

Venture Capital & Private Equity Firms / Domestic Firms

Directorships: BioIQ, HealthChannels, Springbuk, InMediata, Avedro, Venus Concept
David Kabakoff, Partner
Education: BA, Chemistry, Case Western Reserve University; PhD, Yale University
Background: EVP, Dura Pharmaceuticals; CEO, Spiros Development; CEO, Salmedix
Directorships: Lineagen, Castle Biosciences, Biotheranostics

925 HEARST VENTURES
300 West 57th Street
New York, NY 10019

Phone: 212-649-2000
web: www.hearst.com

Mission Statement: Hearst takes minority positions in startups that focus on the intersecting worlds of media and technology.
Founded: 1995
Average Investment: $2 - $10 million
Investment Criteria: Expansion-Stage
Industry Group Preference: Media, Technology
Portfolio Companies: 8i, Acrobatiq, Atzuche, BuzzFeed, Caavo, Drone Racing League, Flash Delivery, HootSuite, Kujiale, LingoChamp, LiveSafe, MobiTV, Otonomo, PowerToFly, RAMP, Relationship Science, Roku, Science, Sharecare, Signal, Spartan Race, Stylus, Swirl, Via, WideOrbit, Wyng, Yoka, Zcool, Zinc, Pandora, XM, Brightcove, E Ink, Sling Media, Local.com, Broadcast.com, Exodus, Netscape, Drugstore.com, Circles, Zip2, I/Pro, Sphere, Medscape, IGG, Nexage, Yieldex

Key Executives:
Steven R. Swartz, President/CEO
Education: Harvard University
Background: President, Hearst Newspapers; President/CEO, SmartMoney; Reporter, The Wall Street Journal

926 HEARTLAND INDUSTRIAL PARTNERS
300 Atlantic Street
7th Floor
Stamford, CT 06901

Phone: 203-327-1200 Fax: 203-327-1201
e-mail: info@heartlandpartners.com
web: www.heartlandpartners.com

Mission Statement: Combines strong financial and operating acumen in order to create a uniquely positioned firm that facilitates growth and significantly increases corporate value.
Founded: 1999
Investment Criteria: Buyouts, Industrial Operations, Debt Financing
Industry Group Preference: Industrial Services, Industrial Equipment
Portfolio Companies: Metaldyne, Springs, Trimas

Key Executives:
Jim McConoughey, Chief Executive Officer
Background: Active Fund Manager, Early Stage Partners; Singapore EDB; Bloomberg LP; Central Illinois Angels; Voice of America; Fox News Channel; NBCUniversal; NPR
Directorships: Zuchem; ViMedicus

927 HELLMAN & FRIEDMAN LLC
415 Mission Street
Suite 5700
San Francisco, CA 94105

Phone: 415-788-5111
e-mail: info@hf.com
web: www.hf.com

Mission Statement: Invests in long-term equity capital to support the strategic and financial objectives of outstanding teams operating businesses with defensible positions in growing markets.
Geographic Preference: United States, Europe
Fund Size: $3.5 billion
Founded: 1984
Average Investment: $300-$1 billion
Minimum Investment: $100 million
Investment Criteria: Leveraged Recapitalization, Acquisition Financing, Buy & Builds, Traditional Buyouts, Financial Restructurings
Industry Group Preference: Business Products & Services, Media, Technology, Marketing, Communications, Information Technology, Financial Services, Healthcare, Software, Internet, Digital Media & Marketing, Industrial Products, Energy, Insurance
Portfolio Companies: Abra, Activamt, Advanstar Communications, Alix Partners, All Funds Bank, Applied, Arch Capital Group Ltd., Artisan Partners, Associated Materials, Axel Springer, Blackbaud, CarProof, Catalina, Change Healthcare, Digitas, Double Click, Edelman Financial Services, Eller Media, Ellucian, Formula 1, Franlin Templeton Investments, Gartmore, Genesys, GTT, GeoVera Insurance, Getty Images, Goodman, Grocery Outlet Bargain Market, GCM Grosvenor, HUB, Intergraph, Internet Brands, Iris, Kronos, LPL Financial, Mitchell, Mondrian Investment Partners Ltd., MultiPlan, Nasdaq, Nielsen, OpenLink, Paris RE, PPD, ProSiebenSat1 Media SE, Renaissance, Scout 24, Sedgwick, Sheridan, Snap Av, SSP, TeamSystem, Texas Genco, Verisure Smart Alarms, Vertafore, Web Reservations International, Wood Mackenzie, Young & Rubicam

Other Locations:
425 Park Avenue
30th Floor
New York, NY 10022
Phone: 212-871-6680

The Brunel Building
2 Canalside Walk
London W2 1DG
United Kingdom
Phone: 44 (0)20 7839 5111

Key Executives:
Brian Powers, Senior Advisor/Chairman Emeritus
Education: Yale University; University of Virginia School of Law
Background: Partner, James D Wolfensohn; Manager/Chief Executive, Jardine Matheson Group; Managing Director/CEO, Consolidated Press Holdings Limited; Managing Director/CEO, Publishing and Broadcasting Limited
Directorships: Blackbaud
Philip Hammarskjold, Executive Chairman
Education: Princeton University; Harvard Business School
Background: Corporate Advisory Department, Dominguez Barry Samuel Montagu; Merchant Banking Department, Morgan Stanley & Company
Directorships: Digitas, Upromise
Patrick Healy, Chief Executive Officer
Education: Harvard College; Harvard Business School
Background: James D Wolfensohn; Consolidated Press Holdings
Directorships: Digitas; Scout24; Verisure; TeamSystem
Jeffrey Goldstein, Advisor Emeritus
Education: Vassar College; PhD, MPhil, MA, Economics, Yale University; London School of Economics
Background: Under Secretary of the Treasury for Domestic Finance, Counselor ot the Secretary of the Treasury; Manging Director/CFO, World Bank; Co-Chairman, BT Wolfensohn
Directorships: AlixPartners, Grosvenor Capital Management Holdings
Stefan Goetz, Partner
Education: MA, Electrical Engineering, RWTH Aachen & Ecole Centrale Paris; MBA, Kellogg School of

Management, Northwestern University
Background: Executive Director, Principal Investments area, Goldman Sachs International; McKinsey & Co.
Judd Sher, Partner/Chief Financial Officer
Education: University of Maine; JD, University of Dayton School of Law; LLM, Taxation, Georgetown University School of Law
Background: Principal, Deloitte Tax LLP
Zita Saurel, Partner
Education: Georgetown University
Background: Investcorp; Leveraged Finance, Lehman Brothers
Directorships: Wood Mackenzie; Web Reservations
Erik Ragatz, Partner
Education: Stanford University; MBA, Stanford Graduate School of Business
Background: Bain Capital; Chairman, SnapAV; Grocery Outlet; ABRA; Associated Materials
Directorships: Sheridan Holdings, LPL Holdings, Goodman Global
Roanne Daniels, Partner & Head, Investor Relations
Education: University of Virginia; MBA, Harvard Business School
Background: Operating Partner, Bain Capital; Consultant, McKingsey & Co.; Correspondent/Editor, Reuters
Allen Thorpe, Partner
Education: Stanford University; MBA, Harvard Business School
Background: Vice President, Pacific Equity Partners; Manager, Bain & Company; Chairman, Sheridan Healthcare
Directorships: MultiPlan; Change Healthcare; Edelman Financial; LPL Financial; Artian Partners; Mondrian Investment Partners; Gartmore Investment Management
David Tunnell, Partner
Education: Harvard University; Harvard Business School
Background: Banking Group, Lazard Freres & Company; Chairman, Applied Systems; Kronos; Activant; GeoVera; Vertafore
Directorships: Genesys; HUB; OpenLink; Arch Capital; Blackbaud; Ellucian; Intergraph; Sedgwick; PARIS RE
Blake Kleinman, Partner
Education: Harvard College
Background: M&A Group, Morgan Stanley & Co.
Directorships: Scout24; TeamSystem; Gartmore; Iris; SSP; Wood Mackenzie
Deepak Advani, Partner
Education: Michigan State University; MS, Computer Engineering, Wright State University; MBA, Wharton School, University of Pennsylvania
Background: IBM; Global Chief Marketing Officer, Lenovo
Directorships: Applied Systems; Renaissance Learning; OpenLink
Arrie Park, Partner/Chief Legal Officer
Education: University of California, Los Angeles; JD, Yale Law School
Background: Corporate Law, Wachtell Lipton Rosen & Katz
Trevor Watt, Partner
Education: Princeton University; MBA, Stanford Graduate School of Business
Background: Executive Director, Morgan Stanley

928 HERCULES TECHNOLOGY GROWTH CAPITAL, INC
400 Hamilton Avenue
Suite 310
Palo Alto, CA 94301

Phone: 650-289-3060
e-mail: info@htgc.com
web: www.htgc.com

Mission Statement: Hercules Capital is a venture lending company with an interest in technology, life science, and sustainable and renewable energy
Geographic Preference: United States, Israel, Canada
Fund Size: $1.6 billion
Founded: 2003
Minimum Investment: $1 million
Industry Group Preference: Technology, Life Sciences, Clean Technology, Renewable Energy
Portfolio Companies: Acceleron Pharma, AcelRx Pharmaceuticals, Achronix Semiconductor, Adiana, Aegerion Pharmaceuticals, Affinity VideoNet, Affinity Express, Agami Systems, Ageia Technologies, Alexza Pharmaceuticals, Althea Technologies, Ancestry.com, Annie's, Anthera Pharmaceuticals, Atrenta, AVEO Pharmaceuticals, BabyUniverse, BARRx, BIND Biosciences, Blurb, Box.Net, Braxton Technologies, BrightSource Energy, Bullhorn, Buzz Media, Calera, Central Desktop, Cha Cha, Chroma Therapeutics, Cittio, ClickFox, Compete, Cornice, Cozi Group, Cradle Technologies, Crux Biomedical, deCODE Genetics, Dicerna Pharmaceuticals, Diomed Holdings, E-Band Communications, EcoMotors, EKOS, Elixir Pharmaceuticals, Enphase Energy, Enpiorion, ENTrique Surgical, EpiCept, Everyday Health, ForeScout Technologies, GameLogic, Glam Media, Gomez, GreatPoint Energy, Guava Technologies, Gynesonics, HedgeStreet, hi5 Networks, HighJump, HighRoads, Horizon Therapeutics, Ikano Communications, InfoLogix, Inotek Pharmaceuticals, IntelePeer, Intelliden, Intelligent Beauty, Interwise, Invoke Solutions, Inxite Software, InXpo, IPA, iWatt, Jab Broadband, Kamada, Kovio, KXEN, Labcyte, LaboPharm, Light Sciences Oncology, Lilliputian Systems, Market Force Information, MaxVision, Memory Pharmaceuticals, Merrimack Pharmaceuticals, Merrion Pharmaceuticals, Nanosolar, Navidea Biopharmaceuticals, NeoNova, Neosil, NeurogesX, NEXX Systems, Novasys Medical, NuGEN Technologies, OATSystems, Occam Networks, Omtrix Biopharmaceuticals, OpSource, Optovia

Other Locations:
31 St. James Avenue
Suite 730
Boston, MA 02116
Phone: 617-314-9973

777 Church Road
Elmhurst, IL 60126
Phone: 847-542-1858

60 E 42nd Street
Suite 1130
New York, NY 10165
Phone: 650-289-3060

4800 Hampden Ln
Suite 200
Bethesda, MD 20814
Phone: 202-446-1634

500 Post Road E
2nd Floor
Westport, CT 06880
Phone: 475-666-0522

Key Executives:
Michael Hara, Managing Director of Investor Relations/Corp. Communications
650-433-5578
e-mail: mhara@htgc.com
Education: BS, Electronics Engineering, DeVry University
Background: VP of Investor Relations/Business Development, Cortina Systems; SVP of Investor Relations, NVIDIA; Wyse Technology; Radius; Verticom Graphics; Vermont Microsystems; GE Healthcare
Scott Bluestein, Chief Executive/Investment Officer
617-314-9976
e-mail: sbluestein@htgc.com
Education: BBA, Finance, Emory University

Venture Capital & Private Equity Firms / Domestic Firms

Background: Founder/Partner, Century Tree Capital Management; Managing Director, Laurus-Valens Capital Management; Financial Technology Coverage Group, UBS

Steve Kuo, Senior Managing Director/Group Head, Technology
650-289-3065
e-mail: skuo@htgc.com
Education: BS, Hass Business School, University of California, Berkeley
Background: Ligthcross; Principal, Comdisco Ventures

Roy Y. Liu, Managing Director
617-314-9982
e-mail: rliu@htgc.com
Education: BS, Electrical Engineering, MBA, University of Michigan
Background: Vice President, GrandBanks Capital; Founding Principal, VantagePoint Structured Investments; Co-Founder of Imperial Bank's Emerging Growth Industries; R&D, IBM

Kristen Kosofsky, Senior Managing Director
617-314-9980
e-mail: kkosofsky@htgc.com
Education: BS, Business, Central Connecticut State University
Background: Managing Director, Horizon Technology Finance; VP, Life Sciences, Comerica Bank; GATX Corporation; Transamerica Technology Finance

April Young, Managing Director
703-245-3184
e-mail: ayoung@htgc.com
Education: BA, MS, Urban & Regional Planning, George Washington University; PhD, Public Policy & Administration, Saint Louis University
Background: Senior Vice President & Managing Director, MMV Financing; Senior Vice President & Managing Director, Comerica Bank; Executive Director, Potomac KnowledgeWay Project; Director, Virginia Department of Economic Development

Lesya Kulchenko, Managing Director, Portfolio Management
650-289-3062
e-mail: lkulchenko@htgc.com
Education: BS, Computer Engineering, Marquette University
Background: Nourish Capital; Hopewell Ventures; Corporate Credit Monitoring Manager, Raiffeisen Bank Ukraine; Product Management, Rockwell Automation

Janice Borque, Managing Director
617-314-9992
e-mail: jborque@htgc.com
Education: BS, Veterinary Science; MBA, Finance & Accounting, University of New Hampshire
Background: Commons Capital; Oxford Bioscience Partners; Senior Vice President/Group Head, Life Sciences, Comerica Bank; President/CEO, Massachusetts Biotechnology Council

Lake McGuire, Managing Director
517-304-0382
e-mail: lmcguire@htgc.com
Education: BS, Construction Management, Michigan State University; MBA, Finance, University of Michigan
Background: Vice President, Business Development, Comerica Bank

R. Bryan Jadot, Senior Managing Director/Group Head, Life Sciences
617-314-9981
e-mail: bjadot@htgc.com
Education: BA, Economics & Government, California State University, Sacramento
Background: 0ice President, Life Sciences Group, Silicon Valley Bank; Corporate Banking, Banque Nationale de Paris

929 HERITAGE PARTNERS
800 Boylston Street
Suite 2200
Boston, MA 02199

Phone: 617-439-0688 Fax: 617-439-0689
e-mail: admin@newheritagecapital.com
web: www.newheritagecapital.com

Mission Statement: Invests preferred and common stock, on a minority or majority basis, in mature, successful manufacturing, distribution and service companies.

Geographic Preference: United States
Fund Size: $1.4 billion
Founded: 1987
Average Investment: $15 - 40 million
Minimum Investment: $15 million
Investment Criteria: Acquisitions, Equity-Based Recapitalizations, Revenues of $4- 20 million EBITDA
Industry Group Preference: Aerospace, Defense and Government, Business Products & Services, Consumer Products, Distribution, Education, Food & Beverage, Healthcare, Healthcare Services, Industrial Products, Manufacturing, Pet Products, Specialty Chemicals, Test & Measurement
Portfolio Companies: Continental, Covalent Health, Centra Industries, Eptam Plastics, The Execu|Search Group, Flying Colours Corp., OneSource Distributors, Reach Air Medical, Rhythmlink, Welcome Dairy

Key Executives:

Mark Jrolf, Managing Senior Partner
617-428-0108
e-mail: mjrolf@newheritagecapital.com
Education: BS, Finance, Babson College; MS, Management, MIT
Background: Equity Partners; McKinsey & Company; Heritage Partners; Bank of Boston
Directorships: Continental; The Execu|Search Group; Eptam Plastics; Covalent Health

Charlie Gifford, Senior Partner
617-428-0104
e-mail: cgifford@newheritagecapital.com
Education: BA, Denison University; MBA, Kellogg School of Management, Northwestern University
Background: Heritage Partners; The New England Revolution; Smith Barney

Nickie Norris, Senior Partner/Chief Operating & Compliance Officer
617-428-3616
e-mail: nnorris@newheritagecapital.com
Education: BS, Business Management, Cornell University
Background: Dolandson Lufkin & Jenrette; Phoenix Private Equity Partners; Heritage Partners
Directorships: Continental; The Execu|Search Group; Eptam Plastics; Covalent Health

Melissa Barry, Partner
617-429-8427
e-mail: mbarry@newheritagecapital.com
Education: BA, University of Virginia
Background: Heritage Partners; Banc of America Securities
Directorships: Continental; Covalent Health

Judson Samuels, Partner
617-428-0106
e-mail: jsamuels@newheritagecapital.com
Education: BA, University of Virginia; MBA, Wharton School, University of Pennsylvania
Background: HIG Capital; Bain & Company; Heritage Partners
Directorships: The Execu|Search Group; Eptma Plastics

Kyle Veatch, Principal
e-mail: kveatch@newheritagecapital.com
Education: BA, Economics, Yale University; MBA, Booth School of Business
Background: Raymond James & Company; PSP Capital Partners

Venture Capital & Private Equity Firms / Domestic Firms

Tristan Velez, Senior Vice President, Finance
617-428-0014
e-mail: tvelez@newheritagecapital.com
Education: BS, MBA, University of Windsor, Ontario
Background: Investors Bank & Trust (Alternative Investments Group); Bisys Hedge Fund Servives

930 HEWLETT PACKARD ENTERPRISE
6280 America Center Drive
San Jose, CA 95002

web: www.hpe.com

Mission Statement: Hewlett Packard identifies and invests in leading startup companies. They invest in disruptive innovation in cybersecurity, analytics and infrastructure.

Key Executives:
  Anhishek Shukla, Managing Director/Global Head of Investing
  Education: MBA, University of California, Berkeley
  Background: Managing Director, GE Ventures

931 HIG CAPITAL
1450 Brickell Avenue
31st Floor
Miami, FL 33131

Phone: 305-379-2322 **Fax:** 305-379-2013
e-mail: info@higcapital.com
web: www.higprivateequity.com

Mission Statement: A leading global private equity firm focused on management buyouts and recapitalizations of leading middle market companies as well as growth equity investments.

Geographic Preference: United States, Europe
Fund Size: $1.75 billion
Founded: 1993
Average Investment: $2 million - $10 million
Minimum Investment: $1 million
Investment Criteria: First Stage, Second Stage, LBO, MBO, Recapitalizations, Growth Equity
Industry Group Preference: Aerospace, Defense and Government, Building Materials & Services, Business Products & Services, Specialty Chemicals, Consumer Products, Distribution, Healthcare, Infrastructure, Manufacturing, Media, Energy, Information Technology, Transportation, Education, Food & Beverage
Portfolio Companies: 37.5, A10 Capital, Accupac, ACG Materials, AERT, Albertville Quality Foods, All American Group, Amerijet International, AMPAC, ARBOC Specialty Vehicles, Arctic Glacier Holdings, ATX Networks, Caraustar Industries, CEL LEP, CFMG, Classmates, Comverge, Constructive Media, Cornerstone Chemical, CPower, Creme Mel, DHISCO, Die Cuts With a View, Eletromidia, Fox River Fiber, Hart InterCivic, HealthSTAR, HelpSystems, Higher Gear Group, Holland Services, Infogix, Innovative Building Systems, Intelius, InterDent, Lexmark, LG Lugar de Gente, Matrixx, Milestone Technologies, Mr. Cat, Net Trans, NextSource, Office Total, Onyx Payments, Pendum, Pro-Pet, Progrexion, Protocol Global Systems, Raymond Express International, Ready Pac Produce, Redfish Rentals, Rennhack Marketing Services, Rolland, Rotorcraft Leasing Company, Ship Supply, Soleo Health, Southern Quality Meats, Stant Corporation, Surgery Partners, T-Bird Restaurant Group, TestAmerica, TLC Vision, TRAKAmerica, Trinity, Universal Fiber Systems, US MED, Valtris Specialty Chemicals, VIP Petcare

Other Locations:
  1380 West Paces Ferry Road
  Suite 1290
  Atlanta, GA 30327
  Phone: 404-504-9333 **Fax:** 404-504-5315

  500 Boylston Street
  20th Floor
  Boston, MA 02116
  Phone: 617-262-8455 **Fax:** 617-262-1505

  One Sansome Street
  37th Floor
  San Francisco, CA 94104
  Phone: 415-439-5500 **Fax:** 415-439-5525

  1271 Avenue of the Americas
  22nd Floor
  New York, NY 10020
  Phone: 212-506-0500 **Fax:** 212-506-0559

  151 N Franklin Street
  21st Floor
  Chicago, IL 60606
  Phone: 312-214-1234 **Fax:** 312-345-5999

  200 Crescent Court
  Suite 1414
  Dallas, TX 75201
  Phone: 214-855-2999 **Fax:** 214-855-2998

  HIG European Capital Partners LLP
  2nd Floor
  London W1K 4QB
  United Kingdom
  Phone: 44-2073185700 **Fax:** 44-2073185749

Key Executives:
  Sami Mnaymneh, Founder/Co-CEO
  Education: BA, Columbia University; JD, Harvard Law School; MBA, Harvard Business School
  Background: Managing Director, The Blackstone Group; VP, Mergers & Acquisitions, Morgan Stanley
  Tony Tamer, Founder/Co-CEO
  Education: Rutgers University; Stanford University; MBA, Harvard Business School
  Background: Partner, Bain & Company; Marketing, Engineering & Manufacturing, Hewlett-Packard; Sprint
  Douglas Berman, Executive Managing Director
  Education: BA, Economics, University of Virginia; MBA, Wharton School, University of Pennsylvania
  Background: Consultant, Bain & Company
  Rick Rosen, Co-President
  Education: Stanford University; MBA, Harvard Business School
  Background: General Electric Company; GE Capital
  Brian D. Schwartz, Co-President
  Education: BS, University of Pennsylvania; MBA, Harvard Business School
  Background: Dillon Read & Co., PepsiCo
  Camilo E. Horvilleur, Managing Director
  Education: BBA, Finance, Texas A&M University; MBA, Harvard Business School
  Background: Associate, Morgan Stanley; Atticus Capital
  Directorships: ATX Networks, PMSI, Capstone Logistics, Safe-Guard Products, Service Net, Align Networks
  Matthew Hankins, Managing Director
  Education: BS, University of Michigan College of Engineering; MBA, Booth School of Business
  Background: Sterling Partners; Co-Founder, Metropolitan Capital Bank; JP Morgan; Accenture
  Michael Gallagher, Managing Director
  Education: BS, Finance & Accounting, Indiana University; MBA, Wharton School
  Background: Apax Partners; Qualitest Pharmaceuticals
  Elliot Maluth, Managing Director
  Education: BBA, University of Washington; MBA, Harvard Business School
  Background: Partner, Behrman Capital; Associate, Golder Thoma Cressey Rauner; Manager, Strategic Consulting Group, Price Waterhouse; Sales Manager, Beverage Division, Procter & Gamble
  Keval Patel, Managing Director
  Education: BA, Economics, Wharton School, University of Pennsylvania
  Background: Graham Partners; Salomon Smith Barney

Venture Capital & Private Equity Firms / Domestic Firms

Richard Stokes, Managing Director
Education: Cornell University
Background: M&A Group, Salomon Smith Barney
Tenno Tsai, Managing Director
Education: Williams College; MBA, Harvard Business School
Background: Principal, Warburg Pincus; Associate, AEA Investors; Consultant, McKinsey & Company
Rob Wolfson, Managing Director
Education: Northwestern University; MBA, Harvard Business School
Background: VP, Sales & Business Development, IPWireless; Consultant, LEK Consulting
Jeff Zanarini, Managing Director
Education: BS, BA, Southern Methodist University; MBA, Harvard Business School
Background: Bain & Company, Goldman Sachs

932 HIGH ALPHA
830 Massachusetts Avenue
Suite 1500, 4th Floor
Indianapolis, IN 46204

web: highalpha.com

Mission Statement: High Alpha creates and funds B2B SaaS companies.

Key Executives:
Scott Dorsey, Managing Director
Education: BA, Indiana University; MBA, Northwestern University
Background: Co-Founder and CEO, Salesforce

933 HIGH COUNTRY VENTURE
Boulder, CO 80302

Mission Statement: To invest in innovative early stage Colorado-based companies, and to work closely with entrepreneurs to drive growth and create profitable businesses.

Fund Size: $50 million
Founded: 2005
Investment Criteria: Early-Stage
Industry Group Preference: Life Sciences, Biotechnology, Clean Technology, Medical Devices, Technology, Software, Internet
Portfolio Companies: AktiVax, BirdBox, Collective IP, Digabit, Endoshape, Full Contact, Kapost, LogRhythm, Mosaic Biosciences, Nutrinsic, QualVu, Sinopsys, Surefire Medical, TheraTogs, ViroCyt

Key Executives:
Mark T Lupa PhD, Managing Director
Education: BSc, Bioengineering, Northwestern University; MPhil, Bioengineering, University of Sussex; PhD, Pharmacology, University of Lund
Background: Founder, CEO & CFO, Tabernash Brewing Company
Directorships: LeftHand/Tabernash, Oberon, TheraTogs, Surefire Medical, Endoshape, Mosaic Biosciences

934 HIGH ROAD CAPITAL PARTNERS
1251 Avenue of the Americas
Suite 4102
New York, NY 10020

Phone: 212-554-3265
web: www.highroadcap.com

Mission Statement: To collaborate with management teams to develop growth plans for portfolio companies. High Road Capital Partners is focused primarily on investing in smaller middle market businesses.

Fund Size: $320 million
Founded: 2007
Average Investment: $3 - $25 million
Investment Criteria: Buyouts, Recapitalizations
Industry Group Preference: Manufacturing, Distribution, Media, Healthcare, Services
Portfolio Companies: Accurate Component Sales, Advanced Sleep Medicine Services, BlueSpire, Cali Bamboo, Celco Controls, The Crown Group, General Tools & Instruments, Guidemark Health, PANOS Brands, SMB Machinery Systems, York Wallcoverings

Key Executives:
Robert J Fitzsimmons, Managing Partner
e-mail: rfitzsimmons@highroadcap.com
Education: BS, Accounting, University of Pennsylvania; MBA, Finance, University of Chicago
Background: Managing Partner, The Riverside Company; Citicorp Venture Capital; Price Waterhouse
Directorships: Advanced Sleep Medicine Services, BlueSpire, The Crown Group, Guidemark Health, PANOS Brands, SMB Machinery Systems
William C Connell, Partner
e-mail: wconnell@highroadcap.com
Education: BA, English, Boston College; MBA, Harvard Business School
Background: Vice President, The Riverside Company; Connell Limited Partnership
Directorships: Advanced Sleep Medicine Services, PANOS Brands, The Crown Group
Jeffrey M Goodrich, Partner
e-mail: jgoodrich@highroadcap.com
Education: BS, Economics, BA, International Relations, University of Pennsylvania; MBA, Finance & Accounting, New York University Stern School of Business
Background: Vice President, The Riverside Company; Corporate Finance, IBJ Whitehall Bank & Trust Company
Directorships: Accurate Component Sales, BlueSpire, Celco, Guidemark Health, General Tools & Instruments
Ben A Schnakenberg, Partner
e-mail: bschnakenberg@highroadcap.com
Education: BA, Political Science & English, Valparaiso University; MBA, Wharton School, University of Pennsylvania; CFA
Background: Senior VP, LaSalle Bank; Madison Capital Funding
Directorships: Accurate Component Sales, Cali Bamboo, Guidemark Health, SMB Machinery Systems

935 HIGH STREET CAPITAL
150 North Wacker Drive
Suite 2420
Chicago, IL 60606

Phone: 312-423-2650 Fax: 312-267-2861
web: www.highstreetcapital.com

Mission Statement: High Street Capital pursues opportunities with lower middle market businesses and implements strategies to build valuable niche manufacturing, outsourced business services, and distribution and logistics companies.

Geographic Preference: Central United States
Fund Size: $100 million
Founded: 1997
Average Investment: $8 million
Minimum Investment: $4 million
Investment Criteria: Revenues up to $100 million, Management-Led Buyouts, Growth Capital, Recapitalizations
Industry Group Preference: Outsourcing & Efficiency, Niche Manufacturing, Distribution, Logistics, Healthcare Services
Portfolio Companies: Applied Process, Avomeen, Banner Services Corporation, BeneSys, Bock & Clark, Can-Do National Tape, Commodity Blenders, Countryside Hospice, CRFS Services, DataSource, DiversiTech, Koontz-Wagner Electronic, Massey Fair, ORB Packing, ShoreMaster, Suburban Team, Superior Fibers, TLC Companies

Key Executives:
Joseph R Katcha, Founder/Principal
312-423-2651
e-mail: joe@highstreetcapital.com

Venture Capital & Private Equity Firms / Domestic Firms

Education: University of Wisconsin, Madison; Harvard University Graduate School of Business
Background: Director, SG Warburg; Partner, Managing Director & COO, KC-CO Investments; Associate, First Atlantic Capital; Associate, M&A, PaineWebber; Peat, Marwick, Mitchell & Co.
Directorships: BeneSys, Countryside Hospice, DataSource, Bock & Clark, MST Analytics, Koontz-Wagner
William J Oberholtzer, Principal
312-423-2652
e-mail: will@highstreetcapital.com
Education: Kalamazoo College; MBA, University of Chicago Graduate School of Business
Background: Alpha Capital; Bank of Nova Scotia; Comerica Bank
Directorships: Superior Fibers, Massey Fair, DiversitTech, DocuForce
Kent C Haeger, Principal
e-mail: kent@highstreetcapital.com
Education: University of Wisconsin, Madison
Background: Managing Director, SG Warburg & Company; Founder & Managing Partner, KC-CO
Directorships: DocuForce, Bock & Clark, MST Analytics, Massey Fair
Richard McClain, Principal
312-423-2654
e-mail: dick@highstreetcapital.com
Education: BS, Engineering, University of Michigan; MBA, University of Texas
Background: VP, Global Business Development & Strategy, Tenneco Automotive; TRW
Directorships: BeneSys, DataSource, Superior Fibers, Koontz-Wagner

936 HIGHBAR PARTNERS
545 Middlefield Road
Suite 175
Menlo Park, CA 94025

e-mail: info@highbarpartners.com
web: www.highbarpartners.com

Mission Statement: HighBAR Partners is an early-stage and structured growth capital firm that helps align Management and Investors to build great companies. HighBAR invests in companies that develop infrastructure software and solutions. HighBAR Partners are hands-on investors and bring significant experience and strategic relationships to every project.

Founded: 1995
Investment Criteria: Early-Stage, Structured Growth Capital
Portfolio Companies: Autotask, Blazent, Clustrix, Janrain, Patientsafe Solutions, Virtual Instruments, Zettaset, Brightmail, Brocade, Cawnetworks, CDS, Dantz, Ingrian, Load Dynamix, Mirapoint, Neopath Networks, Sanlight, Soonr, Tapulous, Tazznet, Vyatta
Key Executives:
  Roy Thiele-Sardina, Managing Partner
  e-mail: roy@highbarpartners.com
  Education: BS, Electrical Engineering & Computer Science, University of Wisconsin, Madison; MBA, Stern School of Business
  Background: Managing Director, Steelpoint Capital; EIR, Mayfield Fund; Co-Founder & CEO, Ingrian Networks; Brocade Communications
  John Kim, Managing Partner
  e-mail: john@highbarpartners.com
  Education: BS, Economics, University of Chicago; MBA, Columbia Business School
  Background: W Capital Partners; Director of Corporate Development, Zeborg; Director of Investments, ISL Managment
  Brian Peters, Managing Director
  Education: BSE, Computer Engineering, University of Michigan, MBA, Columbia Business School
  Background: Investment Banker, Barclays Capital;

Analyst, Rosemounth Capital Management; Software Developer, Nextel Telecomunications
  Chris Kitching, Operating Partner
  Education: BS, MS, Electrical Engineering, Stanford University; MBA, Harvard Business School
  Background: CFO, Sound United; CFO, ClariPhy Communications Inc.; Ethernet

937 HIGHER GROUND LABS
626 W Jackson Boulevard
Suite 600
Chicago, IL 60661

e-mail: info@highergroundlabs.com
web: highergroundlabs.com

Mission Statement: Seeks to discover new techniques for effective campaigning, spark and nurture new collaborations, and strengthen connectivity across progressive tech. Invests in companies building solutions to the most pressing campaign challenges and provides programming and mentorship.

Industry Group Preference: Technology
Portfolio Companies: Avalanche Insights, BallotReady, CallTime, Change Research, Civic Eagle, Civitech, Countable, Deck, FactSquared, Field Day, GroundBase, Grow Progress, Hope, Human Agency, Hustle, Icebreaker, Main Street One, Mobilize, New'Mode, OpenField, Outfox AI, OutreachCircle, Outvote, PredictWise, Qriously, SameSide, Speakeasy Political, Survey 160, Swayable, The tuesday Company, Torch, Victory Guide, Warchest, Wethos
Key Executives:
  Shomik Dutta, Partner
  Education: BA, Williams College; MBA, Wharton School
  Background: Chief Revenue Officer, Romeo Power Technology; Managing Director, Renewable Energy Private Equity
  Directorships: Mobilize
  Betsy Hoover, Partner
  Education: BA, Xavier University
  Background: Partner, 270 Strategies; Online Organizing Director, Obama for America; Regional Director, Democratic National Committee
  Andrew McLaughlin, Partner
  Education: BA, Yale University; JD, Harvard Law School
  Background: President/COO, Assembly OSM; Exec Director, Tsai CITY; Head of Various Bits, Medium.com; CEO/Exec Chairman, Digg; CEO, Instapaper; EVP, Tumblr; Exec Director, Civic Commons; Deputy CTO of the United States; Director of Global Public Policy, Google Inc.; VP/Chief Policy Officer, Internet Corp.

938 HIGHLAND CAPITAL PARTNERS
Boston, MA

web: www.hcp.com

Mission Statement: Invests in seed, early and growth stage companies in the communications, consumer, digital media, healthcare and information technology markets.

Fund Size: $1.8 billion
Founded: 1988
Minimum Investment: $500,000
Investment Criteria: Early, Growth, Seed
Industry Group Preference: Communications, Information Technology, Healthcare, Consumer Products, Internet, Digital Media & Marketing
Portfolio Companies: Aloha, Anova Data, Avidyne, BARonova, Beeswax, BetterLesson, BlueTrap Financial, Bromlum, Cafe Media, Carbon Black, Catlant, Cenx, ClearSky, Datiphy, Disconnect, Enjoy, Exagrid, Fidelis SeniorCare, Freshly, Gigamon, Handy Expert Home Services, Harry's, Iddiction, Infinio, Inxpo, Jaunt, Kascend, Kyruus, Leap Motion, LevelUp, Lovepop, Alwarebytes, Netentsec, Omni, OneSpace, Open Sky, Pharmaca Integrate Pharmacy, Photoboxm QD Vision, Qumulo, Rapidsos, Redbrick Health, Remote Year, Rent The Runway, Rethink Robotics,

Venture Capital & Private Equity Firms / Domestic Firms

RethinkDB, Scopely, Session M, Shift, Signifai, Spartoo, Thred Up, Trilogy Education Services, Tuache.com, Tuniu.com, Turbonomic, US Search, vArmour, Violin Memory, Viva, Weeby.co, Wooga, Xometry, Yipit, ZeroFOX

Other Locations:
537 Hamilton Avenue
Palo Alto, CA 94301
Phone: 650-687-3800

5-9 Union Square West
3rd Floor
New York, NY 10003

451 Jackson Street
San Francisco, CA 94111

Key Executives:
Paul Maeder, Chair/Founding Partner
617-401-4500
e-mail: pmaeder@hcp.com
Education: BSE, Princeton University; MS, Stanford University; MBA, Harvard Business School
Background: Director, Avid Technology/CheckFree/Chipcom HighGround Systems/Mainspring/SCH/SQA/Sybase/WebLine Communications; Novacon; Synemed
Directorships: Imprivata, Performix Technologies, Relicore, Village Ventures, VistaPrint

Daniel Nova, Partner
617-401-4500
e-mail: dnova@hcp.com
Education: BS, Computer Science, Boston College; MBA, Harvard Business School
Background: Former Partner, CMG@Ventures; Sr Associate, Summit Partners; Sales, Wang Laboratories
Directorships: CMI Marketing, Corematrics, GlobalStreams, Gotuit Media, N2 Broadband, Banic Networks, NuGenesis Technologies, Topica, Whole Body

Craig Driscoll, Partner
617-401-4500
Education: BE, Mechanical Engineering, Vanderbilt University
Background: Korn/Kerry International; JacobsRimell; Fidelity Ventures; Beacon Power Corp.; SatCon Technology Corp.
Directorships: Remote Year, Trilogy Education Services, Bullhorn, Quattro

Bob Davis, Partner
617-401-4500
e-mail: bdavis@hcp.com
Education: BS, Northeastern University; MBA, Babson College
Background: CEO, Terra Lycos; Founder, Lycos, Inc.
Directorships: Bullhorn, Genvara, Hangout Industries, NameMedia, OpenSky, Turbine

Corey Mulloy, Partner
650-687-3800
e-mail: cmulloy@hcp.com
Education: BA, Swarthmore College; MBA, Harvard Business School
Background: Corporate Development, ONI; Healthcare Investment, Roberson Stephens & Co; Assistant CEO, Whitman Group
Directorships: AccentCare, Whole Body, Conor Medsystems, NuGenesis Technologies, Radian Medical, US Labs

939 HIGHWAY1
1040 Mariposa Street
San Francisco, CA 94107

e-mail: info@highway1.io
web: www.highway1.io

Mission Statement: Hardware startup accelerator in San Francisco.

Founded: 2013
Average Investment: $50K
Minimum Investment: $50K
Investment Criteria: Seed-Stage
Industry Group Preference: Hardware
Portfolio Companies: Modbot, Navdy, Ringly
Key Executives:
Brady Forrest, Co-Founder

940 HILCO BRANDS
5 Revere Drive
Suite 206
Northbrook, IL 60062

web: www.hilcobrands.com

Mission Statement: A specialized private equity firm with an exclusive focus on investing in successful and struggling consumer brand companies.

Geographic Preference: United States, Canada
Founded: 2006
Average Investment: $25 - $100 million
Investment Criteria: Acquisitions
Industry Group Preference: Consumer Products, Consumer Services, Retailing
Portfolio Companies: Altec, Clipper Marine, Dealgenius.com, Denby, Halston, Haute Hippie, Hillier's, Le Tigre, LetsBab, MadaLuxe Group, Misco, Portico, Powerbilt, Staples, StreetTrend, The Shoe Box, Tradepoint Atlantic, Under the Canopy, Xcel Brands, Xtra-vision

Other Locations:
65 Queen Street West
Thomson Building, Suite 1100
Toronto, ON M5H 2M5
Canada
Phone: 416-361-6336

80 New Bond Street
London W1S 1SB
United Kingdom
Phone: 44-2073172050

Key Executives:
Eric Kaup, Managing Director/General Counsel
e-mail: akaup@hilcoglobal.com
Education: Yale University; JD, Moritz College of Law, Ohio State University
Background: Skadden, Arps, Slate, Meagher & Flom

Edward J Siskin, Executive Vice President
e-mail: esiskin@hilcoglobal.com
Education: BA, Economics, State University of New York at Albany; MBA, Finance & International Business, New York University
Background: Principal, Crystal Financial; President, Back Bay Capital; Managing Director, Bankers Trust; Head of Corporate Development, Red Apple Group; COO, Bank of America Retail Finance Group

Gary C Epstein, Chief Marketing Officer
e-mail: gepstein@hilcoglobal.com
Education: BA, English, Journalism & Political Science, University of Michigan
Background: CEO, Abundant Ventures; CEO/CMO, ReachMD LLC; CMO, American Medical Association; Euro RSCG Worldwide

Jeff Branman, Managing Director
e-mail: jbranman@hilcoglobal.com
Education: University of California, Santa Cruz; University of California, Berkeley; Carnegie Mellon University
Background: President, Interactive Technology Partners; Senior Vice President, Corporate Development, Foot Locker; Investment Banker, Financo; VP, Strategic Planning, May Department Stores Company; Strategy Consultant, Boston Consulting Group
Directorships: Fanatics Inc., Polaroid, Rue La La Inc.

Venture Capital & Private Equity Firms / Domestic Firms

941 HLM VENTURE PARTNERS
116 Huntington Avenue
9th Floor
Boston, MA 02116

Phone: 617-266-0030
web: www.hlmvp.com

Mission Statement: Invests in US-based healthcare technology companies whose products and services provide direct improvements to the organization and distribution of healthcare.

Geographic Preference: United States
Fund Size: $65 million
Founded: 1983
Average Investment: $4 - $10 million
Investment Criteria: Early Stage, Mid-Stage
Industry Group Preference: Healthcare Services, Healthcare Information Technology, Medical Technology, Medical Devices, Diagnostics
Portfolio Companies: AbilTo, ArroHealth, Aventura, Binary Fountain, ClearDATA, Imagine Health, Linkwell Health, Medicalis, mPulse Mobile, Nordic Consulting, OnShift, Payspan, Persivia, Phreesia, Prism Education Group, RedBrick Health, Sanovia Corporation, Spinal Kinetics, Tandem Diabetes Care, Teladoc, Transcend Medical, Valeritas, Vantage Oncology, Vericare, Vets First Choice, Welltok

Key Executives:
Ed Cahill, Partner
e-mail: ecahill@hlmvp.com
Education: Williams College; Yale University
Background: Founding Partner, Cahill Warnock & Company; Managing Director, Alex. Brown & Sons
Directorships: Binary Fountain, Persivia, Phreesia, Tandem Diabetes
Steve Tolle, Partner
Background: SVP/General Manager, Optum, VP of Product Management, Allscripts; Director of Product Management, Pfizer
Vin Fabiani, Partner
e-mail: vfabiani@hlmvp.com
Education: BS, American University
Background: VP & General Manager, First Data Investor Services
Directorships: ClearDATA Networks, Prism Education
Peter Grua, Partner
e-mail: pgrua@hlmvp.com
Education: AB, Bowdoin College; MBA, Columbia University
Background: Managing Director, Alex. Brown & Sons; Research Analyst, William Blair & Company; Strategy Consultant, Booz Allen Hamilton
Directorships: ArroHealth, Imagine Health, Linkwell, Medicalis, Nordic Consulting, OnShift, The Advisory Board Company
Enrico Picozza, Venture Partner
e-mail: epicozza@hlmvp.com
Education: University of Connecticut
Background: Co-Founder, COO & CTO, HTS Biosystems; PerkinElmer; Applied Biosystems
Directorships: Aventura, Transcend Medical, Vericare
Mike Wong, Chief Financial Officer
Education: BSBA, Accounting & Finance, Boston University; MBA, Finance, Boston College
Background: Financial Analyst, Summit Partners; Senior Auditor, Deloitte

942 HMS HAWAII MANAGEMENT
Davies Pacific Center
841 Bishop Street
Suite 860
Honolulu, HI 96813

Phone: 808-545-3755 Fax: 808-531-2611

Mission Statement: Makes venture capital investments in start-up, emerging and established companies with a preference for seed and early-stage Hawaii-based companies and later-stage non-Hawaii-based companies.

Geographic Preference: Hawaii
Founded: 1994
Investment Criteria: Seed-Stage, Early-Stage, Later-Stage with Co-Investors
Industry Group Preference: Telecommunications, Health & Wellness, Biotechnology, Earth Sciences
Portfolio Companies: Firetide, Hawaii Biotech, Hoku Scientific, InterWave, Kona Bay Marine Resources, MobiCom Corporation, Pacific DirectConnect, Pacific Island Resources

Key Executives:
Richard G. Grey, General Partner
Education: BS, MBA, University of California, Los Angeles; JD, University of California, Santa Barbara
Background: Founder, Vidar Corporation; Founder, Transwitch Associates
Directorships: Pacific Island Resources, Kona Bay Marine Resources, Firetide, MedDev Corporation
William K. Richardson, General Partner
Education: University of California, Santa Barbara; Duke University School of Law
Background: Commercial Law & Finance Attorney; Wang Laboratories
Directorships: Pacific DirectConnect, Kona Bay Marine Resources, Hawaii Biotech, HealthScape, Digital Island
John Dean, Special Limited Partner
Education: Holy Cross College; MBA, Finance, Wharton School, University of Pennsylvania
Background: CEO, Silicon Valley Bancshares; CEO, Silicon Valley Bank
Ron Higgins, Special Limited Partners
Background: Founder, CEO, Chairman, Digital Island; CEO, RSHF

943 HOLDING CAPITAL GROUP
104 West 40th Street
19th Floor
New York, NY 10018

Phone: 212-486-6670 Fax: 212-486-0843
web: www.holdingcapital.com

Mission Statement: Holding Capital Group specializes in acquisitions and investments across a variety of industries.

Geographic Preference: United States
Founded: 1975
Average Investment: $2 - $150 million
Investment Criteria: Acquisitions, Recapitalizations, Growth Financing, Management Buyouts
Industry Group Preference: Food Services, Financial Services, Apparel, Distribution, Manufacturing, Retail, Consumer & Leisure
Portfolio Companies: Berkeley Contract Packaging, ChicagoLand Commissary, Haskell Jewels, Haskins Electric, HCG Energy, Innerstave, L&S Industries, Malabar Investments, Premise One, Robert Lee Morris, Samara, Southern States, Star-Glo Industries, Value Partners

Other Locations:
5965 Willow Lane
Dallas, TX 75230

1301 Fifth Avenue
Suite 3405
Seattle, WA 98101
Phone: 206-792-1973

Key Executives:
Steven Leischner, President
e-mail: sleischner@holdingcapital.com
Education: BS, Accounting & Business Administration, Wagner College; CPA
Karl D Dillon, Portfolio Advisor
e-mail: kdillon@holdingcapital.com
Education: BA, Whitman College; MBA, Wharton

Venture Capital & Private Equity Firms / Domestic Firms

School, University of Pennsylvania
Background: Gilliam Joseph & Littlejohn; HAL Investments; Antfactory
Thomas M Galvin, Portfolio Advisor
e-mail: tgalvin@holdingcapital.com
Education: BS, Business Administration, University of Nebraska; CPA
Background: President & Chairman, HCG Energy Corporation

944 HOMEBREW MANAGEMENT
436 Bryant St.
3rd Floor
San Francisco, CA 94107

web: www.homebrew.co

Mission Statement: Focus is on startups supporting the Bottum Up Economy - helping businesses, developers and individuals drive economic growth and innovation through simpler, cheaper and more direct access to technology, information and customers.

Investment Criteria: Seed
Portfolio Companies: Building Connected, Chime, De-Ice, Finix Payments, Honor, Hummingbird, Intellimize, Joymode, Layer, Lumi, Q, Outlier, Primary.com, Pulse Data, Ravti, Ride Report, Seriforge, Shield AI, Stockwell, TheSkimm, Tia, Traptic, Upcounsel, Weave, Winnie

Key Executives:
Hunter Walk, Partner
e-mail: hunter@homebrew.co
Education: BA, History, Vassar; MBA, Stanford University
Background: YouTube; Google; Linden Lab
Satya Patel, Partner
e-mail: satya@homebrew.co
Education: BS in Finance and BS in Psychology from The University of Pennsylvania
Background: Twitter; Battery Ventures; Google; DoubleClick

945 HONE CAPITAL
530 Lytton Avenue
Suite 305
Palo Alto, CA 94301

Phone: 650-251-4930
e-mail: info@honecap.com
web: honecap.com

Mission Statement: A venture capital fund focused on tech-based startup companies.
Fund Size: $150 million
Founded: 2015
Investment Criteria: Seed, Early Stage
Industry Group Preference: Diversified
Portfolio Companies: Aifi, Airtable, Albert, Alto Pharmacy, Amitree, Ample, Apartment List, AspireIQ, Atrium, BetterView, BIOAGE, Blendid, Blockstack, Bluecore, Bolt, Boom, Boon + Gable, Branch, Brave, BuildingConnected, Carbon Black, Catalia Health, Clara, Clover, Cronofy, Cruise, DataRobot, Dia & Co., Dil Mil, Elroy Air, Embark, Emulate, Flexport, Fysical, Grove Collaborative, Guardant Health, Gusto, Haven, Intellimize, June, Juniper Square, Labelbox, Landis, Ledger Investing, Lever, Mattermost, Medisas, Molekule, Nav, Notion, Nurx, Ouster, PayJoy, Protocol Labs, Rappi, Renoviso, Rentlytics, Zrinse, Rippling, Rocksbox Jewelry, Roofstock, Schoolmint, Shift, SketchDeck, Starsky Robotics, Tenjin, Troops, True Facet, uMake, Vantage Robotics, Vesper, Weave, Wigwag, Wonderschool, Woodtric, Your Mechanic, Zeel

Key Executives:
Veronica Wu, Managing Partner
Education: BS, Yale University; MS/PhD, University of California, Berkeley
Background: Tesla Motors; Apple; Motorola; McKinsey & Company
Purvi Gandhi, Partner/Chief Financial Officer
Education: BBA, University of California, Berkeley; CPA
Background: CFO, H&Q Asia Pacific; CFO, MedVantage; Deloitte; Charles Schwab

946 HOPEN LIFE SCIENCE VENTURES
171 Monroe Avenue NW
Grand Rapids, MI 49503

Phone: 616-325-2110
e-mail: info@hopenls.com
web: www.hopenls.com

Mission Statement: Hopen Life Science Ventures is a venture capital firm that invests in early- to mid-stage companies in the life sciences industry.

Geographic Preference: Midwest United States
Fund Size: $65 million
Founded: 2006
Average Investment: $3 - $5 million
Investment Criteria: Seed-Stage, Early-Stage, Mid-Stage
Industry Group Preference: Life Sciences, Therapeutics, Medical Devices, Diagnostics, Healthcare Information Technology
Portfolio Companies: Alphabeta Therapeutics, BjondHealth, ConcertoHealth, Delphinus Medical Technologies, Great Lakes Pharmaceuticals, Intervention Insights, Metabolic Solutions Development Company, NeoChord, Nymirum, ProNAi Therapeutics, Transcorp Spine

Other Locations:
159 Crocker Park Blvd
Suite 400
Westlake, OH 44145
Phone: 440-385-4225

Key Executives:
Mark Olesnavage, Managing Director
Education: BS, Economics & Marketing, MBA, Grand Valley State University
Background: EVP & General Manager, Perrigo Company
Directorships: Michigan Venture Capital Association
Michael Fulton MD, Managing Director
Education: BA, Northwestern University; MD, Cornell University
Background: Founder, Director & CEO, Lanx
Michael Jandernoa, Managing General Partner
Education: University of Michigan
Background: Chairman & CEO, Perrigo Company; Co-Founder, Bridge Street Capital Partners; Co-Founder, Grand Angels
Directorships: Business Leaders for Michigan, Lack Industries, ADAC Corp, Metabolic Solutions Development Company, Grand Valley University Foundation
Jerry Callahan PhD, Venture Partner
Education: PhD, Organizational Leadership
Background: VP, Business Development, Van Andel Research Institute; CIO & VP, Supply Chain, Twinlab/Metabolife

947 HOPEWELL VENTURES
207 East Ohio Street
Suite 248
Chicago, IL 60611

Phone: 312-357-9600
web: www.hopewellventures.com

Mission Statement: Hopewell Ventures partners with strong management teams of high-growth businesses in the Midwest, bringing equity capital, expertise and over a century of experience.

Geographic Preference: Midwest United States
Average Investment: $2 - $7 million

Venture Capital & Private Equity Firms / Domestic Firms

Investment Criteria: Early-Stage, Growth-Stage, Change in Control
Industry Group Preference: Technology, Healthcare, Manufacturing, Medical Devices, Media, Life Sciences, Energy, Information Technology
Portfolio Companies: Pioneer Surgical Technology, INRange Systems, Mersive Technologies, Helios Coatings, SageQuest, Symbios Holdings, National Pasteurized Eggs, VHT, iTRACS Corporation, TLContact, InStadium

Key Executives:
William P. Sutter Jr., Senior Managing Director
Education: BS, Economics, Yale University; MBA, Stanford University
Background: Corporate Finance, Smith Barney; Mesirow Financial
Directorships: Regent Communications
Thomas Parkinson, Partner
Education: BS, Economics, Northwestern University; MBA, Kellogg Graduate School of Management
Background: General Partner, Adena Ventures; Executive Director, Evanston Business Investment Corporation
Craig Overmyer, Principal
Education: Indiana University
Background: Adena Ventures; Regional VP, Ridgewood Capital; VP, Cooper Investment Partners

948 HORIZON PARTNERS, LTD
3838 Tamiami Trail N
Suite 408
Naples, FL 34103

Phone: 239-261-0020 Fax: 239-261-0225
web: www.horizonpartnersltd.com

Mission Statement: A private investment holding company that acquires companies with significant growth prospects and potential for above-average profitability.

Fund Size: $100 million
Founded: 1990
Average Investment: $6 million
Minimum Investment: $10 million
Investment Criteria: Sales between $10-$100 million, gross margins in excess of 25%, medium size companies, privately held or divisions/subsidiaries of larger corporations
Industry Group Preference: Manufacturing, Distribution, Business to Business, Retailing, Packaging, Food & Beverage, Plastics, Consumer Products, Electronics, Financial Services, Specialty Chemicals
Portfolio Companies: TGR Financial Inc., Xymox Technologies Inc.

Other Locations:
9099 West Dean Road
Milwaukee, WI 53224

Key Executives:
Robert M. Feerick, Chairman/Founder
e-mail: rfeerick@horizonpartnersltd.com
Education: Phi Beta Kappa, Georgetown University; MBA, University of Chicago
Background: Chairman, The Corporate Development Group; General Partner, Frontenac Company
Directorships: WinterQuest LLC, Xymox Technologies, Lantor International, Climax Portable Machine Tools, Groeb Farms, Karl's Event Rental
William H. Schaar, Chief Financial Officer
239-261-4588
e-mail: wschaar@horizonpartnersltd.com
Education: DePaul University; MBA, University of Chicago
Background: EVP & CFO, Church Pension Group; ARMCO; Brunswick Corporation; Ford Motor Company; Federal Reserve Bank of Chicago

949 HORIZON TECHNOLOGY FINANCE
312 Farmington Avenue
Farmington, CT 06032

Phone: 860-676-8654 Fax: 860-676-8655
e-mail: jerry@horizontechfinance.com
web: www.horizontechfinance.com

Mission Statement: A venture lending, investment and financial services management company that offers creative financing solutions to technology, life science, healthcare information and services, and cleantech companies.

Founded: 2004
Average Investment: $2 - $25 million
Industry Group Preference: Technology, Life Sciences, Healthcare, Clean Technology, Information Technology
Portfolio Companies: Additech, Aquion Energy, Avalanche Technology, Bolt, Bridge2Solutions, ControlScan, CrowdStar, Decisyon, Digital Signal, eAsic, eBureau, Education Elements, Ekahau, MaaS360, Gwynnie Bee, IgnitionOne, Jump Ramp, Kixeye, Le Tote, Lotame, Luxtera, Mblox, Nanocomp, Nanosteel, Netuitive, NMI, NexPlanar, Optaros, Overture, PebblePost, Powerhouse Dynamics, RazorSight, Receptiv, Rocket Lawyer, SavingStar, Shopkeep, Signix, SilkRoad, Simpletuition, Skyword, Social Intelligence, Soraa, Springcm, Streambase, Systech, Brick, VidSys, WebLinc, Xtera, Xtreme Power, Zinion, AccuVein, Anacor, Argos, Celsion Corp., Direct Flow Medical, Inotek, IntegenX, Lantos Technologies, Mederi, Mitralign, N30 Pharma, Nine Point Medical, OraMetrix, Palatin Technologies Inc., Sample6, Strongbridge Biopharma, Sunesis, Supernus, Titan Pharmaceuticals, Tryton Medical, VTV Therapeutics, Xcovery, Accu Metrics, BioScale, Interleukin Genetics, Genepeeks, Healthedge, Medsphere, Precisi Therapeutics, Radisphere, Recondo, Enphase Energy, Lehigh Technologies, Renmatix, Rypos, Semprius, Tigo Energy

Other Locations:
349 Main Street
Suite 203
Pleasanton, CA 94566
Phone: 925-935-2924 Fax: 925-977-9488

1818 Library Street
Suite 500
Reston, VA 20190
Phone: 703-956-3504

Key Executives:
Rob Pomeroy, Chief Executive Officer/Chairman
860-676-8656
e-mail: rob@horizontechfinance.com
Education: BS, MBA, University of California, Berkeley
Background: President, GATX Ventures; EVP, Transamerica Business Credit; General Manager, Transamerica Technology Finance; Crocker Bank
Gerald A. Michaud, President/Director
860-676-8659
e-mail: jerry@horizontechfinance.com
Education: Northeastern University; Rutgers University; University of Phoenix; Harvard Business School
Background: SVP, GATX Ventures; SVP, Transamerica Business Credit; Senior Business Development Executive, Transamerica Technology Finance; President, Venture Leasing & Capital
Chris Mathieu, Senior Vice President, Chief Financial Officer
860-676-8653
e-mail: chris@horizontechfinance.com
Education: BS, Business Administration, New England College; CPA
Background: VP, Life Sciences, GATX Ventures; VP, Life Sciences, Transamerica Business Credit Technology Finance; VP, Finance, Science International
John C. Bombara, Senior Vice President/General Counsel/Chief Compliance Officer
860-676-8657
e-mail: jay@horizontechfinance.com

Venture Capital & Private Equity Firms / Domestic Firms

Education: BA, Colgate University; JD, Cornell Law School
Background: In House Counsel, GATX Ventures; Partner, Pepe & Hazard LLP
Dan Devorsetz, Senior Vice President/Chief Investment Officer
860-674-1208
e-mail: dan@horizontechfinance.com
Education: BS, Cornell University; MBA, Clark University, CFA
Background: VP, General Electrical Capital Corporation; Credit Manager, GATX Ventures; VP, Director of Analysis for Student Loans, Citigroup; Advest, Inc.; Inronwood Capital
Gregory E. Clark, Managing Director
860-676-8651
e-mail: greg@horizontechfinance.com
Education: BA, Columbia University; JD, MBA, University of Connecticut
Background: VP, GATX Ventures; Business Development, Transamerica Technology Finance; Connecticut Innovations; Attorney, Shipman & Goodwin
Kevin J. May, Senior Managing Director
925-935-2924 x100
e-mail: kevin@horizontechfinance.com
Education: BS, Finance, University of Florida
Background: Director, Credit & Portfolio, Oxford Finance Corporation; VP, Credit & Portfolio Management, GATX Ventures; Finova Capital; Deutsche Financial Services
Mishone B. Donelson, Managing Director
860-674-9949
e-mail: mishone@horizontechfinance.com
Education: BS, Chemical Engineering, MIT; MBA, Kellogg School of Management, Northwestern
Background: Principal, Fairview Capital Partners; Analyst, Ariel Investments
Kevin T. Walsh, Managing Directory
925-935-2924 x101
e-mail: kwalsh@horizontechfinance.com
Education: BS, Business Administration, California State University, Hayward
Background: SVP, Market Manager, Bridge Bank Technology Banking & Capital Finance Division; VP, Relationship Manager, Silicon Valley Bank

950 HORIZON VENTURES LLC
Four Main Street
Suite 20
Los Altos, CA 94022

Phone: 650-917-4100
web: www.horizonvc.com

Mission Statement: A venture capital partnership with exclusive focus on technology-based companies. Offers traditional venture capital strengths to innovative young companies that want to capitalize in the growing information technology market.

Geographic Preference: Northern California
Fund Size: $150 million
Founded: 1999
Average Investment: $2-4 million
Minimum Investment: $1 million
Investment Criteria: Seed, First Round, Second Round, Financing
Industry Group Preference: Software, Wireless Technologies, Technology, Communications, Healthcare Information Technology, Business Products & Services
Portfolio Companies: Chelsio Communications, Identity Engines, Inc., InfiniRoute Networks, Sensys Networks, Venturi Wireless, Applied MicroStructures, Inc., Discera, Inc., iWatt, Inc., LefEngin, Inc., NuCORE Technology, Inc., SpectraLinear, Inc., Theta Microelectronics, Alignment Software, Hipbone, Inc., NativeMinds, Inc., Onstation Corporation, PINC Solutions, Right90, Inc., . Toolwire, Inc., WhiteHat Security, Inc., InterVideo Corp., Knowledge Revolution Inc., SalesLogix, Cholestech Corp., Invivodata, Laser Diagnostics, Neurex Corp., Alien Technology, Photon Dynamics Inc., Silicon Motion Inc., Vertex Networks, AudioTalk Networks, Harmonic Inc., Palm Inc., RapidStream Inc., Sandpiper Networks Inc, SpectraLink Corp.

Key Executives:
Jack Carsten, Managing Director
650-917-4100
e-mail: jack@horizonvc.com
Education: BA, Duke University; MBA, Southern Methodist University
Background: Technology Investments; US Venture Partners; VP, Intel Corporation
John E. Hall, Managing Director
650-917-4100
e-mail: john@horizonvc.com
Education: MBA, BS, San Jose State University; PhD, University of Santa Clara
Background: Newtek Ventures; Intel Corporation
Doug Tsui, Managing Director
650-917-4100
e-mail: doug@horizonvc.com
Education: BSEE, University of California; MBA, Santa Clara University
Background: AudioTalk; VP Marketing, Precept Software; Cisco Systems; 3Com/Bridge Communications; Hewlett-Packard
Art Reidel, Managing Director
650-917-4100
e-mail: art@horizonvc.com
Education: BS, Mathematics, MIT
Background: CEO, Scintera; Chairman/CEO, Pharsight Corp.; President/CEO, Sunrise Test Systems; Venture Partner, Lightspeed Ventures Partners; General Partner, ABS Ventures
Directorships: WhiteHat Security, Eye-Fi, Entelos, Materna Medical

951 HOULIHAN LOKEY
10250 Constellation Boulevard
5th Floor
Los Angeles, CA 90067

Phone: 310-553-8871 Fax: 310-553-2173
web: www.hl.com

Mission Statement: An international, advisory-focused investment bank with expertise in mergers and acquisitions, capital markets, financial restructuring, and valuation.

Geographic Preference: United States
Fund Size: $250 million
Founded: 2001
Average Investment: $6 million
Minimum Investment: $1 million
Investment Criteria: Early Stage, Growth Capital, Acquisition
Industry Group Preference: Manufacturing, Retailing, Education, Healthcare, Financial Services

952 HOUSATONIC PARTNERS
800 Boylston Street
Suite 2220
Boston, MA 02199

Phone: 617-399-9200 Fax: 617-267-5565
e-mail: wthorndike@housatonicpartners.com
web: www.housatonicpartners.com

Mission Statement: A private equity investment firm that has invested in over 25 companies. Seeking to invest in and build companies in cooperation with experienced and entrepreneurial managers. Housatonic plays an active role in their portfolio companies as board members, working with management to formulate company strategy, develop operating budgets, arrange additional financial rounds, and recruit seasons operating executives.

Geographic Preference: United States
Fund Size: $350 million
Founded: 1994
Average Investment: $5 to $20 million
Minimum Investment: $3 million
Investment Criteria: MBO, Recapitalizations, Consolidations
Industry Group Preference: Business Products & Services, Media, Communications
Portfolio Companies: Access, Accurate, Aegis, Aircraft Fasteners, ArchivesOne, Asurion, Beacon Fire & Safety, BirdDog Solutions, Calo, Carillion, CaseCentral, Classic Party Rentals, Continental Fire & Safety, Diamond Rental, Efficient Forms, FDH, FIMC, First American Records Management, HealthWyse, Healthcare Financial Resources Inc., Hema Source, LeadQual, LeMaitre, MedOptions, Oasis, Oneline Radiology, Onramp, Onsite Health, Pro Service Hawaii, Response Linl, Service Source, Sprout Health Group, WCCT, Wind River, ZicroData

Other Locations:
One Post Street
Suite 2600
San Francisco, CA 94104-5203
Phone: 415-955-9020 **Fax:** 415-955-9053

Key Executives:
Barry D. Reynolds, Managing Director
Education: University of California; Stanford Graduate School
Background: Principal, Trident Capital; Manager, Bain & Company; Texas Pacific Group
William N. Thorndike, Managing Director
Education: Harvard University; Stanford Graduate School
Background: T Rowe Price Associates; Walker & Co.
Directorships: Carillon Assisted Living; Lincoln Peak Holdings; OASIS Group; QMC International; ZircoData
Joseph M. Niehaus, Managing Director
Education: Dartmouth College; Harvard Business School
Background: Managing Director, Hellman & Friedman; M&A, Morgan Stanley & Co.
Directorships: Accurate Monitoright; Fastener Distribution Holdings; FIMC; ResponseLinkcircle Graphics; 365 Data Centers; HealthWyse; Calo Programs; ZircoData
Michael C. Jackson, Special Limited Partner
Education: Dartmouth College; Johns Hopkins University
Background: Partner/Managing Director, Lehman Brothers
Directorships: LeMaitre Vascular Inc.; South Florida Media Group; Vox Communications
Eliot Wadsworth II, Special Limited Partner
Education: Harvard University; Harvard Business School
Background: CEO, White Flower Farm; Managing Partner, Boston Common Press
James H. Greene III, Vice President
Education: University of Pennsylvania
Background: Milestone Partners; Financial Sponsors Group, Morgan Stanley & Co.
Directorships: Accurate Monitoring; FIMC
Mark G. Hilderbrand, Managing Director
Education: BS, Boston University; MS, Stanford University; MBA, Harvard Business School
Background: General Partner, Onset Ventures; Summit Partners; Fox Paine & Company; Bain & Company
Jill A. Raimondi, Chief Financial Officer
Education: BS, Business Admin., University of California, Berkeley; CPA
Background: Controller, Trident Capital; Manager, Ernst & Young
Amy L. Laforteza, Controller
Education: BS, Business Admin., Univerity of California, Riverside; CPA
Background: Manager, Ernst & Young
Kirsi Fontenot, Tax Director
Education: BS, Business Admin., San Francisco State University; CPA
Background: Senior Manager, Ernst & Young
H. Irving Grousbeck, Special Limited Partner
Education: Amherst College; Harvard Business School
Background: Consulting Professor, Stanford Business School; Lecturer, Harvard University Graduate School of Business Administration; Co-Founder, Continental Cablevision
Directorships: Alta Colleges; Ancora Capital and Management; Asurion Corporation; Beacon Fire & Safety; Carillon Assisted Living; Rent-Wise; Med-Mart; Wind River Environmental
Mark A. McLaughlin, Principal
Education: Stanford Graduate School of Business
Background: Vice President, Technology Crossover Ventures; TA Associate/Consultant, Oliver Wyman; Sageview Capital; Wealthfront
Stephen M. Johnson, Vice President
Education: BS, Wharton School, University of Pennsylvania; MBA, Kellogg School of Management, Northwestern University
Background: M&A, Credit Suissel Citigroup; General Electric; American International Group
Directorships: Onrad Inc.; Sprout Health; Calo Programs; ZircoData
Charlotte D. MacDonald, Fund Administrator/Executive Assistant
Education: Colby-Sawyer College

953 HOUSTON ANGEL NETWORK
410 Pierce Street
PO Box 12
Houston, TX 77002

web: www.houstonangelnetwork.org

Mission Statement: The Houston Angel Network is a Texas-based angel organization focused on providing capital and support to early stage businesses.

Geographic Preference: Texas, United States
Fund Size: $4 million
Founded: 2001
Investment Criteria: Early Stage
Industry Group Preference: Life Sciences, Information Technology, Healthcare Information Technology, Energy Technology
Portfolio Companies: Adient Medical, Assistant Coach, BiologicsMD, Blausen Medical Communications, Bonfire Wings, Boomerang's, Cerebro Tech Medical Systems, Cinegif, CS Identity, Deep Imaging Technologies, End The Lix, Fairway Medical Technologies, Fannin Partners, Greenling, Houston Health Ventures, Kewl, Kimbia, Mercury Fund, Metric Medical Devices, Molecular Match, Monster Mosquito Systems, Nanospectra Biosciences, Nurtur Me, NutshellMail, On It, Ortho Accel, Personal Wine, Rhythm Superfoods, Rock My Run, Salient Pharmaceuticals, See Forge, Senscient, SioTex, SpringCharts, Strike Brewing Company, Surge, Sweet Leaf Iced Teas, Texas Ventures

Key Executives:
Stephanie Campbell, Managing Director
Education: BASc, Spring Hill College; MBA, Jones Graduate School of Business, Rice University
Background: Government Affairs Consultant, Potomac Partners DC; Independent Research Consultant, Texas Medical Center; Director of Recruiting, Security & Investigative Placement Consultants; General Partner, The Artemis Fund
Directorships: Goodfynd
Mark Leigh, President
Education: BS, University of Illinois; MBA, Kellogg School of Management, Northwestern University
Background: Regional Sales Manager, Evonik Degussa; VP of Pigments, Degussa Engineered Carbons; VP of Marketing/VP/Business Director, Evonik; SVP/GM,

Venture Capital & Private Equity Firms / Domestic Firms

Orion Engineered Carbons; President, Americas, GSE Environmental

954 HOUSTON HEALTH VENTURES
Houston, TX

web: www.houstonhealthventures.com

Mission Statement: Invests in various companies serving the healthcare industry including innovative information technology, medical supplies, and medicinal cannabis.

Founded: 2013
Average Investment: $30,000
Investment Criteria: Seed, Early-Stage
Industry Group Preference: Healthcare, Technology, Medical Supply, Cannabis, Information Technology
Portfolio Companies: INRFOOD, I'm Sick Mobile, myRoundUp, myLAB Box, The Hippo Kitchen, Alltrope Medical, Legworks, Adient Medical, Luminostics

Key Executives:
  David C. Franklin, Co-Founder/Managing Director
  Education: BSE, Bio-Medical/Electrical Engineering, Duke University; MBA, Venture Capital, Anderson School of Management
  Background: Consultant, Accenture; Manager, DaVita; Director of Venture Capital Programs, UCLA Anderson School of Management; Co-Founder, DCF Ventures; EVP, HigherEducation.com; CEO, BestAgents.com; Co-Founder, Joycare Pediatric Day Health Center
  Directorships: Joycare Pediatric Day Health Center; Allotrope Medical
  Huan Le, Co-Founder/Managing Director
  Education: JD, University of Texas School of Law; BA, International Relations/Biology, University of Southern California
  Background: Founder/Director/Advisor, Caphin Inc.; Co-Founder/President, Medifr Inc; CAO/General Counsel, DiCentral Corp.

955 HQ CAPITAL
1290 Avenue of the Americas
10th Floor
New York, NY 10104

Phone: 212-863-2300 Fax: 212-593-2974
web: hqcapital.com

Mission Statement: HQ Capital is a combination of alternative investment managers Auda, Real Estate Capital Partners and Equita.

Geographic Preference: United States
Fund Size: $6.5 Billion
Founded: 2015
Average Investment: $15 million
Investment Criteria: Partnership Investments, Secondary Investments, Co-Investments, Venture Capital and Buyouts
Industry Group Preference: Real Estate

956 HT CAPITAL ADVISORS LLC
437 Madison Avenue
Suite 19D
New York, NY 10022-7001

Phone: 212-759-9080
e-mail: info@htcapital.com
web: www.htcapital.com

Mission Statement: HT Capital offers advice to middle market and closely-held companies that is firmly anchored by decades of experience on Wall Street.

Geographic Preference: United States; International
Founded: 1999
Minimum Investment: $100,000
Investment Criteria: Established, emerging middle market companies
Industry Group Preference: Food & Beverage, Healthcare, Pollution, Industrial Equipment, Electronic Technology, Manufacturing, Electrical Distribution
Portfolio Companies: Cellotape, Cidade, Tablewerks Inc., Hillsidecandy, Richardeyres, Justin's

Key Executives:
  Eric J. Lomas, President
  Education: BS, Business, New York University Graduate School of Administration
  Background: Managing Director/Co-Head of Banking, Gruntal & Co; Deloitte & Touche; Non-Executive Chairman, Rexel; Troster, Singer & Co
  C.A. Burkhardt, Senior Managing Director
  Education: AB, Brown University; MBA, Columbia University Graduate School of Business
  Background: Investment Banker, Janney Montgomery Scott; Financial Analyst, Aetna Life and Casualty; Deloitte Touche & Raquos
  Florence J. Mauchant, Partner/Managing Director
  e-mail: fmauchant@htcapital.com
  Education: Graduate Degree, Institut Commercial de Nancy (France); MBA, Indiana University of Pennsylvania
  Background: Schroders (UK based merchant bank); Generale Bank; Banque Nationale de Paris
  Directorships: NYSSA; FWA
  Thomas Girardi, Managing Director
  Education: BS, Accounting, Montclair State University; MBA, Finance, Rutgers Business School
  Background: Unilever; Reckitt & Colman
  Jean-Damien Perrier, Managing Director
  Education: Sup de Co Tours (France)
  Background: BNP Paribas Corporate Finance Group
  Stephen C. Tardio, Managing Director
  e-mail: stardio@htcapital.com
  Education: MBA, Corporate Finance, The Fuqua School of Business at Duke University; BS, Computer Science, University of Illinois
  Background: Manager of Technology Integration, Andersen Consulting
  David S. Slackman, Managing Director
  Education: BA/MA, Economics, University of Michigan
  Background: President, Commerce Bank; Federal Reserve Bank of New York; The Dime Savings Bank of New York; Atlantic Bank of New York

957 HUDSON VENTURE PARTNERS
545 Fifth Avenue
Suite 401
New York, NY 10017

Phone: 212-644-9797 Fax: 212-371-9305
e-mail: info@hudsonptr.com

Mission Statement: To invest in and advise early stage companies with strong management and good market opportunities in the technology industry.

Geographic Preference: Northeastern United States
Fund Size: $170 million
Founded: 1997
Average Investment: $3 million
Minimum Investment: $1 million
Investment Criteria: Early stage, outstanding business and revenue models, revenues of $2-6 million, a product or service with a proprietary technology
Industry Group Preference: Infrastructure, Information Technology, Software, Enterprise Software, Technology, Communications, Financial Services, Marketing, Advertising, Media, Internet
Portfolio Companies: Acorda, Albridge Solutions, Bigfoot Interactive, Bla-Bla.com, Blue Lobster Software, Centor Software, CertifiedMail, Certpoint, ClientSoft, Comet Systems, Constant Contact, DataMotion, Didera, Dynamic Mobile Data Systmes, E-Tran, Elity Systems, GlobalServe, Greenplum, Guardent, Home Director, iClick, InQ, iHello, iTraffic, Integral, IPI Scrittura, Intellibridge, Knoa

Venture Capital & Private Equity Firms / Domestic Firms

Corporation, LogMatrix, MarketSoft, MIDAS Vision Systems, Marketing Technology Solution: (MTS), Metapa, NetKey, OpenServices, Pathlight Technology, PeanutPress, Peminic, Pivot Solutions, Poindexter Systems, PowerOne Media, PowerSteering Software, Prescient Systems, QualityHealth, QueryObject Systems, Relegence, Roving, ScanBuy, Scrittura, TechRx, TheSquare, TouchCommerce, UGO Networks, Verge Solutions, VuePoint, Wasabi Systems, WebMethods, [x + 1]

Key Executives:
Kim P. Goh, Senior Managing Director
212-644-9797
e-mail: kgoh@hudsonptr.com
Education: BA, Southamptom College, Long Island University; MA, Columbia University; Harvard University; Carnegie-Mellon University
Background: Merck/Medco; Chemical Banking Company; Capital Market Group; Citibank
Directorships: Center Software, Elity Systems, E-Tran Solutions, Peminic

Jay N. Goldberg, Senior Managing Director
212-644-9797
e-mail: jgoldberg@hudsonptr.com
Education: BA, New York University
Background: Opcenter LLC; Lexstra PLC; Business Systems Corporation; Zeitech; Software Design Associates
Directorships: Bigfoot Interactive, GlobalServe, Metapa, i-Hello, PowerSteering, OpenService

Lawrence Howard MD, Senior Managing Director
212-644-9797
Fax: 212-583-1857
e-mail: lhoward@hudsonptr.com
Education: BS, University of New Hampshire; MD, New York Medical College
Background: President/CEO, Presstek; Consultant, The Villages
Directorships: Intellibridge Vuepoint.com, Intuitive Products International, CertifiedMail

Glen Lewy, Senior Managing Director
212-644-9797
e-mail: glewy@hudsonptr.com
Education: BA, Amherst College; JD, University of Chicago Law School
Background: Wolfensohn & Company; Bankers Trust; Debvoise & Plimpton
Directorships: NetKey, Relegence, Intellibridge, Peminic

Bill Carson, Managing Director
212-644-9797
e-mail: bcarson@hudsonptr.com
Education: Undergraduate Degree, Engineering & Economics, University of Notre Dame; MBA, University of Chicago
Background: Citigroup's Strategic Investment Group; IBM

John P. Truehart, Chief Financial Officer
Education: BS, Accounting, State University College of Arts & Sciences
Background: Controller, Charterhouse Group; Manager, Alliance Capital Management Corporation

958 HUMANA VENTURES
500 West Main Street
Louisville, KY 40202

Phone: 502-580-3906
web: www.humana.com

Mission Statement: Humana Ventures fosters innovation in the delivery of healthcare services and the development and use of healthcare information technology, while pursuing financial returns commensurate with the risks of early stage investing.

Geographic Preference: United States
Founded: 1961
Average Investment: $1-$5 million
Minimum Investment: $1 million
Investment Criteria: Early-Stage
Industry Group Preference: Communications, Computer Related, Consumer Services, Distribution, Natural Resources, Industrial Equipment, Medical & Health Related, Energy, Healthcare, Healthcare Services, Healthcare Information Technology
Portfolio Companies: Abaton.com, AirLogix, Aperture Credentialing, BenefitMall.com, CMG Health, CorSolutions Medical Corporation, Essex WoodlandsFund, Healthcare Recoveries, JSA Healthcare Corporation, Latin Healthcare Fund, Paidos Health Management Services, Paradigm Healthcare Corporation, Physics Ventures, Quality Metric, Raytel Medical, TriZetto Group, US Behavioral Health, Workscape

Key Executives:
Paul Kusserow, SVP/Chief Strategy Officer/Corporate Development Officer
Education: Wesleyan University; Master's Degree, Univ. of Oxford
Background: Managing Director, Private Equity, BC Ziegler & Company; Managing Director & CIO, Ziegler HealthVest Fund

Charles W Beckman, Vice President
Education: BBA, University of Texas; MBA, University of Louisville

959 HUMMER WINBLAD VENTURE PARTNERS
50 Francisco Street
Suite 450
San Francisco, CA 94133

Phone: 415-979-9600 **Fax:** 415-979-9601
web: www.hwvp.com

Mission Statement: A venture capital firm focused exclusively on software. HWVP's goal is to provide the capital, experience, and vision that will help companies become leaders in this software-driven economy.

Geographic Preference: United States
Fund Size: $1 billion
Founded: 1989
Investment Criteria: Early-stage, software companies
Industry Group Preference: Applications Software & Services, Consumer Services, Infrastructure, Software, Business to Business, Retailing, Cloud Computing, SaaS, Internet, Enterprise Software
Portfolio Companies: 6connect, AceMetrix, Alpharank, Amberdata, Aria Systems, AspireIQ, Blissfully, Kiip, NeuVector, NuoDB, OptiMine, Sonatype, Stackery, Symbium, TidalScale, XANT

Key Executives:
John Hummer, Founding Partner, Seattle
Education: AB, English, Princeton University; MBA, Stanford Business School

Ann Winblad, Founding Partner
Education: BA, Mathematics & Business Administration, College of St. Catherine; MA, Education & International Economics, University of St. Thomas
Background: Systems Programmer, Federal Reserve Bank; Co-Founder, Open Systems
Directorships: Ace Metricsx, Krillion, MuleSoft, Star Analytics, Voltate Security

Ann Winblad, Founding Partner
Education: BA, Mathematics & Business Administration, St. Catherine University; MA, Education, University of St. Thomas; Honorary Doctorate of Law, University of St. Thomas
Background: Systems Programmer, Federal Reserve Bank; Co-Founder, Open Systems Inc.; Strategy Consultant for various companies: IBM, Microsoft, Price Waterhouse Cooper
Directorships: Hyperion; Mulesoft; The Knot; Net Perceptions; Liquid Audio; AceMetrix; OptiMine; Sonatype

Venture Capital & Private Equity Firms / Domestic Firms

Mitchell Kertzman, Managing Director
Background: Chairman/CEO, Liberate Technologies; CEO, Sybase; CEO, Powersoft
Directorships: AspireIQ; NuoDB; Peerlyst; 6connect
Lars Leckie, Managing Director
Education: Engineering Physics degree, Queen's University; MS, Engineering, Stanford University; MBA, Stanford Graduate School of Business
Background: Co-Founder, Auto-Farm
Directorships: Kiip; InsideSales.com; Innovative Leisure; Aria Systems

960 HUNT INVESTMENT GROUP
1900 North Akard Street
Dallas, TX 75201-2300

Phone: 214-978-8000 Fax: 214-978-8888
e-mail: bjolly@huntinvestment.com
web: www.huntinvestmentgroup.com

Mission Statement: An investment firm seeking to deploy capital with equity and hedge fund managers, private investment funds and select direct co-investments.

Geographic Preference: United States, Western Europe, Japan
Fund Size: $100 million
Founded: 2014
Average Investment: $1 million - $5 million
Minimum Investment: $1 million
Industry Group Preference: Oil & Gas, Real Estate

Key Executives:
McCall Cravens, Senior Vice President/Chief Investment Officer
Education: BA, Economics, BS, Engineering Science, Vanderbilt University; MBA, Harvard Business School
Background: Managing Director, SMU; Pamlico Capital; Lehman Brothers; Analyst, Wachovia
Brian Jolly, Vice President
Education: BBA/MPA, University of Texas, Austin; MBA, Southern Methodist University; CPA
Background: Controller, Hunt Investment Group; Financial Analyst, Hunt Consolidated; Senior Accountant/Advisor, KPMG LLP

961 HUNTINGTON CAPITAL
3636 Nobel Drive
Suite 401
San Diego, CA 92122

Phone: 858-259-7654 Fax: 858-452-2003
web: www.hcapllc.com

Mission Statement: Huntingon Capital seeks to be the best-of-class mezzanine fund serving the lower middle market in the western United States with a particular emphasis on California. We provide capital and strategic assistance to small business entrepreneurs while making a positive and measurable contribution to the community.

Founded: 2000
Investment Criteria: Mezzanine Debt
Portfolio Companies: Advanced Structural Alloys, Altrec, Autumn Years at Newport Mesa, Autumn Years at Ojai, Arosa+LivHome, Burke Williams, CNCdata, Color Labs Enterprises, Cubex, Diamond Contract Services, Eaton Veterinary Pharmaceutical, Environment Furniture, Geary LSF, gen-E, Michael's Bakery Products LLC, Native Foods Café, ONCampus Media, Paragon Technology, PriMetrica, Inc., Progistics Distribution, Protect Plus Air Holdings, Reischling Press, Residential Design Services, RJE International, RPI, Summit Estates, Turbo International, Vertical Management Systems, Wave Technology Solutions Group

Key Executives:
Tim Bubnack, Managing Partner
Background: Managing Director, Silicon Valley Bank; Senior Executive, Comerica Ventures Inc.

Directorships: Cubex Systems, Reischling Press, LLT Corp.
Frank Mora, Partner
Education: B.S. Economics, Wharton School of the University of Pennsylvania, M.B.A. Columbia Business School
Background: DBI Capital, Vice President, Fixed Income Capital Markets team at Citigroup, Venture Capital Officer, Economic Development Bank for Puerto Rico
Directorships: Paragon Technology, Baked In The Sun, PriMetrica, Burke Williams, Progistics Distribution

962 HUNTSMAN GAY GLOBAL CAPITAL
1950 University Avenue
Palo Alto, CA 94303

Phone: 650-321-4910 Fax: 650-321-4911
e-mail: ir@hggc.com
web: www.hggc.com

Mission Statement: A private equity fund focusing on leveraged buyout, recapitalizations and growth transactions in the middle-market.

Geographic Preference: North America
Fund Size: $300 million
Average Investment: $25 - $100 million
Investment Criteria: Leveraged Buyouts, Recapitalizations, Growth Equity, Public To Private, Corporate Carve-Outs
Industry Group Preference: Business Services, Consumer Products, Financial Services, Healthcare, Industrial Services, Information, Software
Portfolio Companies: AutoAlert, Davies Group, Dealer-FX, Denodo, etouches, FPX, Gee Holdings, IDERA, Innovative, Integrity, iQor, MyWebGrocer, Nutraceutical, Pearl, Sandbox, Selligent, SSI, Citadel, GIS, Hollander, Hybris, MaMa Rosa's, Power Holdings, Serena, Sunquest, Turner

Key Executives:
Bob Gay, Executive Director
Education: AB, University of Utah; PhD, Business Economics, Harvard University
Background: Mamaning Director, Bain Capital; Executive Vice President, GE Capital; Engagement Manager, McKinsey & Co.
Greg Benson, Co-Founder/Managing Partner
e-mail: gbenson@hggc.com
Education: BS, Business Administration, University of Minnesota
Background: Bain Capital, General Electric
Directorships: Medical Edge Healthcare Group, ICON Health & Fitness, Nutraceutical International Corp., American Nutritional Casualty Insurance, American Pad & Paper
Gary Crittenden, Executive Director
e-mail: gcrittenden@hggc.com
Education: BS, Brigham Young University; MBA, Harvard Business School
Background: CFO, Citigroup; CFO, American Express; CFO, Monsanto; CFO, Sears Roebuck & Company
Directorships: Chairman, iQor; Pearl Holding Group
Rich Lawson, Co-Founder/CEO
Education: BA, Interdisciplinary Studies, Amherst College; MBA, Harvard Business School
Background: Co-Founder, Sorenson Capital Partners
Directorships: Wasatch Adaptive Sports
Steve Young, Co-Founder/Managing Partner
Education: BS, Finance/Political Science, Brigham Young University; JD, J. Reuben Clark Law School
Background: Co-Founder, Sorenson Capital; NFL

Venture Capital & Private Equity Firms / Domestic Firms

963 HURON CAPITAL PARTNERS LLC
500 Griswold
Suite 2700
Detroit, MI 48226

Phone: 313-962-5800
e-mail: info@huroncapital.com
web: www.huroncapital.com

Mission Statement: A Midwest-based equity investment firm focused on investing in growing, established and profitable companies.

Geographic Preference: United States, Canada
Fund Size: $1.8 billion
Founded: 1999
Average Investment: $20 - $50 million
Minimum Investment: $5 million
Investment Criteria: Corporate spin-offs, family succession transactions, recapitalizations, buy and build strategies, management buyouts
Industry Group Preference: Manufacturing, Consumer Products, Consumer Services, Business Products & Services, Healthcare
Portfolio Companies: Albireo Energy, Aquamar Holdings, Atlantic Beverage Company, B&B Roadway Security Solutions, Direct Connect Lofistix, Drake Automotive, Hansons, High Street Insurance Partners, InterVisions Systems, IQ Brands, Norwest Pallet Supply, Pacific Shoring, Pueblo Mechanical & Controls, Pure Dental Brands, Ronnoco Beverage Solutions, Sciens Building Solutions, StayOnline, Valentus Specialty Chemicals, WD Diamonds, XLerate Group

Key Executives:
Brian Demkowicz, Chair & Founder
313-962-5801
e-mail: bdemkowicz@huroncapital.com
Education: BS, Accounting, Purdue University; MBA, Kellogg School of Management, Northwestern University
Background: Director, Bulkley Capital; Principal, Waud Capital Partners; VP, Heller Equity Capital Corporation; CPA
Directorships: Albireo Energy LLC, Direct Connect Logitix, High Street Insurance Partners, InterVision
Michael Beauregard, Senior Partner
313-962-5802
e-mail: mbeauregard@huroncapital.com
Education: BA, Economics, University of Michigan; MBA, Joseph M. Katz Graduate School of Business, University of Pittsburgh; JD, School of Law, University of Pittsburgh
Background: Managing Director, Macam Corporation; Principal, Japonica Partners; VP, Strategic Planning, Sunbeam Corporation; VP, Finance & Investments, Duchossois Enterprises
Directorships: IQ Brands, Aquamar Holdings, Valentus Specialty Chemicals, Brunder Polymer
Peter Mogk, Senior Partner
313-962-5803
e-mail: pmogk@huroncapital.com
Education: BS, Economics, Miami University of Ohio; MBA, University of Chicago
Background: Vice President, Treasurer, Penske Corporation; Nesbitt Burns Securites; Bank of montreal; Northern Trust Company
Directorships: InterVision Systems, Good Sportsman Marketing, XLerate Group, Pueblo Mechanical & Control, Direct Connect Logistix
James Mahoney, Managing Partner
e-mail: jmahoney@huroncapital.com
Education: BA, Economics & Political Science, Villanova University; MBA, University of Chicago
Background: Conway MacKenzie Inc.; Robert W Baird & Company
Directorships: Sciens Building Solutions, Alireo Energy, XLerate Group, Valentus Specialty Chemicals, Pure Dental Brands, Ronnoco Beverage Solutions

964 HURON RIVER VENTURES
303 Detroit Street
Suite 100
Ann Arbor, MI 48108

web: www.huronrivervc.com

Mission Statement: Huron River Ventures invests in early-stage, Michigan-based, energy technology, Cleanweb, and smart transportation companies offering innovative, cost-effective and higher performing products and solutions to large global problems.

Geographic Preference: United States, Midwest
Average Investment: $1 - $5 million
Investment Criteria: Seed, Series A & B
Industry Group Preference: Energy, Agriculture, Manufacturing, Mobility
Portfolio Companies: Ambiq Micro, ArborMetrix, Cribspot, Deliv, FarmLogs, Opto Atmosphere, PeachWorks, Postmates, Sigh Machine, SkySpecs, Sportsman Tracker, Tachyus, Tackk

Key Executives:
Ryan Waddington, Founding Partner
e-mail: ryan@huronrivervc.com
Education: BS, Aerospace Engineering, University of Michigan; MS, Civil & Environmental Engineering, University of Wisconsin; MBA, Ross School of Business
Background: Ziff Brothers Investments, DTE Energy Corporate Venture Group

965 HYDE PARK VENTURE PARTNERS
415 N LaSalle Street
Suite 502
Chicago, IL 60654

web: hydeparkvp.com

Mission Statement: Hyde Park Venture Partners (HPVP) is an early stage venture capital fund investing in early stage technology companies in the Midwest, with particular focus in Chicago. HPVP draws on its strategic relationship with Hyde Park Angels (HPA) to provide industry and business expertise to its portfolio companies through a network of more than 90 seasoned business executives, entrepreneurs and service professionals. HPVP's principals, Ira Weiss and Guy Turner, and the HPA network take an active role in mentoring and guiding portfolio companies in product development, business strategy, financing and exit through both formal director roles and informal mentorship relationships.

Geographic Preference: Chicago
Average Investment: $750,000 - $1.5 million
Investment Criteria: Early-Stage
Industry Group Preference: Business to Business, Consumer Marketplace
Portfolio Companies: Ahalogy, FarmLogs, FindIt, FoodGenius, InContext Solutions, Iris Mobile, LevelEleven, NoRedInk, ParkWhiz, Protean, SimpleRelevance, Sqrl, TempoDB, Zaranga

Other Locations:
10401 N Meridian Street
Suite 215
Indianapolis, IN 46290

Key Executives:
Ira Weiss, Partner
Education: MBA, PhD, Booth School of Business
Background: Managing Director, RK Ventures; Accountant, Coopers & Lybrand
Directorships: ReTel Technologies
Guy Turner, Partner/Managing Director, Chicago
Education: BS, Mechanical Engineering, Cornell University; MBA, Booth School of Business
Background: Boston Consulting Group; Mechanical Engineer, Raytheon, General Electric
Directorships: InContext Solutions
Tim Kopp, Partner/Managing Director, Indianapolis
Background: Coca-Cola; Procter & Gamble; Webtrends;

Venture Capital & Private Equity Firms / Domestic Firms

ExactTarget
Directorships: Ahalogy, G2Crowd, Level11

966 HYPUR VENTURES
7812 East Acoma Drive
Suite 7
Scottsdale, AZ 85260

Phone: 480-409-4599
web: hypurventures.com

Mission Statement: Invests in various companies within the cannabis industries. Areas of focus include compliance, business intelligence and consumer products.

Founded: 2012
Industry Group Preference: Cannabis, Technology
Portfolio Companies: Blue Line Protection Group, DOPE Magazine, Calyx, Cannasure, Headset, Hypur, Simplifya, Willie's Reserve

967 I-HATCH VENTURES LLC
270 Lafayette Street
Suite 814
New York, NY 10012

Phone: 212-651-1750 Fax: 212-208-4590
e-mail: info@i-hatch.com
web: www.i-hatch.com

Mission Statement: To provide capital and support to early-stage technology companies, with focus on the communications, enabling technology, mobile data services and broadband sectors.

Founded: 1999
Investment Criteria: Early Stage
Industry Group Preference: Communications, Technology, Mobile Data Services, Broadband, Enabling Technology
Portfolio Companies: AtHoc, Datasnap.Io, Equator, M:Metrics, Mobliss, OpenAir, Salsa, SignalSoft, Thumbplay, Vindigo, Widerthan

Key Executives:
Chip Austin, Managing Partner
Education: Duke University; MBA, Harvard Business School
Background: Co-Founder, Interactive Practice, McKinsey & Co.; Morgan Stanley; IBM; President & CEO, Bertelsmann Online; SVP, Sales & Business Development, Prodigy
Brad Farkas, Managing Partner
Education: BA, Harvard College; MBA, Harvard Business School
Background: Founding Partner, Lazard Technology Partners; CFO & Director, Compatible Systems; Founder, Argosy Technology; Director & Principal, pcAnywhere Inc.; Founder, Metropolitan Asset Technology; Co-Founder, Phonetix Inc.; Associate, First Boston

968 I2E
840 Researh Parkway
Suite 250
Oklahoma City, OK 73104

Phone: 405-235-2305
web: i2e.org

Mission Statement: i2E works directly with entrepreneurs, researchers and companies to help them commercialize their technologies.

Fund Size: $88 Million
Founded: 1999
Other Locations:
618 E Third Street
Suite 1
Tulsa, OK 74120
Phone: 918-582-5592

Key Executives:
Scott Meacham, President and CEO
405-813-2401
e-mail: smeacham@i2E.org
Education: BA, MBA, JD, University of Oklahoma
Background: Partner, Meacham & Meacham; CEO and General Counsel, First National Bank & Trust, Elk City; 17th State Treasurer, Oklahoma

969 IA VENTURES
920 Broadway
15th Floor
New York, NY 10010

web: www.iaventures.com

Mission Statement: Invests in companies that create competitive advantage through data.

Investment Criteria: Early-Stage
Industry Group Preference: Software, Digital Media, Healthcare, Consumer Services
Portfolio Companies: Recorded Future, NewsCred, DataRobot, Kinsa, DigitalOcean, MemSQL, Datadog Inc., Drift, Transcriptic, Vectra AI, PlaceIQ, Simple, Next Big Sound, The Trade Desk Inc.

Key Executives:
Roger Ehrenberg, Founder/Managing Partner
Education: BBA, Finance, Economics & Organizational Psychology, University of Michigan; MBA, Finance, Accounting & Management, Columbia Business School
Background: IA Capital Partners; President & CEO, DB Advisors; Investment Banking & Managing Director, Citibank
Directorships: DataSift, Metamarkets, Recorded Future, The Trade Desk, Twice
Brad Gillespie, Partner
Education: PhD, Electrical Engineering, University of Washington
Background: Technology Advisor, Microsoft; Lockheed-Martin

970 IANTHUS CAPITAL MANAGEMENT
420 Lexington Avenue
Suite 414
New York, NY 10170

Phone: 646-518-9411
e-mail: info@ianthuscapital.com
web: www.ianthuscapital.com

Mission Statement: iAnthus operates and invests in cannabis companies.

Geographic Preference: US
Founded: 2014
Industry Group Preference: Cannabis, Agriculture, Financial Services, Healthcare
Portfolio Companies: Citiva, Grassroots Vermont, The Green Solutions, GrowHealthy, Mayflower Medicinals, Organix, Reynold Greenleaf & Associates

Other Locations:
22 Adelaide Street West
Suite 2740
Toronto, ON M5H 4E3
Canada

Key Executives:
Hadley Ford, Director/CEO
Education: BS, Boston University; MBA, Stanford University Graduate School of Business
Background: VP, Goldman Sachs; CFO, Clearway Technologies; Managing Director, Banc of America Securities; CEO, ProCure Treatment Centers
Randy Maslow, Director/President
Education: AB, Government, Cornell University; JD,

Venture Capital & Private Equity Firms / Domestic Firms

Rutgers Law School
Background: SVP, Business Development/General Counsel, XO Communications; Managing Partner, Electric Ventures; SVP/General Counsel, IGE
Julius Kalcevich, Director/CFO
Education: BA, McGill University; MBA, Columbia University
Background: Partner, BG Partners Corp.; Director of Investment Banking, CIBC World Markets
Carlos Perea, Chief Operating Officer
Education: BS, Mechanical Engineering, University of New Mexico; MBA, Stanford University Graduate School of Business
Background: President, Qynergy; Founding Partner, Entrada Ventures; Advisor, Flywheel Ventures; Special Advisor, Verge Fund; Chairman/CEO, MIOX Corp.; President/Director, Nuvita
Directorships: Chairman, YPO New Mexico; InnovateABC; Puralytics
John Henderson, Managing Director/Chief Development Officer
Education: BA, English, Northwestern University; MBA, Tuck School of Business, Dartmouth College
Background: President, George B.H. Macomber Co.; Founding Principal/COO/Development Officer, ProCure Treatment Centers; Founding Partner, Proton International

971 IBM VENTURE CAPITAL GROUP
1 New Orchard Road
Armonk, NY 10504-1722

Phone: 914-499-1900
Toll-Free: 800-426-4968
web: www.ibm.com/innovation/venture-development

Mission Statement: IBM Venture Capital Group's objective is to bring innovation into the venture capital community. Typically, IBM Venture Capital Group does not engage in equity or seed funding, and instead works closely with venture capital firms to discover new technologies and develop business strategies. In 2014, IBM launched the IBM Watson Venture Fund, a venture fund designed to support startups interested in utilizing IBM's own business platform, IBM Watson.

Fund Size: $100 million
Investment Criteria: Startups
Industry Group Preference: Technology, Aerospace and Defense, Automotive, Banking, Education, Electronics, Energy, Healthcare, Insurance, Manufacturing, Metals, Oil & Gas, Retail, Telecommunications & Media, Transportation
Portfolio Companies: BigFix, Claranet, Clearscope, Cloud Temple, Coronado Curragh Pty., CyFir, dan.com, DATEV eG, Deloitte, Elektronabava, Emnotion, Fosen IKT, Geisinger Health System, Veristat

Key Executives:
Angie Grimm, Managing Director
Education: BS, Finance and Marketing, Indiana University, Bloomington; Kelley School of Business, Indiana University
Background: Donaldson, Lufkin & Jenrette
Christoph Auer-Welsbach, Partner
Thomas Whiteaker, Partner
Background: Partner, Propel Venture Partners; Executive Director, BBVA Ventures; Hartford Ventures; Visa Inc.; Omnium Worldwide
Wendy Lung, Director, Corporate Strategy
Education: BBA, Finance & Marketing, University of Washington
Deborah Magid, Director, Software Strategy
Education: University of Pennsylvania; University of Connecticut
Background: Taligent; GE Information Services; AT&T
Savitha Srinivasan, Partner
Education: MS, Computer Science, Pace University

972 ICON VENTURES
505 Hamilton Avenue
Suite 310
Palo Alto, CA 94301

Phone: 650-463-8800
e-mail: info@iconventures.com
web: www.iconventures.com

Mission Statement: An independent venture capital firm investing in emerging technology companies.

Fund Size: $260 million
Founded: 2003
Average Investment: $4 - $8 million
Investment Criteria: Early Stage, Middle Stage
Industry Group Preference: Consumer Internet, Clean Technology, Digital Media & Marketing, Software, Cloud Computing, Communications, Mobile, Security
Portfolio Companies: 41st Parameter, Alation, Aera 1, Aster Data, Attributor, Avnera, Awarepoint, Bill.com, Brion, Calypto, ClairMail, Clicker, Cloud Physics, Cortina, Data Allegro, Delphix, Device Scape, Duetto, Ever, Exabeam, FireEye, Huddle, Infinera, Inkling, Ionic Security, Kixeye, Marketlive, Meebo, Mimosa Systems, Moovweb, Mopub, Ocarina Networks, Oodle, Opcity, Origami Logic, Paloalto, Playstudios, Posterous, PostPath, Proofpoint, Quellan, RedSeal, Reputation.com, Ripcord, Sencha, Si Time, Solidcore, Synack, Teladoc, Thanx, The Muse, True X Media, Trust Arc, Tune, Tunein, Voltage Security, Clip, WGT, Xambala, Yodle, Zephyr Health

Key Executives:
Joe Horowitz, Managing General Partner
e-mail: joe@iconventures.com
Education: BA, Economics, Columbia University; MBA, Wharton School, University of Pennsylvania
Background: US Venture Partners; Exxon Enterprises; Chairman & CEO, Geocast Network Systems
Directorships: Area 1 Security, Devicescape, KIXEYE, Moovweb, PlayStudios, Sencha, Synack, TuneIn, Zephyr Health
Tom Mawhinney, General Partner
e-mail: tom@iconventures.com
Education: BA, Harvard College; MBA, Stanford Graduate School of Business
Background: Canaan Partners; Co-Founder, President & COO, North Systems
Directorships: Area 1 Security, Awarepoint, Bill.com, Huddle, Ionic Security, KIXEYE, MarketLive, Reputation.com, Synack, Teladoc, Yodle, Zephyr Health
Jeb Miller, General Partner
e-mail: jeb@iconventures.com
Education: BA, Economics, Harvard College
Background: The Carlyle Group; Managing Director, Business Development, Scient; Morgan Stanley
Directorships: CloudPhysics, Duetto, Exabeam, Origami Logic, TRUSTe, WGT Sports
Michael Mullany, General Partner
e-mail: michael@iconventures.com
Education: BA, Economics, Harvard College; MBA, Stanford University
Background: CEO, Sencha; VP, Products & Marketing, Engine Yard; PeakStream; Netscape; Loudcloud; VMware
Directorships: Moovweb
Ben Shih, Partner
e-mail: ben@iconventures.com
Education: Massachusetts Institute of Technology; MBA, Stanford Graduate School of Business
Background: Crystal Ventures; Analyst, MDT Advisers; Lotus Development
Peter Yi, Principal
e-mail: peter@iconventures.com
Education: BA, University of California, Berkeley
Background: Worldview Technology Partners

Venture Capital & Private Equity Firms / Domestic Firms

973 ICV PARTNERS
810 7th Avenue
35th Floor
New York, NY 10019

Phone: 212-455-9600 Fax: 212-455-9603
e-mail: emailicv@icvpartners.com
web: www.icvpartners.com

Mission Statement: A private equity firm exclusively investing in companies in the lower end of the middle market, commited to the realities of growing a mid-size business. A certified Minority Business Enterprise (MBE), iCV invests in companies owned by members of ethnic minorities.

Fund Size: $130 million
Average Investment: $5-20 million
Minimum Investment: $5 million
Investment Criteria: Buyouts, recapitalizations, growth equity, corporate Divestitures, family successions and revenues between $25-$250 million
Industry Group Preference: Healthcare, Consumer Products, Processing, Commercial Services, Industrial Equipment, Food & Beverage, Consumer Services, Manufacturing, Business Products & Services
Portfolio Companies: American Alliance Dialysis Holdings, Coverall, LeadingResponse, OneTouchPoint, Physician IMS Control, Safe Security, SG360, SirsiDynix, UTP, AAMP of America, Cargo Airport Services USA, Chung's, Entertainment Cruises, The Hilsinger Company, Innovative, Mallet, Marshall Retail Group, Press A Point, The PFM Group, Stauber Performance Ingredients Inc., Sterling Foods

Other Locations:
1201 West Peachtree
Suite 2800
Atlanta, GA 30309
Phone: 404-682-1401 Fax: 212-504-0842

Key Executives:
Willie E. Woods Jr., President/Managing Director
e-mail: wwoods@icvcapital.com
Education: BA, Accounting, Morehouse College; MBA, Harvard Business School
Background: VP, Deutsche Bank Alex Brown; Levmark Capital; Lehman Brothers; NDB Bank
Lloyd M. Metz, Managing Director
Education: BS, Industrial Engineering, Stanford University; MBA, Harvard Business School
Background: Warburg Pincus; High Yield Capital Markets Group, Morgan Stanley; M&A, JP Morgan
Cory D. Mims, Managing Director
Education: BBA, Howard University; MBA, Harvard Business School
Background: Principal, TSG Capital Group; Salomon Brothers, NY, London
Ira L. Moreland, Managing Director
Education: BS, Accounting, Morehouse College; MBA, University of Chicago
Background: Managing Director, Financial Sponsors Group, SunTrust Robinsin Humphrey; Managing Director, Mid-Cap Investment Banking Group, Banc of America Securities; Citigroup
Directorships: ACG Atlanta
Qian W. Elmore, Principal
Education: BA, Finance, Morehouse College; MBA, Harvard Business School
Background: Principal, Reliant Equity Investors; Senior Associate, Wind Point Partners; Senior Associate, McCown De Leeuw
Zeena Rao, Managing Director
Education: BS, Economics, Wharton School, University of Pennsylvania; MBA, Harvard Business School
Background: Consumer Industrial Group, Lehman Brothers; Investment Banking Division, Deutsche Bank
Sheldon Howell, Principal
Education: BA, Economics & Political Science, Rutgers University; MBA, Ross School of Business, University of Michigan

Background: Churchill Financial, Merrill Lynch, Landenburg Thalmann, American International Group
Jermaine L. Warren, Principal
Education: BS, Business, Hofstra University; MBA, Harvard Business School
Background: Starwood Capital Group, Goldman Sachs

974 ID VENTURES AMERICA LLC
5201 Great America Parkway
Suite 355
Santa Clara, CA 95054

Phone: 408-894-7900 Fax: 408-894-7939
web: www.idsoftcapital.com

Mission Statement: To commit full resources to the building of portfolio companies and the creation of long-term value for these businesses. iD Ventures America, formerly Acer Technology Ventures America, invests primarily in early-stage companies in the United States.

Geographic Preference: United States, Canada
Fund Size: $150 million
Founded: 1998
Average Investment: $500,000 - $3 million
Minimum Investment: $500,000
Investment Criteria: Startups, Seed, First-Round, Second-Round, Early-Stage
Industry Group Preference: Communications, Electronic Technology, Information Technology, Semiconductors, Hardware, Software, Computer Related, Internet Technology, Online Content, Energy Efficiency, Medical Devices, Cloud Computing
Portfolio Companies: Applied Biocode, ATS Advanced Telematic Systems, Bandwidth 10, CoAdna Photonics, CounterPoint Health Solutions, Dragonfly, Ginkgo Bioworks, mCube, Neumitra, Optovue, SiFotonics Technologies, Silicon Frontline Technology, Striiv, Voltafield Technology

Key Executives:
Dr Ronald Chwang, Chairman/President
Education: BEng, Electrical Engineering, McGill University; PhD, Electrical Engineering, University of Southern California
Background: President & CEO, Acer America Corporation; Intel; Bell Northern Research
Directorships: mCube, Striiv, Voltafield Technology, CoAdna, iRobot Corporation, AU Optronics Corporation
Ted Lai, Partner/Chief Financial Officer
Education: BS, MA, Accounting, National Cheng Chi University; MBA, Michigan State University
Background: Controller & CFO, Acer America Corporation; Deloitte & Touche
Ed Yang, Partner
Education: BS, Electrical Engineering, National Cheng-Kung University; Philips International Institute; MS, Electrical Engineering, Oregon State University
Background: Hewlett-Packard Company

975 IDEA FUND PARTNERS
1415 W NC Highway 54
Suite 206
Durham, NC 27707

web: www.ideafundpartners.com

Mission Statement: IDEA Fund Partners invests in seed and early stage technology companies in the Southeast and Mid-Atlantic regions of the United States.

Geographic Preference: North Carolina, Southeast & Mid-Atlantic Regions
Founded: 2006
Minimum Investment: $100,000
Investment Criteria: Seed-Stage, Early-Stage
Industry Group Preference: Information Technology, Materials Technology, Medical Devices, Diagnostics, Software

Venture Capital & Private Equity Firms / Domestic Firms

Portfolio Companies: 71lbs, Antenna, Brightdoor, Canopy, CloudTags, Distil Networks, FilterEasy, First, GradSave, Joicaster, NextRay, Pendo, Physcient, Reveal Mobile, Sarda Technologies, WedPics, Windsor Circle

Key Executives:
Aohn Cambier, Managing Partner
Education: BA, International Relations, Michigan State University; MBA, University of North Carolina at Chapel Hill
Background: CFO, NC IDEA; Microelectronics Center of North Carolina
Directorships: 71lbs, Brightdoor Systems, Sarda Technologies, Royalty Exchange, CloudTags
Lister Delgado, Managing Partner
Education: ScB, Electrical Engineering, Brown University; MS, Computer Engineering, University of Texas, Austin; MBA, University of North Carolina at Chapel Hill
Background: NC IDEA; AT&T Bell Labs; Lucent Technologies
Directorships: Oncoscope, Windsor Circle, GradSave
Richard Fox, Venture Partner
Education: BS, Physics, Massachusetts Institute of Technology
Background: Founding Partner, Astralis Group
Directorships: National Association of Seed and Venture Funds

976 IDEALAB
130 West Union Street
Pasadena, CA 91103

Phone: 626-585-6900 Fax: 626-535-2701
web: www.idealab.com

Mission Statement: Invests in technology companies in the incubation stage.

Geographic Preference: California
Fund Size: $400 million
Founded: 1996
Industry Group Preference: E-Commerce & Manufacturing, Entertainment, Software, Technology, Clean Technology, Communications, Security, Internet, Digital Media & Marketing
Portfolio Companies: aiPod, Branch, Candy Club, CodeSpark, Cool Energy, Edisun Microgrids, Enplug, eSolar, Factual, Flexa, Gem, HelloTech, Kaleo, Lumin, Mightytext, Migo, Mount Wilson Ventures, New Matter, Open, Papaya, Refer.com, Scoutables, Sellbrite, Simbi, Tag Pop, Teliport Me, Tenor, Tint, Trinity Mobile Networks, UberMedia, UCode, WhiteCoat, WorldHaus, X1, Zowdow

Key Executives:
Bill Gross, Chairman
Education: BS, Mechanical Engineering, California Institute of Technology
Background: Solar Devices; GNP Development
Marcia Goodstein, President & CEO
Education: Pomona College
Background: Enfish Corporation; Gemstar Development Corporation; California Institute of Technology Research facility
Alex Maleki, Vice President, Business Development
Education: BA, University of California, Santa Barbra; JD, Southwestern University
Craig Chrisney, Chief Financial Officer
Education: BS, California Polytechnic University
Background: Audit Senior Manager, PricewaterhouseCoopers
Wes Ferrari, Vice President, Information Technologies
Education: BS, Biology & Anthropology, Loma Linda University; MBA, Fisher School of International Business, Monterey Institute of International Studies
Background: Managing Director, IKON Office Solutions

977 IDG CAPITAL
1345 Avenue of Americas
33rd Floor
New York, NY 10105

Phone: 212-337-5200
web: www.idgcapital.com

Mission Statement: An early stage venture capital firm that invests in New Media, E-Commerce and IT companies in the US.

Geographic Preference: United States
Fund Size: $100 million
Founded: 1997
Average Investment: $1 - $5 million
Minimum Investment: $1 million
Investment Criteria: Early-Stage
Industry Group Preference: Infrastructure, Computer Hardware & Software, Enterprise Services, Mobile Communications Devices, Wireless Technologies, E-Commerce & Manufacturing, Healthcare, Information Technology, Internet Technology, New Media
Portfolio Companies: Bilibili, App Annie, Jiguang, Wiseasy, Zapya, Rokid, Tongdun, 5miles, Wecash, Live.Me, CreditEase, Amlogic, Archermind, Iobit, Royole, Pacific Construction, RDA, AsiaTelco Technologies, Anker, Circle, Yixin Group, LongShine, Technology Tarena, Ctrip, Kingdee, Tencent, +360, OriGene, Shenogen Pharma Group, Pai+, Sentieon, Shuangcheng Pharma, China Biologic Products Inc., Funzio G-Bits, Artsy, Sheln, Farfetch, Moncler, Gentle Monster, IGG, Legendary, Apollo Solar, Hyper Strong, Ecovacs Robotics, IDG Energy, HC Semitek, OSRAM, Aikosolar, Xpeng

978 IGNITION PARTNERS
350 106th Avenue NE
1st Floor
Bellevue, WA 98004

Phone: 425-709-0772
e-mail: info@ignitionpartners.com
web: www.ignitionpartners.com

Mission Statement: Ignition invests in emerging and future leaders in communications, internet, software, and services across business and consumer targets.

Investment Criteria: Seed, Series A & B
Industry Group Preference: Machine Learning, Mobile Enterprise, Software, Security, Digital Transformation, Infrastructure, Information Technology
Portfolio Companies: Acalvio, Accompany Beta, Airbiquity, Amplero, Appfog, Apprenda, Aviatrix, Avist, Avvo, Azuqua, Bluedata, BlueStacks, Bromium, Cask, Chef, Cloudmark, Couchbase, DataSphere, Docker, DocuSign, Fire Apps, Glympse, Icertis, KenSci, Korrio, LiveStories, MotifInvesting, Moz, Nymi, Onehub, PaxVax, Previser, Skytap, SnapLogic, Spoken, StreamSets, Talent Sonar, Tempered Networks, Tractable, Trifacta, Verity Solutions, WePay

Other Locations:
108 First Street
Los Altos, CA 94022
Phone: 650-825-6909

Key Executives:
Cameron Myhrvold, Founding Partner
e-mail: cam@ignitionpartners.com
Education: BA, University of California, Berkeley
Background: Microsoft Corporation; Co-Founder, Dynamical Systems
Directorships: Azaleos, Cloudmark, Likewise, Seven, Teranode, Zenprise
Johnathan Roberts, Founding Partner
e-mail: jonro@ignitionpartners.com
Education: BA, History, University of Washington
Background: Microsoft Corporation

Directorships: Docusign, HyperQuality, Spoken Communications, Earth Class Mail
Brad Silverberg, Founding Partner
e-mail: brad@ignitionpartners.com
Education: BS, Computer Science, Brown University; MS, Computer Science, University of Toronto
Background: Senior Vice President, Executive Committee, Microsoft Corporation
Directorships: Avvo, Fotopedia, GlobalScholar, Keas, Seven, SourceLabs, ice.com, Skytap
John Connors, Managing Partner
e-mail: johncon@ignitionpartners.com
Education: BA, Accounting, University of Montana
Background: Microsoft Corporation; PIP Printing; SAFECO Corp; Deloitte, Haskins & Sells
Directorships: Nike, Recruiting.com, FIREapps, AdmitOne, Datasphere, Splunk
Richard Fade, Partner
e-mail: rfade@ignitionpartners.com
Background: Microsoft Corporation
Directorships: Appature, Azaleos, Likewise, InstallFree, One Hub, Talyst, GotVoice
Robert Headley, Administrative Partner
e-mail: rheadley@ignitionpartners.com
Education: MS & BS, Industrial Engineering, Stanford University
Background: Vice President, Finance & Treasurer, Starbucks Corporation; Principal Investment Area & Investment Banking Division, Goldman Sachs
Directorships: Enclarity, Earth Class Mail, FiREapps
Steve Hooper, Founding Partner
e-mail: shooper@ignitionpartners.com
Education: BS, Civil Engineering, Seattle University; MBA, The Wharton School
Background: Chairman & CEO, Netxlink Communications; Co-CEO, Teledesic; CEO, AT&T Wireless
Directorships: Modiv Media, TTMI, SeaMobile, Sparkplub, Airbiquity, AVST, OpenWave, UIEvolution
Michelle Goldberg, Partner
e-mail: michelle@ignitionpartners.com
Education: BA, Columbia University; MA, Harvard University
Background: Consultant, Microsoft's Developer Division; Investment Banking, Ollympic Capital Partners; Management Consultant, A.T. Kearney
Directorships: Visible Technologies, SEOmoz, TrackSimple, Mpire
Adrian Smith, Partner
e-mail: adrian@ignitionpartners.com
Background: Nextlink; AT&T Wireless; McCaw Cellular Communication; British Telecom Research Laboratories
Directorships: SinglePoint, Twisted Pair Solutions, Melodeo, Xeround
Chris Howard, Principal
e-mail: chris@ignitionpartners.com
Education: BS, Psychology, Occidental College; MBA, University of Washington
Background: Advertising & Marketing, Heckler Associates; Pilot + Levy
Directorships: Batch, Hipmunk, Datasphere, Fotopedia, Keas, Parse, SocialEyes

979 ILLINOIS VENTURES
2242 West Harrison Street
Suite 201
Chicago, IL 60612

web: www.illinoisventures.com

Mission Statement: IllinoisVENTURES is a venture capital firm that invests in seed and early-stage companies based on research done in federal laboratories and universities in the Midwest. The firm focuses primarily on businesses in the life sciences, clean technology, physical sciences and information technology sectors.
Geographic Preference: Midwest United States
Founded: 2002
Investment Criteria: Seed-Stage, Early-Stage
Industry Group Preference: Information Technology, Physical Sciences, Life Sciences, Clean Technology
Portfolio Companies: Advanced Diamond Technologies, ANDalyze, Autonomic Materials, Cbana Labs, Chromatin, ClearStream, Cortex Pharmaceuticals, Diagnostic Photonics, EdenPark Illumination, Fluensee, iCYT, Local Offer Network, Mirror.me, Personify, Semprius, ShareThis, SolarBridge Technologies, Solidware Technologies, Tetravitae Bioscience

Other Locations:
60 Hazelwood Drive
Suite 226
Champaign, IL 61820

Key Executives:
Nancy Sullivan, Chief Executive Officer/Senior Managing Director
Education: BBA, Loyola University; MBA, Kellogg School of Management, Masters, Biotechnology, Northwestern University
Background: Director, Office of Technology Management, University of Illinois; Senior Director, Business Development, KeraCure; Director, Northwestern University
Thomas Parkinson, Senior Director
Education: BA, Northwestern University; MBA, Kellogg School of Management

980 ILLUMINATE VENTURES
6114 La Salle Avenue
Unit 323
Oakland, CA 94611

e-mail: contact@illuminate.com
web: www.illuminate.com

Mission Statement: Illuminate Ventures seeks new and innovative business ideas led by committed, talented and diverse teams, particularly those that are inclusive of women entrepreneurs.
Geographic Preference: United States
Investment Criteria: Early-Stage
Industry Group Preference: Internet, SaaS, Information Technology
Portfolio Companies: Allocadia, Bedrock, Brightedge, CafeX Communications, CalmSea, Channeleyes, Coupang, Hoopla, Influitive, Jacobi, Litbit, Nitrio, Opsmatic, Peerlyst, Pex, Red Aril, Sense, Wild Pocketsm Xactly, Yozio, Vivant, DigitalFuel

Key Executives:
Cindy Padnos, Founder/Managing Partner
Education: AB, University of Michigan; MSIA/MBA, Tepper School of Business, Carnegie Mellon University
Background: Director, Outlook Ventures; Founder & CEO, Vivant; President/CEO, Acumen; IDE; Ingres; AT&t
Directorships: BrightEdge, CalmSea, Hoopla, Xactly Corporation
Rebecca Norlander, Venture Partner
Education: BS, Computer Science, Boston University
Background: General Manager, Microsoft
Cliff Higgerson, Strategic Portfolio Advisor
Education: BS, University of Illinois; MBA, University of California, Berkeley
Background: Founding Partner, ComVentures; General Partner, Vanguard Venture Partners; Managing Partner, Hambrecht & Quist
Directorships: Hatteras Networks, Kotura, World of Good, Xtera Communications, Ygnition

981 IMAGINATION CAPITAL
New York, NY

e-mail: info@imaginationvc.com
web: www.imaginationvc.com

Mission Statement: Imagination Capital invests in early-stage companies that are aiming to create change in their industry of choice. They focus in the areas of esports, big data, machine learning, and digital media.

Geographic Preference: United States
Founded: 2017
Average Investment: $250,000 - $500,000
Minimum Investment: $250,000
Investment Criteria: Early-Stage, U.S.-Based
Industry Group Preference: Esports, Big Data, Machine Learning, Digital Media
Portfolio Companies: Boom, Co Star, Epics, Forge, Overtime, Roam, Upcomer, Veritonic

Key Executives:
   Rachel Lam, Co-Founder/Managing Partner
   Education: BS, Industrial Engineering & Operations, University of California Berkeley; MBA, Harvard Business School
   Background: Time Warner Investments Group; Quetzal/Chase Capital Partners; Time Warner Inc.; Credit Suisse First Boston; Morgan Stanley
   Richard D. Parsons, Co-Founder/Partner
   Education: JD, Union University Albany Law School; BA, University of Hawaii
   Background: Citigroup; Time Warner; Dime Bancorp; Patterson Belknap Webb & Tyler

982 IMPLEMENT CAPITAL
17 State Street
40th Floor
New York, NY 10004

Phone: 212-739-0822
e-mail: info@implementcapital.com
web: www.implementcapital.com

Mission Statement: Implement Capital invests in financial technology and services companies focused on the front, middle and back office.

Industry Group Preference: Financial Services, Business Products & Services

Key Executives:
   Jean-Edouard van Praet, Managing Partner
   Education: European Univeristy Brussels
   Background: CFO/Partner/Director, RIMES Technologies; Portfolio Manager, Sofaer Capital; Managing Director, Lawhill Capital

983 IN-Q-TEL
2107 Wilson Boulevard
Suite 1100
Arlington, VA 22201

Phone: 703-248-3000
e-mail: info@iqt.org
web: www.iqt.org

Mission Statement: In-Q-Tel identifies, adapts and delivers innovative technology solutions to support the missions of the Central Intelligence Agency and the broader U.S. intelligence community.

Geographic Preference: United States
Fund Size: $28 million
Founded: 1999
Average Investment: $3 million
Minimum Investment: $1 million
Investment Criteria: Start-Ups, Mezzanine, Emerging and Established companies
Industry Group Preference: Internet Technology, Security, Data Services, Data Communications, Information Technology, Energy, Infrastructure, DNA
Portfolio Companies: 3VR, AdaptivEnergy, Adapx, Advanced Photonix, Alfalight, Arcxis, Asankya, Basis Technology, Bay Microsystems, Biomatrica, Boreal Genomics, CallMiner, Cambrios Technology, Carnegie Speech, Cleversafe, Cloudera, Connectify, Convera, CopperEye, Contour Energy Systems, Decru, Destineer, Digital Reasoning, Digital Solid State Propulsion, Dust Networks, Electro Energy, Elemental Technologies, Ember Corporation, Etherstack, febit, Fetch Technologies, FireEye, Fluidigm, FMS Advanced Systems Group, Gainspan, GATR Technologies, GeoIQ, Geosemble, Genia Photonics, Iatroquest, Idelix Software, Innocentive, iMove, Infinite Power Solutions, Infinate Z, IntegenX, Intelliseek, InView Technology Corporation, Inxight, KZO Innovations, LensVector, Lingotek, Lucid Imagination, MedShape Solutions, Metacarta, Metricstream, MiserWare, MotionDSP, Nanosys, NetBase, Network Chemistry, Nextreme Thermal Solutions, NovoDynamics, Oculis Labs, OpGen, OpenSpan, Palantir Technologies, Paratek Microwave, Pelican Imaging, Perceptive Pixel, Pixim, piXlogic, Platfora, Power Assure, QD Vision, Quantum4D, Quanterix, Qynergy, Recorded Future, RedSeal Systems, ReversingLabs, Seahawk Biosystems Corporation, Semprius, Seventh Sense Biosystems, Skybuilt Power, Signal Innovations Group, SitScape, Silver Tail Systems, Sonitus Medical, SpectraFluidics, SpotterRF, StreamBase Systems, T2 Biosystems, Tendril, Teradici, TerraGo Technologies, Traction Software, Veracode, Visible Technologies, VSee, WiSpry

Other Locations:
   890 Winter Street
   Suite 310
   Waltham, MA 02451
   Phone: 781-529-1100

   800 El Camino Real
   Suite 300
   Menlo Park, CA 94025
   Phone: 650-234-8999

Key Executives:
   Christopher Darby, President & Chief Executive Officer
   Education: University of Western Ontario
   Background: Vice President & General Manager, Intel; President & CEO, Sarvega; Chairman & CEO, @stake; President & CEO, Interpath Communications
   Steve Bowsher, Managing General Partner
   Education: Harvard University; MBA, Stanford University
   Background: General Partner, InterWest Partners; E*TRADE
   Bruce Adams, Legal & General Counsel
   Education: BA, Swarthmore College; JD, Boston University
   Lisbeth Poulos, Chief of Staff
   Education: BA, International Relations, College of William & Mary
   Background: National Security Agency, Central Intelligence Agency; BAE Systems, MicroStrategy
   Lisa Porter, Executive Vice President & IQT Labs
   Education: BS, Nuclear Engineering, MIT; PhD, Applied Physics, Stanford University
   Background: President, Teledyne Scientific & Imaging; Intelligence Advanced Research Projects Activity, ODNI; Associate Administrator, Aeronautics Research Mission Directorate, NASA; Project Manager/Senior Scientist, DARPA
   Matthew Strottman, Chief Operating Officer
   Education: BA, University of Notre Dame; MBA, Georgetown University; CPA
   Background: Technology Investment Banking Group, Friedman Billings Ramsey & Co.; PricewaterhouseCoopers LLP

Venture Capital & Private Equity Firms / Domestic Firms

984 INCUBE VENTURES
2051 Ringwood Avenue
San Jose, CA 95131

Phone: 408-457-3700
e-mail: contact@incubevc.com
web: www.incubevc.com

Mission Statement: InCube Ventures is a life science venture capital firm focused on investing in innovative life sciences companies that can provide solutions to unfulfilled clinical needs.
Founded: 2008
Investment Criteria: Early Stage, Mid-Stage, Late Stage
Industry Group Preference: Life Sciences, Medical Devices, Pharmaceuticals
Portfolio Companies: BodyMedia, Corhythm, Entrack, Fe3 Medical, IntraPace, Neurolink, Nfocus, Python, Rani Therapeutics, Sonoma Orthopedics, Spinal Modulation, WhiteSwell
Key Executives:
  Mir Imran, Chairman/CEO
  Education: BS, Electrical Engineering, MS, Bioengineering, Rutgers University
  Background: Chairman & CEO, InCube Labs LLC
  Directorships: Bodymedia, Corhthym, eGeen, Entrack, Fe2, Intrapace, Modulus, Neurolink, NFocus, Spinal Modulation
  Andrew Farquharson, Managing Director
  Education: University of California, Berkeley; MBA, Harvard University
  Background: Partner, Halo Funds; EVP, Sales, Marketing & Research, Operon Technologies; Genentech
  Wayne Roe, Managing Director
  Background: Founding Officer, Covance Health Economics & Outcomes Services; VP, Economic & Health Policy, Health Industry Manufacturers Association
  Directorships: ISTA Pharmaceuticals, Celera Genomics, Hemaquest, Fe2, Intrapace, Spinal Modulation

985 INCWELL VENTURE CAPITAL
1000 South Old Woodward Avenue
Suite 105
Birmingham, MI 48009

Mission Statement: IncWell Venture Capital is a venture capital firm seeking opportunities with early stage companies in consumer-based and industrial markets.
Geographic Preference: United States, Canada
Founded: 2013
Average Investment: $50,000 - $250,000
Investment Criteria: Startups, Early Stage
Industry Group Preference: Consumer Products, Healthcare, Industrial Technology, Industrial Manufacturing, Software, Enterprise Software, Information Technology, Clean Technology
Portfolio Companies: BeautyTouch, BoostUp, Bridgefy, Bubl, Calendly, Career Now, Clicktivated Video, CoolChip Technologies, CureLauncher, Eve Medical, Everykey, Illumitex, Jewelbots, Kiwi Wearables, KnipBio, LabDoor, Learnmetrics, LocoMobi, Map My Beauty, Meditory, OwnThePlay, OXX, Pavlok, PharmRight Corporation, Plasc Card, Preo, Sentinl, SkySpecs, Stkr.it, Stylekick, Sutro, Theia Interactive, TrackR, Vivid Vision, XOEye Technologies
Key Executives:
  Tom LaSorda, Founder/Managing Partner
  Background: Founder & General Managing Partner, LaSorda Group; Co-Founder, Stage 2 Innovations; CEO, Fisker Automotive; CEO, Chrysler
  Simon Boag, Chief Executive Officer/Managing Partner
  Education: University of Toronto; MS, Management, Stanford University
  Background: CEO, Stage 2 Innovations; Chrysler; Case New Holland; General Motors; CAMI Automotive
  Evonna Karchon, Partner
  Education: BA, Economics & Management/Communication Studies, Albion College
  Background: TechArb; Program Manager, Stage 2 Innovations
  John Melstrom, General Partner
  Education: Michigan State University
  Background: Partner, Fenner Melstrom & Dooling
  Wayne Sales, General Partner
  Education: Harvard Business School
  Background: CEO & President, Canadian Tire Corporation; CEO & President, SUPERVALU Inc.
  Directorships: Tim Hortons, Toys R Us, Albertson's, Canadian Tire

986 INCYTE VENTURES
2911 Turtle Creek Boulevard
Suite 300
Dallas, TX 75219

Phone: 214-599-8700
e-mail: mgineris@incytecapital.com
web: www.incytecapital.com

Mission Statement: Incyte employs a focused, partner-intensive approach intended to result in measurable benefits to the invested capital and management well beyond the initial providing of capital.
Geographic Preference: United States, Canada
Founded: 2000
Average Investment: $20 - $150 million
Minimum Investment: $20 million
Investment Criteria: Early-Stage, Revenues between $25 to $200 million
Industry Group Preference: Telecommunications
Portfolio Companies: American Messaging Services, Paging Network of Canada
Key Executives:
  Marc A. Gineris, Founder & Managing General Partner
  e-mail: mgineris@incytecapital.com
  Education: BA, Pomona College; MBA, Harvard Business School
  Background: M&A; Kidder Peabody & Co.
  Directorships: Aileen, New Dimensions in Medicine, eVIN, Madison Telecommunications

987 INDEPENDENCE EQUITY
2100 Sanders Road
Suite 170
Northbrook, IL 60062

Phone: 847-739-0100 Fax: 224-723-5071
web: www.independence-equity.com

Mission Statement: Independence Equity is an early-stage venture capital firm that invests in companies commercializing technologies that improve resource utilization.
Geographic Preference: United States
Founded: 2010
Average Investment: $500,000 - $1 million
Investment Criteria: Early-Stage
Industry Group Preference: Clean Technology, Material Science
Portfolio Companies: Tagnetics, 10x Technology, Autonomic Materials, Intellihot Green Technologies, NanoStatics, EatStreet, Algal Scientific, Nucurrent, Swapbox, Advanced Diamond Technologies
Key Executives:
  Donald Sackman, Managing Partner
  Education: BS, Mechanical Engineering, Stanford University; MBA, University of Chicago
  Background: Principal, Oryx Capital
  Directorships: Mottahedeh & Co., Advanced Diamond Technology, Digital Acoustics, In-Pipe Technology, Tagnetics
  Michael Gruber, Investment Partner
  Education: BA, International Relations & Economics, University of Pennsylvania; MBA, Kellogg School of

Venture Capital & Private Equity Firms / Domestic Firms

Management
Background: Partner/Co-Founder, G4 Capital; Director, Taproot Ventures
Laurence Hayward, Investment Partner
Education: BS, Psychology, MBA, University of Illinois
Background: Founder, VentureLab; Managing Partner, SCIUS Capital Group
Michael McCullough, Administrative Partner
Education: BBA, Accounting, University of Iowa; MBA, Kellogg School of Management
Background: CFO, Oryx Capital

988 INDEPENDENT BANKERS CAPITAL FUND
1700 Pacific Avenue
Suite 3660
Dallas, TX 75201

Phone: 214-722-6200
e-mail: bconrad@ibcfund.com
web: www.ibcfund.com

Mission Statement: A private equity partnership providing equity capital to established lower-middle-market companies primarily in the Southwestern United States.

Geographic Preference: Southwest
Fund Size: $70 million
Founded: 2000
Average Investment: $2 - $5 million
Minimum Investment: $2 million
Investment Criteria: Recapitalizations, late stage, lower middle market companies and companies with revenues between $10-$50 million
Industry Group Preference: Manufacturing, Distribution
Portfolio Companies: Adao Global, Anthony Machine, Aqueos, Azimuth Technology, Berry Aviation Inc., Burrow Global, Casi, Champion, CPS Houston, DSW Homes, Integrated Advantage Group, Lane Supply Inc., PMA PhotoMetals of Arizona Inc., Raisbeck Engineering, AccuSource Solutions, Alsay Inc., Cohn & Gregory, CareCycle Solutions, Ergo Genesis, GranQuartz, Graco Supply & Integrated Services, Granite & Marble Holdings Inc., Jardine's, Painless, The Finial Company

Key Executives:
Barry B Conrad, Founder/Managing Member
e-mail: bconrad@ibcfund.com
Education: AB, Marshall University
Background: Founder/Managing Partner, Conrad/Collins Merchant Banking Group; Senior VP/Manager of Corporate Finance, Rauscher Pierce Refsnes; CEO, Hart Delta; Partner, Howard, Weil, Labouisse Friedrichs & Company
Thomas B. Hoyt, Managing Member
e-mail: thoyt@ibcfund.com
Education: BA, Economics, University of Virginia; University of Richmond and Virginia Commonwealth University
Background: President & Investment Manager, Hibernia; Founder, Audubon Capital Fund; Managing Director, Rodman & Renshaw; Regional VP, Prudential Capital Corporation; The First National Bank of Chicago; Crestar Financial Corporation
Meg Taylor, Managing Memeber/CFO
e-mail: mtaylor@ibcfund.com
Education: BBA, Accounting, Texas Tech University
Background: Controller, Hicks, Muse, Tate & Furst; Assistant Controller, Nickels & Dimes; Assistant Controller, Sunwestern Investment Group; Ernst & Young
William H. Miltenberger, Managing Member
e-mail: bmiltenberger@ibcfund.com
Education: BBA, Loyola University; MBA, Kellogg School of Management
Background: Portfolio Manager, Highland Capital Management; Venture Capital Officer, Hibernia Capital Corporation

989 INDUSTRIAL GROWTH PARTNERS
101 Mission Street
Suite 1500
San Francisco, CA 94105

Phone: 415-882-4550 Fax: 415-882-4551
web: www.igpequity.com

Mission Statement: A private investment partnership that provides equity capital to private sector, middle-market manufacturing companies, the firm invests equity in a broad range of transactions involving a change of ownership, such as management buyouts, recapitalization, management buy-ins and corporate divestitures. The firm also provides growth capital to privately held companies in the manufacturing sector which require capital in order to expand their businesses.

Geographic Preference: United States
Fund Size: $2.2 billion
Founded: 1997
Average Investment: $10
Minimum Investment: $5 million
Investment Criteria: MBO, Recapitalizations, Growth Financings, Co-Operative, Divesitures, Private Companies/Family Owned and revenues up to $250 million
Industry Group Preference: Manufacturing
Portfolio Companies: Amercable Inc., API Heat Transfer, Associated Chemist Inc., Atlas Material Testing Solutions, Breeze Industrial Products Corp., Cambridge International Inc., Climax Portable Machine Tools, Consolidayed Precision Products Corp., Controls Southeast Inc., Des-Case Corp., Electronic Packaging Products Inc., FMH Aerospace, Global Power Systems, Grakon, Group360 Inc., Ideal-Tridon, Integrated Global Services, Integrated Polymer Solutions, IOTA Engineering, Jonathan Engineered Solutions, Microporous Products, North American Substation Services, O'Brien Corp., Power Protection Products Inc., Q Holding Company, Royal Die and Stamping Co., Seaboard International Inc., SPL, The Felters Group, The TASI Group, Thermal Sensing Products Inc., Weasler Engineering Inc., West American Rubber Company, Xaloy Inc.

Key Executives:
Eric D. Heglie, Managing Director
e-mail: edh@igpequity.com
Education: MBA, Wharton School, University of Pennsylvaniva; BA, University of California, LA
Background: Jeffries & Company; Morgan Stanley Dean Witter
Directorships: Breeze Industrial Products Corporation, Group360
Jeffrey M. Webb, Director
e-mail: jmw@igpequity.com
Education: BA, Economics, Cornell University; MBA, University of Chicago Graduate School of Business
Background: Ridge Capital Partners; Equity Research, William Blair & Company
Directorships: API Heat Transfer, Microporous Products, O'Brien Holding Co., Total Automated Solutions
Daniel L. Delaney, Director
e-mail: dld@igpequity.com
Education: BS, Business Administration, California Polytechnic State University; MBA, Operations & Accounting, University of Chicago Graduate School of Business
Background: Glencoe Capital; Investment Banking, AG Edwards
Directorships: Seaboard Wellhead
Robert M Austin, Vice President
e-mail: rma@igpequity.com
Education: BS, Commerce, University of Virginia; MBA, JL Kellogg School of Management, Northwestern University
Background: Vice President, Lake Capital; The Riverside Company
Matthew P. Antaya, Vice President
e-mail: mpa@igpequity.com

Venture Capital & Private Equity Firms / Domestic Firms

Education: BBA, Finance, College of William & Mary
Background: Analyst, Citigroup

990 INDUSTRY VENTURES
522 Washington Street
San Francisco, CA 94111

web: www.industryventures.com

Mission Statement: A leading investment firm that capitalizes on inefficiencies in venture capital and technology growth equity.

Fund Size: $3 billion
Founded: 2000
Investment Criteria: Seed, Early-Stage
Industry Group Preference: Technology, Communications, Applications, Venture Capital, Pharmaceuticals
Portfolio Companies: Access Closer, Alert Logic, Alibaba, Alphablox, Ancestry.com, AngioScore, AppDynamics, Arch Venture Partners, Arista Networks, ArrowPath Venture Partners, AskMe, Astex Pharmaceuticals, Atherotech, Azure Capital Partners, Baker Communications, Battery Ventures, BitCentral, Blueprint Ventures, Blumberg Capital, BOLDstart Ventures, Boulder Ventures, Broadsoft, Cambridge Display, CellzDirect, CenterPoint Ventures, Chegg, ChemConnect, Chrysalix Venture Capital, ClairMail, ClariPhy, Coleman Swenson Booth, Columbia Capital, CoreOptics, Credant Technologies, Crescendo Ventures, Dejima Inc., DFJ Venture Capital, Draper Espirit, Easton Capital, eBags, Ellie Mae, Eloqua Corp., Enanta Pharmaceuticals, Endforce, Entrade, Envivio, Epocrates, Extended Systems, Facebook, Focus Ventures, Fortinet, Fougera Pharmaceuticals, Foundation Capital, Foundry Group, Frontier Ventures, FT Partner, FTV Capital, Fuse Capital, Garage Technology Ventures, Generation Capital Partners, GetWellNetwork, Green Dot, Horizon Ventures, Ingenuity Systems, Innovation Capital, Instill, Intarcia Therapeutics, InterXion, Jajah Jasper Technologies, JK&B Capital, JMI Equity, Kiodex Inc., LifeLock, Lightspeed Venture Partners, Maveron Equity Partners, MedeAnalytics, Metastorm, Mobius Venture Capital, Model N Inc., Narus, New Enterprise Associates, Newlight Management, Novak Biddle, Once24 Inc., Opsware, Pure Digital, Redpoint Ventures, Rembrandt Venture Partners, Sevin Rosen Funds, Softbank Capital, SoftTech VC, Southern Capitol Ventures, Stephens Investment Mgmt., Storm Ventures, StrongView, Tandem Capital, Teachscape, Technology Partners, Trados, Trialpay, Tripwire, TriReme Systems, True Ventures, Trustwave, Twitter, Varicent Software, Venture Strategy Partners, Vertical Networks, Village Ventures, Virtue, Voltage Security, Voyager Capital, Walden VC, Watchfire Corp., Westin Presidio, Windward Ventures, Xactly, ZipRealty

Other Locations:
225 Reinekers Lane
Suite 216
Alexandria, VA 22314

96 Kensington High Street
London W8 4SG
United Kingdom

Key Executives:
Hans Swildens, Founder/CEO
e-mail: hans@industryventures.com
Education: BA, University of California, Santa Barbara; MBA, Columbia Business School
Background: Co-Founder & President, Microline Software
Justin Burden, Senior Managing Director
e-mail: justin@industryventures.com
Education: BA, University of California, Berkeley; MS, London School of Economics
Background: GE Equity, Wells Fargo
Robert May, Senior Advisor
e-mail: robert@industryventures.com
Education: BS, Finance, San Jose State Uiversity
Background: Consultant, Standish Management; COO/CFO, Founders Fund; CFO, Thomas Weisel Venture Partners; Controller, Mohr Davidow Ventures; Senior Financial Analyst, Hewleet-Packard; Product Control Analyst, Drexler Technologies
Directorships: Financial Executives Alliance
Jonathan Roosevelt, Managing Director
e-mail: jr@industryventures.com
Education: BA, Harvard College; MBA, Harvard Business School
Background: VP of Sales, SoFi; Analyst, Battery Ventures
Victor Hwang, Vice President
e-mail: victor@industryventures.com
Education: BA, Stanford University; MBA, Stanford Graduate School of Business
Background: Managing Partner, Agile Capital Partners; CEP, ICG Asia; Goldman Sachs
Directorships: MyPerfectSale.com
Roland Reynolds, Senior Managing Director
e-mail: roland@industryventures.com
Education: Princeton University; MBA, Harvard Business School
Background: Managing Partner, Little Hawk Capital Management; Principal, Columbia Capital
Directorships: Kearny Venture Partners

991 INETWORKS ADVISORS LLC
820 Evergreen Avenue
Suite 202
Pittsburgh, PA 15209

Phone: 412-904-1014
e-mail: info@inetworkspe.com
web: www.inetworkspe.com

Mission Statement: To provide capital, operational expertise, industry insight, and experienced executives to assist entrepreneurs in accelerating the development of their technology-based product or service.

Founded: 1999
Investment Criteria: Early Stage, Mid-Stage, Late Stage, Restructuring, Leverage Buyouts
Industry Group Preference: Healthcare, Medical Devices, Pharmaceuticals, Diagnostics, Healthcare Information Technology, Healthcare Services, Clean Technology, Energy, Environment, Information Technology, Software, Communications
Portfolio Companies: Cognition Therapeutics Inc., Novian Health, One Logos Education Solutions, PennAlt Organics Inc., Propel IT, Sparkt, Unequal Technologies LLC, Vizsafe, Wenzel Spine

Key Executives:
Anthony M Lacenere, Senior Managing Director
412-927-1793
Fax: 412-294-0492
e-mail: tlacenere@inetworkspe.com
Education: BS, Economics & Finance, University of Dayton; MS, Business Economics, Ohio State University
Background: President, MDX Fund; VP, Financial Affairs & Managing Director, Investments, AMSCO International; Rockwell International; Westinghouse Electric Corporation; Battelle Memorial Institute
Anthony L Tomasello, Senior Managing Director
412-927-1790
Fax: 412-294-0492
e-mail: ttomasello@inetworkspe.com
Education: University of Pittsburgh
Background: Chairman, Novian Health; EVP & CTO, Stericycle
Directorships: Community Schools
Michael T Dieschbourg, Senior Vice President of Investments
Education: BBA, Loyola University
Background: Head of Responsibility & Stewardship, Hermes Investment Management; Co-Founder/CEO of Global Currents Investment Management LLC

Venture Capital & Private Equity Firms / Domestic Firms

992 INFIELD CAPITAL
1002 Walnut Street
Suite 202
Boulder, CO 80302

Phone: 303-449-2921 Fax: 303-449-2936
e-mail: info@infieldcapital.com
web: www.infieldcapital.com

Mission Statement: The Infield Capital model is centered around a unique orientation the firm creates between the Limited Partners and Portfolio Companies in the fund. Infield chose to raise capital from companies that are strategically interested in the transportation industry and can, in turn, create unique opportunities for those companies in which we invest. These opportunities begin with our investment, which is equal parts financial and intellectual capital.

Founded: 2008
Investment Criteria: Early-stage
Industry Group Preference: Clean Technology, Green Technology, Stored Energy, Mobile Energy Transmission, Nontechnology, Alternative Energy, Transportation
Portfolio Companies: Basic 3C, Mission Motors, Pinnacle Engines, Simbol Materials, Solix BioSystems, VanDyne SuperTurbo, Wildcat Discovery Technologies

Key Executives:
David Moll, Founder/Managing Director
Education: Baldwin Wallace College, MBA, Northwestern University
Background: CEO, Webroot Inc.; MTD Products
Directorships: Pinnacle Engines
William Perry, Venture Advisor
Education: Harvard Business School, MIT
Background: President, Precision Visuals Inc.; Co-Founder, Softbridge Advisors

993 INFLECTION POINT VENTURES
Delaware Technology Park
One Innovation Way
Suite 302
Newark, DE 19711

Phone: 302-452-1120
web: www.inflectpoint.com

Mission Statement: Provides venture capital and business support for early-stage telecommunications, information technology, and electronic commerce companies with the potential to generate rapid growth in revenue, profitability, and shareholder value. As of 2010, Inflection Point is managing its current portfolio and is not making new investments.

Geographic Preference: Mid-Atlantic, New England
Average Investment: $2 million
Minimum Investment: $500,000
Investment Criteria: Early Stage
Industry Group Preference: Telecommunications, Information Technology, E-Commerce & Manufacturing
Portfolio Companies: Alternative Fuels Group, CareGain, ComBrio, CurrentAnalysis, Epion, ExoGenesis, Fidelis, Histogenics, Infoether, IntraPoint, LongWatch, LPInnovations, Premise, ReturnCentral, Searchandise Commerce, SkillSurvey, SourceFire, Synchris, Triumfant, TrueLemon

Other Locations:
Delaware Technology Park
One Innovation Way
Suite 302
Newark, DE 19711
Phone: 302-452-1120 Fax: 302-452-1122

Key Executives:
Jeff Davison, General Partner
e-mail: jdavison@inflectpoint.com
Education: Masters, MIT; Bachelor's, Hampshire College
Background: Co-Founder, Tritech Partners; Senior Management, Massachusetts Technology Development Corporation
Mike O'Malley, General Partner
e-mail: momally@inflectpoint.com
Education: JD, Suffolk University; MBA, Babson College; Bachelors, Colby College
Background: MDT Advisers; Massachusetts Technology Development Corporation
Diane Messick, Chief Financial Officer
Education: BS, Accounting, University of Delaware
Background: Student Finance Corporation, Young Conaway Stargatt & Taylor LLP, Solomon & Solomon PC, MBNA America

994 INFLEXION PARTNERS
2156 SW 98th Drive
Gainesville, FL 32608

Phone: 352-339-6669
e-mail: dan@inflexionvc.com
web: www.inflexionvc.com

Mission Statement: An early-venture capital fund organized with an emphasis on company building and harnessing regional, national, and international resources of the fund's managers and strategic partners.

Geographic Preference: Florida
Average Investment: $100,000 - $1 million
Investment Criteria: Seed-Stage, Early-Stage
Industry Group Preference: Communications, Software, Life Sciences
Portfolio Companies: CallMiner, Celsia Technologies, DataBanq, IZEA, Persystent Enterprise, Proximities, RedPath, Visible Assets, WiDeFi

Key Executives:
Jim Boyle, Managing Partner
Education: HBSc, Chemistry, Lakehead University; MBA, Finance & Accounting, McMaster University
Background: Union Carbide Canada Limited; Nortel; Telinvest Management Corporation
Charles Resnick, Managing Partner
Education: AB, MBA, St. Louis University
Background: Danka Business Systems; Tropicana Products; Mellon Bank; PepsiCo; The Procter & Gamble Company; Mimeo, Inc.
Dan Rua, Managing Partner
Education: BS, Computer Engineering, University of Florida; JD, University of North Carolina School of Law; MBA, Kenan-Flagler Business School
Background: Partner, Draper Atlantic; IBM
Michael Barach, Venture Partner
Education: BA, Amherst College; JD, Harvard Law School; MBA, Harvard Business School
Background: General Partner, Village Ventures; Partner, Bessemer Venture Partners; President/CEO, MotherNature.com
Carolyn Ticknor, Venture Partner
Education: BS, Psychology, University of Redlands; MS, Industrial Psychology, San Francisco State University; MBA, Stanford Graduate School of Business
Background: President, Imaging & Printing Business, Hewlett-Packard
Directorships: AT&T Wireless Services, Boise Cascade Corporation

995 INITIALIZED CAPITAL
San Francisco, CA

e-mail: contact@initialized.com
web: initialized.com

Mission Statement: Venture capital firm focused on software startups at seed stage or earlier.

Fund Size: $160 million
Founded: 2012
Investment Criteria: Seed stage or earlier
Industry Group Preference: Software

Venture Capital & Private Equity Firms / Domestic Firms

Portfolio Companies: reddit, patreon, Flexport, Lever, soylent, Triplebyte

Key Executives:
  Garry Tan, Managing Partner
  Education: Stanford University
  Background: Posterous; Palantir
  Alda Leu Dennis, General Partner
  Education: BS, Stanford University; JD, University of California LA
  Background: Associate, Wilson Sonsini Goodrich and Rosati; Associate/General Counsel, Clarium Capital Management; General Counsel, The Founders Fund; COO, Airtime; Founder, Sproutkin Inc.; Managing Partner, 137 Ventures
  Directorships: The Mom Project; Landed; SkySelect; A-Frame Brands
  Brett Gibson, General Partner
  Education: BA, University of California Santa Barbara
  Background: Software Engineer, Grand Central Communications; Developer, Sonific; Co-Founder, Slkinset; Co-Founder, Posterous; Co-Founder, Posthaven
  Jen Wolf, Partner/Chief Operating Officer
  Education: University of Washington
  Background: Director of User Experience, Sapient; Partner, Millimeter Design; VP of Products, Deem Inc.; CEO/Founder, Plumfile Product Consulting; Chief Product Officer, Reserve

996 INITIO GROUP
195 Page Mill Road
Palo Alto, CA 94306

web: www.initiogroupadvisors.com

Mission Statement: An early-stage investment fund that invests in people first. Initio is a 21st century investment and business consulting firm that specializes in emerging and expanding markets focusing on niched forms of real estate and business investment.

Founded: 2010
Investment Criteria: Early-Stage
Industry Group Preference: Real Estate

Key Executives:
  Maria Neal, Chief Executive Officer
  Rahsaan Dean, President
  Education: BA, University of California Berkeley
  Dan Policy, Director, International Finance

997 INLAND TECHSTART FUND
Phone: 561-322-9660

Mission Statement: The Inland TechStart Fund invests seed capital in early stage companies and entrepreneurs with great ideas. The Fund is focused on providing rewarding returns for investors, while building great companies with the next generation of entrepreneurs, and having fun doing it. The Fund invests in technology based companies only.

Geographic Preference: United States, Northwest
Investment Criteria: Early-Stage
Industry Group Preference: Software, Cloud Computing, Internet, E-Commerce & Manufacturing, Mobile, Entertainment, Media, Social Media, Gaming, Energy, Healthcare, Medical Devices, Telecommunications, Clean Technology

Key Executives:
  Scott Broder, Chief Executive Officer
  Education: BS, Computer Science, University of Miami
  Background: CEO, CanAM Internet; CEO, Opalis Software; Citrix Systems
  Steven King Neff, Co-Founder/Senior Manager
  Education: BA, University of Nebraska
  Background: Principal, Revita Institute Northest; Advisor, Signia Capital; Vice President, Marketing, ICM Asset Management

998 INNOSPRING
3401 El Camino Real
Palo Alto, CA 94306

Phone: 408-550-2818
web: www.innospringus.com

Mission Statement: InnoSpring is Silicon Valley's first US-China technology start-up incubator. Its focus is on encouraging startups to expand beyond their home countries to lead huge market opportunities in the US and China. InnoSpring is a joint project between Tsinghua University Science Park (TusPark), Shui On Group (Shui On), Northern Light Venture Capital and Silicon Valley Bank (SVB).

Geographic Preference: United States, China
Fund Size: $405 million
Founded: 2012
Investment Criteria: Seed-Stage, Startup
Industry Group Preference: Consumer Products & Services, Technology, Software
Portfolio Companies: Agentdesks, Akido Labs, Audacy, Cafe X, Celentail.ai, Dine Market, Drive.ai, HackHands, Haitou, Instamotor, Jaunt VR, Jist.tv, Labdoor, Leapmind, Meadow, Meta, Paperspace, Pluralsight, PlushCare, Savioke, Securly, SLIVER.tv, Teaforia, VideoStitch, WiseBanyan

Key Executives:
  Xiao Wang, General Manager, US
  Lara Kwong, Operations & Accounting
  Education: BBA, Accouting, San Jose State University

999 INNOVA MEMPHIS
20 Dudley St.
Suite 620
Memphis, TN 38103

e-mail: info@innovamemphis.com
web: www.innovamemphis.com

Mission Statement: Innova focuses on creating and funding high-growth biotechnology companies, especially in the earliest stages.

Founded: 2007
Investment Criteria: Pre-Seed, Seed, Early-Stage
Industry Group Preference: Biotechnology, Technology, Agriculture, Healthcare, Diagnostics, Medical Devices
Portfolio Companies: Advanced Catheter Therapies, AgriSync, AgSmarts, Ajax Intel, AlwazPro, arGentis, Arkis Biosciences, ArtSquare, BetterWalk, BioNanovations, Bionova, Blood Monitoring Solutions, Cagenix, CareIT, Cast21, Cattlog, Centiba, Cirquest, ClearMedicare, Community Health TV, Compression Kinetics, Coursicle, Cuff-Gard, Dermaflage, Dev/Con Detect, DivorseSecure, EarthSense, EcoSurg, EMBrace Design, EndoInsight, Entac Medical, ExtraOrtho, Fairway Biomed, Feather, FitNexx, FlexSpark, Frontdesk Connect, GlucosAlarm, Growers Holdings, Handminder, Health & Bliss, HelloHome, Hera Health Solutions, HerdDogg, Homey, Innometrix, Inspire Living, IRT, iScreen, iShipdit, Kilimo, L7 Logistics, LawnTap, LendMed, Life Detection Systems, Life Links, LiLoE, Lineus Medical, MedHaul, Mobilizer, Mozak, Nanophthalmics, NCrease, NuscriptRx, Parental Health, Path Ex, Persistence Data Mining, Please Assist Me, Powermet, Preteckt, Pro Hydration Therapy, Prolific Earth Sciences, ProxBox, Quire, Rabbit Tractors, Rantizo, Reemo, Rescue Forensics, Resolute Games, Restore Medical, RistCall, Roundabout Markets, S2 Interactive, SecondKeys, Secure Food Solutions, ServiceBot Software, Shurpa, SILQ, SixFix, Skycision, Soil Nerd, SOMAVAC, SweetBio, SwineTech, Tensor Surgical, Thaddeus Medical Systems, ThroughPut, Tractor Zoom, TradeLanes, TrakLok, Truck Driver Power, Truckish, Urova, Vaxent, View Medical, Vital Metrix, ZoomThru

Key Executives:
  Ken Woody, Partner
  Education: BS, North Carolina State University
  Background: SVP, Global Sales, Smith & Nephew

Orthopedics; VP, Sales, DePuy Spine; GE
Directorships: Cagenix, S2 Interactive, Tensor Surgical, ACT, BioNova Medical
Jan Bouten, Partner
Education: MBA, Duke University
Background: Aurora Funds
Directorships: Quire, iScreen Vision, Restore Medical, Silicone Art Labs, Compression Kinetics
Dean Didato, Partner
Education: BS, Marietta College
Background: Strategic Accounts Manager, The Vincit Group
Directorships: Secure Food Solutions

1000 INNOVATION CATALYST
7117 Florida Boulevard
Suite 202
Baton Rouge, LA 70806

Phone: 225-215-2466
e-mail: info@innovationcatalyst.us
web: www.innovationcatalyst.us

Mission Statement: Innovation Catalyst is a nonprofit venture development organization, formed by community leaders to strengthen and broaden Louisiana's entrepreneurial ecosystem and drive new high-tech company formation through education, connections, and capital.

Geographic Preference: Louisiana
Average Investment: $250K
Industry Group Preference: Diversified
Portfolio Companies: Certification Connect, Dinner Lab, FollowMyCal, Indie Plate, Juicebox, Kinesics, Libricity, Mastery Prep, MobileQubes, Omnidek, PatentDive, Precision Payment Systems, Quarrion, Scholar's First, SellSwipe, SmartPak, Something Borrowed Blooms, Swaybox Studios, Waitr

Key Executives:
Bill Ellison, Chief Executive Director
Education: BA & JD, University of Mississippi
Background: CEO, Red Stick Angel Network

1001 INNOVATION ENDEAVORS
1845 El Camino Real
Palo Alto, CA 94306

e-mail: info@innovationendeavors.com
web: www.innovationendeavors.com

Mission Statement: Innovation Endeavors invests in companies of all sizes in the tech industry.

Founded: 2010
Industry Group Preference: Data, Engineering, Technology
Portfolio Companies: Afresh, AlphaSense, Beamr, Blue River Technology, Bolt Threads, Claroty, Citrine Informatics, Clearmetal, Color, Cropx, Datorama, Dewpointx, Dynamic Yield, Eko, Fabric, FarmerBs Fridge, Form Labs, Freenome, Gatik, GRO Biosciences, Hysolate, Illusive, Karius, Keywee, Planet, Plenty, Rebellion, Replica, SkyTran, Slice, SoFI, Team8, Uber, Ukko, Unbound, Vicarious Surgical, Yotpo, Zymergen

Other Locations:
10 E 53rd Street
14th Floor
New York, NY 10022

121 Menachem Begin Street
57th Floor
Tel Aviv
Israel

Key Executives:
Eric Schmidt, Founding Partner
Education: BS, Electrical Engineering, Princeton University; MS/PhD, Computer Science, University of California, Berkeley
Background: Technical Advisor, Alphabet Inc.; CEO, Google; CEO, Novell; CTO, Sun Microsystems Inc.; Researcher, Xerox Palo Alto Research Center; Bell Laboratories; Zilog
Scott Brady, Partner
Education: BS, Finance, University of Florida; MS, Stanford Grad. School of Business
Background: CEO, Slice; Co-Founder/CEO, FibertTower; CTO, Clarus Corporation; CTO, SQLFinancials; Lecturer in Management, Stanford Grad. School of Business
Sam Smith-Eppsteiner, Partner
Education: BA, Political Science, Stanford University; MBA, Stanford Grad. School of Business
Background: Management Consultant, Bain & Company; Product Manager, Kigali Farms (Rwanda)
Rick Scanlon, Partner
Education: BA, Middlebury College
Background: Morgan Stanley; Credit Suisse
Harpinder Singh, Partner
Education: MS, Computer Science, Indiana University; MBA, Stanford Grad. School of Business
Background: Co-Founder/CEO, Slice Technologies; Co-Founder/Head of Product & Marketing, FiberTower; Software Developer, Oracle; Architect, Bull Honeywell
Dror Berman, Partner
Education: BS, Computer Science, Ben-Gurion University; MBA, Stanford Grad. School of Business
Background: Team Leader of R&D, NICE Systems; Part of Special Forces United of Intelligence Corps of the Israeli Defense Force
Daniel Goldstein, Partner
Education: BA, Communications, IDC Herzliya
Background: Head of Business Development, Red Onion Game
Bridget Storm, Partner/CFO
Education: BA, Gonzaga University; MA, Washington State University
Background: CFO, Makena Capital Management

1002 INNOVATION PLATFORM CAPITAL
2450 Holcombe Blvd
Houston, TX 77021

web: innovationplatformcapital.com

Industry Group Preference: Healthcare, Education, Infrastructure, Energy, Finance, Manufacturing & Distribution, Technology

Key Executives:
Gursh Kundan, CEO
Education: Simon Fraser Univ.
Background: Invesco
Ionel V. Nechiti, President
Background: Platform Management LLC

1003 INNOVATION WORKS
Nova Tower 2
Two Allegheny Center
Suite 100
Pittsburgh, PA 15212

Phone: 412-681-1520
web: www.innovationworks.org

Mission Statement: Innovation Works invests in Southwestern Pennsylvania's technology economy.

Geographic Preference: Southwestern Pennsylvania
Founded: 1999
Average Investment: $340,000
Investment Criteria: Seed
Industry Group Preference: Technology, Life Sciences, Medical Devices, Biotechnology, Information Technology, Software, Internet Infrastructure, Advanced Materials, Consumer Electronics, Energy, Enterprise Software, Mobile, Network Infrastructure, Robotics
Portfolio Companies: AardvarQ, Accipiter Systems, Aethon, Agentase, Alertek, AllFacilities Energy Group, ALung Technologies, American Roadprinting, Appalachian Lighting

Venture Capital & Private Equity Firms / Domestic Firms

Systems, ATRP Solutions, BIOSAFE, BitArmor Systems, Blue Belt Technologies, Bossa Nova Concepts, BPL Global, Bridge Semiconductor, Bueda, Caliber Infosolutions, Carmell Therapeutics, Carnegie Speech Company, CastGrabber, Celluman, Cepstral, Ciespace Corporation, Circadiance, Civic Science, ClearCount Medical Solutions, Cognition Therapeutics, Cohera Medical, Compliance Assurance Corporation, Concurrent Electronic Design Automation, Crono, Crystaplex Corporation, Deeplocal, Diamyd, Epiphany Solar Water Systems, Etcetera Edutainment, FASTTAC, Fluorous Technologies, Health Monitoring Systems, High Performance Building Systems, HyperActive Technologies, Immunetrics, ImpactGames, Industry Weapon, INTEG Process Group, Intimate Bridge 2 Conception, InvestEdge, KeyBay Pharmaceutical, Knopp Neurosciences, Landslide Technologies, LeftRight Studios, Lightfoot, Medallion Anayltics, medSage Technologies, Memory Medallion, Metis Secure Solutions, Mobile Aspects, MobileFusion, ModCloth, mSpoke, My Payment Network, nanoLambda, NeuroInterventions, NuRelm, Penthera Partners, PeriOptimum, PetsDx Imaging, Pittsburgh Iron Oxides, Plextronics, Powercast Corporation, RedPack Logistics, RedPath Integrated Pathology, RedZone Roboticss, ReGear Life Sciences, SEEGRID Corporation, ShowClix, Slim Ops Studios, SMASH, Songwhale, STARR Life Sciences

Key Executives:
Rich Lunak, President & CEO
Education: Carnegie Mellon University; University of Pittsburgh
Background: McKesson

1004 INNOVENTURES CAPITAL PARTNERS
150 South State
Suite 100
Salt Lake City, UT 84111

Phone: 801-243-6674
e-mail: steve@innoventures.com
web: www.innoventurescapitalpartners.com

Mission Statement: A licensed Small Business Investment Company (SBIC) in Salt Lake City, Utah. Innoventures invests in small companies by providing subordinated debt to start-up and growing businesses.

Geographic Preference: Utah, Neighboring States
Fund Size: $9.6 million
Founded: 1983
Average Investment: $50,000 - $250,000
Minimum Investment: $50,000
Investment Criteria: Mezzanine, Start up, Early stage
Industry Group Preference: Information Technology, Manufacturing
Portfolio Companies: BetterBody Foods, Five Star Franchising, Property Solutions

Key Executives:
Steve Grizzell, Managing Director
e-mail: sgrizzell@utfc.biz
Education: MBA, University of Utah; University of Massachusetts; BS, Anthropology, Michigan State
Background: Consultant, World Bank and U.S. Agency for International Development
Robert Lund, General Counsel
Education: JD, Brigham Young University Law School
Background: Utah Technology Finance Corp.
Scott Stenberg, CFO
e-mail: sstenberg@utfc.biz
Education: Master of Professional Accountancy, Weber State University
Background: Internal Auditor, University of Utah

1005 INSIGHT VENTURE PARTNERS
1114 Avenue of the Americas
36th Floor
New York, NY 10036

Phone: 212-230-9200
e-mail: growth@insightpartners.com
web: www.insightpartners.com

Mission Statement: A private equity and venture capital firm that invests in companies in the software-based segments of the information technology industry.

Geographic Preference: United States
Fund Size: $6.3 billion
Founded: 1995
Average Investment: $15 million
Minimum Investment: $5 million
Investment Criteria: Expansion
Industry Group Preference: Infrastructure, Software Services, Applications Software & Services, Consumer Internet, E-Commerce & Manufacturing, Education, Energy, Financial Services, Gaming, Government, Graphics, Healthcare, Marketing, Media, Telecommunications
Portfolio Companies: 1stdibs, 5Nine, 6Waves, Aaptiv, Academic Partnerships, Achieve 3000, Alteryx, AMCS, Anaqua, Appriss, Automattic, Automile, Azuqua, BlaBlaCar, Blinkist, Branding Brand, BrightBytes, BrightEdge, Bullhorn, Bynder, Calm, Campaign Monitor, Caremerge, Cartrawler, CentralReach, CeresImaging, Chargbee, Checkmark, Cherwell, Chrono24, CloudBolt Software, CommunityBrands, Conga, Copado, CoreView, Cylance, DarkTrace, DataCore, Delivery Hero, Despegar.com, Detectify, Devo, Diligent, Divvy, Docker, DocuSign, DrillingInfo, Duco, E2open, Elo7, Ensighten, Episerver, EquipmentShare.co.nz, Everyaction, EzCater, Famous, Fanatics, Fenergo, Film Track, Firemon, Flipboard, Flipp, FloQast, Force, Fourth, Freshly, Gainsight, GoSpotCheck, GraphPad Software, Harver, Hello Fresh, Hinge Health, HomeToGo, Hootsuite, Hotel Urbano, Hustle, Illuminate Education, Ilumno, Indiegogo, Intent Media, Interfolio, Invaluable, iSpot.tv, Jama Software, JFrog, JoyTunes, Kaseya, Kira, Kony, LeanIX, LeanTaaS, Lease Accelerator, Lightricks, LiveAction, Marketing Evolution, Mediaspectrum, Menu Next Door, Mimecast, Ministry Brands, Mirantis, Monday.com, N26, nCino, Nearpod, Nextdoor, NNG, Numetric, Nymbus, OneCommand, OpenEnglish, Optibus, OwnBackup, Parachute Health, Parallels, PicsArt, Pipedrive, Planview, PluralSight, PrecisionLender, Prevalent, Project44, PropertyBrands, Prose, QASymphony, Qualtrics, Quantum Metric, ReceiptBank, Recorded Future, Resolve Systems, Ritual, SalesLoft, Showpad, Sift Science, SimpleNexus, Simplifile, Sisense, Skinny Corp, Skytap, Smart Recruiters, SmartSheet, SMS Assist, Sonarsource, Spacetime Studiios, Spanning, SpareFoot, Spot.im Spot Hero, Studio Moderna, Sysdig, TaxJar, Templafy, Tenable, The Athene Group, The Farmer's Dog, Thycotic, Tigera, Tongal, Tractable, TradingView, Trendy Entertainment, Tricentis, Turnitin, Udemy, Unitends, Veeam, Vela, VTS, Vinted, WalkMe, Wealth-X, Whalerock Industries, Workforce, Yext, Yogome, Yoobic, Zaius, Zenefits, Zumba

Key Executives:
Jeff Horing, Managing Director/Co-Founder
Education: BS, MIT; MBA, Wharton School, University of Pennsylvania
Background: Warburg Pincus; Goldman Sachs
Richard Wells, Managing Director
Education: BS, Economics, Wharton School, University of Pennsylvania; MBA, Harvard Business School
Background: Veritas Software; Paciolan Systems; Associate, Technology Crossover Ventures; Consultant, Mercer Management Consulting
Peter Sobiloff, Managing Director
Background: Datalogix; Ross Systems; Think Systems
Directorships: Achieve3000, DrillingInfo, Duco, Fenergo,

Venture Capital & Private Equity Firms / Domestic Firms

Filmtrack, Kony Sultions, NYMBUS, Planview, Mediaspectrum, Workforce Software

Deven Parekh, Managing Director
Education: BS, Wharton School, University of Pennsylvania
Background: Principal, Berenson Minella & Company; The Blackstone Group
Directorships: Bullhorn, DrillingInfo, Turnitin, Ministry Brands, Apriss, Campaign Monitor, Fanatics, Diligent, 1stdibs, Vela, Chrono24, LetGo, Wallapop

Michael Triplett, Managing Director
Education: BA, Economics, Dartmouth College
Background: Investment Professional, Summit Partners; Financial Analyst, Morgan Stanley & Co.; Midland Data Systems
Directorships: N2W, 5nine Software, Acronis, GFI Software, IKANO/Virtacore, Kaseya, Parrallels, SmartBear, ThreatTrack, Unitrends, Veeam

Jeff Lieberman, Managing Director
Education: Systems Engineering & Finance, Pennsylvania's Moore School of Engineering; Wharton School, University of Pennsylvania
Background: Management Consultant, McKinsey & Company

Ryan Hinkle, Managing Director
Education: BS, Engineering, School of Engineering & Applied Science, University of Pennsylvania; BS, Wharton School
Background: Morgan Stanley; PPL Corporation

1006 INSTITUTIONAL VENTURE PARTNERS
3000 Sand Hill Road
Building 2
Suite 250
Menlo Park, CA 94025

Phone: 650-854-0132
web: www.ivp.com

Mission Statement: One of the premier later-stage venture capital and growth equity firms in the United States. The partnership is focused on later-stage companies, investing in rapidly growing technology and digital media companies.

Geographic Preference: United States, West Coast
Fund Size: $7 billion
Founded: 1980
Average Investment: $25 million
Minimum Investment: $10 million
Investment Criteria: Later-Stage, Expansion, Public
Industry Group Preference: Software, Data Communications, Components & IoT, Technology, Digital Media & Marketing, Internet, Enterprise Software, Information Technology, Mobile, Communications
Portfolio Companies: AddThis, Adroll, Aerohive Networks, Alien Vault, Amplitude, Anomali, App Annie, AppDynamics, Arcsight, Aster Data Systems, Ayasdi, Buddy Media, Business Insider, Business.com, Care.com, Casper, Checkr, Coinbase, Compass, Comscore Networks, Concur Technologies, Cyence, Danger, Datalogix, Dataminr, Domo, DoubleVerify, Dropbox, Dropcam, Fleetmatics, Gaia Interative, General Assembly, Giphy, Github, Glossier, Grammarly, Ground Truth, H5, Hipmunk, HomeAway, Indiegogo, Inspirato, Juniper Networks, Kayak, Klarna, Klout, Legal Zoom, Lifelock, LiveOps, LSI, Marketo, Markmonitor, Masterclass, Mindbody, Mobile 365, Mobileiron, Mulesoft, MYSQL, NerdWallet, Netflix, NGMOCO, Moniture, Ondeck Capital, One Kings Lane, Oportun, Personal Capital, Pindrop, Polycom, Popsugar, Prosper, Pure Storage, Qadium, Qubole, Quigo Technologies, Retail Me Not, Rubrik, Sauce Labs, Seagate Technologies, Shazam, Skytream Networks, Slack, Snapchat, SOFI, Soundcloud, Spiceworks, Steelbrick, Sumo Logic, Supercell, Synchronoss, Tala, Tanium, The Honest Company, The Player's Tribune, Thrive Global, Tivo, Transferwise, Tripwire, Tunein, Twitter, Twyla, Uproxx, Vessel, Voxer, Walker & Company, Whip Networks, Wikia, Yext, Yodlee, Zefr, Zendesk, Zenefits, Zerto, Zipprecruiter, Zynga

Other Locations:
747 Front Street
Suite 100
San Francisco, CA 94111
Phone: 415-432-4660

Key Executives:

Todd C. Chaffee, Advisory Partner
e-mail: tchaffee@ivp.com
Education: BS, University of Minnesota Carlson Business School; Venture Capital Program, Harvard Business School; Advanced Management College, Stanford Graduate Business School
Background: President, Visa International's Venture Capital Group; Norwest; American Express; TRW Information Systems Group; Grand Expeditions

Norman A. Fogelsong, Advisory Partner
e-mail: nfogelsong@ivp.com
Education: BS, Management Science & Engineering, Stanford University; MBA, Harvard Business School; JD, Harvard Law School
Background: Mayfield Fund; McKinsey & Company; Hewlett-Packard Company; Actively Involved in IVP; Integrated Circuit Works; Platinum Software; Polycom/TelCom
Directorships: Aspect Communications, Concur Technology

Steve Harrick, General Partner
e-mail: sharrick@ivp.com
Education: BA, History, Yale University; MBA, Harvard Business School
Background: Internet Capital Group; Highland Capital Partners; Netscape; Morgan Stanley
Directorships: Teros and several other portfolio companies.

Sandy Miller, General Partner
e-mail: smiller@ivp.com
Education: BA, University of Virginia; MBA & JD, Stanford University
Background: Senior Partner, 3i; Co-Founder, Thomas Weisel Partners; Senior Partner, Montgomery Securities; Managing Director, Merrill Lynch; Donaldson Lufkin & Jenrette; Manager, Bain & Company; Securities Lawyer, Pillsbury Winthrop

Dennis Phelps, General Partner
e-mail: dphelps@ivp.com
Education: BA, Government & Economics, Dartmouth College
Background: Battery Ventures; Internet Capital Group; Hambrecht & Quist

Jules Maltz, General Partner
e-mail: jmaltz@ivp.com
Education: BA, Economics, Yale University; MBA, Stanford University
Background: 3i, Admob

1007 INTEGRA VENTURES
300 E Pine Street
2nd Floor
Seattle, WA 98112

Phone: 206-832-1990 **Fax:** 206-832-1991

Mission Statement: To develop a portfolio of outstanding regional and national biomedical companies chosen within the framework of our partner's extensive biomedical, service and device expertise.

Geographic Preference: West Coast United States
Fund Size: $38 million
Founded: 1998
Average Investment: $2 million
Minimum Investment: $500,000
Investment Criteria: Early Stage, Late Stage and Growth Stage

Venture Capital & Private Equity Firms / Domestic Firms

Industry Group Preference: Life Sciences, Healthcare Services, Drug Development, Medical Devices
Portfolio Companies: Acorda Therapeutics, Amnis, Ampla Pharmaceuticals, Blue Heron, Calypso Medical Technologies, Cara Vita, Cardax, ClearMedical, Corus Pharma, Guava Technologies, Hawaii Biotech, HealthHelp, MediQuest, Napo Pharmaceuticals, National Healing, Novasite Pharmaceuticals, PLx Pharmaceutical, Raven Biotechnologies, Targeted Growth, Tepha, WellPartner

Key Executives:
  Joseph Piper JD, Founder/Managing Director
  206-229-5001
  Fax: 206-329-5105
  e-mail: piper@integraventures.net
  Education: BA, Arizona State; JD, Seattle University; MBA, University of Colorado
  Background: President, Capital Services
  Directorships: National Healing, HealthHelp, Physicians Edge, Vara Vita

  Hans Lundin, Chief Financial Officer
  206-229-3814
  Fax: 206-329-5105
  e-mail: lundin@integraventures.net
  Education: BS, US Coast Guard Academy; MBA, University of Colorado
  Background: Chairman, Clear Medical
  Directorships: Blue Heron Biotechnologies, ClearMedical

  Timothy Thompson Black, Partner/Chief Operating Officer
  206-229-3814
  Fax: 206-329-5105
  e-mail: black@integraventures.net
  Education: JD, Seattle University; BA, Colorado College
  Background: SunWest International

  James Nelson MD, Partner
  Education: Harvard University, Harvard Medical School
  Background: Professor of Radiology, UW

1008 INTEGRAL CAPITAL PARTNERS
2750 Sand Hill Road
Menlo Park, CA 94025

e-mail: john@icp.com
web: www.icp.com

Mission Statement: Integral Capital Partners operates a family of partnerships that invests in expansion-stage private and growth-stage public companies in the information and life sciences industries.
Founded: 1991
Investment Criteria: Expansion-Stage, Growth-Stage
Industry Group Preference: Information Technology, Life Sciences
Portfolio Companies: Iolon Inc., Zaffire, Visible Path, Vertical Networks, Tropos Networks, TherOx, Stoke, Silicon Energy, Qpass, Peppers & Rogers, Opsware, OpenTable, Octane Software, NewPort Communications, NetClerk, MyPlay, MetaMatrix, Matrix Semiconductor, Lytx Inc., LogMeIn, Lockdown Networks, Lantern Communications, Ketera, Jasper, Ingenio, Informative, Health Hero Network, Grockit, Event Zero, Drugstore.com, Concept Shopping, Celarix, CareDx, Calix, Blue Nile, Asera, ArcSight, Aragon Surgical, AlphaBlox

Key Executives:
  Pamela Hagenah, Opertations Partner
  Education: BS, University of California, Los Angeles; JD, University of California, Los Ageles
  Background: Attorney, Brobeck Phleger & Harrison
  John Powell, Co-Founder & Managing Director
  Education: BA, University of North Carolina, Chapel Hill; MBA, Darden Graduate School of Business Administration, University of Virginia
  Background: T. Rowe Price
  Brian Stansky, Managing Director
  Education: BS, Accounting, Boston College; MS, Finance & Applied Economics; Sloan School of Management, MIT
  Background: Director, Johns Hopkins Technology Ventures

1009 INTEL CAPITAL
2200 Mission College Boulevard
Santa Clara, CA 95054-1549

Phone: 408-765-8080
web: www.intelcapital.com

Mission Statement: Venture capital arm of Intel invests in mergers, acquisitions and tech startups.
Geographic Preference: Worldwide
Fund Size: $1.28 billion
Founded: 1991
Average Investment: $50-100 million
Investment Criteria: All Stages
Industry Group Preference: Enterprise, Mobility, Consumer Internet, Digital Media & Marketing, Semiconductors, Big Data, Cloud Infrastructure, Aritificial Intelligence, Autonomous Vehicles, IoT, Security, Software, Sports, Entertainment, Health
Portfolio Companies: 99Cloud, Adaptive Mobile, Ad Hawk Microsystems, Aerial, AEye, Airy3D, Alauda.cn, Alcide, Aledia, Almalence, Trace, AlterGeo, Altia Systems, Amenity Analytics, AnD APT Inc., Appionics Holdings, APPScomm, Arcadia Data, ASML, Avaamo, Avegant, Ayar Labs, Awcloud, Beijing UniSoc Technology Ltd., Betaworks, Big Switch Networks, Bigstream, Bluebank, BlueStacks, Borqs, Bossanova, Braigo Labs, Bright Edge, Brit + Co, Bromium, Cafe Communications, CareCloud, Certisign, Cgtrader, Chargifi, Chipsbank, Cloud Genix, Cloudian, Cloudify, Cognitive Scale, CTACCEL, CubeWorks, CYVision, Data Robot, Delair, Denovo, DSC, Dot Product, Dysonics, Eazytec, Echo Pixel, Eclypsium, Element, eLoupes, Embodied, Empathy, Enovix, Eruditor Group, Espressif, Eye Smart Technology, Alcon Computing, Fibocom Wireless, Fictiv, Fileforce, Fino, Flowplay, Forte Media, Fort Scale, Fortumo, Funders Club, Gamalon, Gengo, GenXcomm, Giga Spaces, Goldbely, Good Way Technologies, Good Data, Grameen Intel Social Business, Grand Chip Microelectronics, Griti, Habana, Happist Minds, Help Shift, Here, Horizon Robotics, Huaqin, Huiying Medical Technology, Hungama.com, HY Trust, Ice Tech, Identec Group, Imanis Data Inc., Immersed, InContext Solutions, Indiamart.com, Inpria, Inrix, Interlude, Intezer, Iotas, Jasper Infotech Pvt Ltd., Joby Aviation, KH Connect, KDS China, Kaltura, KM Labs, Kazan Networks, Keyssa, Kinduct, KiraKira3D, KupiVip.ru, Leapmind, Learnmetrics, LegUp, Lintes, Lisnr, Lumiata, Lyncean, Maana, Mango Telecom, MariaDB, Matroid, Mauj Mobile Pvt. Ltd., Maxta, Media Lario Technologies, Megapixel Software Inc., Metaboli, Microprogram, Mighty Ai, Minio Inc., Mirantis, MobiCom, Mocana, Montage Technology, Moovit, Moveable Ink, Movellus Circuits, Myriad Sensors, Nanosys, Nedvia, Netronome, Next Input, Ninebot, Nokta, North, Nuovo Film Inc., NxtGen, Nyansa, Okbuy.com, Orcam, Ossia, Overwolf, Ozon.ru, Panoply, Panorama, Paperspace, Parallels, Paxata, Peloton, Perpetuuiti, Perrone Robotics, Personify, Prafly, Precision Hawk, Preempt, Prep Flash, Prieto Battery, Prism Skylabs, Prophesee S.A., Punchbowl, QNovo, Real Image, R3, Rancard, RASilient, Reconova, Reduxio, Reebonz, Reef for Software Development, Reniac, Reno, Rubikloud, SanJet, Savaari Car Rentals, Savioke, SBA Materials, Schoology, ScienceLogic, Sckipio, Scorestream, Screenovate, Secure Key, SAM, Security Scorecard, Sedona Systems, Selectv, Shenzhen Prafly Technology, SiFive, Sigfox, SilkRoad, Sky Limit Entertainment, Smartzip, SnowCookie

Key Executives:
  Anthony Lin, Vice President/Senior Managing Director
  Education: BA, Economics, University of California Berkeley
  Background: Banc of America Securities; ASAT; Merrill

Venture Capital & Private Equity Firms / Domestic Firms

Lynch; PaineWebber
Directorships: Intel Capital Investment Committee
Dave Flanagan, Vice President/Senior Managing Director
Education: BA, Economics, University of Colorado; MBA, Georgetown University
Background: Van Kasper & Company; Transamerica
Sean Doyle, Managing Director
Education: BA, University of California Berkeley; MBA, UCLA
Background: Laidlaw Equities; Oracle Corporation
Andy Fligel, Senior Managing Director
Education: MBA, Kellogg Graduate School of Management; BS, Commerce, University of Virginia
Background: Robinson-Humphrey
Directorships: ScienceLogic; Maana; Guavus
Dave Johnson, Managing Director
Education: MBA, Cornell University; BA, Vanderbilt University
Background: Procter and Gamble; Chevron Corporation
Mark Rostick, Vice President/Senior Managing Director
Education: JD/MBA, University of South Carolina
Tammi Smorynski, Managing Director
Education: MBA, The Anderson School, UCLA; BA, Accounting/International Management, Georgetown University
Background: J.P. Morgan & Co.
Directorships: Embodied
Tamiko Hutchinson, Vice President/Senior Managing Director
Education: BA, International Relations, University of California; MBA, Finance, Anderson School of Management, UCLA
Background: Solomon Smith Barney
Mark Lydon, Managing Director
Education: BS, Electrical Engineering, California Polytechnic State University
Background: Dialogic Corporation; Engineer, IBM

1010 INTELLECTUAL VENTURES
3150 139th Avenue SE
Building 4
Bellevue, WA 98005

Phone: 425-467-2300
e-mail: info@intven.com
web: www.intellectualventures.com

Mission Statement: Pioneer in the invention capital market with one of the world's largest intellectual property portfolios.

Geographic Preference: Global
Fund Size: $6 billion
Founded: 2000
Industry Group Preference: Invention
Portfolio Companies: Echodyne Corp., Evolv Technologies, Kymeta, TerraPower

Other Locations:
7 Harcourt Street
Dublin 2
Ireland
Phone: 353 0 1 472 0100 **Fax:** 353 1 475 85 82

Intellectual Ventures Lab
14360 SE Eastgate way
Bellevue, WA 98007
Phone: 425-691-3353

19620 Stevens Creek Boulevard
Suite 270
Cupertino, CA 95014
Phone: 650-397-3100

Key Executives:
Nathan Myhrvold, Founder & Chief Executive Officer
Education: UCLA; Princeton University; Cambridge University
Background: Microsoft
Edward Jung, Founder
Background: Deep Thought Group; Microsoft

Peter Detkin, Founder
Education: University of Pennsylvania
Background: Wilson Sonsini
Directorships: Brady Campaign and Center to Prevent Gun Violence

1011 INTERLACE VENTURES
New York, NY 10003

e-mail: hello@interlacevc.com
web: interlaceventures.com

Mission Statement: Interlace Ventures is focused on technology serving the Commerce sector.

Founded: 2019
Average Investment: $200,000 - $600,000
Minimum Investment: $200,000
Industry Group Preference: Consumer, Commerce, Retail, Technology, Artificial Intelligence
Portfolio Companies: Algopix, B8ta, BlueFox.io, Cargo, For Days, French Founders, Goodeed, Hyphen, Oliver, OTO Systems Inc., Presence AI, SelfMade, Senders, Skip

Key Executives:
Vincent Diallo, Managing Partner
Background: Co-Founder, Bleu Capital; CFO, Sinodis; Auditor, Deloitte
Joseph Sartre, Managing Partner
Background: Partner, Bleu Capital; Finance Manager, Evian Asia Pacific; Finance Manager, MinuteBuzz

1012 INTERNATIONAL FINANCE CORPORATION (IFC)
2121 Pennsylvania Avenue NW
NW Washington, DC 20433

web: www.ifc.org

Mission Statement: Promotes sustainable private sector investment in developing countries as a way to reduce poverty and improve people's lives.

Geographic Preference: Worldwide
Fund Size: $2.45 Billion
Founded: 1956
Average Investment: $50.5 Million
Minimum Investment: $1 Million
Industry Group Preference: Agribusiness, Financial Services, Healthcare, Information Technology, Infrastructure, Oil & Gas, Mining, Chemicals, Education, Communications
Portfolio Companies: Arcor Group, Armenia Tomato, Asia Opportunity Fund LP, Baku Coca-Cola Bottlers II, Ciment Blanc d'Algerie, Fushe Kruje Cement, Haripur Power Project, Kabul Serena Hotel, Olam-Africa, LaFarge Surma Cement, Nova Cimangola

Key Executives:
Makhtar Diop, Managing Director
Education: University of Warwick
Background: World Bank

1013 INTERSOUTH PARTNERS
4711 Hope Valley Road
Suite 4F-632
Durham, NC 27707

Phone: 919-493-6640
web: www.intersouth.com

Mission Statement: One of the most active and experienced early-stage venture funds in the Southeast, having invested in more than 75 private companies over the last twenty years.

Geographic Preference: Southeast United States
Fund Size: $780 million
Founded: 1985
Average Investment: $500,000 to $6 million
Minimum Investment: $500,000
Investment Criteria: Early-Stage to Startup

Venture Capital & Private Equity Firms / Domestic Firms

Industry Group Preference: Life Sciences, Information Technology, Communications, Internet, Digital Media & Marketing, Semiconductors, Software, Biotechnology, Medical Technology, Pharmaceuticals
Portfolio Companies: 480 Biomedical, 6fusion, ABT Molecular Imaging, Accipiter, Accordant Health Systems, Adaptify, Advanced Animal Diagnostics, Advanced Biomarker Technologies, AGTC, Aldagen, Alimera Sciences, Applied Genetic Technologies, Argos Therapeutics, Arsenal Medical, Athenix, Azalea, Biolex Therapeutics, ArtiCure, Bright Hub, Burl Software, Calibra Medical, CallMiner, Cellective Therapeutics, Cempra Pharmaceuticals, Clarabridge, Comstock Systems Corporation, Covelight Systems, CSA Medical, Digital Optics, Encelle, Esanex, Extensibility, HexaTech, Infoglide Software, Innocrin, Insmed Inc., Inspire Pharmaceuticals, Integrated Silicon Systems, InvoiceLink, KAI Pharmaceuticals, Lambda Technologies, LOC-AID, Location Smart, Marathon Group, MaxCyte, Microchips Biotech, nContact, Neolinear, New River Innovation, Nitronex, NovaMin Technology, nTouch Research, OpenSite Technologies, Overture Networks, Paradigm Genetics, PeopleMatter, PharmaNetics, Proteon Therpeutics, Row Sham Bow, SciQuest, Semprius, Sentillion, Serenex, SimplifyMD, SmartPath, Snagajob, Sphinx Pharmaceuticals, SunPharm Corporation, TapRoot Systems, Trancept Systems, TransEnterix, Trinity Convergence, UOL Publishing, Vascular Pharmaceuticals, Viamet Pharmaceuticals, Zenoss, Zenph Sound Innovations, Ziptronix

Key Executives:
Dennis Dougherty, Founding Partner
e-mail: dennis@intersouth.com
Education: BA, Oklahoma City University; Postgraduate, Accounting & Finance, Duke University
Background: Office Managing Partner, Accounting Firm
Mitch Mumma, Member Manager
e-mail: mm@intersouth.com
Education: AB, Management Science, Duke University
Background: Manager, Touche Ross & Co.

1014 INTERWEST PARTNERS
2710 Sand Hill Road
Suite 200
Menlo Park, CA 94025

Phone: 650-854-8585 Fax: 650-854-4706
e-mail: info@interwest.com
web: www.interwest.com

Mission Statement: InterWest provides valuable industry, strategic, and corporate development expertise, as well as venture capital, to help young life sciences and IT companies succeed.

Geographic Preference: United States
Fund Size: $650 million
Founded: 1979
Average Investment: $10-15 million
Minimum Investment: $10 million
Investment Criteria: Early-Stage
Industry Group Preference: Information Technology, Healthcare
Portfolio Companies: AGTC, Alt12Apps, Alvine Pharmaceuticals, AMEC, AppMesh, Arcion Therapeutics, Aria, Aryaka, Autonomic Technologies, Badgeville, Biba, Brite Semiconductor, C3 Energy, C9, Carbylan Biosurgery, Cardiac Dimensions, Cebix, Convery Computer, Damballa, Doximity, Drais, Eiger, Empowered, Exalt, Fluidigm, Flurry, GainFitness, Get Satisfaction, Glaukos, Gobiquity Mobile Health, Gojee, Gynesonics, Hangtime, HireArt, iDoneThis, Indi, Invidi, InVisage, Invuity, Joyus, Knotch, Labrys Biologics, Locbox, Lycera, MacroGenics, Marketo, Microfabrica, Mobee, Neuronetics, NeuroPace, NewsCred, NexPlanner, Nuventix, Obalon, Ocera, OnDemand Therapeutics, Optimizely, Pelican Imaging, Pivot, PMW Pharma, PrimeraDx, Quantance, QuatRx, RadioRx, Restoration Robotics, Revision Optics, Sera Prognotics, Splice Machine, Spredfast, Swell, TapJoy, Tesaro, TheRealReal, Transcept, Triposo, USDS, Vendavo, Vidora, Welltok, Xenon, Xirrus

Key Executives:
Flip Gianos, Managing Director, Information Technology
e-mail: flip@interwest.com
Education: BS, Stanford University; MBA, Harvard University
Background: Engineering Manager, IBM
Directorships: Xilinx, T/R Systems
Gil Kliman, Managing Director, Healthcare
e-mail: gkliman@interwest.com
Education: BA, Harvard University; MD, University of Pennsylvania; MBA, Stanford University
Background: LCA Vision; Aris Vision Laser; Norwest VC
Arnie Oronsky, Managing Director, Healthcare
e-mail: aoronsky@interwest.com
Education: BS, New York's University College; PhD, Columbia University's College of Physicians and Surgeons
Background: VP, Drug Discovery, Lederle Lab Division
Directorships: Corixa Corporation, BioTransplant
Khaled Nasr, Partner & COO
Education: BA & MA, Mathematics, Social & Political Sciences, Cambridge University
Background: Alta Partners; President, FlowWise Networks; General Manager, Ipsilon; COO, Advanced Computer Communications
Directorships: Exalt Communications, Gear6, InVisage Technologies, NexPlanar, Xirrus
Stephen Holmes, General Partner Emeritus
Education: BS, Business Administration, Lehigh University; MBA, Harvard Graduate School of Business Administration
Background: Vice President, Finance & Administration, Specialty Brands
Directorships: National Venture Capital Association; International Private Equity & Venture Capital Valuation Guidelines Board
Keval Desai, Partner, Information Technology
Education: BE, Electrical Engineering, University of Mumbai; MS, Computer Science, UC Santa Barbara; MBA, Haas School of Business, UC Berkeley
Background: Director, Product Management, Google; Vice President, Digg
Doug Fisher, Partner, Healthcare
Education: Stanford University; University of Pennsylvania School of Medicine; Wharton School
Background: The Boston Consulting Group; New Leaf Venture Partners
Directorships: Gynesonics; Indi Molecular; Obalon Therapeutics; QuatRx
Drew Harman, Director
Education: Harvard University; INSEAD
Background: TradingDynamics; Ariba
Karen Wilson, Chief Financial Officer
Education: University of California, Berkeley
Background: Frank, Rimerman & Co.

1015 INVENCOR
San Francisco, CA

Phone: 415-531-5003 Fax: 707-257-2196
e-mail: information@invencor.com
web: www.invencor.com

Mission Statement: A seed and early-stage equity provider with an investment focus on high growth rate business opportunities in its prime target markets. An active co-investor and leverages investment opportunities in the ever present gap between the angel investors and larger venture funds.

Geographic Preference: Silicon Valley, Southeast
Founded: 1997
Investment Criteria: Seed, Early Stage, Mezzanine
Portfolio Companies: 4Charity.com, AdOn Network, Arcanvs, AssistGuide, Bioreason, Cardax Pharmaceuticals,

Venture Capital & Private Equity Firms / Domestic Firms

Hawaii Biotech, HotU, Kona Bay Marine Resources, Lumidigm, MyGeek.com, NAPO Pharmaceuticals, Perimeter Labs, Sandpiper Software

Key Executives:
Debra Guerin Beresini, President
e-mail: debra@invencor.com
Education: Dominican College; Global Biotechnology Program, University of California, Berkeley
Background: AR&D Corp; Ford/US Leasing; Hambrecht & Quist; Technology Funding; Senior VP/Manager National Division, Silicon Valley Bank
Kirk Westbrook, President/Chief Financial Officer
e-mail: kirk@invencor.com
Education: San Jose State University
Background: VP, Silicon Valley Bank
Directorships: Hawaii Venture Capital Association; HiBEAM
Richard Harding, Managing Partner
e-mail: richard@invencor.com
Education: BA, University of Montana; Graduate International Management, American Graduate School; MBA, Golden Gate University
Background: Managing Committee, Silicon Valley Bank; First Interstate Bank; American Express International Banking Corporation
Directorships: Founder, Santa Fe Venture Partners; Concise Logic Systems, Lumidigm, Access Anytime Bancorporation/First Bank of New Mexico

1016 INVENT
1930 Ocean Avenue
Suite 305
Santa Monica, CA 90405

web: www.invent.vc

Mission Statement: Invent VC is the only public company in the US that is focused exclusively on building tech startups. The Invent structure provides stakeholders with access to early-stage venture capital through their curated and actively managed portfolio of technology businesses.

Geographic Preference: United States
Average Investment: up to $250,000
Investment Criteria: Early-Stage, Pre-Seed
Industry Group Preference: Technology
Portfolio Companies: Revenue.Com, Sanguine Biosciences

Key Executives:
Demetrios Mallios, Chief Executive Officer
Alan D. Lewis II, Chief Operating Officer

1017 INVENTUS
400 S El Camino Real
Suite 700
San Mateo, CA 94402

Phone: 650-292-2530 Fax: 650-292-2570
e-mail: jk@inventuscap.com
web: www.inventuscap.com

Mission Statement: We seek to support entrepreneurs, first and foremost. Particularly those building disruptive digital services businesses, often integrating consumer or business software into a technology-enabled service. While products have dominated past waves of technology innovation, the industry is in the midst of a transformation from product to service-led businesses. Our team has a highly relevant entrepreneurial and operating background combined with two decades of success partnering with Silicon Valley and Indian entrepreneurs accessing India's natural advantages in adding value to digital services businesses.

Geographic Preference: United States, India
Founded: 1993
Average Investment: $1 - $10 million
Industry Group Preference: Digital Media & Marketing, SaaS, Consumer Internet, Media, Mobile, Technology-Enabled Services, E-Commerce & Manufacturing, Advertising, Software, Financial Services, Communications, Healthcare, Education, Mobile Apps
Portfolio Companies: Aasaan Jobs, Activity Hero, Assured Risk Cover, Avaz, Cbazaar, Credit Sesame, Dhingana, Disco, eDreams Edusoft, Espresso Logic, Farfaria, Funds India, Genwi, Healthify Me, Insta Health Solutions, IntelliVision, Knolskape, Motivo, MoveInSync, Next, Peel-Works, Policy Bazaar, Poshmark, Power2sme, Redbus.in, Resilinc, Savaari Car Rentals, Sensy, Sierra Atlantic, Spotzot Mobile Shopping, Sokrati, StatX, Sys Cloud, Tricog, Truebil, Unbxd, Vivu, Vizury

Other Locations:
Inventus Advisory Service
1st Floor, G.R. Primus
69-1, 1st Cross, Domlur (near Post Office)
Bangalore 560 071
India
Phone: 91-80-4125-6747

Key Executives:
Kanwal Rekhi, Managing Director
Education: BSEE, IIT-Bombay; MSEE, Business & Engineering, Michigan Tech
Background: Co-Founder, Excelan; CEO, Ensim; CEO, Cybermedia
Directorships: Assured Risk Cover, Espresso Logic, GenWi, Funds India, Intellivision, Poshmark, Sierra Atlantic, Statx
Manu Rekhi, Managing Director
Education: BS, Boston University; MBA, Columbia Business School & Haas School of Business
Background: VP, Products, NewsCorp Digital Division; Lolapps; Google
Directorships: Credit Sesame, Dhingana, FarFaria, Genwi, Growbot, Spotzot, Vivu, NextForce
John Dougery, Managing Director
Education: BA, University of California, Berkeley; MBA, Haas School of Business
Background: Sun Microsystems, IBM, Mircosoft, Intel
Directorships: Activity Hero, Credit Sesame, Dhingana, Motiva, Reslinc, Sokrati, Spotzot, Syscloud, Vivu
Samir Kumar, Managing Director, India
Education: BSEE, Indian Institute of Technology; MBA, Indian Institute of Management
Background: Wipro, Acer Technology Ventures
Directorships: Cbazaar, Instahleath Solutions, MoveInSync, Savaari, Sokrati, Knolskape
Parag Dhol, Managing Director, India
Education: BSME, Indian Insitute of Technology; MBA, Indian Institute of Management
Background: Associate Director, Intel Capital
Directorships: Avaz. Funds India, Peel Works, Policy Bazaar, Power2sme, redBus, Tricog, Vizury
Rutvik Doshi, Managing Director, India
Education: BTech, Indian Institute of Technology; MBA, INSEAD
Background: Google; CEO, Taggle
Directorships: Aasaanjobs, Avaz, eDreams Education, HealthifyMe, Sensara, Syscloud, Truebil, Unbxd

1018 INVERNESS GRAHAM INVESTMENTS
3811 West Chester Pike
Building 2, Suite 100
Newtown Square, PA 19073

Phone: 610-722-0300 Fax: 610-251-2880
e-mail: myoung@invernessgraham.com
web: www.invernessgraham.com

Mission Statement: Inverness acquires high growth, innovative manufacturing and service companies through partnership with management and well executed building strategies.

Fund Size: $250 million
Founded: 1997

Venture Capital & Private Equity Firms / Domestic Firms

Investment Criteria: Buyouts, Recapitalizations, Divestitures
Industry Group Preference: Manufacturing, Business Products & Services
Portfolio Companies: Advanced Cath, B+B SmartWorx, Danville, DemandPoint, Energy Solutions International, Extrumed, Faxitron, Global ID Group, ICC Nexergy, Infiltrator Systems Inc., MarginPoint, Mesker, Nobles Worldwide, RacoWireless, SkyBitz, DataSource, GPS Trackit, Kalkomey, SmartFlow Technologies, Spirion, Swipeclock Workforce Management

Key Executives:
Kenneth A. Graham, Founder/Chairman
Education: BA, Dartmouth College; MBA, Amos Tuck School of Business
Background: Senior Vice President, Graham Packaging; Co-Founder, Media Stream
Directorships: Energy Solutions, ExtruMed, Faxitron, Infiltrator, ICCNexergy, SmartFlow, SkyBitz
Scott A. Kehoe, Founder/Managing Principal
Education: BA, Dartmouth College; MBA, Kellogg Graduate School of Management, Northwestern University
Background: President & CEO, MediaStream; Advisor, Graham Group Legacy Businesses; Senior Manager, Ernst & Young
Directorships: B&B Electronics, ExtruMed, Faxitron, Bioptics, TechDevice
Michael B. Morrissey, Managing Principal
Education: BA, University of Pennsylvania; MBA, Wharton School
Background: Vice President, Business Development, Audax Group
Directorships: B&B Electronics, Energy Solutions, FaxitronBioptics, Nobles, SmartFlow, TechDevice
Steven F. Wood, Founder/Vice Chairman
Education: BS, Connecticut State University; CFA
Background: Chairman & CEO, Graham Engineering Corporation; Senior Group Vice President & CFO, Graham Companies and Graham Packaging; Senior Manager, Ernst & Young
Directorships: B&B Electronics, DemandPoint, Energy Solutions, ExtruMed, Nexiant, ICCNexergy, TechDevice
Trey Sykes, Managing Principal
Education: BS, University of California, Berkeley; MBA, Wharton School, University of Pennsylvania
Background: GE Equity, Lehman Brothers Venture Partners, Houlihan Lokey Howard & Zukin
Directorships: ElectriTek AVT, Nexergy

1019 INVESCO PRIVATE CAPITAL
Two Peachtree Pointe
1555 Peachtree Street NE
Suite 1800
Atlanta, GA 30309

Phone: 404-892-0896
e-mail: contactus@invesco.com
web: www.invesco.com

Mission Statement: A private equity firm backing industry leading venture, buyout and other private equity firms and investing directly in private venture capital companies.
Geographic Preference: United States, Worldwide
Fund Size: $3 billion
Founded: 1982
Average Investment: $20 million
Minimum Investment: $10 million
Investment Criteria: Early and Expansion Stage
Industry Group Preference: Information Technology, Life Sciences, E-Commerce & Manufacturing, Communications, Infrastructure

Key Executives:
Marty Flanagan, President & CEO
Education: BBA, Southern Methodist University
Background: EVP/COO, Templeton, Galbraith & Hansberger; Co-President/COO/CFO, Franklin Resources, Inc.

1020 INVESTAMERICA VENTURE GROUP
101 2nd Street SE
Suite 800
Cedar Rapids, IA 52401

Phone: 319-363-8249 **Fax:** 319-363-9683
web: www.investamericaventure.com

Mission Statement: InvestAmerica is a private equity and venture capital management group investing in management buyouts, ownership changes and later-stage growth opportunities. Formerly known as InvestAmerica Investment Advisors.
Geographic Preference: United States
Fund Size: $44 million
Founded: 1985
Average Investment: $1 - $2 million
Minimum Investment: $1 million
Investment Criteria: Management buy-outs, Particular interest in later-stage companies; sales revenues between $10-$50 million
Industry Group Preference: High Technology, Manufacturing, Distribution, Service Industries

Other Locations:
10000 NE 7th Avenue
Suite 330H
Vancouver, WA 98685
Phone: 360-573-5067 **Fax:** 360-573-7462

51 Broadway
Suite 500
Fargo, ND 58102
Phone: 701-298-0003 **Fax:** 701-293-7819

911 Main Street
Commerce Tower
Suite 2424
Kansas City, MO 64105
Phone: 816-842-0114 **Fax:** 816-471-7339

801 Nicollet Mall
Suite 1700W
P.O. Box 2289
Minneapolis, MN 55402
Phone: 651-632-2140

Key Executives:
David R. Schroder, President
319-363-8249
Fax: 319-363-9683
e-mail: david@investam.com
Education: BSFS, Georgetown University; MBA, University of Wisconsin
Background: President, Director, MorAmerica Capital Corporation; VP, Kentucky Highlands Investment Corporation
Robert A. Comey, Executive Vice President
319-363-8249
Fax: 319-363-9683
e-mail: rcomey@investam.com
Education: BA, Economics, Brown University; MBA, Fordham University
Background: Executive VP/Director, MorAmerica Capital Corporation; VP, RIHT Capital Corporation; President, Tower Ventures
Kevin F. Mullane, Senior Vice President
816-842-0114
Fax: 816-471-7339
e-mail: kmullane@investam.com
Education: BSBA, MBA, Rockhurst College
Background: Senior VP, MorAmerica Capital Corporation
Michael H. Reynoldson, Vice President
360-573-5067
Fax: 360-573-7462

e-mail: jcosgriffe@fedc.com
Education: MBA, Finance, University of Iowa; BSBA, Washington State University
Background: Price Waterhouse; Co-Founder, Iowa-Based Fund Company
John G. Cosgriff, Manager
701-298-0003
Education: BS, Business Economics; MS, Economics, North Dakota State University
Background: US Small Business Administration, Minnesota State Univesity, Moorhead

1021 INVESTCORP
280 Park Avenue
New York, NY 10017

Phone: 212-599-4700 **Fax:** 212-983-7073
e-mail: info@investcorp.com
web: www.investcorp.com

Mission Statement: To select and arrange private equity investments in mid to large size companies with capable managers, prominent positions in their industries, a strong track record and potential growth.

Geographic Preference: North America, Western Europe
Fund Size: $2.1 billion
Founded: 1982
Investment Criteria: Company value of $100 million-$1 billion, mid-size, a good established track record, can operate in almost any industry sector
Industry Group Preference: Diversified
Portfolio Companies: Impero, Ageras, Calligo, AlixPartners, Arrowhead, Agromillora, Corneliani, The Wrench Group, SecureLink, NDT CCS, Nobel Learning Communities, Dainese, Arvento, PRO Unlimited, SPGPrints Group B.V., Totes ISOTONER, Namet, AYTB, Paper Source, Leejam, Theeb, Hydrasun, Georg Jensen, Automak Automotive Company, Orka Group, Esmalglass, Archway Marketing Services, Wazee Digital, Sur La Table, Eviivo, Tiryaki Agro, OpSec, Gulf Cryo, L'Azurde, CEME, Kgb, Magnum Semiconductor, TelePacific, Optiv, Fleetmatics, Kentrox, IPH Group, Tyrrells, Armacell, Mania Technologies, Stratus Technologies, CCC, FleetPride, InnerWireless, Mobileway, GL Education Group, Skrill, Moody International, Avecia, Associated Materials, Aero Products, Aurora Systems, Wells-CTI, Veritext, Sophos, American Tire, CSIdentity, Spectel, N&W, Redington Gulf, Platform Solutions, TDX, Asiakastieto, Welcome Break, Randall-Reilly, Softek, Berlin Packaging, Trema, Icopal, Harborside Healthcare, APCOA, Helly Hensen, Hilding Anders, Aspective, Dialogic, Minimax, Stahl, Saks Inc., Autodistribution, ObjectStar, PortalPlayer, US Unwired, Polyconcept, Utimaco, Gerresheimer, ECI, SourceMedia, CSK Auto, Taqua, MW Manufacturers, ZettaCom, Zeta Interactive, Atrenta, Willtek, Neptune, Jostens, 4th Pass, Acta, Carter's, Leica, Main Street Dairy, Chaumet, Falcon, Ebel, SI Corp., Breguet, Star Market, Simmons, Prime Equipment, Dellwood, Circle K, Gucci, Thorn Lighting, Ny Department Stores, Sports & Recreation, Catherines, Fox Photo,

Other Locations:
48 Grosvenor Street
London W1K 3HW
United Kingdom
Phone: 44 (0)20 7629 6600 **Fax:** 44 (0)20 7499 0371

Investcopr House
P.O. Box 5340
Manama
Bahrain
Phone: 973-17-532-000 **Fax:** 973-17-530-816

Qatar Financial Centre - Tower 1
Suite 701
West Bay Area - P.O. Box 24995
Doha
Qatar
Phone: 974-4496-0381 **Fax:** 974-4435-2750

Al Faisaliah Tower
29th Floor
P.O. Box 61992
Riyadh 11575
Saudi Arabia
Phone: 966-11-484-7600 **Fax:** 966-11-273-0771

10 Marina Boulevard
#14-04
Marina Bay Financial Centre Tower 2
Singapore 018983
Phone: 65 69115300

Key Executives:
Mohammed Alardhi, Executive Chairman
Education: BS, Military Science, Royal Air Force UK Staff College; MA, Public Pilicy, John F. Kennedy School of Government, Harvard University
Hazem Ben-Gacem, Co-Chief Executive Officer
Education: BA, Harvard University
Background: Credit Suisse First Boston; Chairman, Corneliani; Chairman, Georg Jensen; Vice-Chair, Dainese
Rishi Kapoor, Co-Chief Executive Officer
Education: BS, Electrical/Computer Engineering, Indian Institute of Technology; MBA, Duke University
Background: CFO, Citigroup
Firas El Amine, Head of Corporate Communications
Education: BA, Communication Arts, Beirut University College; MA, Political Science, Lebanese American University
Background: Corporate Communications Director, Dubai Holdings; Public Relations Director, Alsalam Holding; Public Relations Director, Impact & Echo

1022 INVUS GROUP
750 Lexington Avenue
30th Floor
New York, NY 10022

Phone: 212-371-1717 **Fax:** 212-371-1829
e-mail: nyoffice@invus.com
web: www.invus.com

Mission Statement: Invus looks for transformational opportunities where we can partner with owner-managers to create extraordinary business performance and enjoy the resulting financial rewards. Given this high bar and our small team, we are very selective about the companies with which we get involved. We only make a handful of sizable investments each year.

Geographic Preference: United States, Europe
Investment Criteria: Turnarounds, Growth Capital, Expansion-Stage
Industry Group Preference: Consumer Products, Consumer Services, Food & Beverage, Specialty Retail, Software, Biotechnology, Medical Devices
Portfolio Companies: Avantec Vascular, Blue Buffalo, Bluemercury, The Grow Network, Harry's, Keebler, OdontoPrev, Provalliance-Franck Provost, Weight Watchers

Other Locations:
275 Grove Street
Suite 2-400
Newton, MA 02466
Phone: 617-663-4917

2nd Floor Lansdowne House
57 Berkeley Square
London W1J 6ER
United Kingdom
Phone: 44-20-7493-9133 **Fax:** 44-20-7518-9629

21, Avenue Kléber
Paris 75116

Venture Capital & Private Equity Firms / Domestic Firms

France
Phone: 33-1-56-90-50-00 **Fax:** 33-1-56-90-50-10

22/F, St. George's Building
2 Ice House St.
Central
Hong Kong
Phone: 852-3758-2536 **Fax:** 852-3105-0358

Key Executives:
Raymond Debbane, President/CEO
Education: BS, Agricultural Sciences & Agricultural Engineering, American University of Beirut; MBA, Stanford Graduate School of Business
Background: CEO, Artal Group; Manager, Boston Consulting Group
Christopher Sobecki, Managing Director
Education: BS, Engineering, Purdue University; MBA, Harvard Business School
Background: Engineer, Eastman Kodak Company
Philippe Amouyal, Managing Director
Education: MS, Engineering, DEA, Management, Ecole Centrale de Paris
Background: Vice President & Director, Boston Consulting Group; Research Fellow, Center for Policy Alternatives, MIT
Jonas Fajgenbaum, Managing Director
Education: BS, Wharton School; BA, Economics, University of Pennsylvania
Background: Management Consultant, McKinsey & Company
Aflalo Guimaraes, Managing Director
Education: BA, Economics & Political Science, Yale University; MBA, Wharton School
Background: Manager, Marakon Associates; Federal Reserve
Evren Bilimer, Managing Director
Education: BS, Electrical Engineering & Economics, Yale University
Background: Management Consultant, McKinsey & Company
Benjamin Felt, Managing Director
Education: BA, Economics, Yale University
Background: Management Consultant, The Boston Consulting Group

1023 IRISH ANGELS
Chicago, IL

web: www.irishangels.com

Mission Statement: Founded in September 2012, the new IrishAngels investing group is dedicated to furthering startup growth through early stage investments in which a founder, Board member, or investor is a student, graduate, parent, or faculty member at the University of Notre Dame.

Founded: 2012
Average Investment: under $3 million
Investment Criteria: Notre Dame Affiliation; Seed-Stage, Series A
Industry Group Preference: Internet, Mobile, Healthcare, Social Enterprises, Software, Enterprise Software, Cloud Computing, Manufacturing, Retailing, Business Products & Services
Portfolio Companies: AgenDx, Appcast, Ash & Erie, Baby Scripts, Blue Triangle, Caretaker Medical, CargoSense, Catalyst Orthosience, Chime, Coolfire Solutions, Elevate K-12, Emu Technology, Hatfield & McCoy Whiskey, Kidizen, Genomenon, Groupsense.io, Margin Edge, Micro-LAM, The Mom Project, myCOI, Nurture Life, PageVault, Pattern89, The Renewal Workshop, Rivet Smart Audio, Rivs Digital Interviews, Shot Tracker, Superstar Games, Techstars, Trading View, UpCity, Vagabond, Vapogenix, Vennli, Wolf & Shepherd, Zipfit Denim

Key Executives:
Gale Bowman, Managing Director
Education: BBA, University of Notre Dame; MBA, University of Chicago Booth School of Business
Background: Nielsen; Orbitz.com
Kaitlyn Doyle, Director
Education: BBA, University of Notre Dame; MBA, University of Chicago Booth School of Business
Caroline Yeager, Analyst
Education: BBA, Boston College; MSM, University of Notre Dame

1024 IRON GATE CAPITAL
842 W South Boulder Road
Suite 200
Louisville, CO 80027

Phone: 303-395-1335
e-mail: info@irongatecapital.com
web: www.irongatecapital.com

Mission Statement: Iron Gate Capital is a private equity firm seeking to invest in growth stage companies and assist those businesses in realizing their growth plans.

Founded: 2005
Average Investment: $1 - $5 million
Investment Criteria: Growth Stage
Industry Group Preference: Business to Business, Services, Energy, Healthcare, Real Estate, Retail, Consumer & Leisure
Portfolio Companies: AcuStream, Branded Online, CPX Lone Tree Hotel, Encino Energy, HZO, Kapost, MBH Enterprises, Meritage Energy, Northeastern Ohio Energy Hotel Fund, Smashburger, Syncardia Systems, Techstars

Key Executives:
Doug Fahoury, Founder/Managing Partner
Education: BS, Business Administration, Colorado State University; MBA, California State University, Sacramento
Background: CIO & Principal, Inventure Partners; VP, iBelay; VP, Tango Partners; VP, Consumer Products & Business Development, Exactis.com; Founder & Managing Director, McNatt, Douglas & Co.
Ryan Pollock, Managing Partner
Education: University of Cape Town; Univ. of Oxford; MBA, University of Texas, Austin
Background: Managing Director, Meritage Funds; Investec Asset Management
Directorships: Rocky Mountain Venture Capital Association
Steve McConahey, Co-Founder/Partner
Education: University of Wisconsin; MBA, Harvard Business School
Background: Chairman, SGM Capital; President & COO, EVEREN Securities, EVEREN Capital; President, Kemper Securities
Directorships: Cal Dak International, Great-West Funds, IMA Financial Group, Guaranty BanCorp
Rob Cohen, Co-Founder/Partner
Education: University of Texas, Austin
Background: CEO, IMA Financial Group; Chubb and Son
Directorships: USR, ccintellect

1025 IRONWOOD CAPITAL
45 Nod Road
Suite 2
Avon, CT 06001-3819

Phone: 860-409-2100
web: www.ironwoodcap.com

Mission Statement: Ironwood Capital is a private equity firm based in Connecticut. The firm targets middle market companies and provides growth capital in addition to operational and strategic support.

Fund Size: $300 million
Average Investment: $5 - $20 million
Investment Criteria: Leveraged Buyouts, Growth Financings, Recapitalizations
Industry Group Preference: Business Products & Services, Consumer Products, Education, Environment Products &

Services, Healthcare, Manufacturing, Distribution, Aerospace, Defense and Government
Portfolio Companies: Acelero Learning, Action Carting, Advanced Recycling Systems, Capewell Holdings, City Carting Holding, Curtis Bay Energy, Dancing Deer Baking, Diamond Packaging, DocuLynx, Femco Machine, Fiber-Line, FitLinxx, Flow-Dry, Gold Medal Services, Healthtrax, Hobbs Bonded Fibers, Imperial Machining, iPacesetters, Joliet Equipment, Katahdin Industries, The Learning Experience, MedVantx, Morgan Contracting, My Alarm Center, NEBC, New England Linen, Numet Machining, Pharmaceutic Litho & Label Company, Professional Rental Tools, Red River Waste Solutions, RM Techtronics, Roberts Company, Rostra Tool Company, St. George Warehouse, Tidewater Equipment Company, Tulip Molded Plastics

Key Executives:
Marc Reich, Chairman/Chief Executive Officer
860-409-2101
e-mail: reich@ironwoodcap.com
Education: University of California, Los Angeles; MBA, University of Connecticut
Background: Chairman, Greater Bristol Realty Corporation; Investment Banking, Aetna

Carolyn Galiette, President/Chief Investment Officer
860-409-2105
e-mail: galiette@ironwoodcap.com
Education: BA, English, Dartmouth College
Background: Investment Professional, Aetna; Investment Banking, PaineWebber

Roger Roche, Senior Managing Director
860-409-2129
e-mail: roche@ironwoodcap.com
Education: BS, Accounting & Finance, Babson College
Background: SVP & Managing Director, BankBoston; SwingBridge Capital
Directorships: Action Carting, FEMCO Machine, Tulip Corporation, Katahdin Industries, New England Linen Supply, High Hopes Therapeutic Riding

Victor Budnick, Senior Managing Director
860-409-2108
e-mail: budnick@ironwoodcap.com
Education: Yale University; Harvard Law School; Yale School of Management
Background: President & Executive Director, Connecticut Innovations

Jim Barra, Managing Director
860-409-2113
e-mail: barra@ironwoodcap.com
Education: Bryant University; MBA, University of Connecticut
Background: President, Northeast Regional Association of Small Business Investor Alliance
Directorships: Medport, Advanced Concrete, Genesis Solutions, Columbus House

Dickson Suit, Managing Director
860-409-2128
e-mail: suit@ironwoodcap.com
Education: Brown University; MBA, Columbia Business School
Background: Investment Manager, Environmental Opportunities Fund; Pitney Bowes; PricewaterhouseCoopers
Directorships: Action Carting Environmental Services, VLS Recovery Services

Alex Levental, Managing Director
860-409-2109
e-mail: levental@ironwoodcap.com
Education: BA, Economics & Russian Literature, Colby College
Background: VP, Market Development & Strategic Planning, CCA Global Partners; Analyst, Morgan Stanley; Associate, Advent International
Directorships: Merrill Industries

1026 IRVING PLACE CAPITAL
745 Fifth Avenue
New York, NY 10151

Phone: 212-551-4500
e-mail: info@irvingplacecapital.com
web: www.irvingplacecapital.com

Mission Statement: A private equity firm focused on making equity investments in middle-market companies. The firm partners with talented managers, providing them with the resources they need to sustain growth, build world-class companies and unlock value.

Geographic Preference: North America
Fund Size: $2.7 billion
Founded: 1997
Average Investment: $50 - $250 million
Investment Criteria: Growth Capital, Corporate Divestitures, Byouts, Recapitalizations, Build-Ups, Public-To-Private Transactions
Industry Group Preference: Retail, Consumer & Leisure, Consumer Products, Consumer Services, Industrial Products, Packaging
Portfolio Companies: Alpha Packaging, Bendon, Coker Tire, Dynojet, Mold-Rite Plastics, New York & Company, Rag & Bone

Key Executives:
John Howard, Co-Managing Partner
Education: BA, Trinity College; MBA, Yale School of Management
Background: Co-CEO, Vestar Capital Partners; SVP & Partner, Wesray Capital Corporation
Directorships: Bendon, New York & Co., Rag & Bone, Aeropostale, Dots, Integrated Circuit Systems, Multi Packaging Solutions, Nice-Pak Holdings

Phil Carpenter III, Co-Managing Partner
Education: BS, State University of New York, Binghamton
Background: Brockway Moran & Partners; Bear Stearns & Co.
Directorships: Alpha Packaging Holdings, Dynojet Research, Mold-Rite Plastics, Multi Packaging Solutions, Ohio Transmission Corp., Reddy Ice, Chesapeake

Blake Austin, Principal, Strategic Services
Education: BS, Indiana University
Directorships: Alaris Consulting

David Knoch, Partner/Head of Strategic Services
Education: BBA, MBA, Loyola University of Chicago
Background: Senior Managing Director, Chief Administrative Officer, Alaris Consulting

Bob Bode, Principal, Strategic Services
Education: BBA, University of Iowa; MS, Stuart School of Business, Illinois Institute of Technology
Background: Principal, The Keystone Group; Consultant, Alaris Consulting; Consultant, Crowe Chizek

Paul Lehman, Senior Advisor
Education: BA, Vassar College; MBA, Harvard Business School
Background: COBB Tuning; Edge Products; Bear Stearns Merchant Banking

Michael Hyatt, Senior Advisor
Education: BA, Syracuse University; JD, Emory University School of Law
Background: Senior Managing Director, Bear Stearns & Co.

Joe El Chami, Principal
Education: BS, State University of New York, Binghamton; MBA, Wharton School, University of Pennsylvania
Background: Analyst, Merrill Lynch

Devraj Roy, Partner
Education: BA, Yale University; MBA, Columbia Business School
Background: Associate, Parthenon Capital
Directorships: Caribbean Financial Group Holdings, Pet Supplies Plus Holdings, Ohio Transmission Corp.

Venture Capital & Private Equity Firms / Domestic Firms

Keith Zadourian, Partner
Education: AB, Dartmouth College; MBA, Columbia Business School
Background: Associate, Veritas Capital Management
Directorships: Alpha Packaging Holdings, Chesapeake Holdings, Mold-Rite Plastics, Mold-Rite Plastics, Chromalox

1027 J. BURKE CAPITAL PARTNERS
655 Madison Avenue
25th Floor
New York, NY 10065

web: www.jburkecapital.com

Mission Statement: A private equity firm investing in a wide range of small to mid-size companies.

Average Investment: $3 - $30 million
Investment Criteria: Corporate or Large Spin Offs, Leveraged Recapitalizations, Generational Sales, Industry Consolidations, Under-Performing Companies, Special Situations
Industry Group Preference: Education, Financial Services, Business Products & Services, Consumer Services, Manufacturing, Retail, Consumer & Leisure, Environment Products & Services, Healthcare, Food & Beverage
Portfolio Companies: Apique, Command Health, Leading Edge Innovations, VariBlend Dual Dispensing Systems, Verity Wine Partners

Key Executives:
James J. Burke Jr., Founder
Education: BA, Brown University; MBA, Harvard Business School
Background: Senior Partner & Co-Founder, Stonington Partnerse
Directorships: Ann Taylor Stores Corporation, Lincoln Education Services Corporation
Eric Lauerwald, Partner
Education: BS, Mechanical Engineering, Union College; MBA, Columbia Business School
Background: Principal, Arena Capital Partners; Associate Principal, Churchill Equity & Industrial Equity Partners
Christopher Delaney, Portfolio Manager
Education: BA, Economics, Williams College; MBA, Darden School of Business, University of Virginia
Background: Fixed Income & Commodity Trader, Lehman Brothers

1028 JACKSON SQUARE VENTURES
727 Sansome St.
Suite 300
San Francisco, CA 94111

Phone: 415-229-7100
e-mail: info@jsv.com
web: www.jsv.com

Mission Statement: Jackson Square Ventures is a small venture capital firm leading seed And Series A deaks in SaaS and marketplace companies.

Investment Criteria: Seed, Series A
Industry Group Preference: SaaS, Marketplaces, Consumer, Security, Storage, Enterprise
Portfolio Companies: Alien Vault, Alto Pharmacy, Atrium, Bus.com, Centrify, Contently, Cornershop, Crexi, Crownpeak, Demandbase, DigitalFuel, DocuSign, Doxo, Empyr, EqualLogic, Fortify, Hightail, Intacct, Jackbox Games, Jellyvision, Kace, Kindly Care, Lanetix, Marketlive, Mynd, OfferUp, Omniata, Plume, Rented, Responsys, ScanCafe, Seismic, Sparkcentral, Strava, Talking Blocks, Tapio, ToutApp, Upwork, Vormetric, Waterline Data, Zenput, Zetta

Key Executives:
Josh Breinlinger, Managing Director
e-mail: josh@jsv.com
Education: MIT
Background: oDesk; Rev; Adroll

Directorships: Omniata, OfferUp, rented.com, Contently, Kindly Care, Bus.com, Crexi, Atrium
Greg Gretsch, Managing Director
e-mail: greg@jsv.com
Directorships: Upwork, Responsysm Strava, Toutapp, Equallogic, Jellyvision, Jackbox Games, Sugarsync, Doxo, Talking Blocks
Pete Solvik, Managing Director
e-mail: pete@jsv.com
Directorships: Docusign, Centrify, KACE, Seismic, Topio, Lanetix, Mogl, Scancafe

1029 JAGUAR CAPITAL PARTNERS
PO Box 198
Haverford, PA 19041

Phone: 610-585-0285
web: www.jaguar-capital.com

Mission Statement: Jaguar Capital Partners is a private equity investment firm dedicated to investing in and building companies based in Europe, Asia and the United States.

Geographic Preference: Europe, Asia, United States
Investment Criteria: Early- to Expansion-Stage
Industry Group Preference: Technology, Media, Telecommunications, Financial Services
Portfolio Companies: Arcadian Networks, China Cablecom, Inveshare, Return on Intelligence, UNIRISX, Vizant Technologies

Key Executives:
Jonathan Kalman, Managing Partner
e-mail: jkalman@jaguar-capital.com
Education: BS, Applied Physics, Cornell University; MBA, Kellogg School of Management, Northwestern University
Background: Executive Chairman, UNIRISX; Chairman & CEO, Jaguar Acquisition Corporation; Founder & Managing Partner, Katalyst Venture Partners; IBM
Directorships: Vizant Technologies

1030 JANE VC
Cleveland, OH

e-mail: hello@janevc.com
web: www.janevc.com

Mission Statement: Mission is to invest in early-stage female-founded companies accross a variety of industries.

Geographic Preference: United States
Fund Size: $2 Million
Average Investment: $25,000 - $150,000
Minimum Investment: $25,000
Investment Criteria: Early Stage, Female Founded
Industry Group Preference: All Sectors Considered
Portfolio Companies: Akin, Hatch Apps, Kinside, Proformex, Sown To Grow

Key Executives:
Jennifer Keiser Neundorfer, Founding Partner
Education: BA, Harvard; MBA, Stanford University
Background: 21st Century Fox; YouTube
Maren Thomas Bannon, Founding Partner
Education: BA, Engineering, Dartmouth; MBA, Stanford University
Background: CEO/Co-Founder, LittleLane; Genentech

1031 JARVINIAN VENTURES
One International Place
Suite 1400
Boston, MA 02110

e-mail: info@jarvinian.com
web: www.jarvinian.com

Mission Statement: Jarvinian focuses exclusively on the wireless sector and seeks to support the development of wireless technologies.

Fund Size: $150 million

Venture Capital & Private Equity Firms / Domestic Firms

Average Investment: $1 - $5 million
Investment Criteria: Early Stage
Industry Group Preference: Wireless
Key Executives:
  John Dooley, Founder/Managing Director
  Background: Director, AWS Spectrum Bidco; Founder, Nanoton; FiberTower Corporation
  Tom Eddy, Managing Director
  Education: BS, University of Virginia; JD, Duquesne University School of Law; MBA, Harvard Business School
  Background: COO & Senior General Partner, Atlas Venture; Managing Director, Robertson Stephens & Company; VP, Technology Investment Banking Group, Morgan Stanley & Co.
  Directorships: First Marblehead Corporation

1032 JAVELIN VENTURE PARTNERS
221 Main Street
Suite 1300
San Francisco, CA 94105

Phone: 415-471-1300
web: www.javelinvp.com

Mission Statement: Javelin Venture Partners was founded by former entrepreneurs with a first-hand appreciation of what it takes to develop a company from concept to thriving enterprise.

Geographic Preference: Worldwide
Average Investment: $250,000 - $5 million
Minimum Investment: $250,000
Investment Criteria: Seed, Searies A
Industry Group Preference: Technology, Digital Media & Marketing, Internet, Mobile Communications Devices, Healthcare Information Technology
Portfolio Companies: 3scale, Appvance, Armory, Boost Media, Carbon Health, Clutter, Correlated Magnetics Research, Cyberrinc, Engrade, Estimote, ExecThread, Fair, Famo.us, FEM Inc., Filld, GameCo, ImageVision, Kidpass, KopoKopo, Linqia, Lithium, MasterClass, Netpulse, Nexenta, Niantic Labs, Nuvon, Overstat, Pixalate, Plug.dj, PowerCloud Systems, Prismatic, Rinse, Ritter Pharmaceuticals, Rixty, RxVantage, ScoutLabs, Seismos, Sense Networks, Skytree, Smartasset, Smartzip, Spotsetter, Telerivet, Thanx, The Hunt, Thumbtack, Trumaker, Vacatia, Weddington Way, WellnessFX

Key Executives:
  Noah J. Doyle, Managing Director
  e-mail: ndoyle@javelinvp.com
  Education: BA, Economics; MBA, University of California Berkeley
  Background: Co-Founder, MyPoints.com; Overseas Sales & Marketing, Matsushita's Communications
  Jed Katz, Managing Director
  e-mail: jkatz@javelinvp.com
  Education: BA, Business Economics, UCLA; MBA, Haas School of Business, University of California, Berkeley
  Background: Managing Director, DFJ Gotham Ventures; COO & Founder, Rent Net

1033 JAZZ VENTURE PARTNERS
123 South Park Street
San Francisco, CA 94107

e-mail: info@jazzvp.com
web: jazzvp.com

Mission Statement: Jazz VP seeks breakthroughs in digital technology and neuroscience that influence the human experience. They focus primarily on augumented reality, AI, immersive gaming and closed-loop human-computer systems.

Key Executives:
  John Harris, Managing Partner
  Education: BS, Stanford University; MBA, Northwestern University
  Background: Founder, Heartstream; Co-Founder, ClearFlow; Co-Founder, MDX Partners; Founder, President and CEO, NeuroVista
  Zack Lynch, Managing Partner
  Education: BS, MA, Univerity of California, Los Angelos
  Background: Founder, Neurotechnology Industry Organization; Author; Founder, Experential Technology and NeuroGaming Conference; Founder and CEO, NeuroInsights
  John Spinale, Managing Partner
  Education: Yale University
  Background: Founder, Bitmo; General Manager, Disney Interactive, Mobile and Social Games Division

1034 JB POINDEXTER & COMPANY
600 Travis Street
Suite 400
Houston, TX 77002

Phone: 713-655-9800 **Fax:** 713-951-9038
e-mail: info@jbpco.com
web: www.jbpoindexter.com

Mission Statement: JB Poindexter & Co. aquires companies from private owners and require additional financiaing or operating resources to develop and grow.

Geographic Preference: United States
Fund Size: $500 million
Founded: 1988
Minimum Investment: $2 million
Investment Criteria: Later Stage
Industry Group Preference: Transportation, Machinery, Metals, Industrial Equipment
Portfolio Companies: EFP Corp., MIC Group, Morgan Corp., Morgan Olson, Reading Truck Body, Specialty Vehicles Group, Truck Accessories Group

Key Executives:
  John Poindexter, Chairman/CEO
  e-mail: jpoindexter@jbpco.com
  Education: MBA/PhD in Economics and Finance, New York University
  Background: KD/P Equities; Smith Barney Capital Corporation; Salomon Brothers

1035 JC2 VENTURES
P.O. Box 10195
Dept. 12
Palo Alto, CA 94303

Phone: 650 762-5101
web: www.jc2ventures.com

Mission Statement: JC2 invests in and mentors startup companies dealing with digital technologies in the areas of digital communications, security, agricultural technology, internet, and more.

Geographic Preference: United States
Fund Size: $100 Million
Founded: 2018
Investment Criteria: Startup, Technology
Industry Group Preference: Security, Social Media, Agriculture Technologies, Technology, Internet
Portfolio Companies: Aspire Food Group, Balbix, Bloomenergy, Dedrone, IoTium, Lucideus, Opengov, Pindrop, Privoro, Rubrik, Sparkcognition, Sprinklr, Uniphore

Key Executives:
  John Chambers, CEO/Founder
  Education: BA, BSc, JD, West Virginia University; MBA, Finance/Management, Indiana University
  Background: Cisco

Venture Capital & Private Equity Firms / Domestic Firms

1036 JEFFERIES CAPITAL PARTNERS
520 Madison Avenue
Suite 11
New York, NY 10022

Phone: 212-284-1700
web: www.jefferies.com

Mission Statement: Jefferies provides insight, expertise, and execution to investors, companies and government entitites. The firm offers services in investment banking, equities, fixed income and wealth management.

Geographic Preference: North and South America, Europe, Middle East, Asia
Founded: 1967
Average Investment: $10 to $100 million
Minimum Investment: $10 million
Investment Criteria: LBO, MBO, Industry Consolidation, Recapitalization, Growth
Industry Group Preference: Consumer Products, Education, Energy, Financial Services, Healthcare, Manufacturing, Media, Telecommunications, Transportation, Restaurants, Distribution, Logistics

Key Executives:
Brian P. Friedman, President
Education: BS, Economics, MS, Accounting, Wharton School, University of Pennsylvania; JD, Columbia University School of Law
Background: Attorney, Wachtell Lipton Rosen & Katz
Nicholas Daraviras, Managing Director
Education: BS & MBA, Wharton School, University of Pennsylvania
Background: Equity Research Analyst, Oppenheimer & Co.
James J. Dowling, Managing Director
Education: BS & MBA, Farleigh Dickinson University
Background: Senior Securities Research Analyst, Furman Selz LLC
George R. Hutchinson, Managing Director
Education: BS, Boston University School of Management
Background: Senior Managing Director, Jefferies Randall & Dewey; Friedman Billings & Ramsey
Directorships: Patara Oil & Gas

1037 JEGI CAPITAL The Jordan Edminston Group, Inc.
150 East 52nd Street
18th Floor
New York, NY 10022

Phone: 212-754-0710
e-mail: adamg@jegi.com
web: www.jegi.com

Mission Statement: The leading provider of independent investment banking services for the media, information, marketing services and technology sectors.

Geographic Preference: United States, Europe, Australia
Fund Size: $100 million
Founded: 1987
Average Investment: $1 - 3 million
Minimum Investment: $1 million
Investment Criteria: Early Stage, Late Stage
Industry Group Preference: Publishing, Information Technology, Media, Infrastructure, Marketing, Communications

Other Locations:
One Liberty Square
Boston, MA 02109
Phone: 617-294-6555

90 Long Acre
London WC2E 9RA
United Kingdom
Phone: 44 (0)20 3402 4900

L35, Tower One
International Towers
100 Barangaroo Avenue
Sydney NSW 2000
Australia
Phone: 61 2 8046 6840

Key Executives:
Wilma Jordan, Founder/Chief Executive Officer
e-mail: wilmaj@jegi.com
Education: University of Tennessee
Background: Founder/CEO, The Jordan Edmiston Group; Co-Founder, 13-30 Corporation; COO, Esquire Magazine Group
Directorships: Guideposts; Blyth
Amir Akhavan, Managing Director
Education: BS, Corporate Finance, University of Southern California; MS, University of Virginia
Background: Deloitte Corporate Finance, Deloitte Consulting, Ernst & Young Assurance & Advisory Business
Sam Barthelme, Managing Director
Education: BS & MBA, NY Stern School of Business
Background: AIG; Production Resource Group; Time Warner/CNN
Kathleen Thomas, Managing Director
Education: BA, Architecture, University of North Carolina; MBA, Baruch College
Background: Managing Partner, Drake Star Partners; Marketing, Berkery Noyes; Veronis Suhler Stevenson

1038 JESSELSON CAPITAL CORPORATION
450 Park Avenue
New York, NY 10022-2605

Phone: 212-751-3666

Portfolio Companies: AllCloud, Happy Cloud, Jifiti
Key Executives:
Michael Jesselson, President
Background: Director, American Eagle Outfitters

1039 JETBLUE TECHNOLOGY VENTURES
999 Skyway Road
Suite 350
San Carlos, CA 94070

e-mail: crew@jetblueventures.com
web: www.jetblueventures.com

Mission Statement: JetBlue Technology Ventures focuses investments on aviation technology.

Founded: 2016
Industry Group Preference: Aviation, Technology, Industry
Portfolio Companies: Betterez, Bizly, Claire By 30 Seconds To Fly, Climacell, CoinFlip, Flyr, Gladly, Joby Aviation, Lumo, Miles, Mozio, Node, Redeam, Shape, Slice, Skyhour, Stride, Unicoaero, Volantio

Key Executives:
Bonny Simi, President
Education: BA, Communications; MS, Management; MS, Engineering, Stanford University
Raj Singh, Managing Director, Investments
Education: BS, Imperial College London; MBA, INSEAD, Fontainebleau, France
Background: Mentor, Founder Institute; CEO, Sooqini; General Partner/Co-Founder, Pervasive Technology Ventures; Principal, Investcorp
Amy Burr, Managing Director, Operations & Partnerships
Education: BS, American University; MBA, Moore School of Business, University of Carolina
Background: Founders, Virgin America; Revenue Manager, Continental Airlines

Venture Capital & Private Equity Firms / Domestic Firms

1040 JF SHEA VENTURES
655 Brea Canyon Road
Walnut, CA 91789

Phone: 909-594-9500
web: www.jfshea.com

Geographic Preference: United States
Investment Criteria: Early-Stage
Industry Group Preference: Software, Semiconductors, Biotechnology, Medical Devices

1041 JH WHITNEY & COMPANY
130 Main Street
New Canaan, CT 06840

Phone: 203-716-6100
e-mail: info@whitney.com
web: www.whitney.com

Mission Statement: One of the first US private equity firms. JHW provides private equity capital for small and middle market companies.

Geographic Preference: United States
Fund Size: $750 million
Founded: 1946
Average Investment: $50 to $500 million
Minimum Investment: $50 million
Investment Criteria: Buyouts, Turnarounds, Acquisitions, Recapitalizations, Revenues of $50 - $500 Million
Industry Group Preference: Consumer Products, Retailing, Niche Manufacturing, Business Products & Services, Healthcare
Portfolio Companies: 3B Scientific, Accupac, Aarrowcast, Autosplice, Aveanna Healthcare, Cabi, Caris Life Sciences, CJ Foods Inc., CPG International, Confluence Outdoor, Encanto, FNF Construction Inc., Igloo, Precision for Medicine, Pure Fishing, RBC Bearings, Stevens, TIDI Products, United BioSource, US Bioservices, Uncle Julio's, Wellman Plastics

Key Executives:
Paul R. Vigano, Senior Managing Director
Education: BBA, University of Michigan; MBA, Stanford University Graduate School of Business
Background: M&A, Goldman Sachs & Co.
Robert M. Williams Jr., Senior Managing Director
Education: BA, Bucknell University; MBA, Columbia University
Background: Financial Advisory Services Group, CIBC; Partner, Duff & Phelps
Shaneel D. Patel, Senior Associate
Education: BA, Economics, BS, Commerce, University of Virginia
Background: Hamilton Lane
David J. Zatlukal, Chief Financial Officer
Education: BBA, St. Bonaventure University; CPA
Background: PricewaterhouseCoopers
Kevin J. Curley, Advisor/Chief Compliance Officer
Education: BA, College of the Holy Cross; JD, Columbia Law School
Background: Partner, Morgan Lewis & Bockius; Lord Day & Lord Barrett Smith
Daniel J. O'Brien, Avisor
Education: BS, Fordham University; CPA
Background: Partner/National Chairman, Emerging Business Services Practive, PricewaterhouseCoopers

1042 JK&B CAPITAL
Two Prudential Plaza
180 N Stetson Avenue
Suite 4300
Chicago, IL 60601

Phone: 312-946-1200
web: www.jkbcapital.com

Mission Statement: JK&B Capital is a venture capital firm focused in the software, IT and communications markets.
Geographic Preference: United States
Fund Size: $1.1 billion
Founded: 1996
Industry Group Preference: Telecommunications, Software, Internet Technology, Information Technology, Applications, Pharmaceuticals, Infrastructure, Semiconductors
Portfolio Companies: 21st Century Telecom Group, Actiance, AlterPoint, Anchor Intelligence, Andromedia, Aperto Networks, AppStream, Atrica, Baynote, Bluefire Security Technologies, Cambria Security, Cenzic, Chumby Industries, ClearPoint Metrics, ColdSpark, Commerce One, Continuum Photonics, CoreTek, CounterStorm, Cranite Systems, Daleen Technologies, E2open, Entercept Security Technologies, Exodus Communications, EZ Chip Technologies, FaceTime Communications, Instantis, Intacct Corporation, Interwoven, Intrado, iVivity, Jareva Technologies, Kazeon Systems, Lenslet, Liquidware Labs, Nanochip, nCircle Network Security, NextIO, Novarra, Openwave Systems, Paragon Networks International, Polatix, Reactivity, Scalent Systems, Seaway Networks, Selectica, Sequation, Sheer Networks, SiCortex, Silver Stream Software, SnapTell, Synchrologic, TenXc, Trusted Network Technologies, UNIsite, Ubiquity Software Corporation, UNIsite, Vantrix, Verimatrix, Viewfinity, VMIX Media, Vormetric, XOSoft, Zone Labs

Key Executives:
David Kronfeld, Chairman
e-mail: dkronfeld@jkbcapital.com
Education: BSEE, MS Computer Science, Stevens Institute of Technology; MBA, Wharton School
Background: General Partner, Boston Capital Ventures; VP Acquisitions/Venture Investments, Ameritech; Senior Manager, Booz Allen & Hamilton; Systems Analyst, Electronic Data Systems (EDS)
Thomas Neustaetter, Partner, Software
e-mail: tneustaetter@jkbcapital.com
Education: MBA, MS, University of California, Los Angeles; BA Philosophy, University of California, Berkley
Background: Partner, The Chatterjee Group; Founder/President, Bancroft Capital;Chemical Venture Partners-Northeast of Chemical Bank (now JP Morgan); CFO, First Reserve Corporation; Senior Tax Accountant, Price Waterhouse
Directorships: Cambria Security; Intacct Corporation; FaceTime Communications; Instantis; Selectica; XOSoft
Robert Humes, Partner, Communications
Education: BSEE, Purdue University; MSEE, Polytechnic Institute of Brooklyn
Background: VP Engineering/Technology, Ameritech; VP Operations, Michigan Bell; original design team on cellular tellephony, Bell Labs
Directorships: EZchip Technologies
Tasha Seitz, Partner, Software
e-mail: tseitz@jkbcapital.com
Education: MBA, Stanford Graduate School of Business; BA, Wellesley College
Background: IT Analyst, Gartner Group; Founder, Gartner's Multimedia
Directorships: Bluefire Security Technologies; Cambria Security; Novarra; Trusted Network Technologies; Reactivity; Baynote
Ali Shadman, Partner, Communications
Education: BSEE, MSEE, PhD, Oregon State University
Background: President New Media, Ameritech; Boardmember, Americast; VP Corporate Strategy, Ameritech; Director Technology Development, MCI Telecommunications; Technical Staff, INTELSAT
Directorships: Atrica; Ivivity; Lenslet; Seaway Networks; Sheer Networks; TenXc
Albert DaValle Jr., Partner, Communications
Education: BSEE, Purdue University; MA, Management, Kellogg School of Management

Background: VP Engineering/Construction, Ameritech; VP Technology, Belgacom (Belgium); Senior Planner, Sprint
Directorships: Aperto Networks; Nanochip; Continuum Photonics; SiCortex; Purdue University School of Engineering Advisory Board
Marc Sokol, Partner, Software
Background: SVP/GM Global Marketing, Computer Associates International; Co-Founder, Realia; Co-Author, Realia COBOL compiler; Software Developer, NASA Goddard Space Flight Center
Directorships: AppStream; XOsoft; Cenzic; Cranite Systems; ClearPoint Metrics; Vormetric; Scalent Systems; AlterPoint; CounterStorm
Nancy O'Leary, Partner & CFO
Education: BS, Psychology, Bradley University
Background: Founder, Keystone Associates; Controller, Capital Health Venture Partners; Lanac Technology; Director Finance, CORS

1043 JLL PARTNERS
245 Park Avenue
Suite 1601
New York, NY 10167

Phone: 212-286-8600 Fax: 212-286-8626
web: www.jllpartners.com

Mission Statement: To create value for portfolio companies by providing operational and financial expertise. JLL Partners, a private equity firm with headquarters in New York, targets middle market companies in the financial services, business services, healthcare, industrial, education, aerospace and defense sectors.
Fund Size: $624 million
Founded: 1988
Industry Group Preference: Healthcare, Financial Services, Business Products & Services, Industrial, Education, Aerospace, Defense and Government, Building Materials & Services
Portfolio Companies: ACE Cash Express, American Dental Partners, BioClinica, Builders FirstSource, DPx, Education Affiliates, FC Holdings, IASIS Healthcare, JG Wentworth, Loar Group, Medical Card System, Pioneer Sand Company, Point Blank Enterprises, Ross Education
Key Executives:
Alexander R Castaldi, Managing Director
Education: BA, Central Connecticut State University
Background: CFO & CAO, Remington Products; CFO, Uniroyal Chemical; CFO, Kendall International; Controller, Duracell; KPMG Peat Marwick
Paul S. Levy, Managing Director
Education: BA, Lehigh University; JD, University of Pennsylvania Law School
Background: Managing Director, Drexel Burnham Lambert; CEO, Yves Saint Laurent; VP, Administration, Quality Care; Attorney, Stroock & Stroock & Lavan LLP
Frank J. Rodriguez, Managing Director
Education: BS, Wharton School, University of Pennsylvania
Background: Merchant Banker, Donaldson, Lufkin & Jenrette
Directorships: Mosaic Sales Solutions, Education Affiliates, Motor Coach Industries
Daniel Agroskin, Managing Director
Education: BA, Stanford University; MBA, Wharton School, University of Pennsylvania
Background: Associate, JP Morgan Partners; Analyst, M&A Group, Merrill Lynch
Eugene Hahn, Managing Director
Education: BA, Economics, Cornell University; MBA, Wharton School, University of Pennsylvania
Background: Associate, Warburg Pincus; Analyst, M&A Group, Lazard Freres
Kevin T. Hammond, Managing Director
Education: BS, McIntire School of Commerce, University of Virginia
Background: Analyst, Greenhill & Co.

1044 JMH CAPITAL
155 Federal Street
Suite 502
Boston, MA 02110

Phone: 617-910-2602
web: www.jmhcapital.com

Mission Statement: A private equity firm based in Boston, JMH Capital primarily focuses on growth-oriented companies across a variety of sectors, including food products and services, niche manufacturing, distribution, specialty chemicals and medical devices.
Founded: 2003
Investment Criteria: Recapitalizations, Mangement Buyouts, Leveraged Buyouts, Growth Equity
Industry Group Preference: Niche Manufacturing, Specialty Chemicals, Building Materials & Services, Medical Devices, Business Products & Services, Value-Added Distribution, Analytics & Analytical Instruments, Food Services
Portfolio Companies: Alternative Hose LLC, All4, carlisle Wide Plank Floors, Currie Medical Specialties Inc., Endres Processing, kenexa, MedAssets, Morningside Venture Group, Parterre Flooring Systems, Richard Brady & Associates, Service Radio Rentals, The Signature Group, Spheris, Tri-Star Protector
Key Executives:
John Nies, Managing Partner
781-522-1604
e-mail: jnies@jmhcapital.com
Education: BA, Dartmouth College; MBA, Harvard Business School
Background: Managing Director, Operations, Parthenon Capital; Founding Member & Managing Director, The Parthenon Group; Bain & Co.
Directorships: Carlisle Wide Plank Floors, Service Radio Rentals, Currie Medical Specialties, The Signature Group, Parterre Flooring Systems
Scott Steele, Managing Partner
781-522-1603
e-mail: ssteele@jmhcapital.com
Education: BBA, University of Michigan; MBA, New York University Stern School of Business
Background: Principal, Parthenon Capital; Electra Fleming Americas; Senior Associate, Coopers & Lybrand; Associate, Heller Financial
Directorships: Carlisle Wide Plank Floors, Currie Medical Specialties, Service Radio Rentals, The Signature Group, Parterre Flooring Systems
Michael Stanek, Management Partner
716-870-4298
e-mail: mstanek@jmhcapital.com
Education: BS, Accounting, Rochester Institute of Technology; CPA
Background: CEO, Classifieds Plus; CEO, Northern Group Retail; Akron Manufacturing
Directorships: Carlisle Wide Plank Floors, Parterre Flooring Systems
Tate Bevis, Managing Director
781-522-1613
e-mail: tbevis@jmhcapital.com
Education: BS, MS, Accounting, Carroll School of Management, Boston College
Background: Wachovia Securities; Associate, Deloitte
Directorships: The Signature Group, Parterre Flooring Systems

1045 JMI EQUITY FUND LP
100 International Drive
Suite 19100
Baltimore, MD 21202

Phone: 410-951-0200 Fax: 410-637-8360
web: www.jmi.com

Mission Statement: Focused on enterprise application and infrastructure software and services - investing in companies with rich intellectual property that automates and optimizes business and information technology processes.

Fund Size: $350 million
Founded: 1992
Average Investment: $6 million
Minimum Investment: $1 million
Investment Criteria: Early, Late Stage
Industry Group Preference: E-Commerce & Manufacturing, Software, Internet, Healthcare Information Technology, Business Products & Services
Portfolio Companies: ACI, Activant, Adaptive Insights, Adknowledge, Airclic, Applied, AppNeta, Appriss, Arena, Aarowhead, Attachmate, Automotive Mastermind, Autotask, Avecto, Axeda, Axonify, Benevity, BigMachines, Bindview, Blackbaud, Businessolver, Capsule, Catapult Learning, Classy, Code42, Compusearch, ConfigureSoft, CoreHr, Courion, Double Click, DoubleVerify, eBenx, Ellucian, Eloqua, Empathica, EMS, Gemcom, Global360, Granicus, Halogen Software, Harmony Information Systems Inc., HealthX, Higher Logic, Innovative, Intelex, Intergraph, Internet Brands, Intradiem, Jackson Hewitt Tax Service, Kronos, Level Access, Lytx, Meta Group, Mision Critical Software, Mitchell, Navicure, Neon, Netpro, Network Intelligence Corp., Nimsoft, Paradigm, PointClickCarem PowerPlan, Pros, Quiave, Quic, RSam, Schoology, Seismic, SMT Kingdom, ServiceBench, ServiceNow, Sirius Decisions, Studer Group, TC3, The Search Agency, Triple Point Technology, Trustwave, Undertone, Unica, Vertafore, Vocalocity, Vocus, WhiteHat Security, WorkFront, X Matters, Yello

Other Locations:
7776 Ivanhoe Avenue
Suite 200
La Jolla, CA 92037
Phone: 858-362-9880 Fax: 858-362-9879

Key Executives:
Harry Gruner, Founder & Managing General Partner
410-951-0207
e-mail: hgruner@jmi.com
Education: BA, Yale; MBA, Harvard Business School
Background: Principal, Technology Group, Alex Brown; Marketing, Sigma Design; Investment Banking, Technology Group, Blyth Eastman PaineWebber
Directorships: Appriss, Aptela, Autotask Corp, Catapult Learning, Courion Corp, Halogen Software, Intellitactics, Naivcure
Charles E. Noell, Founder
Education: BA, University of North Carolina; MBA, Harvard Business School
Background: President, John J. Moores; Founder/CEO, BMC Software Inc.; Managing Director, Alex Brown's Technology Group; Associate, American Security Bank; Associate, Pittsburgh National Bank
Directorships: Authentify, Alex Brown Realty Inc., Greystar Real Estate Partners
Paul Barber, Managing General Partner
858-362-9881
e-mail: pbarber@jmi.com
Education: AB, Economics, Stanford University; MBA, Harvard Business School
Background: Manating Director, Alex Brown; Product Marketing, Microsoft; Investment Banker, Merrill Lynch
Directorships: Applied Systems, Healthx, Innovative Interfces, Kronos
Peter Arrowsmith, General Partner
858-362-9882
e-mail: parrowsmith@jmi.com
Education: AB, History/Literature, Harvard University
Background: AEA Investors, Mckinsey & Co.
Directorships: Seismic, The Search Agency, WhiteHat Security, Workfront, xMatters, Yello
Kathy Fields, General Partner/General Counsel
858-362-9884
e-mail: kfields@jmi.com
Education: BS, Business, Indiana University; JD, Stanford Law School
Background: Goodwin Procter LLP; Partner, Testa Hurwitz & Thibeault LLP
David Greenberg, General Partner
410-951-0231
e-mail: dgreenberg@jmi.com
Education: BBA, Finance/Accounting, Goizueta Business School, Emory University
Background: Associate, Cascadia Capital; Analyst, Houlihan Lockey
Directorships: Businessolver, CoreHR, Intelex, Sirius Decisions
Randy Guttman, General Partner & CFO
410-951-0213
e-mail: rguttman@jmi.com
Education: BS, Accounting/Finance, Robert H. Smith School of Business, University of Maryland; CPA
Background: Senior Associate, EY
Brian Hersman, General Partner
858-362-9886
e-mail: bhersman@jmi.com
Education: BA, Economics/Computer Science, MS, Management of Information Systems, Weatherhead School, Case Wetern Reserve University; MBA, Harvard Business School
Background: Senior Associate, Vista Equity Partners; Analyst, McKinsey & Co.
Directorships: Arena, Classy, EMS Software, Innovative Interfaces, Intradiem

Key Executives:
Stacy Feld, Head, Johnson & Johnson Innovation
Education: BA, University of Pennsylvania; JD, Vanderbilt Law School
Background: Former Sr Director of Consumer Scientific Innovation; Partner, Physic Ventures; Business Development, Genentech; Business Development, Third Wave Technologies

1047 JOHNSON & JOHNSON INNOVATION
New Brunswick, NJ 08901

e-mail: jnjinnovation@its.jnj.com
web: jnjinnovation.com

Mission Statement: Johnson & Johnson Innovation, the venture capital arm of Johnson & Johnson, invests in emerging healthcare companies. Johnson & Johnson Development Corporation seeks to generate both financial returns and options for strategic growth for Johnson & Johnson. JJDC targets opportunities with large markets, competitive advantages, and experienced management teams.

Founded: 1973
Investment Criteria: Early-Stage to Advanced Stages
Industry Group Preference: Medical Devices, Diagnostics, Pharmaceuticals, Biotechnology, Consumer Products, Wellness, Prevention
Portfolio Companies: Accelerator Corporation, Asceneuron, Merus, Navitor Pharmaceuticals, NovoCure, Padlock Therapeutics, Protagonist Therapeutics, Vivo Capital

1048 JOHNSTON ASSOCIATES
155 Lambert Drive
Princeton, NJ 08540

Phone: 609-924-2575 Fax: 609-924-3135
e-mail: info@jaivc.com
web: www.jaivc.com

Venture Capital & Private Equity Firms / Domestic Firms

Mission Statement: Provides seed capital to emerging companies in the general Princeton, NJ area for healthcare related businesses. Johnston Associates typically invests in one enterprise a year. The firm invests its own private capital and has no pre-set investment horizons, investment limits or size, or return objectives.

Geographic Preference: New Jersey
Founded: 1968
Investment Criteria: Seed, Startup
Industry Group Preference: Biotechnology, Pharmaceuticals, Healthcare, Therapeutics, Drug Development
Portfolio Companies: Cerus Endovascular, Cytogen Corp., Envirogen, Genex, I-STAT, JDS Therapeutics, Myosotis, PharmaStem, Pharmos, Retrotope, Sepracor, Targent, Zywie LLC

Other Locations:
2205 Trakehner Lane
Reno, NV 89521

Key Executives:
Robert Johnston, Founder
Education: BA, Princeton University; MBA, New York University
Background: Investment Banker: FS Smithers & Company, Smith Barney & Company
Directorships: Envirogen Inc., Vela Pharmaceuticals

1049 JORDAN COMPANY
399 Park Avenue
30th Floor
New York, NY 10022

Phone: 212-572-0800
web: www.thejordancompany.com

Mission Statement: A private investment firm specializing in the buyout and building up of businesses in partnership with management.

Geographic Preference: United States, Europe
Fund Size: $6 billion
Founded: 1982
Investment Criteria: LBO, MBO, Recaps, Private-to-Public, Restructuring, Consolidation, Strategic Buildup, Growth Capital, Established Middle Market Companies with Revenues between $100 Million to $2 Billion
Industry Group Preference: Aerospace, Defense and Government, Building Materials & Services, Consumer Products, Education, Metals, Energy, Transportation, Financial Services, Insurance, Industrial Products, Packaging, Healthcare, Telecommunications, Automotive
Portfolio Companies: ACR Group, Agility, American Freight, Anchor, Arch, Bojangles', Borchers, Bruin II, Capstone, CFS Brands, Dimora, Gulfstream, Harvey Gulf, Odyssey, Parts Authority, Polymer Additives, Production Resource Group, RFJ Auto, Sabre, Silvus, Simpleview, Syndigo, Vantage, Venari, Vertical Bridge, VT Services, Vyne, Watchfire, Worldwide Clinical Trials, Young Innovations

Other Locations:
One North Wacker Drive
Suite 4140
Chicago, IL 60606
Phone: 312-668-0400

680 Washington Boulevard
Suite 1120
Stamford, CT 06901
Phone: 212-572-0800

Key Executives:
Rich Caputo, Chief Executive Partner
Education: BA, Mathematical Economics, Brown University
Background: Analyst, High Yield Department, Prudential-Bache Capital Funding
Directorships: American Fast Freight, American Freight, Borchers, Capstone, Harvey Gulf, Pats Authority, Venari
Dave Butler, Partner
Education: BA, English/Economics, University of Notre Dame; JD, Fordham University School of Law
Directorships: DiversiTech, Watchfire, Worldwide Clinical Trials, Young Innovations
Krisin Custar, Partner
Education: BS, Finance, University of Illinois, Urbana; MBA, University of Chicago Booth School of Business
Background: Director, Investor Relations, First Reserve Corporation; GE Equity; Arthur Andersen
Michael Denvir, Partner
Education: BA, Economics, University of Notre Dame
Directorships: Dimora, Vantage, Worldwide Clinical Trials
Mark Emery, Partner & Co-Head, Operations Management Group
Education: BS, Civil Engineering, Bristol University; MBA, Booth School of Business, University of Chicago
Background: President/CEO, Northstar Aerospace Inc.; President/CEO, Indalez Aluminum Solutions Group; President, Caradon Terrain; President, Hubbard Group; President, Margaux CVC Ltd.; Senior Engagement Manager, McKinsey & Co.
Directorships: Drew Marine, Gulfstream Servives, RFJ Auto, Vantage, VT
Brian Higgins, Partner
Education: BA, Economics, Williams College; CFA
Background: Global Natural Resources Group, Lehman Brothers
Directorships: American Fast Freight, Capstone, Harvey Gulf, Odyssey, Quick
Eion Hu, Partner
Education: AB, Economics, Harvard University; MBA, Harvard Business School
Background: M&A, Salomon Smith Barney
Directorships: RFJ Auto, Vertical Bridge
Joe Linnen, Partner
Education: BBA, Finance, University of Notre Dame
Directorships: Worldwide Clinical Trials
Lisa Ondrula, Partner & Co-Head, Operations Management Group
Education: BS, Accounting, Miami University
Background: Ernst & Young LLP
Directorships: American Freight; Borchers; Parts Authority; Syndigo
Douglas Zych, Partner
Education: BBA, University of Notre Dame
Background: Mergers/Acquisitions Group, Merrill Lynch & Co

1050 JUMP CAPITAL LLC
600 West Chicago Avenue
Suite 625
Chicago, IL 60654

e-mail: info@jumpcap.com
web: jumpcap.com

Mission Statement: Jump Capital is a venture capital firm based in Chicago. The firm pursues opportunities with scalable technology companies and implements long-term investment strategies.

Average Investment: $2 - $15 million
Investment Criteria: Expansion Stage, Growth Capital, Startups
Industry Group Preference: Enterprise Technology, Healthcare Information Technology, Marketing, Financial Services
Portfolio Companies: 4C, AVIA, Booker, Champion Medical Technologies, Doctor on Demand, HealthExpense, LISNR, MediBeacon, NarrativeScience, NowSecure, Opternative, Pangea, ParkWhiz, Personal Capital, Pixability, Procured Health, ProPharma Group, ShareThis, SIM Partners,

Venture Capital & Private Equity Firms / Domestic Firms

Spire, Spring, Swiftpage, True Fit, Tulip Retail, Wholesome Goodness, Zettics, ZipScene

Other Locations:
15 E 26th Street
New York, NY 10010

Key Executives:
Michael McMahon, Managing Partner
Education: BS, Finance, Pennsylvania State University
Background: Co-Founder & Senior Partner, Excelar Group LLC; President, SIRVA; CFO, Rail Services & Card Services, GE Capital
Sach Chitnis, Managing Partner
Education: BS, Chemical Engineering, University of Rochester; MBA, Kellogg School of Management, Northwestern University
Background: Operating Partner, Tarsus Holdings; VP, Consumer Moving & Corporate Development, SIRVA; GE Corporate
Saurabh Sharma, General Partner
Education: Cornell University; MBA, University of Chicago Booth School of Business
Background: Groupon; Lightbank; Barclays Capital; Lehman Brothers; French Institute for Research in Computer Science and Automation; Co-Founder, Benchprep

1051 JUMPSTART INC
6701 Carnegie Avenue
Suite 100
Cleveland, OH 44103

Phone: 216-363-3400 Fax: 216-363-3401
e-mail: askjs@jumpstartinc.org
web: www.jumpstartinc.org

Mission Statement: JumpStart ventures guides Northeast Ohio entrepreneurs with high potential businesses down the path toward wealth creation by providing seed capital, experienced advisors, and a network of vital resources. JumpStart Ventures is the investment arm of JumpStart, Inc., a nationally recognized non-profit transforming the economic impact of entrepreneurial ventures and the ecosystem supporting their growth.

Geographic Preference: Northeastern Ohio
Founded: 2003
Industry Group Preference: Life Sciences, Healthcare, Digital Media, Software
Portfolio Companies: Wiretap, Wisr, StreamLink Software, ExpenseBot, Complion, Markers Workstation, EnosiX, LISNR, 02 RegenTech, Apollo Medical Devices, BioMendics, Vox Mobile, Casentric, BoxCast, eFuneral, Zuga Medical, Movable, Guided Interventions, Sociagram, 7signal, Big River, Amvonet, Intellirod Spine, Milo Biotechnology, Cryothermic Systems, GenomOncology, Enforcer eCoaching, Cureo, Securus Medical Group, Anderson Aerospace, Intelligent Mobile Support, Segmint, SPR Therapeutics, SpearFysh, Caralo Global, MedCity Media, SironRX Therapeutics, CoverMyMeds, Endotronix, Thermalin Diabetes LLC, TheraVasc, Checkpoint Surgical, ABS Materials Inc., Catacel, Myers Motors, Wireless Environment, OnShift, Neuros Medical, IGuiders, Freedom Meditech Inc., Juventas Therapeutics, Inspiron Logistics, CervilLenz, STACK Media, Echogen Power Systems, Great Lakes Pharmaceuticals, AnalizaDX LLC, CardioInsight, MAR Systems, Inspherion, Knotice, Banyan Technology, PreEmptive Solutions, Embrace Pet Insurance, Synapse Biomedical Inc., Ayalogic, Phycal, MesoCoat, Electron Database Company, Amplified Wind Solutions, CFRC Water and Energy Solutions Inc., Design Flux Technologies, Ento Bio, Full Circle Technologies, MET Innovations, Paragon Robotics, Skysun LLC, Body Phyx, Disease Diagnostic Group, iRxReminder, Micro DataStat, Pulmonary Apps, SpireSano, Apply Board, NGageContent, BOLD Guidance, Lauren Loft Social, Enfusen, Flight Deck, Groupmatics, InStore Finance, The Learning Egg LLC, LogiSynn, Projitech, Rabblester, VIPerks, Virteom, Darkside Scientific, Dronewerx, Event 38 Unmanned Systems, Everykey, Hema Imaging, GradSchoolLoans, M.O.M. Tools LLC, Nikola, OcuFreeze, OPTIMA Lender Services, Simply Southern Side, The Wahconah Group, Vintage TeaWorks, Wellness Evolutions, Your Teen Media, Heureka, Talmetrix, hChoices, NEOEx Systems, Eduwear, Micro-Office Systems, Yeu Patch LLC, Micro Fantasy, Connect2Install LLC, CashWorld Automation, College Annex, Case.MD, Aroma Country, 33 Mile Radius, Anexsis, Core Nutrition Planning, Avesta Systems Inc., e-Waste, The CADD Department, Owens Print & Creative Solutions, Connie's Affogato, Making A Difference Consulting, Rust Belt Riders, Studio Stick LLC

Key Executives:
Ray Leach, Chief Executive Officer
e-mail: ray.leach@jumpstartinc.org
Education: University of Akron; MIT Sloan School of Managment
Background: IBM; Founding Member, US Commerce Department's National Advisory Council on Innovation and Entrepreneurship; Chair, National Venture Capital Association
Cathy Belk, President
e-mail: cathy.belk@jumpstartinc.org
Education: BA, Economics, Davidson College; MBA, Duke University
Background: COO, JumpStart Inc.; Director, Innovations, American Greetings; The Coca-Cola Company; Procter and Gamble; Bank of America

1052 JW ASSET MANAGEMENT
515 Madison Avenue
New York, NY 10022

Phone: 212-446-5362

Mission Statement: Specializes in early-stage investments.
Geographic Preference: US, Canada
Industry Group Preference: Cannabis, Healthcare, Pharmaceuticals
Portfolio Companies: TerrAscend, Vensun Pharmaceuticals, Aralez Pharmaceuticals, Establishment Labs, Vitruvias Therapeutics

Key Executives:
Jason Wild, President/CIO
Education: Arnold and Marie Schwartz College of Pharmacy
Background: Chairman, TerrAscend

1053 JW CHILDS ASSOCIATES
500 Totten Pond Rd.
6th Floor
Waltham, MA 02451

Phone: 617-753-1100 Fax: 617-753-1101
e-mail: info@phgrowth.com
web: www.jwchilds.com

Mission Statement: Specializing in leveraged buyouts and recapitalizations of middle-market growth companies.
Geographic Preference: North America
Fund Size: $1.75 billion
Founded: 1995
Average Investment: $600 million
Minimum Investment: $150 million
Investment Criteria: Leveraged buyouts and recapitalizations of middle-market growth companies in partnership with company management
Industry Group Preference: Consumer Products, Healthcare, Retailing, Asset Management
Portfolio Companies: Comoto Holdings, EbLens, Honors Holdings, KeyImpact Sales and Systems, Outward Hound, Shoe Sensation, Siromed, Urology Management Associates, Walker Edison

Key Executives:
Adam L Suttin, Managing Partner
e-mail: asuttin@jwchilds.com

Education: BS magna cum laude, University of Pennsylvania; Bachelor Applied Science magna cum laude, Moore School of Engineering
Background: Associate, Thomas H Lee Company
Directorships: Comoto Holdings, KeyImpact Sales and Systems, Outward Hound, Shoe Sensation, Siromed, Urology Management Associates, Walker Edison
David A Fiorentino, Partner
e-mail: dfiorentino@jwchilds.com
Education: BA, Amherst College; MBA, Harvard Business School
Background: Investment Banking, Morgan Stanley
Directorships: KeyImpact Sales and Systems, Outward Hound, Siromed, Urology Management Associates, Walker Edison
Jeffrey J Teschke, Partner
e-mail: jteschke@jwchilds.com
Education: BA, University of Rochester; MBA, Harvard Business School
Background: Quad-C Management; Merrill Lynch & Co.
Directorships: Comoto Holdings, EbLens, Honors Holdings
William E Watts, Partner
e-mail: bwatts@jwchilds.com
Education: BA, State University of New York, Buffalo
Background: President & CEO, General Nutrition Companies
Directorships: Comoto Holdings, EbLens, Honors Holdings, Shoe Sensation

1054 K9 VENTURES
Palo Alto, CA

web: www.k9ventures.com

Mission Statement: K9 Ventures is a true 'early stage' venture fund that provides funding and support for concept-stage and seed-stage technology companies. We work with entrepreneurs, sometimes even before a company has been formed, to help evaluate, evolve and fund a company in its nascent stages. K9 Ventures focuses on startups in the San Francisco Bay Area that have a strong entrepreneur/team, an idea that has a clear path to revenue, which can be capital efficient and where we can add value.

Geographic Preference: San Francisco Bay Area
Average Investment: $100,000 - $1 million
Investment Criteria: Early-Stage, Seed-Stage
Industry Group Preference: Technology
Portfolio Companies: Auth0, Baydin, Bugsee, Caarbon, CrowdFlower, Dishero, DNAnexus, eShares, Enuma, Everlaw, Gradescope, HighlightCam, KidAdmit, Lucidchart, Lyft, Lytro, Occipital, Osmo, Tapcanvas, Twilio

Key Executives:
  Manu Kumar, Founder
  Education: BS, Electrical & Computer Engineering, MS, Software Engineering, Carnegie Mellon University; Masters & PhD, Computer Science, Stanford University
  Background: Founder/President/CEO, SneakerLabs; Vice President, Interactive Technologies, E.piphany; Chairman/CEO, iMeet; Lecturer, School of Computer Science, Carnegie Mellon University
  Directorships: Auth0, Gradescope, Lyft, KidAdmit, Osmo, Enuma, eShares, Occipital, Boomerang, LucidChart

1055 KAIROS VENTURES
9440 South Santa Monica Boulevard
Suite 710
Beverly Hills, CA 90210

Phone: 310-271-1866
e-mail: info@kairosventures.com
web: www.kairosventures.com

Mission Statement: Kairos Ventures invests in the world's leading scientific discoveries, working with scientists, engineers, and entrepreneurs to help them transform those discoveries into businesses. Kairos is dedicated to invest in projects that will help improve student debt, cost of rent, childcare, and retirement.

Fund Size: $25 million
Founded: 2008
Average Investment: $150,000-$20 million
Industry Group Preference: Energy, Engineering
Portfolio Companies: 1200 Pharma, 3DBio, Actinobac Biomed, Inc., Amorphology, Applaud Medical, Inc., Auspion, Axial Biotherapeutics, Behavioral Signals, Chimera Bioengineering, Compellon, Dear Health, Delpor, El Pharma, Foldax, GeneSciences, Holoclara, KM Labs, Memiray, MemVerge, Mixcomm, NanoClear Technologies, Neuro-Bio, Provivi, Repairogen, Sienza, Symbiotix Biotherapies, Translent Plasma Systems

Key Executives:
  Jim Demetriades, Founder/Manager Partner
  e-mail: jimd@kairosventures.com
  Education: BSc, Economics & Computer Science, Loyola Marymount University
  Background: PHS; Founder, SeeBeyond; Inspero.net
  Alex Andrianopoulos, Chief R&D Officer
  e-mail: alexa@kairosventures.com
  Education: Electrial Engineering; Computer Engineering; MBA, Finance & Marketing
  Background: Oracle
  Nikos Iatropoulos, Regional Partner, Central US
  e-mail: nikosi@kairosventures.com
  Education: BSc, Computer Science, Columbia University; MBA, MIT Sloan School of Management
  Background: CEO, Lingospot; Senior Vice President of Business Development, Piksel; CEO, Upstream

1056 KAISER PERMANENTE VENTURES
One Kaiser Plaza
22nd Floor
Oakland, CA 94612

web: www.kpventures.com

Mission Statement: Supports Kaiser Permanente's mission and brand by investing in products and services that improve the health status of KP members and communities, enhance access to affordable quality health services, innovate ways for providers to organize and deliver healthcare, improve KP's cost structure, and access markets beyond KP's membership.

Geographic Preference: United States
Fund Size: $20 million
Founded: 1945
Average Investment: $1 million
Minimum Investment: $500,000
Investment Criteria: First Stage, Second Stage, Later Stage, Beta Sites, Strategic Alliance
Industry Group Preference: Medical Devices, Healthcare, Information Technology, Therapeutics, Diagnostics, Healthcare Information Technology, Healthcare Services
Portfolio Companies: BigHealth, CollectiveMedical Technologies, Ginger.io, Health Catalust, Ingenious Med, Kitcheck, MetricStream, Omada, Protenus, Proteus Digital Health, Rock Health, Startip + Health, Talix, Validic, Vidyo, BDNA, Concerro, Mageon, Healthline, NexlWeb, Silverlink

Key Executives:
  Chris Grant, Executive Managing Director
  e-mail: chris.m.grant@kp.org
  Education: BA Business/Finance, University of California Santa Barbara
  Background: Rockwell International
  Directorships: Five portfolio companies.
  Amy Belt Raimundo, Managing Director
  e-mail: amy.b.raimundo@kp.org
  Education: BA, Economics, Yale University; MBA, University of California, Berkeley
  Background: Chief Business Officer, Evidation Health; Vice President, Covident Venturesl Vice President,

Venture Capital & Private Equity Firms / Domestic Firms

Advanced Technology Ventures; Management Consultant, APM/CSC Healthcare
Sam Brasch, Senior Managing Dirrection
e-mail: sam.e.brasch@kp.org
Education: BA, Public Policy, Stanford University; MBA, Healthcare Management, Wharton School, University of Pennsylvania
Background: Executive in Residence & Vice President, Frazier Healthcare Ventures; Global Management, Medtronic

1057 KANSAS VENTURE CAPITAL
40 Corporate Woods
Suite 200
9401 Indian Creek Parkway
Overland Park, KS 66210

Phone: 913-262-7117 **Fax:** 913-262-3509
e-mail: mparker@kvci.com
web: www.kvci.com

Mission Statement: An SBIC providing equity and mezzanine capital to Mid-Western based companies with talented management in a variety of industries for expansion, buy-out acquisition or recapitalization.

Geographic Preference: Mid-Western United States
Fund Size: $50 million
Founded: 1977
Average Investment: $1 - 3 million
Minimum Investment: $1 million
Investment Criteria: Mezzanine
Industry Group Preference: Diversified
Portfolio Companies: Airworx Construction Equipment & Supply, ALM Positioners, Arrow Material Handling Products, B12 Transportation Group, Bennett Tool & Die Company, The Carlson Company Inc., Carlson Products, Central States Bus Sales, Crain Hot Old Services, C&W Manufacturing and Sales, Cutler Repaving Inc., Delco Corp., Eagle Precision, English Boiler Tube, Full Vision, High Sierra Energy Partners, In2itive Bsuiness Solutions LLC, KCAS, Legacy Technologies Inc., Perennial Energy LLC, Presence From Innovation, Power I.T. LLC, Remtec Inc., Reynolds Polymer Technologies, Superior Boiler Works Inc., Transfer Tool Products, Vanguard Graphics International

Key Executives:
Marshall D. Parker, President/CEO
Education: BA, Kansas State University; CPA
Background: Marketing, Allen Gibbs and Houlik; Management Services, Ernst & Young; Investment Banker, Blunt Ellis & Loewi; Co-Founder, Snelgrove Parker & Co.
Brian Lueger, Principal
Education: MS, Accountancy, Kansas State University; CPA
Background: Senior Manager, Audit Practice, KPMG

1058 KAPOR CAPITAL
e-mail: info@kaporcapital.com
web: www.kaporcapital.com

Mission Statement: Kapor Capital is an investment fund based in Oakland, CA that invests in seed stage information technology companies which aspire to generate economic value and positive social impact. Investment sectors include but are not limited to education, health and consumer finance.

Geographic Preference: United States
Investment Criteria: Seed-Stage
Industry Group Preference: Information Technology, Education, Healthcare, Consumer Finance
Portfolio Companies: Accredible, Allovue, Always Hired, AngelList, Applauze, Asana, Atipica, BeneStream, Binti, Birdi, Bitly, Blockboard, BlocPower, Blokable, Bloom Technologies, Bolstr, Breakthrough, Brilliant, Call9, Captricity, Catchafire, Citizen, Citrus Lane, ClasDojo, Classkick, Cleanify, Clever, CodeHS, Codespark, Compaas, Compology, Constant Therapy, Desmos, Dropcam, Earn Up, EdCast, Edovo, Educents, Elation Health, Elevate, emocha Mobile Health, Endaga, Engrade, Enuma, Ethic, Fidelis, Flowtown, Formlabs, FounderDating, Front Row, Fundly, FutureAdvisor, Gengo, Genius Plaza, Get Satisfaction, Ginger.io, Glassbreakers, Gojee, Good Eggs, GroupRaise, Handle Financial, Healthify, HealthLoop, Health Sherpa, High Fidelity, Hingeto, Honor, Hopscotch, Human Dx, Hustle, inDinero, Inkling, Interviewing.io, Joonko, Jopwell, Josephine, Junyo, Kairos, Kiverdi, LeadGenius, Learners Guild, LendStreet, LendUp, Life360, Linden Lab, Livestar, Looksharp, Love With Food, Magoosh, Make School, Maker's Row, Managed By Q, Mercaris, Modria, Motion Math, Muzy, Mytonomy, Newsela, NoRedInk, NovoEd, OKpanda, Omada Health, Optimizely, Orchestra, Peel, Piazza, Pigeonly, Plum Perfect, Posterous, Propeller, Prosky, Proven, Rd Rabbit, Regalii, Revivn, SchoolMint, Schoolzilla, SendHub, Shift Payments, ShiftMessenger, Socialize, Sparked, Student Loan Genius, Style Seek, Sweep, Swing Education, Talent Sonar, Talko, Thrive, Tinybop, True Link, Twilio, Uber, UBiome, Uncharted Power, Velano Vascular, Verificient, Via, Visually,

Key Executives:
Mitchell Kapor, Partner
Background: Founder, Lotus Development Corporation; Co-Founder, The Electronic Frontier Foundation; Founding Chair, The Mozilla Foundation; Founding Investor, Linden Lab
Freada Kapor Klein, Partner
Background: Director of Organizational Development, Lotus Development Corporation

1059 KARLIN VENTURES
11755 Wilshire Boulevard
Suite 1400
Los Angeles, CA 90025

Phone: 310-806-9700
e-mail: info@karlinvc.com
web: www.karlinvc.com

Mission Statement: Karlin Ventures is an early-stage venture capital fund based in Los Angeles. Karlin Ventures is compiled of value-add partners helping entrepreneurs who take contrarian approaches to create impactful solutions to big, interesting problems. Karlin Ventures is an affiliate of Karlin Asset Management, a private investment firm managing over $1.4 billion of unleveraged equity capital.

Geographic Preference: United States, West Coast
Fund Size: $145 million
Average Investment: $250,000 - $2 million
Minimum Investment: $250,000
Investment Criteria: Early-Stage
Industry Group Preference: Education, Digital Media & Marketing, Healthcare, Financial Services, Consumer Products
Portfolio Companies: Bark, Bitium, Bridg. Brightfunnel, ChowNow, CREXi, DataRPM, Figs, The Grid, HelloTech, Honk, Investedin, Jukin Media, Kaleo, Laurel & Wolf, Markkit, Noun Project, Pathmatics, Percolata, Pixalate, Policy Genius, Preact, Prevoty, Retention Science, Saygent, ShipHawk, Social Annex, TetraScience, True Link, Verge Genomics, Victorious, Yoi, Cirro Secure, Game Mix, Gyft, Kimono, StrikeAd, Tonx, Walla.by

Key Executives:
TX Zhuo, Managing Partner
Education: BA, Economics & Mathematics, Wesleyan University; MBA, Stanford Graduate School of Business
Background: CFO, Lit Motors; Innovation Endeavors; McKinsey & Co.

Venture Capital & Private Equity Firms / Domestic Firms

1060 KB PARTNERS
600 Central Avenue
Suite 325
Highland Park, IL 60035

Phone: 847-681-1270
e-mail: info@kbpartners.com
web: kbpartners.com

Mission Statement: Established for the purpose of pursuing investment opportunities in the golf and sports worlds. The principals of VSP plan to utilize their diverse entrepreneurial, real estate, financial, investment and management experience, along with extensive industry contacts, to pursue those select opportunities that provide the potential for the greatest return.

Founded: 2010
Industry Group Preference: Golf, Sports, Real Estate, Consumer Products
Portfolio Companies: Club Champion, GAGA, Hammerhead Navigation
Key Executives:
Keith Bank, Founder/Managing Partner
e-mail: keith@versp.com
Education: BS, Economics, Wharton School; MBA, Kellogg Graduate School of Management, Northwestern University
Background: Co-Founder, KB Partners; Principal, Hiffman Shaffer Associates
Directorships: Kirtas Technologies, SteadyMed, Versatile Sports Partners, Club Champion Golf

1061 KB PARTNERS LLC
600 Central Avenue
Suite 390
Highland Park, IL 60035

Phone: 847-681-1270 Fax: 847-681-1370
e-mail: keith@kbpartners.com
web: www.kbpartners.com

Mission Statement: Provides equity financing for early-stage technology companies in the Midwest. KB's objective is to work with talented entrepreneurs and experienced managers to build market leading organizations.

Geographic Preference: Central US, Midwestern US, Chicago
Fund Size: $95 million
Founded: 1996
Average Investment: $1 - $5 million
Minimum Investment: $1 million
Investment Criteria: Seed, Early-Stage, First Round, Second Round
Industry Group Preference: Infrastructure, Information Technology, Telecommunications, Medical Devices, Semiconductors, Computer Hardware & Software, Industrial Services, Communications, Diagnostics, Engineering, Internet Technology
Portfolio Companies: Accumetrics, Active.com, Cadant, Cobotics, Cognitive Concepts, Corona Optical Systems, Data TV Networks, EthnicGrocer.Com, Exacq Technologies, Firefly Energy, iLink Global, Ischemia Technologies, Kirtas Technologies, LeagueLink, Mezzia, Midi, NetRegulus, Orbit Commerce, Performics, Rubicon Technology, Sarvega, Silver Creek, Verax Biomedical
Key Executives:
Keith Bank, Co-Founder/CEO
e-mail: keith@kbpartners.com
Education: BSE, Wharton School, University of Pennsylvania; MBA, Kellogg School of Management, Northwestern University
Background: Principal, Hiffman Shaffer Associates; Co-Founder, deep discount drugstore chain; Turnaround, women's apparel manufacturing & sales company; feature film financing for film - Heaven Is A Playground
Directorships: Chairman, Illinois Venture Capital Association; Chairman/Founder, Chicago Select Golf Invitational; NetRegulus; Data TV Networks; Kirtas Technologies
Raja M. Parvez, Venture Partner
e-mail: raja@kbpartners.com
Education: BS, Mechanical Engineering, University of Peshawar; MS, Industrial Engineering/Management Science, New York University
Background: President/CEO, Rubicon Technology Inc.; President, Optigain Inc.; COO, CyOptics Inc.
Directorships: Xerion Advanced Battery Corp., SiNode Systems Inc., Shasta Crystals Inc.

1062 KBL HEALTHCARE VENTURES
52 East 72nd Street
New York, NY 10021

Phone: 212-319-5555 Fax: 212-319-5591
e-mail: admin@kblvc.com
web: www.kblvc.com

Mission Statement: Physician-run venture capital firm dedicated to discovering and developing innovative companies that create real, lasting value within the U.S. healthcare system.

Geographic Preference: United States
Fund Size: $115 million
Founded: 1991
Minimum Investment: $100,000
Investment Criteria: Seed, Startup, First-Stage, Second-Stage, Early-Stage, Emerging Growth
Industry Group Preference: Biopharmaceuticals, Drug Development, Medical Devices, Healthcare Services, Information Technology
Portfolio Companies: Achillion Pharmaceuticals, Candela, CardioFocus, Magellan Health, Neuronetics, PneumRx, Prolong Pharmaceuticals, Summer
Zachary C. Berk, Managing Director
e-mail: zberk@kblhealthcare.com
Education: BS/Doctorate of Optometry, Pacific University
Background: Concord Health Group; Cambridge Heart; KBL Healthcare Acquisition
Directorships: Lumenos. Comprehensive Medical Management, Gynetics
Marlene R. Krauss, Managing Director
e-mail: mkrauss@kblhealthcare.com
Education: MBA, Harvard Business School; MD, Harvard Medical School; BA, Cornell University
Background: KBL Healthcare Acquisition; Concord Health Group; Cambridge Heart; Lumenos;
Directorships: Lumenos, APS Healthcare, Gynetics

1063 KEARNY VENTURE PARTNERS
One Embarcadero Center
Suite 3700
San Francisco, CA 94111

Phone: 415-875-7777
e-mail: info@kearnyvp.com
web: www.kearnyvp.com

Mission Statement: Kearny Venture Partners is a venture capital firm that invests exclusively in emerging drug and healthcare products. The firm seeks to find solutions to unsolved medical problems, and is willing to invest in innovative companies across a wide range of development stages and medical sectors.

Fund Size: $330 million
Average Investment: $10 - $15 million
Minimum Investment: $2 - $8 million
Investment Criteria: Early-Stage to Late-Stage
Industry Group Preference: Healthcare, Medical Devices, Pharmaceuticals
Portfolio Companies: Aerpio Therapeutics, Akebia Therapeutics, Baxano Surgical, Boreal Genomics, CVRx, Keryx, QuatRx Pharmaceuticals, Repros Therapeutics, SpinalMotion, Tandem Diabetes Care, TriVascular, ViewRay

Key Executives:
Caley Castelein MD, Founder/Managing Member
Education: AB, Harvard College; MD, University of California, San Francisco
Background: Founder & Managing Member, KVP Capital
Directorships: Alivecor, Boreal, Newbridge Pharmaceuticals, Neos Therapeutics, ViewRay, WellPartner, Waterstone Pharmaceuticals
Anupam Dalal MD, Managing Director
Education: BA, Economics, University of California, Berkeley; MD, University of California, San Francisco; MBA, Harvard Business School
Background: Flagship Ventures
Directorships: Aerpio Therapeutics, Akebia Therapeutics, Neurotech, NewBridge Pharmaceuticals, Nora Therapeutics
Jim Shapiro, Managing Director
Education: AB, Princeton University; MBA, Stanford University Graduate School of Business
Background: Co-Founder, SpinalMotion; Investment Banking, Alex. Brown; Associate, Goldman Sachs; Financial Analyst, Bank of America
Directorships: Baxano, CVRx, Hansen Medical, SpinalMotion, Tandem Diabetes Care, TranS1, TriVascular
Dick Spalding, Managing Director
Education: AB, Harvard College; JD, Columbia Law School
Background: Vice President & CFO, Portal Software; CFO, Fusion Medical Technologies; Alex. Brown & Sons; Brobeck Phleger & Harrison
Directorships: Align Technology, Kai Pharmaceuticals, SpinalMotion
Andrew Jensen, Chief Financial Officer
Education: BA, Finance & Accounting, University of California, Berkeley; CPA
Background: CFO, Liquid Realty Partners; Senior Controller, Gryphon Investors; Director, Finance, Sanderling Ventures

1064 KEGONSA CAPITAL PARTNERS
5520 Nobel Drive
Suite 150
Fitchburg, WI 53711

Phone: 308-310-4454
web: www.kegonsapartners.com

Mission Statement: Kegonsa Capital Partners pursues a Money for Minnows strategy. The primary goal of Money for Minnows is to be the first investor in new Wisconsin companies. Money for Minnows promotes new company creation by spreading venture capital across diverse industries, technologies and locations throughout Wisconsin.

Geographic Preference: Wisconsin
Founded: 2005
Investment Criteria: Seed-Stage, Early-Stage
Industry Group Preference: Manufacturing, Biotechnology, Pharmaceuticals, Medical Devices, Internet
Portfolio Companies: Jellyfish, Bio Systems, Idle Free, Semba Biosciences, Networked Insights, Stealth, Brazen, NanoMedex

Key Executives:
Ken Johnson, Managing Director
Background: Associate, Paramount Capital

1065 KEIRETSU FORUM
29 Orinda Way
Suite 415
San Francisco, CA 94563

e-mail: info@keiretsuforum.com
web: www.keiretsuforum.com

Mission Statement: Global investment community of private equity investors, venture capitalists and corporate/institutional investors with 47 chapters on three continents.

Geographic Preference: North America, Europe, Asia
Founded: 2000
Average Investment: $250,000 - $2 million
Investment Criteria: Early-stage
Industry Group Preference: Clean Technology, Consumer, Financial, Healthcare, Real Estate, Technology
Portfolio Companies: 20/20 GeneSystems, 5i Medical, Abom, Acceleration Systems, Agralogics, AlwaysOn, AMHC Healthcare, AnaBios Corporation, Aqueduct Critical Care, Asius Technologies, AttachedApps, BarTrendr, BlueCamroo, Building Energy, BYNDL, CareCap, Clearpath Robotics, Clinovo, Conceptua Math, Corvida Medical, Direct Lending Investments, Drever Capital Management, Embera Neurotherapeutics, EV Connect, Exergyn, Exponential Entertainment, Fairway America, Fingi, Fireman's Brew, Flight Office, Going Green, Graphene Technologies, HeatGenie, HoneyComb, House of Matriach, IBIS Networks, iHealtHome, Immunomic Therapeutics, Infantium, Iomando, Keonn, Kineta, Kiwi Crate, Lightpoint, Linkstorm, LiquidSpace, LumiThera, LYNK Capital, Minetta Brook, MobiCash, MOGL, Ninja Metrics, Nuritas, NuvoMed, Onics, Orpheus Interactive, OtoNexus Medical Technologies, OtoSense, Overlake Capital, Owlized, Pacific West Land, Perfect Point, PetHub, Precision Image Analysis, Plasticity, Plum, Pyatt/Broadmark Management, Quantion, RABBL, Respect Network, Respiratory Motion, RSportz, Safe-H2O, Savara Pharmaceuticals, Schiller Bikes, Scratch-It, Smart Planet Technologies, SnoBar Cocktails, Swyft, SYNQY, Tectonic Audio Labs, Temp Automation, TesoRx Pharma, Tether Technologies, Textile Based Delivery, ThinkSpider, Tilting Motor Works, TranscribeMe, U Grok It, Veristone Capital, VetDC, Viakoo, Voyager Pacific Capital, Wellesley Pharmaceuticals, Worldwise Education, Woven Orthopedics, YouSolar

Key Executives:
Randy Williams, Founder & CEO
415-493-9875
Education: University of California, Berkeley
Background: Co-founder & director, Diablo Valley Bank; President, Pacific Union Commercial Brokerage; Founder, Lamorinda National Bank; Managing Director, Kennedy-Wilson International

1066 KELSO & COMPANY
320 Park Avenue
24th Floor
New York, NY 10022

Phone: 212-350-7700
web: www.kelso.com

Mission Statement: Kelso & Company is a private equity firm that focuses its efforts and resources on investment opportunities in partnership with highly capable management teams in middle market companies.

Geographic Preference: United States, Canada
Fund Size: $5.1 billion
Founded: 1971
Average Investment: $100-250 million
Minimum Investment: $40 million
Investment Criteria: LBO
Industry Group Preference: Manufacturing, Communications, Retailing, Healthcare, Transportation, Chemicals, Media, Consumer Services
Portfolio Companies: 4Refuel, American Beacon, Audio Visual Services Corporation, Augusta Sportswear, Cronos, Delphin Shipping, EACOM Timber, Eagle Foods, Elara Caring, Ellis Communication Group, Foundation Consumer Healthcare, Global Geophysical Services, Harbor Community Bank, Hunt Marcellus, KdocTV Los Angeles, Logan's Roadhouse, Newport Group, Nivel, Oasis Outsourcing, Physicians Endoscopy, The Poseidon Companies, PowerTeam

Venture Capital & Private Equity Firms / Domestic Firms

Services, Premia, Progressive-PMSI, Renfro, Risk Strategies, Sandler O'Neill & Partners, Sentinel Data Centers, Sirius, Southern Carlson, Tallgrass Energy, Tervita, Third Point Re, The Traxys Companies, Truck-Lite, U.S. LBM, Venari Resources, Zenith Energy

Key Executives:
Frank T Nickell, Chairman
212-751-3939
Education: BS Business Administration/Accounting, University of North Carolina
Background: Public Accountant, A.M. Pullen & Company; Member, American Institute of Certified Public Accountants; Director, The Bear Stearns Companies; BlackRock; Earle M. Jorgensen Company; Member, Board of Visitors of the University of North Carolia; Certified Public Accountant
Philip E Berney, Co-Cheif Executive Officer
Education: BS Business Administration, University of North Carolina where he was a Morehead Scholar
Background: Senior Managing Director/Head High Yield Finance, The First Boston Corporation
Directorships: DEL Laboratories, DS Waters, EACOM Timber, Eagle Foods, PowerTeam Services, Sandler O'Neill & Partners, Venari Resources, Wilton Re
Frank J Loverro, Co-Chief Executive Officer
212-751-3939
Education: BA Economics with distinction, University of Virginia
Background: Associate, Private Equity Investing, Clipper Group; High Yield Finance Group, CS First Boston
Directorships: Ajax Resources, Buckeye GP Holdings, Endo, Helios, Oceana Therapeutics, Physicians Endoscopy, Tallgrass Energy, Zenith Energy
Lynn Alexander, Partner, Investor Relations
Education: BBA, Finance & Accounting, Texas Tech University; MBA, University of Michigan
Background: Director, Investment Banking, Merrill Lynch & Co.; Associate, Natural Resources Investment Banking, Kidder Peabody & Co.
Thomas R Wall, IV, Senior Advisory Partner
Education: BS Business Administration with special attainments in Commerce, Washington & Lee University
Background: Lending Officer, Corporate Division, Chemical Bank
Directorships: Augusta Sportswear, B-Way, Charter, Nivel, Renfro, Sandler O'Neill & Partners, Sentinel, Transdigm
George E Matelich, Senior Advisory Partner
Education: MBA Finance/Business Policy, Stanford Grad. School of Business; Holds a Certificate in Management Consulting
Background: Mergers & Acquisitions, Corporate Finance, Lehman Brothers Kuhn Loeb; Consultant, Ernst & Whinney; Certified Public Accountant
Directorships: Charter, CVR Energy, EACOM Timber, Hunt Marcellus, Optigas, Venari Resources, WSI Waste Services
Michael B Goldberg, Senior Advisory Partner
Education: BS Business Administration/Finance with high honors, University of Florida; JD, University of Virginia, member of the Order of the Coif, Law Review
Background: Managing Director/Co-head, Mergers & Acquisitions, The First Boston Corporation; Corporate Law/Partner, Skadden, Arps, Slate, Meagher & Flom; Associate, Cravath, Swaine & Moore; Member, Phoenix House Foundation, Wilson Council of the Woodrow International Center for Scholars
Directorships: Buckeye GP Holdings, Cronos, Delphin Shipping, Eagle Bulk Shipping, Endo, KAR Auction Services, Oceana Therapeutics, Overwatch, Tallgrass Energy
David I Wahrhaftig, Senior Advisory Partner
Education: BA Economics, Western Maryland College; MBA Finance, Wake Forest University; Holds a Certificate in Management Accounting
Background: Associate Director Mergers & Acquisitions/Management Consultant, Arthur Young & Company;
Directorships: Augusta Sportswear, B-Way, DS Waters, Endo, KAR Auction Services, Nivel, Renfro, Transdigm
Frank K Bynum, Jr, Senior Advisory Partner
Education: BA History, University of Virginia
Background: Investment Analyst, New York Life Insurance Company
Directorships: Custom Buildings Products, Nivel, PSAV Presentation Services, Sentinel Data Centers, Sirius, Truck-Lite, U.S. LBM
Steve Dutton, Investment Partner
Education: BS, Commerce, University of Virginia
Background: Investment Banking, Bear Stearns & Co.
Directorships: American Beacon, Newport Group, Oasis Outsourcing, Premia, PSAV Presentation Services, Risk Strategies, Sandler O'Neill & Partners, Third Point Re, Wilton Re
James J Connors II, Senior Advisory Partner
Education: BA, History, College of William & Mary; JD, University of Virginia
Background: Associate, Debevoise & Plimpton
Directorships: Custom Building Products
Matt Edgerton, Investment Partner
Education: BA, Economics & History, Duke University
Background: Investment Banking, Deutsche Bank
Directorships: Augusta Sportswear, EACOM Timber, Eagle Foods, Foundation Consumer Healthcare, Southern Carlson, U.S. LBM
Church M Moore, Investment Partner
Education: BA, English, University of Virginia
Background: Associate, Investcorp International
Directorships: 4Refuel, DEL Laboratories, DS Waters, Elara Caring, Foundation Consumer Healthcare, Helios, KAR Auction Services, Physicians Endoscopy, Truck-Lite
Sandy Osborne, Investment Partner
Education: BA, Government, Dartmouth College
Background: Associate, Summit Partners; Associate, Private Equity Group, JP Morgan & Co
Directorships: Ajax Resources, B-Way, Custom Building Products, CVR Energy, PowerTeam Services, Southern Carlson, Tallgrass Energy, U.S. LBM, Zenith Energy
Christopher L Collins, Investment Partner
Education: BA, English, Duke University; MBA, Stanford Graduate School of Business
Background: Analyst, Stonington Partners
Directorships: American Beacon, Augusta Sportswear, Cronos, Eagle Bulk Shipping, Newport Group, Oasis Outsourcing, Premia, PSAV Presentation Services, Risk Strategies, Third Point Re
Alec Hufnagel, Investment Partner
Education: BA, Economics, Dartmouth College
Background: Leveraged Finance, Deutsche Bank
Directorships: Sirius Computer Solutions, Zenith Energy
Hank Mannix, Investment Partner
Education: BS, Math & Economics, College of the Holy Cross
Background: Investment Banking, Credit Suisse First Boston
Directorships: Custom Building Products, Eagle Bulk Shipping, Elara Caring, Helios, Physicians Endoscopy, Poseidon Containers, PowerTeam Services, Sentinel Data Centers, Sirius
Howard Matlin, Senior Advisory Partner
Education: BA, Political Science, Queens College; MBA, St. John's University
Background: CFO & Principal, Butler Capital Corporation; Deloitte & Touche; Colgate-Palmolive; Riverbank America

Venture Capital & Private Equity Firms / Domestic Firms

1067 KENMONT CAPITAL PARTNERS
401 Louisiana Street
Suite 800
Houston, TX 77002

Phone: 713-223-9922 Fax: 713-223-0930
Toll-Free: 877-337-8499

Mission Statement: Provides creative vehicles to generate attractive returns from opportunities in private equity utilizing disciplined institutional investment processes.

Fund Size: $60 million
Founded: 1998
Average Investment: $5 million
Minimum Investment: $500,000
Investment Criteria: All Stages
Industry Group Preference: Diversified

Key Executives:
Donald R Kendall Jr, Founding Managing Director/CEO
e-mail: dkendall@kenmontcap.com
Education: AB, Hamilton College
Background: Palmetto Partners; Cogen Technologies Capital Company LP; Morgan Stanley; Drexel Burnham; First Boston
Directorships: Cogen Technologies Energy Group, Fremont Partners, Rosecliff, Growth Capital Partners, Murray's Discount Auto Parts, Finalco, MetOx
Laura Dotson, Managing Director
e-mail: ijdotson@kenmontcap.com
Education: BBA, University of Cincinnati
Background: Shells Pension Trust; FBI
John T Harkrider, Managing Director/CFO
e-mail: jkharkrider@kenmontcap.com
Education: BBA, Stephen F Austin State Universtiy
Background: Consolidated Graphics; Hines Interests Limited Partnerhsip; Arthur Andersen, CPA

1068 KENTUCKY HIGHLANDS INVESTMENT CORPORATION
PO Box 1738
362 Old Whitley Road
London, KY 40743-1738

Phone: 606-864-5175 Fax: 606-864-5194
web: www.khic.org

Mission Statement: Locates aspiring entrepreneurs and finances new businesses with capital intended for development; operating in a fiscally conservative manner, makes equity investments, loans, and assists businesses in developing financing packages leveraged by extensive contacts.

Geographic Preference: Southeastern Kentucky
Fund Size: $40 million
Founded: 1968
Average Investment: $2 million
Minimum Investment: $500
Investment Criteria: Startup, Expansion, Buyout, Divestiture
Industry Group Preference: Manufacturing
Jerry Rickett, President/CEO
Education: Cumberland College; MS, Eastern Kentucky University
Background: Chairman, Corbin Planning Commission; Kentucky Tourism Association; Corbin Industrial Commission; Director, Cumberland Valley Area Development District
Brenda McDaniel, EVP/CFO
Education: MBA, Eastern Kentucky University; Accounting, Union College; BS, Business Administration/Accounting, Cumberland College
Background: National Congress for Community Economic Development; Vice Chairman, Rural Local Initiative Support Corporation
Mark Bolinger, Vice President, Business Lending
Education: BS, Business Administration, Berea College
Background: Mountain Association for Community Economic Development

1069 KEPHA PARTNERS
303 Wyman Street
Suite 300
Waltham, MA 02451

web: www.kephapartners.com

Mission Statement: Kepha Partners is a venture capital firm that invests in pre-seed, seed, and early stage companies.

Fund Size: $100 million
Investment Criteria: Seed-Stage, Early Stage
Industry Group Preference: Technology
Portfolio Companies: Azuki, Boundless, Goby, Linkable Networks, Mavrck, NorthPage, OwnerIQ, Paradigm4, Shareaholic, Triblio, Volt DB

Key Executives:
Jo Tango, Founder/Partner
Education: BA, Yale University; MBA, Harvard Business School
Background: General Partner, Highland Capital Partners; Bain & Company
Eric Hjerpe, Partner
Education: Brown University; MS, Management, Massachusetts Institute of Technology Sloan School of Management
Background: Partner, AtlasVenture; Siebel Systems; Center for Information Systems Research

1070 KERN WHELAN CAPITAL
One Ferry Building
Suite 255
San Francisco, CA 94111

Phone: 415-685-0628 Fax: 415-675-8794
e-mail: info@kernwhelan.com
web: www.kernwhelan.com

Mission Statement: Kern Whelan Capital manages a diversified investment portfolio stretching from new ventures to established and profitable businesses across many industry sectors. We invest in only a few companies each year, and partner with outstanding management teams for the long term. While we typically are active members of the board of directors for our businesses, we do not seek involvement in their daily operations. Through a long term approach to the liquidity horizon, Kern Whelan investments are not beholden to a single exit strategy, but are instead opportunistic about investor capital return whether through M&A, IPO, recap, dividend, or otherwise.

Portfolio Companies: Arcadia Communications, Cohera Medical, InvestCloud, Quri, TAB Products, UserTesting, Vignette Wine Country Soda

Key Executives:
Jay Kern, Founder\General Partner
Education: BA, Princeton University; JD, MBA, University of Chicago
Background: Managing Director, Reynolds DeWitt & Co.; McKinsey & Company
J.P. Whelan, General Partner
Education: BA, MA, Stanford University; JD, University of Chicago Law School
Background: M&A Group, JPMorgan, Hambrecht & Quist

1071 KERRY CAPITAL ADVISORS
260 Franklin St.
6th Floor
Boston, MA 02110

Phone: 617-717-8521
e-mail: tjanes@kerrycapital.com
web: www.kerrycapital.com

Venture Capital & Private Equity Firms / Domestic Firms

Mission Statement: Kerry Capital Advisors, Inc., is a principal and advisory firm focused on middle market private equity investment opportunities in the North America and Europe. The firm has been founded by Thomas W. Janes who has a successful 25-year private equity and investment banking track record in working with superior management teams to provide creative capital solutions to a wide variety of financing transactions.

Average Investment: $5 - $50 million
Investment Criteria: Leverage Buyouts, Recapitalizations, Growth Financings
Industry Group Preference: Manufacturing, Consumer Products, Business Products & Services, Healthcare, Logistics, Distribution, Energy, Media, Publishing, Technology, Software
Portfolio Companies: Abbey Healthcare Staffing, Alarmguard Holdings, Ascent Pediatrics, Benchmark, Claricom Solutions, Clark, Cutters Wireline Services, D2Hawkeye, DairyMart, Dalbo, EnvironWorks, Generation Health, Jenzabar, NextWave, Paddock Pools Patios & Spas, PHC, Plymouth Opportunity REIT, Precision Components, Revstone, Rule, Vik Brothers Insurance

Key Executives:
  Thomas Janes, Founder/CEO
  e-mail: tjanes@kerrycapital.com
  Education: AB, Harvard College; MBA, Harvard Business School
  Background: Managing Director, Lincolnshire; Co-Founder/Managing Director, Triumph Capital Group

1072 KESTREL ENERGY PARTNERS
520 Broad Hollow Road
Melville, NY 11747

Phone: 631-421-2711 Fax: 631-214-4238

Industry Group Preference: Energy, Oil & Gas
Portfolio Companies: Downeast LNG, Kestrel Heat
Key Executives:
  Paul A Vermylen Jr, President/Managing Director
  e-mail: vermylen@kestrelenergypartners.com

1073 KHOSLA VENTURES
2128 Sand Hill Road
Menlo Park, CA 94025

Phone: 650-376-8500 Fax: 650-926-9590
e-mail: kv@khoslaventures.com
web: www.khoslaventures.com

Mission Statement: Khosla Ventures is a venture capital firm that invests in innovative technology opportunities across a wide range of industries.

Fund Size: $5 billion
Founded: 2004
Investment Criteria: Early & Late-Stage, Seed Fund, Very Early-Stage Experiments
Industry Group Preference: Consumer, Enterprise, Education, Advertising, Financial Services, Semiconductors, Health, Big Data, Agriculture, Sustainable Energy, Robotics, Chemicals, Storage, Transportation, Space
Portfolio Companies: Affirm, Aguamarina, Akash Systems, AliveCor, Alpine Oral Tech, AltaRock Energy, Apton Biosystems Inc., Arevo, Artrendex, At-Bay, Bay Labs Inc., Berkshire Grey, Bidgely, BigSwitch, BioConsortia, BlockStream, Boku, Boosted Boards, Bridge International Academies, Bungalow, Cadre, Caelux Corporation, Calera, Canary Connect Inc., Carrot Inc., Chain, Citus Data, Coda Project Inc., Color Genomics, Consumer Physics, Cylance, Datera, DB Networks, Deep Genomics Inc., Digital Alloys, DoorDash, eGenesis, Eight, Eligo Bioscience, Ellipsis Health, EtaGen, Ethos Lending, Even, Everlane, Faire, Feetz, Forward, Fundbox, Fundera, Genalyte, Ghost, Giant.AI, Ginger.io, GitLab, Go, Grokker, Guardant Health, HeartVista, Helium Systems, Homebase, Imply, Impossible Foods, Inflammatix Inc., Instacart, Judicata, Just Inc., Karius Inc., Katerra Inc., Kiddom, Koding, Kumu Networks, Lookout, Lumiata, MDalgorithms Inc., Medisas, MemSQL, Mesosphere, MetaMind, Mojo Vision, Momentum Machines, NakedPoppy, Natron Energy, Neurotrack, Nimble Pharmacy, NuTek Salt, Okta, Opendoor, Opentrons, Ori, Owl Cameras Inc., PatternEx, PayNearMe, Pellion, Plastiq, Plum, Pymetrics, Q Bio, Quantopian, QuantumScape, Quartzy, Realm, Replika, Roofstock, Rubrik, Scaled Inference, Scipher Medicine, Scribd, Silicium Energy, Siren Care Inc., Soraa, Spyce Inc., Square, Stripe, Tapingo, TerraPower, Theatro, Tile, Toytalk, True Accord, Truework, Tule, Two Pore Guys Inc., Ukko Inc., Upstart Network, Varentec, Velo3D, Vert, Vibrado,

Key Executives:
  Vinod Khosla, Founding General Partner
  e-mail: ovk@khoslaventures.com
  Education: BS, Electrical Engineering, Indian Institute of Technology; MS, Biomedical Engineering, Carnegie Mellon University; MBA, Stanford University Graduate School of Business
  Background: Founder, Daisy Systems; Sun Microsystems; General Partner, Kleiner Perkins Caufield and Byers
  Samir Kaul, Founding General Partner
  e-mail: sk@khoslaventures.com
  Education: BS, Biology, University of Michigan; University of Maryland; MBA, Harvard Business School
  Background: Flagship Ventures; CEO, Codon Devices; TIGR
  David Weiden, Partner
  e-mail: dw@khoslaventures.com
  Education: BA, Organizational Behavior & Economics, Harvard University; MIT; New York University
  Background: Morgan Stanley; Netscape; SVP, Marketing & Business Development, Tellme Networks; McCaw Cellular; AOL
  Sven Strohband, Chief Technology Officer
  e-mail: sst@khoslaventures.com
  Education: BS, Mechanical Engineering, Purdue University; PhD, Mechanics & Computation, Stanford University
  Background: CTO, Mohr Davidow Ventures; Project Manager, Electronics Research Lab, Volkswagen
  Brian Byun, Venture Partner
  e-mail: bb@khoslaventures.com
  Education: SB, Electrical Engineering & Computer Science, MIT
  Background: Rhapsody Networks; AOL; Netscape; HP; VMware

1074 KICKSTART SEED FUND
2750 East Cottonwood Parkway
Suite 160
Cottonwood Heights, UT 84121

Phone: 801-308-0440
web: www.kickstartseedfund.com

Mission Statement: Kickstart is a seed venture fund dedicated to kickstart companies in the Mountain West by aligning technology creators, industry, entrepreneurs, and capital sources behind the funding and mentoring of seed investments.

Geographic Preference: Mountain West
Fund Size: $8 million
Founded: 2008
Portfolio Companies: Alianza, Artemis, Banyan, Big Squid, Blyncsy, Bookly.co, Brainstorm, Bubble, Catheter Connections, C7 Data Centers, Capshare, Chargeback, Chatbooks, CoNextions, Converus, Cotopaxi, DirectScale, Disco, EcoScraps, Estify, Galileo, Grow, Havenly, Hire Vue, Idaciti, Infusion Soft, In Go, Jack Rabbit, Janiis, Juxta Labs, Lineagen, Lucid Software, Mainframe, Market Dial, Nav, Needle, Nuvi, Omadi Mobile Management, Operational Results, Panoptic Security, Pebble Post, Penblade, PhotoPharmics, Podium, Pop Art, Power Practical, qZZR, Rackware, Radiate Media, Robotic Skies, Room Choice, Ryvers, Sage Bin, Sales Rabbit, Savonix, Self Lender, Simple Citizen, SpinGo, Stance, Studio Design, Suralink, T3S

Venture Capital & Private Equity Firms / Domestic Firms

Technologies, Taskeasy, Teal, Teem, Veritract, VidAngel, Vutara, Vutiliti, Wave, ZenPrint, Cheddar Up, Homie, Monarx, Mountain Hub, Nanobox, Reaction, Trilumina, Zerista, GroSocial, eVisit, Wavelet, Fixes 4 Kids, JSK Therapeutics, Campus Founders Fund, ConexED, Blue Matador, Rags, Cake, Vence, Wastewater Compliance Systems, Fuze Network

Key Executives:
  Gavin Christensen, Managing Director
  Education: BS, Economics, Brigham Young University; MBA, Kellogg School of Management
  Background: Principal, vSpring; Vertical Strategy Associate, Google
  Directorships: Chargeback Guardian, Fuze Network, Grosocial, Jackrabbit Systems, Juxta Labs, NanoMR, Panoptic Security, Symbiot, Zenprint, Zerista
  Dalton Wright, Partner
  Education: BA, Finance, University of Utah; MA, International Studies, Lauder Institute; MBA, Wharton School, University of Pennsylvania
  Background: Alta Ventures
  Directorships: Big Squid, DirectSale
  Alex Soffe, Administrative Partner
  Education: BS, Accounting, University of Utah
  Background: Director of Finance, vSpring/Signal Peak

1075 KIDD & COMPANY
1455 East Putnam Avenue
Old Greenwich, CT 06870

Phone: 203-661-0070 Fax: 203-661-1839
e-mail: wkidd@kiddcompany.com
web: www.kiddcompany.com

Mission Statement: A principal investment firm that designs businesses that transform their industry segments combined with the hands-on involvement required to successfully execute those strategies.

Founded: 1976
Minimum Investment: $10 million
Investment Criteria: LBO
Industry Group Preference: Industrial Services, Consumer Products
Portfolio Companies: Chatham Technologies, Colerain RV, Imaginetics, iPacesetters, Logistyx Technologies, Nexcore Technology, Numet

Key Executives:
  William J Kidd, Founding Partner
  e-mail: wkidd@kiddcompany.com
  Education: BA, MBA, Cornell University
  Gerard A Debiasi, Partner
  e-mail: gdebiasi@kiddcompany.com
  Education: BA, Economics, Summa Cum Laude, Dartmouth College; MBA, Harvard Business School
  Background: Chatham Technologies
  Matthew A Cook, Principal
  e-mail: mcook@kiddcompany.com
  Education: BS, Accounting, BS, Business Administration, Villanova Univeristy; MBA Yale University School of Managemet
  Background: MHT Partners; Canaccord Adams; Braemar Energy Ventures; PricewaterhouseCoopers
  James G Benedict, Principal
  e-mail: jbenedict@kiddcompany.com
  Education: BA, Baylor University; PhD, International Economics, Columbia University
  Background: Senior Managing Director & Chief Talent Officer, Spencer Trask; Managing Director, Diversified Search Companies
  Kenneth J Heuer, Principal
  e-mail: kheuer@kiddcompany.com
  Education: BS, Civil Engineering, Lehigh University; MBA, New York University Stern School of Business
  Background: Managing Director, Spencer Trask; Investment Banker, JPMorgan

1076 KINETIC VENTURES
Two Wisconsin Circle
Suite 660
Chevy Chase, MD 20815

Phone: 301-652-8066
web: www.kineticventures.com

Mission Statement: Seeks partnerships with entrepreneurs dedicated to building the leading companies in high-growth market segments.

Geographic Preference: United States
Fund Size: $100 million
Founded: 1985
Average Investment: $7 million
Minimum Investment: $2 million
Investment Criteria: Early, Growth, Seed, Late-Stages
Industry Group Preference: Internet Technology, Information Technology, Communications, Clean Technology
Portfolio Companies: 9Lenses, AnyPresence, APX, Calix, Cardlytics, Clear Standards, Coraid, Cyan, Genband, HotSchedules, Instant, InterModal Data, ITC Capital Partners, Kwater, Lease Term Solutions, Logic Blox Predictix, Navistone, PlumSilce, ProctorFree, Schoox, Seasoned Staq, Tower Cloud, Vertical Acuity, Virtual Instruments, Vizbee, Weather Analytics, Zift Solutions

Other Locations:
75 Fifth Street NW
Suite 316
Atlanta, GA 30308-1060
Phone: 404-995-8811

Key Executives:
  Jake Tarr Jr., Managing Director
  301-652-8066
  Education: BA, Roanoke College; MBA, Harvard Business School
  Background: Goldman, Sachs and Company; Bank of New York
  Directorships: Mycotech
  William Heflin, Managing Director
  301-652-8066
  Education: MS, BS, Mechanical Engineering, University of Illinois; MSM, MIT, Sloan School of Management
  Background: Research Investment Advisors, Marcam Corporation, IBM
  Nelson Chu, Managing Director
  404-995-8811
  Education: BS, Electrical Engineering, Virginia Tech; MS, Electrical Engineering, MIT; MBA, Harvard Business School
  Background: Management Consultant, McKinsey & Company; Development Manager, Oracle Corporation
  Cam Lanier, Senior Director
  Background: Founding Investor & Chairman, Powertel; Founding Investor, Mindspring
  Directorships: Cardlytics, LeaseTerm Solutions, Tower Cloud, Red Book Connect, LogicBox-Predictix, Chairman, ITC Holdings Company

1077 KINSEY HILLS GROUP
PO Box 999
Menlo Park, CA 94026-0999

e-mail: ekinsey@mac.com

Portfolio Companies: Hotswap, Labmeeting, Mill River Labs, Scribd

Key Executives:
  Michael Hills, Co-Founding Partner
  Education: BS, Political Science, University of Illinois, Urbana-Champaign
  Background: CEO, MJH Capital; SVP Operations, Ariba; Oracle Corporation
  Edward Kinsey, Co-Founding Partner
  Education: BBA, University of Toledo; CPA

Venture Capital & Private Equity Firms / Domestic Firms

Background: CEO, Co-Founder, Quueue; CEO, Determination Ventures

1078 KIRENAGA
66 Palmer Avenue
Suite 49
Bronxville, NY 10708

Phone: 914-202-6046
web: kirenaga.com

Mission Statement: Kirenaga is a Japanese term used to describe a knife or sword blade. Kirenaga represents the principles they aspire to embody as a company - to stay sharp and find and maintain a distinctive edge in everything they do.

Other Locations:
189 S Orange Avenue
Suite 1400
Orlando, FL 32801

Key Executives:
David Scalzo, Founder/Managing Partner
Education: BS, MBA, Northwestern University
Background: Co-Founder/CFO, AdvisorEngine Inc.; COO, Credit Suisse; Managing Director, Bear Stearns; Director, Operations, Precision Plating Company, Chicago
Terrence Berland, Managing Partner
Education: University of Notre Dame; MBA, Northwestern University
Background: CEO, Violet Defense Group; Officer, US Navy; Instructor, Naval Nuclear Power School

1079 KLEINER PERKINS
2750 Sand Hill Road
Menlo Park, CA 94025

e-mail: plans@kpcb.com
web: www.kpcb.com

Mission Statement: Kleiner Perkins is committed to helping entrepreneurs build sustainable technology businesses. For thirty years they have invested in hundreds of market-defining ventures and are constantly on the lookout for promising ideas that either invents new business categories or radically alters existing ones.

Fund Size: $4.6 billion
Founded: 1972
Industry Group Preference: Biotechnology, Communications, Computer Related, Electronic Components, High Technology, Information Technology, Medical & Health Related, Green Technology, Life Sciences
Portfolio Companies: 3-V Biosciences, Aeye, Affectiva, Airbnb, Airtime, Alkira, Ambiqmicro, Amprius, AngelList, Apporbit, Aquion Energy, Area1, Audius, Ayasdi, Beam, Better, BetterWorks, Beyond Meat, Border X Lab, Breathe, Bulletin, Bump, ClearStory, CloudPhysics, Codecademy, CollectiveMedical, Coursera, Crossbar, Datameer, Datastax, DIY, DJI, DoorDash, Drawbridge, Duolingo, Dust Identity, Egnyte, Endame, Enjoy, Epic Games, EssenceHealthcare, Expansion Therapeutics, Farmers Business Network, Feather, Figma, Fleksy, Flipboard, FLX Bio, Fullstory, GeneralRadar, GoEuro, GraphIQ, Gusto, Handshake, Helix, Hixme, Hollar, Houzz, Incorta, Indiegogo, Inspirato, Instacart, Instartlogic, Intercom, Ionic, IronNet Cybersecurity, Jask, Kapwing, Knack, Kinsa, Labelbox, Leanplum, LegalZoom, Livongo, Looker, Magic Leap, Mango Health, Mason Finance, mCube, Mist, Mobcrush, Motiv, N3twork, Nav, Netlify, Newsela, Nextdoor, Nuna, Nurx, Packagd, Paviliondata, Peloton, Pinger, Pinterest, Plaid, Plastiq, Prisma, Productboard, Progyny, Proxy, Puppet, QuantumScape, Qumulo, Remind, Rentmatix, Rent The Runway, Reputation.com, Ripcord, Robinhood, Segment, SessionM, Shape Security, Shoof Technologies, Slack, Smile Direct Club, SpinLaunch, Stance, SoundCloud, SpotAHome, Spruce, Strip, Synack, Tally, Terminal, The Wing, Tmunity, Toss, Tradesy, Trendyol.com, TrueCaller, Trusona, Tulip, Turo, UiPath, Ujet, UntuckIt, Uber, UpStart, Uship, Weem, Victorious, Viz.ai, voloAgri, Willo, Xendit, Zaarly, Zazzle, Zumper

Other Locations:
Unit 2101, BEA Finance Tower
66 Hua Yuan Shi Qiao Road
Pudong
Shanghai 200120
China

Key Executives:
Brook Byers, Founder/Advisor
e-mail: brookb@kpcb.com
Education: MBA, Stanford University; BA, Electrical Engineering, Georgia Tech
Background: Director, Idec Pharmaceuticals; President/Director, Western Association of Venture Capitalists; Contributing Author
Directorships: University of California, SF Medical Foundation; California Healthcare Institute; New Schools Foundation; Stanford Eye Council; USCF Capital Campaign; Asian Art Museum, SF
Bing Gordon, Advisor
e-mail: bingg@kpcb.com
Education: BA, Yale University; MBA, Stanford University
Background: Chief Creative Officer, Electronic Arts
Beth Seidenberg, Advisor
e-mail: beths@kpcb.com
Education: BS, Barnard College; MD, University of Miami
Directorships: 3-V Biosciences, Breathe Technologies, Expansion Therapeutics, FLX Bio, Hixme, Kinsa, Progyny, Tmunity
Ilya Fushman, Partner
Education: PhD, Applied Physics, MS, Electrical Engineering, Stanford University; BS, Physics, Caltech
Background: General Partner, Index Ventures; Head of Product, Dropbox; Principal, Khosla Ventures; Director Of Technology, Solar Junction
Directorships: DUST Identity, Labelbox, Plastiq, Productboard, Robinhood, UiPath
Mamoon Hamid, Partner
Education: BS, Electrical Engineering, Purdue University; MS, Stanford University; MBA, Harvard Business School
Background: Co-Founder & General Partner, Social Capital; Partnerm US Venture Partners; Xilinx
Directorships: Alkira, Figma, Intercom, Kapwing, Mist Systems, Netlify, Prisma, Slack, Tally, Terminal.io, Viz.ai
Wen Hsieh, Partner
e-mail: wenh@kpcb.com
Education: BS, MS, PhD, Electrical Engineering, Caltech
Background: McKinsey & Company; Founder, OnChip Technologies
Directorships: AEye, Ambiq Micro, Amprius, Crossbar, Desktop Metal, DJI, General Radar, mCube, Motiv, Pavilion Data, Proxy Technologies, Qumulo, Ripcord, Shoof Technologies, SpinLaunch
Ted Schlein, Partner
e-mail: teds@kpcb.com
Education: BA, Economics, University of Pennsylvania
Background: Fortify Software; Symantec; DeVenCI
Directorships: App Orbit, Area 1 Security, Ayasdi, Endgame, FullStory, Incorta, Inspirato, Ionic Security, IronNet Cybersecurity, Jask, Reputation.com, Segment, Shape Security, Synack, ujet

1080 KLINE HILL PARTNERS
325 Greenwich Avenue
3rd Floor
Greenwich, CT 06830

Phone: 203-987-6120
e-mail: info@klinehill.com
web: www.klinehill.com

Mission Statement: Kline Hill focuses on the private equity secondary market with sellers of all types.

Fund Size: $1 Billion
Founded: 2015

Venture Capital & Private Equity Firms / Domestic Firms

Key Executives:
Michael Bego, Founder/Managing Partner
203-340-2463
e-mail: mike.bego@klinehill.com
Education: BS, Cornell University; MBA, Columbia University
Background: Partner, Willowridge Partners; Consultant, McKinsey & Co.

1081 KNIGHTSBRIDGE ADVISERS
122 SW Frank Phillips Boulevard
Bartlesville, OK 74003

Phone: 918-336-0978 Fax: 918-336-0824
web: www.knightsbridgeusa.com

Mission Statement: A registered investment adviser that assists European and North American institutional investors to invest in leading early stage venture capital partnerships and specialist public managers that specialize in 'high delta' type companies.

Fund Size: $1.1 billion
Founded: 1983
Minimum Investment: $2, 000, 000
Investment Criteria: Early-Stage
Industry Group Preference: Communications, Computer Related, Internet Technology, Medical & Health Related

Other Locations:
50 Leonard Street
Suite 300
Belmont, MA 02478
Phone: 617-354-0042 Fax: 617-876-0204

Key Executives:
Joel Rommines, Founder
e-mail: jr@knightsbridgeUSA.com
Education: BS, Economics, Drury College
Background: Consultant, Horsley Bridge & Partners; Executive Director, Orion Bank Limited; Citibank NA
Barbara Piette, Managing Principal
Education: BS, Boston College; MBA, Harvard Business School
Background: General Partner, Charles River Ventures; Partner, Schroder Ventures; President, Blackwood Capital
George Arnold, Managing Principal
Education: Swiss Institute of Technology; MS, Electrical Engineering, Stanford University; MBA, Santa Clara University
Background: Director, Citigroup Private Equity
Matthew Ahern, Managing Principal
Education: BA, Boston University; MBA, FW Olin Graduate School of Business, Babson College
Background: Managing Director, Merrill Lynch; Founder & Director, Capitalyst Ventures; Fleet Bank

1082 KNOX CAPITAL
350 N Orleans Street
Suite 9000n
Chicago, IL 60654

web: knox-cap.com

Mission Statement: Knox capital aims to dispense with traditional private equity and prides themmselves on being more nimble and more flexible. They pinpoint where they see potential growth, then seek out partners who match those criteria.

Key Executives:
Alex Gregor, Founder/Partner
312-402-1425
e-mail: aeg@knox-cap.com
Education: BBA, University of Michigan; MBA, Northwestern University, Kellogg School of Management
Background: VP, Pfingsten Partners
Mike Bryant, Partner
708-837-2632
e-mail: mb@knox-cap.com
Education: BBA, University of St. Francis; MBA, MIT Sloan School of Management
Background: Co-Founder/CEO, nSource; President, Legal Services, Integreon
Peter Pacelli, Principal
847-494-4747
e-mail: pjp@knox-cap.com
Education: BA, Yale University; MBA, University of Chicago
Background: Bank of America; Wind Point Partners; Victory Views; Intelligence Officer, US Navy

1083 KODIAK CAPITAL
260 Newport Center Drive
Newport Beach, CA 92660

Phone: 949-432-6900

Mission Statement: A private equity firm investing in pharmaceutical, cannabis, biotech, and Health & Wellness companies.

Geographic Preference: North America
Founded: 2009
Average Investment: $1 million to $25 million
Minimum Investment: $1 million to $5 million
Investment Criteria: Lower Middle Market; $5-$500 Million in Revenue
Industry Group Preference: Cannabis, Agriculture, Pharmaceuticals, Biotech, Health & Wellness
Portfolio Companies: OWCP Pharmaceutical Research, Affinor Growers, Nutritional High, MyDx, Pazoo, C☐r, CannaSys Inc., CannaPharmaRx, UCann, Empire Global, THaT, Rx Safes, Icon Vapor, Soligenix, Uluru, Signal Bay Inc., Upper, Corgreen Technologies, Music Of Your Life

Other Locations:
600 B Street
San Diego, CA 92101

1084 KODIAK VENTURE PARTNERS
PO Box 550225
Waltham, MA 02455

Phone: 781-214-6855 Fax: 978-293-1003
web: www.kodiakvp.com

Mission Statement: Kodiak Venture Partners is a seed and early stage venture capital firm focused on commitment.

Geographic Preference: North America
Fund Size: $681 million
Founded: 1999
Investment Criteria: Seed, Early
Industry Group Preference: Communications, Semiconductors, Software, Information Technology, Wireless, Internet, Digital Media & Marketing, Healthcare Information Technology
Portfolio Companies: Airwide Solutions, ALIS, Allegro Diagnostics, Application Security, AppNexus, Astadia, AuroraNetics, Azimuth Systems, BTI Photonic Systems, ChannelAdvisor Corporation, CXO Systems, Chaoticom, CipherOptics, Cortina Systems, DAFCA, Egenera, Enfora, Extreme Packet Devices, Fluxion Biosciences, GTESS Corporation, GlassHouse Technologies, GreenLight Biosciences, Groove Mobile, High Roads, iAmplify, Ideeli, IE-Engine, IMlogic, Kadient, Legra Systems, Live Gamer, Lumicell, Millennial Net, Mindreef, Motia, Newforma, Potentia Semiconductor, Pragmatech Software, Qvidian, Raza MicroElectronics, RMI Corporation, RulesPower, Sentito Networks, Silicon Dimensions, SIMtone, SpaceClaim Corporation, Symwave, TRA, Taral Networks, TeraConnect, Tiaris, Tropic Networks, uLocate, Vesta Retail Network, Vette, Watchfire, Weather Trends International, WHERE, Wireless China

Key Executives:
Dave Furneaux, Founder/Managing Partner
Education: BA, Colorado College
Background: Furneaux & Company; Chrysalis Symbolic Design; Telecomunications Analyst, Natioal Conference

Venture Capital & Private Equity Firms / Domestic Firms

Directorships: GreenLight Biosciences, Lumicell, Qvidian, Fluxion
Lou Volpe, Managing Partner
Education: BA, Tufts University; MBA, Boston University
Background: ArrowPoint Communications; GeoTel Communications; Parametric Technology
Directorships: Atria, Softdesk
Chip Meakem, Managing Partner
Education: BA, Cornell University; MBA, Columbia University
Background: Draper Fisher Juvetson Gotham; Interactive Imaginations

1085 KOHLBERG & COMPANY LLC
111 Radio Circle
Mount Kisco, NY 10549

Phone: 914-241-7430
e-mail: info@kohlberg.com
web: www.kohlberg.com

Mission Statement: A leading US private equity firm which acquires middle market companies.

Geographic Preference: United States
Fund Size: $3.7 billion
Founded: 1987
Average Investment: $60 million
Minimum Investment: $15 million
Investment Criteria: LBO, MBO, Recaps
Industry Group Preference: Manufacturing, Service Industries, Healthcare Services, Consumer Products, Building Materials & Services, Business Products & Services, Financial Services
Portfolio Companies: AGY Holding Corporation, Alitacare, Aurora Products Group, Bauer Performance Sports Ltd., BioScrip, Inc., Cadence, Chronos Life Group, CIBT, Concrete Technologies Worldwide, e+ Cancer Care, Franklin Energy, Interstate Hotels & Resorts, K2-MDV Holdings, Katy Industries, Inc., Kellermeyer Bergensons Services, MarketCast, Nellson Nutraceutical, Nielsen & Bainbridge, Packaging Dynamics, Inc., Osmose, Phillips-Medisize Corporation, Pittsburgh Glass Works, Risk Strategies Company, Sabre Industries, Inc., Sara Lee Frozen Bakery, Senneca Holdings, SouthernCare, Inc., Specialty Care, Spinal Elements, Stanadyne Corporation, Standard Parking Corporation, SVP Worldwide, Trico Products, Inc., U.S. Retirement & Benefits Partners, U.S. Risk

Key Executives:
James A Kohlberg, Chairman
Education: BA, Golden Gate University; MBA, New York University
Background: Merrill Lynch; Kohlberg Kravis Roberts & Co.
Directorships: Troon Golf, LLC
Samuel P Frieder, Managing Partner
Education: AB, Harvard College
Background: Security Pacific Business Credit
Gordon H Woodward, Partner, Chief Investment Officer
Education: AB, Harvard College
Background: Financial Analyst, James D Wolfensohn
Directorships: Alita Care, Cadence, CIBT Global, e+CancerCare, Franklin Energy Group, Interstate Hotels & Resorts, K2-MDV Holdings, MarketCast, Nellson Nutraceutical, Osmose Utilitie Service
Shant Mardirossian, Partner & Chief Operating Officer
Education: BBA, MBA, Pace University
Background: McKinsey & Company, Senior Staff Accountant, Paneth Haber & Zimmerman
Directorships: Spinal Elements
Benjamin Mao, Partner
Education: AB, Harvard College
Background: Ewing Management Group, Donaldson Lufkin & Jenrette, Credit Suisse First Boston
Directorships: e+CancerCare, Franklin Energy Group, Osmose Utilities Services, Sabre Industries, Senneca Holdings
Seth H Hollander, Partner
Education: BBA, University of Michigan, Ann Arbor
Background: Financial Analyst, Bear Stearns & Co
Directorships: Interstate Hotels & Resorts, Nellson Nutraceutical, Sara Lee Frozen Bakery, Stanadyne Corporation
Andrew P. Bonanno, Partner
Education: BA, Connecticut College; MBA, Washington University
Background: VP of Business Development, New York Butouts Team, American Capital
Christopher Anderson, Partner
Education: BA, Princeton University
Background: Financial Analyst, Warburg Dillon Read
Directorships: Cadence, K2-MDV Holdings LP, Spinal Elements, U.S. Risk Insurance Group
Evan Wildstein, Partner
Education: BBA, University of Michigan
Background: Financial Analyst, Dean Witter Reyolds
Directorships: Alita Care, e+CancerCare, SpecialtyCare, Stanadyne Corporation, U.S. Retirement & Benefit Partners
Ahmed Wahla, Partner
Education: BA, Northwestern University
Background: Lazard Frères & Co.
Directorships: CIBT Global, Interstate Hotels & Resorts, MarketCast, Nellson Nutraceutical, Sabre Industries

1086 KOHLBERG KRAVIS ROBERTS & COMPANY
30 Hudson Yards
New York, NY 10001

Phone: 212-750-8300
web: www.kkr.com

Mission Statement: KKR is an investment firm that makes equity investments in management buyouts on behalf of itself and its investors.

Geographic Preference: North America, Europe, Asia Pacific
Fund Size: $118 billion
Founded: 1976
Minimum Investment: $15, 000, 000
Investment Criteria: LBO, MBO
Industry Group Preference: Chemicals, Consumer Products, Energy, Education, Financial Services, Healthcare, Infrastructure, Media, Communications, Retail, Consumer & Leisure, Technology
Portfolio Companies: 58 Daojia, A-Gas, ACCO Material Handling Solutions, Academy Sports + Outdoors, Accelerated Oil Technologies, Acciona Energia Internacional, Acteon, Activate Capital Ltd., AcuFocus, Ajax Health, Ambea AB, AppLovin, Apple Leisure Group, Arago, Arbor Pharmaceuticals, Associated Partners, Australian Venue Co., Avendus Capital, BMC, Bay Club, Beach, Beijing Capital Juda, Bharti Infratel, Blue Sprig Pediatrics, BridgeBio Pharma, BrightView, CHI Overhead Doors, COFCO Meat, Calabrio, Calsonic Kansei, Calvin Capital, Cardenas, Carter Haston JV, Cascade Sensior Living, Castel Portfolio, Cementos Balboa, Channel Control Marchants, Cherwell Software, China Int'l Capital Corp. Ltd., China Outfitters Holdings, Clarify Health Solutions, Clicktale, Coffee Day Resorts, Cognita Schools, Cohera Medical, Coherus BioSciences, Colonial Pipeline Co., Comstock Resources, Copper, Covenant Surgical Partners, The Crosby Group, Cue & Co., Cylance, Darktrace, Deutsche Glasfaser, DoubleDutch, Drawbridge, Exco Resources, Ebb Therapeutics, EchoNous, Eclipse, Embarcadero Maritime, Emerald Media, Engility, Entellus Medical, Envision Healthcare, Epicor, European Locomotive Leasing, FanDuel, First Data Corp., Focus Financial Partners, ForgeRock, Gambol Pet Group, Gardner Denver, Genesis Energy, GetYourGuide, GfK SE, Global Medical Response, Go

Venture Capital & Private Equity Firms / Domestic Firms

Daddy, Go-Jek, Golden Data, Goodpack, HeTian Hospital Management, Heartland Dental Care, Hensoldt, Hilding Anders, Hipoges, Hitachi Kokusai Electric, Hyperion, Internet Brands, Ivalua, Jiangsu Yuguan, Jitterbit, Joulon, KCF Technologies, KKR Korea Logistics, Koki Holdings, LGC, LS Automotive, Laser Clinics Australia, Latitude Financial Services, Laureate Int'l Universities, Leon Site, Lyft, MMI Holdings, Magic Leap, Mandala Energy, Masan Nutri-Science, Max Financial Services, Maxeda BV, McColl's Transport, Mills Fleet Farm, National Vision, Nature's Bounty, NextEra Energy Partners, OEG, Optimal+, Optiv, Organa, Outsystems, PEMEX Midstream, PRA Health Sciences, Panasonic Healthcare, Papresa, Pepepr Group, PetVet, PharMerica Corp., Pioneer DJ Corp., Privilege Underwriters, Property Guru, Q-Park NV, Qingdao Haier, Quicksilver Resources, RHC Student Housing, Radiant Life Care, Rbmedia, RES, RigNet, River Plaza, Rocky Mountain Midstream, SBI Life Insurance, Santanol, Savant Systems, Sedgwick, Selecta, Sistemia, Slayback Pharma, SoftwareOne, Sonos, Starry, Sundrop Farms, Sunner Development, Tarena, Torq, Trainline, Transphorm, Travelopia, UFC, United Group

Other Locations:
2800 Sand Hill Road
Suite 200
Menlo Park, CA 94025
Phone: 650-233-6560

555 California St.
50th Floor
San Francisco, CA 94104
Phone: 415-315-3620

600 Travis Street
Suite 7200
Houston, TX 77002
Phone: 713-343-5142

Kohlberg Kravis Roberts & Co. SAS
9 Avenue Matignon
Paris 75008
France
Phone: 33-153539600

18 Hanover Square
London W1S 1JY
United Kingdom
Phone: 44-2078399800

KKR Asia Limited
Level 56, Cheung Kong Center
2 Queen's Road
Central
Hong Kong
Phone: 852-63027300

KKR Japan Limited
11F, Meiji Yasuda Seimei Building
2-1-1 Marunouchi, Chiyoda-ku
Tokyo 100-0005
Japan
Phone: 81-362686000

KKR Investment Consultancy (Beijing) Co Ltd
41/F China World Tower 3
No. 1 Jianguomenwai Street, Chaoyang District
Beijing 100004
China
Phone: 86-1058953800

KKR India Advisors Private Limited
2nd Floor, Piramai Tower, Peninsula Corporate Park
Ganpatrao Kadam Marg, Lower Parel West
Mumbai 400 013
India
Phone: 91-2243551300

KKR MENA Limited
Gate Village 4, Levels 5 & 6
DIFC, PO Box 506804
Dubai
United Arab Emirates
Phone: 971-043781500

KKR Korea LLC
36/F, West Tower, Mirae Asset Center 1 Building
26 Eulji-ro 5-gil, Jung-gu
Seoul 100-210
Korea
Phone: 82-263217700

KKR Australia Pty Limited
Level 39, Gateway Building
1 Macquarie Place
Sydney NSW 2000
Australia
Phone: 91-282985500

Key Executives:
Henry R Kravis, Co-Chair & Co-Founder
Education: MBA, Columbia University
George Roberts, Co-Chair & Co-Founder
Education: JD, University of California Law School; BA, Claremont McKenna College
Background: Bear Sterns & Company

1087 KOHLBERG VENTURES
3000 Alpine Road
Portola Valley, CA 94028

Phone: 650-463-1480 **Fax:** 650-463-1481
e-mail: info@kohlbergventures.com
web: www.kohlbergventures.com

Mission Statement: Kohlberg Ventures invests in early stage digital media, consumer product and clean tech companies. Kohlberg Ventures draws on over twenty years experience of bringing patient capital to compelling business opportunities. Since we're investing our own capital, we're equipped to remain active in all market cycles - to take risks in up markets, and to double-down in tighter times. We provide ongoing support with strategic guidance, supplemental talent and an extensive network of domain experts. We recognize that few ventures grow as originally planned, and we're proud of our record in helping entrepreneurs navigate the tactical shifts necessary to thrive.

Fund Size: $35 million
Investment Criteria: Early-Stage
Industry Group Preference: Digital Media & Marketing, Consumer Products, Clean Technology, Advertising, Distribution, Food & Beverage, Power, Energy Efficiency, Enabling Technology
Portfolio Companies: Alibris, Akadémos, Blue Bottle Coffee Company, Business Insider, ClearEdge Power, Current TV, Lunera Lighting, Open Road Integrated Media, Real Gravity, Scharffen Berger Chocolate Maker, Shakti Battery, Social Chorus, Socialmedian, Vintners' Alliance, Wordlock, XQuest

Key Executives:
James A. Kohlberg, Investment Partner
Background: Chairman, Kohlberg & Company
Directorships: Open Road Integrated Media, SocialChorus, The New York Times
John S. Eastburn Jr., Investment Partner
Background: Partner, Kohlberg & Company; Executive, Crystal Dynamics; Vestron; Columbia Pictures; Scovill Fasteners
Greg Shove, Digital Media Partner
Education: Sloan Fellow, Stanford University Graduate School of Business
Background: Founder/CEO, SocialChorus; Executive, America Online; Co-Founder, 2Market; Apple Computer; Sun Microsystems; Digital Equipment
Bill Youstra, Digital Media Partner
Education: MBA, Stanford University; BA, Film, BS, Computer Science, BA, Marketing, University of Maryland; MA, Education, Stanford University
Background: SVP, Marketing & Business Development, Revel Touch

Venture Capital & Private Equity Firms / Domestic Firms

1088 KPG VENTURES
Berkeley, CA 94705

Phone: 925-234-3557
web: www.kpgventures.com

Mission Statement: KPG Ventures provides funding for seed and early stage companies. The firm focuses primarily on tech-centric businesses.

Investment Criteria: Seed-Stage
Industry Group Preference: Consumer Internet, Technology
Portfolio Companies: Bai Du, BrightRoll, Geomagical, Ludic Labs, MindMeld, Nile Guide, Ribbit, Solariat, Sphere, Sportgenic, Teracent, Wowd

Key Executives:
Vince Vannelli, Founder/Managing Partner
Education: BS, MS, Industrial Engineering, Stanford University
Background: SVP & General Manager, Network Products Division, Inktomi Corporation; SVP & General Manager, United States, Hitachi Data Systems; IBM
Directorships: Expect Labs, Sociable Labs, Lingonautics, National Payment Card Association

1089 KPS CAPITAL PARTNERS
485 Lexington Avenue
31st Floor
New York, NY 10017

Phone: 212-338-5100 Fax: 646-307-7100
e-mail: dgray@kpsfund.com
web: www.kpsfund.com

Mission Statement: Focuses on constructive investing in restructurings, turnarounds, and other special situations. KPS invests in companies challenged by the need to effect immediate and significant change.

Geographic Preference: North America, Europe
Founded: 1991
Average Investment: $100 - $500 million
Investment Criteria: Special Situations, Restructurings, Turnarounds; Revenues of $250 Million or higher
Industry Group Preference: Manufacturing, Transportation, Business Products & Services
Portfolio Companies: American & Efird LLC, C&D Technologies, Chassis Breaks International, DexKo Global, Electrical Components International, Expera Specialty Solutions, Heritage Home Group, Interational Equipment Solutions, TaylorMade, Winoa, Anchor Glass Container, United Copper Industries, MCI, WWRD, Waupaca, Global Brass and Copper Inc., North American Breweries, Attends, HHI Holdings LLC, Genesis Worldwide Inc., Blue Ridge Paper Products Inc., Bristol Compressors International Inc., United Road, Cloyes, WRCA, Speedline Technologies, AmeriCast Technologies, Blue Heron Paper Company, Ashcroft Inc., New Flyer, Curtis Papers Inc.

Other Locations:
Barckhausstr 1
Frankfurt D-60325
Germany
Phone: 49-6913814777 Fax: 49-6913814774

Key Executives:
Michael Psaros, Managing Partner
Education: BS, Business Administration, Georgetown University
Background: Investment Banker, Bear Stearns & Co.
Directorships: WWRD Holdings, HHI Group Holdings, Global Brass & Copper, North American Breweries, Motor Coach Industries, United Copper Industries
David Shapiro, Managing Partner
Education: BA, History, University of Michigan; MBA, Finance, University of Chicago Graduate School of Business
Background: Investment Banker, Drexel Burnham Lambert; Dean Witter Reynolds
Directorships: WWRD Holdings, HHI Group Holdings, Global Brass & Copper, North American Breweries, Motor Coach Industries, United Copper Industries
Raquel Palmer, Partner
Education: BS, Political Science, Stanford University
Background: Investment Banker, Kidder Peabody & Co.
Directorships: WWRD Holdings, HHI Group Holdings, Global Brass & Copper, North American Breweries, Motor Coach Industries, United Copper Industries
Jay Bernstein, Partner
Education: BA, Economics, University of Michigan; MBA, Columbia University Graduate School of Business
Background: Investment Banking, Schroders
Directorships: WWRD Holdings, Global Brass & Copper, North American Breweries, Motor Coach Industries, United Copper Industries, International Equipment Solutions

1090 KRG CAPITAL PARTNERS
1800 Larimer Street
Suite 220
Denver, CO 80202

Phone: 303-390-5001 Fax: 303-390-5015
web: www.krgcapital.com

Mission Statement: KRG Capital Partners is a middle market private equity group that partners with entrepreneurs and management teams to build industry-leading companies through organic growth and a customer-centric add-on acquisition strategy

Investment Criteria: Early Stage, Later Stage
Industry Group Preference: Business Products & Services, Financial Services, Healthcare, Industrial, Infrastructure, Life Sciences, Media & Entertainment, Retail, Consumer & Leisure, Energy
Portfolio Companies: Accellent, ANSIRA, Aspen Marketing Services, ATI Physical Therapy, Aurora Diagnostics, Avizent, Case Logic, CCS Medical, Celebrity Inc., Cetero Research, CIVCO, Convergint Technologies, Diversified Foodservice Supply, Federal, Fire & Life Safety America, FMI International, The Focus Corporation, Fort Dearborn Company, Global Employment Solutions, HMS Healthcare, Home Solutions, Interior Specialists, Inventus Power, Liberty Dialysis, Marquette Transportation, Modtech, NCTI, OLSON, PAS Technologies, PetroChoice, Scivex, Specialty Finance Company, The Sun Valley Group, Texta America, The Tensar Corporation, TerraMarc Industries, Trafficware, TransCore, Trinity Hospice, Tronair, UniversalPegasus International, Varel International, Vention Medical, White Cap Industries

Key Executives:
Bruce Rogers, Co-Founder/Managing Director
303-390-5018
Education: Law Degree, Duke University; Rome Center for International Law; Bachelor's of Business in Management & Finance, Stetson University
Background: Partner, Hogan & Hartson LLP; Partner, Kirkland & Ellis LLP
Charles Gwirtsman, Co-Founder/Managing Director
303-390-5019
Education: MBA English, Columbia University
Background: Senior Vice President, Fiduciary Capital Management Company; Corporate Vice President, Paine Weber, Inc.; Investment Banker, E.F. Hutton
Directorships: Friends of Yemin Orde
Christopher Lane, Managing Director
303-390-5006
Education: MBA Management/BA Economics, University of California, Irving
Background: CFO, White Cap
Charles Hamilton, Managing Director
303-390-5031
Education: BS Finance, University of California Berkeley
Background: Managing Director, First Analysis Corporation; Managing Director, Robertson, Stephens & Co,

Bennett Thompson, Managing Director
Education: BA, Economics, Washington and Lee University
Background: Vice President, Heritage Partners; Analyst, Harris Williams & Co.
Colton King, Managing Director
Education: BS, Preprofessional Studies, University of Notre Dame; MBA, Kellogg School of Management
Background: CHS Capital; Analyst, Merrill Lynch
Stewart Fisher, Managing Director
Education: MBA Finance, University of Pennsylvania Wharton School; BS Accounting, Lehigh University
Background: Chief Financial Officer/Executive Vice President of Administration, Accellant; Chief Financial Officer/Vice President GenTek
Ted Nark, Managing Director
Education: BS Business Administration, Washington State University
Background: CEO/Chairman, White Cap Construction Supply; Operating Partner, Leonard Green & Partners; CEO, Corporate Express Australia

1091 KTB VENTURES
1 California St.
Suite 2800
San Francisco, CA 94111

Phone: 650-324-4681

Mission Statement: KTB is recognized as one of the top private equity firms in Korea. With KTB's domestic experience and global investment networks in some of Asia's most important financial centers, KTB aims to become one of Asia's leading private equity firms. KTB focuses on finding undervalued proprietary deals to ensure higher profitability by increasing corporate value.

Geographic Preference: Asia
Industry Group Preference: Information Technology, Digital Media & Marketing, Healthcare
Portfolio Companies: 17 Media, Airespace, Alteon WebSystems, Internet Auction, Babbaco, Beceem, Berkanna Wireless, Big Cafe, Brightstorm, Bitfone, CARsgen Therapeutics, Cell Biologics, Centillium, Chips & Media, China Stem Cell, Cintel, Clobotics, Com2Us, Com21, Coolman Entertainment, Copper Mountain, CrucialTec, Epoch Systems, Focus Media, Fortress Technologies, Gravity, Gushan Environmental, IC Works, IDIS, Il Mare, Inphi Corp., Integrant Technologies, Knowre, Koyj, Lmeca, Lumens, Magnum, MCNex, MCubeWorks, Meebo, Mindray Medical, Moloco, Netro Corporation, Neurotech, NoBroker, Novera Optics, ORIG3N, Palm Commerce, Pantech & Curitel, Park Scientific, Polyfuel, Quickturn Design, Satrec Initiative, Sesil, Seven Media, Sino Forest, SNU Precision, Sonus Networks, Spreadtrum, S&S Tech, Standard Diagnostics, Stoke, Telcom Semicon, Tera Semiconductor, Terawave, Terayon, Todou, Valicert, VeriSilicon, Wayfarer, Wireless Access, WiseNut, Xueersi, Xylan Corporation

1092 L CATTERTON PARTNERS
599 West Putnam Avenue
Greenwich, CT 06830

Phone: 203-629-4901 **Fax:** 203-629-4903
e-mail: info@lcatterton.com
web: www.lcatterton.com

Mission Statement: A leading private equity firm with an exclusive focus on providing equity capital to small to middle market consumer companies in North America who are well positioned for attractive growth.

Geographic Preference: United States, Canada
Fund Size: $1 billion
Founded: 1989
Investment Criteria: Acquisitions, MBO, Recapitalizations, Turnarounds, continued growth and development

Industry Group Preference: Food & Beverage, Retailing, Restaurants, Media, Marketing, Consumer Products, Consumer Services
Portfolio Companies: 2XU, 360 Fly, Ainsworth Pet Nutrition, Alasko, Antenna79, Anthony's Coal Fired Pizza, Artsy, Asiaray Media Group, Baccarat, Ba&sh, Bateel, Beanitos, Bliss, Bodytech, Bruxie, Captain Tortue Group, Caredent, CE LA VI, Cellular Line, Chopt, ClearChoice Holdings LLC, CLIO, Cover FX, CorePower Yoga, Crystal Jade, Donup, Dr. Wu, Edible Arrangements, Elemis, Equinox, El Ganso, Espaçolaser, Ferrara Candy Company, Ganni, Genesis Luxury, Gental Monster, Getaway, Giuseppe Zanotti, Gill Mix Green, Hanna Andersson, HelloWorld, Home Chef, Hopdpddy, 'I and Love And You', Ideal Image, IL MAKIAGE, Innis & Gunn, Intercos, John Hardy, Jones The Grocer Group, JustFoodForDogs, Kopari, Leslie's, Lily's Kitchen, Marubi, Mendocino Farms, Mizzen+Main, Naya, Noodles & Co., Ole & Steen, One Spa World, O Luxe Holdings Limited, Pain Doctor, PatientPoint, Peloton, Pepe Jeans, PetVet Care Centers, PIADA Italian Street Food, Pinarello, PIRCH, Princess Yachtz International, Primanti Bros., Protein Bar and Kitchen, Punch Bowl Social, Pure Barre, Rapsodia, Rhone, R.M. Williams, Sasseur, Seafolly, Snap Kitchen, SteelSeries, Steiner Education Group, St. Marche Group, StriVectin, Sweaty Betty, Trendy International Group, Tula, Uncle Julio's, VER, Velvet Taco, Vroom, Advanced Bio Development, Xin Hee Co. Limited, YG Entertainment, Zarbee's

Other Locations:
1, Rue Euler
Paris 751008
France
Phone: 33-1-44-95-91-22

8 Marina View
Asia Square Tower 1, #41-03 018960
Singapore
Phone: 65-6672-7600

610 5th Avenue
Suite 501
New York, NY 10020
Phone: 212-600-2139

40 Avenue Monterey
Luxembourg L 2163
Luxembourg
Phone: 352-28-86-80-40

Key Executives:
J Michael Chu, Global Co-CEO
Education: BA, Psychology and Economics, Bates College
Background: First Pacific Company; Director Finance, Hagemeyer NV; VP/Treasurer, Hibernia Bank; COO, Comtrad; COO, Doyle Graf Raj
Directorships: Committee of 100
Scott A. Dahnke, Global Co-CEO
Education: BS Mechanical Engineering, University of Notre Dame; MBA, Harvard Business School
Background: Managing Director, Deutsche Bank Capital Partners; Managing Director, AEA Investors; CEO, infoUSA; Partner, McKinsey & Company; Merger Department, Goldman, Sachs & Co; General Motors
Michael J. Farello, Managing Partner
Education: BS, Industrial Engineering, Stanford University; MBA, Harvard Business School
Background: Dell, McKinsey & Company
David Heidecorn, Senior Advisor
Education: BA Economics, Lehigh University; MBA Finance, Columbia Business School
Background: CFO, Alarmguard Holdings; Nantucket Holding; Corporate Finance, GE Capital
Andrew C. Taub, Managing Partner, Buyout Fund
Education: BA, University of Michigan; MBA, Columbia Business School
Background: VP, Nantucket Holding; Senior Associate, Coopers & Lybrand

Venture Capital & Private Equity Firms / Domestic Firms

Jonathan H. Owsley, Managing Partner, Growth Fund
Education: BA Political Science, Middlebury College; JD with Honors, Cornell Law School
Background: Senior Principal, Parthenon Group; Corporate Attorney, Hale & Dorr; Assistant Brew Master, Otter Creek Brewing; College Lacrosse Coach
Nikhil Thukral, Managing Partner, Buyout Fund
Education: BS Finance with High Honors, University of Illinois; MBA, University of Chicago
Background: VP, MidOcean Partners; DB Capital Partners; Associate Healthcare Group, JP Morgan & Co
Marc Magliacano, Managing Partners, Buyout Fund
Education: BS, Economics, Wharton School; MBA, Columbia Business School
Background: Principal, North Castle Partners; NMS Capital
Howard Steyn, Partner, Global Opportunities
Education: AB, Social Studies, Harvard College; MBA, Wharton School
Background: Principal, Bain Capital; McKinsey & Company

1093 LABRADOR VENTURES

Phone: 650-366-6000
e-mail: labrador@labrador.com
web: www.labrador.com

Mission Statement: Labrador Ventures is one of the oldest, premier seed stage funds in Silicone Valley.
Geographic Preference: West Coast
Fund Size: $100 million
Founded: 1989
Average Investment: $2 million
Minimum Investment: $500,000
Investment Criteria: Seed, Startup, First-Stage
Industry Group Preference: Information Technology, Digital Media & Marketing, Software, Communications, Semiconductors
Portfolio Companies: Altierre Corporation, Carsala Inc., Delve Networks, EoPlex Technologies Inc., Infoaxe, Integrated Materials Incorporated, Integrated Photovoltaics, Marrone Bio Innovations, MeeVee Inc., Meteor Solutions, Mi5 Networks, Mixbook, Pandora Media Inc., Phonezoo Communications Inc., PlayPhone Inc., Podaddies Inc., Reveal Technology Inc., Rocketfuel Inc., Shotspotter Inc., Solaicx, Transperra, Traverse Networks Incorporated, Ultriva Inc., UStream, Wiredbenefits Inc., Yardbarker Inc.
Key Executives:
  Larry Kubal, Founder/Partner
  Education: Duke University; MBA Stanford Graduate School of Business
  Background: Founder, Pandora Media; Booz Allen & Hamilton; McGraw-Hill Publications
  Directorships: iPV
  Sean Foote, Venture Partner
  Education: BS, Electrical Engineering, University of Missouri Rolla, MBA, Darden School of Business
  Background: Boston Consulting Group; AT&T Bell Laboratories
  Stuart Davidson, Partner
  Education: Harvard College, Harvard University; Harvard Business School
  Background: Founder/CEO, Combion; President, Alkermes; MCI Communications; Warner Communications
  Directorships: iPV, Shotspotter, Ultriva, Ustream

1094 LACUNA GAP CAPITAL
1100 Spruce Street
Suite 202
Boulder, CO 80302

Phone: 303-447-1700 **Fax:** 303-447-1710

Mission Statement: Lacuna seeks to accelerate the growth of our portfolio companies while mitigating investment risk. We collaboratively invest our unique skill sets and experience in order to help build leading companies of tomorrow and create superior returns for our investing partners.
Average Investment: $500,000 - $3 million
Investment Criteria: Early-Stage
Portfolio Companies: Balihoo, concept3D, IntraOp Medical Corporation, Mocapay, Tribute Direct
Key Executives:
  Rawleigh Ralls, Chief Investor
  Sanford Keziah, Chief Strategist
  JK Hullet, Chief Financial Officer
  Background: CEO, @Last Software; CEO, Net Identity

1095 LAKE CAPITAL
875 N Michigan Avenue
Suite 3520
Chicago, IL 60611-2896

Phone: 312-640-7050 **Fax:** 312-640-7051
e-mail: info@lakecapital.com
web: www.lakecapital.com

Mission Statement: Investing selectively in a limited number of middle-market, service-based companies with the potential for growth.
Geographic Preference: North America, Western Europe
Fund Size: $100 million
Average Investment: $50 - $75 million
Investment Criteria: Buyout, Partnership, Starups
Industry Group Preference: Marketing, Healthcare, Technology, Specialty Servaces, Business Outsourcing, Financial
Portfolio Companies: Driveline Retail, Engine, Viamedia
Key Executives:
  Terrence M. Graunke, Co-Founder/Principal
  Education: BA/MBA, University of Chicago
  Paul G. Yovovich, Co-Founder/Principal
  Education: BA, MBA, University of Chicago; CPA
  Background: Founder, Director, Lighthouse Global Network; President, Advance Ross Corporation; Centel Corporation
  Douglas Rescho, Principal
  Education: BS, Finance, University Of Illinois
  Background: Citigroup Global Markets; Standard & Poor's
  Collin Abert, Principal
  Education: BS, Accountancy, University of Illinois
  Background: JP Morgan

1096 LANCET CAPITAL
100 Technology Drive
Suite 200
Pittsburgh, PA 15219

Phone: 412-402-9914 **Fax:** 412-452-9480
web: www.lancetcapital.com

Mission Statement: Investing in exceptional researchers, clinicians and entrepreneurs to commercialize innovative technologies in the biomedical field.
Founded: 1998
Investment Criteria: Early Stage
Industry Group Preference: Biopharmaceuticals, Medical Devices, Bioinformatics, Therapeutics, Diagnostics
Portfolio Companies: Ardais, Dyax, Enanta, Scion Pharmaceuticals, Stemnion, Stentntor, VivoQuest
Key Executives:
  William J Golden, Managing Director
  617-330-9345
  Fax: 617-330-9349
  e-mail: wgolden@lancetcapital.com
  Education: MBA, Harvard Business School; BS, University of Notre Dame
  Background: Management Consultant, Arthur D. Little; Director, Community Technology Fund

Venture Capital & Private Equity Firms / Domestic Firms

George L Sing, Managing Director
212-332-3220
Fax: 212-332-3221
e-mail: sing@lancetcapital.com
Education: MBA, Harvard Business School; BE, Stevens Institute of Technology
Background: Co-Founder/Senior Partner, Advanced Technology Ventures; Merrill Lynch
Directorships: Regeneron

1097 LASALLE CAPITAL GROUP
70 West Madison Street
Suite 5710
Chicago, IL 60602

Phone: 312-236-7041 **Fax:** 312-236-0720
e-mail: contact@lasallecapital.com
web: www.lasallecapital.com

Mission Statement: To create value for investors by investing in family and entrepreneur-owned businesses in the food and beverage and business services sectors.

Geographic Preference: United States
Fund Size: $210 million
Founded: 1984
Average Investment: $20 million
Minimum Investment: $10 million
Investment Criteria: MBO, Growth, Consolidations, Recaps, LBO
Industry Group Preference: Food & Beverage, Technology, Business Products & Services
Portfolio Companies: Avantech Testing Services, Brown & Joseph, Delorio Foods, Eclipse Advantage, Fresh Origins, Gen3 Marketing, MetaSource, National Gift Card, Processing.com, Westminster Foods

Key Executives:
Rocco J. Martino, Co-Founder/Partner
e-mail: rmartino@lasallecapital.com
Education: BBA, Finance, University of Notre Dame; MBA, Loyola University of Chicago; CPA
Background: Partner, PriceWaterhouseCoopers
Jeffrey M. Walters, Co-Founder/Managing Partner
e-mail: jwalters@lasallecapital.com
Education: BA, Tufts University
Background: Partner, Managing Director, BT Securities Corporation; Chicago/Europe Partners L.P.; Vice President, Citicorp Leveraged Capital Group; American National Bank; Trust Company of Chicago
I. Donald Rosuck, Senior Operating Advisor
e-mail: drosuck@lasallecapital.com
Education: BS, City University of New York
Background: President & CEO, Culligan International; President, Home Products Division, Beatrice Company; Controller, W.R. Grace & Company
Walter G. Freedman, Senior Operating Advisor
e-mail: wfreedman@lasallecapital.com
Education: BA, Dartmouth College; MBA, Tuck School of Business Administration, Dartmouth
Background: COO, Wheels, Inc.; Co-Investor & CEO, Yoplait USA; Presient, Fuller Brush Company; IBM
Steven W. Parks, Senior Operating Advisor
e-mail: sparks@lasallecapital.com
Education: Valparaiso University; MBA, Kellogg School of Management, Northwestern University; CPA
Background: President & COO, HAVI Group LP; EVP & COO, Wico Corporation
Nicholas S. Christopher, Partner
e-mail: nchristopher@lasallecapital.com
Education: BA, Albion College; MBA, University of Chicago Booth School of Business
Background: Senior Associate, UIB Capital; CIVC Partners; Goldman Sachs & Co
Kelly A. Cornelis, Partner
e-mail: kcornelis@lasallecapital.com
Education: BBA, University of Notre Dame; MBA, Kellogg School of Management, Northwestern University
Background: Vice President, SB Partners; William Blair & Company

1098 LATTERELL VENTURE PARTNERS
1603 Camino Ramon
Suite 200
San Ramon, CA 94583

Phone: 925-242-2618
web: www.lvpcapital.com

Mission Statement: To help entrepreneurs create important new healthcare companies treating major diseases and medical disorders.

Geographic Preference: United States
Fund Size: $300 million
Founded: 2001
Average Investment: $50,000 to $10 million
Minimum Investment: $50,000
Investment Criteria: Early Stage, Medium Stage, Late Stage, Spinouts
Industry Group Preference: Biotechnology, Pharmaceuticals, Research & Development, Bio Materials, Medical Devices, Diagnostics, Healthcare, Instrumentation
Portfolio Companies: Aptinyx, Calistoga, Cellective Therapeutics, Ensure Medical, Evoke, ForteBio, Inova Labs, IntegenX, Meritage, Naurex, OncoMed, Pathway, PerceptiMed, ProteinSimple, Proteolix, Pulmonx, Revascular Therapeutics, TetraLogic, Transcend, Viracta

Key Executives:
Patrick Latterell, General Partner
e-mail: pat@lvpcapital.com
Education: SB, MIT; MBA, Stanford Business School
Background: General Partner, Venrock Associates; General Partner, Rotschild Ventures
Peter Fitzgerald, General Partner
e-mail: peter@lvpcapital.com
Education: BS, University Of Santa Clara; RA, Stanford University; MS, Renseelaer Polytechnic Institute; MD, PhD, Dartmouth College
Directorships: Interventional Cardiology Research Laboratory, FDA Medical Device Advisory Panel
Jim Woody, General Partner
e-mail: jim@lvpcapital.com
Education: MD, Loma Linda University; Pediatric Immunology, Duke University & Children's Hospital in Boston (Harvard); PhD in Immunology, University of London, England
Background: CEO, OncoMed; President, General Manager, Roche Bioscience; CSO, Senior VP, Centocor; US Navy Transplant Research Program
Directorships: Viracta Therapeutics, ForteBio, ProteinSimple
Steve Salmon, General Partner
e-mail: steve@lvpcapital.com
Education: BS in Chemical Engineering, University of Maine
Background: Engineering Manager, CVIS; VP of R&D, Boston Scientific; Co-Founder, Integrated Vascular Systems; Co-Founder, Ensure Medical
Ken Widder, General Partner
e-mail: ken@lvpcapital.com
Education: MD, Northwestern University; Pathology, Duke University
Background: Founder, CEO, NovaCardia; Founder, Chairman, CEO, Santarus; Chairman, CEO, Converge Medical; Chairman, CEO, Molecular Biosystems
Directorships: Evoke Pharma, Meritage Pharma, Naurex Inc.
Bob Curry, Venture Consultant
e-mail: bob@lvpcapital.com
Education: Bs, Physics, University of Illinois; MS, PhD, Chemistry, Purdue Univesity
Background: Partner, Alliance Technology Ventures; Partner, Sprout Group; President, Merrill Lynch Venture Capital

Venture Capital & Private Equity Firms / Domestic Firms

1099 LAUDER PARTNERS LLC
Phone: 650-323-5700 Fax: 650-232-2171
e-mail: gary@lauderpartners.com
web: www.lauderpartners.com

Mission Statement: Lauder Partners is an entity investing in various realms of the technology field. We invest both in companies as well as in funds, both venture and others.

Geographic Preference: United States, Canada
Average Investment: $500,000 - $5 million
Industry Group Preference: Technology, Information Technology, Internet
Portfolio Companies: AirVine Scientific, Beyond Meat, Caavo Inc, Cortene, Didi Chuxing, Elevian, Heal, Hidden Level, Hippo Insurance, Hyperloop Transportation Technologies, Kheiron Medical Technologies, Level, LVL Technologies, NaNotics, OpenGov, Openwater, Polystream, Raftr, Solius, SpinLaunch, Uber, UniKey, Via Transportation, Visu, WaterGuru, XCures

Key Executives:
Gary Lauder, Managing Director
e-mail: gary@lauderpartners.com
Education: BA, International Relations, University of Pennsylvania; BS, Economics, Wharton School; MBA, Stanford Graduate School of Business
Background: Aetna, Jacobs & Ramo Technology Ventures, Wolfensohn Associates
Directorships: ActiveVideo Networks, Promptu, MediaFriends, ShotSportter

1100 LAUNCHBOX DIGITAL
76 Cedar Street
Seattle, WA 98121

Mission Statement: LaunchBox Digital is a seed-stage investment firm helping entrepreneurs maximize their chance of success. It is a place for cutting-edge ideas and cutting-edge talent. New entrepreneurs face lots of obstacles in making their vision a reality, and many great ideas and great talent never get out of the starting gate. LaunchBox Digital brings entrepreneurs the seed capital, advice, practical guidance, and connections to help new technology and digital media businesses succeed.

Geographic Preference: North Carolina
Investment Criteria: Early-Stage
Industry Group Preference: Technology, New Media
Portfolio Companies: Altec Lansing, AT&T, Banana Boat, Brunton, Cisco, Costco, Ecova, Hewlett-Packard, IKEA, Johnson & Johnson, Kodak Dental Systems, Lilly, Microsoft, Motorola, neea, NetGear, OfficeMax, Pfizer, Plantronics, Playtex, Samsung, Seagate, Staples, Wacom

Key Executives:
John McKinley, Founding Partner
e-mail: john@launchboxdigital.com
Education: Wharton School
Background: CTO and Founder and President of Digital Services for AOL; Founder and CEO, OurParents; Executive Vice President and head of Global Technology and Services, Merrill Lynch; Senior Vice President and Chief Technology and Information Officer, GE Capital; Partner, Ernst & Young
Mark McDowell
e-mail: mark@launchboxdigital.com
Education: BSEE and MSEE Degrees, MIT
Background: Co-Founder and Managing Partner, Acta Wireless; Manager, MLJ; Officer, United States Air Force
Matthew Jacobson
e-mail: matt@launchboxdigital.com
Education: BA, University of Pennsylvania; MBA, Wharton School
Background: AOL; ABN AMRO; WR Hambrecht; Peter J. Solomon Co.; Toronto Dominion Securities
Steve Lerner, Partner
Education: MA and PhD, University of North Carolina at Chapel Hill
Background: Capstrat; FGI; Yankelovich Partners; KBM; Sterling Cellular; Blue Hill Group
Lee Buck, Partner
Education: BS, Systems Engineering, University of Virginia
Background: Blue Bright Ventures; Near-Time; Extensibility, Inc; Software Designs Unlimited; Arthur Andersen

1101 LAUNCHCAPITAL
195 Church Street
Suite 1700
Cambridge, MA 06510

web: www.launchcapital.com

Mission Statement: LaunchCapital addresses the capital needs of companies that are in the earliest stages of funding by providing a needed source of financing to companies that can quickly advance to the next level of development.

Founded: 2008
Investment Criteria: Seed-Stage
Industry Group Preference: Technology, Consumer Products, Healthcare, Mobile, Software, Internet
Portfolio Companies: Abbey Post, Aerin Medical, Affinimark Technologies, AI Exchange, Amasten, amSTATZ, Apparel Media Group, Apperian, Bluetrain Mobile, C8 Sciences, CardioPhotonics, CardStar, Carsala, Case Continuum, Centri, CMD Bioscience, Collaborate.com, Compology, Continuity, Copiun, Crew, CustomMade, Dailey Grommet, Dekko.co, Diffinity Genomics, Digital Pickle, Domino, Double Dutch, Draker, Eat Club, Eight Spokes, EpiEP, Equityzen, EyelCo, Faraday, Fashion Playres, FMP, FormLabs, Freight Farms, Genomera, Ginger.io, TheGreenBridge.com, Hadapt, Helium, Hodo Soy Beanery, Hyperink, IncentiveTargeting, Innovatient, Intelligent Clearing Network, InterVene, inVino, iQuartic, i-Team, JackCards, Just the Right Book, Karmic Labs, LaunchPad, Leapset, LearnLaunch, Lefora, Life36, LiQuifix, Liquor.com, LittleBorrowedDress, Localytics, LOCJ, LP33, Marlin Mobile, Mayvenn, MerchantAtlas, Mobee, MoMeland Technologies, Nanny Caddy, Niveus Medical, NovaTract, Novogy, Nutrivise, OnFarm, OurStage.com, Ovuline, Paper G, Parelastic, Petnet, Physcient, Play Vs., Profounder, Project Decor, Promoboxx, QDrinks, Quincy, RentJuice, ReportGrid, REsurety, RunKeeper, SafePorche, SecretBuilders, Semantifi, SemiProbe, SKYstream, Socialsci, STR, Supply Hog, Sustainable Real Estate Manager, Techstars, Traackr, Transparent Healthcare, Tripping, True Body, Vicix, Viral Gains, Voltage, Xconomy, Young Broadcasters of America, Your Mechanic, Zadspace, Zagster, Zozi, YouRenew.com

Other Locations:
142 Temple Street
Suite 206
New Haven, CT 06510

500 7th Avneue
17th Floor
New York, NY 10018

Key Executives:
Elon S Broms, Managing Director
Education: BA, Economics, George Washington University; MBA, Yale School of Management
Background: Management Consultant, Fidelity Investments; Corporate Finance, Citigroup
Konstantine Drakonakis, Venture Partner
Education: Civil & Environmental Engineering, University of Vermont; MS, Environmental Management, Yale University
Background: Connecticut Innovations
Bill McCullen, Chief Investment Officer
Education: BS, MS, Electrical Engineering, Worcester Polytechnic Institute; MBA, MIT Sloan School of Business
Background: Sell Side Equity Analyst, Susquehanna Financial Group

Venture Capital & Private Equity Firms / Domestic Firms

Dave Shen, Venture Partner
Background: Yahoo!

1102 LAUNCHCYTE
2403 Sidney Street
Suite 270
Pittsburgh, PA 15203

Phone: 412-481-2200 Fax: 412-592-0349
e-mail: patty@launchcyte.com
web: www.launchcyte.com

Mission Statement: To build value by creating, seeding and harvesting life sciences companies. LaunchCyte's experience, network and resources offer the opportunity to develop early stage technologies into market-leading companies.

Founded: 2000
Investment Criteria: Early-Stage
Industry Group Preference: Life Sciences
Portfolio Companies: Celsense, Crystalplex, Immunetrics, Knopp Biosciences LLC, Reaction Biology

Key Executives:
Tom Petzinger, Founder/Chairman/President/CEO
Education: BS, Journalism, Northwestern University
Background: EVP, Business Development, Knopp Neursciences
Directorships: Knopp Biosciences
Babs Carryer, Co-Founder/Director
Education: Masters, Management, Carnegie Mellon University
Background: President & CEO, RemComm; President, Carryer Consulting
Gregory T Hebrank MD, Director
Education: BS, Biomedical Engineering, Vanderbilt University; MD, Tulane University School of Medicine; MBA, Carnegie Mellon Unversity Tepper School of Business
Background: Founder & Director, Knopp Neurosciences
Directorships: Knopp Biosciences
Robert Unkovic, Director
Education: BS, Ohio State University
Background: Partner, BPU Investment Management

1103 LAUNCHPAD LA
Los Angeles, CA

web: www.launchpad.la

Mission Statement: Launchpad LA is 'the top startup accelerator in Southern California.' We offer each accepted company $25k - $100k, free office space in the heart of Santa Monica (one block from the beach) for four months, a ton of perks and discounts, and most importantly, access to a massive network of mentors, advisors, and investors.

Geographic Preference: Los Angeles
Founded: 2010
Investment Criteria: Seed-Stage
Industry Group Preference: Technology
Portfolio Companies: Adomic, Advocus, Atlas, AudioMicro, BigFrame, ChowNow, Chromatik, CircleSt, Cojoin, Combatant Gentleman, Connectifier, Cramster.com, DanceOn, Datapop, Divshot, Elephant Drive, Fitzroy, Flipgloss, Focus:Trainr, Gendai Games, Guide, Gumgum, Ibeatyou.com, InheritedHealth, JobSync, Jukin Media, Lettuce, Listn, Mark43, Melon, Milk & Honey, Mobile Roadie, Mogreet, Monospace, MoVoxx, Panna, Paratinova.com, Parachute, Periodical, Pop-Up Pantry, Pose, Preact.io, Prevoty, Prospectwise, Ranker, Shopnation, Sometrics, Survly, Swing by Swing, TechForward, Ticket Mob, Totspot, Tradesy, Triptrotting, TrueVault, Tuition.io, Vessix, Victorious, Vow to be Chic, Weilos, Zefr

Key Executives:
Sam Teller, Co-Founder/Managing Director
Education: BA, Harvard College
Background: Charlie, Google AdWords, Credit Suisse

Nicholas Green, Entrepreneur-in-Residence
Education: BA, Economics, Harvard College
Background: Ivy Insiders, Revolution Prep
Chelsea Kent, Entrepreneur-in-Residence
Background: Founder, Scratch

1104 LAUNCHPAD VENTURE GROUP
Boston, MA

web: www.launchpadventuregroup.com

Mission Statement: Launchpad Venture Group, a Boston-based angel investment group, provides funding and advice to early-stage companies. Launchpad looks for innovative, technology-driven startup companies addressing a significant market opportunity where our investment can make a difference. We introduce entrepreneurs to potential investors through business plan presentations at monthly meetings. Launchpad Venture Group consists of individual angel investor members interested in achieving superior returns by financing privately held companies at an early stage of development.

Average Investment: $250,000 - $1 million
Investment Criteria: Early-Stage
Industry Group Preference: High Technology, Financial Services, Industrial, Life Sciences, Healthcare, Software, Information Technology, Internet, E-Commerce & Manufacturing, Media, Social Media, Mobile, Wireless, Medical Devices, Diagnostics
Portfolio Companies: 3Play Media, 7AC Technology, Building Engines, CabinetM, Cambridge Blockchain, CIMCON, Clean Fiber, Cognoptix, Concentric, Content Raven, Crowdly, Electra Vehicles, EnergySage, EveryScape, ezCater, GeoOrbital, Gravyty, Groupsize, InCrowd, Infobionic, iTeam, Kalion, KnipBio, ListenWise, Localytics, ManufactOn, Medumo, MultiSensor Sci., Mobius Imaging, Netra, Parkloco, Peach, Pepperlane, Pixability, Powerhouse Dynamics, Precision Ventures, Prolific Works, Punchbowl, QStream, Repsly, Siamab, Smart Lunches, SmartVid.io, Testive, Tetragenetics, TimeTrade, TruTouch, WeSpire, WindGap, Woo Sports, Zagster, Ziiproom, Zippity

Key Executives:
Hambleton Lord, Chairman
Education: Computer Science, Brown University
Background: Co-Founder, Advanced Visual Systems
Directorships: Cambridge Trust, EveryScape, Netra, Qstream, Repsly
Christopher Mirabile, Managing Director
Education: BA, Colgate University; JD, Boston College Law School
Background: CFO, IONA Technologies; Corporate Lawyer, Testa Hurwitz & Thiebeault; Managment Consultant, Price Waterhouse

1105 LDV CAPITAL
111 East 14th Street
Suite 102
New York, NY 10003

web: www.ldv.co

Mission Statement: LDV Capital seeks to invest in visual technology businesses, such as virtual reality and digital learning.

Geographic Preference: US, Canada, Europe
Founded: 2012
Average Investment: $300, 000 - #500,000
Investment Criteria: Pre-Seed, Seed, Early Stage
Industry Group Preference: Artificial Intelligence, Technology, Consumer, Retail, Robotics, Virtual Reality, Satellite Imaging, Medical Imaging, Security, Photonics, Machine Learning
Portfolio Companies: Camio, Carbon Robotics, Clarifai, Ezra, Fantasmo, Farmeron, Geniachip, Lookmark, Mapillary, Mediachain Labs, Narrative, Newco, Unsplash, Sea Machines, ShopPad, Synthesia, TVision Insights, Uizard, UPSKILL, Voyant Photonics

Venture Capital & Private Equity Firms / Domestic Firms

Key Executives:
Evan Nisselson, Founder/General Partner
Education: University of Vermont
Background: VP of Business Development, Eyetide Media; Founder/CEO, Digital Railroad Inc.; Consultant, Nisselson Co.; Advisor/Mentor, TechPeaks
Abigail Hunter-Syed, Vice President, Operations
Education: BA, University of Rochester; MA, International University, Geneva
Background: Co-Founder, WorldBrain LLC; Economic Researcher, World Trade Organization; Operations, Von Essen Group; Senior Associate, Morgan Stanley

1106 LEAPFROG VENTURES
830 Menlo Avenue
Suite 100
Menlo Park, CA 94025

Phone: 650-926-9900 **Fax:** 650-233-1301

Mission Statement: Our mission is to help our portfolio companies Leapfrog their competitors and achieve industry-leading levels of competitive and market performance as quickly as possible.

Geographic Preference: Western United States
Founded: 2000
Average Investment: $1 - $3 million
Investment Criteria: Seed Stage
Industry Group Preference: Computer Related, Software, Information Technology, Communications, Wireless, Consumer Technology
Portfolio Companies: Avaak, Ace Metrix, Cloud9 Analytics, Global Analytics, HotLink, IronKey, PureWave, RedSeal, SilverTail, Vast, Zebit

Key Executives:
Peter Sinclair, Director
e-mail: pete@leapfrogventures.com
Education: SB, Engineering, MIT; Stanford Business School
Background: Hewlett Packard
Andy Fillat, Director
e-mail: andy@leapfrogventures.com
Education: SB, SM, MIT; MBA, Harvard
Background: Advent International Corp.; Fidelity Investments

1107 LEASING TECHNOLOGIES INTERNATIONAL INC.
221 Danbury Road
Wilton, CT 06897

Phone: 203-563-1100 **Fax:** 203-563-1112
web: www.ltileasing.com

Mission Statement: To preserve working capital through innovative equipment financing. We acquire/lease business equipment essentials like security devices, computers and servers, lab/test equipment, communications equipment, manufacturing/production equipment and office automation equipment.

Fund Size: $30 million
Founded: 1983
Average Investment: $500,000
Minimum Investment: $250,000
Investment Criteria: Seed, Startup, First-Stage, Second-Stage, Mezzanine, LBO
Industry Group Preference: Software, Telecommunications, Biotechnology, Health Related, Internet Technology, Hardware, E-Commerce & Manufacturing, Life Sciences, Education
Portfolio Companies: About.com, Akamai Technology, Array BioPharma, Axolotl, BeFree, Inc. (TriVida Corp.), Carr Separations/Kendro Lab Products, Coordinated Care Solutions, Digitrace/Sleepmed Inc., Earthlink Network Inc., General Bandwidth, Healtheon-WebMD, LTX Corporation, Metavante, National Semiconductor, NetZero Inc., Pyxis -

Helpmate Robotics, Sonexis, SPSS Inc., Superconductor Technologies Inc., TheStreet.com, TransMeta, Triton Network Systems, Virage Logic

Other Locations:
10 Liberty Square
Boston, MA 02109
Phone: 617-426-4116 **Fax:** 617-482-6475

27068 La Paz Road
Suite 270
Aliso Viejo, CA 92656
Phone: 949-290-4312 **Fax:** 949-215-9761

Key Executives:
Jerry Sprole, President/CEO
203-563-1100 ext 212
e-mail: jsprole@LTILeasing.com
Education: BA, Yale University
Background: Founder, President, CEO, LTI Ventures Leasing Corporation; CFO, Intech Capital Corporation; VP, Bank of Boston
William I MacDonald, Senior Vice President
617-426-4116
e-mail: wmacdonald@LTILeasing.com
Education: BA, Tufts University; Advanced Management Program, Harvard University
Background: Senior VP, Bank of Boston; Thirty-one years managing NYC Lending Corresponding Banking and Banking Services Division
Arnold J Hoegler, Executive VP/Founder/COO
203-563-1100 ext 213
e-mail: ahoegler@ltileasing.com
Education: BA, St. John's University
Background: Seven years as leasing and financial services manager at KPMG Peat Marwick; CPA
George A Parker, Executive VP/CFO/Founder
203-563-1100 ext 214
e-mail: gparker@LTILeasing.com
Education: BS Mathematics, Wake Forest; MBA Finance, University of North Carolina
Background: VP, Finance of DPF Computer Leasing; Second VP, Continental Illinois Bank; Founder, LTI Ventures Leasing
Skip Baum, General Counsel/Secretary
203-563-1100
e-mail: sbaum@ltileasing.com
Education: LL.B, Harvard Law School, Yale University

1108 LEE EQUITY PARTNERS
40 West 57th Street
Suite 1620
New York, NY 10019

Phone: 212-906-4900
e-mail: Leeequitypartners@leeequity.com
web: www.leeequity.com

Mission Statement: To work with strong management teams and invest in companies with high growth potential.

Geographic Preference: United States
Founded: 2006
Average Investment: $50 - $150 million
Investment Criteria: Middle Market, Buyouts, Acquisitions, Growth Capital
Industry Group Preference: Business Products & Services, Healthcare Services, Financial Services, Retail, Consumer & Leisure, Consumer, Distribution, Logistics, Media
Portfolio Companies: Aimbridge Hospitality, Captive Resources, Carlile Bancshares, Cross Mediaworks, Deb Shops, Eating Recovery Center, Interluxe Holdings, Midcap Financial, Papa Murphy's International, PDR Network, Skopos Financial, The Edelman Financial Group, Universal American

Key Executives:
Thomas H Lee, Chairman
Education: AB, Economics, Harvard College
Background: Chairman & CEO, Thomas H Lee Partners;

VP, First National Bank of Boston; Analyst, LF Rothschild & Company
Directorships: Aimbridge Hospitality, The Edelman Financial Group, Papa Murphy's International
Mark K Gormley, Partner
Education: BSBA, Finance & Economics, University of Denver; MBA, New York University
Background: Co-Founder & Partner, Capital Z Financial Services Partners; Managing Director, Donaldson Lufkin & Jenrette; Merrill Lynch
Directorships: The Edelman Financial Group, Skopos Financial Group, Captive Resources, Carlile Bancshares, MidCap Financial, PDR Network, Universal American
Benjamin A Hochberg, Partner
Education: AB, Chemistry, Harvard College; MBA, Harvard Business School
Background: Principal, Odyssey Investment Partners; Principal, Bain Capital Partners
Directorships: Aimbridge Hospitality, The Edelman Financial Group, Papa Murphy's International, Skopos Financial Group
Yoo Jin Kim, Partner
Education: AB, Biochemistry, Dartmouth College; MBA, Harvard Business School
Background: Principal, Bain Capital; Consultant, Corporate Decisions Inc.
Directorships: Aimbridge Hospitality, Cross Mediaworks, Eating Recovery Center, Interluxe Holdings, Papa Murphy's International, Paragon Industries
Caitlyn MacDonald, Partner/Head of Investor Relations
Education: BS, Emerson College; MBA, Babson College
Background: Director, First Reserve; Investment Manager, SVG Advisers; Wellington Management
Joseph B Rotberg, Partner/Chief Financial Officer/Chief Compliance Officer
Education: BS, Accounting, School of Professional Accountancy, Long Island University; CPA
Background: CFO, Specialty Consulting, Mercer Management Consulting; Worldwide Director, Internal Audit, Booz Allen Hamilton; Analyst, Salomon Brothers; Senior Auditor, Coopers & Lybrand
Directorships: Captive Resources, Eating Recovery Center

1109 LEEDS EQUITY PARTNERS
590 Madison Ave.
41st Floor
New York, NY 10022

Phone: 212-835-2000 Fax: 212-835-2020
e-mail: info@leedsequity.com
web: www.leedsequity.com

Mission Statement: Leeds Equity partners with successful management teams to invest in established companies with strong track records. Our investment approach is to concentrate on a limited number of high-quality investments, which allows us to devote substantial time and resources to each portfolio company in order to drive the necessary growth that can produce significant capital appreciation.

Industry Group Preference: Education, Training, Information Services, Business Products & Services
Portfolio Companies: Amplifire, BARBRI, Campus Management, CeriFi, Covenant Review, Edcentric, Education Management Corporation, EduK Group, Endeavor Schools, Evanta, Exterro, Fusion, iModules, INTO University Partnerships, Lrn, Knowledge Factor Nobel Learning Communities, Project Management Academy, Prosci, Simplify Compliance

Key Executives:
Jeffrey T Leeds, Co-Founder & Managing Partner
e-mail: jeffrey.leeds@leedsequity.com
Education: BA, History, Yale University; Marshall Scholar, Univ. of Oxford; JD, Harvard Law School
Background: Corporate Finance, Lazard Freres & Co.; Law Clerk, Hon. William J. Brennan Jr, Supreme Court of the United States
Directorships: Amplifire, BARBRI, CeriFi, Endeavor Schools, Exterro, Fusion Education Group, INTO University Partnerships, LRN, Simplify Compliance
Robert A Bernstein, Co-Founder & Managing Partner
e-mail: robert.bernstein@leedsequity.com
Education: BS, Economics, Wharton School
Background: M&A, Lazard Freres & Co.
Directorships: Campus Management, Edcentric, Project Management Academy, Prosci
Jacques V Galante, Partner
e-mail: jacques.galante@leedsequity.com
Education: BS, Finance, University of Illinois Champaign-Urbana
Background: Principal, Buyout Team, The Carlyle Group; Investment Banking, M&A Group, Salomon Smith Barney
Directorships: Amplifire, BARBRI, Campus Management, CeriFi, Edcentric, Exterro, LRN
Peter A Lyons, Partner & Chief Financial Officer
e-mail: peter.lyons@leedsequity.com
Education: BS, Accounting, Saint Michael's College; MBA, Stern School of Business
Background: Senior Manager, Ernst & Young LLP
Scott VanHoy, Partner
e-mail: scott.vanhoy@leedsequity.com
Education: BA, Economics, University of North Carolina; MBA, University of Chicago Graduate School of Business
Background: Vice President, DLJ Merchant Banking Partners; Associate, Quad-C Management; Investment Banking, Banc of America Securities LLC
Directorships: Endeavor Schools, Fusion Education Group, Project Management Academy, Prosci, Simplify Compliance
Eric Gevada, Managing Director
e-mail: eric.geveda@leedsequity.com
Education: BBA, Finance & Economics, University of Notre Dame; MBA, Stanford Graduate School of Business
Background: Senior Associate, Arsenal Capital Partners; Associate, Lightyear Capital
Directorships: Amplifire, BARBRI, CeriFi, Edcentric
Christopher J Mairs, Managing Director
e-mail: christopher.mairs@leedsequity.com
Education: BSc, Mathematics, University of St. Andrews
Background: Greenhill & Co.
Directorships: Endeavor Schools, INTO University Partnerships, Project Management Academy, Prosci, Simplify Compliance
David C Neverson, Principal
e-mail: david.neverson@leedsequity.com
Education: BA, Business Administration, Morehouse College; MBA, Wharton School
Background: ICV Capital Partners
Directorships: Campus Management, Fusion Education Group
Kevin Malone, Principal
e-mail: kevin.malone@leedsequity.com
Education: BSBA, Finance and International Business, Olin Business School at Washington University
Background: Analyst, Harris Williams & Co.
Directorships: Amplifire, BARBRI, Edcentric, Exterro, LRN

1110 LEGACY VENTURE
180 Lytton Avenue
Palo Alto, CA 94301

Phone: 650-324-5980 Fax: 650-324-5982
e-mail: info@legacyventure.com
web: www.legacyventure.com

Mission Statement: Legacy is a unique organization tapping into the financial power of venture capital and combining it with an extensive philanthropic community.

Founded: 1999

Venture Capital & Private Equity Firms / Domestic Firms

Key Executives:
Russell B Hall, Co-Founder & Managing Partner
Education: MBA, Stanford Graduate School; MS, University of California; BS, United States Military
Background: Operator, Merrill Pickard Anderson & Eyre; Sr. Vice President, R. Eliot King & Associates
Kelli Cullinane, Managing Partner & Chief Financial Officer
Education: BA, Economics, MA, Accounting, University of Michigan
Background: HRJ Capital, Ernst & Young
Ben Choi, Managing Partner
Education: BA, Computer Science, Harvard University; MBA, Columbia Business School
Background: Adobe Creative Cloud; Greystripe; Co-Founder, CoffeeTable
Alan Marty, Managing Partner
Education: MBA, Stanford University; Iowa State University
Background: NASA; Hewlett-Packard

1111 LEMHI VENTURES
12800 Whitewater Dr.
Suite 100
Hopkins, MN 55343

Phone: 952-908-9680 Fax: 952-908-9780
e-mail: info@lemhiventures.com
web: www.lemhiventures.com

Mission Statement: Lemhi Ventures invests in companies that disrupt and transform the delivery of health care services. We seek entrepreneurs with market-driven new ideas, competitive assets and experienced teams that promise to create and sustain a more imaginative, more efficient, and more responsible health care system.

Industry Group Preference: Healthcare
Portfolio Companies: Bind, Digital Reasoning, PlanSource, PokitDok, Recondo Technology, Sandlot Solutions, Shareable Ink, TransEngen, Inc.

Key Executives:
Tony Miller, Managing Partner
Education: St. Olaf College; MS, University of Illinois; MBA, Cornell University
Background: UnitedHealth, Deloitte Consulting; CEO, Definity Health
Directorships: Bind
Jodi Hubler, Managing Director
Education: MAIR, BBA, Tillie College of Business, University of Iowa
Background: Cargill, Accoa, Definity Health
Directorships: Bind, Digital Reasoning, PokitDok, PlanSource, Recondo Technology

1112 LEO CAPITAL HOLDINGS, LLC
400 Skokie Blvd.
Suite 410
Northbrook, IL 60062

Phone: 847-418-3240 Fax: 847-418-3424

Mission Statement: Leo Capital Holdings, LLC is a privately funded venture investor making investments in early and later stage private companies. Our focus is primarily on consumer oriented technology and applications. We like ventures that target very large markets, and consider investment opportunities across the United States. Leo maintains a broad network of contacts, investors, and advisors with whom we work after investing to help build value, and usually make investments that allow for our active involvement.

Geographic Preference: United States
Minimum Investment: $1 million - $3 million
Investment Criteria: Early-stage, Late-stage
Industry Group Preference: Entertainment, Internet, Wireless, Technology, Consumer Technology
Portfolio Companies: EpiWorks, FunMobility, GirlSense, GrubHub, JabberSmack, Mighty Cast, NetNearU, PopStarClub, Shoutlet, Starnet Interactive, Tickr

Key Executives:
Randy O. Rissman, Founder and Managing Director
Education: BBA, The University of Michigan; MBA, The Harvard Business School
Background: Founder and CEO, Tiger Electronics

1113 LEONARD GREEN & PARTNERS LP
11111 Santa Monica Boulevard
Suite 2000
Los Angeles, CA 90025

Phone: 310-954-0444 Fax: 310-954-0404
web: www.leonardgreen.com

Mission Statement: To partner with management to enhance the value of companies through operational improvements, acquisitions, financial engineering and other strategic initiatives.

Geographic Preference: United States
Fund Size: $5.3 billion
Founded: 1989
Average Investment: $150 million
Minimum Investment: $50 million
Investment Criteria: LBO, MBO. Focus on companies worth more than $100 million. No start-ups, no technology-centric ventures
Industry Group Preference: Consumer Services, Business Products & Services, Consumer Products, Distribution, Financial Services, Healthcare, Media, Retail, Consumer & Leisure
Portfolio Companies: Advantage Sales & Marketing, AerSale Holdings, Animal Health International, Aspen Dental Management, Authentic Brands Group, BJ's Wholesale Club, Caliber Collision, Cascade Bancorp, CCC Information Services, Charter Nex Films, CHG Healthcare Services, Clean Energy Fuels, The Container Store, CPA Global, David's Bridal, Del Taco Holdings, Ellucian, Equinox Fitness, ExamWorks, HITS, IMS Health, InsightGlobal, IQVia, Jcrew Group, Jetro Cash & Carry, Jo-Ann Stores, LifeTime, Lucky Brand, MD VIP, Mister Car Wash Holdings, Motorsport Aftermarket Group, MultiPlan, North American Partners in Anesthesia, Palms Casino Resort, PDC Brands, Petco Animal Supplies, Promach, Prospect Medical Holdings, Puregym, Restorix Health, Savers, Scitor Corporation, The Shade Store, Shake Shack, Signet Jewelers, SoulCycle, The Sports Authority, SRS Distribution, Tank Holdings Corp., The Tire Rack, Topshop/Topman Holdings, Tourneau, Troon, Union Square Hospitality Group, United States Infrastructure Corporation, US Renal Care, Veritext

Key Executives:
John G Danhakl, Managing Partner
e-mail: danhakl@leonardgreen.com
Education: BA Economics, University of California, Berkeley; MBA, Harvard Business School
Background: Managing Director, DLJ; VP Corporate Finance, Drexel
Directorships: Advantage Solutions, Charter NEX, Genani Corp., Insight Global, IQVIA, J.Crew, Life Time Fitness, Mister Car Wash, MultiPlan, Savers, SRS Distribution
Jonathan Sokoloff, Managing Partner
e-mail: sokoloff@leonardgreen.com
Education: BA Political Economy and History, Williams College
Background: Managing Director, Drexel; Principal, Hambrecht & Quist; Woodman, Kirkpatrick & Gilbreath; Merrill Lynch & Co
Directorships: Advantage Solutions, The Container Store, J.Crew, Jetro Cash & Carry, JOANN Stores, Shake Shack, Signet Jewelers, Topshop/Topman, Union Square Hospitality Group

John M Baumer, Senior Partner
e-mail: baumer@leonardgreen.com
Education: BBA, University of Notre Dame; MBA, Wharton School
Background: VP, DLJ; Fidelity Investments; Arthur Andersen
Directorships: Aspen Dental, CHG Healthcare Services, ExamWorks, Prospect Medical, ResotirxHealth, SoulCycle, U.S. Renal Care

Jonathan Seiffer, Senior Partner
e-mail: seiffer@leonardgreen.com
Education: BS, Bachelor of Applied Science, University of Pennsylvania
Background: Corporate Finance, DLJ
Directorships: Aersale, Authentic Brands Group, BJ's Wholesale Club, Caliber Collision Centers, Mister Car Wash, Savers, SRS Distribution, The Tire Rack

Usama Cortas, Partner
Education: BA, Economics & Political Science, Columbia University
Background: M&A, Retail/Consumer Products Group, Morgan Stanley
Directorships: Authentic Brands Group, CPA Global, Ellucian, Tank Holdings

Timothy J Flynn, Partner
Education: BA, Economics & Political Science, Brown University
Background: Director, Investment Banking, Credit Suisse First Boston; DLJ; M&A, Paine Webber Inc.
Directorships: Authentic Brands Group, CPA Global, Ellucian, Tank Holdings

J Kristofer Galashan, Partner
Education: BA, Business Administration, Richard Ivey School of Business, University of Western Ontario
Background: Investment Banking, Credit Suisse First Boston
Directorships: BJ's Wholesale Club, The Container Store, Life Time Fitness, Mister Car Wash, Pure Gym, The Shade Store, Troon Golf, Union Square Hospitality Group

W. Christian McCollum, Partner
Education: BA, Economics and Government, Cornell University; MBA, Wharton School at University of Pennsylvania
Background: Managing Director, Investcorp; Chemical Securities
Directorships: Charter NEX, Ellucian, ProMach, Veritext

Michael S Solomon, Partner
Education: BA, Economics, Pomona College; CFA
Background: Financial Sponsors Group, Deutsche Banc Alex Brown
Directorships: PDC Brands, Prospect Medical

Alyse Wagner, Partner
Education: BS, Economics, Wharton School
Background: Investment Banking, Credit Suisse First Boston
Directorships: Aersale, Aspen Dental, CHG Healthcare Services, ExamWorks, MDVIP, Prospect Medical, RestorixHealth, U.S. Renal Care

Pete Zippelius, Partner
Education: BS, Finance, Virginia Polytechnic Institute
Background: Managing Director & Co-Head, North American Healthcare Investment Banking, J.P. Morgan

Peter J Nolan, Senior Advisor
e-mail: nolan@leonardgreen.com
Education: BS Agricultural Economics and Finance, Cornell University; MBA, Johnson Graduate School of Management, Cornell University
Background: Managing Director/Co-Head, DLJ Investment Banking; First VP, Drexel; VP, Prudential Securities; Associate, Manufacturers Hanover Trust
Directorships: Activision, Aersale

1114 LERER HIPPEAU VENTURES
100 Crosby St.
Suite 308
New York, NY 10013

Phone: 646-237-4837
e-mail: contact@lererhippeau.com
web: www.lererhippeau.com

Mission Statement: Lerer Hippeau Ventures is a seed stage venture capital fund. We invest in founders in the earliest stages of a startup's life. We respect and seek out entrepreneurs with product vision, consumer insight, focused execution, and unwavering ambition. Lerer Ventures also operates SohoTechLabs, an incubator that builds start-ups from the idea up. When we are lucky enough to meet founders with these qualities, our hope is that they will choose us as a partner. Everyone here starts and runs companies for a living. Lerer Ventures is where we invest in our peers.

Investment Criteria: Seed-Stage
Industry Group Preference: Consumer, Digital Media, eCommerce, Technology, Enterprise Software
Portfolio Companies: Abra, Adaptly, Airtime, Allbirds, Ample Hills, Augury, AutoFi, Ava, Axial, Axios, Bark Box, BaubleBar, Bench, Betaworks, Bkstg, Blade, Block, Bloglovin', Bowery, Brami, Brat, Brit+Co, BuzzFeed, Camp, Casa, Casper, Chartbeat, Chubbies, Class Dojo, Clique Media Group, Clubhosue, Code Climate, Confide, Conversion Logic, Cotopaxi, Crexi, Crypt, CultureIQ, Dering Hall, Dia & Co., Digital Genius, DocSend, Doctor on Demand, Dragon Innovation, Drift, DRL, Even Financial, Everlane, Everytable, Expa, Fancy Hands, Fatherly, Fitplan, Food 52, FoxTrot, Fresh Nation, Friendsly, Fundera, Furnishare, Genies, Genius, Giphy, Glamsquad, Glossier, Goby, Good Uncle, Green Matters, Group Nine, Grovo, Guideline, Heartbeat, Herb, Heyday, Homer, Hungry Root, IFTTT, Inturn, JanusVR, Jibe, Joor, Jott, June, Keezy. K Health, Klara, Leaf Link, Le Tote, Little Bits, LiveIntent, Lola, Maxwell Health, Metric Insights, Mic, Mirror, Namely, Neighborhood Fuel, Neighborland, NewsCred, Ollie, Opentrons, OrderGroove, Ordway, Oscar, OwnLocal, Paintzen, Palmetto, Pando, Panna, Parsec, Percolate, Plus One Robotics, Poncho, Pop Dust, Power to Fly, Properly, Prose, Quartzy, Realm, Rebel Mouse, Refinery 29, Resy, Revere, Revolution Credit, Rockets of Awesome, Rubica, Sailthru, Science Exchange, Scout Mob, SeatGeek, Seller Crowd, Sfara, Skift, Social Sentinel, Soma, Soylent, Spacious, Spectrum, Splash, Splice, Sportsrocket, Spring, Stitch, Studypool, The Black Tux, The Inside, Thrive Global, Tikl, Tracksmith, Transfix, Tr

Key Executives:
Kenneth Lerer, Managing Partner
Background: Co-Founder, Huffington Post
Directorships: Buzzfeed, Group Nine Media, Blade, Thrive Global

Ben Lerer, Managing Partner
Education: University of Pennsylvania
Directorships: Group Nine Media, Casper, RaisedByUs, Refinery29

Eric Hippeau, Managing Partner
Education: Sorbonne University
Background: CEO, Huffington Post; Managing Partner, Softbank Capital
Directorships: Buzzfeed, Marriott International

1115 LEVINE LEICHTMAN CAPITAL PARTNERS
345 N Maple Drive
Suite 300
Beverly Hills, CA 90210

Phone: 310-275-5335 Fax: 310-275-1441
e-mail: main@llcp.com
web: www.llcp.com

Venture Capital & Private Equity Firms / Domestic Firms

Mission Statement: To provide capital to industry leading companies owned and managed by entrepreneurs.
Geographic Preference: United States
Fund Size: $452 million
Founded: 1984
Average Investment: $25 million
Minimum Investment: $10 million
Investment Criteria: Late Stage Venture, Growth/Expansion Capital, Recaps
Industry Group Preference: Aerospace, Defense and Government, Consumer Products, Entertainment, Equipment, Financial Services, Processing, Franchising, Healthcare, Radio, Real Estate, Security, Software, Food & Beverage, Telecommunications
Portfolio Companies: Allied Aerofoam Products, Beef 'O' Brady's, Bertucci's Corporation, Best Lawyers, Brass Smith Innovations, Capsa Healthcare, Caring Brands International, Champion Manufacturing, CJ Fallon, Deter Magnetic Technologies, FASTSIGNS International, FlexRay, Genova Diagnostics, GL Education, Global Franchise Group, Hand & Stone, HomeVestors, Jonathan Engineered Solutions, Law Business Research, Lawn Doctor, Magnolia Bluffs Casino, Mander Portman Woodward Limite, Mckenzie Sports Products, Monte Nido, Nobles Worldwide, Nothing Bundt Cakes, Pacific Handy Cutter, Pacific Wave Systems, Pacific World Corporation, The Poma Companies, Polyform Products Company, Regional Rail, Revenew International, Senior Helpers, SFERRA, Smith System Driver Improvement Institute, Squla, Synyron Maerial Handling, Therapeutic Research Center, Trinity Consultants, Tronair, Inc., Werner Holdings, West Academic, Wetzel's Pretzels, Zorg Domein

Key Executives:
Lauren B Leichtman, CEO/Founding Partner
Education: JD, Southwestern University; LLM, Columbia Law School
Background: Law, Public/Private Sectors; Securities and Exhange Commission
Arthur Levine, President/Founding Partner
Education: MBA, Anderson School of Management; JD, Columbia Law School
Background: Principal, Westwood One
Paul W. Drury, Senior Managing Director
Education: BS, Finances and Accounting, Texas Tech University; MBA, Booth School of Business at University of Chicago
Background: Vice President, The CIT Group; Bank of America
Monica J. Holec, Senior Managing Director
Education: HBA, Richard Ivey School of Business at University of Western Ontario
Background: Partner, Triago; Private Equity Funds, Merrill Lynch; Analyst, Investment Banking, DLJ Securities
Andrew M. Schwartz, Senior Managing Director
Education: BS, Economics, Wharton School; BSE, Computer Science and Engineering, University of Pennsylvania
Background: Vice President, Liberty Partners; Investment Banking Analyst, Jefferies & Company
David Wolmer, Senior Managing Director
Education: BA, University of Michigan; JD, Fordham University School of Law
Background: Associate, Milbank Tweed Hadley & McCloy LLP
John O'Neill, Senior Managing Director
Education: BComm, MA, Accounting, University College Dublin
Background: Partner, Graphite Capital; Hawkpoint Partners; Deloitte

1116 LEXINGTON PARTNERS
399 Park Avenue
20th Floor
New York, NY 10022
Phone: 212-754-0411
e-mail: info@lexpartners.com
web: www.lexingtonpartners.com

Mission Statement: Lexington Partners is the leading manager of secondary private equity fund investments and co-investments in leveraged equity transactions. Focus to provide liquidity to private equity investors interested in selling limited partnership interests.
Geographic Preference: United States, United Kingdom, Western Europe, Asia-Pacific
Fund Size: $15 billion
Founded: 1994
Minimum Investment: $1,000,000
Investment Criteria: Newly formed buyout, mezzanine, venture capital and international partnerships
Industry Group Preference: Diversified
Portfolio Companies: CardioKinetix, Emerald Solutions, Forcepoint, Movik Networks, PowerVision, Sovrn, Websense

Other Locations:
111 Huntington Avenue
Suite 2920
Boston, MA 02199
Phone: 617-247-7010

3000 Sand Hill Road
Building 1, Suite 220
Menlo Park, CA 94025
Phone: 650-561-9600

Lexington Partners UK LLP
1 Medici Courtyard
2nd Floor
London W1S 1BR
United Kingdom
Phone: 44-20-7399-3940

Lexington Partners Asia Limited
Suites 2903-2909, 29/F, Two IFC
8 Finance Street
Central
Hong Kong
Phone: 852-3987-1600

Lexington Partners Chile SpA
3477 Isidora Goyenechea Ave.
17th Floor, Suite 170 B
Las Condes, Santiago
Chile
Phone: 56-2-2487-6700

Key Executives:
Brent Nicklas, Founder & Non-Executive Chairman
212-754-0411
e-mail: brnicklas@lexpartners.com
Education: BA, Amherst College; MBA, Stanford Business School
Background: Founding Partner, Landmark Partners; Vice President, Merrill Lynch Capital Markets
Wilson S Warren, Partner & President
212-754-0411
e-mail: wswarren@lexpartners.com
Education: BA, Economics, Williams College
Background: Associate, Landmark Partners; Analyst, LaSalle Partners
Mark M Andrew, Partner, Boston
617-247-7010
e-mail: mmandrew@lexpartners.com
Education: BS, Management, University of Massachusetts Amherst
Background: Principal, Banc of America Securities
Lee J Tesconi, Senior Advisor, Boston
617-247-7010
e-mail: ljtesconi@lexpartners.com

Venture Capital & Private Equity Firms / Domestic Firms

Education: BS, Boston College; MBA, MIT Sloan School of Management
Background: Managing Director, BancBoston Capital; Vice President, BankBoston's LBO Lending Group
Duncan A Chapman, Senior Advisor, New York
212-754-0411
e-mail: dachapman@lexpartners.com
Education: BA, Economics, Columbia University
Background: President, Butler Chapman & Co; Senior Vice President, Lehman Brothers
Thomas Giannetti, Partner, New York
212-754-0411
e-mail: tgiannetti@lexpartners.com
Education: BS, Accounting, New York University
Background: Senior Manager, Audit, Ernst & Young
John G Loverro, Partner, New York
212-754-0411
e-mail: jloverro@lexpartners.com
Education: BA, Economics, Fairfield University; MBA, Darden School, University of Virginia
Background: Vice President, Investment Banking, JPMorgan; Portfolio Manager, PIMCO/Oppenheimer Capital; InverMexico
Bart D Osman, Partner, New York
212-754-0411
e-mail: bdosman@lexpartners.com
Education: BA, History, Dartmouth College; MBA, Tuck School of Business, Dartmouth College
Background: Director of Acquisitions & Investments, Reuters America; Analyst, Merrill Lynch
David B Outcalt, Partner, New York
212-754-0411
e-mail: dboutcalt@lexpartners.com
Education: BA, Economics, Williams College; MBA, The Wharton School
Background: Associate, Landmark Partners; Analyst, Bear Stearns
John G Rudge, Partner, New York
212-754-0411
e-mail: jgrudge@lexpartners.com
Education: BA, American Civilizations, Middlebury College; MBA, Tuck School of Business, Dartmouth
Background: Associate, Investment Banking, Morgan Stanley
Victor L Wu, Partner, New York
212-754-0411
e-mail: vlwu@lexpartners.com
Education: BBA, University of Michigan Busines School; MBA, The Wharton School
Background: Analyst, Investment Banking, Goldman Sachs
Tom Newby, Partner, Menlo Park
650-561-9600
e-mail: tnewby@lexpartners.com
Education: BS, Business Administration, University of North Carolina; MBA, Stanford Graduate School of Business
Background: Managing Director, Montgomery & Co; General Partner, Technology Crossover Ventures
Jennifer W Kheng, Partner, Menlo Park
650-561-9600
e-mail: jwkheng@lexpartners.com
Education: BS, Biological Sciences, MS, Management Science & Engineering, Stanford University
Background: Analyst, Morgan Stanley
James D.C. Pitt, Partner, London
44-20-7399-3940
e-mail: jpitt@lexpartners.com
Education: BSc, Management Science, City University, London; MBA, INSEAD, France
Background: Managing Director, AXA Private Equity; Managing Director, Whitney & Co; Vice President, Morgan Stanley's Leveraged Finance Group
Anthony W. Garton, Partner, London
44-20-7399-3940
e-mail: agarton@lexpartners.com
Education: BA, Hispanic and Latin American Studies, University of Bristol
Background: Principal, Conven; Vice President, Investment Banking, Credit Suisse; Associate Director, UBS Investment Bank
Pal B Ristvedt, Partner, London
44-20-7399-3940
e-mail: pbristvedt@lexpartners.com
Education: BS, Business Administration, University of California Berkeley; MBA, INSEAD, France
Background: Investment Banking, Morgan Stanley
Kirk M. Beaton, Partner, Hong Kong
852-3987-1600
e-mail: kbeaton@lexpartners.com
Education: LLB, University of Strathclyde; Universität Hamburg; Universidad Complutense de Madrid
Background: Analyst, Investment Banking, Morgan Stanley
Timothy Huang, Partner, Hong Kong
852-3987-1600
e-mail: thuang@lexpartners.com
Education: BS, Business Administration, Cornell University; MBA, Booth School of Business at University of Chicago
Background: Executive Director, LGT Capital Partners; Engagement Manager, Investment AB Kinnevik
Jose M. Sosa del Valle, Partner, Santiago
56-2-2487-6700
e-mail: jsosadelvalle@lexpartners.com
Education: MS, Industrial Engineering, Instituto Technologico de Buenos Aires; MBA, Columbia Business School
Background: Associate, Investment Banking, Goldman Sachs

1117 LFE CAPITAL
319 Barry Ave. South
Suite 215
Wayzata, MN 55391

Phone: 612-752-1809 **Fax:** 612-752-1800
e-mail: laurent@lfecapital.com
web: www.lfecapital.com

Mission Statement: LFE Capital invests in businesses with revenues of $5 to $50 million that need capital to support a plan of rapid growth.

Geographic Preference: Upper Midwest Region
Founded: 1999
Average Investment: $2 - $5 million
Industry Group Preference: Business Products & Services, Healthcare, Medical Devices, Consumer Services, Consumer Products
Portfolio Companies: API Outsourcinv, Avant Healthcare Professionals, The Big Know, Coolibar, eMindful, Fitness on Request, M.A. Gedney, Gentra Systems, Global ID Group, Halo Innovations, Immaculate Baking Co., Inlet Medical, Jackson's Honest, JobDig, Portero, SimonDelivers, Wellbeats
Other Locations:
649 Fifth Ave. South
Suite 226
Naples, FL 34102
Key Executives:
Leslie Frécon, Founder & Managing Partner
Education: BA, Stanford University; MBA, Finance, UCLA
Background: SVP, Corporate Finance, General Mills; Corporate Lending Officer, Bank of America

1118 LIBERTY CAPITAL PARTNERS
Naples, FL

Phone: 203-323-6666
e-mail: info@libertycapitalpartners.com
web: www.libertycapitalpartners.com

Venture Capital & Private Equity Firms / Domestic Firms

Mission Statement: Liberty Capital Partners provides wealth management services, private equity opportunities, and corporate advisory services to its clients.
Founded: 1994
Investment Criteria: Early-Stage, Growth-Stage
Industry Group Preference: Software, Equipment, Financial Services, Food & Beverage
Portfolio Companies: All Seasons Services, Armstrong Franklin, ASP, Asure Software, ConnectEDU, Dynadec, Finale, GCA Services Group, Global Asset Alternatives, Heartlab, Impact, Liberty Tire Recycling, Meyer Materials, Nattagansett Beer, Portfolio Solutions, Remotely, Rentbits, Spada Media, Windward Petroleum

Other Locations:
Stamford, CT
Troy, MI

Key Executives:
James S Gladney, Founder/Managing Partner
e-mail: jgladney@libertycapitalpartners.com
Education: BS, University of Rhode Island
Background: Managing Partner, Park Avenue Equity Partners
Directorships: All Seasons Services, Rentbits, Remotely

1119 LIBERTY CITY VENTURES
East 45th St.
New York, NY 10017

e-mail: info@libertycityventures.com
web: www.libertycityventures.com

Mission Statement: Liberty City Ventures is a seed stage fund headquartered in New York City. We invest in startups that are innovating at the cross-sections of technology, media and commerce. We began operations in the summer of 2012 and are led by experienced technology executives and investors.
Founded: 2012
Investment Criteria: Seed
Industry Group Preference: Technology, Media, Commerce
Portfolio Companies: BitGo, Boost, BRD, Faith Street, Farm Hill, Hullabalu, itBit, LibraTax, Parcel, Parenthoods, Paxos, Pickie, Solid Partners, TripleLift

Key Executives:
Charles Cascarilla, CFA, Founding Partner
Education: BBA, Finance, Univesity of Notre Dame
Background: Co-Founder, Cedar Hill Capital Partners; Portfolio Manager, Claiborne Capital; Analyst, Bank of America Securities; Analyst, Goldman Sachs
Andrew Chang, Founding Partner
Education: BS, Operation and Technology Management, Boston College; MBA, New York University
Background: COO, ConditionOne; Associate, TechStars; Operations, Kantar Video; Consumer Insights and Research Division, 360i
Dorothy Jean Chang, Founding Partner
Education: Yale University
Background: VP, Brew Media Relations; Edelman; Text 100
Emil Woods, Founding Partner
Education: BSE, Wharton School
Background: Portfolio Manager (Current) And Co-Founder, Cedar Hill Capital Partners, LLC; Portfolio Manager, SAC Capital Management; Equities and Asset Management Division, Goldman Sachs

1120 LIFE SCIENCES GREENHOUSE OF CENTRAL PA
225 Market Street
Suite 500
Harrisburg, PA 17101

Phone: 717-635-2100 **Fax:** 717-635-2010
web: www.lsgpa.com

Mission Statement: The Life Sciences Greenhouse is a public/private venture whose mission is to commercialize bioscience technologies.
Geographic Preference: Pennsylvania
Investment Criteria: Early-Stage
Industry Group Preference: Life Sciences, Biosciences
Portfolio Companies: Azevan Pharmaceuticals, Chromatan, Immunomic Therapeutics, Indigo Biosciences, INRange Systems, MacuLogix, Micro Inverventional Devices, NanoHorizons, Novasentis, QuantumBio, Ras Therapeautics, Saladax Biomedical

Key Executives:
Mel Billingsley PhD, President & CEO
Education: BS, Biophysics & Microbiology, University of Pittsburgh; Doctoral Degree, Pharmacology, George Washington University; Postdoctoral Degree, Neuropharmacology, Yale School of Medicine
Background: Professor, Pharmacology, Pennsylvania State University Milton S Hershey College of Medicine
Ronald P Thiboutot PhD, Executive Vice President
717-635-2102
Education: BS, MS, PhD, Massachusetts College of Pharmacy
Background: President, RT Consultants; Plant Director, Wyeth Pharmaceuticals
Steve Carpenter, Vice President, Venture Operations
717-635-2131
Education: BS, Mechanical Engineering, Lehigh University; MBA, Pennsylvania State University
Background: DuPont, Berg Electronics, FCI USA

1121 LIGHTBANK
600 West Chicago Avenue
Suite 775
Chicago, IL 60654

e-mail: press@lightbank.com
web: www.lightbank.com

Mission Statement: Provides a solid business model, technology that works, top talend and an experienced connected partner.
Investment Criteria: Early-Stage
Industry Group Preference: Social Media, Consumer Internet, Business to Business, Consumer Products
Portfolio Companies: Ark, Babba Co., BeachMint, Beautylish, Belly, BenchPrep, Benzinga, Betterfly, Beyond Games, Bonfaire, Boom, Carlease, Catalytic, Classkick, Clearcover, Cleversense, Coffee Meets Bagel, Contently, Crowdrise, Doubledutch, Dough, Draft Day, Drivin, ElaCarte, Eventup, Expel, Fiverr, Fooda, Frank & Oak, FreeAgent, GameFlip, GetGoing, HDVI, HighGround, Hipster, Hireology, Ionic, Lifecrowd, Lightswitch, Locality, Locu, Markkit, Needle, Neumob, Nubundle, Obaz, Onswipe, Ovia Health, Ovuline, Paladin Cyber, Pawngo, PerBlue, Qwiki, Reverb, Riskmatch, SkyVu, Snapsheet, SnapTravel, Socialkaty, SoCore Energy, Soundsupply, SpotHero, Sprout Social, Tagkast, Take Lessons, Talent Bin, TastyTrade, TastyWorks, Team Liquid, Tempus, Udemy, Uptake, Vettery, Whos Here, Zaarly, Zeel, Zero, Zest Health

Key Executives:
Eric Lefkofsky, Partner & Co-Founder
Education: JD, University of Michigan Law School
Background: Founder & CEO, Tempus; Co-Founder & Chairman, Groupon
Brad Keywell, Partner & Co-Founder
Education: BBA, JD, University of Michigan
Background: Founder, Echo Global Logistics, MediaBank, Groupon
Vic Pascucci III, Managing Partner
Background: USAA; Partner, Munich Re/HSB Ventures
Directorships: Clearcover, Snapsheet, Carlease, Sprout Social, Fooda, Paladin Cyber, Hireology, Ionic, Hatch Loyalty, Benchprep, Udemy, NuBundle, Billtrim

Venture Capital & Private Equity Firms / Domestic Firms

1122 LIGHTHOUSE CAPITAL PARTNERS
3555 Alameda de las Pulgas
Suite 200
Menlo Park, CA 94025

Phone: 650-233-1001
e-mail: info@lcpartners.com
web: lcpartners.com

Mission Statement: A private venture capital partnership specializing in providing debt financing to technology based start-up companies which have already received financing commitments from top tier venture capital firms.

Geographic Preference: United States
Fund Size: $650 million
Founded: 1994
Average Investment: $5 million
Minimum Investment: $1 million
Investment Criteria: Startups, Early-Stage, Growth Capital, Equipment Financing
Industry Group Preference: Technology, Life Sciences
Portfolio Companies: Angie's List, ARYx Therapeutics, Azelon Pharmaceuticals, BiPar Sciences, Cogit.com, DiVitas Networks, HDmessaging, if(we), iHear Medical, Kala Pharmaceuticals, Life360, LVL7 Systems, Mimosa Systems, NanoH2O, Rafter, Responsys, Revivio, Santur Corporation, Shansong (FlashEX), Shixianghui, Transera Communications, ZestFinance

Other Locations:
255 Main St.
Kendall Center
Cambridge, MA 02142
Phone: 617-441-9192 Fax: 617-354-4374

303 Wyman St.
Suite 300
Waltham, MA 02451
Phone: 617-441-9192

336 Bon Air Center
Suite 527
Greenbrae, CA 94904
Phone: 415-464-5900

Key Executives:
Richard Stubblefield, Co-Founder/Managing Director
415-484-5977
e-mail: rick@lcpartners.com
Education: BS, University of California; MBA, Golden Gate University
Background: Senior VP, Comdisco Ventures
Gwill York, Co-Founder/Managing Director
617-441-9192 ext 601
e-mail: gwill@lcpartners.com
Education: AB, Harvard University; MBA, Harvard Business School
Background: Senior VP, Comdisco Ventures
Cristy Barnes, Managing Director
650-233-1007
Education: BA Psychology, University of California, Los Angeles
Background: Senior Associate, Highland Capital Partners; Internet Research Group, Robertson Stephens
Jeff Griffor, Managing Director
617-441-9192 x 604
e-mail: jeff@lcpartners.com
Education: BS Business Economics/Finance, Ohio University; MBA, Loyola University Chicago
Background: Commercial/Technology Lending Experience, Fleet Boston; Loan/Credit Analysis, CIT Groupo/First Chicago National Bank
Ned Hazen, Mangaging Director
617-441-9192 x 603
e-mail: ned@lcpartners.com
Education: AB Political Science, Brown University; MBA Harvard Business School
Background: Investment Banker, Venture Capitalist, Senior Finance Operations Executive, Avid Technology/Robertson Stephens and Company
Damian Arroyo, Managing Director
Background: Manager, Private Banking, Banc Sabadell Banco Banif and Banco Madrid

1123 LIGHTHOUSE PARTNERS
3801 PGA Boulevard
Suite 500
Palm Beach Gardens, FL 33410

Phone: 561-741-0820 Fax: 561-748-9046
web: www.lighthousepartners.com

Mission Statement: Lighthouse Partners provide an alternative to traditional fixed income investments to offer flexibility to companies.

Geographic Preference: North America
Fund Size: $5 billion
Founded: 1996
Industry Group Preference: All Sectors Considers

Other Locations:
71 S Wacker Drive
Suite 1860
Chicago, IL 60606
Phone: 312-592-1820 Fax: 312-592-1839

437 Madison Avenue
21st Floor
New York, NY 10022
Phone: 212-588-0342 Fax: 212-588-0338

2nd Floor
48 Pall Mall
London SW1Y 5JG
United Kingdom
Phone: 44-0-203-189-9470

76th Floor, Suite 7609
The Center
99 Queen's Road
Central
Hong Kong
Phone: 852-2159-9612 Fax: 852-2159-9688

W22F Sjibuya Mark City
1-12-1 Dogenzaka
Shibuya-ku
Tokyo 150-0043
Japan
Phone: 81-0-3-4360-5415 Fax: 81-0-3-4360-5301

Key Executives:
Sean McGould, President/Co-Chief Investment Officer
Education: BSc, Accounting, Butler University
Directorships: Outside Trader Investment Program, Trout Trading Management Co.; HFA Holdings Ltd.; Price Waterhouse
Ben Browning, President
Education: BA, University of Michigan; JD, Duke University
Background: K2 Advisors
Robert Swan, Chief Operating Officer
Education: BA, Business Economics, University of California
Background: Senior Treasury Consultant, Computer Sciences Corp.; Ernst & Young
Directorships: Accounting, Trout Trading Management Co.
Scott Perkins, Executive Managing Director
Education: BBA, Accounting, College of William and Mary; JD, Washington & Lee University School of Law
Background: Corporate Attorney, Mays & Valentine LLP; Coopers & Lybrand LLP
Clark Prickett, Executive Managing Director
Education: BA, University of Richmond; MBA, University of Chicago; CFA
Background: SunTrust Bank

Venture Capital & Private Equity Firms / Domestic Firms

Kensington Pavilion
96 Kensington High Street
Penthouse Floor
London W8 4SG
United Kingdom
Phone: 44 2036 408676

1125 LIGHTSPEED VENTURE PARTNERS
2200 Sand Hill Road
Menlo Park, CA 94025
Phone: 650-234-8300 **Fax:** 650-234-8333
web: lsvp.com

Mission Statement: To serve as lead investors on early stage consumer and enterprise ventures in the areas of fintech, media, commerce, security, infrastructure, saas, big data, analytics, and more.
Geographic Preference: United States, Israel, China, India
Fund Size: $4 Billion
Founded: 1971
Average Investment: $5 million
Minimum Investment: $2 million
Investment Criteria: Early
Industry Group Preference: Enterprise, Big Data, Analytics, Infrastructure, Security, Social, Consumer, Fintech, E-Commerce & Manufacturing, Media, SaaS
Portfolio Companies: 51VR, 99Bill, Aerohive, Affirm, Affirmed Networks, Airbug, Alooma, Amec, AppDynamics, Aqua Security, Aquantia, Arbor Networks, Arctic Wolf, Athos, Audius, Avamar, Avere Systems, Avi Networksm Barefoot Networks, Basis.io, Beme, Betterup, Binaris, Bitmain, Blend, Blockchain, Bloomreach, Blue Nile Bluevine, Bonobos, Brandable, Brocade, Bromium, BTCC, Building Connected, BYJU's, Calista Technologies, Candis, Celequest, Che101, Cheddar, Ciena, Citadel, Clark, Clever, Cloud Moment, Cloudbees, Coding, Cohere Technologies, Companion, Comprehend, Craftsvilla, Crowdamp, Daily Harvest, Darwinbox, Datastax, Datorama, Datos IO, Datrium, Delphix, Dianping, Docker, DOTC United, Dote, Double Click, Dr.2, Dremio, EastMachinery, Edaijia, Edgespring, Ehealth, Elastifile, Elementum, Ensilo, Epic Games, Epsagon, Evariant, Eve.com, Everstring, Evolv, Exabeam, Extensity, Eyeview, Face U, Faire, FangDD, Fashionara, Fastfox, Fireglass, Fivestars, Flip, Flixster, Forty Seven, Freight Tiger, FreshMenu, Fushion-IO, Gainsight, Galileo Technology, Giphy, Girlboss, Global Peersafe, GMedia, Goop, Grab, Growth Networks, GrubHub, Guardant Health, Handshake, Hanshow, Heptio, HighFive, Hollar, Hongchizhineng, HungryRoot, IEver, IfChange, IHaveU, Illumix, Indian Energy Exchange, Influitive, Informatica, Innolight, Innovaccer, Insightera, IO Turbine, Iplas, Itzcash Card, Karius, Kenandy, Kespry, Kiva Software, Kixeye, KJK, Kodiak Robotics, Kongregate, Kosmix, Ladder, Laiye, Ledgerx, Lele Global, Lian Luo, LightLogic, Liking Fit, Limeroad, Link-A-Media, LiveProfile, LiveU, LuckyPai, Lulutrip, Magicpin, Maker Comms, Mamadav, Man Bang Group, Mapr, Masergy, Mediav, Meilele, Memoir Systems, Mend, Metasolv Software, Mic Networks, Millenial Fox, Million Warehouse, Mist, Mulesoft, MyBuys, MYND, Natera, Nemo, Nest, Netskope, Nexttao, Nicira Networks, Nimble Storage, Numerify, Nutanix, One Assist, Orbis Education, Origami Logic, Outbrain, Overops, Oyo Rooms, Parsable, PDD, People.ai, Percolate, Pernixdata, Personalis, Personetics, Phone.com, Pixel Technologies, Playdom, Plexistor, Plexxi, Pliant Technology, Poncho, PPDAI, PredictHQ, Priority Vendor, Provigent, PSS Systems, Pulse, Pushpins, QingCloud, Quantum Effect Dev., Quantumscape, Qubole, Rapshere, Real Time Genomics, Recordgram, Redcarpet, Reflektive, Reliable Robotics, Ripple, Riverbed Technology, Rockyou!, Rong360, Roofstock, Rothy's, Rubrik, Saga, Sagreen, Sailpoint, Scodix, Serverless, ShareChate, ShoeDazzle, Shookit, Shuttl, Sirocco

Other Locations:
1st Floor, Studio No. 63
Tower A, Worldmark 1, Asset Area 11
Indira Gandhi International Airport
New Dehli 110037
India
Phone: 91 11 4251 9619

Sarona
4 Zvi Strachilevich Street
Tel Aviv 6473957
Israel
Phone: 972 3 974 6800 **Fax:** 972 3 974 6851

21/F, Suite 2105
Platinum Building, No. 233 Tai Cang Road
Huang Pu District
Shanghai 200020
China
Phone: 86 21 5386-6500 **Fax:** 86 21 5386-6668

Unit 3007, Tower 2
China Central Place, No. 79 Jian Guo Road
Chaoyang District
Beijing 100025
China
Phone: 86 10 5969-5980 **Fax:** 86 10 5969-6690

2nd Floor, Avinash Chambers
80 Ft. Rd, 4th Block Koramangala
Bengaluru 560034
India
Phone: 91 80 46239797

Key Executives:
Andrew Moley, Operating Partner & CFO
e-mail: andrew@lsvp.com
Education: The Wharton School; Stanford University
Background: eGreetings Network; CMC Industries; Mercer Management Consulting
Arif Janmohamed, Partner
e-mail: arif@lsvp.com
Education: University of Waterloo; The Wharton School
Background: Cisco Systems; WebTV; Andes Network
Barry Eggers, Founding Partner
Education: BA Economics/Business, UCLA; MBA, Stanford University
Background: Weiss, Peck & Greer Venture Partners; Director Business Development, Cisco Systems
Bipul Sinha, Venture Partner
Education: Indian Institute of Technology; The Wharton School
Background: Blumberg Capital; Oracle Corporation; American Megatrends; IBM
David Gussarsky, Partner
Education: BA, Economics, LLB, Tel Aviv University; MBA, Insead, Fountainebleu, France
Background: Partner, BRM Capital; CEO, Paspar2; Corporate Attorney, Rosensweig & Company; Israeli Defense Forces; Eudentics
Jeremy Liew, Partner
e-mail: jeremy@lsvp.com
Education: BA/BSc, Australian National University; MBA, Stanford University
Background: SVP, Corporate Development, AOL; Chief of Staff, Netscape; CitySearch; Interactive Corp.
John Vrionis, Venture Partner
Education: BA, Harvard University; MS, Computer Science, University of Chicago; MBA, Stanford University
Background: Product Management, Determina; Freedom Financial Network
Peter Nieh, Partner
Education: BS Electrical Engineering, AB Economics, MBA, Stanford University
Background: Weiss, Peck & Greer Venture Partners; Business Development/Product Marketing, General Magic; Acer; Strategy Consultant, Bain & Comapny
Ravi Mhatre, Partner
Education: BS Electrical Engineering, BA Economics, MBA, Stanford University
Background: Weiss, Peck & Greer Venture Partners;

Bessemer Venture Partners; Market Development, Silicon Graphics; Lehman Brothers; Booz Allen Hamilton; BDIS
Yoni Chiefetz, Partner
e-mail: yoni@lightspeedvp.com
Education: MSc, Applied Mathematics & Computer Science, Weizmann Institue of Science; BSc, Applied Mathematics, Tel-Aviv University
Background: Partner, Star Ventures

1126 LIGHTSTONE VENTURES
2884 Sand Hill Road
Suite 121
Menlo Park, CA 94025

Phone: 650-388-3676 Fax: 650-388-3675
web: www.lightstonevc.com

Mission Statement: Lightstone Ventures, formed by the life science teams of Advanced Technology Ventures and Morgenthaler Ventures, targets early stage life sciences companies with the potential to transform medicine.

Fund Size: $172 million
Founded: 2012
Investment Criteria: Early Stage
Industry Group Preference: Life Sciences, Biotechnology, Medical Devices, Biopharmaceuticals, Therapeutics
Portfolio Companies: Acceleron, Alexo Therapeutics, Calithera, Catabasis, Catalyst Biosciences, Claret Medical, EarLens, Elcelyx, EndoGastric Solutions, FIRE1, Flex Pharma, ForSight VISION4, ForSight VISIONS, Galleon, GlobeImmune, Holaira, Hydra Biosciences, Kona Medical, Miramar Labs, Mosaic Biosciences, Moximed, Nexis Vision, Nimbus Therapeutics, OncoMed, Optiscan, Powervision, Principia, Promedior, Ra Pharma, Relievant Medsystems, Scioderm, Second Genome, SetPoint Medical, Spine Wave, Stemgent, Thrasos Therapeutics, Tragara, Transcend Medical, Twelve, Vapotherm

Other Locations:
500 Boylston Street
Suite 1380
Boston, MA 02116
Phone: 617-933-3770 **Fax:** 617-933-3769

9 Pembrook Street
Dublin 2
Ireland

OCBC Centre #27-07
65 Chulia Street 049513
Singapore

Key Executives:
Mike Carusi, General Partner
e-mail: mcarusi@lightstonevc.com
Education: BS, Mechanical Engineering, Lehigh University; MBA, Amos Tuck School of Business Administration, Dartmouth College
Background: Director, Business Development, Inhale Therapeutic Systems; Principal, The Wilkerson Group
Directorships: National Venture Capital Association
Chris Christoffersen PhD, Special Partner
e-mail: rchris@lightstonevc.com
Education: BS, Chemistry & Mathematics, Cornell College; PhD, Chemistry, Indiana University
Background: President & CEO, Ribozyme Pharmaceuticals; Senior VP, Research, SmithKline Beecham; VP, Discovery Research, The Upjohn Company; President, Colorado State University
Directorships: GlobeImmune, Catalyst Biosciences, Galleon Pharmaceuticals, Tragara Pharmaceuticals, Stemgent, Elcelyx, Calithera Biosciences
Jean George, General Partner
e-mail: jgeorge@lightstonevc.com
Education: BS, University of Maine; MBA, Simmons College Graduate School of Management
Background: VP, Global Sales & Marketing, Genzyme Corporation; BancBoston Ventures
Hank Plain, General Partner
e-mail: hplain@lightstonevc.com
Education: BS, Finance, University of Missouri
Background: Founder, Ardian; President & CEO, Perclose; Chairman, Embolic Protection; Director, TransVascular
Directorships: EarLens, Claret
Jason Lettmann, General Partner
e-mail: jason@lightstonevc.com
Education: BA, University of Iowa; MBA, Ross School of Business, University of Michigan
Background: VP, Split Rock Partners; Co-Founder, Tarsus Medical; Guidant Corporation; Accenture; Genetic Research Analyst, University of Iowa
Directorships: Alexo Therapeutics, FIRE1, Promedior, Ra Pharmaceuticals, Relievant Medsystems, Second Genome, Spinewave, Vapotherm

1127 LIGHTYEAR CAPITAL
9 West 57th Street
New York, NY 10019

Phone: 212-328-0555
e-mail: proposals@lycap.com
web: www.lycap.com

Mission Statement: Lightyear Capital is a leading private equity firm providing buyout and growth capital to companies across the financial services industry.

Fund Size: $3 billion
Founded: 2000
Investment Criteria: Buyouts, Growth Capital
Industry Group Preference: Financial Services
Portfolio Companies: Advisor Group, Alegus Technologies, Antares Holdings Limited, ARGUS Software, Athilon Group Holdings Corp., Augeo FI, BakerCorp, Cascade Bancorp, Cerity Partners, Cetera Financial Group, Clarion Partners, Collegiate Funding Services, Community & Southern Bank Holdings, Datalot, eCommission, Ed., First Sun Capital, Flagstone Reinsurance Holdings Limited, Goldleaf Financial Solutions, Kepler Equities, NAU Country Insurance Company, Paradigm Management Services, Ridgeworth Investments, Therapy Brands, Ygrene Energy Fund, Wealth Enhancement Group

Key Executives:
Chris C Casciato, Managing Director
Education: BS, Civil Engineering, United States Military Academy; MBA, Harvard Business School
Background: Partner, Goldman Sachs & Co.
Stewart KP Gross, Managing Director
Education: BA, Government, Harvard University; MBA, Columbia Business School
Background: Warburg Pincus
Michal Petrzela, Managing Director
Education: BS, Accounting and Finance, Syracuse University; MBA, Stanford Graduate School of Business
Background: Barclays, Credit Suisse, Arthur Andersen
Mark F Vassallo, Managing Partner
Education: BA, Economics, Harvard University; MBA, Columbia Business School
Background: Managing Director, PaineWebber

1128 LILLY VENTURES
115 West Washington Street
Suite 1680 - South
Indianapolis, IN 46204

Phone: 317-429-0140 **Fax:** 317-75928191
web: www.lillyventures.com

Mission Statement: Lilly Ventures is the venture capital arm of Eli Lilly and Company responsible for life science investing in North America and Europe. Our primary goal is to facilitate the success of companies in our areas of focus through early to expansion stage investments and value-adding resources.

Geographic Preference: North America, Europe

Venture Capital & Private Equity Firms / Domestic Firms

Fund Size: $200 million
Founded: 2001
Investment Criteria: Early - Expansion Stage, Start-Up
Industry Group Preference: Biotechnology, Pharmaceuticals
Portfolio Companies: Aeglea Biotherapeutics, Aileron Therapeutics, Avid Radiopharmaceuticals, Cavion, Cerulean Pharma, CGI Pharmaceuticals, Coherus Biosciences, esanx, Esanex, Forma Therapeutics, GlobeImmune, Hydra Biosciences, InCube Ventures, InnoCentive, Innocrin, Intradigm Corporation, Kymera Therapeutics, Lysomal Therapeutics, Nimbus Discovery, Numerate, Protagonist Therapeutics, Receptos, Surface Oncology, Sutro Biopharma, Symic Biomedical, Viamet Pharmaceuticals

Key Executives:
　S Edward Torres, Managing Director
　e-mail: ed@lillyventures.com
　Education: BA, Creighton University; MBA, University of Michigan Business School
　Background: CFO, Lilly Argentina
　Directorships: Innocrin Pharmaceuticals, Viamet Pharmaceuticals
　Steven E Hall, General Partner
　e-mail: steve@lillyventures.com
　Education: BS, Chemistry, Central Michigan University; PhD, Organic Chemistry, MIT
　Background: Co-Founder & Senior Vice President, R&D, Serenex; Site Director, Sphinx Labs
　Directorships: Cavion Pharma, Esanex, FORMA Therapeutics, Hydra Biosciences, Kymera Therapeutics, Lysosomal Therapeutics, Nimbus Therapeutics
　Armen B Shanafelt, General Partner
　e-mail: armen@lillyventures.com
　Education: BS, Chemistry & Physics, Pacific Lutheran University; PhD, Chemistry, University of California, Berkeley
　Background: CSO, Biotherpeutic Pipeline, Eli Lilly & Company; DNAS Research Insitute; Director of Research, Roche Diagnostic Corporation; Bayer Corporation
　Directorships: Aeglea BioTherapeutics, Aileron Therapeutics, Protagonist Therapeutics, Surface Oncology, Sutro Biopharma, Symic Biomedical

1129 LIME ROCK PARTNERS
Heritage Plaza
Suite 4600
1111 Bagby Street
Houston, TX 77002

Phone: 713-292-9500
web: www.lrpartners.com

Mission Statement: Private equity firm focused on the oil and gas sector.

Fund Size: $9 billion
Founded: 1998
Industry Group Preference: Energy, Engineering, Oil & Gas, Mining
Portfolio Companies: AccessESP, Airis Wellsite Services, Archer, Ardyne, Arena Gulf, Augustus Energy Partners II, Axis Energy Services, Basin Properties, Blackjewel, Capstone Natural Resources II, Cor4 Oil, CrownRock, CrownRock Minerals, OilSERV, Prime Rock Resources, Reelwell, Reveal Energy Services, San Jacinto Minerals, SDI Gas, Shelf Drilling, Silixa, Silvertip Completion Services, TGT Oilfield Services, Wayfinder Resources

Other Locations:
274 Riverside Avenue
Suite 3
Westport, CT 06880
Phone: 203-293-2750

Key Executives:
　Will Franklin, Managing Director
　Education: University of Texas, Austin; Harvard Business School
　Background: Riverstone Holdings
　Directorships: Airis, GEODynamics, OilSERV, Shelf Drilling, Xtreme Drilling
　Jonathan Farber, Co-Founder & Managing Director
　Education: School of Foreign Service of Georgetown University
　Background: Goldman Sachs
　Directorships: Augustus Energy Partners II; Cor4 Oil; CrownRock; CrownRock Minerals; San Jacinto Minerals; Arena Exploration; Black Shire Energy; Coronado Resources; Deer Creek Energy
　John Reynolds, Co-Founder & Managing Director
　Education: BA, Bucknell University
　Background: Goldman Sachs
　Directorships: Blackjewel; Shelf Drilling; Archer; Eastern Drilling; EnerMech; Hercules Offshore; IPEC; Noble Tesco; Torch Offshore; VEDCO Holdings
　Trevor Burgess, Managing Director
　Education: Oxford University
　Background: Director of Global Business Units & Group Director of Marketing and Technology, Expro; VP of Sales, Baker Hughes
　Directorships: Acoustic Zoom; Ardyne; Reelwell; Reveal Energy Services; Silixa; TGT Oilfield Services; Gas2; Senscient; TerraSpark; Geosciences

1130 LIMESTONE VENTURES
98 San Jacinto Blvd.
Suite 320
Austin, TX 78701

Phone: 512-346-7111 **Fax:** 512-346-2111
e-mail: info@limestonevc.com
web: www.limestonevc.com

Mission Statement: To grow innovative high technology companies.

Founded: 1999
Investment Criteria: Seed-Stage, Early-Stage
Industry Group Preference: High Technology
Portfolio Companies: BlueSpace Software, Collider, CTS, Kionix, Metreos Corporation, Mimix Broadband, MobiTV, NetSpend, Sharklet Technologies, SiVerion, Rheonix, Wimba

Key Executives:
　Bob Inman, Chairman
　Education: BA, University of Texas, Austin
　Background: Managing Director, Gefinor Ventures; Managing Director, Inman Ventures
　Tom Inman, Managing Director
　Education: BS, Electrical Engineering, MBA, University of Texas, Austin
　Background: Principal, Gefinor Ventures

1131 LINCOLNSHIRE MANAGEMENT
780 Third Avenue
40th Floor
New York, NY 10017

Phone: 212-319-3633
e-mail: info@lmi780.com
web: www.lincolnshiremgmt.com

Mission Statement: A private equity firm focused on acquiring and growing small and middle market companies.

Geographic Preference: Worldwide
Fund Size: $835 million
Founded: 1986
Average Investment: $25 million
Minimum Investment: $3 million
Investment Criteria: LBO, Recaps
Industry Group Preference: Niche Manufacturing, Distribution
Portfolio Companies: The Alaska Club, Allison Marine, Cutters, Dalbo Holdings, Desch Plantpak, Fallon Visual Products, Flight Training Acquisitions, Holley, Latite

Holdings, National Pen, Nursery Supplies Inc., PADI, Phoenix Brands, True Temper Sports, Wireline

Key Executives:
TJ Maloney, Chairman & CEO
Education: BA, Boston College; JD, Fordham University School of Law
Background: Managing Director, Lincolnshire; Attorney/Founder, Maloney Mehlman Katz
Michael J Lyons, President
e-mail: mlyons@lincolnshiremgmt.com
Education: BS, BA, Boston University; MBA, Harvard University
Background: CPA, PriceWaterhouse
Vineet Pruthi, Senior Managing Director
e-mail: vpruthi@lincolnshiremgmt.com
Education: BS, Bombay University; MBA, Rutgers University
Background: CFO, Credentials Services International
Thomas R Callahan, Managing Director
e-mail: tcallahan@lincolnshiremgmt.com
Education: AB, Harvard University
Background: Executive Managing Director, Equity Capital Markets HSBC Securities; Treasurer/The China Fund
George J Henry, Managing Director
e-mail: ghenry@lincolnshiremgmt.com
Education: BA, Harvard University; MBA, Darden Graduate School of Business Administration, University of Virginia
Background: Associate, Bowles Hollowell Conner; GAMA Corporation
Philip Kim, Managing Director
Education: AB, Economics, Harvard University
Background: Associate, Knickerbocker LLC; Analyst, Fortress Investment Group LLC
James G Binch, Senior Advisor
e-mail: jbinch@lincolnshiremgmt.com
Education: BScE, Princeton University; MBA, Wharton School, University of Pennsylvania
Background: President & CEO, Memry Corporation; Combustion Engineering; Cresap McCormick & Paget Inc.
Phil Jakeway, Managing Director
Education: BA, Georgetown University; MBA, Columbia University
Background: CEO, American Business Institute; Founder & CEO, The Supporting Cast
James McLaughlin, Managing Director
e-mail: jmclaughlin@lincolnshiremgmt.com
Education: BA, Bucknell University; JD, Cornell Law School
Background: Partner, Pillsbury Winthrop LLP
Pieter Kodde, Managing Director
Education: Amsterdam School of Business
Background: Rabobank International, ABN AMRO
John O'Connor, Managing Director
Education: BA, University College Dublin; Tuck School of Business
Background: Managing Director, Barclays Bank Ireland; Nat West; KPMG
Ottavio Serena, Managing Director
Education: Universita' degli Studi di Roma
Background: Citicorp Venture Capital; Italian Armed Forces

1132 LINDEN LLC
150 N. Riverside Plaza
Suite 5100
Chicago, IL 60606

Phone: 312-506-5600 Fax: 312-506-5601
e-mail: info@lindenllc.com
web: www.lindenllc.com

Mission Statement: Linden is a healthcare and life science private equity firm that builds exceptional value in mature businesses. We specialize in traditional management buyouts of independent companies as well as investments in non-core businesses owned by large corporations.

Founded: 2002
Investment Criteria: Management Buyouts
Industry Group Preference: Healthcare, Life Sciences
Portfolio Companies: Ability One, Advarra, Avalign Technologies, BarrierSafe Solutions International, Behavioural Centers of America, Corpak Medsystems, Drayer Physical Therapy Institute, ERG, Flexan, Focused Health Solutions, Hycor, The Hydrafacial Company, Inovision, Kendro Laboratory, LifeStream, Merical, Northwestern Management Services, Pinnacle Treatment Centers, ProPharma Group, Ranir, SeraCare Life Sciences, Smile Doctors Braces, Strata Dx, SutureExpress, Virtus Pharmaceuticals, Young Innovations, Z-Medica

Key Executives:
Anthony B Davis, President & Managing Partner
e-mail: tdavis@lindenllc.com
Education: BA, Economics, Northwestern University; MBA, University of Chicago Graduate School of Business
Background: Partner, One Equity Partners; Strategy Consultant, Cresap McCormick & Paget
Directorships: ProPharma, Smile Doctors, Spear Education, Advarra, Sage Dental, Virtus Pharmaceuticals
Brian C Miller, Managing Partner
e-mail: bmiller@lindenllc.com
Education: BA, Princeton University; MBA, Harvard Business School
Background: First Chicago Equity Capital, Salomon Brothers
Directorships: Flexan, HydraFacial, MeriCal, Solara, Z-Medica
Michael Farah, Partner
e-mail: mfarah@lindenllc.com
Education: BA, Finance, Carnegie Mellon University; MBA, Harvard Business School
Background: VP, Metalmark Capital; Private Equity Associate, Summit Partners
Michael Watts, Partner
e-mail: mwatts@lindenllc.com
Education: BA, Economics and History, Washington & Lee University; MBA, Kellogg School of Management
Background: Brockway Moran & Partners; Stephens Inc.

1133 LINDSAY GOLDBERG
630 Fifth Avenue
30th Floor
New York, NY 10111

Phone: 212-651-1100 Fax: 212-651-1101
e-mail: contact@lindsaygoldbergllc.com
web: www.lindsaygoldbergllc.com

Mission Statement: Lindsay Goldberg seeks to become long-term partners with family business owners, management teams and experienced CEOs who have as their goal significant long-term growth in their enterprise.

Geographic Preference: Worldwide
Investment Criteria: Growth Equity
Portfolio Companies: Alliant Insurance Services, Ambulatory Services of America, Aptitude Investment Management, Aviv REIT, Bell Nursery Holdings, Bluegrass Materials Company, Brightstar Corp., Continental Energy Systems LLC, Crane & Co., Dealer Tire, ECS Federal, EnergySolutions, First American Payment Systems, Formation Energy, FSB Global Holdings, Intermex Holdings, Keystone Foods Holdings, Klöckner & Co. AG, Maine Beverage Company, MBI Energy Services, Pacific Architects and Engineers, PetroLogistics, Pike Electric Corporation, PL Midstream, PSC Holdings I, RECON Holdings III, Rosetta LLC, Scandza AS, The Brock Group, Vitruvian LC, Wacker Construction Equipment AG, Weener Plastic GmbH, WoodSpring Hotels Holdings

Venture Capital & Private Equity Firms / Domestic Firms

Key Executives:
Alan E Goldberg, CEO & Co-Founder
Education: BA, Philosophy & Economics, New York University; MBA, New York University Graduate School of Business; JD, Yeshiva University
Background: Chairman & CEO, Morgan Stanley Private Equity
Directorships: Aptitude Investment Management, Crown Point International, Odfjell Termials BV, Stelco
Robert D Lindsay, Chairman & Co-Founder
Education: BA, English & American Literature, Harvard College; MBA, Stanford University
Background: Managing General Partner, Bessemer Holdings; Managing Director, Morgan Stanely Private Equity
Directorships: The Bessemer Group
Krishna K Agrawal, Managing Director
Education: BS, Finance and Information Systems, New York University; MBA, Stanford Graduate School of Business
Background: Investment Banking Analyst, Morgan Stanley
Directorships: Odfjell Terminals, Intermodal Holdings, Stelco
Megan Lundy, Managing Director
Education: BA, History, Columbia University
Background: DLJ Investment Partners, Barclays
Michael W Dees, Partner
Education: BA, Economics, Harvard College; MBA, Harvard Business School
Background: M&A, Morgan Stanley
Directorships: Odfjell Terminals BV, Paccor, Schur Flexibles GmbH, VDM Metals, Stelco
J Russell Triedman, Partner
Education: ScB, Applied Mathematics, Brown University; JD, University of Chicago Law School
Background: Principal, Bessemer Holidings; Director, Fox Paine & Company
Directorships: Golden West Packaging Group, BA Solutions, Crown Point International, Crown Paper Group, Second Spring Healthcare Investments
John F Aiello, Partner
Education: BA, Political Science, New York Univerity; JD, Georgetown University
Background: Managing Director, Goldman Sachs; Weil Gotshal & Manges LLP
Directorships: Aptitude Asset Management, Trygg Pharma Group AS
Jeffrey B Bunder, Partner
Education: BA, Emory University; MBA, New York Univerity; CPA
Background: Ernst & Young
Directorships: Stelco
Stephen P DeFalco, Partner
Education: BS, Mechanical Engineering, MIT; MS, Computer Engineering, Syracuse University; MBA, MIT Sloan School of Management
Background: CEO, Crance & Co.; CEO, MDS; CEO, Senseonics; CEO, PathoGenetix; Strategy Consultant, McKinsey & Company;
Eric T Fry, Partner
Education: BA, Economics, Wharton School; MBA, Harvard Business School
Background: Managing Director, Morgan Stanley Private Equity
Brian P Kelley, Partner
Education: BA, Economics, College of the Holy Cross
Background: CEO, Keurig Green Mountain; President, North American Operations, Coca-Cola Company; General Electric; Proctor & Gamble
Directorships: Keurig Green Mountain, Blue Apron, BA Solutions
Christopher M Laitala, Partner
Education: BA, Government, Harvard College; MBA, Harvard Business School

Background: Managing Director, HIG Capital; JH Whitney & Co.; Great Point Partners
Directorships: PT Solutions, Women's Care Holdings, Refresh Mental Health
Jacob J Lew, Partner
Background: United States Senate; Managing Director, Citigroup; Executive VP & COO, New York University
Directorships: Stelco

1134 LINLEY CAPITAL
601 Lexington Avenue
43rd Floor
New York, NY 10022

Phone: 646-863-7200 **Fax:** 646-863-7201
e-mail: info@linleycapital.com
web: www.linleycapital.com

Mission Statement: Linley Capital is a New York-based private equity firm that invests in mid-sized companies, in the United States, Europe and Latin America, through leveraged buyouts, recapitalizations and growth equity investments. The company invests in a wide variety of industries and sectors that include branded consumer products as well as selected subsectors of industrial and manufacturing businesses. Linley Capital has an investment strategy that is both long-term and conservative and works in close partnership with the management team to develop comprehensive and sustainable operating and growth strategies.

Geographic Preference: United States, Europe, Latin America
Founded: 1993
Investment Criteria: Linley Capital generally invests in companies with a $100 million to $2 billion range in revenue.
Industry Group Preference: Technology, Financial Services, Business Products & Services, Energy, Clean Technology, Industrial, Manufacturing, Aerospace, Defense and Government, Retail, Consumer & Leisure, Consumer

Key Executives:
John R Jonge Poernik, Founder & Managing Partner
Education: MA, Marketing & Communications, University of Amsterdam; MBA, Finance, Wharton School
Background: Partner, Circle Peak Capital; Vice President, Limited Brands
Sebastian C. Widmann, Senior Associatie
Education: BA, Tufts University
Matthew Croft, Senior Associate
Education: BA, Finance, Baruch College

1135 LINN GROVE VENTURES
5012 53rd St. S
Fargo, ND 58104

Phone: 701-356-5655
web: www.linngroveventures.com

Mission Statement: Linn Grove Ventures seeks to identify the best early and mid-stage life science companies with outstanding technology that can benefit from our strategic capital and business strategies, while creating growth within the Corridor.

Geographic Preference: Upper Midwest Region
Investment Criteria: Early-Stage, Mid-Stage
Industry Group Preference: Life Sciences, Agriculture
Portfolio Companies: FarmQA, Next Healthcre, Virgin Plants

Key Executives:
Dan Hodgson, Managing Partner
Education: BS, English, Bemidji State University
Directorships: FarmQA, Next Health Care, Virgin Plants
Dennis O'Brien, Managing Partner
Education: BS, Chemical Engineering, Rensselaer Polytechnic Institute; Simon School, University of Rochester; Columbia Business School
Directorships: Next Health Care

Steve Polski, Managing Director
Education: BA, Marketing, University of St. Thomas
Background: Andersen Windows; Cargill; Enerfo USA
Directorships: Living Well Disability Services, Clean Energy Economy Minnesota

1136 LINSALATA CAPITAL PARTNERS
5900 Landerbrook Drive
Suite 280
Mayfield Heights, OH 44124

Phone: 440-684-1400 Fax: 440-684-0984
e-mail: info@linsalatacapital.com
web: www.linsalatacapital.com

Mission Statement: Private equity firm focused on middle market leveraged and management buyouts.
Geographic Preference: United States
Fund Size: $425 million
Founded: 1984
Average Investment: $25 million
Minimum Investment: $10 million
Investment Criteria: LBO, MBO
Industry Group Preference: Building Materials & Services, Plastics, Distribution, Automotive, Business to Business, Direct Marketing, Convergent Technologies
Portfolio Companies: Eatem Foods Co., Glynlyon, Happy Floors, Harden Manufacturing, The Home Decor Companies, Home Helpers, Hospitality Mints, Manhattan Beachwear LLC, NeuroTherm, Paradigm Packaging, Randy's Worldwide Automotive, Signature Systems Group, Spartan Foods of America, Stag-Parkway, Transpac, U-Line, Wellborn Forest Products, Whitcraft Group

Key Executives:
Frank Linsalata, Chairman
e-mail: flinsalata@linsalatacapital.com
Education: BS, Case Western Reserve University; MBA, Harvard Business School
Background: Founder/Edgecliff Investment; Executive VP/COO, Midland-Ross
Directorships: Home Helpers, Randy's Worldwide Automotive
Eric V Bacon, Senior Managing Director
e-mail: ebacon@linsalatacapital.com
Education: Albion College; MBA, Stanford University
Background: Consultant, McKinsey & Company; Allied-Signal
Directorships: Randy's Worldwide Automotive, Signature Systems Group, Manhattan Beachwear Holding Company, Hospitality Mints
Stephen B Perry, Senior Managing Director
e-mail: sperry@linsalatacapital.com
Education: Lake Erie College
Background: Senior VP/CFO, CFA Window Group; Auditor, Touche Ross; Controller, Elektrapak; Director Planning/Analysis, FL Industries; VP Finance, CMS Holding
Directorships: Glynlyon Holding Company, Happy Floors, Wellborn Forest Products

1137 LIQUID CAPITAL GROUP
1420 Spring Hill Rd.
Suite 600
McLean, VA 22102

Phone: 703-626-3757
e-mail: info@liquidcapitalgroup.com
web: www.liquidcapitalgroup.com

Mission Statement: Offers accredited investors and families access to a diversified portfolio of superior emerging information technology companies and top venture capital funds.
Founded: 2000
Investment Criteria: Early-Stage

Industry Group Preference: Information Technology, Digital Security, Mobile Computing, Communications, Digital Rights Management, E-Commerce & Manufacturing, Networking
Portfolio Companies: InterSAN, Lightningcast, MaterialNet, Matrics, MortgageIT.com, netForensics, Object Video, Overture Technologies, Parature, ServiceBench, Visto, WiderThan

Key Executives:
Randolph C Domolky, Managing Director
Education: BA, Economics & Environmental Studies, University of Pennsylvania
Background: Managing Director, GKM Newport; Pricipal, NextStep Partners; Vice President, NEON Communications; General Manager, Carrier Sales Division, Winstar Communications

1138 LITTLEJOHN & COMPANY LLC
8 Sound Shore Drive
Suite 303
Greenwich, CT 06830

Phone: 203-552-3500
e-mail: info@littlejohnllc.com
web: www.littlejohnllc.com

Mission Statement: A private equity firm that makes control equity investments in mid-sized companies that are underperforming their potential or struggling with financial or operational challenges.
Geographic Preference: Canada, Europe, United States
Fund Size: $1.3 billion
Founded: 1996
Average Investment: $75 million
Minimum Investment: $50 million
Investment Criteria: LBO, MBO
Industry Group Preference: Industrial Equipment, Chemicals, Automotive, Food & Beverage, Healthcare, Plastics, Textiles, Distribution, Consumer Products, Processing
Portfolio Companies: Accuride, Alvogen, Angiotech, ASG Technologies, Alphabroder, Ameriqual, Aquilex, Benevis Practice Services, Brown Jordan International, Chemtura, Clean Earth, CoActive Technologies, Contech Engineered Solutions, Cook & Boardman Group, Cornerstone Chemical Company, Cosmetic Essence Innovations, CTI Foods, Cunningham Lindsey, Direct Chassis Link Inc., Dex One, Diamond Innovations, Eliokem Materials & Concepts, Erickson, Evergreen, Express Energy Services, General Trailers, GSE Environmental, Gulf Coast Shipyard Group, Hanleywood, HDT Global, Hennings Automotive, Horsehead, Hostway, HydroChemPSC, Installed Building Products, Interior Logic Group, Jerr-Dan, Joerns Healthcare, Kenan Advantage Group, Keystone Automotive Operations, Latham International, Luxfer, Motion Recruitment, Nellson, Newgistics, NewCold, Noranda, Northwest Hardwoods, Pameco Corp., Penda Corporation, Perfect Fit, Pernix Therapeutics, PlayPower, Prince, PSC, Sequa, Sitel, Smile Brands Inc., Sotera Defense Solutions, Soundview Maritime LLC, Stallion, Stolle Machinery, Strategic Materials, Sun Source, Synchronous Aerospace Group, Synventive, S&S Industries, Tidel, Total Safety, Tronox, Unitek, Universal Lighting Technologies, Van Houtte Cafe, vRad, Wastequip, WireCo WorldGroup, Weight Watchers, World and Main, Wyle

Key Executives:
Angus C Littlejohn Jr., Chairman
Education: BS Economics, University of Pennsylvania
Background: Joseph, Littlejohn & Levy; Quadrex Securities
Michael I Klein, Chief Executive Officer
Education: MBA, Harvard Business School; BS Accounting, New York University
Background: S&S Industries; Senior Associate, Joseph, Littlejohn & Levy; Sumitomo Corporation

Venture Capital & Private Equity Firms / Domestic Firms

Directorships: Brown Jordan, PlayPower, Cornerstone Chemicals

Edmund J Feeley, Managing Director
Education: MBA, College of William & Mary; BSE, Naval Architecture, University of Michigan
Background: President/COO, Fleer Corporation; Timberland Company; Booz Allen & Hamilton
Directorships: Northwest Hardwoods, Cornerstone Chemicals Corp.

Brian W Michaud, Managing Director
Education: BA, Economics and Spanish, Middlebury College
Background: Analyst, CIBC World Markets
Directorships: Total Safety, HydroChemPSC, Strategic Materials Group

Robert E Davis, Managing Director
Education: BA, Economics, Northwestern University; MBA, JL Kellogg School of Management, Northwestern University
Background: Managing Director, Oaktree Capital Management's Mezzanine Fund; Principal, Halcyon Asset Management; Prudential Insurance Company
Directorships: Alphabroder, Interior Logic Inc.

Michael B Kaplan, Managing Director
Education: BA, Communications, SUNY Albany
Background: Senior Associate, Ripplewood Holdings; Associate Attoney, Cravath Swaine & Moore
Directorships: Hostway, Unitek, Total Safety, HydroChemPSC

Richard E Maybaum, Managing Director
Education: BA, Philosophy & Political Science, University of Rochester; JD, American University
Background: Portolio Manager, Ramius Capital Group; Managing Director, Alpine Associates; Chase Securities

Antonio Miranda, Managing Director
Education: AB, Harvard College; MBA, Stanford Graduate School of Business
Background: Associate, Clayton Dubillier & Rice; JP Morgan & Co
Directorships: Tidel

Steven G Raich, Managing Director
Education: BA, Duke University; MBA, Stern School of Business, New York University
Background: Golub Associates; Ernst & Young LLP
Directorships: Strategic Materials Inc., Stallion Oilfield Services, Interior Logic Inc., Cook & Boardman

Gentry S Klein, Managing Director
Education: BS, Economics, Wharton School
Background: Associate, Rothschild; Credit Analyst, Rock Hill Partners; Analyst, Chanin Capital Partners
Directorships: Total Safety

1139 LIZADA CAPITAL LLC
8259 East Alameda Road
Scottsdale, AZ 85255

web: www.lizadacapital.com

Mission Statement: Invests in the cannabis industry. Areas of interest include research & data, dispensaries & retail, cultivation, lab testing, packaging, equipment, paraphernalia, security, business services, and information management.

Geographic Preference: United States, Canada
Fund Size: $5 million
Founded: 1998
Average Investment: $100,000
Minimum Investment: $10,000
Industry Group Preference: Cannabis, Information Technology, Consumer Products
Portfolio Companies: AmeriCann, Aphria, Auntie Dolores, The Arcview Group, Budding Enterprise Fund, BDS, Calyx, CDX, CannLabs, Canopy Boulder, CannaRoyalty Corp., Elixirs, DigiPath Inc., Electrum Partners, Ebbu, FLRish, GW Pharmaceuticals, Growcentia, GrowBLOX Science, GFarmalabs, Green Flower Media, Green Thumb Industries, Harborside Health Center, Healthy Headie Lifestyle, Herban Planet, High Times, Jane West, Lexaria Energy, Las Vegas Cannaplex, Mass Roots, Medicine Man Technologies, MJIC, Mirth Provisions, MedBox, MedMen, NeWAY, New Frontier, Noble Blends, Notis Global, Nutritional High, Peter Tosh, PROHBTD, Quigley's, Steep Hill, Therabis, Sunniva, Temescal Wellness, Treatibles, Tech Holdings, Panther Capital, Vapor Slide

Key Executives:
Steve Trenk, Founder/Managing Member

1140 LLR PARTNERS INC
2929 Arch Street, Cira Center
Philadelphia, PA 19104

Phone: 215-717-2900
web: www.llrpartners.com

Mission Statement: LLR is opportunistic, investing in companies with strong growth potential, proven business models and outstanding management.

Geographic Preference: Mid Atlantic & Eastern United States
Fund Size: $800 billion
Founded: 1999
Average Investment: $15 million
Minimum Investment: $10 million
Investment Criteria: Growth, Acquisition, Buyouts, Recapitalizations
Industry Group Preference: Business Products & Services, Information Technology, Healthcare Services, Financial Services, Retailing, Processing, Consumer Services, Software, Education, Manufacturing
Portfolio Companies: 3SI Security Systems, Agility Recovery, Alsbridge, American Renal Associates, Avenues: The World School, Benefit Express, BluVector, BrightHeart, Brightside Academy, Cedar Capital, Celero Accelerated Commerce, Cigital, Codiscope, CollabNet, ComNet, CompoSecure, Coredial, Crothall Healthcare, CyberShift, Digital Guardian, Edlio, Edmund & Associates, EKR Therapeutics, eLocal, eOriginal, eResearch Technology, excelleRx, Eye Health America, Eyewitness Surveillance, Five Below, Fleet One, Gestalt, Healthcare Finance Group, Heartland Payment Systems, HighPoint Solutions, Illuminate Education, InfoHighway, InnaPhase, IO Education, IOD, JGWPT Holdings, Kemberton, Key2Act, Learn Behavioural, Logi Analytics, Maxwell Systems, Medbridge, Medical Science & Computing, Medmark, Mercury Security, Midigator, Numotion, Onapsis, Opinion Research Corporation, Orbis Education, Pet 360, Phish Labs, Phreesia, Physicians Immediate Care, Princeton Softech, Professional Capital Services, Prophet 21, Quintiq, Rapid Ratings, Reading Truck Body, Relias Learning, Revitas, Rizing, Schweiger Dermatology Group, SDI Health, SDI Inc., Sicom, Singer Equities, Spark Post, Sterling Trading Tech, Sun Behavioural Health, Taratec, Tribridge, Ultimus Fund Solutions, UltiSat, Vanderbilt, Vector Solutions, Vivere Health, Welocalize, World Aware

Key Executives:
Mitchell L Hollin, Partner
e-mail: mhollin@llrpartners.com
Education: BS, Economics, University of Pennsylvania; MBA, Finance, Wharton School
Background: Co-Founder/Managing Director, Advanta Partners; Patricof & Co Ventures (Apax)
Directorships: Celero Commerce, CompoSecure, Midigator, Professional Capital Services, Sterling Trading Tech, Ultimus Fund Solutions

Seth J Lehr, Partner
e-mail: slehr@llrpartners.com
Education: BS, Economics, University of Pennsylvania; MBA, Finance, Wharton School
Background: Managing Director, Legg Mason; Co-Founding Partner, The Middle Market Group; Investment Banking VP, Lehman Brothers; Investment Banking Analyst, First Boston; Sales, IBM

Venture Capital & Private Equity Firms / Domestic Firms

Directorships: Avenues: The World School, IO Education, Mercury Security, SDI Inc., Vanderbilt
Ira M Lubert, Partner
e-mail: ilubert@llrpartners.com
Education: BS Human Development, Pennsylvania State University
Background: Principal/Founder, Independence Capital Partners; Managing Director/Co-Founder, TL Ventures; Founder, Radnor Venture Partners; Chairman/President, CompuCom Systems; Sales, IBMA
Directorships: Safeguard Scientifics, The Franklin Institute, National Constitution Center
Howard D Ross, Partner
e-mail: hross@llrpartners.com
Education: BA, University of Pennsylvania
Background: Senior Partner, Arthur Andersen LLP; CPA
Directorships: Agility Recovery, Key2Act, Numotion, Rapid Ratings, Rizing
Jack Slye, Partner
e-mail: jslye@llrpartners.com
Education: BS, University of Maryland; MBA, Wharton School
Background: Principal, Sterling Partners; COO & Vice President of Corporate Development, Sylvan Learning
Directorships: Edlio, Illuminate Education, Learn Behavioural, MedBridge, Orbis Education, Sun Behavioural Health
Scott A Perricelli, Partner
e-mail: sperricelli@llrpartners.com
Education: BS, Accounting, Bucknell University; MBA, Finance & Entrepreneurship, JL Kellogg School of Management, Northwestern University
Background: Investment Banker, William Blair & Co
Directorships: BenefitExpress, Eye Health America, Kemberton Healthcare Services, Learn Behavioural, Orbis Education, Phreesia, Physicians Immediate Care, Schweiger Dermatology Group
David J Reuter, Partner
e-mail: dreuter@llrpartners.com
Education: BS, Business & Economics, Lehigh University; CPA
Background: Arthur Andersen
Directorships: CollabNet, CoreDial, Edmunds & Associates, eLocal, eOriginal, SparkPost
David A Stienes, Partner
e-mail: dsteines@llrpartners.com
Education: BBA, Accounting, James Madison University; CPA
Background: Arthur Andersen
Directorships: 3SI Security Systems, Agility Recovery, BluVector, ComNet, Digital Guardian, Eyewitness Surveillance, Onapsis, Vanderbilt Industries, WorldAware

1141 LM CAPITAL SECURITIES
2385 NW Executive Center Drive
Suite 100
Boca Raton, FL 33431

Phone: 561-351-4114
e-mail: info@lmcap.net
web: lmcapitalcorp.com

Mission Statement: Dedicated to providing high quality investment management and investment banking services to private and public entities. Built on the cornerstones of integrity, professionalism and superior performance, LM Capital Securities, is an emerging full service investment firm.

Founded: 1993
Minimum Investment: $1 million
Investment Criteria: Strong Management Team; 5-Year Record of Profitability; Above Average Investment Returns of 20%
Industry Group Preference: Consumer Products, Distribution, Industrial Equipment, Medical & Health Related

Key Executives:
Leslie M Corley, President/CEO
e-mail: LeslieCorley@LMCapitalSecurities.com
Education: BS, University of Illinois; MBA, Harvard Graduate School of Business Administration
Background: Founder, LM Capital; Kelso & Company; Fidelity Investments, Boston; Norton Simon, Inc.

1142 LOCUS VENTURES
Redwood City, CA 94065

web: www.locus.vc

Mission Statement: A tech-based venture capital firm that offers its portfolio companies insights on product design, professional development and team-building.

Geographic Preference: US, Asia
Fund Size: $300 million
Founded: 2016
Industry Group Preference: Artificial Intelligence, Information Technology, Software, Applications
Portfolio Companies: Allure Systems, Blue Bottle Coffee, Branch, Brilliant, CareerTu, Cattle Care, Convictional, Digi-Prex, Doorstead, Framer, Glowing.io, Grabb-It, Grin Scooters, HomeCourt.ai, Interative.ai, LemonBox, Lob, Masterclass, Matternet, Meesho, Miso, Notable Labs, One Medical, Orchid Labs, Oxygen, Panther Labs, Passport, Portside, Precious, Proper, Razorpay, Recko, Simple Habit, Standard Cognition, Uber, Vahan, Very Good Security, VideoSlick

Key Executives:
Eric Kwan, Managing Partner
Education: BS/MS, Carnegie Mellon University; MS, Stanford University
Background: Senior Member of Technical Staff, Oracle; Senior Technical Yahoo, Yahoo!; Software Engineer, Facebook; Founding Engineer, Operator; Advisor, Cozymeal Inc.; Investor, Panther Labs
Tommy Tsai, Managing Partner
Education: BS, Stanford University
Background: Director of Engineering, Loopt; Founding Engineer, Shopkick; Co-Founder, Shopular; Co-Founder, Coefficient
William Chan, Managing Partner
Education: BS/MS, Stanford University
Background: Software Engineer, NeoPath Networks; Tech Lead, Google; Co-Founder, S Loyalty; Co-Founder, Wave Commerce

1143 LOMBARD INVESTMENTS
950 John Daly Boulevard
Suite 260
San Francisco, CA 94015

Phone: 415-397-5900 Fax: 415-397-5820
web: www.lombardinvestments.com

Mission Statement: Lombard provides strategic advice to its portfolio companies, adds further value through introducing innovations and improved business practices and by leveraging its extensive relationships in North America and Asia.

Geographic Preference: North America, Asia
Fund Size: $1 billion
Founded: 1985
Average Investment: $30 million
Minimum Investment: $5 million
Investment Criteria: Acquisition, LBO, MBO, Recapitalization
Industry Group Preference: Business to Business, Education, Financial Services, Industrial Equipment, Manufacturing, Materials Technology, Chemicals, Wholesale, Distribution, Retailing, Media, Entertainment, Healthcare, Energy
Portfolio Companies: Asia Books, Asiasoft, Career Choices, Centara Hotels and Resorts, Central Pattana, Concung, Dakota Minnesota & Eastern Railroad, Easy Buy, Express

Venture Capital & Private Equity Firms / Domestic Firms

Food Group, Fu Sheng Industrial, Good Morning Shinhan Securities, Hansol Gyoyook Company, JWD, Kantana Group, Krungthep Land, KSNET, MC Group, Mega Lifesciences, Mermaid Maritime, Mithmitree, Nok Airlines, Overseas Dragon China, Pomelo, Pruska Real Estate, Robinson Department Store, S. Pack & Print, San Shing Fastech Corporation, S&P Syndicate, Silkspan, SNC Former, Somboom Advance Technology, Syn Mun Kong Insurance, The Medical City, TICON Industrial, Trinity Watthana, Viet-UC Group, Workpoint Creative TV

Other Locations:
Room 1107, 11/F
Tower 2, Lippo Center
89 Queensway
Hong Kong
Phone: 852-28787388 **Fax:** 852-28787288

Key Executives:
Thomas Smith, Managing Director
e-mail: tsmith@lombardinvestments.com
Education: Graduated Cum Laude From Harvard College
Background: CEO/CFo ACI

1144 LONE STAR FUNDS
2711 North Haskell Avenue
Suite 1700
Dallas, TX 75204

Phone: 214-754-8300
e-mail: investorrelations@lonestarfunds.com
web: www.lonestarfunds.com

Mission Statement: Invests globally in secured and corporate unsecured debt instruments, real estate related assets and select corporate opportunities.
Fund Size: $24 billion
Founded: 1995
Industry Group Preference: Diversified

Other Locations:
888 7th Avenue
11th Floor
New York, NY 10019
Phone: 917-286-3300

1441 Brickell Avenue
Suite 1750
Miami, FL 33131
Phone: 786-482-2100

800 de la Gauchetiere West
South East Portal - Suite 9400
P.O. Box 1458
Montréal, QC H5A 1K6
Canada
Phone: 514-879-6310

Washington Mall
Suite 304
7 Reid Street
Hamilton HM11
Bermuda
Phone: 441-2961754

Marunouchi Kitaguchi Building
12th Floor
1-6-5 Marunouchi, Chiyoda-ku
Tokyo 100-0005
Japan
Phone: 81-352245300

Suite 2003, York House
The Landmark
15 Queen's Road
Central
Hong Kong
Phone: 852-3700-6900

10 Collyer Quay
#05-08, Ocean Financial Centre 049315
Singapore
Phone: 65-6800-9520

Lone Star Europe Acquisitions Lts.
12 Queen Anne St.
London W1G 9LF
England
Phone: 44-2076166800

Niedenau 61-63
Frankfurt am Main 60325
Germany
Phone: 49-69710422600

5 rue de Castiglione
Paris 75001
France
Phone: 33-1-8565-9020

Calle de Velazquez 34
1st Floor
Madrid 28001
Spain
Phone: 34-917-931-705

Key Executives:
John Patrick Grayken, Founder & Chairman
Education: MBA, Harvard University
Directorships: Patriot Equities

1145 LONG POINT CAPITAL
26700 Woodward Avenue
Royal Oak, MI 48067

Phone: 248-591-6000 **Fax:** 248-591-6001
web: www.longpointcapital.com

Mission Statement: Focuses on partnering with successful entrepreneurs of middle market businesses to help them achieve their financial goals.
Geographic Preference: North America
Fund Size: $315 million
Average Investment: $10-20 million
Minimum Investment: $10 million
Investment Criteria: Recaps, MBO, Consolidations
Industry Group Preference: Manufacturing, Distribution, Business Products & Services
Portfolio Companies: Arch Aluminum and Glass, Arrow Tru-Line, Artistic Holdings, Atlantic Plywood, Broadcasting Partners, CentriLogic, CHI Overhead Doors, CHA Consulting, Corsicana Mattress Company, Cumming Group, EuroDesign Cabinets, EYP Architecture & Design, Gradall, Haynes International, Hire Counsel & Mestel, Interlogix, National Print Group, Outdoor Seasons, Precision Products Group, Quaker Fabric, Savage Sports, St. George Logistics, Sunbury Textile Mills, The Saxton Group, Therma-Tru Doors, Torrent Resources, UMA Enterprises, Woolpert

Other Locations:
747 Third Avenue
22nd Floor
New York, NY 10017
Phone: 212-593-1800 **Fax:** 212-593-1888

Key Executives:
Eric Von Stroh, Partner
e-mail: evonstroh@longpointcapital.com
Education: BA, Economics and Political Science, Colgate University
Background: CFO, Five Star Food Service; Vice President, SG Capital Partners LLC; Chase Securities
Ira Starr, Partner
e-mail: istarr@longpointcapital.com
Education: BSE, Princeton University; MBA, Harvard Business School
Background: Partner, MLG&A; Investment Banker, Merrill Lynch; Management Consultant, Booz, Allen & Hamilton

1146 LONG RIVER VENTURES
50 Milk St
Boston, MA 02109

Phone: 617-326-3770
e-mail: tpeake@longriverventures.com
web: www.lrvhealth.com

Mission Statement: Long River Ventures invests in seed and early stage companies in healthcare, IT, and other technology-driven sectors. Formed by a group of experienced entrepreneurs and venture capitalist, Long River is designed and structured to invest smaller amounts of capital with typically initial investments of $500,000 to $1MM. We back exceptional entrepreneurs who are focused on building capital efficient businesses.

Geographic Preference: Northeast: Boston, New York
Fund Size: $50 million
Average Investment: $500,000 - $1 million
Investment Criteria: Seed-Stage, Early-Stage
Industry Group Preference: Healthcare Information Technology, Medical Devices, Diagnostics, Information Technology, Software, Telecommunications, Media, Internet, Clean Technology, Business Products & Services
Portfolio Companies: Convergent Dental, Eggrock, Extreme Reach, Health Guru, Healthrageous, Gate Rocket, GetWellNetwork, LifeIMAGE, M2S, MedVentive, Omedix, Optasite, Pervacio, Phreesia, Profile Systems, Protedyne, Qteros, Reconda International, Retail Optimization, Solais Lighting, Verax BioMedical

Key Executives:
  Tripp Peake, Managing Partner
  e-mail: tpeake@longriverventures.com
  Education: BA, Dartmouth College; MBA, Yale University
  Background: Partner, Kestrel Venture Management; Co-Founder, Mass Ventures; Co-Founder, Science Park Associates
  Directorships: Extreme Reach, Health Guru, Optasite, Profile Systems, Protedyne, Qteros, Sovereign Hill Software
  Will Cowen, Managing Partner
  e-mail: wcowen@longriverventures.com
  Education: BA, University of Colorado; MBA, MIT
  Background: Founder, NaviNet; CEO, Pegasus Medical Technologies
  Directorships: Eggrock, GetWellNetwork, Healthrageous, LifeIMAGE, Medical Metrx Systems, MedVenture, Phreesia, Solais, Verax Biomedical
  Mike Cataldo, Venture Partner
  e-mail: mcataldo@longriverventures.com
  Education: BA, Economics, Columbia University
  Background: CEO, Convergent Dental; CEO, Cambridge Semantics; Founder, MediVation
  John Kole, Venture Partner
  e-mail: jkole@longriverventures.com
  Education: BA, Princeton University's Woodrow Wilson School of Public & Internaitonal Affairs; JD, University of Michigan Law School
  Background: President, Merrimack Capital; Managing Director, Comcast Interactive Capital

1147 LONGITUDE CAPITAL
2740 Sand Hill Rd.
2nd Floor
Menlo Park, CA 94025

Phone: 650-854-5700
web: www.longitudecapital.com

Mission Statement: Longitude Capital is a life sciences venture capital firm specializing in investments in medical devices, biotechnology, pharmaceutical product development, and diagnostics and R&D tools.

Founded: 2006
Average Investment: $10 - $30 million
Industry Group Preference: Life Sciences, Medical Devices, Biotechnology, Pharmaceuticals, Diagnostics
Portfolio Companies: 89bio, Aimmune Therapeutics, Akebia Therapeutics, Alphaeon, Amphora Medical, Aptinyx, Axonics Modulation Technologies, Baronova, California Cryobank, CardioDX, CrownWheel Partners, Curasen Therapeutics, Cydan, Encore Dermatology, Inflazome, Inozyme Pharma, Kala Pharmaceuticals, KaNDy Therapeutics, Molecular Templates, Murj, Nabriva, Nalu Medical, Neurana Pharmaceuticals, Orbus Therapeutics, Poseida Therapeutics, Rapid Micro Biosystems, Renew Inserts, RxSight, Sublimity Therapeutics, Sutrovax, Tricida, Velicept Therapeutics, Venus Concept, Welbe Health

Other Locations:
One Fawcett Place
Greenwich, CT 06830
Phone: 203-769-5200

Key Executives:
  Juliet Tammenoms Bakker, Managing Director, Greenwich
  e-mail: jbakker@longitudecapital.com
  Education: BS, Biological Sciences, Cornell University; MPA, Kennedy School of Government, Harvard University
  Background: Managing Director, Pequot Ventures; Director, Strategic Planning, Waste Management Internationa
  Directorships: Alphaeon, Axonics Modulation Technologies, Encore Dermatology, Nalu, RxSight, Venus Concept
  Patrick Enright, Managing Director, Menlo Park
  e-mail: penright@longitudecapital.com
  Education: BS, Biological Sciences, Stanford University; MBA, Wharton School
  Background: Managing Director, Pequot Ventures; Managing Member, Delta Opportunity Fund; PaineWebber Development Corporation
  Directorships: Aimmune, Aptinyx, CardioDx, CuraSen Therapeutics, Jazz Pharmaceuticals, Orbus Therapeutics, SutroVax
  Marc-Henri Galletti, Managing Director, Menlo Park
  e-mail: mgalletti@longitudecapital.com
  Education: AB, Princeton University; MBA, Kellogg School of Management
  Background: SVP, Pequot Ventures; Amerindo Investment Advisors; Vector Fund Management
  Directorships: Amphora, Medical, Murj
  David Hirsch MD, PhD, Managing Director, Greenwich
  e-mail: dhirsch@longitudecapital.com
  Education: BA, Biology, Johns Hopkins University; MD, Harvard Medical School; PhD, Biology, MIT
  Background: VP, Pequot Ventures; Engagement Manager, McKinsey & Company
  Directorships: Inflazome, Molecular Templates, Poseida Therapeutics, Rapid Micro Biosystems, Tricida, Velicept
  Sandip Agarwala, Managing Director, Greenwich
  Education: BSE, Systems Engineering, University of Pennsylvania; MBA, Wharton School
  Background: VP, Auven Therapeutics; Consultant, Boston Consulting Group
  Directorships: Cydan Development, Inozyme, Aptinyx
  Gregory Grunberg, Managing Director, Menlo Park
  Education: AB, Amherst College; MD, MBA, Duke University
  Background: Principal, Rho Ventures; Engagement Manager, McKinsey & Company
  Directorships: 89bio, BaroNova, Kala Pharmaceuticals, WelbeHealth, Sydnexis
  Josh Richardson, Managing Director, Greenwich
  Education: BS, University of South Florida; MD, University of Virginia
  Background: Engagement Manager, McKinsey & Company
  Directorships: KaNDy Therapeutics; Neurana Pharmaceuticals; Sublimity Therapeutics

Venture Capital & Private Equity Firms / Domestic Firms

1148 LONGUEVUE CAPITAL LLC
111 Veterans Boulevard
Suite 1020
Metairie, LA 70005

Phone: 504-293-3600 Fax: 504-293-3636
web: www.lvcpartners.com

Mission Statement: Our goal is to realize substantial long-term capital gains through investments in a diversified portfolio of companies by leveraging our experience, creativity, capital and network of resources.

Fund Size: $82 million
Founded: 2001
Investment Criteria: Recaps, Distressed, Turnarounds, MBO
Portfolio Companies: Advanced Metering Data Systems, Ardent Services, Arnold Logistics, Ascent Aviation Services Corporation, Azimuth Technology, Blue Dot Energy Services, ECA Medical Instruments, Jackson Offshore Holdings, Pod Pack International, Premier Store Fixtures, Prime Health Services, Professional Rental Tools, Quality Senior Living Partners, St. George Logistics, Zavation Medical Products

Other Locations:
733 Third Ave.
15th Floor
New York, NY 10017
Phone: 646-660-3994 Fax: 504-293-3636

136 Herber Ave.
Suite 204
P.O. Box 8000
Park City, UT 84060
Phone: 435-655-3605 Fax: 435-655-7676

Key Executives:
Rick S Rees, Co-Founder & Managing Partner
e-mail: rrees@lvcpartners.com
Education: BA & MBA, Tulane University
Background: CFO, Halter Marine Group; CFO, FGI; President, Texas Drydock; Principal, Maritime Capital
John C McNamara II, Co-Founder & Managing Partner
e-mail: jmcnamara@lvcpartners.com
Education: BS, Georgetown University; MBA, Harvard Business School
Background: President & CEO, Stewart Capital; Investment Banking, Drexel Burnham Lambert; Donaldson Lufkin & Jenrette
Charles A Cox, Director
e-mail: ccox@lvcpartners.com
Education: BA, University of Georgia; JD, Cumberland School of Law, Samford University; MBA, Kenan-Flagler School, University of North Carolina
Background: Covey Capital Management; Attorney, Allen Kopet & Associates
Raymond J Jeandron III, Partner
e-mail: rjeandron@lvcpartners.com
Education: BS, Management, Boston College
Background: Investment Banking, Jeffries & Company; Global Hunter Securities
Ryan K Nagim, Partner
e-mail: rnagim@lvcpartners.com
Education: BBA, Finance, Southern Methodist University; MBA, Wharton School
Background: Principal, American Capital; Investment Banking Analyst, J.P. Morgan

1149 LONGWOOD FUND
The Prudential Tower
800 Boylston Street
Suite 1555
Boston, MA 02199

Phone: 617-351-2590
e-mail: info@longwoodfund.com
web: www.longwoodfund.com

Mission Statement: Longwood's mission is to identify technologies and to found companies that will advance new therapeutics that can not only make a difference in the lives of patients worldwide, but also create significant value for investors. This is achieved by leveraging the management team's history of successful healthcare company formation and operational leadership.

Industry Group Preference: Healthcare, Therapeutics, Pharmaceuticals
Portfolio Companies: Alnara Pharmaceuticals, ArcherDX, Axial Biotherapeutics, Bicycle Therapeutics, Calithera Biosciences, Channel Medsystems, Colorescience, Flex Pharma, GRAIL, IlluminOss, KalVista Pharmaceuticals, Millendo Therapeutics, Mitobridge, OvaScience, PTC Therapeutics, Pulmocide, Recros Medica, Renovia, Scan Therapeutics, Sitryx Therapeutics, Twentyeight-Seven, Verastem

Key Executives:
Rich Aldrich, Co-Founder & General Partner
Education: Boston College; MBA, Amos Tuck School
Background: Co-Founder, Sirtis Pharmaceuticals, Concert Pharmaceuticals; Founding Employee, Vertex Pharmaceuticals
Directorships: KalVista Pharmaceuticals, Colorescience, Axial, Renovia, Sitryx Therapeutics
Christoph Westphal, Co-Founder & General Partner
Education: BA, Columbia University; MD, Harvard Medical School; PhD, Genetics, Harvard University
Background: Co-Founder/CEO, Alnlam Pharmaceuticals, Momenta Pharmaceuticals
David H Donabedian, Partner
Education: BA, Chemistry, St. Anselm College; PhD, Polymer Chemistry, University of Massachusetts; MBA, University of North Carolina
Background: VP & Global Head of Ventures, AbbVie; VP Global New Deal Strategy and Development, GlaxoSmithKline; Sr. Manager, Accenture's Strategic Services Consulting Group
Directorships: Alcyone Life Sciences, Axial Biotherapeutics, Millendo Therapeutics

1150 LONGWORTH VENTURE PARTNERS
303 Wyman St.
Suite 300
Waltham, MA 02451

Phone: 781-663-3600 Fax: 781-663-3619
e-mail: info@longworth.com
web: www.longworth.com

Mission Statement: Build leading technology companies in conjunction with top entrepreneurs by leveraging our extensive industry expertise and contacts.

Geographic Preference: United States
Fund Size: $130 million
Average Investment: $2 - $3 milllion
Minimum Investment: $250,000
Investment Criteria: Early and expansion-stage
Industry Group Preference: Enterprise Services, Infrastructure, Business to Business, Applications Software & Services, Internet, Digital Media & Marketing
Portfolio Companies: Applause, Constant Contact, Creative Market, DFA Capital Management, Estimize, Fliptop, Genesis Networks, Grab Media, Hospital IQ, iJet, Innovectra, Kaon, Kitsy Lane, Jibe, Marathon, MCA Solutions, Mobiquity, Moodlerooms, NuoDB, Olapic, OwnerIQ, Parlano, PLUMgrid, Power Inbox, RAIDCore, Rapid Miner, Rivermine, Rize, Scanbuy, Scarpblog, Sermo, Softricity, StraighterLine, Swirl, Symform, Thinking Screen Media, Thor Technologies, TrackVia, Triblio, Tylted, Varolii, VeloBit, Viewfinity, VKernel

Key Executives:
Paul Margolis, Founding Partner
e-mail: p.margolis@longworth.com
Education: BA, Brown University; MBA, Harvard Business School
Background: Founder/Chairman/CEO/President of

Marcam Corporation; Co-Founder/ Chairmanlications Group
Directorships: Mobiquity, VeloBit
Jim Savage, Founding Partner
e-mail: j.savage@longworth.com
Education: BA, Harvard University
Background: Founder and General Manager of ZD-Net; CEO of PlanetAll.com; Executive VP, Simon & Schuster/Prentice Hall; Digital Media, Mcgraw-Hill
Directorships: Constant Contact, Triblio, Grab Media, Softricity, Sermo, Moodlerooms, Applause
John Lawrence, Partner & CFO
e-mail: j.lawrence@longworth.com
Education: BA Accounting, Assumpton College
Background: CFO, Quail Piping Products; Assistant VP/M&A/SEC/IR, Asani/America; Auditor, Arthur Andersen
Nilanjana Bhowmik, Partner
e-mail: n.bhowmik@longworth.com
Education: BE Computer Science, Indian Institute of Technology; MS Computer Science, University of South Carolina; MBA, INSEAD
Background: VP Mergers/Acquisitions, Broadview International; Director Professional Services, eXcelon Corporation; Technical/Managament, Object Design
Directorships: Jibe, NuoDB, PLUMgrid, RapidMiner, Swirl, TrackVia

1151 LOVELL MINNICK PARTNERS LLC
215 Manhattan Beach Boulevard
2nd Floor
Manhattan Beach, CA 90266

Phone: 310-414-6160
web: www.lovellminnick.com

Mission Statement: An independent, management-controlled private equity firm formed to provide buyout capital and growth capital to developing companies in the financial services industry.

Fund Size: $800 million
Founded: 1999
Average Investment: $10-$40 million
Minimum Investment: $5 million
Investment Criteria: Leveraged Buyouts, Recapitalizations, Growth Capital
Industry Group Preference: Financial Services, Business Products & Services
Portfolio Companies: 361 Capital, Alps, AssetMark, Atlantic Asset Management, Attom Data Solutions, Berkeley Capital Management, Center Square Investment Management, Centurion Capital Group, ClariVest Asset Management, Commercial Credit, Currency, Dahlam Rose & Co., Duff & Phelps, Engage, First Allied, Foreside, Global Financial, HD Vest Financial Services, JS Held, Kanaly Trust, Keane, Leerink, Lincoln Investment, LSQ Funding, Matthews Asia, Mercer Advisors, National Auto Care, Plan Member Services, Powell Johnson, Seaside National Bank & Trust, SRS Acquiom, Stein Rose Investment Counsel, Tortoise, Trea Asset Management, TriState Capital, UNX, Worldwide Facilities

Other Locations:
555 E. Lancaster Ave.
Suite 510
Radnor, PA 19087
Phone: 610-995-9660

1155 Avenue of the Americas
Suite 2550
New York, NY 10036
Phone: 646-971-3230

Key Executives:
Jeffrey D Lovell, Co-Chairman
Education: BS, Business Administration, University of Colorado; University of Southern California
Background: Co-Founder, Putnam Lovell Securities; SEI Investments
James Minnick, Co-Chairman
Education: United States Air Force Academy; BA, Economics, University of Denver
Background: President/CEO, Morgan Grenfell Capital Managment; Executive VP, SEI Investments
Robert M Belke, Managing Partner
Education: BBA, Finance & Accounting, University of Wisconsin; MBA, Finance & Accounting, University of Chicago
Background: Associate, Direct Private Equity Group, TIAA-CREF; Senior Analyst, Wilshire Associates
Directorships: Keane Holdings, JS Held Holdings, Tortoise Investments, Worldwide Facilities
Steven C Pierson, Managing Partner
Education: BS, Finance & Management, Virginia Tech University; MBA, Fuqua School, Duke University
Background: UBS, Credit Suisse, Putnam Lovell Securities
Directorships: Global Financial Credit, National Auto Care, SRS Acquiom, Trea Asset Management
Spencer P Hoffman, Partner
Education: BA, African American Studies, Brown University; MBA, Private Equity, Wharton School, University of Pennsylvania
Background: Principal, Safeguard Scientifics; Associate, Mellon Ventures; Global Investment Banking Group, Merrill Lynch; Manager, Corporate Affairs, MicroStrategy
Directorships: Engage People, Foreside Financial Group, Worldwide Facilities
John D Cochran, Partner
Education: BA, English, University of California, Los Angeles; MS & MBA, Manufacturing Systems Engineering, Stanford University
Background: Principal, SV Investment Partners; Analyst JW Childs Associates; Financial Analyst, Salomon Brothers
Directorships: Seaside National Bank & Trust, Commercial Credit, LSQ Group Holding, Currency Capital, ATTOM Data Solutions
Brad Armstrong, Partner
Education: BS, Business Administration, Kenan-Flagler Business School, University of North Carolina; MBA, Finance & Accounting, Kellogg School of Management, Northwestern University
Background: Financial Institutions Group, Bank of America Merrill Lynch
Directorships: ATTOM Data Solutions, Commercial Credit, Global Financial Credit, LSQ Group Holding, Tortoise Investments
Jason S Barg, Partner
Education: BS, Accounting, Schreyer Honors College, Pennsylvania State University; MBA, Wharton School
Background: Financial Institutions Group, Goldman Sachs; Senior Associate, Forensics, PricewaterhouseCoopers
Directorships: ATTOM Data Solutions, CenterSquare Investment Management, Foreside Financial Group, JS Held Holdings
Trevor C Rich, Partner
Education: BA, Economics, Brigham Young University; MBA, Wharton School
Background: Corporate Development, Morgan Stanley; Analyst, JP Morgan
Directorships: National Auto Care, Worldwide Facilities

1152 LOVETT MILLER & COMPANY
Phone: 813-222-1477 **Fax:** 813-222-1478
e-mail: info@lovettmiller.com
web: www.lovettmiller.com

Mission Statement: Provides growth capital and shareholder liquidity for rapidly-growing, privately-held companies, with a

Venture Capital & Private Equity Firms / Domestic Firms

particular emphasis on technology-enhanced services and healthcare companies.

Geographic Preference: Southeastern United States
Fund Size: $175 million
Founded: 1997
Average Investment: $3 - $10 million
Minimum Investment: $2 million
Investment Criteria: Early-stage, growth capital, growth buyouts.
Industry Group Preference: Communications, Consumer Services, Financial Services, Information Technology, Medical Devices, Technology, Software, Healthcare, SaaS, Healthcare Services, Business Products & Services, Telecommunications, Retailing
Portfolio Companies: 360Commerce, Alphamed, Careanyware, Centennial Healthcare Corporation, Cybex Computer Products Corporation, Docufree Corporation, Employease, Everbank Financial Coporation, Florida Bank Group, Go Software, Healthcare Solutions, Inc., K&G Men's Centers, Inc., Key-Trak, Inc., Kinetic Books Company, Main Bank Corporation, Med3000 Group, Peopleclick, Powertel, Proxima Therapeutics RXStrategies, Sigma International General Medical Apparatus, Southcoast-Boca Associates, Southeast Healthplan, Telovations, Towercom Development, Towercom Enterprises, Towercom Limited, United Dental Care

Key Executives:
   W Scott Miller, Co-Founder & Managing Partner
   e-mail: Scott@LovettMiller.com
   Education: MBA, Harvard Business School; BA, University of the South
   Background: Global Trade Technologies; South Atlantic Venture Partners II; Bowles Hollowell Conner & Company; Morgan Stanley & Company
   Directorships: 360 Commerce, Centennial HealthCare, K&G Men's Centers, PeopleClick, United Dental Care, Sigma International, Med 3000, Employease, Proxima Therapeutics
   Rad Lovett, Co-Founder
   e-mail: Rad@LovettMiller.com
   Education: AB, Harvard University
   Background: Founder/Chairman/CEO, TowerCom Enterprises/Development/Limited; President, Southcoast Capital; Corporate Finance, Merrill Lynch; Lincoln Property
   Directorships: Healthcare Solutions, EverBank Financial, RxStrategies, CareAnyware, DocuFree, TowerCom V

1153 LOWERCASE CAPITAL
San Francisco, CA

web: www.lowercasellc.com

Mission Statement: At Lowercase Capital, we invest in startups, acquire later stage companies and advise businesses and funds of all sizes on strategy and execution.

Geographic Preference: United States
Fund Size: $40 million
Founded: 2007
Investment Criteria: Seed-Stage, Startup, Later-Stage Acquisitions
Portfolio Companies: 9gag, Automattic, Bee Free Honee, Bellhops, Binti, Brightwheel, Bytegain, ChartBeat, Common, Comparably, DigitalGenius, Digital Objects, Docker, Dubsmash, Envoy, Electric Imp, Fanbridge, Flirtey, Gimlet Media, Grove, Handshake, Happy Returns, Hatch Baby, Heavybit, Hodinkee, Joymode, Kickstarter, Liftopia, Little Labs, Lookout, LTSE, Lumi, MakeSpace, Mark43, Medium, Mobcrush, Mux, Noun Project, Nurx, Omnity, Optimizely, Poll Everywhere, Radish, Ranker, RecordSetter, RescueTime, Shape, Slack, Smash.gg, Snowshoe, Stensul, Streak, Stripe, StyleSeat, Synervoz, Tala, TalentWorks, Toymail, Tred, Triller, Uber, Urban Airship, Viro Media, Veggie Grill, VidIQ, VoiceOps, Waggle, Webshots, Wizeline, Women.com

Key Executives:
   Chris Sacca, Founder
   Education: Georgetown University Law Center
   Background: Head of Special Initiatives, Google; Speedera Networks; Attorney, Fenwick & West

1154 LUDLOW VENTURES
Detroit, MI 48226

web: www.ludlowventures.com

Mission Statement: To help entrepreneurs transform startups into industry leading companies.

Geographic Preference: United States
Fund Size: $15 million
Founded: 2010
Investment Criteria: Startups, Seed Stage, Early Stage
Industry Group Preference: Technology, Consumer Products
Portfolio Companies: Alpha Outpost, Ambassador, AngelList, Boxbee, Campaign, Canvs, Circa, Cleanly, Density, Final, Flud, Flywheel, Fundly, Gather, Giftcard Zen, HeadOut, Honey, Hooked, Instore, Kickback, Launchkey, Lob, Luka, Lumi, MinBox, Mirror, Navdy, Nestio, NetPlenish, Notarize, Ordr.In, Paperspace, Point, Product Hunt, Quikly, Rentabilities, Roadtrippers, Roximity, Scentbird, Shots, Snowshoe, SpokenLayer, Sprig, Sqwiggle, Stealth, Stem, Tribe, Try, uBeam, UpTo, Videolicious, Vive, Wag, Wantworthy, WorkLife

Key Executives:
   Jonathon Triest, Founder/Managing Partner
   Education: BS, University of Michigan
   Background: Founder & Managing Partner, Sandwich Fund; Creative Director, Discovery Productions; Founder, Triest Group
   Directorships: The Trico Foundation, Venture for America
   Brett deMarrais, Partner
   Education: University of Michigan
   Background: Founder, Wedit; Out of the Blue Entertainment
   Blake Robins, Partner
   Education: BS, Michigan State University
   Background: Campus CEO, Zaarly Inc.; Community Manager, General Assembly

1155 LUX CAPITAL
1600 El Camino Real
Suite 290
Menlo Park, CA 94025

Phone: 650-681-0183 Fax: 650-618-0372
e-mail: info@luxcapital.com
web: www.luxcapital.com

Mission Statement: To find outstanding early stage companies and support them as a long-term partner. To build lasting companies while providing superior rates of return to our investors.

Founded: 2000
Minimum Investment: $100,000
Investment Criteria: Seed & Early-Stage
Industry Group Preference: Nanotechnology, Life Sciences, Energy, Technology, Healthcare
Portfolio Companies: 3scan, Aeva, Aira.io, Airmap, Alluvium, AltspaceVR, Applied Intuition, Aptible, Aria Insights, Arraiy, Astranis, Auransa, Auris, Authorea, Blockstack, Bright Machines, Cala Health, Cape Analytics, Cerulean, Citizen, Clarifai, Cloud MedX, Common Networks, Computable, Crystal IS, CTRL-Labs, Deep Sentinel, Desktop Metal, Drone Racing League, Echodyne, Embodied Intelligence, Everspin Technologies, Evolv Technology, Flex Logix, G2X Energy, Geocea Biosciences, Halo Neuroscience, Hangar Technology, Happiest Baby, Hometeam, Kala Pharmaceuticals, Kallyope, Kurion, Kymeta, Kyruus, Latch, LightForm, Looking Glass, Loom Vision, Lux Research, Luxtera, Madaket, Magen Biosciences, Mahana Therapeutics,

Matterport, Molecular Imprints, Moment, Mythic, Nanosys, Nervana Systems, New Knowledge, Noon, Novel Effect, Nozomi Networks, Oasis Labs, OpenSpace, Orbital Insight, Pager, Pinscreen, Pivotal Commware, Planet Las, Plethora, Primer, RDMD, Recursion Pharmaceuticals, Rigetti Computing, Ripcord, Saildrone, Scaled Inference, Scatter, Science 37, SentiBiosciences, Shapeways, SiBeam, Silicon Clocks, Siluria Technologies, SOLS Systems, Subspace, Survios, Tempo Automation, Transphorm, Veo Robotics, Visla, Visor, Visterra, Vium, Workit Health, Zipdrug, Zoox

Other Locations:
920 Broadway
11th Floor
New York, NY 10010
Phone: 646-475-4385 **Fax:** 646-349-2960

Key Executives:
Peter Hébert, Co-Founder/Managing Partner
Education: BS Communications, Syracuse University Newhouse School
Background: Lehman Brothers Equity Research; American Express International, London; DMB&B; Sports Illustrated
Directorships: Auris Health, Bright Machines, Cape Analytics, Everyspin Technologies, Flex Logix, G2X Energy, Halo Neuroscience, Lux Research, Luxtera, Matterport, Pivotal Commware, Ripcord
Robert Paull, Co-Founder/Venture Partner
Education: University of Virginia
Background: CEO, Rob Paull Consulting; CTO, VMDO Architects; Co-Founder, Virtucom; Author
Directorships: Cala Health, Cerulean Pharma, Genocea Biosciences, Kala Pharmaceuticals, Kyruus, Magen, Molecular Imprints, Visterra
Josh Wolfe, Co-Founder/Managing Partner
Education: BS Economics and Finance with Honors, Cornell University
Background: Investment Banker, Salomon Smith Barney; Merrill Lynch; Prudential Securities; AIDS Research, Cell Vision; Journal of Leukocyte Biology; Co-Founder, NanoBusiness Alliance; Author
Directorships: 3Scan, Aira.io, CTRL-Labs, Crystal IS, Echodyne, Kallyope, Kurion, Kymeta, Looking Glass, Lux Research, Nanosys, Shapeways, Silicon Clocks, Siluria Technologies
Adam Kalish, General Partner
e-mail: adam.kalish@luxcapital.com
Education: BS, Economics & Communications, University of Miami; University of Westminster
Background: Director, Everest Capital; Quellos Capital Management; DreamWorks SKG

1156 LYNWOOD CAPITAL PARTNERS
Denver, CO

Phone: 303-885-7166 **Fax:** 303-573-7810
e-mail: dh@lynwoodcapital.com
web: www.lynwoodcapital.com

Mission Statement: Lynwood Capital is a private equity investment firm based in the Rocky Mountain Region that acquires and invests in businesses with initial values from $5 million to $100 million.
Geographic Preference: United States
Industry Group Preference: Natural Resources, Distribution, Food & Beverage, Business Products & Services, Manufacturing
Portfolio Companies: Avalara, Chieftain Sand and Proppant, Communications Products and Services, Dickinson Frozen Foods, Owl Cybersecurity, Rocket Seals, UPF Services, Work Options Group

Key Executives:
David Hanson, Partner
e-mail: dh@lynwoodcapital.com
Education: BS, Economics & Engineering, Yale University

Ned Doubleday, Advisor
Education: BA, East Asian Studies, Yale University; MBA, UCLA

1157 M/C PARTNERS
53 State Street
Suite 2602
Boston, MA 02109

Phone: 617-345-7200 **Fax:** 617-345-7201
e-mail: mcp@mcpartners.com
web: www.mcpartners.com

Mission Statement: Invests in early-stage companies in the emerging segments of the communications industry, as well as telecom-related information technology services.
Geographic Preference: North America, Europe
Fund Size: $550 million
Founded: 1976
Average Investment: $50 million
Minimum Investment: $5 million
Investment Criteria: Early-Stage
Industry Group Preference: Communications, Media, Infrastructure, Technology, Software, Wireless Technologies, Advertising
Portfolio Companies: AccentHealth, Attenda, Baja Broadband, Benestra, Carbon60, Cavalier Telephone, CellularOne, CoreLink Data Centers, CSDVRS, Denovo, Ensono, Everstream, Fusepoint, Involta, GTS, Legendary, Lightower, Melita, MetroPCS, Mobi PCS, Neutral Connect Networks, Nuvox, Omega Wirless, Plum Choice, PR Wireless, Public Mobile, SpeechCycle, Thrive Networks, Triad 700, Zayo Bandwidth

Key Executives:
James F Wade, Managing Partner
e-mail: jwade@mcpartners.com
Education: BBA, University of Notre Dame; MBA, Harvard Business School
Background: Harris Bank
Directorships: Involta, Neutral Connect Networks, Thrive Networks
David D Croll, Managing Partner
e-mail: dcroll@mcpartners.com
Education: BS, Cornell University; MBA, Harvard Business School
Background: TA Associates
Gillis C Cashman, Managing Partner
e-mail: gcashman@mcpartners.com
Education: AB, Economics, Duke University
Background: Salomon Smith Barney
Directorships: Carbon60, Denovo, Ensono, Involta, Thrive Networks
Brian M Clark, Managing Partner
e-mail: bclark@mcpartners.com
Education: BBA, Finance & Accounting, University of Michigan
Background: Salomon Smith Barney
Directorships: Neutral Connect Networks, PR Wireless
Edward J Keefe, Chief Financial Officer & Chief Compliance Officer
e-mail: ekeefe@mcpartners.com
Education: BS, Business Administration, University of Maine; MBA, Suffolk University; MS, Taxation, Bentley College
Background: VP of Finance, Atlas Venture; Instrumentation Laboratory; Tax Consultant, Coopers & Lybrand; Senior Financial Analyst, Raytheon Company

1158 M12
San Francisco, CA

web: m12.vc

Mission Statement: Invests in the areas of artificial intelligence, machine learning, automotive, big data, analysis,

Venture Capital & Private Equity Firms / Domestic Firms

business SaaS, cloud infrastructire, emerging trends, productivity, communications, and security.

Geographic Preference: North America, Europe, Israel
Fund Size: $65 Million
Founded: 2016
Investment Criteria: Series A-D
Industry Group Preference: Artificial Intelligence, Machine Learning, Automotive, Big Data, Analysis, Cloud Infrastructure, Productivity, Communications, Security, Emerging Markets, Sectors & Technologies, SaaS
Portfolio Companies: Acerta, Agolo, Airmap, Airobotics, Aqua, Beamery, BlueVine, Bonsai, Cerebri, ClearMotion, CloudLanes, Cloud Simple, CNEX Labs, Code Fresh, Cognitive Scale, Comfy, Contract Security, Directly, Dynamic Signal, Element, Envisagenics, Figure Eight, Frame, Ground Truth, Hazy, Help Shift, HYAS, i3 Equity Partners, Illusive, Incorta, Inter Ana, Kahoot!, Layer, Livongo, Login Radius, Make.tv, Markforged, Mental Canvas, Netradyne, Onfido, Outreach, PandaDoc, Paxata, Pickit, Pixvana, Prevedere, Rapidsos, Rescale, Snaproute, Synack, Syntiant, Tact.ai, Team8, Trusona, Twentybn, Unbabel, Unravel, Voiceitt, Voicera, Volterra, White Source, Work Board, Zencity, Zipwhip

Key Executives:
Nagraj Kashyap, Corporate VP/Global Head
Education: BEng, Computer Science, University of Mysore; MS, Computer Science, University of Texas; MBA, J.L. Kellogg Graduate School of Management, Northwestern University
Background: Qualcomm Ventures
Leo de Luna, General Manager/Managing Director
Education: BBA, University of Texas; MBA, Haass School of Business, University of California Berkeley
Background: Principal, Split Rock Ventures; Saints Capital; AMD; St. Paul Venture Capital; Lehman Brothers; Singapore Armed Forces
Rashmi Gopinath, Partner
Education: BEng, University of Mumbai; MBA, J.L. Kellogg Graduate School of Management, Northwestern University
Background: Investment Director, Intel Capital; Couchbase; BlueData; GE; Oracle
Mony Hassid, General Manager/Managing Director
Education: BSc/MSc, Electrical Engineering, Tel Aviv University; MBA, Tel Aviv University
Directorships: Managing Director, Qualcomm Ventures; Managing Director, Motorola Ventures
Samir Kumar, Managing Director
Education: BSc, Mechanical Engineering, Cornell University
Background: Qualcomm; Microsoft; Enterprise Mobility; Palm; Samsung
Lisa Nelson, Managing Director
Education: BA, Univeristy of Washington
Background: Microsoft

1159 M25 GROUP
Chicago, IL

web: m25group.com

Mission Statement: Chicago-based, early-stage micro-VC fund investing solely in the Midwest.
Geographic Preference: Midwest
Founded: 2015
Average Investment: $500K to $2 million
Investment Criteria: Early-Stage
Industry Group Preference: Agriculture, E-Commerce & Manufacturing, Education, Fashion, Finance, Food & Beverage, Health, Logistics, Manufacturing, Marketing, Materials, Media, Legal, Social Media, Software
Portfolio Companies: Anglr, Ballot Ready, Block Six Analytics, BoxFox, branch, Chowly Inc., Cladwell, ConceptDrop, dabble, DATTUS, The Eastman Egg Company, EXPLORER, Jetpack Workflow, KnowledgeHound, Luna Lights, PactSafe, PAGEVAULT, PrintWithMe, realync, regroup, REWARDS21, Scanalytics Inc., SPATIAL, Sportsman Tracker

Key Executives:
Victor Gutwein, Managing Director
Education: University of Chicago
Mike Asem, Partner
Education: Purdue University

1160 MADISON DEARBORN PARTNERS
70 West Madison St.
Suite 4600
Chicago, IL 60602

Phone: 312-895-1000 Fax: 312-895-1001
e-mail: info@mdcp.com
web: www.mdcp.com

Mission Statement: The objective is to invest in companies in partnership with outstanding management teams to achieve significant long term appreciation in equity value. A flexible investment approach, encompassing both management buyouts and structured minority investments, has been a key tenet to MDP's investment philosophy for several decades.

Geographic Preference: United States
Fund Size: $8 billion
Founded: 1992
Average Investment: $100-$600 million
Minimum Investment: $50 million
Investment Criteria: MBO, LBO, Recapitalizations, Growth Capital, Acquisition Financing
Industry Group Preference: Financial Services, Healthcare, Consumer Services, Communications, Energy, Manufacturing, Consumer Products, Telecommunications, Media, Technology-Enabled Services
Portfolio Companies: Aderant Holdings, Alcami, Amynta Group, Ankura, Ardonagh Group, Asurion Corporation, BlueCat Networks, Boise Cascade Company, Bolthouse Farms, Buckeye Cellulose Corporation, B-Way Holding, CapitalSource, Cbeyond, CDW, Centennial Towers, Cinemark, Cornerstone Brands, EVO Payments International, Fieldglass, First Wind Holdings, Fleet Complete, Great Lakes Dredge & Dock Corporation, Ikaria, Intelsat, Intermedia, Kaufman Hall & Associates, LA Fitness International, LGS Innovations, LinQuest Corporation, Liquid Web, Magellan Midstream Partners, MetroPCS, Multi Packaging Solutions, National Mentor Holdings, Navacord, Nextel Partners, NextG Networks, NFP Corporation, Nordic Packaging and Container International, Nuveen Investments, Option Care, Packaging Corporation of America, PayPal, Performance Health, Q9 Networks, QuickPlay Media, RDX, Ruth's Hospitality Group, Ryder TRS, Sage Products, Schrader International, Sirona Dental Systems, SIRVA, Smurfit Kappa, Solis Mammography, Sorenson Communications, Stericycle, Team Health Holdings, The Topps Company, Things Remembered, TransUnion, Tuesday Morning, U.S. Lumber, U.S. Power Generating Company, Univision Communications, Valitas Health Services, VWR International, Wind Telecom S.p.A., XM Satellite Radio Holdings, Yankee Candle

Key Executives:
John A Canning Jr, Chairman
Education: AB, Denison University; JD, Duke University
Background: Executive Vice President, The First National Bank; President, First Chicago Venture Capital
Directorships: Corning Inc., Milwaukee Brewers Baseball Club
Paul J Finnegan, Co-CEO
Education: AB, Harvard College; MBA, Harvard Graduate School of Business Administration
Background: First Chicago Venture Capital
Directorships: CDW Corp., AIA Corp., Government Sourcing Solutions
Samuel M Mencoff, Co-CEO
Education: AB, Brown; MBA, Harvard Business School
Background: First Chicago Venture Capital; Industrial

National Bank
Directorships: Packaging Corporation of America, World Business Chicago
Zaid F Alsikafi, Managing Director
Education: BS, Wharton School; MBA, Harvard Business School
Background: Goldman Sachs
Directorships: Centennial Towers, Intermedia, Liquid Web, RDX, Univision Communications
Elizabeth Q Betten, Managing Director
Education: AB, Brown University; MBA, Stanford University Graduate School of Business
Background: JPMorgan
Directorships: Option Care, Solis Mammography
Karla J Bullard, Managing Director & CFO
Education: BS, CPA, University of Illinois; MBA, University of Chicago
Background: Managing Director & CFO, Deerfield Capital Management; VP, Finance, JP Morgan Chase; Arthur Andersen LLP
Richard H Copans, Managing Director
Education: BA, Duke University; MBA, Northwestern University Kellogg Graduate School of Management
Background: Thomas H Lee Partners, Morgan Stanley & Co.
Directorships: Nordic Packaging and Container International, SIRVA, U.S. Lumber
Vahe A Dombalagian, Managing Director
Education: BS, Georgetown University; MBA, Harvard School of Business Administration
Background: Texas Pacific Group; Bear Stearns & Co.
Directorships: Amynta Group, Ankura, Ardonagh Group, EVO Payments, Navacord, NFP Corporation
James N Perry, Jr, Managing Director
Education: BA, University of Pennsylvania; MBA, University of Chicago
Background: First Chicago Venture Capital
Directorships: Asurion Corporation, Centennial Towers, Intermedia, Liquid Web, The Topps Company, Univision Communications
Timothy P Sullivan, Co-President
Education: BS, United States Navy; MS, University of Southern California;, MBA, Stanford University Graduate School of Business
Background: First Chicago Venture Capital, United States Navy
Directorships: Alcami, Kaufman Hall & Associates, Option Care, Performance Health, Solis Mammography
Thomas S Souleles, Co-President
Education: AB, Princeton University; JD, Harvard Law School; MBA, Harvard School of Business Administration
Background: Wasserstein Perella & Co Inc.
Directorships: Nordic Packaging and Container International, SIRVA, U.S. Lumber
Michael J Dolce, Managing Director & Head, Capital Markets
Education: BS, Babson College
Background: Bank of America Merrill Lynch
Jason Shideler, Managing Director
Education: BS, University of Texas; MBA, Stanford Graduate School of Business
Background: Investment Banking Analyst, Health Care Group, JP Morgan
Directorships: Alcami, Kaufman Hall & Associates, Performance Health
Annie S Terry, Managing Director, General Counsel & Chief Compliance Officer
Education: BS, Accountancy, University of Illinois; JD, Georgetown University Law Center
Background: Associate, Kirkland & Ellis LLP
Douglas C Grissom, Managing Director
Education: BA, Amherst College; MBA, Harvard School of Business Administration
Background: Bain Capital; McKinsey & Company; Goldman Sachs & Co.
Directorships: BlueCat Networks, Fleet Complete, LGS Innovations, LinQuest Corporation
John E Knutsen, Managing Director
Education: BS, Boston University
Background: Managing Director, Private Fund Group, Credit Suisse; Goldman Sachs & Co.; Donaldson Lufkin & Jenrette
Matthew W Norton, Managing Director
Education: BS, Wharton School; MBA, Wharton School
Background: Merrill Lynch
Directorships: BlueCat Networks, Fleet Complete, Kaufman Hall & Associates, LGS Innovations, LinQuest Corporation, NFP Corporation
Scott G Pasquini, Managing Director
Education: BSE, Princeton University; MBA, Harvard Business School
Background: Associate, GTCR Golder Rauner; M&A Group, Merrill Lynch
Directorships: Centennial Towers, Liquid Web, RDX, The Topps Company
David E Pequet, Managing Director
Education: BS, Indiana University
Background: Private Fund Group, Credit Suisse
Matthew W Raino, Managing Director
Education: BBA, University of Michigan; MBA, Northwestern University Kellogg School of Management
Background: Credit Suisse First Boston
Directorships: Amynta Group, Ankura, Ardonagh Group, EVO Payments, Navacord, NFP Corporation

1161 MADISON PARKER CAPITAL
715 Boylston St.
Boston, MA 02116

Phone: 650-229-8676
e-mail: info@madisonparkercapital.com
web: www.madisonparkercapital.com

Mission Statement: Madison Parker Capital provides liquidity and growth capital to select middle-market enterprises. We provide the value-added capital and resources to help these firms realize their maximum potential. In addition, we seek to provide attractive exit opportunities for owners and operators and divestiture opportunities for divisions of corporate parent companies that no longer reflect the overall strategic focus. Madison Parker Capital endeavors to partner with management and execute seamless transactions.

Average Investment: up to $50 million
Investment Criteria: MBO, Expansion Financings, Recapitalizations
Industry Group Preference: Advanced Materials, Enabling Technology, Business Products & Services, Consumer Products, Retailing, Restaurants, Manufacturing
Portfolio Companies: A123 Systems, Aquis, beRecruited, Boloco, Ceramem, ChargePoint, InnerProduct Partners, IPATH, Klone Lab, Paper House Productions, SonicCloud, Utrecht Art Supplies, Venyu, Village Power Finance

1162 MADRONA VENTURE GROUP
999 Third Avenue
34th Floor
Seattle, WA 98104

Phone: 206-674-3000 Fax: 206-674-8703
web: www.madrona.com

Mission Statement: Madrona's investment approach is to make early-stage investments in promising ventures and build long-term relationships, actively assisting its portfolio companies.

Geographic Preference: Pacific Northwest
Fund Size: $650 million
Founded: 1995
Investment Criteria: Seed, Start-up, Early Stage
Industry Group Preference: Internet Technology, Infrastructure, Technology, Consumer Services, Software Services, Business Products & Services, Wireless

Venture Capital & Private Equity Firms / Domestic Firms

Technologies, Consumer Internet, Digital Media & Marketing, Advertising, Networking, Infrastructure
Portfolio Companies: 2nd Watch, Accolade, Algorithmia, Amperity, Animoto, Answer IQ, Atsu, Boomerang Commerce, Booster, Branch, Cape, Chatitive, Crowd Cow, Datacoral, Domicile, Echodyne, Eclypsium, Envisagenics, Eventbase, Evocalize, ExtraHop, GawkBox, HelloTech, Highspot, Igneous, Indochino, Integris Software, IO Pipe, iSpot.tv, Jama, JinTronix, Jobalign, Lumatax, M87, Mato-Erno.com, Mighty AI, MobileWalla, Moz, Opal, Peach, Pixvana, Player Tokens, Pluto, Pro.com, Pulselabs, Pulumi, Qumulo, Renew, Rigado, Rover.com, Saykara, Seeq, Shippable, Shyft, Skytap, Smartsheet, Snowflake, Spruce Up, Suplari, Terraclear, The Riveter, Tigera, TraceMe, UiPath, Unearth, Wicket Labs, WildTangent, Wonder Workshop, Wrench, Xnor.Ai

Key Executives:
Thomas A Alberg, Co-Founder/Managing Director
e-mail: thomas@madrona.com
Education: Harvard College; Law Degree, Columbia Law School
Background: Partner, Perkins Cole; Cravath, Swain & Moore; President, LIN Broadcasting Corporation; Executive VP, McCaw Cellular Communications
Directorships: Impinj, Amazon.com, ACES Northwest Network, TechNet Northwest, Pacific Science Center, Challenge Seattle

Paul Goodrich, Co-Founder/Managing Director
e-mail: paul@madrona.com
Education: Amherst College; University of Utah Law School
Background: Partner, Perkins Cole Law Firm; Co-Founder, William D. Ruckelshaus Associates; General Partner, Environmental Venture Fund
Directorships: Evenbase, Jintronix

S Somasegar, Managing Director
e-mail: soma@madrona.com
Education: BS, Electronics and Communication Engineering, Anna University; MS, Computer Engineering, Louisiana State University
Background: SVP, Developer Division, Microsoft Corporation
Directorships: AnswerIQ, Branch, Envisagenics, Might Ai, Pixvana, Pulumi, Shyft, Snowflake, Suplari, Tigera, UIPath, Unearth

Matt McIlwain, Managing Director
e-mail: matt@madrona.com
Education: Dartmouth College; MBA, Harvard Business School; MA, Public Policy, Harvard's Kennedy School of Government
Background: Vice President, Genuine Parts Company; Engagement Manager, Mckinsey & Company; CS First Boston
Directorships: 2nd Watch, Accolade, Amperity, Animoto, Booster, ExtraHop, Igneous, Pluto, Qumulo, SkyTap, Smartsheet, Suplari, TraceMe, Xnor.Ai

Scott Jacobson, Managing Director
e-mail: scott@madrona.com
Education: BS, Applied Mathematics & Economics, Northwestern University; MBA, Stanford Graduate School of Business
Background: Senior Product Manager, Amazon.com
Directorships: Boomerang Commerce, Chatitive, Crowd Cow, Evocalize, Indochino, Mighty AI, MobileWalla, Peach, Player Tokens, Pro.com, Rover, Wonder Workshop

Tim Porter, Managing Director
e-mail: tim@madrona.com
Education: BS, Mechanical Engineering, MIT; MBA, Stanford Graduate School of Business
Background: Corporate Development, Microsoft
Directorships: Algorithmia, Echodyne, Eclypsium, HighSpot, Integris, Jama Software, JobAlign, Pixvana, Saykara, Shippable

Len Jordan, Managing Director
e-mail: len@madrona.com
Education: BS, Finance & Economics, Eccles School of Business, University of Utah
Background: General Partner, Frazier Technology Ventures
Directorships: HelloTech, iSpot.tv, M87, Opal, Rigado, Wicket Labs, Wrench

1163 MAIN STREET CAPITAL HOLDINGS LLC
301 Grant Street
14th Floor
Pittsburgh, PA 15219

Phone: 412-904-4020 **Fax:** 412-904-1794
web: www.mainstcap.com

Mission Statement: A private equity firm that has an outstanding track record of creating value with its entrepreneur partners. Our solid performance has been achieved by carefully selecting unique, well-positioned middle-market companies with superior management teams and then providing the proper incentives and resources required to maximize value.

Geographic Preference: Eastern United States
Average Investment: $3 - $25 million
Industry Group Preference: Manufacturing, Food & Beverage, Homeland Security, Niche Manufacturing, Distribution
Portfolio Companies: AccuSpec Electronics, C&K, Coining of America, Conelec, Harry's Fresh Foods, Hi-Rel Group, I-Deal Optics, Lloyd's Barbeque Company, LTS Scale Company, NABCO Inc., Pinnacle Electronics, Sajar Plastics, Steak-ummm, Stiffel, W&W Dairy, Wisconsin Cheese Group

Key Executives:
Dennis G Prado, Managing Partner
412-904-3561
e-mail: dprado@mainstcap.com
Education: BA, Economics, Bucknell University; MS, Information Systems, MBA, University of Pittsburgh
Background: Fortune Brands; Manager, Price Waterhouse LLP Corporate Finance Group
Directorships: Conelec of Florida, I-Deal Optics, W&W Dairy

W Ryan Davis, Managing Partner
412-224-2734
e-mail: wrdavis@mainstcap.com
Education: BS, Physics, Dickinson College; JD, Dickinson School of Law, Pennsylvania State University
Background: Partner, Morgan Lewis & Bockius LLP
Directorships: I-Deal Optics, W&W Dairy

1164 MAINE ANGELS
e-mail: contactmaineangels@gmail.com
web: www.maineangels.org

Mission Statement: The Maine Angels is a group of accredited investors who provide financial resources and mentorship to early stage companies and entrepreneurs in New England, with particular focus on Maine-based businesses.

Geographic Preference: Maine, New England
Founded: 2003
Average Investment: $10,000 - $710,000
Investment Criteria: Early Stage
Industry Group Preference: Biotechnology, Diagnostics, Therapeutics, Clean Technology, Software, Internet, Consumer Products, Financial Services, Media, IT Services, Nanotechnology, Retail, Consumer & Leisure
Portfolio Companies: Abierto Networks, AboGen, Academic Merit, Avaxia Biologics, Broadcast Pix, CEI Coastal Ventures III, Cerahelix, Cognoptix, Corbus Pharmaceuticals, Digital Life Technologies, ezCater, Gelato Fiasco, Goodlux Technology, HoneyTree Films, Introspective Systems, IW Financial, Jam Hub, LeaseQ, Linkstorm, Maine Wealth Partners, Morpheus Technologies, Nanocomp, NetClarity, Newfield Design, Northern Equity Investments, Ocean Renewable Power Co., Pika Energy, Pixability, Playrific, Regroup, Respiratory Motion, Siamab Therapeutics, Tego, Zylo Media

Key Executives:
Ralph Nodine, Chair
Matt Ware, Vice Chair
Background: Senior Partner, Partners In Performance; Mentor, Top Gun Startup Accelerator Program

1165 MAINE VENTURE FUND
PO Box 63
Newport, ME 04953

Phone: 207-924-3800
e-mail: terri@maineventurefund.com
web: maineventurefund.com

Mission Statement: The Maine Venture Fund is a Maine-based fund that focuses exclusively on investing in promising growth companies. The fund considers Maine based companies in almost all industry sectors, though the return potential of the investment must be high enough to justify the risk taken.

Geographic Preference: Maine
Founded: 1996
Industry Group Preference: All Sectors Considered
Portfolio Companies: Abierto Networks, Aiko Biotechnology, Bar Harbor Biotechnology, BlueTarp Financial, Bourgeois Guitars, Cerahelix, Certify, Chemogen, Chimani, Coast of Maine, CourseStorm, DreamLocal, Emergent Discovery, Finetune, Fly The Wave, Gelato Fiasco, Genextropy, HarborTechnologies, Hyperlite Mountain Gear, InterSpec, Looks Gourmet Food Company, LulaWed, Maine Craft Distilling, MedRhythms, Mingle Healthcare Solutions, Mobile Price Card, Mousam Valley, NBT Solutions, Newfield Design, Nyle Systems, Ocean Approved, Orono Spectral Solutions, PenBay Solutions, Pika Energy, R.E.D.D., RedZone, Sea Bags, Wentorth Technology

Key Executives:
Joe Powers, Managing Director
e-mail: joe@maineventurefund.com
Education: BA, Middlebury College; MA, Tuck University
Background: Tesla; Zoox; Clean Marine Energy
Nina Scheepers, Investment Manager
e-mail: nina@maineventurefund.com
Education: Tuck University
Background: Product Manager, Unum
John Burns, Strategic Advisor
e-mail: john@maineventurefund.com
Education: Undergraduate Degree, University of Maine; MS, Resource Economics, Penn State; MBA, Babson College
Background: Adjunct Faculty, University of Maine

1166 MANHATTAN INVESTMENT PARTNERS
200 Park Avenue
Suite 1700
New York, NY 10166

Phone: 646-354-6520 Fax: 646-349-1987
e-mail: info@manhattaninvest.com
web: www.manhattaninvest.com

Mission Statement: Private investment and merchant firm providing advisory services and investment capital to leading middle market companies, emerging-growth enterprises, and entrepreneurial ventures.

Geographic Preference: East Coast
Fund Size: $5 billion
Founded: 1990
Average Investment: $13 million
Minimum Investment: $5 million
Investment Criteria: Mezzanine, Second Stage, MBO, Common Stock, Convertible Debt, Senior Debt, Growth Financing, Management Buyouts, Platform Build-Ups, Special Situations
Industry Group Preference: Industrial Equipment, Broadcasting, Communications, Computer Related, Electronic Components, Energy, Entertainment, Internet Technology, Medical, Pharmaceuticals, Consumer Products, Real Estate

Key Executives:
David J Machlica, Managing Partner
Education: University of Massachusetts, Pennsylvania State University
Background: Laventhol and Howath, Dunn Corporation

1167 MANSA CAPITAL
5444 Westheimer
Suite 1000
Houston, TX 77056

Phone: 713-974-9327
e-mail: info@mansallc.com
web: www.mansallc.info

Mission Statement: Mansa Capital seeks to become key stakeholder in the economic development of Ghana through strategic alliance with established global companies.

Geographic Preference: Ghana, Global
Investment Criteria: Project Development, Mezzanine
Industry Group Preference: All Sectors Considered
Portfolio Companies: HydroDive, Intership, Kavin Engineering, Ocean Installer, Van Dyke Energy Company, Wyndham Garden, Zomay Marine and Logistics
Other Locations:
307/308 3rd Floor, Emporium Section
Movenpick Ambassador Hotel
Independence Ave.
Accra
Ghana
Phone: 233-030-3961305

Key Executives:
George Y Owusu, Founder/CEO

1168 MANSA EQUITY PARTNERS
500 Boylston Street
5th Floor
Boston, MA 02116

Phone: 617-424-4940 Fax: 617-977-9162

Mission Statement: Mansa Equity Partners is a health care private equity investment firm specializing in high growth companies in the health care services and health care technology sectors. Mansa focuses on companies as they prepare for expansion, acquisition, privatization or IPO. We integrate strong expertise in health care policy, regulation, and reimbursement with vast experience in health care operations, marketing, finance, and medical administration.

Investment Criteria: Early-Stage
Industry Group Preference: Healthcare
Portfolio Companies: Accreon, E4 Health, HealthPrize Technologies, HealthSense, Independent Living Systems, Skipta

Key Executives:
Ruben J King-Shaw Jr, Managing Partner/CIO
Education: BS, Industrial & Labor Relations, Cornell University; MS, Health Services Administration, Florida International University; Master of International Business, Center for Industrial Studies, Madrid
Background: COO & Deputy Administrator, Centers for Medicare & Medicaid Services; Senior Advisor, Secretary of the Treasury
Directorships: Independent Living Systems
Jason P Torres, Partner/COO
Education: BS, Finance & Information Systems, Rensselaer Polytechnic Institute; MBA, Stanford Graduate School of Business
Background: Deutsche Bank High Yield Group, Salomon Smith Barney Asset Finance Group
James Renna, Partner

Venture Capital & Private Equity Firms / Domestic Firms

1169 MARANON CAPITAL
303 West Medison St.
Suite 2500
Chicago, IL 60606

Phone: 312-646-1200 Fax: 312-578-0047
e-mail: info@maranoncapital.com
web: www.maranoncapital.com

Mission Statement: Maranon Capital provides senior financing, mezzanine debt and equity co-investments for both private equity-backed as well as entrepreneur-owned middle market transactions. We have the flexibility to structure a one-stop financing solution or provide stand-alone senior or mezzanine debt. Maranon Capital does not take control equity positions, but will consider a minority equity role in conjunction with a financing relationship.

Geographic Preference: North America
Investment Criteria: Middle-Market Businesses
Industry Group Preference: Consumer Products, Business Products & Services, Consumer Services, Healthcare Services, Distribution, Manufacturing
Portfolio Companies: Affinitiv, Aircraft Technical Publishers, All States Ag Parts, Ameda, Ancile Solutions, AquaChem, Aristotle Corporation, Atlantic Beverage Company, BBJ Rentals, Bix Produce, Care Hospice, CHA Consulting, Clearant, Coastal Companies, Counsel On Call, CRS Temporary Housing, Dermatology Group, Digital Room, DirectPath, Drillinginfo, Dunn Paper, edriving, EMPG, Engage2Excell, Enviro Vac, EyeSouth, Fidelity Payment Services, Fisher Unitech, Global Knowledge, Gold Standard Baking, GPRS, Haystack, Health & Safety Institute, Hunt Valve, Idaho Pacific, Infogroup, Innovative Chemical Products, J.S. Held, Jensen Hughes, Keane, Kepro, Kronos, Laces, Lakeview Health, LBP Manufacturing, Lionbridge, Magnate Worldwide, Mercer Advisors, Mid Atlantic Capital, Millennium Trust, Miller Heiman, Milton Industries, Momentum, Monroe Truck Equipment, National Spine & Pain Centers, New Era Technology, Niacet, Northstar Travel, Nuvei, OnePath, PathGroup, Phillips & Temro, PKWare, PowerStop, PRV Metals, Sage Hospice, Simplify Compliance, Smile Doctors, Specialty Sales, Spinrite, Tax Guard, Tender Greens, Top Rx, US Salt, Vision Group, Wedgewood Pharmacy, Women's Care Florida, World 50, Young America

Key Executives:
Ian Larkin, Co-Founder/Managing Director
312-646-1202
e-mail: iml@maranoncapital.com
Education: BBA, University of Notre Dame
Background: American Capital Strategies, William Blair Capital Partners, Dean Witter & Company
Laura Albrecht, Managing Director
312-646-1214
e-mail: lka@marnoncapital.com
Education: BS, Indiana University; MBA, Kellogg Graduate School of Management
Background: American Capital Strategies, Adams Street Partners
Rich Jander, Managing Director
312-646-1216
e-mail: rtg@maranoncapital.com
Education: BSBA, Miami University; MBA, Kellogg Graduate School of Management
Background: CapitalSource, LaSalle Bank, PNC Bank
Demian Kircher, Managing Director
312-646-1203
e-mail: dk@maranoncapital.com
Education: BBA, University of Michigan; MBA, Kellogg School of Management
Background: American Capital Strategies, Franklin Street Equity Partners, DocuSystems, Arthur Andersen
Greg Long, Managing Director
312-646-1204
e-mail: gml@maranoncapital.com
Education: BBA, University of Notre Dame; MBA, Harvard Business School
Background: American Capital Strategies, LEK Consulting, William Blair Capital Partners, Morgan Stanley Group
Mike Parilla, Managing Director/Chief Compliance Officer
312-646-1205
e-mail: msp@maranoncapital.com
Education: BS, Finance, University of Illinois, Urbana; MBA, University of Chicago Graduate School of Business; CPA
Background: Heller Financial, Ernst & Young
Rommel Garcia, Managing Director
312-646-1211
e-mail: rpg@maranoncapital.com
Education: AB, University of Chicago; MBA, University of Chicago Graduate School of Business
Background: LaSalle Bank, JP Morgan Chase

1170 MARKPOINT VENTURE PARTNERS
15770 Dallas Pkwy
Suite 800
Dallas, TX 75248

Phone: 972-490-1976 Fax: 972-490-1980
Toll-Free: 888-627-5764

Mission Statement: To provide individual investors an affordable opportunity to participate in the same high quality venture capital investment opportunities that have historically been restricted to only large institutional investors.

Geographic Preference: Southwestern United States
Founded: 1996
Average Investment: $250,000 - $1 million
Portfolio Companies: Airwide Solutions, Aether Partners, Dataside, L.I.T. Surgical, Maystreams, Vizionware, Softricity, Spatial Wireless, SyChip, X-EMI, Xtera Communications

Key Executives:
Tex Sekhon, Managing Partner
e-mail: tsekhon@markpt.com
Education: BBA, University of North Texas
Background: Co-Founder, Markpoint Company; Founder & Managing Partner, Markpoint Realty Group
Kirk Fichtner, Managing Director
e-mail: kfichtner@markpt.com
Education: BBA, Texas Tech University; MBA, Finance & Investments, George Washington University
Background: Dillon Read & Co.; NationsBank; DuPont

1171 MARWIT CAPITAL LLC
100 Bayview Circle
Suite 550
Newport Beach, CA 92660

Phone: 949-861-3636 Fax: 949-861-3637
e-mail: info@marwit.com
web: www.marwit.com

Mission Statement: Marwit is a private investment firm that partners with management teams to build industry leading companies in the lower middle market.

Geographic Preference: Western United States
Fund Size: $184 million
Founded: 1962
Average Investment: $10 - $30 million
Minimum Investment: $10 million
Investment Criteria: MBO, LBO, Recaps, Expansion, Growth Equity
Industry Group Preference: Manufacturing, Distribution, Services, Infrastructure, Healthcare, Retail, Consumer & Leisure, Entertainment, Business Products & Services, Renewable Resources
Portfolio Companies: ARC Machines, Driftwood Dairy Holding, Fire Grill, Granite Seed Company, Promax Nutrition, Solis Women's Health, Western Emulsions

Venture Capital & Private Equity Firms / Domestic Firms

Key Executives:
Matthew L Witte, Managing Partner
e-mail: mwitte@marwit.com
Education: Cornell University
Background: IndX Software; The Related Companies
Directorships: Solis Women's Health, Promax Nutrition, ARC Machines, Granite Seed, Fire Grill, STEC, Paciolan, IndX Software, Marina Medical, Infotec, New West Communications
Chris L Britt, Managing Partner
e-mail: britt@marwit.com
Education: BA, Economics, Stanford University; MBA, Finance, Anderson Graduate School of Management at UCLA
Background: Levine Leichtman Capital Partners; Partner, BCC Capital Partners
Directorships: Boot Barn, Western Emulsions, Storyteller Theatres, Driftwood Dairy, Fire Grill, Nupla, Signature Theatres, Gregg Gift Co., Columbia Aluminum Products, T and T Industries

1172 MARYLAND VENTURE FUND
7021 Columbia Gateway Dr.
Suite 200
Columbia, MD 21046

Phone: 410-715-4191
web: www.marylandventurefund.com

Mission Statement: The Maryland Venture Fund (MVF) is a regionally recognized leader in seed and early-stage investing and a national model for state-supported investment programs. With nearly two decades of experience and numerous successful investments, MVF invests in highly innovative technology companies across the full range of industry sectors including software, communications, cybersecurity and life sciences companies in the areas of healthcare IT, medical devices and diagnostics.

Geographic Preference: Maryland
Fund Size: $84 million
Investment Criteria: Seed-Stage, Early-Stage
Industry Group Preference: Technology, Software, Communications, Cyber Security, Life Sciences, Healthcare Information Technology, Medical Devices, Diagnostics
Portfolio Companies: 20/20 GeneSystems, 3C Logic, 410Labs, 6th Treet Inc., A&G Pharmaceutical, Advanced BioNutrition, Akonni Biosystems, Aledade, Apkudo, Ashvattha, Bambecco, BrainScope Company, CoFoundersLab, Cover My Test, Curbio, Cytimune Sciences, Cytomedix, Fidelis Security Systems, Fugue, Geostellar, Gold Lasso, Gray Bug, Groupsite.com, Harpoon Medical, HomeCare.com, iLearning Engines, KoolSpan, LifeSprout, Luminal, Maxtena, Moodlerooms, Naviscan PET Systems, Optoro, Paratek, Pathsenors, Personal Genome Diagnostics, Plasmonix, Pulse 8, Racktop, Reel Genie, Sensics, Sequella, Social Toaster, StayNTouch, Tales2Go, Theranostics Health, TRX Systems, Vorbeck Materials, Weather Analytics, Xometry, Zenoss, ZeroChroma, Zeuss

Key Executives:
Andy Jones, Managing Director
Education: BS, MS, Electrical Engineering, Cornell University; MBA, Chicago Booth School of Business
Background: Chief Investment Officer, Maryland Technology Development Corporation; General Partner, Boulder Ventures

1173 MASCHMEYER GROUP VENTURES
46 South Park Street
San Francisco, CA 94107

web: www.mgv.vc

Mission Statement: MGV is an early stage venture capital firm investing in emerging tech companies.
Average Investment: Up to $500,000

Key Executives:
Marc Schroder, Managing Partner/Co-Founder
Background: Investor, Seed + Speed Ventures
Carsten Marschmeyer, Founding Partner

1174 MASON WELLS
411 E Wisconsin Avenue
Suite 1280
Milwaukee, WI 53202

Phone: 414-727-6400 **Fax:** 414-727-6410
web: www.masonwells.com

Mission Statement: Creates value for investors by organizing, acquiring and strategically repositioning privately held businesses in partnership with management. Helps entrepreneurial managers build successful private companies by providing investment capital for the purchase of an existing business or the expansion of its operations by internal improvements and/or acquisition.

Geographic Preference: Midwest
Fund Size: $500 million
Founded: 1982
Average Investment: $15 million
Minimum Investment: $5 million
Investment Criteria: Later-Stage, LBO, MBO, Recapitalization
Industry Group Preference: Packaging, Information Technology, Printing, Software, Materials Technology, Business Products & Services
Portfolio Companies: A&R Logistics, AWT Labels & Packaging, Aquion, Buffalo Games, Charter NEX Films, Coating Excellence International, Converting, Creative Forming, Dedicated Computing, EastPoint Sports, Eddy Packing, GAMFG Precision, General American, HyperEdge, InterBay Technologies, King Juice Company, L.B. White Company, MGS Manufacturing, Mullinix Packages, Nelipak, NGI Holdings, Oilgear Company, Oliver Products, Pacon Corp., Paragon Development Systems, Paris Presents, Premix, Prime Distribution, Qualas Power Services, Structural Concepts, Sturm Foods, Whitehall Specialties

Key Executives:
Tom Smith, Executive Managing Director/Chairman
414-727-6416
e-mail: tgsmith@masonwells.com
Education: BA, University of Wisconsin, Madison
Background: Marshall & Illsley Corp
Directorships: Aquion, Buffalo Games, Coating Excellence International, Pacon Corporation, Mullinix Packages
Jay Radtke, Senior Managing Director
414-727-6405
e-mail: jradtke@masonwells.com
Education: BA, Vanderbilt University; MBA, Columbia Business School
Background: Cornerstone Equity Investors, Lehman Brothers
Directorships: AWT Labels & Packaging, L.B. White Company, Nelipak Healthcare Packaging, Structural Concepts, Charter NEX Films, Mullinix Packaging, Oliver Products, Pacon Corp.
Greg Myers, Senior Managing Director
414-727-6404
e-mail: gmyers@masonwells.com
Education: MBA, Marquette University; BS, University of Iowa
Background: Marshall & Illsley
Directorships: EastPoint Sports, Eddy Packing, MGS Manufacturing, Nelipak Healthcare Packaging, Whitehall Specialties
Kevin P Kenealey, Senior Managing Director
414-727-6417
e-mail: kkenealey@masonwells.com
Education: BS, University of Minnesota; JD, Northwestern School of Law
Background: Kirland & Ellis

Directorships: A&R Logistics, King Juice Co., NGI Holdings Corp., Paris Presents, Qualus Power Services
Ben Holbrook, Senior Managing Director
414-727-6422
e-mail: bholbrook@masonwells.com
Education: BS, Psychology, Brown University
Background: Research Associate, Janney Montgomery Scott; Corporate Finance Analyst, Thomas Weisel Partners
Directorships: A&R Logistics, Buffalo Games, Eddy Packing, King Juice Co., Paris Presents, Whitehall Specialties
Jim Domach, Chief Financial Officer
414-727-6412
e-mail: jdomach@masonwells.com
Education: BS, Business Administration, St. Norbert College; MBA, Marquette University
Background: Loan Audit Manager, Marshall & Ilsley Corporation Commercial Audit Group
Directorships: Eddy Packing, Dedicated Computing, General American, Premix, Oilgear

1175 MASS VENTURES
308 Congress Street
5th Floor
Boston, MA 02210

Phone: 617-723-4920 Fax: 617-723-5983
web: www.mass-ventures.com

Mission Statement: The Massachusetts Technology Development Corporation, a leading edge venture capital firm that addresses the 'capital gap' for start-up and expansion of early stage technology companies operating in the Commonwealth of Massachusetts.
Geographic Preference: Massachusetts
Fund Size: $62 million
Founded: 1978
Average Investment: $250,000
Minimum Investment: $100,000
Investment Criteria: Seed, Startup, First-Stage, Second-Stage
Industry Group Preference: Systems & Software, Industrial, Robotics, Internet, Digital Media & Marketing, Healthcare Information Technology, Clean Technology, Energy, Mobile, Medical Devices, Hardware
Portfolio Companies: Applause, Armored Things, BoardOnTrack, ClearGov, Edaris Health, Fairmarkit, Ginkgo Bioworks, Grapevine, Harvest Automation, HorsePower, Inside Tracker, Jebbit, Life Image, Machine Metrics, OwnerIQ, Raven360, Spiro Technologies, Veritas,
Key Executives:
Walter M (Jerry) Bird, President
617-226-2822
e-mail: jbird@mass-ventures.com
Education: BA, Dartmouth College; MBA Tuck School at Dartmouth
Background: Brook Venture Partners; Nova MedVentures; Claflin Capital Management
Directorships: Forerun, lifeIMAGE, uTest
Jason Allen, Vice President
617-207-5576
e-mail: jallen@mass-ventures.com
Education: BA, Denison University; MA, Theological Studies, Harvard Divinity School; JD, Northeastern University School of Law
Background: Launch Capital; General Manager, Ovia Insights
Charlie Hipwood, Vice President
617-306-4512
e-mail: chipwood@mass-ventures.com
Education: BA, Boston College; MBA, Booth School of Business, University of Chicago
Background: JP Morgan

1176 MASSACHUSETTS CAPITAL RESOURCE COMPANY
420 Boylston Street
5th Floor
Boston, MA 02116

Phone: 617-536-3900
web: www.masscapital.com

Mission Statement: MCRC is a source of risk capital for Massachusetts' business and invests across the entire range of business development financings.
Geographic Preference: Massachusetts
Founded: 1977
Average Investment: $5 million
Minimum Investment: $1 million
Investment Criteria: Second-Stage, Mezzanine, LBO, Growth Capital, Acquisitions, Recapitalizations
Industry Group Preference: Communications, Computer Related, Electronic Components, Instrumentation, Genetic Engineering, Industrial Equipment, Equipment, Internet Technology, Medical & Health Related, Consumer Products, Healthcare, Manufacturing, Software, Technology
Portfolio Companies: Advanced Practice Strategies, Aquent, Aspen Tech, Bainbridge, Baynes Electric Supply, Bigbelly Solar, Curaspan Health Group, Exergen, Harbar, Harmonix Music Systems, Litecontrol, Lytron, Magnemotion, Marshall Tube, Medtouch, Network Allies, Phillips Screw Company, Polar Beverages, Pure Incubation, Quadrant Software, Rypos, Seaman Paper, Tri-Wire, Valet Park, WTE Corporation
Key Executives:
Suzanne L Dwyer, Managing Director
617-536-8251
e-mail: sdwyer@masscapital.com
Education: BS/BA, Bridgewater State College; MBA, Babson Graduate School of Bussiness
Background: State Street Bank & Trust Company; Brown Brothers Harriman & Co
Dan Corcoran, Managing Director
617-536-5323
e-mail: dcorcoran@masscapital.com
Education: BA, Economics, Boston College; MBA, Babson College
Background: Bank of New England; BankBoston; Citizens Financial Group

1177 MASSACHUSETTS GROWTH CAPITAL CORPORATION
529 Main Street
Schrafft Center
Suite 201
Charlestown, MA 02129

Phone: 617-523-6262 Fax: 617-523-7676
web: www.massgcc.com

Mission Statement: To provide financing to small businesses in Massachusetts to which private capital is not readily available with the purpose of creating or preserving jobs and promoting economic development.
Geographic Preference: Massachusetts
Founded: 1975
Average Investment: $300, 000
Minimum Investment: $100,000
Investment Criteria: Seed, Startup, First-Stage, Second-Stage, LBO, MBO
Industry Group Preference: Communications, Computer Related, Electronic Components, Instrumentation, Genetic Engineering, Industrial Equipment, Equipment, Internet Technology, Medical & Health Related
Key Executives:
Lawrence D Andrews, President & CEO
617-337-2800
e-mail: landrews@massgcc.com

Venture Capital & Private Equity Firms / Domestic Firms

1178 MASTHEAD VENTURE PARTNERS
301 Newbury St.
Suite 241
Danvers, MA 01923

Phone: 617-621-3000 Fax: 617-621-3055
e-mail: info@mvpartners.com
web: www.mvpartners.com

Mission Statement: Masthead's partners possess successful track records creating long-term value in early-stage companies. We seek market-making ventures with strong teams and powerful intellectual property in high-growth segments.

Investment Criteria: Early Stage
Industry Group Preference: Software, Internet Technology, Communication Technology, IT-Intensive Life Science Applications, Internet Infrastructure
Portfolio Companies: AEP Networks, Bitpipe, Ecount, Centric Software, Chumby, ExpoTV, Genesis Networks, Intercasting Corporation, Liquid Machines, NewsGator Technologies, Nexaweb Technologies, Packet Design, RuleStream Corporation, Scanbuy, Tremor Media, TripConnect

Key Executives:
Braden M (Brady) Bohrmann, General Partner
Education: BS, Finance & Communications, Babson College
Background: COO, Watson Technologies; CFO, Alpha-Beta Technology
Directorships: ExpoTV, inOvate Communications, RuleStream
Daniel K Flatley, General Partner
Education: AB, University of Notre Dame; JD, Georgetown University School of Law
Background: Managing Director, Credit Suisse First Boston And Donaldson
Directorships: AEP Networks, Genesis Networks, Newsgator, Scanbuy, Tacoda Systems, TripConnect, Phillips Plywood, Nuron, Mail.com
Richard W Levandov, General Partner
Education: BS, Binghamton University
Background: Partner, Softbank Technology Ventures
Directorships: Chumby, Liquid Machines, Newsgator, Nexaweb, Tacoda, Tremor
Stephen K Smith, General Partner
Education: First Class Honors Degree, Computer Science, Brighton Polytechnic University; MBA Harvard Business School
Background: Analyst, PaineWebber
Directorships: Maine Technology Institute
Timothy P Agnew, Principal
Education: University of Virginia School of Law; Vassar College
Background: CEO, Finance Authority of Maine
Directorships: CEI Community Ventures, the Great Schools Partnership, the Maine Trust for People with Disabilities, HealthInfoNet, Senator George J. Mitchell Scholarship Reserach Institute
Mary M Shannon, Principal
Education: Holy Cross; MBA, Boston College
Background: Director of Planning & Analysis, Sefer; Liberty Mutual Group

1179 MATCHSTICK VENTURES
Twin Cities, MN

web: www.matchstickventures.com

Mission Statement: To support innovation and diverse entrepreneurs in startup communities.

Geographic Preference: The Rockies
Average Investment: $50,000 - $1,000,000
Investment Criteria: Early-Stage, Seed
Industry Group Preference: Technology
Portfolio Companies: Addstructure, AdHawk, Air Tailor, Ambassador, Blueprint Registry, Branch, Bybe, Ilos, Inspectorio, Itsbyu, Kapta, Kidizen, Kipsu, Kokko, Learn To Live, Local Crate, Localize, Nexosis, Savitude, Scale Factor, Shopturn, Spot Crowd, Sprucebot, Story Xpress, Structural, Upsie

Key Executives:
Ryan Broshar, Founder & Managing Partner
e-mail: ryan@matchstickventures.com
Education: BSB, Entrepreneurship and Marketing, University of Minnesota; MBA, University of Colorado Boulder
Background: Managing Partner, Confluence Energy; Co-Founder, Beta.MN; Managing Partner, Confluence Capital Partners; Managing Director, Techstars
Natty Zola, Managing Partner
e-mail: natty@matchstickventures.com
Education: BA, Finance, University of Maryland - Robert H. Smith School of Business
Background: Managing Director, Techstars; Sr. Director, MapQuest; Co-Founder & CEO, Everlater

1180 MATERIAL IMPACT
131 Dartmouth Street
3rd Floor
Boston, MA 02116

web: materialimpact.com

Mission Statement: Material Impact transforms materials into companies that makes an impact. They focus on quantum leap advancements in technology and material technologies that will impact basic human needs and quality of life.

Fund Size: $200 Million

Key Executives:
Carmichael Roberts, Co-Founder and Managing Partner
Education: BS, PhD, Duke University; MBA, Massachussets Institute of Technology
Background: General Partner, North Bridge Venture Partners; Co-Founder, Diagnostics For All; President and CEO, Arsenal Medical
Adam Sharkawy, Co-Founder and Managing Partner
Education: PhD, Duke University
Background: VP, Research, Ventrica Inc.; VP, Research, Abbott Ventures; SVP, The Medicines Company

1181 MATH VENTURE PARTNERS
Chicago, IL 60654

web: www.mathventurepartners.com

Mission Statement: MATH Venture Partners is a venture capital fund investing in early to growth-stage technology companies. MATH seeks to create partnerships with talented and committed digital entrepreneurs.

Geographic Preference: United States
Fund Size: $28 million
Founded: 2014
Average Investment: $500,000 - $1 million
Investment Criteria: Startups, Seed Stage, Early Stage, Expansion Stage, Growth Stage
Industry Group Preference: Technology
Portfolio Companies: Acorns, All4Staff, Apervita, CardFlight, Digital Golf Technologies, GameWisp, InRentive, MightyNest, Music Audience Exchange, NoRedInk, NowSecure, RedSeal, Roost, SocialSignIn, Spoon University, Telnyx, ThinkCERCA

Key Executives:
Mark Achler, Managing Director
Education: BA, History & Economics, Purdue University
Background: Senior VP, New Business, Strategy & Innovation, Redbox; President, Emmi Solutions; Founding Partner, Kettle Partners; President, Kinesoft Development; CEO & Co-Founder, The Whitewater Group
Troy Henikoff, Managing Director
Education: BS, Engineering, Brown University; Northwestern University
Background: Lecturer, Kellogg School of Management;

Venture Capital & Private Equity Firms / Domestic Firms

Managing Director, Techstars; Co-Founder, Excelerate Labs; CEO, OneWed.com; President, Amacal; Co-Founder & CEO, SurePayroll.com; President, Systemetrics

1182 MATLINPATTERSON
70 East 55th St.
9th Floor
New York, NY 10022

Phone: 212-651-9500
web: www.matlinpatterson.com

Mission Statement: A global distressed private equity firm.

Key Executives:
David J Matlin, Chief Executive Officer
Education: BA, Wharton School; JD, University of California
Directorships: Flagstar Bank, Standard Pacific

1183 MATON VENTURE
1601 S De Anza Boulevard
Suite 115
Cupertino, CA 95014

Phone: 408-786-5168 **Fax:** 408-996-0728
web: www.maton.com

Mission Statement: To help new entrepreneurs by investing in privately owned companies offering promising new technologies.
Geographic Preference: United States, Taiwan, Japan, Germany
Investment Criteria: All Stages
Industry Group Preference: Technology
Portfolio Companies: Advanced Analogic Technologies, Analogic Tech, Apherma Corporation, Bit Bliz, Breveon, Broadband Communications, Crosslayer Networks, eBest, Envivio, Innovative Robotics, Intelligent Epitaxy Technology, Martsoft, Octasoft, OmniVision, Oplink, Ortega Innfosystems, PicoNetics, Primanex Corporation, Storactive, Syscan, Tsunami Visual Technologies, ZYNX Networks

Key Executives:
Connie Chuang, Co-Founder
Jesse Chen, Co-Founder
Background: Co-Founder, President & CEO, BusLogic
Jaff Linn, Co-Founder
Background: Vice President, Engineering, BusLogic

1184 MATRIX PARTNERS
101 Main Street
17th Floor
Cambridge, MA 02142

Phone: 617-494-1223
e-mail: info@matrixpartners.com
web: www.matrixpartners.com

Mission Statement: Committed to building long-term relationships with outstanding entrepreneurs and helping them build significant, industry-leading companies.
Geographic Preference: United States, India, China
Founded: 1977
Average Investment: $2 to $10 million
Minimum Investment: $2 million
Investment Criteria: All Stages
Industry Group Preference: Enterprise Software, Communications, Semiconductors, Internet Technology, Wireless Technologies, Consumer Internet, Networking, Clean Technology, Energy
Portfolio Companies: Acacia, Adelphic, Affirmed, Aibang.com, Almond Systems, Ambarella, Anjuke.com, ApartmentList, Aquto, Aylus Networks, BabyTree, Canopy, Canva, Carbon Black, Carbon Design, Care.com, Circle, CloudBees, Conductor, Confer, Crossbeam Systems, Cyphort, Didi Chuxing, Digital Fountain, Digium, Earnin, Ele.me, Emphirix, Enservio, The Flatiron School, Fuze Network, Gilt Groupe, GOAT, GrabCad, HubSpot, Huddle, Hyper9, Inflection, Intent Media, Jetsetter, JustFabulous, Kalido, Klip, Koding, Koudai, Lever, Locality, MarkForged, minuteKEY, Mitro, Momo, Namely, Oculus VR, Ola, OpenSpan, Panzura, Plexx, Polyvore, Poynt, Qihoo, QPID Health, Qualtré, Quora, Quri, Rocksbox, Salsify, Sila, SpiderCloud Wireless, Storiant, Taulia, TechStyle, textPlus, The Echo Nest, TribeHR, UniDesk, VeriVue, VeVeo, VideoIQ, Xiaomi, Xtalic, Zaius, Zendesk, ZestFinance

Other Locations:
535 Mission St.
Suite 2600
San Francisco, CA 94105
Phone: 650-798-1600

Key Executives:
Timothy A Barrows, Partner
617-494-1223
e-mail: tbarrows@matrixpartners.com
Education: Williams College; MBA, Stanford University
Background: Merrill Lynch Capital Markets
Directorships: Affirmed Networks, Carbon Black, Cloud Zero, nference, Qrativ
Paul J Ferri, Co-Founder
e-mail: pjf@matrixpartners.com
Education: MBA, Columbia University; MSEE, Polytechnic University of New York; BSEE, Cornell University
Background: Founder, Hellman Ferri Investment Associates; General Partner, WestVen Management
Directorships: Airvana, Aylus Networks, Empirix, Netezza, VeriVue, Veveo
Stan J Reiss, Partner
617-494-1223
e-mail: sreiss@matrixpartners.com
Education: BSEE, Cornell University; SMEE, SMOR, Massachusetts Institute of Technology
Background: McKinsey & Company
Directorships: Acacia Communications, LogRocket, RightHand Robotics, Xtalic, Lightmatter
David R Skok, Partner
781-890-2244
e-mail: dskok@matrixpartners.com
Education: BSc, Computer Science, University of Sussex (England)
Background: SilverStream Software; President/CEO, Watermark Software
Directorships: Apollo GraphQL, CloudBees, Conductor, Digium, Enservio, GrabCAD, Hubspot, Meteor, Namely, OpenSpan, SageCloud, Salsify, Video IQ, Zaius
Andrew W Verhalen, Partner
650-796-1600
e-mail: averhalen@matrixpartners.com
Education: MBA, MSEE, BSEE, Cornell University
Background: Divisional VP, 3Com Corporation; Intel Corporation
Directorships: Panzura, Sila Nanotechnologies
Antonio Rodriguez, Partner
e-mail: antonio@matrixpartners.com
Education: AB, Social Studies, Harvard University; MBA, Stanford Graduate School of Business; Graduate Studies, Computer Science, Stanford University
Background: CTO, HP; Founder & CEO, Tabblo; VP, Engineering, MyPublisher; Memora; Abuzz; The Boston Consulting Group
Directorships: Adelphic, Canopy, Care.com, Ctrl Labs, Echo Nest, Intent Media, Koding, MarkForged, Oculus VR, Owl Labs, Sqrrl, TalkTo
Dana Stalder, Partner
650-798-1600
e-mail: dana@matrixpartners.com
Education: BS, Commerce, Santa Clara University
Background: Senior Vice President, Product Sales, PayPay; Vice President, Internet Marketing, eBay; Founding Executive, Respond.com; Vice President, Finance, Netscape

Venture Capital & Private Equity Firms / Domestic Firms

Directorships: Afterpay, ApartmentList, Bugsnag, Earnin, Gilt Groupe, iRise, Lever, minuteKEY, Polyvore, Poynt, Quin Street, textPlus, Work4Labs, Zendesk, ZestFinance
Ilya Sukhar, Partner
Education: BS, MEng, Computer Science, Cornell University
Background: Ooyala, Etacts, Parse, Facebook
Directorships: Fivetran, Flock Safety, Height, Hustle, Mashgin, Parabola, Slab

1185 MAVERICK VENTURES
1 Letterman Drive
Building D
San Francisco, CA 94129

Phone: 415-343-1900
web: www.maverickventures.com

Mission Statement: Maverick Ventures invests in entrepreneurs across the healthcare and technology sectors.
Founded: 1993
Key Executives:
 Lee Ainslie, Founder
 Education: BS, University of Virginia; MBA, University of North Carolina
 Background: Managing Director, Tiger Management

1186 MAVERON LLC

Phone: 206-288-1700
e-mail: maveron@maveron.com
web: www.maveron.com

Mission Statement: A financial and strategic partner to those companies who demonstrate both passion and vision in transforming the consumer experience.
Geographic Preference: United States
Fund Size: $600 million
Founded: 1997
Industry Group Preference: Consumer Services
Portfolio Companies: Against Gravity, Allbirds, Arivale, August, Axius, Big Box, Boon + Gable, Booster, Bread, Capella Education, CircleUp, Clarity Money, Common, Course Hero, Cover, Cranium, Crowd Cow, Darby Smart, Decide.com, Dia & Co., Direct Buy, Dolls Kill, Dolly, Drugstore.com, Dwellable, Eargo, Earnest, eBay, Elysium, Everlane, Fabric, Fit XR, Flywire, General Assembly, Genies, Good, Groupon, Handle, Happy Returns, Homeroom, HopSkipDrive, iBeat, Illumix, Imperfect Produce, Inkbox, JetClosing, Jott, Jumpcut, Keeps, Kids on 45th, Kinetix Living, KonMari, Koru, Leaftail Labs, Lovevery, Lucy, Madison Reed, Masse, MegaBots, Mode.ai, Modern Fertility, Moment, Naja, Nécessaire, Neighborhood Goods, Newsle, Nextfoods, Nomadic, NovoED, Panna, Peach, Periscope, PetCoach, Pinkberry, Pioneer Square Labs, Pluto, Potbelly, Pro.com, Prose, Quellos, Red Tricycle, SafeTrek, Sana, Scoot, Seatme, Service, Shutterfly, Simbi, Splash, Spyce, Study Edge, Svrf, The Guild, The Wrap, Tile, True Facet, Trupanion, Vacatia, Vhoto, Vicarious, Virtuix Omni, Visor, Wander Beauty, Way Up, Zulily, Zume Pizza
Key Executives:
 Dan Levitan, Co-Founder/Partner
 Education: Horace Mann School, Duke University, Harvard Business School
 Background: Managing Director, Schroders
 Directorships: Allbirds, Arivale, CircleUp, Peach, Pluto VR, Pro.com, Spyce, The Wrap, Trupanion
 Anarghya Vardhana, Partner
 e-mail: anarghya@maveron.com
 Directorships: Masse, Illumix, Imperfect Produce, Inkbox, Pluto VR, Spyce, The Guild Hotels
 David Wu, Partner
 e-mail: dave@maveron.com
 Directorships: Booster, Darby Smart, Eargo, Illumix, Inkbox, Modern Fertility

 Pete McCormick, Partner
 e-mail: pmccormick@maveron.com
 Education: BA, Economics, University of Washington
 Background: Partner, Graham & Dunn Law Firm
 Directorships: Madison Reed
 Jason Stoffer, Partner
 e-mail: jstoffer@maveron.com
 Education: BA, Economics, University of Michigan; MBA, Wharton School
 Background: Senior Director, Career Education Corp.
 Directorships: Common, Course Hero, Dolls Kill, Dolly, Everlane, Flywire, General Assembly, Imperfect Produce, Keeps, The Guild Hotels, TrueFacet

1187 MAYFIELD FUND
2484 Sand Hill Road
Menlo Park, CA 94025

Phone: 650-854-5560
web: www.mayfield.com

Mission Statement: Mayfield has always been about the people - experienced, committed partners; smart, innovative entrepreneurs; loyal, knowledgeable investors -all working together to build sustainable technology companies that solve tough customer problems.
Geographic Preference: United States
Fund Size: $2.7 billion
Founded: 1969
Average Investment: $3 million
Minimum Investment: $500,000
Investment Criteria: Seed, Startup, First-Stage, Second-Stage, Third-Stage, Series A, Growth Stage, Later Stage
Industry Group Preference: Communications, Computer Related, E-Commerce & Manufacturing, Electronic Components, Education, Media, Software, Internet Technology, Biotechnology, Medical & Health Related, Life Sciences, Environment Products & Services, Consumer Services, Energy Technology, Telecommunications
Portfolio Companies: 3DRobotics, AgilOne, Alignable, Alfresco, Appcelerator, Arcadia Data, AudienceScience, Baihe.com, Balbix, BigPanda, Blackarrow, Brighter, C9, Centrify, ClassPass, CloudGenix, CloudPhysics, CloudVelox, Couchbase, Crunchbase, Earny, EasilyDo, Edison, Elatica, Electric Cloud, Fab, fitmob, Fixya, Fungible, Gigya, GroundWork, Grove, HashiCorp, HealthTap, if(we), IndiaProperty.com, InfluxDB, Jawbone, Lantern, LatticePower, Lyft, Mammoth Biosciences, MapR Technologies, Massdrop, Matrimony.com, Mission Bio, Moat, NewsCred, Outreach, OUYA, Portworx, Poshmark, Qunar.com, Qventus, Rancher, Rubicon Project, ServiceMax, ShiftLeft, ShineOn, Skilljar, SmartRecruiters, SMiT, Stockpile, SwiftStack, Tejas Networks, Tonal, Tripp, TrustRadius, Versa Networks, Vexata, Viralheat, Webroot, WideOrbit, WorkSpan, Zipongo
Key Executives:
 Navin Chaddha, Managing Director
 e-mail: nchaddha@mayfield.com
 Education: MS, Electrical Engineering, Stanford University
 Background: Partner, Gabriel Venture Partners; CTO, VXtreme; Co-Founder, iBeam Broadcasting
 Rajeev Batra, Partner
 e-mail: rbarta@mayfield.com
 Education: MEng, Electrical Engineering, Cornell University; BSEE Honors, University of Maryland, College Park; MBA, Harvard Business School
 Background: Siebel Systems, Scopus Technology, Open Environment Corporation

1188 MAYFLY CAPITAL

web: www.mayflycapital.com

Mission Statement: Mayfly Capital LLC invests and partners with entrepreneurs developing innovative, environmentally

Venture Capital & Private Equity Firms / Domestic Firms

conscious technologies for the graphic arts and printing industries. Before it emerged as an independent firm in 2009, Mayfly was the internal investment and development arm of a family-owned commercial printing company based in Cleveland, Ohio. Now, as a standalone firm, Mayfly can provide its investments the support and resources needed to achieve their near-term goals while increasing their long-term value by developing operational and financial strategies.

Founded: 2009
Industry Group Preference: Graphic Arts, Printing
Portfolio Companies: Ross PPD Corporation, 121nexus

Key Executives:
 Charlie Kim, Managing Partner/Founder
 Education: BS, Economics & Finance, Ohio Northern University; MS, Accounting, Boston College
 Background: Intervale Capital; Merrill Lynch

1190 MB VENTURE PARTNERS
17 West Pontotoc Ave.
Suite 101
Memphis, TN 38103

Phone: 901-322-0330 Fax: 901-322-0339
web: www.mbventures.com

Mission Statement: MB Venture Partners is a Memphis, Tennessee venture capital firm that provides equity capital and strategic direction to life science companies.

Fund Size: $76 million
Founded: 2001
Investment Criteria: Seed-State, Early-Stage, Later-Stage
Industry Group Preference: Life Sciences, Biotechnology, Medical Devices
Portfolio Companies: AxioMed Spine, Better Walk, Biomimetic, BioNanovations, BioSet, Blood Montoring Solutions, Calosyn Pharma, Cayenne Medical, Compression Kinetics, CrossRoads, Cuff-Mate, EcoSurg, Endoinsight, Expanding Orthopedics, Focal Point Pharmaceuticals, GTx, Handminder, Hapten Sciences, Health & Bliss, Hubble Telemedical, Innometrix, iScreen Vision, Jumpstart Foundy, Kereos, KFx Medical, MB Innovations, Mobilizer, Nanopthalmics, Ortho Kinematics, Protein Discovery, Restore Medical Solutions, S2 Interactive, Salient Surgical, Spine Wave, Sweetbio, Tidal Wave Technology, Urova Medical, Veracity Medical Solutions, View Medical, Visioneering Technologies, Zyga

Key Executives:
 Gary Stevenson, Co-Founder/Managing Partner
 Education: University of Missouri; MBA, Kellogg School of Business
 Background: Abbott Laboratories
 Directorships: AxioMed Spine, BioSET, Kereos, KFx Medical, Hapten Sciences, S2 Interactive, Visioneering, Focal Point Pharmaceuticals, iScreen, Restore Medical Solutions, MB Innovations
 Mike Sherman, Partner
 Education: BS, Biomedical Engineering, University of Texas
 Background: Sofamor Danek
 Directorships: Anulex Technologies, Cayenne Medical, Calosyn Pharma, Expanding Orthopedics, Hubble Telemedical, Tidal Wave Technology, Veracity Medical, Urova Medical, Nanopthalmics, Zyga

1191 MBF CAPITAL CORPORATION
12 East 49th Street
28th Floor
New York, NY 10017

Phone: 212-339-2861 Fax: 212-339-2834
web: www.mbfcapital.com

Mission Statement: An investment firm specializing in making private equity investments principally in technology driven, early stage information technology and medical technology companies.

Investment Criteria: Early Stage, Turnarounds, Growth Capital
Industry Group Preference: Information Technology, Medical Devices, Telecommunications, Networking, Software, Semiconductors, Biopharmaceuticals, Healthcare Services, Drug Development
Portfolio Companies: eMotion, ExSar Corporation, Gunther International, IQ Systems, Lamar, Network-1 Software & Technology, Network Specialists, Syntonix Pharmaceuticals, Vela Pharmaceuticals

Key Executives:
 Mark Fisher, President
 Background: Principal, Alex Brown; Senior Vice President/Investments, Lehman Brothers; Vice President, Merrill Lynch Futures
 Directorships: Vela Pharmaceuticals, ExSar Corporation

1192 MCG CAPITAL CORPORATION
1001 19th Street North
10th Floor
Arlington, VA 22209

Phone: 703-247-7500 Fax: 703-247-7505
e-mail: mcg@mcgcapital.com

Mission Statement: A provider of capital and strategic advice to small to mid-size companies, focusing on growth and value creation.

Geographic Preference: United States
Founded: 1990
Investment Criteria: Revenue between $20-$200 million, $3-$25 million in EBITDA, Proven business models, Operating leverage
Industry Group Preference: Communications, Information Technology, Media, Technology, Broadcasting, Plastics, Business Products & Services, Consumer Products, Healthcare, Entertainment, Education
Portfolio Companies: Accurate Group Holdings, Broadview Networks Holdings, C7 Data Centers, Community Investors, GMC Television Broadcasting, IDOC, Industrial Saffety Technologies, Intrafusion Holding Corporation, Legacy Cabinets Holdings II, Maverick Healthcare Equity, RadioPharmacy Investors, South Bay Mental Health Center, Surefire Medical, Velocity Technology Solutions

Key Executives:
 B Hagen Saville, President/COO
 e-mail: hsaville@mcgcapital.com
 Background: First Union National Bank, Signet Bank
 E Peter Malekian, Managing Director
 e-mail: pmalekian@mcgcapital.com
 Education: BS, George Mason University; MBA, Cornell University, Johnson School of Management
 Background: Ferris Baker Watts; Financial Analyst, Arthur Andersen; Consultant, Hoffman Morison & Fitzgerald
 Keith Kennedy, CFO/Managing Director
 Background: GE Capital; Earnst & Young LLP

1193 MCG CAPITAL MANAGEMENT
750 Kearns Blvd.
Suite 295
Park City, UT 84060

Phone: 435-214-7127
web: www.mcgcapitalmgt.com

Mission Statement: MCG Capital Management is committed to producing consistent profitability for clients.

Key Executives:
 Michael C Giese, President
 e-mail: mgiese@mcgcapitalmgt.com
 Education: BS, Astronautical Engineering, US Air Force Academy

Venture Capital & Private Equity Firms / Domestic Firms

1194 MCGOVERN CAPITAL
230 West 56th Street
New York, NY 10019

Phone: 212-688-9840
e-mail: katey@mcgoverncapital.com
web: www.mcgoverncapital.com

Mission Statement: Invests in startup companies in various industries, including Health & Wellness, Food & Beverage, medicinal cannabis, air & water purification, eSports, and media.

Investment Criteria: Seed, Early-Stage
Industry Group Preference: Health & Wellness, Skincare, Food & Beverage, eSports, Cannabis, Technology, Media, Communications
Portfolio Companies: Sobe, The Water Initiative, K&A Water, KX Industries, Narragansett Beer, Beverage Innovations, Celsius, Rise Brewing Co., Neostrata, Skinphonic, Regimend MD, Optigenex, Isreal Plant Sciences, PlantEXT, Intiva, Intiva Biopharma, WeedMD, Wellness Centers, Esports, iItoo, Clean Coal Technologies Inc., Perimeter Internetworking, Wealthtracking, Angstrom Publishing, Counsel Press,

Key Executives:
Kevin M. McGovern, Chairman/CEO
Education: AB, Cornell University; JD, Saint John's University School of Law
Background: Chairman/CEO, The Water Initiative

1195 MCGOWAN CAPITAL GROUP
101 North Main Avenue
Suite 325
Sioux Falls, SD 57104

Phone: 605-357-5302 Fax: 605-357-5303
e-mail: info@mcgowancapitalgroup.com
web: www.mcgowancapitalgroup.com

Mission Statement: To provide private equity opportunities for investors and to assist with the building of successful enterprises.

Geographic Preference: Midwest
Founded: 2004
Investment Criteria: Early Stage, Mid-Stage
Industry Group Preference: Diversified
Portfolio Companies: Classified Verticals, Dakotaland Autoglass, Grand Prairie Foods, Granite City Food & Brewery, Maverick Air Center, NB Golf Cars, Progressive Acute Care, Sajan, Savigent, South Dakota Innovation Partners, The Prairie Club, ZeaChem

Key Executives:
Gene McGowan Sr, Founder/Chief Executive Officer
Background: Entrepreneur in Residence, Bluestem Capital Company; COO, Individual Investor Services; Piper Jaffray

1196 MEAKEM/BECKER VENTURE CAPITAL
603 Beaver Street
Suite 201
Sewickley, PA 15143

Phone: 412-749-5720 Fax: 412-749-5721
e-mail: info@mbvc.com
web: www.mbvc.com

Mission Statement: To help build leading, next-generation companies of significant value.

Geographic Preference: Eastern & Midwestern United States
Founded: 2005
Investment Criteria: Early-Stage
Industry Group Preference: Life Sciences, Information Technology
Portfolio Companies: Spreecast, Schoology, Shipwire, Cloudmeter, HotPads, Kiva Systems, CollegeProwler.com, Leostream, RapidBuyr, 3form, BeatBox, Tiversa

Key Executives:
David Becker, Co-Founder/Managing Director
e-mail: dbecker@mbvc.com
Education: BS, Chemical & Petroleum Refining Engineering, Colorado School of Mines; MS, Chemical Engineering, West Virginia College of Graduate Studies (Marshall University); MBA, Harvard University
Background: President & Chief Investment Officer, Clearwater Capital Management; COO, FreeMarkets; Dole Fresh Fruit International
Directorships: Hotpads, Shipwire, Leostream, Kiva, Schoology
Mark G Miller, Senior Director
e-mail: mmiller@mbvc.com
Education: BS, Chemical Engineering, MS, Metallurgy, Georgia Tech; MBA, University of Pittsburgh Katz School of Business
Background: Chairman, CEO & President, Solutions Consulting; Accenture
David Koegler, Principal/CFO
e-mail: dkoegler@mbvc.com
Education: BA, Slippery Rock University
Background: VP, Finance & Administration, Meakem Venture Partners; Senior Manager, FreeMarkets

1197 MEDIA VENTURE PARTNERS
255 California Street
Suite 850
San Francisco, CA 94111

Phone: 415-391-4877 Fax: 415-549-0515
web: www.mvpcapital.com

Mission Statement: Media Venture Partners identifies opportunities and makes the vital connections necessary to expedite successful transactions and maximize value for its clients.

Geographic Preference: Worldwide
Founded: 1987
Minimum Investment: Less than $100,000
Investment Criteria: Seed, Startup, First-Stage, Second-Stage, LBO, MBO
Industry Group Preference: Communications, Computer Related, Publishing, Consumer Products, Technology, Wireless Technologies, Infrastructure, Radio, Television, Broadcasting

Other Locations:
420 Nichols Road
Kansas City, MO 64112
Phone: 816-249-1630 Fax: 415-549-0515

3 Allied Drive
Suite 120
Dedham, MA 02026
Phone: 617-345-7316 Fax: 415-549-0515

2033 11th Street
Suite 6
Boulder, CO 80302
Phone: 303-284-3965 Fax: 415-549-0515

Key Executives:
Elliot B Evers, Managing Director & Co-Founder
e-mail: eevers@mediaventurepartners.com
Education: BA, Journalism, University of California, Berkeley; JD, Hastings College of the Law, University of California; Diplome Semestriel, University of Paris
Jason Hill, Managing Director
e-mail: jhill@mediaventurepartners.com
Education: BS, Finance & Economics, Boston College
Background: Associate, Amsterdam Pacifi Securities; Analyst, Investment Banking Division, Goldman Sachs & Co
Brian Pryor, Managing Director
Education: BS, Finance & Economics, Boston College
Gred Widroe, Managing Director
e-mail: gwidroe@mediaventurepartners.com
Education: BS, Agricultural & Managerial Economics,

Venture Capital & Private Equity Firms / Domestic Firms

University of California, Davis; MBA, Cornell University
Background: Amsterdam Pacific Securities; COO, Apollo Communications; Product Management, Pacific Bell
R Clayton Funk, Managing Director
e-mail: cfunk@mediaventurepartners.com
Education: BA, Communications, Washburn University
Background: Nations Media Partners

1198 MEDIPHASE VENTURE PARTNERS
2150 Washington St.
Suite 200
Newton, MA 02462

Phone: 617-332-3408 Fax: 617-332-8463
e-mail: administration@mediphasefunds.com

Mission Statement: A venture capital firm focusing on health care/life sciences companies. We seek rapidly growing companies with outstanding market opportunities.

Investment Criteria: Early Stage
Industry Group Preference: Healthcare, Life Sciences, Biopharmaceuticals
Portfolio Companies: Concert Pharmaceuticals, DiscoveRx, PatientKeeper, Relypsa, STARTech, Supplemental Health Care, Tetraphase Pharmaceuticals, Wellpartner

Key Executives:
Lawrence G Miller, MD, Founding Partner
Education: Harvard College, Cambridge University, Harvard Medical School
Background: Senior Vice President, Hambrecht & Quist Capital Management; Exectutive Vice President & Director, Internal Operations, Avicenna Systems Corp; Vice President, HPR; Physician & Pharmacologist, Faculty Member, Department of Pharmacology & Experimental Therapeutics, Tufts University School of Medicine
Paul A Howard, Founding Partner
Education: AB, Bowdoin College; MS, University of Massachusetts, Amherst; SM, Sloan School of Management, MIT
Background: Senior Vice President, Hambrecht & Quist Capital Management; Senior Technical Sales Executive, Miles Biotechnology Division, Bayer AG
W Lambert Welling, Managing Director
e-mail: bert.welling@gmail.com
Education: MBA, Columbia Business School; BA, Middlebury College
Background: Pace Consulting Group; VP, Federal Street Capital Corporation
Edward B Marsh, MD, Managing Director
e-mail: emarsh@medtechcapital.com
Education: AB, Princeton University; MD, Johns Hopkins University
Robert W Macleod, Managing Director
e-mail: bmacleod@medtechcapital.com
Education: BA, Trinity College; Harvard Business School
Background: Kendall Company; Eliot Bank; CFO, Foster Medical Supply

1200 MEIDLINGER PARTNERS
3401 Market Street
Suite 200
Philadelphia, PA 19104

Phone: 215-701-3299 Fax: 215-557-0912
e-mail: kmeidlinger@meidlingerpartners.net
web: www.meidlingerpartners.net

Mission Statement: A private equity firm with operational expertise in the water and wastewater sectors.

Geographic Preference: United States, Western Europe
Investment Criteria: Later-Stage, Growth Equity
Industry Group Preference: Water
Portfolio Companies: ANDalyze, Environmental Operating Solutions, Liberty Hydro, RedZone Robotics, Triton Water

Key Executives:
Karen Meidlinger, Principal
e-mail: kmeidlinger@meidlingerpartners.net
Education: BSc, Marine Biology, University of Liverpool; MBA, University of Cape Town
Background: University City Science Center, Johnson & Johnson
Michael Lynch, Senior Associate
Education: Cornell University, Pennsylvania State University Dickinson School of Law
Background: Contract Attorney

1201 MEKETA INVESTMENT GROUP
80 University Avenue
Westwood, MA 02090

Phone: 781-471-3500
web: www.meketagroup.com

Mission Statement: Investment partners who think strategically and execute with integrity to secure the future for institutions and individuals

Founded: 1978
Industry Group Preference: Finances, Healthcare

Key Executives:
James E Meketa, Managing Principal/Chairman
Education: AB, Harvard University

1202 MENDOZA VENTURES
359 Newbury Street
5th Floor
Boston, MA 02115

Phone: 617-505-6070
web: mendoza-ventures.com

Mission Statement: Mendoza Ventures is a Fintech, AI, and Cybersecurity venture capital. It is both woman and minority owned and is the first latinx founded venture on the east coast.

Key Executives:
Adrian Mendoza, Founder/General Partner
Education: University of Southern California; Harvard University
Background: Co-Founder and CTO, Apptient
Senofer Mendoza, Founder/General Partner
Education: University of Massachussetts; Suffolk University
Background: Investor, Listo Unlimited; Investor, Senso.ai

1203 MENLO VENTURES
1300 El Camino Real
Suite 150
Menlo Park, CA 94025

Phone: 650-854-8540 Fax: 650-854-7059
e-mail: contact@menlovc.com
web: www.menlovc.com

Mission Statement: Seeking combinations of talented management, superior products or services, and market opportunities that create the potential for exceptional returns on their investment, typical investment ranges from $4 million to $10 million.

Geographic Preference: United States
Fund Size: $3 billion
Founded: 1976
Average Investment: $10 million
Minimum Investment: $250K
Investment Criteria: All Stages
Industry Group Preference: Communications, Internet Technology, Semiconductors, Data Services, Computer Hardware & Software, Infrastructure, Information Technology, Enterprise Software, Mobile & Internet, Networking, Storage & Computing, Security
Portfolio Companies: 3T Biosciences, 6 River Systems, AeroScout, Aisera, Alloy, AppDome, Aquera, Aevere Systems, AVI Networks, Benchling, Betterment,

BeyondCore, BitPay, BitSight Technologies, BlueVine, Bread, Breather, Carbonite Inc., Carta, Cellfire, Chime Bank, Cyras Systems, Cinemagram, Clarifai, Clear Labs, Cofactor Genomics, CouchSurfing, Credit Sesame, DataXu, Encoded Therapeutics, Envoy, Epiodyne, Everclaw, Fleetsmith, Getaround, Gilead Sciences Inc., Glide, Harness, HomeLight, Indio, INVIDI Technologies, JUMP, Kalpana, Keaton Row, Kidaptive, LiveOps, Livingly Media, Lumosity, MailFrontier, MealPal, Minted, NCircle Entertainment, Open Solutions, PillPack, Pixable, Platform9, Pliant Therapeutics, Pluribus Networks, Qualia, Recursion Pharmaceuticals, RightHand Robotics, Roku, Rover.com, Scality, Sellpoints, Scenti Bio, ShipBob, Signifyd, Spinnaker Networks, STANCE, StrataCom Inc., Synthego, Talari Networks, tCell, Telenav, The Black Tux, Uber, Unravel Data, UrbanSitter, Usermind, Veriflow, Vidyo, Voltage Security, Warby Parker, Waterline Data, Yellowbrick, YuMe, Zylo

Other Locations:
524 2nd Street
San Francisco, CA 94107

Key Executives:
Douglas C. Carlisle, Partner Emeritus
Education: BS, Electrical Engineering, University of California, Berkeley; MBA, Stanford University Graduate School of Business; JD, Stanford University Law School
Background: Design Engineer, ROLM Corporation
Directorships: Cellfire, Check, LiveOps, Lytx, Nexxo, Nlight Photonics, Readyforce, RF Surgical, Vidyo
John W. Jarve, Partner Emeritus
Education: BS/MS, Electrical Engineering, MIT; MBA, Stanford University
Background: Charles Stark Draper Laboratory at Harvard Medical School; Booze Allen and Hamilton; Intel Corporation
Directorships: Avere Systems, Betterment, BeyondCore, Coraid, Credit Sesame, DataXu, Livingly Media
Mark A. Siegel, Partner
e-mail: mark@menloventures.com
Education: BS, Physics/Electrical Engineering, Massachusetts Institute of Technology; MBA, Stanford Graduate School of Business
Background: Oracle Corporation, Netscape Communications Corporation.
Directorships: Dropcam, Dstillery, eXelate, Invidi, Pluribus Networks, Tintri, Voltage Security
Venky Ganesan, Partner
Education: Reed College, California Institute of Technology
Background: Vice President, JAFCO Ventures, Program Manager, Encarta Group, Microsoft
Directorships: Avi Networks, BitSight, Dedrone, Machine Zone, OverOps, Rover, UpCounsel, Waterline Data Science
Shawn T. Carolan, Partner
e-mail: shawn@menloventures.com
Education: MBA, Stanford University Graduate School of Business; BS, MS, Electrical Engineering, University of Illinois
Background: Management Consultant, Booz-Allen & Hamilton; Open Port Technology; Motorola's Cellular Infrastructure Group; Wireless Data Group; Sprint PCS; University of Illinois' Center for Computational Electromagnetics
Directorships: IMVU, PlayPhone, Roku, TeleNav, Uber, YuMe
J.P. Sanday, Partner
e-mail: jp@menlovc.com
Education: Carroll School of Management, Boston College; MBA, Stanford Grad. School of Business
Background: Summit Partners; VP of Growth, CreativeLive; VP of Growth, Kiwi; Product Manager, Amazon
H. DuBose Montgomery, Founder/Partner Emeritus
e-mail: dubose@menlovc.com

Education: MIT; Harvard Business School
Background: Bell Labs
Matt Murphy, Partner
e-mail: matt@menlovc.com
Education: Tufts University; Stanford Graduate School of Business
Background: Kleiner Perkins Caufield & Byers
Steve Sloane, Partner
e-mail: steve@menlovc.com
Education: Princeton University
Background: Oliver Wyman; Insight Venture Partners
Tyler Sosin, Partner
e-mail: tyler@menlovc.com
Education: Stanford University
Background: Accel Partners
Jordan Ormont, Talent Partner
e-mail: jordan@menlovc.com
Education: Bloomsburg University
Background: Century Associates; Howard Fischer Associates; Kleiner Perkins Caufield & Byers
Grace Ge, Principal
e-mail: grace@menlovc.com
Education: BA, Rice University
Background: Associate, RRE Ventures; Consultant, Accenture
Kirsten A. Mello, Chief Financial Officer
Education: Santa Clara University
Background: Ernst and Young
Croom Beatty, Partner
Education: BA, History, Princeton University
Background: Payoneer; Susquehanna Growth Equity
Naomi Pilosof, Partner
e-mail: naomi@menlovc.com
Education: BSc, Industrial Engineering, Northwestern University; MBA, Stanford University Graduate School of Business
Background: Vice President of Growth, Invoice2go; Product Lead, Evernote

---

1204 MENTOR CAPITAL PARTNERS LTD
PO Box 560
Yardley, PA 19067

Phone: 215-736-8882 Fax: 215-736-8882
e-mail: sager@mentorcapitalpartners.com
web: www.mentorcapitalpartners.com

Mission Statement: Engaging with management in a leadership role by leveraging operations to create sustaining value.

Fund Size: $50 million
Founded: 1994
Investment Criteria: Early Stage, Mezzanine Expansion, Leveraged Transactions
Industry Group Preference: Business Products & Services, Distribution, Financial Services, Healthcare, Industrial Technology, Information Technology
Portfolio Companies: Collect America, CoreCare Systems, JADE Equipment Corporation, KNF Corporation, Neoware Systems, North America Cable Equipment, PeerView, Veltek Associates

Key Executives:
Edward F Sager Jr, Co-Founder/President
215-736-8882
Fax: 215-736-8882
Education: BS, Mechanical Engineering, Lafayette College; MBA, Finance & Marketing, New York University Graduate School of Business
Background: VP, Sprout Group; Officer, CoreStates/First Pennsylvania Bank; Westinghouse Electric Corporation; Duriron Company; Colgate-Palmolive Company

Venture Capital & Private Equity Firms / Domestic Firms

1205 MERCATO PARTNERS
2750 E. Cottonwood Pkwy.
Suite 500
Cottonwood Heights, UT 84121
Phone: 801-220-0055 Fax: 801-220-0056
e-mail: info@mercatopartners.com
web: www.mercatopartners.com

Mission Statement: Mercato invests growth capital and brings world-class sales and marketing execution to emerging technology companies.
Investment Criteria: Later Stage, Growth Stage
Industry Group Preference: Technology, Consumer
Portfolio Companies: Alliance Health, Altitude Digital, Central Logic, Control4, CradlePoint, Cymphonix, Domo, Ephesoft, Fusio-Io, Gailileo Processing, Goal Zero, MediConnect Global, ObservePoint, Primary Data, SaltStack, Skullcandy, Sphero, Stance, SteelHouse, Untangle, upwell, Venafi

Key Executives:
Greg Warnock, Managing Director
Education: PhD, Entrepreneurship & Venture Finance, University of Utah
Background: Co-Founder, vSpring Capital
Directorships: Altitude Digital, Cymphonix, DOMO, Skullcandy, Stance
Ryan Sanders, Director
Education: BS, Brigham Young University; MBA, University of Texas
Background: Escalate Capital Partners
Directorships: ObservePoint, Galileo, Central Logic, Altitude Digital
Joe Kaiser, Director
Education: BSBA, Saint Louis University; MBA, Kellogg School of Management
Background: Director of Capital Markets, Vivint Solar; Blackstone Group; Analyst, A.G. Edwards & Sons

1206 MERCK GLOBAL HEALTH INNOVATION FUND
One Merck Dr.
Whitehouse Station, NJ 08889
web: merckghifund.com

Mission Statement: To identify new business models and adjacency opportunities in healthcare.
Fund Size: $125 million
Founded: 2011
Industry Group Preference: Healthcare, Diagnostics
Portfolio Companies: AdvanDx, AsuraGen, ClearDATA Networks, Cleveland HeartLab, Daktari, EHealth Technologies, ElectroCore, GenomeDx, Healthsnese, Humedica, Liaison, MedCPU, Medivo, PatientSafe Solutions, Preventice, Prophecy, Remedy Informatics, TelerX, VirtualScopics, WellDoc

Key Executives:
Bill Taranto, President & General Partner
Education: BBA, St. Bonaventure University
Background: Johnson & Johnson
David Rubin, Managing Director
Education: BA, Biology, Binghamton University; PhD, Molecular Biology, Temple University
Background: CEO, Cognia Corporation
Dave Stevenson, Managing Director
Education: BA, Washington University; MBA, Vanderbilt University
Background: Sanofi-Aventis; Ernst & Young
Joe Volpe, Managing Director
Education: BS, University of South Florida
Background: J&J Corporate Innovations
Joel Krikston, Managing Director
Education: BA, Fairfield University; MBA, NYU Stern School of Business
Background: Johnson & Johnson Development Corporation; JP Morgan

1207 MERCURY FUND
3737 Buffalo Speedway
Suite 1750
Houston, TX 77098
Phone: 713-715-6820
e-mail: info@mercuryfund.com
web: www.mercuryfund.com

Mission Statement: Mercury Fund is a seed-stage venture capital firm that makes equity investments in compelling and novel software and science-based startup opportunities. Mercury partners with extraordinary entrepreneurs to build globally competitive businesses, focusing on technology innovation originating in the U.S. Midcontinent. Our firm has a particular interest in startups associated with seed accelerators, incubators and universities. We frequently invest prior to the formation of a business plan or complete management team.
Geographic Preference: United States
Founded: 2005
Average Investment: $50,000 - $1.5 million
Investment Criteria: Seed-Stage, Early-Stage
Industry Group Preference: Software, Digital Media & Marketing, Mobile, Internet, SaaS, Cloud Computing, Life Sciences
Portfolio Companies: Ambiq Micro, Ambyint, Apto, Benson Hill Biosystems, BlackThorn Therapeutics, Datical, Deep Imaging, DNAtrix Therapeutics, GameSalad, Graylog, Koupon, Label Insight, Lisnr, Mobify, Optimizely, PactSafe, Resonant, ShareThis, Sight Machine, Sinopsys Surgical, Swift Biosciences, TrackX, Trendkite, Vistarmedia

Other Locations:
303 Detroit St.
Suite 105
Ann Arbor, MI 48104

106 E 6th Street
Suite 900
Austin, TX 78701

Key Executives:
Blair Garrou, Managing Director
Education: BS, Management, Washington & Lee University
Background: CEO, Intermat; Principal, Genesis Park
Directorships: Alert Logic, GameSalad, Graphicly, Koupon Media, ShareThis
Dan Watkins, Venture Partner
Education: BS, Materials Science, Engineering, Rice University; MS, PhD, Materials Science, Engineering, Carnegie Mellon University
Background: Founder & Managing Partner, A3 Associates; Co-Founder, Nanospectra Biosciences
Directorships: Deep Imaging, DNAtrix, GlycosBio, Illumitex
Aziz Gilani, Managing Director
Education: BBA, University of Texas; MBA, Kellogg School of Management
Background: Senior Enagagement Leader, Infosys Consulting; ABB Performance Services
Directorships: Black Locus, Datical, Epic Playground, GameSalad, Infochimps, Koupon Media, ShareThis
Adrian Fortino, Managing Director
Education: BSE, Mechanical Engineering, University of Michigan; MBA, Ross School of Business, University of Michigan
Background: Managing Director, Detroit Innovate; Managing Director, First Step Fund
Directorships: Ambiq Micro, Ambyint, Benson Hill, Lisnr, Sight Machine

Venture Capital & Private Equity Firms / Domestic Firms

1208 MERIDA CAPITAL PARTNERS
641 Lexington Avenue
18th Floor
New York, NY 10022

e-mail: info@meridacap.com
web: www.meridacap.com

Mission Statement: Invests in several aspects of the cannabis industry, including cultivation technology, products and services associated with cannabis as a agriculture product, medicinal cannabis, and recreational consumer products.

Founded: 2009
Industry Group Preference: Cannabis
Portfolio Companies: Grow Generation, Canndescent, Kush Bottles, Lumigrow, Manna Molecular Science LLC, Mainstem, New Frontier Data, Simplifya, Steep Hill, Valley Agriceuticals

Key Executives:
   Mitch Baruchowitz, Managing Partner
   Education: BA, History, Brandeis University; JD, Boston University School of Law
   Background: Managing Director, Boo Trade; Attorney, Incloode; CCO, MarketAxess; Corp. counsel, Axiom Legal; Deputy General Counsel, Pali Capital; Sr. Managing Director, ACGM Inc.; Sr. Managing Director, Cavu Securities
   Kevin Gibbs, Partner
   Education: Old Dominion University
   Background: Palace Investment Company; Principal, Grow West
   David Goldburg, Partner
   Education: BA, History, Brown University
   Background: M&A Analyst, First Boston Corp.; Portfolio Manager, Oak Hill Advisors; Manager, Morgan Stanley; Manager, Bear Steams; Managing Director, Goldman Sachs
   Peter Rosenberg, Partner
   Education: BBA, University of Colorado Boulder
   Background: Director, Salomon Brothers; Managing Director, Barrington Associates; Managing Director, Wells Fargo Securities; Managing Director, Duff & Phelps
   Jeff Monat, Partner
   Education: University Of Pennsylvania; Wharton School
   Background: Analyst, Goldman Sachs; Sr. Analyst, Rockbay Capital; Sr. Analyst, Seven Locks Capital; Investment Professional, Sage Rock Capital
   Directorships: Steep Hill
   Daisy Mellet, Partner
   Education: BA, International Relations, St. Joseph's University; MA, New School for Social Research
   Background: Sr. Guide, Venture Europe GmbH; Operations Associate, FrontPoint Partners; Client Advisory Associate, Massif Partners; Operations Analyst/Investor Relations Manager, Seawolf Capital
   Howard Glynn, Director of Investor Relations
   Education: Tulane University
   Background: Account Manager, Sony Signatures; OTC Trader, Cowen & Co.; Equity Sales Trading, Pali Capital; Sr. VP Institutional Sales Trading, Maxim Group; VP, Business Development, The Araca Group; Managing Director, Managing Director, Connecticut Family Office Association
   Robert Swartz, Director of Relationship Management
   Education: BS, Finance/Investment Management, Duquesne University; MS, Accounting, Saint Vincent College
   Background: Officer & Securities Trader, PNC; VP/Investment Advisor, PNC; VP/Portfolio Advisor, FNB Corp.
   Steven Ritterbush, Operating Partner
   Education: BS, Engineering/BA, Political Science, Union College; MS, Oceanography, University of Hawaii; MA, Law & Diplomacy, Fletcher School Of Law and Diplomacy, Tufts University; PhD, International Economics, Harvard University
   Background: Founder/Managing Partner, Fairfax Partners; Founder, HealthASPex Inc.; Founder, APACHE Medical Systems Inc.

1209 MERIDIAN MANAGEMENT GROUP
826 E Baltimore Street
Baltimore, MD 21202

Phone: 410-333-2548 Fax: 410-333-2552
web: mmgcapitalgroup.com

Mission Statement: Professional asset manager for economic development and private equity funds.

Geographic Preference: Mid-Atlantic
Fund Size: $75 million
Average Investment: $1 million
Minimum Investment: $500,000
Investment Criteria: First-Stage, Second-Stage, Mezzanine
Industry Group Preference: Computer Related, Healthcare, Communications
Portfolio Companies: EEC Incorporated, EZCertify.com, MidAtlantic Broadband, Odyssey Technologies, Stella May Contracting, The Great Gourmet

Key Executives:
   Stanley W Tucker, President/CEO/Co-Founder
   Education: BA, Science, Morgan State University; MA, Science, Carnegie-Mellon University
   Background: Executive Director, Maryland Small Business Development Financing Authority; Vice President, Park Heights Development Corporation; Credit Analyst, The Equitable Trust Company
   R Randy Croxton, Senior VP/Chief Information Officer
   Education: BS, Morgan State University
   Background: VP, Developing Systems Limited; Baltimore Economic Development Corporation
   Timothy L Smoot, Senior VP/CFO
   Education: BS, Morgan State University
   Background: Deputy Director, Maryland Small Business Development Financing Authority
   Anthony L Williams, VP Senior Investment Officer
   Education: BA, University of California
   Background: Capital Fund; Syndicated Communications; Fulcrum Venture Capital Corporation

1210 MERIT CAPITAL PARTNERS
303 West Madison Street
Suite 2100
Chicago, IL 60606

Phone: 312-592-6111 Fax: 312-592-6112
e-mail: mcp@meritcapital.com
web: www.meritcapital.com

Mission Statement: Formerly William Blair Mezzanine Capital Partners, Merit Capital invests alongside management and shareholders to effect a change in company's ownership structure, to provide capital for growth or acquisitions, or to sponsor and provide capital to effect a buyout of a business.

Geographic Preference: United States
Fund Size: $612 million
Founded: 1993
Average Investment: $15 million - 30 million
Minimum Investment: $15 million
Investment Criteria: Middle-market companies with consistent earning and healthy cash flow
Industry Group Preference: Manufacturing, Distribution, Business to Business, Logistics
Portfolio Companies: Active Minerals International, Advanced H2O, Advantaged Sintered Metals & Contact, Alliance, Bakewise Brands, B.E.T. - er Mix, Bluegrass Dairy and Food, Carex Health Brands, Carter-Waters, Choice Brands Adhesives, Cobra Waire & Cable, Crown Products & Services, Design Space, Digney York Associates, Dr. Comfort, E-Conolight, Engendren Corporation, Ferrara Fire Apparatus, Flunt Industries, Gartner, Glunt Industries, Green Creative, Icon Identity Solutions, Identity Group Holdings

Venture Capital & Private Equity Firms / Domestic Firms

Corporation, ISI Detention Contracting Group, Kinex Medical Company, Kinex R&M Rehabilitation, Knights Apparel, Manistique Papers, Manitowoc Tool & Machining, Nedway Air Ambulance, Midwest Iron & Metals, Midwestern Manufacturing Company, Monarch Industries Limited, MTI International, Nester Hosiery, PVI Industries, Reliant Home Health, Rose Paving, RSA Engineered Products, Sales Performance International, Skyline Windows, Slocum Adhesives, Steele Solutions, Structural and Steel Products, TGR Industrial Services, U.S. Minerals, Versatile Processing Group, VTI Instruments

Key Executives:
Thomas F Campion, Managing Director
Education: BBA, Accountancy, St. Norbert College; MBA, University of Wisconsin, Madison
Background: Director, Prudential Asset Management Asia; Vice President, Prudential Capital Corporation
Directorships: MTI International, The Plastics Group, Active Minerals International, Ferrara Fire Apparatus, Bluegrass Dairy and Food, U.S. Minerals, Crown Products & Services, Engendren
David M Jones, Managing Director
Education: BBA, University of Notre Dame; MBA, University of Chicago
Background: Senior Consultant, Peterson Consulting
Timothy J MacKenzie, Managing Director
Education: BA, Northwestern University; MBA, University of Illinois
Background: SVP, Fiduciary Capital; Prudential Capital Corporation
Directorships: Digney York, Skyline Windows, Alden Industries, RSA Engineered Products, Structural and Steel Products
Daniel E Pansing, Managing Director
Education: BS, Political Science, Miami University, Ohio; MBA, Anderson School, UCLA
Background: First National Bank of Omaha; LaSalle Bank
Directorships: Knights Apparel, Skyline Windows, Monarch Industries Limited
Terrance M Shipp, Managing Director
Education: BS, University of Colorado; MBA, Kellogg School of Management, Northwestern University
Background: Partner, LaSalle Capital Group; Prudential Capital Corporation
Directorships: MTI International, The Plastics Group, Bakewise Brands, Versatile Processing Group, Carex Health Brands
Marc J Walfish, Managing Director
Education: BS, Business Administration, MBA, Boston University
Background: Prudential Insurance Company of America; SVP, Prudential Capital Corporation
Directorships: AAR Corporatin, B.E.T.-er Mix, VTI Instruments, Bakewise Brands, WeCare
Evan R Gallinson, Managing Director
Education: BBA, University of Michigan; MBA, Northwestern University Kellogg School of Management
Background: M&A Group, BMO Capital; Corporate Finance, William Blair & Company
Directorships: Digney York, Glunt Industries, RSA Engineered Products
Benjamin W Yarborough, Managing Director
Education: BA, Economics, University of Pennsylvania; MBA, University of Chicago Graduate School of Business
Background: Consultant, Marakon Associates
Directorships: Ferrara Fire Apparatus, Carex Health Brands, Knights Apparel, WeCare, Monarch Industries, Structural and Steel Products

1211 MERIT ENERGY COMPANY
13727 Noel Road
Suite 1200
Tower 2
Dallas, TX 75240

Phone: 972-701-8377 Fax: 972-960-1252
e-mail: info@meritenergy.com
web: www.meritenergy.com

Mission Statement: A private firm specializing in direct investments in mature oil and gas assets. Merit acquires, operates and develops producing oil and gas properties on behalf of equity-based, reinvestment oriented limited partnerships.

Geographic Preference: United States, Canada, Gulf of Mexico
Fund Size: $4 billion
Founded: 1989
Average Investment: $10 million
Minimum Investment: $5 million
Industry Group Preference: Industrial Equipment, Energy, Oil & Gas

1212 MERITAGE FUNDS
1530 Blake Street
Suite 200
Denver, CO 80202

Phone: 303-352-2040 Fax: 303-352-2050
e-mail: info@meritagefunds.com
web: meritagefunds.com

Mission Statement: Meritage is a Denver-based manager of private investment funds. Contributes both capital and expertise to every investment, working as a partner with entrepreneurs to accelerate the growth of their businesses.

Geographic Preference: U.S.
Fund Size: $600 million
Founded: 1998
Average Investment: $500K
Minimum Investment: $100K
Investment Criteria: Growth Equity
Industry Group Preference: Technology-Enabled Services
Portfolio Companies: Brooks Fiber Properties Inc., Cencom Cable, Completel, Conner Perphirals, Crown Castle International, Crisp Media, Datavail, Digital Fortress, Diveo, Newpath Network, Edgeconnex, Faction, Masergy, McCaw Cellular, P2Binvestor, Nuvox, Smartsky, Verio

Key Executives:
David Solomon, Founder/Managing Director
Background: Executive Chairman, NuVox; CFO, Brooks Fiber Properties; KPMG
Directorships: NuVox

1213 MERITECH CAPITAL PARTNERS
245 Lytton Avenue
Suite 125
Palo Alto, CA 94301

Phone: 650-475-2200
e-mail: info@meritechcapital.com
web: www.meritechcapital.com

Mission Statement: Meritech is a late-stage venture capital firm dedicated to building technology companies of lasting value.

Geographic Preference: United States
Fund Size: $2.6 billion
Founded: 1999
Average Investment: $25 million
Minimum Investment: $10 million
Investment Criteria: Late Stage, Buy-outs, Spin-offs
Industry Group Preference: Information Technology, Communications, Enterprise Software, Internet Technology, Semiconductors, Infrastructure, Consumer Internet, Digital

Venture Capital & Private Equity Firms / Domestic Firms

Media & Marketing, Wireless Technologies, SaaS, Medical Devices
Portfolio Companies: 10X Genomics, 2Wire, Acclarent, Alteryx, Amplitude, Anaplan, Ancestry, Ariosa Diagnostics, Auth0, BigFix, Box, Braze, Broadsoft, Bromium, CAN Capital, Cloudera, CloudHealth Technologies, CloudPassage, Cornerstone OnDemand, Coupa, Danger, DataDog, Datastax, DealerSocket, Duo, Evernote, ExtraHop, Facebook, Force10, ForeScout, Forgerock, Fortinet, Fusion-io, Glaukos, Glint, GoDundMe, Greenplum, GuideSpark, Icertis Applied, iMPERVA, Ionic, Kinetica, Lifesize, Looker, Lucid, Lynda.com, Model N, MuleSoft, Netezza, NetSuite, Nextdoor, Niantic, Panzura, Pendo, Pop Cap, Presidio, Proofpoint, Prosper, Rally Software, Riverbed, Roblox, Ruckus Wireless, Salesforce, Servicemax, Simplivity, Snapchat, Sonedo, Sourcefire, Spring by Pivetal, Tableau Software, Tele Atlas, Tensilica, UiPath, Veracode, Wonga.com, Yammer, Yapstone, Zipcar, Zulily

Key Executives:
Paul Madera, Co-Founder & Partner
Education: MBA, Stanford Graduate School of Business; BS, US Air Force Academy
Background: Managing Director, Montgomery Securities; Morgan Stanley; US Air Force Pilot/Congressional Liaison to Senate/House Armed Services Committees
Robert Ward, Co-Founder & Partner
Education: BA, Williams College; MS, MIT
Background: VP/Private Equity Placement Group, Montgomery Securities; Corporate Finance Department, Smith Barney
George Bischof, Partner
Education: BA, Stanford University; MBA, Kellogg School of Management, Northwestern University
Background: General Partner, Focus Ventures; Robertson Stephens
Joel Backman, Chief Operating Officer
Education: BS, Business Administration, University of Arizona
Background: Senior Director of Business Development, IPWireless; Co-Founder, Ultimate Inc.; Sunterra Corporation
Craig Sherman, Partner
Education: Princeton University
Background: CEO, Gaia Interactive; Entrepreneur-in-Residence, Benchmark Capital; COO, Ancestry.com; American International Group; CEO, Cendant Japan

1214 MERITURN PARTNERS
234 Fayetteville Street
6th Floor
Raleigh, NC 27601

Phone: 919-821-1550
web: www.meriturn.com

Mission Statement: Meriturn invests in control-oriented stakes in middle-market companies experiencing financial or operational challenges. In addition, we pursue minority investments in undercapitalized financial institutions. Our mission is to enhance value for our investors and portfolio companies by utilizing our experience, relationships, and resources to deliver the best solutions to complex middle-market corporate problems.
Investment Criteria: Restructurings, Turnarounds, Special Situations, Chapter 11 Bankruptcy, 363 Asset Purchases, Stalking Horse Bidder, Reorganizations, Out-of-Court Restructurings, Distressed Debt Purchases
Industry Group Preference: Agriculture, Chemicals, Consumer Products, Distribution, Energy, Financial Services, Forestry, Mining, Life Sciences, Manufacturing, Metals, Packaging, Paper, Processing, Publishing
Portfolio Companies: Barnacle Seafood, Captain Ed's Lobster Trap, Cudahy Tanning Co., Dunn Paper, Irving Tanning, Johnston Fabrics & Finishing, Madvapes, Prime Leather, SSI, Valentine Paper, Vermont Smoke & Cure

Other Locations:
One Montgomery Street
Suite 2500
San Francisco, CA 94104
Phone: 415-595-5000

Key Executives:
Lee C Hansen, Partner
e-mail: lee@meriturn.com
Education: BS, Business Administration, Bucknell University; MBA, J.L. Kellogg School, Northwestern University
Background: President, Stonepath Group; SVP Strategy & Corporate Development, Bank of America
Mark W Kehaya, Partner
e-mail: mark@meriturn.com
Education: MA, Economics, Cambridge University; Fuqua School, Duke University
Background: President, Eturn Communications; Stanard Commercial Corporation
Directorships: Standard Commerical Corporation

1215 MERITUS VENTURES
362 Old Whitley Road
PO Box 1738
London, KY 40743-1738

Phone: 606-864-5175 Fax: 606-864-5194
e-mail: questions@meritusventures.com
web: www.meritusventures.com

Mission Statement: To generate market-rate returns for its investors while promoting shared and sustainable business growth and wealth creation throughout its target region.
Geographic Preference: Rural Regions of Southern & Central Appalachia
Fund Size: $36.4 million
Founded: 2002
Average Investment: $250,000 - $2.5 million
Investment Criteria: Expansion-Stage
Industry Group Preference: Manufacturing, Technology, Software
Portfolio Companies: Arkansas Automatic Sprinklers, Gridsmart Technologies, Pinnacle Medical Solutions, SinglePipe Communications, Superior Fabrication, Virtulytix, Wazoo Sports, Zipit

Other Locations:
10426 Jackson Oaks Way
Suite 103
Knoxville, TN 37922
Phone: 865-220-1715 Fax: 865-220-1711

Key Executives:
Ray Moncrief, Fund Manager
Background: President, Eclipse Management
Grady Vanderhoofven, Fund Manager
Background: Executive Vice President, Eclipse Management

1216 MERIWETHER CAPITAL CORPORATION
30 Rockefeller Plaza
Room 5600
New York, NY 10112

Phone: 212-649-5890 Fax: 212-649-5615
web: www.meriwethercapital.net

Mission Statement: Providing equity and desire to be the controlling shareholder in mergers and acquisitions.
Geographic Preference: Eastern United States
Founded: 1976
Average Investment: $4 million
Minimum Investment: $1,000,000
Investment Criteria: Second Stage, LBO, MBO, Middle-Market companies, Revenues ranging from $10-$100 million
Industry Group Preference: Manufacturing, Distribution

Venture Capital & Private Equity Firms / Domestic Firms

Portfolio Companies: Custom Wholesale Floors, Segrest, Tonka Equipment Company, Wood Pro

Key Executives:
  Robert W Petit, Partner
  e-mail: rpetit@meriwethercap.com
  Education: Boston College; MBA, Wharton School of the University of Pennsylvania
  Background: Dyson-Kissner-Moran Corporation; President/CFO, Furigas International
  George D O'Neill, Founder
  Education: Harvard University
  Background: Train-Cabot & Associates; Equity Corporation; Chase Manhattan Bank

1217 MERLIN NEXUS
424 West 33rd Street
Suite 330
New York, NY 10001

web: www.merlinnexus.com

Mission Statement: Merlin Nexus invests globally in private and public healthcare companies, and is among the most successful healthcare investment companies in the US.

Geographic Preference: Worldwide
Fund Size: $200 million
Founded: 2001
Investment Criteria: Late-Stage Private Companies, Private Investments in Public Equity (PIPEs), Long-Term Open Market Investments
Industry Group Preference: Healthcare, Life Sciences

Key Executives:
  Dominique Semon, Chief Investment Officer
  Education: Master in Economics, New York University; License in Science, Molecular Biology, University of Neuchatel, Switzerland; CFA
  Background: Head, Healthcare Private Capital Markets Group, Robertson Stephens; Portfolio Manager, New York Life; Biotechnology Research Analyst, Citibank; Head of Sequencing Lab, Biogen
  Alberto Bianchinotti, Chief Financial Officer
  Education: BS, Accounting, Binghamton University; CPA
  Background: Healthcare Analyst, Merlin BioMed Group; Audit & Tax Supervisor, Anchin Block & Anchin LLP

1218 MERRILL LYNCH VENTURE CAPITAL
4 World Financial Center
250 Vesey Street
New York, NY 10080

web: www.ml.com

Mission Statement: Provides capital markets services, investment banking and advisory services, wealth management, asset management, insurance, banking and related products and services on a global basis. Merrill Lynch has over 14,000 advisors in offices across the United States and internationally.

Geographic Preference: Global
Fund Size: $1.1 billion
Founded: 1914
Industry Group Preference: Diversified

1219 MERUS CAPITAL
505 Hamilton Avenue
Suite 315
Palo Alto, CA 94301

e-mail: info@meruscap.com
web: www.meruscap.com

Mission Statement: We partner with founders who have the passion and ability to build lasting, dynamic businesses. Merus invests in seed and Series A stage iEnterprise startups in Silicon Valley. Our typical investment ranges from $200K to $2.5M. As a company's first institutional investor, we play an active role and believe in a deeply collaborative approach to business-building.

Geographic Preference: Silicon Valley
Average Investment: $200,000 - $2.5 million
Investment Criteria: Seed-Stage, Series A
Industry Group Preference: Software
Portfolio Companies: AdRoll, Alice, Alucid Technologies, Amplitude, Apptimize, Arch, Aromyx, Authentic8, Chai Labs, Corona Labs, Fixed, Indio, IOTurbine, Iterable, Kamcord, Modewalk, Natero, Nuvoloso, Omnity, Omny, Outward, Parabola, Periscope, Runa, SensorTower, Shelter Luv, Silexica, Splashtop, Symphony, TerrAvion, Womply, Xcalar

Key Executives:
  Sean Dempsey, Managing Partner
  Education: Claremont McKenna College
  Background: Principal, Corporate Development, Google; Corporate Development, Microsoft; M&A, Deutsche Morgan Grenfel
  Peter Hsing, Managing Partner
  Education: BS, Industrial Engineering, Columbia University; MBA, Wharton School
  Background: Managing Director, Corporate Strategy Group, Microsoft; Associate, JP Morgan Telecom
  Directorships: Authentic8
  Salman Ullah, Managing Partner
  Education: BS, Physics, University of Oxford; PhD, Theoretical Physics, Stanford University
  Background: Vice President, Corporate Development, Google; General Manager, Corporate Strategy, Microsoft
  Directorships: Corona Labs, Runa

1220 MESA CAPITAL PARTNERS
3060 Peachtree Road, NW
Suite 970
Atlanta, GA 30305

Phone: 678-904-3223 Fax: 678-904-3226
web: www.mesacp.com

Mission Statement: Mesa Capital Partners invests in high-potential small businesses in industries and geographic areas underserved by other capital providers.

Founded: 2003
Average Investment: $500,000 - $2 million
Investment Criteria: Early-Stage
Industry Group Preference: Manufacturing, Services
Portfolio Companies: 555 Mansell, 860 South, 900 Dwell, 1322 North, Ansley Commons, Ansley at Roberts Lake, Bentley Place, Canopy at Belford Park, Cobblestone Fayette, Crestmark, Edgemont, Legacy at Sandhill, Legacy Ridge, Liv Riverale, Majestic Oaks, Montage Embry Hills, Palmetto Exchange, Riverstone, Sea Island Lake Cottages, Skyland Exchange, Spring Lake, Terramar, The Ace, The Gallery, The Mill at New Holland, The Overlook, The Paramont, The Phoenix at James Creek, The Retreat at Grand Lake, Town Place, Vista Ridge

Key Executives:
  Thomas D. Bell, Jr., Chairman
  e-mail: tbell@mesacp.com
  Background: Cousins Properties
  Directorships: Regal Entertainment Group, AGL Resources, Norfolk Southern Corporation, Emory University, Grady Memorial Hospital Corporation, Metro Atlanta Chamber of Commerce
  Jeff S Tucker, Managing Partner
  e-mail: jtucker@mesacp.com
  Background: Land South Development
  Zach E Schaumburg, Partner
  Education: Bachelors Journalism & Advertising, University of Colorado; Masters Massachusetts Institute of Technology
  Background: Vice President, J. Tucker Development Partners

1221 MESA GLOBAL
85 Fifth Avenue
Sixth Floor
New York, NY 10003

Phone: 212-792-3950

Mission Statement: Offers full-service investment banking capabilities and strategic advisory services to an international roster of clients

Fund Size: $4.3 billion
Industry Group Preference: Digital Media & Marketing

1222 MESA VERDE PARTNERS
4225 Executive Square
Suite 600
La Jolla, CA 92037

Phone: 619-289-7428
e-mail: info@mesaverdevp.com
web: www.mesaverdevp.com

Mission Statement: To invest in a diversified portfolio of early-stage biotechnology and medical technology companies in the Southwest.

Geographic Preference: Southwestern United States
Fund Size: $40 million
Founded: 2006
Average Investment: $1.5 million
Minimum Investment: $250,000
Investment Criteria: Seed, Startup, Early
Industry Group Preference: Life Sciences, Drug Development, Medical Devices, Diagnostics, Healthcare Information Technology
Portfolio Companies: Biomatrica, Elevation Pharma, Exagen Diagnostics, Independa, Lineagen, Mediapacs, Retrosense, Satiogen, Tokalas

Key Executives:
Carey Ng, Managing Director
Education: MBA, Rady School, UCSD; PhD, UCLA
Background: Abbott Laboratories
Directorships: Satiogen Pharmaceuticals, Medipacs, Biomatrica, Exagen Diagnostics, Tokalas, Independa, Retrosense Therapeutics
Fred A Middleton, Managing Director
Education: BS, MIT; MBA, Harvard Business School
Background: CFO, Genentech; Morgan Stanley Ventures; Sanderling; McKinsey & Co.

1223 MESA+
85 Fifth Avenue
6th Floor
New York, NY 10003

Phone: 212-792-3950
e-mail: sayhi@mesa.vc
web: www.mesa.vc

Mission Statement: MESA+ is an early stage venture fund focused on e-commerce, advertising technology and digital content. We co-invest between $50,000 and $250,000 in Seed and Series A rounds alongside established early stage venture firms (we never lead a financing). We concentrate on the New York digital media market but are able to invest in companies headquartered in other cities across the country and around the world.

Geographic Preference: New York
Investment Criteria: Seed-Stage, Series A
Industry Group Preference: Digital Media & Marketing, E-Commerce & Manufacturing, Advertising
Portfolio Companies: Abra, Basno, BetterDoctor, Bezar, BitVault, Bread, Button, Carmera, Clique Media Group, Codefights, Consumr, Culinary Agents, DJZ, EasyPost, Emissary, FEM, FitStar, Fuisz Media, Gem, Grand st., Hopscotch, Hungry Root, InVenture, Iodine, Keychain Logistics, KISI, MakersKit, Moonfrye, Nativo, Navdy, Panjo, Parachute, Pickie, Plan Vanilla, QuizUp, Republic Project, Ringly, Rinse, Seedling, Shake, Skift, Snowshoe, Soma, The Noun Project, Triage, TripleLift, Tution.io, Vrideo, Wedgies, Who What Wear, Yoshirt, Zillabyte

Key Executives:
Mark Patricof, Special Advisor
Education: BA, Emory University
Background: Co-Founder/CEO, Creative Arts Agency
Directorships: Rockwell Group, New York Cruise Lines, New Heights
Andrew Montgomery, Managing Partner
Education: BA, Georgetown University
Background: Analyst, Merrill Lynch; Co-Founder, New York Code & Design Academy
Directorships: Nonprofit Management Systems

1224 METAFUND
2545 S Kelly Avenue
Edmond, OK 73013

Phone: 405-949-0001 Fax: 405-949-9005
e-mail: info@metafund.org
web: www.metafund.org

Mission Statement: MetaFund is engaged in private equity, tax credits, credit enhancement, and portfolios of mortgage loans for Habitat for Humanity. Its private equity investments are targeted towards businesses with the goal of creating financial, social and environmental returns on investment.

Geographic Preference: Oklahoma, Arizona, Nebraska, Kansas, Colorado
Founded: 1999
Portfolio Companies: Custom Composites, Geophysical Research Company, Ideal Crane

Key Executives:
A. Thomas Loy, Founder, Chair & CEO
e-mail: tloy@metafund.org
Education: BA, Master of Liberal Studies, University of Oklahoma
Background: Oklahoma City University; U.S. Treasury Department; KPMG
Directorships: First Bethany Bank, Community Development Venture Capital Alliance
Blake Trippet, President
e-mail: btrippet@metafund.org
Education: University of Oklahoma
Background: Goldman Sachs

1225 METAPOINT PARTNERS
Three Centennial Drive
Peabody, MA 01960-7906

Phone: 978-531-1398
web: www.metapoint.com

Mission Statement: Focused primarily on acquiring new platform or stand-alone portfolio companies.

Geographic Preference: United States, Canada
Fund Size: $25 million
Founded: 1988
Average Investment: $2.4 million
Minimum Investment: $1.5 million
Investment Criteria: $8-$30 million in revenues, $750m in EBITDA, Industrial/Commercial; Low-Medium Tech products, Leadership In Niche Markets, Differentiated, Management Continuity preferred
Industry Group Preference: Industrial Equipment, Manufacturing
Portfolio Companies: Kochek, Nickson Industries, Northeastern Nonwovens, Nylon Corporation of America, Spaulding Composites, Stone Panels

Key Executives:
Keith C Shaughnessy, Chairman/CEO
978-531-4444
e-mail: keith@metapoint.com
Education: BS, Management, Boston College
Background: VP, Bank of Boston

Venture Capital & Private Equity Firms / Domestic Firms

Stuart I Mathews, President
978-531-1398 ext 4
e-mail: stuart@metapoint.com
Education: BA, Political Science, Tufts University
Background: Assistant VP, Bank of Boston

1226 METROPOLITAN PARTNERS GROUP
70 East 55th St.
19th Floor
New York, NY 10022

Phone: 212-561-1250 **Fax:** 212-561-1201
e-mail: info@metpg.com
web: www.metpg.com

Mission Statement: Metropolitan Venture Partners is a private equity investment manager with offices in New York and London. Our experienced team works in partnership with our portfolio companies and takes an active role in helping entrepreneurs create value and build their businesses.

Geographic Preference: United States, United Kingdom
Average Investment: $3 million
Minimum Investment: $500,000
Investment Criteria: Seed, First, Recapitalizations, High Growth companies
Industry Group Preference: Software, Communications, Internet Technology, Technology, Infrastructure

Key Executives:
Paul Lisiak, Managing Partner
Education: BA, Economics, University of Pennsylvania
Background: Lazard Asset Management; Metropolitan Venture Partners
Directorships: Playbox Corp., New Credit America, Next Level Finance Partners
Arvind Krishnamurthy, Managing Director
Education: BA, Harvard College; MBA, Harvard Business School
Background: Principal, Paragon Outcomes; Principal, CAM Capital; Goldman Sachs

1227 MHS CAPITAL
333 Bush Street
Suite 2250
San Francisco, CA 94104

Phone: 415-655-2800
e-mail: info@mhscapital.com
web: www.mhscapital.com

Mission Statement: We are early-stage investors backed by tech entrepreneurs. We work closely with visionary founders building the next-generation of category defining companies.

Investment Criteria: Early-Stage
Industry Group Preference: Advertising, Consumer Products, Digital Media & Marketing, Distribution, E-Commerce & Manufacturing, Education, Energy, Enterprise Software, Financial Services, Marketing, Mobile, SaaS, Social Media
Portfolio Companies: Applifier, Bizible, Bridge, Candex, Combatant Gentlemen, Convertro, CourtTrax, Fonality, GiftCertificates.com, Guidebook, HandShake, HowAboutWe.com, IndieGoGo, Julep, LifeShield Security, Magnify360, Mind Lab, MOAT, Nexleaf Analytics, OPOWER, Out of Milk, Ownza, Platfora, Pulpo Media, ShiftPlanning, Simply Measured, Thumbtack, Udemy, VentureBeat, WeHeartIt

Key Executives:
Mark Sugarman, Founder/Managing Partner
Background: Internet Capital Group, VerticalNet
Directorships: Applifier, Candex, Indegogo, Opower, Pulpo Media, Simply Measured, Thumbtack, Udemy
Vijay Nagappan, Principal
Education: BS, Economics, Wharton School
Background: Evercore Partners, Wired Gamez
Directorships: Simply Measured

1228 MIDATLANTIC FUND
e-mail: info@midatlanticfund.com
web: www.midatlanticfund.com

Mission Statement: The MidAtlantic Fund seeks start-up opportunities that are producing innovative technologies.

Investment Criteria: Seed-Stage, Early-Stage
Industry Group Preference: Mobile Technology, Healthcare, Healthcare Services
Portfolio Companies: 5Medical Marketing, Acton Pharmaceuticals, Axiom CME, HLine Digital Media, Hudson Medical Communications, Performax Physical Therapy, Propel Orthodontics, QED, SNDR, TechDerm, Teladoc, Vertos Medical

Key Executives:
Richard Johnson, Managing Director
Education: BA, New York University; MD, Mount Sinai School of Medicine; Columbia University
Directorships: Propel Orthodontics

1229 MIDDLEBURG CAPITAL DEVELOPMENT
Liberty House
7 South Liberty Street
Middleburg, VA 20117

Phone: 540-687-7134
web: www.mcapd.com

Mission Statement: Middleburg Capital Development is a private equity investment firm. We partner with entrepreneurs, growing businesses, private banking groups, university incubation centers, funds, and other private equity groups. We are involved with new technologies, data and information sectors, the service sectors, core manufacturing and natural resources. Our partners and our Advisory Board members support interest in global opportunities.

Industry Group Preference: Information Technology, Big Data, Consumer Services, Business Products & Services, Manufacturing, Natural Resources
Portfolio Companies: CargoSense, Emu Technology, Horizon Packaging, Horizon Systems, Inovateus Solar, Ionic Liquid Solutions, MyBurger, SCP Ltd., Thermalin Diabetes, Trion Coating, Vagabond

Key Executives:
Timothy F. Sutherland, Chairman/CEO
540-687-7134
e-mail: tfsutherland@mcapd.com
Education: BA, Knox College; MBA, New York University
Background: Founder/Chairman/CEO, Pace Global Energy Services
David Sutherland, President
540-687-7314
e-mail: dsutherland@mcapd.com
Education: BA, MBA, University of Notre Dame
Background: Deputy Director, Operations, Pace Global Energy Services

1230 MIDMARK CAPITAL LP
177 Madison Avenue
Morristown, NJ 07960

Phone: 973-971-9960
web: www.midmarkcapital.com

Mission Statement: Combines financial resources and business capabilities to acquire significant ownership positions and strategic buy-outs in privately and publicly owned middle-market companies with the objective to increase the value of those positions over the long term.

Geographic Preference: United States, Europe, Latin America, Asia
Fund Size: $300 million under management
Founded: 1989
Average Investment: $10 million
Minimum Investment: $5 million

Investment Criteria: Strong management team, businesses which do not involve very high rapidly changing technology, revenues from $20 to $150 million
Industry Group Preference: Manufacturing, Distribution, Service Industries, Retailing, Industrial Services
Portfolio Companies: AVO Carbon Holdings, Avista Oil, Cinedigm Digital Cinema, Fetco Home Decor, General Products, MRI Flexible Packaging, Pediatria, The PromptCare Companies, Strategic Legal Solutions, TCR
Key Executives:
  Denis Newman, Managing Director
  Education: BA, Yale University; MBA, Harvard Business School
  Background: Managing Director, First Boston; President, The Dunmore Group; Financial Officer, International Bank for Reconstruction & Development-World Bank
  Joseph R Robinson, Managing Director
  Education: BA, Cornell University; Wharton School of Finance
  Background: President, CEO Vendex International's Brazilian; Vice President, Lexington Investment Company
  Matthew W Finlay, Managing Director
  Education: BA, Philosophy, Yale University; MBA, Columbia Business School
  Background: Juno Partners; Mille Capital; Southport Partners
  Douglas A Parker, Managing Director
  Education: BA, Electrical Engineering & Economics, Yale University; MBA, Columbia Business School
  Background: Regent Capital Partners LP; Sales, Thomson Financial Services/Truesdell Company
  Larry A Colangelo, Director
  Education: BA, Rowan University; MBA, Xavier University
  Background: President/CEO, SPD Technologies; Executive Positions, RCA/Rockwell Internatioinal

1231 MIDOCEAN PARTNERS
320 Park Avenue
Suite 1600
New York, NY 10022

Phone: 212-497-1407
web: www.midoceanpartners.com

Mission Statement: A private investment firm that specializes in middle market investments in the US and Europe. MidOcean targets control investments with minimum equity contribution of $25 million.

Geographic Preference: United States, Europe
Minimum Investment: $25 million
Industry Group Preference: Business Products & Services, Consumer, Media & Telecommunications, Niche Manufacturing, Industrial Services
Portfolio Companies: Affinity Dental Management, Agilex Fragrances, Alpha Guardian, Allant, BH Cosmetics, Fairway, Florida Food Products, Freshpet, Global Knowledge, Grandpoint, Hanley Wood/Meyers Research, Hunter Fan, Image Skincare, Jones & Frank, KidKraft, LegalShield, Noranco, Nutrabolt, Penton Media, The Planet Group, Questex, South Beach Diet, System One, Travelpro Group, Water Pik
Key Executives:
  Ted Virtue, CEO
  e-mail: tvirtue@midoceanpartners.com
  Education: Middlebury College
  Background: Chief Executive Officer, DB Capital Partners; President, BT Alex Brown Inc; Bankers Trust
  Steve Miller, Chairman
  e-mail: rsmiller@midoceanpartners.com
  Background: Chairman, Delphi Corporation; Federal Mogul; Bethlehem Steel; Waste Management; Morrison Kudson; Ford Motor Company
  Deborah Hodges, Managing Director, Chief Operating Officer
  e-mail: dhodges@midoceanpartners.com
  Education: BA, Princeton University; MBA, Kellogg Graduate School of Mangement
  Background: Chief Operating Officer, DB Capital Partners; Capital Management Group, Bankers Trust
  Andrew Spring, Managing Director, Chief Financial Officer
  e-mail: aspring@midoceanpartners.com
  Education: BS, The Wharton School; JD, Cornell Law School
  Background: Director, DB Capital Partners; Associate, White & Case
  Frank Schiff, Managing Director
  e-mail: fschiff@midoceanpartners.com
  Education: BS, University of Colorado; JD, Cornell Law School
  Background: Managing Director, DB Capital Partners; Partner, White & Case LLP
  Elias Dokas, Managing Director
  e-mail: edokas@midoceanpartners.com
  Education: BA, Economics, Columbia University; MBA, Harvard Business School
  Background: Managing Director, Blackstone Group; Investment Professional, Merrill Lynch Capital Partners

1232 MIDWEST MEZZANINE FUNDS
55 West Monroe Street
Suite 3650
Chicago, IL 60603

Phone: 312-291-7300 **Fax:** 312-345-0665
e-mail: info@mmfcapital.com
web: www.mmfcapital.com

Mission Statement: Since its inception, Midwest Mezzanine has partnered with private equity sponsors, fundless sponsors, and management teams by providing junior capital to U.S. and Canadian companies in the lower-end of the middle-market.

Geographic Preference: United States, Canada
Fund Size: $450 million
Founded: 1992
Average Investment: $15 million
Minimum Investment: $5 million
Investment Criteria: Buyouts, Acquisition, Recapitalizations, Growth Capital
Industry Group Preference: Manufacturing, Distribution, Business Products & Services, Consumer Products, Industrial Services, Food & Beverage, Education
Portfolio Companies: Allied 100 All Island Media, Apex Microtecnology, Driven Performance Brands, Capsa Solutions, Currie Medical, Denion Pharmaceuticals, FB Brands, Fiber Composites, Hughes, Premium Franchise Brands, Kadel's Auto Body, LeadingResponse, Merit Service Solutions, Microdynamics Group, Packaging Concepts & Design, Potter Electric, The RapcoHorizon Company, Sentient Medical Systems, OneTouchPoint, TS3 Technology, Uncle Milton, Vapor Power, Appied Adhesives, Water Co. Holding
Key Executives:
  David A Gezon, Senior Managing Director
  e-mail: dgezon@mmfcapital.com
  Education: MBA, Northwestern University; BS, Miami University
  Background: GE Capital; Kleinwort Benson Limited
  J Allan Kayler, Advisor
  e-mail: jkayler@mmfcapital.com
  Education: BA, DePaul University; MBA, Indiana University
  Background: MNC Capital Corporation, Sherry Lane Partners, Midwest Mezzanine
  Directorships: Hunter's Specialties, Potter Electric Signal, EB Brands
  C Michael Foster, Senior Managing Director
  e-mail: mfoster@mmfcapital.com
  Education: MBA, DePaul University; BS, Georgetown University

Venture Capital & Private Equity Firms / Domestic Firms

Background: Senior VP, LaSalle Bank; VP, Bank of Boston
Paul Kreie, Senior Managing Director
e-mail: pkreie@mmfcapital.com
Education: BS, Finance, Marquette University; MBA, University of Chicago
Background: Longterm Credit Bank of Japan; Heller Financial
Ana M Winters, Managing Director
312-291-7302
e-mail: awinters@mmfcapital.com
Education: BS, Accounting, DePaul University; MBA, University of Chicago Graduate School of Business; CPA
Background: LaSalle Bank; Manager, Ernst & Young

1233 MILESTONE GROWTH FUND
401 Second Avenue South
Suite 1032
Minneapolis, MN 55401-2393

Phone: 612-338-0090
web: www.milestonegrowth.com

Mission Statement: Funds ethnic minority businesses to create wealth for their owners, generate jobs and contribute to improving the community. The goal is a permanent revolving investment fund that provides equity-type financing to facilitate and accelerate the formation of capital in minority-owned businesses.

Geographic Preference: United States
Fund Size: $200 million
Founded: 1990
Average Investment: $500,000
Minimum Investment: $200,000
Investment Criteria: Seed, Startup, Expansion, Minority-owned companies
Industry Group Preference: All Sectors Considered
Portfolio Companies: Armor Security, EMPO Corporation, Latino Communications Network, Manny's Tortas, Martinez Geospatial, Painting by Nakasone, Touching Lives Adult Day Services, Synico

Key Executives:
  Judy Romlin, President/CEO
  Education: University of Minnesota; Venture Capital Institute
  Background: National City Bank; Norwest Bank; Marquette Bank Minneapolis
  Directorships: St. Louis Park Dollars for Schools

1234 MILESTONE PARTNERS
555 East Lancaster Avenue
Suite 500
Radnor, PA 19087

Phone: 610-526-2700 **Fax:** 610-526-2701
web: www.milestonepartners.com

Mission Statement: Provides liquidity to non-management shareholders of family-owned businesses, facilitates the transition of ownership to key managers and capitalizes on growth opportunities while maintaining the legacy of the founding entrepreneurs.

Geographic Preference: United States, Canada
Fund Size: $360 million
Founded: 1995
Average Investment: $5 - $40 million
Minimum Investment: $5 million
Investment Criteria: LBO, MBO, Recapitalizations, Buy-and-Build Strategies
Industry Group Preference: Manufacturing, Distribution, Services
Portfolio Companies: Avure Food Processing, Black Letter Discovery, Blaschak Coal Corporation, Cafe Enterprises, CODi, Dydacomp, EB Brands, eCommission Financial Services, Eliason Corporation, EnterpriseDB, Freestyle Solutions, G5, Global Connection, Good Health Natural Products, H3 Sportgear, Higher Power Nutrition, Image API, Interconnect Devices, Knights Apparel, Learn It Systems, Machine Laboratory, Mariner Finance, Martex Fiber, mTAB, Neutronics, Occasion Brands, Outlook Group, Pancon, PayLink Payment Plans, Precision Partners Holding Company, Quintus Technologies, RedZone Robotics, Safemark Systems, Southern Management Corporation, Stravina, Trans-Trade, United Road Towing, US Auto Sales

Key Executives:
  Scott Warren, Managing Partner
  610-526-2702
  e-mail: swarren@milestonepartners.com
  Education: BS, Finance, University of Virginia
  Background: Managing Director, Philadelphia First Group/Beacon Capital; VP Mergers Aacquisitions, Lehman Brothers; Private Placement, Philadelphia National Bank
  John P Shoemaker, Managing Partner
  610-526-2708
  e-mail: jshoemaker@milestonepartners.com
  Education: BA, University of Pennsylvania; JD, Boston College School of Law
  Background: Managing Director, Internet Capital Group; Managing Director, Mellon Ventures-Philadelphia Office; VP Corporate Development, RAF Industries; Corporate Attorney, Reed Smith Shaw & McClay-Philadelphia; Investment Banker, Morgan Stanley
  David G Proctor, Partner
  610-306-6590
  e-mail: dproctor@milestonepartners.com
  Education: BSc, Economics, Wharton School, University of Pennsylvania; MSE, EMTM Program, University of Pennsylvania
  Background: Senior Vice President, Wind River Holdings; VP, Sales & Marketing, Philadelphia Mixing Solutions
  Adam H Curtin, Partner
  610-526-2711
  e-mail: acurtin@milestonepartners.com
  Education: BS, Finance, Pennsylvania State University
  Background: Analyst, Merrill Lynch
  John J Nowaczyk, Partner & Chief Compliance Officer
  610-526-2712
  e-mail: jnowaczyk@milestonepartners.com
  Education: BA, Harvard College
  Background: Financial Analyst, Kidder Peabody & Co.; Associate, Paine Webber; Legg Manson Wood Walker
  Paul Slaats, Partner
  e-mail: pslaats@milestonepartners.com
  Education: BS, Purdue University; MBA, University of Chicago
  Background: Managing Director, Internet Capital Group; Co-Founder, Spyglass Partners; Associate, Safeguard Scientifics

1235 MILLENIUM TECHNOLOGY VALUE PARTNERS
60 East 42nd St.
New York, NY 10165

Phone: 646-521-7800
e-mail: info@mtvlp.com
web: www.mtvlp.com

Mission Statement: Invests primarily in communications infrastructure, systems, tools and enabling technologies. Currently emphasizing later-stage investments and a range of promising new technologies and businesses with strong revenue growth and customer traction. Ready to commit not only our capital but our time, advice and relationships to build sound, successful businesses.

Fund Size: $1 billion
Founded: 2000
Investment Criteria: Growth Equity, Secondary & Alternative Liquidity, Venture Debt & Permanent Capital

Industry Group Preference: Communications, Networking, Enabling Technology, Infrastructure, Internet, Digital Media & Marketing, Fintech, Software
Portfolio Companies: 1st Virtual Communications, Acronis, Airvana, Agility, Alfresco, Alibaba Group, ArcSight, Art.com, Aventail, Axsun Technologies, BeachMint, BetterCloud, Bigcommerce, Chef, Chegg, Cloudreach, Datapipe, eHarmony, Epocrates, ETF Securities, Facebook, Fonality, Glam Media, Good, Green Dot, Hautelook, HootSuite, ID Analytics, Inspirato, iPass, Iron Planet, Janrain, Jumio, Kik, LegalZoom.com, LifeLock, LiveOps, Lookout, MarkLogic, NetSpend, Ning, OnX, Pentaho, Pinterest, Playspan, Precision Hawk, Rearden Commerce, Reply.com, Requisite Technology, RigNet, Spotify, SugarCRM, Surun, Telaria, TellMe, Tumblr, Twitter, Verilume, WatchDox, Wayport, WildTangent, Yodle, Zappos

Key Executives:
  Daniel L Burstein, Founder/Managing Partner
  e-mail: burstein@mtvlp.com
  Background: CIO, Ps Capital Holdings; PS Capital Ventures; Senior Advisor, Blackstone Group; Consultant, Sony; Toyota; Microsoft; Sun Microsystems; Author
  Samuel L Schwerin, Founder/Managing Partner
  e-mail: schwerin@mtvlp.com
  Education: BS, Lehigh University; MBA, Wharton School
  Background: VP Finance, StorageApps; Blackstone Group; M&A, Salomon Brothers; Founder, OpenPeak
  Ray Cheng, Partner
  Education: BS, Economics, Wharton School; BS, Electrical Systems Engineering, University of Pennsylvania
  Background: Rho Ventures
  Directorships: Pentaho, PrecisionHawk, Blackmore Sensor & Analytics, Phantom AI, BigCommerce
  Jonathan Glass, Chief Financial Officer
  e-mail: glass@mtvlp.com
  Education: BS, Boston University; MBA, Fordham University
  Background: Vice President, Finace, Venrock; Controller, Greenbriar Equity Group; Tax Manager, Deloitte & Touche

1236 MINDFULL INVESTORS
2 Mallard Rd.
Belvedere, CA 94920

Phone: 415-847-2949
e-mail: connect@mindfullinvestors.com
web: www.mindfullinvestors.com

Mission Statement: Mindful Investors is the leading private equity fund which invests exclusively in companies providing sustainable and healthy living focused products to consumers.

Investment Criteria: Invests exclusively in the natural, organic and sustainable consumer products and consumer services marketplace.
Industry Group Preference: Consumer Products, Consumer Services, Clean Technology, Environment, Renewable Energy, Sustainability
Portfolio Companies: Atheer Labs, BINA, CleanFish, Marketwired, Next Thing Co., Retailigence, Scanadu, SOL Republic, Soma, Yerdle

Key Executives:
  Stuart L Rudick, Founding Partner
  Education: BS, Business Administration, University of Colorado
  Background: Founding Partner, Uplift Equity; Associate Director, Bear Stearns; Partner, Shearson Lehman/Davis Skaggs

1237 MIRAMAR VENTURE PARTNERS
2101 E Coast Highway
Suite 300
Corona del Mar, CA 92625

Phone: 949-760-4450 Fax: 949-760-4451
web: www.miramarvp.com

Mission Statement: Miramar invests in early-stage information technology opportunities, with an emphasis on projects based in Southern California. We partner with leading entrepreneurs to transform game changing ideas into capital efficient, profitable businesses.

Geographic Preference: Southern California
Investment Criteria: Early-Stage
Industry Group Preference: Information Technology, Data Storage, Semiconductors, Networking, SaaS, Internet
Portfolio Companies: AccelOps, Aktino, Arradiance, Azuro, Berkana Wireless, Brand Affinity Technologies, Cirro, Coradiant, Factual, FastSoft, HyperQuality, Independa, Innovative Micro Technology, Jeda Networks, Load Dynamix, Matrix Sensors, OptionEase, Predixion Software, Protego Networks, Rachio, RealPractice, Scopely, Silicon Systems, Solarflare Communications, Tarari, Tempo AI, Veritone, Welltok

Key Executives:
  Bruce Hallett, Managing Director
  949-760-4455
  e-mail: bhallett@miramarvp.com
  Education: BA, University of California, Irvine; JD, UCLA
  Background: Managing Partner, Brobeck Phleger & Harrison
  Directorships: OCTANe
  Sherman Atkinson, Managing Director
  Education: BA, Purdue University
  Background: CEO-In-Residence, Austin Ventures; COO, Intermix Media

1238 MISSION BAY CAPITAL
953 Indiana St.
San Francisco, CA 94107

Phone: 415-347-8287
e-mail: info@missionbaycapital.com
web: www.missionbaycapital.com

Mission Statement: Mission Bay Capital LLC uses capital and expertise to help entrepreneurs emerging from the University of California change the world. Its success will address social challenges, replenish future funds, and ultimately build a research and educational endowment the California Institute of Quantitative Biosciences will drive the development of the next generation of innovations.

Geographic Preference: California
Fund Size: $11.3 million
Founded: 2009
Investment Criteria: Seed, Startups
Industry Group Preference: Biotechnology, Healthcare
Portfolio Companies: Alector, Applaud Medical, Atreca, Avexegen, Bell Biosystems, Bolt Threads, Calithera, Caribou Biosciences, Cell Design Labs, Chrono Therapeutics, Circle Pharma, Droplet, eFFECTOR Therapeutics, Epiodyne, Fluxion, Graphwear, Invenio Imaging, Logic.ink, Magnamosis, Magnap, Mammoth Biosciences, Mitokinin, Ocular Dynamics, Perlara, Photoswitch Biosciences, Pionyr Immunotherapeutics, Principia, SiteOne Therapeutics, Sound Agriculture, Symicbio, Tangible Science, TrueNorth Therapeutics, Viewpoint Therapeutics, Vivace Therapeutics, Wild Type, Zephyrus, Zymergen

Key Executives:
  Douglas Crawford PhD, Managing Partner
  e-mail: douglas.crawford@missionbaycapital.com
  Education: PhD, Biochemistry, University of California, San Francisco

Venture Capital & Private Equity Firms / Domestic Firms

Directorships: Redwood Biosciences, Delpor, BayBio Institute
Robert Blazej, PhD, Partner
e-mail: robert.blazej@missionbaycapital.com
Education: PhD, Bioengineering, University of California
Background: Director, Novozyme's Digital Biotechnology Unit; CEO, Allopartis Biotechnologies
Regis B Kelly PhD, Senior Advisor
Education: University of Edinburgh; PhD, Biosciences, California Institute of Technology
Background: Executive Vice-Chancellor, University of California, San Francisco
Directorships: Bay Area Scientific Innovation Consortium

1239 MISSION VENTURES
9255 Towne Centre Dr.
Suite 350
San Diego, CA 92121

Phone: 858-350-2100 **Fax:** 858-350-2101
e-mail: donna@missionventures.com
web: www.missionventures.com

Mission Statement: Mission Ventures helps build successful enterprises in Southern California and creates superior returns on investment for its investors. This is accomplished by investing in the most promising early stage companies in high growth emerging markets and providing significant assistance to those companies as they develop.
Geographic Preference: Southern California
Fund Size: $225 million
Founded: 1997
Average Investment: $10 million
Minimum Investment: $2 million
Investment Criteria: Early, Startup
Industry Group Preference: Communications, E-Commerce & Manufacturing, Enterprise Software, Infrastructure, Internet Technology, Technology, Software
Portfolio Companies: CalAmp, Enevate, Entropic Communications, MaxLinear, Networks in Motion, TransChip, Verimatrix, Wildcomm, Zyray Wireless, EVEO, ID Analytics, MarginPoint, Sitematic, Alpine Data Labs, Digital Island, Greenplum, Ortiva Wireless, 3E Company, Access Sports Media, BMS Reimbursement, Cogent Healthcare, Image Metrics, LeisureLink, NetSeer, RockeTalk, Slacker, SodaHead, Transaction Wireless, VMIX, WorkWell Systems, Zui.com
Key Executives:
   Robert Kibble, Co-Founder/Managing Partner
   Education: BA, Natural Sciences, Univ. of Oxford; MBA, Darden School, University of Virginia
   Background: Founder/General Partner, Paragon Venture Partners; VP, Citicorp Venture Capital; VP, Citicorp Merchant Banking Group; Investment Banking, Wall Street
   Directorships: Eveo, Nexiant, SodaHead
   David Ryan, Managing Partner
   e-mail: DavidR@missionventures.com
   Education: BA, Northeastern University; MBA, Case Western Reserve University
   Background: General Partner, Copley Venture Partners; Medusa Corporation
   Directorships: Access360 Media, Active Storage, BMS Reimbursement Management, NetSeer, Nirvanix, WorkWell Systems
   Ted Alexander, Managing Partner
   e-mail: ted@missionventures.com
   Education: MBA, Duke Uiversity; BS Engineering, United States Naval Academy
   Background: Business Development/Market Analysis, Sandpiper Networks; GE Information Services
   Directorships: Enevate, ID Analytics, Ortiva Wireless, Rocketalk, Verimatrix, LeisureLink
   Leo Spiegel, Managing Partner
   e-mail: leo@missionventures.com
   Education: BA, Management Services, University of California, San Diego
   Background: President, Digital Island; CEO, Sandpiper Networks; Senior VP/CTO, Donnelley Enterprise Solutions; Co-Founder/CTO, LANSystems
   Directorships: Alpine Data Labs, Eveo, Zui.com, MaestroDev, RotoHog, Slacker, Transaction Wireless
   Caroline Barberio, Chief Financial Officer
   Education: BS, Business Adminstration, San Diego State University
   Background: Auditor, Deloitte & Touche; Gray Cary Ware & Freidenrich; Sisthe Energies; Applied Molecular Evolution; Vice President, Finance, Sorrento Associates

1240 MISSIONOG
1760 Market St.
Suite 902
Philadelphia, PA 19103

e-mail: info@missionog.com
web: www.missionog.com

Mission Statement: We partner with high-growth businesses in segments where we have had prior success as operators, including financial services and payments, data platforms, and software. We apply our experience and capabilities to a group of highly skilled and passionate entrepreneurs whose businesses are on the cusp of exponential growth.
Minimum Investment: $100,000 - $500,000
Industry Group Preference: Enterprise Software, Technology, Business Products & Services, Software, Data & Analytics, Financial Services, Payments & Financial Services
Portfolio Companies: Accurate Group, Alkami, Behalf, Bento for Business, Bridge, Clip, Cloudamize, Deko, DemystData, DivvyCloud, Factor Trust, Frontline Selling, GAN Integrity, Ingo Money, Journey Sales, OneTwoSee, Revolution Credit, Solovis, Syncapay, Tethr, Venminder, Zibby
Key Executives:
   Andy Newcomb, Managing Partner
   e-mail: andy@missionog.com
   Education: BA, History, Trinity College
   Background: Co-Founder, Relay Network; Group Head of Sales and Corporate Development, Citi Prepaid Services; Founding Team Member, Ecount; Portfolio Manager, Chartwell Investment Partners
   Directorships: PeopleLinx, Softgate Systems, RewardsNOW, OneTwoSee
   Gene Lockhart, Chairman and Managing Partner
   e-mail: gene@missionog.com
   Education: BS, University of Virginia; MBA, The Darden School at the University of Virginia
   Background: Special Advisor, General Atlantic; Venture Partner, Oak Investment Partners; President and CEO, MasterCard International; CEO, Midland Bank Plc; President of the Global Retail Bank of BankAmerica Corporation; President of Consumer Services, AT&T
   George Krautzel, Managing Partner
   e-mail: george@missionog.com
   Education: BS, Finance, Villanova University
   Background: Co-Founder, ITtoolbox

1241 MITSUI GLOBAL INVESTMENT
535 Middlefield Road
Suite 100
Menlo Park, CA 94025

Phone: 650-234-5000 **Fax:** 650-323-1516
e-mail: mgicontactsjfvz@mitsui.com
web: www.mitsui-global.com

Mission Statement: Mitsui Global Investment is committed to helping entrepreneurs build businesses from the early stages through global expansion. We wish to partner with exceptional individuals who are reinventing industries while improving human welfare all over the world.

Portfolio Companies: 4info, Actimis, AdBrite, Aeluros, Anaeropharma Science, ArmaGen, ArraVasc, ASA

Venture Capital & Private Equity Firms / Domestic Firms

Foodnesia, Asthmatx, Autotalks, Axikin Pharma, Beceem Firetide, BioAmber, Bioelectron, Boingo Wireless, Boston Biomedical, Broncus Technologies, Calypso Medical Technologies, Cappella, Cardeus Pharmaceuticals, Cardiovascular Systems, Change Healthcare, ContinuumRx, Convenient Power HK Limited, CounterTack, Cylene Pharmaceuticals, Ekos Corporation, EnerVault, Etonenet, EyeSight Mobile Technologies, Fewmo Tech Limited, Garapon, Glamour Sales Holding, Global Consumer Products, GMZ Energy, goBalto, GTI Capital, Hainan Hailing Chemipharma Corporation, Halation Photonics, HelloSoft, IAT Automobile Technology, Infomart International, InnoPath Software, Inventys Thermal, Kaiima Bio Agritech, Kaltura, Kaminario, Kineto Wireless, Kovio, Laszlo Systems, LensVector, Leyou, Life Media, Location Labs, Marrone Bio Innovations, MC10, MoBeam, Mo'Minis, NanoGram, NapaJen Pharma, NetMotion Wireless, Neul, NovoStent Corporation, NxThera, On-Chip Biotechnologies, OpenX Software, OptiScan Biomedical, Palamida, Panacos, Pica 8, Pinnacle Energies, Promethera Biosciences, Protein Simple, Proterra, Prudent Energy, QD Laser, Redwood Systems, Rive Technology, RGB Networks, Ruckus Wireless, S*BIO Pte., SenSage, Shanghai Global Baby Products, Shanghai Yi Shang Network Information Company, Sirrus, Six Rooms Holdings, Solaria Corporation, Spire Global, Symic, Valens Semiconductor, Virident Systems, YPX Caman Holdings

Other Locations:
Nippon Life Marunouchi Garden Tower 11F
1-3, Marunouchi 1-Chome
Chiyoda-Ku
Tokyo 100-8631
Japan
Phone: 81-3-3285-3166 **Fax:** 81-3-3285-9156

Room 810, China World Tower A
1 Jian Guo Men Wai Avenue
Beijing 100004
China
Phone: 86-10-5965-3560 **Fax:** 86-10-6505-3128

5F Asia House
4 Weizman St.
Tel Aviv 6423904
Israel
Phone: 972-3-696-0503 **Fax:** 972-3-696-0423

Key Executives:
Shinya Imai, President & CEO
Education: Bachelor of Law, Waseda University
Kenichi Kimura, Managing Director
Education: Bachelor of Mechanical Engineering, University of Tokyo

1242 MK CAPITAL
40 Skokie Blvd
Suite 430
Northbrook, IL 60062

Phone: 312-324-7700
e-mail: kris@mkcapital.com
web: www.mkcapital.com

Mission Statement: Offers multi-stage growth equity and venture capital to companies. MK Capital assists management teams in developing corporate strategy, generating business development opportunities and raising additional capital.

Investment Criteria: All Stages
Industry Group Preference: Digital Media & Marketing, Data Center, Software, Education Technology
Portfolio Companies: ADAR IT, Apex Learning, AwesomenessTV, BidPal, Bladelogic, Brightmont Academy, Carbon Media Group, CellTrak, Datapop, DramaFever, eSpark, Eved, GameFly, HealthiNation, Junction Solutions, Kollective, Kontiki, LLamasoft, Machinima, Multicast Media, Nerdio, Netuitive, OneCause, Passport, PECO Pallet, Playcast, Poptent, Quark Games, ReachForce, SimpleReach, Smoothstone, Unitas Global, Wellspring Worldwide, Zefr

Other Locations:
535 W. William
Suite 303
Ann Arbor, MI 48103
Phone: 734-663-6500

Key Executives:
Bret Maxwell, Managing General Partner
e-mail: bmaxwell@mkcapital.com
Education: McCormick School of Engineering, Northwestern University; Kellogg Graduate School of Management
Background: Co-Founder, First Analysis' Venture Capital Practice
Mark Koulogeorge, Managing General Partner
e-mail: mark@mkcapital.com
Education: Dartmouth College; Stanford Graduate School of Business
Background: Managing Director, First Analysis Corporation; Booz Allen Hamilton
Karen Buckner, Partner/COO
e-mail: kbuckner@mkcapital.com
Education: University of Michigan; Kellogg School of Management
Background: VP, Operations, I-Works
Directorships: TopSchool, Apex Learning, Smoothstone Communications, Retention Education, Enhancescape
Kirk Wolfe, Partner
e-mail: kwolfe@mkcapital.com
Education: BS, Industrial & Operations Engineering, University of Michigan; MBA, Stanford University
Background: Field Operations, Ariba; Motorola

1243 MOBILE FOUNDATION VENTURES
137 Forest Avenue
Palo Alto, CA 94301

e-mail: contact@MFVPartners.com
web: www.mfvpartners.com

Mission Statement: A venture capital fund focused on tech-based companies, such as AI, neural computing, big data, and shared mobility.

Founded: 2017
Investment Criteria: Pre-Series A, Series A
Industry Group Preference: Artificial Intelligence, Computing, Big Data, Data Analytics, Automotive, Mobility
Portfolio Companies: Analog Inference, Summary Analytics, TwentyBN
Key Executives:
Karthee Madasamy, Managing Partner
Education: BS, College of Engineering, Guindy; MS, University of Michigan; MBA, University of Chicago
Background: Managing Director/VP, Qualcomm Ventures

1244 MOBILITY VENTURES
P.O. Box 1597
Addison, TX 75001

Phone: 972-991-9942 **Fax:** 972-669-7873
e-mail: email@mobilityventures.com
web: www.mobilityventures.com

Mission Statement: Mobility Ventures focuses on early-stage, cutting edge companies that enable Mobility and promote a mobile lifestyle. We define Mobility as solutions that leverage the convergence of wireless infrastructures, the Internet, applications and services which result in anytime, anywhere connectivity. Ours franchise is Mobility. We invest across the Wireless Ecosystem in technologies, applications, services and medias that enable and promote a mobile society. These include areas such as, mobile marketing, mobile health, mobile commerce, location based services and energy/ power management.

Investment Criteria: Early-Stage
Industry Group Preference: Mobile, Wireless, Internet

Venture Capital & Private Equity Firms / Domestic Firms

Portfolio Companies: 10C Technologies, AdMarvel, Alereon, Always Market, B2X, Bakcell, Blue Calypso, Caribe, Command Audio, EnerAge, EntegraBlu, Genesis, GoldStar, Haxiot, Indoor Atlas, IndoTraq, Inner Wireless, InnoPath, Liquidmetal Technologies, Magnolia Broadband, Mobiserve, Mobixell, Navini Networks, Neonode, Now Public, Orpiva, Phenometrix, PulseWave, PWRF, Renren, Santerra, Sirific, Solarwinds, Tele Atlas, TelRock, Uniscon, VeriSign, VMX, Zebek

Key Executives:
Roman Kikta, Founder/Managing Partner
Education: BA, Rutgers University
Background: Nokia, Panasonic, GoldStar, OKI; Founder, Global Wireless Holdings
Mark Fruehan, Venture Partner
Education: BS, Economics, Pennsylvania State University
Background: Vice President, VeriSign
Arlan Harris, Partner
Education: BS, University of Texas, Dallas
Background: Austin Ventures, Genesis Campus Funds, LifeGate Ventures

1245 MOBIUS VENTURE CAPITAL
1050 Walnut Street
Suite 210
Boulder, CO 80302

e-mail: jill@mobiusvc.com
web: www.mobiusvc.com

Founded: 1996
Investment Criteria: Early-Stage
Industry Group Preference: Communications Software, Communications, Components & IoT, Consumer Services, Enterprise Applications, Healthcare Information Technology, Infrastructure, Infrastructure Software, Professional Services
Portfolio Companies: Bloom Energy, deCarta, Impinj, Rally Software, ReaMetrix, Return Path, Sitrion, Techorati
Key Executives:
Brad Feld, Co-Founder, Managing Director
Education: BS, MS, Management Science, MIT
Background: Chief Technology Officer, AmeriData Technologies; Feld Technologies
Directorships: National Center for Women & Information Technology
Seth Levine, Principal
Education: Macalester College
Background: FirstWorld Communications; Business Development Group, ICG Communications

1246 MODERNE VENTURES
410 N Michigan Avenue
Suite 740
Chicago, IL 60611

web: www.moderneventures.com

Mission Statement: Moderne Ventures invests in early stage companies centering in and around real-estate, insurance, finance, hospitality and home service industries.
Key Executives:
Constance Freedman, Founder/Managing Partner
Education: BS, Boston University; MBA, Harvard University
Background: Head, Strategic Investments, National Association of Realtors; Founder, REach; Investor, Cue Ball

1247 MOHR-DAVIDOW VENTURES
777 Mariners Island Boulevard
Suite 550
San Mateo, CA 94404

Phone: 650-854-7236
e-mail: mdvinfo@mdv.com
web: www.mdv.com

Mission Statement: We are committed to helping new companies build great teams, devise winning product and marketing strategies, run smooth operations, establish effective distribution strategies, and create successful business models.
Geographic Preference: United States
Fund Size: $2 billion
Founded: 1983
Average Investment: $3 million
Minimum Investment: $500,000
Investment Criteria: Early Stage
Industry Group Preference: Software, Infrastructure, Life Sciences, Communications, Semiconductors, Information Technology, Clean Technology
Portfolio Companies: Actuate, Adamas, Agile, AirPR, Aryaka, Analyte Health, Aryaka, Audience Science, Balance Therapeutics, BandPage, Brickstream, Broadbase Software, Brocase, BuildDirect, CardioDX, Carrier IQ, Cenzic, Corventis, Coupa, Crescendo Biosciences, Critical Path, Doxo, DS-IQ, DVS Sciences, Echelon, Employee Channel, Epigram, Figs, Finsphere Corporation, FormFactor, Gain Credit, Genius Genomatics, Gordon Murray Design, Healthtap, Honest Buildings, Hotchalk, Infusionsoft, Ipsilon, iRhythm, Kabbage, Lagrange Systems, Marble, Massive, Medio, Neon, nLight, Numerical Technologies, One Spot, ONI Systems, Opxbio, Pacific Biosciences, Panasas, ParAllele, PB Works, People Pattern, Personalis, Pluribus Networks, Proofpoint, PunchTab, RainDance, Rally, RainDance, Rambus, Recurrent Energy, ReSci, Retention Science, Reverb, Rocketfuel, Ruby Ribbon, Sabrix, Sensity, Sequenta, Shutterfly, Simbol Materials, Sipx, SodaHead, Splice Machine, Ticketfly, Tuition.io, Verinata Health, Virtuoz, Visible Measures, Vitesse, WebScale, WorkFusion, Xambala, Xicato, ZeaChem, Zebit, Zip2

Key Executives:
William Ericson, Managing Partner
Education: BSFS, Georgetown University of Foreign Service; JD, Northwestern University School of Law
Background: Managing Partner, Founder, Venture Law Group's Pacific Northwest office

1248 MONITOR CLIPPER PARTNERS
25 Whiting Road
Wellesley, MA 02481

Phone: 617-638-1100 Fax: 617-638-1110
e-mail: mcp@monitorclipper.com
web: www.monitorclipper.com

Mission Statement: Seeks to make private equity investments in middle-market companies to which we can add significant value through the combined skills of our principals and our privileged access to the proprietary resources of The Monitor Group.
Geographic Preference: United States, Western Europe
Fund Size: $2 billion
Founded: 1998
Average Investment: $20 - $200 million
Investment Criteria: Management Buyouts, Recapitalizations, Growth Equity Investments
Industry Group Preference: Diversified
Portfolio Companies: The Access Group, CMC Biologics, Colford Capital, Higher Education Partners, Kanetix, LaserShip, Market Force Information, Merrick Pet Care, Microgame, MyEyeDr., National Entertainment Network, Palladium Group, Pharmetics, Reverse Logistics GmbH, Roger Garments, W2 Group, WoodPellets.com

1249 MONITOR VENTURES
5050 El Camino Real
Suite 228
Los Altos, CA 94022

Phone: 650-475-7300
web: www.monitorventures.com

Venture Capital & Private Equity Firms / Domestic Firms

Mission Statement: We are committed to creating value by identifying strong entrepreneurs and building successful companies from the ground up.

Average Investment: $250,000 - $1 million
Investment Criteria: Early-Stage
Industry Group Preference: Software, Networking, Communications, Consumer Products
Portfolio Companies: Adaptive Planning, Greystripe, HydroPoint Data Systems, Limeelife, Local Response, Media Platform, Meru, Verdezyne

Key Executives:

Neal Bhadkamkar, Co-Founder & Managing Partner
Education: Indian Institute of Technology; MBA, Harvard Business School; PhD, Electrical Engineering, Stanford University
Background: VP Manufacturing, Zowie Intertainment; Interval Research

Teymour Boutros-Ghali, Co-Founder & Managing Partner
Education: Electrical Engineering, Cambridge University; PhD, Physics, SM, Management, MIT
Background: AllBusiness; Zowie Intertainment; Thrive Online; Pubisher, Time International

Jerry Engel, General Partner
Education: Bachelors, Penn State; Masters, Wharton School
Background: Founder, Entrepreneurial Services Group, Arthur Young; General Partner, Kline Hawkes

Fern Mandelbaum, Partner
Education: BA, Economics, Brown University; MBA, Stanford Graduate School of Business
Background: Co-Founder, Skyline; SRI International

1250 MONTLAKE CAPITAL
1200 Fifth Avenue
Suite 1800
Seattle, WA 98101

Phone: 206-956-0898
e-mail: montlake@montlakecapital.com
web: www.montlakecapital.com

Mission Statement: Montlake Capital is a leading growth equity form dedicated to delivering superior returns for our investors by partnering with private companies that have solid growth potential.

Geographic Preference: Northwestern United States
Fund Size: $100 million
Founded: 1999
Industry Group Preference: Consumer Products, Healthcare, Retailing, Technology, Financial Services, Business Products & Services
Portfolio Companies: AA Asphalting, Blue Dog Bakery, Coastal Community Bank, Fresca Mexican Foods, HerbPharm, i4cp, Intrepid Learning Solutions, SmartRG, SOG Specialty Knives & Tools, Specified Fittings, Wellpartner

Key Executives:

Andy Dale, Managing Director
Education: AB, Harvard College; MBA, Harvard Business School
Background: M&A Group, Smith Barney; First Century Partners
Directorships: Coastal Community Bank, i4cp, Intrepid Learning Solutions, PayScale, SmartRG, WellPartner

Noel de Turenne, Managing Director
Education: BA, University of Washington; MBA, Foster School of Business
Directorships: AA Asphalting, Specified Fittings, SOG Specialty Knives & Tools, Herbpharm, i4cp

1251 MONTREUX EQUITY PARTNERS
Four Embarcadero Center
Suite 3720
San Francisco, CA 94111

Phone: 650-234-1200 Fax: 650-234-1250
e-mail: info@mepvc.com
web: www.mepvc.com

Mission Statement: A private equity firm focused o building great life science and healthcare companies. The goal is to generate significant long-term capital gain by investing in superior businesses with high quality management teams.

Fund Size: $250 million
Founded: 1993
Average Investment: $5 million
Minimum Investment: $2 million
Investment Criteria: All stages
Industry Group Preference: Life Sciences, Healthcare, Biopharmaceuticals, Medical Devices
Portfolio Companies: Asthmatx, Avantis Medical Systems, Best Health, Cerexa, Coalescent Surgical, Colore Science, Crown Laboratories, Enteric Medical Technologies, Epirus Biopharmaceuticals, GC Aesthetics, Glaukos, Great Lakes Health Plan, Integrated Biosystems, Kareo, KFX Medical, Know Better Foods, Mako Surgical Corp., MindBody, Moksha8, Nova Cardia, Novostent, Orexigen, Paymap, Peninsula, Percsys, Pivot Medical, Product Health, PulmonX, Pure Life Renal, Questcor Pharma, Renal Care Partners, Si-Bone, Skin Medica, Somaxon Pharma, Sonoma Pharma, Tiger Connect, Tobira Therapeutics, Transcept

Key Executives:

Daniel K Turner III, Managing Director
e-mail: dan@mepvc.com
Education: BS, Sacramento State University; MBA, Haas School of Business, University of California, Berkeley
Background: Turnaround Group Manager, Berkeley International; Founding CFO, Oclassen Pharmaceuticals; High Technology Group, Price Waterhouse
Directorships: GC Aesthetics, Moksha8, Epirus, Glaukos, Tobira Therapeutics

Michael Matly, MD, Managing Director
Education: BS, Cornell University; MD, Mayo Clinic; MBA, Harvard Business School
Background: Mayo Clinic
Directorships: Tiger Connect, Kareo, Pure Life Renal, Pulmonx

Michael Mayer, Managing Director
Education: BA, Washington State University
Background: Partner, PricewaterhouseCoopers

1252 MONUMENT ADVISORS
255 North Alabama
Suite 333
Indianapolis, IN 46204

Phone: 317-656-5065 Fax: 317-656-5060
e-mail: request@monument-capital.com
web: www.monumentadv.com

Mission Statement: A private equity firm focused on management buyins, management buyouts, leveraged buyouts and recapitalizations in the microcap market. We partner with management teams to acquire and help build companies within niche service, distribution and manufacturing industries with enterprise values between $8 and $20 million.

Geographic Preference: Midwestern United States
Fund Size: $22.5 million
Average Investment: $1 - $3 million
Industry Group Preference: Industrial Services, Distribution, Niche Manufacturing
Portfolio Companies: Citadel Architectural Products, CT Acquisition Corp., Dronen Consulting, Instrument Development Corporation, Insurance Auto Auctions, Felins USA, Foam Rubber Products, HETSCO, Lake City Acquisition, Mountain Muffler, Nationwide Distribution,

Venture Capital & Private Equity Firms / Domestic Firms

New Polar, Presidential Holdings, Presidential, Separators, Service Design Associates

Key Executives:
Joseph P Schaffer, Managing Director
e-mail: jschaffer@monumentadv.com
Education: BS, Finance, Butler University; MBA, Indiana University
Background: Assistant Vice President, First Chicago Capital Markets
Directorships: Foam Rubber, Felins USA, Instrument Development Corporation

1253 MOORE VENTURE PARTNERS
La Jolla, CA

web: www.moorevp.com

Mission Statement: MVP Funds is a group of entrepreneurs and seasoned investors that are passionate about building the next generation of companies related to human longevity, high technology and life sciences.

Key Executives:
Terry Moore, Founder/Managing Partner
Education: MBA
Background: Founder/Chair, VC Roundtable; Founder/Executive Director, Morrison & Forrester Venture Network; Managing Director, HamiltonTech Capital Partners

1254 MORADO VENTURE PARTNERS
web: www.moradoventures.com

Mission Statement: Morado Venture Partners provides the resources entrepreneurs need to launch successful enterprises. Our partnership with our portfolio companies goes far beyond simply offering seed funding. We offer companies insights gained from experience, share their passion, and connect them to industry leaders who can help them.

Geographic Preference: San Francisco Bay Area, West Coast, New York City Area
Founded: 2011
Average Investment: $150,000
Investment Criteria: Seed-Stage
Industry Group Preference: Internet, E-Commerce & Manufacturing, Consumer Internet, Mobile, SaaS
Portfolio Companies: Active Mind Technology, Amitree, Apportable, Apsalar, Arterys, August Lock, Bagcheck, Betable, Betabrand, BitYota, BoarwalkTech, Boostable, Breakthrough, Bunndle, Cardspring, Cargomatic, Citrine Informatics, Class Dojo, Clef, Clover, Colingo, Colourlovers, Context Logic, CPUsage, Dasher, DataTorrent, Dot & Bo, Emmerge, eVenues, Evernote, Getaround, Gobble, GraphSQL, GreenGoose, Grid, Hiku, HipGeo, Impermium, Jetpac, JustOne, Layer, LitBit, Livestar, Local Motion, Lumo, ModBot, NeuMitra, Nuzzel, Onswipe, Openbucks, Opsclarity, Opsmatic, Optimus Ride, Osaro, Pen.io, Pepperdata, Polar, Proven.com, Puddle, Rainforest, RewardsPay, Rigetti, Romotive, Sano, Sapho, Savioke, Science Exchange, ShoCard, Sourcery, Space Monkey, Stackhut, Story Magic, Sunshine, Talech, ThinAir, Thislife, Tinfoil Security, Tomfoolery, Trnql, Trumo, Trusted Insight, Viewics, VIMOC, Watchsend, Wello, Whitetruffle, Wholeshare, Wittlebee, Xockets, Yozio

Key Executives:
Ash Patel, Founding Partner
Education: BSc, Computer Science, Kings College, University of London
Background: Senior Vice President, Platform Engineering, Yahoo!
Michael Marquez, Founding Partner
Education: BS, Managerial Economics, University of California, Davis; MBA, University of North Carolina, Chapel Hill
Background: Co-Founder, CODE Advisors; EVP, CBS Interactive

1255 MORGAN STANLEY EXPANSION CAPITAL
web: www.morganstanley.com

Mission Statement: Our goal is to use the experience of our team and the strength of Morgan Stanley to help build successful companies, generate superior returns for our investors and create wealth for entrepreneurs.

Geographic Preference: United States, Western Europe
Fund Size: $1.2 billion
Founded: 1986
Average Investment: $30 million
Minimum Investment: $5 million
Investment Criteria: Expansion Stage, Late, Growth Buyout
Industry Group Preference: Information Technology, Healthcare, Enterprise Software, Communication Technology, Infrastructure, Semiconductors, Healthcare Information Technology, Healthcare Services, Biopharmaceuticals
Portfolio Companies: Airespace, Allscripts, Anasazi, Arcadian Management, Aurum Software, Avamar, Bachman Information Systems, Benefit Mall, Biex, BizBuyer.Com, Blaze Software, Blue Star Solutions, Bowstreet, Business Engine, Buzzsaw.com, CallFire, Cambridge Heart, Cardiac Pathways, ChemConnect, Children's Discovery Center, Chip Express Corporation, Chromatic Research, Ciphergen Biosystems, Clinipace Worldwide, Cohesity, Comergent, Commerce One, Compucare, Concentra, Connect South, Constant Contact, Control Delivery Systems, Core Security Technologies, DicoverRx, DocuWare, eCentria, EcoIntense, Elevate, Eska, Ethertronics, Fuhu, Global Custom Commerce, Good Technology, GumGum, High Q, Instapage, Integral, Internap, iRise, Mojo, Mondee, Motionpoint, Motive Medical Intelligence, NanoString Technologies, Nutanix, Perceptive Software, Plateau, Rocket Lawyer, Sendmail, Smart Pants Vitamins, Socialware, Southern Care Hospice Services, Spinal Kinetics, Sprout, ThruPoint, Tiff's Treats Cookie Delivery, VBrick Systems, Vigilant Solutions, VizExplorer, Voices.com, XSInc

Key Executives:
Peter Chung, Head of Expansion Capital
Education: Dartmouth College, Stanford Graduate School
Background: Investment Banking Professional, Morgan Stanley
Melissa Daniels, Managing Director
Education: BA, Economics, University of North Carolina at Chapel Hill; MBA, Haas School of Business at the University of California at Berkeley
Background: Product/Software Development Manager, National Director of Fulfillment Operations, Southeast Regional Manager at Commerce Clearing House; Staff of Aviation Subcommittee, U.S. House of Representatives and University of North Carolina.
Directorships: Arcadian Management Services, Clinipace Worldwide, Discoverx, EKOS, IDeas, National Healing, PeopleClick, SouthernCare
Bill Reiland, Managing Director
Education: BA, Economics, Yale University; MBA, Tuck School of Business
Background: Leerink Swann
Lincoln Isetta, Managing Director
Education: Boston College

1256 MORGAN STANLEY PRIVATE EQUITY
e-mail: private.equity@morganstanley.com
web: www.morganstanley.com

Mission Statement: Morgan Stanley Private Equity is the firm's primary business for investing in large and middle-market private equity transactions globally on behalf of its clients.

Geographic Preference: Worldwide
Average Investment: $100 million - $500 million
Portfolio Companies: McKechnie Aerospace, Tops Markets, Learning Care Group, Breitenfeld, Triana Energy, Trinity CO2, Zenith, ReachOut Healthcare America, EmployBridge, Sterling Energy, Access Cash, Creative Circle

Venture Capital & Private Equity Firms / Domestic Firms

Key Executives:
Mark Bye, Managing Director
Education: BS & MS, MIT
Background: President & CEO, Dystar GmbH; Group Vice President, Air Products & Chemicals
Directorships: Carus Chemical Corporation, Breitenfeld AG, Trinity CO2
James Howland, Managing Director
Education: BA, Bucknell University; MBA, Stanford University Graduate School of Business
Background: President, Dun & Bradstreet International; CEO, Edison Schools Educational Services Group; CEO, Regus Business Center; American Express; McKinsey & Company
Directorships: Learning Care Group, EmployBridge, Access Cash, ReachOut
Gary S Matthews, Managing Director
Education: BA, Princeton University; MBA, Harvard Business School
Background: Simmons Bedding Company; Sleep Innovations; Derby Cycle Corporation; Worldwide Consumer Medicines, Bristol Myers Squibb; Managing Director, UK, Diageo/Guinness Limited
Directorships: Van Wagner, Lagunitas, Learning Care Group
John Moon, Managing Director
Education: AB, Harvard College; AM & PhD, Business Economics, Harvard University
Background: Managing Director, Riverstone Holdings
Directorships: Sterling Energy, Triana Energy Investments, Trinity CO2
Aaron Sack, Managing Director
Education: Dartmouth College; MBA, Wharton School, University of Pennsylvania
Background: Vice President, Goldman Sachs
Directorships: EmployBridge, Learning Care Group, Access Cash, Creative Circle

1257 MORGENTHALER VENTURES
3200 Alpine Road
Portola Valley, CA 94028

Phone: 650-388-3676 Fax: 650-388-3675
web: www.morgenthaler.com

Mission Statement: To partner with industry leading management teams and provide them with the highest possible level of support as they build their companies and create long term shareholder value.

Geographic Preference: United States
Fund Size: $3 billion
Founded: 1968
Average Investment: $5-$15 million
Minimum Investment: $500,000
Investment Criteria: Early-Stage
Industry Group Preference: Life Sciences, Information Technology, Internet, Enterprise Software, Biotechnology, Medical Devices
Portfolio Companies: Adara Media, Amati, Apple Computers, Aptis, Atria, Big Switch Networks, BilltoMobile, BlueAc, BlueGill Technologies, Brion Technologies, Catena Networks, Check, Chrysalis, CLK Design Automation, Convo, Cortina Systems, Crossbow Technology, Doximity, Endwave, Evans and Sutherland, Evernote, Fiber Optic Network Systems, FiveStar, Force 10 Networks, Fundly, Illustra, Imeem, Intelleflex, Jaspersoft, KnowledgeNet, LendingClub, Microchip, MuleSoft, NBX Corporation, Netli, New Foxus, NEXTEL, Nominum, Nuance Communications, NuoDB, OneChip Photonics, Orb Networks, Overture Networks, Paratek Microwave, PeopleMater, Peregrine Semiconductor, Planet Soho, Practice Fusion, Premiys, QuickLogic, R2 Semiconductor, Rhythm NewMedia, Siri, Socrata, Sonatype, Synopsys, TimesTen, Unity Semiconductor, VeriFone, Vitesse, Voltage Security, Volterra Semiconductor, Webspective, Wize Commerce

Key Executives:
Robin Bellas, Partner
Ralph E Chrisoffersen, Partner
Jason Lettmann, Partner
Hank Plain, Partner
Nassim Usman, Venture Partner

1258 MOTIV PARTNERS
755 Sansome Street
Suite 450
San Francisco, CA 94111

e-mail: info@motivpartners.com
web: www.motivpartners.com

Mission Statement: MOTIV is an ecosystem built to support leaders and company founders. MOTIV sources high quality deal flow, conduct diligence, make investments, and provide expertise to portfolio companies. MOTIV brings a network of aligned family offices and capital providers, many of whom also have deep industry insights and customer and supplier relationships.

Founded: 2016
Industry Group Preference: Clean Technology, Finance, Application Software, Food Services, Technology, Data Analytics, Healthcare
Portfolio Companies: Community Investment Management, The Cranemere Group Ltd., Good Eggs, Lending Club, Lyft, Peer IQ, Uprising, Virta, XL Hybrids

Key Executives:
Oliver Guinness, Co-Founder/Managing Director
Education: BS, Economics, Cornell University; MS, International Affairs & Business, Emerging Markets, Columbia University
Background: Merril Lynch; Greyrock Capital; Co-Founder, Clearpoint Ventures
Bill Tarr, Co-Founder/Managing Director
Education: BA, Dartmouth College
Background: Co-Founder, Aquillian Investments; Management Consultant, Origo Global Business Partners
Directorships: New Sector Alliance

1259 MOTLEY FOOL VENTURES
Alexandria, VA 22314

web: foolventures.com

Mission Statement: A venture capital fund seeking to invest in early stage Fintech companies.

Fund Size: $150 million
Founded: 2018
Average Investment: $1-$2 million
Minimum Investment: $500,000
Investment Criteria: Early Stage, Annual Revenue between $500,000 to $5 million
Industry Group Preference: Fintech, Artificial Intelligence, Information Technology
Portfolio Companies: Affectiva, Bitwise, Blockable, Eyrus, HomeCare.com, HUNGRY Marketplace, InHerSight, LegalMation, Microshare, MotoRefi, MyWallSt, PostProcess, RoundTrip, tEQuitable, Territory Foods, Upskill, UrbanStems, WealthForge, YouEarnedIt, Runpath

Key Executives:
Olleb Douglass, Managing Director
Education: BA, Accounting, University of Baltimore
Background: CFO, The Motley Fool Holdings Inc.; Auditor, KPMG
Directorships: Eyrus; InHerSight; Young Artists of America
Brendan Mathews, Vice President
Education: BA, Economics, University of Virginia; MBA, University of California, Berkeley
Background: Accenture
Rob Runett, Vice President
Education: BA, Journalism, University of Maryland

Venture Capital & Private Equity Firms / Domestic Firms

Background: Director of Retail Operations, Motley Fool Asset Management LLC

1260 MOTOROLA SOLUTIONS VENTURE CAPITAL
500 West Monroe Street
Suite 4400
Chicago, IL 60661-3781

Phone: 847-576-5000
web: www.motorolasolutions.com

Mission Statement: As part of the Chief Technology Office of Motorola, Motorola Solutions Venture Capital invests in applications and technologies that complement and enhance the fund's ability to keep public safety personal safe and effective at their jobs, by letting them focus on the mission, not the technology.

Geographic Preference: United States
Fund Size: $11.3 billion
Founded: 1999
Average Investment: $5 million
Minimum Investment: $3 million
Investment Criteria: Startup, Growth, Expansion
Industry Group Preference: Entertainment, Information Technology, Communications, Electronic Components, Security, Healthcare, Wireless Technologies, Telecommunications, Digital Media & Marketing, Government, Networking, Mobile Broadband, Social Media
Portfolio Companies: Agent, BlueLine Grid, Boundless, Cyphy, Devmynd, Neurala, Nok Nok Lab, Nubo, Orion, Pellion, SceneDoc, Seamless Docs, RapidSOS, TRX Systems, VocalZoom, SST

Key Executives:
  Eduardo Conrado, Chief Strategy & Innovation Officer
  Background: VP, Marketing/IT, Motorola Solutions

1261 MOUNTAIN GROUP CAPITAL
3835 Cleghorn Avenue
Suite 300
Nashville, TN 37215

Phone: 615-843-9100 **Fax:** 615-313-9996
web: mtngp.com

Mission Statement: Mountain Group Capital is an investment firm dedicated to investing in and actively guiding transformational businesses in the Life Sciences and Technology sectors. Founded in 2002, MGC principals have invested in more than 20 companies in these sectors.

Founded: 2002
Investment Criteria: Seed-Stage, Early-Stage
Industry Group Preference: Life Sciences, Medical Devices, Diagnostics, Nutraceuticals, Technology, Business Products & Services, Consumer Services, Healthcare Services
Portfolio Companies: Apire Health, Castle Biosciences, Cerebrotech, Clearside Biomedical, Diabetes Care Group, Diagnovus, G1 Therapeutics, MedCenterDisplay, Myomo, NeuroTronik Limited, NuSirt, Cyber Physical Systems, ABT Molecular Imaging Evermind, Industrial Ceramic Solutions, InvisionHeart, Just A Pinch Recipe Club, OnFocus, Pathfinder Therepeutics, SwingPal, Streamweaver, VenX, Concept Therapeutics, DirectVetMarketing, Clinical Products, DeviceFidelity, Ironwood Pharmaceuticals, Panopto, PharmMD, Value Payment Systems

Key Executives:
  Joe Cook Jr, Managing Director
  Education: BS, Engineering, University of Tennessee
  Background: Founder, Ironwood Pharmaceuticals; Group Vice President, Eli Lilly & Company
  Directorships: Ironwood Pharmaceuticals, Corcept Therapeutics, Amylin Pharmaceuticals
  Byron Smith, Managing Director
  Education: MBA, University of Chicago
  Background: Procter & Gamble, Pepsico, GTE Wireless, AT&T, EVP/CMO, Excite @ Home
  Directorships: NuSirt Sciences, MedCenter Display, Value Payment Systems, Streamweaver
  Joe Cook III, Managing Director
  Education: BA, Economics, Davidson College
  Background: Director, Private Placements, Robert W Baird & Co.; Vice President, JC Bradford & Co.
  Directorships: Pathfinder Therapeutics, VenX Medical, Industrial Ceramic Solutions, DPS Healthcare
  Steven D Singleton, Managing Director
  Education: BS, Finance, University of South Florida; Stetson University College of Law
  Background: Corporate Law, Trenam Kemker

1262 MOUNTAINEER CAPITAL
107 Capitol Street
Charleston, WV 25301

Phone: 304-347-7519 **Fax:** 304-347-0072

Mission Statement: To provide venture capital to promising new and existing businesses located in West Virginia and surrounding states.

Geographic Preference: West Virginia
Average Investment: $250,000 - $1 million
Investment Criteria: Early-Stage
Industry Group Preference: Technology, Information Technology, Communication Technology, Specialty Chemicals, Environmental Science, Forensic Science, Advance Polymers, Toxic Materials Handling, Hardwood Products, Coal Processes, Natural Gas, Medical Devices, Software, Education Technology
Portfolio Companies: Aero Corporation, Frontier Firewood, Game Plan, JBLCo, MetalWood Bats, New Carbon, Plethora, ThinOptX, Threewide, Troy, Vandalia Research, Vested Health

Key Executives:
  William H Taylor II, Managing General Partner
  Education: BS, Engineering Science, Johns Hopkins University; MS, Princeton University; PhD, Princeton University
  Background: Partner, Taylor & Turner Associates; Founder & Vice President, Data Science Ventures
  J Rudy Henley, Partner
  e-mail: jrhenley@mtncap.com
  Education: BS, Business Administration, West Virginia University
  Background: Senior Managing Director, McCabe-Henley Properties
  Patrick A Bond, General Partner
  e-mail: pabond@mtncap.com
  Education: BS, MS, Industrial Engineering, West Virginia University
  Background: Managing Director, McCabe Henley LP, Consulting, Growth Management Group

1263 MOUSSE PARTNERS
9 West 57th St.
Suite 4605
New York, NY 10019-2701

Mission Statement: Mousse Partners specializes in venture capital investments.

Investment Criteria: Growth-Stage
Portfolio Companies: Beautycounter, Everplans, Harmless Harvest, Mavin, Memebox Corporation, Paddle8, SeatGeek, Teforia, WHOOP

Other Locations:
  Beijing
  China

Key Executives:
  Charles Heilbronn, Founder & President
  Education: Master in Law, Universite de Paris V, Law School; LLM, New York University Law School
  Background: Chanel Inc.; Willkie Farr & Gallagher

Venture Capital & Private Equity Firms / Domestic Firms

1264 MOZART VENTURE PARTNERS
web: www.linkedin.com/in/rainerdechet

Mission Statement: Mozart Venture Partners is US-American seed venture capital company (in formation) that invests in tech startups.
Founded: 2014
Investment Criteria: Seed-Stage
Industry Group Preference: Technology
Key Executives:
Rainer Dechet, Founder

1266 MPE PARTNERS
Fifth Third Center
600 Superior Ave. East
Suite 2500
Cleveland, OH 44114

Phone: 216-416-7500
web: www.mpepartners.com

Mission Statement: Morgenthaler Private Equity (MPE) Partners focuses on the lower middle market, specifically on industry-leading companies with transaction values from $25 million to $150 million.
Geographic Preference: North America
Industry Group Preference: Manufacturing, Commercial Services, Industrial
Portfolio Companies: B&E Group, Bettcher Industries, dlhBowles, DreamLine, Plastic Components, Trachte, United Pipe & Steel Corp.
Other Locations:
One Liberty Square
Suite 620
Boston, MA 02109
Phone: 617-587-7800
Key Executives:
Peter Taft, Partner
e-mail: ptaft@mpepartners.com
Education: BA, Amherst College; MBA, Harvard Business School
Background: McDonald & Company Securities
Directorships: B&E Groups, Bettcher Industries, dlhBowles, Plastic Components
Karen Tuleta, Partner
e-mail: ktuleta@mpepartners.com
Education: BA, Baldwin-Wallace College
Background: Carnegie Capital Management Company
Directorships: Bettcher Industries, dlhBowles, Plastic Components, Trachte
Joe Machado, Partner
e-mail: jmachado@mpepartners.com
Education: BA, Princeton University; MBA, Harvard Business School
Background: American Capital Strategies; HCI/Thayer Capital Partners
Directorships: DreamLine, Trachte, United Pipe & Steel
Matt Yohe, Partner
e-mail: myohe@mpepartners.com
Education: BA, Washington & Lee University; MBA, Harvard Business School
Background: American Capital Strategies; HCI/Thayer Capital Partners
Directorships: Bettcher Industries, Plastic Components, Trachte
Graham Schena, Partner
e-mail: gschena@mpepartners.com
Education: BA, Colgate University; MBA, MIT Sloan School
Background: Windjammer Capital; Sentinel Capital Partners; HIG Capital
Directorships: DreamLine

1267 MPG EQUITY PARTNERS
17 East Monroe Street
#219
Chicago, IL 60603

Phone: 630-334-8131
e-mail: mgoy@mpgequity.com
web: www.mpgequity.com

Mission Statement: MPG Equity Partners is seeking to acquire profitable, privately held businesses in the Midwestern US where owners are seeking liquidity and a transition out of daily management.
Geographic Preference: Midwest
Investment Criteria: Ownership Transitions
Industry Group Preference: Healthcare, Information Technology, Business Products & Services, Consumer Services, Niche Manufacturing, Value-Added Distribution
Portfolio Companies: BrainBits, Clear Contract, Clear NDA, Health iPASS, MedService Repair, MouseHouse, Power Hour Fitness
Key Executives:
Michael Goy, Managing Partner
630-334-8131
e-mail: mgoy@mpgequity.com
Education: BS, Finance, Kelley School of Business, Indiana University; MBA, Booth School of Business
Background: Founding Member, Foros Group; Associate, Sterling Partners

1268 MPM CAPITAL
450 Kendall St.
Cambridge, MA 02142

Phone: 617-425-9200
web: www.mpmcapital.com

Mission Statement: We seek to maximize value creation by focusing on inflection points in the development of companies, such as the achievement of clinical proof-of-concept data, the achievement of early commercial success, and by reinvigorating commercial platforms with potentially high growth assets.
Geographic Preference: United States, Europe
Fund Size: $900 million
Average Investment: $1 million
Minimum Investment: $500,000
Investment Criteria: All Stages
Industry Group Preference: Biotechnology, Healthcare, Medical Devices, Pharmaceuticals, Medical Technology
Portfolio Companies: 23andMe, 28-7, Alnara Pharmaceuticals, Amphivena Therapeutics, Anthera Pharmaceuticals, Aratana Therapeutics, Astute Medical, Biomarin, Blade, Celladon, Cerecor, Chiasma, Coda, Conatus Pharmaceuticals, CoStim Pharmaceuticals, Cullinan Oncology, DigiTx Partners, EKR Therapeutics, Endologix, Entrada, Epizyme, FortéBio, Harpoon, Iconic Therapeutics, Idenix, IOMX, iPerian, iTeos, Maverick, Mitokyne, Naked Biome, Nevro, Oncorus, Oxagen, Pacira Pharmaceuticals, Peplin, Pharmasset, Potenza Therapeutics, Proteon Therapeutics, Radius, Raze Therapeutics, Repare, Rhythm, Sai, Selexys Pharmaceuticals, Semma, Sideris Pharmaceuticals, Solasia, Syndax, TCR2, Tetherex, Tizona, Trieza, TriNetX, Trivascular, True North Therapeutics, Valeritas, Vascular Pharmaceuticals, Verastem, Werewolf
Other Locations:
2000 Sierra Point Pkwy.
Suite 701
Brisbane, CA 94005
Phone: 650-533-3300 Fax: 650-553-3301
Key Executives:
Luke B Evnin, Managing Director
650-553-3300
Fax: 650-553-3301
e-mail: levnin@mpmcapital.com
Education: PhD, University of California; BA, Princeton

Venture Capital & Private Equity Firms / Domestic Firms

University
Background: Accel Partners
Directorships: Epic Therapeutics; Metabasis; PiMedical; Venturi Group
Todd Foley, Managing Director
617-425-9200
Fax: 617-425-9201
Education: BS, Chemistry, MIT; MBA, Harvard Business School
Background: Business Development, Genentech; Management Consulting, Arthur D Little
Directorships: Chiasma, CombinatoRx, Rhythym Pharmaceuticals
Ansbert K Gadicke MD, Managing Director
617-425-9200
Fax: 617-425-9201
Education: MD, JW Goethe University
Background: Boston Consulting Group; Research positions in Biochemistry and Molecular Biology, Whitehead Institute/MIT, Harvard University, German Cancer Research Center
Directorships: Cerimon Pharmaceuticals, Dragonfly Sciences, Elixir Pharmaceuticals, Radius Health, Solasia Pharma KK

1269 MS&AD VENTURES
2730 Sand Hill Road
Menlo Park, CA 94025

web: msad.vc

Mission Statement: MS&AD Ventures is funded by MS&AD Insurance Group Holdings. The firm seeks to invest in tech-based innovations.
Industry Group Preference: Technology, Insurance, FinTech, Mobility, Cyber Security, Security, Automation, IoT, Data Mangement, Healthcare
Portfolio Companies: Akinova, Averon, ClearedIn, Dathena Science, Element, FinLeap, Geosite, i2X, Jupiter Intelligence, Lucideus, Node, Qunomedical, Rubrick, SkopeNow, Skycatch, Socotra, Spot, Taiger, Tide, Tomorrow, Vdoo, Voyage, WorldCover
Key Executives:
  Jon Soberg, Managing Partner
  Education: BS, Harvey Mudd College; MS, Robotics, Northwestern University; MBA, Wharton School
  Background: Managing Director, Blumberg Capital; Managing Partner, Expansive Ventures; COO, REEF Technology; Co-Founder/Partner, Early Impact Ventures; Venture Partner, CerraCap Ventures; Co-Founder, FlexCap Partners; Lecturer, The Wharton School
  Directorships: Lucideus; WorldCover; True Link Financial
  Tak Sato, Managing Partner
  Education: MBA, Chuo University Graduate School
  Background: General Manager, Cholamandalam MS General Insurance Co.; Head of Investment, MS&AD Insurance
  Tiffine Wang, Partner
  Education: BA, University of California, Davis
  Background: Marketing Manager, Alchemist Accelerator; HACKcelerator Program Manager, AngelHack; Co-Founder/Marketing, Akiva Health Systems; Co-Founder, Entrepreneurcareer.com; Head of Mentoring Program, European Innovation Academy; Sr. Investment Manager, Singtel Innov8 Ventures

1270 MSOUTH EQUITY PARTNERS
Two Buckhead Plaza
3050 Peachtree Road NW
Suite 550
Atlanta, GA 30305

Phone: 404-816-3255 Fax: 404-816-3258
e-mail: info@msouth.com
web: www.msouth.com

Mission Statement: Provides equity capital and expertise to support management teams in acquisitions and recapitalizations of lower middle market companies.
Geographic Preference: Southern United States
Fund Size: $1 billion
Founded: 1984
Investment Criteria: Acquisitions, Recapitalizations
Industry Group Preference: Distribution, Business Products & Services, Manufacturing
Portfolio Companies: BC Technical, Building Products & Services Company, Capstone Logistics, Children & Teen Dental Group, Coastal Companies, Coastal Sunbelt, Community & Southern Bank, Crom, Diversified, Eagle Quest International, Eco-Site, Education Networks of America, Employ Bridge, EnergyCo. Holdings, Fischben, GaiaTech, Hire Dynamics, Interior Logic Group, One Path, PetroLiance, Signal Outdoor Advertising, Southern HVAC, Tachyon, Technical Innovation, The Intersect Group, Thompson Industrial Services, The Right People Construction Group, United Telephone Company, USA Television Holdings, Vectorply
Key Executives:
  Mark L Feidler, Partner
  e-mail: mfeidler@msouth.com
  Education: BA, Economics, Duke University; JD, Vanderbilt Law School
  Background: President & COO, BellSouth Corporation; COO, Cingular Wireless; Head of Corporate Development, BellSouth; Investment Banking, The Robinson-Humphrey Company
  Michael D Long, Partner
  e-mail: mlong@msouth.com
  Education: BS Finance/Accounting, MBA, Oklahoma State University
  Background: CEO, Pac Pizza LLC; NationsBank
  Bart A McLean, Senior Advisor
  e-mail: bmclean@msouth.com
  Education: BS, University of Delaware; MBA, Indiana University
  Background: Principal, Allsop Venture Partners; VP, Republic Venture Group; Lending Officer, Republic Bank
  Peter S Pettit, Partner
  e-mail: ppetit@msouth.com
  Education: BS, Commerce, McIntire School of Commerce, University of Virginia; MBA, Kellogg School of Management, Northwestern University
  Background: Vice President, Code Hennessy & Simmons; The Robinson-Humphrey Company
  Wanda R Morgan, Chief Financial Officer
  e-mail: wmorgan@msouth.com
  Education: BS, Accounting, University of Alabama; CPA

1271 MTS HEALTH INVESTORS
623 Fifth Avenue
14th Floor
New York, NY 10022

Phone: 212-887-2100 Fax: 212-887-2111
e-mail: info@mtspartners.com
web: www.mtspartners.com

Mission Statement: A principal investor that partners with seasoned, highly motivated management teams to significantly enhance the overall equity value in the companies in which it invests; believes firmly in equity-based incentives for management teams; builds discernible value through both the experienced guidance of its principals and investing in operating companies with sound fundamentals.
Founded: 2000
Investment Criteria: LBO, Corporate Divestitures, MBO, Growth Financing, Recapitalizations
Industry Group Preference: Healthcare Services, Outsourcing & Efficiency, Medical Devices
Portfolio Companies: Activate Healthcare, Acorda Therapeutics, Addex Therapeutics, Adynxx, AeroCare

444

Venture Capital & Private Equity Firms / Domestic Firms

Holdings, Alliance Healthcare Services, Ameritox, Apollo Global Management, Aprecia Pharma, Arbutus Biopharma, ARCA Biopharma, Arizona Center for Cancer Care, Arsenal Capital Partners, Baxter International, Bloom Health, Boston Children's Hospital, Caladrius Biosciences, Celator Pharma, Celerion Holdings, Celsus Therapeutics, Champions Oncolody, Churchill Pharma, Cold Spring Harbor Laboratory, CoLucid Pharma, Cyteir Therapeutics, Dana-Farber Cancer Institute, Data Driven Delivery Systems, Diffusion Pharma, Dimension Therapeutics, DNA Diagnostics Center, Envisia Therapeutics, Examination Management Services, Health Diagnostic Laboratory, HealthHelp, Horizon Pharma, IASIS Healthcare Corporation, Immunogen, ImmusanT, Ipsen, Jazz Pharma, Keryx Biopharma, Laurel Health Care Co., Ligand Pharma, Loving Care Agency, Madrigal Pharma, myNEXUS, Novozymes, Ocera Therapeutics, Ocular Technologies, OncoGenex Pharma, Otsuka Pharma, PathGroup, Physicians Dialysis, Poxel, Promise Healthcare, pSivida, Psyadon Pharma, Protalix Biotherapeutics, Realm Therapeutics, Shionogi & Co., Shire, Signature Hospice and Home Health, Starmount, StrataDx, Strongbridge Biopharma, Synta Pharma, Tarveda Therapeutics, TeamHealth, Tripex Pharma, Universal American, University of Massachusetts Medical School, Velicept Therapeutics, Verona Pharma, Vital Decisions, Walter and Eliza Hall Institute, Woodbury Health Products, Zymeworks

Key Executives:
  Curtis S Lane, Founding Partner
  e-mail: lane@mtspartners.com
  Education: MBA, Wharton School
  Background: Evercore Capital Partners; Manager Healthcare Investment, Bear Stearns & Co; Corporate Finance, Smith Barney, Harris Upham & Co
  Directorships: Lifeline Center for Child Development
  Mark E Epstein, Managing Partner
  e-mail: epstein@mtspartners.com
  Education: BS, Wharton School
  Background: Managing Director, Banc of America Securities' Private Equity Placements Group; VP, Private Equity Placements, Merrill Lynch & Co.
  Andrew J Weisenfeld, Managing Partner
  e-mail: weisenfeld@mtspartners.com
  Education: BS, Cornell University; MBA, Wharton School
  Background: Managing Director, Banc of America Securities' Corporate and Investment Banking Healthcare Group; Managing Director, JP Morgan; Merrill Lynch

1272 MUNICH REINSURANCE AMERICA, INC
555 College Road E
PO Box 5241
Princeton, NJ 08543

Phone: 609-243-4200 **Fax:** 609-243-4257
web: www.munichreamerica.com

Mission Statement: Offers stability, financial security, and expertise to clients; as a member of Munich Re Group, investments are backed by Munich Re's financial strength and commitment to reinsurance.

Geographic Preference: United States
Fund Size: $3.5 billion
Founded: 1917
Average Investment: $2.5 million
Investment Criteria: Second Round
Industry Group Preference: Insurance
Key Executives:
  Anthony J Kuczinski, President & CEO
  Philip Roeper, SVP/Chief Information Officer
  609-243-4711
  Education: BSEE, University of Southampton, UK
  Background: Director Global Network Services, DHL Systems; Comtext; ITT; Marconi Communications

1273 MURPHREE VENTURE PARTNERS
1221 Lamar
Suite 1136
Houston, TX 77010

Phone: 713-655-8500 **Fax:** 713-655-8503
web: www.murphreeventures.com

Mission Statement: Privately owned investment company that makes very early stage direct equity investments into entrepreneurial enterprises, and aligns itself with entrepreneurs and management groups, acting in concert with them as an owner and investor. In all instances, the company will operate to the highest standards of professionalism and ethical behavior. Quality of service and reputation will ultimately define the success of the firm's endeavors and the goal is to be worthy of the highest.

Geographic Preference: Southeastern United States
Fund Size: $60 million
Founded: 1987
Average Investment: $5 million
Minimum Investment: $250,000
Investment Criteria: Seed, Early-Stage, Quality management team, national or international market scope, definable exit within 3-7 years
Industry Group Preference: Business to Business, E-Commerce & Manufacturing, Semiconductors, Photonics, Life Sciences, Medical Devices, Telecommunications, Energy, High Technology
Portfolio Companies: Anark Corporation, Accello, Aldis, Dowley Security, Intrinergy, Object Reservoir, Smart Furniture, Square 1 Bank

Other Locations:
  1 Swiftwater Trail
  The Hills, TX 78738

  3104 Blue Lake Drive
  Suite 120
  Birmingham, AL 35243

Key Executives:
  Dennis E Murphree, Managing General Partner
  e-mail: dmurphree@murphreeventures.com
  Education: BA, Southern Methodist University; MBA, Wharton School
  Background: President/CEO, Murphree & Company; Faculty, Jones Graduate School, Rice University; Founder, Vail National Bank
  Directorships: Avent Networks, Unico Corporation, FiberDynamics, Journee Software
  John White, General Partner
  e-mail: jwhite@murphreeventures.com
  Education: BS, Political Science, Texas A&M University; JD, University of Texas School of Law
  Background: Private Law Practice; Co-Founder, Standard Renewable Energy Group; Managing Director, The Wind Alliance

1274 MURPHY & PARTNERS FUND LP
708 Third Avenue
Suite 1910
New York, NY 10017

Phone: 212-209-3879 **Fax:** 212-209-7148
e-mail: john@murphy-partners.com

Mission Statement: A private equity fund that, when fully invested, expects to hold a diversified portfolio of privately owned equity securities in profitable manufacturing, distribution and service companies. The fund typically invests in circumstances where it is the lead or controlling investor, where debt can be used along with equity to maximize growth, and where management seeks to have a significant equity share of the business.

Geographic Preference: United States
Founded: 1988
Average Investment: $1 - $10 million
Minimum Investment: $1 million

Venture Capital & Private Equity Firms / Domestic Firms

Investment Criteria: LBO, MBO, Growth, Early Stage
Industry Group Preference: Education, Healthcare, Media, Business Products & Services
Portfolio Companies: Mosaica Education Inc., N B Education
Key Executives:
  John J Murphy Jr, Managing General Partner
  212-209-3879 x1129
  Fax: 212-209-7148
  e-mail: john@murphy-partners.com
  Education: MBA, Amos Tuck School of Business Administration; AB, College of the Holy Cross College
  Background: 25-year investment track record with a lifetime IRR of over 30%; substantial investment experience in media/healthcare/education; Founder Fund I and II; Founding General Partner, Adler & Shaykin
  Directorships: Board position on all M&P portfolio companies

1275 MVP CAPITAL PARTNERS
259 N. Radnor-Chester Road
Suite 130
Radnor, PA 19087

Phone: 610-254-2999
e-mail: info@mvpcap.com
web: www.mvpcap.com

Mission Statement: Private equity investment firms that provide capital for later-stage growth companies and to finance acquisitions and recapitalizations.
Geographic Preference: Central & Eastern United States
Fund Size: $150 million
Founded: 1987
Average Investment: $3-10 million
Minimum Investment: $1 million
Investment Criteria: Later-Stage, Buy-Outs, Recapitalizations, Roll-Ups
Industry Group Preference: Publishing, Database Services, Media, Retailing, Distribution, Niche Manufacturing, Computer Hardware & Software, Life Sciences, Infrastructure, Business Products & Services, Healthcare Services, Consumer Products, Aviation
Portfolio Companies: Air Chef, Air Medical Group Holdings, American Bath Group, Andrews International Holdings, ANI Pharmaceuticals, Cadence Capital Management, Coffin Turbo Pump, Compass Water Solutions, Composite Technologies, Comprehensive Addiction Programs, Destination Maternity, Dorland Health, Expert Plan, GCA Service Solutions, Implex Corporation, Index Stock Imagery, Keystone Ranger Holdings, Legal Communications, MCMC, Mothers Work, Northern Contours, Omega Health Systems, Planalytics, Professional Press, Saxbys Coffee, Soft-Switch, SupplyOne Holding, Swiss Farm Stores, The Fairways Group, The Praxis Companies, York Risk Services
Key Executives:
  Bob Brown, Managing Partner
  Education: Princeton University; MBA, Wharton Graduate School; JD, University of Pennsylvania
  Background: Principal, Venture Capital firm; Founding Member, Greater Philadelphia Venture Group; Founding Director, Penn Venture Fund
  Tom Penn, Partner
  Education: BS, MIT; MBA, Stanford University
  Background: Partner, Boston Millennia Partners; President/CEO, Tektagen; President, Independence Ventures

1276 McCARTHY CAPITAL
1601 Dodge Street
Suite 3800
Omaha, NE 68102

Phone: 402-932-8600 Fax: 402-991-0020
e-mail: info@mccarthycapital.com
web: www.mccarthycapital.com

Mission Statement: McCarthy Capital uses its disciplined investment strategy to focus on investing in businesses in partnership with established management teams. This philosophy has enabled our portfolio companies to exceed their growth expectations for more than two decades.
Fund Size: $475 million
Founded: 1999
Minimum Investment: $10 million
Portfolio Companies: 365 Retail Markets, Advantor Systems Corporation, Altair Global, Alpha Comm Enterprises, AmeriSphere, Bamboo Rose, Bearence Management Group, Benaissance, Bigger Pockets, DSCI, Environmental Planning Group, Guild Mortage Company, HHA eXchange, Honey Smoked Fish, Life Care Services, Medical Solutions, Prospect Brands, Quantum Workplace, Remi, Rx Savings Solutions, SAFE Boats International, Scooter's Coffee, Seven10, Signal 88 Security, SKC Communication Products, Southwest Value Partners, The Remi Group, Triage Staffing, TriMech, United Real Estate Group
Other Locations:
  20 William St.
  Suite 160
  Wellesley, MA 02481
  Phone: 617-330-9700
Key Executives:
  Michael R McCarthy, Partner
  402-991-8414
  e-mail: mmccarthy@mccarthycapital.com
  Education: BA, St. John's University
  Background: Founder, McCarthy Organization
  Directorships: Cabela's Incorporated, Election Systems & Software, SAFE Boats
  Patrick J Duffy, President and Managing Partner
  402-991-8405
  e-mail: pduffy@mccarthycapital.com
  Education: BS, University of Southern California; JD, Creighton University School of Law
  Background: Partner, Fraser Stryker
  Directorships: Bearence Management Group, Benaissance, CoSentry.net, Life Care Services
  Robert Y Emmert, Managing Partner
  617-330-9710
  e-mail: bemmert@mccarthycapital.com
  Education: BA, Georgetown University
  Directorships: NRG Media, Advantor Systems Corporation

1277 NASSAU CAPITAL
12 Vanderventer Avenue
PO Box 1475
Princeton, NJ 08542

Phone: 609-430-9700
e-mail: rspowell@nassaucap.com
web: www.nassaucap.com

Mission Statement: Specializes in real estate financial strategies.
Founded: 1997
Key Executives:
  Robert S Powell Jr, Managing Director
  e-mail: rspowell@nassaucap.com
  Education: University of North Carolina; MA, PhD, Economics, Princeton University
  Background: President/CEO, DKM Properties; New Jerseye Economic Development Authority

Venture Capital & Private Equity Firms / Domestic Firms

Gerry Doherty, Senior Associate
Education: BA, Economics, University of Connecticut; MBA, Economics, University of Delaware
Ian J Mount, Senior Associate
Education: Vanderbilt University; MBA, Finance, American University
Background: Director of Development, Hekemian Kasparian Troast Group; Project Manager, Nassau HKT Urban Renewal Associates

1278 NAUTIC PARTNERS
50 Kennedy Plaza
Providence, RI 02903

Phone: 401-278-6770
web: www.nautic.com

Mission Statement: Nautic's mission is to achieve superior long-term investment returns for investors while preserving a strong culture that is based on partnership, humility and respect.
Geographic Preference: United States
Fund Size: $2.5 billion
Founded: 1986
Average Investment: $75 - $250 million
Minimum Investment: $50 million
Investment Criteria: Buyouts, Recapitalizations, Consolidations, Growth Financiings
Industry Group Preference: Business Products & Services, Manufacturing, Healthcare, Communications
Portfolio Companies: 1105 Media Holdings, All Metro Health Care Services, Applied Consultants, CCD Holdings, Curtis Industries Holdings, Custom Window Systems, Design/Craft Fabric Holdings, HB Performance Systems Holdings, HPS Holding Company, Milestone Aviation Group, NLS Holdings, Oasis Outsourcing, PEP Industries, QoL Meds, Reliant Hospital Partners, Respond2 Communications Holdings, Simonds Industries, Superior Vision Holding Company, Theorem Clinical Research Holdings

Key Executives:
Bernie Buonanno, Managing Director
401-278-5670
e-mail: bbuonanno@nautic.com
Education: AB, Brown University; MBA, Harvard Business School
Background: Fleet Equity Partners; Prudential-Bache Capital Funding
Habib Y Gorgi, Managing Director
401-278-6770
e-mail: hgorgi@nautic.com
Education: AB, Brown University; MBA, Columbia University
Background: Fleet Equity Partners; BankAmerica; Fleet Bank
Chris J. Crosby, Managing Director
401-278-6770
e-mail: ccrosby@nautic.com
Education: BS, Boston College; MBA, Harvard Business School
Background: McCown De Leeuw & Co., Kidder Peabody & Co.
Scott Hilinski, Managing Director
401-278-6770
e-mail: shilinski@nautic.com
Education: AB, Harvard University
Background: Fleet Equity Partners; TA Associates; Deloitte & Touche
Chris F. Corey, Managing Director
e-mail: ccorey@nautic.com
Education: BA, Assumption College; MBA, Columbia Business School
Background: JH Whitney & Co., Lehman Brothers
James A. Beakey, Managing Director, Business Development
e-mail: jbeakey@nautic.com
Education: BA, Trinity College; MBA, Northwestern University
Background: Capstone Partners, Adams Harkness & Hill
Chris A. Pierce, Managing Director
e-mail: cpierce@nautic.com
Education: BA, Yale University; MBA, Stanford Graduate School of Business
Background: Greenhill Capital Partners, Saloman Smith Barney/Citigroup Global Markets

1279 NAVIGATION CAPITAL PARTNERS
1175 Peachtree Street NE
10th Floor
Atlanta, GA 30361

Phone: 404-264-9180 **Fax:** 404-264-9305
e-mail: deals@navigationcapital.com
web: www.navigationcapital.com

Mission Statement: Works in close collaboration with the senior management of our portfolio companies, providing the benefit of our operating experience, insight and relationships.
Geographic Preference: United States
Fund Size: $2 billion
Founded: 2006
Average Investment: $10 - $40 million
Investment Criteria: $20 to $200 million in revenue
Industry Group Preference: Distribution, Business Products & Services, Financial Services, Healthcare Services, Transportation, Logistics, Automotive, Building Materials & Services, Manufacturing, Infrastructure, Media, Food & Beverage, Government
Portfolio Companies: Brightwell Payments, Brown Integrated Logistics, Computex Technology Solutions, Definition 6, Exeter Finance Corporation

Key Executives:
Lawrence Mock, Managing Partner, Co-Founder
404-583-0425
e-mail: lmock@navigationcapital.com
Education: BA, Harvard College; MS, Florida State University; London School of Economics
Background: President & CEO, Mellon Ventures; Co-Founder, River Capital; COO, Hangar One
Directorships: Brown Integrated Logistics, Exeter Finance, Definition 6, Brightwell Payments, Computex Technology Solutions
John Richardson, Managing Partner, Co-Founder
Education: BA, Princeton University; MBA, University of Pittsburgh
Background: Managing Director, Mellon Ventures; CFO, Unibev
Directorships: Pecora Corp.
Mark Downs, Partner, Co-Founder
Education: BA, University of Pittsburgh; MBA, Northwestern University, JL Kellogg School of Management
Background: Senior Vice President, Mellon Ventures
Directorships: AH Harris, Brightwell Payments, Definition 6, Five Star Food Service, Quantapoint
Eerik Giles, Partner, Co-Founder
Education: BS, Economics, Pennsylvania State University
Background: Vice President, Mellon Ventures; Legg Mason
Directorships: Pecora Corporation, Computex Technology Solutions, Technical Innovation
Dennis Lockhart, Partner
Education: BA, Economics and Political Science, Stanford Universy; MS, International Economics and American Foreign Policy, Johns Hopkins University
Background: CEO, President, Federal Reserve Bank of Atlanta; Managing Partner, Zephyr Management; President of Heller International Group, Heller International; Citibank
Directorships: Metro Atlanta Chamber of Commerce, Georgia Research Alliance

Venture Capital & Private Equity Firms / Domestic Firms

1280 NAVIGATOR PARTNERS LLC
P.O. Box 159
Summit, NJ 07901

Phone: 908-273-7733 Fax: 908-273-5566
e-mail: info@navigatorpartners.com
web: www.navigatorpartners.com

Mission Statement: Navigator is a private equity firm, a related entity is the manager for Navigator Growth Partners LP, a private equity investment fund organized as an SBIC, which created a diversified portfolio with a focus on manufacturers and marketers of basic consumer products and services.

Geographic Preference: Mid-Atlantic
Fund Size: $100 million
Founded: 1999
Average Investment: $2 million
Minimum Investment: $500,000
Investment Criteria: Later-Stage, Acquisitions, Growth Capital
Industry Group Preference: Diversified
Portfolio Companies: Compass Water Solutions, Crestcom, FirstLight HomeCare, Jon M Hall Company, K9 Resorts, Molecular Imaging Technology, Nelson Pipeline, Revere

Key Executives:
W Joseph Imhoff, Co-Founder/Managing Partner
Education: Northwestern University
Background: Chairman, Hebi Health Care AB; Founder/CEO, Hagemeyer Foods; VP/CIO, Jim Walter Corp; VP, W.R. Grace & Co; Senior Marketing/Operations Officer, Borden
Directorships: Nelson Pipeline, K9 Resorts
Bernard B Markey, Co-Founder/Managing Partner
Education: Villanova University; MM, Kellogg School of Management Northwestern University
Background: Chairman, Greater Philadelphia Venture Group
Directorships: CK Franchising, Universal Envrionmental Services, Lumeta Corporation
William H Stewart, Co-Founder/Managing Partner
Education: BS, Villanova University; MBA, New York University
Background: Managing Director, Nassau Captical; CFO, KMC Telecom; KDC Solar; KDC Agribusiness
Directorships: FirstLight HomeCare, K9 Resorts, Nelson Popeline, Jon M Hall Company

1281 NAVITAS CAPITAL
1111 Broadway Avenue
Oakland, CA 94607

web: www.navitascap.com

Mission Statement: Navitas Capital is a cleantech venture capital firm focused on investing in next generation energy efficiency and green building technology companies.

Founded: 2008
Industry Group Preference: Clean Technology, Building Materials & Services, Software
Portfolio Companies: Aquicore, Bowery, Cherre, Comfy, Gridium, HappyCo, Harbour, Honest Buildings, HqO, Katerra, Livly, Matter Port, OpenSpace, Orchard, PeerStreet, PiinPoint, Powermat, Procore, Ravti, Sweeten, Truss, View Dynamic Glass

Other Locations:
9460 Wilshire Boulevard
Suite 850
Beverly Hills, CA 90212

Key Executives:
Travis Putnam, Co-Founder/Managing Partner
Education: BS, Economics, Wharton School
Background: Founder, Genesis Management Group; Murphy & Associates Capital
Jim Pettit, Co-Founder/Managing Partner
Education: BS, Haas School of Business, University of California, Berkeley
Background: Principal, Bancroft Capital; Managing Director, JP Morgan
Directorships: Optimum Energy, Gridium, Enmetric Systems, Lunera Lighting
Gary Dillabough, Managing Partner
Education: BS, Civil Engineering, California Polytechnic State University, San Luis Obispo
Background: Managing Partner, Westly Group; EBay; Vistro Corporation; Improvenet; Media Arts Group
Directorships: View Dynamic Glass, Lunera Lighting, Building Robotics, Honest Buildings, MyHealthTeams

1282 NAVY CAPITAL
575 Lexington Avenue
4th Floor
New York, NY 10022

Phone: 646-512-8748
e-mail: ir@navycapital.com
web: www.navycapital.com

Mission Statement: Invests in new opportunities within the legal cannabis industry, including consumer, healthcare and agriculture.

Founded: 2017
Industry Group Preference: Cannabis, Consumer Products, Healthcare, Technology, Agriculture
Portfolio Companies: CLS Holdings USA, GrowGeneration, MariMed, PLUS

Key Executives:
Kevin Gahwyler, President/Chief Financial Officer
Education: BS, Biology, Fairfield University; MIM, International Finance, Thunderbird School of Global Management
Background: Investment Analyst, GM Asset Management; Director of Investor Relations, Sagamore Hill; SVP, Pequot Capital; Managing Director, CDG Holdings; President, KenCole Capital LLC; COO/Director, Business Development, Twin Capital Management
Directorships: A Little Hope Foundation; Team Racing for Veterans (RV4)
Jeffrey Schultz, General Counsel/Chief Compliance Officer
Education: BA, English, University of Michigan; JD, Cardozo School of Law
Background: Legal & Compliance, K2 Advisor; Legal Counsel, BNP Paribas Investment Partners; Chief Legal/Compliance Officer, Phoenix Investment Advisor; Managing Director/Sr. Counsel/CCO, GPB Capital; Sr. Advisor, GPB Capital
Sean Stiefel, Principal
Education: University of St. Gallen (Switzerland); BBA, Marshall School of Business, University of Southern California
Background: Analyst, Barclays Capital; Associate, Millenium Management; Trader, Northwoods Capital
John T. Kaden, Principal
Education: AB, Harvard University; JD, Yale Law School
Background: Founder/Chief Investment Officer, Cynthion Partners; Co-Manager/Chief Investment Officer, Northwoods Capital; Manager/Chief Investment Offer, Navy Capital Green Fund LP

1283 NAXURI CAPITAL
425 Broadway St.
Redwood City, CA 94062

Mission Statement: Naxuri Capital is the premier seed fund investing in early stage companies at the intersection of fashion, retail, and technology. The Naxuri Capital Investment strategy is focused on early stage companies in the fashion and technology market. We are very selective when choosing our investment opportunities and we are very confident that we can add significant value to the companies we invest in.

Investment Criteria: Early Stage

Venture Capital & Private Equity Firms / Domestic Firms

Industry Group Preference: Fashion, Retail, Consumer & Leisure

Key Executives:
Enrico Beltramini, Managing Director
Background: Corporate Executive and Global Advisor at Gucci, Fiat, Rinascente Group, and PA Consulting Group
Patrick Chung, Managing Director
Background: Co-Founding Managing Director, SK Telecom Ventures; Corporate Attorney, Wilson Sonsini Goodrich & Rosati; Advior, Kim & Chang; Director of Business Development, Dialpad Communications

1284 NAYA VENTURES
222 W Las Colinas Boulevard
Suite 755E
Irving, TX 75039

e-mail: info@nayaventures.com
web: www.nayaventures.com

Mission Statement: Naya Ventures invests in companies located in the US and India in technology, focusing on mobile and cloud services.

Geographic Preference: United States, India
Average Investment: $250,000 - $3 million
Investment Criteria: Early-Stage
Industry Group Preference: Mobile, SaaS, Cloud Computing, Big Data, Business to Business, B2B, AI, Emerging Technology
Portfolio Companies: Altia Systems, Appnique, autoGraph, Boxfish, DocSynk, GlobalOutlook, Glympse, HyperVerge, KeepTrax, Kore.ai, Motivity Labs, PDHI

Other Locations:
710 Second Avenue
Suite 400
Seattle, WA 98104

Floor-3, Block-1
My Home Hub
Madhapur
Hyderabad 500081
India

Key Executives:
Dayakar Puskoor, Co-Founder/General Partner
Education: Stephen F. Austin University; MS, Computer Science, Nova University
Background: Hosting & Mobility Solutions, Microsoft; Founder & CEO, JP Mobile
Directorships: Altia Systems, SnapOne, Zoomingo
Pabhakar Reddy, Co-Founder/Managing Partner
Education: BS, Engineering, Andhra University; MBA, Booth School of Business
Background: Managing Director, ANSR Group; CIO, Risesmart.com
Directorships: GlobalOutlook, Motivity Labs

1285 NCT VENTURES
One Marconi Place
274 Marconi Boulevard
Suite 400
Columbus, OH 43215

e-mail: info@nctventures.com
web: www.nctventures.com

Mission Statement: NCT incvests in early-stage businesses, and they focus on helping entrepreneurs build lasting buisness.

Geographic Preference: Midwestern United States
Industry Group Preference: Marketing, Logistics, Research, Industrial Products, Economics
Portfolio Companies: 10X Engineered Materials, Aver, Azoti, Buzz Solutions, Data Inventions, DOmedia, Ethex, Exacter, FactGem, HAAS Alert, Healthy Roster, Heureka Software, Impact Economics, Imperva Bot Management, inTouch, iUNU, JadeTrack, LevelEleven, Mentored, Nikola Labs, Nimia, Olive, OnSeen, OROS, PopCom, PriorAuthNow, SHARE

Key Executives:
Rich Langdale, Managing Partner
Education: Ohio State University
Background: Co-Founder, Digital Storage
Bill Frank
Background: United States Army; Co-Founder, Prometheus Group; Co-Founder, MuniNET
Lindsay Karas, Partner
Education: BA, Political Science, Canisius College; JD, MBA, Ohio State University
Michael Butler, Partner
Education: BS, Accounting, Ohio State University; MBA, Ashland University; CPA
Background: President, Nationwide Fund Distributors; CFO, Ernst & Whinney

1286 NDI MEDICAL
22901 Millcreek Boulevard
Suite 110
Cleveland, OH 44122

Phone: 216-378-9106 Fax: 216-378-9116
e-mail: info@ndimedical.com
web: www.ndimedical.com

Mission Statement: NDI is a leading venture capital and commercialization firm that focuses on innovative neurodevice technologies to address significant unmet health conditions.

Founded: 2002
Industry Group Preference: Medical Devices
Portfolio Companies: Checkpoint Surgical, Deep Brain Innovations, MEDSTIM, SPR Therapeutics

Other Locations:
308 W Rosemary Street
Suite 308
Chapel Hill, NC 27516
Phone: 919-928-8005 Fax: 919-928-8006

601 Carlson Parkway
Suite 1050
Minneapolis, MN 55305
Phone: 612-770-0390 Fax: 216-378-9116

Key Executives:
Geoffrey B Thrope, Founder/CEO
Education: BS, Biomedical Engineering, Case Western Reserve University
Background: Vice President, New Business Development, NeuroControl Corporation
Leonard M Cosentino, Managing Director
Education: JD, Case Western Reserve University School of Law
Robert Strother, Vice Presiden of Engineering/CTO
Education: BEng, Electrical Engineering, Case Western Reserve University
Background: Research Instrumentation Associates

1287 NEEDHAM CAPITAL PARTNERS
250 Park Avenue
New York, NY 10177

Phone: 212-371-8300 Fax: 212-705-0411
web: www.needhamco.com

Mission Statement: Provides private equity capital for the expansion of private and smaller public growth companies; liquidity for longer-term shareholders in private and smaller public growth companies; strategic acquisitions and management-led buyouts of growth companies.

Geographic Preference: United States
Fund Size: $1 billion
Founded: 1985
Average Investment: $2-$10 million
Investment Criteria: Mezzanine, LBO, Special Situations, Expansion, MBO, Recaps

Venture Capital & Private Equity Firms / Domestic Firms

Industry Group Preference: Computer Related, Consumer Services, Information Technology, Medical Devices, Software, Semiconductors, Retailing, Technology, Telecommunications, Clean Technology, Communications, Infrastructure, Financial Services
Portfolio Companies: Agile Software, Alacritech Inc., Athena Semiconductors, Atherotech, Auust Technology Corporation, Bay MicroSystems, Biocept, Blue Pumpkin Software/Witness Systems, Boxer Cross, Capital SLI Group, CenterRun, Ceon Corporation/Convergys Corporation, Ceradyne, Chip X Corp (Chip Express), Clarity Visual Systems/Planar Systems, Collectors Universe, College Enterprises/Blackboard, Color Kinetics, Conventor, CoWare, diCarta/Emptoris, Displaytech, ePartners, Fatbrain.com/Barnesandnoble.com, Favrille, Hot Rail/Conexant/Skyworks, Innovion, Kanisa/Knova, Lara Networks, Loadstar Sensors, Logic Vision, Nascentric, Neophotonics, Nextest/Teradyne, Obsidian/Applied Materials, Peregrine Semiconductor, Persistence Software, Pharsight, Rebar, Sensis, Silicon Metrics, SOFTEK Storage Solutions, Southwall Technologies, SpaceClaim, Stanford Microdevices/Sirenza, TestQuest, Trinity Convergence, ViewLogic Systems, Wind River Systems/Rapid Logic

Other Locations:
Two International Place
Suite 2610
Boston, MA 02110
Phone: 617-457-0910 **Fax:** 617-457-5777

701 Carlson Parkway
Suite 250
Minnetonka, MN 55305
Phone: 612-474-2963

535 Mission Street
San Francisco, CA 94105
Phone: 415-262-4860 **Fax:** 650-854-9853

180 North LaSalle
Suite 3700
Chicago, IL 60601
Phone: 312-981-0412 **Fax:** 312-377-0278

Key Executives:
Kevin McGrath, Managing Director & Head, Corporate and Venture Services
e-mail: corporateservices@needhamco.com
Education: BA, Southern Connecticut University
Background: JP Morgan; Merrill Lynch; Smith Barney; Banc of America Securities
Jack Iacovone, Chief Executive Officer
212-705-0297
e-mail: jiacovone@needhamco.com
Education: BS, Accounting, Pace University
Background: KPMG Peat Marwick LLP

1288 NEMO CAPITAL PARTNERS
28819 Franklin Road
Southfield, MI 48034

Phone: 248-213-9899
web: www.nemohealth.com

Mission Statement: NEMO Capital Partners is a private equity firm that targets companies in the medical technology sector.

Industry Group Preference: Healthcare, Healthcare Information Technology, Medical Technology
Portfolio Companies: Collaborative Practice Solutions, DirectEHR, SmartSheet10 Technology, TRAKnet

Key Executives:
Ali Safiedine DPM, Chief Executive Officer
Education: BA, Biology, Wayne State University; DPM, Barry University; MBA, University of Michigan
Background: President, Michigan Podiatric Medical Association
John Guiliana DPM, Executive Vice President
Education: BS, Pharmacy, St. John's University; MS, Healthcare Management, College of Saint Elizabeth; DPM, Temple University
Background: Owner, Foot Care Associates
Jeff Frederick DPM, Executive Vice President
Education: Michigan State University
Background: President, Michigan Podiatric Medical Association; American Academy of Podiatric Practice Management

1289 NEST VENTURES
3104 Camelback Road
Suite 144
Phoenix, AZ 85016-4595

Phone: 602-315-9550
e-mail: info@nestventures.com
web: www.nestventures.com

Mission Statement: A consulting boutique that offers customized solutions to its client companies. The company was formed with the purpose of advising both public and private companies focusing on capital formation, strategic alliances, mergers and acquisitions, and other operational issues.

Geographic Preference: International
Fund Size: $600 million
Founded: 1997
Average Investment: $7-$8 million
Minimum Investment: $5 million
Investment Criteria: Later Stage
Industry Group Preference: Biotechnology, Software, Communications, Digital Media & Marketing, Wireless Technologies, Energy

Key Executives:
Glenn Williamson, Managing Partner
Background: Founder/CEO, Canada Arizona Business Council; Director, Obsidian Strategies

1290 NEW ATLANTIC VENTURES
11911 Freedom Drive
Suite 1080
Reston, VA 20190

Phone: 703-563-4100 **Fax:** 703-563-4111
web: www.navfund.com

Mission Statement: To make seed and early-stage investments in businesses targeting high-growth emerging mass markets.

Fund Size: $117 million
Founded: 2006
Average Investment: $500,000 - $5 million
Investment Criteria: Seed-Stage, Early-Stage
Industry Group Preference: Mobile, New Media, Online Services, Technology, SaaS, Advertising, Software, Consumer, Entertainment, E-Commerce & Manufacturing
Portfolio Companies: AppTap, Bambecco, BlockScore, Brand Yourself, CivicScience, CrashMob, Crossboard Mobil, EveryScape, ExecOnline, HealthWarehouse.com, Invincea, Moda Operandi, Nantero, PokitDok, PulsePoint, Qliance, Quad Learning, Scoutmob, Solve Media, Spotflux, Tap 'n Tap, Truveris, TVU Networks, YieldBot, Zady, Zerve

Other Locations:
One Mifflin Place
Suite 400
Cambridge, MA 02138

Key Executives:
John Backus, Founder/Managing Partner
703-563-4101
e-mail: john@navfund.com
Education: BA, Economics, MBA, Stanford University
Background: President & CEO, InteliData Technologies
Directorships: AppTap, Invincea, Spotflux, PokitDok
Thanasis Delistathis, Founder/Managing Partner
703-563-4106
e-mail: thanasis@navfund.com
Education: BSE, Electrical Engineering, Princeton University; BCert, Public Policy, Princeton University Woodrow Wilson School; MBA, Harvard Business School

Venture Capital & Private Equity Firms / Domestic Firms

Background: Investment Banking, Thermo Electron Corp.; McKinsey & Co.
Todd Hixon, Founder/Managing Partner/Chief Financial Officer
617-758-4213
e-mail: todd@navfund.com
Education: BA, Princeton University; MBA, Harvard Business School
Background: Managing Partner, DFJ New England Fund; SVP, The Boston Consulting Group
Directorships: Qliance, CivicScience, Tap-n-Tap, EveryScape
Scott Johnson, Founder/Managing Partner
617-758-4234
e-mail: scott@navfund.com
Education: BS, Operations Research, Cornell University; MBA, MIT Sloan School of Management
Background: DFJ New England; East Coast Partner, Cambridge Technology Capital Fund
Directorships: Fashion Playtes, Solve Media, Truveris, Yieldbot, Spotflux

1291 NEW CAPITAL FUND
2100 Freedom Road
Suite A
Little Chute, WI 54140

web: www.newcapitalfund.com

Mission Statement: Focused on making early-stage life and material science, information technology and growth-stage niche/advanced manufacturing investments.

Geographic Preference: Wisconsin
Fund Size: $45 million
Founded: 2006
Average Investment: $500,000 to $1.5 million
Minimum Investment: $500,000
Investment Criteria: Early-Stage, Growth Stage
Industry Group Preference: Niche Manufacturing, Information Technology, Life Sciences
Portfolio Companies: Aurizon Ultrasonics, Magma Flooring, Phoenix Nuclear Labs, Ro-Flow Compressors, Simply Incredible Foods, Forte Research Systems, Hopster, Huterra, Optimine, TrafficCast International, Invenra, Rapid Diagnostek, Renovar, Silatronix, Swallow Solutions, Xolve
Key Executives:
   Robert DeBruin, Managing Director
   e-mail: bob.debruin@newcapitalfund.com
   Education: BBA, Accounting, University of Wisconsin, Madison
   Background: President, Schenck Corporate Finance Group; Arthur Young & Co.
   Directorships: NEW Capital Fund, Master Mold, National Tissue Company, Werner Electric
   Charlie Goff, Managing Director
   e-mail: charlie@newcapitalfund.com
   Education: Math & Computer Science, University of Wisconsin, Oshkosh; MBA, University of Wisconsin, Madison
   Background: Staff Accountant, Arthur Anderson LLP; Founder, Forward Enterprises
   Directorships: Azco, Keller, Inc., HuTerra, De Pere, Rapid Diagnostek, Xolve, Renovar, Aurizon Ultrasonics
   David Gitter, Managing Director
   e-mail: dave.gitter@newcapitalfund.com
   Education: BBA, MBA, University of Wisconsin, Oshkosh
   Background: M&I Marshal & Isley Corporation
   Directorships: Azco, Network Health Plan, Valley Packaging, Fox Valley Residency Clinic, Community Real Estate, Personal Property Foundation
   Steve Predayna, Managing Director
   e-mail: steve.predayna@newcapitalfund.com
   Education: BBA, Accounting, University of Wisconsin, Oshkosh

   Background: Vice President, Schenck Corporate Finance Group; Great Northern Corporation

1292 NEW CAPITAL PARTNERS
2101 Highland Avenue South
Suite 700
Birmingham, AL 35205

web: www.newcapitalpartners.com

Mission Statement: To acquire and/or partner with businesses and management teams who are focused on building sustainable businesses of exceptional value.

Geographic Preference: Texas, Southeastern United States
Fund Size: $225 million
Founded: 2001
Investment Criteria: Buyouts, Acquisitions, Recapitalizations, Growth Equity
Industry Group Preference: Healthcare Services, Healthcare Information Technology, Financial Services, Insurance, Business Products & Services
Portfolio Companies: ACES Quality Management, Care Services LLC, Collect Rx, ControlCase, Dotcom Therapy, GeoVera Insurance, Healthfuse, Medsurant Health, P&R Dental Strategies, Precision, Sequence Health, Sprout, Telehealth Solutions, Volly

Other Locations:
   2101 Cedar Springs Road
   Suite 1200
   Dallas, TX 75201
   Phone: 214-871-5408 **Fax:** 214-871-5401
Key Executives:
   Jim Little, Managing Partner & Founder
   Education: BS, Engineering, Auburn University
   Directorships: Cogent Partners, Safe Harbour Underwriters
   James Outland, Managing Partner
   Education: BA, Political Science, BFA, Advertising, Southern Methodist University
   Background: Officer, UnitedHealth Group
   Directorships: Repay Holdings, MDnet Solutions, Medsurant Holdings, Teladoc Medical Services
   Adam Cranford, Managing Director
   Education: BS/MS, Georgia Institute of Technology; MBA, Booth School of Business, University of Chicago
   Background: Executive Group Analyst, Dollar General Corporation
   Directorships: Collect Rx; Medsurant Holdings; P&R Dental; Volly; ACES Quality Management; Precision; Healthfuse
Key Executives:
   John Whorf, Managing Director
   781-799-9474
   Education: BS, Massachusetts Maritime Academy; MBA, FW Olin Graduate School of Business, Babson College

1294 NEW ENGLAND BUSINESS EXCHANGE
Wellesley, MA 02481

Phone: 781-801-4429
e-mail: jwhorf@nebex.com
web: www.nebex.com

Mission Statement: Focus on building strong relationships, paying attention to detail, recognizing value, delivering excellent service, and negotiating from a position of strength.

Founded: 1988
Average Investment: $500,000
Minimum Investment: $100,000
Investment Criteria: Open
Portfolio Companies: Accumeter Labs, Adams Brush Manufacturing, Aerovox, AET, American Candy, American Felt & Filter, Avista, BancBoston Capital, BAI Global, CLT Research, CML Group, Commonwealth Sprague, Contact East, Creative Solutions Group, General Electric, Geo Mcquesten, Goldner Hawn, Guideline Research, Harmony

Venture Capital & Private Equity Firms / Domestic Firms

Toy, Infrasoft, Interlacken Capital, Jilcraft, Judson Technologies, The Langley Corporation, Language Management, International, The Leather Shop, Merlin Metalworks, Missouri Metals, New England Envelope, New England Growth Fund, Norsun Foods, Opticon, Pentzer Corporation, Perkin Elmer, Rad Locks, Retail Associated Mgt., Safeguard America, Standex International, The Stanley Works, Store Fixtures Group, Syon, Tech Pak, TEK Supply, Teradyne, Tra-con, Tripifoods, Westcoast Entertainment, Whistler, Williams Healthcare, Wilton Corporation, Worcester Brush, Xtra-Vision PLC, Videosmith, Voltarc

1295 NEW ENGLAND CAPITAL PARTNERS
One Gateway Center
Suite 405
Newton, MA 02458

Phone: 617-964-7300 Fax: 617-964-7301
web: www.necapitalpartners.com

Mission Statement: A private equity investment firm focused on acquiring lower middle-market operating companies. NECP is a successor to and affiliate of New England Capital Management.

Geographic Preference: Northeastern United States
Founded: 1991
Average Investment: $10 - 30 million
Minimum Investment: $2 million
Industry Group Preference: Manufacturing, Distribution, Business Products & Services, Consumer Products

Key Executives:
  Aevin M McCafferty, Chairman
  e-mail: kevin@necapitalpartners.com
  Education: AB, Harvard College; MBA, University of Chicago
  Background: General Partner, Madison Dearborn Partners; Vice President, First Chicago Venture Capital; Partner, Catalyst Health; Partner, Technology Partners
  Robert D Winneg, President
  e-mail: rwinneg@necapitalpartners.com
  Education: BA, Economics, Tufts University; MBA, Tuck School of Business Administration, Dartmouth College
  Background: Principal Investor, BancBoston Capital
  Directorships: Wild Planet
  Brendan McCafferty, Principal
  e-mail: bmccafferty@necapitalpartners.com
  Education: AB, Harvard University
  Background: President, Dustless Floor Sanding

1296 NEW ENTERPRISE ASSOCIATES
1954 Greenspring Drive
Suite 600
Timonium, MD 21093

Phone: 410-842-4000 Fax: 410-842-4100
e-mail: LPRelations@nea.com
web: www.nea.com

Mission Statement: A leading venture capital firm investing in information technology, energy technology and healthcare companies. Practicing classic venture capital for over 25 years, NEA focuses on early stage investments, playing an active role in assisting management to build companies of lasting value. With $6 billion under management, NEA's experienced management team has invested in over 500 companies, of which more than 135 have gone public and more than 150 have been acquired. NEA has offices in across the U.S.

Geographic Preference: Global
Fund Size: $18 billion
Average Investment: $10 million
Minimum Investment: $200,000
Investment Criteria: All Stages
Industry Group Preference: Electronics, Consumer Technology, Enterprise Mobility, Virtualization, Technology-Enabled Services, SaaS, Cloud Computing, Biopharmaceuticals, Healthcare Devices, Healthcare Services

Portfolio Companies: Anyscale, Black Diamond Therapeutics, Branch, Built Robotics, Clock Work, Coursera, Crispr Therapeutics, Databricks, Datarobot, Delta Stream, Everside Health, Fizz, Forethought, Genies, Goodleap, Masterclass, Moonpay, Opendoor, Patreon, Radiology Partners, Robinhood, Strive Health, Tempus, Transfix, Uniphore

Other Locations:
  5425 Wisconsin Avenue
  Suite 800
  Chevy Chase, MD 20815
  Phone: 301-272-2300 Fax: 301-272-1700

  2855 Sand Hill Road
  Menlo Park, CA 94025
  Phone: 650-854-9499 Fax: 650-854-1854

  104 5th Avenue
  19th Floor
  New York, NY 10001
  Phone: 646-677-2777

Key Executives:
  Peter Barris, Chairman
  Education: MBA, Dartmouth College; BSEE, Northwestern University
  Background: President/COO, LEGENT; Senior VP/General Manager, UCCEL; VP/General Manger, GE
  Forest Baskett, General Partner
  Education: BA, Mathematics, Rice University; PhD, Computer Science, University of Texas, Austin
  Background: Senior Vice President of R&D, Silicon Graphics; Founder, Western Research Laboratory; Professor of Computer Science & Electrical Engineering, Stanford University
  Tony Florence, Managing General Partner, Technology
  Education: AB & MBA, Economics, Dartmouth College
  Background: Managing Director, Morgan Stanley
  Mohamad Makhzoumi, Managing General Partner, Healthcare
  Education: BS, International Relations, University of Pennsylvania
  Background: UBS Investment Bank; Associate, Summit Partners
  Directorships: Aetion, American Pathology Partners, Bright Health, Collective Health, Curisium, Docent Healths, Nuvolo, Pager, Paladina Health, Radiology Partners, SCI Solutions, etc.
  Josh Makower, General Partner
  Education: BS, Mechanical Engineering, MIT; MBA, Columbia University; MD, NYU School of Medicine
  Background: ExploraMed
  Scott Sandell, Managing General Partner
  Education: MBA, Stanford University; AB, Engineering Sciences, Dartmouth College
  Background: Boston Consulting Group; C-ATS Software; Microsoft
  Directorships: Bloom Energy. Branch Metrics, CareZone, Cloudflare, Coursera, Datrium, Enigma, Hello Alfred, One Concern, Qadium, Robinhood, Transfix, UnifyID
  Peter Sonsini, General Partner
  Education: BA, Political Economy, University of California, Berkeley; MBA, Kellogg School of Management, Northwestern University
  Background: VMware; Mirapoint; Hewlett-Packard; Montgomery Securities
  Directorships: Conviva, Databricks, GuideSpark, Instabase, Lattice Engines, MapR Technologies, Matroid, Nefeli, Nginx, Splashtop, Yubico

1297 NEW LEAF VENTURE PARTNERS
420 Lexington Avenue
Suite 408
New York, NY 10170

Phone: 646-871-6400 Fax: 646-871-6450
e-mail: info@nlvpartners.com
web: www.nlvpartners.com

Mission Statement: A leading healthcare technology investor, our goal is to build strong companies by supporting exceptional teams in the development of clinically important and commercially attractive products.

Fund Size: $1.3 billion
Founded: 2005
Industry Group Preference: Biopharmaceuticals, Medical Devices, Diagnostics
Portfolio Companies: Afferent Pharmaceuticals, Calchan Holdings, Calithera Biosciences, Chimerix, Concert Pharmaceuticals, Convergence Pharmaceuticals, Intarcia Therapeutics, Karos Pharmaceuticals, Karus Therapeutics, MEI Pharma, Principia Biopharma, Relypsa, Sopherion Therapeutics, Tioga Pharmaceuticals, VaxInnate, Versartis, Awarepoint, Irhythm Technnologies, Kit Check, QPID Health, Tigertext, Treato, Truveris, Altura Medical, Cardiokinetix, Direct Flow, Illuminoss Medical, Intrinsic Therapeutics, Neuronetics, Reshape Medical, Spine Wave, Spiracur, Advanced Cell Diagnostics, Caredx, Labcyte, Oxord Immunotec

Other Locations:
1200 Park Place
Suite 300
San Mateo, CA 94403
Phone: 650-234-2700 Fax: 650-234-2704

Ron Hunt, Managing Director
646-871-6400
e-mail: ron@nlvpartners.com
Education: BS, Cornell University; MBA, Wharton School
Background: Sprout Group; Consultant, Coopers & Lybrand Consulting; Johnson & Johnson; SmithKline Beecham Pharmaceuticals
Directorships: Durata Therapeutics, Spine Wave, IlluminOss Medical, Relypsa

Vijay Lathi, Managing Director
650-234-2700
e-mail: vijay@nlvpartners.com
Education: BS, Chemical Engineering, MIT; MS, Chemical Engineering, Stanford University
Background: Sprout Group; Analyst, Healthcare Venture Capital Group, Robertson Stephens & Co.; Cornerstone Research
Directorships: Expression Diagnostics, iRhythm Technologies, Kit Check, Oxford Immunotec, TigerText

James Niedel, Managing Partner
646-871-6400
e-mail: jim@nlvpartners.com
Education: MD, PhD, Biochemistry, University of Miami; Fellow, Royal College of Physicians
Background: Venture Parter, Sprout Group; Chief Science & Technology Officer, GlaxoSmithKline; Board Member, Glaxo Wellcome plc; Professor of Medicine & Chief of the division of Clinical Pharmacology, Duke Medical School
Directorships: Intarcia Therapeutics, Tioga Pharmaceuticals, Chimerix

Rebecca Luse, Principal
e-mail: rebecca@nlvpartners.com
Education: BS, Biochemistry & Mathematics, Indiana University
Background: Research Senior Associate, Biotechnology, Jefferies; Research Associate, Specialty Pharmaceuticals, Piper Jaffray; Analyst, Bay City Capital; Healthcare Investment Banking Analyst, Bank of America Securities

Craig Slutzkin, Chief Operating Officer/Chief Financial Officer
e-mail: craig@nlvpartners.com
Education: BA, Accounting, Queens College; MBA, Columbia Business School
Background: CFO, Sprout Group; Senior Manager, Ernst & Young

1298 NEW MARKETS VENTURE PARTNERS
8161 Maple Lawn Blvd
Suite 350
Fulton, MD 20759

Phone: 301-362-5511 Fax: 301-362-5517
web: www.newmarketsvp.com

Mission Statement: New Markets Venture Partners is a leading early stage venture capital firm that invests in and actively assists innovative information technology, education and healthcare companies.

Geographic Preference: Mid-Atlantic United States
Investment Criteria: Early-Stage
Industry Group Preference: Information Technology, Education, Healthcare
Portfolio Companies: American Honors, Authntk, BetterLesson, BioSet, Calvert Education Services, Civitas Learning, CSA Medical, eCoast Marketing, Fishtree, Graduation Alliance, Innovative Biosensors, K2 Intelligence, Kickboard, Kroll BondRatings, Mashable, MediaSolv, Orchestro, Overture Technologies, PresenceLearning, Questar Assesment, Regent, Snappcloud, Starfish Retention Solutions, StraighterLine, Think Through Learning, Three Ring, Videology, Workspace.com

Key Executives:
Robb Doub, General Partner
e-mail: rdoub@newmarketsvp.com
Education: University of Vermont; MBA, Georgetown University
Background: Managing Director, Small Enterprise Assistance Funds; Associate, Calvert Group
Directorships: eCoast Sales Solutions, PresenceLearning

Mark Grovic, General Partner
e-mail: mgrovic@newmarketsvp.com
Education: University of California, Berkeley; JD, Georgetown University
Background: Portfolio Manager, Small Enterprise Assistance Funds; Director, Baltic Small Equity Fund; Co-Founder & Principal, Templeton Emerging Europe Fund; Principal, Templeton Direct Advisors; Portfolio Manager, Calvert Group
Directorships: Graduation Alliance, Innovation Biosensors, Lightningcast, Moodlerooms, Workspace.com

Donald Spero, Founding Partner
e-mail: dspero@newmarketsvp.com
Education: Cornell University; PhD, Physics, Columbia University
Background: Director, Dingman Center for Entrepreneurship; Founder, Spero Quality Strategies; Founder, President & CEO, Fusion Systems Corporation

1299 NEW MEXICO COMMUNITY CAPITAL
801 University Blvd SE
Suite 102
Albuquerque, NM 87106

Phone: 505-924-2820 Fax: 505-213-0333
Toll-Free: 866-222-1552
e-mail: info@nmccap.org
web: nmccap.org

Mission Statement: Through targeted financial investments and entrepreneurial support, NMCC produces two primary results: positive social returns as the direct consequence of new job opportunities and a well-trained, well-compensated workforce in the local community; along with solid financial returns for our investors.

Geographic Preference: New Mexico
Fund Size: $14.65 million

Venture Capital & Private Equity Firms / Domestic Firms

Founded: 2004
Investment Criteria: At least 5 employees; in operation for more than 2 years; at least $500,000 in sales; pattern of sustained revenue growth; cash flow postive for at least one year; strong management team
Industry Group Preference: Manufacturing, Consumer Products, Energy, Environment, Food & Beverage, Tourism, Consumer Services, Business Products & Services
Portfolio Companies: Aspen Avionics, IntelliCyt, American Clay, Wellkeeper, Armed Response Team, MIOX Corporation, Aero Mechanical Industries, TruTouch Technologies

Key Executives:
  Elizabeth Gamboa, Executive Director
  e-mail: liz@nmccap.org
  Education: BS, San Francisco State University; MBA, Presidio Graduate School
  Background: Morgan Stanley; Project Manager, Quokka Sports
  J Michael Schafer, Managing Director
  e-mail: michael@nmccap.com
  Education: BS, Davidson College; MBA, University of Michigan
  Background: General Partner & Principal, Tullis-Dickerson & Company; Founder & President, Ventures UNC

1300 NEW MOUNTAIN CAPITAL
1633 Broadway
48th Floor
New York, NY 10019

Phone: 212-720-0300 Fax: 212-582-2277
e-mail: NMC-GeneralInquiry@newmountaincapital.com
web: www.newmountaincapital.com

Mission Statement: To acquire the highest quality leaders in key growth industries and seek companies which are characterized by: market leadership in sustainable growth niches; high barriers to competitive entry, as demonstrated by high operating margins; strong 'downside' protection in all reasonable worst-case scenarios; and the opportunity for extraordinary returns due to rapid growth or to special factors existing at the time of investment.

Fund Size: $5.1 billion
Founded: 2000
Average Investment: $100 - $500 million
Minimum Investment: $50 million
Investment Criteria: Mid-Market with enterprise value of $100-500 million, LBO, Buildups, Recapitalizations, MBO, Growth Equity Transactions
Industry Group Preference: Education, Communications, Media, Healthcare, Business to Business, Power Technologies, Capital Goods, Consumer Products, Software, Logistics, Business Products & Services, Financial Services, Infrastructure, Energy
Portfolio Companies: ABB Optical Group, ACA Compliance Group, Alexander Mann Solutions, AmWINS Group, Apptis Holdings, Aventor Performance Materials Holdings, Bellerophone Therapeutics, Camber, Connextions, Deltek, EverBank Financial Corporation, Ikaria, Inmar, Intermarine, IRI, JDA Software Group, MailSouth, National Medical Health Card Systems, Medical Specialties Distributors, NuSil Technology, Overland Solutions, Paris, Re Holdings, SNL Financial, Strayer Education, Stroz Friedberg, Surgis, Valet Waste, Validus Holdings, Western Dentral

Key Executives:
  Steven B Klinsky, Founder & CEO
  Education: BA Economics, University of Michigan; MBA, Harvard Business School; JD with Honors, Harvard Law School
  Background: Co-Founder LBO Group, Goldman, Sachs & Co; Associate Partner/General Partner, Forstmann Little & Co
  Andrew D. Barous, Managing Director
  Education: BA, Economics, Hamilton College
  Matthew M. Bennett, Managing Director
  Education: AB, Political Science, Princeton University; JD, Villanova University School of Law
  Background: CEO, CIOX Health; EVP, Global Medical Operations; Chief Legal Officer, Ikaria Inc.; EVP/CAO/Chief Business Officer, VIASYS Healthcare Inc.; Litigator, Stradley Ronon Stevens & Young
  Directorships: CIOX Health; Gelest; Cytel; Sparta Systems; Bellerophon Therapeutics
  Prasad Chintamaneni, Managing Director
  Background: Oresident, Global Industries; Consultant, Cognizant
  David C. Coquillette, Managing Director
  Education: BA, DePauw University; MBA, Wharton School, University of Pennsylvania
  Background: Oak Hill Advisors; Goldman Sachs; Lehman Brothers
  Directorships: Goodwill Industries of Greater New York; Goodwill Industries of New Jersey
  Robert A. Hamwee, Managing Director & CEO, NMFC
  Education: BBA, Finance & Accounting, University of Michigan
  Background: President, GSC Group; Greenwich Street Capital Partners; The Blackstone Group
  Directorships: Purina Mills; Envirosource; Viasystems
  Laura C. Holson, Managing Director & COO, Credit
  Education: BS, Economics, Wharton School, University of Pennsylvania
  Background: Healthcare Investment Banking, Morgan Stanley
  Teddy Kaplan, Managing Director & Portfolio Manager, Net Lease
  Education: BS, McIntire School of Commerce, University of Virginia; MBA, Columbia Business School
  Background: Managing Director, Angelo Gordon & Co.; W.P. Carey Inc.; Meyer Duffy & Associates; Brown Brothers Harriman
  Lewis S. Klessel, Managing Director
  Education: BS, Wharton School, University of Pennsylvania; MBA, Harvard Business School
  Background: Bain Capital; Home Depot; McKinsey & Company; Ernst & Young
  John R. Kline, Managing Director & President, NMFC
  Education: MS, Mechanical Engineering, Polytechnic Institute of New York; PhD, University of Illinois, Urbana-Champaign; MBA, University of Chicago
  Background: JP Morgan Partners; Managing Director, CCMP Capital Advisors; McKinsey & Company; AT Kearney
  Peter N. Masucci, Managing Director
  Education: BA, University of Iowa; MBA, Stanford Grad. School of Business
  Background: M&A Analyst, Goldman Sachs
  Directorships: Deltek; InComm Holdings; Inmar; Valet Waste
  Matthew S. Holt, Managing Director & President, Private Equity
  Education: AB, English & American Literature, Harvard College
  Background: M&A Group, Lehman Brothers
  Directorships: Avantor Performance Materials Holdings, Ikaria Holdings, NuSil Technology
  Andre V. Moura, Managing Director
  Education: AB, Computer Science, Harvard College; MBA, Harvard Business School
  Background: ABC Group, Goldman Sachs & Co.
  Directorships: Aceto; Alteon Health; Avantor; Bellerophon; Gelest; Sparta Systems; Topixs Pharmaceuticals; ACA Compliance Group; Medical Specialties Distributors; NuSil
  Robert W. Mulcare, Managing Director
  Education: AB, Woodrow Wilson School, Princeton University; MA, Economics, National University of

Venture Capital & Private Equity Firms / Domestic Firms

Ireland
Background: McKinsey & Company
Directorships: OneDigital; MAG Aerospace; ACA Compliance Group; AmWINS Group; Alight Solutions
Albert A. Notini, Managing Director & Lead, Operating Partner Group
Education: AB, Boston College; MA, Boston University
Background: President & Chief Operating Officer, Sonus Network Inc.; CFO, Manufacturers' Services Ltd.; Senior Partner, Hale and Door LLP; Law Clerk to the Chief Justice of the Massachusetts Supreme Judical Court
Jack W. Qian, Managing Director
Education: BA, Economics & Mathematics, Yale University
Background: Global Technology Group, Morgan Stanley
Directorships: Ciox Health; Convey Health; Quian; IRI; JDA Software; Sparta Systems; DRB Systems; Revint Solutions

1301 NEW RHEIN HEALTHCARE INVESTORS
100 n 18th street
Two Logan Square, Suite 1930
Philidelphia, PA 19103

Phone: 215-419-7830
web: newrhein.com

Mission Statement: New Rhein is a venture capital fund manager focused on healthcare therapeutics and medical devices. Their investment strategies focus on proven molecules used in new ways.

Geographic Preference: Global
Average Investment: $10-30 Million
Investment Criteria: Unmet Medical Need; Proof of Scientific Concept; Health-Economic Value; Clear Clinical and Regulatory Plan; IP/Market Exclusivity

Other Locations:
Blokhuisstraat 47J
B-2800
Mechelen
Belgium
Phone: 32 15-48-08-00

Birch House, Fairfield Avenue
Staines upon Thames
Middlesex TW18 4AB
England
Phone: 44 1279-755-775

Key Executives:
Ivan Gergel, Founder/Managing Partner
Education: MD, University of London
Background: Chief Medical Officer, Nektar Therapeutics Inc.; EVP/Chief Scientific Officer, Endo Health Solutions; President, Forest Research Institute
Greg Parekh, Founder/Managing Partner
Education: PhD, Northwestern University
Background: CEO, Biocartis NV
Subhanu Saxena, Managing Partner
Education: MBA, INSEAD; MA, Oxford University
Background: Managing Director, Cipla; CEO, Novartis UK

1302 NEW SCIENCE VENTURES
299 Park Avenue
41st Floor
New York, NY 10171

Phone: 212-688-5100 Fax: 212-308-9196
e-mail: info@newscienceventures.com
web: www.newscienceventures.com

Mission Statement: New Science Ventures, LLC (NSV) is a New York-based venture capital firm which invests in companies using novel scientific approaches in the Life Sciences sector and the Information Technology sector.

Geographic Preference: United States, Europe, India, China
Fund Size: $300 million
Founded: 2004
Investment Criteria: Early-Stage, Later-Stage
Industry Group Preference: Information Technology, Life Sciences, Biotechnology, Pharmaceuticals, Medical Devices, Therapeutics
Portfolio Companies: Achronix, Alexar Therapeutics, Ario Pharma, BioScale, Caringo, CEGX, Celleration, Dali Wireless, Dezima Pharma, DirectedSensing, Ferric Semiconductor, GTxcel, iCAD, Juventas Therapeutics, Kateeva, Mangstor, Oxyrane, PerceptiMed, Resolve Therapeutics, RFArrays, Seahorse Bioscience, Silicon Space Technology, SoliCore, Svelte, Symphogen, Therox, Tigertext, Trellis Bioscience, Vaultive

Key Executives:
Somu Subramaniam, Managing Partner
212-661-3497
e-mail: somu@newscienceventures.com
Education: BTech, Indian Institute of Technology; MBA, Harvard Business School
Background: Director, McKinsey & Company
Directorships: Achronix Semiconductor, Silicon Space Technology, Dali Wireless, Oxyrane, Juventas Therapeutics, Resolve Therapeutics, Dexima Pharma, Vaultive, TigerText, iCAD
Tom Lavin, Partner
212-661-3498
e-mail: tom@newscienceventures.com
Education: AB, Government, Wesleyan University; MBA, Harvard Business School
Background: Head, Real Estate Investment Banking, First Boston, Smith Barney; Head, Commercial Mortgage Lending, MetLife
Directorships: Achronix Semiconductor, Celleration, RF Arrays Systems
Andrew Abrams, Partner
e-mail: andrew@newscienceventures.com
Education: BA/MA/MS, Natural Sciences & Biochemistry, University of Cambridge; MBA, Harvard Business School
Background: Associate, JP Morgan
Directorships: Paradigm Diagnostics
Brenda Marex, Chief Financial Officer
e-mail: brenda@newscienceventures.com
Education: BA, Accounting/Information Systems, Queens College; CPA
Background: Controller, Cerberus Capital; Controller/VP, Citigroup Alternative Investments

1303 NEW VANTAGE GROUP
1616 Anderson Road
McLean, VA 22102

Phone: 703-255-4930
web: www.newvantagegroup.com

Mission Statement: Managers of five angel funds and angel groups for early-stage venture funds for active investors.

Geographic Preference: District of Columbia, East Coast
Founded: 1997
Average Investment: $ 500,000-1 million
Minimum Investment: $500,000
Investment Criteria: Seed, Early Stage
Industry Group Preference: All Sectors Considered

Key Executives:
John May, Founder/Managing Partner
e-mail: john@newvantagegroup.com
Education: BA, Earlham College; MPA, Maxwell School, Syracuse University
Background: Co-Founder, Investors' Circle; Co-Founder/Executive Director, Private Investors Network; General Partner, Calvert Social Venture Partners; Author
Jeremy Bauman, Associate
e-mail: mba@newvantagegroup.com

Venture Capital & Private Equity Firms / Domestic Firms

Education: BA, Kenyon College; International MBA, University of South Carolina

1304 NEW VENTURE PARTNERS
PO Box 881
New Providence, NJ 07974

Phone: 908-464-0900 **Fax:** 908-655-9142
web: www.nvpllc.com

Mission Statement: Establishes close, long-term relationships with global technology corporations to commercialize innovations through spin-out ventures.

Geographic Preference: North America, Asia
Founded: 1997
Investment Criteria: Spin-Outs
Industry Group Preference: Networking, Communications, Software, Semiconductors, Hardware, Clean Technology, Nanotechnology, Storage, Bioinformatics
Portfolio Companies: @Roads, AetherPal, Airclic, Alverix, Andrew, AraLight, Azure Solutions, BLiNQ Networks, brisbane Materials, Celiant, CrossFiber, DAFCA, Elemedia, Everspin Technologies, Flarion, GainSpan, GeoVideo Networks, GlobalCast, iBiquity Digital, iCRTec, Intelleflex, Internet Photonics, ISPsoft, Liquavista, Lucent Digital Video, Lumeta, Maps on Us, Microwave Photonics, Neohapsis, NextG Networks, Novinda, NVMdurance, Own Products, Procelerate Technologies, PsyTechnics, Real Time Content, SavaJe Technologies, ShopWell, Silicon Hive, SiPort, Subex, SyChip, Valent, Vasona Networks, Vidus, VPI Systems

Key Executives:
  Andrew Garman, Managing Partner
  Education: AB, Engineering & Applied Physics, Harvard College; MS, Mechanical Engineering, Stanford University; MBA, Stanford University
  Background: Vice President, Lucent Technologies; Managing Director, BT Ventures; Vice President, Xerox New Enterprise Group
  Stephen Socolof, Managing Partner
  Education: BA, Economics, BS, Mathematical Sciences, Stanford University; MBA, Amos Tuck School, Dartmouth College
  Background: Lucent Technologies; Booz Allen & Hamilton
  Directorships: Center for the Study of Private Equity at the Tuck School
  Tom Uhlman, Managing Partner
  Education: BA, Political Science, University of Rochester; PhD, Political Science, University of North Carolina, Chapel Hill; Masters Degree, Stanford University School of Business
  Background: President, Lucent Technologies New Venture Group; AT&T; Director, Corporate Development, Hewlett-Packard
  Directorships: iBiquity Digital, Lumeta, AetherPal
  Marc Rappoport, Chief Financial Officer/Partner
  Education: BS, Economics, New York University; MBA, Columbia Business School
  Background: CFO/General Partner, Lucent Venture Partners

1305 NEW YORK ANGELS
1216 Broadway
2nd Floor
New York, NY 10001

web: www.newyorkangels.com

Mission Statement: An independent consortium of individual accredited angel investors. Incorporated by the former members of NYNMA Angel Investor Program to provide opportunities for its members to obtain outstanding financial returns by investing in early-stage technology and new media companies in the New York city area and accelerating them to market leadership.

Founded: 1997
Average Investment: $250,000 - $750,000
Minimum Investment: $250,000
Investment Criteria: Seed, Early Stage
Industry Group Preference: Technology, Media
Portfolio Companies: Adapt Media, SignStorey, Linkstorm, MediaTile, Good Health Advertising, uKnow, Sociocast, C3 Metrics, Ministore, Crowdly, Rockerbox, Snakblox, eJammingAudiiO, Synergy Beverages, DesignBuddy, Cookstr, Pinterest, AudioVroom, 1000 Museums, Brain Sentry, Sportsvite, Happy Toy Machine, Movio Network, Zenplaya, Antengo, Tripshare, 72Lux.com, Mouth, HeTexted, AllTheRooms, Concert Window, Librify, Slyce, Nito, PhotoKharma, Authorea, School Loop, Aristotle Circle, Timbuktu, CourseHorse, Citelighter, Metaphor, Zero G, Koolspan, GridPlex Networks, Email Data Source, Anvato, Magnify.net, TalkShoe, innRoad, Pond5, MPoint, StandoutJobs, Viddler, FastTrac, Live Look, SalesconX, Localytics, Altruik, PublicStuff, Greenhouse, Field Lens, Carnegie Speech, WhiteSource, Critical Mention, SureDone, Dash, CrowdTangle, Seamless Docs, iSpeech, Meddle, StoryVine, SocialSign.in, CreativeWorx, Minds'Eye, Better Mobile Security, Keaton Row, Style for Hire, Tommy John, The RunThrough, Beauty Booke, Payoneer, Recognia, Transactis, EasyCopay, Payperks, PEX Card, Moven, Vestorly, Kasisto, DIGIT Wireless, Chromis Fiberoptics, Ambient, Clear Align, Senscient, SocialBicycles, goTenna, Vital Herd, Canary, ImagineAir, BioScale, UROValve, CogRx

Key Executives:
  David S Rose, Founder
  Education: BA, Yale University; MBA, Finance, Columbia University
  Background: Chairman/CEO, Angelsoft; Co-Founder/Chairman, The Computer Classroom; Rose Associates
  Brian Cohen, Chairman Emeritus
  Education: BS, Biology & Speech Communications, Syracuse University; MS, Science Communications, Boston University School of Public Communications
  Background: Founder, iFluence; Founder, Good Cause Communications

1306 NEW YORK CITY ENTREPRENEURIAL FUND New York City Economic Development Corporation
One Liberty Plaza
New York, NY 10006

web: www.nycedc.com

Mission Statement: To provide capital to promising New York City-based technology startup companies.

Fund Size: $22 million
Average Investment: $750,000
Minimum Investment: $100,000
Investment Criteria: Early Stage, New York City based companies
Industry Group Preference: Internet Technology, Biotechnology, Software, Telecommunications

Key Executives:
  James Patchett, President/CEO
  Education: BA, Economics, Amherst College; MBA, Stanford University
  Background: VP, Urban Investment Group, Goldman Sachs

1308 NEW YORK LIFE CAPITAL PARTNERS
30 Hudson Street
Jersey City, NJ 07302

e-mail: MainStayShareholderServices@nylim.com
web: www.newyorklifeinvestments.com

Mission Statement: An integrated asset management enterprise serving a variety of sectors. Manages two private equity co-investment funds and a mezzanine fund, by concentrating investments around Core Partners, a select group of veteran LBO sponsors with a history of strong performance, discipline across market cycles, a proven ability to create value, the co-investment funds are well positioned across all market cycles.

Fund Size: $8 billion
Founded: 1984
Average Investment: $15 - $25 million
Minimum Investment: $500,000
Investment Criteria: Leveraged Acquisitions, Recapitalizations, Growth Capital, Mezzanine
Industry Group Preference: Biotechnology, Communications, Computer Related, Electronic Technology, High Technology, Medical & Health Related, Software

1309 NEW YORK VENTURE PARTNERS
New York, NY

e-mail: t@nyvp.com
web: www.nyvp.com

Mission Statement: A venture capital firm seeking to invest in tech-based companies in New York.

Founded: 2014
Industry Group Preference: Technology, Artificial Intelligence, Software, Health & Wellness, Applications
Portfolio Companies: 1000 Museums, AllTheRooms, Authorea, Bandwagon, Bon Voyaging, Boundless Mind, BrandYourself, Collectively, ComiXology, CourseHorse, Fi Smart Dog Collar, FutureStay, GameCo, goTenna, Gust, HeTexted, Heymama, Imagine Air, Journey Meditation, Media Armor, Peel Away Labs, Pinterest, PublicStaff, Rogue, Salido, School Loop Inc., Secfi, Tommy John, Uizard, VincePair Inc., Visual Vocal

Key Executives:
 Brian Cohen, Founding Partner
 Education: BS, Syracuse University; MS, Boston University
 Background: CEO, TSI Communications Worldwide; CEO, Mindstorm Communications; CEO, Focus Technology; CEO, Globalcomm; Co-Founder/CEO, Launch.it; Founder/President, Good Cause Communications
 Trace Cohen, Managing Director
 Education: BW, Syracuse University; MBA, Columbia Business School
 Background: Founder/CMO, Brand-Yourself.com; Co-Founder/SVP, iFluence PR; Advisor, Pivot; Co-Founder/Head of Product, Launch.it

1310 NEWBURY VENTURES
600 Menlo Avenue
Menlo Park, CA 94025

web: www.newburyven.com

Mission Statement: Newbury Ventures specializes in identifying opportunities for significant capital appreacation, by investing in promising entrepreneurial companies at early stages of their corporate development.

Fund Size: $500 million
Founded: 1992
Average Investment: $5-10 million
Minimum Investment: $2 million
Investment Criteria: High Growth in technology, communications and IT industries
Industry Group Preference: Telecommunications, Data Communications, Information Technology, Internet Technology, Technology, Wireless Technologies, IT Security
Portfolio Companies: Clourdera, Quanergy, Womply, DeliveryAgent, Skully Helmets, AdStage, Fuel Powered, Wishabi, Lucibel, B DNA, Xtera, Zozi

Other Locations:
 255 Shoreline Drive
 Suite 520
 Redwood Shores, CA 94065
 Phone: 650-486-2444

Key Executives:
 Ossama Hassanein, Senior Managing Director
 e-mail: ossama@newburyven.com
 Education: BSc, Electrical Engineering, University of Alexandria; MSc, Electrical Engineering & MBA, University of British Columbia
 Background: EVP, Berkeley International; Chairman, Technocom Ventures; President, Newbridge Holdings
 Joe Kell, Chief Financial Officer
 e-mail: joe@newburyven.com
 Education: BS, Business Admnistration, Saint Mary's College; CPA
 Background: Audit Manager, Technology Assurance & Advisory Group

1311 NEWBURY, PIRET & COMPANY
One Boston Place
Suite 2600
Boston, MA 02108

Phone: 617-367-7300 **Fax:** 781-268-5081
web: www.newburypiret.com

Mission Statement: To provide investment banking services to middle market growth companies. Clients often have a technology focus which differentiates their products and services.

Geographic Preference: US and Europe
Founded: 1981
Average Investment: $3-$100 million
Minimum Investment: $3 million
Industry Group Preference: Business to Business, Healthcare, Manufacturing, Technology

Key Executives:
 Marguerite A Piret, President/CEO
 e-mail: mpiret@newburypiret.com
 Education: MBA, AB, Harvard University
 Background: Managing Director, Kridel Securities Corporation; Commercial Loan Officer, New England Merchants National Bank
 Marvin W Ritchie, Managing Director, Valuations
 e-mail: mritchie@newburypiret.com
 Education: BS, West Virginia University; MBA, Wharton School
 Background: Principal, Real Estate Investments Group, Northfield Capital; Vice President, Adams, Harkness & Hill; Vice President, Bear, Stearns
 John Piret, Managing Director
 e-mail: jpiret@newburypiret.com
 Education: DSc, Physical Sciences, Ecole des Mines de Paris; MS, Chemical Engineering, MIT; AB, Applied Mathematics, Harvard College
 Background: President/Founder, Corion Technologies

1312 NEWFIELD CAPITAL
555 5th Avenue
14th Floor
New York, NY 10017

Phone: 212-599-5000
e-mail: gcamp@newfieldcapital.com
web: www.newfieldcapital.com

Geographic Preference: United States, Canada, United Kingdom, France, Germany, Europe
Founded: 1991
Minimum Investment: $10 million
Investment Criteria: LBO, MBO
Industry Group Preference: Consumer Services, Financial Services, Media, Telecommunications, Real Estate, Consumer Products

Key Executives:
 Gregory T. Camp, Managing Director

Venture Capital & Private Equity Firms / Domestic Firms

1313 NEWLIGHT MANAGEMENT
500 N Broadway
Suite 144
Jericho, NY 11753

Mission Statement: The Newlight Management family of funds seeks to achieve consistently superior returns for its stakeholders through investments in public and private technology companies.

Geographic Preference: United States
Fund Size: $120 million
Founded: 1997
Average Investment: $1 - $4 million
Minimum Investment: $1 million
Investment Criteria: High growth potential, strong management
Industry Group Preference: Semiconductors, Communications, Software, Services, Internet Technology, Business to Business, Infrastructure, E-Commerce & Manufacturing
Portfolio Companies: Acrodyne Communications, AuthenTec, CareGain, etrials, FatWire, GigOptix, Invision, Massive, NetOps, Newpoint Technologies, Parago, Peregrine Semicondutor, Raketu, SilverCarrot, Sonics, VideoNext, VitalStream

Key Executives:
  Robert M Brill, Managing Partner
  516-433-0090
  Fax: 516-433-0412
  e-mail: brill@nlventures.com
  Education: PhD, Nuclear Physics, Brown University
  Robert F Raucci, Managing Partner
  e-mail: raucci@nlventures.com
  Education: MBA, Columbia University

1314 NEWLIGHT PARTNERS
320 Park Avenue
25th Floor
New York, NY 10022

Phone: 212-205-2660
e-mail: info@newlightpartners.com
web: www.newlightpartners.com

Mission Statement: Partners with founders and management teams to build and grow businesses, providing them with the capital and support needed to execute on their vision. Unlike traditional private equity, Newlight invests over time with the flexibility to start with a platform buyout or de novo.

Founded: 2018
Average Investment: Up to $200 million
Industry Group Preference: Digital Infrastructure, Insurance, Specialty Lending, Energy, Healthcare, B2B
Portfolio Companies: APR Energy, Aurigen, Bay Tech, Bioenergy Development Company, Crystal Financial, Essent Group, Extenet Systems, Hyperoptic, Leyline, Liberty Pressure Pumping, Narragansett Bay, Oak Street Health, OneWest Bank, Pondurance, Propeller Industries, RITC, Sail Internet, Syndicate, TowerCo, Waypoint Leasing, Zenium

Key Executives:
  David Wassong, Co-Managing Partner
  Education: BA, University of Pennsylvania; MBA, Wharton School
  Background: Co-Head of Strategic Investments Group, Soros Fund Management; Partner, Soros Private Equity Partners; VP, Lauder Gaspar Ventures
  Ravi Yadav, Co-Managing Partner
  Education: BS, Rutgers University; MBA, Harvard Business School
  Background: Co-Head of Strategic Investments Group, Soros Fund Management; Managing Partner, Sunaria Group; VP, Warburg Pincus
  Ruairi Grant, Managign Director/Chief Financial Officer
  Education: LLB, Queen's University of Belfast; Postgrad in Accounting, University of Ulster
  Background: Financial Controller/SVP, EIG Global Energy Partners; Manager of Assurance Services, Pricewaterhouse Coopers
  Joshua Ho-Walker, Managing Director
  Education: BS, Leonard N Stern School of Business, New York University
  Background: Principal, Soros Fund Management; Analyst, Investment Banking, Merrill Lynch

1315 NEWSCHOOLS VENTURE FUND
1616 Franklin Street
2nd Floor
Oakland, CA 94612

Phone: 415-615-6860 **Fax:** 415-615-6861
e-mail: info@newschools.org
web: www.newschools.org

Mission Statement: NewSchools invests in both non-profit and for-profit organizations that are working to improve public education in a variety of ways. Our venture portfolio includes more than 100 highly effective organizations working to change the lives of low-income children across the country.

Geographic Preference: United States
Investment Criteria: Early-Stage, Seed-Stage
Industry Group Preference: Education
Portfolio Companies: 100Kin10, Academy for Urban School Leadership, Achievement Preparatory Academy, Alliance for College-Ready Public Schools, Appletree Institute for Education Innovation, Aspire Public Schools, AspireU, BetterLesson, Beyond 12, Blendspace, BrightBytes, Camelback Ventures Fellowship Program, Capital Teaching Residency, Center to Support Excellence in Teaching, Character Lab, Charter Board Partners, City on a Hill, ClassDojo, ClassWallet, CodeHS, CodeNow, Concentric Educational Solutions, CoreSpring, Crescent City Schools, Curriculet, Dc Preparatory Academy, DC Public Charter School Board, DC School Reform Now, Democrcy Prep Public School, District of Columbia International School, DSST Public Schools, E.L. Haynes Public Charter School, Edcamp Foundation, EdSurge, Education Elements, Educreations, Edward W. Brooke Charter School, Ellevation, EnCorps, Engrade, Equal Opportunity Schools, eSpark, Excel Academy Charter Schools, The Expectations Project, Explore Schools, Families for Excellent Schools, Fellowship for Race and Equity in Education, FreshGrade, Friends of Choice in Urban Schools, Friendship Public Charter Schools, Future Is Now Schools, Goalbook, Great Oakland Public Schools Leadership Center, GreatSchools, Grockit, Hapara, Ingenuityprep, Inspired Teaching Demonstration School, Junyo, Khan Academy, Kidaptive, KIPP DC, KIPP MA, Leadership Public Schools, Leading Educators, Learning Games Network, LearnZillion, Lighthouse Community Charter School, Listen Current, Locomotive Labs, MasteryConnect, Match Education, MATCH Teacher Residency, Matchbook Learning, Motion Match, Mundo Verde PCS, Mystery Science, Mytonomy, Nearpod, Nepris, New Classrooms, New Leaders, New Paradigm for Education, New Schools for New Orleans, New Teacher Center, Newsela, NoRedInk, North Star Academy Charter School of Newark, Paul Public Charter School, Presence Learning, Reading Partners, Readworks, Relay Graudate School of Education, ReNEW Charter Management Organization, Rocketship Education, Roxbur Preparatory Charter School, Scholar Academies, SchoolMint, Schoolzilla, Securly, Seneca Family of Agencies All-In Partnership, Shining Stars Montessori Academy, Socrative, Sposato Graduate School Of Education, Student for Education Reform, Tales2Go, Teach For America Oakland, Teaching Channel, TeachingWorks, TeachLive, Teachscape, TEAM Charter Schools, TNTP, TuvaLabs, Tynker, Uncommon Schools, UP Education Network, Urban Strategies Council, Urban Teacher Center, YES Prep Teaching

Key Executives:
  Stacey Childress, Chief Executive Officer
  Background: Faculty Member, Harvard Business School

Venture Capital & Private Equity Firms / Domestic Firms

Frances Messano, Senior Managing Partner
Education: AB, Harvard College; MBA, Harvard Business School
Background: VP, Teach for America; Associate Partner, Monitor Institute
Scott Benson, Managing Partner
Education: BSBA, University of North Carolina; MBA, Harvard Business School
Background: Sr Program Officer, Gates Foundation; Director of Strategic Academic Initiatives, DC Public Schools

1316 NEWSPRING CAPITAL
Radnor Financial Center
555 East Lancaster Avenue
3rd Floor
Radnor, PA 19087

Phone: 610-567-2380 Fax: 610-567-2388
e-mail: aveverka@newspringcapital.com
web: www.newspringcapital.com

Mission Statement: NewSpring Capital's experienced and skilled investment professionals aim to partner with outstanding entrepreneurial management teams to build companies that are leaders in their fields.

Geographic Preference: Mid-Atlantic Region
Fund Size: $600 million
Investment Criteria: NewSpring Growth: Equity Capital for Growth & Expansion Stage; NewSpring Healthcare: Equity Capital; NewSpring Mezzanine: Mezzanine Capital for Expansion Stage & Buyout Opportunities
Industry Group Preference: Business Products & Services, Enabling Technology, Information Technology, Healthcare, Pharmaceuticals, Healthcare Services, Medical Devices, Specialty Manufacturing
Portfolio Companies: 3Pillar Global, Bluenog, BCG, Clutch, Dstillery, Enterprises DB, Exegy, Exelate, FirstBest, Ifbyphone, iPipeline, Market Street Advisors, Message Systems, Mobiquity, Open Road, Raritan, Relay, Smart Destinations, Star2Star Communications, Velocidata, VidSys, XOS Digital

Other Locations:
575 5th Avenue
18th Floor
New York, NY 10017
Phone: 610-567-2380 Fax: 610-567-2388

120 S Riverside Plaza
Chicago, IL 60606
Phone: 312-342-2700 Fax: 610-567-2388

100 West Road
Suite 325
Towson, MD 21204
Phone: 410-832-7586 Fax: 610-567-2388

Key Executives:
Michael DiPiano, Managing General Partner
e-mail: mdipiano@newspringcapital.com
Education: BS, Penn State University; MBA, Stern School of Business
Background: Safeguard Scientifics; CEO, Chemical Leaman Corporation; Baxter Healthcare Corporation
Marc Lederman, General Partner, NewSpring Growth
e-mail: mlederman@newspringcapital.com
Education: BS, Accountancy, Villanova University; MBA, Wharton School
Background: Manager, Business Assurance & Advisory Services Group, Deloitte & Touche
Glenn Rieger, General Partner, NewSpring Growth
e-mail: grieger@newspringcapital.com
Education: Colby College; MBA, Wharton School
Background: Co-Founder & Managing Director, Cross Atlantic Partners
Brian G. Murphy, General Partner, NewSpring Healthcare
e-mail: bmurphy@newspringcapital.com
Education: BS, Science, State University of New York, Cortland
Background: Founder, Acquisition Management Services; NovaCare; Heritage Health Systems; Partners National Health Plans
Bruce Downey, Advisory Partner
e-mail: bdowney@newspringcapital.com
Education: Miami University; Law Degree, Ohio State University
Background: Chairman & CEO, Barr Pharmaceuticals; Capital Partner, Winston & Strawn
Steven Hobman, General Partner, NewSpring Mezzanine
e-mail: shobman@newspringcapital.com
Education: AB, Franklin & Mashall College; MBA, West Chester University
Background: Meridian Bank, Progress Bank, Comerica Bank; Founder, TechBanc; Co-Founder, Ben Franklin/Progress Capital Fund
Greg Barger, General Partner, NewSpring Mezzanine
e-mail: gbarger@newspringcapital.com
Education: BS, Finance, University of Connecticut; MBA, Loyola College
Background: Managing Director, Calvert Street Capital Partners; SVP, Mercantile Bank

1317 NEXT FRONTIER CAPITAL
544 E Main Street
Suite A
Bozeman, MT 59715

e-mail: investment@nextfrontiercapital.com
web: www.nextfrontiercapital.com

Mission Statement: Next Frontier Capital partners with mission-driven, talented entrepreneurs to build Rocky Mountain technology companies of national impact, utility, and value.

Geographic Preference: Montana, Colorado, Utah, Wyoming, Nevada, Arizona, Idaho
Founded: 2015
Average Investment: $2 - 5 million
Investment Criteria: Early-Stage, Series A
Industry Group Preference: Technology
Portfolio Companies: Advsir, Alpin, Ataata, Aumni, Bandwango, BioSqueeze, Blackmore, Blocky, Bonusly, Chargeback, Claravine, Clearas, Demoflow, Emmersion, EveryoneSocial, Gravwell, Getro, Halp, IronCore, LumenAd, MeatEater, OnX, OptioSurgical, Ortibal Shift, PatientOne, Phoenix Labs, PurCellBio, Quiq, Remix Labs, S2 Corporation, Section, SiteOne Therapeutics, Submittable, TrustLab, TwinThread, VIRIS Detection Systems

Other Locations:
1131 E Broadway
Suite 136
Missoula, MT 59802

Key Executives:
Will Price, Founder & General Partner
Education: MBA, Northwestern University
Background: CEO, Flite; Managing Director, Hummer Winblad Venture Partners; Pequot Capital; Morgan Stanley
Directorships: SiteOne Therapeutics; Submittable; Quiq; Halp; OptioSurgical
Richard Harjes, Founder & General Partner
Background: Co-Founder, Willow Spring Ranch Montana; Managing Director, Citadel Investment Group; Partner, Numeric Investors
Directorships: Blackmore; IronCore Labs; Ataata; Clearas
Les Graig, General Partner
Background: Executive Director, Montana State University Innovation Campus; Co-Founder, The Twenty; Co-Founder, RedOwl Analytics; Technical Operations Officer, Central Intelligence Agency
Directorships: S2 Corporation; Bandwango; EveryoneSocial; Gravwell

Venture Capital & Private Equity Firms / Domestic Firms

1318 NEXT VENTURES

e-mail: info@nextventures.com
web: nextventures.com

Mission Statement: Next Ventures is a venture capital firm created to grow opportunities in rising sports, fitness, nutrition and wellness markets.

Key Executives:
   Lance Armstrong, Founder/Managing Partner
   Background: Cyclist; Athlete; Host, THEMOVE Podcast; Host, THE FORWARD Podcast
   Lionel Conacher, Managing Partner
   Background: Co-Founder, Westwind Partners Inc.; CEO, Westwind; President, Thomas Weisel Partners; Senior Advisor/Operating Partner, Altramont Capital Partners
   Melanie Strong, Managing Partner
   Background: VP/General Manager, Nike Skateboarding; Nike

1319 NEXT WORLD CAPITAL
836 Montgomery Street
San Francisco, CA 94133

Phone: 415-202-5450 Fax: 415-358-8233
e-mail: businessplan@nextworldcap.com
web: www.nextworldcap.com

Mission Statement: Next World Capital is an international expansion-stage venture capital firm with $200 million of assets. Headquartered in San Francisco, NWC is the only Silicon Valley VC managing a sales and business development platform to help its companies expand in Europe.

Geographic Preference: Worldwide
Fund Size: $200 million
Investment Criteria: Expansion Stage
Industry Group Preference: Software, Internet, Mobile
Portfolio Companies: AgilOne, BrightRoll, Datameer, Datastax, DynamicOps, GoodData, Host Analytics, iDeeli, Nexgen Storage, Virtual Instruments, Zuora

Other Locations:
11 Avenue Myron Herrick
Paris 75008
France
Phone: 33-155359920 Fax: 33-145636098

The Stanley Building
7 Pancras Square
London NIC 4AG
United Kingdom
Phone: 44-2037145102

Craig Hanson, Co-Founder/General Partner
Education: BA, Carleton College; MS, Stanford Graduate School of Business
Background: Vice President, FTV Capital; Pricipal, Vista Ventures; Vice President, Berenson Minella & Company; Credit Suisse First Boston
Ben Fu, General Partner
Education: BS, Electrical Engineering & Computer Science, MEng, MIT
Background: Principal, Scale Venture Partners; Senior Sales Engineer, Symantec, IMlogic, Akamai
Frederic Halley, Operating Partner
Education: MS, Telecommunication Engineering, Telecom Paris; MBA, Kellogg School of Management
Background: Managing Partner, Tioga Venture; COO, Netsize; GM, Pertinence; Sales Director, SLP Infoware; Consultant, Boston Consulting Group

1320 NEXTGEN ANGELS
5404 Wisconsin Avenue
Suite 1000
Chevy Chase, MD 20815

e-mail: nextgenangels@gmail.com
web: www.nextgenangels.com

Mission Statement: Companies considered will have at least a few of the following characteristics: seed or early-stage with opportunity for explosive growth; web, mobile, SAAS; located in Greater Washington, DC region.

Geographic Preference: Greater Washington, DC Region
Investment Criteria: Seed, Early Stage
Industry Group Preference: Web Related, Mobile, SaaS
Portfolio Companies: Disruption Corporation, Socialradar, Speek, APX Labs, Spinnakr, uKnow, EncoreAlert, Nvite, Revmetrix, Avizia, CustomVine

1321 NEXTSTAGE CAPITAL
2570 Boulevard of Generals
Building 100, Second Floor
Audubon, PA 19403

Phone: 610-539-2297
web: nextstagecap.com

Mission Statement: NextStage Capital focuses on finding undiscovered early stage investment opportunities in the Mid-Atlantic region. With an emphasis on technology, software, hardware and services, our goal is to find talented entrepreneurs with a compelling and validated technology offering and help them build company value.

Geographic Preference: Mid-Atlantic Region
Fund Size: $175 million
Investment Criteria: Early-Stage
Industry Group Preference: Technology
Portfolio Companies: HigherNext, Lumesis, Sidecar, Certes Networks, Ticketleap, Savana, Evident Software, Dayak, Anysource Media, MODA Technology Partners, Orbius, Agilence, HX Technologies, Waywire (Magnify Networks), Hardmetrics, Visinex

Key Executives:
   Terry Williams, Co-Founder/Managing Partner
   e-mail: terry@nextstagecapital.com
   Education: Indiana University of Pennsylvania
   Background: Founder, TWC Group; Strategic Consultant, Dialogic Corporation
   Directorships: Movitas, Cross X Platform
   Dan McKinney, Co-Founder/Managing Partner
   e-mail: dan@nextstagecapital.com
   Education: University of Cincinnati
   Background: Officer, Safeguard Scientifics; Sales & Marketing, IBM
   Directorships: TicketLeap, Savana, Sidecar, Magnify Networks, Ben Franklin Technology Investment Advisory Committee, New Jersey Technology Advisory Board
   Rob Adams, Co-Founder/Managing Partner
   e-mail: rob@nextstagecapital.com
   Education: BS, Economics, Skidmore College; MBA, University of Michigan
   Background: VP & Officer, Safeguard Scientifics; Co-Founder, Ascendigm; Rascoff/Zysblatt; Entrepreneurial Services, Ernst & Young

1322 NEXTVIEW VENTURES
179 Lincoln Street
Suite 404
Boston, MA 02111

web: www.nextviewventures.com

Mission Statement: Dedicated seed stage investors building transforming internet businesses.

Geographic Preference: East Coast US
Average Investment: $250,000 - $500,000
Investment Criteria: Seed-Stage
Industry Group Preference: Internet
Portfolio Companies: Alignable, BookBub, Boundless, Bridj, Change Collective, Cloze, Code Climate, CustomMade, Dunwello, Emissary, Farmeron, Goodsie, Insight Squared, Mojo Motors, Objective Logistics, Paintzen, Platiq, Shareaholic, Skillz, SkyVu, Sunrise, Swipely, TaskRabbit, Thred Up, TripleLift, Turning Art, YesGraph

Venture Capital & Private Equity Firms / Domestic Firms

Key Executives:
Rob Go, Co-Founder/Partner
Education: Duke University; MBA, Harvard Business School
Background: Spark Capital; Business Product Leader, Ebay; Consultant, The Parthenon Group
Lee Hower, Co-Founder/Partner
Education: BAS, Systems Engineering, University of Pennsylvania; BS, Economics, Wharton School
Background: PayPal; Co-Founder, LinkedIn; Principal, Point Judity Capital
David Biesel, Co-Founder/Partner
Education: AB, Economics, Duke University; MBA, Stanford Graduate School of Business
Background: Vice President, Venrock; Co-Founder, Sombasa Media; Vice President, Marketing, About.com

1323 NFX
604 Mission Street
Suite 200
San Francisco, CA 94105

e-mail: qed@nfx.com
web: www.nfx.com

Mission Statement: NFX approach early-startup investments through the eyes of founders.

Geographic Preference: Silicon Valley, Isreal
Average Investment: $500,000 - 5 million
Minimum Investment: $250,000
Industry Group Preference: Technology, Software, Travel, Entertainment, Healthcare, Commercial Software, Big Data & Analytics, Retail, Social Media
Portfolio Companies: Lyft, Patreon, Doordash, Trulia, Poshmark, Houseparty, Honeybook, Outdoorsy, SmilarWeb, Good Readers, Wanelo, LiveRamp, Path, Playtika, 3DR, Feedly, Crackle, Flickr, Second Life, Life 360, Tickle, Lastminute.com, Wonderhill, Solv, Stella, Plenty, Honor, Virta Health, Ivy, Grabr, Ozzy, Mammoth Diagnostics, Fitmob, AngelList, Mapillary, Amino, Friend.ly, Splacer, Circle Up, Skout, Crossrider, iAngel, MyHeritage, Plarium, MyThings, Fuse.it, Worthy, Graduway, R2Net, Zula, Bizzabo, NanoRep, Tradeo, Kenshoo, Ava, Riptide, Hippo, Chatalytic, SweetIM, Viv, Saltside, Storyhunter, Peekk Travel, Gogo Bot, Swell, Iron Pearl, Red Bubble, Leap, Jiff, Branchout, Zinch, Affinity Labs, Maya's Mom, Zeus, Motivate, Rooster, MarketMan, Wheelhouse, LiquidSpace, Genome Compiler, Crowdcast, The Hotels Network, Cricket Health, Wheelwell, Jet Insight, Blueberry, KimKim, Kwik, Finrise, Leaders, Headnote, Mission Mark, Brightcrowd, Travel Joy, Golden Key, Fairly, Hipdot, Incredible Health, Materialist, Crater

Other Locations:
400 Florence Street
Palo Alto, CA 94301

8 Hachoshlim Street
Herzliya 1369377
Isreal

Key Executives:
James Currier, Managing Partner
Education: BA, Political Economics, Princeton University; MBA, Harvard Business School
Background: Co-Founder/CEO, Tickle; Co-Founder, Wonderhill; Co-Founder, IronPearl; Co-Founder, Jiff
Pete Flint, Managing Partner
Education: MS, Physics, University of Oxford; MBA, Stanford Grad. School of Business
Background: Co-Founder/CEO, Trulia; Co-Founder, lastminute.com
Gigi Levy-Weiss, Managing Partner
Education: MBA, Kellogg School of Management, Northwestern University
Background: CEO, 888 Holdingsl Division President, Amdocs
Directorships: EMEA Client Advisory Council, Facebook

1324 NGEN PARTNERS
733 Third Avenue
New York, NY 10017

Phone: 212-450-9700
web: www.ngenpartners.com

Mission Statement: NGEN Partners is a pioneering investor in the cleantech sector. They invest in businesses that offer economically valuable products and services that positiviely affect the environment.

Geographic Preference: United States, Canada
Fund Size: $500 million
Founded: 2001
Average Investment: $5 - $25 million
Investment Criteria: Early-Stage to Late-Stage
Industry Group Preference: Clean Technology, Environment, Alternative Energy, Energy Efficiency, Pollution, Advanced Materials, Green Technology, Energy Storage
Portfolio Companies: Adura Technologies, Alterra Power Corp., Artificial Muscle, Bare Snacks, Brightfarms, Catalytic Solutions, Choose Energy, DIRTT Environmental Solutions, eIQ Energy, ENXSuite, Enzymedica, eRecyclingCorps, evandtec, Fallbrook Technologies, Greengate, Hycrete, MokaFive, Nanosphere, Native Foods Cafe, nlyte Software, Powerspan, Pure Energies Group, Rayne, REGEN Energy, Renaissance Lighting, Renewable Funding, Sensicore, Solaria, SolFocus, Soraa, Textronics, Threshold Power, Tioga Energy, Two Moms in the RAW, Zevia

Other Locations:
1114 State Street
Suite 247
Santa Barbara, CA 93101
Phone: 805-564-3156 **Fax:** 805-564-1669

733 Third Avenue
18th Floor
New York, NY 10017
Phone: 212-450-9700

Key Executives:
Peter S.H. Grubstein, Founder/Managing Member
Education: Yale University
Directorships: Renewable Funding, BrightFarms, Native Foods Cafe
Shay Murphy, Partner
Education: BA, Columbia University; MBA, NYU Stern School of Business
Background: DG Energy Partners; Citigroup
Directorships: Encycle
Rosemary Ripley, Managing Director
Education: BA, MBA, Yale University
Background: Corporate Business Development, Altria Group; Managing Director, Furman Selz; Co-Founder, Circle Financial Group
Directorships: MokaFive, nlyte, Zevia, Bare Snacks, Two Moms in the Raw

1325 NGN CAPITAL
60 Long Ridge Road
Suite 402
Stamford, CT 06902

Phone: 212-972-0077 **Fax:** 212-972-0080
e-mail: investorrelations@ngncapital.com
web: www.ngncapital.com

Mission Statement: NGN Capital is a venture capital firm dedicated to healthcare investing, focusing on ventures with the potential to achieve above average private equity returns with an emphasis on later stage investments.

Geographic Preference: United States, Europe
Investment Criteria: Early-Stage to Later-Stage
Industry Group Preference: Healthcare, Biotechnology, Medical Devices
Portfolio Companies: Aerovance, Artisan Pharma, BeneChill, BioArray Solutions, EKOS, Horizon Pharma,

Venture Capital & Private Equity Firms / Domestic Firms

Javelin Pharmaceuticals, Jerini AG, KIKA Medical, Micromet, MultiPlan, PIN Pharma, OptiScan Biomedical, Power Medical Interventions, Santhera Pharmaceuticals AG, Sightline Technologies, Small Bone Innovations, Tigris Pharmaceuticals, ACT Biotech, Cerapedics, Endosense SA, Exosome Diagnostics, Medrium, NOXXON Pharma AG, Resverlogix, SpineView, Valtech Cardio, Vivaldi Biosciences

Other Locations:
c/o Oracle Partners
200 Greenwich Avenue
Greenwich, CT 06830
Phone: 203-862-7900 **Fax:** 203-862-1613

Bergheimer Str. 89a
Heidelberg 69115
Germany
Phone: 49-6221893760 **Fax:** 49-62218937625

Key Executives:
Kenneth S Abramowitz, Co-Founder/Managing General Partner
Education: BA, Columbia University; MBA, Harvard Business School
Background: Managing Director, The Carlyle Group; Analyst, Sanford C Bernstein & Co.
Directorships: Valtech Cardio, Small Bone Innovations, Akorn
John R Costantino, Managing General Partner
Education: BS, JD, Fordham University; CPA
Background: Partner, Walden Partners; Partner, Constantino Melamede & Geenberg; EVP, COO, Director, Conair
Directorships: ACT Biotech, Vivaldi Biosciences
Peter Johann PhD, Managing General Partner
Education: PhD, Technical University of Munich
Background: Division Head, Corporate Development, Boehringer Ingelheim; Global Business Leader, F. Hoffman-La Roche
Directorships: Horizon Pharma, Exosome Diagnostics
Alexander Cuomo, Chief Financial Officer
Education: BA, Ithaca College; MS, Finance, Lubin School of Business, Pace University

1326 NGP
2850 North Harwood Street
19th Floor
Dallas, TX 75201

Phone: 972-432-1440
e-mail: inquiries@ngptrs.com
web: ngpenergycapital.com

Mission Statement: Energy sector investment fund.

Fund Size: $17 billion
Founded: 1988
Industry Group Preference: Oil & Gas
Portfolio Companies: 89 Energy, Aspen Energy Partners, Avad Energy, Axia Energy, Blackbeard Operating LLC, Black Mountain Sand, BlueStone Natural Resources, Bravo Natural Resources LLC, Caltex Resources, Castell Oil Company, Castlerock, Catapult, CH4 Energy, Colgate Energy, Conexus Energy, Confluence Resources, Crimson Pipeline LP, Crossing Rocks Energy, Fifth Creek Energy, Hibernia Energy, Highmark Energy, Iron Horse Midstream, Juniper Resources, Infinity Natural Resources, Luxe Energy, Mallard Exploration, Massif Oil & Gas II, Mettle Midstream Partners, Oilfield Water Logistics, Outrigger Energy, Petrus Resources, Prairie Storm Energy Corp, Rebllion Energy, Remora Petroleum, Springbok Energy, Steppe Resources Inc., Titus Oil & Gas LLC, Torrent Oil, Trilogy Midstream, World Oil Properties Inc.

Other Locations:
717 Texas Avenue
Suite 1650
Houston, TX 77002
Phone: 713-579-5700
Key Executives:
Chris G. Carter, Managing Partner
Education: BBA & MPA, University of Texas; MBA, Stanford University
Background: Associate, McKinsey & Company; Analyst, Deutsche Bank
Tony R. Weber, Advisory Partner
Education: BBA, Finance, Texas A&M University
Background: CFO, Merit Energy Company; SVP & Division Head of Energy, Union Bank of California

1327 NGP CAPITAL
418 Florence Street
Palo Alto, CA 94301

web: www.ngpcap.com

Mission Statement: Focusing exclusively on the mobile industry, NGP Capital brings a global perspective and deep understanding of global trends to every engagement. NGP are active investors adding value through strategic insight, operational excellence and its vast network of contacts in the mobile industry.

Geographic Preference: Worldwide
Fund Size: $250 million
Founded: 2005
Industry Group Preference: Mobile Technology
Portfolio Companies: Adknowledge, Babbel, Cloudmark, Dealsandyou.com, Digital Lumens, Fashion and You, Fyber, Ganji, Gigwalk, Grand Cru, Gridsum, Heptagon, Hipmunk, Innovis, Inside Secure, Intermedia, InVisage, Kaltura, MVD House, MAG Interactive, Meican, PubMatic, Quikr, RetailNext, Rocketfuel, SolarVista Media, TechProcess, Verve, Vizury, Wei Chai Shi, YPlan, Zubie
No. 1 Jianquomenwai Avenue
Room 710, Office Tower II
China World Trade Centre
Beijing 100004
China

1328 NGP ENERGY CAPITAL
2850 N Harwood Street
19th Floor
Dallas, TX 75201

Phone: 972-432-1440
e-mail: inquiries@ngptrs.com
web: www.naturalgaspartners.com

Mission Statement: Invests in the energy and related industries, with particular emphasis on young companies that acquire and exploit producing oil and gas properties. NGP Energy Capital will generate superior risk-adjusted investment returns while forming and maintaining the highest quality industry relationships and will conduct its business according to the highest standards of honesty, integrity and fairness.

Geographic Preference: North America
Fund Size: $7.3 billion
Founded: 1988
Average Investment: $50 million
Minimum Investment: $10 million
Investment Criteria: Startup, First Stage, Mezzanine
Industry Group Preference: Oil & Gas, Natural Gas, Energy
Portfolio Companies: 89 Energy, Aspen Energy Partners, Avad Energy, Axia Energy, Black Mountain Sand, Blackbeard Operating LLC, Boaz Energy LLC, Caltex Resources, Camino Natural Resources, Castlerock Exploration, Catapult Services, Centennial Resource Development LLC, CH4 Energy, Colgate Energy, Conexus Energy, Confluence Resources, Crimson Pipeline LP, Enlink Midstream, Fifth Creek Energy, Hibernia Energy, Infinity Natural Resources, Iron Horse Midstream, Luxe Energy, Luze Minerals, Mallard Exploration, Massif Oil & Gas, Mettle

Venture Capital & Private Equity Firms / Domestic Firms

Midstream Partners, Outrigger Energy, Petrus Resources, Prairie Storm Energy Corp., Rebllion Energy, Springbok Energy, Switchback Energy Acquisition, Tap Rock Resources, Teal Natural Resources, Titus Oil & Gas LLC, Torrent Oil, Trilogy Midstream, World Energy Partners

Other Locations:
717 Texas Avenue
Suite 1650
Houston, TX 77002
Phone: 713-579-5700

Key Executives:
Chris G Carter, Managing Partner
Education: BBA & MPA, Accounting, University of Texas at Austin; MBA, Stanford University
Background: Associate, McKinsey & Company; Analyst, Deutsche Bank's Energy Investment Banking Group

1329 NJTC VENTURE FUND
**1001 Briggs Road
Suite 280
Mount Laurel, NJ 08054**

Phone: 856-273-6800 **Fax:** 856-273-0990
e-mail: info@njtcvc.com

Mission Statement: Catalytic seed, startup, and early stage venture capital investments. The firm actively partners with entrepreneurs to build unique, leading-edge businesses that drive superior returns for investors and economic growth in the community. NJTC Venture Fund is fully invested and closed to new investment opportunities.

Fund Size: $80 million
Founded: 2001
Investment Criteria: Fully Invested
Portfolio Companies: Achieve3000, Archive Systems, InstaMed, IntegriChain, RightAnswers, V12 Group, Andrew Technologies, Colby Pharmaceuticals, CytoSorbents, Intra-Cellular Therapies, Redpoint Bio, Sword Diagnostics, Power Survey

Key Executives:
Jim Gunton, General Partner
856-273-6800 x233
e-mail: jim@njtcvc.com
Education: BS, Stanford University; MBA, Fuqua School of Business
Background: Promoter Manager, Oracle Corporation; VP/Principal, Edison Venture Fund
Joseph Falkenstein, General Partner
856-273-6800 x 226
e-mail: joe@njtcvc.com
Education: CPA, Temple University
Background: Partner, Andersen's Growth Company and Technology Practice
Directorships: Archive Systems, V12 Group, Sword Diagnostics, Power Survey, Cylex
Robert Chefitz, General Partner
973-994-0606
e-mail: robert@njtcvc.com
Education: Northwestern University; Columbia University
Background: General Partner, Apax Partners; Golder Thoma Cressey

1330 NKM CAPITAL
Boston, MA

e-mail: info@nkmcap.com
web: www.nkmcap.com

Mission Statement: A venture capital firm that focuses on early stage tech-based companies across the US. NKM Capital has offices in Boston, New York, and Silicon Valley.

Founded: 2012
Investment Criteria: Early Stage
Industry Group Preference: Technology, Artificial Intelligence, Consumer, Software, Applications

Portfolio Companies: Analytical Space, Astranis, Bluesmart, Boom, Carta, Copia, Cruise, Deepgram, Eight Sleep, Flirtey, Hyperloop One, Instavest, Interviewed, Lyft, Mogul, Numerai, Relativity Space, Revlo, Ripple, Robinhood, Smarking, Tesorio, Truebill, Wakie Inc., WorldCover, Zenysis, ZoomCar India

Key Executives:
Nurzhas Makishev, Partner
Education: BS, MIT; MS, John F. Kennedy School of Government, Harvard University; MBA, Wharton School
Background: Researcher, MIT Media Lab; Investment Banker, Banc of America Securities; Investment Banker, JP Morgan; Software Engineer, Oracle; Angel Investor

Other Locations:
Maria 01
Lapinlahdenkatu 16
Building 3
Helsinki 00180
Finland

12, Avenue des Morgines
1213 Petit-Lancy
Geneva
Switzerland

Key Executives:
John Gardner, Venture Partner
Education: MBA, University of Chicago; JD, University of Cincinnati
Background: BlueRun Ventures; Senior Business Development, Nokia
Directorships: Adknowledge, Cloudmark, PubMatic, RetailNext, Rocketfuel, Verve Wireless, Vizury
Paul Asel, Partner
Education: BA, Dartmouth College; MBA, Stanford Graduate School of Business
Background: International Finance Corporation; General Partner, Telos Ventures; Senior Vice President, Delta Capital
Directorships: Intermedia, Luminate, Gangi.com, Gridsum, KongZhong, Madhouse, Network 18, SolarVista Media, Techprocess Solutions, UC Web
Bo Ilsoe, Partner
Education: MS, Electronics Engineering, Aalborg University, Denmark
Background: Alcatel, Nokia, Vertex Management
Directorships: Heptagon, Innovis, Inside Secure, InVisage, Pelican Imaging, Sponsorpay, Voddler
Upal Basu, Partner
Education: BS, Engineering, Imperial College, London; MS, Engineering, Stanford University; MBA, Harvard Business School
Background: Founder & CEO, Mformation Technologies; McKinsey & Company
Directorships: Deals and You, Fashion and You, Innovis, Kaltura, Network 18, Quikr

1332 NORO-MOSELEY PARTNERS
**Medici Building
3284 Northside Parkway NW
Suite 525
Atlanta, GA 30327-2337**

Phone: 404-233-1966
web: www.noromoseley.com

Mission Statement: Helps emerging and growth companies realize their long-term vision by providing the appropriate financial resources, experience and foresight to take them to the next level. It's mission is to create strong relationships with our portfolio companies and entrepreneurs and to add value where needed to produce superior returns for the company, its employees and shareholders.

Geographic Preference: Southeastern US
Fund Size: $580 million
Founded: 1983
Average Investment: $3-$5 million

Venture Capital & Private Equity Firms / Domestic Firms

Minimum Investment: $2 million
Investment Criteria: Startup, First-Stage, Second-Stage
Industry Group Preference: Technology, Fintech, Broadband, Security, Digital Media & Marketing, Logistics, Healthcare, Healthcare Services, Information Technology, Business Outsourcing, Financial Services, Technology-Enabled Services
Portfolio Companies: Array Health, Appia, Change Healthcare, ClearLeap, Diabetes Care Group, Direct General, FrontStream Payments, Hospice Link, Liaison, Navitas Lease, nCrowd, Outbound Engine, PeopleMatter, PlayOn, Pure Life Renal, PureWRX, RemitDATA, SalesFusion, Streamline Health, Tower Cloud, Virtustream, Wellcentive

Key Executives:
Mike Elliott, Venture Partner
Education: BS, Mathematics, MBA, University of North Carolina
Background: Managing Director, The Wakefield Group; Managing Director, NationsBank Capital
Directorships: Appia, Frontstream Payments, PeopleMatter, TowerCloud
Allen S Moseley, General Partner
Education: BA, University of North Carolina; MBA, Harvard Business School
Background: Associate, Robinson-Humphrey Company; Bowles Hollowell Conner & Company; Merrill Lynch; James River Corporation
Alan J Taetle, General Partner
Education: BA, Economics, University of Michigan; MBA, Harvard University
Background: Executive VP Marketing & Business Development, MindSpring
Spence McCelland, General Partner
Education: BA, Vanderbilt University; MBA, Kellogg School of Management at Northwestern University
William L Hudson, Administrative Partner/Chief Financial Officer
Education: CPA, BS, University of Virginia
Background: Equifax; nBank.com; Arthur Andersen

1333 NORTH AMERICAN FUND
135 S LaSalle Street
Suite 3225
Chicago, IL 60603

Phone: 312-332-4950 **Fax:** 312-332-1540
e-mail: dbergonia@northamericanfund.com
web: www.northamericanfund.com

Mission Statement: North American's perspective is long term. Its goal is to build companies through internal growth and/or additional acquisitions into significantly larger enterprises that are leading participants in their market niches.
Geographic Preference: Midwestern, Southeastern
Fund Size: $115 million
Founded: 1989
Average Investment: $5-$15 million
Investment Criteria: Buyouts or Growth Capital
Industry Group Preference: Manufacturing, Food & Beverage, Medical Products & Services, Consumer Products, Distribution, Business Products & Services, Education, Financial Services
Portfolio Companies: ACR Electronics, Actown-Electrocoil, Amtec Precision Products, Culinary Standards, Gateway Healthcare, Minnesota Educational Computing, Polymer Corporation, Valley Meats

Other Locations:
312 SE 17th Street
Suite 300
Fort Lauderdale, FL 33305
Phone: 954-463-0681 **Fax:** 954-527-0904

Key Executives:
Charles L Palmer, Managing Partner
954-463-0681
Fax: 954-527-0904

Education: BSBA, Georgetown University; MBA, Northwestern University
Background: Co-founder/VP, Heizer Corporation; Director, National Venture Capital Association; Managing Partner, North American Company
Robert L Underwood, Managing Partner
312-332-4950
Fax: 312-332-1540
e-mail: runderwood@northamericanfund.com
Education: BS in Mechanical Engineering, MS, PhD in Engineering Sciences, Stanford University; MBA, Santa Clara University
Background: General Partner, ISSS Ventures; President, Northern Trust Venture Capital; VP, Heizer Corporation
R David Bergonia, Managing Partner
312-332-4950
Fax: 312-332-1540
e-mail: dbergonia@northamericanfund.com
Education: JD, Harvard University; BBA, University of Notre Dame
Background: VP Corporate Finance, Chicago Corporation; VP, Legal Administration, Heizer Corporation

1334 NORTH ATLANTIC CAPITAL CORPORATION
Two City Center
Fifth Floor
Portland, ME 04101

Phone: 207-772-4470 **Fax:** 207-772-3257
e-mail: ccoyne@northatlanticcapital.com
web: www.northatlanticcapital.com

Mission Statement: A later-stage fund manager that provides risk capital to privately owned businesses in the Northeastern United States. Through active board participation, annual executive education for CEOs and complimentary strategic advisory services, North Atlantic Capital Corporation helps entrepreneurs amplify their competitive advantages and grow their businesses.
Geographic Preference: East Coast
Fund Size: $100 million
Founded: 1986
Average Investment: $4 - 8 million
Minimum Investment: $1 million
Investment Criteria: To fund the expansion of existing growth businesses and management buyouts of established companies
Industry Group Preference: Computer Related, Financial Services, Wholesale, Health Related, Information Services, Internet Technology, Materials Technology, Software, Retailing, Telecommunications, Waste & Recycling, Business Products & Services, Technology-Enabled Services
Portfolio Companies: Academic Management Systems, Appia, Autotask Corporation, iContact, KickApps (KIT Digital), OnForce, Synacor, Triggit, Voxeo, Zmags

Key Executives:
David M Coit, Managing Director
207-772-4470
Fax: 207-772-3257
e-mail: dcoit@northatlanticcapital.com
Education: BA, Yale University; MBA, Harard Business School
Background: President, Maine Capital Corporation; First National Bank Boston
Mark J Morrissette, Managing Director
207-772-4470
Fax: 207-772-3257
e-mail: mark@northatlanticcapital.com
Education: BA, Dartmouth; MBA, Harvard Business School
Background: Strategic Consulting, CSC Index;

Venture Capital & Private Equity Firms / Domestic Firms

1335 NORTH BRIDGE VENTURE PARTNERS
60 William Street
Suite 350
Waltham, MA 02481

Phone: 781-290-0004 Fax: 781-290-0999
e-mail: info@northbridge.com
web: www.northbridge.com

Mission Statement: North Bridge invests in exceptional people whose ideas have the potential to disrupt the way we live and work. Its Seed, Venture and Growth Equity strategies help transform those ideas into companies and those companies into market leaders.

Geographic Preference: East Coast
Founded: 1994
Average Investment: $20 million
Minimum Investment: $100-$200,000
Investment Criteria: Early Stage; Special Situations
Industry Group Preference: Communications, Healthcare, Distribution, Electronic Components, Genetic Engineering, Software, Infrastructure, Digital Media & Marketing
Portfolio Companies: O3b Networks, 1366 Technologies, 45M, 480 Biomedical, A123 Systems, Acquia, Actifio, Active Endpoints, Active.com, Aeropost, Akiban Technologies, Akorri, Allegro, Antenna Software, Apperian, AppIQ, Aquto, Archivas, Argon Networks, Arris, ArrowPoint Communications, Arsenal Medical, Aushon Biosystems, Authentica, Awareness, Aylus Networks, Azimuth, Belmont Technology, Bigfoot Networks, Black Sand Technologies, BlueShift, Bluespec, Bright Tiger Technologies, BrightTalk, Broadband Access Systems, Cadia Networks, Camiant, Centra, Clarity Health, Clothia, Cognio, Compass EOS, Connance, Contact Solutions, CoolPlanet, Couchbase, Currensee, Demandware, Disqus, DYM, DYN, Embrane, eRoom Technology, Excelligence, Firm 58, FirstSense Software, Foro Energy, Fring, Gridco Systems, Healthrageous, Humedica, I-Logix, Idiom, IMN, Infineta, Infomedics, IP Mobile, Jive, kSaria, Leapfrog, LiveRamp, Lumigent, Lytro, Macheen, Mavenir Systems, Mc10, MessageBus, MFormation, Mitotix, Moasis, Movik, Mozes, My Perfect Gig, Nasuni, NaviNet, NetCore, New Oak, Newforma, NOCpulse, Notifymd, ID, Paydiant, PHARMetrics, Oracle, Philo, Plexxi, Proto Labs, QD Vision, Quallaby, Quora, Qvidian, Radview, RagingMobile, Ravel, Redstone Communications, Reva Systems, Reval, Revit Technology, Revolution Analytics, Rpath, RuffaloCODY, Salsify, SambaCloud, Seniorlink, SensAble, Sharethrough, Signiant, Silverback Technologies, SilverStream, Smartassel, SmartPark Equine, SolidWorks, Sonus Networks, SoundBite, Spaceclaim

Key Executives:
Ed Anderson, Managing Director
Education: University of Denver, Columbia University Graduate School of Business
Richard A D'Amore, General Partner
Education: Northeastern University; Harvard University Graduate School of Business Administration
Background: Consultant, Bain and Company; CPA, Arthur Young & Company
Mikel Pehl, Managing Director
Background: Partner, Advent International; President & COO, Razorfish; Chairman & CEO, i-Cube
Paul A Santinelli, Partner
Education: BS, Emerson College
Background: Director, Red Hat Network; Founder & CEO, NOCpulse; Chief Technology Officer, Global Crossing

1336 NORTH CASTLE PARTNERS
183 East Putnam Avenue
Greenwich, CT 06830

Phone: 203-862-3200
web: www.northcastlepartners.com

Mission Statement: A leading smallcap consumer private equity firm focused on consumer-driven product and service businesses in the health, wellness and active living sector.

Geographic Preference: North America
Industry Group Preference: Consumer Products, Consumer Services, Nutrition
Portfolio Companies: Flatout Flatbread, Ibex, Jenny Craig, Palladio, Doctor's Best, Octane Fitness, Curves, Performance Bicycles, Red Door Spa, Mineral Fusion

Key Executives:
Charles F Baird Jr, Founder & Managing Director
Education: AB, Harvard College; MBA, Harvard Business School
Background: Managing Director, AEA Investors; Bain & Company
Directorships: Ignite, International Fitness, Red Door Spas
Jon Canarick, Managing Director
Education: B.B.A. University of Michigan, M.B.A. Columbia Business School
Background: Financial Sponsors Coverage and Leveraged Finance groups, Bear, Stearns, & Co.
Directorships: Curves, Mineral Fusion, Flatout, Palladio Beauty Group, International Fitness, Performance Bicycle
Alison Minter, Managing Partner
Education: A.B. Economics, Princeton University
Background: Evolution Global Partners, Insurance and Leveraged Finance groups at Donaldson, Lufkin & Jenrette
Directorships: Ignite, Doctor's Best, Ibex, Red Door Spas, Octane Fitness
Alyse Skidmore, Partner/Chief Financial Officer/Chief Operating Officer
Education: L.L.M. Taxation, New York University School of Law; Juris Doctorate, Hofstra University School of Law; Bachelor of Science Accounting, University of Massachusetts Amherst
Background: Senior Manager, Ernst & Young

1337 NORTH COAST TECHNOLOGY INVESTORS LP
300 Rodd Street
Suite 201
Midland, MI 48640

Phone: 734-662-7667
e-mail: partners@northcoastvc.com
web: www.northcoastvc.com

Mission Statement: Backs entrepreneurs who seek to build major enterprises in the Midwest. North Coast welcomes the opportunity to meet with entrepreneurs and discuss their business plans.

Geographic Preference: Midwest
Fund Size: $100 million
Founded: 1999
Average Investment: $4 million
Portfolio Companies: Advanced Material Process Corporation, Approach Software, Arbortext, Avidimer Therapeutics, BalaDyne, Camile Products, Chromatic Research, Colorbok, CytoPherx, Everex Systems, Excera Materials Group, Fulcrum Composites, Gema Diagnostics, Intelligence Controls, MaxFunds.com, Mechanical Dynamics, Nematron Corporation, Open Networks Engineering, Procite, RenaMed Biologics, Shertrack, Solidica, Virtela Communications

Other Locations:
206 S Fifth Avenue
Suite 550
Ann Arbor, MI 48104
Phone: 734-662-7667 Fax: 734-662-6261

Key Executives:
Lindsay Aspegren, Co-Founder
e-mail: lindsay@northcoastvc.com

Venture Capital & Private Equity Firms / Domestic Firms

Education: MBA, Harvard Business School; Graduated magna cum laude with distinction, BA in History, Yale University
Hugo Braun, Co-Founder
e-mail: hugo@northcoastvc.com
Education: MS, Management, Sloan School of Management at MIT; Graduated cum laude with distinction, BA in Economics, Yale University

1338 NORTH DAKOTA DEVELOPMENT FUND
1600 E. Century Avenue
Suite 2
PO Box 2057
Bismarck, ND 58503

Phone: 701-328-5300
web: www.business.nd.gov

Mission Statement: A statewide, non-profit development corporation, the Fund provides flexible gap financing through debt and equity investments for new or expanding primary sector businesses.
Geographic Preference: North Dakota
Fund Size: $25 million
Founded: 1991
Average Investment: Up to $300,000
Investment Criteria: Based in North Dakota, the enentrepreneur must generally have a minimum of 15% equity in the project. Loans must be secured with a 1st or 2nd mortage in fixed assets, equipment, inventory, collateral.
Industry Group Preference: Manufacturing, Business to Business, Information Technology, Processing, Consumer Services
Key Executives:
   James Leiman, Director
   701-328-5388
   e-mail: jleiman@nd.gov

1339 NORTH HILL VENTURES
535 Boylston Street
6th Floor
Boston, MA 02116

Phone: 617-835-9719
e-mail: brettj.rome@northhillventures.com
web: www.northhillventures.com

Mission Statement: Focused exclusively on early-stage financial technology and marketing technology investments.
Fund Size: $125 million
Founded: 1999
Investment Criteria: Early-Stage
Industry Group Preference: Fintech, Marketing
Portfolio Companies: Exchange Solutions, Smart Destinations, Simple Tuition, Interactions, Tervela, Live Well Financial, CashStar, MX, Saylent
Key Executives:
   Brett J Rome, General Partner
   e-mail: brettj.rome@northhillventures.com
   Education: AB, Princeton University; MBA, Amos Tuck School, Dartmouth College
   Background: Principal, Westbury Capital Partners; Principal, The Parthenon Group

1340 NORTHERN LIGHT VENTURE CAPITAL
2855 Sand Hill Road
Menlo Park, CA 94025

Phone: 650-585-5450 **Fax:** 650-585-5451
e-mail: www.nlvc.com
web: www.nlightvc.com

Mission Statement: Northern Light Venture Capital is a leading China-focused venture capital firm targeting early and growth stage opportunities. Partners with select entrepreneurs with groundbreaking ideas and exceptional vision to build world-class companies.
Geographic Preference: China
Fund Size: $1 billion
Founded: 2005
Industry Group Preference: Technology, Media, Telecommunications, Clean Technology, Healthcare, Manufacturing, Consumer Products, Consumer Services, Wireless Technologies
Portfolio Companies: AbMart, Advanced Solar Power, Aerohive, Anji, Anquanbao, Austri, Baihe, BGI, C-Platform, Caerphilly, Chukong Technologies, City Media, Crossbar, CSALC, Daojia, Denovo, DerbySoft, Dianrong, DinoDirect, Dream Square, EpiTop, GigaDevice, Gogo, Grandoil, Green Bio, Halathion, Hengxin Electric, Hillstone, Hoodong, iAppPay, iFreecomm, Kaixin001, Keduo, Koowo, LianLian, LineKong, M15, Macrosan, Masa Maso, Meituan, Micropoint, Nuovo Film, Pearl Hydrogen, Pipilu, Prudent Energy, Sentons, SGE, Shanghai iRay, Shineon, Sinldo, Solarvista, Spreadtrum, SPS, Starrino, Sunlit, TalkingData, Telegent Systems, ThunderSoft, Tidal Systems, TimesLED, TrustGo, Velo, Viatime, Xixun, Zamplus Technology, Zonton

Other Locations:
   Two Pacific Place
   88 Queensway Admiralty
   Suite 2210
   Hong Kong
   Phone: 852-2281-6200 **Fax:** 852-2537-3299

   China Central Place
   32F, Tower 2
   No. 79 Jianguo Road, Chaoyang District
   Beijing 100025
   China
   Phone: (8610) 57696500 **Fax:** (8610) 5969185

   1539 Nanjing West Road
   Unit 1701, Tower 2
   Kerry Centre
   Shanghai 200040
   China
   Phone: (8621) 61034800 **Fax:** (8621) 60671991

   Room 302, Building 13
   Sandlake VC/PE Community
   183 East Suhong Rd., Suzhou Industrial Park
   Jiangsu 215026
   China
   Phone: (86512) 66969911 **Fax:** (86512) 6699916

   Unit 1407
   East Block, Coastal Building
   Hai De San Dao, Nanshan District
   Shenzhen 518054
   China
   Phone: (86755) 36992780 **Fax:** (86755) 36882155

Key Executives:
   Feng Deng, Founding Managing Director
   Education: BS, MS, Electrical Engineering, Tsinghua University; MS, Computer Engineering, University of Southern California; MBA, Wharton School
   Background: Co-Founder, NetScreen Technologies
   Yan Ke, Founding Venture Partner
   Education: BS, Electrical Engineering, Tsinghua University; MS, PhD, Computer Science, Johns Hopkins University
   Background: Co-Founder, NetScreen Technologies; Senior Software Engineer, Cisco Systems
   Lixin Li, Venture Partner
   Education: BS, Electrical Engineering, MA, School of Economics & Management, Tsinghua University
   Jeffrey Lee, Partner
   Education: BA, Economics, Harvard College; MBA, Wharton School
   Background: Strategic Marketing Manager, Agilent Technologies Wireless Semiconductor Division; Director,

Venture Capital & Private Equity Firms / Domestic Firms

US Operations, Wavics; Founding Partner, Newton Technology Partners
Zhi Tan PhD, Venture Partner
Education: Computer Science & Technology Department, Jilin University; PhD, Computer Science, Worcester Polytechnic Institute of Massachusetts
Background: President, Shanghai Framedia Advertising Development Ltd; Senior Advisor, Tom Group Limited; CEO, 8848.net; Vice President, Microsoft China; Senior Vice President, UTStarcom
He Huang PhD, Partner
Education: BS, Thermal Engineering & Environmental Engineering; MS, PhD, Thermodynamics, Tsinghua University
Background: Vice President, Hina Group; US Department of Energy
Tony Wu, Partner
Education: ME, Power Engineering, Huazhong University of Science & Technology; MBA, Cheung Kong Graduate School of Business
Background: DFJ China, Shanda Strategic Investment

1341 NORTHGATE
649 San Ramon Valley Blvd
Danville, CA 94526

Phone: 925-820-9970 Fax: 925-820-9994
e-mail: info@northgate.com
web: www.northgatecapital.com

Mission Statement: Northgate's proven investment approach is predicated on the fact that tremendous investment opportunities exist within the alternative asset arena, specifically within sub-classes like private equity and venture capital, where the recognition of market changing innovation and active management dictates exceptional returns. To identify and gain access to the highest performing funds, Northgate capitalizes on its proprietary and rigorous processes, in addition to its deep industry relationships. Northgate's investment focus includes a mix of investments in funds operating in both developed markets and emerging markets.

Geographic Preference: North America, Europe, Asia, Latin America
Founded: 2000
Industry Group Preference: Technologies
Portfolio Companies: Ambarella, Adams Pharma, AdMob, Aoptix, Arresto Biosciences, Bloom Energy, Clearwell, Drobo, eMeter, FourSquare, Jive Software, Meraki, Palo Alto, Proofpoint, RingCentral, Rocketfuel, Root Music, Silver Peak, Silverspring Networks, Stoke, Tethys Bioscience, Verinata Health, Visible Measures, Xoom, Yelp, Zazzle.com

Other Locations:
Paseo de las Palmas 405
18th Floor
Mexico DF 11000
Mexico
Phone: 52-55-5202-3200

150 California Street
San Francisco, CA 94111
Phone: 415-417-6000 Fax: 415-417-3978

Key Executives:
Casey Gordon, Managing Partner
Education: BA, Sociology, Johns Hopkins University; MBA, Sloan School of Management, MIT
Background: Head, Private Investments, The Capital Partnership Group of Companies
Directorships: Atia Vision; Supira Medical; NuVera Medical
Brent Jones, Co-Founder/Managing Director
Education: BS, Economics, University of Santa Clara
Background: National Football League
Directorships: Zazzle
Allan Chou, Partner
Education: MBA, Amos Tuck School of Business, Dartmouth College; CFA
Background: Analyst, Cambridge Associates
Oscar Alvarado, Partner
Education: MBA, Kent Business School, University of Kent
Background: Managing Director, Diversified & Private Equity LatAm Coverage Group, Scotiabank Global Banking; Division Head, Banamex
Thomas Vardell, Co-Founder/Managing Director
Education: BS, Industrial Engineering, Stanford University
Background: National Football League
Jana Vazé, Chief Financial Officer
Education: MS, Accounting, University of Illinois; MBA, University of Pune, India
Background: Acountant, Shea Labagh Dobberstein; Finance Operations, Standard Chartered Mutual Fund, Mumbai, India

1342 NORTHPOND VENTURES
7500 Old Georgetown Road
Suite 850
Bethesda, MD 20814

Phone: 240-800-1200
web: northpondventures.com

Mission Statement: Northpond Ventures funds companies and management teams creating solutions for some of society's greatest needs in life sciences and technology.

Other Locations:
4 Brattle Street
3rd Floor
Cambridge, MA 02138

Key Executives:
Michael Rubin, Founder/CEO
Education: Harvard University; MBA, University of Massachusetts, Amherst; CFA
Background: Co-Founder/Managing Partner, Sands Capital Ventures
Sharon Kedar, Co-Founder/Partner
Education: BA, Rice University; MBA, Harvard University; CFA
Background: CFO, Sands Capital Management; Consultant, McKinsey & Co.

1343 NORTHSTAR CAPITAL
2310 Plaza Seven
45 South 7th Street
Minneapolis, MN 55402

Phone: 612-371-5700 Fax: 612-371-5710
web: www.northstarcapital.com

Mission Statement: Focused on junior capital lending.

Geographic Preference: United States, Canada
Founded: 1993
Average Investment: $5 - $30 million
Industry Group Preference: Distribution, Manufacturing, Business Products & Services, Financial Services, Education, Healthcare
Portfolio Companies: Advanced Duplication Services, KP Holdings, Techno-Aide, Keystone Retaining Wall Systems, Security American Financial Enterprises, LA Fitness International, CanGen Holdings, Bix Produce Company, MBH Settlement Group, Integrated Turf Solutions, Lucent Polymers, Paradigm Group, Synteract, Continental Structural Plastics, Comm-Works Holdings, Spectrum Lubricants, A&D Environmental Services, EMS Management & Consultants, RollEase, JL Darling, Bioreclamation, Clowe & Cowan of El Paso, JMH International, Accurate Component Sales, Trim Parts, Citadel Outsource Group, Control Device, Quick Attach Attachments, Indo-European Foods, Receivables Management Partners, Gary Platt Manufacturing, Persante, Industrial Magnetics, Omega Environmental Technologies, Huskie Tools, Union Tractor, GPA Acquisition Company,

Venture Capital & Private Equity Firms / Domestic Firms

Pyramid Healthcare, SP Industries, ShurCo Acquisition, Lifesafer, Vectorply, All Tech/IESCO, Cash Management Solutions, United Rotary Brush Corporation, Kieffer & Co., Stant Corporation, World Wide Packaging, Contract Land Staff, Intelliteach, Mosquito Control Services, TMI International, Workhorse Rail, Specified Fittings, Atronix, Windy City Wire, St. Croix Hospice

Other Locations:
216 N Broadway
Suite 203
Fargo, ND 58102

Key Executives:
Douglas E Mark, Managing Partner
612-371-5703
e-mail: dmark@northstarcapital.com
Education: BBA, University of North Dakota
Background: Churchill Capital; Charles Bailly & Company

Scott L Becker, Founder/Advisory Partner
612-371-5704
e-mail: sbecker@northstarcapital.com
Education: BA, St. John's University; MBA, University of Minnesota; JD, William Mitchell College of Law
Background: Manager of Investments, Adler Management; General Mills; Control Data Business Centers

Charles L Schroeder, Founder/Advisory Partner
612-371-5706
Education: BA, Reed College; MA, Tufts University
Background: Investment Manager, Churchill Capital; Salomon Brothers

1344 NORTHWOOD VENTURES
485 Underhill Boulevard
Syosset, NY 11791

Phone: 516-364-5544
e-mail: info@northwoodventures.com
web: www.northwoodventures.com

Mission Statement: Private equity firm which invests in venture capital opportunities, management buyouts and industry consolidations.

Geographic Preference: United States
Fund Size: $200 million
Founded: 1983
Average Investment: $2-10 million
Minimum Investment: $2 million
Investment Criteria: Wide Range Industries, Management Buyouts, Industry Consolidations
Industry Group Preference: Telecommunications, Consumer Services, Internet Technology, Manufacturing, Retailing, Broadcasting, Financial Services, Health Related, Service Industries, Wireless
Portfolio Companies: abc Financial, Air Waves Inc., Celebration Restaurant Group, Centerline Communications, Charge Point, Community Broadcasters LLC, Designer Protein, DSG, Gifnote, Jack Rogers, JVC, Man Crates, pdv Wireless, Red Built, Rudy's Barbershop, Spectrum Five, Stone Goff Partners, Tstar 600, Zevia

Key Executives:
Paul Homer, Managing Director
Education: MBA, Zarb School of Business at Hofstra University; BS Finance, Bentley College
Background: Financial Analyst

Jamie Schiff, Managing Director
Education: BA, History, Trinity College; Masters, Real Estate, Columbia University
Background: Acquisitions group, HFZ Capital; Groton Partners

Peter G. Schiff, Managing Partner/Founder
Education: Lake Forest College; MBA, University of Chicago, Booth School of Business
Background: Warburg Pincus Co.; Chemical Bank (JPMorgan Chase & Co.)

1345 NORWEST EQUITY PARTNERS
80 South 8th Street
Suite 3600
Minneapolis, MN 55402

Phone: 612-215-1600
web: www.nep.com

Mission Statement: Norwest Equity Partners (NEP) is a leading private equity firm focused on building companies into industry leaders. NEP manages $4.6 billion of capital through a series of equity and mezzanine funds. The firm is currently investing in NEP IX, a $1.2 billion fund.

Fund Size: $1.2 billion
Founded: 1961
Investment Criteria: Management Buyouts, Recapitalizations, Growth Financing
Industry Group Preference: Industrial Services, Business to Business, Healthcare, Consumer Services, Consumer Products, Distribution, Financial Services, Manufacturing, Technology
Portfolio Companies: Apothecary Products, Arteriors, Actex, Bailiwick, Bix Produce, Bowtech, Clover Imaging Group, Edge Fitness Clubs, Eyebobs, Focal Point Data Risk, GoHealth, Institute For Integrative Nutrition, Marco, Movati Athletic, Old Hickory Smokehouse, Pentec Health, Ramsey Industries, Surgical Information Systems, Unitah Engineering & Land Serveying, Wahoo Fitness, Welocalize, West Star Aviation

Other Locations:
360 Rosemary Avenue
Suite 1500
West Palm Beach, FL 33401

Key Executives:
Tim DeVries, Managing Partner
612-215-1679
Fax: 612-215-1601
e-mail: tdevries@nmp.com
Education: BA, Bethel College; MBA, Cornell University
Background: Churchill Companies
Directorships: BowTech, Gopher Resource, Minnesota Rubber & Plastics

Timothy Kuehl, Partner
612-215-1668
Fax: 612-215-1601
e-mail: tkuehl@nep.com
Education: BBA, University of Notre Dame; MBA, Wharton School of the University of Pennsylvania
Background: Investment Advisors Inc.; Professional Hockey Player (Sweden)
Directorships: Momentum Group, Pentec Health, Shock Doctor, Surgical Information Systems

Todd Solow, Partner
612-215-1671
e-mail: tsolow@nep.com
Education: BBA, University of Michigan; MBA, Kellogg School of Management Northwestern University
Background: First Union Securities; Jacobson Companies
Directorships: Actagro, Jacobson Companies, Shock Doctor, Stanton Carpet Corp., Trilliant Food & Nutrition, Wealth Enhancement Group

1346 NORWEST VENTURE PARTNERS
525 University Avenue
Suite 800
Palo Alto, CA 94301

Phone: 650-321-8000
web: www.nvp.com

Mission Statement: Norwest Venture Partners (NVP) is a global venture and growth equity investment firm that manages more than $3.7 billion in capital and has funded over 450 companies since inception. It has offices in Palo Alto, California, Mumbai and Bangalore, India and Herzelia, Israel.

Fund Size: $3.7 billion

Venture Capital & Private Equity Firms / Domestic Firms

Founded: 1961
Average Investment: $10-$15 million
Minimum Investment: $1-$5 million
Investment Criteria: Multi-Stage
Industry Group Preference: Software, Services, Internet, Systems & Hardware, IT Infrastructure, Information Technology, Technology-Enabled Business, Business Products & Services, Financial Services, Consumer Products, Healthcare
Portfolio Companies: 6 River Systems, ACL, ActOn, Agari, Alma Campus, American Endovascular, Aporeto, Appnomic, Appriss, Attune, Avetta, Bailey 44, Birdies, Bitglass, BlueJeans, Boost Insurance, Brite, Button, Capillary, CareCloud, Casper, ClearDATA, CognitiveScale, Common, Copper, Cority, CRMnext, CyberX, Cynet, Dremio, Dtex Systems, ElasticRun, Angagio, Ess Kay Finance, Exabeam, Extole, Five Star Finance, Gong.io, Grove Collaborative, Health Catalyst, Hobnob, HoneyBook, IFTTT, Impel NeuroPharma, Infutor, Jolyn, JoyRun, Karat, Kendra Scott, Kishlay Snacks, Knotel, Kwik, Leanplum, Legion, Lending Club, Lumosity, Madison Reed, Manthan Systems, Minted, Mist, MobileIron, Modsy, Motif Investing, National Stock Exchange of India, NationWide Healthcare, NextHealth Technologies, Ninth Decimal, Nueclear, Omada Health, Onsite Dental, Opendoor, Ovum Hospitals, Owler, PCH International, Pepperfry, Perfint, Personali, Phiar, Plaid, Policygenius, Prevedere, Propel, Qubole, Quikr, Qventus, Rainmaker, RevX, Ritual, RiverMend Health, Sadbhav, Science Exchange, Second Measure, Shape Security, Silk Road Medical, Simpplr, Singular, SlashNext, Smilo, SnapRoute, Socrates AI, Sojern, Spotify, StellaService, Sulekha, SundaySky, Suvidhaa, Swiggy, Talkspace, Target PharmaSolutions, Thyrocare, TigerConnect, Topo Athletic, Turnitin, Uber, Udemy, Vast, Veritas Finance, VisitPay, WekaIO, Wiliot, Wine Access, World View, Zenoti

Other Locations:
Two South Park St.
3rd Floor
San Francisco, CA 94107
Phone: 415-918-5010

6 Hachoshlim Street
7th Floor
PO Box 12242
Herzliya 46724
Israel
Phone: 972-774107090

15th Floor, Express Tower
Nariman Point
Mumbai 400021
India
Phone: 91-2261501111

Key Executives:
Promod Haque, Managing Partner
Education: BS, Electrical Engineering, University of Delhi, India; PhD Electrical Engineering, Northwestern University; MBA, Northwestern Kellogg Graduate School of Management
Background: COO/CEO, Siemens International, Thorn EMI, Emergent Technologies, Dimensional Medicine
Jon Kossow, Managing Partner
Education: BA, Harvard College
Background: Goldman Sachs
Directorships: ACL, Appriss, Avetta, Cority, Infutor, Rainmaker, Topo Athletic, Turnitin, Wine Access
Matthew D Howard, General Partner
Background: VP Marketing, Vertical Networks; Digital Equipment Corporation; BDM International; Bolt, Beranek
Jeffrey M Crowe, Senior Managing Partner
Education: MBA, Stanford Graduate School of Business; BA, Dartmouth College
Background: DoveBid, Edify Corporation, ROLM Corporation, Siemens, IBM,

Dror Nahumi, General Partner
Education: BSc, Electrical Engineering, Technion-Israel Institute of Technology, Haifa
Background: EVP & Chief Strategy Officer, ECI; CEO, Axonlink; Senior Research Engineer, AT&T Bell Labs
Directorships: Pontis, SolarEdge, SundaySky
Dr. Ryan A Harris, General Partner
Education: BA, Psychology, Stanford University; MS, Health Research & Policy, Stanford University; MD, University of California, San Francisco School of Medicine
Background: Principal, The Carlyle Group; Industry Ventures
Casper de Clercq, General Partner
Education: BA, Biochemistry, Dartmouth College; MS, Biological Science, Stanford University; MBA, Stanford University Graduate School of Business
Background: Partner, U.S. Venture Partners; Vice President, Business Development, Sales & Marketing, Aerogen; Co-Founder, Epicor; Marketing, Heartpoint
Directorships: Basis, Simpirica Spine
Sonya Brown, General Partner
Education: BS, Northwestern University; MBA, Harvard Busienss School; CFA
Background: Summit Partners
Directorships: Aramsco, Airborne Health, Central Security Group, Physicians Formula Holdings, Snap Fitness, Sparta Systems
Niren Shah, Managing Director, NVP India

1347 NORWICH VENTURES
1210 Broadcasting Road
Suite 201
Wyomissing, PA 19610
Phone: 610-373-5320 **Fax:** 610-373-5520
web: www.norwichventures.com

Mission Statement: Norwich Ventures is a venture capital firm committed to helping entrepreneurs, healthcare professionals and inventors build innovative medical device companies.

Investment Criteria: Early-Stage
Industry Group Preference: Medical Devices
Portfolio Companies: Affera, Arterys, Daktari Diagnostics, Intelligent Bio-Systems, Lexington Medical, Pelvalon, Podimetrics, ReThink Medical, Rhythmia Medical, Soffio Medical, Svelte Medical Systems, Syncro Medical Innovations, Vaxess Technologies

Other Locations:
303 Wyman Street
Suite 300
Waltham, MA 02451
Phone: 781-890-2161 **Fax:** 781-207-8526

Key Executives:
Philip Fleck, Director
e-mail: phil@norwichventures.com
Education: BS, Mechanical Engineering, Lehigh University; University of Pennsylvania
Background: President/COO, Arrow International
Marlin Miller, Co-Founder/Senior Advisor
e-mail: mm@norwichventures.com
Education: MBA, Harvard Business School; BS, Ceramic Engineering, Alfred University
Background: Chairman/CEO, Arrow International; VP, Connors Investor Services
Aaron Sandoski, Co-Founder/Managing Director
e-mail: aaron@norwichventures.com
Education: AB, Chemistry & Economics, Dartmouth College; MBA, Harvard Business School
Background: DEKA; Consultant, McKinsey & Company

Venture Capital & Private Equity Firms / Domestic Firms

1348 NOVAK BIDDLE VENTURE PARTNERS
PO Box 341877
Bethesda, MD 20827

Phone: 240-497-1910
e-mail: info@novakbiddle.com
web: www.novakbiddle.com

Mission Statement: To provide equity financing and assistance to the management of young, information technology companies.

Geographic Preference: East Coast
Fund Size: $580 million
Founded: 1997
Minimum Investment: $100,000
Investment Criteria: Early Stage through First Round, will consider Later Stage & Spinouts
Industry Group Preference: Communications, Computer Related, Education, Electronic Components, Instrumentation, Internet Technology, Optical Technology, Information Technology, Consumer Internet, Security, Software
Portfolio Companies: 2U, AddThis, AnswerLogic, Appfluent Technology, Appian, Approva, Blackboard, Capital Education Group, Centice, Cetrifuge Systems, Clear Standards, Command Information, Copiun, CorasWorks, CounterStorm, Digital Signal, DigitalBridge Communications, Educational Initiatives, Emotive Communications, Entevo, FiberZone Networks, Fidelis Education, Giga Information Group, Infoblox, Intelliworks, LifeMinders, LifeShield Security, LogicLibrary, Luna Technologies, Matrics, N.E.W. Customer Service, ObjectVideo, Optinel Systems, Orchestro, Panasas, Paratek, Parchment, PlaySay, Previstar, Princeton Optronics, ReverbNation, SafeView, Shoeboxed, Simplexity, Social Gaming Network, SolidFire, Spectrum K12 School Solutions, SS8, Starfish Retention Solutions, Synchris, Tantivy Communications, Telogy Networks, Torrent Systems, Triumfant, Trusted Computer Solutions, Trusted Edge, UniversityNow, Vubiquity, WealthEngine, Webs, Woodwing Communications Systems, XtremeSpectrum, Ztar Mobile

Key Executives:
A.G.W. Biddle III, Co-Founder/General Partner
e-mail: jack@novakbiddle.com
Education: University of Virginia
Background: InterCAP; Partner, Vanguard Atlantic; Executive Assistant, Gartner Group; Business Development Partners
E. Rogers Novak, Jr., General Partner
Background: Co-Founder, Grotech Partners; Investment Banking, Baker, Watts & Co
Directorships: Blackboard, SpectrumK12, Trusted Computer Solutions, Digital Signal Corporation, Intelliworks, Centrifuge Systems
Philip L. Bronner, General Partner
Education: BS, Computer Science, Carnegie Mellon University; JD, University of Pennsylvania School of Law; MBA, The Wharton School
Background: Management Consultant, McKinsey & Co
Directorships: Approva, Vision Chain, InGrid, Netcordia, Freewebs, Clearspring, Social Gaming Network, 2Tor
Tom Scholl, General Partner
e-mail: tom@novakbiddle.com
Education: Purdue University
Background: Founded Telogy Networks; VP, Hughes Network Systems; Co-Founder, Cognio; Author of 'Packet Switching' in McGraw Hill's Communications Handbook
Simita Bose, Partner
Education: BS, Northwestern University; MBA, Harvard Business School
Background: The Boeing Company; Booz Allen Hamilton
Joy E. Binford, Chief Financial Officer
e-mail: joy@novakbiddle.com
Education: BA, American University; Certified Public Accountant
Background: CFO, InterCAP Graphics

Prashanth V. Boccasam, General Partner
Education: Computer Science, University of Pune; University of Cincinnati; Executive Management Program, Sloan School, MIT
Background: Founder & CEO, Approva Corporation
Directorships: Copiun, Approva, Appfluent, Appian, Centrifuge Systems

1349 NOVAQUEST CAPITAL MANAGEMENT
4208 Six Forks Road
Suite 920
Raleigh, NC 27609

Phone: 919-459-8620 Fax: 919-516-0580
e-mail: NQinfo@nqcapital.com
web: www.nqcapital.com

Mission Statement: NovaQuest Capital Management manages private equity and other investments in the global biopharmaceutical sector, where its principal focus is investing in late-stage clinical assets and commercial phase biopharmaceutical products. NovaQuest contracts with global biopharmaceutical corporations to invest side-by-side in their most strategic development and commercialization programs. Side-by-side investing means that NovaQuest invests in the products that biopharmaceuticals intend to develop and commercialize while the biopharmaceutical continues to invest its own capital in the same products.

Founded: 2000
Industry Group Preference: Biopharmaceuticals
Portfolio Companies: Allergan, Azurity, california Cryobank, Catalyst Clinical Research, Clinical Ink, Eisai, Global european Pharma, Hospira, Informed DNA, Lilly, Pfizer Inc., Pharmaxis, ProStrakan, sanofi, Shionogi Inc., Takeda

Key Executives:
Ron Wooten, Founder/Managing Partner
Education: BS, Chemistry, University of North Carolina; MBA, Boston University
Background: EVP, Quintiles; First Union Securities
John Bradley, Founder/Partner/Chief Operating Officer
Education: BBA, MBA, Wake Forest University; CPA
Background: SVP, Quintiles' Corporate Development Group
Jonathan Tunnicliff, Founder/Partner/Chief Investment Officer
Education: BS, Mathematical Statistics, University of Liverpool; MS, Medical Statistics, University of Newcastle; MBa, Sheffield Hallam University
Background: Director of Operations, S-Cubed
Robert Hester, Chief Financial Officer
Education: BA, Accounting, North Carolina State University; CPA
Background: Sr Finance Director, NovaQuest unit, Quintiles; Director/Controller, Misys Healthcare; Public Accountant, KPMG

1350 NOVARTIS VENTURE FUNDS
100 Technology Square
Cambridge, MA 02139

Phone: 617-871-3536
e-mail: claire.mcnulty@nvfund.com
web: www.nvfund.com

Mission Statement: Investing in innovative life science concepts for patient benefit creating attractive returns for entrepreneurs and investors.

Geographic Preference: United States, Canada, Europe, Switzerland, Asia/Pacific
Fund Size: $800 million
Founded: 1996
Average Investment: $15-30 million
Minimum Investment: $100,000
Investment Criteria: Seed Stage, All Stages Considered

Industry Group Preference: New Therapeutics & Platforms, Medical Devices & Implants, Diagnostics, Drug Delivery, Life Sciences, Healthcare, Biopolymers
Portfolio Companies: Aelin Therapeutics, AAD, Adicet Bio, Akouos, Artios, Annexon Bioscience, Anokion, AGL, Bicycle Therapeutics, Cavion, eFFECTOR, Enterprise Therapeutics, E-Scape Bio, Expansion Therapeutics, Forendo Pharma, Forma Therapeutics, Galera Therapeutics Inc., Genedata, ImaginAb, Inflazome, Kanyos Bio, LemonAid Health, Macrolide Pharmaceuticals, Myopowers, Oculis, Rox, Selenity Therapeutics, Scan Therapeutics, Twentyeight Seven, Vivet Therapeutics

Other Locations:
Novartis International AG
Postfach CH-4002
Basel
Switzerland
Phone: 41-61-324-37-14
Simone Forrer, Office Manager

Key Executives:
Dr. Markus Goebel, Managing Director, Cambridge
Education: MD, PhD, Ludwig Maximilians University in Munich; MBA, Henley Management College
Background: Pharmaceutical Corporate M&A; Head Nervous System Business Development & Licensing; Farmitalia Germany; Roche
Michal Silverberg, Managing Director, Cambridge
Education: BA, Economics & Business Management, Haifa University; MBA, Tel Aviv University; MA, Biotechnology, Columbia University
Background: Senior Partner, Takeda Ventures; Novo Nordisk; MGVS; OSI Pharmaceuticals
Dr. Campbell Murray, Managing Director, Cambridge
Education: MPP, John F. Kennedy School of Government; MBA, Harvard Business School
Background: Novartis Institutes for BioMedical Research; Auckland Hospital
Dr. Anja König, Global Head, Basel
Education: PhD, Cornell Univeristy
Background: Associate Partner, McKinsey and Company
Florent Gros, Managing Director, Basel
Education: MA, Biotechnology Engineering, in France
Background: Nestlé; Pasteur Merieux Connaught

1351 NOVELTEK CAPITAL CORPORATION
521 5th Avenue
Suite 1700
New York, NY 10175

Phone: 646-244-0098 **Fax:** 212-370-0925
e-mail: info@noveltek.com
web: www.noveltek.com

Mission Statement: Synergistic services revolving around emerging growth strategic business development and financing, exit strategies in the US and Europe (including dual listings), and post exit financial strategies.

Founded: 1983
Minimum Investment: $1 million
Investment Criteria: Emerging Growth
Industry Group Preference: Information Technology, Telecommunications, Healthcare, Energy, Transportation, Consumer Services, Biotechnology

Key Executives:
Gabor (Gabe) Baumann, President
212-286-1963
Fax: 212-661-7606
Background: Mitsubishi, Pfizer, Asahi, American Optical, ITW, Solomon Smith Barney, Natexis Banque Populaire, Gruntal and National Securities, President's White House Task Force

1352 NOVENTI VENTURES
Newark, CA 94560

web: noventi.net

Mission Statement: An early-stage venture capital firm focused on building successful companies through the partnership we establish with our entrepreneurs. By leveraging our decades of operating experience, a global network of resources, and a proven approach to venture investing, we help guide our companies through the many seen and unseen challenges of growth.

Founded: 2002
Investment Criteria: Early-Stage
Industry Group Preference: Technology, Clean Technology
Portfolio Companies: Active Optical MEMS, Auror Algae, Bitfone, Celltick, Dishcarft, Easy Market, Ercio, IrisCube, Kasenna, M7, Minerva Networks, Neato Robotics, Nextlabs, Sygate, Velomat Assembly Automation, Waterguru

Key Executives:
Giacomo Marini, Founder & Managing Director
Background: Chairman, Marini Investments; Chairman, TES Automation; Chairman, Cosmo Industrie; CEO, FutureTel; President & CEO, Common Ground Software; Co-Founder, Logitech; IBM; Olivetti
Directorships: Marini Investments, Velomat, PCTEL

Other Locations:
15 Bonnie Way
Allendale, NJ 07401
Phone: 610-254-4286 **Fax:** 610-254-4240

1354 NOVUS VENTURES LP
Cupertino, CA 95014

Mission Statement: To provide funding for promising early-stage companies and contribute Novus resources and participation to these ventures to help them grow and flourish in the dynamic, challenging high-tech business world.

Geographic Preference: Western United States
Fund Size: $150 million
Founded: 1994
Minimum Investment: $200,000
Investment Criteria: Early-Stage
Industry Group Preference: Information Technology, Enterprise Software, Infrastructure, Semiconductors
Portfolio Companies: ADECN, Encirq, FlyteComm, Inapac Technologies, expresso, Invivo Data, mBlox, Rainmaker Systems, PropertyView Solutions, Pathwork Diagnostics, Tidal Software, Venturi Wireless, Toolwire, Zantaz

Key Executives:
Shirley Cerrudo, General Partner
e-mail: scerrudo@novusventures.com
Background: Burr Egan Deleage & Company, Wells Fargo Investment Company, McKinsey & Company
Daniel Tompkins, Managing Partner
e-mail: ddtompkins@novusventures.com
Education: BA & BSEE, Rice University; MBA Stanford University
Background: Fairchild Semiconductor, DSC Ventures, Wells Fargo Investment Company
Stewart Schuster, Managing Director
e-mail: eschuster@novusventures.com
Education: B.Math, Washington University; M.Math, PhD, Computer Science, University of Illinois
Background: Vice President, Sybase Incorporated; Technical and Marketing Management at Ingres; Tandem Computers; and Intel

1355 NTH POWER TECHNOLOGIES
555 Mission Street
Suite 3300
San Francisco, CA 94105

Phone: 415-983-9983
e-mail: info@nthpower.com
web: www.nthpower.com

Venture Capital & Private Equity Firms / Domestic Firms

Mission Statement: Focusing on investment opportunities derived from the transition to competitive and global energy service markets.

Geographic Preference: United States
Fund Size: $420 million
Founded: 1997
Average Investment: $1-$2.5 million
Minimum Investment: $500,000
Investment Criteria: First-Stage, Second-Stage, Energy Sector
Industry Group Preference: Distribution, Utilities, Consumer Services, Power Technologies, Energy, Outsourcing & Efficiency, Storage, Business to Business, Information Technology, Energy Technology
Portfolio Companies: Accelergy, AllConnect, ARXX, BPL Global, Calstar, Capstone Turbine, Comverge, Evergreen Solar, FirstFuel Software, Glasspoint Solar, Hara, Nanogram Devices, Nexant, Northern Power Systems, Precursor Energetics, Propel Biofuels, Proton Energy Systems, RSI, Rive Technology, Silicon Energy, SmartSynch, SpectraSensors, SynapSense, Terrapass, Tempronics, Thetus, Topanga, Tioga Energy

Key Executives:
   Nancy C Floyd, Founder/Managing Director
   Education: MA, Political Science, Rutgers University; BA, Political Science, Franklin and Marshall College
   Background: Founder, NFC Energy Corporation; Co-Founder, Pac Tel Spectrum; Launched Spectrum Services
   Directorships: Silicon Energy, Evergreen Solar, Smartsynch, Serveron, SpectraSensors, Propel Biofuels, Thetus
   Tim Woodward, Managing Director
   Education: MBA, UCLA; BS, Resource Economics, Berkeley University
   Background: Liberty Environmental Partners; Chairman, Monitoring Technology Corporation; Senior Management, First Source
   Bryant J Tong, Managing Director
   Education: BS, Accounting, University of California at Berkeley
   Background: Co-Founder, ReSourcePhoenix Inc.; Senior Management, Phoenix American; Ernst & Young
   Directorships: Accelergy, Arxx, Calstar
   Matt Jones, Partner
   Education: Duke University's Fuqua School of Business; BA, Mechanical Engineering, University of California at Davis
   Background: Accenture (Andersen Consulting)
   Directorships: Tempronics, Topanga, REEl Solar, Precursor Energetics

1356 NUVEEN
730 Third Avenue
New York, NY 10017

web: www.nuveen.com

Mission Statement: Managing assets across diverse asset classes, geographies, and investment styles, offers solutions for a range of investors including pension funds, insurance companies, sovereign wealth funds, banks and family offices.

Geographic Preference: Worldwide
Fund Size: $989 billion
Founded: 1898
Industry Group Preference: Diversified
Key Executives:
   Jose Minaya, Chief Executive Officer
   Education: BS, Finance, Manhattan College; MBA, Amos Tuck School of Business, Dartmouth College
   Background: President, TIAA Global Real Assets; Merrill Lynch; JP Morgan
   Seun Salami, Chief Financial Officer
   Education: Obafemi Awolowo University; Ohio University
   Background: Jones Lang LaSalle Inc; Deloitte; KPMG

1357 NVIDIA INCEPTION
2788 San Tomas Expressway
Santa Clara, CA 95051

Phone: 408-486-2000
web: www.nvidia.com

Mission Statement: NVIDIA looks for partners that are using their GPU platforms to pursue breakthroughs in data analytics, self-driving cars, healthcare, Smart Cities, high performance computing, virtual reality and more.

1358 NYC SEED
Six MetroTech Center
Brooklyn, NY 11201

Phone: 707-469-3669
e-mail: apply@nycseed.com

Mission Statement: NYC Seed was formed to provide deserving New York City seed stage entrepreneurs with the capital and support they need to move from idea to product launch. NYC Seed has brought together many New York organizations to provide funding and support for young companies in New York City. The NYC Seed Partners include ITAC, The New York City Economic Development Corporation, The New York City Investment Fund, NYSTAR, and Polytechnic Institute of NYU.

Investment Criteria: Seed stage
Industry Group Preference: Software, Technology
Portfolio Companies: Magnetic, Valign, Ticketfly, SeatGeek, Enterproid, How About We, Datadog, ToutApp, Zipmark, Eachscape, Contently, Silver Lining, Amicus, See.me, Singly, Fieldiens, Powhow, Zeel, SoMoLend, Ufora, 10sheet, CourseHorse, Clothes Horse, Little Borrowed Dress, Bounce Exchange, Enigma

Key Executives:
   Owen Davis, Managing Director
   Education: BA, Brown University; MBA, Columbia Business School
   Background: General Partner, Contour Venture Partners; Adjunct Professor, Columbia Business School; Private Equity Consultant, PC LLC; CEO, Petal Computing; CEO, Sonata; CEO, Thinking Media

1359 O'REILLY ALPHATECH VENTURES
1 Lombard Street
Suite 303
San Francisco, CA 94111

Phone: 415-693-0200
e-mail: plans@oatv.com
web: www.oatv.com

Mission Statement: As seed investors, our focus is to help founders find clarity around their product and market in the most cash efficient way possible. This is a critical stage of development and one that can easily be misguided should a company raise too much or too little capital.

Average Investment: $250,000 - $2 million
Investment Criteria: Seed Stage
Industry Group Preference: Internet, Big Data, Mobile, Networking
Portfolio Companies: 3D Robotics, Cquia, Amee, Artists Wanted, Betabrand, Bitly, Bloom, Chairish, Chartbeat, Chumby, Codeacademy, Cover, Devver, Fastyl, Fidelis, Fitnesskeeper, Foursquare, Gamelayers, Get Satisfaction, Good Data, Grouply, Instructables, Jirafe, Learnzillon, littleBits Electronics, Localdirt, Maker Meia, Makespace, Misfit Wearables, Openx, Opensignal, Parakey, Path Intelligence, Peerj, Planet Labs, Science Exchange, Seeclickfix, Sherpaa, Sight Machine, Signal Sciences, Sonicliving, Spark, Strobe, Sweetlabs, Timehop, Tripit, Wesabe

Venture Capital & Private Equity Firms / Domestic Firms

Key Executives:
Bryce Roberts, Managing Director
Education: Brigham Young University
Directorships: 3D Robotics, Bit.ly, Bloom, Chartbeat, Codeacademy, Cover, Devver, Fidelis, FitnessKeeper, Foursquare, Gamelayers, Get Satisfaction, Kirafe, OpenX, Parakey
Mark Jacobsen, Managing Director
Education: BA, St. Olaf College; JD, Georgetown University Law Center
Background: Executive VP, New Ventures, O'Reilly Media; Business Affairs Director, Colossal Pictures
Directorships: AMEE, Betabrand, CollabNet, Planet Labs, Fast.ly, LocalDirt, LearnZillion, OpenSignal, Path Intelligence, SeeClickFix

1360 OAK HILL CAPITAL PARTNERS
One Stamford Plaza
263 Tresser Boulevard
15th Floor
Stamford, CT 06901

Phone: 203-328-1600
web: www.oakhillcapital.com

Mission Statement: Oak Hill Capital Partners is a leading private equity firm with a unique family-office heritage. Oak Hill targets opportunities to partner with exceptional entrepreneurs, management teams and corporations who share the firm's vision for value creation and philosophy of aligning interests.

Fund Size: $8 billion
Founded: 1985
Investment Criteria: Middle-Market
Industry Group Preference: Business Products & Services, Financial Services, Distribution, Healthcare, Media, Telecommunications, Technology
Portfolio Companies: Ability, AccentCare, Align Technology, American Skiing Company, Anchor Media Investors, Arder Holdings, Atlantic Broadband Group, Avolon Aerospace Limited, Berlin Packaging, Blackboard, Butler Schein Animal Health, Caribbean Restaurants, Cincinnati Bell, Dave & Buster's, Duane Reade, Earth Fare, eGain Communications, Exl Services, Financial Engines, Firth Rixson, FNB United, GATX Logistics, Genpact Limited, Hillman Group, Intermedia.net, IPWireless, Jacobson Companies, Local TV, MeriStar Investment Partners Lesee, Metrika, Monsoon Commerce, NSA International, OH Aircraft Acquisition, Oversee.net, Primus International, Progressive Moulded Products, Pulsant Limited, RSC Holdings, Security Networks, SmartPak Equine, Southern Air Holdings, SVTC Technologies, SWS Group, Telecity Group, The Container Store, TravelCenters of America, Vantage Oncology, Vertex Data Science, ViaWest, WaveDivision Holdings, WideOpenWest

Other Locations:
3000 Sand Hill Road
Bldg 2, Suite 160
Menlo Park, CA 94025
Phone: 650-234-0500

65 East 55th Street
32nd Floor
New York, NY 10022
Phone: 212-527-8400

Tyler Wolfram, Managing Partner
Education: AB, Brown University; MBA, Wharton School, University of Pennsylvania
Background: Managing Director, J.H. Whitney & Co. LLC; Managing Director, Cornerstone Equity Investors LLC; VP, Donaldson Lufkin & Jenrette Inc.
Brian Cherry, Managing Partner
Education: AB, Princeton University; MBA, Wharton School, University of Pennsylvania
Background: Senior Managing Director, J.H. Whitney & Co. LLC; Merchant Banker, Donald Lufkin & Jenrette Inc.
Steven Puccinelli, Managing Partner
Education: BS, University of California, Berkeley; MBA, Harvard Business School
Background: Investcorp International Inc.; Donaldson Lufkin & Jenrette Inc.

1361 OAK INVESTMENT PARTNERS
901 Main Avenue
Suite 600
Norwalk, CT 06851

Phone: 203-226-8346
web: www.oakvc.com

Mission Statement: OAK invests in rapidly growing companies that address large or expanding markets. These companies ideally can establish a leading market position in an equity-efficient manner, and protect that position once established.

Geographic Preference: United States, Worldwide
Fund Size: $5.8 billion
Founded: 1978
Average Investment: late stage $30-75 million; early $10-25 million
Minimum Investment: $5 million
Investment Criteria: Invest across a spectrum, in proven management teams, source deals from a refined referral network.
Industry Group Preference: Enterprise Services, Telecommunications, Storage, Financial Services, Outsourcing & Efficiency, Healthcare, Retailing, Infrastructure, Software, Information Technology, Internet, Consumer Products, E-Commerce & Manufacturing, Healthcare Information Technology, Energy
Portfolio Companies: Acculynk, Airspan Networks, Aspect Software, Attivio, Aurora Algae, Benefitfocus, Boston-Power, Brit Media, Catlight Health, Centric Software, Chamate, Cheddars, Circle Internet Financial Limited, Cloud Technology Partners, CommVerge Solutions, Deem, Demand Media, Dot & Bo, Duedil, Enjoy Technology, eSolar, FirstRain, FreshBooks, FRS, Gazillion Entertainment, GENBAND, Geotrace Technologies, Giosis, Good Technology, Great Gate Network, GTS CE Holdings, Hipmunk, IMI Exchange, Independent Living Solutions, iZENEtech, Keep Holdings/AdKeeper, Kinetic Social, Kratos Defense & Security Solutions, Kuaipay, Lianlian Pay, Limelight Networks, LumaSense Technologies, Major League Gaming, Milyoni, Mimosa Networks, MobiTV, Mojix, Movik Networks, Moxie Software, MyLife.com, NeoPhotonics Corporation, Nexant, NextNav, nLight Photonics, Nomorerack.com, Norse, NowThisMedia, One Medical Group, Photonic Devices, Photobucket, Plastic Logic, Precision fOr Medicine Holdings, Protean Electric, Radisphere National Radiology Group, RazorGator, Rebel Mouse, SmartDrive Systems, Solarflare Communications, sovrn Holdings, Sunrop Fuels, SunSun Lighting, Thrillist Media Group, Tikona Digital Networks, U.S. Auto Parts Network, Vesta, Wonga.com, xG Health Solutions, XIO, Ybrant, YoYi Media, Zayo Group, Zumobi

Other Locations:
3000 Sand Hill Road
Suite 3-245
Menlo Park, CA 94025
Phone: 650-614-3700

Key Executives:
Edward F. Glassmeyer, Managing Partner
e-mail: ed@oakvc.com
Education: MBA, The Tuck School; Princeton University
Background: Managing Director, Citicorp Venture Capital; Managing Director, The Sprout Capital Group
Directorships: Collabera, Enterprist Sourcing Services, Geotrace, Major League Gaming, Xiotech

Bandel L. Carano, Managing Partner
e-mail: bandel@oakvc.com
Education: BS/MS Electrical Engineering, Stanford University
Background: Morgan Stanley
Directorships: Stanford Engineering Venture Fund
Fred Harman, Managing Partner
650-614-3700
e-mail: fred@oakvc.com
Education: BS & MS, Electrical Engineering, Stanford University; MBA, Harvard Graduate School of Business
Background: Morgan Stanley's Venture Capital Group
Directorships: AdKeeper, Aspect Software, Demand Media, Federated Media, FRS, Knowledge Networks, Limelight Networks, MyLife.com, RazorGator, Rearden Commerce, Shop.com, Sutherland Global
Ann Lamont, Managing Partner
203-226-8346
e-mail: annie@oakvc.com
Education: BA, Political Science, Stanford University
Background: Research Associate, Hambrecht & Quist
Directorships: Acculynk, Argus Information & Advisory Services, Benefitfocus, Castlight Health, iHealth Technologies, NetSpend, PayFlex, PharMEDium Healthcare, Radisphere, TxVia, Vesta
Grace Ames, General Partner & Chief Operating Officer
e-mail: grace@oakvc.com
Education: BA Government, Smith College
Background: Harvard Management Company; VP, Barclay Investments
Ren Riley, Venture Partner
650-614-3700
e-mail: ren@oakvc.com
Education: BA, Government, Dartmouth College
Background: Senior Associate, Robertson Stephens
Directorships: Centric Software, Gazillion Entertainment, MyLife.com, Moxie Software, Sutherland Global Services, YoYi Media
Andrew Adams, General Partner
Education: BA, History, Princeton University
Background: Senior Associate, Capital Resource Partners
Directorships: iHealth Technologies, NetSpend, Radisphere, National Radiology Group, XG Health Solutions

1362 OAKTREE CAPITAL MANAGEMENT LLC
333 South Grand Avenue
28th Floor
Los Angeles, CA 90071

Phone: 213-830-6300 **Fax:** 213-830-6293
e-mail: investorrelations@oaktreecapital.com
web: www.oaktreecapital.com

Mission Statement: Seeks to purchase senior and secured debt and make short and long term investments.
Geographic Preference: United States, Canada, Western Europe
Fund Size: $13.3 billion
Founded: 1995
Average Investment: $100 million
Minimum Investment: $5 million
Investment Criteria: Mezzanine, Acquisition, Recapitalization, Special Situations, Distressed Debt
Industry Group Preference: All markets considered
Other Locations:
Oaktree Capital Management LP
1301 Avenue of the Americas
34th Floor
New York, NY 10019
Phone: 212-284-1900 **Fax:** 212-284-1901

Oaktree Capital Management LP
680 Washington Blvd
6th Floor
Stamford, CT 06901
Phone: 203-363-3200 **Fax:** 203-363-3210

Oaktree GmbH
Frankfurter Welle
An Der Welle 3, 9th Floor
Frankfurt am Main 60322
Germany
Phone: 49-692443393000 **Fax:** 49-692443393199

Oaktree Capital Management (UK)
10 Bressenden Place
London SW1E 5DH
United Kingdom
Phone: 44-2072014600 **Fax:** 44-2072014601

Oaktree Capital Management Pte Ltd
80 Raffles Place #51-03
UOB Plaza 1
Singapore 048624
Singapore
Phone: 65-63056550 **Fax:** 65-63056551

Oaktree Japan Inc
Atago Green Hills Mori Tower
37th Floor, 2-5-1 Atago, Minato-ku
Tokyo 105-6237
Japan
Phone: 81-357766760 **Fax:** 81-357766761

Barbara Strozzilaan 201
1083 HN
Amsterdam 1083 HN
Netherlands
Phone: 31-205792128 **Fax:** 31-205792129

Oaktree France SAS
39, rue de Courcelles
Paris 75008
France
Phone: 33-142991515 **Fax:** 33-142991511

Oaktree Capital (Seoul) Limited
Suite 2203, 22/F Trade Tower
511 Yeongdong-daero, Gangnam-gu
Seoul 06164
Korea
Phone: 82-221918000 **Fax:** 82-221918080

Suite 2001, 20/F, Champion Tower
3 Garden Road
Hong Kong
China
Phone: 852-36556800 **Fax:** 852-36556900

26A Boulevard Royal
7th Floor
Luxembourg L-2449
Luxembourg
Phone: 352-2663254700 **Fax:** 352-26632599

Room 36, 28th Floor
China World Office 1
No. 1 Jianguomenwai Avenue, Chaoyang District
Beijing 100004
China
Phone: 86-1065350208 **Fax:** 86-1065350209

Key Executives:
Howard Marks, Co-Chairman
Education: BSEc, Wharton School, University of Pennsylvania; MBA, University of Chicago
Background: TCW Group; CIO, Domestic Fixed Income of Trust Company; President, TCW Asset Management Company; Citicorp Investment Management
Bruce Karsh, Co-Chairman & Chief Investment Officer
Education: AB, Economics, Duke University; JD, University of Virginia School of Law
Background: Managing Director, TCW; Associate, O'Melveny and Myers; Judicial Clerk, Honorable Anthony M Kennedy
Jay Wintrob, Chief Executive Officer
Education: BA & JD, University of California, Berkeley

Background: President & CEO, AIG Life & Retirement; President, SunAmerica Investments Inc.; O'Melveny & Myers
Sheldon Stone, Principal & Co-Portfolio Manager
Education: BA, Bowdoin College; MBA, Accounting & Finance, Columbia University
Background: Citibank; Prudential Insurance Company

1363 OBVIOUS VENTURES
220 Halleck Street
Suite 120
San Francisco, CA 94129

e-mail: info@obvious.com
web: obvious.com

Mission Statement: Obvious Ventures seeks to work with companies dedicated to solving universal problems such as health and wellness and clean energy.

Founded: 2014
Industry Group Preference: Energy, Mobility, Healthcare, Wellness, Agriculture, Fintech, Education
Portfolio Companies: Amply, Bakpax, Beam, Beyond Meat, Block Renovation, Boon Supply, CareZone, Change.org, Computable, Corvus Insurance, DarwinAI, Devoted Health, Diamond Foundry, Enbala, Enervee, Fair, Good Eggs, Gusto, Happiest Baby, Hedvig, Incredible Health, Inspire, Joy, Keyo, LabGenius, Lilium, Long Game, Long-Term Stock Exchange, Lyric, Magic Leap, Medium, Mixt, Miyoko's Kitchen, Mosaic, Myro, Octave, Olly, Planet, Plant Prefab, Proterra, Recursion Pharmaceuticals, RenoRun, Seriforge, Sighten, Tentrr, Urban Remedy, Virta, Visor, VSCO, Welly, Workpop, XpertSea, Zymergen

Key Executives:
Ev Williams, Co-Founder
Background: Co-Founder of several companies including: Pyra Labs; Odeo; Obvious Corp; Twitter; CEO, Medium
James Joaquin, Co-Founder/Managing Director
Education: Brown University
Background: Co-Founder, Clearview Software; Co-Founder, When.com; President/CEO, Ofoto; President/CEO, Xoom.com
Vishal Vasishth, Co-Founder/Managing Director
Education: MS, North Carolina State University; MBA, Anderson School of Management
Background: Founding Partner, SONG Investment Advisors; Senior Executive, Steve Case's Revolution LLC; Chief Strategy Officer, Patagonia
Andrew Beebe, Managing Director
Education: BA, Dartmouth College
Background: Chief Commercial Officer, Suntech; VP of Distributed Generation, Nextera Energy; Co-Founder, Bigstep.com
Nan Li, Managing Director
Education: BS, Computer Science Engineering, University of Michigan
Background: Investment Manager, Innovation Endeavors; Head of Product/Operations/Finance, Gigwalk; Venture Capitalist, Bain Capital Ventures; Management Consultant, Bain & Company; PM, Microsoft

1364 OCA VENTURES
351 West Hubbard Street
Suite 600
Chicago, IL 60654

Phone: 312-327-8400 Fax: 312-542-8952
web: www.ocaventures.com

Mission Statement: OCA Ventures is a venture capital firm focused on investments in companies with dramatic growth potential, primarily in technology, financial services, for-profit education and technology-enabled services businesses.

Geographic Preference: United States
Founded: 2001
Average Investment: $3 - $5 million

Investment Criteria: Seed-Stage to Expansion-Stage
Industry Group Preference: Technology, Mobile Commerce, Financial Services, Education
Portfolio Companies: 71lbs, Alert Logic, Apparel Media Group, Automated Insights, Base, Base-2 Capital, BrightNest, Brill Street, Campus Explorer, Cartavi, Cleversafe, CohesiveFT, Ed Map, Excelerate Labs, FeeFighters, Fitocracy, Healthfinch, Iris Mobile, Javlin Capital, Midi Compliance & Ethics Solutions, Net-Hopper, National Billing Partners, OpenMarkets, Pangea, Pinpoint Care, Power 2 Switch, Red Foundry, Safe Shepherd, Sales Beach, Snapsheet, SpotHero, Sumridge Partners, Supplyhog, SwipeSense, TechSkills, TradeKing, Univa, WedPics, Whittl

Key Executives:
Jim Dugan, CEO/Co-Founder/Managing Partner
Education: BA, Economics, University of Rochester; MBA, JL Kellogg Graduate School of Management
Background: Continental Bank; Illinois Venture Capital Association
John Dugan, Chair Emeritus/Co-Founder
Education: BA, Business Administration, Pace College; US Naval Academy
Background: Americas for Swiss Bank Corporation; Purcell, Graham & Company; Controller, Baker, Weeks & Company
Peter Ianello, Chair/Co-Founder
Education: BA, Mount St. Mary College
Background: President & CEO, SBC Capital Markets; General Partner & Member, O'Connor & Associates
Mark Berman, Special Advisor
Education: BA, Accounting, Baruch College; JD, Brooklyn Law School
Background: Partner, O'Connor Partners Investment Office; Managing Director, Swiss Bank Corporation
Directorships: Techskills, Cohesive FT

1365 OCEANSHORE VENTURES
1350 Bayshore Highway
#920
Burlingame, CA 94010

Phone: 415-309-6752

Mission Statement: Oceanshore Ventures helps private companies get the early stage operating capital and access to world-class, international networks of suppliers, technologists and business leaders that they need to develop successfully. We are committed to making investments in early stage companies that develop breakthrough advanced materials-based technologies in renewable energy, energy storage, and energy efficiencies, and that hold the promise of delivering highly competitive solutions to the global market.

Investment Criteria: Early-Stage
Industry Group Preference: Technology, Energy Storage
Portfolio Companies: Confluence Solar, Skyline Solar, Lumiette, EnerVault, Crystal Solar

Key Executives:
Ken Pearlman, Founding Partner/Managing Director
e-mail: ken@oceanshorevc.com
Education: BS, Biology, University of California, Riverside; MBA, Santa Clara University
Background: Firsthand Capital; Executive Director, CIBC World Markets; Dean Witter Reynolds, Robertson Stephens & Company
Directorships: Crystal Solar, EnerVault, Lumiette
Eva Bjorseth, Founding Partner/Managing Director
e-mail: eva@oceanshorevc.com
Education: BBA, MBA, California State University
Background: Trade Commissioner, Innovation Norway; Presdio Ventures Partners

Venture Capital & Private Equity Firms / Domestic Firms

1366 OCTANe
65 Enterprise
Aliso Viejo, CA 92656

Phone: 949-330-6569 Fax: 949-330-6561
e-mail: info@octaneoc.org
web: www.octaneoc.org

Mission Statement: OCTANe connects people and ideas with capital and resources to fuel technology growth in Orange County. Our members represent Orange County technology executive leaders, entrepreneurs, investors, venture capitalists, academicians, and strategic advisors.

1367 ODEON CAPITAL PARTNERS
750 Lexington Avenue
27th Floor
New York, NY 10022

Phone: 212-257-6970 Fax: 212-504-3012
web: www.odeoncap.com

Mission Statement: To fund private and select public growth and expansion stage companies with established business franchises and solid financial metrics. The fund seeks to take either control or significant minority positions and to obtain board representation or board observer rights in each company in which it invests.

Fund Size: $250 million
Founded: 1999
Average Investment: $8 million
Industry Group Preference: Enterprise Services, Business to Business, Manufacturing, Distribution, Healthcare Services, Outsourcing & Efficiency

Key Executives:
Evan Schwartzberg, Managing Partner
Background: Merrill Lynch & Co., Louis Dreyfus Corporation, Pursuit Parners, Solomon Smith Barney, Bank of America Securities
Matthew Van Alstyne, Co-Founder/Managing Partner
Background: Ore Hill Partners LLC, Royal Bank of Scotland, Deutsche Bank, DebtTraders

1368 ODYSSEY INVESTMENT PARTNERS
590 Madison Avenue
39th Floor
New York, NY 10022

Phone: 212-351-7900
web: www.odysseyinvestment.com

Mission Statement: Odyssey makes majority, controlled investments primarily in established middle-market companies in a variety of industries.

Fund Size: $2 billion
Founded: 1998
Investment Criteria: Leveraged Acquisitions, Growth Financings, Recapitalizations
Industry Group Preference: Industrial Manufacturing, Business Products & Services, Insurance, Aerospace, Defense and Government, Energy, Supply Chain Management
Portfolio Companies: 4Wall Entertainment Inc., Addison Group, AeroPrecision, Aramsco, Aviation Technologies, Barcodes, BarrierSafe Solutions International, Cross-Country Infrastructure Services Inc., Dayton Superior Corporation, Dresser, Duravant, EAG Laboratories, Evergreen Tank Solutions, Integrated Power Services, Integro, Monarch Marking Systems, Montpelier Re Holdings, Neff Corp., Norcross Safety Products, One Call Medical, Peninsula Packaging Company, Pexco, Pro Mach, Ranpak, Safway Group Holding, SM&A Holdings, Testek Inc., TNT Crane & Rigging, TransDigm, TrialCard, tri-Star Aerospace, United Site Services, Wastequip, Wencor, Williams Scotsman, York Insurance Services

Other Locations:
401 Wilshire Boulevard
Suite 900
Santa Monica, CA 90401
Phone: 818-737-1111

Key Executives:
Stephen Berger, Chairman
Education: Brandeis University; University of Chicago
Background: Executive Vice President, GE Capital Corporation; Chairman & CEO, Financial Guaranty Insurance Company
Brian Kwait, Chief Executive Director
Education: University of Michigan; MBA, Wharton School
Background: Associate, Bear Stearns & Co.; CPA, Ernst & Whinney
William Hopkins, Vice-President
Education: University of California, San Diego; MBA, University of Southern California
Background: Merchant Banking Group, GE Capital Corporation; Wells Fargo Bank
Doug Hitchner, Managing Principal & COO
Education: Bucknell University
Background: Vice President, Goldman Sachs & Co.; Marine Midland Bank
Randy Paulson, Special Advisor
Education: BSB, Accounting, University of Minnesota; MBA, Kellogg Graduate School, Northwestern University
Background: Executive Vice President, National Financial Partners; Bear Stearns & Co.; GE Capital Corporation
Jeffrey McKibben, Senior Managing Principal
Education: BS, Economics, Wharton School; MBA, Harvard Business School
Background: Associate, Saugatuck Capital; Associate, Marakon Associates
Craig Staub, Senior Managing Principal
Education: BA, Economics, MPP, Public Policy, College of William & Mary
Background: Vice President, Westbury Equity Partners; Vice President, The Shattan Group; Associate, Marakon Associates

1369 OEM CAPITAL
2507 Post Road
Southport, CT 06890

Phone: 203-254-0200 Fax: 203-259-4041
e-mail: rjk@oemcapital.com
web: www.oemcapital.com

Mission Statement: Specializes in sale or divestiture of electronics, communications and computer companies. Also secure capital to complete an acquisition or restructure a company and secure merger acquisition candidates.

Geographic Preference: United States
Fund Size: $50 million
Founded: 1985
Average Investment: $5-50 million
Minimum Investment: $500,000
Investment Criteria: Smaller Size, Technical Orientation
Industry Group Preference: Electronic Components, Computer Related, Communications, Information Technology

Other Locations:
1875 Century Park E
Suite 1220
Los Angeles, CA 90067
Phone: 310-432-8585 Fax: 310-432-8576

Key Executives:
Ronald J. Klammer, President/Managing Director
e-mail: rjk@oemcapital.com
Education: MBA, Harvard Business School; MS, University of Pennsylvania; BA, Electrical Engineering, Villanova University
Background: Corporate VP, Gulton Industries; VP, Cross River Products Inc; Management/Technical, General Electric's Missile and Space Division
Michael Cohen, Managing Director
e-mail: mc@oemcapital.com

Venture Capital & Private Equity Firms / Domestic Firms

Education: MSc, Electrical Engineering, Drexel University; MBA, Wharton School of Business, University of Pennsylvania
Background: Diamond Capital Advisors; Johnson & Johnson; Hewlett Packard; General Electric; Honeywell International; Norwest Equity Partners; 3i Capital; Kulicke & Soffa
Shawn Thompson, Managing Director
e-mail: st@oemcapital.com
Education: BS, Economics, Wharton School of Business, University of Pennsylvania
Background: Diamond Capital Advisors; Barrington Associates
Tom Kastner, Managing Director
e-mail: tk@oemcapital.com
Education: BA, University of California at Berkeley; MBA, Yale University
Background: GP Ventures
Steve Klammer, Managing Director
e-mail: jsk@oemcapital.com
Education: BSc, Economics, Northeastern University; MBA, Booth School of Business, University of Chicago
Background: OEM Capital; Highbar Capital Management; Whitebox Advisors; Walleye Trading
Lori L. Murphree, Managing Director
e-mail: lm@oemcapital.com
Education: BA, California State University; MBA, International Management, Thunderbird Graduate School of Global Management
Background: Diamond Capital Advisors; Sapient; WPP; IBM; CACI; GXS; Silicon Valley Bank; Grant Thornton UK; Results International; McCracken Advisory Partners; Bacchus Capital Management
Mike Brunell, Managing Director
e-mail: mjb@oemcapital.com
Education: BA, University of California San Diego; MBA, Finance, Wharton School of Business, University of Pennsylvania
Background: Diamond Capital Advisors; Networks; Celgene; Abraxis Bioscience; American BioScience; Dillon, Read & Co.
Mark R. Ross, Managing Director
e-mail: mrr@oemcapital.com
Education: BSc, Finance, Lehigh University
Background: Diamond Capital Advisors; Mosaic Capital; Cogito Capital Partners; Chatsworth Securities
Directorships: Autobytel Inc.; AutoWeb; On Word Information
Chris Whitcomb, Managing Director
e-mail: cjw@oemcapital.com
Education: Economics, Lawrence University
Background: OEM Capital; Oppenheimer; Dain Bosworth; Piper Jaffray; William Blair; ThinkEquity Partners
Kristopher Prakash, Managing Director
e-mail: kp@oemcapital.com
Education: BS, Accounting, University of Southern California; Master's, Business Taxation, London School of Business
Background: Diamond Capital Advisors; Federal Reserve Bank of San Francisco
Wayne Platt, Managing Director
e-mail: wp@oemcapital.com
Education: MBA, Wharton School of Business, University of Pennsylvania; Finance, University of Cape Town
Background: Diamond Capital Advisors; Cappello Global; Houlihan Lokey

1370 OFF THE GRID VENTURES
2nd Street
San Francisco, CA 94111

e-mail: info@otgventures.com
web: www.otgventures.com

Mission Statement: Seeks to invest in "off the grid" entrepreneurs such as women and minority founders.
Founded: 2016
Investment Criteria: Seed, Early Stage
Industry Group Preference: Enterprise Tech, Fintech
Portfolio Companies: Aingel, Alchemy, AON3D, Barrel Park Investments, Base Venture, Bitesize, CreditStacks, DevCon Detect, Flexport, Fr8, OneKloud, OptionWay, Presence.ai, RankMyApp, Savitude, Skylights, Swarm Vision, Voxeet, Walnut Algorithms, WittyCircle, Zerply

Key Executives:
David Mes, General Partner
Education: Wharton School; La Sorbonne
Ben Orthlieb, General Partner
Education: Wharton School
Background: Tech Executive, LinkedIn; Boston Consulting Group
Mat Peyron, Co-Founder/Advisor
Education: MS, Imperial College; MBA, Wharton School
Background: Senior Director, Quinstreet; CEO, Wheelhouse Enterprises; VP of Venture Development, Aegon
Amber Caska, Advisor
Education: BS, University of Sydney
Background: Audit Senior, KPMG; GAAP Technical Lead, GE Capital; Controller, Safeco Insurance; Treasurer, Vulcan Inc.; VP of Private Banking, JP Morgan; CFO, Hillspire LLC; Leadership Council, Cinequest; Co-Founder/Venture Partner, Portfolia; CEO/Managing Partner, NEXT Family Office
Directorships: Portland Trail Blazers; The Hospital Club

1371 OKAPI VENTURE CAPITAL
1590 S Coast Highway
Suite 10
Laguna Beach, CA 92651

Phone: 949-715-5555 **Fax:** 949-715-5556
web: www.okapivc.com

Mission Statement: Okapi Venture Capital provides long-term capital and management support to start-ups. We take pride in partnering with exceptionally talented entrepreneurs and operational executives to develop their emerging businesses.

Geographic Preference: Southern California, Orange County
Investment Criteria: Seed-Stage, Early-Stage
Industry Group Preference: Life Sciences, Information Technology, Biotechnology, Diagnostics, Internet, Healthcare Information Technology, Healthcare Services, Materials Technology, Medical Devices, Semiconductors, Software, Wireless
Portfolio Companies: OmniVision Entertainment, Helixis, Transaction Wireless, OrthAlign, Obalon Therapeutics, WellTok, SignNow, BabyList, CrowdStrike, BioTrace Medical, Qualaroo, Pegasus Solar, Focal Therapeutics

Key Executives:
B Marc Averitt, Co-Founder/Managing Director
949-715-5555
e-mail: averitt@okapivc.com
Education: Philosophy & Business Administration, University of Southern California; JD, Pepperdine University School of Law
Background: Managing Director, Strategic Business Development, Intel Corporation; Sun Microsystems
Directorships: My Damn Channel, RF Nano Corporation, Transaction Wireless, SecondVoice
Sharon Stevenson DVM, PhD, Co-Founder/Managing Director
949-715-5557
e-mail: stevenson@okapivc.com
Education: MS, Veterinary Pathology, DVM, Ohio State University; PhD, Comparative Pathology, University of California, Davis; MBA, UCLA Anderson Graduate School of Management

Venture Capital & Private Equity Firms / Domestic Firms

Background: SVP, Technology & Planning, SkinMedical; Principal, Domain Associates; President & CFO, Volcano Therapeutics
Directorships: MicroVention, Neuropace, NuVasive, Santarus, SkinMedica, GenVault

1372 OLYMPUS PARTNERS
Metro Center
One Station Place
4th Floor
Stamford, CT 06902

Phone: 203-353-5900
web: www.olympuspartners.com

Mission Statement: To build a diversified portfolio by making investments in growth companies, acquisitions, financings and restructurings.

Geographic Preference: United States
Fund Size: $1.7 billion
Founded: 1988
Average Investment: $75 million
Minimum Investment: $25 million
Investment Criteria: Growth Capital to LBO and Restructuring
Industry Group Preference: Healthcare, Software, Financial Services, Business to Business
Portfolio Companies: 3D Corporation Solutions, American Residential, AMN Healthcare, AmSpec, Ann's House of Nuts, Ariel Re, Aspen Re, Centerplate Inc., Churchill Financial Group, Client Distribution Services, Club Staffing, CountryBanc, Eldorado Bancshares, Ennis-Flint, Foodware Group, FrontierVision Partners LP, Global Link Logistics, Heniff Transportation Systems LLC, Homax, IXS, K-MAC, Liqui-Box, Lyft, Meridian Rail Services, Nebraska Book Company, Norwesco, NPC International, Pennant Foods Corp., Pepper Dining, Petmate, Pharma Marketing Ltd., Phoenix Services LLC, PLZ Aeroscience Corporation, Pregis, Prime Advantage, The Princeton Review, PSAV, Professional Service Industries, Rise Baking Company, The Ritedose Corporation, Shemin, Siffron, Snyder Industries Inc., Soliant, Symmetry Medical, Talbot Underwriting, Tanenbaum-Harber Insurance Group, Tempest Re, TravelCenters of America, The Waddington Group, Woodcraft Industries

Key Executives:
  Rob Morris, Chair & CEO
  Education: AB, Hamilton College; MBA, Tuck School of Business
  Background: Senior VP, General Electric Investment Corporation; Management, GE, Manufacturing and Financial Service
  Directorships: Churchill Financial, The Ritedose Corporation, Tank Holding Corp., Homax Products, Professional Service Industries, Woodcraft Industries
  Lou Mischianti, Managing Partner
  Education: BS, Yale University
  Background: The Clippergroup, Odyssey Partners, First Boston
  Directorships: The Ritedose Corporation, Tank Holding Corp., Homax Products, Pepper Dining, Professional Service Industries, Woodcraft Industries
  Jim Conroy, Managing Partney
  Education: BA, University of Virginia; MBA, Tuck School of Business
  Background: Bain & Company, Goldman Sachs, General Elecrtic Investment Corporation
  Directorships: The Ritedose Corporation, Ariel Re

1373 OMEGA FUNDS
185 Dartmouth St.
Boston, MA 02116

web: omegafunds.net

Mission Statement: Omega Funds focuses on addressing severe, unmet medical needs by investing in biotechnology and medical device companies, therapeutics, and disruptive technologies.

Geographic Preference: North America, Western Europe
Investment Criteria: Early-, Mid-, and Late-Stage
Industry Group Preference: Healthcare, Biotechnology, Medical Devices, Therapeutics

Key Executives:
  Richard Lim, Managing Director
  Education: AB, MBA, Harvard University
  Background: General Partner, MVM Life Science Partners; Vice President, Saunders Karp & Megrue; Manager, LEK Consulting
  Claudio Nessi, Managing Director
  Education: MBA, Erasmus University; PhD, Genetics, University of Pavia
  Background: Managing Partner, NeoMed Management
  Anne-Mari Paster, Managing Director/CFO
  Education: BS, Engineering, Turku Institute of Technology; Boston University
  Background: CFO, Third Rock Ventures; CFO, MPM Capital; Founder & CFO, APS Material Services
  Otello Stampacchia, Managing Director
  Education: MS, Genetics, University of Pavia; PhD, Molecular Biology, University of Geneva
  Background: AlpInvest Partners; Portfolio Manager, Lombard Odier Immunology Fund; Goldman Sachs; Index Securities

1374 OMIDYAR NETWORK
1991 Broadway Street
Suite 200
Redwood City, CA 94063

Phone: 650-482-2500
web: www.omidyar.com

Mission Statement: Omidyar Network is a philanthropic investment firm dedicated to harnessing the power of markets to create opportunity for people to improve their lives. We invest in and help scale innovative organizations to catalyze economic, social and political change.

Geographic Preference: Worldwide
Minimum Investment: $1 million
Industry Group Preference: Consumer Internet, Mobile, Government
Portfolio Companies: Alliance for Affordable Internet, Amicus, Change.org, Couchsurfing, DoSomething.org, GSMA Mobile for Development Intelligence, HealthKart, Linden Lab, Meetup, Mimoni, NationBuilder, Neoteny Labs, Quikr, Range Networks, sovrn, Versé, Wikia, African Leadership Academy, Akshara Foundation, Anudip Foundation, Aspiring Minds, Bridge International Academies, EnglishHelper, IkamvaYouth, Kalibrr, RLabs, Teach for India, Tree House, Better Than Cash Alliance, BRAC, Center for Financial Services Innovation, Cignifi, Consultative Group to Assist the Poor, Core Innovation Capital, Elevar Equity, GSMA Mobile Money for the Unbanked, IntelleGrow, Kiva, LeapFrog Investments, Lenddo, MFX Solutions, MicroEnsure, MicroSave, Off.Grid:Electric, Paga, Prosper, Rev, Ruma, SOLIDUS Investment Fund, Vistaar Finance, Zoona, Africa Check, African Media Initiative, Association for Democratic Reforms, BudgIT, Center for Global Development, Center for Research and Teaching in Economics, Center on Democracy, Development and the Rule of Law, Code for America, Committee to Protect Journalists, ePanstwo Foundation, Fundacion Ciudadano Inteligente, Pundar, Global Integrity, Global Voices, IMCO, Instituto Cidade Democratica, International Budget Partnership, Janaagraha, Livity Africa, Media Development Investment Fund, Meu Rio, Mideast Youth, Myanmar Innovation Greenhouse, mySociety, New Citizen (Centre UA), ONE Campaign, Open Data Institute, Open Government Partnership, Open Knowledge, Praekelt Foundation, Project on Government Oversight, Publica, Sahara Reporters, SeeClickFix, Sunlight Foundation, The XYZ Show,

Venture Capital & Private Equity Firms / Domestic Firms

Transparency & Accountability Initiative, Tumml, Ushahidi, Versa, BRAC, Foundation for Ecological Security, Indian Institute for Human Settlements, Intitute for Liberty and Democracy, Landesa, icroBuild, Red Tierras, Artemisia, Bridges Ventures, Co-Creation Hub, Endeavor, Global Impact Investing Network, IGNIA, Nesta, Pymwymic, The Bridgespan Group, Toniic, d.light Design, iMerit, SONG Investment Company

Other Locations:
1333 New Hampshire Avenue SW
Suite 730
Washington, DC 20036
Phone: 202-448-4505

61B, 2 North Avenue
Maker Maxity, Bandra-Kurla Complex
Bandra (E), Mumbai
Mumbai 400 051
India
Phone: 91-02261187300

Charlotte House, 1st Floor
47-49 Charlotte Road
London EC2 3QT
United Kingdom
Phone: 44-02077299997

Key Executives:
Pierre Omidyar, Co-Founder/Managing Partner
Education: BS, Computer Science, Tufts University
Background: Founder, eBay; Co-Founder, Ink Development Corp.

1375 OMNICAPITAL GROUP
800 West Main Street
Suite 204
Freehold, NJ 07728

Phone: 908-497-6807 **Fax:** 908-502-0424
web: theomnicapitalgroup.com

Mission Statement: A venture capital firm dedicated to helping entrepreneurs build the best next-generation communication and information technologies for rapidly growing markets.

Portfolio Companies: Catheter Robotics, Personalized Media, Veveo, One On One Ads, eZuce, Flowonix Medical

Key Executives:
Dr. Arun Netravali, Managing Partner
908-497-6807
Background: President, Bell Laboratories
Directorships: Level 3 Communications, LSI, Sezmi, Knewco
JD Gardner, General Partner
908-497-6807
e-mail: jdgardner@omnivc.com
Background: Telecom
John Harrington, Venture Partner
Background: Managing Partner, Accenture Communication
Doug Eby, General Partner
908-497-6807
Directorships: Level 3 Comminications, Markel

1376 ONE EQUITY PARTNERS
510 Madison Avenue
19th Floor
New York, NY 10022

Phone: 212-277-1500
e-mail: oep.info@oneequity.com
web: www.oneequity.com

Mission Statement: To combine the strengths of an independent global private equity firm with the resources of a leading global bank.

Geographic Preference: Worldwide
Fund Size: $2 billion
Founded: 2001
Average Investment: $150 million
Minimum Investment: $50 million
Investment Criteria: MBO, Growth Capital
Industry Group Preference: Chemicals, Healthcare, Manufacturing, Technology, Travel & Leisure, Energy, Food & Beverage, Media
Portfolio Companies: Aligned Energy/Inertech, Allied S/A, AnexBusiness, Celltrion Healthcare, China Medicine, Cless Cosméticos, Constantia Flexibles, Duropak, East Balt Bakeries, Engineering Ingegneria Informatica, Expert Global Solutions, Genband, Grupo Phoenix, Library Solutions, M*Modal, Merfish Pipe and Supply and Pipe Exchange, Netas, Portal de Documentos, Schoeller Arca Systems, Smartrac Technology, Sonneborn Refined Products, Unicoba, Voltyre-Prom, Wilbanks Trucking and Wilbanks Leasing, Wow! Nutrition

Other Locations:
330 N Wabash Avenue
Suite 3750
Chicago, IL 60611
Phone: 312-517-3750

Herengracht 466
Amsterdam CA 1017
Netherlands
Phone: 31-204203000

Neue Mainzer Str. 84
Frankfurt am Main 60311
Germany
Phone: 49-6950607470

David Lippin, Managing Director/Head, Investor Relations
Education: BA, Economics, Harvard College
Background: Sun Capital Partners; GoldPoint Partners; First Manhattan Consulting Group
Carlo Padovano, Managing Director
Education: BS, Engineering & Management Systems, Columbia University
Background: GP Investimentos; JP Morgan
Directorships: Cless Comestics; Orion; Rizing; Wow! Nutrition; Portal; Unicoba; Allied
Steve Rappaport, Director of Research
Education: BA, Colby College; MA & MPhil, Columbia University; Executive Certificate In Management & Technology, Sloan School of Management, MIT
Background: SVP, Lazard Frères & Co.; SVP, Prudential Securities; Captain, US Air Force
Joseph Huffsmith, Managing Director
Education: BS, Mathematics & Economics, Duke University; MBA, University of Chicago
Background: Asia Capital Markets, JPMorgan
Directorships: GENBRAND, Netas, Precision Gear Holdings
Andrew Dunn, Managing Director
Education: BA, Modern History, University of Oxford; MPP, International Trade & Finance, Harvard Kennedy School of Government
Background: Boston Consulting Group

1377 ONEX FALCON
21 Custom House Street
10th Floor
Boston, MA 02110

Phone: 617-412-2700
e-mail: info@onexfalcon.com
web: www.falconinvestments.com

Mission Statement: Onex Falcon was formed in December 2020 through the acquisition of Falcon Investment Advisors by a subsidiary of Toronto-based Onex Corporation, a global investment firm focused in private equity, credit, and wealth management. Today, Onex Falcon has approximately $4.0 billion of capital under management and has invested $5.2 billion on behalf of investors since its founding.

Founded: 2020

Venture Capital & Private Equity Firms / Domestic Firms

Investment Criteria: Acquisition Financings, Recapitalizations, MBO, LBO, Growth Capital Financings, Liquidity, Structured Finance
Industry Group Preference: Diversified
Portfolio Companies: Accurate Metal Fabrications, Allion Healthcare, American Institute of Technology, AMPAC Packaging, Anton Capital Entertainment SCA, Bellisio Foods, BrightStar, Capital Sports Holdings, Capitain D's, Connect America Holdings, Dearborn Mid-West Conveyor Company, Digital Domain, EcoATM, Education One D/B/A Penn Foster, Gas Station TV, Ignition Group, Jason Incorporated, Jobson Healthcare Information, Kendrick Electric, Lapmaster International, LVI Services, MSX International, Northcentral University, One On One, Protect America, Purchasing Power, RFS Goldings, RoadSafe Traffic Systems, Rook Media, Saveology, Shari's Restaurants, Triad Retail Media, Village Roadshow Entertainment Group, WealthTrust, WL Plastics

Key Executives:

Sandeep D Alva, Managing Partner
617-412-2701
Education: BComm, Bombay University; MBA, Cornell University
Background: President, Hancock Mezzanine Investments; Joseph Littlejohn & Levy

William J Kennedy Jr, Managing Partner & Chief Operating Officer
617-412-2702
Education: BS, Business Management, Susquehanna University; CFA
Background: John Hancock Life Insurance Company

John S Schnabel, Managing Partner & Chief Investment Officer
212-300-0206
Education: BS, Chemistry, Adelphi University; MBA, Operations Research, Hofstra University
Background: Partner, Canterbury Capital Partners

Matthew J Hurley, Managing Director & Chief Financial Officer
617-412-2703
Education: BS, Business Administration, Bryant University
Background: John Hancock Financial Services

Eric Y Rogoff, Managing Director
212-300-0207
Education: BBA, University of Michigan School of Business
Background: Executive Director, Leveraged Finance, CIBC World Markets Corp.

Sven K. Grasshoff, Managing Director
617-412-2712
Education: BS, Business Administration, University of Colorado; MBA, Johnson School at Cornell University
Background: Corporate Development Group, Fischer Scientific International; Latona Associates; Citigroup Global Markets

1378 ONONDAGA VENTURE CAPITAL FUND
241 West Fayette Street
Syracuse, NY 13202

Phone: 315-478-0157
web: www.ovcfund.com

Geographic Preference: Northeast, Middle Atlantic
Fund Size: $2.5 million
Founded: 1985
Average Investment: $200,000
Minimum Investment: $100,000
Portfolio Companies: Accuracy Microsensors, AnAerobics, Appro Healthcare, Bioworks, Impact Technologies, Kiomix, UStec

Key Executives:
Michael Schattner, President
315-478-0157
Fax: 315-478-0158
Education: BS, University of Virginia; MBA, Syracuse University

1379 ONSET VENTURES
2490 Sand Hill Road
Menlo Park, CA 94025

Phone: 650-529-0700 Fax: 650-529-0777
e-mail: mp@onset.com
web: www.onset.com

Mission Statement: Focuses on seed and early-stage investing in medical technology and information technology markets.
Geographic Preference: Silicon Valley
Fund Size: $205 million
Founded: 1984
Average Investment: $5 million
Minimum Investment: $1 million
Investment Criteria: All Stages
Industry Group Preference: Medical Technology, Information Technology, New Media, Mobility, Infrastructure Software, Medical Devices, Drug Delivery, Diagnostics, Healthcare Information Technology
Portfolio Companies: Accelerated Networks, Access Closure, Adaptive Insights, Adara, Ads Native, Alteon WebSystems, AneuRx, APX, Arcot, Baronova, Buysight, Callidus Software, Clarify, ClariPhy, Cloud Cruiser, Conceptus, Corvita Corporation, Curon Medical, CytoPherx, Eloquent, Embollic Protection, Endocardial Solutions, Endotex, Ensim, EnteroMedics, Euphonix, Fleux Pine, Gadzoox Networks, Gale Technologies, Glimmerglass, Gridstore, Hotspur Technologies, Invarium, Nektar, NetSeer, Neuronetics, Nok Nok Labs, Novasys Medical, Obopay, Packeteer, Pancetera, Penederm, Placecast, Presidio Systems, Relievant, SS8, Sadra Medical, Securent, Sentilla, Spinal Concepts, Trilogy, Truviso, Uptake Medical, Valeritas, Vertos Medical, Vidder, Vindicia, VisionCare

Key Executives:

Terry Opdendyk, Founder/Partner, Information & Medical Technologies
e-mail: terry@onset.com
Education: BS, Michigan State University; MS, Stanford University
Background: VP, VisiCorp; Technical Manager, Hewlett-Packard; Intel Corporation
Directorships: Adaptive Planning, APX, Arcot Systems, Callidus Software, Nektak Therapeutics (formerly Inhal Therapeutics), NetSeer, Sentilla, Truviso

Robert Kuhling, Partner, Information & Medical Technologies
e-mail: rob@onset.com
Education: BA, Hamilton College; MBA, Harvard Business School
Background: Director Marketing, Sun Microsystems, VP, Manager, General Electric-Calma's, Team Leader, Bostons Consulting Group
Directorships: Access Closure, Aperion, BARNova, Hotspur Technologies, Uptake Medical

David Lane, Partner, Information Technology
e-mail: lane@onset.com
Education: BSEE, University of Southern California; MBA, Harvard Business School
Background: Diamondhead Ventures; Harvard Management Company; IBM
Directorships: Truviso, UPEK, Vindicia

Shomit Ghose, Partner, Information Technology
e-mail: shomit@onset.com
Education: BS, Computer Science, University of California, Berkeley
Background: SVP Operations, Tumbleweed Communications; VP, Worldwide Professional Services Organization, BroadVision

Steve LaPorte, Venture Partner, Medical Technology
e-mail: slaporte@onset.com
Education: BS, Mathematics & Computer Science, University of Wisonsin, Stevens Point; MBA, University

Venture Capital & Private Equity Firms / Domestic Firms

of Minnesota
Background: VP, NeuroVentures; Business Development, Medtronic
David Pann, Venture Advisor, Information Technology
e-mail: dpann@onset.com
Education: Computer Science, Business Administration, University of Vermont
Background: General Manager, Microsoft's Search Business Group
Rick Schell, Venture Partner, Information Technology
e-mail: rick@onset.com
Education: BA, Mathematics & Computer Science, MS & PhD, Computer Science, University of Illinois
Background: Chief Technologist, NetIQ; Founder, iSharp; Intel; Sun Microsystems; Borland

1380 OPEN PRAIRIE VENTURES
400 East Jefferson
Effingham, IL 62401

Phone: 217-347-1000
e-mail: info@openprairie.com
web: www.openprairie.com

Mission Statement: An Illinois based venture capital firm that invests in early stage, technology companies in the midwest region.

Geographic Preference: Midwest Region
Founded: 2000
Average Investment: $3 million
Investment Criteria: Early Stage
Industry Group Preference: Biotechnology, Technology
Portfolio Companies: Infoblox, TomoTherapy, iNest, MedVenture, Vestaron, Compact Particle Acceleration, Metactive, NewLeaf Symbiotics, iCyt, Innara Health, FlowForward Medical, Axonia Medical, Metabolic Solutions Development Company, Monteris, Tolera, Vestaron

Key Executives:
Jim Schultz, Founder/Managing Partner
e-mail: jim@openprairie.com
Education: BA, Business Administration, Southern Methodist University; JD, DePaul University College of Law; MBA, J.L. Kellogg Graduate School of Management at Northwestern University
Background: Founder/Chairman, Telemind Captial Corporation; Chairman, Prime Banc Corporation; Chairman/CEO, Physicians Clinical Laboratories;
Directorships: Vestaron
Dennis Beard, General Partner
217-819-5202
e-mail: dennis@openprairie.com
Education: BS, Accounting, Millikin University, Decatur; MBA, University of Illinois, Urbana-Champaign
Background: Adjunct Lecturer, College of Business, University of Illinois; EPL BioAnalytical Systems; Controller, SLM Instruments
Mike Peck, General Partner
913-492-3636
e-mail: mike@openprairie.com
Education: BS, Mechanical Engineering, University of Kansas; MBA, Kellogg School, Northwestern University
Background: Fund Manager, Kansas Technology Enterprise Corporation; Manager, Accenture
Directorships: Cernium, Infoblox, KCBioMediX

1381 OPENVIEW VENTURE PARTNERS
303 Congress Street
7th Floor
Boston, MA 02210

Phone: 617-478-7500
e-mail: info@openviewpartners.com
web: www.openviewpartners.com

Mission Statement: An expansion-stage venture capital fund, with a focus on high-growth software, internet and technology-enabled companies. Much of the team's success has been driven by its active role in providing its portfolio companies with strategic value-add services and highly practical operating expertise.

Geographic Preference: Worldwide
Fund Size: $240 million
Founded: 2006
Average Investment: $5 to $15 million
Minimum Investment: $5 million
Investment Criteria: Expansion-Stage
Industry Group Preference: Technology, Software, Internet, Digital Media & Marketing, Technology-Enabled Services
Portfolio Companies: SwiftStack, DataDog, Field Lens, Signpost, Pantheon, Smashfly, FieldAware, Socrata, Spredfast, Sonian, UnboundID, Xtium, Nextdocs, Monetate, Canvas, Skytap, Kareo, uSamp, Balihoo, Intronis, Open-E, VersionONe, AtTask, Exinda

Key Executives:
Scott Maxwell, Founder/Senior Managing Director
e-mail: smaxwell@openviewpartners.com
Education: BS, MS, Mechanical Engineering, University of California, Davis; PhD, Mechanical Engineering, MIT; MBA, MIT Sloan School of Management
Background: Senior Managing Director, Insight Venture Partners; Partner, Putnam Investments
George Roberts, Venture Partner
e-mail: groberts@openviewpartners.com
Education: BA, Marketing & Finance, University of Wisconsin
Background: EVP, North American Sales, Oracle Corporation; System5; Applied Data Research

1382 OPUS CAPITAL
Menlo Park, CA

Phone: 650-543-2900
e-mail: info@opuscapital.com
web: www.opuscapital.com

Mission Statement: Opus Capital works to accelerate growth, helping entrepreneurs build strong, sustainable enterprises. Aims to facilitate key relationships, provide access to critical resources and offer counsel on strategy, finance and operations.

Geographic Preference: Central United States
Fund Size: $1 billion
Founded: 1993
Average Investment: $5-$10 million
Minimum Investment: $5 million
Investment Criteria: Early Stage, Seed
Industry Group Preference: Communications, Software, Technology, Enterprise Software, Infrastructure, Internet, Semiconductors, Wireless
Portfolio Companies: AlertEnterprise, Cloud4Wi, Devpost, Dome9, Edunav, Jivox, Panzura, Payfone, Sequent Software, Sisense, SolarEdge, TrapX Security, Workboard

Key Executives:
Dan Avida, General Partner
e-mail: davida@opuscapital.com
Education: BSc, Computer Engineering, Technion, The Israel Institute of Technology
Background: President/CEO, Decru Inc.; Officer, Israel Defense Force
Gill Cogan, General Partner
e-mail: gill@opuscapital.com
Education: MBA, University of California, LA
Background: Founding General Partner, LightSpeed Venture Partners; Managing Partner, Weiss-Peck & Greer Venture Partners Fund; Adler & Company; CEO, Formtek
Directorships: EFI; Exigen; Personeta; Royalty Services; Softier; Telespree; Transparency
Joseph Cutts, Administrative Partner & CFO
e-mail: joe@opuscapital.com
Education: BS, Finance, Pennsylvania State University; MS, Finance/Marketing/International Business, Kellogg School of Management
Background: Executive Officer, Electronics for Imaging;

Venture Capital & Private Equity Firms / Domestic Firms

CFO/COO, EFI; Hills Bros. Coffee; Nestle Beverage Company
Phil Greer, Special Limited Partner
e-mail: phil@opuscapital.com
Education: AB, Princeton University; MBA, Harvard Business School
Background: Founding Partner, Weiss, Peck & Greer
Serge Plotkin, Venture Partner
e-mail: serge@opuscapital.com
Education: BSc, MSc, Electrical Engineering, Ben Gurion University; PhD, Computer Science, MIT
Background: Associate Professor, Computer Science, Stanford University; Co-Founder, Decru

1383 ORBIMED HEALTHCARE FUND MANAGEMENT
601 Lexington Avenue
54th Floor
New York, NY 10022-4629

Phone: 212-739-6400
web: www.orbimed.com

Mission Statement: An asset management firm focused exclusively on the global health sciences industry with a family of private equity funds, hedge funds and other investment vehicles.

Fund Size: $5 billion
Founded: 1993
Average Investment: $15 million
Minimum Investment: $5 million
Investment Criteria: All Stages with emphasis on Mid-Later Stage private companies
Industry Group Preference: Life Sciences, Medical Devices, Drug Development
Portfolio Companies: Acutus, Adaptimmune, Adimab, Aerocrine AB, Aerpio, Affirmed, AIMS, Alector, Amarin, Ambit Biosciences, arGEN-X, ARMO Biosciences, Arsanis Biosciences, Audentes Therapeutics, Avitide, Bacterin, Bharat Serums and Vaccines, BioLineRx, Bonovo Orthopedics, CardiAQ, Cardioxyl, CCAM Biotherapeutics, Cerapedics, Cerenis Therapeutics, Cleave Biosciences, Clementia, Crown Bioscience, DFine, Dimension Therapeutics, Domain Surgical, EA, Ecron Acunova, Eddingpharm, GC Aesthetics, GC-Rise Pharmaceutical, Glaukos, Good Start Genetics, Igenica, Inspire Medical Systems, Intercept, Invitae, Iroko Pharmaceuticals, Keystone Heart, KIMS GCC, KIMS India, Loxo Oncology, Medigus, MID Labs, Mirati Therapeutics, Natera, OmniGuide Surgical, Ornim Medical, Otic Pharma, Otonomy, OxOnc Development, PharmAcbine, Pieris AG, Practice Fusion, Principia Biopharma, ProNAi, RDD Pharma, Realton Corporation, Redhill Biopharma, Relypsa, Response BioMedical, Roka BioScience, Sage Therapeutics, Selecta Biosciences, Shasun, SI-Bone, Sientra, Ingulex, Sonnendo, Surya, Symbiomix Therapeutics, TELA Bio, TigerText, Treato, Unilife, ViewRay, Waterstone Pharmaceuticals, Whale Imaging

Other Locations:
1700 Owens Street
Suite 540
San Francisco, CA 94158
Phone: 415-294-8740

Suite F 27, Grand Hyatt Plaza
Santacruz East
Mumbai 400055
India
Phone: 91-2261403000

1 Shankar Street
Herzliya 4672501
Israel
Phone: 972-732822600

Unit 4706, Raffles City
Shanghai Office Tower
268 Xizang Middle Road
Shanghai 200001
China
Phone: 86-2163351700

Key Executives:
Sven H. Borho, Managing Partner
Education: University of Bayreuth; Msc Economics, London School Of Economics
Background: Senior Analyst, Mehta and Isaly
Carl L. Gordon PhD, Managing Partner
Education: Harvard College; Fellow, Rockefeller University; PhD Molecular Biology, MIT; CFA
Background: Senior Biotechnology, Mehta and Isaly
W. Carter Neild, Managing Partner
Education: BA Economics, Emory University; CEP, Institute D'Etudes Politiques, Paris; MBA, University of Chicago; CFA
Background: Director, UBS Alternative Investments Group; Investment Management, First Chicago Bank
Geoffrey C. Hsu, General Partner
Education: Harvard Medical School; MBA, Harvard Business School
Background: Financial Analyst, Lehman Brothers; Manager, Business Development, Veritas Medicine

1384 OREGON ANGEL FUND
760 SW 9th Avenue
Suite 2380
Portland, OR 97205

Phone: 503-727-2197

Mission Statement: The Oregon Angel Fund (OAF) is a community supported, professionally managed, investor driven angel fund. The fund provides investors privileged access to the most promising startups and early-stage growth companies in Oregon and SW Washington. OAF is the most active local venue for funding startups in terms of both participants and dollars invested.

Geographic Preference: Oregon, Southwest Washington
Founded: 2007
Average Investment: $100, 00 - $2 million
Minimum Investment: $100,000
Investment Criteria: Early-Stage
Industry Group Preference: All Sectors Considered
Portfolio Companies: AbSci, ActionSprout, BigLeaf, Networks, Brandlive, Bright.md, Cascade Prodrug, Celly, Chinook Book, ClearAccess, ClearFlow, Columbia Power Technologies, CrowdCompass, Customer.io, Daverci, DesignMedix, Diabetomics, Elemental Technologies, Farmhouse Culture, Giftango, GlobeSherpa, Green Zebra Grocery, Hubb, Inpria, IOTAS, Jama Software, Little Bird, Lumen Learning, Lumencor, Meridian, MobileRQ, Muut, Northshore Bio, Notion, Opal, Outdoor Project, Pacific Light Technologies, Paydici, Perfect Company, Poached Jobs, RNA Networks, RYNO Motors, Second Porch, Senrio, SmartRG, The Clymb, Veelo, Wicked Quick, Wild VR, Wildfang

Key Executives:
Eric Rosenfeld, Co-Founder
Education: Stanford Univ.; Institute for Management Development, Switzerland
Background: Co-Founder, Capybara Ventures; Principal Owner, Second Story Interactive Studios; Director, Corporate Development, Mentor Graphics; Analyst, SRI International; Research Fellow, Stanford Graduate School of Business
Scott Sandler, Fund Manager
Education: BS, Computer Systems Engineering, University of Massachusetts, Amherst
Background: CEO, Novas Software; Intel

Venture Capital & Private Equity Firms / Domestic Firms

1385 ORIGIN VENTURES
549 W Randolph Street
Suite 601
Chicago, IL 60061

Phone: 312-644-6449
e-mail: inquire@originventures.com
web: www.originventures.com

Mission Statement: Origin looks for companies in large, growing categories which have demonstrated product/market fit. They also back exceptional entrepreneurs in earlier stages who disrupt or create markets through unconventional, innovative approaches.

Geographic Preference: U.S.A., Canada
Fund Size: $80 million
Founded: 1999
Average Investment: $0.5-4 million
Investment Criteria: Early-Stage and Series A
Industry Group Preference: Technology, Marketplaces, SaaS, Business to Business
Portfolio Companies: 15Five, Ahalogy, Aisle50, AppDetex, Apptentive, Archer Education, Atavium, Avant, Backlot Cars, Bottlenose, Bound, Cameo, Cityscan, ClaimForce, Curiosity, DialogTech, DirectScale, Doggyloot, Fountain, Gamer Sensei, GrubHub, Idelic, Inest, Kidizen, Measured, Mighty, MyAlerts, Persio, Neat Work, Shoutlet, Teem, Tock, Tovala, Trala, ViralGains, Voxpopme, Whittl, Windsor Circle, Wove

Other Locations:
Salt Lake City, UT

Key Executives:
  Steven N. Miller, Founding Partner
  Education: BS, Business Administration/Marketing, University of Illinois, Urbana-Champaign
  Background: Quill Corporation
  Directorships: Backlot Cars, Impact Engine, VHT
  Bruce N. Barron, Founding Partner
  Education: BS, Accounting, University of Illinois, Urbana-Champaign; CPA
  Background: Board Member, Applied NeuroSolutions; CEO, APNS
  Directorships: DialogTech, MyAlerts, Bound, Tock
  Brent Hill, Managing Partner
  Education: BS, Finance, Bradley University; MBA, Booth School of Business
  Background: Leader, Central Region Sales Organization, Twitter; Head of Financial Services, Google; FeedBurner
  Directorships: Ahalogy, Apptentive, Bound, Curiosity, Fountain, Kidizen, AppDetex, DirectScale, Teem
  Jason Heltzer, Managing Partner
  Education: BS, Computer Science, University of Michigan; MBA, Booth School of Business, University of Chicago
  Background: Partner, OCA Ventures; Software Engineer, Deloitte Consulting
  Directorships: Ahalogy, Atavium, Base, MyAlerts, Tock, Tovala
  Alex Meyer, Managing Partner
  Education: BS, Mechanical Engineering, University of Illinois; MBA, Harvard Business School; Theater, Second City Conservatory
  Background: Vice President, Global Business Development, SAP; Senior roles with Deloitte and House of Blues
  Directorships: Founder and Chair, Harvard Business School Alumni Angels and Entrepreneurship Council of Chicago; HBS Alumni Angels Association; HBSCC Charitable Fund

1386 ORIGINATE VENTURES
205 Webster Street
Bethlehem, PA 18015

Phone: 610-866-5588 Fax: 610-866-5688
e-mail: shannon.morin@originateventures.com
web: www.originateventures.com

Mission Statement: Originate Ventures is a venture capital investment firm, targeting early stage product and services companies located in Pennsylvania and the Mid-Atlantic region.

Geographic Preference: Pennsylvania, Mid-Atlantic Region
Average Investment: $500,000 - $4 million
Investment Criteria: Early-Stage
Industry Group Preference: Medical Devices, Healthcare, Consumer, Information Technology, Internet
Portfolio Companies: Adhezion Biomedical, BA Insight, Care Kinesis, Clickpay Services, CMP.LY, Collections Marketing Center, FSA Store, Holganix, Medallion Analytics, Micro Interventional Devices, NaturalInsight, Proton Media, RightsFlow, TB Biosciences

Key Executives:
  Mike Gausling, Managing Partner
  Education: BS, Mechanical Engineering, Rensselaer Polytechnic Institute; MBA, Finance, Miami University, Ohio
  Background: Co-Founder & CEO, OraSure Technologies; Proctor & Gamble
  Glen R Bressner, Managing Partner
  Education: BSBA, Boston University; MBA, Babson College
  Background: Partner, Mid-Atlantic Venture Funds
  Eric Arnson, Managing Partner
  Education: University of Michigan
  Background: Founder, ENVISION; Proctor & Gamble

1387 ORIX
1717 Main Street
Suite 1100
Dallas, TX 75201

Phone: 214-237-2000
web: www.orix.com

Mission Statement: ORIX provides equity capital to lower middle market and middle market companies throughout the United States. Investments are made from $5-25 million for a variety of growth strategies, buyouts, recapitalizations, and strategic acquisitions. ORIX typically targets minority interests (10-49% ownership), allowing existing owners or sponsors to retain control.

Geographic Preference: United States
Average Investment: $5 - $25 million
Investment Criteria: Buyouts, Acquisitions, Co-Investments, Management-led Buyouts, Recapitalizations

Key Executives:
  Terry Suzuki, President and CEO
  Education: Keio University; MBA, University of Chicago
  Background: Co-CEO, Cerberus Japan; Partner, KPMG
  Jorge Jaramillo, Chief of Staff/Managing Director
  Education: Butler University; MBA, Washington University
  Background: Highland Capital Management; Wells Fargo, Capital Markets

1388 OSAGE PARTNERS
50 Monument Road
Suite 201
Bala Cynwyd, PA 19004

Phone: 484-434-2255 Fax: 484-434-2256
web: osageventurepartners.com

Mission Statement: Osage Partners is a family of venture capital funds that includes Osage Venture Partners and Osage University Partners. Each fund has a dedicated professional staff and a distinct investment strategy. We seek to invest in determined and creative entrepreneurs and assist them in building high growth businesses with consistent revenue streams.

Geographic Preference: Mid-Atlantic Region
Fund Size: $100 million
Founded: 1990

Average Investment: $1 - $2 million
Investment Criteria: Early-Stage
Industry Group Preference: Enterprise Applications, Healthcare Information Technology, Software, SaaS, Internet, Business Products & Services, Healthcare Services, Information Technology
Portfolio Companies: Automated Insights, BA-Insight, Canvas, Ceptaris, CMC, Earnest Research Company, ExecOnline, FieldView Solutions, Halfpenny Technologies, HardMetrics, Identropy, InstaMed, Medallion Analytics, Moda Technology Partners, PeopleLinx, Pneuron, ProtonMedia, RackWare, SevOne, Sidecar

Other Locations:
10 County Line Road
Branchburg, NJ 08876
Phone: 484-434-2255 **Fax:** 484-434-2256

Key Executives:
Robert S Adelson, Managing Partner
Education: Yale University, Yale University Law School
Background: Clerk, Third Circuit Court of Appeals; Corporate Law, Wolf Block Schorr & Solis-Cohen
Directorships: Melior Discovery, SevOne
Nathaniel V Lentz, Managing Partner
Education: Brown University, Stanford Graduate School of Business
Background: President & CEO, Verticalnet; Partner, Mercer Management Consulting
Directorships: Carnegie Speech, Landslide Technologies, InstaMed, Hard Metrics, Proton Media, FieldView
David Drahms, Principal
Education: Mechanical Engineering, University of Rochester; MBA, Wharton School
Background: Teradyne
Directorships: Halfpenny Technologies, Yaupon Therapeutics

1389 OUTCOME CAPITAL
11911 Freedom Drive
Suite 1010
Reston, VA 20190
Phone: 703-225-1500 **Fax:** 703-225-1515
web: www.outcomecapital.com

Mission Statement: Outcome Capital's investment strategy is to invest in sectors where we have knowledge, experience and a successful track record. These sectors are driven by fundamental economic and business trends that create attractive investment opportunities and are often supported by proprietary technology.

Average Investment: $1 - $3 million
Investment Criteria: All Stages
Industry Group Preference: Government, Aerospace, Defense and Government, Homeland Security, Communications, Internet, New Media, Technology, Life Sciences, Healthcare, Financial Services
Portfolio Companies: Alltrust Networks, Brightdoor, DoublePositive, Earth Networks, Genesis Financial Solutions, Preferred Systems Solutions, RFID Global Solutions, Saylent Technologies, Social Solutions

Other Locations:
80 William Street
Suite 250
Wellesley, MA 02481
Phone: 703-225-1500 **Fax:** 703-225-1515

Key Executives:
Jonathan R Wallace, Managing Director
e-mail: jwallace@outcomcapital.com
Education: BS, Commerce, University of Virginia McIntire School of Commerce; MBa, Darden School of Business
Directorships: Double Positive, RFID Global, AllTrust, Saylent, PerformLife
Michael J Cromwell III, Managing Director
e-mail: mcromwell@outcomecapital.com
Education: BA, Yale University; JD, Georgetown University
Directorships: BrightDoor Systems, Social Solutions, Preferred Systems
Oded Ben-Joseph PhD, Managing Director
e-mail: oben-joseph@outcomecapital.com
Education: Imperial College of Science, Technology & Medicine (UK); PhD, University of Cambridge
Background: Managing Director, Boston Equity Advisors
Arnie Freedman, Managing Director
e-mail: afreedman@outcomecapital.com
Education: University of Massachusetts
Background: Co-Founder/Principal, Boston Equity Advisors; Founder & CEO, Rustel

1390 OUTLOOK VENTURES
3000F Danville Boulevard
Suite 110
Alamo, CA 94507
Phone: 415-547-0000

Mission Statement: Actively invests in promising early and growth stage industry-transforming information technology companies.

Geographic Preference: West Coast United States
Fund Size: $140 million
Founded: 1996
Investment Criteria: Early-Stage, Growth-Stage
Industry Group Preference: Consumer Internet, Business to Business, Information Technology, Infrastructure, Internet
Portfolio Companies: The Active Network, ClairMail, Digital Chocolate, Echopass, Loyalty Lab, nSite Software, Overture, Reply, Soundview Technology, Toolwire, Vantos, Xactly

Key Executives:
Randy Haykin, Managing Director
Education: BA, Organizational Studies, Brown University; MBA, Harvard Business School
Background: Senior Sales & Marketing Positions at Yahoo!, Viacom, Paramount, BBN, IBM, Apple Computer
Directorships: Digital Chocolate, Reply.com, Reconnex, Loyalty Lab, Bridgestream, NetBrowser Communications, nSite Software, Impulse Network, eTeamz, Voquette, Obiquity, Logilent
Carl Nichols, Managing Director
Education: BS, Computer Science, Brown University; MBA, Harvard Business School
Background: SBC/Pacific Bell, Scrivner, Booz Allen & Hamilton
Directorships: ClairMail, Lasso Logic, Epicentric, MarketHome, Arthas, Toolwire, Vantos, Kinecta

1391 OUTPOST CAPITAL
355 Berry Street
San Francisco, CA 94158
web: outpostvc.com

Mission Statement: Outpost Capital is a venture vapital fund focused on Virtual Reality and Artificial Intelligence, as well as blockchain technology.

Geographic Preference: US, China
Founded: 2016
Investment Criteria: Early Stage
Industry Group Preference: Artificial Intelligence, Virtual Reality, Blockchain, Technology, Robotics
Portfolio Companies: Aconite, Big Box, Fable, Humense, Jido, Jingtum, Kite & Lightning, MOAC, Modal, Natilus, Pingpad, The Rogue Initiative, Supermedium, TheWaveVR, UploadVR, Visby

Key Executives:
Ryan Wang, Co-Founder/General Partner
Background: Venture Partner, CLI Ventures; Investment Banker, Citigroup

Venture Capital & Private Equity Firms / Domestic Firms

Sha Zhou, Co-Founder/General Partner
Background: HP; Alteon; NetScaler; NetScreen; Juniper
Cherie Liu, Vice President, Investment
Education: MS, Columbia University

1392 OVP VENTURE PARTNERS
Kirkland, WA

Phone: 425-889-9192
e-mail: hoban@ovp.com

Mission Statement: Makes equity investments in early stage technology-based companies primarily in the Western third of North America, while maintaining a leading market share position in the Pacific Northwest.

Fund Size: $185 million
Founded: 1983
Average Investment: $1-$5 million
Minimum Investment: $100,000
Investment Criteria: Seed, Startup, First-stage, Second-stage
Industry Group Preference: Software, Communications, Life Sciences
Portfolio Companies: Adapx, Cradlepoint Technology, Datsphere Technologies, EnerG2, Fate Therapeutics, GenoLogics, NanoString Technologies, Novomer, OncoFactor, RedSeal, Talyst, Tigo Energy, Verdezyne

Other Locations:
One SW Columbia
Suite 1675
Portland, OR 97258
Phone: 503-697-8766

Key Executives:
Gerry Langeler, Managing Director
Education: AB Chemistry, Cornell University; MBA, Harvard University
Background: Co-Founder & President Mentor Graphics, Author 'Vision Trap'
Directorships: Advanced Inquiry Systems, Carbonflow, Collaborative Software Initiative, EnerG2, GainSpan, Max-Viz, Viral Logic Systems Technology
Bill Funcannon, Managing Director
Background: Venture Fund Controller, Hambrecht & Quist
Directorships: LeMond Fitness, M2E

1393 OWL VENTURES
400 Pacific Avenue
3rd Floor
San Francisco, CA 94133

Phone: 415-277-0300
web: owlvc.com

Mission Statement: Owl Ventures is a global venture capital firm focused on the merger of K-12 education and technology.

Founded: 2014
Industry Group Preference: Software, Applications, Education, Healthcare, Technology, Child Care
Portfolio Companies: Abl, Accelerate Learning, Amira Learning, Bakpax, Benchprep, BetterLesson, Byju's, Degreed, Dreambox, Hazel Health, Imbellus, Kiddom, Kuali, Labster, LearnZillion, Lele Ketang, Lingo Live, Newsela, Noodle Partners, Panorama Education, Piper, Quizlet, Raftr, RaiseMe, Remind, Securly, SV Academy, Swing Education, Thinkful, Tinkergarden, Whitehat Jr.

Other Locations:
300 Sand Hill Road
Building 3
Suite 180
Menlo Park, CA 94025

Key Executives:
Ian Chiu, Managing Director
Education: BS/MS, Industrial Engineering, Stanford University; MBA, Stanford Grad. School of Business
Background: Warburg Pincus; Silver Lake Partners; Bain & Company
Directorships: Liaison International; Dude Solutions; Civitas Learning
Tom Costin, Managing Director
Education: BA, Bowdoin College; MBA, Stanford Grad. School of Business
Background: Private Investment Specialist, Cambridge Associates; Managing Director, SoleTech; Associate, FLAG Capital
Amit A. Patel, Managing Director
Education: BA, Mathematical Economic Analysis, Rice University; MBA, Stanford Grad. School of Business; MA, Education, Stanford Grad. School of Education
Background: Founder, Perfonal Academic Trainers; Director of Technology, Success Academy Charter Schools
Tory Patterson, Co-Founder/Managing Director
Education: BA, Economics, Williams College; MBA, Stanford Grad. School of Business
Background: Partner, Catamount Ventures
Jed Smith, Co-Founder/Advisor
Education: BA, Middlebury College; MBA, Harvard Business School
Background: Founder/Managing Partner, Catamount Ventures; Fouunder, Drugstore.com
Directorships: Linden Labs; Revolutions; Abl.; Piper; RaiseMe; Amour Vert; Banyan Water; Plum Organics; Seventh Generation

1394 OXANTIUM VENTURES
2600 Virginia Ave NW
Suite 512
Washington, DC 20037

e-mail: info@oxantium.com
web: www.oxantium.com

Mission Statement: Oxantium Ventures invests worldwide in a diversified range of companies, distributed across three stages of enterprise development - seed, early stage, and growth. This is done for two primary reasons. One is to follow a balanced portfolio strategy and minimize risk. The other is to offer a 'lifecycle' of support to promising companies and to have the capacity to fund them from the early idea stage to well after they are out of incubation and require financing to sustain growth

Geographic Preference: Worldwide
Investment Criteria: Seed-Stage, Early-Stage, Later-Stage
Industry Group Preference: Software, Hardware, Wireless, Information Technology, Enabling Technology, Advanced Materials, Nanotechnology, Power
Portfolio Companies: Anvato, RFnano, EnerTech Environmental, iMove, E.A.R.T.H., Make a Mind Co., Solar Array Ventures, Wireless World Net

Key Executives:
Newton Howard, Managing Director
Education: PhD
Background: Chairman, Center for Advanced Defense Studies
Richard Wirt, Managing Director
Education: PhD
Background: Vice President/General Manager, Intel Corporation Software & Solutions Group; Chief Scientist & EVP, In-Q-Tel

1395 OXFORD BIOSCIENCE PARTNERS
535 Boylston Street
Suite 402
Boston, MA 02116

Phone: 617-357-7474 Fax: 617-357-7476

Mission Statement: To generate long-term capital gains for both the investors in the Fund and the entrepreneurs that we support. To meet this goal, we invest in businesses capable of improving the diagnosis and treatment of disease, as well as the companies with technologies that accelerate drug discovery and

Venture Capital & Private Equity Firms / Domestic Firms

development. We have achieved considerable success and above average returns in the bioscience field.

Geographic Preference: United States, Europe
Fund Size: $850 million
Founded: 1992
Average Investment: $5 million
Minimum Investment: $1 million
Investment Criteria: Healthcare
Industry Group Preference: Biotechnology, Genomics, Medical Devices, Research & Development, Therapeutics, Life Sciences
Portfolio Companies: Gene Logic, Human Genome Sciences, Exelixis, Genset S.A., ACADIA Pharmaceuticals, Inc., AVEO Pharmaceuticals, Cardiome Pharma, Ceres, Dicerna Pharmaceuticals, Enata Pharmaceuticals, ExonHit Therapeutics, Genetic Therapy, Geron Corporation, Glori Energy, Illumina, Inkine Pharmaceutical Company, Inverness Medical Innovations, Orchid BioSciences, QuadraMed, Salix Pharmaceuticals, Santhera Pharmaceuticals, Sosei, Targacept, VIVUS, Xencor

Other Locations:
30765 Pacific Coast Highway
Suite 370
Malibu, CA 90265
Phone: 310-589-0025 **Fax:** 310-589-0099

1396 OYSTER VENTURES
1355 Market Street
Suite 488
San Francisco, CA 94103

e-mail: partners@oyster.vc
web: oyster.vc

Mission Statement: Oyster Ventures invests in exceptional new-frontier technology companies. Targets companies that bring liquidity and efficiency to antiquated industries, companies that enable globalization, and with the leverage to massively scale.

Geographic Preference: North America, Asia
Fund Size: $30MM
Founded: 2016
Average Investment: $250K
Minimum Investment: $100K
Industry Group Preference: Fintech, Vertical, SaaS, Marketplace, Blockchain
Portfolio Companies: Blockstack, Equipmentshare, Forge Global, LogDNA, MasterClass, Postmates, Republic.co

Key Executives:
Sophie Liao, General Partner
Background: Managing Director, Rothenberg Ventures; Venture Partner, Draper Dragon; M&A Manager, Eight Solutions; M&A Manager, FFD Labs; Anchor, CCTV; Anchor, Travel Channel; Head of Business Development, Cameron Pace Group
Kenneth Ballenegger, Managing Partner
Background: Co-Founder/Chief Strategy Officer, Republic Crypto; Co-Founder/CTO, FreshPay; Architect/Head of Mobile Engineering, Chartboost; Engineer, Tapulous

1397 PACIFIC COMMUNITY VENTURES
51 Federal Street
San Francisco, CA 94107

Phone: 415-442-4300 **Fax:** 415-442-4313
e-mail: info@pcvmail.org
web: www.pacificcommunityventures.com

Mission Statement: Focused exclusively on growing small businesses in California. We seek to invest in and build companies in partnership with experienced and entrepreneurial managers who share our vision and passion for growth.

Geographic Preference: California
Founded: 1999
Average Investment: $1-4 million

Investment Criteria: Growth Equity, Management Led Buy-Outs, Liquidity for Family-Owned or Closely-Held Companies, Recapitalizations/Restructurings
Industry Group Preference: Specialty Food Products, Ethnic Products & Services, Health Related, Low-Capital Intensity Manufacturing, Environment Products & Services
Portfolio Companies: Adina, Beacon Fire & Safety, Bentek Corporation, Evergreen Lodge, Fresh Dining, Galaxy Desserts, Mercados SUVIANDA, Moving Solutions, New Leaf Paper, Niman Ranch, Pacific Pharmacy Group, SABEResPODER, Timbuk2

Other Locations:
2448 Historic Decatur Road
Suite 200
San Diego, CA 92106
Phone: 619-818-6872 **Fax:** 619-516-2295

Key Executives:
Bulbul Gupta, President and CEO
Education: George Washington University; University of Michigan
Background: Global Entrepreneurship Advisor, Clinton Campaign; Founding Advisor, Socos Labs;Adjunct Lecturer, NYU
Patrick Teixeira, Chief Financial Officer
Education: BSBA, Sonoma State University
Background: CEO, Abilene Partners; Managing Director, PCV Finance

1398 PACIFIC CORPORATE GROUP
Phone: 619-522-0100 **Fax:** 619-522-0099
e-mail: info@pcgfunds.com
web: www.pcgfunds.com

Mission Statement: A research driven investment management firm focused solely on private equity.

Geographic Preference: United States, Western Europe, Japan
Fund Size: $350 million
Founded: 1979
Investment Criteria: All Stages
Portfolio Companies: Armonix, Spectrawatt, SolarReserve, Allied Resource Corporation, ReliOn, Range Fuels, Odersun, Fat Spaniel Technologies

Key Executives:
Christopher J Bower, CEO/Founder
Education: BS, University of Colorado; JD, University of San Diego
Background: Arthur Young & Company

1399 PACIFIC HORIZON VENTURES
500 Union Street
Suit 835
Seattle, WA 98101

Phone: 206-682-1181 **Fax:** 206-682-8077
e-mail: phv@pacifichorizon.com
web: www.pacifichorizon.com

Mission Statement: A Seattle-based venture capital firm with national presence, focused on the life science and healthcare industries. With a successful track record of over ten years, as demonstrated in our first two funds, we invest in validation phase, early and mid stage private companies across North America with a particular focus on the Pacific Northwest region.

Geographic Preference: North America, Northwest Region
Fund Size: $75 million
Founded: 1993
Minimum Investment: $250,000
Investment Criteria: Early Stage
Industry Group Preference: Health Related, Life Sciences
Portfolio Companies: Koronis Pharma, ViaCyte, Argos Therapeutics, AtheroGenics, CareWise, CellPathways, Diametrics Medical, Focal, Health Systems Technologies, Illumigen Biosciences, Inhibitex, iScience Interventional,

NeoPath, Norian Corporation, Orquest, Rasiris, Sapient Health Networks, SleepMed, Tandem Medical, Therion Biologicals Corporation, Tissue Repair Company, Transmolecular, Trimeris, VirtGen, Coral Systems, Creative Multimedia, Edmark Corporation, Innova Corporation, Proxim, RTIME

Key Executives:
  Donald J Elmer, Managing General Partner
  206-682-1181
  Fax: 206-682-807
  e-mail: elmer@pacifichorizon.com
  Education: MA, Economics, University of Pennsylvania; BA, Economics, Western Washington University
  Directorships: ViaCyte, Koronis Pharmaceuticals
  David A Krekel, Principal
  Education: BS, Chemistry, Harvey Mudd College; MBA, University of Washington
  Background: Virginia Mason Medical Center
  William Robbins, Business Relations Principal
  e-mail: phv@pacifichorizon.com
  Education: BA, Catholic University of America

1400 PACIFIC VENTURES GROUP
Los Angeles, CA 90015

Phone: 310-800-4556
e-mail: info@pacvgroup.com

Mission Statement: Privately-held venture capital partnership focused exclusively on investments in food, beverage and alcohol related industries.

Geographic Preference: United States
Fund Size: $100 million
Founded: 1995
Average Investment: $2-$5 million
Minimum Investment: $250,000
Investment Criteria: Seed, Startup, First-Stage, Second-Stage, Mezzanine, LBO, Special situations, Buy-ins, Consolidations, Recapitalization
Industry Group Preference: Food & Beverage Related

Key Executives:
  Shannon Masjedi, CEO and President
  Education: Arizona State University

1401 PALADIN CAPITAL GROUP
2020 K Street NW
Suite 620
Washington, DC 20006

Phone: 202-293-5590
e-mail: info@paladincapgroup.com
web: www.paladincapgroup.com

Mission Statement: Paladin Capital Group is a leading multi-stage private equity firm that provides funding to growing companies. Across the globe, from Silicon Valley to Brazil, Paladin invests in best-of-breed companies with technologies, products, and services that meet the challenging demands of commercial, federal, and international customers.

Geographic Preference: North America, Brazil
Fund Size: $950 million
Founded: 2001
Average Investment: $10-$30 million
Minimum Investment: $5 million
Investment Criteria: Up to $250 million in annual sales, Small to mid-size, Consolidations, Restructurings, Growth Equity
Industry Group Preference: Homeland Security, Security, Alternative Energy, Technology
Portfolio Companies: 10x Technologies, Accubuilt, Adapx, Application Security, Arxan, BAInsight, BugCrowd, BuildingIQ, Clearcube, Cloudshield, Command Information, Courion, Crossbow, CyberCore Technologies, Damballa, DigitalBridge Communications, Digital Signal Corporation, Endgame, Fixmo, FPMI Solutions, HealthTell, HelioVOlt, Initiate, Luminus, Modius, Neohapsis, Newlanis, Nexidia, Orchestra, Paladin Ethanal Acquistion, PerspecSys, PhishMe, Previstar, Quantalife, Racemi, Renewable Energy Products, Royalty Pharma, SafeView, Shadow Networks, SOA Software, ThreatStream, TOMA Biosciences, Twist Bioscience, UniTrends, VREC, White Ops., WiSpry

Other Locations:
  295 Madison Avenue
  12th Floor
  New York, NY 10017
  Phone: 202-293-5590

  3000 Sand Hill Road
  Suite 2-145
  West Menlo Park, CA 94025

  20 North Audley Street
  London W1K 6WE
  United Kingdom
  Phone: 44-0203-931-9704

Key Executives:
  Michael Steed, Founder/Managing Partner
  Education: Loyola Marymount University; JD, Loyola University School of Law
  Background: Senior VP of Investments, Washington, DC Financial Company
  Mark Maloney, Founder/Managing Director/Chief Compliance Officer
  Education: BS, Towson University
  Directorships: Adaptx, FPMI Solutions
  Dr. Alf L. Andreassen, Global Security Expert
  Education: PhD, Physical Chemistry, Cornell University
  Background: Founding Member, AT&T Solutions; Technical Advisor, Naval Warfare; Bell Laboratories
  Directorships: AgION, CloudShield, Digital Signal, Oryxe Energy, Previstar
  Kenneth A. Minihan, Managing Director
  Education: BA, Florida State University; MA, Naval Postgraduate School
  Background: Lt. General (Ret), United States Air Force; Director, National Security Agency/Central Security Service; Chairman & President, Security Affairs Support Association
  Directorships: Arxan, Command Information, GlassHouse, Neohapsis, Nexidia
  E. Kenneth Pentimonti, Principal
  Education: BA, Economics & Political Science, Stanford University; MBA, Anderson School at UCLA
  Background: Investment Banker, JP Morgan Chase; Senior Consultant/Auditor, Arthur Andersen & Co.
  Paul Conley, Managing Director/Venture Studio Director
  Education: BS, MS, Mechanical & Aerospace Engineering, University of Virginia; PhD, Computational Physics, MS, Bioengineering, University of California, San Diego
  Background: Founding CEO, BrightScale; Los Alamos National Laboratory
  Philip Eliot, Venture Partner
  Education: AB, Physics, Harvard University
  Background: FBR Technology Venture Partners

1402 PALISADE CAPITAL MANAGEMENT
One Bridge Plaza
Suite 695
Fort Lee, NJ 07024

Phone: 201-585-7733
Toll-Free: 800-330-9966
web: www.palisadecapital.com

Mission Statement: Provide investment management services to large institutions through our Small-Cap Equity and Convertible Security strategies. Through the proper balancing of risk and reward we endeavor to provide meaningful returns while preserving clients' capital.

Fund Size: $400 million
Founded: 1997
Average Investment: $5 to $30 million

Venture Capital & Private Equity Firms / Domestic Firms

Minimum Investment: $2 million
Investment Criteria: All Stages
Portfolio Companies: Brickell Biotech, Everlaw, Neurologix, Send Word Now, RAD Technologies
Other Locations:
  251 Royal Palm Way
  Suite 601
  Palm Beach, FL 33480
  Phone: 561-832-3558
Key Executives:
  Alison Berman, President and CEO/Chair
  e-mail: aberman@palcap.com
  Education: Brown University; JD, Benjamin N. Cordozo School of Law
  Background: Attorney, Skadden, Arps, Slate & Flom LLP
  Jack Feiler, Vice Chair
  Education: BA, City College of New York; JD, Brooklyn Law School
  Background: Account Executive, Burnham & Co.; Senior Executive VP, Broad Street Investment Management; Senior VP of Investments, Smith Barney
  Steven E Berman, Vice Chair
  Education: BA, Syracuse University; JD, Brooklyn College Law School
  Background: Executive Vice President, Drexel Burnham; Attorney/CEO, Manufacturing Company; Senior Vice President, Smith Barney
  Jeffrey D Serkes, Chief Operating Officer
  Education: BBA, Accounting, George Washington University
  Background: Senior Vice President & CFO, Allegheny Energy; Vice President & Treasurer, IBM Corporation; RJR Nabisco
  Dennison T Veru, Chief Investment Officer
  Education: Franklin & Marshall College
  Background: President & Director of Research, Awad Asset Management; Drexel Burnham Lambert; Smith Barney Harris Upham

1403 PALISADES VENTURES
11726 San Vicente Blvd
Suite 450
Los Angeles, CA 90049

Phone: 310-571-6214
web: www.palisadesgrowth.com

Mission Statement: A Los Angeles-based VC firm making growth stage investments in systems, services, software, and hardware companies that are driving the adoption of leading edge IT, communications, and media technologies.
Average Investment: $2.5 - $7 million
Investment Criteria: Growth-Stage
Industry Group Preference: Information Technology, Software, Media, Communications
Portfolio Companies: Apacheta Corporation, Language Weaver, Lucix, MegaPath Networks, Micro Power, Omneon, Peregrine Semiconductor, Polaris Wireless, SOA Software, xAD, Visage Mobile, Zinio Systems
Key Executives:
  Paul D'Addario, Co-Founder, Partner
  Education: BA, Boston College; MSc, London School of Economics, JD, Villanova Law School
  Background: Managing Director, Donaldson Lufkin & Jenrette
  Anders Richardson, Co-Founder, Partner
  Education: BA, Harvard College; MBA, Harvard Business School
  Background: Investment Banking, Donaldson Lufkin & Jenrette
  Directorships: SOA Software, V-Enable

1404 PALLADIUM EQUITY PARTNERS
Rockefeller Center
1270 Avenue of the Americas
31st Floor
New York, NY 10020

Phone: 212-218-5150 Fax: 212-218-5155
e-mail: palladium@palladiumequity.com
web: www.palladiumequity.com

Mission Statement: Provides equity to companies seeking to grow, restructure or provide liquidity for shareholders. Palladium principals have invested more than $2 billion of equity in over 60 companies in the last two decades while developing a distinguished track record of successful partnerships with management teams.
Fund Size: $1 billion
Founded: 1997
Average Investment: $15 - 75 million
Investment Criteria: Leveraged Buyouts, Recapitalizations, Corporate Spin-Outs, Growth Financing, Restructurings
Industry Group Preference: Business Products & Services, Financial Services, Consumer Products, Food Services, Healthcare, Manufacturing, Media, Retail, Consumer & Leisure
Portfolio Companies: ABRA Auto Body & Glass, American Gilsonite, BankUnited, Cannella Media, Capital Contractors Inc., Castro Cheese, CircusTrix, Clarion Industries, DailyMe, Daniel's Jewelers, Del Real Foods, DolEx Dollar Express Inc., Fora Financial, GoodWest Industries Inc., HealthSun, Hy Cite Enterprises LLC, Jordan Health Services, Kar's Nuts, Kymera International, Mission Community Bank, Prince International Corporation, Pronto Insurance, QMax, Quirch, Raben Tire, Regional Management Corp., Sahale Snacks, Spice World, Taco Bueno, Teasdale Foods Inc., TransForce Inc., Wise Foods Inc.
Other Locations:
  1 Station Place
  Suite 501
  Stamford, CT 06902
Key Executives:
  Marcos A Rodriguez, Chair & CEO
  Education: BS, Mechanical Engineering, Columbia University; MA, International Studies, Lauder Institute, University of Pennsylvania; MBA, Wharton School
  Background: Partner, Oseph Littlejohn & Levy (Jll)
  Chris Allen, Partner
  Education: BS, Mathematics, Morehouse College; BS, Electrical Engineering, Georgia Institute of Technology; MBA, Harvard Business School
  Background: Arlon Capital Partners; GenNx360 Capital Partners; Windjammer Capital Investors; Bain & Co.
  Directorships: Del Real; Kar's Nuts
  Christina Bushey, Chief Operating Officer
  Education: BA, Finance-Economics, Manhattanville College
  Background: Marketing/Corporate Access Coordinator, Wunderlich Securities Inc.; Institutional Equity Sales & Trading Departments, Kaufman Bros. L.P., & Brean Murray, Carret & Co.

1405 PALMS & COMPANY
Palms Bayshore Building
West Wing Penthouse #408
6421 Lake Washington Boulevard NE
Kirkland, WA 98033-6876

Phone: 425-828-6774 Fax: 425-827-5528
e-mail: palms@peterpalms.com
web: www.peterpalms.com

Mission Statement: Transition from resources that will become seriously devalued due to Global Economic Meltdown of 2011 including hyper inflation, soaring gold prices, collapse of

banking industry, collapse of real estate market, oil priced in other than dollars, other currencies becoming gold backed, etc.
Geographic Preference: Europe, Russia, China, Eastern Europe, United States, Canada, Mexico
Founded: 1934
Average Investment: $30 million
Minimum Investment: $1 million
Investment Criteria: Management team in place, simple solution for a big problem, defined exit strategy
Industry Group Preference: Pharmaceuticals, Agriculture, Mining, Construction, Oil & Gas, Machinery
Portfolio Companies: Congress Inns, Deltona Corporation, Eastern Elevator, Golf In Corporation, Gulf American Land Corporation, JSC Krasalkor Aluminiystroi Krasnoyarsk, Lummi Indian Nation, Mackle Brothers, Mechanical Rubber Products, Riva Boats

Other Locations:
1001 Oakwod Boulevard
Fairfield, IA 52556
Phone: 641-472-0262 **Fax:** 641-469-6360

Key Executives:
Dr. Peter J Palm IV, President
425-828-6774

1406 PALO ALTO VENTURE PARTNERS
300 Hamilton Avenue
4th Floor
Palo Alto, CA 94301

Phone: 650-462-1221
e-mail: judy@pavp.com
web: www.pavp.com

Mission Statement: An early stage, information technology, venture capital firm producing stellar returns by helping entrepreneurs lead new markets in enterprise communications and computing into proven companies.
Geographic Preference: United States, West Coast
Fund Size: $150 million
Founded: 1996
Investment Criteria: Seed, Early Stage, First Stage, Mezzanine, Second Stage, Seed, Startup
Industry Group Preference: Information Technology, Enterprise Services, Computer Related, Online Content, Software
Portfolio Companies: Adforce, Aspectrics, AGIS, AvantGo, CareerBuilder, Gemandforce, Empolyease, Esurance, More.com, Nextance, PostX, Semagtx, Vicinity, When.com

Key Executives:
Peter Ziebelman, Founding Partner
Education: MSC Computer Science, Yale Unversity
Background: Marketing Executive, Texas Instruments; Ryan McFarland

1407 PALO ALTO VENTURE SCIENCE
501 Forest Ave
Palo Alto, CA 94301

Phone: 650-530-0040
e-mail: info@venture-science.com
web: www.venture-science.com

Mission Statement: We invest in leading startups using model based approaches to venture capital. Our objective is to achieve a superior rate of return by following a systematic approach to investing and applying proprietary analytical models.
Investment Criteria: Early Stage
Industry Group Preference: Mobile, E-Commerce & Manufacturing, Consumer Technology, Education Technology, Healthcare Information Technology
Portfolio Companies: Appetas, Safe-Guard, Zipmark, Olapic, The Visual Revenue Platform, Vipit, TIO Networks Corporation, Clinipace Worldwide, KnowledgeTree, Lineagen, Quantenna Communcations, Ooma, Luxtera, Aggregate Knowledge

Key Executives:
Matt Oguz, Founding Partner
e-mail: matt@venture-tech.com
Education: MBA, Decision Science, GSU
Selahattin Onen, Managing Partner
Education: BSEE, University of Denver; Stanford University
Background: CEO, G101; CEO, AGE Energy Group

1408 PALOMAR VENTURES
1881 Von Karman Avenue
Suite 220
Irvine, CA 92612

Phone: 949-475-9455 **Fax:** 949-475-9456
e-mail: jgauer@palomarventures.com
web: www.palomarventures.com

Mission Statement: Focuses on early stage information technology companies that demonstrate the potential for exceptional growth and market leadership.
Fund Size: $225 million
Founded: 1999
Average Investment: $5 million
Minimum Investment: $2-$5 million
Investment Criteria: Early-Stage
Industry Group Preference: Broadband, Infrastructure, Business to Business, Telecommunications, Software, Technology
Portfolio Companies: Ace Metrix, Akonix Systems, AlterPoint, Applimation, Attensite Corporation, Biscotti, Bubbly, Cerebra, Composite Software, Continuous Computing, CoreObjects, Damballa, DATAllegro, Dorado, Edgewater Networks, Entone Technologies, Efficient Networks, ExteNet Systems, Fulcrum, Gluecode Software, Incuity Software, Inovys Corporation, Interperse, Lombardi Software, Mixed Signals, MyBuys, Netcontinuum, Netork Physics, Paymetrics, Predixion Software, Ravenflow, RealOps, Silver Creek Systems, Strix Systems, Utique, Virtela, Voxify

Other Locations:
18881 Von Karman Avenue
Suite 960
Irvine, CA 92612
Phone: 949-475-9455 **Fax:** 949-475-9456

1200 Park Place
Suite 300
San Mateo, CA 94403
Phone: 650-566-1100 **Fax:** 650-510-6836

Key Executives:
Jim Gauer, Managing Director
Education: BA, Mathematics, UCLA; PhD Candidate, Mathematics & Philosophy, Johns Hopkins University
Background: General Partner, Enterprise Partners Venture Capital
Directorships: Ace Metrix, Composite Software, CoreObjects, Dorado, Lombardi Software, Paymetric
Lisa Riedmiller, Chief Financial Officer
Education: BA, California State University
Background: OSCCO Ventures

1409 PALOMINO CAPITAL
2525 Knight Street
Suite 275
Dallas, TX 75219

Phone: 214-269-3400
e-mail: info@palominocap.com
web: www.palominocap.com

Mission Statement: Palomino Capital partners with management teams to invest in middle-market buyouts, industry consolidations, and recapitalizations.
Geographic Preference: United States
Fund Size: $2 billion

Venture Capital & Private Equity Firms / Domestic Firms

Investment Criteria: Buyouts, Industry Consolidations, Recapitalizations
Industry Group Preference: Niche Manufacturing, Distribution, Building Materials & Services, Business Products & Services

Key Executives:
  Chuck Butler, Partner
  Education: BA, University of Texas, Dallas
  Background: Barrier Advisors, Convergent Communications, PricewaterhouseCoopers Corporate Finance
  John Toomay, Partner
  Education: BA, Economics, Brown University; AVA
  Background: Associate, Mercer Management Consulting; United Airliens

1410 PAMLICO CAPITAL
150 North College Street
Suite 2400
Charlotte, NC 28202
Phone: 704-414-7150
web: www.pamlicocapital.com

Mission Statement: To generate exceptional investment returns by providing talented managers and growing companies with capital, ideas and encouragement. Formerly Wachovia Capital Partners and First Union Capital, Pamlico Capital provides flexible capital and strategic advice to companies whose management teams have a vision for their business and operating expertise to implement their strategies.

Geographic Preference: United States
Fund Size: $1.1 billion
Founded: 1988
Average Investment: $15 million - $100 million
Minimum Investment: $1 million
Investment Criteria: Management or Leveraged Buyouts, Recapitalziations, Growth or Acquisition Financings, Mezzanine Financings, Special Situations
Industry Group Preference: Communications, Consumer Products, Distribution, Industrial Services, Medical & Health Related, Information Technology, Media, E-Commerce & Manufacturing, Manufacturing, Energy, Financial Services, Business Products & Services, Healthcare
Portfolio Companies: 10th Magnitude, A4 Health Systems, ACIST Medical Systems, Airwavz Solutions, American Community Newspapers, American Renal Associates, ATX Networks, BeckerBs Healthcare, BNI, Cartegraph, Clearlink, Coastal Drilling, Comsys, Constella, Daxko, DayNine, Dexter + Chaney, Digitech, excellRx, GreatAmerica, Greenway, Healthcare First, HelioCampus, Hosting, Inner City Broadcasting, iBBS, IntraLinks, JAG-ONE, Lightower, Mactec, MedCap, MetaMetrics, MetroPCS, NewWave Communications, NuVox, Office Practicum, Personify, Physicians Endoscopy, PrizeLogic, Prometheus, Randall-Reilly, Securadyne Systems, Secure-24, Service Express, Silverline, Sonitrol Corporation, Symplr, T2 Systems, TekLinks, Three Eagles Communications Company, TNW Systems, TRG Screen, USA Compression Partners, US Eye, US Radiosurgery, VRI, Vast Broadland, Veston Nautical, Veterinary Practice Partners, Wilcon, Winsight, World 50, WorldStrides

Key Executives:
  Scott B. Perper, Partner
  704-383-0000
  Fax: 704-374-6711
  Education: Undergraduate Degree, Bowdin College; MBA, Harvard Business School
  Background: VP, Kidder, Peabody & Company
  Directorships: HOB Entertainment; NuVox Communications; US Salt Holdings; VIVAX
  Frederick W. Eubank II, Partner
  704-383-0000
  Fax: 704-374-4709
  Education: Undergraduate Degree, Wake Forest University; MBA with honors, Duke University
  Background: CIO, First Union's Specialized Industries
  Directorships: CapitalSource; COMSYS IT Partners; Constella Group
  L. Watts Hamrick III, Partner
  704-383-0000
  Fax: 704-383-6538
  Education: Undergraduate Degree; MBA, Duke University;
  Background: Tax Consultant, Price Waterhouse
  Directorships: American Community Newspapers; Piedmont Television; Three Eagles Communications; BullsEye Telecom; Utilicom Networks; Heartland Publications; NewWave Communications; MACTEC
  Brian F. Chambers, Partner
  704-414-7177
  e-mail: brian.chambers@pamlicocapital.com
  Education: BBA, University of Wisconsin; MBA, Booth School of Business
  Background: Principal, Beecken Petty O'Keefe; Analyst, Piper Jaffray
  Directorships: JAG-ONE; US Eye; Veterinary Practice Partners
  Arthur C. Roselle, Partner
  Education: Undergraduate Degree, MS Mathematics, University of Virginia
  Background: EVP, R-H Capital Partners, VP, The Robinson-Humphrey Company
  Directorships: COMSYS IT Partners; NewWave Communications; Worldstrides Holdings
  Walker C. Simmons, Partner
  Education: BS Commerce, University of Virginia; Masters of Management, JL Kellogg Graduate School
  Background: VP, Bruckmann, Rosser, Sherrill & Company; Associate, The Robinson-Humphrey Company; Chartered Financial Analyst
  Directorships: American Community Newspapers; Heartland Publications; Sonitrol; Three Eagles Communications; TMW Systems; MetroPCS; NuVox Communications
  Scott R. Stevens, Partner
  Education: Undergraduate, University of North Carolina, MB, Stanford University
  Background: Analyst, First Union Securities' Communications And Media Finance Group
  Eric J. Wilkins, Partner
  704-715-4554
  e-mail: eric.wilkins@wachovia.com
  Education: BA, University of North Carolina, Chapel Hill; MBA, Columbia Business School
  Background: Associate, DLJ Merchant Banking Partners; Associate, McCown De Leeuw & Company; Analyst, Bowles Hollowell Conner & Company
  Directorships: Integrated Broadband Services
  R. Scott Glass, Jr., Principal
  701-414-7121
  e-mail: scott.glass@pamlicocapital.com
  Education: BS, Wake Forest University; MBA, Wharton School
  Background: Associate, Tailwind Capital Partners; Associate, American Capital; Analyst, Wachovia Securities
  Directorships: Digitech; Office Practicum; Veterinary Practice Partners
  Jay R. Henry, Principal
  704-414-7184
  e-mail: jay.henry@pamlicocapital.com
  Education: BS, West Virginia University; MBA, Kellogg School of Management
  Background: Senior Associate, Saw Mill Capital; Analyst, Edgeview Partners
  Directorships: Becker's Healthcare; BNI; HelioCampus; PrizeLogic; TRG Screen; Winsight; World 50
  Andrew B. Tindel, Principal
  704-414-7180

e-mail: andrew.tindel@pamlicocapital.com
Education: BE, Vanderbilt University; MBA, Harvard Business School
Background: Associate, GTCR LLC; Analyst, Goldman Sachs
Directorships: 10th Magnitude; Airwavez Solutions; Silverline; Vast Broadband

1411 PANORAMA CAPITAL
1999 S. Beascom Avenue
Suite 700
Campbell, CA 95008

Phone: 650-234-1420
web: www.panoramacapital.com

Mission Statement: Panorama Capital invests in passionate entrepreneurs building leading companies in life sciences and technology.

Industry Group Preference: Life Sciences, Technology
Portfolio Companies: Alvine Pharmaceuticals, Axiom, Auspex, Belair Networks, Beyond the Rack, CardioKinetix, Federated Media Publishing, Fixmo, Hyperion Therapeutics, Itero, NinthDecimal, Neoconix, NextWave Pharmaceuticals, Powervision, Presidio Pharmaceuticals, Shoedazzle, Skyfire, Syncapse, Tynt, Validity, Vyatta, World Golf Tour, Zoove

Key Executives:
Christopher J Albinson, Managing Director
Education: BS, MBA, University of Western Ontario
Background: General Partner, JP Morgan Partners
Directorships: Federated Media, Jiwire, Belair Networks, Tynt, Vyatta
Shahan D Soghikian, Managing Director
Education: BA, Pitzer College; MBA, UCLA Anderson School of Management
Background: Chemical Venture Partners, Bankers Trust, Prudential Equity Group
Directorships: Narus, Tagsys RFID, Squaretrade
Rod Ferguson, Managing Director
Education: BS, University of Illinois; PhD, State University of New York; JD, Northwestern University
Background: Partner, InterWest Partners; Genentech Inc.; Mccutchen, Doyle, Brown, & Enersen
Damion Wicker, Managing Director
Education: BS, Massachussets Institute of Technology; MD, Johns Hopkins School of Medicine; MBA, Wharton School
Background: President, Adams Scientific; MBW Venture Partners; Alexon Inc.

1412 PANORAMIC VENTURES
3575 Piedmont Road NE
Building 15, Suite 730
Atlanta, GA 30305

Phone: 404-410-6476
e-mail: hello@panoramic.vc
web: panoramic.vc

Mission Statement: Panoramic Ventures is a venture capital firm that seeks to open new doors for entrepreneurs in overlooked regions.

Founded: 2021
Industry Group Preference: Diversified
Portfolio Companies: Acclivity Health Solutions, Achievelt, Acivilate, Aspirion Health Resources, Car360, Case Status, ChartSpan, CheckAction, Cleverly, ConnexPay, Cypress, Defy Trends, DemandJump, Digital Assent, EmpowHR, FullScaleNANO, GameDriver, GigLabs, GPA Learn, Gro, Ingenious Med, Inked, Kobiton, LeaseQuery, Luma, MaterialsXchange, Microf, Monsieur, NexDefense, OncoLens, Pya, Otto, PlayOn! Sports, Pointivo, PriorAuthNow, ReachHealth, RelayOne, ShareholdInSite, StrataCloud, ThingTech, Trella Health, Tricentis, UserIQ, Vendormate, Vibenomics, Virtual Badge, VoApps, Wellview

Key Executives:
Mark Buffington, Managing Partner
Paul Judge, Managing Partner
Paul Iaffaldano, General Partner
Dan Drechsel, General Partner
Mark Flickinger, General Partner & Chief Operating Officer
Todd Knudsen, Chief Financial Officer

1413 PANTHEON VENTURES (US) LP
555 California Street
Suite 3450
San Francisco, CA 94104

Phone: 415-249-6200
e-mail: san.francisco@pantheon.com
web: www.pantheon.com

Mission Statement: Pantheon is a pioneer in private equity with a history of consistent performance and client service reflected in our continued success and reputation as an industry leader.

Geographic Preference: United States, Europe, Asia
Fund Size: $2.2 Billion
Founded: 1982
Investment Criteria: Leveraged Buyouts, Early-Stage & Later-Stage Venture Capital, Special Situations, Distressed Debt, Turnaround, Mezzanine Funds
Industry Group Preference: Manufacturing, Services, Information Technology, Healthcare, Energy, Communications, Consumer Products

Other Locations:
10 Finsbury Square
4th Floor
London EC2A 1AF
United Kingdom
Phone: 44-02033561800

33 Des Voeux Road
21st Floor
Central
Hong Kong
Phone: 85-237189600

11 Times Square
35th Floor
New York, NY 10036
Phone: 212-205-2000

Key Executives:
Brian J. Buenneke, Partner
Education: AB, Government, Dartmouth College; MBA, Kellogg School of Management, Northwestern University
Background: HarbourVest Partners; Duke Street Capital; Paul Capital Partners; Lehman Brothers Investment Banking Division
Dennis McCrary, Partner
Education: BA, Michigan State University; MBA, University of Michigan
Background: Adams Street Partners; Bank of America; Continental Bank
Kevin Dunwoodie, Partner
Education: University of Notre Dame; MBA, Harvard Business School
Background: Associate, Morgan Stanley; Private Equity Analyst, Pacific Corporate Group
Matt Garfunkle, Partner
Education: BA, History & Economics, Brown University
Background: Cambridge Associates
Jeff Miller, Partner
Education: BA, Economics & Mathematics, Gustavus Adolphus College; MBA, Northwestern University
Background: Vice President, Lehman Brothers; Associate, Wells Fargo
Kathryn Leaf, Partner
Education: BA, Modern Languages, Oxford University; MA, Modern Languages, Oxford University

Venture Capital & Private Equity Firms / Domestic Firms

Background: GIC Special Investments; Centre Partners; Morgan Stanley's Investment Banking Division
Evan Corley, Partner
Education: BS, Business Administation, Boston University
Background: Polaris Venture Partners; JPMorgan

1414 PAPPAS VENTURES
2520 Meridian Parkway
Suite 400
Durham, NC 27713

Phone: 919-998-3300 Fax: 919-998-3301
web: www.pappasventures.com

Mission Statement: Pappas Ventures invests exclusively in the life sciences sectory - biotechnology, specialty pharmaceuticals, drug delivery, diagnostics, medical devices, and related ventures - across the United States and Canada. Pappas Ventures has more than $350 million in capital under management, and has guided the launch and/or development of 56 companies.
Geographic Preference: Southeast, Mid-Atlantic Region
Fund Size: $350 million
Founded: 1994
Minimum Investment: $100,000
Investment Criteria: Seed, Early-Stage, Mezzanine
Industry Group Preference: Biopharmaceuticals, Biotechnology, Medical Devices, Drug Development, Health Related, Life Sciences, Technology
Portfolio Companies: Achillion, Aclara Biosciences, Afferent Pharmaceuticals, Anthera Pharmaceuticals, Arena, ArgoMed, Athersys, Balance Therapeutics, Barosense, Bayhill Therapeutics, Biosyntech, BrainCells, Calyx Therapeutics, CadrioDx, CeNeRx, Cequent Pharmaceuticals, Cerexa, Chimerix, Cognetix, CoLucid, Dynogen, EBM Solutions, Elitra, Emerald, Envisia, FlowCardia, Gentis, IlluminOss, LEAD, LipoScience, Liquida Technologies, Lumena, Marina, Milestone Pharmaceuticals, Mirati, Nereus, NuVasive, Optherion, Panacos, Peninsula Pharmaceuticals, Plexigen, Plexxikon, Reprogenesis, Rotation Medical, Selventa, Sensys, Signase, Spherics, Syndax, Syntonix, TargeGen, TESARO, Thrasos, TYRX, Ultragenyx, Variagenics, X-Ceptor
Key Executives:
  Ford Worthy, Partner
  919-998-3300
  Education: BA Interdisciplinary Studies, University of North Carolina; JD, University of Chicago
  Background: Corporate and securities attorney, Womble Carlyle Sandridge & Rice. Writer and associate editor, Fortune Magazine

1415 PAR CAPITAL MANAGEMENT
One International Place
Suite 2401
Boston, MA 02110

web: www.parcapital.com

Mission Statement: PAR Capital Management manages a private investment fund. The firm was founded in 1990 and is located in Boston, Massachusetts. Our philosophy is based on the belief that long term investment success can be achieved through narrowly focused and rigorous fundamental research, disciplined portfolio management, and the alignment of incentives between manager and client.

1416 PARADIGM CAPITAL LTD
155 North Wacker Drive
Suite 4400
Chicago, IL 60606

Phone: 312-474-1901 Fax: 312-277-2011

Mission Statement: Paradigm seeks to reconcile the dilemma that often occurs between investors and entrepreneurs. Entrepreneurs seek to retain the ownership, control and capital appreciation of the firm they operate. To achieve this goal entrepreneurs will need assistance in evaluating the capital raising alternatives and negotiating with institutional investors. Investors seek to control and maximize thee returns on each transaction. They have highly sophisticated financial talent and frequently must review many transactions to find investments that meet their criteria. By serving as a strategic conduit between these two parties, Paradigm Capital creates an optimal situation for both the company and potential investors.
Geographic Preference: United States
Founded: 1996
Investment Criteria: Seed Stage, Early Stage
Industry Group Preference: Business to Business, Logistics
Key Executives:
  Edward J Condon Jr, Founder
  Education: College of the Holy Cross
  Background: Vice President, Sears Roebuck & Company

1417 PARALLEL INVESTMENT PARTNERS
3889 Maple Avenue
Parkland Hall, Suite 220
Dallas, TX 75219

Phone: 214-740-3610 Fax: 214-740-3630
web: www.parallelip.com

Mission Statement: Parallel Investment Partners is an institutional private equity firm focused exclusively on investing in North American middle-market growth companies.
Geographic Preference: North America
Fund Size: $400 Million
Founded: 1992
Investment Criteria: Lower Middle-Market
Industry Group Preference: Business to Business, Consumer Products, Education, Energy, Healthcare, Specialty Consumer Products
Portfolio Companies: Marmalade Café, Mealey's Furniture, Moosejaw Mountaineering, Superior Automotive Group, Superior Automotive Group, The Fragrance Outlet, USA Discounters, Accelerated Companies, Offshore Inland Marine & Oilfield Services
Key Executives:
  F. Barron Fletcher III, Managing Director
  e-mail: bfletcher@parallelip.com
  Education: BA in Mathematics & Economics, Yale University
  Background: Merchant Banking & Mergers and Acquisitions, Wasserstein Perella & Co.
  Jared L. Johnson, Managing Director
  e-mail: jjohnson@parallelip.com
  Education: BA in American Studies, Stanford University
  Background: Vice President, Summit Partners

1418 PARTECH INTERNATIONAL
200 California Street
San Francisco, CA 94111

Phone: 415-788-2929
e-mail: media@partechpartners.com
web: partechpartners.com

Mission Statement: To provide financing for startup and emerging growth companies in the US and Europe, mostly in the field of infrastructure software, E-business, solutions and wireless communication.
Geographic Preference: United States, Europe
Fund Size: $1 billion
Founded: 1982
Average Investment: $1 million
Minimum Investment: $500,000
Investment Criteria: Early-Stage, Mid-Stage
Industry Group Preference: Communications, Software, Electronic Components, Medical & Health Related, Environment Products & Services, Industrial Equipment, Internet, E-Commerce & Manufacturing, Digital Media & Marketing, Information Technology, Energy

Venture Capital & Private Equity Firms / Domestic Firms

Portfolio Companies: Acco, Akimbi, Alephd, Alltricks.com, Attune, Atlantis Computing, Auxmoney, BugCrowd, Bolt, BrandsforFriends.com, Cartesis, Caarbon, Dailymotion, Dymant, DemanderJustice.com, Evergig, Fluxus, EverTeam, Getinsured.com, HeartThis, Goom Radio, Intalio, Leara, LED Engin, Lima, Meninvest Kantox, Moodbyme, OpenSesame, NovaSparks, Plae, PricingAssistant, PriceMatch, Prysm, Qapa.fr, Pulse.io, Riplay, Scoop.it, Rockyou, SecretSales.com, Sensopia, Sensee, Sigfox, Tapfwd, Fketchfab, Teads.tv, Touch Commerce, Total Immersion, TouchOfModern, TVTY, TVtrip, Venteala propriete.com, Voxeet, Vodkaster, WunderCar, Yieldr

Other Locations:
33 Rue du Mail
Paris 75002
France
Phone: 33-153656553

Schröderstrabe 11
Berlin 10115
Germany

442 Rue de Kaolack
Point E
Dakar
Senegal

Key Executives:
Jean-Marc Patouillaud, General Partner
Education: BA, Public Policy, Stanford University
Background: SPO Partners; Goldman, Sachs & Company
Philippe Collombel, General Partner
Education: Northwestern University; Masters, Law & Economics, University of Paris
Background: Carrefour; Andersen Consulting
Directorships: Netsize, Pertinence, Semagix/Protege
Mark Menell, Senior Partner
Education: BA, Economics, University of Pennsylvania; BS/MBA, Wharton School
Background: SVP of Business Development, Wanderful Media; Founding COO/CFO, ShopRunner; Founding Partner, Rustic Canyon; Investment Banker, Morgan Stanley
Directorships: FreedomPop; The Bouqs
Nicolase El Baze, General Partner
Education: MBA, Ecole Des Hautes Etudes Commerciales; Graduate Degree in International Management, UC Berkeley & University of Cologne, Germany
Background: Co-Founder, Softway International; ISDnet; Bigstep.Com; MultiMania
Jai Choi, Partner
Education: BS, Finance & Business Economics, Marshall School of Business, University of Southern California
Background: Principal, IGNITE Group; OnePage Software; Co-Founder, On-Air Networks; PA Consulting Group
Karen Noel, General Partner
Education: LLM, University Panthéon Assas; ESSEC Business School
Background: Partner, Gide Loyrette Nouel

1419 PARTHENON CAPITAL
399 Boylston Street
13th Floor
Boston, MA 02116

Phone: 617-961-4000
web: www.parthenoncapital.com

Mission Statement: A private equity investment firm with $1.1 billion of capital under management. The firm focuses on investing in select middle market companies with revenues of $50-$500 million.

Fund Size: $2.2 billion
Founded: 1998
Average Investment: $60 million
Minimum Investment: $20 million

Investment Criteria: Leveraged Recapitalizations, MBO, Growth Capital
Industry Group Preference: Business Products & Services, Financial Services, Food & Beverage, Consumer Products, Consumer Services, Distribution, Manufacturing, Healthcare, Logistics, Technology-Enabled Services
Portfolio Companies: Abeo, Altegra Health, Ascension Insurance, ASG Security, BlueSnap, Bracket, Bryant & Stratton College, Coastal Credit, Eliza Corporation, Enyvision, eSecLending, HD Vest, loanDepot, Merchant Warehouse, Performant Financial Corporation, Periscope Holdings, Seaside National Bank & Trust, Social Service Coordinators, Triad Isotopes

Other Locations:
Four Embarcadero Center
Suite 3610
San Francisco, CA 94111
Phone: 415-913-3900

1400 Lavaca Street
Suite 1300
Austin, TX 78701
Phone: 512-813-4900

Key Executives:
Dave Ament, Managing Partner/Co-CEO
617-960-4088
Education: BA, Harvard University
Background: Princiapl, Audax Group; Apollo Advisors; Financial Analyst, Morgan Stanley & Company
Brian P Golson, Managing Partner/Co-CEO
415-913-3960
e-mail: bgolson@parthenoncapital.com
Education: BS with Honors and Distinction, University of North Carolina; MBA with High Distinction, Harvard Business School
Background: CFO/VP Operations, Everdream; Prometheus Partners; GE Capital Strategic Planning and Acquisition
Directorships: Rackable Systems; Arrow Financial Services
William C. Kessinger, Chief Investment Officer
415-913-3990
Education: BS, MS, Industrial Engineering, Stanford University; MBA, Harvard Business School
Background: Partner, GTCR Golder Rauner; Golder, Thoma, Cressey, Rauner; Parthenon Group; AnswerThink Consulting Group; National Equipment Services; Global Imaging Systems; Cambridge Protection Industries; Transaction Network Services; Associate, Prudential Asset Management Asia
Bill Winterer, Partner, Capital Markets
617-960-4060
e-mail: williamw@parthenoncapital.com
Education: BA, Williams College; MBA, New York University; CPA
Background: Director, FleetBoston Debt Capital Markets; Audit/M&A, KPMG; SPP Capital
Andrew C. Dodson, Managing Partner
e-mail: andrewd@parthenoncapital.com
Education: BA, Duke University; MBA, Harvard Business School
Background: Consultant, Bain & Company; Financial Analyst, Enron Corp.; Trilogy
Zachary Sadek, Partner
617-960-4083
e-mail: zachs@parthenoncapital.com
Education: BA, History, MS, Social Sciences, University of Chicago
Background: Investment Banking, Dresdner Kleinwort Wasserstein
Directorships: Restaurant Technologies, Tier Technologies
Kurt A. Brumme, Partner
617-960-4059
Education: BA, Economics/Mathematics, Williams

Venture Capital & Private Equity Firms / Domestic Firms

College; MBA, Harvard Business School
Background: Finance/Corporate Development Manager, Grupo Qualicorp; General Atlantic; Morgan Stanley
Directorships: RedCard Systems; Trinity Partners; Zelis Health
Anthony J. Orazio, Partner
617-960-4066
Education: BA, Economics, Swarthmore College
Background: Oak Hill Capital Partners; Blackstone
G. Thomas Hough, Principal
617-960-4043
Education: BS/MS, Wake Forest University
Background: Analyst, BlackArch Partners

1420 PARTISAN MANAGEMENT GROUP
293 Pearl St.
Boulder, CO 80302

Phone: 303-589-0019
web: www.partisanmgmt.com

Mission Statement: Partisan Management Group identifies unmet medical needs and invests in medical device and drug delivery companies that will meet those needs.

Investment Criteria: Early Stage
Industry Group Preference: Medical Devices, Drug Delivery
Portfolio Companies: Ash Access, Enable Injections, Neuronetics, Ponce de Leon Pharmaceuticals, Preceptis Medical, Surefire Medical

Other Locations:
6 Ocean Club Dr.
Amelia Island, FL 32034
Phone: 904-491-8619

Key Executives:
Karen Cassidy, Principal
e-mail: kjcassidy@partisanmgmt.com
Norman Weldon, Principal
e-mail: nrweldon@partisanmgmt.com

1421 PARTNERS HEALTHCARE RESEARCH VENTURES
101 Huntington Avenue
4th Floor
Boston, MA 02199

Phone: 617-954-9500
web: innovation.partners.org

Mission Statement: Partners HealthCare Research Ventures & Licensing is advancing commercialization of new medical technologies from Partners' academic medical centers. Bringing together specialists in medical technology licensing, research contracts, ventures and business development, we partner with investigators, scientists and clinicians to translate new medical technology into healthcare practice. Representing Brigham and Women's Hospital, Massachusetts General Hospital, and McLean Hospital, Partners HealthCare is the largest academic biomedical research enterprise in the US. We are committed to a creative, solutions-oriented approach to licensing, ventures and research that delivers opportunities to improve patient care around the world.

Geographic Preference: United States
Investment Criteria: Early-Stage
Industry Group Preference: Healthcare, Life Sciences, Diagnostics, Medical Devices, Pharmaceuticals
Portfolio Companies: Alopexx Pharmaceuticals, Annovation Biopharma, BIND Biosciences, BioBehavioral Diagnostics, CoStim, Daktari Diagnostics, Editas Medicine, Exosome Diagnostics, Fate Therapeutics, Life Image, MoMelan Technologies, NinePoint Medical, NKT Therapeutics, Provasculon, QPID, RaNA, Spero Therapeutics, Resolvyx, Sebacia, Selecta Biosciences, Synovex, T2 Biosystems, TargAnox, VisionScope Technologies, ZELTIQ

Key Executives:
Chris Coburn, Chief Innovation Officer
Background: Executive Director, Cleveland Clinic Innovations; Vice President/General Manager, Battell Memorial Institute
Directorships: Automatic Technologies, Explorys, U.S. Enrichment Corporation
Trung Q. Do, Vice President, Business Development
Education: BS, University of California, Irvine; MA, MBA, Boston University
Background: Director of Operations, PharMetrics; Consultant, Arthur Andersen; Boston Biomedical Consultants
Roger Kitterman, Vice President, Venture
e-mail: rkitterman@partners.org
Education: AB, Harvard College; MBA, Finance, Columbia Business School
Background: Founder, Mass Medical Angels; General Partner, Mi3 Venture Partners; Managing Director, Lee Munder Venture Partners

1422 PARTNERSHIP FUND FOR NEW YORK CITY
One Battery Park Plaza
5th Floor
New York, NY 10004

web: partnershipfundnyc.org

Mission Statement: A private fund with a civic mission in the vision of Henry R Kravis, to mobilize the city's financial and business leaders to help build a stronger and more diversified local economy, identifying and supporting New York City's most promising entrepreneurs in both the for-profit and nonprofit sectors.

Fund Size: $95 million
Founded: 1996
Average Investment: $1.5 million
Minimum Investment: $500,000
Investment Criteria: All Stages, Job Creation, Revitalization
Industry Group Preference: Healthcare, Retailing, Tourism, Information Technology, Media, Entertainment, Communications, Clean Technology
Portfolio Companies: Bien Cuit, Bionic Sight, Centripetal, Cureatr, Digital Reasoning, Dual Therapeutics, Freelancers Union, Grameen America, Hot Bread Kitchen, Independence Care System, Intra-Cellular Therapies, Karos Pharmaceuticals, Kasisto, Kings County Distillery, Marketing Technology Solutions, NY Accelarator Corp., New York Genome Center, OwnEnergy, PIN Pharma, Red Rabbit, Repairogen, Scratch Music Group, Trey Whitfield School, trueEx, True Office, Vivaldi Biosciences, Voxy

Key Executives:
Maria Gotsch, President & CEO
Education: BA, Wellesley College; MBA, Harvard Business School
Background: Managing Director, BT Wolfensohn; LaSalle Partners; Merrill Lynch Capital Markets, NY and London

1423 PATHBREAKER VENTURES
San Francisco, CA

web: www.pathbreakervc.com

Mission Statement: Pathbreaker Ventures seeks to invest in tech companies with a specialization and a common goal to solve problems.

Founded: 2016
Investment Criteria: Early Stage
Industry Group Preference: Artificial Intelligence, Machine Learning, Deep Learning, Language Processing, Virtual Reality, Robotics
Portfolio Companies: Addressable, Apprente, Beyond View, Biobot Analytics, Catalog Technologies, Cinchapi, CryptoMove, Diligent Robotics, Difter Entertainment, Edify, Esper, Fathom Computing, Iron Ox, Limbix Health, Ono

Venture Capital & Private Equity Firms / Domestic Firms

Food Co., OptimoRoute, Orderful, Reliable Robotics, Rheo, Safely You, Simbe Robotics, Spiketrap, Superhuman, Text IQ, Vergesense, Visby

Key Executives:
Ryan Gembala, Managing Partner
Education: BBA, University of Georgia; MBA, Booth School of Business
Background: Co-Founder/Executive Director, H.E.R.O. for Children; Lead Associate, Hyde Park Angels; VP of Business Development, Telly; Early Stage Investor, Azure Capital Partners; Deal Lead, Corporate Development, Facebook

1424 PATRIOT CAPITAL
509 S Exeter Street
Suite 210
Baltimore, MD 21202

Phone: 443-573-3010 Fax: 443-573-3020
web: www.patriot-capital.com

Mission Statement: A leading source of growth capital for middle-market companies seeking to finance business expansion, acquisitions, management buyouts or balance sheet recapitalizations.

Fund Size: $270 million
Average Investment: $3 - $15 million
Investment Criteria: Business Expansion, Acquisition Financing, Major Capital Expenditures, Recapitalizations, Management Buyouts
Portfolio Companies: Vita Nonwovens, Metaltec Steel Abrasive, MetroGistics, Carthage Specialty Paperboard, Horizon Mud Comapny, AAA Slaes & Engineering, PCN Network, Red River Waste, The Sandbox Group, Food Distributor, McCubbin Hosiery, Orbital Tool Technologies, ErgoGenesis, Custom Control Concepts, Inspection Oilfield Services, Auburn Armature, CSP Business Media, ALON and XL Associates, GroupAero, Vantage Media, Mimeo.com, Chandler Industries, R&D Circuits, PPI-Time Zero, Cutex, Cyalume Technologies, STx Healthcare Services, The Motley Fool, Southeast Directional Drilling, Terracare Associates, CommutAir, International Development, R&H Supply, Instrument Sales and Service, AWS Convergence Technologies, eServices, Home Health Holdings, Fairfield Collectibles, PRI Group, Controlled Contamination Services, Expert Janitorial Services, D&S Residential Services, Dedicate Transport

Other Locations:
225 West Washington
Suite 2200
Chicago, IL 60606
Phone: 847-867-1299 Fax: 847-574-1285

Key Executives:
Thomas O Holland Jr, Managing Partner
e-mail: tholland@patriot-capital.com
Education: BA, University of Florida
Background: Founder, Allegiance Capital; Banc of America Corporation
Charles P McCusker, Managing Partner
e-mail: cmccusker@patriot-capital.com
Education: BS, Engineering, Virgina Tech; MBA, University of Chicago
Background: General Partner, ServiceMaster Venture Fund
Directorships: Dedicated Transport, Terminal Transportation, ExpertJMS, PRI Group
Daniel Yardley, Managing Director
e-mail: dyardley@patriot-capital.com
Education: Mount St. Mary's College; MBA, Johns Hopkins University
Background: Associate, Allegiance Capital; Analyst, M&A Group, Allegis Group
Charles A Bryan, Senior Principal & Adviser
e-mail: cbryan@patriot-capital.com
Education: BS, University of North Carolina; Harvard Business School; CPA
Background: Co-Founder & President, Bengur Bryan & Co.; VP, Alex. Brown & Sons
Directorships: PJPA LLC
Tom Kurtz, Managing Director - Midwest
e-mail: tkurtz@patriot-capital.com
Education: BS, Accounting, Western Michigan University
Background: Textron Financials Business Credit Division; GE Capital, Citicorp, Bank oF America, Chase/JP Morgan
Patrick Hamner, Managing Director - Southwest
e-mail: phamner@patriot-capital.com
Education: Southern Methodist University; BS, MBA, University of Texas
Background: Capital Southwest Corporation; Founding Chair, Heelys Inc.
Directorships: NASBIC
David Christopher, Managing Director - Southeast
e-mail: dchristopher@patriot-capital.com
Education: BBA, University of Michigan; MBA, University of Chicago
Background: Co-Founder/Partner, Peachtree Equity Partners; VP, Wachovia Bank; CIVC Partners; Kidder, Peabody & Co.; JP Morgan

1425 PEACHTREE EQUITY PARTNERS
1230 Peachtree Street NE
Suite 1900
Atlanta, GA 30309

Phone: 404-870-8900 Fax: 404-870-8191
e-mail: info@peachtreeequity.com
web: www.peachtreeequity.com

Mission Statement: Provides junior capital for small businesses.

Geographic Preference: United States
Fund Size: $60 million
Founded: 2002
Average Investment: $3 - $10 million
Minimum Investment: $3 million
Investment Criteria: Subordinate Debt with Cash Interest & Warrants
Industry Group Preference: Manufacturing, Healthcare, Business Products & Services, Consumer Products, Consumer Services, Government, Education, Financial Services, Media, Communications
Portfolio Companies: CV Holdings, Imagimed, Marlin Business Services Corp., Mertz Manufacturing, National P.E.T., American BioCare, Butler, Conger & Elsea, Convergent, DTI Transportation, Emtec, Expert NJS, FutureTech Holdings, Technical Innovation, Tech Rentals, The Roof

Key Executives:
David Christopher, Partner
Education: BBA, University of Michigan; MBA, University of Chicago
Background: Vice President, Wachovia Capital Associates; Continental Illinois Venture Corporation; Investment Banking Analyst, Kidder Peabody & Co.
Wendell Reilly, Partner
Education: BA, English, Emory University; MBA, Finance, Vanderbilt University
Background: Founder, Grapevine Communications; CFO, Lamar Advertising Company
Matt Sullivan, Partner
Education: University of Pennsylvania; Harvard Business School
Background: Managing Director, Wachovia Capital Associates; Corporate Finance, Kidder Peabody & Co.
John McCarty, Partner
Education: BS, Wharton School
Background: Senior Investment Officer, Roswell Capital Partners; Investment Banking, Banc of America Securities

Venture Capital & Private Equity Firms / Domestic Firms

1426 PEAR VC
158 South Park Street
San Francisco, CA 94107

web: www.pear.vc

Mission Statement: Helps entrepreneurs lay the foundations of a defensible, category-defining company.

Founded: 2013
Average Investment: $750K - $3 million
Minimum Investment: $250K - $1 million
Investment Criteria: Pre-Seed; Seed; Series-A
Portfolio Companies: Aaptiv, Affinity, Akko, Allocate, Anycart, AspireIQ, Atticus, Aurora, Axle Health, Bioage, Beyond Trucks, Boxbot, Branch, Capella Space, Cardless, Clearbrain, Cooby, Covalent, Darwin, Doordash, Doxel, EdgeDB, Elevate, EmCasa, Emburse, Expedock, Exporta, FairStreet, Fam, Fanimal, FarmRaise, Faves, Federato, Flexport, Firefly, Fitbod, Flock, Flok, Foresight Diagnostics, Freewill, Frubana, Fure Inventory, Gatsby, Going Merry, GroveXR, Gryps, Guardant, Gusto, Heap, Hoodline, Imprimed, IncludeAI, Infinite Uptime, Instaread, Intellimize, Interface Biosciences, Inventa, Ixlayer, JetInsight, June, Juni Learning, Keebo, Ladder, Learn to Win, Local Kitchens, LocateAI, Maker, Melonn, Memebox, Metawork, Millibatt, Mirra, Mulu, Muni, NeuraHealth, NeuroNav, Newton, Nightfall, Nabell, Nova, Onramp, One Concern, Osmind, Osmos, Pando Labs, Pando, Playbook, Polar, Polygon, Pragli, Prenav, Quadric, Quansa, rePurpose, Recora, Reduct.Video, Run the World, SavviAI, SensorTower, Senti Bio, Sequel, Siren, Smarty, Sniffspot, SnoutID, Solvvy, Switchmate, Sympto, TeachFX, The Custom Movement, TownHound, True & Co., Twine, Vanta, Viz.AI, Wagr, WeShare, Wedding Party, WindBorne, Xillis, Yada, Young Alfred, Zippin

Key Executives:
Mar Hershenson, Founding Managing Partner
Education: BEng, Stanford University
Pejman Nozad, Founding Managing Partner

1427 PEGASUS CAPITAL GROUP
3250 Ocean Park Blvd
Suite 203
Santa Monica, CA 90405

Phone: 310-392-9100 Fax: 310-392-9101
e-mail: info@pegasuscapgroup.com
web: www.pegasuscapgroup.com

Mission Statement: We invest in simple businesses with proven track records and clear opportunities for growth. Acquisition candidates include privately-held companies and divisions of larger corporations that are currently, or have the potential to become, leaders in their industry niche.

Geographic Preference: North America
Founded: 1997
Average Investment: $5 million
Minimum Investment: $2 million
Investment Criteria: Leveraged Buyouts, Management Buyouts, Corporate Divestitures, Recapitalizations, Growth Equity
Industry Group Preference: Low Technology, Manufacturing, Distribution, Specialty Services
Portfolio Companies: Midwest Automotive Designs, Jackrabbit, SANTIER, SPG International, American Piping Products

Key Executives:
Patrick F Whelan, Managing Partner
310-392-0100
e-mail: pwhelan@pegasuscapgroup.com
Education: Economics/Computer Science, Vanderbilt University; MBA, Wharton School
Background: Co-Managing Director Mergers/Acquisitions, Broadview International; Abacus Ventures; InterFirst Ventures; Co-Founder/Board Member, TranSwitch Corporation; Teleos Communications; Board Member, TelWatch Corporation; Quality Components
Directorships: WeatherGuard Building Products, Shield Pack, SPG, Design Space
Luke Sage, Partner
e-mail: lsage@pegasuscapgroup.com
Education: BS, Western Michigan University; MBA, Saint Louis University
Background: President, Health Capital Group

1428 PELION VENTURE PARTNERS
2755 E Cottonwood Parkway
Suite 520
Salt Lake City, UT 84121

Phone: 801-365-0262 Fax: 801-365-0233
e-mail: info@pelionvp.com
web: www.pelionvp.com

Mission Statement: We look constantly to discover innovative opportunities with visionary entrepreneurs who have a strong desire to succeed and the discipline to execute, and we help them launch their great ideas and achieve exciting new journeys in the marketplace.

Geographic Preference: Western U.S.
Fund Size: $200 million
Founded: 1986
Investment Criteria: Early stage
Industry Group Preference: Information Technology, Digital Media & Marketing, Software, Infrastructure, Communications, Medical Devices, Nanotechnology, Networking, Wireless, Internet
Portfolio Companies: 33across, Adapx, AngioScore, Bitcasa, Bloxr, CloudFlare, CloudVelocity, CONVIVA, Domo Technologies, DotNetNuke, Formation Data Systems, gazillion, Integral, Keen IO, MetaCloud, Mojiva, Moki Mobility, Primary Data, Skylight Healthcare Systems, Soasta, Stormpath, Venafi

Key Executives:
Jeff Kearl, General Partner
Education: BA, Brigham Young University
Background: Logoworks; vSpring Capital
Directorships: Scopely; Just Water
Matt Mosman, General Partner
Background: Founder, College Heights Partners; SVP, Oracle Corporation; CEO, Unifi Software
Blake Modersitzki, General Partner
Education: BS, Brigham Young University
Background: Novell, WordPerfect
Chris Cooper, General Partner
Education: University of Utah, University of Phoenix
Background: Director, Partner Engineering & Developer Services, Novell
Ben Lambert, General Partner
Education: BA, MBA, Brigham Young University
Background: Jefferies Financial Group; Sears Holding Co.
Chad Packard, General Partner
Education: BA, Brigham Young University; JD, Santa Clara University; MBA, Brigham Young University
Background: Director, Marich Confectionary

1429 PENINSULA CAPITAL PARTNERS LLC
One Detroit Center
500 Woodward Avenue
Suite 2800
Detroit, MI 48226

Phone: 313-237-5100 Fax: 313-237-5111
e-mail: campbell@peninsulafunds.com
web: www.peninsulafunds.com

Mission Statement: An investment company specializing in subordinated debt and structured equity investments in superior middle market companies.

Fund Size: $390 million
Founded: 1995
Minimum Investment: $4 million
Investment Criteria: MBO, LBO, Growth Capital

Venture Capital & Private Equity Firms / Domestic Firms

Industry Group Preference: Industrial Services, Consumer Products, Retailing, Food & Beverage, Distribution

Key Executives:

William Y Campbell, Chairman/Founder
e-mail: campbell@peninsulafunds.com
Education: BA, Albion College; MBA, Bowling Green State University
Background: Campbell & Company; First of Michigan Corporation; Standard Federal Bank; Michigan National Corporation & W.Y.

Scott A Reilly CFA, President/CIO/Founder
e-mail: reilly@peninsulafunds.com
Education: BBA, University of North Dakota; MBA, Fuqua School of Business at Duke University
Background: Churchill Capital; Northstar Capital Ltd.; Security Pacific Bank

William F McKinley, Executive VP/Founder
e-mail: mckinley@peninsulafunds.com
Education: BS, Babson College; MBA, Fuqua School of Business at Duke University
Background: WY Campbell & Company; First of Michigan Corporation

James A Illikman CFA, Partner
e-mail: illikman@peninsulafunds.com
Education: BBA/MBA, University of Michigan
Background: Talon Equity Partners LLC; Freudenberg-NOK General Partnership; United Technologies; Delphi Corporation

Karle E LaPeer PE CFA, Partner
e-mail: lapeer@peninsulafunds.com
Education: BS, Mechanical Engineering, Michigan Technological University; MBA, University of Michigan
Background: First of Michigan Corporation; Harrell & Associates; GMFanuc Robotics Corporation

Steven S Beckett, Partner
e-mail: beckett@peninsulafunds.com
Education: BA, California Polytechnic State University; MBA, Fuqua School of Business At Duke University
Background: Commercial Banking, Societe Generale; Citibank

1430 PENINSULA VENTURES
1500 Fashion Island Boulevard
Suite 102
San Mateo, CA 94404

Phone: 650-517-1900 **Fax:** 650-517-1999
e-mail: info@peninsulaventures.com
web: www.peninsulaequity.com

Mission Statement: At Peninsula Ventures, we believe in creativity, innovation, and the entrepreneurial spirit. Because the ones who matter most are the entrepreneurs whose ideas keep moving the world ahead. We're constantly searching for the next great market. We leverage our experience with past investments and the insights we gain from working with different companies to help identify these markets and the new technologies that emerge. To us, being and investor means being an active part of an ecosystem that is changing right before our eyes.

Geographic Preference: United States
Investment Criteria: Early-Stage
Industry Group Preference: Software, Infrastructure, Technology
Portfolio Companies: Axcient, Alianza, Basis, BroadHop, Flint, Lucid, Lumenetix, Marketo, Net Power & Lighting, Plastc Card, Pramata, Radius Intelligence, Response Analytics, Ribbit, Scinfiniti, SeeControl, Keyssa

Key Executives:

Greg Ennis, Partner
Education: BA, Economics & Political Science, Stanford University; MBA, Anderson School of Management
Background: Managing Director, Thompson Clive & Partners

Ryan Keating, Partner
Education: Boston University
Background: Microsoft; Salomon Smith Barney; PricewaterhouseCoopers

1431 PENN VENTURE PARTNERS
132 State Street
Suite 200
Harrisburg, PA 17101

Phone: 717-236-2300 **Fax:** 717-236-2350
web: www.pennventures.com

Mission Statement: Penn Venture Partners is focused on growth and expansion stage venture capital investment within certain underserved markets located in the Commonwealth of Pennsylvania.

Geographic Preference: Central & Northern Pennsylvania
Average Investment: $500,000 - $1.25 million
Investment Criteria: Growth-Stage, Expansion-Stage
Industry Group Preference: Agribusiness, Manufacturing, Biotechnology, Life Sciences, Computer Hardware & Software, Software, Media, Education, Business Products & Services, Energy, Environmental Technology, Marketing, Distribution, Networking, Telecommunications
Portfolio Companies: BioHitech America, Benten Bio Services, The Corporate University Xchange, Cyber-Patrol, NanoHorizons, Probity Medical Transcription, The Harrisburg Senators, Thermacore

Key Executives:

Thomas A Penn, Managing Director
Education: BS, Metallurgy & Materials Science, MIT; MBA, Stanford; JD, University of Pennsylvania
Background: Senior Partner, Meridian Capital Partners; Partner, Boston Millennia Partners; President & CEO, Tektagen

Dean M Kline, Managing Director
Education: MPhil, Cambridge University; BA, Wheaton College
Directorships: Journal Publications, Corporate University Xchange, Probity Medical Transcription, Senators Partners, Thermacore

Robert Graham, Managing Director
Education: BA, LaSalle University; MBA, Saint Joseph's University
Background: President, RG Consulting; President and CEO, Dorland Healthcare Information; EVP and CFO, Broadreach Consulting; VP and COO, Legal Communications Ltd.
Directorships: CyberPatrol Inc.

1432 PENNELL VENTURE PARTNERS LLC
332 Bleecker Street
#K-67
New York, NY 10014

Phone: 718-855-7087
e-mail: info@pennell.com
web: pennell.com

Mission Statement: An early-stage venture investor formed to meet the need for professional early-stage risk capital in New York and help bridge the gap in the investor marketplace between angel investors and institutional venture capital funds. PVP backs exceptional entrepreneurs who demonstrate the ability, creativity and drive necessary to develop leading companies.

Geographic Preference: New York
Fund Size: $5 million
Founded: 1996
Average Investment: $750,000
Investment Criteria: Early-Stage
Industry Group Preference: Software, Business to Business, Information Technology

Venture Capital & Private Equity Firms / Domestic Firms

Key Executives:
Thomas B Pennell, President
e-mail: thomas@pennell.com
Education: BA, University of Pennsylvania; MBA, New York University
Background: Chase Manhattan Bank; Endeavor Capital Management; Access Capital

1433 PENTA MEZZANINE FUND
20 N Orange Avenue
Suite 1550
Orlando, FL 32801

Phone: 407-648-5097 **Fax:** 407-650-3311
web: www.pentamezz.com

Mission Statement: Penta Mezzanine Fund is a private investment firm providing customized growth capital solutions to profitable, lower-middle-market companies nationwide. We look to invest our funds in established companies operated by experienced and proven management teams with a history of building enterprise value. Penta Mezzanine Fund was created by former industry executives and experienced investors who place a high value on their relationships with management teams.

Geographic Preference: United States
Average Investment: $2 - $25 million
Investment Criteria: Lower Middle Market, Growth Capital
Industry Group Preference: All Sectors Considered
Portfolio Companies: Twinlab Consolidated Holdings, Alexander Tank, Level Four Orthotics and Prosthetics, Green Distribution, Organic Holdings, Aviaion Inflatables, Method Holdings, Margaritaville, Orion Technologies, The Pub, KBP Foods, Great HealthWorks, Association Financial Services

Key Executives:
John Morgan, Founding Partner/Senior Advisor
e-mail: jmorgan@pentamezz.com
Education: BA, JD, University of Florida
Background: Principal, Florida Mezzanine Fund; WonderWorks Attractions; Morgan & Morgan
Rebecca Irish, Managing Partner
e-mail: rirish@pentamezz.com
Education: BS, Accounting, Mississippi College; CPA
Background: Co-Founder, RVR Consulting Group; CFO, Arcadia Resources; CFO, Rotech Medical Corporation
Jeff Black, Managing Partner
e-mail: jblack@pentamezz.com
Education: Goizueta Business School
Background: Managing Director, Cantaro Capital; Financial Network Investment Corporation; CEO, MidCap
Grant Hill, Senior Advisor
e-mail: ghill@pentamezz.com
Education: BA, History, Duke University
Background: Founder, Hill Ventures
Seth Ellis, Senior Advisor
e-mail: sellis@pentamezz.com
Education: BS, Accounting, University of Florida; CPA
Background: Principal/Co-Founder, Florida Mezzanine Fund; CEO, Digital Imaging; Co-Founder, Florida Regional Emergency Services

1434 PERFORMANCE EQUITY MANAGEMENT, LLC
5 Greenwhich Office Park
3rd Floor
Greenwich, CT 06831

Phone: 203-742-2400
e-mail: info@peqm.com
web: www.peqm.com

Mission Statement: Performance Equity Management is a leading global private equity firm with approximately $9 billion in AUM, as of December 2018. The firm's mission is to provide high quality private equity investment access, both partnership and direct, to institutional clients worldwide.

Geographic Preference: United States, Europe, Asia

Fund Size: $9 billion
Founded: 2005
Investment Criteria: Buyouts, Venture Capital, Asset/Portfolio Restructuring, Distressed For Control, Distressed Trading, Equity-Oriented, Mezzanine Debt
Industry Group Preference: All markets considered

Key Executives:
John Clark, President
Education: BA & MBA, Brigham Young University
Background: MetLife; KPMG Peat Marwick
Jeffrey Barman, Chief Investment Officer
Education: BA, Stanford University; MBA, Columbia University
Background: Portfolio Manager, General Motors Investment Management (GMIMCo) Private Equity Group; Operations Manager, Oracle Corporation
Marcia Haydel, Managing Director
Education: BA, Louisiana State University; MBA, Tulane Freeman School of Business
Background: VP of Fixed Income, Alliance Capital Management; Director of Investments, MetLife Investments Ltd.
Frank Brenninkmeyer, Managing Director
Education: BBA, University of Notre Dame; MBA, Anderson School of Management
Background: VP, GE Asset Management
Jeffrey Reals, Managing Director
Education: BA, Colgate University
Background: Portfolio Manager, General Motors Investment Management (GMIMCo) Private Equity Group; Advent International; Liberty Mutual Insurance
Lawrence Rusoff, Managing Director
Education: BA, Cornell University; MBA, Kellogg School of Management, Northwestern University
Background: Portfolio Manager, General Motors Investment Management (GMIMCo) Private Equity Group; Salomon Brothers, Inc.; Chairman, Private Equity Subcommittee, Cornell University Endowment
James Tybur, Managing Director
Education: Systems Engineering degree, University of Virginia; MBA, Harvard Business School
Background: Principal, Trinity Ventures; VERITAS Software; Boston Consulting Group

1435 PERMAL CAPITAL MANAGEMENT
The Prudential Tower
800 Boylston Street
Suite 1325
Boston, MA 02199-7610

Phone: 617-587-5300 **Fax:** 617-587-5301
web: www.permalcapital.com

Mission Statement: Established to formalize the US private equity activities of Permal Group to enhance risk/return investment profile versus other public and private equity alternatives.

Fund Size: $900 million
Founded: 1994
Minimum Investment: $500,000
Investment Criteria: Second-Stage, Mezzanine, LBO, MBO
Industry Group Preference: Communications, Computer Related, Consumer Products, Distribution, Electronic Components, Genetic Engineering, Industrial Equipment, Medical & Health Related

Other Locations:
900 Third Avenue
28th Floor
New York, NY 10022
Phone: 212-418-6500 **Fax:** 212-418-6510

Key Executives:
Redington Barrett III, Senior Managing Partner, Investment Committee
e-mail: rbarrett@permal.com
Education: Princeton University; MBA, Amos Tuck

School of Business, Dartmouth
Background: Managing Director, Gemini Investors; Analyst, Fidelity Management & Research; Keefe, Bruyette & Woods
Robert Di Geronimo, Managing Director, Investment Committee
e-mail: rdg@permal.com
Education: BS Accounting, University of Delaware
Background: Senior Associate, Price Waterhouse
Benjamin Marino, Managing Director/CFO/CCO
e-mail: bmarino@permal.com
Education: BS Accounting, University of Massachusetts; MBA, Northeastern University; CPA
Background: Assistant Controller, Summit Partners; Accounting Manager, Real Estate Company; Senior Associate, Price Waterhouse
Michael D'Agostino, Managing Partner, Investment Committee
Education: BA, Economics, Colby College; MBA, Case Western Reserve University
Background: COO, Andesite LLC; President, Hartland & Co.
Aaron Bright, Principal
Education: BS, Accounting, Washington University; MBA, MSF, Boston College, Carroll School of Management
Background: Kendall Investments; Senior Associate, Cambridge Associates

1436 PEROT JAIN
8235 Douglas Avenue
Suite 200
Dallas, TX 75225

web: www.perotjain.com

Mission Statement: Perot Jain's mission is to provide timely capital and resources and high quality strategic advice to assist companies in achieving their maximum potential.

Geographic Preference: US-Based
Founded: 2014
Average Investment: Up to $500,000
Investment Criteria: Technology critical to Scalability; Leadership; Early Stage/Seed Focused; B2B/Business Services/Mobility/Healthcare

Key Executives:
Ross Perot, Jr., Co-Founder
Education: Vanderbilt University
Background: Captain, United States Air Force
Anurag Jain, Co-Founder/Managing Partner
Education: MBA, University of Michigan
Background: Founder, Brigade Corporationl VP, Dell; Director, WorldHaus

Other Locations:
1325 Avenue of the Americas
25th Floor
New York, NY 10019
Phone: 212-651-6400 **Fax:** 212-651-6399

4350 East-West Highway
Suite 202
Bethesda 20814
Germany
Phone: 301-6523200 **Fax:** 301-6523800

1438 PFINGSTEN PARTNERS LLC
300 N LaSalle Street
Suite 5400
Chicago, IL 60654

Phone: 312-222-8707 **Fax:** 312-222-8708
e-mail: pfingstenpartners@pfingsten.com
web: www.pfingstenpartners.com

Mission Statement: Provides equity capital to acquire and grow Midwest and Mid-Atlantic based middle market companies in partnership with management. Pfingsten Partners was formed on the concept of blending senior operating management and financial transaction expertise in its investment activities. Pfingsten Partners operates under four guiding principals: creation of shareholder value; responsible ownership; integrity; and professional conduct.

Geographic Preference: United States, China, India
Fund Size: $525 million
Founded: 1989
Average Investment: $15-$100 millionn
Minimum Investment: $15 million
Investment Criteria: Acquisition of growth companies, consolidations, leveraged buyouts, management buyouts, and recapitalizations
Industry Group Preference: Manufacturing, Distribution, Business Products & Services
Portfolio Companies: 4Wheel Drive Hardware, Allied Reliability Group, AllPoints, American Academic Suppliers, Ap+m, Arrowhead Electrical Products, Bailey International, Barjan, Burton Saw & Supply, Closet Works, Crane 1, CURT Manufacturing, Des-Case Corporation, Diamond Assets LLC, Dynapower, Environmental Lights, FireKing Security Group, Full Spectrum, Garretson Resolution Group, Hallcrest, Hy-Bon Engineering Company, Industrial Lighting Products, Kith Kitchen, Lumenier, Marlen International, MPE, Norcraft Companies, Oliver Printing & Packaging Co., Park Foods, Pfingsten Publishing, Premiere Global Sports, Powervar, Quality Valve, RapidAir, Rx Label Technology, Sign-Zone, South-Tek Systems, Suzo-Happ, SpeeCo, Superior Recreational Products, Technibus, TPC Wire & Cable, Tropitone, Unified Power, WoodallBs, ZSi-Foster

Other Locations:
5th Floor, Block A
Lucky Commercial Building
Second Road, Zhendi District
Changan Town, Dongguan, Guangdong 523850
China
Phone: 86-76981663655

335, Udyog Vihar, Phase IV
Near Delhi International Airport
Gurgoan
Haryana 122012
India
Phone: 91-1244308204

Key Executives:
Thomas S. Bagley, Founder/Senior Managing Director
e-mail: tbagley@pfingsten.com
Education: BA, North Park College; DePaul University
Background: Citicorp North America; Continental Bank
James J. Norton, Senior Managing Director
e-mail: jnorton@pfingsten.com
Education: University of Illinois
Background: Director, Cooper Lybrand
John H. Underwood, Senior Managing Director
e-mail: junderwood@pfingsten.com
Education: BBA, MBA, University of Wisconsin
Background: Heller Equity; VP, Citicorp North America
Denio R. Bolzan, Managing Director
e-mail: dbolzan@pfingsten.com
Education: BS, DePaul University
Background: Operations VP, Ryerson Tull; Washington Steele; Lukens; Coopers & Lybrand
Scott A. Finegan, Managing Director
e-mail: sfinegan@pfingsten.com
Education: BS, Marquette University; MBA, Northwestern University
Background: VP, American National Bank and Trust Company; Analysis, Horizon Partners Ltd
John J. Starcevich, Managing Director
e-mail: jstarcevich@pfingsten.com
Education: BS, DePaul University
Background: Lukens; Jupiter Mechanical Construction; Jupiter Industries; Lybrands
Phil D. Bronsteatter, Managing Director
Education: BBA, Finance, Economics & Mathematics,

Venture Capital & Private Equity Firms / Domestic Firms

Marquette University
Background: Analyst, Investment Banking Group, Lazard Middle Market; Analyst, Investment Banking Group, Cleary Gull; Associate, American Appraisal Associates

1439 PFIZER VENTURE INVESTMENTS
235 East 42nd Street
New York, NY 10017

Phone: 212-733-2323
web: www.pfizer.com/partners/venture-investments

Mission Statement: Pfizer Venture Investments, the venture capital arm of Pfizer, Inc., invests for return in areas of current or future strategic interest to Pfizer. PVI seeks to remain at the forefront of life science advances, looking to identify and invest in emerging companies that are developing compounds and technologies that have the potential to enhance Pfizer's pipeline and shape the future of our industry.

Geographic Preference: United States
Fund Size: $50 million
Founded: 2004
Investment Criteria: All Stages
Industry Group Preference: Healthcare, Life Sciences, Therapeutics, Diagnostics, Drug Delivery, Pharmaceutical Services, Healthcare Information Technology
Portfolio Companies: Ablexis, Aquinox, Autifony, Biodesy, Celladon, Clovis Oncology, Cydan, DVS Sciences, Epic Sciences, Flexion Therapeutics, HD Biosciences, M2S, Merus, Mersana Therapeutics, MIRNA Therapeutics, MISSION Therapeutics, Neuronetics, Nodality, NovoCure, Rhythm Pharmaceuticals, TetraLogic

Key Executives:
  Barbara J Dalton PhD, Vice President/Senior Management Partner
  Education: Penn State University; PhD, Microbiology & Immunology, The Medical College of Pennsylvania
  Background: Research Scientist, Immunology, SmithKline & Frenh Laboratories; SR One; General Partner, EuclidSR Partners
  Bill Burkoth, Executive Director/Senior Partner
  Education: BS, Chemistry, Whitman College
  Background: Business Development, Galileo Pharmaceuticals; Analyst, Bay City Capital

1440 PGIM PRIVATE CAPITAL
180 North Stetson Avenue
Suite 5600
Chicago, IL 60601

web: www.pgim.com/private-capital

Mission Statement: PGIM Private Capital structures creative financial solutions that meet a variety of client needs. Formerly known as Prudential Capital Group.

Fund Size: $60 billion
Average Investment: $10 - $75 million
Investment Criteria: Recapitalizations, Growth Capital, Buyouts, Acquistions
Industry Group Preference: All markets considered

Key Executives:
  Allen A Weaver, Senior Managing Director
  312-540-4212
  e-mail: allen.weaver@pgim.com
  Education: BS, Stanford University; MBA, Wharton School

1441 PHILQUO VENTURES
PO Box 721
Palo Alto, CA 94302-0721

e-mail: info@philquo.com
web: www.philquo.com

Mission Statement: Founded, funded and managed by a team of seasoned executives from Wall Street, Silicon Valley and Hollywood, we strive to bring financing, mentoring and managerial guidance to bright minds with relevant and timely new products or services.

Investment Criteria: Early-Stage
Industry Group Preference: Consumer Products, Consumer Services
Portfolio Companies: Anchange Productions, Cliptone, Crimson Hexagon, Fab, Fido Labs, Loudr, Mobile Commons, My Damn Channel, Parallel Geometry, Pixelux Entertainment, Ribbit, The Plunge, Wello

Key Executives:
  Philip Engelhardt, Managing Partner
  Background: Senior Advisor/Angel Investor, Plug and Play Tech Center

1442 PHYSIC VENTURES
200 California Street
5th Floor
San Francisco, CA 94111

Phone: 415-354-4901 Fax: 415-354-4915
e-mail: info@physicventures.com
web: physicventures.com

Mission Statement: Physic Ventures provides capital and support to entrepreneurs focused on building exceptional science-based, consumer-directed health and sustainable living companies.

Geographic Preference: United States, Canada
Investment Criteria: Seed-Stage to Growth-Equity Stage
Industry Group Preference: Enabling Technology, Consumer Products, Sustainable Living
Portfolio Companies: Alliance Health, Chromatin, Elixir, EnergyHub, Gazelle, GoodGuide, HalSource, HealthLoop, Impinj, Merrimack, Novomer, Pharmaca, Rayne, Recyclebank, Revolutions Foods, Surface Logix, T2 Biosystems, Textronics, WaterSmart, Yummly

Key Executives:
  Dion Madsen, Co-Founder/Managing Director
  Education: BComm, Finance, University of Saskatchewan
  Background: Managing Director, Unilever Technology Ventures; Partner, RBC Capital Partners
  Directorships: Elixer Pharmaceuticals, HaloSource, On-Q-Ity, Pharmaca, SurfaceLogix
  William Rosenzweig, Co-Founder/Managing Director
  Background: Founding CEO, Republic of Tea; Faculty, Haas School of Business
  Andy Donner, Director
  Education: Duke University; MBA, Haas School of Business, UC Berkeley
  Background: Senior Associate, Great Spirit Ventures; Technology M&A Group, Wasserstein Perella
  Andrew Williamson PhD, Director
  Education: BA, PhD, Physics, University of Cambridge; MBA, Haas School of Business, UC Berkeley
  Background: National Renewable Energy Laboratory, Department of Energy
  Directorships: Chromatin, EnergyHub, Gazelle, Halosource, Impinj, Novomer
  Stacy Feld, Director
  Education: BA, Sociology, University of Pennsylvania; JD, Vanderbilt Law School
  Background: Associate Director, Business Development, Genentech; Director, Licensing & Corporate Development, Third Wave Technologies
  Directorships: T2 Biosystems

1443 PHYTO PARTNERS
2080 NW Boca Raton Blvd.
Suite 6
Boca Raton, FL 33431

Phone: 561-542-6090
e-mail: larry@phytopartners.com
web: www.phytopartners.com

Venture Capital & Private Equity Firms / Domestic Firms

Mission Statement: Invests in companies within the cannabis industry focused on business solutions and services, including grow technology, packaging, data analytics, testing, research & development, distribution logistics, and consulting services.

Geographic Preference: US
Investment Criteria: Early-Stage; Companies not directly exposed to supply/demand/pricing; 6-9 months monitoring of management/operations; Visible exit strategy
Industry Group Preference: Cannabis, Technology, Data Analytics, Infrastructure
Portfolio Companies: New Frontier Data, Steep Hill, Leaf, Grownetics, Gatekeeper Innovation Inc., Baker Technologies, Flow Hub, Leaf Link, W☐rk, Front Range Biosciences, Marijuana Doctor, Vangst, Sail, Green Flower, Lucid Green

Key Executives:
Larry Schnurmacher, Managing Partner
Education: BBA, George Washington University
Background: Financial Advisor, Shearson Lehman Brothers; Financial Advisor, Oppenheimer & Co.; Financial Advisor, Morgan Stanley Wealth Management; Founder/CEO, Phyto Advisors
Directorships: New Frontier Data
Brett Finkelstein, Managing Director
Education: BBA, University of Hartford
Background: Managing Director, Skywest Partners

1444 PI CAPITAL GROUP LLC
6507 Wilkins Avenue
Pittsburgh, PA 15217

e-mail: info@picapitalgroup.com
web: www.picapitalgroup.com

Mission Statement: Pi capitalizes those early-stage ventures who create unique technology in the areas of Internet, software, information technologies, telecommunications, life sciences, advanced materials, and semiconductor.

Geographic Preference: Western Pennsylvania, Eastern United States
Founded: 2001
Investment Criteria: Early-Stage
Industry Group Preference: Technology, Internet, Software, Information Technology, Telecommunications, Life Sciences, Advanced Materials, Semiconductors
Portfolio Companies: Ondotek, CompAS Controls, Aethon, medSage Technologies, mSpoke, NewCare Solutions, CastGrabber

Key Executives:
John R Hammer, Chairman
Background: Chief Investment Officer & CFO, Innovations Works; President & Director of Corporate Finance, Capital Access Partners; VP, Weatherly Private Capital; VP, MMC Group; Gulf Oil Corporation

1445 PIDC PHILADELPHIA
1500 Market Street
Suite 2600
Philadelphia, PA 19102

Phone: 215-496-8020 Fax: 215-977-9618
web: www.pidc-pa.org

Mission Statement: PIDC plans and implements economic development initiatives which enhance the competitive environment, generate jobs and produce higher tax ratables throughout the city of Philadelphia.

Geographic Preference: Philadelphia, PA
Founded: 1957
Average Investment: $200,000
Industry Group Preference: Aerospace, Defense and Government, Biotechnology, Communications, Computer Related, Electronic Components, Natural Resources, Environment Products & Services, High Technology, Medical & Health Related, Energy

Key Executives:
Anne Bovaird Nevins, President
Education: MBA, Wharton School; University of Pennsylvania
Background: Director, Development, Historic Philadelphia; White House Office of Cabinet Affairs
Thomas Queenan, Chief Operating Officer/ Senior Vice President
Education: Syracuse University; Columbia University; MBA, Wharton School
Background: City Treasurer, Rendell Administration; Temple University Health System; Dickenson College

1446 PIEDMONT ANGEL NETWORK
243 S Marshall Street
Winston-Salem, NC 27101

e-mail: dgrein@piedmontangelnetwork.com
web: www.piedmontangelnetwork.com

Mission Statement: An angel investment group managed by its own members and operates on a fund resource for investments. The group focuses on investment opportunities with companies in the early stage of development and has a high potential for rapid growth.

Geographic Preference: North Carolina, South Carolina, Virginia
Investment Criteria: Early-Stage
Industry Group Preference: Life Sciences, Software, Technology
Portfolio Companies: Guerilla RF, Entigral Systems, Virtual Event Bags, ClearEdge 3D, Phthisis Diagnostics, Southeast TechInventures, Raw Essentials, Protochips, Pique Therapeutics, Bioptigen, Arbovax, Sensory Analytics, Sandbox Learning, Piedmont Pharmaceuticals, Optivia Medical, SpermCheck, Batanga, AvidXchange, Aldagen

Key Executives:
Andy Dreyfuss, Fund Executive
e-mail: adreyfuss@piedmontangelnetwork.com

1447 PINE BROOK ROAD PARTNERS
60 East 42nd Street
50th Floor
New York, NY 10165

Phone: 212-847-4333 Fax: 212-847-4334
e-mail: info@pinebrookpartners.com
web: www.pinebrookpartners.com

Mission Statement: To make business building and growth capital investments.

Founded: 2006
Industry Group Preference: Energy, Financial Services
Portfolio Companies: Brigham Resources, Comet Ridge Resources, Common Resources III, Elevation Resource Holdings, Forge Energy, GR Energy Services Holdings, High Ground Energy, Saguaro Resources, Serafina Energy, Source Energy Partners, Stonegate Production Company, Stonegate Production Company II, Wagon Wheel Exploration, AloStar Bank of Commerce, Amedeo Capital Limited, Aurigen Capital Limited, Community Trust Financial Corp., Essent Group, Global Atlantic Financial Group, Green Bancorp, NBIC Holdings, Strategic Funding Source, Third Point Reinsurance, United PanAm Financial Corporation

Key Executives:
Howard H Newman, Managing Partner
Education: Cambridge University; PhD, Business Economics, Harvard University
Background: Vice Chairman, Warburg Pincus; Morgan Stanley
Richard Aube, Managing Partner
Education: BA, Dartmouth College
Background: DE Shaw & Company; Partner, JP Morgan Partners; Beacon Group
Joseph M Gantz, Executive Advisor
Education: BA, History, University of Pennsylvania;

Venture Capital & Private Equity Firms / Domestic Firms

MBA, Columbia University Business School
Background: Chairman & CEO, Empire Brushes; Fitz & Floyd; Seymour Housewares Corp.; Founding Partner, Walnut Investment Partners

1448 PINEBRIDGE INVESTMENTS
Park Avenue Tower
65 East 55th Street
New York, NY 10022

Phone: 646-857-8000
web: www.pinebridge.com

Mission Statement: Seeks to provide mezzanine and private equity capital to middle market and emerging growth companies based in North America and Western Europe. Funding is provided to facilitate leveraged buyouts, recapitalizations, consolidations, acquisition growth, and growth capital requirements. The firm manages $96.9 billion in global assets as of September 2019.

Geographic Preference: North America, Western Europe
Fund Size: $83 billion
Founded: 1960s
Average Investment: $50 million
Minimum Investment: $10 million
Investment Criteria: Second Stage, Mezzanine, Consolidations, Acquisition, LBO, MBO, Recapitalization, Privatizations
Industry Group Preference: All markets considered

Key Executives:
Gregory A. Ehret, Chief Executive Officer & Executive Director
Education: BA, Economics, Bates College; MBA, Boston University
Background: President, State Street Global Advisors (SSGA)
Tracie E. Ahern, Chief Financial Officer & Chief Risk Officer
Education: BS, Accounting, Manhattan College; MBA, Finance & International Business, NYU Stern School of Business
Background: CFO, Soros Fund Management; VP of Capital Markets Accounting, Freddie Mac; Lord Abbett & Co.; Beutsche Bank; Goldman Sachs

1449 PINNACLE VENTURES
160 El Camino Real
Suite 250
Palo Alto, CA 94025

Phone: 650-926-7800
web: www.pinnacleven.com

Mission Statement: A private venture capital fund focused on providing debt and equity financing to early-stage companies across information technology, cleantech and healthcare. Pinnacle differentiates itself through the strength and diversity of its team, its creative and flexible financing alternatives and its unique approach to helping its portfolio companies achieve success.

Investment Criteria: Early-Stage
Industry Group Preference: Information Technology, Clean Technology, Healthcare
Portfolio Companies: 1Life Healthcare, AcelRx Pharmaceuticals, Access Closure, APT Pharmaceuticals, Aquantia Corporation, Avnera Corporation, Baxano, BlueKat, Broadbus Technologies, Calistoga Pharmaceuticals, Cameron Health, Chegg, Cobalt Technologies, Confluent Surgical, Conformative Systems, eBureau, Farecast, Flixster, Gilt Groupe, Glu Mobile, Intersect ENT, Jasper Wireless, JBoss, Kaai, Kazeon Systems, Kerberos Proximal Solutions, Kontiki, Lanzatech NZ, LifeSize Communications, LipoSonix, Lotame Solutions, Lutonix, M-Factor, Mascoma Corporation, Miasole, Movius, MySpace, Newport Media, Ocular Therapeutix, Pandora Media, Pluck Corporation, Quidsi, Quorum Systems, Qumranet, Reliant Technologies, RGB Networks, Right Media, SentreHEART, Siliquent Technologies, Silver Peak Systems, SiPort, Solyndra, Spiracur, StumbleUpon, SVNetwork, The Fanfare Group, Topanga Technologies, Trapeze Networks, TriVascular, Troux Technologies, Visiogen, Vocalocity, WiChorus, Zazzle.com, Ze-Gen, ZeaChem, Zecter, ZING Systems, ZipCar

Key Executives:
Kenneth R Pelowski, Founder & Managing Partner
650-926-7802
e-mail: kpelowski@pinnacleventures.com
Education: BSE, Electrical Engiering, MBA, University of Michigan
Background: Redpoint Ventures; Founder & Board Member, Currenex; COO, CFO & Board Member, GetThere; EVP & CFO, Preview Travel; Corporate Vice President, General Instruments; Sun Microsystems; Intel
Robert H Savoie, Partner, Chief Operating Officer
650-926-7805
e-mail: rsavoie@pinnacleventures.com
Education: BBA, University of Michigan; CPA
Background: VP, Finance, Comdisco Ventures; CFO, H&Q Fund Management; Access Technology Partners; Arthur Anderson
Arun Ramamoorthy, Principal
650-926-7811
e-mail: aramamoorthy@pinnacleventures.com
Education: BTech, Indian Institute of Technology; MS, Electrical Engieering, University of Michigan; MBA, Haas School of Business, University of California, Berkeley
Background: Corporate Branding & Strategic Marketing, Intel

1450 PIONEER CAPITAL
Five Tower Bridge
300 Barr Harbor Drive
Suite 280
West Conshohocken, PA 19428

Phone: 610-862-2100 Fax: 610-862-2120
web: www.pioneercapital.com

Founded: 2000
Portfolio Companies: Seattle Shellfish, MIM-Hayen, Evol Foods, WineCare Storage, Relay

Key Executives:
J Peter Pierce, Founder & Chief Executive Officer
Education: University of Pennsylvania
Background: President & CEO, Pierce Leahy
J Peter Pierce Jr, Partner
Education: Tulane University
Background: Cross Atlantic Capital Partners

1451 PITTSBURGH EQUITY PARTNERS
6507 Wilkins Avenue
Pittsburgh, PA 15217

Phone: 412-265-1325
e-mail: info@pghpep.com
web: www.pghpep.com

Mission Statement: Pittsburgh Equity Partners is a venture capital fund specifically formed to grow Western Pennsylvania's most promising early-stage companies in the life sciences and information technology industries.

Geographic Preference: Western Pennsylvania
Investment Criteria: Early-Stage
Industry Group Preference: Life Sciences, Information Technology
Portfolio Companies: Encentiv Energy, Intelligent Mobile Support, Industry Weapon, ShowClix, StatEasy, Voci Technologies, Wombat, Wright Therapy Products

Key Executives:
Edward R Engler, Managing Partner
e-mail: ed@pghpep.com
Education: BS, Applied Mathematics & Computer

Venture Capital & Private Equity Firms / Domestic Firms

Science, Carnegie Mellon University
Background: Transarc Corporation; Founder, Summa Technologies
Directorships: JumpStart Wireless, mSpoke, Brainstage, Summa Technologies

Stephen G Robinson, Managing Partner
e-mail: steve@pghpep.com
Education: Political Science, University of Pittsburgh
Background: Managing General Partner, Robinson Properties; Director, Gateway Travel Management
Directorships: mSpoke, BitArmor, Webmedx, Automated Cell, Precision Therapeutics

1452 PITTSBURGH LIFE SCIENCES GREENHOUSE
2403 Sidney Street
Suite 285
Pittsburgh, PA 15203

Phone: 412-201-7370 Fax: 412-770-1276
e-mail: info@plsg.com
web: www.plsg.com

Mission Statement: The Pittsburgh Life Sciences Greenhouse provides capital investments and customized company formation and business growth services to our region's life sciences enterprises.

Geographic Preference: Western Pennsylvania
Founded: 2002
Investment Criteria: Seed-Stage, Early-Stage
Industry Group Preference: Life Sciences, Biotechnology, Diagnostics, Healthcare Information Technology, Medical Devices, Therapeutics
Portfolio Companies: Applied Isotope Technologies, Celsense, Crystalplex, Falcon Genomics, Immunetrics, MS2 Array, SpectraGenetics, Advanced Technology Healthcare Solutions, Cernostics, Intelomed, NanoHealth, ReddPath Integrated Pathology, Almadtrac, Blenderhouse, Caliber Infosolutions, Chronic Health Metrics, Health Monitoring Systems, Iagnosis, MedRespond, MedSage Technologies, Mymedcoupons.com, NewCare Solutions, PHRQL, Well Bridge Health, ALung Technologies, BioSafe, Carmell Therapeutics, ChemDAQ, Circadiance, ClearCount, Cohera Medical, Flexicath, Medrobotics, Quantum Ops, ReGear Life Sciences, Renal Solutions, Rinovum, Rubitection Separation Design Group, Spinal MetRX, Starr Life Sciences, Vytrace, Wright Therapy Products, ATRP Solutions, Cognition Therapeutics, Complexa, Knopp Biosciences, Launchcyte, Lipella Pharmaceuticals, Washburn Therapeutics

Key Executives:
John W Manzetti, President & CEO
e-mail: jwmanzetti@plsg.com
Education: BSBA, Geneva College; MBA, University of Akron
Background: President & CEO, NOMOS Corporation; EVP & CFO, Carnegie Group
James Jordon, Vice President, Chief Investment Officer
e-mail: jjordon@plsg.com
Education: BS, Business Administration, Merrimack College; MBA, Boston University
Background: SVP, McKesson Corporation; VP, Marketing, Johnson & Johnson

1453 PIVA
4 Embarcadero Center
Suite 3950
San Francisco, CA 94111

Phone: 650-420-7800 Fax: 650-209-8266
web: www.piva.vc

Mission Statement: Piva is an independent vC firm that makes big bets and has the perserverance to turn big ideas into reality.

Investment Criteria: Future Industries (AI, Automation); Future Materials/Production (Specialty Chemicals, Alternative Materials; Future Energy (Decarbonization, Electrification, Digitilization)

Key Executives:
Ricardo Angel, CEO/Managing Partner
Education: BS, MS, PhD, University of Illinois; MBA, Northwestern University
Background: SVP, GE Energy Financial; Managing Director, GE Ventures
Adzmel Adznan, Partner/Operating Manager
Education: MBA, Harvard University
Background: Chief of Staff, Petronas
Bennett Cohen, Partner
Education: BA, Columbia University; Oxford University
Background: Venture Principal, Shell; Investor, Aurora

1454 PIVOTNORTH CAPITAL
Palo Alto, CA

web: twitter.com/pivotnorth

Mission Statement: An early-stage capital fund for extraordinary founders.

Fund Size: $35 million
Founded: 2011
Investment Criteria: Seed-Stage, Series A
Industry Group Preference: Consumer Services, Business Products & Services

Key Executives:
Tim Connors, Founder/General Partner
Background: Sequoia Capital, US Venture Partners

1455 PLATINUM EQUITY
360 N Crescent Drive
Beverly Hills, CA 90210

Phone: 310-712-1850
web: www.platinumequity.com

Mission Statement: Platinum Equity specializes in mergers, acquisitions and operations of companies that provide mission-critical products, services and solutions in diverse industries.

Other Locations:
3 Allied Drive
Suite 109
Dedham, MA 02026
Phone: 781-461-8888

1 Greenwich Office Park
N Building, 2nd Floor
Greenwich, CT 06831
Phone: 203-930-2010

52 Vanderbilt Avenue
21st Floor
New York, NY 10017
Phone: 212-905-0010

5 Hanover Square
1st Floor
London W1S 1HQ
United Kingdom
Phone: 44 20-3535-0899

12 Marina View #21-05
Tower 2, Asia Square
Singapore 018961
Singapore
Phone: 65 6709-4090

Key Executives:
Tom Gores, Founder and CEO
Education: BSc, Michigan State University
Mary Ann Sigler, Partner and CFO
Education: BA, California State University; MA, University of Southern California
Background: Senior Partner, Ernst & Young LLP

Venture Capital & Private Equity Firms / Domestic Firms

1456 PLEXUS VENTURES
1701 Waterford Way
Maple Glen, PA 19002

Phone: 215-542-2727 Fax: 215-542-2288
e-mail: bob_moran@plexusventures.com
web: www.plexusventures.com

Mission Statement: Consulting services to the Life Sciences industry. Our vision is to provide a global network of professional consultants to augment the internal capabilities of Life Science companies. Our team consists of pharmaceutical industry trained and experienced entrepreneurs.

Founded: 1990
Investment Criteria: Seed, Startup, First-Stage
Industry Group Preference: Industrial Equipment, Biotechnology, Genetic Engineering, Medical
Portfolio Companies: ACADIA Pharmaceuticals, Inc., Advanced Scientifics, Albany Molecular Research, Angelini Group, Ansaris, Antares Pharma, ArBlast, AstraZeneca, Auden McKenzie, BioControl Limited, Bentley Pharmaceuticals, BRAIncoBiopharma, Britannia Pharmaceuticals Limited, Can-Fite BioPharma, Thermo Fisher Scientific, Celon Pharma, Cephalon, Consilient Health, Cubist Pharmaceuticals, Derma Sciences, Destiny Pharma, Diasome, Eisai, Elan, Elona Bio Technologies, Elusys Therapeutics, EUSA Pharma, Ferring Pharmaceuticals, GlaxoSmithKline, Jelfa SA, HRA Pharma, Kirin Pharmaceutical, Kun Wha Pharmaceutical, Kyowa Hakko Kirin, Labormed, Locus, Lorus Therapeutics, Mabion, MDM, Meda Pharmaceuticals, Mocuis, Nanjing Kingfriend Biochemical Pharmaceutical Co., Nektar Therapeutics, Neuronyx, Nosan, Noscira, NovaDel Pharma, Noscira, NovaDel Pharma, Novartis, NPS Pharmaceuticals, Opocrin, Orbona, Par Pharmaceutical, Permatec, West Pharmaceuticals, Pierre Fabre, Primus Pharmaceuticals, Polfa Kutno SA, Reckitt Benckiser, Recordati S.p.A., Salix Pharmaceuticals, Seikagaku, Sigma-Tau Pharmaceutical, Taisho Pharmaceutical Co., Teva, Becton, Dickinson and Company, Traslational Cancer Drugs Pharma, US Pharmcia, Xoma

Other Locations:
1223 Wilshire Boulevard
Suite 941
Santa Monica, CA 90403
Phone: 310-584-7480 Fax: 310-388-5572

Hancocks Mount
Sunningdale
Berkshire SL5 9PQ
United Kingdom
Phone: 44-1344873077 Fax: 44-1344624903

Via Stephenson 94
Milan 20157
Italy
Phone: 39-02-390-30807 Fax: 39-02-390-30820

Kompanii Kordian 38
Warsaw 02-495
Poland
Phone: 48-228391199 x 104 Fax: 48-228825194

Voltastrasse 35
Zurich CH-8044
Switzerland
Phone: 41-432680155 Fax: 41-432680155

Ahornweg 16
Oberursel D61440
Germany
Phone: 49-6172-32110 Fax: 49-3172-32129

Alameda Venezuela 69
Jandira SP 06648-040
Brazil
Phone: 55-1146180504 Fax: 55-1146175419

7F Toranomon 40MT Building
5-13-1, Toranomon
Minato-ku
Tokyo 105-0001
Japan
Phone: 81-05058068475 Fax: 81-367451759

Key Executives:
Robert P Moran, President
215-542-2727
e-mail: bob_moran@plexusventures.com
Education: BBA, Villanova University; CPA
Background: Corporate Development Consultant, Hybridon; Business Development, SmithKline Beecham; Deloitte, Haskins & Sells
Michael P O'Sullivan, Managing Partner
44-1344-873-077
e-mail: michael_osullivan@plexusventures.com
Background: CFO, Ethical Holdings; VP Finance, SmithKline Beecham
Pino N Modica, Managing Partner
310-315-7106
e-mail: pino_modica@plexusventures.com
Background: International Marketing Manager, Recordati SA; A Menarini Srl; Product Manager, American Cyanamid Corporation/Lederle; Lawyer; Financial Consultant, Sanpaolo Bank of Italy
Richard A Brown, Partner & Head, Tokyo Office
81-3-6279-3570
e-mail: richard_brown@plexusventures.com
Background: Business Development, Eli Lilly & Company
John F Chappell, Founder, Special Advisor
e-mail: john_chappell@plexusventures.com
Education: BA, Harvard University
Background: SmithKlineBeecham
Directorships: Salix Pharmaceuticals

1457 PLUG AND PLAY VENTURES
Silicon Valley, CA

web: www.plugandplaytechcenter.com/ventures

Mission Statement: Plug and Play Ventures funds the teams that build defensible businesses of the future. Each investment is a case-by-case basis.
Fund Size: $30 Million
Average Investment: $114, 000

1458 PLUM ALLEY
New York, NY

Phone: 347-348-7901
e-mail: info@plumalley.co
web: plumalley.co

Mission Statement: Plum Alley invests in advanced technology and healthcare that will improve our lives and the planet.

Fund Size: $25 million
Average Investment: $500,000-$1.5 million
Investment Criteria: Early Stage; Advanced Tech and Medical Breakthroughs; Women Founders or Women and Men Founders in STEM; Massive Impact at Scale Business Models

Key Executives:
Deborah Jackson, Founder and CEO
Education: MBA, University of Columbia
Background: Founder, Women Innovate Mobile
Andrea Turner Moffitt, Co-Founder and General Partner
Education: BA, Tulane University; MBA, University of Columbia
Background: Founder, Wealthrive Inc.; Author
Avantika Daing, Managing Director and Partner
Background: Senior Director, Global Marketing, Bristol-Myers Squibb; Senior Global Director, Marketing, Eyetech Pharmaceuticals; Co-Founder/CEO, SquareKey.com; Chief Revenue Officer, Jopwell

1459 PLYMOUTH MANAGEMENT COMPANY
555 Briarwood Circle
Suite 210
Ann Arbor, MI 48108

Phone: 743-747-9401
e-mail: info@plymouthvc.com
web: www.plymouthvc.com

Mission Statement: To realize superior returns through the long term appreciation of investments. Funds managed by PMC invest in small growth companies. We generally invest in revenue producing companies with the potential for growth through a defined, catalytic event or milestone whose achievement will be financed, at least in part, by PMC managed funds.

Geographic Preference: Michigan, Great Lakes Region
Founded: 2003
Average Investment: $500,000 - $2 million
Portfolio Companies: Certified Security Solutions, CloudOne, InContext Solutions, 365 Retail Markets, XanEdu, IDV Solutions, Lynx Network Group, UICO, FutureNet Group, Weathershield, Solulink, Neuromonics, Janeeva, Eagle River Homes

Key Executives:
Ian Bund, Chairman/Senior Advisor
e-mail: ibund@plymouthvc.com
Education: Bachelor of Economics, University of Sydney; MBA, Harvard University
Mark Horne, Operating Partner
e-mail: mhorne@plymouthvc.com
Education: BA, Business Administration, Cedarville University; MBA, Wharton School
Jeff Barry, Partner
e-mail: jbarry@plymouthvc.com
Education: BA, Economics, Trinity College; MBA, Finance, Vanderbilt University
Background: Senior Economist, Overseas Private Investment Corporation; Consultant, Oakland University Incubator

1460 PNC ERIEVIEW CAPITAL
1900 East 9th Street
17th Floor
Cleveland, OH 44114

Phone: 216-222-3763
web: www.pnc.com/erieview/english/home.html

Mission Statement: PNC Erieview Capital, formerly National City Equity Partners, is a Cleveland, Ohio-based investment firm that is currently managing approximately 50 investments. PNC Erieview Capital has actively invested junior capital in over 160 middle market transactions alongside successful private equity sponsors.

Geographic Preference: North America
Fund Size: $1 billion
Founded: 1979
Average Investment: $5 - 20 million
Minimum Investment: $1 million
Investment Criteria: Leverage Buyouts, Recapitalizations, Growth Capital, Aquisition Capital, Shareholder Liquidity
Industry Group Preference: Distribution, Food & Beverage, Healthcare, Manufacturing, Services
Portfolio Companies: Abrisa Industrial Glass, Accessories Marketing, Altech Inspections, Arrow Tru-Line, Associated Materials, ATI, Atrium Companies, Autosplice, Burton Flower & Garden, Connor Bros, CorePharma Holdings, Cumming Acquisition, DSI Holding Company, Eatem Foods, Energy Manufacturing, Excelsior Medical, Experient, Fasteners for Retail, FCX Performance, Franklin Energy Services, Gila, Group Dekko, Harden Manufacturing, Hardware Resources, Healthcare Management Systems, HealthTech Holdings, HGI Holdings, Hilite Industries, Hoffmaster Group, Home Decor Holdings, Hopkins Manufacturing, Hospitality Mints, Hygenic, Infiltrator Systems, Innerpac, Juice Tyme Acquisition Corp, LDiscovery, Liberty Safe & Security Products, Manhattan Beachwear, MicroGroup, Moss Holding Company, NeuroTherm, Nielsen & Bainbridge, Olon Industries, Paradigm Packaging, Radiac Abrasives, Royal Adhesives, Royal Baths Manufacturing, Savage Sports, SmartSource Holdings, Spartan Foods of America, Standadyne Corporation, Stanton Carpet Corp, The ServiceMaster Company, The Tranzonic Co, Titan Fitness, Transpac Imports, Transtar Industries, Tronair Holdings, Truck Bodies & Equipment International, Truck-Lite, US Foodservice, U-Line Corporation, UMA Enterprises, Vendormate, Veritext Holding Company, Vitex Packaging Group, Wellborn Forest Products, Whitcraft Group

Key Executives:
Edward S. Pentecost, Managing Director/President
e-mail: ed.pentecost@pncerieview.com
Education: BA, Economics & Management, Albion College; MBA, Case Western University
Background: Investment Banking, McDonald Investments; National City Corporation
Carl E. Baldassarre, Senior Advisor
e-mail: carl.baldassarre@pncerieview.com
Education: BS, Finance, John Carroll University
Background: National City Corporation
David A. Sands, Director
e-mail: david.sands@pncerieview.com
Education: BSBA, Ohio State University
Background: Brown Gibbons Lang & Company
Eric C. Morgan, Managing Director
e-mail: eric.morgan@pncerieview.com
Education: BS, Finance, Boston College; London School of Economics
Background: Investment Banking, Saloman Smith Barney
Steve G. Pattison, Managing Director
e-mail: steve.pattison@pncerieview.com
Education: BS, Business Administration, Miami University; MBA, University of Chicago
Background: Investment Banking, McDonald Investments; Ernst & Young
Jason R. Cornacchione, Principal
e-mail: jason.cornacchione@pncerieview.com
Education: BSBA, Miami University; MBA, Case Western Reserve University
Background: Public Accounting, PricewaterhouseCoopers

1461 PNC RIVERARCH CAPITAL
Two PNC Plaza
620 Liberty Avenue
22nd Floor
Pittsburgh, PA 15222

web: www.pncriverarch.com

Mission Statement: A private equity firm with over $500 million of capital under management. We make investments to provide growth capital or to assist in ownership transitions such as leveraged buyouts or recapitalizations.

Geographic Preference: Eastern two-thirds of the United States
Fund Size: $500 million
Founded: 1982
Average Investment: $10-$30 million
Minimum Investment: $10 million
Investment Criteria: Growth Equity, Buyouts
Industry Group Preference: Telecommunications, Business Products & Services, Manufacturing, Distribution
Portfolio Companies: Custom Molded Products, Environmental Express, Goldco, LawLogix, Precision Aviation Group, The Cleaning Authority, Women's Marketing

Venture Capital & Private Equity Firms / Domestic Firms

1462 POINT B CAPITAL
300 East Pine Street
Seattle, WA 98122

Phone: 206-577-7221
e-mail: info@pointbcap.com
web: www.pointbcap.com

Mission Statement: In addition to decades of diverse investment experience, we provide proven strategic, operational and leadership skills that come from being part of Point B. Companies that we invest in know they have a partner that understands their industry and shares the practical business know-how to get things done. Only Point B Capital provides the connections that come with being part of the Point B brand and having Point B as our parent company. Our network of client and industry relationships includes hundreds of companies and strategic partners that value Point B's business perspective and track record of creating mutually beneficial relationships among our portfolio companies and Point B clients.

Portfolio Companies: appAttach, Calico Energy Services, Carrum Health, Cartavi, ClearEdge Partners, Earshot, Inovus Solar, Post.Bid.Ship., QwikCart, RoundPegg, Sales Portal, Telnyx

Other Locations:
1637 Wazee Street
Suite 200
Denver, CO 80202

Key Executives:
Mike Pongon, Chief Executive Officer
Education: Harvard University; University of Chicago; BA, University of Washington
Background: Business Analyst; Project Leader; Program Manager
EJ Blanchfield, Chief Operating Officer
Education: BA, University of Washington

1463 POINT JUDITH CAPITAL
211 Congress Street
Suite 210
Boston, MA 01220

Phone: 617-600-6260
e-mail: info@pointjudithcapital.com
web: pjc.vc

Mission Statement: At Point Judith Capital, we seek to unite innovative founders with serial entrepreneurs to build world class companies.

Founded: 2001
Industry Group Preference: Internet, Mobile Technology, Healthcare Information Technology, Clean Technology
Portfolio Companies: Coachup, Sittercity, Retroficiency, Tesora, Anover.net, SnapGear, TicketManager.com, Evergage, Envista, Ve24, Medical Metrix Solutions, Rndex, Nexamp, Curoverse, Kitsy Lane, Multiply, MyEnergy, GetWellNetwork, Nest, 3Tier, Powerhouse Dynamics, Pixability, AetherPal, Taqua, Antenna, Nabsys, MedOptions, FSA Store, Ozon.ru, Optasite, Expensify, Novare, Fidelis, Kalpan Hydro, Tower Ventures, Spirus Medical

David Martirano, Co-Founder, General Partner
e-mail: david@pointjudithcapital.com
Education: BS, University of Rhode Island; MBA, Columbia Business School
Background: Co-Founder, Rex Capital; Investment Banking, Cowen & Company
Directorships: Antenna Software, Envista, FanIQ, Fidelis Security Systems, GetWellNetwork, MedOptions, NABsys, Optasite, Taqua
Zaid Ashai, Venture Partner
e-mail: zaid@pointjudithcapital.com
Education: AB, International Relations & Economics, Brown University; MBA, Harvard Business School; MPA, JFK School of Government, Harvard University
Background: Good Energies; Associate, HarbourVest Partners; Investment Banking, Credit Suisse
Directorships: Nexamp, Power Assure
Rob May, General Partner
e-mail: dmixer@pointjudithcapital.com
Education: BA, Union College; MBA, Harvard Business School
Background: Founding Partner, Columbia Capital; Founder, Rex Capital; President, Providence Cellular

1464 POLARIS VENTURE PARTNERS
One Marina Park Drive
Boston, MA 02210

Phone: 781-290-0770
e-mail: partnership@polarispartners.com
web: www.polarispartners.com

Mission Statement: To indentify and invest in seed, first round, and early stage technology and life sciences businesses with exceptional promise and help them grow into sustainable, market-leading companies.

Geographic Preference: United States, Europe
Fund Size: $4.3 billion
Founded: 1996
Investment Criteria: Seed-Stage, First Round, Early-Stage
Industry Group Preference: Technology, Life Sciences, Information Technology, Digital Media & Marketing, Consumer Services, Business Products & Services, Healthcare
Portfolio Companies: 1366 Technologies, 480 Biomedical, Acceleron Pharma, Adimab, Advion, Aepona, Aerodesigns, Alimera Sciences, Antenna Software, Aria, Arsanis, Arsenal Medical, Art.com, Athletes' Performance, Atyr Pharma, Automattic, Balconytv, Barkbox, Best Doctors, Bind Therapeutics, Blackarrow, Botanical Labs, Bridgepoint Medical, Calorics, Cardiac Dimensions, Cardlytics, Cerulean Pharma, Confluence Technologies, Data Sciences, deCODE Genetics, Digicert, Doctrakr, Earth Networks, Egnyte, Ella Health, Erewards, Fancy Hands, Fate Therapeutics, Focus Financial, Follica, Formspring.Me, Genocea Biosciences, Hydra Biosciences, Ice.Com, Impinj, Imprivata, Infinian Corp, Infinite Power Solutions, InMobi, Inseal Medical, Iora, Ironwood Pharmaceuticals, Jibe, Jibjab, Kala Pharmaceuticals, Kissmetrics, Legalzoom, Liaison International, Life Line Screening, Living Proof, Localytics, Logentries, LogMeIn, Medvantx, Message Bus, Microchips, Mixel, Nanosys, Nea, Neuronetics, Noetix, Ocular Therapeutix, Partssource, Phreesia, Phytel, Postrocket, Promedior, Pulmatrix, Qualaroo, Quantcast, Readyforzero, Receptos, Recurly, Remedy Health, Respicardia, Roundbox, Selecta Biosciences, Seventh Sense Biosystems, Shoedazzle.Com, Sionyx, Six Waves, Snappcloud, Sosh, Space Monkey, Spindle Labs, Sun Catalytix, Sustainx, T2 Biosystems, Taris Biomedical, Teeology, Trevena, Trulia, Turntable.Fm, Vets First Choice, Visterra, Wantful, Wikicell, Xactly, Xpressdocs, Xtuit Pharmaceuticals

Other Locations:
150 W 28th Street
Suite 904
New York, NY 10001

One Letterman Drive
Building C, Floor 3
The Presidio of San Francisco
San Francisco, CA 94129
Phone: 855-787-3500

Key Executives:
Dave Barrett, Partner
e-mail: dbarrett@polarisventures.com
Education: BS, University of Rhode Island
Background: COO, Calico Commerce; SVP, Worldwide Operations, Pure Atria
Directorships: Confluence, Egnyte, FREEjit, Imprivata, LogMeIn, MarkMonitor, Phytel, VKernel
Brian Chee, Managing Partner
e-mail: bchee@polarisventures.com

Venture Capital & Private Equity Firms / Domestic Firms

Education: BS, United States Military Academy, West Point; MBA, Amos Tuck School of Business, Dartmouth College
Background: Captain, US Army Corps of Engineers; Baxter Healthcare
Directorships: Apnex Medical, Ascend Health, Botanical Laboratories, BridgePoint Medical, Cardiac Concepts, Data Sciences International, MedVantx
Jon Flint, Founding Partner
e-mail: jflint@polarisventures.com
Education: BA, Hobart College; JD, University of Virginia Law School
Background: Partner, Burr Engan Deleage & Co; Associate, Testa Hurwitz & Thiebault; Watergate Special Prosecution Force
Directorships: Athlete's Performance, JibJab Media, Living Proof
Alan Crane, Entrepreneur Partner
e-mail: acrane@polarisventures.com
Education: BA, MA, MBA, Harvard University
Background: Co-Founder & CEO, Cerulean Pharma; Co-Founder, Visterra; President & CEO, Momenta Pharmaceuticals; Senior Vice President, Corporate Development, Millennium Pharmaceuticals
Directorships: Momenta Pharmaceuticals, T2 Biosystems, Hydra Biosciences, Seventh Sense Biosystems, Vaccinex, Cerulean Pharma, Visterra
Terry McGuire, Founding Partner
e-mail: tmcguire@polarisventures.com
Education: BS, Physics & Economics, Hobart College; MS, Engineering, Thayer School, Dartmouth College; MBA, Harvard Business School
Background: Burr Egan Deleage & Co.; Golder Thoma & Cressey
Directorships: Acceleron Pharma, Adimab, Arsenal Medical, Ironwood Pharmaceuticals, Life Line Screening, MicroCHIPS, Pulmatrix, Trevena
Amir Nashat, Executive Partner
e-mail: anashat@polarisventures.com
Education: BS, Mechanical Engineering, MS, Materials Science, University of Califnornia, Berkeley; PhD, MIT
Directorships: aTyr Pharmaceuticals, Avila Therapeutics, BIND Biosciences, Fate Therapeutics, Living Proof, Pervasis Therapeutics, Promedior Pharmaceuticals

1465 POLESTAR CAPITAL
180 N Michigan Avenue
Suite 1905
Chicago, IL 60601

Phone: 312-984-9090 **Fax:** 312-984-9877
e-mail: dkcollins@polestarvc.com
web: www.polestarvc.com

Mission Statement: To bring technologies/innovations developed in the finance and capital markets to Tenant Improvement financing, focusing on commercial lease transactions.

Founded: 1970
Minimum Investment: $250,000
Investment Criteria: Startup, Early-Stage, First-Stage, Second-Stage
Industry Group Preference: Communications, Computer Related, Consumer Services, Education, Electronic Components, Instrumentation, Information Technology
Portfolio Companies: Adamation, BridgeStream, Bayview Systems, Kids123.com, Kinetic Computer Corporation, NetNoir, Network Commerce, Unisource Network Services, ViaNovus

Key Executives:
Derrick K Collins, General Partner
Education: BS, Texas A&M University; MBA, University of Chicago
Background: President of Shorebank Capital Corporation; South Shore Bank ; Ameritech Illinois
Directorships: Currently on Board of Directors of ViaNovus, Bridgestream, Adamation, National Association of Investment Companies
John W Doerer, General Partner
Education: BBA, University of Michigan, MBA, Indiana University
Background: Vice President of Amaco Venture Capital
Directorships: Curently serves on the Board of Directors off Vianovus, Adamation and Kids123.com
Wally Lennox, General Partner
Education: BS, Citadel; MBA, Ohio State University
Background: President, Amoco Venture Capital

1466 POMONA CAPITAL
780 Third Avenue
New York, NY 10017-7076

Phone: 212-593-3639
web: www.pomonacapital.com

Mission Statement: A global private equity investment firm focused on the purchase of primary, secondary interests in top performing venture capital and buyout funds.

Geographic Preference: United States, Europe, Israel
Fund Size: $6.7 billion
Founded: 1994
Minimum Investment: $10 million
Investment Criteria: Seed, Startup, First-Stage, Second-Stage, Mezzanine, LBO, MBO, Secondaries, Co-Investments
Industry Group Preference: Communications, Computer Related, Consumer Services, Equipment, Information Services, Media, Medical & Health Related, Industrial Services

Other Locations:
80 Brook Street
London W1K 5EG
United Kingdom
Phone: 44-2072686350

10 Chater Road
Suite 1506-7, 15th Floor
Prince's Building
Central
Hong Kong
Phone: 852-36283629

Key Executives:
Michael D. Granoff, CEO
Education: JD, Georgetown University; BA, University of Pennsylvania
Background: Golodetz Ventures, TEI Industries
Frances N. Janis, Senior Partner
Education: MBA, Northeastern University; BS, State University of New York
Background: General Partner, Hambro International Equity Partners
Lorraine Hliboki, Partner
Education: BS, Fairfield University; MBA, NYU Stern School of Business
Background: Senior Managing Director, GE Equity, General Electrical Company; Senior Financial Analyst, Financial Guaranty Insurance Company
Jim Rorer, Partner
Education: BA, Duke University; MBA, Harvard Business School
Background: U.S. Trust; Bain & Co.; Credit Suisse

1467 PORTLAND SEED FUND
805 SW Broadway
Suite 2440
Portland, OR 97205

Phone: 503-419-3007
e-mail: info@portlandseedfund.com
web: www.portlandseedfund.com

Venture Capital & Private Equity Firms / Domestic Firms

Mission Statement: We find and surround the most promising seed-stage companies with capital, mentoring and contacts to nurture vigorous economic growth in Oregon.
Geographic Preference: Oregon
Average Investment: $25, 000
Industry Group Preference: Diversified
Portfolio Companies: 4Tell, Appthwack, AuthO, Brandlive, Bright.md, Cloudability, Droplr, Energy Storage Systmes, Glider, GraphAlchemist, Hone Comb, Measureful, Minettabrook, MUUT, NurseGrid, Opal, PrestoBox, SERPs.com, Simple Emotion, Smart Mocha, Snapflow, Tellagence, Vadio, Cel.ly, Geoloqi, Globe Sherpa, Mobilitus, Alum.ni, Beeminder, Comic Rocket, Show Kicker, Surefield, Vizify, Better Bean, Homeschool, Indow Windows

Key Executives:
Jim Huston, Founder/Managing Director
503-780-1952
e-mail: jim@portlandseedfund.com
Education: MBA, Kellogg School of Management
Background: Managing Director, Blueprint Ventures; Intel Capital

Angela Jackson, Managing Director
e-mail: angela@portlandseedfund.com
Education: BA, English & History, Boston University; MA, Environmental Studies, University of Oregon
Background: AB Jackson Group, Portland State University Business Accelerator; Principal, Emergent

1468 POSEIDON ASSET MANAGEMENT
330 Fell Street
San Francisco, CA

Phone: 617-571-7114
web: poseidonassetmanagement.com

Mission Statement: Invests in seed, early-stage companies within the cannabis industry.
Founded: 2013
Industry Group Preference: Cannabis
Portfolio Companies: Ascend Wellness, Baker Technologies, Flow Kana

Key Executives:
Emily Paxhia, Managing Partner
e-mail: epaxhia@poseidonassetmanagement.com
Education: BA, Psychology, Skidmore College; MA, Psychology, New York University
Background: Market Research Analyst, Houghton Mifflin; Sr. Research Consultant, Sachs Insights; Research Consultant, Miner & Co. Studio
Directorships: Marijuana Policy Project, Athletes for CARE

Morgan Pahxia, Managing Partner
Education: BS, Applied Mathematics, University of Rhode Island
Background: Financial Advisor Associate, UBS Wealth Management; Investment Counselor, Providence Based Investment Advisor; Principal/Managing Director, Paxhia Investment Management
Directorships: Baker Technologies, Wurk, Surna Inc.

Michael Boniello, Managing Director
Education: BA, Marketing, Miami University
Background: Bond Analyst/Assist Portfolio Manager, Hunterview; Associate, Thomas Weisel Partners; Assistant VP, Barclays Wealth & Investment Management; Analyst, Merrill Lynch

Andy Roche, Investment Analyst
Education: BS, Accounting, SUNY Geneseo
Background: Associate, Deloitte

1469 POST CAPITAL PARTNERS
805 Third Avenue
8th Floor
New York, NY 10022

Phone: 212-888-5700 **Fax:** 206-222-2518
e-mail: mpfeffer@postcp.com
web: www.postcp.com

Mission Statement: A private investment firm that invests in small and lower middle-market businesses with solid fundamentals and a history of stable cash flow and/or attractive growth prospects.
Geographic Preference: North America
Investment Criteria: Leveraged Buyouts, Recapitalizations, Corporate Divestitures, Consolidations, Acquisitions, Growth Capital
Industry Group Preference: Business Products & Services, Financial Services, Consumer Products, Healthcare Services, Media, Publishing, Manufacturing, Transportation, Logistics
Portfolio Companies: EC Waste, Invo Healthcare, TBA Global, BHS Specialty Chemicals, DTT Surveillance, Amigo Insurance Holding Corporation, Agent Media Corporation, American Disposal Services, Abra, United Road Services, StatementOne

Key Executives:
Mitchell Davidson, Managing Director
Education: BA, Tufts University; JD, New York University School of Law
Background: Financial Sponsors Group, Merrill Lynch; M&A, Skadden Arps Slate Meagher & Florn LLP

Michael S Pfeffer, Managing Director
Education: BSEE, Tufts University; MBA, Finance, Columbia University
Background: Managing Director & Partner, Charterhouse Group International; Senior Vice President, GE Capital

Christopher PH Cheang, Director, Head of Business Development
Education: BA, Middlebury College; MBA, Stern School of Business, New York University
Background: Cabot China Limited; Adams Harkness

1470 POUSCHINE COOK CAPITAL MANAGEMENT LLC
375 Park Avenue
Suite 3408
New York, NY 10152

Phone: 212-784-0620 **Fax:** 212-784-0621
web: www.pouschinecook.com

Mission Statement: A private equity firm whose mission is to transition companies to significantly higher growth and profitability, and to generate superior returns for investors and management-team partners.
Geographic Preference: United States
Fund Size: $175 million
Founded: 1997
Average Investment: $5-$25 million
Minimum Investment: $5 million
Investment Criteria: EBITDA $5 Million
Industry Group Preference: Business Products & Services, Consumer Products, Consumer Services, Education, Environment Products & Services, Manufacturing, Media, Restaurants, Specialty Chemicals, Financial Services, Retail, Consumer & Leisure, Healthcare Services
Portfolio Companies: Griswold, Latex International, SDI, Financial Health Services

Key Executives:
John L Pouschine, Founder/Managing Director
212-784-0624
Fax: 212-784-0621
e-mail: jpouschine@pouschinecook.com
Education: Princeton University, Harvard Business School
Background: Senior VP, Electra; VP, Ventures Ltd

Venture Capital & Private Equity Firms / Domestic Firms

Directorships: MedPay Corproation, Latex Foam International, MasterCraft Boat Company, Spring Air Partners, Doc & Ingalls, Great Lakes Home Health & Hospice
Everett R Cook, Founder/Managing Director
212-784-0622
Fax: 212-784-0621
e-mail: ecook@pouschinecook.com
Education: Dartmouth College; Tuck School of Business at Dartmouth
Background: Managing Director, Ampton Investments; Chairman/CEO, Bake Rite Foods; Vice President/Director, Cook International; Vice President/Director, Terminix International; Director, PBCM; Chairman, Cook Flexner; Mortgage Securities Professional, First Pennco Securities
Directorships: MedPay Corporation, Interplan Corporation, Ampac Packaging, Harlem Furniture
Robert Jenkins, Principal
212-784-0625
Fax: 212-784-0621
e-mail: rjenkins@pouschinecook.com
Education: Middlebury College, New York University Leonard N Stern School of Business
Background: Senior VP, S.N. Phelps; Principal, Head & Company; Senior Auditor, KPMG Peat Marwick
Directorships: Latex Foam International, Spring Air Partners, Harlem Furniture, Doc & Ingalls
Brian Harrison, Principal
212-784-0627
Education: BS, Vanderbilt School of Engineering
Background: Brown Brothers Harriman's Merchant Banking Group; VP, Altpoint Capital Partners; Associate, MacQuarie's Industrials

1471 PPM AMERICA CAPITAL PARTNERS
225 W Wacker Drive
Suite 1200
Chicago, IL 60606

Phone: 312-634-2500
web: www.ppmamerica.com

Mission Statement: Providing private equity capital for co-investments in buyouts with equity sponsors, management buyouts, recapitalizations, industry build-ups and growth equity.
Geographic Preference: Worldwide
Fund Size: $2.2 billion
Founded: 1982
Minimum Investment: $5 million
Investment Criteria: MBO, Recapitalizations, Build-Ups, Growth Equity
Industry Group Preference: Diversified
Key Executives:
  Craig Smith, President, CEO & CIO
  Education: BEng & MBA, Cornell University
  Background: VP & Senior Portfolio Manager, Loomis Sayles & Co.
  Mary Capasso, EVP, COO & General Counsel
  Education: BS, Elmhurst College; JD, Chicago-Kent College of Law
  Background: General Counsel, Harris Associates; Executive Director & Deputy General Counsel, UBS Global Asset Management; Associate, Bell, Boyd & Lloyd
  Champ Raju, Managing Partner & Head, Prviate Equity
  Education: MBA, Kellogg Graduate School of Management; BS, Accounting and Finance, Indiana University
  Background: PricewaterhouseCoopers LP; Audit Group
  Directorships: Capital H Group, HCG Holdings, LLC

1472 PRAESIDIAN CAPITAL
419 Park Avenue South
New York, NY 10016

Phone: 212-520-2600 Fax: 212-520-2601
e-mail: info@praesidian.com
web: www.praesidian.com

Mission Statement: Praesidian Capital is an innovative private investment firm focused on providing senior and subordinated debt along with growth capital to private lower middle market businesses in the United States.
Geographic Preference: United States
Average Investment: $5 - $20 million
Investment Criteria: Growth & Acqustion Financings, Management & Sponsored Buyouts, Recapitalizations, Refinancings
Key Executives:
  Jason D Drattell, Founder/Managing Partner
  212-520-2620
  e-mail: jdrattell@praesidian.com
  Education: BBA, Finance, Pace University
  Background: Founding Partner, The Blackstone Group; Heller Financial; Chemical Bank
  Glenn C Harrison, Partner
  212-520-2612
  e-mail: gharrison@praesidian.com
  Education: BA, Economics, Rutgers University
  Background: Vice President, Merrill Lynch Middle Market Finance; Assistant Vice President, Fleet National Bank

1473 PRAIRIE CAPITAL
191 North Wacker Drive
Suite 800
Chicago, IL 60606

Phone: 312-360-1133 Fax: 312-360-1193
web: www.prairie-capital.com

Mission Statement: To facilitate ownership transitions for companies in the lower middle market.
Fund Size: $300 million
Founded: 1997
Industry Group Preference: Niche Manufacturing, Business Products & Services, Financial Services, Education, Consumer Products, Industrial Services
Portfolio Companies: Captek Softgel, Industrial Water Treatment Solutions, Swiss-American Products, Damac Products, Messenger, Riverchase Dermatology, TeacherMatch, DRB Systems, Forthfield, StyleCraft Home Collection, Specialized Education Services, FCA Packaging, Pioneer Metal Finishing, Statlab Medical Products, Chicago Deferred Exchange, Insource Contract Services, R3 Education, ProVest, Regency Beauty Institute
Key Executives:
  C Bryan Daniels, Founding Partner
  e-mail: bdaniels@prairie-capital.com
  Education: BA, Mathematics & Chemistry, Wabash College; MBA, University of Chicago; MS, Computer Science, University of Chicago
  Background: SVP, Commercial Banking, American National Bank & Trust Company; Investment Committee, ANB Mezzanine
  Directorships: Chicago Deferred Exchange Corp., Creditors Interchange, ProVest, R3 Education, Security Technologies, Taylor Capital Group, Titanium Solutions
  Stephen V King, Founding Partner
  e-mail: sking@prairie-capital.com
  Education: BS, Finance, University of Illinois; MBA, Finance, University of Chicago; JD, Loyola University
  Background: President, ANB Mezzanine Corporation; VP, American National Bank & Trust Company
  Directorships: FCA Packaging Products, Insource Contract Services, Pioneer Metal Finishing, R3 Education, Specialized Education Services

Venture Capital & Private Equity Firms / Domestic Firms

Darren M Snyder, Partner
e-mail: dmsnyder@prairie-capital.com
Education: BA, Economics, Drake University; MBA, University of Chicago
Background: VP, American National Bank & Trust Company
Directorships: Fortis, GPA, Messenger, Pioneer Metal Finishing, Plastimayd
Christopher T Killackey, Partner
e-mail: ckillackey@prairie-capital.com
Education: BS, Finance, University of Illinois; MBA, University of Chicago
Background: Director, Banc One Mezzanine Corporation; VP, American National Bank
Directorships: ProVest, Titanium Solutions, Plastimayd, Navman, Double E, StatLap
Nathan J Good, Vice President
e-mail: ngood@prairie-capital.com
Education: BA, Accountancy, University of Illinois; MBA, University of Chicago Booth School of Business
Background: Senior Analyst, BMO Nesbitt Burns Equity Partners; Analyst, Credit Suisse First Boston
Directorships: Messenger, StatLab, FCA, Fortis, Navman Wireless
Sean M McNally, Vice President
e-mail: smcnally@prairie-capital.com
Education: BS, Finance, University of Illinois; MBA, University of Chicago Booth School of Business
Background: Analyst, William Blair & Company
Directorships: Chicago Deferred Exchange, Double E

1474 PRAIRIEGOLD VENTURE PARTNERS
5708 South Remington Place
Suite 600
Sioux Falls, SD 57108

Phone: 605-275-2999
e-mail: info@pgvp.com
web: www.pgvp.com

Mission Statement: We prefer to invest in early-stage opportunities in the Midwest; this allows us to take meaningful ownership positions with less capital and play an active role in formulating company strategy. we seek to add value through our network of contacts and our experience.
Investment Criteria: Early-Stage
Industry Group Preference: Biotechnology, Clean Technology, Industrial, Life Sciences, Medical Devices and Equipment, Technology, Energy
Portfolio Companies: PrarieGold Solar, Virtual Incision Corporation, Lineagen, tenKsolar, ZeaChem, General Compression, Augusta Systems, Agrivida, Chronix Biomedical, Game Plan Technologies, iCentera
Key Executives:
 Paul Batcheller, Partner
 Education: B.A. Economics, Macalester College
 Background: Advisor to Senator Tom Daschle
 Directorships: tenKsolar, ZeaChem, Agrivida, General Compression, South Dakota Rural Enterprise
 Mike Jerstad, Partner
 e-mail: jerstad@pgvp.com
 Education: B.A. Tufts University; J.D. Georgetown University; M.B.A. University of Chicago
 Background: Pip Jaffray Healthcare Investment Banking Group, Attorney, Briggs and Morgan, P.A.
 Directorships: Grand Prairie Goods, Chronix Biomedical, Orasi Medical, Virtual Incision, Lineagen
 Susan Simko, Chief Financial Officer
 e-mail: simko@pgvp.com
 Education: B.B.A. Finance, University of Iowa; M.B.A. University of South Dakota
 Background: Director of Planning, Verio; Finance Manager, Andersen Consulting

1475 PRECURSOR VENTURES
170 Grant Avenue
4th Floor
San Francisco, CA 94108

e-mail: hello@precursorvc.com
web: precursorvc.com

Mission Statement: Precursor Ventures believes that all entrepreneurs benefit from having an institutional investor to help them scale their company from the beginning.
Geographic Preference: San Francisco Bay Area, New York and Toronto
Average Investment: $100,000-$250,000
Investment Criteria: First Institutional Round of Investment; First-Time Entrepreneurs; Diversity
Key Executives:
 Charles Hudson, Managing Partner/Founder
 Background: Partner, SoftTech VC

1476 PRELUDE VENTURES
1 Ferry Building
San Francisco, CA 94111

Phone: 415-729-1270
web: www.preludeventures.com

Mission Statement: Prelude Ventures is a VC firm seeking to address climate change. They have a long-term commitment to the sector and accept well-informed risks.
Founded: 2013
Key Executives:
 Nat Simmons, Co-Founder
 Education: BA, MA, University of California, Berkeley
 Background: Co-Founder, Sea Change Foundation; Principal, Renaissance Technologies
 Laura Baxter-Simmons, Co-Founder
 Education: BA, MA, University of California, Berkeley; JD, Stanford University
 Background: Co-Founder, Sea Change Foundation; General Counsel/Chief Compliance Officer, Meritage Group LP

1477 PRESENCE CAPITAL

e-mail: hello@presencecap.com
web: www.presencecap.com

Mission Statement: Virtual and Augmented Reality venture fund.
Fund Size: $10 million
Industry Group Preference: Virtual Reality & Augmented Reality
Portfolio Companies: Baobab Studies, BeyondView, Bigscreen, Blue Vision, Byte, Camera IQ, Drifter Entertainment, Escher Reality, Experiment 7, Floreo, Harmonix, Lightform, Limbix, Loom.AI, Nomadic, Osso VR, The Rogue Initiative, Sandbox VR, Scope AR, Simbe, SkyLights, Thalmic Labs, TRIPP, Upload, Visbit, Wave VR
Key Executives:
 Amitt Mahajan, Managing Partner
 Education: University of Illinois - Urbana/Champaign
 Background: Epic Games; Toro; MyMiniLife
 Paul Bragiel, Managing Partner
 Education: BS, University of Illinois
 Background: Managing Partner, i/o Ventures; Co-Founder, GameFounders; Founding Partner, Sisu Game Ventures; Savannah Fund; Golden Gate Ventures; Managing Partner, Bragiel Brothers; CEO, Paragon Five; CEO, Meetro; CEO, Lefora
 Phil Chen, Managing Partner
 Education: UCSD; Fuller Seminary
 Background: Alex eReader; Glo Bible; HTC

1478 PRESIDIO VENTURES
3979 Freedom Circle
Suite 340
Santa Clara, CA 95054

Phone: 408-845-9458
e-mail: info@presidio-ventures.com
web: www.presidio-ventures.com

Mission Statement: As an investor and a partner, we assist outstanding technology and media companies in expanding their business throughout Japan and Asia by leveraging our best assets: technology expertise, international business development experience, and a cross-industry network.

Geographic Preference: United States
Founded: 1998
Investment Criteria: Early-Stage
Industry Group Preference: Software, Consumer Internet, Media, Clean Technology, Semiconductors, Advanced Materials
Portfolio Companies: Adknowledge, Agrivida, Alta Devices, Appcelerator, Arbor Networks, ArcSight, Aryaka, Atheros Communications, Aurora Networks, Axxana, Azul Systems, BitTorrent, BlueLane, BlueStacks, Calient Technologies, Cambrios, Carrier IQ, Catalytic Solutions, Cleversafe, Cloudmark, CommVerge Solutions, Coskata, Cotendo, Embrane, Enevate, Engine Yard, ExtendMedia, Extensity, Extreme Networks, Fortinet, Fusion-io, Glympse, GreatPoint Energy, Ikanos Communications, Intermatix, Intrinsa, Karmasphere, Lastline, Liquid Audio, LiveScribe, Locamoda, mCube, Movius Interactive, MySQL, NetScreen, Nexenta, Nominum, Ocarina Network, ONI Systems, OpenX, Prism Skylabs, Revolution Analytics, RightScale, SEEO, Siara Systems, Siluria, SINA Corporation, Solantro, SoonR, Splashtop, Spring Tide Networks, Stoke, Tealium, Terracotta, Topspin Communications, VA Linux Systems, View Point, Vina Technologies XenSource, Xsigo Systems, Zimbra

Key Executives:
  Doug Kuribayashi, CEO
  Education: MBA, University of Virginia
  Background: President and CEO, Sumisho E-Commerce

1479 PRIMARY VENTURE PARTNERS
48 West 21st Street
4th Floor
New York, NY 10010

e-mail: info@primary.vc
web: www.primary.vc

Mission Statement: Primary Venture Partners, formerly High Peaks Venture Partners, makes early-stage investments in industry transforming technology companies.

Geographic Preference: Northeast United States
Founded: 2004
Average Investment: $500,000 - $2 million
Investment Criteria: Early-Stage
Industry Group Preference: SaaS, E-Commerce & Manufacturing, Information Technology
Portfolio Companies: Accela, Allworx, Amicus, Apprenda, Auterra, Bench, Bounce Exchange, Clothes Horse, Coupang, CredSimple, DerbyJackpot, Divide, Drawbridge Networks, Fashion Project, FieldLens, FlatWorld Knowledge, Greats, Handshake, iQ License, Jet, Keychain Logistics, Kohort, MakeSpace, Maple, PS Dept, Pump Audio, RealDirect, Reonomy, ReQuest, Routehappy, SimpleReach, Synaptic Digital, TheSquareFoot, Ticketfly, Vnomics, VYou, WhoSay, Widetronix, Yipit, Zipmark

Key Executives:
  Brad Svrluga, General Partner
  e-mail: brad@primary.vc
  Education: Williams College
  Background: The Berkshires Capital Investors; Strategy Consultant, Monitor Group
  Ben Sun, General Partner
  e-mail: ben@primary.vc
  Education: University of Michigan
  Background: Co-Founder, LaunchTime

1480 PRIMUS CAPITAL
5900 Landerbrook Drive
Suite 200
Cleveland, OH 44124-4020

Phone: 440-684-7300 Fax: 440-684-7342
e-mail: info@primuscapital.com
web: www.primuscapital.com

Mission Statement: Primus Capital is a venture capital firm committed to funding private companies with exceptional growth potential.

Geographic Preference: United States, Canada
Fund Size: $620 million
Founded: 1983
Average Investment: $10 million
Investment Criteria: Proprietary Product Advantage, Seasoned Management, Early-Stage to Mature
Industry Group Preference: Business to Business, Education, Communications, Healthcare
Portfolio Companies: AOD Software, Cardinal Commerce, EMMI Solutions, G2 Web Services, Hyperwallet Systems, Medhost, PartsSource, PathGroup, SkillSurvey, Vondormate

Key Executives:
  Phillip C Molner, Managing Partner
  e-mail: pmolner@primuscapital.com
  Education: BA, Economics & Mathematics, Yale University; JD, Yale Law School
  Background: McKinsey & Company; Boston Consulting Group
  Directorships: Encore Legal Solutions, Focus Receivables Management, Healthcare Management Systems, MedHost, Passport Health Communications, PathGroup
  Jonathan E Dick, Managing Director
  e-mail: jdick@primuscapital.com
  Education: Bs Mathematics and Economics, Brown University, MBA Harvard University
  Background: Sales Management, Lotus Development; IBM; McKinsey & Company
  Directorships: Carrier International, Entek IRD International, Ingredients.Com, Paycor Inc, PlanSoft Corp, Wireless
  Ronald C Hess Jr, Managing Director
  e-mail: rhess@primuscapital.com
  Education: BA, Economics & History, Middlebury College
  Background: Investment Banking Analyst, Global M&A Group, Lehman Brothers
  Directorships: G2 Web Services, Vendormate
  William C Mulligan, Senior Advisor
  e-mail: bmulligan@primuscapital.com
  Education: BA, Economics, Denison University; MBA, University of Chicago
  Background: McKinsey & Company; Deere and Company; First National Bank of Chicago
  Directorships: Bioanalytical Systems, Brulin Corporation, HUEBCORE Communications, Isolab

1481 PRISM CAPITAL
444 North Michigan Avenue
Suite 1910
Chicago, IL 60611

Phone: 312-464-7900 Fax: 312-464-7915
e-mail: robert@prismfund.com
web: www.prismfund.com

Mission Statement: Prism Capital provides subordinated debt to lower middle market companies through the Prism Mezzanine Fund and expansion capital to smaller growing companies through the Prism Opportunity Fund. We partner

Venture Capital & Private Equity Firms / Domestic Firms

with superior management teams and private equity professionals to finance growth, recapitalizations and buyouts.

Fund Size: $50 million
Average Investment: $2 - $15 million
Investment Criteria: Growth Equity, Recapitalizations, Buyouts
Industry Group Preference: Information Technology, Healthcare, Manufacturing, Services
Portfolio Companies: Banner Services, Celleration, Newser, Trustwave, 3-D Machining, Angie's List, Bell Automotive Products, Private Company, Craftsmen Industries, Destination Cinema, EZE Trucking, FCA, Fusion, Hill & Valley, Hi-Tech Manufacturing, McCoy Sales, Optical Experts Manufacturing, Ott-Lite, TCI, Vandor, VIA, Violet Packing

Key Executives:
Robert Finkel, Managing Partner
e-mail: robert@prismfund.com
Education: BA, Social & Beharioral Sciences, Johns Hopkins University; MBA, Harvard Business School
Background: Investment Manager, Wind Point Partners; Corporate Associate, Paine Webber
Directorships: Artromick Internationa, SteriMed Holdings
Steve Vivian, Partner
e-mail: steve@prismfund.com
Education: BS, General Engineering, MBA, University of Illinois
Background: Associate, BancAmerica Securities; Territory Manager, Parker Hannifin Corporation
Directorships: Fitzroy Dearborn Publishing, ClearSource
John Hoesley, Partner
e-mail: john@prismfund.com
Education: BS, Chemistry, University of Illinois; MBA, Kellogg School of Management
Background: CFO, Legato Partneres; Co-Founder & CEO, eVincio Corporation
Directorships: SteriMed Holdings, ISD Holdings, Trustwave, Celleration
Blaine Crissman, Partner
e-mail: blaine@prismfund.com
Education: BA, Economics & Finance, Augustana College; MBA, Fuqua School of Business, Duke University
Background: Principal, Bank of America Capital Investors; BancAmerica Securities; VP, First Bank Systems
Directorships: Optical Experts Manufacturing, VIA, Fusion Specialties, Violet Packing
Bill Harlan, Partner
e-mail: bill@prismfund.com
Education: BA, Economics & Political Science, University of Notre Dame; MBA, University of Chicago
Background: Golub Associates Incorporated; Principal, CID Equity Partners
Directorships: Braxton-Bragg Corporation, 3-D Machining, Craftsmen Industries, Bell Automotive Products, McCoy Sales Corporation

1482 PRITZKER GROUP PRIVATE CAPITAL
111 South Wacker Drive
Suite 4000
Chicago, IL 60606

Phone: 312-447-6000
web: www.pritzkergroup.com/private-capital/

Mission Statement: Pritzker Group Private Capital acquires middle-market companies based in North America, and focuses primarily on businesses in the manufactured products, services and healthcare sectors. The firm seeks to create long-term value through its permanent capital base, which brings such advantages as flexibility with transaction structure, efficiency in decision-making, and partnership with management teams. Pritzker Group provides resources and expertise with the objective of helping to build companies, and is a potential partner for family- and entrepreneur-owned businesses.

Geographic Preference: United States, Canada
Founded: 2002
Investment Criteria: Middle Market, Mature Companies, Buyouts, Recapitalizations, Growth Capital, Industry Consolidations, Corporate Divestitures, Enterprise Value $100 - $500 million, EBITDA $15 million or greater
Industry Group Preference: Manufacturing, Services, Healthcare
Portfolio Companies: Clinical Innovations, ENTACT, Entertainment Cruises, LBP Manufacturing, Milestone AV Technologies, PECO Pallet, PLZ Aeroscience, Signicast, Technimark

Other Locations:
11150 Santa Monica Blvd
Suite 1500
Los Angeles, CA 90025
Phone: 310-575-9400

Key Executives:
JB Pritzker, Co-Founder/Managing Partner
Education: AB, Political Science, Duke University; JD, Northwestern University School of Law
Background: Founding Member, Illinois Venture Capital Association
Tony Pritzker, Co-Founder/Managing Partner
Education: BA, Engineering, Dartmouth College; MBA, University of Chicago
Background: Chairman, AmSafe Partners; President, Baker Tanks; Regional VP, Operations, Getz Bros & Co.; Group Executive, Marmon Group
Directorships: Heal The Bay
Paul Carbone, Managing Partner, Private Capital
Education: University of Chicago; MBA, Harvard Business School
Background: Director & Managing Partner, Private Equity Group, Robert W. Baird & Co.; Senior VP, Investment Banking Group, Kidder, Peabody & Co.
Directorships: Lyric Opera of Chicago, Misericordia Endowment Fund, Shedd Aquarium, University of Chicago Medical Center

1483 PRITZKER GROUP VENTURE CAPITAL
110 North Wacker Drive
Suite 4350
Chicago, IL 60606

Phone: 312-447-6001
web: www.pritzkergroup.com/venture-capital

Mission Statement: Pritzker Group Venture Capital is a premier, early-stage venture capital firm investing in a broad range of technology and telecommunications companies that combine innovation and experience to take advantage of unique market opportunities. The firm dedicates all its resources to the pursuit of excellence.

Geographic Preference: United States
Fund Size: +$106 million
Founded: 1996
Average Investment: $500,000 - $50 million
Minimum Investment: $500,000
Investment Criteria: Early Stage, US-based
Industry Group Preference: Technology, Telecommunications, Enterprise Software, Healthcare, Energy, Emerging Technology, Consumer
Portfolio Companies: Active Network, AiCure, Aircell, Air Map, Analyte Health, Apervita, Apprentice, Augury, Avia, Away.com, Awesomeness TV, Baselayer, Big Frame, Bird, Bright.md, Built In, Cameo, Cartavi, Casper, Catalytic, Cleversafe, Cloud Technology Partners, CultureiQ, Curiosity.com, Dollar Shave Club, DroneBase, eCollege, egreetings.com, eSpark, Eved, Everdream, EverTrue, Firm58, FleetMatics, G2 Crowd, FreightWaves, Good Uncle, GraphicIQ, HelloGiggles, HopSkipDrive, Hollar, HqO, HyperQuest, Industrial Toys, Interior Define, InterOptic, IO,

Venture Capital & Private Equity Firms / Domestic Firms

Iris, Journera, Kollective, LeftHand Networks, Level Ex, Maisonette, Mapbox, Mindshow, Lightstream, OpenPath, Opternative, Outcome Health, Pin Drop Security, Playdom, Plus One Robotics, Pluto.TV, PreparedHealth, project44, PureWow, Red Balloon Security, Retention Science, Retrofit, Scopely, Seebo, SevenFifty, Shiftgig, Signal, SilverVue, SinglePlatform, Sittercity, Smartvid.io, SMS Assist, Snap Sheet, Sportvision, SpotHero, Spring Labs, SwipeSense, The Honest Company, Tock, Tovala, TicketsNow, Upserver, Vettery, Viv, Vow to be Chic, VTS, Wander Beauty, Wise Apple, X.ai, Zinch

Other Locations:
11150 Santa Monica Boulevard
Suite 1500
Los Angeles, CA 90025
Phone: 310-575-9400

Key Executives:
Tony Pritzker, Co-Founder
Education: BA, Engineering, Dartmouth College; MBA, University of Chicago
Background: Chairman, AmSafe Partners; President, Baker Tanks; Regional VP, Operations, Getz Bros & Co.; Group Executive, Marmon Group
Directorships: Heal The Bay
J.B. Pritzker, Co-Founder
Education: AB, Political Science, Duke University; JD, Northwestern University School of Law
Background: Founding Member, Illinois Venture Capital Association; Chicago Ventures
Chris Girgenti, Managing Partner
Education: BS, Applied Mathematics & Economics, Brown University; MBA, Finance & Accounting, Columbia Business School; CFA
Background: Corporate Finance, Chicago Corporation; Kemper Securities; Mergers & Acquisitions Group, KPMG Peat Marwick
Directorships: Advantage Optics, BASELAYER Technology, IO Data Centers; Chicago Botanic Garden; The Brown University Sports Foundation; National Venture Capital Association
Adam Koopersmith, Managing Partner
Education: BS, Economics, Wharton School, University of Pennsylvania; MBA, Kellogg School of Management, Northwestern University
Background: Sportvision; Berkshire Partners; Investment Banker, Alex Brown
Directorships: Analyte Health, Apervita, G2 Crowd, Interoptic, Kollective, SilverVue
Matt McCall, Partner
Education: BA, Economics & History, Williams College; MBA, Kellogg School of Management, Northwestern University; McCormick School of Engineering, Northwestern University
Background: Boston Consulting Group; Bankers Trust; Merrill Lynch; US Trust

1484 PRIVATEER HOLDINGS
2701 Eastlake Avenue East
Seattle, WA 98102

Phone: 206-432-9325
web: www.privateerholdings.com

Mission Statement: Invests in the cannabis industry.

Founded: 2010
Industry Group Preference: Cannabis
Portfolio Companies: Tilray, Leafly, High Park, Marley Natural, Goodship, Irisa, Grail, Head Light
Key Executives:
Brendan Kennedy, Executive Chairman
Education: BA, University of California, Berkeley; MS, Engineering, University of Washington; MBA, Yale School of Management
Background: President/CEO, Mindability Inc.; COO, SVB Analytics
Michael Blue, Managing Partner
Education: BBA, Harding University; MBA, Yale School of Management
Background: VP, de Visscher & Co.; Principal, Herrington Inc.
Christian Groh, Partner
Background: Director of Sales, SVB Analytics
Directorships: Nextel Communications

1485 PRO-RATA OPPORTUNITY FUND
11911 Freedom Drive
Suite 1080
Reston, VA 20190

Phone: 703-563-4100 **Fax:** 703-563-4111
web: proof.vc

Mission Statement: PROOF invests strategic capital alongside early stage VC firms.

Founded: 2015
Key Executives:
John Backus, Co-Founder/Managing Partner
Education: BA, MBA, Stanford University
Background: Co-Founder, US Order; Bain & Co.; Bain Capital
John Burke, Co-Founder/Managing Partner
Education: BA, University of California, Santa Cruz; BS, University of California, Berkeley; MBA, Harvard Business School
Thanasis Delistathis, Co-Founder/Managing Partner
Education: BSE, Princeton University; MBA, Harvard Business School
Background: Mckinley & Co.

1486 PROCYON VENTURES
14/F, One Broadway
Cambridge, MA 02142

e-mail: contact@procyonventures.com
web: www.procyonventures.com

Mission Statement: Procyon Ventures focuses on early stage technology companies, with particular interest in innovations involving data, analytics and IT infrastructure.

Geographic Preference: North America, Asia
Fund Size: $10 million
Founded: 2014
Average Investment: $50,000 - $500,000
Investment Criteria: Startups, Seed, Series A, Series B, Early Stage
Industry Group Preference: Big Data, Analytics & Analytical Instruments, IT Infrastructure, SaaS, Networking
Portfolio Companies: APX Labs, Contastic, Essess, Infinite Analytics, Oculii, Reniac, Seven Bridges Genomics, Smarking, Speedy Packets, Weft
Key Executives:
Malcolm Sweeney, Partner
Drew Volpe, Partner
Education: AB, Computer Science, Harvard University
Background: VP, Product Development, Semantic Machines; Co-Founder & CTO, Locately; Director, Product Development, Endeca Technologies

1487 PROGRESS EQUITY PARTNERS
2200 Ross Avenue
Suite 3838
Dallas, TX 75201

Phone: 214-978-3838 **Fax:** 214-978-3848
web: www.progressequity.com

Mission Statement: A private equity investment firm that acquires majority control of well-managed, entrepreneurial, service-based businesses.

Industry Group Preference: Healthcare, Pharmaceuticals, Food & Beverage, Communications, Marketing

Venture Capital & Private Equity Firms / Domestic Firms

Portfolio Companies: American Exteriors, COCAT, Crestcom International, Diversified Machine Systems, D&S Residential Services, EnAqua Solutions, Oncology Molecular Imaging, Terracare Associates, Revere Packaging

Other Locations:
7887 E Belleview Avenue
Suite 1100
Englewood, CO 80111
Phone: 303-297-1701 **Fax:** 303-228-1638

Key Executives:
Michael L Bailey, Founding Partner
Education: BS, Business Administration, University of Chattanooga; MS, Management, Georgia State University
Background: Partner, Transition Capital Partners; Co-Founder, Specialty Dessers LLC
Directorships: American Exteriors, Cambridge Home Healthcare Holdings, COCAT, D&S Residential Holdings, Diversified Machine Systems Holdings, Revere Packaging Holdings
Stephen N Sangalis, Founding Partner
Education: BS, Business Administration, University of Colorado, Boulder; MBA, Finance, Indiana University Kelley School of Business
Background: Founding Partner, Rocky Mountain Capital Partners; Hanifen Imhoff Capital Partners
Directorships: Diversified Machine Systems, Terracare Associates, Westcon, American Exteriors, COCAT
Paul A Yeoham, Founding Partner
Education: BS, Business Administration & Finance, University of Texas, Arlington; MS, Business, Southern Methodist University
Background: Senior Partner, Transition Capital Partners; Westcott Communications
Directorships: Terracare Associates, Westcon, Oncology Molecular Imaging
Carolina B Hensley, Principal
Education: BS, Business Administration, University of Denver
Background: Guaranty Bank & Trust, Highline Equity Partners

1488 PROGRESS VENTURES
One Broadway
14th Floor
Cambridge, MA 02142

Phone: 617-401-2711
web: www.progressventures.com

Mission Statement: Progress Ventures seeks to finance early-stage business-to-business platforms, with exclusive focus on media and marketing technology companies.

Fund Size: $20 million
Founded: 2008
Average Investment: $2 - $4 million
Investment Criteria: Startups, Early Stage
Industry Group Preference: Business to Business, Media Technology, Marketing Technology, Data & Analytics, Analytics & Analytical Instruments, Online Advertising, Mobile
Portfolio Companies: Crave Labs, Dstillery, Integral Ad Science, Iris.TV, Lisnr, Localytics, MediaMath, Pixability, Qualia, Simpli.fi, Skyword, Tru Optik, Trust Metrics

Other Locations:
245 Park Avenue
27th Floor
New York, NY 10167
Phone: 212-609-6914

Key Executives:
Sam Thompson, Founding Partner
Education: BA, Lewis & Clark College; MBA, FW Olin Graduate School of Business, Babson College
Background: Pod Consulting; Procter & Gamble; Phoenix Media/Communications Group; IGN Entertainment; Snowball.com
Directorships: MassBike
Nick MacShane, Founding Partner
Education: BA, Government & History, Skidmore College
Background: Virtual Access Networks; MyWay.com; Scotia Pharmaceuticals
Adriaan Zur Muhlen, Managing Partner
Education: BS, Miami University; MBA, Harvard Business School
Background: Partner, Glouston Capital Partners; Procter & Gamble
Chris Legg, Partner
Education: BCom, Queen's University; MBA, Harvard Business School
Background: Tandem Expansion Fund; Argo Global Capital; Credit Suisse; Merrill Lynch
Rick Gallagher, Managing Partner/Chief Financial Officer
Education: BBA, Accounting, Isenberg School of Management, University of Massachusetts, Amherst
Background: EVP, COO & CFO, Phoenix Media Group; CFO, WebGen Systems

1489 PROJECT 11 VENTURES
Boston, MA

web: www.project11.com

Mission Statement: Project 11 Ventures is a seed stage fund aiming to partner with entrepreneurs and work alongside them to build great software and technology businesses.

Fund Size: $30 million
Investment Criteria: Startups, Seed Stage
Industry Group Preference: Software, Technology
Portfolio Companies: Airmada, Alchemista, Alpha Sheets, Dataquest, DipJar, LibertyX, MoveWith, Sentenai, TVision Insights, Volta Networks

Key Executives:
Bob Mason, Managing Director
e-mail: bob@project11.com
Education: BS, Worcester Polytechnic Institute
Background: Co-Founder & CTO, Brightcove; Software Architect, ATG; Program Manager, Microsoft
Katie Rae, Managing Director
e-mail: katie@project11.com
Background: Managing Director, Techstars Boston; Microsoft; Co-Founder, Startup Institute
Reed Sturtevant, Managing Director
e-mail: reed@project11.com
Background: Managing Director, Techstars Boston; Microsoft; Managing Director & VP, Technology, Idealab; CTO, Eons; Co-Founder, Startup Institute

1490 PROLOG VENTURES
7701 Forsyth Boulevard
Suite 1095
St Louis, MO 63105

Phone: 314-743-2400
e-mail: prolog@prologventures.com
web: www.prologventures.com

Mission Statement: Venture Capital Firm specializing in life sciences.

Founded: 2001
Industry Group Preference: Life Sciences
Portfolio Companies: Divergence, IntelliCyt, Moleculera Labs, Plum Organics, Singulex, Spindrift, Zeel, AirXpanders, Attune, EndoStim, EraGen, Neurolutions, NxThera, ShopWell, TOMA Biosciences, Veniti, Veran

Key Executives:
Brian Clevinger, Founder/Managing Director
Education: Washington University
Background: Alafai Capital

Venture Capital & Private Equity Firms / Domestic Firms

Ilya Nykin, Founder/Managing Director
Education: Odessa University
Gregory Johnson, Founder/Managing Director
Education: MIT
Teddy Shalon, Managing Director
Education: BA, BS, MS, Washington University
Background: Co-Founder, Ivy Technologies; Co-Founder, Metaphase; Founder, ThinOptics, Waterpods, Airxpanders, Osteogenix and BioPolymetrix

1491 PROMUS VENTURES
Chicago, IL

e-mail: info@promusventures.com
web: www.promusventures.com

Mission Statement: Investing in early-stage software companies that are changing the world.

Investment Criteria: Early-Stage
Industry Group Preference: Software
Portfolio Companies: Virool, NewHound, BackOps, Storify, Kahuna, Getable, Prism Skylabs, YourMechanic, Chromatik, Owner Listens, Airware, First Opinion, Prizeo, Embarke, Solve Media, Audiodraft, Binpress, Sqwiggle, Layer, AngelList, Seamless Toy Company, Kensho, Vires Aero, Kurbo Health, Vaurum, Ambition, See Me, Bellabeat, Whoop, Tulip Retail, Gauss Surgical, Standard Treasury, Spire, Navdy

Key Executives:
Mike Collett, Managing Partner/Founder
e-mail: mcollett@promusventures.com
Education: BS, BA, Vanderbilt University; MBA, Washington University
Background: VP, Merrill Lynch M&A Group; Analyst, Masters Capital Management; Co-Founder/Managing Director, Masters Capital Nanotechnology Fund

1492 PROQUEST INVESTMENTS
2430 Vanderbilt Beach Road
Unit 108-190
Naples, FL 34109

Phone: 609-919-3560 Fax: 609-919-3570
web: www.proquestvc.com

Mission Statement: ProQuest Investments invests in healthcare companies ranging from seed stage to late-stage. The company is devoted to the advancement of developing businesses in the healthcare industry.

Geographic Preference: United States, North America, Europe
Fund Size: $900 million
Founded: 1998
Average Investment: $250,000 - $25 million
Investment Criteria: Seed to Late-Stage
Industry Group Preference: Healthcare
Portfolio Companies: Achillion Pharmaceuticals, Agile Therapeutics, Clarus Therapeutics, Eagle Pharmaceutical, Immune Design, Mast Therapeutics, Mersana Therapeutics, NovaDel Pharma, Revision, SomaLogic, Sopherion Therapeutics, TeLoRmedix, Tragara Pharmaceuticals, Zosano Pharma

Other Locations:
12626 High Bluff Drive
Suite 325
San Diego, CA 92130
Phone: 858-847-0315 Fax: 858-847-0316

380 Rue St-Antoine Ouest
Bureau 2020
Montreal, QC H2Y 3X7
Canada
Phone: 514-842-1625 Fax: 514-842-1379

Key Executives:
Jay Moorin, Partner
609-919-3565
Education: BA, Economics, University of Michigan
Background: Chairman & CEO, Maganin Pharmaceuticals; Managing Director, Healthcare Banking, Bear Stearns & Co. Inc.; VP, Marketing & Business Development, ER Squibb Pharmaceutical Company
Directorships: ACMI, Acurian, Aires Pharmaceuticals, Eagle Pharmaceuticals, Epic Therapeutics, Gloucester Pharmaceticals, Guava Technologies, Mersana Therapeutics, MethlyGene, Novacea
Alain Schreiber, MD, Partner
609-919-3568
Education: BS, MD, Free University of Brussels
Background: President & CEO, Vical; Senior VP, Research, Rhone-Poulenc Rorer
Directorships: Eagle Pharmaceuticals, Immune Design Corporation, Revision Optics, Telormedix, Tragara Pharmaceuticals
Pasquale DeAngelis, CFO/Administrative Partner
609-919-3567
Education: BS, Accounting, St. Peter's College; MS, Taxation, Pace University; CPA
Background: Partner, KPMG; Co-Founder/Managing Partner, DeAngelis & Higgins, Adjunct Professor, Seton Hall University & Rider University
Stuart Holden, MD, Chairman, Scientific Advisory Board
Education: University Of Winsconsin-Madison; MD, Cornell University
Background: Surgeon, Cedars-Sinai Medical Center; Assistant Professor of Surgery, Georgetown University School of Medicine
Directorships: Louis Warschaw Prostate Cancer Center, Prostate Cancer Foundation

1493 PROSPECT CAPITAL CORPORATION
10 E 40th Street
42nd Floor
New York, NY 10016

Phone: 212-792-2095
e-mail: investorrelations@prospectstreet.com
web: www.prospectstreet.com

Mission Statement: An mezzanine debt and private equity firm that manages a publicly-traded, closed-end, dividend-focuses investment company.

Fund Size: $1 billion
Founded: 1988
Average Investment: $10-50 million
Investment Criteria: Mezzanine Debt, Acquisitions, Growth, Development, Financings, Recapitalizations
Industry Group Preference: All sectors considered
Portfolio Companies: Adernant, Aircraft Fasteners, ALG USA Holdings, Allied Defense Group, American Broadband, American Gilsonite, AMU Holdings, APH Property Holdings, Apidos CLO, Arctic Glacier, Arctic Oilfield Equipment, Ark-La-Tex Wireline Services, Armor Holding II, ARRM Holdings, Atlantis Healthcare Group, Babson CLO, Blue Coat Systems, BNN Holdings, Broder Bros., Brookside Mill CLO, Byrider Systems, BXM Holding Company, Caleel and Hayden, Capston Logistics, Cargo Airport Services, CCPI Holdings, Cent 17 CLO, Cinedigm DC, Coverall, CP Well Testing, Credit Central, Crossman Corporation, CRT Midco, Deltek, Diamondback, Echelon Aviation, Edmentum, Learning, Empire Today, Energy Solutons, First Tower, Fischbein, Fleetwash, Focus Brands, FPG, Galaxy II, Global Employment Solutions, Grocery Outlet, GTP Operations, Gulf Coast Machine and Supply, Halcyon Loan Advisors, Harbortouch Holdings of Delaware, Harley Marine Services, ICON Health & Fitness, IDQ Holdings, Ikaria, Injured Workers Pharmacy, Instant Web, Interdent, JAC Holding Corporation, Laserhip, LCM XIV CLO, LHC Holdings, Madison Park Funding IX, Manx, Matrixx Initiatives, Maverick Healthcare, MITY Holdings of Delaware, Mountain View CLO, Nationwide Acceptance Holdings, NCP Finance, New Century Transportation, Nixon, NPH Property Holdings, Octagon Investment Partners, Onyx Payments, Pacfic World,

Venture Capital & Private Equity Firms / Domestic Firms

Pelican Products, Photonic Technologies SAS, Pinnacle Treatment, PrimeSport, Prince Mineral Holding Corporation, Progrexion Holdings, Royal Adhesives, RV, Ryan, Sandow Media, Small Business Whole Loan Portfolio, Snacks Parent, Spartan Energy Services, Speedy Group Holdings, Sport Helmets Holdings, Stauber Performance, STI Holdings, Stryker Energy, Sudbury Mill, Symphony CLO IX, System One Holdings, Targus Group, TB Corp., Tectum Holdings, The Copernicus Group, The Healing Staff, Therakos, Tolt Solution, Traeger Pellete Grills, Transaction Network Services, Trinity Services Group, TriMark USA, United Sporting Company, United States Environmental Services, UPH Property Holdings, Valley Electric, Venio, Water Pik, Wheel Pros, Wind River Resources, Wolf Energy Holdings

Key Executives:
John F. Barry III, Chairman/CEO
Education: AB History, Princeton University; JD Degree, Harvard Law School
Background: VP, Corporate Finance, Merrill Lynch; Chairman & CEO, BondNet Trading Systems; Managing Director, LF Rothschild & Company; Director, Prudential Securities
Directorships: CT Financial Developments, Prospect St. NYC Discovery Fund, Prospect St. NYC Vp-Investment Fund
Michael G. Eliasek, President/COO
Education: MBA, Harvard Business; BS, University of Virginia
Background: Bain & Company
David L. Belzer, Managing Director
Education: MBA, Washington University; BA, Indiana University
Background: Fieldstone Private Capital Group; Blaylock & Partners, GE Capital; Wheelabrator Technologies
Daria Becker, Chief Administrative Officer
Education: BA, Wellesley College; Massachusetts Institute of Technology
Background: CitiBank NA
David Moszer, Managing Director
Education: BA, University of Virginia; MBA, Columbia University
Background: GSO Capital Partners; Principal, FriedbergMilstein; Principal, GarMark Partners; Bear Stearns
Jason Wilson, Managing Director
Education: BS, Mechanical Engineering, University of Notre Dame; MBA, University of Chicago Graduate School of Business
Background: Investment Banking, Lehman Brotherse; UBS Investment Bank
Directorships: Yatesville Coal Holdings; Ajax Rolled Ring & Machine; Veterans Securing America

1494 PROSPECT PARTNERS LLC
200 W Madison Street
Suite 2710
Chicago, IL 60606

Phone: 312-782-7400 Fax: 312-782-7410
web: www.prospect-partners.com

Mission Statement: Manages two funds totaling $270 million focused exclusively on management-led leveraged acquisitions of lower middle market companies with niche strategies; partnering with management teams to acquire and help build companies whose base revenue is typically between $10 and $30 million at the time of our investment, and pursue add-on acquisitions with as little as $2 million in revenue.

Geographic Preference: United States
Fund Size: $270 million
Founded: 1998
Average Investment: $1-$7 million
Minimum Investment: $1 million
Investment Criteria: MBO, Recapitalizations in the lower middle market

Industry Group Preference: Household Goods, Consumer Products, Leisure, Food & Beverage, Education, Automotive, Marine Services, Sports, Information Technology, Health Related, Packaging

Portfolio Companies: Absolutely Custom Group, Codel Holding Company, Cyclonaire Holding Corporation, Education Futures Group, ESI Lighting, ICI Holding Company, Knight Packaging Group, Kronos Foods, Landmark Irrigation Holding Services, Navix Holdings Corporation, Owen Equipment Holdings, Polymer Holding, Prospect Pools Group, Prospect Water, Summit Fire Protetcion, Superior Tool Holding Company, SurePoint Holdings, Tender Products, Velocity Aerospace Holding Group, Velvac Holdings, WDP Holdings Corporation, Wedgewood Hospitality Group

Louis W Kenter, Partner
e-mail: lkenter@prospect-partners.com
Education: BS Mechanical Engineering, University of Illinois; MBA University of Chicago
Background: Kenter & Company; Marquette Venture Partners; McKinsey & Company; Skidmore, Owings & Merrill
Directorships: Education Corporation of America, GameMark Products, V4 Group, John Boos Company, Revere Group, Kifco
Richard C Tuttle, Partner
e-mail: rtuttle@prospect-partners.com
Education: BA Economics, Stanford University; MBA Stanford Graduate School of Business
Background: Health Care & Retirement Corporation; Golder, Thoma & Cressey; McKinsey & Company
Directorships: Office Resources, Excello Products LLC, Optronics Products, Remuda Ranch Company, Cobler Origin Technologies
Erik E Maurer, Partner
e-mail: emauer@prospect-partners.com
Education: BA, Stanford University; MBA, Northwestern JL Kellogg Graduate School of Management
Background: Northern Trust Company; Inroads Capital Partners
Directorships: PAC Holding Company, First Texas Products Company, Optronics Products, Wrap Pack Products Corporation, V4 Group
Brett P Holcomb, Partner
e-mail: bholcomb@prospect-partners.com
Education: BA, Kenyon College; MBA, Kellogg School of Management, Northwestern University
Background: Associate, American Capital; Analyst, Bear Stearns & Co
Bradley C O'Dell, Partner
e-mail: bodell@prospect-partners.com
Education: BS, University of Richmond; MBA, Kellogg School of Business, Northwestern University
Background: Vice President, Silver Oak Services Partners; Associate, Willis Stein & Partners
Directorships: Kronos Foods, Gold Star Food Service, Summit Fire Protection, Tender Products

1495 PROSPECT VENTURE PARTNERS
525 University Avenue
Suite 1350
Palo Alto, CA 94301

Phone: 650-327-8800
web: www.prospectventures.com

Mission Statement: Prospect Venture Partners is dedicated to investing in outstanding biopharmaceutical and medical device companies. Prospect targets commercially attractive biomedical enterprises with outstanding entrepreneurial management teams, proprietary products, and innovative technologies with the potential for significant investment returns.

Fund Size: $1 billion
Average Investment: $10 - $20 million

Venture Capital & Private Equity Firms / Domestic Firms

Investment Criteria: New Company Incubations, First and Second Financing Rounds, Late-Stage
Industry Group Preference: Biopharmaceuticals, Medical Devices
Portfolio Companies: Alvine Pharmaceuticals, Amicus Therapeutics, Amira Pharmaceuticals, AVEO Pharmaceuticals, Baxano Surgical, Cabochon Aesthetics, CHG Healthcare, Complete Genomics, DFine, Gloucester Pharmaceuticals, Hansen Medical, Idun Pharmaceuticals, Infinity Pharmaceuticals, Jazz Pharmaceuticals, Kythera Biopharmaceuticals, Nanosys, Neomend, NGM Biopharmaceuticals, NinePoint Medical, Nora Therapeutics, Novacept, Novavax, Opus Medical, Pamira, PCI Holding Corporation, Portola Pharmaceuticals, Rinant Neuroscience, ROXRO Pharma, Sapphire Therapeutics, Senomyx, SentreHEART, SGX Pharmaceuticals, Somaxon Pharmaceuticals, SurgRx, Tercica, Tinea Pharmaceuticals, Topica Pharmaceuticals, Transave, Trubion Pharmaceuticals, Vanda Pharmaceuticals, Visiogen, Vitae Pharmaceutcals

Key Executives:
  Russell Hirsch MD, PhD, Managing Director
  Education: BA, Chemistry, University of Chicago; MD & PhD, Biochemistry, University of California, San Francisco
  Background: General Partner, Mayfield; Biomedical Research, University of California, San Francisco
  Directorships: Intuitive Surgial, Hansen Medical, Opus Medical, Orquest, AVEO Pharmaceuticals, Visiogen, Baxano, Dfine, SentreHEART, Portola Pharmaceuticals
  David Schnell MD, Managing Director
  Education: BS, Biological Sciences, Stanford University; MA, Health Services Research, Stanford University School of Medicine; MD, Harvard Medical School
  Background: Partner, Kleiner Perkins Caufield & Byers; Sandoz Pharmaceuticals; Co-Founder & CEO, Healtheon Corporation

1496 PROVCO GROUP
795 E Lancaster Avenue
Suite 200
Villanova, PA 19085

Phone: 610-520-2010 **Fax:** 610-520-1905
web: www.provcogroup.com

Mission Statement: Provco facilitates early-stage and mature financing on a select basis.
Average Investment: $1,000,000-$10,000,000
Minimum Investment: $100,000
Investment Criteria: First-Stage, Second-Stage
Industry Group Preference: Communications, Computer Related, Consumer Products, Distribution, Electronic Components, Instrumentation, Genetic Engineering, Medical & Health Related
Portfolio Companies: Integra Life Sciences, Prime Bank, Ballard Leasing, Interactive Investor International, Hooters Restaurants, HAL Trust, Medicus Technologies

Key Executives:
  Richard E Caruso PhD, Founder
  Education: BS, Susquehanna University; MSBA, Bucknell University; PhD, London School of Economics, University of London
  Background: Principal, LFC Financial Corp.; Pricewaterhouse & Co.
  Directorships: Integra Life Sciences Corporation
  Gary R DiLella, Vice President
  Education: BS, Pennsylvania State University; MS, Villanova University
  Background: Finance Department, LFC Financial Corp.
  Gerald Holtz, Vice President
  610-520-2010
  Fax: 610-520-1905
  Education: MBA, Duke University; BS, Villanova University
  Background: Co-Founder, Hoot Owl Restaurants LLC; PepsiCo; Price Waterhouse & Company

1497 PROVENANCE VENTURES
e-mail: bbiniak@yahoo.com
web: www.provenanceventures.com

Mission Statement: A venture capital firm focused on developing seed and early-stage social technology companies. The firm places value on the building of sustainable, high growth businesses through partnerships with entrepreneurs and operational execution.
Geographic Preference: United States
Fund Size: $10 million
Founded: 2006
Investment Criteria: Seed-Stage, Early-Stage
Industry Group Preference: Media, Digital Media & Marketing, Communications

Key Executives:
  Bryan Biniak, Founder/Managing Director
  Education: BA, International Relations, Business & Economics, Boston University
  Background: Senior Vice President, AG Interactive Gem M Division; COO, Vivendi Universal Moviso Division; Founding Member, Harmonix Music Systems

1498 PROVIDENCE EQUITY PARTNERS
50 Kennedy Plaza
18th Floor
Providence, RI 02903

Phone: 401-751-1700
e-mail: info@provequity.com
web: www.provequity.com

Mission Statement: A private investment firm specializing in equity investments in communications and media companies around the world. To create value by building lasting partnerships with talented entrepreneurs and by providing them with the capital, industry expertise and broad network of relationships necessary to build companies that will shape the future of the communications and media industries.
Fund Size: $22 billion
Founded: 1989
Average Investment: $75 million
Minimum Investment: $10 million
Investment Criteria: Growth capital
Industry Group Preference: Telecommunications, Media, Entertainment, Information Services
Portfolio Companies: ABTL, AcadeMedia, Altegrity, Ambassador Theatre Group, Ascend Learning, Asurion, Blackboard, CDW, Chernin Group, CSDVRS, Digiturk, EDMC, Galileo Global Education, GlobalTranz, Grupo TorreSur, Hathway, HSE24, Idea Cellular, ikaSystems, Ironman, ITT Educational Services, KIN, Learfield Sports, M7 Group, Miller Heiman, MLS Media, OpenSky, Q Networks, RentPath, SRA International, Star CJ, Study Group, SunGard, Survey Sampling International, Trilogy International Partners, TVB, UFO Movies India, Univision Communications, VectorLearning, VendorSafe Technologies, Volia, vRad, Wize Commerce, ZeniMax Media

Other Locations:
31 West 52nd Street
Suite 2400
New York, NY 10019
Phone: 212-588-6700 **Fax:** 212-588-6701

28 St. George Street
London W1S 2FA
United Kingdom
Phone: 44-2075148800 **Fax:** 44-2076292778

Key Executives:
  Glenn M. Creamer, Senior Managing Director Emeritus
  Education: MBA, Harvard Business School; BA, Brown University
  Directorships: Transwestern Publishing

Venture Capital & Private Equity Firms / Domestic Firms

Michael J. Dominguez, Chief Investment Officer
Education: MBA, Harvard Business School; BA, Bucknell University
Directorships: Bresnan Communications; F&W Publications
Edward A. Chestnut, Managing Director, Investor Relations
Education: BA, University of Notre Dame
Background: Managing Director, Fortress; Founder, Atlantic-Pacific Capital Chicago Office; Northern Trust Company
Patrick D. Dunn, Managing Director, Providence Public
Education: BA, Bowdoin College
Background: Portfolio Manager, Northern Pines; Raptor Group; Tudor Investment Corporation; Morgan Stanley
Joshua C. Empson, Senior Advisor
Education: BA, Princeton University
Background: Partner, NantCapital; Managing Director, Forstmann Little & Co.; United Online; NBC
Directorships: Influence Media Partners; Learfield Sports; MLS Media
Jonathan M. Nelson, Founder & Executive Chair
Education: MBA, Harvard Business School; BA, Brown University
Directorships: Bresnan Broadband, eircom ltd., Language Life Services, Western Wireless Corp., Yankees Entertainment and Sports Network LLC, VoiceStream Wireless Corp.
Michael N. Gray, Managing Director
Education: BS & MS, University of North Carolina; MBA, Stanford Grad. School of Business
Background: First Union Capital Partners
Directorships: Grupo TorreSur; Univision Communications
William S. Hughes, Managing Director
Education: BA, Dartmouth College; MBA, Harvard Business School
Background: Associate, Summit Partners; CEO, Netdecisions Group; Analyst, Lehman Brothers
Directorships: KPa; n2Y; TimeClock Plus; Vistage
Lisa M. Lee, Managing Director, Investor Relations
Education: BA, Stanford University; MBA, Harvard University
Background: Managing Director, CVC Capital Partners; Merrill Lynch; A.T. Kearney
Karim A. Tabet, Senior Managing Director
Education: Ecole Polytechnique; MBA, Wharton School
Background: Associate, Goldman Sachs
Directorships: Catalpa
Andrew A. Tisdale, Senior Managing Director
Education: BA, Vanderbilt University; MBA, University of North Carolina
Background: Morgan Stanley
Scott M. Marimow, Managing Director
Education: BS, Wharton School, University of Pennsylvania
Background: Analyst, Deutsche Bank
Directorships: RentPath; TAIT; Topgolf; EZLinks Golf; ZeniMax Media; AutoTrader Group; Hulu; Learfield Sports; MLS Media; Newport Television
Peter O. Wilde, Chairman, PSG
Education: BA, Colorado College; MBA, Harvard Business School
Background: General Partner, BCI Partners
Directorships: Archipelago Learning, Ascend Learning, Decision Resources, Edline, Education Management Corp., NEW Asurion, Study Group

1499 PSG
401 Park Drive
Suite 204
Boston, MA 02215

Phone: 617-544-8800
e-mail: info@psgequity.com
web: www.psgequity.com

Mission Statement: PSG invests in growth-stage software companies that are ready to step on the accelerator, as they've reached an inflection point through demonstrated product-market fit, rapid organic growth and customer focus.
Investment Criteria: Growth-Stage
Industry Group Preference: Software, Technology
Portfolio Companies: 2ndWave Software, Abacusnext, Anju Software, Arcoro, Artur'in, Assembly, Billwerk, Burning Glass Technologies, Centrl, Chatmeter, Conversica, Copysmith AI Inc., Dental Intelligence, DigitalED, Divvy Cloud, EverCommerce, FluentStream Technologies, Foreground, Formstack, Government Brands, Hornetsecurity, Imaweb, Impact, INE, Inhabit IQ, Introhive, Jobcase, Kenect, LegitScript, LivTech, LogDNA, LogicGate, LogicMonitor, Lumaverse Technologies, Lusha, MAPAL Group, Meal Ticket, Ministry Brands, nalanda Global, Netsurion, Next Glass, NoFraud, Nomentia, NXTsoft, OfColor, PatientNow, Patron Technology, Payrix, Pinapple Payments, Propertybase, Quilt, School Status, Semarchy, SevenRooms, Signaturit Solutions, Singlewire Software, Skeepers, Skybox Security, Snap! Raise, SnapApp, Sovereign Sportsman Solutions, Stack Sports, Sympa, Talos Systems, Tentacle, Therapy Brands, ThreatConnect, Traliant, Transit Technologies, Tribute Technology, Untangle, Validity, Vehlo, Vertical Knowledge, Visualfabriq, Wagepoint, Worldwide Express, Your Cause

Other Locations:
4900 Main Street
Suite 330
Kansas City, MO 64112
Phone: 816-895-4300

15 Sloane Square
London SW1W 8ER
United Kingdom
Phone: 44-20-3997-1500

Key Executives:
Lori Ali, Managing Director/Head of Talent
617-544-8804
e-mail: lori.ali@psgequity.com
Bill Aliber, Managing Director
816-895-4301
e-mail: william.aliber@psgequity.com
Skip Besthoff, Managing Director
617-544-8852
e-mail: skip.besthoff@psgequity.com
Edward Chestnut, Managing Director
212-588-1327
e-mail: edward.chestnut@psgequity.com
John Clancy, Managing Director/Head of Portfolio Operations
617-544-8807
e-mail: john.clancy@psgequity.com
Rick Essex, Managing Director
617-544-8867
e-mail: rick.essex@psgequity.com
Marco Ferrari, Managing Director
617-544-8802
e-mail: marco.ferrari@psgequity.com
Edward Hughes, Managing Director
44-20-7514-8830
e-mail: edward.hughes@psgequity.co.uk
Sinisa Krnic, Managing Director, European Tax & Compliance
44-20-7514-8846
e-mail: sinisa.krnic@psgequity.co.uk
Charlotte Lawrence, Managing Director
44-20-3997-1525
e-mail: charlotte.lawrence@psgequity.co.uk
Lisa Lee, Managing Director
212-588-1328
e-mail: lisa.lee@psgequity.com
Adam Marcus, Managing Director
617-544-8853
e-mail: adam.marcus@psgequity.com

Venture Capital & Private Equity Firms / Domestic Firms

Aldo Mareuse, Managing Director
44-20-3997-1508
e-mail: aldo.mareuse@psgequity.co.uk
John Marquis, Managing Director
617-544-8808
e-mail: john.marquis@psgequity.com
Chip Pollard, Managing Director
617-544-8806
e-mail: chip.pollard@psgequity.com
Marc Puglia, Managing Director/Chief Financial Officer
401-277-5621
e-mail: marc.puglia@psgequity.com
Romain Railhac, Managing Director
44-20-3997-1522
e-mail: romain.railhac@psgequity.co.uk
Danny Rammal, Managing Director/Head of Europe
44-20-3997-1501
e-mail: dany.rammal@psgequity.co.uk
Tom Reardon, Managing Director
617-544-8803
e-mail: thomas.reardon@psgequity.com
Bill Skarinka, Managing Director
617-544-8809
e-mail: bill.skarinka@psgequity.com
Christian Stein, Managing Director
44-20-3997-1523
e-mail: christian.stein@psgequity.co.uk
Matt Stone, Managing Director
617-544-8810
e-mail: matthew.stone@psgequity.com
Peter Troost, Managing Director
617-544-8868
e-mail: peter.troost@psgequity.com
Charles Vernudachi, Managing Director, Business Development
44-20-7514-8808
e-mail: charles.vernudachi@psgequity.co.uk

1500 PSILOS GROUP
165 Broadway
Suite 2301
New York, NY 10006

Phone: 212-242-8844
web: www.psilos.com

Mission Statement: Seeks to investment time, energy and relationships into each opportunity, helping entrepreneurial partners to put in place operating capital structures that will support and enhance the quality and value of the businesses over the long-term and navigate through the normal ups and downs.

Geographic Preference: United States
Fund Size: $580 million
Founded: 1998
Average Investment: $20 - $25 million
Minimum Investment: $8 million
Investment Criteria: Revenue Stage, Later Stage
Industry Group Preference: Healthcare, Medical Technology, Healthcare Services, Healthcare Information Technology
Portfolio Companies: AngioScore, Caregiver Services, Gamma Medica-Ideas, HealthEdge, Mauna Kea Technologies, OmniGuide, PatientSafe Solutions, SeeChange Health

Other Locations:
21 Tamal Vista Boulevard
Suite 194
Corte Madera, CA 94925
Phone: 415-945-7010 **Fax:** 415-945-7011

100 N Guadalupe Street
Suite 203
Santa Fe, NM 87501
Phone: 505-995-8500 **Fax:** 505-995-8501

Key Executives:
Stephen M. Krupa, Managing Partner/CEO/COO
Education: BS, Mechanical Engineering, University of South Florida; MBA, Wharton School
Background: VP, Wasserstein Perella & Co; Associate, Kidder Peabody & Co; Mechanical Engineer/Manager New Business, Johnson Controls
Directorships: Active Health Management; ARTISTdirect.com; HealthScribe; Caregiver Services
David Eichler, Managing Partner
Education: MBA, Darden Graduate School of Business Administration, University of Virginia; MA, National Security, Georgetown University; Undergraduate, Government & International Relations, Cornell University
Background: Investment Banker, Wasserstein Perella & Company; Defense Policy Analyst, DynCorp

1501 PSL VENTURES
240 2nd Avenue South
Suite 300
Seattle, WA 98104

Phone: 206-202-2227
web: www.psl.com/ventures

Mission Statement: Aims to invest in early-stage, pre-seed, seed, and series A companies in the area of technology.

Geographic Preference: Pacific Northwest, United States
Fund Size: $80 Million
Average Investment: $500,000 - $2,000,000
Minimum Investment: $500,000
Investment Criteria: Technology, Pacific Northwest, Early Stage, Seed, Series A
Industry Group Preference: Technology
Portfolio Companies: Canotic, Inspo Network, JetClosing, Shukinko, StopDDoS, Taunt

Key Executives:
Greg Gottesman, Managing Director/Co-Founder
Education: Stanford University; Harvard Busines School; Harvard Law School
Background: Managing Director, Madrona Venture Group; Co-Founder, Madrona Venture Labs
Directorships: Board Member, Rover.com; Board Member, Mighty Ai; President Evergreen Venture Capital Association
Julie Sandler, Managing Director
Education: BA, MA, Psychology, Stanford University; MBA, Harvard Business School
Background: Partner, Madrona Venture Group; Senior Product Manager, Amazon; Product Management, Accenture; TechStreet.com
Directorships: University of Washington Foster School of Business; Washington Roundtable; Washington State Opportunity Scholarship
Geoff Entress, Managing Director/Co-Founder
Education: University of Michigan Law School; Tepper School of Business, Carnegie Mellon University; University of Notre Dame
Background: Voyager Capital; Madrona Venture; Perkins Coie; Jones Day; UrbanEarth.com; Salomon Brothers; The Prudential Home Mortgage Company; Mellon Bank; Priority Investment Management; Dusquesne Capital Management
Directorships: JettClosing; Hiya; Meritage Soups; Bonanza; Foodee; LiquidPlanner; Alliance of Angels

1502 PTV SCIENCES
3600 N. Capital of Texas Highway
Suite B180
Austin, TX 78746

Phone: 512-872-4000
e-mail: bplans@ptvsciences.com
web: www.ptvsciences.com

Venture Capital & Private Equity Firms / Domestic Firms

Mission Statement: PTV Sciences is a healthcare venture capital and growth equity firm focused on enabling healthcare entrepreneurs and global innovation.
Geographic Preference: United States
Fund Size: $191 million
Founded: 2003
Industry Group Preference: Healthcare, Life Sciences, Medical Devices, Biotechnology, Pharmaceuticals, Diagnostics
Portfolio Companies: Apollo Endosurgery, AsuraGen, Bioform Medical, Biomimetic, Cameron Health, Cardiva Medical, Corventis, GlycoMimetics, IDEV, Intersect, LDR, Mirna Therapeutics, Osteobiologics, On-X Life Technologies, Ortho Kinematics, Tryton Medical

Other Locations:
1000 Main
Suite 3250
Houston, TX 77002
Phone: 713-209-7555 **Fax:** 713-209-7599

Matthew S Crawford, Founding Managing Director
Education: BA, MBA, Wake Forest University
Background: Partner, Academy Funds; First Union Capital Markets Corporation
Directorships: Apollo Endosurgery, IDEV Technologies, LDR Spine, On-X-Life Technologies

1503 PURETECH VENTURES
500 Boylston Street
Suite 1600
Boston, MA 02116

Phone: 617-482-2333 **Fax:** 617-482-3337
web: www.puretechhealth.com

Mission Statement: Focuses on major unmet medical needs that have yet to be addressed by emerging science, and looks for cutting edge discoveries and technologies that have the potential to yield products with considerable market differentiation.
Investment Criteria: Early-Stage
Industry Group Preference: Therapeutics, Medical Devices, Diagnostics

Daphne Zohar, Founder/CEO
e-mail: dzohar@puretechventures.com
Directorships: Enlight Biosciences, Follica, Libra Biosciences, Vendanta Bioscience, Mandara Sciences, Karuna Pharmaceuticals, Tal Medical, Satori Pharmaceuticals
Stephen Muniz, COO
e-mail: smuniz@puretechventures.com
Education: BA, Economics & Accounting, College of the Holy Cross; JD, New England School of Law
Background: Partner, Edwards Angell Palmer & Dodge LLP
Eric Elenko, CIO
e-mail: eelenko@puretechventures.com
Education: BA, Biology, Swarthmore College; PhD, Biomedical Sciences, University of California, San Diego
Background: Consultant, McKinsey & Company; President, Technology Evaluation Group

1504 QED INVESTORS
web: www.qedinvestors.com

Mission Statement: QED Investors actively supports high-growth businesses that use information to compete - and win. While our support is tailored to the specific needs of each portfolio company, we typically provide a combination of both capital and capability. With operationally-oriented skills that we believe are both fundamentally applicable and broadly transferable, we enjoy working closely with a small set of carefully selected companies that range in size and style. But common to all of our partnerships is a shared conviction that information plays a decisive role in the success of the company, a mutual desire for a high degree of direct engagement, and a shared enthusiasm for experimentation and learning.
Industry Group Preference: Information Technology
Portfolio Companies: 2U, 33across, AddThis, ApplePie Capital, Audience Partners, Avant Credit, BlueYield, Borro, Can Capial, Card.com, China Rapid Finance, Credit Karma, Drive Factor, Fundera, Future Finance, Global Analytics, GreenSky, Klarna, L2C, LendUp, MediaMath, Mobile Posse, OnSwipe, Optoro, NU Bank, Orchard, peerTransfer, Privlo, Propane Taxi, Prosper, Red Ventures, Remitly, Signifyd, SoFi, Spruce Media, The Americas Card, Valen Analytics, Video Blocks, Videology, Vubiquity, WealthEngine

Key Executives:
Nigel Morris, Partner
Education: MBA, London Business School
Background: Co-Founder, Capital One Financial Services
Frank Rotman, Founding Partner
Education: BS, MS, University of Virginia
Background: Capital One

1505 QUABBIN CAPITAL
160 Federal Street
Boston, MA 02110

Phone: 617-330-9041
e-mail: info@quabbincapital.com
web: www.quabbincapital.com

Mission Statement: Is a privately held firm, concentrating, since 1990, in the private equity market. Boston Projects develops investment opportunities directly and through affiliated sponsors and intermediaries that include investment bankers, attorneys, and co-investor partners.
Portfolio Companies: Advanced Duplication Services, Ascendant Advisors Group, Archon Woodworks, Dan-Loc Bolt & Gasket, Inventus, Library Systems & Services, Mozido, Porter Group, RIMCO Royalty Partners, SAMBASafety, Southwaste Serivces, SPC TelEquip, Upper Crust

Key Executives:
John I Snow III, President/Managing Director
Education: BA, Economics, Amherst College; MS, Accounting, New York University
Background: Auditor, KPMG Peat Marwick
Directorships: Advanced Duplication Services, Hoffco, Inc., Purater Group Library Systems & Services, Remco Royalty Partners
Steven A Leese, Managing Director
Education: BA Economics, Amherst College; MBA, Harvard University
Background: Investment Banking, Merrill Lynch
Directorships: Dan-Lol; Bolt & Gasket; SPL Telegroup; Southwaste, Inc.; Onecare, Inc.

1506 QUAD PARTNERS
570 Lexington Avenue
36th Floor
New York, NY 10022

Phone: 212-724-2200
web: www.quadpartners.com

Mission Statement: Quad Partners was founded to make value-added private investments in the education industry.
Fund Size: $200 million
Founded: 1999
Industry Group Preference: Education
Portfolio Companies: B&H Education, Beckfield College, Blue Cliff College, Dorsey Schools, Noel-Levitz, Pacific College of Oriental Medicine, Stratford School, Swedish Institute, TargetX, The Learning Experience, Trillium College, ILSC Education Group, Inside Higher Ed, RuffaloCODY

Venture Capital & Private Equity Firms / Domestic Firms

Key Executives:
Lincoln E Frank, Managing Partner
Education: LL.M, Cambridge University; JD, University of Pennsylvania Law School; BA, Wesleyan University
Background: COO, JP Morgan; Banker, Goldman, Sachs & Company; Skadden Arps
Thomas H Kean, Advisory Partner
Education: MA, Columbia University Teachers College; BA, Princeton University
Background: President, Drew University; Governor, New Jersey
Daniel P Neuwirth, General Partner
Education: MBA, Amos Tuck School, Dartmouth; BA, Williams College
Background: Donaldson, Lufkin & Jenrette; Goldman, Sachs & Company
Stephen H Spahn, General Partner
Education: PhD, Columbia University; Univ. of Oxford; BA, Dartmouth College
Background: Headmaster/Owner, Dwight School; Founder, International School of London; John Catt Education Ltd.
Russell S Dritz, Principal
Education: BS, The Wharton School, University of Pennsylvania
Background: Banker, Credit Suisse First Boston

1507 QUAD-C MANAGEMENT
200 Garrett Street
Suite M
Charlottesville, VA 22902

Phone: 434-979-2070
e-mail: info@qc-inc.com
web: www.quadcmanagement.com

Mission Statement: To invest in profitable middle market companies with attractive growth opportunities where the firm can add value by providing capital and supporting the company's management and employees.

Geographic Preference: North America
Fund Size: $1 billion
Founded: 1989
Average Investment: $75 million
Minimum Investment: $25 million
Investment Criteria: LBO, Growth Capital
Industry Group Preference: Manufacturing, Distribution, Services
Portfolio Companies: @properties, A Stucki Company, Accoustical Material Services, AIT Worldwide Logistics, Asset Acceptance Capital Corp., Augusta Sportswear Group, Balboa Water Group, Behavioral Interventions, Boulder Scientific Company, Capital Tool & Design, Caribeean Restaurants, Century Graphics Corporation, Cloverhill Bakery, Colibri, Compassion-First Pet Hospitals, Curvature, Dental Care Alliance, Document Technologies, Durcon, EFC International, Galleher, Generation Brands, Heartland Automotive Services, Huddle House, Inmark, InterWrap, Joerns Healthcare, Krayden, Lexicon Marketing, MW Industries, Network Global Logistics, NuSil Technology, Pharm-Olam, Polaris Pool Holdings, Prism Vision Group, Rainbow Early Education, Red Robin Gourmet Burgers, Royal Adhesives & Sealants, Service Partners, Staff Leasing, Stanton Carpet, Stauber, Stimsonite Corporation, Tandus Flooring, TDS Logistics, Technimark, Transport Labor Contract, United Piece Dye Works, Universal Fiber Systems, Vaco, VMG Health, Wolf, Worldwide Express

Key Executives:
Terry Daniels, Chairman
Education: BA, University of Virginia; MBA, Colgate Darden School, University of Virginia
Background: Vice Chairman, WR Grace & Co; President, Western Publishing; Senior Vice President, Matel
Tony Ignaczak, Managing Partner
Education: BS, Wharton School; MBA, Harvard Business School
Background: Merrill Lynch; Bacus Communications
Steve Burns, Managing Partner
Education: BS, Boston College; MBA, Wharton School
Thad Jones, Partner
Education: BS, McIntire School of Commerce, University of Virginia
Background: Corporate Finance, Robinson-Humphrey; Croft & Bender
Directorships: Augusta Sportswear Group; Spa & Bath Holdings; Assset Acceptance Capital Corp
Tim Billings, Partner
Education: BS, Business Administration, Georgetown University
Background: Principal, MidOcean Partners
Directorships: Classic Party Rentals, Document Technologies, Generation Brands
Frank Winslow, Partner
Education: AB, Princeton University
Background: Consultant, Quantitative Strategies Group, Public Financial Management
Tom Hickey, Partner
Education: BA, Economics & English, University of Virginia; MBA, Harvard Business School
Background: Managing Director, Castle Harlan
Directorships: TLC Companies, Heartland Automotive Services
Michael Brooks, Partner
Education: BA, Bucknell University
Background: Leveraged Finance Group, Bear Stearns & Co.

1508 QUADRANGLE GROUP
New York, NY 10001

Phone: 212-418-1700
e-mail: info@quadranglegroup.com
web: www.quadranglegroup.com

Mission Statement: Quadrangle is a private investment fund that specializes in the global media and communications industry.

Geographic Preference: United States, Asia
Fund Size: $3 billion
Founded: 2000
Industry Group Preference: Information Services, Communications, Media
Portfolio Companies: Access Spectrum LLC, Bresnan Broadband, Cequel Communications, Cinemark, DataNet Communications, DHI Group Inc., Get AS, Grupo Corporativo Ono, Hargray Holdings, Lumos Networks, Mobility, NTELOS Holdings, NuVox Communications, PMC, Protection One, Publishing Group of America, Tower Vision, US LEC, West Corporation

Key Executives:
Michael Huber, President/Managing Principal
Education: BA magna cum laude Mathematics, Macalester College; MBA, Sloan School of Management
Background: Media and Communications, Donaldson, Lufkin & Jenrette; BellSouth
Directorships: Access Spectrum, Cequel Communications, DAVE Holdings, Hargray Holdings, NTELOS Holdings

1509 QUAKE CAPITAL PARTNERS
100 Congress Avenue
Suite 2000
Austin, TX 78701

web: www.quakecapital.com

Mission Statement: A venture capital fund and startup accelerator seeking to build startup ecosystems and enhance innovation across multiple industry verticals and geographies.

Geographic Preference: US, Europe
Average Investment: $100K - $150K

Venture Capital & Private Equity Firms / Domestic Firms

Industry Group Preference: Blockchain, AdTech, AgTech, Virtual Reality, Artificial Intelligence, Cellular Communications, Cyber Security, Energy, Robotics, Infrastructure, SaaS, Social Media, Logistics, Machine Learning, Manufacturing

Portfolio Companies: 17TeraWatts, 70 Millions Staffing, A la Carte Delivery, Abravax, Axle.AI, Adventr, Adway, AimSteady, Alteria Automation, Ampathy, AptivIO, AquaSprouts, BBy Inc., BC3 Technologies, Baarb, Baby Quip, CarServ, Cartogram, CatapultX, ChatQuery, CitySmart, CityGrowsm Contentplace, Data Gram, Dentidesk, Digital Claim, Doctors, Dripkit, Drofika, Elliegrid, Endorsify, EsportsOne, Everlasting Wardrobe, Family Plan, FenSense, Five to Nine, Flatlay, Gluetech, GoTRIBE, Good Boy Studies, Good Company, Hava Health, Health Hero, Informu, Junkless, Kericure, Kittery, Lilu, Locus Insights, Love Goodly, Man Outfitters, Marquii, Mickey Forest, MicroEra Power, Mirow, Morbax, Node Capital, Open Health Network, Ormigga, Partify, Pebby, QuickBRCare, Randian, Radial3D, Rain Systems, Ranked Media & Technologies, Rebus, Recoup Fitness, RideKleen, Saasuma, SeaProducts, SeeRoseGo, Socionado, SolePower, Sonic Sleep, Steereo, Stemless, ToMarket, Tracks N Teeth, Trainers Vault, University Beyond, Upside Health, Versusgame, Vetty, ViaHero, Voiceitt, VueBox, WearWorks, Whoseyourlandlord, Yip Yap

Key Executives:
  Glenn Argenbright, Founder/General Partner
  Education: LLB, University of San Diego
  Amy Coveny, Managing Partner
  Jason Fernandez, Managing Partner
  Dr Kai Buehler, Managing Partner

1510 QUAKER BIOVENTURES
Cira Centre
2929 Arch Street
Philadelphia, PA 19104-2868

Phone: 215-988-6800 Fax: 215-988-6801
e-mail: info@quakerpartners.com
web: www.quakerbio.com

Mission Statement: A venture capital firm dedicated to investing in life science companies located in the Mid-Atlantic region.

Geographic Preference: United States, Mid-Atlantic
Fund Size: $420 million
Founded: 2003
Average Investment: $5-$20 million
Minimum Investment: $2.5
Investment Criteria: All Stages, Superior Technology, Large market attraction
Industry Group Preference: Life Sciences, Medical Devices, Healthcare, Biopharmaceuticals, Healthcare Services
Portfolio Companies: Achillion, Amicus Therapeutics, Bioleap, Biolex, BioRexis, Celator Pharmaceuticals, Cellatope, Cempra, CorridorPharma, Diasome, DiscoveryLabs, Durata Therapeutics, EKR Therapeutics, Eximias, Horizon Pharma, Insmed, Intact Vascular, MedMark, NB Therapeutics, Neotropix, Neuronetics, NovaSom, NuPathe, New York Digital Health Accelerator, Optherion, Precision Dermatology, Precision Therapeutics, Protez Pharmaceuticals, RainDance Technologies, Regado, RapidMicro Biosystems, Semprae, TargetRx, Tarsa Therapeutics, TearScience, Tengion, TetraLogic, TransEnterix, Tranzyme Pharma

Key Executives:
  Brenda D Gavin, Founding Partner
  Education: Biology, Baylor University; DVM, University of Missouri; MBA, University of Texas
  Background: President, S.R. One; Director of Business Development, SmithKline Beecham Animal Health Products; Epidemiologist, Centers for Disease Control and Prevention
  Ira M Lubert, Founding Partner
  Education: BS, Pennsylvania State University;
  Background: Safeguard Scientifics; Founder, Radnor Venture Partners; Chairman/President, CompuCom Systems; IBM; Principal/Co-Founder, Independence Capital Partners
  P Sherrill Neff, Founding Partner
  Education: Wesleyan University; University of Michigan Law School
  Background: President/CEO/Director, Neose Technologies; Senior VP Corporate Development, U.S. Healthcare; Managing Director, Alex-Brown & Sons; Attorney, Morgan-Lewis & Brockius
  Directorships: Amicus Therapeutics; BioRexis; Regado Biosciences; Resource Capital Corporation; Greater Philadelphia Venture Group
  Richard S Kollender, Partner
  Education: BA, Franklin and Marshall College; MBA, Health Administration & Policy, University of Chicago
  Background: GlaxoSmithKline; CPA, KPMG Peat Marwick
  Directorships: Transport Pharmaceuticals; TargetRx
  Adele C Oliva, Partner
  Education: BSc, Finance, St. Joseph University; MBA, Marketing, Cornell University
  Background: Partner, Apax Partners; Baxter Healthcare; CoreStates Financial Corp.
  Directorships: EKR Therapeutics, NovaSom, Prometheus Labs, Semprea Laboratories

1511 QUALCOMM VENTURES
5775 Morehouse Drive
San Diego, CA 92121

web: www.qualcommventures.com

Mission Statement: Qualcomm Ventures is the investment arm of Qualcomm Inc., a Fortune 500 company with operations across the globe.

Geographic Preference: Worldwide
Fund Size: $100 million
Founded: 2000
Investment Criteria: Early- to Late-Stage
Industry Group Preference: Artificial Intelligence, Automotive, Data Center, Enterprise, Digital Health, IoT, Mobile
Portfolio Companies: Accuvally Inc., AirMap, Airspace Technologies, Airspan, Airstrip, AliveCor, Alo7, Amec, Amionx, Anteryon, Any Vision, AttackIQ, Attune Technologies, Bell Robotics, Bitbar, Bluestacks, Boohee, Borqs, Brain Corporation, Cambridge Wowo, Capillary Technologies, Carbon Robotics, CargoX, Cavendish Kinetics, Chukong Technologies, Clarifi, ClearMotion, Clinitron, CloudFare, Cohesity, Common Sensing, Creatcomm, Cyanogen, Doctor On Demand, Dover Microsystems, Dunamu, Earn, Elevoc, Enovix, Eques, Even, Excelero, FabHotels, Farmeasy, Flirtey, Foneric, Formula E, Gift Talk, Gizwits, goBalto, GouKW, GWC, Hi Technologies, Housejoy, ideaForge, IguanaFix, Ineda Systems, Ingresse, InnoMake, Innovium, inPlug, Jana, JobPlanet, Kaleo, Kneron, Loggi, Lookout, M87, Magic AI, Magic Leap, Magisto, Maketion, Mandaˆ, MangoPlate, Mantis Vision, MapMyIndia, MapR, Matterport, Medisafe, Memblaze, Memed, Meus Pedidos, Microduino, MindTickle, MoveInSync, NeoBear, Ninjacart, Noom, OneWeb, OpenSignal, Particle, Pitch Deck, Portea, PropTiger, Prospera, QuintoAndar, Reach Robotics, RetailNext, Reverie Language Technologies, Ridlr, ScyllaDB, Sense360, SenseTime, SevenInvensun, SEWORKS, Shadowfax, Siklu, SJ Semi, Skycatch, Sparta Science, Spire, Splacer, Spyce, Steelhouse Stellapps Technologies, Stratoscale, Swift Navigation, TabTale, Tango, Team 8, thatgamecompany, The Void, Tonbo Imaging, Toss Lab, Unisound, Verve, Viva Republica, Voluntis, WebRadar, weka.io, Welltok, Wha Tap, Wiliot, Workspot, XHoogee, XIMMERSE

Venture Capital & Private Equity Firms / Domestic Firms

Other Locations:
85 Cidade Moncoes
Sao Paulo CEP 045760-010
Brazil

6F Tower C, Beijing Global Trade Center
No. 36 North Third Ring Road East
Dongcheng District
Beijing 100013
China

1 Sutter Street
Suite 600
San Francisco, CA 94104

Doddanekudi Village Circle
Marathalli Outer Ring Road
Bangalore KA 560 037
India

4 HaHarash St
Neve Ne'eman
Hod HaSharon 4524075
Israel

3135 Kifer Road
Santa Clara, CA 95051

Key Executives:
Quinn Li, Senior Vice President/Global Head
Education: MBA, Cornell University; BS, MS, PhD, Electrical Engineering, Washington University, St. Louis
Background: IBM Systems; Lucent Technologies
Directorships: Airspan, Cohesity, Eero, Innovium, OneWeb, RetailNext, Verve, Zoom
Carlos Kokron, Vice President/Managing Director, North America
Education: BS, MS, Chemical Engineering; MBA, Haas School of Business, UC Berkeley
Background: Director, Intel Capital; Unilever; Unocal 76; Partner, Stratus Group
Directorships: Matterport, Spire, Particle, CargoX, Loggi, Ingresse, WebRadar
James Shen, Vice President/Managing Director, China
Education: BS, Electrical Engineering, Zhejiang University; MS, Communication Management, University of Southern California
Background: Head of QIS China, Qualcomm; GM, Tiani-BREW; Co-Founder, NeTrue Communications; VP, General Photonics
Merav Weinryb, Vice President/Managing Director, Israel
Education: BSc, Information Systems Engineering, the Technion; MBA, INSEAD
Background: Director, Intel Capital; Principal, Pitango Venture Capital
Directorships: Excelero, Magisto, Mantis Vision, Medisafe, ScyllaDB, Splacer, Stratoscale, Tab Tale, Tapingo, Weka.io, Zeek
Varsha Tagare, Managing Director, India
Education: MS, Electrical Engineering, University of Wisconsin, Madison; BE, Electrical Engineering, University of Bombay
Background: Intel Capital

1512 QUANTUM CAPITAL PARTNERS
1511 North Westshore Blvd.
Sutie 700
Tampa, FL 33607

Phone: 813-280-1720
e-mail: information@quantumcapitalpartners.com
web: www.quantumcapitalpartners.com

Mission Statement: Provides capital for privately owned, rapidly-growing businesses, primarily in the Southeastern United States.

Geographic Preference: Southeastern United States
Founded: 1998
Average Investment: $1 - $5 million
Minimum Investment: $500,000
Investment Criteria: Experience, laterstage, mezzanine
Industry Group Preference: Technology, Retailing, Manufacturing, Service Industries, Hospitals, Financial Services, Wholesale, Business to Business
Key Executives:
Stuart G Lasher, Managing Director
Background: CPA, KPMG Peat Marwick; CFO, Silk Greenhouse Inc; Co-Founder, National Business Solutions
Tyler Lasher, Partner
Education: University of South Florida
Background: Fitlife Foods; Co-Founder, Positive Lifestyle International
William J Schifino Jr, Director
Background: Williams, Reed, Weinstein, Schifino & Mangione P.A.

1513 QUARRY CAPITAL MANAGEMENT
2 Pleasant Street
Natick, MA 01760

Phone: 508-655-3540
web: www.quarrycapital.com

Mission Statement: A private investment firm that specializes in providing capital and/or advisory services to lower middle-market companies.

Geographic Preference: North America
Industry Group Preference: Manufacturing, Distribution, Business Products & Services, Retailing, Healthcare
Portfolio Companies: Royal Pet Supplies
Key Executives:
Brent P Johnstone, Managing Director
e-mail: bjohnstone@quarrycapital.com
Education: BA, Harvard College; MBA, Harvard Business School
Background: Thomson Financial; General Manager, TheMarketsPro; Founder, BulldogResearch.com

1514 QUEEN CITY ANGELS
4555 Lake Forest Drive
Suite 650
Cincinnati, OH 45242

Phone: 513-373-6972
e-mail: info@qca.com
web: www.qca.com

Mission Statement: The Queen City Angels (QCA) is the first group of experienced, accredited investors committed to accelerating the growth of outstanding early-stage businesses in the Cincinnati area and the surrounding region, via smart investments capable of producing a substantial return.

Geographic Preference: Cincinnati & Surrounding Region
Average Investment: $200,000 - $1 million
Investment Criteria: Early-Stage
Industry Group Preference: All Sectors Considered
Portfolio Companies: Akebia Therapeutics, Alliance Business Lending, AssureRx, Bioformix, Business Backers, CHMack, Collabornet, Copper Mountain Beverages, CoupSmart, EndoSphere, Define My Style, Ischemia Care, Miminally Invasive Devices, OnTrak Software, RhinoCyte, Safeway Safety Step, SoMoLend, SonarMed, Spine Form

1515 QUEST VENTURE PARTNERS
Menlo Park, CA

web: www.questvp.com

Mission Statement: Quest Venture Partners believes in entrepreneurism and the magnificent achievements the right team of individuals can accomplish.

Founded: 2007
Average Investment: $100,000 - $1.5 million
Investment Criteria: Early-Stage
Portfolio Companies: 500friends, App.ic, Crowdbooster, CrodFlower, Expect Labs, Genwi, HighlightCam, Ifeelgoods,

Venture Capital & Private Equity Firms / Domestic Firms

iSocket, PicCollage, Retailigence, Sociable Labs Stipple, Testmunk, theBouqs.com, Tripping, Whodini

Key Executives:
  Andrew Ogawa, Managing Partner
  e-mail: andrew@questvp.com
  Education: BA, Economics & East Asian Studies, University of California, Santa Barbara; MBA, International Management, Thunderbird
  Background: Manager, Daimler AG
  Directorships: Highlightcam, Fididel
  Marcus Ogawa, Managing Partner
  e-mail: marcus@questvp.com
  Education: BS, Computer Information Systems, Bentley University
  Directorships: Qik, Retailigence, Fididel
  Maarten 't Hooft, Managing Partner
  Background: Google; Android Team, Google; Mercury Software

1516 QUESTA CAPITAL
1156 15th Street NW
Suite 1101
Washington, DC 20005

e-mail: info@questacapital.com
web: www.questacapital.com

Mission Statement: Questa Capital invests and supports outstanding healthcare leaders who are striving to build the next generation of growth companies.

Founded: 1996
Average Investment: $15-40 million
Investment Criteria: Sectors: Healthcare Services, Healthcare Technology and Medical Devices

Other Locations:
  274 Brannan Street
  San Francisco, CA 94107

Key Executives:
  Ryan Drant, Founder/Managing Partner
  Education: BA, Stanford University
  Background: General Partner, New Enterprise Associates; Health Care Investment Banking Group
  Bradley Sloan, Founder/Managing Partner
  Education: BA, University of North Carolina
  Background: Senior Investment Professional, Parthenon Capital; Broadlane Inc.; Evercore Partners; MTS Health Partners

1517 QUESTMARK PARTNERS LP
2850 Quarry Lake Drive
Suite 301
Baltimore, MD 21209

web: www.questm.com

Mission Statement: Invest in emerging growth companies with exceptional management teams and proven products and services.

Geographic Preference: United States
Fund Size: $750 million
Founded: 1998
Average Investment: $5 - $15 million
Minimum Investment: $5 million
Investment Criteria: Late Stage growth companies in emerging markets
Industry Group Preference: Software, Medical Devices, E-Commerce & Manufacturing, Healthcare, Consumer Services
Portfolio Companies: Adara, Applause, Courion, Discover Books, Guavus, IntegenX, iStreamPlanet, Kodiak Networks, NComputing, Overture Networks, ServiceMax, Taulia, Teladoc, TrialPay, Vapotherm, Vidyo, Virtustream, Xirrus

Key Executives:
  Benjamin Schapiro, Founder/Partner
  410-895-5811
  Fax: 410-895-5808
  e-mail: bschapiro@questm.com
  Education: Economics, Randolph-Macon College
  Background: Alex Brown & Sons
  Directorships: Align, Aspect Medical, eHealthinsurance, Tisslink, Zaplet
  Mike Ward, Partner
  Education: Northwestern University; MBA, Harvard Business School
  Background: Management Consultant, Boston Consulting Group
  Directorships: Vapotherm, MedManage Systems

1518 QUILVEST CAPITAL PARTNERS
65 E 55th Street
25th Floor
New York, NY 10022

Phone: 212-920-3800
e-mail: communication@quilvestcapital.com
web: www.quilvestcapitalpartners.com

Mission Statement: Quilvest Capital Partners, with nearly 100 seasoned professionals, offers independent, global private equity and real estate solutions to private investors, families, and institutions around the world. During the past four decades, Quilvest has invested approximately $5B in over 300 private equity and real estate funds and 150 direct investments and remains dedicated to leveraging the experience, insights, and resources of the Quilvest Group to achieve superior returns. Formerly known as Quilvest Private Equity.

Geographic Preference: Worldwide
Fund Size: $5 billion
Founded: 2002
Industry Group Preference: Real Estate, Emerging Markets, Sectors & Technologies
Portfolio Companies: 5asec, Acrotec, Alliant Group, Aminoagro, Anthony's Pizza, Appirio, Bci Broadband, Bjb Education/Jade, Buzzparadise, The Chia Co., Command Alkon, Del Monte Foods, Deltek, Fci, Findis, Gamo, Hill And Valley, Igps, Innate Pharma, Intarcia, Intrinsic, Kadent/Landau, Laney Drilling, Marco Aldany, Masterskill, Matthews, Metro Franchising, Multiplan, Myriad, Neotract, Net4, Nocibe, Pashas, Pay-O-Matic, P.F. Chang's, Photobox, Poof-Slinky, Performance Food Group, Royalty Pharma, Schur Flexible, Smi, Stp, Thermasys, Tiendas 3b, Tiway Oil, Tortilla, Towry, Ubique, Vansken, Wholesome Sweetners, Yo! Sushi

Key Executives:
  Benton Cummings, Partner
  Education: BA, History, Dartmouth College; MBA, Kenan-Flagler Business School
  Background: Managing Director, Prospect Capital; Managing Director, Allied Capital
  Henrik Falktoft, Partner
  Education: MBA, Harvard Business School
  Background: Morgan Stanley, ZS Fund, Deutsche Bank
  Carlos Heneine, Senior Executive Officer, Quilvest Dubai
  Education: BS, Aeronautical Engineering, Imperial College of Science & Technology, London University; MBA, INSEAD
  Background: British Aerospace/BAE Systems; Consultant, Booz Allen & Hamilton; Mercer Management; Head of Strategy, Banque Sarador
  Michele Kinner, Senior Advisor
  Education: AB, Economics & Psychology, Smith College; MBA, Whittemore School, University of New Hampshire
  Background: Royal Bank of Canada; JPMorgan Chase; Chase Alternative Asset Management
  Marc Manasterski, Senior Partner
  Education: HND, Marketing, College of the Distributive Trades; MBA, INSEAD
  Background: CEO, Alliance Hospitality Group; Real Estate Development

Lawrence Neubauer, Partner
Education: AB, Woodrow Wilson School, Princeton University; JD, MBA, University of Chicago
Background: Centre Partners; Founding Member, Malakand Capital; SG Capital Partners; White & Case; Bankers Trust Company; U.S. Department of Commerce, The White House
Maninder Saluja, Partner & Head, Private Equity Funds
Education: BBA, Finance, University of Michigan; MBA, Harvard Business School
Background: Alvarez & Marsal; DLJ
Jean-Francois Le Ruyet, Partner
Education: HEC; MBA, Columbia Business School
Background: Senior Associate Consultant, Bain & Company; Junior Engagement Manager, McKinsey & Company

1520 QUINBROOK INFRASTRUCTURE PARTNERS
1330 Post Oak Blvd
Suite 1350
Houston, TX 77056

web: www.quinbrook.com

Mission Statement: Investors in low carbon and renewable energy infrastructure.
Geographic Preference: North America, UK, Australia
Average Investment: $25-150 million
Industry Group Preference: Low Carbon and Renewable Energy Infrastructure
Portfolio Companies: Cape byron Power, Energy Trade, Gemini Solar and Battery Storage Project, Glidepath Power Solutions, Lockyer, Scout Clean Energy, Velox Power
Other Locations:
53/54 Grosvenor Street
5th Floor
London W1K 3HU
United Kingdom
Phone: 44 207 818 8600

Suite 1.303
15-21 Via Roma
Isle of Capri, Queensland 4217
Australia
Phone: 61 7 5592 6669
Key Executives:
David Scaysbrook, Co-Founder & Managing Partner
Education: University of Sydney
Rory Quinlan, Co-Founder & Managing Partner
Education: Queensland University of Technology

1521 QUOTIDIAN VENTURES
New York, NY 10010

e-mail: hi@quotidian.co
web: www.quotidianventures.com

Mission Statement: Quotidian Ventures is a seed to early-stage investment fund that invests in great visionaries building global companies whose services we want to incorporate into our everyday life.
Founded: 2010
Average Investment: $100,000 - $200,000
Investment Criteria: Early-Stage, Seed-Stage
Industry Group Preference: Digital Media & Marketing, Entertainment, Advertising, Mobile, E-Commerce & Manufacturing, Publishing
Portfolio Companies: Admitted.ly, Artsicl, Amicus, Adcade, August, Bench, Brass Monkey, BringMeThat, Circa, Clip, Clothia, Comprehend, Disruption, Docracy, FaithStreet, FieldLens, Idea.me, IMRSV, Keychain Logistics, Knodes, Launchrock, Loverly, Matchbook, Memoir, Moveline, Nestio, PaintZen, SmartAsset, SmileBack, SponsorHub, SupplyHog, Tagstand, Tapad, Thinkful, Thinkup, Versa, Videolicious, Wallaby, WePow, YesGraph, Zerply

Key Executives:
Pedro Torres Picon, Managing Director

1522 RA CAPITAL MANAGEMENT
20 Park Plaza
Suite 1200
Boston, MA 02116

Phone: 617-778-2500
web: www.racap.com

Mission Statement: RA Capital Management invests in public and private healthcare and life science companies that are developing medications, devices, and diagnostics. RA Capital has a flexible approach and invests at multiple stages.
Industry Group Preference: Healthcare, Drug Development, Life Sciences, Medical Devices, Diagnostics
Portfolio Companies: 89bio, Aclaris Therapeutics, Adeo Health Science, Aeglea Biotherapeutics, Aimmune Therapeutics, Agrimetis, Akouos, Arvinas, Ascendis Pharma, Attune Pharmaceuticals, Audentes, Avexis, Bellicum Pharmaceuticals, Biohaven Pharmaceuticals, Black Diamond Therapeutics, BlueBirdBio, Blueprint Medicines, Braeburn, CalmImmune, Carnot, Cidara Therapeutics, Civitas Therapeutics, Clementia, Coherus Biosciences, Collegium Pharmaceutical, Crinetics, Dicerna, Dimension Therapeutics, Eidos, Eiger Biopharmaceuticals, Expansion Therapeutics, G1 Therapeutics, Galera Therapeutics, GBT, Imbria Pharmaceuticals, InflaRx, InhibRx, Intarcia, Ivantis, Juno Therapeutics, Kala Pharmaceuticals, KalVista, Lantos Technologies, Lumena Pharmaceuticals, Lyra Therapeutics, Medeor Therapeutics, Merus, Mitra Biotech, Moderna, Natera, Nivalis, Orchard Therapeutics, Ova Science, Precision Biosciences, Prevail Therapeutics, Protagonist Therapeutics, RaPharma, Reneo, RxSight, Satsuma, SeluxDx, Seres Therapeutics, Shockwave Medical, Sierra Oncology, Solid Biosciences, Sojournix, Spero Therapeutics, Stoke Therapeutics, SynthOrx, Taris, Terapore, Theriana Pharmaceuticals, Vella, Versartis, ViaCyte, Wave Life Sciences, WhiteSwell, Xenikos, Zafgen, ZS Pharma
Key Executives:
Peter Kolchinsky, Portfolio Manager/Managing Director
Education: BS, Cornell University; PhD, Virology, Harvard University
Directorships: Dicerna Pharmaceuticals, Wave Life Sciences
Rajeev Shah, Portfolio Manager/Managing Director
Education: BA, Cornell University
Background: Senior Project Leader, Altus Pharmaceuticals
Andrew Levin, Managing Director
Education: BSE, Princeton University; PhD, MIT; MD, Harvard Medical School
Background: Vice President, H.I.G. BioVentures
Josh Resnick, Managing Director
Education: BA, Williams College; MD; University of Pennsylvania; MBA, Wharton School
Background: President & Managing Partner, MRL Ventures Fund; Venture Partner, Atlas Venture; Partner, Prism Venture Partners

1523 RADIUS VENTURES
680 Fifth Avenue
Suite 1202
New York, NY 10019

web: www.radiusventures.com

Mission Statement: Radius Ventures is a venture capital firm that invests exclusively in leading edge healthcare companies. Radius searches for the winners of tomorrow - entrepreneurs whose ideas and talents qualify them to pursue large market opportunities successfully.
Fund Size: $200 million
Founded: 1997
Average Investment: $5-10 million

Venture Capital & Private Equity Firms / Domestic Firms

Investment Criteria: Mid-Late Stage
Industry Group Preference: Healthcare
Portfolio Companies: Aethon, Ambit Biosciences, Amicus Therapeutics, Athersys, BioStorage Technologies, Carekinesis, EndoGastric Solutions, Esionic, Healthsense, Management Health Solutions, Minimally Invasive Devices, Nugen Technologies, Tactile Systems Technology

Key Executives:
Jordan S Davis, Managing Partner
Education: MBA, JL Kellogg Graduate School; BA, State University of New York
Background: Managing Director, KBL Healthcare Acquisition Corporation; Private Client Services, Morgan Stanley;
Directorships: Health Language
Daniel C Lubin, Managing Partner
Education: BS Foreign Service, Georgetown University; MBA, Harvard Business School
Background: Director/Investment Banking Division, Schroder Wertheim & Company; Co-Founder/Managing Director, KBL Healthcare; Lending Officer, International Division, Manufacturers Hanover Trust
Directorships: Management Health Solutions, Healthsense
George M Milne, Jr. PhD, Venture Partner
Education: BS, Yale University; PhD, MIT
Background: Executive Vice President, Pfizer
Directorships: Mettler-Toledo, Inc.; MedImmune, Inc.; Charles River Laboratories, Inc.; Athersys, Inc.; Mystic Aquarium-Institute for Exploration; New York Botanical Gardens; BioStorage Tech
Vincent S Conti, Venture Partner
Background: President & CEO, Maine Medical Center; Board of Trustees, Dartmouth-Hitchcock Medical Center & Health System
Directorships: Healthscan
James M Mead, Venture Partner
Education: BS & MA, Penn State University
Background: Vice Chairman, BOD BlueCross Blue Shield Association; President & CEO, BlueCross Blue Shield Association
Directorships: Hershey Trust, Vitality Group LLC, Lebanon Valley College, Management Health Solutions, Milton Hershey School, Milton S Hershey Foundation, Greater Harrisburg Foundation
Neenah Jain, Chief Financial Officer
Education: BA, Southern Methodist University
Background: Senior Associate, Pricewaterhouse Coopers LLP; Controller, Capital Analytics

1524 RAF INDUSTRIES
50 Momentum Road
Suite 303
Bala Cynwyd, PA 19004

Phone: 215-572-0738 **Fax:** 215-576-1640
e-mail: acquisitions@rafind.com
web: www.rafind.com

Mission Statement: Acquires and operates a diversified group of middle market manufacturing companies located across the United States. Our acquisition focus is on Giftware and Promotional Products, Industrial Products and Building and D-I-Y Products. RAF Ventures invests in early-stage companies with unique niche products.

Geographic Preference: United States
Founded: 1979
Average Investment: $500,000-$5 million
Minimum Investment: $250,000
Investment Criteria: Early-stage, Unique products, Strong management
Industry Group Preference: Computer Related, Consumer Products, Electronic Components, Instrumentation, Industrial Equipment, Equipment, Medical & Health Related, Manufacturing
Portfolio Companies: Earth Tech, Geo-Solutions, American Millwork Corporation, Ferche Millwork, Materials Marketing, Steamist, U.S. Tape, Freedom Medical, Pine Environmental Services, Technical Gas Products, Campania International, Lazart Production, Cool Gear International, Thirstystone Resources, Bar-Plate Manufacturing, Disston Precision, MILSPRAY Military Technologies

Key Executives:
Robert A Fox, Chairman/CEO
Education: BS, Economics, University of Pennsylvania
Background: CEO, Warner Company
Directorships: InPhonic, Inc.; Wistar Institute; Foreign Policy Research Institute
Richard M Horowitz, President/COO
Education: JD, Harvard Law School; BA, Economics & Political Science, University of Pennsylvania
Background: Wolf, Block, Schorr and Solis-Cohen Law Firm
Directorships: Children's Crisis Treatment Center; Wistar Institute; UPenn's Center for Community Partnerships
Michael F Daly, VP/CFO
Education: MBA, BS, Business Management, Temple University
Background: CPA, Laventhol & Horwath
Andrew Souder, VP, Acquistions
Education: JD, Villanova University; MM, JL Kellogg Graduate School of Management; BBA, University of Notre Dame
Background: Corporate Law, Reed Smith Shaw McClay; Corporate Banking, Continental Bank NA

1525 RALLY VENTURES
702 Oak Grove Avenue
Menlo Park, CA 94025

Phone: 650-854-1200
web: www.rallyventures.com

Mission Statement: Rally Ventures is a venture capital firm focused on investing in early-stage companies in the business technology industry.

Fund Size: $100 million
Founded: 2012
Investment Criteria: Early Stage
Industry Group Preference: Business Technology, Enterprise Software
Portfolio Companies: 9Lenses, Appboy, Atlantis Computing, Backtrace, Badgeville, Beckon, Bugcrowd, Cloud Elements, Corvil, Coupa, DecisionNext, Edgewater Networks, Elevate, GutCheck, HiveIO, InsideTrack, Joyent, Kapta, Lithium, LockPath, Qubell, ReadyPulse, Sport Ngin, Sqrrl, VentureBeat, VisiTrend, Zipongo

Other Locations:
100 Washington Avenue S
Suite 1310
Minneapolis, MN 55401
Phone: 952-995-7450

Key Executives:
Charles Beeler, Managing Director
e-mail: charles@rallyventures.com
Education: BA, Colby College; MBA, Wharton School, University of Pennsylvania
Background: General Partner, El Dorado Ventures; Scripps Ventures; Piper Jaffray
Directorships: Atlantis Computing, Backtrace, Bugcrowd, Coupa, Joyent, Luxury Link, Qubell, Ready Pulse, Camp Chippewa Foundation
Jeff Hinck, Managing Director
e-mail: jeff@rallyventures.com
Education: BA, Economics, Northwestern University; JD, Harvard Law School
Background: General Partner, El Dorado Ventures; McKinsey & Company; Crescendo Ventures; CEO, Sistina Software
Directorships: Cloud Elements, Elevate, GutCheck, LockPath, Sport Ngin

Venture Capital & Private Equity Firms / Domestic Firms

Zenas Hutcheson, Venture Partner
e-mail: zenas@rallyventures.com
Background: Co-Founder, Vesbridge Partners; Co-Managing Partner, SPVC; CEO, Vivo Networks; CAECO; Control Automation
Directorships: Corvil, Kwicr, TA Labs, Visitrend, SaltDNA
Tom Peterson, Venture Partner
e-mail: tom@rallyventures.com
Background: Union Venture Corp.; El Dorado Ventures
Directorships: Appboy, Badgeville, Edgewater Networks, InsideTrack
Stephanie McCoy, Chief Financial Officer
e-mail: stephanie@rallyventures.com
Education: BA, Business & Accounting, University of St. Thomas
Background: PricewaterhouseCoopers; Crescendo Ventures; Decathlon Capital Partners

1526 RAND CAPITAL CORPORATION
2200 Rand Building
Buffalo, NY 14203

Phone: 716-853-0802 Fax: 716-854-8480
web: www.randcapital.com

Mission Statement: The primary focus of our investment strategy is to provide venture capital funds to small- to mid-sized companies headquartered in the Western and Upstate New York region.
Geographic Preference: Western & Upstate New York
Fund Size: $20 million
Founded: 1969
Average Investment: $50,000-$5 million
Investment Criteria: Private held companies, Unique or possess proprietary right (s), Membership on the company's Board of Directors, Duration of investment from 3-5 years
Industry Group Preference: Healthcare, Technology, Communications, Industrial Services
Portfolio Companies: BinOptics, Carolina Skiff, Chequed.com, First Wave Products Group, Gemcor II, G-TEC Natural Gas Systems, Knoa Software, Mercantile Adjustment Bureau, Mezmeriz, Microcision, QuaDPharma, Rheonix, SocialFlow, Somerset Gas Transmission Company, SOMS Technologies, Synacor

Key Executives:
Allen F Grum, President & CEO
Education: BA, Eisenhower College; MBA, Rochester Institute of Technology
Background: Executive VP, Hamilton Financial Corporation; Senior VP, Marine Midland Mortgage Corporation
Margaret Whalen Brechtel, Vice President, Finance
Education: BS, MBA, State University of New York, Buffalo
Background: Operations Finance Manager, Cellular One
Daniel P Penberthy, CFO/Executive Vice President
Education: MBA, State University of New Yor, Buffalo
Background: CFO, Greater Buffalo Partnership; Greater Buffalo Convention and Visitors Bureau; Senior Associate, Greater Buffalo Development Foundation; KPMG

1527 RAPTOR GROUP
401 W 14th Street
4th Floor
New York, NY 10014

Phone: 212-266-6900
web: www.raptorgroup.com

Mission Statement: Raptor Group is the venture capital arm of Raptor Capital Management LP. Partners with and deploy capital to early-stage, market disrupting technology and media companies to build the next generation of market leaders.
Investment Criteria: Early-Stage
Industry Group Preference: Technology, Media, Music, Advertising, Branded Goods, E-Commerce & Manufacturing, Digital Media & Marketing, Broadcasting, Sports, Gaming, Social Media, Travel & Leisure, Hospitality, Entertainment
Portfolio Companies: AS Roma, Boston Celtics, Raptor Sports Properties, Blue Bottle, FIGS, Hulafrog, Julep, Moven, Narragansett Beer, Nic and Zoe, Normal, Quirky, Room77, Reebok Spartan Race, Twine Health, Unreal Candy, Yasso, Zhena's, Airbnb, Artsy, Backplane, Biobeats, Bluefin Labs, Datapop, Depict, E 1023, The Echonest, Fliptop, General Assembly, GraphScience, IfOnly, Krush, Layer Vault, Magnitude Software, Matter, Media Spike, Metamarkets, NumberFire, Openbay, Open Sky, PlaceIQ, Qualia, Securitypoint Media, Velos, Sonic Notify, Spongecell, Spotify, Fancy, Ticket Evolution, Twitter, Uber, Workpop

Other Locations:
280 Congress Street
12th Floor
Boston, MA 02210
Phone: 617-772-4600

Key Executives:
James J Pallotta, Chairman/Managing Director
Education: BBA, Finance, University of Massachusetts; MBA, Northeastern University
Background: Essex Investment Management Company, Tudor Investment Management
Directorships: Boston Celtics, AS Roma
Harry DeMott, Managing Director
Education: BS, Economics, Princeton University; MBA, Stern School of Business
Background: Founder, Gothic Capital Management; King Street Capital Management; Knighthead Capital Management

1529 RAYMOND JAMES CAPITAL
Phone: 727-567-5066
e-mail: cindy.ford@raymondjames.com
web: www.raymondjames.com/ecm/rjcapital

Mission Statement: Raymond James Capital is the private equity subsidiary of Raymond James Financial.
Average Investment: $15 - $50 million
Investment Criteria: Recapitalizations, Management-Led Buyouts
Industry Group Preference: Consumer Products, Energy, Financial Services, Healthcare, Manufacturing
Portfolio Companies: Albion Medical Holdings, Event Photography Group, Sirchie Fingerprint Laboratories, Gabriel Logan, HVT Group, Southern Assisted Living, Souther Lithoplate

Key Executives:
David E Thomas Jr, Managing Director
Education: University of Richmond; JD, MBA, Emory University
Background: Chairman & CEO, Safety-Kleen Corp.; Head of Investment Banking, Raymond James Financial
Directorships: Albion Medical Holdings, Event Photography, Sirchie Acquisition Company
Gene J Ostrow, Managing Director
Education: University of Albany
Background: CFO, NationsRent; CFO, OHM Corp.; Senior Manager, KPMG
Directorships: Albion Medical Holdings, Event Photography Group, Sirchie Acquistion Company

1530 REACH CAPITAL
Palo Alto, CA

web: reachcapital.com

Mission Statement: Reach Capital invests in technology that helps improve classroom learning, digital learning, and takes education to new heights.
Founded: 2015

Venture Capital & Private Equity Firms / Domestic Firms

Industry Group Preference: Technology, Applications, Software, Education, Digital Learning
Portfolio Companies: Abl, AdmitHub, Atlas, Aura, Betterlesson, Bitwise Industries, BookNook, Breathe for Change, ClassDojo, Collegebacker, Crash, Desmos, Ellevation, Epic, eSpark Learning, Frank, Freshgrade, Future Fuel, Gradescope, GradeSlam, Handshake, Holberton, Hone, InClassToday, Kaymbu, Kickup, LAB4U, Lightneer, Lingokids, Lovevery, Mathpix, Mrs Wordsmith, Mystery Science, Nearpod, Newsela, Outschool, Padlet, PeopleGrove, Piper, Replit, Riipen, SchoolMint, Schoolzilla, Stellic, Sunlight, TeachFX, The Podcast App, Tinkergarten, Tynker, Winnie, WriteLab

Key Executives:
   Jennifer Carolan, General Partner
   Education: BA, Loyola University of Chicago; MA, Stanford University
   Background: Managing Director of Seed Fund, NewSchools Ventures Fund
   Directorships: Equal Opportunity Schools; Education Elements; Bullis Charter School; WriteLab; Nearpod; EdSurge; BetterLesson; FreshGrade; PeopleGrove; Outschool; Ellevation Education
   Shauntel Garvey, General Partner
   Education: BS, Chemical Engineering, MIT; MEd, Stanford Grad. School of Education; MBA, Stanford Grad. School of Business
   Background: Senior Engineer, Procter & Gamble; Partner, NewSchools Venture Fund
   Directorships: Tales2Go; Schoolzilla; Abl; Holberton School; Riipen
   Wayee Chu, General Partner
   Education: BA, University of Michigan
   Background: Financial Analyst, Morgan Stanley; Assistant VP, Merrill Lynch; Director of Finance, Lifestyle Media; Co-Founder, NewSchools Seed Fund
   Directorships: Wishbone.org
   Esteban Sosnik, General Partner
   Education: BA, University of Virginia
   Background: Analyst, JP Morgan; Associate, Innova Capital; CEO, Penguin Holdings; Co-Founder/CEO, Wanako Games; VP of Business Development, Vivendi; Co-Founder/CEO, Atakama Labs; VP, DeNa; Executive Director, co.lab
   Directorships: Farmacity SA

1531 RECIPROCAL VENTURES
100 Crosby Street
Suite 605
New York, NY 10012

e-mail: info@recinv.com
web: recvc.com

Mission Statement: A venture capital fund interested in tech-based companies.
Geographic Preference: US, Canada, UK
Average Investment: Up to $3 million
Investment Criteria: Seed, Early Stage
Industry Group Preference: Infrastructure, Software, Technology, Consumer, FinTech
Portfolio Companies: Baton, Extend, Fanbank, The Graph, Mindbridge, Qwil, Radar Relay, Tallarium, TradeIt

Key Executives:
   Michael Steinberg, Managing Partner
   Education: BA, University of Wisconsin
   Background: Portfolio Manager, SAC Capital Management
   Josh Kuzon, Managing Partner
   Education: BS, Lehigh University
   Background: Silicon Valley Bank; JP Morgan
   Craig Bural, Partner
   Education: Lafayette College
   Background: FiscalNote; Morgan Stanley

1532 RED CLAY CAPITAL HOLDINGS
1401 Peachtree Street
Suite 500
Atlanta, GA 30309-3142

Phone: 615-697-9144
e-mail: info@redclaycapital.com
web: redclaycapital.com

Mission Statement: A private investment firm focused on investing in and supporting the long-term development of growth-stage companies.
Geographic Preference: Southeastern US
Investment Criteria: Large Business (Fortune 1000); Government (Federal, State or Local; Revenue of $10 million to $50 million
Industry Group Preference: Manufacturing, Transportation, Infrastructure, B2B, Distribution Services
Portfolio Companies: Gray Line of Tennessee, Knowledge Architechts

Other Locations:
3200 West End Avenue
Suite 500
Nashville, TN 37203
Phone: 615-212-9136

Key Executives:
   C Mark Arnold, Partner
   e-mail: marnold@redclaycapital.com
   Education: BA, Brown University; MM, Finance, Northwestern University
   Background: VP of Operations, Gray Line of Tennessee; Founder/Chair, Nuestro Bano; Exec Dir. of Corp Development, BellSouth Corporation
   H Beecher Hicks, III, Partner
   e-mail: hhicks@redclaycapital.com
   Education: BA, Marketing, Morehouse College; MBA, Finance, University of North Carolina
   Background: Operating Principal, Onyx Capital Ventures; Investment Banker, Bank of America; Former White House Fellow
   H Bryan Britt, Principal
   e-mail: bbritt@redclaycapital.com
   Education: BBA, Clark Atlanta University
   Background: Analyst, Wachovia Securities; Member, Loan Syndications Group, Regions Capital Markets

1533 RED SEA VENTURES
120 East 23rd Street
New York, NY 10010

e-mail: hello@redseaventures.com
web: redseaventures.com

Mission Statement: A venture capital firm investing in early-stage startups focused on innovative technology.
Geographic Preference: New York
Founded: 2013
Investment Criteria: Early-Stage
Industry Group Preference: Technology
Portfolio Companies: Allbirds, Alwaysprepped, Ample Hills Creamery, Back To The Roots, Buster, Casetext, Convoy, Eargo, Elite Daily, Fabric, Fancy, FeVo, Fly, Genies, Goby, Insidehack, JanusRV, Joor, LeagueApps, Nest, Nucleus, Outdoor Voices, The Outline, Paintzen, Get Point, Prose, SkySafe, Smart Vision Labs, Solid X Partners Inc., Sweet Green, Tracksmith, Splash, Universal Standard, Violet Grey, Way Up, Zipdrug

Key Executives:
   Scott Birnbaum, Founder
   Education: Georgetown University; Fordham University Law School
   Background: Co-Founder, EPOL; Corporate Attorney, White & Case; Strategy & Business Development, CBS Local
   Directorships: Peace

Venture Capital & Private Equity Firms / Domestic Firms

Jason Fiedler, Principal
Education: BA, Economics, University of Pennsylvania
Background: Co-Founder, Splash.FM; Uber
Paul Strachman, Venture Partner
Education: BS, MS, Engineering, Ecole des Points et Chausees, France; MS, Finance & Economics, London School of Economics; MBA, Stanford Grad. School of Business
Background: Bain & Co.; Equinox

1534 RED SWAN VENTURES

Mission Statement: Red Swan invests in entrepreneurs who delight customers, create culture, and disrupt industries.

Portfolio Companies: Bonobos, Oscar, Birchbox, Warby Parker, Hailo, Wanelo, Floored, Scopely, Coinbase, RJMetrics, Harry's, Chloe + Isabel, TaskRabbit, 42 Floors, Matterport, Days, Grovo, Sunglass, Weddington Way, ID.me, Modern Meadow, AidIn, Thanx, RelayRides, SeatGeek, Help, OrderAhead, Betterment, Keychain Logistics, Whistle, Nomi, Cabify, Trumaker, Artivest, Cover, LayerVault, Evertrue, Spree Commerce, Hinge, Cambrian Genomics, PolicyMic, Building Robotics, Hightower, AltSchool

Key Executives:
Andy Dunn, Managing Director
Dave Eisenberg, General Partner
Chris Travers, General Partner

1535 REDHILLS VENTURES
PO Box 370369
Las Vegas, NV 89137-0369

Phone: 702-233-2160
e-mail: info@redhillsventures.com
web: www.redhillsventures.com

Mission Statement: To work with healthcare companies that clearly exhibit high growth potential.

Average Investment: $250,000 - $7 million
Industry Group Preference: Healthcare
Portfolio Companies: Adore Me, Communication Science, Global Medical Isotope Systems, Health Data Insights, Health Data Vision Inc., Intellicare, ItsMyNews, Ozonator, SimSuite, Trustifi, Velos

Key Executives:
Victor Chaltiel, Founder
e-mail: vchaltiel@redhillsventures.com
Education: Ecole Superieure des Sciences Economiques et Commercials; MBA, Harvard Business School
Background: Chairman & CEO, Total Renal Care Holdings; Chairman & CEO, Total Pharmaceutical Care; Baster International
Antoinette "Toni" Chaltiel, Founder/Manager
Education: Dublin City University
Background: President, Total Insurance and Planning Corporation

1536 REDMONT VENTURE PARTNERS
820 Shades Creek Parkway
Suite 1200
Birmingham, AL 35209

web: www.redmontcapital.com

Mission Statement: A private equity firm providing capital for early-stage and expansion stage opportunities.

Geographic Preference: Southeastern United States
Investment Criteria: Early-Stage, Expansion-Stage
Industry Group Preference: Business Products & Services, Financial Services, Healthcare, Information Technology, Industrial Manufacturing
Portfolio Companies: Aero-Mark MRO, America Rotor Company, Atherotech, Chlorogen, ContinuumRx, Emageon, Entegrat, FreeTextbooks.Com, High Ground Solutions, Hoffman Media, Locox, Ocera Therapeutics, Optimal IMX, Pennant Sp, PeopleTec, Reliant Medical Products, Source Medical, Vaxin, Wadley Crushed Stone Company, Water Science Technologies

Key Executives:
Roddy JH Clark, Partner Emeritus
e-mail: rclark@redmontvp.com
Education: BA, Political Science & History, Mercer University
Background: American Hospital Supply Corporation, Medfusion, Norell Healthcare, Horizon Medical Products, Myelotec, Gynecare
Directorships: Emageon, Folia, Reliant Medical Products, Chlorogen
Philip L Hodges, Managing Partner
e-mail: phodges@redmontvp.com
Education: BS, Business Administration, Samford University
Background: HealthSouth, Tubular Products Corporation, Atherotech
Directorships: American Legal Search, EnteGreat, Vaxin
Doug Sellers, Partner
Education: BS, Commerce & Business Administration, University of Alabama
Background: Co-Founder/EVP/CFO, Merchant Capital
Directorships: Children's Harbor; Brantwood Children's Home; American Red Cross of Central Alabama

1537 REDPOINT VENTURES
2969 Woodside Road
Woodside, CA 94062

Phone: 650-926-5600
web: www.redpoint.com

Mission Statement: Redpoint Ventures takes a three-tiered approach to starting businesses that bring value to young companies at every level.

Founded: 1999
Investment Criteria: Early Stage
Industry Group Preference: Communications, Enterprise Services, Storage, Mobile Communications Devices, Internet Technology, Infrastructure, Wireless Technologies, Software
Portfolio Companies: LaunchDarkly, Light Step, AppZen, TruSignal, Gigster, Bright Health, Essential Products, Cockroach Labs, RaiseMe, Astro, Chorus, Sentinel One, Nubank, Brandless, Sourcegraph, HashiCorp, Guild, Clara, Flexe, Justworks, Lifesize, Eero, Dremio, Duo Security, Collective Health, Nextdoor, Spring Path, Button Inc., Tenor, LuxeValet, Snowflake Computing, Vurb, Platform9, Victorious, Yunshan Networks, BitGo, RenRench.com, Just Eat, DraftKings, PocketGems, Qwilt, Caspida, RelateIQ, Pindrop Security, Apus, Tact.ai, Memoir, Acompli, Arista, Igneous, Refresh, 9Tong, Jauni, Bangcle, Looker, 117go.com, Lastline, Scripted, Twilio, Wochit, Curious.com, Bingdian, PSafe, Artic Wolf, Cyanogen, Pulse, Big Switch Networks, Zendesk, Tastemade, Sonos, IDreamSky, Open English, Stripe, Electric Imp, Axial, LoopNet, QuantiFind, Yixia, Moogsoft, Apple Toon, Trip.com, Intent Media, Mapr, Pure Storage, ThredUp, IntoNow, Viajanet.com.br, MMC Networks, Concur, Zuora, Xango, BlueFin Labs, Kabam, Machinima, Peel, Expensify, Miaozhen Systems, Posterous Spaces, Erply, Extole, Datameer, Tantalus, CouchDB Relax, 2U, Storsimple, NextG Networks, Gravity, Auditude, Internet Brands, Clicker, Cloud.com, Answers.com, Impact Radius, Heroku, BlueKai, True X Media, Hark, eBureau, FraudSciences, Adap.tv, Scribd., Innofidei, Qihoo 360, Fan.tv, KaDang, Gaia Online, Clearwell, Cgen, Jumptap, WiChorus, Right Media, Myspace, HomeAway, Intermolecular, Amec, Lead Point, Mobitv Inc., Zimbra, BCD Semiconductor, EfficientFrontier,

Other Locations:
27 Maiden Lane
7th Floor

Venture Capital & Private Equity Firms / Domestic Firms

San Francisco, CA 94108
Phone: 415-604-4100

1539 Nanjin Road West
Kerry Center, Tower 2
Suite 1801
Shanghai 200040
China
Phone: 86-21-6288-7757 **Fax:** 86-21-6288-7797

79 Jianguo Road
Hua Mao Center, Tower 2
9th Floor
Beijing 100025
China

Diamond Tower, Rue Joaquim Floriano
1120A, cj.92
Itaim Bibi
Sao Paulo, SP 04534-004
Brazil

Key Executives:
Allen Beasley, Partner Emeritus
Education: BA, Stanford University; MBA, Stanford Graduate School of Business
Background: Ipsilon Networks; Synopsys; Alex Brown & Sons
Directorships: Amp'd Mobile; OuterBay; Orbital Data; AirPlay; eNet
Jeff Brody, Founding Partner
Education: BS Engineering, University of California; MBA, Stanford School of Business
Background: General Partner, Brentwood Venture Capital; Comdisco Venture Leasing; Associate, Crosspoint Venture Partners; Schlumberger
Directorships: Anger, ePeople, Lets Talk, Loopnet, KMV, Kodiak
Tim Haley, Founding Partner
Education: BA, Philosophy, Santa Clara University
Background: Principal, Haley Associates
Directorships: Homestead Technologies, Movaris, M7, Netflix, Reflect.com
Tom Dyal, Founding Partner
Education: BS Electrical Engineering, Georgia Institute of Technology; MS Electrical Engineering, Stanford University
Background: Product Management, Bay Networks; Systems Engineer, AT&T Bell Labaoratories;
Directorships: Cortina Systems, Santera Systems, TopSpin Communications, Velio Communications, Vivace Network Tellabs
Chris Moore, Partner Emeritus
Education: BA, Mathematics/Economics, Dartmouth College; MBA, Stanford School of Business
Background: IVP, Business Development, wine.com; Management, Peapod; Ameritech; Financial Analyst, Wasserstein Perella & Co
Scott Raney, Managing Director
Education: BSEE, Duke University; MBA, Harvard Business School
Background: Senior Managing Partner, New Products/NorthPoint; Management Consultant, Bain & Company; Director Engineering, VideoPort Technologies; Advanced Technology Group, Andersen Consulting
John Walecka, Founding Partner
Education: BS, MS Engineering, Stanford University; MBA, Stanford University Graduate School of Business
Background: Director, Western Association of Venture Capitalists; Director, Stanford Business School Venture Capital Trust; Atherton Education Foundation; Management, Stanford University Smart Product Design Laboratory
Directorships: Stanford Business School Venture Capital Trust; Menlo Park Atherton Education Foundation
Geoff Yang, Founding Partner
Education: BSE Engineering/Management Systems/AB Economics, Princeton University; MBA, Stanford Graduate School of Business
Background: General Partner, IVP; Associate, First Century Partners; IBM
Directorships: Ask Jeeves, TiVo, Turnstone, Azul, BigBand Networks, Procket Networks, SyStream, Tahoe Networks, President's Information Technology Advisory Committee
Satish Dharmaraj, Managing Director
Education: BS, MS, Computer Science, Harvard University
Background: Founder/CEO, Zimbra; VP, Messaging Products Division, Openwave Systems
David Yuan, Partner, Head of Redpoint China
Education: BS, Electrical Engineering, MIT
Background: CEO, iTelco Communications
Annie Kadavy, Managing Director
Education: BA, MA, Biology & Organizational Business, Stanford University; MBA, Stanford Graduate School of Business
Background: Charles River Ventures; Bain & Company; Warby Parker; Uber Freight

1538 REDWOOD CAPITAL CORPORATION
PO Box 475668
San Francisco, CA 94147
Phone: 415-397-3800 **Fax:** 415-563-2127

Mission Statement: A family owned business that is well acquainted with the challenges facing the early stage company and its entrepreneurs, and is skilled at how to go about addressing those challenges.

Geographic Preference: San Francisco Bay Area
Founded: 1982
Average Investment: $10 - $25MM
Minimum Investment: $100,000
Investment Criteria: Early Stage
Industry Group Preference: Consumer Products
Portfolio Companies: eKnitting, GetRelevant, Airtreks, LeaseExchange, Native Minds, nextResort, ProClarity Corporation, TrueSAN Networks, Inc.

Key Executives:
Krist Jake, Founder/President
Education: BSE, Princeton University; MBA/MSE, Stanford University
Background: Co-Founder/Chairman, Denali National Park; Founder, San Francisco Ocean Film Festival

1539 REDWOOD CAPITAL GROUP
1 East Wacker Drive
Suite 1600
Chicago, IL 60601
Phone: 312-995-7300
web: redwoodcapgroup.com

Mission Statement: To be the foremost choice of institutional and private equity in pursuit of strategic multifamily investments.

Industry Group Preference: Real Estate, Property Management

Key Executives:
David Carlson, Co-Founder/Managing Director
Education: BS, Finance, University of Illinois; MBA, DePaul University
Background: Equity Residential; Onyx Capital International; Draper & Kramer
Mark Isaacson, Co-Founder/Managing Director
Background: EVP/CFO, Alliance Holdings; EVP/CFO, The Laramar Group; National Real Estate Division, Altschuler Melvoin and Glasser; Auditor, Deloitte and Touche
Bob Flannery, EVP/Chief Operating Officer
Education: BS, Northern Illinois University; MBA, Wayne State University
Background: President/COO, CA Residential; COO, JRG

Venture Capital & Private Equity Firms / Domestic Firms

Capital Partners; Partner/CFO, Jameson Sotheby's International Realty

1540 REEFI CAPITAL
555 West 5th Street
Los Angeles, CA 90013

Phone: 323-406-6892
e-mail: SBlumenthal@ReeFi.com
web: www.reefi.com

Mission Statement: ReeFi is a private equity firm specializing in real estate financing for the cannabis industry. ReeFi clients including greenhouse facilities, processing, warehouse, testing, & distribution facilities, and retail & dispensary locations.

Geographic Preference: US
Average Investment: $500,000-$10 million
Minimum Investment: $500,000
Industry Group Preference: Cannabis, Real Estate

Other Locations:
5727 South Lewis Avenue
Suite 210
Tulsa, OK 74105
Phone: 918-392-3200 **Fax:** 918-392-2861

1542 RELATIVITY CAPITAL
1040 Founders Row
Suite D
Greensboro, GA 30642

Phone: 706-352-4112 **Fax:** 706-453-0042
e-mail: info@relativitycap.com
web: relativitycap.com

Mission Statement: An independent fee-only registered investment advisory firm focused on providing portfolios constructed from its top down review process to seek out superior returns while striving to reduce portfolio risk along the way.

Industry Group Preference: Diversified

Other Locations:
85 Third Avenue
36th Floor
New York, NY 10022
Phone: 212-350-1540

Key Executives:
G Thomas Lackey, Jr, Managing Partner/Portfolio Manager
Education: BBA, University of Georgia
Background: Partner, Presidium Capital; Partner, Barber Lackey Financial Group
Jennifer D Lackey, Founder/Chief Compliance Officer
Education: Terry College of Business, University of Georgia
Background: Chief Compliance Officer, Barber Lackey Financial Group

1543 REMBRANDT VENTURE PARTNERS
San Francisco, CA 94111

Phone: 415-528-2900 **Fax:** 415-528-2901
web: www.rembrandtvc.com

Mission Statement: Rembrandt focuses on early stage technology companies, where it plays an active role in helping entrepreneurs grow companies.

Geographic Preference: Silicon Valley
Fund Size: $230 million
Founded: 2004
Investment Criteria: Early-Stage
Industry Group Preference: Technology, Internet, Infrastructure, Applications Software & Services, Communications, Wireless, New Media
Portfolio Companies: Allegiance, Appcelerator, Autopilot, Avaamo, Cavium Networks, CloudOn, Concurrent, Convio, Coveroo, Dynamic Signal, Electric Cloud, Good Technology, InsideView, IronPort, LiveRamp, LotLinx, Lytics, MetaLINCS, Needle, Netuitive, Ooyala, Pipedrive, Proximetry, Quark Games, RadialPoint, Rhythm NewMedia, SensorTower, Skybox Security, Smart Recruiters, Xactly Corporation, Zenprise

Key Executives:
Douglas Schrier, General Partner
Education: Economics/Pre-Med, DePauw University; MBA, Columbia Business School
Background: Senior Partner, Argo Global Capital; Senior Vice President, Acquisitions, SAIC
Directorships: Solect Technology Group, Multium Information Systems, VocalDAta, ODS Networks, Ceon, Narad Networks, Digital Bridges, World Wide Packets, Cosmocom, uReach
Gerald S Casilli, General Partner
Education: BS, Electrical Engineering, University of Pittsburgh
Background: Chairman, IKOS Systems; General Partner, Trinity Ventures; Founder & General Partner, Genesis Capital
Directorships: InsideView, Xactly Corporation
Scott Irwin, General Partner
Education: B.S., Systems Engineering, University of Virginia; MBA, UCLA Anderson School of Management
Background: General Partner, El Dorado Ventures
Directorships: Allegiance, Convio, InsideView, Lytics, Pipedrive, SensorTower, Tower Cloud, Webtrends
Pauline Duffy, Chief Financial Officer
Education: BS, Accounting, San Jose State University
Background: Controller, Prospero Ventures; Controller, CAD Solutions; Controller, Celtrix Pharmaceuticals

1544 RENAISSANCE VENTURES
33 South 13th Street
3rd Floor
Richmond, VA 23219

Phone: 804-643-5500
e-mail: info@renventures.com
web: www.renventures.com

Mission Statement: Renaissance Ventures and its affiliates invest in special situations across classes including mis-priced equity and debit securities and buy-out in both public and private markets.

Geographic Preference: Mid-Atlantic Region
Founded: 1997
Investment Criteria: Mis-priced equity and debt securities in the public markets.

Key Executives:
Herbert W Jackson, Managing Director
Education: BS, Business Administration, UNC-Chapel Hill
Background: Avanti Partners

1545 RENEWABLETECH VENTURES
Salt Lake City, UT 84111

e-mail: info@renewablevc.com
web: www.renewablevc.com

Mission Statement: RenewableTech Ventures is an early stage and growth stage venture fund investing in renewable energy, clean technology, energy conservation, green materials and other technologies. Entrepreneurs with innovative technology and green solutions should seek financing from RenewableTech Ventures.

Geographic Preference: Rocky Mountain Region of United States & Canada
Industry Group Preference: Renewable Energy, Clean Technology, Energy Efficiency, Information Technology, Life Sciences
Portfolio Companies: ACTR (GeoStrut), Ashtech, Consolidated Energy Systems, Solid Carbon Products, Waterton Polymer Products

Venture Capital & Private Equity Firms / Domestic Firms

Other Locations:
301 North End East
Suite 113
Rexburg, ID 83440

301 Main Street
Cardston, AB T0K 0K0
Canada

Key Executives:
Todd Stevens, Managing Director
Education: BS, Accounting & Management, University of Utah; MBA, Harvard Business School
Background: Founder & Managing Director, EPIC Ventures; Manager, Zions Bank Venture Capital Department
Directorships: Netcentives, i-Central, O'Currance, Vertical Technologies, MyFamily/The Generations Network, Cirque, ZARS Pharma
Dal Zemp, Venture Partner
Education: BA, Educational Psychology, MA, Brigham Young University; MBA, NYU Stern School of Business
Background: Founder, Ashtech Industries; Founder, Kodiak Mountain Stone; Founder, Whisper Creek Log Homes; Founder, Paradise Canyon Golf Resort & Land Corporation
Directorships: ACTR, Kodiak Mountain Stone, Whisper Creek Log Homes, Paradise Canyon Land Corporation, Recycle Wear USA
Robert Pothier, Venture Partner
Education: BS, Finance, Brigham Young University; Executive Program, Stanford University
Background: Venture Partner, EPIC Ventures; Partner, Wasatch Venture Fund III
Directorships: Rockford Corporation, CopperKey, Exagen Diagnostics, Lumidigm, Lytek, MyGeek, Yellowstone Hotel Systems

1546 RESEARCH CORPORATION TECHNOLOGIES
6440 N Swan Road
Suite 200
Tucson, AZ 85718

Phone: 520-748-4400 Fax: 520-748-0025
e-mail: communique@rctech.com
web: www.rctech.com

Founded: 1987
Investment Criteria: Early-Stage
Industry Group Preference: Biotechnology, Life Sciences, Medical Devices, Therapeutics
Portfolio Companies: APT Pharmaceuticals, BioCision, Catalyst Biosciences, Cylene Pharmaceuticals, Esperance Pharmaceuticals, Jenrin Discovery, OncoGenex Technologies, ParinGenix, Peptech, Sertoli Technologies, Spirogen, Therapeutic Human Polyclonals, Alerion Biomedical, Clear Catheter Systems, Kerberos Proximal Solutions, Option 3, OrthAlign, Varix Medical Corp., Vasonova

Key Executives:
Chad W Souvignier, Vice President
520-748-4400
e-mail: csouvignier@rctech.com
Education: BS, Chemistry, University of Wisconsin, Eau Claire; MS, Polymer Science, University of Akron; MBA, PhD, Materials Science & Engineering, University of Arizona
Background: Manager, International Marketing, Guilford Pharmaceuticals; Product Development, Proctor & Gamble

1547 RESERVOIR VENTURE PARTNERS
735 Ceramic Place
Suite 120
Westerville, OH 43081

Phone: 614-846-7241

Mission Statement: Reservoir Venture Partners is a Columbus, Ohio based venture capital firm bringing capital, business building acumen, and a strong network of advisors to entrepreneurs and their teams. RVP supports portfolio companies with dynamic guidance to our entrepreneurs in all key aspects of operations, governance and strategy. We genuinely believe that teams succeed.

Average Investment: $500,000 - $1 million
Investment Criteria: Early-Stage
Industry Group Preference: Information Technology, Healthcare, Clean Technology
Portfolio Companies: AxioMed Spine, Juventas Therapeutics, Imalux, Minimally Invasive Devices, Cine-tal Systems, iSqFt, Manta Media, Scale Computing, Nextumi, WebLinc, Xcelerate Media

Key Executives:
Curtis D Crocker, Managing Partner
e-mail: ccrocker@reservoirvp.com
Education: BS, Olivet Nazarene University; MBA, Indiana University
Background: Partner, Alpha Capital Partners; Partner, Northwest Ohio Venture Fund

1548 RESILIENCE CAPITAL PARTNERS
25101 Chagrin Boulevard
Suite 350
Cleveland, OH 44122

Phone: 216-292-0200 Fax: 216-292-4750
web: www.resiliencecapital.com

Mission Statement: A merchant banking firm focused on principal investing/investment banking services for companies in distressed and restructuring situations.

Geographic Preference: Midwest, Great Lakes Regions
Fund Size: $300 million
Founded: 2001
Average Investment: $25 million - $250 million
Industry Group Preference: Automotive, Manufacturing, Capital Goods, Chemicals, Plastics, Metals, Retailing, Transportation, Packaging, Distribution
Portfolio Companies: Aero Communications, Aerospace Products International, Affinity Specialty Apparel, ASC Signal, CR Brands, Flight Options, Hynes Industries, North Coast Minerals, PendaForm, Thermal Product Solutions, Thermal Solutions Manufacturing, WT Hardwoods Group

Key Executives:
Bassem A Mansour, Co-CEO
216-292-4748
Fax: 216-292-4750
e-mail: bmonsour@resiliencecapital.com
Education: MBA, Case Western Reserve University; BS, University of Dayton
Background: SVP, McDonald Investments Restructuring Group; Operations Manager, Northwest Micrographics
Steven H Rosen, Co-CEO
216-292-4535
Fax: 216-292-4750
e-mail: srosen@resiliencecapital.com
Education: BS, University of Maryland; MBA, Case Western Reserve University
Background: Management, Merrill Lynch & Company
David Glickman, Partner
e-mail: dglickman@resiliencecapital.com
Education: BA, Political Science, Washington & Jefferson College; MBA, University of Southern California
Background: Partner, Edgewater Capital
Ki Mixon, Partner
216-292-0503
Fax: 216-292-4750
e-mail: kmixon@resiliencecapital.com
Education: History, Wittenberg University; MBA, Weatherhead School of Management, Case Western Reserve University
Background: Associate, McDonald Investments;

1549 RESOLUTE.VC
San Francisco, CA

web: www.resolute.vc

Mission Statement: Resolute is focused on finding extraordinary entrepreneurs and helping them succeed over the course of their career. Resolute invests as little as $50K and as much as $750K in a company's initial financing. Resolute guides entrepreneurs to the key milestones for a successful venture round.

Portfolio Companies: BarkBox, Bitium, Blippy, Card.com, DJZ, DocRun, EidoSearch, Fancy Hands, Greenhouse, Gympact, Happier, Homejoy, Hopscotch, Influitive, iSocket, Kissmetrics, MessageMe, OKpanda, People.co, Reonomy, Rollbar, Runnable, Shop Hers, Signifyd, Webshots, Sunrise, TidePool, Vayable, Yardsale, Zenbox

Key Executives:
  Mike Hirshland, Founder

1550 RESONANT VENTURE PARTNERS
Ann Arbor, MI 48104

web: www.resonantvc.com

Mission Statement: Resonant Venture Partners is a venture capital firm focused on investing in seed stage companies in the software, services, and cloud infrastructure sectors.

Geographic Preference: United States
Founded: 2010
Average Investment: $500,000
Investment Criteria: Seed Stage, Early Stage
Industry Group Preference: Information Technology, Cloud Infrastructure, Software, Services
Portfolio Companies: Accio Energy, Bitfusion, Cargo, Deepfield, Duo Security, Filament, Orchestrate, Precog, Search Lateral, Sookasa, Stratos, Virta Labs, ZeroVM

Key Executives:
  Michael Godwin, Managing Director
  e-mail: michael@resonantvc.com
  Education: Berklee College of Music; MBA, University of Michigan
  Background: Managing Director, Wolverine Venture Fund, University of Michigan; Consultant & Software Engineer, Menlo Innovations; Independent Online Distribution Alliance; WebCrawler
  Directorships: Accio Energy, Pinoccio
  Jason Townsend, Managing Director
  e-mail: jason@resonantvc.com
  Education: BS, Computer Engineering, MBA, University of Michigan
  Background: Managing Director, Wolverine Venture Fund, University of Michigan; CEO, Life Magnetics; Founder & CEO, Ikanos Power; CEO, Townsend Investments; ITT Automotive; Chrysler
  Directorships: Protean, ZeroVM

1551 RESOURCE CAPITAL FUNDS
1400 Wewatta Street
Suite 850
Denver, CO 80202

Phone: 720-946-1444
web: www.resourcecapitalfunds.com

Mission Statement: Resource Capital Funds is a private equity firm specializing in the mining industry. RCF seeks to build successful companies with the ability to generate strong returns.

Geographic Preference: Worldwide
Fund Size: $2 billion
Founded: 1998
Average Investment: $10 - $300 million
Minimum Investment: $1 million
Industry Group Preference: Mining, Minerals, Metals, Energy
Portfolio Companies: AlloyCorp Mining, Ascot Resources, Atico Mining, Ausenco, Bannerman Resources, Blast Movement Technologies, Buffalo Coal, Coastal Ventures, Drummond Gold Limited, Firestone Diamonds, First Bauxite, First Nickel, Geopacific Resources, Global Advanced Metals, Gold Road Resources, IC Potash, India Resources Limited, Jolimont Global Mining Systems, Kingsgate Consolidated, Lighthouse Resources, Metalicity, MZI Resources, New Age Exploration, Noront Resources, NovaCopper, Nyota Minerals, Peninsula Energy, Piney Woods Resources, ProVale, Riversdale Resources, TMAC Resources, Toro Gold Limited, Uranium Resources, Vendetta Mining, Vimy Resources Limited, Wolf Minerals Limited

Other Locations:
  RCF Management LLC
  2 Jericho Plaza
  Suite 103
  Jericho, NY 11753
  Phone: 631-692-0043

  Resource Capital Funds Management Pty Ltd
  24 Kings Park Road
  Level 1
  West Perth WA 6004
  Australia
  Phone: 61-0864761900

  RCF Management (Toronto) Inc.
  25 York Street
  Suite 610
  Toronto, ON M5J 2V5
  Canada
  Phone: 647-726-0640

  RCF Management LLC
  Oficina de Representacion en Chile
  Nueva Costanera 4040, #31
  Vitacura, Santiago 7630000
  Chile
  Phone: 56-222454361

  RCF Management (UK) Ltd.
  33 St. James's Square
  St. James
  London SW1Y 5JS
  United Kingdom
  Phone: 44-2081327672

Key Executives:
  James McClements, Managing Partner
  e-mail: jtm@rcflp.com
  Education: University of Western Australia
  Background: NM Rothschild; Standard Chartered Bank
  Directorships: Global Advanced Metals Pty Ltd
  Ross Bhappu, Partner & Head, Mature Funds
  e-mail: rbhappu@rcflp.com
  Education: BS, MS, Metallurgical Engineering, University of Arizona; PhD, Mineral Economics, Colorado School of Mines
  Background: Director, Business Development, Newmont Mining Corporation; Cyprus Minerals Company
  Directorships: Lighthouse Resources, Piney Woods
  Russ Cranswick, Partner & Head, Fund
  e-mail: rcranswick@rcflp.com
  Education: BSc, Geology, University of British Columbia
  Background: Freeport McMoRan Gold Company; Kennecott Canada Inc.
  Directorships: Coastal Ventures, TMAC Resources Inc.
  Mason Hills, Chair of Partners & General Counsel
  e-mail: mhills@rcflp.com
  Education: BEc, University of Western Australia; LLB, Murdoch University
  Directorships: Global Advanced Metals, First Bauxite Corporation, First Drilling Group
  Michele Valenti, Partner & COO
  e-mail: mvalenti@rcflp.com

Venture Capital & Private Equity Firms / Domestic Firms

Education: BS, Accounting & International Business, New York University
Background: COO, Deutsche Bank; Nomura Securities; Merrill Lynch; Mahoney Cohen & Company

1552 RETAIL & RESTAURANT GROWTH CAPITAL LP
11700 Preston Road
Suite 660 PMB 411
Dallas, TX 75230

Phone: 214-766-8173 Fax: 469-533-1982
e-mail: rrgc@rrgcsbic.com
web: www.rrgcsbic.com

Mission Statement: Provides debt capital and strategic counsel to businesses operating in the retail and restaurant industry that have exhibited a potential for accelerated growth and expansion. The four general partners collectively have over 60 years of private investment, management, consulting and operating experience in the retail and restaurant industries.

Geographic Preference: United States
Fund Size: $60 million
Founded: 1996
Average Investment: $1-$3 million
Investment Criteria: Growth, Acquisition, Recapitalization, Buyouts
Industry Group Preference: Retailing, Restaurants, Services
Portfolio Companies: Quizno's, Elizabeth Arden, Texas Land & Cattle, Left at Albuquerque, The Art Store, Le Gourmet Chef, Walking Co., Cafe Express, Progressive Concepts, Beauty First, Uncle Julio's

Key Executives:
Raymond C Hemmig, General Partner
e-mail: rhemmig@rrgcsbic.com
Background: Chairman, ACE Cash Express; Executive, Hickory Farms; JC Penny; Grandy's Restaurant; Founding Partner, Hemmig & Martin
Directorships: Restoration Hardware; Elizabeth Arden Holdings; NASC Enterprises

J Eric Lawrence, General Partener
e-mail: elawrence@rrgcsbic.com
Background: Senior Consultant, Arthur Andersen, LLP; VP, Strategic Retail Ventures; Director Quizno's, Blue Cafe and Advisory Director, NASC Enterprises
Directorships: Progressive Concepts, Beauty First

Mark L Masinter, General Partener
e-mail: mmasinter@rrgcsbic.com
Education: BS, Political Science, Southern Methodist University
Background: Harber Masinter Company; Strategic Retail Ventures
Directorships: Le Gourmet Chef, Beauty First, The Walking Company, Shoes.com

Joseph L Harberg, President
e-mail: jharberg@rrgcsbic.com
Education: JD, University of Houston; BA, Business Administration, University of Texas
Background: Licensed Attorney; Harberg Masinter Company; Strategic Retail Ventures
Directorships: The Art Store, NASBIC, SoRASBIC

1553 RETHINK COMMUNITY
707 Westchester Ave.
Suite 401
White Plains, NY 10604

Phone: 914-269-0921
e-mail: info@rethink.vc
web: rethink.vc/community

Mission Statement: Rethink Community is focused on reinvigorating American communities through investments in real estate that maximize economic and civic growth. Investments center on improving education, housing, healthcare, and workforce opportunities.

Industry Group Preference: Housing, Education, Healthcare, Industry

Key Executives:
Michael Walden, Managing Partner
Education: BS, University of Richmond
Background: COO, Seavest Investment Group; Managing Director, Potomac Media Partners
Directorships: EverFi, Neverware

1554 RETHINK EDUCATION
707 Westchester Ave.
Suite 401
White Plains, NY 10604

Phone: 914-269-0921
e-mail: info@rethink.vc
web: rethink.vc/education

Mission Statement: Our education system is one of the last places to be remade by technology. That's about to change. We are investing in the people, ideas and companies that are rethinking the way we learn and teach. Rethink Education seeks to invest in progressive growth-stage companies that are at the forefront of the education technology industry and have the capacity to make positive impacts on our communities.

Investment Criteria: Growth-Stage
Industry Group Preference: Education
Portfolio Companies: 2U, Abl, Ace Learning, AdmitHub, AllHere, Allovue, American Prison Data Systems, Bridge International Academies, Bear, Bridge International Academy, BrightBytes, Burning Glass, CareAcademy, Civitas Learning, Clark, Cognitive Toy Box, Course Report, Crehana, Degreed, Edmit, Education Elements, Ellevation, Engrade, Entangled Ventures, EverFi, Flocabulary, Formative, General Assembly, Guild, Hapara, Hickory, Intellus Learning, Invibed, Kenzie Academy, KiraKira3D, Knowledge to Practice, Lessonly, McGraw-Hill, MedAux, MissionU, Neverware, NoodleMarkets, NoRedInk, Pathbrite, PathStream, Plianced, Pluralsight, Rethink, Rethink Autism, Second Accent, Sixup, Smarterer, StraighterLine, Student Opportunity Center, SV Academy, Trilogy Education Services, Toot, Upswing, VidCode, Voxy, Wonda VR, Wonderschool

Key Executives:
Rick Segal, Managing Partner
Education: BA, English, Wesleyan University
Background: Founder, Seavest
Directorships: Advanced Prison Data Systems, Flocabulary, Knowlege to Practice, Noodle Markets, Voxy, Civitas, Speakaboos

Matt Greenfield, Managing Partner
Education: BA, MA, PhD, English, Yale University
Background: Founder, Stonework Capital; Associate, ABS Ventures
Directorships: Allovue, Brightgytes, CareAcademy, Kenzie Academy, NoRedInk

Michael Walden, Managing Partner, Rethink
Background: COO, Seavest Financial Group; Managing Director, Potomac Media Partners; EVP, InPhonic
Directorships: EverFi, Neverware

Brandon Avrutin, Venture Partner
Education: BA, Philosphy & Economics, Middlebury College
Background: Investment Associate, Seavest Capital Partners; Investmant Banking Analyst, Lazard

Venture Capital & Private Equity Firms / Domestic Firms

1555 RETHINK IMPACT
707 Westchester Ave.
Suite 401
White Plains, NY 10604

Phone: 914-269-0921
e-mail: info@rethink.vc
web: rethink.vc/impact

Mission Statement: Rethink Impact is a venture capital firm that invests in female leaders in technology.

Industry Group Preference: Technology
Portfolio Companies: Aclime, Angaza, Catchafire, Change.org, Classy, Everfi, Evidation, Ketos, Neurotrack, Purpose, Sempre Health, Spring, Univfy, Winnie

Key Executives:
  Jenny Abramson, Founder/Managing Partner
  Education: BA, MA, Stanford University; MBA, Harvard Business School
  Background: CEO, LiveSafe
  Heidi Patel, Partner
  Education: AB, Princeton University; MBA, Stanford Graduate School of Business
  Background: Director, Pacific Community Ventures; Founding Member, AOL Time Warner Ventures; Credit Suisse First Boston
  Kate Castle, Partner/Chief Marketing Officer
  Education: BA, Wheaton College
  Background: Marketing Partner, Flybridge Capital Partners; Co-Founder/Operating Partner, XFactor Ventures

1556 REV1 VENTURES
1275 Kinnear Road
Columbus, OH 43212

Phone: 614-487-3700
e-mail: info@rev1ventures.com
web: www.rev1ventures.com

Mission Statement: Rev1 Ventures provides investment capital for commercialization of innovations in information technology, advanced materials and medical technology. Supports early-stage, Ohio-based entities by facilitating risk sharing on opportunities with high upside potential.

Geographic Preference: Ohio
Industry Group Preference: Information Technology, Advanced Materials, Medical Technology
Portfolio Companies: 7signal Solutions, Acceptd, AircraftLogs, AquaBlok, AssureRx Health, Brand Thunder, BringShare, Capture Education, CardiOx, Clarivoy, ClearSaleing, Cryothermic Systems, Ecolibrium Solar, EndoSphere, Exacter, Great Lakes Pharmaceuticals, HTP, l2C Technologies, IncludeFitness, inmobly, Intelligent Mobile Support, Midwest MicroDevices, Minimally Invasive Devices, NanoStatics, nChannel, Neuros Medical, PreEmptive Solutions, SageQuest, SeeMore Interactive, Seen Digital Media, SironRx Therapeutics, SparkBase, T-Pro Solutions, TheraVase, Traycer Systems, Znode

Other Locations:
  Rev1 Gateway
  1590 North High Street
  Columbus, OH 43201

Key Executives:
  Tom Walker, President/CEO
  Education: BS, University of Oklahoma; MBA, Oklahoma City University
  Background: Business Development Manager, Battelle; CEO/Executive Director, Oklahoma Investment Forum; Founder, SeedStep Angels; President/CEO, i2E Inc.
  Kristy Campbell, Chief Operating Officer
  Education: BS, Ohio University; MBA, Ashland University
  Background: Marketing Manager, Logica; EC Outlook Inc.; Evolving Systems; Director of Marketing, Title First Agency; Saama; Director of Digital Marketing, Manta; Chief Marketing Officer, Rev1 Ventures
  David Dillman, Chief Financial Officer/Chief Compliance Officer
  Education: BS, University of Montana
  Background: Accounting Manager, Boone and Crockett Club; Controller, Enterprise Holdings

1557 REVEL PARTNERS
110 Greene Street
Suite 703
New York, NY 10012

web: www.revelpartners.com

Mission Statement: Revel Partners is a team of experienced entrepreneurs and investors that provides growth capital to exceptional management teams and helps them build leading digital media businesses.

Average Investment: $500,000 - $3 million
Investment Criteria: Early-Expansion Stage
Industry Group Preference: Digital Media & Marketing, Internet, Software, Consumer Services, Social Media
Portfolio Companies: Acre Trader, Akorda, Augmented Radar Imaging, Cadence, Curacity, Fetcher, Instnt, Lawmatics, Lawyaw, Lending Front, MarketMuse, Native Voice, Nexosis, Omnichain, Populus, Sourcify, STAQ, SupplyAI, Tenovos, Zylo Tech, Zype

Key Executives:
  Joe Apprendi, Partner
  Education: BA, Economics, Oberlin College
  Background: Founder & CEO, Collective; K2 Digital; CLIQNOW! Sales Group, 24/7 Media, Eyeblaster; Klipmart; Falk eSolutions
  Thomas Falk, Partner
  Background: CEO, eValue Group; Founder, Falk & Partners
  Chris Young, Partner
  Education: BS, Business, Skidmore College; MBA, Rensselaer Polytechnic Institute
  Background: Chairman & CEO, Digital Broadcasting Group; Co-Founder, Klipmart
  John Vincent, Partner
  Education: BA, Psychology, Vanderbilt University
  Background: CEO/Co-Founder, EyeWonder; Leap Online; Magellan TSA; Place Space Media; Captive Concepts

1558 REVOLUTION LLC
1717 Rhode Island Avenue NW
Suite 1000
Washington, DC 20036

Phone: 202-776-1400
web: www.revolution.com

Mission Statement: Revolution invests in companies attacking traditional industries on the brink of disruptive change.

Geographic Preference: Eastern U.S.
Fund Size: $200 million
Average Investment: $4-8 million
Investment Criteria: Startups; Early Stage
Industry Group Preference: Education, Financial Services, Sports, Media & Entertainment, Marketplaces, Software & Services, Transportation, Hospitality & Travel, E-Commerce & Manufacturing, Health
Portfolio Companies: Aura, BenchPrep, Bloomscape, Bright Cellars, Busbud, eSUB Construction Software, Good Buy Gear, Homesnap, Member Suite, Mint House, Paro, Policy Genius, Resolute AI

Key Executives:
  Tige Savage, Managing Partner
  Education: BBA, James Madison University; MBA, University of Michigan Ross School of Business
  Background: Vice President, Time Warner Ventures; Founding Team, Riggs Capital Partners
  Directorships: AddThis, Homeshap, Booker, Flexcar, HelloWallet, LivingSocial, NewBrand Analytics, Personal, Revolution Money, Snagfilms, UberMedia

Venture Capital & Private Equity Firms / Domestic Firms

David Golden, Managing Partner
Education: AB, Harvard University; JD, Harvard Law School
Background: JPMorgan, Hambrecht & Quist, Code Advisors
Directorships: Barnes & Noble, Blackbaud, Everyday Health, Vinfolio
Clara Sieg, Partner
Education: Stanford University
Background: UBS Investment Bank; Probitas Partners
Directorships: Busbud; Framebridge; PolicyGenius

1559 REX HEALTH VENTURES
310 S Harrington Street
Raleigh, NC 27603

web: www.rexhealthventures.com

Mission Statement: Rex Health Ventures is part of Rex Healthcare's groundbreaking innovation platform, Rex Strategic Innovation. RHV features an early stage venture fund, a team of healthcare and investment professionals and a commitment to improving patient care.

Average Investment: $250,000 - $2 million
Investment Criteria: All Stages Considered
Industry Group Preference: Healthcare Information Technology, Healthcare Services, Medical Devices, Biopharmaceuticals
Portfolio Companies: Aerial Biopharma, Arrive BioVentures, Awarepoint, Baebies, BardyDX, Emergo Therapeutics, Gauss Surgical, Kit Check, Midnight Pharma LLC, Phononic, Phynd Technologies, Target Pharmasolutions, Veran Medical Technologies

Key Executives:

Bobby Helmedag, Managing Director
Education: BS, Finance, University of Notre Dame
Background: BlueCross BlueShield of Tennessee, Citigroup, KPMG
Directorships: Aerial BioPharma
Anita Watkins, Director, Strategic Innovation
Education: MS/JD, University of North Carolina
Background: VP, Government Relations, University of North Carolina
Ray Jang, Associate
Education: BS, Biochemistry & Economics, University of California San Diego; MBA, University of North Carolina

1560 RFE INVESTMENT PARTNERS
36 Grove Street
New Canaan, CT 06840

Phone: 203-966-2800
e-mail: info@rfeip.com
web: www.rfeip.com

Mission Statement: A private equity investment firm focusing on smaller middle-market service, manufacturing and distribution businesses.

Geographic Preference: United States
Fund Size: $300 million
Founded: 1979
Average Investment: $10-$25 million
Minimum Investment: $5 million
Investment Criteria: Partner with management to acquire majority interests in smaller middle market companies, that passes leading marketShare positions in their care niche market.
Industry Group Preference: Manufacturing, Distribution, Services
Portfolio Companies: AbelConn Holdings, Advanced Technology Services, Baxter Manufacturing, Brooks & Whittle Limited, Camino Modular Systems, Cattron Group, CBT Technology, Commonwealth Business Media, ConsoliDent, DelStar Technologies, Flow Solutions, Great Clips, Hastings Holdings Corporation, Health Watch Holdings, HTI Technologies Holding Corporation, iMedX Holdings, JSI Store Fixtures, Kenan Advantage Group, Lectrus Corporation, McKenzie Sports Products, Metalico, Nudo Products, OK Indutries, PCX Aerostructures, Pro Active Therapy, PureRed Integrated Marketing, Rescare, Scandura Holdings, Seed Holdings, ShelterLogic Investment, Sun Healthcare, Washington Inventory Service

Key Executives:

Michael J Foster, Senior Managing Director/Chief Compliance Officer
e-mail: mfoster@rfeip.com
Education: BS, Doctor of Jurisprudence, Cornell University
Background: Partner, O'Sullivan Graev & Karabell
Directorships: Brook & Whittle Ltd, Extrusion Technology Inc., iMedX Inc, Lectrus, Plantation Products Inc.
James A Parsons, Senior Managing Director
e-mail: jparsons@rfeip.com
Education: MBA, University of Michigan; BA, Williams College
Background: Michigan Capital; NBD Bancorp, Inc.
Directorships: AbelComm LLC, Brook & Whittle Ltd, iMedX Inc., Lectrus Corp., Plantation Products
Donald A Juricic, Managing Director/Chief Financial Officer
e-mail: djuricic@rfeip.com
Education: BS, Villanova University; MBA, New York University
Background: Control Data Corporation
Ned Truslow, Managing Director
e-mail: ntruslow@rfeip.com
Education: MA, University of St Andrews, Scotland; MBA, University of Texas
Background: Columbia Naples Capital
Directorships: AbelConn LLC, Nudo Products, TradeSource Inc.
R Peter Reiter, Jr, Managing Director, Business Development
e-mail: preiter@rfeip.com
Education: BBA, Iona College; MBA, New York University
Background: KPMG Peat Marwick
Directorships: Extrusion Technology Inc., iMedX Inc., Lectrus Corp, Plantation Products Inc.
Michael W Rubel, Managing Director
e-mail: mrubel@rfeip.com
Education: BBA, James Madison University; MBA, Duke University
Background: Weston Presido
Directorships: iMedX Inc., Plantation Products Inc.

1561 RHO VENTURES
Carnigie Hall Tower
152 W 57th Street
23rd Floor
New York, NY 10019

Phone: 212-751-6677 Fax: 212-751-3613
web: www.rhoventures.com

Mission Statement: Rho Ventures invests in innovators that redefine the status quo. RhoBs investment philosphy does not fit a conventional model. Rho believes that formulaic approaches to investing lead to risk adverse strategies that stifle innovation. As a result, Rho is not bound by a particular stage of investment and do not shy away from contrarian ideas.

Fund Size: Rho Ventures VI: $510 million
Founded: 1981
Average Investment: $10 million
Minimum Investment: $1 million
Investment Criteria: All stages
Industry Group Preference: Electronic Technology, Internet Technology, Telecommunications, Computer Hardware & Software, Biotechnology, Healthcare, New Media, Healthcare, New Energy, Information Technology, Biopharmaceuticals, Medical Devices, Communications

Portfolio Companies: 3DP, Active Power, AddThis, Advancis/Middle Brook, Airspan Networks, Alibre, Alien Technology, AlleWin Technologies, Amp'd Mobile, Ample Communications, Anacor Pharmaceuticals, Ansa, AnswerSoft, Applied Science Fiction, AqueSys, Archemix, Archimede Technology Group, Aristacom, Aristotle Circle, August, Auto Data Network, Avolent, BioTransplant, Bluefly, BroadLogic, Calera, Capstone Turbine Corporation, Cara Therapeutics, Carparts/ADN, Celtro, Celunol, Cesura, ChaCha, Channel Insight, ChargePoint, Chiaro Networks, Chorum Technologies, Ciena, Ciris Energy, Claremont, Clear Urban Energy, CloudPay, COM21, Commerce One, Compaq, ComSpace, Constellar, Convercent, Convex, Convey Computer, Copper Mountain, Coral Network, Corton Precision Optical Company, CRB Innovations, Crosstrees Medical, Crystal Semi, Cypress Semiconductor, CytoMed, Dashlane, Delsys Pharmaceutical, Dendreon, diaDexus, Differential Diagnostics, Dyax, EAI-Vista, Eclat, Effective Measure, eMachines, Emerald Solutions, EndoMedix, Enerkem, enherent, Enmass, Eracom, eTang, Everdream, Everyday Health, Excara, Eziba, Fintech Lab, Fractal Systems, Feneral Paramterics, Genetic Therapy, GenVec, GetGlue, Global Exchange Services, Gloucester Pharmaceuticals, GynoPharma, Health Allies, HealthSynq, Human Genome Science, IdenTrust, Ingenuity, InnerWireless, Innova Dynamics, Inotek, inPowered, Integral Wave, IntraLinks, Intransa, Ipsum Networks, ItzBig, iVillage, JustFav, Kana Software, KD 1, Landmark Graphics, LeukoSite, Lightpointe, Longwall, LucidLogix, Lukens, Magainin, Main Control, Mandalay Sports Media, Market 6, Medigene, MedImmune, Megapath, Memory Pharmaceuticals, Meriton, Mersana, Metropolitan, Miniscribe, Minster, MIPS Computer, MM Companies, Monterey Design Systems, more.com, MPV, Multispectral Imaging, MyBuys, National Pain Institute, NeoWorld, NephroGenex, NEXTEC, NGM, NitroMed, Nora Therapeutics, Now Public, NuMega, Nuventix, nuvoTV, Oloop, OMGPOP, ON24, OnCart, Oncologix, Optical Micro-Machines, Potilink, Orametrix, Orqis Medical, Osteo Arthritis Sciences, Osteotech, Parlo, Pediatric Pharma, Peranet, Perfect Commerce, Pharmagenics, Pharmavene, Philo, Phone-Orr, PHT, Powerful Media, Precision Demand, Premier Allergy, Premier Ambulatory, Premier Anesthesia, Principia, Procept, Proteon Networks, Public Mobile, Quintessant Communications, Quovadx, Raycer, Reachable, ReachLocal, Ripe Digital Entertainment, RIT, SARcode Bioscience, Savelli, Senomyx, Senesonics Medicine and Science

Other Locations:
525 University Avenue
Suite 1350
Palo Alto, CA 94301
Phone: 650-463-0300 **Fax:** 650-463-0311

Rho Canada
1800 McGill College Avenue
Suite 840
Montreal, QC H3A 3J6
Canada
Phone: 514-844-5605 **Fax:** 514-844-9004

Key Executives:
Habib Kairouz, Managing Partner
Education: BS, Engineering, BA, Economics, Cornell University; MBA, Finance, Columbia University
Background: Reich & Co., Jesup & Lamont
Directorships: Bluefly, Everyday Health, InnerWireless, IntraLinks, Public Mobile, ReachLocal, Travel Ad Network, Verified Person
Mark Leschly, Managing Partner
212-848-0414
Fax: 212-751-3613
e-mail: mleschly@rhomanagement.com
Education: MBA, Stanford Graduate School of Business
Background: General Partner, Healthcare Ventures; Consultant, McKinsey & Company
Directorships: Anacor, Diversa, Memory Pharmaceuticals, MPV, NitroMed, Orametrix, Orquis, Senomyx, Tercica, Vicuron
Joshua Ruch, Managing Partner
Education: MBA, Harvard Business School
Background: Investment Banker, Salomon Brothers
Directorships: 3-D Pharmaceuticals, Applied Science Fiction, Diacrin, Diversa, Human Genome Sciences, Sionex, TechSmart, Yantra
Martin Vogelbaum, Partner
Education: AB, Biology and History, Columbia University
Background: General Partner, Apple Tree Partners; General Partner, Oxford Bioscience Partners
Directorships: Gloucester Pharmaceuticals, Nuvelo
Doug McCormick, Venture Partner
Education: MBA, Columbia University School of Business
Background: NBC Universal ; CEO, Lifetime Entertainment Services
Directorships: Marketwatch, Lin Television, Wayport, Waterfront Media
Patrick Wack, Venture Partner
Education: BSE, Princeton University
Background: CEO, IntraLinks; COO, Professional Sports Care Management
Directorships: IntraLinks, MPV, Patersons, Xora
Mark Roehrenbeck, Principal
Education: BS, Fisher College of Business, Ohio State University
Background: PricewaterhouseCoopers
Peter Kalkanis, Chief Financial Officer
Education: BS, Accounting, Lehman College
Background: CPA, Eisner LLP

1562 RHYTHM VENTURE CAPITAL
1350 6th Avenue
New York, NY 10019

e-mail: info@rhythmvc.com
web: rhythmvc.com

Mission Statement: Rhythm invests in and partners with early stage companies taking transformational appraoches to healthcare.

Other Locations:
1350 6th Avenue
Palo Alto, CA 94022

Key Executives:
Jordan Ryan, Founder/Managing Partner
Education: BA, Stanford University
Background: Partner, Avalon Capital; Strategic Partner, Hardee Brothers
Anwar Hussain, General Partner
Education: AB, MHA, Cornell University; MD, Stony Brook University
Background: Physician; Chief Medical Information Officer, UHS Hospitals; Chief Medical Information Officer, Community Health Systems; Venture Advisor, New Leaf Venture Partners

1563 RIBBIT CAPITAL
Palo Alto, CA 94301

web: www.ribbitcap.com

Mission Statement: Ribbit Capital, a Silicon Valley-based venture capital firm with its sights on raising a significant amount of venture funding that will be aimed singularly at driving innovation around the world in lending, payments, insurance, accounting, tax preparation and personal financial management. Ribbit targets disruptive, early stage companies that leverage technology to reimagine and reinvent what financial services can be for people and businesses.

Fund Size: $100 million
Founded: 2013

Venture Capital & Private Equity Firms / Domestic Firms

Industry Group Preference: Financial Services
Portfolio Companies: Activehours, Borro, BTC Jam, CAN Capital, Coinbase, Comparaonline.com, ContaAzul, CreditKarma, Funding Circle, Invoice2go, Parasut, Policy Bazaar.com, Robinhood, Wealthfront, Xapo, Zest
Key Executives:
  Meyer Malka, Founder
  Background: Co-Founder/Chairman, Lemon
  Directorships: Wonga, Peixe Urbano
  Nick Shalek, General Partner
  Education: BA, Yale University; MA, Stanford University School of Education; MBA, Stanford Graduate School of Business
  Background: Senior Analyst, Yale Investment Office; Director of Business Operations, Verne Capital; Founding Member, Sutter LLC

1564 RICHMOND GLOBAL
20 W 55th Street
New York, NY 10019

e-mail: peter.kellner@rglobal.com
web: www.rglobal.com

Mission Statement: Ricmond Global are active, early stage investors in the U.S. and active, growth stage investors in global markets. Managing partners Peter Kellner and David Frazee have worked together for a decade growing companies that span five continents. Their strategy has permitted them to be diversified by sector and geography, achieving strong returns throughout cycles.

Geographic Preference: United States, Global
Investment Criteria: Early stage, Growth stage
Industry Group Preference: All Sectors Considered
Key Executives:
  Peter Kellner, Managing Partner
  e-mail: peter.kellner@rglobal.com
  Education: BA, Princeton University; JD, Yale Law School; MBA, Harvard Business School
  Background: Co-Founder, Endeavor; Founder, EMLA Association; Co-Founder, Richmond Global Sciences
  Directorships: Richmond Global Sciences
  David Frazee, Managing Partner
  e-mail: david.frazee@rglobal.com
  Education: AB, Stanford University; JD, University of Michigan Law School
  Background: Equity Partner, K&L Gates; Founder/CEO, Demystifying Silicon Valley

1565 RIDGE CAPITAL PARTNERS LLC
107 W Federal Street
Unit 4
PO Box 2056
Middleburg, VA 20118

Phone: 540-687-8161 Fax: 540-687-8164
e-mail: bdavis@ridgecapital.com
web: www.ridgecapital.com

Mission Statement: A private equity investment firm focused on partnering with outstanding managers to pursue platform build-ups and growth investments in companies in the smaller end of the middle market.

Geographic Preference: United States
Founded: 1992
Average Investment: $3-$8 million
Minimum Investment: $1 million
Investment Criteria: Recapitalizations, Management-Led Platform Build-Ups, Management-Led Buyouts, Take-Private Transactions, Growth Equity
Industry Group Preference: Niche Manufacturing, Distribution, Business Products & Services, Consumer Products
Portfolio Companies: Cavalier Fire Protection LLC, Equibrand Holding Corporation, LAT Apparel, Pumps and Controls, Wincore Window Company, Zamma Corporation

Key Executives:
  J. Bradley Davis, Managing Partner
  Education: BA, Pennsylvania State University
  Background: Trivest; LaSalle Partners; Chemical Bank
  Directorships: LAT Apparel, Wincore Windows and Doors, Cavalier Fire Protection, HELLEN Systems
  Clark F. Davis, Managing Partner
  Education: BS, Finance & Marketing, University of Richmond
  Background: Trivest
  Directorships: LAT apparel, Wincore Windows and Doors, Pumps and Controls, Equibrand Holdings, Zamma Corporation

1566 RIDGE VENTURES
One Letterman Dr.
Building D, Suite P100
San Francisco, CA 94129

Phone: 415-439-4420
e-mail: info@ridge.vc
web: ridge.vc

Mission Statement: Ridge Ventures is an early stage venture capital fund that invests in founders who redefine software using advanced technologies, new distribution models, and innovative user experience.

Investment Criteria: Early Stage
Industry Group Preference: Software, SaaS, Technology
Portfolio Companies: AlphaDraft, Andromedia, Babycenter, BandPage, BlueBox, Braze, cClearly, Chubbies, Datanyze, Discord, Espresa, F5, Fastly, Flowdock, FreeRange Games, FreeForm, FreshPlanet, Funzio, Grabango, GuideSpark, HeyMarket, IndieGoGo, JumpCloud, Jyve, Kixeye, Krux, Leaplife, Loup, MindMeld, Minted, Next Games, Nuzzel, nWay, Orion Labs, Outlier, ParkMe, Phoenix Labs, Plain Vanilla, Prism, Revcascade, SafeGraph, Sapho, Sense, Service Metrics, Simply Hired, Smartling, Soothe, Spinner, Splitwise, Super Bit Machines, Survata, Telltale, Tempered Networks, The League, Thirdlove, Tinfoil Security, Trifacta, Triller, UpLift, UpOut, UXPin, VA Linux, Vidible, WatchGuard, WeHeartIt, Yesware, YouEarnedIt
Key Executives:
  Alexander Rosen, Co-Founder/Managing Director
  Education: BS, MIT; MBA, Stanford University Graduate School of Business
  Background: Analyst, Credit Suisse; General Partner, Sprout Group
  Directorships: Minted, ThirdLove, Smartling, Braze, UpLift, Chubbies, Fastly, Tempered Networks, YouEarnedIt, SafeGraph
  Pat Kenealy, Co-Founder/Managing Director
  Education: BA, Economics, Harvard University
  Background: Managing General Partner, IDG Ventures San Francisco
  Gil Penchina, Partner
  Education: BS, University of Massachusetts; MBA, Kellogg School of Management
  Background: Vice President and General Manager, eBay
  Directorships: Fastly, Civic, Ripple, Brave

1567 RIDGEWOOD CAPITAL
14 Philips Parkway
Montvale, NJ 07645

Phone: 201-447-9000
e-mail: support@ridgewoodcapital.com
web: www.ridgewoodcapital.com

Mission Statement: Was formed to take advantage of the dramatic growth in the technology sector.

Fund Size: $2.7 billion
Founded: 1998
Average Investment: $7 million
Minimum Investment: $3 million
Investment Criteria: Expansion

Venture Capital & Private Equity Firms / Domestic Firms

Industry Group Preference: Semiconductors, Communications, Software, Energy, Wireless Technologies, Energy Technology, Renewable Energy, Oil & Gas

Key Executives:
Matthew E. Swanson, Senior Managing Director
Education: BA, Harvard University; JD, Harvard Law School
Background: Investment Management Division, Securities & Exchange Commission; Tax Department, Chadbourne & Parke
Daniel Gulino, SVP/Legal & Corporate Secretary
Education: Farleigh Dickinson University; Rutgers University School of Law
Background: In-House Counsel, GPU; PPL Resources; Alumax

1568 RIDGEWOOD ENERGY
1254 Enclave Parkway
Houston, TX 77077

Fax: 201-447-0474
Toll-Free: 800-942-5550
e-mail: info@ridgewoodenergy.com
web: www.ridgewoodenergy.com

Mission Statement: Houston private equity firm focused on energy.

Geographic Preference: Gulf of Mexico
Founded: 2008
Industry Group Preference: Energy

Key Executives:
Robert Gold, Senior Managing Director

1569 RINCON VENTURE PARTNERS
803 Chapala Street
Santa Barbara, CA 93101

Phone: 805-969-5484
web: www.rinconvp.com

Mission Statement: Rincon Venture Partners seeks to partner with extraordinary entrepreneurs and assist them as they build world class businesses. Rincon Venture Partners serve in supporting roles, helping entrepreneurs achieve success.

Geographic Preference: Southern California
Average Investment: $500,000 - $1 million
Investment Criteria: Early-Stage
Industry Group Preference: Internet
Portfolio Companies: Campus Explorer, Connectivity, Datapop, Digital Performance, Divshot, Earnest, ElephantDrive, HGData, Invoca, Keen IO, Launchpad.la, Local Market Launch, Promt.ly, Ranker, The Resumator, Rentlytics, Shift, Sideqik, Steelhouse, Tradesy, Worksteady

Other Locations:
1217 2nd Street
Santa Monica, CA 90401

Key Executives:
Jim Andelman, Managing Partner
Education: BS, Economics, Wharton School; MBA, Amos Tuck School of Business, Dartmouth
Background: Broadview Capital Partners; Technology Investment Banking Group, Deutsche Banc Alex Brown; Symmetrix
Ryan A Smiley, Managing Director
e-mail: rsmiley@rlhequity.com
Education: BS, Finance, Wharton School; MBA, UCLA Anderson School of Management

1571 RISE OF THE REST
1717 Rhode Island Avenue NW
Suite 1000
Washington, DC 20036

Phone: 202-776-1400
web: revolution.com

Mission Statement: Revolution seeks to partner with passionate entrepreneurs upending traditional industries with innovative products and services where we believe our unique areas of specialized expertise will help create significant value.

Geographic Preference: United States
Founded: 2005
Investment Criteria: Seed
Industry Group Preference: Education, Financial Services, Entertainment, Marketplace, Software, Transportation, Hospitality, Travel, eCommerce, Manufacturing, Healthcare, Food, Consumer

1572 RITTENHOUSE VENTURES
Building 100 Innovation Center
4801 South Broad Street
Suite 340
Philadelphia, PA 19112

Phone: 215-972-1502
web: www.rittenhouseventures.com

Mission Statement: Rittenhouse Ventures invests in early stage companies across a range of technology sectors, and primarily seeks opportunities in Pennsylvania and the Mid-Atlantic region. Rittenhouse Ventures was formerly known as Emerald Stage2 Ventures.

Geographic Preference: Pennsylvania, Mid-Atlantic Region, Washington to New York Corridor
Founded: 2006
Average Investment: $500,000 - $750,000
Investment Criteria: Early-Stage
Industry Group Preference: Technology, Technology-Enabled Services, Healthcare Information Technology, Pharmaceuticals, Outsourcing & Efficiency, Financial Services, Fintech
Portfolio Companies: AlignAlytics, Core Solutions, GSI Health, Halfpenny Technologies, Kynectiv, Life.io, Miria Systems, Noble Biomaterials, Tabula Rasa Healthcare, Take the Interview, Vcopious

Key Executives:
Saul Richter, Managing Partner
Education: BA, Economics, Columbia University; MBA, Columbia Business School
Background: Principal, Himalaya Capital; Lucent Technologies; Softbank Ventures; Jerusalem Global Ventures; Flatiron Partners; Founder, US Operations, Zapper Technologies
Directorships: Take the Interview, Miria Systems, Vcopious
Bruce Luehrs, Managing Partner
Education: BA, Economics, Duke University; MBA, Kellogg School of Management, Northwestern University
Background: General Partner, Edison Venture Fund; VP, Columbia Capital; Principal, PNC Equity Management; President, SBIC Unit, Fidelcor Capital; Officer, United States Air Force
Directorships: Tabula Rasa Healthcare, Miria Systems, Core Solutions
Britton Murdoch, Principal
Education: BS, University of Pennsylvania; MBA, New York University
Background: Founder/Managing Director, Strattech Partners LLC
Directorships: Fiberlink; Internet Capital Group; Airgas; V-Span

1573 RIVER ASSOCIATES INVESTMENTS LLC
633 Chestnut Street
Suite 1640
Chattanooga, TN 37450

Phone: 423-755-0888 Fax: 423-755-0870
e-mail: ccudd@riverassociatesllc.com
web: www.riverassociatesllc.com

Venture Capital & Private Equity Firms / Domestic Firms

Mission Statement: Exclusively focused on control buyouts of lower middle market companies in the United States and Canada.
Geographic Preference: United States, Canada
Fund Size: $222 million
Founded: 1989
Average Investment: $10-$30 million
Minimum Investment: $10 million
Investment Criteria: Buyouts, Recapitalizations, Divestures
Industry Group Preference: Manufacturing, Distribution, Industrial Services, Business Products & Services, Select Retail
Portfolio Companies: Boxercraft, CMS Management Solutions, Industrial Magnetics, National Deli, Omega Environmental Technologies, Rose City Printing and Packaging, TrueNet Communications

Key Executives:
  Jim Baker, Managing Partner
  e-mail: jbaker@riverassociatesllc.com
  Education: MBA/BS, University of Tennessee, Knoxville
  Background: President/COO, CONSTAR International; President, Baker Dixon Packaging; Arthur Andersen & Company
  Mike Brookshire, Managing Partner
  e-mail: mbrookshire@riverassociatesllc.com
  Education: BS, University of Tennessee, Chattanooga
  Background: Arthur Andersen & Company
  Mark Jones, Partner
  e-mail: mjones@riverassociatesllc.com
  Education: BA, Economics, Vanderbilt University; MBA, Samford University
  Background: South Trust Bank
  Directorships: Several Private companies and charitable organizations
  Patten Pettway, Partner
  e-mail: pprettway@riverassociatesllc.com
  Education: BA, University of Colorado; MBA, The Wharton School
  Background: Joseph Decosimo & Company
  Craig Baker, Partner
  e-mail: cbaker@riverassociatesllc.com
  Education: MBA, Emory University; B.ChE., Georgia Institute of Technology
  Background: Finance Manager, General Chemical Corporation; Operations Manager, Marsulex
  Blake Lewis, Vice President
  e-mail: blewis@riverassociatesllc.com
  Education: BS, Finance & Accounting, University of Tennessee
  Background: Avondale Partners
  Stuart Vyule, Vice President
  e-mail: svyule@riverassociatesllc.com
  Education: BS, Finance, Virginia Tech.
  Background: Bank of America Merrill Lynch

1574 RIVER CAPITAL
4200 Northside Parkway
Building 14
Suite 250
Atlanta, GA 30327

Phone: 404-873-2166
e-mail: info@river-capital.com
web: www.river-capital.com

Mission Statement: An Atlanta-based private investment firm which provides capital for management buy-outs, recapitalizations and growth capital needs of well-established middle market companies.
Geographic Preference: South, Midwest, Mid Atlantic
Fund Size: $600 million
Founded: 1983
Average Investment: $10-$50 million
Minimum Investment: $10 million
Investment Criteria: Recapitalizations, Management Buy-outs, Growth Capital
Industry Group Preference: Distribution, Manufacturing, Business Products & Services
Portfolio Companies: American Threshold Industries, Blue Wave, Can-Do National Tape, DéCor Gravure, Five Start Manufacturing, Hometown Communications, New Image Group, Piedmont Aviation Services, Tronair, Winston Furniture Company

Key Executives:
  Jerry D. Wethington, President
  e-mail: jwethington@river-capital.com
  Education: BA, Economics, University of Kentucky; MA, Economics, Western Kentucky University; MBA, University of Louisville
  Background: COO, Mitchell Steel; Senior Manager, Fuqua Industries, Teledyne
  Directorships: Blue Wave Products, Inc., CDNT, Five Star Manufacturing, New Image Group
  Bryan M. Wethington, Vice President
  e-mail: bwethington@river-capital.com
  Education: BS, Managerial Finance, University of Mississippi
  Background: Founder, Southern Setup; Founder, Rebel Yell Inc.
  Directorships: Five Star Manufacturing

1575 RIVER CITIES CAPITAL FUNDS
221 East Fourth Street
Suite 2400
Cincinnati, OH 45202-4151

Phone: 513-621-9700
web: www.rccf.com

Mission Statement: A family of three venture capital funds based in Cincinnati, Ohio, with an office in Raleigh, NC. Invests primarily in early stage to middle stage companies, located in the Midwest and Southeast, that operate in a variety of high growth industries.
Geographic Preference: Midwest, Southwest
Fund Size: $300 million
Founded: 1994
Average Investment: $2 million
Minimum Investment: $2 million
Investment Criteria: First-stage, Second-stage
Industry Group Preference: Diversified
Portfolio Companies: Advanced Biomarker, Canvas, Continuity Control, EndoChoice, Health Integrated, Ifbyphone, Intradiem, Knowledge Tree, MedPlast, NICO, NineSigma, Orthalign, PerfectServce, SIM Partners, StepLeader, Surgiquest, Tissuetech, Trax, Univa, Urgent Team

Other Locations:
  2501 Blue Ridge Road
  Suite 220
  Raleigh, NC 27607
  Phone: 919-374-5600

Key Executives:
  R Glen Mayfield, Co-Founder
  Education: BA, DePauw University
  Background: Founder, Mayfield & Robinson; VP, First National Bank
  Edwin T Robinson, Co-Founder
  Education: AB, Thomas More College; JD, University of Cincinnati College of Law
  Background: Mayfield & Robinson; Arthur Andersen & Company
  Daniel T Fleming, Managing Director
  Education: BSME, Ohio State University; MBA Harvard University
  Edward C McCarthy, Managing Director
  Education: BSEE, Northeastern University; MSEE, Florida Institute of Technology; MBA, Stetson University
  Background: Harris Corporation

J Carter McNabb, Managing Director
Education: BA, Trinity College; MBA, Owen School at Vanderbilt
Background: JC Bradford & Company; Paine Webber Group
Robert A Heimann, Managing Director
Education: BS, Accounting, University of Virginia; MBA, J.L. Kellogg School of Business at Northwestern University
Background: VP Corporate Development, Intelliseek, Inc.
Rurik G Vandevenne, Managing Director
Education: BE, Mechanical Engineering, Vanderbilt University
Background: Scient, Accenture

1576 RIVERSIDE COMPANY
45 Rockefeller Center
630 Fifth Avenue
Suite 400
New York, NY 10111

web: www.riversidecompany.com

Mission Statement: Private equity firm investing in premier companies at the smaller end of the middle market, focusing on industry-leading companies.

Fund Size: $1.3 billion
Founded: 1988
Minimum Investment: $3 million
Investment Criteria: LBO, MBO
Industry Group Preference: Business Services, Consumer, Education, Healthcare, Software & IT, Technology, Manufacturing, Retail
Portfolio Companies: ActiveStyle, Alchemy, Alcholo Monitoring Systems, American Hospice, American Stock Transfer & Trust Company, Anitox, ARCOS, Avatar International, Be Green Packaging, BeneSys, Blue Microphones, Bohemia Interactive Simulations, Brandmuscle, Brookson, Camelot Education, Censis, CorporateRewards, Crioestaminal, :DentalPlans, Diatron Group, DMA, DPA Microphones, Drex-Chem Malaysia, The Dwyer Group, Eemax, Emergency Communications Network, Fisher/Unitech, G&H Orthodontics, Global Orthopaedic Technologies, Grace Hill, Harvey Tool, H-D Manufacturing, HRA Pharma, iAutomation, IDOC, Insurance Claims Management, It's Just Lunch, Keycast, Keymile, Kyjen, Learning Seat, Lexipol, MEC3, Medical Payment Exchange, Mintra Trainingportal, MNX, Orliman, Paradigm Tax Group, PharmMD, Physicians Pharmacy Alliance, Polar Windows, PPS, ProSites, Rameder, Reima, Rutland Plastics, SAFEbuilt, SIGG, Simcro, Specialized Medical Services, Spectrio, Summit Medical Group, Sunless, Sunrise Windows, Tate's Bake Shop, Team Technologies, Tensator, Transporeon, Tropikal Pet, Uinta Brewing Company, Water-Jel, WhatCounts, Wiz Korea, Y International, YourMembership.com

Other Locations:
575 Market Street
Suite 3050
San Francisco, CA 94105
Phone: 415-348-9560

3333 Lee Parkway
Suite 700
Dallas, TX 75219-5111

Terminal Tower
50 Public Square
29th Floor
Cleveland, OH 44113

Alter Hof 5
Munich 80331
Germany

St. Martin's Courtyard
17 Slingsby Place
5th Floor
London WC2E 9AB
United Kingdom

1453 - 3rd Street Promenade
Suite 305
Santa Monica, CA 90401
Phone: 310-499-5080

Lloyd Georgelaan 7
Brussels 1000
Belgium

C/O Riverside Europe Partners Ab
Box 1126 11181
Stockholm
Sweden

13-15 Avenue De La Liberté
Luxembourg L-1931
Luxembourg
Phone: 352-2717291

P De La Castellana N 140 7b
Madrid 28046
Spain
Phone: 34-915901337

4/F Lee Garden Three
1 Sunning Road, Causeway Bay
Causeway Bay, Hong Kong
China
Phone: 852-3769-6117

Level 21, 101 Collins Street
Melbourne VIC 3000
Australia
Phone: 61-3-8672-2000

12 Marina View
Asia Square Tower 2 #23-01, Suite 67
Republic Plaza
Singapore 018961
Singapore
Phone: 65-6317-8563

Key Executives:
Béla Szigethy, Co-CEO, New York
Education: BA, Oberlin College; Masters of International Affairs, Columbia University
Background: Citibank, NA
Stuart Baxter, Managing Partner, San Francisco
Education: BA, Economics, Stanford University
Background: Director of Crimson Capital's Czech Restructuring and Privatization Group; President, AI International Corporation; Credit Suisse First Boston
Suzanne Kriscunas, Managing Partner, Dallas
214-871-9640
Fax: 214-871-9620
e-mail: skriscunas@riversidecompany.com
Education: BA, French, Denison University; MA, MBA, Indiana University
Background: Managing Director & Co-Founder, Legacy Private Capital Partners; Managing Director, Banc One Capital Corporation
Ron Sansom, Managing Partner, Cleveland
216-344-1040
Fax: 216-244-1330
Education: BS, Industrial Engineering, Auburn University; MS, Management, Krannert Graduate School of Management, Purdue University
Background: President, Sensing & Control, Honeywell Automation & Control Products; President & CEO, Kinetek
Loren Schlachet, Managing Partner, Los Angeles
310-499-5080
Fax: 310-499-5090
e-mail: lschlachet@riversidecompany.com
Education: BA, History, University of Pennsylvania; MBA, Finance, Stern School of Business, New York University

Venture Capital & Private Equity Firms / Domestic Firms

Background: Associate, Claremont Capital Corporation; Associate, TCW Capital
Timothy Gosline, Partner, Cleveland
216-344-1040
Fax: 216-344-1330
e-mail: tgosline@riversidecompany.com
Education: BBA, Business Administration, Kent State University; MBA, Finance, Case Western Reserve University
Background: Sea-Tech; Manager of Financial Analysis, Midland Ross Corporation; Senior Accountant, Deloitte & Touche

1577 RIVERSTONE
712 Fifth Avenue
36th Floor
New York, NY 10019

Phone: 212-993-0076 **Fax:** 212-993-0077
web: www.riverstonellc.com

Mission Statement: Since 2000 Riverstone has pursued a four-sector approach within the energy and power industry, targeting investments in the exploration & production, midstream, energy services and power & coal sectors. The Firm believes that a strategic allocation across the energy industry's main sectors results in superior rick-adjusted returns for Limited Partners.

Geographic Preference: North America, Latin America, Europe, Africa, Asia
Fund Size: $27 billion
Founded: 2000
Investment Criteria: Buyout, Growth Capital
Industry Group Preference: Conventional Energy, Renewable Energy
Portfolio Companies: 4Gas Holding B.V., Abasco Energy Technologies, AG Global, Bara Energia do Brasil Petroleo e Gás, Belden & Blake Corporation, Bottle Rock Power, Bridger, Buckeye Partners, C/R Energy Jade, CanEra Resources, Carrier Energy Partners, CDM Resource Management, CNDAA, Coastal Carolina Clean Power, Cobalt International Energy, CODA Holdings, Cuadrilla Resources Holdings, Davenport Newberry Holdings, Dresser, Dynamic Industries, Dynamic Offshore Resources, Eagle Energy Company of Oklahoma, Eagle Energy Exploration, Emerald Clean Power, Enduro Resource Partners II, Enduro Resource Partners, Ensus Ethanol, Enviva Holdings, EP Energy, Fairfield Energy, Fieldwood Energy, Foresight Reserves, Frontier Drilling, Gibson Energy, Green Earth Fuels, Heysta Energy, HongHua Co., Hudson Products Corporation, ILX Holdings, ILX Holdings II, InTANK, International Logging, Kerogen Energy Holdings, Kinder Morgan, Kramerk Junction, Legend Natural Gas, Legend Production Holdings, Liberty Oilfield Services, Liberty Resources, Liberty Resources II, Magellan Midstream Services II, Mistral Energy, Niska Gas Storage, Northern Blizzard Resources, Patagonia BioEnergia, Patriot Storage, Pattern Energy Group, Permian Tank & Manufacturing, Petroplus Holdings, Phoenix Exploration Company, PVR Partners, Quintana Shipping, Quorum Business Solutions, R/c Sugarkane, Raven Power Holdings, Red Technology Alliance, ReEnergy Holdings, Ridgebury Tankers, Sage Midstream, Sapphire Power Holdings, Seabulk International, Seajacks International, SemGroup, Shelter Bay Enery, Silver Ridge Power, Stallion Oilfield Services, Talos Energy, Targe Energy, ThermaSource, Three Rivers Operating Company, Titan Operating, Titan Specialties, Topaz Power Group, Trail Ridge Energy Partners, TrailStone, Turbine Air Systems, USA Compression, UTEX Industries, Vantage Energy, Velocita Energy Developments, Venada Oil & Gas, White Rose Energy Ventures

Other Locations:
2744 Sand Hill Road
Suite 100
Menlo Park, CA 94025
Phone: 650-540-2800
48 Dover Street
London W1S 4FFU
England
Phone: 44 20 3206 6300 **Fax:** 44 20 3206 6301
1000 Louisiana
Suite 1450
Houston, TX 77002
Phone: 713-357-1400 **Fax:** 713-357-1399
Javier Barros Sierra 540 Torre 2
Piso 2 Colonia Lomas de Santa Fe
Mexico City, DF 01210
Phone: 52-55-9177-2030
Herengracht 450
Amsterdam 1017 CA
The Netherlands
Phone: 31-20-240-4447

Key Executives:
Baran Tekkora, Partner
Education: BA, Hamilton College
Background: Goldman Sachs
Robert M Tichio, Partner
Education: AB, Dartmouth College; MBA, Harvard Business School
Background: Goldman Sachs; JP Morgan
Jamie M Brodsky, Partner
Education: BA, Duke University; MBA, Columbia University
Background: UBS Investment Bank

1578 RIVERVEST VENTURE PARTNERS
101 S. Hanley Road
Suite 1850
St Louis, MO 63105

Phone: 314-726-6700
e-mail: info@rivervest.com
web: www.rivervest.com

Mission Statement: Focuses exclusively on innovations in life sciences, a field in which our team has significant research, clinical, operational and investment expertise.

Geographic Preference: United States
Fund Size: $75 million
Founded: 2000
Average Investment: $500,000 - $6 million
Minimum Investment: $500,000
Industry Group Preference: Life Sciences
Portfolio Companies: Accumetrics, Allakos, CGI Pharmaceuticals, Cabrellis Pharmaceuticals, Calypso Medical Technologies, Cameron Health, Centerre Healthcare, Conforma Therapeutics, CyDex Pharmaceuticals, Excaliard Pharmaceuticals, IDev Techologies, Kaperio, Kereos, Lumena Pharmaceuticals, Luminous Medical, Lutonix, MacroGenics, Mpex Pharmaceuticals, Neuros Medical, Otonomy, Salient Surgical Technologies, Securus Medical Group, Tryton Medical, Velocimed, Xcyte, Xoft, ZS Pharma

Other Locations:
11000 Cedar Avenue
Suite 100
Cleveland, OH 44106
Phone: 212-658-3982

Key Executives:
Thomas C Melzer, Co-Founder/Managing Director
Education: BS, Stanford University; MBA, Stanford Graduate School of Business
Background: Managing Director, Morgan Stanley; President/CEO, Federal Reserve Bank of St. Louis
Jay W Schemelter, Co-Founder/Managing Director
Education: BA, Michigan State University; MBA, Booth School of Business, University of Chicago
Background: Sr Financial Analyst, General Mills;

Venture Capital & Private Equity Firms / Domestic Firms

Marketing Manager, Medtronic; Equity Research Analyst, Piper Jaffray; Principal, Cresendo Ventures
John McKearn PhD, Managing Director
Education: BS, Biology, Northern Illinois University
Background: GD Searle & Co.; EI Dupont de Nemours and Company
Niall A O'Donnell PhD, Managing Director
Education: MA, University of Oxford; PhD, University of Dundee; MBA, Rady School of Management, University of California San Diego
Background: Interim Chief Medical Officer, Lumena Pharmaceuticals Inc.; President/Interim CEO, Reneo Pharmaceuticals; Principal, Rivervest Venture Partners
Karen Spilizewski, Vice President
Education: BS/MS/MBA, Case Western Reserve University
Background: Business Development Manager, Avery Dennison; VP, Business Development, BioEntreprise
Directorships: Neuros Medical Inc.; Securus Medical Group; Standard Bariatrics Inc.

1579 RLH EQUITY PARTNERS
10900 Wilshire Blvd
Suite 850
Los Angeles, CA 90024

Phone: 310-405-7200 Fax: 310-405-7222
web: www.rlhequity.com

Mission Statement: To be the preferred private equity partner of exceptional high growth middle-market companies. Formerly known as Riordan, Lewis & Haden.

Geographic Preference: United States
Fund Size: $265 million
Founded: 1979
Average Investment: $15M - $40M
Minimum Investment: $10 million
Investment Criteria: Equity growth financing, MBO, Recapitalization
Industry Group Preference: Business Products & Services, Healthcare, Government Services
Portfolio Companies: Avella Specialty Pharmacy, Bluewolf, Clarity Solution Group, Mondo, RGM Group, Silverado Senior Living, Siteworx, The Chartis Group, Total Woman

Other Locations:
18300 Von Karman Avenue
Suite 730
Irvine, CA 92612
Phone: 949-428-2200 **Fax:** 949-428-2210

300 East 5th Avenue
Suite 390
Naperville, IL 60563
Phone: 312-281-7987

Key Executives:
J Christopher Lewis, Co-Founder/Managing Director
310-405-7200
e-mail: clewis@rlhinvestors.com
Education: BS, Finance, MBA, University of Southern California
Murray E Rudin, Managing Director
Education: BS, Electrical Engineering, University of Rochester; JD, Harvard Law School
Michel Glouchevitch, Managing Director
e-mail: mg@rlhequity.com
Education: BA, Political Science, Swarthmore College; MBA, Hautes Etudes Commerciales, Paris
Michael J Orend, Managing Director
e-mail: morend@rlhequity.com
Education: BA, University of Virginia
Background: Sales Executive, Digital Equipment Corptortation; Business Development Manager, PricewaterhouseCoopers
Directorships: Arthur Andersen & Co.; Lake Capital
Robert Rodin, Managing Director
e-mail: rrodin@rlhequity.com
Education: University of Connecticut
Background: CEO, Marshall Industries; Vice Chairman, CommerceNet; CEO/Chairman, RND Group Inc.
Directorships: Napster; CyberCoders; Collabrx; CareerBliss; ALS Therapy Development Institute; Siteworx LLC; Clarity Insights; Inspirage; Biorasi; SupplyFrame
Kevin D Cantrell, Managing Director
e-mail: kcantrell@rlhequity.com
Education: BS, Finance, Auburn University; MBA, Kellogg School of Management, Northwestern University

1580 ROARK CAPITAL GROUP
1180 Peachstreet Street NE
Suite 2500
Atlanta, GA 30309

Phone: 404-591-5200
web: www.roarkcapital.com

Mission Statement: Roark Capital Group is an Atlanta-based private equity firm that specializes in consumer, business and environmental services companies with attractive growth prospects and revenues ranging from $20 million to $1.0 billion. Roark focuses on middle-market investment opportunities through family-owned business transfers, management and corporate buyouts, recapitalizations, going-private transactions and corporate divestitures. Roark has acquired 20 franchise/consumer brands that operate in 50 states and 43 countries.

Geographic Preference: Worldwide
Fund Size: $1.5 billion
Average Investment: $25-$250 million
Investment Criteria: Family-Owned Business Transfers, Management & Corporate Buyouts, Recapitalizations, Going-Private Transactions, Corporate Divestitures
Industry Group Preference: Consumer Services, Business Products & Services, Environment Products & Services
Portfolio Companies: 1-800 Radiator, Anytime Fitness, Arby's, Auntie Anne's, Basecamp Fitness, Batteries Plus Bulbs, Bosley's, Buffalo Wild Wings, CARSTAR, Carvel, Cinnabon, CKE Restaurants, Corner Bakery Cafe, Culver's, Driven Brands, Drybar, Fitness Connection, FOCUS Brands, Great Expressions Dental Centers, Inspire Brands, Installation Made Easy, International Car Wash Group, Jamba Juice, Jim 'N Nick's Bar-B-Q, Jimmy John's, Maaco, Massage Envy, McAlister's Deli, Meineke, Miller's Ale House, Moe's Southwest Grill, Naf Naf, Orangetheory Fitness, Pet Supermarket, Pet Valu, Primrose Schools, R Taco, Schlotzsky's, Seattle's Best International, Self Esteem Brands, Solterra Recycling Solutions, Sonic, Take 5 Oil Change, Waxing the City

Other Locations:
540 Madison Avenue
37th Floor
New York, NY 10022
Phone: 212-806-6000

Key Executives:
Neal K. Aronson, Founder & Managing Partner
404-591-3333
e-mail: nealaronson@roarkcapital.com
Background: Co-Founder/CFO/Executive VP, US Franchise Systems; Principal, Odyssey Partners LP; Principal/General Partner, Acadia Partners LP
Directorships: FOCUS Brands, Money Mailer, FastSigns, McAlisters, Batteries Plus
Paul D. Ginsberg, President
404-591-3331
e-mail: pginsberg@roarkcapital.com
Education: BA, Union College; JD, University of Chicago Law School
Background: Paul Weiss Rifkind Wharton & Garrison LLP
Stephen D. Aronson, Managing Director & General Counsel

Venture Capital & Private Equity Firms / Domestic Firms

404-591-5210
e-mail: saronson@roarkcapital.com
Education: BA, Government, Lehigh University; JD, University of Chicago Law School
Background: SVP, General Counsel, Executive Committee, US Franchise Systems
Timothy B. Armstrong, Managing Director
212-518-0712
e-mail: tarmstrong@roarkcapital.com
Education: Undergraduate Degree, Yale University
Background: Saunders Karp & Megrue
Erik O. Morris, Chief Investment Officer
404-591-5205
e-mail: emorris@roarkcapital.com
Education: BS, Business Administration, University of North Carolina, Chapel Hill
Background: Partner, Grotech Capital Group, Deutsche Bank
Directorships: Primrose Schools, Waste Pro, Wingstop
Steve Romaniello, Senior Advisor
404-591-5215
e-mail: stever@roarkcapital.com
Education: Tufts University
Background: President & CEO, FOCUS Brands; President & COO, US Franchise Systems; VP, Holiday Inn Worldwide
Directorships: FOCUS Brands, FastSigns
Geoff A. Hill, Managing Director
404-591-3330
e-mail: ghill@roarkcapital.com
Education: BA, Cornell University School of Hotel Administration
Background: President, Cinnabon; VP, USFS; Director of Sales, Bristol Hotel Company
Directorships: FOCUS Brands
Kevin Hofmann, Managing Director
404-591-3322
e-mail: khofmann@roarkcapital.com
Education: BS, Computer Science, Central Michigan University
Background: President/Chief Marketing Officer, Home Depot; CIO/CTO, GE; Dow Chemical

1581 ROBIN HOOD VENTURES
3675 Market Street
Philadelphia, PA 19104

Phone: 215-839-6256 Fax: 484-214-0114
e-mail: info@robinhoodventures.com
web: www.robinhoodventures.com

Mission Statement: Robin Hood Ventures consists of Greater Philadelphia Region entrepreneurs/investors who have joined together to fund and aid the development of local companies through their collective business experience and contacts. Skill sets include depth in all functional areas, including general management, marketing, sales, product development, marketing communications, and finance.

Investment Criteria: Seed-Stage
Industry Group Preference: Energy, Information Technology, Business Products & Services, Financial Services, Insurance, Entertainment, Real Estate, Manufacturing, Healthcare, Consumer Products, Restaurants, Biopharmaceuticals, Medical Devices, Diagnostics
Portfolio Companies: ATRIN Pharmaceuticals, AlphaPoint, Biologics, Biomeme, Burrow, ChargeItSpot, Core Solutions, Document Depository Corp., ExpressCells, GenPro, FemSelect, Grassroots Unwired, Illumine Radiopharmaceuticals, Immunome, Inpensa, Intrommune, LIA Diagnostics, LoanLogics, Luxtech, NanoPack Inc., Ophidion, OWIT Global, Peeractive, Proscia, ReturnLogic, Sidecar, Simply Good Jars, TASSL, Thermalin, Thrupore, Virion Therapeutics, Wash Cycle Laundry, WizeHive, Yellowdig

Key Executives:
Ellen Weber, Executive Director
Education: BS, Economics, Wharton School, University of Pennsylvania
Background: Executive Director, Fox School of Business Innovation, Temple University; COO/Co-Founder, VisionMine; Managing Director/Founder, Antiphony Partners LLC; Sr Consultant, Andersen Consulting

1582 ROCK ISLAND CAPITAL
1415 W 22nd Street
Suite 1250
Oak Brook, IL 60523

Phone: 630-413-9136 Fax: 630-574-0213
web: www.rockislandcapital.com

Mission Statement: Rock Island Capital LLC is a private equity fund that provides equity and mezzanine capital to middle market companies. Rock Island has over $150 million in committed capital under management and makes majority and minority investments in leading middle market manufacturing, distribution or service companies with enterprise values up to $100 million. Our firm is focused on building long-term relationships with business owners, management teams, investors, lenders and referral sources. These relationships are the cornerstones of our firm and are built on honesty, loyalty and fairness.

Fund Size: $150 million
Investment Criteria: Middle Market
Industry Group Preference: Manufacturing, Distribution, Business Products & Services
Portfolio Companies: Advanced Industrial Devices, Atlas Connectivity, Baker Manufacturing, Central Power, Continental Services, DGS Retail, Environmental Recovery Corporation, Esmark, Excel Engineering, ERC midwest, Kemco Systems, Lake Shore Group, Mascara Sales & Marketing, Piedmont Candy Company, Pumps and Controls, Runyon Equipment Rental, Thorco, Valley Fastener Group, Venture Sales Group, Welch ATM

Key Executives:
Alfred M. Mattaliano, Partner
e-mail: mattaliano@rockislandcapital.com
Education: BBA, Finance, University of Notre Dame; MM, Finance & Accounting, Northwestern University Kellogg Graduate School of Management
Background: Principal, Catalyst/Hall; Founder & Partner, Vine Street Partners; Vice President, Corporate Finance, Bankers Trust Company; Second Vice President, American National Bank
Michael E. Nugent, Partner
e-mail: nugent@rockislandcapital.com
Education: BBA, Accounting, University of Notre Dame; CPA
Background: Vice President, Dresner Capital; Director, Vine Street Partners; KPMG Peat Marwick LLP
Daniel K. Alport, Vice President
e-mail: alport@rockislandcapital.com
Education: BS, Finance, University of Illinois
Background: Vice President, Deloitte Corporate Finance
Brian Bastedo, Vice President
e-mail: bastedo@rockislandcapital.com
Education: BBA, Accounting, University of Notre Dame; MBA, Finance, Indiana University; CPA
Background: Managing Director, RedRidge Finance Group; Associte Director, Bridge Finance Group; Manager, PriceWaterhouseCoopers LLP

1583 ROCKPORT CAPITAL
160 Federal Street
18th Floor
Boston, MA 02210-1700

web: www.rockportcap.com

Mission Statement: A leading venture capital firm that partners with cleantech entrepreneurs around the world. Collaborates

Venture Capital & Private Equity Firms / Domestic Firms

with management teams to foster growth and create value, building innovative companies that bring disruptive technologies and products to the 21st century.

Geographic Preference: Worldwide
Average Investment: $500,000 - $25 million
Minimum Investment: $500,000
Investment Criteria: All Stages
Industry Group Preference: Clean Technology, Energy, Resource Efficiency, Transportation, Advanced Materials, Green Building
Portfolio Companies: Achates Power, Aspen Aerogels, Clean Diesel Technologies, Comverge, Deerpath Energy, drillMap, EcoFactor, EcoSMART Technologies, Eka Systems, Enki Technology, Enlightened, Enovix, Enphase Energy, Evergreen Solar, Exclara, FirstFuel Software, Flywheel Software, GaN Systems, Gazelle, GlassPoint, Gridco Systems, Honest Buildings, Hycrete, HydroPoint Data Systems, InVisage, Luxim, MicroSeismic, NanoGram Devices, Nectar Power, NeoPhotonics, NewLeaf Symbiotics, Northern Power Systems, Project Frog, Qnovo, Rayne Water, Recurve, Renaissance Lighting, Renovate America, Solar Universe, Soliant, Southwest Windpower, Streetline, SustainX

Key Executives:
  William E James, Managing General Partner
  Education: BA, History, Colorado College
  Background: Chairman & CEO, Citizens Corporation; Founder, Citizens Lehman Power
  Directorships: MicroSeismic, Think Holdings AS
  Alexander Ellis III, General Partner
  Education: BA, Political Science, Colorado College; MBA, Yale School of Management
  Background: Knoll International; Kenetech Corporation
  Janet James, General Partner/COO
  Education: BA, Govenment, Dartmouth College; MBA, Columbia Business School
  Background: EVP, Citizens Corporation; CEO, Citizens Gas Supply Corporation
  Stoddard M Wilson, General Partner
  Education: BA, Economics & History, Brown University; MBA, Harvard Business School
  Background: AT&T; Director External Affairs, Wilbraham & Monson Academy

1584 RODA GROUP
2217 5th Street
Berkeley, CA 94710

Phone: 510-649-1900
e-mail: info@rodagroup.com
web: www.rodagroup.com

Mission Statement: Provides entrepreneurs the resources, environment, and guidance to launch and grow their high technology businesses.

Founded: 1997
Investment Criteria: Seed Stage
Industry Group Preference: High Technology
Portfolio Companies: Axine, Game Ready, Gridtential, Inventys, mOasis

Key Executives:
  Roger A Strauch, Chairman
  e-mail: roger@rodagroup.com
  Education: BS, Electrical Engineering, Cornell University; MS, Electrical Engineering, Stanford University
  Background: CEO, Chairman, Ask Jeeves; Board Member, CEO, Symmetricom; Co-Founder, TCSI Corp.
  Directorships: Cool Systems
  Daniel H Miller, Managing Director
  e-mail: dan@rodagroup.com
  Education: BS, Electrical Engineering, Cornell University; MS, Electrical Engineering, Stanford University
  Background: President, Board Member, Ask Jeeves; EVP, TCSI Corp.
  Directorships: Solazyme

1585 ROMULUS CAPITAL
101 Arch Street
Boston, MA 02110

web: www.romuluscap.com

Mission Statement: Romulus Capital invests in seed-stage technology companies that seek to become industry leaders. The firm is young, entrepreneurial, and global, while retaining deep experience at the earliest stages of company formation.

Founded: 2008
Average Investment: $50,000 - $500,000
Investment Criteria: Seed-Stage
Portfolio Companies: Aidin, Allurion Technologies, Bombfell, Classpass, Cohealo, Crocodoc, DashBin, Disrupt Beam, Docphin, ElaCarte, Estify, Fitocracy, Giner.io, Gyft, Placester, Scholar Locker, Smart Lunches, Soundtracker, TheTapLab, Zigfu

Key Executives:
  Neil Chheda, Co-Founder/General Partner
  Education: BA, Political Science, Yale University; MBA, Harvard Business School
  Background: Product Manager, Zynga; McKinsey & Company; Kleiner Perkins
  Krishna K Gupta, Co-Founder/General Partner
  Education: BS, Materials Science & Engineering, MIT
  Background: Management Consultant, McKinsey & Company; JPMorgan

1586 ROOT CAPITAL
130 Bishop Allen Drive
2nd Floor
Cambridge, MA 02139

Phone: 617-661-5792
web: www.rootcapital.org

Mission Statement: Root Capital is a non-profit social investment fund that is pioneering finance for grassroots businesses in rural areas of developing countries. Provides capital, delivers financial training and strengthen market connections for small and growing businesses that build sustainable livelihoods and transforms rural communities.

Geographic Preference: Latin America, Africa
Founded: 1999
Industry Group Preference: Food & Beverage, Agriculture
Other Locations:
  225 metros Norte del BCR
  Paseo Colon
  San José
  Costa Rica
  Phone: 506-2258-7094

  Methodist Ministries Centre
  Oloitoktok Road
  Lavington, Nairobi
  Kenya
  Phone: 254-736-864892

  Ma. Adelina Flores No. 20
  Zona Centro
  San Cristobal de las Casas
  Chiapas
  Mexico
  Phone: (52) 967-674-0465 **Fax:** (52) 967-631-5615

Key Executives:
  William F Foote, Founder & CEO
  Education: BA, Yale University; MSc, Development Economics, London School of Economics
  Background: Financial Analyst, Latin American Corporate Finance Group, Lehman Brothers

Venture Capital & Private Equity Firms / Domestic Firms

1587 ROPART ASSET MANAGEMENT
3 Greenwich Office Park
2nd Floor
Greenwich, CT 06831

Phone: 203-552-6697
e-mail: contact@ropart.com
web: www.ropart.com

Mission Statement: The Ropart Asset Management Funds is a private equity firm that invests directly in small to midsize companies. The firm pursues a flexible strategy, investing throughout the capital structure and in multiple industries, including Business Services, Healthcare Services, Consumer Products, Financial Services, and Software/Technology.

Average Investment: $3 - $15 millin
Investment Criteria: Control Investments, Mezzanine Lending, Growth Capital, Distressed or Special Situations
Industry Group Preference: Business Products & Services, Healthcare Services, Consumer Products, Financial Services, Software, Technology
Portfolio Companies: ALC Concierge Service, Crexendo, Digital Traffic Systems, Elite Daily, Fragmob, iCentris, Liftoff Mobile, Protein Sciences, QCL Holdings, Root Wireless

Key Executives:
   Todd A Goergen, Managing Partner
   e-mail: tgoergen@ropart.com
   Education: BA, Economics & Political Science, Wake Forest University
   Background: M&A, Donaldson, Lufkin & Jenrette; Director, M&A, Blyth
   Directorships: QCL Holdings, Digital Traffic Systems, Crexendo, FragMob, ViSalus

1588 ROSE TECH VENTURES
158 West 29th Street
11th Floor
New York, NY 10001

web: www.rose.vc

Mission Statement: Rose Tech Ventures is an early stage investment fund, incubator, and all-around support infrastructure dedicated to finding, nurturing and launching the next generation of world class ventures.

Investment Criteria: Early-Stage
Portfolio Companies: Ambient Devices, Bioscale, Catalist, Challenge Post, Chromis Fiberoptics, CircleUp, Comixology, Crimson Hexagon, Concierge Choice, Critical Mention, Domdex, eJamming, Email Data Source, FASTTAC, GridPlex, Gust, iGuitar, Inn Road, Instinctiv, Kidzui, KoolSpan, LearnVest, LinkStorm, LiveLOOK, Luxology, Magnify Networks, Mashery, MediaTile, Metaphor Solutions, Monetate, Nimbit, Panjiva, Performline, Pond5, Por ti, Familia, Postling, Rocket Racing League, School Loop, Senscient, SetJam, SocialBomb, Space Adventures/Zero-G, TalkShoe, Trazzler, Vidler, Say Media, 33across, Wellgood

Key Executives:
   David S Rose, Managing Director
   Education: BA, Yale University; MBA, Finance, Columbia Business School
   Background: Chairman & CEO, Angelsoft; Chairman, New York Angels, Chairman, Egret Capital Partners
   Directorships: KoolSpan, Pond5, Comixology, Magnifiy Networks

1589 ROSECLIFF VENTURES
245 Fifth Avenue
14th Floor
New York, NY 10016

Phone: 212-492-3000 Fax: 212-586-7695
e-mail: contact@rosecliffvc.com
web: www.rosecliffvc.com

Mission Statement: A venture capital firm interested in startup and early stage companies with substantial growth potential.
Founded: 2010
Average Investment: Up to $250,000
Investment Criteria: Seed, Series A Round
Portfolio Companies: Allbirds, Banza, Brad's Raw Foods, Brewpublik, Cargo, Create1, CYC Fitness, Edufii, FanAI, Goby, Heyday, Homer, Jack Threds, Juice Press, Leo Health, Lyon and Post, Neutun, Nuzzel, Open Sponsorhip, Ollie, Petal, Pure Growth Organics, Raden, RecoverX, RTS, Riide, Roomi, SelfMade, Sidedolla, Tout, TraceME, Trustify, Twist, Wheels Up, Viyet, Voyajoy, WSC, YellowDig, Youstake

Key Executives:
   Michael P. Murphy, Founder/Managing Partner
   Education: Hofstra University; D'Amore-Mckim School of Business, Northeastern University
   Directorships: Ample Hills Creamery, KARR Group of Companies, Cargo,
   Michael V. Caso, Principal
   Education: BS, Mathematics & Economics, Gabelli School of Business, Fordham University
   Background: Sales & Trading Division, Merrill Lynch; Investment Banker, Rosecliff Ventures

1590 ROSER VENTURES LLC
1105 Spruce Street
Boulder, CO 80302

Phone: 303-443-6436
e-mail: roserventures@roserventures.com
web: www.roserventures.com

Mission Statement: A venture firm established to invest in private offerings of companies that exhibit the potential for superior long term returns.

Geographic Preference: Rocky Mountain
Fund Size: $75 million
Founded: 1987
Average Investment: $2 million
Minimum Investment: $250,000
Investment Criteria: Early Stage
Industry Group Preference: Communications, Electronic Technology, Software, Manufacturing, Low Technology, Information Technology

Key Executives:
   Christopher W Roser, Partner
   303-443-7935
   Education: University of Colorado; MBA, New York University
   Background: Main Hurdman KMG; Equity Research Associates; Associate, Ladenburg
   James LD Roser, General Partner
   303-443-7924
   e-mail: jroser@roserventures.com
   Education: BA, Economics, Bucknell University; MBA, Harvard University
   Background: Smith, Barney & Company; Brown Brothers Harriman; Cyrus J Lawrence & Company

1591 ROSEWOOD CAPITAL
One Maritime Plaza
Suite 1575
San Francisco, CA 94111

Phone: 415-362-5526 Fax: 415-362-1192

Mission Statement: Rosewood invests exclusively in a small number of high-quality, consumer-oriented, growth companies.

Fund Size: $80 million
Founded: 1985
Average Investment: $10 - $40 million
Minimum Investment: $3 million
Investment Criteria: Small-Medium size businesses, Experienced Management, Superior Market, Strong Growth, Proven Profitability

Venture Capital & Private Equity Firms / Domestic Firms

Industry Group Preference: Consumer Products, Consumer Services, Restaurants, Retail, Consumer & Leisure, Outsourcing & Efficiency, Financial Services
Portfolio Companies: Cobalt Boats, Jamba Juice, 3 Day Blinds, Noah's Bagels, New York Sports Clubs, Anna's Linens, Alternative, CapitalSource, Under Armour

1592 ROTH CAPITAL PARTNERS
888 San Clemente Drive
Newport Beach, CA 92660

Fax: 949-720-7215
Toll-Free: 800-678-9147
web: ww.roth.com

Mission Statement: Roth Capital Partners is dedicated to the micro-cap marketplace. Provides institutional quality investment banking, research and distribution services to high quality micro-cap companies and offers investment guidance and current market information to their investors. Professional investment counselors have the experience to help clients identify and achieve financial goals through solid investments that include an array of proprietary and third-party products.

Founded: 1984
Minimum Investment: $2 million
Industry Group Preference: Business Products & Services, Clean Technology, Consumer Products, Gaming, Healthcare, Technology, Media

Other Locations:
730 Fifth Avenue
25th Floor
New York, NY 10019

470 Atlantic Avenue
4th Floor, Office #4062A
Boston, MA 02210
Phone: 949-720-5745

11150 Santa Monica Boulevard
Suite 480
Los Angeles, CA 90025 **Fax:** 310-445-5864

6183 Paseo del Norte
Carlsbad, CA 92011
Phone: 858-509-2500 **Fax:** 858-509-0790

155 North Wacker Drive
Suite 1900
Chicago, IL 60606
Phone: 312-564-8100

888 San Clemente Drive
Suite 3103-04, K Wah Centre, 1010 Huai Hai Zhong Road
Xuhui District
Newport Beach, CA 92660
Phone: 86-21-6141-5757 **Fax:** 949-7207215

Hong Kong Limited
Two International Finance Centre
8 Finance Street, 19/F
Central
Hong Kong
Phone: 852-22518585

Key Executives:
Bryon C Roth, Chairman/CEO
949-720-5721
Fax: 949-720-7223
e-mail: broth@rothcp.com
Education: Undergraduate Degree, University of San Diego; MBA, Cornell University
Gordon Roth, Chief Operating Officer & CFO
949-720-5774
e-mail: groth@roth.com
Education: WM Penn University, Drake University
Background: Deloitte & Touche
Ted Roth, President/Head of Institutional Sales
858-509-2502
e-mail: troth@roth.com
Education: Iowa Wesleyan College; JD, Washburn University; LLM, University of Missouri Kansas City
Background: Biotech R&D, Plastics Manufacturing
Aaron M Gurewitz, Managing Director, Equity Capital Markets
949-720-5703
e-mail: agurewitz@roth.com
Education: San Diego State University
Background: Friedman Billings Ramsey; Wedbush Morgan Securities; Prudential Securities; Wells Fargo Bank

1593 ROUGH DRAFT VENTURES
20 University Road
4th Floor
Cambridge, MA 02138

web: www.roughdraft.vc

Mission Statement: Student-led fund backs student founders in Boston, Mass.

Geographic Preference: Greater Boston Area Colleges and Universities
Average Investment: $5,000 - $25,000
Investment Criteria: Early Stage
Industry Group Preference: Financial Services, Software, E-Commerce & Manufacturing
Portfolio Companies: Beepi, Bowery, Charitweet, Cloudstitch, DeskConnect, Downtyme, Findit, Grove Labs, Healogram, INDICO, Life Guard Games, Lilypad Scales, Local Lift, Mark43, Mercaux, Nightingale, Pegasense, Pluto Mail, Request Now, Sand Hill Exchange, Smarking, Speech4Good, Technical Machine, Valet.io, Valued Investing, Vaska Tech, WatchSend

1594 ROUNDTABLE HEALTHCARE PARTNERS
272 East Deerpath Road
Suite 350
Lake Forest, IL 60045

Phone: 847-739-3200 **Fax:** 847-482-9215
web: www.roundtablehp.com

Mission Statement: RoundTable Healthcare Partners seeks to leverage its healthcare industry knowledge, operational experience, and financial expertise to generate outstanding investment returns.

Geographic Preference: United States, Canada, Europe
Fund Size: $650 million
Founded: 2001
Investment Criteria: Buyouts, Acquisitions, Consolidations
Industry Group Preference: Healthcare, Medical Devices, Medical Products, Pharmaceuticals
Portfolio Companies: Advantice Health, AMI Holdings Inc., Aqua Pharmaceuticals, Ascent Healthcare Solutions, Argon Medical Devices, Aspen Surgical, Avalign Technologies, Beaver Visitec, Bioniche Pharma, Clinical Innovations, Core Pharma, Deerland, Excelsior Medical, MedAssist, Renaissance Pharma, Revision Skincare, Sabex, Salter Labs, Santa Cruz Nutritionals, Symmetry Surgical, TIDI, Vesta

Key Executives:
Lester B. Knight, Founding Partner
Education: BS, Industrial Engineering, MBA, Cornell University
Background: Vice Chairman, Cardinal Health; Chairman & CEO, Allegiance
Directorships: AdvaMed
Joseph F. Damico, Founding Partner/Senior Advisor
Education: MBA, James Madison University
Background: Executive VP, Cardinal Health; President & COO, Allegiance; Baxter; American Hospital Supply Corporation
Directorships: Renaissance Pharma, Salter Labs, Santa Cruz Nutritionals
R. Craig Collister, Managing Partner
Education: University of Michigan; MBA, Harvard University Graduate School of Business Administration

Venture Capital & Private Equity Firms / Domestic Firms

Background: Credit Suisse First Boston
Directorships: Argon Medical Devices, Salter Labs, TIDI Products
David J. Koo, Senior Advisor
Education: BBA, Accountancy, University of Notre Dame; CPA
Background: VP, US Healthcare Investment Banking Group, Credit Suisse First Boston; KPMG Peat Marwick
Directorships: Renaissance Acquisition Holdings, Santa Cruz Nutritionals
Pierre FréChette, Managing Partner
Education: BS, Mechanical Engineering & Diploma in Business Administration, University of Sherbrooke
Background: VP of Marketing/Business Development, Baxter; President/COO, Sabex; Vice-Chair, Canadian Generic Pharmaceutical Association; President/CEO, Sandoz Canada Inc.; CEO, Renaissance Acquisition Holdings
Andrew B. Hochman, Senior Partner
Education: BS, Economics, Wharton School, University of Pennsylvania
Background: VP, Business Development, Graceway Pharmaceuticals
Directorships: Santa Cruz Nutritionals

1595 ROYALTY CAPITAL MANAGEMENT
Royalty Capital Management LLC
Lexington, MA 02420

Phone: 781-861-8490
e-mail: alf@royaltycapital.us
web: www.royaltycapital.us

Mission Statement: Actively seeking new investments where a royalty against gross revenue can return original capital within 18 months.

Founded: 1994
Average Investment: $200,000
Minimum Investment: Less than $100,000
Investment Criteria: All Stages
Industry Group Preference: Communications, Computer Related, Consumer Products, Electronic Components, Energy, Genetic Engineering, Industrial Equipment, Medical & Health Related, Natural Resources
Key Executives:
  Arthur L Fox, President
  Education: BSEE, University of Maryland; MSEE, Massachusetts Institute of Technology
  Background: Hewlett Packard Co., Westinghouse Corporation; Co-founder, Octek, Inc., Lexidata Corporation, Medicel, Inc.

1596 RPM VENTURES
320 N Main Street
Suite 400
Ann Arbor, MI 48104

Phone: 734-332-1700
web: www.rpmvc.com

Mission Statement: Provides sound guidance and support to entrepreneurs and technology startups, helping transform their ideas into the next generation of new economy companies. Investments concentrates on IT or Software firms selling to the Midwest Manufacturing or Automotive customer Base and Midwest University spin-outs.

Geographic Preference: Midwest, California
Fund Size: $275 million
Founded: 2000
Average Investment: $2 million
Minimum Investment: $250,000
Investment Criteria: Seed, Early Stage, Startup
Industry Group Preference: Wireless Technologies, Infrastructure, Technology, Software, Semiconductors, Manufacturing, Materials Technology, Energy
Portfolio Companies: ArborMetrix, Automatics, BountyJobs, Deepfield, Deliv, Eden Park Illmination, Glyde, Janrain, Mojo Motors, Oxlo Systems, ShareThis, Social Finance, BlueLeaf, Boom! Studios, Bloud Tecnology Partners, Filament Labs, Getaround, Giftly, Gobbler, Karmic Labs, Navdy, QZZR, SupportPay, Collabrify
Key Executives:
  Marc Weiser, Managing Director
  Education: BS, Aerospace Engineering, University of Michigan; MBA, University of Michigan Business School
  Background: Founder, QuantumShift; MessageMedia; Associate, Arbor Partners
  Tony Grover, Managing Director
  Education: BS, Mechanical Engineering, University of Michigan; MS, Industrial Engineering, Purdue University; MBA, Kellogg Graduate School of Business
  Background: VP, White Pines Ventures
  Directorships: Performix, Arbor Photoics, Eden Park, JanRain

1597 RRE VENTURES
130 E 59th Street
New York, NY 10022

Phone: 212-418-5100
e-mail: info@rre.com
web: www.rre.com

Mission Statement: RRE Ventures is an early-stage venture capital firm headquartered in New York City. Partners with extraordinary entrepreneurs who seek to disrupt and transform industries. RRE is a long-term lead investor.

Fund Size: $850 million
Founded: 1994
Average Investment: $5-10 million
Investment Criteria: Seed-Stage, Early-Stage
Industry Group Preference: Internet Technology, Software, Communications, Information Technology, Financial Services, Mobile, Enterprise Software, Consumer Products, Media
Portfolio Companies: AvantCredit, Bark & Co., Base, Betaworks, Bitly, Bitpay, Boom, Breather, Business Insider, BuzzFeed, Chain, CoverHound, Crossboard Mobiel, Drobo, Electric Cloud, Floored, HYLA, imIX, K2 Global, Kik, Kroll BondRatings, Mod Operandi, Netsertive, Noom, Odyssey, Ojo, OnDeck, Open Peak, Palantir Technologies, Paperless, PayFone, PrimeRevenue, Quirky, Rave Mobile Safety, Recyclebank, Roundbox, Sailthru, Shake, Socialflow, Spire, Tendril, Tinybop, Trumaker & Co., VigLink, YieldBot, Yipit
Key Executives:
  Stuart Ellman, Founder/General Partner
  e-mail: sje@rre.com
  Education: BA Economics, Wesleyan University; MBA, Harvard University
  Background: Advisory Capital Partners; Associate, Morgan Stanley & Company; Analyst, Dillon, Read & Company; McKinsey & Company
  James Robinson, Founder/General Partner
  e-mail: jim@rre.com
  Education: MBA, Harvard University
  Background: Hambrecht & Quist Venture Capital
  James Robinson, III, Founder/General Partner
  e-mail: jdriv@rre.com
  Education: MBA, Harvard University; BS Industrial Management, Georgia Institute of Technology
  Background: Computer Entrepreneur; Investment Banking; Venture Capital
  Directorships: On Deck Capital, Prime Revenue, SkyGrid, Visprise
  Will Porteous, General Partner/COO
  e-mail: will@rre.com
  Education: BA, Stanford University; MSc, London School of Economics, MBA, Harvard University
  Background: SupplyWorks, NetMarket

Venture Capital & Private Equity Firms / Domestic Firms

Directorships: BuzzFeed, Data Robotics, HowAboutWe, Peek, Skyhook Wireless, Xobni
Raju Rishi, General Partner
Education: BS & MS, MIT
Background: Venture Partner, Sigma Prime Ventures; Executive, AT&T; Executive, Lucent
Jay Hass, Partner
Education: BA, Politics, Princeton University; Completed CFA Institute's Investment Management Program, Harvard Business School
Background: Managing Director, Brown Brothers Harriman; Advisor to the M. Night Shyamalan Foundation
Directorships: Cheetah Korea Value Fund
Jason Black, Principal
Education: BA, Psychology, Harvard University

1598 RTP VENTURES
885 Third Avenue
24th Floor
New York, NY 10022

Phone: 646-568-7206
e-mail: info@rtp.vc
web: www.rtp.vc

Mission Statement: Building companies takes time and resources. Having experienced investors who, instead of watching from the sidelines, built companies themselves can make all the difference.

Geographic Preference: United States, Israel, Turkey
Investment Criteria: Seed-Stage, Early-Stage, Later-Stage
Industry Group Preference: Big Data, Cloud Computing, E-Commerce & Manufacturing, Automation, SaaS
Portfolio Companies: Datadog, Fab, GridGain, Koding, Lidyana, Liftopia, RichRelevance, SiSense, Techstars, Tinfoil Security, Tutum, WorkFusion, Zerto

Key Executives:
Kirill Sheynkman, Co-Founder/Partner Emeritus
Education: Electrical Engineering & Computer Science, Stanford University; MBA, Haas School of Business

1599 RUBICON VENTURE CAPITAL
One Little West Twelfth Street
3rd Floor
New York, NY 10014

e-mail: info@rubicon.vc
web: rubicon.vc

Mission Statement: The mission of Georgetown Angels is to invest in high potential early stage disruptive technology companies while leveraging our network and relationships to accelerate the growth of our portfolio companies.

Investment Criteria: Later Stage Seed, Series A & B Rounds Co-Investing
Industry Group Preference: Fintech, Human Resource Technology, Marketplaces, New Service Models, Transformational Businesses, SaaS, Big Data, Cloud Computing, Advertising Technology, Media Technology, Mobility, Consumer Internet, Commerce, Social Services
Portfolio Companies: AgentIQ, Boom Fantasy, Canvs, Carpe, Daily Harvest, Dealflicks, Domio, Easyship, Honeycommb, Iotera, Lenda, LISNR, Maestro, Navdy, NodePrime, Nylas, One Page, Partender, Percolata, PremFina, Privus, Sourcery, Student Loan Genius, Superhuman, Tackk, The Block, Today Tix, True Anthem, Trumaker & Co., Unikrn, Zylotech

Other Locations:
44 Tehama St.
San Francisco, CA 94105

Key Executives:
Joshua B. Siegel, General Partner - New York
Education: BA, Boston University; MBA, Georgetown University
Background: Managing Member, Fantastia Partners; Manager, Eastern European Banking Systems, Citibank; Director of Market Intelligence, Citicorp Debt Capital Markets
Andrew C. Romans, General Partner - San Francisco
Education: BA, UVM; MBA, Georgetown University
Background: General Partner, The Founders Club; Director, Rainmaker Securities; Founder & President, The Global TeleExchange

1600 RUNTIDE CAPITAL
250 Park Avenue
7th Floor
New York, NY 10177

Phone: 212-572-4857
web: www.runtidecapital.com

Mission Statement: RunTide invests in growth stage businesses addressing the connected digital economy.

Geographic Preference: North America, Europe
Average Investment: $15 - $35 million
Minimum Investment: $15 million
Investment Criteria: Early-Stage, Revenues of a minimum $5 million, Operating History of 3 to 10 years
Industry Group Preference: Digital Media, Mobile Services, Data Analytics, Digital Marketing, E-Commerce, Communications, Cloud Computing
Portfolio Companies: Adaptix, Antenna, Binwise, Canal+, Interxion, Mobile Embrace, Model Metrics, Intent, PlusTV, Wine.com

Key Executives:
Charles Auster, Partner
e-mail: causter@runtidecapital.com
Education: Tufts University; JD, National Law Center George Washington University
Background: Partner/Managing Director, One Equity Partners; Founder, Auster Capital Partners
Directorships: Global Packaging Corporation
Robert Manning, Partner
e-mail: rmanning@runtidecapital.com
Education: Williams College
Background: Partner, Baker Capital; Founding Executive, DMX Inc.L CFO, Intermedia Communications Inc.; Director, Digex Inc.
Directorships: Interxion, Wine.com, Adaptix Inc., CoreValue Software, Canal+, Broadview Networks, Turin Networks
Kerri Ford, Partner
e-mail: kford@runtidecapital.com
Education: MBA, Wharton School, University of Pennsylvania
Background: Baker Capital; Cabletron Systems
Directorships: Canal+, Adaptix, Broadview Networks, MediaNet
Matt Auster, Principal
e-mail: mauster@runtidecapital.com
Education: Colgate University
Background: Auster Capital Partners; Carl Marks Advisory Group; Citigroup
Directorships: Assure Space LLC, Binwise Inc., Wilcoms Ltd.

1601 S3 VENTURES
6300 Bridgepoint Parkway
Building One, Suite 405
Austin, TX 78730

Phone: 512-258-1759
web: www.s3vc.com

Mission Statement: To help talented entrepreneurs take their technology and market knowledge and form valuable businesses.

Geographic Preference: Texas, Southwest United States
Fund Size: $60 million
Investment Criteria: Early-Stage

Venture Capital & Private Equity Firms / Domestic Firms

Industry Group Preference: Technology, Infrastructure, Software
Portfolio Companies: Alkami, Bluecava, Complex Media Network, Gravitant, Invodo, Kimbia, Metal Networks, OrthoAccel Technologies, Packet Design, Phunware, Pivot3, Pristine, Tango, TVA Medical, VUV Analytics
Key Executives:
   Brian R Smith, Managing Director
   Education: BSEE, University of Cincinnati; MSEE, Purdue University
   Background: Co-Founder, Convergent Investors Fund; Managing Director, Convergent Investors; Founder, Chairman & CEO, Crossroads Systems; Product Development, IBM Corporation
   Directorships: Callvine, Digby, Invodo, LibreDigital, OrthoAccel, Sipera, StoredIQ, Tango Health
   Charlie Plauche, Partner
   Education: BS, Finance, University of Mississippi; MBA, Red McCombs School of Business, University of Texas
   Background: Commercial Portfolio Manager, Regions Bank; Associate, Private Equity Group, Harbert Management Corporation;
   Directorships: Pristine Inc.; Kimbia; Favor; TVA Medical Inc.; Tango Health Inc.; BrainCheck; Atmosphere; LevelSet; OutboundEngine; Interplay Learning; LeanDNA; IFM Restoration; Alkami Tech

1602 SABAN CAPITAL GROUP
Phone: 310-557-5100
web: www.saban.com

Mission Statement: Through its private equity activitites, the firm makes both controlling and minority investments in public and private companies. The firm looks to drive growth, profitability and significant shareholder value of its investments through its solid track record and a unique blend of hands-on operating success with private equity investment expertise. SCG takes and active role in its portfolio companies in partnership with strong management.

Founded: 2001
Industry Group Preference: Media, Entertainment, Communications
Portfolio Companies: Celestial Tiger Entertainment, ironSource, Media Nusantara Citra, MNC Sky Vision, Partner Communications, Saban Brands LLC, Saban Films, Taomee, Univision Communications
Key Executives:
   Haim Saban, Chairman and Chief Executive Officer
   Adam Chesnoff, President and Chief Operating Officer
   Education: MBA, Anderson School of Management; BA, Economics and Management, Tel Aviv University's Recanatl School of Business Administration
   Joel Andryc, Managing Director, Private Equity
   Education: BA, Marquette University
   Philip Han, Senior Vice President and Chief Investment Officer
   Education: BA, Economics/Business, UCLA; MBA, Anderson School
   Sumeet Jaisinghani, Managing Director, Private Equity
   Education: BS, Finance and Management, Kelley School of Business, Indiana University

1603 SACHS CAPITAL
web: www.sachscapital.com

Mission Statement: Sachs Capital is a patient and value-add investor that acquires equity positions in private operating companies in the Mid-Atlantic region. Sachs Capital targets private investment opportunities that are too small or do not meet the investment criteria for, or are otherwise overlooked by, larger, institutional venture capital and private equity funds.

Geographic Preference: Mid-Atlantic United States
Founded: 2007
Average Investment: $1 - $5 million
Industry Group Preference: Diversified
Portfolio Companies: Highline Wealth Management, The Cleaning Authority, Motista, Empire Petroleum Holdings, Source 4 Teachers, TLK Group, Interaction Laboratories, BizTel One, Core Commnications, Bluemercury, Community of Science, Congressional Bank, Corus Health Realty, Cvent, eGain, Underground Solutions, LifeLinkMD, Lucidmedia, Matrics, P&A, Skye Chesapeake Bay Roating Company, Viztec
Key Executives:
   Andrew Sachs, Managing Member
   Education: BS, Foreign Service, Georgetown University; MBA, Georgetown University's McDonough School of Business
   Background: Analyst, Morgan Stanley; Co-Founder, KMS Investments; President, Capital Investors II; Co-Founder, Bethany Partners
   Directorships: Chesapeake Bay Roasting, Cleaning Authority, Empire Petroleum Holdings, Frontier Strategy Group, Source 4 Teachers, 1A Labs
   Stuart Bassin, Managing Partner
   Education: BS, Accounting & Finance, Washington University
   Background: Auditor, KPMG; Portfolio Analyst, The Zitelman Group; Co-Founder, Valuation Services Inc.; Arbitrator, American Arbitration Association

1604 SACRAMENTO ANGELS
Sacramento, CA

web: www.sacangels.com

Mission Statement: The Sacramento Angels and their Venture Capital strategic members believe in the journey of the entrepreneur and startups; the journey to make the world a better place, to create jobs and to keep America strong, competitive and at the forefront of innovation. We believe in this journey because we have traveled the path ourselves, either as entrepreneurs, working as executives in onetime startup companies, or as investors in the venture capital industry.

Geographic Preference: Northern California
Average Investment: up to $2 million
Portfolio Companies: Clinovo, ReovoRX, Revolights, Dynaoptics, TranscribeMe, Phyllom Bioproducts, On Farm Systems, Ecotensil, iSnap, Clean World Partners, LifeWave, Aperia, WellDog, Vokle, Glue Networks, Cloud Cruiser, Critical Perfusion, Reframe It, Vinperfect, Enkata Technologies, Freepath, NexGen Medical Systems, Visicon Technologies, Alter G, Clario Medical, Idapted, Revionics, Kovars, Prolacta Bioscience, Regenemed, Uptake Medical, American LegalNet, Novostent, PatientSafe Solutions, Mobius Technologies

1605 SAFEGUARD SCIENTIFICS
170 North Radnor-Chester Rd.
Suite 200
Radnor, PA 19087

Phone: 610-293-0600
e-mail: webmaster@safeguard.com
web: www.safeguard.com

Average Investment: $5-25 million
Investment Criteria: Seed Stage, Series A, Series B
Industry Group Preference: Technology, Healthcare, Financial Services, Digital Media
Portfolio Companies: Aktana, Clutch, Flashtalking, Hoopla, InfoBionic, Lumesis, Medcrypt, MediaMath, Mequilibrium, Moxe, NovaSom, Prognos, Quantic Mind, Sonobi, Syapse, T-Rex, The One Health Company, Transactis, Trice Medical, Velano Vascular, Vitaltrax, WebLinc, Zipnosis
Key Executives:
   Gary J Kurtzman, SVP & Managing Director
   Education: MD
   Steven J Grenfall, SVP & Managing Director
   Education: CPA

Venture Capital & Private Equity Firms / Domestic Firms

1606 SAGEVIEW CAPITAL
245 Lytton Ave.
Suite 250
Palo Alto, CA 94301

Phone: 650-473-5400
e-mail: info@sageviewcapital.com
web: www.sageviewcapital.com

Mission Statement: Sageview Capital combines active ownership, industry experience, and a partnership approach to provide growth capital to small and mid-size companies involved in the technology, financial services, and business services sectors.

Founded: 2005
Investment Criteria: Small and Mid-Sized Companies
Industry Group Preference: Technology, Financial Services, Business Services
Portfolio Companies: 360insights, Aceable, Avalara, Brandwatch, CallRail, Demandbase, DMT, Elastic Path, Exaro Energy III, MetricStream, NAM, Reflexis, Sageview-Wolff Real Estate, United Capital, Womply

Other Locations:
55 Railroad Ave.
Greenwich, CT 06830
Phone: 203-625-4200

Key Executives:
Ned Gilhuly, Co-Founder/Managing Partner
650-473-5410
e-mail: christine@sageviewcapital.com
Education: BA, Duke University; MBA, Stanford University
Background: Partner, KKR; Merrill Lynch Capital Markets
Directorships: Avalara, Elastic Path, Demandbase, Exaro Energy III, MetricStream
Scott Stuart, Co-Founder/Managing Partner
203-625-4255
e-mail: kathy@sageviewcapital.com
Education: AB, Dartmouth College; MBA, Stanford University
Background: Partner, KKR; Lehman Brothers Kuhn Leob
Directorships: NAM, Reflexis, United Capital, DMT Development Systems Group
Jeff Klemens, Partner
650-473-5430
e-mail: jeff@sageviewcapital.com
Education: BS, Business Administration, University of Southern California
Background: Associate, SPO Partners & Co.; Analyst, Goldman Sachs
Directorships: Avalara, Elastic Path, MetricStream, Reflexis, Sageview-Wolff Real Estate, DMT Development Systems Group
Andrew Korn, Partner
203-625-4217
e-mail: korn@sageviewcapital.com
Education: BA, Economics, Yale University
Background: Consultant, Boston Consulting Group
Directorships: Brandwatch, 360insights
Dean Nelson, Partner
Education: BS, Purdue University; MBA, University of Chicago
Background: Founder, KKR Capstone; Partner, Boston Consulting Group
Directorships: Reflexis, Brandwatch, 360insights, Womply, CallRail, Aceable

1607 SAIL VENTURE PARTNERS
3161 Michaelson Drive
Suite 750
Irvine, CA 92612

Phone: 949-398-5100 **Fax:** 949-398-5101
web: www.sailcapital.com

Mission Statement: A national venture capital firm specializing in early-stage companies.

Founded: 2002
Investment Criteria: Early Stage
Industry Group Preference: Clean Technology, Energy, Water
Portfolio Companies: Enerpulse, Ener-core, Ice Energy, SN Tech, Xtreme Power, Dow Kokam, Paragon, Kokam, WaterHealth International, M2 Renewables, Cleantech Group, CNS Response, Clean Technology Solutions

Other Locations:
2900 S Quincy Street
Suite 410
Arlington, VA 22206
Phone: 703-379-2713

1441 Canal Street
Suite 324
New Orleans, LA 70112
Phone: 504-598-5244

79 Wellington Street West
PO Box 37, 21st Floor
Toronto, ON M5K 1B7
Canada

1608 SAINTS CAPITAL
Phone: 415-773-2080
e-mail: info@sainstcapital.com
web: saintscapital.com

Mission Statement: Saints is a leading direct secondary acquirer of venture capital and private equity investments in emerging growth companies around the globe.

Geographic Preference: United States
Fund Size: $1 billion
Founded: 2000
Industry Group Preference: Technology, Healthcare, Consumer, Industrial, Communications, Consumer Services, Retail, Consumer & Leisure, Semiconductors, Software, Internet
Portfolio Companies: Acsis, Actelis Networks, Art.com, AtTask, Bay Microsystems, Beta O2, Blurb, Capella Photonics, CardioFocus, Cascade, Cidra, Coloredge, Conviva, Deem, Factual, Fulcrum Bioenergy, Gem, Genband, GigaComm, GigaTrust, GlassPoint, Illumina, Imgur, Infra, InnoGraft, InnoPath, Innovative Technology, Innovia, Interactive Media Holdings, Into Networks, Kaleo, Kik, Kona Medical, Linden Lab, Lithium, Medallia, Microchip, Minerva, Mitralign, Nanomix, ON24, One Medical, OrSense, Porch, Radisys, Reunion, RibX, Siano, SnugMug, Thinkwell, Tissuemed, Toolwire, Trion, TVU Networks, Verance, Viron, VivaReal, Webroot, Zazzle

Key Executives:
Kenneth B Sawyer, Managing Director
Education: BS, Industrial Engineering, Stanford University; MBA, Stanford Graduate School of Business
Background: Head of M&A, Prudential Volpe Technology Group; Head, Strategic Advisory Services, Volpe Brown Whelan & Co.
Directorships: Clearguage, Continuous Computing, HK Systems, Travel Intelligence, Laureate Pharmaceuticals, Acsis, Alliance
David P Quinlivan, Managing Director
Education: BA, Physics, Harvard University; MBA, Stanford University
Background: SVP, Finance, Insweb; Investment Banking, Credit Suisse First Boston

1609 SALEM INVESTMENT PARTNERS
4064 Colony Rd.
Suite 430
Charlotte, NC 28211

Phone: 704-684-4700
web: www.salemip.com

Venture Capital & Private Equity Firms / Domestic Firms

Mission Statement: Provides mezzanine debt and equity capital to lower middle-market companies.
Geographic Preference: Southwest & Mid-Atlantic Regions
Founded: 1999
Investment Criteria: Growth Financing, Acquisitions, Buyouts, Recapitalizations, Ownership Transitions
Industry Group Preference: Business Products & Services, Information Services, Communications, Media, Consumer Products, Distribution, Manufacturing, Healthcare Services
Portfolio Companies: A Touch of Country Magic, Acme Finishing Company, Apogee Translite, BW Manufacturing, Catalyte, Century Resources, ClassOne Group, Connectivity Wireless, Data Display Systems, DeWayne's Quality Metal, Dewey's Bakery, Edge Technologies, Global Value Commerce, Himalayan Handmade Candles, Honor Medical Staffing, Independent Imaging, Insight 2 Design, Instadium, Lamination Services, Linuxx Global Solutions, Mason Steel, Protochips, PSA Worldwide, Quality Alumnum Products, Reeves Extruded Products, Rugs Direct, Southeast Guardrail, Sunbelt Medical, US Tarp, Village Realty

Other Locations:
7900 Triad Center Dr.
Suite 333
Greensboro, NC 27409
Phone: 336-245-4747 **Fax:** 336-768-6471

Key Executives:
David M Faris, Partner
e-mail: dfaris@salemip.com
Education: BA, International Studies, University of South Carolina; MBA, University of South Carolina Moore School of Business
Background: SVP, Commercial Banking Group, RBC Bank; Principal, Banc of America Securities
Kevin B Jessup, Partner
e-mail: kjessup@salemip.com
Education: BS, Finance, University of North Carolina, Greensboro
Background: Partner, Blue Ridge Investors II; M&A, Wachovia Corporation
Philip W Martin, Partner
e-mail: pmartin@salemip.com
Education: Lenoir-Rhyne University
Background: Founder, Salem Capital Partners; VP Finance/CFO, Central Air Conditioning Distriburos; Corporate Treasurer, Douglas Battery Manufacturing Company

1610 SALESFORCE VENTURES
Salesforce Tower
415 Mission Street
3rd Floor
San Francisco, CA 94105

web: www.salesforce.com/company/ventures

Mission Statement: Salesforce Ventures, the venture capital arm of Salesforce, is dedicated to investing in and building the next generation of enterprise technology companies.
Geographic Preference: United States, Europe, Japan, Global
Fund Size: $100 million
Founded: 2009
Investment Criteria: Startups, Early Stage, Late Stage
Industry Group Preference: Enterprise Applications, Enterprise Software, Mobile Apps, Mobile Communications Devices, Cloud Computing
Portfolio Companies: 6Sense, 7Summits, A-SaaS, Abeja, AirPR, Aislelabs, All Turtles, Amplero, Andela, Andpad, Angaza, Appiphony, Arxxus, Astadia, AttackIQ, Augment, Automile, Autopilot, Bizer, BizReach, Bloomreach, Bringg, Bugcrowd, Carto, ChatBook, Classy, CloudSense, Cogito, Conga, Cooladata, Crunchbase, Crystal, Cydas, DEG, DemandBase, Devenson, Digital Genius, Dispatch, Empaua, Ellevest, Evariant, Evernote, Figure Eight, FinancialForce, Flect, FollowAnalytics, Forter, Free, Full Circle Insights, Fullstory, Gainsight, GetFeedback, GoCo, Goodpatch, Gospel, Govini, Guild, Guru, Gusto, HelpShift, HighSpot, Hoopla, Hustle, IFTTT, Informatica, Innova, InsideSales.com, InsightSquared, Introhive, Invoca, Janrain, Jazz, Jitterbit, Kakehashi, Kapost, Kitalive, Kooltra, Kyruus, Layer, LeadSift, LevelEleven, Loop & Tie, Madaket, MapAnything, Measurabl, Moneytree, Msg.ai, Narvar, Ncino, Novidea, NS1, Nymi, neMob, Onfido, PenDataSoft, Optimizely, OSF Commerce, OwnBackup, Pendo, Pieberry, Privitar, Propel, Pymetrics, Qubit, Quovo, RaiseMe, Relationship Science, Resilinc, Revup, Rootstock Software, RoundCorner, Runa, Samanage, Saucelabs, ScopeAI, SessionM, Sigfox, Silverline, Simplus, Simpplr, Sitetracker, Skuid, Smart Recruiter, SocialSafeGuard, , Splice, Squirro, Stripe, Tact.aI, Talkdesk, TechSee, Tectonic, TierICRM, Thousand Eyes, Torchlite, Traction Guest, Tulip, Unbabel, Universal Avenue, Up Skill, Vidyard, Viridis, Virsys12, Vlocity, Voicea, VSee, Wefox, Westbrook, Workato, Wootric, Wyng, Zylo

Key Executives:
Marc Benioff, Chairman/CEO
Education: BS, Business Administration, University of Southern California
Background: Oracle Corporation; Founder, Liberty Software; Apple Computer
Parker Harris, Chief Technology Officer
Education: BA, English Literature, Middlebury College
Background: Left Coast Software; Metropolis Software

1611 SALMON RIVER CAPITAL
1345 Avenue of the Americas
31st Floor
New York, NY 10105

Phone: 646-291-8831
e-mail: requestforinformation@salmonrivercapital.com
web: www.salmonrivercapital.com

Mission Statement: We have a single objective: working in active partnerships with entrepreneurial teams to build exceptional technology-enabled enterprises across a set of industries we know well.
Minimum Investment: $1 million
Industry Group Preference: Education, Healthcare Information Technology, Fintech, Online Media, Information Technology
Portfolio Companies: Axioma, Big Fish Games, Capella Education Company, eVestment, Moldflow Corporation, Netsmart Technologies, Parchment, PeriGen

Key Executives:
Joshua Lewis, Founder and Managing Principal
Education: PhD, Univ. of Oxford; AB, Princeton University
Background: General Partner, Warburg Pincus; General Partner, Forstmann Little

1612 SALT CREEK CAPITAL
2055 Woodside Road
Suite 250
Woodside, CA 94061

Phone: 415-238-4876
e-mail: info@saltcreekcap.com
web: www.saltcreekcap.com

Mission Statement: A private equity firm focused on lower middle market companies.
Geographic Preference: United States
Investment Criteria: Recapitalizations, Growth Capital, Buyouts, Management Led Buyouts, Corporate Divestitures
Industry Group Preference: Business Products & Services, Distribution, Energy Services, Franchising, Logistics, Specialty Finance
Portfolio Companies: Aquamar Holdings, Blue Ribbon Dispatch, Boyd Industries, Drake Equipment, Electro-Motion Inc., Extranomical Tours, The Flavor of california LLC, Four

Venture Capital & Private Equity Firms / Domestic Firms

Wheel Campers, Garrison Manufacturing, Griplock Systems, IT Assist Inc., King Tester Corporation, michigan Landscape Professionals, Network Distributors, Pacific Paper, Pacific Shoring, Roman Products LLC, Safe In Sound Hearing, Sound Building Supply, Sperry & Rice, Warne Scope Mounts, WorkWell Medical Group

Key Executives:
Dan Phelps, Founder & Managing Director
e-mail: dan@saltcreekcap.com
Education: BSBA, Ohio State University; MBA, University of Chicago; CPA
Background: General Partner, Duchossois Technology Partners; Pritzker Family
Dan Mytels, Founding Member & Managing Director
Education: B.S. Management Science, University of California San Diego

1613 SALVEO CAPITAL
2100 Sanders Road
Suite 170
Northbrook, IL 60062

Phone: 312-260-1125
web: www.salveocapital.com

Mission Statement: Invests in companies serving the cannabis industry, including software & technology, support services, dispensaries, and cultivation centres.

Industry Group Preference: Cannabis
Portfolio Companies: Headset, Front Range Biosciences, W☐rk, Tokyo Smoke, Treez, Purissima, Flow Kana, PathogenDx, Harborside Health Center, Ascend Wellness, Baker Technologies

Key Executives:
Michael C. Gruber, Managing Partner
Education: BA, Enconomics/International Relations, University of Pennsylvania; MBA, Finance/Accounting/Marketing, Kellogg School of Management, Northwestern University
Background: Mentor, The Founder Institute; Manager Partner, VentureLab; Investor/Mentor, TechStars Chicago; Founder/Managiner Partner/CEO, Cornerstone Opportunity Partners; Partner, Independence Equity
Directorships: Front Range Biosciences, Algal Scientific, KitoTech Medical
Jeffrey Howard, Managing Partner
Education: BA, Philosophy, Westminster College; MBA, Charles H. Kellstadt Graduate School of Business, DePaul University
Background: Managing Director/Head of Americas Futures & Options, Merrill Lynch; Managing Director/Global Head of Prime Services, Royal Bank of Scotland
Sean Doyle, Senior Associate
Education: BBA, Eller College of Management, University of Arizona; MBA, Booth School of Business, University of Chicago
Background: Co-Founder, InsightDrive; Sales Analyst, Vestas

1614 SAMSUNG NEXT
2 Embarcadero Center
San Francisco, CA 94111

web: samsungnext.com

Mission Statement: Samsung NEXT is the venture capital arm of Samsung Group.

Geographic Preference: US, Canada, Europe, Israel, Korea
Founded: 2012
Industry Group Preference: Artificial Intelligence, Virtual Reality, Blockchain, Data Analytics, Digital Health, Robotics, IoT, Mobility, Security, Cryptocurrency
Portfolio Companies: 2sens, 8i, After School, Baobab Studios, Bayshore Networks, Beekeeper, BioBeats, BlazingDB, Branch, Brodmann17, Cohero Health, Converge, Covariant AI, Cylera, Dapper Labs, Dashbot, Data.World, Dataguise, Directly, Edgeworx, Eko Studio, Entrypoint VR, Famous, Figure 1, Filament, FloydHub, Glooko, Grover, HealthifyMe, Healthy.io, Home.is, HYPR, Intezer, Intuition Robotics, Juvo, Life360, LiquidSky, Mobidoo, Nexar, Packet, PlayVS, Puls, RapidDeploy, SafeDK, SignalWire, Sixense, Sliver.tv, Sorenson Media, Spatial Stae, StreamElements, Survios, Swiftly, Terapede, Tetrate, Unbabel, Unikey, VeeR, Vicarious, Vidrovr, Vinli, Virtru, WeVR, Zimperium

Other Locations:
30 West 26th Street
New York, NY 10010

Neue Schonhauser Street 3-5
Berlin 10178
Germany

129 Samsung-ro
Yeongtong-gu
Suwon
Gyeonggi-do
Korea

Tel Aviv
Israel

Key Executives:
Gary Coover, General Manager/Head of Operations
Education: BA, Santa Clara University; MBA, Haas School of Business
Background: Consultant, Navigant Consulting
Gus Warren, Managing Director, New York
Education: BA, Cornell University
Background: Venture Partner, FirstMark Capital; Co-Founder/COO, Disconnect; SVP/GM, Spot Runner; Portfolio Manager, Granite Ventures; Time Warner Ventures; Product Manager, Internet Profiles
Jamie Choi, VP/Head of Samsung NEXT Korea
Education: BA, Syracuse University; MBA, Yonsei University
Background: VP, Goldman Sachs
Eyal Miller, VP/Managing Director, Israel
Education: MBA, Recanati School of Business, Tel Aviv University
Background: Co-Founder, Google Cample, Tel Aviv; Head of New Business & Corporate Development, Google Israel

1615 SAN DIEGO VENTURE GROUP
10996 Torreyana Road
Suite 285
San Diego, CA 92121

Phone: 858-558-8750
e-mail: info@sdvg.org
web: www.sdvg.org

Mission Statement: To provide a networking forum for entrepreneurs, venture capitalists and advisors in an informal atmosphere where human expertise can foster new ventures.

Founded: 1986

Key Executives:
Mike Krenn, President
Background: DLA Piper; Founder, Venture Pipeline Group; Founder, Tech Coast Angels; Founder, CommNexus

1616 SAND HILL ANGELS
Mountain View, CA 94043

web: www.sandhillangels.com

Mission Statement: Makes early stage investments in promising startups and provides expertise and assistance in fledgling enterprises.

Geographic Preference: San Francisco Bay Area
Founded: 2000
Average Investment: $100,000 - $500,000
Investment Criteria: Early stage

Venture Capital & Private Equity Firms / Domestic Firms

Industry Group Preference: Information Technology, Software, Communications, Networking, Semiconductors, Life Sciences, Bioinformatics, Medical Devices, Pharmaceuticals, Diagnostics, Clean Technology
Portfolio Companies: Aligned Carbon, Ampaire, Apponboard, Arcadia, Archer Aviation, Armory, Ashvattha, Astra Augmedix, Axiom Space, Banzai, Beast Brands, Bryte, Carbon 38, Carbon Health, Carta, Chooch AI, ClearFlame Engines, ClearLaw AI, Connected Signals, Diatomix, EquipmentShare, FiscalNote, Front Range Biosciences, Greenlight Guideline, HitRecord, Hungry, HyperScience, IDbyDNA, Imprint Energy, Inhalon Biopharma, Invenia, Isabl, Jackpocket, KidsToPros, LeaseLock, Lex Markets, Lottery Now, madison Reed, Masterclass, Mati, Matrix Industries, Mission Bio, Mojo Vision, MycoTechnology, Nanomedical Diagnostics, New Age Meats, New Wave Foods, Nines, OnScale, Orbit Fab, Overtime, Owl AI, Parsley Health, Peloton Technology, Petal, Philo, PlusPlus, Prodigy, PROFUSA, Quip, Qurasense Relativity Space, Samba TV, ShellHound, Senti Biosciences, Sentinel Healthcare, Shiprocket, Skillz, Sonavi Labs, Subspace, The Guild, Thirty madison, Trash Warrior, Volumetric Biotechnologies, WaterSmart Software, Xplore

1617 SANDALPHON CAPITAL
111 W Illinois Street
WeWork River North, 5th Floor
Chicago, IL 60654

e-mail: info@sandalphoncapital.com
web: sandalphoncapital.com

Mission Statement: Sandalphon seeks to be a helpgul partner to entrepreneurs to maximize the probability of a good outcome for all stakeholders.
Geographic Preference: Chicago and Midwest US
Founded: 2016
Average Investment: $100,000-300,000

Key Executives:
Jonathan Ellis, Founder/Managing Director
Education: BSc, University of Manchester; INSEAD
Background: SVP, MacQuarie Principal Finance Group

1618 SANDBOX INDUSTRIES
1000 West Fulton Market
Suite 213
Chicago, IL 60607

Phone: 312-243-4100
e-mail: info@sandboxindustries.com
web: www.sandboxindustries.com

Mission Statement: Sandbox Industries creates, invests in and explores new businesses. The firm pursues early-stage investment opportunities and aims to leverage its experience, expertise, and resources to drive the success of its portfolio companies. Sandbox Industries has partnered with Cultivian Ventures through the venture capital firm Cultivian Sandbox Ventures, which invests in agricultural technology companies.
Fund Size: $18.8 million
Average Investment: $50,000 - $2 million
Investment Criteria: Seed-Stage, Early Stage
Industry Group Preference: Software, Technology-Enabled Services
Portfolio Companies: 71LBS, Fresh Squeeze, Aavya Health, AbioGenix, Allituition, Allylix, Aquaspy, Aratana, Babbaco, BFF GEMZ, Bloom Health, Bluelight, Bon'App, Bookyap, Buzz Referrals, CakeStyle, Capson, Cara Health, CareCentrix, CareHubs, CareSimply, CareWire, Change Healthcare, Connection Brands, Cookitfor.us, Corengi, Cureeo, Defy, Dermlink, Desktop Geneti, Divergence, Doggyloot, Embodi, Eosi, Essence Group, EveryMove, Fango, Feefighters, Fibroblast, Food Genius, Foodini, Frintit, GeckoCap, Get Fresh Kit, Getafive, GiveForward, Goshi, Gweepi Medical, Harvery Automation, HealthClinicPlus, Healthspring, HealthDelivery, HeartFlow, HomeTouch, Initiate, IntroFly, Invivolink, iquartic, Lab42, Lasso, Lost Crates, Marbles, Mathzee, Medopad, Mira Rehab, Morgan Street, MoxieJean, My Coupon Doc, Myca, NaviHealth, Nexidia, Noblivity, Orbeus, Orggit, PatientCo, Phreesia, Pictarine, Portable Medic, Power2Switch, Push Wellness, PVPower, Readeo, ScholarPro, Shortlist, Smart Scheduling, Soma Analytics, Spothero, SwiftPay MD, SwipeSense, Exchangery, United Preference, Uprise Medical, WeGather, WhimseyBox, Yosko, Zeomega

Other Locations:
444 Townsend Street
Suite 3
San Francisco, CA 91407
Phone: 312-243-4100

Key Executives:
Robert Shapiro, Chairman/Managing Director
Education: AB, Harvard College; JD, Columbia University School of Law
Background: Chairman & CEO, Monsanto Agriculture Group; CEO, The NutraSweet Company; VP & General Counsel, GD Searle & Co.
Directorships: Chromatin, Elevance Renewable Sciences, Intrexon Corporation, Conservis Corp., Advanced Animal Diagnostics
Nick Rosa, Co-CEO
Education: BS, Political Science, Northern Illinois University; MBA, DePaul University
Background: CEO, NutraSweet Company; Senior Executive, Monsanto
Matt Downs, Co-CEO
Education: BA, Brigham Young University; MBA, Stanford Graduate School of Business
Background: Associate, Highland Capital Partners; Analyst, M&A, Morgan Stanley
Directorships: Aspire Health, Capson, Essence Group, Lumiata, Medsave, Myca
Anna Haghgooie, Managing Director
Education: BBA, University of Michigan Ross School of Business; MBA, University of Chicago Booth School of Business
Background: Financial Management Program, General Electric; Associate Director, Fitch Ratings; General Manager, Pulling Down the Moon
Steve Engelberg, Managing Director
Education: BA, University of Michigan; MA, Georgetown University; JD, Harvard Law School
Background: SVP, Monsanto Company; Managing Partner, Keck, Mahin & Cate; Legislative Council, Senator Walter F. Mondale

1619 SANDERLING VENTURES
1300 S El Camino Real
Suite 203
San Mateo, CA 94402

Phone: 650-401-2000 Fax: 650-375-7077
e-mail: info@sanderling.com
web: www.sanderling.com

Mission Statement: To be the partner of choice for entrepreneurs and investors in building biomedical companies that improve the treatment of human diseases.
Fund Size: $318 million
Founded: 1979
Average Investment: $1 million
Minimum Investment: $250,000
Investment Criteria: Seed, Early-Stage, Later-Stage
Industry Group Preference: Biotechnology, Medical & Health Related, Pharmaceuticals, Therapeutics
Portfolio Companies: Altor BioScience, Artielle, Asteres, Axikin Pharmaceuticals, CalciMedica, CoMentis, Cylene Pharmaceuticals, Dynatherm Medical, InfraReDx, LineaGen, Naviscan, NovoStent, Pulsar Vascular, Sotera Wireless, Tenex Greenhouse, TheraVida, Theregen Corporation, Tomophase, Torax, ViaCyte, Atherogenics, CardioNet, Chimerix,

Dendreon, Digirad, Dynavax Technologies, Endocyte, InterMune Pharmaceuticals, ISTA Pharmaceuticals, Pacira Pharmaceuticals, ReGen Biologics, Regeneron Pharmaceuticals, SkyePharma, Stereotaxis, Vical, Xoma

Other Locations:
1010 Sherbrooke Street W
Suite 408
Montreal, QC H3A 2R7
Canada
Phone: 515-564-6474

Key Executives:
Fred A Middleton, Managing Director
Education: BS Chemistry, MIT; MBA, Harvard Business School
Background: Consultant, McKinsey & Company; Vice President, Chase Manhattan Bank; President Finance/Administration, Genentech; Co- Founder, Morgan Stanley Ventures
Robert G McNeil PhD, Managing Director
Education: PhD, Molecular Biology, Biochemistry, Genetics, University of California, Irvine
Background: Portfolio Manager, Shuman Agnew & Co; Co-founder/CEO, CoCensys; Chairman/CEO, Acea; Chairman, Peregrine Pharmaceuticals
Paulette Taylor, General Counsel/Principal
Education: JD, University of California Hastings College of Law; BA, University of Washington
Background: Counsel, Alumax; Associate, Farella, Braun & Martel; Executive VP, National Insurance Group
Timothy C Mills PhD, Managing Director
Education: BSEE, University of Colorado; MSEE and Computer Science, PhD Bioengineering, University of California, Berkeley; San Francisco School of Medicine
Background: Corporate VP New Business/Chief Scientific Officer, Target Therapeutics; Director, Prograft Medical; Director Interventional Cardiology, Baxter Healthcare
Directorships: Artifical Heart Program, Irvine Medical Center
Timothy Wollaeger, Managing Director Emeritus
Education: BA Economics, Yale University; MBA, Stanford Graduate School of Business
Background: VP/General Manager Mexico, Baxter International; VP/CFO, Hybritech; Founding General Partner, Biovest; Co-Founder, Columbia Hospital Corporation; Founder, Kingsbury Capital Partners
Peter C McWilliams PhD, Venture Partner
Education: PhD, MA, Chemistry, Princeton University; BA Natural Sciences, Cambridge University; MBA, Columbia Business School
Background: Product Manager, Genentech, Associate, Booz, Allen & Hamilton; Oxford Molecular

1620 SANDLER CAPITAL MANAGEMENT
711 5th Avenue
15th Floor
New York, NY 10022

Phone: 212-754-8100 **Fax:** 212-826-0280/0281
web: www.sandlercap.com

Mission Statement: To identify, invest and create value in companies that operate in the communications industries.

Geographic Preference: United States, Europe
Fund Size: $750 Million
Founded: 1990
Average Investment: $5 - $60 million
Minimum Investment: $5 Million
Investment Criteria: Early Stage, Growth Stage, Established
Industry Group Preference: Communications, Media, Entertainment

Key Executives:
Michael Marocco, Managing Director/Head, Private Equity
Education: BA, University of Southern Maine; MBA, New York University
Background: Research Analyst, Morgan Stanley
John Kornreich, Senior Advisor
Education: BA, University of Pennsylvania; MBA, Columbia Business School
Background: Investment Analyst, CBWL Hayden Stone; Portfolio Manager, Neuberger & Bermain
William Bianco, Managing Director
Education: BA, Brown University; JD, Harvard Law School
Background: Associate/Partner, Akin Gump Strauss Hauer & Feld LLP
Directorships: Farelogix; Modulant Solutions; Wizmo
Andrew Sandler, Managing Director/Portfolio Manager, Head of Hedge Funds
Education: B.S. Finance, University of Wisconsin at Madison

1621 SANOFI-GENZYME BIOVENTURES
50 Binney Street
Cambridge, MA 02142

web: www.sanofigenzymebioventures.com

Mission Statement: SGBV is different from traditional venture capital firms. SGBV provies portfolio companies with guidance and advice by leveraging established expertise in science, preclinical and clinical development, regulatory, manufacturing, market access, commercialization, and more. In return, SBV expects an ongoing window into the company's progress and future products, through advisory committee membership, technical update meetings, board observers and/or director positions.

Investment Criteria: Private early-stage
Industry Group Preference: Biotechnology, Healthcare Innovation, Oncology, Vaccines, Integrated Health Solutions, Life Sciences
Portfolio Companies: Unum Therapeutics, LTI, Immune Design, Common Sensing, Edimer, Ultrageny Pharmaceutical, Esperance, Kahr Medical, Fate Therapeutics, GlycoMimetics, KaloBios, Proteostasis, Valerion Therapeutics

Other Locations:
54-56 Rue La Boétie
Paris 75008
France

Jason P Hafler, Managing Director
Education: BA, Bowdoin College; PhD, University of Cambridge
Background: Director of Corporate Development, RaNA Therapeutics; Associate, Life Sciences Group, Atlas Ventures; Entrepreneurial Fellow, Flagship Ventures; Analyst, JSB Partners LP
Directorships: Escient Pharmaceuticals; Icosavax; Expansion Therapeutics; Amathus Therapeutics
Jim Tenkle, Head of Investments
Education: BS, University of Michigan; PhD, Organic Chemistry, MIT; MBA, University of California Berkeley
Background: VP of Investments, Pivotal bioVenture Partners; Gilead Sciences

1622 SANTE VENTURES
300 West 6th Street
Suite 2300
Austin, TX 78701

Phone: 512-721-1200
e-mail: press@santeventures.com
web: www.santeventures.com

Mission Statement: Focused on developing lasting, well-aligned partnerships with exceptional entrepreneurs and executives to build valuable companies. In addition to capital, Sante Ventures provides deep healthcare domain expertise and extensive background of industry contacts and resources.

Geographic Preference: United States

Venture Capital & Private Equity Firms / Domestic Firms

Fund Size: $14.5 million
Founded: 2006
Average Investment: $4 - $12 million
Investment Criteria: Early-Stage, Seed-Stage
Industry Group Preference: Life Sciences, Medical Technology, Healthcare Services, Healthcare Information Technology
Portfolio Companies: BARonova, BetaCat Pharmaceuticals, BioStable Science & Engineering, Claret Medical, Endo Stim, Iowa Approach, Lumos Pharma, Lyric Pharmaceuticals, Millipede, Mirna Therapeutics, Molecular Templates Inc., Terapio, TVA Medical, Healthcare Highways, HNI Healthcare, AbVitro, Accuro, Emageon, Explorys Medical, Healthspring, LDR Spine, Rise Health, Stereotaxis, TomoTherapy

Other Locations:
4203 Montrose Boulevard
Suite 300
Houston, TX 77006
Phone: 713-904-1926

Key Executives:
Kevin M. Lalande, Managing Director
Education: BS, Electrical & Computer Engineering; MBA, Harvard Business School
Background: Austin Ventures; Management Consultant, McKinsey & Company; Co-Founder, Netopia; Co-Founder, TimeMarker
Joe Cunningham MD, Managing Director
Education: BS, MD, Texas A&M University; MBA, Baylor University
Background: Healthcare Venture Partner, Austin Ventures; Vice Chair, Ascension Health Venture Investment Committee; Chief Medical Officer, Providence Health System; Executive Director, Providence Health Alliance
Douglas D. French, Managing Director
Background: President & CEO, Ascension Health System; Venture Partner, Austin Ventures
Directorships: Herman Miller, Emageon, Ascension Health, Diginity Health
Casey Cunningham, MD, Chief Scientific Officer
Education: MD, University of Texas Southwestern Medical School; Fellowship, Oncology & Hematology; Harvard Medical School
Background: Chief Medical Officer, Terapio; Chief Medical Officer, Molecular Templates; Founding Member, Division of Experimental Medicine, Brigham & Women's Hopsital; Associate Director, Mary Crowley Cancer Research Center
Billy Cohn, MD, Venture Partner
Education: Oberlin College; Baylor College of Medicine
Background: Associate Professor, Harvard Medical School; Director, Minimally Invasive Surgical Technology, Texas Heart Institute; Associate Professor, Surgery, Baylor College of Medicine; Adjunct Professor, Bioengineering, University of Houston
James Eadie, MD, Partner
Education: BS, Bioengineering, University of Michigan; MBA, University of Texas McCombs School of Business; MD, Harvard Medical School
Background: Air Force, Medical Director & Vice-Chair of Emergency Medicine, Wilford Hall Medical Center

1623 SAPPHIRE VENTURES
3408 Hillview Avenue
Building 5
Palo Alto, CA 94304

Phone: 650-382-1110
e-mail: info@sapphireventures.com
web: www.sapphireventures.com

Mission Statement: Sapphire Ventures is focused on helping today's most innovative expansion-stage technology companies become global category-defining leaders.

Geographic Preference: United States, Europe, Israel
Fund Size: $353 million
Founded: 1996
Average Investment: $5 - $12 million
Investment Criteria: Early- and Growth-Stage
Industry Group Preference: Information Technology
Portfolio Companies: Alfresco Software Alteryx, Apigee, Black Duck, Box, Convercent, DocuSign, Fitbit, GroundWork, iovation, iTAC Software AG, iYogi, Jibe, Kaltura, Krux, Lavante, Lithium Technologies, Mirantis, MuleSoft, Narrative Science, Newgen Software, Nutanix, OnDeck, One97, Onventis, OpenX, Ping Identity, Recommind, Retail Solutions, Return Path, SAVO, Scytl, Socrata, Splashtop, Spring Mobile, Square, Ticketfly, Zend

Key Executives:
Nino Marakovic, CEO and Managing Director
Education: Williams College; Stanford Grad. School of Business
Background: meVC Draper Fisher Jurvetson
Directorships: Inkling; Integral Ad Science; OpenX; Tidalscale

1624 SARATOGA PARTNERS
535 Madison Avenue
4th Floor
New York, NY 10022

Phone: 212-906-7800 **Fax:** 212-750-3343
e-mail: saratoga@saratogapartners.com
web: www.saratogapartners.com

Mission Statement: Saratoga partners has achieved attractive rates of return by consistently following a three-pronged investment strategy: add value through partnership with outstanding management; invest for growth in middle market companies; and customize capital structures to minimize risk and optimize return. Saratoga believes that its disciplined investment approach, based on time honored principals, will continue to provide the superior returns it has historically achieved.

Geographic Preference: United States
Fund Size: $750 million
Founded: 1984
Average Investment: $10-$400 million
Minimum Investment: $5 million
Investment Criteria: LBO, MBO, Recaps
Industry Group Preference: Communications, Distribution, Natural Resources, Financial Services, Industrial Equipment, Publishing, Energy
Portfolio Companies: Advanced Lighting Technologies Inc., Atlantic Cellular Company LP, The Bowery Saving Bank, CapMAC, Cannell Communications LP, Commsoft, Data Return LLC, Datavantage Corporation, Emeritus Corporation, Equality Specialities Inc., EUR Systems Inc., Formica Corporation, Gulf Coast Coca-Cola Bottling Company, Hawaiian Wireless Inc., Hi-Lo Automotive Inc., J&W Scientific Inc., James Communications, Koppers Inc., NAT Inc., Scovill Fasteners Inc., Sericol Inc., STC Wireless Resources Inc., USI Insurance Services Corp., Viking Office Products

Key Executives:
John P. Birkelund, Senior Advisor
Education: AB, Princeton University; Northwestern University
Background: Dillon Reed & Company; Co-Founder New Court Securities Corporation; Chief Executive Officer of N.M. Rothschild & Sons; Past Director New York Stock Exchange
Charles P. Durkin, Jr., Senior Advisor
Education: BS, Princeton University; MBA, Columbia University
Background: Director of the following companies, Atlantic Cellular; Datavantage Corporation, Koppers, Inc; Scovill Fasteners; USI Holdings; CapMSC, Formica Coproration, Hi-Lo Automotive; Viking Office Products

Venture Capital & Private Equity Firms / Domestic Firms

Christian L. Oberbeck, Managing Director
Education: BS in Physics and BA in Mathematics, Brown University; MBA, Columbia University
Background: Corporate Development Group of Arthur Young; Blyth Eastman Paine Webber; Castle Harlan
John F. MacMurray, Managing Director
Education: AB, Princeton University; MBA, Columbia Business School
Background: EuroConsult
Charles G. Phillips, IV, Managing Director
Education: AB, Harvard College; MBA, Harvard Business School
Background: Dillon Read's; McCown De Leeuw & Company; Equality Specialties; Datavantage Corporation
Richard A. Petrocelli, Managing Director
Education: BS, Georgetown University; MBA, New York University
Background: Gabelli; BDO Siedman
Maria F Costanzo, Controller
Education: BS, Iona College
Background: Compass Global Group; Gabelli Asset Management; Tax Consultant for Arthur Andersen
David W. Niemiec, Senior Advisor
Education: Graduated Harvard College; MBA, Harvard Business School
Background: Vice Chairman of Dillon, Read & Company;

1625 SATORI CAPITAL
2501 North Hardwood Street
20th Floor
Dallas, TX 75201

Phone: 214-390-6270
Toll-Free: 888-972-8674
e-mail: info@satoricapital.com
web: www.satoricapital.com

Mission Statement: Satori is the preferred partner for companies that are building significant long-term value through a sustainable approach.

Geographic Preference: Southwestern United States
Investment Criteria: Middle Market: Revenues from $25 to $200 million
Industry Group Preference: Business Products & Services, Consumer Products, E-Commerce & Manufacturing, Financial Services, Manufacturing, Software, Information Technology, Telecommunications
Portfolio Companies: 24 Hour Fitness, Aspen Heigths, Gibraltar Capital Holdings, Hodges Ward Elliott, Longhorn Health Solutions, The Lovesac Company, Nomacorc, Purple Land Management, Ranger Wireless Solutions, SunTree Snack Foods, Zorch International

Other Locations:
2821 West 7th Street
Suite 285
Fort Worth, TX 76107

Key Executives:
Sunny Vanderbeck, Managing Partner
Background: Co-Founder/CEO, Data Return; Team Leader, Microsoft; U.S. Special Operations Command
Randy Eisenman, Managing Partner
817-200-7805
Education: BS, Business Administration, University of Texas
Background: Partner, Q Investments; Financial Analyst, Goldman Sachs & Co.
Rugger Burke, Principal
214-390-6274
Education: BS, JD, Southern Methodist University
Background: Master in Chancery; FINRA Arbitrator
John Grafer, Principal
214-390-6284
Education: BBA, Accounting, University of Notre Dame; MBA, Finance, University of Chicago Booth School of Business

Background: Senior Vice President, Giuliana Partners; M&A Group, Credit Suisse First Boston; Proprietary Trading Group, JP Morgan Chase & Co.

1626 SATURN PARTNERS
75 Federal Street
Suite 1320
Boston, MA 02110

Phone: 617-574-3330 Fax: 617-574-3331
e-mail: saturnasset@saturnpartnersvc.com
web: www.saturnasset.com

Mission Statement: A venture capital and private equity firm committed to generating significant returns for its investors.

Geographic Preference: Northeastern United States
Founded: 1994
Investment Criteria: Early-Stage
Industry Group Preference: Biotechnology, Information Technology, E-Commerce & Manufacturing, Fintech, Advanced Materials
Portfolio Companies: 3form, Alignable, American Made, Applied CleanTech, Axioma, BioWish Technologies, Bodymedia, Boston Duck Tours, Chirpify, Constant Contact, CORE Outdoor Power, Express KCS, FreeMarkets, Good Technology, Knopp Biosciences, Marathon, Mismi, Omaze, Pavève, Panopto, SureLogic, The Ride, Think Through Math, Twin Rivers Technologies, Xpress Natural Gas

Key Executives:
Jeffrey S McCormick, Chairman/Managing Partner
Education: BS, Biology; MBA, Finance, Syracuse University
Background: Bariston Associates
Directorships: MooBella, American Made, SureLogic, Knopp Neurosciences, Applied Clean Tech, NHXS
Bill Guttman, Partner
Education: MA/PhD, Oxford University
Background: Co-Founder, CyLab; CEO, Printcafe; CEO, Axioma
Directorships: American Made LLC; Express KCS; Panopto; Trunomi; YieldStree
Edward A Lafferty, Partner/Chief Financial Officer
Education: BS, Business Administration, Northeastern University; MBA, Bentley College
Background: Controller, Berkshire Partners
Directorships: Applied CleanTech, ModelGolf

1627 SAUGATUCK CAPITAL COMPANY
4 Armstrong Road
Suite 230
Shelton, CT 06484

Phone: 203-348-6669 Fax: 203-324-6995
e-mail: saugatuck@saugatuckcapital.com
web: www.saugatuckcapital.com

Mission Statement: Private investment firm specializing in middle market acquisitions and growth equity investments.

Geographic Preference: United States, Canada
Fund Size: $126 million
Founded: 1982
Average Investment: $6 million
Minimum Investment: $3 million
Investment Criteria: Later-Stage, LBO, MBO, Consolidation, Growth, Recaps; Companies with prominent positions in niche markets, proprietary products and services or high-engineering and/or service content
Industry Group Preference: Diversified
Portfolio Companies: American Pipe & Plastics, APCT, Exocor, FEMCO Machine Co., Floor & DéCor Outlets of America, Lunada Bay Corp., Pharmaceutic Litho & Label Company, PPI/Time Zero Inc., The TharpeRobbins Company, TradeSource, Tulip Corporation

Key Executives:
Gary L Goldberg, Managing Director
e-mail: ggoldberg@saugatuckcapital.com

Venture Capital & Private Equity Firms / Domestic Firms

Education: BA, Philosophy, Colgate University; MBA, Cornell University Johnson Graduate School of Management
Background: Founder & Managing Partner, Arch Investment Management; VP Operations, Priceline.com
Stuart W Hawley, Managing Director
e-mail: shawley@saugatuckcapital.com
Education: BS, University of North Carolina; MBA, Kenan-Flagler Business School, University of North Carolina, Chapel Hill
Background: VP, Prudential Securities, Fidelity Investments
Frank J Hawley Jr, Senior Advisor
Education: Phi Beta Kappa, BS, Physics, University of North Carolina; MBA, Harvard Business School
Background: General Partner, Foster Management Company; Executive Vice President, Laidlaw-Coggeshall, Inc., Lazard Freres, Eaton & Howard, Inc.

1628 SAVANO CAPITAL PARTNERS
6 East Eager St.
Suite 4A
Baltimore, MD 21202

Phone: 443-873-3561
e-mail: info@savanocapital.com
web: www.savanocapital.com

Mission Statement: Savano Capital partners with private shareholders and exceptional growth companies.

Portfolio Companies: Actifio, Clarabridge, DrFirst, Endgame, Everquote, Hearsay, Ignition One, JobCase, Kaltura, Lotame, Nintex, Parallels, Silver Peak, UpWork, Vestmark

Other Locations:
1775 Tysons Blvd.
5th Floor
Tysons, VA 22102
Phone: 443-873-3561

Key Executives:
Tom Smith, Managing Partner
e-mail: tom@savanocapital.com
Education: BS, Elizabethtown College; MBA, University of North Carolina, Chapel Hill
Background: General Partner, Edison Ventures; General Partner, Mid-Atlantic Venture Funds

1629 SCALE VENTURE PARTNERS
950 Tower Lane
Suite 1150
Foster City, CA 94404

Phone: 650-378-6000 Fax: 650-378-6040
e-mail: businessplan@scalevp.com
web: www.scalevp.com

Mission Statement: A venture capital fund for all stages of a company's growth with a focus on innovative technologies.

Fund Size: $25 million
Founded: 1960
Average Investment: $5 - $15 million
Minimum Investment: $3 million
Investment Criteria: Early-Stage, Mid-Stage, Late-Stage
Industry Group Preference: Broadband, Enterprise Services, Semiconductors, Optical Technology, Software, Biotechnology, Medical Devices, Networking, Technology, Healthcare, Media, Marketing
Portfolio Companies: Actiance, Agari, Alimera Sciences, Applause, Apteligent, Arena, Ascenta Therapeutics, Aurum, Aviso, Bill.com, Obizible, Boundary, Box, BrightRoll, Chef Code Can, Circle Ci, Cloud Health Technologies, Connect, E-Data Sift, Datastax, Demand Base, DiaDexus, DocuSign, Drone Deploy, eGroups, Entone, Everyday Health, Exact Target, Extole, Forter, Front Bridge, Glu, Good, Healogics, Horizon Pharma, Hubspan, Hubspot, Imt, Jasper Soft, JFrog, Katch, Keep Truckin, Lever, Liaison, Livescribe, LivHome, Locus, Lumension, MBlox, Namely, Net6, NetGenesis, New Century Hospice, Omniture, Onelogin, Oraya Therapeutics, Orexigen, OuterBay, Pentheon, People Matter, Real-Time Collaboration Solutions By PlaceWare, PubNub, Realm, Ring Central, SailTthru, Scale Computing, ScanSafe, Solvvy, Sonexa, Speechworks, Spinal Kinetics, Stormpath, Sylantro, TalkIQ, Teros, Textio, Threat Stack, Treasure Data, Tripwire, Unifi, Vitrue, Walk Me, Wayport, Wrike, Zogenix, Zone Labs

Key Executives:
Mark Brooks, Venture Partner
e-mail: mark@scalevp.com
Education: BA, Economics, Dartmouth College; MBA, Finance & Entrepreneurial Managment, Wharton School
Background: Senior Associate, Mercer Management Consulting; Loan Officer, Media Group, Manufacturers Hanover Trust Company
Directorships: Alimera Sciences, Century Hospice, In-Patient Consultants Management, LivHome, National Healing Holding Corporation, Oraya Therapeutics, Spinal Kintetics
Kate Mitchell, Partner
e-mail: kate@scalevp.com
Education: BA, Stanford University; MBA, Executive Program, Golden Gate University
Background: Senior Vice President, Bank of America
Rory O'Driscoll, Managing Director
e-mail: rory@scalevp.com
Education: BSc, London School of Economics
Directorships: Arena Solutions, Box.net, DocuSign, ExactTarget, Hubspan, Innovion, LiveScribe, Lumension Security, Vantage Media
Stacey Bishop, Partner
e-mail: stacey@scalevp.com
Education: BA, University of Michigan; MBA, Columbia Business School
Background: M&A, Bank of America's Corporate Development Group; Account Manager, Syntel
Sharon Weinbar, Venture Partner
e-mail: sharon@scalevp.com
Education: BA, MA, Engineering, Harvard University; MBA, Stanford Graduate School of Business
Background: Critical Path, Amplitude Software, Adobe Systems, Bain & Company
Directorships: Actiance, Everyday Health, MerchantCircle, PlayPhone, Reply!Com, uTest
Andy Vitus, Partner
e-mail: andy@scalevp.com
Education: MS, Electrical Engineering, Stanford University; BS, Electrical Engineering;, University of Cape Town
Background: Hardware Engineer, Electronics for Imaging
Directorships: Entone, Innovion
Rob Herb, Venture Partner
e-mail: rob@scalevp.com
Education: BS, Electrical Engineering, University of Illinois
Background: Executive Vice President/Chief Marketing Officer, AMD
Directorships: Enpirion, NComputing, Siimpel Corporation

1630 SCHOONER CAPITAL LLC
Two Financial Center
60 South Street
1th Floor
Boston, MA 02111

Phone: 617-963-5200 Fax: 617-963-5201
e-mail: info@schoonercapital.com
web: www.schoonercapital.com

Mission Statement: Seeks growth equity investments and alternative assets with a long-term perspective.

Geographic Preference: United States
Fund Size: $300 million
Founded: 1971

Minimum Investment: $250,000
Investment Criteria: Startup, First-Stage, Second-Stage, Mezzanine
Industry Group Preference: Communications, Education, Training, Business to Business, Leisure, Consumer Services
Portfolio Companies: Best Doctors, Custom Made, COLO, Emerald Therapeutics, Exithera Pharmaceuticals, Fashion Project, F&B Asias, IndoStar Capital Finance, iiWisdom, Millstone, Mediasilo, Mimetogen, Moonshine Farms, Nanoscale Powders, Orthocare Innovations, Railcomm, StyleFeeder, SRS Medical, Seventh Generation, Topokine, Zixi

Key Executives:

Vin Ryan, Founder/Chairman
Education: Boston University
Background: Founder, National Hydro; Founder, Arch Mobile Communications
Directorships: Iron Mountain, Continental Cablevision

Peter Binas, Managing Director
Education: AB, Harvard University; JD, Harvard Law School; MBA, Harvard Business School
Background: Management Consultant, McKinsey & Company
Directorships: RailComm, Colo Railroad Builders, Orthocare Innovations

Ted Henderson, Managing Director
Education: Dartmouth College; MBA, Harvard Business School
Background: General Manager, The Washington Post Company
Directorships: Best Doctors, Orthocare Innovations, Seventh Generation, SRS Medical, Millstone Medical Outsourcing

---

1631 SCHRODER VENTURES HEALTH INVESTORS
One Boston Place
201 Washington Street
Suite 3900
Boston, MA 02108

Phone: 617-367-8100
web: www.svhealthinvestors.com

Mission Statement: SV Health Investors is a venture capital adviser and manager that makes selected investments in businesses with experienced entrepreneurs and management teams.

Geographic Preference: United States, Europe
Fund Size: $2.0 billion
Founded: 1993
Average Investment: $4-$15 million
Minimum Investment: $1 million
Investment Criteria: Seed, Startup, First-Stage, Second-Stage, Late-Stage, Buyouts, Turnarounds, Expansion
Industry Group Preference: Biotechnology, Pharmaceuticals, Medical Devices, Healthcare Information Technology, Life Sciences, Healthcare Services
Portfolio Companies: Accelecare Holdings, AcuFocus, Adimab, AeroCare, Alba Therapeutics, Aligned Telehealth, Alinea Pharma, Allegiance Hospice Group, AllianceCare, Aptiv Solutions, Arsais, Artios, Autifony Therapeutics, Avitide, AvroBio, BardyDx, Bicycle Therapeutics, BioCore Holdings, Broadlane, Cadent Technologies, Calchan Holdings, CardioFocus, Catabasis, Celerion, Centauri Health Solutions, Cibiem, Coral Therapeutics, CoreLab Partners, CRI Worldwide, CSA Medical, Deciphera, EBR Systems, Endotronix, ErVaxx Limited, Evidation, Jet Health, Juvaris BioTherapeutics, Kalvista Pharma, Karus Therapeutics, Kesios Therapeutics, Leiters, NKT Therapeutics, Nordic Consulting Partners, Ocular Therapeutix, Oxagen Limited, PanOptica, Pionyr Immunotherapeutics, Pulmocide, Remita Health, ReShape, Ribometrix, Schweiger Dermatology Group, Sitryx Therapeutics, Soffio Medical, Solsys Medical, Spectrum Professional Services, Spinal Kinetics, Stim Wave, Sun Behavioural Health, Sutro Biopharma, Thesan Pharma, TopiVert, TransEnterix, UrgentTeam, US Renal Care, ValenTx, Vantia Pharma, VHSquared, Ximedica, Zarodex

Other Locations:
71 Kingsway
London WC2B 6ST
United Kingdom
Phone: 44-2074217070

Eugene Hill, Chairman
Education: BA, Middlebury College; MBA, Boston University
Background: President, United Healthcare Behavioral Division; President/Chairman, Sierra Health and Life Insurance Company
Directorships: Accelecare Wound Centers, Cadent, ISG Holdings, Medifacts, Patient Care, Socios Mayores, US Renal Care

Kate Bingham, Managing Partner, Biotechnology
44-20-7421-7071
Education: Biochemistry, Univ. of Oxford; MBA, Harvard Business School
Background: Business Development, Vertex Pharmaceuticals; Monitor Company
Directorships: Alantos, Auxillium, ESBATech, Hexagen, Kinetix, KuDos, Leukosite, Mednova, Micromet, PowderMed, Bicycle, EUSA, RespiVert

Michael Ross PhD, Managing Partner, Biotechnology
Education: AB, Dartmouth College; PhD, Chemistry, Caltech, Post Doctorate, Molecular Biology, Harvard University
Background: Vice President Development, Genetech; Founding CEO, Arris Pharmaceutical; Managing Partner, Didyma LLC
Directorships: Aderis Pharmaceuticals, Arris Pharmaceutical, Carta Proteomics, CyThera, Glycofi, Epimune, Genencor, MetaXen, Rinat, Xenova

Paul LaViolette, COO/Managing Partner, Medical Devices
Education: BA, Psychology, Fairfield University; MBA, Boston College
Background: COO, Boston Scientific Corporation; CR Bard; Kendall/Tyco
Directorships: Urolgix, Percutaneous Valve Technologies, Advarned; Cameron Health, Conceptus, DC Devices, Direct Flow Media, DJO Global, Thoratec, Trans1, ValenTx

Michael Balmuth, Managing Partner, Healthcare
Background: General Partner, Summit Partners; General Partner, Edison Partners
Directorships: AeroCare, Aligned Telehealth, Cantauri Health Solutions, Evidation, Ximedica

Houman Ashrafian, Managing Partner, Biotechnology
Background: Co-Founder, Cardiac Report; Co-Founder, Heart Metabolics; VP, Clinical Science Group, UCB
Directorships: ErVaxx, TRexBio

Tom Flynn, Managing Partner, Healthcare
Background: Partner, Ferrer Freeman & Co.; GE Capital; Prudential Investment Corporation
Directorships: AeroCare, Jet Health, Leiters, Nordic, Remita Health, Schweiger Dermatology Group, Sun Behavioural Health, Urgent Team

---

1632 SCHULTZE ASSET MANAGEMENT
800 Westchester Ave
Suite 632
Rye Brook, NY 10573

Phone: 914-701-5260 **Fax:** 914-701-5269
e-mail: info@samco.net
web: www.samco.net

Mission Statement: Special situation investing in financially troubled and distressed credits.

Geographic Preference: United States
Fund Size: $170 million

Venture Capital & Private Equity Firms / Domestic Firms

Key Executives:
  George J Schultze, Managing Member/Portfolio Management
  e-mail: schultze@samco.net
  Education: BA, Rutgers College; MBA/JD, Columbia University
  Background: Resurgence Asset Management, MD Sass; Mayer Brown & Platt

1633 SCIENCEVEST

  e-mail: info@sciencevest.com
  web: www.sciencevest.com

Mission Statement: ScienceVest is a venture capital fund investing in tech-based companies. Special interests include biotechnology, batteries, drones, sensors, and bacteriphages.

Founded: 2016
Average Investment: $125, 000
Industry Group Preference: Biotechnology, Robotics, Green Technology, Blockchain, Artificial Intelligence
Portfolio Companies: Avro Life Science, Advano, Calyx, ExplORer Surgical, Filecoin, Greensight Agronomics

Key Executives:
  Javier Noris, Partner
  e-mail: javier@sciencevest.com
  Education: BS, California State University
  Background: Venture Partner, Deep Science Ventures; Founder, NorisTalent
  Directorships: Life Extension Advocacy Foundation
  Ramphis Castro, Partner
  e-mail: ramphis@sciencevest.com
  Education: University of Puerto Rico
  Background: Software Engineer, Rock Solid Technologies; President/Chief Software Engineer, Simple Engineer Corporation; Principal Technology Advisor, Relisc Corporation; Co-Founder, TainoApp Inc.; Global Facilitator, Techstars; Co-Founder/Managing Partner, Mindchemy

1634 SCIFI VC
San Francisco, CA

  e-mail: info@scifi.vc
  web: scifi.vc

Mission Statement: SciFi invests in early-stage data-related projects.

Founded: 2017
Investment Criteria: Pre-Seed, Seed
Industry Group Preference: Data & Analytics, Technology
Portfolio Companies: Artivest, Blend Labs, Ellevest, Glow and Affirm, Gusto, OpenDoor, True Accord

Key Executives:
  Max Levchin, Founder
  Education: BS, Computer Science, University of Illinois
  Background: VP, Engineering, Google; Co-Founder/CTO, PayPal; Founder/CEO, Slide; Founder/CEO, Affirm; Chairman, Yelp
  Directorships: Yahoo!; Kaggle; Evernote
  Nellie Levchin, Partner
  Education: BA, Business Admin., California State University
  Background: Chief Risk Officer, Clarium Capital Management; Financial Systems Product Manager, PayPal; Financial Planning Analyst, eBay
  Directorships: Glow Inc.

1635 SCOUT VENTURES
New York, NY 10007

  web: www.scoutventures.com

Mission Statement: Scout Ventures works with transformational technologies that disrupt an established business model. BHV's primary focus is where media and entertainment companies (content distribution hubs) impact consumers and their rapidly evolving tech-enhanced lifestyle. BHV's secondary focus is content creation. By analyzing consumer behavior through proprietary technology platforms, BHV understands the challenges brands have connecting and communicating with their increasingly fragmented and unfocused audience. At this intersection, BHV leverages operational experience and strategic relationships to aggregate audience and/or monetization.

Investment Criteria: Early-Stage
Industry Group Preference: Media, Entertainment, Consumer Internet, Mobile, Advertising Technology
Portfolio Companies: Borer City Media, FreshTemp, Local Motors, Circa, Cody, Olapic, Sverve, Kanvas, rFactr, BlackBook, Fliptu, Flow, TIDBT, Adcade, bContext, Signpost, inSparq, Villagize, Free Awesome, Plyfe, 1000 Museums, LeagueApps, Brainscape, GateGuru, Everplans, Legacy Connect, Zipmark, ClearServe, RedOwl Analytics, Bespoke Post, HealthyOut, Scoot, SeedInvest, Assurely, Speakr, IML, Portalarium, Hullabalu, NetPlenih, BuyFi, Vengo, Plexus Entertainment, SocialWeekend, Nestio, CirrusWorks, VOYAT, Unite US, ID.me, Mayvien, Virtuix

Key Executives:
  Bradley C Harrison, Managing Partner
  e-mail: brad@bhv.vc
  Education: BSE, Quantitative Economics, United State Military Academy, West Point; MBA, Sloan School of Management, MIT
  Background: Partner, ITU Ventures; Business Affairs, AOL; United States Army
  Wes Blackwell, Partner
  Education: BS, United States Naval Academy; MBA, Darden School of Business, University of Virginia
  Background: Aviator, US Navy; Director of Marketing, US Navy Academy; VP of Business Development & Strategy, Jacksonville JetPort; Sr Implementation Manager, LiveSafe; Angel Investor
  Directorships: DataTribe

1636 SCP PARTNERS
7 Great Valley Parkway
Suite 190
Malvern, PA 19355

  Phone: 610-995-2900 **Fax:** 610-975-9546
  e-mail: info@scppartners.com
  web: www.scppartners.com

Mission Statement: A multi-stage venture capital firm focused on investments in Information and Communication Technology, Life Sciences, Services, Defense and Security.

Geographic Preference: United States
Fund Size: $1 Billion
Founded: 1996
Average Investment: $2 - 10 million
Minimum Investment: $2 million
Investment Criteria: Expansion Stage, Early Stage, Later Stage Middle Market Buyout Opportunitites
Industry Group Preference: Information Technology, Telecommunications, Financial Services, Medical Devices, Media, Life Sciences, Aerospace, Defense and Government, Security, Communications, Pharmaceuticals, Diagnostics
Portfolio Companies: Amg, Amkor Technology, Echo 360, Fourthwall Media, Deep Breeze, Dvtel, Giftcertificates.Com, Gigared, Grab Networks, Hospitality Associates, Magnolia Broadband, Pentech, Q Group, Selway Partners, Software Technology, Tammac, Trig, Vertex Management Israel, Vitalife, Xvionics

Other Locations:
  74 Grand Avenue
  Englewood, NJ 07631
  Phone: 201-541-1080 **Fax:** 201-541-1084

Key Executives:
  Wayne B Weisman, Partner
  Education: BA, cum laude, University of Pennsylvania; MBA, New York University Graduate School of Business Administration

Venture Capital & Private Equity Firms / Domestic Firms

Background: Managing Director, Churchill Investment Partners; CIP Capital Management; Executive VP, Affinity Biotech; Saul, Ewing, Remick & Saul
Directorships: Grab Networks; Echo 360; Deap Breeze, Ltd.
Thomas G Rebar, Partner
Education: BS, summa cum laude, University of Scranton; MBA, New York University Graduate School of Business
Background: Senior VP, Cvharterhouse; Bankers Trust Company
Directorships: Pentech Financial Services; DVTel, Inc.
Yaron Eitan, Partner
Education: MBA, Wharton School of Business, University of Pennsylvania
Background: Co-Founder/President/CEO, Selway Partners LLC
Directorships: DVTel, Magnolia Broadband, Cyalumax Technology, Inc.
Winston J Churchill, Managing General Partner
Education: BS, Fordham University; MA, University of Oxford; JD, Yale Law School
Background: Founded Churchill Investment Partners; Bessemer Securities Corporation; Practiced Law at Saul Eqing LLP
Directorships: Trustee of Immaculate University, American Friends of New College Oxford, England and the Gesu School; AkmerTechnology, Inc.; Cylumax Technology, Inc.
Roger Carolin, Venture Partner
Education: BBE, Duke University; MBA, Harvard Business School
Background: Co-Founded CFM Technologies; Honeywell Inc; General Electric Company
Directorships: Chairman of Franklin Fuel Cells
Charles C Freyer, General Counsel & Chief Administrative Officer
Education: AB, Princeton University; JD, Yale Law School
Background: Miller Investment Management; Saul Ewing, LLP; Lieutenant Colonel, Retired in the US Army Judge Advocate General's Corps
Directorships: Admitted to practice in Pennsylvania and New York, has completed his Series 65
Richard L Sherman, Venture Partner
Education: University of Nebraska; JD, New York University School of Law
Background: Deputy General Counsel, SmithKline Beckman Corporation; Founder & Managing Officer, QED Technologies
Directorships: CytoMed, IBAH, Kenna Technologies, Mera Pharmaceuticals, Sparta Pharmaceuticals
Gen. John M Keane, Venture Partner
Education: BS, Fordham University; MA, Philosophy, Western Kentucky University; Army War College; Command & General Staff College
Background: Vice Chief of Staff, US Army
Directorships: MetLife, General Dynamics, MacAndrews & Forbes, Cyalume Technologies Holdings

1637 SCRUM VENTURES
575 Marsket Street
PO 1600
San Francisco, CA 94105

web: scrum.vc

Mission Statement: Scrum Ventures is an early stage venture capital based in Silicon valley. We invest in entrepreneurs who are creating startups in the high growth mobile sector. We help companies accelerate growth with our expertise and powerful network in Asia.
Average Investment: $100,000 - $1MM
Investment Criteria: Early Stage
Industry Group Preference: Mobile
Portfolio Companies: Kidaptive, App.io, Prizeo, Aarki, First Opinion, Binpress, SharePractice, Spire, Le Tote, Lob, Mobileworks, Placemeter, Koemei, Noom, Boostable, Panna, Vidpresso, Focus Motion, LivBlends, Pantry, Altitude
Key Executives:
Tak Miyata, Founding Partner
Education: Master's Degree in nano Science from Waseda University

1638 SCULPTOR CAPITAL MANAGEMENT
9 W 57th Street
39th Floor
New York, NY 10019

Phone: 212-790-0000
e-mail: investorrelations@sculptor.com
web: www.sculptor.com

Mission Statement: Alternative asset manager serving global base of institutional investors.
Fund Size: $33 billion
Founded: 1994
Industry Group Preference: Real Estate
Other Locations:
Sculptor Capital Management Europe Limited
2nd Floor
London W1F 7EB
United Kingdom
Phone: 44 207-758-4400

Sculptor Capital Management Hong Kong Limited
Level 20, Suite 2002
88 Queensway
Hong Kong

Sculptor Overseas Investment Fund Management Co., Ltd.
Shanghai International Finance Center Tower II
8 Century Avenue, Pudong New Area
Shanghai 200120
China
Phone: 86 2160626186

Key Executives:
Jimmy Levin, Chief Executive Officer & Chief Investment Officer
Education: BA, Harvard University
Wayne Cohen, President & Chief Operating Officer
Education: BA, International Relations, Tulane University; JD, New York University School of Law
Background: Attorney & General Counsel, Sculptor Capital Management; Attorney, Schulte Roth & Zabel LLP
Dava Ritchea, Chief Financial Officer
Education: BBA, Carnegie Mellon University
Background: CFO, Assured Investment Management

1639 SEACOAST CAPITAL CORPORATION
55 Ferncroft Road
Suite 110
Danvers, MA 01923

Phone: 978-750-1300 Fax: 978-750-1301
web: www.seacoastcapital.com

Mission Statement: Invests mezzanine and equity capital in small, growing companies led by strong, entrepreneurial management teams.
Geographic Preference: United States
Fund Size: $200 million
Founded: 1990
Average Investment: $2-$10 million
Minimum Investment: $500,000
Investment Criteria: Second-Stage, Mezzanine, LBO, Special Situations
Industry Group Preference: Communications, Computer Related, Consumer Products, Distribution, Electronic Components, Industrial Equipment, Medical & Health Related, Electronic Components, Manufacturing, Business Products & Services

Venture Capital & Private Equity Firms / Domestic Firms

Portfolio Companies: BISCO Environmental, Cinetopia, ElectroCraft, FAPS, Frank Entertainment Group, The Jay Group, Matlet Group, Mearthane Products, Mountain Alarm, Northwest Cascade, Patriot Environmental Services, QK Holdings, QuVis, UX Specialized Logistics, Walden Behavioral Health

Other Locations:
One Bush Street
Suite 650
San Francisco, CA 94104
Phone: 415-956-1400

Key Executives:
Timothy P Fay, Partner
e-mail: tfay@seacoastcapital.com
Education: BA, Economics, University of Texas, Dallas; MBA, University of Chicago
Background: Co-Founder, Key Mezzanine Fund, Key Principal Partners; The Barclasy Group; The Federal Reserve Bank

Thomas W Gorman, Partner
e-mail: tgorman@seacoastcapital.com
Education: AB, Holy Cross College; MBA, Amos Tuck School of Business Administration
Background: General Motors Corporation; Lending Officer, Shawmut Bank of Boston

Jeffrey J Holland, Partner
e-mail: jholland@seacoastcapital.com
Education: BS, Stanford University; MBA, Harvard Business School
Background: Consultant, MAC Group; Andersen Consulting

Eben S Moulton, Senior Advisor
e-mail: emoulton@seacoastcapital.com
Education: BS, Colorado College; PhD, Vanderbilt; MBA, Columbia University Trustee of Colorado College
Background: Bank of New England
Directorships: Unitil Corporation

James T Donelan, Principal
e-mail: jdonelan@seacoastcapital.com
Education: BA, Economics, Middlebury College
Background: Analyst, Investment Banking, Adams Harkness & Hill

1640 SEAPOINT VENTURES
777 108th Ave. NE
Suite 1895
Bellevue, WA 98004

Phone: 425-455-0879
e-mail: info@seapointventures.com

Mission Statement: To generate unique insights that help portfolio companies lead market trends and build value in early stage companies. Seapoint stays focused on solid business models, intelligent fundraising, assembling exceptional teams and staying collaborative with our internal and external partners.

Founded: 1997
Investment Criteria: Early-Stage
Industry Group Preference: Communications, Wireless, Broadband, Network Infrastructure
Portfolio Companies: Airspan, aQuantive, BridgeWave Communications, Dantz, Entomo, Hubspan, Internap, Kineto, Modiv Media, Mojix, NetMotion, Ontela, PhoneSpots, PocketThis, PowerTech Group, Qpass, SinglePoint, SNAPin Software, Talisma, Tegic, Telecom Transport Management, Trumba, Vayusa, Wireless Services Corporation, Zumobi

Key Executives:
Thomas S Huseby, Managing Partner
Education: BS, Economics, BS, Industrial Engineering, Columbia University; MBA, Stanford University
Background: Co-Founder & CEO, Metawave Communications Corporation; President & CEO, Innova Corporation; Raychem Corporation
Directorships: Airspan, Ground Truth, Zumobi, Hubspan, Kineto Wireless, Modiv Media, Mojix, Photobucket, SinglePoint

Melissa Widner, General Partner
Education: Bachelor's Degree, University of Washington; MA, Stanford University
Background: Co-Founder, 7Software; CEO, Northwest Supply
Directorships: Hubspan, Powertech, PhoneSpots, NetMotion

1641 SEAPORT CAPITAL
40 Fulton Street
27th Floor
New York, NY 10038

Phone: 212-847-8900 **Fax:** 212-320-0270
e-mail: info@seaportcapital.com
web: www.seaportcapital.com

Mission Statement: Works with talented management teams to create valuable companies that are leaders in their market segments.

Geographic Preference: United States
Fund Size: $400 million
Founded: 1991
Average Investment: $10-35 million over the life of the investment
Minimum Investment: $5 million
Investment Criteria: Late Stage. Growth, Recapitalizations, Buy-Outs
Industry Group Preference: Business to Business, Communications, Media, Technology, Information Services, Business Products & Services
Portfolio Companies: All Traffic Data, Atmosera, B Media Group, EoStar, Exacom, Filmwerks LLC, i3 Broadband, Keg Logistics, Linen King, Municipal Communications II, Quality Uptime Services, Quatris Healthco

Key Executives:
Bill Luby, Founding Partner
e-mail: bluby@seaportcapital.com
Education: BA Economics, Trinity College; MBA, Fuqua School of Business, Duke University
Background: CEA Capital Partners; Managing Director, Chase Capital; Managing Director LBO, Chase Merchant Banking Group

Jim Collis, Founding Partner
e-mail: jcollis@seaportcapital.com
Education: BSEE, Rensselaer Polytechnic Institute; MBA, Columbia Business School
Background: CEA Capital Partners; Principal, Chase Capital Partners; Associate/VP, Chase Merchant Banking Group; Principal Engineer, National Teleconsultants

Scott McCormack, Partner
e-mail: smccormack@seaportcapital.com
Education: AB, Economics, Harvard College
Background: BancBoston Capital
Directorships: Independence Media, SCDC Holdings, Peak 10

Bob Tamashunas, Partner
e-mail: btamashunas@seaportcapital.com
Education: BS, Science, Georgetown University; MBA, Columbia Business School
Background: Leveraged Bank Loan Group, Prudential Capital Group
Directorships: Bay Communications, Municipal Communications, Worley Claim Service

Howard Kaufman, Chief Financial Officer
e-mail: hkaufman@seaportcapital.com
Education: BS, Accounting, University of Scranton
Background: SVP & CFO, Lynch & Mayer; Financial Vice President, Carteret Financial Group

1642 SEAWAY VALLEY CAPITAL CORPORATION
10 Park St., Fl. 2
Gouverneur, NY 13642-1052

Phone: 315-287-1122 **Fax:** 302-636-5454

Mission Statement: Seaway Valley Capital Corporation was formed to provide companies access to capital for growth, expansion and restructuring. Seaway Valley has a particular, but not exclusive, focus of providing capital solutions to the underserved region of Northern New York.

Geographic Preference: Northern New York
Investment Criteria: Early-Stage, Mid & Later-Stage, Management Buyouts
Industry Group Preference: Manufacturing, Technology, Agriculture, Restaurants, Real Estate, Consumer Products
Portfolio Companies: Patrick Hackett Hardware Company, Altieri Bakery, Sackets Harbor Brewing Company, Seaway Restaurant Group

Key Executives:
  Thomas W Scozzafava, President & CEO
  Education: BA, Economics & Mathematics, Hamilton College
  Background: Co-Founder, GS AgriFuels Corporation; Director, Prudential's Merchant Banking Group; Lehman Brothers' Merchant Banking Group; GE Capital Corporation
  Directorships: New York State Power Authority

1643 SECOND ALPHA
276 Fifth Avenue
Suite 204
New York, NY 10001

Phone: 212-446-1600
web: www.secondalpha.com

Mission Statement: Second Alpha crafts innovative capital solutions that allow founders, managers and investors in private companies to achieve liquidity prior to company sales or IPOs. Second Alpha buys shares and convertible securities on a secondary basis and also invests capital directly into growth companies.

Geographic Preference: United States, Canada
Investment Criteria: Growth Stage
Industry Group Preference: Technology, Media, Telecommunications
Portfolio Companies: 23andme, AccessData, Artful Home, Avst, Bolt Insurance, Buffer, Code42, Coursera, DailyPay, Everbridge, Everquote, Healthcare.Com, Netmotion Wireless, On24, OpenX, Prove Inc., Sixth Sense Media, Sportvision, Terago, Touch Commerce, UserTesting

Key Executives:
  Richard Brekka, Co-Founder/Managing Partner
  e-mail: rbrekka@secondalpha.com
  Education: BS, University of Southern California; MBA, University of Chicago
  Background: President/Managing Partner/Founder, Dolphin Equity Partners; Managing Director, CIBC; Chase Capital
  Jim Sanger, Co-Founder/Managing Partner
  e-mail: jim@secondalpha.com
  Education: BS, University of Pennsylvania
  Background: General Partner, ABS Ventures; Managing Director, Deutsche Bank's DB Capital Venture Partners
  Directorships: June Media, Terago Networks
  Eugene Galantini, Chief Financial Officer
  e-mail: egalantini@secondalpha.com
  Education: BS, Accounting, University of Scranton; CPA
  Background: CFO, Dolphin Equity Partners; Assistant Controller, New York Life Capital Partners

1644 SECOND AVENUE PARTNERS
1301 Second Avenue
Suite 2850
Seattle, WA 98101

Phone: 206-332-1200 **Fax:** 206-332-1201
web: www.secondave.com

Mission Statement: Second Avenue Partners is a Seattle-based provider of management, strategy, and capital for early stage companies. The partners invest their own money, typically directed at emerging Internet businesses in the high-tech field. Second Avenue Partners' investment approach is to make early-stage investments in promising ventures and build long-term relationships, actively assisting its portfolio companies in becoming market leaders.

Investment Criteria: Early-Stage
Industry Group Preference: High Technology
Portfolio Companies: AudienceScience, Azaleos, CoolSpotter, Essention, FanNation, Fantasy Moguls, FLEXE, Front Desk, Glassnetic Inc., HealthSlate, Inkd, Insitu Group, JeNu, Locationlabs, Market Leader, Modumetal, Newsvine, Qliance, RealSelf, Seeq, Slope, TreeRing, WISErg

Key Executives:
  Mike Slade, Founding Partner
  Education: BA, Economics, Colordo College; MBA, Stanford Graduate School of Business
  Background: Director, Corporate Marketing, Microsoft; Starwave; NeXt Computer
  Nick Hanauer, Founding Partner
  Education: BS, Philosophy, University of Washington
  Background: Board Advisor, Amazon; Founder & CEO, aQuantive; Founder, Gear.com
  Pete Higgins, Founding Partner
  Education: BS, Economics, History, MBA, Stanford University
  Background: Microsoft
  Directorships: Ice Energy, Modumetal, Rubicon Interactive, Insitu Group, Market Leader

1645 SECOND CENTURY VENTURES
Chicago, IL 60611

e-mail: hello@secondcenturyventures.com
web: www.secondcenturyventures.com

Mission Statement: Second Century Ventures is the strategic investment arm of the National Association of Realtors. We build companies using our extensive industry knowledge and experience, vast membership base and the power of the Realtor brand. We are a catalyst for building relationships among new technologies, new opportunities and new talent to help deliver the future of the industry.

Industry Group Preference: Real Estate
Portfolio Companies: Back At You Media, BombBomb, Deduct, Desktime, DocuSign, EndHub, EPropertyData, FundWell, Ifbyphone, Lumentus, Move, NAR REach, Planwise, Reach150, SeaSuite By Goby, SentriLock, SmartZip, Treater, Updater, WeVideo, Workface, xceligent, Ziplogix

Key Executives:
  Tyler Thompson, Managing Partner
  Education: BA, Brigham Young University; MS, Real Estate Development, MIT
  Background: Director of Metrics, Business Software Alliance; CEO, CaptureQuest Inc.; CEO/Director, Avalon Digital Marketing Systems Inc.; VP of Business Development, Deductr; Managing Partner, Black Shamrock
  Mark Birschbach, Managing Director
  Education: BBA, Finance, University of Notre Dame
  Background: VP of Banking Investments, Citigroup; President/COO, Active Radius LLC; COO, Monthlys; Managing Director REach; SVP of Strategic Business, Innovation & Technology, National Association of Realtors

Venture Capital & Private Equity Firms / Domestic Firms

1646 SECTION 32

e-mail: info@section32.com
web: www.section32.com

Mission Statement: Section 32 invests in a wide range of projects from robotics and digital currencies to medical research and agriculture to the music industry and more.

Fund Size: $150 million
Founded: 2016
Industry Group Preference: Robotics, Technology, Medical Research, Medical Equipment, Music, Health
Portfolio Companies: Arsanis, Auris, BloomAPI, Celularity, Coinbase, Dave, Dialpad, Eatsa, Embark, Freenome, Kobalt, LimeBike, Neocis, Norquin, Teckro, Vir

Key Executives:
  Bill Maris, Founder
  Education: Middlebury College
  Background: Investor AB, Burlee.com, Web.com, Google Ventures, Calico
  Mike Pellini, Managing Director
  Education: BA, Boston College; MBA, Drexel University; MD, Jefferson Medical College
  Background: CEO/Chairman, Foundation Medicine; President/COO, Clarient

1647 SEED MILESTONE FUND
1 Ferry Building
Suite 201
San Francisco, CA 94111

Phone: 415-479-6080
e-mail: contact@seedmilestone.com
web: www.seedmilestone.com

Mission Statement: Seed Milestone Fund is a new fund dedicated to core technology, B2B, foundational tech, platforms, IoT, information systems, SaaS, logistics and digital transformation.

Founded: 2020

Key Executives:
  Peter Henry, Founder/General Partner
  Education: Stanford University
  Background: Managing Partner, Perspectrum LLC; Managing Director, Canard Sauvage LLC; Founder/Managing Partner, Act 5 Ventures LLC
  Neal Strickberger, Founder/General Partner
  Background: Principal, Dangerous Knowledge, Applied; Angel Investor, Keiretsu Forum

1648 SEIDLER EQUITY PARTNERS
4640 Admiralty Way
Suite 1200
Marina del Rey, CA 90292

Phone: 213-683-4622 Fax: 213-624-0691
e-mail: info@sepfunds.com
web: www.sepfunds.com

Mission Statement: A private equity investment firm that partners with visionary executives to grow their businesses.

Founded: 1992
Investment Criteria: Growth Capital Financing, Management or Partner Buyouts, Recapitalizations
Industry Group Preference: Education, Specialty Retail, Distribution, Gaming, Railroad Services, Medical Products, Mobility
Portfolio Companies: LA Fitness International, Aden & Anais, Sportsman's Warehouse, Tonoga, Korvis, Sunny Sky Products, Emergency Essentials

Key Executives:
  Peter Seidler, Managing Partner
  Education: BS, Finance, University of Virginia; MS, Business Administration, University of California, Los Angeles
  Robert Seidler, Managing Partner
  Education: BA, Georgetown University; MBA, University of California, Los Angeles
  Eric Kutsenda, Managing Partner
  Education: BS, Accounting, University of Illinois; MS, Taxation, DePaul University

1649 SELBY VENTURE PARTNERS
3500 Alameda De Las Pulgas
Suite 200
Menlo Park, CA 94025

Phone: 650-854-7399 Fax: 650-854-7039
web: www.selbyventures.com

Mission Statement: To invest in passionate entrepreneurs who want to build the next generation of category defining companies.

Geographic Preference: West Coast
Fund Size: $135 million
Founded: 1998
Average Investment: $1-$2.5 million
Minimum Investment: $250,000
Investment Criteria: Early, Expansion, Seed
Industry Group Preference: Communications, Electronic Technology, Software, Manufacturing, Wireless Technologies, Hardware, Semiconductors, Internet, Sustainable Technologies, Digital Media & Marketing, Information Technology
Portfolio Companies: Attributor, BigFix, BigStage, Blue Pumpkin Software, ConsumerReview, Coremetrics, LiveCapital, ModViz, Pandora Media, Panopticon, SugarSync, Size Technologies, Tempo Payments, Visage Mobile, 3ware, 4INFO, Active-Semi, Bay Microsystems, Clairvoyante, HotRail, Intelleflex, Silicon Packets, SkyPilot Networks, Triformix, Active Semiconductors, Clairvoyante, Ecohaus

Key Executives:
  Bob Marshall, Managing Director
  e-mail: bob@selbyventures.com
  Education: BEE, Heald Engineering; MBA, Pepperdine University
  Background: Tandem Computers; Diablo Systems; InfoGear Technology
  Directorships: 3Ware, Bay Microsystems, Blue Pumpkin Software, Quicksilver Technology, Sierra Monitor Corp., Wytec
  Jim Marshall, Managing Director
  e-mail: jim@selbyventures.com
  Education: BS, Finance, Santa Clara University; MBA, Pepperdine University
  Background: VP, Commercial Software Practice
  Directorships: Live Capital, ConsumerReview, Panopticon, SkyPilot Network, Zenasis Technologies
  Doug Barry, Managing Director
  e-mail: doug@selbyventures.com
  Education: BS, UC Berkeley; MBA, Harvard University
  Background: Co-Founder, CobaltCard; Senior Executive, Electronic Arts; Mavio Communications; Turner Broadcasting
  Directorships: BigFix, Clairvoyante Laboratories, Cranite Systems, Size Technology, SkyPilot Network, Visage Mobile

1650 SELWAY CAPITAL
38 Ridge Road
Tenalfy, NJ 07670

web: www.selwaycapital.com

Mission Statement: To provide companies with a unique blend of capital, expertise, commitment and operational management at the earliest stages to a select number of promising ideas and projects within information technology and telecommunication markets.

Investment Criteria: Early Stage

Industry Group Preference: Information Technology, Telecommunications
Portfolio Companies: DVTEL, STI, Magonlia Broadband
Key Executives:
  Yaron Eitan, Founder
  Education: BA, Economics, Haifa University; MBA, Wharton School
  Background: Co-Founder, Reshef Technologies; Founder/CEO, Geotek Communications; Co-Founder/Chairman, Marpai Health; Co-Founder/Chairman, DeepCube; Co-Founder/Chairman, Emporus Technologies
Key Executives:
  Michael C Skaff, Co-Founder/Managing Director
  e-mail: mikes@senecapartners.com
  Education: BS, Economics & Mathematics, MBA, University of Michigan
  Background: Managing Director, Manchester Capital; VP, Home Care Operations, MedMax
  Anthony W Zambelli, Co-Founder/Managing Director
  e-mail: tonyz@senecapartners.com
  Education: Ross School of Business, University of Michigan
  Background: Managing Director, Manchester Capital; Great Lakes Region Corporate Finance, Deloitte & Touche

1652 SENECA PARTNERS
Two Towne Square
Suite 810
Southfield, MI 48076

Phone: 248-723-6650
e-mail: info@senecapartners.com
web: www.senecapartners.com

Mission Statement: A venture capital fund focused on providing growth capital to companies in the healthcare industry that are located in Middle America.
Geographic Preference: Midwest United States
Founded: 2002
Average Investment: $500,000 - $2.5 million
Investment Criteria: Early-Stage to Later-Stage
Industry Group Preference: Healthcare Services, Healthcare Information Technology, Medical Devices

1653 SENTIENT VENTURES
11412 Bee Caves Road
Suite 300
Austin, TX 78738

Phone: 512-402-1717 Fax: 512-402-1616
e-mail: info@senven.com
web: www.sentientventures.com

Mission Statement: Sentient Ventures is a private equity firm that invests in seed, early, and expansion stage companies using the following fund types: early stage venture capital, middle market private equity and subordinated debt.
Geographic Preference: Texas
Average Investment: $500,000 - $7.5 million
Investment Criteria: Seed-Stage, Early-Stage, Expansion Stage
Portfolio Companies: Austin Entrepreneurs Foundation, Texchange (Austin), Austin Technology Incubator, Venture Fellows, College of Natural Sciences Advisory Council, School of Management and Business Advisory Council, TXEntre
Key Executives:
  David Lee, Managing Partner
  Background: Managing Partner, Murphree Venture Partners; Viasoft; Tivoli Systems
  Jonathan Ring, Venture Partner
  Background: Founder & President, Caringo; VP, Engineering, Siebel Systems; Comdisco
  James Wells, Venture Partner
  Background: VP, Sales, RealNetworks; Dazel Corporation; Apple Computer
  Mansoor Ghori, Venture Partner

1654 SENTINEL CAPITAL PARTNERS
330 Madison Avenue
27th Floor
New York, NY 10017

Phone: 212-688-3100 Fax: 212-688-6513
e-mail: info@sentinelpartners.com
web: www.sentinelpartners.com

Mission Statement: To generate superior investment returns by enabling talented executives to build great businesses.
Geographic Preference: United States
Fund Size: $200 million
Founded: 1995
Average Investment: $20 million
Investment Criteria: MBO, Late Stage, Recapitalizations, Growth Financing
Industry Group Preference: Aerospace, Defense and Government, Industrial Manufacturing, Business Products & Services, Consumer Products, Consumer Services, Food Services, Franchising, Healthcare Services
Portfolio Companies: Checkers Drive-In Restaurants, Colson Group, Credit Infonet Group, Critical Solutions International, Hollander Sleep Products, Hospice Advantage Holdings, Huddle House, IEP Technologies, National Spine & Pain Centers, Newk's Eatery, North American Rescue, Northeast Dental Management, PlayCore, Power Products, RotoMetrics, Spinrite, TGI Fridays, Vintage Holdings, WellSpring Pharmaceutical Corporation
Key Executives:
  Eric D Bommer, Partner
  e-mail: Bommer@sentinelpartners.com
  Education: BA, Brown University
  John F McCormack, Co-Founder/Senior Partner
  e-mail: McCormack@sentinelpartners.com
  Education: BS, Boston College
  David S Lobel, Co-Founder/Managing Partner
  Education: MBA, MS, Stanford University; BS, University of Witwatersrand
  Background: Office Depot, Entre Computer Center, Rocky Mountain Saving Bank, Smith Barney, Bain and Company
  Paul F Murphy, Partner
  Education: MBA, Georgetown University; BS, US Military Academy
  Background: Vice President at NationsBanc Capital Markets; Merchant Banking Group, Chase Manhattan Bank
  Thomas P Fitzpatrick, Operating Partner
  Education: BBA, St. John's University; Certified Public Accountant
  Background: Coopers & Lybrand; Senior Vice President, Englehard Corp
  James D Coady, Partner
  Education: BA, Harvard University; MBA, Northwestern University
  Background: First Chicago Equity Capital, Analyst at Alex, Brown & Sons
  Sidney J Feltenstein, Operating Partner
  Education: BA, Boston University
  Background: EVP, Worldwide Marketing, Burger King Corporation; Operations & Marketing, Dunkin' Donuts
  Directorships: Interim Healthcare, Inscape Publishing, Massage Envy, Southern California Pizza Company
  Edward L Kuntz, Operating Partner
  Education: BA, JD, Master of Law, Temple University
  Background: CEO, Kindred Healthcare; CEO, Living Centers of America; Associate General Counsel, ARA Services
  Directorships: Kindred Healthcare, Rotech Healthcare

Venture Capital & Private Equity Firms / Domestic Firms

1655 SENTRY FINANCIAL CORPORATION
201 S Main Street
Suite 1400
Salt Lake City, UT 84111

Phone: 801-596-9600
e-mail: info@sentry.financial
web: www.sentryfinancial.com

Mission Statement: Invest growth capital with businesses under $10 million in revenue. Add value to portfolio companies through hands-on counsel in areas of marketing, finance, accounting and information systems processing. Provide in-house capability to finance sales to portfolio company customers where appropriate.

Geographic Preference: United States
Fund Size: $15 million
Founded: 2002
Average Investment: $500,000
Minimum Investment: $200,000
Investment Criteria: Second Stage, Mezzanine, MBO
Industry Group Preference: Financial Services, Conservation, Distribution, Health Related, Outsourcing & Efficiency, Energy, Entertainment, Internet, Healthcare Information Technology

Key Executives:
Jonathan M Ruga, Founder/CEO
801-303-1108
e-mail: jruga@sentryfinancial.com
Education: Graduated, magna cum laude, University of Utah with Undergraduate Degress in Accounting, Finance; MBA, Obtained a Law Degree
Background: Chairman, Sentry's Investment Committee; Attorney, Parr, Waddoups, Brown, Gee & Loveless; Lease Education/Consulting, Amembal, Deane & Associates
Scott F Young, COO
Education: Graduated Finance Degree, Obtained a Law Degree, University of Utah
Background: Partner, Parr, Waddoups, Brown, Gee & Loveless; Judicial Clerkship, Utah Supreme Court
G Stephen Browning, Chief Accounting Officer/Chief Information Officer
Education: BA Accounting, Masters in Information Systems, Brigham Young University
Background: Senior Manager, Browning, Creer & Associates; Accounting/Consulting, KPMG Peat Marwick

1656 SEQUEL VENTURE PARTNERS
4430 Arapahoe Avenue
Suite 220
Boulder, CO 80303

Phone: 303-546-0400
web: www.sequelvc.com

Mission Statement: Seeks to provide exceptional return to investors by combining knowledge, experience, and relationships to enhance the likelihood of substantial success for portfolio companies.

Geographic Preference: Rocky Mountain Region
Fund Size: $400 million
Average Investment: $3 million
Minimum Investment: $2 million
Investment Criteria: Seed, Early-stage
Industry Group Preference: Health Related, Information Technology, Telecommunications, Computer Related, Genetic Engineering, Internet Technology, Technology, Clean Technology, Healthcare

Key Executives:
Dan Mitchell, Partner
Education: BS, University of Illinois; MBA, University of California, Berkeley
Background: Founder, Capital Health Management; Institutional Venture Capital Fund, First National Bank of Chicago
Directorships: GlobeImmune, Kalypto Medical

Tom Washing, Partner
Education: BA, Dartmouth College; JD, University of Michigan Law School
Background: Founding General Partner, Horsley Keogh Associates; General Partner, Hill Carman & Washing
Directorships: SkyeTek, YieldEx
John Greff, Partner/CFO
Education: BS, Business Administration, Colorado State University; MBA, University of Denver
Background: CFO, Allos Therapeutics; CFO, Somatogen
Kinney Johnson, Partner
Education: BA, Mathematics/Business Administration, Augsburg College; MS, Mathematical Computer Science, University of Iowa
Background: Founder, Capital Health Management; Founder/President, Fischer Imaging Corporation
Directorships: Evolutionary Genomics, HomeSphere, Intio
Tim Connor, Partner
Education: BA, Washington College; MBA, Harvard Business School
Background: Managing Director, Lehman Brothers Technology Investment Banking Group; Senior VP Operations/CFO, Access Health
Directorships: Aztek Networks, Datalogic, InfoNow Corporation, Quova
Chris Scoggins, Venture Partner
Education: BS, Trinity University; MBA, Stanford Graduate School of Business
Background: Associate, The Sprout Group; Co-Founder, Internet Reports
Directorships: YieldEx

1657 SEQUOIA CAPITAL
web: www.sequoiacap.com

Mission Statement: Provides start-up venture capital funding for seed-stage, early-stage and growth companies.

Geographic Preference: United States, Israel, China, India
Fund Size: $400 million
Founded: 1972
Average Investment: $5 million
Minimum Investment: $50,000
Investment Criteria: Seed Stage, Early Stage, Growth Stage
Industry Group Preference: Electronic Technology, Components & IoT, Software, Energy, Financial Services, Healthcare Services, Internet, Mobile, Outsourcing & Efficiency
Portfolio Companies: 100 Thieves, 23andMe, 3Com, [24]7.ai, ActionIQ, AdMob, Against Gravity, Agile Software, AgilOne, Airbnb, AirStrip, Altiscale, AMCC, Ameritox, Amplitude, Amylin, App Annie, Appirio, Apple, Arbor/Hyperion, Aruba, Aspect Development, Assurex Health, Aster Data, Atari, Athelas, Avanex, Barefoot Networks, Barracuda Networks, bebop, Berkeley Lights, Bird, Blue Danube Systems, Brud, Cafepress, Carbon, Carbon Black, CEGX, CenterRun Software, Charlotte Tillbury, Chartboost, Cisco, Citizen, Clari, Clearwell Systems, Clever, Clickatell, Clover Health, Clutter, Cobalt Robotics, Cohesity, Comprehend, Confluent, Cortexyme, Crew, Cumulus Networks, Cypress, Decolar, Dia&Co, Docker, Domino Data Lab, DoorDash, Drawbridge, Drift, Dropbox, Druva, Electronic Arts, Elevate, Elevate Credit, Embark Trucks, EndoChoice, Ethos, Eventbrite, Evernote, Everwise, Faire, FireEye, First Republic Bank, Flex, Front, FutureAdvisor, GameFly, GenEdit, GitHub, Good Eggs, Google, Graphcore, Green Dot, Guardant Health, Hayneedle, Health Catalyst, Hearsay Systems, HireVue, Houseparty, Houzz, HubSpot, Humble Bundle, Infoblox, Inkling, INS, Inside.Com, Instacart, Instagram, IPG, Isilon Systems, Jasper, Jawbone, Jive, Kahuna, KAYAK, Kenshoo, Kiwi, Klarna, Lattive Engines, Lifecode, LightStep, Lilt, Limbix, Linear Technology, LinkedIn, LitePoint, LSI Logic, Luminate, Mapillary, MarkLogic, Maven, Medallia, MedExpress, Mellanox, Meraki, Merlin Securities, Metanautix,

Venture Capital & Private Equity Firms / Domestic Firms

MetaStable, Metaswitch Networks, Microchip Technology, Mobileron, MongoDB, Moovit, Mu Sigma, Namely, Natera, NetApp, Netezza, NetScreen, NEXT Trucking, Nimble, Nimble Storage, Nubank, Numerify, NVIDIA, Okta, Onyx Pharmaceuticals, OpenDNS, Oracle, Orbital Insight, Orchid Labs, Palo Alto Networks, PayPal, Peakstream, Percolate, PicsArt, Pixelworks, PlanGrid, PMC-Sierra, Pocket Gems, Polychain Capital, POPSUGAR, Progress Software, Prosper, Qualtrics, Quantenna, Quantum Circuits, Quidd, R2 Semiconductor, Rackspace, Rappi, Re:store, Redback Networks, reddit, Remix, RideOS, RingCentral, Robinhood, Rockset, Ruckus Wireless, Rylo, Saba Software, Scanntech, SecurityScorecard, ServiceNow, Setter SimpliSafe, Skyhigh Networks, Skyscanner, Snowflake, Sourcefire, Springpath, Square, StackRox, StarkWare Stella & Dot, Stemcentrx, Strava, Streamlabs, Stripe, Sumo Logic, Sunrun, Symantex, Telcare, Thanx, The Wing, ThousandEyes, Thumbtack, Tourlane, Trulia, Trupo, Tula Tech., Tumblr, TuneIn, UiPath, Unity Tech., VA Linux/SourceForge, Varage Sale, Vector

Other Locations:
Room 3606
China Central Place Tower 3
77 Jianguo Road Chaoyang District
Beijing 100025
China
Phone: 86 10 8447 5668 **Fax:** 86 10 8447 5669

Suite 3613, 36/F
Two Pacific Place
88 Queensway
Hong Kong
China
Phone: 852 2501 8989

Room 3006
Plaza 66 Tower 2
1366 Nanjing West Road
Shanghai 200040
China
Phone: 86 21 6288 4222

Sequoia Capital India Advisors
6th Floor, East Wing, Block B
77 Town Centre, Off Hal Airport Road, Yemlur
Bengaluru 560037
India
Phone: 91 0 80 412 458 80

Sequoia Capital India Advisors
Peninsula Corporate Park
Ganpatrao Kadam Marg, Lower Parel
Mumbai 400013
India
Phone: 91 0 22 4074 7272

Sequoia Capital India Advisors Pvt. Ltd.
JW Marriott, Asset Area 4
Delhi Aerocity
New Delhi 110037
India
Phone: 91 0 11 4956 7200

Sequoia Capital India Advisors
26-12 South Beach Tower
Singapore 189767
Singapore
Phone: 65 6812 9162

50 Eli Landau Boulevard
Orchid Oceanus Hotel
Herzelia 4685150
Israel
Phone: 972 9 9579440

Roelof Botha, Partner
Education: BS, Actuarial Science/Economics/Statistics, University of Cape Town; MBA, Stanford Graduate School of Business
Background: CFO, PayPal; Management Consultant, McKinsey & Company
Directorships: Luxim
Jim Goetz, Partner
Education: BSEE, University of Cincinnati; MSEE, Stanford University
Background: General Partner, Accel Partners; Entrepreneur, VitalSigns; VP/GM, VitalSoft/Lucent, VP Network Management, Bay Networks; SynOptics; Marketing, AT&T; AT&T Bell Labs; Digital Equipment
Douglas Leone, Partner
Education: BS, Mechanical Engineering, Cornell University; MS, Industrial Engineering, Columbia University; MS, Management, MIT
Background: Sales Management, Sun Microsystems; Hewlet-Packard; Prime Computer
Michael Moritz, Partner
Background: Time Warner; Founder, Technologic Partners
Alfred Lin, Partner
Education: BA, Applied Mathematics, Harvard University; MS, Statistics, Stanford University
Background: Chairman/COO/CFQ, Zappos.com; VP, Finance, Tellme Networks; Co-Founder & General Manager, Venture Frogs
Bryan Schreier, Partner
Education: BS, Computer Science, Princeton University
Background: Senior Director, International Online Sales & Operations, Google; Technology Banking Group, Morgan Stanley
Bill Coughran, Partner
Background: Bell Labs; Google; Entrisphere
Jess Lee, Partner
Education: Stanford University
Background: Google; Polyvore
Mike Vernal, Partner
Background: Facebook
Stephanie Zhan, Partner
Education: BS, Stanford University
Directorships: Sunday; Linear; Middesk; Rec Room Inc.; Brud; PicsArt; Ethos Life

1658 SERAPH GROUP

e-mail: paul@seraphgroup.net
web: www.seraphgroup.net

Mission Statement: Founded in 2005, Seraph Group is a super angel fund that invests between $50,000 and $1,000,000 in high-growth start-ups, bridging the funding 'gap' left by individual angels and institutional VCs. Our growing network of 180 members offers an unparalleled breadth of expertise and a unified passion for helping founders build great companies. As dedicated early-stage investors, we understand how a compelling product becomes a powerful business and commit strategic guidance from the Seraph members best suited to help our companies grow. We also understand the value of time: Seraph Group manages funds and operates with a single Managing Partner that makes quick investment decisions, eliminating the challenge of syndicating angel investors.

Founded: 2005
Average Investment: $50,000 - $1 million
Investment Criteria: Seed-Stage, Early-Stage
Industry Group Preference: Information Technology, Web Services, Communications, Life Sciences, Mobile, Consumer Internet, Consumer Products, Enterprise Software, Industrial Products, Mobile Apps
Portfolio Companies: Aarki, AfterSteps, Appbistro, Alsalar, Asankya, BringIt, Catch, Cc:Betty, Charles Chocolates, Creative Market, Digital Health Department, Fliggo, Fundly, Life360, Marble, Midverse Studios, Mixrank, Neurotic Media, nVision, Gopago, PBWorks, People Power, Primeloop, Prompt.ly, Qwiki, RallyOn, Second Genome, SendHub, SilverTail, Site Jabber, Stem Cell Theranostics, Suddenly Social, TalentBin, Tasting Room, Trip Trotting, UCT Coatings, Urbantag, Victrio, Wakemate, Wifi Slam

Venture Capital & Private Equity Firms / Domestic Firms

Key Executives:
Tuff Yen, Founder/CEO
Education: BA, University of California, Berkeley; MBA, Yale School of Management
Jake Moilanen, General Partner
Education: BS, University of Michigan; MBA, University of Texas

1659 SEVEN PEAKS VENTURES
1001 Southwest Emkay Drive
Suite 140
Bend, OR 97702

e-mail: contactus@sevenpeaksventures.com
web: www.sevenpeaksventures.com

Mission Statement: Seven Peaks Ventures seeks to invest in innovative technology companies with the potential to make an impact on the world.
Fund Size: $15 million
Founded: 2013
Average Investment: $50,000 - $500,000
Investment Criteria: Early Stage
Industry Group Preference: Technology, Consumer Software, Cloud Computing, Digital Health Technology
Portfolio Companies: Amplion, Bright.md, ClientSuccess, CodeHS, Cozy, Cricket Health, CrowdStreet, Crowd Supply, Customer.io, Droplr, Enlitic, Kindara, Manzama, Opal, Scratch-it, SlamData, Upstream Health, Vungle, ZapInfo, Zembula

Key Executives:
Dino Vendetti, Managing Director
Education: BSEE, San Diego State University; MSEE, MBA, University of Washington
Background: Managing Director, Formative Ventures; General Partner, Bay Partners; Vulcan Ventures
Corey Schmid, General Partner
Education: BA, Human Development & Psychology, Boston College; MBA, Business Administration & Management, Portland State University School of Business
Background: Respironics; Invizeon Corporation; Invivodata
Directorships: Oregon Bioscience Association
Tom Gonser, General Partner
Education: BA, Economics, University of Washington
Background: Channel Development, Mccaw Cellular; VP of Business Development, Point.com; Founder/President, NetUPDATE; Founder, GPSflight Inc.; Managing Partner, TMD Ventures; Investment Partner, Seven Peaks Ventures; Founder, DocuSign Inc.
Directorships: Metricstory; Amitree; Trusona; Liveoak Technologies Inc.; NAVIS
Sara Leggat, Chief Financial Officer
Education: BComm., University of British Columbia; MBA, MIT
Background: Sr Research Analyst, Thomas Weisel Partners; Partner/Ressearch Analyst, Longwood Investment Advisor; Head of Business Development, Galt Investment Partners; Chief Marketing Officer, Longwood Investment Advisors; Founder/Managing Partner, BayPeak Partners LLC

1660 SEVENTYSIX CAPITAL
375 E Elm Street
Suite 100
Conshohocken, OA 19428

web: www.seventysixcapital.com

Mission Statement: SeventySix Capital invests in entrepreneurs who have 're-imagined' how we eat, play, drive, entertain, date, search, and stay healthy.
Geographic Preference: Eastern Corridor
Fund Size: $90 million
Average Investment: $4 million
Minimum Investment: $500,000
Industry Group Preference: Technology, Healthcare
Portfolio Companies: BBox, C360 Live, Diamond Kinetics, FORTE, Maestro, Nerd Street Gamers, Play By Play Sports Broadcasting Camps, ShotTracker, Swish Analytics, U.S. Intergrity, Vigtory Sportsbook, VSIN

Key Executives:
Wayne D Kimmel, Managing Partner
610-825-0250
Fax: 610-825-0205
Education: University of Maryland College Park; LLD, Widener University School of Law
Background: Founder/Manager, atPhilly Internet Email Newsletter; CEO, KimmelCorp.com; Attorney, Kimmel/Carter/Roman & Peltz
Directorships: OrganizedWisdom, Ryzing, meetMoi, KGRA Energy, SeamlessWeb
Jon Powell, Managing Partner
Education: BA, University of Maryland; JD, Delaware Law School
Background: Co-Founder, Microsoft Reactor Philadelphia; Strategic Partner, Rubicon Talent

1661 SEVIN ROSEN FUNDS
PO Box 192128
Dallas, TX 75219

Phone: 972-702-1100 Fax: 972-702-1103
web: www.srfunds.com

Mission Statement: Focused on early-stage investing for information sciences and life sciences companies.
Fund Size: $1.9 billion
Founded: 1981
Average Investment: $2 million
Minimum Investment: $500,000
Investment Criteria: Research and Development, Seed, Startup, First-Stage
Industry Group Preference: Internet, Media, Software, Technology, Communications, Infrastructure, Life Sciences, Healthcare, Advanced Materials, Energy
Portfolio Companies: Alder Biopharmaceuticals, BioBehavioral Diagnostics, Cube Optics, Ethertronics, Extennet, GENBAND, HexaTech, Hightail, Invodo, Luminescent, Luxtera, Market6, Metabolon, NetSocket, Scintera, Verified Person, Vidyo, Xtera

Key Executives:
Jon W Bayless, General Partner
Education: BSEE, University of Oklahoma; MEE, University of Alabama; PhD, Electrical Engineering, Arizona State University
Background: Arthur A Collins, E-Systems, Motorola
Stephen M Dow, General Partner
Education: BA, MBA, Stanford University
Background: Booz Allen and Hamilton
John Jaggers, General Partner
Education: BA, MEE, Rice University, MBA, Harvard University
Background: Rotan Mosle
Jackie Kimzey, General Partner
Dave Mclean, General Partner
e-mail: djm@srfunds.com
Background: IBM
Directorships: BioBehavioral Diagnostics, HexaTech, Market6, MetaCarta, SensorLogic
John Oxaal, General Partner
e-mail: jto@srfunds.com
Background: Co-Founder & CEO, Volumetrics Medical Imaging
Directorships: Astute Networks, Cadtel, Ethertronics, Luminescent, Luxtera, Metabolon, Scintera
Charles Phipps, General Partner
Education: BSEE, Case; MBA, Harvard University
Background: Texas Instruments

Venture Capital & Private Equity Firms / Domestic Firms

Nick Sturiale, General Partner
e-mail: nick.sturiale@carlyle.com
Education: BS, California State University, Chico; MBA, University of California, Berkeley
Background: Jafco Ventures, The Carlyle Groupo, Co-Founder, Timbre Technologies
Directorships: Bill.com, Groundwork Open Source, RedSeal Systems, ReputationDefender, SocialVibe, Vuclip

1662 SEYMOUR ASSET MANAGEMENT
150 East 58th St.
17th Floor
New York, NY 10155

Phone: 212-341-4030
e-mail: admin@seymourasset.com
web: seymouram.com

Mission Statement: Seymour Asset Management is a team of professionals who have managed allocations and assets for some of the worlds largest institutions. They offer clients a tailored investment strategy that aligns with best industry practices.

Key Executives:
 Tim Seymour, Chief Investment Officer
 Background: CIO, Triogem Asset Management; Managing Partner, Red Star Asset Management; Managing Director, Troia Dialog

1663 SHAMROCK CAPITAL ADVISORS
1100 Glendon Avenue
Suite 1600
Los Angeles, CA 90024

Phone: 310-974-6600 Fax: 310-734-4540
e-mail: contact@shamrockcap.com
web: www.shamrockcap.com

Mission Statement: Shamrock Capital Advisors is a private equity firm with over $700 million of capital under management. Investing exclusively in the media, entertainment, and communications sectors, Shamrock partners with strong management teams and takes an active, collaborative approach to creating value in each investment.

Fund Size: $700 million
Founded: 1978
Average Investment: $15 - $50 million
Investment Criteria: Growth Equity, Management & Leverage Buyout, Leveraged Recapitalizations
Industry Group Preference: Media, Entertainment, Communications
Portfolio Companies: FanDuel, Giant, Isolation Network, Mobilite, PGOA Media, Questex, Screenvision, T3Media

Key Executives:
 Stephen D. Royer, Partner
 Education: Stanford University; MBA, Anderson School of Management
 Background: Investment Banking, Lehman Brothers
 Directorships: Mobilitie, Learfield Communications, Screenvision, INgrooves
 Michael A. LaSalle, Partner
 Education: University of Notre Dame; MBA, Anderson School of Management
 Background: Associate, Putnam Lovell Securities
 Directorships: Harlem Globetrotters, INgrooves, Mojiva
 William J. Wynperle, Partner
 Education: Dartmouth College; MBA, Anderson School of Management
 Background: M&A Group, Smith Barney
 Directorships: MarketCast, Learfield Communications, Mojiva
 Andrew J. Howard, Partner
 Education: Stanford University
 Background: Vice President, Clarity Partners
 Directorships: Screenvision, MarketCast, Mobilitie

 Alan H. Resnikoff, Partner
 Education: Stanford University; MBA, Stanford Graduate School of Business
 Background: Associate Consultant, Bain & Company
 Directorships: Learfield Communications, Screenvision

1664 SHAMROCK HOLDINGS
3500 West Olive Avenue
Suite 700
Burbank, CA 91505

Phone: 818-845-4444
web: www.shamrock.com

Mission Statement: Shamrock Holdings, Inc. was founded by the late Roy E. Disney in 1978 and serves as the investment vehicle for certain members of the Roy E. Disney Family. Shamrock's tenet's are straightforward - invest and act with integrity, responsibility, and transparency. In addition to investing and providing services to the Disney Family, Shamrock, through a subsidiary, manages several real estate investment programs.

Founded: 1978

1665 SHARESPOST
555 Montgomery Street
Suite 1400
San Francisco, CA 94111

Fax: 650-492-6871
Toll-Free: 800-279-7754
e-mail: info@sharespost.com
web: sharespost.com

Mission Statement: The SharesPost marketplace makes it easy to explore private growth companies, access investment opportunities and find liquidity.

Founded: 2009
Investment Criteria: Late-Stage
Industry Group Preference: Diversified
Portfolio Companies: 23andMe, Circle Internet Financial, DoorDash, Getaround, Grab, instacart, Nextdoor, Planet, Postmates, Ripple, Robinhood, Virgin Hyperloop One

Key Executives:
 Nick Grabowski, Chief Technology Officer
 Education: BS, Florida State University
 Background: VP of Application Architecture, Charles Schwab & Co.; Managing Director, Software Architecture
 Erika McKiernan, Chief Financial Officer
 Education: BS, Califronia Polytechnic State University
 Background: CFO, PENSCO Trust Company
 Chris Setaro, Global Chief Compliance Officer
 Education: BS, Syracuse University
 Background: CCO, Nasdaq Inc.; CCO, Instinet LLC

1666 SHASTA VENTURES
2440 Sand Hill Road
Suite 300
Menlo Park, CA 94025

Phone: 650-543-1700
e-mail: info@shastaventures.com
web: www.shastaventures.com

Mission Statement: Shasta was formed to back brilliant entrepreneurs with an unwavering commitment to the customer experience. They seek passionate, hardworking entrepreneurs of early stage companies in the areas of enterprise, consumer, and emerging platforms.

Geographic Preference: United States
Investment Criteria: Early-Stage, Seed, Series A
Industry Group Preference: Software, Infrastructure, Business to Business, Wireless Technologies, Marketing, E-Commerce & Manufacturing, Semiconductors, Consumer Services, Internet
Portfolio Companies: 6D.ai, 8th Wall, ACC Systems, Adometry, Airspace, Aloha, Anaplan, Apptio, Apteligent,

Venture Capital & Private Equity Firms / Domestic Firms

Aquera, Archrock, Athelas, Atrium, Aviso, Beautiful AI, Big Box, Bloc, Boomerage Commerce, Brandcast, Camera IQ, Canva, Caring.com, Cequence Security, Chartcube, ClassDojo, CloudPassage, Color, Cover, Data.World, Deep Sentinal, Demdex, Digital Air Strike, Dr. On Demand, Dollar Shave Club, Eero, Elroy Air, Entelo, Extole, Fable Studio, Fetch Robotics, Flyhomes, FogLogic, Frame.io, Glint, Grin, Highspot, Hinge, Hobo Labs, iConclude, Imperfect Produce, Isara, Jack Erwin, Kapwing, Leaftail Labs, LeanData, Leanplum, LearnUp, Let's Do This, Lightbend, Liquidspace, Lithium, LiveIntent, Logoworks, Lucidworks, Macro Meta, Makara, Mint, Mocana, Mochi, Needle, Nest, Neumob, Nextdoor, NodeFly, Noon, Numina, Octi, Outright, Path, Plays.tv, Poppin., Rd.Md, Resilinc, Rosie, SayNow, Scalyr, Second Measure, SendBird, Simple, Skilljar, Skycure, SlamData, Smule, Snap Strat, Socratic, Spiceworks, Spire, Squelch, Stance, Starship, Starsky Robotics, Steel Brick, StrongLoop, Suplari, Survios, Tally, TaskRabbit, The Farmer's Dog, The Pill Club, Tiger Connect, Timehop, Tonal, Tumri, Turn, Turo, Umuse, Unblockable, Upserve, Vailmail, Vector, vFunction, VoloMetrix, WatchDox, Whisper, Zefr, Zenprise, Zuora, Zwift

Other Locations:
27 South Park Street
Suite 101
San Francisco, CA 94107

Key Executives:
Robert Coneybeer, Founder/Managing Director
Education: BS, Mechanical Engineering, University of Virginia; MS, Mechanical Engineering, Georgia Institute of Technology; MBA, Wharton School
Background: General Partner, New Enterprise Associates; Lead Integration/Test Engineer Astro Space, Martin Marietta
Tod Francis, Managing Director
Education: BA, Economics, Northwestern University; MBA, Kellogg School of Management
Background: General Partner, Trinity Ventures; Partner, Ram Group Marketing Management; Product Manager, Johnson & Johnson
Ravi Mohan, Managing Director
Education: BS, Operations Research/Industrial Engineering, Cornell University; MBA, University of Michigan School of Business
Background: General Partner, Battery Ventures; Transaction Processing Systems, Accenture; Software Applications, Hyperion Software Corp; MIC; Co-Founder, Silicon Valley Chapter Indian Venture Capital Association; McKinsey & Company
Directorships: The Indus Entrepreneurs
Jason Pressman, Managing Director
Education: BS, Finance, University of Maryland; MBA, Stanford Graduate School of Business
Background: VP Strategy/Business Development/Operations, Walmart.com; Associate, Selby Venture Partners; Associate, Alex.Brown
Doug Pepper, Managing Director
Education: BA, Dartmouth College; MBA, Stanford University
Background: General Partner, InterWest Partners; Financial Analyst, Goldman Sachs; Amazom.com
Nikhil Basu Trivedi, Managing Director
Education: AB, Molecular Biology, Princeton University
Background: Artsy; Insight Venture Partners
Directorships: ClassDojo, Fram.io, Hinge, Imperfect Produce, Plays.tv, Tally, The Farmer's Dog, The Pill Club

1667 SHEPHERD VENTURES
11696 Sorrento Valley Road
Suite F
San Diego, CA 92121

Phone: 858-509-4744
e-mail: info@shepherdventures.com
web: www.shepherdventures.com

Mission Statement: A venture capital fund that generates significant capital appreciation through carefully selected and wisely shepherded investments. As an SBIC, Shepherd Ventures partners with the US Small Business Administration to help fund and grow America's small businesses.

Geographic Preference: Southern California, San Diego, Southwest
Investment Criteria: First Stage/Disruptive Technology; Later Stage
Industry Group Preference: Information Technology, Life Sciences, Software, Enterprise Applications, Wireless, Mobile Computing, Networking, Infrastructure, Medical Devices, Biotherapeutics, Diagnostics, Healthcare Information Technology
Portfolio Companies: Andigilog, CEYX Technologies, Digital Orchid, Emergent Respiratory Products, Lighting Technologies International, Lucix Corporation, MedManage Systems, NP Photonics, OCULIR, Planet ATE, Quickoffice, Revance Therapeutics, Sendio, SiliconSystems, Skylight Healthcare Systems, SpecificMEDIA, Voyager Systems, wiSpry

Key Executives:
George C Kenney, Managing Partner
Education: BSEE, Rensselaer Polytechnic Institute; MSEE, Stanford University; MBA, Columbia University; Optic's Program, London Imperial College; Industrial Management Program, Harvard University
Background: CTO/Partner, Nicholas-Applegate; CTO/Managing Director, Kidder Peabody; Swiss Bank; Salomon Brothers; American Stock Exchange; Director Research, North American Philips; Co-Founder, Digital Measurements Corp; Patentholder; Keynote Speaker
Tom W Siegel, Managing Director
Education: BA Economics, MBA, University of Illinois; CPA; CFA
Background: Senior VP, Advantage Capital Partners; Founder, National Association of Venture Forums; Publisher, Dealmaker's Digest; Founder, software/systems integrator; Management Consultant, KPMG Peat Marwick
Richard P Kuntz, Managing Director
Education: BS, MS, MIT; MBA, JL Kellogg Graduate School of Management at Northwestern University
Background: Senior Managing Director, Premier Medical Partner Fund; Principal, Senmed Medical Ventures; 3i Group; Prudential Insurance Company of America
John R Nelson, Venture Partner
Education: BA, University of Wisconsin; MA Economics, Washington State University; PhD work, doctoral skill certification in computer sciences, University of Oregon
Background: Managing Director: California Capital Partners, Terra Nova Capital Can-Am Fund, Consortium Capital Partners, Ventana Global Funds Technology Gateway, Venture Management Group; Investment Director, Commonwealth of Australia; Senior VP Marketing, National Computer Systems

1668 SHERBROOKE CAPITAL
e-mail: info@sherbrookecapital.com
web: www.sherbrookecapital.com

Mission Statement: Dedicated exclusively to providing growth and expansion capital to emerging companies in the health and wellness industry.

Founded: 1999
Average Investment: $1 - $4 million
Industry Group Preference: Food & Beverage, Healthcare, Medical Devices
Portfolio Companies: Advanced BioNutrition, Affinnova, Angie's, Boathouse Sports, Ciao Bella, Farmigo, Food Should Taste Good, Halfpops, HeartBar, Immaculate Baking Co., IZZE, Kill Cliff, Outside The Classroom, oregon Chai, TransMedics, VetCentric

Key Executives:
John K Giannuzzi, Managing General Partner
e-mail: giannuzzi@sherbrookecapital.com
Education: West Virginia University, American University
Background: Managing Director, BankBoston
Directorships: Outside The Classroom, Advanced BioNutrition, VetCentric, Polymerix, Affinova, Boathouse Sports, FoodShouldTasteGood, Adina, Ciao Bella

1669 SHERPALO VENTURES
Menlo Park, CA 94025

e-mail: info@sherpalo.com
web: www.sherpalo.com

Mission Statement: Sherpalo guides and mentors exceptional entrepreneurs as they take their innovative ideas and disruptive technologies and turn them into successful businesses.

Founded: 2000
Investment Criteria: Early-Stage
Industry Group Preference: Consumer Internet
Portfolio Companies: Abacus.AI, AbCellera, Aisera, Alphabet Inc., Antheia, CaaStle, EasyPost, Filecoin, Flexport, GoForward Inc., Gusto, Hexagon Bio, Hypersonix, InMobi, Metabase Inc., Mix, Mosaic, Next Jump, Notion, Paperless Post, Protocol Labs, Robust Intelligence, Scalyr Inc., Stripe, Upwork, WishFin, Yubico

Key Executives:
Ram Shiriam, Founder/Managing Partner

1670 SHORE CAPITAL PARTNERS
1 East Wacker Drive
Suite 2900
Chicago, IL 60601

Phone: 312-348-7580 **Fax:** 312-348-7669
web: www.shorecp.com

Mission Statement: Shore Capital Partners is a private equity firm aiming to provide capital, business development guidance, and industry insight to lower middle market healthcare companies.

Geographic Preference: North America
Fund Size: $112.5 million
Investment Criteria: Management Buyouts, Leveraged Buyouts, Successions, Consolidations, Recapitalizations, Corporate Divestitures
Industry Group Preference: Healthcare
Portfolio Companies: Chicagoland Smile Group, ClearPath Diagnostics, Cumberland Therapy Services, Fast Pace Urgent Care, Florida Autism Center, My Therapy Company, RapidCare Clinic, Shippert Medical, Southern Veterinary Partners, Specialdocs Consultants, Summit Medical

Key Executives:
Justin Ishbia, Managing Partner
e-mail: jishbia@shorecp.com
Education: BA, Accounting, Michigan State University; JD, Vanderbilt University Law School
Background: Valor Equity Partners; Kirkland & Ellis
Directorships: Fast Pace Urgent Care, Pediatric Therapy Services, Southern Veterinary Partners, Summit Medical, Florida Autism Center, Specialdocs Consultants
Ryan Kelley, Partner
e-mail: rkelley@shorecp.com
Education: BA, Accounting, Honors College, Michigan State University; MBA, Kellogg School of Management, Northwestern University
Background: Water Street Healthcare Partners; Bank of America
Directorships: ClearPath Diagnostics, Fast Pace Urgent Care, Pediatric Therapy Staffing
Mike Cooper, Partner
e-mail: mcooper@shorecp.com
Education: BSBA, Finance & Management, McDonough School of Business, Georgetown University
Background: Wind Point Partners; UBS Investment Bank
Directorships: Southern Veterinary Partners, Specialdocs Consultants
John Hennegan, Partner
e-mail: jhennegan@shorecp.com
Education: BS, University of Illinois; MBA, Kellogg School of Management, Northwestern University
Background: Henry Crown & Company; Citigroup
Directorships: ClearPath Diagnostics, Fast Pace Urgent Care, Pediatric Therapy Services
Don Pierce, Partner
e-mail: dpierce@shorecp.com
Education: BBA, Finance, University of Notre Dame
Background: Baxter International; RoundTable Healthcare Partners; UBS Investment Bank
Directorships: Summit Medical Products, Shippert Medical Technologies

1671 SIERRA ANGELS
PO Box 3215
Incline Village, NV 89450

web: www.sierraangels.com

Mission Statement: As a result of the extensive operational experience of our members, many entrepreneurs have found our high value-added model to be enormously helpful in both their strategic and operational development. Our thoughtful selectivity of companies in which to invest combined with our proactive collaboration with other funding and partnering entities helps to ensure that the chosen companies get the focus, support and funding required for success.

Geographic Preference: Northern Nevada, Northern California
Industry Group Preference: Clean Energy, Green Technology, Computing, Communications, Healthcare, Mobile, Software, Technology
Portfolio Companies: Animated Speech Corporation, Aperia Technologies, Cloud Cruiser, DynaOptics, Gatekeepr Innovation, Glue Networks, Jopari Solutions, Marrone Organic Innovators, OptiComp Corporation, Reframe It, RevoLights, Sierra Nevada Solar, TranscribeMe, Up Out, Vokle, Zippy App

1672 SIERRA VENTURES
1400 Fashion Island Boulevard
Suite 1010
San Mateo, CA 94404

Phone: 650-854-1000
e-mail: info@sierraventures.com
web: www.sierraventures.com

Mission Statement: Works with entrepreneurs and management teams to originate and build new companies into large, profitable businesses. Seeks to find the right combination of investment and expertise to help companies grow and deliver on their promise.

Geographic Preference: United States, India, China
Fund Size: $600 million
Founded: 1982
Average Investment: $10-$15 million
Minimum Investment: $1 million
Investment Criteria: Seed to Mid Stage
Industry Group Preference: Internet Technology, Communications, Computer Related, Consumer Services, Electronic Technology, Financial Services, High Technology, Information Technology, Service Industries, Software, Consumer Technology, Semiconductors
Portfolio Companies: Agent IQ, Appcues, Applitools, Astronomer, CNEX Labs, Core Tigo, Deep Lens, Drop, Falcon Computing, Headspin, Hired, Interplay Learning, K4Connect, Kinnek, Krisp, LeadGenius, Movandi, NextInput, Omniex, Phenom TRM Cloud Platform, Q-CTRL, Qeexo, Quadratic 3D, Radius, Regulus, Shape Security, Sikka Software Corporation, SiSense, SK Spruce, SkyDeck Accelerator, SkyDrop, Sliver.tv, Support Logic, Text IQ,

Venture Capital & Private Equity Firms / Domestic Firms

VeeR, Yalo, Zaloni, Zeta Global, Zimperium, Zycada Delivery Network

Key Executives:
Peter Wendell, Founder/Advisor
e-mail: peter@sierraventures.com
Education: BA, Princeton University; MBA, Harvard University
Background: Executive Manager, IBM; McKinsey & Company; Faculty, Stanford University
Directorships: Centex Telemanagement
Tim Guleri, Managing Director
e-mail: tim@sierraventures.com
Education: BS, Electrical Engineering, Punjab Engineering College; MS, Robotics/Industrial Engineering, Virginia Polytechnic Institute
Background: LSI Logic; VP Technical Field Operations/Product Marketing, Scopus Technology; Co-Founder/CEO, Octane Software; Vice Chairman/Executive VP, Epiphany
Directorships: Approva, CodeGreen Networks, DotNetNuke, Everest Software, Greenplum, MakeMyTrip, Sourcefire, CarWale
Mark Fernandes, Managing Director
e-mail: mfernandes@sierraventures.com
Education: BS Mechanical Engineering, Bangalore University; MS Mechanical Engineering, University of California, Berkeley; MBA, Harvard University
Background: Director Infrastructure Software, Merrill Lynch; Research Analyst, Robertson Stephens; Product Manager, Cisco Systems; Product Manager, Seagate Technology; Founding Team, PanoCorp Displays
Directorships: Ooyala, Opalis Software, Spotzer Media Group
Ben Yu, Managing Director
e-mail: byu@sierraventures.com
Education: BSEE, University of Western Australia; MA, PhD, Princeton University
Background: Managing Engineer/Corporate R&D, 3Com Corporation; Business Development, Merz Australia
Directorships: AuthenTec, MicroPower, Paracer, SyChip

1673 SIGHTLINE PARTNERS
8500 Normandale Lake Boulevard
Suite 1070
Bloomington, MN 55437

Phone: 952-641-0300 Fax: 952-641-0310
e-mail: buzz@sightlinepartners.com
web: www.sightlinepartners.com

Mission Statement: SightLine Partners manages venture funds that invest in promising emerging growth companies in the medical technology sector and the healthcare industry.

Geographic Preference: United States
Founded: 1992
Average Investment: $2 - $8 million
Investment Criteria: Later Stage
Industry Group Preference: Medical Devices, Medical Technology, Healthcare

Key Executives:
Buzz Benson, Managing Director
Education: St. Johns University; CPA
Background: Piper Jaffray, Partner, Stonebridge Capital; Investment Officer, Cherry Tree Ventures
Directorships: Acorn Cardiovascular, Anulex, Broncus, LipoScience, Verax Biomedical
Kunal Paymaster, Managing Director
Background: Scientific Cardiac Rhytm Management, Boston

1674 SIGMA PARTNERS
Phone: 650-853-1700 Fax: 650-853-1717
e-mail: info@sigmapartners.com
web: www.sigmapartners.com

Mission Statement: To identify, invest in, and provide support and constructive counsel to companies with exceptional management strength and growth prospects. Seeks to combine their capital, experience, and active involvement with the ideas and capabilities of outstanding entrepreneurial teams to develop substantial and profitable businesses.

Geographic Preference: United States
Fund Size: $1 billion
Founded: 1984
Average Investment: $2 to $8 million
Minimum Investment: $2 million
Investment Criteria: Early-Stage
Industry Group Preference: Computer Related, Electronic Technology, Software, Communications, Clean Technology, Semiconductors, Wireless Technologies, Data Storage, Mobile Computing, Electronics, Internet, SaaS, Business Products & Services, Enterprise Software
Portfolio Companies: Acquia, Aprimo, aPriori, Arasys Technologies, Atrributor, AutoVirt, Azuik, Birthday Express, Blackwave, Blue Agave Software, Broadware Technologies, CallMiner, CaseNET, Centrify, Certeon, CiRBA, CrownPeak Technology, Damballa, Demandbase, Dexterra, Digital Fuel Technologies, Digital Music Network, DocuSign, EasyAsk, Emagia, Encover, EndWave, Enkata Technologies, EqualLogic, Envis Corp, Everspin Technologies, ExaGrid Systems, Expressor Software Corp, FieldCentrix, Fogbreak Software, Fortify Software, GainSpan Corp, GlassHouse Technologies, Idiom Technologies, Incipient, Initiate Systems, Inovis, Instill, Intacct Corporation, Interactions, iWatt, Jellyvision, Kana Software, Kateeva, Laser Diagnostic Technology, Leyden Energy, MarketLive, Menara Networks, Nasuni Corporation, Nexx Systems, Nimblefish Technologies, Noetix, Nucore Technology, O-In Design Automation, oDesk Corporation, OnExchange, OpenPages, OpenSpan, OutStart, Oversight Systems, POET Software, Quantenna Communications, QuickSilver Technology, R2 Semiconductor, Rave Wireless, RecycleBank, Reflectent Software, Replay Solutions, Responsys, Retica Systems, Savantis Systems, ScanCafe, Sequence Design, Silverlink Communications, SkillSoft, Soladigm, Solaria, Steelwedge, SugarSync, Sunchron, SupplySolution, Svaya Nanotechnologies, Tervela, Toolwire, Topio, Tradebeam, Trustwave, Vendavo, Vericept, Versata, Vettro, Vicom Systems, Vignette, Vinusa, Visual Mining, Vormetric, World Power Technology Senasis Technologies

Key Executives:
Lawrence G Finch, Managing Director
e-mail: lgf@sigmapartners.com
Background: President and CEO, Paradise Systems, Inc.; Founder, President and CEO, Shasta General Systems, Inc.; Singer Business Machines; Friden, Inc.
Directorships: Acumos, Global Village Communications, International Network Services IPNet Solutions, iWatt, Nimblefish, Nucore, Paradis Tech, Phoenix Tech, Quicksilver Tech, Ray Dream

1675 SIGMA PRIME VENTURES
20 Custom House Street
Suite 830
Boston, MA 02110

Phone: 617-330-7872
web: www.sigmaprime.com

Mission Statement: Our first-hand experience allows us to give early-stage companies both tactical and strategic guidance and access to a powerful business network. Our team has founded or cofounded 10 companies, helped run 10 companies, and collectively been responsible for exits worth over $4.2B in companies where we were operators. We invest in early stage technology companies focusing on SaaS, Cloud, Mobile, disruptive technologies and technology-enabled service companies.

Geographic Preference: East Coast
Investment Criteria: Early-Stage

Venture Capital & Private Equity Firms / Domestic Firms

Industry Group Preference: SaaS, Cloud Computing, Mobile, Technology-Enabled Services
Portfolio Companies: Acquia, aPriori, BiOM, BlueConic, CallMiner, Ceros, Cirba, CloudHealth Technologies, Codeship, Coherent Path, Contently, Damballa, eCommHub, ExaGrid Systems, Interactions, Kwicr, Mobiquity, Nasuni, OpenSpan, Oversight Systems, Paradigm4, RAVE, Recyclebank, Rethink Robotics, Silverlink, Tervela, VoltDB, Wordstream

Key Executives:

   Robert E Davoli, Managing Director
   Education: BA, History, Ricker College
   Background: President & CEO, Epoch Systems; Founder, SQL Solutions

   Paul Flanagan, Managing Director
   Education: BS, Accounting, Bentley College
   Background: EVP/CFO, VistaPrint; President/CEO, StorageNetworks

   John Mandile, Managing Director
   Education: BSE, Engineering Science & Mathematics, Tufts University; MS, Computer Science, Worcester Polytechnic University
   Background: President/CEO, Vermeer Technologies; Principal, SQL Solutions

   Jere Doyle, Managing Director
   Education: BS, Boston College; MBA, Harvard Business School
   Background: Founder, Prospectiv; Oyster Angel Fund; Doyle Enterprises

   John Simon, Managing Director
   Education: BA, History & Science, Harvard University; MA, Politics, Univ. of Oxford
   Background: Co-Founder/Managing Director, General Catalyst Partners; Founder/CEO, UroMed Corporation

1676 SIGNAL EQUITY PARTNERS
805 Third Avenue
Suite 1202
New York City, NY 10022

Phone: 860-479-1186 **Fax:** 212-208-4433
web: www.signal-equity.com

Mission Statement: Signal Equity Partners invests in capital, time and effort to grow our portfolio companies into enduring, large scale businesses.

Founded: 1996
Investment Criteria: Leveraged Buyouts, Roll-Ups, Restructurings, Secondary Purchases of Investment Portfolios
Industry Group Preference: Communications, Media, Technology

Key Executives:

   Timothy P Bradley, Co-Founder/Managing Director
   Education: BA, Yale University, JD, New York University, MBA, Columbia Business School
   Background: Partner, Exeter Group

   Charles T Lake II, Managing Director
   Education: BS, Trinity College, MBA, Northwestern University
   Background: Director Of Budget & Finance, Telular Corporation, Transworld Communications

   Malcolm C Nolen, Managing Director
   Education: BA, Yale University, MBA, Columbia Business School
   Background: Director, Evoke Software Corporation, Overseer Of Securities, Bank Of New York

1677 SIGNAL FIRE
501 - 2nd Street
Suite 100
San Francisco, CA 94107

e-mail: startups@signalfire.com
web: www.signalfire.com

Mission Statement: A venture capital firm funding startup data companies.

Fund Size: $375 million
Average Investment: Seed, $1-5 million; Breakout, up to $15 million
Industry Group Preference: Data & Analytics, Entertainment, Technology, Applications, Retail, Consumer & Leisure
Portfolio Companies: ClassDojo, Color Genomics, Frame.io, Grabr, Grammarly, Hawthorne Effect, Juve, Jyve, Ledge Investing, Lighthouse, OneSignal, Osso VR, PropelPLM, Rocksbox, SafeGraph, ScopeAR, SmartSpot, TextRecruit, Yodas, Zume Pizza

Key Executives:

   Chris Farmer, Managing Director/CEO
   Education: BA, International Relations/Business, Tufts University & the Fletcher School of Diplomacy
   Background: Cowen & Company; Venture Partner, General Catalyst Partners; VP, Bessemer Venture Partners; Consultant, Bain & Company

   Ilya Kirnos, Managing Director/CTO
   Education: BSE, Computer Science, Princeton University
   Background: Software Engineer, Google; Technical Lead, Gmail Ads; Technical Lead, AdWords Performance and Scalability; Founder/Technical Lead, Google Prediction Markets; CardSpring; Bell Labs; Oracle

   Walter Kortschak, Executive Chairman/CIO
   Education: BS, Engineering, Oregon State University; MS, Engineering, California Institute of Technology; MBA, University of California, LA
   Background: Co-Founder, EndCue; Managing Partner, Summit Partners; VP/Associate, Crosspoint Venture Partners
   Directorships: National Venture Capital Association

   Tony Huie, Venture Partner
   Education: BS, MS, Electircal Engineering, Stanford University
   Background: Executive, Dropbox; Investor, Technology Crossover Ventures; Consultant, McKinsey & Company

1678 SIGNAL LAKE
606 Post Road East
Suite 667
Westport, CT 06880-4549

Phone: 203-454-1133 **Fax:** 203-454-7142
e-mail: info@signallake.com
web: signallake.com

Mission Statement: To generate significant capital growth through early stage investments in the broadband telecom and networking infrastructure being built for the global economy over the next several decades.

Industry Group Preference: Broadband, Telecommunications, Networking, Infrastructure
Portfolio Companies: RemoTV, HVault Storage, InPhase, RFMD, Cradle Techologies, SLT Logic, Hermois, GlobalSoft, Force10, Corredge Networks, SeraStar, Oracle/Skywire, NET Technologies, Intellectual Ventures, Avail Media

Other Locations:
50 Commonwealth Avenue
Suite 504
Boston, MA 02116
Phone: 617-267-5205 **Fax:** 617-262-7037

Key Executives:

   Bart Stuck, Founder/Managing Director
   e-mail: bartstuck@signallake.com
   Education: BS, MS, Doctorate, Electrical Engineering & Computer Science, MIT
   Directorships: CorEdge Group, CorEdge Networks, Hermios, SeraStar, SLT Logic

   Michael Weingarten, Director
   e-mail: mikew@signallake.com
   Education: BS, MS, Columbia University; MBA, Harvard Business School

Venture Capital & Private Equity Firms / Domestic Firms

Background: Boston Consulting Group, Monitor Group
Directorships: CorEdge Networks, SLT Logic

1679 SIGNAL PEAK VENTURES
2755 E Cottonwood Parkway
Suite 520
Salt Lake City, UT 84121

Phone: 801-942-8999 Fax: 801-942-1636
e-mail: info@vsp.com
web: www.vsp.com

Mission Statement: To help passionate entrepreneurs build leading companies with enduring value.

Fund Size: $400 million
Average Investment: $2 - $3 million
Investment Criteria: Seed-Stage, Early-Stage, Later-Stage (under special circumstances)
Industry Group Preference: Enterprise Software, Networking, Communications, Security, Internet, Mobile Computing, Drug Delivery, Diagnostics, Medical Devices, Information Technology, Life Sciences
Portfolio Companies: Agilix, Alianza, Altiris, Alpha Bay, Ancestry.com, Aspen Avionics, Athena Feminine Technologies, BDNA, C7, Cerberian, Coherex Medical, ComScore, Control4, EFileCabinet, Experticity, Fat Pipe, Footnote, GlobalSim, Graduation Alliance, Helius, Infusionsoft, iTOKiNET, LANDesk Software, Lingotek, Luxul, MaxStream, MediConnect Global, Mirabilis Medica, Nano MR, Netaphor Software, NetVision, Numira, Penguin Computing, Power Innovations, PublicEngines, Q Therapeutics, Radiate Media, Senforce, Smile Reminder, Solera Networks, Solutionreach, Symbiot Business Group, True Fit, Verismic, Viawest, Voonami, Wildworks, ZARS Pharma

Key Executives:
Ben Dahl, Managing Director
Education: AB, Princeton University; JD, University of California Berkeley; MBA, Columbia Business School
Background: Partner, Pelion Venture Partners
Brandon Tidwell, Managing Director
Education: BS/MS, Accounting, Brigham Young University; JD, Columbia Law School
Background: Managing Director, Canopy Ventures
Scott Petty, Managing Director
Education: BS, Economics, Brigham Young University; MBA, Harvard Business School
Background: COO, Board Director, Zuka Juice; Consultant, Bain & Company

1680 SIGNIA VENTURE PARTNERS
2055 Woodside Road
Suite 270
Redwood City, CA 94061

Phone: 650-614-5800
web: www.signiaventurepartners.com

Mission Statement: To be the most helpful investor an entrepreneur will ever have.

Founded: 2012
Industry Group Preference: Blockchain, E-Commerce, Fitness, Transportation, Virtual Reality, Data Security, Fintech, Health, SaaS
Portfolio Companies: Alibaba.com, Boxed Wholesale, Cruise, Fun+, Kurbo Health, PepperData, Playdom, Super Evil Megacorp

Key Executives:
Ed Cluss, Managing Director
Education: BS/MS, Engineering, MIT; MBA, Harvard Business School
Background: VP of Marketing, Aspect Telecommunications; President/COO/CEO, Aveo; President/CEO, InfoGear Technology; VP/GM, Cisco; President/CEO, NextHop Technologies
Directorships: Schoop Technologies Inc.; ApplePie Capital; Pensa Systems; Fortem Technologies; Nativo; MomentFeed; Pepperdata; BlueTalon; Kauna Ventures
Sunny Dhillon, Managing Director
Education: BS, University of Oxford; MS, London School of Economics & Political Sciences; MBA, Kellogg School of Management, Northwestern University
Background: Investment Banking Analyst, Rothschild; VC Associate, Pritzker Group; Co-Founder/Head of Product, BarSchool
Directorships: GBx
Rick Thompson, Managing Director
Education: MBA, Wharton School
Background: Program Manager, Octel; Founding CEO/Chair, Flycast; Founding Chairman, Dogtime Media; Funzio; Idle Games; Wild Needle Inc.; Playdom; Adify

1681 SIGULER GUFF & COMPANY
200 Park Avenue
23rd Floor
New York, NY 10166

Phone: 212-332-5100 Fax: 212-332-5120
web: www.sigulerguff.com

Mission Statement: To generate high absolute rates of return by capitalizing on the inefficient allocations of capital that regularly occur in the financial markets.

Fund Size: $1.3 billion
Founded: 1995
Investment Criteria: Multi-strategy (distressed, venture, LBO, mezzanine, energy)
Industry Group Preference: Diversified

Other Locations:
One International Place
Suite 2710
Boston, MA 02110
Phone: 617-648-2100 Fax: 617-648-2121

2205 CITIC Square
1168 Nanjing Road West
Shanghai 200041
China
Phone: 86-2152925256 Fax: 86-2152925575

Siguler Guff India Advisers Private Limited
Suite C-1607, One BKC, Bandra-Kurla Complex
Bandra East
Mumbai 400 051
India
Phone: 91-2242154830

Brookfield House, 4th Floor
44 Davies Street
London W1K EJA
United Kingdom
Phone: 44 (20) 3771-4910 Fax: 44 (20) 3070-0435

160 Horacio Lafer Avenue
Suite 42, 4th Floor
Sao Paulo 04538-000
Brazil
Phone: 555-1134769992

Level 20 Marunouchi Trust Tower Main
1-8-3 Marunouchi Chiyoda-Ku
Tokyo 100-0005
Japan

11F, 28 Saemunan-Ro 5ga-Gil
Jongno-Gu

Venture Capital & Private Equity Firms / Domestic Firms

Seoul 13170
South Korea

3730 Kirby Drive
Suite 1200
Houston, TX 77098

38/F, Infinitus Plaza
Sheung Wan
Hong Kong

Key Executives:
Drew Guff, Co-Managing Partner & Chief Investment Officer
212-332-5108
Fax: 212-332-5120
e-mail: drewg@sigulerguff.com
Education: AB, Harvard University
Background: Principal, Paine Webber Merchant Banking Group; Assistant to the President, Paine Webber; Founder, Pacific Media KK
Directorships: Eurasia Foundation, Phillips Academy Institute for the Recruitment of Teachers, NPV Russia
George W. Siguler, Executive Chairman
212-332-5111
Fax: 212-332-5120
Education: BA, Amherst College; MBA, Harvard Business School
Background: Founding Partner, Harvard Management Company; Founder, Paine Webber's Private Equity Group; Chief of Staff, US Department of Health and Human Services
Directorships: Board of Oversees Visiting Committee of the Harvard Medical School, Trustee of the Bement School
Donald Spencer, Managing Director & Senior Advisor
212-332-5105
Fax: 212-332-5120
e-mail: donalds@sigulerguff.com
Education: BA, Wesleyan University; JD, New York University School of Law
Background: First VP/Associate General Counsel, Mitchell Hutchins; Sr VP/General Counsel, Atalanta/Sosnoff Capital Corporation; Sullivan & Cromwell; Shereff Friedman, Hoffman & Goodman
Kenneth Burns, Co-Managing Partner & COO
212-332-5102
Fax: 212-332-5120
e-mail: kenb@sigulerguff.com
Education: BS, State University of New York at Oneonta; MBA, St. Johns University
Background: CFO, Odyssey Investment Partners; Controller, Odyssey Partners; Controller, Buffalo Partners
Directorships: Frowen Holdings Limited (a Cyprus holding company)
Kevin Kester, Managing Partner
Education: BA, Government, Hamilton College; MBA, Finance, University of Colorado, Boulder
Background: Investment Division, Colorado Public Employees' Retirement Association
Cesar Collier, Partner & Head, Latin America
Education: Law Degree, Universidade Catolica de Pernambuci; MBA, Funacao Getulio Vargas
Background: SVP, Standard Bank Private Equity; Senior Management Positions Wal-Mart, Carrefour, Royal Ahold, Bompreco

1682 SILICON ALLEY VENTURE PARTNERS
300 Park Avenue
18t Floor GCP
New York, NY 10022

web: www.savp.com

Mission Statement: Founded 1998 in NYC by Steve Brotman, the successful Web 1.0 founder of AdOne, SAVP is entrepreneur centric. SAVP is making early and growth stage investments in its fourth fund. SAVP was the among the first institutional investors in two successful IPOs - Live Person and Medidata - and has many profitable exits in its portfolio. SAVP's investment focus continues to be on East Coast, post-revenue early and growth stage ventures in business software and information services, health care, e-commerce, and new networks enabled by mobile, social and data. SAVP makes a handful of North East, early stage investments per year, mostly as a co-investor.

Geographic Preference: East Coasts
Founded: 1998
Average Investment: $25,000 - $1 million
Investment Criteria: Early-Stage, Growth Stage
Industry Group Preference: Business Software, Information Services, Health Care, E-Commerce & Manufacturing, Mobile, Networking
Portfolio Companies: Critical Mention, Data Synapse, GameTrust, Headliner, Knovel, Live Person, Medidata, Navtrck, PartStore, Rewind.me, Ugo, You Now

Key Executives:
Steve Brotman, Managing Partner
Education: Duke University; JD/MBA, Washington University
Background: Founder, AdOne; Advisor, New World Ventures

1683 SILKROAD EQUITY
Chicago, IL 60654

e-mail: info@silkroadequity.com
web: www.silkroadequity.com

Mission Statement: SilkRoad Equity is a global private investment firm with interests in a diversified portfolio of public and private companies. SilkRoad Equity invests its own capital in companies with strong market positions, recognized brands and enormous growth potential. SilkRoad Equity's investment philosophy centers around a core set of principles focused on partnering with management to execute strategies for long term value creation.

Geographic Preference: Worldwide
Founded: 2003
Investment Criteria: Start-ups, Buy-outs, Build-ups, Spin-offs, Privatizations and Industry Consolidations
Industry Group Preference: Technology, Gaming, Media & Entertainment, Healthcare, Energy, Real Estate
Portfolio Companies: AffiliateShop, CardZee, ChatBlazer, ExpressCoin, GoCoin, InterAct911, MissionMode, MooMee, Onramp Branding, Pendulab, SilkRoad Technology, SolidSpace, TrueLook, Viwawa, Barefoot Landing, Harbourgate Resort & Marina, Liberty Plaza, SilkRoad Realty Capital, Jimmy Buffet's Margaritaville, Levy Acq., ONE Group, Sunda, EBOOST, Primo Water, Alabama Theater, House of Blues, Cryo-Cell

Key Executives:
Andrew "Flip" Filipowski, Co-Founder & Executive Chairman
e-mail: flip@silkroadequity.com
Background: COO, Cullinet; CEO, PLATINUM Technology
Directorships: SilkRoad Technology, InterAct 911, SilkRoad Realty Capital
Matthew Roszak, Co-Founder & Vice Chairman
e-mail: matt@silkroadequity.com
Education: BA, Economics, Lake Forest College
Background: Co-Founder & CFO, SilkRoad Technology; Principal, Advent International; Keystone Capital Partners

1684 SILVER CREEK VENTURES
5949 Sherry Lane
Suite 1515
Dallas, TX 75225

Phone: 214-265-2020 **Fax:** 214-692-6233
web: www.silvercreekfund.com

Venture Capital & Private Equity Firms / Domestic Firms

Mission Statement: Invests in companies and markets where there is industry expertise and opportunity for significant value. Areas of concentration are telecommunications carrier infrastructure, Internet, data networking, wireless services, infrastructure.

Geographic Preference: Texas, California
Fund Size: $75 million
Founded: 1989
Investment Criteria: Early Stage
Industry Group Preference: Communications, Computer Related, Electronic Components, Instrumentation, Information Technology
Portfolio Companies: Aktino, Alteon WebSystems, Bivio, Bloomfire, Cellfire, Centennial Communications, Corsair Communications, Credence Systems, Crystal Semiconductor, Diamond Lane, Egnyte, Gazzang, MetroPCS, NetSocket, Nimbix, OneSpot, ONI Systems, OpenConnect Systems, Optical Data Systems, Pivot3, Powerfile, ProNet, Sensity, Shomiti Systems, Talari Networks, Theatro, Traxo, WaferScale Integration, Xillinx, Yvolver

Key Executives:
   Mark C Masur, General Partner
   Education: BS, Weber State University; MBA, University of Denver
   Background: General Partner, Trailhead Ventures/Sherry Lane Partners/O'Donnell & Masur; InterFirst Venture Corporation
   Michael T Segrest, General Partner
   Education: Undergraduate Degree/MBA Finance, University of Texas Austin
   Background: General Partner, Trailhead Ventures; O'Donnell & Masur; Sherry Lane Partners

1685 SILVER LAKE
2775 Sand Hill Road
Suite 100
Menlo Park, CA 94025

Phone: 650-233-8120
web: www.silverlake.com

Mission Statement: Invests in leading technology businesses around the world.
Geographic Preference: North America, Europe, Asia
Fund Size: $10.3 billion
Founded: 1999
Industry Group Preference: Technology, Technology-Enabled Businesses
Portfolio Companies: Alibaba Group, Avago, Avaya, AVI-SPL, BlackLine, Cast & Crew, Dell, Fanatics, ForeFlight, Global Blue, GoDaddy, Influence Health, Intelsat, Locaweb, Motorola Solutions, Opera Solutions, Qunar, Quorum Business Solutions, Red Ventures, Sabre, SMART Modular, Talend, Vantage Data Centers, Velocity Technology Solutions, WME/IMG

Other Locations:
   220 Halleck Street
   Suite 100
   San Francisco, CA 94129

   55 Hudson Yards
   550 W 34th Street
   40th Floor
   New York, NY 10001
   Phone: 212-981-5600

   10080 North Wolfe Road
   Suite SW3-190
   Cupertino, CA 95014
   Phone: 408-454-4732

   Silver Lake Europe LLP
   Broadbent House
   65 Grosvenor Street
   London W1K 3JH
   United Kingdom
   Phone: 44-2032058400

   Silver Lake Asia Limited
   33/F Two IFC
   8 Finance Street
   Central
   Hong Kong
   Phone: 852-36643300 Fax: 852-36643456

Key Executives:
   Kenneth Hao, Chairman/Managing Partner
   Education: AB, Economics, Harvard College
   Background: Managing Director, Hambrecht & Quist
   Directorships: Avago Technologies Limited, SMART Modular Technologies
   Mike Bingle, Vice Chairman
   Education: BSE, Biomedical Engineering, Duke University
   Background: Principal, Apollo Advisors; Investment Banker, Leveraged Finance Group, Goldman Sachs & Co.
   Directorships: Fanatics, Gartner
   Egon Durban, Co-CEO
   Education: BS, Finance, Georgetown University
   Background: Investment Banking Division, Corporate Finance Technology Group & Equity Capital Markets Group, Morgan Stanley
   Directorships: Dell, Intelsat SA, Motorola Solutions
   Greg Mondre, Co-CEO
   Education: BS, Economics, Wharton School, University of Pennsylvania
   Background: Principal, Texas Pacific Group; Investment Banker, Communications, Media & Entertainment Group, Goldman Sachs & Co.
   Directorships: Avaya, Fanatics, GoDaddy, Motorola Solutions, Red Ventures, Sabre Holdings, Vantage Data Centers
   Joe Osnoss, Managing Partner/Managing Director
   Education: AB, Harvard College
   Background: Goldman Sachs & Co.; Coopers & Lybrand Consulting; Bracebridge Capital
   Directorships: Cegid; Cornerstone OnDemand; EverCommerce; First Advantage; Global Blue; LightBox; Sabre

1686 SILVER OAK SERVICES PARTNERS
1560 Sherman Avenue
Suite 1200
Evanston, IL 60201

Phone: 847-332-0400 Fax: 847-492-1717
e-mail: info@silveroaksp.com
web: www.silveroaksp.com

Mission Statement: Silver Oak Services Partners is a lower middle market private equity firm focused exclusively on services businesses. We seek to partner with exceptional management teams to build industry leading businesses, consumer and healthcare service companies.

Geographic Preference: United States
Average Investment: $10 - $30 million
Investment Criteria: Control Investments in Leveraged Acquistions, Recapitalizations, Build-Ups and Growth Transactions
Industry Group Preference: Business Products & Services, Healthcare Services, Consumer Services
Portfolio Companies: Accent Ood Services, Altura Communication Solutions, Construction Labor Contractors, Direct Tavel, Glazer-Kennedy Insider's Circle, iSystems, National Distribution & Contracting, Physical Rehabilitation Network, Tranzonic, VASA Fitness

Key Executives:
   Daniel M Gill, Managing Partner
   847-332-0410
   e-mail: dgill@silveroaksp.com
   Education: BA, Economics, Bucknell University; MBA, University of Chicago Graduate School of Business

Background: Founding Partner & Managing Director, Willis Stein & Partners; CIVC/Bank of America; Corporate Finance Department, Kidder Peabody & Co
Directorships: Physicians Endoscopy, Convergent Resources, CompuPay, Education Corporation of America, Merit Health Systems Corporation
Gregory M Barr, Managing Partner
847-332-0401
e-mail: gbarr@silveroaksp.com
Education: BA, Economics & English, Wesleyan University; MBA, Harvard Business School
Background: Managing Director, Nautic Partners; Fleet Equity Partners; Management Consultant, McKinsey & Company
Directorships: VeriClaim, Accent Food Services, National Distribution & Contracting
Andrew S Gustafson, Partner
Education: BA, Middlebury College; MBA, Kellogg School of Management, Northwestern University
Background: VP, Thoma Bravo LLC; Boston Consulting Group; Associate, Wind Point Partners; Investment Banker, Goldman Sachs & Co.
Directorships: Convergent Resources; Direct Travel; iSystems; Porter & Chester Institute
Wade D Glisson, Partner
847-332-0408
e-mail: wglisson@silveroaksp.com
Education: BS, Finance, University of Illinois, Urbana-Champaign; MBA, Northwestern University Kellogg School of Management
Background: Private Equity Investments, Lake Capital; Associate, Advent Internaitonal; Investment Banking, AG Edwards
Directorships: Physicians Endoscopy, National Distribution & Contracting

1687 SILVERTON PARTNERS
600 W 7th Street
Austin, TX 78701

Phone: 512-476-6700 Fax: 512-477-0025
e-mail: businessplans@silvertonpartners.com
web: www.silvertonpartners.com

Mission Statement: An early-stage venture capital firm focused on Texas-based companies. Aspires to partner with exceptional entrepreneurs who are committed to attacking growth markets with proprietary products or services.
Geographic Preference: Texas
Average Investment: $200,000 - $1 million
Investment Criteria: Early-Stage
Industry Group Preference: Semiconductors, Advanced Materials, Consumer Internet, Mobile, Enterprise Software, Technology-Enabled Services
Portfolio Companies: 360pi, Boundless Network, Equipboard, Famigo, Favor, FibeRio, Nuve, OutboundEngine, Pingboard, PureWRX, Sailpoint, Silicon Laboratories, Socialware, SpareFoot, StackEngine, StepOne, Tk20, TrendKite, TurnKey, UnboundID, uShip, WP Engine, The Zebra
Key Executives:
Roger Chen, Partner
Education: BS, University of Michigan; MBA, Wharton School
Background: Principal, Genacast Ventures
Directorships: Apprentice; Billie; Cooper Cow Coffee; Fetch; Kronologic; Literati; Living Security; Mobile Tech RX; Novo Labs; OneDay; Popspots; Restream; RouteFusion; Wheel
Morgan Flager, Partner
Education: BS, Stanford University
Background: FTV Capital, Ingrian Networks, Kintana
Directorships: BlackLocus, CopperEgg, Famigo, Socialware, UnboundID
Kip McClanahan, Partner
Education: BS, Electrical Engineering, University of Texas
Background: BroadJump, TippingPoint, NetSpeed
Directorships: CopperEgg, OutboundEngine, Socialware, Sparefoot, WPEngine

1688 SIMON SCHOOL VENTURE CAPITAL FUND

e-mail: ssvcf@simon.rochester.edu

Mission Statement: The purpose of the Simon School Venture Capital Fund is to create unique and experiential learning opportunities for students with respect to entrepreneurship and venture capital investment. The Fund will provided a unique educational experience for Simon students through hands-on due diligence, interaction with entrepreneurs, presentations to advisory board members, direct participation in investment decisions based on comprehensive due diligence and investment analysis with the intent to perpetuate the life of the fund. The SSCVF will serve as a hallmark activity for the Simon School and increase the School's visibility and participation in Rochester's entrepreneurial ecosytem.

Investment Criteria: Early Stage
Portfolio Companies: StormBlok, Forsake, FINsix, FastCAP Systems

1689 SINEWAVE VENTURES
18th Street
South Arlington, VA

web: sinewave.vc

Mission Statement: A venture capital firm interested in early-stage investments in commercial companies with a focus on technology.

Founded: 2014
Industry Group Preference: Cloud, Cybersecurity, Big Data, Networking, Infrastructure, SaaS, Preventative Health and Services, Finance, Education, Technology
Portfolio Companies: APX Labs, SentinelOne, Tamr
Key Executives:
Yanev Suissa, Founding General Partner
Education: BA, Yale University; JD, Harvard Law School; MBA, Oxford Said School of Business; MA, Sydney Law School
Background: Investor, NEA; Senior Investment Officer, Bush & Obama Administrations
Christopher Gaughan, General Partner
Education: BA, Economics & Political Science, Yale University; CFA
Background: Co-Founder/President, Big Sky Capital; CEO, Condesa Financiera; Co-Founder/President, Illumination Asset Management; Principal, Matlin Patterson Asset Management
Vivek Ladsariya, Partner
Education: BA, Electrical Engineering, University of Mumbai; MBA, Yale University
Background: Partner, Fenox VC; Founder, GameGarage; Founder, Moyyer Research
Patricia Muoio, Venture Partner
Education: BA, Philosophy, Fordham University; PhD, Philosophy, Yale University
Background: National Security Agency
Karen Evans, Venture Partner
Education: BS, Chemistry; MBA, West Virginia University
Background: Administrator for E-Goverment/IT, Office of Management & Budget; Chief Information Officer, Department of Energy
Directorships: US Cyber Challenge
Oliver Libby, Venture Partner
Education: Harvard College
Background: Founding Partner/Managing Director, Hatzimemos/Libby; Consultant, Guiliani Partners LLC; Co-Founder, The Resolution Project Inc.
Eric Hatzimemos, Venture Partner
Education: New York Law School

Venture Capital & Private Equity Firms / Domestic Firms

Background: Co-Founder, Giuliani Partners LLC; Assistant Counsel to Mayor Giuliani; Assistant Criminal Justice Coordinator in the Mayor's Office; Associate, Weg and Myers; Assistant District Attorney
Brian Hibblen, Venture Partner
Education: BS, Physics, United States Airforce Academy; MS, Engineering Physics, US Air Force Institute of Technology
Background: Chairman, US Government Cyby S&T Working Group; Assistant Deputy Undersecretary of Defense
Directorships: Remote Sensing Center, Naval Postgraduate School

1690 SIXTHIRTY
911 Washington Avenue
Suite 816
St. Louis, MO 63101

Phone: 314-669-6803
e-mail: hello@sixthirty.co
web: www.sixthirty.co

Mission Statement: SixThirty provides fintech startups with $100K in funding, mentors, and connections to the top financial services companies in the country. Backed by the St. Louis Regional Chamber and venture capital firm Cultivation Capital, SixThirty selects eight financial-based technology startup companies each year, four for the Fall class and four in the spring. Those companies selected to take part in the four-month accelerator program will receive hands-on training, mentoring, and networking opportunities with the top financial services companies in the region.

Geographic Preference: St. Louis
Founded: 2013
Average Investment: $100,000
Investment Criteria: Start-Up, Seed-Stage
Industry Group Preference: Financial Services
Portfolio Companies: Davo Technologies, Gremlin, Hedgeable, Lending Standard, MiiCard, MyMoneyButler, New Constructs, PromisePay, Public Funds Investment Tracking and Reporting, Upside, Wealth Access, XY Verify

Key Executives:
Atul Kamra, Managing Director
Education: MComm., Bombay University; MBA, Duke Fuqua School of Business
Background: Partner, Booz & Company; President, First Clearing; Sr Managing Director, Wells Fargo Advisors

1691 SJF VENTURES
200 N Magnum Street
Suite 203
Durham, NC 27701

Phone: 919-530-1177 **Fax:** 919-530-1178
web: www.sjfventures.com

Mission Statement: SJF Ventures invests and assists high-growth companies that positively impact the world.

Fund Size: $17 Million; $28 Million
Founded: 1999
Average Investment: $1 - $10 Million
Minimum Investment: $1 Million
Investment Criteria: Expansion Stage
Industry Group Preference: Clean Technology, Web-Enabled Services, Premium Consumer Products, Sustainability, Business Products & Services
Portfolio Companies: YieldBot, Ayla Networks, Validic, EnTouch Controls, Easy Metrics, Think Through Learning, Versify, Vital Farms, Aseptia, BioSurplus, Living Earth Technology, Optoro, Community Energy, HYLA Mobile, FieldView, MediaMath, ServiceChannel, Truist, CleanScapes, Rustic Crust, MedPage Today, Telkore, Intechra, groSolar, Preclick, B.B. Hobbs, ED MAP, Home Bistro, Sun & Earth, Salvage Direct, Ryla, Evco Research, DDF, RealWinWin, Spectral Dimensions, CitySoft, Foxfire, Brightside Academy, SelecTec, R24 Lumber, Zap, Delta Systems

Other Locations:
85 Broad Street
28th Floor
New York, NY 10004
Phone: 917-693-4858

700 Larkspur Landing Circle
Suite 199
Larkspur, CA 94939
Phone: 415-646-4965

Key Executives:
Rick Defieux, Founder/Investment Committee Chair
Education: BA & MA, Boston University; MBA, Columbia University
Background: Venture Partner, Batelle Ventures; General Partner, Allegra Partners IV; General Partner, Edison Venture Funds I, II & III
Directorships: Silicon Power
David Griest, Managing Director
Education: MBA, Yale School of Management; BBA, Finance, University of Georgia
Background: Croft & Bender; C&B Capital
Alan Kelley, Managing Director
415-659-8277
e-mail: akelley@sjfventures.com
Education: MBA, Emory University; BA, Public Policy, Duke University
Background: Milestone Venture Partners; Program Director, Hands On Atlanta; Project Manager, The Landmarks Group in Berlin, Germany
Directorships: ServiceChannel, Ryla
David Kirkpatrick, Founder/Managing Director
919-530-1177 x407
e-mail: dkirk@sjfventures.com
Education: BA, Physics & History, Duke University; MBA, UNC Kenan Flagler School of Business
Background: Founder, KirkWorks; Founder, SunShares
Directorships: Community Energy, groSolar, B.B. Hobbs, EdMap
Arrun Kapoor, Managing Director
212-209-3063
e-mail: akapoor@sjfventures.com
Education: BA, New York University; Master's, International Political Economics, London School of Economics
Background: Bain & Company
Directorships: FieldView Solutions, ServiceChannel
Cody Nystrom, Managing Director
919-530-1177 x406
e-mail: cnystrom@sjfventures.com
Education: BS, Systems & Information Engineering, University of Virginia
Background: Ewing Bermiss & Co.
Directorships: Community Energy

1692 SK TELECOM VENTURES
310 De Guigne Drive
Sunnyvale, CA 94085

Phone: 408-328-2900 **Fax:** 408-328-2931
web: www.skta.com

Mission Statement: A dedicated venture capital fund that looks to make financial returns on investments through funding internet, mobile and digital media companies that can leverage the funds sole limited partner, SK Telecom.

Geographic Preference: Worldwide
Fund Size: $100 million
Investment Criteria: Seed-Stage, Early-Stage, Growth Stage
Industry Group Preference: Internet, Mobile, Digital Media & Marketing
Portfolio Companies: Skyera, Argyle Data, ChartBoost, Kabam, Tsumobi, deCarta, English Central, RockYou

Venture Capital & Private Equity Firms / Domestic Firms

Key Executives:
Min H. Park, General Partner
Background: Motorola
David Kim, Vice President/CFO

1693 SKYLINE VENTURES
525 University Avenue
Suite 1350
Palo Alto, CA 94301

Phone: 650-462-5800 Fax: 650-329-1090
web: www.skylineventures.com

Mission Statement: Specializes in investing in outstanding product-focused healthcare companies.
Geographic Preference: United States
Fund Size: $350 million
Founded: 1997
Average Investment: $15 - $35 million
Investment Criteria: Seed-Stage, Startup
Industry Group Preference: Industrial Equipment, Medical, Biotechnology, Medical Devices, Healthcare, Medical & Health Related
Portfolio Companies: AcelRx Pharmaceuticals, Advion BioSciences, Avidia, Collegium Pharmaceutical, Crescendo Biosciene, Concert Pharmaceuticals, Dicerna Pharmaceuticals, DiscoveRx, Dow Pharmaceutical Sciences, Genocea Biosciences, Hansen Medical, iBalance Medical, Intuitive Surgical, KAI Pharmaceuticals, MAKO Surgical, MAP Pharmaceuticals, Medivance, NimbleGen, NovaCardia, Theravance, Proteon Therapeutics, SI-BONE, Sirtris Pharmaceuticals, SpinalMotion, Sutro Biopharma, Tetraphase Pharmaceuticals, XenoPort

Key Executives:
John F Freund, Partner
Education: BA, Harvard College, MD, Harvard Medical School, MBA, Harvard Business School
Background: Partner, Morgan Stanley Venture Partners, Executive Vice President, Acuson Corporation
Eric M Gordon, Partner
Education: PH.D & MS, University of Wisconsin
Background: Director Of Medicinal Chemistry At The Squibb Institute For Medical Research, Bristol Myers Squibb Pharmaceutical Institute In Princeton,
Stephen J Hoffman MD, Partner
Education: MD, University of Colorado; PhD, Chemistry, Northwestern University
Background: General Partner, TVM Capital; Founding President, Allos Therapeutics
Yasunori Kaneko MD, Partner
Education: MD, Keio University School of Medicine; MBA, Stanford Graduate School of Business
Background: Genetech; Paribas Capital Markets; SVP/CFO, Isis Pharmaceuticals

1694 SKYTREE CAPITAL PARTNERS
1980 Festival Plaza Drive
Suite 425
Las Vegas, NV 89135

e-mail: info@skytreepartners.com
web: www.skytreepartners.com

Mission Statement: Invests in various sectors including technology, healthcare, energy, agriculture, and cannabis.
Industry Group Preference: Healthcare, Cannabis, Technology, Energy, Agriculture
Other Locations:
15260 Ventura Boulevard
Suite 1700
Sherman Oaks, CA 91403

Key Executives:
Matthew Neely, Co-Founder/Managing Partner
Education: Lee Business School, University of Nevada Las Vegas
Background: Owner, Matthew Neely Insurance Agency; Owner, Asher Macrae Insurance Services; Owner, Cannabis Risk Management; Founder, paTh.Media
Erik Allison, Co-Founder/Managing Partner
Education: William Woods University; University of Missouri-Columbia
Background: Financial Advisor, Morgan Stanley Smith Barney; Investment Advisor, United Capital Financial Partners; Investment Advisor, Cambridge Investment Research; Sr. Financial Advisor, Fountainhead Wealth; Founder/CEO, EA Wealth Management
Luke K. Stanton, Managing Director
Education: BA, Political Science, University of Notre Dame; JD, Pepperdine University School of Law
Background: Co-Founder/Principal, Frontera Entertainment; Founder/Executive Chairman, Frontera Law Group; Executive Director/US Operations, Sunniva Inc.

1695 SLATER TECHNOLOGY FUND
3 Davol Square
Providence, RI 02903

e-mail: info@slaterfund.com
web: www.slaterfund.com

Mission Statement: Focuses on the support of entrepreneurs who have the vision, leadership and commitment to build substantial business enterprises.
Geographic Preference: Rhode Island
Founded: 1997
Investment Criteria: Seed-Stage
Industry Group Preference: Life Sciences, Information Technology
Portfolio Companies: Illuminoss, Lucidux, Mnemosyne, Nabsys, ProThera Biologics, Neurotech, MyOmics, Cytosolv, EpiVax, Medrobotics, Dominion Diagnostics, Selva Medical, Concordia Fibers, Sentient Biosciences, Slater Technology Fund, Vitrimark, Cyberkinetics, Absolute Commerce, Care Thread, Andera, RxVantage, Mobile Fusion, Dynadec, GeneSpectrum, Location, Far Sounder, MTI Film, Tizra, Insight Health Solutions, Traction Software, Swyx, Advanced Image Enhancement, Enhanced Energy Group, VoltServer, vCharge, Alektrona, eGO, Modular Energy Devices, WeatherPredict, Bioprocess H2O

Key Executives:
Thorne Sparkman, Managing Director
Education: BA, Biological Anthropology, Harvard University; MBA, University of California, Berkeley, Haas School of Business
Background: Founder & CEO, Incubator, Inc.; CEO, EScribe Corporation
Bob Chatham, Director
Education: BA, Colgate University
Background: Industry Analyst, Forrester Research

1696 SLOW VENTURES
1006 Kearny Street
San Francisco, CA 94133

web: www.slow.co

Mission Statement: Dedicated to helping innovative projects reach their potential.
Founded: 2009
Industry Group Preference: Technology, Applications, Digital Media, Cannabis
Portfolio Companies: Breather, Wag, Eaze, Cadre, Meadow, Common, Verge Genomics, Collective Retreats, Phylos, Tile, WayUp, uBiome, Nexar, Brandless, allbirds, Boosted, Brain.fm, Domino Data Lab, Dwell, Eero, Gusto, Bloom Farms, Honor, Livongo Health, Perlara PBC, Airtable, Ro, Tempest, Angellist, Nextdoor, Postmates, Wealthfront, Everlane, Blue Bottle Coffee, Nest, Xapo, Amplitude, Evernote, Percolate, Pinterest, Codecademy, Managed by Q, Casper, Hipcamp, Resy Network, Slack, PillPack, ClassPass, Accion Systems, Front, Giphy, Robinhood, Houseparty

Venture Capital & Private Equity Firms / Domestic Firms

Key Executives:
Dave Morin, Founder/Partner
Education: BA, Economics, University of Colorado at Boulder
Background: Product & Marketing, Apple; Platform & Connect, Facebook; Special Partner, Kleiner Perkins Caufield & Buyers; Co-Founder/CEO, Path; Co-Founder/CEO, Sunrise Bio
Directorships: Dwell Media; Evenbrite
Sam Lessin, Partner
Education: AB, Social Studies, Harvard University
Background: Associate Consultant, Bain & Co.; CEO, Drop.io; VP of Product Management, Facebook; Co-Founder, Fin
Will Quist, Partner
Education: University of California, Berkeley
Background: Editor, AlwaysOn Network; Analyst, Banc of America Securities; VP/Managing Director, Industry Ventures
Scott Marlette, Partner
Education: BS EE, Networks/Security/Communications, Georgia Institute of Technology; MS EE, Networks/Distributed Systems, Stanford University
Background: Engineer/Product Manager, Facebook; Co-Founder, GoodRx
Kevin Colleran, Managing Director
Education: BA, Management & Marketing, Babson College
Background: Global Advertising Sales, Facebook; Columnist, The Wall Street Journal; Venture Partner/Advisor, General Catalyst Partners

1697 SMARTINVEST VENTURES
1007 North Orange Street
Wilmington, DE 19801

e-mail: gerry@smartinvestventures.com
web: www.smartinvestventures.com

Mission Statement: SmartInvest Ventures is an Early Stage accelerator fund.

Founded: 2015
Investment Criteria: Early Stage
Industry Group Preference: Artificial Intelligence, Technology, Software

Key Executives:
Fred Hosaisy, Co-Founder/General Partner
Education: BS, Accounting/Finance, Temple University; MBA, Wharton School
Background: CEO, CFL-LLC E-Commerce; Director of Operations, NLdH Law; CFO/Controller, Hotwire Communications & Business Solutions LLC; Assistant COO/Director, Fox Chase Cancer Center
Gerry Moan, Managing Partner
Charles Kerrigan, General Partner
Education: MBA, Fox School of Business & Management, Temple University
Background: VP, Jefferson Bank; CFO, Archdiocese of Philadelphia; VP/Manager, Allied Irish Bank; SVP, Wells Fargo Private Bank; Director of Marketing, Legacy Adivsor; SVP/Financial Consultant, First Cornerstone Bank

1698 SOCIAL CAPITAL

e-mail: inbox@socialcapital.com
web: www.socialcapital.com

Mission Statement: Company seeks to advance humanity by harnessing technology to address human needs.

Fund Size: $1.2 Billion
Founded: 2011
Investment Criteria: Lifecycle
Industry Group Preference: Consumer, Education, Enterprise, Financial Services, Frontier, Healthcare
Portfolio Companies: Aclima, AIRMAP, Athos, Autonomic, Base, Bitoya, Bluenose Analytics, Box, Breakthrough, Brilliant, Bustle, Captricity, Carta, ClearSide, CloudOn, CollectiveHealth, CommonBond, Confer Health, Coolan, Cover, Cozy, CreativeLIVE, Cryptomove, Datacoral, Descomplica, Digital Currency Group, DroneSeed, Ezetap, Forge, Fresno, Front, Glooko, Greenhouse, Groq, Harvey, HubHaus, Hustle, InstaEDU, Intercom, Lema21, LotusFlare, Lumity, Mango Games, MeMed, mParticle, MPHARMA, NetSkope, Neurotrack, NiYO, OneLogin, Penny, Premise, Propeller Health, Relativity, Remind, Replicon, SAILDRONE, Secret Cinema, SEMRE, SFOX, Simplee, Slack, Slang, SurveyMonkey, Swarm, Swing Education, Syapse, Treehouse, UrbanFootprint, Wave, Wealthfront, WeeCare, Yammer

Key Executives:
Chamath Palihapitiya, Founder & CEO
Education: BA, Electrical Engineering, University of Waterloo
Background: Facebook; BMO Nesbitt Burns; AOL; Mayfield Fund

1699 SOCIAL SECTOR VENTURES
855 East Collins Boulevard
Richardson, TX 75081

Phone: 972-852-2411
e-mail: connect@socialsectorventures.com
web: www.socialsectorventures.com

Mission Statement: The mission of Social Sector Ventures is to support the entrepreneurial activity most likely to benefit Nonprofit Organizations (NPOs) in initiating and developing the relationships needed to create a better world. Social Sector Ventures believes that entrepreneurship and technology innovation must be directed at the problems of the changing world within the context of private funding and investment. Capital funding and entrepreneurship are necessary if organizations are to unlock 21st century giving opportunities and guide donor relationships in a world of rapidly changing technology.

Portfolio Companies: 2DIALOG, Affinaquest, Call2Action

Key Executives:
John E Walvoord, Chief Executive Director
Education: PhD, Columbua University

1700 SOFINNOVA VENTURES
3000 Sand Hill Road
Building 4
Suite 250
Menlo Park, CA 94025

Phone: 650-681-8420 **Fax:** 650-322-2037
e-mail: info@sofinnova.com
web: www.sofinnova.com

Mission Statement: Seeks to create value by providing entrepreneurs with the resources, experience, and network necessary to grow early stage companies into profitable businesses.

Geographic Preference: San Francisco Bay Area, San Diego, Seattle, Europe
Fund Size: $1 billion
Founded: 1974
Average Investment: $5 - $7 million
Minimum Investment: $500,000
Investment Criteria: Seed, Early Stage, Startup
Industry Group Preference: Information Technology, Life Sciences, Therapeutics, Pharmaceuticals
Portfolio Companies: Aclaris Therapeutics, Aerie Pharmaceuticals, Alimera Sciences, Alvine, Amarin, Anthera Pharmaceuticals, Ascendis Pharma, Ascenta Therapeutics, Audentes Therapeutics, Auris Medica, Catalyst Biosciences, Cebix, Civitas Therapeutics, Coherus Biosciences, Durata Therapeutics, First Aid Shot Therapy, Histogenics Hyperion Therapeutics, Innocoli, KaloBios, Marinus Pharmaceuticals, Mirna Therapeutics, NuCana, ObsEba, Ocera, Ophthotech

Corporation, Principia Biopharma, Prothena Corporation, Salveo, Spark Therapeutics, TESARO, Versartis, ZS Pharma

Other Locations:
1250 Prospect Street
Ocean Level-4
La Jolla, CA 92037
Phone: 858-551-4880

3, Place Ville Marie
Bureau 12350
Montreal, QC H3B 0E7

Key Executives:
James Healy, Managing Partner
415-228-3396
Fax: 415-228-3390
e-mail: jim@sofinnova.com
Education: BA, Molecular Biology, Scandinavian Studies, University of California, Berkeley; MD, PhD, Immunology, Stanford University
Background: Partner, Sabdering Ventures; Miles (Bayer) Pharmceuticals; Lawrence Berkeley Laboratory; Howard Hugh Medical Institute
Directorships: InterMune Pharmaceuticals, BioSpace.com
Maha Katabi, General Partner
Education: BS, Biology/PhD, Pharmacology, McGill University
Background: Managing Partner, Oxalis Capital; Partner, Sectoral Asset Management; VP, Ventures West Management; T2C2 Capital Bio
Directorships: Chair, Exactis Innovation; BIOQuéBec
David Kabakoff, Executive Partner, Private Equity
858-550-0959 x101
e-mail: david@sofinnova.com
Education: BA, Case Western Reserve University; PhD, Yale University
Background: Co-Founder, Salmedix; CEO, Spiros Development Corp
Directorships: Trius Therapeutics, Amplimmune, InterMune, Avalon Pharmaceuticals, Alylix
Lars Ekman, Executive Partner, Private Equity
858-405-1653
Education: PhD & MD, University of Gothenburg, Sweden
Background: President of Research & Development, Elan
Directorships: ARYx Therapeutics, InterMune

1701 SOFTBANK CAPITAL
38 Glen Avenue
Newton, MA 02459

Phone: 617-928-9300 **Fax:** 617-928-9304
e-mail: contactus@softbank.com
web: www.softbank.com

Mission Statement: An independent venture capital firm focused on early stage high growth technology based businesses benefiting from the rapid deployment and adoption of broadband and mobile technologies.

Geographic Preference: United States
Founded: 1995
Average Investment: $2 million
Minimum Investment: $500,000
Investment Criteria: Early-Stage
Industry Group Preference: Digital Media & Marketing, E-Commerce & Manufacturing, Business to Business, Media, Networking
Portfolio Companies: Action X, Associated Content, Betaworks, Bigcommerce, Bluefin Labs, Boxee, Buddy Media, Burstly, BuzzFeed, Celtra, Cheezburger, Chloe + Isabel, Criteo, CrowdTwist, Dering Hall, Desktone, Echo360, EdCast, FieldLens, Fitbit, Flashnotes, FlightCar, Genius, Gilt Groupe, GLAMSQUAD, Grab Media, Grind Networks, The Huffington Post, Hyperpulic, IgnitionOne, Interactions, Jump Ramp Games, Kabbage, Keychain Logistics, KickApps, Kony, Lerer Ventures, LiteScape, Loverly/Dubblee Media, MobileDay, Moat, Mobile Posse, MocoSpace, NatureBox, Nellymoser, NowThis News, OMGPOP, Paper.li/Smallrivers, Pivot, Pogoplug/Cloud Engines, Popdust, Poptip, RebelMouse, Reonomy, Rivermine, Schematic Labs, SellerCrowd, Sermo, Shake, Shareablee, Sherpaa, Sidecar, SocialFlow, Spanfeller Media Group, Swirl Networks, Synaptic Digital, Talkspace, Taykey, TechStars, The Dodo, Thumb, True & Co., Updater, Vertical Performance Partners, Wildcard, X.ai, xAd, YouAre.TV, Zady, ZipList, Zynga

Other Locations:
One News Plaza
Suite 10
Buffalo, NY 14203
Phone: 716-845-7520 **Fax:** 716-845-7539

130 West 25th Street
8th Floor
New York, NY 10001
Phone: 617-558-6770 **Fax:** 617-928-9304

1 Circle Star Way
4th Floor
San Carlos, CA 94070
Phone: 617-928-9300 **Fax:** 617-928-9304

Key Executives:
Ronald D Fisher, Vice Chair
e-mail: ron_fisher@softbank.com
Education: MBA, Columbia University; Bachelor of Commerce, University of Witwatersand in South Africa
Background: CEO, Phoenix Technology; Interactive Systems Corporation; Visicorp; TRW; ICL
Directorships: ETrade Group, GSI Commerce, InsWeb Corporation, Terabeam Corporation, Vie Financial Group

1702 SOFTTECH VC
Palo Alto, CA 94301

web: www.softtechvc.com

Mission Statement: An early stage venture capital firm managing seed stage funds.

Average Investment: $200,000 - $750,000
Investment Criteria: Seed-Stage, Early-Stage
Industry Group Preference: Consumer Internet, Social Media, Mobile, Infrastructure
Portfolio Companies: 6SensorLabs, 8tracks, About.me, ADstruc, Animoto, August, Better Finance, BetterDoctor, Bit.ly, Blekko, Breezy, Chartbeat, ClassDojo, Clever, Coin, Curse, DNANexus, Docsend, DroneDeploy, Estately, Fab, FanBridge, Farmeron, Fitbit, FounderDating, FreshPlanet, Front, Get Satisfaction, Gigwalk, Grovo, Halo Neuroscience, Handshake, Hired, Kahuna, KissMetrics, Lantern, Mission Motors, MobileDay, Next Big Sound, Niche, Nuzzel, Panorama Education, Poshmark, PostMates, RedCap, Reputation.com, RJ Metrics, Sapho, SendGrid, Shippo, SmartShoot, SocialWire, Soldsie, Songkick, Stitch, StrikeAd, StyleSeat, Survata, TakeLessons, Teads, Thanx, Top Hat, True&Co., Tulip Retail, Ustream, Vidyard, VigLink, Visual.Ly, Vungle, YourMechanic, ZEFR

Key Executives:
Jeff Clavier, Founder/Managing Partner
Education: MS, Computer Science; Research Degree, Distributed Computing
Background: President, RVC Capital
Stephanie Palmeri, Partner
Education: BS, Villanova University; MBA, Columbia Business School

1703 SOGAL VENTURES
New York, NY

e-mail: hello@sogalventures.com
web: www.sogalventures.com

Mission Statement: SoGal Ventures is a female-led millennial venture capital firm investing in early stage startups in the US and Asia with diverse founding teams.

Geographic Preference: US, Asia

Venture Capital & Private Equity Firms / Domestic Firms

Investment Criteria: Seed-Stage
Portfolio Companies: AK Valley, Archer Rppse, ASAY, birdi, ClassTracks, emocha, Everly Well, Function of Beauty, Girls Labs, GiveCampus, Glidian, GuavaPass, Helium, HelloAva, Hidrate Spark, Insilico Medicine, Kairos, Kids on 45th, Kitt.ai, Kylie.ai, Little Spoon, Lovevery, Mindshare Medical, Moby Mart, Mogul, Motiva, NailSnaps, Nebulab, Negotiatus, Osmosis, Progressly, Proscia, Refresh Body, Siren Care, Sonavex Surgical, SWAAY, The Right.Fit, Torigen, Trustify, Tueo Health, Unbound, Voga Coffee, Werk, Wheelys, Winky Lux, Wisebanyan, Yet Analytics

Key Executives:
  Pocket Sun, Founding Partner
  Education: MS, University of Southern California
  Elizabeth Galbut, Founding Partner
  Education: MBA/MA Johns Hopkins University and Maryland Institute college of Art; Georgetown University; London School of Economics
  Background: Founder, A-Level Capital

1704 SOLSTICE CAPITAL LP
81 Washington Street
Suite 303
Salem, MA 01970

Phone: 617-523-7733
e-mail: info@solcap.com
web: www.solcap.com

Mission Statement: Seeks superior venture capital returns for limited partners through investments in seed and early-stage companies in the industry areas of alternative energy, education, environment, life science, and information technology; demonstrates commitment to provide both capital and expert guidance to assist portfolio companies as they deal with the challenges and opportunities of growth. Not currently making investments in new companies.

Geographic Preference: Northeast, Southwest
Fund Size: $85 million
Founded: 1995
Minimum Investment: $500,000
Investment Criteria: Seed, Startup, First-Stage, Second-Stage
Industry Group Preference: Information Technology, Alternative Energy, Life Sciences, Environment Products & Services, Education, Clean Technology
Portfolio Companies: Abuzz Technologies, Archivas, Arzan, Carefx, CodeRyte, Connected, MetaCarta, Okena, Optimax Systems, Pharsight, Q1 Labs, Angstrom Pharmaceuticals, CellzDirect, HTG Molecular Diagnostics, Regenesis Biomedical, Evergreen Solar, Proton Energy Systems, Protonex, StrionAir, Active Control eXperts, E Ink, Lipton Corporate Child Care Centers, Lumidigm, OutStart

Key Executives:
  Harry A George, Managing General Partner
  Education: AB, Bowdoin College
  Background: Co-Founder/Director/VP Finance, Interleaf; Co-Founder/Director/VP Finance, Kurzweil Computer Products
  Directorships: ImaRx Therapeutics, Lumidigm, High Throughput Genomics, CellzDirect, Regenesis Biomedical
  Henry W Newman, General Partner
  Education: Bowdoin College; MBA, Wharton School
  Background: VP, BancBoston Ventures; Financial Management, Bank of Boston; CPA, Coopers & Lybrand
  Directorships: CodeRyte, Quelsys, Lipton Corp Childcare, Intrak Wireless

1705 SONY INNOVATION FUND
1730 N 1st Street
San Jose, CA 95112

web: www.sonyinnovationfund.com

Mission Statement: The venture capital branch of Sony Corporation, Sony Innovation Fund actively invests in the technology industry.
Geographic Preference: US, Japan, Europe, Israel
Founded: 2016
Investment Criteria: Seed, Early Stage, Middle-Stage
Industry Group Preference: Technology, Artificial Intelligence, Entertainment, Gaming, Health & Wellness, Industry, Logistics, Manufacturing, Mobility, Fintech, Robotics, IoT, Virtual Reality, Security
Portfolio Companies: Activ Surgical, AdHawk, Adrich, Agility Robotics, AirMap, AWAKENS, DefinedCrowd, Digilens, Embodied, Exo Imaging, Little Star Media, Matternet, Miles, Ridecell, Shimmur, Sight Machine, sliver.tv, StrongArm Technologies

Other Locations:
2207 Bridgepointe Parkway
San Mateo, CA 94404

6 Ha'harash Street
Central District
Hod Hasharon 45240
Israel

1-7-1 Konan Minato-ku
Tokyo 108-0075
Japan

Key Executives:
  Joseph Tou, Managing Director
  Education: BS, University of Michigan; MS/MEng, Northwestern Univesity; MBA, Kellogg School of Management
  Background: Software Engineer, Ford Motor Company; Sr. Marketing/Product Manager, Intel; Sr. Research Analyst, Pacific Crest Securities; VP, Bertram Capital; Managing Director, Mavent Partners; VP of Corporate Development, Sony Corporation of America

1706 SONY STRATEGIC TECHNOLOGY PARTNERSHIPS
1730 North 1st Street
San Jose, CA 95112

Phone: 408-352-4636 Fax: 408-352-4640
e-mail: austin.noronha@am.sony.com

Mission Statement: Provides a window into emerging technology and business opportunities and helps establish strategic partnerships with innovative startups.
Geographic Preference: Worldwide
Founded: 1998
Average Investment: $3-5 million
Investment Criteria: Differentiated Core Enabling Technologies
Industry Group Preference: Infrastructure, Internet Technology, Audio & Video Distribution, Advanced Data Compression Technologies, Digital Rights Management, Image-Recognition, Reconfigurable Processors, Display Technologies, Wireless Technologies, Video Gaming
Portfolio Companies: ACCESS, ArrayComm, Digital Founatin, IP Unity, Internet Number Corporation, NTRU Cryptosystems, Oren Semiconductor, Reflectivity, SecureMedia, Sandcraft, Tao, TeraLogic, Time Domain, Transmeta, 727 Solutions, Equator Technologies, i3 Mobile, IFILM, Intrinsic Graphics, Lightspan, Montavista, PacketVideo, TiVo, WildTangent

Key Executives:
  Austin Noronha
  408-352-4636
  Fax: 408-352-4640
  e-mail: austin.noronha@am.sony.com
  Shoichi Osawa
  408-352-4779
  Fax: 408-352-4640
  e-mail: shoichi.osawa@am.sony.com

1707 SORENSON CAPITAL
3400 N Ashton Blvd
Suite 400
Lehi, UT 84043

Phone: 801-407-8400
e-mail: info@sorensoncapital.com
web: www.sorensoncapital.com

Mission Statement: Sorenson Capital is a private equity firm headquartered in Salt Lake City, Utah. Provides small to middle-market buyout and growth equity investments, with a particular focus on opportunities in selected states in the Mountain and Western regions of the United States.

Geographic Preference: Mountain & Western United States
Average Investment: $3 - 25 million
Portfolio Companies: Pluralsight, Zerbee's, Excel Manufacturing, AtTask, Nexmo, Empathica, Suncrest Solar, JWD Machine, Wilson Electronics, AccessData, CustomControl Concepts, Roberts Tool Company, HealthCatalyst, Tru Hearing, Bamboo HR, Mindshare Technologies, Goal Zero, NCS Energy Services, Imagine Learning, MM Pipeline Services, Southeast Directional Drilling, HGB, Jetset Sports, IDC, MITY Enterprises, RWI Construction, LifePort, Omniture, Vitron, Atlas Aerospace, WASI, Provocraft, LS, Dickson Construction

Key Executives:
   Fraser Bullock, Founder/Managing Director
   Education: BA, Economics, MBA, Brigham Young University
   Background: Partner, Bain Capital; Founder, Alpine Consolidated
   Tim Layton, Founder/Managing Director
   Education: BS, Statistics, MBA, Brigham Young University
   Background: Co-Founder, InStar Services; Managing Director, Alpine Consolidated
   Ron Mika, Founder/Managing Director
   Education: BS, Chemical Engineering; Brigham Young University; MBA, Harvard Business School
   Background: Bain Capital, Bain & Company
   Luke Sorenson, Managing Director
   Education: BS, Accounting, Brigham Young University; MBA, Wharton School
   Background: Director, Sorenson Media; Vice President, Sorenson Real Estate
   Mark Ludwig, Managing Director
   Education: BA, Russian, Brigham Young University; MBA, Wharton School
   Background: Associate, Bain & Company
   Legrand Lewis, Advisor
   Education: BS, Accounting, Brigham Young University; MBA, Harvard Business School
   Background: Consultant, Bain & Company; Capmark Financial Group

1708 SORRENTO VENTURES
2211 Encinitas Boulevard
Suite 200
Encinitas, CA 92024

Phone: 858-792-2700 Fax: 858-792-5070
e-mail: aking@sorrentoventures.com
web: www.sorrentoventures.com

Mission Statement: Sorrento Ventures is committed to providing strategic capital and vision to promising emerging growth companies.

Geographic Preference: Southern California
Fund Size: $115 million
Founded: 1985
Average Investment: $1 to $5 million
Minimum Investment: $500,000
Investment Criteria: Startup, First-Stage, Second-Stage, Mezzanine, LBO
Industry Group Preference: Healthcare, Medical Devices, Biotechnology, Technology, Communications, Enterprise Software, Electronics, Internet, Internet Technology, E-Commerce & Manufacturing, Retailing, Consumer Products, Distribution
Portfolio Companies: Cameron Health, Digirad, Idun Pharmaceuticals, Neurogenetics, Perlan Therapeutics, A-Life Medical, Idetic, IP MobileNet, SeatAdvisor, V-Enable, Catheter Innovations, CombiChem, Corvas International, DepoTech, Endonetics, Gensia Pharmaceuticals, IDEC Pharmaceuticals, Infrasonics, La Jolla Pharmaceutical Company, Laser Diagnostic Technologies, Medication Delivery Devices, Mikotor, Mycogen Corporation, Viagene, Vical, ESI Software, FieldCentrix, Keylime Software, LAM Research Company, Pacific Communications Sciences, Primary Access Corporation, University Netcasting, Garden Fresh Restaurant, Hot Topic

Key Executives:
   Robert M Jaffe, Co-Founder/President
   Education: MBA, Harvard Business School; MS Electrical Engineering, California Institute of Technology; BS Electrical Engineering/Computer Science, University of California Berkeley
   Background: Merrill Lynch Capital Markets; Salomon Brothers; Goldman Sachs; Hughes Aircraft Company; McKinsey & Co
   Directorships: A-Life Medical, Bebe Stores, Digirad, IPMobileNet, Perlan Therapeutics

1709 SOSV
174 Nassau Street
Suite 3000
Princeton, NJ 08542

e-mail: press@sosv.com
web: sosv.com

Mission Statement: The firm's strategy is to invest in a small number of highly promising startups and use its deeply resourced programs to accelerate product development, acquire customers, and scale.

Average Investment: $150K - $250K
Investment Criteria: Pre-Seed; Seed; Series A
Industry Group Preference: Diversified
Portfolio Companies: API3, BitMEX, NotCo, Opentrons, Perfect Day, Shopal, Snapask, Upside Foods, Yeelight

Other Locations:
   1230 York Avenue
   16th Floor
   New York, NY 10065

   479 Jessie Street
   San Francisco, CA 94103

   Republic of Work
   12 South Mall
   Cork T12 RD43
   Ireland

   7F, Black Ark
   2070 Shennan Middle Road
   Futian District
   Shenzhen 518028
   China

   Hero Center, Level 1, Bldg 3, West Entrance
   28 East YuYuan Road
   Shanghai 200040
   China

   No. 1 Yumen Street
   Zhongshan District
   Taipei City 10491
   Taiwan

Key Executives:
   Bill Liao, General Partner
   Background: Co-Founder, WeForest; Co-Founder, CoderDojo; Founder & CEO, Finaxis AG

Venture Capital & Private Equity Firms / Domestic Firms

Cyril Ebersweiler, General Partner
Background: Managing Director, HAX; Founder & Managing Director, Chinaccelerator
Duncan Turner, General Partner
Background: Managing Director, HAX;
Po Bronson, General Partner
Background: Founder & Partner, The Writers Grotto
Sean O'Sullivan, Managing General Partner
Background: Founder, Open Ireland; Managing Director, Carma
Shawn Broderick, General Manager
Background: Principal, TechVibe; Managing Director, TechStars
William Bao Bean, General Partner
Background: Managing Director, SOSV MOX; Managing Director, Chinaccelerator; Managing Director, Singtel; Partner, SoftBank China & India Holdings
Stephen McCann, General Partner & Chief Financial Officer
Background: Company Director, The Huntsman (Tower) Ltd.; Financial Controller, Travel Focus Ltd.

1710 SOURCE CAPITAL GROUP
276 Post Road West
Westport, CT 06880
Phone: 203-341-3500 **Fax:** 203-241-3515

Mission Statement: Offers equity and other debt financing to help further the growth of companies that are often overlooked by the larger investment banking firms.
Geographic Preference: Arizona, California
Fund Size: $17.2 million
Founded: 1992
Average Investment: $250,000
Minimum Investment: $50,000
Investment Criteria: First-stage, Second-stage, Mezzanine, Special situations
Industry Group Preference: Communications, Computer Related, Consumer Products, Distribution, Electronic Components, Electronic Technology, Energy, Natural Resources, Genetic Engineering, Industrial Equipment, Forestry, Medical & Health Related, Financial Services, Oil & Gas

Other Locations:
7377 East Doubletree Ranch Road
Suite 290
Scottsdale, AZ 85258
Phone: 480-368-1488 **Fax:** 480-368-1319

790 East Colorado Blvd
Pasadena, CA 91101
Phone: 626-240-0872 **Fax:** 626-240-0882

433 South Main Street
Suite 117
West Hartford, CT 06110
Phone: 866-433-0600 **Fax:** 860-313-0319

3170 North Federal Highway
Suite 103A
Lighthouse Point, FL 33064
Phone: 954-785-1990 **Fax:** 954-785-6579

98-1277 Kaahumanu Street
Aiea, HI 96701
Phone: 808-483-5005 **Fax:** 808-483-5020

632 Adams Street
Suite 210
Bowling Green, KY 42101
Phone: 270-843-8985 **Fax:** 270-842-3028

211 Main Street
Marlborough, MA 01752
Phone: 508-480-8383 **Fax:** 508-485-8161

708 Third Avenue
5th Floor
New York, NY 10017
Phone: 212-286-0890 **Fax:** 212-286-0891

245 Park Avenue
24th Floor
New York, NY 10167
Phone: 212-372-8840 **Fax:** 212-372-8839

2130 Headquarters Plaza
East Tower 2nd Floor
Morristown, NJ 07960
Phone: 973-590-2650 **Fax:** 973-590-2649

Key Executives:
David W Harris, President
Education: BA, University of Pennsylvania
Background: Smith Barney Harris Upham & Company; Oppenheimer & Company
Bruce C Ryan, Vice Chairman
Education: BS, Northeastern University
Background: Vice President, Private Capital Investment Group, Chemical Bank

1711 SOUTHEAST INTERACTIVE TECHNOLOGY FUNDS
1500 Perimeter Park Drive
Suite 310
Morrisville, NC 27560
Phone: 919-558-8324 **Fax:** 919-655-0541

Mission Statement: A venture stage investor who focuses exclusively on information technology and communications investments across industry verticals.
Geographic Preference: Southeast
Fund Size: $180 million
Founded: 1995
Average Investment: $4 million
Minimum Investment: $2 million
Investment Criteria: Early Stage
Industry Group Preference: Services, Technology, Telecommunications, Infrastructure, Enterprise Software, Business Products & Services, Software, Information Technology, Media
Portfolio Companies: Allconnect, BuildCraft Homes, BuildLinks, Nitronex, TerraServer, XS, OpenSite Technologies, Accipiter, Wave Systems, iEntertainment Network, ChanneLogics, GadgetSpace, Red Storm Entertainment, HAHT Commerce, Chatfish, HowStuffWorks, Pixel Magic Imaging, Arsenal Digital Studios, Waveguide Solutions, VisionAIR, MediaSpan Group

Key Executives:
Norvell E Miller IV, Managing General Partner
919-558-8324
Education: MBA/BA, Duke University
Background: EMS Financial; Triangle Assets Consulting; Mobius Group; Dental Care Partners;
Directorships: AllConnect, Arsenal, Digital Solutions, MediaSpan Group, Pixel Magic Imaging, VisionAIR, WaveGuide, Elumens
Steve Rakes, General Partner/CFO
Education: BA, English & Radio/Television Production, MS, Accounting, University of North Carolina, Chapel Hill
Background: Ernst & Young; Sloan Financial Group
Rami Elkhatib, Venture Consultant
Education: BS, Purdue University; MIT Sloan School
Background: Senior Director, Oneworld Software; Proctor & Gamble; UBS Warburg; Merrill Lynch

1712 SOUTHERN CAPITOL VENTURES
100 E Six Forks Road
Suite 200
Raleigh, NC 27609
Phone: 919-858-7580
web: www.southcap.com

Venture Capital & Private Equity Firms / Domestic Firms

Mission Statement: Southern Capitol Ventures is dedicated to helping outstanding entrepreneurs build market-leading companies.
Geographic Preference: Southeast, Mid-Atlantic United States
Founded: 2000
Average Investment: $500,000 - $1.5 million
Minimum Investment: $35, 000
Investment Criteria: Early-Stage
Industry Group Preference: Software, E-Commerce & Manufacturing, Digital Media & Marketing, Mobile, Healthcare Information Technology
Portfolio Companies: Art.com, ArtusLabs, AZVIcode, AudienceFUEL, Batanga, BrightContext, ChannelAdvisor, DoublePositive, ETix, FullSeven Technologies, Global Value Commerce, Motricity, ReverbNation, Synthematix, WeddingWire, Zift Solutions
Key Executives:
   Ben Brooks, Founding Partner
   e-mail: ben@southcap.com
   Education: University of North Carolina, Chapel Hill; MBA, Fuqua School of Business, Duke University
   Background: Director, Strategy, Capital Investment Group; SVP, Josephthal & Co.; CEO, Marion Bass Securities
   Directorships: FullSeven Technologies
   Jason Caplain, General Partner
   e-mail: jason@southcap.com
   Education: BS, Finance, Bentley College
   Background: Red Hat, Harrison Hurley & Company
   Directorships: ReverbNation, Zift Solutions
   David Jones, Partner
   e-mail: david@southcap.com
   Education: BS, Electrical Engineering, US Naval Academy; MS, Management Information Systems, University of Virginia; MBA, UNC Chapel Hill
   Background: Deloitte Consulting; Co-Founder, CTO, Orthocopia.com
   Directorships: ArtusLabs

1713 SOUTHERN CROSS VENTURE PARTNERS
420 Florence Street
Suite 210
Palo Alto, CA 94301

web: www.sxvp.com

Mission Statement: Assists early stage companies that demonstrate the potential for exceptional growth and market leadership.
Founded: 2006
Average Investment: $2 to $5 million
Industry Group Preference: Software Services, Telecommunications, Advanced Materials, Semiconductors, Digital Media & Marketing, Internet, Security, Nanotechnology, Environment, Energy, Mining, Water, Agriculture
Portfolio Companies: Autopilot, Brandscreen, CrossFiber, Effective Measure, Mantara, Mesaplexx, Mocana, Nitero, Pygg, Quantenna Communications, RIO, RMSS, SBA Materials, Shoes of Prey, Virsto, Wave Semiconductor, Woodboard, Precise Light Surgical, Brisbane Materials, Hydrexia, Boulder Ionics, Sunverge
Other Locations:
   PO Box 5084
   Elanora Heights NSW 2101
   Australia
   Phone: 61-0283147400
Key Executives:
   Bob Christiansen, Managing Director
   Education: Bachelor of Economics, Diploma of Information Processing, University of Queensland
   Background: General Partner, Allen & Buckenridge
   John Scull, Managing Director
   Education: Bachelor's Degree, University of Oklahoma; MBA, Harvard University
   Background: Venture Partner, Allen & Buckenridge
   Directorships: Aurema, ekit, Wedgetail/Vintela, Fultec Semiconductor, Fiberom, VaST Systems
   Mark Bonnar, Managing Director
   Education: BS/PhD, Heriot-Watt University
   Directorships: Sunman Energy; Wattwatchers; Greensync; BenAn Energy; Octillion Energy; Hydrexia; Mojo Power; Ecoult

1714 SOUTHPORT PARTNERS
2425 Post Road
Southport, CT 06490

Phone: 203-292-0019
e-mail: dm@southportpartners.com
web: www.southportpartners.com

Mission Statement: Southport Partners is a technology investment banking firm, specializing in mergers and acquisitions, as well as raising equity from institutional sources with over $2 billion of transactions completed over the last ten years.
Geographic Preference: United States
Founded: 1986
Average Investment: $12 million
Minimum Investment: $5 million
Investment Criteria: Second-Stage, Mezzanine, LBO, MBO
Industry Group Preference: Communications, Computer Related, Education, Electronic Components, Instrumentation, Financial Services, Insurance, Medical & Health Related, Internet Technology, Publishing, Transportation
Key Executives:
   Dale McIvor, Founding Partner
   Education: BSEE, University of Michigan; MSEE, University of Maryland; MBA, Harvard Business School
   Background: Boston Consulting Group; Mitre Corp.; Research Engineer, National Security Agency
   Katherine Watts, Founding Partner
   Education: BA, Washington University, MBA, New York University
   Background: Manager, Norton Simon; Merrill Lynch
   Mathew Veedon, Affiliate
   Education: BCom, Syndenham College, University of Mumbai; MBA, Yale University
   Background: Consultant, Redding Consultants; Principal, NGV Partners Fund; Senior Consultant, Accenture

1715 SOUTHWEST MICHIGAN FIRST LIFE SCIENCE FUND Southwest Michigan First
2700 Stadium Drive
Kalamazoo, MI 49008

Phone: 269-553-9588
web: www.southwestmichiganfirst.com

Mission Statement: The Southwest Michigan First Life Science Fund is a limited partnership venture fund interested in early stage life science opportunities in the Kalamazoo Region that have demonstrably viable technologies.
Geographic Preference: Kalamazoo Region
Fund Size: $50 million
Investment Criteria: Early-Stage
Industry Group Preference: Life Sciences
Portfolio Companies: Axonia Medical, Metabolic Solutions Development Company, Monteris Medical, NephRx, Toera Therapeutics, Vestaron
Key Executives:
   Ron Kitchens, Senior Partner
   e-mail: rkitchens@southwestmichiganfirst.com

Venture Capital & Private Equity Firms / Domestic Firms

1716 SOZO VENTURES
900 Veterans Boulevard
Suite 330
Redwood City, CA 94063

web: sozo.ventures

Mission Statement: Invests and supports technology enabled ventures with their global expansion. Aims to connect the most ambitious entrepreneurial teams with the world's most advanced and respected customers and distributors.

Founded: 2012
Industry Group Preference: Data Technology, eCommerce, Enterprise Cloud, Fintech, IoT, Healthcare Technology
Portfolio Companies: Anduril, Anomali, Applied Intuition, Aromyx, Attentive, Carta, Chainalysis, Chorus, Clearco, CloudPassage, Cohesity, Coinbase, Deel, Drishti, Fastly, Flexport, Grammarly, Handshake, Insighly, Kargo, Lotame, MongoDB, Neurotrack, One Concern, Opower, Palantir, Playco, Project 44, Revinate, Servicemax, Square, Tessian, Twitter, Zoom

Other Locations:
EGG JAPAN, 9th Floor
Shi-Marunouchi Building, 1-5-1 Marunouchi
Chiyoda-ku
Tokyo 100-6509
Japan

Key Executives:
Phil Wickham, Senior Managing Director
Background: Co-Founder, Reference Media; General Partner, JAFCO America Ventures; Executive Chairman, Kauffman Fellows
Koichiro Nakamura, Senior Managing Director
Education: BA, Waseda University; MBA, University of Chicago
Background: Mitsubishi Corporation
Masayuki Fuji, Senior Director
Education: BA, Waseda University
Background: Nomura Securities; CEO, Nomura Bank International

1717 SPACEVEST

web: www.spacevest.com

Mission Statement: Provides new business initiatives, strategic development, capital resource planning and investment management.

Geographic Preference: United States
Fund Size: $300 million
Founded: 1991
Average Investment: $3-$5 million
Minimum Investment: $500,000
Investment Criteria: Second Round or Later
Industry Group Preference: Components & IoT, Equipment, Software, Satellite Communications, Cable, Optical Technology, Copper, Applications Software & Services, Networking, Enterprise Services, Aerospace, Defense and Government

Key Executives:
John B Higginbotham, Founder/Chairman/Managing Director
703-904-9800
Fax: 703-904-0571
e-mail: jbh@spacevest.com
Education: BS Civil Engineering with Honors, Virginia Tech; MBA, Harvard Business School
Background: Co-Founder, Director, Sr VP, International Technology Underwriters; Satellite Systems Analyst, Corroon, Black/Inspace; President, Marketing Manager, Hewlett Packard
Directorships: Space Foundation, Virginia Tech Alumni Association

1718 SPARK CAPITAL
137 Newbury Street
8th Floor
Boston, MA 02116

Phone: 617-830-2000
e-mail: info@sparkcapital.com
web: www.sparkcapital.com

Mission Statement: Spark Capital is a venture capital firm that partners with exceptional entrepreneurs seeking to build disruptive, world-changing companies. Spark works to leverage their experiences, honed product & business instincts and extensive networks to help entrepreneurs build great companies.

Geographic Preference: Worldwide
Fund Size: $3 billion
Founded: 2005
Average Investment: $25,000 - $25 million
Investment Criteria: Early Stage
Industry Group Preference: Interactive Media, Mobile, Online Applications, Web Platforms, Infrastructure, Advertising, Cloud Computing, Social Media
Portfolio Companies: 1stdibs, 5minMedia, 8D World, Academia.edu, Accelera, Adap.TV, Adkeeper, Admeld, AltiusEd, Aviary, Benu, BloomNation, Boxee, Bug Labs, Close.io, Consumerunited, Contextin, Covestor, DIY, Etoro, Exfm, Fitorbit, Foursquare, Frontier Strategy Group, FundersClub, GDGT, Getyourguide, Hey, Inc., Intune Networks, IP Wireless, i-Wireless, JANA, Jelly in the News, Kateeva, KickApps, Kik, Kitchen Surfing, Lexity, Lift, LinkWell Health, Mark43, Enara Networks, Nextnew Networks, Nimble Commerce, Oculus VR, OMGPOP, OneRiot, Onswipe, Orchard, Panjo, peerTransfer, Picturelife, Plaid, Priceonomics, Qriously, Quantopian, RunKeeper, Sendme, Senr.net, Singpost, Sincerely, Skillshare, Socratic, StackExchange, StoreNVY, SuperPedestrian, Svpply, Thalmic Labs, thePlatform, Timehop, Triggit, tumblr, Twitter, Upworthy, VeriVue, Warby Parker, Wayfair, WorkMarter, Zazma

Other Locations:
165 Mercer Street
New York, NY 10012
Phone: 917-243-4200

332 Pine Street
Floor 7
San Francisco, CA 94104
Phone: 415-593-9002

Key Executives:
Alex Finkelstein, General Partner
Education: BA, Political Science, Middlebury College
Background: Principal, Seed Capital Partners; Associate, GrandBanks Capital; Cambridge Associates
Directorships: 5min, 8D World
Bijan Sabet, General Partner
Education: BS, Boston College
Background: Senior Vice President, Corporate Development, GameLogic; Entrepreneur-in-Residence, Charles River Ventures; Business Development, WebTV
Directorships: Tumbler, ThePlatform, Twitter, Sendme
Jeremy G. Philips, General Partner
Education: University of New South Wales; Harvard Kennedy School
Background: News Corporation; Photon Group
Directorships: TripAdvisor
Kevin Thau, General Partner
Education: UC, Santa Barbara
Background: Silicon Graphics; Software.com; Twitter
Nabeel Hyatt, General Partner
Education: Maryland Institute; Purdue University
Background: Conduit Labs; Zynga
Directorships: Cruise; Fig; Harmonix; Postmates; Proletariat; DIY; Sonder; Thalmic Labs
Santo Politi, Co-Founder & General Partner
Education: BS, Physics, Bogazici University, Istanbul;

Venture Capital & Private Equity Firms / Domestic Firms

MS, Electrical Engineering, NJIT; MBA, Finance, Wharton School, University of Pennsylvania
Background: yPartner, Charles River Ventures; President, New Media, Blockbuster Entertainment; Co-Founder, BT Venture Partners; Matsushita Electric Industrial
Directorships: KickApps, OneRiot, IWireless Home
Todd Dagres, Co-Founder & General Partner
Education: BS, Psychology, Trinity College; MBA, Boston University
Background: General Partner, Battery Ventures; Senior Lecturer, MIT Sloan School of Management; Principal & Senior Technology Anaylst, Montgomery Securities; Senior Technology Anaylst, Smith Barney/Robinson Humphrey; Business Development Manager, Networks & Communications, Digital Equipment Corporation
Directorships: Verivue, Akamai Technologies, Covestor

1719 SPARKLABS GLOBAL VENTURES
Palo Alto, CA

web: www.sparklabsglobal.com

Mission Statement: Business is now truly global. Exceptional entrepreneurs, that are building strong, category defining companies at highly advantageous valuations - can be found anywhere.

Geographic Preference: Worldwide
Investment Criteria: Seed-Stage
Industry Group Preference: Enterprise Software, Consumer Internet
Portfolio Companies: Andela, Blend, Good.co, Codekingdoms, Flow State Media, Hullabalu, Iodine, Knowre, LawPal, Lifesum, Mango Plate, Memebox, My GO Games, The Orange Chef Co., Parko, PayByGroup, Payoff, Petnet, Quarterly, SelfScore, Soundwave, Stitch, Timecast, WOO, Zanbato, 42

Key Executives:
Frank Meehan, Co-Founder/General Partner
Background: Horizons Ventures; Founder, Kuato Studios; Ericsson; Hutchison Whampoa
Bernard Moon, Co-Founder/General Partner
Education: BA, English & Psychology, University of Wisconsin-Madison; MPA, Telecom & New Media Policy, Columbia University
Background: Co-Founder, SparkLabs; Co-Founder & CEO, Vidquik; Managing Director, Lunsford Group; Co-Founder, GoingOn Networks; Director, IRG
John Lee, Co-Founder/Partner
Education: BA, Biology, University of Chicago
Background: Co-Founder, Hostway

1720 SPECTRUM EQUITY INVESTORS LP
One International Place
35th Floor
Boston, MA 02110

Phone: 617-464-4600
web: www.spectrumequity.com

Mission Statement: Provide equity capital to companies in the communications, information, media, entertainment and interactive industries; with each investment our goals are the same, to build premier businesses and achieve substantial long term capital appreciation for shareholders.

Geographic Preference: North America, Western Europe, Australia
Fund Size: $4.7 billion
Founded: 1994
Average Investment: $25-$100 million
Minimum Investment: $1 million
Investment Criteria: Seed, First-stage, Second-stage, Mezzanine; Leveraged Buyouts, Recapitalizations, Acquisition Financings, Secondary Share Purchases
Industry Group Preference: Communications, Entertainment, Information Technology, Media, Business Products & Services, Online Advertising, Software, Internet, Digital Media & Marketing
Portfolio Companies: AllTrails, Ancestry, Animoto, Bats, Bitly, Business Monitor International, B-Stock, Choice, DataCamp, Definitive Healthcare, Digital Marketing Institute, EagleView Technologies, Ethoca, Exactbid, ExamSoft, Extreme Reach, Finalsite, GoodRx, Grubhub, Headspace, HealthMedX, Ibfx.com, iPay Technologies, iSelect.com.au, Ita Software, Jagex Games Studio, Jimdo, Lead Group, Litmus, Lucid, Lynda.com, MedHok, Mortgagebot, Net Health, NetQuote, NetScreen, Offensive Security, Origami Risk, Passport Health Communications, Payer Compass, PicMonkey, Prezi, QTC Medical Services, RainKing, RCN, Rightside, RiskMetrics Group, Seisint, Survey Monkey, Teachers Pay Tachers, Tenstreet, The Expert Institute, Trintech, Verafin, Verisys, Weddingwire, World-Check

Other Locations:
140 New Montgomery
20th Floor
San Francisco, CA 94105
Phone: 415-464-4600

Key Executives:
Brion B Applegate, Co-Founder
Education: BA, Colgate University; MBA, Harvard Business School
Background: TA Associates
Ronan Cunningham, Managing Director
Education: BComm, University College Dublin; MBA, INSEAD
Background: SVP, Capital Partnering, General Atlantic; Partner, Adam Street Partners
Directorships: Institutional Limited Partners Association
Mike Farrell, Managing Director
Education: BA, Bowdoin College; MBA, Harvard Business School
Background: Tudor Investment Corporation
Chris Mitchell, Managing Director
e-mail: chris@spectrumequity.com
Education: AB, Princeton University
Background: TA Associates; Monitor Clipper Partners; SG Warburg;
Directorships: Chartered Marketing Services; RiskMetrics Group, Seisint; Surebridge, Inc; United Asset Coverage
Jeff Haywood, Managing Director
Education: BA, Duke University
Background: Thoma Cressey Equity Partners; Goldman Sachs
Brian Regan, Managing Director
Education: BS, Bucknell University
Background: PricewaterhouseCoopers
Victor E Parker, Managing Director
e-mail: vic@spectrumequity.com
Education: BA, Dartmouth College; MBA, Stanford Graduate School of Business
Background: Summit Partners; Product Manager, ONYX Software; Consultant, Andersen Consulting
Benjamin M Spero, Managing Director
e-mail: bspero@spectrumequity.com
Education: AB, History & Economics, Duke University
Background: Consultant, Bain & Company; Co-Founder, TouchPak
Peter T Jensen, Managing Director
e-mail: pete@spectrumequity.com
Education: BA, Stanford University; MBA, Wharton School
Background: Technology, Media & Telecom Investment Banking Group, JPMorgan
Stephen M LeSieur, Managing Director
e-mail: steve@spectrumequity.com
Education: BA, Princeton University; MBA, Dartmouth College
Background: Associate, Trident Capital; Analsyst, Media & Communications Group, Thomas Weisel Partners
Adam J Margolin, Managing Director
e-mail: adam@spectrumequity.com

Venture Capital & Private Equity Firms / Domestic Firms

Education: AB, Harvard University
Background: Vice President, Media & Telecom Investment Banking Group, Citigroup

1721 SPEKTRA CAPITAL
620 Kirkland Way
Suite 204
Kirkland, WA 98033

Phone: 425-307-1299
e-mail: info@spektracapital.com
web: www.spektracapital.com

Mission Statement: Interested in companies operating in large markets or traditional segments underserved by emerging technologies. Prefers defined revenue models, a short path to profitability and straightforward value propostions.

Founded: 2012
Investment Criteria: Early Stage
Industry Group Preference: Mobile Apps, SaaS, Platform As A Service

1722 SPELL CAPITAL PARTNERS LLC
222 South Ninth Street
Suite 2880
Minneapolis, MN 55402

Phone: 612-371-9650 **Fax:** 612-371-9651
e-mail: info@spellcapital.com
web: www.spellcapital.com

Mission Statement: To sponsor a strong management team with a proven track record in a LBO situation. Focuses on industrial businesses and help industries to achieve goals.

Geographic Preference: Midwest
Fund Size: $75 million
Founded: 1988
Average Investment: $3 - $12 million
Minimum Investment: $2 million
Industry Group Preference: Chemicals, Manufacturing, Plastics, Metals
Portfolio Companies: American Card Services, Tech Cast Holdings, Animal Adventure, Valley Vessel Fabricators, Midwest Plastic Products, NPI Medical, Thermoforming Technology Group, Falls Fabricating, Filter Minder, Norshield Security Products, Premier Precision Group, Smartlink, Apartment Data Services, AC Busines Media, Las Vegas Color Graphics, Arandell, Learn It Systems, Alliance Steel Service, Adler Hot Oil Service, All Safe, Sellars

Key Executives:
William H Spell, President
612-371-9650
Fax: 612-371-9651
e-mail: williamspell@spellcapital.com
Education: BS, University of Minnesota; MBA, Carlson School of Management, University of Minnesota
Background: Former Investment Banker
Directorships: A number of private/public companies and non-profits
Darren Brathol, Managing Director
e-mail: darren@spellcapital.com
Education: BS, University of Wisconsin; MBA, Carlson School of Business, University of Minnesota
Background: Investment Banking Analyst, Lazard Middle Market
James W Rikkers, Senior Managing Director
Education: BA, Economics & Finance, University of St. Thomas
Background: Mezzanine Capital Group, Wells Fargo
Andrea R Nelson, Chief Operating Officer/Chief Financial Officer
Education: BSB, Carlson School of Management, University of Minnesota, CPA
Background: Tax Director, PricewaterhouseCoopers LLP

1723 SPENCER TRASK VENTURES
1140 Avenue of the Americas
New York, NY 10036

Toll-Free: 800-622-7078
web: spencertraskco.com

Mission Statement: Spencer Trask is a leading private equity firm discovering idea to shape the 21st century. With our network of co-investors and business leaders, we provide visionary entrepreneurs with both financial and intellectual capital to transform bright ideas into world-changing companies.

Geographic Preference: United States
Founded: 1991
Investment Criteria: Startup, Early-Stage
Industry Group Preference: Healthcare, Life Sciences, Software, Media, Information Technology, Telecommunications, Mobile Communications Devices, Genomics, Optical Technology, Stem Cell Therapy
Portfolio Companies: Fastcase, Casemaker, El Super, Sessions.edu, Aperture, Innocentive, Ciena, Myriad, Health Dialog

Other Locations:
1700 East Putnam Avenue
Suite 306
Old Greenwich, CT 06870

1724 SPERO VENTURES
1991 Broadway Street
Suite 110
Redwood City, CA 94063

web: spero.vc

Mission Statement: Spero Ventures invests in late Seed tech companies.

Founded: 2018
Average Investment: $3 million - $12 million
Investment Criteria: Late Seed, Series A
Industry Group Preference: Artificial Intelligence, Technology, Applications, Software, Consumer, Health & Wellness
Portfolio Companies: Anchor, Base, Bunker, Core, Crew, DroneSeed, Fathom, Gencove, Huckleberry, Hustle, Indus, Jopwell, Koko, Markov, RevUp, Roam Robotics, SafeTraces, Shelfmint, Skillshare, Tortuga AgTech

Key Executives:
Shripriya Mahesh, Partner
Background: Omidyar Network; eBay; NextCard
Rob Veres, Partner
Education: MBA, Kellogg School of Management
Background: Omidyar Network
Ha Nguyen, Partner
Education: BS, Wharton School; MBA, Harvard Business School
Background: eBay; Oodle; Co-Founder, Product Leader Summit

1725 SPINDLETOP CAPITAL
7000 N Mopac Expy
Suite 315
Austin, TX 78731

Phone: 512-961-4633
e-mail: admin@spindletopcapital.com
web: www.spindletopcapital.com

Mission Statement: Spindletop Capital is a private equity and venture capital firm specializing in the healthcare industry.

Geographic Preference: United States
Founded: 2011
Average Investment: $10 - $50 million
Investment Criteria: Late Stage, Growth Equity, Expansion Capital
Industry Group Preference: Life Sciences, Healthcare Services, Healthcare Information Technology,

Venture Capital & Private Equity Firms / Domestic Firms

Pharmaceuticals, Biopharmaceuticals, Medical Devices, Diagnostics
Portfolio Companies: Avanzar Medical, Bioventus, Castle Biosciences, Hospitalists Now, Navigating Cancer, QSpex Technologies
Key Executives:
  Dr Evan Melrose, Founding Managing Director
  Education: BA, University of Pennsylvania; MD, Indiana University School of Medicine; MBA, Wharton School
  Background: Founding Managing Director, PTV Sciences; Director, Burrill & Company
  Directorships: Texas Business Hall of Fame Foundation
  Steve Whitlock, Managing Director
  Education: BS, Mechanical Engineering, Texas A&M University; MBA, Embry-Riddle Aeronautical University
  Background: Co-Founder, Path4 Ventures; Operating Venture Partner, PTV Sciences; Co-Founder, Spinal Restoration; President, LDR Spine USA; Centerpulse Orthopedics
  Directorships: Spinal Restoration, Ortho Kinematics
  Dr Robert McDonald, Venture Partner
  Education: MD, University of Texas Southwestern Medical School; MBA, Wharton School of Business, University of Pennsylvania
  Background: President & Founder, Aledo Consulting; Anthem Blue Cross and Blue Shield; Eli Lilly & Company
  Shannon Rothschild, Venture Partner
  Education: BA, Tulane University; MBA, MHA, Indiana University
  Background: Venture Partner, Heron Capital; Manager, Product Design & Development, Humana Inc.; RealMed; Anthem Alliance

1726 SPINNAKER CAPITAL PARTNERS
Southport, CT 06890

Phone: 203-255-8828
web: www.spinnakercapital.com

Mission Statement: Spinnaker Capital Partners LLC is a private equity fund investing in various equity and debt instruments in non-public small and middle market consumer oriented businesses.

Geographic Preference: Northeast Corridor, Boston to Washington DC
Investment Criteria: Leveraged Buyouts, Management Buyouts, Expansion Financing, Early-Stage Venture Rounds, Distressed Situations

1727 SPIRE CAPITAL PARTNERS
1500 Broadway
Suite 1811
New York, NY 10036

Phone: 212-218-5454 **Fax:** 212-218-5455
web: www.spirecapital.com

Mission Statement: An active and experienced private equity firm with an investment focus in small market companies within the business services, information services, media and communications sectors.

Geographic Preference: United States
Fund Size: $600 milion
Founded: 2000
Average Investment: $20 million
Minimum Investment: $15 million
Investment Criteria: Seed, Growth, Expansion, Later
Industry Group Preference: Media, Communications, Business Products & Services, Information Services, Education
Portfolio Companies: American Community Newspapers, Ariston Global, AssetNation, Carpathia Hosting, Certiport, Dynamic Quest, Encoda Systems, ERI Solutions, Highline Financial, Highline Media, Inflow Inc., iNNERHOST, Just Marketing International, Lighthouse, Nassau Broadcasting Partners LP, NetFortris, O2B Kids, On Campus Marketing, Patriot Media, Performance Assessment Network Inc., Professional Bull Riders, Rainbow Child Care Centre, SkyMall, Sonitrol Inc., Surgent Professional Education, Tarpon Towers, Trax Group, Vector Media, Velocity, Vivax
Other Locations:
  Five Tower Bridge
  300 Barr Harbor Drive
  Suite 400
  Conshohocken, PA 19428
  Phone: 610-397-1700
Key Executives:
  Andrew J. Armstrong. Jr., Partner
  Education: AB, Economics, Duke University
  Background: Co-Founder, Waller-Sutton Media Partners; President, Waller Capital Corporation; Philadelphia National Bank and Manufacturers Hanover Trust
  Bruce M. Hernandez, Partner
  e-mail: bhernandez@spirecapital.com
  Education: BS, University of Vermont; MBA, New York University
  Background: Co-Founder & CEO, Waller-Sutton Media Partners; CFO, Horizon Cellular Group
  Directorships: Certiport, Just Marketing International, Nassau Broadcasting Partners
  Sean C. White, Partner
  e-mail: swhite@spirecapital.com
  Education: BS, Binghamton University; MBA, New York University
  Background: Vice Presdient, Waller-Sutton Media Partners; Waller Capital Corporation
  Directorships: Carpathia Hosting, SalvageSale, Certiport, SkyMall
  David K. Schaible, Partner
  e-mail: dschaible@spirecapital.com
  Education: BS, Indiana University
  Background: Financial Analyst, Bear Stearns & Co
  Directorships: Ariston Global, Just Marketing International, PBR
  Donald E. Stewart, Chief Financial/Compliance Officer
  e-mail: dstewart@spirecapital.com
  Education: BS, Accounting, Widener University
  Background: CFO, Iron Oak Development; CFO/COO, Specialty Brands; Regional Controller, Wawa Food Markets
  Directorships: On Campus Marketing

1728 SPLIT ROCK PARTNERS
16526 West 78th St.
Suite 504
Eden Prairie, MN 55346

Phone: 952-995-7474 **Fax:** 952-995-7475
web: www.splitrock.com

Mission Statement: A venture capital firm dedicated to building productive partnerships with entrepreneurs who have the vision and ability to create companies of enduring value.

Geographic Preference: West Coast
Fund Size: $750 million
Founded: 1988
Average Investment: $1-$10 million
Minimum Investment: $1 million
Investment Criteria: Seed, First-stage, Second-stage, Mezzanine
Industry Group Preference: Information Technology, Healthcare, Consumer Services, Retailing, Service Industries, Manufacturing, Life Sciences, Software, Internet, Medical Devices, Enterprise Software, Business Products & Services
Portfolio Companies: Acquia, Adaytum, AmCom, Anuluex Technologies, Ardian, Aritech, Auxilium, Bigcommerce, Bigfix, Black Duck, BlueKai, Calabrio, Calix, Caring.com, Cayenna Medical, Code42, Colorescience, Compete, DemandBase, DexCom, DFine, EBR Systems, eBureau, Entellus Medical, Evalve, Flycast, ForSight Newco II, Gravie, Guardian Analytics, Help Systems, HighJump,

Venture Capital & Private Equity Firms / Domestic Firms

HireRight, Histogenics, Holaira, Ideas, InsideView, Intacct, Internet Broadcasting, Janrain, Kspine, Lawson, LowerMyBills, MyNewPlace, Net Perceptions, NextCard, Novologix, Nuvaira, Prometheus Laboratories, Quin Street, RF Surgical, Santarus, Sentillion, SkinMedica, Snagajob, Sonoma Orthpedic, Spanlink, Sparkcentral, Spine-Tech, SPS Commerce, Tarsus Medical, Tornier, Transcend Medical, TruSignal, Twelve, Vendavo, Volo Metrix, Vormetric, Xora, Zyga Technology

Key Executives:
Michael Gorman, Managing Partner
e-mail: michael@splitrock.com
Education: BA Economics/Public Policy, Duke University; MBA/JD, Harvard University
Background: Harvard Management Company; Bain & Co
Directorships: Adaytum Software, Auxilium, Bravanta, HighJump Software, IDeaS, Information Advantage, Lawson Software, Net Perceptions, Optical Solutions, SPS Commerce, Vendavo, XIOtech
Dave Stassen, Managing Director
e-mail: dave@splitrock.com
Education: Graduate, University of St. Thomas
Background: Spine-Tech; North Star Ventures; IBM
Directorships: Ancillary Care Management, Atritech, Avecor, Avera Pharmaceuticals, Converge Medical, DexCom, Disc Dynamics, Evalve, GeoDigm MiraMedica, Myocor, Sinus Rhythm Technologies
James R Simons, Managing Director
952-995-7488
e-mail: jim@splitrock.com
Education: BA, Economics, History, Stanford University; MBA, JL Kellogg Graduate School of Management of Northwestern University
Background: General Partner, Marquette Venture Partners; Associate, Trammell Crow Compnay; Analyst First Boston Corporation
Directorships: Aleri, BigFix, CarParts Technologies, Command Audio, Compete, Ecast, firstRain, Flycast Communications, HireRight, Internet Broadcasting, Lexar Media, LowerMyBills, NEW
Josh Baltzell, Venture Partner
e-mail: josh@splitrock.com
Education: St. Olaf College; MBA, University of Minnesota Carlson School of Management
Background: Principal, St. Paul Venture Capital; Vice President, Piper Jaffray
Steve Schwen, Chief Financial Officer
e-mail: steve@splitrock.com
Education: BA, Business Administration/Accounting, University of St. Thomas
Background: CFO, St. Paul Venture Capital; KPMG LLP

1729 SPP CAPITAL
550 Fifth Avenue
12th Floor
New York, NY 10036

Phone: 212-455-4500
web: www.sppcapital.com

Mission Statement: Dedicated to the proposition that every client is entitled to the highest standard of service: to execute every transaction in a diligent, comprehensive manner; to demonstrate integrity and vigilance in representing the best client interests; to exercise leadership and promote ethical standards in the securities industry; to assure clients achieve terms and conditions which reflect aggressive pricing and flexible structures.

Founded: 1989
Portfolio Companies: ACCT Holdings, Ambient Air, Angelle, Blueberry Broadcasting, EServices, Industrial Piping, Island Oasis, TCSC, Tulsa Inspection Resources, Wholesale Floors

Key Executives:
Robin Ellis Busch, Managing Partner
212-455-4504
e-mail: rbusch@sppcapital.com
Education: Graduate, New York University
Background: Bankers Trust
Stefan L Shaffer, Co-Founder/Managing Partner
212-455-4502
e-mail: sshaffer@sppcapital.com
Education: JD, Cornell Law School; Graduate, Colgate University
Background: Bankers Trust Company; White & Case; White House Intern
Amy S Lazarus, Chief Operating Officer
212-455-45115
e-mail: alazarus@sppcapital.com
Education: MBA Finance, Columbia Graduate School of Business; BS Business Administration, University of Vermont
Background: Bankers Trust Company; CPA, Arthur Andersen
C Todd Kumble, Managing Partner
212-455-4508
e-mail: tkumble@sppcapital.com
Education: BA, Yale University; MBA, Wharton School
Background: Home Box Office; Allen Group Inc; Manufacturers Hanover
John Cable, Partner
Education: BA, Economics & Art History, Stanford University; MBA, Amos Tuck School of Business Administration
Background: Corporate Finance Positions at Nike, Coach; Investment Banking Analyst,

1730 SPRING CAPITAL PARTNERS LP
The Foxleigh Building, Suite 340
2330 W Joppa Road
Lutherville-Timonium, MD 21093

Phone: 410-685-8000 **Fax:** 410-545-0015
web: www.springcap.com

Mission Statement: Spring Capital's mission is to contribute to the success of small and medium-sized businesses by providing mezzanine financing, and critical component of investment capital for growing companies.

Geographic Preference: Eastern United States
Fund Size: $75 million
Founded: 1999
Average Investment: $2 - $7 million
Minimum Investment: $2 million
Investment Criteria: Expansion, Acquisition, LBO, MBO, Recapitalization
Industry Group Preference: Technology, Communications, Business to Business
Portfolio Companies: Cybera, Cyberpoint, Dermatology Associates of Tyler, Enefco, eServices, GI Plastek, HomeCentric Healthcare, iPacesetters, Jawbone, MC MC, Monster Media, Numet Machining Techniques, Portadam, PSS, Quantem, QuantumClean, Swiss Farms, Tzetzo Bros., Xand

Other Locations:
170 N Radnor Chester Road
Suite 101
Radnor, PA 19087
Phone: 610-964-7972

Key Executives:
Robert M. Stewart, Co-Founder/General Partner
e-mail: rms@springcap.com
Education: Graduate, Hampden-Sydney College; MBA, Wake Forest University
Background: Armata; Cross Hill Financial; Legg Mason; Board Service, DIGEX/Cidera/Network Technologies Group

Venture Capital & Private Equity Firms / Domestic Firms

Michael F. Donoghue, Co-Founder/General Partner
e-mail: mfd@springcap.com
Education: Graduate, Georgetown University; MBA, University of Virginia
Background: Corestates
Directorships: MathSoft Engineering and Education, Vocollect

John C. Acker, General Partner
e-mail: jca@springcap.com
Education: Gettysburg College
Background: Vice President, Capital Markets Group, Allfirst Bank

Peter B. Orthwein, Jr., General Partner
e-mail: pbo@springcap.com
Education: BS, MBA, Cornell University
Background: Priceline.com, Starwood Hotels & Resorts Worldwide, Brooks, Houghton & Company

Brian C. McDaid, General Partner
e-mail: bcm@springcap.com
Education: Haverford College; CFA
Background: Navigant Capital Advisors, KPMG Corp. Finance

1731 SPRING LAKE EQUITY PARTNERS
125 High St.
Suite 2211
Boston, MA 02110

Phone: 617-391-6300 Fax: 617-391-6390
e-mail: info@springlep.com
web: springlakeequitypartners.com

Mission Statement: Spring Lake Equity Partners is a Boston-based private equity firm. We invest equity capital primarily in later-stage, technology-oriented companies. Our investment philosophy is simple and has remained consistent over time - we seek to partner with great management teams to take their businesses to the next level, creating value for all stakeholders. Spring Lake strives to add value to our portfolio companies through active Board participation and accessing our network of contacts which includes our own and those of our key strategic partners, WestRiver Equity Partners, Tudor Investment Corp., and the George Kaiser Family Foundation.

Founded: 2013
Average Investment: $7-$15 million
Investment Criteria: Later-Stage Growth Equity, Recapitalizations, Acquisitions
Industry Group Preference: Software, Digital Media & Marketing, Mobile, Data Center, Healthcare Information Technology, Business & Financial Services
Portfolio Companies: Adaptive Computing, Advanced Fibre Communication, Allegro Development Corp, Arcsoft, Art Technology Group, Aspect Ratio, Assistive Technologies, Astadia, Avici Systems, Batanga, Benu Networks, Brio Technology, Captura Software, Chordiant Software, Classic Sports Network, Crossbeam Systems, Digital Island, Dorado, Fidelis Security Systems, Force10 Networks, Gain Capital Group, Global Cash Access, Gravy Analytics, Gray Peak Technologies, Icom Cmt, InsideView, Intelligrated, International Components, Lightspeed Financial, Matrixx, Mediamath, Mediaplatform, Meteor Learning, N2 Broadband, N2K, Neocera, Netbase Solutions, Netprospex, Observeit, One Door, Plated, Remedy Partners, Roberts Radio, Shoebuy, Single Digits, SmarterHQ, Sqrrl, Switch & Data Facilities, Thorne Research, TractManager, Transmeta Corporation, Transwitch, Turbine, Vantage Media, Vantrix Corporation, Velocity Technology Solutions, Virtify, Vurv Technology, Wavelink Corporation, Wimba, Wired Ventures

Key Executives:

Bob Forlenza, Managing Partner
Education: BS, Accounting & Business Administration, Washingtion & Lee University; MBA, Harvard Business School
Background: Managing Partner, Tudor Investment Corporation; Vice President, Carlisle Capital; Executive, American Management Company; Management Consultant, Bain & Company
Directorships: Virtify, Allegro Development, Thorne Research

Carmen Scarpa, Managing Partner
Education: BA, Economics, Harvard University; MBA, Harvard Business School
Background: Partner, Tudor Investment Corporation; Associate, Triumph Capital Group; Corporate Finance Analyst, Drexel Burnham Lambert
Directorships: Batanga

Dan MacKeigan, Partner
Education: BS, Biology, Trinity College
Background: Partner, Tutor Investment Corporation; Vice President and Senior Public Equity Research Analyst, Friedman, Billings, Ramsey; Financial Consultant, Zurich Investments
Directorships: Vantage, Vantrix, ArcSoft

Jeff Williams, Partner
Education: BA, History, Yale University; MBA, MIT Sloan School of Management
Background: Partner, Tudor Investment Corporation; Associate, Downer & Company; Strategic Consultant, Oplab; Financial Analyst, Fox-Pitt, Kelton Ltd.
Directorships: Single Digits, Thorne Research, Virtify

1732 SPRING LANE CAPITAL
50 Milk St.
16th Floor
Boston, MA 02109

Phone: 514-761-4150
e-mail: info@springlanecapital.com
web: www.springlanecapital.com

Mission Statement: Spring Lane Capital partners with strong management teams who are involved in creating sustainable solutions in the energy, water, food and waste sectors.

Industry Group Preference: Environment, Sustainability, Water, Waste & Recycling, Food & Beverage, Energy, Renewable Energy

Other Locations:
1200 Ave. McGill College
Sutie 1100
Montreal, QC H3B 4G7
Canada

Key Executives:

Christian Zabbal, Managing Partner
Education: MBA, McGill University
Background: Managing Partner, Black Coral Capital; Partner, ghSMART & Company

Rob Day, General Partner
Education: BA, Swarthmore College; MBA, Kellogg School of Management
Background: Consultant, Bain & Company
Directorships: New England Clean Energy Council

Nikhil Garg, General Partner
Education: BS, Stanford University; MBA, MIT Sloan School of Management
Background: Partner, Black Coral Capital; Climate Change Capital; Core Carbon Group; Bain & Company

1733 SPRING MOUNTAIN CAPITAL
650 Madison Avenue
20th Floor
New York, NY 10022

Phone: 212-292-8300
web: www.springmountaincapital.com

Mission Statement: Spring Mountain Capital's private equity group focuses on providing growth capital to small companies in both active co-investment and lead capacities.

Founded: 2001
Investment Criteria: All Stages
Industry Group Preference: All Sectors Considered

Venture Capital & Private Equity Firms / Domestic Firms

Portfolio Companies: Applied Genetics, Alphatec, Aton Pharma, BAWAG, BHS Specialty Chemical Products, Chrysler Holdings, Cleaire Advanced Emissions Control, Coolerado Corporation, Eletrobras, Foresight Reserves, Giga-Tronics, GlucoVista, GreenMan Technologies, IRON Solutions, MedAvante, Outrigger Media, Patriot National Bancorp, Perquest, Powermat, Perferred Pet Care, Whip Tail Technologies

Key Executives:
  Raymond L.M. Wong, Managing Director/Head of Growth Equity
  Education: BA, Political Science, Yale College; MBA, Harvard Business School
  Background: Managing Director, Merrill Lynch & Co.; Managing Member, DeFee Lee Pond Capital
  Directorships: Alleghany Corporation, Merrill Lynch Ventures
  Jamie Weston, Managing Director
  Education: BA, Economics, Drew University; MBA, Fordham University
  Background: Partner, The Wicks Group of Companies; IBJ Whitehall Bank & Trust; National Wesmnister Bancorp
  John L Steffens, Founder/Senior Managing Director
  Education: BA, Economics, Dartmouth College
  Background: President, Consumer Markets, Merrill Lynch & Co.
  Directorships: Colony Financial, Cicero
  Gregory P Ho, President
  Education: BS, Administrative Science, Yale College; JD, Columbia Law School
  Background: Principal/CFO, McKinsey & Company; Donovan Leisure Newton & Irvine

1734 SR ONE LTD
985 Old Eagle School Road
Suite 511
Wayne, PA 19087

web: www.srone.com

Mission Statement: Invest globally in early-stage healthcare companies pursuing innovative, breakthrough science. Their expanded remit also focuses on maximizing the value of GSK technological innovation to establish new businesses and revenue opportunities.

Geographic Preference: North America, Europe
Fund Size: $560 million
Founded: 1985
Average Investment: $5-8 million
Minimum Investment: $100,000
Investment Criteria: Seed, Startup, First-Stage, Second-Stage, Mezzanine, LBO
Industry Group Preference: Medical & Health Related, Biotechnology
Portfolio Companies: AGTC, Aileron, Arcellx, Asceneuron, Ato Bio, AvhanaHealth, Bicycle Therapeutics, Bird Rock Bio, CalciMedica, Constellation Pharmaceuticals, Crispr Therapeutics, Decibel Therapeutics, Dicerna Pharmeceuticals, eFFECTOR, F-Star, Genocea, Gladius Pharmaceuticals, Gotham Therapeutics, HTG, Illuminoss, Macrolide Pharmaceuticals, Mission Therapeutics, Morphic Therapeutic, Navitor Pharmaceuticals, Nimbus Therapeutics, Nkarta Therapeutics, Palleon Pharmaceuticals, Pandion Therapeutics, Princepa Biopharma, Princeps Therapeutics, Progyny, Propeller, PSIOxus, Pulmocide, Scynexis, Second Genome, Spero Therapeutics, TP Therapeutics, Tranquis Therapeutics Inc., TranslateBio, VHsquared, ZappPx

Other Locations:
29 Farm Street
London W1J 5RL
United Kingdom

San Francisco, CA 94158

Key Executives:
  Rajeev Dadoo, Managing Partner
  Education: BA, Chemistry & Mathematics, Knox College; PhD, Chemistry, Stanford University; MBA, The Wharton School of Business
  Background: Genentech; BioRad; Unimicro Technologies
  Simeon J. George, Chief Executive Officer
  Education: BA, Neuroscience, Johns Hopkins University; MBA, Wharton School of Business; MD, University of Pennsylvania, School of Medicine
  Background: Consultant, Bain & Company; Investment Banking, Goldman Sachs; Merrill Lynch
  Directorships: Anaphore
  Matthew Foy, Partner
  Education: BA, Molecular Biology/Genetics/Statistics, Univeristy of Oxford; Corporate Finance, London Business School; Drug Discovery, University College London
  Background: Greenhill & Co

1735 SSM PARTNERS
Triad III Building
6070 Poplar Avenue
Suite 560
Memphis, TN 38119

Phone: 901-767-1131
web: www.ssmpartners.com

Mission Statement: To invest in private companies distinguished by exceptional management, a unique business model and prospects for high growth: We view each investment as a partnership with management in developing a successful business. SSM invests in Internet businesses, typically software solutions and business-to-business e-commerce, high technology, telecommunications and other business service companies.

Geographic Preference: Southeastern United States, Texas
Fund Size: $250 million
Founded: 1973
Average Investment: $5-$20 million
Minimum Investment: $3 million
Investment Criteria: High growth companies with proven business models. Companies typically have $10 million of revenue and are profitable at the point of investment.
Industry Group Preference: Technology-Enabled Businesses, Healthcare Services, Business Products & Services, Consumer Services
Portfolio Companies: Bulldog Solutions, Complete Holdings Group, Connecture, FrontStream Payments, HealthTeacher, Ifbyphone, New Era Portfolio, OpinionLab, RemitDATA

Key Executives:
  James D Witherington Jr, Advisory Partner
  Education: BA Economics, Vanderbilt University; MBA, University of Chicago
  Background: SSM Since 1973
  Directorships: Plan Express; DataCert
  R Wilson Orr III, Managing Partner
  Education: BA Economics/Business Administration, Vanderbilt University
  Background: JP Morgan
  Directorships: Kirkland's, All Web Leads; Bulldog Solutions; Chronicity
  Casey West, Managing Partner
  Education: BA, History, Virginia Military Institute; MBA, Harvard Business School
  Background: Petra Capital; Donaldson, Lufkin & Genrette (DLJ)
  Directorships: FrontStream Payments; RemitDATA

Venture Capital & Private Equity Firms / Domestic Firms

Hunter Witherington, Managing Partner
Education: BA, Economics, Vanderbilt University
Background: Stephens, Inc.

1736 STAENBERG VENTURE PARTNERS
308 9th Avenue N
Seattle, WA 98109

Phone: 206-264-0784
e-mail: info@staenberg.com
web: www.staenberg.com

Mission Statement: Staenberg Ventures is a Seattle-based firm focused on venture capital funding, strategic consulting and entrepreneurship in the technology, business social media, and consumer products arenas. By leveraging an extensive partner network in the Silicon Valley, the Pacific Northwest, New York and South America, our firm provides a unique and important bridge between these business centers.

Geographic Preference: Silicon Valley, Pacific Northwest, New York, South America
Industry Group Preference: Communications, Network Infrastructure & Security, Business Products & Services, Software, Consumer Services, Medical Technology
Portfolio Companies: Airbiquity, Aprimo, Business.com, Care2, CaseCentral, Command Audio, Corrigo, ENA, ezboard, Lydian Trust, Mimio, mInfo, NapaStyle, New Vine Logistics, PAR3, Prime Advantage, Revenue Science, Salu, Seagate, SquareTrade, StubHub, Syncronex, Time Domain, VetCentric, Vista

Key Executives:
Jon Staenberg, Managing Partner
e-mail: jon@staenberg.com
Education: BS, MS, MBA, Stanford University
Directorships: Hand of God Wines

1737 STAGE 1 VENTURES
890 Winter Street
Suite 208
Waltham, MA 02451

Phone: 781-772-1010 Fax: 941-847-7121
e-mail: info@stage1ventures.com
web: www.stage1ventures.com

Mission Statement: Stage 1 Ventures works hard every day to earn its reputation as a quality partner for visionary entrepreneurs who date to innovate, challenge and fundamentally change the dynamics of new and existing markets.

Geographic Preference: Mid-Atlantic Region
Investment Criteria: Early-Stage
Industry Group Preference: Mobile, Internet, SaaS, Internet Technology, Marketing, Advertising, Security
Portfolio Companies: Paydiant, Marxent, AdelaVoice, OnePIN, Connect Towers, dondeEsta, xPeerient, Veloxum, Innerpass, Carbonite, Nimbit, Myxer, Zapoint, Interactive Television, Magnify.net, Parelastic, Deep, Dashbell, Vivox, Flashnotes, Nexercise, PhantomAlert, Autonet Mobile, Openbay, PureCars, Carvoyant, Maple Farm Media, InStream Media, OwnerIQ, Myxer, Promoboxx, Ditto, Mobee, Sitewit, Coherent Path, shareThat, LocusPlay, Delfigo Security, DropFire, Wing Power Energy, Banshee Wines, Newburyport Brewing Company, Glanola

Other Locations:
5580 La Jolla Boulevard
Unit 80
La Jolla, CA 92037
Phone: 650-336-3778

2F 242 Yang-Guang Street
NeiHu, Taipei 11491
Taiwan
Phone: 886-975726772

Key Executives:
David William Baum, Managing Director
e-mail: dwbaum@stage1ventures.com
Education: BS, Computer Science, Drexel University; MBA, Harvard Business School
Background: Founder, Pensoft Corporation; Manager, Prism Venture Partners
Jonathan Gordon, Managing Director
e-mail: jgordon@stage1ventures.com
Background: Founder, Ametron Technologies; CEO, mGen; CEO & Founder, EndPoints

1738 STARBOARD CAPITAL PARTNERS
30 Jelliff Lane
Southport, CT 06890

Phone: 203-259-8855 Fax: 203-259-8287
web: www.starboardcapital.net

Mission Statement: A financial sponsor that initiates, finances and partners with management and private equity investors in the acquisition of companies with enterprise values of $20 million to $250 million.

Fund Size: $85 million
Founded: 2004
Average Investment: $1,750,000
Minimum Investment: $500,000
Industry Group Preference: Biotechnology, Computer Related, Electronic Technology, Energy, Industrial Equipment, Real Estate, Natural Resources, Automotive, Consumer Products, Building Materials & Services, Construction, Distribution, E-Commerce & Manufacturing, Manufacturing, Healthcare
Portfolio Companies: Apothecare LLC, CV Properties LLC, JPC Holdings LLC, PureRED, PursueCare LLC, TheraPlay

Key Executives:
Dean E Fenton, Managing Member/Chairman
Education: Harvard College; Graduate School of Business at Columbia University; Officer, USAF
Background: Founding Partner, Prime Capital Management Company; General Partner, Sprout Group
Marc C Bergschneider, Managing Member
Education: AB, Brown University; MBA, University of Chicago
Background: CEO/Chairman, National Fairways; Managing Partner, New Charleston Capital; Managing Director, Lehman Brothers
Directorships: Brown University Sports Foundation; National Rowing Foundation
Peter H Smith Jr, Managing Director
e-mail: pjs@starboardcapital.net
Education: Middlebury College
Background: President & Founder, Canwell Capital; Birinyi Associates, Vice President, Bear Stearns
Brian E Stern, Operating Partner
e-mail: brians@starboardcapital.net
Education: University of East Anglia, Norwich England; Harvard University Graduate School of Business
Background: Director, ESP; Director, HNI Corporation; Senior Vice President, Xerox Corporation; Chief Strategy Officer, President, Office Document Products; President, Xerox Technology Enterprisees

1739 START GARDEN

e-mail: hello@startgarden.com
web: www.startgarden.com

Mission Statement: Start Garden invests $5,000 in a new idea each week. At the $50,000-$500,000 level of an investment, Start Garden works closely with their entrepreneurs to help identify new business models and develop their people and network. Start Garden offers an alternative experience to the traditional venture capital firms.

Fund Size: $15 million
Founded: 2012
Average Investment: $5,000
Minimum Investment: $5,000
Industry Group Preference: Diversified
Portfolio Companies: Hip Shot Dot, Varsity News Network, GinkgoTree, GreenLancer, IMSRV, Local Orbit, FetchNotes, NxtMile Sports Insoles, Blue Medora, Chalkfly, Breakup Goods, Benefit, Ambassador, Sol, EXO, Conpoto, Xcess Able, Alsentis, Eidex Education Analytics, VerifyValid, Silikids

Key Executives:
 Rick DeVos, Founder & CEO
 e-mail: rick@startgarden.com
 Paul Moore, Director
 e-mail: paul@startgarden.com
 Mike Morin, Director
 e-mail: mike@startgarden.com

1740 STARTUP CAPITAL VENTURES
535 Middlefield Road
Suite 280
Menlo Park, CA 94025

Phone: 650-461-8100
web: www.startupcapitalventures.com

Mission Statement: To build a supportive partnership around an outstanding entrepreneurial team, with a clear market vision for its product or service. To focus on investing in strong management teams, not just technologies. To strive to help build companies based on proven principals of integrity, patience and flexibility.

Geographic Preference: Silicon Valley, Hawaii, Texas, Oklahoma, China
Average Investment: $250,000 - $1 million
Investment Criteria: Early-Stage
Industry Group Preference: Software
Portfolio Companies: Adama Materials, AGIS, Attainia, Central Pacific Bank, Dali Wireless Systems, DeviceVM, Switchfly, TagArray, Think Finance, TuneIn, WhiteHat Security, Winery Exchange, Xignite, Zero2IPO

 2800 Woodlawn Drive
 Suite 156
 Honolulu, HI 96822
 Phone: 808-202-2538

Key Executives:
 John C Dean, Managing Partner
 Background: CEO, Silicon Valley Bank; Managing Director, Tupetele Ventures Fund; Investment Director, Advanced Technology Ventures; Walden International; Authosis Capital
 Timothy Dick, Managing Partner
 Education: BS, Electrical Engineering, University of California, Irvine; MBA, Stanford University
 Background: Founder, Hawaii Superferry; Co-Founder, Grassroots.com; Founder, WorldPages.com; Principal, Boston Consulting Group
 Directorships: Adama Materials, Dali Wireless, TRUSTe, Silvertail Systems, TagArray, RadioTime, Hawaii Superferry
 Bob Rees, Venture Partner
 Education: BA, Business, Principia College; MBA, New York University Stern School of Business
 Background: Special Limited Partner, Woodside Fund; Access Venture Partners
 Directorships: WhiteHat Security, Xignite

1741 STARVEST PARTNERS
650 Madison Avenue
20th Floor
New York, NY 10022

Phone: 212-863-2500 **Fax:** 212-863-2520
e-mail: info@starvestpartners.com
web: www.starvestpartners.com

Mission Statement: To invest in technology-enabled business services companies at the expansion stage.

Geographic Preference: United States
Fund Size: $150 million (Fund I) and $245 million (Fund II)
Average Investment: $5 million
Minimum Investment: $2 million
Investment Criteria: 2nd, 3rd, 4th Institutional Rounds
Industry Group Preference: Electronic Technology, Business to Business, Enterprise Services, Software
Portfolio Companies: Accept Software, AppDirect, Bluestreak, Ceros, Connected, CrowdTwist, Fieldglass, Host Analytics, iCrossing, Ideeli, Insurance.com, Iron Solutions, Mazu Networks, MessageOne, NetSuite, NewComLink, Newgistics, Outrigger, PeopleMatter, Perquest, PivotLink, PrecisionDemand, RAMP, Receivables Exchange, RetailNet, Switchfly, Take the Interview, Transactis, Travora Media, UrbanBound, Veracode, Xignite

Key Executives:
 Laura Belle Sachar, Co-Founder/Managing Partner
 e-mail: laura@starvestpartners.com
 Education: BA, Barnard College; Columbia University; MBA, Columbia University Graduate School of Business
 Background: Gabelli Securities; Founder, Sachar Capital; Founding Chairman, NYNMA Angel Investors Program; Associate Editor, Financial World magazine; Financial Analyst, Prudential Securities
 Directorships: Newgistics, Ideeli, Veracode
 Jeanne Mariani Sullivan, Co-Founder
 212-863-2530
 e-mail: jeanne@starvestpartners.com
 Education: BS, University of Illinois; JD, Creighton University
 Background: Managing Director, Olivetti Ventures; Managing Director, 4C Ventures; AT&T; Product Director, Bell Laboratories; Business Marketing/Production Director, Bozell Worldwide
 Directorships: Iron Solutions, Transactis
 Deborah A Farrington, Co-Founder/Managing Partner
 Education: Smith College; MBA, Harvard Business School
 Background: President/CEO, Victory Ventures; Senior Executive, Asian Oceanic Group; Merrill Lynch & Co
 Directorships: NetSuite, Fieldglass, Insurance.com, Pivot Link, Host Analytics
 Robert E Kelly, Chief Financial Officer
 e-mail: bob@starvestpartners.com
 Education: BBA, Manhattan College; MBA, Baruch College; CPA
 Background: Senior VP Strategic Planning, Paradyme Human Resources Corporation; CFO, Hertz Corporation; Audit Manager, PricewaterhouseCoopers

1742 STARWOOD CAPITAL GROUP LLC
2340 Collins Avenue
Miami Beach, FL 33139

Phone: 305-695-5200
web: www.starwoodcapital.com

Mission Statement: Starwood Capital Group is a privately held investment management firm that specializes in real estate related investments on behalf of select private and institutional investor partners. It aligns its interests with those of its investment partners, placing its own capital at risk on every transaction and receiving returns only when its partners receive theirs.

Fund Size: $6.5 billion
Founded: 1991

Venture Capital & Private Equity Firms / Domestic Firms

Average Investment: $10-$100 million
Minimum Investment: $5 million
Investment Criteria: Seed, First-stage, Second-stage, Mezzanine
Industry Group Preference: Real Estate, Hotels, Property Management, Industrial Equipment
Other Locations:
100 Pine Street
Suite 3000
San Francisco, CA 94111
Phone: 415-247-1220

One East Wacker Drive
Suite 3600
Chicago, IL 60601
Phone: 312-242-3200

Starwood Asset Management
400 Galleria Parkway
Suite 1450
Atlanta, GA 30339
Phone: 770-541-9046

1255 23rd Street NW
Suite 250
Washington, DC 20037
Phone: 202-507-6710

1640 S Sepulveda Boulevard
Los Angeles, CA 90025
Phone: 310-893-2781

1 Eagle Place
2nd Floor
London SW1Y 6AF
United Kingdom
Phone: 44-2070163650

2-4, rue Eugene Ruppert
Luxembourg L-2453
Luxembourg
Phone: 352-26645121

Beechavenue 54
Schiphol-Rijk 1119 PW
The Netherlands
Phone: 31-206586520

Starwood Capital Asia
Somptueux Central, 20/F
52-54 Wellington Street
Hong Kong
Phone: 852-3792-0349

Key Executives:
Barry S. Sternlicht, Chairman & CEO
Education: BA, Brown University, MBA, Harvard Business School
Background: i Star Financial
Jeffrey G. Dishner, President & COO
Education: BA Economics, Wharton School; MBA, Amos Tuck School, Dartmouth
Background: Commercial Mortgage Finance Group JP Morgan; JMB Realty Corporation
Madison F. Grose, Senior Managing Director/Co-General Counsel
Education: BS, Stanford University; JD, University of California, LA
Background: Senior Partner, Pircher Nichols & Meek
Directorships: i Star Financial
Christopher D. Graham, Managing Director/Head, Real Estate Acquisitions for the Americas
Education: BBA, Finance, James Madison University; MBA, Harvard Business School
Background: Director, Financial Consulting Group, CB Richards Ellis
Ellis F. Rinaldi, Senior Managing Director/Co-General Counsel
Education: JD, Georgetown University; BA Accounting, University of Massachusetts
Background: Winthrop Stimson Putnam & Roberts; Pircher Nichold & Meeks
Directorships: RFF
Laura M. Rubin, Managing Director/Head, Portfolio Management
Education: BS, Economics, Wharton School; MBA, Kellogg School of Management
Background: VP, Goldman Sachs; JMB Realty; Urban Development Corp.

1743 STATELINE ANGELS
Rockford, IL

web: www.statelineangels.com

Mission Statement: Stateline Angels is an Angel investor organization that provides investment capital to start-up and early stage companies. Members who choose to invest may also lend their operational experience to enhance the chance of success to the ventures. We are dedicated to fostering growth in the Stateline area and upper Midwest region by assisting individuals in the development of successful businesses.

Geographic Preference: Midwest
Founded: 2004
Investment Criteria: Early-Stage
Industry Group Preference: Biotechnology, Business Products & Services, Computers & Peripherals, Peripherals, Consumer Products, Electronics, Financial Services, Energy, Information Technology, Medical Devices, Networking, Retailing, Distribution, Semiconductors, Software
Portfolio Companies: 10X, LiftSeat Corporation, Bias Power, Advanced Diamond Technologies, Ratio, Traycer Systems, Lumec Control Products, IMCO Technologies, Akoya

1744 STEELPOINT CAPITAL PARTNERS
215 S Highway 101
Suite 211
Solana Beach, CA 92075

e-mail: info@steelpointcp.com
web: www.steelpointcp.com

Mission Statement: Steelpoint Capital invests in growing consumer companies in the health, wellness and fitness sectors. Headquartered in San Diego, CA, Steelpoint looks to partner with companies that possess authentic brands and clear opportunities for growth. Steelpoint's team draws on extensive operating and investment experience to provide value-added support to portfolio companies and their management teams.

Geographic Preference: Southern California
Industry Group Preference: Health & Wellness, Fitness
Portfolio Companies: Acorns, Bag Borrow or Steal, Boingo Wireless, GreatCall, Hookit, Hylete, Kidrobot, Matuse, Orion Telescopes & Bionoculars, Sealand Natural Resources, Tasti D-Lite, SKLZ, X-1 Audio
Key Executives:
James Caccavo, Founder/Managing General Partner
Education: BS, Economics & Finance, University of Scranton
Background: Managing Director, Moore Capital Management's Private Equity Group

1745 STERLING PARTNERS
650 S Exeter Street
Suite 1000
Baltimore, MD 21202

Phone: 443-703-1700 **Fax:** 443-703-1750
web: www.sterlingpartners.com

Mission Statement: Sterling Partners focus is on distinctive or products, favorable prospects for growth, a sustainable advantage, predictable cash flow and low inventories that turn quickly. Favor non-cyclical industries that are least vulnerable to recession. Focuses on buyouts, venture capital and real estate.

Geographic Preference: United States, Northeast, Mid-Atlantic, Midwest

Venture Capital & Private Equity Firms / Domestic Firms

Fund Size: $700 million
Founded: 1983
Investment Criteria: EBITDA $5-25mm; majority ownership opportunity; strong fit with Sterling's industry experience; competitive advantage; distinctive product/service; superior industry fundamentals
Industry Group Preference: Direct Marketing, Education, Distribution, Manufacturing, Healthcare, Business Products & Services, Technology
Portfolio Companies: Adeptus Health, Ameritox, Ashworth, Brace Industrial Gorup, Conversant, Educate Online, Educate, Foundation Partners Group, Gem Mobile Treatment Services, Infilaw, Innotrac, IO, Kids Care Dental Group, Laureate International Universities, Livingston International, Longitude Licensing, Meritas, Optimer, Pingora Asset Management, Plattform Advertising, Progressus Therapy, Prospect Mortgage, Q-Centrix, Remedi Seniorcare, Results Physiotherapy, Savo, School of Rock, Spartan College of Aeronautics and Technology, Surgical Solutions, Susiecakes, Tribeca Flashpoint Media Arts Academy

Other Locations:
401 North Michigan Avenue
Suite 3300
Chicago, IL 60611
Phone: 312-465-7000 **Fax:** 312-465-7001

701 Brickell Avenue
Suite 1700
Miami, FL 33131
Phone: 305-808-2970 **Fax:** 305-808-2900

Key Executives:
Eric Becker, Co-Founder
e-mail: ebecker@sterlingpartners.com
Education: University of Chicago
Background: Tango Communications
Directorships: Ashworth, Avectra, Connections Academy, Optimer Brands, Progressus Therapy
Steven Taslitz, Co-Founder/Chairman
e-mail: staslitz@sterlingpartners.us
Education: BS Accountancy, University of Illinois
Directorships: Many Boards in which Sterling has invested, as well as Sterling Venture Partners (a venture capital fund) and Sterling Real Estate Partners
Christopher Hoehn-Saric, Co-Founder/Managing Director
e-mail: choehn-saric@sterlingpartners.com
Directorships: Connections Academy, Educate Online, Educate, i/o Data Centers, The InfiLaw System, Livingston International, Meritas, Smarterville
Doug Becker, Co-Founder/Managing Director
Background: Founder, Laureate Education Inc.; Chairman/CEO, Sylvan Learning Systems
Jeff Elburn, Managing Director
Education: BBA, Salisbury University
Background: Finance Principal, ABS Capital Partners
Alv Epstein, Managing Director
Education: BA, Political Science, Ohio State University; JD, Harvard Law School
Background: General Counsel/VP of Business Affairs, Kaplan Inc.; Corporate Attorney, Katten Michin Rosenman LLP
Jason Rosenberg, Managing Director
Education: BA, Northwestern University; JD, Northwestern University School of Law; MBA, Kellogg School of Management
Background: Found, Inc.
Directorships: Ashworth, Cornerstone, The Leman International School
Shoshana Vernick, Managing Director
Education: BS, Indiana University
Background: One Equity Partners, Razorfish
Directorships: School of Rock, Securenet, Progressus
Rick Elfman, Managing Director
Education: BA Economics/Political Science, Tufts University; MBA Finance, University of Chicago

Background: Institutional Sales, Goldman Sachs; Owned/Operated Chain of Pharmacies-Boston; Founder, Little Elves
Directorships: Numerous portfolio companies
Jeff Schechter, Senior Advisor
e-mail: jschechter@sterlingpartners.com
Education: BS, Accounting, University of Maryland; MS, Finance, Loyola University
Background: Grotech Capital Group, Ernst & Young

1746 STONE POINT CAPITAL LLC
20 Horseneck Lane
Greenwich, CT 06830

Phone: 203-862-2900
web: www.stonepointcapital.com

Mission Statement: Stone Point Capital is a private equity firm that makes investments in the global financial services industry.

Geographic Preference: United States
Fund Size: $3.5 billion
Founded: 1993
Average Investment: $50-250 million
Minimum Investment: $50 million
Investment Criteria: Startup, LBO, MBO
Industry Group Preference: Insurance, Financial Services
Portfolio Companies: Access Point Financial, AloStar Bank of Commerce, The ARC Group, Atrium Underwriting Group, C3/CustomerContactChannels, Citco III, Duff & Phelps, Eagle Point Credit Management, Enhanced Capital/Tree Line, Enstar Group, Freepoint Commodities, First Data Holdings, HCBF Holding Company, Hodges-Mace, Lancaster Pollard Holdings, LTCG, Merchant Capital Solutions, NEBCO Insurance Services, New Point IV/V/VI, New Ocean Capital Management, NXT Capital, Prima Capital Advisors, Standcard Bancshares, SKY Harbor Capital Management, SCS Financial Serices, Sedgwick, Torus Insurance Holdings, Trident V Credit Holdings, Verisight, Amberst Holdings, Asset Allocation & Management Company, Atlantic Capital Bancshares, Auction.com, Automobile Protection Coporation, Carlile Bancshares, Cunningham Lindsey Group Limited, Edgewood Partners Holdings, Grandpoint Capital, Higginbotham Insurance Agency, NXT Capital, OneWest Bank Group, Pierpoint Securities, StoneRiver Holdings, Symbion, Yadkin Financial, Preferred Concepts, Privilege Unerwriters, Vanbridge

Other Locations:
1 Vanderbilt Avenue
50th Floor
New York, NY 10017
Phone: 203-862-2900

205 Datura Street
Suite 400
West Palm Beach, FL 33401

Key Executives:
Charles A. Davis, Chief Executive Officer
e-mail: CDavis@stonepoint.com
Education: BA, University of Vermont; MBA, Columbia University
Background: Investment Banking Services, Goldman, Sachs & Company
Directorships: AMS Services, AXIS Capital Holdings Limited, Sedgwick CMS Holdings, Media General, Merchants Bancshares, Progressive Corporation, MMC Capital Foundation
Kurt E. Bolin, Managing Director
e-mail: KBolin@stonepoint.com
Education: BS, Wake Forest University; MBA, Wharton School
Background: Managing Director, GE Capital
Directorships: BLC Holdings LLC
Stephen Friedman, Chairman
e-mail: SFriedman@stonepoint.com
Education: BA, Cornell University; LLB, Columbia Law School

Venture Capital & Private Equity Firms / Domestic Firms

Background: Goldman-Sachs & Co., Law Clerk
Directorships: Goldman-Sachs & Company
James D. Carey, Managing Director
e-mail: JCarey@stonepoint.com
Education: BS, Boston College; JD, Boston College Law School; MBA, Duku University Fuqua School of Business
Background: Associate, Merrill Lynch & Co.; Corporate Attorney, Kelley Drye & Warren LLP
Directorships: Asset Allocation & Management Company, Cunningham Lindsey Group Limited, Lane McVicker, Locton International Holdings Limited, Privilege Underwriters
David J. Wermuth, Managing Director & General Counsel
e-mail: DWermuth@stonepoint.com
Education: BA, Yale University; MBA, New York University Stern School of Business; JD, Cornell Law School
Background: Corporate Attorney, Cleary Gottlieb Steen & Hamilton LLP; Auditor, KPMG Peat Marwick
Directorships: Amherst Holdings, Asset Allocation & Management Company, Edgewood Partners Holdings, OneWest Bank Group, StoneRiver Holdings
Nicolas D. Zerbib, Managing Director
e-mail: nzerbib@stonepoint.com
Education: BA, Amherst College; MBA, Harvard Graduate School of Business Administration
Background: Analyst, Goldman Sachs & Co.; Catamount Capital Management; Boston Consulting Group
Darran A. Baird, Managing Director
e-mail: dbaird@stonepoint.com
Education: BA, Stanford University
Background: Deputy Head of Strategic Development, Marsh & McLennan Companies; Managing Director, Securitas Capital; Associate, Smith Barney
Christopher M. Doody, Managing Director
e-mail: Cdoody@stonepoint.com
Education: BA, Middlebury College; MBA, Columbia University Graduate School of Business
Background: Analyst, Merrill Lynch & Co.
Directorships: GENEX Services
Michael D. Gregorich, Managing Director
e-mail: Mgregorich@stonepoint.com
Education: BA, Middlebury College; MBA, New York University Leonard N Stern School of Business
Background: Senior Vice President, Donaldson Lufkin & Jenrette
Directorships: APCO Holdings, Cyprexx Services, NOVA Group Services, Real Estate Disposition Corporation
Agha Khan, Managing Director
e-mail: AKhan@stonepoint.com
Education: BA, Cornell University
Background: Analyst, Salomon Smith Barney
Directorships: The ARC Group, Cyprexx Services, Real Estate Disposition Corporation
Peter M. Mundheim, Managing Director & Counsel
e-mail: Pmundheim@stonepoint.com
Education: AB, Duke University; JD, University of Pennsylvania Law School
Background: Attorney, Cleary Gottlieb Steen & Hamilton LLP; Law Clerk, Chancellor William T Allen, Delaware Court of Chancery; Assistant Product Manager, Commerce Clearing House
Directorships: APCO Holdings, Cunningham Lindsey Group Limited, Cyprexx Services, NOVA Group Services, Privilege Underwriters, Real Estate Disposition Corporation
Sally A. DeVino, Managing Director & CFO
Education: BS, Manhattan College; CPA
Background: Senior Manager, BDO Seidmen
Fayez S. Muhtadie, Managing Director
e-mail: Fmuhtadie@stonepoint.com
Education: BSBA, Ohio State University; MBA, Columiba University Graduate School of Business
Background: Analyst, Credit Suisse First Boston; Financial Analyst, Aon Capital Markets
Directorships: NOVA Group Services
Eric L. Rosenzweig, Managing Director
e-mail: Erosenzweig@stonepoint.com
Education: BS, Wharton School, University of Pennsylvania
Background: Analyst, UBS Investment Bank

1747 STONEBRIDGE PARTNERS
81 Main Street
Suite 505
White Plains, NY 10601

Phone: 914-682-2700 Fax: 914-682-0834
e-mail: info@stonebridgepartners.com
web: www.stonebridgepartners.com

Mission Statement: Provides returns through leveraged recapitalizations of smaller, privately held companies or divisions of public companies.

Fund Size: $500 million
Founded: 1986
Average Investment: $10 million
Minimum Investment: $7 million
Investment Criteria: LBO, MBO
Industry Group Preference: Industrial Services, Specialty Packaging, Niche Manufacturing, Specialty Manufacturing, Building Materials & Services, Infrastructure
Portfolio Companies: American Dryer Corporation, BrandFX, Exal Group, Hydraulex Global, Safety Infrastructure Solutions, Specialty Bakers

Key Executives:
Michael S Bruno Jr, Managing Partner
e-mail: msb@stonebridgepartners.com
Education: BS, Economics, Allegheny College; MBA, Columbia Business School
Background: Mergers/Acquisitions, Salomon Brothers
Andrew A Thomas, General Partner
Education: BS, Engineering, Purdue University; MS, Engineering, Illinois Institute of Technology; MBA, University of Chicago Business School
Background: Partner, Hawthorne Partners; Senior Member, Bank America; Managerial/Engineering, Inland Steel Company/Airco Industrial Gases
William G. Connors, Manaing Director
e-mail: wconnors@stonebridgepartners.com
Education: BA, Business Administration, State University of New York; CPA
Background: Manager, Accounting/Auditing Group, Prince Waterhouse, LLP
Stephen A. Hanna, Managing Director
e-mail: shanna@stonebridgepartners.com
Education: BA, Economics, Lafayette College; MBA, Finance & Accounting, Stern School of Business, New York University
Background: Director, Corporate Finance Group, IBJ Whitehall
David R Schopp, Operating Partner
Education: MS, Engineering, Rensselaer Polytechnic Institute
Background: President & CEO, Orbis Corporation; General Manager, Promo Edge
Directorships: American Dryer Corporation, Attica Hydraulic Exchange, Specialty Bakers
Michael A Steinbeck, Operating Partner
Education: Indiana University, DeVry Institute of Technology
Background: CEO, CII Technologies; EVP, Sales & Marketing Operations, CP Clare
Directorships: BondCote Corporation

1748 STONEHENGE GROWTH CAPITAL
236 Third Street
Baton Rouge, LA 70801

Phone: 225-408-3000 Fax: 225-408-3090

Venture Capital & Private Equity Firms / Domestic Firms

Mission Statement: Stonehenge Growth Capital manages the venture capital, private equity and mezzanine investment activities of Stonehenge Capital Company. Stonehenge is a perfect match for companies with a long-term vision focused on pursuing new, exciting and high growth opportunities, and for entrepreneurs with a passion for innovation and achievement.

Geographic Preference: Southeast, Northeast, Texas
Fund Size: $80 million
Founded: 1999
Average Investment: $4 million - $6 million
Minimum Investment: $1 million
Investment Criteria: Growth Equity
Industry Group Preference: Technology, Business Products & Services, Healthcare, Life Sciences, Manufacturing, Distribution
Portfolio Companies: 7thOnline, AuthenTec, Bulldog Solutions, Critical Mention, DataSynapse, eHealth Global Technologies, iCardiac Technologies, In.vision Research, Knovel, Lorica Solutions, Lumetrics, Medidata Solutions, Partsearch Technologies, Payformance, Pilgrim Software, PixFusion, SensorTran, TouchPay Holdings, Alinean, Dowley Security Systems, Electronic Data Resources, Integrated Portfolio Management Services, Proficient Auto, Red Vector, Health Integrated, Image-Guided Neurologics, ZetrOZ, Dixie Southern, Environmental Lighting Concepts, Iron Horse Tools, T&K Machine, Twin Vee, American Scholar, COCAT, Moran Printing, Classic Events, Evolve, Oxford Collection Agenecy, AXIS Industrial Services, Coastal Drilling Company, Dolphine Marine International, Edgen Corporation, Florida Marine Group, Genesis Offshore, Gulfstream Services, H2X, Kim Susan, Louisiana Crane Company, Louisiana Tuggs, Rotorcraft Leasing Company, Technical Compression Services, Astro Electroplating, Avanti Marble & Granite, Barvista Homes, Col-Met Spray Booths, D'Lisi Food Systems, Ecoboard Holdings, Hornet Group, MB Industries, Millennium Outdoors, MilMar Food Group, Niagara Thermal Products, PECO Pallet, Petersen Pet Provisions, Sasun, Sunbelt Steel, The Metropolitan Switch Board Company, Trans American Rubber, Filco Carting, Rocky Mountain Portable Storage

Other Locations:
707 West Azeele Street
Tampa, FL 33606
Phone: 813-221-4413 **Fax:** 813-221-6453

152 W 57th Street
20th Floor
New York, NY 10019
Phone: 212-265-9380 **Fax:** 212-656-1344

7887 E Belleview Avenue
Suite 1100
Denver, CO 80111
Phone: 720-956-0235 **Fax:** 720-956-0209

191 W Nationwide Boulevard
Suite 600
Columbus, OH 43215
Phone: 614-246-2456 **Fax:** 614-246-2461

3424 North Shepard Avenue
Milwaukee, WI 53211
Phone: 414-906-1702 **Fax:** 414-906-1703

2001 Park Place
Suite 320
Birmingham, AL 35203
Phone: 205-458-2778 **Fax:** 866-539-9881

3625 N Hall Street
Suite 520
Dallas, TX 75219
Phone: 214-599-8850 **Fax:** 214-442-5626

8000 Maryland Avenue
Suite 1190
St. Louis, MO 63105
Phone: 314-721-5707 **Fax:** 314-721-5135

1020 Highland Colony Parkway
c/o Matt Thornton
Ridgeland, MS 39157
Phone: 601-985-4251 **Fax:** 601-985-4500

Brent T Sacha, Director, Growth Capital
e-mail: btsacha@stonehengegc.com
Education: BA, Economics, University of Virginia; MBA, Kellogg School of Management, Northwestern University
Background: Manager, M&A and Corporate Finance, AGL Resources; Townsend Frew & Company

Stephen A Bennett, Managing Director
Dallas Office
e-mail: sabennett@stonehengegc.com
Education: MBA, JL Kellogg Graduate School; BBA, University of Texas
Background: Banking Officer, Bank One; Manager Telecommunications/Media Practice, Deloitte Consultling
Directorships: Bulldog Solutions, TouchPay Holdings, Alinean, T&K Machine

1749 STONEWOOD CAPITAL MANAGEMENT
209 4th Avenue
Pittsburgh, PA 15222

Phone: 412-391-0300 **Fax:** 412-391-0500
e-mail: info@stonewoodcapital.com
web: www.stonewoodcapital.com

Mission Statement: To act as institutional angel investors, providing not only capital, but business expertise and advice to companies that are in the early phase of their development.

Geographic Preference: Eastern United States, Canada
Fund Size: $100 million
Founded: 1994
Average Investment: $2 million
Minimum Investment: $1 million
Investment Criteria: Seed, First Round Equity Capital, LBO, MBO
Industry Group Preference: Manufacturing, Distribution, Technology, Healthcare, Drug Development, Media, Business Products & Services
Portfolio Companies: Addressograph-Bartizan, C-K Composites Co., NewBold, Tank Services, Ardica Technologies, Demegen, Plan4Demand, Precision Therapeutics, ReGear, TimeSys

Key Executives:
J. Kenneth Moritz, President
Education: BS, University of Pennsylvania; JD, University of Pittsbugh School of Law; MSIA, Carnegie Mellon University

John Tippins, Managing Director
Education: BE, Electrical Engineering, Vanderbilt University; MBA, University of Pittsburgh Katz School of Business
Background: Director, Tippins Incorporated

Peter J Muth, Senior Vice President
Education: BS, Business, University of Dayton; MBA, University of Pittsburgh Katz School of Business
Background: Birchmere Capital; PNC Bank

1750 STORM VENTURES
3000 Sand Hill Road
Building 4, Suite 210
Menlo Park, CA 94025

Phone: 650-926-8800
web: www.stormventures.com

Mission Statement: Storm Ventures was founded by a seasoned group of industry veterans with the common vision of sharing a collective experience, passion and energy to help talented and driven entrepreneurs build great companies of enduring value.

Fund Size: $500 million
Founded: 1997

Industry Group Preference: Information Technology, Networking, Semiconductors, Software, Wireless, Security, Enterprise Applications, Hardware, Virtualization
Portfolio Companies: Acces 360, AdMobius, Airespace, AirPlug, Algolia, Amber Networks, Appcelerator, Asoka, AtScale, Averail, Berkana Wireless, BlackStratus, Catamaran, Cellfire, Cloudwords, Com2uS, Crowd Factory, DVDO, EchoSign, Flint Mobile, Greenlight Technologies, GuideSpark, HubPages, iML, JetCell, Kidaro, Kineto, Lightera, Marketo, Mcube Works, MetaCloud, Micel, MobileIron, Modo Labs, NetScaler, OSA Technologies, Parklet, Pipedrive, Qumu, Rafter, RainStor, Restorando, RiseSmart, SandForce, Sanera Systems, Sierra Monolithics, Silego, Splashtop, SwiftStack, TalkDesk, Telera, Transera, TrueSpan, Venturi Wireless

Key Executives:
Ryan Floyd, Managing Director
e-mail: ryan@stormventures.com
Education: BS, MS, Earth Systems, Stanford University
Background: Business Development, E-TEK Dynamics; Summit Partners
Directorships: 3Crowd, Appcelerator, Crowd Factory, HubPages, NetForensics, SandForce, Splashtop
Josef Friedman, Venture Partner
e-mail: josef@stormventures.com
Education: MS, Electrical Engineering, San Diego State University; MBA, National University
Background: Co-Founder & CEO, Expression; Apple Computers
Directorships: Anchor Bay Technologies, TrueSpan, Nuelight, Auvitek, Kidaro, Inovys

1751 STRIPES GROUP
402 West 13th Street
New York, NY 10014

Phone: 212-823-0720
e-mail: info@stripesgroup.com
web: www.stripesgroup.com

Mission Statement: Stripes Group delivers more than capital. By leveraging their resources, contacts and experience, their partner companies are able to increase profitability to grow faster and maximise value while maintaining the independence that defines an entrepreneul's success.

Founded: 2003
Average Investment: $10 - $100 million
Minimum Investment: $10 million
Industry Group Preference: Business to Business, Consumer Internet, SaaS, Consumer Products
Portfolio Companies: Art.com, Audio Network, Blue Apron, Craftsy, Elance ODek, EMarketer, Folica, GrubHub, Kareo, Kinetic Social, MyWebGrocer, Netbiscuits, NetQuote, Pond5, Refinery29, Sandata, SilverSky, SmartWool, Stella & Chewy's, Turtle Beach

Key Executives:
Ken Fox, Managing Partner
22-823-0730
Education: BS, Economics, Pennsylvania State University
Background: Managing Director, Internet Capital Group; Director, Safeguard Scientifics; Co-Founder, A-10 Capital; Co-Founder, Sentinel Fund
Karen Kenworthy, Vice President, Consumer Investments
212-823-0725
Education: BS, Biomedical Engineering, BA, Economics, Yale University; MBA, Stanford Graduate School of Business
Background: Bain & Company, UBS
Ron Shah, Vice President
212-823-0724
Education: BA, Philosophy, Duke University
Background: Co-Founder, Endgame Capital; M&A Group, Citigroup Global Markets

Jason Santiago, Partner/Chief Technology Officer
212-823-0731
Education: BA, Architecture & Planning, Columbia University; MBA, Columbia Business School
Background: Investment Banking, Cowen & Company; Director, Primedia
Wayne Marino, Partner/Chief Financial Officer
212-823-0733
Education: BS, Finance, Rutgers University; MS, Accountancy, Mendoza College of Business, University of Notre Dame
Background: Controller, Veronis Suhler Stevenson; Vice President, Aetos Capital; Ernst & Young

1752 STRUCTURE CAPITAL
e-mail: info@structure.vc
web: structure.vc

Mission Statement: Invests in entrepreneurs who desire to pass on their wealth, wisdom, and expertise as they grow over time.

Industry Group Preference: Waste & Recycling
Portfolio Companies: Uber, Shyp, MoviePass, SurfAir, Chicory, KangaDo, Gigit, PogoSeat, Boatbound, Peerspace, The Dating Ring, DJZ, Vessel, MakeSpace, Neighbor.ly, Stitch, Zaranga, DOZ, Popexpert, Willcall, Noble Transmission, Equidate, GoGoGab, Partnered, Mattermark, Lovely, Bohemian Guitars, AirHelp, ProductBIO, Beyond, Mavatar, Zootrock, Feastly, Totspot, Laurel & Wolf, Cross Fader, 15Five, Sumazi, Honk, Fixed, Ongig, Cambly, Breathometer, Cargomatic, Poliogg, Merchbar, Near Me, Knotch

1753 SUMMER STREET CAPITAL PARTNERS
60 School Street
Suite 1420
Orchard Park, NY 14127

Phone: 716-566-2900 **Fax:** 716-566-2910
web: www.summerstreetcapital.com

Mission Statement: In addition to offering the capital companies need, Summer Street Capital Partners provides expertise, vast resources, and hands-on approach, all aimed at helping companies thrive like never before.

Geographic Preference: United States
Founded: 1997
Investment Criteria: Buyouts, MBO, Growth Financing, Family Transition, Corporate Divestiture, Recapitalization
Industry Group Preference: Education, Environment Products & Services, Healthcare, Niche Manufacturing
Portfolio Companies: Commonwealth Sprague Capacitor, UStec, IWS, Palladian, USA Datanet, Action, Graphic Controls, Pacific Pools, Praxis, Reichert, Belmont Meat Products, WillCare, ICE, Healthtrax, Sarolina Staff, la Madeline, Tulsa Welding School, RSI, Apple Valley Waste, Curtis Bay Medical Waste Services, New England Orthotic & Prosthetic Systems, Midwest Technical Institute, Multisorb Technologies, FSL 3D

Key Executives:
Michael P McQueeney, Managing Partner
e-mail: mmcqueeney@summerstreetcapital.com
Education: MBA, Amos Tuck School of Business, Bowdoin College
Background: Founder & President, Buffalo Ventures
Brian D'Amico, Managing Partner
e-mail: bdamico@summerstreetcapital.com
Education: BS, Finance, Cansius College
Background: Vice President, Buffalo Ventures
Jennifer Chalmers Balbach, Partner
e-mail: jbalbach@summerstreetcapital.com
Education: Harvard College; MBA, Amos Tuck School of Business
Background: Vice President, Buffalo Ventures; Management Consultant, Bain & Company
John Collins, Partner
Education: BA, Economics, Cornell University

Venture Capital & Private Equity Firms / Domestic Firms

Background: Investment Banking Analyst, Deutsche Bank's Leveraged Finance Group

1754 SUMMIT PARTNERS
222 Berkley Street
18th Floor
Boston, MA 02216

Phone: 617-824-1000
web: www.summitpartners.com

Mission Statement: Summit Partners provides growth equity for exceptional companies. Founded in 1984, Summit has raised more than $11 billion in capital and has provided growth equity, recapitalization and management buyout financing to more than 300 companies across a wide range of industries and geographies. The firm supports outstanding management teams that have self-financed their companies to market leadership. Summit Partners enhances the value of these companies through infrastructure development, executive and board recruiting, and strategic and operational advice. The firm also brings extensive experience in helping companies navigate the complex process of public offerings or strategic sales or mergers.

Geographic Preference: United States, Canada, Europe, Asia
Fund Size: $11 billion capital base
Founded: 1984
Average Investment: $25 million-$75 million
Minimum Investment: $5 million
Investment Criteria: Growth Equity, Recapitalizations, Management Buyouts
Industry Group Preference: Business Products & Services, Communication Technology, Communications, Consumer Products, Education, Energy, Financial Services, Healthcare, Life Sciences, Industrial Products, Internet, Information Services, Media, Entertainment, Semiconductors
Portfolio Companies: 3 Day Blinds, 360T Group, A+ Network, A10 Networks, ABILITY Network, Acacia Communications, Academic Management Services, Accedian Networks, Access Information Management, Active Voice, Actix, Acturis, AdvaCare, Advancce Health, Advance Medical, Advanced Cell Diagnotics, Aehr Text Systems, Aeryon Labs, Alert 360, Alpha Smart, AltoCom, Answers, ApoCell, Associa, Aurora Diagnostics, AVAST Software BV, AvePoint, Belkin International, Bigpoint GmbH, CareCentrix, Casa Systems, Central Security Group, Champion Windows, Clarabridge, Clearwater Analytics, Cloudmark, Commercial Defeasance, COMS Interactive, Continuum, Delphix, Empower RF Systems, FleetCor Technologies, Flow Traders BV, Focus Financial Partners, Fortegra Financial, Gainsight, Globe Wirelss, Heart to Heart Hospice, Help/Systems, Hiperos, Infor Global Solutions, JAMF Software, Logi Analytics, M/A-COM Technology Solutions Holdings, MEDITECH, Modernizing Medicine, Multifonds (IGEFI Group Sarl), National Veterinary Associates, Nomacorc, Paris Town, Peak Well Systems, PeerApp, PeopleAdmin, Philz Coffee, Progressive Finance, RiskIQ, Rocket Fuel, RuffaloCODY, Salient Partners, Solid State Equipment, Solutionreach, Sparta Systems, Systems Maintenance Services, Telerik, TeleSign Holdings, Tivoli Audio, Trident University International, Ubiquiti Networks, Vente-Privee, Visier, WebAction, Welltec International, Winshuttle Holdings, Wowza Media Systems, Zenoss

Other Locations:
200 Middlefield Road
Suite 200
Menlo Park, CA 94025
Phone: 650-321-1166

11-12 Hanover Square
London W1S 1JJ
United Kingdom
Phone: 44-02076597500

Summit Luxembourg S.a.r.l.
33, rue du Puits Romain
Bertange L-8070
Luxembourg
Phone: 352-2648-0048 **Fax:** 352-2736-5159

Key Executives:
John R Carroll, Managing Director
617-824-1052
e-mail: john@summitpartners.com
Education: AB, Dartmouth College; MM, Kellogg School of Management, Northwestern University
Background: Bain & Company; BayBank
Directorships: Associa, Cetero Research, ComPsych, FleetCor Technologies, Fortegra Financial

Matthias G Allgaier, Managing Director
44-0-20-7659-7505
e-mail: mallgaier@summitpartners.com
Education: MBA, Mannheim University; PhD, Business Administration, Karl Franzens University
Background: Managing Director, H.I.G. Capital Europe; Apax Partners, General Atlantic Partners
Directorships: Elatec, Market Logic, Signavio, Zahneins

David W Averett, Managing Director, Peak Performance Group
617-824-1021
e-mail: daverett@summitpartners.com
Education: BS, US Military Academy at West Point; MBA, Goizueta Business School, Emory University
Directorships: MedOptions, NetBrain Technologies, Parts Town

Darren M Black, Managing Director
617-824-1011
e-mail: dblack@summitpartners.com
Education: AB, Harvard College; MBA, Wharton School
Background: Managing Partner, SV Life Sciences
Directorships: ABILITY Network, Advance Health, DMG Practice Management Solutions, HealthSun, Paradigm Outcomes, PharmScript, Sound Physicians

Andrew J Collins, Managing Director
650-614-6652
e-mail: acollins@summitpartners.com
Education: BS, Finance, Miami University
Background: Banc of America Securities; ABN Amro Financial Services
Directorships: Arista, Delphix, Gainsight, InfoArmor, NetWitness, Podium, Reverb.com, RiskIQ, Striim, Uber, Ubiquiti, Wildfire Interactive, Winshuttle, Wowza Media Systems

Peter Y Chung, Managing Director & CEO
650-614-6701
e-mail: pchung@summitpartners.com
Education: AB, Harvard University; MBA, Stanford University
Background: Goldman, Sachs & Company; Patagonia
Directorships: Coast Asset Management, Empower RF Systems, M/A-COM Technology Solutions Holdings, Trident University International (TUI), Ubiquiti Networks

Scott C Collins, Managing Director & COO
617-824-1012
Education: AB, Harvard University; JD, Harvard Law School
Background: McKinsey and Company; US Department of Justice; The White House
Directorships: B&W TEK, My Dentist Holdings, NetWitness, OB Hospitalist Group

Christopher J Dean, Managing Director
617-824-1067
e-mail: cdean@summitpartners.com
Education: BA, University of Notre Dame; MBA, Harvard Business School
Background: Morgan Stanley; JH Whitney & Co; Sun Microsystems
Directorships: Aurora Diagnostics, Champion Windows, Commercial Defeasance, Focus Financial Partners, Salient Partners, Sun Trading

Craig D Frances MD, Managing Director
650-614-6602
e-mail: cfrances@summitpartners.com

Education: BA, Cornell University; MD, Cornell University Medical College
Background: Chief Medical Resident, University of California, San Francisco
Directorships: HealthCare Partners, National Veterinary Associates

Robin W Devereux, Managing Director & CAO
617-824-1606
e-mail: rdevereux@summitpartners.com
Education: BS, Accounting, Northeastern University
Background: National Development; Property Capital Trust; RM Bradley & Co.; Deloitte & Touche

Leonard C Ferrington, Managing Director
650-614-6643
e-mail: lferrington@summitpartners.com
Education: BS, Accounting, Leventhal School of Accounting, University of Southern California
Background: Celerity Partners; Baxter Healthcare International
Directorships: A10 Networks, Access Information Management, Aeryon Labs, Ascentis, Heald College, Ruffalo Noel Levitz, Smartsheet, Teaching Strategies, Trident University Int'l, Ubiquiti

Greg S Goldfarb, Managing Director
650-614-6653
e-mail: ggoldfarb@summitpartners.com
Education: AB, Harvard University
Directorships: Clearwater Analytics, Cloudmark, Gainsight, IntelliChem, Jamf, LiveOffice, onXmaps, PatSnap, Philz Coffee, ProClarity Corp., RiskIQ, Rocket Fuel, TeleSign, Tiny Prints, Visier

Thomas H Jennings, Managing Director
617-824-1053
e-mail: tj@summitpartners.com
Education: AB, Boston College
Background: Andersen Consulting (now Accenture)
Directorships: Accedian Networks, ApoCell, AvePoint, Hiperos, NameMedia, Teleik

Mark A deLaar, Managing Director
617-824-1027
e-mail: mdelaar@summitpartners.com
Education: BS, United States Military Academy; MBA, MIT Sloan School of Management
Background: DB Alex Brown, Banc of America Securities & Public Financial Management, United States Army
Directorships: IMMCO Diagnostics, My Dentist Holdings, OB Hospitalist Group

Matthew G Hamilton, Managing Director
617-824-1073
e-mail: mhamilton@summitpartners.com
Education: BA, Economics, Colby College
Directorships: Flow Traders, Focus Financial Partners, Invoice Cloud, Patriot Growth Insurance Services, Progressive Finance, Salient Partners, Telerik, Vestmark

Jay D Pauley, Managing Director
617-824-1070
e-mail: jpauley@summitpartners.com
Education: BS, Ohio State University; MBA, Wharton School
Background: Apax Partners; GE Capital
Directorships: Alert 360, FineLine Technologies, Grand Design RV, Harvey Performance Co., Parts Town, Vivint, Vivint Solar

Alexander D Whittemore, Managing Director, Capital Markets
617-824-1025
e-mail: awhittemore@summitpartners.com
Education: BA, Carleton College; MBA, University of Virginia Darden School
Background: Morgan Stanley, Chase Manhattan Corporation, Chemical Banking Corporation

Peter L Rottier, Managing Director
650-614-6624
e-mail: prottier@summitpartners.com
Education: BS, Carlson School of Management, University of Minnesota; MBA, Stanford Grad. School of Business
Background: KSL Capital Partners; Stone Arch Capital; RBC Capital Markets
Directorships: Answers, Ascentis, Healthline Media, HelpSystems, Infor, ISH, MercuryGate, Perforce Software, Rocket Fuel, Salient Partners, Snap Fitness, Solid State Equipment, Trintech

Hans Sikkens, Managing Director & Head, Europe
44-0-20-7659-7500
e-mail: hsikkens@summitpartners.com
Education: BS, MSc, University of Groningen; MSc, CERAM Graduate School of Management & Technology
Background: Scotia Capital; IBM Corporation
Directorships: 360T Group, Acturis, Avast, Darktrace, Flow Traders, Masternaut, Multifonds, OnRobot, RELEX Solutions, SafeBoot, Siteimprove, Syncron, Welltec International

Christian R Strain, Managing Director
44-0-20-7659-7504
e-mail: cstrain@summitpartners.com
Education: BA, Yale University; MBA, Harvard Business School
Background: Apax Partners
Directorships: Normec, Ogone, Peak Well Systems, Sézane, Sipartech, vente-privee.com, Westwing Group

Thomas M Tarnowski, Managing Director
44-0-20-7659-7503
e-mail: ttarnowski@summitpartners.com
Education: BBA, Valdosta State University; MBA, Harvard Business School
Background: Triton; Credit Suisse First Boston; Citigroup
Directorships: Advance Medical, DentalPro, Independent Vetcare, zahneins

1755 SUN CAPITAL PARTNERS
5200 Town Center Circle
4th Floor
Boca Raton, FL 33486

Phone: 561-394-0550
web: www.suncappart.com

Mission Statement: Our mission is consistent, top decile returns for our LPs, to protect and enhance our reputation, continued growth & improvement, to provide outstanding people with great careers, and allow our stakeholder partners to share in our success.

Founded: 1995
Investment Criteria: Control Equity Investments, Leveraged Buyouts, Bank Debt, Trade Claims, Seller Notes, High Yield Securities
Industry Group Preference: Automotive, Business Products & Services, Distribution, Flexible Packaging, Manufacturing, Natural Resources, Restaurants, Retailing, Technology, Transportation, Food & Beverage, Financial Services, Healthcare, Media, Communications
Portfolio Companies: Aclara, ADTI, AlbéA, America Golf, American Rec, Ames, Arrow Tru-Line. Bar Louie, Bonmarché, Boston Market, BTX Group, Bundy Refrigeration, BWGS, C&K, Clear Choice, Coveris, Creekstone Farms, Demilec, Dreams, ELIX Polymers, Esim Chemicals, Famosa, Fazoli's, FFO Home, Flabeg, Flamingo Horticulture, Flavor1, Flexitech, Franchise, Freshpak, Friendly's Garden Fresh Restaurant Corp., Gem Shopping Network, Gordmans, Hanna Anderson, Heartland, Hickory Farms, Horizon Services, Hweden, Innocor, Jacques Vert Group, Johnny Rockets, Kellwood Company, Kraco, La Place, Lexington Home Brands, LOUD Technologies, Marsh, NextPharma, NFP Automotive, O&S Doors, PaperWorks, Parker, PEMCO, Perfect Timing, Performance Fibers, Point Blank Enterprises, Polestar, Pop Displays, Rebecca Taylor, Restaurants Unlimited, Robertshaw, Rowe, S&N Communications, Scotch & Soda, Sofa Carpet Specialist, Sharps, Shopko, Smokey Bones, Spectralink, Stake Center,

Venture Capital & Private Equity Firms / Domestic Firms

Stone Point Materials, The Limited, Tier One Relocations, True, Trulite, Unico, V&D, Vari-Form, VPS, Vince, Windsor

Other Locations:
11111 Santa Monica Blvd
Suite 1050
Los Angeles, CA 90025
Phone: 310-473-1116

100 Park Avenue
Suite 2900
New York, NY 10017
Phone: 212-588-9156

Sun European Partners LLP
2 Park St.
1st Floor
London W1K 2HX
United Kingdom
Phone: 44-0-207-318-1100

Sun Capital Partners Sourcing LLC
Block A, World Finance Center
4003 Shennan East Road
Luohu District, Shenzhen 518001
China
Phone: 86-75525981628

Key Executives:
Rodger R Krouse, Co-CEO
Education: BS, Economics, The Wharton School
Background: Senior Vice President, Lehman Brothers
Marc J Leder, Co-CEO
Education: BS, Economics, The Wharton School
Background: Senior Vice President, Lehman Brothers
M Steven Liff, Senior Managing Director
Background: NationsBank; Bank of America Commercial Finance
Bruce Roberson, Senior Managing Director
Tim Stubbs, Senior Managing Director
Education: BA, Oxford University; MBA, London Business School
Background: Sapa Group
C Deryl Couch, Managing Director & General Counsel
Education: BA, Political Science, Furman University; JD, Cornell Law School
Background: White & Case, Partner, Greenberg Traurig
Scott W Edwards, Managing Director
Education: BS, Finance, Georgetown University; MBA, Tuck School of Business
Background: Principal, Henderson Private Capital; Associte, GE Equity
Matthew N Garff, Managing Director
Education: BS, Finance, University of Utah; MBA, Finance, University of Chicago
Background: The Carlyle Group, KSL Fairways
Aaron P Wolfe, Managing Director
Education: BA, Economics, University of Virginia
Background: Harris Williams & Co.
Paul Daccus, Managing Director
Education: Dundee University
Background: Director, Deloitte & Touche; Arthur Andersen
Kevin J Calhoun, Managing Director & CFO
Education: BS, Accounting, University of Florida
Background: Ernst & Young; Chief Financial Officer, Atlas Companies

1756 SUN MOUNTAIN CAPITAL
527 Don Gasper Avenue
Santa Fe, NM 87505

Phone: 505-780-4218
e-mail: info@sunmountaincapital.com
web: sunmountaincapital.com

Mission Statement: A private equity and venture capital investment firm that provides fund investment advisory services for public and private entities as well as manages direct investment funds.
Geographic Preference: Rocky Mountain & Southwest Regions
Fund Size: $500 million
Founded: 2006
Average Investment: $300, 000 - $10 million
Investment Criteria: Venture Capital, Mezzanine Debt, Growth Equity
Industry Group Preference: Diversified
Key Executives:
Brian Birk, Managing Partner
Education: BS, Economics, Carleton College; MBA, Kellogg School of Management
Background: VP & Director, Fort Washington Capital Partners; Founder, MetaWeb
Directorships: Aspen Avionics, American Clay, Exagen Diagnostics, Lumidigm, Puente Partners
Sally Corning, Partner
Education: BSBA, Finance, Georgetown University; MBA, Columbia University Graduate School of Business
Background: Investment Banking, Dean Witter Reynolds; Morgan Stanley; Credit Suisse First Boston
Directorships: nanoMR
Lee Rand, Partner
Education: BA, Computer Science & Mathematics, Cornell University; MBA, Harvard Business School
Background: Founder, Knogee; Ernst & Young
Directorships: Skorpios Technologies, JackRabbit Systems

1757 SUNBRIDGE PARTNERS
3659 Green Road
Suite 100
Beachwood, OH 44122

Phone: 216-360-0151
web: www.sunbridgepartners.com

Mission Statement: To make a difference with entrepreneurs, by sharing their vision to change the world.
Geographic Preference: United States, Japan
Investment Criteria: Early-Stage
Industry Group Preference: Information Technology, SaaS, Cloud Computing, Wireless, Open Source, Clean Technology, Enterprise Software, Digital Media & Marketing, Semiconductors, Business Products & Services
Portfolio Companies: Accela Technology, Alien Technology, AucSale, Avec Lab, BeTrend, Bloom Energy, Blue Spark Technologies, bydsign, Class Technology, Concur Japan, e-Medical System, FAOPEN, FiBest, Fun-Life, G-Mode, GaiaX, Hamster, Horizon Digital Enterprise, istyle, ITMedia, LT Solutions, MacroMill, Miracle Linux, Net Asia, New IT Venture, OKWave, Roonets, RouteLambda, Salesforce Japan, Salesforce.com, Shicoh Engineering, SilkRoad Japan, Smarts Japan, VistaPoint Technology, Yap, Zipit Wireless

Other Locations:
179 Jefferson Drive
Menlo Park, CA 94025
Phone: 650-353-5401

11f, JR Ebisu Building
1-5-5 Minami, Ebisu
Shibuya-ku
Tokyo 150-0022
Japan

222 South Church Street
Suite 100
Charlotte, NC 28202
Phone: 704-443-8369

Key Executives:
Allen Miner, Founder/General Partner
Education: Computer Science, Asian Studies, Brigham Young University

Venture Capital & Private Equity Firms / Domestic Firms

Background: CEO, SunBridge Corporation; Oracle Corporation; Founder, Oracle Japan
Directorships: Salesforce Japan
John Gannon, Founder/General Partner
Education: BS, Aerospace Engineering, Penn State University; MBA, University of Chicago
Background: Co-Founder, Equitek Capital; Engineer, General Electric Astro-Space Division; Associate, Merrill Lynch; SVP, NationsBank
Directorships: Embedded Planet, Blue Spark Technologies
Ken Ehrhart, Founder/General Partner
Education: University of California, Berkeley
Background: Co-Founder, Equitek Capital; Director of Research, Forbes' Gilder Technology Report; Founder, E-Consulting
Directorships: Alien Technology, NITV
Paul Grim, Founder/General Partner
Education: BSc, Mechanical Engineering, MIT; MBA, MIT Sloan School of Management
Background: Co-Founder, Equitek Capital; Gemini Consulting; Coopers & Lybrand
Directorships: Zipit Wireless, Yap

1758 SUNRISE CAPITAL PARTNERS
16950 Via de Santa Fe
Suite 5060-153
Rancho Santa Fe, CA 92067

Phone: 858-259-8911
e-mail: info@sunrisecapital.com
web: www.sunrisecapital.com

Mission Statement: Sunrise Capital Partners is a Systematic Global macro trading firm found in 1980. Sunrise brings an informed, long-term perspective, an adaptive and evolutionary research platform and responsive client-focused delivery to investors seeking the best opportunities in today's global financial markets. For more than 30 years, Sunrise has followed a thorough, methodical and highly risk-attuned course in developing and applying dynamic insights and innovations.

Key Executives:
Rick Slaughter, Founding Partner
Education: B.S. Finance San Diego State University, Systems Management University of Southern California
Background: Founder of Commodity Monitors, Inc.
Jason Gerlach, Managing Partner/CEO
Education: M.A. Public Policy Analysis and Public Administration University of Wisconsin; B.A. Government Cornell University
Background: Attorney with Hale and Dorr LLP and Howard Rice Nemerovski Canady Falk & Rabkin.

1759 SUPPLY CHAIN VENTURES
Boston, MA

Phone: 207-286-6464
e-mail: dave@supplychainventure.com
web: supplychainventure.com

Mission Statement: Invests in marketing, sales, and supply chain innovators.
Industry Group Preference: Manufacturing, Marketing, Media, Robotics, Industry
Portfolio Companies: ActualMeds, Blank Label, Bow & Drape, CabinetM, Cohealo, Crimson Hexagon, Descartes Systems Group, Foxtrot, Jebbit, LevaData, Little Passports, Llamasoft, Logistics Marketplace, NBD, NextShift Robotics, Paradigm4, Placester, Resilinc, Sandymount Technologies, Shipmonk, SupplyAI, Supply Shift, Transporeon, Work Truck Solutions

Key Executives:
David L. Anderson, Managing General Partner
Education: BA, University of Connecticut; PhD, Boston College
Background: Managing Partner of Supply Chain Consulting, Accenture; VP of Logistics Consulting, Temple Barker & Sloane Inc.; VP, Data Resources Inc.
Directorships: Placester; NextShift Robotics; NBD Nanotechnology
Dan Dershem, General Partner
Directorships: Transplace; Transporeon; Llamasoft

1760 SUSA VENTURES
Mission District
San Francisco, CA

web: susaventures.com

Mission Statement: Seeks to invest in tech-based companies with a focus on proprietary data.
Founded: 2013
Investment Criteria: Seed
Industry Group Preference: Big Data, Technology, Consumer, Industry, Virtual Reality, Artificial Intelligence
Portfolio Companies: AMI, Andela, Aquera, Avro Life Science, Bright, Casetext, Chatdesk, Clutch, Cortex, CrowdAI, Drivezy.com, Elliot, Expanse, Flexport, Fourpost, Fuzzbuzz, Guilded, Hodinkee, Honeybee, Human Interest, Humble Dot, HYAS, Interviewing.io, Intricately, Juvena Therapeutics, LendUp, Locale, Lyst, Mashgin, Merit, Modsy, Mux, MycoWorks, Naborly, Namo Media, Newfront, Outlier, Pachyderm, Parachute, People Data Labs, Percolata, Periscope, Persephone Biome, Pex, Plan, PolicyGenius, Rigetti, Roam, Robin Care, Robinhood, Rockbot, RunaHR, Scalyr, Scope AR, SimpleLegal, Smile Identity, Spring Discovery, Stedi, Stord, Sundae, TigerGraph, Tortuga AgTech, Treasury Prime, TrendMD, Troops, Union Crate, VeriSIM Life, Viz, Wurb, Whisper, WorkRamp

Key Executives:
Chad Byers, Co-Founder/General Partner
Education: BA, Environmental Science, University of Colorado
Directorships: Robinhood; Flexport
Leo Polovets, Partner
Education: BS, California Institute of Technology
Background: Software Engineer, LinkedIn; Software Engineer, Google; Sr. Software Engineer, Factual; Angel Investor
Seth Berman, General Partner
Education: BS, University of Colorado
Background: VP of Strategic Marketing, Richmont; Angel Investor
Natalie Fleming Arora, Head of Operations
Education: BA, Arizona State University
Background: Director of Partnerships, JUST; Director of Business Development, Juicero

1761 SUSQUEHANNA GROWTH EQUITY
401 City Avenue
Bala Cynwyd, PA 19004

Phone: 610-617-2600
e-mail: info@sgep.com
web: www.sgep.com

Mission Statement: SGE is the US-based private equity arm of The Susquehanna International Group of Companies (SIG), a global financial institution still owned and operated by several of its founders. The culture they established drives our management-centric approach to private equity. We support operators, not run their businesses. Working behind the scenes, we reach new customers, introduce key partnerships, and recruit executive talent. We are open to a wide variety of transaction structures and are not subject to the vagaries of the private equity fundraising cycle.

Geographic Preference: North America, Europe, Israel
Average Investment: $5 - $50 million
Investment Criteria: Growth Capital, Buyouts, Recapitalizations, Divestitures, Acquisition Financing
Industry Group Preference: SaaS, E-Commerce & Manufacturing, Financial Services, Internet

Venture Capital & Private Equity Firms / Domestic Firms

Portfolio Companies: BoomTown, B-Stock Solutions, CallApp, Clearleap, Credit Karma, ETF Securities, Global Tranz, HMP, iCims, JK Group, MMIT, Netformx, Offers.com, Payoneer, PaySimple, Skybox Security, The Logic Group, Zyme

Key Executives:
  Scott Feldmen, Director
  e-mail: scott.feldman@sgep.com
  Education: BS, Finance, Boston College
  Background: Co-Founder, Superior Street Capital Markets
  Directorships: Credit Karma, HMP Communications, iCIMS, JK Group, MMIT
  Amir Goldman, Director
  e-mail: amir.goldman@sgep.com
  Education: BS, Economics, University of Pennsylvania; MBA, Harvard Business School
  Background: TL Ventures, BRM Capital
  Directorships: iCIMS, JK Group, MMIT, Netformx, PaySimple, Zyme
  Jonathan Klahr, Director
  e-mail: jonathan.klahr@sgep.com
  Education: BA, War Studies, Kings College; MBA, Hebrew University
  Background: BRM Capital
  Directorships: iCIMS, Netformx, Offers.com, Skybox, The Logic Group, Versafe

1762 SUTTER HILL VENTURES
755 Page Mill Road
Suite A-200
Palo Alto, CA 94304

web: www.shv.com

Mission Statement: We invest in technology based start-ups that pioneer important products/services and devote our time, money and expertise to building these companies into industry leaders.

Fund Size: $200 million
Founded: 1962
Average Investment: $100,000 - $5 million
Minimum Investment: $100,000
Investment Criteria: Seed, startup, First-stage, Second-stage, Management buy-out
Industry Group Preference: Biotechnology, Computer Related, Education, High Technology, Medical & Health Related
Portfolio Companies: @Mobile.com, AAC Acoustic, ACACIA Venture Partners, Acceleron Pharma, Actiance, AkaRx, Aksys, AllBusiness, Alteon WebSystems, AmberPoint, Amerigroup Real Solutions, Ameritox, Amira, Amylin, Apollo Computers, Artisan Partners, Aspect Medical Systems, Avant!, Avid, Barrx Medical, Benu, Biovest International, Bix, Blue Ridge Pharmaceuticals, Boxer, Brierley + Partners, BroadVision, C3 Energy, Cardica, Celeritek, Chengwei Capital, Clarus, Closedloop Solutions, Clover, Connection Engine, Consorte Media, Copper Mountain, COR, Corcept Therapeutics, Corixa, Costanoa Venture Capital, Data Domain, DemandBase, Digidesign, Digital Chocolate, Dionex, Drais, Drobo, e-Rewards, Farecast, FeedBurner, Forte Tools, Foundation DB, Free Monee, Glassdoor.com, GLMX, Golden Gate Capital, Grain Communications Group, Grand Junction, Guardian Analytics, Helion, Horizon Pharma, Hybritech, Idexx, iDun, Infinera, Inflection, InQuira, Instart Logic, Intacct, Ideas Revenue Organization, ISIS, Interventional Technologies, Kalypto Medical, Kineto Wireless, Legato, Lifescan, LifeSize, Line 6, Linear Technology, LinkSmart, LSI Logic, Lucky, Lynk, Makena Capital, Mattersight, Mentor Graphics, Merced Systems, Metronome Therapeutics, Mips, Molecular Devices, MyNewPlace, Network Appliance, Networks in Motion, Neurex, Nexxo, Nimsoft, NuGen, nVidia, Omnicell, OnStream Networks, OpenDNS, Pacific Biosciences, Palm, PINC Solutions, Platfora, PMC-Sierra, Portola, Primary Access, PureStorage, Pyxis, QuinStreet, Redseal Systems, Restoration Robotics, Return Path, Right Hemisphere, Room 77 Hotel Search, Roxro, Ruckus Wireless, Satmetrix, Shutterfly, SILA, Silverrail, SpinMedia, StreetLine, Sumologic, Swift Financial, Symmetricom, Tellabs, Therma-Wave, Threshold Pharmaceuticals, TOA Technologies, Tomfoolery, Tower Cloud, Venture TDF China, Verinata Health, Vical, Virage, Virobay, Vitria, Vivace Networks, Wildcard Systems, Xoft, Yaolan, Yext, Youku

Key Executives:
  David L Anderson, Managing Director
  Education: BS Electrical Engineering, MIT; MBA, Harvard University
  Background: Watkins-Johnson; Past Board Seats: Palm Computing/Appollo Computing/Neurex/Hybritech; Responsible for start-up funding for LSI Logic/Quantum Corporation/Mentor Graphics/Linear Technology
  Directorships: Dionex, Brierley & Partners, E-Rewards, Concept Shopping
  Jeff Bird, Limited Partner
  Education: Biology Degree, Stanford; PhD Cancer Biology/MD, Stanford Medical School
  Background: Senior Vice President, Gilead Sciences
  Directorships: Artemis Health, Drais Pharmaceuticals, Horizon Therapeutics, MacuSight, NuGen Technologies, Portola Pharmaceuticals, Restoration Robotics, Roxro Pharma, Threshhold Pharma
  Mike Speiser, Managing Director
  Education: BA, University of Arizona; MBA, Harvard Business School
  Background: Vice President, Community Products, Yahoo!; President & CEO, Bix; Vice President, Symantec; Vice President, Product Management, Veritas; Co-Founder, Epinions.com
  James N White, Limited Partner
  e-mail: jwhite@shv.com
  Education: BS, Industrial Engineering, Northwestern University; MBA, Harvard University
  Background: Vice President, Marketing, Macromedia; Vice President, Marketing, Silicon Graphics; Hewlett-Packard
  Directorships: Digital Chocolate, Glassdoor.com, Inquira, Object Reservoir, Right Hemisphere, Satmetrix, Shutterfly, SilverRail Technologies, Streetline Networks, WebVisible

1763 SV ANGEL
San Francisco, CA 94102

web: svangel.com

Mission Statement: Angel investor in San Francisco offers advice on business development, financing and M&A.

Geographic Preference: California
Fund Size: $20 million
Investment Criteria: Seed-Stage, Early-Stage
Industry Group Preference: Information Technology, E-Commerce & Manufacturing, Consumer Internet, Gaming, Enterprise Software, Social Media
Portfolio Companies: Airbnb, Amplitude, Coinbase, Databricks, DoorDash, Dropbox, Gusto, Headspace, Instacart, Opendoor, Pagerduty, Pinterest, Slack, Square Space, TransferWise, Twilio, Twitch, Warby Parker

Key Executives:
  Ron Conway, Founder & Co-Managing Partner
  Education: BS, Political Science, San Jose State University
  Background: National Semiconductor Corporation, Altos Computer Systems, Personal Training Systems
  Topher Conway, Co-Managing Partner
  Education: UCLA
  Background: eCost; EQAL
  Brian Pokorny, Advisor
  Education: Santa Clara University
  Background: Airbnb

Venture Capital & Private Equity Firms / Domestic Firms

Kevin Carter, Advisor
Education: Santa Clara University
Background: Silicon Valley Bank
Robert Pollak, Advisor
Education: University of Virginia
Background: Morgan Stanley

1764 SV HEALTH INVESTORS
One Boston Place
201 Washington St.
Suite 3900
Boston, MA 02108

Phone: 617-367-8100 Fax: 617-367-1590
web: svhealthinvestors.com

Mission Statement: SV Health Investors seeks to transform healthcare by investing in entrepreneurs who create disruptive companies and treatments.

Industry Group Preference: Biotechnology, Medical Devices, Healthcare, Digital Health
Portfolio Companies: AcuFocus, Adimab, AeroCare, Aligned Teleheath, Arsanis, Artios, Autifony, Avitide, Avrobio, BardyDx, Bicycle Therapeutics, CardioFocus, Catabasis, Centauri Health Solutions, Cibiem, CSA Medical, EBR Systems, Endotronix, Evidation, Deciphera, Jet Health, Leiters, Nordic, Ocular Therapeutix, Remita Health, ReShape, Schweiger Dermatology Group, Solsys Medical, Spectrum, Stim Wave, Sun Behavioural Health, Urgent Team, US Renal Care

Other Locations:
71 Kingsway
London WC2B 6ST
United Kingdom
Phone: 44-20-7421-7070 Fax: 44-20-7421-7077

Key Executives:
Houman Ashrafian, Managing Partner, Biotechnology
Education: University of Cambridge; BM BCh, DPhil, University of Oxford
Background: Co-Founder, Cardiac Report, Heart Metabolics; VP, Clinical Science Group, UCB Pharma
Directorships: Ervaxx, Sitryx
Michael Balmuth, Managing Partner, Healthcare
Education: AB, Dartmouth College; MBA, Harvard Business School
Background: General Partner, Summit Partners; General Partner, Edison Parters
Directorships: Aerocare, Aligned Telehealth, Centauri Health Solutions, Evidation, Ximedica
Kate Bingham, Managing Partner, Biotechnology
Education: First Class Degree, Biochemistry, Oxford University; MBA, Harvard Business School
Background: Vertex Pharmaceuticals; Monitor Company
Directorships: Artios, Autifony, Bicycle, Calchan, Delenex, Arvaxxm KalVista, Karus, Pulmocide, Sitryx, TopiVert, Vantia, VHsquared, Zarodex
Tom Flynn, Managing Partner, Healthcare
Education: AB, Economics, Holy Cross College; MBA, Harvard Business School
Background: Partner, Ferrer Freeman & Co.; GE Capital; Prudential Investment Corporation
Directorships: AeroCare, Jet Health, Leiters, Nordic, Remita Health, Schweiger Dermatology Group, Sun Behavioural Health, UrgentTeam
Paul LaViolette, COO & Managing Partner, Medical Devices
Education: BA, Psychology, Fairfield University; MBA, Boston College
Background: COO, Boston Scientific; CR Bard; Kendall
Directorships: BardyDx, CardioFocus, Cibiem, CSA Medical, EBR Systems, Endotronix, Soffio Medical, Solsys Medical, Stim Wave, TransEnterix, ValenTx, Ximedica
Mike Ross, Managing Partner, Biotechnology
Education: AB, Dartmouth College; PhD, Caltech; Post-Doctoral Fellowship, Harvard
Background: Genentech; Managing Partner, Didyma
Directorships: Adimab, Alba, Alinea, Archemix, Arsanis, Avitide, AvroBio, Catabasis, Deciphera, Juvaris, NKTT, Pionyr, Ribometrix, Sutro Biopharma, Thesan Pharmaceuticals

1765 SV INVESTMENT PARTNERS
1700 East Putnam Avenue
Greenwich, CT 06870

Phone: 212-735-0700 Fax: 203-990-0714
e-mail: nsomers@svip.com
web: www.svip.com

Mission Statement: SV Investment Partners, formerly known as Schroder Ventures US, is a private equity firm specializing in buyouts and buildups of business services companies.

Geographic Preference: United States
Fund Size: $270 million
Founded: 1999
Average Investment: $25 million
Minimum Investment: $10 million
Investment Criteria: Later Stage
Industry Group Preference: Business Products & Services
Portfolio Companies: International Decision Systems

Other Locations:
500 West Putnam
Suite 400
Greenwich, CT 06830
Phone: 203-987-3021 Fax: 203-738-1138

Key Executives:
Nicholas Somers, Partner
212-735-0700
Fax: 212-735-0702
e-mail: nsomers@svip.com
Education: MBA, University of Chicago; BA, Washington University, St. Louis
Background: Founder/Partner, Greenwich Street Capital Partners; Travelers; Morgan Stanley
Directorships: Mesa Communications, ThoughtWorks, Market Place Media
Philip Cole, Principal
Education: BA, Kingston University
Background: CFO, PrecisionIR
Will Sale, Vice President
Education: BA, Yale University
Background: Investment Banking Analyst, Bank of America Merrill Lynch

1766 SVB CAPITAL
3003 Tasman Drive
Santa Clara, CA 95054

web: www.svb.com/gaining-traction/capital-strategies-solutions

Mission Statement: SVB Capital's deep industry knowledge and multi-faceted industry relationships provide us with extensive access to and knowledge of private equity at both the firm and portfolio company levels. SVB Capital's investment expertise allows us to leverage this unrivaled access, insight and proprietary deal flow to create a unique competitive advantage and superior investment selection ability.

Geographic Preference: United States
Fund Size: $1 Billion
Founded: 1983
Average Investment: $200,000
Minimum Investment: $50,000
Industry Group Preference: Biotechnology, Communications, Electronic Technology, Information Technology, Medical, Software, Clean Technology, Hardware, Life Sciences, Internet
Portfolio Companies: Adore, AtlEn Opportunity, Brickwood NYC, CAMSIE Leasing, Card Compliant, Clinical Research Investments, iLight, Muzik, Orange Groves/OCP Holding

Venture Capital & Private Equity Firms / Domestic Firms

Company, Orbis Biosciences, Paradise Rentals, Ridgewood Energy Fund, SelectQuote, StoreFinancial, Spectrum Motors, The Wireless Stores, Worldwide Wireless

Key Executives:
Aaron Gershenberg, Managing Partner
Education: BA, Economics, Wesleyan University; MA, Finance, John F Kennedy School of Government, Harvard University
Background: FirstCorp; Investment Banking, Union Bank of California
Sulu Mamdani, Managing Partner
Education: BA, Applied Mathematics, Harvard College; MBA, Harvard Business School
Background: Co-founder of Mazu Networks, manager of venture capital investments at The Carlyle Group

1767 SVOBODA CAPITAL PARTNERS
One North Franklin Street
Suite 1500
Chicago, IL 60606

Phone: 312-267-8750 Fax: 312-267-6025
e-mail: info@svoco.com
web: www.svoco.com

Mission Statement: A private equity firm that invests in and helps build value-added distribution, business services and consumer products businesses.
Fund Size: $250 million
Average Investment: $10 - $25 million
Investment Criteria: Management Buyouts, Leveraged Recapitalizations, Growth Equity Investments
Industry Group Preference: Distribution, Business Products & Services, Consumer Products
Portfolio Companies: SWC Technology Partners, Reliable Parts, Blake & Pendleton, Strategic Marketing, MEI Labels Holdings, GPA, Monroe Engineering, DataBank, Applied Adhesives, Cape Electrical Supply, Border Construction Specialties

Key Executives:
John A Svoboda, Senior Managing Director
e-mail: jas@svoco.com
Education: BA, Williams College; MBA, Stanford Graduate School of Business
Background: Corporate Finance Department, William Blair & Company
Directorships: Glover Park Group, OPT Holdings, Cape Electrical Supply, GPA Holdings
Andrew B Albert, Managing Director
e-mail: aalbert@svoco.com
Education: BA, Washington University; MBA, University of Wisconsin
Background: CEO, Nashua Corporation; Chairman/CEO, Rittenhouse
Directorships: Border Construction Specialties, Forsythe Technologies, Transco

1768 SWAN & LEGEND VENTURES
P.O. Box 6247
Leesburg, VA 20178

web: www.swanandlegend.com

Mission Statement: Swan & Legend invests in tech-enabled consumer brands and the business-to-business companies that support them.
Industry Group Preference: Consumer Brands, Restaurants, Digital Commerce, Retail Services, Wellness
Portfolio Companies: Airbnb, Allegro Venture Partners, Anonymous Content, Bedrock, Beefsteak, Big Teams, Capital Sports Ventures, Cava, China Senior Care, Custom Ink, Duratap, Echo360, Evergreen Transport, Framebridge, Fyrfly, Glidr, Gwynnie Bee, Ideeli, José Andrés ThinkFoodGroup, Kind, La Lumière, MusiCapital, MyOwnMed, Noodle, Optoro, OrderGrove, Pinterest, Quad Learning, Revsite, Showfields, Soapbox, Social Radar, Square, Sugar23. SV Angel, Tango Card, Urbanstems, Veritonic, Wthn

Other Locations:
154 Grand St.
New York, NY 10013

Key Executives:
Fredrick D. Schaufeld, Co-Founder & Managing Director
Education: BA, Government, Lehigh University
Background: Partner, Monumental Sports and Entertainment; Founder, NEW Corp.
Directorships: Noodle, CustomInk, Frambridge, KIND Healthy Snacks, Quad Learning, José Andrés' ThinkFoodGroup, Cava, UrbanStems, DuraTap
Anthony Nader, Co-Founder & Managing Director
Education: John Carroll University; MBA Weatherhead School of Management at Case Western Reserve University
Background: Partner, Monumental Sports and Entertainment; Senior Management, NEW Corp.
Directorships: Cranemere Group; Optoro, BigTeams, DuraTap, KIND Healthy Snacks
David Strasser, Managing Director
Education: BS, Hotel Administration, Cornell University; MBA, Fuqua School of Business at Duke University
Background: Salomon Brothers; Citigroup; Bank of America Securities; Janney Montgomery Scott; Andor Capital
Directorships: Seeds of Peace

1769 SWANDER PACE CAPITAL
101 Mission Street
Suite 1900
San Francisco, CA 94105

Phone: 415-477-8500 Fax: 415-477-8510
e-mail: info@spcap.com
web: www.spcap.com

Mission Statement: Focuses on management-led buyouts, company recapitalizations, industry consolidation, changes of ownership, growth companies needing capital, turnarounds in select situations.
Fund Size: $600 million
Founded: 1996
Minimum Investment: $3 million
Investment Criteria: Second-Stage, LBO
Industry Group Preference: Consumer Products, Food & Beverage, Food Services, Retailing, Hardware, Health Related, Leisure, Sports, Consumer Services
Portfolio Companies: Kicking Horse Coffee, Lavo, Recochem, Frozen Specialties, Applegate, Branch Brook Holdings, Oregon Ice Cream, Clarion Brands, Aden & Anais, Incase Deigns, Kooba, Raj Manufacturing, Gilchrist & Soames, gloProfessional, Merrick Pet Care, Wholesome Pet Care, Bravo Sports

Other Locations:
550 Hills Drive
Suite 106
Bedminster, NJ 07921
Phone: 908-719-2322 Fax: 908-719-9311

81273 North Service Road East
Oakville, ON L6H 1A7
Canada
Phone: 416-573-6098

Andrew Richards, Co-Founder/CEO
e-mail: andrew@spcap.com
Education: AB Fine Arts, Harvard University; MBA, Harvard Business School
Background: VP, William E Simon & Sons; Investment Banker, PaineWebber
Directorships: Nonni's Food Company, Frozen Specialties, S T Specialty Foods

Venture Capital & Private Equity Firms / Domestic Firms

Mark Poff, Managing Director, San Francisco
Education: BA, University of California, Davis; MSc, London School of Economics
Background: Bain & Co; Consultant, LEK Consulting
Directorships: Bravo Sports, Incase Designs, Kooba, Fresh Food Concepts, Insight Pharmaceuticals, Lavo, Liberty Brand Products, Pineridge Bakery, Raj Manufacturing, ReNew Life Formulas
Corby Reese, Managing Director, New Jersey Office
Education: BA, Yale University; MBA, Harvard Business School
Background: BancBoston Capital
Directorships: Bravo Sports, Frozen Specialities, Ideal Snacks, Insight Pharmaceuticals Corporation, ReNew Life Formulas, Santa Cruz Nutritionals
C Morris Stout, Managing Director, San Francisco
Education: BA, Vanderbilt University; MBA, Stanford Business School
Background: Vice President, Lonbard Investments
Directorships: Gilchrist & Soames, Good Source Solutions, Insight Pharmaceuticals, Border Foods, International Fiber Corporation, Lavo, Prepared Meal Holdingds, Santa Cruz Nutritionals
Robert DesMarais, Managing Director
Education: BS, Michigan State University; MBA, Northwestern University
Background: Principal, Banc of America Secruties' Consumer & Retail Group
Directorships: Lavo, Marketfare Foods, Raj Manufacturing
Tyler Matlock, Managing Director
Education: BA, University of Wisconsin-Madison

1770 SWITCH VENTURES
San Francisco, CA

e-mail: pitch@switch.vc
web: www.switch.vc

Mission Statement: A venture capital fund seeking to invest in companies based in the software and internet sector.

Founded: 2016
Investment Criteria: Seed, Early Stage
Industry Group Preference: Software, Applications, IoT, Technology
Portfolio Companies: Aaptiv, Allay, Altostra, The Athletic, Audm, Bulk MRO, Coinbunble, Floravere, Goodpath, Instaread, Jupiter, Luxuery Presence, NewtonX, NextRequest, PolicyGenius, SketchDeck, Tolemi, Unbound

Key Executives:
Paul Arnold, Founder/Partner
Education: BS, University of Utah; JD, University of Michigan Law School
Background: Consultant, McKinsey & Co.; Senior Director, AppDirect; Founder/Partner, Arnold Capital

1771 SYCAMORE VENTURES
731 Alexander Road
Suite 303
Princeton, NJ 08540

Phone: 609-759-8888 Fax: 609-759-8900
web: www.sycaventures.com

Mission Statement: Sycamore Ventures is a team of dedicated investment professionals with a broad range of industry experiences in communication, software, and life sciences.

Geographic Preference: US, the greater China region, India
Fund Size: $550 Million
Founded: 1995
Average Investment: $10-25 Million
Minimum Investment: $5 Million
Industry Group Preference: Semiconductors, Telecommunications, Internet Technology, Software, Healthcare, Media, Financial Services, Networking, E-Commerce & Manufacturing, Biotechnology, Broadcasting

Portfolio Companies: Acer Group, ACM Research Corporation, Advanced Analogic Technologies, AirCell, Airspan Networks, Applied Optoelectronics, ASUSTek Computer, Avalent Technologies, BizLink Holdings, Brightcord Investment, CapMAC Holdings, Cardiva Medical, Cellink, Clear Technology, Corrigo, Co-Tech Copper Foil, C-Pro, DVN Holdings, eAccess, EASYLINK, Epitomics, Equity Broadcasting, Exclaim, FloNetwork, Global Sun Technology, Hayes Medical, HOLA Home Furnishing, Home Inns & Hotel Management, International Media Group, IPCore Tecnologies, Juno Online Services, Landune International, LogicVision, MAKO Surgical, Marketech International, Net263 Holdings, NWP Services, Ortodisc Technology, Ortega InfoSystems, OSA Technologies, Osteotech, Outlast Technologies, People's Motor International, Premier Pacific Pharmaceutical Industries, Ralink Technology, Redgate Media, RIM China Company, RxHope, Sakura Enterprises, Semiconductor Manufacturing International Corporation, Shin Kong Mitsukoshi Department Store, SOURCEBYNET, StemCyte, Taiwan IC Packaging, TeleNav, United Platform Technologies, Universal Media Group, Univision Technology, U-Systems, Wistron NeWeb, Xin Hua Media Coldings, Xylos, z-kat

Other Locations:
19925 Stevens Creek Boulevard
Cupertino, CA 95014-2358
Phone: 408-973-7861 Fax: 408-973-7261

3 Columbus Circle
Suite 1402
New York, NY 10019
Phone: 212-247-4590 x 5 Fax: 212-247-4801

Key Executives:
Stephen Chiao, Managing Partner
e-mail: sschiao@sycaventures.com
Education: Masters Degree in Electrical Engineering from Princeton University, and an MBA from the Wharton School at The University Pennsylvania
Background: Philips Electronics, RCA Corporation, AT&T Corporatio
Peter Gerry, Managing Partner
e-mail: pgerry@sycaventures.com
Kilin To, Managing Partner
e-mail: kto@sycaventures.com

1772 SYMMETRIC CAPITAL
950 Winter Street
Suite 2500
Waltham, MA 02451

Phone: 781-419-1100 Fax: 781-419-1101
web: www.symmetriccapital.com

Mission Statement: Symmetric Capital focuses on established businesses led by proven management teams, to create real partnerships to help them reach even greater success.

Geographic Preference: United States, Canada
Average Investment: $5 - $20 million
Investment Criteria: Growth-Stage, Expansion-Stage
Industry Group Preference: Business Products & Services, Consumer Products, Healthcare Services, Applied Technology, Industrial Products, Financial Services, Software
Portfolio Companies: Academic Management Services, Acurex, Air Serv, Appro Systems, Astech, Belkin, Biomedical Structures, BioRx, CBS Payroll Services, ChanTest, Cido, Complete Innovations, EMED, First Marketing, The Galtney Group, Gryphon Networks, Hemophelia Resources of America, Insperity, K-Tek, NewStar Financial, P&H Solutions, Pacer Electronics, Poorman-Douglas, Quote.com, Sanitors, School Imrpovement Network, Somero Enterprises, TekLinks

Key Executives:
Daniel K Doyle, Managing Partner
781-419-1120
e-mail: ddoyle@symmetriccapital.com
Education: AB, Economics, Harvard College

Venture Capital & Private Equity Firms / Domestic Firms

Background: Managing Partner, Shawmut Capital
Directorships: AirServ, Complete Innovations, Gryphon Networks
Rob Walsh, General Partner
e-mail: rwalsh@symmetriccapital.com
Education: BS, Yale University; MBA, Harvard Business School
Background: Principal, Texas Growth Fund

1773 SYNCOM VENTURE PARTNERS
4800 Hampden Lane
Suite 200
Bethesda, MD 20814

Phone: 301-608-3203 Fax: 301-608-3307
e-mail: info@syncom.com
web: www.syncom.com

Mission Statement: Syncom Venture Partners is aggressively focused on creating the next generation of market leaders within the rapidly growing sectors of digital media, mobile technology, and web based services.

Fund Size: $400 million
Founded: 1977
Average Investment: $5 - $15 million
Investment Criteria: Growth Stage
Industry Group Preference: Multimedia, License Communications, Digital Business Services
Portfolio Companies: AppTap, LikeList, Dub, Heatwave Interactive, Indoor Direct, Maya Entertainment Group, Outspark, Proclivity Systems, ShowUHow, Thought Equity Motion, V-ME Media, Voyages, WDT

Terry L. Jones, Managing Partner
Education: BS, Electrical Engineering, Trinity College; MS, Electrical Engineering, George Washington University; MBA, Harvard University Graduate School of Business Administration
Background: Co-Founder and Vice President, Klambere Savings and Loan; Senior Electrical Engineer, Westinghouse Aerospace and Litton Industries
Directorships: V-me Media, Weather Decisions, TV One
Kateri Jones, Analyst
Education: BA, English and Economics, Spelman College
Roy Kosuge, Principal
Education: BA, Harvard University
Background: Vice President of International Strategy and Operations, Faith Inc; Director of Business Development, Universal Music Group; Strategy Analyst, AT&t Broadband
Stanley T. Smith, Principal
Education: BA, History, Dartmouth College
Background: Director of Corporate Development, Yahoo!'s Search Marketing Group; Director of Mergers and Acquisitions, Overture Inc.; Vivendi Universal; Paine Webber; Merrill Lynch
Directorships: Alikelist; Heatwave Interactive; Outspark; Proclivity Systems
Herbert P. Wilkins, Jr., General Partner
Education: BS, Marketing, University of Maryland; MBA, F.W. Olin School of Business at Babson College
Background: IVT; SI-TV; TMX Interactive
Tyrone Wilson, Chief Financial Officer
Education: BBA, Temple University

1774 SYNERGY LIFE SCIENCE PARTNERS
PO Box 22489
San Francisco, CA 94122

Phone: 650-854-7155 Fax: 650-332-1581
web: www.synergylsp.com

Mission Statement: Focused on investing in private, early-stage medical device companies or emerging companies who are combining a medical device with a therapeutic payload.

Geographic Preference: United States
Investment Criteria: Early-Stage
Industry Group Preference: Life Sciences, Therapeutics, Medical Devices
Portfolio Companies: Aptus Endosystems, Inspire Medical Systems, iRhythm Technologies, Oraya Therapeutics, Synecor

Key Executives:
Richard Stack MD, Managing Director
e-mail: rstack@synergylsp.com
Background: President, Synecor; Professor Emeritus of Medicine in Cardiology, Duke University
Directorships: BaroSense
William Starling, Managing Director
e-mail: wstarling@synergylsp.com
Education: BS, University of North Carolina, Chapel Hill; MBA, University of Southern California
Background: CEO, Synecor; American Edwards Laboratories; Founding Management Team, Advanced Cardiovascular Systems; Vice President, Ventritex; President/CEO, Cardiac Pathways Corporation
Directorships: iRhythm Technologies
Mudit Jain PhD, Partner
e-mail: mjain@synergylsp.com
Education: BE, Electrical Engineering, Regional Engineering College; PhD, Biomedical Engineering, Duke University; MBA, Wharton School
Background: Executive Director, Johnson & Johnson Development Corporation; Chief Science Officer, Johnson & Johnson; Cardiac Rhythm Management Division, Guidant Corporation
Directorships: Inspire Medical Systems
Tracy Pappas, Chief Financial Officer
e-mail: tpappas@synergylsp.com
Education: BA, Economics, University of California, Berkeley; CPA
Background: CFO, Scale Venture Partners; CFO, Saints; KPMG

1775 SYNERGY VENTURES
545 Middlefield Road
Suite 205
Menlo Park, CA 94025

Phone: 650-322-3475
web: www.synergyventures.net

Mission Statement: Synergy Ventures invests in medical device companies in the United States.

Geographic Preference: United States
Fund Size: $25 million
Founded: 1996
Average Investment: $250,000 - $1 million
Minimum Investment: $250,000
Industry Group Preference: Medical Devices
Portfolio Companies: Breathe Technologies, C2 Therapeutics, Chestnut Medical, CV Ingenuity, Promethean Surgical Devices, RetroVascular, Spiracur, Uptake Medical

Key Executives:
Allan Johnston PhD, Co-Founder & Managing Director
Education: PhD, Bioinorganic Chemistry, University of Guelph
Background: Program Manager, Center for Medical Technology, SRI International
Directorships: Three Oaks Innovations
Robert Okun MIM, Co-Founder & Managing Director
Education: BA, Japanese, MA, International Management, American Graduate School of Management
Background: Director, Berkeley/NED Development Capital Limited

1776 SYNGENTA VENTURES
629 Davis Drive
Research Triangle Park
Durham, NC 27709

Phone: 919-226-7302
web: www.syngentaventures.com

Mission Statement: Syngenta Ventures, the venture capital arm of Syngenta, is seeking to indentify early stage companies with a strong technology base or new business model, or both, where our team of investment professionals, together with the support of our 26, 000 colleagues across the world, can help build valuable businesses benefitting both Syngenta and the investee company stakeholders.

Geographic Preference: North America, Europe, Asia, South America
Average Investment: $500,000 - $5 million
Investment Criteria: Early-Stage
Portfolio Companies: Agrinos, Agrivida, Biognosys, BioLeap, BoMill, Brandtone, Edenspace, EuroFem, Illumitex, Marrone Bio Innovations, Metabolon, Nemgenix, Population Genetics

Key Executives:
   Shiri Ailons, Head
   Education: MBA, Oxford Business School; LLB, Tel Aviv University
   Background: ADAMA Agricultural Solution
   Jason Gabriel, Managing Director
   Education: MBA, University of Virginia
   Background: Managing Director, Third Security LLC
   David Pierson, Managing Director
   Education: BS, United States Military Academy; MBA, Duke University
   Background: Lieutenant, 82nd Airborne Division, Carolina; Captain, 2nd Infantry Division, Korea; Eneral Partner, Intersouth Partners
   Michael Lee, Managing Director
   Education: BSc, PhD, University of Durham; MBA, RSM Erasmus, Rotterdam
   Background: Unilever
   Shubhang Shankar, Managing Director
   Education: Indian Institute of Technology, New Delhi; MBA, Indian Institute of Management, Ahmedabad
   Background: Management Consultant, Boston Consulting Group

1777 SYNTHESIS CAPITAL
184 High Street
4th Floor
Boston, MA 02110

Phone: 857-366-8456 Fax: 857-366-8466
web: www.synthesis.capital

Mission Statement: Synthesis Capital is a Boston-based firm led by a team of investment professionals who previously managed the healthcare venture practice within Advent International for over 14 years. Collectively, the Synthesis Capital Team has led or helped manage over 35 private equity and venture investments in biotechnology, medical device companies and healthcare services at all stages of development.

Geographic Preference: United States, Europe
Average Investment: $10 - $15 million
Investment Criteria: Growth Financing, Special Situations, Spin Outs
Industry Group Preference: Biotechnology, Medical Technology, Medical Devices, Healthcare Services, Healthcare Information Technology, Biopharmaceuticals
Portfolio Companies: Achillion Pharmaceuticals, Aegerion Pharmaceuticals, Alcala Farma, Ampla Pharmaceuticals, Anadys Pharmaceuticals, Anesiva, Array BioPharma, Artemis Pharmaceuticals, Astex Therapeutics, Cellzone, Crucell, Cubist Pharmaceuticals, CV Therapeutics, deCODE Genetics, Enanta Pharmaceuticals, Exelixis, GPC Biotech, ILEX Oncology, Nereus Pharmaceuticals, Pharming, Prexa Pharmaceuticals, Raptor Pharmaceuticals, ReVision Therapeutics, Sirion Therapeutics, Spear Therapeutics, Tecan, Telik, Trident Pharmaceuticals, Variagenics, Viatris

Key Executives:
   Jason Fisherman, Co-Founder
   Education: BA, Molecular Biophysics & Biochemistry, Yale University; MD, University of Pennsylvania; MBA, Wharton School
   Background: Managing Director, Advent International; National Cancer Institute
   Directorships: Achillion Pharmaceuticals, Ampla Pharmaceuticals, Cellzome, Nereus Pharmaceuticals, Prexa Pharmaceuticals, Spear Therapeutics
   Charles Cohen, Co-Founder
   Education: BA, University of New York, Buffalo; PhD, New York University School of Medicine; Post Doctoral Fellowship, University of Virginia
   Background: Partner, Advent International; Co-Founder, Creative BioMolecules
   Directorships: Ampla Pharmaceuticals, Cellzome, Exelixis, Prexa Pharmaceuticals, Trident Pharmaceuticals, ReVision Therapeutics, Sirion Therapeutics
   Tom Needham, Co-Founder
   Education: BA, Bowdoin College; MBA, Olin Graduate School of Business
   Background: Principal, Advent International; Vice President, GPC Biotech
   Directorships: Prexa Pharmaceuticals, Spear Therapeutics, Trident Pharmaceuticals

1778 TA ASSOCIATES
200 Calrendon St.
56th Floor
Boston, MA 02116

Phone: 617-574-6700
web: www.ta.com

Mission Statement: TA Associates invests in private companies in growth industries to help management teams build significant value. The firm has invested in and supported more than 400 companies as a long-term partner through a variety of economic and financial market cycles. In addition to providing financial support, TA Associates offers strategic guidance, industry knowledge and contacts in the financial community.

Fund Size: $16 billion
Founded: 1968
Minimum Investment: $60 million
Investment Criteria: Seeks investment opportunities in growing profitable, private companies. We will also provide capital for management-led buyouts and recapitalization of growth companies.
Industry Group Preference: Technology, Financial Services, Healthcare, Business Products & Services, Consumer
Portfolio Companies: 5.11, Accruent, Aicent, Amann Girrbach AG, Answers, Arxan Technologies, AVG Technologies, BATS Global Markets, Bigpoint GmbH, BluePay Processing, Cath Kidston, CMOSIS, Cosentry, Dealer Tire, DigiCert, DNCA Finance SA, Dr Lal PathLabs, Dutch, e-Rewards, Evanston Capital Management, First Eagle Investment Management, Flashtalking, Forgame Holdings Limited, Fotolia Holdings, Fractal Analytics Private Limited, FreeWave Technologies, Full Sail University, Indialdeas.com, Internationella Engelska Skolan, IntraLinks, ION Investment Group, Jupiter Fund Management, Keeley Asset Management, Kinetic Social, M and M Direct, Med Solutions, Micromax Informatics Limited, MicroSeismic, Millenium Laboratories, MIS Implants Technologies, Nintex Group, Numeric Investors, Onlineprinters GmbH, Professional Warranty Service, Prometheus Group, Radialpoint, RGM Advisors, Senior Whole Health, SoftWriters, SpeedCast, Stadion Money Management, Tega Industries, TEOCO, The Los Angeles Film Schook, The Rocky Mountain School of Design, Towne Park, Twin Med, Vatterott Educational Centers, Viewpoint, Zadig & Voltaire

Other Locations:
   64 Willow Place
   Suite 100

Menlo Park, CA 94025
Phone: 650-473-2200

TA Associates Ltd
3rd Floor, Devonshire House
1 Mayfair Place
London W1J 8AJ
United Kingdom
Phone: 44-2078320200

TA Associates Advisory Pvt. Ltd.
13th Floor, Birla Aurora
Dr. Annie Besant Rd.
Worli, Mumbai 400 030
India
Phone: 91-2261443100

TA Associates Asia Pacific Ltd.
One Exchange Square
16th Floor, 8 Connaught Place
Central
Hong Kong
Phone: 852-3656-6300

Key Executives:
Jeffrey S Barber, Managing Director
617-574-6795
e-mail: jbarber@ta.com
Education: BA Political Science, Johns Hopkins University; MBA, Columbia Business School
Background: Weiss Peck & Greer; Vestar Capital Partners; Financial Analyst/Global Power Utilities, Morgan Stanley & Co
Michael S Berk, Managing Director
617-574-6709
e-mail: mberk@ta.com
Education: AB, East Asian Studies, Harvard College; MBA, Harvard Business School; JD, Harvard Law School
Background: Joseph Littlejohn & Levy, Frontenac Company
Jeffrey T Chambers, Senior Advisor
650-473-2201
e-mail: jchambers@ta.com
Education: BA, Harvard University; MBA, Stanford University
Background: Meredith Associates
Todd R Crockett, Managing Director
650-473-2227
e-mail: tcrockett@ta.com
Education: BA, Princeton University; MBA, Harvard Business School
Background: Salomon Brothers
Brian J Conway, Chair
617-574-6705
e-mail: bconway@ta.com
Education: BA, Amherst College; MBA, Stanford University
Background: Merrill Lynch
Johnathan M Goldstein, Senior Advisor
617-574-6773
e-mail: jgoldstein@ta.com
Education: SB Biology/Chemical Engineering, SM Biochemical Engineering, MIT; MBA, Harvard Business School
Background: Biogen
Kurt R Jaggers, Senior Advisor
650-473-2203
e-mail: kjaggers@ta.com
Education: BS/MS Electrical Engineering, Stanford University; MBA, Stanford University Graduate School of Business
Background: Network Equipment Technologies; ROLM Corporation; Business Computer Corporation; Boston Consulting Group
A. Bruce Johnston, Advisor
617-574-6706
e-mail: bjohnston@ta.com
Education: BS, Electrical Engineering, Duke University; MBA, Pennsylvania State University
Background: President, idealab! Boston; General Manager, Lotus Development Corporation; Research Analyst, First Boston Corporation; Sales & Engineering, AT&T Communications
Roger B Kafker, Senior Advisor
617-574-6785
e-mail: rkafker@ta.com
Education: BA, History, Haverford College; MBA, Harvard Business School
Background: Bakers Trust Company
Kenneth T Schiciano, Managing Director
617-574-6768
e-mail: kts@ta.com
Education: BS, Electrical Engineering & Computer Science, Duke University; MS, Electrical Engineering, Stanford University; SM Management, MIT Sloan School of Management
Background: AT&T Bell Laboratories
Richard D Tadler, Senior Advisor
617-574-6708
e-mail: rtadler@ta.com
Education: BS, Finance, University of Virginia; MBA, Wharton School, University of Pennsylvania
Background: General Partner, Investments Oraange Nassau; ARMCO
Jonathan W Meeks, Managing Director
650-473-2238
e-mail: jmeeks@ta.com
Education: BS, Mathematics, Yale University
Background: Robertson Stephens
Jennifer M Mulloy, Managing Director
650-473-2229
e-mail: jmulloy@ta.com
Education: AB, Economics, Stanford University; MBA, Harvard Business School
Background: Robertson Stephens
Ajit Nedungadi, Chief Executive Officer
011-44-20-7823-0210
e-mail: ajit@ta.com
Education: BS, Electrical Engineering & Economics, Yale University; MBA, Harvard Business School
Background: Trilogy Software, Investcorp International, Credit Suisse First Boston
M Roy Burns, Managing Director
617-574-6732
e-mail: rburns@ta.com
Education: BS, Business Administration, Washington & Lee University; MBA, Stanford Graduate School of Business
Background: Equity Investments, Davidson Kempner Partners; Leveraged Finance, Banc of America Securities
Mark H Carter, Managing Director
617-574-6739
e-mail: mcarter@ta.com
Education: BE, Mechanical Engineering, Vanderbilt University; MBA, Columbia Business School
Background: Parthenon Capital, FdG Associates, The Halifax Group, Lehman Brothers
Hythem T El-Nazer, Managing Director
617-574-6776
e-mail: hte@ta.com
Education: London School of Economics; AB, Economics, Brown University; MBA, Columbia Business School
Background: McKinsey & Company; Investment Banking, Donaldson Lufkin & Jenrette
Harry D Taylor, Managing Director
617-574-6767
e-mail: htaylor@ta.com
Education: AB, Economics, Hamilton College; MBA, Harvard Business School
Background: Associate, Stone Point Capital; Financial Analyst, Goldman Sachs & Co.
Directorships: e-Rewards, IntraLinks, Numara Software

Venture Capital & Private Equity Firms / Domestic Firms

William D Christ, Managing Director
617-574-6769
e-mail: bchrist@ta.com
Education: BS, Business Administration, Washington & Lee University; MBA, Tuck School of Business, Dartmouth College
Background: Global Real Estate Group, Lehman Brothers

1779 TAILWIND CAPITAL
485 Lexington Avenue
New York, NY 10017

Phone: 212-271-3800
e-mail: info@tailwind.com
web: www.tailwind.com

Mission Statement: Tailwind focuses on growing middle market companies in the healthcare and business & communications sectors.

Fund Size: $775 million
Founded: 2000
Average Investment: $25 million - $100 million
Investment Criteria: Enterprise Value of Up to $300 Million; EBITA of $10 Million to $50 Million
Industry Group Preference: Healthcare, Business Products & Services, Telecommunications
Portfolio Companies: Adobe Healthcare, Acertus, Anvil International, Apex Companies, Archway Marketing Services, AST, Banner Solutions, Benevis, Brawler Industries, Colony Hardware, Core BTS, Cumberland Consulting Group, Cumming Group, DermaRite, Diamondback Drugs, Diversified, Edenbridge, Freedom Innovations, Hamilton State Bancshares, HMT, Lieberman Research Worldwide, Loenbro, Lone Peak, Invatron Systems, Longs Pharmacy Solutions, National HME, Nautilus Neurosciences, Nsight, Oceus Networks, Optimal Solutions Integration, PetMedicus Laboratories, Pillar Processing, PremierXD, RANDYS Worldwide Automotive, ReTrans, SDI Health, Stratix, TowerCo, Transit Wireless, Ventiv Technology, VersaPharm

Key Executives:
Lawrence B. Sorrel, Managing Partner
e-mail: lsorrel@tailwind.com
Education: Brown University, Harvard Law School, Harvard Business School
Background: Welsh Carson Anderson & Stowe, Morgan Stanley
James S. Hoch, Partner
e-mail: jhoch@tailwind.com
Education: Williams College, Harvard Business School
Background: Morgan Stanley Capital Partners
Frank V. Sica, Partner
e-mail: fsica@tailwind.com
Education: Wesleyan University, Amos Tuck School of Business, Dartmouth College
Background: President, Soros Private Funds Management
Brian S. Berkin, Partner
e-mail: bberkin@tailwind.com
Education: University of Michigan; Wharton School
Background: Pacific Founders; LLR Partners; RoundTable Healthcare Partners; Credit Suisse
Jeffrey M. Calhoun, Partner
e-mail: jcalhoun@tailwind.com
Education: Tufts University, University of California, Berkeley Haas School of Business
Background: Montgomery Securities, Thomas Weisel Partners
Geoffrey S. Raker, Partner
e-mail: graker@tailwind.com
Education: Brown University; Harvard Business School
Background: Warburg Pincus, Morgan Stanley, Bain & Company
Adam F. Stulberger, Partner
e-mail: astulberger@tailwind.com
Education: Lafayette College, New York University School of Law
Background: SpectraSite Communications, Morgan Stanley, Credit Suisse
David S. Gorton, Partner
e-mail: dgorton@tailwind.com
Education: Vanderbilt University; Emory University School of Law
Background: Investment Banker, Lehman Brothers; Lawyer, Skadden Arps Slate Meagher & Flom
Andrew R. Mayer, Partner
e-mail: amayer@tailwind.com
Education: Dartmouth College; Wharton School
Background: Thomas H. Lee Partners; Deutsche Bank
Sanjay Swani, Partner
e-mail: sswani@tailwind.com
Education: Princeton University; Harvard Law School; MIT Sloan School of Management
Background: Welsh Carson Anderson & Stowe; Morgan Stanley

1780 TAKEDA VENTURES
435 Tasso St.
Suite 300
Palo Alto, CA 94301

Phone: 650-328-2900 Fax: 650-328-2922
e-mail: contact@tri-takeda.com
web: www.takedaventures.com

Mission Statement: Takeda Ventures, Inc. is the corporate venture arm of Takeda Pharmaceutical Company Ltd. that supports therapeutic innovation in the biopharmaceutical sector and academic sectors.

Founded: 2001
Investment Criteria: Early Stage, Late Stage
Industry Group Preference: Biopharmaceuticals, Healthcare, Pharmaceuticals
Portfolio Companies: Ambys Medicines, Cortexyme, Crescendo Biologics, Hookipa Biotech AG, Obsidian, Outpost Medicine, Palleon Pharmaceuticals, Presage Biosciences, Ribon Therapeutics, StrideBio

Key Executives:
Michael Martin, Head of Takeda Ventures
Education: PhD
Background: Takeda Pharmaceuticals
Karen Hong, Senior Partner
Education: BS, Chemistry, BA, Molecular Biology, University of California, Berkeley; PhD, Biology, MIT
Background: Partner, ProQuest Investments
Directorships: Agile Therapeutics, Mersana Therapeutics, Clarus Therapeutics
David A Shaywitz, Senior Partner
Education: MD, Harvard Medical School; PhD, MIT
Background: Chief Medical Officer, DNAnexus; Merck; Boston Consulting Group; Theravance
Robbie Woodman, Senior Partner
Education: MSc, Biochemistry, University of Oxford; PhD, Oncology, University of Cambridge
Background: Principal, Sofinnova Partners

1781 TALLWOOD VENTURE CAPITAL
325 Lytton Avenue
Suite 4A
Palo Alto, CA 94301

Phone: 650-473-6750
e-mail: information@tallwoodvc.com
web: www.tallwoodvc.com

Mission Statement: Focuses on investments in differential technologies and products that will have a significant impact on the semiconductor industry.

Fund Size: $600 million
Industry Group Preference: Semiconductors
Portfolio Companies: Accent, Alphion Corp., Audience, Axiom Microdevices, Calypto Design Systems Inc., Cavendish Kinetics, Crossing Automation Inc., Cyras

Venture Capital & Private Equity Firms / Domestic Firms

Systems, Iknaos, Inphi Corp., Marvell Technology Group, NewPort Communications, Ozmo Devices, Pixim Inc., Qspeed Semiconductor, Quintic, Redfern Integrated Optics, Sandbridge Technologies Inc., SiRF Technology Holdings Inc., Silicon Clocks, Stream Machine, TrueSpan, Wave Computing, Wilocity

Other Locations:
Tallwood (WuXi) Venture Capital
#1002, #21-1 Chang Jiang Road
WuXi New District, WuXi
JiangSu Provice 214028
China
Phone: 86-051081816335 **Fax:** 86-051081814997

Key Executives:
Luis Arzubi, General Partner
Education: BS/MS, Electrical Engineering, National University of Littoral, Argentina
Background: VP/GM, Microelectronics Division, IBM; Lab Director, General Technology Division, IBM
Directorships: Cavendish Kinetics
Dado Banatao, Managing Partner
Education: BEng, Mapua Institute of Technology, Philippines; MS, Electrical Engineering, Stanford University
Background: Partner, Mayfield Fund; Co-Founder, Chips & Technologies; Co-Founder, Mostron; GM, National Semiconductor, GM, Seeq Technologies; GM, Intersil; GM, Commodore International

1782 TAO VENTURE CAPITAL PARTNERS
e-mail: info@taovp.com
web: www.taocap.com

Mission Statement: TAO Venture Capital Partners provides capital and advisory services to entrepreneurs pursuing global market opportunities in Information Technology, Internet, Media, and Consumer Services.

Industry Group Preference: Information Technology, Internet, Media, Consumer Services, Clean Technology, Security, SaaS
Portfolio Companies: Active.com, Active Network, BrightCloud, EcoATM, Par Accel, TradeBeam

1783 TAYRONA VENTURES
8411 Market Street
San Francisco, CA 94103

web: tayronaventures.wordpress.com

Mission Statement: Tayrona Ventures is a hands-on fund that invests in and works closely with early stage startups in Colombia and throughout Latin America. We take a Silicon Valley approach to venture capital, with a team of seasoned mentors and partners in the region. Our ultimate mission is to create and accelerate the next generation of technology companies in Latin America's rapidly emerging markets.

Geographic Preference: Latin America
Investment Criteria: Early-Stage
Industry Group Preference: Technology
Key Executives:
Paul Bragiel, General Partner
Alan Colmenares, General Partner
William Hsu, General Partner

1784 TDF
2 Wisconsin Circle
Suite 920
Chevy Chase, MD 20815
Phone: 240-483-4286 **Fax:** 301-907-8850
web: www.tdfventures.com

Mission Statement: To partner with talented entrepreneurs and build competitive and innovative technology and services companies.

Geographic Preference: North America
Average Investment: $500,000 - $5 million
Investment Criteria: Early-Stage, Later-Stage
Industry Group Preference: Communications, Media, Technology
Portfolio Companies: American Honors, AppMesh, Arxan Technologies, Aztek Networks, Booker, Colubris Networks, Cyan, EdgeConneX, HelloWallet, IEX Group, Inlet Technologies, Insightpool, Mindshift Technologies, Ooma, Punchh, Quantance, Spectrum Bridge, SpinMedia, Stellar Loyalty, Valencell, Virtustream

Key Executives:
Jim Pastoriza, Partner
Education: BS, Columbia University; MS, MIT
Background: Partner, JP Morgan Communications Partners LP; Partner, AT&T Ventures; AT&T; Lucent Technologies
Randall Brouckman, Operating Partner
Education: BS, University of Michigan; MS, Electrical Engineering, Stanford University
Background: CEO, EdgeConneX; Founder, Wade Capital Group

1785 TEAKWOOD CAPITAL
8226 Douglas Avenue
Suite 355
Dallas, TX 75225
Phone: 214-750-1590 **Fax:** 214-750-1468
e-mail: contact@teakwoodcapital.com
web: www.teakwoodcapital.com

Mission Statement: Teakwood Capital is a Dallas, Texas private equity firm. We make equity investments in profitable companies and strong management teams seeking growth.

Geographic Preference: Texas, Arizona, Arkansas, New Mexico, Louisiana, Oklahoma, Tennessee
Average Investment: $2 million
Investment Criteria: Growth, Buyouts, Recapitalization, Corporate Divestitures
Industry Group Preference: Technology-Enabled Services, Software
Portfolio Companies: Prodagio Software, SigmaFlow, Long Range Systems, Clockwork Solutions, MyOpenJobs, InReach, TWG Plus

Key Executives:
Ed Olkkola, Managing Director
Education: University of Massachusetts; MBA, Northeastern University
Background: SVP, A.H. Belo Corporation; General Partner, Austin Ventures; Compaq
Vinse Davidson, Managing Director, Finance/CFO/COO
Education: BS, Accounting, University of Tennessee, Martin; MPA, University of Texas, Austin
Background: Partner & CFO, STARTech Early Ventures

1786 TECH COAST ANGELS
Santa Monica Blvd
Los Angeles, CA 90034
web: www.techcoastangels.com

Mission Statement: Tech Coast Angels is an angel investment organization consisting of over 300 members in five networks across California. TCA focuses on funding startups in a number of industries, including life sciences, information technology, media, consumer products, financial, software, retail and Internet.

Geographic Preference: Southern California
Founded: 1997
Investment Criteria: Startups, Early Stage
Industry Group Preference: Life Sciences, Biotechnology, Information Technology, Services, Retail, Consumer & Leisure, Internet, Software, Media, Consumer Products, Technology, Industrial, Clean Technology
Portfolio Companies: Accuscore, Active Live Scientific, Adventrx Pharmaceuticals, Aggregate, AgileNano,

Venture Capital & Private Equity Firms / Domestic Firms

Airborne1, Airsis, Akiva, Allylix, Althea, AnaBios Corporation, Angstrom, AnyMeeting, Apeel Sciences, Ascendant Spirits, Atlas Apps, Avaxia Biologics, Axitron, Banshee Bungee, Beacon Healthcare, Benchmark Revenue Management, BikeStation, Bitvore Corporation, Bizbuyer, Bluebeam Software, Brain X, BrandAmerica, Business Backers, CardioCreate, CargoTech, CaseStack, Cashie Commerce, Cognition Therapeutics, Continental Windpower, Controltec, Cosemi Technologies, Crisi Medical Systems, Cyber Rain, Dax Solutions, DealCurrent, DermTech International, Dispatch Tracking Solutions, Docufide, EDN, Edufii, Eefoof, eGuardian, ElephantDrive, Enstigo, eTeamz, Etronica, ExtendCredit, EZ Apps, Fitn, Garden Organics, GazelleLab, Gemmus Pharma, GetThis, Ginni Designs, Gremln, GroundMetrics, H2O Audio, H2Scan, Heartland Resources, HitFix, Image Searcher, Immuno Gum, InfoBionic, Inhance Media Audiofile, Inlustra, Innozen, IPourIt, ISpeech, Iyia Technologies, JobSync, JointlyHealth, Kalyra, Landroller, Language Weaver, Larada Sciences, Leaselock, LeisureLink, Lendamend, Liquid Grids Swarmology, Luxim, Make It Work, Makucell, Mamoca, Masher Media, Media Matchmaker, Micropower, Mindbody Software, Mobile Cause, MobileXL, Mogl, MojoPages, Molecular Detection, MyShape, Neural Analytics, Nine Star, Ninja Metrics, Numira Biosciences, Olfactor Laboratories, Olive Medical, Ombitron, One Stop Systems, Opposing Views, Opticon Medical, Optionease, Orfid, Organic Go, Orion Data Analysis, P4RC, Paradigm Select Assets, Parcel Pending, Park Tours, Pedalign, Pediatric Biosciences, Perfectna, PharmaSecure, Phone Halo, Portfolium, Practice Technologies, Procore, Property Bureau, Proxy Debt Buyer, Ranker, Respiratory Motion, RetroSense Therapeutics, Ring Router, Rock My World, Rx Timer Cap, Savara, Schlep Fetch, SeniorQuote, ShareDesk, Sleepsafe Drivers, Social Rewards, Sockwa, Soda Head, Somabar, Sonoma Beverage Works, Sponge Tech, TextPower, TradeYa, TrueVault, TrustEgg, V-Enable, Vigilistics, Virtual Metrix, Vokle, Voyager Systems, Wasatch Microfluids, Wispry, Wonder Technologies, Yapert, YouMail, Yowza

1787 TECHNOLOGY CROSSOVER VENTURES
250 Middlefield Road
Menlo Park, CA 94025

Phone: 650-614-8200
web: www.tcv.com

Mission Statement: Technology Crossover Ventures (TCV) invests in public companies through private and public transactions. In evaluating technology companies, TCV looks for proven business models, demonstrated revenue traction and a solid path to profitability.

Geographic Preference: United States, Canada
Fund Size: $3.3 billion
Founded: 1995
Average Investment: $35 million
Minimum Investment: $15 million
Investment Criteria: Expansions, Late Stage
Industry Group Preference: Information Technology, Internet, Software, Fintech, Infrastructure
Portfolio Companies: Act-On, Actifio, Adknowledge, Alarm.cOm, Appnexus, Dollar Shave Club, Dough.com, eBags, eHarmony, Electronic Arts, Elevate Credit, ExtraHop Networks, Facebook, Genesys, Go Daddy, iPipeline, IQMS, Just Fabulous, K12, kgb, Merkle Group, Minted, Netflix, New Voice Media, NexTag, Open English, Origin Holdings, OSIsoft, Rapid7, Rent the Runway, Sitecore Corporation, SiteMinder, Spotify, Swagbucks, Tastytrade, TechTarget, TheStreet.com, Think Finance, ThinkingPhones, TradingScreen, Travelport, VICE Media, Webroot Software

Other Locations:
7 Bryant Park
1045 - 6th Avenue
24th Floor
New York, NY 10018
Phone: 212-808-0200

11 Charles II Street
1st Floor
London SW1Y 4QU
United Kingdom
Phone: 44-2070042620

Key Executives:
Jay Hoag, Founding General Partner
650-614-8200
Fax: 650-475-1229
Education: BA, Economics and Political Science, Northwestern University; MBA, University of Michigan
Background: Managing Director, Chancellor Capital Mangement

Rick Kimball, Founding General Partner
650-614-8200
Fax: 650-475-1229
Education: Cum Laude, AB degree History, Dartmouth College; MBA Finance, University of Chicago
Background: Managing Director, Montgomery Securities

Kapil Venkatachalam, General Partner
Education: MS, Electrical Engineering, Dartmouth College
Background: CIO, Goldman Sachs
Directorships: EtQ; Rave Mobile Safety

John Drew, General Partner
650-614-8200
Fax: 650-475-1229
Education: BS, United States Military Academy; MS, Columbia University
Background: President, CEO, International Network Services

Woody Marshall, General Partner
Education: BA, Hamilton College; MBA, JL Kellogg Graduate School of Management, Northwestern University
Background: Trident Capital; Associate, Leveraged Capital Group, Banque Paribas; Financial Analyst, Chase Manhattan Bank

Jake Reynolds, General Partner
650-614-8200
Fax: 650-475-1229
Education: AB, Dartmouth College; MBA, Columbia Business School
Background: Associate, General Atlantic Partners

Robert Trudeau, General Partner
Education: BAH, Political Science, Queen's University; MBA, University of Western Ontario
Background: Principal, General Atlantic Partners; Managing Director, iFormation Group

Tim McAdam, General Partner
Education: BA, Dartmouth College; MBA, Stanford Graduate School of Business
Background: Trinity Ventures, GTCR

David Yuan, Senior Advisor
Education: AB, Harvard University; MBA, Stanford Graduate School of Business
Background: JPMorgan Partners; Management Consultant, Bain & Company

1788 TECHNOLOGY PARTNERS
550 University Avenue
Palo Alto, CA 94301

Phone: 650-289-9000 **Fax:** 650-289-9001
e-mail: admin@technologypartners.com
web: www.technologypartners.com

Mission Statement: Technology Partners teams with visionary entrepreneurs to create successful new companies.

Geographic Preference: Western United States
Fund Size: $300 million
Founded: 1980
Average Investment: $1-$25 million

Venture Capital & Private Equity Firms / Domestic Firms

Minimum Investment: $100,000
Investment Criteria: Seed, Startup, First-stage
Industry Group Preference: Clean Technology, Energy Technology, Water Technology, Advanced Materials, Life Sciences, Consumer Medicine, Cost-Effective Medicine, Neurotechnology
Portfolio Companies: Accelergy, Akeros Silicon, G2X Energy, IMERGY Power Systems, Imperium Renewables, KAIAM Corporation, NYSE Blue, Ogin, PolyFuel, PowerGenix Systems, Sensicore, Solexel, Tesla Motors, Benvenue Medical, BrainCells, Cadence Pharmaceuticals, Calypte Biomedical, Cardax Pharmaceuticals, Cell Pathways, Cereve, Cholestech, Corcept Therapeutics, CryoCor, Cryogen, Ekos, Neura, Elcely Therapeutics, Essentialis, ForSight VISIONS, HeartStent, Incline Therapeutics, Inncercool Therapies, Iomai, Iridex, Leptos Biomedical, Mewave, NeuroPace, Nfocus Neuromedical, PercuSurge, Revance Therapeutics, Rinat Neuroscience, Saegis Pharmaceuticals, Scioderm, Solta Medical, Spinal Dynamics, TONIX Pharmaceuticals, Transcend Medical, Tria Beauty, Ventritex, Visiogen

Other Locations:
100 Shoreline Highway
Building B, Suite 282
Mill Valley, CA 94941
Phone: 415-332-9999 **Fax:** 415-332-9998

Key Executives:
Roger J Quy PhD, General Partner
e-mail: roger@technologypartners.com
Education: MBA, Hass School of Business, UC Berkeley; PhD, University of Keele; BA, Psychology, Law, University of Keele
Background: Hewlett-Packard Corporation, Oxford Instrument Group
Ted Ardell, Partner
e-mail: ted@technologypartners.com
Education: Graduate with Distinction, United States Naval Academy
Background: Impell Corporation, Bechtel Corporation
Ira M Ehrenpreis, General Partner
e-mail: ira@technologypartners.com
Education: JD, MBA, Stanford Graduate School of Business; Stanford University Law School; Graduate, UCLA
Background: Goldman, Sachs & Company, Juniper Partners
Jim Glasheen, General Partner
e-mail: jim@technologypartners.com
Education: BS, Duke University; MA/PhD, Harvard University; Deutsche Akademische Austauschdienst fellow at Universitaet des Saarlandes, Germany
Background: McKinsey & Company's Pharmaceutical and Medical Products Practice
Sheila Mutter, General Partner/CFO
e-mail: sheila@technologypartners.com
Education: BS in Accounting, University of Akron; Certified Public Accountant
Background: Coopers & Lybrand

1789 TECHNOLOGY VENTURES CORPORATION
1115 University Boulevard SE
2nd Floor
Albuquerque, NM 87106-4320

Phone: 505-246-2882
e-mail: contactus@techventures.org
web: www.techventures.org

Mission Statement: To facilitate the commercialization of technology in New Mexico, primarily from the national laboratories, and the research universities in the region. A primary focus of Technology Venture Corporation (TVC) is attracting risk investment money, and it assists technology-based companies by facilitating technology transfer and coordinating management and business assistance.
Geographic Preference: California, Nevada, New Mexico
Founded: 1993
Minimum Investment: Less than $100,000
Industry Group Preference: Technology

Key Executives:
John Freisinger, President & CEO
505-246-2882
Bob McCarty, CFO/Director of Operations
Background: GE, Avery Denison, Arthur Andersen, Sandia National Labs

1790 TECHOPERATORS
One Buckhead Plaza
3600 Peachtree Road NW
Suite 720
Atlanta, GA 30305

Phone: 404-537-2525
e-mail: info@techoperators.com
web: www.techoperators.com

Mission Statement: The TechOperators mission is straightforward: Helping seriously smart people turn game-changing ideas into great companies. We love taking a role in that rocket launch from early stage to widespread adoption, accelerated growth, and serious market share in a seriously competitive world. Today's software climate is ripe for innovation, and customers are ready to discover and purchase next-generation solutions. TechOperators makes smart investments that help innovative solutions reach those customers at scale. Our difference? Decades of hard-fought operating success and experience running at venture speed to keep you from being left in the dust. Because we're not just VCs, and great companies aren't built on just cool ideas and money.

Geographic Preference: Southeast United States
Fund Size: $450 million
Founded: 2008
Investment Criteria: Early-Stage
Industry Group Preference: Technology, Cloud Computing, Social Media, Technology-Enabled Software, Business to Business
Portfolio Companies: Vorstack, Siftit, Predikto, Hire IQ, Immunet, Endgame, Vocalocity, Joulex, Interactive Advisory Software, Ionic Security, Springbot

Key Executives:
Dave Gould, Operating Partner
Education: BS, Economics, University of Pennsylvania; MBA, Emory University
Background: Chairman & CEO, Witness Systems
Glenn McGonnigle, General Partner
Education: BS, Mechanical Engineering, University of Virginia
Background: CEO, VistaScape Security Systems; Co-Founder, Internet Security Systems
Said Mohammadioun, Managing Partner
Education: BS, MS, Electrical Engineering, Georgia Institute of Technology; MBA, Georgia State University
Background: CEO & Chairman, Synchrologic; Founder & CEO, Samna Corporation
Tom Noonan, Operating Partner
Education: Mechanical Engineering, Georgia Tech; MBA, Harvard University
Background: Chairman, President & CEO, Internet Security Systems; Senior Management, Dun & Bradstreet Sotware; National Infrastructure Advisory Council

1791 TECHSTARS
1050 Walnut Street
Boulder, CO 80302

web: www.techstars.com

Venture Capital & Private Equity Firms / Domestic Firms

Mission Statement: International network of startup accelerator programs.
Average Investment: $100K
Investment Criteria: Seed
Portfolio Companies: Digital Ocean, Localytics, Sendgrid, Contently, Occipital, Next Big Sound, Kapost, Orbotix, FullContact, Simple Energy, Mocavo, GrabCAD, Kinvey, Placester, Crowdtwist, OnSwipe, Everymove, Remitly, Remotive, Cloudability, Distil Networks, Moveline, Pivotdesk, Revolv, Coachup, Pillpack, Plated

Key Executives:
David Cohen, Founder/Chairman
Background: Pinpoint Technologies; earFeeder.com
Brad Feld, Co-Founder
Education: MIT
Background: Intensity Ventures; Mobius Venture Capital
David Brown, Co-Founder
Education: McGill University
Background: Pinpoint Technologies

1792 TEDCO
5565 Sterrett Place
Suite 214
Columbia, MD 21044

Phone: 410-740-9442 Fax: 410-740-9422
Toll-Free: 800-305-5556
e-mail: info@tedco.md
web: www.tedco.md

Mission Statement: TEDCO is a resource of mentoring, funding and networking for entrepreneurs and start-ups that need guidance as they bring innovative concepts to the market.
Fund Size: $550 million
Founded: 1998
Investment Criteria: Startup/Seed, Early State, Expansion, Later Stage Funding

Troy LeMaile-Stovall, CEO and Executive Director
Education: BS, Southern Methodist University; MS, Stanford University; MBA, Harvard University
Background: COO, University of the District of Columbia; Founder, LeMaile-Stovall LLC; Founder, GTMS Partners LLC
Stephen Auvil, Executive Vice President, Programs
e-mail: sauvil@tedco.md
Education: BS Biology & Engineering Science, Loyola College; MBA Administration, University of Baltimore; Masters of Science in Biotechnology, Johns Hopkins University
Background: Co-Principal Investigator, National Science Foundation; Director, UMBC Office of Technology Development; Assistant Director, Office of Technology Licensing at the Johns Hopkins University

1793 TEL VENTURE CAPITAL
3100 West Warren Avenue
Fremont, CA 94538

Phone: 510-624-3450 Fax: 510-624-3451
web: www.tel.com/about/tel_vc

Mission Statement: Our investments cover a range of technologies from those impacting Tokyo Electron's core semiconductor, flat panel display and PV businesses, to renewable energy, energy storage, water treatment, life science, healthcare, medical electronics, lighting, photonics, printable electronics and other areas of emerging innovation.
Geographic Preference: United States, Japan
Industry Group Preference: Semiconductors, Renewable Energy, Energy Storage, Water, Life Sciences, Healthcare, Electronics
Portfolio Companies: Molecular Imprints, Liola, Genalyte, MIOX, EnterVault, Luxtera, Crystal Solar, Vista Therapeutics, Quantum14, NanoGram, Unidym, Invarium

Other Locations:
Akasaka Biz Tower
3-1 Akasaka 5-Chome
Minato-ku
Tokyo 107-6325
Japan
Phone: 81-355617270 Fax: 81-355617066

Key Executives:
Kay Enjoji, President
Education: BA, Economis, Keio University
Background: Director, MEMS Division, TEL; TEL Corporate Marketing
Ted Hirose, Group Director
Education: BA, Keio University; MBA, New York University

1794 TELEGRAPH HILL PARTNERS
360 Post Street
Suite 601
San Francisco, CA 94108

Phone: 415-765-6980 Fax: 415-765-6983
e-mail: info@thpartners.net
web: www.thpartners.net

Mission Statement: A private equity firm dedicated to helping life science, medical device and healthcare companies achieve their growth objectives

Investment Criteria: Growth Equity
Industry Group Preference: Healthcare, Life Sciences, Medical Devices, Chemistry, Reagent Suppliers, Healthcare Services, Information Services
Portfolio Companies: Accumetrics, AcroMetrix, Agena Bioscience, Althea Technologies, AltheaDx, Ambion, AngioScore, Apppplied Precision, Asuragen, Aurora Discovery, BioVentrix, Confirma, Dharmacon, Estech, Freedom Innovations, Interface, Kinetikos Medical, LDR, MedPricer, NEXUS Biosystems, PneumRx, RareCyte, SAGE, SwitchGear, VidaCare

Key Executives:
J Matthew Mackowski, Chairman, Managing Director
e-mail: jmm@thpartners.net
Education: BA, Duke University; MBA, The Wharton School
Background: Citicorp Venture Capital; Roberton, Stephens & Co
Directorships: Kinetikos Medical, Ambion, Aurora Discovery, Interface Associates, Asuragen, Althea Technologies, AltheaDx, MedPricer
Thomas A Raffin MD, Venture Partner
e-mail: tar@thpartners.net
Education: BA, Stanford University; MD, Stanford University School of Medicine
Background: Faculty, Stanford Univeristy School of Medicine; Co-Founder, Stanford University Center for Biomedical Ethics
Deval A Lashkari PhD, Senior Partner
e-mail: dal@thpartners.net
Education: BA, University of California, Berkeley; PhD, Stanford University
Background: Research Director, Synteni; Operon Technologies
Jeanette M Welsh JD, Partner, COO
e-mail: jmw@thpartners.net
Education: BA, Philosophy & France, Hunter College, City University of New York; JD, Fordham University School of Law
Background: Three Cities Research; Practiced Law, Epsten, Becker & Green PC
Rob C Hart CFA, Partner
e-mail: rch@thpartners.net
Education: BS, University of California, Santa Barbara; JD/MBA, Northwestern University School of Law/Kellogg School of Management

Background: Citigroup's Financial Entrepreneurs & Healthcare Investment Banking Groups

1795 TELESOFT PARTNERS
601 California Street
19th Floor
San Francisco, CA 94111

Phone: 415-757-5650
web: www.telesoftvc.com

Mission Statement: Telesoft provides value-added capital for technology, communications and energy value chain companies, including wireless, software, systems, applications, services and components companies.

Geographic Preference: United States, Europe, Israel, India
Fund Size: $625 million
Founded: 1996
Average Investment: $1-15 million
Minimum Investment: $500,000
Investment Criteria: Seed, Startup, First-stage, Second-stage, Mezzanine
Industry Group Preference: Technology, Communications, Energy, Software, Information Technology, Wireless
Portfolio Companies: Aarohi Communications, AmberWave, BayPackets, BPL Mobile Comunications, Calient Networks, Calix, Catamaran, Cerent, ConvergeNet, CoSine Communications, CreekPath Systems, Education.com, empowertel, Ikanos Communications, Internet Photonics, iWitness/Zantaz, Jungo, Knowledge Adventure, Kymata, Lara Networks, LiteScape, LogLogic, Lynx Photonic Networks, Matrix Semiconductor, Nexant, Omnipoint, OnFiber, Promatory, Provide Commerce, Sierra Design, SigmaTel, Tele Atlas, Triton, Validity Sensors, Versatile, Vina Technologies, VoiceObjects, VxTel, Xambala, Xpedion Design Systems

Key Executives:
 Arjun Gupta, Chief Executive
  e-mail: arjun@telesoftvc.com
  Education: BS, MS, Washington State University; MBA, Stanford University
  Background: Strategy Consultant, McKinsey & Company; Software Engineer, Tektronix Inc
 George Schmitt, Managing Director
  e-mail: georges@telesoftvc.com
  Education: BA, Saint Mary's College; MS, Stanford University
  Background: Chairman/CEO, Espire Communications; President/Director, Omnipoint Communication Services
 Alan Howard, Chief Financial Officer
  Education: BS, Colorado State University
  Background: CFO, Creative Communications, Vice President Finance/Administration, Hydro Agri
 Alan Foster, Managing Director
  Education: BS, MS, Mechanical Engineering, Stanford University; MBA, The Anderson School, UCLA
  Background: Principal, Berkeley International Capital Corporation; Silicon Graphics; Apple Computer
 Chris LeBlanc, Industry Research
  Education: BS, Mechanical Engineering, San Jose State University; MBA, Santa Clara University
  Background: Vice President, Banc of America; Senior Research Analyst, RHK; Intel; Hewlett Packard
 Gary Cuccio, Operating Partner
  e-mail: garyc@telesoftvc.com
  Education: BA, Political Science, California State University Los Angeles; MBA, St. Mary's College; AMP, Harvard University
  Background: CEO, ATG; CEO, LHS Group; COO, Omnipoint; VP, Airtouch Europe & Asia; President, Airtouch Paging; Pacific Tel
 Paul Unruh, Managing Director
  e-mail: paulu@telesoftvc.com
  Education: BSBA, MS, Accounting, University of North Dakota
  Background: Vice Chairman, Bechtel Group; Founding President, Oracle Applications Users Group

1796 TEN ELEVEN VENTURES
250 Northern Avenue
Suite 300
Boston, MA 02210

Phone: 617-986-5040
web: www.1011vc.com

Industry Group Preference: Artificial Intelligence, Software, Applications, Technology, Cyber Security
Portfolio Companies: BlackHorse Solutions, CyberGRX, Cylance, Darktrace, Digital Shadows, GoSecure, Hexadite, Ionic Security, JASK, KnowBe4, Offensive Security, Optiv, Ordr, Ping Indentity, Sonrai Security, Twistlock, Verodin, Vulcan Cyber

Other Locations:
 345 Lorton Avenue
 Suite 401
 Burlingame, CA 94010
 Phone: 855-910-1011

 777 Pearl Street
 Suite 211
 Boulder, CO 80302
 Phone: 303-909-8873

Key Executives:
 Alex Doll, Founder/Managing General Partner
  Education: BS, Financial, Wharton School; BS, Systems Engineering, Moore School, University of Pennsylvania; MBA, Stanford Grad. School of Business
  Background: PGP Corporation; Embark; PeopleSoft; OneID; Investment Banker, Robertson Stephens & Co.
 Mark Hatfield, Founder/General Partner
  Education: BA, McMaster University; MBA, York University
  Background: Partner, Fairhaven Capital; Managing Director, Motorola Ventures; Various Corporate Business Development Roles, Bell Canada Enterprise; Bank of Montreal
 Brian Draves, Partner/COO
  Education: JD, University of California, Los Angeles
  Background: General Counsel, Techstars

1797 TENASKA CAPITAL MANAGEMENT
14302 FNB Parkway
Omaha, NE 68154-5212

Phone: 402-691-9700 Fax: 402-691-9727
e-mail: info@tenaskacapital.com
web: www.tenaskacapital.com

Mission Statement: Private equity investor in the power and energy sectors.

Founded: 2003
Industry Group Preference: Energy
Portfolio Companies: Armstrong Energy, Big Sandy Peaker, Calumet Energy, Commonwealth Chesapeake, Crete Energy, High Desert Power, Holland Energy, Lincoln Generating, New Covert Generating, Pleasants Energy, Rio Nogales Power, Rolling Hills Generating, Troy Energy, US Power Generating, University Park Energy, Wolf Hills Energy

Key Executives:
 Paul G Smith, Senior Managing Director

1798 TENAYA CAPITAL
3101 Park Boulevard
Palo Alto, CA 94306

web: www.tenayacapital.com

Mission Statement: Tenaya Capital is a leading venture capital firm that invests in early growth venture-backed technology companies. Tenaya Capital is an equal partnership and work as a team to evaluate investments and support their portfolio companies.

Fund Size: $1 billion
Founded: 2009
Average Investment: $5 - $10 million

Investment Criteria: Second or Third Instituional Round; Early or Later-Stage
Industry Group Preference: Software, Consumer Internet, Communications, Semiconductors, Electronics, Clean Technology, Consumer Internet, Information Technology
Portfolio Companies: Acquia, Active-Semi, AgilOne, Avere Systems, Baihe, Baixing, Bigcommerce, Bluebox Security, Brighter, CareCloud, CastIron, CloudPassage, Composite Software, Contendo, Cyan, Digium, Druva, eBureau, Edmodo, Empirix, Endeca Technologies, Eventbrite, ExaGrid Systems, GameFly, GoodData, Green Dot, GupShup, Health Language, Hortonworks, HubSpot, Infoblox, Inkling, Instart Logic, Isilon Systems, ItsOn, Kaminario, Kayak.com, Kenshoo Kodiak Networks, Kontera, LifeSize Communications, Lithium Technologies, Lucky Pai, Lyft, Mark Logic, Maxta, Meru Networks, Mobilygen, Navini Networks, New Relic, Overture Networks, Palo Alto Networks, Platfora, PowerReviews, Qunar, Raptr, ResearchGate, Righscale, ShoreTel, SideStep, SilkRoad Technology, Smartling, Spiceworks, Storwize, Taykey, Tealium, TeleNav, ThreatMATRIX, Tidemark, Valere Power, VeriSilicon, VideoIQ, Wintegra, Wooga, Zappos.com, Zuora

Key Executives:
Tom Banahan, Partner
Education: BA, University of California, Santa Barbara
Background: VP, Business Development, Marimba; VP, Worldwide Sales, Spyglass; Comdisco
Stewart Gollmer, Partner
Education: BA, Johns Hopkins University; JD, Brigham Young University; MBA, University of Chicago Graduate School of Business
Background: Technology Investment Banking Group, Lehman Brothers
Brian Melton, Partner
Education: BS, Wake Forest University; MBA, Stanford University
Background: Merchant Banking Group, Lehman Brothers
Brian Paul, Partner
Education: BS, Economics, Wharton School, University of Pennsylvania; MBA, Northwestern University Kellogg School of Management
Background: Global Technology & Healthcare Investment Banking Groups, Lehman Brothers; First Boston
Dorian Merritt, Chief Financial Officer
Education: BA, Economics, University of California; MS, Accountancy, San Jose State University
Background: PricewaterhouseCoopers; Lightspeed Venture Partners; Sierra Ventures; ONSET Ventures

1799 TENNESSEE COMMUNITY VENTURES
3841 Green Hills Village Drive
Suite 400
Nashville, TN 37215

e-mail: bizplan@tncvfund.com
web: www.tncvfund.com

Mission Statement: TNCV is focused on technology transfer, seed and early stage investment opportunities. TNCV seeks to identify technologies, products and/or services that offer a unique solution to a specific point of pain or opportunity for their respective industries, lend themselves to business models that offer a clear path to profitability with modest capital needs and promote scalable cost structures that create competitive advantages. Each investment opportunity will be evaluated based on an ability to deliver exceptional financial returns while transforming and diversifying Tennessee's economic base through the creation of quality jobs and community wealth.

Average Investment: $50,000 - $750,000
Investment Criteria: Seed-Stage, Early-Stage
Industry Group Preference: Technology-Enabled Products, E-Commerce & Manufacturing, Digital Media & Marketing, Manufacturing, Advanced Materials, Food & Beverage, Business Products & Services, Retailing
Portfolio Companies: Pro Player Connect, VoicesHeard Media

Key Executives:
William Guttman, Partner
Education: PhD
Background: Founding Group, Carnegie Mellon CyLab; Co-Founder, Printcafe; Partner, Saturn Asset Management, TL Ventures
Directorships: Alphacet, Axioma, ExpressKCS, Panopto, Mismi, Northstar

1800 TENONETEN VENTURES
Los Angeles, CA

web: www.tenoneten.net

Mission Statement: We are technologists who believe technology can make the world a better place. We are decision makers who believe 'having the data' leads to the best decisions. We live in Los Angeles and believe L.A. is a world-class technology hub that's getting stronger every day. And we believe in audacious ideas and the people with the conviction to make them happen.

Geographic Preference: Southern California
Investment Criteria: Early-Stage
Industry Group Preference: Technology
Portfolio Companies: Curbide, Connectivity, Wit.AI, Kixer, Second Spectrum, Honk, ConnectHQ, Mapsense, Zirtual, Misfit Wearables, Pipeline DB, Alation, Burner, Weotta, Divshot, Ranker, Cambrian Genomics, SRCH2, Nearwoo, Vurb, Bottlenose, StrikeAd, Kaggle, Kaleo, Wavii, Trippy, Triggit, Goodreads, SurfAir, The Climate Corporation, Zest Finance, Prismatic, Wish, Scopely, SodaHead, ProCore, PLYmedia, Movato, MomentFeed, Locu, Howcast, Expect Labs, eXist db

Key Executives:
David Waxman, Managing Partner
Education: MS, MIT Media Lab
Background: Co-Founder, Firefly; Co-Founder, PeoplePC; Co-Founder, SpotRunner
Gil Elbaz, Founding Partner
Education: BS, Engineering/Applied Science & Economics, Caltech
Background: IBM, Sybase, SGI; Co-Founder, Applied Semantics; Google

1801 TEXADA CAPITAL CORPORATION
62 Greenwood Shoals
Suite A
Grasonville, MD 21638

Fax: 443-782-0248
Toll-Free: 866-595-6224
e-mail: info@texada.com
web: www.texada.com

Mission Statement: An investment banking firm serving direct marketing companies: telemarketing, direct mail, printing, fulfillment, data base management and e-commerce. We assist the owners and officers of such companies to achieve their corporate development objectives. We offer a broad range of merger and acquisition services overseen by its principal who have extensive experience in investment banking. We maintain and constantly update its database on direct marketing companies.

Fund Size: $9 million
Founded: 1996
Average Investment: $2 million
Minimum Investment: $1 million
Investment Criteria: LBO, MBO, Acquisitions
Industry Group Preference: Database Services, Direct Marketing, Outsourcing & Efficiency, E-Commerce & Manufacturing

Key Executives:
Laurie G. Kolbeins, Managing Director
e-mail: lkolbeins@texada.com
Education: University of British Columbia; Harvard Business School

Venture Capital & Private Equity Firms / Domestic Firms

Background: Officer, Compass Capital Advisors; Manager of Business Advisory Services, Mellon Bank Corporate Finance Group
Bluette N. Blinoff, Managing Director
e-mail: bblinoff@texada.com
Education: Cornell University; University of Denver College of Law
Background: VP of Corporate Finance, EF Hutton & Company; Acting President, Patten Mortgage Company; Partner, Kutak, Rock & Huie; Practiced Law, Holme, Roberts & Owen

1802 TEXAS EMERGING TECHNOLOGY FUND
17919 Waterview Pkwy.
Suite 1.50
Dallas, TX 75252

Phone: 972-883-4920 Fax: 972-883-4919

Mission Statement: The Texas Emerging Technology Fund (TETF) was created by the 79th Texas Legislature in 2005 at the urging of Gov. Perry to provide Texas with an unparalleled advantage in the research, development, and commercialization of emerging technologies.

Geographic Preference: Texas
Founded: 2005
Investment Criteria: Early Stage
Industry Group Preference: Emerging Markets, Sectors & Technologies
Key Executives:
  Laurie M. Rich, Special Advisor on Higher Education
  512-936-8434
  e-mail: laurie.rich@gov.texas.gov
  Jonathon W Taylor, Director
  Robert Crisalis, Investment Manager
  Patrick Boswell, Investment Manager
  David Morrow, Investment Manager

1803 TEXO VENTURES
6101 W Courtyard Drive
Suite 2-225
Austin, TX 78730

Toll-Free: 877-488-8396
web: www.texoventures.com

Mission Statement: Dedicated to investing in and building innovative healthcare companies. We work side-by-side with entrepreneurs, providing both the capital and collaboration needed for successful commercialization.

Geographic Preference: United States
Fund Size: $300 million
Investment Criteria: Early-Stage
Industry Group Preference: Healthcare, Healthcare Information Technology, Technology-Enabled Services, Medical Devices, Diagnostics
Portfolio Companies: Wenzel Spine, Televero Health, Ortho Kinematics, PrecedentHealth, EmployerDirect, AlaFair, IsoStem, SwipeSense, OpenMarkets
Key Executives:
  Jerry DeVries, Partner
  Education: BS, Mechanical Engineering, Louisiana State University; MBA, Baylor University
  Background: General Partner, Path4 Ventures
  Directorships: Wenzel Spine, OrthoKinematics, Alafair, IsoStem
  Philip Sanger MD, Partner
  Education: BA, Political Science, University of Texas, Austin; MD, Texas Tech; Internal Medicine Internship & Residency, Baylor School of Medicine; Chief Pulmonary Fellow, University of California, San Francisco
  Background: Chief of Pulmonary Medicine, Texas Tech School of Medicine
  Randall Crowder, Partner
  e-mail: crowder@texoventures.com
  Education: BS, General Management & Environmental Engineering, United States Military Academy; MBA, McCombs School of Business, University of Texas, Austin
  Background: CEO, Texas Venture Labs

1804 TGAP VENTURES
7117 Stadium Drive
Kalamazoo, MI 49009

Phone: 269-217-1999 Fax: 269-381-7620
e-mail: pete@farner.net
web: tgapvcfunds.com

Mission Statement: TGap Ventures serves entrepreneurs through the Midwest by assisting them define, develop, grow and build value in their businesses.

Geographic Preference: Midwest Region
Average Investment: $500,000 - $1 million
Industry Group Preference: Software, Life Sciences, Internet Infrastructure, Specialty Manufacturing, Plastics, Communication Technology
Portfolio Companies: HistoSonics, Inspire Medical Systems, InStadium, Interrad Medical, MedVantx, NeoChord, Regesis Biomedical, ValenTx
Key Executives:
  Jack K Ahrens II, General Partner
  269-760-4570
  Fax: 413-832-4838
  e-mail: jahrens620@aol.com
  Education: Indiana University
  Background: President, United Capital Corporation of Illinois; General Partner, Parthfinder Venture Capital Funds
  Peter W Farner, General Partner
  269-217-1999
  Fax: 269-381-7620
  e-mail: pete@farner.net
  Education: Duke University; MBA, University of Michigan
  Background: Senior VP, Ryan Partnership; Stroh Brewery

1805 TGF MANAGEMENT
111 Congress Avenue
Suite 2900
Austin, TX 78701

Phone: 512-322-3100

Mission Statement: One of the largest and most active middle market buyout firms in the Southwest.

Geographic Preference: Southwest United States
Fund Size: $700 million
Founded: 1992
Average Investment: $25-$100 million
Investment Criteria: Later Stage
Industry Group Preference: Manufacturing, Distribution, Construction, Industrial Services, Outsourcing & Efficiency, Food & Beverage, Consumer Products
Portfolio Companies: ENTACT, M&M Manufacturing, Sterling Foods

1806 TH LEE PUTNAM VENTURES
1120 Avenue of the Americas
Suite 1807
New York, NY 10036

Mission Statement: TH Lee Putnam Ventures is a technology-focused private equity firm affiliated with Thomas H. Lee Partners, a leading buyout firm, and Putnam Investments, a leading global money management firm.

Fund Size: $1.1 billion
Founded: 1999
Average Investment: $20 - 50 million
Investment Criteria: Later-Stage, Public Entities, Middle Market Buyouts, Recapitalizations, Spinouts

Industry Group Preference: Technology, Financial Services, Retail, Consumer & Leisure, Consumer Products, Distribution, Logistics, Business Outsourcing
Portfolio Companies: Symphony Services, 4R Systems, LN Holdings, Parago

1807 THAYER STREET PARTNERS
41 Madison Ave.
34th Floor
New York, NY 10010

Phone: 212-256-8740
web: www.thayerstreet.com

Mission Statement: A boutique private investment firm with an emphasis on the specialty finance, technology, media and business services industries.
Founded: 2011
Average Investment: $5-50 Million
Investment Criteria: Middle-Market, Late Stage, Growth Stage
Industry Group Preference: Business Products & Services, Technology, Media, Technology-Enabled Services, Financial Services, Insurance
Key Executives:
  Alexandra Prima, Vice President
  212-253-3942
  e-mail: alexandrap@thayerstreet.com
  Education: BBA, Finance, Southern Methodist University; MBA, NYU Stern School of Business
  Background: Associate, Silver Point Capital; Senior Associate, Cedar Street Capital

1808 THAYER VENTURES
PO Box 7775
San Francisco, CA 94120

Phone: 415-782-1414
web: www.thayerventures.com

Mission Statement: Thayer Ventures partners with entrepreneurs to create, develop and build technology companies that will revolutionize the hospitality industry.
Founded: 2009
Industry Group Preference: Hospitality, Restaurants, Lodging, Gaming, Airlines
Portfolio Companies: Liftopia, TripBam, Traxo, Sphere, Hipmunk, Nor1, SocialTables, ID90, Posiq, Groupize, Duetto, Viridis, New Brand Analytics, Adara, Switchfly
Key Executives:
  Christopher R Hemmeter, Managing Director
  e-mail: chris@thayerventures.com
  Education: Cornell University, Harvard Business School
  Background: Founder & CEO, Dynamic Payment Ventures; Founder & CEO, CriticalArc Technologies
  Directorships: Capton
  Mark E Farrell, Managing Director
  e-mail: mark@thayerventures.com
  Education: BA, Loyola Marymount University; MA, University College Dublin; JD, University of Pennsylvania Law School
  Background: Investment Banker, Thomas Weisel Partners; Lawyer, Wilson Sonsini Goodrich & Rosati
  Jeff Jackson, Managing Director
  e-mail: jeff@thayerventures.com
  Education: Dartmouth College; MBA, Kellogg Business School
  Background: American Airlines, Sabre Inc.
  Directorships: Rent-A-Center
  Lee Pillsbury, Managing Director
  Education: BS, Cornell University; MBA, Northwestern University

1809 THE ALCHEMIST ACCELERATOR
San Francisco, CA

web: www.alchemistaccelerator.com

Mission Statement: A venture-backed initiative focused on accelerating the development of seed-stage ventures that monetize from enterprises (not consumers).
Founded: 2012
Investment Criteria: Seed
Industry Group Preference: Technology
Portfolio Companies: Carta Healthcare, Cobalt.Io, Farmwise, Foresight, Launch Darkly, Moengage, Privacera, Rigetti Quantum Computing, Unwrinkly Inc., Yotascale

1810 THE ARCVIEW GROUP
169 11th Street
San Francisco, CA 94103

Toll-Free: 855-892-1951
e-mail: info@arcviewgroup.com
web: arcviewgroup.com

Mission Statement: Invests in the cannabis industry.
Founded: 2010
Investment Criteria: Seed, Early-Stage
Industry Group Preference: Cannabis
Portfolio Companies: Tokyo Smoke, 4Front, Aqualitas, Eaze, Ebbu, Gatekeeper Innovation, Green Flower, Meadow, MJ Freeway, Chooze, Toke With, MJardin, SPARC, Mirth, Flowhub, Leaf, W☐rk, Medicine Man, The Goodship, Steep Hill, Growcentia
Key Executives:
  Troy Dayton, Chief Executive Officer
  Education: American University
  Background: Associate Director, Interfaith Drug Policy Initiative; Director of Development, Multidisciplinary Association for Psychedelic Studies; Co-Founder, Students for Sensible Drug Policy; Sr. Development Officer, Marijuana Policy Project; Partner, Canopy Boulder
  Directorships: Marijuana Policy Project; National Cannabis Industry Association
  Steve DeAngelo, President
  Education: University of Maryland
  Background: Co-Founder/Executive Director, Harborside; Co-Founder, Steep Hill
  Jeanne M. Sullivan, General Partner
  Education: BS, Marketing/Advertising, University of Illinois at Urbana-Champaign; JD, Creighton University School of Law
  Background: Product Management, AT&T/Bell Labs; Managing Director, Olivetti Ventures; Chief Inspiration Officer, Sullivan Adventures; Co-Founder, StarVest Partners
  Directorships: Astia; Women's Leadership Board, Harvard Kennedy School
  Brian Sheng, General Partner
  Education: Princeton University
  Background: Founder, IvyBound; Analyst, Shenzhen Capital Group Co.; Partner, DreamTech Ventures; Foreign Investment Advisor, URI Investment Fund; Co-Founder/Managing Partner, Fresh VC
  Directorships: Eaze
  Michael Brosgart, VP, Sales & Marketing
  Education: George Washington University
  Background: Executive Director, LatinFinance; Director of Sales/Special Projects, Luxury Brand Partners
  Directorships: Frecuencia Latinoamerica Publications

1811 THE CHANNEL GROUP
576 Fifth Avenue
Suite 903
New York, NY 10036

Phone: 212-330-8076 Fax: 212-627-8877
e-mail: info@thechannelgroup.com
web: www.thechannelgroup.com

Venture Capital & Private Equity Firms / Domestic Firms

Mission Statement: A New York-based life sciences venture development and management firm, that engages in two types of activities, venture formation and venture transactions.
Geographic Preference: North America, Europe, Pacific Rim
Founded: 2001
Industry Group Preference: Life Sciences, Biotechnology, Pharmaceuticals, Diagnostics, Medical Devices, Reagent Suppliers, Biologicals
Other Locations:
   Pacific Channel Ltd.
   101 Customs Street E
   PO Box 106818
   Auckland 1143
   New Zealand
   Phone: 64 9 377 9689 **Fax:** 64 9 337 0710
Key Executives:
   Robert J. Beckman, Co-Founder/Managing Partner
   e-mail: rbeckman@thechannelgroup.com
   Education: BS, Pharmaceutical Sciences, Columbia University
   Background: Co-Founder, Intergen Company; VP, Marketing Services, Revlon Health Care Group
   Directorships: Lesanne Life Sciences, LLC
   Allan R. Goldberg, PhD, Co-Founder/Partner Emeritus
   e-mail: agoldberg@thechannelgroup.com
   Education: BA, English & Mathematics, Cornell University; PhD, Biochemistry/Biology, Princeton University
   Background: Co-Founder, Innovir Laboratories, Professor of Virology, The Rockefeller University
   Directorships: Astex Pharmaceuticals
   Philip N. Sussman, Managing Partner
   e-mail: psussman@thechannelgroup.com
   Education: BS, Physics, SUNY Stony Brook; MS, Biotechnology, Manhattan College; SM, Management, Sloan School of Management, MIT
   Background: Senior Management, Perlegen Sciences; Memory Pharmaceuticals; Cadus Pharmaceutical Corp; Director, Strategy & Business Development, Ciba-Gelgy Corp's Pharmaceuticals Division
   Directorships: Lesanne Life Sciences, Thar Pharmaceuticals
   Vijay Aggarwal, PhD, Managing Partner
   Education: BA, Chemistry, Case Western Reserve University; PhD, Pharmacology/Toxicology, Medical College of Virginia
   Background: CEO, VaxiGenix; President & CEO, Aureon Laboratories; President, AAI Development Services
   Directorships: AccuGenomics, Genisphere, Hycor Biomedical, Mitomics, Targeted Diagnostics and Therapeutics, Viracor-IBT Laboratories
   Shmuel Einav, PhD, Advisory Partner
   Education: BSc, MSc, Mechanical & Nulcear Engineering, Technion; PhD, Biomechanical Engineering, Stony Brook University
   Background: Professor, Biomedical Engineering, Stony Brook University; Director, Medical Technologies, Center of Excellence for Wireless & Information Technology

1812 THE HIVE
720 University Avenue
Suite 200
Palo Alto, CA 94301

e-mail: info@hivedata.com
web: hivedata.com

Mission Statement: The Hive is a venture capital fund and co-creation studio working with AI-based companies.
Average Investment: $1.5 million - $2 million
Investment Criteria: Seed, Early Stage
Industry Group Preference: Artificial Intelligence, Industry, Finance, Insurance, Health & Wellness, Blockchain
Portfolio Companies: 8 Security, Astound, Augmented Pixels, Blockstream, Colabot, Decision Engines, Deep Forest Media, Dojo Madness, FogHorn, Geminus, Jobr, Lightning Network, Live Objects, Nurego, Percolata, Perspica, Peritus AI, Snips, Staq, Trusted Insight, TruU, Xage Security
Key Executives:
   T.M. Ravi, Co-Founder/Managing Director
   Education: PhD, University of California, Los Angeles
   Background: President/CEO, Media Blitz Inc.; VP, Cheyenne Software; VP, Computer Associates, President/CEO, Peakstone Corporation; Founder/President/CEO, Mimosa Systems; CMO, Iron Mountain Digital; Co-Creator, FogHorn Systems Inc.
   Sumant Mandal, Co-Founder
   Education: Michigan State University; MBA, Kellogg School of Management
   Background: Managing Director, Clearstone Venture Partners; Co-Founder, The Fabric; Managing Director, March Capital Partners
   Directorships: BillDesk; 8 Security; Rubicon Project

1813 THINKTIV VENTURES
1011 San Jacinto Blvd
Suite 202
Austin, TX 78701

Phone: 512-745-8100 Fax: 512-857-7751
web: www.thinktiv.com

Mission Statement: Thinktiv revolutionizes the process of building businesses that win. In a world where the cost of launching products and companies continues to plummet, we believe lethal talent is more valuable than cash capital. Like most people investing in early-stage businesses, we also believe that finding and hiring the right talent represents the greatest risk factor to an early-stage company's ultimate success.
Founded: 2007
Investment Criteria: Early-Stage
Industry Group Preference: SaaS, E-Commerce & Manufacturing, Social Media, Digital Media & Marketing, Internet
Portfolio Companies: Adlucent, Affinergy, AlertTech, Attivio, BP3, Bazaarvoice, BlackLogus, Bloodbuy, Boundless Network, Bulldog, Burst, College Portfolio, Collider Media, Common Assets, CopperEgg, Democracy.com, Energytics, Experts Exchange, GasBuddy, Icon.me, LookNook, OnPulse, OtherInbox, PayGo, Prysm, QuickGifts, SharePost, Shopatron, Socialware, Spredfast, Stylefy, TrueCar, Vast
Other Locations:
   111 N Whitfield Street
   Third Floor
   Pittsburgh, PA 15206
   Phone: 412-404-2745
Key Executives:
   Jonathan Berkowitz, Chief Executive Officer
   Education: BS, MS, Information Systems, Carnegie Mellon University
   Background: Vice President, Product Strategy, B-Side Entertainment; Director, Product Stategy, Trilogy
   Justin B. Petro, Chief Product Officer/Co-Founder
   Education: BFA, Carnegie Mellon University
   Background: Director, User Experience, Design Edge; Trilogy Software
   Paul Burke, Managing Partner/Co-Founder
   Education: BFA, Carnegie Mellon University
   Background: Design Director, Trilogy Software; Creative Director, CollegeHire.com; Founder, Inkwell Studios
   Steve Waters, Chief Ventures Officer
   Education: BA, Organizational Behavior, Stanford University
   Background: Founder/CEO, Triggerbox; Trilogy; Firepond; RightNow Technologies; BetweenMarkets; B-Side Entertainment; M&A Analyst, Bear Stearns

1814 THIRD ROCK VENTURES
29 Newbury Street
3rd Floor
Boston, MA 02116

Phone: 617-585-2000
web: www.thirdrockventures.com

Mission Statement: Building of valuable and transformational life science companies that show high growth potential and are well-positioned to make a difference in the marketplace.

Fund Size: $800 million
Founded: 2007
Industry Group Preference: Life Sciences, Therapeutics, Diagnostics, Medical Devices
Portfolio Companies: Ablexis, Afferent Pharmaceuticals, Agios Pharmaceuticals, Alcresta, Allena Pharmaceutials, Alnara Pharmaceuticals, Bluebird Bio, Blueprint Medicines, Cibiem, Constellation Pharmaceuticals, CytomX Therapeutics, DC Devices, Edimer, Editas, Element Science, Eleven Biotherapeutics, Foundation Medicine, Global Blood Therapeutics, Ingenica, Jounce Therapeutics, Kala Pharamaceuticals, Lotus Tissue Repair, MyKardia, NinePoint Medical, Nurix, PanOptica, Rhythm, Sage Therepeutics, SeventhSense Biosystems, Taris Biomedical, Topica Pharmaceuticals, Voyager Therapeutics, WarpDrive Bio, Zafgen,

Other Locations:
499 Illinois Street
Suite 110
San Francisco, CA 94158
Phone: 415-766-3600

Key Executives:
Mark Levin, Partner
e-mail: mark@thirdrockventures.com
Education: MS, Chemical & Biomedical Engineering, Washington University
Background: Co-Founder, Mayfield Funds' Life Sciences effort; Founding CEO of Tularik, Cell Genesys/Abgenix, Focal, Stem Cells, Millennium Pharmaceuticals
Directorships: Blueprint Medicines, Constellation Pharmaceuticals, DC Devices, Eleven Biotherapeutics, Foundation Medicine, NinePoint Medical, Warp Drive
Kevin Starr, Partner
e-mail: kevin@thirdrockventures.com
Education: BA, Mathematics & Business, Colby College; MS, Corporate Finance, Boston College
Background: COO & CFO, Millennium Pharmaceuticals; Millennium BioTherapeutics; Biogen; Digital Equipment Corporation
Directorships: SAGE Therapeutics, Afferent Pharmaceuticals, Agios Pharmaceuticals, Global Blood Therapeutics, MyoKardia, PanOptica, Zafgen Pharmaceuticals
Robert Tepper, MD, Partner
e-mail: bob@thirdrockventures.com
Education: AB, Biochemistry, Princeton University; MD, Harvard Medical School
Background: President of R&D, Millennium Pharmaceuticals; Co-Founder, Cell Genesys/Abgenix
Directorships: Jounce Therapeutics, Alcresta, Allena, Bluebird.bio, Constellation Pharmaceuticals, Kala Pharmaceuticals
Abbie Celniker, Partner
Education: BA, Biology, University of California, San Diego; PhD, Molecular Biology, University of Arizona
Background: CEO, Eleven Biotherapeutics; CEO, Taligen Therapeutics Inc.; SVP of Pharmaceutical Sciences & Operations, Millennium Pharmaceuticals Inc.; Associate Director of Biological Assay Development, Genentech
Directorships: MassBio
Neil Exter, Partner
e-mail: neil@thirdrockventures.com
Education: BS, Cornell University; MS, Stanford University; MBA, Harvard Business School
Background: CBO, Alantos Pharmaceuticals; VP, Millennium Pharmaceuticals
Directorships: CytomX Therapeutics, Cibiem
Kevin Gillis, Partner/COO
e-mail: kgillis@thirdrockventures.com
Education: BA, Brandeis University; MBA, Bentley University
Background: VP, Finance, Coley Pharmaceutical Group; Millennium Pharmaceuticals, The Coca-Cola Company
Craig Muir, Partner, San Francisco
e-mail: craig@thirdrockventures.com
Education: BS, Animal Physiology, University of California, Davis
Background: SVP, Technical Operations, Codon Devices; Millennium Pharmaceuticals
Cary Pfeffer MD, Partner
e-mail: cary@thirdrockventures.com
Education: BA, Biochemistry, Columbia University; MD, University of Pennsylvania; MBA, Wharton School
Background: Founder, The Pfeffer Group; Biogen
Charles Homcy, MD, Partner
Education: AB/MD, John Hopkins University
Background: Professor of Medicine, San Francisco Medical School, University of California; Attending Physician, San Francisco VA Medical Center; Co-Founded, Portola Pharmaceuticals
Christoph Lengauer, PhD, Partner
Education: MS, Human Genetics, University of Salzburg; PhD, Biology, Heidelberg University; MBA, Medical Services Management, John Hopkins University

1815 THIRD SECURITY
The Governor Tyler
1881 Grove Avenue
Radford, VA 24141

Phone: 540-633-7900 Fax: 540-633-7939
web: www.thirdsecurity.com

Mission Statement: Third Security is a venture capital firm characterized by an expanding global perspective and a distinctively patient approach. We evaluate opportunities in a wide range of industries, but principally focus on emerging through late-stage investments in life-sciences and communications technology.

Investment Criteria: Expansion, Later Stage
Industry Group Preference: Life Sciences, Communication Technology
Portfolio Companies: Heyo, OvaScience, Agilis, Soligenix, AmpliPhi, Genopaver, Synethic Biologics, Oragenics, Intrexon, Halozyme, Fibrocell Science, Avexis, Persea Bio, Fitnet

Other Locations:
735 Market Street
3rd Floor
San Francisco, CA 94103
Phone: 415-644-5365 **Fax:** 415-344-0677

2875 South Ocean Boulevard
Suite 214
Palm Beach, FL 33480
Phone: 561-855-7831 **Fax:** 561-355-0627

Key Executives:
Randal J. Kirk, Senior Managing Director/Chief Executive Officer
Education: B.A. Business, Radford University; J.D., University of Virginia
Background: New River Pharmaceuticals
Directorships: Halozyme Therapeutics, ZIOPHARM Oncology, Intrexon
Marcus Smith, Senior Managing Director/General Counsel/Chief Compliance Officer
Education: B.B.A./J.D., University of Georgia
Background: Senior Vice President/General Counsel/Secretary, New River Pharmaceuticals; Attorney, The Southland Corporation and Occidental Oil & Gas

Venture Capital & Private Equity Firms / Domestic Firms

Corporation
Directorships: Fibrocell Science

1816 THIRD WAVE DIGITAL
web: thirdwavedigital.vc

Mission Statement: Los Angeles company invests in early-stage media and technology entrepreneurs.
Investment Criteria: Early-Stage
Industry Group Preference: Media, Mobile
Portfolio Companies: 88Rising, All Def Digital, BeautyCon, Canvas, DanceOn, DigiTour, Drone Racing League, FameBit, Greenfly, Gunslinger Studios, Hello Giggles, Immortals, IndMusic, Insurrection Media, IRIS.TV, Jukin Media, Merry Jane, Mitu, Mondo Media, Naritiv, Pluto.TV, Rocket Jump, Stem, TasteMade, Tubular Labs, Vessel, VideoAmp, WeVR, ZEFR

1817 THOMA BRAVO LLC
300 North La Salle Street
Suite 4350
Chicago, IL 60654

Phone: 312-254-3300
web: www.thomabravo.com

Mission Statement: Thoma Bravo targets control investments in companies with strong business franchises led by experienced executives who aspire to achieve industry leadership.
Geographic Preference: United States
Fund Size: $2 billion
Founded: 1990
Average Investment: $60 million
Minimum Investment: $5 million
Investment Criteria: LBO, MBO, Later Stage
Industry Group Preference: Business Products & Services, Healthcare, Consumer Products, Software, Financial Services, Education, Technology
Portfolio Companies: Attachmate, Blue Coat Systems, Compuware Corporation, Deltek, Dynatrace, Edmentum, Embarcadero Technologies, Empirix, Flexera Software, Global Healthcare Exchange, Hyland Software, InfoVista S.A., Keynote Systems, LANDESK Software, Local Media of America, Mediware Information Systems, Porter & Chester Institute, SailPoint Technologies, Segall Bryant & Hamill, Sirius Computer Solutions, Sparta Systems, SRS Software, Telestream, TravelClick, Tripwire, Vision Solutions

Other Locations:
600 Montgomery Street
32nd Floor
San Francisco, CA 94111
Phone: 415-263-3660 Fax: 415-392-6480

Key Executives:
Carl D Thoma, Managing Partner/Founder
312-777-4420
e-mail: cthoma@thomabravo.com
Education: Graduate, Oklahoma State University; MBA, Stanford Graduate School of Business
Background: Implemented Growth, First Chicago Equity Group; Founder, Golder, Thoma & C
Orlando Bravo, Managing Partner/Founder
415-263-3665
e-mail: obravo@thomabravo.com
Education: BA, Brown University; MBA, Stanford Graduate School of Business; JD, Stanford Law School
Background: Mergers/Acquisitions, Morgan Stanley
Directorships: Embarcadero Technologies, Sirius Comuter Solutions, LANDesk Software, Blue Coat Systems, Deltek, Digital Insight, Keynote Systems
Lee M Mitchell, Managing Partner
312-777-4450
e-mail: lmitchell@thomabravo.com
Education: Wesleyan University; University of Chicago Law School
Background: Principal, Golder; Partner, Sidley & Austin;

CEO, Field Enterprises
Directorships: Porter & Chester Institute, Local Media of America
Scott Crabill, Managing Partner
415-263-3662
e-mail: scrabill@thomabravo.com
Education: BS, Industrial Engineering, Stanford University; MBA, Stanford University
Background: Summit Partners, Hewlett-Packard, JH Whitney & Co., Alex Brown & Sons
Directorships: Attachmate Corporation, Vision Solutions, Edmentum, Tripwire, Mediware Systems, SRS Software
Seth Boro, Managing Partner
415-249-6719
e-mail: sboro@thomabravo.com
Education: BComm, Queen's University School of Business; MBA, Stanford Graduate School of Busienss
Background: Summit Partners, ServiceSource, CreditSuisse, First Marathon Securities
Directorships: Hyland Software, Vision Solutions, LANDesk Software, Tripwire, Blue Coat Systems, InfoVista S.A., Mediware Systems, Keynote Systems, Empirix
Holden Spaht, Managing Partner
415-263-3667
e-mail: hspaht@thomabravo.com
Education: BA, Economics, Dartmouth College; MBA, Harvard Business School
Background: Morgan Stanley Capital Partners, Thomas H Lee Partners, Morgan Stanley
Directorships: Embarcadero Technologies, Sirius Computer Solutions, Edmentum, Telestream, Deltek, Digital Insight

1818 THOMAS H LEE PARTNERS
100 Federal Street
Boston, MA 02110

Phone: 617-227-1050
web: www.thl.com

Mission Statement: Only pursues companies that want to be pursued with a leveraged buyout. Typical acquisitions are middle market companies with growth potential, which are revamped and either sold or are taken public.
Fund Size: $12 billion under management
Founded: 1974
Investment Criteria: Growth Buyouts
Industry Group Preference: Business Products & Services, Financial Services, Consumer, Healthcare, Media, Information Services
Portfolio Companies: 1-800-CONTACTS, Agencyport Software, Aramark, Black Knight Financial Services, Ceridian, CompuCom Systems, CTI Foods, Cumulus Media, First Bancorp, Fogo De Chao, Hawkeye Renewables, iHeartMedia, Intermedix, inVentiv Health, MoneyGram International, Party City, Phillips Pet Food & Supplies, Prime Risk Partners, ServiceLink, Systems Maintenance Services, The Nielsen Company, Umpqua Holdings Corporation, Univision Communications, West Corporation

Key Executives:
Scott M. Sperling, Co-CEO
Education: BS, Purdue University; MBA, Harvard Business School
Background: Managing Partner, The Aeneas Group; Senior Consultant, Boston Consulting Group
Todd M. Abbrecht, Co-CEO
Education: BSE, Finance, Wharton School; MBA, Harvard Business School
Background: M&A, Credit Suisse First Boston
Directorships: Aramark, Fogo de Chao, Intermedix, inVentiv Health, Party City
Anthony J. DiNovi, Chair
Education: AB, Harvard College; MBA, Harvard Graduate School

Background: Corporate Finance, Goldman Sachs & Company; Wertheim Schroeder & Company
Michael A. Bell, Managing Director
Education: BS, Wharton School; MBA, Harvard Business School
Background: Exec. Chairman, Syneos Health; President, Commercial Division, INC Research, Syneos Health
Directorships: Agiliti Health Inc.; Centria Healthcare; Healthcare Staffing Services; Professional Physical Therapy
Mark L. Benaquista, Managing Director
Education: BS, Management Science Information Systems, Rutgers University; MS, Management Systems Analysis, Kean University
Background: SVP & Co-CIO Warner Music Group; Senior Director, Merck & Co.; JP Morgan; Chelsea Consulting
Henry J. Boye, Managing Director
Education: BA, International Studies, Dickinson College; MBA, Wharton School
Background: Managing Director, Blue Ridge Partners; Publisher, Harvard Business Review; COO & SVP of Corporate Development, Mass Insight
Thomas M. Hagerty, Managing Director
Education: BBA, University of Notre Dame; MBA, Harvard Business School
Background: M&A, Morgan Stanley & Co
Directorships: Fidelity National Financial, Fidelity National Information Services, Black Knight Financial Services, ServiceLink H9oldings, MoneyGram International, First Bancorp, Ceridian
Vincente Piedrahita, Managing Director
Education: BA, Sociology, Princeton University; MBA, Harvard Business School
Background: Director of Strategic Projects, Clear Channel Outdoor; Consultant, Monitor Group
James C. Carlisle, Managing Director & Head, Technology & Business Solutions
Education: BSE, Operations Research, Princeton University; MBA, Harvard Business School
Background: Financial Institutions Group, Goldman Sachs & Co.
Directorships: Univision Communications, Clear Channel Outdoor Holdings, Agencyport Software
Joshua M. Nelson, Managing Director & Head, Healthcare
Education: AB, Politics, Princeton University; MBA, Harvard Business School
Background: JPMorgan Partners; McKinsey & Co; The Beacon Group
Directorships: 1-800-CONTACTS, inVentiv Health, Party City, Hawkeye Energy Holdings
Soren L. Oberg, Advisory Partner
Education: AB, Applied Mathematics, Harvard College; MBA, Harvard Business School
Background: Morgan Stanley & Co; Hicks Muse Tate & Furst Inc
Directorships: Ceridian Corporation, CompuCom Systems, Grupo Corporativo Ono, S.A., Systems Maintenance Services, West Corporation
Kent R. Weldon, Advisory Partner
Education: BA, Economics, University of Notre Dame; MBA, Harvard Business School
Background: Morgan Stanley & Co; Wellington Management Company
Gregory A. White, Managing Director & Head, Investor Relations
Education: BNE, Georgia Insitute of Technology; MBA, Harvard Business School
Background: Thomas Weisel Partners; TA Associates; Morgan Stanley & Co; Smith Barney; UNC Ventures
Daniel G. Jones, Managing Director & Head, SRG
Education: BA, Dartmouth College; MBA, MIT Sloan School of Management
Background: Management Consultant, Monitor Group; Financial Project Manager, Deputy to CFO, Lan Airlines

Shari H. Wolkon, Managing Director & General Counsel
Education: AB, Economics, Princeton University; MBA, Johnson Graduate School of Management, Cornell University; JD, Cornell Law School
Background: Corporate Partner, Ropes & Gray LLP
Ganesh B. Rao, Managing Director & Head, Financial Technology & Services
Education: BA, Economics, Duke University; MBA, Harvard Business School
Background: M&A, Morgan Stanley & Co.; Greenlight Capital
Directorships: Black Knight Financial Services, Ceridian HCM Holding, Comdata, MoneyGram International, ServiceLink Holdings, The Nielsen Company
Jeff T. Swenson, Managing Director & Head, Vertical Software
Education: BA, Economics, Northwestern University; MBA, Harvard Business School
Background: Private Equity Group, Bain Capital; Management Consultant, Bain & Company
Directorships: 1-800-CONTACTS, Acosta, CTI Foods, Fogo de Chao, Intermedix Corporation, Phillips Pet Food & Supplies and Seamless Holdings

1819 THOMAS WEISEL VENTURE PARTNERS
One Montgomery Street
Suite 3700
San Francisco, CA 94104

Phone: 415-364-2500 **Fax:** 415-364-2695
Toll-Free: 888-267-3700
web: www.tweisel.com

Mission Statement: An early-stage venture capital firm that invests in emerging information technology companies. As a partner with a long-term perspective, TWVP plays an active role in helping entrepreneurs turn ideas into sustainable businesses.

Industry Group Preference: Information Technology

1820 THOMAS, MCNERNEY & PARTNERS
One Landmark Square
Suite 1920
Stamford, CT 06901

Phone: 203-978-2000 **Fax:** 203-978-2005
web: www.tm-partners.com

Mission Statement: A healthcare private equity firm with over 60 years combined healthcare private equity and venture capital experience.

Geographic Preference: East Coast, Midwest, West Coast
Fund Size: $375 million
Average Investment: $20 million
Minimum Investment: $5 million
Investment Criteria: All Stages
Industry Group Preference: Healthcare, Life Sciences, Pharmaceuticals, Medical Devices, Biotechnology, Diagnostics
Portfolio Companies: Apptec Laboratory Services, Altair Therapeutics, Cebix, Coley Pharmaceutical Group, Invitae, SGB, Tranzyme Pharma, Virdante Pharmaceuticals, Arkal Medical, Asante Solutions, Atritech, AxioMed Spine, Bausch & Lomb, CAS Medical Systems, Galil Medical, Intuity Medical, Keystone Dental, Osteobiologics, Softscope Medical Technologies, Torax Medical, Vertiflex, Amarin, Auspex Pharmaceuticals, Celator Pharmaceuticals, Clarus Therapeutics, CNS Therapeutics, InnoPharma, Neurotherapeutics Pharma, Ocera Therapeutics, Oriel Therapeutics, Packaging Coordinators, Quinnova Pharmaceuticals, Solstice Neurosciences, Tioga Pharmaceuticals, Zogenix

Other Locations:
60 South 6th Street
Suite 3620

Venture Capital & Private Equity Firms / Domestic Firms

Minneapolis, MN 55402
Phone: 612-465-8660 **Fax:** 612-465-8661

3366 N. Torrey Pines Court
Suite 220
La Jolla, CA 92037
Phone: 858-373-5800 **Fax:** 858-228-5751

Key Executives:
James E Thomas, Partner
Education: BS, Wharton School; MS, London School of Economics
Background: Leader Healthcare Technology, Warburg Pincus; VP, Goldman Sachs International, London
Directorships: CAS Medical Systems, Clarus Therapeutics, Galil Medical, InnoPharma, Keystone Dental, Packaging Coordinators
Peter H McNerney, Partner
Education: BA, Yale University; MBA, Stanford University; CPA
Background: Co-Founder, Thomas, McNerney & Partners; Co-Founder/Managing Partner, Kensington Group; Founder/CEO, Memtec North America; Baxter Healthcare Corporation; President, Minnesota Venture Capital Association
Directorships: Asante Solutions, Torax Medical
Alex Zisson, Partner
Education: Brown University
Background: Managing Director/Health Care Strategist, Hambrecht & Quist
Directorships: Auspex Pharmaceuticals, Clarus Therapeutics, InnoPharma
Kathleen A Tune, Partner
Education: MS, Microbiology, University of Minnesota; MBA, University of Minnesota Carlson School of Management
Background: Health Care Analyst, Piper Jaffray; Solvay, SA; Senior Scientist, Molecular Biology, University of Minnesota
Directorships: AxioMed Spine, CAS Medical Systems, VertiFlex

1821 THOMVEST VENTURES
203 Redwood Shores Parkway
Suite 680
Redwood City, CA 94065

Phone: 350-965-4700 **Fax:** 350-618-1509
e-mail: info@thomvest.com
web: www.thomvest.com

Mission Statement: Our focus is working with entrepreneurs to make every company we invest in a success. We deliberately invest in a smaller number of select companies, making perhaps three to four new investments per year. We then bring the diverse talents of our team to bear, helping entrepreneurs in everything from strategy to marketing, sales, business development, to structuring and financing transactions. We are long-term partners with the companies we invest in, and encourage you to get in touch with us if you think our firm might be a good fit for yours.

Geographic Preference: Silicon Valley
Fund Size: $250 million
Investment Criteria: Early-Stage to Growth-Stage
Portfolio Companies: Apsalar, Axcient, DataXu, Kabbage, LendingClub, LendUp, Milyoni, NetBase, SoFi, Tactus, Virool, Vungle, YottaMark, Avalanche Technology, Inxent, SoonR

Key Executives:
Don Butler, Managing Director
Education: BA, Chinese, UCLA; MA, East Asian Studies & Political Science, Stanford University
Background: Asia Pacific Ventures; Analyst, Lehman Brothers
Directorships: Apsalar, Avalanche, Axcient, Kabbage, Milyoni, Netbase, Vungle, YottaMark

1822 THREE CITIES RESEARCH
135 East 57th Street
Suite 15-103
New York, NY 10022

Phone: 212-838-9660 **Fax:** 212-980-1142
e-mail: info@tcr-ny.com
web: www.tcr-ny.com

Mission Statement: Focused on businesses that are substantially underperforming their potential. To deploy dedicated resources to deeply understand the value proposition and competitive environment of its portfolio companies, and partner with management teams to develop and execute winning strategies.

Fund Size: $700 million
Founded: 1976
Minimum Investment: $10 million
Investment Criteria: Unexploited Growth, Underperforming companies, Complicated transactions
Industry Group Preference: Manufacturing, Service Industries, Distribution, Industrial Equipment, Retailing, Publishing
Portfolio Companies: Agrileum, Bluefish Holdings LLC, Finn Corp, Parallel Products

Key Executives:
J. William Uhrig, Partner
212-605-3206
e-mail: uhrigb@tcr-ny.com
Education: Purdue University, University of Chicago
Christopher Erickson, Partner
e-mail: christopher.erickson@tcr-ny.com
Education: BS, University of Wisconsin, Madison; PhD, Physics, Princeton University
Background: McKinsey & Co
Jason Stein, Partner
e-mail: jason.stein@tcr-ny.com
Education: BA, University of San Diego; MBA, UC Berkeley
Background: Vendio Corporation; Quantum Corporation
Christian Schwartz, Principal
e-mail: schwartzc@tcr-ny.com
Education: BA, Duke University; MBA, Wharton School
Background: Associate, Unisphere

1823 THRIVE CAPITAL
New York, NY

e-mail: info@thrivecap.com
web: www.thrivecap.com

Mission Statement: Thrive Capital is a venture capital investment firm focused on media and internet investments.

Founded: 2009
Industry Group Preference: Media, Internet
Portfolio Companies: Twitch, Tutorspree, Summly, Spree Commerce, Simple, Shift, Reddit, OnSwipe, Memoir, Maple, Jet, Instagram, Hyperpublic, Hot Potato, Hightower, GroupMe, Flatiron School, FabFitFun, Fab, Dispatch, Cue, Baby.com.br,

Key Executives:
Joshua Kushner, Founder/Managing Partner
Education: Harvard University
Background: Co-Founder, Oscar Health
Directorships: VTS, Hightower
Kareem Zaki, Investor
Education: AB, Economics & Healthcare Policy, Harvard University
Background: Private Equity Invest, The Blackstone Group; Business Analyst, McKinsey & Company; Investment Banking Analyst, JP Morgan

1824 THUNDERBIRD ANGEL NETWORK
Phoenix, AZ

Phone: 385-232-4226
e-mail: z.c.mckinney@global.t-bird.edu

Venture Capital & Private Equity Firms / Domestic Firms

Mission Statement: The Thunderbird Angel Network (TAN) is a dynamic group of accredited investors who are affiliated with the Thunderbird School of Global Management. Our members are Tbird alumni, professors, friends and members of the Phoenix startup community. TAN serves as a source to its members for early-stage companies that have the potential to grow rapidly. The Network is based at the Thunderbird School of Global Management, a hotspot for global business; thus, its members are interested in both domestic and international deals. TAN members typically seek to invest between $50,000 and $500,000,

Minimum Investment: $50,000
Investment Criteria: Early-Stage
  Tanaha Hairston, Managing Director
  Lacey Yoder, Managing Director

1825 TI VENTURE CAPITAL Texas Instruments Incorporated
12500 TI Boulevard
Dallas, TX 75243

Phone: 972-995-2011
e-mail: ti_venture@list.ti.com
web: www.ti.com/tiventures

Mission Statement: To provide Texas Instruments with strategic awareness of new technologies and markets, allow close partnering with our business teams and external venture capital firms on investment and alliance opportunities, and provide financial return for TI.

Founded: 1996
Investment Criteria: Startup, Early-Stage
Industry Group Preference: Emerging Markets, Sectors & Technologies, Semiconductors, Wireless Architectures, Power Management, Medical Devices, Networking, Wireless Technologies, Energy Management

Key Executives:
  Jean-Louis Trochu, Managing Director
  Tom Shackelford, Managing Director

1826 TICONDEROGA PRIVATE EQUITY
2305 Broadway Street
Boulder, CO 80304

Phone: 303-938-3768 Fax: 650-384-5811
e-mail: craig@ticcap.com
web: www.ticcap.com

Mission Statement: Focus on private equity investments in SaaS and healthcare services.

Fund Size: $20 million
Founded: 2010
Average Investment: $500K
Minimum Investment: $400K
Investment Criteria: LBO, MBO, Later
Industry Group Preference: Enterprise Software, SaaS, Healthcare Services
Portfolio Companies: The Neck and Back Clinics, National Research Institute, Construction Software Technologies, FastSpring, Damac, Park Place Technologies, Aileron Solutions, Memorial MRI & Diagnostic, Samba Safety

Other Locations:
  25 Braintree Hill Park
  Suite 200
  Braintree, MA 02184
  Phone: 781-930-3142

Key Executives:
  Craig A.T. Jones, Co-Founder/Managing Partner
  e-mail: craig@ticcap.com
  Education: BA, California State University; JD Magna Cum Laude, Harvard Law School
  Background: Co-Founder, Ticonderoga Capital; Partner, Dillon Read Venture Capital and Advent International; Associate, Centennial Funds; Management Consultant, Bain & Company
  Directorships: eStudySite; National Research Institute; CloudXPartners; InnoCentive; Blue Sky Networks; TransXSystems
  James E Vandervelden, Co-Founder/Partner
  e-mail: james@ticcap.com
  Education: BA Economics/Organizational Behavior & Management, Brown University
  Background: Principal, Dillon Reed; T A Associates; APM Inc
  Robert M. Hannon, Administrative Director
  781-416-3409
  e-mail: bob@ticcap.com
  Education: BA, Economics, Harvard College; MBA, Finance, Wharton School, University of Pennsylvania
  Background: Treasurer, Town & Country Corporation; Data General Corporation; Ford Motor Company; Leesona Corporation

1827 TIE ANGELS GROUP SEATTLE
PO Box 821
Redmond, WA 98073

web: www.tieangels.com

Mission Statement: TiE Angels Group Seattle or TAGS is an angel investment group formed by Charter Members of TiE Seattle to cater to the funding needs of startups primarily in Seattle and the Northwest region. The mission of TAGS is to act as an intermediary to provide entrepreneurs a means to raise funds for their ventures. TAGS provides strategic early stage investment and support, by leveraging the invaluable experience and network of TiE Charter Members. TAGS will provide a high quality deal flow, and early stage, typically seed or Series A round, funding and investment opportunities to its members, and access to funds, mentorship and guidance from an elite group of TAGS members and TiE Seattle Charter Members.

Geographic Preference: Seattle, Northwest
Investment Criteria: Seed-Stage, Early-Stage
Industry Group Preference: Software, Infrastructure, Internet, Mobile, Clean Technology, Healthcare, Education, Medical Devices
Portfolio Companies: Byndl, Exponential Entertainment, Movie Pong, Minettabrook, Knewsapp, Unify2, Versium, TrueFacet

Key Executives:
  Kumar Sripadam, Chair

1828 TIGER GLOBAL MANAGEMENT
9 West 57th St.
35th Floor
New York, NY 10019

Phone: 212-843-8030
web: www.tigerglobal.com

Mission Statement: Tiger Global Management is an investment firm that deploys capital globally. The firm launches and manages hedge funds and manages private equity.

Founded: 2001
Investment Criteria: Early-Stage, Growth-Stage
Industry Group Preference: Technology, Internet, Industrial, Consumer, Media, Telecommunications
Portfolio Companies: GaiaWorks, Guidelines, Ola, Olo, Postmastes, Procore, Roposo, Stripe, Taimei Medical Technology, Yaoshibang

Key Executives:
  Charles P Coleman III, Co-Founder/Managing Partner
  Education: BA, Williams College
  Anil L Crasto, Chief Operating Officer
  Background: Sr Accountant, Ernst & Young; Sr Manager, Price Waterhouse Coopers; Partner/COO/CFO, Compass Group; Partner/CFO, R6 Capital Management; Managing Director/COO, Mount Kellett Capital Management
  Scott Schleifer, Partner
  Education: BS, Wharton School

Venture Capital & Private Equity Firms / Domestic Firms

Background: Private Equity Investor, The Blackstone Group

1829 TIME WARNER INVESTMENT CORPORATION
1 Time Warner Center
New York, NY 10019-8016

Phone: 212-484-7819
e-mail: ir@timewarner.com
web: www.timewarner.com/our-company/tw-investments/

Mission Statement: The Time Warner Investments group focuses on investment opportunities that directly enhance Time Warner's ability to meet specific strategic goals. These strategic goals include the delivery of new services, enhancement of an existing product, entry or expansion into a key strategic market, completion of a strategic partnership, and critical research and development.

Geographic Preference: United States, Western Europe
Fund Size: $100 million
Founded: 2001
Average Investment: $10 million
Minimum Investment: $2 million
Investment Criteria: All Stages
Industry Group Preference: Broadcasting, Cable, Radio, Computer Hardware & Software, Internet Technology, Networking, Publishing, Telecommunications, Networking, Advertising
Portfolio Companies: Adaptly, BroadLogic, Bustle, Conviva, CrowdStar, Double Fusion, Dynamic Sinal, Epoxy, Exent, Gaia Online, Hammer & Chisel, Joyus, Krux, Nuvo TV, Simulmedia, Trion, Visible World, WeHeartIt, YieldMo
Jason Kilar, CEO

1830 TL VENTURES
435 Devon Park Drive
700 Building
Wayne, PA 19087

Phone: 610-971-1515
e-mail: info@tlventures.com
web: www.tlventures.com

Mission Statement: Focused on venture investing in category-defining, early-stage companies in software, communications, information infrastructure and business services, TL Ventures provides portfolio companies with operational, entrepreneurial and financial expertise and a global network of resources and contacts. Actively seeking new investments.

Geographic Preference: United States, Worldwide
Fund Size: $1.5 billion
Founded: 1988
Average Investment: $3 - 10 million
Minimum Investment: $3 million
Industry Group Preference: Biotechnology, Information Technology, Communications, Software, Networking, Business Products & Services
Portfolio Companies: Axiom, Celator Pharmaceuticals, Donuts, Finite Carbon, FIRE Solutions, Global Education Learning Holdings, iSpot, Noble BioMaterials, OEwaves, Pivotal Systems, QuatRx Pharmaceuticals, Salem International University, Schiller International University, SkyCross, Sopherion Therapeutics, Translarity

Key Executives:
  Mark DeNino, Managing Director
  e-mail: mdenino@tlventures.com
  Education: BA, Finance, Accounting, Boston College; MBA, Harvard Business School
  Background: President, CMS Corporate Finance
  Directorships: Celarix; Coastal Security Systems; aRealty.com; Hire.com; MediaBrians.com; Mobility Technologies
  Robert Keith, Managing Director
  e-mail: rkeith@tlventures.com
  Education: BS, American History, Amherst College; JD, Temple University
  Background: Managing Director, Radnor Venture Partners; Fidelity Bank
  Robert N. Verratti, Operating Partner
  Education: US Naval Academy
  Background: CEO, Nationa; Media; CEO, Total Core Systems; CEO, Great Western Cities; CEO, Global Ticket; EDS
  Robert J. McParland, Financial Partner
  Education: BS, Accountancy, University of North Carolina, Chapel Hill
  Background: Safeguard Scientifics; Senior Manager, PricewaterhouseCoopers
  Janet L. Stott, Chief Financial Officer
  Education: BS, Accounting, Philadelphia University; CPA
  Background: Controller, Katalyst LLC; Senior Manager, KPMG LLP

1831 TOBA CAPITAL
San Francisco, CA

e-mail: hello@tobacapital.com
web: www.tobacapital.com

Mission Statement: Toba Capital is a venture firm founded by Vinny Smith. We are a small team with twice the per capita operating experience of traditional VCs, investing in the markets we know firsthand: business applications and IT & internet infrastructure. Our background enables us to provide portfolio companies with unique operational support. We know what it takes to build a billion dollar software company and have seen both sides of over a hundred investments and M&A transactions.

Industry Group Preference: Business Products & Services, Information Technology, Internet, Infrastructure
Portfolio Companies: Clear Slide, Alteryx, Catavolt, Cirro, Codenvy, Dataguise, Directly, FloQast, Liquidware Labs, Maven Link, Parsec, Paxata, Predixion, Stratos, Quorum, Reach150, Sauce Labs, Seal, Secureauth, SHIFTMobility, Smarsh, Smartbear, Speakr, Stealthbits, Synoptek, Team Snap, Transifex, WSO2

Key Executives:
  Vinny Smith, Founder

1832 TOMORROW VENTURES
e-mail: info@tomorrowvc.com
web: www.tomorrowvc.com

Mission Statement: A hybrid, opportunistic venture capital firm developing innovative ideas with the power to change the way we live.

Geographic Preference: Worldwide
Industry Group Preference: Technology
Portfolio Companies: Legend Pictures, Humin, Maskd, Bitsqr, Doctor on Demand, Beautycounter, Shape Security, Remitly, LYFE Kitchen, Relay Foods, biNu, Stamped, Sharecare, Maker Studios, HealthLoop, Events.com, Remedy Systems, Sightly, Forbes Travel Guide, The Backplane, Prism Skylabs, Newhound, PowerGen Renewable Energy, Instructure, Appia, Ness Computing, DailyWOrth, Cortera, The BondFactor Company, Signal, Fanaticall, Prosper, Ciqual Limited, EverFi, Fullbridge, Scientific Media, Playsino, News Distribution Network, TomorrowInnovations, Welcu, Intern, Xfire, Cx, GTI Capital Group, GTI Medivenures

1833 TONIIC
901 Mission Street
Suite 205
San Francisco, CA 94103

Phone: 415-746-9925
web: www.toniic.com

Mission Statement: Toniic is an international impact investor network promoting a sustainable global economy by investing

Venture Capital & Private Equity Firms / Domestic Firms

in entrepreneurs addressing the fundamental needs of people and planet.

Geographic Preference: Worldwide
Industry Group Preference: Healthcare, Education, Environment, Housing
Key Executives:
    Adam Bendell, Chief Executive Officer
    Education: Cornell University; University of Chicago Law School
    Background: FTI Consulting

1834 TOPSPIN PARTNERS
Three Expressway Plaza
Suite 100
Roslyn Heights, NY 11577

Phone: 516-625-9400 Fax: 516-625-9499
e-mail: info@topspinpartners.com
web: www.topspinpartners.com

Mission Statement: To generate superior returns by partnering with management to build great companies.
Fund Size: $213 million
Average Investment: $1 - $15 million
Portfolio Companies: Patch Products, Brighter Dental, Care, GHS Interactive, Security, Hart Systems, HCOA Fitness, New Whey Nutrition, Pulse Veterinary Technologies, Stagnito Business Information, 2-20 Records Management, Utrecht Manufacturing
Key Executives:
    Leo Guthart, Founding Partner
    Education: AB, Physics, Harvard College; MBA, Harvard Business School; Doctorate, Corporate Finance, Harvard Business School
    Background: President, CEO & Chairman, Ademco
    Directorships: Aptar Group
    Leigh Randall, Managing Partner
    Education: AB, Duke University; JD, Harvard Law School
    Background: CFO, Stonewater Spas; vP, Corporate Development, Small World Media; Consultant, McKinsey & Company

1835 TORNANTE COMPANY
Phone: 212-981-5216
web: tornante.com

Mission Statement: Founded in 2005 by Michael Eisner, The Tornante Company is a privately-held company that invests in, acquires and operates companies in media and entertainment.
Founded: 2005
Industry Group Preference: Media, Entertainment
Portfolio Companies: Airtime, Omaze, TaskRabbit, Topps, Tornate Animation, Vuguru, Who What Wear
Key Executives:
    Michael Traub, Media Contact

1836 TOYOTA AI VENTURES
4440 El Camino Real
Los Altos, CA 94022

e-mail: info@toyota-ai.ventures
web: toyota-ai.ventures

Mission Statement: A subsidiary of the Toyota Research Institute, this venture capital firm seeks to invest in entrepreneurs committed to innovation in the AI sector. Toyota AI Ventures focuses on autonomous mobility, robotics, and data.
Founded: 2017
Minimum Investment: $100 million
Industry Group Preference: Artificial Intelligence, Autonomous Mobility, Robotics, Data Analytics
Portfolio Companies: Apex.AI, Blackmore, Boxbot, Bumblebee Spaces, Cartica AI, Cobalt Robotics, Connected Signals, Elementary Robotics, Embodied, Freedom Robotics, Intuition Robotics, Joby Aviation, May Mobility, Metawave, Moodify, Nauto, Parallel Domain, Perceptive Automata, Realtime Robotics, Recogni, Revel, Sea Machines Robotics, SLAMcore, Skip, Third Wave Automation
Key Executives:
    Jim Adler, Managing Director
    Education: BS, Electrical Engineer, University of Florida; MS, Electrical/Computer Enginerring, University of California, San Diego
    Background: VP of Data & Business Development, Metanautix; VP of Data Systems & Chief Privacy Officer, Intelius; Founder, VoteHere; Engineer, Lockheed Martin
    Natalie Fonseca Licciardi, Operating Partner/VP, Platform & Marketing
    Education: BComm, University of California, Los Angeles
    Background: Consultant, Toyota Research Institute; Founder/CEO, SageScape; Co-Founder, Tech Privacy Summit; Executive Producer, Privacy Identity Innovation; Head of Conference Development & Marketing, Vox Media; Head of Marketing & Audience Development, Recode

1837 TPG CAPITAL
345 California St
Suite 3300
San Francisco, CA 94104

Phone: 415-743-1500 Fax: 415-743-1501
web: www.tpg.com

Mission Statement: TPG Capital is one of the largest private equity investment firms in the world.
Geographic Preference: Global
Fund Size: $75 Billion
Founded: 1992
Investment Criteria: Leveraged buyouts, growth capital, fund management
Industry Group Preference: Consumer/Retail, Media & Telecommunications, Industrials, Technology, Travel/Leisure, Healthcare
Portfolio Companies: Adare Pharmaceuticals, Advent Software, Alinta Energy, ALLTELL, American Beacon, Aptalis Pharma, Armstrong, Axip Energy Services, Beaver-Visitec International, Beringer, Diomet, Burger King, Catellus, CCC Information Services, Chobani, Cirque Du Soleil, Continental Airlines, Copano Energy, Creative Artists Agency, Cushman & Wakefield, Ducati Motor Holding Spa, Ellucian, Enlink Midstream, Enlivant, EnvisionRX, Exactech, Eze Software Group, Fenwal, Fidelity National Financial Services, Fleetpride Inc., Gelson's Market, Grohe, Healthscope, Hotwire.com, Iasis Healthcare, Immucor, Ims Health, Intergraph, J. Crew, Jonah Energy LLC, Kindred Healthcare, Kudu, Lenta, Life Time, Llamasoft, LPL Financial, Lynda.com, McAffee, Memc Electronic Materials, Mey Alcoholic Beverages, Neiman Marcus, Nexeo Solutions, Northern Tier Energy, Norwegian Cruise Line, Ontex International, Oxford Health Plans, P3 Logistic Parks, Par Pharmaceutical, Parkway Properties, Petco Animal Supplies, Petro Harvester, Poundworld Retail LTD, Prezzo, Prosight Specialty Insurance, Quintiles, RCN Grande, Rentpath Inc., Sabre, Saxo Bank, Seagate Technology, St Residental, Sungard, Surgical Care Affiliates, Taylor Morrison Home Corporation, TES Global, Texas Genco, The Warranty Group, Transplace, Transporeon, Univision Communications, Vertafore, Vice, Viking Cruises, WellSky, Wind River
Other Locations:
    900 - 16th Street NW
    Suite 200
    Washington, DC 20006
    Phone: 202-375-2733

    301 Commercial Street
    Suite 3300

Venture Capital & Private Equity Firms / Domestic Firms

Fort Worth, TX 76102
Phone: 817-871-4000 Fax: 817-871-4001
888 7th Avenue
(between 56th & 57th Sts.)
35th Floor
New York, NY 10106
Phone: 212-601-4700 Fax: 212-601-4701
20th Floor, Parnas Tower
521 Teheran-ro, Gangnam-gu
Seoul 06164
Korea
Phone: 82 2 6944 7888
Suite 3801, China World Tower 3
No.1, Jianguomenwai Avenue
Chaoyang District
Beijing 100004
China
Phone: 86-10 5965-3888 Fax: 86-10 5965-3999
Units 1201-1204
Level 12, Cyberport 1
100 Cyberport Road
Hong Kong
China
Phone: 852 3515-8888 Fax: 852 3515-8999
1004, The Capital
Plot No. C-70, G-Block
Bandra Kurla Complex, Bandra (E)
Mumbai 400 051
India
Phone: 91-22 6136-1900 Fax: 91-22 6136-1901
The Goldbell Centre
5 rue Eugene Ruppert
Luxembourg L-2453
Luxembourg
Phone: 352 2700-41251 Fax: 352 2700-412599
5th Floor, Park House
116 Park Street
London W1K 6AF
United Kingdom
Phone: 44 0 20 7544 6500 Fax: 44 0 20 7544 6565
Level 38
80 Collins Street
Melbourne 3000
Australia
Phone: 61-3 9664-4444 Fax: 61-3 9663-7005

Key Executives:
David Bonderman, Chairman
Education: Harvard Law School; University of Washington
Background: Co-Founder, Hotwire.com; Co-Founder, CoStar Group Inc.; Chairman, Continental Airlines Inc.; COO, Robert M. Bass Group Inc.; Partner, Arnold & Porter; Special Assistant to the U.S. Attorney General in the Civil Rights Division; Assistant Professor, Tulane University School
Directorships: Kite Pharma Inc.
Karl Peterson, President & CEO
Education: BBA, University of Notre Dame
Background: Director/President/CEO, Pace-I; Managing Partner, TPG Europe LLP
Directorships: Sabre; Caesars Acquisition Company; Playa Hotels & Resorts; Saxo Bank; TES Global; Pace-I

1838 TRANSCENDENT CAPITAL
447 Broadway
New York, NY 10002

e-mail: hello@transcendent.capital
web: www.transcendent.capital

Mission Statement: Transcendent Capital focuses on tech-based companies across all sectors.
Geographic Preference: North America
Founded: 2017
Investment Criteria: Early Stage, Growth Stage
Industry Group Preference: Technology
Key Executives:
Tarik Abbas, Managing Partner
Education: BA, Fordham University
Background: FinTech Mentor, Startupbootcamp; Venture Partner, NextGen Venture Partners

1839 TRANSITION PARTNERS LTD
1942 Broadway
Suite 314
Boulder, CO 80302

Phone: 303-938-6834 Fax: 303-938-6850
e-mail: terry@transitionpartnersltd.com
web: www.transitionpartnersltd.com

Mission Statement: We provide senior level transitional support to companies requiring capital, management, and or planning to achieve targeted business objectives. At our very essence, we provide transition to firms which find themselves at a crossroads.
Geographic Preference: United States, Worldwide
Fund Size: $98 million
Founded: 1994
Average Investment: $7 million
Minimum Investment: $500,000
Investment Criteria: Healthcare/High Technology Fields
Industry Group Preference: Biotechnology, Computer Related, Software, Financial Services, Medical & Health Related, Pharmaceuticals
Portfolio Companies: WAVi, Signal Storage Innovations, iSatori, X-COM, Lucid Dimensions, NavStar, Adaptive Ozone Solutions, FiberForge, Omni, TechPubs, 3QMatrix, Trimac Industries, One Cavo, PureTech Systems, WhiteDove Herbals, Adventure Sports Products, BSI2000, Crystal Packaging, Royal Sign Supply, TeamMates, comCables, Networth Services, Amorfix Life Sciences, dataQorp, Polar Molecular Corporation, Subscription Services, Aspen Laser & Technologies, Deciphera Pharmaceuticals, LAB InterLink, SimplyWell, BeyondNow Technologies, Concepts Direct, INF Tech Enterprises, International Medical Group, ZymeTx, Amarillo Biosciences, e-infoda.com, LANtech, US Medical, Cannect Communications, Corgenix, Integrated Spatial Information Solutions, Dataview Solutions, eSfot, NovaDx, Vidatron, Care Concepts, COMgroup International, Command Security Corporation, Conception Technology, CST Images, EnviroSolutions, Healthcare Funding Corp., H.J. Meyers & Co., Lifestream Diagnostics, Reaads, Ryan Murphy Inc., Dennis Conncer Sports, The Village Green Bookstore, Reality Female Condom, Hippocrates Associates, Hospital Therapy Services, Lutheran Family Services, Children's Cable Network, Primus, Biostar, DCX, Ferrell Companies, 1Mage Software, MainTech, NEON, OMNI Design, Jade Solutions, H.C. Berger Brewing Company
Key Executives:
W Terrence Schreier, President/Managing Director
303-938-6834
Fax: 303-938-6850
e-mail: terry@transitionpartnersltd.com
Background: Corporate Counsel, Hoechst Roussel AG(Marion Laboratories); Director/COO, Continental Healthcare Systems; Director/CEO, Cell Technology; Director/CEO, Air Methods; Outside Director, Recontek(PS Group)
Charles Holcomb, Managing Director
303-882-2425
Fax: 303-973-5020
e-mail: cnhol@aol.com
Gene Copeland, Managing Director
970-547-1879
Fax: 970-453-0773
e-mail: copelandcgi@aol.com

1840 TRANSLINK CAPITAL
228 Hamilton Avenue
Suite 210
Palo Alto, CA 94301

Phone: 650-330-7353 Fax: 650-330-7351
e-mail: info@translinkcapital.com
web: www.translinkcapital.com

Mission Statement: Build strong, long-lasting relationships between high technology start-ups in the United States and industry leaders in the technology markets of Japan, Korea and Greater China.

Geographic Preference: United States, Japan, Korea, Greater China
Industry Group Preference: Technology
Portfolio Companies: Adwo, AirPlug, Appcelerator, Carbonite, Chartboost, CloudOn, deCarta, Enterprise DB, Eye-Fi, Guavus, HZO, Kamcord, Livescribe, Luxul Technology, Memo Right, Montage Technology, MusicShake, Nexenta, Noom, nWay, Peel, Quixey, SandForce, SoundHound, Tango, Ubooly, Wildfire, Winking Entertainment, Workspot, Xsigo Systems, YuMe

Other Locations:
2fl, Ilsin Bldg
714 Hannam 2-dong
Yangsan-gu
Seoul 140-894
Korea
Phone: 82-25685029 Fax: 82-25685013

14/F, T2, China Central Place
No. 79 Jian Guo Road
Chaoyang District
Beijing 100020
China
Phone: 86-10-8588-9000 x667 Fax: 86-10-8588-9001

5th Floor, Tokio Marine Nichido Building
Shinkan 1-2-1 Marunouchi
Chiyoga-ku
Tokyo 100-0005
Japan
Phone: 81-3-3284-1711 Fax: 81-3-3284-1885

Toshi Otani, Co-Founder/Managing Director
Education: MBA, Stanford Business School
Background: Senior VP, Everypath
Jackie Yang, Co-Founder/Managing Director
Education: MBA, University of Missouri; BS, Mechanical Engineering, National Tsinghua University
Background: Founding Investor, Maxlin Montage Technology Group, Parade Technologies

1841 TRANSMEDIA CAPITAL
717 Market Street
Suite 100
San Francisco, CA 94103

web: www.transmediacapital.com

Mission Statement: Transmedia Capital helps build digital media and marketing businesses, bridging the gap between new and traditional media. We've started companies, raised venture capital, taken companies public, sold companies, and mentored many young entrepreneurs. We have a tremendous network of advisers and venture partners that can provide our portfolio companies the assistance to help accelerate their growth. Transmedia Capital is the only seed fund investing in specifically the new media and online advertising sector providing deep domain expertise, operating experience, and expert advisory relationships for entrepreneurs.

Average Investment: $250,000 - $2 million
Investment Criteria: Seed-Stage
Industry Group Preference: Digital Media & Marketing, Marketing, Advertising
Portfolio Companies: AngelList, Ark, Bottlenose, Buddy, Clypd, DOMO, Genius, Kiip, LevelUp, Lover.ly, Merchant Atlas, MyLikes, Optilly/Install Monitizer, Percolate, Rally, Relevvant, RolePoint, Traction, TrialPay, Two Tap, Wish, LinkedIn, Share This, Snapchat, Tagged, Twitter Urban Airship

Key Executives:
Chris Redlitz, General Partner
Background: Managing Partner, Kicklabs; Co-Founder, AdAuction; Co-Founder, OnVillage; Reebock Int'l
Peter Boboff, General Partner
Education: BS, Mathematics, Western Australia Institute of Technology
Background: Founder, Axis Consulting; Charles Schwab & Co.

1842 TRASK INNOVATIONS FUND Purdue Research Foundation
1801 Newman Road
Purdue Technology Center Aerospace
West Lafayette, IN 47906

Phone: 765-588-3475 Fax: 765-463-3486
e-mail: otcip@prf.org
web: www.prf.org/otc

Mission Statement: The Purdue Research Foundation-managed Trask Innovation Fund (TIF) is a Purdue University development mechanism to assist faculty with work to further commercial potential of technologies disclosed to the Office of Technology Commercialization (OTC). The fund's objective is provide financial support designed to provide an individual technology portfolio up to $50,000 for a period of six months. Formerly known as the Emerging Innovations Fund.

Geographic Preference: Indiana
Founded: 2008
Average Investment: $20, 000 - $500,000
Investment Criteria: Early-Stage/Pre-Series A
Industry Group Preference: Life Sciences, Technology
Key Executives:
Brooke Beier, Executive Director
765-588-3464
e-mail: blbeier@prf.org
Education: BS, MS, PhD, Biomedical Engineering, Weldon School of Biomedical Engineering, Purdue University

1843 TRELLIS PARTNERS
138 Trinity Street
Cedar Creek, TX 78612

Phone: 512-330-9200
e-mail: businessplans@trellis.com
web: www.trellis.com

Mission Statement: Venture capital professionals whose focus is on helping build leading technology companies through early-stage investment.

Geographic Preference: Texas
Founded: 1997
Portfolio Companies: WiseGate, Other Inbox, Debix, Genband, Xtera, FRH Consumer Services, Encoding.com, CPO Commerce, Zilliant, Ziften, TabbedOut

Key Executives:
John L Long Jr, General Partner
Education: BS Electrical Engineering, Georgia Institute of Technology; MBA, University of Texas
Background: Partner, Dakota Venture Management; General Partner, Southwest Venture Partners
Directorships: Zilliant, Ziften
Alexander C Broeker, General Partner
Background: Director, Ernst & Young; Management, Deloitte & Touche; Director, Works; CPA
Directorships: Debix, TabbedOut

Venture Capital & Private Equity Firms / Domestic Firms

1844 TRELYS FUNDS
PO Box 5066
Cary, NC 27512-5066

Phone: 919-459-4650 Fax: 919-459-4670
web: www.trelys.com

Mission Statement: To invest in entrepreneurial teams who combine vision and creativity in addressing opportunities in growing markets.

Geographic Preference: South Carolina
Founded: 2001
Average Investment: $500,000 - $3 million
Investment Criteria: Early-Stage, Middle-Stage
Industry Group Preference: Information Technology, Communication Technology, Biotechnology, Life Sciences, All Sectors Considered
Portfolio Companies: Aldagen, Biolex Therapeutics, Metabolon, MiMedx, Ometric, TriVirix, UniTrends

Key Executives:
Adrian Wilson, Managing General Partner
e-mail: awilson@trelys.com
Education: JD, MBA, University of North Carolina
Background: Fund Manager, Coastal Growth Partners; Private Practice, Helms Mulliss & Johnston

1845 TRESS CAPITAL LLC
3 Columbus Circle
15th Floor
New York, NY 10019

e-mail: invest@tresscapital.com
web: www.tresscapital.com

Mission Statement: A venture capital and private equity firm investing in companies focused on the cannabis industry.

Founded: 2013
Industry Group Preference: Cannabis
Portfolio Companies: Baker Technologies, Cannabis Now, Headset, Infusion Biosciences, SC Labs, Grownetics, Northburd

Key Executives:
Asher Troppe, Co-Founder/CEO
e-mail: asher@tresscapital.com
Background: Founder/Managing Director, Capital Objectives; Founder/Managing Director, Capital Objects Alpha Balance
David Hess, President
e-mail: dhess@tresscapital.com
Background: Director of New Client Services, MetTel; VP, Business Property Finance Corp.; Director of Business Development, OccuNomix International; President/Founder, Luminosity International
Jonathan Eisenberg, Partner
e-mail: jeisenberg@tresscapital.com
Steven Peterson, Partner, Solutions
e-mail: speterson@tresscapital.com
Education: BS, Accounting, Villanova University; MBA, Golden Gate University
Background: VP of Finance, Rovi Corp.; SVP of Finance, Access Information Management; Chief Financial Officer, Borelli Investment Co.; Co-Founder, webKPI; VP of Marketing/Sales, CellarStone Inc.; General Manager, Elemental Wellness Center; Co-Founder, Turning Points Global; Partner, Cukierman & Co.
Anthony Davis, Operating Partner
Education: Silver Lake All Nations Bible College
Background: VP of Operations, Mactus Group; Co-Founder/Managing Partner, Anslinger Capital; Advisor/Investor, DOPE Magazine; Advisor/Investor, Headset; Investor/Partner, Saint Marie Records; Co-Owner/Advisor, Quantum Power Munich; Co-Founder/Managing Partner, Monition Partners; CEO, ALTO

1846 TREVI HEALTH CAPITAL
600 Madison Avenue
15th Floor
New York, NY 10065

Phone: 212-813-9201
e-mail: info@trevihealth.com
web: www.trevihealth.com

Mission Statement: Trevi Health Capital is a specialist investment firm that provides healthcare-focused alternative asset management through private equity and hedge funds on a global scale. The investment team combines experienced investment professionals and senior-level executives and entrepreneurs with proven track records.

Investment Criteria: Growth Stage
Industry Group Preference: Healthcare, Medical Devices, Biopharmaceuticals, Healthcare Services
Portfolio Companies: AGI Dermatics, Flynn Pharma, Manhattan Physicians Laboratories, MedAvante, Omeros, Optovue, Paradigm Spine, Small Bone Innovations, Salient Surgical Technologies, CareWell Urgent Care, US HealthVest, Home Skinovations, EasyLap

Other Locations:
52 Conduit Street
3rd Floor
London W1S 2YX
United Kingdom
Phone: 44-02072922570

Key Executives:
David Robbins, Co-Founder/CIO
Education: Wharton School, New York University School of Law
Background: Corporate Law, Cahill Gordon & Reindel; Strategic Advisor, Elan Corporation; Advisor, Barr Pharmaceuticals
Directorships: Paradigm Spine, Optovue, Home Skinovations, Bally Technologies
Andrew Fink, Co-Founder
Education: AB, Columbia College; JD, Columbia School of Law
Background: Healthcare & Life Sciences Group, Dresdner Kleinwort Wasserstein; Corporate Law, Paul Weiss Rifkind Wharton & Garrison

1847 TRIANGLE ANGEL PARTNERS
PO Box 110062
Research Triangle Park, NC 27709

Phone: 919-904-4565
web: www.triangleangelpartners.com

Mission Statement: Triangle Angel Partners (TAP) is an experienced group of angel investors who invest their time, analysis and money into early life cycle companies in the high tech and life services industries. Our members are executives, PhDs, successful entrepreneurs and professional investors. With TAP's exclusive network, we get the first look at the best new ideas coming our of the Raleigh, Durham, Chapel Hill and the Research Triangle Park areas.

Geographic Preference: North Carolina
Investment Criteria: Early-Stage
Industry Group Preference: High Technology, Life Sciences
Portfolio Companies: Adzerk, Entigral Systems, Physcient, SEAL, Stealz, WedPics, Windsor Circle

1848 TRIANGLE PEAK PARTNERS
505 Hamilton Avenue
Suite 300
Palo Alto, CA 94301

Phone: 650-561-4415
web: www.trianglepeakpartners.com

Mission Statement: Triangle Peak Partners conducts private investments in companies where we can work with management and help create value. We have a deep background in venture

Venture Capital & Private Equity Firms / Domestic Firms

capital and private equity investing in private and public technology, energy, and alternative energy companies.

Minimum Investment: $2 - $15 million
Investment Criteria: Early-Stage, Later-Stage, Public
Industry Group Preference: Technology, Energy, Alternative Energy
Portfolio Companies: Achates Power, Agent Ace, Astroboundary, Bunchball, Coupons.com, FineLine Technologies, Fliaz, Framehawk, Fusion-io, Getaround, Guardian Analytics, Kurtosys, LibreDigital, Lytx, Machinima, Marlin Software, Optify, PCH International, Ping Identity, Prism Skylabs, Puppet Labs, SCIenergy, Send Me Mobile, Sojern, snapLogic, TakeLessons, Tremor Video, Vidyo, Yieldex, Aereon, American Energy Partners, Arc Terminals, Brawler, Chesapeake Energy, Copano Energy, Crestwood, Eclipse Resources, Endeavour, Plains GP Holdings, PXP, Regency, SandRidge, Seven Generations, Sunnova, Tallgrass Energy, Teekay, WireCo

Other Locations:
11 Greenway Plaza
Suite 2000
Houston, TX 77046
Phone: 713-439-1097

Key Executives:
Dain F DeGroff, Co-Founding Partner
Education: BS, Mechanical Engineering, Stanford University; MBA, Wharton School
Background: Managing Director, Fort Mason Capital; Investment Banking, Hambrecht & Quist; JP Morgan
Directorships: Yieldex
Michael C Morgan, Co-Founding Partner
Education: BA, Economics, MA, Sociology, Stanford University; MBA, Harvard Business School
Background: President/CEO, Portcullis Partners; President, Kinder Morgan
Directorships: Bunchball, DriveCam, SCIenergy
David L Pesikoff, Co-Founding Partner
Education: BA, Mathematics, Williams College; MBA, Stanford University
Background: Principal, Fayez Sarofim & Co.; Management Consultant, Gemini Consulting, Bain & Company
Directorships: Guardian Analytics, Optify

1849 TRIATHLON MEDICAL VENTURES
300 East Business Way
Suite 200
Cincinnati, OH 45241

Phone: 513-247-6122
web: www.tmvp.com

Mission Statement: Triathlon Medical Ventures is a Midwest-based venture capital firm that invests exclusively in the life sciences. We provide equity capital to early and expansion state companies with proprietary biomedical technology platforms or products addressing significant human healthcare needs.

Geographic Preference: Midwest United States
Founded: 2004
Average Investment: $500,000 - $7 million
Investment Criteria: Early-Stage, Expansion-Stage
Industry Group Preference: Life Sciences, Healthcare, Biopharmaceuticals, Medical Devices
Portfolio Companies: Aerpio Therapeutics, Akebia Therapeutics, Biovex, CoLucid Pharmaceuticals, Endocyte, Juventas Therapeutics, Kereos, SironRx Therapeutics, Tolera Therapeutics, Celleration, Expanding Orthopedics, Hydrocision, Lonestar Heart, Mitralighn, Remon Medical Technologies, Renal Solutions, Suturtek

Other Locations:
201 North Illinois Street
16th Floor
South Tower
Indianapolis, IN 46204
Phone: 317-280-8233 **Fax:** 317-328-9743

222 South First Street
Suite 200
Louisville, KY 40202
Phone: 502-410-1652 **Fax:** 502-584-6335

Key Executives:
Dennis B Costello, Co-Founder/Managing Partner
Education: BS, United States Naval Academy; MBA, Harvard Business School
Background: Senmed Medical Ventures, American Crital Care, Clonetics, Regent Hospital Products, Hana Biologics
Suzette Dutch, Managing Partner
Education: BA, Economics, Case Western Reserve University; MBA, Wharton School
Background: Senmet, Sentron
Directorships: Tolera Therapeutics, Akebia, BioVex
John M Rice PhD, Co-Founder/Managing Partner
Education: BS, MS, PhD, Microbiology & Virology, Ohio State University
Background: Managing Director, Senmed Medical Ventures
Directorships: Akebia Therapeutics, Syntherix, Kereos
Carrie Bates, Managing Partner
317-280-8233
Fax: 317-328-9743
Education: BS, Finance, BS, Computer Science, MBA, Stanford University
Background: Guidant Corporation, Eli Lilly
Directorships: CS-Keys, Mitralign, Pradama

1850 TRIBE CAPITAL
Menlo Park, CA

web: www.tribecap.co

Mission Statement: Investments focus on internet and software leveraging data and technology.

Geographic Preference: United States
Fund Size: $22.7 Million
Founded: 2018
Investment Criteria: Seed, Series A
Industry Group Preference: Software & Internet
Portfolio Companies: Applied Intuition, Carta, Cover, Dataform, Front, GiveLegacy, Sfox, Snark.ai, Toko

Key Executives:
Arjun Sethi, Co-Founder/Partner
Education: BA, Economics, Boston University; BA, BS, University of Maryland College Park
Background: 6waves; MessageMe; Yahoo!; Social Capital LP
Directorships: Carta; Cover; Sfox
Jonathan Hsu, Co-Founder/Partner
Education: BS, Engineering Physics, University of California, Berkeley; MS, PhD, Stanford Univeristy
Background: Microsoft; SuperPoke; Slide, Inc.; Facebook; Social Capital LP
Directorships: Insight Data Science
Ted Maidenberg, Co-Founder/Partner
Education: BSBA, Finance, Washington University in St. Louis
Background: Credit Suisse; Time Warner Ventures; Warner Bros; USVP; Social Capital LP
Directorships: Simplee

1851 TRIBECA VENTURE PARTNERS
13-17 Laight Street
Suite 606B
New York, NY 10013

Phone: 212-966-9333
web: www.tribecavp.com

Mission Statement: TVP is an early-stage venture capital firm that partners with world class entrepreneurs in the NYC area

Venture Capital & Private Equity Firms / Domestic Firms

leveraging emerging technologies and business models to create and disrupt huge markets.

Average Investment: $100,000 - $4 million
Investment Criteria: Early-Stage, Seed-Stage
Industry Group Preference: Digital Media & Marketing, E-Commerce & Manufacturing, Financial Services, Advertising, Mobile, Software
Portfolio Companies: AppNexus, Backtrace I/O, BetterCloud, clypd, Cognical, Coinsetter, CommonBond, Crowdtap, Flat World Knowledge, Forever, FTRANS, HomeSphere, LeadiD, Lendio, Live Gamer, MakersKit, Maxwell Health, Opternative, RealDirect, Shopkeep, Spanfeller Media, Truveris, Virsex, Vook

Key Executives:
   Brian Hirsch, Co-Founder/Managing Partner
   212-389-1601
   e-mail: brian@tribecavp.com
   Education: BA, Economics & American Studies, Brandeis University
   Background: Founder & Managing Director, GSA Venture Partners; Principal, Sterling Venture Partners
   Directorships: Coinsetter, CommonBond, CrowdTap, Flat World Knowledge, FTRANS, HomeSphere, Just Sing It, Lendio, Mobile Commons, Pontiflex, RealDirect, ShopKeep, Spanfeller Media Group, Vook
   Chip Meakem, Co-Founder/Managing Partner
   212-389-1604
   e-mail: chip@tribecavp.com
   Education: BA, Cornell University; MBA, Columbia Business School
   Background: Managing Partner, Kodiak Venture Partners; DFJ Gotham; Founding Employee, Interactive Imaginations
   Directorships: Appnexus, Ideeli, LiveGamer, TRA Global

1852 TRIDENT CAPITAL
400 S. El Camino Real
Suite 300
San Mateo, CA 94402

Phone: 650-289-4400 **Fax:** 650-289-4444
e-mail: info@tridentcap.com
web: www.tridentcap.com

Mission Statement: A venture capital firm founded to invest in information and business services companies.

Fund Size: $1.5+ billion
Founded: 1993
Average Investment: $3-20 million
Investment Criteria: Multi-Stage Venture Capital
Industry Group Preference: Information Technology, Enterprise Software, SaaS, Business Products & Services, Information Services, Consumer Services, Digital Media & Marketing, Social Media
Portfolio Companies: 2CheckOut, 8thBridge, Acclaris, AccountNow, Advanced ICU Care, Advanced Payment Solutions, Aethon, AirTight Networks, AlienVault, Amprius, Appia, Arxas Technologies, BlueCat Networks, BrightRoll, Bytemobile, Chamberlin Edmonds & Associates, CSG Systems International, Datatel, eGistics, Epicor Software, eXelate, Extole, Fruition Partners, HealthMEDX, Hip Digital, HomeAway, Host Analytics, HyTrust, Iconic Labs, Infotrieve, Internet Profiles, JiWire, Jobvite, Kayak, Mapquest.com, mBlox, Medicode, MedSave, MegaPath Networks, Merchant eSolutions, Microland, Mocana, Mustang Ventures, Neilsoft, Neohapsis, Odyssey Logistics & Technology, PAL, PeriGen, PivotLink, Profex, Prolexic, Qualys, Resolution Health, RezSolutions, RoyaltyShare, Sabre Holdings, Sidestep, Signio, Siva Power, Sojern, Solera Networks, Sygate Technologies, Tablus, Teladoc, Thismoment, THOR Technologies, Tiandi Energy, Turn, Voltage Security, XRS, Xunlight

Key Executives:
   Donald R. Dixon, Co-Founder/Senior Managing Director
   e-mail: ddixon@tridentcap.com
   Education: BSE, Princeton University; MBA, Stanford Graduate School of Business
   Background: Co-President, Partech International; Managing Director, Alex Brown & Sons; VP, Morgan Stanley & Company; Sr Account, Citibank NA
   Directorships: 2Checkout, AccountNow, Advanced Payment Solutions, Amprius, eGistics, Infotrieve, Neohapsis, Odyssey Logistics, Qualys, RoyaltyShare, SivaPower, Tiandi Energy, XRS
   John H. Moragne, Co-Founder/Managing Director
   e-mail: jmoragne@tridentcap.com
   Education: BA, Dartmouth College; MS, Stanford University
   Background: Principal, Bain Capital; Principal, Information Partners Capital Fund
   Directorships: Turn, Sojern, Appia, JiWire, Perigen, ArrayPower, Jobvite
   Arneek Multani, Managing Director
   e-mail: amultani@tridentcap.com
   Education: BS, Wharton School of Business, BAS Moore School of Engineering, University of Pennsylvania; MBA, Stanford Graduate School of Business
   Background: Product Management, Network Storage Software Products Group, Sun Microsystems; Health & Fitness Industries, McCown De Leeuw & Co.; Media & Telecommunications, M&A Group, Morgan Stanley & Co.
   Directorships: MedSave, HealthMEDX, Acclaris, Teladoc, Neilsoft, Microland
   J. Alberto Yepez, Managing Director
   e-mail: ayepez@tridentcap.com
   Education: BS, Kellogg School of Management, Northwestern University; BS, University of San Francisco
   Background: VP, Indentity Management & Security, Oracle; Chairman, President & CEO, Thor Technologies; EIR, Warburg Pincus; Co-CEO, Entrust; Chairman & CEO, enCommerce; Senior Management Positions, Apple Computer
   Directorships: AlientVault, Mocana, Neohapsis, AirTight Networks, BlueCat Networks, HyTrust, Mocana
   Howard S. Zeprun, Chief Operating Officer & General Counsel
   e-mail: hzeprun@tridentcap.com
   Education: BS, Systems Engineering, University of Pennsylvania School of Engineering & Applied Science; BS, Finance, Wharton School of Commerce & Finance; JD, Harvard Law School
   Background: Corporate & Securities Partner, Wilson Sonsini Goodrich & Rosati; Corporate Counsel, Apple Computer
   Michael Biggee, Managing Director
   e-mail: mbiggee@tridentcap.com
   Education: MS, Engineering, Cornell University; BS, Chemical Engineering, Cornell University
   Background: Dolphin Equity Partners; Global Technology Banking, Merrill Lynch; Chemical Engineer, Procter & Gamble & General Mills

1853 TRILANTIC CAPITAL PARTNERS
399 Park Avenue
39th Floor
New York, NY 10022

Phone: 212-607-8450
e-mail: ir@trilantic.com
web: www.trilantic.com

Mission Statement: Trilantic Capital Partners was formed by the former principals of Lehman Brothers Merchant Banking. Trilantic Capital Partners seeks to partner with management teams with a compelling strategy, a well-developed framework for execution, extensive industry and operating experience and an established performance record.

Geographic Preference: North America, Western Europe
Fund Size: $7 billion
Founded: 2009
Average Investment: $50 - $180 million

Venture Capital & Private Equity Firms / Domestic Firms

Investment Criteria: Management Buyouts, Recapitalizations, Growth Equity, Corporate Divestitures, Generational Transitions
Industry Group Preference: Business Products & Services, Consumer Services, Energy Services, Financial Services
Portfolio Companies: 24-7 Intouch Inc., Asset Living, Djr Energy LLC, Elephant Oil & Gas, Fluid Delivery Solutions LLC, Highgate Hotels, Indigo Natural Resources LLC, M5 Midstream LLC, Ortholite Holdings LLC, Solaris Midstream Holdings LLC, Sunbelt-Solomon Solutions, Sunrise Strategic Partners LLC, Taymax Group Holdings LLC, Traeger Pellet Grills LLC, TRP Energy LLC, Velvet Energy LTD, Ward Energy Partners

Other Locations:
35 Portman Square
London W1H 6LR
United Kingdom

26 Bd Royal
Luxembourg L-2449
Luxembourg

Key Executives:
Charles Ayres, Managing Partner & Chairman
212-607-8440
Education: BA, Economics, Duke University; MBA, Amos Tuck School, Dartmouth College
Background: Founding Partners, MidOcean Partners; Head, DB Capital Partners North America
Daniel James, Managing Partner, Head/North America
212-607-8410
Education: BA, Chemistry, College of the Holy Cross
Background: Lehman Brothers M&A Group
Directorships: Angelica Corporation, Blount International, Houston International Insurance Group, VantaCore Partners
Christopher Manning, Senior Advisor
212-607-8484
Education: BBA, University of Texas, Austin; MBA, Wharton School
Background: Head, Lehman Brothers' Investment Management Division
Charles Fleischmann, Partner
212-607-8466
Education: BA, Colgate University
Background: Investcorp International Inc.; JP Morgan; Shearman and Sterling; Chairman, Home Franchise Concepts Parents
Directorships: Sunbelt-Solomon Solutions; United Subcontractors Inc.
Jeremy Lynch, Partner
212-607-8448
Education: BS, Applied Mathematics, Union College
Background: Principal, Lehman Brothers Merchant Banking; Analyst & Associate, Lehman Brothers
Directorships: Addison Group; MicroStar Logistics; 24-7 InTouch Inc.; Asset
James Manges, Partner & Head of Consumer
212-607-8424
e-mail: jmanges@trilanticpartners.com
Education: BA, Yale University; MBA, Columbia Business School
Background: Principal, Lehman Brothers Merchant Bankingl Chairman, Sunrise Strategic Partners; President, Vice; Lazard Alternative Investments; Leveraged Finance Group; Merrill Lynch
Directorships: Kodiak Cakes; Ortholite Holdings; Taymax Group Holdings; Traeger Pellet Grills; Implus Corporation; Fortitech; Home Franchise Concepts Parents; SRAM
Grant Palmer, Senior Advisor
212-607-8415
Education: BA, Economics & History, Duke University; MBA, Columbia Business School
Background: Senior Associate, Lehman Brothers Merchant Banking
Directorships: Ortholite Holdings; Sunrise Strategic Partners; Traeger Pellet Grills; Implus Corporations
Elliot Attie, Partner & CFO
212-607-8423
Education: BS, Accounting, State University of New York
Background: VP, Lehman Brothers Merchant Banking; Senior Manager, PricewaterhouseCoopers
Directorships: New York Chapter of the Private Equity CFO Association
Andrew Hopping, Senior Advisor
512-362-6250
Education: BS & BA, University of Colorado
Background: Analyst, Lehman Brothers Merchant Banking
Directorships: DJR Energy; Elephant Oil & Gas
Glenn Jacobson, Senior Advisor
212-607-8420
Education: Dartmouth College
Background: Lehman Brothers

1854 TRILOGY PARTNERSHIP
155 108th Avenue NE
Suite 400
Bellevue, WA 98004

Phone: 425-458-5900
web: trilogyequity.com

Mission Statement: Trilogy Partnership seeks high growth opportunities in both developed and emerging countries.

Industry Group Preference: Wireless Technologies, Communications, Technology
Portfolio Companies: Alert1, Asurion, Farmstr, FireApps, GameChanger, Globys, Haiku Deck, Hola, Jobaline, Lookout, Mits, PrePlay, Red Tricycle, Remitly, SignalSense, Tellwise, Viva Bolivia, Viva Dominican Republic, 2degrees

---

1855 TRINITY VENTURES
2480 Sand Hill Road
Suite 200
Menlo Park, CA 94025

Phone: 650-854-9500
e-mail: info@trinityventures.com
web: www.trinityventures.com

Mission Statement: Trinity invests in companies where the business experience of its professionals can add significant value to the entrepreneur and the company, early stage companies, and more established businesses with high growth potential.

Fund Size: $300 million
Founded: 1986
Average Investment: $1-$5 million
Minimum Investment: $250,000
Investment Criteria: Seed, Startup, First-stage, Second-stage
Industry Group Preference: E-Commerce & Manufacturing, Communications, Software
Portfolio Companies: 21vianet.com, 24/7 Real Media, Act-On Software, Affinity Jobs, Ankeena, Aruba Networks, Aryaka, Aventail, BabyCenter, BackWeb, Badgeville, BeachMint, Biba, Bix, Blue Nile, BlueStripe, BlueTarp Financial, Bonfaire, Bright Horizons, Care.com, Clearleap, Cloudability, Cloudscaling, Connected, Conner, Crescendo Communications, CrowdFlower, CubeTree, Deliv, Digital Market, Digital Research, Docker, Dot & Bo, Dot Loop, DynamicSignal, EggDrop, Enovix, Exalt, Extreme Networks, Fitstar, Forté, Fuego, Getinsured.com, Gigi Hill, Green Patch, GreenThrottle, GridIron, Hoopla, ID Analytics, IKOS, Illustra, Infoblox, IntruVert Networks, Jama, Jamba Juice, Kiva Software, KIXEYE, Likewise, Loggly LoopNet, Marmot, MaxPoint, Mobile Messenger, Modulus Video, mSpot, MyNewPlace, Net Effect Systems, NetFlip, Network Alchemy, New Relic, NextGreatPlace, NextCard, Orative, Owler, P.F. Chang's, PayScale, PerfectMarket, Photobucket, PlayFirst, Posterous, RadiumOne, Red Aril, RiverMuse,

Venture Capital & Private Equity Firms / Domestic Firms

RJMetrics, Ruby Ribbon, Sabrix, ScaleArc, SciQuest, ServiceMax, SevenSpace, ShopIgniter, Skyfire, Speedera Networks, StackMob, Starbucks Coffee, Sygate, Taulia, ThredUp, Torbit, Trion, Truaxis, TrustID, TubeMogul, Uptake, Virage, Wall Data, WeddingChannel.com, Weddington Way

Other Locations:
One Market Plaza
Steuart Tower, #1208
San Francisco, CA 94105

Key Executives:
Noel J Fenton, Founding Partner
e-mail: noel@trinityventures.com
Education: BS Chemistry, Cornell University; MBA, Stanford Graduate School of Business
Background: Chief Executive Officer, Acurex and Covalent Systems
Directorships: BlueStripe Software, Blue Tarp Financial, DotLoop, SciQuest, ServiceMax, Taulia, TrustID
Patricia Nakache, General Partner
e-mail: patricia@trinityventures.com
Education: MBA, Stanford Graduate School of Business, AB, Harvard University
Background: McKinsey & Company
Directorships: BeachMint, Care.com, KIXEYE, Owler, PayScale, Ruby Ribbon, thredUP, Weddington Way, Whisper
Ajay Chopra, General Partner
e-mail: ajay@trinityventures.com
Education: BSEE, Birla Institute of Technology & Science, India; MSEE, Stony Brook University
Background: Co-Founder, Pinnacle Systems; Mindset Corporation; Atari Corporation; Unisys Corporation
Directorships: Bonfaire, CrowdFlower, Dynamic Signal, FitStar, Mobile Messenger, RadiumOne, TubeMogul, White Sky
Larry Orr, General Partner
e-mail: larry@trinityventures.com
Education: AB, Mathematics, Harvard University; MBA, Stanford Graduate School of Business
Background: Hewlett-Packard; Neiderhoffer Cross & Zeckhauser
Directorships: GetInsured, Perfect Market, ShopIgniter, ProtectWise, Hoopla Software
Gus Tai, Venture Partner
e-mail: gus@trinityventures.com
Education: AB, Applied Mathematics, Harvard University; MS, Materials Science & Engineering, MIT; MBA, MIT Sloan School of Management
Background: Digital Equipment Corporation, Bain & Company
Directorships: Callisto Media, Dot & Bo, MaxPoint Interactive, Moovweb, PlayFirst, Trion Worlds, WetPaint, Zulily

1856 TRIPLETREE LLC
3600 Minnesota Drive
Suite 200
Edina, MN 55435

Phone: 952-223-8400
web: www.triple-tree.com

Mission Statement: TripleTree is led by a team of former operating executives, bankers, entrepreneurs, and venture capitalists. Our services include mergers & acquisitions, principal investing and strategic advisory.

Industry Group Preference: Healthcare, Technology
Kevin R Green, Founding Managing Director
e-mail: kgreen@triple-tree.com
Education: BA, MBA, University of San Diego
Background: CEO, Summit Medical; CEO, Integrated Medical Systems
David A Henderson, Founding Managing Director
e-mail: dhenderson@triple-tree.com

Education: Morehead State University; CPA
Background: Arthur Andersen

1857 TRITON VENTURES
6300 Bridge Point Parkway
Building 1
Suite 500
Austin, TX 78730

Phone: 512-795-5820 **Fax:** 512-795-5828
e-mail: laura@tritonventures.com
web: www.tritonventures.com

Mission Statement: Established with the belief that significant opportunities exist to transfer technology from corporate or institutional development environments into new entrepreneurial companies focused on rapid growth.

Investment Criteria: Spinouts, Early Stage
Industry Group Preference: Enterprise Services, Information Technology, Communications, Advanced Materials, Software
Portfolio Companies: Applied Science Fiction, ClearOrbit, Exterprise, Gallery Watch, Charitygift, Greenmountain, Hart InterCivic, Innovalight, MindFlow Technologies, Vincera

Key Executives:
Laura J Kilcrease, Managing Director
e-mail: laura@tritonventures.com
Education: MBA, University of Texas; Chartered Management Accountant
Background: Director, Center for Commercialization & Enterprise; Founding Director, Austin Technology Incubator; Capital Network; Austin Software Council
Directorships: Women's Leadership Advisory Board; Beyster Institute
Scott Collier, Managing Director
e-mail: scott@tritonventures.com
Education: BS Engineering, Texas A&M University; MBA, University of Texas; Engineering Management Program, California Institute of Technology
Background: VP, Capital Southwest Corporation; Aircraft Engineer/Project Manager, Northrop Grumman

1858 TRIVE CAPITAL
2021 McKinney Avenue
Suite 1200
Dallas, TX 75201

Phone: 214-499-9715 **Fax:** 469-310-9961
e-mail: info@trivecapital.com
web: www.trivecapital.com

Mission Statement: Trive Capital is a Dallas, Texas-based private equity firm investing in equity and debt securities with approximately $900 million in capital under management.

Geographic Preference: North America
Fund Size: $900 million
Average Investment: $10-150 million
Investment Criteria: Lower Middle Market
Industry Group Preference: Diversified
Portfolio Companies: AGM Automotive, Chicago Miniature Lighting, Valence Surface Technologies, Huron, Precise Packaging, Southern Towing Company

Key Executives:
Conner Searcy, Managing Partner
e-mail: connersearcy@trivecapital.com
Education: BA, Vanderbilt University; MBA, Harvard Business School
Background: Partner, Insight Equity; Stonegate; Bain & Company
Chris Zugaro, Partner
e-mail: chriszugaro@trivecapital.com
Education: BS, Computer Engineering, Texas A&M University; MBA, Stanford Graduate School of Business
Background: Principal, Insight Equity; Bain & Company
David Stinnett, Partner
e-mail: davidstinnett@trivecapital.com

Venture Capital & Private Equity Firms / Domestic Firms

Education: BA, Economics & Philosophy, Vanderbilt University
Background: Insight Equity; Associate, Pamlico Capital; Analyst, M&A Group, McGladrey Capital Markets
Desmond Henry, Managing Director
e-mail: desmondhenry@trivecapital.com
Education: BS, Finance, University of Southern California
Background: Managing Director, Black Canyon Capital; Vice President, Merrill Lynch European M&A Group
Blake Bonner, Partner
e-mail: blakebonner@trivecapital.com
Education: BBA, Finance & Entrepreneurial Management, Neeley School of Business, Texas Christian University
Background: Insight Equity; Analyst, Houlihan Lokey
Shravan Thadani, Managing Director
e-mail: shravanthadani@trivecapital.com
Education: MPA, McCombs School of Business, University of Texas
Background: VP, Sequel Holdings; Associate, Goldman Sachs; Analyst, Houlihan Lokey

1859 TRIVEST PARTNERS
550 South Dixie Highway
Suite 300
Coral Gables, FL 33146

Phone: 305-858-2200 Fax: 305-285-0102
e-mail: info@trivest.com
web: www.trivest.com

Mission Statement: A leading provider of equity for middle market corporate acquisitions, recapitalizations and growth capital financings, always co-investing with company management and pursues transactions which are supported by the management and Boards of Directors of the investee companies.

Geographic Preference: Southeast, Midwest, United States
Fund Size: $325 million
Founded: 1981
Minimum Investment: $5 million
Investment Criteria: Middle Market Acquisitions, Recapitalizations, Growth Financing
Industry Group Preference: Niche Manufacturing, Business Products & Services, Consumer Products
Portfolio Companies: Advanced Discovery, AM Conservation Group, Columbus Recycling, Ellery Homestyles, Endeavor, HandStands, National Auto Care, North Star Seafood, Northfield Industries, OnePath Systems, Pelican Water Systems, Ryko, SRS, Take 5, Twin-Star International, Wise Company

Key Executives:
Troy D Templeton, Managing Partner
e-mail: ttempleton@trivest.com
Education: BBA, MBA, Stetson University
Background: Southeast Bank, NA
Directorships: Endeavor Telecom
Jamie E Elias, Partner
e-mail: jelias@trivest.com
Education: BS, Boston College; MBA, Harvard Business School; CPA
Background: Audit/Advisory Group, Price Waterhouse, Miami
Directorships: Twin-Star, DirectBuy, Ryko Solutions, AM Conservation
David Gershman, Partner & General Counsel
e-mail: dgershman@trivest.com
Education: BA, Union College; JD, New York University School of Law; NY and Florida Bar
Background: Akerman, Senterfitt & Edison, PA; M&A Counsel, Automatic Data Processing; Practicing Lawyer, Morgan Lewis, NY
Directorships: Onepath Systems, Hazmasters, Endeavor, Onepath, Group III, Take 5
Russ Wilson, Partner
e-mail: rwilson@trivest.com
Education: BA, Business Management & Economics, Eckerd College
Background: Associate, PNC Equity; Associate, Raymond James' Investment Banking Division
Directorships: Twin-Star International, Ryko Solutions, Take 5 Oil Change, Ellery Homestyles
Forest Wester, Partner
e-mail: fwester@trivest.com
Education: Dartmouth College; MBA, Harvard Business School
Background: Associate, Lehman Brothers' Private Equity Division
Directorships: Group III International, Endeavor Telecom, Onepath Systems
Jorge Gross Jr, Partner
e-mail: jgross@trivest.com
Education: BA, Economics, Columbia University; MBA, Wharton School, University of Pennsylvania
Background: Associate, Credit Suisse First Boston
Directorships: AM Conservation, Hazmasters

1860 TRU MANAGEMENT
141 South 6th Avenue
Suite 1025
Tucson, AZ 85702-1025

Phone: 520-328-7443
web: www.trugroup.com

Mission Statement: To help build successful companies through fine tuning business strategies, building the right management team, finding resources, and introducing portfolio companies to corporate alliances to expand internationally. Tru Management provides their portfolio companies with services to help them succeed in a competitive and rapidly changing tech environment.

Geographic Preference: United States, Canada, Mexico, Europe, Middle East, China
Fund Size: $1 billion
Average Investment: $1 million - 10 million
Investment Criteria: Early, Expansion, Late
Industry Group Preference: Communications, Electronic Technology, Information Technology, Software

Other Locations:
95 Prince Arthur Avenue
Suite 117
Toronto, ON M5R 3P6
Canada
Phone: 416-935-1754

Key Executives:
Edward R. Anderson, President & CEO
e-mail: anderson@trugroup.com
Education: BSc, Dpl, Marketing Research, MBA

1861 TRUE NORTH VENTURE PARTNERS
205 North Michigan Avenue
Suite 2930
Chicago, IL 60601

Phone: 312-574-1700
web: www.truenorthvp.com

Mission Statement: True North Venture Partners invests in and supports early stage businesses that have the potential to transform, expand and lead global industries. Our goal is to indentify exceptionally talented entrepreneurs with the vision, drive and business potential to significantly improve the world and help them realize their dreams by providing capital and expertise.

Average Investment: $100,000 - $25 million
Minimum Investment: $100,000
Investment Criteria: Early-Stage
Industry Group Preference: Energy, Water, Agriculture, Waste & Recycling

Venture Capital & Private Equity Firms / Domestic Firms

Other Locations:
2390 E Camelback Road
Suite 203
Phoeniz, AZ 85016
Phone: 602-476-5800

Key Executives:
Michael J Ahearn, Founder
Education: BS, JD, Arizona State University
Background: Co-Founder, First Solar; Partner & President, True North Partners
Matthew S Ahearn, Founder
Education: BS, Political Science & Economics, Northwestern University
Background: BDT Capital Partners, Goldman Sachs & Co.
Steven D Kloos PhD
Education: BS, Chemistry, University of Wisconsin, River Falls; PhD, Chemistry, North Dakota State University
Background: Advanced Technolgy Leader, GE Water & Porocess Technologies

1862 TRUE VENTURES
575 High Street
Suite 400
Palo Alto, CA 94301

web: www.trueventures.com

Mission Statement: True is a venture firm for very early stage entrepreneurs that partners with promising entrepreneurs at the earliest stages in the highest-growth segments of the technology market, where history demonstrates the best rates of return.

Investment Criteria: Seed-Stage, Early-Stage, Later-Stage, Private Equity, Debt Financing
Industry Group Preference: Digital Media & Marketing, Online Publishing, Internet Communications, Mobile Technology, Mobile Entertainment, Internet Advertising, Software, Gaming, E-Commerce & Manufacturing, SaaS, Media, Internet, Enterprise Software, Infrastructure, Mobile Services
Portfolio Companies: 3D Robotics, 410 Labs, 9GAG, About.me, Academia.edu, Adku, Airstone Labs, Always Prepped, AOptix, Apcera, Appconomy, Applauze, Apply Financial, appssavvy, Automatic, B-Stock Solutions, Bandcamp, Betable, bLife, Blue Bottel Coffee, BraceAbility, BrightRoll, Concurrent, Datacraft Solutions, Dinamundo, Directly, DJZ, Duo Security, EdgeConnex, Evident.io, Finderly, Fitbit, Flint, GigaOM, Ginger.io, Hedvig, Helpshift, High Fidelity, Inventables, Keep Holdings, Kicksend, Kiip, KISSmetrics, Kurtosys, littleBits Electronics, Loggly, Madefire, Madison Reed, Message Bus, Metamarkets, Mindbites, MobileSpan, MoviePass, Namely, Narrative, Nearstream, Neighborland, Neon, Orabrush, Orchestrate.io, Ovelin, PayNearMe, Piston Cloud, POSE, Puppet Labs, Qualaroo, Quarterly, RescueTimy, Runscope, SaveUp, Schematic Labs, Showyou, Sifteo, Singly, Smarterer, SocialPandas, Socrative, Soundhawk, Sparked, Spectrum Bridge, Splice, Spree Commerce, Stitch Labs, StockTwits, Streetline, TastemakerX, Technical Machine, tenXer, TerraEchos, ToyTalk, TripleLift, Urban Airship, Valencell, Webshots, WhoBet

Other Locations:
501 3rd Street
San Francisco, CA 94107

Phil Black, Founder
Education: AB, Economics, Stanford University
Background: Founder, Blacksmith Capital; General Partner, ABS Ventures; General Partner, Weiss Peck & Greer; General Partner, Greer Venture Partners
Jon Callaghan, Founder
Education: BA, Government, Dartmouth College; MBA, Harvard Business School
Background: Summit Partners; AOL Greenhouse; Managing Partner, @Ventures; Managing Director, Globespan

Tony Conrad, Partner
Education: BS, Telecommunications, Indiana University; BA, Economics, Indiana University
Background: Sphere; about.me
Toni Schneider, Founder
Education: BS, Computer Science, Stanford University
Background: Yahoo!; Automattic

1863 TSG CONSUMER PARTNERS
600 Montgomery Street
Suite 2900
San Francisco, CA 94111

Phone: 415-398-2300 Fax: 415-421-2350
web: www.tsgconsumer.com

Mission Statement: The leader in the U.S. in building and investing in leading middle-market branded consumer companies.

Geographic Preference: United States
Founded: 1987
Average Investment: $15-$100 million
Investment Criteria: Internal Growth & Acquisitions, Full or Partial Liquidity, Mangement Buyouts, Corporate Divestitures
Industry Group Preference: Consumer Products, Distribution, Industrial Equipment, Beauty & Personal Care, Food & Beverage, Restaurants
Portfolio Companies: Alexis Bittar, Paige, REVOLV, Alterna, Dentek, e.l.f. Cosmetics, IT Cosmetics, Kenra, Perricone MD, Pevonia, Sexy Hair, Cytosport, Gardein, Raybern's, thinkThin, Dogswell, My Fit Foods, Planet Fitness

Other Locations:
712 Fifth Avenue
46th Floor
New York, NY 10019
Phone: 212-265-4111 Fax: 212-265-4845

Key Executives:
Charles H Esserman, Founder/Managing Director, President & CEO
Education: BS, MIT; MBA, Stanford University
Background: Bain & Company

1864 TSG EQUITY PARTNERS
636 Great Road
Stow, MA 01775

Phone: 978-461-9900 x116
e-mail: tns@tsgequity.com
web: www.tsgequity.com

Mission Statement: A private equity investment firm providing growth and acquisition financing to expansion stage and middle market companies.

Geographic Preference: Mid-Atlantic, Northeast
Fund Size: $250 million under management
Founded: 1996
Average Investment: $1 to $2.25 million
Minimum Investment: $1 million
Investment Criteria: Growth Capital, Expansion Stage, Middle Market, Recapitalizations
Industry Group Preference: Communications, Consumer Services, Electronic Technology, Information Technology, Manufacturing, Software
Portfolio Companies: VA Linux Systems, Tower Ventures, Vermont Teddy Bear, SolarOne Solutions, Katahdin Inc., Optasite, Marketmax, 4R Systems

Key Executives:
T Nathanael Shepherd, Co-Founder, Principal
Education: MBA, Clark University Graduate School of Management
Background: Associate Director, PCS; Director Development, Perkins
Directorships: Katahdin Industries, Vermont Teddy Bear Co., SolarOne Solutions

Thomas R Shepherd, Co-Founder, Principal
Education: BA Economics, Washington & Lee University; Master of Industrial and Labor Relations, Cornell University; Executive Program, Amos Tuck School, Dartmouth College
Background: Managing Director, Thomas H Lee Company; President, GTE Lighting Products Group; President NA, Phillips Commercial Electronics Corporation
Directorships: 4R Systems, Amerace, General Nutrition Companies, Optasite, PNC - New England, Thermoscan, Vermont Teddy Bear Co.

1865 TTV CAPITAL
1230 Peachtree Street
Suite 1150
Atlanta, GA 30309

Phone: 404-347-8400 Fax: 404-347-8420
e-mail: info@ttvcapital.com
web: www.ttvcapital.com

Mission Statement: TTV Capital is an Atlanta-based investment firm focused on providing capital to early-to-late stage privately held companies in the financial services industry and IT driven businesses with products that serve the financial services industry.

Founded: 2000
Investment Criteria: Early-Stage to Later-Stage
Industry Group Preference: Financial Services, Information Technology
Portfolio Companies: 3V, ALI Solutions, Bill.com, Bitpay, Bluepoint Solutions, Cardlytics, Connecture, ControlScan, CRESecure, EquityLock Solutions, eWise, EXACTUALS, Financelt, Ftrans, FX Bridge, Green Dot, Interactive Advisory Software, IP Commerce, KnowledgeStorm, Lendkey, Magnet Banking, MicroBilt, moneydesktop, Neovest, PayCycle, Perimeter eSecurity, ShopKeep, Silverpop, Springbot

Key Executives:
Gardiner W Garrard III, Founder/Partner
Education: BA, University of North Carolina, Chapel Hill; MBA, Goizueta Business School, Emory University
Directorships: Bluepoint Solutions, EquityLockSolutions, FTRANS, FX Bridge, Perimeter Security, ShopKeep
W Thomas Smith Jr, Founder/Partner
Education: BS, Industrial Management, Georgia Institute of Technology
Background: Vice President, IBM
Directorships: 3V, eWise, Silverpop, IP Commerce
Mark A Johnson, Partner
Education: Miami University; MBA, Ohio State University
Background: Founder, CheckFree Corporation; Founder, e-RM Ventures
Directorships: Bill.com, Cardlytics, ControlScan, Fleetcor, FX Bridge
Sean Banks, Partner
Education: BS, Economics, United States Naval Academy; JD, University of San Diego; MBA, Emory University
Directorships: ControlScan

1866 TUATARA CAPITAL
New York, NY

e-mail: info@tuataracap.com
web: www.tuataracapital.com

Mission Statement: Invests in companies across the supply chain for the cannabis industry, including research & testing, cultivation, processing, and retail.

Founded: 2014
Industry Group Preference: Cannabis
Portfolio Companies: Teewinot Life Sciences, Willie's Reserve, Green Dot, Enlighten, CanAscen Group

Key Executives:
Mark Zittman, Partner/Chairman
Education: BBA, University of Florida
Background: Sr. Managing Director, Guggenheim Partners
Al Foreman, Partner/Chief Investment Officer
Education: BS, Finance, University of Connecticut; JD, Arizona State University; MBA, W.P. Carey School of Business, Arizona State University
Background: Associate/VP, Citigroup; Sr. Business Development Manager, Virtual Growth Inc.; Managing Director, JP Morgan
Directorships: Vitech Systems Group
Marc Riiska, Partner/Chief Operating Officer
Education: BS, Finance, University of Connecticut
Background: Partner, Ilios Partners; Director of Business Development, SS&C Technologies
Richard Taney, Managing Director
Education: BA, History/Biology, Tufts University; JD, James E. Beasley School of Law, Temple University; JD, Boston University School of Law
Background: Managing Partner, Sandpiper Capital Partners; President/CEO, Delcath Systems Inc.; President/CEO, Curaleaf Inc.; Managing Partner, T2 Capital
Directorships: Veridian Capital Advisors, MGT Capital Investments, Medicsight, Delcath Systems Inc.
Adrienne Foo, Managing Director
Education: BS, Accounting, Northern Illinois University
Background: Sr. Auditor, Arthur Andersen; Sr. Auditor, KPMG; Accounting Supervisor, Spectrum Global Fund Administration; VP, Deutsche Asset Management; VP, JPMorgan Chase & Co.; Managing Director, Pinebridge Investment
Young Yeo, Vice President
Education: BS, Chemistry, Carnegie Mellon University
Background: Associate, China Momentum Fund; Scientist/Researcher, Carnegie Mellon University

1867 TUGBOAT VENTURES
306 Cambridge Avenue
Palo Alto, CA 94306

Phone: 650-470-1400
web: www.tugboatventures.com

Mission Statement: To help the highest potential entrepreneurs bring their dreams to life.

Investment Criteria: Seed-Stage, Early-Stage
Industry Group Preference: SaaS, Enterprise Software, Consumer Internet, Internet, Advertising
Portfolio Companies: Alminder, Amazon, Applied Silver, Business Signatures, Citrus Lane, Cranium, Drugstore.com, E.Piphany, Education Elements, Five Apes, Good, Google, Hapara, healthTap, HoneyApps, Ifeelgoods, Mahoot, Mamapedia, Matrixx, NewSchools Venture Fund, Peloton, Red Herring, RepairPal, RichRelevance, Risk I/O, SayNow, Savvymoney, Shop It To Me, Stella & Dot, SuccessFactors, Tapjoy, Wikia, Nine Plus

Key Executives:
Dave Whorton, Founder
Education: BS, Mechanical Engineering, University of California, Berkeley; MBA, Stanford Graduate School of Business
Background: Kleiner Perkins Caufield & Byers; Texas Pacific Group Ventures; Founding CEO, Good Technology; Co-Founder, Drugstore.com

1868 TULLIS HEALTH INVESTORS
55 Old Field Point Road
Stamford, CT 06830

Phone: 203-629-8700
web: www.thi-funds.com

Venture Capital & Private Equity Firms / Domestic Firms

Mission Statement: Provides capital to healthcare companies at all stages of growth with creative, committed management teams.
Geographic Preference: United States
Fund Size: $350 million
Founded: 1986
Average Investment: $500,000 - $10,000,000
Minimum Investment: $250,000
Investment Criteria: All Stages
Industry Group Preference: Biotechnology, Life Sciences, Healthcare, Medical Devices, Information Technology, Pharmaceuticals
Portfolio Companies: VidaCare, Impulse Monitoring, Physician Sales & Service, QuadraMed, BioRexis
Other Locations:
  11760 U.S. Highway 1
  Suite 502W
  North Palm Beach, FL 33408
  Phone: 561-799-7762
Key Executives:
  Jim Tullis, Founder/General Partner
  Education: BA, Stanford University; MBA, Harvard Business School
  Background: Morgan Stanley
  John Tullis, Managing General Partner
  Education: DePauw University; University of Virginia; MBA, University of Miami
  Background: Senior Director, Ryder System Inc.; Associate, MJ Meehan & Co.
  Neil Ryan, Venture Partner
  Education: BA, University of Ottawa; MBA, Wharton School
  Background: Co-Founder, Oxford Partners; Co-Founder, Oxford Bioscience Partners; Co-Founder & President, Randolph Computer Corporation; President, GTE New Ventures Corporation; SVP, GTE Corporation

1869 TULLY & HOLLAND
20 William Street
Suite 135
Wellesey, MA 02481

Phone: 781-239-2900 **Fax:** 781-239-2901
web: www.tullyandholland.com

Mission Statement: Tully & Holland specializes in highly complex transactions, custom designing financial solutions for the unique needs of each client.
Geographic Preference: United States
Founded: 1992
Minimum Investment: $5 million
Investment Criteria: Mezzanine, LBO, MBO
Industry Group Preference: Consumer Products, Distribution, Medical & Health Related, Food & Beverage, Retail, Consumer & Leisure
Key Executives:
  Timothy Tully, President, Food & Consumer Groups
  e-mail: ttully@tullyandholland.com
  Education: BA, Harvard University
  Background: Advising, Proctor & Gamble, General Mills Inc, Management Positions At H.J.Heinz, RJR Nabisco, Marketing, Dancer, Fitzgerald & Sample Inc
  Jamie Lane, Managing Director
  e-mail: jlane@tullyandholland.com
  Education: BA, Colgate University; JD, Northwestern University
  Background: Strategic Advisor, Merrill Lynch; Director, William Blair & Co.

1870 TUSK VENTURES
251 Park Avenue S
8th Floor
New York, NY 10010

e-mail: info@tusk.vc
web: tusk.vc

Mission Statement: TVP invests in early stage tecnology startups operating in heavily regulated markets or new businesses where no regulatory framework exists. They provide regulatory, political and media support to their founders.
Key Executives:
  Bradley Tusk, Co-Founder/Managing Partner
  Education: BA, University of Pennsylvania; JD, University of Chicago
  Background: Deputy Governor, Illinois; Communications Director, US Senator, Chuck Schumer; Author; Adjunct Professor, Columbia Business School
  Jordan Nof, Co-Founder/Managing Partner
  Education: BS, Florida State University; MBA, Rollins Graduate School of Business
  Background: Director, Blackstone; AllianceBernstein

1871 TVC CAPITAL
11260 El Camino Real
Suite 220
San Diego, CA 92130

Phone: 858-704-3261 **Fax:** 858-523-9560
web: www.tvccapital.com

Mission Statement: TVC Capital is a private equity firm focused on investments in and acquisitions of software companies and software-enabled service firms. We target a wide spectrum of software sectors and industry verticals that are poised for growth and consolidation. Our Partners have 60+ years of experience in technology leadership, executive management, public and private board participation, and strategic transaction advisory. In partnering with exceptional management teams, we work 'in the trenches' with our portfolio companies to accelerate growth, maximize value and position for a profitable M&A exit.
Geographic Preference: United States
Investment Criteria: Growth Equity, Recapitalizations, Buyouts
Industry Group Preference: Software
Portfolio Companies: Centage, EdgeWave, LiquidPlanner, ReverseVision, Levels Beyond, Limeade, Mercent, Halo Business Intelligence, MeetingSense Software, Digital Map Products, LocationSmart
Key Executives:
  Steven J Hamerslag, Co-Founder/Managing Partner
  Education: BA, Economics, University of California, Berkeley
  Background: President & CEO, J2 Global Communications; Founder, MTI Technology
  Jeb S Spencer, Co-Founder/Managing Partner
  Education: Boston College; MBA, Harvard Business School
  Background: Co-Founder/President, Backwire; Finance Division, Republican National Committee
  Directorships: Ellie Mae, ReverseVision, Levels Beyond, TechnoCom, Halo Business Intelligence

1872 TVV CAPITAL
201 Fourth Avenue North
Suite 1250
Nashville, TN 37219

Phone: 615-256-8061 **Fax:** 615-256-7057
web: www.tvvcapital.com

Mission Statement: A value-oriented, lower middle-market focused private equity firm that makes control leveraged buyout investments in established, private and profitable companies

Venture Capital & Private Equity Firms / Domestic Firms

with strong management teams and enterprise values in the range of $10-100 million.
Geographic Preference: Southeastern United States
Fund Size: $10 million
Founded: 1998
Average Investment: $20 - 100 million
Minimum Investment: $5 million
Investment Criteria: Acquisition, LBO, MBO, Expansion, Recaps
Industry Group Preference: Telecommunications, Niche Manufacturing, Distribution, Industrial Services, Food & Beverage
Portfolio Companies: Design Molded Plastics, Critical Solutions International, IDI, Bigham Brothers, Indco, Big 3 Precision Products
Key Executives:
  Andrew Byrd, Founder/President
  615-256-8061
  Fax: 615-256-7057
  Education: BA, Vanderbilt University; JD, Vanderbilt University; Master of Taxation, Georgetown University
  Background: Director & EVP, GenCap America
  Andrew Byrd, Jr., Managing Director
  Education: BS, MS, Cornell University; JD, Vanderbilt University
  Background: National Security Agency

1873 TWIN BRIDGE CAPITAL PARTNERS
30 South Wacker Drive
Suite 1740
Chicago, IL 60606

Phone: 312-284-5600 **Fax:** 312-284-5599
e-mail: bgallagher@twinbridgecapital.com
web: www.twinbridgecapital.com

Mission Statement: Investor in LBO funds and co-investments.
Geographic Preference: North America
Fund Size: $1 billion
Founded: 2005
Average Investment: $20 Million
Minimum Investment: $10 Million
Investment Criteria: LBO Funds in North America
Industry Group Preference: All Sectors Considered
Portfolio Companies: Blue Coat, Bumble Bee Seafoods, American Industrial Partners, Carousel Capital, DrivenBrands, EN Engineering, Civic Partners, Lovell Minnick Partners, Gilchrist & Soames, LANDesk Software, Odyssey Investment Partners, Sentinel Capital Partners, Matthews, RenewLife, Swander Pace Capital, Thoma Bravo
Key Executives:
  F. Matthew Petronzio, Partner
  Education: BA, Bucknell University; MBA, Vanderbilt University
  Background: Partner, Five Points Capital; SunTrust Equity Partners
  Brian Gallagher, CFA, Partner
  312-284-5602
  e-mail: bgallagher@twinbridgecapital.com
  Education: MBA, Northwestern University; BA Accounting, University of Notre Dame
  Background: Principal, UIB Capital; Partner, PPM America Capital Partners
  Directorships: Renew Life, Grosvenor Registered Multi-Strategy Fund, HFS Chicago Scholars
  Joe Dimberio, Partner
  312-284-5605
  e-mail: jdimberio@twinbridgecapital.com
  Education: BA, Marketing, University of Notre Dame; MBA, University of Notre Dame
  Background: Senior Partner, PPM America Capital Partners
  Directorships: Gilchrist & Soames
  Pat Lanigan, Partner
  312-284-5606
  e-mail: planigan@twinbridgecapital.com
  Education: BA, Mechanical Engineering, University of Notre Dame; MBA, University of Chicago
  Background: Senior Partner, PPM Capital Partners
  Directorships: Pace Corporation

1874 TWIN CITIES ANGELS
web: tcangels.com

Mission Statement: To achieve an outstanding financial return on members' time commitment and invested capital.
Geographic Preference: Minneapolis/St. Paul. Minnesota, Wisconsin, Iowa, the Dakotas
Founded: 2006
Average Investment: $25, 000 - $2 million
Investment Criteria: Seed-Stage, Early-Stage
Industry Group Preference: Medical Technology, Medical Devices, Diagnostics, Pharmaceuticals, Biotechnology, Veterinary Medicine, Information Technology
Portfolio Companies: Alvarri, Amphora Medical, Ativa Medical, Bard's Tale Beer, Cardia Access, Cardialen, EcoEnvelopes, Engineered Propulsion Systems, MainStay Medical, Marner, Once Innovations, Perk Health, PlaCor, ReconRobotics, TST Media, UnityWorks Media, Vixar

1875 TWJ CAPITAL
Six Landmark Square
Suite 404
Stamford, CT 06901

Phone: 203-359-5610 **Fax:** 203-359-5810
e-mail: twjones@twjcapital.com
web: www.twjcapital.com

Mission Statement: TWJ Capital makes growth equity investments in expansion stage companies which need 'acceleration capital' to achieve growth inflection, and venture capital investments in start-up and early stage investments.
Average Investment: $500,000 - $5 million
Investment Criteria: Start-Up, Early-Stage, Expansion-Stage
Industry Group Preference: Telecommunications, Internet Technology, Business Products & Services, Specialty Retail
Portfolio Companies: Acoustic Technologies, eData Source, Floor & Decor Outlets of America, Tango Networks, KoolSpan, NetNumber, Game Trust, MVP Group International
Other Locations:
  7272 Wisconsin Avenue
  Suite 300
  Bethesda, MD 20814
  Phone: 301-941-1959 **Fax:** 301-941-1265
Key Executives:
  Thomas W Jones, Founder/Senior Partner
  e-mail: twjones@twjcapital.com
  Education: BA, MS, Cornell University; MBA, Boston University
  Background: Chairman & CEO, Citigroup Asset Management; Vice Chairman & Director, TIAA-CREF; SVP, John Hancock Mutual Life Insurance Company
  Nigel W Jones, Partner
  e-mail: nigel@twjcapital.com
  Education: BA, Harvard University; MBA, Stanford University Graduate School of Business
  Background: Principal, Carlyle Group; Associate, Goldman Sachs & Co.; Communications Officer, Captain, Force Reconnaissance Company, United States Marine Corps

1876 TWO SIGMA VENTURES
100 Avenue of the Americas
16th Floor
New York, NY 10013

e-mail: ventures@twosigma.com
web: www.twosigmaventures.com

Venture Capital & Private Equity Firms / Domestic Firms

Mission Statement: Two Sigma Ventures, a division of Two Sigma Investments, LLC, invests in companies run by highly driven people with potentially world-changing ideas. We seek out people using technology, computing, mathematics, or data to tackle hard problems, and we aim to help them thrive.

Founded: 2001
Investment Criteria: All Stages
Industry Group Preference: Technology, High Technology
Portfolio Companies: 3DRobotics, Anki, Floored, Kickboard, littleBits Electronics, Rethink Robotics, Symcat.com, Experiment, Placed, Renthop, Tinybop, Ufora, Canary

1877 TXV PARTNERS
Austin, TX 75201

e-mail: connect@txvpartners.com
web: txvpartners.com

Mission Statement: TXV Partners is dedicated to the collaborative process with its portfolio companies.

Founded: 2015
Industry Group Preference: Healthcare, Enterprise Software, Consumer
Portfolio Companies: Future.Fit, Kambr, NameCoach

Key Executives:
Brandon Allen, Founding Partner
Education: Princeton University
Background: Consultant, Stax; Consultant, Chartic
Marcus Stroud, Founding Partner
Education: Princeton University
Background: Analyst, MarketAxess; Vida Capital; Clubhouse Investment Club
Directorships: Trey Athletes

1878 TYLT LAB
1158 26th Street
Suite 325
Santa Monica, CA 90403

Phone: 310-331-8797 Fax: 310-870-7039
web: www.tyltlab.com

Mission Statement: Our focus is identifying, capitalizing, and building innovative, high growth companies. We are entrepreneurs ourselves, and have a hands-on approach to working with founders. Put simply, we believe in adding value, not just adding capital.

Investment Criteria: Early-Stage
Industry Group Preference: Consumer Electronics, Technology, Telecommunications, Consumer Products, Clean Technology, Healthcare, Entertainment, Fashion
Portfolio Companies: Cargomatic, Flexport, Moveline, Normal Ears, Paper Battery Company, PogoSeat, Tixr, Toguh, VNTANA, TodayTix

Key Executives:
Rami Rostami, Chairman/Co-Founder
Education: BS, Managment, California State University, Northridge
Background: Founder/CEO, Technocel Wireless Products; American Investment Group; Information Control Company
Gerard N. Casale, Managing Director/Co-Founder
Education: BA, Economics, Fairfield University; JD, Pepperdine University School of Law
Background: Founder, X-Laboratories

1879 UBIQUITY VENTURES
Palo Alto, CA 94301

e-mail: sunil@ubiquity.vc
web: www.ubiquity.vc

Mission Statement: A venture capital fund investing in machine learning and smart hardware companies.

Founded: 2017
Industry Group Preference: Machine Learning, Artificial Intelligence
Portfolio Companies: Diligent Robotics, Eclypsium, Elementary Robotics, Esper, Halter, Jargon, Loft Orbital, Parallel Domain, Windborne

Key Executives:
Sunil Nagaraj, Founder/Managing Partner
Education: BS, University of North Carolina; MBA, Harvard Business School
Background: Bessemer Venture Partners; Bain & Company; Cisco; Microsoft
Directorships: Diligent Robotics; Esper; Halter; Jargon; Levl; Parallel Domain

1880 UBS GLOBAL ASSET MANAGEMENT
One North Wacker Drive
Chicago, IL 60606

Phone: 312-525-7300
web: www.ubs.com

Mission Statement: UBS Global Asset Management believes that value-added investment returns are primarily function asset management decisions made within an integrated view of global capital markets, world economies and financial markets. Thus, investment management both within and across global stock markets, must be based upon comprehensive knowledge and analyses of integrated investment fundamentals.

Geographic Preference: North America, Asia Pacific, Switzerland, Europe
Fund Size: $10 billion
Founded: 1972
Average Investment: $1- $30 million
Minimum Investment: $1 million
Investment Criteria: Early-stage, Growth Equity Financings, MBO, Restructurings
Industry Group Preference: Global Industries

Key Executives:
Ralph Hamers, Group Chief Executive Officer
Education: Tilburg University
Background: ING; ING Belgium; ING Netherlands
Kirt Gardner, Group Chief Financial Officer
Education: BS, Economics, Williams College; MBA, Wharton School
Background: CFO, Citigroup; Global Head of Financial Services Strategy, BearingPoint; Managing Director, Barents Group

1881 UNCORK CAPITAL
Palo Alto, CA

web: uncorkcapital.com

Mission Statement: Founded under the name SoftTech VC, Uncork Capital is a lead investor in the micro-VC market.

Fund Size: $100 Million
Founded: 2004
Average Investment: $1.2 million
Minimum Investment: $750,000
Investment Criteria: Seed
Industry Group Preference: Artificial Intelligence, Robotics, Information Technology, Applications, Software, Data Analysis
Portfolio Companies: ClassDoko, DroneDeploy, Fountain, Front, LaunchDarkly, Joya Communications Inc., Molekule, Panorama Education, Poshmark, Postmates, Shippo, Tempo Automation, Top Hat, Widyard, Zefr

Key Executives:
Jeff Clavier, Founder/Managing Partner
Education: MS, Computer Science, Université Paris Descartes
Background: Head of Development, Effix Systems; Head of Development, Reuters Plc.; Co-Producer, RVC SoftEdge Conference; Partner, RVC Capital
Directorships: Curse Inc.; Pathfire; Tacit; UltraDNS

Stephanie Palmeri, Partner
Education: BS, Marketing/Management Information Systems, Villanova University; MBA, Columbia Business School
Background: NYC Seedl Accenture; Estee Lauder
Directorships: ClassDojo
Andy McLoughlin, Partner
Education: BA, Economics, University of Sheffield
Background: Intercom; Pipedrive; Bugsnag; Apiary; Buffer; Postmates
Ashley Cravens, Director of Operations
Education: BS, Business Administration/Marketing, University of Oregon
Background: Securities Assistant, Rosenbaum Financial; Licensed Broker, Morgan Stanley; Associate, Smith Barney

1882 UNDERDOG VENTURES
23 Route 105, E Brighton Road
PO Box 443
Island Pond, VT 05846

Phone: 802-723-9909 Fax: 802-723-9933
e-mail: info@underdogventures.com
web: www.underdogventures.com

Mission Statement: Underdog Ventures creates innovative and customized investments to meet the specific needs of each of our investors, each of whom has a dedicated fund that invests in areas that they choose.

Investment Criteria: Socially Responsible Companies
Industry Group Preference: Environment, Conservation, Consumer Products, Food & Beverage
Key Executives:
David Berge, Founder/President/Managing Partner
e-mail: david@underdogventures.com
Background: Director, Vermont National Bank's Socially Responsible Banking Fund

1883 UNION CAPITAL CORPORATION
445 Park Avenue
14th Floor
New York, NY 10022

Phone: 212-832-1141 Fax: 212-832-0554
e-mail: ucc@unioncapitalcorp.com
web: www.unioncapitalcorp.com

Mission Statement: Union pursues a highly selective investment policy and as a general rule, will only invest in companies which combine an active, highly capable management team with a healthy business that is characterized by stable and modestly growing cash flow. We will also consider turnaround situations that could be combined with our existing portfolio companies.

Geographic Preference: United States
Founded: 1968
Average Investment: $5 - $50 million
Minimum Investment: $3 million
Investment Criteria: Leveraged Buyouts, Management Buyouts, Corporate Divestitures, Recapitalizations, Lower and Middle Markets
Industry Group Preference: Advertising, Commercial Services, Household Goods, Direct Marketing, Tourism, Distribution, Business Products & Services, Printing, Food & Beverage, Marketing, Printing, Manufacturing
Portfolio Companies: Caps Visual Communications, MKTG, MultiAd, Ventura Associates
Key Executives:
James Marlas, Founding Partner
Education: JD, University of Chicago; MA, Univ. of Oxford; BA, Harvard University
Background: CEO, Mickelberry Food Products, Associate, Baker & McKenzie
Directorships: New York City Opera, The Young Presidents Organization, The Chairman's Council of The Metropolitan Museum of Art, Commanderie De Bordeaux
Gina E. Molano, Director of Administration
Education: BA Advertising/Marketing, Universidad de Bogota Jorge Tadeo Lozano, Columbia
Arthur G Murray, Operating Partner
Background: President/CEO, Salerno-Mcgowan; Sunshine Biscuits
Directorships: Factset Research Systems
Jay F Laudauer, Managing Partner
Education: BBA, Baruch College; MBA, MIT Sloan School
Background: Ortech International
Kevin Delaplane, Finance Partner
Education: BBA, University of Notre Dame; MBA, DePaul University
Background: Asset Based Lending, Harris Bank/Bank oF Montreal
William Ogden, Managing Partner
Education: BA, Dartmouth College; MBA, University of Virginia
Background: Granite Capital Partners; Prudential Financial; Inter-Atlantic Capital Partners
Reis L Alfond, Managing Partner
Education: BA, Dartmouth College
Background: Management Consulting

1884 UNION SQUARE VENTURES
915 Broadway
19th Floor
New York, NY 10010

Phone: 212-994-7880 Fax: 212-994-7399
e-mail: info@usv.com
web: www.usv.com

Mission Statement: Union Square Ventures is an early stage venture capital fund focused on web services. Seeks to invest in passionate, experienced entrepreneurs who are focused on creating highly scalable services and significant value propositions for their end users.

Geographic Preference: United States, Europe
Fund Size: $1 billion
Founded: 2003
Average Investment: $250,000 - $25 million
Investment Criteria: Early-Stage
Industry Group Preference: Internet, Internet Technology
Portfolio Companies: Abridge, Algorand, Amino, Arweave, Assembly, Autonomous Partners, Auxmoney, Blockstack, Blocktower Capital, Cloudflare, CoverWallet, Codecademy, Code Climate, Coinbase, CrowdRise, Dapper Labs, Dronebase, DuckDuckGo, Duolingo, Etsy, Foursquare, GoTenna, Indeed, Kickstarter, Marley Spoon, MetaStabble Capital, Modern Fertility, Multicoin Capital, Onefootball, Payjoy, Placeholder, Polychain Capital, Protocol Labs, Quizlet, RealtyShares, Recount Media, Science Exchange, Shippo, ShopShops, Simscale, Sofar Sounds, SoundCloud, Top Hat, Twitter, Tucows, Veniam, Wattpad, YouNow, Zynga

Key Executives:
Brad Burnham, Partner
Education: BA, Political Science, Wesleyan University
Background: AT&T; Executive-in-Residence, AT&T Ventures
Directorships: Indeed, Pinch Media, Tumblr, Wesabe, Adaptive Blue, SimulMedia, Tracked.com, Meetup, Bug Labs
Fred Wilson, Partner
Education: BS, Mechanical Engineering, MIT, MBA, Wharton School
Background: Founder, Flatiron Partners
Albert Wenger, Partner
Education: Harvard College; PhD, Information Technology, MIT
Background: Founder, DailyLit; President, del.icio.us
John Buttrick, Partner
Education: American Studies, Northwestern University;

Venture Capital & Private Equity Firms / Domestic Firms

JD, Villanova University School of Law
Background: Corporate Law, Davis Polk & Wardwell; Partner, Livewire; Board of Directors, Agfa-Gevaert NV; Advisor, Eckford Group
Directorships: Environmental Advocates of New York, Hirondelle USA
Andy Weissman, Partner
Education: BA, Wesleyan University; JD, Georgetown University
Background: AOL, Dawntreader Ventures
Rebecca Kaden, Partner
Education: BA, English & American Literature, Harvard; MBA, Stanford University
Background: Partner, Mavreon

1885 UNITED TALENT AGENCY VENTURES
9336 Civic Center Drive
Beverly Hills, CA 90210

Phone: 310-273-6700
e-mail: utaventures@unitedtalent.com
web: ventures.unitedtalent.com

Mission Statement: The early-stage and startup investment arm of United Talent Agency with an interest in media, sports, entertainment, and technology.

Founded: 2013
Investment Criteria: Seed, Early-Stage, Startup
Industry Group Preference: Media, Communications, Sports, Entertainment, Technology
Portfolio Companies: Art19, Awesomeness TV, Captiv8, Chorus, Cloud9, CrowdRise, Dreamscape, Fatherly, Figtagram, Hello Giggles, Houseparty, Lyft, MasterClass, MikMak, Pocket Watch, One Up Sports, Pluto, Patreon, The Players Tribune, Radish, Raze, Rex, Splash, Statmuse, Stem, Thrive Market, True Anthem, Uproxx, Victorious, Waggle

Other Locations:
888 7th Avenue
New York, NY 10106
Phone: 212-659-2600

Key Executives:
Brent Weinstein, Head of Digital Media
Education: University of Southern California; University of San Diego School of Law
Background: Corporate Law
Sam Wick, Head of Ventures
Background: MySpace, AOL, Mp3.com, Sony
Kosha Shah, Executive
Education: BA, Economics & Political Science, Stanford University
Background: Management Consulting/Strategic Planning, Mattel

1886 UNIVERSITY VENTURE FUND
299 South Main Street
Suite 310
Salt Lake City, UT 84111

Phone: 801-326-3590 Fax: 801-326-3598
e-mail: info@uventurefund.com
web: www.uventurefund.com

Mission Statement: University Venture Fund invests in compelling new technologies, high growth opportunities and stable cash flow businesses across a broad range of industries and sectors. This opportunistic approach allows UVF to take advantage of the latest trends and market dynamics, and leverage the diverse backgrounds of our students. UVF only co-invests alongside our other reputable institutional investors.

Geographic Preference: United States
Industry Group Preference: Consumer Products, Consumer Services, Internet, Technology, Healthcare
Portfolio Companies: Alianza, American Achievement Corporation, Ancora, Barosense, Catheter Connections, Coherex Medical, Control4, CompleteXrm, Daz3d, Handi Quilter, Infinera, Instructure, Intelisum, Lineagen, Merrimack Pharmaceuticals, Omniture, Socialtext, Transpond, TrustedID, Veritract

Key Executives:
Paul Brown, Managing Director

1887 UNSHACKLED VENTURES
435 Hamilton Avenue
Palo Alto, CA 94301

web: www.unshackledvc.com

Mission Statement: Unshackled is a venture capital fund providing capital, support and resources to immigrant entrepreneurs.

Geographic Preference: United States
Fund Size: $3.5 million
Founded: 2014
Average Investment: $300,000
Investment Criteria: Startups, Early Stage
Industry Group Preference: Diversified
Portfolio Companies: Geospago, Bluefield, OnTarget, Pluto, Shortlist, SensiHub, Togg, Gridraster, Lily, Sporple, Starskyrobotics, Brite Health, Pod Foods, CaaScade, Sote Logistics, Immediately

Key Executives:
Manan Mehta, Founding Partner
Education: BS & BA, Engineering & Economics, University of California, Los Angeles
Background: Co-Founder, Fanery; Head, Marketing, Kno; RBC Capital Markets
Nitin Pachisia, Founding Partner
Education: BComm, Finance & Accounting, Delhi University
Background: VP, Finance, Kno; Manager, Deloitte & Touche; ABB Limited

1888 UPDATA VENTURE PARTNERS
2099 Pennsylvania Avenue NW
8th Floor
Washington, DC 20006

Phone: 202-618-8750 Fax: 202-315-2668
web: www.updatapartners.com

Mission Statement: To invest in leading companies with outstanding management operating in large markets with an ascertainable technological advantage.

Geographic Preference: East Coast
Fund Size: $100 million
Founded: 1987
Average Investment: $5 - $20 million
Minimum Investment: $5 million
Investment Criteria: Growth Capital, LBO
Industry Group Preference: Enterprise Services, Information Technology, Financial Services, Healthcare, Business Products & Services, Outsourcing & Efficiency, Software, Internet
Portfolio Companies: Acclaris, Alert Logic, Amber Road, Appfluent, Bradford Networks, BRIDGE Energy Group, CMWare, Collective Bias, CoreStreet, DataCore Software, e-Security, Everest Software, ForeSee, GETPAID, Harmony Information Systems, iContact, Interactions, iSheriff, jobs2web, July Systems, The Kernel Group, LendKey, Logi Analytics, M86 Security, Mashable, Merlin Technologies, NetKey, Nimaya, Nintex, Numara Software, ObjectVideo, OrderMotion, OTG Software, Pet360, PulsePoint, RedVision Systems, RES Software, Secure Software, Softek, Spectrum K12, Trustwave, V3 Systems, Video Blocks, Viewpoint, XebiaLabs

Key Executives:
John Burton, Operating Partner
e-mail: jburton@updata.com
Education: Boston College
Background: President, Legent Corporation
Barry M Goldsmith, General Partner
Background: CGA Computer, Updata Software,

Venture Capital & Private Equity Firms / Domestic Firms

Carter Griffin, General Partner
e-mail: cgriffin@updata.com
Education: BS, Business Administration, University of North Carolina, Chapel Hill; MBA, JL Kellog School of Management
Background: Co-Founder, Brivo Systems; Senior Vice President, Kaiser Associates

James Socas, General Partner
e-mail: jsocas@updata.com
Education: University of Virgina; Harvard Business School
Background: Senior Vice President, Symantec

Ira D Cohen, Venture Partner
e-mail: icohen@updata.com
Education: BS, Accounting, City University; MS, Banking & Financial Services, Boston University; Executive Education Program, Harvard Business School
Background: CFO/CGA Computer; CFO/Tridex; Director of Internal Audit/MetPath;
Directorships: Director and Chair/Audit Committee Datastream Systems, Inc.

Jon Seeber, Principal
e-mail: jseeber@updata.com
Education: BA, Computer Science & History, Duke University; MBA, Harard Business School
Background: Busines Development, IBM Global Services

Kevin Zhang, Partner
Education: Harvard College
Background: The Boston Consulting Group; Verscend Technologies

1890 UPFRONT VENTURES
1314 7th Street
Suite 600
Santa Monica, CA 90401

web: www.upfront.com

Mission Statement: Formerly known as GRP Partners, UpFront Ventures invests in innovative technologies in relation to digital media, commercial and consumer goods and services.

Geographic Preference: United States, Europe
Fund Size: $300 million
Founded: 1996
Average Investment: $3 - $12 million
Minimum Investment: $3 million
Investment Criteria: First-Stage, Second-Stage
Industry Group Preference: Consumer Services, Retailing, Financial Services, Mobile Infrastructure, Distribution, Digital Media & Marketing, Marketing, SaaS, Cloud Computing, Mobile Apps
Portfolio Companies: 11 Honore, Adly, Adore Me, Alpha Draft, Apeel Sciences, Awe.sm, BillMeLater, Burstly, ChowNow, Comparably, Copilot, Cordial, CyberSource, DailyLook, eData Sift, Dealertrack Technologies, Deliv, Density, Digital Air Strike, Draft, Drone Base, Eagle Crest Energy, Emida, Envestnet, Epoxy, FabFitFun, Factual, Fame and Partners, Ferris, Goat, GoodRx, Gravity, Grove, Gumgum, Happy Returns, Health Data Insights, Health Data Vision Inc., HelloTech, HopSkipDrive, Imbellus, Inboard, Infosum, Invoca, Jiko, Kyriba, Lastminute.com, Luxe, Maker, MakeSpace, Mitu, MongoLab, Mytime, Nanit, Navdy, Nexkey, Nextplus, Nima, NuOrder, Osmo, Overture, Parachute, Pathmatics, Qualys, ReScie, Ring, Ritual, Rubica, Seedling, Seriously, Shots, Silversheet, Skurt, Skyline Home Loans, Stem, Tact.ai, Territory, The Mighty, The Wave VR, Thred Up, Token, Troopwork, TrueCar, uBeam, GUD, Ulta Beauty, Vemba, Vidme, Vreal, Waldo, Walker & Co., Zest Finance

Key Executives:
Mark Suster, Managing Partner
Education: BA, Economics, University of California, San Diego; MBA, University of Chicago
Background: VP, Product Management, Salesforce.com; Founder/CEO, Koral; Founder/CEO, BuildOnline; Accenture
Directorships: Density, Imbellus, Invoca, MakeSpace, Mitu, MyTime, Nanit, Osmo, Skurt, Tact, uBeam, Vidme, InfoSum, Vemba, Burstly, Gravity, Maker Studio

Yves Sisteron, Managing Partner
Education: JD/LLM, University of Law-Lyon France; LLM, New York University School of Law
Background: Fourcar BV, Carrefour SA
Directorships: Adore Me, Apeel Sciences, DailyLook, Fame and Partners, GumGum, Health Data Vision, Jiko, Kyriba, Nima, Health Data Insights, Ugo, Ulta

Greg Bettinelli, Partner
Education: BA, Political Science, University of San Diego; MBA, Graziadio School of Business & Management, Pepperdine University
Background: Chief Marketing Officer, HauteLook; EVP, Business Development & Strategy, Live Nation; Sr. Director, Business Development, StubHub
Directorships: 11 Honore, Deliv, DroneBase, Goat, Happy Returns, HopSkipDrive, Rention Science, Ring, Ritual, Rubica, Sense360, Silversheet, ThredUp, Walker and Company

Kara Nortman, Partner
Education: BA, Politics, Princeton University; MBA, Stanford University
Background: Co-Founder, Moonfrye, SVP/General Manager, Urbanspoon/Citysearch; M&A, IAC
Directorships: Hatch Labs, Parachute, Qordoba, Seddling, Stem, Territory, Waldo

Aditi Maliwal, Partner
Education: BA, Stanford University
Background: Product Manager, Next Billion Users Team, Google; Crosslink Capital; Deutsche Bank

Kobie Fuller, Partner
Education: Harvard College
Background: Investor, Accel; Chief Marketing Officer, REVOLVE; Co-Founder, OpenView Venture Partners; Investor, Insight Venture Partners

Michael Carney, Partner
Education: BS, University of California, Santa Barbara
Background: Editor, Pandoldaily; Founding Team Member, Worldvest

Key Executives:
Steven Florsheim, Partner
Education: Yale University; University of Michigan Law School
Background: Founder/Partner, Byron Marsh Capital; Managing Partner, Sperling & Slater; Chief Acquisitions Officer, Levy Acquisition Corp.

1892 UPHEAVAL INVESTMENTS
444 W Lake Street
Chicago, IL 60606

web: upheavalinvestments.com

Mission Statement: An early-stage venture capital fund focused on the tech industry.

Founded: 2018
Investment Criteria: Seed, Early Stage, Growth Stage
Industry Group Preference: Technology, Infrastructure
Portfolio Companies: Aktive, Atomos Nuclear and Space, Chowly, HaptX, LiveMetric, Passbase, Reniac, SpaceX

Key Executives:
Riley Florsheim, Partner
Background: CIO, Byron Marsh Capital; CEO, RF School Tech; Analyst, Levy Family Partners

1893 UPS STRATEGIC ENTERPRISE FUND
55 Glenlake Parkway NE
Building 1, 4th Floor
Atlanta, GA 30328

e-mail: sef@ups.com

Mission Statement: The Strategic Enterprise Fund (the "SEF") is the private equity strategic investment arm of UPS. The Fund

Venture Capital & Private Equity Firms / Domestic Firms

is a corporate venture capital group which focuses on developing critical partnerships and acquiring knowledge returns from its investments in information technology companies and emerging market-spaces. The Fund invests in companies that are strategically relevant to UPS, and reflects the strong emphasis that UPS places on becoming the leading provider of technologically advanced services in the transportation and logistics industry.

Geographic Preference: United States and select foreign locations.
Founded: 1997
Average Investment: $250,000-1,500,000
Investment Criteria: Strategic Relevance and Knowledge Returns, Co-Investment and Early Stage Investing, Strong Management, Board Meeting Observation Rights, Investment Range and Geographic Location.
Portfolio Companies: Cold PackSystem, DemandPoint, Deposco, Docufree, Impinj, Kabbage, Liaison Technologies, Shutl, Skytree, United Villages

1894 UPWELLING CAPITAL GROUP
2800 Fifth Street
Suite 120
Davis, CA 95618

Phone: 530-758-7888
e-mail: contact@upwellingcapital.com
web: upwellingcapital.com

Mission Statement: The Principals have cumulatively overseen over $50 billion in global private equity commitments and have successfully managed over $5 billion in legacy, tail-end commitments, transfers and workouts for leading institutional investors.

Fund Size: $50 billion
Founded: 2011
Industry Group Preference: All markets considered
Key Executives:
Joncarlo Mark, Founder
Education: UC, Davis; UC, San Diego
Background: California Public Employees Retirement System

1895 URBAN INNOVATION FUND

e-mail: info@urbaninnovationfund.com
web: www.urbaninnovationfund.com

Mission Statement: Urban Innovation Fund is a venture capital firm that invests in seed capital and entrepreneurs shaping the future of cities.

Investment Criteria: Seed-Stage
Industry Group Preference: Energy, Sustainability, Renewable Energy, Housing, Transportation, Education, Financial Services, Arts, Recreation, Health
Portfolio Companies: APANA, BookNook, Bumblebee Spaces, Catch, codeSpark, curbFlow, DropCountr, Ethic, Local Bushel, Milk Stork, Ride Report, Stop Breathe & Think, The Town Kitchen, udelv, Valor Water Analytics, Visage, Voatz

Key Executives:
Julie Lein, Managing Partner
Education: BA, Stanford University; MBA, MIT Sloan School
Background: Co-Founder, Tumml
Directorships: Tumml, Empower Work
Clara Brenner, Managing Partner
Education: BA, New York University; MBA, MIT Sloan School
Background: Co-Founder, Tumml
Directorships: Tumml

1896 URBAN US
29 Norman Avenue
Brooklyn, NY 11222

web: urban.us

Mission Statement: The Urban Us fund is focused on early stage investments to help businesses go from concept to reality.
Geographic Preference: US, Canada, Europe, Israel
Founded: 2013
Investment Criteria: Seed, Pre-Series A
Industry Group Preference: Real Estate, Energy, Finance, Fintech, GovTech, Infrastructure, Industry, Public Health & Safety, Transportation, Mobility, Workforce Development
Portfolio Companies: 3AM Innovations, Architizer, Avvir, BlocPower, Blockable, Blueprint Power, Borrow, Bowery, BRCK, Build Stream, Bumblebee, Circuit, ClearRoad, CityMart, CoInspec, Coord, Cove.tool, Dash, GreenQ, Evolve Energy, Ecomo, Flair, Food For All, Haas Alert, Hubster, KIWI, LiveStories, LogCheck, Lunewave, Mark43, Miles, One Concern, Onewheel, Open Data Nation, Park & Diamond, Perl Street, Pi Variables, Qucit, Rachio, Radiator Labs, Revivn, RoadBotics, Sapient Industries, SeamlessDocs, Skycatch, Social Construct, Starcity, Swell Energy, Swiftera, Thrilling, Toggle, Treau, Upshift, Urbint, Varuna, Versatile Natures, Wright Electric

Other Locations:
Ferry Building, One
Suite 201
San Francisco, CA 94111

2747 Glendon Avenue
Los Angeles, CA 90064

Key Executives:
Shaun Abrahamson, Managing Partner
Education: BS, University of Cape Town; MS, MIT; MBA, Berlin School of Creative Leadership
Background: Angel Investor
Stonly Baptiste, Partner
Background: Founder, Veddio Cloud Solutions
Mark Paris, Partner
Education: BA, Johns Hopkins University; MA, Public Policy, Harvard University
Background: Managing Director, Citigroup Urban Innovation Initiative

1897 US RENEWABLES GROUP
2425 Olympic Boulevard
Suite 4050 West
Santa Monica, CA 90404

web: www.usregroup.com

Mission Statement: US Renewables Group is one of the largest investment firms focused exclusively on the renewable energy industry.

Fund Size: $750 million
Founded: 2003
Average Investment: $30 to $70 million
Investment Criteria: Early-Stage to Acquisitions of Operating Assets
Industry Group Preference: Renewable Energy, Energy, Power Generation, Biofuels
Portfolio Companies: ASAlliances Biofuels, Bottle Rocket Power, Free Flow Power, Fulcrum Bioenergy, General Compression, Integral Energy Management, Newberry Geothermal, Niagara Generation, NOVO Energy, OPX Biotechnologies, Oski Energy, Penrose Landfill Gas Conversion LLC, Pipestem Energy Group, Recovery Technology Solutions, Renewable Energy Group, SolarReserve, ThermaSource, Tracy Biomass, Westeryly Wind

Other Locations:
10 Bank Street
Suite 580
White Plains, NY 10606
Phone: 914-390-9610

Key Executives:
Lee Bailey, Managing Director
Education: BA, St. Lawrence University; MS, Northwestern University; Law Degree, Washington

Venture Capital & Private Equity Firms / Domestic Firms

University School of Law
Background: Partner, Rustic Canyon Partners; Energy Conversion Devices; White House Director for International Science & Technology Commercialization
Directorships: Bottle Rock Power, SolarReserve
James McDermott, Managing Director
Education: BA, Philosophy, Colorado College; MBA, Anderson School, UCLA
Background: Municipal Finance Group, First Boston; Private Capital Group, Prudential; Allen & Company
Directorships: BioEnergy, General Compression, Novo Development Corporation, Oski Energy, SolarReserve

1898 US VENTURE PARTNERS
1460 El Camino Real
Suite 100
Menlo Park, CA 94025

Phone: 650-854-9080 Fax: 650-854-3018
e-mail: contact@usvp.com
web: www.usvp.com

Mission Statement: USVP is active in all aspects of a young company's development including strategy, recruiting, partnerships, financing and operational advice. Works as a partnership to make initial investment decisions to make every investment successful in their portfolio. Primarily interested in helping a company make the decisions and investments it needs to become a leader in its industry. Increasing competitiveness and aggressiveness of mature companies requires knowledge and access at high levels in order to avoid head on collisions with market leaders. Comfortable making an initial $500,000 seed investment to a $10 million later stage investment.

Geographic Preference: California
Fund Size: $1.1 billion
Founded: 1981
Average Investment: $4-$5 million
Minimum Investment: $500,000
Investment Criteria: Seed, Startup, First-Stage, Second-Stage, LBO, Market Opportunity, Geography
Industry Group Preference: Internet Technology, Communications, Software, Semiconductors, Health Related, Consumer Products, Life Sciences, Energy, Web-Enabled Services, Data Storage, Wireless Technologies, Agriculture, Medical Devices, Drug Development
Portfolio Companies: Akros Silicon, AltoBeam, Adify, Accelops, Act On, Aerogen, Applied Biosystems, Applied Micro, Appthority, Aptus Endosystems, Articulinx, Artisan Components, Ascenta Therapeutics, Asempra, Ask, Astute Networks, AtheroMed, AtriCure, Avenue A Razorfish, Axiom, Bayhill Therapeutics, Bevocal, Blekko, Blue Coat, Box, Calithera Biosciences, Callaway Golf, CardioKinetix, Castlight Health, Centillium Communications, Check Point, Chute, Cipher Trust, Clear Shape Technologies, Cleave Biosciences, Clustrix, Comilion, Commerce 5, Compugen, Contour Energy Systems, Crescendo Communications, CryoVascular Systems, Determina, Devax, Diablo Technologies, DMO Systems, Dotomi, Dstillery, Dune Networks, EasilyDo, eFFECTOR Therapeutics, Elentec Semiconductor, Electric Cloud, Ensure Medical, Exablox, Force 10, Fresh Choice, Genta, Genus, Glycomed, GoPro, Grokr, Guidewire, Harmonic, Headway Technologies, HeartFlow, Hooked Media Group, Hotel Tonight, IC Works, Ilypsa, iMPERVA, Inadco, Inceptus, Insidesales.com, Inspire Medical Systems, Instantis, Integrated Vascular Systems, Intellikine, InterMolecular, Intersect Enterprises, Intransa, Intuity Medical, Iomega, Jeda Networks, Kaiam Corporation, Karma Sphere, Kilopass Klocwork, Lasso, LineStream Technologies, Livefyre, Living Social, Lutonix, LVL7, M-Factor, Matritech, MaxLinear, MegaPath, Mellanox Technologies, Micro Linear, MicroHeart, Microvention, Military Advantage, Minerva Networks, MMC Networks, Mobbles, Montavista, MyYearbook, Nanostim, Neoconix, Object Reservoir, Occam Networks, ON24, OncoMed Pharmaceuticals, Optichron, PetsMart, Photon Dynamics, Proteclix, Qnovo, Quixey, ReadyForce, Redline Communications, Redwood Systems, RelayHealth, ReShape Medical, Revolution Money, Right90, Sagent Technologies, Sanarus Medical, SanDisk, Savings.com, ScoreBig, SentreHEART, Sequent Medical, SiBEAM, Sierra Monolithics, Silego Technology, Simprius Spine, Smartling, SocialShield, Spectranetics, St. Francis Medical Technologies, Stratacom, StrataLight, Sun Mircosystems, SupplyFrame, Synarc, Synfora, Talima Therapeutics, Tap11, Teknovus, Teranetics, think3, ThreatMetrix, Total Beauty, T-RAM, Trovix, Trunk Club, Trusteer, Valeritas, Ventritex, Verity, Vical, Victro, Vontu, Winster, X1 Technologies, Xicato, Ximus, Xoma, Xylan, Yammer

Key Executives:
Irwin Federman, Advisor
e-mail: federman@usvp.com
Education: Honorary Doctorate, Engineering Science, Santa Clara University; BS, Economics, Brooklyn College
Background: CEO, Monolithic Memories; Chariman, Seniconductor Industry Association
Directorships: Check Point, Centillium, Nuance Communications, Lightspeed Semiconductor, ON24, Astute Networks, Mellanox
Philip M Young, Advisor
e-mail: pyoung@usvp.com
Education: BME, Cornell University; MS in engineering Physics, George Washington University, MBA, Harvard University
Background: President & CEO, Oximetrix, Inc.; Concord Partners; Venture Capital & Corporaate Finance, New Court Securities; Management Consultant, McKinsey & Company; Boards: CoCensys, Penederm, Cardiovascular Imaging Systems
Directorships: Aerogen, Zoran, Bayhill Therapeutics, Caspian Networks, Gator, Healink, MicroHeart, RelayHealth, St. Francis Medical, Synarc, Time3
Steven M Krausz, General Partner
e-mail: skrausz@usvp.com
Education: MBA, Stanford Graduate School of Business; BS, Electrical Engineering, Stanford University
Background: NASA Ames; BTI Computers; Direct; Daisy Systems; Boards: EPIC Design Technologies, Photon Dynamics
Directorships: Agility Communications, New Focus, Exponent, Megapath, Sierra Monolithics, Object Reservoir, StrataLight, Vontu, Gluon Networks, Performance Retail, Kasenna, Notiva, WebCohort
Jonathan D Root MD, General Partner
e-mail: jroot@usvp.com
Education: MBA, Columbia University; MD, College of Medicine, University of Florida; AB, Economics, Government, Darthmouth College
Background: Assistant Professor of Neurology & Director of the Neurosurgery Intensive Care Unit, New York Hospital-Cornell Medical Center;
Directorships: Altus Biologics, CryoVascular Systems, Integrated Vascular Systems, MicroVention, Raven Biotechnologies
Casey Tansey, General Partner
Education: BS & MBA, College of Notre Dame
Background: CEO & President, Heartpoint; Baxter Edward's Cardiovascular Division
Directorships: Epicor Medical, Heartport
Rick Lewis, General Partner
Education: BS, Computer Science & Engineering, University of California, Davis; MS, Computer Science, University of California, Berkeley; MBA, Harvard Business School
Background: Autodesk, Walt Disney Imagineering; Co-Founder, Design Variations; Co-Founder, Common Point Technologies; Sun Microsystems
Directorships: Act-On Software, Victrio, Yammer
Jacques Benkowski PhD, General Partner
Education: BSc, Computer Engineering, Technion Israel Institute of Technology; MS & PhD, Computer Engineering, Carnegie Mellon University

Background: CEO & President, Monterey Design Systems; Founder & General Manager, Epic Design Technology
Dafina Toncheva, General Partner
e-mail: dafina.t@usvp.com
Education: BA, Harvard University; MBA, Stanford Grad. School of Business
Background: Bain & Co.; Venrock
Directorships: Apptimize, Arkose Labs, Insidesales.com, Luma Health, Prevoty, Raken

1899 VALAR VENTURES
915 Broadway
Suite 1101
New York, NY 10010

web: www.valarventures.com

Mission Statement: Valar Ventures welcomes ideas from start-ups globally that dare to push to great what others would only push to good enough. We're looking for those who go their own way - entrepreneurs outside of the United States with groundbreaking ideas and the determination to see them to reality. With your passion and our capital, we can build the next great global company.

Geographic Preference: Worldwide
Investment Criteria: Early-Stage
Industry Group Preference: Enterprise Software, Internet, Education, Consumer Internet, Cloud Computing, Software
Portfolio Companies: Xero, Transferwise, Vend, Dinda, Granify, Canopy Labs, ScriptRock
  Andrew McCormack, Partner
  Education: BA, Political Science, University of Pennsylvania
  Background: eCount, Yahoo!, PayPal, Clarium Capital Management
  James Fitzgerald, Partner
  Education: JD, University of California, Los Angeles
  Background: COO, Thiel Capital; Skadden, Arps, Slate, Meagher & Flom LLP

1900 VALENCE LIFE SCIENCES
500 Park Avenue
New York, NY 10022

Phone: 212-891-1100
web: www.valencefund.com

Mission Statement: Valence Life Sciences is a leading life sciences investment firm focused on late-stage private and micro-cap public drug development companies. Valence Advantage Life Sciences Fund II's targeted late-stage investment strategy - in conjunction with the team's experience, insight, and disciplined approach - has produced successful results for both its investors and portfolio companies.

Founded: 2012
Investment Criteria: Later-Stage
Industry Group Preference: Life Sciences
Portfolio Companies: Anthera Pharmaceuticals, ArQule, Celator Pharmaceuticals, Corthera, Geminx, Gentium, Invuity, Regado Biosciences, Sunesis, Vivus
Key Executives:
  A. Rachel Laheny, Managing Director
  Education: AB, Harvard College; PhD, Columbia University
  Background: Head, Biotech Research Team & SVP, Lehman Brothers; Hambrecht & Quist
  Eric Roberts, Managing Director
  Education: BS, Wharton School, University of Pennsylvania
  Background: Managing Director & Co-Head, Global Investment Group, Lehman Brothers; Managing Director, Partner & Founder, Life Sciences Department, Dillon, Read & Co. Inc.

1901 VALHALLA PARTNERS
8000 Towers Crescent Drive
Suite 1050
Vienna, VA 22182

Phone: 703-448-1400 Fax: 703-448-1441
e-mail: info@valhallapartners.com
web: www.valhallapartners.com

Mission Statement: To help talented entrepreneurs build world-class companies, by choosing to focus on business models and geographies that are well known.

Geographic Preference: United States
Fund Size: VP I: $177 million; VP II: $264 million
Founded: 2002
Average Investment: $10 million
Minimum Investment: $100,000
Investment Criteria: Seed to Later-Stage
Industry Group Preference: Information Technology, Infrastructure, Digital Media & Marketing, Education, SaaS
Portfolio Companies: Adaptly, App47, Automated Insights, BlueStripe, Custora, DomainHoldings, EnterpriseDB, Exchange Solutions, Fishbowl, Flat World, Geomagic, Getwell Network, Jumptap, KZO, LeftHand Networks, MiserWare, My Docket, Nirvanix, Parature, Place IQ, Qumulo, RealOps, Register.com, Rivermine, SafeNet, Sepaton, Shareablee, ShopSocial.ly, Solidfire, Speek, Swoop, Upfront Digital Media, Verical, Videology, Vistar Media, Vubiquity, WellAWARE Systems, Zonoff
Key Executives:
  Arthur J Marks, Managing General Partner
  e-mail: art@valhallapartners.com
  Education: BS Industrial Engineering, University of Michigan; MBA with High Distinction, Harvard University Graduate School of Business
  Background: General Partner, New Enterprise Associates; General Electric; Marketing/Sales, Baxter Laboratories
  Directorships: Domain Holdings, EnterpriseDB, Jumptap, Parature, SafeNet, Sepaton, SolidFire, Videology, Vubiquity
  Kiran Hebbar, Partner
  e-mail: kiran@valhallapartners.com
  Education: Bachelor's Degree, Indian Institute of Technology; MS, University of Maryland; MBA, Wharton School, University of Pennsylvania
  Background: Director, Product Management, Siebel Systems; Software Engineer, Bentley Systems; Mellon Ventures
  Directorships: Adaptly, Custora, Fishbowl, Flat World Knowledge, PlaceIQ, ShopSocially, Upfront Digital Media, Vistar Media, Vubiquity, Yelli, Zonoff
  Harry D'Andrea, Administrative General Partner
  e-mail: harry@valhallapartners.com
  Education: BA Foreign Service, Pennsylvania State University; MBA, Drexel University
  Background: CFO, Advanced Switching Communications; CFO, Call Technologies; CFO, Yurie Systems; CFO, American Communication Services
  Directorships: ExaDigm, Exchange Solutions, Safenet, Qumulo

1902 VALIA
875 Washington Street
New York, NY 10014

web: www.valia.vc

Mission Statement: Valia is a venture capital firm that backs founders building futuristic and iconic companies.

Other Locations:
  595 Pacific Avenue
  Jackson Square
  San Francisco, CA 94133

  72-74 Dean Street
  SoHo

Venture Capital & Private Equity Firms / Domestic Firms

London W1D 3SG
England

Key Executives:
Khaled Jalanbo, Managing Partner
Education: BS, Boston University; MS, Columbia University
Background: Entrepreneur; Angel Investor

1903 VALLEY VENTURES LP
1275 W Washington Street
Suite 101
Tempe, AZ 85281

Phone: 480-661-6600 Fax: 602-286-5284
web: valleyventures.org

Mission Statement: Focused on creating sustained high market-value companies that will dominate their industry niches while achieving fast-growing revenues and earnings.

Geographic Preference: Southwestern United States-Arizona, New Mexico, Southern California
Fund Size: $95 million
Founded: 1995
Average Investment: $5 million
Minimum Investment: $500,000
Investment Criteria: Second-Stage, Mezzanine, LBO
Industry Group Preference: Communications, Electronic Components, Electronic Technology, Medical & Health Related, Software, Industrial Equipment, Financial Services, Life Sciences, Information Technology, Microelectronics, Pharmaceuticals, Diagnostics
Portfolio Companies: Amplimed Corporation, Ascent Healthcare Solutions, Azerx, Cellzdirect, Delinea, HTG Molecular Diagnostics, Innovasic Semiconductor, Quasar, Regenesis Biomedical, Siverion, Vital Therapies

Other Locations:
PO Box 62798
Phoenix, AZ 85082

1904 VALOR EQUITY PARTNERS
875 North Michigan Avenue
Suite 3214
Chicago, IL 60611

Phone: 312-683-1900 Fax: 312-683-1881
e-mail: info@valorep.com
web: www.valorep.com

Mission Statement: A Chicago-based, middle market private equity firm dedicated to building great businesses in partnership with proven managers.

Founded: 1995
Average Investment: $10 - 30 million
Investment Criteria: New Platforms, Equity Investment, Add-On Investments, Special Situations
Industry Group Preference: Industrial Products, Specialty Distribution, Infrastructure, Manufacturing, Healthcare, Business Products & Services, Consumer Products, Energy Services
Portfolio Companies: Addepar, Family Home Health Services, Fooda, Marathon Pharmaceuticals, Renovate America, Sizzling Platter, Space Exploration Technologies

Key Executives:
Antonio Gracias, Chief Executive/Investment Officer
Education: BS & MSFS, International Finance & Economics, Georgetown University School of Foreign Service; JD, University of Chicago Law School
Background: Founder; MG Capital; Associate, Goldman Sachs
Juan Sabater, Partner
Education: A.B. History, Princeton University; J.D. Stanford Law School
Background: Managing Director, Goldman, Sachs & Co.
Jonathan K. Shulkin, Partner
Education: B.B.A. Accounting, University of Texas at Austin
Background: Investment & Portfolio team, MG Capital; President of Electronic Plating Service and Chief Operating Officer, Amax Plating, Electronic Plating Service, And Associated Plating Company
Timothy Watkins, Partner
e-mail: twatkins@valorep.com
Education: BS, Mechanical Engineering, Bradford University; MS, Industial Robotics, Cranfield Institute of Technology
Background: Vice President, MG Capital; Principal Consultant, Westworks Ltd
Bradley Sheftel, Managing Director
e-mail: bsheftel@valorep.com
Education: BA, Political Science, Tulane University
Background: JP Morgan Securities

1905 VALUEACT CAPITAL
San Francisco, CA

Phone: 415-362-3700 Fax: 415-362-5727
e-mail: info@valueact.com
web: www.valueact.com

Mission Statement: Valueact Capital's overall investment strategy takes a buy-the-whole-business or private equity approach as it seeks to take advantage of increasing structural inefficiencies in the small-capitalization sector of the public markets.

Fund Size: $5 billion
Founded: 2000
Industry Group Preference: Information Technology, Industry, Energy, Finance, Consumer, Healthcare
Portfolio Companies: Adobe Systems Inc., Alliance Data Systems Corp., Allison Transmission Holdings Inc., Arcosa Inc., Armstrong Flooring Inc., Armstrong World Industries Inc., Baker Hughes Inc., CBRE Group Inc., Citigroup Inc., Dresser-Rand Group; Exterran Energy Corp., Element Fleet Management Corp., Equifax, Fidelity National Financial Inc., Gartner Inc., Gevity HR Inc., Gardner Denver Inc., Intergraph Corp., Invensys Plc., Halliburton Co., Insurance Auto Auctions Inc., Immucor Inc., Life Technologies Corp., Lifeline Systems Inc., Lincare Holdings Inc., MDS Inc., MedQuist Inc., Mentor Corp., MSC Software Corp., Martha Stewart Living Omnimedia Inc., Merlin Enterainments Plc., Moody's Corp., Morgan Stanley, Rockwell Collins Inc., Rolls-Royce Holdings Plc., Redwood Trust Inc., Rentokil Initial Plc., Reynolds & Reynolds Co., Siebel Systems Inc., Seagate Technology Plc., Sara Lee Corp., Snap-On Inc., SLM Corporation, Seitel Inc., Tektronix Inc., Trinity Industries Inc., Twenty-First Century Fox Inc., TriZetto Group Inc., Warner Chilcott Plc., Williams Scotsman International Inc., Willis Towers Watson Plc.

Key Executives:
G. Mason Morfit, CEO & CIO
Education: BA, Princeton University
Background: Credit Swisse First Boston
Brandon B. Boze, Partner & President
Education: BE, Mechanical Engineering, Vanderbilt University
Background: Lehman Brothers; Chair, CBRE Group Inc.
Directorships: Valeant Pharmaceuticals International; ValueAct Capital
Briana J. Zelaya, Partner & Head, Marketing and Investor Relations
Education: BA, Loyola Marymount University
Background: Marketing, Blum Capital Partners

1906 VANCE STREET CAPITAL
11150 Santa Monica Blvd
Suite 750
Los Angeles, CA 90025

Phone: 310-231-7100
web: www.vancestreetcapital.com

Venture Capital & Private Equity Firms / Domestic Firms

Mission Statement: Invests in profitable middle market companies with enterprise values ranging from $50 to $200 million.
Geographic Preference: United States
Industry Group Preference: Aerospace, Defense and Government, Medical Products, Manufacturing
Portfolio Companies: Micronics Filtration Holdings, International Aerospace Coatings, Klune Industries, Micross Components, Process Fab, Semicoa
Key Executives:
  Richard R Crowell, Founding Partner
  Education: BA, University of California, Santa Cruz; MBA, Anderson School of Business
  Background: Co-Founder & President, Aurora Capital Group; Managing Partner, Acadia Partners; Managing Director, Corporate Finance, Drexel Burnham Lambert
  Michael Janish, Managing Partner
  e-mail: mjanish@vancestreetcapital.com
  Education: BS, MBA, Michigan State University
  Background: President and CEO, Avalon Laboratories; President and CEO, Precitech
  Brian D Martin, Managing Partner
  Education: BS, Business Administration, Haas School of Business, University of California, Berkeley
  Background: Vice President, Leveraged Buyouts Group, American Capital; Robertson Stephens

1907 VANDAELE CAPITAL
web: www.vandaelecapital.com

Mission Statement: At Vandaele Capital, we invest in startups, acquire and turnaround distressed companies, and advise businesses of all sizes on strategy and execution by forming partnerships. We also offer the expertise necessary to take any business to the next level. We focus on the challenges that emerging companies face, and we deliver proven, practical, customized solutions geared towards making companies more profitable. Our diverse portfolio of companies offers unique collaboration with businesses that demonstrates early success and high future potential.
Investment Criteria: Early-Stage
Portfolio Companies: EventReviews.com, Willa Skincare, Events.com, My Event Insurance, Qnary, Little Ducks Organics, Bump, Peeled Snacks
Key Executives:
  Christophe Vandaele, Founder
  Education: Masters Degree, Political Science & Military, Chateau d'Arenberg Military Academy
  Background: CEO, Redline Diplomatic Relocation

1908 VANTAGEPOINT CAPITAL PARTNERS
1001 Bayhill Drive
Suite 220
San Bruno, CA 94066

Phone: 650-866-3100 Fax: 650-338-1919
web: www.vpcp.com

Mission Statement: One of the leading venture capital firms in the world. With an interest in companies ranging from start-ups to pre-IPO, an active multi-stage investor. Providing long-term capital, with more than $4 billion under management and available for companies.
Founded: 1996
Average Investment: $20-$100 million
Investment Criteria: Multi-Stages
Industry Group Preference: Technology, Healthcare, Clean Technology, Information Technology, Energy, Energy Efficiency, Internet, Digital Media & Marketing
Portfolio Companies: 1366 Technologies, 3VR Security, Adura Technologies, AlertMe, Allbusiness.com, Allvoices, Amprius, Angstrom Power, Anthera Pharmaceuticals, Axsun Technologies, BlueWhale, Bridgelux, BrightSource Energy, Cbeyond Communications, CGI Pharmaceuticals, ChaCha, Chemrec AB, ChipX, Cobalt Technologies, Conceptus, CymaBay Therapeutics, Datran Media, Definity Health, Direct Flow Medical, DNS Services, E-One Moli, edo Interactive, EndPlay, Entrisphere, Evolv, FanIQ, GAIN Capital Group, Genomatica, glo AB, Global Financial Technology, Goldwind, Grocery Shopping Network, Healthline Networks, HengFu Logistics, Huga Optotech, iBAHN, Identified, InnoPath Software, Innovari, IntelePeer, InvestLab, Inxight Software, iWatt, Kagoor Networks, Klipsch Audio, Liquid Light, Liquid Robotics, Livescribe, Mascoma, Mayi, Meritron Networks, MiaSolé, Mobile 365, Multiply, MyFP, Myspace/Intermix Media, Neuraltus Pharmaceuticals, Nexsan Technologies, Next Step Living, Ogin, Ostara, OZ Communications, Phreesia, Pica8, Premium Power, PulsePoint, Pure Digital Technologies, ReachLocal, Safe Life, Santur, Savvion, Scribd, Serious Energy, Solarcentury, Solazyme, Spanfeller Media Group, Spatial Wireless, Switch, TargeGen, Tendril, Tesla Motors, TIDAL Software, TouchTunes Interactive Networks, TransMedics, Transport Technology Systems, Trilliant, VeriSilicon, Vook, WageWorks, Widevine Technologies, Xcellerex, YouMail, Zvents

Other Locations:
Unit 601, 6th floor, Tower 3
China Central Place
No. 77 Jian Guo Road, Chao Yang District
Beijing 100025
China
Phone: 86-1065989650 Fax: 86-1065989884

Key Executives:
  Alan E Salzman, CEO & Managing Partner
  Education: GC, London School of Economics; BA, University of Toronto; JD, Stanford Law School; lLM, Vrije Universiteit Brussel
  Tom Bevilacqua, Managing Director
  Education: BA, University of California, Berkeley; JD, University of California, Hastings College of the Law
  Background: Executive Vice President, E*Trade; Founder, ArrowPath Venture Partners
  David Fries, Managing Director
  Education: BS, Florida Atlantic University; PhD, Physical Chemistry, Case Western Reserve University
  Background: President, General Electric Ceramics
  Bill Harding, Managing Director
  Education: BS, MS, University of Arizona; PhD, Arizona State University; Officer, Military Intelligence Branch, United States Army Reserve
  Background: Managing Director, Morgan Stanley & Co.; President, Morgan Stanley Venture Partners
  Jim Marver, Managing Director
  Education: BA, Williams College; MPP, PhD, University of California, Berkeley
  Patricia Splinter, COO & Managing Director
  Background: Intel Corporation
  Richard Harroch, Managing Director
  Education: BA, University of California, Berkeley; JD, University of Californa, Los Angeles
  Background: Orrick, Herrington & Sutcliffe LLP

1909 VARDE PARTNERS
901 Marquette Avenue South
Suite 3300
Minneapolis, MN 55402

Phone: 952-893-1554 Fax: 952-893-9613
e-mail: investor.services@varde.com
web: www.varde.com

Mission Statement: Varde Partners has employed a diversity of event-driven investment strategies, earning its investors attractive risk-adjusted rates of return. Investments have centered on debt obligations of financially-troubled companies and, in more than 100 private transactions, nonperforming and sub-performing commercial real estate, commercial and industrial loans, residential mortgages, and consumer debt. Varde Partners manages several different investment funds that provide varying investment strategies and include multi-year lock up, annual redemption and offshore vehicles.

Fund Size: $300 million
Founded: 1993
Minimum Investment: $1 million
Industry Group Preference: Financial Services, Real Estate, Infrastructure, Mortgages
Other Locations:
Varde Partners Europe Limited
2 St. James's Market
London SW1Y 4AH
United Kingdom
Phone: 44-02078083370 **Fax:** 44-02078083371

Varde Partners Asia Pte Ltd
6 Battery Road
#21-01 049909
Singapore
Phone: 65-65790800 **Fax:** 35-65790801

510 Madison Avenue
12th Floor
New York, NY 10022
Phone: 212-321-3780 **Fax:** 212-321-3799

Key Executives:
Marcia L. Page, Co-Founder/Executive Chair
Education: BA, Economics, Gustavus Adolphus College; MBA, University of Minnesota
Background: VP, EBF & Associates; Portfolio Manager, Cargill
George G. Hicks, Co-Founder/Co-CEO
Education: BA, Gustavus Adolphus College; JD, University of Minnsota Law School
Background: SVP, Cargill Financial
Ilfryn Carstair, Partner/Chief Investment Officer/Co-CEO
Education: BC, University of Queensland, Australia; MBA, INSEAD, France
Background: Deutsche Bank London; Pacific Equity Partners
Dave Marple, Partner/General Counsel
Education: BA, Colgate University; JD, New York University School of Law
Background: Sr. Managing Director/General Counsel, Residential Capital; Lawyer, Structured Finance Department, Orrick Herrington & Sutcliffe

1910 VCFA GROUP
509 Madison Avenue
Suite 812
New York, NY 10022

Phone: 212-838-5577 **Fax:** 212-838-7614
e-mail: sharris@vcfa.com
web: www.vcfa.com

Mission Statement: VCFA Group provides liquidity to private equity investors. VCFA purchases, on a secondary basis, single interests or entire portfolios of interests in venture capital funds and venture backed companies. VCFA also purchases interests in other private equity funds, including mezzanine and buyout funds.

Geographic Preference: Worldwide
Fund Size: $230 million
Founded: 1982
Minimum Investment: $250,000
Investment Criteria: Existing limited partnership interests or existing interests in venture backed companies.
Other Locations:
One Sansome Street
Suite 3680
San Francisco, CA 94104
Phone: 415-296-0660 **Fax:** 415-296-0990

Key Executives:
David B Tom, Managing Director
e-mail: dtom@vcfa.com
Education: MBA, Harvard Business School
Background: Investment Banker, Goldman Sachs High Technology Group
Steven J Taubman, Director - San Francisco
415-296-0660
e-mail: taubman@vcfa.com
Education: MBA, Leonard M Stern School of Business; MS, Meteorology, Pennsylvania State University; BS, Atmospheric Science, University of California
Background: Standard & Poors
Andrew Riley, Managing Director
e-mail: areilly@vcfa.com
Education: BS, Boston College
Background: Director, Business Development, KVH Industries; Managing Director, Accretive Exit Capital LLC; Managing Director, Thomas Keenan Ventures

1911 VEBER PARTNERS LLC
605 NW 11th Avenue
Portland, OR 97209-3235

Phone: 503-229-4400 **Fax:** 503-224-0949
e-mail: gveber@veber.com
web: www.veber.com

Mission Statement: Veber Partners' goal is to develop and maintain long-term relationships through quality service and a record of performance raising new capital, assisting in corporate strategic alliances, and successfully closing acquisitions and ownership transitions. Veber also purchases middle market companies using its own equity and the equity of its strategic investors.

Geographic Preference: Pacific Northwest
Founded: 1994
Average Investment: $5-10 million
Minimum Investment: $2 million
Investment Criteria: Mezzanine, Equity
Industry Group Preference: Manufacturing, Distribution, Technology, Business Products & Services, Consumer Retail, Healthcare
Portfolio Companies: Veber Solar I, NWPolymers, CRU-DataPort, Pony Lumber, Pacific Interpreters, Tradewinds Forest Products, Associated Chemists, Tactix

Key Executives:
Gayle L Veber, Managing Partner/CEO
e-mail: gveber@veber.com
Education: BS, Massachusetts Institute of Technology; MBA, Columbia University
Background: Founder & CEO Of Nova Northwest, Inc., Chairman & CEO of PacifiCorp Financial Services Group, Mobil Oil, Caltex Petroleum, Halcon Int
Directorships: CRU-Data Port, Pacific Interpreters
Rodger P Adams, Senior Partner
e-mail: radams@veber.com
Education: BA, Humboldt State University; MA, MBA, University of Oregon
Background: PacifiCorp Financial Services, Security Pacific Bank Oregon Bank
Directorships: NW Polymers, CrossCurrent, CRU-Data Port
Nicholas J Stanley, Senior Partner
e-mail: nstanley@veber.com
Education: B.A. Finance/Psychology, Georgetown University
Background: Fine Arts Graphics; Stanley Investment Management; Titan Group
Directorships: OHSU Foundation, St. Anthony Village Enterprise, Services for All Generations, Oregon Entrepreneurs Network

Venture Capital & Private Equity Firms / Domestic Firms

1912 VECTOR CAPITAL
One Market Street
Steuart Tower
23rd Floor
San Francisco, CA 94105

Phone: 415-293-5000
web: www.vectorcapital.com

Mission Statement: A private equity boutique specializing in spinouts, buyouts and recapitalizations of established technology businesses. Vector identifies and pursues these complex investments in both the public and private markets.

Geographic Preference: Mainly outside of Silicon Valley
Fund Size: $2 billion
Founded: 1997
Average Investment: $20-$100 million
Minimum Investment: $10 million
Investment Criteria: Buy-outs, Recapitalizations, Spin-outs
Industry Group Preference: Technology
Portfolio Companies: 2020, Aladdin, Allegro, Aspect, Cambium Networks, Certara, Cheetah Digital, ChyronHego, CloudSense, CollabNet VersionOne, Corel, Emarsys, Extricity, Gerber Scientific, Host Analytics, IPVALUE Management, iVita Financial, LANDesk, Meltwater, MoxiWorks, Niku, Open Solutions, ProcessClaims, RAE Systems, RealNetworks, Register.com, Saba, SafeNet, Savi Technology, SourceHOV, Synamedia, Technicolor, Tekelec, Teletrac, The Kela Group, Tidel, Triton Digital, Vesta, Vispero, WatchGuard, WinZip

Key Executives:
  Alex Slusky, Managing Director & Founder
  Education: BA, Economics, Harvard University; MBA, Harvard Business School
  Background: ZiffBrothers; Partner, New Enterprise Associates; Consultant, McKinsey & Company; Product Manager, Microsoft Corporation
  David Fishman, Managing Director
  Education: BA, Economics, Duke University; MBA, JL Kellogg School of Management
  Background: Managing Director, M&A, Goldman Sachs & Co.
  David Baylor, Managing Director & COO
  Education: BS, Arizona State University; JD, Berkeley School of Law, University of California
  Background: COO/CFO, Thomas Weisel Partners Group; Managing Director, Montgomery Securities; Securities Attorney, Howard Rise Nemerovski Canady Falk & Rabkin; CPA, Deloitte & Touche
  Robert Amen, Managing Director
  Education: BA, History & Economics, Stanford University; MBA, Wharton School
  Background: Business Development, Microsoft Corporation; Finance Analyst, Montgomery Securities
  Directorships: Precise Software Solutions

1913 VEDANTA CAPITAL LP
540 Madison Ave.
30th Floor
New York, NY 10022

Phone: 212-710-5220 Fax: 212-710-5221
web: vedacap.com

Investment Criteria: Growth stage
Industry Group Preference: Information Technology, Life Sciences, Biotechnology, Medical Devices, Healthcare Services, Retail, Consumer & Leisure, E-Commerce & Manufacturing, Transaction Processing, Financial Services
Portfolio Companies: Litescape, Cast Iron, Consentry, Cortina Systems, Touchdown Technologies, Genband, Wayport, Omneon, Callidus, Arcot, Placeware, E2open

Key Executives:
  Michael Patterson, General Partner
  Education: BA, Latin American Studies, Wesleyan University; MBA, Columbia Business School
  Background: Principal, Invesco Private Capital; Corporate Associate, AMVESCAP; Executive Recruiter, Russell Reynolds
  Shrikant Sathe, General Partner
  Education: BT, Engineering, The Indian Institute of Technology; Masters, Electrical Engineering, Virginia Polytechnic Institute; MBA, Wharton Business School, University of Pennsylvania
  Background: Customer Marketing Manager, Daisy Systems; Director of Product Marketing and Director of Strategic Vendor Partnerships, Cadence Design Systems; Senior Vice President of Marketing, Infineon Technologies; Co-Founder and Vice President Of Marketing and Operations, SiNett Corporation
  Directorships: Erasmic Ventures, Harbinger Systems
  Parag Saxena, Co-Founder
  Education: BT, The Indian Institute of Technology, Bombay; MS, Chemical Engineering, West Virginia College of Graduate Studies; MBA, Wharton School, University of Pennsylvania
  Background: Citigroup Investment Management; Managing Partner and Founder, Invesco Private Capital (IPC); Product Manager, Becton Dickinson; Business Strategy Development, Booz, Allen, and Hamilton
  Howard Goldstein, Venture & Operating Partner
  Education: JD, Brooklyn Law School; BA, Sociology and Government, Clark University
  Background: General Partner and Co-founder, Invesco Private Capita
  Directorships: Make-A-Wish
  Gonzalo Cordova, Partner
  Education: BA and MA, Economics, University of Florida; Diplome d'Etudes Approfondies, Economic Policy, Institut d'Etudes Politiques
  Background: Senior Portfolio Manager, Citigroup Asset Management
  Andrew L. Dworkin, Partner
  Education: JD, New York University's School of Law; MA, Clinical Psychology, New York University; BA, Clinical Psychology and International Relations, University of Pennsylvania
  Background: Administrative Partner, INVESCO Private Capital; General Counsel, Chancellor Capital Management; Corporate Associate, Debevoise & Plimpton
  Margaret Riley, Partner
  Education: BS, Accounting, University of Wisconsin at Eau Claire
  Background: CFO, Invesco Private Capital; Auditor, Carlson Companies

1914 VEGAS TECHFUND
Las Vegas, NV

web: www.vegastechfund.com

Mission Statement: VegasTechFund is a seed stage investment fund focused on empowering amazing founders and startups passionate about building community in downtown Las Vegas.

Geographic Preference: Las Vegas
Investment Criteria: Seed-Stage
Portfolio Companies: Walls 360, Fancred, Understory, Ticketbase, Bow & Drape, Zirtual, AdEspresso, CoolChip Technolgies, Primeloop, Travelnuts, Mizzen & Main, CultureIQ, Tealet, Freak'n Genius, CheckiO, Mouth, World View, OrderWithMe, Spree Commerce, Fluencr, Local Motors, Moveline, Banjo, True&Co., Ministry of Supply, Quarterly, SurfAir, Combat Gent, CrowdHall, Umba, RecordSetter, Hachi, iDoneThis, Wildfang, Skillshare, Original, teamly, LaunchKey, General Assembly, Bluefields, wedgies, Rolltech, The SPIRIT Project, Fandeavor, Digital Royalty, LaunchBit, Local Motion, Romotive

Key Executives:
  Tony Hsieh, Partner
  Background: CEO, Zappos.com
  Fred Mossler, General Partner
  Background: Zappos.com

Venture Capital & Private Equity Firms / Domestic Firms

Will Young, General Partner
Background: Director of Engineering, Zappos.com
Zach Ware, Managing Partner
Background: Zappos.com, Founder, WorkInProgress

1915 VELOCITY EQUITY PARTNERS LLC
10 Liberty Square
Boston, MA 02109

Phone: 617-338-2545 **Fax:** 617-261-3864
e-mail: info@velocityep.com

Mission Statement: Creates value by identifying and supporting outstanding entrepreneurs with unique innovations and a powerful drive to build market-leading companies; works with management teams to create premier companies in their field with the help of capital, expertise in building companies, and access to key networks.

Geographic Preference: New England, New York, Washington DC Corridor
Average Investment: $1 million - $5 million
Investment Criteria: Early Stage
Industry Group Preference: Information Technology, Enterprise Software, Communications, Infrastructure, Wireless Technologies, Software, Manufacturing, Industrial Products
Portfolio Companies: AccuRev, BEZ Systems, CiDRA, CyVera, Dotomi Direct Messaging, Exmplar, The Feedroom, InnoPad, LP Innovations, Metatomix, Nexaweb, ProFind, Reflectent, Retail Solutions, Sonexis, WebDialogs

1916 VENBIO
1700 Owens Street
Suite 595
San Francisco, CA 94158

Phone: 415-800-0800
e-mail: info@venbio.com
web: www.venbio.com

Mission Statement: A unique private equity firm formed from many different backgrounds, experiences and disciplines. Our common belief is that life science investing has changed dramatically over the past decade and so the investment platform needed to change. venBio is the culmination of our vision to integrate finance, science, commercial and clinical experiences into all stages and forms of life science investing.

Industry Group Preference: Life Sciences, Therapeutics, Medical Technology

Other Locations:
1350 Avenue of the Americas
20th Floor
New York, NY 10019
Phone: 212-937-4970

Key Executives:
Corey Goodman, Co-Founder/Managing Partner
Background: President, Biotherpeutics & Bioinnovation, Pfizer; Co-Founder, Exelisis, Renovis, Second Genome & Ossianix
Directorships: Solstice Biologics, Labrys Biologics, Oligasis, Ossianix, Second Genome
Robert Adelman, Co-Founder/Managing Partner
Background: Private Equity Partner, OrbiMed Advisors; Founder, Operon Technologies & Roka Bioscience
Directorships: Seragon Pharmaceuticals, Solstice Biologics

1917 VENCORE CAPITAL
4500 SW Kruse Way
Suite 350
Lake Oswego, OR 97035

Phone: 503-699-4997 **Fax:** 503-675-3136
Toll-Free: 800-890-4992
web: www.vencorecapital.com

Mission Statement: With our unique approach to venture debt financing, Vencore Capital helps early-stage, emerging growth companies extend their operating cash runway, and move towards profitability and increased valuation.

Geographic Preference: United States
Average Investment: $50,000 to $2 million
Minimum Investment: $50,000
Investment Criteria: Early-Stage Growth Capital
Industry Group Preference: Computer Related, Consumer Products, Life Sciences, Semiconductors, Business Products & Services, Software, Media, Telecommunications, Wireless Technologies
Portfolio Companies: Absorbent Technologies, AdventureLink, Afiniti Ventures, Agoura Technologies, Airborne 1, Apex Construction Systems, Audiomojo, Axcel Photonics, Axial Biotech, Be Jane, Bella Pictures, Black Rock Systems, Blink Twice, Blue Heron Technologies, Blue Lava Group, Bossa Nova Beverages Group, Brainshark, Cadforce, Calypte, CardioKinetix, Catalyst Oncology, Caveon, Chartone, Chockstone, Clupedia, Commrail, Confirma, Control Works, Criteria Labs, Dakota Arms, Dynamic Organic Light, Efficere, Endurance International, Engine Yard, Farralon Medical, Foundationworks, Galileo Processing, Health Carechain, iLinkMD, Intelligent Medical Devices, Inlustra Technologies, iSense, Isonics, IsoRay Medical, iWorlds Simulations, KBI Biopharma, Kimomex Markets, Kyma Technologies, Layered Technologies, LeisureLink, Lipomics, LensVector, Luxine, MEC Dynamics, Melior Discovery, Microphage, Missions Controls Automation, Morrone Organic Innovations, Motoczysz, MultiGEN Diagnostics, NBS Design, Neato Robotics, Neptune, Neuroptix, Nextreme Thermal Solutions, Northwave Technology, Novalux, NxGen Electronics, Ondax, Orphgen Pharmaceuticals, Oxysure Systems, Pacific GMP, Pathwork Diagnostics, Piedmont Pharmaceuticals, Prolacta Bioscience, Proteogenix, PTRx, Quantumsphere, Quick Study Radiology, Rogue Valley Microdevices, Rubicon Technology, S3C, SensAble, Sirigen, SMT Dynamics, Sword Diagnostics, Texas Advanced Optoelectronic, Thorley Industries, Touchdown Technologies, Trius Therapeutics, Vesta Therapeutics, Motoczysz, Neptune Networks, New Vine Logistics, Novinium, Organic Holding Company, PerceptiS, Phoenix Gold, Organic Holding Company, Progressive Beverages, Quintek Technologies, RealWinWin, SBBnet, Socrates Media, Softlayer Technologies, Synodon, The Water Company, WAG Hotels, Wavepoint Ventures, Accept Software, Adapx, Agilence, Aras, Arcot Systems, Buyingshow Solutions, Care2.com, Colorep, CYA Technologies, DAVE Networks, Daverci Solutions, Digital Map Products, Drivesafety, e-Dialog, Evident Software, eZCom Software, Flytecomm, Green Builder Media, Grid Network Systems, hi5 Networks, iArchives, Incuity Software, Infocrossing iConnection, Isolation Networks, Kaon Interactive, Klir Technologies, Kontera Technologies, Liquidus, Live Cargo, Magnify.net, Mesoft, Miria Systems, Mobile Content Networks, MODA Technology Partners, Navio Systems, Nexus Energy Software, Nimbit, nQueue, OnMeta, Ostendo Technologies, Piczo, Reality Digital, RightAnsers, ShowingTime, Soundflavor, Transware

Key Executives:
John Saefke, Chief Executive Officer
Education: BS, Finance & Management, University of Oregon; Post-Baccalaureate Degree, Accounting, Portland State University
Background: Controller, FirstCorp
Jim Johnson, Chief Operating Officer
Education: BS, Finance, California State University; Defense Language Institute
Background: Venture Leasing Division, FirstCorp; Household International
David Dolezal, Managing Director, Rocky Mountain Region
303-410-4495
e-mail: dave@vencorecapital.com
Education: BS, Business Administration, Portland State

Venture Capital & Private Equity Firms / Domestic Firms

University
Background: Vice President, Silicon Valley Bank

1918 VENROCK ASSOCIATES
7 Bryant Park
23rd Floor
New York, NY 10018
Phone: 212-444-4100 Fax: 212-444-4101
web: www.venrock.com

Mission Statement: Provides funding and services for entrepreneurs with breakthrough ideas in technology, healthcare, media and energy.

Geographic Preference: United States
Fund Size: $1+ billion
Founded: 1969
Minimum Investment: $5 million
Investment Criteria: Early Stage
Industry Group Preference: Technology, Healthcare, Media, Energy, Healthcare Information Technology, Social Media, Biofuels, Distributed Electricity, Vehicle Technology, Biopharmaceuticals, Diagnostics, Medical Devices, Advertising Technology, Consumer Technology
Portfolio Companies: 6sense, 10X Genomics, Acceleron Pharma, Achaogen, Adavium Medical, ADiFY, Adnexus, Aha, Aledadem Amino, Alimera Sciences, Anacor Pharma, Appia, Appthority, AppNexus, Aria Systems, Ariosa Diagnostics, Atom Computing, Avalanche Biotech, BCD, B-Hive, Bizo, Beckon, BlogHer, Boston Power, Boundless, Burner, Castlight Health, Celladon, Chisel, Ciclon Semiconductor, Cloudflare, CodeRyte, Constellation Pharma, CoreTrace, Crunchyroll, Ctera, Cygilant, Cymabay Therapeutics, Cyteir Therapeutics, Dapper, DATAllegro, Dataminr, Devoted Health, Doctor on Demand, Dollar Shave Club, Dstillery, Dynamic Signal, Encoded Genomics, Evident.io, Extend Media, Fate Therapeutics, FINsix, Gazelle, Grand Rounds, Happier, Hua Medicine, Hyper9, Ikaria, Impopharma, INRIX, Inscripta, Intuityy Medical, Jiff, Juno Therapeutics, Klout, Kwicr, Kyruus, Lavante, Lucid, Luxe, Lyra, Misty Robotics, Niara, Nest, Newport Media, Numerated, Optinuity, P.A. Semi, PEAK Surgical, Percipient.ai, Personal Capital, Phononic, PowerVision, Quantenna, QuatRx, Quip, Receptos, Redbeacon, RedSeal, RegenXBio, Reflexion, Renew, Retail Solutions, Salsify, Sapphire Energy, Semtek, Shape, Shockwave Medical, Simple Star, Skyryse, SlideShare, SmartBix, Smartling, SocialShield, Socrates.ai, Spirox, Stride, Suki, Targeted Genetics Corp., Threadbox, Transonic Combustion, Tri Alpha Energy, Trubion Pharma, Tudou, Twofish, Unity Biotechnology, VeloCloud, Virdante Pharma, Virta, Where, Workframe, World Heart Corp., YouNow, Zeltiq, ZoomInfo

Other Locations:
3340 Hillview Avenue
Palo Alto, CA 94304
Phone: 650-561-9580 Fax: 650-561-9180

34 Farnsworth St.
3rd Floor
Boston, MA 02210
Phone: 617-995-2000 Fax: 617-995-2001

Key Executives:
Brian Ascher, Partner
e-mail: bda@venrock.com
Education: BA, Magna Cum Laude, Princeton University; MBA, Stanford University
Background: Senior Product Manager, Intuit; Strategy Consultant, Monitor Group
Directorships: Awarepoint, Vocera
Nick Beim, Partner
e-mail: nick@venrock.com
Education: Stanford University; University of Oxford
Background: Associate, McKinsey; Associate, Goldman Sachs; General Partner, Matrix Partners
Directorships: Dataminr, Workframe, Quip Inc., Chisel.ai, Percipient.ai

Camille Samuels, Partner
e-mail: cami@venrock.com
Education: BA, Duke University; MBA, Harvard Business School
Background: Managing Director, Versant Ventures
Directorships: Spirox Medical, Unity Biotechnology
Bob Kocher MD, Partner
e-mail: bkocher@venrock.com
Education: University of Washington; MD, George Washington University
Background: Special Assistant to the President, Healthcare & Economic Policy, Obama Administration, Member, National Economic Council; Partner, McKinsey & Company
Directorships: Castlight Health
Bryan Roberts, Partner
650-475-3750
Fax: 650-561-9180
e-mail: broberts@venrock.com
Education: BA, Dartmouth College; PhD, Chemistry/Biology, Harvard University
Background: Investment Banking, Kidder Peabody & Company
Directorships: Achaogen, Castlight Health, Ironwood Pharmaceuticals
Mike Tyrrell, Partner
617-679-0365
Fax: 617-679-0301
e-mail: mft@venrock.com
Education: BS, University of New Hampshire
Background: Spyglass; Multiflow Computer; Celerity Computing; Prime Computing
Directorships: Appia, Aria Systems

1919 VENSANA CAPITAL
3601 W 76th Street
Suite 20
Minneapolis, MN 55435
Phone: 612-217-8680
e-mail: info@vensanacap.com
web: www.vensanacap.com

Mission Statement: Vensana Capital is a venture capital and growth equity investment firm that partbers with entrepreneurs who will trasnform healthcare with breakthrough innovations in medical technology.

Fund Size: $225 Million
Founded: 2019
Average Investment: $10-30 Million
Investment Criteria: Medical Devices; Diagnostics and Data Science; Digital Health and Tech-Enabled Services

Other Locations:
101 Church Street
Suite D
Vienna, VA 22180

Key Executives:
Justin Klein, Co-Founder/Managing Partner
Education: AB, BS, MD, Duke University; JD, Harvard Law School
Background: Partner, NEA
Kirk Nelson, Co-Founder/Managing Partner
e-mail: kirk@vensanacap.com
Education: BA, MBA, Harvard University
Background: Consultant, Bain & Co.; Pro Hockey Player

1920 VENTANA CAPITAL MANAGEMENT LP
22431 Antonio Parkway
Suite B160-1002
Rancho Santa Margarita, CA 92688
Phone: 949-766-4486 Fax: 949-766-4487
web: ventanainnovation.wordpress.com

Mission Statement: Ventana likes to fund global expansion, especially in regards to China. It also concentrates efforts on first and second stage enterprises, technology developed by the aerospace, quasi-governmental industries, university-based scientific spin-outs, institutional research and private entrepreneurial opportunities in the areas of the environment, health services and medical devices, biotechnology and biopharmaceutical and technology.

Geographic Preference: Southern California, Worldwide
Fund Size: $230 million
Founded: 1974
Average Investment: +$5 million
Minimum Investment: $2 million
Investment Criteria: First and Second-Stage Including Growth Stage
Industry Group Preference: Environmental Protection, High Technology, Biotechnology, Biopharmaceuticals, Technology, Telecommunications, Pollution, Energy, Hazardous Waste, Medical & Health Related, Therapeutics, Research & Development, Aerospace, Defense and Government, Wireless Technologies, Digital Media & Marketing
Portfolio Companies: Advanced Photonix, Aktino, Brooktree Corporation, California Linear Devices, Cymer, Fidelica Microsystems, Innovent Systems, Neophotonics, PairGain Technology, Pathlight Technologies, Proxima, Sequoia Communications, Soma Networks, Alliance Pharmaceutical, Agouron Pharmaceuticals, BioCryst Pharmaceuticals, Corvas International, GalaGen, Idun Pharmaceuticals, Integra Life Sciences, Maxim Pharmaceuticals, R-2solid to Warburg Pincus, La Jolla Pharmaceutical Company

Other Locations:
11673-202 Charter Oak
Reston, VA 20190
Phone: 405-824-5549

Key Executives:
Thomas O Gephart, Founder/Managing Partner
Education: BA, Engineering, University of Southern California
Background: Executive Positions: AMP Inc., Bunker-Ramo Corporation, Hughes Aircraft; Founder, Interlink Company; Chariman: Advantix Inc., APTA Group Inc., Cellnet Corporation, HemaCare Coroporation, Infrasonics Inc., QTRON Inc.

1921 VENTURE ASSOCIATES PARTNERS LLC
355 Sweetbriar Road
Memphis, TN 38120-2515

Phone: 901-763-1434 **Fax:** 901-763-1428
e-mail: email@venture-associates.com
web: www.venture-associates.com

Mission Statement: Primarily underperforming situations in growth industries, primarily manufacturing; looking for new platform company as well as synergistic acquisitions.

Geographic Preference: United States, Canada, Mexico
Founded: 1985
Average Investment: $5 - $15 million
Minimum Investment: $1 million
Investment Criteria: Revenue $20-$200 million; Underperforming situations in growth industry
Industry Group Preference: Components & IoT, Aerospace, Defense and Government, Plastics, Electronic Technology
Portfolio Companies: Applied Composites, Crown Fiberglass, Diversified Composites, Applied Aerospace Structures, Century Wheel @ Rim, Applied Molded Products, Agena Technologies

Key Executives:
Burton B Weil, Chairman
e-mail: bweil@venture-associates.com
Education: BS, University of Tennessee; MBA, University of Memphis; JD, Vanderbilt University; CPA

1922 VENTURE CAPITAL FUND OF NEW ENGLAND
30 Washington Street
Wellesley, MA 02481

Phone: 781-431-8400 **Fax:** 781-237-6578
e-mail: inquiries@vcfne.com
web: www.vcfne.com

Mission Statement: The Venture Capital Fund of New England's investment activities are characterized by: a focus on early stage companies; a geographic concentration in the New England region; an emphasis on technology based enterprises; and an additional interest in direct marketing - related businesses. VCFNE prefers New England-based companies in the early stage investment category, though it is also willing to consider on an occasional basis a seed or expansion stage investment and companies located outside the Northeastern US.

Geographic Preference: New England
Fund Size: $80 million
Founded: 1981
Average Investment: $500,000 - $1.5 million
Minimum Investment: $500,000
Investment Criteria: Early-Stage
Industry Group Preference: E-Commerce & Manufacturing, Broadcasting, Communications, Computer Related, Electronic Technology, High Technology, Industrial Equipment, Information Technology, Software, Cable, Radio, Direct Marketing
Portfolio Companies: Protonex, First Equity, Tibersoft, Nutfield Technology, Texterity, NextMark, Aircuity, ComBrio, Redtail Solutions, ExoGenesis, EMO Labs, LP Innovations, Cartera Commerce, Saylent Technologies, Air-Inc

Key Executives:
Carl Novotny, Managing Director
e-mail: cnovotny@vcfne.com
Education: B.A. Rice University; MBA, Harvard Business School
Background: First USA Partners; First USA Bank; Trans National Financial Services
Directorships: Associates in Internation Research, Saylent Technologies, Next Mark, EMO Labs
Gordon R Penman, Managing Director
e-mail: gordon.penman@wbd-us.com
Education: B.A., College of William and Mary; J.D., University of Virginia Law School
Background: Brown Rudnick; Boston Bar Association
E Jack Stewart, Managing Director
e-mail: jstewart@vcfne.com
Education: BS, Yale University; MBA, Harvard Business School
Background: Partner, Corning Venture Management; Founder, Kestral Venture Management
Chad Novotny, Managing Director
e-mail: chad.novotny@vcfne.com
Education: BA, Amherst College; MBA, Babson College
Background: Principal and CTO; The Support Group Inc.

1923 VENTURE INVESTORS LLC
University Research Park
505 South Rosa Road
Suite 201
Madison, WI 53719

Phone: 608-441-2700 **Fax:** 608-441-2727
web: www.ventureinvestors.com

Mission Statement: Although the Midwest is home to many of the nation's leading research institutions, it possesses just a small fraction of the nation's venture capital. Venture Investors is filling this void with patient capital and the experience of building companies. We are investors that are willing to become actively involved in building the team and organization that are necessary to lead a company to success.

Geographic Preference: Midwest

Fund Size: $118 million
Founded: 1982
Average Investment: $5-7 million
Minimum Investment: $250,000
Investment Criteria: Focus is on the stage of company development rather than specific industries. In general, Venture Investors looks to invest in companies with proprietary products that offer distinct competiveness.
Industry Group Preference: Healthcare, Technology, Clean Technology
Portfolio Companies: Aerpio Therapeutics, Akebia Therapeutics, Cellectar Biosciences, Celleration, Deltanoid Pharmaceuticals, EBI Life Sciences, Euthymics Bioscience, Gala Biotech, Great Lakes Pharmaceuticals, HistoSonics, IntraLase, Inviragen, Juventas Therapeutics, LenSx, Madison Vaccines Inc., NanoBio, Nerites, NeuMoDx, Neurovance, NeuWave, NimbleGen Systems, Procertus, Promega, ReShape Medical, Third Wave Technologies, Tissue Regeneration Systems, TomoTherapy, ZyStor Therapeutics, AlfaLight, Guild, NetSocket, Pattern Insight, Thalchemy, UpTo, Chromatin, Silatronix, Virent

Other Locations:
201 South Main Street
Suite 900
Ann Arbor, MI 48104
Phone: 734-274-2904 **Fax:** 734-214-3006

John Neis, Executive Managing Director
e-mail: john@ventureinvestors.com
Education: BS Finance, University of Utah; MS Marketing & Financing, University of Wisconsin
Background: Chartered Financial Analyst
Directorships: Deltanoid Pharmaceuticals, Virent Energy Systems

Scott Button, Managing Director
e-mail: scott@ventureinvestors.com
Education: BS Mechanical Engineering, University of Wisconsin; MBA, University of Chicago
Background: Sales Engineer Rockwell International; Operations Manager, McDonalds Corporation
Directorships: SoftSwitching Technologies, Inc., NeuWave Medical, Silatronix

Paul Weiss, Managing Director
e-mail: paul@ventureinvestors.com
Education: BS, Biochemistry, Carleton University, Ottawa; PhD, Biochemistry, MBA, University of Wisconsin, Madison
Background: President, Gala Biotech Division of Cardinal Health; VP, Business Development, 3-Dimensional Pharmaceuticals; Director of Licensing, Wyeth-Ayerst Pharamaceuticals
Directorships: Akebia Therapeutics, Euthymics Bioscience, Mithridion, ProCertus

Jim Adox, Managing Director
e-mail: jim@ventureinvestors.com
Education: BS, Mechanical Engineering, MS, Mechanical Engineering, MBA, University of Michigan
Background: RidgeLine Ventures; EDF Ventures
Directorships: HistoSonics, Incept BioSystems, Michigan Venture Capital Association, Tissue Regeneration Systems

1924 VENTURE TECH ALLIANCE
2585 Junction Avenue
San Jose, CA 95134

Phone: 408-382-7927 **Fax:** 408-382-8004
web: www.vtalliance.com

Mission Statement: A venture investment management company targeting early-stage business investments in the semiconductor industry and other emerging technology areas.

Fund Size: $165 million
Founded: 2001
Minimum Investment: $1-$3 million
Investment Criteria: Early to Mid-Stage
Industry Group Preference: Semiconductors, Emerging Markets, Sectors & Technologies
Portfolio Companies: 5V Technologies, Aiconn Technology, AMCC, Apache, Aquantia, Audience, Auramicro, Axiom, Beceem, Bridgelux, Exclara, Gemfire, Ikanos, Impinq, IvenSense, Leadtrend, LiquidLEDs, MediaTek, Mutual-Pak, Maxim, Eoconix, NetLogic, NextIO, Nvidia, Optichron, Pixim, Power Analog, Microelectronics, Powervation, QUALCOM, Quellan, RichWave, Sentelic, SiRF Technology, SVTC, Synopsys, Teknovus, POWERPRECISE, Reflectivity, Thales, Tilera, Touch Micro-System, Tech, Validity, Xceive, YoBon

Other Locations:
615 West Prospect Street
Seattle, WA 98119

No. 10, Li-Hsin 6th Road
Hsin-Chu Science-Based Industrial Park
Hsin-Chu
Taiwan 300
China
Phone: 03-6669980 **Fax:** 03-6669970

Key Executives:
Ron Norris, Managing Partner
206-441-8080
Fax: 206-441-7373
e-mail: morris@vtalliance.com
Education: BS, Physics, Sam Houston State University; MS, Physics, University of Arkansas
Background: SVP, Worldwide Marketing & Sales, TSMC; President, TSMC USA; VP & General Manager, Data I/O Corporation

Kai Tsang, Managing Partner
408-382-7927
Fax: 408-382-8004
e-mail: ktsang@vtalliance.com
Education: BS, Physics, National Taiwan University; PhD, Physics, University of Illinois
Background: Senior Director, Cypress Semiconductor Company; VP Operations, Galvantech; VP Technology/Development, IC Works; Director Technology Development, Paradigm Technology
Directorships: RichWave Technology, Sentelic, 5V Technologies, Power Analog Microelectronics, Aiconn Technology, LiquidLEDs

Christy Chou, Managing Partner
408-382-8086
Fax: 408-382-8004
e-mail: cchou@vtalliance.com
Education: BA, Finance, MBA, Finance & International Business, National Taiwan University
Background: Hewlett Packard Company; Finance Manager, TSMC North America

1925 VENTURESOUTH
225 S Pleasantburg Drive
Suite C-5
Greenville, SC 29607

web: venturesouth.vc

Mission Statement: VentureSouth is an Angel investment group that work to develop and manage various angel grounds and funds across the Southeast.

Geographic Preference: Southeastern United States, The Carolinas
Fund Size: $20 million
Portfolio Companies: Actived, ATW, Atlas Organics, Avadim Technologies Inc., Babies, Booster, Brightfield, CharlestonPharma, Cirtemo, Emrgy, Farmshots, Grow Journey, Kiyatec, Kwipped, New York Butcher Shoppe, Nirvana Science, OBMedical, Pandoodle, Pharmright, Physcient, Plum Print, Proaxion, ProctorFree, Proterra, Rival Health, Sensory Analytics, Servosity, Southeast TechInventures, Target Pharma Solutions, TIO, Tip Hive, Uvision360, Vendor Registry, Work America, Zipit, The Iron

Venture Capital & Private Equity Firms / Domestic Firms

Yard, Lien Nation, Sabal Medical, Selah Genomics, Verdeeco, Virtual Event Bags

Key Executives:

Matt Dunbar, Managing Director
Education: MBA, MA, Education, Stanford University; BSc, Chemical Engineering, Clemson University
Background: Management Consultant, Boston Consulting Group; Engineer, Eastman Chemical Company
Directorships: UCAN, Angel Capital Accosiation, Entegra Financial Corp.

Charlie Banks, Managing Director
Education: BS, Business Admin., Newberry College
Background: Portfolio Manager

Paul Clark, Managing Director
Education: MA, Medieval History, Fordham University; BA, History, Durham University
Background: Senior Vice President of M&A; Principal, BC Partners; M&A Advisory Experience, NM Rothschild & Sons

1926 VERGE FUND
317 Commercial Street NE
Albuquerque, NM 87102

Phone: 505-247-1038 Fax: 505-244-8040
e-mail: information@vergefund.com
web: www.vergefund.com

Mission Statement: Verge Fund is a highly motivated venture capital fund that invests in seed-stage, high-growth ventures in the Southwest.

Geographic Preference: New Mexico, Southwest United States
Investment Criteria: Seed-Stage
Industry Group Preference: Technology, Clean Technology, Electronics, SaaS
Portfolio Companies: Altela, AttachedApps, BoomTime, Exemplify, IntelliCyt, Nuvita, Nuvita Professional, Pajarito Powder, Sportxast, Trutouch, Vertical Power, Vibrant, Wellkeeper, ZTEC Instruments

Key Executives:

William F Bice, Founding Partner
Background: Founder & CEO, ProLaw Software; West km; Founder, BoomTime
Directorships: Vertical Power, Nuvita

Thomas J Stephenson, Managing Partner
Education: BA, Physics, Rice University; MBA, Information Management & Technology, McCombs School of Business, University of Texas, Austin
Background: General Parnter, Murphree Venture Partneres
Directorships: Altaview, Altela, Metaphor, Nanocrystal, Wellkeeper

Ron J McPhee, Partner
Education: Computer Engineering, University of New Mexico
Background: Founder, HealthFirst Corporation; Founder, Nuvita
Directorships: AltaView Technologies, Boomtime

Larry Lujan, Partner
Education: BA, New Mexico State University
Background: Manuel Lujan Agencies; HUB International
Directorships: Santa Miria el Mirrador Foundation; Albuquerque Hispano Chamber of Commerce

1927 VERITAS CAPITAL FUND LP
9 West 57th St.
29th Floor
New York, NY 10019

Phone: 212-415-6700
e-mail: info@veritascapital.com
web: www.veritascapital.com

Mission Statement: Veritas Capital Fund is a private equity firm that partners with experienced and motivated management teams to acquire and develop middle market companies.

Geographic Preference: North America
Fund Size: Fund I - $175 million, Fund II - $200 milion
Founded: 1992
Minimum Investment: $1, 000, 000
Investment Criteria: Later Stage Growth, LBO, MBO
Industry Group Preference: Aerospace, Defense and Government, Consumer Products, Telecommunications, Electronic Technology, Manufacturing
Portfolio Companies: Abaco Systems, Aeroflex, Alion, Anaren, Aptim, Athena, BeyondTrust, Cambium Learning Group, Contintental Electronics Corp., Cotiviti, CPI International, DynCorp International, Enterprise Electronics Corporation, Excelitas Technologies, Global Tel Link, Guidehouse, Integrated Defense Technologies, KeyPoint Government Solutions, McNeil Technologies, Onsolve, Peraton, Perspecta, Salient CRGT, SolAero Technologies, Standard Aero, Trak Communications, Truven Health Analytics, Vangent, Vencore, Vertex Aerospace, Virence, Wornick Company

Key Executives:

Ramzi M Musallam, CEO/Managing Partner
212-688-0020
Fax: 212-688-9411
e-mail: rmusallam@veritascapital.com
Education: BA in Economics & Mathematics, Colgate University; MBA, University of Chicago Graduate School of Business
Background: Associate, Pritzker & Pritzker; Berkshire Partners; Chemical Bank

Hugh D. Evans, Managing Partner
Education: B.A. Harvard University; M.B.A. University of Chicago
Background: Partner/member of Investment Committee at Falconhead Capital; Principal at Stonington Partners
Directorships: Aeroflex Holding Corp., Excelitas Technologies, CPI International, Truven Health Analytics, The SI Organiztion Holding Corp., KepPoint Government Solutions, CRGT

Ashish Chandarana, Partner
Education: BA, Brown University; M.Phil, Cambridge University; MBA, University of Chicago Booth School of Business; CFA
Background: Partner, McKinsey & Co.; Investment Principal, Aureos Capital

James Dimitri, Partner
Education: BS, Vanderbilt University; MBA, Kellogg School of Management
Background: Principal, Welsh Carson Anderson & Stowe

Brian Gorczynski, Partner
Education: BS, Boston College; MBA, Harvard Business School
Background: Managing Partner, North Cove Partners; Managing Director, BAML Capital Partners; Managing Director, Merrill Lynch Global Private Equity

Benjamin M. Polk, Partner
Education: J.D. Cornell Law School; B.A. Hobart College
Background: Senior Partner, Schulte Roth & Zabel LLP
Directorships: Aeroflex Holding Corp., CPI International, CRGT, Excelitas Technologies, KeyPoint Government Solutions, The SI Organization Holding Corp., Truven Health Analytics.

Daniel Sugar, Partner
Education: BSE, Princeton University; MBA, Wharton School
Background: Miller Buckfire & Co.

1928 VERIZON VENTURES
1 Verizon Way
Basking Ridge, NJ 07920

web: www.verizonventures.com

Venture Capital & Private Equity Firms / Domestic Firms

Mission Statement: A tech-based venture capital fund interested in various technology sectors, including: connected devices and hardware, media and entertainment, commerce and advertising, data and analytics, and infrastructure. Verizon is a long-term investor.

Founded: 2013
Industry Group Preference: Commerce, Advertising, Software, Data & Analytics, Infrastructure, Networking, Media, Entertainment, Technology, Information Technology, Artificial Intelligence, Virtual Reality, Security
Portfolio Companies: 4Home, 8i, ActionX, AdStage, AdTheorent, Airborne Entertainment, Airship, Beamr, Benbria, BL Healthcare, BlueKai, Brit + Co., Bug Labs, CardStar, Cellfire, CENX, Civis Analytics, ClipCall, CloudBees, Consert, ConteXtream, Edgybees, Entropic, Filament, Flash Networks, Globetouch, Glympse, Iguazio, Invidi, Jana, Kiip, Kinvey, Kumu Networks, Light Field Lab, Lumina Networks, Medio, MobileRQ, Networks in Motion, OmniSci, Open Garden, Optibus, Payfone, PlaySight, PrecisionHawk, Q-Sensei, Renovo, Sfara, SimplyTapp, SparkCognition, Swiftmile, The Fabric, The Hive, The VOID, Thumbplay Music, Urgent.ly, Veniam, Verdigris, Versa Networks, VOOM, YourMechanic, Zenverge

Other Locations:
1095 6th Avenue
New York, NY 10036

499 Hamilton Avenue
Palo Alto, CA 94301

201 Spear Street
San Francisco, CA 94105

Rothschild Boulevard 22
Tel Aviv-Yafo
Israel

Key Executives:
Samy Ben Aissa, Managing Director
Education: MS, université de Technologie de Compiègne; MS, Gannon University; MBA, NYU Stern School of Business
Background: AT&T; JP Morgan; GE Transportation Systems; K. Hovnanian Homes; Avaya
Jeffrey Black, Managing Director
Education: BBA, University of North Carolina; MBA, Goizueta Business School, Emory University
Background: JP Morgan; Delta Air Lines
Alex Khalin, Managing Director
Education: MBA, MIT
Background: HP; Boston Consulting Group; Schlumberger
Michelle McCarthy, Managing Director
Education: BA, American University; MBA, Georgetown University
Background: Verizon Capital
Kristina Serafim, Managing Director
Education: BEng, Kettering University; MBA, Harvard Business School
Background: Director, Intellectual Ventures; Corporate Development, IBM; NAGRA Innovations

1929 VERONIS SUHLER STEVENSON
400 Park Ave.
17th Floor
New York, NY 10022

Phone: 212-935-4990
e-mail: mehranl@vss.com
web: www.vss.com

Mission Statement: Veronis Suhler Stevenson is a leading middle-market private investment firm that makes private equity, mezzanine and senior credit investments within the information, education, media and communications and business services industries.

Geographic Preference: North America, Europe
Fund Size: $3.1 billion
Founded: 1981
Average Investment: $10 - $150 million
Investment Criteria: Buyouts, Recapitalizations, Growth Financings, Strategic Acquisitions
Industry Group Preference: Media, Communications, Business Products & Services, Education, Marketing
Portfolio Companies: Access Intelligence, Acrisure, Advanstar, Ascend Media, Avatar International, B&B Merger Corp., Berliner Verlag, Birch Telecom, Brand Connections, Broadcasting Partners, Cable Management Ireland, Cambium Learning Group, Cannella Response Television, Canon Communications, Caravan Health, Cast & Crew, Centaur Communications, Chemical Week, Clarion Events, Connexion Point, Contexo Media, Coretelligent, CSC Media Group, DeTelefoongids BV, DOAR Communications, DTN, Ebiquity, Executive Health Resources, Eyewitness News, Fonecta Oy, Gallo Holdings, Golden State Towers, Granada Learning Group, Greenslate, Hanley-Wood, Hostway, Hughes Broadcasting Partners, Infobase, International Media Partners, Ipreco, ITE Group, IT-Ernity, ITN Networks, Market Strategies International, MediaResponseGroup, Mediatel, MetSchools, Navtech, Pepcom GmbH, PJS Publications, Quadranet, Red 7 Media, Remedy Health Media, Rifkin Acquisition Partners, Riviera Broadcast Group, Sandow Media, Schofield Media Group, SHL, SNL Securities, Solucient, SourceMedical, Southern Theaters, Spectrum Resources Towers, Strata Decision, SureSource, System One, Tax Credit, The Official Information Company, Thomsons Online Benefits, TMP Worldwide Advertising & Communications, TRANZACT, Triax Midwest Associates, Triax Southeast Assocites, Trover Solutions, User Friendly Media, Vault.com, VKidz, Writtle, YBR Group, Yellow Book USA, Zed Group

Key Executives:
Jeffrey T Stevenson, Managing Partner
212-381-8122
e-mail: stevensonj@vss.com
Education: BA, Rutgers College
Background: Executive VP Corporate Finance, VSS
David Bainbridge, Managing Director
e-mail: bainbridged@vss.com
Education: Cornell University; Stern School of Business at New York University
Background: Investment Banking, Berkery Noyes & Co.; Scott-Macon
R Trent Hickman, Managing Director
212-381-8454
e-mail: hickmant@vss.com
Education: AB, History & French Literature, Duke University; MBA, Finance, Wharton School, University of Pennsylvania
Background: First Union Securities
Directorships: Brand Connections, Market Strategies, Souther Theatres, TMP Worldwide, Tranzact
Patrick N.W. Turner, Managing Director
e-mail: turnerp@vss.com
Background: Managing Director, Crescent Capital Group LP; Crimson Capital; Managing Partner, Canterbury Capital Partners
Directorships: IT-Ernity; MRG

1930 VERSANT VENTURES
One Sansome St.
Suite 3630
San Francisco, CA 94104

Phone: 415-801-8100
web: www.versantventures.com

Mission Statement: Partners with entrepreneurs to finance young medical device, bio-pharmaceutical, healthcare service, and e-Health companies, helping them grow to become pre-eminent companies in their field.

Fund Size: $1.6 billion
Founded: 1999
Average Investment: $1 - $10 million

Minimum Investment: $1 million
Investment Criteria: Early-Stage
Industry Group Preference: Medical Devices, Pharmaceuticals, Healthcare, Biotechnology, Healthcare Services, Healthcare Information Technology
Portfolio Companies: Adverum, Akero, Aligos, Alter G, Amira Pharma, Anokion, Aprea, Audentes, Biotie, Black Diamond, Blue Rock, Bright Peak, Cadence, CardiAQ Valve Technologies, Ceterix Orthopaedics, Clovis Oncology, Crispr, Crinetics, CymaBay, Ebb, Enterprise Therapeutics, FivePrime, Flexion, ForSight Vision 4, ForSight Vision 5, GenSight, Glaukos, Gotham Therapeutics, Gritston Oncology, Inari, Inception 4, Inception 5, Inception IBD, Intuity Medical, Jecure, Jnana, Kanyos Bio, Lava, Metavention, Minerva Surgical, Monteris Medical, Monte Rosa, NeuWave Medical, Northern Biologics, NousCom, Novira, Nuvaira, Oculeve, Okairos, Oyster Point Pharma, Pandion, Passage Bio, Pipeline, Piqur, Quanticel, Quentis, Repare, Sebacia, Sirocco, Tarveda, Tempest, Therachon, Turnstone, Twelve, VenatoRx, Veran, Vividion, WaveTec Vision

Other Locations:
  6175 Nancy Ridge Dr.
  San Diego, CA 92121
  Phone: 619-323-3463

  920 Broadway
  16th Floor
  New York, NY 10010
  Phone: 646-357-1286

  Aeschenvorstadt 36
  Basel CH - 4051
  Switzerland
  Phone: 41-61-225-4600

  887 Great Northern Way
  Suite 210
  Vancouver, BC V5T 4T5
  Canada
  Phone: 604-424-9913

  101 College Street
  Heritage Building, Suite 340
  Toronto, ON M5G 1L7
  Canada
  Phone: 416-649-5646

Key Executives:
  Brad Bolzon, Chair/Managing Director
  Education: PhD, MS Pharmacology, University of Toronto; Post Doctoral Research training, Ottawa Heart Institute, Ottawa
  Background: Executive VP, F. Hoffmann-La Roche; Management, Eli Lilly and Company
  Jerel Davis, Managing Director
  Education: PhD, Stanford University
  Background: Associate Principal, McKinsey & Co.
  Directorships: Quantical, Novira, Cripr, Inception 4, Inception 5, Northern, Turnstone, BlueRock, Repare, VenatoRx, Akero
  Clare Ozawa, Managing Director
  Education: BS, Stanford University; PhD, Stanford University Medical School
  Background: Inception Sciences; Novartis Pharma; McKinsey & Co.
  Directorships: Inception IBD, Oyster Point Pharma, Pipeline, Sirocco
  Tom Woiwode, Managing Director
  Education: PhD, Stanford University
  Background: XenoPort
  Directorships: Adverum, Aligos, Anokion, CODA, Crispr, Gritstone, Kanyos, Passage Bio, Tempest, Therachon, Vividion
  Robin Praeger, Managing Director & Advisor
  Education: BS, Political Economics of Industrial Societies, University of California, Berkeley; MS, Taxation, Golden Gate University
  Background: Tax Partner, Arthur Andersen

1931 VERTICAL GROUP
106 Allen Road
Suite 207
Basking Ridge, NJ 07920

Phone: 908-277-3737
e-mail: info@vertical-group.com
web: www.vertical-group.com

Mission Statement: Acts as a venture capital firm focused on the fields of medical technology and biotechnology; principals act as founders, early-stage investors, major shareholders and executives of many of the medical technology industry's most successful companies; manages partnerships with a vertical range of investments including: early and late-stage venture companies; private operating companies of all sizes.

Geographic Preference: United States
Fund Size: $200 million
Founded: 1988
Average Investment: $500,000 - $10 million
Minimum Investment: $500,000
Investment Criteria: Seed, First-stage, Second-stage, Mezzanine
Industry Group Preference: Medical Devices, Technology, Biotechnology, Healthcare
Portfolio Companies: Atheromed, Biosurface Technologies, Flexuspine, Galil Medical, Home Dialysis Plus, Incumed, InPhenix, Meritage Pharma, Omada, Oncomed, ProteinSimple, Silk Road Medical, Singular BIO, Tepha, TetraLogic Pharmaceuticals, Tornier, ViaCyte

Other Locations:
  530 Lytton Avenue
  Suite 304
  Palo Alto, CA 94301
  Phone: 650-566-9060

Key Executives:
  Richard B Emmitt, General Partner
  e-mail: REmmitt@vertical-group.com
  Education: BA, Economics, Bucknell University; MBA, Rutgers College
  Background: Investment Analyst, Cyrus J Lawrence; F Eberstadt
  Directorships: American Medical Systems, BioSet, ENTrigue Surgical, ev3 Inc., Galil Medical, Incumed, Tepha, Tornier
  Jack W Lasersohn, General Partner
  e-mail: JLasersohn@vertical-group.com
  Education: JD, Yale Law School; MA, Fletcher School of Law & Diplomacy; BS, Physics, Tufts University
  Background: F Eberstadt; Corporate Attorney, Cravath, Swaine & Moore
  Directorships: Anova, Masimo Corporation, Oncomed, Phothera, Silk Road Medical
  John E Runnells, General Partner
  e-mail: JRunnells@vertical-group.com
  Education: JD, Harvard Law School; BS, Business Administration, Pennsylvania State University
  Background: Co-Founder, Paddington Partners; Partner, Wabster & Sheffield
  Directorships: Anova, Dynamic Implants, Flexuspine, Incumed
  Tony M Chou, General Partner
  Education: BS, Physics & Electrical Engineering, Carnegie Mellon University; MD, Case Western Reserve University
  Background: Abbott Vascular Division, Abbott Labotories; Vice President & General Manager, Vascular Closure; Director, Adult Cardiac Catheterization Laboratory

1932 VESEY STREET CAPITAL PARTNERS LLC
101 Avenue of the Americas
New York, NY 10013

Phone: 212-213-4156
web: www.vscpllc.com

Venture Capital & Private Equity Firms / Domestic Firms

Mission Statement: Vesey Street Capital Partners seeks to invest in businesses that can create value for hospitals, payors, and healthcare providers.
Geographic Preference: United States
Founded: 2014
Investment Criteria: Middle Market
Industry Group Preference: Healthcare Services
Portfolio Companies: Imedex, ScribeAmerica
Key Executives:
  Adam Feinstein, Co-Founder/Managing Partner
  Education: BS, Business Management, University of Maryland, College Park; CFA
  Background: Senior VP, Corporate Development & Strategic Planning, Laboratory Corporation of America Holdings; Managing Director, Equity Research, Barclays Capital; Lehman Brothers

1933 VESTAR CAPITAL PARTNERS
520 Madison Avenue
33rd Floor
New York, NY 10022

Phone: 212-351-1600
e-mail: info@vestarcapital.com
web: www.vestarcapital.com

Mission Statement: Most successful opportunities are created by management teams, who respond positively to having increased operating autonomy and a meaningful ownership position in their companies.
Fund Size: $7 billion
Founded: 1988
Average Investment: $100 million - $3 billion
Minimum Investment: $50 million
Investment Criteria: LBO, MBO
Industry Group Preference: Consumer Products, Consumer Services, Financial Services, Healthcare, Media, Communications
Portfolio Companies: American Roland Foods, Big Heart Pet Brands, Civitas Solutions, DeVilbiss Healthcare, Gleason, Healthgrades, Hearthside Food Solutions, Institutional Shareholder Services, MediMedia USA, Press Ganey Associates, Radiation Therapy Services, St. John Knits, Sun Products, Tervita, Triton Container

Other Locations:
  1555 Blake Street
  #200
  Denver, CO 80202
  Phone: 303-292-6300

Key Executives:
  Daniel S. O'Connell, Founder & CEO
  Education: BA, Brown University, MBA, Yale Univeresity School of Management
  Background: Management Buyout Group, First Boston Corporation
  Robert L. Rosner, Founding Partner & Chair, Investment Committee
  Education: BA, Economics, Trinity College; MBA, Wharton School
  Background: Management Buyout Group, The First Boston Corporation
  James P. Kelley, Founding Partner & Managing Director
  e-mail: jkelley@vestarden.com
  Education: BS, University of Northern Colorado; JD, University of Notre Dame, MBA, Yale University School of Management
  Background: Senior Executive, Management Buyout Group, First Boston Corporation
  James L. Elrod Jr., Senior Advisor
  Education: AB, Colgate University; MBA, Harvard Business School
  Background: Executive VP Finance/Operations, Physicians Health Services; Managing Director/Partner, Dillon, Read & Company

  Nikhil J. Bhat, Managing Director & Co-Head, Investments
  Education: BS, Economics, Wharton School; MBA, Stanford Grad. School of Business
  Background: Advent International; Bain & Company
  Kevin A. Mundt, Managing Director
  Education: BA, Brown University; MBA, Harvard Business School
  Background: Consultant, Bain & Company; Managing Director, Marsh & McLennan; Mercer Oliver Wyman
  Roger C. Holstein, Managing Director
  Education: BA, Swarthmore College
  Background: CEO & President, WebMD Corporation; CEO, Consumer Health Services
  Chris A. Durbin, Managing Director
  Education: BBA, University of Notre Dame; MBA, Kellogg Graduate School of Management
  Background: Managing Director, Strategy & Business Development, Bank of America's Global Wealth & Investment Management
  Kenneth O'Keefe, Managing Director, COO & Head, Investor Relations
  Education: AB, Economics, Brown University
  Background: Executive Vice President & CFO, Pyramid Communications; CEO & President, AMFM; President & COO, Clear Channel Radio Group
  Norman W. Alpert, Founding Partner, President & Co-Head, Investments
  Education: AB, Brown University
  Background: Senior Executive, Management Buyout Group, First Boston Corporation

1934 VIDA VENTURES
40 Broad Street
Suite 201
Boston, MA 02109

e-mail: info@vidaventures.com
web: vidaventures.com

Mission Statement: A venture capital firm specializing in growth capital investments in the healthcare sector.
Fund Size: $255 million
Founded: 2017
Industry Group Preference: Healthcare, Biotechnology
Portfolio Companies: A2 Biotherapeutics, Aktis Oncology, Allogene Therapeutics, AskBio, Centessa, Dyne Therapeutics, Homology Medicines, IconOvir, InnoSkel, Kadiant, Kinnate Biopharma, Kronos Bio, Kyverna Therapeutics, Locana, neogene Therapeutics, Oyster Point, PACT Pharma, Pioneer Immunotherapeutics, Praxis Precision Medicines, Precision Medicine Group, Protego Biopharma, Quanta Therapeutics, Recode Therapeutics, Scorpion Therapeutics, Sutro Biopharma, Tectonic Therapeutics, Vigil Neuroscience, Volastra Therapeutics
Key Executives:
  Tefan Vitorovic, Co-Founder/Managing Director
  Education: BS, Biological Sciences, MS, Biology, Stanford University; MBA, Harvard Business School
  Background: Principal, Third Rock Ventures; Associate, TPG Capital; Investment Bankinf Analyst, Credit Suisse; Research Associate, Stanford University Medical Center
  Arie S. Belldegrun, Co-Founder/Senior Managing Director
  Education: MD, Hebrew University of Jerusalem
  Background: Chairman/President/CEO, Kite Pharma; Chairman, Cougar Biotechnology; Chairman/Partner, Two River;
  Directorships: UCLA Institute of Urology Oncology; Cell Design Labs; Teva; SonaCare Medical; Talon Therapeutics; Paramount Aquisition; Chem Rx Corp.; Email Real Estate.com
  Fred Cohen, Co-Founder/Senior Advisor
  Education: MD, Stanford University School of Medicine
  Background: Senior Advisor, TPG Capital

Venture Capital & Private Equity Firms / Domestic Firms

1935 VILLAGE GLOBAL
440 Davis Street
San Francisco, CA 94111

web: www.villageglobal.vc

Mission Statement: Non-traditional venture capital network of successful founders providing capital to startups.

Investment Criteria: Early-Stage

Industry Group Preference: Digital Health, Fintech, SaaS, Consumer Internet

Portfolio Companies: ADDI, Airbase, Bumblebee Spaces, Certain Lending, Compound, Darkstore, Forethought, Kapwing, Ontic, Shipwell, Superplastic, Traptic

Key Executives:
Ben Casnocha, Co-Founder & Partner
Background: Co-Founder, New Anchor Foundation; Co-Founder & Partner, Allied Talent; Chief of Staff to Ried Hoffman; CEO, Start-Up of You; Partner, Wasabi Ventures; Co-Founder, Silicon Valley Junto; Founder & Chair, Comcate
Anne Dwane, Co-Founder & Partner
Education: BSBA, Georgetown University; MBA, Harvard Business School
Background: Co-Founder & Partner, GSV Acceleration Fund; Chief Business Officer, Chegg; CEO, Zinch; General Manager, Monster Worldwide; Co-Founder, Military.com; Business Development, Interval Research
Directorships: Harvard Business Publishing
Peter Torenberg, Partner
Education: BA, Economics & English Literature, University of Michigan
Background: Founder & Chair, On Deck; Co-Founder & Chair, Token Daily; Community & Business Development, Product Hunt; Co-Founder & CEO, Rapt.fm; Product Marketing, Seelio; Business Development, Direct Brands

1936 VINE ST VENTURES
e-mail: info@vinestventures.com
web: www.vinestventures.com

Mission Statement: Vine Street Ventures is a venture capital investment firm dedicated to investing in internet and mobile businesses.

Industry Group Preference: Internet, Mobile, Consumer Internet

Key Executives:
Dave Knox, Partner
Background: Co-Founder, The Brandery; CMO, Rockfish; Brand Manager, P&G
Robert McDonald, Managing Member
Background: VC Attorney, Taft Stettinius & Hollister LLP; Co-Founder, The Brandery
JB Kropp, Founder
Background: Twitter, The Brandery
Marina Dedes Gallagher, Managing Member

1937 VINTAGE CAPITAL MANAGEMENT
4705 S Apopka Vineland Road
Suite 210
Orlando, FL 32819

Phone: 407-506-7085
web: www.vintagecapitalmanagement.com

Mission Statement: Vintage Capital Management is a private equity investor specializing in aerospace and defense, manufacturing and consumer sectors. They seek investment opportunities where they can project investment strategies that can be executed in a short amount of time.

Investment Criteria: Corporate Spinoffs; Consolidations and build-ups; Family Owned Businesses; Bankruptcy Acquisitions; Recapitalizations; Private Acquisitions; Management Buyouts; Toehold Public Company Investments

Other Locations:
627 Harland Street
Milton, MA 02186
Phone: 617-690-2580

Key Executives:
Brian Kahn, Founder/Managing Partner
e-mail: bkahn@vintcap.com
Education: BA, Harvard University
Background: Chair, White Electronic Designs Corporation; Chair, API Technologies Corporation; Director, Integral Systems Inc.; Director, Aarons Inc.
Directorships: Buddy Newco LLC; Good to Go Wheels and Tires; Flexi Compras
Andrew Laurence, Partner
e-mail: alaurence@vintcap.com
Education: BA, Harvard University
Background: Triumph Capital; Managing Director, Causeway Partners; Partner, Coral Reef Capital Partners

1938 VIRGINIA SMALL BUSINESS FINANCING AUTHORITY
101 N 14th Street
11th Floor
Richmond, VA 23219

Phone: 804-786-6585
e-mail: sbsd@sbsd.virginia.gov
web: www.sbsd.virginia.gov

Mission Statement: Ready to assist those businesses and non-profit organizations looking to grow in Virginia, the local economic development authorities and municipalities needing debt financing to attract businesses into their jurisdictions, as well as bankers seeking to find creative ways in which to make that next loan to a small business.

Investment Criteria: Fewer than 250 employees, less than $10 million in annual gross revenues for each of its last three fiscal years or has a net worth of $2 million or less

Other Locations:
851 French Moore, Jr. Boulevard
Suite 110
Abingdon, VA 24210
Phone: 276-676-3768

Key Executives:
Jennifer Mayton, Executive Director
804-593-2007
e-mail: jennifer.mayton@sbsd.virginia.gov
Anna Mackley, Chief Credit Officer & Operations Manager
804-371-8255
e-mail: anna.mackley@vdba.virginia.gov
Lawrence Wilder, Senior Policy Advisor
804-371-2064
e-mail: lawrence.wilder@sbsd.virginia.gov

1939 VISION CAPITAL
681 Fifth Avenue
14th Floor
New York, NY 10022

Phone: 212-303-6200
web: www.visioncapital.com

Mission Statement: Structured to provide investment and growth capital for companies with products and technologies appropriate for rapid expansion into global markets; targets European-based technology companies who are seeking to enter the US capital and product markets and US companies with premier venture backing seeking to enter the European market. Has an established network of partners and investors in Europe and the US to execute this Trans-Atlantic investment strategy. Seeks technology companies that have proven the innovation and commercial validity of their products by reaching a significant level of strength, recognition, market acceptance and material revenues, but have not yet been able to achieve their full international potential.

Geographic Preference: United States, Europe
Fund Size: $78 million
Founded: 1994
Average Investment: $3 million
Investment Criteria: Companies with expansion capital to accelerate the global expansion and growth process.
Industry Group Preference: Communications, Computer Related, Consumer Services, Distribution, Electronic Components, Instrumentation, Financial Services, Insurance, Industrial Services, High Technology, Software, Internet
Portfolio Companies: Education Corporation of America, Strategic Materials, Velocitel, Vitopel, United Initiators, Pantex International, Bormioli Rocco, New Evolution Ventures, ABL Technic, Metallwarenfabrik Gemmingen, Swisshaus, The Service Companies, Nordax Finans, JDR, BrightHouse, Pirtek Europe, Park Cake, Pork Farms, Portman Travel, DeltaRail, NuVision Engineering, Kinectrics, CPL Industries, Elegant Hotels Group

Key Executives:
   William Wick, Managing Director & CFO
   Education: AB, Economics, Stanford University; MBA, Kellogg Graduate School of Management
   Background: CFO, ZoZa.com; CFO, QuickPower

1940 VISTA EQUITY PARTNERS
401 Congress Avenue
Suite 3100
Austin, TX 78701

Phone: 512-730-2400
web: www.vistaequitypartners.com

Mission Statement: Vista Equity Partners invests in enterprise software. They partner with organizations at every phase of growth to rise to the next level.

Other Locations:
   180 North Stetson Avenue
   Suite 4000
   Chicago, IL 60601
   Phone: 312-229-9500

   55 Hudson Yards
   Floor 23
   New York, NY 10001
   Phone: 212-804-9100

   4 Embarcadero Center
   Floor 20
   San Francisco, CA 94111
   Phone: 415-765-6500

   1111 Broadway
   Suite 1980
   Oakland, CA 94607

Key Executives:
   Robert Smith, Founder, Chair and CEO
   Education: BS, Cornell University; MBA, Columbia Business School
   Background: Co-Head, Enterprise Systems, Goldman Sachs
   David Breach, COO/Chief Legal Officer
   Education: BBA, Eastern Michigan University; JD, University of Michigan
   Background: Senior Corporate Partner, Kirkland & Ellis

1941 VISTA VENTURE PARTNERS
306 Cambridge Avenue
Palo Alto, CA 94306

Phone: 650-252-0550
e-mail: info@vistavp.com
web: vistavp.com

Mission Statement: Vista VP is an early stage Venture Capital fund firm.

Key Executives:
   Michael Spector, Founder
   e-mail: michael@vistavp.com
   Education: University of California; CPA; PFS
   Background: Partner, Burr Pilger Mayer Inc.
   Fern Mandelbaum, Managing Member
   e-mail: fern@vistavp.com
   Education: BA, Brown University; MBA, Stanford University
   Background: Co-Founder and CEO, Skyline Products; Metcal, Bain and Co.; SRI International; Hewlett Packard
   Aaron White
   e-mail: aaron@vistavp.com
   Education: University of San Francisco; CFP
   Background: Consultant

1942 VITAL FINANCIAL LLC
7101 Wisconsin Avenue
Suite 1210
Bethesda, MD 20814

Phone: 415-297-6451
e-mail: casher@vitalfin.com
web: www.vitalfin.com

Mission Statement: To use our talents, insights, knowledge and experience to find, analyze and structure private equity and venture capital investments in companies so as to provide significantly above-market returns on our own capital and on the funds that co-investors entrust to our stewardship.

Founded: 2007
Average Investment: $1 - $5 million
Investment Criteria: Early-Stage, Later-Stage
Industry Group Preference: Software, Technology, Financial Services
Portfolio Companies: 10X Technologies, AxioMx, Booker Software, CD Dignostics, Certicom, Clinverse, Halfpenny Technologies, HealthTell, Lookingglass Cyber Solutions, NovaTract Surgical, Pervacio, QuantaLife, SchoolChapters, Shoefitr, Sparqd, Twist Bioscience, Spikes Security, TOMA Biosciences

Other Locations:
   92 Hopmeadow Street
   3rd Floor
   Simsbury, CT 06809
   Phone: 860-729-3247

Key Executives:
   A Craig Asher, Principal
   e-mail: casher@vitalfin.com
   Education: Stanford University; MBA & MS, Industrial Engineering, Northwestern University
   Background: Director, Product Management, Trigo Technologies; Consultant, Andersen Consulting
   Nathaniel C Brinn, Principal
   e-mail: nbrinn@vitalfin.com
   Education: University of Delaware; MBA, Finance & Accounting, Fuqua School of Business, Duke University
   Background: CEO, CR Certification Corporation; EVP, Corporate Development, Webster Bank; CEO, HSA Bank

1943 VIVO CAPITAL
192 Lytton Avenue
Palo Alto, CA 94301

Phone: 650-688-0818
e-mail: info@vivocapital.com
web: www.vivocapital.com

Mission Statement: At Vivo Capital, we leverage our internal expertise in evaluating data to generate outsized returns for company founders and employees as well as for our investors. The majority of Vivo's investments are in U.S. based companies with therapeutic products in clinical development.

Geographic Preference: West Coast

Fund Size: $200 million
Founded: 1996
Average Investment: $2 million
Minimum Investment: $500,000
Investment Criteria: Seed, Start-Up, Later Stage, Mezzanine, PIPE
Industry Group Preference: Biotechnology, Health
Portfolio Companies: Aclaris Therapeutics, Agile Therapeutics, AirXpanders, Akari Therapeutics, Apellis Pharma, Ascendis Pharma, Aurinia, Biohaven Pharma, BioPharmX, Capnia, Carbylan Therapeutics, Durata Therapeutics, Eiger, Essentialis, Foamix, Harmony Biosciences, Impel NeuroPharma, Kadmon, Kala Pharmaceuticals, KalVista Pharma, MacroGenics, Medeor Therapeutics, MEI Pharma, Menlo Therapeutics, Minerva Surgical, Nabriva Therapeutics, Nora Therapeutics, Ocera Therapeutics, OncoGenex Pharma, Outpost Medicine, Palatin, ProNAi Therapeutics, REGENXBIO, Revance Therapeutics, Sagent Pharmaceuticals, Selecta Biosciences, Semnur Pharma, SentreHEART, Sierra Oncology, Soleno Therapeutics, Strongbridge Biopharma, Surgical Specialties, Synapse BioMedical, Trevena, TRIA Beauty, Tricida, Verona Pharma

Other Locations:
Suite 2805, HKRI Centre Two
No. 288, Shimen Road
Shanghai 200041
China
Phone: 86-21-6888-0039

Suite 1801, West Tower, Twin Towers
B12 Jianguomenwai Avenue
Chaoyang District
Beijing 100022
China
Phone: 86-10-5764-2288

Rm B3, 5f, No.335, Sec.2, Dunhua S. Rd.
Da'an District
Taipei 10669
Taiwan
Phone: 886-2-2378-2268

Key Executives:
Dr. Edgar G Engleman, Partner/Chief Scientific Advisor
Education: BA, Harvard University; MD, Columbia University
Background: Cetus Immunie; Genlabs Technologies; National Medical Audit; Dendreon Corporation; CellGate Technologies
Dr. Frank Kung, Partner
Education: BS, National Tsing Hua University; MBA, University of California
Background: Cetus Immune; Genlabs Technologies
Shan Fu, Partner
Education: BA, MA, Peking University
Background: Senior Managing Director, Blackstone

1944 VOLITION CAPITAL
111 Huntington Avenue
Suite 2700
Boston, MA 02199

Phone: 617-830-2100
e-mail: info@volitioncapital.com
web: www.volitioncapital.com

Mission Statement: Volition Capital is a growth equity firm that principally invests in high potential, founder-owned companies across different technology sectors. Our firm specializes in partnering with founders to help them achieve their fullest aspirations for their business.

Geographic Preference: United States & London
Founded: 2010
Average Investment: $5 - 10 million
Minimum Investment: $3 million
Investment Criteria: Growth Capital, Acquisition Capital
Industry Group Preference: Internet, SaaS, Information Services, Technology-Enabled Business, Infrastructure
Portfolio Companies: Chewy.com, Ensighten, G5, GlobalTranz, iPipeline, LoanLogics, The Resumator, Velocify, Visual IQ

Key Executives:
Larry Cheng, Managing Partner & Founder
617-830-2305
Fax: 617-203-1270
e-mail: lcheng@volitioncapital.com
Education: BA, Psychology, Harvard College
Background: Partner, Fidelity Ventures; Senior Associate, Battery Ventures; Associate, Bessemer Venture Partners
Directorships: Cortera, Ensighten, GlobalTranz, MFG.com
Roger Hurwitz, Managing Partner & Founder
617-830-2306
Fax: 617-203-1275
e-mail: roger@volitioncapital.com
Education: BS, Accounting, Syracuse University; MBA, The Wharton School
Background: Partner, Fidelity Ventures; Partner, Apax Partners; Vice President GE Equity, GE Capital
Sean Cantwell, Managing Partner & Founder
617-830-2318
Fax: 617-203-1269
e-mail: sean@volitioncapital.com
Education: BBA, University of Notre Dame; MBA, Harvard Business School
Background: Vice President, Fidelity Ventures; Summit Partners; Arthur Andersen, Principal, The Parthenon Group
Andy Flaster, Managing Partner & COO
Education: BS, Wharton School, University of Pennsylvania; Boston College
Background: CFO, Fidelity Ventures; VP, Thomas H. Lee Partners; Consultant, Coopers & Lybrand

1945 VOODOO VENTURES, LLC
643 Magazine
Suite 102
New Orleans, LA 70130

Phone: 504-298-8884
web: www.voodooventures.com

Mission Statement: Our core philosophy revolves around matching talented partners with great ideas to build businesses. By providing resources and expertise, we work with people wo make ideas into reality.

Portfolio Companies: Launchpad, Flatstack, Niko Niko, BarNotes, Federated Sample, Neighborland

Key Executives:
Chris Schultz, Founder

1946 VORTEX PARTNERS
2626 Cole Avenue
Dallas, TX 75204

Phone: 214-849-9806

Mission Statement: Venture capital firm committed to providing critical resources, contacts and capital to promising startups.

Founded: 1999
Investment Criteria: Startups
Industry Group Preference: Business Products & Services, Software
Portfolio Companies: OpsTechnology, Real Foundations, RealManage

Key Executives:
Christopher O'Neill, Founder/General Partner
e-mail: coneill@vortexpartners.com
Education: MBA, Stanford University; BS Chemical Engineering, BA Economics, Rice University

Venture Capital & Private Equity Firms / Domestic Firms

Background: General Partner, EFO Holdings; Investment Banking, Paine Webber
Tom Hedrick, Senior Partner
Education: BS, University of Notre Dame; MBA, Harvard Business School
Background: Senior Partner, McKinsey & Company; Co-Director, North American High Tech Practice; Texas Venture Capital & Private Equity Practice

1947 VOYAGER CAPITAL
719 Second Avenue
Suite 1400
Seattle, WA 98104

Phone: 206-438-1800 Fax: 206-438-1900
e-mail: joanne@smartconnectionspr.com
web: www.voyagercapital.com

Mission Statement: Voyager Capital is a leading West Coast information technology venture firm, providing entrepreneurs with the resources, experience, and connections to build successful companies. Voyager invests primarily in early-stage clean IT, digital media, software and services, wireless, and web infrastructure companies, where the firm's domain expertise and 'Go-to-Market' resources help build market leaders. Voyager Capital has $370 million under management with offices in Seattle, Washington; Menlo Park, California; and Portland, Oregon.

Geographic Preference: Pacific Northwest, Northern California
Fund Size: $370 million
Founded: 1997
Average Investment: $6 million over life of company
Minimum Investment: Early: $1-2.5 million; Growth: $3-5 million
Investment Criteria: Early-Stage, Growth
Industry Group Preference: Enterprise Services, Internet Technology, Business to Business, Wireless Technologies, Software, Infrastructure, Digital Media & Marketing
Portfolio Companies: Act-On Software, Alliance Health Networks, AnswerDash, aQuantive, Art2Wave, Attenex, Attensa, autoGraph, AutoGrid, Ayla Networks, Blue Box Group, Bonanza, Capital Stream, Captura Software, ChargePoint, Chirpify, ClearCare, ClearCommerce, Coolr, Covario, Elemental Technologies, Geoloqi, Global Market Insie, GoAhead Software, Kadiri, Kryptiq, Lighter Capital, Lytics, Medify, Melodeo, MindSumo, NetPodium, Nusym Technology, Photobucket, Placecast, Qsent, Rio SEO, SeeCommerce, Sensys Networks, Skyward, Tegic Communications, Tropos Networks, UBIX, Vidder, WellnessFX, Wise.io, Yapta, Zebra Imaging, Zettics

Other Locations:
3000 Sand Hill Road, 3-100
Menlo Park, CA 94025
Phone: 650-854-4300 Fax: 650-854-4399

1044 NW 9th Avenue
Portland, OR 97209
Phone: 503-621-6668

Key Executives:
Erik Benson, Managing Director
e-mail: benson@voyagercapital.com
Education: Graduate Pacific Lutheran University; Harvard Business School
Background: President, Mimix; JP Morgan Chase
Directorships: Act-On Software, Chirpify, Covario, Elemental Technologies, Lighter Capital, Lytics, UBIX, Zettics
Diane Fraiman, Managing Director
Education: Vanderbilt University; MBA, INSEAD
Background: Sequent Computer; Tektronix Video and Networking; Informix Software; Sanctum

1948 VULCAN CAPITAL
Phone: 206-342-2000
e-mail: press@vulcan.com
web: capital.vulcan.com

Mission Statement: A leading private equity firm that creates long-term value by applying extensive industry knowledge, operational expertise and flexible financial resources to attractive investment opportunities.

Founded: 2003
Investment Criteria: Early-Stage
Portfolio Companies: Asentium Capital, Enhanced Capital Partners, Makena Capital Management, Silvercrest, 4info, Audience, Avalanche Technology, Bizo, Flipkart.com, Gilt Groupe, Gist, Magic Leap, Redfin, Sand9, Scytl, SiOnyx, TrueCar, Zuora, Applied Proteomics, BiPar Sciences, Omeros, PTC Therapeutics, Charter Communications, DreamWorks Animation SKG, Laureate Education, Tower Co.

Key Executives:
Chris Orndorff, Chief Investment Officer
Education: BS, Miami University; MBA, University of Chicago; CFA
Background: Portfolio Manager, Western Asset; Portfolio Manager, Payden & Rygel; Portfolio Manager, Northern Trust

1949 W CAPITAL PARTNERS
400 Park Avenue
New York, NY 10022

Phone: 212-561-5240 Fax: 212-561-5241
web: www.wcapgroup.com

Mission Statement: W Capital Partners invests in companies to execute long-term growth plans.

Geographic Preference: USA and Europe
Fund Size: $2.3 Billion
Founded: 2001
Average Investment: $15 Million
Industry Group Preference: Consumer, Enterprise, Software, Fintech, Healthcare, Industry, Business Services, Media, Retail, Semiconductors, Communication
Portfolio Companies: Acquia, Adam Aircraft, American Traffic Solutions, Amphastar, Ancestry.Com, Aoptix Technologies, Ascent Energy, Bay Microsystems, Bigfix, Blackboard, Brainlab, Coinmatch, Collegenet, Compbenefits, Conduit, Corementrics, Credit Karma, Demand Media, Dentistry For Children, Double-Take Software, Dynacast, Eroom, Everfi, Financial Engines, Fios, First Utility, Freshdirect, Green Dot, Hemosense, Hertz, High Technology Solutions, Hydro Resources, Icontact, Infinera, Integrated Systems Engineering, Intranets.Com, Jordan Health Services, Kb Alloys, Khimetrics, Kony, M*Modal, Markettools, Metastorm, Merchant E-Solutions, Milk Specialties, Mindbody, Moosejaw, Mzinga, Neolane, Nibc Bank, Opentable, Oriental Trading, Partminer, Ping Identity, Playeau Systems, Primarion, Prodigy Health Group, Quickarrow, Quinstreet, Ravn Alaska, Reliant Pharmaceuticals, Riskmetrics, Sensitech, Sige Semiconductor, Ss8 Networks, Standard Bancshares, Techprocess Solutions, Telaria, Thayer Aerospace, Thousandeyes, Travelcenters Of America, Tunnel Hill, Universal Studios Escape, Vanguard Health Systems, Yodlee, Workfront, World Kitchen, Wrc Media

Key Executives:
David Wachter, Co-Founder/Managing Partner
e-mail: dwachter@wcapgroup.com
Education: BS, Tufts University; MBA, New York University
Background: Investment Banker/Private Equity Investor, Lehman Brothers
Robert Migliorino, Co-Founder
e-mail: migs@wcapgroup.com
Education: BS, Drexel University

Background: Founding Partner, Canaan Partners; GE Information Services
Stephen Wertheimer, Co-Founder
e-mail: swertheimer@wcapgroup.com
Education: BS, Indiana University; MM, Northwestern University
Background: Head, Paine Webber Investments, Tokyo; Founder, Water Capital Management

1950 WACHTEL & CO. INC
1701 K Street NW
Suite 615
Washington, DC 20006

Phone: 202-898-1144
web: www.wachtelco.com

Geographic Preference: Greater Washington DC
Founded: 1961
Average Investment: $100,000 - $300, 000
Investment Criteria: Startups, First Stage, Second Stage, Recapitalizations
Industry Group Preference: Technology

Key Executives:
Bonnie K Wachtel, CEO
Education: BA, MBA, University of Chicago; JD, University of Virginia
Background: Information Analysis; Intergrated Systems; VSE Corportaion

1951 WAFRA CAPITAL PARTNERS INC
350 Park Avenue
16th Floor
New York, NY 10022

Phone: 212-377-0030 **Fax:** 212-293-6345
web: www.wafracapital.com

Mission Statement: An affiliate of Wafra Inc., Wafra Capital Partners is a seperate operating entity and a US registered investment adviser. WCP specializes in structuring, leasing, finance and real estate products.

Founded: 2012

Key Executives:
Robert Toan, Chief Executive Officer
Education: JD, LLM, New York University
Background: Partner, Hughes Hubbard & Reed LLP; Partner, Baker & MacKenzie
Michael Gontar, Chief Investment Officer
Education: New York University
Background: Experienced Associate, KPMG LLP; President and Co-Founder, NY based real estate investment firm

1952 WAFRA INC
345 Park Avenue
41st Floor
New York, NY 10154-0101

Phone: 212-759-3700 **Fax:** 212-813-9488
web: wafra.com

Mission Statement: Wafra's private equity strategy targets middle-market investments, co-investments and club deals, seeking to leverage their network and partnerships. Their venture capital strategy seeks to invest in leading venture capital funds and companies where they have a strategic edge.

Fund Size: $14 billion
Founded: 1986
Average Investment: $300 million
Industry Group Preference: Real Estate

Other Locations:
27 Knightsbridge
London SW1X 7LY
England
Phone: 44 203-966-9865

1703 W 5th Street
Suite 800
Austin, TX 78703
Phone: 212-759-3700

Al Soor Street
Twin Towers, 21st Floor, Block A
Mirqab
Kuwait
Phone: 965 222-663-52

Ideation House, 94 Pitts Bay Road
1st Floor
Pembroke HM 08
Bermuda
Phone: 441-824-3700

Key Executives:
Fawaz Al-Mubaraki, Chief Executive Officer
Education: BS, Kuwait University
Background: Portfolio Manager, Wafra; Analyst, Department of Public Institution, Kuwait
Adel A Alderbas, Chief Investment Officer
Education: BS, Purdue University; MBA, Harvard Business School

1953 WALDEN VENTURE CAPITAL
750 Battery Street
Suite 700
San Francisco, CA 94111

Phone: 415-391-7225
web: www.waldenvc.com

Mission Statement: Walden Capital Partners L.P. is a Small Business Investment Company (SBIC) which targets companies in need of growth capital. Walden Capital invests in companies that have strong, proven management teams have passed the early stages of business development, and are positioned for expansion.

Geographic Preference: United States, Worldwide
Fund Size: $500 million
Founded: 1974
Average Investment: $1 million
Minimum Investment: $500,000
Investment Criteria: Seed, First-stage, Second-stage, Mezzanine
Industry Group Preference: Digital Media & Marketing, Cloud-Based IT Services, Software, Infrastructure
Portfolio Companies: Aarki, Blazent, Blue Lithium, BoomBotix, The Clymb, Comedy.com, Glam.com, Gump's, H5, Iconoculture, Image Vision Labs, Niku, Palamida, Pandora, PowerCloud Systems, SoundHound Inc., Telekenex, Terayon, VitalStream

Other Locations:
2105 Woodside Road
Woodside, CA 94062

Key Executives:
Arthur Berliner, Managing Director
Education: BA, University of California, Berkeley
Background: Founded, Walden Group, Sutro & Company
Larry Marcus, Managing Director
Education: BA, University of California, Berkeley
Background: Deutsche Bank Alex Brown, Roberston Stephens
Bill McDonagh, Venture Partner
Education: BBA, University of Notre Dame; MBA, Golden Gate University
Background: President & COO, Broderbund Software
Directorships: Apollo International
George Sarlo, Venture Partner
Education: BA, Harvard Graduate School of Business, BS, University of Arizona
Background: Vice President, William D Witter Inc, Portfolio Manager, Capital Research Inc

Venture Capital & Private Equity Firms / Domestic Firms

Matt Miller, Managing Director
Education: BA, Cornell University; MBA, Columbia University
Background: CEO, Moai Technologies; VP, Marketing, Remedy; Gupta Group
Directorships: H5 Technologies, Iconoculture, Ignite Technologies, Palamida, Market Insight
Robert Raynard, Chief Financial Officer
Education: BA, American University; MBA, Boston University
Background: Chief Financial Officer, Robertson Stephens Asset Management; Senior Manager, PricewaterhouseCoopers LLP

1954 WALL STREET VENTURE CAPITAL
110 Wall Street
11th Floor
New York, NY 10005

Phone: 877-748-4468 **Fax:** 800-860-9489
e-mail: wallstreetventurecapital@yahoo.com

Mission Statement: A venture capital firm dedicated to helping entrepreneurs realize their dreams of building world class companies that will become leaders in their field. We believe deeply in the value created by the entrepreneurial process and in the relentless pursuit of opportunity. We enjoy the challenge of aiming high and believe that by pursuing lofty goals, we will ultimately generate the highest returns of our investors.

Geographic Preference: Worldwide
Fund Size: $800 million
Founded: 1984
Average Investment: $1 - $5 million
Minimum Investment: $1 million
Investment Criteria: Business Plan, Board in Place
Industry Group Preference: Business to Business
Other Locations:
28 East Jackson Building
10th Floor
Chicago, IL 60604
Phone: 877-748-4468

75 State Street
Boston, MA 02109
Phone: 877-748-4468

23 Nanjing E Road
Shanghi 200002
China
Phone: 8621-63295787 **Fax:** 8621-63295787

1955 WALNUT GROUP
312 Walnut Street
Suite 1151
Cincinnati, OH 45202

Phone: 513-651-3300 **Fax:** 513-651-1084

Mission Statement: The Walnut Group makes capital investments across a broad range of industry sectors and also facilitates transactions throughout North America.

Geographic Preference: North America
Investment Criteria: Acquisitions, Growth Equity, Recapitalizations, Late-Stage Ventures, Mergers, Alliances
Industry Group Preference: Retail, Consumer & Leisure, Consumer Products, Media, Communications, Consumer Services, Business Products & Services, Manufacturing, Real Estate, Entertainment, Restaurants, Aerospace, Defense and Government, Security
Portfolio Companies: Adspace Networks, Ameristop, Argo Tea, Build-a-Bear Workshop, CAP (Children at Play) Toys, Changing Paradigms, Conserv, CWK Network, Deal$ Nothing Over a Dollar, Duke Realty, Empire Brushes, Goliath Solutions, Home Products International, Horizon Development, Imagitas, ITC, Logo Athletics, LoveSac, Marian Heath Greeting Cards, M Cubed Technologies, Medsite, Nelson Communications, North American Baking, PECO Pallet, Pinnacle Direct Marketing, Reborn Beauty, Renaissance Mark, Rookwood Pavillion, Seed Media Group, SimonDelivers, Sleek Medspa, Skylight.net, Sovereign Brands, Tapper Candies, Total Management & Earlybird Courier, Wild Things, WMI Holdings, Work 'n Gear
Key Executives:
Frederic H Mayerson, Chairman/Managing General Partner
Education: Miami University; University of Michigan Law School
Background: Chairman, United Sports Ventures; Principal, Frederic H Mayerson Group

1956 WAND PARTNERS
1 Union Square West
Suite 208
New York, NY 10003

Phone: 212-909-2620 **Fax:** 212-307-5599
web: www.wandpartners.com

Mission Statement: An active private equity sponsor and investor focused on specialty financial services. In all of our investments, database analysis and feed-back driven decision-making are central to the management's approach to business.

Fund Size: $250 million
Founded: 1985
Minimum Investment: $3 million
Investment Criteria: Seed, First-stage, Second-stage, Mezzanine
Industry Group Preference: Distribution, Energy, Natural Resources, Financial Services, Food & Beverage, Insurance, Industrial Services
Portfolio Companies: American Independent Companies, Paraline Group
Key Executives:
Bruce W Schnitzer, Managing Director & Chairman
212-949-1729
Education: University of Texas, Austin; MBA, University of Texas, Austin
Background: Director, Marsh & McLennan Companies; President & CEO, Marsh & McLennan Incorporated; Vice President, JP Morgan/Morgan Guaranty Trust Company
John S Struck, Managing Director
212-909-2620
e-mail: jstruck@wandpartners.com
Education: BA, Economics, University of Rhode Island
Background: Principal, Friday Holdings; President, BIS Strategic Decisions; Director, Prudential Bache Securities, Corporate Finance; General Electric Corporation

1957 WARBURG PINCUS LLC
450 Lexington Avenue
New York, NY 10017

Phone: 212-878-0600 **Fax:** 212-878-9351
e-mail: info@warburgpincus.com
web: www.warburgpincus.com

Mission Statement: Warburg Pincus' private equity investment activities combine human and capital resources to make long-term investments. The firm takes an active role in the development of its investments and employs its professional, financial, and business skills to enhance investment results. Warburg Pincus does not itself run businesses on a day-to-day basis; rather it works in partnership with managements and makes its knowledge, experience, and relationships available to the companies in which it invests in a positive and supportive manner. In every case in which the firm makes a direct equity investment, the portfolio company's management also holds a significant equity stake to ensure that its interests are parallel to those of Warburg Pincus.

Geographic Preference: Worldwide
Fund Size: $5 billion
Founded: 1939

Minimum Investment: $10 million
Investment Criteria: Late-Stage, Developing, Expanding, Startup, Early-Stage, Recapitalizations, Buy-Outs
Industry Group Preference: Information Technology, Healthcare, Media, Communications, Energy, Financial Services, Business Products & Services
Portfolio Companies: 58.com, A Place for Mom, AAG Energy Limited, ACB (India), Accriva Diagnostics, Aeolus Re, AmRest, Amtek Auto, Antero Resources, Aramark, Association of Certified Anti-Money Laundering Specialists, Au Financiers, AVTEC, Banco Indusval & Partners, Beijing Amcare Women's & Children's Hospital, Beijing Tianyu Communications Equipment, Biba Apparels, Black Swan Energy, Bridgepoint Education, Brigham Resources, Builders FirstSource, Canbriam Energy, Capital First Limited, Ceres, China Auto Rental, China Biologic Products, China Kidswant, Clondalkin, Competitive Power Ventures Holdings, ComplexCare Solutions, Consolidated Precision Products, Continental Warehousing, Coyote Logistics, Crossmark, CrowdStrike, Delonex Energy, Diligent Power Private, e-Sharing, Endurance Energy, Evidon, Explora Petroleum, Extant Components, FacilitySource, Fairfield Energy, First Green Partners, Franshion Properties, Gangavaram Port, GrubHub Seamless, GT Nexus, Gulf Coast Energy Resources, Hawkwood Energy, Home Dialysis, IMC Limited, InComm, INEA, Interactive Data, International Asset Systems, iParadigms, JHP Pharmaceuticals, Jida Pharmaceuticals, Keystone Dental, Kontron, Kosmos Energy, Koudai Shopping, Laredo Petroleum Holdings, Lemon Tree, Liaison International, MBIA, MEG Energy, Melinta Therapeutics, Metropolis Healthcare Limited, MultiView, National Penn Bancshares, New Breed Logistics, Omega Energia Renovael S.A., onTargetjobs, Osum Oil Sands, Pet Center Comercio and Participacoes S.A., Poundland, Premier Foods, PW Medtech Group, QuEST, Quikr, RDA Microelectronics, Red Star Macalline, RegionalCare Hospital Partners, Resolution II, Safetykleen, Sand Hill Petroleum B.V., Santander Asset Management, Silk Road Medical, Sterling Financial, Stratford School, Suniva, Sunnywell Group, Survitec, Synutra International, The Gordian Group, The Mutual Fund Store, Tornier, Total Safety, Triton Container International, Tulip Media, Velvet Energy, Venari Resources, Vincom Retail, West Valley Energy, Xueda Education Group, Yodlee

Other Locations:
One Market Plaza
Spear Tower, Suite 1700
San Francisco, CA 94105
Phone: 415-796-5200 **Fax:** 415-659-0045

4400 Post Oak Pkwy
Suite 1900
Houston, TX 77027
Phone: 713-325-5360 **Fax:** 713-583-9309

Warburg Pincus Investment Consulting Co Ltd
26th Floor, China World Tower A
1 Jianguomenwai Avenue
Beijing 100004
China
Phone: 86-1085292688 **Fax:** 86-1085292677

Warburg Pincus India Ptv Ltd
7th Floor, Express Towers
Nariman Point
Mumbai 400021
India
Phone: 91-2266500000 **Fax:** 91-2266500001

Warburg Pincus Asia LLC
Suite 6703
Two International Finance Center, 8 Finance Street
Hong Kong
Phone: 852-25366183 **Fax:** 852-25213869

Almnack House
28 King Street, St. James's
London SW1Y 6QW
United Kingdom
Phone: 44-2073060306 **Fax:** 44-2073210881

Warburg Pincus Shanghai Branch
45/F, HKRI Center One, HKRI Taikoo Hui
No. 288 Shimen Yi Rd.
Shanghai 200041
China
Phone: 86-2160577388 **Fax:** 86-2160577310

Warburg Pincus do Brasil Ltda.
Av. Brig. Faria Lima 2277- 9 andar
Jd. Paulistano
Sao Paulo 01451-001
Brazil
Phone: +55 11 3096 3500 **Fax:** +55 11 3096 3509

Warburg Pincus Singapore Pte Ltd.
50 Collyer Quay
#06-04, OUE Bayfront
Singapore 049321
Singapore
Phone: +65 6320-7500 **Fax:** +65 6634-0119

Key Executives:
Charles R Kaye, Chief Executive Officer
Education: University of Texas
Directorships: Partnership for New York City
Joseph P Landy, Special Limited Partner
Education: BS, Economics, Wharton School; MBA, Leonard N Stern School of Business, New York University
Julian Cheng, Managing Director
Education: BA, Harvard University
Background: Salomon Smith Barney; Bankers Trust
Mark M Colodny, Managing Director & Head, Technology
Education: AB, Harvard University; MBA, Harvard Business School; JD, Harvard Law School
Background: SVP Corporate Development, Primedia
Directorships: Helix, Liaison International, MultiView
Steven G Glenn, Managing Director, CFO & COO
Education: BS, Binghamton University; MS, SUNY Albany; JD, Fordham University
Background: Partner, Ernst & Young
Peter Kagan, Managing Director & Head, Energy
Education: AB, Harvard College; JD & MBA, University of Chicago
Background: Investment Banking, Salomon Brothers
Directorships: Antero Resources, Broad Oak Energy, Fairfield Energy, Laredo Petroleum, MEG Energy, Targa Resources
Robert B Knauss, Managing Director, Policy & Compliance
Education: Harvard University; University of Michigan Law School
Background: Partner, Munger Tolles & Olson LLP
Vishal Mahadevia, Managing Director, Head of India
Education: BS, University of Pennsylvania
Background: Principal, Greenbriar Equity Group
Michael Martin, Managing Director & Head, Financial Services
Education: BS, Economics, Claremont Men's College; JD, Columbia University School of Law
Background: President, Brooklyn NY Holdings; Managing Director, UBS Investment Bank
Directorships: Sallie Mae, Aeolus Re, Cortview Capital, National Penn Bancshares, Primerica, The Mutual Fund Store
James Neary, Managing Director
Education: BA, Tufts University; MBA, Kellogg School of Management
Background: Managing Director, Chase Securities
John W Shearburn, Managing Director
Education: Vanderbilt University; University of North Carolina
Background: Managing Director, Goldman Sachs

Venture Capital & Private Equity Firms / Domestic Firms

Christopher Turner, Managing Director, Head, Capital Markets
Education: BS, Cornell University; MBA, Finance, Leonard N Stern School of Business, New York University
Background: Managing Director, Goldman Sachs; Bankers Trust Company
Frank Z Wei, Managing Director, Head of China
Education: BS, University of Texas; MBA, Harvard Business School
Background: Morgan Stanley; McKinsey & Co.
Daniel Zilberman, Managing Director & Head, Capital Solutions
Education: BA, Tufts University; MBA, Wharton School
Background: Evercore Capital Partners; Lehman Brothers

1958 WARWICK GROUP
51 Locust Avenue
Suite 202
New Cannan, CT 06840

Phone: 203-966-7447 **Fax:** 203-966-2199
e-mail: info@warwickgroup.com
web: www.warwickgroup.com

Mission Statement: A private equity firm specializing in the acquisition and recapitalization of profitable businesses with revenues up to $100 million.
Founded: 1970
Investment Criteria: Mergers, Acquisitions, Leveraged Buy-outs, Recapitalization
Industry Group Preference: Proprietary Products, Services, Distribution, Manufacturing
Portfolio Companies: CMG Holdings, e-Government Solutions, Premier Kids Care

1959 WASABI VENTURES
San Mateo, CA

web: www.wasabiventures.com

Mission Statement: Wasabi Ventures is a venture capital, incubator, and consulting firm that specializes in building and advising early stage technology companies. In the last 10 years, Wasabi Ventures has built, financed, and advised over 200 start-ups including some wildly successful ventures like Right Now Technologies, PBworks, Ustream, and Etherpad.
Geographic Preference: United States
Industry Group Preference: Advertising, E-Commerce & Manufacturing, Energy, Gaming, Healthcare Information Technology, Media, Mobile, Social Media, Technology
Portfolio Companies: Caplinked, UserTesting, Statisfy, Vidfall, Motion Math, Appglu, Apply Kit, Canvs+, CreativeGig, Cube26, Funsherpa, Gizmo, Haystagg, Humanoid, inVino, LawPivot, LSAT, Lutebox, Monstrous, Mosaic, Motifworks, PathSource, PBWorks, PEKU Publications, Postling, Proven.com, QuickAirLink, RepairPal, SalesGoose, SocialToaster, Roomi, SpeakerText, Immediatelyapp.com, SwitchNote, 500friends, Takeoff, TestSoup, Trove, TrackR, TrustEgg, Uconnect, UStream, Vidstructor, Wanderu

Key Executives:
Tom Kuegler, Co-Founder/Managing Partner
e-mail: tk@wasabiventures.com
Background: Co-Founder, SNT & SpinBox
Chris Yeh, Co-Founder/Managing Partner
e-mail: chris@wasabiventures.com
Education: Stanford University, MBA, Harvard Business School
Background: Founding Team, United Online Services, Merrill Lynch Intelligent Technologies Group

1960 WASHINGTON CAPITAL VENTURES
PO Box 9929
McLean, VA 22102

Fax: 703-827-0522
e-mail: info@wcvonline.com

Mission Statement: Venture capital firm investing in early stage and Mid-Atlantic based technology companies.
Geographic Preference: East Coast
Founded: 2001
Investment Criteria: Early Stage
Industry Group Preference: Technology, High Technology, Networking, Communications

Key Executives:
Lev Volftsun, Co-Founder & Managing Partner
Background: General Manager/Vice President, Cisco Systems, Co-Founded Lightspeed International, MCI, Stratus, British Telecom And Concert

1961 WASSERSTEIN & CO.
1185 Avenue of the Americas
39th Floor
New York, NY 10036

Phone: 212-702-5602
e-mail: contact@wasserco.com
web: www.wasserco.com

Mission Statement: A leading independent private equity and investment firm focused on middle-market leveraged buyout investments and related investment activities.
Fund Size: $2 billion
Founded: 1996
Minimum Investment: $2 million
Investment Criteria: Leveraged Buy-outs, Middle-Market
Industry Group Preference: Communications, Computer Related, Consumer Services, Genetic Engineering, Internet Technology, Medical & Health Related, Media, Consumer Products, Water
Portfolio Companies: ALM Media, Globecomm Systems, High Pressure Equipment Company, Paris Presents, Penton Media, Recorded Books

Key Executives:
Ellis Jones, Chairman
Education: Yale School of Management; University of California at Berkeley
Background: Wasserstein Perella & Co.; Managing Director, Salomon Brothers; Vice President Investment Banking, The First Boston Corporation
Directorships: Element K; True Advantage; Phoenix House; Cate School
Rajay Bagaria, President & Chief Investment Officer
Education: BA, Individualized Study, New York University; London School of Economics
Background: Partner, Apollo Investment Management; Goldman Sachs
Directorships: LVI Services Inc.; Generation Brands; Playpower Inc.; The Manitou School
Joseph Dutton, Chief Financial Officer & Chief Compliance Officer
Education: MS, Economics, University College Dublin; Joint Honors degree, Business & Economics, Trinity College Dublin
Background: Senior Product Manager, JP Morgan
Andrew McLellan, Managing Director
Education: BS, Finance & Government, University of Notre Dame
Background: SVP, Sheffield Asset Management; Apollo Global Management; Analyst, Deutsche Bank
Ralph Montana, Controller
Education: BS, Finance & Economics, City University of New York
Background: State Street Investment Management Services

Sean O'Keefe, Director
Education: BBA, Western New England University
Background: S&P Capitala

1962 WATER STREET HEALTHCARE PARTNERS
333 West Wacker Drive
Suite 2800
Chicago, IL 60606

Phone: 312-506-2900
e-mail: info@wshp.com
web: waterstreet.com

Mission Statement: A strategic private equity firm focused exclusively on healthcare. Our team of healthcare executives invest their experience and insight to build market-leading companies of lasting value.

Founded: 2005
Average Investment: $50 - $500 million
Investment Criteria: Middle-Market Companies
Industry Group Preference: Healthcare, Diagnostics, Medical Products & Services, Pharmaceuticals, Specialty Distribution, Life Sciences, Healthcare Services
Portfolio Companies: Access MediQuip, BioClinica, Breg, CareCentrix, Celerity Pharmaceuticals, HealthPlan Holdings, MarketLab, New Century Health, Orgentec, Premise Health, RTI Surgical, Sarnova, Temptime

Key Executives:
Tim Dugan, Managing Partner
Education: Stanford University; MBA, University of Chicago Graduate School of Business
Background: Founder & Partner, First Chicago Equity Capital; Director, One Equity Partners
Directorships: AAIPharma, HealthPlan Holdings, Sarnova
Kevin Swan, Founding Partner
Education: University of Southern Illinois
Background: President & CEO, Health Alliance; Group President, McKesson Medical Distribution; President & CEO, Griffith Micro Science/Sterigenics; Operating Partner, One Equity Partners
Directorships: Precision Dynamics Corporation, Sarnova
Chris Sweeney, Founding Partner
Education: Williams College
Background: Principal, Cleary & Oxford
Directorships: Precision Dynamcis Corporation, Sarnova
Robert Womsley, Partner
Education: Vanderbilt University; MBA, University of Chicago Graduate School of Business
Background: Senior Partner, Citi Private Equity
Directorships: Medical Specialties Distributors

1963 WATERMILL GROUP
One Cranberry Hill
750 Marrett Road
Suite 401
Lexington, MA 02421

Phone: 781-891-6660
e-mail: kurstell@watermill.com
web: www.watermill.com

Mission Statement: Invests in a variety of industries, with a preference for medium-growth companies which are experiencing structural change due to new competitive market dynamics, new technologies, consolidation or shifts in demand.

Geographic Preference: United States
Founded: 1978
Minimum Investment: $1,000,000
Investment Criteria: Middle-market, manufacturing and value-added distribution, moderate industry growth, reasonable industry margins, market or segment leadership
Industry Group Preference: Metals, Building Materials & Services, Manufacturing, Environmental Protection, Chemicals, Wood Industries, Transportation, Distribution, Business Products & Services
Portfolio Companies: Fine Tubes, Superior Tube, FutureMark Group Manistique, Multilayer Coating Technologies, C&M Corporation, Tenere, The Plastics Group

Key Executives:
Steven E Karol, Managing Partner & Founder
e-mail: skarol@watermill.com
Education: BS, Tufts University, President's Program on Leadership, Harvard Business School
Directorships: HMK Enterprises
Julia Karol, President and COO
e-mail: jkarol@watermill.com
Education: BA, Tufts University; MA, Stanford University; Harvard Business School
Background: Jumpstart; Partner, Social Venture Partners, Boston
Dale S Okonow, Senior Partner
e-mail: dokonow@watermill.com
Education: BS, Cornell University; JD & MBA, Cornell University
Background: Partner, President & COO, Sawyer Realty Holdings; General Counsel & CFO, HMK Enterprises
Benjamin P Procter, Senior Partner
e-mail: bprocter@watermill.com
Education: BA, Economics, Trinity College; MS, Accounting, Northeastern University
Background: Director Financial Planning, HMK Enterprises
Robert W Ackerman, Senior Partner
e-mail: backerman@watermill.com
Education: Yale University; MBA & DBA, Harvard Business School
Background: Chairman & CEO, Sheffield Steel Corporation; President & CEO, Lincoln Pulp & Paper Company; President, Premoid Corporation

1964 WAUD CAPITAL PARTNERS LLC
300 North LaSalle Street
Suite 4900
Chicago, IL 60654

Phone: 312-676-8400
web: www.waudcapital.com

Mission Statement: Waud Capital Partners is a leading middle-market private equity firm that partners with exceptional management teams to create, acquire, and/or grow companies that address significant, inefficient, highly fragmented and underserved industry segments. Invests primarily through control-oriented growth equity investments, industry consolidations, buyouts, or recapitalizations and seek companies that generate strong cash flow and can be grown both organically and through add-on acquisitions.

Geographic Preference: United States
Fund Size: $1 billion
Founded: 1993
Average Investment: $20-100 million
Minimum Investment: $20-100 million
Investment Criteria: Exceptional Management Teams, Market Niches, Strong Market, Growth Potential, Record of Historical Profitability
Industry Group Preference: Manufacturing, Distribution, Services
Portfolio Companies: Acadia Healthcare, Adreima, Adult & Pediatric Dermatology, ASG Security, Aquion Water Treatment, CarePoint Partners, The Center for Vein Restoration, Chirotouch, Cogent Healthcare, Compex, Cordant, CyberGrants, Dimensional Dental, DS Medical, Heart & Paw, iOffice, Ivy Rehab, Jazz Pharmaceuticals, National Security Partners, Optimum Outcomes, Parish Publishing Solutions, Pharmacy Partners, Pilot Thomas Logistics, ProNerve, PSI, Regency Hospital Company, Sphere, The GI Alliance, True Partners, Unifeye Vision Partners

Venture Capital & Private Equity Firms / Domestic Firms

Key Executives:
Reeve B Waud, Founder/Managing Partner
312-676-8450
Education: BA, Economics, Middlebury College; MA, Management, JL Kellogg Graduate School, Northwestern University
Background: Founder, Sovereign Specialty Chemicals; Founder, Pacer Propane LP; Investment Professional, Golder, Thoma, Cressey & Rauner; Corporate Finance, Salomon Brothers
Directorships: Alarm Security Group LLC, Whitehall Products, Christiana Industries, Parish Publications
Matt Clary, Partner
312-676-8406
Education: BA, Economics, University of Washington; MBA, Kellogg School of Management, Northwestern University
Background: Partner, Banc of America Capital Investors; Senior Associate, Corporate Banking Group, Bank of America
Directorships: Aquion Water Treatment Products, CarePoint Partners, Hospitalists Management Group
David Neighbors, Partner, Healthcare Services
312-676-8407
Education: BBA, Finance, University of Notre Dame
Background: Citigroup Investments, Salomon Smith Barney
Directorships: Hospitalists Management Group, Regency Hospital Company, True Partners Consulting
Justin C Dupere, Partner, Software & Technology
Education: BS, Wharton School; MBA, Kellogg School of Management
Background: GTCR; Morgan Stanley
Directorships: ChiroTouch, CuberGrants, iOffice, PSI Services, Sphere Payments
Christopher J Garber, Partner, Healthcare Services
Education: BA, Duke University; MBA, Kellogg School of Management
Background: Baird & Co.
Directorships: Cordant Health Solutions, Pharmacy Partners, Unifeye Vision Partners
Mark Flower, Chief Financial Officer & Chief Compliance Officer
312-676-8425
Education: BBA, Accounting & Finance, University of Wisconsin; CPA
Background: Vector Fund Management, Arthur Andersen, Kemper Financial Services, Kemper Asset Management, Iowa Grain Company

1965 WAVELAND INVESTMENTS LLC
900 North Michigan Avenue
Suite 1100
Chicago, IL 60611

Phone: 312-506-6450
web: wvlnd.com

Mission Statement: Waveland Investments targets lower middle market companies based in the United States, with focus on the manufacturing, distribution and service industries. Waveland pursues profitable businesses with talented management teams.

Geographic Preference: United States
Founded: 2000
Average Investment: $5 - $10 million
Investment Criteria: Buyouts, Growth Stage
Industry Group Preference: Manufacturing, Distribution, Business Products & Services, Consumer Services, Financial Services
Portfolio Companies: Better Things, CCS, Clark Brands, Daddies Board Shop, Doodad, Fluidmesh Networks, Hudson Lock LLC, Indiana Business Bank, Justice Design Group, NTE Aviation LLC, O2 Cool

Other Locations:
1850 Second Street
Suite 201
Highland Park, IL 60035

Key Executives:
Dennis Zaslavsky, Founder/Partner
312-506-6460
e-mail: dzas@wavelandinvestments.com
Education: BBA, University of Michigan; JD, Stanford University; CPA
Background: COO, Urban Shopping Centers; JMB Realty Corporation; Katten Muchin & Zavis
Meghan Otis, Partner
312-506-6470
e-mail: motis@wavelandinvestments.com
Education: BA, Mathematics, Northwestern University; MBA, Harvard Business School
Background: Goldman Sachs & Co.; LaSalle Partners
Phil Calian, Operating Partner
312-506-6490
e-mail: pcalian@wavelandinvestments.com
Education: BA, Chemistry, Brown University
Background: Founder & Managing Partner, Kingsbury Partners; American Classic Voyages Co.; CFI Industries Inc.

1966 WAVEMAKER PARTNERS
1333 Second Street
Suite 600
Santa Monica, CA 90401

Phone: 310-861-2100
Toll-Free: 800-875-0757
web: www.wavemaker.vc

Mission Statement: We invest in a broad range of technology-driven companies that are catalysts for change.

Industry Group Preference: Seed, Technology
Portfolio Companies: 500 Startups, Adly, Adomic, Advent, Affinity Neworks, Amplify, Art of Click, Ayannah, BeTheBeast.com, Breaker, Bridg, Buzzstarter, Caplinked, Card.com, Cloud Access, Club W, Craftyful, Dealflicks, DFR, DSTLD, East Club, Eko, Ellie, Exist, Fanbread, FGL, FloQast, Four Eyes, Frenzoo, Gem, Gimmie, Groupsite, Gushcloud, Healint, HipVan, Investedin, Kalibrr, Laurel & Wolf, Leagues, Lingia, Luxola, Maestrodev, Markkit, MCN, Morph Labs, My New Financial Advisor, Naritiv, Nativo, OpenX, P4RC, Phunware, PicoCandy, Pie, Playsino, Pollenizer, Praized, Prospect Medical, RadPad, Ranker, Rexter, Ribbon, RxVantage, Science, Shift, ShipHawk, ShopYourWorld.com, Shop Genius, Simple Reach, SKOut, Smove, SOA Software, SocialAnnex, Squabbler, Stack Commerce, StaffRanker, StrikeAd, Strong Ventures, Structo, SurfAir, Takelessons, Technorati, Telly, TheBouqs.com, Trade Gecko, Trade Sparq, TransferSoft, Twitmusic, Uncovet, Vator.tv, Viagogo, VideoAmp, Vow To Be Chic, Webtide, Whisk, Xyleme, YouMail, Zap, Zumata

Key Executives:
Eric Manlunas, Founder/Managing Partner
Education: BS, Communications, Florida International University; MBA, Pepperdine University
Background: Frontera Group; Founder, Sitestar; Siemer Ventures

1967 WAVEPOINT VENTURES
535 Middlefield Road
Suite 280
Menlo Park, CA 94025

Phone: 650-331-7393 Fax: 650-331-7393
e-mail: info@wavepointventures.com
web: www.wavepointventures.com

Mission Statement: Wavepoint helps committed teams bring unique innovations to market faster and more efficiently,

Venture Capital & Private Equity Firms / Domestic Firms

resulting in more wealth creation for entrepreneurs and investors.

Average Investment: $15 Million
Investment Criteria: Seed, Early-Stage
Industry Group Preference: Information Technology, Clean Technology, Medical
Portfolio Companies: Cloud Cruiser, dotFX, Marrone Bio Innovations, Second Genome, Sentilla, Sevenly, Vandolay, Velomedix, Vertascale Software

Other Locations:
535 Middlefield Road
Suite 280
Menlo Park, CA 94025
Phone: 650-331-7393 **Fax:** 650-331-7393

1968 WAYZATA INVESTMENT PARTNERS
One Carlson Parkway North
Suite 220
Plymouth, MN 55447

Phone: 952-345-0700
web: www.wayzatainvestmentpartners.com

Mission Statement: At Wayzata, we uncover and actively manage unique alternative investment opportunities, consistently delivering success for our investors.

Founded: 2004
Portfolio Companies: Perkins Restaurant & Bakery, MasterCraft, Grede Casting, Merisant, Star Tribune Media Holdings, Lazydays, Arrow Storage Products, Key Plastics, Majestic Star, Portola, SuperService, Tembec, Stallion, Propex, Topack Fittings, Caraustar, Anchor Glass, Hawkeye Renewables, SDI Special Devices, RathGibson, US Corrugated, Pliant, AMES, Smurfit-Stone, Guadalupe Power, Minnetonka Tankers, Sundevil Power, Midgard, Sea Transportation-Dry Bulk, East Shore Aircraft, Mint Farm Energy, Cascade Pacific Pulp, California Power, CityNorth, Cobalt Office Park

---

1969 WEBB INVESTMENT NETWORK
web: www.winfunding.com

Mission Statement: Our goal is to invest in companies that aim to change the world, particularly in the fields of cloud computing, enterprise software, mobile, marketplaces, e-commerce, crowdsourcing, and consumer internet.

Average Investment: $350,000
Minimum Investment: $250,000
Investment Criteria: Seed, Later Stage
Industry Group Preference: Information Technology
Portfolio Companies: Aero, AppLovin, Badgeville, Bitnet, BitYota, Boost CTR, CloudHelix, Diffbot, Epic, Everwise, Grubwithus, Hangtime, Hellosign, Hipmunk, Indiegogo, Ionic Security, LiveLoop, Local Response, Lockpath, Meteor, Nebula, Okta, Opscode, Pagerduty, Panorama, Pepperdata, Pindrop Security, Quixey, RelayRides, Respondly, RethinkDB, Science Exchange, StarMobile, Takelessons, Tapsense, Tenxer, TrueAccord, Upstream Commerce, Voxer, Vungle, Wavefront, We Pay, Workspot, Yozio, Zanbato, Zuora

Key Executives:
Maynard Webb, Founder
Education: Florida Atlantic University
Background: COO, eBay; CEO, LiveOps; Co-Founder, Everwise; Author

---

1970 WEDBUSH CAPITAL PARTNERS
1000 Wilshire Boulevard
Suite 830
Los Angeles, CA 90017

Phone: 213-688-8018 **Fax:** 213-688-8095
web: www.wedbushcapital.com

Mission Statement: Our objective is to make sound investments in profitable companies that are rapidly growing or poised for growth.

Geographic Preference: Western United States
Fund Size: $120 million
Founded: 1980
Average Investment: $5-$10 million
Minimum Investment: $2 million
Investment Criteria: Growth Investments, Recapitalizations, Management-Led Buyouts
Industry Group Preference: Business to Business, Consumer Products, Manufacturing
Portfolio Companies: Criterion Brock, Critical Alert Systems, Passport Food Group, VCC Optoelectronics

Key Executives:
Eric D Wedbush, Managing Director
e-mail: eric.wedbush@wedbushcapital.com
Education: MBA, Anderson School; BS, San Diego State University
Background: Wedbush Morgan Securities
Directorships: Reyn Spooner, BATS Trading, ONE Industries, Wedbush Inc., Wedbush Bank
Geoff Bland, Managing Director
e-mail: geoff.bland@wedbushcapital.com
Education: BA in Economics, Stanford University; MBA, JL Kellogg Graduate School
Background: Co-Founder ShareWave, a fabless wireless semiconductor company
Directorships: CriterionBrock, ONE Industries, Critical Alert Systems

---

1971 WELLS FARGO CAPITAL FINANCE
2450 Colorado Avenue
3rd Floor
Santa Monica, CA 90404

Phone: 310-453-7300 **Fax:** 310-453-7444
Toll-Free: 877-770-1222
web: www.wellsfargocapitalfinance.com

Mission Statement: We are a specialty secured lender with an entrepreneurial spirit and the backing of our parent company, Wells Fargo, one of the nation's strongest financial services companies.

Geographic Preference: North America
Fund Size: $50 million
Average Investment: $50-$750 million
Minimum Investment: $15 million
Investment Criteria: Recapitalizations, Turnarounds, Debtor-in-Possession Financings, Rediscount Lines, Leveraged Acquisitions and Middle-Market for Growth Companies
Industry Group Preference: Manufacturing, Retailing, Communications, Technology, Distribution, Transportation, Wholesale, Specialty Finance, Restaurants, Healthcare, Real Estate
Portfolio Companies: Affordable Interior Systems, Allied Alloys, Curtis Screw Company, Emcore, ES Robbins, Freedom Group, HomeCare, Marcegaglia, MEGA Brands, Milacron, National Spinning Company, PolyOne, Sage Automotive, Solar Plastics, Tree Island Industries, Alliance Tire Company, Building Material Distributors, Building Materials Holding Corporation, Delek Refining, Design Ideas, Goodmans, Knights Apparel, MMS - A Medical Supply Company, Nash Finch, TriMas, Wave Electronics, Wellman, Wythe Will Distributing, Alaska Airlines, Aquent, Douglas Steel Supply, GLS Companies, Nortech Sytems, Perkins & Marie Callender's, SecurAmerica, Stream Global Services, API Healthcare, Bullhorn, Ex Libris Global Holdings, Insurity, PROS, Telogis, BeyondTrust Software, Calypso Technology, FleetMatics USA, Network Instruments, BJ's Wholesale Club, Brookstone, City Sports, Destination Maternity, Dick's Sporting Goods, Floor & Décor, Gander Mountain, Harbor Freight, Kitchen Collection, Marvin's, Pet Smart, Raley's, Sears Canada, Advance Group, APF - WFCF,

Venture Capital & Private Equity Firms / Domestic Firms

Alliance Business Lending, Axis Capital Funding II, Cavalry Investments, Continental Business Credit, Direct Capital, Fast Pay Partners, Gemcap Lending I, JFIN Business Credit Fund, Mackinac Commercial Credit, Marquette Business Credit SPE I, Marquette Transportation Finance, MidCap Funding IV, National Funding, NXT Capital Funding IV, Rapid Financial Services, Siena Funding, ABRH, Arby's Restaurant Group, Mastro's Restaurants, Orion Healthcorp, Infusystem

Other Locations:

1100 Albernathy Road
Suite 1600
Atlanta, GA 30328-5657

14241 Dallas Parkway
Suite 1300
Dallas, TX 75254

601 California Street
7th Floor
San Francisco, CA 94108
Phone: 415-403-1100

10 South Wacker Drive
13th Floor
Chicago, IL 60606-7453

One Boston Place
18th Floor
Boston, MA 02108

100 Park Avenue
3rd Floor
New York, NY 10017
Phone: 212-703-3500

22 Adelaide St. West
Toronto, ON M5H 4E3
Canada

5901 Priestly Dr.
3rd Floor
Suite 306
Carlsbad, CA 92008-8825

116 Inverness Dr. E
3rd Floor
Suite 375
Englewood, CA 80112-5149

301 South College Street
5th Floor
Charlotte, NC 28202
Phone: 704-715-5417

1000 Louisiana St.
3rd Floor
Houston, TX 77002-5027

1700 Lincoln Street
6th & 21st Floor
Denver, CO 80203

333 South Grand Avenue
Suite 4150
Los Angeles, CA 90071
Phone: 213-443-6000

110 East Broward Boulevard
11th Floor
Suite 1100
Ft. Lauderdale, FL 33301-3503

200 South Biscayne Boulevard
14th Floor
Miami, FL 33131
Phone: 305-789-6982

730 Second Avenue South
8th Floor
Minneapolis, MN 55402
Phone: 612-673-8500

1 South Broad Street
3rd Floor
Philadelphia, PA 19107
Phone: 267-321-6692

100 West Washington Street
15th Floor
Phoenix, AZ 85003
Phone: 602-378-2478

1300 SW 6th Avenue
14th Floor
Portland, OR 97201
Phone: 503-886-2664

601 California St.
7th Floor
San Francisco, CA 94108
Phone: 415-403-1100

999 3rd Avenue
10th Floor
Seattle, WA 98104
Phone: 206-343-6402

1753 Pinnacle Drive
6th Floor
McLean, VA 22102-3833
Phone: 703-760-6100

2200 N. Commerce Pkwy.
2nd Floor
Suite 206
Weston, FL 33326-3258

800 N. Magnolia Ave.
7th Floor
Orlando, FL 32803-3264

Key Executives:
James Marasco, Senior Managing Director
e-mail: jim.marasco@wellsfargo.com
Education: BA, Accounting, Michigan State University
Background: GE Capital, Citicorp
Holly Kaczmarczyk, Senior Managing Director
Education: Millikin University; Thunderbird School of Global Management
Background: CEO, Wells Fargo Bank, N.A.

1972 WELLSPRING CAPITAL MANAGEMENT LLC
605 Third Avenue
44th Floor
New York, NY 10158

web: www.wellspringcapital.com

Mission Statement: Aims to increase the profitability of promising companies which can benefit from the firm's extensive experience in management, investment strategies, and business productivity.

Fund Size: $3 billion
Founded: 1995
Minimum Investment: $25 million
Investment Criteria: Acquisition, LBO, MBO
Industry Group Preference: Aerospace, Defense and Government, Consumer Services, Distribution, Financial Services, Food & Beverage, Insurance, Industrial Services
Portfolio Companies: Airswift, API Heat Transfer Inc., Chemaid Laboratories, Checkers Drive-In Restaurants Inc., Cleaver Brooks Inc., Crosman Corporation, Dave & Buster's Inc., Diagnostic Imaging, Edwin Watts Golf Shops, Great Lakes Caring Home Health & Hospice, Help At Home Inc., Hess Print Solutions Inc., Hoffmaster Group Inc., JW Aluminum Company, Lucky Strikes Entertainment, National Seating & Molbility, Neucel Specialty Cellulose LTD., Omni Energy Services Corp., Paragon Films, Performance Food Group, Proampac, Prolamina Corporation, Qualitor, Resco Products Inc., Residential Services Group Inc., Stripes Holdings LLC, Tradesmen, Tube City IMS Corporation, Vatterott College, Vistar Corporation

Venture Capital & Private Equity Firms / Domestic Firms

Key Executives:
Alexander E. Carles, Managing Partner & Co-President
Education: BA, Economics, College of William & Mary
Background: Whitney & Company; Research Analyst, Lehman Brothers
John E. Morningstar, Managing Partner & Co-President
Education: BS, University of Virginia; MBA, Wharton School
Background: Castle Harlan; Merrill Lynch

1973 WELSH, CARSON, ANDERSON & STOWE
599 Lexington Ave.
Suite 1800
New York, NY 10022

Phone: 212-893-9500
web: www.wcas.com

Mission Statement: Focuses investments in information/business services and healthcare. Its strategy is to buy growth businesses, partner with outstanding management teams and build value for investors through a combination of operational improvements, internal growth initiatives and strategic acquisitions.

Geographic Preference: United States
Fund Size: $20 billion
Founded: 1979
Average Investment: $50 to $100 million
Industry Group Preference: Healthcare, Information Technology, Business Products & Services
Portfolio Companies: Abzena, Accredo Health, Accuro, AGA Medical, AIM Software, Alert Logic, Alliance Data Systems, Amdocs Ltd., American Residential, AmeriPath, Aptuit, Ardent Health Services, Asurion, Avetta, Bausch & Lomb, BISYS Group, Card Establishment Services, CareSpot Express Healthcare, Ceridian, Clearwater, Cohesive Network Systems, Concentra, Decision One, Dex Media, Emerus, FISERV, GetWellNetwork, Global Knowledge Network, GlobalCollect, Hawk Medical, Headstrong, Identifix/SRS, InnovAge, Intoxalock, K2M, Kindred at Home, Kindred Healthcare, LabOne, Lytx, Magella, Matrix Medical Network, MedAssets America, MedCath, MedE America, MemberHealth, MMIT, MultiPlan, National Dentex, NaviHealth, Onward Healthcare, Oxford Finance, Paycom, Peak10, Quick Base, Quorum Health Group, Renal Advantage, Revel Systems, Ruesch Systems, SAVVIS, Select Medical, Simeio Solutions, Smile Brands, Solstas Lab Partners, Springstone, TransFirst, Triple Point Technology, United Surgical Partners International, Universal American, US Acute Care Solutions, US Anesthesia Partners, US Investigation Services, US Oncology, US Radiology Specialist, Valeritas, Westminster Healthcare

Other Locations:
580 California St.
Suite 1700
San Francisco, CA 94104
Phone: 415-375-4110

Key Executives:
Russell Carson, Founder & General Partner
Education: Dartmouth College; MBA, Columbia Business School
Background: Chairman/CEO, Citicorp Venture Capital
Bruce Anderson, Founder & General Partner
Education: University of Minnesota
Background: Executive VP, Automatic Data Processing
Patrick J Welsh, Founder & General Partner
Education: Rutgers University; MBA, University of California, Los Angeles
Background: President, Citicorp Venture Capital
Anthony J de Nicola, Chair
Education: DePauw University; MBA, Harvard Business School
Background: William Blair & Company; Goldman Sachs & Company
D Scott Mackesy, Managing Partner
Education: College of William & Mary
Background: Investment Research Department, Morgan Stanley Dean Witter
Brian T Regan, General Partner & Head, Healthcare Group
Education: Yale College
Background: Investment Banking, Merrill Lynch
Eric J Lee, General Partner & Head, Diversity & Inclusion
Education: Harvard University
Background: M&A & High Technology, Goldman Sachs & Co
Jonathan M Rather, General Partner
Education: BS, Accounting, Boston College; MS, Taxation, Pace University
Background: COO & CFO, Goelet Investment Office
Thomas A Scully, General Partner
Education: BA, University of Virginia; JD, Catholic University
Background: Administrator, Centers for Medicare & Medicaid Services; President & CEO, Federation of American Hospitals
Sean M Traynor, General Partner
Education: Villanova University; MBA, Wharton School, University of Pennsylvania
Background: BT Alex, Coopers & Lybrand
Michael E Donovan, General Partner & Head, Technology Group
Education: Yale College
Background: Windward Capital Partners
Christopher Hooper, General Partner
e-mail: chooper@wcas.com
Education: BA, Colgate University
Background: Golden Gate Capital
Directorships: Avetta, Clearwater Analytics, Quick Base, Revel Systems
Gregory G Lau, General Partner
Education: AB, Harvard College; MBA, Harvard Business School
Background: FFL Partners
Edward P Sobol, General Partner
e-mail: esobol@wcas.com
Education: BA, Stanford University; MBA, Harvard Business School
Background: FFL Partners
Directorships: Emerus, InnovAge, Kindred Healthcare, Kindred at Home, MMIT, National Dentex
Christopher W Solomon, General Partner & Director, Capital Markets
Education: BA, Wake Forest University; MBA, Ross School of Business, University of Michigan
Background: JP Morgan

1974 WEST HEALTH INVESTMENT FUND
10350 North Torrey Pines Road
La Jolla, CA 92037

Phone: 858-535-7000
Toll-Free: 855-937-8100
web: www.westhealth.org

Mission Statement: The West Health Investment Fund was established with a unique mission - to lower health care costs - by providing risk capital for companies with cutting-edge health care technologies and services.

Fund Size: $100 million
Industry Group Preference: Healthcare, Healthcare Information Technology
Key Executives:
Shelley Lyford, President and CEO
Education: University of San Diego
Zia Agha, Chief Medical Officer and EVP
Education: MS, Medical College of Wisconsin; MD, Aga Khan University

Venture Capital & Private Equity Firms / Domestic Firms

Background: Director, San Diego Healthcare System; Professor, University of California

1975 WESTERN STATES INVESTMENT GROUP
4025 Sorrento Valley Boulevard
San Diego, CA 92121

Phone: 858-678-0800 Fax: 858-678-0900
web: www.wsig.com

Mission Statement: Invests in a portfolio of companies involved in sectors of industry ranging from networking to software to life sciences, in the interests of producing beneficial financial returns. Not actively seeking investment opportunities.

Geographic Preference: West Coast
Fund Size: $30 million
Founded: 1976
Average Investment: $2 million
Minimum Investment: $1 million
Investment Criteria: Seed, First-Stage, Second-Stage, Mezzanine
Industry Group Preference: Communications, Computer Related, E-Commerce & Manufacturing, Electronic Components, Electronic Technology, Internet Technology, Medical & Health Related
Portfolio Companies: Lpath, DermTech International, Vaxiion Therapeutics
Key Executives:
Terry Trzcinka, Investment Liaison

1976 WESTERN TECHNOLOGY INVESTMENT
104 La Mesa Drive
Suite 102
Portola Valley, CA 94028

Phone: 650-234-4300 Fax: 650-234-4343
e-mail: info@westerntech.com
web: www.westerntech.com

Mission Statement: Focused on expanding the productive partnership between venture capital investors and venture lenders. Asset-based investments enable venture capital investors and management to maximize their equity investment through leverage.

Fund Size: $400 million
Founded: 1980
Average Investment: $250,000 to $30 million
Minimum Investment: $250,000
Investment Criteria: Experienced management, high growth potential
Industry Group Preference: Communications, Computer Related, Electronic Components, Instrumentation, Internet Technology, Genetic Engineering, Medical & Health Related, Life Sciences, Biotechnology, Medical Devices, Healthcare, Security, Semiconductors, Wireless Technologies
Portfolio Companies: 0-In Design, 3PARdata, 5Square Systems, Ablathion Frontiers, Abrizio, Access360, Accruent, Accuri Cytometers, Aceva, Actelis, Active Software, AcuFocus, Acusphere, Adaptive Planning, Adforce, Adomo, AdRoll, Advanced ICU Care, Aeluros, Aerogen, AeroScout, Aesgen, Afara Websystems, Agistics, Airgo Networks, Akimbo Systems, Alere Medical, Alopa Networks, Altierre, Amber Networks, Ample Communications, Ample Medical, Ampulse, Analogix Semiconductor, Anchor Intelligence, Andale, Andigilog, Apere, Arena Solutions, Aristos Logic, Arroyo Video Solutions, Asera, Askola USA Corporation, Aspire Medical, Astral Point Communications, Astro Gaming, Athena Design Systems, Athersys, Atlantis Computing, Atrica, Avamar, Azuro, Berkeley Design Automation, Bevocal, BigFix, BioAbsorbable Therapeutics, Biometrix, Bitwave Semiconductor, Bivio Networks, Biz360, Blackfoot, Blaze Entertainment, Blekko, BlueRoads, BlueSocket, Bluestar Solutions, Bocada, Bridgespan, Brion Technologies, Broad Daylight, Brocade Communications, Broncus Technologies, Business Engine, BuzzLogic, Calico Commerce, Calient Networks, Calista Technologies, Calix Networks, Cameron Health, CancerVax, Cardica, Cardio Focus, CardioNOW, Cardiva Medical, Catamaran Communications, Causes, Caymas Systemts, Cellfire, CellGate, Cellscape, Cerent, Ceres, Chakshu Research, Chameleon Systems, Ciphergen Biosystems, CipherOptics, CiraNova, Circle of Moms, Cloudmark, CloudShield, Coalescent Surgical, Collarity, Commerce One, Confirma, ConforMIS, Corvis, CoSine Communications, Counterpane Internet Security, CoWare, Crimson Microsystems, Cswitch, Cull, CV Ingenuity, CyberHeart, Cyclone Commerce, Cyras Systems, Daylight Solutions, Delve Networks, DemandBase, diCarta, Digex, Digital Generation Systems, Discera, Dragnet Solutions, E2O Communications, EchoPass, EcoSMART Technologies, eduFire, EForce Media, Ellacoya Networks, Emergent Game Technologies, Emergent Respiratory Products, Emotive Communications, Emphasys Medical, Encelle, Enigma Semiconductor, Enkata Technologies, EnteroMedics, Envivio, EoPlex, Equinix, Ethertronics, Evalve, Evera Medical, Evincii, Exodus, Fabric Networks, FaceBook, fastmobile, Feedster, FilmLoop, firstRain, Flock, Friendster, Future Point Systems, Fwix, Fyre Storm, Gear6, General Bandwith, Genius, Genteric, Gizmo5 Technologies, Gluon Networks, Goodmail Systems, Google, Green Border Technologies, GridNetworks, Guardian Analytics, HandyLab, Headway Technologies, Zenverge, Zoove, Zyomyx

Key Executives:
Maurice Werdegar, Investment Partner/CEO
e-mail: mauricew@westerntech.com
Education: BA, MBA, Stanford Universtiy
Background: iMinds Ventures; CFO, MetaMarkets; Corporate Finance, Robertson Stephens
Jay Cohan, Investment Partner
e-mail: jayc@westerntech.com
Education: BS, MS, Electrical Engineering, MIT; MBA, Harvard Business School
Background: Puma Technology; Orcale Corporation; SoftMagic
David Wanek, Investment Partner
e-mail: davidw@westerntech.com
Education: BS, University of Kansas, MBA, University of Mexico, JD, Santa Clara University
Background: Marketing, Verisign, Wilson Sonsini Goodrich And Rosati, And Os Alamos National Laboratories
Dave Gravano, Investment Partner
e-mail: daveg@westerntech.com
Education: BA, Duke University
Background: Silicon Valley Bank, Fortress Investment Group, Meier Mitchell/GATX Ventures
Rudy Ruano, Investment Partner
e-mail: rudy@westerntech.com
Education: BS, Finance, San Jose State University
Background: CEO, ScanRx; VP, Business Development, iMeditation SA
Hagi Schwartz, Venture Partner
e-mail: hagi@westerntech.com
Background: Founder, Magnolia Capital; CFO, Check Point Software Technologies
Directorships: Silicon Graphics, BigFix, TUI University

1977 WESTLAKE SECURITIES
2700 Via Fortuna
Suite 250
Austin, TX 78746

Phone: 512-314-0711 Fax: 512-306-1651
web: www.westlakesecurities.com

Mission Statement: Promotes economic growth by matching promising ventures to potential investors, educating companies and investors on business financing issues, and linking emerging companies with appropriate professional business expertise.

Fund Size: $275 million
Founded: 1992

Venture Capital & Private Equity Firms / Domestic Firms

Average Investment: $25 million
Minimum Investment: $5 million
Investment Criteria: Seed, Research & Development, Start-Up, First-stage, Second-stage, Mezzanine, LBO
Industry Group Preference: Business Products & Services, Communications, Consumer Products, Consumer Services, Distribution, Logistics, Energy Services, Healthcare, Information Services, Insurance, Financial Services, Manufacturing, Oil & Gas, Semiconductors, Software

Other Locations:
6363 Woodway
Suite 1000
Houston, TX 77057
Phone: 713-590-9690 **Fax:** 713-590-9601

11676 US Highway One
North Palm Beach, FL 33408
Phone: 561-352-8815

2000 Kaliste Saloom Road
Suite 400
Lafayette, LA 70508
Phone: 337-291-1260 **Fax:** 337-291-1265

Key Executives:
Matt Anderson, CEO/Managing Director
e-mail: andersend@westlakesecurities.com
Education: MBA, Sam Houston State University; University of Chicago; Harvard University
Wilson Allen, Partner/Managing Director
e-mail: wilson@westlakesecurities.com
Education: BA, Economics, University of Texas; MBA, Pepperdine University
Background: President, Signature Capital Securities, LLC; Co-Founder, Wind River Capital Company; Online Editor, Hoover's; Sr Equity Trader/Member of Equity Asset Allocation Committee, Eagle Management & Trust Company
Jon D'Andrea, Managing Director
e-mail: jdandrea@westlakesecurities.com
Education: University of Texas
Grant Pritchard, Managing Director
e-mail: gpritchard@westlakesecurities.com
Education: BS, University of Southern California; MBA, Columbia Business School
Mark Austin, Managing Director
e-mail: maustin@westlakesecurities.com
Education: BBA, MBA, University of Texas, Austin
Kevin Brady, Managing Director
e-mail: kbrady@westlakesecurities.com
Education: BS, Texas A&M University
Brian Hawkins, Managing Director
e-mail: bhawkins@westlakesecurities.com
Education: CPA, MBA, Sam Houston State University

1978 WESTLY GROUP
2200 Sand Hill Road
Suite 250
Menlo Park, CA 94025

Phone: 650-275-7420 **Fax:** 650-362-2338
e-mail: plans@westlygroup.com
web: www.westlygroup.com

Mission Statement: The Westly Group is a clean technology-oriented venture capital firm. We focus primarily on companies with proven revenue streams but are open to investments in all stages of growth.

Founded: 2007
Investment Criteria: All Stages
Industry Group Preference: Clean Technology
Portfolio Companies: Building Robotics, Enerkem, Ioxus, Revolution Foods, Solexel, Calstar Products, Feastly, Lunera, SCIenergy, View, Clean Well, Good Eggs, My Health Terms, Sentinel, WaterSmart, Cooliris, GreenWave Systems, Recyclebank, Simple Energy, Yerdle, Edeniq, Honest Buildings

Key Executives:
Steve Westly, Managing Partner
Education: Stanford University; MBA, Stanford Graduate School of Business
Background: Controller & Chief Fiscal Officer, State of California; Senior Vice President of Marketing, eBay; Office of Conservation and Solar, US Department of Energy
Timothy Wang, Partner
Education: BA, Brown University; MBA, USC Marshall School of Business
Background: Co-Founder, ChinaScope; Analyst, S&P Capital IQ
Dave Coglizer, Principal
Education: University of California, Davis; MBA, Stanford Graduate School of Business
Background: Bancomer; Senior Category Manager, eBay; CB Richard Ellis
Directorships: Amonix

1979 WESTVIEW CAPITAL PARTNERS
125 High Street
High Street Tower
26th Floor
Boston, MA 02110

Phone: 617-261-2050 **Fax:** 617-261-2060
e-mail: cvs@wvcapital.com
web: www.wvcapital.com

Mission Statement: WestView Capital Partners is a Boston-based private equity firm focused exclusively on lower middle market companies.

Fund Size: $500 million
Founded: 1990
Average Investment: $5 - $30 million
Investment Criteria: Recapitalizations, Growth Equity, Buyouts, Consolidations
Industry Group Preference: Business Products & Services, Software, Information Technology, Healthcare Services, Logistics, Distribution, Industrial, Manufacturing, Consumer Products, Retail, Consumer & Leisure, Media, Publishing
Portfolio Companies: Abacus Group LLC, Accountabil IT, Advanced Technology Services UK Limited, Alku, Alpha II, Apex Revenue Technologies, Bell and Howell, Body Central, CloudWave, Collaborative Solutions, L'Anza, English Color, eSolutions, Executive Health Resources, Fitness Connection, Graphic Controls, Health Monitor Network, Jopari Solutions, KLDiscovery, Mintz Group, Northwest Plan Services, Nwestco, OneNeck IT Services, Park Place Technologies, Peerless Industrial Group, Providea Conferencing, Radiac Abrasives, Receivable Solutions, Resource Ammirati, RuffaloCODY, Snow Companies, The Paper Store, The Phia Group, The Shelby Group, Thorne Research, TriTech Software Systems, Unified Patents, VaultLogix, VC3, Veriato, Wavelink Corporation, Xtend Healthcare

Key Executives:
Carlo A. von Schroeter, Managing Partner
617-261-2051
Education: BS, Mechanical Engineering, Queen's University; MBA, Harvard Business School
Background: General Partner, Weston Presidio; Vice President, Security Pacific Capital; District Engineering Manager, Shell Canada Limited
Directorships: American Asphalt & Grading, Star International Holdings, Geosystems, Delstar, Lion Brewery, Medscape
Richard J. Williams, Managing Partner
617-261-2052
e-mail: rjw@wvcapital.com
Education: BS, Computer Science, Yale University; MBA, Wharton School
Background: Partner, Tudor Investment Corporation; Managing Director, Triumph Capigal Group; Associate, Drexel Burnham Lambert
Directorships: Ameridata Technologies, United Natural

Venture Capital & Private Equity Firms / Domestic Firms

Foods, Hatten Communications, Claricom Holdings, Longview Group, International Computer Graphics, OutSource International
John H. Turner, General Partner
617-261-2053
e-mail: jht@wvcapital.com
Education: BA, Economics, University of New Hampshire; MBA, Wharton School
Background: General Partner, Norwest Mezzanine Partners; Managing Director, Triumph Capital Group; Heller Financial
Matthew T. Carroll, General Partner
617-261-2054
e-mail: mtc@wvcapital.com
Education: BS, Finance, Boston College
Background: VP, Corporate Development, LogistiCare; Associate, Triumph Capital Group; Analyst, Dean Witter Reynolds
Directorships: LogistiCare
Jonathan E. Hunnicutt, General Partner
e-mail: jeh@wvcapital.com
Education: AB, Government/Geography, Dartmouth College; MBA, Tuck School of Business
Background: Associate, Weston Presidio; Associate, Fleet Equity Partners; Analyst, Merrill Lynch

1980 WGI GROUP
New York, NY

e-mail: contact@wgifund.com
web: www.wgifund.com

Mission Statement: WGI Group provides early stage capital to internet entrepreneurs.
Average Investment: $500,000
Investment Criteria: Seed-Stage, Early-Stage
Industry Group Preference: Internet
Key Executives:
  Michael Walrath, Partner
  Education: BA, English, University of Richmond
  Background: Founder & CEO, Right Media
  Directorships: Meteor Games, MOAT, GuideMe, Yext, InAdCo
  Noah Goodhart, Partner
  Education: BA, Cornell University; MA, Yale University
  Background: Founder, Colonize.com; Co-CEO, Ad Group; Founding Investor, Right Media
  Jonah Goodhart, Partner
  Education: BA, Cornell University
  Background: Co-CEO, Smarter Ad Group; Founding Investor, Right Media

1981 WHEATLEY PARTNERS
80 Cuttermill Road
Great Neck, NY 11021

Phone: 516-773-1024 Fax: 516-773-0996
e-mail: info@wheatleypartners.com

Mission Statement: To work closely with entrepreneurs to build successful businesses and typically support portfolio companies at all stages of development.
Founded: 1992
Investment Criteria: All Stages
Industry Group Preference: Software, Business Products & Services, Information Technology, Life Sciences, Medical Devices, Communications, Networking, Education, Healthcare, Healthcare Information Technology

Other Locations:
  747 Third Avenue
  24th Floor
  New York, NY 10017

1982 WHITE STAR CAPITAL
331 Park Avenue S
New York, NY 10010

e-mail: info@whitestarvc.com
web: www.whitestarcapital.com

Mission Statement: White Star Capital, is an investment vehicle that deploys between $250k and $2.5M in startups in North America, Western Europe and other selective markets.
Geographic Preference: Europe, North America
Average Investment: $250,000 - $2.5 million
Investment Criteria: Early-Stage
Industry Group Preference: Mobile, Social Media, Gaming, E-Commerce & Manufacturing
Portfolio Companies: Salesfloor, adglow, Echo, aire, Gymtrack, KeyMe, Red Sift, Borrowell, Hole 19, Dice, Vention, Freshly, drop, mnubb, digg, Klaxoon, TheGuarantors, Bloglovin', Safello, Meero
Other Locations:
  407 McGill
  Suite 808
  Montreal, QC
  Canada

  37-41 Mortimer Street
  Fitzrovia
  United Kingdom

  40 Rue Francois
  1st Floor
  Paris 75008
  France

  20th Floor On Building
  158-164 Queen's Road Central
  Hong Kong
  Hong Kong

  Level 3, Sanno Park Tower
  2-11-1 Nagata-Cho, Chiyoda-Ku
  Tokyo 100-6162
  Japan

Key Executives:
  Eric Martineau-Fortin, Founder/Managing Partner
  Education: HEC Canada; MSc
  Background: ABN AMRO, Paris; Merrill Lynch International, New York
  Jean-Francois Marcoux, Co-Founder/Managing Partner
  Education: HEC Montreal; MSc, University of Sherbrooke; CFA
  Background: Co-Founder, Ludia; Senior M&A, Scotia Bank; Deutsche Bank; CDPQ; TC Transcontinental

1983 WI HARPER GROUP
50 California Street
Suite 2580
San Francisco, CA 94111

Phone: 415-397-6200 Fax: 415-397-6280
web: www.wiharper.com

Mission Statement: Seeks to help talented entrepreneurs, engineers and scientists create world-class technology companies by providing them with valuable resources and guidance.
Geographic Preference: United States, Asia, Central Europe
Fund Size: $225 million
Founded: 1993
Average Investment: $7 million
Minimum Investment: $500,000
Investment Criteria: Early Stage, Early-Expansion Stage
Industry Group Preference: E-Commerce & Manufacturing, Digital Media & Marketing, Wireless

Technologies, Broadband, Optical Technology, Biotechnology, Clean Technology, Healthcare, Technology
Portfolio Companies: Aicent, Airy:3D, Alpha Ring, Avaamo, Blossom, Coffee Meets Bagel, Cold Genesys, Commerce One, Divx, Drop, DynoSense, Epic!, Flutter, GCT, Holor, Kloudless, Momentum Machines, nway, Ooma, PAVmed, Percolata, Playswell, PMC, Polly Portfolio, Poshly, Shots Studio, Signma, Synthego, Thunder, ViSenze, Vizio, Walla.by, Wonder Workshop, Wynd

Other Locations:
10F-2 Ruentex Banking Tower
76 Tun Hua South Road
Sec. 2
Taipei
Taiwan
Phone: 886-2-2755-6033 **Fax:** 886-2-2709-2127

806 Tower A
Pacific Century Place
Beijing 100027
China
Phone: 86-10-6539-1366 **Fax:** 86-10-6539-1367

Key Executives:
Paul Chau, Senior Partner
e-mail: pchau@wiharper.com
Education: MS, Business Administration/Finance, University of California, Berkeley; BS, Electrical Engineering, University of Canterbury, New Zealand
Background: VP, Walden International; VP, GIC Special Investment Private Limited; Senior Consultant, BARRA
Shahi Ghanem, Senior Partner
Education: BS, Economics, University of California, Irvine
Background: Chief Strategy Officer/EVP, Corporate Development, BitTorrent Inc.; President, DivX. Chairman/CEO, Brickfish; CEO, EmpoweHER; SVP, Technology, Greens.com
Y.K. Chu, Senior Partner
Education: BS, National Cheng-Kung University; MS, Drexel University
Background: President, Sasson International; General Manager, Iridium Taiwan Gateway
Directorships: YesHealth; iStaging; Codementor; SNSPlus

1984 WICKS GROUP OF COMPANIES, LLC
400 Park Avenue
New York, NY 10022
Phone: 212-838-2100 **Fax:** 212-223-2109
e-mail: info@wicksgroup.com
web: www.wicksgroup.com

Mission Statement: Focused private equity firm that specializes in selected segments of the communications, information and media industries in the United States.

Geographic Preference: United States
Fund Size: fund I $62m, fund II $383m, fund III $535m
Founded: 1989
Average Investment: $5-$25 million
Investment Criteria: LBO, MBO
Industry Group Preference: Business to Business, Publishing, Radio, Advertising, Cable, Communications, Media, Information Technology, Broadcasting, Education, Media
Portfolio Companies: New Mountain Learning, Wicks Educational Publishing, CFM Religion Publishing Group, NewBay Media, Northstar Travel Media, SCI Solutions, Southern Technical College, Verse Music Group, Wilks Broadcast Group, Mcmurry/TMG, Jobson Healthcare Information, Harris Connect, Bonded Services Group, Bendon, Antenna International

Key Executives:
Craig B Klosk, Co-Founder/Managing Partner
212-407-2202
e-mail: craig.klosk@wicksgroup.com
Education: BS, Labor Relations, JD, Cornell University
Background: Attorney, Paul, Weiss, Rifkind, Wharton & Garrison; Senior Editor, Cornell Law Review
Daniel L Black, Managing Partner
212-407-2212
e-mail: daniel.black@wicksgroup.com
Education: AB, Dartmouth College
Background: Managing Director/Co-head, Merchant Banking; Senior VP/Co-head, US Corporate Banking; Trustee, Bank Street College
Matthew E Gormly III, Managing Partner
212-407-2205
e-mail: matt.gormly@wicksgroup.com
Education: BA, Economics, Hampden-Sydney College; MBA, Babcock School of Management, Wake Forest University
Background: Managing Director, BC Advisors
Daniel M Kortick, Managing Partner
212-407-2207
e-mail: daniel.kortick@wicksgroup.com
Education: MBA, Finance, Bryant College; BA, Hobart College
Background: Fleet Bank; BankBoston
Max von Zuben, Managing Partner
212-407-2210
Education: BA, English & American Literature, Harvard College; MBA, Columbia Business School
Background: Associate, Dubiler & Company; Investment Banking, Donaldson, Lufkin & Jenrette Securities

1985 WILDCAT VENTURE PARTNERS
777 Mariners Island Boulevard
Suite 550
San Mateo, CA 94404
Phone: 650-234-4840
e-mail: ideas@wildcat.vc
web: wildcat.vc

Mission Statement: Wildcat Venture Partners invests in Business-to-Business startups emerging in the tech industry.

Founded: 2015
Industry Group Preference: Technology, Machine Learning, Artificial Intelligence, IoT, Cloud, Mobility, Digital Health, EdTech, Education, SaaS, Software, FinTech
Portfolio Companies: Aceable, Amplero, C3.ai, Carrum Health, Clover, Drum, Green Fig, Key, LeaseLock, Obo, Olono, Reach, Remarkable, Ritual, Tuition.io, Vlocity, What 3 Words, Zebit

Key Executives:
Bill Ericson, Founding Partner
Education: BS, Georgetown University School of Foreign Service; JD, Northwestern University School of Law
Background: Managing Partner, Mohr Davidow Ventures
Bryan Stolle, Founding Partner
Education: BBA/MBA, University of Texas at Austin
Background: General Partner, Mohr Davidow Ventures; Founder/CEO, Agile Software
Jennifer Trzepacz, Partner/COO
Education: BA, Bryant University; MBA, Simmons Grad. School of Management
Background: EVP, RocketFuel; LivingSocial; Salesforce; Electronic Arts; Yahoo!
Bruce Cleveland, Partner
Education: BBA, California State University
Background: Founder, GreenFig; Apple; AT&T; Oracle; Siebel Systems
Geoffrey Moore, Partner
Education: BA, Literature, Stanford University; PhD, Literature, University of Washington
Background: Author; Speaker; Advisor
Phyllis Whiteley, Partner
Education: BA, Chemistry; PhD, Pharmacology, Washington University
Background: Partner, Mohr Davidow Ventures; Officer/SVP of Business Development, Perlegen Sciences

Venture Capital & Private Equity Firms / Domestic Firms

Inc.; VP of Strategic Portfolio Management, Roche; Senior Research Immunology, Merck
Randall Ussery, Partner
Education: BA, History, James Madison University; MBA, Babson College
Background: Herman Miller

1986 WILLOWRIDGE PARTNERS
122 East 42nd Street
37th Floor
New York, NY 10017

Phone: 212-369-4700 **Fax:** 212-369-5661
e-mail: info@willowridge.com
web: www.willowridge.com

Mission Statement: Willowridge Partners buys limited partnership interests in buyout and venture capital funds on a secondary basis.

Fund Size: $535 million
Founded: 1995
Average Investment: $20 million
Investment Criteria: Buyouts, Mezzanine
Industry Group Preference: Diversified

Key Executives:
Jerrold Newman, Partner
212-369-2888
e-mail: jnewman@willowridgeinc.com
Education: MBA, Amos Tuck School, Dartmouth; BS, Cornell University
Background: CPA, Price Waterhouse; CPA, Acquisitions, Booz, Allen & Hamilton
Luisa Hunnewell, Partner
212-369-1220
e-mail: lhunnewell@willowridge.com
Education: MBA, Amos Tuck School, Dartmouth; BA, University of Pennsylvania
Background: Insurance, Chemical Bank
James O'Mara, Partner
212-369-3211
e-mail: jomara@willowridge.com
Education: BA, Hamilton College
Background: Office of Investments, Hamilton College
Lawrence Fang, Partner
212-369-8922
e-mail: lfang@willowridge.com
Education: BBA, University of Michigan
Background: Principal, Pomona Capital; AIG Global Investment Group
Michael Kenny, Controller
212-369-8844
e-mail: mkenny@willowridge.com
Education: BS, Accountancy, St. John's University
Background: Vice President, Goldman Sachs & Co.; RSM McGladrey; Merrill Lynch

1987 WILMINGTON INVESTOR NETWORK
1802 South Churchill Drive
Wilmington, NC 28403

Phone: 910-538-6641
e-mail: info@wilmingtoninvestor.com
web: www.wilmingtoninvestor.com

Mission Statement: WIN is a private equity fund interested in high-growth companies from all areas of business.

Geographic Preference: Eastern North Carolina & Eastern South Carolina
Industry Group Preference: Technology, Biotechnology, Medical Devices
Portfolio Companies: 3Derm, ABK Biomedical, Affinergy, Arbovax, Axial Exchange, Basho, CARS, Chaologix, Ecolibrium Solar, Gemmus Pharma, Mobee, Oculis Labs, Onco Health, Pique Therapeutics, Physcient, Protochips, Public Relay, Respiratory Motion, Sensory Analytics, Stimwave, TranscribeMe, Trusted Metrics, Validic, Wilmington Pharmaceuticals, WindGap Medical

1988 WILSHIRE PRIVATE MARKETS
1299 Ocean Avenue
Suite 700
Santa Monica, CA 90401

Phone: 310-451-3051
web: www.wilshire.com

Mission Statement: Provides customized investment solutions to institutional clients worldwide.

Geographic Preference: Worldwide
Fund Size: $5.5 Billion
Founded: 1984
Investment Criteria: LBOs, Distressed, Special Situations, Growth Capital, Venture Capital
Industry Group Preference: All markets considered

Other Locations:
210 Sixth Avenue
Suite 3720
Pittsburgh, PA 15222
Phone: 412-434-1580

222 West Adams Street
Suite 1880
Chicago, IL 60606
Phone: 312-762-5500

Wilshire Associated Europe B.V.
World Trade Center - Tower H, 25th Floor
Zuidplein 204
Amsterdam 1077 XV
Netherlands
Phone: 31-203057530

370 Interlocken Boulevard
Suite 620
Broomfield, CO 80021
Phone: 303-626-7444

525 Washington Boulevard
Suite 2410
Jersey City, NJ 07310
Phone: 201-984-4899

3 Pickering Street
#02-39 Nankin Row
China Square Central
Singapore 048660
Singapore
Phone: 65-6435-2169

1 Connaught Place
Suite 3412
37F Jardine House
Hong Kong
China
Phone: 852-2832-6601

Landmark, 1 Giltspur Street
London EC1A 9DD
United Kingdom
Phone: 44-20-7920-3100

Key Executives:
Mark Meakpeace, Chief Executive Officer
Background: Group Director of Information Services, London Stock Exchange Group; Chief Executive, FTSE Russell
Andy Stewart, Deputy CEO
Background: Industry Partner, Motive Partners; President & COO, Man Investments
Scott Condron, Chief Operating Officer
Education: Rochester Institute of Technology
Background: Blackrock; Aladdin Wealth Tech; Republic National Bank of New York; Mercadian Capital; Drexel Burnham Lambert

Venture Capital & Private Equity Firms / Domestic Firms

Jason Schwarz, President
Education: Hamilton College, New York; Marshall School of Business, University of Southern California

1990 WIND POINT PARTNERS
676 North Michigan Avenue
Suite 3700
Chicago, IL 60611

Phone: 312-255-4800 **Fax:** 312-255-4820
web: www.wppartners.com

Mission Statement: Acquires middle market businesses in partnership with outstanding management teams that possess a clear vision for creating value over a five year time period.

Geographic Preference: United States
Fund Size: $400 million
Founded: 1983
Average Investment: $30 - $150 million
Minimum Investment: $8 million
Investment Criteria: LBO, Recapitalizations, Industry Consolidations, Expansion Capital
Industry Group Preference: Business to Business, Healthcare, Industrial Services, Consumer Services
Portfolio Companies: Active Interest Media, America's PowerSports, Argotec, Dicom Transportation Group, Interface Solutions, Knape & Vogt, Nelson Global Products, Nonni's, Novolex, Pelss, Petmate, RailWorks, Rupari Foods, Shearer's Foods, Taylor-Wharton International, Vertellus Specialties

Key Executives:
Nathan Brown, Managing Director
Education: BA, Philosophy with distinction, Queen's University; MBA with honors, University of Chicago
Background: Analyst, Corporate Finance/Mergers & Acquisitions, ScotiaMcLeod
Directorships: America's PowerSports, Marshfield DoorSystems, United Subcontractors
Joe Lawler, Managing Director
Education: BS, Boston College; MBA, Kellogg School of Management, Northwestern University
Background: Analyst, William Blair & Company
Bob Cummings, Managing Director/Co-Founder
e-mail: rlc@wppartners.com
Education: BSME, Rensselaer Polytechnic Institute; MBA, Harvard Business School
Background: General Partner, Robertson, Colman & Stephens; Consultant, McKinsey & Company
Directorships: Bakery Chef, Procyon Technologies, VICORP Restaurants
Richard R Kracum, Managing Director/Co-Founder
e-mail: rrk@wppartners.com
Education: MBA, MS, Chemistry, University of Chicago; BA, Carleton College
Background: Principal, Booz, Allen & Hamilton; Chairman, Prange Way
Directorships: Pacific Cycle, Bushnell Performance Optics, America's PowerSports, Benchmark Medical, Ames True Temper, AIR-Serv Holdings
Alex Washington, Managing Director
Education: BA Finance, Morehouse College; MBA, Harvard Business School
Background: Senior Associate, Whitney & Company; Business Analyst, McKinsey & Company; Member, Class VI Kauffman Fellows
Directorships: Arr-Maz Custom Chemicals
Paul Peterson, Managing Director
Education: BBA Finance, University of Iowa; MBA, Harvard Business School
Background: Associate, Wind Point; Financial Analyst, Houlihan Lokey Howard & Zukin; Management, Harley-Davidson Motor Company
David Stott, Managing Director
Education: BBA, Finance & Accounting, University of Michigan; MBA, Kellogg School of Management, Northwestern University

Background: Financial Analyst, Investment Banking Division, Citigroup
Konrad Salaber, Managing Director
e-mail: kas@wppartners.com
Education: BA, English, Washington University, St. Louis; MBA, Booth School of Business
Background: Analyst, AG Edwards Capital Markets
Directorships: Knape & Vogt, Nonni's, Rupari Foods

1991 WINDCREST PARTNERS
750 Third Avenue
33rd Floor
New York, NY 10017

Phone: 212-257-6704
e-mail: info@windcrestpartners.com
web: www.windcrestpartners.com

Mission Statement: Through WINDCREST PARTNERS II, we invest in private companies at all stages of development and seek to partner with talented management teams and innovative entrepreneurs. We pride ourselves on providing the financial support and guidance that management teams require to build strong, sustainable businesses.

Geographic Preference: United States
Investment Criteria: All Stages
Portfolio Companies: GoodData, Offerpop, Violin Memory, Mobilize.me, Voxer, Micro Office, Axial, Appriss, eNNOV, Dalet, GSO, HigherOne, Metropolitan National Bank, Syncsort, uTest, Clementon Park Splash Worlld, Nasville Shores Water Park, Ocean Breeze Water Park, Regent, SmartRecruiters, Monark, Wavemark Technologies

Key Executives:
James Gellert, Partner
212-257-6704
e-mail: jgellert@windcrestpartners.com
Education: AB, Harvard College
Background: Partner, Windcrest Discovery Investments; Oakes Fitzwilliams & Co.
Michael Gellert, Partner
212-599-3630
e-mail: mgellert@windcrestpartners.com
Education: AB, Harvard College
Directorships: Dalet Technologies, Seacor Holdings, Devon Energy, Humana, Six Flags, Regal Cinemas
William Fitzgerald, Partner
212-257-6705
e-mail: wfitzgerald@windcrestpartners.com
Education: AB, Harvard College; CFA
Background: Analyst, JP Morgan Investment Management

1992 WINDFORCE VENTURES, LLC
40 West 25th Street
New York, NY 10010

web: www.windforceventures.com

Mission Statement: Windforce Ventures is a venture capital firm specializing in early-stage social media and mobile technology investments. Headquartered in NYC, the firm is spearheaded by investment wizards and social media technology entrepreneurs. We couple exceptional entrepreneurs and cutting edge technologies with in-house advisorship to help them build thriving companies.

Investment Criteria: Early-Stage
Industry Group Preference: Social Media, Mobile Technology
Portfolio Companies: BetterCompany, Sightly, Navdy, Food Genius, Reactor Labs, Mobile Roadie, Mashwork, Social Chorus, Kloudless, Freak'n Genius

Key Executives:
Mario Montoya, Founder & President
Education: Wharton School of Business
Background: Renaissance Technologies; BEA Associates
Jason Stein, Founding & Managing Partner
Education: New York University

Venture Capital & Private Equity Firms / Domestic Firms

Background: Founder & President, Laundry Service
Directorships: Reactor, Inc; Kloudless
Michoel Ogince, Founding & Managing Partner
Background: Director of Platform and Product Strategy, Big Fuel
Directorships: Mashwork; Nexgate, Mass Relevance; Video Genie; Social Chorus
Waiman Leung, Advising Partner
Education: BA, Economics, New York University
Background: Founding Partner, LyonRoss Capital Management; Portfolio Manager, BEA Associates; Equity Research Analsyt, Lehman Brothers
Brian Sullivan, Advising Partner
Education: St. Johns University
Background: Founder and Executive Producer, Movie Loft Productions

1993 WINDHAM VENTURE PARTNERS
1325 Ave. of the Americas
27th Floor
New York, NY 10019

Phone: 212-763-8525
e-mail: info@windhamventures.com
web: www.windhamvp.com

Mission Statement: Windham Venture Partners takes advantage of its unique relationships to access and build disruptive life science companies that will change the healthcare industry.

Industry Group Preference: Healthcare, Medical Technology, Digital Health
Portfolio Companies: BehaveCare, Blueprint Health, Cartiva, ClarVista Medical, Coravin, CredSimple, CuraSeal, CureAtr, CVRx, Dots, Earlens, GlySens, Help Around, InSleep Technologies, Invuity, Locemia Solutions, mc10, Nebula Genomics, Neotract, Neuspera, NovellusDx, Novocure, Nuelle, Nuvaira, Personal Genome Diagnostics, Science Exchange, Tales2Go, VytronUs, WellDoc, Willow

Key Executives:
Adam E Fine, General Partner & CEO
Education: BA, Boston University; MBA, New York University
Background: VP & General Manager, I-many Inc.; Analyst, Cordis Corp.; Analyst, Coopers & Lybrand
Directorships: Coravin, GlySens, CuraSeal, HelpAround, SpineView, MC10, Holaira, VytronUS
Roger S Fine, General Partner & Chairman
Education: Columbia University; New York University School of Law
Background: VP & General Counsel, Johnson & Johnson

1994 WINDSPEED VENTURES
52 Waltham Street
Lexington, MA 02421

Phone: 781-860-8888 Fax: 781-860-0493
e-mail: info@wsventures.com
web: www.windspeed.com

Mission Statement: Actively helps build high technology companies, communications, security, media and internet services industries.

Geographic Preference: Northeast United States
Founded: 1999
Investment Criteria: Early-Stage
Industry Group Preference: Communications, Security, Media, Internet
Portfolio Companies: Active Network, Bradford Networks, BurstPoint Networks, Future Point Systems, Zipit Wireless, Apps.com, Bitfone, Fidelia Technology, Gracenote, OnFiber Communications, THINQ Learning Solutions, VistaPrint

Key Executives:
Daniel H Bathon Jr, General Partner/Chairman
Education: Villanova University
Background: Partner, Drexel Burnham Lambert; FINATECH Inc.
Directorships: Future Point Systems, BurstPoint Networks
John W Bullock, Managing Partner
Education: BS, Computer Science, Fitchburg State College
Background: Bay Networks; Wellfleet Communications; Development Engineer, Codex/Motorola Corp.
Directorships: Bradford Networks, BurstPoint Networks
Steven E Karlson, General Partner
Education: BS, Electrical Engineer, Brown University
Background: Co-Founder/President, Accordance Corporation; OpenWave; Data General Corporation
Directorships: Zipit Wireless

1995 WINDWARD VENTURES
San Diego, CA 92101

Phone: 619-435-5600
web: www.windwardventures.com

Mission Statement: A classic venture capital partnership organized to produce superior investment returns by providing capital and management assistance to early-stage, high growth companies. The firm manages a dedicated pool of capital provided by a group of institutional investors, individuals, and successful entrepreneurs; in addition, the firm occasionally manages direct investments on behalf of its limited partners. No longer making new investments.

Geographic Preference: Southern California
Fund Size: $90 million
Founded: 1997
Average Investment: $3 - $5 million
Minimum Investment: $250,000
Investment Criteria: Seed, Startup, First-Stage, Second-Stage, Early Stage, High Growth
Industry Group Preference: Data Communications, Electronic Technology, Semiconductors, Software, Internet Technology, Infrastructure, Medical Devices, Telecommunications
Portfolio Companies: Proximetry, SynergEyes, Syntricity

Other Locations:
PO Box 7688
Thousand Oaks, CA 91359
Phone: 805-499-7338

Key Executives:
David Titus, Managing Director
e-mail: titus@windwardventures.com
Education: BA, University of California, Santa Barbara
Background: General Partner/Managing Director Corporate Finance, Technology Funding; Co-Founder/Senior VP, Silicon Valley Bank
James A Cole, Managing Director
e-mail: cole@windwardventures.com
Background: Founding General Partner, Spectra Enterprise Associates; Partner, New Enterprise Associates; Co-Founder/Executive VP, Amplica
Directorships: Vitesse Semiconductor Corporation, Gigatronics

1996 WING VENTURE PARTNERS
2061 Avy Avenue
Second Floor
Menlo Park, CA 94025

Phone: 650-316-8300
e-mail: info@wing.vc
web: wing.vc

Mission Statement: A next generation venture capital firm. Our sole focus is the transformation of Business Technology. Businesses of all sizes are embracing Data, Mobile and Cloud. The DMC paradigm shift is reshaping every corner of IT.

Investment Criteria: Early-Stage
Industry Group Preference: Business Technology, Data & Analytics, Mobile Computing, Cloud Computing, Information Technology

Venture Capital & Private Equity Firms / Domestic Firms

Portfolio Companies: Blue Jeans Networks, Jasper Wireless, Cumulus Networks, Redback Networks, Opower, Nimble Storage

Key Executives:
Gaurav Garg, Founding Partner
Education: BS, MS, Electrical Engineering, BS, Computer Science, Washington University, St. Louis
Background: Partner, Sequoia Capital; Founder, Redback Networks; Synoptics; Bay Networks
Directorships: Ruckus Wireless, FireEye, Mobileiron, Jasper, Shape Security, Instart Logic, Cohesity, Netscaler
Peter Wagner, Founding Partner
Education: AB, Physics, Harvard College; MBA, Harvard Business School
Background: Managing Partner, Accel Partners; Line Manager, Silicon Graphics
Directorships: Blue Jeans Network, OPOWER, Qwilt, Cumulus Networks, Jut, Platfora, CloudPhysics, Primary Data

1997 WINGATE PARTNERS
750 N St. Paul
Suite 1200
Dallas, TX 75201

Phone: 214-720-1313 Fax: 214-871-8799
web: www.wingatepartners.com

Mission Statement: To purchase controlling equity interests in companies where there is the opportunity to create value through superior operational and strategic execution.

Fund Size: $200 million
Founded: 1987
Average Investment: $250 million
Minimum Investment: $25 million
Investment Criteria: Controlling equity investments in manufacturing, distribution and service businesses undergoing significant transition, with revenues between $50 million and $500 million
Industry Group Preference: Consumer Services, Distribution, Electronic Components, Electronic Technology, Industrial Equipment, Business to Business, Manufacturing
Portfolio Companies: Strata Worldwide, MPI Products, Nekoosa, Preferred Compounding, Western Marketing, Dunn Paper, Stein World, Sunrise Oilfield Supply, USA Environment, Cal Pacific

Key Executives:
Jay I Applebaum, Partner
Education: BBA, University of Texas
Background: Founded, Plexus Financial Services; Merger & Acquisitions, Salomon Brothers; Management, Arthur Andersen & Company
Directorships: Corrpro; Pro Parts Xpress; Loomis, Fargo & Company
James A Johnson, Partner
Education: BS Industrial Engineering, Stanford University; MBA, Stanford Grad. School of Business
Background: Principal, Booz, Allen & Hamilton
Directorships: Corrpro; AmerCable; S&N Communications; Redmand Building Products; Century Products; AmeriStat; United Stationers; Pro Parts Xpress; Kevco
Jason Reed, Partner
Education: BS Economics/Finance, Oklahoma State University; MS Finance, London School of Economics; MBA, Harvard Business School
Background: Case Leader, Boston Consulting Group
Directorships: ENSR; AmerCable/Corrpro

1998 WINKLEVOSS CAPITAL
e-mail: press@winklevosscapital.com
web: www.winklevosscapital.com

Mission Statement: At Winklevoss Capital, we believe in determined entrepreneurs. Risk-taking is just in their blood. By providing guidance, relationships and capital, we reinforce their pursuit of a frictionless world and a better human experience. Because those who dare to fail greatly, dare to achieve greatly.

Portfolio Companies: Addy, ALOHA, AngelList, Astro, August, Authy, Bitcoin, BoxC, Cabify, Cambrian Genomics, Carbon38, Cargomatic, Changetip, Fedora, FiscalNote, Flexport, Keepy, Kimono, Lenda, Matternet, Memebox, MeUndies, Minibar, One Month, Paddle8, Partender, People.co, Regalii, Shyp, Sumzero, Sunshine, Taptalk, Vero, Xapo, Zuli

Key Executives:
Tyler Winklevoss, Founder
Cameron Winklevoss, Founder

1999 WINNEBAGO SEED FUND
124 W Wisconsin Avenue
Suite 240F
Neenah, WI 54956

web: www.winnebagoseedfund.com

Mission Statement: Winnebago Seed Fund seeks to generate investor return by partnering with talented entrepreneurs in Wisconsin to rapidly grow their businesses.

Geographic Preference: Wisconsin
Founded: 2016
Industry Group Preference: Diversified

Key Executives:
David Trotter, Managing Director
Education: BS, Marquette University

2000 WINONA CAPITAL MANAGEMENT
980 North Michigan Avenue
Suite 1950
Chicago, IL 60611

Phone: 312-334-8800 Fax: 312-223-9484
e-mail: info@winonacapital.com
web: www.winonacapital.com

Mission Statement: Winona Capital Management is a unique private investment firm. We create lasting value by investing in consumer driven businesses operating in the lower end of the middle market.

Fund Size: $125 million
Industry Group Preference: Consumer Products, Consumer Services
Portfolio Companies: Boloco, CIRCA, Fusion Education Group, Johnny's Fine Foods, KJUS, Petsense, Top Driver
Luke Reese, Managing Director
e-mail: lreese@winonacapital.com
Education: DePauw University, University of Michigan Law School
Background: Senior Manager, Amer Sports; Corporate Law, Lathan & Watkins
Directorships: Peter Millar, Dragon Alliance, Johnny's Fine Foods, Top Driver
Laird Koldyke, Managing Director
e-mail: lkoldyke@winonacapital.com
Education: Northwestern University; Kellogg Graduate School of Management
Background: Founding Partner, Triple Tree Capital; General Partner, Frontenac Company
Directorships: Chipolte Mexican Grille, Einstein's Bagels, Wild Oats Markets, Home Fashions, Marks Bros. Jewelers, Leewards Crafts
Jason Sowers, Director
e-mail: jsowers@winonacapital.com
Education: Amherst College; MBA, University of Chicago Booth School of Business
Background: Global Strategic & Commercial Intelligence Group, KPMG
Directorships: Dragon Alliance

Venture Capital & Private Equity Firms / Domestic Firms

2001 WIREFRAME VENTURES
San Francisco, CA

web: www.wireframevc.com

Mission Statement: Wireframe Ventures seeks mission-driven entrepreneurs emerging in constantly growing tech industry.

Founded: 2016
Industry Group Preference: Technology, Fintech, Healthcare, Wellness
Portfolio Companies: Assurex Health, Astronomer, DNAnexus, Full Harvest, Geneticure, Level 10 Energy, Mammoth Biosciences, Misty Robotics, Near Space Labs, OpenInvest, Palantir, Renew Financial, Reverie Labs, Xtelligent

Key Executives:
  Harsh Patel, Co-Founder/Managing Partner
  Education: BS, University of Illinois; MBA, Stanford Grad. School of Business
  Background: Manager, Accenture; Co-Founder/CTO, Orbit Commerce Inc.; General Partner, RRE Ventures; President, Bina Technologies; General Partner, Claremont Creek Ventures; Affiliate, Webb Investment Network
  Directorships: CareMessage; DNAnexus; Assurex Health; NuMedii

2002 WISCONSIN INVESTMENT PARTNERS
PO Box 45919
Madison, WI 53744

Phone: 608-692-7481
e-mail: info@wisinvpartners.com
web: www.wisinvpartners.com

Mission Statement: Wisconsin Investment Partners is a life science- and technology-focused angel investment firm.

Geographic Preference: Wisconsin
Founded: 2000
Investment Criteria: Early Stage
Industry Group Preference: Life Sciences, Technology
Portfolio Companies: AquaMost, Aver Informatics, BeeKeeper Labs, BellBrook Labs, Biolonix, Carson Life, Cellectar, ConjuGon, Deltanoid Pharmaceuticals, Forward Health Group, HarQen, Health eFilings, Invenra, iVMD, Kiio, Lumec, Madison Vaccines, Murfie, Needls, NeoClone, nPoint, OptiMine, Phoenix Nuclear Labs, Pinpoint Software, Quintessence Biosciences, SHINE Medical Technologies, Silatronix, Skin Analytics, Snowshoe Stamps, SOLOMO, Stemina Biomarker Discovery, Stratatech Corporation, Swallow Solutions, TrackIF, Virent, Xolve, Zurex Pharma Inc.

Key Executives:
  Brad Bodden, Co-Manager
  Education: University of Washington
  Michael Thorson, Co-Manager
  Education: BS, Economics, United States Military Academy; Brasenose College, Univ. of Oxford
  Background: Founder & Managing Director, Inventure Capital; Bank of America, London; President, Banc of America Securities, Japan; Soros Funds Limited; Bankers Trust Company
  Bob Wood, Co-Manager
  Background: Space-Metrics; American Players Theatre
  Andrea Dlugos, Co-Manager
  Background: Project Manager; Business Analyst; Financial Analyst

2003 WOMEN'S VENTURE CAPITAL FUND
9720 Wilhire Boulevard
Fifth Floor
Beverly Hills, CA 90212

Phone: 323-496-6424
e-mail: monica@womensvcfund.com
web: www.womensvcfund.com

Mission Statement: The Fund capitalizes on the expanding pipeline of women entrepeneurs leading gender diverse teams and creating capital efficient, high growth companies in digital media and sustainable products and services. We believe that this unique investment strategy now provides the potential for extraordinary returns.

Industry Group Preference: Digital Media & Marketing, Environment, Mobile, Social Media
Portfolio Companies: OMNI Retail Group, EdSurge, NVoicePay, Proxio, Ivycorp
  Edith Dorsen, Founder & Managing Director
  e-mail: edith@womensvcfund.com
  Education: BS, Economics, Wharton School; MBA, Harvard Business School; MPA, Kennedy School of Government
  Background: Business Development, Children's Television Workshop; Investment Banking, Salomon Brothers; McKinsey & Company

2004 WOODBRIDGE GROUP
1764 Litchfield Turnpike
Suite 250
New Haven, CT 06525

Toll-Free: 800-567-1119
e-mail: headquarters@woodbridgegrp.com
web: www.woodbridgegrp.com

Mission Statement: To professionally represent middle market companies in the mergers and acquisitions arena.

Geographic Preference: Worldwide
Investment Criteria: Middle-market companies with $5 to $100 million in revenue
Industry Group Preference: Business Products & Services, Consumer Products, Distribution, Franchising, Logistics, Manufacturing, Software, Waste & Recycling

Key Executives:
  Robert Koenig, Chief Executive Officer
  e-mail: robert@woodbridgegrp.com
  Background: President, Koenig Corporation
  Donald A Krier, Senior Managing Director/Partner
  e-mail: donald@woodbridgegrp.com
  Education: BS in Business/Systems, Taylor University
  Larry Reinharz, Senior Managing Director/Partner
  Education: BA, Political Science & Economics, Manhattanville College
  Background: Commercial Finance, JP Morgan Chase; Merrill Lynch

2005 WOODSIDE FUND
303 Twin Dolphin Rive
Suite 600
Redwood Shores, CA 94065

Phone: 650-610-8050 Fax: 650-610-8051
e-mail: info@woodsidefund.com

Mission Statement: Woodside Fund is a venture capital firm. The firm has grown to four funds and over $110 million under management. The Fund is distinctive in that each partner has founded, built and served as CEO in at least one company prior to joining the Fund. As former entrepreneurs, we understand the difficulties of raising venture capital and the challenges of launching a new enterprise. Our practical knowledge and firsthand experience enable us to develop unusually close, long-term relationships with the founders and managers of our portfolio companies. As a result, we typically serve as the lead investor and have co-founded a number of our portfolio companies. We also balance our early-stage emphasis with selective investments in emerging companies.

Fund Size: $110 million
Founded: 1983
Average Investment: $5-10 million
Investment Criteria: Seed, Startup, First-stage, Second-stage

Industry Group Preference: Biotechnology, Software, Electronic Technology, Energy, Natural Resources, Industrial Services, Medical & Health Related, Networking, Telecommunications, Semiconductors, Enterprise Software
Portfolio Companies: Analogix Semiconductor, APX, Aristos Logic, Athena Design, Azaire Networks, BeFree, Berkeley Design Automation, Borderware, Conexant Systems, Evans & Sutherland, Firepond, Intalio, Intellefex, Intelligent Markets, InterTrust, Matisse Networks, Merant, Nanoconduction, New Era of Networks, Novell, Onsite Systems, SS8 Networks, DMC Stratex Networks, Stream Processors, Tacit Software, Veriware, Zenverge, PowerReviews

Key Executives:
  Vincent M Occhipinti, Co-Founder, Managing Director
  Education: Graduate, Stanford University and Graduate School of Business, University of California, Berkeley
  Background: Founder, President, & CEO, Logisticon Inc.; Vice President of Marketing, Mobility Systems
  Robert E Larson, Co-Founder, Managing Partner
  Education: BS, MIT; Master of Science and PhD Degrees, Electrical Engineering, Stanford Unviersity
  Background: Co-Founder, President, & CEO, Systems Control; President, International Institute of Electrical & Electronic Engineers
  Directorships: Consulting Professor, Stanford University - Engineering/Economic Systems Department

2006 WORK-BENCH
110 Fifth Avenue
5th Floor
New York, NY 10011

Phone: 646-494-6231
e-mail: hello@work-bench.com
web: www.work-bench.com

Mission Statement: A venture capital firm investing in early-stage startups in the field of enterprise software.

Founded: 2012
Investment Criteria: Series A & B
Industry Group Preference: Big Data & Analytics, Cloud Native Infrastructure, Data-Defined Security
Portfolio Companies: Algorithmia, Alluvium, Blacktrace, Cockroach Labs, Core OS, Dialpad, Merlon Intelligence, Metric Insights, RA EL, Socure, Tamr, Trapezoid, True, UpLevel, UpSkill, vArmour, Versive, VTS, X.

Key Executives:
  Jonathan Lehr, Co-Founder/General Partner
  Education: BSE, Bioengineering, University of Pennsylvania
  Background: Founder, NY Enterprise Technology Meetup; IT, Morgan Stanley
  Jessica Lin, Co-Founder/General Partner
  Education: BA, Government & African Studies, Harvard University
  Background: Learning & Development Manager, Cisco Systems

2007 WRF CAPITAL
2815 Eastlake Avenue E
Suite 300
Seattle, WA 98102

Phone: 206-336-5600
e-mail: info@wrfcapital.com
web: www.wrfseattle.org

Mission Statement: Manages Washington Research Foundation's seed venture fund by creating and investing primarily in technology-based start-up companies that have strong ties to the University of Washington and other non-profit research institutions in Washington State.

Geographic Preference: Washington
Founded: 1981
Average Investment: $1-$2 million
Minimum Investment: $500,000
Investment Criteria: Early Stage
Industry Group Preference: Biomedical, Biotechnology, Infrastructure, Information Technology, Advanced Materials, Healthcare, Industrial Services, Software, Internet
Portfolio Companies: AbSci, Accelerator Corp., Accium Biosciences, Acylin Therapeutics, Alder Biopharmaceuticals, AnswerDash, Apogen, AppAttach, Aqueduct, Arzeda Corp., Bellwether Bio, Cardeas Pharma, Cardiac Insight, Corensic, EnerG2, Epithany, Faraday, FlexMinder, GlobeImmune, Groove Biopharma, Group14, Hyperion Therpeutics, Ikaria, Juno Therapeutics, MicroGREEN Polymers, Mirador Biomedical, Mobisante, Modumetal, Nexgenia, Nimbic, NLIGHT, Nohla, Oncofactor, One Radio, Phase Genomics, Phytelligence, Protemo, Qazzow, Resolve Therapeutics, Rodeo Therapeutics, Shippable, Skytap, SNUPI Technologies, Targeted Growth, TransformativeMed, Uptake Medical, VLST, Wibotic

Key Executives:
  Ronald S Howell, CEO
  Education: BS, Biochemistry, Washington State University
  Background: Medical sales and operations
  Jeff Eby, CFO
  Education: AB/B.Arch, Rice University; MBA, Finance & Accounting, Northwestern University's Kellogg Graduate School of Management
  Background: CFO, Seattle Art Museum; Consultant, Arthur Andersen & Christopher J. Brown and Associates
  Loretta Little, Managing Director
  Education: AB, Zoology, Pomona College; MA, Business Administration, University of Arizona
  Background: Marketing Manager/Market Consultant
  William J Canestaro, Managing Director
  Education: AB, Dartmouth College; MSc, Oxford University; PhD, University of Washington
  Background: National Pharmaceutical Council; Genetech; AstraZeneca
  Directorships: Arzeda, Bellwether Bio, Phase Genomics, Icosavax, EpiThany, Wibotic

2008 WYNNCHURCH CAPITAL
6250 North River Road
Suite 10-100
Rosemont, IL 60018

Phone: 847-604-6100 Fax: 847-604-6105
Toll-Free: 877-604-6111
web: www.wynnchurch.com

Mission Statement: To partner with management by capitalizing on the company's strength to achieve revenue growth and profit improvement.

Geographic Preference: United States, Canada
Fund Size: $500 million
Founded: 1999
Investment Criteria: Buyouts, Corporate Carve-Outs, Recapitalizations, Joint Ventures, Restructurings, Growth Capital, Going Private, Bankruptcies
Industry Group Preference: Niche Manufacturing, Distribution, Transportation, Logistics, Energy, Power Technologies, Business Products & Services, Industrial Services
Portfolio Companies: Burtek Enterprises, Calyx Transportation Group, Fabco Automotive, Foss Manufacturing Company, Groupe Moreau, Henniges Automotice Holdings, Indiana Limestone Company, Ironform Holdings, JAC Products, Loadmaster Derrick & Equipment, Northstar Aerospace, Pro-Fab Group, Senco Brands, Surepoint Technologies Group, United States Pipe and Foundry Company, US Manufacturing Corporation, Vista-Pro Automotive, Wolverine Advanced Materials

Other Locations:
  2121 Rosecrans Avenue
  Suite 2370

Venture Capital & Private Equity Firms / Domestic Firms

El Segundo, CA 90245
Phone: 310-492-4068

Wynnchurch Capital Canada LLC
150 York Street
Suite 801
Toronto, ON M5H 3S5
Canada
Phone: 416-363-1423
Key Executives:
John A. Hatherly, Managing Partner
e-mail: jhatherly@wynnchurch.com
Education: BA, University of Notre Dame; MBA, University of Wisconsin
Background: Senior Executive, GE Capital; First National Bank of Chicago
Directorships: Android Industries, Connection Concepts, SafeWorks, Calyx Transporation Group, 4Front Engineered Solutions, The Surepoint Group
Duncan S. Bourne, Managing Director
847-604-6104
e-mail: dbourne@wynnchurch.com
Education: BS, Chemical Engineering, Northwestern University; MBA, University of Chicago
Background: Parter, BDO Seidman LLP; Senior Manager, Ernst & Young
Steve M. Welborn, Managing Director
847-604-6129
e-mail: swelborn@wynnchurch.com
Education: BSBA, Finance, University of Missouri; MBA, St. Louis University
Background: COO, Gateway Marketing International; AT&T; Adams Harris Inc.
Morty White, Managing Director
416-363-1423
e-mail: mwhite@wynnchurch.com
Education: BComm, McGill University; MBA, University of Michigan
Background: GE Capital

2009 XG VENTURES

e-mail: info@xg-ventures.com
web: www.xg-ventures.com

Mission Statement: XG Ventures was founded in March 2008 by ex-Googlers, who were early hires in strategic roles at Google. Pietro Dova and Andrea Zurek are the managing members of XG Ventures and are dedicated to advising and investing in supremely talented early stage teams. We learned a great deal at Google, including how its unique culture shaped a dynamic and fun enterprise. Together, with our complementary expertise, our goal is to help successfully guide the start-up teams, in which we invest and advise, to the next stage. We provide operational and strategic expertise, mentorship, global networking contacts, and access to seed capital and beyond.

Founded: 2008
Investment Criteria: Early-Stage
Industry Group Preference: Consumer Internet, Mobile, Gaming, Social Media, Digital Media & Marketing
Portfolio Companies: AdStage, AirHelp, Altitude, Apiary.io, Apptimize, Blend, Chartboost, Chobo Labs, Dealflicks, eShares, Euclid, Facecake, Glympse, Graffiti Labs, Kamcord, Keen IO, Kloudless, LivBlends, Mighty Meeting, MNectar, Mylikes, NoRedInk, nWay, OLSet, PicCollage, Piqora, Pogoseat, Prediction IO, Rapt Media, Rockbot, Science Exchange, Shift, Shots, Shyp, Small Demons, Starmaker, Tangible Play, Tapsense, Telly, Thanx, Thirdlove, Tok.tv, Tsumobi, Tynker, Verious, Wizeline, Wish, Yango.com, Zesta, Zuli
Key Executives:
Pietro Dova, Partner
Education: Civil Engineering, Imperial College; MS, Management, MIT Sloan School of Management
Background: Corporate Controller & Finance Director, Google

Andrea Zurek, Partner
Background: Google, Computerworld

2010 XSEED CAPITAL MANAGEMENT
3130 Alpine Road
Suite 200
Portola Valley, CA 94028

Phone: 650-331-1230
e-mail: info@xseedcap.com
web: www.xseedcap.com

Mission Statement: Founded in 2006 as one of the pioneers of the new venture industry, XSeed Capital works with entrepreneurs to build differentiated technology startups that dramatically change markets. We are serial entrepreneurs who appreciate the dedication, passion, anxiety and sleepless nights it takes to build something valuable from scratch.

Fund Size: $110 million
Founded: 2006
Investment Criteria: Seed-Stage
Industry Group Preference: Information Technology, Clean Technology, Life Sciences
Portfolio Companies: StackStorm, Cirro Secure, Trifacta, Zooz, @Scale, Chatous, Lex Machina, Biota Technology, Citrine, Cape Productions, Dispatcher, Breezeworks, DropThought, Neon, BrightBox, Sipx, The League, Pixlee, Playnomics, GeneWeave, ZipLine Medical, HMicro, Allopartis, MuseAmi, OpxBio, Siva
Key Executives:
Michael Borrus, Founding General Partner
e-mail: mborrus@xseedcap.com
Education: BA, Princeton University; MA, UC Berkeley; JD, Harvard Law School
Background: Technology Banking, The Petkevich Group; Adjunct Professor, UC Berkeley's College of Engineering
Rob Siegel, General Partner
e-mail: rsiegel@xseedcap.com
Education: BA, UC Berkeley; MBA, Stanford University
Background: General Manager, GE Security; EVP, Pixim; Co-Founder & CEO, Weave Innovations
Alan Chiu, Partner
e-mail: dhanzel@xseedcap.com
Education: BASc, Electrical & Computer Engineering, University of British Columbia; MS, Management, Stanford Graduate School of Business
Background: Vice President, Product Marketing & Reagent Development, Pacific Biosciences; Principal Scientist, Molecular Dynamics
Jeff Thermond, Venture Partner
e-mail: jthermond@xseedcap.com
Education: BA, Philosophy & Psychology, Yale University; MBA, Marketing, Indiana University
Background: CEO, Woven Systems; CEO, Epigram; VP & General Manager, 3Com
Damon Cronkey, Partner
Background: SurveyMonkey; Yahoo

2011 Y COMBINATOR
335 Pioneer Way
Mountain View, CA 94041

web: www.ycombinator.com

Mission Statement: Y Combinator funds large numbers of startups in two batches each year, in winter and summer.

Founded: 2005
Average Investment: $120K
Investment Criteria: Seed
Industry Group Preference: Web/Mobile Applications
Portfolio Companies: Stripe, Vidyard, Optimizely, Checkr, Coinbase, PlanGrid, Weebly, Gusto, DoorDash, Clever, LendUp, Dropbox, Teespring, Mixpanel, Machine Zone, Segment, CoreOS, Twitch, Reddit, FiveStars, Genius, Tilt, Docker, Matterport, Airbnb, PagerDuty, Memebox, Heroku, WePay, Instacart

Venture Capital & Private Equity Firms / Domestic Firms

Key Executives:
   Jessica Livingston, Co-Founder
   Education: Bucknell University
   Background: Adams Harkness

2012 YELLOWSTONE CAPITAL
1177 West Loop S.
Suite 1425
Houston, TX 77027

            Phone: 713-650-0065 **Fax:** 713-650-0055
            e-mail: info@yellowstonecapital.com
            web: www.yellowstonecapital.com

Mission Statement: A Houston-based, private equity and venture capital investment firm, focused on acquiring and/or investing in small to medium-sized businesses.
Geographic Preference: North America, Europe, Middle East, Asia
Founded: 1993
Investment Criteria: Buy-outs
Industry Group Preference: Energy Technology, Industrial Manufacturing, Healthcare, Life Sciences, Food & Beverage
Key Executives:
   Omar A Sawaf, Chairman/CEO
   Education: BA, Ohio State University; MBA, Harvard University
   Background: President, Capital Guidance Corporation
   Sami Sawaf, Principal
   Education: BBA, MBA, Methodist University
   Background: Director, FTI Corporate Finance; MENA Solar Energy; White River Energy

2013 YES VC
San Francisco, CA

            e-mail: partners@yes.vc
            web: yes.vc

Mission Statement: Yes VC is an pre-seed and seed-stage venture capital firm investing in infrastructure, internet, and other technologies.
Geographic Preference: United States, Europe
Fund Size: $50 million
Founded: 2018
Average Investment: $250,000 - $1 million
Minimum Investment: $250,000
Industry Group Preference: Technology, Infrastructure, Internet, Applications, Security, AI
Portfolio Companies: Gaze, Orchid, Spell
Key Executives:
   Caterina Fake, Co-Founder
   Education: BA, English, Vassar College
   Background: Co-Founder, Flickr; Co-Founder, Hunch
   Jyri Engestrom, Co-Founder
   Education: MA, University of Helsinki; PhD, Lancaster University
   Background: Senior Product Manager, Internet Handhelds, Nokia; Product Manager, Google; Co-Founder/Chairman, Jaiku; Co-Founder/CEO, Ditto.me; Director of Product Management, Groupon; Head of Product, Boosted Inc.; Entrepreneur in Residence, True Ventures
   Directorships: ICEYE

2014 YORK STREET CAPITAL PARTNERS LLC
Bedminster, NJ 07921

            e-mail: golding@yorkstreetcapital.com

Mission Statement: An investment firm that provides mezzanine and equity capital to private equity sponsors for acquisitions, buyouts, growth capital and recapitalizations of middle market companies.
Geographic Preference: United States
Fund Size: $557 million
Founded: 2002
Average Investment: $10-$35 million
Minimum Investment: $10 million
Investment Criteria: Acquistions, Buyouts, Growth Capital, Recapitalizations, Mezzanine
Industry Group Preference: Healthcare, Manufacturing, Industrial Services, Consumer Products, Food & Beverage
Portfolio Companies: Bare Escentuals, Brickman Group, Easton-Bell Sports, Hudson Products, i2, Lexington Home Brands, Managed Health Care Associates, MD Beauty, Miller Heiman, Motorsport Aftermarket Group, Neptune Technology Group, Panther Expedited Services, Performance, Powermat, Prestige Brands International, River Ranch Fresh Foods, Sunshine Restaurant Partners, Targus Group International, World Health Club
Key Executives:
   Robert M Golding, Managing Partner
   908-658-3714
   e-mail: golding@yorkstreetcapital.com
   Education: BA, Trinity College
   Background: Managing Director, CIT's Corporate Finance Group; Salomon Brothers; Merrill Lynch; Irving Trust Company
   Directorships: Lexington Furniture, Easton-Bell Sports, Miller Heiman, Panther Expedited Services, Performance, Targus Group International
   Christopher A Layden, Managing Partner
   908-658-3713
   e-mail: layden@yorkstreetcapital.com
   Education: BA, Fairfield University; MBA, The George Washington University
   Background: Senior Director/Founding Member, CIT's Corporate Finance Group; Reuben H. Donnelly Corp.; Xerox Credit Corporation
   Directorships: Targus Group International
   Logan V. O'Connor, Vice President
   908-658-9944
   e-mail: logal@yorkstreetcapital.com
   Education: B.A. Economics, Trinity College
   Background: Targus Group International, Lexington Furniture, World Health Club

2015 YUCAIPA COMPANIES
Los Angeles, CA

            Phone: 310-789-7200
            e-mail: investorrelations@yucaipaco.com
            web: www.yucaipaco.com

Mission Statement: A premier investment firm that has established a record of fostering economic value through the growth and responsible development of companies.
Founded: 1986
Key Executives:
   Ron Burkle, Managing Partner

2016 ZELKOVA VENTURES
667 Madison Avenue
New York, NY 10065

            web: www.zelkovavc.com

Mission Statement: At Zelkova Ventures, we are passionate about assisting in the growth of businesses. We roll up our sleeves and partner with our portfolio companies for success. Zelkova Ventures is a venture capital firm committed to helping talented entrepreneurs build incredible companies. Primarily we look to invest in early stage companies, many times pre-revenue. In many instances we provide a company's first outside/institutional capital. As former entrepreneurs, we understand the highs and lows of launching a new company. We look to take an active role and partner with the companies we invest in. Along with our capital Zelkova brings expertise, insight and execution to all of our portfolio companies.
Investment Criteria: Early-Stage
Industry Group Preference: SaaS, Internet, Media, Green Technology

Venture Capital & Private Equity Firms / Domestic Firms

Portfolio Companies: Ribbit, Locus Energy, Crimson Hexagon, My Damn Channel, Fynaz, Altruik, Encoding.com, JIBE, Livefyre, Kapost, Fab.com, GameChanger, Kohort, Spring Metrics, GreenGoose, FullContact, HelpScout, RedRover, BrandYourself, Ambassador, Dispatch.io, Space Monkey, Lettuce, RJ Metrics, Reachli, Customer.io, Postmaster, Crowdly, FlyCleaners

Key Executives:
   Jay Levy, Partner
   Education: Rutgers University
   Background: Morgan Stanley; Founder, MPI Professionals; Founding Partner, Trueview Services
   Larry Scheinfeld, Partner
   Background: Principal, Quellos Group; Partner, Uproot Wines

2017 ZEPHYR MANAGEMENT LP
12 E 49th Street
41st Floor
New York, NY 10017

Phone: 212-508-9400 **Fax:** 212-508-9494
web: www.zmlp.com

Mission Statement: Zephyr Management LP is a global private equity and marketable securities firm. The firm specializes in the creation and management of highly focused and value added investment funds. Since its founding, Zephyr has sponsored twenty-two investment funds representing approximately $1.8 billion in capital commitments. Each Zephyr fund has a discrete management team which has skills matched to the particular investment opportunity.

Geographic Preference: Asia, Africa, Latin America, Europe, Middle East
Fund Size: $1 billion
Founded: 1994
Investment Criteria: Consolidations, Management Buy-outs, Recapitaizations, Growth Capital
Industry Group Preference: Diversified

Other Locations:
   1st Floor, Aleph Primero
   613, 12th Main Rd, Hal 2nd Stage
   Indiranagar, Bengaluru
   Karnataka 560008
   India
   Phone: 91-80-4681-8300

   No. 48/5/1 (West Wing)
   Parkway Building
   Park Street
   Colombo 2
   Sri Lanka
   Phone: 94-11-2303810 **Fax:** 94-11-2303811

Key Executives:
   Thomas C. Barry, Founder & Chair
   Education: MBA, Harvard Business School; BA, Latin American Studies, Yale University
   Background: President/CEO, Rockefeller & Company; President, T. Rowe Price; CFA, Institute of Chartered Financial Analysts
   Mukul Gulati, Managing Partner
   Education: BA, Economics, University of Maryland; MBA, Columbia Business School
   Background: VP of Quantitative Research, Reuters
   Directorships: Multex
   Stephen E. Canter, Managing Director
   Education: AB, Cornell University; MBA, Columbia University Gradudate School of Business
   Background: Chairman & CEO, The Dreyfus Corporation; Vice Chairman, Mellon Financial Corporation

2018 ZETTA VENTURE PARTNERS
473 Jackson Street
Suite 200
San Francisco, CA 94111

e-mail: info@zettavp.com
web: www.zettavp.com

Mission Statement: Zetta Venture Partners is a tech-based venture capital firm with a specialty in Artificial Intelligence.

Average Investment: $1-3 million
Minimum Investment: $1 million
Industry Group Preference: Artificial Intelligence, Technology
Portfolio Companies: Allure Security, Aptology, Clearbit, Constructor, Crate.io, Domino Data Lab, Domo, Dor, Falkonry, Finite State, Focal Systems, FollowAnalytics, Galley, InsideSales.com, Invenia, Kaggle, Lilt, Marketing Evolution, Myia, Opsani, OptiMine, Promethium, Rever, Test.ai, Tractable, Verusen, VideaHealth

Key Executives:
   Mark Gorenberg, Managing Director
   Education: BS, MIT; MS, University of Minnesota; MS, Standford University
   Background: Sun Microsystems
   Ash Fontana, Managing Director
   Education: University of Sydney
   Background: Co-Founded, Topguest; Private Equity Analyst, MacQuarie Capital
   Jocelyn Goldfein, Managing Director
   Education: BS, Stanford University
   Background: Software Engineer, Facebook; Software Engineer, VMware

2019 ZM CAPITAL
19 West 44th Street
18th Floor
New York, NY 10036

Phone: 212-223-1383 **Fax:** 212-223-1384
web: zmclp.com

Mission Statement: ZM Capital is the private equity investment fund of ZelnickMedia. The fund invests in media companies in which the partnership's capital resources, industry contacts and operational experience can meaningfully enhance growth and value.

Industry Group Preference: Media, Software, Publishing, Advertising, Direct Marketing, Networking & Equipment, Marketing, Music
Portfolio Companies: 9 Story Limited, Airvana, Alloy, Cannella Response Television, Cast & Crew, ITN Networks, Take-Two Interactive

Key Executives:
   Strauss Zelnick, Co-Founder
   Education: BA, Wesleyan University; JD, Harvard Law School; MBA, Harvard Business School
   Background: President & CEO, BMG Entertainment; President & CEO, Crystal Dynamics; President & CEO, 20th Century Fox
   Directorships: Take Two Interactive Software
   Karl Slatoff, Managing Partner
   Education: BA, Kenyon College; MBA, Harvard Business School
   Background: Vice President, New Media, BMG Entertainment; Strategic Planning, Walt Disney Company
   Directorships: Cannella Response Television
   Jordan Turkewitz, Managing Partner/Chief Investment Officer
   Education: BA, Government, Cornell University; MBA, Columbia Business School
   Background: Senior Director, Acquisitions, JupiterMedia Corporation; Associate, Merrill Lynch
   Andrew Vogel, Managaing Partner/Chief Investment Officer
   Education: BA, Mathematics & Economics, Wesleyan

Venture Capital & Private Equity Firms / Domestic Firms

University; MBA, Harvard Business School
Background: Ripplewood Holdings; McCown De Leeuw & Co.; Lehman Brothers

2020 ZONE VENTURES
2882 Sand Hill Road
Suite 150
Menlo Park, CA 94025

Phone: 650-233-9000
web: www.zonevc.com

Mission Statement: A partnership funded by institutional investors for the purpose of providing equity capital to young, high growth companies, while achieving superior returns to its investors.

Geographic Preference: United States, California
Fund Size: $135 million
Founded: 1998
Average Investment: $1-$2 million
Minimum Investment: $1 million
Investment Criteria: Seed, First Stage
Industry Group Preference: Software, Communications, Information Technology, Manufacturing, Media, Wireless Technologies, Networking, Technology
Portfolio Companies: 3GA, Advanced, Akimbo Systems, Allpets.com, Biger Boat, Copper Key, Digital Campaigns, DivX, eStyle, hiwire, Lumexis, Microfabrica, Neven Vision, Showbizdata, Siimpel, Traffic Station, Vizional, Zkey.com, Zone Reactor

Key Executives:
Frank M. Creer, Founder/Managing Director
Education: Finance, University of Utah
Directorships: Akimbo; DivX; emWare; e-Style; Packet Air Networks; Vizional Technologies; ZKey
Dr. N. Darius Sankey, Partner
Education: BS, Physics & Electrical Engineering, MIT; PhD, Optical Engineering, The Institute of Optics at the University of Rochester
Background: Management Consultant, McKinsey & Company; Rand, At&T Bell Laboratories; Adju
William Lewis, Partner
Education: BS, Engineering Physics, University of California, Berkeley; MS, PhD, Materials Science & Engineering, Stanford University
Background: JP Morgan, Intevac

Timothy Draper, Founder/Managing Director
Education: BS, Electrical Engineering, Stanford University; MBA, Harvard Business School

2021 ZS FUND LP
1133 Avenue of the Americas
New York, NY 10036

Phone: 212-398-6200 **Fax:** 212-398-1808
web: www.zsfundlp.com

Mission Statement: A private equity firm engaged in making long-term investments in successful middle-market companies.

Geographic Preference: United States
Fund Size: $150 million
Founded: 1985
Minimum Investment: $5 million
Investment Criteria: LBO, MBO
Industry Group Preference: Business to Business, Consumer Products, Distribution, Retailing, Instrumentation, Medical & Health Related, Insurance, Industrial Equipment
Portfolio Companies: Casabella Holdings, ECS Refining, Industrial Air Tool, L.P., Research Horizons, SOS Security, Transervice Logistics

Key Executives:
Ned Sherwood, Co-Founder
e-mail: nsherwood@zsfundlp.com
Education: Wharton School at the University of Pennsylvania
Background: Principal, AEA Investors; VP, W.R. Grace & Company; Assistant to President, Hazeltine Corporation
Shahzad Pirvani
e-mail: spirvani@zsfundlp.com
Education: BBA, University of Warwick; University of Georgia
Background: Battery Ventures; Blackford Capital; Arctaris Impact Investors
Bob Horne
e-mail: bhorne@zsfundlp.com
Education: BA, Harvard College; MBA, Stanford Graduate School of Business
Background: Vice President, Salomon Brothers
Nick Burger
e-mail: nburger@zsfundlp.com
Education: BA, Yale University
Background: Analyst, Merrill Lynch; MLC Funds Management

Canadian Firms

2022 32 DEGREES CAPITAL
635 8th Avenue SW
Suite 650
Calgary, AB T2P 3M3
Canada

Phone: 403-695-1069 Fax: 403-695-1069
e-mail: info@32degrees.ca
web: www.32degrees.ca

Mission Statement: Private equity firm focused on developing crude oil and natural gas reserves and production.

Geographic Preference: Canada, United States
Fund Size: $105 million
Founded: 2004
Average Investment: $5 - $25 million
Investment Criteria: Early-Stage
Industry Group Preference: Oil & Gas
Portfolio Companies: Sphere Energy, Corval Energy, Sitka Exploration, Canamax Energy, Western Oilfield Equipment Rentals, Core Line Pipe, HPC Energy Services, Vertex Resource Group, Artis Exploration, Rising Star Resources, Summerland Energy, Karve Energy

Key Executives:
  Larry Evans, Founder & Managing Partner
  Education: University of Manitoba
  Background: Glacier Energy; Ice Energy; Avalanche Energy; Colony Energy
  Directorships: Artis Exploration; Corval Energy; Vertex Resource Group
  Mitch Putnam, Founder & Managing Partner
  Education: University of Alberta
  Background: Glacier Energy; Ice Energy; Avalanche Energy; Colony Energy
  Directorships: Canamax Energy; Summerland Energy; Karve Energy; Rising Star Resources; Sitka Exploration; HPC Energy Services
  Trent Baker, Managing Partner
  Education: Queen's University
  Background: KPMG
  Directorships: Vertex Resource Group; CORE Linepipe; Sphere Energy

2023 4FRONT CAPITAL PARTNERS
47 Colborne Street
Suite 303
Toronto, ON M5E 1P8
Canada

Phone: 416-861-1100
web: www.4frontcapitalpartners.com

Mission Statement: 4Front Capital Partners us an independent investment bank focused on the growth of their companies in knowledge-based industries.

Key Executives:
  John Travaglini, Chief Executive Officer
  Education: Wilfred Laurier University
  Raj Natarajan, Partner/Vice President
  Education: MBA, University of Toronto
  Mark Kennedy, Managing Director
  Education: Wilfred Laurier University; MBA, York University

2024 500 STARTUPS CANADA
Calgary, AB
Canada

web: 500canada.ca

Mission Statement: Seed stage venture capital fund.

Geographic Preference: Canada
Fund Size: $30 million
Founded: 2017
Investment Criteria: Early-Stage, Seed
Portfolio Companies: AmpMe, ApplyBoard, Attendease, Avidbots, BenchSci, Chatkit, Chatter Research, Creative Market, Cot Blockchain Music, Element AI, Finaeo, Fluent.ai, Homigo, Humi HR, Hysko, Innerspace, Keatext, Knotet, Local Logic, Logojoy, Lumotune, Mejuri, Meya.ai, Motorleaf, NestReady, Obie.ai, Play the Future, reDock, Shoelace, Smart Reno, Synervoz, Swept, Unito, Urbanlogiq, WayPay, Welltrack

2025 7 GATE VENTURES
68 Water Street
Suite 401
Vancouver, BC V6B 1A4
Canada

e-mail: info@7gate.vc
web: 7gate.vc

Mission Statement: 7 Gate Ventures funds technical founders to help them grow into billion-user companies.

Founded: 2015

Other Locations:
  2 Embarcadero Center
  8th Floor
  San Francisco, CA 94111

Key Executives:
  Amir Vohooshi, Founding Managing Partner
  Background: Founder, Beeptunes.com; Founder/CEO, Rahnema
  Alireza Rahnema, Managing Partner
  Education: BSc, McGill University; MBA, Schulich School of Business
  Background: Co-Founder, ALCK Entertainment

2026 ACCESS CAPITAL CORPORATION
3080 Yonge St.
Suite 4070
Toronto, ON M4N 3N1
Canada

Phone: 416-366-4820
e-mail: robmcl@access-capital.com
web: www.access-capital.com

Mission Statement: Offers guidance to companies that are major buyers and sellers of electric power projects.

Geographic Preference: North America, Canada
Fund Size: $2.6 billion
Founded: 1990
Investment Criteria: Acquisitions, Divestitures, Expansion Capital, Management Buyouts
Industry Group Preference: Power Technologies, Financial Services, Engineering

Key Executives:
  Robert S. McLeese, Founder & President
  Education: BSc, University of Western Ontario; MBA, McMaster University
  Directorships: ACI Energy
  George H. Cholakis, Senior Vice President
  Education: BSc, University of Toronto; MBA, York University
  Background: Vice President, Corporate Finance, Midland Doherty (subsequently Midland Walwyn and later Merrill Lynch), Toronto; Manager Corporate Finance and Manager Merchant Banking, Bank of Montreal, Toronto; Manager, Financial Planning.
  Directorships: Vice Chairman, Toronto Board of Trade Electricity Task Force;Executive Committee, Stakeholders Alliance For Competition and Customer Choice ("SAC").

Venture Capital & Private Equity Firms / Canadian Firms

2027 AIP PRIVATE CAPITAL
Royal Bank Plaza, South Tower
200 Bay Street
Suite 3240
Toronto, ON M5J 2J1
Canada

Phone: 416-601-0808 Fax: 888-900-4123
Toll-Free: 855-275-0868
e-mail: info@aipprivatecapital.com
web: aipprivatecapital.com

Mission Statement: AIP Private Capital is an investment firm focused on providing private equity and venture debt financing to emerging growth businesses.
Geographic Preference: Canada, United States, South America, Europe
Founded: 2010
Average Investment: $1 - $5 million
Investment Criteria: Emerging, Management Buyouts, Recapitalizations, Turnarounds, Corporate Divestitures, Acquisitions, Growth Capital
Industry Group Preference: Financial Services, Business Products & Services, Clean Technology, Information Technology, Transportation, Oil & Gas
Portfolio Companies: Arkados Group, BioGanix, Carl Data Solutions, Cannabix Technologies, Next Door Lending, Relevium Technologies, Smart Autonomous Solutions, SolBright Renewable Energy, Torino Power Solutions, West Point Resources

Other Locations:
　Moscow Embankment Tower
　10 Presnenskaya
　Naberezhnaya Block C
　Moscow 123317
　Russia

　Korea Teachers Pension, 9th Floor
　Yeouido-dong
　Yeongdeungpo-Gu
　Seoul 150-742
　South Korea

　Dubai Trade, 10th Floor
　Limitless Galleries Building 4
　Downtown Jebel Ali
　Dubai
　United Arab Emirates

Key Executives:
Alex Kanayev, Managing Partner
Education: San Diego State University; MBA, York University; CPA
Background: Senior VP, Sprott Asset Management; Portfolio Manager, BMO Financial Group; Managing Partner, Goldman & Partners; Managing Director, RUS Communications
Directorships: Capital Guardian

2028 ALBERTA ENTERPRISE
Suite 1405, TD Tower
10088 102 Avenue
Edmonton, AB T5J 2Z2
Canada

Phone: 587-402-6601 Fax: 587-402-6612
e-mail: info@alberta-enterprise.ca
web: www.alberta-enterprise.ca

Mission Statement: Alberta Enterprise partners with proven VC technology funds investing in Alberta.
Geographic Preference: Alberta
Fund Size: $440 million
Founded: 2008
Industry Group Preference: Software, Internet, Media, Manufacturing, Clean Technology, Energy, Medical Devices, Life Sciences, Pharmaceuticals, Electronics
Portfolio Companies: 32 Degrees Capital, Accelerate Fund, Avrio Capital, Azure Capital Partners, Builders VC, Chrysalix, EnrTech Capital, iNovia Capital, McRock Capital, Panache Ventures, Relay Ventures, Yaletown

Key Executives:
Kristina Williams, President & CEO
Education: Master of Laws, Uppsala University; MBA, University of Alberta
Background: Director of Marketing, Cevena Bioproducts; VP Marketing, Natraceutical Canada
Directorships: TEC Edmonton
Rebecca Giffen, Vice President, Investments
Education: BComm, Haskayne School of Business, University of Calgary
Background: Director of Fund Investments, BDC Venture Capital
Paul Godman, Vice President, Investments
Education: University of Waterloo; University of Calgary
Background: EnCana

2029 ALBERTA INVESTMENT MANAGEMENT CORP.
10250 101 Street NW
Suite 1600
Edmonton, AB T5J 3P4
Canada

Phone: 780-392-3600
e-mail: info@aimco.ca
web: www.aimco.ca

Mission Statement: Alberta Investment Management Corp. is one of the largest institutional investment managers in Canada. A Crown corporation of the Province of Alberta, AIMCo seeks to produce superior, long-term investment results through good governance and the pursuit of the best investment opportunities around the world.
Fund Size: $108.2 billion
Founded: 2008
Industry Group Preference: Real Estate, Infrastructure
Portfolio Companies: Axcan Pharma, CCS, Cengage, Ceridian, DGAM, Generac, GLM Industries, KMC Mining, RTL-Westcan, TransAlta Corp.

Other Locations:
　100 King Street West
　Suite 5120
　PO Box 51
　Toronto, ON M5X 1B1
　Canada
　Phone: 647-789-5700

　72 Welbeck Street
　4th Floor
　London W1G 0AY
　United Kingdom
　Phone: 44 (0)20 3102 1900

Key Executives:
Evan Siddal, CEO
Education: B.A., Management Economics, University of Guelph; B.LL., Osgoode Hall Law School
Background: President & CEO, Canada Mortgage and Housing Corp. (CMHC);
Paul Langill, Chief Financial Officer
Education: MA, Accounting, University of Waterloo
Background: Special Advisor to the Chairman & CEO, TD Bank Financial Group; EVP, TD Bank Group; COO, TD Securities; Partner, Ernst & Young
Sandra Lau, Co-Chief Investment Officer & Head, Public Investments
Background: Senior Portfolio Manager
Directorships: Co-Founder & Co-Chair, Edmonton Women in Finance

2030 ALTAS PARTNERS
79 Wellington Street West
Suite 3500
PO Box 357
Toronto, ON M5K 1K7
Canada

Phone: 416-306-9800
e-mail: contact@altaspartners.com
web: altaspartners.com

Mission Statement: Seeks to invest in only one or two businesses each year.

Fund Size: $5 billion
Founded: 2012
Average Investment: $400 million - $1 billion
Industry Group Preference: Healthcare, Services, Industrial
Portfolio Companies: Capital Vision Services, Dubois Chemicals, Hub International, Medforth Global Healthcare Education, Nsc Minerals, Padi, Pye-Barker Fire & Safety, Tecta America, United Women's Healthcare, University Of St. Augustine For Health Sciences

Key Executives:
   Andrew Sheiner, Founder/Managing Partner
   Education: McGill University; Harvard University
   Background: Onex Corp.
   Directorships: Hospital for Sick Children (Toronto); Canadian Advisory Board (Harvard Business School)
   Scott Werry, Managing Partner
   Education: University of North Carolina; Harvard Business School
   Background: McColl Partners
   Directorships: Capital Vision Services; PADI
   Christopher McElhone, Managing Partner
   Education: Harvard University; MBA, Wilfred Laurier University
   Background: Director, Husky Injection Molding Systems; Onex Corp.

2031 AMORCHEM
4 Westmount Square
Suite 160
Westmount, QC H3Z 2S6
Canada

Phone: 514-849-7696
e-mail: info@amorchem.com
web: amorchem.com

Mission Statement: AmorChem is an early stage venture fund dedicated to biotech companies and academic research.

Fund Size: $87 Million
Founded: 2011
Industry Group Preference: Life Science, Biotech, Pharmaceuticals
Portfolio Companies: Arna Therapeutics, Corbin Therapeutics Inc., Giiant Pharma Inc., Inversago Pharma Inc., Liminal Biosciences Inc., Neurasic Therapeutics, Semathera Inc.

Key Executives:
   Elizabeth Douville, Founder & Managing Partner
   e-mail: elizabeth@amorchem.com
   Education: PhD, Biochemistry, University of Ottawa
   Background: Senior Partner, GeneChem
   Inès Holzbaur, Founder & Managing Partner
   e-mail: ines@amorchem.com
   Education: PhD, Chemistry, University of Cambridge
   Background: Senior Associate, GeneChem
   Kevin McBride, Partner & CSO
   e-mail: kevin@amorchem.com
   Education: MSc, Analytical Chemistry, Queen's University
   Background: CEO, ARNA Therapeutics

2032 AMPLITUDE
3, Place Ville-Marie
Espace CDPQ, Suite 12350
Montreal, QC H3b 0E7
Canada

Phone: 514-298-4222
e-mail: info@amplitudevc.com
web: amplitudevc.com

Mission Statement: Amplitude is a venture capital firm dedicated to bringing the best healthcare innovations to market to help improve the lives of patients.

Other Locations:
   180 John Street
   Toronto, ON M5T 1X5
   Canada

   2015 Main Street
   Vancouver, BC V5T 3C2
   Canada

Key Executives:
   Jean-Francois Pariseau, Partner
   e-mail: jfpariseau@amplitudevc.com
   Dion Madsen, Partner
   e-mail: dmadsen@amplitudevc.com
   Nancy Harrison, Venture Partner
   e-mail: neharrison@amplitudevc.com

2033 ANCIENT STRAINS
2702 - 401 Bay Street
Toronto, ON M5H 2Y4

Phone: 416-545-7214
web: www.ancientstrains.ca

Mission Statement: Invests in the global cannabis industry.

Geographic Preference: Canada, USA, India
Founded: 2014
Industry Group Preference: Cannabis

Key Executives:
   Daryl Hodges, Chairman/CEO
   Education: HBSc, Enconomic Geology; MSc, Geochemistry, University of Waterloo
   Background: Founder/Mining Analyst/CEO/Chairman, Jennings Capital Inc.; President, Ladykirk Capital Advisors Inc.
   Directorships: Executive Chairman, Minera IRL Limited
   Samir Biswas, President/Director
   Education: BCom, Finance; MBA, Agriculture
   Background: CFO, MedCann Access; Has served as VP, CFO, Strategic Advisor, Deputy to CEO, Treasurer, and GM to 12 private/public Canadian companies.

2034 ANNAPOLIS CAPITAL
140, 4 Avenue SW
Calgary, AB T2P 3N3
Canada

Phone: 403-231-4430
e-mail: info@anncap.com
web: www.annapoliscapital.ca

Mission Statement: A creative, value-adding, and long-term investor of growth capital in the Canadian energy sector. From its head office in Calgary, the Annapolis team uses its interdisciplinary expertise, Canadian network of relationships, and track record of value-creation to help its investors and portfolio company management teams profit.

Geographic Preference: Canada
Fund Size: $650 million
Founded: 2006
Average Investment: $15-60 million
Investment Criteria: Early-Stage
Industry Group Preference: Energy, Oil & Gas

Venture Capital & Private Equity Firms / Canadian Firms

Key Executives:
Peter Williams, Managing Partner & CEO
403-231-4434
e-mail: pwilliams@anncap.com
Education: BA, LLB, Dalhousie University
Background: CEO & Chairman, Krang Energy; CEO, Passage Energy; Governor, Canadian Association of Petroleum Producers
Directorships: Avalanche Energy, Caltex Energy, Evolve Exploration, HighRock Energy, Bulldog Oil & Gas, Corintian Energy, Caltex Energy
Jody Forsyth, Managing Partner
403-231-4433
e-mail: jforsyth@anncap.com
Education: BSc, Dip.Eng., LLB, MBA, Dalhousie University; LLM, Osgoode Hall Law School
Background: Vice President, Krang Energy; Vice President, Berland Exploration; Corporate Secretary, Avalanche Energy
Directorships: Evolve Exploration
Mark Poelzer, Managing Partner
403-231-4431
e-mail: mpoelzer@anncap.com
Education: BComm, University of Saskatchewan
Background: Vice President, Finance & CFO, Vigilant Exploration; CFO, Berland Exploration; CFO, Questor Technologies; CFO, Passage Energy
Directorships: Breton Energy

2035 APECTEC
3911 Trasimene Cr. SW
Calgary, AB T3E 7J6
Canada

Phone: 403-685-1888 Fax: 403-685-1880
web: www.apectec.com

Mission Statement: To help oil and gas and petroleum entrepreneurs to joint venture, partner and start, grow and finance promising investment opportunities, promising early-stage companies and companies employing technologies to enhance oil and gas operations.

Geographic Preference: Global
Founded: 1989
Average Investment: $1 Million
Investment Criteria: Startups, Seed-Stage, Early-Stage, Joint Venture Funding
Industry Group Preference: Oil & Gas, Natural Gas
Key Executives:
Barclay W. Hambrook, Chief Executive Officer
Education: University of Calgary; University of Toronto
Background: Enercana Capital

2036 ARC FINANCIAL
4300, 400 - 3 Avenue SW
Calgary, AB T2P 4H2
Canada

Phone: 403-292-0680
e-mail: genfeedback@arcfinancial.com
web: www.arcfinancial.com

Mission Statement: To invest in partnerships with outstanding management teams to grow energy companies and create shareholder value.

Geographic Preference: Canada
Fund Size: CDN $6 billion
Founded: 1989
Average Investment: CDN $25 - $100 million
Investment Criteria: Early stage
Industry Group Preference: Energy, Oilfield Services, Infrastructure, Power Generation, Oil & Gas
Portfolio Companies: Beringer Energy, BluEarth Renewables, C&C Energia, Canbriam Energy, Canyon Services Group, Capio Exploration, Cequence Energy, Chinook Energy, Global Tubing, Huron Energy Corporation, Nexterra Systems, Tesla Exploration Ltd., Seven Generations Energy, Sitka Exploration, Shiningstar Energy, STEP Energy Services, Tangle Creek Energy, Unconventional Gas Resources

Key Executives:
Kevin Brown, Co-Chair & Director
403-292-0687
e-mail: kbrown@arcfinancial.com
Education: BSc, Chemical Engineering; MA, Economics, University of Alberta
Background: Canadian Energy Research Institute
Directorships: Unconventional Resources Canada, Seven Generations Energy Ltd
Lauchlan Currie, Co-Chair & Director
403-292-0431
e-mail: lcurrie@arcfinancial.com
Education: BSc, Geology, University of Calgary; MBA, Queen's University
Directorships: Capio Exploration Ltd., Tangle Creek Energy Ltd.
Brian Boulanger, Chief Executive Officer & Director
e-mail: bboulanger@arcfinancial.com
Education: University of Western Ontario
Directorships: Modern Resources Inc.; Rifle Shot Oil Corp.
Peter Tertzakian, Managing Director
403-292-0809
e-mail: ptertzakian@arcfinancial.com
Education: BSc, Geophysics, University of Alberta; MSc, Management of Technology, Sloan School of Management, MIT
Directorships: Nexterra Systems Corp.
Tanya Causgrove, Chief Financial Officer & Managing Director
Education: BComm, University of Alberta
Mac Van Wielingen, Founder & Partner
403-292-0686
e-mail: mvanwielingen@arcfinancial.com
Education: BA, Business, Richard Ivey School of Business, University of Western Ontario
Directorships: BluEartch Renewables
John Dielwart, Partner
e-mail: jdielwart@arcfinancial.com
Education: University of Calgary
Chris Seasons, Partner
e-mail: cseasons@arcfinancial.com
Education: Queen's University

2037 ARCTERN VENTURES
101 College Street
Suite 155
Toronto, ON M5G 1L7
Canada

e-mail: info@arcternventures.com
web: www.arcternventures.com

Mission Statement: Provides early-stage 'seed' funding to cleantech companies with significant growth potential.

Geographic Preference: Canada
Fund Size: $30 million
Founded: 2006
Average Investment: $1 - $3 million
Investment Criteria: Startup
Industry Group Preference: Clean Energy, Energy Storage, Mobility, Advanced Manufacturing & Materials, Resource Use & Efficiency, Foodtech
Portfolio Companies: Aquabyte, CircuitMeter, Clir, Emitwise, GreenMantra, Hydrostor, Kebotix, Mighty Buildings, MMB Networks, Morgan Solar, Mosa Meat, Palmetto, Parity, Polar Sapphire, Rethought Insurance, Sheertex, Smart Energy Instruments, Smarter Alloys, Sparq, Terramera, ThinkIQ, Woodland, Xeal, Zoomo

Venture Capital & Private Equity Firms / Canadian Firms

Key Executives:
  Tom Rand, Co-Founder & Partner
  Education: BSc, Electrical Engineering, University of Waterloo; MSc, Philosophy of Science, University of London; MA, PhD, University of Toronto
  Background: Founder, Voice Courier
  Murray McCaig, Co-Founder & Managing Partner
  Education: MBA, University of Western Ontario
  Background: McKenna Group; RSL Investments

2038 ARDENTON
1021 West Hastings Street
Suite 2400
Vancouver, BC V6E 0C3
Canada

Phone: 833-416-1490
web: www.ardenton.com

Mission Statement: Ardenton is a private equity corporation focused on long term growth. They nurture management teams and expand into new markets.

Other Locations:
  18 King Street E
  Suite 515
  Toronto, ON M5C 1C4
  Canada
  Phone: 416-304-9454

  120 Research Lane
  Suite 202
  Guelph, ON N1G 0B4
  Canada
  Phone: 833-416-1490

  100 Crescent Court
  Suite 595
  Dallas, TX 75201
  Phone: 214-390-7455

  3 Hardman Square
  2nd Floor
  Manchester
  United Kingdom
  Phone: 44 161-457-0117

2039 ARGOSY PARTNERS
141 Adelaide Street West
Suite 760
Toronto, ON M5H 3L5
Canada

Phone: 416-367-3617 Fax: 416-367-3895
e-mail: info@argosypartners.com
web: www.argosypartners.com

Mission Statement: Argosy Partners is a private equity firm that provides capital to successful entrepreneurs and institutional investors to deliver a range of effective financial solutions for tough business situations.

Geographic Preference: Canada
Founded: 1995
Minimum Investment: $2 Million
Portfolio Companies: Art For Everyday, Bayview Hospitality Group, Carego, Celtrade, CAST Software, Eratech, Gourmet Settings, iMarketing Solutions Group, Insception Lifebank, Level Platforms, Logistik Unicorp, TCDS.com, Westmount Storefront Systems

Key Executives:
  Richard Reid, Founder & Partner
  Background: Burn Fry; Gordon Capital Corp.; Wood Gundy
  Larry Klar, Partner
  Background: KPMG; Canadian General Capital

2040 ARVA LIMITED
4120 Yonge Street
Suite 310
Toronto, ON M2P 2B8
Canada

Phone: 416-222-0842 Fax: 416-222-6243
web: arva.ca

Mission Statement: Arva looks for long-term opportunities in companies whose owners are seeking an exit, or who require ongoing financial and strategic support.

Geographic Preference: Canada
Founded: 1956
Investment Criteria: Long-Term, Later-Stage
Industry Group Preference: Communications, Manufacturing, Telecommunications, Construction
Portfolio Companies: MLL Telecom, Normerica Building Systems, Trylon-TSF, Ultra-Fit Manufacturing

Key Executives:
  Mike Stevens, President
  Background: President, Waltec Components; President, S.W. Fleming
  John Stevens, Executive Vice President
  Background: Managing Partner, Osler, Hoskin & Harcourt
  Bill Smith, Vice President, Finance & Corporate Secretary
  Background: Cott Corporation; Molson Breweries; Apple Computer

2041 ASHBRIDGE PARTNERS
31 Wingold Avenue
Toronto, ON M6B 1P8

e-mail: info@ashbridgepartners.ca
web: www.ashbridgepartners.ca

Mission Statement: Ashbridge is a private, entrepreneurial investment firm that seeks to acquire and manage small to medium-sized businesses by partnering with existing management teams.

Geographic Preference: Canada
Founded: 2013
Investment Criteria: Early-Stage, Mid-Stage
Industry Group Preference: Personal Care, Packaging, Manufacturing
Portfolio Companies: Caryl Baker Visage, Bagwell Supply, Geroline

Key Executives:
  Nathan Tam, Partner
  Education: Richard Ivey School of Business, University of Western Ontario
  Background: Co-Founder, Offleash Media; Onex Corporation; Morgan Stanley
  Jordan Goodman, Partner
  Education: University of Western Ontario
  Background: VP, Authentic Brands Group; Hilco Consumer Capital
  Ryan DeCaire, Partner
  Education: Richard Ivey School of Business, University of Western Ontario
  Background: Onex Corporation; Bank of America Merrill Lynch

2042 AUXO MANAGEMENT
3198 Orlando Drive
Mississauga, ON L4V 1J2

web: www.auxomanagement.com

Mission Statement: Auxo is a private, entrepreneurial investment firm focused on small to medium-sized businesses whose owners are considering retirement.

Founded: 2010
Investment Criteria: Later-Stage
Industry Group Preference: Video Surveillance, Security

Venture Capital & Private Equity Firms / Canadian Firms

Portfolio Companies: Meglan, Stealth Monitoring, Trask Contracting, UCIT

Key Executives:
  Robert Cherun, Co-Founder & Managing Partner
  e-mail: rob@auxomanagement.com
  Education: MBA, Stanford Graduate School of Business; HBA, Richard Ivey School of Business, University of Western Ontario
  Background: Morgan Stanley; McKinsey & Company
  Erik Mikkelsen, Co-Founder & Managing Partner
  e-mail: erik@auxomanagement.com
  Education: HBA, Richard Ivey School of Business, University of Western Ontario
  Background: President & SRO, Stealth Monitoring; Regent Properties; Barclays Capital; Ink Media

2043 AVAC
220, 6815-8 Street NE
Calgary, AB T2E 7H7
Canada

Phone: 403-274-2774
web: avacgrp.com

Mission Statement: AVAC Ltd. is an Alberta-based investment company investing in promising early-stage commercial ventures in value-added agri-business, information and communications technologies, life sciences, and other industrial technology sectors. AVAC also manages an active early-stage venture capital fund-of-funds investment pool, and the Accelerate angel co-investment Fund. AVAC's mandate is to help bridge the critical investment gap that exists between innovative ideas and commercial business success.

Geographic Preference: Alberta
Fund Size: $15 million
Founded: 1997
Investment Criteria: Early-Stage, Startup, Exit
Industry Group Preference: Agricultural Technologies, Technology
Portfolio Companies: Afinity Life Sciences, Antibe Therapeutics, Baby Gourmet, Botaneco, Business Infusions, Calgary Scientific, CanBiocin, Ceapro, CoolIT Systems, Decisive Farming, Enterprise Macay, Enthrill Distribution, eThor, Himark Bogas, iKingdom, InnerVision Medical Technologies, IntelliView Technologies, Lethbridge Biogas, Livestock Water Recycling, Mobovivo, Radient Technologies, SBI Fine Chemicals, Sustainable Produce Urban Delivery, Tynt Multimedia, Under the Roof Decorating, Userful, Waggers Pet Products, Wedge Networks

Key Executives:
  Warren Bergen, President
  e-mail: wbergen@avacltd.com
  Education: BComm, University of Saskatchewan; Pepperdine University
  Mark Carlson, Managing Director
  e-mail: mcarlson@avacltd.com
  Education: MBA
  Directorships: Accelerate Fund Limited Partnership
  Martin Vetter, Senior Investment Manager
  e-mail: mvetter@avacltd.com
  Education: Memorial University of Newfoundland; MBA, University of Calgary
  Background: Acceleware; Hemisphere GPS; Novatel Wireless; Nortel
  Jim Hardin, Senior Investment Manager
  e-mail: jhardin@avacltd.com
  Education: BSc, Zoology, PhD, Gastrointestinal Physiology, University of Calgary

2044 AZIMUTH CAPITAL MANAGEMENT
Centennial Place East
3110, 520 - 3rd Avenue SW
Calgary, AB T2P 0R3
Canada

Phone: 403-517-1500
e-mail: info@navigatingenergy.com
web: navigatingenergy.com

Mission Statement: Focused on building long-term franchise value through partnership relationships with Limited Partners, portfolio companies, service providers and members of the Firm.

Geographic Preference: Canada
Fund Size: $1.6 billion
Founded: 2003
Investment Criteria: Startup, Early-Stage
Industry Group Preference: Energy, Oil & Gas, Infrastructure
Portfolio Companies: Altex Energy, Enoflex, Entrada Resources, Karve Energy Inc., M-Flow, Magma, Monolith, Recover Energy Services, Steelhead Lng, Tourmaline, Whitecap Resources Inc.

Key Executives:
  Jim Nieuwenburg, Operating Partner
  Education: BS, Electrical Engineering; Executive Program, University of Western Ontario
  Background: CEO, Petromet Resources; VP, Norcan Energy; Amoco Canada
  Directorships: Amarone Oil & Gas, Fairborne Energy, Black Swan Energy, Legacy Oil & Gas, Rifco
  Jeff Van Steenbergen, Co-Founder & Managing Partner
  Education: Bachelor of Applied Science, Civil Engineering, Queen's University; MBA, Dalhousie University
  Background: Co-Head, North American Oil & Gas, JP Morgan & Co.; Mobil; Hibernia; Sable Offshore Energy
  Directorships: Aduro Resources, Altex Energy, Cobal International Energy, Fairfield Energy, Magma Global, Seven Generations Energy
  Dave Pearce, Deputy Managing Partner
  Education: BS, Mechanical Engineering, University of Calgary
  Background: President & CEO, Northrock Resources; VP, Corporate Development, Fletcher Challenge Canada; Dome Petroleum
  Directorships: Fairfield Energy, Black Swan Energy, Cutpick Energy, All Points Energy
  Francesco Mele, Chief Operating Officer & Partner
  Education: BS, MBA, Bachelor of Laws, University of Alberta
  Jim Farnsworth, Operating Partner
  Education: BSc, Geology, Indiana University; MSc, Geology, Western Michigan University
  Background: Co-Founder & President, Cobalt International Energy; SVP, British Petroleum
  Directorships: Indiana University Advisory Board; Jackson School of Geosciences, University Of Texas
  Howard Mayson, Operating Partner & Senior Advisor
  Education: MSc, Mechanical Engineering, MIT; BEng, University of Sheffield; Advanced Management Program, Wharton Business School
  Background: SVP, British Petroleum
  Directorships: Corex Resources; Encana

2045 BANYAN CAPITAL PARTNERS
1400 - 130 King Street W
PO Box 240
Toronto, ON M5X 1C8
Canada

web: www.cclgroup.com/banyan/en

Venture Capital & Private Equity Firms / Canadian Firms

Mission Statement: Banyan Capital Partners is a boutique private equity firm investing in mid-sized companies in North America.
Geographic Preference: North America
Investment Criteria: Growth Stage, Mergers, MBO, LBO, Spin-Offs, Going Private, Recapitalizations, Succession
Industry Group Preference: Diversified
Portfolio Companies: Bevo Agro, Corix Group, Dental Technologies, Fios, Foundstone, Genoa Healthcare, GW Anglin Manufacturing, ISR, KOS Corp, MIP, Newcrete, Oakcreek Golf, Party Packagers, Premium Brands, Qmax Solutions, Purity Life Health Produts, Q'Max Solutions, Rack Attack, Shanahan's, Syscon Justice Systems, Tartan Canada Corporation
Key Executives:
   Jeff Wigle, Managing Director
   416-216-7076
   e-mail: jwigle@banyancp.com
   Education: BA, Economics, University of Western Ontario
   Background: Vice President, Richardson Capital Limited
   Directorships: Party Packagers, GW Anglin Manufacturing
   Simon Gelinas, Managing Director
   416-364-2801
   e-mail: sgelinas@banyancp.com
   Education: BComm, McGill Univ.; MBA, University of British Columbia
   Directorships: G.W. Anglin Mfg., Oakcreek Golf & Turf, Rack Attack

2046 BAYSHORE CAPITAL
Commerce Court W
199 Bay Street, Suite 2900
PO Box 459
Toronto, ON M5L 1G4
Canada

Phone: 416-214-6851 **Fax:** 416-214-9895
web: bayshore.com

Mission Statement: Bayshore finances and builds companies in real estate, financial services, and information technology.
Founded: 1995
Industry Group Preference: Real Estate, Financial Services, Information Technology
Portfolio Companies: Armel Corporation, RPM Technologies, Secure Key, Fenix Opportunity
Key Executives:
   Henry Wolfond, Chair & CEO
   Background: Osler Hoskin & Harcourt
   Directorships: Canadian Jewish Political Affairs Ctee, University Hospital Foundation, UJA Federation Community Advisory Council, Faculty of Law University of Alberta Advisory Ctee
   Andrew Brown, President & Co-Founder
   Education: BComm, Queen's University; LLB, University of Toronto
   Background: i-money; Osler, Hoskin & Harcourt

2047 BCF VENTURES
1100 Boulevard René-Lévesque Ouest
Montreal, QC H3B 4N4
Canada

e-mail: info@bcfventures.vc
web: bcfventures.vc

Mission Statement: BCF Ventures invests at the seed and series A stage of technology-based start-ups.
Geographic Preference: Canada, USA, Israel, China, Western Europe
Founded: 2018
Average Investment: $1-5 Million
Investment Criteria: Up to $10 Million Valuation; Technology-Based; Low Cash Burn; At Least 2 Full-time Founders, one technical
Key Executives:
   Sergio Escobar, Chief Executive Officer

2048 BDC CAPITAL
5, Place Ville Marie
Ground Floor
Montreal, QC H3B 5E7
Canada

Fax: 877-329-9232
Toll-Free: 877-232-2269
web: www.bdc.ca

Mission Statement: Crown corporation supports Canadian entrepreneurs with a focus on small and medium-sized businesses.
Geographic Preference: Canada
Founded: 1944
Industry Group Preference: Technology
Key Executives:
   Jerome Nycz, Executive Vice President, BDC Capital
   Education: BA, Concordia Univ.; IMBA, Hartford Univ.
   Background: BDC Senior VP, Corporate Strategy & Subordinate Financing
   Directorships: Canadian Venture Capital and Private Equity Association
   Alison Nankivell, Senior Vice President, Fund Investment & Global Scaling
   Education: BComm, University of Toronto; MA, London School of Economics & Political Science
   Karl Reckziegel, Senior Vice President
   Education: BEng, University of New Brunswick; MBA, Concordia University

2049 BEDFORD CAPITAL
130 Adelaide St. West
Suite 2900
Toronto, ON M5H 3P5
Canada

Phone: 416-947-1492 **Fax:** 416-947-9673
web: www.bedfordcapital.ca

Mission Statement: Bedford partners with management teams to build industry leading companies. All investment decisions are made internally by the principals of Bedford Capital, with a team comprised diverse backgrounds and direct operating experience.
Geographic Preference: Eastern Canada
Founded: 1982
Average Investment: $5 - $15 million
Investment Criteria: Management Buyouts, Recapitalizations, Growth Capital
Portfolio Companies: B+H International LP, Champion Petfoods LP, Elmira Pet Products, IPD Global, L.B. Maple Treat Corporation, Noranco, Spring Air Sommex Corporation
Key Executives:
   Tim Bowman, Managing Director
   416-947-1492 x310
   e-mail: tbowman@bedfordcapital.ca
   Education: BEng, MBA, LLB
   Background: Corporate Lawyer, Davies Ward & Beck; Vice President, Corporate Dvelopment, Magna International; Co-Founder, Apex Capital; Managing Director, BMO Nesbitt Burns
   Elliott Knox, Managing Director
   416-947-1492 x238
   e-mail: eknox@bedfordcapital.ca
   Education: BMath, Certified Management Accountant
   Background: Andersen Consulting; Co-Founder, Janna Systems; Co-Founder, Lealand Group
   David Hass, Partner
   416-947-1492 x312

Venture Capital & Private Equity Firms / Canadian Firms

e-mail: dhass@bedfordcapital.ca
Education: BA, MBA
Background: Senior Account Manager, Royal Bank; Vice President, Lenbrook; Managing Director, Venture Debt Fund; Managing Director, Small Business Venture Fund, Royal Bank Ventures
Sheila Murray-Tateishi, Senior Vice President & CFO
416-947-1492 x320
e-mail: sheilamt@bedfordcapital.ca
Education: BA, MBA
Background: CFO, Techbanc; SVP/CFO, Nalvana Limited; CFO, Security Pacific Bank

2050 BERINGER CAPITAL
141 Adelaide Street W
Suite 750
Toronto, ON M5H 3L5

Phone: 416-928-2166
e-mail: hello@beringercapital.com
web: www.beringercapital.com

Mission Statement: Beringer partners with growing technology companies that have strong management teams and where there is an opportunity to create value.

Investment Criteria: Mid-Stage
Industry Group Preference: Technology
Portfolio Companies: AdWeek, Blue Acorn, Benzinga, Brand Shop, BrandWeek, Hyper Giant, ICi Digital, Inman, Mediotype, Perform
Other Locations:
261 Madison Avenue
Floor 8
New York, NY 10016
Key Executives:
  Perry Miele, Chair & Managing Partner
  e-mail: pmiele@beringercapital.com
  Background: Chief of Staff to the Minister of International Trade; Gingko Group; DraftWorldwide
  Directorships: Andrew Peller Wines, Canadian Heart & Stroke Foundation, Trilliam Health Partners, LCBO, Match Marketing, Budco
  Bill Kostenko, Vice Chair & Managing Partner
  e-mail: bkostenko@beringercapital.com
  Education: MBA, McMaster University
  Background: CFO, Sherwood; Genesis Microchip; Mitel; Rolm Canada; Rockwell International
  Lu Cacioppo, Vice Chair & Managing Partner
  e-mail: lcacioppo@beringercapital.com
  Background: Leader, Deloitte Private; National Managing Partner, Deloitte SME Program
  Gil Ozir, Managing Partner
  Education: JD, New York University School of Law; Lafayette College
  Background: Managing Director, AMR International; McKinsey & Company
  Directorships: SEED Impact

2051 BEST FUNDS
56 The Esplanade
Suite 503
Toronto, ON M5E 1A7
Canada

Phone: 416-203-7331 Fax: 416-203-6630
e-mail: info@bestfunds.ca
web: bestfunds.ca

Mission Statement: BEST Fund invests in traditional industries with the objective of generating interest income and long term capital.

Geographic Preference: Ontario
Fund Size: $80 million
Founded: 1996
Investment Criteria: Seed-Stage, Early-Stage, Later-Stage
Industry Group Preference: Software, Cloud Computing, Financial Services, Clean Technology, SaaS
Portfolio Companies: 01 Communique, Acuity, Agile Systems, AIM Health Group, Apeks, ArcticDX, ARXX ICF, Asset Matrix, Axentra Corporation, Azonic, BitHeads, BSM Wireless, CNSX Markets, Cognivue Corporation, ComPower Systems, ComponentArt, Cymat, Bulldog Group, ChangePoint, Choreo, Chrysalis, Claymore Capital Management, Canadian National Stock Exchange, Cognivue Corporation, Combat Networks, ComponentArt, Compower Systems, Cygnal Technologies, Cymat, Dejero Labs, Delego, DisclosureNet, DragonWave, Echoworx Corporation, Eco Logic, Electrovaya, ERMS Corporation, Evault, FileTrek, Garner, Geminare, Grantium, Hatsize, Impath Networks, Indigo, Industrios Software, Infonaut, IMS, Internet Secure, Iogen Corporation, Kaval Wireless, Kneebone, Life Imaging Systems, Momentum, MKS, N-Dimension Solutions, Necho Systems, Newstep Networks, Novus Health, OnX Enterprise Solutions, Optessa, PitchPoint Solutions, Pixelink, Polyphalt, Powerband Global, Protus IP Solutions, Questrade, Sand Tech, Sensory Technologies, Signifi, Skura, Soliton, Spectra Securities Software, T-Base Communications, Teambuy.ca, Telos Entertainment, Transgaming, Triple G Systems, Vision Max, X2O Media, XipLink, XPi

Key Executives:
  John Richardson, CEO & Director
  416-203-7331 x228
  Education: University of Western Ontario; State University of New York
  Tom Lunan, Chief Financial Officer
  416-203-7331 x230
  Education: Wilfrid Laurier University
  Background: Toronto Stock Exchange; Ontario Securities Commission
  Mark Donatelli, Vice President
  416-203-7331 x227
  e-mail: mdonatelli@bestfunds.ca
  Background: Wave Financial; Northbridge Financial; PricewaterhouseCoopers; OpenText

2052 BINGLEY CAPITAL
20 Richmond Street E
Suite 600
Toronto, ON M5C 2R9
Canada

web: www.bingleycapital.com

Mission Statement: Bingley focuses on mid-market companies where the founder is seeking an exit, and where long-term value can be built. The firm also offers advisory services.

Geographic Preference: Ontario & Quebec
Investment Criteria: Mid-Market; Sales of $10 million to $100 million; EBITDA of at least $2 million
Industry Group Preference: Industrial, Consumer
Portfolio Companies: Mansour Mining Technologies, Gregg Drilling & Testing
Key Executives:
  Stephan Bey, Principal
  647-930-9556
  e-mail: stephan.bey@bingleycapital.com
  Education: BBA, Wilfried Laurier University; MBA, London School of Business; CA
  Background: Managing Director, Investment Banking, Lehman Brothers; Corporate Controller, Tsubaki of Canada; Deloitte & Touche
  Andrew Bishop, Principal
  e-mail: andrew.bishop@bingleycapital.com
  Education: BA, Political Science & Economics, McGill University; MBA, Schulich School of Business, York University; CFA
  Background: HSBC Securities
  Directorships: Willow Breat & Hereditary Cancer Support

2053 BIOENTERPRISE
The Jaral Corporate Centre
120 Research Lane
Suite 202
Guelph, ON N1G 0B4
Canada

Phone: 519-821-2960 Fax: 519-821-2960
Toll-Free: 866-464-4524
e-mail: info@bioenterprise.ca
web: www.bioenterprise.ca

Mission Statement: A not-for-profit business accelerator. Bioenterprise provides commercialization services to help with the growth of agri-technology businesses ranging from early start-ups to expanding established companies.

Geographic Preference: Canada
Founded: 2003
Investment Criteria: Start-ups to well-established
Industry Group Preference: Agricultural Technologies

Other Locations:
Innovacorp
1 Research Drive
Dartmouth, NS B2Y 4M9
Canada

Key Executives:
Dave Smardon, President & CEO
Background: Co-Founder, Learning Connections; Co-Founder, Commcorp Technologies; Co-Founder, Nibiru Investments; Co-Founder, Capital Management Ltd.
Italo Cerra, Vice President, Finance
Background: Accountant, Deloitte & Touche; Vice President, Finance, Teltone Limited

2054 BIOINDUSTRIAL INNOVATION CANADA
1086 Modeland Road
Sarnia, ON N7S 6L2
Canada

Phone: 226-778-0020
e-mail: info@bincanada.ca
web: www.bincanada.ca

Mission Statement: Sarnia-based business accelerator focused on industrial bioproducts.

Geographic Preference: Sarnia-Lambton
Founded: 2008
Industry Group Preference: Bioenergy, Biofuel, Biochemicals & Biomaterials
Portfolio Companies: 3E Nano, Benefuel, CO2 GRO, Cellulosic Sugar Producers Co-Operative, Comet Bio, EcoSynthetic, FireRein, Forward Water Technologies, GreenCore, GreenMantra Technologies, Greyter Water Systems, KMX, Li-Cycle, Origin Materials, Polar Sapphire, Renix, Ubiquity Solar, Vive Crop Protection, Woodland Biofuels

Key Executives:
A.J. (Sandy) Marshall, Executive Director
Education: BASc, MASc, Univ. of Waterloo
Background: Lanxess Canada
Directorships: Lambton College, Biorefinery Research Inst. at Lakehead Univ.

2055 BIOMINDS LABS INC.
Brookfield Place
181 Bay Street
Suite 1800
Toronto, ON M5J 2T3
Canada

web: www.biomindlabs.co

Mission Statement: Formerly known as Crosswinds Holdings, Biomind is biotech research and development company aimed at transforming biomedical sciences knowledge from natural psychotropic plants into novel pharmaceutical drugs and innovative nanotech delivery systems for a variety of psychiatric and neurological conditions.

Geographic Preference: Canada
Industry Group Preference: Pharmaceuticals, Biotech, Research & Development

Key Executives:
Alejandro Antalich, Chief Executive Officer & Director
Background: CEO, ICC Labs; President, Latam, Aurora Cannabis

2056 BIRCH HILL EQUITY PARTNERS
4510-81 Bay Street
PO Box 45
Toronto, ON M5J 0E7
Canada

Phone: 416-775-3815 Fax: 416-775-3859
e-mail: info@birchhillequity.com
web: www.birchhillequity.com

Mission Statement: Mid-market private equity firm focused on companies valued between $30 million and $600 million, across a range of industries.

Geographic Preference: Canada, United States
Fund Size: CDN $3 billion
Founded: 1994
Investment Criteria: Middle-Market Companies
Portfolio Companies: Bio Agri Mix, Campus Energy, CCM Hockey, Citron Hygiene, Cozzini Bros, FlexNetworks, GDI, Greenfield Global, HomeEquity Bank, Marsulex Environmental Technologies, Mastermind Toys, Motion Specialties, Softchoice, Terrapure Environmental, Tidewater Midstream and Infrastructure

Key Executives:
Stephen J. Dent, Partner
Education: BBA, Wilfred Laurier University; MBA, Richard Ivey School of Business, University of Western Ontario
Background: TD Capital; Founding Partner, Merchant Private Trust
Matthew B. Kunica, Partner
Education: Bachelor of Applied Science, Mineral Engineering, University of Toronto
Background: TD Capital; Associate, Credit Suisse First Boston; Analyst, BMO Nesbitt Burns
Felix-Etienne Lebel, Partner
Education: BComm, McGill University; CFA
Background: CIBC World Markets
Directorships: Citron Hygiene; Softchoice Corporation
John Loh, Partner, Capital Markets
Education: HBA, Richard Ivey School of Business, Western University
Background: Director, Asian Media and Telecom Group, TD; TD Securities
Directorships: Bluewave Energy, Carson Dellosa Publishing, Cookie Jar Entertainment, DHX Media, Novadent, GlobeNet Communications Group, Vector Intermediaries, WNI Holdings
John B. MacIntyre, Partner
Education: BComm, Queen's University; Chartered Accountant
Background: President, TD Capital
Michael J. Salamon, Partner
Education: BS, Applied Science, Electrical Engineering, University of Toronto; MBA, University of Chicago
Background: TD Capital; Vice President, Harrowston Inc.
David G. Samuel, Partner
Education: HBA, Richard Ivey School of Business, University of Western Ontario; MBA, Harvard Business School
Background: President, Rogers High Speed Internet Access; McKinsey & Company; Morgan Stanley
Pierre J. Schuurmans, Partner & COO
Education: MBA, Stanford University; HBA, Richard Ivey School of Business, Western University

Venture Capital & Private Equity Firms / Canadian Firms

Background: CFO & Vice President at various companies; Consultant, McKinsey & Company; Monitor Company
Directorships: Hanlan Boat Club

2057 BMO CAPITAL MARKETS
100 King Street W
Toronto, ON M5X 1H3
Canada

Phone: 416-359-4000
web: capitalmarkets.bmo.com

Mission Statement: Invests in and works closely with exceptional management teams in companies with defensible market positions and franchise characteristics which generate strong cash flow and operate in attractive growth markets. The primary goal is long-term value creation, thus partnering with experienced management in compelling industry segments to identify and develop platform companies. In 2015, BMO co-invested in OMERS Ventures Fund II, a venture capital fund managed by OMERS Ventures.

Geographic Preference: North America
Fund Size: $647 billion
Founded: 2000
Minimum Investment: $500,000
Investment Criteria: Middle-Market Leveraged Buyouts, Growth Equity, Structured Equity Investments

Other Locations:
3 Times Square
New York, NY 10036

Key Executives:
Dan Barclay, CEO & Group Head
Education: BSc(Hons.), Unversity of Alberta; MBA, University of Calgary
Summer Hinton, Chief Operating Officer
Education: BS, Northwestern University; MBA, Wharton Business School
Background: COO of Enterprise Initiatives, Infrustructure & Innovation

2058 BOND CAPITAL
1100 Melville Street
Suite 1160
Vancouver, BC V6E 4A6
Canada

Phone: 604-687-2663
web: www.bondcapital.ca

Mission Statement: Offers capital in the form of debt or equity to entrepreneurs.

Geographic Preference: Western Canada, Northwestern U.S.A.
Founded: 2002
Average Investment: $2 to $30 million
Investment Criteria: Later-Stage
Industry Group Preference: Oil & Gas Services, Manufacturing, Distribution, Wholesale, Transportation, Agriculture, Food & Beverage, Financial Services, Healthcare, Consumer Products, Private Education

Key Executives:
Davis Vaitkunas, President & Founder
e-mail: davis@bondcapital.ca
Education: Univ. of Alberta
Jim Elliott, CFO
Education: University of Alberta
Background: Mercer Intl., Westcoast Energy/Duke Energy, Ernst & Young
Corry J. Silbernagel, Managing Director, Originations
Education: University of British Columbia; INSEAD

2059 BONNEFIELD FINANCIAL
141 Adelaide Street W
Suite 510
Toronto, ON M5H 3L5

Phone: 613-230-3854
Toll-Free: 877-695-3854
e-mail: info@bonnefield.com
web: bonnefield.com

Mission Statement: Bonnefield provides land-lease funding exclusively to farmers.

Founded: 2009
Investment Criteria: Farm Land
Industry Group Preference: Farming, Agriculture

Other Locations:
14 Concourse Gate
Suite 100
Ottawa, ON K2E 7S6

Key Executives:
Tom Eisenhauer, President & CEO
Education: BA, University of King's College; Dalhousie University; MA, Queen's University; PDO, Canadian Securities Institute; ICDD, Institute of Corporate Directors; Rotman School of Business
Background: Managing Partner, Latitude Partners; Managing Director, TD Securities; Managing Director, Lancaster Financial
Directorships: University of King's College
Jeff McAllister, Vice President, Investments
Education: BS, University of Western Ontario; BBA, Richard Ivey School of Business, University of Wesntern Ontario; CFA; CPA
Background: Senior Accounting, Ernst & Young

2060 BRIGHTSPARK VENTURES
21 Bedford Road
3rd Floor
Toronto, ON M5R 2J9
Canada

e-mail: invest@brightspark.com
web: www.brightspark.com

Mission Statement: A venture capital firm dedicated to development Canadian-rooted companies.

Geographic Preference: Canada
Fund Size: $200 Million
Founded: 1999
Average Investment: $3 Million
Minimum Investment: $1 Million
Investment Criteria: Start-up, Seed-Stage, Early-Stage
Industry Group Preference: Information Technology, Wireless Technologies, Mobile, Software, Artificial Intelligence
Portfolio Companies: AdHawk Microsystems, AOMS, Buy Back Booth, Classcraft, Hopper, Hubba, InVivo AI, Jazinga, Jewlr, Nano Magnetics, nGUVU, Nudge Rewards, Potloc, Sabse Technologies, Wysdom AI

Other Locations:
Espace CDPQ
3 Place Ville-Marie
Bureau 12350
Montreal, QC H3B 0E7
Canada

Key Executives:
Mark Skapinker, Co-Founder & Managing Partner
e-mail: marks@brightspark.com
Background: President, Delrina
Directorships: Upside Fdn. of Canada
Sophie Forest, Managing Partner
e-mail: sophie@brightspark.com
Education: BA, Finance, University of Sherbrooke
Background: CDP Capital Technology
Directorships: Jewlr Inc., Hopper, nGUVU

2061 BRISIO INNOVATIONS INC.
409 Granville Street
Suite 1052
Vancouver, BC V6C 1T2
Canada

Phone: 604-644-0072
e-mail: support@brisio.com
web: brisio.com

Mission Statement: Brisio Innovations Inc. invests its capital in companies and opportunities which management believe are undervalued and have potential for significant appreciation. The company makes investments in both public and private markets and focuses on opportunities in a wide variety of industries excluding the resource and resource service sectors. Brisio does not invest on behalf of any third party and it does not offer investment advice.

Geographic Preference: Canada
Industry Group Preference: Healthcare, Industry, Services, Technology
Portfolio Companies: Allur Group Inc., Atlas Engineered Products, Gatekeeper Systems Inc., Immunoprecise, Innovotech Inc., Lite Access Technologies Inc., Namsys, Nanalysis, Pioneering Technology, Renoworks Software Inc., Total Telcom Inc., Vigil Health Solutions Inc.

Key Executives:
Paul Andreola, CEO & President
Background: CEO & President, NameSilo; Editor & Publisher, SmallCap Discoveries; CEO & President, Netco Silver Inc.; President, Canadian Nexus Capital Markets; President, Burrard Street Capital Co.
Directorships: ImmunoPrecise; Atlas Engineering Products
Natasha Tsai, Chief Financial Officer
Education: University of British Columbia
Background: Controller, Dejour Enterprises Ltd.; Senior Accountant, Grant Thornton LLP

2062 BROOKFIELD ASSET MANAGEMENT
Brookfield Place
181 Bay Street
Suite 300
Toronto, ON M5J 2T3
Canada

Phone: 416-363-9491
web: www.brookfield.com

Mission Statement: Global alternative asset manager focused on property, renewable power, infrastructure and private equity.

Geographic Preference: Canada, United States, Europe, India, Australia, South America
Fund Size: $500 billion
Industry Group Preference: Real Estate, Infrastructure, Renewable Power, Private Equity
Portfolio Companies: Ainsworth Lumber, Armtec Limited, Brookfield Real Estate & Relocation Services, Concert Industries, CWC Well Services, Ember Resources, Grande Cashe Coal, Hammerstone Corp., Hudson Bay Company, Insignia Energy, Longview Fibre Paper & Packaging, MAAX, Norbord, Stelco, Tecumseh Products, Vicwest, Western Forest Products

Other Locations:
Brookfield Place
250 Vesey Street
15th Floor
New York, NY 10281-1023
Phone: 212-417-7000

One Canada Square
Level 25, Canary Warf
London E14 5AAD
United Kingdom
Phone: 44 20 7659 3500

Avenida Das Naçoes Unidas, 14.261
EdifiCio Wt Morumbi - Ala B
20§ Andar, Morumbi
Sao Paulo 04794-000
Brazil
Phone: 55 11 2540 9150

Level 19
10 Carrington Street
Sydney NSW 2000
Australia
Phone: 61 2 9158 5100

Level 24
Al Mustaqbal Street, DIFC
PO Box 507234
Dubai
United Arab Emirates
Phone: 971 4 597 0100

Unit 1
4th Floor, Godrej BKC
Bandra Kurla Complex
Mumbai 400 051
India
Phone: 91 22 6600 0700

Suite 1201, Tower B, One East
No. 736 South Zhongshan 1st Road
Huangpu District
Shanghai 200021
China
Phone: 86 21 2306 0700

Key Executives:
Bruce Flatt, Chief Executive Officer
Justin Beber, Managing Partner, Head of Corporate Strategy, Chief Legal Officer
Education: BEcon, McGill University; MBA/LLB, Schulich School of Business & Osgoode Hall Law School, York University
Barry Blattman, Vice Chair
Education: University of Michigan; New York University
Background: Salomon Brothers; Merrill Lynch
Jeff Blidner, Vice Chair
Marcus Day, Managing Partner, Real Estate
Munish Dayal, Managing Director, Private Equity
Brian Kingston, Managing Partner & CEO, Real Estate
Background: CEO, Prime Infrastructure; CFO, Multiplex
Brian Lawson, Vice Chair
Directorships: Governing Council, University of Toronto; Community Food Centers Canada
Natalie Adomait, Managing Director, Renewable Power
Luiz Lopes, Executive Chair, Latin America
Background: Magliano CTVM; Fiat Leasing; Banco Fiat
Directorships: Brazilian Symphonic Orchestra; Brazil-Canada Chamber of Commerce; Fundacao Dom Cabral; Fundacao Getulio Vargas
Cyrus Madon, Managing Partner & CEO, Private Equity
Background: PricewaterhouseCoopers
Craig Noble, Managing Partner & CEO, Alternative Investments
Education: Mount Allison University; Schulich School of Business
Background: Bank of Montreal
Lori Pearson, Managing Partner & COO
Directorships: Brookfield Foundation; Pathways to Education in Canada
Sam Pollock, Managing Partner & CEO, Infrastructure
Education: Queen's University
Directorships: TWC Enterprises
William Powell, Managing Partner, Real Estate
Education: University of Richmond; Darden School of Business
Anuj Ranjan, Managing Partner & Head of Business Development
Education: BSc, University of Alberta; MBA, Richard Ivey School of Business

Venture Capital & Private Equity Firms / Canadian Firms

Sachin Shah, Managing Partner & Chief Investment Officer
Education: University of Toronto
Ben Vaughan, Managing Partner, Infrastructure
Education: Queen's University

2063 BUILD VENTURES
1505 Barrington St
2nd Floor
Halifax, NS B3J 3K5
Canada

web: www.buildventures.ca

Mission Statement: Build Ventures works with dedicated management teams to help build early stage technology companies in the Atlantic region.

Fund Size: $50 million
Founded: 2013
Investment Criteria: Early Stage
Industry Group Preference: Technology
Portfolio Companies: Affinio, Celtx, Introhive, Resson Aerospace, Smart Skin Technologies, Interaxon, AirVM, icejam, Fiddlehead, Dash Hudson, Spring Loaded, The Money Finder, Manifold, Radient 360, ProcedureFlow

Key Executives:
Patrick Keefe, General Partner
e-mail: patrick@buildventures.ca
Education: MPhil, Univ. of Oxford; MBA, Harvard Business School
Background: VP, Investment, Innovacorp; Founder, CVAI; Atlas Venture; The Boston Consulting Group
Rob Barbara, General Partner
e-mail: rob@buildventures.ca
Education: Queen's University; MBA, Richard Ivey School of Business, University of Western Ontario
Background: SVP, Burgundy Asset Management; Founder, Beaujolais Private Investment Management; TD Securities; President & Co-Founder, eSalveo

2064 CAISSE DE DEPOT ET PLACEMENT DU QUEBEC
Édifice Jacques-Parizeau
1000, place Jean-Paul-Riopelle
Montréal, QC H2Z 2B3
Canada

Phone: 514-842-3261 **Fax:** 514-842-4833
Toll-Free: 866-330-4833
e-mail: info@cdpq.com
web: cdpq.com

Mission Statement: Fund manager for pension and insurance plans.

Fund Size: $326.7 Billion
Founded: 1965
Key Executives:
Charles Emond, President & CEO
Education: BBA, HEC Montreal
Background: Partner, Grant Thornton LLP; Manager, PricewaterCooper; EVP, Scotiabank

2065 CANADIAN BUSINESS GROWTH FUND
730-145 King Street West
Toronto, ON M5H 1J8
Canada

Phone: 416-364-2243
Toll-Free: 833-459-2243
web: cbgf.com

Mission Statement: Growth capital investor formed by Canada's leading banks and insurance companies.

Fund Size: $545 million
Minimum Investment: $3-20 million
Portfolio Companies: Amelia, Appnovation, Believeco, Busbud, Cold Bore Technology, Felix, Homestyle Selections, Kudos, Librestream, LifeRaft, Lift Auto Group, MaxSold, Neovation, Paystone, ProcedureFlow, Prodigy, Proposity, Shopper+, Stephano Group, STN Video, Unyte, Xello

Key Executives:
George Rossolatos, CEO & Managing Partner
e-mail: george.rossolatos@cbgf.com
Education: Queen's Univ.; Kellogg School of Management
Background: Avante Logixx; TorQuest Partners

2066 CARPEDIA INTERNATIONAL
75 Navy St.
Oakville, ON L6J 2Z1
Canada

Phone: 905-337-3407
web: www.carpediacapital.com

Mission Statement: Carpedia International manages various investments on behalf of founding shareholders, financial institutions, and individuals. The Carpedia approach focuses on identifying and implementing sustainable, financially accretive change without capital expenditure, examining changes to product, process, system and behaviour.

Geographic Preference: Canada
Average Investment: $8 to $20 million
Minimum Investment: $8 million
Investment Criteria: Succession Sales, Recapitalizations, Management Buy-Outs/Buy-Ins, Carve-Outs, Growth Capital
Industry Group Preference: Manufacturing, Food & Beverage, Transportation, Distribution, Consumer Services, Business Products & Services, Hotels, Restaurants, Retailing

Other Locations:
305 Tarpon Drive
Fort Lauderdale, FL 33301
USA

230 Park Avenue
3rd Floor W
New York, NY 10169
USA

Key Executives:
Mark Follows, President
e-mail: mfollows@carpedia.com
Education: BA, Harvard University
Daniel Lee, Managing Director
e-mail: dlee@carpedia.com
Education: BA & MBA, Dalhousie University

2067 CATALYST CAPITAL GROUP
181 Bay Street, Suite 4700
PO Box 762
Bay Wellington Tower, Brookfield Place
Toronto, ON M5J 2T3
Canada

Phone: 416-945-3000 **Fax:** 416-945-3060
e-mail: info@catcapital.com
web: catcapital.com

Mission Statement: Catalyst specializes in control and/or influence investments in distressed and undervalued Canadian situations.

Geographic Preference: Canada
Fund Size: $4.3 billion
Founded: 2002
Portfolio Companies: Advantage, Allstream, Brushstrokes, Cabovisao, Callidus Capital Corporation, Call-Net Enterprises Inc., Calpine Co., Canwest, Countryside Power Income Fund, Frontera Energy, Gateway Casinos & Entertainment, Geneba Properties N.V., Hollinger, Imax, Mobilicity, Natural Markets Food Group, Quad/Graphics, Royal Group Technologies Limited, Snowbear, Sonar Entertainment Inc., SR Telecom & Co., Stelco Inc., Therapure Biopharma Inc., YRC Worldwide

Venture Capital & Private Equity Firms / Canadian Firms

Key Executives:
  Newton Glassman, Managing Partner
  Education: MBA, Wharton School of the University of Pennsylvania
  Directorships: FrontPoint Partners, LLC., Gateway Casinos & Entertainment Ltd., Cable Satisfaction International Inc., Natural Markets Restaurant Corp., Ceberus Capital Management LP
  Gabriel de Alba, Managing Director & Partner
  Education: BSc, NYU Stern School of Business; MBA, Columbia University
  Background: Bank of American International Merchant Banking Group, Banker's Trust New York Merchant Brank Group
  Directorships: Geneba Properties, Advantage Rent-A-Car, Gateway Casinos & Entertainment, Therapure Biopharma, World Color Press, Sonar Entertainment
  Rocco DiPucchio, Managing Director & COO
  Education: Osgood Hall Law School, York University
  Background: Senior Partner, Lax O'Sullivan Lisus Gottlieb LLP; Associate, Blake, Cassels & Graydon LLP
  James Riley, Managing Director
  Education: Masters of Law, Harvard University; University of Toronto
  Background: Banking and Finance Law Group, Goodmans LLP; Norton Rose Filbright Canada; Stikeman Elliott LLP
  Steven Rostowsky, CFO
  Education: University of Cape Town
  Background: Sprott Inc.

2068 CBI2 CAPITAL
4300 Bankers Hall W
888 - 3rd Street SW
Calgary, AB T2P 5C5

Phone: 403-351-1779
e-mail: contact@cbi2.com
web: cbi2.com

Mission Statement: Formerly known as Target Capital, CBI2 Capital invests in early-stage companies within the expanding cannabis industry.
Geographic Preference: Canada, Europe, US
Founded: 2017
Investment Criteria: Early-Stage
Industry Group Preference: Cannabis
Portfolio Companies: LivWell International Corp.

Key Executives:
  Sonny Mottahed, Chairman/President/CEO
  Education: University of Calgary
  Background: Chairman/CEO, 51st Parallel Life Sciences; Business Development, Nexen Inc.; Institutional Sales, Salman Partners Inc.; Investment Banking, Canaccord Financial; Managing Director, Raymond James & Associates; CEO, Black Spruce Merchant Capital
  Directorships: IR Optimizer; Iridium Risk Services; Razor Energy Corp.
  Bill MacDonald, Executive VP/Director
  Directorships: Grunewahl Organics; Inner Spirit Holdings
  David Cheadle, Chief Financial Officer
  Education: BCom, University of Manitoba
  Background: VP, Canaccord Genuity Inc.; VP, Raymond James & Associates; Managing Partner, Black Spruce Merchant Capital
  Gregory G. Turnbull, Director
  Education: BA, Philosophy/English, Queen's University; LLB, Law, University of Toronto
  Background: Sr. Partner, McCarthy Tetrault LLP
  Directorships: Hawk Exploration; Online Energy Inc.; Heritage Oil Plc.; Sonde Resources Corp.; Porto Energy Corp.; Sunshine Oilsands; Marquee Energy; Crescent Point Energy; Storm Resources
  Matteo Volpi, Director
  Education: BA, International Management, Franklin College; London Business School
  Background: Business Development, INTELS Nigeria Ltd.; Business Development Manager, Olrean Invest Africa; Business Development Manager, Ocean Alliance Consultancy; CEO, IOMS
  Directorships: Gaia Consulting Ltd.

2069 CCEI
10 Adelaide Street E
Toronto, ON M5C 1J3
Canada

Phone: 416-572-8526
e-mail: info@cc-ei.ca
web: www.cc-ei.ca

Mission Statement: CCEI invests equity in renewable energy and infrastructure assets in oECD and developing, high-yield markets.

Founded: 2019

Key Executives:
  Okan Altug, Managing Director
  Education: BA, Bogazixi University, Istanbul; MBA, Pace University
  Background: Founder, Daruma Corporate Finance
  Sasha Jacob, Managing Director
  Education: BA, Bishop's University; MBA, Sir Wilfred Laurier University; GP LLM, University of Toronto
  Background: CEO, Jacob Capital Management
  Axel Goldenberg, Managing Director
  Education: Richmond University, London
  Background: Co-Founder/Managing Partner, Dem-Al Autogas; Founder, Naturelgaz
  Warren Smulowitz, Managing Director
  Background: Bank of Montreal
  Ugur Kilic, Managing Director
  Education: MBA, Boston University
  Background: Country Manager, Yingli Solar, Istanbul
  Ruchan Hamamci, Managing Director
  Education: BSc, MSc, PhD, Bosphorus University
  Background: Eksim Investment Holding; Sancak Energy Holding

2070 CELTIC HOUSE VENTURE PARTNERS
239 Argyle Avenue
Ottawa, ON K2P 1B8
Canada

web: www.celtic-house.com

Mission Statement: Celtic House Venture Partners is an independent Canadian investment firm actively pursuing and investing in innovative technology businesses. The company works closely with management teams to produce successful results for its investors. From offices in Toronto and Ottawa, Celtic House manages three funds.

Geographic Preference: Canada, United Kingdom
Fund Size: $425 million
Founded: 1994
Investment Criteria: Early-Stage
Industry Group Preference: Communications, Networking, Information Technology, Infrastructure, SaaS
Portfolio Companies: Auvik, Canvaspop, Corsa, Envenio, FileFacets, Graphite Software, KodaCloud, Nuvyyo, Peraso Technologies, Rare, Raven, Vleepo

Key Executives:
  David Adderley, Partner
  Education: BA, Queen's University; LLB, University of Western Ontario
  Background: Gowlings LLP
  Directorships: Avvasi, Diablo Technologies, Graphite Software, Nuvyyo
  Tomas Valis, Partner
  Education: PhD, University of Toronto; Postdoctoral Researcher, MIT

Venture Capital & Private Equity Firms / Canadian Firms

Cory Michalyshyn, Chief Financial Officer
Education: BComm., Queen's University
Background: CFO & COO, Solink

2071 CENTRESTONE VENTURES
7-1250 Waverley Street
Winnipeg, MB R3T 6C6
Canada

Phone: 204-453-1230 Fax: 204-453-1293
web: www.centrestoneventures.com

Mission Statement: CentreStone Ventures is a life sciences focused private venture capital fund investing primarily in companies developing early stage therapeutics, medical devices, diagnostics and new drug delivery methods.
Geographic Preference: Western Canada, Midwest United States
Investment Criteria: Early-Stage
Industry Group Preference: Life Sciences, Therapeutics, Medical Devices, Diagnostics
Portfolio Companies: Diamedica, Medicure, Verista Imaging, LED Medical Diagnostics, Orasi Medical, Sanommune, Ardeo Imaging, Marsala Biotech, Limestone Pharma

Key Executives:
Albert D. Friesen, Chief Executive Officer
Education: PhD, Protein Chemistry, University of Manitoba
Background: President, Winnipeg Rh Institute
Marcus Enns, Venture Partner
Education: B.Comm, University of Manitoba
Background: VP, Corporate Affairs, Genesys Venture Inc.
Directorships: Miraculins, Kane Biotech
James Kinley, Vice President, Finance & Operations
Education: BComm, University of Manitoba
Background: Manitoba Telecom

2072 CHRYSALIX
1111 West Hastings St.
Suite 333
Vancouver, BC V6E 2J3
Canada

Phone: 604-659-5499 Fax: 604-659-5479
e-mail: info@chrysalix.com
web: www.chrysalix.com

Mission Statement: The Chrysalix Global Network is a premier alliance of independent, top-tier clean energy venture capital firms - globally linked but locally managed - with the primary goal to better address the global nature of the cleantech industry. Spanning three continents, the CGN firms discuss local deal flow, exchange knowledge, and share networks resulting in faster geographical expansion for their portfolio companies, lowered investment risk, and superior fund performance.
Geographic Preference: Global
Founded: 2001
Investment Criteria: Early-Stage
Industry Group Preference: Oil & Gas, Metals & Mining, Manufacturing, Logistics, Construction, Transportation, Chemicals & Advanced Materials, Agriculture, Utilities & Electric Power, Asset Management, Artificial Intelligence, Data Analytics, Internet of Things, Robotic Systems, Blockchain
Portfolio Companies: Angstrom, Applied Impact Robotics, Axine Water Technologies, Brammo Motorsports, Bridgelux, Day4, DTE, Enbala, Enerworks, Epyon, Fat Spaniel, Feasible, GAN Systems, General Fusion, H2Gen, Haila Technologies Inc., Lilliputian, Liquid Light, Minehub Technologies Inc., Minesense, Novamera Inc., Relion, Rithmik Solutions, Sortera Alloys, Svante, VerAI

Key Executives:
Fred van Beuningen, Managing Partner
Education: Erasmus University
Directorships: Director of Innovation & Strategic Marketing, AkzoNobel
Wal van Lierop, Executive Chair/Founding Partner
e-mail: wvlierop@chrysalix.com
Education: PhD, Economics, Vrije Universiteit, Amsterdam
Background: VP Strategic Planning, Westcoast Energy; McKinsey & Company
Charles Haythornthwaite, Senior Partner
e-mail: chaythornthwaite@chrysalix.com
Education: MBA, Berkeley; PhD, Laser Physics & Materials Science, University of Southhampton
Background: Soliant Energy

2073 CIBC CAPITAL MARKETS
161 Bay St.
Brookfield Place
Toronto, ON M5J 2S8
Canada

web: www.cibccm.com

Mission Statement: Focuses on growth-oriented businesses and looks to help founders and management teams take their company to the next level, committed to providing steady support through all economic cycles.
Geographic Preference: Canada
Fund Size: $200 million
Founded: 1989
Average Investment: $10-20 million
Minimum Investment: $2 million
Investment Criteria: Later-Stage, Growth Equity, Acquisitions, Management/Leveraged Buy-Outs, Recapitalizations
Industry Group Preference: Software, Energy, Financial Services, Technology, Manufacturing, Pharmaceuticals, Medical Devices, Healthcare, Hardware, Communications, Mining, Oil & Gas, Power, Real Estate, Telecommunications
Portfolio Companies: AKQA, Adaytum, Advanced Interactive Systems, Algorithmics, Almonde, Arriva Pharmaceuticals, Avere, B2eMarkets, Bell ActiMedia, Broadband Services, Cardikine, CashEdge, CCS, Chrysalis, Clean Air Partners, Cornice Corporation, Creation Technologies, Datawire Communication Networks, Definiens AG, DirectBuy, eAssist Global Solutions, Eontec Limited, Equator Technologies, Esurg Corporation, Everypath, Firm AS, First Asset Management, FreshDirect, FuelQuest, Groupe Lucien Barriere, GCAN Insurance Company, GT Nexus, HAHT Commerce, Herbal Magic, Hubspan, Hydrogenics Corporation, InfoTalk Corporation, InQuira, Interwise, iSuppli Corporation, iVillage, Juniper Financial, Kaval Wireless Technologies, Keystone Communications, Lavalife, MetricStream, MicroMed Technology, Molecular Staging, Multi-Channel Communications, NetByTel, Nextpage, Nursefinders, Nuvelo, OnePath Networks, Otis Spunkmeyer, PerformanceRetail, Persona, Points International, PortalPlayer, Prepaid Direct, Prior Data Sciences, Progressive Group, Proton Energy Systems, Qpass, QUMAS, Realstar Management, Seisint, SemperCare, Servicesoft Technologies, SiGe Semiconductor, Silicon Bandwidth, Silicon Energy Corp, Soltrus, Syrrx, THINQ Learning Solutions, TheBrain Technologies Corporation, Totality, Triversity, US HealthWorks, ValiCert, Venturion Limited Partnership, Vigilance, Visiprise, Vividence Corporation, Vytek Corporation, Western Forest Products, Wild Tangent, Workbrain, Wysdom, Yantra

Key Executives:
Harry Culham, Sr. Exec. VP and Group Head, CIBC Capital Markets
Education: Sauder School of Business, University of British Columbia
Directorships: CIBC Children's Foundation; Faculty Advisory Board, Saunder School of Business; Mount Sinai Hospital
Roman S. Dubczak, Managing Dir., Global Investment Banking, CIBC Capital Markets

Venture Capital & Private Equity Firms / Canadian Firms

Education: BComm, University of Toronto; MBA, Schulich School of Business
Directorships: Fraser Institut, CIBC Children's Foundation
Christian Exshaw, Managing Dir. and Head, Global Markets, CIBC Capital Markets
Education: Master of Science, Risk Management & Financial Instruments, Insitut d'Administration des Entreprise, France

2074 CIBC INNOVATION BANKING
Toronto, ON
Canada

e-mail: Mailbox.CIBCInnovationBanking@cibc.com
web: www.cibc.com/en/commercial/areas-of-specialization/innovation-banking.html

Mission Statement: This branch of CIBC invests in clients who are in the innovation economy, from startups to later-stage businesses.

Founded: 2018
Investment Criteria: Early Stage, Middle Stage, Later Stage, Startups, Mature Companies
Industry Group Preference: Technology, Software, Innovation
Portfolio Companies: 7 Shifts, Active Campaign, Active State, Adthena, Aktana, AlyaaCare, Allbound, Altia, Altus Assessments, apptegy, Quatic Informatics, ARInsights, Assent, ATC, Avoxi, Azalea Health, Backstop Solutions, Benevity, Bera Outsmart, Bidgely, Bloomerang, Blue J, Bridgit, Calytera, Canalyst, Cinchy, CipherHealth, Clarius, Coconut Software, Complion, Confidant, CoPilot AI, Credly, Crunchbase, DefenceStorm, Dext, E2Open, Edsby, Egress, Embotics, Emovi, EPact, Epion Health, Eventus, Exari, EzTexting, Finch, First Ascent Ventures, FleetComplete, Fulcrum, Geoforce, Ginger, Gravy Analytics, Hardent, Health Fidelity, Health Joy, Hive9, Hootsuite, Informed DNA, Infutor, Innovate MR, Intellijoin, Intradiem, Invixium, Jane, Karbon, Keyfactor, Karbyte, Librestream, Lifespeak, Lightspeed, Liongard, Liqid, Management Controls, Maverix Private Equity, MayStreet, Medfar Clinical Solutions, Medtrainer, Mindful Health Solutions, Narrative Science, Ninjacat, NuMat, Onsite Dental, OpSens, Parchment, Pender Growth Fund, PitchPoint Solutions, Plotly, Point Predictive, Pomelo, Practice Ignition, Praemo, Proctoru, Profound, ProNavigator, prophix, Prusm Capital, PulmonX, Q4, Redica Systems, Relatient, RemoteLock, Rose Rocket, Rubikloud, Ruby, Sampler, Semior, Sensibill, SingleOps, SiteDocs, Solink, Stratifyd, Taplytics, Tehama, Terminus, Tractable, Tricentis, Vanedge Capital, Vapotherm, Vbrick, VeeAM, Vena, Vertu Capital, Voyant, Webair, Webware.io, Whitecap Venture Partners, White Star Capital, Worximity,

Key Executives:
Mark McQueen, President/Executive Managing Director
e-mail: mark.mcqueen@cibc.com
Education: BA, Western University
Background: President & CEO, Wellington Financial LP;
Directorships: Algoma Central Corp
Amy Olah, Managing Director
e-mail: amy.olah@cibc.com
Education: BComm, University of Guelph
Background: VP of Business Development, Wellington Financial LP
Mark Usher, Managing Director/North American Market Leader
e-mail: mark.usher@cibc.com
Education: BA, Western University; MBA, Queen's University
Background: VP of Knowledge Based Industries, RBC; Partner, INVISION Inc.; Partner, Wellington Financial LP

2075 CLAIRVEST GROUP
22 St. Clair Avenue East
Suite 1700
Toronto, ON M4T 2S3
Canada

Phone: 416-925-9270
e-mail: info@clairvest.com
web: www.clairvest.com

Mission Statement: Clairvest partners with management to invest in profitable small and mid-sized North American companies with the goal of helping to build value in the business and generate superior long term financial returns for investors.

Geographic Preference: North America
Fund Size: $1 billion
Founded: 1987
Average Investment: $15 - 100 million
Minimum Investment: $5 million
Investment Criteria: Expansion, Acquisition or Buy-out, Turnaround
Industry Group Preference: All Sectors Considered
Portfolio Companies: Accel Entertainment, ace2three.com, Also Energy, Digital Media Solutions, Elements Casino, Meriplex Communications, Right Time Heating and Air Conditioning, Winter Bros. Waste Systems

Key Executives:
Jeff Parr, Vice Chair and Managing Director
Education: University of Western Ontario
Background: Partner, Canadian Mezzanine Fund; Coopers & Lybrand
Directorships: N-Brook Mortgage Group, Casino Marina del Sol, Casino New Brunswick, Midwest Gaming
Ken Rotman, CEO and Managing Director
Education: BA, Tufts University; MSc, London School of Economics; MBA, New York University
Background: EM Warburg Pincus & Co.
Directorships: Wellington Finanaical, Light Tower Rentals, PEER 1, Discovery Air
Michael Wagman, President and Managing Director
Education: HBA, Richard Ivey School of Business; CFA
Background: BMO Nesbitt Burns Equity Partners
Directorships: Casino Marina del Sol, Latin Gaming Osorno, KUBRA, Sonco Gaming
Michael Castellarin, Managing Director
Education: BComm, Queen's University; MBA, Northwestern University Kellogg School of Management
Background: Management Consultant, Monitor Company
Directorships: Light Tower Rentals, Sonco Gaming
Mitch Green, Managing Director
Education: BS, Cornell University; MBA, University of Michigan School of Business
Background: Leveraged Finance, BNP Capital Markets; Corporate Finance, Bank of America
Directorships: KUBRA, PEER 1
Robbie Isenberg, Managing Director
Education: MBA, Northwestern Univeristy's Kellogg School of Management; HBA, Richard Ivey School of Business
Background: Sr. Case Team Leader, Monitor Group; Investment Banking, Credit Suisse
Sebastien Dhonte, Managing Director
416-413-6026
e-mail: sdhonte@clairvest.com
Education: BComm, McGill University; MBA, INSEAD
Background: Consultant, McKinsey & Company

2076 CLEARSPRING CAPITAL PARTNERS
30 Wellington Street W
Suite 500
Toronto, ON M5L 1E2
Canada

Phone: 416-868-4900
e-mail: info@cscap.ca
web: www.cscap.ca

Venture Capital & Private Equity Firms / Canadian Firms

Mission Statement: A private equity team with a focus on creating value and success for middle market Canadian companies. Formerly known as Callisto Capital.
Geographic Preference: Canada
Fund Size: $600 million
Founded: 2002
Average Investment: $20 - $50 million
Investment Criteria: Middle Market, Acquisitions, Buyouts, Consolidations, Restructurings, Recapitalizations
Industry Group Preference: Technology, Healthcare, Manufacturing, Consumer Products, Business Products & Services
Portfolio Companies: Cbi Health Group, Creation Technologies, Demers Ambulances, Diversified Metal Engineering, Dynacare Kasper, Homewood Health, Logistik, Maxxam Analytics, Medical Pharmacies, Mini-Skool, Spectrum Health Care, Telecon, Town Shoes, Voyages Traditours
Other Locations:
   1575, De l'Avenir Boulevard
   Bureau 100
   Laval, QC H7S 2N5
   Canada
   Phone: 416-868-4900
Key Executives:
   Lawrence Stevenson, Managing Director
   416-868-4512
   e-mail: lstevenson@cscap.ca
   Education: Royal Military College; MBA, Harvard Business School
   Background: CEO, Chapters; Co-Founder, Bain & Company Canada; CEO, Pep Boys
   Jim Probert, Chief Financial Officer
   416-868-4911
   e-mail: jprobert@cscap.ca
   Education: BA, University of Toronto
   Background: Director, Finance, CARGO Cosmetics Corp.; PricewaterhouseCoopers
   John Veitch, Principal
   e-mail: jveitch@cscap.ca
   Education: BComm, Queen's University
   Background: Scotiabank
   Directorships: Logistik Unicorp, Demers Ambulances
   Joseph Shlesinger, Senior Advisor
   416-868-4516
   e-mail: jshlesinger@cscap.ca
   Education: Ryerson Polytechnic University; MBA, Richard Ivey School of Business, University of Western Ontario
   Background: Strategy Consultant, Bain & Company Canada
   Directorships: Medical Pharmacies Group, Town Shoes, Alpine Canada Alpin
   Marie-Claude Boisvert, Affiliated Advisor
   e-mail: mcboisvert@cscap.ca
   Education: Ecoles des Hautes Etudes Commerciales de Montreal; MBA, INSEAD
   Background: Managing Partner, Kilmer Capital; CFO, Greiche & Scaff; Goldman Sachs; KPMG

2077 CM PARTNERS
1021 West Hastings Street
Suite 1200
Vancouver, BC V6E 0C3
Canada

Phone: 604-558-6168
e-mail: info@cm-canada.com
web: cmpartners.ca

Mission Statement: CM Partners is a private equity firm that invests in profitable, well-managed, small to medium sized businesses.
Geographic Preference: Canada, USA
Fund Size: $200 Million
Founded: 2017
Average Investment: $5-30 Million
Key Executives:
   Kenny Zou, Founder and CEO
   Education: BA, University of California, Berkeley
   Background: Hana Financial Group
   Regan Li, Co-Founder and Managing Partner
   Education: BS, Duke University; MBA, University of Pennsylvania
   Background: HIG Capital; Macquarie Capital

2078 COBALT CAPITAL
1464 Cornwall Rd.
Suite 7
Oakville, ON L6J 7W5
Canada

Phone: 905-815-9755
e-mail: pkeane@cobaltcapital.ca
web: www.cobaltcapital.ca

Mission Statement: Cobalt Capital is a boutique private equity firm made up of former business owners and operators seeking to help private companies grow and innovate by investing their capital and contributing their operating expertise. The partners of Cobalt Capital have significant business and entrepreneurial experience in a wide range of disciplines, sectors, and geographies and they work closely with the companies they invest in to help them achieve their goal of growth activities.
Geographic Preference: Canada, United States
Average Investment: $2 - $5 million
Minimum Investment: $2 million
Investment Criteria: Ownership Succession, Expansion Capital, Acquisition Financing, Management Buy-Out/Buy-In, Divisional Spin Off, Recapitalization
Industry Group Preference: Diversified
Portfolio Companies: Pyrotek Special Effects, Phoenix Innovations Corp.
Key Executives:
   Patrick Keane, President & CEO
   905-815-9755 x222
   e-mail: pkeane@cobaltcapital.ca
   Background: Keanall Group of Comanies
   Scott Dunlop, Managing Director
   905-815-9755 x231
   e-mail: sdunlop@cobaltcapital.ca
   Background: Vice President/General Manager, Specialty Home Products, CFM Corporation
   Brian Hogan, Director & CFO
   905-815-9755 x223
   e-mail: bhogan@cobaltcapital.ca
   Background: CFO, Iovate Health Sciences; Corporate Finance, CFM Corporation

2079 COPPERLION CAPITAL
2600 - 200 Granville Street
Vancouver, BC V6C 1S4

Phone: 604-637-1112 **Fax:** 604-637-1113
e-mail: info@copperlioncapital.com
web: www.copperlioncapital.com

Mission Statement: CopperLion performs corporate development and special projects on behalf of the Washington Companies.
Industry Group Preference: Marine Transportation, Construction, Engineering, Environmental, Mining, Aviation, Rail Transportation
Portfolio Companies: Aviation Partners, Envirocon, Modern Machinery, Montana Rail & Southern Railway of British columbia, Montana Resources, Seaspan Marine Corp
Key Executives:
   Kyle Washington, Executive Chair
   Education: BBA, University of Montana
   Directorships: Seaspan Corporation, Seaspan Marine Corporation, Envirocon, Modern Machinery, Montana

Rail Link, Montana Resources, Southern Railway of British Columbia

2080 CORDIANT CAPITAL
1002 Sherbrooke Street West
Suite 2800
Montreal, QC H3A 3L6
Canada

Phone: 514-286-1142
web: www.cordiantcap.com

Mission Statement: Focused on infrastructure debt in emerging markets.

Geographic Preference: Asia, Eastern Europe, Latin America, Africa
Fund Size: $1.5 billion
Founded: 1999
Portfolio Companies: Tecon Rio Grande SA, Real People Investment Holdings, SREI Infrastructure Finance Ltd, Latapack, ProCredit Group, Vicentin SAIC, Eleme Petrochemical

Key Executives:
  Benn Mikula, Co-CEO
  Education: BA & MA, McGill University
  Background: Coradiant; Fibermedia; CEO, CloudOps; Montreal Neurological Hospital & Research Institut; Montreal Children's Hospital; President, Acorn Society
  Jean-François Sauvé, Co-CEO
  Education: Business Administration, L'École des Hautes études Commerciales; MBA, INSEAD
  Background: Barclays Bank; President, Pictet Canada LP
  James T. Kiernan, Honorary Chairman
  Education: BA, Brown University; MBA, Harvard University
  Background: President, Goldman Sachs Canada Inc.

2081 COVINGTON CAPITAL CORP.
340 King Street
4th Floor
North Elevator
Toronto, ON M5A 1K8
Canada

Phone: 416-365-0060
Toll-Free: 888-746-4751
e-mail: info@covingtonfunds.com
web: www.covingtonfunds.com

Mission Statement: Covington Capital is a Canadian venture capital investment firm focused on supporting the growth and success of visionary entrepreneurs within Canada. Lead by a team of seasoned venture capitalists, Covington has invested in over 100 enterprises throughout Canada. Covington invests in small to medium sized Canadian enterprises that hold strong growth potential.

Geographic Preference: Canada
Fund Size: $300 Million
Founded: 1994
Average Investment: $500,000 to $7 million
Minimum Investment: $500,000
Investment Criteria: Mid to Later Stage
Industry Group Preference: Manufacturing, Distribution, Information Technology, Healthcare
Portfolio Companies: Clek Inc., Interface Biologics, MMIST, PowerBand Global, Wire IE

Key Executives:
  Scott Clark, Managing Partner
  e-mail: scott@covingtoncap.com
  Education: HBA, Richard Ivey School of Business
  Background: Vice President, Harrowston; Business Development Bank of Canada
  Phil Reddon, Managing Partner
  e-mail: phil@covingtoncap.com
  Education: HBA
  Background: Business Development, Bank of Canada
  Directorships: Bank of Montreal Capital Corporation
  Matt Hall, SVP, Investments
  e-mail: matt@covingtoncap.com
  Education: BACS, Business Administration, Huron College University; CBV
  Background: Great-West Life Co.
  Lisa Low, VP, Finance
  e-mail: lisa@covingtoncap.com
  Education: MA, BA, BSc, University of Waterloo
  Background: IBM Canada, Deloitte, Touche
  Stephen Campbell, CFO and Director, Valuations
  e-mail: steve@covingtoncap.com

2082 CREDIT MUTUEL EQUITY
600 de Maisonneuve W
Suite 2810
Montreal, QC H3A 3J2
Canada

Phone: 514-281-2286
web: www.creditmutuelequity.com

Mission Statement: A venture capital firm that supports business leaders by providing equity at all stages of their companies' development, from seed phase to buyout. Crédit Mutuel Equity is the Private Equity branch of Crédit Mutuel Alliance Fédérale.

Geographic Preference: France, Canada, USA, Germany, Switzerland
Investment Criteria: Seed, Start-up, Expansion
Industry Group Preference: Agriculture, Farming, Consumer Goods, E-Commerce, Energy, Real Estate, Industry, Engineering, Software, IT, Media, Health, Transportation, Logistics

Other Locations:
  TD Canada Trust Tower
  161 Bay Street
  Suite 2440
  Toronto, ON M5J 2S1
  Canada
  Phone: 647-699-7401

  520 Madison Avenue
  37th Floor
  New York, NY 10022
  Phone: 917-515-0974

  28, Avenue de l'Opera
  Paris 75002
  France
  Phone: 33(0)1 53 48 53 00

  32, avenue Camus
  BP 50416
  Nantes 44004 Cedex 01
  France
  Phone: 33(0)2 40 35 75 31

  23, parvis des Chartrons
  Bordeaux 33058
  France
  Phone: 33(0)5 56 99 58 81

  33, avenue Le Corbusier
  Lille 59000
  France
  Phone: 33(0)3 20 12 65 97

  Espace Cordeliers
  2, rue du President Carnot
  Lyon 69293 Cedex 02
  France
  Phone: 33(0)4 72 56 91 00

  31, rue Jean Wenger-Valentin
  Strasbourg 67000

France
Phone: 44(0)3 88 37 74 85

Avenue de Champel 29
Geneva CH-1206
Switzerland
Phone: 41 22 347 66 35

Schutzengasse 30
Zurich CH-8001
Switzerland
Phone: 41 43 543 64 27

c/o BECM
9-11 Wilhelm-Leuschner Strasse
Frankfurt 60329
Germany
Phone: 49 69 274 021 87

Key Executives:
Ludovic André, Managing Director
e-mail: ludovic.andre@creditmutuel.eu
Education: MS, Grenoble Inst. of Techology; MBA, HEC - Paris
Background: Air Liquide
Raghu Bharat, Principal
e-mail: raghu.bharat@emerilloncapital.com
Education: MBA, McGill University
Background: Nokia Siemens Networks
Directorships: lvl Studio, CM Labs Simulations

2083 CROSBIE & COMPANY
150 King Street West
15th Floor
PO Box 95
Toronto, ON M5H 1J9
Canada

Phone: 416-362-7726 Fax: 416-362-3447
e-mail: info@crosbieco.com
web: www.crosbieco.com

Mission Statement: Crosbie excels at creating customized market-based solutions to help clients meet their objectives. They bring experience, expertise and knowledge of markets, as well as specialized professional resources. They're known for developing and aggressively implementing creative approaches that produced successful client outcomes.

Geographic Preference: Canada
Founded: 1971
Investment Criteria: Restructurings, Management Buyouts
Portfolio Companies: ACI, Belmont Meat Products, CDI Computer Dealers, CFN, Circuit World, Construction Control, HMR Foods, Quint, Rumble Automation, Wolf Medical Systems

Key Executives:
Allan Crosbie, Chairman Emeritus
416-362-4217
e-mail: acrosbie@crosbieco.com
Education: MBA, Harvard Business School; BA, University of Toronto
Background: Wood Gundy
Ed Giacomelli, Vice Chair
416-362-0020
e-mail: egiacomelli@crosbieco.com
Education: BA, MBA, Ivey School of Business, Western University
Background: Wood Gundy, Rothschild
Directorships: WIC Communications, Prostate Cancer Canada, St. Michael's Hospital Foundation
Ian Macdonell, Managing Director
416-362-1953
e-mail: imacdonell@crosbieco.com
Education: BSc, Chemical Engineering, Queen's University; MBA, Richard Ivey School of Business, Western University
Background: CIBC Wood Gundy; RBC Capital Market
Directorships: Zeton International

Colin Walker, Managing Director
416-362-7016
e-mail: cwalker@crosbieco.com
Education: BEng, Management degree, McMaster University; MBA, Michael G. DeGroote School of Business
Background: Portfolio Manager, First Ontario Fund; Vice President, Swiss Bank Corporation
Directorships: Toronto Chapter of the Turnaround Manager
Richard Betsalel, Managing Director
416-362-4882
e-mail: rbetsalel@crosbieco.com
Education: BSc, Biology, McMaster University; MBA, Schulich School of Business, York University
Background: Financial Analyst, Bank of Nova Scotia
Michael Duncan, Vice President
e-mail: mduncan@crosbieco.com
Education: Richard Ivey Business School

2084 CROSS-BORDER IMPACT VENTURES
MaRS Centre, West Tower
Suite 1720
661 University Avenue
Toronto, ON M5G 1M1
Canada

Phone: 416-583-5821
e-mail: info@crossborder.ventures
web: www.crossborder.ventures

Mission Statement: Cross Border Impact Ventures aims to be the preferred investor for transformative health technology companies with the potential of meeting the needs of women, children and adolescents across global markets.

Fund Size: $30 million
Industry Group Preference: Healthcare, Health Technology
Key Executives:
Annie Thériault, Managing Partner
Education: BS, Mount Allison University; MBA, Wilfrid Laurier University
Background: Northwater Capital Management Inc; Grenville Strategic Royalty Corp; Grand Challenges Canada
Donna Parr, Managing Director
Education: MS, University of Toronto; MBA, York University
Background: Senior Portfolio Manager, OMERS; Private Equity Fund Manager, Canada Pension Plan; Executive Director, CellAegis Devices; President, Crimson Capital Inc
Directorships: Constellation Software Inc; Topicus.com

2085 CROWN CAPITAL PARTNERS
333 Bay Street
Suite 2730
Toronto, ON M5H 2R2
Canada

web: crowncapital.ca

Mission Statement: A specialty investment manager providing alternative debt financing for private equity backed and non-sponsored middle market transactions from offices in Toronto and Calgary. Crown Capital was founded as a successor company of Crown Life Insurance Company and is wholly owned by its management partners. For its investors, Crown Capital provides a strong track record of effective investment management in the alternative debt space. In 2011, Crown Capital entered into a strategic partnership with Hesperian Capital Management Ltd., portfolio manager of Norrep Group of Funds, whereby Hesperian will, pending regulatory and other approvals, acquire an equity interest in Crown Capital.

Geographic Preference: Canada
Founded: 2000
Average Investment: $5 to $25 million

Minimum Investment: $5 million
Investment Criteria: Acquisitions, Management Buy-Outs, Growth Financings, Recapitalizations
Portfolio Companies: Genalta Power, Touchstone Exploration, Landdrill International, Contac Services, Petrowest Energy Services Trust
Other Locations:
150 - 9th Avenue SW
23rd Floor
Calgary, AB T2P 3H9
Canada
Key Executives:
Christopher A. Johnson, President and CEO
e-mail: chris.johnson@crowncapital.ca
Education: BComm, University of Guelph; CFA, CBV
Background: Investment Manager, Crown Life Insurance Company
Michael Overvelde, SVP, Finance and CFO
e-mail: michael.overvelde@crowncapital.ca
Education: BComm, Queen's University; CPA; CFA
Background: VP, Raymond James; roles at TD Securities
Adam Jenkins, Vice President
e-mail: adam.jenkins@crowncapital.ca
Education: BS, University of Calgary
Background: VP of Corporate Development, Marquee Energy

2086 CTI LIFE SCIENCES
1 Place Ville-Marie
Suite 1050
Montreal, QC H3B 4S6
Canada

Phone: 514-798-2333
e-mail: info@ctisciences.com
web: www.ctisciences.com

Mission Statement: CTI Life Sciences invests in pre-clinical and clinical development stage life sciences companies.
Geographic Preference: Canada, USA
Fund Size: $245 million
Founded: 2006
Industry Group Preference: Life Sciences, Biopharmaceuticals
Portfolio Companies: XTUIT, Sutrovax, Phemi, Dalcor Pharmaceuticals, Immunovaccine Inc., Visterra, Ilkos Therapeutics, Profound Medical Corp., Cellaegis Devices, Zymeworks, Precithera
Key Executives:
Ken Pastor, Managin Partner
514-798-2333
e-mail: kpastor@ctisciences.com
Background: Merrill Lynch Canada; Porfolio Manager, Federation des Caisses Desjardins
Jean-Francois Leprince, Managing Partner
514-787-1619
e-mail: jfleprince@ctisciences.com
Background: President & CEO, Aventis Pharma Canada; Marion Merrell Dow
Directorships: Somnus Therapeutics Inc., IRICoR (Insititue for Research in Immunology and Cancer), AllerGen NCE Inc.
Shermaine Tilley, Managing Partner
e-mail: stilley@ctisciences.com
Education: MBA, University of Toronto; PhD, John Hopkins University
Laurence Rulleau, Managing Partner
e-mail: lrulleau@ctisciences.com
Education: Universite du Quebec a Montreal; PhD, Montreal University

2087 CYCLE CAPITAL MANAGEMENT
1000 Sherbrooke St. W
Suite 1610
Montreal, QC H3A 3G4
Canada

Phone: 514-495-1022
e-mail: info@cyclecapital.com
web: www.cyclecapital.com

Mission Statement: A cleantech venture capital fund manager.
Geographic Preference: Canada
Founded: 2009
Investment Criteria: Seed-Stage, Early Stage
Industry Group Preference: Clean Technology, Renewable Energy
Portfolio Companies: Agrisoma Biosciences, Airex Energy, CVT Corp., Energate, Enerkem, Eocycle, GaN Systems, Greenmantra Technologies, Inocucor Technologies, Laboratoire M2, LED Roadway Lighting, Local Logic, Lufa Farms, MineSense, Polystyvert, Power Survey, ESS Inc.
Other Locations:
MaRS Centre, West Tower
661 University Avenue
Suite 450
Toronto, ON M5G 1M1
Canada

Building 9, 14th Floor
No. 195 Hongkong E Street
Laoshan District
Qingdao
China

Key Executives:
Andree-Lise Methot, Founder & Managing Partner
e-mail: amethot@cyclecapital.com
Education: MS, University of Montreal; BS, Geological Engineering, University Laval
Background: Founder, Fonds d'investissement en developpement durable/FIDD
Directorships: Ecotech Quebec, Reseau Capital, Natural Gas Technologies Centre
Claude Vachet, Managing Partner
e-mail: cvachet@cyclecapital.com
Education: Chemical Engineering, Ecole Polytechnique; MBA, Finance, HEC Montreal
Background: Innovatech, Kirchner, Multiple Capital

2088 DANCAP PRIVATE EQUITY
197 Sheppard Ave. W
Toronto, ON M2N 1M9
Canada

Phone: 416-590-9444 **Fax:** 416-590-7444
e-mail: elias@dancap.ca
web: www.dancap.ca

Mission Statement: Provides direct investments to Canadian mid-market businesses that require private equity financing in the form of equity or subordinate debt. Participates in co-investment partnerships in medium to large sized Canadian companies and international co-investment opportunities alongside private equity and institutional investors.
Geographic Preference: Canada
Fund Size: $50 Million
Founded: 2002
Average Investment: $1 to $10 million
Minimum Investment: $1 million
Investment Criteria: Acquisitions, Management Buyouts, Recapitalizations, Capital Expansion
Industry Group Preference: Manufacturing, Healthcare, Consumer Products, Technology, Consumer Services
Portfolio Companies: Cann Trust Direct, Flyp Technologies Inc., IOU Financial Inc., GreenField Ethanol, Key Brandon Entertainment Inc., Porter Aviation Holdings, Christmas Tradition, Millennium Care Inc., BC Decker Inc., Victess Capital Corp., Hetworth Corp., Gavel & Gown, Jancee Screw

Products, Newbury Equity Partners LP, Portfolio Litigation Fund, Direct Marketing Company, Madison Dearborn Capital Partners VII LP, Landmark Equity Partners XV LP, Blue Point Capital Partners III(A) LP, Brentwood Associates Private Equity V LP, MHR Institutional Partners IV LP, CTP Offshore-C Feeder Fund Ltd., Court Square Capital Partners III LP, GC Partners Interational Ltd., Landmark Equity Partners XIV LP, LODH Private Equity Euro Choice III LP, CEREP II Mezzanine Loan Partners LP, NYLIM Jacob Ballas India Fund III LLC, Carlyle Asia Partners III LP, Madison Dearborn Capital Partners VI LP, PAI Erope V LP, Newbury Second Fund LP, European Secondary Development Fund IV LP, Clearview Capital Fund II LP, Primus Pacfic Partners I LP, Brentwood Associates Private Equity IV LP, Lyceum Capital Fund II, Rosemont Solebury Co-Investment Fund LP, Tenaska Poer Fund II LP, The Resolute Fund II, MatlinPatterson Global Opportunities Partners III LP, CVCI Growth Partnership II, MHR Institutional Partners III, GCM Grosvenor LS Power Equity Partners II, Excellere Capital Partners LP, LODH Private Equity Euro Choice III, Eureka II LP, The Succession Fund LP, Quadriga Capital III, Terra Firma Capital Partners III, Carlyle Japan International Partners II, Court Square Capital Partners II, Blue Point Capital Partners II, Madison Dearborn Capital Partners V, Tenaska Power Fund LP, Carlyle Europe Real Estate Partners II, MacQuarie European Infrastructure Fund LP

Key Executives:
Aubrey Dan, Principal
e-mail: aubreydan@dancap.ca
Education: University of Western Ontario; Honorary Doctorate of Laws, Assumption University
Background: Wampole Canada, Dancap Productions
Elias Toby, COO, CFO
e-mail: elias@dancap.ca
Background: Anderson Quick, Deloitte & Touche

2089 DESJARDINS CAPITAL
2, complexe Desjardins
bureau 1717
CP 760
Montreal, QC H5B 1B8
Canada

Phone: 514-281-7131
Toll-Free: 866-866-7000
web: www.desjardinscapital.com

Mission Statement: Desjardins Capital invests in dynamic and innovative businesses in diverse sectors across Quebec.
Geographic Preference: Quebec
Fund Size: $1.25 billion
Founded: 2001
Minimum Investment: $50,000 - $750,000
Investment Criteria: All stages and possible exit strategies
Industry Group Preference: Manufacturing, Business Products & Services, Information Technology, Telecommunications
Portfolio Companies: 20-20 Technologies, 3ci, A. & D. Prevost, A.T.L.A.S. Aeronautique, Acceo Solutions, Acema Importations, Acier Majeau, Action Mecanique, Agence De Securite Mirado, Albert Perron, Alimentation Francis Gravel, Alutrans Canada, Alyotech Canada, Amaya Gaming Group, Ambulance Medilac, Anderson Group, Andre Potvin Cuisine/Salle De Bain, Approvisionnement Populaire, Arbell Electronics, Ateliers Cfi Metal, Attraction Media, Autobus Dionne, Autobus Dufresne, Avjet Holding, Axesnetwork Solutions, Azentic, Balances M. Dodier, Batitech, Beaudry & Theroux, Behaviour Interactive, Boisaco, Bonneterie Richelieu, Bouffard Sanitaire Et Acier Bouffard, Boutique Le Pentagone, Budget Propane, C.R.O.I., C.R.S/Vamic, Cables Ben-Mor, Cactus Commerce, Camoplast Solideal, Cam-Trac Sag-Lac, Canmec Group, Cavalia, Centre De Tri, Centre Des Congres De Sept-Œles, Centre Medical Le Mesnil, Cervo-Polygaz, Charcuterie L. Fortin Ltee, Chariots Elevateurs Du Quebec, Cheq Fm, Chlorophylle, Chocolat Jean-Talon, Cif Metal Ltd, Clic, Climatisation Mixair, Clinique D'Optometrie Vu, Cls Info, Cogiscan, Collection Papillon Gemme, Comact Equipment, Complexe Funeraire Ste-Bernadette, Complexe Sportif Interplus, Concept Mat, Conception Gsr, Congebec, Construction L.F.G., Construction Leclerc Et Pelletier, Cooperative De Travailleurs Actionnaire De Negotium Technologies, Cooperative De Travailleurs Actionnaire De Tec, Cooperative Forestiere De Girardville, Cooperative Forestiere De L'Outaouais, Cooperative Funeraire De L'Estrie, Cooptel, Coractive, Corporation Developpement Knowlton, Creaform, Cta De Magnus Poirier, Cuisines G.B.M., Decoplex, Dek Canada, Demolition Et Excavation Demex, Demtec, Distribution Eugene Gagnon, Dynagram Software, Ebi-Tech, Echaufadage Industriel, Eco-Pak, Editions Gladius International, Electro-5, Emballages Deltapac, Emile Bilodeau Et Fils, Enobia Pharma, Entreprises Alfred Boivin, Entreprises D'Auteuil & Fils, Entreprises Rodrigue Piquette Inc, Environnement Sanivac, Eocycle Technologies, Equipements De Piscine Carvin, Equipements Julien Achard & Conception Gsr, Equipements Polytek, Evolutel, Excavation Vallier Ouellet, Exo-S, Expertronic, Exploration Midland, Express Havre St-Pierre Ltee, Farinart, Fempro Inc, Fenetres Selection, Filspec, Flexo Labels, Fonderie Bsl, Formedica Ltee, Frima Studio, Fromagerie Boivin, Galenova, Garage Georges Beaudoin, Gesdix, Gestion Alain Hebert, Gestion C.T.M.A., Gestion Gilles D'Amours, Gestion P.R.N. Vigneault, Gestion Patrick Firreri

Key Executives:
Guy Cormier, Chair, President and CEO
Education: Bachelors of Business Administration, MBA, École des Hautes Études Commerciales
Marie-Hélène Nolet, Chief Operating Officer

2090 DIAGRAM VENTURES
2200 Stanley Street
Maison Atholstan
Montreal, QC H3A 1R6
Canada

web: diagram.ca

Mission Statement: Diagram is a venture builder that fosters and de-risks ideas to build conviction in the opportunity. The firm matches entrepreneurs with vetted ideas and larger capital investment.
Geographic Preference: Canada, United States
Industry Group Preference: Financial Services, Insurance, Software, Healthcare, Blockchain, Cryptocurrency
Portfolio Companies: Baselane, Breathe Life, Clearestate, Collage, Conduit, Dialogue, Nesto, Novisto, Pillar Financial, Retirable, Streamingfast, Synctera, Wingocard
Other Locations:
77 King Street W
Suite 400
Toronto, ON M5K 0A1

Key Executives:
Francois Lafortune, Co-Founder & CEO
Education: BEng, McGill University; MBA, Stanford Graduate School of Business
Background: Co-Leader of Canadian Technology, McKinsey & Company
Paul Desmarais III, Co-Founder & Chair
Education: BA, Harvard College; MBA, INSEAD
Background: Portag3 Ventures; Great-West Lifeco; Imerys
Directorships: Great-West Life; Investors Group; Mackenzie; Pargesa; Groupe Bruxelles Lambert
Guillaume Marion, Partner & COO
Background: Financial Institutions Group, HSBC; PSP Investments; Genuity Capital Markets
Directorships: Montreal Economic Institute

Venture Capital & Private Equity Firms / Canadian Firms

2091 DISCOVERY CAPITAL
43-1238 Eastern Drive
Port Coquitlam, BC V3C 6C5
Canada

Phone: 604-683-3000 Fax: 604-941-0010
e-mail: info@discoverycapital.com
web: www.discoverycapital.com

Mission Statement: Discovery Capital is one of Canada's most experienced technology venture capital firms. Discovery Capital focuses primarily on the enhancement of BC-based technology ventures, in the areas of information technology, communications, health & life sciences and environmental & energy technologies.

Geographic Preference: British Columbia
Founded: 1986
Investment Criteria: Early-Stage
Industry Group Preference: Information Technology, Healthcare Information Technology, Advanced Technologies, Communications, Life Sciences, Technology, Environment, Energy
Portfolio Companies: Asprevea Pharmaceuticals, ALI Technologies, Cardiocomm Solutions Inc, Circon Systems Corp, Day4 Energy, Idelix Software, Photochannel Networks, Sierra Wireless, Tantalus Systems Corp, Texada Software Inc, TIR Systems, Tri-Link Technologies Inc, Vigil Health Management, Vision2Hire Solutions Inc

Key Executives:
  John McEwen, Chief Executive Officer
  e-mail: jmcewen@discoverycapital.com
  Education: BComm, University of British Columbia
  Background: Tantalus Systems Corp., IBM Canada Ltd.
  Harry Jaako, President
  e-mail: hjaako@discoverycapital.com
  Education: B.Eng., Lakehead University
  Background: TSX Group , Inc., Vancouver Stock Exchange, DMR Group, TSX Venture Exchange, Toronto Stock Exchange, IBM Canada Ltd.
  Directorships: Texada Software Inc., Leading Edge, TIR Systems Ltd., Exceptional Technologies Fund 5 Inc., Vigil Health Solutions Inc., NRC-IRAP & BC Discovery Fund Inc.
  Charles Cook, Vice President/CFO
  e-mail: ccook@discoverycapital.com
  Education: MBA, University of British Columbia; CMA
  Background: Director, Dundee Securities Corporation

2092 DISRUPTION VENTURES
446 Spadina Road
Suite 303
Toronto, ON M5P 3M2
Canada

e-mail: info@disruption-ventures.com
web: disruption-ventures.com

Mission Statement: Disruption Ventures funds companies with female-led businesses.

Investment Criteria: Seed-Stage; Companies must be female-led
Industry Group Preference: Digital Technology, Fintech
Portfolio Companies: ePact Network, Fafle Tech Labs, Hostfully

Key Executives:
  Elaine Kunda, Managing Partner
  Education: McMaster University
  Background: President & CEO, b5media; President & CEO, ZipLocal; Managing Director, Toronto.com; Business Development Manager, Grey Interactive
  Directorships: G(irls)20 Summit

2093 DISTRICT VENTURES CAPITAL
2540 Kensington Road NW
Calgary, AB T2N 3S3
Canada

e-mail: contact@districtventurescapital.com
web: www.districtventurescapital.com

Mission Statement: Provides VC funding for innovative Canadian companies in the food & beverage and health & wellness sectors.

Geographic Preference: Canada
Fund Size: $30 million
Average Investment: $150K
Industry Group Preference: Consumer Products
Portfolio Companies: Chickapea Pasta, Balzac's Coffee, RTHM, Nada Moo!, Bow Valley BBQ, Drizzle, One World Foods, Cook It, Healthy Pets, Torill's Table, Prairie Fava, Little Tucker, Farm Fresh Pet Foods, Culcherd

Key Executives:
  Arlene Dickinson, President & CEO
  Jason Berenstein, Partner & CFO
  Education: Univ. of Toronto

2094 DMZ VENTURES
Toronto, ON
Canada

web: dmzventures.com

Mission Statement: Network of accelerator programs under the brand name Zone Startups. Formerly known as Ryerson Futures.

Portfolio Companies: Ada, Beam, Borrowell, Buyproperly, Chatter, Click.ai, Crowdbabble, Domio Health Audio, Erplain, Evichat, Figure1, Flipd, Flybits, Flyshot, Halp, Hubbli, Intel Sports, Level Jump, Litmus, Livegauge, Maple Assist, Mio, Optimity, Remitr, Repable, Sampler, Sensibill, Sensorsuite, Shoelace, SmartTones Media, Smooth Commerce, Snapscreen, Soapbox, Staffy, Swift, Switchboard, Thrive, Wave, Zensurance

2095 DOVENTI CAPITAL
Vancouver, BC

web: www.doventi.com

Mission Statement: Invests in companies serving the cannabis industry. Areas of focus include production, research, bio-pharmaceuticals, health sciences, and phytoceuticals.

Founded: 2015
Industry Group Preference: Cannabis
Portfolio Companies: Altaire, BC Naturals, Cannera Consulting, GreenTec Bio-Pharmaceuticals, Qstrios, Vitalis Extraction Technology, Zenalytic Laboratories

Key Executives:
  Norton Singhavon, Founder/Managing Director
  Education: Kwantlen Polytechnic University
  Background: Investor/Advisor, Permanent Construction & Project Management LTD; President, Syndicate Ventures; Consultant, Cronos Group; Advisor to CEO/Business Development, Invictus MD Strategies Corp.; Founder/Chairman/CEO, GTEC Holdings

2096 DREAM MAKER VENTURES
16 McAdam Avenue
Toronto, ON M6A 0B9
Canada

Phone: 905-553-7326
e-mail: info@dreammaker.vc
web: www.dreammaker.vc

Mission Statement: Dream Maker Ventures is the investment segment of Dream Maker Corp., an asset management firm in

Venture Capital & Private Equity Firms / Canadian Firms

Toronto. Their goal is to fund early stage companies that use technology to transform the way businesses operate.

2097 DRI CAPITAL
100 King Street W
Suite 7250
PO Box 62
Toronto, ON M5X 1B1
Canada

Phone: 416-863-1865
e-mail: info@dricapital.com
web: www.dricapital.com

Mission Statement: DRI Capital manages funds that purchase royalties from pharmaceutical and biotechnology companies, research institutions, universities, and inventors. It is an indirect subsidiary of Persis Holdings Ltd.

Fund Size: $2 billion
Founded: 1992
Industry Group Preference: Healthcare, Biopharmaceuticals, Drug Development
Portfolio Companies: Enbrel, Keytruda, Myozyme, Remicade, Sensipar, Simponi, Stelara, Tysabri, Zytiga

Key Executives:
Behzad Khosrowshahi, Chief Executive Officer
e-mail: bk@dricapital.com
Education: BA, History, Reed College; CA
Background: Future Shop Ltd., Deloitte & Touche LLP
Chris Anastasopoulos, EVP & CFO
e-mail: ca@dricapital.com
Education: BComm, Univ. of Toronto; MBA, Rotman School of Management
Background: Ontario Municipal Employees Retirement System

2098 EDGESTONE CAPITAL PARTNERS
175 Bloor St. E
Suite 801
North Tower
Toronto, ON M4W 3R8
Canada

Phone: 416-860-3740 Fax: 416-860-9838
e-mail: info@edgestone.com
web: www.edgestone.com

Mission Statement: EdgeStone provides capital, strategic direction and business and financial advice to help promising mid-market and early-stage companies achieve their full potential. EdgeStone leverages the resources of its broad business network and ensures an alignment of interests to achieve superior returns for all stakeholders.

Geographic Preference: Canada
Fund Size: $2 Billion
Founded: 2000
Investment Criteria: Management Buyouts, Leveraged Buyouts, Recapitalizations, Expansion Capial
Industry Group Preference: Information Technology, Software, Telecommunications, Data Services, Internet Technology, Infrastructure, Energy, Manufacturing, Business Products & Services, Consumer Services
Portfolio Companies: Aurigen, Eurospect Manufacturing Inc., EZShield, Porter Aviation Holdings, Stephen's Rental Servies Inc., Specialty Commerce Corp.

Key Executives:
Samuel L. Duboc, Partner
Education: BS, Chemical Engineering, Tufts University; MBA, Harvard Business School
Background: Deals Review Committee, CIBC Capital Partners; Co-Founder, Loyalty Group; COO, Holzman Jewellers
Directorships: EZShield, New Food Classics, Porter Aviation Holdings, Stephenson's Rental Services, Bryker Techology Partners

Gilbert S. Palter, Managing Partner and Chief Investment Officer
Education: University of Toronto; MBA, Harvard Business School
Background: Founder/CEO/Managing Director, Eladdan Capital Partners; Founder, Eladdan Enterprises; Morgan Stanley; Smith Barney; McKinsey & Company; Clairvest Group
Directorships: Aurigen Capital Limited, Continental Alloys & Services, Specialty Catalog Corporation, Eurospec Manufacturing, Mitel Networks Corporation
Stephen O. Marshall, Managing Partner and Chief Operating Officer
Education: LLB, University of Western Ontario; MBA, MIT Sloan School of Management
Background: EVP, MDC Corporation; Managing Partner, Torys
Directorships: EZShield, Eurospec Manufacturing, Porter Aviation Holdings, Continental Alloys & Services

2099 ELGNER GROUP INVESTMENTS
3280 Bloor Street West
Suite 902
Toronto, ON M8X 2X3
Canada

Phone: 647-426-0380 Fax: 647-426-0376
e-mail: csinclair@elgnergroup.com
web: www.elgnergroup.com

Mission Statement: A privately held, self-funded investment group focused on small to medium sized fundamentally sound businesses that face operational, financial or business stress. Elgner Group will invest in fundamentally sound businesses that are either growing profitably or face operational, financial or business stress. We are particularly attracted to companies that offer significant opportunities to improve operating costs and markets that face substantial business change, foreign competition or industry consolidation.

Geographic Preference: Canada, United States
Founded: 1993
Average Investment: $2 to $25 million
Minimum Investment: $2 million
Investment Criteria: Distressed Situations, Corporate Divestitures, Recapitalizations, Family Successions, Unique Situations
Industry Group Preference: Manufacturing, Real Estate, Industrial Services, Automotive, Information Technology, Transportation, Capital Equipment, Distribution

Key Executives:
Claude Elgner, Managing Director
Education: P.Eng.
Roger Elgner, Managing Director
Education: P.Eng.
Craig Sinclair, Investment Director
Education: B.Comm.
Tim Chapman, Investment Director
Education: P.Eng.

2100 ELNOS
ELNOS Corporation for Business Development
31 Nova Scotia Walk
Suite 306, Third Floor
Elliot Lake, ON P5A 1Y9
Canada

Phone: 705-848-0229
web: www.elnos.com

Mission Statement: A full-service business development corporation that was established to stimulate economic growth in the ELNOS Region through new business development and investment.

Geographic Preference: Canada
Fund Size: $23 Million
Founded: 1993

Venture Capital & Private Equity Firms / Canadian Firms

Average Investment: Up to $250,000
Minimum Investment: $10,000
Investment Criteria: Start Up, Expansion, Financial Restructuring
Key Executives:
  William Elliott, General Manager
  e-mail: welliott@elnos.com
  Sharon Farquhar, Director of Financial Services
  e-mail: sfarquhar@elnos.com

2101 EMERALD TECHNOLOGY VENTURES
1320 - 161 Bay Street
Toronto, ON M5J 2S1
Canada

Phone: 416-900-3453 Fax: 416-900-3457
e-mail: info@emerald-ventures.com
web: www.emerald-ventures.com

Mission Statement: Global industrial technology investor.
Geographic Preference: Europe, North America
Fund Size: $450 million
Founded: 2000
Investment Criteria: Early-Stage, Expansion-Stage
Industry Group Preference: Clean Technology, Energy, Advanced Materials, Water
Portfolio Companies: Advanced BioNutrition, AlphaICs, EWT, Enocean, GeoDigital, HydroPoint, Identec Solutions, Librestream, Lucintech, Metgen, Open Mineral, P97, Powerhouse Dynamics, TaKaDu, Tropic Biosciences, Ushr

Other Locations:
  Emerald Technology Ventures AG
  Seefeldstrasse 215
  Zurich 8008
  Switzerland
  Phone: 41-442696100 **Fax:** 41-442696101

  Emerald Technology Ventures Pte. Ltd
  80 Raffles Place, Uob Plaza 1, #59-02
  Singapore 048624
  Singapore
  Phone: 65 9749 6900

Key Executives:
  Gina Domanig, Managing Partner
  Education: MBA, Thunderbird; ESADE
  Background: Senior Vice President, Sulzer
  Directorships: Identec Solutions, Inge, Pelamis
  Markus Moor, Senior Partner & CTO
  Education: Mechanical Engineering, University of Applied Sciences Solothum, Switzerland; MS, Economics & Technology, University of St. Gallen
  Background: Investment Director, SAM Private Equity; Miteco
  Directorships: Xunlight Corp., Enocean GmbH, O-Flexx Technologies
  Hans Dellenbach, Senior Partner & CFO
  Education: School of Business Administration, Zurich
  Background: Financial Controller, Kuoni Trave
  Directorships: Identec Solutions
  Charles Vaslet, Senior Partner
  Education: Electrical & Electronics Engineering, University of Leeds; MBA, Henley Management College
  Background: Vice President, ABB Equity Ventures; National Power LLC

2102 EPIC CAPITAL MANAGEMENT
2 Toronto Street
Toronto, ON M5C 2B6
Canada

e-mail: info@epiccapital.ca
web: epiccapitalmanagement.ca

Mission Statement: Boutique asset manager with a focus on Canada.
Geographic Preference: Canada
Founded: 2000
Industry Group Preference: Healthcare
Key Executives:
  David Fawcett, Founding Partner & Portfolio Manager
  e-mail: dfawcett@epiccapital.ca
  Background: Deutsche Bank Securities; First Marathon Securities
  Sabrina Hao, Partner
  e-mail: shao@epiccapital.ca
  Education: BS, University of Toronto
  Background: CEO, Reciprocity Asia
  Gordon Cheung, Venture Partner
  e-mail: gcheung@epiccapital.ca
  Background: Clinical Director, MRI & CT, CML Healthcare
  Scott Kaplanis, Venture Partner
  e-mail: skaplanis@epiccapital.ca
  Education: HBA, Richard Ivey School of Business
  Background: Macquarie Capital Markets
  Directorships: Memex Inc.

2103 ESPRESSO CAPITAL
8 King St. E
Suite 300
Toronto, ON M5C 1B5
Canada

Phone: 877-605-2021
e-mail: info@espressocapital.com
web: www.espressocapital.com

Mission Statement: Espresso Capital is partnered with private investors from the high technology community. They have built relationships with institutional finance companies, venture capital groups and professional service firms. Espresso Capital was founded by veteran technology company executives who understand first-hand the challenges faced by founders and entrepreneurs in funding the growth of their businesses.
Geographic Preference: Canada
Founded: 2009
Average Investment: $200,000
Industry Group Preference: Digital Media & Marketing, High Technology
Portfolio Companies: Algolux, Centah, Colligo, Coreworx, Detacratic, Grouby, HomeStars, OM Signal, Pressly, Q4, Strongpoint, Staftfl, Unbounce

Other Locations:
  125 S Clark Street
  Chicago, IL 60603
  USA

  700 N San Vicente Blvd
  7th Floor
  West Hollywood
  Los Angeles, CA 90069
  USA

  156 - 2nd Street
  San Francisco, CA 94105
  USA

Key Executives:
  Will Hutchins, Managing Director
  e-mail: will@espressocapital.com
  Background: TD Securities, Stikeman Elliott, Paul Weisse
  Enio Lazzer, Chief Operating & Financial Officer
  e-mail: enio@espressocapital.com
  Background: CIBC World Markets, Northern Trust Company Canada
  Alkarim Jivraj, Chief Executive Officer
  e-mail: alkarim@espressocapital.com
  Background: Managing Partner, Intrepid Business Acceleration Fund; Yorkton Securities
  Directorships: eSentire, SCI Marketview
  Will Jin, Managing Director
  Background: Covington Capital; Hathaway Corp.

Venture Capital & Private Equity Firms / Canadian Firms

2104 EVENTI CAPITAL PARTNERS
250 Yonge Street
Suite 1602
Toronto, ON M5B 2L7
Canada

web: www.eventi.com

Mission Statement: Toronto-based investment group specializing in SaaS, Internet infrastructure services and medical devices.

Founded: 2002
Investment Criteria: Early-Stage, Later-Stage
Industry Group Preference: SaaS, Internet Infrastructure Services, Medical Devices
Portfolio Companies: Base Pair Biotechnologies, Ceryx, Environics, Kinetic Commerce, Tenzing, Thindata, Visualase

Key Executives:
  Bill Di Nardo, Managing Partner
  Education: Richard Ivey School of Business
  Background: President & CEO, Grocery Gateway
  Directorships: Kinetic Commerce, Tenzing
  Scott Bryan, Managing Partner
  Background: General Counsel, Grocery Gateway; Miller Thomson; Star Data Systems
  Derek Ruston, Co-Founder/Partner
  Background: President, B&R Associates; General Partner, Catalina Southwest Investments; Management Consultant, McKinsey & Company; Senior Partner, Peter Barnard Associates

2105 EVOK INNOVATIONS
1410-1130 West Pender St.
Vancouver, BC V6B 2L3
Canada

e-mail: info@evokinnovations.com
web: www.evokinnovations.com

Mission Statement: Partnership between BC Cleantech CEO Alliance, Cenovus Energy and Suncor Energy invests in the commercialization of clean technology.

Fund Size: $100 million
Industry Group Preference: Clean Technology
Portfolio Companies: Allonnia LLC, ARIX Technologies, DarkVision Technologies, Ekona Power, Expeto Wireless, HARBO Technologies, Kelvin Inc., Mosaic Materials, Osperity, Quidnet Energy, Rotoliptic Technologies, Sanctuary AI, SensorUp, Syzygy Plasmonics, Twelve, Veerum

Key Executives:
  Marty Reed, Partner
  Background: The Roda Group
  Mike Biddle, Partner
  Education: BSc, University of Louisville; PhD, Case Western Reserve University
  Background: Dow Chemical; Cummins Engine Company; Founder, MBA Polymers
  Naynika Chaubey, Partner
  Education: AB, Princeton University

2106 EXPORT DEVELOPMENT CANADA
150 Slater Street
Ottawa, ON K1A 1K3
Canada

Toll-Free: 800-229-0575
web: www.edc.ca

Mission Statement: Offers financial and risk management solutions to help Canadian businesses expand into the international market.

Geographic Preference: North America, South America
Founded: 1944
Industry Group Preference: Industrial Equipment, Transportation, Engineering, Information Technology, Manufacturing, Telecommunications, Energy

Key Executives:
  Mairead Lavery, President and CEO
  Education: Queen's University Belfast
  Background: Bombardier
  Carl Burlock, EVP and Chief Business Officer
  Education: MBA, Dalhousie Univ.
  Background: Nova Scotia Power
  Lorraine Audsley, SVP and Chief Risk Officer, Global Risk Management
  Education: Henley Business School; University of Reading
  Ken Kember, SVP, Finance and Technology & CFO
  Education: BA, Master of Accounting, University of Waterloo; CA; CMA
  Background: Senior Manager, Accounting Group, PricewaterhouseCoopers
  Stephanie Butt Thibodeau, SVP, People and Culture
  Education: BComm, University of Ottawa; CFA

2107 EXTREME VENTURE PARTNERS
Toronto, ON
Canada

e-mail: info@evp.vc
web: evp.vc

Mission Statement: Focuses on providing early stage venture capital and management expertise to startup businesses to help propel them into the big leagues. Beyond the financial resources, EVP takes a hands-on approach to supporting startups, bringing a depth of technical and business expertise to the project.

Geographic Preference: Canada, United States
Average Investment: $300K
Minimum Investment: $250K
Investment Criteria: Pre-seed/Seed Stage
Industry Group Preference: Mobile, Data & Analytics, Internet of Things
Portfolio Companies: ACTO, Airstream, Beam Messenger, Blanc Labs, Blanclink, Chatter Research, CRG, Crowdcare, D1G1T, Damon X Labs, Dentem, DirectedAI, Dot Health, Eve Tab, Evree, Extreme Innovations, Flixel, Foxquilt Insurance, Granify, Groupie, Guardly, Hackworks, Influitive, Linkett, Lokafy, Mavencare, Minbox, National Prostaff, Nekso, Palette, Pitstop, Play The Future, Qualia, Revlo, RiverPay, Sensorsuite, Spently, Statflo, Stem Village, ThinkData Webware, Ubique, Uken, Upsight, Wagepoint, World Of Angus, Works, Zoom.AI

Key Executives:
  Ian Ainsworth, Managing Partner
  Directorships: Altamira, Fields Institute for Mathematical Science
  Ray Sharma, Founding Partner/CEO
  Education: Business Administration, Richard Ivey School of Business
  Background: CSFB Technology Group, BMO Nesbitt Burns, GMP Capital Trust
  Imran Bashir, Founding Partner/COO
  Education: MS, Electrical Engineering, University of Toronto
  Background: President & CEO, Envision Mobile; President & COO, Octanewave Software
  Ken Teslia, Founding Partner/Chairman
  Education: MBA, York University
  Background: RBC Capital Markets, Credit Suisse First Boston, GMP Capital Trust

2108 FARM CREDIT CANADA
3700 Victoria Ave. E
Regina, SK S4Z 1A5
Canada

Phone: 306-780-5616 Fax: 306-780-5611
Toll-Free: 855-230-6821
e-mail: skregina@fcc-fac.ca
web: www.fcc-fac.ca

Venture Capital & Private Equity Firms / Canadian Firms

Mission Statement: Provides venture capital financing to small and medium-sized businesses in value-added food processing, manufacturing of agricultural equipment, commercial processing and ag biotech.

Geographic Preference: Canada
Fund Size: $36 billion
Founded: 2002
Average Investment: $2.75 Million
Minimum Investment: $0.5 Million
Investment Criteria: Early-Stage, Growth-Stage, Mature-Stage Companies
Industry Group Preference: Agriculture, Forestry, Fishing, Food & Beverage, Nutraceuticals, Life Sciences, Biotechnology
Portfolio Companies: A&A Trading, Agribiotics Inc., Atlantic Horticulture, BIOX Corporation, Ensyn Technologies, MCN Bioproducts, Poss, Sembiosys Genetics Inc., Walker Seeds

Key Executives:
Michael Hoffort, President/Chief Executive Officer
Education: P.Ag., University of Saskatchewan
Directorships: STARS Air Ambulance
Sophie Perreault, Executive Vice President/Chief Operating Officer
Education: P.Ag., Laval University
Directorships: Regina Food Bank

2109 FASTBREAK VENTURES
Toronto, ON
Canada

web: www.fastbreak.co

Mission Statement: Fastbreak ventures focuses on enterprise software opportunities across FinTech, PropTech, Digital Health, and other industries where there's a growing customer base.

Founded: 2008
Investment Criteria: Pre-Seed/Seed Stage

Key Executives:
Matt Saunders, Co-Founder and Partner
Education: BA, MBA, Northeastern University
Background: COO, Millennium Data Systems; Partner, DVG Consulting; President, Ryerson Futures Inc.; Partner, Zone Startups Ventures
Alan Lysne, Co-Founder and Partner
Education: BEng, Queen's University
Background: Co-Founder/CTO, Davinci Technologies; CEO, Cascada Mobile; COO, Grapple Mobile; COO/Managing Partner, Ryerson Futures Inc.

2110 FENGATE
77 King Street W
Suite 3410
Toronto, ON M5K 1H1
Canada

Phone: 416-488-4184
web: fengate.com

Mission Statement: Fengate invests in long-life, high-quality assets and businesses on behalf of their clients.

Founded: 2016
Average Investment: $20-75 Million

Other Locations:
2275 Upper Middle Road E
Suite 700
Oakville, ON L6H 0C3
Canada
Phone: 905-491-6599

PO Box 30540
Houston, TX 77229
Phone: 346-241-0648

Key Executives:
Justin Catalano, Managing Director/Group Head of Private Equity
Education: BBA, Wilfred Laurier University; CFA
Background: Birch Hill Equity Partners; TD Capital; TD Securities
Omar Khalifa, Managing Director/Head of Private Equity Investments
Education: BBA, Wilfred Laurier University; CFA
Background: Director, Private Markets Group, OPTrust; BMO Capital Markets

2111 FIBERNETICS VENTURES
96 Grand Avenue S
Suite 203
Cambridge, ON N1S 2L9
Canada

Phone: 519-489-6700
e-mail: info@fibernetics.ca
web: www.fibernetics.ca/fibernetics-ventures

Mission Statement: Fibernetics looks for unique start-ups and early stage companies with innovative approaches to fiberoptic technology and telecommunications.

Founded: 2004
Investment Criteria: Start-Up, Early Stage
Industry Group Preference: Telecommunications

Key Executives:
Jody Schnarr, Chair & Executive Officer
Education: University of Toronto

2112 FIRST ASCENT VENTURES
10 King Street E
Suite 900
Toronto, ON M5C 1C3
Canada

Phone: 416-306-3021
e-mail: deals@firstascent.vc
web: www.firstascentventures.com

Mission Statement: Invests in emerging Canadian technology companies.

Founded: 2015
Average Investment: $5 - 10 Million
Investment Criteria: Series A and later
Industry Group Preference: Machine Learning, Big Data, Cloud Computing, Analytics, Mobile, Artificial Intelligence
Portfolio Companies: Assent, DailyPay, Dialogue, Q4, Rubikloud, ScribbleLive, Sensibill, SportlogiQ, ThinkData, Upchain

Other Locations:
3 Place Ville Marie
Suite 12350
Montreal, QC H3B 0E7
Canada

1 Ferry Building
San Francisco, CA 94111
USA

Key Executives:
Richard Black, Co-Founder & Managing Partner
Tony Van Marken, Co-Founder & Managing Partner
Nicole Vivaldi, Chief Financial Officer

Venture Capital & Private Equity Firms / Canadian Firms

2113 FONDACTION
2175, boul. De Maisonneuve Est
Bureau 103
Montreal, QC H2K 4S3
Canada

Phone: 514-525-5505
e-mail: investissement@fondaction.com
web: www.fondaction.com

Mission Statement: Labor-sponsored retirement savings management fund.
Geographic Preference: Quebec
Fund Size: $1.7 Billion
Founded: 1996
Other Locations:
125, boul. Charest Est
Bureau 501
Quebec, QC G1K 3G5
Canada
Phone: 418-522-8650
Key Executives:
Genevieve Morin, President & CEO
Education: BA, Concordia University; MBA, HEC Montreal
Background: Anges Quebec Capital

2114 FONDS DE SOLIDARITE FTQ
CP 1000, Succ. Chabanel
Montreal, QC H2N 0B5
Canada

Phone: 514-383-3663 Fax: 514-383-2501
Toll-Free: 800-567-3663
e-mail: comm@fondsftq.com
web: www.fondsftq.com

Mission Statement: Invests in companies impacting the Quebec economy and offer them services to further their development and create, maintain or protect jobs. Promotes economic training for workers so they can increase their influence on the economic development of Quebec. Stimulates the Quebec economy through strategic investments that benefit both Quebec workers and companies alike.
Geographic Preference: Quebec
Fund Size: $14.3 billion
Founded: 1983
Investment Criteria: Growing markets, Niches, Management buyouts
Industry Group Preference: All Sectors Considered
Portfolio Companies: A. & L. Pinard, A.S. Nettoyage, Abc Environnement, Abipa Canada, Acceo Solutions, Acier Fastech, Acier Majeau, Acquisio, Addenda Capital, Adelard Soucy, Adventure Gold, Aeroport International De Mont-Tremblant, AGF Group, Agora Communication, Agritibi R.H., Agro-100 Ltee, Agro-Bio Controle, Agrocentre Belcan, Alary, St-Pierre Et Durocher Arpenteurs Geometres, Alimentation Coop Port-Cartier, Alimentation L'epicier, Aliments Urbains, Amecci, Amh Canada Ltee, Andy Transport, Ani-Mat, Armeco, Asmacure, Atelier D'Usinage Quenneville, Atelier Progun, Atelier Tangente, Athos Services Commemoratifs, Atrium Innovations, Auberge Et Spa Le Nordik, Auberge Relais Lac Cache, Aurizon Mines Ltd, Aurvista Gold Corporation, Autobus Lion, Auvents W. Lecours, Avior Integrated Products, Azimut Exploration, B.M.B., Bercomac Limitee, Bertrand Ducks, Bestar, Bioniche Life Sciences, Bmi Canada, Bombardier, Boreal - Informations Strategiques, Boreal Drilling, Boutique La Vie En Rose, Brome Financial Corporation, BSL Wood Products, Cactus Commerce, Cafe Faro, Camoplast Solideal, Canada Moteurs Importations, Canadian Helicopters, Cape By The Sea, Carriere Neigette, Carrosserie Pro 2010, Cartier Resouces, Casavant Brothers, Centre De Peinture L.B.G., Centre Jardin Lac Pelletier, Ch Group Limited Partnership, Chateau Bonne Entente, Chateau M.T., Chemco

Key Executives:
Janie C. Béique, President and CEO
Education: MBA, Georgetown University; MBA, ESADE University
Directorships: Groupe CH; Groupe Functionalab; The Orchestre Symphonique de Montréal; Aéro Montréal

2115 FORAGE CAPITAL PARTNERS
400 Crowfoot Crescent NW
Suite 502
Calgary, AB T3G 5H6
Canada

Phone: 403-215-5492
e-mail: rlethebe@foragecapitalpartners.com
web: foragecapitalpartners.com

Mission Statement: Forage Capital Partners provides growth capital to businesses along the entire agriculture and food industry value chain. Forage offers both growth equity and subordinated debt. The Forage team works closely with entrepreneurs and management on the type of capital required to help them grow and prosper in a global marketplace.
Fund Size: $100 Million
Industry Group Preference: AgTech, Agriculture, Food
Portfolio Companies: Alasko Foods Inc., Awake Chocolate, Big Marble Farms, Croptimistic Technology Inc., Evoco Ltd., Fieldless Farms, Food 4 Pets Canada, Just Solutions Agriculture, LHG Foods Inc., Mother Raw, Ostara Nutrient Recovery Technologies Inc., Perlite Canada Inc., Red Dog Deli Raw Food Company, S3 Enterprises Inc.
Key Executives:
Jim Taylor, Managing Director
Education: MBA, Rotman School of Management, University of Toronto; BA, University of Alberta
Steven Leakos, Managing Director
Education: BComm, University of Saskatchewan
Daniel McCrimmon, Managing Director
Background: Manager, Ernst & Young

2116 FOUNDATION EQUITY CORPORATION
Canada

web: www.foundationequity.com

Mission Statement: Provides capital to entrepreneurs in the areas of energy services, manufacturing, and B2B software.
Industry Group Preference: Energy Services, Manufacturing, B2B Software
Portfolio Companies: Circle Cardiovascular Imaging, DriveAble Assessment Centres, Trajectory IQ, McCoy Global
Key Executives:
Kerry Brown, Founder & Chair
Education: University of Alberta; CA
Directorships: McCoy Global, DriveAble Assessment Centres, First Yellowhead Equities
Mike Cabigon, President
Education: BComm, University of Alberta
Background: VP & General Manager, Persona Communications

2117 FOUNDATION MARKETS
77 King Street West
Suite 2905
P.O. Box 121 Toronto Dominion
Toronto, ON M5K 1H1

Phone: 416-777-7300
e-mail: info@foundationmarkets.com
web: www.foundationmarkets.com

Mission Statement: A private merchant bank investing in early-stage public & private companies.
Geographic Preference: Canada
Founded: 2005
Investment Criteria: Early-Stage

Industry Group Preference: Cannabis, Technology, Food & Beverage, Natural Resources
Portfolio Companies: Aquamiel Tequilla, Aura Health Corp., Blockchain Innovations Inc., California Gold Inc., Harborside Inc., Irri-Al-Tal Ltd., Lineage Grow Co., Platinex Inc., Nutritional High, Snow Lakes Resources Ltd.
Key Executives:
  Adam Szweras, Chairman
  Education: LLB, Osgoode Hall Law School, York University
  Background: Partner, Fogler Rubinoff
  Directorships: Nutritional High; Aurora Cannabis
  Peter Bilodeau, President/CEO
  Education: MBA, Dalhousie University
  Alex Storcheus, Managing Director, Corporate Finances
  Education: BBA, Finance, Schulich School of Business, York University
  Directorships: Capricorn Business Acquisitions Inc.; BlockChain Innovations Corp.

2118 FOUNDERS GROUP OF FOOD COMPANIES
1111 West Hastings St
Suite 200
Vancouver, BC V6E 2J3
Canada

web: www.foundersfoodgroup.com

Mission Statement: Family-owned company solely focused on food businesses.
Geographic Preference: Canada; Midwest/Western US
Average Investment: $15-75 million
Investment Criteria: Mature
Industry Group Preference: Food
Portfolio Companies: Armand Agra, Freshstone Brands, Ganache Brands, Presteve Foods
Key Executives:
  Rod Senft, Partner
  e-mail: rod.senft@foundersfoodgroup.com
  Education: Univ. of Manitoba
  Background: Tricor Pacific Capital; Pender West Capital Partners
  Richard Harris, Partner
  e-mail: richard.harris@foundersfoodgroup.com
  Education: Univ. of Oxford; Univ. of London
  Background: Golden Boy Foods; Coca-Cola Drikker AS
  Trevor Johnstone, Partner
  e-mail: trevor.johnstone@foundersfoodgroup.com
  Education: UC Berkeley
  Background: Tricor Pacific Capital
  Derek Senft, Partner
  e-mail: derek.senft@foundersfoodgroup.com
  Education: Dartmouth College; London Business School
  Background: Pender West Capital Partners
  Directorships: Pender West Capital Partners; Canada Film Capital; Overland Container Transportation Services

2119 FRAMEWORK VENTURE PARTNERS
47 Front Street E
Suite 400
Toronto, ON M5E 1B3
Canada

web: www.framework.vc

Mission Statement: Framework invests in software companies with a focus on re-imagining everyday financial services applications or appling AI solutions to industry-specific datasets.
Other Locations:
  415 W Cordova Street
  Suite 203
  Vancouver, BC V6B 1E5
  Canada
Key Executives:
  Peter Misek, Co-Founder and Partner
  Education: CA, CPA, Illinois University
  Background: Venture Partner, DN Capital; Partner, BDC IT Venture Fund; Founder, SoundPays Inc.; Managing Director/Co-Head, Global Technology Research, Jefferies
  Andrew Lugsdin, Co-Founder and Partner
  Education: BSc, McGill University
  Background: Partner, BDC IT Venture Fund; Founder and President; Software Engineer, Nortel Networks

2120 FREYCINET INVESTMENTS
Toronto, ON
Canada

e-mail: info@freycinetinvestments.com
web: freycinetventures.com

Mission Statement: Freycinet Investments is a venture capital firm that invests in high potential technology companies, with particular focus on early stage ventures in the Toronto-Waterloo area.
Geographic Preference: Canada
Founded: 2013
Investment Criteria: Seed, Early Stage
Industry Group Preference: Technology, Water, Human Wellness, Artificial Intelligence
Portfolio Companies: Borrowell, Canopy Labs, Football For Good, GrowSumo, Hubba, Lucent Sky, Lucent Sky, Mosaic Manufacturing, Hashtag Paid, Proteocyte AI, PumpUp, PUSH, Sampler, Set Scouter, TrendMD, WatrHub
Key Executives:
  James Appleyard, Founder/President
  Education: BA, MBA, Rotman School of Management, University of Toronto; MSc, London School of Economics
  Background: Artez Interactive

2121 FULCRUM CAPITAL PARTNERS
885 West Georgia St
Suite 1020
Vancouver, BC V6C 3E8
Canada

Phone: 604-631-8088
e-mail: info@fulcrumcapital.ca
web: fulcrumcapital.ca

Mission Statement: Fulcrum Capital Partners provides flexible private equity and mezzanine financing to the Canadian middle market. They have helped build and grow more than 120 mid-market companies while generating superior, consistent returns for investors.
Geographic Preference: Canada
Fund Size: $750 million
Founded: 2011
Average Investment: $5 to $30 million
Minimum Investment: $5 million
Investment Criteria: Succession Planning, Growth Equity, Consolidations, Acquisitions, Management or Leveraged Buy-Outs, Privitization, Recapitalization, Pre-IPO Financing
Industry Group Preference: Manufacturing, Services, Distribution & Logistics, Consumer Products
Portfolio Companies: Accucam Machining, Aci Brands, Arctic Chiller Group, Athletica Sport Systems, Canstar Restorations, Dana Hospitality, G.I. Group, Jnm Group, Mobile Parts, National Logistics Services, Nilex, Tradesmen Enterprises, Verdant, Vitalus, Weatherhaven
Other Locations:
  79 Wellington St W
  Suite 3510
  Toronto, ON M5K 1K7

Venture Capital & Private Equity Firms / Canadian Firms

Canada
Phone: 416-864-2761

Key Executives:
Graham Flater, Partner
604-631-8078
e-mail: graham.flater@fulcrumcapital.ca
Education: BComm, University of British Columbia; CFA
John Philp, Partner
416-864-2705
e-mail: john.philp@fulcrumcapital.ca
Education: BA, Economics, Queen's University; MBA, Finance & Accounting, McGill University; ICC.D
Background: Richardson Greenshields, TD Securities, HSBC Securities, Managing Director, HSBC Capital
Johan Lemmer, Partner & CFO
604-631-8060
e-mail: johan.lemmer@fulcrumcapital.ca
Education: BComm, Bachelor of Accountancy, University of Witwatersrand; Business Economics Postgraduate Degree, University of South Africa
Background: CFO, HSBC Capital; CFO/VP Finance, Vancity
Paul Eldridge, Partner
416-864-2709
e-mail: paul.eldridge@fulcrumcapital.ca
Education: BComm, University of Guelph; MBA, University of Toronto
Background: HSBC Securities, Clairvest
Directorships: Allied, ACI, Astley Gilbert, G Adventures
Paul Rowe, Partner
604-631-8093
e-mail: paul.rowe@fulcrumcapital.ca
Education: BBA, St. Francis Xavier University; CFA
Background: HSBC Bank Canada; HSBC Capital
Directorships: A&B Rail Services, JAG Flocomponents, Petrospec Engineering
Greg Collings, Partner
416-864-3194
e-mail: greg.collings@fulcrumcapital.ca
Education: BBA, Wilfrid Laurier University; CA
Background: Audit Division, Collins Barrow Toronto
Directorships: Alumicor

2122 GARAGECAPITAL
Waterloo, ON
Canada

web: www.garage.vc

Mission Statement: GarageCapital is a Venture capital firm built by founders for founders.

Portfolio Companies: Acerta, Ada, Aide, Alert Labs, Alt Tex, Applyboard, Astranis, Avro Life Science, Bansho, Betterup, Binsentry, Blitzen, Bloom, Bonfire, Buf, Careerlist, Careguide, Caribou Wealth, Census, Chargespot, Chitter, Clearpath Robotics, Clew, Coconft, Codegem, Cognito, Commercebear, Commit, Contentfly, Convictional, Convox, Crescendo, Darwinai, Databox, Diagram Ventures, Disco, Dozr, Drifting In Space, Dwelling, Easypost, Embark Trucks, Evolved Meats, Fellow, Fiix, Flashbox, Float, Gecko Robotics, Grobo, Groq, Headroom, Helpwear, Humi, Hypercomply, Infra, Interaptix, Kenota, Kepler Communications, Kindred, Koble, Kritik, Lilia, Lugg, Manifest Climate, Moment Energy, Multiply Labs, Notch, Nurx, Okhi, Openphone, Openunit, Parallelz, Panther, Parlor, Pela, Perl Street, Phenomical Ai, Piinpoint, Placenote, Poka, Preemadonna, Ross, Relay, Ritual, Roadmunk, Roundtrip, Routethis, Sandylane, Sbx Robotics, Secoda, Shakudo, Skip Scooters, Snack, Sortable, Spatial, Statflo, Street Contxt, Substack, Superpowered, Taplytics, Terminus, Tertill, Tiggy, Toric, Tribe, Trunk, Trusscore, Utvate, Uvaro, Vanhawks, Vendr, Vinn Auto, Vital Biosciences, Voyage Labs, Wrk, Zenbase, Ziplunch

Key Executives:
Mike McCauley, Founder/General Partner
Education: BASc, University of Waterloo
Background: Co-Founder, BufferBox; Product Manager, Google Fi; Product Manager, Google X
Devon Galloway, Co-Founder/General Partner
Education: BASc, University of Waterloo
Background: Co-Founder, Redwoods Media; Co-Founder/CEO, Vidyard

2123 GCI CAPITAL
4789 Yonge Street
Unit 706
Toronto, ON M2N 0G3
Canada

Phone: 416-218-8828
e-mail: info@gci.vc
web: www.gci.vc

Mission Statement: Toronto-based early stage venture capital firm with two funds, including GCI Ventures.

Geographic Preference: Canada, China
Investment Criteria: Early Stage; Seed
Industry Group Preference: Information Technology, SaaS, Digital Health, B2B
Portfolio Companies: Alongside, ApplyBoard, C2RO, DreamPayments, ECO Technologies, Envenio, Eigen Innovations, EwayTech, Fantuan Delivery, FileFacets, Genecis, Graphite Software, GrubMarket, Insuranceforchildren.ca, Juix, MappedIn, O2 Canada, Peraso, Repable, Sinitic, Tacit Innovations, TritonWear

Other Locations:
Unit 1001, Bld. 5, EFC
Dist. Yuhang
Hangzhou City, Zhejiang Province
China

42514 Albrae Street
Fremont, CA 94538
USA

239 Argyle Avenue
Suite 100
Ottawa, ON K2P 1B8
Canada

Key Executives:
Larry Y. Liu, Founding Partner
e-mail: larry@gciventures.com
Education: Rotman School of Management, University of Toronto; University of Portsmouth
Background: EffiSolar Energy Corporation

2124 GENESIS CAPITAL CORPORATION
8 King Street E
Suite 1410
Toronto, ON M5C 1B5

Phone: 416-214-2225
web: www.genesiscapitalcorp.com

Mission Statement: Genesis acquires and grows companies that can benefit from the firm's experience, in a range of industries and deal sizes.

Founded: 2010
Industry Group Preference: Manufacturing, Construction, Energy Services, Industrial Services, Environmental & Waste Management

Venture Capital & Private Equity Firms / Canadian Firms

2125 GENESYS CAPITAL
123 Front St W
Suite 1503
PO Box 34
Toronto, ON M5J 2M2
Canada

Phone: 416-598-4900
e-mail: info@genesyscapital.com
web: www.genesyscapital.com

Mission Statement: Genesys Capital is focused on building companies in the high-growth sectors of healthcare and biotechnology. Through its expertise and network, Genesys accelerates the development of commercially viable emerging companies that represent promising life science investment opportunities.

Geographic Preference: Canada
Fund Size: $200 million
Founded: 2000
Average Investment: $3 Million
Minimum Investment: $1 Million
Investment Criteria: Seed, Early, Expansion
Industry Group Preference: Biotechnology, Healthcare, Life Sciences
Portfolio Companies: Adapsyn Bioscience, Aptinyx, Fairhaven Pharmaceuticals, Flosonics Medical, Functional Neuromodulation, Fusion Pharmaceuticals, Impopharma, Inversago Pharma, Invitae Corp., Profound Medical, Therapeutic Monitoring Systems, Tioga Pharmaceuticals

Key Executives:
  Kelly Holman, Managing Director
  Education: BS, Biochemistry, MBA, Queen's University
  Background: Senior Investment Manager, MDS Capital Corp.
  Damian Lamb, Managing Director
  Education: McMaster University; MS, Molecular Neurobiology, MBA, Queen's University
  Background: Investment Manager, MDS Capital Corp.
  Directorships: Affinium Pharmaceuticals, Profound Medical
  Jamie Stiff, Managing Director
  Education: BS, Queen's University; MBA, Rotman School of Management
  Background: Samuel Lunenfield Research Institute, Mount Sinai Hospital
  Directorships: glcare Pharma

2126 GEORGIAN PARTNERS
2 St Clair Ave West
Suite 1400
Toronto, ON M4V 1L5
Canada

Phone: 416-868-9696
e-mail: info@georgian.io
web: georgian.io

Mission Statement: Investors in growth-stage software companies.

Geographic Preference: North America
Founded: 2008
Investment Criteria: Expansion-Stage, Growth-Stage
Industry Group Preference: Enterprise Software, Digital Media & Marketing, Information Technology, Internet, Cloud Computing, Artificial Intelligence
Portfolio Companies: Aera, Beam Dental, Bidgely, Bluecore, Chorus.ai, Cority, DataCandy, DefenseStorm, DISCO, eSentire, Fiix, Flashpoint, FreshBooks, Glooko, IEX Group, Influitive, Integrate.ai, Polar, Reonomy, RiskIQ, Ritual, Scribble, SentientScience, Shipwell, Siemplify, SignPost, Stratifyd, Tealium, Top Hat, TotalExpert, TraceLink, TrackTik, True Fit, Vision Critical, Welltok, WorkFusion, Xanadu

Key Executives:
  John Berton, Head of Operations
  Education: BA, Queen's University; Computer Science, University of Calgary; CFA
  Background: VRG Capital
  Justin Lafayette, Lead Investor, Head of Firm
  Background: Vice President, Information Platform & Solutions, IBM; Co-Founder, DWL
  Simon Chong, Lead Investor, Head of Customer Operations
  Education: MBA, Henley Management School
  Background: Worldwide Director of Sales, Information Solutions, IBM Software Group; DWL

2127 GIBRALTAR & COMPANY
100 Adelaide Street West
28th Floor
Toronto, ON M5H 1S3
Canada

e-mail: contact@gibraltarcompany.ca
web: www.gibraltarcompany.ca

Founded: 2013
Industry Group Preference: Consumer Products
Portfolio Companies: Blue Ant Media, CivicConnect, CrowdRiff, fanxchange, LXR and Co., Lunata Hair, Sheerly Genius, Tilley, VisionCritical

Key Executives:
  Cam Di Prata, CEO and Managing Partner
  Education: Concordia Univ.; Richard Ivey School of Business
  Background: Nesbitt Burns, Citigroup, Scotia Capital, National Bank of Canada
  Directorships: Crowdriff, FanXchange, LXRandCo
  Joe Mimran, Co-Founder and Chairman
  Background: Alfred Sung, Club Monaco, Joe Fresh
  Luigi Fraquelli, Co-Founder and Managing Director
  Education: McGill Univ.
  Background: BMO Capital Markets

2128 GLOBALIVE
48 Yonge Street
Suite 1200
Toronto, ON M5E 1G6
Canada

Phone: 416-204-7559
e-mail: info@globalive.com
web: www.globalive.com

Mission Statement: Startup studio and global investment firm.

Founded: 1998
Investment Criteria: Seed, Pre-Seed, Series A
Industry Group Preference: Telecommunications, Media, Real Estate, Artificial Intelligence, Healthcare
Portfolio Companies: Alignvest Management Corp., Dragonfly, Flexiti Financial, Founders Advantage Capital, Gibraltar, GlobaliveXMG, Nuuvera, Pitchpoint Solutions, Time Play, Touch Bistro, Trilogy International Partners, Zoocasa

Other Locations:
  11 North Moore 6B
  New York, NY 10013

  318 Spear St, #8G
  San Francisco, CA 94105

Key Executives:
  Anthony Lacavera, Founder & Chairman
  e-mail: anthonylacavera@globalive.com
  Education: Univ. of Toronto
  Background: WIND Mobile
  Brice Scheschuk, Managing Partner
  e-mail: bricescheschuk@globalive.com
  Education: BComm, Dalhousie Univ.
  Background: WIND Mobile

Venture Capital & Private Equity Firms / Canadian Firms

Simon Lockie, Partner
e-mail: simonlockie@globalive.com
Education: BA, University of Toronto; LLB, McGill University
Background: Partner, Davies Ward Phillips & Vineberg LLP
Directorships: WIND Mobile, Canadian Sea Turtle Network
David Roff, Partner
e-mail: davidroff@globalive.com
Education: BA, University of Western Ontario

2129 GOLDEN OPPORTUNITIES FUND
830, 410 22nd Street East
Saskatoon, SK S7K 5T6

Phone: 888-866-4494
e-mail: info@goldenopportunities.ca
web: goldenopportunities.ca

Mission Statement: Provincial retail venture capital fund invests in Saskatchewan companies.
Geographic Preference: Saskatchewan
Industry Group Preference: Cannabis, Infrastructure, Construction, Healthcare, Innovation, Technology, Hospitality
Portfolio Companies: Superior Group of Companies, Aurora Cannabis Inc., Performance Plants, Western Building Centres Limited, Warman Home Centre, P.M. Power Group Inc., Gold Health Cre, Cova, DynaIndustrial, Fluid Clarification, Dyna Crane Services, TORC Oil & Gas, Safety Seven, Fort Garry Brewing Co., Librestream Technologies Inc., Terra Grain Fuels Inc., Credence Resources, LEX Energy Partners, Avalon, The Goal Group

Key Executives:
  Grant J. Kook, President/CEO
  Background: President/CEO, Cheung On; President/CEO, Ramada Hotels

2130 GOLDEN VENTURE PARTNERS
20 Maud Street
Suite 306
Toronto, ON M5V 2M5
Canada

web: goldenvp.com

Mission Statement: Golden Venture Partners provides funding and support to early stage companies focused on developing mobile products and services. The firm seeks to foster the next generation of breakthrough mobile technologies.
Geographic Preference: North America
Fund Size: $100 million
Founded: 2011
Average Investment: $750,000
Investment Criteria: Seed, Early Stage
Industry Group Preference: Mobile, Technology, Artificial Intelligence, Fintech, Robotics, SaaS
Portfolio Companies: Action X, Alyce, AppHero, ApplyBoard, Apptentive, Avidbots, BenchSci, Brightwheel, Carbonated, ChefHero, Clearbanc, Delphia, Ecopackers, Faire, Gallop, Helpful, Infinity Quick, Influitive, Inkbox, Jiffy, Joist, KitchenMate, Lentil, mParticle, Medchart, Plooto, Properly, ProteinQure, ResQ, Ritual, RoadMunk, Set.fm, Skip the Dishes, SkyWatch, Snowball, SoapBox, Tempo, TimeHero, Top Hat, Toucan, TVision, Upverter, Wattpad, WAVE, Xanadu, Yesware

Key Executives:
  Matt Golden, Founder & Managing Partner
  Education: BA, Economics, York University; Law/MBA, University of Ottawa
  Background: Partner, BlackBerry Partners; Director, New Ventures, BrightsparkVentures; Co-Founder, Tira Wireless; Osler
  Ameet Shah, General Partner
  Education: BSc, Computer Science & Economics, University of Toronto
  Background: Managing Director, Zynga; Co-Founder, Five Mobile; Director, Systems Engineering & Strategic Accounts, Tira Wireless; IBM; Grey Interactive
  Bert Amato, Venture Partner
  Education: BSc, Engineering, University of Toronto
  Background: Co-Founder & CTO, Delrina Corporation; VP, Symantec Corporation; IBM Canada Research Laboratory; Co-Founder, Schematix Computer Systems
  Jamie Rosenblatt, Partner
  Education: BA, Univ. of Western Ontario; JD, MBA Univ. of Toronto
  Background: Avid Life Media

2131 GOLDEN VENTURES
20 Maud Street
Suite 306
Toronto, ON M5V 2M5
Canada

web: www.golden.venture

Mission Statement: Golden Ventures was founded with the belief that early stage founders in Canada were underserved by financial options. The firm offers specialized support for all aspects of a business.
Geographic Preference: Canada, United States
Fund Size: $100 million
Founded: 2011
Average Investment: $500K - $2M
Investment Criteria: Seed
Industry Group Preference: All Sectors Considered
Portfolio Companies: Actionx, Aikido, Alyce, Applyboard, Apptentive, Arteria Ai, Auto Hauler Exchange, Autumn Ai, Avidbots, Barley, Basil, Benchsci, Big Brain, Bluedot, Boostsecurity.Io, Brightwheel, Buildable, Bunch, Callia, Carbonated, Chatlink, Clearco, Composer, Configure8, Crux Ocm, Cybrid, Daylight, Delphia, Disco, Diversio, Emerge, Empowered, Erthos, Faire, Float, Forma.Ai, Gadze Finance, Good Good, Helpful, Horizon Blockchain Games, Hypercomply, Hypercontext, Infinity Quick, Influitive, Inkbox, Jiffy, Joist, Kitchenmate, Lumeto, Mparticle, Manifest Climate, Marble, Minervaai, Mymentor, Nautical Commerce, Neo Financial, Notch, Odyssey Interactive, Plooto, Powered By People, Properly, Proteinqure, Pulse, Ramper, Ratio, Reblink, Resq, Ritual, Roadmunk, Secoda, Set Fm, Shakepay, Shakudo, Sherpa, Skip The Dishes, Skywatch, Snack, Snowball, Stacked, Stadium Live, Swyft, Sylva, Tvision, Tempo Smart Calendar, Time Hero, Tiny Mile, Top Hat, Toucan, Tribe, Umamicart, Underground Cellar, Vetted, Waabi, Wattpad, Xanadu, Yesware, Yuhu, Zero Acre Farms

Key Executives:
  Matt Golden, Founder & Managing Partner
  Education: LLB & MBA, University of Ottawa; BA, York University
  Background: Lawyer, Osler; Partner, BlackBerry Partners Fund; Partner, Brightspark Ventures; Co-Founder, Tira Wireless
  Ameet Shah, General Partner
  Education: BSc, University of Toronto
  Background: Co-Founder, Five Movile; General Manager, Zynga; Director of Systems Engineering & Strategic Accounts, Tira Wireless

2132 GOOD NEWS VENTURES
Toronto, ON
Canada

e-mail: info@goodnewsventures.com
web: goodnewsventures.com

Mission Statement: Early-stage investor in all sectors.
Investment Criteria: Early-Stage
Industry Group Preference: Artificial Intelligence, Internet of Things, Big Data, B2B, Cloud/SaaS, Mobile, Marketplaces, Finance, Healthcare, Applications,

Venture Capital & Private Equity Firms / Canadian Firms

Infrastructure, Networking, Security, Space Technology, Storage
Portfolio Companies: ACTO, Axis, Bruha, Claim Compass, Cuboh, Darwin AI, Doorr, eleven-x, Envoi, Fleetops, GoWrench, Hockeystick, HTBASE, Intelocate, iRestify, KitchenMate, Hashtag Paid, Rally, Sampler, Stay22, Voiceflow, Zoom.ai
Key Executives:
   Marat Mukhamedyarov, Founding Partner
   Education: Gubkin Russian State University of Oil & Gas; Internaitonal Business School; Georgian College; George Brown College
   Background: Masters Alliance; Alumoplast
   Directorships: York Angel Investors
   Mohan Markandaier, Managing Partner
   Education: University of Toronto
   Background: Pulse Voice
   Directorships: York Angel Investors
   Mona Kung, Partner
   Education: BSS, University of Ottawa; MBA, University of Ottawa; Rotman School of Management, University of Toronto; MiF, London Business School
   Background: External Panel Reviewer, Ontario Centres of Excellence; Teaching Assistant, York University; Bankers Trust
   Directorships: York Angel Investors; East Gate Capital Management

2133 GRANITE PARTNERS
Toronto, ON
Canada

Phone: 416-720-8776
e-mail: reidbuchanan@granitepartners.ca
web: www.granitepartners.ca

Mission Statement: A Canadian private equity firm that targets profitable, well-managed manufacturing and service companies with sales in the $10 million to $100 million range. Granite's goal is to help entrepreneurs and owner-managers build upon and unlock the value they have created in their businesses.

Geographic Preference: Canada
Founded: 1996
Investment Criteria: Estate Planning Transactions, Management Buy-Outs, Shotguns
Industry Group Preference: Manufacturing, Business Products & Services
Portfolio Companies: Chair-Man Mills, Chainsaw, Ecom Food Industries, Event Rental Group, Mike & Mike's Organics, Pixel Underground, Post Factory NY, PS Production Services, SIM Digital, Tattersall Sound & Picture
Key Executives:
   Doug Buchanan, Managing Director
   Education: MBA
   Background: President & CEO, Granite Venture Partners; Leveraged Capital Group, Citicorp; Corporate Finance Unit, CIBC

2134 GREEN ACRE CAPITAL
2 Bloor St W
Suite 1805
Toronto, ON M4W 3E2
Canada

e-mail: info@greenacrecapital.ca
web: greenacrecapital.ca

Mission Statement: Investment fund focused on the Canadian medical and recreational cannabis industry.
Geographic Preference: Canada
Industry Group Preference: Cannabis
Portfolio Companies: Ample Organics, Anandia Labs, Aqualitas, The Friendly Stranger, Green Tank Technologies, Humble & Fume, Leaf Forward, Solo Growth Corp., Tokyo Smoke, Trait Biosciences

933 - 17th Avenue SW
7th Floor
Calgary, AB T2T 5R6
Canada
Key Executives:
   Matt Shalhoub, Managing Partner, Toronto
   Education: HBA, Richard Ivey School of Business
   Tyler Stuart, Managing Partner, Calgary
   Education: BComm, Univ. of Saskatchewan

2135 GREENSKY CAPITAL INC
6 Adelaide Street E
Suite 500
Toronto, ON M5C 1H6
Canada

Phone: 416-585-7850
e-mail: info@greenskycapital.com
web: greenskycapital.com

Mission Statement: GreenSky is a group of affiliated organizations based in Toronto working with entrepreneurs across North America.

Founded: 2010
Key Executives:
   Greg Stewart, Principal
   Education: BSBA, University of Florida; MBA, University of Toronto
   Background: Equity Analyst, Neuberger Berman; CFO, American Strategic Insurance
   Michael List, Principal
   Education: BAH, LLB, Queen's University

2136 GREENSOIL INVESTMENTS
2345 Younge Street
Suite 804
Toronto, ON M4P 2E5
Canada

e-mail: info@greensoil-investments.com
web: www.greensoil-investments.com

Mission Statement: Greensoil Building Innovation Fund invests in products, services and technologies related to real estate.

Geographic Preference: Canada; U.S.
Industry Group Preference: Building Innovation
Portfolio Companies: Amatis, Carbon Cure, ElectrIQ Power, Goby, Honest Buildings, Illuma Drive, Kaarta, Lunera, SensorSuite
Key Executives:
   Alan Greenberg, Co-Founder and Chairman
   Education: Univ. of Toronto
   Background: Minto Group of Companies
   Directorships: BridgeGreen Capital; BioHarvest Inc.; Goby Inc.; Haldor Inc.
   Gideon Soesman, Co-Founder and Managing Partner
   Education: Hebrew Univ.; Boston Univ.; Ben Gurion Univ.
   Background: GMS Capital
   Dave Harris Kolada, Managing Partner
   Education: BComm., Queen's University
   Background: Oracle; Cognos; Jefferson Partners
   Directorships: Great West Lifeco; Investors Group; Power Financial Corp.
   Jamie James, Managing Partner
   Background: Tridel

2137 HARDY CAPITAL PARTNERS
510 Seymour Street
Suite 1020
Vancouver, BC V6B 3J5
Canada

Phone: 604-235-5550
e-mail: invest@hardycapital.com
web: www.hardycapital.com

Mission Statement: Hardy focuses on companies that are positioned for growth and threaten to disrupt existing major players.

Fund Size: $100 million
Founded: 2014
Average Investment: $500,000 - $5 million
Investment Criteria: High Growth
Industry Group Preference: Optical, Fintech, Real Estate, Insurance
Portfolio Companies: Clearly.ca, Coastal.com, Cotopaxi, Cymax, Flexday, Flexitive, Foodee, Indi, Jive Software, LD Vision Group, Lensway.com, Lensway.se, Liquidity Wines, Merrco Payments, Mogo, Naborly, Privé Revaux, RDM Corporation, Solink, Sonder, Surkus, Tangoe

Key Executives:
Roger Hardy, CEO & Chair
Background: Co-Founder & CEO, Coastal Contacts

2138 HEADWATER EQUITY PARTNERS
1890 - 1111 West Georgia Street
Vancouver, BC V6E 4M3
Canada

Phone: 604-694-8063
e-mail: info@headwaterequity.com
web: www.headwaterequity.com

Mission Statement: Headwater Equity Partners is a private equity fund that targets lower middle market companies based in Western Canada.

Geographic Preference: Canada
Investment Criteria: Lower Middle Market, Growth Capital, Buyouts, Acquisitions, Divestitures, Successions
Industry Group Preference: Manufacturing
Portfolio Companies: Interior Heavy Equipment Operator School, Frost Fighter, 911 Industrial Response, Mormak, Precision Mounting, Pumps & Pressure

Key Executives:
Dan Jacques, Managing Partner
604-694-8064
e-mail: dan_jacques@headwaterequity.com
Education: BBA, Simon Fraser University; MBA, Richard Ivey School of Business, University of Western Ontario; CA
Background: Senior Director, Merchant Banking, HSBC Capital; Morgan Stanley; Donaldson Lufkin & Jenrette; KPMG Corporate Finance
Simon Koch, Managing Partner
604-694-8063
e-mail: simon_koch@headwaterequity.com
Education: BA, English Literature, University of British Columbia; CA
Background: Senior Director & CFO, HSBC Capital; KPMG

2139 HIGHLAND WEST CAPITAL
1508-999 West Hastings St
Vancouver, BC V6C 2W2
Canada

Phone: 604-558-4925
e-mail: info@hwcl.ca
web: hwcl.ca

Geographic Preference: Western North America (Western Canada)
Industry Group Preference: Industry, Manufacturing, Financial Services
Portfolio Companies: AllWest Insurance Services, BID Group

Key Executives:
David Rowntree, Founder & Managing Director
Background: Co-Founder/Managing Director, Tricor Pacific Capital Inc.
David A. Schellenberg, Managing Director
Background: Managing Director, Jim Pattison Group; President/CEO, Conair Group
Dave Mullen, Managing Director
Education: BComm.; MBA
Background: Head of Private Equity for the Americas, HSBC; Managing Director, Graycliff Partners

2140 HIGHLINE BETA
372 Bay Street
2nd Floor
Toronto, ON M5H 2W9
Canada

e-mail: info@highlinebeta.com
web: highlinebeta.com

Mission Statement: Highline BETA works with corporations in the areas of Corporate Innovation Programming, New Venture Development and Investment Funds.

Portfolio Companies: Andela, Breather, Drop, FameBit, Hurrier, LocalMind

Other Locations:
135 Madison Avenue
5th Floor
New York, NY 10016
USA

4 Place Ville-Marie
3rd Floor
Montreal, QC H3B 2E7
Canada

30 S Wacker Drive
22nd Floor
Chicago, IL 60606
USA

151 West Hastings Street
Vancouver, BC V6B 1H4
Canada

Key Executives:
Marcus Daniels, Founding Partner & CEO
Education: BA, Psychology & Economics, McGill University; MBA, Smith School of Business, Queen's University
Background: Founder & Exec. Chair, MeshSquared Ventures; Co-Founder & CEO, HIGHLINE.vc; Managing Director, Extreme Startups; COO, Trend Hunter; VP, Operations, Frameworks; VP, AME Learning; Co-Founder & President, FLUID eNovations
Directorships: SDEVM
Ben Yoskovitz, Founding Partner & CPO
Education: BSc, Psychology, McGill University
Background: VP, Product, VarageSale; Director, Product Management, Salesforce.com; VP, Product, GoInstant; Founder & Publisher, NextMontreal; Founding Partner, Year One Labs; Co-Founder, Standout Jobs; Director, Operations, Grasshopper New Media; Director, Operations, Standpipe Studios
Directorships: Proposify, LocalMind
Lauren Robinson, General Partner
Education: BComm, Finance & Entrepreneurship, McGill University; General Assembly
Background: Executive Director, Female Funders; Global Operations Director, HIHLINE.vc; Head of Operations, Extreme Startups; National Bank Financial
Directorships: National Angel Capital Organization;

Vancouver Entrepreneurs Forum; Canadian Acceleration and Business Incubation Association

2141 IGAN PARTNERS
60 Bloor Street W
9th Floor
Toronto, ON M4W 3B8
Canada

Phone: 416-925-2433
e-mail: info@iganpartners.com
web: iganpartners.com

Mission Statement: iGan Partners is an early-stage investor in health technology companies.
Geographic Preference: Canada
Fund Size: $26 million
Founded: 2011
Investment Criteria: Early-stage
Industry Group Preference: Internet, Software, Healthcare Information Technology, Artificial Intelligence
Portfolio Companies: Adracare, Augur, BrainFx, CBx, Cosm Care, eSight, Exact Imaging, Finaeo, FlipGive, Flosonics Medical, Limelight, MedChart, Meta, MolucLight, Quandl, ResQ, RetiSpec, Rhythem Xience, Right Health, Rna Diagnostics, SceneDoc, SomaDetect, Think Research, Triage
Key Executives:
　Sam Ifergan, Founder & Managing Partner
　Education: BEng, McGill University; MBA, John Molson School of Business, Concordia University
　Background: Co-Founder, Visualsonics; Tri-Link Technologies; Brighter Minds; Strategy Consultant, Mercer Management Consulting
　Joel Finlayson, Partner
　Education: Dalhousie University; MBA, Cambridge University; Berkeley School of Public Health
　Background: Co-Founder & Managing Director, WellNovation; Middle East Healthcare Partner, PWc; MONITOR Group
　Directorships: Creative Destruction Lab; Royal College of Physicians & Surgeons of Canada
　Gregory Ogorek, Partner
　Education: BBA, ICS Business School
　Background: VP of Sales & Business Development for various startups

2142 IMPERIAL CAPITAL
200 King Street W
PO Box 57
Suite 1701
Toronto, ON M5H 3T4
Canada

Phone: 416-362-3658
e-mail: icl@imperialcap.com
web: imperialcap.com

Mission Statement: A private fund manager that focuses on buy-out opportunities in the Canadian and American mid-market. Imperial Capital has earned a reputation for: (i) identifying recession-resistant industries; (ii) undertaking extensive due diligence, (iii) strategic value creation; and (iv) creative liquidity events.
Geographic Preference: Canada, United States
Fund Size: $800 Million
Founded: 1989
Average Investment: $50-150 Million
Investment Criteria: Management Buy-Out Opportunities, Take-Private Opportunities, Leveraged Recapitalizations
Industry Group Preference: Healthcare, Business & Consumer Services
Portfolio Companies: AIM Health Group, Associated Freezers Corporation, Beefeaters, E.D. Smith & Sons, Kenra, Lise Watier, Pacific Coast Publishing, Procaps, Schulman Associates, Stantec
Key Executives:
　Jeffrey Rosenthal, Managing Partner
　416-362-3658 x226
　e-mail: jr@imperialcap.com
　Education: BA, Commerce & Economics, University of Toronto; MBA, Finance & Entrepreneurial Studies, Schulich of Business, York University
　Directorships: Schulman Associates Institutional Review Board, AIM Health Group
　Justin MacCormack, Managing Partner
　e-mail: jmaccormack@imperialcap.com
　Education: BSc, Environmental Engineering, University of Guelph; MBA, Richard Ivey School of Business, University of Western Ontario
　Background: McKinsey & Cmopany; Trafalgar Securities
　Directorships: Onex Corporation
　Christopher Harris, Partner
　416-362-3658 x235
　e-mail: charris@imperialcap.com
　Education: BComm, Queen's University
　Background: Transaction Services, KPMG
　Gene Shkolnik, Partner
　416-362-3658 x245
　e-mail: gs@imperialcap.com
　Education: Shulich School of Business; CPA
　Background: KPMG; Canadian Army

2143 IMPRESSION VENTURES
2300 Yonge St
PO Box 2398
Toronto, ON M4P 1E4
Canada

Phone: 647-725-3355
e-mail: info@impression.ventures
web: impression.ventures

Mission Statement: Late-seed/early Series A Fintech investors.
Investment Criteria: Late-seed, Early Series A
Industry Group Preference: Fintech
Portfolio Companies: Brim, Sensibill, Wealthsimple, Zoocasa
Key Executives:
　Christian Lassonde, Founder & Managing Partner
　Education: BSc, BESc, Univ. of Western Ontario; MBA, Univ. of South Florida
　Background: Virtual Greats, Millions of Us
　Directorships: SickKids Foundation
　Maor Amar, Managing Partner
　Education: McGill Univ.; ESC Nice

2144 INBC INVESTMENT CORP
Victoria, BC
Canada

e-mail: info@inbcinvestment.ca
web: www.inbcinvestment.ca

Mission Statement: InBC Investment Corp. (InBC) is a strategic investment fund created by the Government of British Columbia. Formerly known as BC Renaissance Capital Fund.
Geographic Preference: British Columbia, North America
Fund Size: $2 billion
Founded: 2008
Industry Group Preference: Digital Media & Marketing, Information Technology, Life Sciences, Clean Technology
Portfolio Companies: Angstrom Power, Boreal Genomics, CoolEdge Lighting, Delta-Q Technologies Corp., Endurance Wind Power, E-One Moli Energy, GrowLab Ventures, Indicee, LaCima, Light Based Technologies, Mingleverse Laboratories, Nexterra Systems, NGRAIN, Ostara Nutrient Recovery Techologies, Partnerpedia Solutions
Key Executives:
　Jill Earthy, Chief Executive Officer
　Education: BA, Western University; MBA, University of

Victoria
Background: Co-Founder, Frontline Staff; Founder, Momcafe Network Inc.; CEO, Forum for Women Entrepreneurs (FWE) BC, now called WEC BC
Leah Nguyen, Chief Investment Officer
Education: BBA, Beedie School of Business, Simon Fraser University
Background: Manager, Accenture; Project Manager, Lululemon Athletica; Investment Director, TELLUS Pollinator Fund for Good; Business Enablement Director, TELLUS Ventures
David Mortimer, Chief Financial Officer
Education: BA, University of Victoria
Background: Sr. Auditor, Office of the Auditor General of British Columbia; Executive Director, Investment Capital, Province of B.C.; CFO, Province of B.C.; Director of Financial Planning, Province of B.C.

2145 INDURAN VENTURES INC.
PO Box 26
Kingston, ON K7L 4V6
Canada

web: www.induranventures.com

Mission Statement: Induran Ventures invests in Canadian companies in the biotechnology sector.

Geographic Preference: Canada
Average Investment: $5-15MM
Investment Criteria: Seed-Stage, Start-Up, First-Stage, Second-Stage, Mezzanine, Buyout
Industry Group Preference: Biotechnology
Portfolio Companies: Biox, Defryus Inc., GraySpace Therapeutics Inc., Performance Plants, SignPost Cancer Dx Inc.

Key Executives:
J. Peter Blaney, Founder & CEO
e-mail: peterblaney@induranventures.com
Education: MBA, MPA, Queen's University
Background: Founder & CEO, Dynex Capital Corp.; Founder & CEO, Tancho Advisors Group
Barry Markowsky
Education: BSc, MSc, Microbiology, MBA, University of Toronto
Background: General Manager, ViiV Healthcare ULC; VP, Business Development & Director, Specialty Care Division, Glaxo Wellcome Inc.; GlaxoSmithKline
Paul Lucas
Education: Queen's University; Columbia University
Background: President & CEO, GlaxoSmithKline

2146 INFORMATION VENTURE PARTNERS
1 University Ave
Suite 1901
Toronto, ON M5J 2P1
Canada

e-mail: info@informationvp.com
web: www.informationvp.com

Mission Statement: Venture capital investors focused on the FinTech market.

Geographic Preference: Canada, United States
Fund Size: $106 million
Founded: 2014
Investment Criteria: Early-stage
Industry Group Preference: Core Financial Applications, Financial Security & Crime Prevention, Financial Data Applications, Capital Markets, Payments & Financial Services, SaaS
Portfolio Companies: Adaptive Insights, BigID, Coconut Software, Esentire, Flybits, Infobright, Igloo, Knowtions Research, LendingFront, Placemark Investments, Procurifiy, PostBeyond, Q4, Sensibill, Thor Technologies, Thoughtexchange, Varicent, Verafin, Viigo, YayPay

Key Executives:
Robert Antoniades, Co-Founder & General Partner
Education: BBA, Wilfrid Laurier University; CFA
Background: Managing Director, RBC Venture Partners; VP, BMO Nesbitt Burns Equity Partners; Executive Director, CIBC Capital Partners
Directorships: Infobright Software, Adaptive Insights, Brickstream, Igloo Software
David Unsworth, Co-Founder & General Partner
Education: BA, Economics, Wilfrid Laurier University; MBA, Queen's University
Background: RBC Venture Partners
Directorships: Verafin, Igloo Software, eSentire, Jana Mobile
Kerri Golden, Venture Partner
Education: HBA, Richard Ivey School of Business, University of Western Ontario
Background: Director & Co-Owner, Urban Flats Toronto; CFO, Primaxis Technology Ventures; COO, SeaWell Networks; CFO, Infobright; Rogers Wireless; CFO, Alliance Atlantis Communications; Lorus Therapeutics; CEO, Paging Division, Bell Mobility
Sara Defina, Director of Finance
Education: BComm, University of Toronto
Background: SurePath Capital Partners

2147 INITIATIVE CAPITAL LIMITED
141 Adelaide Street West
Suite 1200
Toronto, ON M5H 3L5

Phone: 416-307-3271 Fax: 416-363-2010
web: initiativecapital.com

Mission Statement: Invests in the cannabis industry.

Investment Criteria: Seed, Early-Stage
Industry Group Preference: Cannabis, Technology, Biotechnology, Data Management

Key Executives:
Hamish Sutherland, President/CEO
e-mail: hamish@initiativecapital.com
Education: BEng, McMaster University; MBA, Schulich School of Business, York University
Background: VP of Marketing, Strike Technologies; Director of Business Development, Research Now; President, Porcupine Goldor Mines; President/CEO, Hunter Porcupine Gold; Managing Partner, The Marketing Partners; COO, Kaypok Inc.; COO, Bedrocan Canada; COO, Asterio Cannabis Inc.; President/CEO, White Sheep Corp
Directorships: Chair, Little Geeks Foundation
Loudon Owen, Managing Partner
e-mail: lowen@initiativecapital.com
Education: BA, University of Toronto; JD, Osgoode Hall Law School; MBA, INSEAD
Background: Co-Founder, McLean Watson Capital

2148 INNOVACORP
400-1871 Hollis Street
Halifax, NS B3J 0C3
Canada

Phone: 902-424-8670 Fax: 902-424-4679
Toll-Free: 800-565-7051
e-mail: info@innovacorp.ca
web: innovacorp.ca

Mission Statement: Innovacorp helps high potential early stage companies commercialize their technologies and succeed in the global marketplace.

Geographic Preference: Nova Scotia
Fund Size: $40 million
Founded: 1995
Average Investment: $100,000 - $3 million
Investment Criteria: Early-Stage
Industry Group Preference: Technology

Portfolio Companies: ABK Biomedical, Agada Bioscience, Aiotv, Alentic Miscroscience, Appili Therapeutics, Apptonomy Mobile Technologies, Atlantic Motor Labs, Aqualitas, Carboncure, Cellufuel, Clinical Logistics, Conquer Mobile, covina Biomedical, Dash Hudson, Daxsonics Ultrasound, Densitas, DeCell Technologies, DeNovaMed, DGI Clinical, DMF Medical, EagleBurgmann, Eosense, Emagix, Green Power Labs, Health QR, Health Outcomes Worldwide, InNetwork, Immunovaccine, Island Water Technologies, Jetasonic, Kivuto, LeadSift, Light Sail Energy, Livenlenz, Maritime Biologgers, Medusa Medical Technologies Inc., Metamaterial Technologies Inc., The Money Finder, MouseStats, Mimir Networks, Novonix, Ocean Executive, Photo Dynamic, Proposify, QRA, Rend, The Rounds, SabrTech Inc., Show Battery, Spring Loaded, Sky Squirrel Technologies, Skyline, Solid State Pharma Inc., SimplyCast, Swell Advantage, Swept, TrueLeaf, TitanFil, Tesla, Up My Game, Ubique Networks, Woodscamp

Key Executives:
Malcolm Fraser, President & CEO
Education: BComm, Mount Allison University
Background: Founder, ISL Internet Solutions Ltd.,
Directorships: Art Gallery of Nova Scotia, Dalhousie Medical Research Foundation, Sobeyart Foundation, Digital Nova Scotia
Andrew Ray, Vice President, Investment
Education: BSc, Saint Mary's Univ.; MSc, Intl. Space Univ.; MBA, Brigham Young Univ.
Background: Bazari
Dawn House, Vice President, Client Engagement & Communications
Education: Mount Saint Vincent Univ.
Background: Health Canada
Donna Bourque, Vice President, Finance & Operations
Background: Nova Scotia Power; Saint Mary's Univ. School of Business

---

2149 INNOVOBOT
4297-B Sherbrooke Street W
Westmount, QC H3Z 1H2
Canada

Phone: 514-487-5557
e-mail: info@innovobot.com
web: www.innovobot.com

Mission Statement: Innovobot helps companies use technology to build stronger businesses.

Key Executives:
Zoya Shcuhpak, Managing Partner, Innovobot Fund
Education: Concordia University; MBA, McGill University
Background: CFO, Fairstone Financial; Desjardins Venture Capital; CIBC World Markets; Scotia Capital Markets
Mario Venditti, CEO
Education: MSc, MBA, McGill University
Background: COO, Above Security

2150 INOVIA CAPITAL
3 Place Ville-Marie
Suite 12350
Montreal, QC H3B 0E7
Canada

web: www.inovia.vc

Mission Statement: Investors in early-stage technology companies.
Geographic Preference: Canada, United States
Fund Size: $110 million
Investment Criteria: Seed-Stage, Early-Stage
Industry Group Preference: Technology, Life Sciences, Artificial Intelligence
Portfolio Companies: 33Across, AlayaCare, Allocadia, AppDirect, Armored Things, Bench, BenchSci, Boosted, Busbud, CareGuide, Clearblanc, Clearpath, Community Sift, CoolIT Systems, Darwin AI, Drivewyze, Eideticom, Fellow, FutureFamily, LightSpeed, North, Peraso, PEX Card, Poka, RenoRun, Resonate Networks, Ross, Rubikloud, SnapTravel, Sonder, Spatial, Street Contxt, Swept, Top Hat, TrackTik, TripleLift, Tulip Retail, Vidyard, WorkFusion

Other Locations:
130 Bloor Street W
Toronto, ON M5S 1N5
Canada

168 South Park
San Francisco, CA 94107

15-19 Bloomsbury Way
London WC1A 2TH
United Kingdom

Key Executives:
Patrick Pichette, Partner
Education: MA, Philosophy, Politics, Economics, Oxford University; BBA, Université du Québec ... Montréal
Background: Google; McKinsey; Sprint Canada
Shawn Abbott, Partner
Education: BS, Physics, University of Alberta
Background: CTO/President, Rainbow Technologies
Directorships: CoolIT Systems, Peraso, Top Hat, Drivewyze, WorkFusion, Solium
Karamdeep Nijjar, Partner
Education: MBA, Richard Ivey School of Business, University of Western Ontario; BMath, Computer Sciences, University of Waterloo
Background: RBC; Platform Solutions Inc.
Chris Arsenault, Partner
Background: Founder & CEO, SIT
Directorships: Fixmo, Gamerizon, Localmind, Reflex Photonics, Ryma, Well.ca, Woozworld
Todd Simpson, Partner
Directorships: Collective, PEX

2151 INSTARAGF
66 Wellington Street W
Toronto-Dominion Bank Tower, 31st Floor
Toronto, ON M5K 1E9
Canada

Phone: 416-815-6224
e-mail: info@instaragf.com
web: instaragf.com

Mission Statement: InstarAGF promotes an entrepreneurial, collegial environment built on open communication and transparency. They offer opportunities for professional grwoth and partnerships.

Founded: 2014

Key Executives:
Gregory Smith, President and CEO
Education: Queen's University
Background: Managing Partner, Brookfield Financial Global Infrasturcture Advisory Group; President, Maccuarie Capital Funds Canada Ltd.; Managing Director, RBC Capital Partners
George So, Managing Partner
Education: University of Waterloo
Background: Founder/Managing Partner, Kindle Capital Group Inc.; Senior Member, Canada Pension Plan Investment Board

---

2152 INTRINSIC VENTURE CAPITAL
37 Richard Way SW
Suite 301
Calgary, AB T3E 7M8
Canada

e-mail: info@intrinsicvc.com
web: www.intrinsicvc.com

Venture Capital & Private Equity Firms / Canadian Firms

Mission Statement: Intrinsic Ventures is an early-stage venture fund uniquely positioned to support international teams gain a place in North America.

Geographic Preference: International

2153 INVESTECO
70 The Esplanade
Suite 400
Toronto, ON M5E 1R2
Canada

Phone: 416-304-1750 **Fax:** 416-362-2387
e-mail: info@investeco.com
web: investeco.com

Mission Statement: InvestEco focuses on sustainable food and agriculture.

Geographic Preference: North America
Fund Size: $35 million
Founded: 2002
Investment Criteria: Expansion Stage
Industry Group Preference: Sustainable Food and Agriculture, Renewable Energy, Water Technologies, Resource Productivity Technologies, Transportation Solutions
Portfolio Companies: Maison Le Grand, Lesser Evil, Sol Cuisine, Nada Moo!, Kuli Kuli, MamaEarth Organics, 100KM Foods Inc., Vital Farms, Maple Hill Creamery, GeoDigital, miovision technologies, Woodland Biofuels, Ensyn, Rowe Farms

Key Executives:
    Andrew Heintzman, Managing Partner
    Education: BA, MA, McGill University
    Background: Co-Founder & Publisher, Shift Magazine
    Directorships: Lotek Wireless, Triton Logging, Horizon Distributors
    Alex Chamberlain, Managing Partner
    Education: LLB, MBA, CFA
    Background: Attorney, Smith Lyons; Corporate Finance, PricewaterhouseCoopers Securites
    Directorships: UV Pure Technologies, EnerWorks, Rowe Farms
    Michael Curry, Partner/Director
    Education: BA
    Directorships: 100km Foods Inc.
    Charles Holt, Partner
    Education: LLM, London School of Economics; JD, University of Ottawa
    Background: Corporate Law

2154 INVESTX
999 Canada Place
Suite 654
Vancouver, BC V6C 3E1

Phone: 844-246-4556
e-mail: info@investx.com
web: www.investx.com

Mission Statement: InvestX was founded on a commitment to provide access to the growing private markets.

Industry Group Preference: Technology, Social Media, IoT
Portfolio Companies: 23 and Me, Airbnb, Dataminr, DocuSign, Instacart, Lyft, Nerd Wallet, Palantir, Pinterest, Hootsuite, Indigo, SoFi, Spotify, Turo, Uber

Other Locations:
    19 Fulton Street
    Suite 307
    New York, NY 10038
    Phone: 212-390-9270

Key Executives:
    Marcus New, Founder & CEO
    Patrick E. Brake, Jr., U.S. Corporate Counsel & COO
    Colin Wrinch, Chief Technology Officer

2155 INVICO CAPITAL CORPORATION
209 8th Avenue SW
Suite 600
Calgary, AB T2P 1B8
Canada

Phone: 403-538-4771 **Fax:** 403-538-4770
e-mail: info@invicocapital.com
web: www.invicocapital.com

Mission Statement: Alternative investment fund management firm.

Geographic Preference: Canada
Fund Size: $350 million
Founded: 2006
Industry Group Preference: Energy, Real Estate

Key Executives:
    Jason Brooks, President
    Education: BComm, Haskayne School of Business; CFA
    Background: Vice President, Ernst & Young
    Allison M. Taylor, Chief Executive Officer/Portfolio Manager
    Education: BS, Actuarial Science & Statistics, University of Western Ontario; MBA, Finance, Haskayne School of Business
    Background: Senior Associate, Ernst & Young

2156 IRONBRIDGE EQUITY PARTNERS
Bay Adelaide Centre - East Tower
22 Adelaide Street West
Suite 3520
Toronto, ON M5H 4E3
Canada

Phone: 416-863-0105
e-mail: info@ironbridgeequity.com
web: ironbridgeequity.com

Mission Statement: Ironbridge is a Toronto-based private equity firm focused exclusively on investing in companies in the Canadian lower middle-market. Ironbridge specializes on traditional industry businesses in the manufacturing, distribution, consumer products and services.

Geographic Preference: Canada
Fund Size: $400 million
Average Investment: $15 to $40 million
Minimum Investment: $15 million
Investment Criteria: Management Buyouts, Expansions, Recapitalizations, Restructurings
Industry Group Preference: Manufacturing, Distribution, Consumer Products, Consumer Services, Business Products & Services
Portfolio Companies: Canada Metal (Pacific), midland appliances, A.V. Gauge & Fixture, Brooklin Concrete, Avena Foods, Thermogenics, Back in Motion, Advance Engineered Products, Dumur Industries, Alliance Corp., M&M Resources, Hank's Maintenance, L&C Trucking, MBRP, Alumni Educational Solutions

Key Executives:
    Alan G. Sellery, President/Managing Partner
    Education: BBA, University of Western Ontario; MBA, Harvard Business School
    Background: Partner, EdgeStone Capital Partners; Bain & Company
    Directorships: Gesco Industries, Gaspard LP, Global Railway Industries
    Peter Samson, Managing Partner
    Education: BBA, University of Western Ontario
    Background: Bain & Company
    Peter Dowse, Managing Partner
    Education: BComm, BA, Queen's University; CFA
    Background: VP, EdgeStone Capital Partners
    Directorships: Gesco Industries
    Jeffrey N. Murphy, Managing Partner
    Education: BS, Materials & Metallurgical Engineering, Queen's University; MS, University of British Columbia

Venture Capital & Private Equity Firms / Canadian Firms

Background: Co-Founder, Blackmore Partners; Marketing Executive, Noranda; Engineering Consultant, Hatch Associates
Andrew Walton, Managing Partner
Education: BComm, University of Cape Town; Rotman School of Management, University of Toronto
Background: Partner, Signal Hill Equity Partners; Partner, EdgeStone Capital Partners; Partner, PWc Transaction Services Group; CEO, Westridge Cabinets Ltd.; CFO, New Food Classics Partnership
Directorships: Alliance Corporation, Midland Appliance, OEL Projects, Romet Limited, C&V Portable Accommodations, Westridge Cabinets, Continental Alloys & Services, Eurospec Manufacturing

2157 ISLAND CAPITAL PARTNERS
31 Queen Street
Charlottetown, PE C1A 4A4
Canada

e-mail: info@peislandcapitalpartners.com
web: peislandcapitalpartners.com

Mission Statement: Island Capital is an early stage VC Fund investing in high growth potential PEI companies.

Geographic Preference: PEI
Fund Size: $4.25 million
Average Investment: $100,000-500,000

Key Executives:
Alex MacBeath, Managing Partner
Education: BSc, University of Prince Edward Island; MBA, Dalhousie University
Background: CEO, Grant Thornton LLP

2158 InstarAGF
Toronto Dominion Bank Tower
66 Wellington Street West
31st Floor
Toronto, ON M5K 1E9
Canada

Phone: 416-815-6224
web: www.instaragf.com

Mission Statement: Manages alternative investments in the North American middle market.

Geographic Preference: North America
Founded: 2014
Industry Group Preference: Industry, Manufacturing
Portfolio Companies: AllWest Insurance Services, BID Group

Key Executives:
Gregory J. Smith, President & CEO
Education: Queen's Univ.
Background: Brookfield Financial; Macquarie Capital Funds Canada
Directorships: Canadian Council of Public-Private Partnerships; Lighthouse Equity Partners; Avrio Ventures
George So, Managing Partner
Education: Univ. of Waterloo
Background: Kindle Capital Group; Canada Pension Plan

2159 JOG CAPITAL
440 - 2nd Avenue SW
Suite 2370
Calgary, AB T2P 5E9
Canada

Phone: 403-232-3340 Fax: 403-705-3341
e-mail: info@jogcapital.com
web: jogcapital.com

Mission Statement: Calgary-based PE firm focused on light oil assets in Western Canada.

Geographic Preference: Western Canada
Fund Size: $350 million
Founded: 2002
Average Investment: C$75-150 million
Investment Criteria: Early-Stage
Industry Group Preference: Energy, Oil & Gas

Key Executives:
Ryan Crawford, Chair
Education: BComm, Finance, University of Saskatchewan; CFA
Background: Relationship Manager, ATB Financial; Associate, Bank of America
Craig Golinowski, President
Education: MBA, University of Western Ontario; BComm, Finance, University of Alberta; CFA
Background: Investment Banking, RBC Capital Markets
Daryl Gilbert, Managing Director
Background: President & CEO, GLJ Associates; Great Northern Oil Ltd.
Kel Johnston, Managing Director
Education: BSc, Univ. of Manitoba; Univ. of Calgary
Background: Alberta Clipper Energy
Directorships: Leucrotta Exploration
Jason White, Managing Director
Education: Haskayne School of Business; Univ. of Alberta
Background: CIBC World Markets
Directorships: Karve Energy

2160 KENSINGTON CAPITAL PARTNERS
95 St. Clair Avenue West
Suite 905
Toronto, ON M4V 1N6
Canada

Phone: 416-362-9000 Fax: 416-362-0939
e-mail: info@kcpl.ca
web: www.kcpl.ca

Mission Statement: Employee-owned alternative investment fund focused on the North American market.

Geographic Preference: Canada, United States
Fund Size: $1.1 billion
Founded: 1996
Industry Group Preference: Technology, Retailing, Consumer Products, Financial Services, Manufacturing, Media, Telecommunications, Healthcare, Information Technology, Energy, Industrial Services
Portfolio Companies: CGL Manufacturing Inc., Oncap, Novacap, Prodomax Automation Ltd., Protenergy, Providence Equityt, Parallel49 Equity, Trrivest, TriWest Capital Partners, Turtle Island Recycling, White Swan Environmental Ltd.

Other Locations:
221-10th Avenue SE
Suite 203
Calgary, AB T2G 0V9
Canada
Phone: 587-351-4122

675 West Hastings St
Suite 200
Vancouver, BC V6B 1N2
Canada
Phone: 604-565-2188

Key Executives:
Thomas Kennedy, Chair & Senior Managing Director
Education: BSc, Engineering, Queen's University; DBA, University of Edinburgh
Background: Consolidation Coal Co., Alberta Energy Company, Bunting Warburg, Lancaster, TD Securities
Directorships: Triax Growth Fund
Richard Nathan, Senior Managing Director
Education: BA, Computer Science, Dartmouth College; LLB, University of Toronto, Faculty of Law
Background: Founding Partner, Brightspark Ventures; Managing Director, Goodmans Venture Group; Corporate Law, Osler Hoskin & Harcourt LLP
Eamonn McConnell, Senior Managing Director/Chief Investment Officer

Education: MBA, McGill University & HEC France; CAIA
Background: Barclays Global Investors, Deutsche Bank, Merrill Lynch
Matthew Cross, Managing Director (Vancouver)
Education: BA, Queen's University; HBA, Richard Ivey School of Business; MBA, Harvard Business School
Background: VP, Parallel49 Equity; Deloitte Consulting; Teekay Corporation
Directorships: White Swan Environment; Horseshoe Power
Harold Huber, Managing Director (Calgary)
e-mail: hhuber@kcpl.ca
Education: LL.B., University of Saskatchewan College of Law; B.Admin, University of Regina]
Background: Infrastruture & Energy Group of Torys LLP, McCarthy Tétrault LLP
Martin Kent, Managing Director
Education: B.Admin, Harvard University; BComm, Queen's University
Background: CFO, Quantum Murray LP, ONCAP, EdgeStone, Morgan Stanley, J.P. Morgan
Directorships: Newport Partners, RBC Dominion Securities

2161 KILLICK CAPITAL
95 Water Street
2nd Floor
PO Box 5383, Stn. C
St. John's, NL A1C 5W2
Canada

Phone: 709-738-5513 Fax: 709-738-5578
e-mail: inquiries@killickcapital.com
web: killickcapital.com

Mission Statement: Killick Capital invests in venture businesses, aerospace businesses, and businesses located in Newfoundland & Labrador specifically.
Geographic Preference: Atlantic Canada
Founded: 2004
Industry Group Preference: Aerospace, Technology
Portfolio Companies: Canadian Northern Outfitters, Carta Worldwide, Celtx, Clockwork Fox, CoLab Software, Coloursmith, Firecraft Products, Harbr, HeyOrca, Killick Aerospace, MAX, Mysa, PathFactory, radient360, Rally, Seaformatics, Sequence Bio, St. John's Hop On Hop Off, SucSeed, Turbine Engine Specialists, Verafin

Key Executives:
Mark Dobbin, Founder & President
Background: CEO, Vector Aerospace Corporation
Directorships: CHC Helicopter Corporation; Innovation & Business Investment Corporation; Business & Arts NL
Tom Williams, Partner & Vice President, Investments
Education: CA; CBV
Background: CHC Helicopter Corporation; Vector Aerospace Corporation; Grant Thornton
Joe McKenna, Partner & CFO
Background: CFO, Research & Development Corporation; Deloitte

2162 KILMER CAPITAL PARTNERS
Scotia Plaza
40 King Street West
Toronto, ON M5H 3Y2
Canada

e-mail: info@kilmergroup.com
web: www.kilmergroup.com

Mission Statement: A leader in making private equity investments in small to mid-sized businesses undergoing periods of rapid growth, significant change or ownership transition.
Geographic Preference: Canada
Fund Size: $1 billion
Average Investment: $5 to $50 million
Minimum Investment: $5 million
Investment Criteria: Later-Stage, Growth Equity
Industry Group Preference: Electronics, Communications, Technology, Food & Beverage, Apparel, Healthcare, Consumer Products, Media, Entertainment
Portfolio Companies: Altasciences Clinical Research, Atelka, Cmc Interconnect Technologies, Coalision, Compact Power Equipment Centers, Coretec, Cypress Five Star, English Bay Batter, Give & Go Prepared Foods Corp., McGregor Industries, Smtc Corporation, Tribal Sportswear, Unisync Group, Vansco Electronics

Key Executives:
Larry Tanenbaum, Chair & CEO
Education: BS, Economics, Cornell University
Michael Griffiths, President & COO
Education: BComm, Loyola College/Concordia University; MBA, York University
Background: President/COO, KVN; Manager, Clarkson Gordon Chartered Accountants
Doug Peel, Vice Chair & Managing Partner
Background: President & CEO, KVN; Twin Dolphin Technologies; President, Newstar Technologies; Bryker Data Systems; Cygnet Storage Solutions
Directorships: Unisync, Algorithme

2163 KLASS CAPITAL
MaRS Centre, Heritage Building
101 College Street
Suite 145
Toronto, ON M5G 1L7
Canada

Phone: 674-494-9881
web: www.klass.com

Mission Statement: A growth equity investment company targeting small software or web enabled post revenue companies.
Geographic Preference: Canada, United States
Fund Size: $50 million
Founded: 2010
Average Investment: $1 to $5 million
Minimum Investment: $500,000
Investment Criteria: Early-Stage
Industry Group Preference: Software, Web Applications & Services, SaaS, Enterprise Software
Portfolio Companies: Plex, Resolver, TrackTik, Nulogy, 360 Insights, Condo Control Central, Docebo, AlayaCare, Method CRM, Vena Solutions, Granify

Key Executives:
Daniel Klass, Founder/Managing Director
e-mail: daniel@klasscapital.com
Education: BSc, Mathematics; MBA, Finance/Accounting; CPA
Background: TD Capital, EdgeStone Capital Partners

2164 KNIGHT'S BRIDGE CAPITAL PARTNERS
Toronto, ON
Canada

Phone: 416-866-3132
e-mail: info@kbcpartners.com
web: www.kbcpartners.com

Mission Statement: Family office and private equity manager in Toronto.
Founded: 2008
Average Investment: $6 - $10 million
Investment Criteria: Later-Stage
Industry Group Preference: Consumer Products, Retailing, Internet, New Media
Portfolio Companies: Authentic Brands Group, Ellen Tracy, Polaroid, Robert Graham, TubeMogul, The Works

Venture Capital & Private Equity Firms / Canadian Firms

Key Executives:
Kenny Finkelstein, Co-Founder & CEO
Background: Co-Founder, Gen-X Sports; Co-Founder, Lifestyle Brands

2165 LAURENCE CAPITAL
150 Caroline St South
Suite 403
Waterloo, ON N2L 0A5
Canada

Phone: 226-476-1374 Fax: 519-340-0325
e-mail: info@laurencecapital.com
web: www.laurencecapital.com

Mission Statement: Waterloo-based private capital firm invests in public and private Canadian companies and real estate.
Geographic Preference: Canada
Founded: 2004
Investment Criteria: Late stage
Industry Group Preference: Technology, Financial Services, Real Estate
Portfolio Companies: Bauer Marketplace, Cellwand Communications, Charcoal Group, Clearpath Robotics, Deer Ridge Centre, Fiix, Kognitiv Corporation, Langhaus Financial, Onco-Screen, Oviinbyrd Forest, Oviinbyrd Golf Club, Relay Ventures, Waterloo Brewing, Wealthpoint Health Services, XMG Studio
Key Executives:
Peter Schwartz, Chair & Partner
Education: MBA, University of Western Ontario
Background: Descartes Systems Group
Directorships: Kognitiv Corp.
Paul Laufert, Managing Director
Education: BA, LLB, Queen's University

2166 LEX CAPITAL MANAGEMENT
2530 Sandra Schmirler Way
Regina, SK S4W 0M7
Canada

Phone: 306-790-8676
e-mail: info@lexcapital.ca
web: lexcapital.ca

Mission Statement: Private equity firm makes early-stage investments in the Canadian energy sector.
Geographic Preference: Western Canada
Fund Size: $90 million
Investment Criteria: Early-Stage
Industry Group Preference: Energy, Oil & Gas
Key Executives:
E. Craig Lothian, Executive Chair
306-790-4152
Education: BA, LLB, University of Saskatchewan
Background: President, Keystone Royalty Corp.; Founder, Villanova Oil Corp.; Chairman & CEO, Flatland Exploration
Directorships: PetroBakken Energy, Smart Completions
Dean Popil, Managing Partner & CEO
306-790-8658
Education: BAdmin, University of Regina; CBV; CFA
Directorships: CanGas Solutions, Wyatt Oil + Gas
Curtis Armstrong, Managing Partner & CFO
306-790-8660
Education: BS, Management & Finance, Minot State University; CFA

2167 LGC CAPITAL
800 rue du square-Victoria
Suite 3700
Montreal, QC H4Z 1A1

web: www.lgc-capital.com

Mission Statement: Invests in the global cannabis industry.
Geographic Preference: Canada, Jamaica, Europe, Australia
Founded: 2015
Industry Group Preference: Cannabis
Portfolio Companies: Tricho-Med Corp.; Global Canna Labs; Etea Sicurezza Ltd.; Viridi Unit SA; CLV Frontier Brands; Evolution BNK, Little Green Pharma
Key Executives:
John McMullen, Chief Executive Officer
Education: BA, Political Science, University of Western Ontario
Background: Investment Advisor, Canaccord Genuity; Investment Banking, Stratigis Capital Advisors

2168 LIGHTHEART MANAGEMENT PARTNERS
1040 West Georgia Street
15th Floor
Vancouver, BC V6E 4H1
Canada

e-mail: info@lightheartmanagement.com
web: www.lightheartmanagement.com

Mission Statement: LightHeart management partners looks to preserve and grow the legacy, heritage and culture of every business that they invest in.
Key Executives:
Laing Henshall, Partner
Education: BA, University of Western Ontario; JD, University of Calgary
Background: Principal, CPS Capital; General Counsel, Premier Exhibitions
Wei Lin, Partner
Education: University of British Columbia
Background: Engagement Manager, McKinsey & Co.
Shay Nulman, Partner
Education: BBA, York University; MBA, Western University
Background: CFO, Gibraltar Ventures

2169 LIGHTHOUSE EQUITY PARTNERS
1333 W Broadway
Suite 750
Vancouver, BC V6H 4C1
Canada

e-mail: info@lhequitypartners.com
web: www.lhequitypartners.com

Mission Statement: Lighthouse invests in Western-based businesses that are currently profitable, looking for full or partial stakeholder liquidity, and want an investment partner to drive growth.
Geographic Preference: Western Canada, Western United States
Fund Size: $500 million
Founded: 2012
Industry Group Preference: Technology, SaaS
Portfolio Companies: Adperfect, Primex Technologies
Key Executives:
Steve Hnatiuk, Co-Founder & Managing Partner
Background: Yaletown Venture Partners; TD Bank; Accenture; PricewaterhouseCoopers
Directorships: Entrepreneurship@UBC, Canadian Venture Capital & Private Equity Association; CapitalRoad Foundation, Pacific Parklands Foundation
Joe Lucke, Co-Founder & Managing Partner
Background: Tricor Pacific Capital; Credit Suisse Private Equity; JP Morgan & Co.; Morgan Stanley & Co.; M.K. Wong & Associates
Directorships: Canadian Private Equity & Venture Capital Association; Association for Corporate Growth; Young Presidents' Association

Venture Capital & Private Equity Firms / Canadian Firms

2170 LIONHART CAPITAL LTD
Calgary, AB
Canada

Fax: 1-888-287-7949
Toll-Free: 1-888-287-2807
web: www.lionhartcapital.com

Mission Statement: Lionhart Capital invests in Canadian business in the primary sector: forestry, mining, transportation, construction. They are commited to flexible financing solutions for startups and established companies alike.

Geographic Preference: Canada
Fund Size: $300 million
Founded: 1990
Average Investment: $10,000 - $30 million
Minimum Investment: $10,000
Investment Criteria: Startup, Early Stage, Middle Stage, Later Stage
Industry Group Preference: Commercial Transportation, Construction, Mining, Forestry, Oil & Gas

2171 LONGBOW CAPITAL
421 7th Avenue SW
Calgary, AB T2P 4K9
Canada

Phone: 403-264-1888 Fax: 403-264-1855
e-mail: communications@longbowcapital.com
web: www.longbowcapital.com

Mission Statement: Longbow invests in the energy sector, specifically in oil and gas. Longbow is run by energy experts who partner with companies who are doing their business efficiently, effectively, and responibly for long-term, high-growth investments.

Geographic Preference: North America
Founded: 1997
Investment Criteria: High-Growth, Long-Term Investment
Industry Group Preference: Oilfield Services, Energy, Infrastructure, Oil & Gas

Key Executives:
  Larry Birchall, Executive Chairman
  403-767-7362
  e-mail: lbirchall@longbowcapital.com
  Education: University Of Calgary
  Tyson Birchall, Managing Director
  403-767-7367
  e-mail: tbirchall@longbowcapital.com
  Education: BBA, Business Administration, Acadia University; CFA
  Background: VP of Investment Banking, Tristone Capital Inc.
  Directorships: North West Refining, North 40 Resources
  Art Robinson, Managing Director
  403-767-7368
  e-mail: arobinson@longbowcapital.com
  Education: BMgt, University of Lethbridge; MBA, Queen's University
  Background: VP of Corporate Development, EnerMax Services; Vice President, SCF Partners
  Directorships: Air Drilling Asscoiates, Moore Pipe, Tecton Energy Services, Xoleum Services
  Chandra Henry, CFO/CCO
  403-767-7359
  e-mail: chenry@longbowcapital.com
  Education: BComm, University of Calgary; CPA; CFA
  Background: CFO, FirstEnergy Captial Corp.
  Directorships: Pengrowth Energy Corporation, Alberta Ballet Company
  Matt Cunning, Vice President
  403-767-7374
  e-mail: mcunning@longbowcapital.com
  Education: BComm, Sauder School of Business, University Of British Columbia
  Background: Director of Commercial Strategy, Parkland Fuel Corporation
  Directorships: Drillform Technical Services

2172 LUGE CAPITAL
3 Place Ville Marie
Espace CDPQ, Office 12350, Floor L
Suite 50
Montreal, QC H3B 0E7
Canada

web: www.luge.vc

Mission Statement: Luge Capital is a fintech focused venture capital fund looking to invest in Canadian companies in the areas of data security, insurtech, lending algorithms, robo advisors, next gen payments, blockchain, merchant services, wealth management tools, alternative lending solutions, process automation, bots, regtech, and more.

Geographic Preference: Canada
Fund Size: $75 Million
Founded: 2017
Minimum Investment: $250,000
Investment Criteria: Early Stage, Seed, Series A
Industry Group Preference: Fintech, Artificial Intelligence, Data Security, Insurance, Blockchain, Wealth & Asset Management
Portfolio Companies: Flinks

Other Locations:
  439 University Avenue
  5th Floor
  Toronto, ON M5G 2H6
  Canada

Key Executives:
  David Nault, General Partner
  Education: BCom, Marketing, Concordia University
  Background: Investor, iNovia Capital; President, Callio Technologies; Pivotal Payments
  Karim Gillani, General Partner
  Education: BASc, Systems Design Engineering, University of Waterloo; MSc, Finance/Economic Policy, University of London; LLM Master of Laws, University of Toronto
  Background: Xoom; BlackBerry; Redknee Solutions

Other Locations:
  303 Wyman Street
  Suite 300
  Waltham, MA 02451-1208
  Phone: 781-530-3868

  Espace CDPQ
  3, Place Ville Marie
  Bureau 12350, Niveau L
  Montreal, QC H3B 0E7
  Canada
  Phone: 514-844-6927

  1021 W Hastings St
  9th Floor
  Vancouver, BC V6E 0C3
  Canada
  Phone: 604-558-5156

Key Executives:
  Peter van der Velden, Managing General Partner
  Education: BSc, MSc, Queen's University; MBA, Schulich School of Business
  Background: Co-founder Fusion Capital Partners; Vencap Equities Alberta Ltd as Vice President, Business Development
  Beni Rovinski, Managing Director
  Education: BSc, Biochemistry, Rice University; PhD, Biochemistry, McGill University
  Background: Senior Scientist, Sanofi Pasteur
  Directorships: Aegera Pharmaceuticals, Avalon Pharmaceuticals, Cervelo Pharmaceuticals, Health Hero Network, Immunicon, IMMC, Inovise Medical, KAI Pharmaceuticals, Morphotek, Protana

Daniel Hetu, Managing Director
Education: MD, University of Sherbrook Quebec; MBA, Ecole des Hautes Etudes
Gerry Brunk, Managing Director
Education: BA, University of Virginia; MBA, Stanford University Graduate School of Business
Background: Founder and COO of a private bioinformatics company, and earlier was an executive at two venture-backed health care technology firms; Engagement Manager, The Boston Consulting Group
Directorships: ActivBiotics, AdipoGenix, LaConner Technologies, Targanta Therapeutics, Pharmasset

2174 LUMIRA VENTURES
141 Adelaide Street
Suite 770
Toronto, ON M5H 3L5
Canada

Phone: 416-213-4223
web: www.lumiraventures.com

Mission Statement: LUMIRA invests in later stage biopharmaceutical and medical device companies.

Geographic Preference: United States, Canada
Fund Size: $450 million
Average Investment: $5 - $10 million
Investment Criteria: Later-Stage
Industry Group Preference: Biopharmaceuticals, Therapeutics, Pharmaceuticals, Life Sciences
Portfolio Companies: AmacaThera, Antio Therapeutics, Antiva Biosciences, Aurinia Pharmaceuticals, Bardy Diagnostics, BAROnova, Cardiac Dimensions, Celtaxsys, Corvia Medical, Edesa Biotech, Endotronix, Engage Therapeutics, enGene, Exact Imaging, Forbius, G1 Therapeutics, Gladius Pharmaceuticals, HistoSonics, KalGene Pharmaceuticals, KisoJi Biotechnology, Medexus Pharmaceuticals, Notch Therapeutics, Opsens, OsteoQC, Satsuma Pharmaceuticals, Swift Medical, Think Research, Zymeworks

2175 MACKINNON, BENNETT & CO.
1 Place Ville Marie
Suite 3670
Montreal, QC H3B 3P2
Canada

Phone: 514-876-3939 Fax: 514-876-3956
e-mail: info@mkbandco.com
web: www.mkbandco.com

Founded: 2007
Investment Criteria: Growth
Industry Group Preference: Clean Energy, Transportation, Smart Cities
Portfolio Companies: Miovision, Communauto, BBOXX, Meteo Protect, Potentia Renewables

Key Executives:
Kenneth MacKinnon, Managing Partner
Education: McGill Univ.; Ivey Business School
Background: Merrill Lynch
Directorships: Miovision Technologies

2176 MANTELLA VENTURE PARTNERS
488 Wellington Street West
Suite 304
Toronto, ON M5V 1E3
Canada

Phone: 416-479-0779
e-mail: info@mantellavp.com
web: mantellavp.com

Mission Statement: Early-stage investors in mobile and Internet software businesses.

Geographic Preference: Canada
Fund Size: $35 million
Average Investment: $500,000
Investment Criteria: Early-Stage
Industry Group Preference: Wireless Technologies, Consumer Internet, Information Technology, Software, Artificial Intelligence
Portfolio Companies: Brave Commerce, Chango, Chatkit, Curbo, Enso Connect, Felix, Flixel, Gallop, Joist, PebblePost, Pushlife, Ritual, Shopcaster, Shopistry, SurfEasy, Unata, Wisk, Wysdom

Key Executives:
Robin Axon, Co-Founder & General Partner
Education: BAS, Aerospace Engineering, University of Toronto; MBA, Queen's University
Background: Partner, Ventures West; MD Robotics
Directorships: Brave Commerce, Unata, HipSell
Duncan Hill, Co-Founder & General Partner
Education: BMath, Computer Science & Combinatronics/Optimization, University of Waterloo
Background: Entrepreneur in Residence, Ventures West; Founder & Chief Technology Officer, Think Dynamics
Directorships: Chango, SurfEasy, Brave Commerce, HipSell

2177 MANULIFE CAPITAL
200 Bloor Street East
NT-6
Toronto, ON M4W 1E6
Canada

web: www.manulifecapital.com

Mission Statement: Invests junior capital in Canada and the United States to support growing middle market businesses and specialty real estate opportunities.

Geographic Preference: North America
Fund Size: $1.5 billion
Founded: 1998
Average Investment: $15 - $50 million fund investments
Investment Criteria: MBO, M&A, LBO, Growth
Industry Group Preference: Manufacturing, Retailing, Life Sciences, Financial Services, Real Estate, Oil & Gas
Portfolio Companies: Bradshaw International, English Bay Batter, Envirosystems, Flynn Restaurant Group, GoodLife Fitness, HOMEQ Corp., Knowlton Development Corporation, Marketwired, NSC Minerals, Recochem, Shred-It, Sleep Country Canada, Softchoice

Key Executives:
Vipon Ghai, Global Head, Private Equity & Credit
416-852-8468
e-mail: Vipon_Ghai@manulife.com
Education: BBA, Wilfrid Laurier University; CMA, CFA
Background: Bank of Montreal Capital, Bank of Nova Scotia
Rajiv Bakshi, Managing Director
416-852-5228
e-mail: Rajiv_Bakshi@manulife.com
Education: BComm, University of Toronto; CA, CBV, CFA
Background: KPMG
Liam Coppinger, Managing Director, Private Equity - Asia
e-mail: Liam_Coppinger@manulife.com
Rob Scully, Managing Director, Venture Capital
e-mail: Robert_Scully@manulife.com

2178 MAPLE LEAF ANGELS
47 Colborne Street
Suite 403
Toronto, ON M5E 1E3
Canada

Phone: 416-646-6235
e-mail: info@mapleleafangels.com
web: mapleleafangels.com

Venture Capital & Private Equity Firms / Canadian Firms

Mission Statement: Not-for-profit organization connects high net worth investors with seed and early stage technology companies.
Geographic Preference: Canada
Founded: 2007
Average Investment: $120K
Investment Criteria: Seed-Stage, Early-Stage
Industry Group Preference: Technology, Artificial Intelligence
Portfolio Companies: Acto, AlayaCare, Bus.com, Chalk, ChipCare, Cinnos, Cybeats, Cybernetiq, Encycle, ExpertFile, Film Monkey, Fluent.AI, Futurestate IT, GotGame, Hangry, Intelivote Systems, iRestify, Jaza, Kenzington Brewing Company, Koomi, LifeHive Systems, Locketgo, Madcap Learning Adventure, Moregidge, Nicoya Lifesciences, OMX, Orchard, Quench, Raven, Red Wolf Security, ReDeTec, Spartatn, SportlogiQ, Stdlib, SuitedMedia, Suncayr, Suometry, Top Hat, Transit Labs, TritonWear, Ubisoft, UCIC, Wealthsimple, Wisely
Key Executives:
  Vihangi Mehta, Managing Director
  Education: BS, University of Waterloo
  Prathna Ramesh, Chief Compliance Officer
  Education: BComm, University of Toronto
  Sanjana Muthanna, Operations Manager
  Education: BS, McMaster University

2179 MARIGOLD CAPITAL
366 Adelaide Street W
Suite 606
Toronto, ON M5V 1R9
Canada

Phone: 647-783-7725
e-mail: info@marigold-capital.com
web: marigold-capital.com

Mission Statement: Marigold Capital invests in overlooked and undervalued teams and companies in sectors, industries and communities that can tranform the future.
Key Executives:
  Jonathan Hera, Founder/Managing Partner
  Background: Sarona Asset Management; Royal Bank of Canada
  Narinder Dhami, Managing Partner
  Background: Managing Director, LEAP

2180 MARKET SQUARE EQUITY PARTNERS
36 Distillery Lane
Suite 440
Toronto, ON M5A 3C4
Canada

web: marketsquarepartners.ca

Mission Statement: Toronto-based private equity firm focused on buyouts in the lower middle market.
Geographic Preference: Canada
Investment Criteria: Buyouts
Industry Group Preference: Infrastructure Services
Portfolio Companies: Ontario Excavac, D.M. Robichaud, Clean Water Works, Intelligent Soil Recycling
Key Executives:
  Matt Hall, Managing Partner
  Background: Great-West Life; Marcus Evans; Covington Capital
  Derrick Ho, Partner
  Background: PricewaterhouseCoopers; Wolseley plc; VenGrowth Private Equity; Covington Capital

2181 MARS INVESTMENT ACCELERATOR FUND
MaRS Discovery District
101 College Street
Suite 125
Toronto, ON M5G 1L7
Canada

Phone: 647-255-1080
e-mail: iaf@marsdd.com
web: www.marsiaf.com

Mission Statement: Helps accelerate the growth of new technology companies being established in Ontario and positions them for further investments by angels and venture capitalists.
Geographic Preference: Ontario
Average Investment: $500,000
Investment Criteria: Seed-Stage, Early-Stage
Industry Group Preference: Life Sciences, Information Technology, Communications, Entertainment, Healthcare, Clean Technology, Advanced Materials
Portfolio Companies: ACTO, Chatter, Klashwerks, Maple, MedChart, Ecamion, Encycle, GreenMantra, MetaFlo, Peak Power, Polar Sapphire, Pond Biofuels, Si-Cat, SPARQ, Temporal, Client Outlook, Encycle Therapeutics, eSight, figure 1, Flosonics Medical, Forbius, Intellijoint, Nicoya Lifesciences, OpenCare, Profound Medical, Swift Medical, VitaSound
Key Executives:
  Larry LaKing, Managing Director
  Education: BA, University of Waterloo; Queen's University; University of Western Ontario
  Background: Executive Chair, Granite Networks; President and CEO, BTI Systems

2182 MCCAIN CAPITAL PARTNERS
95 St. Clair Avenue W
Suite 200
Toronto, ON M4V 1N6
Canada

Phone: 416-643-0702
e-mail: info@mccaincapital.com
web: mccaincapital.com

Geographic Preference: North America
Key Executives:
  Zac McIsaac
  Education: Mount Allison Univ.; Queen's Univ.
  James Dent
  Education: Queen's Univ.
  Background: CIBC Capital Markets

2183 MCROCK CAPITAL
219 Dufferin Street
Suite 303B
Toronto, ON M6K 3J1
Canada

web: www.mcrockcapital.com

Mission Statement: McRock Capital is an Industrial Internet of Things venture capital fund focused on investing in companies that intersect Internet-related technologies with large industrial markets.
Geographic Preference: Canada, United States
Fund Size: $65 million
Founded: 2012
Investment Criteria: Early Stage
Industry Group Preference: Power, Water, Oil & Gas, Transportation, Manufacturing, Software, Hardware
Portfolio Companies: Praemo, Miovision, Worldsensing, Decisive Farming, Serious Integrated, Invixium, Mnubo, RtTech Software

Venture Capital & Private Equity Firms / Canadian Firms

Other Locations:
2540 Kensington Road NW
Calgary, AB T2N 3S3
Canada

Key Executives:
Scott MacDonald, Co-Founder & Managing Partner
e-mail: scott@mcrockcapital.com
Background: Managing Director, Venture Capital Subsidiary, Ontario Power Generation
Directorships: RtTech Software, Invixium, Pure Technologies, SynapSense, Pressure Pipe Inspection Company, RuggedCom
Whitney Rockley, Co-Founder & Managing Partner
e-mail: whitney@mcrockcapital.com
Education: BComm, Ryerson University; MBA, University of Calgary
Background: Partner, Nomura New Energy Ventures; Partner, Emerald Technology Ventures; Encana; Revolve Technologies
Directorships: RtTech Software, Mnubo, Invixium
Ha Nguyen, Vice President
e-mail: ha@mcrockcapital.com
Education: BA, Foreign Trade Univ., Hanoi; MSc, Aston Business School
Background: IDG Ventures Vietnam
Siddharth Srivastava, Vice President
e-mail: siddharth@mcrockcapital.com
Education: BA, Economics, Grinnell College; MSc, Finance, London School of Economics
Background: EY; Rothschild

2184 MEDTEQ+
740 Notre-Dame Street W
Suite 1400
Montreal, QC H3C 3X6
Canada

Phone: 514-398-0896
e-mail: info@medteq.ca
web: www.medteq.ca

Mission Statement: MEDTEQ+ strives to accelarate innovation and position, on a global scale, Canadian medical technologies, services and products.

Fund Size: $63 Million

Key Executives:
Diane Cote, Chief Executive Officer

2185 MINK CAPITAL
120 Adelaide Street W
Suite 2500
Toronto, ON M5H 1T1
Canada

e-mail: info@minkcapital.ca
web: www.minkcapital.ca

Mission Statement: Mink Capital is a consulting firm for Family Offices, providing education on investing in Private Equity.

Geographic Preference: North America
Founded: 2011

Key Executives:
Steve Balaban, Founder & Chief Investment Officer
Education: University of Waterloo; Wilfrid Laurier University; CFA
Background: President, Stellar Outdoor Advertising
Bruce Yang, Private Equity Associate
Education: MBA, Rotman School of Management, University of Toronto
Background: Impulsivity; Tokyo Star Bank; Atos

2186 MIRALTA
51 York Street
Westmount, QC H3Z 1N7
Canada

Phone: 514-484-9806
e-mail: miralta@miralta.com
web: www.miralta.com

Geographic Preference: Ontario; Quebec
Average Investment: $2-10 million
Industry Group Preference: Technology
Portfolio Companies: Ignis Innovation

Key Executives:
Eric Baker
Education: Queen's Univ.; MIT
Background: Innocan; Union Carbide Canada
Christopher Winn, CFO
Education: McGill Univ.
Background: Innocan
Thomas Kaneb
Education: Queen's Univ.; Harvard Business School
Background: Universal Terminals

2187 MISTRAL VENTURE PARTNERS
Ottawa, ON
Canada

web: www.mistralvp.com

Mission Statement: The company invests in startups that focus on business to business solutions.

Geographic Preference: Eastern Canada
Investment Criteria: Startup, Seed Stage, B2B
Industry Group Preference: B2B, Online Marketplaces, Marketplace, Software, Blockchain, Artificial Intelligence
Portfolio Companies: Banter, Better Software Company, BlocWatch, Blue J Legal, Buckzy, Ceipal, CENX, CloudCheckr, edly, Expeto, Foko, Klipfolio, OMsignal, Quidbit, Rare.io, Relogix, Ritual, Sensibill, Soundpays, Stockpile, Symend, Unito, Zepheira

Key Executives:
Code Cubitt, Managing Director
Education: BSc, University of Alberta; MBA, Robert H. Smith School of Business, University of Maryland
Background: COO, Zephyr Technology; Partner, Motorola Ventures; Principal, Gabriel Venture Partners
Bernie Zeisig, Managing Partner
Education: BA, Economics, Carleton University; BA, Economics, Université de Chambéry; MSc, Entrepreneurial Studies, Stirling Univerity
Background: Senior Managing Partner, Cycle Capital; Senior Partner, VIMAC Ventures
Mike Scanlin, Venture Partner
Education: BS, Management Science, University of California, San Diego
Background: Partner, Battery Ventures; Sierra Ventures
Directorships: Axentis, DBS Communications, Element Labs, Vykor, Zebra Imaging
Gordon Smythe, Venture Partner
Education: BA, International Business, California State University, Fullerton; MBA, Entrepreneurial Studies and Finance, Marshall School of Business, University of Southern California
Background: Founder, The VC Forum; Founder, Pelna Inc.; Toshiba
Tianpeng Wang, Venture Partner
Education: LLB, International Economic Law, University of International Business and Economics, Beijing; JD, Bradeis School of Law, University of Louisville
Background: Partner, Jingtian & Gongcheng; PE/VC Lawyer, Clifford Chance; PE/VC Lawyer, Morrison & Foerster; PE/VC Lawyer, Linklaters
Pablo Srugo, Principal
Education: BA, Economics, Carleton University
Background: Co-Founder/COO, Gymtrack

2188 MMV CAPITAL PARTNERS
370 King Street West
Suite 442
Toronto, ON M5V 1J9
Canada

Phone: 416-977-9718 Fax: 416-591-1393
web: www.mmvf.com

Mission Statement: MMV Capital Partners is focused on providing growth capital to emerging technology and life sciences companies throughout North America. It has financed over 200 companies that range from being very early stage to established enterprises. MMV's creative financing solutions have helped the entrepreneurs of these companies realize their growth potential and reach critical milestones at all stages of development.

Geographic Preference: North America
Fund Size: $400 million
Founded: 1998
Average Investment: $1.5 to $10 million
Minimum Investment: $1.5 million
Investment Criteria: Growth Capital
Industry Group Preference: Technology, Life Sciences, Communications, Software, Clean Technology
Portfolio Companies: Abridean, Acclaris, Agilence, Airband, Andrew Davidson & Company, AgnioChem, Antares Pharma, Arxx Building Products, Avisena, Axeda, Axela, BelAir Networks, BeliefNet, Beyond The Rack, Blueprint, BTI Systems, Camillion Solutions, Canadian Bureau of Investigations & Adjustments, Chancery Software, CheckPoint HR, Chronogen, CiRBA, Cita Neuro Pharmaceutical, Clickability, ClickSquared, CorrectNet, Datawire Communication Networks, Decision Dynamics, Device Anywhere, DFT Microsystems, Diablo Technologies, Digital Payment Technologies, DMTI Spatial, eChalk, Ellumniate, EM4, EnterpriseDB, Epocal, ESP Technologies, Espial Group, Exchange Solutions, Exclaim, Exposoft Solutions, FitLinxx, Five Star Technologies, Foresee Results, Frantic Films, FullTilt Solutions, Generation5, GeoCom TMS, Globalserve, Health Integrated, HighRoads, HNW, Hubspan, Icera, iJET Intelligent Risk Systems, iKobo, Innovectra Corporation, Inception Biosciences, Integral Development Corporation, Intelliworks, Invivodata, Laszlo Systems, LogicTree, LucidMedia, Maptuit, MarketingIsland.com, Maximum Throughput, Merlin Technologies, Mistral Pharma, Momentum Healthware, Nakina Systems, Natural Convergence, Neat Receipts, NeoEdge Networks, NetBase Solutions, NetKey, NileGuide, NineSigma, Nistica, NOVX Systems, Ooma, OrderMotion, Osprey, PacketMotion, Pivot, Portico Systems, PowerSteering Software, PrimeRevenue, Quickhit, Qumu, Razorsight, Redknee, Reflex Photonics, Resonant Medical, ResponseTek Networks, Ryma Technologies Solutions, Safe Life Corp., SellPoint, SenSage, Sentx, Sermo, Side Effects Software, Skila, SkyWave Mobile Communications, Smart Destinations, Software Technology, Solbright, Spectralinera, Spectrum K12 School Solutions, SpeedDate.com, Stretch, Sutus, Teachscape, Tira Wireless, Topigen Pharmaceuticals, TrustDigital, Tutor.com, UIEvolution, Unitrends, US HIFU, Vantrix Corporation, Verified Person, Veris Health Sciences, WaveSat, Xceed Molecular Corp., Xeye, xMatters, Xora, Z-Tech

Key Executives:
 Minhas Mohamed, Co-Founder & CEO
 Education: University of Western Ontario, CA, CFA
 Background: Senior Partner, Quorum Funding Corporation; Ernst & Young

2189 MONTECO STRATEGIC CAPITAL
2300 Yonge Street
Suite 1600
Toronto, ON M4P 1E4
Canada

Phone: 416-960-9968
Toll-Free: 866-960-9968
e-mail: info@monteco.com
web: monteco.com

Mission Statement: Provides management experience, technical and product development infrastructure, and capital resources to startups and acquired properties.

Portfolio Companies: AutoServe1, Good Harbour Laboratories, Imtex, Riptide Tek

Key Executives:
 Scott Monteith, President & CEO
 Education: Ryerson University
 Roland DuBois, Chief Operating Officer
 Education: BS, University of New Hampshire
 Background: President, Green Turtle Technologies; President, Imbrium Systems

2190 MOSAIC CAPITAL PARTNERS
6300 Northam Drive
Mississauga, ON L4V 1H7
Canada

Phone: 416-367-2888 Fax: 416-367-8146
e-mail: info@mosaicvp.com
web: www.mosaicvp.com

Mission Statement: Mosaic Capital Partners is a Toronto-based private investment firm.

Geographic Preference: Canada, United States
Fund Size: $135 Million
Founded: 1997
Average Investment: $2 - $10 million
Investment Criteria: Seed, Early-Stage, Expansion
Industry Group Preference: Internet Technology, Information Technology

Key Executives:
 Vernon Lobo, Managing Director
 Education: BSc, Engineering, University of Waterloo; MBA, Harvard University
 Background: McKinsey & Company, Nortel Networks
 Directorships: Cyberplex, AirIQ, Silanis Technologies, Tecsys
 Ron Farmer, Managing Director
 Education: BA, MBA, University of Western Ontario
 Background: McKinsey & Company
 Directorships: Bank of Montreal, Valeant Pharmaceuticals

2191 McLEAN WATSON CAPITAL
141 Adelaide Street W
Suite 1002
Toronto, ON M5H 3L5
Canada

Phone: 416-363-2000 Fax: 416-363-2010
e-mail: ATong@mcleanwatson.com
web: www.mcleanwatson.com

Mission Statement: A venture capital firm with an interest in all espects of the technology and sector.

Geographic Preference: North America, Far East
Founded: 1992
Average Investment: $1 - $5 million
Investment Criteria: Seed-Stage, Early-Stage, Later-Stage
Industry Group Preference: Information Technology, Communications, Hardware Technology, Software Services, Energy Technology
Portfolio Companies: i4i, Signiant, Quantec

Key Executives:
 John Eckert, Partner
 e-mail: john@round13capital.com

Education: BA, MBA, University of Western Ontario
Background: Joint COO, Softimage; VP, Director, Corporate Finance, Wood Gundy; CIBC Wood Gundy
Directorships: Echelon, SkyWave Mobile Communications, Sitebrand, Activplant, Fortiva
Loudon Mclean Owen, Partner
e-mail: lowen@mcleanwatson.com
Education: BA, University of Toronto; LLB, Osgoode Hall, Toronto; MBA, INSEAD
Background: Joint COO, Softimage
Directorships: i4i, Vismand Exploration, Amplus Communications, Ntegrator International, Quantec

2192 NEW BRUNSWICK INNOVATION FOUNDATION
440 King Street
Suite 602
King Tower
Fredericton, NB E3B 5H8
Canada

Toll-Free: 877-554-6668
web: nbif.ca

Mission Statement: Private, not-for-profit corporation invests in startups and R&D.

Geographic Preference: New Brunswick
Fund Size: $100 million
Founded: 2003
Average Investment: $25,000 to $1 million
Minimum Investment: $25,000
Investment Criteria: Early-Stage
Industry Group Preference: Energy, Environmental Technology, Information Technology, Life Sciences, Natural Resources, Manufacturing, Aerospace, Defense and Government, Food & Beverage
Portfolio Companies: Alongside, Anessa, Avrij, Beauceron Security, Eigen Innovations, Encore Interactive, Fiddlehead Technology, Flixel Cinemagraph, Gemba, HotSpot Merchants, Introhive, Inversa Systems, Kognitiv Spark, MycoDev Group, PatriotOne Technologies, Populus Global, Porpoise, Repable, Resson Aerospace, Rise, Scene Sharp, Selectbidder, SimpTek Technologies, Smartpods, Smart Skin, SomaDetect, Sonrai, Soricimed, Stash Energy, Total Pave, WellTrack

Key Executives:
Jeff White, CEO
e-mail: jeff.white@nbif.ca
Education: BBA, St. Francis Xavier University; CPA
Background: COO, East Valley Ventures; CFO, Radian6; CFO, Q1 Labs; CFO, Genesys Laboratories Canada; Interim CEO, Canada's Ocean Supercluster
Laura Richard, Director of Research
Education: BSc, University of New Brunswick; PhD, Inorganic Chemistry, University of Oxford
Background: Procter & Gamble; Velocys

2193 NEXT CANADA
175 Bloor Street East
Suite 1800
South Building
Toronto, ON M4W 3R8
Canada

e-mail: info@nextcanada.com
web: www.nextcanada.com

Mission Statement: A national, non-profit organization that focuses on four main streams of startups: Next 36, for students and grads launching startups; Next Founders, for founders of high growth ventures; Next AI, for artificial intelligence-related ventures; and Next ED for Canadian business looking to utilize AI.

Geographic Preference: Canada
Founded: 2010
Investment Criteria: Student/recent grad startups, high growth ventures, AI-related ventures.
Industry Group Preference: Artificial Intelligence

Key Executives:
Joe Canavan, Principal
Education: BBA, Concordia University; OPM, Business, Harvard Business School
Background: CEO, Assante Wealth Management; CEO, Synergy Asset Management; Founder, GT Global (Canada); VP, National Sales, Fidelity Investment Canada, CEO, Children's Aid Foundation
Directorships: Jays Care Foundation; Singularity University
Kyle Winters, Chief Executive Officer
Education: Omnium Global MBA, Rotman School of Management, University of Toronto; EMBA, University of St. Gallen; Executive Education Certificates, Harvard University
Background: Executive Director, Corporate & Foundation Relations, University of Toronto; National VP, Corporate Partnerships, Heart & Stroke Foundation of Canada; President, Canadian Foundation for AIDS Research

2194 NEXT EQUITIES
17511 - 107 Avenue NW
Suite 102
Edmonton, AB T5S 1E5
Canada

Phone: 780-986-0095 ext 301
web: nextequities.com

Mission Statement: Targets promising companies looking for funding and complementary expertise to accelerate growth and profitability.

Geographic Preference: North America
Investment Criteria: Growth; Companies Size between $500K to $5M
Industry Group Preference: Industrials, Real Estate, Facial Analysis, Childcare
Portfolio Companies: Block 45, Doorstat, Henry The Dentist, Kepler Academy, Nuwest Communities, Fiberex, Most Oil, The Press Gallery, Troverie, Vytalize Health

Key Executives:
Sikandar Atiq, President
Education: BComm, Univ. of Alberta; MBA, NYU Stern School of Business
Background: Goldman Sachs

2195 NIAGARA BUSINESS & INNOVATION FUND
55 Clarence St
PO Box 519
Port Colborne, ON L3K 5X7
Canada

Phone: 905-834-2173
web: www.niagarafund.com

Geographic Preference: Niagara Region/Southern Ontario
Founded: 2014
Average Investment: $150K

2196 NORTHLEAF CAPITAL PARTNERS
79 Wellington Street West
6th Floor, Box 120
Toronto, ON M5K 1N9
Canada

Toll-Free: 866-964-4141
e-mail: contact@northleafcapital.com
web: www.northleafcapital.com

Mission Statement: Founded as TD Capital, Northleaf is a global private equity, infrastructure and private credit manager.

Geographic Preference: North America, Europe, Asia
Fund Size: $21 Billion

Venture Capital & Private Equity Firms / Canadian Firms

Founded: 2009
Investment Criteria: Venture & Growth Equity, Buyouts, Special Situations, Infrastructure
Portfolio Companies: BLS Revecore, Can Art Aluminum Extrusion, Cushman & Wakefield, Ecobee, Emerald Textiles, FreshBooks, Lenskart, Mercer Advisors, Pinova, Polycor, Randall & Reilly, Refresco, Vision Critical

Other Locations:
1155 rue Metcalfe
Suite 1500
Montréal, QC H3B 2V6
Canada
Phone: 866-964-4141

48 Dover Street
4th Floor
London W1S 4FF
United Kingdom
Phone: 44 (0) 20 7321 5750

One North Franklin Street
Suite 3340
Chicago, IL 60606
Phone: 312-871-4832

228 Hamilton Avenue
3rd Floor
Palo Alto, CA 94301

299 Park Avenue
41st Floor
New York, NY 10171
Phone: 646-512-9600

120 Collins Street
Level 50
Melbourne 3000
Australia
Phone: 61 3 9900 6229

Key Executives:
Rob MacLellan, Chairman
e-mail: rob.maclellan@northleafcapital.com
Education: BComm, Carleton University; MBA, Harvard University; CA
Background: Managing Director, Lancaster Financial Holding
Stephen Foote, Managing Director, Sales
e-mail: stephen.foote@northleafcapital.com
Education: BA, York Univ.
Background: UBS Global Asset Management
Jeff Lucassen, Chief Financial Officer & Chief Operating Officer
e-mail: jeff.lucassen@northleafcapital.com
Education: BComm, Univ. of Windsor; BA, Univ. of Western Ontario
Background: The Carlyle Group
Gavin Foo, Managing Director, Investor Operations
e-mail: gavin.foo@northleafcapital.com
Education: BComm, University of Toronto; CA
Background: TD Capital Private Equity; SVP/CFO, IA Clarington Investments; Trimark Financial Corporation; Coopers & Lybrand
Stuart Waugh, Managing Director & Managing Partner
e-mail: stuart.waugh@northleafcapital.com
Education: BA, Trinity College, University of Toronto; LLB, Faculty of Law, University of Toronto
Background: TD Capital Private Equity; Management Consultant, McKinsey & Company; BPI Financial Corporation; McCarthy Tetrault

2197 NOVA SCOTIA BUSINESS INC.
World Trade & Convention Center
1800 Argyle St
Suite 701
Halifax, NS B3J 3N8
Canada

Phone: 902-424-6650
Toll-Free: 800-260-6682
e-mail: info@nsbi.ca
web: www.novascotiabusiness.com

Mission Statement: Invests in companies seeking growth capital, and looks for venture capital investors as partners in Nova Scotia's knowledge-based economy.
Geographic Preference: Nova Scotia
Fund Size: $55 million
Founded: 2001
Average Investment: $1 to $3 million
Minimum Investment: $1 million
Investment Criteria: Mid- to Late-Stage
Industry Group Preference: Financial Services, Aerospace, Defense and Government, Manufacturing, Security, Gaming, Life Sciences, Clean Technology
Portfolio Companies: Azorus, DynaGen, Halifax Biomedical, Health Outcomes Worldwide, Impath Networks, Intellivote Systems, Kytogenics, LED Roadway Lighting, Origin BioMed, Oris4, Techlink Entertainment, Unique Ltd.

Key Executives:
Laurel C. Broten, President & CEO
Education: BA, BSc, McMaster Univ.; JD, University of Western Ontario
Peter MacAskill, Chief Operating Officer
Education: BSc, St. Francis Xavier University
Michael Branchflower, Vice President, Sales & Strategic Marketing
Background: Execution Specialists Group
Directorships: Embrace Hope

2198 NOVACAP
3400, rue de l'Eclipse
Bureau 700
Brossard, QC L4Z 0P3
Canada

Phone: 450-651-5000 **Fax:** 450-651-7585
e-mail: info@novacap.ca
web: www.novacap.ca

Mission Statement: Novacap Industries invests in middle-market companies within traditional industries that have the potential to become world leaders by developing their market, technology and operations or through industry consolidations. Novacap technologies invests in companies focusing on growth and market leadership in information and communications technologies sectors. It partners with first rate management teams and actively works with them to build leading organizations in their markets.

Geographic Preference: North America
Fund Size: $3.6 Billion
Founded: 1981
Average Investment: $5-50 Million
Minimum Investment: $5 Million
Investment Criteria: Growth, Buyout
Industry Group Preference: Industry, Technology, Media & Telecommunications
Portfolio Companies: Bestar, Foliot Furniture, GHP Group, GTI, Hallcon, Horizon, Intelerad, Joseph Ribkoff, Kingsdown, Leading Edge Geomatics, Malhot Industries, Master, Mobile Storage Systems, Mucci Farms, Nautilus Plus, Nitrex, Noble Foods, Nuvei, Octasic, Pkware, Royal Mat, Spectrum Health Care, Smyth, Synergx, Syntax, Windmill Farms

Other Locations:
1 University Avenue
Suite 1600

Venture Capital & Private Equity Firms / Canadian Firms

Toronto, ON M5J 2P1
Canada
Phone: 416-536-2222 **Fax:** 450-651-7585

Key Executives:
Pascal Tremblay, President, CEO & Managing Partner
Education: BBA, University of Sherbrooke; MBA, McGill University
Background: Partner, Argo Global Capital; CDP Capital
Directorships: Ryma Technologies Solutions, LiquidxStream Systems, Creaform, Stingray Digital, Tenrox, PKWare

Jacques Foisy, Chair & Managing Partner
Background: KPMG, Montreal; Olympia Group
Directorships: KDC, Octasic, Royal Mat, BGR Saws, Tradition Foods, Demers Ambulances, Metro Supply Group, Rosmar Packaging Corporation

2199 OMERS PRIVATE EQUITY
900 - 100 Adelaide Street W
Toronto, ON M5H 0E2
Canada

Phone: 416-369-2400
web: www.omersprivateequity.com

Mission Statement: Pension administrator for municipal employees in the province of Ontario invests in high-quality private equity and infrastructure assets.

Geographic Preference: Global
Fund Size: $85 billion
Founded: 1962
Industry Group Preference: Infrastructure, Energy, Transportation
Portfolio Companies: Alexander Mann Solutions, Caliber Collision, CBI Health Group, CEDA, Epiq, ERM, Forefront Dermatology, Inmar, Kenan Advantage, Lifeways, National Veterinary Associates, Paradigm, Premise Health, Trescal, V.Group, Vue International

Other Locations:
450 Park Avenue
9th Floor
New York, NY 10022
Phone: 646-376-3100

The Leadenhall Building
122 Leadenhall Street
London EC3V 4AB
United Kingdom
Phone: 44 (0)20 7822 8300

One Raffles Quay
#41-01, North Tower 048583
Singapore
Phone: 65 6540 9350

Key Executives:
Michael Graham, Global Head of Private Equity
Education: BComm, Queen's University; MBA, Schulich School of Business, York University
Background: HSBC
Directorships: Kenan Advantage Group, EPIQ, Great Expressions Dental Centers, United States Infrastructure Corporation, Nordco, CHG Healthcare, Marketwired

2200 ONCAP
161 Bay Street
49th Floor
Toronto, ON M5J 2S1
Canada

Phone: 416-214-4300
e-mail: info@oncap.com
web: www.oncap.com

Mission Statement: Invests in and builds shareholder value in North American small and mid-sized companies that are leaders in their defined market niche and possess meaningful growth potential.

Geographic Preference: North America
Fund Size: $1.1 billion
Founded: 1999
Average Investment: $20 - $200 million
Investment Criteria: Equity Capital, Going Private Transactions
Portfolio Companies: AutoSource Motors, Bradshaw Home, Chatters, Davis-Standard, Enertech, Englobe, Hopkins Manufacturing, ILAC, IntraPac, Laces Group, Pinnacle Renewable Energy, Precision Global, Pure Canadian Gaming, Venanpri Group, Walter Surface Technologies, Wyse Meter Solutions

Other Locations:
712 Fifth Ave
40th Floor
New York, NY 10019
Phone: 212-582-2211

Key Executives:
Michael Lay, Managing Partner
e-mail: mlay@oncap.com
Education: Richard Ivey School of Business
Background: Ontario Teachers' Pension Plan Board; Versus Technologies

Gregory Baylin, Managing Director
e-mail: gbaylin@oncap.com
Education: Queen's University
Background: Scotia Capital

Mark Gordon, Senior Partner
e-mail: mgordon@oncap.com
Education: Boston College; MBA, Richard Ivey School of Business
Background: Goldman Sachs & Co., BMO Nesbitt Burns

2201 ONEX PARTNERS
161 Bay Street
Toronto, ON M5J 2S1
Canada

Phone: 416-362-7711
e-mail: info@onex.com
web: www.onex.com

Mission Statement: Onex is one of North America's oldest and most successful private equity firms committed to acquiring and building high-quality businesses in partnership with talented management teams. The Company is guided by an ownership culture focused on achieving strong absolute growth, with an emphasis on capital preservation. With an experienced management team, significant financial resources and no debt at the parent company, Onex is well-positioned to continue to acquire and build businesses.

Geographic Preference: North America
Fund Size: $6.9 billion
Founded: 1984
Investment Criteria: Acquisitions, Carve-Outs, Restructurings, Consolidations
Industry Group Preference: Aerospace, Defense and Government, Healthcare, Industrial Products, Entertainment
Portfolio Companies: AIT, AutoSource, BBAM, BradshawHome, BrightSpring, Carestream, Celestica, Chatters, Clarivate Analytics, Davis Standard, Emerald Expositions, Englobe, Hopkins, IntraPac, Jack's, Jeld-Wen, Laces, Parkdean Resorts, Pinnacle, PowerSchool, Precision, Pure Canadian Gaming, Ryan, RSG, Save a Lot Food Stores, Schumacher, SGS Co., SIG, SMG, Survitec, Tecta America, Venanpri Group, Walter Surface Technologies, WireCo, York

Other Locations:
712 Fifth Avenue
New York, NY 10019
Phone: 212-582-2211

8 St. James's Square
London SW1Y 4JU

Venture Capital & Private Equity Firms / Canadian Firms

United Kingdom
Phone: 44 (0)20-7389-1540

930 Sylvan Avenue
Englewood Cliffs, NJ 07632
Phone: 201-541-2121

21 Custom House Street
10th Floor
Boston, MA 02110
Phone: 617-412-2700

Key Executives:
Gerry Schwartz, Chair & CEO
Education: MBA, Harvard Business School; LLB, BComm, University of Manitoba
Background: Co-Founder/President, CanWest Capital
Ewout Heersink, Vice Chair
Education: MBA, Queen's University; BBA, Richard Ivey School of Business
Background: CanWest Capital, KPMG
Robert Le Blanc, President & Head of Onex Partners
Education: BS, Bucknell University; MBA, New York University
Background: Berkshire Hataway, General Electric
Directorships: Magellan Health Services, Emergency Medical Services, Res-Care, Center for Diagnostic Imaging, Skilled Healthcare Group, The Warranty Group, Cypress Insurance
Chris Govan, Senior Managing Director & CFO
Education: BA, MA, University of Waterloo
Background: Senior Tax Manager
Anthony Munk, Vice Chair
Education: BA, Queen's University
Background: Vice President, First Boston Corporation; Portfolio Manager, Guardian Capital
Directorships: Cineplex, Barrick Gold Corporation, RSI Home Products, Tomkins Building Products, JELD-WEN Holding

2202 ONPOINT VENTURES
Toronto, ON
Canada

Mission Statement: OnPoint Ventures supports the advancement of Canadian start-up and scale-up businesses relating to health, medtech and commercialization.

Geographic Preference: Canada

Key Executives:
Paul Weber, Managing Director
647-504-4260
e-mail: weberpaul112c@gmail.com
Background: Founder, Toronto Medtech CEO Round Table
Susan So, Partner
e-mail: susanso416@gmail.com

2203 ONTARIO CAPITAL GROWTH CORPORATION
700 Bay Street
Suite 2401
Toronto, ON M5G 1Z6
Canada

Phone: 416-325-6874
Toll-Free: 877-422-5818
web: www.ocgc.gov.on.ca

Mission Statement: A joint initiative between the Government of Ontario and leading institutional investors to invest primarily in Ontario-based and Ontario-focused venture capital and growth equity funds that support innovative, high-growth companies.

Geographic Preference: Ontario
Fund Size: $455 million
Founded: 2009

Industry Group Preference: Clean Technology, Life Sciences, Media, Communications, Information Technology, Digital Media & Marketing

Key Executives:
Steve Romanyshyn, President & CEO
Education: MA, Economics, University of Victoria
Background: Government of Ontario

2204 PANACHE VENTURES
3 Place Ville Marie
Bureau 12350
Montreal, QC H3B 0E7
Canada

web: www.panache.vc

Mission Statement: Seed stage venture capital fund.

Geographic Preference: Canada
Investment Criteria: Seed
Industry Group Preference: 3D Technology, AI, Blockchain, Cleantech, Cyber Security, Digital Media, E-Commerce, Energy, Healthcare, Fintech, IoT, Marketing Technology, SaaS, Telecommunications, Social Media
Portfolio Companies: Acto, Aon3d, Audible Reality, Dooly, Certn, Colab Software, Communo, Cto.Ai, Evree, Fightcamp, Fispan, Fleetops, Flinks, Green-Eye Technology, Harbr, Humanfirst, Invivo Ai, Lane, Lexop, Marketmuse, Masterpiecevr, Medstack, Mobsquad, Orchard, Redock, Securicy, Spocket, Vyrill, Wisk Bar Inventory, Wize

Other Locations:
150 9 Avenue SW
Suite 2100
Calgary, AB T2P 1B4
Canada

1040 Hamilton Street
Vancouver, BC V6B 5T4
Canada

373 King Street SW
Suite 301
Toronto, ON M5V 1K1
Canada

Key Executives:
Mike Cegelski, Chair
Background: Founder, iBeware; Founder, Beltron Technologies; Partner, 500 Startups Canada
Patrick Lor, Partner
Education: University of Calgary
Background: Co-Founder, iStockphoto; Managing Partner, 500 Startups Canada

2205 PANGAEA VENTURES LTD
1500 West Georgia Street
Suite 1520
Vancouver, BC V6G 2Z6
Canada

web: www.pangaeaventures.com

Mission Statement: Advanced materials venture capital.

Geographic Preference: North America, Europe, Asia
Fund Size: $157 million
Founded: 2000
Average Investment: $3 million
Minimum Investment: $250K
Investment Criteria: Commercial Products Based on Physical Science Innovations, Early Commercial Stage, Strong Management Team
Industry Group Preference: Advanced Materials, Clean Technology, Energy, Electronics, Health, Sustainability, Agriculture
Portfolio Companies: Airborne Intl., ESS Inc., A2M, Tivra Corp., Aspect Biosystems, Correlia Biosystems, NewLeaf Symbiotics, Redlen Technologies, Vestaron, Calysta, CarbonCure, polySpectra, Switch Materials

Venture Capital & Private Equity Firms / Canadian Firms

Other Locations:
5080 N 40th Street
Unit 105
Phoenix, AZ 85018

Key Executives:
Chris Erickson, Founder & General Partner
e-mail: cerickson@pangaeaventures.com
Education: BComm, University of Calgary; JD, University of Toronto
Background: Partner, Osler Hoskin & Harcourt
Purnesh Seegopaul, General Partner
e-mail: pseegopaul@pangaeaventures.com
Education: BSc, Chemistry, University of Guyana; PhD, Chemistry, University of New South Wales
Andrew Haughian, General Partner
e-mail: ahaughian@pangaeaventures.com
Education: Bachelor of Applied Science, Mechanical Engineering, University of Toronto; MBA, Sauder School of Business, University of British Columbia

2206 PARALLEL49 EQUITY
1055 West Hastings Street
Suite 1060
Vancouver, BC V6E 2E9
Canada

Phone: 847-295-4410
web: www.p49equity.com

Mission Statement: A leading private equity firm that invests in profitable, well-managed, middle-market companies in Canada and the United States.

Geographic Preference: Canada, United States
Fund Size: $1.2 Billion
Founded: 1996
Investment Criteria: Acquisitions, MBO, Recapitalizations, Sales of Subsidiaries
Industry Group Preference: Manufacturing, Business Products & Services, Distribution, Consumer Products, Food & Beverage, Consumer Services, Waste & Recycling, Education, Financial Services, Healthcare, Logistics
Portfolio Companies: Certified Recycling, Gold Standard Baking, Kinetrex Energy, Questco, Tiger Calcium, BFG Supply, CPI Card Group, MedTorque

Other Locations:
225 East Deerpath Road
Suite 200
Lake Forest, IL 60045
Phone: 847-295-4410 Fax: 847-295-4243

Key Executives:
Brad Seaman, Managing Partner
847-295-4427
e-mail: bseaman@p49equity.com
Education: BBA, Bowling Green State University; MBA, University of Dallas
Background: Senior Vice President, Merchant Banking Business, General Electric Company
Directorships: CPI Card Group, Keyes Packaging Group, Strong Precision Technologies
Rod Senft, Founder & Investment Committee Member
604-646-4363
e-mail: rsenft@p49equity.com
Education: BComm, LLB, University of Manitoba
Background: Tricor Pacific Capital; Macluan Capital Corporation; Hines Nurseries; SunGro Horticulture; Davis & Company; Cargill (Canada) Inc.; Thompson, Dorftman, Sweatman
Directorships: Golden Boy Foods

2207 PARKVIEW CAPITAL PARTNERS
105 Bedford Road
Toronto, ON M5R 2K4
Canada

Phone: 416-947-0123 Fax: 416-947-1877
e-mail: info@parkviewcapital.com
web: parkviewcapital.com

Mission Statement: Mid-market private investment firm in Toronto.

Geographic Preference: Canada
Founded: 1993
Average Investment: $10 to $30 million
Minimum Investment: $10 million
Industry Group Preference: Manufacturing, Business Products & Services, Energy, Aerospace, Defense and Government, Transportation, Financial Services, Education, Marketing
Portfolio Companies: Active Industrial Solutions, KV Custom Window and Doors, Labelink

Key Executives:
Donald Jackson, Chair & Founder
Education: BA, University of Alberta; MBA, University of Western Ontario Ivey School of Business
Background: President & CEO, Laidlaw
Directorships: Vector Aerospace, Northstar, Laidlaw, ADT, Attwoods, Trimac Limited, Derlan Industries
Robert Bramer, Managing Director
Education: BComm, Queen's Univ.
Background: Ernst & Young

2208 PELORUS VENTURE CAPITAL
St. John's, NL
Canada

web: www.pelorusventure.com

Mission Statement: Venture capital company dedicated to building the Atlantic Canada ecosystem.

Geographic Preference: Atlantic Canada
Founded: 2015
Portfolio Companies: Hey Orca!, Clockwork Fox, Sentinal Alert, Sequence Bio

Key Executives:
Chris Moyer, Director
e-mail: chris@pelorusventure.com
Education: BComm, Dalhousie Univ.; MBA, Saint Mary's Univ.
Background: GrowthWorks

2209 PELOTON CAPITAL MANAGEMENT
8 King Street E
Suite 1100
Toronto, ON M5C 1B5
Canada

Phone: 647-957-8320
e-mail: info@pelotoncapitalmanagement.com
web: www.pelotoncapitalmanagement.com

Mission Statement: Peloton Capital Management is a Private Equity firm with long-term capital and investment orientation.

Key Executives:
Steve Faraone, Managing Partner
Education: BComm, University of British Columbia
Background: Managing Director, OTPP; BMO Capital Markets
Mike Murray, Managing Partner
Education: BComm, Queen's University; MBA, Tuck School of Business, Dartmouth
Background: Managing Director, OTPP; Bain & Co.

Venture Capital & Private Equity Firms / Canadian Firms

2210 PENDER WEST CAPITAL PARTNERS
Vancouver, BC
Canada

Mission Statement: Pender West invests in small- to medium-sized businesses in Canada. The company partners with no set hold periods or investment horizons
Geographic Preference: Canada, Western United States
Founded: 2000
Investment Criteria: Small Business, Medium Business, Buyout, Co-Investment
Industry Group Preference: Transportation, Logistics, Packaging, Recycling, Business Services, Manufacturing & Distribution
Portfolio Companies: Base 10 Group, Canada Film Capital, Dinoflex, EP Canada Film Services, Overland Container Transportation Services, Premium Brands, Tapp Label Technologies

Key Executives:
Bruce Hodge, Managing Director
Education: MA, Economics, Queen's University; MBA, University of Western Ontario
Background: Founding Partner, CWC Capital; Vice President/Director, Pemberton Securites
Directorships: Base 10 Group, Canada Film Capital, Dinoflex, EP Film Services, Overland Container Transportation Services, Tapp Label Technologies
Wade Flemons, Managing Director
Education: BEng, Industrial Engineering, Stanford University; MBA, University of Western Ontario
Background: Partner, CWC Capital; Pemberton Securites; Price Waterhouse
Directorships: Base 10 Group, Canada Film Capital, Dinoflex, EP Film Services, Overland Container Transportation Services, Tapp Label Technologies
Derek Senft, Vice President
Education: BA, Dartmouth College; MBA, London Business School
Background: Principal, Tricor Pacific Founders Capital; Senior Associate, Tricor Pacific Capital; CIBC World Markets
Directorships: Base 10 Group, Canada Film Capital, Dinoflex, EP Film Services, Overland Container Transportation Services, Tapp Label Technologies
Rod Senft, Director
Education: Law, Business Administration, University of Manitoba
Background: Founder/Principal, Tricor Pacific Capital; Davis & Co.; Cargill Canada; Thompson, Dorfman, Sweatman
John Zaplatynsky, Director
Education: BSc, University of Manitoba
Directorships: Retail Merchants Association of BC, BC Landscape and Nursery Association, Premium Brands Holdings Corporation, Contech International Inc.
Carsten Sorensen, Director
Education: BSc, Finance, University of California, Berkeley
Background: CEO, The Orphanage; Proxicom

2211 PENFUND
Bay Adelaide Centre
333 Bay Street
Suite 610
Toronto, ON M5H 2R2
Canada

Phone: 416-865-0707 Fax: 416-364-4149
web: penfund.com

Mission Statement: Provider of junior capital to mid-market companies in North America.
Geographic Preference: North America
Fund Size: $1.8 Billion
Founded: 1979
Investment Criteria: Acquisitions, Recapitalizations, MBO, LBO, Reorganizations
Industry Group Preference: Consumer, Business Services, Healthcare
Portfolio Companies: 24-7 Intouch, Aveanna Healthcare, Caliber Collision, CBI Health Group, Forefront Dermatology, Give & Go, GoodLife Fitness, Hopkins, Mevotech, Mister, Pet Supermarket, Plews & Edelmann

Key Executives:
Richard Bradlow, Partner
416-645-3794
e-mail: richard@penfund.com
Education: BA, University of Western Ontario; MBA, Harvard University
Background: Scotia Capital
Adam Breslin, Partner
416-645-3796
e-mail: abreslin@penfund.com
Education: BA, McGill University; MBA, Wharton School
Background: Boston Consulting Group, C Bernstein & Co., CEO, Excentia, Imperial Capital
Directorships: Gesco Industries
Jeremy Thompson, Partner
416-645-3790
e-mail: jthompson@penfund.com
Education: BA, Economics, Queen's University
Background: Leveraged Finance, Goldman Sachs & Co.; Oak Hill Capital Management
Nicole Fich, Partner
e-mail: nfich@penfund.com
Education: HBA, Richard Ivey School of Business
Background: Onex Partners, GRI Capital
Joe Mattina, Partner
e-mail: jmattina@penfund.com
Education: BComm, McMaster University; CPA
Background: Apollo Management; MacQuarie Canada; Fortress Investment Group; GE Capital; KPMG

2212 PERSISTENCE CAPITAL PARTNERS
600 de Maisonneuve Boulevard W
Suite 2000
Montreal, QC H3A 3J2
Canada

Toll-Free: 866-379-5842
e-mail: info@persistencecapital.com
web: www.persistencecapital.com

Mission Statement: Private equity firm focused exclusively on healthcare.
Geographic Preference: Canada
Founded: 2008
Average Investment: $5 to $10 million
Minimum Investment: $5 million
Investment Criteria: MBO, Recapitalizations, Divestitures/Carve Outs, Distress Situations, Growth Equity, Consolidations, Roll-Ups
Industry Group Preference: Healthcare
Portfolio Companies: AnimaPlus, Anova Fertility & Reproductive Health, functionability, kDa Group, LMC Diabetes & Endocrinology, MCA Dental Group, mdBriefCase, Medspa Partners, Rx Drug Mart

Other Locations:
60 Bloor Street W
Suite 404
Toronto, ON M4W 2B8
Canada

Key Executives:
Dr. Sheldon Elman, Founding Partner
Education: McGill University Faculty of Medicine
Background: Founder, Medisys Health Group
Stuart M. Elman, Managing Partner
Education: HBA, Richard Ivey School of Business

Venture Capital & Private Equity Firms / Canadian Firms

Background: President, Medisys Health Group; Trader Classified Media
Adrianna Czornyj, Partner
Education: HBBA, Business Administration & Accounting, Wilfrid Laurier University
Background: Deloitte; BDO Dunwoody LLP
Directorships: Canadian Women in Private Equity
John Trang, Partner
Education: BComm, Queen's University
Background: TorQuest Partners; Lloyds Banking Group; UBS
Directorships: Lift Investments

2213 PFM CAPITAL
2nd Fl., The Assiniboia Club Bldg.
1925 Victoria Avenue
Regina, SK S4P 0R3
Canada

Phone: 306-791-4855 Fax: 306-791-4848
e-mail: pfm@pfm.ca
web: www.pfm.ca

Mission Statement: PFM aims to work with Saskatchewan businesses with a focus on growth capital, management buyout and expansion financing transactions.

Geographic Preference: Saskatchewan
Fund Size: $728 million
Founded: 1989
Average Investment: $5-20 million
Industry Group Preference: Industry, Energy, Agriculture
Portfolio Companies: Harbour Landing Village, Hi-Tec Profiles, Prairie Soil Services, Steel Reef Infrastructure Corp.

Key Executives:
Randy Beattie, President & Founding Partner
e-mail: randybeattie@pfm.ca
Directorships: Factory Optical, Hospitality Network, Hi-Tec Profiles
Rob Duguid, CEO & Founding Partner
e-mail: robduguid@pfm.ca
Background: Crown Capital Partners
Directorships: Steel Reef Infrastructure Corp., Auctus Property Fund, StorageVault Canada

2214 PINNACLE MERCHANT CAPITAL
Brookfield Place, TD Canada Trust Tower
181 Bay Street, Suite 2830
Toronto, ON M5J 2T3
Canada

Phone: 416-601-2270
web: www.pincap.com

Mission Statement: Independent investor and financial advisory firm invests at all stages of the company life cycle.

Geographic Preference: Canada
Founded: 1998
Average Investment: $1 million
Investment Criteria: All Stages
Industry Group Preference: Information Technology, Software, Digital Media & Marketing, Internet

Key Executives:
Arif N. Bhalwani, Managing Director
Education: MBA, Queen's University; CFA
Background: Managing Director, Third Eye Capital

2215 PIQUE VENTURES
Vancouver, BC
Canada

web: piqueventures.com

Mission Statement: Pique Ventures is an impact investment and management company.

Founded: 2012
Industry Group Preference: Fashion, Digital Content, Digital Media & Marketing
Portfolio Companies: Beanworks, Careteam, ePACT Network, FoodMesh, MuseFind, myBestHelper

Key Executives:
Bonnie Foley-Wong, Founder
e-mail: bonnie@piqueventures.com
Education: BS, Mathematics, MS, Accounting, Univ. of Waterloo

2216 PLAZA VENTURES
10 Wanless Avenue
Suite 206
Toronto, ON M4N 1V6
Canada

Phone: 416-481-2222 Fax: 416-481-8000
web: plaza.ventures

Mission Statement: Plaza Ventures focuses on high-growth, seed-stage technology companies looking for value-added capital, and micro-cap public technology companies looking for a breakout strategy.

Average Investment: $500K to $1.5M
Investment Criteria: Seed-Stage
Industry Group Preference: Real Estate, Enterprise Software, Digital Media, Mobile Technology, Artificial Intelligence
Portfolio Companies: 411.ca, Busbud, CareGuide, CareWorx, Dejero, Drop, FanXchange, Findspace, Hubba, Iguazio, Key Living, LANDR, Miovision, MMB Networks, Mobify, PostBeyond, Q4, StackAdapt, SweetIQ

Key Executives:
Daniel Brothman, General Partner
e-mail: danielbrothman@plazacorp.com
Education: BA, York University; JD, Osgoode Hall Law School; MBA, Schulich School of Business
Background: Corporate M&A
Matthew Leibowitz, General Partner
e-mail: matthew@plaza.ventures
Education: HBA, Univ. of Toronto; MSc, Univ. of New South Wales; LLM, Oxford Univ.
Daniel Israelsohn, Vice President
e-mail: dan@plaza.ventures
Education: HBA, MBA, Richard Ivey School of Business

2217 PORTAG3 VENTURES
Toronto, ON
Canada

e-mail: info@p3vc.com
web: p3vc.com

Mission Statement: Invests in early stage financial tech companies with a potential for global impact.

Geographic Preference: Global
Fund Size: $400 Million
Founded: 2016
Investment Criteria: Early Stage, Financial Technology, Global
Industry Group Preference: Fintech, Artificial Intelligence, Data, Insurance, Wealth, Personal Finance, Banking
Portfolio Companies: Alan, Albert, Borrowell, Clark, ClearBanc, Collage, D1g1t, Dialogue, Drop, Flybits, Hellas Direct, Integrate.ai, Kin, Koho, League, LimelightHealth, Loot, Multiple, Neat, Planto, Quovo, Seed, Street Contxt, Stride Health, Wave, Wealthsimple

Key Executives:
Paul Desmarais III, Partner
Education: BA, Economics, Harvard College; MBA, INSEAD
Background: Risk Management Group, Great-West Lifeco; Imerys; Goldman Sachs
Adam Felesky, Partner
Education: BEng, Civil Engineering, BA, Political Science, McMaster University
Background: Horizons Exchange Traded Funds;

Venture Capital & Private Equity Firms / Canadian Firms

JPMorgan Canada; CIBC World Markets; JPMorgan Derivative's Group
Samuel Robinson, President
Education: MA, English, MPhil, Modern Middle Eastern Studies, Christ Church
Background: Goldman Sachs
Directorships: Sagard Capital
Stephan Klee, Chief Financial Officer
Education: BA, Wilfrid Laurier University; MBA, Richard Ivey School of Business; AMP, Harvard Business School
Background: SoFi Banking Division

2218 PRIVEQ CAPITAL FUNDS
1500 Don Mills Road
Toronto, ON M3B 3K4
Canada

Phone: 416-447-3330
web: www.priveq.ca

Mission Statement: Private equity portfolio manager invests in niche service, distribution and manufacturing companies within 5 hours travel of Toronto, Canada.

Geographic Preference: Toronto Area
Fund Size: $85 Million
Founded: 1994
Average Investment: $3 to $7 Million
Minimum Investment: $3 Million
Investment Criteria: Expansion, Acquisition, Buy-out
Industry Group Preference: Niche Manufacturing, Distribution, Business Products & Services
Portfolio Companies: Integracare, Kraus Global, Accipiter, Frantic Films

Key Executives:
Bradley W. Ashley, Managing Partner
Education: JD, Osgoode Hall Law School; MBA, Schulich School of Business
Background: Senior Manager, Ernst & Young Corporate Finance; Assitant Treasurer, JP Morgan
Lee M. Grunberg, Partner
Education: BA, Economics & Political Science, McGill University; MBA, Schulich School of Business
Background: Associate Director, Merchant Banking
Directorships: R Nicholls Distributors, Frantic Films Corporation

2219 PRIVITI CAPITAL
850, 444 5th Avenue SW
Calgary, AB T2P 2T8
Canada

Phone: 403-263-9943 Fax: 403-265-1134
Toll-Free: 855-333-9943
e-mail: info@priviticapital.com
web: www.priviticapital.com

Mission Statement: Private equity firm specializing in the Canadian energy market.

Geographic Preference: Canada
Fund Size: $360 Million
Founded: 2007
Industry Group Preference: Energy, Oil & Gas, Natural Gas

Key Executives:
Ward Mallabone, President & CEO
e-mail: wmallabone@priviticapital.com
Education: BComm, University of British Columbia; Law Degree, University of Calgary
Background: COO/VP Law, Enervest Management Ltd

2220 QUANTUM VALLEY INVESTMENTS
560 Westmount Road North
Waterloo, ON N2L 0A9
Canada

e-mail: contact@quantumvalleyinvestments.com
web: quantumvalleyinvestments.com

Mission Statement: Private fund focused on the commercialization of breakthroughs in Quantum Information Science.

Geographic Preference: Canada
Fund Size: $100 million
Founded: 2013
Investment Criteria: Early-Stage
Industry Group Preference: Communications, Information Technology

Key Executives:
Mike Lazaridis, Co-Founder & Managing Partner
Education: University of Waterloo
Background: Co-Chairman/Co-CEO, Research In Motion/BlackBerry
Doug Fregin, Co-Founder & Managing Partner
Education: Electrical Engineering, University of Windsor
Background: Co-Founder, Research in Motion/BlackBerry

2221 QUARK VENTURE
2500-1075 West Georgia Street
Vancouver, BC V6E 3C9
Canada

Phone: 604-262-8818
web: www.quarkventure.com

Mission Statement: Vancouver VC firm focused on biotechnology and health sciences companies.

Founded: 2015
Industry Group Preference: Biotechnology, Health Science
Portfolio Companies: ARTMS, Biscayne Neurotherapeutics, Canary Medical, CathWorks, Eloxx Pharmaceuticals, Eyevensys, Iome, Keros Therapeutics, Lyndra, Microbion Corporation, Phemi, PhysIQ, Pi Therapeutics, ReSolutionTx, Sitka Biopharma, SQZ Biotech, V-Wave

Other Locations:
17th Floor, Suite 199
Third Tianfu Street
High-Tech District
Chengdu 610000
China
Phone: 86-13666152158

Key Executives:
Jesson Chen, Chair & General Partner
Education: Sichuan University; Sichuan MBA College; Southwest University
Karimah Es Sabar, CEO & General Partner
Education: BSc, University of Salford; MSc, University of London; Cert., Sloan School of Management
Directorships: Triumf Innovations; Health & Biosciences Economic Strategy Table, Govt. of Canada
Franklin Jiang, COO & General Partner
Education: BSc, Shanghai Jiotong University; MSc, University of Regina; PhD, UBC
Directorships: Stealth Energy, Sun Oil
Zafrira Avnur, Chief Scientific Officer & General Partner
Background: Roche Partnering
Kaley Wilson, Director, Business Development
Education: PhD, University of British Columbia
Background: Centre for Drug Research and Development

Venture Capital & Private Equity Firms / Canadian Firms

2222 RADAR CAPITAL
150 King Street W
Suite 1720
PO Box 47
Toronto, ON M5H 1J9
Canada

Phone: 416-800-6733 Fax: 416-862-2498
e-mail: info@radarcapital.ca
web: www.radarcapital.ca

Geographic Preference: Canada
Investment Criteria: Pre-IPO
Portfolio Companies: Kognitiv, Metamaterial Technologies, Bonne O
Key Executives:
  Mark Lerohl, President
  Education: Univ. of Alberta; Ivey Business School
  Background: Canaccord Capital Corp.
  Directorships: Big Brother Big Sisters

2223 RBC CAPITAL MARKETS
Royal Bank Plaza
200 Bay Street
Toronto, ON M5J 2W7
Canada

Phone: 416-842-7575
web: www.rbccm.com

Mission Statement: RBC Capital Markets is an international corporate and investment bank, offering customized products and services to institutions, corporations, governments and high net worth clients around the world.
Geographic Preference: North America, the UK, Europe, Asia-Pacific
Average Investment: $10 - $20 million
Investment Criteria: Mezzanine financing to mid-market
Industry Group Preference: Life Sciences, Technology, Telecommunications, Manufacturing, Business Products & Services, Consumer Products, Information Technology, Restaurants, Retail, Consumer & Leisure, Oil & Gas, Artificial Intelligence
Key Executives:
  Derek Neldner, CEO & Group Head
  Education: BComm, Finance, University of Alberta; CFA
  Directorships: Hospital for Sick Children Foundation, United Way of Toronto & York Region

2224 REAL VENTURES
Notman House
51 Sherbrooke Street West
Montreal, QC H2X 1X2
Canada

web: realventures.com

Mission Statement: A seed stage Venture Fund investing in web, mobile and digital media.
Geographic Preference: Canada
Investment Criteria: Seed-Stage
Industry Group Preference: Internet, Digital Media & Marketing, Wireless Technologies, SaaS, Mobile
Portfolio Companies: Canvass, Mejuri, MindBridge, ROSS, Swift Medical
Other Locations:
  MaRS Centre
  101 College Street
  Suite 140
  Toronto, ON M5G 1L7
  Canada
Key Executives:
  JS Cournoyer, Board Partner
  Background: Co-Founder, Montreal Startup
  Alan MacIntosh, Board Partner
  Background: President, OSMO Foundation
  Directorships: McCord Museum, Quartier de l'Innovation, Mobile Giving Foundation Canada
  John Stokes, Managing Partner

2225 RECAPHEALTH VENTURES
Vancouver, BC
Canada

web: recaphealthventures.com

Mission Statement: RecapHealth Ventures supports opportunities that provide innovative solutions to the challenges facing health and social care systems around the world.
Geographic Preference: Canada, United States, Europe
Founded: 2011
Industry Group Preference: Healthcare
Portfolio Companies: AlayaCare, Change Heroes, CML Healthcare, CoPatient, Ethelo, HealthEJourney, Health Innovations Group, KLUE, Medeo, QHR Technologies, ThoughtWire, Tyze, Vision Critical, Yyoga
Key Executives:
  Richard Osborn, Managing Partner
  Education: University of British Columbia; Queen's University
  Background: Co-Founder & Partner, Greenstone Venture Partners; Business Development Bank of Canada; Multiactive; Founder, BC Social Venture Partners

2226 RED LEAF CAPITAL
441 - 100 Innovation Drive
Winnipeg, MB R3T 6G2
Canada

Phone: 204-451-5243
web: www.redleafcapital.ca

Mission Statement: Red Leaf Capital is the first CVCA member based in Manitoba. They are a hybrid venture capital and management consulting firm in Manitoba.
Founded: 2009
Key Executives:
  Stuart Henrickson, Founder
  Background: Managing Director, National Bank of Abu Dhabi; CEO, Standard Bank, Dubai
  Candy Dong, Investment Manager
  Education: MBA, University of Manitoba
  Background: AstraZenca

2227 REGIMEN PARTNERS
1285 West Pender Street
Suite 570
Vancouver, BC V6E 4B1
Canada

Phone: 778-379-1000
e-mail: info@regimenpartners.com
web: www.regimenpartners.com

Mission Statement: Private equity firm focused on buying and holding small businesses.
Portfolio Companies: Radial Engineering, CRS CraneSystems, Plastifab Industries, Central Technology Services, All Gold Imports
Other Locations:
  151 Yonge Street
  Suite 1100
  Toronto, ON M5C 2W7
  Canada

  10072 Jasper Avenue
  Suite 239
  Edmonton, AB T5J 1V8
  Canada
Key Executives:
  Cooper Seeman, Managing Director
  Education: Univ. of British Columbia
  Background: Abacus Private Equity; Highgate Holdings

Venture Capital & Private Equity Firms / Canadian Firms

Gerry Bellerive, Managing Director
Education: Simon Fraser University
Background: Capital West Partners
David Eisler, Managing Director
Education: Queen's Univ.; Univ. of British Columbia
Background: Stern Partners; Banyan Capital Partners

2228 RELAY VENTURES
446 Spedina Road
Suite 303
Toronto, ON M5P 3M2
Canada

e-mail: toronto@relayventures.com
web: relayventures.com

Mission Statement: Relay Ventures makes early-stage investments in mobile technology and services.

Fund Size: $800 million
Founded: 2008
Investment Criteria: Early Stage
Industry Group Preference: Mobile Technology, Mobile, SaaS, Digital Media & Marketing, Enterprise Software
Portfolio Companies: 7shifts, AdmitHub, Alate Partners, AngelList, Automat, Bird, Blue Ant Media, Blue J Legal, Circle, ecobee, FreshGrade, Good Buy Gear, Greenlight, Influitive, inPowered, Kira Talent, MobSquad, Mojio, Nymi, Payfone, Populus, PubNub, Quid, Rally Rd., Sherpa, Swift Medical, theScore, TouchBistro, Ujet

Other Locations:
150 - 9 Avenue SW
Suite 2100
Calgary, AB T2P 3H9
Canada

474 Bryant Street
San Francisco, CA 94107
USA
Phone: 650-627-7749

Key Executives:
Geoff Beattie, Chair
Education: JD, University of Western Ontario
Background: Torys LLP, Woodbridge Company, Thomson Reuters
Directorships: General Electric, Maple Leaf Foods, Acasta Enterprises
John Albright, Co-Founder & Managing Partner
Education: BBA, Schulich School of Business
Directorships: OCAD University, Centre for Aging and Brain Health Innovation
Alex Baker, Managing Partner
e-mail: alex@relayventures.com
Education: Schulich School of Business
Background: Management Consultant, BearingPoint; PWC Consulting
Directorships: Influitive, ClearFit, TribeHR, Payfone, Wiewdle, Neuralitic
Kevin Talbot, Co-Founder & Managing Partner
e-mail: kevin@relayventures.com
Education: BA, Strategic Studies, Rotman School of Management, University of Toronto; MBA, York University
Background: Royal Bank of Canada
Directorships: Kiip, Xobni, Payfone, WorldMate, Appia
Jeannette Wiltse, Partner & CFO
e-mail: jeannette@relayventures.com
Background: Director of Finance & Administration, RBC Venture Partners; Secretary-Treasurer, Euro Brokers Canada
Jake Cassaday, Venture Partner
e-mail: jake@relayventures.com
Education: BA, McGill University; MBA, Rotman School of Management, University of Toronto
Background: Rotman Entrepreneurship & Venture Capital Association; Spin Master

2229 RELENTLESS PURSUIT PARTNERS
Canada

web: www.relentlesspursuitpartners.com

Investment Criteria: Early-Stage
Industry Group Preference: Health Technology
Portfolio Companies: Canary Medical

Key Executives:
Brenda Irwin, Managing Partner

2230 RENEWAL FUNDS
The Flack Block
500-163 West Hastings Street
Vancouver, BC V6B 1H5
Canada

Phone: 604-424-9930
e-mail: hello@renewalfunds.com
web: www.renewalfunds.com

Mission Statement: Mission venture capital firm investing in companies producing social and environmental change.

Geographic Preference: Canada, USA
Investment Criteria: Early Stage
Portfolio Companies: Back to the Roots, Cascadia Windows & Doors, Farmhouse Culture, FoodLogiQ, Goddess Garden, Ian's Natural Foods, Lotek, Mama Earth Organics, Miovision, Opti, Opus One Solutions, Prana, Rustic Crust, Sensible Organics, SPUD, Swiftly, Terramera

Key Executives:
Carol Newell, Co-Founder
Education: St. Lawrence University
Paul Richardson, Managing & Founding Partner
Education: Queen's University; University of Toronto
Background: Fasken Martineau, Strathy & Richardson, Renewal Partners
Directorships: Mama Earth Organics
Joel Solomon, Founding Partner
Background: Renewal Partners, Endswell Foundation
Directorships: RSF Social Finance, Social Venture Network, Business for Social Responsibility, Tides Canada Foundation, Hollyhock

2231 RHO CANADA VENTURES
Montreal, QC
Canada

web: www.rhocanada.com

Mission Statement: A division of Rho Capital Partners investing in Canadian technology companies.

Geographic Preference: Canada
Fund Size: $100 Million
Founded: 2006
Investment Criteria: Early Stage
Industry Group Preference: New Media, Mobile Apps, Wireless Infrastructure, Semiconductors & Materials, Software (incl. SaaS)
Portfolio Companies: Acalvio, Aislelabs, Auvik, BounceX, Confirm.io, Exact Media, Fevo, Figure 1, Frank & Oak, Highline, Hyalto, Karma Gaming, LiveBarn, Plotly, Resson Aerospace, Smart Skin, Sociable Labs, SportlogiQ

Key Executives:
Sean Brownlee, Partner
Education: BA, MBA, Carleton Univ.
Background: JMH Capital, 3i Corporation
Roger Chabra, Partner
Education: BA, Univ. of Western Ontario; MBA, Richard Ivey School of Business
Background: GrowthWorks Capital
Jeff Grammer, Partner
Education: BA, MA, Boston Univ.
Background: Intel, Chips and Technologies, N*Able Technologies, Ember Corp.

Venture Capital & Private Equity Firms / Canadian Firms

Habib Kairouz, Managing Partner
Education: BA, BS, Cornell Univ.; MBA, Columbia Univ.
Background: Reich & Co., Jesup & Lamont
Peter Kalkanis, Chief Financial Officer
Education: BS, City Univ. of New York
Background: Eisner LLP

2232 RIPPLE VENTURES
410 Adelaide Street West
Toronto, ON M5V 1S8
Canada

web: www.rippleventures.ca

Mission Statement: Early-stage venture fund focused on "frontier technologies" in North America.

Geographic Preference: Toronto, Waterloo, Montreal, Boston
Average Investment: $250-500K
Minimum Investment: $250K
Investment Criteria: Early-Stage
Industry Group Preference: Enterprise Software, Healthcare Technology, Industrial Technology, Enterprise Blockchain, Media Technology
Portfolio Companies: OnúCall, Tread, voiceflow, Pitstop, omelas, Cybeats

Key Executives:
Matt Cohen, Managing Partner
Background: Turnstyle Solutions
Michael Garbe, General Partner
Background: Accelerated Connections

2233 RIV CAPITAL
40 King Street W
Suite 2504
Toronto, ON M5H 3Y2

Phone: 416-583-5945
Toll-Free: 855-227-8639
e-mail: info@rivcapital.com
web: www.rivcapital.com

Mission Statement: Venture capital firm specializing in cannabis. Formerly named Canopy Rivers.

Geographic Preference: Global
Founded: 2017
Investment Criteria: Market Size, Market Need, Traction, Return on Investment, Leadership Team
Industry Group Preference: Cannabis
Portfolio Companies: Agripharm, BioLumic, Canapar, Civilized, Greenhouse Juice, Headset, Herbert, High Beauty, James E. Wagner Cultivation Corporation, LeafLink International, PharmHouse, Radicle, TerrAscend, Tweed Tree Lot, Vert Mirabel, YSS, ZeaKal

Key Executives:
Mark Sims, President & CEO
Education: Wharton School, University of Pennsylvania; MSc, Cleveland State University; BEng, University of Michigan
Background: SVP of Strategy and M&A, The Scotts Miracle-Gro Company
Eddie Lucarelli, Chief Financial Officer
Education: BComm, Smith School of Business, Queen's University; CPA
Background: VP, M&A Group, TD Securities; Senior Manager, Deloitte LLP
Matthew Mundy, Chief Strategy Officer & General Counsel
Education: BA, University of Southern California; JD, University of Toronto
Background: Associate, Blake Cassels & Graydon

2234 ROADMAP CAPITAL INC.
130 Bloor Street W
Suite 603
Toronto, ON M5S 1N5
Canada

Phone: 647-748-0052
e-mail: info@roadmapcapitalinc.com
web: roadmapcapitalinc.com

Mission Statement: Roadmap Capital pursues high growth investment opportunities and seeks to create partnerships with outstanding companies.

Geographic Preference: Canada, United States
Founded: 2013
Industry Group Preference: Technology, Information Technology, Clean Technology, Healthcare, Life Sciences
Portfolio Companies: Corsa Technology, LiquiGlide, MMB Networks, Peraso Technologies, Perimeter Medical Imaging

Key Executives:
Riadh Zine, Co-Founder & Principal
Education: MSc, Financial Engineering, Ecole des Hautes Etudes Commerciales, University of Montreal
Background: Managing Director, Global Investment Banking, RBC Capital Markets; Royal Bank of Canada
Hugh Cleland, Co-Founder & Principal
Education: BA, Harvard University; CFA
Background: Research Associate, Midland Walwyn Capital; Analyst & Associate Portfolio Manager, Interward Capital Corporation; Portfolio Manager, Northern Rivers Capital Management
Imed Zine, Principal
Education: MSc, PhD, Electrical & Computer Engineering, University of Calgary
Background: Senior Engineer & Technology Advisor, CMC Microsystems; Research Associate, TRTech

2235 ROUND 13 CAPITAL
100 Broadview Avenue
Suite 300
Toronto, ON M4M 3H3
Canada

e-mail: info@round13capital.com
web: www.round13capital.com

Mission Statement: VC firm invests in growth-stage Canadian companies.

Geographic Preference: Canada
Investment Criteria: Growth Stage
Portfolio Companies: Affinio, Aislelabs, Article, Bluerush, Bold, HiMama, Hubdoc, Kooltra, Limelight, RouteThis, Sourced, Statflo, ThoughtWire, TouchBistro

Key Executives:
Bruce Croxon, Managing Partner
Background: Lavalife
John Eckert, Managing Partner
Background: McLean Watson Capital
Craig Strong, General Partner
Education: MBA, Rotman School of Management
Background: Fitzii, Deloitte, Ethos

2236 RUSSELL SQUARE PARTNERS
2 St. Clair Avenue W
Suite 1004
Toronto, ON M4V 1L5
Canada

e-mail: dbaum@russellsquarepartners.com
web: www.russellsquarepartners.com

Mission Statement: Russell Square Partners invest in Canadian businesses with growth opportunities.

Geographic Preference: Canada
Investment Criteria: Buyout, Recapitalizations, Transitions, Succession Plans
Industry Group Preference: Technology, Coding, Consumer

Venture Capital & Private Equity Firms / Canadian Firms

Portfolio Companies: Bitmaker, Pluck Tea
Key Executives:
  Dan Baum, Managing Partner
  Education: BA, McGill University; MBA, Harvard Business School
  Background: Birch Hill Equity Partners; McKinsey & Co.
  Directorships: Sleep Country Canada
  Andy Burgess, Managing Partner
  Education: BA, Princeton University; MBA, INSEAD
  Background: CEO/Co-Founder, Somerset Entertainment; McKinsey & Co.; Loblaws
  Directorships: Upper Canada College, Repath Industries, Alasko Foods, Hamburg Honda

2237 SAF GROUP
1900 Dome Tower
333 7th Ave SW
Calgary, AB T2P 2Z1
Canada

Phone: 403-984-1941
e-mail: info@safgroup.ca
web: safgroup.ca

Mission Statement: The SAF Group is a private equity firm that provides financing to companies in the energy, metals & mining, and commodities & marketing industries.
Geographic Preference: Canada
Fund Size: $2 billion
Founded: 2014
Industry Group Preference: Energy, Metals & Mining, Commodities, Marketing
Other Locations:
  450 Commerce Place
  400 Burrard Street
  Vancouver, BC V6C 3A6
  Canada
Key Executives:
  Ryan Dunfield, CEO & Managing Principal
  Education: BA, Economics, University of Calgary
  Background: Principal, Second City Capital Partners; Gibralt Capital Corp.
  Aaron Bunting, Principal, COO & CFO
  Education: BComm, Haskayne School of Business, University of Calgary; CFA; CA
  Background: VP, K2 & Associates Investment Management; Director, Funds Management, Canoe Financial; VP, Mustang Capital Partners; Analyst, KPMG Advisory
  Ryan Haughn, Managing Director
  Education: MBA, Carleton University; CFA
  Kyle Hickey, Managing Director
  Education: BComm, McGill University; MA, University of Oxford
  Background: BMO; JPMorgan

2238 SANDPIPER VENTURES
Canada

e-mail: hello@sandpiper.vc
web: sandpiper.vc

Mission Statement: Sandpiper Ventures is focused on investing in initiatives developed and led by women.
Founded: 2020
Investment Criteria: Women-Led or Founded
Key Executives:
  Cathy Bennett, Founding and Managing Partner
  Background: CEO, Bennett Group; CEO, TaskForce NL
  Rhiannon Davies, Founding and Managing Partner
  Background: GrandVision NV
  Sarah Young, Founding and Managing Partner
  Background: Managing Partner, NATIONAL Public Relations; Avenir Global

2239 SARONA ASSET MANAGEMENT
137 Glasgow Street
Suite 210, Unit 148
Kitchener, ON N2G 4X8
Canada

Phone: 519-883-7557
e-mail: sarona@saronafund.com
web: www.saronafund.com

Mission Statement: The company invests in businesses and markets that allow for profitable growth and sustainable development.
Geographic Preference: Africa, Asia, Latin America, Emerging Europe
Fund Size: 500 million
Founded: 2010
Investment Criteria: Growth Stage, Mid Market,
Industry Group Preference: Healthcare, Financial Services, Consumer Goods & Services, Light Manufacturing, Transportation, Logistics, Communication Technology, Energy, Education
Other Locations:
  46 Claude Debussylaan
  Amsterdam, MD 1082
  The Netherlands
  Phone: 31.207981311

  80 State Street
  Albany, NY 12207
  Phone: 519-883-7557
Key Executives:
  Gerhard Pries, Founder & Executive Chair
  Education: CPA
  Background: MEDA; PricewaterhouseCoopers
  Directorships: Grand Challenges Canada, ImpactAssets
  Paulus J Ingram, Co-Managing Partner
  Education: BA, Amherst College; MSc, International Finance, University of Amsterdam; LLM, Vrije University; LLM, Univerity of Amsterdam; CFA
  Background: APG Asset Management; Opportunity Fund; Capricorn Investment Group; Skoll Foundation
  Menno Derks, Managing Director, Private Equity
  Education: MA, Business Engineering, University of Twente; CFA
  Background: Senior Investment Manager, Investment Committeee Member, PGGM; FMO; ABN AMRO Asset Management
  Serge LeVert-Chiasson, Co-Managing Partner
  Education: MSc, Accounting and Finance, London School of Economics; MBA, Schulich School of Business; CFA
  Background: Export Development Canada; Crédit Lyonnais; Founding Chair, Argo Captial Management
  Deborah de Rooij, Managing Director, Private Debt
  Education: BA, Economics, Amsterdam Schoool of Economics; RBA
  Background: Head of Emerging Market Debt, Head of Global Manager Selection, APG Asset Management; Senior Portfolio Manager, Achmea Gloal Investors

2240 SCALEUP VENTURES
114-250 The Esplanade
Toronto, ON M5A 1J2
Canada

web: suv.vc

Geographic Preference: Canada
Fund Size: $106 million
Founded: 2016
Investment Criteria: Early-Stage
Industry Group Preference: Technology
Portfolio Companies: autograph, Coconut Calendar, dooly, Flextive, FundThrough, fusebill, mavencare, naborly, plooto, Revlo, roserocket, SoLink, Sonder, SortSpoke, Splash, Wysdom AI

Venture Capital & Private Equity Firms / Canadian Firms

Other Locations:
3450 W 27th Ave
Vancouver, BC V6S 1P6
Canada

Kevin Kimsa, Managing Partner
Education: Univ. of Waterloo
Background: Omers Ventures

2241 SCOTIABANK PRIVATE EQUITY
Scotia Plaza
40 King Street West
Toronto, ON M5H 3Y2
Canada

Phone: 416-866-6506

Mission Statement: Private investment arm of Scotiabank.

Geographic Preference: Global
Average Investment: $5 to $25 million
Minimum Investment: $5 million
Investment Criteria: Mid- to Late-Stage
Industry Group Preference: Manufacturing, Industrial Goods, Finance, Consumer Products & Services, Technology, Building Materials & Resources

2242 SEAFORT CAPITAL
CIBC Building
1201 - 1809 Barrington Street
Halifax, NS B3J 3K8
Canada

e-mail: info@seafortcapital.com
web: seafortcapital.com

Mission Statement: Halifax-based investment firm with a diverse portfolio.

Geographic Preference: Canada
Founded: 2012
Industry Group Preference: Manufacturing, Distribution, Infrastructure
Portfolio Companies: AW Leil, Cooper Equipment Rentals, Jardine Transport, Mecfor, Titanium Energy Services

Key Executives:
Rob Normandeau, President & Managing Partner
Education: BA, University of Western Ontario; MBA, University of Toronto
Background: President & CEO, Clarke Inc.
Directorships: IWK Children's Hospital Foundation, Canadian Venture Capital & Private Equity Association, Rocky Mountain Liquor
Matthew Towns, Partner
Education: BBA, Wilfrid Laurier University; MBA, St. Mary's University
Background: RBC Capital Markets; Imperial Oil Limited
Stephen Denton, Partner
Education: BBA, MBA, Dalhousie University; CFA
Background: Manager, Commercial Banking, CIBC; Director, Research, Clarke Inc.
Directorships: Phoenix Youth Programs

2243 SEARCHLIGHT
22 Adelaide Street West
35th Floor
Toronto, ON M5H 4E3
Canada

Phone: 416-687-6590
web: www.searchlightcap.com

Geographic Preference: North America; Europe
Investment Criteria: Leveraged buyouts, growth equity, recapitalizations
Portfolio Companies: Ardent Hire Solutions, Cengage Learning, EOLO, Global Eagle, Gymboree, Hemisphere Media Group, Hunter Boot, Liberty Latin America, M&M Food Market, Mitel, Octave Group, PatientPoint, RackSpace, Roots, Shift4 Payments, Uniti

Other Locations:
745 Fifth Avenue
27th Floor
New York, NY 10151
Phone: 212-293-3730

56 Conduit Street
4th Floor
London W1S 2YZ
United Kingdom
Phone: 44 (0)20 7290 7910

Key Executives:
Oliver Haarmaan, Founding Partner
Education: Brown Univ.; Harvard Business School
Background: KKR & Co.
Directorships: Hunter Boot, EOLO
Erol Uzumeri, Founding Partner
Education: Univ. of Toronto; London Business School
Background: Ontario Teachers' Pension Plan
Directorships: M&M Food Market, Roots
Eric Zinterhofer, Founding Partner
Education: Univ. of Pennsylvania; Harvard Business School
Background: Apollo Management
Directorships: Charter Communications

2244 SECOND CITY REAL ESTATE
666 Burrard Street
Suite 3210
Vancouver, BC V6C 2X8
Canada

Phone: 604-806-3350 Fax: 604-661-4873
e-mail: info@secondcityrealestate.com
web: www.secondcityrealestate.com

Mission Statement: Private equity partnership focused on mid-market commercial real estate transactions.

Geographic Preference: North America
Founded: 2011
Industry Group Preference: Commercial Real Estate

Key Executives:
James Farrar, Managing Director
Education: CPA; CFA
Greg Tylee, Managing Director
Education: CA
Background: President, Bosa Properties
Ryan Chan, Chief Financial Officer
Education: BS, State University of New York; CGA
Background: Real Estate Investment Manager, Gibralt; Anthem Properties & Parklane Homes

2245 SERRUYA PRIVATE EQUITY
210 Shields Court
Markham, ON L3R 8V2

web: www.serruyaprivateequity.com

Mission Statement: Invests in various including retail, food & beverage, and cannabis. Commonly known as SPE.

Founded: 2010
Investment Criteria: $5M-$1B revenue
Industry Group Preference: Retail, Food & Beverage, Cannabis
Portfolio Companies: Global Franchise Group, Yogen Fruz, Pinkberry, Swensen's, Yogurty's, Second Cup Coffee Co., STK, The Dirty Bird, Hydrofarm, Things Engraved, The Canadian National Institute of Health Inc., Persian Acceptance Corp., Chip and Pepper, Promenade, The Templar Hotel, Blue Mountain Village, Édifice Aldred, Jamba Juice, Famoso, Milestones, CoolBrands International, Kahala Brands, Fairweather, Tivoli Audio, Freedom Mobile, Sani-Service, The King Edward, The Town of Wasaga Beach, Laredo Hospitality, Aleafia, Verano Holdings, F/ELD, PROHBTED, Isodiol International, PLUS, Aphria

Venture Capital & Private Equity Firms / Canadian Firms

Key Executives:
  Michael Serruya, Managing Director
  Education: Ryerson University
  Background: Chairman/CEO, Kahala Brands
  Aaron Serruya, Managing Director
  Education: Western University
  Background: CEO, SU&BU
  Simon Serruya, Managing Director
  Directorships: Yogurty's Froyo; Swensen's Ice Cream; Yogen Fruz
  Gurion De Zwirek, Managing Director
  Education: BA, Business Admin./Political Science, University of Haifa; MA, International Relations/Business, University of Toronto
  Background: Former Naval Officer; Interim CEO, Things Engraved Inc.
  Directorships: Tivoli Audio
  Patrick Chung, VP, Finance
  Education: BAFM, Accounting/Financial Management; MAcc, University of Waterloo
  Background: Associate, Fuller Landau; Experienced Associate, PwC Canada; Assistant Manager of Finance Advisory, Deloitte; Director of Finance, Inside Edge Properties

2246 SIGNAL HILL EQUITY PARTNERS
2 Carlton Street
Suite 1700
Toronto, ON M5B 1J3
Canada

Phone: 416-847-1168
e-mail: admin@signalhillequity.com
web: www.signalhillequity.com

Mission Statement: Private equity firm focused on Canadian mid-market companies.

Geographic Preference: Canada
Fund Size: $300 million
Average Investment: $5 to $20 million
Minimum Investment: $5 million
Investment Criteria: Management Transitions, Restructurings, Acquisitions, Growth Equity
Industry Group Preference: Business & Consumer Services, Specialty Manufacturing, Building Products, Food & Consumer Products, Resource Services
Portfolio Companies: City Wide Towing, McIntosh Perry, C&V Portable, Romet, Westridge Cabinets, Shnier, Orbit Garant

Key Executives:
  Patrick W.A. Handreke, Chair
  Education: BA, Commerce & Economics, University of Toronto
  Background: President & CEO, Northam Realty Advisors Limited
  James C. Johnson, Co-Founder & CEO
  e-mail: jjohnson@signalhillequity.com
  Education: BComm, MBA, LLB, University of Windsor
  Background: Senior Executive, Newcourt Credit Group; Co-Founder, Ironbridge Equity Partners
  Directorships: Westridge Cabinets, Construction Control, Gesco Industries
  Fred Creasey, Chief Financial Officer
  416-847-1501

2247 SKYPOINT CAPITAL
1371 E Woodroffe Avenue
Nepean, ON K2G 1V7
Canada

Phone: 613-727-5073 Fax: 613-727-8768
e-mail: info@skypointcorp.com
web: www.skypointcorp.com

Mission Statement: Early-stage investor in telecommunications and information technology.
Geographic Preference: Canada
Investment Criteria: Early Stage
Industry Group Preference: Telecommunications, Wireless Technologies

2248 STANDUP VENTURES
101 College Street
MaRS Discovery District, Suite 125
Toronto, ON M5G 1L7
Canada

e-mail: info@standupvc.com
web: standupvc.com

Mission Statement: StandUp Ventures champions breakthrough companies led by women.

Investment Criteria: At least 1 woman in a C-Level Leadership position and an equitable amount of ownership; enterprise software and digital health; seed stage

Key Executives:
  Michelle McBane, Managing Director
  Education: University of Ottawa; MBA, McMaster University
  Background: Principal, Michelle McBane Consulting; Sr. Investment Director, MaRS Investment Accelerator Fund

2249 STERN PARTNERS
650 W Georgia Street
Suite 2900
Vancouver, BC V6B 4N8
Canada

Phone: 604-681-8817 Fax: 604-681-8861
e-mail: inquiries@sternpartners.com
web: www.sternpartners.com

Mission Statement: Stern Partners invest in companies from North America that have the potential for growth.

Geographic Preference: North America
Investment Criteria: Long-Term, Growth
Industry Group Preference: Manufacturing, Publishing & Printing, Distribution, Retail, Services
Portfolio Companies: Alberta Newsprint Company, Auld Phillips, Bootlegger Clothing, cleo fashions, Comark Services, Derksen Printers, FP Newspapers, Greenstar Plant Products, McMynn Leasing, McRae's Environmental Services, National Energy Equipment, OUTtv Network, Parian Capital Corporation, Parian Logistics, Port Hawkesbury Paper, Ricki's Fashions, Silver Jeans Co., TerraLink Horticulture, The Portables Exhibit Systems, Thinkingbox, Urban Barn, Warehouse One Clothing, Weskey Graphics, Western Glove Works

Key Executives:
  Ronald N Stern, President
  Background: Corporate and Commercial Law
  Directorships: Vancouver Airport Authority, Vancouver East Cultural Centre, Vancouver General Hospital, Canadian Council For Israel and Jewish Advocacy
  Norm Drewlo, Vice President
  Background: Controller, Gas Equipment Supplies; President, National Energy Equipment
  Shamsh Kassam, SVP/Chief Financial Officer
  Education: BComm, University of British Columbia; CA
  Background: Vice President/CFO, Western International Communications; CanWest Global Communications
  Caroline Sanche, Vice President
  Education: BBA, Marketing and Finance, Simon Fraser University; CA; CPA
  Background: Associate Partner, KPMG; Interim CFO, Vancouver Board of Trade; Vice President, Finance, Rick Hansen Foundation
  Peter Roberts, Vice President, Technology
  Background: Methanex; SK Group; Senior Consultant, Spectra Energy; SAP Managing Consultant, ISM;

Venture Capital & Private Equity Firms / Canadian Firms

Managing Director, SAP Services, TELUS; Director of Consulting, Sierra Systems

2250 SUMMERHILL VENTURE PARTNERS
1 St. Clair Avenue W
Suite 403
Toronto, ON M4V 1K6
Canada

Phone: 416-408-0700

Mission Statement: Early-stage investor focused on the wireless, digital media and information technology sectors.

Geographic Preference: North America
Fund Size: $175 million
Founded: 1993
Investment Criteria: Early-Stage
Industry Group Preference: Mobility, Digital Media & Marketing, Enterprise Applications, Cloud Computing, Social Media
Portfolio Companies: Vantrix, BLiNQ, ScribbleLive, Sonian, C2FO

Key Executives:
  Gary Rubinoff, Managing Partner
  e-mail: grubinoff@summerhillvp.com
  Education: LLP, University of Western Ontario School of Law; MBA, Richard Ivey School of Business
  Background: Partner, JL Albright Venture Partners; Jefferson Partners LP

2251 TACTICO
486 Saint-Catherine Street W
Suite 409
Montreal, QC H3B 1A6
Canada

e-mail: info@tactico.com
web: www.tactico.com

Mission Statement: Tactico is a hands-on venture capital firm focusing on start-ups and post-seed through Series A stage deals in technology-focused verticals, including FinTech and SaaS.

Geographic Preference: Canada, United States
Founded: 2008
Average Investment: $1 - 3 million
Minimum Investment: $10,000
Investment Criteria: Startups, Seed, Series A
Industry Group Preference: Fintech, Financial Services, Technology, SaaS Businesses, MarTech, Real Estate Tech
Portfolio Companies: Auticon, IRYStec, Moka, Pointus Partners, Soundskrit, Sportlogiq, StoneLock, Willful

Key Executives:
  Rick Ness, Managing Partner
  Education: BA, Economics, McGill University
  Background: Director, Link Energy Supply; Director, Sportlogiq; CEO/Director, Fidelit Clearing Canada ULC; President, Embanet; President/CEO, Penson Financial Services
  Liam Cheung, Managing Partner
  Education: BMath, MSc, Management, PhD, Economics, McGill University
  Background: Exec. Chairman, Mylo; CEO/COO/PM, Tactex; Managing Partner/Founder, Pointus Partners; COO, Embanet; SVP of Strategic Development; COO, Penson; President/Founder, LOC Info; EVP of Fixed Income Trading, Marleau Lemire Securities; Actuarial Specialist/Expert System Tech Developer, Towers Perrin
  Philippe Leroux, Partner/Legal Counsel
  Education: BSc/LLB, University of Montreal; MBA, HEC Montreal
  Background: VP/Associate General Counsel, Penson Financial Services Canada

2252 TANDEM EXPANSION FUND
460 McGill St
Suite 500
Montreal, QC H2Y 2H2
Canada

Phone: 514-510-8900
e-mail: info@tandemexpansion.com
web: www.tandemexpansion.com

Mission Statement: A growth equity investor in Canadian technology companies.

Geographic Preference: Canada
Fund Size: $300 million
Founded: 2009
Average Investment: $10 - $30 million
Minimum Investment: $10 million
Investment Criteria: Later-Stage
Industry Group Preference: Information Technology, Clean Technology, Energy Technology, Advanced Materials, Life Sciences
Portfolio Companies: Anaergia, Averna, Blueprint Software Systems, Coveo Solutions, Densify, Solace, Vertex Downhole

Key Executives:
  André Gauthier, Managing Partner
  514-510-8909
  Education: BBA, HEC Montreal; CA
  Background: EVP/CFO, Telesystem International Wireless
  Brent Belzberg, Co-Founder
  Education: BComm, Queen's University; JD, University of Toronto
  Background: Founder & Senior Managing Partner, TorQuest Partners
  Charles Sirois, Co-Founder
  Education: BS, Finance, University of Sherbrooke; MS, Finance, Laval University
  Background: Founder, Chairman & CEO, Telesystem; Chairman, Enablis Foundation Canada
  Directorships: Zone3 Inc., Propulsion Ventures Inc., ID Capital Management Inc., Argo Global Capital Inc., Rogers Communications

2253 TECH CAPITAL PARTNERS
8 Erb Street West
Waterloo, ON N2L 1S7
Canada

Phone: 519-883-8255 **Fax:** 519-883-1265
web: techcapital.com

Mission Statement: Venture capital firm focused on technology.

Geographic Preference: Waterloo Region
Fund Size: $95 Million
Founded: 2001
Average Investment: $500K - $2MM
Minimum Investment: $500,000
Investment Criteria: Seed, Early-Stage
Industry Group Preference: Communications, Electronic Technology, Information Technology, Photonics, Semiconductors, Telecommunications, Video Industry, Wireless Technologies, Infrastructure, Technology
Portfolio Companies: Avvasi, Bering Media, Ecobee, Fongo, Overlay.tv, Sidense

Key Executives:
  Andrew Abouchar, Co-Founder & Partner
  519-883-8416
  e-mail: abouchar@techcapital.com
  Education: Bachelor of Applied Science, BA, University of Waterloo; CFA, CA
  Background: Working Ventures Canadian Fund; Founder, Waterloo Ventures
  Directorships: Avvasi, Coverity, Sidense
  Tim Jackson, Co-Founder & Partner
  519-883-0959

Venture Capital & Private Equity Firms / Canadian Firms

Education: BA, University of Waterloo; CA
Background: CEO, Accelerator Center; Associate Vice President Commercialization, University of Waterloo; CEO/CFO, PixStream
Directorships: Bering Media, Ecobee, FibreTech Telecommunications, LiveHive Systems, Metranome, PostRank, Q9 Networks, Sandvine, VideoLocus

2254 TECHNOCAP
4028 Marlowe
Montreal, NS H4A 3M2
Canada

Phone: 514-483-6000
e-mail: cpedroso@technocap.com
web: www.technocap.com

Mission Statement: Venture capital firm has been investing in small businesses since 1993.
Geographic Preference: Quebec, Ontario, Western Canada
Fund Size: $250 million
Founded: 1993
Average Investment: $6.5 Million
Minimum Investment: $3 Million
Investment Criteria: Startup, Expansion Stages, Proven Management, Management Style, 100% Dedication
Industry Group Preference: Technology, Telecommunications, Computer Related, Software, Electronic Technology, Instrumentation, Energy, Environmental Protection, Health Related
Portfolio Companies: Kinaxis, FreeBalance, BiblioMondo, DreamWater, SpaceWatts, Hyperchip, Yotta Yotta, GlobalMedic, telweb

Key Executives:
Richard Prytula, Chair & Founder
Education: BSc, Electrical Engineering, University of Saskatchewan; MBA, University of Western Ontario
Background: Owner, LNS Group

2255 TELESYSTEM
460 McGill Street
5th Floor
Montreal, QC H2Y 2H2
Canada

Phone: 514-397-9797 Fax: 514-397-1569
e-mail: info@telesystem.ca
web: telesystem.ca

Mission Statement: Family-owned media and technology investor since 1972.
Geographic Preference: Worldwide
Founded: 1972
Industry Group Preference: Healthcare, Environment Products & Services, Media, Entertainment, Internet, Software, Industrial Services, Digital Media & Marketing
Portfolio Companies: CVTCORP, CiPerceptions, Coveo, OnMobile, Prevtec Microbia, Stingray, Zone3

Key Executives:
Francois-Charles Sirois, President & CEO
Background: Founder & President, Up2 Technologies, Microcell i5, Masq Inc.
Directorships: Stingray Digital, Plexo, iPerceptions, Zone3
Charles Sirois, Chair & Founder
Background: BCE Mobile Communications; Teleglobe; Telesystem International Wireless; Microcell Communications
Directorships: Rogers Communications; Fondation de l'entrepreneurship
Denis M. Sirois, Vice President, Investments
Background: President, BCCL; Exaclan
Directorships: Exaclan, Plexo, iPerceptions, Opsens

2256 TELUS VENTURES
Telus Garden
510 W. Georgia Street
Vancouver, BC V6B 0M3
Canada

Fax: 604-438-0325
web: ventures.telus.com

Mission Statement: Investment arm of TELUS invests in innovative network technologies.
Geographic Preference: Canada, United States
Founded: 2001
Average Investment: $1 to $3 million
Minimum Investment: $1 Million
Investment Criteria: Early- to Late-Stage, Post-Beta Development
Industry Group Preference: Data Services, Internet Technology, Wireless Technologies, Telecommunications, Digital Media & Marketing, Networking
Portfolio Companies: Alithya, Beacon, DOmedic, Enstream, Fathom, Fortius Sport & Health, Get Real Health, League, MDS, Mojio, PatientSafe, Right Health, SecureKey Technologies, Sprout, Taulia, Vigilent, Vox Mobile
Richard Osborn, Managing Partner
Education: UBC; Queen's University
Background: RecapHealth Ventures
Directorships: Continuum, Fortius, Mojio, Right Health, ScaleUp Ventures, Vision Critical

2257 TENX VENTURES
4623 West 8th Avenue
Vancouver, BC V6R 2A6

e-mail: peter@tenx.biz
web: www.tenx.biz

Mission Statement: Invests in various Canadian industries.
Investment Criteria: Early-Stage
Industry Group Preference: Software, Robotics, Fintech, Cannabis
Portfolio Companies: Allocadia, QxMD, InvestX, Tagga, Immersive Media, Jones Rail Industries, Light Integra Technology, Lyft, Digital Domain, Campaign Monitor, CareCru, InsureCert Systems, CANBank, Chain Bureau, First National Digital Currency, Poseidon, Alphablock

Key Executives:
Mahala McCullagh, Managing Partner

2258 TERA CAPITAL CORPORATION
2678 St. Johns Siderd
Stouffville, ON L4A 2T4
Canada

Phone: 416-368-8372 Fax: 416-368-1427
Toll-Free: 1-888-368-8372
e-mail: info@teracap.com
web: www.teracap.com

Mission Statement: The company focuses on small capital equities room for growth in natural resources, clean energy, biotechnology and financial services.
Founded: 1996
Investment Criteria: Early Stage, Growth Markets, Mid Stage, Later Stage
Industry Group Preference: Natural Resources, Industrials, Clean Energy, Biotechnology, Financial Services
Portfolio Companies: Astound Inc., Electrophotonics, embotics, MKS, Opentext Corporation, Sierra Wireless, Truearc, VIQ Solutions, Vivecrop

Key Executives:
Howard Sutton, President
Education: PEng; MBA; CFA
Background: Partner, Goodman and Company
Directorships: Tera Capital, PESA

Venture Capital & Private Equity Firms / Canadian Firms

2259 TERALYS CAPITAL
999 Boulevard de Maisonneuve Ouest
Suite 1700
Montreal, QC H3A 3L4
Canada

Phone: 514-509-2080
e-mail: info@teralyscapital.com
web: www.teralyscapital.com

Mission Statement: Teralys Capital finances venture capital funds investing in information technology, life sciences and industrial innovations.

Geographic Preference: Canada
Fund Size: $2 Billion
Founded: 2009
Investment Criteria: Early-Stage, Growth & Expansion Stage
Industry Group Preference: Life Sciences, Clean Technology, Information Technology

Key Executives:
Jacques Bernier, Managing Partner
e-mail: jbernier@teralyscapital.com
Background: Senior Vice President, Solidarity Fund QFL
Eric Legault, Managing Partner
e-mail: elegault@teralyscapital.com
Background: Venture Capital Program, Caisse de depot et placements du Quebec
Luc Couture, Partner
e-mail: lcouture@teralyscapital.com
Background: Senior Investment Advisor, Solidarity Fund QFL
Cédric Bisson, Partner
Education: MD, McGill University; JD, University of Montreal
Background: McKinsey & Company
Directorships: ProCure, Montreal InVivo, Montreal Biennale of Art

2260 THE WESTERN INVESTMENT COMPANY OF CANADA
1010 24 Street SE
High River, AB T1V 2A7
Canada

web: winv.ca

Mission Statement: Publicly traded private equity company based in Western Canada.

Geographic Preference: Western Canada
Founded: 2015
Portfolio Companies: GlassMasters Autoglass, Golden Health Care, Ocean Sales, Foothills Creamery

Key Executives:
Scott Tannas, President and Chief Executive Officer
Background: Western Financial Group
Shafeen Mawani, Chief Operating Officer
Education: Simon Fraser Univ.; Ivey Business School
Background: CIBC World Markets; UBS Securities Canada
Directorships: GlassMasters Autoglass, Golden Health Care, Ocean Sales, Foothills Creamery
Stacey Cross, Chief Financial Officer
Directorships: GlassMasters Autoglass

2261 THERILIA
1010 Sherbrooke Street W
Suite 408
Montreal, QC H3A 2R7
Canada

Phone: 514-564-6474 Fax: 514-564-6424
e-mail: info@therillia.com
web: therillia.com

Mission Statement: Therilia is an autonomous company of Sanderling Ventures. It aims to cost effectively develop novel drug candidates from preclinical to clinical stages.

Key Executives:
Michael Dixon, President and CEO
Education: BComm, University of Toronto
Background: Chief Financial Officer, Gemin X Pharmaceuticals; VP, Finance, Morphometrix Technologies
Pierre Beauparlant, Chief Business Officer
Education: PhD, McGill University
Background: Medical Therapeutic Head, Hematology, Novartis Pharmaceuticals Canada; VP, Research and Development, Gemin X Pharmaceuticals

2262 TIMIA CAPITAL
1100 Melville Street
Suite 835
Vancouver, BC V6E 4A6
Canada

Phone: 604-398-8839
e-mail: info@timiacapital.com
web: timiacapital.com

Mission Statement: Timia Capital offers a tech-enabled lending platform to provide founder-friendly capital to growing recurring revenue technology businesses.

Founded: 2015
Average Investment: $2M
Minimum Investment: $1M
Portfolio Companies: Actionfigure, Agentis, Aprio, Attendease, Avenue, Beanworks, Clariti, Cova, Echosec, Daylight, Fleet Hoster, Icompass, Karbon, Lasso, Lead Genius, Measured, Metazoa, Myagi, Parkbench.Com, Predictable Revenue, Quickmobile, Realsavvy, Resilio, Rocketrez, Surefire Local, Syxsense, Vonigo, Wagepoint, Watch Wire, Ziva, Zmags

Key Executives:
Mike Walkinshaw, CEO & Director
e-mail: mikew@timiacapital.com
Education: University of British Columbia
Background: Co-Founder & Managing Partner, Fronterra Capital; Managing Partner & CFO, Chrysalix Energy
Andrew Abouchar, CFO & Chief Credit Officer
e-mail: andrewa@timiacapital.com
Background: Co-Founder & Partner, Tech Capital Partners Inc.; Founder, TCP Property Inc.; Investment Manager, Working Ventures

2263 TOP RENERGY INC.
1111 West Hastings St
Suite 790
Vancouver, BC V6E 2J3
Canada

Phone: 778-379-2891
e-mail: bp@toprenergy.com
web: www.toprenergy.com

Mission Statement: Investor in start-ups and early- and middle-stage companies in a broad range of industries including clean energy, education and manufacturing.

Geographic Preference: Canada, China
Founded: 2010
Investment Criteria: Startups, Early-Stage, Middle-Stage
Industry Group Preference: Technology, IT & Software, Social Media, Clean Energy, Supply Chain Management, Education, Healthcare, Manufacturing
Portfolio Companies: Srckode, Atiti, EraPlay, Cyclodes, Hausway, XParcels, Tabcon, Top in Nature, Eco Digitec, Top Canventure, Quality HVAC

Key Executives:
Chris Xie, President & Chief Executive Officer
Education: Wenzhou University; MBA, Schiller International University, Germany; MS, Financial

Venture Capital & Private Equity Firms / Canadian Firms

Engineering & Risk Management, New York University
Background: Deputy of Business Administration Manager, Siemens
Stephan Siegel, Advisor
Education: BSc, University of Bayreuth, Germany; PhD, Finance, Columbia University
Background: Associate Professor, Department of Finance & Business Economics, University of Washington; Project Manager & Consultant, GCI Management

2264 TORQUEST PARTNERS
Brookfield Place
161 Bay St
Suite 4240
Toronto, ON M5J 2S1
Canada

Phone: 416-956-7022
e-mail: brock@torquest.com
web: www.torquest.com

Mission Statement: Private equity firm focused on the middle market.
Geographic Preference: Canada
Fund Size: $1 billion
Founded: 2002
Average Investment: $20 to $80 million
Minimum Investment: $20 million
Investment Criteria: Middle-Market; Entrepreneur or Family Successions, Corporate Carve-Outs, Public to Private, Management Buyouts, Recapitalizations
Industry Group Preference: Financial Services, Business Products & Services, Chemicals, Food & Beverage, Consumer Products, Manufacturing
Portfolio Companies: A&W, Bartek, Can Art Aluminum Extrusion, Cando Rail Services, Joriki, Maviro, McKeil Marine, Polycor, Prepac, Rubicon Pharmacies, SCM Insurance Services, The TEAM Companies, Universal Rail Systems

Key Executives:
Brent Belzberg, Senior Managing Partner
416-956-7006
e-mail: belzberg@torquest.com
Education: BComm, Queen's University; JD, University of Toronto
Background: Founder, Harrowston
Directorships: CIBC, Tandem Expansion Fund
Eric Berke, Managing Partner
416-956-7034
e-mail: berke@torquest.com
Education: BA, University of Vermont; MBA, Boston University
Background: President/CEO, Gustin Kramer
Daniel Sonshine, Partner
416-867-2482
e-mail: sonshine@torquest.com
Education: AB, Economics, Harvard University; JD, MBA, University of Toronto
Background: CIBC Capital Partners, CIBC World Markets
Directorships: Associated Brands, Herbal Magic
Craig Rankine, Partner & CFO
416-867-2484
e-mail: rankine@torquest.com
Education: BComm, University of Toronto
Background: Deloitte & Touche LLP
Matthew Chapman, Partner
416-867-2480
e-mail: chapman@torquest.com
Education: BSc, MSc, McGill University; MBA, Rotman School of Management, University of Toronto
Background: Workbrain, RBC Capital Markets
Directorships: Pinova Holdings
Michael Hollend, Partner
416-867-2487
e-mail: hollend@torquest.com
Education: LLB, MBA, University of Toronto; BA, Economics, University of Western Ontario
Background: Partner, EdgeStone Capital Partners; Goodmans LLP; Investment Banking, Griffiths McBurney & Partners
Directorships: 4Refuel

2265 TRELLIS CAPITAL CORPORATION
333 Wilson Avenue
Suite 600
North York, ON M3H 1T2
Canada

Phone: 416-398-2299
e-mail: info@trelliscapital.com
web: www.trelliscapital.com

Mission Statement: Trellis invests in Canadian growth technology companies.
Geographic Preference: Canada
Fund Size: $10 Million
Founded: 2000
Average Investment: $500,000 to $2 million
Minimum Investment: $500,000
Investment Criteria: Early- to Mid-Stage
Industry Group Preference: Industrial Products, Manufacturing, Alternative Energy, Infrastructure, Advanced Materials, Clean Technology, Semiconductors, Robotics, Technology
Portfolio Companies: BioAstra Technologies, Datec Coating Corporation, Flybits, Funnel Cake, Handshake VR, iS5 Communications, Rank, Teraspan Networks, Think Data Works, TrendMD, Volante System

Key Executives:
Sunil Selby, Founder & Managing Partner
Education: Richard Ivey School of Business, University of Western Ontario, MBA
Background: President, Volante systems
Directorships: Advanced Technology Fund of Royal Bank Equity Partners
Dominic Talalla, Managing Partner
Background: CEO, Datec Coating Corp.; Investment Director, BDC Venture Capital; General Manager, GE Industrial Systems Canada
Directorships: Volante; IS5 Communications; Datec Coating Corp.; Teraspan

2266 TRICOR PACIFIC CAPITAL
1111 West Hastings Street
Suite 200
Vancouver, BC V6E 2J3
Canada

Phone: 604-646-4365
e-mail: opportunities@tricorpacific.com
web: www.tricorpacific.com

Mission Statement: Tricor Pacific is a leading Canadian family office investing in manufacturing, districution, business services, food, real estate and private equity.
Geographic Preference: Canada and Mid-West to Western US
Founded: 1996
Investment Criteria: Mature Business; Generating EBITDA of $3-25 million; Seasoned Partners

Key Executives:
Shawn Lewis, President and Managing Director
604-646-4370
e-mail: slewis@tricorpacific.com
Education: BSc, LLB, McGill University
Background: VP/General Counsel, Stern Partners
Derek Senft, Managing Director
604-726-5051
e-mail: derek.senft@tricorpacific.com
Education: BA, Dartmouth College; MBA, London Business School
Background: Co-Founder, Founders Group of Food

Companies; Owner, Presteve Foods, Totally Chocolate and Armand Agra; Owner/Director, Frontline Real Estate Services

2267 TRIWEST
4600, 400 - 3rd Avenue
Calgary, AB T2P 4H2
Canada

Phone: 403-225-1144 Fax: 403-225-3547
e-mail: info@triwest.ca
web: triwest.ca

Mission Statement: Western Canadian private equity firm.

Geographic Preference: Western Canada
Fund Size: $1.25 Billion
Founded: 1998
Average Investment: $15 to $50 million
Investment Criteria: Buy-Outs, Growth Financings, Corporate Divestitures, Special Situations
Industry Group Preference: Manufacturing, Distribution, Business Products & Services
Portfolio Companies: Broda Group, Bull Moose Capital, California Trusframe, Coast Appliances, Colter Energy, Fraser River Pile & Dredge, International Fitness Holdings, Kayden Industries, Lithion Power Group, Northern Mat & Bridge, Peloton Computer Enterprises, Prostar Energy, PRT Growing Services, Source Energy Services, Strike Group, Trimlite Manufacturing, Triple M Housing, Zytech Building Systems

Key Executives:
  Jeff Belford, Senior Managing Director
  Education: BComm, University of Toronto; CA
  Background: CFO, Swiss Water Decafeinated Coffee Company; Director of Finance & Operations, Descente North America
  Ron Jackson, Co-Founder
  Background: President, Burns Foods
  Lorne Jacobson, Co-Founder & Vice Chair
  Background: Vice President, Corporate Development, General Counsel, Burns Foods Limited; Partner, Bennet Jones
  Mick MacBean, Senior Managing Director
  Education: BComm, University of Saskatchewan; CA
  Background: CEO, Diamond Energy Services; ARC Financial Corporation
  Norman Rokosh, Senior Managing Director
  Education: Engineering Degree, University of British Columbia; MBA, London Business School
  Dino DeLuca, Chief Operating Officer
  Background: Burnet, Duckworth & Palmer
  Chad Danard, Senior Managing Director
  Education: BComm, Queen's University School of Business
  Background: Global Energy Group, Morgan Stanley
  Ryan Giles, Senior Managing Director
  Education: Business Administration, Richard Ivey School of Business; AB, Economics & Mathematics, Bowdoin College
  Background: Associate, Onex Corporation

2268 TVM LIFE SCIENCE MANAGEMENT
2 Place Alexis Nihon
Suite 902
3500 Boulevard de Maisonneuve W
Montreal, QC H3Z 3C1
Canada

Phone: 514-931-4111
web: www.tvm-capital.com

Mission Statement: Founded in Germany in 1983, TVM is now an international affiliation of PE and VC firms.

Key Executives:
  Hubert Birner, Managing Partner
  Education: MBA, Harvard Business School; PhD, Ludwig Maximilian University
  Background: Zeneca Agrochemicals; McKinsey & Company
  Directorships: CENTOGENE AG, SpePharm Holdings BV, leon nanodrugs GmbH, AL-S Pharma AG, Proteon Therapeutics, Acer Therapeutics
  Luc Marengere, Managing Partner
  Education: PhD, University of Toronto
  Background: Managing Partner, VG Partners; La Caisse De Depot; MDS Capital; MedTech Partners; Amgen
  Directorships: Emovi, Acanthas Pharma, Occelaris Pharma, Ixchelsis, PRCL Pharma, Panthera Dental, FAAH Pharma, Kaneq Biosciences, Acer Therapeutics, Rapid Micro Biosciences

2269 VANCITY CAPITAL
Vancouver, BC V6B 5R8
Canada

e-mail: kalen_stewart@vancity.com
web: www.vancity.com/BusinessBanking/Financing/GrowthCapital

Mission Statement: A branch of Vancouver City Savings Credit Union, Vancity Capital invests in small- to medium-sized companies that have a positive influence in BC.

Geographic Preference: British Columbia
Average Investment: $500,000 - $5 million
Minimum Investment: $500,000
Investment Criteria: Subordinated Debt, Mezzanine Financing, Convertible Debentures
Industry Group Preference: Social Impact, Environment, Innovation

Key Executives:
  Kalen Stewart, Investment Manager
  e-mail: kalen_stewart@vancity.com
  Education: BComm, University of Victoria; CFA
  Background: Analyst, Capital Street Group; Analyst, Trilogy Properties; ARC Resources

2270 VANEDGE CAPITAL PARTNERS
1333 West Broadway
Suite 750
Vancouver, BC V6H 4C1
Canada

Phone: 604-569-3883
e-mail: info@vanedgecapital.com
web: www.vanedgecapital.com

Mission Statement: Vanedge is a Vancouver-based, early-stage venture capital fund.

Geographic Preference: Canada, United States
Fund Size: $296MM
Founded: 2010
Investment Criteria: Early-Stage, Later-Stage
Industry Group Preference: Cloud Computing, Artificial Intelligence, Cyber Security, SaaS, Digital Media
Portfolio Companies: AVA, Bitfusion, Bridgit, Boundless, Canalyst, Echodyne, Femtosense, GO-JEK, Hytrust, Illusense, Mediacore, Metafor, Omnisci, Plantiga, Playnomics, Plotly, Privacy Analytics, Quantum Benchmark, Recon Instruments, Rigado, RoosterBio, SensorUp, SpaceX, vArmour, Vendasta, Vodasafe, Wurldtech, xCures

Key Executives:
  V. Paul Lee, Managing Partner
  Background: President, Electronic Arts (EA)
  Directorships: DigiBC
  Moe Kermani, Managing Partner
  Education: MSc, PhD, Physics, University of British Columbia
  Background: Vice President, NetApp
  Micah Siegel, Partner
  Education: PhD, California Institute of Technology
  Background: C2C Ventures, Stanford Univ.

Venture Capital & Private Equity Firms / Canadian Firms

Todd Tessier, Acting CFO
Education: BComm, Univ. of Saskatchewan
Background: Recon Instruments, BC Renaissance Capital Fund

2271 VERDEXUS
137 Glasgow Street
Suite 210
Kitchener, ON N2G 4X8
Canada

Phone: 519-957-2230 Fax: 519-957-2239
Toll-Free: 888-713-4090
e-mail: canada@verdexus.com
web: www.verdexus.com

Mission Statement: Boutique firm focused on management buyouts and corporate divestitures.
Geographic Preference: Canada, United States, Europe
Founded: 2001
Investment Criteria: Management buyouts, corporate divestitures
Industry Group Preference: Information Technology, New Media, Mobile, Cyber Security, Software

Key Executives:
Randall Howard, General Partner
e-mail: rhoward@verdexus.com
Education: B.Math, University of Waterloo
Background: Founder, MKS
Directorships: iotum
Ray Simonson, General Partner
e-mail: rsimonson@verdexus.com
Education: Systems Designs Engineering, University of Waterloo; Finance Program, Queen's University
Background: Coreworx, Bluegill Technologies
Suresh Patel, Senior Advisor, Europe
e-mail: spatel@verdexus.com
Education: Artificial Intelligence, University of Brighton
Background: Head of European Investments, Compaq Computer Corp.; Director, Netscape Communications Europe

2272 VERSION ONE VENTURES
Vancouver, BC
Canada

web: versionone.vc

Mission Statement: Version One Ventures is an early-stage fund investing in consumer internet, SaaS and mobile entrepreneurs.
Geographic Preference: North America
Average Investment: $200,000 - $500,000
Investment Criteria: Early-Stage
Industry Group Preference: Consumer Internet, Mobile, E-Commerce & Manufacturing, SaaS
Portfolio Companies: Abstract, Ada Support, AngelList, Blockstack, Booster Fuels, Celo, Chefit, Citizen Hex, Coinbase, Clio, Dapper, Dolly, Drover, Figure 1, Frank & Oak, Gencove, Guesser, Headout, Indiegogo, Indochino, Jobber, Kobalt, Lolli, Manifold, MetaStable Capital, Nexus Mutual, Outreach, Placenote, Pickle Robot, Polychain Capital, Preemadonna, Qurasense, Roost, Scanwell, Shippo, Smore, Top Hat, Trim, Unbounce, Wattpad, Yapta, Zenput

Key Executives:
Boriz Wertz, Founding Partner
e-mail: boris@versionone.vc
Education: PhD, Graduate School of Management, Koblenz
Background: AbeBooks.com
Directorships: Andreesen Horowitz
Angela Tran, General Partner
e-mail: angela@versionone.vc
Education: Univ. of Toronto
Background: Insight Data Science
Directorships: Computer History Museum

2273 VERTU CAPITAL
150 King Street W
Suite 212
Toronto, ON M5H 1J9
Canada

web: vertucapital.ca

Mission Statement: Vertu Capital seeks to collaborate with teams in the Canadian technology industry that are building to go global.
Geographic Preference: Canada
Investment Criteria: Less than $20M Revenue; Enterprise Value between $75-250M

Key Executives:
Lisa Melchior, Founder/Managing Partner
Education: BA, Western University; MBA, York University
Background: CIBC World Markets; OMERS Private Equity
Kim Davis, Partner and COO
Education: BComm, York University
Background: Co-Founder, David Cornfield Melanoma Fund; CFO, TorQuest Partners; Senior Manager, Deloitte

2274 VRG CAPITAL
145 Wellington Street W
Suite 900
Toronto, ON M5J 1H8
Canada

Phone: 416-581-8850 Fax: 416-581-0020
e-mail: info@vrgcapital.com
web: www.vrgcapital.com

Mission Statement: VRG Capital Corp. is a Toronto-based private equity firm focused on investing in companies needing capital for growth, buyouts and mergers.
Geographic Preference: Canada
Founded: 1982
Investment Criteria: Acquisitions, Financings, Roll-Ups, Public Offerings
Industry Group Preference: Healthcare, Financial Services, Information Technology, Logistics, Insurance, Marketing/Sales Services

Other Locations:
777 Dunsmuir Street
Suite 1700
Vancouver, BC V7Y 1K4
Canada

Key Executives:
Gordon Feeney, Chair
Directorships: Finance Corp. of Bahamas, Moneris Solutions, Royal Mutual Funds
J.R. Kingsley Ward, Managing Partner
Education: BA, BComm
Background: President, VRG; Chairman, Pareto Corporation
Brock Bundy, Managing Partner
Education: CMA, B.Soc.Sc.
Background: Royal Bank of Canada
Merv Simpson, Managing Partner
Background: Senior Manager, Chartered Accounting Firm
Greg Cochrane, Managing Partner
Background: Co-Owner, Mariposa Communications & Promotions
Directorships: Wheels Group
Rod Campbell, Managing Partner
Education: MBA, Univ. of British Columbia
Background: Clarus
Directorships: Jones Brown, Clarus Securities
Michael Egan, Family Office Partner
Background: InSystems Technologies
Directorships: Real Matters
Kerry Shapansky, Family Office Partner
Background: Pareto

Venture Capital & Private Equity Firms / Canadian Firms

Deborah McDonald, Chief Financial Officer
Background: Royal Bank of Canada

2275 WATERTON GLOBAL RESOURCE MANAGEMENT
Commerce Court West
199 Bay Street
Suite 5050
Toronto, ON M5L 1E2
Canada

Phone: 416-504-3505 Fax: 416-504-3200
e-mail: info@watertonglobal.com
web: www.watertonglobal.com

Mission Statement: Waterton Global Resource Management is a private equity firm that specializes in the mining and metals sectors.
Geographic Preference: Canada, United States, South America
Fund Size: $1.75 billion
Founded: 2009
Average Investment: $10 - $300 million
Industry Group Preference: Mining, Metals
Key Executives:
 Isser Elishis, Managing Partner & Chief Investment Officer
 Background: Senior VP & Director, HSBC
 James Hennessy, Chair
 Background: President & CEO, ING Mutual Funds
 Directorships: Allis Chalmers Oil & Gas Services
 Cheryl Brandon, Partner, Investment Management
 Education: CFA
 Background: Leeward Hedge Funds; Duff Capital Advisors
 Jack McMahon, Partner, Head of Mining Operations
 Background: Tethyan Copper
 Richard Wells, Partner & Chief Financial Officer
 Education: CA
 Background: Manager, Financial Reporting, Magna International; PricewaterhouseCoopers

2276 WESLEY CLOVER
390 March Road
Suite 110
Ottawa, ON K2K 0G7
Canada

Phone: 613-271-6305
web: www.wesleyclover.com

Mission Statement: Ottawa-based super angel investor focused on information and communications technologies, and real estate and leisure properties.
Geographic Preference: Worldwide
Founded: 2000
Investment Criteria: Seed, Early-Stage, Follow-On
Industry Group Preference: Information Technology, Telecommunications, Digital Media & Marketing, Real Estate, Entertainment, Networking, Leisure, Cloud Computing, Mobile, SaaS
Portfolio Companies: Aydanaya, Benbria Loop, Brookstreet, Career JSM, Celtic Manor, Certn, Cliniconex, Codeherent, CounterPath, CreatorDen, CulturVate, Diskyver, Ecosec, Encepta, Encore Networks, English Ninjas, Enjovia, Filefacets, Hut Six Security, Hyalto, Hyas, ICC Wales, Init Live, Iven, KRP Properties, Learnium, Lota.cloud, Martello, Mydoma Studio, Pisano, Pretio Interactive, ProntoForms, ReactEvent, Referral Saasquatch, Reliving, Segmentify, Solace, Solink, SumoShift, Surple, Talkative, Taraspan, Teldio, ThinkRF, Twentify, WCS Europe, Wesley Clover Solutions
Key Executives:
 Terry Matthews, Chair
 Education: University of Wales
 Background: Mitel, Newbridge Networks

Paul Chiarelli, President & COO
Background: Director, Finance, Tundra Semiconductor Corporation; Deloitte

2277 WESTCAP
409 3rd Avenue South
Suite 601
Saskatoon, SK S7K 5R5
Canada

Phone: 306-652-5557 Fax: 306-652-8186
e-mail: info@westcapmgt.ca
web: westcapmgt.ca

Mission Statement: Manager of niche investment funds.
Geographic Preference: Canada
Fund Size: $500 million
Founded: 1991
Industry Group Preference: Agriculture, Healthcare, Hospitality, Infrastructure, Innovation, Management Buyouts, Resources
Portfolio Companies: Aria, The Brixton, Canpro Ingredients, The Cayman, Dyna Crane Services, Dynaindustrial, Daxton, Fluid Clarification, Golden Health Care, Hjr Asphalt, Jump.Ca, Kensington Flats, Parliament Pointe, Prairie Meats, Ramada Plaza, Sequoia, Shangri-La, Superior Group Of Companies, Tackpoint, Warman Home Centre
Key Executives:
 Grant J. Kook, President, CEO and Founder
 Background: President & CEO, Cheung On; President & CEO, Ramada Hotels

2278 WESTERN AMERICA CAPITAL GROUP
10025-102A Avenue
Suite 1500
Edmonton, AB T5J 2Z2
Canada

Phone: 780-496-9171 Fax: 780-496-9172
web: www.wacapital.com

Mission Statement: Private management and corporate buyout firm focused on mid-market manufacturing, distribution and service companies.
Geographic Preference: Western United States, Canada
Founded: 1987
Average Investment: Up to $50 million
Investment Criteria: Succession, Leveraged Buyouts, Management Buyouts, Acquisitions
Industry Group Preference: Manufacturing, Distribution, Business Products & Services, Oil & Gas, Construction, Software
Portfolio Companies: Canadian Forestry Equipment, Custom Welding Services, United Roadbuilders, Commercial Bearing Service, Northland Material Handling, Garneau Welding and Fabricating, Bri-Chem Supply, Sodium Solutions
Key Executives:
 Richard Caron, Partner
 e-mail: rcaron@wacapital.com
 Don Caron, Partner
 e-mail: dcaron@wacapital.com

2279 WHITE SHEEP CORP
141 Adelaide Street West
Suite 1200
Toronto, ON M5H 3L5

web: whitesheepcorp.com

Mission Statement: Invests and operates facilities that cultivate, process, extract, package, and distribute cannabis for medicinal & recreational use.
Geographic Preference: Canada, US
Founded: 2013
Industry Group Preference: Cannabis

Portfolio Companies: Altopa Inc., Oblend, Ample Organics, Cannabis Big Data, Biomedican

Key Executives:
Hamish Sutherland, President/Co-CEO
Education: BEng, McMaster University; MBA, Schulich School of Business, York University
Background: VP of Marketing, Strike Technologies; Director of Business Development, Research Now; President, Porcupine Goldor Mines; President/CEO, Hunter Porcupine Gold; Managing Partner, The Marketing Partners; COO, Kaypok Inc.; COO, Bedrocan Canada; COO, Asterio Cannabis Inc.
Michael Siltala, Co-CEO and Chief Legal Officer
Education: Queen's University; JD, Dalhousie University
Background: Professional NHL Player; Torys LLP
Bharat Choudhary, Chief Financial Officer
Education: University of Waterloo; CPA, CA, KPMG
Background: VP, Finance, TerrAscend Corp.; Director, Finance, Novadaq Technologies Inc.

2280 WHITECAP VENTURE PARTNERS
22 St. Clair Avenue E
Suite 1010
Toronto, ON M4T 2S3
Canada

Phone: 416-961-5355 Fax: 416-961-3232
e-mail: info@whitecapvp.com
web: www.whitecapvp.com

Mission Statement: Early-stage venture capital fund focused on information and communications technologies, food tech, and med tech.
Geographic Preference: Canada
Fund Size: $100 million
Average Investment: $2 to $5 million
Minimum Investment: $2 million
Investment Criteria: Early-Stage
Industry Group Preference: Healthcare, Medical Technology, Information Technology, Communications, Food & Beverage
Portfolio Companies: Bold Commerce, Bolt Logistics, Felix, Nicoya, PartnerStack, Silofit, Vetster

Key Executives:
Carey Diamond, Partner
e-mail: carey@whitecapvp.com
Education: BA, Economics, University of Western Ontario; LLB, Osgoode Hall Law School
Directorships: Broadband Networks, PC Docs Group, iMagicTV, Loran International, Protenergy
Blaine Hobson, Chair, Investment Committee
e-mail: blaine@whitecapvp.com
Education: Richard Ivey School of Business, University of Western Ontario
Directorships: Qvella, Real Matters
Russell Samuels, Partner
e-mail: russell@whitecapvp.com
Education: HBA, Richard Ivey School of Business; JD, University of Western Ontario
Background: Senior Manager, Corporate & Business Development, Freshbooks; Associate, Mantella Venture Partners; Analyst, Canada Pension Plan Investment Board
Shayn Diamond, Partner
e-mail: shayn@whitecapvp.com
Education: BA, Philosophy, University of Western Ontario; MBA, JD, Queen's University
Background: Wildeboer Dellelce LLP
Kim Coote, Vice President, Finance
e-mail: kim@whitecastle.ca
Education: BA, Economics, York University; CPA; CGA

2281 WHITEHORSE LIQUIDITY PARTNERS
200 Wellington Street West
Suite 600
Toronto, ON M5V 3C7
Canada

web: www.whitehorseliquidity.com

Key Executives:
Yann Robard, Managing Partner
Education: Dalhousie Univ.
Background: Canada Pension Plan Investment Board
Michael Gubbels, Partner
Education: Wilfrid Laurier Univ.
Background: Ontario Teachers' Pension Plan; OMERS Private Equity
Giorgio Riva, Partner
Education: McGill Univ.
Background: Scotiabank
Rob Gavin, Partner
Education: Ivey Buesiness School, Western University
Background: Denham Capital Management; BMO Capital Markets

2282 XPV WATER PARTNERS
40 University Ave
Suite 801
Toronto, ON M5J 1T1
Canada

Phone: 416-864-0475 Fax: 416-864-0514
e-mail: info@xpvwaterpartners.com
web: www.xpvwaterpartners.com

Mission Statement: XPV invests in and advises water-related companies.
Geographic Preference: Canada
Fund Size: $400 Million
Average Investment: Up to $25 million
Industry Group Preference: Water, Semiconductors, Building Materials & Services, Oil & Gas, Food & Beverage
Portfolio Companies: Aquatic Informatics, Atlas-SSI, BCR Solid Solutions, EOSi, FATHOM, Isle Utilities, LuminUltra, Metasphere Ltd., Mobiltex, Natural Systems Utilities, Newterra, Nexom, Organica, Shenandoah Growers, SmartCover Systems

Key Executives:
David Henderson, Founder & Managing Partner
Education: Ryerson Univ.
Background: Kinghaven Capital Corp.
Directorships: FATHOM Water Holdings, Newterra Group
Khalil Maalouf, Partner
Education: BComm, Concordia Univ.
Background: VenGrowth Capital Partners
Directorships: BCR Environmental Corp., Organica Water
Sam Saintonge, Partner
Education: BBA, Bishop's University

2283 YALETOWN VENTURE PARTNERS
1122 Mainland Street
Suite 510
Vancouver, BC V6B 5L1
Canada

Phone: 604-688-7807
e-mail: info@yaletown.com
web: www.yaletown.com

Mission Statement: Yaletown leverages an extensive on-the-ground network to seek out the most promising cleantech and IT investment opportunities.
Geographic Preference: Western Canada, United States
Fund Size: $160 million
Founded: 2001
Average Investment: $2 - $4 million
Investment Criteria: Early-Stage, Seed-Stage

Venture Capital & Private Equity Firms / Canadian Firms

Industry Group Preference: Clean Technology, Information Technology, Artificial Intelligence
Portfolio Companies: Circle Cardiovascular Imaging, Chaordix, Charli, Columbia Green Techologies, Cooledge, CTO.ai, Elastic Path, ePact, Equicare Health, Good Natured, Highline, Finn AI, Fluids Inc., Food.ee, LoginRadius, Mixpo, Mover, Redlen Technologies, Phemi Health Systems, Pretio Interactive, Showbie, Sokanu, Tasktop, ThoughtExchange, ThoughtWire, Tutela, Vizimax

Other Locations:
150 - 9th Avenue SW
26th Floor
Calgary, AB T2P 3H9
Canada
Phone: 403-444-8300

290 Lakeshore Drive
Suite 205
Pointe-Claire, QC H9S 4L3
Canada
Phone: 514-548-2084

100 King Street W
Suite 5600
Toronto, ON M5X 1C9
Canada

Key Executives:
Salil Munjal, Managing Partner
604-800-2209
Education: BSc, University of Toronto; Law Degree, Queen's University
Background: COO, Leitch Technology
Directorships: Vizimax
Hans Knapp, Partner
Background: Brigill Investments
Shyam Gupta, Partner
Education: PhD
Background: SDP Telecom, Somel Investments
Brad Johns, Partner
Background: Moneta Capital, Nortel
Eric Bukovinsky, Partner
Background: Jefferies & Company
Sophie Gupta, Principal, Operations
Education: BComm, University of Ottawa; LLB, Laval University
Background: McCarthy Tetrault

2284 YELLOW POINT EQUITY PARTNERS
1285 West Pender Street
Suite 900
Vancouver, BC V6E 4B1
Canada

e-mail: admin@ypoint.ca
web: www.ypoint.ca

Mission Statement: Mid-market investor now on its fourth fund.
Geographic Preference: Western Canada, Pacific Northwest United States
Founded: 2004
Average Investment: $5 to $25 million
Minimum Investment: $5 million
Investment Criteria: MBO, Going Private Transactions, Growth Capital Funding, Recapitalizations, Spin-Offs, Succession Planning
Industry Group Preference: Manufacturing, Technology, Communications, Energy, Financial Services, Healthcare, Business Products & Services
Portfolio Companies: Bravo Target Safety, Canadian Appliance Source, CBI Health Group, CIMS, Cast Steel Products, Edo Japan, Foley's, MacKay CEO Forums, RAMMP Hospitality, Remcan, Securiguard, Seymour Investment Management, The State Group, Viper

Key Executives:
Brian Begert, Co-Founder & Managing Partner
e-mail: bbegert@ypoint.ca
Education: BS, Economics, University of Southern California; MBA, University of British Columbia
Background: Founding Partner, Goepel Shields & Partners; Managing Director, Raymond James
Directorships: Prism Medical, Shanahan's, RAMMP, Seymour, CIMS
Dave Chapman, Co-Founder & Managing Partner
e-mail: dchapman@ypoint.ca
Education: BComm, Finance, University of Calgary; MBA, University of Western Ontario
Background: CEO, Greenlight Power Technologies; SVP, Merrill Lynch
Directorships: Crossroads C&I, We Care, CBV Collection Services

International Firms

Venture Capital & Private Equity Firms / International Firms

2285 21 PARTNERS
Via G. Felissent, 90
Treviso 31100
Italy

Phone: 39-0422316611 Fax: 39-0422316600
e-mail: info@21investimenti.it
web: www.21investimenti.it

Mission Statement: European private equity group providing capital, support and expertise to mid-market companies.
Geographic Preference: France, Southern Europe
Fund Size: $730 million
Founded: 1992
Average Investment: $1.22 - $111.44 million
Investment Criteria: LBO, Expansion, Development and Growth, Middle Market
Industry Group Preference: All Sectors Considered
Portfolio Companies: Adesso, Assicom, Cleor, CMG Silhouette Sports Club, Daltys, Digital Virgo, DGF, EGB Investments, Ethical Coffee Company, Farnese Vini, Forma-Dis, Forno d'Asolo, Ligier-Microcar, Nadella, Oberthur, Palmers, PittaRosso, Poligof, Potel & Chabot, SIFI, Sirti, Stroili Oro Group, Synerlab, Viabizzuno

Other Locations:
Via Montenapoleone 8
Milan 20121
Italy
Phone: 39-0277121311 Fax: 39-0277121333

9 Avenue Hoche
Paris 75008
France
Phone: 33-0156883300 Fax: 33-0156883320

37 Route du Creux de Genthod
Geneva 1294
Switzerland

Aleje Jerozolimskie 65/79
Warsaw 00-697
Poland
Phone: 48-226307575 Fax: 48-226307576

Key Executives:
Alessandro Benetton, Founding Managing Partner
Education: BS, Business Administration, Boston University; MBA, Harvard University
Background: Goldman Sachs
Directorships: Benetton Group, Edizione Srl, Autogrill
Gérard Pluvinet, Founding Managing Partner
Education: Institut d'Etudes Politiques
Background: Managing Director & Chairman, Societe Centrale pour l'Industrie
Dino Furlan, Managing Partner
Education: Ca' Foscari University of Venice
Background: Finance Department, Fiat Auto
Cedric Abitbol, Managing Partner
Background: Director, Private Equity, Capstone Palomar; VP, Private Equity, Unigestion
Francois Barbier, Managing Partner
Education: Ecole Superieure de Commerce
Background: Executive, Societe Centrale pour l'Industrie; CFO, Siaco
Henry Huyghues Despointes, Senior Advisor
Background: Executive, Societe Centrale pour l'Industrie
Matteo Chieregato, Partner
Education: University of Bologna
Background: Paladin Capital Partners; Fincomit
Andrea Mazzucato, Partner
Education: University of Padova
Background: Private Equity Partners; ABN Amro
Caroline Giral, Principal
Education: EMYLON Business School; Paris-Dauphine University
Background: KPMG

Giovanni Bonandini, Principal
Education: Bocconi University; CA
Background: 3i Group; KPMG

2286 212 CAPITAL PARTNERS
Eglence Sokak, No. 19
Arnavutkoy, Besiktas
Istanbul 34345
Turkey

e-mail: info@212ltd.com
web: www.212ltd.com

Mission Statement: 212 Capital Partners is a venture capital fund committed to investing in early stage Internet and technology companies in Turkey.
Geographic Preference: Turkey
Average Investment: $500,000 - $3 million
Investment Criteria: Early-Stage
Industry Group Preference: Internet, Technology, Communications, Software, Digital Media & Marketing, Cloud Computing
Portfolio Companies: ArcadeMonk, Hazinem, Hemen Kiralik, HotelRunner, IyziCo, Parca Deposu, Solvoyo, VizeraLabs

Key Executives:
Numan Numan, Managing Director
Education: BSc, Computer Science, Ege University
Background: Vice President, Goldman Sachs; CS First Boston; Dun & Bradstreet, GTE
Directorships: HemenKiralik.com, HotelRunner, IyziCo
Ali H Karabey, Managing Director
Education: University of Michigan
Background: Arthur Andersen; Morgan Stanley Capital International; Deutsche Bank
Directorships: Solvoyo, Hazinem.com, Parcadeposu.com
Dilek Dayinlari, Vice President
Education: BS, Mechanical Engineering, Yildiz Technical University; MBA, Strategy, Johnson & Wales University
Background: Director, Strategy & Analysis, Groupon; Senior Management Consultant, Communications & High Technology, Accenture; Business Developer, Koc Holding
Emre Kurttepeli, Investment Committee Member
Education: Columbia University
Background: Founder, Mynet Group; Founder, Fornet
Directorships: Endeavor
Mahmut L Unlu, Investment Committee Member
Education: Georgia Institute of Technology; MBA, Rice University
Background: Associate, Iktisat Bankasi; Assistant General Manager, Yatirim Bank; Co-Founder, Dundas Unlu

2287 350 INVESTMENT PARTNERS
4th Floor
Dorset House
27-45 Stamford Street
London SE1 9NT
United Kingdom

Phone: 44-02078324601
e-mail: invest@ctip.co.uk
web: www.ctip.co.uk

Mission Statement: CT Investment Partners LLP actively engages with entrepreneurs to build successful clean energy businesses. We invest in innovative, high-growth companies early in their lifecycles. At CT Investment Partners, our team knows that it's difficult to grow a business on your own. Since 2001, we have completed investments in 27 UK-based cleantech businesses, which have raised nearly £200 million in venture capital, making us one of the most active cleantech investors in Europe.
Geographic Preference: United Kingdom
Fund Size: £200 million
Founded: 2006
Average Investment: £500,000 - £10 million

Venture Capital & Private Equity Firms / International Firms

Investment Criteria: Early-Stage
Industry Group Preference: Clean Technology
Portfolio Companies: 4 Energy, CamSemi, Arieso, New Earth Solutions, Open Energi, Intamac, Helveta, Oxsensis, Aero Thermal, Acal Energy, Pelamis, Green Biologics, Imperative Energy, Senselogix, Cable Sense, Placefirst, EcoLogicLiving, Ultromex, Acoustic Sensing Technology

Key Executives:
Peter Linthwaite, Managing Partner
Education: Oxford University
Background: Founding Director, Royal London Private Equtiy Limited; Managing Director, Murray Johnstone Private Equity

2288 360 CAPITAL PARTNERS 360 Capital Management SA
13 Avenue de l'Opéra
Paris 75001
France

Phone: +33-01-7118-2912
e-mail: info@360capitalpartners.com
web: www.360capitalpartners.com

Mission Statement: 360 Capital Partners is a Venture Capital firm, investing in Innovation at full scale, in Europe and more particularly in France and Italy.
Geographic Preference: Europe, France, Italy
Fund Size: 350 million Euro
Founded: 1997
Average Investment: 2 million Euro
Minimum Investment: 500K Euro
Investment Criteria: Early-Stage, Seed-Stage
Industry Group Preference: Internet, Telecommunications, Clean Technology, Medical Technology, Media, Entertainment, Financial Services, New Materials, Engineering, Industrial Services, E-Commerce & Manufacturing, Robotics, Information Technology
Portfolio Companies: 21 Buttons, Alci, Alsid, Arbe Robotics, Balyo, BeMyEye, Bergamotte, Birdly, Brainiac, Casavo, CharityStars, Chronocam, Cubyn, Doveconviene/Shopfully, EarthCube, Eatalynet, Enerbee, Exotec, Exotrail, EZ-WHEEL, Fotokyte, HeyCater, Hi Bruno, ID5, Innoviz, Jobdisabili, LeSlipFrançais, Milkman, Musement, Neurala, Neutrino, Newlisi, Otherwise, PIQ, Qapa, Qopius, Seedcamp, Sophia Genetics, Supermercato 24, Tediber, The Socialite Family, Tiller, Traefik, TVTY, Unilend

Other Locations:
Via Brisa 3
Milan 20123
Italy
Phone: 39-0236560950

Key Executives:
Fausto Boni, General Partner, Milan
Education: BA, Economics, Bocconi University; MBA, INSEAD
Background: Co-Founder, Net Partners Ventures; McKinsey & Co.; L'Air Liquide
François Tison, General Partner, Paris
Education: ENST; MBA, Columbia University
Background: France Telecom; Assocate Director, Nomura; SVP, Europ@web
Emanuele Levi, General Partner, Paris
Education: University of Turin
Background: Unicredito Italiano Group; Bain & Co.; Lazard Investment Banking
Cesare Maifredi, General Partner, Milan
Education: MBA, Darden School of Business Administration, University of Virginia; MEng, University of Brescia
Background: McKinsey & Co.; Bain & Co.
Dominique Rencurel, General Partner, Paris
Education: MA, Université de Paris Dauphine
Background: BNP Paribas; Co-Founder, Orkos Capital
Nader Sabbaghian, General Partner, Paris
Education: MEng, MIT
Background: Accenture; McKinsey & Co.; CEO, BravoSolution; Founder, Bakeca

2289 3I ASIA PACIFIC 3i Group
6 Battery Road
Level 42, Unit 07
Singapore 049909
Singapore

Phone: 65-62322937 Fax: 65-62322943
e-mail: singapore@3i.com
web: www.3i.com

Mission Statement: Provides a comprehensive range of private equity and venture capital solutions across all funding stages, from start-ups through growth capital to buyouts.
Geographic Preference: Singapore, Southeast Asia, Hong Kong, Japan, Korea, Taiwan, India
Fund Size: $1.18 Billion
Founded: 1945
Average Investment: $95.04 Million
Minimum Investment: $2.37 Million
Investment Criteria: Early Stage, Growth Capital, MBO, MB, IBO
Industry Group Preference: Leisure, Engineering, Healthcare, Software Services, Manufacturing, Telecommunications, Information Technology, Oil & Gas, Transportation
Portfolio Companies: Focus Media, GST Holdings Ltd, Asia Renal Care

Key Executives:
Lisa Johnson, Director
Oliver Wong, Director

2290 3I AUSTRIA BETEILGUNG GmbH 3i Group
16 Palace St
London SW1E 5JD
United Kingdom

Phone: 44-2079753131 Fax: 44-2079753232
e-mail: vienna@3i.com
web: www.3i.com

Mission Statement: Actively seeking new investments.
Geographic Preference: Austria, Germany, London
Fund Size: $11 Billion
Founded: 1945
Average Investment: $95.04 Million
Minimum Investment: $2.37 Million
Investment Criteria: Seed, Early Stage, Start-up, Growth Capital
Industry Group Preference: Communications, Computer Related, Software, Electronic Technology, Private Equity, Infrastructure, Debt Management
Portfolio Companies: Hyperwave

Key Executives:
Simon Borrows, Chief Executive

2291 3I DEUTSCHLAND GESELLSCHAFT FUR 3i Group
Bockenheimer Landstraäe 2-4
Frankfurt am Main
Frankfurt 60306
Germany

Phone: 49-697100000 Fax: 49-69710000113
e-mail: frankfurt@3i.com
web: www.3i.com

Mission Statement: Investment activities range from early phase financing up to the financing of buyouts.
Geographic Preference: Germany
Fund Size: £15 Million
Founded: 1984

Venture Capital & Private Equity Firms / International Firms

Average Investment: $95.04 Million
Minimum Investment: $2.37 Million
Investment Criteria: Concentrates on start up and early growth enterprises
Industry Group Preference: Communications, Healthcare, Software, Electronic Technology, Semiconductors, Information Technology
Portfolio Companies: Gries Deco, DTMS, Epigenomics, Kontron Embedded AG, Igeneon, Element 5, SR Technics

Key Executives:
 Ulf von Haacke, Partner, Managing Director, Head of Industrial
 e-mail: london@3i.com
 Education: Degree in economics, PhD
 Background: serving on the boards of MVC MobilVideoCommunication AG,
 Directorships: Member of the Josef A. Schumpeter Gesellschaft.
 Peter Wirtz, Partner, Managing Director

2292 3I EUROPE PLC 3i Group
16 Palace St
London SW1E 5JD
United Kingdom

Phone: 44-2079283131 Fax: 44-2079753232
e-mail: kathryn.vanderkroft@3i.com
web: www.3i.com

Mission Statement: Investment activities: private equity, infrastructure, debt management.
Geographic Preference: UK, North America, Asia, Continental Europe
Fund Size: o14 billion
Founded: 1945
Investment Criteria: Private Equity, Infrastructure, Debt Management
Industry Group Preference: Business Products & Services, Healthcare, Consumer, General Industrial
Portfolio Companies: ACR Capital Holdings, Norma Group, Foster + Partners, Memora Services Funerarias, Mayborn Group, Quntiles, Transnational Corporation

Key Executives:
 Menno Antal, Managing Partner, Private Equity
 Julia Wilson, Group Finance Director

2293 3I GERMANY GmbH 3i Group
Bockenheimer Landstraäe 2-4
Frankfurt am Main
Frankfurt 60306
Germany

Phone: 49-697100000 Fax: 49-69710000113
e-mail: frankfurt@3i.com
web: www.3i.com

Mission Statement: Investment activities range from early phase financing up to the financing of buyouts.
Geographic Preference: Germany, Switzerland, Austria
Fund Size: £15 Million
Founded: 1984
Average Investment: $95.04 Million
Minimum Investment: $2.37 Million
Investment Criteria: Expansion, Leveraged Buyout, Management Buyout
Industry Group Preference: Communications, Healthcare, Software, Electronic Technology, Semiconductors, Information Technology
Portfolio Companies: Gries Deco, DTMS, Epigenomics, Kontron Embedded AG, Igeneon, Element 5, SR Technics

Key Executives:
 Laura Boeck, Associate Germany

2294 3I GESTION SA 3i Group
3 rue Paul Cezanne
Paris 75008
France

Phone: 33-173151100 Fax: 33-173151124
e-mail: paris@3i.com
web: www.3i.com

Mission Statement: 3i is an international leader in Private Equity. We focus on Buyouts, Growth Capital and Infrastructure and invest across Europe, Asia and North America. Our competitive advantage comes from our international network and the strength and breadth of our business relationships. These underpin the value that we deliver to our portfolio, shareholders and fund investors.
Geographic Preference: France
Fund Size: £15 Million
Founded: 1984
Average Investment: $95.04 Million
Minimum Investment: $2.37 Million
Investment Criteria: Expansion, Development, Mid-Market Buyout
Industry Group Preference: Healthcare, Industrial Products, Business Products & Services, Financial Services, TMT, Consumer Products
Portfolio Companies: Galva Union, Goto Software, Grands Vins De Girande, Meristem Therapeutics, None Networks, Repetto International, Tartine et Chocolat

Key Executives:
 David Fewtrell, Director
 Remi Carnimolla, Partner, Managing Director
 Denis Ribon, Partner, Managing Director, Head of Healthcare
 e-mail: paris@3i.com
 Education: MBA, HEC; University Veterinary surgeon de Lyon.
 Background: Veterinary surgeon
 Directorships: Consulting
 Stéphane Duhr, Director

2295 3I ITALY 3i Group
16 Palace Street
London SW1E 5JD
United Kingdom

Phone: 44-2079283131 Fax: 44-2079753232
e-mail: milan@3i.com
web: www.3i.com

Mission Statement: Actively seeking new investments.
Geographic Preference: Italy
Fund Size: Euro 500 million
Founded: 1945
Average Investment: Euro 200 Million
Minimum Investment: $2.39 Million
Investment Criteria: Expansion & Development Capital, Replacement Capital, Buyout & Buy in, All Stages
Industry Group Preference: Business Products & Services, Consumer, Healthcare, Industrial

Key Executives:
 Andrew Cox, Director
 e-mail: london@3i.com
 Education: ME, MBA
 Background: Sambonet. TTED (Table Top Engineering and Design). FEME,
 Directorships: Board member of AIFI, the Italian Venture Capital Association.
 Jonathan Crane, Director
 e-mail: london@3i.com
 Education: Electronic Engineering, MBA from INSEAD
 Background: Andersen Consulting, dealt with planning and development of information systems, and later at Arthur D. Little,
 Michael Curtis, Director
 e-mail: london@3i.com

Venture Capital & Private Equity Firms / International Firms

Education: Electrical Engineering/Industrial Automation, ENSEEIHT; IT Degree, ENSAE; MBA, Bocconi University in Milan
Background: management consultant at Andersen Consulting for four years (in London and Milan) focusing on business processes engineering and post merger integration projects.
Directorships: he worked in applied research in France
Anna Dellis, Director
e-mail: london@3i.com
Education: Doctorate, Business Economy
Background: Worked near the office of Bristol in England
Directorships: Auditor near KPMG

2296 3I SPAIN 3i Group
Calle Ruiz de Alarco n 12 - 20 .BM
Madrid 28014
Spain

Phone: 34-915214419 Fax: 34-915219819
e-mail: madrid@3i.com
web: www.3i.com

Mission Statement: Actively seeking new investments.
Geographic Preference: Spain
Fund Size: $1.18 Billion
Founded: 1995
Average Investment: $95.04 Million
Minimum Investment: $2.37 Million
Investment Criteria: Invests in buyouts in all sectors
Industry Group Preference: Diversified

Key Executives:
Javier Martin, Senior Associate
Education: MBA
Background: Booz Allen and Consulting Hamilton
Maite Ballester, Partner, Managing Director
Education: MBA, Engineer of Mines
Background: Executive of Investments in the office of Birmingham
Directorships: Member of the committee of direction of the Spanish Association of Capital Risk .

2297 3I TEUPSCHLAND GmbH 3i Group
Bockenheimer Landstraáe 2-4
Frankfurt am Main
Frankfurt 60306
Germany

Phone: 49-697100000 Fax: 49-69710000113
web: www.3i.com

Mission Statement: A private equity and venture capital enterprise, leading world-wide, investment activities from early phase financing up to the financing of buyouts.
Geographic Preference: Germany
Fund Size: £15 Million
Founded: 1984
Average Investment: $95.04 Million
Minimum Investment: $2.37 Million
Investment Criteria: Seed, Startup, Early-Stage, First-Stage, Second-Stage, Expansion and Development
Industry Group Preference: Chemicals, Communications, Computer Related, Distribution, Electronic Components, Industrial Equipment, Life Sciences, Information Technology, Healthcare
Portfolio Companies: Gries Deco, DTMS, Epigenomics, Kontron Embedded AG, Igeneon, Element 5, SR Technics

Key Executives:
Laura Boeck, Associate
Education: Degree in Business
Background: Lukas Hydraulik GmbH.
Directorships: Board member of bwcon (Baden-Württemberg Connected). He is member of Rotary Stuttgart and also a fellow of the Alumni of St. Gallen University

Heiko Geissler, Associate Director
Education: MBA , Phd
Background: Bertelsmann AG as Executive Vice President for Corporate Development

2298 3I UK 3i Group
16 Palace Street
London SW1E 5JD
United Kingdom

Phone: 44-2079283131 Fax: 44-2079753232
e-mail: london@3i.com
web: www.3i.com

Mission Statement: Actively seeking new investments.
Geographic Preference: United Kingdom, USA, Asia, Europe
Fund Size: $1.18 Billion
Founded: 1995
Average Investment: $95.04 Million
Minimum Investment: $2.37 Million
Investment Criteria: Start-up and Early-Stage
Industry Group Preference: All Sectors Considered
Portfolio Companies: National Car Parks, Fairline Boats Holdings Ltd, Sparrowhawk Media, Hobbs, Bowater Building Products Limited, Bowater Home Improvements Limited, Huntswood CTC Ltd, Fairways Group (UK), Adande Refrigeration, Variable Message Signs, PD Services Ltd, Pap

Key Executives:
Masaaki Fudeuchi, Senior Director
e-mail: london@3i.com
Education: MBA , Degree in Politics, Philosophy and Economics
Background: Financial and strategy consultant for Arthur Andersen, RSM Robson Rhodes and the Kalchas Group
Rowena Gracey, Senior Associate
e-mail: london@3i.com
Education: Degree in Mathematics and Management, CPA
Background: Birmingham
Directorships: Member of the Growth Capital leadership team and UK Growth Capital management group.

2299 3M UNITEK
Hermeslaan 7
Diegem 1831
Belgium

Phone: 02-7225111 Fax: 02-7200225
e-mail: 3munitek.be@mmm.com
web: www.3m.com

Mission Statement: A diversified technology company serving customers and communities with innovative products and services. Each of our seven businesses has earned leading global market positions.
Industry Group Preference: Consumer Products, Electronics, Health Related, Industrial, Safety and Graphics, Energy

Key Executives:
Inge G. Thulin, Chairman, President & Chief Executive Officer
Education: MBA, Economics & Marketing, Gothenburg University/IHM Business School;
David W. Meline, Senior Vice President & Chief Financial Officer

2300 3T CAPITAL
46, rue Barrault
Paris 75634
France

e-mail: contact@3tcapital.com
web: www.3tcapital.com

Mission Statement: Focusing on technology transfer and innovative companies within the Information Technology and

Communication sector from their seed, start-up and early-stage phases, and a partner with Institut Mines Telecom, Telecom Technologies Transfert (3T) is funded by the European Investment Fund, CDC Entreprises, within the framework of FSI France Investissement program, and Institut Mines Telecom. Founded by seasoned entrepreneurs with strong track record launching and growing technology companies, including successful transaction sales, Telecom Technologies Transfert (3T) is an independently managed Investment Fund.

Investment Criteria: Seed-Stage, Startup, Early-Stage
Industry Group Preference: Information Technology, Communications
Portfolio Companies: Recommerce Solutions, Ubicast, Go2mo, Luceor Wimesh Systems, Skerou, MuteeGaming.com, Plan Me Up, Green Bureau, Izypeo, Innes

Key Executives:
  Daniel Caclin, Managing Partner
  e-mail: daniel.caclin@3tcapital.com

2301 3TS CAPITAL PARTNERS 3i Group plc
web: www.3tscapital.com

Mission Statement: 3TS Capital Partners identifies, evaluates and recommends investments for the Funds it is advising. After the investment is made, 3TS represents the Fund either directly and/or with non-executive directors with positions on the Board and works with the management to fully support the development of the investee companies. Investors in the Funds include 3i, Cisco, Sitra, EBRD, and KfW among others.

Geographic Preference: Central Europe, Eastern Europe
Fund Size: $330 million Euro
Average Investment: $2 - $10 million Euro
Investment Criteria: Expansion Capital, Buyouts
Industry Group Preference: Technology, Telecommunications, Media, Marketing, Business Products & Services, Financial Services, Healthcare Services, Environment, Energy, Retail, Consumer & Leisure, Clean Technology, Pharmaceuticals, Software, Information Technology
Portfolio Companies: Expander, TMS Brokers, Romprest Service SA, Mobiltel EAD, Orange Slovensko, Elit Teknoloji, BKS Cable, InternetCorp, STK, ClickAd, Avangate, SolveDirect Service Management, LogMeIn, Systinet Corporation, PXP Group, Centrul Medical Unirea, Cycleenergy, Netretail Holding, Komex

Other Locations:
  Wahringer Strasse 3/15 A
  A-1090 Vienna
  Austria
  Phone: +43 1 402 36 79

  Americka 23
  Prague 2 120 00
  Czech Republic
  Phone: +420 225 990 847 **Fax:** +420 225 990 857

  ul.Sienna 72/7
  00-833 Warsaw
  Poland
  Phone: +48 22 890 22 15

  50-52 Putul lui Zamfir St.
  Et.2, Ap.5
  Bucharest 1, RO-011367
  Romania
  Phone: +40 3 1100 0259

  Buyukdere Caddesi Ecza
  Sokak Safter Is Merkezi
  Kat:6
  Levent 34430 Istanbul
  Turkey
  Phone: +90 212 325 7653

Key Executives:
  Pekka Santeri Maki, Managing Partner, Budapest/Vienna
  e-mail: pmaki@3tscapital.com
  Education: Helsinki University of Technology; Universidad Cumplutense in Madrid; Wirschaftsuniversitat Vienna
  Background: Managing Partner, Red Catalyst Ltd
  Jiri Benes, Partner
  e-mail: jbenes@3tscapital.com
  Education: BA and MA, Prague School of Economics
  Zbigniew Lapinski, Partner
  e-mail: zlapinski@3tscapital.com
  Education: M.Sc., Warsaw School of Economics
  Mihai Sfintescu, Partner
  e-mail: msfintescu@3tscapital.com
  Education: MBA, University of Washington
  Elbruz Yilmaz, Investment Manager
  e-mail: eyilmaz@3tscapital.com
  Education: Economics, Ege University (Turkey); MBA, Pittsburg State University

2302 3W VENTURES Latour & Zuberbuhler GmbH
Oberdorfstrasse 124
Herisau 9100
Switzerland

web: www.3wventures.com

Mission Statement: We are funding or co-funding international internet startups up to USD 250,000.

Geographic Preference: Switzerland
Average Investment: CHF50'000 - CHF500'000
Industry Group Preference: Healthcare, Information Technology, Telecommunications, Gaming, New Media
Portfolio Companies: ForAtable.com, Lunchgate.ch, Inverstiere.ch, Blankpage AG, UEPAA!!, Shadow Government, Youblisher.com, Nanotion, Quitt.ch, Domo Safety, Hyperweek.net, Fontself.com, Medudem.com, Touchtown.ch, Annularspace, Store-Locator.com,

Key Executives:
  Yves Latour, Founding Partner
  Arvin Zuberbuehler, Founding Partner

2303 3i GROUP PLC
16 Palace Street
London SW1E 5JD
United Kingdom

Phone: 44-2079753131 **Fax:** 44-2079753232
web: www.3i.com

Mission Statement: An international investor, 3i Group PLC works with talented management teams to develop businesses that have potential for significant growth.

Geographic Preference: Worldwide
Fund Size: $1.3 billion
Average Investment: $100 - $300 million
Investment Criteria: High Growth, Mid-Market
Industry Group Preference: Business Products & Services, Financial Services, Industrial Services, Energy, Consumer Products, Consumer Services, Healthcare, Technology, Media, Telecommunications, Infrastructure
Portfolio Companies: ACR Capital Holdings, Action, AESSEAL, Agent Provocateur Limited, Amor GmbH, Aspen Pumps, Basic-Fit, BVG India, Cerenicimo, Christ, Dynatect Manufacturing, Element Materials Technology, Eltel Networks Oy, ESG, Etanco, EURO-DIESEL, GEKA GmbH, GIF, GO Outdoors, Hobbs, JMJ Associates, Lekolar, Loxam, Mayborn Group, Memora Inversiones Funerarias, MKM Building Supplies, Navayuga Engineering Company, OneMed Group, Polyconcept, Q Holding, Quintiles Transnational, Refresco Gerber, Scandlines, SLR Consulting Limited, UFO Movietz Pvt, Weener Plastic Packaging Group
  Calle Ruiz de Alarcon n 12-2-B
  Madrid 28014

Spain
Phone: 34-915214419 Fax: 34-915219819

Cornelis Schuytstraat 72
Amsterdam 1071 JL
Netherlands
Phone: 31-203057444 Fax: 31-203057455

3 Rue Paul Cezanne
Paris 75008
France
Phone: 33-173151100

OpernTurm
Bockenheimer Landstrabe 2-4
Frankfurt 60306
Germany

PO Box 7847
Stockholm 10399
Sweden
Phone: 46-850610100 Fax: 46-850621130

6 Battery Road
Level 42, Unit 7
Singapore 049909
Singapore
Phone: 65-62322937 Fax: 65-62322943

3rd Floor, Nicholas Piramal Tower
Peninsula Park
Ganpatrao Kadam Marg
Mumbai 400 013
India
Phone: 91-22-66523131 Fax: 91-22-66523141

One Grand Central Place
60 East 42nd Street
Suite 4100
New York, NY 10165
Phone: 212-848-1400 Fax: 212-848-1401

Key Executives:
Simon Borrows, Chief Executive
Education: University of London; MBA, London Business School
Background: Founder/Co-President, Greenhill; CEO, Baring Brothers International Limited; Corporate Finance, Morgan Grenfell
Directorships: The British Land Company PLC
Julia Wilson, Group Finance Director
Background: Arthur Andersen; Harrison PLC; Tomkins PLC; Group Tax Director, Cable & Wireless PLC
Directorships: Legal & General Group PLC
Menno Antal, Managing Partner/Co-Head, Private Equity
Education: MSc, Electrical Engineering, Delft University of Technology; MBA, IMD Switzerland
Background: Managing Director, Benelux; Heineken
Jeremy Ghose, Managing Partner/Debt Management CEO
Education: BA, Business Administration
Background: Executive Officer, Mizuho Corporate Bank
Alan Giddins, Managing Partner/Co-Head, Private Equity
Background: Managing Director, Societe Generale; Accountant, KPMG
Phil White, Managing Partner, Infrastructure
Education: MBA, London Business School
Background: Division Director, Infrastructure Funds, MacQuarie Group; Barclays; WestLB
Directorships: Anglian Water Group, Elenia
Ben Loomes, Managing Partner, Infrastructure/Group Strategy Director
Education: BA, Masters of Science, Experimental & Theoretical Physics, University of Cambridge
Background: Goldman Sachs; Greenhill; Morgan Stanley

2304 AAC CAPITAL PARTNERS
ITO Tower, 21st Floor
Gustav Mahlerplein 106
MA Amsterdam 1082
Netherlands

Phone: 31-203331326
e-mail: info@aaccapitalpartners.com

Mission Statement: AAC Capital Partners Holding is an investment management company with 1.7 billion Euro under management and two specialized investment funds, dedicated to mid-market buyouts in North-Western Europe.

Geographic Preference: Europe
Fund Size: 1.7 Billion Euro
Investment Criteria: Middle-Market Buyouts
Portfolio Companies: Exie, iRex Technologies, PIERIS Proteolab, NexWave Solutions

Key Executives:
Gerben Kujiper, Chairman
e-mail: gerben.kuijper@aaccapitalpartners.com
Education: Masters, Business Economics, Erasmus University
Background: ABN AMRO
John de Die, CFO/COO
e-mail: john.de.die@aaccapitalpartners.com
Education: MS, Econometrics & Mathematical Economics, Tirburg University
Background: SVP, Finance, KLM Royal Dutch Airlines

2305 AAVISHKAAR
13B, 6th Floor, Techniplex II, IT Park
Off Veer Sarvarkar Fly Over, Goregaon West
Mumbai 400 062
India

Phone: 91-2261248900 Fax: 91-2261248930
e-mail: funds@aavishkaar.org
web: www.aavishkaar.in

Mission Statement: Aavishkaar is a pioneer in early stage investing in the country and has been active in the space for over a decade. We are guided by the fundamental belief that investing in early stage entrepreneurial ventures can not only deliver commercial returns, but also bring about significant efficiencies and developmental impact to rural and underserved communities. Over time, Aavishkaar has built a track record of high impact scalable enterprises in its portfolio that span across seven key sectors, namely Agriculture and Dairy, Education, Energy, Handicrafts, Health, Water and Sanitation, Technology for Development and Microfinance and Financial Inclusion.

Geographic Preference: India
Investment Criteria: Early-Stage
Industry Group Preference: Agriculture, Education, Energy, Healthcare, Water, Sanitation, Technology, Rural Innovations, Handicrafts, Agriculture
Portfolio Companies: Mantra Dairy, INI Farms, Zameen Organic, Vaatsalya, GV Meditech, Swas Healthcare, MeraDoctor, Waterlife, Saraplast, B2R Technologies, Net Systems Informatics, Shree Kamdhenu Electronics, Vortex Engineering, Butterfly Fields, Karadi Tales Company, Rangusutra, Desert Artisans, Servals Automation, Vana Vidyut Private Ltd, Share Microfin, BASIX Group, Equitas, Grameen Koota, Utkarsh Microfinance, Suryoday Micro Finance, Belstar Investment

Key Executives:
Vineet Rai, Partner/Managing Director
Education: Indian Institute of Forest Management
Background: Co-Founder, Intellecap
P Pradeep, Partner/Executive Director
Education: MBA, Finance, Bachelor of Applied Science
Directorships: Belstar, Vaatsayla, Grameen Koota, Servals Automation

Venture Capital & Private Equity Firms / International Firms

2306 AB CAPITAL & INVESTMENT CORPORATION The Phinma Group
Units 1401-1403, 14th Floor Tower One & Excha
Ayala Triangle, Ayala Avenue
Metro Manila
Makati City 1226
Philippines

Phone: 632-8987555 Fax: 632-8987596
e-mail: customerservice@abcapital.com.ph
web: www.abcapitalonline.com

Mission Statement: Actively seeking new investments.
Geographic Preference: Philippines
Fund Size: $990 Million
Founded: 1980
Investment Criteria: Early Stage, Expansion, Startup
Industry Group Preference: Computer Hardware & Software, Consumer Services, Telecommunications

Key Executives:
Frank S. Gaisano, Chairman & Chief Executive Officer
e-mail: customerservice@abcapitalonline.com
Education: ME
Background: Director Cebu Holdings, Inc., Mapfre Asian Insurance Corporation, Governor and EVP of the Phil. Assoc.
Directorships: Trustee and Treasurer of the Phil. Stock Exhange Foundation, Inc
Senen L. Matoto, President and Chief Operating Officer

2307 ABB TECHNOLOGY VENTURES
Affolternstrasse 44
PO Box 8131
Zurich CH-8050
Switzerland

Phone: 41-43 317 7111 Fax: 41-43317 4420
web: new.abb.com/us

Mission Statement: Headquartered in Zurich, with offices in Silicon Valley and Washington, D.C., ABB Technology Ventures (ATV) invests in companies of strategic interest to ABB at all stages and in all parts of the world. Comprised of ABB veterans and seasoned venture capitalist professionals, ATV invests in high potential energy technology companies that improve performance while lowering environmental impact and which can benefit from ABB's technology development resources and global market access.

Geographic Preference: North America, Switzerland
Founded: 1988
Average Investment: $1 - $20 million
Industry Group Preference: Energy, Clean Technology, Wind Power
Portfolio Companies: Trilliant, Industrial Defender, Power Assure, Pentalum, Aquamarine Power, ECOtality, Validus DC Systems, TaKaDu, GreenVolts

Key Executives:
Alanna Abrahamson, Head of Investors Relations
Education: University of Bombay; LLM, University of Virginia School of Law; MBA, Harvard Business School
Background: Prudential, GE Capital

2308 ABINGWORTH MANAGEMENT LIMITED
38 Jermyn Street
London SW1Y 6DN
United Kingdom

Phone: 44-02075341500 Fax: 44-02072870480
e-mail: info@abingworth.com
web: www.abingworth.com

Mission Statement: Active investor in biotechnology and healthcare.
Geographic Preference: US, UK and Europe
Fund Size: $700 Million
Founded: 1973
Average Investment: $20-80 million
Minimum Investment: $1-20 Million
Investment Criteria: Seed, Startup, Other Early Stage, Expansion and Development, Purchase of Quoted Shares
Industry Group Preference: Biotechnology, Medical, Life Sciences
Portfolio Companies: Ablynx, Akubio, Alexza Molecular Delivery Corporation, Dynogen Pharmaceuticals, Fovea, Gynesonics, Novexel, Portola Pharmaceuticals, PowderMed, Syntaxin

Other Locations:
3000 Sand Hill Road
B1-145
Menlo Park, CA 94025
Phone: 650-9260600 Fax: 650-9269782

890 Winter Street
Suite 150
Waltham, MA 02451
Phone: 781-4668800 Fax: 781-4668813

Key Executives:
Stephen Bunting, Managing Partner
Education: Degree in Biological Chemistry
Background: Biotechnology Editor, PJB Publications
David Leathers, Special Partner
e-mail: leathers@abingworth.com
Education: Chartered Accountant
Background: Director, Rothschild Asset Management; Biotechnology Investments Limited, GeneMedicine, GenPharm International and Pharming
Jonathan MacQuitty, Partner
e-mail: abingwthus@aol.com
Education: MA, Chemistry, Oxford University; PhD, University of Sussex; MBA, Stanford University
Background: Board of the Biotechnology Industry Organisation and is a Director of a number of biotech companies
Directorships: President of US Location
James Abell, Partner and CFO
e-mail: abell@abingworth.com
Education: Biology Degree, Chartered accountant
Background: KPMA; Consultant, Medical Research Council; Director, Cambridge Genetics; Chief Financial Officer, Prolifix Limited
Directorships: CFO
David Mayer, Partner
Education: PhD in biochemistry from Aston University, Birmingham, and a BSc in biology from Queen Mary College, London
Background: Pan-European Pharmaceuticals Analyst at investment bank, Dresdner Kleinwort Benson, Head of the Policy Unit at the Wellcome Trust
John Heard, Executive Partner and General Counsel
e-mail: info@abingworth.com
Education: PhD in Biological Sciences
Background: N M Rothschild & Sons as Advisor to Investments Limited
Directorships: Astex Technology, Aurora Biosciences, Cantab Pharmaceuticals, Devgen, Genetic Therapy, Hexagen and 3-Dimensional Pharmaceuticals.
John Shields, Executive Partner, Science and Technology
Education: PhD in Immunology, University of Glasgow
Background: Senior VP, Research, Cantab Pharmaceuticals; Glaxo Institute for Molecular Biology; Research Positions, Institute of Child Health, the University of London

2309 ABM AMRO CAPITAL FRANCE ABN AMRO Group
9 Avenue Matignon
Paris 75008
France

Phone: 33-0153936900 Fax: 33-0153936925

Venture Capital & Private Equity Firms / International Firms

Mission Statement: Actively seeking new investments. All sectors considered except banking, defense, real estate.
Geographic Preference: France
Fund Size: $118 Million
Founded: 2001
Average Investment: $59 Million
Minimum Investment: $35.6 Million
Investment Criteria: LBO, MBI
Industry Group Preference: All Sectors Considered
Portfolio Companies: Acteon, Tergal, Fibers, Cotterlaz, Bonna Sabla, JEC, Retif, Groupe Doucet, Salins

2310 ABOA VENTURE MANAGEMENT OY
Kluuvikatu 5
Helsinki 00100
Finland

Phone: 020-7798620 Fax: 358-24107779
e-mail: info@aboaventure.fi

Mission Statement: Aboa Venture has established itself as Western Finland's leading venture capital company. Aboa Venture offers equity financing and financing solutions, and a commitment to development work, and the shared risk with the entrepreneur.
Geographic Preference: Finland
Fund Size: $100 Million
Founded: 1994
Average Investment: $1.18 Million
Minimum Investment: $0.23 Million
Investment Criteria: Invests in unlisted Finnish small and medium-sized companies
Industry Group Preference: Life Sciences, Electronic Technology, Metals, Engineering
Portfolio Companies: Bio-Nobile Oy, BioTie Therapies Oyj, FIT Biotech Oyj, Hormos Medical Ltd Oy, Juvantia Pharma Ltd Oy, Bitboys Oy, Sanako Corporation, Mios e-Solutions Oy, Nisamest Oy, TR-Tech. Int Oy, Dino Lift Oy, DWT-Engineering Oy, Finn Lamex Safety Glass Oy, Hydrovoima

2311 ABRIS CAPITAL
Grzybowska Park
ul. Grzybowska 5A
Warsaw 00-132
Poland

Phone: 48-225645858 Fax: 48-225645859
e-mail: warsaw@abris-capital.com
web: www.abris-capital.com

Key Executives:
Neil Milne, Managing Partner

2312 ABRT VENTURE FUND
5, Building 4, Bersenevskaya
emb. Golden Island
Moscow 119072
Russia

Phone: 7-812-335-5545
e-mail: project@abrtfund.com
web: www.abrtfund.com

Mission Statement: ABRT Venture Fund helps entrepreneurs build world-class software companies.
Investment Criteria: Seed, Startup, Early-Stage, Growth-Stage
Industry Group Preference: Software, Consumer Software, SaaS, Internet, New Media, Mobility
Portfolio Companies: HomeMe.ru, StarWind Software, Acronis, InvisibleCRM, OKTOGO, Drimmi, Veeam Software, KupiVIP, AutomationQA
Key Executives:
Andrei Baronov, Partner
Education: Master's Degree, PhD, Physics & Technology, Moscow Institute of Physics & Technology
Background: R&D Director, Microsoft Business Unit, Quest

2313 ABU DHABI INVESTMENT AUTHORITY
211 Corniche Street
P.O. Box 3600
Abu Dhabi
United Arab Emirates

Phone: 971-24150000 Fax: 971-24151000
web: www.adia.ae

Mission Statement: Actively seeking new investments.
Geographic Preference: UAE
Fund Size: $2 Billion
Founded: 1977
Investment Criteria: Leveraged Buyout, Management Buyout, Recapitalization, Second Stage
Industry Group Preference: Advertising, Broadcasting, Business to Business, Communications, Equipment, Computer Related, Computer Hardware & Software, Consumer Services, Diversified, Electronic Technology, Entertainment, Film, Financial Services, Food Services
Key Executives:
Sheikh Khalifa bin Zayed Al Nahyan, Chairman
Sheikh Hamed bin Zayed Al Nahyan, Managing Director

2314 ACACIA CAPITAL PARTNERS
CPCI, Capital Park
Fullbourn, Cambridge CB21 5XE
United Kingdom

Phone: 44-2072997399
e-mail: info@acaciacp.com
web: www.acaciacp.com

Mission Statement: Acacia Capital Partners is an independent management company made up of experienced venture capitalists with in-depth operational and investment management experience. We invest in later stage innovative technology companies both directly and indirectly.
Investment Criteria: Later-Stage
Industry Group Preference: Technology
Portfolio Companies: Skinkers, Mirics Semiconductor, Xmos, Lionhead Studios, Solarflame Communications, Shazam, Empower, Automsoft, Clariteam
Key Executives:
Christopher Smart, General Partner
Education: MSc, Physics, Durban University; MSc, Management, Imperial College, London University
Directorships: Automsoft International, Mirics Semiconductor, Shazam, Solarflare

2315 ACCEDE CAPITAL
Level 11, 1 Chifley Square
Sydney NSW 2000
Australia

Phone: 61-282330030 Fax: 61-282330031

Mission Statement: Accede Capital is an early stage focused venture capital firm committed to backing our entrepreneurs build great companies. Our team has over 60 years collective experience in venture capital and working with early stage technology companies, so we understand what it takes to build great technology companies and create significant shareholder value.
Investment Criteria: Early-Stage
Industry Group Preference: Technology
Portfolio Companies: Dilithium Networks, G2 Microsystems, Sensory Networks, ManageSoft, Finisar
Key Executives:
Chris Beare, Chairman/General Partner
Education: BSc, BE, PhD, Adelaide University; MBA,

Harvard Business School
Background: CEO, Hambros; CEO, Radiata

2316 ACCELMED
6 Hachoshilm St
6 Floor
PO Box 2014
Herzliya Pituach 46120
Israel

Phone: 972-97885599 **Fax:** 972-99588594
e-mail: Amir@accelmed.com
web: www.accelmed.co.il

Mission Statement: Accelmed is a private equity investment firm focused on long-term value creation for medical device companies. Accelmed invests in small and mid-cap private and public companies.

Geographic Preference: Israel
Industry Group Preference: Medical Devices, Life Sciences
Portfolio Companies: Cardiapex, CariHeal, EndoSpan, Eximo Medical, MCS/Medical Compression Systems, NLT Spine, PeerMedical, Pi-R Squared, Valcare Medical

Key Executives:
Mori Arkin, Chairman
Education: Tel Aviv University
Background: Chairman, Agis Industries

2317 ACCENT EQUITY PARTNERS
Lime Grove House
Green Street, St Helier
Jersey JE1 2ST
Channel Islands

Phone: 46-8-545-07300 **Fax:** 46-8-545-07329
e-mail: info@accentequityfunds.com
web: www.accentequity.se

Mission Statement: Accent is a group of private equity funds focusing on investments in lower mid-market buyout and later-stage expansion capital transactions in the Nordic region.

Geographic Preference: Nordic Region
Founded: 1994
Investment Criteria: Mid-Market Buyouts
Industry Group Preference: Diversified
Portfolio Companies: AR Carton, Autotube, Aviator, Bergteamet, Candyking, Corvara, DJO, Hooks, Jetul, Mont Blanc, NSS, RenoNorden, ScandBook, Scandic Hotels, Troax

Key Executives:
Ian Lambert, Director
Education: BSc, English & Social Sciences, Stockholm University; BSc, Journalism & Communcation, Stockhold School of Journalism
Background: Vice President, KF Industri AB

2318 ACCENTURE TECHNOLOGY VENTURES
1 Plantation Place
30 Fenchurch Street
London EC3M 3BD
United Kingdom

Phone: 44-2078444000 **Fax:** 44-2078444444
web: www.accenture.com

Mission Statement: Accenture Technology Ventures is the venture capital unit of Accenture. Our mission is to help entrepreneurs build great companies that can transform entire industries, create new markets and generate superior economic returns.

Geographic Preference: Americas, Asia Pacific, Europe / Middle East / Africa (EMEA)
Fund Size: $1.5 Billion
Average Investment: $7.5 Million
Minimum Investment: $2 Million
Investment Criteria: Early Stage, Expansion/Development
Industry Group Preference: Consumer Services, Business to Business, Wireless Technologies, Technology, Infrastructure, Management, Marketing

Key Executives:
Pierre Nanterme, Chairman & CEO
Background: Managing partner of ventures and alliances in Accenture's Communications & High Tech operating group, managing partner of Accenture's outsourcing group in the Americas.
Directorships: Roup director-sales development, managing partner of Accenture's corporate development activities in the Americas.
Jo Deblaere, Chief Operating Officer
Background: HSBC Midland Montagu
Directorships: Marketing Director, Global Financial Markets .
Gianfranco Casati, Group Chief Executive-Growth Markets
Background: Group chief executive of the Communications & High Tech Operating group, Managing partner for Accenture's operations.
Directorships: Chief Operating Officer-Client Services.
Stephen J Rohleder, Group Chief Executive-Health & Public Service
Background: Managing partner - Accenture's Government Operating Group U.S , Accenture's U.S. Federal operating unit.
Directorships: Group Chief Executive of Accenture's global Government operating group.
Michael J. Salvino, Group Chief Executive-Business Process Outsourcing
Background: Managing partner-Practice Process and Quality, Country Managing Partner & Regional managing Partner for Italy, Greece and Turkey.
Directorships: Chief Financial Officer, capital risk officer, chief risk officer, treasurer and managing partner of corporate matters.
Shawn Collinson, Chief Strategy Officer
Education: Oxford University
Background: Managing Partner of the Products-Europe operating unit, global managing partner for our Automotive, Industrial and Travel & Transportation industry groups, Pharmaceuticals & Medical Products group in Europe.

2319 ACCERA AG
Weinheimer Str. 64a
Mannheim 68309
Germany

Phone: 49-6211815370 **Fax:** 49-62118153799
e-mail: info@accera.de
web: www.accera.de

Mission Statement: Specializes in investments in the renewable energy sector.

Founded: 2001
Industry Group Preference: Renewable Energy, Energy
Portfolio Companies: EPV Solar

Key Executives:
Marcus Rist, Executive Board Member
Education: MSc, Electrical Engineering
Background: MVV Energie AG

2320 ACCESS MEDICAL VENTURES
35 Windsor Road
North Haven, CT 06473-3045

Phone: 203-281-4585
e-mail: webinfo@accessmv.com
web: accessmv.com

Mission Statement: Access Medical Ventures is a U.S based venture capital fund that focuses specifically on investing and advancing medical device start-ups.

Geographic Preference: United States

Venture Capital & Private Equity Firms / International Firms

Investment Criteria: Early-Stage
Industry Group Preference: Medical Devices
Portfolio Companies: CartiHeal, MinInvasive Orthopedic Solutions, AVMedical Dialysis Access Management, Tradeo, E-Motion Medical Ltd., Nitiloop, Samson Neuro Sciences, Latrima Medical
Key Executives:
  Michael Tal, Partner
  Education: MD, Hadassah Medical School, MCP, Hahnemann University, Yale University; MBA, Yale University
  Background: Associate Professor of Radiology, Yale University School of Medicine
  Limor Sandach, Partner
  Education: BSc, Chemical Engineering, Master of Engineering, Technion, Israel Institute
  Background: Partner, 7health Ventures

2321 ACE & COMPANY
30 Rue du Rhone
Geneva 1204
Switzerland

Phone: 41-223113333 Fax: 41-223116666
e-mail: info@aceandcompany.com
web: www.aceandcompany.com

Mission Statement: ACE & Company Development Group Ltd., is a diversified investment and advisory group specialized in direct investments in emerging markets and emerging industries.
Geographic Preference: United States, Europe, Middle East
Founded: 2005
Investment Criteria: Angel, Growth-Stage, Buyout Stage, Private Equity Secondaries
Industry Group Preference: Consumer Products, Consumer Services, Technology, Financial Services
Portfolio Companies: Acunote, Alpha Networks, Adgrok, Aerofs, Airlease, Apportable, Carthage Agricultural Company, Carwoo!, DotCloud, Gazillion Entertainment, Etacts, FlightCaster, Genagro, GoCardless, Global Blue, HighlightCam, Inpulse, Libero, Lucidity Lights, MidNox, Minomonsters, Movity, PayPlug, Paystack, PlanGrid, Priceonomics, Rescale, StepStone, Philadelphia Energy Solutions, Tok & Stok, RethinkDB, Terra Firma, Skysheet, StudyEdge, Taptolearn, Vayable, Verbling, Virool, Sensible Organics, Seventh Generation, Union Agriculture Group, Y Combinator
Key Executives:
  Adam Said, Co-Founder
  Christopher Kile, Co-Founder
  Sherif Elhalwagy, Co-Founder

2322 ACE VENTURE CAPITAL LIMITED
Dongwoo B/D
Mirae Asset Venture Tower, 16th Floor
Kangnam-Gu
Seoul 135-280
Korea

Phone: 82-234522202 Fax: 82-234522566
web: www.acecapventures.com

Mission Statement: Actively seeking new investments.
Geographic Preference: Korea, Japan
Founded: 2000
Investment Criteria: Seed, Start-Up, Expansion, Buyouts
Industry Group Preference: Information Technology, Biotechnology, Services, Semiconductors, Telecommunications, Electronic Technology, Internet Technology
Key Executives:
  Howard Greenberg, President & Founder
  Background: Board of Director of KSIA (Korea Semiconductor Industry Association)
  Directorships: Chairman of SEMI (Semiconductor Equipment's and Materials International).

2323 ACELERADORA
Contour Avenue
6594-17 Floor
Savassi-Belo Horizonte/MG 30110-044
Brazil

Mission Statement: Aceleradora supports startups with seed capital and management, and help companies in their innovation strategy.
Founded: 2008
Investment Criteria: Seed-Stage, Startup
Portfolio Companies: Acessozero, Anuncie La, Crowdtest, Ningo, Pligus
Key Executives:
  Yuri Gitahy, Founder
  Background: CTO, Vetta Technologies; Systems Engineering Manager, UOL

2324 ACKERMANS & VAN HAAREN
Begijnenvest 113
Antwerpen 2000
Belgium

Phone: 32-32318770 Fax: 32-32252533
e-mail: info@avh.be
web: en.avh.be/home.aspx

Mission Statement: Actively seeking new investments.
Geographic Preference: Belgium, France, Luxembourg, Netherlands
Fund Size: 3.1 Billion
Founded: 1994
Investment Criteria: Bridge, Expansion - development, Replacement, Small buyout (£m equity), Mid market buyout (15M-150m equity), Large buyout (150m-300m equity), Public to private, Privatisation
Industry Group Preference: All Sectors Considered
Portfolio Companies: Alural Group, Cindu International, Corn. Van Loocke, Hertel Holding, IDOC, IlloSpear, NMC, Oleon Holding, Synvest.
Key Executives:
  Luc Bertrand, Executive director, Chairman EC
  e-mail: marc.depauw@sofinim.be
  Education: Master of Economics
  Background: Societe Nationale d'Investissement (General Manager), Civil Service.
  Andre-Xavier Cooreman, Chief Operating Officer

2325 ACME LABS
Pauler utca 12
IV/1
Budapest H-1013
Hungary

Mission Statement: ACME Labs provides not just funding, but the advice, expertise, and relationships to help entrepreneurs shape and realize their vision. ACME Labs is not just an accelerator, but an integrated strategic advisory, corporate finance, and venture capital practice.
Geographic Preference: Europe
Investment Criteria: Early-Stage
Industry Group Preference: Digital Media & Marketing, Financial Services, Clean Technology, Life Sciences
Portfolio Companies: Secure Directory, Stereocake, Crossway Media Solutions, Shinrai
Key Executives:
  Gyuri Karady, Chairman
  Education: McGill University; Doctorate in Engineering, Harvard University
  Background: Baring Private Equity/Baring Crilius, Julius Baer Capital

Venture Capital & Private Equity Firms / International Firms

2326 ACONCAGUA VENTURES
Humboldt 1967
2§ Floor
Buenos Aires C1414CTU
Argentina

Phone: 54-1155562673
web: www.aconcaguaventures.com

Mission Statement: Aconcagua Ventures is an early-stage hi-tech venture capital firm investing in Argentina and Latinamerica. Our goal is to generate outstanding returns for our investors and, by developing our portfolio, to help transform the regional economical landscape towards a more competitive model generating value from knowledge.

Geographic Preference: Argentina, Latin America
Investment Criteria: Early-Stage
Industry Group Preference: High Technology, Software, Internet, Communications, Medical Devices
Portfolio Companies: Container Consultants & Systems, Core Security Technologies, Keepcon, Popego

Key Executives:
Jonatan Altszul, Co-Founder/Managing Partner
Background: Co-Founder, Core Security Technologies; Special Projects Group, Argentine Tax Agency

2327 ACRUX LIMITED
103-113 Stanley Street
West Melbourne VIC 3003
Australia

Phone: 61-383790100 Fax: 61-383790101
web: www.acrux.com.au

Mission Statement: Actively seeking new investments in specialty pharmaceutical business products.

Geographic Preference: Australia
Fund Size: $30 Million
Founded: 1998
Average Investment: $1-5 Million
Minimum Investment: $500,000
Investment Criteria: Early Stage, Expansion
Industry Group Preference: Biotechnology, Pharmaceuticals

Key Executives:
Ross Dobinson Bbus, Executive Chairman
e-mail: info@acrux.com.au
Education: PhD
Background: Research and teaching appointments at universities in England, Australia and the USA and was on the founding Board of Directors of the International Pharmaceutical Aerosol Consortium - Regulatory Science.
Tony Di Pietro, Chief Financial Officer and Company Secretary

2328 ACT VENTURE CAPITAL LIMITED
Richview Office Park, Clonskeagh
Dublin 14
Ireland

Phone: 353-12600966 Fax: 353-12600538
e-mail: info@actvc.ie
web: www.actventure.ie

Mission Statement: ACT Venture Capital is Ireland's leading independent venture capital company.

Geographic Preference: Ireland & the UK
Fund Size: $415 Million
Founded: 1994
Average Investment: $200,000 - $10 million
Minimum Investment: $890,000
Investment Criteria: Invests in growth-oriented companies led by exceptional entrepreneurs with strong management team
Industry Group Preference: Software, Communications, Internet Technology, Hardware, Life Sciences
Portfolio Companies: Raidtec Corporation, MDS Gateways, Intense Photonics, Massana, Kymata, Stockbyte, CR2, Cape Clear, ACRA Control, Piercom, Scietific Systems, QUMAS, ASH Technologies, TV Three, Life Style, ODENBERG

Key Executives:
Niall Carroll, Managing Partner
Education: BE, FMCA, FIMC, FIBI, Electrical Engineering, University College, Dublin; Fellow, Chartered Institute of Management Accountants; Fellow, Institute of Management Consultants
Background: Consumer Electronics Division of General Electric of the USA and became Manager - Quality Control in the United States and Ireland, general management and financial divisions of PA Management Consultants in Ireland, Managing Director of AIB Venture Capital
Directorships: Founder.
John Flynn, Managing Director
Education: Commerce, Chartered Accountant, Business Strategy
Background: KPMG in Dublin from 1976 to 1987, Director of AIB Corporate Finance from 1987 to 1984,
John O'Sullivan, Director of ACT Venture Capital
Education: BE, Chemical Engineering, MIE
Background: Director of AIB Venture Capital and Allied Combined Trust
Debbie Rennick, Director of ACT
Education: Communications, DPA, FCA, Chartered Accountant
Background: Director of AIB Capital Markets Holdings (U.K.) and also acted as Operations and Finance Director of a large, AIB associated

2329 ACTIS
2 More London Riverside
London SE1 2JT
United Kingdom

Phone: 44-2072345000 Fax: 44-2072345010
e-mail: info@act.is
web: www.act.is

Mission Statement: Actively seeking new investments.

Geographic Preference: Africa, China, Malaysia, South Asia
Fund Size: $5.0 Billion
Founded: 1948
Average Investment: $100 Million
Minimum Investment: $5 Million
Investment Criteria: Early Stage, Expansion and Development Capital, Replacement Capital, Buyout and Buyin
Industry Group Preference: Energy, Information Technology, Financial Services, Chemicals, Transportation, Telecommunications, Leisure, Manufacturing, Logistics, Tourism
Portfolio Companies: Glenmark Pharmaceuticals, Globeleq, Grain Bulk Handlers, Grameenphone, Housing Development Finance Corporation, Jyothy Laboratories, Lenco, Mengniu Dairy, Nitrex Chemicals, Orascom Telecom Algeria, Pacific Rim Palm Oil, Persianas, Platmin, Powercom

Key Executives:
Jonathon Bond, Partner
e-mail: info@act.is
Background: Head of HR for Citibank's commercial banking division in South Asia and Asia Pacific
Directorships: Head of Actis's Operations Group.
Torbjorn Caesar, Partner

2330 ACTIVA CAPITAL
203, Rue du Faubourg Saint-Honore
Paris 75008
France

Phone: 31-143125012 Fax: 31-143125013
web: www.activacapital.com

Venture Capital & Private Equity Firms / International Firms

Mission Statement: Activa Capital is an independent private equity company with a strong entrepreneurial spirit.
Fund Size: 500 million Euro
Average Investment: $30 Million - $200 Million
Investment Criteria: MBO, Spin-Off, Owner Buyout, Growth Capital, Build-Ups
Industry Group Preference: Consumer Products, Distribution, Business Products & Services, Healthcare, Pharmaceuticals, Media, Information Technology
Portfolio Companies: Armatis-Laser Contact, Privamista Group, Findis, Abrisud, Ergalis-Selpro-Plus RH, Albarelle, Bruno Saint Hilarie, Sport 2000, Creal, Logitrade, ProNatura

Key Executives:
   Charles Diehl, Partner
    Education: University of Geneva; MBA, Wharton School
    Background: Co-Founder, Barclays Private Equity France

2331 ACTIVE VENTURE PARTNERS
Paseo de Gracia 35
Atico
Barcelona 08007
Spain

Phone: 34-93-178-6868 **Fax:** 34-93-272-2436
web: www.active-vp.com

Mission Statement: ACTIVE was founded in Barcelona in 2002. We manage two funds, Molins Capital Inversion SCR SA and Amerigo Innvierte Spain Ventures FCR RS, whose vintage years are 2004 and 2010 respectively. Both are early stage venture capital funds that invest in technology related businesses.
Geographic Preference: Spain, Germany, Switzerland, Austria, Scandinavia
Founded: 2002
Average Investment: 500,000 - 4 million Euro
Investment Criteria: Early-Stage
Industry Group Preference: Technology, Tech Enabled Services, Enterprise Software, Consumer Internet, Consumer Media, Communications, Wireless, Security, Clean Technology
Portfolio Companies: Banebys, PackLink, Review Pro, SanaExpert, Uzerzoom, YD, Offerton Liveshopping, Restalo, Whisbi, Zyncro

Key Executives:
   Christopher Pommerening, Founding Partner
    Education: European Business School, London
    Background: Co-Founder, AutoScout24 Spain

2332 ACTOMEZZ Groupama Private Equity SA
49 avenue d'Iena
Paris 75116
France

Phone: 33-153935151 **Fax:** 33-153935154

Mission Statement: ActoMezz primarily acts as an arranger of mezzanine financing and sometimes as a minority shareholder in two areas: investment alongside private equity funds, and investment alongside management teams who wish to increase their ownership position following an initial successful LBO.
Fund Size: 187 million Euro
Average Investment: $5 and $30 million
Investment Criteria: Buyouts, Acquisitions, Later-Stage/Expansion Financing
Portfolio Companies: Emeraude International, Domidep, Lagarrique, Forma-Dis, Abrisud, Groupe Rougnon, Editions Oberthur, Sotralu, Marie-Laure PLV, Emeraude Chimie International, Ionisos, Faab-Fabicauto, World Freight Company International

Key Executives:
   Stephane Bergez, Head
   01-53-9351-71
   e-mail: sbergez@groupama-pe.fr
   Education: Master's Degree, Essec; Engineering Degree, Sup'Meca
   Background: Euler-Hermes SFAC

2333 ACUMEN VENTURES
Australia

web: www.acumenvc.com

Mission Statement: An early stage venture capital fund investing in world class startups emerging from South East Asia and Australia.
Geographic Preference: South East Asia, Australia
Average Investment: $100,000 - $2 million
Investment Criteria: Seed Stage, Series A
Industry Group Preference: Software, Internet, Mobile, E-Commerce & Manufacturing, Cloud Computing, Infrastructure, Enterprise Software, Technology-Enabled Services

Key Executives:
   Shane Cheek, Managing Partner
    Background: Founder, Method Advisory; Playford Capital

2334 ADARA VENTURE PARTNERS
Calle Jose Abascal, 58
Madrid 28003
Spain

Phone: 34-914517070 **Fax:** 34-91-451-7090
web: www.adaravp.com

Mission Statement: The creation of Adara was driven by our partners' belief that venture capital needs to bring more than money to the table. We have a strong focus on bringing in-house expertise to portfolio companies, helping them successfully develop and reach ambitious business objectives. We believe this results-orientated approach combined with strict opportunity selection optimizes success for our partners - both investors and entrepreneurs.
Industry Group Preference: Software Services, Mobile Services, Semiconductors, Telecommunications, Clean Technology
Portfolio Companies: ADD, AlienVault, Arque, Berggi, Cambridge Broadband Networks, Ecutronic, Elastix, Eyesquad, Genasys, Illuminate, OpenBravo, Polymita Technologies, Ring2Conferencing

Key Executives:
   Jesus Sainz, Chairman
    Background: CEO, Ogden Corp.; Parcque Tematico de Madrid SA

2335 ADASTRA
Schafflerstrabe 4
Munchen D-80333
Germany

Phone: 49-8971040850
e-mail: info@adastra.de
web: www.adastra.de

Mission Statement: AdAstra actively accompanies its portfolio companies towards the capital markets or other means of realizing their value potential. In this process, we see ourselves as a reliable and business-oriented investor. It is our aim to be integrated in the business concept as a genuine partner not only through our capital but also through active involvement, guidance and support.
Founded: 2000
Investment Criteria: Growth Capital
Industry Group Preference: Information Technology, Internet, E-Commerce & Manufacturing, Telecommunications
Portfolio Companies: Ask, Ask|Net, Baurer, Gomez, Suse, Trados

Key Executives:
   Ulrich Clemm, Founder/Managing Partner
    Background: Managing Director, HVB Beteiligungs GmbH

Venture Capital & Private Equity Firms / International Firms

2336 ADD VENTURE
Bersenevskaya Naberezhnaya 6
Resident Digital October, bg
Moscow
Russia

Phone: 8-9263398250
web: www.addventure.to

Mission Statement: AddVenture provides start-up investments for a quick launch, 'smart money' and business contacts. Internet grows fast as so does our appetite for web projects: AddVenture III fund will invest $50k to $1 mln, the most promising ones will get even more.
Geographic Preference: Russia
Founded: 2008
Minimum Investment: $50,000
Investment Criteria: Seed-Stage
Industry Group Preference: Internet, SaaS
Portfolio Companies: Delivery-club.ru, Pixonic, AlterGeo, Insales, Minibanda, Easyfinance.ru, Timetovisit.ru
Key Executives:
  Maxim Medvedev, Founder'/Managing Partner
  Background: Co-Founder, Pixonic
  Directorships: Pixonic

2337 ADLEVO CAPITAL CIM Fund Services
Les Cascades Building
Edith Cavell Street
Port Louis
Mauritius

Phone: 230-2129800
e-mail: info@adlevocapital.com
web: www.adlevocapital.com

Mission Statement: Adlevo Capital is a Mauritius-based private equity fund manager founded on the conviction that meaningful development in sub-Saharan Africa will be driven by the increasing application of technology to business processes across all sectors.
Geographic Preference: Africa
Industry Group Preference: Infrastructure, Consumer Services, Business Products & Services
Portfolio Companies: InterSwitch Limited, Paga, Rancard Solutions
Key Executives:
  Yemi Lalude, Managing Partner

2338 ADVANCE PROPERTY FUND
Level 5, 182 George Street
Sydney 2000
Australia

Phone: 61-894155655 Fax: 61- 292311673
Toll-Free: 1800-819935
e-mail: investorservices@advance.com.au
web: www.advance.com.au

Mission Statement: Actively seeking new investments.
Geographic Preference: Australia
Fund Size: $75 billion
Founded: 1999
Key Executives:
  Patrick Farrell, Head of Advance Investment Solutions

2339 ADVANTAGE PARTNERS
12F Sanno Park Tower
2-11-1 Nagata-cho
Minato-ku Tokyo 105-0001
Japan

Phone: 81-351570183 Fax: 81-351-570187
e-mail: master@advantagegroup.co.jp
web: www.advantagegroup.co.jp

Mission Statement: Investing in acquisitions, buy-outs, buy-ins and other private equity opportunities.
Geographic Preference: Japan
Fund Size: $387 Million
Founded: 1992
Average Investment: $20.85 Million
Minimum Investment: $8.34 Million
Investment Criteria: Early Stage, Expansion and Development Capital
Industry Group Preference: All Sectors Considered
Portfolio Companies: BMB Corp, Fuji Machinery Mfg. & Electronics Co. Ltd., Polygon Pictures Inc., ICREO Co. Ltd., KISCO Solutions, BrainyWorks, Hiramatsu Inc., AiCO Technologies Co. Ltd, Actus Corporation, Keyport Solutions, Inc., Kokunai Shi
Key Executives:
  Shinichiro Kita, Manager
  e-mail: master@advantagegroup.co.jp
  Education: BA in Economics
  Background: McKinsey & Company (Tokyo)
  Hideo Nagatsuyu, Partner

2340 ADVENT VENTURE PARTNERS
158-160 North Gower Street
London NW1 2ND
United Kingdom

Phone: 44-2079322100 Fax: 44-2079322174
e-mail: info@adventventures.com

Mission Statement: Maintains a close hands-on management style and seeks to form a strong working relationship with each of its investees.
Geographic Preference: United Kingdom, USA, Western Europe
Fund Size: $885 Million
Founded: 1981
Average Investment: $17 Million
Minimum Investment: $3.54 Million
Investment Criteria: Start-up, Early Stage, Expansion/Development, Secondary purchase/replacement capital, MBO, MBI
Industry Group Preference: Electronic Technology, Software, Communications, Biotechnology, Medical Devices
Portfolio Companies: Adeptra, AM-BEO, Ask, Axion, Casella, Cartesis, Celoxia, Citel Tech, EQOS, INCA, K2 Optronic, Netik, Pelican, Phyworks, Snell and Wilcox
Key Executives:
  Fiona MacLaughlin, Associate
  Education: Metallurgy, Oxford University
  Background: Industrial Engineer, De La Rue; Manufacturing Operations, Formica International; After steering through a management buy-out of a Formica subsidiary in 1971, ran the resulting company for 10 years.
  Directorships: Founding Chairman, British Capital Venture Association
  Peter Baines, General Partner
  e-mail: info@adventventures.com
  Education: BSC, MSC, London University; MBA, INSEAD
  Background: Picker International, PricewaterhouseCoopers, Investment Director Schroder Ventures France
  Alain Huriez, Venture Partner
  e-mail: info@adventventures.com
  Education: Electrical Engineer
  Background: Honeywell, Case & Variany/Univac, Director of High Technology Unit 3i
  Mike Chalfen, General Partner
  e-mail: info@adventventures.com
  Education: Software Engineer
  Background: UNISYS; ICL/Managing Director, INSAC Group

Venture Capital & Private Equity Firms / International Firms

Les Gabb, Finance Director
e-mail: info@adventventures.com
Education: Biochemistry, Oxford University; Chartered Accountant
Background: Credit Industrial et Commercial et UEI for 3 years. Head of Accounts, London Branch of French Bank; Managing Director, Bemuda International Investment Management (Europe); Chartered Accountant, KPMG Peat Marwick McClintock
Dale Pfost, General Partner
e-mail: info@adventventures.com
Education: BSC Economics, London School of Economics
Background: Black & Decker; Innotech Investment; 3i
Ian J. Nicholson, Operating Partner
e-mail: info@adventventures.com
Education: Chemical engineering, Biotechnology
Background: Director Venture Capital, Monsato Healthcare/Petrochemical
Directorships: Non-executive Director, Dura Pharmaceuticals, Oxford Glycosciences, Othofix International NV, Professional Staff plc, Vernalis Group plc
Kaasim Mahmood, Partner
e-mail: info@adventventures.com
Education: BA, Biology, Vassar; MBA, Stanford University
Background: Group VP M&A, Rhone Poulenc
Andrew J Wood, Venture Partner
e-mail: info@adventventures.com
Education: Physics, Oxford University
Background: Managing Director, Mowlem; Technology Venture Capital Fund Manager, MTI
Raj Parekh, General Partner
Shahzad Malik, General Partner
e-mail: info@adventventures.com
Education: Oxford University; Cambridge University; Specialized in International Cardiology, while pursuing research in heart muscle disorders
Background: McKinsey & Company

2341 AEM CAPITAL
Av. Nilo Pecanha, 50/1512 Centro
Rio de Janeiro 20020-906
Brazil

Phone: 21-25321592 Fax: 21-22927538
web: www.aembr.com.br

Mission Statement: Invests in high-growth markets with a highly specialized team.
Industry Group Preference: Energy, Infrastructure, Oil & Gas
Portfolio Companies: Starfish Oil & Gas, Tridemensional Engenharia
Key Executives:
Antonio E.F. Muller, Partner
Education: BS, Engineering, State University of Rio de Janeiro
Background: VP, Business Development, ABB Setal Lummus

2342 AESCAP VENTURE
Barbara Strozzilaan 101
Aescap Venture, Spaces
Amsterdam 1083 HN
Netherlands

Phone: 31-205702940 Fax: 31-206737846
e-mail: pkrol@asecap.com
web: www.aescap.com

Mission Statement: Aescap Venture is a venture capital company investing in private medical companies in Europe. We invest in high-potential companies with realistic product opportunities. This involves investments in all phases of development.
Geographic Preference: Europe
Industry Group Preference: Healthcare, Medical Devices
Portfolio Companies: ActoGeniX, Affectis Pharmaceuticals AG, Aquapharm BioDiscovery, Avantium BV, to-BBB BV, Biocartis SA, EOS SpA, f-Star GmbH, i-Optics BV, Orphazyme ApS, ProtAffin Biotechnologic AG, Vivendy Therpeutics
Key Executives:
Patrick Krol, Managing Partner
e-mail: pkrol@aescap.com
Background: Founder & Managing Director, Firm United Healthcare; Co-Founder, Interactive Healthcare; Co-Founder, Healthcare Management School
Directorships: Shire Pharmaceuticals, Aquapharm, i-Optics, to-BBB, f-Star

2343 AFC MERCHANT BANK
180 Cecil Street,
Bangkok Bank Building
Suite 17-00
Singapore 69546
Singapore

Phone: 65-622247155 Fax: 65-622250727
web: www.afcmerchantbank.com

Mission Statement: Finances projects and assists in promoting industrialisation and overall economic development in the Asian region.
Geographic Preference: Asia
Fund Size: $200 Million
Founded: 1981
Investment Criteria: Early Stage, Expansion, Startup
Industry Group Preference: Diversified
Key Executives:
Jeronimo U Kilayko, Chairman
Adilaksana Putranto, President Director

2344 AFTERDOX
7 Nachlieli Street
Kfar Sava 44246
Israel

Phone: 972-545511688
e-mail: info@afterdox.com
web: www.afterdox.com

Mission Statement: AfterDox is a 'smart' angels investment group, comprised of 50 present and former top executives, mostly from Amdocs. Smart - because our partners are involved in the management and strategic planning of its portfolio companies, supporting the management in the initial business development, building the company and marketing it, participate in decision making processes and daily management.
Founded: 2007
Investment Criteria: Pre-Seed, Seed-Stage, Startup
Industry Group Preference: Telecommunications, Internet, Advertising, Information Technology, Software
Portfolio Companies: Bizzabo, RingYa, Donaza, FlixWagon, IMScouting, Fenavic, TodaCell, Internet Is Fun
Key Executives:
Menahem Shalgi, Chairman
Education: BA, Business Administration, New York Technology University
Background: President/CEO/Founder, cVidya Networks

Venture Capital & Private Equity Firms / International Firms

2345 AGATE MEDICAL INVESTMENTS
Toyota Tower B, 7th Floor
67 Igal Alon St
Tel-Aviv 67443
Israel

Phone: 972-35652285 Fax: 972-35652284
e-mail: agate@agate-invest.com
web: www.agate-invest.com

Mission Statement: Agate Medical investments LP is a group of funds, specialized in providing growth capital to mature Medtech companies. Agate, as one of Israel's leading healthcare investors, has established a leading position in the healthcare VC industry, resulting in quality deal-flow and investor partnerships.
Geographic Preference: Israel
Founded: 2007
Investment Criteria: Later-Stage
Industry Group Preference: Healthcare, Health Related, Medical Technology, Medical Devices
Portfolio Companies: VisionCare, Tulip Medical, Navotek Medical, BrainsGate, Angioslide, Iscare AS, Lumenis, Sensimed, Valeritas
Key Executives:
  Dani Haveh, Co-Founder/Managing General Partner
  e-mail: danin@agate-invest.com
  Education: LLB, Hebrew University
  Background: Minister of Health, Israel

2346 AGF PRIVATE EQUITY Allianz Group
117, avenue des Champs-Élysées
Paris 75008
France

Phone: 33-0158185656 Fax: 33-158185689
e-mail: contact@agfpe.com

Mission Statement: Works with the best partnerships worldwide and invests in the best emerging companies in France.
Geographic Preference: France, Europe
Fund Size: $120 Million
Founded: 1995
Average Investment: Euro50 - Euro70 Million
Minimum Investment: $1.8 Million
Investment Criteria: Early Stage
Industry Group Preference: Software, Telecommunications, Infrastructure, Life Sciences
Portfolio Companies: A.S. Group, Arisem, Cosmosbay, Diatos, Eolring Dynamic Cell Network, Exonhit, Fluxus, Leacom, Mediapps, NetGraph Information Technology SA, Neurotech, NexGen, PS Soft, Sefas, StreamCore, Travelprice.com, iProgress, Aptanomics, Bmd, Celectis, Elbion, Faust Pharma, Integragen, Meristem Therapeutics, SpineVision, Zealand Pharma, Alchimer, Everbee, Valiosys, BVRP, Dalet, Ever, Grid Expert, AS Groupe, Vizelia, Cril Telecom Software, Lea com, ONE Access Networks, Stepmind, Telisma, Cosmosbay Vectis, Kiala, Meetic
Key Executives:
  Christophe Bavaria, CEO & Managing Partner
  e-mail: contact@agfprivatequity.com
  Education: Diploma of Secretary
  Background: Bank Clerk
  Benoist Grossmann, Managing Partner
  Luc Maruenda, Partner
  e-mail: contact@agfprivatequity.com
  Education: Master degree in Accounting and Finance, Master degree in Business Law, Nantes University
  Background: Asset Mnagement; Head of Fixed Income portfolio, Allianz France
  Directorships: Investment Manager, Member
  Sophie Cadorel, Communication Manager
  e-mail: contact@agfprivatequity.com
  Education: Masters in Corporate Communication amd Information Research, Paris University
  Background: Information Researcher, IT Firm, Corporate Communication

2347 AIB SEED CAPITAL FUND Dublin Business Innovation Centre
The Tower, Trinity Tech & Enterprise Centre
Pearse Street
Dublin 2
Ireland

Phone: 353-1-6713111 Fax: 353-1-6713330
web: www.aibseedcapitalfund.ie

Mission Statement: Invests in seed-stage companies across Ireland.
Geographic Preference: Ireland
Founded: 2007
Investment Criteria: Seed-Stage, Startup
Portfolio Companies: AccountsIQ, Almotech, Arann Healthcare, Benetel, Cambus Medical, Clevamama, CrescentDx, DataKraft, Davra Networks, Donseed, Endeco, Episensor, Eventovate, Fantom, Ferfics, ICAP Media, Ideal Binary, ImeeGolf, Insulcheck, Kemartek, Kidspotter, Marvaomedical, MicksGarage, Mingoa, Movidius, Nortev, Onformonics, OnlineTradesmen.ie, Openplain, MeaningMine, Phorest, Reading Bridges, Sensl, Swrve, Smartbin, TerminalFour, Tvrecheck, VisibleThread, Zartis

2348 AIG INVESTMENT CORPORATION (ASIA) LIMITED
Peninsula Corporate Park
Piramal Tower
9th Floor, G.K. Marg
Mumbai 400013

Phone: 852-28321200 Fax: 852-28939530
Toll-Free: 1800-2667780
web: www.aig.com

Mission Statement: Provides insurance and financial services.
Geographic Preference: Worldwide
Industry Group Preference: Insurance, Financial Services
Key Executives:
  Martin S. Feldstein, President & Chief Executive Officer
  Education: MBA, Bachelor of Arts, Accounting.
  Background: Deputy Director General of the Economics Staff to the President of the Philippines
  Directorships: Senior Vice President, Investments.
  Richard C. Holbrooke, Vice Chairman

2349 AITEC
23 Duke of Avila Avenue
Lisbon 1000-138
Portugal

Phone: 351-213100013 Fax: 351-213526314
e-mail: info@aitec.pt

Mission Statement: Invests in new technology based companies.
Geographic Preference: Lisbon.
Founded: 1987
Investment Criteria: Seed, Startup, Early-stage, Expansion & Development
Industry Group Preference: Computer Related, Software, Electronic Technology
Key Executives:
  Manuel Alves, Director

2350 AJU CAPITAL COMPANY
1329 Seocho-dong Secho-gu
Kangnam-Gu
Seoul NV
South Korea

Phone: 82-234717546 Fax: 82-234843400
web: www.aju.co.kr

Venture Capital & Private Equity Firms / International Firms

Mission Statement: Investment strategy focused on core industry segments including electricity and electronics and information technology.
Geographic Preference: South Korea
Founded: 1997
Industry Group Preference: Electronic Technology, Information Technology

Key Executives:
   Kyu Young Moon, Chairman

2351 AKSOY INTERNET VENTURES
Mill Sk. Nida Tower No. 18
Kat 5 34 742
Kozyatagi Kadikoy
Istanbul
Turkey

Mission Statement: Seeks to invest in companies producing consumer internet products.
Industry Group Preference: Consumer Internet
Portfolio Companies: MarketPage, Tinypay.me

2352 ALBEMARLE PRIVATE EQUITY LIMITED
1 Albemarle Street
London W1X 3HF
United Kingdom

Phone: 020-74919555 **Fax:** 020-74917245

Mission Statement: A private equity firm that has three funds that are managed on a discretionary basis. We invest in well established unquoted companies with current profits of $750,000 Euro per annual or more.
Geographic Preference: United Kingdom
Fund Size: $160 Million
Average Investment: $5 Million
Minimum Investment: $2.5 Million
Investment Criteria: Expansion and Development, Bridge finance, Refinancing bank debt, Secondary purchase/replacement capital, Rescue/turnaround, MBO, MBI
Industry Group Preference: Agriculture, Biotechnology, Chemicals, Communications, Computer Related, Consumer Services, Energy, Financial Services, Industrial Services, Industrial Products, Medical & Health Related, Materials Technology

2353 ALCHEMY PARTNERS
21 Palmer Street
London SW1H 0AD
United Kingdom

Phone: 44-2072409596 **Fax:** 44-2072409594
web: www.alchemypartners.co.uk

Mission Statement: Offers speed and flexibility in private equity.
Geographic Preference: United Kingdom, Austria, Germany, Republic of Ireland, Switzerland
Fund Size: $226 Million
Founded: 1997
Average Investment: Euro 2.7 Billion
Minimum Investment: $35.5 Million
Investment Criteria: Refinancing bank debt, Secondary purchase/replacement capital, Rescue/turnaround, MBO, MBI, Public-to-Private
Industry Group Preference: All Sectors Considered
Portfolio Companies: Paramount Hotels, Inspired Group Ltd, Anglian PLC, Four Seasons Health Care, Air-sea Survival Equipment, Alcentra, Anglian Group, ASSE, Blagden, Brooks Service Group, CedarCrestone, Centric, compare, Datapoint, ICS, Jacques Vert, Just Learning

Key Executives:
   Dominic Slade, Managing Partner
   e-mail: dslade@alchemypartners.co.uk
   Education: MBA, International Relations, Harvard University
   Background: Director, Apax; Managing Partner, Schroder Ventures; Citicorp Venture Capital
   Ian Cash, Partner
   Background: Senior Manager, Coopers & Lybrand
   Frits Prakke, Partner
   e-mail: pbridges@alchemypartners.co.uk
   Background: Associate Director, Lonrho Plc
   John Rowland, COO & CFO
   e-mail: jbostock@alchemypartners.co.uk
   Education: Chartered Management Accountant
   Background: Medical/Aerospace Division, Vickers plc; Perkins Diesels and Rolls Royce Motors
   Bob Hewson, Director
   e-mail: steve@bodger.net
   Education: Economics, Cambridge University; Chartered Accountant
   Background: Finance Director, EWS; Armour Group
   Thomas Boszko, Director
   e-mail: pcasey@alchemypartners.com
   Education: Business graduate, Chartered Accountant
   Background: Career Venture Capitalist and Entrepreneur with a special interest in the Irish market; Director, DCC; Director, Apax Partners
   Alex Leicester, Partner
   e-mail: jmoulton@alchemypartners.co.uk
   Background: Apax; Schroder Ventures; Citicorp Venture Capital

2354 ALCUIN CAPITAL PARTNERS LLP
2 Eaton Gate
London SW1W 9BJ
United Kingdom

Phone: 44-2031784089 **Fax:** 44-2031784090
e-mail: info@alcuincapital.com
web: www.alcuincapital.com

Mission Statement: Alcuin Capital Partners specialises in making growth capital, or development capital investments in profitable smaller-middle market companies.
Geographic Preference: United Kingdom
Average Investment: £2-10 million
Investment Criteria: Buyouts, Buy-Ins, Recapitalizations, Growth Capital
Portfolio Companies: AVM, AudioGo, Agrivert, Alpine Risk Services, Cafe Nero, CW Environmental, Domus, Krispy Kreme UK, Osprey Publishing, Tasker Ventures, TTA

Key Executives:
   Mark Storey, Partner
   Education: BA, History, Balliol College; MA, Birkbeck
   Background: BancBoston Capital

2355 ALFA CAPITAL Alfa Group
ul. Garden Kudrinskaya, 32
page 1 Bronnaya Plaza
Moscow 123001
Russia

Phone: 7-0957973152 **Fax:** 7-0957973151
e-mail: info@alfacapital.ru
web: www.alfacapital.ru

Mission Statement: Focuses on companies with potential to become market leaders.
Geographic Preference: Ukraine, Russia
Fund Size: $236 Million
Founded: 1996
Investment Criteria: Early to mid stage
Industry Group Preference: Biotechnology, Health Related, Medical Devices, Pharmaceuticals, Telecommunications, Oil & Gas

Key Executives:
   Irina Krivosheeva, Chairman of the Board
   e-mail: info@alfacapital.ru
   Education: BA, University of Michigan; Senior Executive Program, Columbia University

Background: Founder and Principal of Troika Dialog, Director of both the US-Russia Business Council and Moscow's American Chamber of Commerce
Yakov Galperin, Member of the Board, Deputy General Director, Head of Multifamily

2356 ALICE VENTURES SRL
1 Piazzale F Baracca
Milan 20123
Italy

Phone: 39-024998171 Fax: 39-0248517583
e-mail: info@aliceventures.it
web: www.aliceventures.it

Mission Statement: Multinational venture capital management team comprised of partners.

Geographic Preference: Italy, Israel, United Kingdom
Fund Size: $203 Million
Average Investment: Euro 170 Million
Minimum Investment: $1.2 Million
Investment Criteria: Early - Mid Stage, Seed Capital, Start-Up Capital
Industry Group Preference: Communications, Information Technology, Internet Technology, Life Sciences, Semiconductors, Medical

Key Executives:
Ilaria Rajevich, Chief Financial Officer
Background: 3C Communications, Cardcast,
Elisa Candeloro, Financial Controller
John Gonzalez, Life Sciences
e-mail: john.gonzalez@aliceventures.it
Background: Telcordia Technologies, Smithkline Beecham
Edoardo Lecaldano, Information Technologies
e-mail: edoardo.lecaldano@aliceventures.it
Background: Bank of Italy; Mediobanca
Francesco Torelli, General Counsel
Background: Major Italian and international law firms.
Directorships: In charge of legal affair.
Hillel Milo, Medical Devices and Communication Technologies
Background: Zoran Microelectronics;Walden Israel VC Fund, Clal Venture Capital, Infinity
Elisa Candeloro, Financial Controller
e-mail: elisa.candeloro@aliceventures.it
Education: Degree in Accounting
Background: Stanleyworks Group; Caterpillar Group
Cesare Luigi Sironi, Telecommunication and Data Networking
Education: Telecommunications, internet infrastructure
Background: Cisco Systems, Iunet, Lucent Technologies, Zhone Technologies

2357 ALIVE IDEAS
27 rue de Charonne
Paris 75011
France

Phone: 33-184166258
e-mail: contact@aliveideas.fr
web: www.aliveideas.fr

Mission Statement: The mission of Alive Ideas is right there in our name: we bring ideas to life. To achieve this mission, we seek passionate teams with fun or revolutionnary ideas, and try to help them with some of the ingredients of success: business tips and smart money. We also develop our own ideas, gathering code-gurus and marketing genius together.

Portfolio Companies: Deolan, Doctrackr, Infinit, Recisio, Declicmedia, Groupement JV, Mapado, La Cuisine du Web

Key Executives:
Jerry Nieuviarts, Partner
Nicolas Rosset, Partner

2358 ALLEGRO INVESTMENT FUND
Research Park Haasrode
Esperantolaan 4
Heverlee, Leuven B-3001
Belgium

Phone: 32-485664650
e-mail: info@allegroinvestmentfund.com
web: www.allegroinvestmentfund.com

Mission Statement: Allegro Investment Fund (AIF) is a Leuven-based investment group that provides funding to early stage high-tech companies primarily in Flanders. We are looking for innovative, technology-driven spin-off companies addressing a significant world-wide market opportunity managed by skilled and highly motivated teams.

Average Investment: 200,000 - 1 million Euro
Investment Criteria: Early-Stage
Industry Group Preference: Technology
Portfolio Companies: ICsense, EconCore, Formac Pharmaceuticals, Visys, GreenPeak, Leuven Air, EqcoLogic, Rmoni, Excico, Triphase, Pharma Diagnostics, Elytra, @Mire, ICMS, Zenso, Vision++, MagCam, Mindcet

Key Executives:
Geert Everaert, Founder
Background: CFO, Pension Fund Manager, Tenneco Monroe

2359 ALLELE FUNDS
5-8 The Sanctuary
London SW1P 3JS
United Kingdom

Phone: 020-30110360 Fax: 020-30111288

Mission Statement: Allele Funds are investment funds which invest in high-growth healthcare and technology companies worldwide.

Geographic Preference: Worldwide
Industry Group Preference: Healthcare, Technology

Key Executives:
Gail Lese, Founder/CEO/Portfolio Manager
Education: MD, Cornell University; MBA, Harvard Business School
Background: Founder, Lese Investments LLC

2360 ALLIANCE ENTREPRENDRE
5-7 rue de Monttessu
Paris 75007
France

Phone: 33-158193208 Fax: 01-53648765
web: www.allianceentreprendre.com

Mission Statement: An investment company set up by the French savings banks and Caisse des Depots Group, takes a minority share in bigger SMEs, especially in companies at the transfer stage.

Fund Size: $60.5 Million
Founded: 1995
Average Investment: $1.5-$2.7 Million
Industry Group Preference: All Sectors Considered

Key Executives:
Lionnel Thomas, Chief Executive Officer
Jean-Pierre Léger, Associate director

2361 ALLIANCE VENTURE
Stranden 57, Aker Brygge
Oslo N-0250
Norway

Phone: 47-22944020 Fax: 47-22471221
e-mail: info@allianceventure.com
web: www.allianceventure.com

Venture Capital & Private Equity Firms / International Firms

Mission Statement: Alliance Venture invests in emerging technology companies at an early stage and supports their global expansion through our international network.
Geographic Preference: Norway/Scandinavia
Fund Size: $75 million
Founded: 2001
Investment Criteria: Seed-Stage, Early-Stage
Industry Group Preference: Technology, Information Technology, Semiconductors, Software, Media, Mobile
Portfolio Companies: Capnia, FXI Technologies, HYPRES, Interagon, bMenu, Intergrasco, PagePlanner, poLight, 3D Perception, Encap, Never.no, MemfoACT, Novelda, Optosense, Phonofile, Ping Communications, Edvantage Group AS, TiFiC AB, Owera, Net4Call AS, Falanx AS, Network Electronics ASA

Key Executives:
Jan-Erik Hareid, Managing Partner
e-mail: hareid@allianceventure.com
Education: MSc, Physics & Industrial Engineering, Norwegian University of Science; IEP, INSEAD
Background: Head, Innovation Norway

2362 ALLIANZ CAPITAL PARTNERS GmbH
Theresienstr. 6-8
Munich 80333
Germany

Phone: 49-8938007010 Fax: 49-8938007586
e-mail: contact@allianzcapitalpartners.com
web: www.allianzcapitalpartners.com

Mission Statement: Allianz Capital Partners offers financing solutions to meet the diverse capital requirements of unlisted companies.
Geographic Preference: Western Europe, Africa, Americas, Europe, Germany
Fund Size: $1.01 Billion
Founded: 1998
Minimum Investment: $30 Million
Investment Criteria: Growth Capital, MBO, Management Buy-in, Shareholder Restructuring, Mezzanine
Industry Group Preference: All Sectors Considered

Key Executives:
Rainer Husmann, Executive manager
Education: Business Administration, Economics, Law and Social Sciences University of St. Gallen;Harvard Business School:ISP
Background: Bain & Co., Boston ;Goldman Sachs & Co., New York;Goldman Sachs International, London;Goldman Sachs & Co. OHG, Frankfurt

2363 ALMI FORETAGSPARTNER AB
Liljeholmsvägen 32, Box 47631
Stockholm 117 94
Sweden

Phone: 46-087098900 Fax: 46-840-60300
e-mail: info@almi.se
web: www.almi.se

Mission Statement: Actively seeking new investments.
Geographic Preference: Sweden
Founded: 1994
Industry Group Preference: All Sectors Considered

Key Executives:
Goran Lundwall, Chief Executive Officer/Koncernchef
Maroun Aoun, Chief Executive Officer

2364 ALOE PRIVATE EQUITY
34 Boulevard Malesherbes
Paris 75008
France

web: www.aloe-group.com

Mission Statement: A dynamic team of people with high integrity and a passion for investing in proven environmental technologies that have an end market focused on Asia.
Geographic Preference: Asia
Founded: 2003
Portfolio Companies: Allied Technologies, AgroGeneration, Environcom, Greenko Group Plc, Longmen Group, Maxsys Ltd, MBA Polymers, Polygenta, Recupyl, Vertaris

Other Locations:
8 High Street
Twyford RG10 9AE
United Kingdom

Executive Suite 2
International Business Park Westin
Oberoi Garden City
Goregaeon East, Mumbai
India

Huan Teng Edifice
Room 1808, Chaoyang
Beijing 100021
China

Key Executives:
Vivek Tandon, Co-Founder/General Partner
Education: BSc, Physics, Imperial College; PhD, University College, London
Background: Managing Director, Viventures

2365 ALPHA ASSOCIATES
Talstrasse 80, PO Box 2038
Zurich 2038
Switzerland

Phone: 41-432443100 Fax: 41-432443101
web: www.alpha-associates.ch

Mission Statement: Alpha Associates is an independent private equity fund-of-funds manager and advisor based in Zurich, Switzerland. We manage globally diversified and geographically focused private equity funds-of-funds and customized private equity accounts for a global institutional and private client base.
Founded: 1999
Investment Criteria: Early-Stage Growth Financing, Late Stage Expansion Financing, Buyout Transactions, Distressed/Turnaround Investments

Key Executives:
Peter Derendinger, CEO/Partner
Education: PhD, Law, University of Fribourg; Master of Laws, Northwestern University
Background: Swiss Life Private Equity Partners; Credit Suisse

2366 ALPHA BANK
105, Athinon Avenue
Maroussi
Athens 104 47
Greece

Phone: 801-113260000 Fax: 30-6199170
e-mail: complaints@alpha.gr
web: www.alpha.gr

Mission Statement: A group of companies with highly demanding goals and objectives in shoosing companies to invest in.
Geographic Preference: Greece
Founded: 1907
Investment Criteria: Early Stage, Expansion & Development Capital, Seed Capital, Start-Up Capital.
Industry Group Preference: All Sectors Considered

Key Executives:
Leonidas A Zonnios, General Manager
Directorships: Banker, Executive Member

Nicholas Beis, General Manager
Directorships: Banker, Executive Member

2367 ALPHA BETEILIGUNGSBERATUNG GmbH
49 Avenue Hoche
Paris 75008
France

Phone: 33-156602020 Fax: 33-156601022
e-mail: secretariat@groupealpha.fr
web: www.alphagruppe.com

Mission Statement: Alpha specialises in mid-size LBOs and concentrates on well managed family-owned companies and fast growing companies with build-up opportunities in France, Germany and the Netherlands.

Geographic Preference: France, Germany, USA, Belgium, Netherlands, Switzerland, Austria
Fund Size: $1.5 Billion
Founded: 1985
Minimum Investment: $11.8 Million
Investment Criteria: Expansion and Development Capital, Buyout and Buyin
Industry Group Preference: All Sectors Considered
Portfolio Companies: Basler, BFM, CDC, Gortz & Schiele, Retif, Neuf Telecom, Histoire d'Or, Hyva, KP1, Loxam, Business Materis, Offset Gerhard Kaiser, Seloger, Protegys Group, RMC, Rue du Commerce, Safic Alcan, Salins du Midi, Stokomani, Tom Tailor, Trans-o-Flex, HarbourVest Partners

Key Executives:
Alain Blanc-Brude, Chairman
Thomas Mulliez, Managing Director

2368 ALPHAMUNDI GROUP LTD
Bahnhofstrasse 54
4th Floor
Zurich 8001
Switzerland

Phone: 41-44-5080-556 Fax: 41-44-5080-543
e-mail: info@alphamundi.ch
web: www.alphamundi.ch

Mission Statement: AlphaMundi Group Ltd is a commercial entity based in Switzerland and exclusively dedicated to Impact Investing: profitable investments that generate net benefits to society. AlphaMundi provides debt and equity financing to profitable and scalable ventures in strategic Sustainable Human Development sectors such as Microfinance, Affordable Education, Fairtrade Agriculture and Renewable Energy. AlphaMundi also contributes to the emergence of Impact Investing through education events, publications, and industry associations.

Founded: 2007
Industry Group Preference: Microfinance, Education, Agriculture, Renewable Energy

Key Executives:
Tim Radjy, Founding CEO
Education: Master of Arts, Political Science, University of Geneva
Background: Morgan Stanley Capital International, UBS

2369 ALPINVEST GmbH
701 Citibank Tower
3 Garden Road
Hong Kong 60325
China

Phone: 85-228787099 Fax: 85-228787009
web: www.alpinvest.com

Mission Statement: AlpInvest Partners is a private equity investment manager with a global focus on a full spectrum of investment products.

Geographic Preference: Germany, Switzerland, Austria
Fund Size: $23.74 Billion
Founded: 1999
Investment Criteria: Buyouts, Fund to Fund Investment, Expansion Financing, Bridging Finance, Replacement, MBO, MBI, Takeover Financing
Industry Group Preference: Technology, Life Sciences
Portfolio Companies: Alfabet, Impress, Infitel, VPI Systems, Axxima, Brahms, co.don, Coley, Curacyte

Key Executives:
Volkert Doeksen, Chairman, Managing Partner
Education: MBA, Columbia University; Tax Law, University of Amsterdam; Civil Law, University of Utrecht
Background: ABN AMRO
Paul de Klerk, Chief Financial Officer & Chief Operating Officer
e-mail: volkert.doeksen@alpinvest.com
Education: MA, Law, University of Leiden
Background: Dresdner Kleinwort Benson, Mezzanine Fund , US Buy-Out Fund, Dillon Read (Mergers & Acquisitions),
Directorships: Managing Partner

2370 ALPINVEST HOLDING NV Alpinvest
Jachthavenweg 118
Amsterdam 1081 KJ
Netherlands

Phone: 31-205407575 Fax: 31-205407500
e-mail: wim.borgdorff@alpinvest.com
web: www.alpinvest.com

Mission Statement: Actively seeking new investments.
Geographic Preference: Europe, Worldwide
Fund Size: $100 Million
Founded: 1999
Investment Criteria: MBO/LBO mid-market, Venture Capital technology, Mezzanine and industrial holding on long-term
Industry Group Preference: Technology, Life Sciences
Portfolio Companies: Raet, ReMark, IMCD, FanoFineFood, Spring Flower, Itho, Krauthammer, Novagraaf, Driessen Aerospace, Vetus den Ouden, Halin, Euromate, Nijgh Periodieken, Avantium, Crucell, Galapagos, IsoTis

Key Executives:
Volkert Doeksen, Chairman, Managing Director
Education: MBA, Brunel University
Background: Dresdner Kleinwort Benson Private Equity, Kleinwort Benson
Directorships: Head of Investments
Wim Borgdorff, Managing Partner
Education: BA, MA , Science, Delft University of Technology; MBA, Erasmus University; MA, Real Estate, University of Amsterdam
Background: ABP Investments, ING Asset Management
Maarten Vervoort, Partner
e-mail: maarten.vervoort@alpinvest.com
Education: London Business School; MBE, Erasmus University
Background: PricewaterhouseCoopers Management Consultants (PWC);Corporate & Operations Strategy team of PWC;NIB Capital Bank

2371 ALPINVEST PARTNERS B.V.
Jachthavenweg 118
Amsterdam 1081 KJ
Netherlands

Phone: 31 20 540 7575 Fax: 31 20 540 7500

Other Locations:
AlpInvest U.S. Holdings, LLC

35th Floor

Venture Capital & Private Equity Firms / International Firms

New York, NY 10171
Phone: 212-332-6240 **Fax:** 212-332-6241
701 Citibank Tower
3 Garden Road
Hong Kong
China
Phone: 852-28787099 **Fax:** 852-28787009
Key Executives:
   Paul de Klerk, Managing Director
   e-mail: paul.de.klerk@alpinvest.com
   Education: MBA, Columbia University
   Tatiana Chopova, Managing Director
   e-mail: tatiana.chopova@alpinvest.com
   Education: BS, University of Bristol; MBA, INSEAD
   Background: Consultant, McKinsey & Co.
   Peter Cornelius, Managing Director
   e-mail: peter.cornelius@alpinvest.com
   Education: London School of Economics; MD, Economics, University of Gottingen
   Background: ING Asset Management
   Rob de Jong, Managing Director
   e-mail: rob.de.jong@alpinvest.com
   Education: MSc, Business Economics, Erasmus University Rotterdam
   Background: Senior Consultant, PricewaterhouseCoopers
   Marek Herchel, Managing Director
   e-mail: marek.herchel@alpinvest.com
   Education: BS, Business Administration, MS, Finance, Suffolk University
   Background: Senior Analyst, State Street
   Wouter Moerel, Managing Director
   e-mail: wouter.moerel@alpinvest.com
   Education: MS, Business Administration, University of Groningen
   Background: The Carlyle Group; Vice President, Corporate Finance, JPMorgan; Director, Corporate Finance, Lehman Brothers
   Directorships: Lyceum Capital; Paragon Partners
   Christophe Nicolas, Managing Director
   e-mail: christophe.nicolas@alpinvest.com
   Education: MBA, Ecole Superieure de Commerce de Paris
   Background: Morgan Stanley
   Chris Perriello, Managing Director
   e-mail: chris.perriello@alpinvest.com
   Education: BA, Economics, University of Pittsburgh; MBA, Georgia Institute of Technology
   Background: Principal, Paul Capital Investments
   Sander van Maanen, Managing Director
   e-mail: sander.van.maanen@alpinvest.com
   Education: MS, Chemical Engineering, Delft University of Technology; MBA, INSEAD
   Background: Boston Consulting Group; Product Development Manager, Procter & Gamble
   Maarten Vervoort, Managing Director
   e-mail: maarten.vervoort@alpinvest.com
   Education: Master, Business Economics, Erasmus University in Rotterdam
   Background: PricewaterhouseCoopers Management Consultants; PWC; NIB Capital Bank
   Directorships: Advent, Alpha, Atlas, Varclays, PE, B&S, Bain Capital Europe, Candover, CVC, Charterhouse, Cinven, Nordic Capital, Quadriga
   George Westerkamp, Managing Director
   e-mail: george.westerkamp@alpinvest.com
   Education: MA, Economics, Erasmus University in Rotterdam
   Background: Parnib; NIB Capital Bank
   Directorships: Rayner Food Group, Baxi Group, Nycomed
   Wendy Zhu, Managing Director
   e-mail: wendy.zhu@alpinvest.com
   Education: BS, Business Administration, University of Southern California; CFA
   Background: Senior Vice President, Macquarie Funds Management

2372 ALTA BERKELEY ASSOCIATES
42 Berkeley Square
London W1J 5AW
United Kingdom
Phone: 44-2033931107 **Fax:** 44-2030700797
e-mail: tb@altaberkeley.com

Mission Statement: Actively seeking new investments.
Geographic Preference: US , Europe , Israel
Founded: 1982
Average Investment: $15.05 Million
Minimum Investment: $2.65 Million
Investment Criteria: Seed, Startup, Other Early Stage, Expansion and Development
Industry Group Preference: Components & IoT, Data Communications, Software Services, Technology, Biotechnology, Semiconductors
Portfolio Companies: Elantec Semiconductors, Frontier Silicon, Inside Contactless, Polatis, Siliquent, Synad, Syquest, Teradici, Xtellus, Cambridge Positioning Systems, Castify Networks, Dune Networks, Native Networks, Araccel, C-Dilla, Emme, Improveline, ioBox, M-Spatial, SBS Broadcasting, Scoo
Key Executives:
   Bryan Wood, Partner
   e-mail: bw@alta-berkeley.com
   Education: MBA, Harvard Business School; BS, Industrial Engineering, Virginia Polytechnic Institute
   Background: European Finance Vice President, Gould Inc; several other European and US finance and operating roles
   Directorships: Founder
   Tim Brown, Partner
   Education: Degree in Physics, Manchester University; MBA, Cranfield School of Management
   Background: Eight years technology venture capital, Alta Berkeley and 3i Cambridge; consultant project management in RF division of the JET European Nuclear Fusion programme; technical sales management, Leybold; product management, Surface Technology Systems; semicon
   Hugh Smith, Partner
   Education: Degree in Accountancy and Statistics, Southampton University
   Background: Chartered Accountant with Arthur Young, managing client portfolio covering a wide range of industries
   Directorships: Chief Operating Officer

2373 ALTA GROWTH CAPITAL
Bosque de Duraznos 127
4th floor
Bosques de las Lomas
D.F. 11700
Mexico
Phone: 52-5552543280
e-mail: info@agcmexico.com
web: www.agcmexico.com

Mission Statement: Alta Growth Capital manages a private equity fund focused on investments in middle market companies in Mexico. Our private equity, transactional, and operational experience, both in Mexico and internationally, makes us well-positioned to provide attractive returns for our investors and help our portfolio companies achieve success.
Geographic Preference: Mexico
Average Investment: $10-20 million
Investment Criteria: Middle-Market Companies
Portfolio Companies: Amerimed, ARG, Bunker's Group, Medicus

Venture Capital & Private Equity Firms / International Firms

Key Executives:
Erik Carlberg, Managing Director
Education: BA, MS, Business Administration, Ivey School of Business, University of Western Ontario
Background: Partner, Baring Latin American Partners

2374 ALTA VENTURES MEXICO
Avenida Gomex Morin 955 Sur
Suite 315
Colonia Montbello
San Pedro Garza Garcia, Nuevo Leon 66279
Mexico

Phone: 52-8114779014
e-mail: info@altaventures.com
web: www.altaventures.com

Mission Statement: Alta Ventures Mexico is an early-stage venture capital fund. Based in Monterrey Mexico we provide seed, venture and growth capital to companies targeting high-growth markets. The Alta team has directly founded startups and as investors helped launch more than 80 companies.

Geographic Preference: Mexico
Fund Size: $70 million
Average Investment: $5 - $10 million
Minimum Investment: $50,000
Investment Criteria: Early-Stage
Industry Group Preference: Internet, SaaS, Mobile Computing, Consumer Services, Security, Communications, Healthcare
Portfolio Companies: AeroPRISE, Altiris, The American Academy, Amerimed, Ancestry.com, Grupo ARG, Bunker's, Certifacame.com, Convert.com, Dalus, Diverza, Energyn Corporation, Familylink, GlobalSIM, JSK Therapeutics, Juxta Labs, Kickstart Seed Fund, Knowlix, Master Financial Management, Murally, Panoptic Security, Public Engines, Reachable, Rhomobile, Senforce, Xtreme Cinemas

Other Locations:
3315 Mayflower Avenue
Suite 1
Lehi, UT 84043
Phone: 801-653-3926

Key Executives:
Paul Ahlstrom, Managing Director
Education: BA, Communications, Brigham Young University
Background: Co-Founder, vSpring Capital

2375 ALTO INVEST
65, rue du Marechal Foch
Versailles 78000
France

Phone: 01-39543567 Fax: 01-39545376
e-mail: contact@altoinvest.fr
web: www.altoinvest.fr

Mission Statement: Alto Invest is a portfolio management company independently approved by the AMF, specializes in investing in SMEs . ALTO INVEST offers a range of FCIC, FIP and venture capital for private and institutional clients.

Geographic Preference: Europe, North America, Asia
Founded: 1994
Portfolio Companies: Akamedia, Cedip Infared Systems, Decalog, Dmailer, iORGA Group, Ma-Papaterie, Memobox, Netflective Technology, TalentSoft, TXCOM

2376 ALTOR EQUITY PARTNERS
Jakobsgatan 6
Stockholm 111 52
Sweden

Phone: 46-86789100 Fax: 46-86789101
e-mail: info@altor.com
web: www.altor.com

Mission Statement: Altor is a private equity firm focused on investing in and developing medium sized companies anchored in the Nordic region. Our ambition is to make a real difference as a valuable partner for owners and managers in building world class companies.

Geographic Preference: Nordic Region
Fund Size: 3.8 billion Euro
Founded: 2003
Portfolio Companies: AGR Group, Akers Group, Alo, Apotek Hjartat, Byggmax, Carnegie, Constructor, CTEK Creator Group, Dustin, ELIXIA, Eltek Group, Euro Carter, Ferrosan Medical Devices, Haarslev Industries, Helly Hansen, Lindorff Group, Max Matthiessen, Navico, Njorsk Gjenvinning, NorthStar, ONE, Orchid Orthopedic Solutions, Papyrus, Piab, Qmatic, Sonion, Wrist

Key Executives:
Bengt Maunsbach, Partner

2377 ALVEN CAPITAL
1 Place Andre Malraux
Paris 75001
France

Phone: 33-155343838 Fax: 33-155343839
e-mail: contact@alvencapital.com
web: www.alvencapital.com

Mission Statement: Alven Capital assists companies and the leaders of its portfolio in the long term, particularly in terms of strategy, acquisitions and exit.

Geographic Preference: France
Fund Size: 100 million Euro
Founded: 2000
Average Investment: £1 Million - £5 Million
Industry Group Preference: Internet, Media, Information Technology
Portfolio Companies: AntVoice Group, Aquarelle.com, BirchBox, Commerce Guys, Coupling Wave Solutions, Digibonus, EBlink, EntropySoft, Ercom, Happyview.fr, iAdvise, Jobintree, Koala.ch, Lengow, Mailjet, Makemereach, MeilleursAgents.com, Metaboli, Mobiletag, MobPartner, Myfab, Novapost, Planetveo, Qosmos, Quelleenergie.fr, SimpleIT, Smallable, SoCloz, Splendia, Startingdot, TextMaster, Urban Rivals, Voiturelib

Key Executives:
Guillaume Aubin, Managing Partner
Education: Ecole Polytechnique
Background: Banking Division, Paribas

2378 AMADEUS CAPITAL PARTNERS LIMITED
Mount Pleasant Housex
2 Mount Pleasant
Cambridge CB3 0RN
United Kingdom

Phone: 44-01223707000 Fax: 44-01223707070
e-mail: info@amadeuscapital.com

Mission Statement: Amadeus is a private venture capital firm specializing in high-technology firms who have global aspirations, defensible technology and a strong management team.

Geographic Preference: United Kingdom, Western Europe, Ireland
Fund Size: $489 million
Founded: 1997
Average Investment: $244 million
Minimum Investment: $17 million
Investment Criteria: Seed, Start-up, Other early stage, Expansion and Development, Bridge finance, Secondary purchase/replacement capital, Rescue/turnaround, MBI
Industry Group Preference: Medical & Health Related, Chemicals, Communications, Internet Technology, Electronic Technology, Networking, E-Commerce & Manufacturing
Portfolio Companies: Cambridge Silicon Radio, Clearswift, Optos PLC, Southampton Photonics, Enigmatec,

Venture Capital & Private Equity Firms / International Firms

ArtimiCambridge Broadband, CSR, E14, Level 5 Networks, Nujira, PacketFrpont, Red-M, Xelerated, AePONA, Axiom, End2End, Orchestream, Smartner, Valista, Nanomagnetics, Plastic Logic, Power Paper, TeraView, Mediasurface, Quadstone, Ridgeway, Riskclick, Whereonearch, Lastminute, LeatherXchange, Leisure-Hunt, Silicon Media, Optos, Solexa

Key Executives:
   Anne Glover, Co-Founder & Chief Executive
   e-mail: info@amadeuscapital.com
   Education: Andrea holds a BSc in Economics from the London School of Economics and an MBA from Cambridge University
   Background: Financial Auditor, Executive Vice President of Villa Playa Dorada SA,
   Hermann Hauser PhD, Partner, Co-Founder
   e-mail: info@amadeuscapital.com
   Education: Vienna Univ.; Univ. of Cambridge
   Peter Wynn, Partner, Co-Founder
   e-mail: info@amadeuscapital.com
   Education: Chartered accountant
   Background: Director of Finance for Acorn Computers, International Computers.
   Directorships: co-founder
   Simon Cornwell, Partner
   e-mail: info@amadeuscapital.com
   Background: Apax Partners & Co. Ventures Ltd.

2379 AMALFI CAPITAL MANAGEMENT
Suite 804 No. 233 Weihai Road
Shanghai 200040
China

Phone: 8621-6165-9399

Mission Statement: Amalfi Capital is an investment fund focused on China with a long-short concentrated portfolio strategy. The fund offers differentiation in its approach to investing in Asia, its understanding of the impact and influence of technology and its assessment of the risks and opportunities associated with emerging markets.

Geographic Preference: Asia
Portfolio Companies: Qriously

Key Executives:
   Paul A Waide, Co-Founder/Chief Investment Officer
   Education: BA, Economics & Asian Studies, University of Melbourne
   Background: Vice President, Winnington Capital

2380 AMANAH VENTURES SDN BHD
19th Floor, Menara MIDF
82, Jalan Raja Chulan
21st Floor
Kuala Lumpur 50200
Malaysia

Phone: 603-21738888 Fax: 603-21738877
e-mail: gcc@midf.com.my
web: www.midf.com.my

Mission Statement: Promotes the development of the manufacturing industry in Malaysia through the provision of medium and long-term loans.

Geographic Preference: Malaysia
Fund Size: $1.58 Million
Founded: 1960
Average Investment: $1.32 Million
Minimum Investment: $0.8 Million
Investment Criteria: All Stages, including Expansion, Mezzanine
Industry Group Preference: Industrial Services, Pharmaceuticals, Biotechnology, Advanced Manufacturing, Brokering, Retailing, Property Management, Asset Management

Key Executives:
   Tan Sri Dato Mahmood Bin Taib, Chairman
   Foo Wei Hoong, Chief Financial Officer

2381 AMANET TECHNOLOGIES LIMITED
34 Iron Street
Tel Aviv 69710
Israel

Phone: 972-37659555 Fax: 972-36440125
e-mail: amanet@amanet.co.il
web: www.amanet.co.il

Mission Statement: Provides in-depth services, working together with customers to identify needs and identify solution options.

Geographic Preference: Israel, UK, France, Germany, Norway, Switzerland, Australia, Czech Rep
Founded: 1970
Industry Group Preference: Technology, Computer Related, Electronic Technology, Pharmaceuticals, Telecommunications, Financial Services, Insurance, Tourism, Oil & Gas, Life Sciences, Marketing
Portfolio Companies: Avgol (Plastics), Amcor, A.S.T. Soldering Technologies, A.A. Kachtan, Arit Optronics, Atifon (Packaging prod.), Ashot Ashkelon (metal), Brom compositions, Coca-Cola, Deutsch-Dagan (Elect.), Dead Sea Industries (Chemicals), Echtman Engineering Co., EL-OP (Optics), Elbi

Key Executives:
   Avraham Assaf, Investor Relations
   e-mail: amanet@amanet.co.il
   Prisma Finance, Market Maker

2382 AMBIENT SOUND INVESTMENTS
Tallinn
Estonia

e-mail: info@asi.ee
web: www.asi.ee

Mission Statement: We are a unique seed investment company, investing in people and ideas in technology and across the industry spectrum. Our team is made up of founding engineers at Skype and professionals with tech, operational and finance backgrounds.

Geographic Preference: Asia, Europe, United States
Fund Size: 100 million Euro
Founded: 2003
Investment Criteria: Seed-Stage, Startup
Industry Group Preference: Enterprise Software, Computer Hardware & Software, Healthcare, Life Sciences, Internet, Consumer Services, Networking, Communications, Semiconductors
Portfolio Companies: Armorize, Blaast, Blip.tv, Clifton, DailyPerfect, Drimki, EGeen, Eleutian, Evikon, Flowplay, Frenzoo, Guardtime, InkSpin1, Markit, Mendeley, My Heritage, Oskando, Progeniq, Senseg, Wahanda

Key Executives:
   Tauno Tats, Chief Executive Officer
   e-mail: tauno@asi.ee
   Education: MSc, Tallinn Technical University
   Background: Vice-Chancellor for the Ministry of Finance of Estonia

2383 AMBIENTA ENVIRONMENTAL ASSETS
Piazza Fontana, 6
Milan 20122
Italy

Phone: 39-027217461
e-mail: info@ambientasgr.com
web: www.ambientasgr.com

Mission Statement: An independent growth private equity investor, focused on industrial growth investing.

Geographic Preference: Europe
Founded: 2007
Industry Group Preference: Environment, Energy, Waste & Recycling, Renewable Energy

Venture Capital & Private Equity Firms / International Firms

Portfolio Companies: Tattile, Found Ocean, Tower Light, Amplio Filtration Group, MBA Polymers, Spig, Ravelli, Icq Holding, Ambienta Biomasse

Key Executives:
Nino Tronchetti Provera, Managing Partner
Education: Business Adminstration, Luiss University; MBA, INSEAD
Background: CEO, Finsiel; Founder, Cam Technolgie

2384 AMICUS CAPITAL PARTNERS
Stone Lodge, Clare Road
Ballycastle BT54 6DJ
Northern Ireland

Phone: 44-2820769322

Mission Statement: Amicus Capital Partners Ltd is a private equity network that specialises in unusual investment opportunities. Amicus Capital Partners have an appetite for MBO's, BIMBO's, unpopular sectors and tough turnaround situations.

Geographic Preference: United Kingdom, North America, Ireland, Turkey
Investment Criteria: MBO, Turnarounds
Industry Group Preference: Industrial Services, Media, Retail, Consumer & Leisure, Healthcare, Technology
Portfolio Companies: ACS, Adria, AP Technical Textiles, APW Yarn Technologies, Glenaden Shirts Limited, Global Armour, Origin Fertility Care, Rombah Wallace

Key Executives:
John Beddows, Partne5r
Background: Vice President, Worldwide, UK Managing Director, Kurt Salmon Associates

2385 AMMER PARTNERS
Schauenburgstrasse 27
Hamburb 20095
Germany

Phone: 49-40-2000-3960
e-mail: info@ammerpartners.vc
web: www.ammerpartners.vc

Mission Statement: Ammer Partners' multi-disciplinary team supports start-ups and established companies with capital, know-how and networks on the basis of long-standing experience as a CEO, investor and advisor. Our focus is on companies which offer security-relevant services or products. For us the term 'security' contains all areas in which persons, infomations or objects are protected - no matter whether in a private or commercial environment.

Geographic Preference: Germany
Industry Group Preference: Security, Consumer Services, Retail, Consumer & Leisure, Clean Technology, Communications, High Technology
Portfolio Companies: Netbreeze, Secusmart

Key Executives:
Dieter Ammer, Founder/Senior Partner
Background: Partner, Arthur Andersen & Co.; CEO, Zucker AG

2386 AMOREPACIFIC VENTURES
181, 2ga Hangang-ro
Yongsan-gu
Seoul 140-777
South Korea

web: ventures.amorepacific.com

Mission Statement: AMOREPACIFIC Ventures is the AMOREPACIFIC group's corporate venture capital arm. We invest in early and later stage opportunities which are strategically relevant to AMOREPACIFIC.

Founded: 2011
Investment Criteria: All-Stages
Industry Group Preference: Health & Wellness

2387 AMP PRIVATE CAPITAL NEW ZEALAND LIMITED AMP Capital
Level 14, HP Tower, 171 Featherston Street
Wellington NV
New Zealand

Phone: 64-449-42200 Fax: 64-449-42123
web: www.ampcapital.co.nz

Mission Statement: AMP Capital Investors (New Zealand) Limited is AMP's specialist fund manager; it identifies financial market opportunities that investment managers actively turn into enhanced returns for their clients.

Geographic Preference: Australia, New Zealand
Fund Size: $7.1 Billion

Key Executives:
Graham Law, Managing Director
Background: Treasury Manager, Natural Gas Corporation
Nick Dobson, Principal

2388 AMPEZZO PARTNERS
36 Upper Brook Street
London W1K 7QJ
United Kingdom

Phone: 44-2074999081
e-mail: info@ampezzo.co.uk
web: www.ampezzo.co.uk

Mission Statement: Ampezzo Capital is a private equity firm specialised in online growth stage businesses. Ampezzo I currently has a portfolio of 7 investments employing over 100 employees.

Founded: 2010
Investment Criteria: Growth Equity, Later-Stage
Industry Group Preference: Internet

Other Locations:
Ampezzo Capital PCC Ltd.
Ogier House, St. Julian's Avenue
St. Peter Port
Guernsey GY1 1WA
United Kingdom

Key Executives:
Henrik Ljung, Co-Founding Partner
Background: CEO/Partner, Siguiente Capital AB

2389 AMPHION CAPITAL PARTNERS
19 Buckingham Gate
London W1J 8DJ
United Kingdom

Phone: 44-2086303843 Fax: 44-2070-169100
e-mail: info@amphionplc.com
web: www.amphionplc.com

Mission Statement: Amphion creates, operates and finances life science and technology companies in partnership with corporations, governments, universities and entrepreneurs.

Geographic Preference: UK, USA, Asia, Western Europe
Fund Size: $1.6 Billion
Founded: 1998
Average Investment: $20 Million
Minimum Investment: $15 Million
Investment Criteria: Public and private early-stage investments
Industry Group Preference: Life Sciences, Technology, Pharmaceuticals, Genetic Engineering
Portfolio Companies: Motif Biosciences Inc., WellGen Inc., Beijing Med-Pharm Co. Ltd., Beijing Med-Pharm Co. Ltd., Firestar Software Inc., AXCESS International Inc., Durham Scientific Crystals Limited (DSC), Supertron Technologies, Inc.

Key Executives:
R. James Macaleer, Non-executive Chairman
Robert J. Bertoldi, President and Chief Financial Officer

Venture Capital & Private Equity Firms / International Firms

2390 AMWIN MANAGEMENT PTY LIMITED
66 Mamre Road
St Mary's
Level 4
New South Wales 2760
Australia

Phone: 02-98332100 Fax: 02-98337900
e-mail: melinda@asims.com.au
web: www.amwin.com.au

Mission Statement: AMWIN Management is an international partnership between CHAMP Ventures and the Walden International Investment Group.

Geographic Preference: Australia, New Zealand
Fund Size: $42 Million
Founded: 1997
Average Investment: $2.5 Million
Minimum Investment: $1 Million
Investment Criteria: Start-up, Mezzanine, Expansions
Industry Group Preference: Electronic Technology, Medical, Manufacturing, Internet Technology, Health Related, Semiconductors, Infrastructure
Portfolio Companies: Seek Communications Limited, Gekko Systems Pty Limited, Austal Ships, Medical Imaging Australasia Group Limited, Looksmar

Key Executives:
   Chon C Tang, Director
   Education: Bachelor of Business Accounting, University of Western Sydney
   Background: Australian Mezzanine Investments
   Hock Voon Loo, Director

2391 ANACACIA CAPITAL
Level 2, 4-10 Bay Street
Double Bay
Sydney NSW 2028
Australia

Phone: 612-93631222 Fax: 612-85804600
e-mail: contact@anacacia.com.au
web: www.anacacia.com.au

Mission Statement: Anacacia Capital is a leading Australian private equity firm that focuses on small-medium enterprises (SMEs) in the mid-market. Our business is investing private equity into established companies that are managing ownership change, succession, management buyouts and new acquisitions. We provide strategic insight and capital to outstanding management teams to help these businesses to grow.

Geographic Preference: Australia, New Zealand
Fund Size: $125 million
Founded: 2007
Portfolio Companies: Appen Butler Hill, Home Appliances, Lomb Scientific, Muir Engineering Group, Norwest Productions, Planet Services, Rafferty's Garden, Roofsafe

Key Executives:
   Jeremy A Samuel, Founder/Managing Director
   Education: BA, Bachelor of Law, University of New South Wales; MBA, Yale University School of Management
   Directorships: Appen, Home Appliances, Rafferty's Garden

2392 ANGEL COFUND
Angel CoFund Foundry House
3 Millsands
Sheffield S3 8NH
United Kingdom

e-mail: info@angelcofund.co.uk
web: www.angelcofund.co.uk

Mission Statement: The fund has been designed and established by a consortium of private and public bodies with expertise in business angel investment. It is a private sector body with clear objectives to boost the quality and quantity of business angel investing in England, and to support long-term, high quality jobs in growing companies.

Geographic Preference: United Kingdom
Fund Size: £50 million
Founded: 2011
Average Investment: £100 Million
Minimum Investment: £100,000
Portfolio Companies: Phase Vision, Style-Passport.com, Future Drinks, Enval, PlayJam, Leanworks, Non-Linear Dynamics, CrowdVision, MoBank, Micrima, HipSnip, Ebury Partners, Advanced LEDs, Gcrypt, Sanona, Upad, LumeJet

2393 ANGELAB VENTURES
Via P. Mascagni 14
Milan 20122
Italy

e-mail: info@angelabventures.com
web: www.angelabventures.com

Mission Statement: Founded by Angelo Moratti, AngeLab's Group focuses on Value Investing and Building Companies. We seek innovative ventures in the areas of lifestyle, new media and life sciences.

Industry Group Preference: New Media, Life Sciences
Portfolio Companies: Applix, Dal Bolognese Ristorante, Desantis, Emjag Digital, Golazo, Kensington & Sons, Lovin' Scoopful, Privategriffe, Telecom Design, Tommie Cooper, Viagogo, Wat-Aah

Key Executives:
   Angelo Moratti, Chairman/CEO
   Background: Chairman, Saras SpA; Chairman, Sarlux
   Lorenzo Pozza, Vice Chairman
   Education: L Bocconi University
   Background: Founding Partner, Partners CPA
   Paolo Gualdani, Investment Director
   Education: BS, MS, Business Administration, L Bocconi University

2394 ANGLO CHINESE INVESTMENT COMPANY LIMITED
40th Floor
Two Exchange Square
8 Connaught
Central
Hong Kong

Phone: 852-28454400 Fax: 852-28451162
e-mail: accf@anglochinesegroup.com
web: www.anglochinesegroup.com

Mission Statement: Provides advisory services for mergers and acquisitions, raising capital, corporate reorganisation and rescue, litigation support and regulatory compliance.

Geographic Preference: Hong Kong, China
Founded: 1988
Investment Criteria: Value driven or Event driven opportunities
Portfolio Companies: Melco International Development Limited, K.Wah International Holdings Limited, MediaNation Inc., Pacific Coffee (Holdings) Limited, RT Sourcing Asia Limited, China Resources Cement Holdings Limited, Fandango Inc., Tse Sui Luen Jewellery Limited

Key Executives:
   Stephen Clark, Managing director and co-founder
   Background: Wardley Limited;Citicorp International Limited; First National Bank of Boston
   Christopher Howe, Managing director & Co-Founder
   Background: Hong Kong Securities Institute;Listing Committee of The Stock Exchange of Hong Kong;Wardley Limited;Citicorp International Limited;Standard Merchant Bank Limited

2395 ANNAPURNA VENTURES
Piazzale Biacamano 2
Milan 20121
Italy

e-mail: info@annapurnaventures.com
web: www.annapurnaventures.com

Mission Statement: The mission of Annapurna Ventures is to identify and support disruptive innovations in the digital media industry, creating great companies with a proactive investment process.

Founded: 2009
Investment Criteria: Seed-Stage, Early-Stage, First-Stage, Second-Round
Industry Group Preference: Consumer Internet, Enterprise Software, Mobile, Digital Media & Marketing, E-Commerce & Manufacturing
Portfolio Companies: Appsbuilder, Paperlit, Pharmawizard, Plugg, MoneyFarm
Key Executives:
  Massimiliano Magrini, Founder/Managing Partner
  Background: Publitalia, Rusconi, Sole 24 Ore, Altavista, Google Italy

2396 ANT FINANCIAL
Z Space
No. 556 Xixi Road
Hangzhou
China

Phone: 86 571-2688-8888 Fax: 86 571-8643-2811
web: www.antfin.com

Mission Statement: A technology company that aims to create inclusive financial services to the world through technology innovations and an open, shared credit system.

Geographic Preference: China, Global
Fund Size: $150 Billion
Founded: 2014
Investment Criteria: Financial Technology
Industry Group Preference: Financial, Technology
Portfolio Companies: Alipay, Ant Financial Cloud, Ant Fortune, MYbank, Zhima Credit
Key Executives:
  Eric Jing, Executive Chairman/CEO
  Education: MBA, Carlson School of Management, University of Minnesota; BEng, College of Economics & Management, Shanghai Jiao Tong University
  Background: CFO, Guangzhou Pepsi Cola Beverage Co; Senior Finance Director/Vice President, Alibaba Group; Chief Financial Officer, Alipay
  Simon Hu, President
  Education: EMBA, China Europe International Business School
  Background: China Construction Bank; China Everbright Bank
  Leiming Chen, General Counsel
  Education: JD, Osgoode Hall Law School, York University
  Background: Partner, Simpson Thacher & Bartlett

2397 ANTERRA CAPITAL
Herengracht 450
Amsterdam 1017 CA
Netherlands

Phone: +31 202 051 034
e-mail: office@anterracapital.com
web: www.anterracapital.com

Mission Statement: Anterra Capital is an independent growth capital fund. We invest in fast growing companies that are working to make the global food supply chain safer, more efficient and more sustainable. Our focus is on supporting the growth of companies who are commercializing novel technologies and services. We invest across the food supply chain from novel agro inputs and precision farming through to smarter logistics and consumer safety. We do not invest in other funds, land, operating assets, or other capital intensive businesses.

Average Investment: EUR 2M to EUR 12M
Industry Group Preference: Agriculture, Farming
Portfolio Companies: Voltea, Food Freshness Technology, Ceradis, BluWrap
Key Executives:
  Adam Anders, Managing Partner
  Education: Bachelors Degree in Commerce, University of Adelaide, Australia; MBA, Cambridge University
  Background: Rabobank; Ironbridge Capital; Bain & Co.
  Koen van Engelen, Partner
  Education: Masters, Financial Economics, University of Amsterdam
  Background: Rabobank Private Equity; Alpinvest
  Philip Austin, Partner
  Education: Masters, Chemical Engineerng and Pharmaceutical Chemistry, Heriot Watt University in Edinburgh
  Background: Rabo Ventures; Atlas Ventures; McKinsey & Company; ICI
  Maarten Goossens, Principal
  Education: Masters of Business Administration, Free University of Amsterdam
  Background: Rabo Ventures

2398 ANTHEMIS GROUP
25 Soho Square
3rd Floor
London W1D 3QK
United Kingdom

Phone: 44-20-3653-0100
e-mail: info@anthemis.com
web: www.anthemis.com

Mission Statement: Anthemis Group is the leading digital financial services investment and advisory firm focused on re-inventing financial services through technology for the 21st century. We advise, transform and invest in businesses that are building better ways to design, consume and distribute financial services in the Information Economy.

Founded: 2010
Investment Criteria: Growth Stage
Industry Group Preference: Financial Services
Portfolio Companies: Abaka, Alaffia Health, Alt Bank, Allocate, Amplify, Apis Partners, Apollo, Arthena, Artivest, Atom, Atomic, Automatic, Azimo, Axle, Aya, Backstage Capital, Balance Re, Bento for Business, Betterment, BigchainDB, Blueleaf, Branch, Brandwatch, Carta, Chronomics, Cledara, The Climate Corporation, Currencycloud, Daylight, Demex, DwellWell, EasyHealth, Eigen Technologies, Ejara, Ember, eToro, Feel, Fidor Bank, First Boulevard, Flo, Flat-mx, Flock, Fluidly, Flux, Goin, Goji, Greenspark, Happy Money, Hedvig, Hokodo, Hometree, Hoptroff, Humanizing Autonomy, Imandra, Indix, Insurdata, Joshin, JUMO, Kaiko, Kettle, Kindur, Koffie, KWh Analytics, LocoNav, Matic, Mansa, Maxwell, Meniga, Messari, Metamarkets, Monax, Monese, Moven, Mporium, Neptune Networks, Nivelo, Novoic, Now Money, Numan, Omni:Us, OnSiteIQ, PayPerks, Pipe, Premise, Proportunity, Qapital, Qover, Quantemplate, Quantopian, Rally Rd., REalyse, ScribbleLive, Seedcamp, Sentimoto, Simple, Skuad, Stable, Stepex, Stepladder, StockTwits, Stowga, StratiFi, Super, Swaypay, Taina Tech, Tide, Timetric, Tremor, Treasury Spring, Trov, TrueLayer, Unifi Health, Unmind, VERiCASH, Wayhome, Weavr, Wollit, Xapix, Yulife, ZyFin, +Simple

Other Locations:
  122 Hudson Street
  3rd Floor

Venture Capital & Private Equity Firms / International Firms

New York, NY 10013
Phone: 646-757-1310

15, Boulevard F.W. Raiffeisen
Luxembourg L-2411
Luxembourg

Quai de l'Ile 13
Geneva 1204
Switzerland

Key Executives:
Sean Park, Founder & Chief Investment Officer
Education: Rice University
Background: Dresdner Kleinwort
Directorships: Arthena; Blueleaf; Happy Money; Kaiko; Kindur; Maxwell; Stratifi; Tide; Tremor; Trov; Bettermen
Amy Nauiokas, Founder & Chief Executive Officer
Education: Dickinson College; Columbia University
Background: Archer Gray
Directorships: Matic; Trov; Arthena; Koffie; EasyHealth

2399 ANTRAK CAPITAL
Marc House
13/14 Great Saint Thomas Apsolte
London EC4V 2BB
United Kingdom

Phone: 44-2071834858

Mission Statement: Antrak Capital contributes growth capital and our time, targeted at helping businesses address the barriers to expansion thereby speeding up the achievement of the common goal.

Geographic Preference: United Kingdom
Industry Group Preference: Internet, SaaS, Digital Media & Marketing, Mobile
Portfolio Companies: Cognitive Match, CommonTime, i-Nexus, PeerIndex, weComm

Key Executives:
Kevin Douglas, Partner
Directorships: CommonTime

2400 ANVAR
27-31, avenue du Général Leclerc
Cedex 09
Paris 94710
France

Phone: 33-141-798000 Fax: 33-142660220
web: www.bpifrance.fr

Mission Statement: Promoting and financing technological innovation, especially for small and medium-sized companies and research and development partnerships.

Geographic Preference: Europe
Investment Criteria: Small and Medium Enterprises

Key Executives:
Michael Guilbad, Delegate General Manager
Jean-Marie Sepulchre, General Secretary

2401 ANZ GRINDLAYS 31 INVESTMENT SERVICES LIMITED
15 Kasturba Gandhi Marg
New Delhi 110 001
India

Phone: 91-1123721232 Fax: 91-1123721249

Mission Statement: Actively seeking new investments.
Fund Size: $13.5 Million
Founded: 1835

2402 ANZ PRIVATE EQUITY Private Equity Media
Level 8, ANZ Centre, 23-29 Albert Street
Auckland
New Zealand

Phone: 64-800-151393 Fax: 64-937-44121
e-mail: anzprivatenz@anz.com
web: www.anz.com

Mission Statement: Actively seeking new investments.
Geographic Preference: New Zealand, Austrailia
Fund Size: $302 Million
Founded: 1835
Minimum Investment: $0.75 Million
Investment Criteria: Development and Growth, Expansion, Late-Stage, Management BuyOuts or Management Buy-Ins
Portfolio Companies: Argent (Ford Alloy Wheel Plant), Motion Industries (Saeco and Precision Bearings), Alto Plastics, Securimax, Pacific Print Group

Key Executives:
Michael Smith, Chief Executive Officer
Education: Dumfries Academy;MA from the University of Edinburgh;MBA- Cranfield School of Management;London Business School
Background: Ford of Europe;Citibank;Standard Chartered Plc.;International Monetary Conference;Business Council of Australia and the Australian Graduate School of Management; London Stock Exchange, Capital Radio Plc., the Auditing Practices Board, Cranfield School of
Directorships: Member of the Foreign Affairs Council & The Business Regulation Advisory Group
Shayne Elliott, Chief Financial Officer

2403 AON JAUCH & HUBENER GmbH Aon Corporation
Lyonerstrasse 15 (ATRICOM)
Frankfurt 60528
Germany

Phone: 49-69297270 Fax: 49-692-97276200
Toll-Free: 1877-3844276
web: www.aon.com

Mission Statement: AON Mergers & Acquisitions Group (AMAG) provides risk, insurance & human capital advisory services to private equity investors through due diligence leading to transaction solutions.

Geographic Preference: Worldwide
Founded: 1982

Key Executives:
Michael O'Halleran, Chairman
Education: Undergraduate, Kansas State University; MBA, Harvard Business School
Background: Head Financial Services Practice, McKinsey & Company; Investment Banker, Piper Jaffray and Hopwood; Investment Banker, Federal Reserve Bank of Kansas City
Directorships: International Insurance Society; Financial Services Roundtable; Economic Club of Chicago
Axel Heitkamp, Chief Executive Officer
Background: CEO, Aon Corporation
Directorships: Board of Trustees, Northwestern University; Life Trustee, Rush University Medical Center; Director, Chicago Bears Football Club
Michael O'Halleran, Senior Executive VP
Education: BA Accounting & Finance, University of Wisconsin-Whitewater
Background: Chairman/CEO, Aon Global Re and Wholesale; Senior Executive, Wausau Insurance; Senior Executive, General Reinsurance; Senior Executive, Alexander Re
Directorships: Economic Club of Chicago; World Presidents Organization; World Business Chicago; Cardinal Health Board of Directors;

Venture Capital & Private Equity Firms / International Firms

2404 AON MERGERS & ACQUISITIONS GROUP
8 Devonshire Square
London EC2M 4PL
England

Phone: 44-2076235500 Fax: 33-158-777777
Toll-Free: 1877-3844276
web: www.aon.com

Mission Statement: Aon's merger and acquisition experts provide a range of services and access to a global network of integrated resources to help you manoeuvre safely through your transaction. By providing in-depth due diligence and transaction solutions, we will help enhance your value creation and enable your management to identify the hidden opportunities and financial value so crucial to your portfolio company or corporate acquisition.

Founded: 1982

Key Executives:
Gregory C. Case, President & Chief Executive Officer
Patrick G. Ryan, Executive Chairman

2405 AON RISK SOLUTIONS Aon Corporation
Rue Jules Cockxstraat 8-10
Brussels BE-1160
Belgium

Phone: 32-027309511 Fax: 32-27309888
Toll-Free: 1877-3844276
web: www.aon.com

Mission Statement: Aon Corporation is a leading provider of risk management services, insurance and reinsurance brokerage, human capital and management consulting, and specialty insurance underwriting.

Geographic Preference: Belgium
Founded: 1982
Industry Group Preference: Insurance Brokerage, Risk Management, Human Capital Consulting

Key Executives:
Aon Benfield, Executive Chairman
e-mail: herman_kerremans@aon.be

2406 APAX GLOBIS PARTNERS & COMPANY
Globis Capital Partners/Apax
Sumitomo Realty & Development Kojimachi Build
5-1 Nibancho
Chiyoda-ku
Tokyo 102-0084
Japan

Phone: 81-352753939 Fax: 81-352753825
e-mail: info-gcp@globis.co.jp
web: www.globiscapital.co.jp

Mission Statement: A joint venture between Globis and Apax Partners that targets companies residing in the technology, retail, and health care sectors.

Geographic Preference: Japan
Fund Size: $166 Million
Founded: 1996
Average Investment: $5 Million
Minimum Investment: $1.6 Million
Investment Criteria: Early Stage, Expansion Stage, Later Stage
Industry Group Preference: Technology, Software, Information Technology, Digital Media & Marketing, Retailing, Healthcare
Portfolio Companies: AcuteLogic Corporation, Embedded Linux Technology Inc., Link Evolution, Lumin-oZ Co. Ltd., Nozomi Photonics Co. Ltd., Optware Corporation, PhotoniXnet Corporation, e-trees Japan Inc., C-guys Inc, ZMP Inc., Digital Media Professionals Inc., Wide Corporat

Key Executives:
Yoshito Hori, Representative partners, Globis President
Education: BA, Economics, Hitotsubashi University; MBA, Harvard Business School
Background: Canon Inc
Shoichi Kariyazono, Partner
Education: BA, Law, Keio University; MBA, University of Pittsburgh
Background: Management Strategy Division of Sanwa Research Institute Corporation
Yumiko Hatori, Senior Associate
Education: BS, Engineering, Tokyo University
Background: Arthur D. Little, Inc
Keisuke Ide, Principal
Education: BA, Economics, Keio University; MBA, Stanford University
Background: Sumitomo Bank, NEC
Tetshushi Kawaguchi, Partner
Education: BS, MS, Tokyo University
Background: Arthur D. Little
Akihiro Higashi, Senior Associate
Education: MBA, London Business School, Masters, Policy and Management, Doshisha Graduate Unversity
Background: Management Strategy Division of Sanwa Research Institute Corporation
Shinichi Takamiya, Partner, Chief Strategy Officer
Education: BA, Economics, Sophia University; MBA, New York University; CPA
Background: Worked with 5 big audit firms in New York and Tokyo
Minoru Imano, Partner, Chief Operating Officer
Education: BS, Engineering, University of Waterloo; MBA, Japan American Institute of Management Science
Background: Turbolinux's Embedded Division, Metrowerks Corporation

2407 APIDC-VENTURE CAPITAL LIMITED
8-2-546, Plot No.140, Sheesh Mahal
Road No 7
Banjara Hills
Hyderabad 500 034
India

Phone: 91-4023351044 Fax: 91-4023351047
e-mail: info@ventureast.net
web: www.ventureast.net

Mission Statement: Actively seeking new investments.
Fund Size: $300 million

Key Executives:
Ramesh Alur, General Partner
Sameer Sawarkar, Chief Executive Officer

2408 AQUAGRO FUND
6 Kaufman Street
Beit Gibor
14th Floor, PO Box 17
Tel Aviv 68012
Israel

Phone: 972-37954111 Fax: 972-37954122
web: www.aquagrofund.com

Mission Statement: AquAgro Fund, L.P. is a venture capital fund focused on Israel's innovative water and agriculture technologies, as well as other innovative clean technologies. The fundamental problems in the water, energy and food sectors globally are growing steadily in gravity and magnitude and present a series of challenges to all of us. Along with these challenges come very big opportunities to companies which will create new cost effective and groundbreaking technologies that will provide solutions on a global scale to these very real problems which will stay with us in decades to come.

Geographic Preference: Israel
Industry Group Preference: Water, Agriculture, Clean Technology
Portfolio Companies: AquAgro Lab, Desalitech, Computerized Electricity Systems, Evogene, Impel

Venture Capital & Private Equity Firms / International Firms

Microchip, Transbiodiesel, Tomaisins, Variable Wind Solutions, ZoOpt

Key Executives:
Benjamin Gaon, Chairman
Background: President/Chairman, B. Gaon Holdings Ltd.; President/CEO, Koor Industries

2409 AQUITAINE INVESTMENT ADVISORS LIMITED
Suite 1905 ING Tower, 308 Des Voeux Road
Far East Financial Centre
Central
Hong Kong
Phone: 852-25281600 Fax: 852-25281900
web: www.aquitaine.com.hk

Mission Statement: Aquitaine Investment Advisors Ltd, an investment management firm, specialising in alternative investments targeted to Asia and Japan on behalf of institutional investors.

Geographic Preference: US, Europe and Asia
Founded: 1999
Investment Criteria: Early Stages

Key Executives:
Marlene R Wittman, Group Managing Director
Education: AB International Economics & MBA International Finance, Princeton University's Woodrow Wilson School of International/Public Affairs; Fudan University; Institute of International Relations of National Chengchi University
Background: Headed, Nikko Europe's Asian Equities; Director, Nikko Securities
Directorships: Investment Advisor, Securities and Futures Commission
Arthur E Yama, Managing Director
Education: BS Economics, Dartmouth College; MAR (Real Estate), Harvard University
Background: Director, Managing Partners Limited; Senior Regional Analyst, Nikko Securites; VP, Batterymarch Real Estate Advisors; VP, Liberty Properties
Directorships: Investment Advisor, Securities and Futures Commission

2410 ARAVIS VENTURES
Merkurstrasse 70
Zurich CH-8032
Switzerland
Phone: 41-434992000 Fax: 41-434992001
e-mail: info@aravis.ch
web: www.aravis.ch

Mission Statement: Aravis is the first independent Swiss on-shore private equity house, an established investor in the renewable energy and life science spaces.

Fund Size: 250 million Swiss francs
Founded: 2001
Industry Group Preference: Renewable Energy, Life Sciences
Portfolio Companies: Ambrx, Athelas, Biotie Therapies, Borean Pharma, Donnadolce Service SRL, Energy Life One SRL, EntreMed, Evolva, HF2 SRL, Ikaria, IMVision, Kalypsys, LuciaWind AG, Marino Med, Merlion Pharma, Miikana Therpeutics, Mundus Energia SRL, NovImmune, Nura, Omeros, Panomics, RuiYi, S*Bio, SOGEM, Symetis, Synosia Therpeutics, Telormedix

Key Executives:
Jean-Philippe Tripet, Founder/Managing Partner
e-mail: jeanphillippe@aravis.ch
Education: Business Administration, University of Geneva
Background: Senior Executive Vice President, Head of Sector, Lombard Odier & Cie
Directorships: Telormedix, Symetis, S Bio, Merlion, Maison Takuya Pte Ltd, Evolva, Synosia, Omeros

2411 ARCHER CAPITAL
13 Hickson Road
Suite 7, Pier 2/3
Dawes Point
Sydney NSW 2000
Australia
Phone: 61-282433333 Fax: 61-292413151
web: www.archercapital.com.au

Mission Statement: Leading private equity investment house in Australia.

Geographic Preference: Australia, New Zealand
Fund Size: $3 Billion
Founded: 1986
Investment Criteria: LBO, Middle Market
Portfolio Companies: Amart All Sports, Australian Geographics, Dome Coffees, Emeco, Hirequip Projex, John West Foods, MCK Group, Red Paper Group, Repco Group, Signature Security Group, SULO, Tasman Building Products

Key Executives:
Andrew Gray, Managing Director
Education: BS Engineering, BS Economics, University of Queensland; MBA, IMD Switzerland
Background: General Manager, CSR Limited; Management Consultant, McKinsey & Co
Peter Gold, Managing Director
Education: Bachelor of Commerce, University of Melbourne
Background: Analyst, Greenchip Funds Management; Financial Analyst, Morgan Stanley & Co; Superannuation/Investment Actuarial Analyst, Sedgwick Noble Lowndes
Justin Punch, Senior Advisor
Education: Bachelor of Commerce, Bachelor of Laws, University of NSW; MBA, Harvard Business School
Background: Co-Founder/Manager, The Spot; Executive General Manager, Simplot; Executive General Manager, Shelf Stable Foods Division; Management Consultant, Boston Consulting Group
Craig Cartner, Managing Partner
Education: Bachelor of Commerce, Melbourne University; MBA with distinction, Harvard University
Background: Director, MacQuarie Direct Investment Ltd; Funds Manager, Platinum Asset Management; Retail, Just Jeans
Adam Foster, Investment Director
Education: Ecole Superieure des Sciences Economiques et Commerciales (ESSEC)
Background: Financial Analyst, Morgan Stanley
Ben Frewin, Investment Manager
Education: Commerce, University of Adelaide; MBA, Kellogg School of Management
Background: Business Development Manager, Network Ten; Equity Analyst, MacQuarie Equities; PricewaterhouseCoopers

2412 ARCIS GROUP
30 rue Galile
Paris 75116
France
Phone: 33-0147238862 Fax: 33-147238855
e-mail: mail@arcisgroup.com
web: www.arcisgroup.com

Mission Statement: ARCIS is an international asset management firm, and a member of the Association Française des Investisseurs en Capital (AFIC) and the European Private Equity & Venture Capital Association (EVCA).

Geographic Preference: Europe, Asia, USA
Fund Size: $836 Million
Founded: 1993
Investment Criteria: Early Stage, Development Capital, LBO, Secondary basis
Industry Group Preference: All Sectors Considered

Venture Capital & Private Equity Firms / International Firms

Key Executives:
  Romain Bouché, Co-Founder & Managing Partner
  Henri Isnard, Co-founder & Managing Partner

2413 ARGAN CAPITAL
15-17 Grosvenor Gardens
London SW1W 0BD
United Kingdom

Phone: 44-2076476970 Fax: 44-2076476999
web: www.argancapital.com

Mission Statement: Argan Capital is a leading independent European private equity fund focused on acquiring and developing European mid-market companies.
Geographic Preference: Nordic Region, Europe, Italy and France
Investment Criteria: Mid-Market Companies
Portfolio Companies: AAT, Delsey, Faster, Gas Control Equipment, Hortex, Humana, Janton
Key Executives:
  Wojciech Goc, Managing Partner
  e-mail: wgoc@argancapital.com
  Education: MA, Economics, Akademia Ekonomiczna; MBA, Texas Christian University
  Background: Managing Director, Investment Advisory Firm; JMAI; IBM

2414 ARGOS SODITIC SA
Rue du Rhone, 118
Geneva CH-1204
Switzerland

Phone: 41-228496633 Fax: 41-228496627
e-mail: gsemmens@argos-soditic.com
web: www.argos-soditic.com

Mission Statement: Argos Soditic is an independent European private equity which focuses on investing in small to medium sized companies; acts as exclusive advisor to the Euroknights group of Funds
Geographic Preference: Italy, Portugal, France, Switzerland
Founded: 1989
Investment Criteria: Small to Medium sized companies, Strong position on its markets, Potential for growth
Industry Group Preference: Insurance, Pensions
Portfolio Companies: Ceramic/Apolo Group, Chabert-Duval, De Vecchi Group, Du Pareil Au Meme, Eau Ecarlate, Eider, Fillattice, Le Bronze Industriel, Serap, Starline, Tipico
Key Executives:
  Cédric Bruix, Partner
  e-mail: ebugnone@argos-soditic.com
  Education: University of Geneva
  Background: SG Warburg Soditic
  Directorships: Chairman of the EVCA (European Venture Capital Association)
  Guy Semmens, Partner
  e-mail: gsemmens@argos-soditic.com
  Education: Law, Durham University
  Background: Clifford Chance,
  Directorships: Member of EVCA working committee

2415 ARGOS SODITIC SPAIN
Piazza Diaz 5
Milan 20122
Italy

Phone: 39-0200660700 Fax: 39-0200660799
web: www.argos-soditic.com

Mission Statement: Actively seeking new investments.

2416 ARGUS CAPITAL LTD
33 Cavendish Square
36 Poland Street
London W1G 0PW
United Kingdom

Phone: 44-2071824620 Fax: 44-2071824150
e-mail: ali.artunkal@arguscapitalgroup.com
web: www.arguscapitalgroup.com

Mission Statement: We seek companies that have high quality management teams that posses the requisite managerial skills and an entrepreneurial approach. Our investee companies will have products or services with distinct competitive advantage and strong growth prospects.
Fund Size: £ 263 million
Founded: 1998
Average Investment: £10 - £40 million
Investment Criteria: Buyouts, Mergers, Acquisitions, Roll-Ups, Restructurings
Key Executives:
  Ali Artunkal, Managing Partner
  Background: Director, Chase Investment Bank

2417 ARKAFUND MEDIA & ICT
Gossetlaan 30
1702 Groot-Bijgaarden

Belgium

Phone: 32-2464911 Fax: 32-24633706
web: www.arkafund.be

Mission Statement: Arkafund provides support to its portfolio companies, combining operational insight with entrepreneurial understanding. The fund provided growth capital to mainly early stage media and internet innovators.
Founded: 2006
Investment Criteria: Early-Stage
Industry Group Preference: Internet, Digital Media & Marketing, Media
Portfolio Companies: Adam Software, Arco, Domaininvest, European Directory Assistance, Larian Studios, Mifratel, Netmining, Nieuws.Be, One Agency, Oxynade, Papillon D'Or, Queromedia, Quick Sensor, Wataro, Xpertize, Yuntaa
Key Executives:
  Luc De Vos, Chairman

2418 ARMADA INVESTMENT GROUP
Seestrasse 39
Kusnacht CH-8700
Switzerland

Phone: 41-449149000 Fax: 41-449149001
e-mail: office@armada.com
web: www.armada.com

Mission Statement: Armada Investment Group is committed to helping exceptional entrepreneurs build innovative technology companies that will change the way people work and communicate.
Fund Size: $120 million
Founded: 2000
Average Investment: $3 - $7 million
Minimum Investment: $750,000
Investment Criteria: Early Stage, Spin Outs, or Later Stage with early attributes.
Industry Group Preference: Technology, Diversified
Portfolio Companies: Alegra AG, GoingOn Networks Inc., Oanda Coorperation, Overture Networks, Skyway, Wave7 Optics Inc., Celeris AG, edocs, Inc., Helvetic.com AG,
Key Executives:
  Daniel S Aegerter, Chairman
  Education: BS Business Administration, Winterthur

Venture Capital & Private Equity Firms / International Firms

School, Switzerland
Background: DYNABIT AG; Swiss Bank Corporation; Chairman/CEO TRADEX
Directorships: Higher Markets, DYNABIT
Simon Koenig, Managing Director

2419 ARTS ALLIANCE
5 Young Street
London W8 5EH
United Kingdom

Phone: 44-0-20-7361-7720 Fax: 44-0-20-7361-7766
e-mail: info@artsalliance.co.uk
web: www.artsalliance.co.uk

Mission Statement: Arts Alliance is a venture capital organization dedicated to entrepreneurship in Europe. We advise on investments on behalf of the Hoegh family. All of Arts Alliance's activities focus on technology-enabled service companies. We are interested in companies that provide services to both consumers and business users, and we invest in a number of sectors including film, and online marketing & advertising.

Geographic Preference: Europe
Founded: 1996
Industry Group Preference: Technology-Enabled Services, Film, Online Marketing, Advertising
Portfolio Companies: Arts Alliance Media, Brainient, CreativeLIVE, Kebony, Kenshoo, Ledlight Group, Lucky Voice Private Karaoke, Metfilmschool, Mr Wolf, Mydeco.com, Povo, Shazam, We Are Pop Up, YCD Multimedia

Key Executives:
Thomas Hoegh, Founder & CEO
Education: BS, Fine Arts, Theatre, Northwestern University; MBA, Harvard Business School
Directorships: Kenshoo, Kebony, Arts Alliance Media

2420 ARX
Kronberg Building
Ehlenuv dum, 28. rijna 12
Praha 11000
Czech Republic

Phone: 420-224235399 Fax: 420-224239424
e-mail: praha@arxequity.com

Mission Statement: ARX can assist entrepreneurs in buy outs or buy ins.

Geographic Preference: Europe
Fund Size: $120 Million
Founded: 1996
Average Investment: $9 Million
Minimum Investment: $3.6 Million
Investment Criteria: Expansion and Development, Mezzanine and Bridge
Industry Group Preference: All Sectors Considered
Portfolio Companies: Flanco International, Ergis, Cenega N.V., Print Polska, Hungarocamion Rt., Czech On Line, Scientific Publishers

2421 ASAHI BANK INVESTMENT COMPANY LIMITED
1-3-1 Kyobashi, Chuo-ku
Tokyo 104-0031
Japan

Phone: 81-3-3270-3311 Fax: 81-3-3270-3315

Mission Statement: Investment and financing for small and medium sized businesses.

Geographic Preference: Tokyo, Northern Japan
Fund Size: $4.4 million
Founded: 1988
Industry Group Preference: Information Technology

2422 ASAHI LIFE CAPITAL COMPANY LIMITED
1-7-3 Nishi Shinjuku, Shinjuku ku
Tokyo 163-8611
Japan

Phone: 81-423-383111 Fax: 81-333468246
web: www.asahi-life.co.jp

Mission Statement: Provides investment trust products mainly consist of Japanese equity.

Founded: 1888

Key Executives:
Yuzuru Huzita, President & Chief Executive Officer

2423 ASCENSION VENTURES
14 Fulwood Place
Floral Street
Covent Garden
London WC1V 6HZ
United Kingdom

Phone: 44-2074301800
e-mail: info@ascensionventures.com
web: www.ascensionventures.com

Mission Statement: Ascension Ventures is the investment arm of Ascension Media Group, one of the UK's leading investment and business services groups in the creative industries and digital technology sectors. At Ascension Ventures we invest behind entrepreneurs and talent in the creative industries and related digital technology sectors providing capital to help build businesses that own and exploit intellectual property rights in content and brands.

Industry Group Preference: Digital Media & Marketing, Creative Industries

Key Executives:
Sanjay Wadhwani, Founder/CEO
Education: BSc, Economics, University of Bristol

2424 ASCLEPIOS BIORESEARCH
10 Philpot Lane
5th Floor
London EC3M 8AA
United Kingdom

Phone: 44-2073985680 Fax: 44-2073985681

Mission Statement: A life science venture capital business offering ethically driven investment opportunities in mid-stage pharmaceutical testing and technologies.

Founded: 2009
Investment Criteria: Early-Stage, Mid-Stage
Industry Group Preference: Pharmaceuticals, Life Sciences, Diagnostics
Portfolio Companies: Genmedica Therapeutics

Key Executives:
Simon A Conder, Managing Director
Background: Registered Securities Representative, London Stock Exchange

2425 ASIAN INFRASTRUCTURE FUND ADVISERS LIMITED AIF Capital
Suite 3401, Jardine House, 1 Connaught Place
Central
Hong Kong

Phone: 852-29127888 Fax: 852-28450786
e-mail: info@aifcapital.com
web: www.aifcapital.com

Mission Statement: One of the largest Asia based independent private equity firms that provides growth capital for expansion, buy-outs or recapitalizations.

Geographic Preference: Asia, Australia
Fund Size: $1 billion
Founded: 1994

Venture Capital & Private Equity Firms / International Firms

Investment Criteria: Buy-outs, Recapitalizations, Expansion
Industry Group Preference: Financial Services, Manufacturing
Portfolio Companies: Bayantel, Bharti Tele-Ventures, CNK Telecom, DeMaT TransAsia, Excelcom, GVK Power, Meiya Power Company, Olam International, PT Marga Mandalasaki, SeAH Besteel, Sichuan Tomorrow Fine Chemical Co., Wison Chemical Engineering, Yes Bank

Key Executives:
Peter Amour, Chief Executive Officer

2426 ASIAN STRATEGIC INVESTMENTS CORPORATION
Fangyuan West Road
Chao Yang District
China Parkview Center on the 5th four
Beijing 100015
China

Phone: 86-1064382750 Fax: 86-1064382734
e-mail: general@asimco.com.cn
web: www.asimco.com.cn

Mission Statement: Actively seeking new investments.
Geographic Preference: US, China, Europe
Founded: 1994

Key Executives:
John F Perkowski, Chairman & Chief Executive Officer
Gary Ding, Vice President

2427 ASIAVEST PARTNERS
11/F, 318 Ruei Guang Road
Nei Hu District
Taipei
Taiwan 114
China

Phone: 886-227972989 Fax: 886-227978289

Mission Statement: AsiaVest Partners, TCW/YFY Ltd. is a leading venture capital firm investing in private companies in the Greater China Region, namely Taiwan, China, and Hong Kong. Since its founding in 1995, the Firm has been nurturing companies with innovative technologies, competitive market positions, and strong management teams to develop high growth business.
Geographic Preference: Taiwan, China, Hong Kong
Fund Size: $980 million
Founded: 1995
Industry Group Preference: Semiconductors, Information Technology, Wireless Technologies, Manufacturing, Consumer Products
Portfolio Companies: Acer, Amtran, Anyka, Askey, ATT, Basso, Bei Jing Lepro Seva, Cems, Champtek, Chipbond, Chipmore, CMI, CMW, Coretronic, Coxon, Dac, Egistec, Eva Airways, Falconstor, Formosa International, Fubon Financial, Grand Cathay Securities, Holiday Enterainment, Inapac, Infrant, Isoftstone, Lattice Power, Leyou, Montage, Monterey, Opulan, Parade, Princo, Rf Magic, Scientech, Silitech, Smic, Solargigia, Solomon Systech, Stic, Sundia, Superalloy, Tpo, Tsmc, ULi, UTAC, Wischip, Wistron, Wpg Holding, Yieh United Steel

Other Locations:
865 South Figaroa Street
Los Angeles, CA 90017
Phone: 1213-2441065 Fax: 1213-2440821

Key Executives:
T.J. Huang, Founder/Managing Parnter
Education: National Taiwan University; PhD, Computer Sciences, University of Wisconsin, Madison
Background: CFO/Managing Director, YFY Paper Mfg. Co.

2428 ASLANOBA CAPITAL
Saray Mah. Dr. Adnan Buyukdeniz Cad. No. 2
Akkom Ofis Park.3 Blok Kat. 4
34768 Umraniye
Turkey

Phone: 0216-6921284 Fax: 0216-6921265
e-mail: contact@aslanobacapital.com
web: www.aslanobacapital.com

Mission Statement: Aslanoba Capital is responsible for the early stage technology investments of Hasan Aslanoba, the leading angel investor in Turkey. We invest in ambitious teams pursuing disruptive ideas in areas such as marketplaces, e-commerce, mobile, and SaaS. Following investment, we apply our domain knowledge, business experiences, and relationships to help grow our companies.
Geographic Preference: Turkey
Investment Criteria: Early Stage
Industry Group Preference: E-Commerce & Manufacturing, Mobile, SaaS
Portfolio Companies: Metrekare, Modanisa, InfoDif, Fitc&Color, OnlineMarket, Sopsy, Guvenrehberi, Lilakutu, Idemama, Hazinem Pirlanta, Dugun.com, CloudArena, BuldumBuldum.com, MailMag, Ininal, Vivense, Bitaksi, Tasit.Com, Hemen Kiralikm, Etohum

Key Executives:
Hasan Aslanoba, Founder
Education: Instanbul University Management Program; MBA, San Diego National University
Background: CEO, Erikli Water
Cankut Durgun, Managing Director
Education: Degrees in Economics and Management Science, Massachusetts Institue of Technology; MBA, Stanford Univeristy
Background: Co-Founder, Romulus Capital; McKinsey & Company; Bain & Company; Goldman Sachs; AT&T; Pfizer

2429 ASTELLA INVESTMENTS
Rua Gomes de Carvalho
1666-19 Walk
Sao Paulo SP 04547-006
Brazil

e-mail: site@astellainvest.com
web: www.astellainvest.com

Mission Statement: Astella invests capital, culture and capabilities in entrepreneurial daring and determined to change the world by building extraordinary companies.
Geographic Preference: Brazil
Industry Group Preference: Education, Healthcare, Financial Services, Business Products & Services, Technology
Portfolio Companies: Dualtec, HelpSaude, Imobox, Mobilife, Navegg, Portal Educacao, SmartKids, Tryoop, Tuilux

Key Executives:
Edson Rigonatati, Partner
Education: Business Administration, University Mackenzie; MBA, Columbia Business School
Background: ICT Management

2430 ASTER CAPITAL
26 avenue de l'Opera
Paris 75001
France

Phone: 33-1-45613095
e-mail: contact@aster.com
web: www.aster.com

Mission Statement: Aster Capital is a leading cleantech venture capital fund, sponsored by Alstom, Rhodia and Schneider Electric. Aster's mission is to support innovative start-ups by accelerating their growth. We focus on highly

Venture Capital & Private Equity Firms / International Firms

promising companies that have developed superior solutions to solve global challenges in the energy and environment sectors.
Geographic Preference: Worldwide
Founded: 2000
Investment Criteria: Early-Stage, Late-Stage
Industry Group Preference: Clean Technology, Energy, Environment, Mobility, Transportation
Portfolio Companies: Digital Lumens, Airbnb, Cpower, Casanov@, Cosmotech, Solairdirect, FraudMetrix, Jet Metal, Sun Culture, OpenDataSoft, D.Light, PEG, Atlantium, Aventium, Worktile, Optireno, Iceotope, IronSource, Easy Bike, Uber, Ping++, Open Wide, InspiraFarms, Teem Photonics, Planet, Eficia, Habiteo, BuildingIQ, Paygo Energy, EcoFactor, Element Analytics, NetasQ, LinkDoc, Alauda.io, Docker, Aligence, ekWateur, Finalcad, ConnectBlue, ZingBox, Ioxus, Ordinal, Entouch, Lucibel, Customer Matrix, Tronics

Other Locations:
7 bd Malesherbes
4th Floor
Paris 75008
France
Phone: 33-145613095 **Fax:** 33-145613450

10th Floor, ChangFeng
International Tower
89 YunLing Road E
Shanghai 200062
China
Phone: 86-2160656507 **Fax:** 86-2160768988

Sagid House, Industrial Park Hasaron
PO Box 1800
Kadima 60920
Israel
Phone: 972-98305552 **Fax:** 972-98996105

Key Executives:
Jean-Marc Bally, Managing Partner
e-mail: jmbally@aster.com
Education: MS, Business Management, Grenoble Graduate School of Business; INSEAD
Background: Co-Founder, Investment Partner, Aster
Directorships: SolaireDirect, Tronics Microsystems, ConnectBlue, Jet Metal Technologies, Optireno, Lucibel
Todd Dauphinais, Investment Partner
e-mail: tdauphinais@aster.com
Education: BBA, Finance, Texas A&M University; MBA, University of Notre Dame
Background: President, EFI Electronics
Alexander Schlaepfer, Investment Partner
e-mail: aschlaepfer@aster.com
Education: BA, Sciences, University of St. Gallen; MSc, Finance, London Business School
Background: BU Power Service
Directorships: Ioxus
Pascal Siegwart, Investment Partner
e-mail: psiegwart@aster.com
Education: MSc, Biotechnology, Ecole Polytechnique, Montreal
Background: CO2 Operations Director, Rhodia & Orbeo; Energy Purchasing Director, Rhodia Energy

2431 ASTOR CAPITAL GROUP
Moscow City, Naberezhayna Tower
Block C, Floor 4, Office 404
10, Presneskaya, Nabrezhnaya
Moscow 123317
Russia
Phone: 7-4955077980 **Fax:** 7-495-926-7315
e-mail: info@astorcg.com
Mission Statement: Specializes in business turn-around, special situaltions, conflict resoluton and growth boosting investment strategies.
Investment Criteria: Special Situations, Turnarounds
Industry Group Preference: Real Estate, Oil & Gas, Manufacturing, Distribution, Retail, Consumer & Leisure, Construction, Financial Services, Transportation
Key Executives:
Will Andrich, President
Education: MSc, Finance, London Business School; International Business Degree, University of Copenhagen
Background: HSBC, European Bank for Reconstruction

2432 ASTUTIA VENTURES
Maximilianstrasse 45
Munchen D-80538
Germany
Phone: 49-89189083880 **Fax:** 49-891890838888
web: www.astutia.de
Mission Statement: Founded in 2006, ASTUTIA is an owner-controlled, independent investment company with headquarters in Munich and an office in Berlin. The main focus of our investments lies in the areas of digital media and the internet in the early and growth stages. We offer venture capital, an outstanding international network, and industry-related know-how to support your growth.
Founded: 2006
Investment Criteria: Early-Stage, Growth Stage
Industry Group Preference: Digital Media & Marketing, Internet
Portfolio Companies: Commercetools, Dreamlines, Fashionette, Flaconi, InterNations, Mornin' Glory, Mister Spex, Mysportbrands & Mysportworld, Pactas, Quest.ii, V-Bank
Key Executives:
Benedict Rodenstock, Founder/CEO
Education: MBA, University St. Gallen; University Bologna
Background: Hurbert Burda Media, WEB.DE, Roland Berger Strategy Consultants

2433 ATILA VENTURES
Par La Ville Place
14 Par-la-Ville Road
Hamilton HM08
Bermuda
Phone: 441-2956081 **Fax:** 441-2921373
Mission Statement: ATILAVENTURES was founded in 1999 with the goal of providing capital, operating and other value adding resources to entrepreneurs in Europe. Our experience gained in Silicon Valley, Europe and Asia in the high growth technology sector is used to provide entrepreneurs primarily in Switzerland, France, Germany, Austria and other European countries with venture capital, advice and networking.
Geographic Preference: Western Europe
Founded: 1999
Industry Group Preference: Information Technology, Telecommunications, Electronics, E-Commerce & Manufacturing
Key Executives:
James Keyes, Chairman

2434 ATLANTIC BRIDGE
31 Kildare Street
Dublin 2
Ireland
Phone: 353-16034450 **Fax:** 353-16425661
web: www.abven.com
Mission Statement: Atlantic Bridge is a growth equity fund focused on technology investments with offices in Dublin, London and Silicon Valley. We believe in the entrepreneur and support management teams that have the vision and ambition to exploit major growth opportunities. Our team of seasoned entrepreneurs, experienced managers, finance professionals and investment experts possess decades of experience growing

successful technology businesses globally. This wealth of experience and extensive industry contacts adds value above and beyond a purely financial investment.

Geographic Preference: Ireland, United Kingdom, United States
Investment Criteria: Growth Stage
Industry Group Preference: Cloud Computing, Virtualization, Infrastructure, Semiconductors, Wireless Technologies, Information Technology
Portfolio Companies: Accuris, Acision, BioSensia, Envivio, Panda Security, Maginaatics, Metaio, Nero, Openmind, Ozmo Devices, Quixey, Swrve

Other Locations:
33 St James's Square
London SW1Y 4JS
United Kingdom
Phone: 44-2076619304 **Fax:** 44-2076619594

Key Executives:
Peter McManamon, Chairman
Education: Business Studies, Trinity College
Background: Co-Founder, Parthus Technologies

2435 ATLANTIC VENTURES
Sempacherstrasse 1
Luzern 6002
Switzerland

Phone: 550-0049010
web: www.atlanticventures.com

Mission Statement: Atlantic Ventures in a Berlin and Zurich based vehicle focused on building lean startups and fostering talented entrepreneurs. Leveraging our network and experience, we invest in media and technology companies from their early stages and we make them become market leaders.

Industry Group Preference: Technology, Consumer Internet
Portfolio Companies: A., Barcoo, Bonusbox, EyeEm, Gate5, Gidsy, Loopcam, MangirKart, Monoqi, Phonedeck, Plazes, Plista, Readmill, Soundcloud, StudiVZ, Too.Step, Txtr

Key Executives:
Christophe Maire, Partner
Background: CEO, Txtr; Co-Founder, Gate5

2436 ATLAS VENTURE: FRANCE
25 First Street
Suite 303
Cambridge, MA 02141

Phone: 617-5882600 **Fax:** 33-158365960
web: www.atlasventure.com

Mission Statement: Atlas Venture takes an integrated, international team approach to building success for portfolio companies on the world stage.

Geographic Preference: USA, UK, France, Germany
Fund Size: $2.1 Billion
Founded: 1980
Average Investment: $15 Million
Minimum Investment: $5 Million
Investment Criteria: Technology and Life Sciences companies in US and Europe
Industry Group Preference: Technology, Components & IoT, Software, Life Sciences, Drug Development, Medical Devices, Tools
Portfolio Companies: Achillion, Active Endpoints, AEB, Alnylam, Anadigm, Anadys, Archemix, Arqule, Aureon Labrotories, Bit9, BlueShift, Bluespec, LK DEsign Automation, Compund Therapeutics, Dynogen, Ellacoya, Gotuit Media, Helicos, Isilon, Ivrea Pharmaceuticals, Jaulna, Kalid

Key Executives:
Fred Destin, Partner
Education: MS, University of Toulouse; Ecoie Nationale Superieure de l'Aeronautique et de l'Espace
Background: Arthur Anderson, Credit Lyonnais, SED Ventures.
Dustin Dolginow, Principal
Education: PhD, University Rene Descartes; Masters in Strategic Management, Ecole des Hautes Etudes Commerciales
Background: CDP Capital, Deutsche Bank and Merrill Lynch.
Jeff Fagnan, Partner
Education: MD, Paris School of Medicine; Masters in Management, Sloan School at MIT
Background: BioServe Ltd, Genset, Ipsen Beaufour.
Barry Fidelman, Partner
Education: MS, EM Lyon, London Business School; Materials Physics and Advanced Chemistry, Ecole Centrale
Background: Credit Lyonnais Private Equity, Clinvest.

2437 ATOMICO
50 New Bond Street
London W1S 1BJ
United Kingdom

e-mail: contact@atomico.com
web: www.atomico.com

Mission Statement: Atomico is an international technology investment firm, focused on helping the world's most disruptive technology companies reach their full potential on a global scale.

Geographic Preference: Europe, North America, South America, Asia
Fund Size: $1.5 billion
Founded: 2006
Industry Group Preference: Technology, Consumer Internet
Portfolio Companies: 6wunderkinder, Bitmovin, Bossa Studios, Chemist Direct, Drivetribe, Everything, Equal Media, FON, Farmdrop, GoEuro, Graphcore, Habito, Hail, Hem, Hinge Health, IMA, Jobandtalent, Klarna, Last.flicloud, Klarna, Kyte, Last.Fm, LendInvest, Lilium Aviation, Mapillary, MessageBird, Mydeco, Onetwotrip, OnTruck, Ostrovok, Pipdrive, Playfire, Quipper, Rovio, Scandit, Seesmic, Siine, Silk, Skype, Supercell, Teralytics, Truecaller, UniPlaces, Viagogo, Wrapp, Clutter, Compas, Deca, Fab, Heysan, Jawbone, Knewton, Memphis Meats, Power Reviews, Quid, Rdio, Stripe, Technorati, The Climate Corp., Xobni, ZocDoc, Bebestore, Cinemaki, Connect Part, S Gympass, Pedidos Ya, Restorando, Cmune, Gengo, SmartNews, iBoxPay, Ofo

Other Locations:
Av. Brigadeiro Faria Lima
3729, 5 Andar
Sao Paulo 04538-905
Brazil

Regeringsgatan 65
Stockholm 111 56
Sweden

#1015, 1-9-7
Kita-Shinagawa
Shinagawa-ku
Tokyo 104-0001
Japan

15/F China World Tower 3
1 Jiangumenwai Avenue
Chaoyang District
Beijing 100020
China

Key Executives:
Niklas Zennstrom, CEO/Founding Partner
Education: Business, MSc, Engineering Physics, Uppsala University
Background: Co-Founder, Skype, Kazaa, Joltid, Joost
Directorships: Fon, Jolicloud, Rovio

Venture Capital & Private Equity Firms / International Firms

Carter Adamson, Venture Partner
Background: Head of Product, Skype; Senior Program Manager, ICQ; Director of Product Strategy, AOL
Alexis Bonte, Venture Partner
Background: CEO, eRepublik Labs; Lastminute.com
Chris Barnes, Partner/Chief Operating Officer
Education: Double First, Economics & History, Cambridge University; CFA
Background: CFO, Terra Firma; Private Equity Group, Arthur Andersen

2438 ATP PRIVATE EQUITY PARTNERS
2 Sjaeleboderne, 1 Floor
Copenhagen K DK-1122
Denmark

Phone: 45-33193070 Fax: 45-33193071
e-mail: info@atp-pep.com
web: www.atp-pep.com

Mission Statement: Dedicated to global private equity investment management.

Geographic Preference: Europe, USA
Fund Size: $7 Billion
Founded: 2001
Average Investment: $500 Million
Minimum Investment: $5.9 Million
Investment Criteria: Early stage venture capital, Buyout
Industry Group Preference: Food Services, Heating, Automotive, Healthcare, Industrial Services, Transportation
Portfolio Companies: Nordic Capital IV, Symbion, Axel, Bank Invest, Novi, Polaris, Dansk Erhvervsinvestering, Health Cap, Nordic Mezzanine, IT Provider, Nordic Venture Partners, BC Partners VIII

Key Executives:
Torben Vangstrup, Partner
45 33 19 30 81
e-mail: tva@atp-pep.com
Education: MS Economics, Aarhus University
Background: HealthCap IV, Nordic Capital V, Lindsay Goldberg & Abingworth IV
Susanne Forsingdal, Partner
45 33 19 30 77
e-mail: sus@atp-pep.com
Education: MS Economics, Finance, Accounting, Copenhagen Business School; Political Science, Luther College
Background: Senior VP, Danske Bank
Klaus Ruhne, Partner
45 33 19 30 76
e-mail: klr@atp-pep.com
Education: MS Economics, Copenhagen University
Background: Director at Danske Bank, Senior Equity Analyst at Erskilda Securities

2439 ATRIA CAPITAL PARTENAIRES
5-7, rue de
Monttessuy 75007
France

Phone: 33-158194581 Fax: 33-158192641

Mission Statement: LBO and development capital specialist which takes equity stakes in French middle market companies.

Geographic Preference: France
Fund Size: 496 million Euros
Founded: 1999
Average Investment: 25 million Euros
Minimum Investment: 15 million Euros
Investment Criteria: French mid-cap growth companies with EV of 30 million to 200 million Euros
Industry Group Preference: Industrial Services, Consumer Products, Retailing, Healthcare, Information Technology, Insurance
Portfolio Companies: Abcd, Abrisud, Altead, Cap Vert Finance, Ekkia, European Homes, FPEE, Ionisos, LPR, Mc2i, Parcours, Phythea, Shark, Trigo, Un Jour Aileurs

Key Executives:
Dominique Oger, Chairman
e-mail: atria@atria-partenaires.com
Education: IEP Paris, DES Economy Paris
Background: Sefinnova (Madrid) Founder & CEO; Sofinindex Chairman, Coparis Founder & CEO, Cfi Chairman
Eric Aveillan, CEO
e-mail: atria@atria-partenaires.com
Education: Ecole Polytechnique Paris; MBA, Wharton School, University of Pennsylvania
Background: Worms & Cie, Pechel Industries Co-Founder, Warburg Dillon Read Executive Director
Patrick Bertiaux, Member Management Board
e-mail: atria@atria-partenaires.com
Education: MBA, Paris Dauphine, DECS
Background: Director of SCR Vecteur, Investment manager of Cfi

2440 AUGMENTA
Zinkgatan 2
Lomma 234 21
Sweden

Phone: 46-705-94-84-76

Mission Statement: Augmenta invests in early stages in companies that have unique products and great growth potential. We focus on companies in southern Sweden.

Geographic Preference: Sweden
Founded: 2003
Investment Criteria: Early-Stage
Portfolio Companies: Exini Diagnostics, Emstone Engineering, All of It IT, Pastair, Adenovir Pharma, CanlmGuide

Key Executives:
Conny Bjarnram, CEO
e-mail: conny.bjarnram@augmenta.se

2441 AUGMENTUM CAPITAL
27 St James's Place
London SW1A 1NR
United Kingdom

Phone: 44-2075141998
e-mail: info@augmentumcapital.com
web: www.augmentumcapital.com

Mission Statement: Augmentum Capital is an investor with a wealth of international entrepreneurial experience. We invest in growth stage businesses in the e-commerce and technology sectors worldwide. We are a fund run by entrepreneurs who want to work with entrepreneurs.

Geographic Preference: Worldwide
Founded: 2009
Investment Criteria: Growth Stage
Industry Group Preference: E-Commerce & Manufacturing, Technology
Portfolio Companies: Borro, BuillionVault.com, SRL Global, Persistent Sentinel, Bathrooms.com, Zopa

Key Executives:
Tim Levene, Co-Founder

2442 AURA CAPITAL OY Auratum Group
Aurakatu 8
Southampton 20100
Finland

Phone: 358-265166600 Fax: 358-265166621
e-mail: forename.surname@auratum.com
web: www.auracapital.com

Mission Statement: Venture capital company that makes investments in internationalising high tech companies
Geographic Preference: Finland
Founded: 1997
Average Investment: 500K - $1.5Million
Investment Criteria: Start-ups and early-stage growth companies.
Industry Group Preference: High Technology, Software, Media, Telecommunications, Mobile Communications Devices, Internet Technology
Portfolio Companies: Emic, First Orange Contact, Commit, Avset, Delfoi, Agentum Technologies, Bluegiga Technologies, Mforma, Oplayp, Mobilemode, AdaptaMat, Incap, Chip-Man Technologies, Stick Tech
Key Executives:
  ARI Siponmaa, Managing Partner
  e-mail: ari.spionmaa@auratum.com
  Education: MS
  Background: Consultant at Andersen Consulting
  Petri Salonen, Partner
  e-mail: jukka.harju@auratum.com
  Education: MS, Helsinki University of Technology
  Background: Senior management positions at AtBusiness Communications and Hewlett Packard

2443 AURELIA PRIVATE EQUITY
Kurhessenstrasse 1-3
Frankfurt am Main 60431
Germany

Phone: 069-80900 Fax: 069-8090109
e-mail: info@aurelia-pe.de
web: www.aurelia-pe.de

Mission Statement: AURELIA participates in the funds it manages as a financier of innovative early-stage technology companies in Germany. We provide capital for research and development, launch of the products, the production structure and internationalization. Our engagement is in the order of 0.5 to 3 million euro. AURELIA is a partner in time, introduces the strategic know-how and capital to the company. With our experience and contacts we accompany the management and create the basis for further expansion. The aim is to develop our investments into successful companies with strong market positions.
Industry Group Preference: Life Sciences, Information Technology, Communications
Portfolio Companies: Cooee, EMBL Technology Fund, GILUPI, Hematris Wound Care, jCatalog Software, MovingIMAGE24, MerLion Pharmaceuticals, PC-Soft,
Key Executives:
  Jurgen Leschke, Managing Partner
  Background: Corporate Banking, Dresdner Bank AG; Founder, TFG Venture Capital Group

2444 AURIGA PARTNERS
18 Matignon Avenue
Paris 75008
France

Phone: 33-153300707 Fax: 33-153300700
e-mail: auriga@aurigapartners.com
web: www.aurigapartners.com/

Mission Statement: Independent Venture Capital firm managing several early stage funds specializing in Information Technology and Life Sciences
Geographic Preference: France, Western Europe, North America, Israel
Fund Size: $136 Million
Founded: 1998
Average Investment: $5.9 Million
Minimum Investment: $1.18 Million
Investment Criteria: Seed, Start-up, First Stage, invest primarily in the European Union, with a minor focus on North America and Israel.
Industry Group Preference: Information Technology, Medical & Health Related, Life Sciences
Key Executives:
  Bernard Daugeras, Chairman
  Education: Finance Mnaagement/Advanced Accounting, Institut Superieur de Gestion
  Background: Financial control for an industrial group
  Directorships: Analyzing business models & administrative and financial follow-up of portfolio companies
  Patrick Bamas, Founder, General Partner
  Education: Ecole Superieure d'Electricite; Institut d'Administration des Enterprises de Paris
  Background: IT and strategy consultant, Director of Finovelec
  Directorships: Information Technology, Scientific Instrumentation and Industrial Processes.
  Jacques Chatain, Founder, General Partner
  Education: Paris Chamber of Commerce and Industry
  Background: IDI Group, investor and Secretary General of Finovelec
  Directorships: Information Technology and the Internet
  Philippe Granger, Partner
  Education: Doctorate in Information Technology, Ecole Polytechnique
  Background: IT researcher, Professor
  Directorships: Information Technology, Electronics and the Telecommunication
  Philippe Peltier, Partner
  Education: Masters in Molecular Biology, University of Paris; Masters in Finance, ESSEC
  Background: Equity analyst at CCF Securities
  Directorships: Life Sciences

2445 AURUM VENTURES MKI
16 Abba Hillel Silver Street
Aurec House
Ramat Gan 52506
Israel

Phone: 972-35762420 Fax: 972-35762605
e-mail: info@aurum.co.il
web: www.aurum.co.il

Mission Statement: Aurum Ventures MKI provides value added growth capital to exceptional entrepreneurs within the fields of life-sciences and clean-tech. While we focus on investing in unique, cutting edge technologies that will mature into successful business companies, our investments reflect our own values, so we prefer investing in companies that, through their sound commercial propositions, also contribute to the well-being of mankind.
Industry Group Preference: Life Sciences, Clean Technology
Portfolio Companies: Nephera, LifeBond, I20 Pharma, VBL Therapeutics, Vecta, Corassist, Fertiseeds, Proteologics, Alantium, N-Triq, Elcom Technologies, OnePath Networks, Dune
Key Executives:
  Nili Lesnick, CEO
  Education: BA, Economics, MSc, Industrial Engineering, Ben-Gurion University
  Background: Elbit Sytems Ltd.

2446 AUSTRAL CAPITAL PARTNERS
El Bosque North 0123
Suite 601
Santiago
Chile

Phone: 56-2-246-0808 Fax: 56-2-246-0809
web: www.australcap.com

Venture Capital & Private Equity Firms / International Firms

Mission Statement: Austral Capital Partners is a venture capital firm focused on indentifying globally scalable, high growth entrepreneurs and technologies.
Founded: 2007
Industry Group Preference: Technology, Life Sciences
Portfolio Companies: Andes Biotechnologies, Atakama Labs, BAL, Fiscalia Privada, Green Pacific Biologicals, Junar, Multicaja, Nimbic, Paperless, Producto Protegido, Scanntech, Scopix

Key Executives:
Gonzalo Miranda, Managing Partner
Education: BSc, MSc, Mechanical Engineering, Catholic University of Chile; MBA, MOT, Haas School of Business
Background: Managing Director, Endeavor Chile
Directorships: Scopix Solutions, Paperless, Multicaja, Producto Protegido
Matias Errazuriz, Managing Director
Background: Founding Partner, Genera4
Directorships: AEON Biogroup, Coaniquem

2447 AUSTRALIAN ETHICAL INVESTMENT LIMITED
130 Pitt Street
Level 8
Sydney NSW 2000
Australia

Phone: 61-262011988 Fax: 61-0262011987
Toll-Free: 1800- 021227

Mission Statement: Australian Ethical Investment Ltd is an independent funds manager based in Canberra specialising in environmental and socially responsible investment.

Geographic Preference: Australia
Fund Size: $350 Million
Founded: 1986
Average Investment: $5 Million
Minimum Investment: $2.5 Million
Investment Criteria: Invests in environmental and socially positive activities
Industry Group Preference: Education, Conservation, Energy, Food & Beverage, Healthcare, Financial Services, Telecommunications, Information Technology, Investment Analysis and Research, Sales and Marketing, Administration and Accounting, Superannuation, Efficient Transport, Biotechnology, Recycling
Portfolio Companies: ABC Learning Centres Ltd, Ansell Ltd, Australian Pipeline Trust, Adeliade Bank Ltd, Australian Central Credit Union, Alinta Ltd, Australian Education, Baldor Electric Co, Bank of Qeensland, Bank of Western Australia, Baxter Group Ltd, Bendigo Bank Ltd, Blackmores Ltd

Key Executives:
Phillip Vernon, Managing Director
Education: BS
Background: Trustee of an award superannuation fund for the credit union industry, Faculties of economics, environmental studies and geography at the University of New South Wales
Directorships: Director
David Barton, Chief Financial Officer

2448 AUTHOSIS VENTURES
Room 2101, 21st Floor Westlands Centre
20 Westlands Road
Quarry Bay Hong Kong
China

Phone: 852-29604611 Fax: 852-29600185
e-mail: info@authosisvc.com
web: www.authosis.com

Mission Statement: With our extensive operational background, we have both the breadth and depth of professional experience to nurture companies from an initial concept to healthy growth and, ultimate commercial success.

Geographic Preference: Silicon Valley, China
Founded: 2000
Investment Criteria: Seed-Stage, Early-Stage
Industry Group Preference: Information Technology, Software, Internet, E-Commerce & Manufacturing, Wireless Technologies, Mobile Technology, Fabless IC, Communication Technology
Portfolio Companies: Affinity Engiens, AssistGuide, BioImagene, BitAuto, Dali Wireless, Ensenta, Erlang Technology, EzRez Software, H5 Technologies, Inphi Corp., Kahala Code Factory, MyETone, PayDay One, Pericom Technology, Radio Time, Sitoa, Solus Biosystems, Telegent Systems, United Platform Technologies, Uniwave, Voicesoft, WhiteHat Security, Xi'an Supermicro, Zero2IPO

Key Executives:
Danny Lui, Chairman
Education: Bachelor's Degree, Computing Science, Imperial College, University of London
Background: Co-Founder, Legend Group; Founder, APTG Ventures

2449 AVANTI CAPITAL
25 Harley Street
London W1G 9BR
United Kingdom

Phone: 44-2072991459 Fax: 44-2072991451
e-mail: richard.kleiner@avanticap.com
web: www.avanticap.com

Mission Statement: Avanti Capital is a private equity company, with a strategy of investing in businesses, using a combination of debt and equity.

Geographic Preference: Europe
Industry Group Preference: Consumer Products, Leisure, Retail, Consumer & Leisure
Portfolio Companies: Eclectic Bars Limited, Expresso Education Limited, mBlox, Medcenter

Key Executives:
Richard Kleiner, Director
Background: Founder, Odyssey Partners; Managing Partner, Gerald Edelman Chartered Accountants

2450 AVENIR TOURISME
32 Bld de
Strasbourg 75468
France

Phone: 33-144540391 Fax: 33-144540392
e-mail: avenir.tourisme@orange.fr

Mission Statement: Actively seeking new investments.

Fund Size: Ffr 38.9 million
Founded: 1986
Minimum Investment: Ffr1 million
Industry Group Preference: Tourism

Key Executives:
Cécile Legeais, Manager

2451 AVIGO CAPITAL
503-504 DLF Place (Office Tower)
A4 District Center, Saket
New Delhi 110017
India

Phone: 91-1143683300 Fax: 91-1143683335

Mission Statement: Avigo Capital, a Private Equity Fund Manager was formed in Sep 2003 with a focus on Private Equity Investments in the SME, and emerging sectors in emerging markets, mainly India. The Investment Team at Avigo has a cumulative experience of over 200 years in Private Equity, Investment/Corporate Banking, Consulting, and Operations. AVIGO's philosophy is to be the first or amongst the early

Venture Capital & Private Equity Firms / International Firms

institutional investors primarily providing growth capital to fast growing SME companies in the industrial/ emerging sectors in India. AVIGO has built up and demonstrated extensive on-the-ground expertise as well as experience in building businesses in the growth stage and handling various investment related issues.

Geographic Preference: India
Founded: 2003
Investment Criteria: Growth Stage
Portfolio Companies: Tecpro Systems, Hythro Power Corporation, GET Power, Spykar, Bharat Box Factory, Rinac India, Aeroflex, Comat

Other Locations:
355, NexTeracon Tower 1
3rd Floor, Cybercity
Ebene
Mauritius
Phone: 230-4647275 **Fax:** 230-4643290

161/162 A Wing
Mittal Court
Nariman Point
Mumbai 400 021
India
Phone: 91-2249154242 **Fax:** 91-22-4915-4242

Key Executives:
Achai Ghai, Founder/Managing Director
Education: BComm, MBA
Background: Corporate & Investment Banking, American Express, HSBC, EBIL, Canadian Imperial Bank of Commerce

2452 AVISTA PARTNERS
78 Pall Mall
London SW1Y 5ES
United Kingdom

Phone: 44-207-193-6780 **Fax:** 44-207-691-7112
e-mail: info@avistapartners.com
web: www.avistapartners.com

Mission Statement: Avista Partners is an independent investment banking firm focusing on the digital media and luxury & lifestyle industries. We bring deep sector expertise, global relationships, and world class transaction experience. Our global network is based on strong relationships with founders and senior management, as well as investors including venture capitalists, private equity firms, hedge funds, family offices and institutional investors.

Founded: 2007
Industry Group Preference: Digital Media & Marketing, Luxury/Lifestyle

Key Executives:
Paul Heydon, Managing Director
e-mail: paul.heydon@avistapartners.com
Education: MBA, HBA, Richard Ivey School of Business, University of Western Ontario
Background: Partner, London Venture Partners; Managing Director, Unity Capital; Head of Interactive Entertainment, Commerzbank Securities
Valerie Blin, Managing Director
e-mail: valerie.blin@avistapartners.com
Education: BA, Northwestern University; CEP, Insitut d'Etudes Politques, Paris
Background: Morgan Stanley, JP Morgan, Deutsche Bank
Marianne Okland, Managing Director
e-mail: marianne.okland@avistapartners.com
Education: MSc, Finance & Economics, Norwegian School of Economics & Business Administration
Background: JP Morgan, UBS

2453 AVIV VENTURE CAPITAL
36 Shacham Street
Ram Building, 5th Floor
Petach Tikva 49517
Israel

Phone: 972-39761111 **Fax:** 972-39199300
e-mail: info@avivvc.com
web: www.avivvc.com

Mission Statement: Aviv invests in Israel related, revenue stage companies that bring breakthrough technologies to large established industries. We have a preference for companies offering 'Hi-Tech solutions for Low-Tech industries' such as security, clean-tech, automotive, printing, and medical devices.

Geographic Preference: Israel
Founded: 2001
Investment Criteria: Later-Stage
Industry Group Preference: Security, Clean Technology, Automotive, Printing, Medical Devices
Portfolio Companies: Actona, Bitband, DeepBreeze, MCS, M.G.V.S, BeInSync, FriCSo, Ozvision, BriefCam, Jettable, ScaleMP, Minicom Digital, Apos, Tipa, Optimal Test, Valens Semiconductor, LGC Wireless

Key Executives:
Dov Tadmor, Chairman
Background: Founder & Chairmain, Israel Equity Limited

2454 AVLAR BIOVENTURES
Highfield Court
Church Lane
Madingley
Cambs CB23 8AG
United Kingdom

Phone: 44-1954211515 **Fax:** 44-1954211516
web: www.avlar.com

Mission Statement: Active investment in seed and early stage biotechnology and healthcare opportunities. The differentiating philosophy of Avlar is not only in the selection of excellent opportunities but in the active development and management of its ventures, particularly those in the embryonic stages of their growth.

Founded: 1999
Industry Group Preference: Healthcare, Medical Devices, Diagnostics
Portfolio Companies: Amura, Cambridge Biotechnology, CeNeS, Cozart, Crescendo Biologics, De Novo Pharmaceuticals, ImmunoBiology, Medical Device Innovation, PAION, Paradigm Therapeutics, Proteom, Purely Proteins, Sangamo Biosciences, Sterix Limited

Key Executives:
Alan Goodman, Co-Founder
Daniel Roach, Co-Founder

2455 AVONMORE DEVELOPMENTS
6 Snow Hill
London EC1A 2AY
United Kingdom

Phone: +44 20 7002 7118
e-mail: contactus@avonmoredevelopments.com
web: www.avonmoredevelopments.com

Mission Statement: Avonmore's investments cover a number of different areas and consideration is given to all investment opportunities we receive. However, it should be noted that we currently only invest in UK based businesses and generally those with sub £3 million pre-money valuations. Experienced management teams, with defendable technology and a proven market demand are also key investment criteria.

Geographic Preference: United Kingdom
Founded: 2000
Average Investment: £100,000 - £250,000
Investment Criteria: Seed and early stage equity capital financing

Industry Group Preference: All Sectors Considered
Portfolio Companies: Tagman, Specle, Socialbro, OC Robotics Ltd, Languagelabs.com, Groupspaces, Glow Digital Media, ByBox, Bac2 Ltd, Virtual IT

Key Executives:
Simon Blakey
Michael Blakey

2456 AWAY REALTY
3rd Syromyatnicheskiy lane, 3/9, page 6
Moscow 105120
Russia

Phone: 7-495-2588866 Fax: 7-499-6782182
web: www.away.ru

Mission Statement: Delta Capital Management is a leading private equity manager dedicated to developing and funding emerging growth companies.
Geographic Preference: Russia
Fund Size: $300 Million
Founded: 1994
Average Investment: $7.5 Million
Minimum Investment: $5 Million
Investment Criteria: Focuses on Emerging Growth and Long-term Companies
Industry Group Preference: Telecommunications, Media, Technology, Research & Development, Energy, Consumer Products, Financial Services, Utilities
Portfolio Companies: CompuLink, DeltaBank, DeltaCredit, DeltaLease-Far East, EGAR Technology, Independent Network Television Holdings, Lomonosov Porcelain Plant, National Cable Networks, Polygrafoformlenie, Saint Springs, SPAR Middle Volga, SPAR Moscow Holdings, StoryFirst Co

Key Executives:
Patricia Cloherty, Chairman & Chief Executive Officer
Education: B.A. from the San Francisco College, M.A. and M.I.A. from Columbia University.
Background: Apax Partners, Inc., National Venture Capital Association, Chairman of an Investment Advisory Council, Lexicon Genetics, Inc., Independent Network Television Holdings (Moscow), the U.S. Russia Center for Entrepreneurship, and the EastWest Institute.
Roman Simonov, Managing Director
Education: BA Economics with Honors from Stanford University; MBA from Harvard Business School
Background: Deputy General Director, IBS, Moscow; Investment Banking, Goldman Sachs; Consultant, McKinsey & Company, Los Angeles/Moscow/Prague
Paul Price, Managing Director
Education: Irish Institute of Chartered Accountants
Background: Russia Country Inns/Rezidor SAS; SPAR Moscow/Middle Volga; Senior Management, Tetra Pack; Coca-Cola
Natalie Polischuk, Vice President
Education: BA in Economics from the University of Kiev-Mohyla, MBA from Harvard University.
Background: Western NIS Enterprise Fund in Kiev, Ukraine, CIS.
Anton Titov, Vice President
Education: MD from St. Petersburg State Medical Academy, PhD in Cell and Molecular Biology from The Rockefeller University and MBA from Harvard Business School in Boston.
Background: Neurological Surgery resident at Children's Hospital in Boston, University in New York.

2457 AXA INVESTMENT MANAGERS PRIVATE EQUITY EUROPE
20 Vendome Place
75001 Paris 75001
France

Phone: 33-144459200 Fax: 33-144459300
e-mail: sylvie.deneubourg@axa-im.com
web: www.axaprivateequity.com

Mission Statement: Focuses on investment opportunities where we have a distinct competitive advantage and can deliver both product and service excellence for our clients
Geographic Preference: Europe, Asia, USA
Founded: 1994
Average Investment: $458 Billion
Investment Criteria: Seed, Start-up, LBO Distress
Industry Group Preference: Internet Technology, Information Technology, Electronic Technology, Software, Telecommunications
Portfolio Companies: ianet, Poliris, Axialog, ConsortNT, FRA/Business Interactif, MediaDev, Quatermove, Coronis Systems, Europe Technologies, Finsecur, Tagsys, iRoc, Venture/Life Sciences Agendia, Coletica, Cytheris, Innate Pharma, Mutabilis, Neuro 3D, Proteus, Catalliances, Ever

Key Executives:
Dominique Senequier, President
e-mail: vincent.gombault@axa-im.com
Education: MS, Financial Techniques, ESSEC; DESS, Banking and Finance; Degrees in Law and Economics
Background: French Trade Commission in Detroit (USA), Investment Managers at the M&A department of Societe Generale,
Directorships: Member of the Executive Committee
Dominique Gaillard, Managing Director
e-mail: dominique.gaillard@axa-im.com
Education: Ecole Polytechnique; Ecole Nationale des Ponts et Chaussées; Institut d'Administration des Entreprises; MS, UC Berkeley
Background: Péchiney group, Member of the Executive Board - Charterhouse (now Chequers)
Directorships: Member of the Executive Committee

2458 AXIS PARTICIPATIONES EMPRESARIALES
C/ Los Madrazo, 38 2a
Madrid 28014
Spain

Phone: 34-91523165437 Fax: 34-915321933
e-mail: axis@axispart.com
web: www.axispart.com

Mission Statement: Invests in SMEs with a profitable high growth potential
Geographic Preference: Spain
Founded: 1986
Average Investment: $6.28 Million
Minimum Investment: $0.6 Million
Investment Criteria: Profitable working companies - or those with potential profits in the short term.

Key Executives:
Guillermo Jimenez, General Director
Emilio Ramos Gorostiza, Operations Manager

2459 AXM VENTURE CAPITAL
57g Randolph Avenue
London W9 1BQ
United Kingdom

Phone: 5089856
e-mail: info@axmvc.co.uk
web: www.axmvc.co.uk

Mission Statement: Manages the Creative Capital Fund and Northwest Fund 4 Digital Creative.
Geographic Preference: United Kingdom

Venture Capital & Private Equity Firms / International Firms

Investment Criteria: Early-Stage
Portfolio Companies: First Active Media, Autology World, Mydish
Key Executives:
Fred Mendelsohn, Investment Director

2460 AXON PARTNERS GROUP
Jose Ortega y Gasset, 25
Madrid 28006
Spain

Phone: 34-913102894
web: www.axonpartnersgroup.com

Mission Statement: Axon Partners Group (Axon) is an international firm dedicated to value creation through investing and consulting services in the broad technology sector, from ICT to Energy. We manage early to growth capital funds of over 130 Million USD in technology and innovation, supported by prestigious investors from all over the world.

Geographic Preference: Spain, Latin America, India
Average Investment: $100,000K to $25M
Portfolio Companies: Aqua Mobile, Captronic Systems, DocOnYou, Enigma, Nanobiomatters, Nice People At Work, Virgin Play, Wuaki.tv, Zinkia
Other Locations:
801 Brickell Avenue
9th Floor
Miami, FL 33131
Phone: 786-6001462

Calle 87 No. 10 - 93 Of 701
Piso 15
Edifocio Av. Chile
Bogota
Chile
Phone: 571-6353007

Key Executives:
Francisco Velazquez de Cuellar, CEO/Managing Director

2461 AXVENTURES
Republica de Eslovenia 1970
Piso 8 B
Buenos Aires C1426CZH
Argentina

Phone: 54-91154517555
e-mail: lbril@axventures.com
web: www.axventures.com

Mission Statement: Ax Ventures SRL is the Local Manager of Pymar Fund LP, in Argentina. The aim of PYMAR is to invest in Argentine innovative and technology companies that target regional and global markets.

Geographic Preference: Argentina
Industry Group Preference: Technology, Software, Biotechnology, Clean Technology
Portfolio Companies: Bioscience, Keclon, Cupoint, Zauber

Key Executives:
Juan Jose Zaballa, General Partner

2462 AXXESS CAPITAL
33 Aviatorilor Blvd
Bucharest 011853
Romania

Phone: 4021-2077100 Fax: 4021-2228503
e-mail: office@axxesscapital.net
web: www.axxesscapital.net

Mission Statement: Investment Manager of Romanian-American Enterprise Fund and Balkan Accession Fund
Average Investment: $5 Million - $15 Million
Portfolio Companies: EDY International, EELF, Capa Finance, Iceline/Darko, Industrial Access, Frigotechnica, BitDefender, Noriel, Banca Romenesca, Ralfi/Estima Finance, Motoractive, Domenia Credit, Jet Finance, Domo Retail, Policolor

Other Locations:
3 Ohridskoezero Street
Floor 4
Sofia 1330
Bulgaria
Phone: 3592-9269743 Fax: 3592-944-1475

545 Fifth Avenue
Suite 300
New York, NY 10017
Phone: 212-6975766 Fax: 212-8180445

Key Executives:
Horia D Manda, Managing Partner
Education: MBA, University of Quebec
Background: CIO, RAEF

2463 AZINI CAPITAL PARTNERS
29 Farm Street
London W1J 5RL
United Kingdom

Phone: 44-2031783388
e-mail: paul.hill@azini.com
web: www.azini.com

Mission Statement: Azini Capital is a UK based private equity firm that specialises in acquiring portfolios of private and public technology companies from historical investors and shareholders. Azini Capital typically acquires significant minority stakes and prefers to hold investments for a number of years - providing additional funding if required - in order to maximize the growth, development and ultimate value of the companies.

Geographic Preference: United Kingdom
Founded: 2007
Industry Group Preference: Software, Technology, Materials Technology, High Technology
Portfolio Companies: Amino Technologies, Antenova, Bluearc, Aim Technology, Bolero, Centerbeam, Corvil, Crescendo Networks, Digital Fuel, Focus Solutions, Frontier Silicon, Iforce, Investis, Keronite, Mobixell Networks, Ob10, Oberon Media, Onespin, Picochip, Pond Ventures, Portrait Software, Raysat, Shazam, Sonim, Starhome, Streamserve, Transitive

Key Executives:
Michael Bennett, Co-Founder
Education: BSc, Electronic Engineering, Southampton University
Background: British Telecom, IBM, LMS Capital

2464 AZIONE CAPITAL
46 East Coast Rd
#07-03, Eastgate
Singapore 428766
Singapore

Phone: 65-31121688
e-mail: startup@azionecapital.com
web: www.azionecapital.com

Mission Statement: An early stage venture capital investment company and startup incubator.

Geographic Preference: Asia
Founded: 2006
Investment Criteria: Early-Stage
Industry Group Preference: Digital Media & Marketing, Mobile Communications Devices, Wireless Technologies, Energy, Maritime Industry
Portfolio Companies: LocAsian Networks, Who Works Around You Pte Ltd, Hibernator, Events Core, myWobile Pte Ltd, e994, ClickingHouse Pte Ltd, Talenz, Fusion Ads, GameMo

Venture Capital & Private Equity Firms / International Firms

2465 B DASH VENTURES
Holland Hills Mori Tower
No. 11, No. 2, 5-chome
Toranomon, Minato-ku
Tokyo
Japan

e-mail: info@bdashventures.com
web: www.bdashventures.com

Mission Statement: B Dash Ventures invests in promising startups and leading Internet industry entrepreneurs.

Portfolio Companies: Enter Crews, Lindoc, Mr Taddy, (es) Corporation, ScaleOut, FCV, Fresvii, Cubie Messenger

Key Executives:
Hiroyuki Watanabe, President/CEO

2466 B-TO-V PARTNERS
Blumenaustrasse 36
St. Gallen 9000
Switzerland

Phone: 41-71-242-2000 Fax: 41-71-242-2001
e-mail: info@b-to-v.com
web: www.b-to-v.com

Mission Statement: b-to-v is both venture capital firm and a leading investor network. To our members, we provide an incomparable deal flow, in the form of lead- and co-investment-opportunities, collaborative investment processes and access to a unique network of like-minded entrepreneurs. To companies we are a reliable partner when it comes to capital access, entrepreneurial intelligence and professional support.

Geographic Preference: Germany, Europe
Average Investment: 50,000 - 2 million Euro
Industry Group Preference: Advanced Technologies, Internet, Mobile
Portfolio Companies: ArmedAngels, IWAtech, Campanda, Fantasy Shopper, Winlocal, Cycleon, Sum Up, Qype, Highdef, Cellity, Hitmeister, Curefab, ONTOPx, Mobile City, Fab, Flaconi, Angela Bruderer, Happify, Urbanara, Spinelab, Sharewise, Orcamp, Blacklane Limiusines, Ondeso, Xing, Quanta, Linguee, Cod Farmers, Zynga, W.I.S.E., Immatics, Carsablanca, Facebook, CellEra, Luxodo, HengZhi, Studitemps, Reille24, Voss, Finanzchek, Ixigo, Loxi, RomoWind, Alatest, Massiv Konzept, Nanda Tech, Plazes, Mybet.com, eCift, TVSmiles

Other Locations:
Barerstrasse 1
Munich 80333
Germany

Meinekestrasse 5
Berlin 10719
Germany

Key Executives:
Florian Schweitzer, Co-Founder/Partner
Education: University of St. Gallen

2467 BAEKELAND FUNDS
Bollebergen 2 B
Gent-Zwijnaarde 9052
Belgium

Phone: 32-09-264-8987
e-mail: patrick.dhaese@ugent.be

Mission Statement: Invests in growing, innovative companies that are commercializing technology developed within Ghent University.

Fund Size: 3.6 million Euro
Founded: 1999
Average Investment: 500,000 Euro
Investment Criteria: Seed-Stage, Startup
Industry Group Preference: High Technology
Portfolio Companies: ActoGeniX, Arcarios, Artisto Music, Caliopa, Complix Alphabody Therapeutics, Pronota, Sigasi, Spartanova, Trinean

Key Executives:
Patrick Dhaese

2468 BAF SPECTRUM
30 Biopolis Street
#09-02 Matrix
Singapore 138671
Singapore

Phone: 65-6777-7139
e-mail: info@bafspectrum.com

Mission Statement: We are a Singapore-based angel fund investing in Asia-based technology startups with a compelling value proposition and a global high-growth potential. We like to work with entrepreneurs who can demonstrate both creative fervor and execution flair. We look at the feasibility of their innovative ideas, review their execution skills and assess their commitment & competency to grow the company to a global brand with our experienced investment team.

Geographic Preference: Asia
Founded: 2006
Average Investment: $1.5 million
Minimum Investment: $75, 000
Investment Criteria: Startup, Seed-Stage
Industry Group Preference: Digital Media & Marketing, Internet, Consumer Internet, Mobile, Information Technology
Portfolio Companies: Anacle, Anafore, Game Ventures, Healthtrends Medical Investments, IXIGO, Mozat, ProgenIQ

Key Executives:
Sanjeev Shah, Managing Director
Education: BS, International Business, Loyola Marymount University
Background: Founder, Rollon Hydraulics

2469 BALDERTON CAPITAL
28 Britannia Street
The Stables
London WC1X 9JF
United Kingdom

Phone: 4 020 701 668 00
web: www.balderton.com

Mission Statement: An early stage venture capital investor that focuses on European technology comanies.

Geographic Preference: Europe, United States, Asia
Fund Size: $2.2 Billion
Founded: 2000
Average Investment: $5-15 million
Minimum Investment: $100,000
Investment Criteria: Early-Stage, Series A, Seed
Industry Group Preference: E-Commerce & Manufacturing, Consumer Internet, Software, Communications, Security, Semiconductors, Consumer Services, Media, Financial Services
Portfolio Companies: 3D Hubs, Adludio, Aircall, Andjaro, Appear [here], Banjo, Carwow, Citymapper, Cleo, Comply Advantage, Contentful, Credit Benchmark, Crowdcube, Curious AI Company, Dalia Research, Depop, Dinghy, Display Link, Dubsmash, Eqise, Ezoic, Funnel, Furhat Robotics, Globoforce, GoCardless, Healx, Hiya, Infarm, Instabridge, InterResolve, Kobalt, Kupivip.ru, Labaster, Lovecrafts, Luno, Lyst, Memrise, Mojoworks, MyTomorrows, Nlyte Software, Nutmeg, Openet, Patients Know Best, Pay With My Bank, Peakon, Prodigy Finance, Pusher, Qubit, Rebtel, Recorded Future, Rentify, Revolut, ROLI, Scytl, Simple Feast, Sketchfab, Sophia Genetics, Soundtrack Your Brand, Tapdaq, Tempow, Tessian, The Hut Group, The Tab, Thread, Tictail, Touch Surgery, Trademark

Venture Capital & Private Equity Firms / International Firms

Now, Vestiaire Collective, Virtuo, Vivino, VOI, Wooga, Workable, Zego, Zopa

Key Executives:
  Tim Bunting, Senior Advisor
  44 020 7016 6800
  e-mail: tim@balderton.com
  Education: University of Cambridge
  Background: Goldman Sachs
  Bernard Liautaud, Managing Partner
  44 020 7016 6800
  e-mail: bernard@balderton.com
  Education: MS, Engineering Management, Stanford University; Ecole Centrale de Paris
  Background: Dashlane; Business Objects
  Jerome Misso, Senior Advisor
  44 020 7016 6800
  e-mail: contact_jerome@balderton.com
  Education: University of Hull
  Background: Nabarro; Eversheds
  Adrian Rainey, Operating Partner
  e-mail: arainey@balderton.com
  Education: BA, Oxford University
  Background: Taylor Wessing

2470 BALLPARK VENTURES
159/165 Great Portland Street
5th Floor
Tennyson House
London W1W 5PA
United Kingdom

e-mail: info@ballparkventures.com
web: www.ballparkventures.com

Mission Statement: Ballpark Ventures is a small, boutique fund investing in early stage technology startups.
Geographic Preference: Europe
Industry Group Preference: Technology, Mobile, Retail, Consumer & Leisure, Media
Portfolio Companies: Blismedia, Eyequant, Tadaa, Dbvu, Sales Gossip, Loop Me, Future Ad Labs, Blink, Bluefields, On Device Research, Springboard, Pipe

Key Executives:
  Ollie Bishop
  e-mail: ollie@ballparkventures.com
  Background: Founder, STEAK

2471 BALTCAP MANAGEMENT LTD
Tartu mnt. 2
Tallinn 10145
Estonia

Phone: 372-6650280 Fax: 372-6650281
web: www.baltcap.com

Mission Statement: Delivers superior return on equity for investors via invetsment in unlisted advanced stage growth oriented Baltic companies.
Geographic Preference: Baltic Countries
Fund Size: $90 million
Founded: 1995
Average Investment: $3 million
Minimum Investment: $ 300, 000
Investment Criteria: Expansion Stage companies with good grwoth capabilities
Industry Group Preference: Telecommunications, Toys, Clinical Development, Food & Beverage, Information Technology, Machinery, Electronic Technology, Automotive

Key Executives:
  Peeter Saks, Managing Partner
  e-mail: vygandas.juras@BaltCap.com
  Matts Andersson, Senior Adviser, Partner
  e-mail: martin.kodar@BaltCap.com
  Education: BA Economics, Tallinn Technical University
  Background: Administrator in a machinery trading company Nava.
  Directorships: supervisory board member in AS Vipex and AS Ecometal.
  Dagnis Dreimanis, Partner
  e-mail: dagnis.dreimanis@BaltCap.com
  Education: BSBA Finance and Economics, Slippery Rock University of Pennsylvania
  Background: Financial Advisory Services Manager in PricewaterhouseCoopers.
  Directorships: supervisory board member in SIA Hansa Electronics, INTRAC Group AB, SIA DT Mobile, SIA Adam Auto, SIA DEPO DIY, SIA V.L.T.
  Oliver Kullman, Investment Director
  e-mail: ruth.laatre@BaltCap.com

2472 BANEXI VENTURES PARTNERS
13-15 rue Taitbout
Paris 75009
France

Phone: 33-173028969 Fax: 33-140143896

Mission Statement: Focuses on emerging and early stage companies with a priority given to high growth companies with high technology.
Geographic Preference: France
Founded: 1983
Investment Criteria: Emerging and Early Stage companies
Industry Group Preference: Life Sciences, Information Technology, Optical Technology, Semiconductors, Electronic Technology, Medical Technology
Portfolio Companies: Avertec, Iroc, Impact, LDL Technology, Lumilog, Novasic, WSI, Mesatronic, SI Auto, Humirel, TEEM PH, Coronis, Infusio, Kelkoo, Masa, Webdyn, Quotatis

Key Executives:
  Michel Dahan, Chairman
  Education: Ecole Polytechnique; ENSAE
  Background: CEO - SAARI
  Directorships: Chairman
  Philippe Mere, General Partner, Electronics
  Education: MS Engineering, Ecole des Mines de Paris
  Background: Genset, a French Biotech company
  Sophie Pierrin-Lepinard, General Partner
  Education: PhD, Pharmacy, Toulouse University; MA, Finance, ESCP
  Background: Marketing, Proctor & Gamble Pharmaceuticals; Investment Manager, Credit Agricole
  Philippe Herbert, Partner, Internet
  Education: Graduate, SUPELEC
  Background: Director of Marketing, Schlumberger

2473 BANK J VONTOBEL COMPANY AG
Gotthardstrasse 43
Zurich CH-8022
Switzerland

Phone: 41-0582837111 Fax: 4-0582837650
e-mail: vontobel.group@vontobel.ch
web: www.vontobel.com

Mission Statement: Actively seeking new investments.
Founded: 1924

Key Executives:
  Herbert J. Scheidt, Chairman
  Dr. Frank Schnewlin, Vice-Chairman of the Board of Directors, Chairman of the Risk and

2474 BARCELONA EMPREN
Gran Via de les Corts Catalanes
635 6th floor
1 Planta
Barcelona 08010
Spain

Phone: 34-902227237 Fax: 34-934019709

Venture Capital & Private Equity Firms / International Firms

Mission Statement: Actively seeking new investments in the Barcelona VC market.
Geographic Preference: Spain
Founded: 1999
Average Investment: $3 million - $15 million
Minimum Investment: $350,000
Investment Criteria: Invests in innovative companies with a technological base
Industry Group Preference: Biotechnology, Internet Technology, Software, Telecommunications, Media
Portfolio Companies: Xcellsyz, Advancell, Era-plantech, Crystax, Isoco, Net Translations, Nonstopyacht, Agents Inspired, Amr Systems, Fractus, Voz Telecom

Key Executives:
Christian Fernández, Chief Executive Officer
Emilio Gómez, Director Operations

2475 BARCLAYS LEVERAGED FINANCE
1 Churchill Place
London E14 5HP
United Kingdom

Phone: 44-2476-842100 Fax: 44-02071167636
web: www.barclays.co.uk

Mission Statement: Actively seeking new investments.
Geographic Preference: United Kingdom, Western Europe
Investment Criteria: Expansion and Development, Bridge Finance, Refinancing Bank Debt, Secondary Purchase/Replacement Capital, Rescue/Turnaround
Industry Group Preference: All Sectors Considered

Key Executives:
John Varley, Chief Executive Officer
Bob Diamond, President

2476 BARCLAYS PRIVATE EQUITY FRANCE
34 / 36 Avenue de Friedland
Cedex 8
Paris 75383
France

Phone: 33-144583232 Fax: 33-0156694344
web: www.barcap.com

Mission Statement: Actively seeking new investments.
Geographic Preference: France
Founded: 1991
Investment Criteria: MBO, MBI, Capital Expansion

Key Executives:
Eric Bommensath, Co-Chief Executive, Corporate and Investment Banking
e-mail: julie-lorin.meurisse@barclayscapital.com
Education: Graduation at Dauphine University Paris
Justin Bull, Chief Operating Officer
e-mail: gonzague.debligniers@barclayscapital.com
Background: Investor in capital in Banexi & Charterhouse
Patrick Clackson, Chief Executive
e-mail: laurent.chauvois@barclayscapital.com
Education: IEP
Background: Agricultural credit Indosuez
Justin Bull, Chief Operating Officer
e-mail: guillaume.jacqueau@barclayscapital.com
Education: Economics, Business, Finance Graduate.Masters in Finance
Patrick Clackson, Chief Executive
e-mail: cedric.sicard@barclayscapital.com
Education: MBA, University of Texas
Background: Banexi, BNP Kuwait

2477 BARCLAYS VENTURES Barclays
1 Churchill Place
1st Floor
London E14 5HP
United Kingdom

Phone: 1-02124124096 Fax: 44-2075-994691
web: www.barclayscorporate.com

Mission Statement: Invests as a strategic partner alongside management teams, working together to build and realise shareholder value.
Geographic Preference: United Kingdom, Republic of Ireland
Fund Size: $124 Million
Founded: 1997
Average Investment: $6.20 Million
Minimum Investment: $1.77 Million
Investment Criteria: Expansion and Development, Secondary purchase/replacement capital, MBO, MBI, Buy and Build, Roll-out
Industry Group Preference: Business to Business, Leisure, Media, Retailing, Education, Financial Services, Healthcare, Manufacturing, Technology, Telecommunications, Logistics
Portfolio Companies: Benlowe Group Ltd, Diesel Marine International Ltd, System C Healthcare Ltd, Le Monde Holdings Ltd, Esprit Holidays Ltd, VJ Technology, Sovereign Woodmet

Key Executives:
Khilan Dodhia, Director
Alex Brebbia, Director

2478 BARING CORILIUS PRIVATE EQUITY
ul. Wspolna 47/49
Warsaw 00-684
Poland

Phone: 48-226274000 Fax: 48-226274001

Mission Statement: Manages the Baring Central European Fund. A private equity fund manager focused on central Europe. BCPE is a member of Baring Private Equity International.
Geographic Preference: Central Europe, Poland, Hungary, Romania, Bulgaria
Founded: 1997
Minimum Investment: $10 Million
Investment Criteria: Growth, Development, Consolidation
Portfolio Companies: Allami Nyomda, Baoya Estates, CR Media Group, Falcon-Vision, Infopress, Poligrafia SA, Topway Industries

Key Executives:
György Karády, Managing Partner
Education: PhD, Harvard University
Background: Director, European Bank for Reconstruction & Development; Strategy Consultant, US/France
Jacek Pogonowski, Partner
Education: BS Finance, St. John's University
Background: Managing Director, IB Austria Financial Advisors; Arthur Andersen, Warsaw
William R Watson, Partner
Education: MBA, INSEAD
Background: Telecom Team, EBRD; Corporate Finance, Salomon Brothers

2479 BARING PRIVATE EQUITY PARTNERS ASIA
8 Finance Street
Two International Finance Centre
Suite 3801
Central
Hong Kong

Phone: 85-228439300 Fax: 852-28439372
e-mail: hongkong@bpeasia.com

Mission Statement: Actively seeking new investments.
Geographic Preference: India, Singapore, China, Hong Kong, Taiwan, Korea
Fund Size: $257 Million
Founded: 1997
Key Executives:
  Dar Chen, Managing Director
  e-mail: info@bpepasia.com
  Malcolm Lai, Managing Director

2480 BARING PRIVATE EQUITY PARTNERS ESPANA SA
Hermosilla
11-5a Planta
Madrid 28001
Spain
Phone: 34-917818870 Fax: 34-917818877
e-mail: bpepmadrid@bpep.es
web: www.bpep.es

Mission Statement: Provides equity to private Spanish and Portuguese companies, with the objective of financing and contributing to their expansion, shareholder restructuring or management-buy-out.
Geographic Preference: Spain, Portugal
Fund Size: $240 Million
Founded: 1987
Investment Criteria: Expansion, Consolidations, Restructuring, Middle Market
Industry Group Preference: Medical & Health Related, Construction, Heating, Engineering, Media, Automotive
Portfolio Companies: Losán, Aricam, Manuel, Iturmo, Climastar, Ingemas, Novatex, Socinser, Selenis, Sedal, Elite, Marcanet, Aguamur, Iberchem, Autoequip, Bioferma, Euro-atomizado.
Key Executives:
  José Angel Sarasa, Managing Partner

2481 BARING PRIVATE EQUITY PARTNERS INDIA
9th Floor, Infinity Tower A, DLF Phase II
Gurgoan 122002
India
Phone: 91-124-4321100 Fax: 91-124-4321155
e-mail: rahul.bhasin@bpepindia.com
web: www.bpepindia.com

Mission Statement: Partner with exceptional entrepreneurs to build outstanding businesses by providing growth capital and assistance in scaling up through access to relevant industry and management expertise.
Geographic Preference: India
Fund Size: $1 Billion
Founded: 1984
Average Investment: $100 Million
Minimum Investment: $15 million
Investment Criteria: Mid-market transactions, Management buy-out, Significant Minority, Minority
Industry Group Preference: Information Technology, Infrastructure, Banking, Financial Services, Healthcare, Telecommunications, Real Estate, Media, Education, Consumer Products
Portfolio Companies: Mphasis, Molecular Connections, JRG Securities, AuroMira Energy, Infrasoft Technologies, Integra Securities, Secova Services, PharmArc Analytics, Rea Metrix, Maples, Molecular Connections, Sphaera Pharma, Shilpa Medicare, Muthoot Finance, Cethar Vessels
Other Locations:
  1 Royal Plaza
  Royal Avenue
  St Peter Port
  Guernsey, Channel Island GY1 2HL
  United Kingdom
  Phone: 44-14817-35814
Key Executives:
  Gyuri Karady, Managing Partner
  e-mail: rahul.bhasin@bpepindia.com
  SM Sundaram, Partner, Director
  408-690-4014
  e-mail: sundaram@bpepusa.com
  Education: MBA, Indian Institute of Management, Ahmedabad
  Background: Partner & CFO
  Directorships: Infrasoft Technologies, Infrasoft Tech, Secova e-Services, Maples, Auro Mira Energy, Sphaera Pharma

2482 BARING VOSTOK CAPITAL PARTNERS
125047, Moscow, ul. Forest, 9
Business Center White Gardens, Building B, 6 fl.
Gasheka Str. 7, Building 1
Moscow 123056
Russia
Phone: 7-0959671307 Fax: 7-0959671308
e-mail: info@bvcp.ru
web: www.bvcp.ru

Fund Size: $400 Million
Founded: 1994
Investment Criteria: Medium sized
Industry Group Preference: Oil & Gas, Energy, Media, Services, Telecommunications, Branded Goods, Technology
Portfolio Companies: Airln Space, Burren Energy, DalRybProm, GCMW, Golden Telecom, Promopost Holding, Rostik Restaurants Ltd, ru-Net Holdings, riskdata, Sakhinterlesprom, StoryFirst, Syktyvkar, United Confectioneries
Key Executives:
  Arkady Volozh, CEO of Yandex
  Background: European Bank for Reconstruction & Development (EBRD); Salomon Brothers
  Directorships: NIS Fund
  Vyacheslav Zarenkov, Chairman
  Education: BS, PhD, Moscow Power Engineering Institute
  Background: Professor/Researcher, Moscow Power Engineering Institute; CEO, Alfa Asset Management; Director, Alfa Capital
  Directorships: Tops BI, AirInSpace

2483 BASF VENTURE CAPITAL
4, Gartenweg
Gebaude Z 025
Ludwigshafen 67063
Germany
Phone: 49-6216076801 Fax: 49-6216076819
web: www.basf-vc.de

Mission Statement: The corporate venture capital company of BASF Group, investing globally in promising start-up companies and funds. BASF invests in start-up companies and venture capital funds worldwide. Its investments focus on innovative technologies with a high growth potential where chemistry plays an important role, as well as new materials and substances with significant market opportunities. BASF not only invests venture capital, but also supports its investments through targeted interaction between BASF Group's worldwide know-how and research network and its portfolio companies.
Geographic Preference: Worldwide
Investment Criteria: Startup, Early-Stage
Industry Group Preference: Chemicals, Plastics, Agriculture, Oil & Gas, Energy, Biotechnology, Nanotechnology
Portfolio Companies: Advanced BioNutrition, Allylix, Arcadia Biosciences, ARCH Venture Partners, Aspen Aerogels, Baseclick, Chrysalix, Clean Diesel Technologies,

Venture Capital & Private Equity Firms / International Firms

Datalase, Deutsche Rohstoff AG, Fintech, FloDesign, Heliatek, Luca Technologies, NanoMas Technologies, NGen Enabling Technologies Funds, Oxonica, Pangaea Ventures, Plastic Logic, Sciessent, SDC Materials, Solidia Technologies

Other Locations:
46820 Fremont Blvd
Fremont, CA 94538
Phone: 510-4456140

45th Floor, Jardine House
No. 1, Connaught Place
Central
Hong Kong
Phone: 852-27313755

Roppongi Hills Mori Tower 21F
6-10-1, Roppongi, Minato-ku
Tokyo 106-6121
Japan
Phone: 81-337964117 Fax: 81-337965947

Key Executives:
Dirk Nachtigal, Managing Director
49-621-60-76813
Education: University of Gottingen, University of Hamburg
Background: Head of Finance, Accounting & Control, BASF Schwarzheide GmbH

2484 BASIL PARTNERS Kross Border Trust Services Limited
St. Louis Business Centre
Onr Desroches & St. Louis Streets
Port Louis
Mauritius

Phone: 230-2031100 Fax: 230-2031150
e-mail: info@basilpartners.com
web: www.basilpartners.com

Mission Statement: Basil Partners is a venture capital fund focused on investing in either Indian / Asian companies which seek to expand into Global markets or US / European companies which have an India / Asia centric offshore based model. Basil's investment philosophy is to Partner with the Portfolio company and 'Actively Build' world class companies. Our capital comes from 'Basil Growth Corporation', a closed-end Venture Capital Fund incorporated in Mauritius.

Geographic Preference: India, Asia, United States, Europe
Industry Group Preference: Information Technology
Portfolio Companies: Cignex, Endeavour, GGVS, IT Convergence, Karmic, Netscribes, SDG

Key Executives:
Rajeev Srivastava, CEO/Managing Partner
Education: BS, Engineering, MBA, Mumbai University
Background: Founder, Apar Infotech

2485 BAY BG BAVARIAN VENTURE CAPITAL CORP
Queen Street 23
PO Box 1155
Munich 80539
Germany

Phone: 089-122280100 Fax: 089-122280101
e-mail: info@baybg.de
web: www.baybg.de

Mission Statement: Invests in medium-sized companies
Geographic Preference: Germany
Investment Criteria: Growth, Innovation, MBO, MBI, Bridging loans
Industry Group Preference: Consumer Products, Wholesale, High Technology, Industrial Services, Retailing, Life Sciences
Portfolio Companies: Baierl & Demmelhuber Innenausbau GmbH, Töging am Inn, Balnea Erlebnisbäder GmbH & Co. Chieming/Obb, Cottan Cosmetic GmbH, München, Dinghartinger Apfelstrudel Productions-UND Vertriebs, Landsham, Dobler Metallbau GmbH, München, ES-Plastic GmbH

Key Executives:
Guenther Henrich, Managing Director
Peter Pauli, Managing Director

2486 BAYERN KAPITAL
Landgasse 135 a
Landshut 84028
Bavaria

Phone: 49-8719232555 Fax: 49-8719232555
e-mail: info@bayernkapital.de
web: www.bayernkapital.de

Mission Statement: Bayern Kapital GmbH is a public Bavarian venture capital company and was founded as part of the 'Bavarian Future Initiative' as a wholly-owned subsidiary of the LfA Foerderbank Bayern (Bavaria's development bank) at the end of 1995. The objective of Bayern Kapital is to finance research and development and market launch of new products. In this effort Bayern Kapital usually acts as co-investor in cooperation with a private lead investor. The 'Bayern Kapital model' is unique in Germany. Bayern Kapital has now developed into an essential location factor and driver of private financing in Bavaria.

Geographic Preference: Bavaria
Founded: 1995
Average Investment: 250,000-500,000 Euro
Investment Criteria: Seed-Stage, Startup, Early-Stage
Industry Group Preference: High Technology

Key Executives:
Roman Huber, Managing Director
Rudolf Mayr, Managing Director

2487 BB BIOTECH VENTURES
Seestrasse 16
Kusnacht 8700
Switzerland

Phone: 41-442676700 Fax: 41-442676701
e-mail: info@bellevue.ch

Mission Statement: BB Biotech Ventures is a healthcare-dedicated venture capital fund, focused on companies that develop and market drugs and medical devices. The Guernsey-based fund is advised by the Bellevue Asset Management Group, which has operations in Curaçao, Boston/USA and Kusnacht/Zurich, Switzerland.

Industry Group Preference: Healthcare, Medical Devices
Portfolio Companies: Aerovance, Aleva Neurotherpeutics, Alpex Pharma, AM Pharma, Anteis, Atlas Genetics, BioVascular, Cadence Pharmaceuticals, Calypso Medical Technologies, Cameron Health, Cervelo Pharmaceuticals, Lumavita, Molecular Partners, NEOSE Technologies, Natural Dental Implants, Optimer Pharmaceuticals, Orthocon, Palyon, Pevion Biotech, Radius Health, Sonetik, Swiss Smile, TargeGen, Tioga Pharmaceuticals, Vaximm

Key Executives:
Klaus Breiner, Senior Investment Advisor Private Equity
Background: Business Consultant, Booz Allen & Hamilton
Directorships: Agendia, Alpex Pharma, Cadence Pharmaceuticals, Cervelo Pharmaceuticals, Glycart Biotechnology, Orthocon
Jurg Eckhardt, Senior Investment Advisor Private Equity
Education: MBA, INSEAD; MD, University of Basel
Background: Associate Partner, McKinsey & Company
Directorships: Anteis, Calypso Medical Technologies, TargeGen, Swiss Smile Holding

Venture Capital & Private Equity Firms / International Firms

2488 BC PARTNERS LIMITED
40 Portman Square
London W1H 6DA
United Kingdom

Phone: 44-2070094800 Fax: 44-2070094899
e-mail: london@bcpartners.com
web: www.bcpartners.com

Mission Statement: Actively seeking new investments.
Geographic Preference: United Kingdom, Western Europe
Fund Size: $87.2 billion
Founded: 1986
Average Investment: $264 Million
Minimum Investment: $21.6 Million
Investment Criteria: Secondary purchase/replacement capital, MBO, MBI, Institutional BO, Leveraged Build Up, Public-to-Private
Industry Group Preference: Technology, Healthcare, Heating, Publishing, Automotive, Hospitals
Portfolio Companies: Amadeus, Dometic, Picard, Centro Médico Teknon, Baxi Group, SEAT, Telecolumbus, Hirslanden Holdings, Elis II, Galbani, LD COM, Mark IV Industries, General Healthcare Group
Key Executives:
Fahim Ahmed, Partner
Education: MBA from Stanford University and an economics degree from Cambridge
Background: Boston Consulting Group
Justin Bateman, Senior Partner
Education: MBA from the University of Chicago, Graduate of both the Ecole Polytechnique and the Ecole Nationale Supérieure des Télécommunications
Background: Director, Finapol Sarl, Manager, Finapol Sarl, Vice Chairman, Wasserstein Perella & Co.
Directorships: Executive
Michael Chang, Partner
Education: MBA from The Wharton School in Pennsylvania and an economics degree from Cambridge.
Background: Bankers Trust, Bain & Co in Boston and London,

2489 BECO CAPITAL

web: www.becocapital.com

Mission Statement: Based in Egypt, BECO Capital gives companies the two vital ingredients that they most need in their early development stage: growth capital and hands-on operational mentorship. BECO tries to to strike a balance between the bottom line and benefiting local communities. BECO aspires to give VSMEs the boost they need to make giant leaps for the Middle East.
Geographic Preference: Middle East
Key Executives:
Dany Farha, Founder/CEO
Background: Co-Founder, Bayt.com

2490 BEIJING HIGH TECHNOLOGY INVESTMENT COMPANY
Center Gate Technologies Building
12th floor
Haidian District
Beijing 100081
China

Phone: 86-1062140588 Fax: 86-1062142499
web: www.bhti.com.cn

Mission Statement: Committed to investing in strong, growing companies.
Geographic Preference: China
Fund Size: $31 Million
Founded: 1998
Investment Criteria: Making investment in high-tech enterprises
Industry Group Preference: Information Technology, Life Sciences, Energy, Environmental Protection
Portfolio Companies: Altan China Co Ltd, Shenzhen Tsinghua Tongfang Co Ltd, Tsinghua Tongfang Artificial Environment Co Ltd, Beijing Ibase Software Co Ltd, Capital Biochip Corporation, Beijing Phylion Battery Co Ltd, Beijing King's Orient Hi-Tech Group Co Ltd
Key Executives:
Qi Rong, General Manager
Xing Hualou, Chairman

2491 BEIJING VENTURE CAPITAL COMPANY LIMITED
10th Floor, Haidian Science Technology Tower
Haidian District
No.3 Nada Street, Zhongguancun
Beijing 100081
China

Phone: 86-1068943739 Fax: 86-1068943779

Mission Statement: Committed to investing in strong, growing companies.
Geographic Preference: China
Fund Size: $465 Million
Founded: 1998
Average Investment: $40 million
Minimum Investment: $1 Million
Investment Criteria: Expansion Capital, Development Capital, Buyout
Industry Group Preference: Information Technology, Environmental Protection, Materials Technology
Portfolio Companies: Beijing International Trust and Investment Co, Beijing International Power Development & Investment Corp, China CYTS Tours Holding Co Ltd.,
Key Executives:
Xu Zhe, Chairman
Rongzi Wang, Vice President & Supervisor

2492 BENCIS CAPITAL PARTNERS
World Trade Center Amsterdam
Zuidplein 76
Amsterdam 1077 XV
Netherlands

Phone: 31-205400940 Fax: 31-205400941
e-mail: info@bencis.com
web: www.bencis.nl

Mission Statement: Bencis Capital Partners is an independent private equity firm targeting medium sized companies in the Benelux countries. Bencis Capital Partners is fully independent and is owned by its partners. Bencis Capital Partners is responsible for the management of Bencis Buyout Fund I (established in 2000) and is fund manager of Bencis Buyout Fund II (2004), Bencis Buyout Fund III (2007) and Bencis Buyout Fund IV (2011).
Geographic Preference: Benelux
Industry Group Preference: Manufacturing, Food & Beverage, Leisure, Media, Wholesale, Retail, Consumer & Leisure
Portfolio Companies: AXA Stenman, Baert, CMI-Dutchview, Desso, Florimex Group, Itho Daalderop, Neroc, Royal Sanders, Shoeby - Lakeside, SK FireSafety Group, Smulders Group, Stork Prints, Tandvitaal, Teidem - Jomo, The Employment Group, Unlimited Sports Group, Verelst, Winsol
Key Executives:
Zoran van Gessel, Co-Founder
Education: MSc, Economics, University of Amsterdam
Background: Senior Executive, MeesPierson Corporate Finance
Directorships: Jomo, Teidem, Axa Stenman, Tandvitaal

Venture Capital & Private Equity Firms / International Firms

2493 BERENBERG PRIVATE CAPITAL
Neuer Jungfernstieg 20
Hamburg 20354
Germany

Phone: 49-40350600 Fax: 49-4035060900
e-mail: info@berenberg.de
web: www.berenbergbank.de

Mission Statement: Actively seeking new investments.

Founded: 1590
Minimum Investment: 25, 000 Euro
Investment Criteria: All Stages
Industry Group Preference: All Sectors Considered

Key Executives:
   Claus-G. Budelmann, General Partner
   49 4035060212
   Hans-Walter Peters, General Partner
   49 4035060214

2494 BERLIN TECHNOLOGIE
Unter den Linden 16
Berlin 10117
Germany

Phone: 49-0-30-408-173-214
e-mail: info@berlinholding.com
web: www.berlinholding.com

Mission Statement: Berlin Technologie Holding focuses exclusively on growth capital and special opportunity situations in technology and technology-enabled businesses. BTH was founded by successful entrepreneurs and investors who invest in companies with significant growth potential.

Investment Criteria: Growth Stage, Special Situations
Industry Group Preference: Technology, Technology-Enabled Services
Portfolio Companies: Sevenval, Sensorberg, Realytics, Europe Apotheek, Viagogo

Key Executives:
   Joern-Carlos Kuntze, Founder/Managing Partner
   e-mail: joern.kuntze@berlinholding.com
   Education: BA, International Finance, Regents College; MBA, London Business School
   Background: Senior Partner, Oliver Wyman; Venturepark AG

2495 BERRIER CAPITAL
Via Manzoni, 16
Milan 20121
Italy

Phone: 39-0236644120 Fax: 39-0236644129
web: private-equity.berriercapital.com

Mission Statement: The Company researches, selects and evaluates investment in both the majority and the minority in SMEs, manages the due diligence , negotiate the terms and conditions investments, supports the management of investee companies in developing strategies and processes of growth and value creation, manages the processes of disinvestment. corporate structure is that of a holding company independent under Italian law. The Company does not use , if only marginally and, in any case, very contained, of leverage in the operations of acquisition, in the conviction of the total alignment between creating value for its members and creating value for the subsidiaries.

Portfolio Companies: Greentech Innovation, Mediamo

Key Executives:
   Alberto Craici, Founding Partner
   Alessandro Marina, Partner
   Francesco Saibene, Investment Manager

2496 BERTI INVESTMENTS
7 Cavendish Square
London W1G 0PE
United Kingdom

Phone: 44-02076129362
web: www.bertiinvestments.com

Mission Statement: Berti is an environmental impact investment company. We invest in innovative, growing, entrepreneurial businesses in the UK whose strategy focuses on reducing carbon emissions.

Geographic Preference: United Kingdom
Industry Group Preference: Energy, Clean Technology, Renewable Energy
Portfolio Companies: Ecovision Renewables, Firefly Solar Generators, Ecometrica, HomeSun

2497 BERYTECH FUND
Berytech Technological Pole
Mkalles
Lebanon

Phone: 961-4533040 Fax: 961-4533070

Mission Statement: Berytech fund is a Lebanese start up fund. Its mission is to invest in early growth Lebanese companies whose business is in the information and communication technology (ICT) in exchange for equity ownership. With over USD6 million under management, the Fund focuses on technology companies in Lebanon with proven commercial viability. We have the operational experience to nurture the right management team to make the vision a reality, helping fast growing companies avoid pitfalls. We offer vision, imagination, experience and a network of contacts across the globe through the Fund partners.

Geographic Preference: Lebanon
Founded: 2008
Average Investment: $100,000 - $1.2 million
Investment Criteria: Startup, Seed-Stage

Key Executives:
   Maroun N Chammas, Chairman
   Background: Director, Chammas Group; Co-Founder, Teleinvest Holdings

2498 BESTPORT VENTURES
29 Gloucester Place
London W1U 8HX
United Kingdom

Phone: 44-2074872555 Fax: 44-2074875535
e-mail: asimmons@bestport.co.uk
web: www.bestport.co.uk

Mission Statement: Bestport draws on the strong track record and experience of the founders and our accomplished advisory board to invest in and assist fast-growing, ambitious companies through to profitable exits.

Geographic Preference: United Kingdom
Founded: 2005
Average Investment: £250,000 - 3 million
Investment Criteria: Growth/Expansion Capital, MBO, MBI
Industry Group Preference: Business Products & Services, Healthcare, Technology
Portfolio Companies: CreditCall Limited, Healthcall Optical Services, Hotelscene Limited, Intela Global Limited, Mfuse Limited, Oracle Care Limited

Key Executives:
   Ole Bettum, Co-Founder
   e-mail: obettum@bestport.co.uk
   Education: BSc, Economics, London School of Economics; MBA, Columbia Business School
   Background: Price Waterhouse, Close Brothers Group

Venture Capital & Private Equity Firms / International Firms

2499 BI WALDEN MANAGEMENT SDN Walden International
One California St.
Suite 2800
San Francisco, California
San Francisco, CA 94111

Phone: 415-7657100 Fax: 415-7657200
e-mail: usa@waldenintl.com
web: www.waldenintl.com

Mission Statement: Actively seeking new investments.
Geographic Preference: China, Malaysia, Taiwan, India, Singapore, USA
Fund Size: $1.6 Billion
Founded: 1987
Investment Criteria: Start Up
Industry Group Preference: Communications, Electronic Technology, Software, Semiconductors, Digital Media & Marketing, Information Technology
Portfolio Companies: 2bSURE.com Pte Ltd, Actelis Networks, Inc, AirTight Networks, Inc, Archway Digital Solutions Inc, BeamReach Networks, Broadxent Pte Ltd, Cameo Communications, Inc., Celestial Semiconductor, Ltd., Centillium Communications, Inc., Centrum Communic

Key Executives:
Brian Chiang, Managing Director
e-mail: akau@waldenintl.com
Education: BS, Electrical Engineering, Brown University; MBA, University of Virginia
Background: President of Chemical Technologies Ventures, Management consultant at Strategic Planning Associates and Booz
Lip-Bu Tan, Chairman

2500 BIG SOCIETY CAPITAL
72-78 Fleet Street
London EC4Y 1HY
United Kingdom

Phone: 020-7186-2500
e-mail: enquiries@bigsocietycapital.com
web: www.bigsocietycapital.com

Mission Statement: Big Society Capital is the world's first social investment wholesaler. Big Society Capital was launched in April 2012 with up to £600 million of capital to develop the social investment market in the UK by improving access to finance for social sector organizations and by raising investor awareness of investment opportunities that provide a social as well as a financial return.
Geographic Preference: United Kingdom
Fund Size: £600 million
Founded: 2012
Minimum Investment: £500,000
Industry Group Preference: Social Enterprises, Education, Wellness, Conservation, Environment
Portfolio Companies: Iaam, Resonance, Big Issue Invest, Bridges Ventures, ClearlySo, Ethical Property, Francising Works, LGT, Nesta Impact Investments, Pure Leapfrog, Social Stock Exchange

Key Executives:
Nick O'Donohoe, Chief Executive Officer
Background: Global Head of Research, JP Morgan; Goldman Sachs
Directorships: Global Impact Investing Network

2501 BIG SUR VENTURES
Fdez. de la Hoz 33
5 cto-dcha
Madrid 28010
Spain

Phone: 34-916237731
e-mail: jm@bigsurventures.es
web: www.bigsurventures.es

Mission Statement: Big Sur, based in Madrid, is an investor in companies early stage companies and working with passionate teams that seek to transform their markets with great ideas.
Investment Criteria: Seed-Stage, Early-Stage
Industry Group Preference: Internet, New Media, Technology-Enabled Services, Information Technology, Clean Technology, Digital Media & Marketing, Cloud Computing

Key Executives:
Jose Miguel Herrero, Founder
e-mail: jm@bigsurventures.es
Education: BSEECS, MSEE, Santa Clara University; MBA, Berkeley's Haas School of Business
Background: LaNetro

2502 BIGFOOT VENTURES
13th Floor C. Wisdom Centre
37 Hollywood Road
Causeway Bay
Central
Hong Kong

Phone: 852-58083400 Fax: 852-30158536
e-mail: info@bigfootventures.com
web: www.bigfoot.com/oc-bigfoot-ventures.php

Mission Statement: Bigfoot Ventures is a wholly-owned international private venture capital subsidiary of the Bigfoot Group of Companies. With operations in Hong Kong, Singapore, Cebu (Philippines), New York, Los Angeles and Antwerpen (Belgium), the company manages and implements the Group's investment plans and strategies, focusing on sectors operating in communications, technology, education, entertainment, and new media.
Geographic Preference: Asia, Europe, United States
Founded: 2004
Industry Group Preference: Communications, Technology, Education, Entertainment, New Media
Portfolio Companies: Fashion One

Other Locations:
BigFoot Entertainment
1451 Ocean Drive
Suite 200
Miami Beach, FL 33139
Phone: 305-5045000

2503 BIO FUND MANAGEMENT OY
4 Mikonkatu, 3rd Floor, PO Box 164
Helsinki 101
Finland

Phone: 358-92514460 Fax: 358-92514620
web: www.biofund.fi

Mission Statement: The company manages the Bio Fund I, II, III and BFV II
Geographic Preference: Worldwide
Fund Size: $ 234 Million
Founded: 1998
Minimum Investment: $1.2 Million
Investment Criteria: Early Stage, Expansion, Development Capital, Start-Up Capital, Turnaround, Restructuring, Buyout/Buyin
Industry Group Preference: Agriculture, Biotechnology, Chemicals, Medical & Health Related, Food & Beverage, Forestry, Fishing

Key Executives:
Kalevi Kurkijärvi, Senior Partner, Chairman & Chief Executive Officer
e-mail: erkki.pekkarinen@biofund.fi
Education: MBA, Helsinki School of Economics & Business Administration
Background: Director of finance at the Local Government Pensions Institution

Venture Capital & Private Equity Firms / International Firms

Directorships: In charge of funding work and investor relations
Seppo Mäkinen, Senior Partner
e-mail: kalevi.kurkijarvi@biofund.fi
Education: PhD in Biochemistry and Molecular Biology, University of Turku
Background: Director of venture capital group in the Finnish National Fund of Research and Development Sitra, executive vice president at Wallac Oy and as president and CEO at Pharmacia Diagnostics Production Oy.
Directorships: Chairman of the board at BioTie Therapies Oy, MAP Medical Oy, Bio Orbit Oy, Admin Technologies Oy, FibroGen Europe Oy, Pribori Oy, Hormos Medical Oy and Rados Technology Oy

2504 BIO*ONE CAPITAL EDMI
250 North Bridge Road
#28-00 Raffles City Tower
179101
Singapore

Phone: 65-68326832 Fax: 65-68326838
e-mail: infoHQ@edbi.com
web: www.edbi.com

Mission Statement: Through EDBI's dedicated fund manager for Biomedical Sciences, Bio*One Capital invests in innovative healthcare IT, services, devices and therapeutics companies; and played an instrumental role in growing Singapore's Biomedical Sciences industry over the last 10 years. With over 40 portfolio companies globally, we continue to back innovative fast-growing companies that target significant market opportunities with a clear exit strategy. With our support, they are able to leverage on Singapore's position as the leading Biomedical Sciences center in Asia to access Asia's rapid-growing markets and competitive resources in fuelling their global growth.

Geographic Preference: Asia
Industry Group Preference: Healthcare Information Technology
Portfolio Companies: Adamas Pharmaceuticals, Addex Pharmaceuticals, Artisan Pharma, Cylacel Pharmaceuticals, Five Prime Therapeutics, FORMA Therapeutics, goBalto, Idenix, Invaragen, Ironwood, KaloBios Pharmaceuticals, Kalypsys, Lonza Biologics, Maccine, MerLion, Perlegen, Renovis, Revance, S*Bio, Sotera Wireless, Vanda Pharmaceuticals

2505 BIOGENERATION VENTURES
Gooimeer 2-35
Naarden 1411 DC
Netherlands

Phone: 31-356993000 Fax: 31-356993001
web: www.biogenerationventures.com

Mission Statement: BioGeneration Ventures manages funds that are actively investing venture capital in the next generation of successful life sciences companies in The Netherlands, Belgium and Germany.

Geographic Preference: The Netherlands, Belgium, Germany
Founded: 1995
Industry Group Preference: Healthcare, Therapeutics, Medical Devices, Diagnostics, Food & Beverage
Portfolio Companies: Arcarios, arGEN-X, BioCeros, Cristal Delivery, Dezima Pharma, EPD-visionk, FlexGen, Lanthio Pharma, Medisse, Mucosis, NovioGendix, Progentix Orthobiology, Revisios, Simibio

Key Executives:
Edward van Wezel, Managing Partner
31-35-699-3011
e-mail: edward@biogeneration.vc
Education: MSc, Chemistry, University of Utrecht; MSc, Biochemical Engineering, Delft University of Technology
Background: Process Engineer, Chiron; Project Manager, Johnson & Johnson
Directorships: Arcarios, NovioGendix, Progentix, Orthobiology, Cristal Delivery

2506 BIOMED PARTNERS
Elisabethenstr. 23
Basel CH-4051
Switzerland

Phone: 41-612703535 Fax: 41-612703500
e-mail: info@biomedvc.com
web: www.biomedvc.com

Mission Statement: BioMedPartners is one of the leading European venture capital firms providing private equity and mezzanine financing to early- and mid-stage healthcare and human life science companies. We target the entire industry with special focus on pharmaceuticals, biotechnology, diagnostics and medical technology.

Geographic Preference: Europe
Fund Size: CHF 250 million
Investment Criteria: Early-Stage, Mid-Stage
Industry Group Preference: Healthcare, Life Sciences, Pharmaceuticals, Biotechnology, Diagnostics, Medical Technology
Portfolio Companies: Activaero, Aleva, Anergis, Curetis, Evolva, Sequana Medical, Vaximm, Ventaleon

Key Executives:
Gerhard Ries, Co-Founder/General Partner
41-61-270-3580
e-mail: ries@biomedvc.com
Education: MS, PhD, Molecular Biology, University of Basel
Background: Partner, InterPharmaLink

2507 BIOPACIFIC VENTURES
Level 6
2 Kitchener Street
Auckland 1010
New Zealand

Phone: 64-93072562 Fax: 64-93072349

Mission Statement: BioPacificVentures concentrates on making selective investments in a small number of companies that are exceptionally innovative, have a sound business model and possess an experienced management team. Portfolio companies are actively supported by BioPacificVentures at all development stages, from R&D and clinical trial design to product launch and international expansion.

Geographic Preference: New Zealand, Australia
Founded: 2005
Industry Group Preference: Nutrition, Pharmaceuticals, Cosmetics, Food & Beverage, Biotechnology, Life Sciences
Portfolio Companies: Anzamune, CoDa Therapeutics, Focus Genetics, Horizon Science, New Zealand King Salmon, New Zealand Pharmaceuticals, Vital Foods

Key Executives:
Andrew Kelly, Co-Founder/Executive Director
Education: PhD, Life Sciences
Background: Founding Executive, Celentis; General Manager, Investment, AgResearch

2508 BIOPROCESS CAPITAL PARTNERS
Bldg 1, 8, Nauchny Proezd
Moscow 117246
Russia

Phone: 7-4954118594 Fax: 7-4956443797

Mission Statement: Bioprocess Capital Partners LLP mostly invests in venture projects in two areas of modern high-tech industry - Live Systems / Biotechnology and Fine Chemistry and in selected biotechnological and pharmaceutical start-up projects from Russia and other countries.

Geographic Preference: Russia
Fund Size: 3 billion rubles

Venture Capital & Private Equity Firms / International Firms

Founded: 2001
Investment Criteria: Early-Stage
Industry Group Preference: High Technology, Biotechnology, Pharmaceuticals

2509 BIOVEDA CAPITAL
50 Cuscaden Road
#07-02 HPL House
249724
Singapore

Phone: 65-62389200 **Fax:** 65-6733383
e-mail: info@biovedacapital.com

Mission Statement: BioVeda is a Singapore based firm. We invest in companies in the healthcare sector with leading market positions, proprietary technologies, and outstanding scientific and management talent. We are a crucial business and scientific bridge between companies in the East and West, linking business and technology between two very diverse markets.

Investment Criteria: Early-Stage to Development Stage
Industry Group Preference: Healthcare, Life Sciences, Pharmaceuticals
Portfolio Companies: Agilix Corporation, ASLAN Pharmaceuticals, Clearbridge BioMedics, Dynavax Technologies, Idun Pharmaceuticals, Kiadis Pharma, Memory Pharmaceuticals, MerLion Pharmaceuticals, NeuroVision, NOD Pharmaceuticals, Paratek Pharmaceuticals, Renovis, Renovo, Singapore Advanced Biologics

Key Executives:
  Damien Lin, General Partner
  Background: PrimePartners, Vickers Ballas, Morgan Grenfell Asia

2510 BIRK VENTURE
Karenslyst alle 8b
Oslo 0278
Norway

Phone: 47-90871483
e-mail: post@birkventure.no
web: www.birkventure.no

Mission Statement: Birk Venture is a Scandinavian venture company exclusively focusing on the life science industry. The company was founded in 2010 by Hans Ivar Robinson. Our vision is to be a preferred business partner in the life science sector. We offer venture capital to young companies with significant growth prospects. Our broad industrial experience from the pharmaceutical and biotechnology industry and international network, are the foundation for our strategic and long-term investments in life science.

Geographic Preference: Scandinavia
Founded: 2010
Industry Group Preference: Life Sciences
Portfolio Companies: Algeta, APIM Therapeutics, BerGenBio, Nextera, Nordic Nanovector AS, PCI Biotech, Pronova BioPharma, Targovax

Key Executives:
  Hans Ivar Robinson, Managing Director/Chairman
  Background: AstraZeneca, Pfizer, Pronova BioPharma

2511 BLACKBIRD VENTURES
Level 5
80 Mount Street
North Sydney NSW 2060
Australia

Phone: 61-0-2-8314-7400
e-mail: contact@blackbird.vc
web: www.blackbird.vc

Mission Statement: Blackbird Ventures is a venture capital firm that invests in inherently global Internet businesses formed by Australians. We back world-class founders who are setting out to make a difference in the world. Blackbird Ventures itself is a collection of Australia's most successful startup founders and Silicon Valley's top investors who want to help you succeed on a global stage.

Geographic Preference: Australia
Investment Criteria: Seed-Stage, Series A, Later-Stage
Industry Group Preference: Internet, Consumer Internet, Social Media, SaaS, Mobile, E-Commerce & Manufacturing, Software
Portfolio Companies: Canva, Coinjar, Elto.com, Ninja Blocks, Safety Culture, Sessions, Shoes of Prey, Startmate

Key Executives:
  Niki Scevak, Managing Director
  Education: University of New South Wales
  Background: Founder, Startmate; Founder, Homethinking

2512 BLACKFIN CAPITAL PARTNERS
127, avenue des Champs Elysees
Paris 750008
France

Phone: 01-75000230 **Fax:** 01-75000239
web: www.blackfincp.com

Mission Statement: BlackFin is a private equity firm dedicated to financial services: distribution and brokerage of financial products, asset management, electronic banking, BPO, internet finance and capital markets.

Average Investment: 10-30 million Euros
Industry Group Preference: Financial Services
Portfolio Companies: Applicam, Chiarezza, Groupe Cyrus, Kepler Capital Markets, MisterAssur, Owliance

Key Executives:
  Sabine Mathis, Chief Financial Officer
  Education: Ecole Polytechnique, Ecole de la Statistique de l'Administration Economique
  Background: Aquiline Capital Partners, ProCapital

2513 BLOOM EQUITY
25-27 Fitzwilliam Pl
Ballsbridge
Dublin 2
Ireland

Phone: 01-669-4700
e-mail: sarah@hban.org

Mission Statement: Experienced entrepreneurs investing in early stage Irish Technology companies.

Geographic Preference: Ireland
Investment Criteria: Early-Stage
Industry Group Preference: Technology
Portfolio Companies: Boxever, Phorest, ManageCO2, InishTech, Fantom, SourceDogg, Scrazzl, B-Sm@rk

Key Executives:
  Anthony Bermingham, Group Chairperson
  Education: Chartered Accountant
  Background: Director, Atlanta International Ltd

2514 BLUE COVE VENTURES
60 Hawker Street
2607 Torrens
2607
Australia

Phone: 61-413227711
web: www.bluecoveventures.net

Mission Statement: Blue Cove Ventures invests in innovation focusing on early expansion opportunities. We love web and software opportunities and invest in entrepreneurs who have great, commercially viable ideas with significant global potential. We like entrepreneurs with passion and persistence who go that extra mile to get the job done.

Geographic Preference: Australia
Founded: 2007
Investment Criteria: Early-Stage
Industry Group Preference: Internet

Venture Capital & Private Equity Firms / International Firms

Portfolio Companies: Simmerson Holdings, Windlab Systems

Key Executives:
   Nick McNaughton, Chief Operating Officer
   e-mail: nick@bluecoveventures.net

2515 BLUEGEM CAPITAL PARTNERS
16 Berkeley Street
London W1J 8DZ
United Kingdom

Phone: 44-02076479710 Fax: 44-02076811304
e-mail: enquiries@bluegemcp.com

Mission Statement: An independent London based private equity fund, BlueGem seeks to invest in sector specific mid-market companies based in Western Europe.

Geographic Preference: Western Europe
Fund Size: £200 million
Founded: 2006
Average Investment: £10-40 million
Industry Group Preference: Retail, Consumer & Leisure, Consumer Products, Distribution, Business Products & Services
Portfolio Companies: Enotria, Fintyre, Liberty, Management Consulting Group, Neomobile, Olicar, The Private Clinic Group

Key Executives:
   Marco Capello, Founder/Managing Partner
   Education: Politecnico di Torino; MBA, Columbia University
   Background: Managing Director, Merrill Lynch Global Private Equity
   Directorships: Olicar, The Private Clinic, Fintyre, Neomobile, Management Consulting Group, Libery, Ufi Filters, Enotria

2516 BLUESHIFT INTERNET VENTURES
Blueshift
21, Abdul Razack Street
Dignity Centre
Saidapet
Chennai 600 015
India

Phone: 91-4442272583 Fax: 91-4442272582
web: www.blueshift.com

Mission Statement: Blueshift's suite of services includes Offshore Software Development for diverse industries and verticals, Consulting and Business Solutions (which include Knowledge Discovery and technology driven Recruitment services) and IT services.

Geographic Preference: USA, India
Founded: 1993
Investment Criteria: Blueshift's mission is to provide quality solutions and services with scalable, cost-effective resources, to reduce time-to-market for clients worldwide
Industry Group Preference: Software, Information Technology

Key Executives:
   Prashant Sankaran, Chief Executive Officer
   e-mail: sankaran@sankaran.com
   Education: Ph.D, Temple University; MBA, XLRI
   Background: Information systems industry
   Dr. Sankaran P. Raghunathan, Chief Operating Officer

2517 BLUME VENTURES
Blume Venture Advisors
Unit 4, Jetha Compound, Opp Nirmal Park
Byculla (East)
Mumbai
India

e-mail: jobs@blumeventures.com

Mission Statement: Blume Ventures provides seed funding in the range of $50K-$250K to early-stage tech-focused/tech-enabled ventures. We are proponents of a collaborative approach and like to co-invest with like-minded angels and seed funds. We then provide follow0on investments to our stellar portfolio companies, ranging between $500K and $1.5 million.

Geographic Preference: India
Fund Size: 100 Crore
Average Investment: $500,000 - $1.5 million
Investment Criteria: Seed-Stage, Early-Stage
Industry Group Preference: Technology, Technology-Enabled Services
Portfolio Companies: CallRecall, E2E Networks, Mettl, Moneysights, Proptec Renewables, Remma Consulting, Sparsha Learning, SportsNest, Trolly, Valgen

Key Executives:
   Karthik Reddy, Managing Partner
   Education: MBA, IIM Bangalore & Wharton School
   Background: SSKI, Brand Capital/Private Treaties, Times Group
   Sanjay Nath, Managing Partner
   Education: MBA, UCLA Anderson School of Graduate Management
   Background: IBM Global Services, Pricewaterhouse Coopers

2518 BM-T BETEILIGUNGS MANAGEMENT THURINGEN GmbH
Gorkistrasse 9
Erfurt 99084
Germany

Phone: 49-3617447601 Fax: 49-3617447635
e-mail: info@bm-t.com
web: www.bm-t.com

Mission Statement: Strengthens Thüringen's Economy through targeted Investments in innovative and growth-oriented companies with high potential.

Geographic Preference: Germany
Fund Size: $0.3 Billion
Founded: 2003
Average Investment: $1 Million
Minimum Investment: $0.2 Million
Investment Criteria: Germany Based, All Stages Considered
Industry Group Preference: Life Sciences, Electronics, Information Technology, Media, Engineering, Automation, All Sectors Considered
Portfolio Companies: APPsolute Mobility, Axsol, BianoGMP, c-LEcta, Crowd Architects, Devie Medical, Enginsight, Ezono, FBGS, Hacker Automation, Hapila, Hasec, Heyfair, Ifesca, InflaRX, Intercept Technology, Intercus, JeNaCell, Jenetric, jenID Solutions, Jenoptik, KAHLA Porzellan, Lean Plastics, Leyhs Pharma, Lynatox, Magnitude Internet, Master PIM, Mi-Factory, MITEC Automotive, Music DNA, NovaPump, oncgnostics, Paketin, Pamyra, PDV-Systeme, Pflegeplatz-manager, Plazz Entertainment, Preventicus, Q-Sensei, QSIL, Redwave Medical, SAMAG Group, Scienova, SecondSol, siOPTICA, SmartDyeLivery, TrophpSYS, Ucandoo, Zeilenwert

Key Executives:
   Rudolf Humer, Chairman

2519 BMP AKTIENGESELLSCHAFT BMP
Venture Capital
Schlterstrae 38
Berlin 10629
Germany

Phone: 49-30203050 Fax: 49-3020305555
e-mail: bmp@bmp.com
web: www.bmp.com

Venture Capital & Private Equity Firms / International Firms

Mission Statement: One of the leading venture capital companies, we specialise in start-up and expansion financing strong growing companies.
Geographic Preference: Germany, Western Europe, Osteuropa
Fund Size: $59.3 Million
Founded: 1997
Investment Criteria: Early Stage, High-growth markets
Industry Group Preference: Business to Business, Life Sciences, Financial Services, Marketing, Publishing, Software, Technology, Telecommunications
Portfolio Companies: Newtron AG, Bankier, eHedge AG, eprofessional GmbH, ergoTrade AG, European Telecommunication Holding E.T.H. AG, Gamigo AG, Heliocentris Energiesysteme GmbH, Jerini AG, K2 Internet S.A., Revotar Biopharmaceuticals AG, Salt of Life AG, Shotgun Picture
Key Executives:
Oliver Borrmann, Chief Executive Officer
e-mail: bmp@bmp.com
Gerd Schmitz-Morkramer, Chairman
e-mail: bmp@bmp.com

2520 BOCI DIRECT INVESTMENT MANAGEMENT LIMITED Bank of China
1 Garden Road
Bank of China Tower Suite 35F
Central
Seoul
Hong Kong

Phone: 852-22308888 Fax: 852-28109736
web: www.bocgroup.com

Mission Statement: BOCI is a wholly owned subsidiary of the Bank of China and aims to provide a full range of investment banking services to its clients.
Geographic Preference: Hong Kong, UK
Fund Size: $1 Billion
Founded: 1998
Investment Criteria: State-owned companies, Medium and Small size listed companies
Industry Group Preference: Energy, Transportation, Infrastructure, Real Estate, Manufacturing
Key Executives:
Kwok Leung Lee, Managing Director

2521 BOEHRINGER INGELHEIM VENTURE FUND
Binger Strasse 173
Ingelheim am Rhein 55216
Germany

Phone: 49-6132778740
web: www.boehringer-ingelheim-venture.com

Mission Statement: Our primary aim is to activate success for those companies and entrepreneurs we support and to earn a reputation as a long-term trusted partner. Beyond capital investment, we intend to take an active role with our portfolio companies - delivering significant added value through our own extensive drug discovery, scientific and managerial expertise and access to selected relevant experts and knowledge. Nevertheless, we also attach significant importance to confidentiality, establishing ethical walls to protect our portfolio companies and entrepreneurs.
Average Investment: 10-15 million Euros
Investment Criteria: Early-Stage
Industry Group Preference: Healthcare, Life Sciences, Pharmaceuticals
Portfolio Companies: AMP Therapeutics, ArmaGen Technologies, Inserm Transfert Initiative, Okairos, Promethera

Key Executives:
Frank Kalkbrenner, Vice President
Background: Senior Scientist, Director, Boehringer Ingelheim

2522 BONVENTURE
Pettenkoferstrasse 37
Munchen D-80336
Germany

Phone: 49-89200012531 Fax: 49-89-200-01-2539
e-mail: info@bonventure.de
web: www.bonventure.de

Mission Statement: BonVenture is a social venture capital fund that was established by comitted individuals willing to take responsibility for the community. They believe, that with individual prosperity comes a social obligation to improve society. Our investors dedicate their material and intellectual resources in order to leverage efficent social or ecological solutions that cannot be provided by the public sector.
Geographic Preference: German-Speaking Countries
Industry Group Preference: Education, Social Services
Portfolio Companies: Atempo Group, Abotic, Bettermarks, Chancenwerk, DialogMuseum, Flachsland Zukunftsschulen, Hand In Gag, Kunterbunt, Moving Image 24, Rock Your Life, Violence Prevention Network

2523 BOTTS & COMPANY LIMITED
2nd Floor
103 Mount Street
44 Davies Street
London W1K 2TJ
United Kingdom

Phone: 44-2070161202 Fax: 44-87 01343714
e-mail: postmaster@bottscompany.com

Mission Statement: Actively seeking new investments.
Geographic Preference: United Kingdom, Western Europe
Fund Size: $176 Million
Founded: 1987
Average Investment: $17.6 Million
Minimum Investment: $48.82 Million
Investment Criteria: Expansion and Development, Bridge Finance, Refinancing Bank Debt, Secondary Purchase/Replacement Capital, Rescue/Turnaround, MBO, MBI, Institutional BO
Industry Group Preference: Communications, Media, Leisure, Financial Services, Industrial Services, Entertainment
Key Executives:
John Botts, Non-Executive Director
Education: Columbia University
Background: Kuhn Loeb Lehman Brothers; Kidder Peabody; CSFB
Andrew Haining, Managing Director
Education: MA, Economics, Cambridge University
Background: Bank of America; Natwest Markets
Robin Black, Director
e-mail: r.black@bottscompany.com
Education: BA, Politics, Exeter University
Background: Vice President In the Structured Debt and Private Equity Division, Bankers Trust Company

2524 BR OPPORTUNITIES
Av. Ibirapuera 2.907
Conj. 509
Sao Paulo 04029-200
Brazil

Phone: 55-23377126 Fax: +55-1123727430
web: www.bropportunities.com.br

Mission Statement: BR Opportunities - Growth Capital Investments is a private equity fund manager that drives emerging, high-impact companies for the improvement of

Venture Capital & Private Equity Firms / International Firms

Brazil. Its mission is to invest in high-impact organizations, accelerate their growth and transform them into effective leaders in their markets of operation. In pursuit of this goal, its strategy is to bring to these organizations management and professional governance, while enhancing their visibility, transparency, and network of relationships. Based on this approach, we implement successful models of high added value.

Geographic Preference: Brazil
Founded: 2010
Key Executives:
  Carlos Miranda, Founder
  Education: BA, Architecture & Urban Planning; MBA, Finance, IBMEC-RJ
  Background: Ernst & Young
  Vitor Horibe, Partner
  Education: BA, Business Administration EAESP/FGV; MBA, Finance UCLA Anderson School of Management
  Background: Roland Berger

2525 BRABANTSE ONTWIKKELINGSMIJ NV (BOM)
Goirlese Weg 15
5026 PB Tilburg
PO Box 3240
Tilburg 5003 DE
Netherlands

Phone: 31-135311120 Fax: 31-135311121
e-mail: bom@bom.nl
web: www.bom.nl

Mission Statement: Actively seeking new investments.
Investment Criteria: Startup, Early-Stage, Expansion, Development, MBO, Management Buy-in
Industry Group Preference: All Sectors Considered
Key Executives:
  Matthijs Van Miltenburg, Project Foreign Investments
  Ben Engel, Senior project manager

2526 BRAINSPARK PLC
12/16 Laystall Street
The Lightwell
Clerkenwell
London EC1R 4PF
United Kingdom

Phone: 44-2078436600 Fax: 44-2078436601
web: www.brainspark.com

Mission Statement: Brainspark Plc is an AIM listed company, focusing on investments in best-of-breed Information & Communication Technology (I&CT) primarily in Europe and Israel.

Geographic Preference: Europe, Israel
Founded: 1998
Investment Criteria: New investments
Industry Group Preference: Information Technology, Communications
Portfolio Companies: Advanced Computer Systems, Easyart.com, Fortune Cookie, Geosim Systems, Kerb, MetaPack, San Vicente Group, TraderServe
Key Executives:
  Francesco Gardin, chairman
  David Meacher, Non-Executive Board Member
  e-mail: email@brainspark.com
  Education: MBA, INSEAD; Durham University
  Background: Director of Strategic and Financial Planning for Bass PLC
  Directorships: Partner
  Steward Dodd, Founder and CEO

2527 BRANDON CAPITAL PARTNERS
Level 9
278 Collins Street
Melbourne, Victoria 3000
Australia

Phone: 61-396570700 Fax: 61-396570777
e-mail: info@brandoncapital.com.au
web: www.brandoncapital.com.au

Mission Statement: Brandon Capital Partners makes seed and venture capital investments to support the development and international growth of Australian life science companies. We work collaboratively with entrepreneurs to demonstrate the benefit of their technology, thereby creating value for them, their teams and our investors.

Geographic Preference: Australia
Fund Size: AUD$50 million, AUD$51 million
Industry Group Preference: Life Sciences, Drug Development, Medical Devices
Portfolio Companies: Elastagen, Fibrotech, Global Kinetics, Osprey Medical, PolyActiva, Signostics, Spinifex, Vaxxas, Verva

Other Locations:
Level 7
210 George Street
Sydney, NSW 2010
Australia
Phone: 61-292472577 Fax: 61-292477344

Key Executives:
  Chris Nave, Managing Director
  Education: PhD, Endocrinology & Physiology, University of Melbourne
  Background: Manager, Biotechnology Team, Melbourne Ventures
  Directorships: BACE Therapeutics, Fibrotech Therapeutics, Fluorotrop, Global Kinetics Corporation

2528 BRIDGEPOINT CAPITAL GmbH
Neue Mainzer Straße 28
Frankfurt 60311
Germany

Phone: 49-692108770 Fax: 49-6921087777
e-mail: Frankfurt@bridgepoint.eu
web: www.bridgepoint-capital.com

Mission Statement: Bridgepoint is a leading provider of private equity with a 25-year track record of investing in businesses that will achieve long-term capital growth.

Geographic Preference: Europe, UK, France, Sweden, Italy, Germany
Fund Size: $12 billion
Founded: 1980
Average Investment: $162.7 Million
Minimum Investment: $29.75 Million
Investment Criteria: Expansion Financing, Bridging Finance, Replacement, MBO, MBI
Industry Group Preference: Consumer Services, Financial Services, Healthcare, Media, Chemicals, Manufacturing, Services, Beverages, Software, Automotive, Materials Technology, Computer Related
Portfolio Companies: 1st Credit, Adams Childrenswear, All3Media, Alliance Medical, Arco Bodegas, Attendo, Aura Light International AB, Autinform GmbH, Betterware, Capula, CarPark, CESA, CFP Flexible Packaging, Clinical Assessment Services, CompuTrain Europe B.V, Concent
Key Executives:
  Bernie Schuler, Diretor
  Marc Zugel, Diretor

Venture Capital & Private Equity Firms / International Firms

2529 BRIDGEPOINT CAPITAL LIMITED
95 Wigmore Street
London W1U 1FB
United Kingdom

Phone: 44-2074323500 Fax: 44-2074-323600
e-mail: London@bridgepoint.eu
web: www.bridgepoint-capital.com

Mission Statement: Bridgepoint is a leading provider of private equity with a 25-year track record of investing in businesses that will achieve long-term capital growth.

Geographic Preference: Europe, UK, France, Sweden, Italy, Germany
Fund Size: $6.17 Billion
Founded: 1980
Average Investment: $162.8 Million
Minimum Investment: $30 Million
Investment Criteria: Expansion Financing, Bridging Finance, Replacement, MBO, MBI
Industry Group Preference: Consumer Services, Financial Services, Healthcare, Media, Chemicals, Manufacturing, Services, Beverages, Software, Automotive, Materials Technology, Computer Related
Portfolio Companies: 1st Credit, Adams Childrenswear, All3Media, Alliance Medical, Arco Bodegas, Attendo, Aura Light International AB, Autinform GmbH, Betterware, Capula, CarPark, CESA, CFP Flexible Packaging, Clinical Assessment Services, CompuTrain Europe B.V, Concent

Key Executives:
Benoit Alteirac, Director
Background: Carnaud Group
Chris Bell, Partner, Head of Manufacturing & Industrials sector

2530 BRIDGES VENTURES
1 Craven Hill
London W2 3EN
United Kingdom

Phone: 020-72625566 Fax: 020-72626389
e-mail: info@bridgesventures.com
web: www.bridgesventures.com

Mission Statement: Bridges Ventures is a specialist fund manager, dedicated to using an impact-driven investment approach to create superior returns for both investors and society at-large. We believe that market forces and entrepreneurship can be harnessed to do well by doing good.

Fund Size: £340 million
Founded: 2002
Portfolio Companies: Carduus, CloudIQ, Historic Futures, Ardenham Energy, TEG, Aerothermal Group, Babington, Halo, New Career Skills, Credential, SealSkinz, The Gym, Bagnali Court, Triage, School Stickers, Chill Factor, Whelan Refining Ltd, Smart Storage, Holiday Inn Express, Action For Children, Teens and Toddlers, New Horizons Program, Community Links, Auto22, Casa, HCT Group, Callbritannia

Key Executives:
Philip Newborough, Co-Founder/Managing Partner
Education: BA, York University
Background: General Manager, Aiwa; Managing Director, MWB Business Exchange

2531 BRIGHT CAPITAL
6/2 Bersenevskaya Emb.
Moscow 119072
Russia

Phone: 7-4959898540 Fax: 7-4959823309
web: www.bright-capital.com

Mission Statement: Bright Capital is an independent venture capital firm that invests globally in a wide range of promising companies solving problems in energy efficiency and resource scarcity.

Industry Group Preference: Energy, Renewable Energy, Energy Efficiency, Advanced Materials
Portfolio Companies: Cardiodx, Epuramat, Fotoshkola, RRT Global, Suvolta, Quantenna Communications

Other Locations:
3000 Sand Hill Road
Bldg 2, Suite 180
Menlo Park, CA 94025
Phone: 650-6277750

Key Executives:
Boris Ryabov, Managing Partner
Education: International Institute of Economic Relations; MBA, Warwick University
Background: Deputy Director General, RU-COM

2532 BRM SEED
10 Nissim Aloni Street
Tzameret Park
Herzliya
Tel Aviv 6291924
Israel

Phone: 972-39715100 Fax: 972-39715101
e-mail: info@brm.com
web: www.brm.com

Mission Statement: BRM Capital is a venture capital firm that invests primarily in Israel-related seed and early stage companies in the Software, Communications and Components domains.

Geographic Preference: US, Israel
Founded: 1988
Investment Criteria: Israel-related seed and early stage companies
Industry Group Preference: Infrastructure Software, Communications, Components & IoT
Portfolio Companies: GigaSpaces, Human Eyes, NPX Technologies Ltd., Pando Networks, ProSight, Whale Communications, Oplus Technologies, Passave, Schema, Wavion

Key Executives:
Eli Barkat, Chairman and Co-Founder
e-mail: eli@brm.com
Education: BS, Computer Science and Mathematics, Hebrew University of Jerusalem
Background: CEO of BackWeb Technologies Ltd.
Yuval Rakavy, Venture Partner and Co-Founder

2533 BROADLINE PRINCIPAL CAPITAL
360 Pudong Nan Lu
Suite 26C
Shanghai 200120
China

Mission Statement: Broadline Principle Capital is a leading multi-industry private equity firm with global capabilities and China expertise. BPC selectively invests in companies that are industry leaders and rising stars that can benefit from BPC's platform, relationships, and expertise to expand operations, gain efficiencies, and grow earnings.

Industry Group Preference: Diversified
Portfolio Companies: Xi'an Longi Silicon, Beijing Odyssey Chemicals, Befar Group, Shida Shenghua Chemical, Show Long Fashion Gourmet Co, Sunrain Energy, Billions Chemicals, Xinya Paper Group, Jinhe Industrial, MySteel.com, Trendzone Construction, Shanghai Chunge Glass Co., South Memory Restaurant Co., Shanghai Shen-Li High Tech, Hisoar Pharma, Crystal Optech, Yotrio Group, Taizhou Reflecting Materials, Haihong Hydraulic Science, Tadelon Holding Group, Jiangxi Guohong Group, Lier Chemical Co., Guangdong Yashii Group

Venture Capital & Private Equity Firms / International Firms

Key Executives:
  Lin-Lin Zhou, Founding CEO
  Education: MBA, PhD

2534 BROOKLYN VENTURES
Nyenrode Business Universiteit
Straatweg 25
PO Box 130
Breukelen 3621
Netherlands

e-mail: info@brooklyn-ventures.com
web: www.brooklyn-ventures.com

Mission Statement: Brooklyn Ventures brings together seasoned executives with various backgrounds. We have a joint commitment to help companies with great potential and ideas to succeed. Each of us has a proven track record in our own field.
Portfolio Companies: RBN, IRM Systems, Blivio, SoSocio, Valuewait, Needs & Senses
Key Executives:
  Hans Osnabrugge, Partner
  Education: BA, MSc
  Background: Relationship Manager, Schretlen & Co.

2535 BRYAN GARNIER & COMPANY
53 Chandos Place
London WC2N 4HS
United Kingdom

Phone: 44-2073322500 Fax: 44-2073322559
e-mail: bede@bryangarnier.com
web: www.bryangarnier.com

Mission Statement: Providing fast-growing, independent partnership of experienced finance professionals servicing the needs of large corporations, venture capitalists, institutional investors and private clients.
Geographic Preference: Europe
Founded: 1996
Investment Criteria: Growing European companies and growth-oriented investors.
Industry Group Preference: Technology, Media & Telecommunications, Life Sciences, Branded Goods, Retailing, Outsourcing & Efficiency, Media, Healthcare, Renewable Energy & Environment, Business Products & Services
Portfolio Companies: Transgene, Centrale Partners, Carrere Group, MAPI, 21 Centrale Partners, ASK, Telisma, CAST, SCORT, Job partners, OMNITICKET network, DOUBLE Trade, Reef, Attol, Stella, Reef, SCORT, ActiveCard.
Key Executives:
  Greg Revenu, Corporate Contact

2536 BRZTECH
Av. das Nacoes Unidas, 11541
14 Andar CJ 141
Brooklin
Sao Paulo
Brazil

Phone: 55-11975255282

Mission Statement: BRZtech is an investment group oriented to developing tech solutions and support tech companies with a future vision.
Portfolio Companies: Realtime, Mobbit Systems, HIS

2537 BT FUNDS MANAGEMENT LIMITED
Level 7, Westpac on Takutai Square
16 Takutai Square
Auckland 1141
New Zealand

Phone: 649-3673300 Fax: 64-936-73302
Toll-Free: 0800-800661

Mission Statement: Helping New Zealanders create and manage their wealth since 1989. Providing a diverse range of investment options including funds managed by our teams as well as alliances with global investment managers.
Geographic Preference: New Zealand, Australia
Fund Size: $1.6 billion
Founded: 1989
Key Executives:
  Fiona Oliver, Chief Operating Officer
  Chris Caton, Chief Economist

2538 BULL VENTURES
TC Gulliver, 27 Floor
Sportivnaya, Square 1
Kiev 01023
Ukraine

Phone: 044-500-6868

Mission Statement: We are interested in building long-term relationships with experienced and active partners who can bring into the team not only money, but also a deep understanding of business processes.
Geographic Preference: Ukraine, Central & Eastern Europe
Fund Size: $10 million
Founded: 2013
Industry Group Preference: E-Commerce & Manufacturing, Media, Marketing, Logistics
Key Executives:
  Dmitry Smirnov, Managing Partner
  Background: Managing Partner, FlintCap; Deputy Director, Finam Investment Fund

2539 BULLNET
Parque Empresarial La Finca
Paseo del Club Deportivo, 1
1 - Edificio 3 - Pozuelo de Alarcon
Madrid 28223
Spain

Phone: 34-917997206 Fax: 34-917995372
e-mail: julecia@bullnetcapital.com
web: www.grupobullnet.com

Mission Statement: Bullnet Gestion is a Spanish independent venture capital firm specialized in technology projects.
Geographic Preference: Spain
Average Investment: $2 - $4 Million
Investment Criteria: Early-Stage
Industry Group Preference: Information Services, Telecommunications, Media, Healthcare
Portfolio Companies: Anafocus, Onco Vision, Multiwave, NetSpira, Arvirago, Visure, Digital Legends, Zhilabs, Codice Software, UAV Navigation, POF
Key Executives:
  Javier Ulecia, Partner
  Education: Universidad Politecnica, Madrid; MBA, HEC
  Background: Co-Founder/CEO, Doing; Senior Manager, Bain & Company

2540 BURAN VENTURE CAPITAL
Khlebny Lane 8
Moscow 121069
Russia

Phone: 7-495-5404842
e-mail: info@buranvc.com
web: www.buranvc.com

Mission Statement: Buran Venture Capital is a venture fund founded in 2010 targeting to invest US$50m over the course of the next 4-5 years in Russia, CIS and Israel.
Geographic Preference: Russia, CIS, Israel
Fund Size: $50 million
Founded: 2010
Average Investment: $300, 000 - $3 million

Venture Capital & Private Equity Firms / International Firms

Industry Group Preference: E-Commerce & Manufacturing, Digital Media & Marketing, Mobile & Internet, Communications, SaaS
Portfolio Companies: EpistoGraph, JustEva.ru
Key Executives:
  Alexander Konoplyasty, Managing Partner

2541 BUSINESS GROWTH FUND
45 Church Street
Birmingham B3 2RT
United Kingdom

Phone: 0845-2668862
e-mail: enquiries@bgf.co.uk
web: www.businessgrowthfund.co.uk

Mission Statement: BGF provides long-term capital for fast growing British companies.
Geographic Preference: United Kingdom
Average Investment: £2-10 million
Industry Group Preference: High Technology, Software, Electronics, Leisure & Hospitality, Tourism, Retail, Consumer & Leisure, Renewable Energy, Clean Technology, Healthcare, Life Sciences, Business Products & Services, Outsourcing & Efficiency, Consumer Goods
Portfolio Companies: Bulitt, Celaton, Magma Global, Boost Juice Bars

Key Executives:
  Richard Bishop, Head of Investments
  e-mail: richard.bishop@bgf.co.uk
  Education: Birmingham University
  Background: 3i

2542 BUTLER CAPITAL PARTNERS FRANCE
30, cours Albert 1er
1st Floor
Paris 75008
France

Phone: 33-145615580 Fax: 33-145619794
e-mail: contact@butlercapitalpartners.com
web: www.butlercapitalpartners.com

Mission Statement: Butler Capital Partners is the leading independent private equity partnership in France.
Geographic Preference: France, Eastern Europe
Fund Size: 500 Million Euros
Founded: 1991
Investment Criteria: LBO and turnarounds
Industry Group Preference: Information Technology, Distribution, Logistics, Advertising, Publishing, Marketing
Portfolio Companies: 1001 Listes, Abrium, Atys, AutoDistribution, Cesar, Exlinea, Flo, France Champignon, Giraud International, Press Index, REP

Key Executives:
  Laurent Parquet, Director
  Education: ESSEC
  Background: Andersen Consulting
  Pierre Costes, Director
  Education: ESSEC, Chartered Accountant
  Background: Arthur Andersen
  Walter Butler, Partner and Chairman of BCP
  Education: Polytechnique X, Ecole Nationale des Mines de Paris
  Background: Advisor to the Minister of Economy and Finance, French Treasury; Energy/Telecommunications/Raw Materials Advisor, Minister of Industry
  Frédéric Favreau, Director
  Education: Ecole Centrale de Paris, Master of Science MII
  Background: Bankers Trust, Paribes
  Marc-Eric Flory, CFO
  Education: Master Degree in Tax and Business Law
  Background: Lawyer

2543 BUTZOW NORDIA ADVOCATES LTD
Fabianinkatu 29 B
Helsinki FI-00100
Finland

Phone: 358-106841300 Fax: 358-106841700

Mission Statement: A full service law firm with expertise in mergers and acquisitions among other areas. Providing competent and extensive services in various kinds of transactions; corporate acquisition, capital investment and outsourcing.
Geographic Preference: Finland, Russia, Sweden, Germany, France, United States
Founded: 1999
Industry Group Preference: Commercial Contracts, Private Equity, Property Transactions, Labour Law, Company Law, Financial Services, Corporate Insolvency, Restructuring, Litigation

Key Executives:
  Marja-Leena Kangasrääsiö, Office Manager

2544 CAIXA CAPITAL RISC
Av. Diagonal
613 3 Planta
Barcelona B 08028
Spain

Phone: 93-4094060
e-mail: info@caixacapitalrisc.es
web: www.caixacapitalrisc.es

Mission Statement: Through its area for entrepreneurs, 'la Caixa' has developed a combination of tools to support, finance and accompany new business initiatives with a high growth potential in Spain. Among the main ones, those that stand out are the unique set of venture capital tools that invest in the early stages of innovative projects through Caixa Capital Risc, and the creation of instruments that promote the entrepreneurial spirit and accompaniment in the development of new innovative business initiatives through Iniciativa Emprendedor XXI.

Fund Size: $73 million
Investment Criteria: Early-Stage
Portfolio Companies: Onmia Molecular, Laboratorios Sanifit, Sabimedical, Sagetis Biotech, Genmedica Therapeutics, Medlumics, Privalla, Groupalia, I-Neumaticos, Syncro, Good Deal, Apesoft

2545 CAMPUS COMPANIES VENTURE CAPITAL FUND
Molesworth House, Molesworth Street
Dublin
Ireland

Phone: 353-16790818 Fax: 353-16799014
web: www.campuscapital.com

Mission Statement: Operates an active, value added style of investment that provides valuable commercial experience to the early stage enterprise.
Geographic Preference: Ireland
Founded: 1998
Investment Criteria: Seed, Early Stage Irish Businesses, Commercial Sector Businesses including services
Industry Group Preference: Communications, Digital Media & Marketing, Biotechnology, Software, Education
Portfolio Companies: Kappoki Games LTD, Baydon Solutions Ltd, Cinario Ltd, Tridelta plc, Pharmatrin Ltd, Martialone Ltd.

Key Executives:
  Brian Flavin, Associate
  Dr. Pat Ryan, Managing Partner
  Background: Appian Technology plc

Venture Capital & Private Equity Firms / International Firms

2546 CANALIS CAPITAL
Calle 50
13th Floor
Panama City 00000
Panama

e-mail: team@canaliscapital.com
web: www.canaliscapital.com

Mission Statement: A venture capital and acceleration firm investing in the global cannabis industry.

Founded: 2018
Industry Group Preference: Cannabis
Key Executives:
  Raymond H., Founder
  Education: The Hebrew University; University of Pennsylvania
  Background: Analyst, Nomura; Innovation Director, Regency Group; Intern, Merrill Lynch; Nike Intern, Northbay International
  Steven Haddadian, Partner
  Education: Business Admin., Biola University
  Background: Founder, Sr. Talent Manager, Hungry Mind Entertainment; Project Coordinator, STX Entertainment; Angel Investor, Founder Institute; Investor, Crypto; Co-Founder/Partner, The Future Party; Co-Founder/CEO, viva.ai

2547 CANDOVER
34 Lime Street
London EC3M 7AT
United Kingdom

Phone: 44-2074899848 Fax: 44-2072485483
e-mail: info@candover.com
web: www.candoverinvestments.com

Mission Statement: Candover specialises in arranging and leading large buy-outs and buy-ins across Europe.

Geographic Preference: United Kingdom, Western Europe
Fund Size: $6.7 Billion
Founded: 1980
Average Investment: $180 Million
Minimum Investment: $36 Million
Investment Criteria: MBO, MBI, Leveraged Build Up, Public-to-Private
Industry Group Preference: Chemicals, Financial Services, Manufacturing, Communications, Media, Information Technology, Software, Leisure, Materials Technology, Computer Related, Entertainment
Portfolio Companies: Wood Mackenzie, Bureau van Dijk, Electronic, Publishing, Alcontrol, Vetco International, Pipeline Integrity, International, Equity Trust, Aspen Insurance, SPA, Eversholt Leasing, Gala Group, Bourne Leisure, Jarvis Hotels, Inveresk
Key Executives:
  John Arney ACA, Managing Director
  e-mail: j.delano@candover.com
  Education: LLB
  Background: PricewaterHouse, Bank of Scotland
  Doug Fairservice, Joint Deputy Chairman
  e-mail: d.fairservice@candover.com
  Education: Bachelor of Science, MBA
  Background: ICFC
  Colin Buffin, Managing Director
  e-mail: c.buffin@candover.com
  Education: Natural Sciences, Oxford Trinity College
  Background: Investigations and Corporate Finance Departments at Deloitte Haskins & Sells.
  Directorships: Business Manager
  Marek Gumienny, Managing Director
  e-mail: m.gumienny@candover.com
  Education: ACA
  Background: Chartered Accountant, PWC
  Richard Stone, Chairman
  e-mail: j.tonn@candover.com
  Education: European Business School
  Background: Citicorp, Deutsche Bank, Deutsche Handelsbank
  John Arney, Managing Partner
  e-mail: j.arney@candover.com
  Education: Chartered Accountant
  Background: JP Morgan Partners, European buyouts in the support services, media & communications, chemicals and leisure sectors. During
  Malcolm Fallen, Chief Executive Officer
  e-mail: c.green@candover.com
  Background: Director in Deutsche Morgan Grenfell, He gained experience in a number of areas including emerging markets, project finance and structured finance.
  Lord Jay Ewelme, Senior Independent Director
  e-mail: i.gray@candover.com
  Education: CA
  Background: Managing director of Bank of Scotland
  Jan Oosterveld, Non-executive Director
  e-mail: s.leefe@candover.com
  Background: Arthur Andersen
  Scott Longhurst, Non-executive Director
  e-mail: i.gray@candover.com
  Education: Chartered Accountant
  Background: Managing director of Bank of Scotland.
  Brian Mercer, Director
  e-mail: b.mercer@candover.com
  Education: Masters in Business Administration
  Background: Broadview International, Non-executive director of Kennet Capital.

2548 CANTON VENTURE CAPITAL COMPANY LIMITED
Room 1101
11/F 183 Tianhebei Road
Guangzhou
China

web: www.c-vcc.com

Fund Size: $300 million
Founded: 1999

2549 CAPITAL 18
Express Trade Tower
Plot No. 15 & 16, Sector 16A
Noida
Uttar Pradesh 201 301
India

Phone: 91-1204341818 Fax: 91-1166173955

Mission Statement: We believe in the power of Indian entrepreneurs and their ability to build successful, world class businesses. With our experience as founders, entrepreneurs and investors, we bring an ability to accelerate business growth through operational, strategic and financial improvements. We believe return on capital is the best measure of our expertise in investing and serving our entrepreneurs.

Geographic Preference: India
Average Investment: INR5 Crores to INR20 Crores
Investment Criteria: Growth Stage
Portfolio Companies: 24x7 Learning, Colosceum, Ubona, Greycells18, Wespro, Stargaze, Webchutney, Yatra, NetworkPlay, DEN
Key Executives:
  Raghav Bahl, Managing Director
  Education: St. Stephens College; MBA, University of Delhi
  Background: Founder & Managing Director, Network 18

Venture Capital & Private Equity Firms / International Firms

2550 CAPITAL INTERNATIONAL Capital Group Companies
40 Grosvenor Place
London SW1X 7GG
United Kingdom
Phone: 44-2078645000 Fax: 352-227443

Mission Statement: Capital International Funds is part of The Capital Group Companies, an independent global investment management organisation with over 70 years of experience managing money for individuals and institutions.

Founded: 1931
Investment Criteria: Long-term growth prospects
Key Executives:
Philip Winston, Senior Vice President
e-mail: steven_watson@capgroup.com
Habib I. Annous, Manager

2551 CAPITAL TODAY
Suite 3808
Jin Mao Tower, 88 Century Boulevard
Shanghai 200121
China
Phone: 86-2150988886 Fax: 96-2150988050
e-mail: info@capitaltoday.com
web: www.capitaltoday.com

Mission Statement: Capital Today manages dedicated China country funds. It is one of the first independent private equity firms in China. Founded by Kathy Xu in 2005, Capital Today is committed to provide growth capital to small and medium-sized Chinese companies and helps them build sustainable businessess and No. 1 brands in China.

Geographic Preference: China
Fund Size: $680 million
Founded: 2005
Industry Group Preference: Consumer Products, Retail, Consumer & Leisure, Internet
Portfolio Companies: Kung Fu Fast Food Chain, YiFeng Pharmacy Chain, Sinoway Herbal Skin Care, JingDong 360 Buy Online, Zbird Online Diamonds
Key Executives:
Kathy Xu, Founder

2552 CAPITON AG
33 Bleibtreustr
Berlin 10707
Germany
Phone: 49-303159450 Fax: 49-3031594557
e-mail: info@capiton.de
web: www.capiton.de

Mission Statement: Partners with many small and medium-sized enterprises and invests in promising, future-proof markets

Geographic Preference: Germany, Austria, Switzerland
Founded: 1992
Average Investment: $5 million - 100 million
Minimum Investment: $15 Million
Investment Criteria: Expansion Financing, Bridging Finance, Replacement, MBO.
Key Executives:
Stefan Theis, Senior Partner
Andreas Kogler, Senior Partner

2553 CAPMAN CAPITAL MANAGEMENT OY
32 Korkeavuorenkatu
Helsinki 130
Finland
Phone: 358-207207500 Fax: 358-207207510
web: www.capman.com

Mission Statement: CapMan's operations are divided into two business units, CapMan Private Equity and CapMan Real Estate.

Geographic Preference: Finland, Nordic region, EU, Baltic countries
Fund Size: $2.65 Billion
Founded: 1989
Average Investment: $31.9 Million
Minimum Investment: $3.61 Million
Investment Criteria: Expansion, MBO/MBI
Industry Group Preference: Technology, Life Sciences, Real Estate, Fund Management, Fundraising, Legal and Compliance, Investor Relations, Communications, Group Finances, Human Resources, Information Technology
Portfolio Companies: AffectoGenimap, Animex, Ascade Telecom Software, Atbusiness, Avitec, Distocraft, Eco-Dan, EM4, Eoidio, Aerocrine, Eutech Medical, InDex, Inion, Jolife, Millicore, Prostalund, Silex.
Key Executives:
Kaisa Arovaara, Deputy CFO
e-mail: tuomo.raasio@capman.com
Education: LL.M.
Background: Kansallis Banking Group, Finnish companies
Directorships: Head of CapMan Buyout
Olli Liitola, Senior Partner
e-mail: olli.liitola@capman.com
Education: MS, Enginering
Background: Haly Invest Oy, Vihti Savings Bank, Industrialisation Fund of Finland Ltd.
Directorships: CFO, Deputy CEO (CapMan Plc)
Peter Buch Lund, Senior Partner
e-mail: peter.buch.lund@capman.com
Education: Technical License
Background: Cultor Oy, Grafica Oy
Vesa Vanha-Honko, Senior Partner
e-mail: vesa.vanha-honko@capman.com
Education: MS, English, BS, Economics
Background: Instrumentarium Ltd, Author of Several Scientific Publications, Finnish and international companies.
Directorships: Head of Group Development
Heikki Westerlund, CEO, Senior Partner
e-mail: heikki.westerlund@capman.com
Education: MS, Economics
Background: Sitra in Private Equity and Research, Finnish Venture Capital Association
Directorships: CEO

2554 CAPRICORN VENTURE PARTNERS NV
Jonge St. Jacob, Lei 19/1 - B-3000
Leuven 3000
Belgium
Phone: 32-16284100 Fax: 32-16284108
e-mail: capricorn@capricorn.be
web: www.capricorn.be

Mission Statement: Capricorn Venture Partners was established in 1993 as an advisor of venture capital funds that invest in technology-based growth companies in Western Europe.

Geographic Preference: Belgium, France, Netherland, Finland, Germany, United Kingdom.
Fund Size: $22.3 Million
Founded: 1993
Investment Criteria: Seed, Start-up, Other early stage.
Industry Group Preference: Biotechnology, Energy, Environment Products & Services, Internet Technology, Medical, Electronic Technology, Healthcare
Portfolio Companies: BioAlliance Pharma, Omrix Biopharmaceuticals, Orthovita, 4AZA Bioscience, UroGene, TiGenix, Amplexor, i-merge, Ortec International, Xplanation International, EcoPhos, Orthovita.

Venture Capital & Private Equity Firms / International Firms

Key Executives:
Philippe Haspeslagh, Chairman
Education: Ph.D. Solid State Physics, University of Leuven.
Background: Founder of Quest For Growth N.V., Co-Founder and Vice Chairman of EASDAQ, Managing Director of BeneVent Management, Managing Director, Belgian VC.
Directorships: Managing Director,
Paul Decraemer, Executive Director

2555 CAPVIS EQUITY PARTNERS
Grabenstrasse 17
Baar/Zug CH-6340
Switzerland

Phone: 41-433005858 Fax: 41-433005859
e-mail: pr@capvis.com
web: www.capvis.com

Mission Statement: Actively seeking new investments, concentrating on well established medium-sized companies.
Geographic Preference: Switzerland, Austria, Southern Germany.
Fund Size: $480 Million
Founded: 1999
Average Investment: EUR900 million
Minimum Investment: $7.7 Million
Investment Criteria: Invests in Medium-sized Companies, MBO's, Expansion and Fast-growing Companies
Industry Group Preference: Textiles, Chemicals, Automotive, Electronic Technology
Portfolio Companies: KCS, Polytec Holding AG, REMP AG, RMB SA, Soudsonic, Tobles AG, Phonak, Disetronic, Saia-Burgess, Komax, SIA Abrasives

Key Executives:
Daniel Flaig, Partner
e-mail: felix.rohner@capvis.com
Background: UBS AG ,
Directorships: Partner, Advisory Board (Beirat): Findlay Industries
Rolf Friedli, Partner
e-mail: rolf.friedli@capvis.com
Education: MBA
Background: Investment Banking bei Goldman Sachs, Clariden Bank
Directorships: RMB SA, REMP AG, Soudsonic, Melches
Felix Rohner, Partner
Education: HSG, PhD
Background: Swiss Private Equity & Venture Capital Association
Directorships: Komax, sia Abrasives, Tobler AG, Saia-Burgess Electronics
Ueli Eckhardt, Partner
Education: PhD, Attorney at Law
Background: Worked the legal division of STG
Directorships: Feintool, Freetraders, Sandherr
Stephan Lauer, Partner
e-mail: yves.dudli@capvis.com
Education: MBA, PhD
Background: SBC Warburg , Citibank and Swiss Bank Corporation/SBC, Corporate Finance/Investment Banking.
Directorships: Polytec Holding AG, Soudsonic, Sia Abraoives, Saia Burgess Electronics
Ricarda Demarmels, Investment Director
e-mail: daniel.flaig@capvis.com
Education: HSG, Master of Science in Management
Background: Arthur Andersen Business Consulting Zurich
Directorships: Board of directors mandates include: Clinique Bois Cerf, Uster Technologies
Marc Battenfeld, Associate Director
e-mail: marc.battenfeld@capvis.com
Education: HSG
Background: Phoenix Aktiengesellschaft
Directorships: Tobler AG, Polytec Holding AG

Boris Zoller, Investment Director
e-mail: info@capvis.com
Education: lic. oec. publ., University of Zurich, Switzerland
Background: Procter & Gamble SA in Geneva, Volkswagen de México S. A. de C. V. in Puebla/Mexico, Siemens Business Services AG in Zurich-Kloten and Heidrick & Struggles AG in Zurich

2556 CARLYLE ASIA INVESTMENT ADVISORS LIMITED Carlyle Group
2 Pacific Place
Suite 88
Queensway 88
Hong Kong

Phone: 852-28787000 Fax: 852-28787007
e-mail: inquiries@carlyle.com
web: www.carlyle.com

Mission Statement: Actively seeking new investments.
Geographic Preference: U.S., Europe, and Asia
Fund Size: $400 Million
Founded: 1987
Investment Criteria: Buyouts, venture capital, real estate and leveraged finance
Industry Group Preference: Aerospace, Defense and Government, Automotive, Consumer Services, Healthcare, Industrial Services, Real Estate, Technology, Telecommunications, Media, Transportation, Retailing, Business to Business
Portfolio Companies: Actelis Networks, Inc., AcuFocus, Adesso Systems, Inc., Aerostructures Corporation, Airport Technology Center, Ballston Plaza II, Belden & Blake Corporation, Beru AG, Bfinance, Blackboard, Inc., BNX Systems, Boto International, CAMECA, Canes.

Key Executives:
Tamotsu Adachi, Managing Director
Julia Adam, Associate Director

2557 CARMEL VENTURES
12 Abba Eban Avenue
Ackerstein Towers Bldg. D
Herzeliya 46725
Israel

Phone: 972-99720400 Fax: 972-99720401
e-mail: info@carmelventures.com
web: www.carmelventures.com

Mission Statement: Carmel Ventures helps build great ideas into exceptional companies and talented entrepreneurs into genuine leaders. As investors with a significant track record, we have individually and collectively gone through every stage of the company building lifecycle, and our perspective - drawn from both sides of the investment equation - is based on real life experiences.

Fund Size: $235 million
Founded: 2000
Investment Criteria: Early-Stage
Industry Group Preference: Semiconductors, Communications, Software, SaaS, Internet, Media, Wireless, Mobile
Portfolio Companies: Abe's Market, Amadesa, Axxana, bTendo, C2 Microsystems, Clarizen, cVidya Networks, DesignArt Networks, eXelate, Group Commerce, Imagine Communications, ironSource, Kampyle, Kontera Technologies, LiveU, Multiphy, MyThings, OpTier, Optimal Test, Outbrain, Oversi Networks, Payoneer, Perfecto Mobile, Personetics, RealMatch, Red Bend Software, SAManage, Shunra Software, Skybox Security, SundaySky, Tapingo, TradAir, Wanova, YCD-Multimedia

Key Executives:
Eylon Penchas, General Partner
e-mail: sdovrat@carmelventures.com
Background: Co-Founder, Viola Group

Venture Capital & Private Equity Firms / International Firms

Directorships: Outbrain, GroupCommerce, cVidya, eXelate, ECI Telecom, Amadesa, Wanova

2558 CASS ENTREPRENEURSHIP FUND Cass Business School
106 Bunhill Row
London EC1Y 8TZ
United Kingdom

Phone: 44-02070408600
e-mail: jan.reoch.1@city.ac.uk
web: www.cass.city.ac.uk

Mission Statement: The Cass Entrepreneurship Fund is a £10 million venture capital fund, providing growth equity to start-up and early stage companies. Established in 2010, The Fund has already financed a number of Cass entrepreneurs, as well as providing general support and incubation facilities.

Geographic Preference: United Kingdom
Fund Size: £10 million
Founded: 2010
Average Investment: £50,000 - £500,000
Investment Criteria: Early-Stage, Startup
Portfolio Companies: Alva, Cloud Business, Contego Fraud Solutions, Accutrainee, BuildaBrand

Key Executives:
Cliff Oswick, Chairman
e-mail: jane.reoch.1@city.ac.uk

2559 CASTROL INNOVENTURES
Castrol Technology Centre, Whitchurch Hill
Pangbourne
Berkshire RG8 7QR
United Kingdom

Phone: 44-1189843311

Mission Statement: Building on Castrol's strengths and heritage we want to invest in and create material businesses beyond lubricants. Our focus is on developing innovative technologies and business models in: Smart Mobility, Responsible Castrol, Next Gen Engineering and Intelligent Operations.

Founded: 2010
Industry Group Preference: Mobility, Sustainable Energy, Technology

Key Executives:
Roy Williamson, Founder
Education: Herriott Watt University
Background: Global Market Space Manager, Castrol; Unilever

2560 CATAGONIA CAPITAL
Rosenthaler Str. 42
Berlin 10178
Germany

Phone: 49-30398313030 Fax: 49-30398213031
web: www.catagonia.com

Mission Statement: We invest in software and service companies that make use of online and mobile technologies. In so doing, we rely on disruptive business ideas with the potential to redefine established markets. We actively support our founding teams with resources and comprehensive knowledge. We also apply our experiences to founding our own new companies in the areas of mobile Internet, social and local network applications, as well as other online business models.

Founded: 2009
Investment Criteria: Start-Up, Early-Stage
Industry Group Preference: Internet, Mobile
Portfolio Companies: Tynec, Deutsche Messe Interactive, BeLocal, Jamii, Autoda, Ubertweek, Bio.Logis

Key Executives:
Ralph Eric Kunz, Founder/Managing Partner
Education: University of Chicago; PhD
Background: Nokia Corporation, Bertelsmann AG

2561 CATALANA D'INICIATIVES CR SA
Valencia, 225, Entlo. Int
Barcelona 8007
Spain

Phone: 34-933178161 Fax: 34-933189287
web: www.iniciatives.es

Mission Statement: The main goal is to foment investment in existing companies, promote new business projects and manage third party funds invested in business initiatives with remarkable growth potential.

Geographic Preference: Spain, Europe
Fund Size: $50 million
Founded: 1985
Average Investment: $1.5 million
Industry Group Preference: All Sectors Considered

Key Executives:
Antoni Trallero Vilar, Manager
Background: Economist
Josep-Ramon Sanroma Celma, Chief Executive Officer
e-mail: malbanell@iniciatives.es

2562 CATALYST FUND LP
3 Daniel Frish Street
Tel Aviv 64731
Israel

Phone: 972-36950666
e-mail: audreyg@catalyst-fund.com
web: www.catalyst-fund.com

Mission Statement: Catalyst Fund, LP is an Israel-based venture capital fund investing in maturing companies.

Geographic Preference: Israel
Founded: 1995
Average Investment: $2.5 Million
Minimum Investment: $1 Million
Investment Criteria: Maturing companies, High-technology industry.
Industry Group Preference: Telecommunications, Information Technology, Medical Devices, Enterprise Services, Biopharmaceuticals, Software, Real Estate
Portfolio Companies: Omrix, Bos, Corex, On-set, PowerDsine, MTI Wireless Edge, Ltd., Surf Communication Solutions, Scopus, VCON.

Key Executives:
Edouard Cukierman, CEO & Managing Partner
e-mail: edouardc@catalyst-fund.com
Education: MBA, INSEAD; BS, Israel Institute of Technology
Background: President and CEO of the Astra Fund, Vice Chairman of Citec-Environment and Services.
Directorships: Partner
Boaz Harel, Senior Partner

2563 CATALYST FUND MANAGEMENT & RESEARCH LIMITED
4th Floor, 20 Old Street
London EC1V 9AB
United Kingdom

Phone: 44-02074909520 Fax: 44-2072-811873
e-mail: info@catfund.com

Mission Statement: Actively seeking new investments.

Geographic Preference: United Kingdom, Eastern Europe, Western Europe
Fund Size: $91.39 Million
Founded: 1997
Average Investment: $6.85 Million

Venture Capital & Private Equity Firms / International Firms

Minimum Investment: $571, 000
Investment Criteria: Seed, Start-up, Other early stage, Expansion and Development, Refinancing bank debt, Secondary purchase/replacement capital, Rescue/turnaround, MBO, MBI
Industry Group Preference: Financial Services
Portfolio Companies: Avanza, EPO.com, Firstquote Masson Financial Services, Knowledge Power, Propero, Safeonline, Spiritsoft

Key Executives:
  Tim Farazmand, Non-Executive Director
  e-mail: tim@catfund.com
  Education: MBA
  Background: Royal Bank Development Capital
  Directorships: CEO
  Rodney Schwartz, Chief Executive Officer
  e-mail: rod@catfund.com
  Education: MBA
  Background: PaineWebber, Lehman Brothers, Paribas
  Directorships: CEO

2564 CATALYST INVESTMENT MANAGERS PTY LIMITED PPM Capital
Level 9, 151-153 Macquarie Street
Sydney 2000
Australia

Phone: 61-292701200 Fax: 61-292701222
e-mail: enquiries@catalystinvest.com.au
web: catalystinvest.com.au

Mission Statement: Catalyst is a wholly owned subsidiary of PPM Capital, the global private equity investing arm of Prudential Plc.

Geographic Preference: Australia, New Zealand
Fund Size: $1 billion
Founded: 1989
Average Investment: $135 Million
Minimum Investment: $20.0 Million
Investment Criteria: MBO, MBI
Industry Group Preference: Information Technology, Healthcare, Industrial Services, Agribusiness, Distribution, Education, Entertainment, Financial Services, Food & Beverage, Manufacturing, Retailing, Contracting, Life Sciences, Transportation, Business to Business

Key Executives:
  Brian Gatfield, Chairman
  e-mail: justinryan@catalystinvest.com.au
  Background: Lawyer
  John Story, Managing Director
  e-mail: gwindeyer@catalystinvest.com.au
  Background: NRMA, Ciba-Gigy, BLE Capital

2565 CATALYST VENTURE PARTNERS
The Innovation Centre
Carpenter House
Bath BA1 1UD
United Kingdom

Phone: 44-0-1225-331498 Fax: 44-0-1225-318568
e-mail: hello@catvp.com
web: www.catvp.com

Mission Statement: Catalyst Venture Partners was founded in 1999 when a group of technology entrepreneurs got together to create a networked accelerator and specialist corporate finance boutique. The genesis of the company lay in the partners experience as private investors who regularly came across technology companies, frequently with great IP, who were seeking funds but who were lacking the necessary commercial expertise and management firepower to be credible to potential sources of finance.

Founded: 1999
Average Investment: £500,000 - 5 million
Investment Criteria: Early-Stage, Later-Stage

Portfolio Companies: OCM Print Management Solutions, Oilstudios.com, Green Motion, EVRS, Classwatch, Azure Films, Pedalite, FTL, Firebrand Media, The Business Software Center, Claritum, Realflair, Euroflow, Yellowtag, Iken, The Sceptre Group

Other Locations:
  Paragon House
  Lyncombe Vale Road
  Bath BA2 4LS
  United Kingdom

Key Executives:
  Richard Turner, Founder
  e-mail: rjt@catvp.com
  Education: MSc, Economics, University of Reading
  Background: World Bank, African Development Bank, UN, Partner, East European Consulantcy Practice, KPMG

2566 CATAPULT VENTURE MANAGERS
11 Burrough Court
Burrough on the Hill, Melton Mowbray
Leicestershire LE14 2QS
United Kingdom

Phone: 0116-2388200 Fax: 0116-239-6997
web: www.catapult-vm.co.uk

Mission Statement: Catapult specializes in providing equity capital for businesses.

Fund Size: £100 Million
Founded: 1999
Average Investment: £200,000 - £2 million
Investment Criteria: Early Stage, Development Capital, MBO/MBI

Other Locations:
  11 Burrough Court
  Burrough on the Hill, Melton Mowbray
  Leicestershire LE14 2QS
  United Kingdom
  Phone: 0116-2388200 Fax: 0121-616-0181

Key Executives:
  Rob Caroll, Managing Director
  0116-238-8200
  e-mail: rob@catapult-vm.co.uk
  Education: BA, Pharmacy, Kings College London; MBA, Bradford University Management School
  Background: 3i PLC
  Directorships: Charles Lawrence Group PLC
  Ed Wass, Chief Investment Officer
  0116-238-8200
  e-mail: robin@catapult-vm.co.uk
  Education: Chemical Engineering, Bath University
  Background: BP, Blue Circle, 3i PLC
  Directorships: Melton Mowbray Building Society
  Graham Mold, Position Director
  0116-238-8200
  e-mail: graham@catapult-vm.co.uk
  Background: KPMG
  Ray Harris, Investment Director
  0121-616-0180
  Education: First Class Honours Degree in Economics, UEA
  Background: Corporate Finance Advisor

2567 CATHAYA CAPITAL
2105B, Financial Square
333 Jiujiang Road
Shaghai
China

Phone: 8621-60452690

Mission Statement: Cathaya Capital is a Cross Border Private Equity Fund investing in Chinese companies in the area of Clean Tech and Health Care. The fund targets companies that can benefit from cross border alliances to gain access to international markets and advanced technologies. Cathaya

Capital works closely with the companies to help strengthen its operational and financial team, and helps the companies develop strategic partnerships and international market presence.
Geographic Preference: China
Industry Group Preference: Clean Technology, Healthcare
Portfolio Companies: Jonway Automobile, APMG, Zap China JV, Better World
Key Executives:
  Priscilla M Lu, Managing Partner
  Education: BS, MS, Computer Science, University of Wisconsin, Madison; PhD, Electrical Engineering & Computer Science, Northwestern University
  Background: China Advisor, Mayfield Fund; Founder, Interwave Communications

2568 CAZENOVE PRIVATE EQUITY Cazenove Capital
12 Moorgate
London EC2R 6DA
United Kingdom
Phone: 44-02034791000 Fax: 44-02034790010
web: www.cazenoveprivateequity.com

Mission Statement: CPE operates as a division of Cazenove Capital Management Limited, with the sole objective of producing superior returns for its investors.
Geographic Preference: United Kingdom, Western Europe
Fund Size: $414.5 Million
Founded: 2000
Average Investment: $24.8 Million
Minimum Investment: $10.63 Million
Investment Criteria: Expansion and Development, Bridge finance
Industry Group Preference: Communications, Media, Information Technology, Software, Internet Technology, Electronic Technology, Hardware, Computer Related
Portfolio Companies: Axiom, Clearswift Corporation, Empower, iOra, K-Vault Software Ltd (KVS), Metapack, Callserve, Cityspace, European Telecommunications & Technology, Fluency Voice Technology, Imagine, Avantium International B.V., BlackSpider Technologies, Celoxica

Key Executives:
  Mary-Anne Daly, Head of Wealth Management
  e-mail: info@cazenoveprivateequity.com
  Education: Graduate of Dartmouth College
  Background: IPOs of hundreds of companies worldwide.
  Jeremy Hervey, Head of Charities

2569 CDC CAPITAL PARTNER CDC Group
123 Victoria Street
80 Victoria Street
London SW1E 6DE
United Kingdom
Phone: 44-2079634700 Fax: 44-2079634750
e-mail: enquiries@cdcgroup.com
web: www.cdcgroup.com

Mission Statement: Actively seeking new investments.
Geographic Preference: Africa, Asia, Latin America
Founded: 1948
Investment Criteria: Start-up, Early Stage
Key Executives:
  Graham Wrigley, Chairman
  e-mail: enquiries@cdcgroup.com
  Education: Bachelor of Science, MBA
  Background: Director On the Board of Directors, IPDC
  Ian Goldin, Non-executive Director

2570 CDH INVESTMENTS
China
e-mail: cdhpe@cdhfund.com
web: www.cdhfund.com

Mission Statement: CDH Private Equity was established in 2002 by an experienced team of senior investment professionals who have been working and investing together since 1995. During this period of time, the CDH founding partners have built a strong culture of transparency and rigorous discipline that has generated an enviable level of consistency of investment performance. Today, CDH Private Equity has more than US$4 billion assets under management and has invested in more than 50 portfolio companies, many of which are well-known brands and industry leaders in China. CDH Private Equity focuses on partnering with superior management teams who aspire to grow their companies into world-class, industry leaders in China's growing domestic market.
Geographic Preference: China
Fund Size: $900 million
Founded: 2002
Investment Criteria: Early-Stage, Growth Stage
Industry Group Preference: Information Technology, Healthcare, Education, Clean Technology, High Technology
Portfolio Companies: 360, CDG, Yoho.com, Ether Optronics, Blue Ocean Network, Xiron, LDK, GCL, AOSP, Joyoung, Kanchli, Alltech

2571 CEDAR (ISRAEL) FINANCIAL ADVISORS LIMITED Cedar Fund
9 Keren Hayesod Street, PO Box 505
Herzelia 46105
Israel
Phone: 972-99577227 Fax: 972-99577228

Mission Statement: A leading provider of investment and financial advice for high technology companies.
Geographic Preference: Israel
Fund Size: $225 Million
Founded: 1997
Average Investment: $10 Million
Investment Criteria: Early stage
Industry Group Preference: Telecommunications, Networking, Enterprise Services, Internet Technology, Software, Infrastructure, Communications, Wireless Technologies
Portfolio Companies: Animon, Appilog Inc., BigBand Networks, Celtro, ClickFox, e-Glue, Guardium Inc., MessageVine Montilio, Onaro, Orsus Solutions, PeerApp, Red-C, Silver Kite, WebCollage Inc., WiNetworks

Key Executives:
  Gal Israely, Co-Founder
  e-mail: info@cedar.co.il
  Education: MBA Finance, Tel Aviv University
  Background: Managing Director in the High Tech Investment Banking group of Bear Stearns in NY
  Directorships: Active Board Member
  Amnon Shoham, Co-Founder
  e-mail: info@cedar.co.il
  Education: CPA, BA, Tel Aviv University
  Background: Assistant Controller for Champion Motors,
  Motti Vaknin, CEO
  e-mail: info@cedar.co.il
  Education: BS, Computer Science, Ben-Gurion University
  Background: President, CEO and founder of Exactium Ltd
  Dorin Miller, Venture Partner
  e-mail: info@cedar.co.il
  Education: Bachelor's degree in computer science and MIS from from Tel Aviv University
  Background: member of the R&D team-BigBand Networks

Venture Capital & Private Equity Firms / International Firms

2572 CEDRUS INVESTMENTS
Grand Pavilion
802 West Bay Road
Grand Cayman
Cayman Islands

Phone: 345-7697100
web: www.cedrusinvestments.com

Mission Statement: Cedrus Investments' Private Equity Group makes venture capital, growth capital and mezzanine capital investments in companies located in the Greater China Region, Southeast Asia, Korea, Indonesia, Japan and Australia or elsewhere but with their business focusing on these geographical areas, and these companies are engaged in the following industries: clean technology, biotechnology, energy, nanotechnology, nature resources, consumer and media.

Geographic Preference: Asia, Australia
Industry Group Preference: Clean Technology, Biotechnology, Energy, Nanotechnology, Natural Resources, Consumer, Media

Key Executives:
Rani Jarkas, Chairman

2573 CELADON CAPITAL GROUP
Suite 22-7
Wisma UOA II
21 Jalan Pinang
Kuala Lumpur 50450
Malaysia

Phone: 60-327117211 Fax: 60-327155211
e-mail: celadon@celadon.asia

Mission Statement: Investment Banking, specializing in M&A, PE and VC.

Geographic Preference: Malaysia, Southeast Asia, India
Founded: 1996
Investment Criteria: All States
Industry Group Preference: Clean Technology, Biotechnology, Healthcare, Innovative Technology, Services, Manufacturing

Key Executives:
Nicholas C. Ashby, Founder & CEO
e-mail: nick@celadoncapital.com
Education: University of Cambridge
Background: Investment & Securities Research, Portfolio Management, M&A, Privitizations, Corporate Finance

2574 CENTRALWAY
Binzstrasse 18
Zurich
Switzerland

Phone: 41-44-578-4000
e-mail: info@centralway.com
web: www.centralway.com

Mission Statement: Every year, Centralway Ventures funds numerous early stage companies, which are redefining the future of their respective industry. Based in Zurich and London, Centralway Ventures partners with leading investors to identify, fund and support innovative ventures across the globe. For 15 years, Centralway has been investing in online companies, helping them to develop. Our experience shows that company value can only be generated through a strong product focus, operative excellence and constant innovation.

Founded: 1999
Investment Criteria: Early-Stage
Industry Group Preference: Internet
Portfolio Companies: Numbrs, Buttercoin, Standard Treasury, LendingClub, Sandbox, Securesafe

Other Locations:
Somerset House
New Wing
Strand
London WC2R 1LA
United Kingdom

Key Executives:
Martin Saidler, CEO/Founder
Background: Founder, Jobinteractive.com; Management Group, Beisheim Holding AG
Severin Jan Ruegger, Managing Partner, Investments
Education: BA, University of St. Gallen; MSc, London School of Economics
Background: Founder, Solosso; Co-Founder, Dealicious
Nicolas Ruflin, Managing Partner, Technology
Education: MS, Computer Science, University of Basel
Background: Co-Founder, Technical Lead, useKit

2575 CEYUAN
Qiniao Hutong
Number 35
Dongcheng District
Beijing 50450
China

Phone: +86 10 84028800 Fax: +86 10 84020999
e-mail: info@ceyuan.com
web: www.ceyuan.com

Mission Statement: Ceyuan is a Beijing-based early stage venture capital firm focused on IT and emerging growth companies. We emphasize backing great teams, technology and business innovation. Our mission is to assist entrepreneurs in creating and building world-class businesses. Our conviction, network of relationships and grass roots culture give us the opportunity to discover the next big idea early.

Investment Criteria: Early-Stage
Industry Group Preference: Information Technology, Internet, Wireless
Portfolio Companies: 360 Safe, 3GPP, CVT, Douban, ETSolar, HaoDF, iSpeak, Jiayuan, Letao, Light In The Box, NetWin, PPS, R2G, TX, UC, Vancl, Venustech, WE Magazine, Wuhan Groce Nordic New Energy, Yicha, Zbird, Zhongdian Biotech, Zunlei

Key Executives:
Bo Feng, Co-Founder/Partner
Education: College of Marin, San Francisco State University
Background: Founder/Partner, Chengwei Ventures; Chief Representative, ChinaVest; Vice President, Robertson Stephens & Co.

2576 CHALLENGE FUNDS - ETGAR LP
20 Lincoln Street
Rubenstein House
20th Floor
Tel Aviv 67134
Israel

Phone: 972-35628555 Fax: 972-35621999
e-mail: etgar@challenge.co.il

Mission Statement: The Challenge Funds are two Delaware limited partnerships focused on equity investments in Israel-related privately held and publicly traded companies.

Geographic Preference: Israel
Fund Size: $250 Million
Founded: 1995
Investment Criteria: All stages
Industry Group Preference: Communications, Media, Medical Devices, Real Estate, Industrial Services, Software, Biotechnology, Semiconductors, Internet Technology, Healthcare
Portfolio Companies: Alvarion, Atrica, Comgates, Congruency, DSP Group Inc, Liberate, PowerDsine, Schema Ltd, FlashNetworks Ltd, Orckit Communications Ltd, Radware, MATE Ltd, Demantra Ltd., BitBand Ltd, RT-SET Ltd, Viryanet Inc., CBD Tech Ltd, D-Pharm, Sol-Gel, XTL, ASI, M.T.R.E, Smartlight Ltd

Venture Capital & Private Equity Firms / International Firms

Key Executives:
Yossi Ciechanover, Founder and Consultant
e-mail: joseph@challenge.co.il
Education: Ph.D. in Philosophy from Boston University, L.L.M. from the University of California at Berkeley, Magister Juris degree from the Hebrew University of Jerusalem, member of the New York and Israeli Bar Associations
Background: Chairman of the Board of El Al Israel Airlines. President of PEC Israel Economic Corporation
Directorships: Bank of Israel Advisory Committee, Board of Israel Discount Bank
Yossi Pastel, Chief Financial Officer & Vice President

2577 CHARLOTTE STREET CAPITAL
20 Portman Square
City of Westminster
London W1H 6LW
United Kingdom

web: www.charlottestreetcapital.com

Mission Statement: Invests up to £200,000 in early stage UK technology businesses that have barriers to entry and 'market validation' usually by way of initial sales.

Geographic Preference: United Kingdom
Average Investment: £20k to £200k
Investment Criteria: Early-Stage
Industry Group Preference: Technology
Portfolio Companies: Appshed, Culturelabel.com, GoSquared, HybridCluster, Last Second Tickets, Likely, Loveholidays.com, Ondevice Research, Retronaut, Seedcamp, Simpletax

Key Executives:
Bo Pedersen, Partner
e-mail: bo@sharlottestreetcapital.com

2578 CHARTERHOUSE CAPITAL PARTNERS I
Charterhouse
7th Floor Paternoster Square
Warwick Court
Paternoster Square
London EC4M 7DX
United Kingdom

Phone: 44-2073345300 Fax: 44-2073345333
web: www.charterhouse.co.uk

Mission Statement: Actively seeking new investments.

Geographic Preference: United Kingdom, Europe
Fund Size: $26.1 Billion
Founded: 1980
Average Investment: $400 million and $4 billion
Minimum Investment: $356.5 Million
Investment Criteria: All stages
Industry Group Preference: All Sectors Considered
Portfolio Companies: Barracuda, Avent, Autobar, Saga, TDF, Coral Eurobet, Cegelec Holdings, PreCon, Lucite International

Key Executives:
Duncan Aldred, Partner

2579 CHASE CAPITAL PARTNERS
One Exchange Square
8 Connaught Place

Hong Kong

Phone: 852-82288030 Fax: 852-82288031
web: www.chase.com

Founded: 1984
Industry Group Preference: Life Sciences, Healthcare, Media, Telecommunications, Technology, Consumer Services, Financial Services

Key Executives:
Peter DeMaria, Senior Vice President
John Goldthorpe, Head
Education: Bsc in Physics from Bristol University
Background: Life Assurance Holding Company Limited, M&H Plastics Limited, TIW Czech NV, Mobifon SA, SiTeco, JPMorgan Italian Fund III, Pemco and Chase Mittel Fund II
Derek A. Holley, Senior Vice President / National Field Exam Manager
Dan Lane, Senior Vice President / West Region Head
Education: Language from university of paris, bachelors of arts, economics & finance form university of north london
Background: The Chase Manhattan Bank
Mary Reasoner, Senior Vice President / Southeast Region Head
Education: Nijenrode Bachelor, HEC Master
Background: Greenwich Technology Partners Incorporated , Apax Partners , Botts & Company , Bain & Company
Jeffrey A. Stern, Senior Vice President / South Region Head
Education: Founder of J.P. Morgan plc, New York, Founder of IndustriKapital
Joseph J. Virzi, Senior Vice President / Midwest Region Head
Peter York, Senior Vice President / ABL-IB Region Head
Education: Bachelor of arts from Oxford university
Background: jpmp

2580 CHELSFIELD PARTNERS
67 Brook Street
London W1K 4NJ
United Kingdom

Phone: 44-02072902388
e-mail: enquiries@chelsfield.com
web: www.chelsfield.com

Mission Statement: Chelsfield Partners LLP invests in real estate and related businesses in the UK and Europe. We bring together businesses and individuals with the financial weight, track record, industry network and vision to identify exceptional opportunities. We create significant added value and deliver large scale projects and corporate investments across the real estate sector.

Geographic Preference: United Kingdom, Europe
Fund Size: £1.5 billion
Industry Group Preference: Real Estate

Key Executives:
Elliott Bernerd, Co-Founder/Chairman
e-mail: ebernerd@chelsfield.com
Background: Founder/Chairman, Chelsfield PLC; Co-Founder, Stockley PLC; Chairmain/CEO, Michael Laurie & Partners

2581 CHENGWEI VENTURES
Lane 672, Suite 33C, Changle Road
Shanghai 200040
China

Phone: 86-2154048566 Fax: 86-2154048766
e-mail: General@Chengwei.com
web: www.chengwei.com

Mission Statement: Chengwei Ventures seeks to create entrepreneurial returns on capital by investing in and helping build companies that have scalable business opportunities in the global Chinese economy.

Geographic Preference: China
Average Investment: $11 million
Minimum Investment: $1 Million
Investment Criteria: Early stages
Industry Group Preference: Communications, Enterprise Services, Branded Goods, Manufacturing, Healthcare, Media, Software, Consumer Products, Education, Oil & Gas

Venture Capital & Private Equity Firms / International Firms

Portfolio Companies: OneWave Inc, BabyCare, AAC Acoustic, Huaya Technology, BMI Asia, Oval Technologies, Digital Chocolate, Agape Package Manufacturing, Antig Technology Co, HDT Inc, Shengtang Entertainment, CNC, Asia Info, InfoSec, IEI Technologies.

Key Executives:
Steve Xiangdong Zou, President & CEO
e-mail: General@Chengwei.com
Education: B.A. from University of California, Berkeley and his M.B.A. from Stanford Business School
Background: Partner of Orchid Asia Holdings, Perot Systems Corporation in Texas
Directorships: Managing Partner
Bo Feng, Special Partner & Co-Founder

2582 CHEUNG KONG INFRASTRUCTURE HOLDINGS LIMITED
12/F Cheung Kong Centre
2 Queen's Road Central
Central
Hong Kong

Phone: 852-21223133 Fax: 852-25014550
e-mail: contact@cki.com.hk
web: www.cki.com.hk

Mission Statement: Diversified infrastructure company with a focus in the development, investment and operation of infrastructure businesses.
Geographic Preference: Hong Kong, China, Australia, UK, Canada, Philippines
Fund Size: $300 Million
Industry Group Preference: Infrastructure, Power Technologies, Utilities
Portfolio Companies: North of England Gas Distribution Network, CitiPower I Pty Ltd, Envestra Limited, ETSA Utilities, Powercor Australia Ltd, Hongkong Electric, Zhuhai Power Plant, Qinyang Power Plants, Henan, Siping Cogen Power Plants, Fushun Cogen Power Plants,

Key Executives:
Canning FOK Kin Ning, Deputy Chairman
e-mail: contact@cki.com.hk
Education: BSc in Engineering and MBA
KAM Hing Lam, Group Managing Director

2583 CHINA DEVELOPMENT INDUSTRIAL BANK CDFH
10504 125 Nanjing East Road
Taipei 10570
Taiwan

Phone: 886-227638800 Fax: 886-227562144
e-mail: ir@cdibh.com

Mission Statement: Actively seeking investments.
Geographic Preference: US, Japan, Korea, Southeast Asia, Taiwan
Fund Size: $58 Billion
Founded: 1959
Investment Criteria: all stages
Industry Group Preference: Electronic Technology, Telecommunications, Semiconductors, Wireless Technologies, Biotechnology, Medical Devices, Automotive

Key Executives:
Mu-Tsai Chen, Chairman
Mr. Paul Yang, President & Chief Executive Officer

2584 CHINA ISRAEL VALUE CAPITAL
Room 801, Central Tower
No. 88 Fuhua First Road
Fultan District
Shenzhen
China

Phone: 86-75533359986 Fax: 86-75533359970
e-mail: steven@civcfund.com

Mission Statement: China-Israel Value Capital L.P., is a China-focused, Private Equity Fund headquartered in Shenzhen, China, with 13 offices in China and Herzeliya, Israel. CIVC mainly focuses on Medium sized Chinese companies with: Exceptional and experianced management teams; Established sales operations, typically with revenues between $30M-$100M; and a Rapidly growing market.
Geographic Preference: China, Israel
Founded: 2005
Industry Group Preference: Information Technology, Consumer Electronics, Healthcare, Clean Technology
Portfolio Companies: C2 Micro, KeenHigh Technologies, Vtion Wireless, JinkoSolar Holdings, LuHua Chemical Co., Celgen Biopharmaceutical Co., China Dredging, Juli, Huji

Other Locations:
4 Shenkar Street
Belt Graph 1st Floor
POB 12549
Herzeliya 46725
Israel
Phone: 972-99505478 Fax: 972-99505475

Key Executives:
Jin Haitao, Co-Founder/General Partner
Education: Huazhong University
Background: Chairman, Shenzhen-Hong Kong Investment Association

2585 CHINA MERCHANTS CHINA DIRECT INVESTMENTS LTD.
168-200 Connaught Place
1803 China Merchants Tower
Shun Tak Centre
Central
Hong Kong

Phone: 852-28589089 Fax: 852-28588455
web: www.cmcdi.com.hk

Mission Statement: China Merchants Group, the major shareholder of CMCIM, operated directly under the Ministry of Communications of China before the PRC implemented the policy of separation of enterprises from government organizations.
Geographic Preference: Hong Kong, Beijing, Nanjing, Bangkok
Fund Size: $33 Billion
Founded: 1993
Average Investment: $10 Million
Minimum Investment: $120, 000
Investment Criteria: Bridge, Early Stage, Expansion & Development Capital, Buyout
Industry Group Preference: Financial Services, Brokering, Insurance, Banking, Management, Culture and Media, Manufacturing, Energy and Resources, Information Technology, Agriculture
Portfolio Companies: China Merchants Bank, Industrial Bank Co. Ltd, Industrial Securities Co. Ltd, Jutian Fund Management Co, Ltd. Jutian Securities Co. Ltd, China Merchants Securities Co. Ltd.

Key Executives:
Li Yinquan, Chairman

2586 CHINA MERCHANTS CHINA INVESTMENT MANAGEMENT
1803 China Merchants
Shun Tak Centre
168 - 200 Connaught Road
Central
Hong Kong

Phone: 852-28589089 Fax: 852-28588455
web: www.cmcdi.com.hk

Venture Capital & Private Equity Firms / International Firms

Mission Statement: Specializes in investing in China based businesses. Its investment objective is to acquire quality investments in China principally in unlisted enterprises.
Geographic Preference: China
Fund Size: $100 Million
Founded: 1993
Average Investment: US$10 million
Minimum Investment: $10 Million
Investment Criteria: Start up seed, early stages
Industry Group Preference: Financial Services, Real Estate, Manufacturing, Infrastructure
Portfolio Companies: China Merchants Bank Co. Ltd, Industrial Bank Co. Ltd, Industrial Securities Co. LtdChina Merchants Securities Co. Ltd, Jutian Securities Co. LtdHoulder China Insurance Broker Ltd, Jutian Fund Management Co. Ltd, China Merchants Plaza (Shanghai) Property C
Key Executives:
    Li Yinquan, Chairman
    Hong Xiaoyuan, Executive Director

2587 CHINA VEST LIMITED
Beijing China Resources Building
5th Floor, No. 8 Jian Guo Men Bei Avenue
Suite 508B
Beijing 100005
China

    Phone: 86-1085191535 **Fax:** 86-1085191530
    e-mail: info@chinavest.com.cn
    web: www.chinavest.com

Mission Statement: The firm functions as a bridge to Chinese companies and foreign multi-national corporations.
Geographic Preference: China
Founded: 1981
Average Investment: $212 Million
Minimum Investment: $25 Million
Investment Criteria: growing middle market
Industry Group Preference: Logistics, Healthcare, Media, Textiles, Machinery, Information Technology, Financial Services, Private Equity, Research Provider
Key Executives:
    Robert A. Theleen, Chairman & Chief Executive Officer
    Directorships: Vice President and Beijing Representative
    Jenny Hsui, President

2588 CHINA WALDEN MANAGEMENT LIMITED Walden Group
Beijing China Resources Bldg.
No. 8 Jianguomenbei Avenue, Ste. 1702, 17/F
Dongcheng District
Beijing 100005
China

    Phone: 86-1085192519 **Fax:** 86-1085192520
    e-mail: chinahk@waldenintl.com
    web: www.waldenintl.com

Mission Statement: Invests in entrepreneurs and companies that demonstrate an ability to gain a competitive advantage in the markets they serve.
Geographic Preference: China
Fund Size: $1.6 Billion
Founded: 1987
Investment Criteria: early stages
Industry Group Preference: Communications, Electronic Technology, Software, Semiconductors, Consumer Services, Information Technology
Portfolio Companies: Celestial Semiconductor, Ltd, ChannelSoft Holdings, China Motion Telecom International ltd, CommVerge Solutions, Accel Semiconductor Corporation
Key Executives:
    Lip-Bu Tan, Chairman/Founder
    Brian Chiang, Managing Director

2589 CHORD CAPITAL
Harston Mill
Harston
Cambridge CB22 7GG
United Kingdom

    Phone: 440-1223875598
    e-mail: info@chordcapital.co.uk
    web: www.chordcapital.co.uk

Mission Statement: Chord Capital is a venture investment company based in Cambridge and London. We work with entrepreneurs to drive our portfolio companies from technology projects to commercial enterprises.
Geographic Preference: United Kingdom
Industry Group Preference: Energy, Advanced Materials, Environment, Renewable Energy, Energy Efficiency, Medical Technology, Biometrics
Portfolio Companies: Altraverda, ImmunoBiology, Metalysis, FreeHand Surgical, Sensortec, CIP Technologies
Key Executives:
    John Townsend, Managing Director
    Education: BA, Economics, University of Manchester
    Background: CEO, Vesta Capital Partners
    Directorships: Altravarda, Metalysis, Prosurgics

2590 CHRYSALIS CAPITAL ChrysCapital
Suit 504, St. James Court
Room 101
Port Louis 110003
Mauritius

    Phone: 23-02115410 **Fax:** 23-02086413
    e-mail: kenny.chryscapital@intnet.mu
    web: www.chryscapital.com

Mission Statement: ChrysCapital is a principal investment firm with Mission Partnering with passionate leaders to build world-class companies.
Geographic Preference: India, USA, Mauritius
Fund Size: $2.5 Billion
Founded: 1999
Average Investment: $50 Million - $1 Billion
Minimum Investment: $10 Million
Investment Criteria: Growth investments, carve-outs, joint ventures, buy-outs/buy-ins
Industry Group Preference: Outsourcing & Efficiency, Business to Business, Healthcare, Software Services, Information Technology, Financial Services, Business Products & Services, Manufacturing, Consumer Products, Infrastructure
Portfolio Companies: Balkrishna Industries, Gammon, Global Vantedge, ING Vysya Bank, Micro Inks, Moser Baer, New Path, The Shriram Group, Suzlon, Yes Bank
Key Executives:
    Brahmal Vasudevan, Director
    e-mail: ashish.dhawan@rediffmail.com
    Education: Dual Bachelor (Bachelor of Science and Bachelor of Arts), Yale University . Harvard University , MBA With Distinction
    Background: Goldman Sachs , McCown De Leeuw & Co.
    Ashish Dhawan, Senior Managing Director

2591 CHRYSCAPITAL MANAGEMENT COMPANIES ChrysCapital
IFS Court, TwentyEight, Cybercity
Les Cascades
3rd Floor
Ebene
Mauritius

    Phone: 230-4673000 **Fax:** 230-4674000
    e-mail: kenny.chryscapital@intnet.mu
    web: www.chryscapital.com

Venture Capital & Private Equity Firms / International Firms

Mission Statement: Supports passionate leaders in building world class companies.
Geographic Preference: India, USA, Mauritius
Fund Size: $450 Million
Founded: 1999
Average Investment: $2.5 Billion
Minimum Investment: $8 Million
Investment Criteria: Focuses on companies with defensible market positions and strong underlying organic growth potential including Management Buy-Outs, Recapitalization, Carve-outs, Joint Ventures, PIPEs
Industry Group Preference: Outsourcing & Efficiency, Business to Business, Healthcare, Software Services, Information Technology, Financial Services
Portfolio Companies: Balkrishna Industries, Gammon, Global Vantedge, ING Vysya Bank, Micro Inks, Moser Baer, New Path, The Shriram Group, Suzlon, Yes Bank
Key Executives:
    Ashish Dhawan, Senior Managing Director
    e-mail: info@chryscapital.com
    Education: MBA, IIM Bangalore, Bachelors degree in accounting from Delhi University
    Sanjiv Kaul, Managing Director
    e-mail: info@chryscapital.com
    Education: Pharmacy graduate with an M.B.A.-IIM Ahmedabad, AMP from Harvard Business School, Boston.
    Background: Managing Director of Ranbaxy, China
    Brahmal Vasudevan, Managing Director
    e-mail: info@chryscapital.com
    Education: M.B.A. from the Harvard Business School and graduated in aeronautical engineering from Imperial College, London
    Background: Director of Marketing at ASTRO
    Kunal Shroff, Managing Director
    Education: BA, Knox College; MBA, University of Chicago
    Background: Radiowave; McCown De Leeuw & Company
    Kushal Agarwal, Associate
    e-mail: info@chryscapital.com
    Education: Bachelors degree in accounting from Mumbai University, CA
    Background: KPMG
    Gulpreet Kohli, Principal
    e-mail: info@chryscapital.com
    Education: MBA, Clark University; B.A Delhi University
    Background: GE Capital
    Ashish Agarwal, Associate
    e-mail: info@chryscapital.com
    Education: M.B.A. in finance from Mumbai University, B.Com from Garhwal University
    Background: Global Research division of McKinsey & Company

2592 CIC FINANCE CIC Group
6 Avenue of Provence
Cedex 9
Paris 75452
France

Phone: 33-145969696 **Fax:** 33-145969666
e-mail: filbprod@cic.fr
web: www.cic.fr

Mission Statement: CIC delivers high quality and specialist services to expatriate communities in France.
Geographic Preference: France
Fund Size: $293.5 Million
Founded: 1940
Average Investment: $3.7 - 5.5 Million
Minimum Investment: $0.9 Million
Investment Criteria: Expansion and Development, LBO, MBO, Venture Capital
Industry Group Preference: Retailing, Media, Communications, Industrial Services, Medical & Health Related
Portfolio Companies: Adhersis, Chantemor, Coficern/Sagem, Cote Sud Invetissement, Esi Group SA, Fenwick, Frans Bonhomme, Groupe De Presse Michel Hommell, Le Figano, Nature et D'couvertes, Right Vision, Sebia, Sucriere De Bernevil, Tabur/Bricogite
Key Executives:
    Bruno Julien-Laferrière, Chief Executive Officer
    e-mail: arnouca@cic.fr
    Education: IEP Paris, Maitrise en droit
    Hubert Veltz, Chief Operating Officer
    e-mail: messagfr@cic.fr
    Education: IEP Paris, Maitrise d'economie
    René Pastant, Director of logistics and organisation
    Education: DEA de mathematiques

2593 CICLAD
22 Avenue Franklin Roosevelt
Roosevelt
Paris 75008
France

Phone: 33-156597733 **Fax:** 33-153762210
e-mail: info@ciclad.com
web: www.ciclad.com

Mission Statement: Actively seeking new investments.
Fund Size: $135 Million
Founded: 1988
Average Investment: $30 Million
Minimum Investment: $10 Million
Industry Group Preference: All Sectors Considered
Portfolio Companies: Arthus-Bertrand, Dalie, Garard Pasquier, IMV, ITM, Mogarde, Calectro, Satelec, Siraga, Terres, Aventure, VSD, Vermed
Key Executives:
    Lionel Lambert, Associate
    e-mail: llambert@ciclad.com
    Education: MBA Politics, Paris Institute of Politics
    Background: Boston Consulting Group
    Thierry Thomann, Associate
    e-mail: tthomann@ciclad.com
    Jean-Francois Vaury, Founder/Associate
    e-mail: jtvaury@ciclad.com

2594 CID GROUP
19F, Tower B, CCIG International Plaza
333 Cao Xi North Road
Shanghai 200030
China

Phone: 86-21-3397-3678 **Fax:** 86-21-3397-3599
e-mail: inquiries@cidgroup.com
web: www.cidgroup.com

Mission Statement: Founded in 1998, The CID Group was established by a seasoned and professional team with more than 200 years of direct investment experiences. Since inception, the team has been fully committed to carrying out the mission of 'Integrating Global Resources to Create Synergistic Businesses'. Today, CID has become one of the fastest growing Asia-headquartered private equity firms.
Geographic Preference: Greater China
Fund Size: $1 billion
Industry Group Preference: Semiconductors, Wireless, Telecommunications
Portfolio Companies: Advanced Analogic Technologies, Advanced Power Electronics Corporation, eGalax, Global Mixed-Mode Technology, Prolific Technology, Richtek Technology, Semiconductor Manufacturing International Corporation, STATs ChipPac Taiwan Semiconductor Corporation, Techwell, Worldwide Semiconductor, Flexium Interconnect, Inpaq Technology, Kinsus Interconnect Technology Corporation, Mstar Semiconductor, Shun On

Electronic, Solomon Systech, Taiflex Scientific, Young Fast Optoelectronics, Entire Technology, Formosa Epitaxy, Gamma Optical, Quanta Display, Wiseware Technology, WSE Corporation, Elite Advanced Laser Corporation, Quanta Storage, Skymedi Corporation, Topray Technologies, Alpha Networks, Meru Networks, Tainet Communcation Systems, Aiptek International, Ambow Education, Asia Vital Components, Brighton Best International, Chenming Mold Industrial Corporation, Fullterton Technology, Rotam Global AgroSciences, Super Dragon Technology, Univacco Technology

Key Executives:
Steven Chang, Managing Partner
Education: BS, Electrical Engineering, National Taipei Institute of Technology; BS, Management, National Chung Hsing University; MBA, National Cheng Chi University; PhD, Management, Shanghai Jiao Tong University
Background: Investment Manager, China Development Industrial Bank; Founder, Taiflex Scientific

2595 CINCO CAPITAL
Gänsemarkt 43
Hamburg 20354
Germany

Phone: 49-4044191700 Fax: 49-40228211699
e-mail: contact@cinco-capital.com

Mission Statement: Cinco Capital is building a portfolio of holdings in private companies. Currently Cinco Capital holds investments in Europe and the U.S. in different industries such as technology, financial services, telecommunications, wholesale, marketing, media and others.

Geographic Preference: Europe, United States
Industry Group Preference: Technology, Financial Services, Telecommunications, Wholesale, Marketing, Media
Portfolio Companies: Adconion Media Group, Agarrius, Brille24, Cliqz.com, Dopplr.com, Fab.com, Facebook Investment Fund LLC, Getmobile, Impossible Software, IWATech, Jameslist.com, Lifebond, Lofty, Mobileye.com, Nikoma, Numberfour AG, Offbeatguides, Pixsta, Prezi.inc, PublicStuff, Qype, Samedi.de, Supreme NewMedia, Xing AG, Zynga

2596 CINVEN LIMITED
Warwick Court
Paternoster Square
London EC4M 7AG
United Kingdom

Phone: 44-2076613333 Fax: 44-2076613888
e-mail: info@cinven.com
web: www.cinven.com

Mission Statement: Applies effective strategies to our businesses, creating value and long-term growth.

Geographic Preference: Europe
Fund Size: $9.02 Billion
Founded: 1977
Average Investment: $601 Million
Minimum Investment: $300 Million
Investment Criteria: All stages of funding
Industry Group Preference: Business to Business, Consumer Services, Healthcare, Industrial Services, Retailing, Leisure
Portfolio Companies: Approvia, Gala, MediMedia, NCP, Unique Pubs, Springer, Fitness First, Amadeus, Eutelsat, CBR, Foseco, Klöckner Pentaplast, Foseco, Newsquest, William Hill, General Healthcare

Key Executives:
Hugh Langmuir, Partner
e-mail: info@cinven.com
Education: Graduate of Glasgow University
Background: The Royal Bank of Scotland in their Leveraged Finance Group, Ernst & Young- worked in Boston and London
Adam Prindis, Associate
e-mail: info@cinven.com
Education: Degree in Economics from LUISS in Rome and an MBA from INSEAD
Background: Henderson Private Capital- Partner and Managing director
Yagnish Chotai, Director
e-mail: info@cinven.com
Education: Degree in Economics and Accountancy from Edinburgh University
Background: Director with Hill Samuel Development Capital
Jonathan Clarke, Partner
e-mail: info@cinven.com
Education: He has a degree in Physiology from Oxford University
Background: Advisor-KPMG
Guy Davison, Partner
e-mail: info@cinven.com
Education: Guy has a History degree from Cambridge University.
Background: Larpent Newton, KPMG
Andrew Joy, Senior Adviser
e-mail: info@cinven.com
Education: A degree in Politics, Philosophy and Economics from Oxford University
Background: Managing Director of Hill Samuel Development Capital, Chairman of the British Venture Capital Association.
Alex Leslie, Principal
e-mail: info@cinven.com
Education: Degree in History from Cambridge University and has a doctorate in Medieval Politics.
Background: Board Director of research and planning at Valin Pollen, Board Director of planning at Gavin Anderson.
Hugh Langmuir, Managing Partner
Education: Hugh is a graduate of Edinburgh University, Harvard and London Business School
Background: Bain & Co, Citicorp in London and Paris.
Directorships: partner
Brian Linden, Director
e-mail: info@cinven.com
Education: Business Finance graduate
Background: Deloitte & Touche.
Andrew Joy, Senior Adviser
e-mail: info@cinven.com
Education: Degree in Politics, Philosophy and Economics from Oxford University
Background: Managing Director of Hill Samuel Development Capital, Chairman of the British Venture Capital Association,
Ben Osnabrug, Principal
e-mail: info@cinven.com
Education: Graduate of Oxford University -studied Politics, Philosophy and Economics.
Background: Bain & Co, - worked on numerous strategy projects across a variety of sectors in the UK and South Africa
Simon Rowlands, Senior Adviser
e-mail: info@cinven.com
Education: Degree in Engineering, is a chartered engineer, MBA from Cranfield School of Management
Background: Simon worked with an international consulting firm on multidisciplinary engineering projects in the UK and Southern Africa.

Venture Capital & Private Equity Firms / International Firms

2597 CIPIO PARTNERS
Palais am Lenbachplatz
Ottostrasse 8
Munich D-80333
Germany

Phone: 49-895506960 Fax: 49-8955069699
e-mail: info@cipiopartners.com
web: www.cipiopartners.com

Mission Statement: Cipio Partners is known as a leading international investment management firm in the secondary direct market. We were founded in June 2003 and are managing several funds of early and later-stage venture capital and mid-market investments worldwide. Our staff is based in Munich and San Jose, CA. Cipio Partners pursues the acquisition of portfolios of direct private equity investments in the secondary market. We consider transactions ranging from single-company shareholdings to large and well diversified portfolios across all stages of the investing life-cycle, from early to late-stage venture capital through mid-market and smaller buy-out investments. Securities purchased may include equity, mezzanine and debt.

Geographic Preference: Worldwide
Founded: 2003
Investment Criteria: Early-Stage to Late-Stage

Other Locations:
560 S Winchester Blvd
Suite 500
San Jose, CA 95128
Phone: 408-2367654 Fax: 408-2367651

Key Executives:
Tom S Anthofer, Managing Partner
e-mail: tanthofer@cipiopartners.com
Education: MBA, Duke University, Fuqua School of Business
Background: Partner, Broadview Holdings

2598 CITA GESTION
11bis rue Balzac
Paris 75008
France

Phone: 01-42257676 Fax: 33-145012429
e-mail: info@cita.fr
web: www.cita.fr

Mission Statement: CITA invests side to side with a management team, to support a company plan.

Geographic Preference: France
Fund Size: $336 Million
Founded: 1985
Average Investment: 1 to 12 million Euros
Minimum Investment: $1 Million
Investment Criteria: Startup, Development, Buyout, Leveraged buy outs (LBO)
Industry Group Preference: Pharmaceuticals, Software Services, Biotechnology, Media, Advertising, Textiles
Portfolio Companies: Actelion, Etam, Freesbee, Infodustry, Partenaires Livres, Porcher, REP, Sidel, Solsoft, Actelioln, Adelior, Allocine, Arpida, CB News, Locamex, Synerway

Key Executives:
Philippe Queveau, Managing Director
e-mail: info@cita.fr
Education: Queveau graduated from the Ecole Polytechnique.
Background: Managing Director of the Société Financière Heuliez, CEO of the SA Henri Heuliez
Patrick Plouvier, Investments Manager
e-mail: info@cita.fr
Education: Graduated Ecole Nationale Supérieure des Mines de Saint-Etienne, MBA Degree from the Wharton School (Pennsylvania).
Background: Executive at Coparis

2599 CITY OF LONDON INVESTMENT GROUP PLC
77 Gracechurch Street
London EC3V 0AS
United Kingdom

Phone: 44-2077111566 Fax: 44-2077110772
e-mail: ukclientservicing@citlon.co.uk
web: www.citlon.co.uk

Mission Statement: Provides long term capital growth via active Country Asset Allocation and Stock Selection in emerging markets.

Geographic Preference: London, Europe, Africa, Middle East, USA, Latin America, Canada, Singa
Fund Size: $1.5 Billion
Founded: 1991
Investment Criteria: emerging market

Key Executives:
Glenn Lee, Marketing

2600 CLAL ELECTRONICS INDUSTRIES LIMITED
3 Azrieli Center, 45th Floor
The Triangular Tower
Tel Aviv 67023
Israel

Phone: 972-36075777 Fax: 972-36075778
e-mail: cii@cii.co.il
web: www.cii.co.il

Mission Statement: Actively seeking new investments.

Geographic Preference: Israel
Fund Size: $3149 Million
Founded: 1998
Investment Criteria: Early stage
Industry Group Preference: Electronic Technology, Communications, Semiconductors, Graphic Arts
Portfolio Companies: Mashav, Nesher1, Taavura1, American Israeli Paper Mills2, Kitan Consolidated, Jafora, Cargal, Scitex3, ECI, Nova, Saifun, Main Venture Capital Funds, CBI (ARTE), ECTel, Viryanet

Key Executives:
Gonen Bieber, Vice President Finance
e-mail: cbi@cbi.co.il
Education: Tel Aviv University, L.L.B. & Political Science
Background: Ganden Group - Founder and Chairman
Avi Fischer, CEO & Chairman of the Board
e-mail: cbi@cbi.co.il
Education: Tel Aviv University, L.L.B
Background: IDB Holdings Corp. Ltd, Ganden Holdings Ltd, Fischer, Behar, Chen & Co

2601 CLARENDON FUND MANAGERS
8th Floor
City Exchange
11-13 Gloucester Street
Belfast BT1 4LS
Ireland

Phone: 028-90326465 Fax: 028-90326473
e-mail: info@clarendon-fm.co.uk
web: www.clarendon-fm.co.uk

Mission Statement: Clarendon Fund Managers Limited is venture capital fund manager based in Belfast, which is authorised and regulated by the Financial Services Authority. Clarendon manage £20m of regional VC Funds in Northern ireland including £13m of fully invested Funds (Viridian Growth Fund and Nitech Growth Fund) and the recently established Co-Fund NI, a £7.2m fund that will co-invest with business angel/private investor lead deals which when matched to the private investment on a deal by deal basis will equate to a £16m Fund.

Geographic Preference: Ireland

Fund Size: £16 million
Founded: 2001
Industry Group Preference: Medical Devices, Biotechnology, Communications, Food & Beverage, Waste & Recycling, Renewable Energy, Gaming
Portfolio Companies: Lagan Technologies, Bluechip Technologies, Bittware, Art Technology Group, Fusion Antibodies, Datacitics, TraceAssured, AxisThree, Heartsine Technologies, Dark Water Studios, Biomass CHP, Intelesens, Vertical Wind Energy, Kelsius Limited, Biznet Solutions

Key Executives:
 Alan Mawson, Chairman
 Education: MBA, MIT; PhD, University of Lancaster
 Background: Founding Director, Electra Innvotec

2602 CLARITY CAPITAL
28 Old Brompton Road
Suite 256
South Kensington
London SW7 3SS
United Kingdom

Phone: 44-2075914438
e-mail: info@claritycapital.com

Mission Statement: Long-term investor, focusing on private investments in entrepreneurial companies with leading-edge technology and motivated management teams. The firm provides guidance and accelerated time to market.
Geographic Preference: Canada, Mexico, Brazil, Africa, United Kingdom
Founded: 1996
Average Investment: $5.0 million
Minimum Investment: $1 million
Investment Criteria: Seed, Startup, First-Stage
Industry Group Preference: Minerals, Life Sciences, Energy, Creative Industries
Portfolio Companies: Lobby7, Raindance

Other Locations:
 6235B 86 Avenue
 Southest
 Calgary, AB
 Canada
 Phone: 403-258-3680

 Box 9422, Sonpark
 Nelspruit, Mpumalanga
 Box 9422, Sonpark
 Mpumalanga 1206
 South Africa
 Phone: 27-13-755-1892 Fax: 27-13-755-1994

 105 Plumtree Road
 Belmont
 Bulawayo
 Zimbabwe
 Phone: 263-94603612 Fax: 263-99460376

Key Executives:
 Allan Dolan, Managing Director, Founder
 Background: Founder, African Minerals Limited

2603 CLEANTECH INVEST
Malminrinne 1 B
Helsinki 00100
Finland

Phone: 358-405015127
e-mail: lassi.noponen@cleantechinvest.com
web: www.cleantechinvest.com

Mission Statement: We are a private equity fund management company focusing on cleantech. We create success stories by combining capital, technology & sector know-how and access to key players in the cleantech sector, globally. Our Nordic presence gives us access to some of the world's most exciting deals.
Industry Group Preference: Clean Technology
Portfolio Companies: Savo-Solar, Netcycler, Enersize, MetGen, BT Wood, Ultranat, Enercomp, Matox, Onel

Key Executives:
 Lassi Noponen, Chairman/Partner
 Education: LLM, MBA
 Background: Co-Founder/CEO, Proventia Group Oy

2604 CLEANTECH VENTURES
Level 2, 710 Collins Street
Docklands
Victoria 3008
Australia

Phone: 61-439268350

Mission Statement: Cleantech Ventures is a specialist venture capital fund manager focused on investments in companies developing clean technologies. Cleantech Ventures Pty Ltd is an Australian-owned and managed venture capital company. Our highly experienced investment team has an extensive track record in venture capital investing in companies from pre-seed to expansion stage and a deep understanding of the cleantech sector.
Investment Criteria: Pre-Seed to Expansion-Stage
Industry Group Preference: Clean Technology
Portfolio Companies: Ilum-A-Lite, Lang Technologies, Netsol, MIGfast, Nu Energy, Oceanlinx, Renex Holdings, Semitech Semiconductor, Active Reactor Company, Ecoult, Ember Technologies, Hardwear, Worldwide Coatings

Key Executives:
 Jan Dekker, Managing Director
 Education: Masters Degree, Environmental Law, Sydney University; Graduate Diploma, Environmental Studies, Macquarie University
 Background: Founding Managing Director, Centre for Energy & Greenhouse Technologies

2605 CLIFFORD CHANCE PUNDER
46 Mainzer Landsrasse
Frankfurt 60325
Germany

Phone: 49-69719901 Fax: 49-6971994000
e-mail: daniela.weber-rey@cliffordchance.com
web: www.cliffordchance.com

Mission Statement: Provides advice, technical expertise, and an understanding of the commercial environment in which our clients operate.
Geographic Preference: Americas, Asia, Europe, Middle East
Investment Criteria: All stages
Industry Group Preference: Air Transportation, Automotive, Beverages, Chemicals, Construction, Energy, Pharmaceuticals, Financial Services, Food Services, Healthcare, Restaurants, Household Goods, Insurance, Information Technology, Media
Portfolio Companies: Altria, Safeway plc, Merrill Lynch, Carrefour, China Netcom, Metro Group

Key Executives:
 Andreas Dietzel, Regional Managing Partner
 Sebastian Maerker, Partner

2606 CLIMATE CHANGE CAPITAL
3 More London Riverside
London SE1 2AQ
United Kingdom

Phone: 44-02073935000 Fax: 44-02079395030

Mission Statement: A pre-eminent European cleantech private equity fund which invests expansion capital in high growth, later stage companies and buy outs in the areas of clean power, clean transport, energy efficiency, waste recovery and water. Our goal is to back exceptional companies that contribute to a

lower carbon economy, a more sustainable environment and generate attractive returns for our investors.
Fund Size: £200 million
Average Investment: £10 - 20 million
Minimum Investment: £5 million
Investment Criteria: Later-Stage, Expansion Capital, Buy-Outs
Industry Group Preference: Clean Technology, Power, Transportation, Energy Efficiency, Waste & Recycling, Water
Portfolio Companies: Climate Energy, Enecsys, Enerqos, Metallkraft, Neura, Nualight, Nujira, Orege, Power Plus Communications
Key Executives:
  James Cameron, Chairman
  Education: BA, University of London; MA, Oxford University
  Background: Senior Partner, Graphite Capital

2607 CLOSE BROTHERS EQUITY MARKETS
Close Brothers Group
Neue Mainzer Str. 1
Frankfurt 60311
Germany
Phone: 49-699720040 Fax: 49-6997200415
e-mail: info@closebrothers.de
web: www.dcadvisory.com

Mission Statement: Close Brothers, a Frankfurt based Investment Bank, specializes in providing corporate finance advice for medium sized transactions in Germany and its neighboring countries.
Geographic Preference: Germany
Founded: 1991
Investment Criteria: Medium sized transactions
Portfolio Companies: Klockner Pentaplast, Equivest, Schneidersohne, ELAXY, Elektronik+Kabeltechnik Gmbh & Co., RedDot, Lisi group, PCI Group, FTE, SIG Holding, DIEL
Key Executives:
  Stefan Jaecker, Chief Executive
  Dr. Wolfgang Kazmierowski, Managing Director

2608 CLOSE BROTHERS PRIVATE EQUITY
Close Brothers Group
2 George Yard
London EC3V 9DH
United Kingdom
Phone: 44-2070651100 Fax: 44-2075886815
e-mail: enquiries@cbpel.com

Mission Statement: Invests in UK management buy-outs.
Geographic Preference: United Kingdon
Fund Size: $780.9 Million
Founded: 1984
Average Investment: $61 Million
Minimum Investment: $11.15 Million
Investment Criteria: Expansion and Development, Bridge finance, Refinancing bank debt, Secondary purchase/replacement capital, Rescue/turnaround, MBO, MBI, Institutional BO, Public-to-Private
Industry Group Preference: Business to Business, Transportation, Manufacturing, Leisure, Tourism, Consumer Services, Logistics
Portfolio Companies: Minova International, V Ships, Allied Glass Containers, Park Resorts, Hillary's Group, IDIS, Walton Garden Buildings, Aqualisa
Key Executives:
  Ben Alexander, Investment Director
  e-mail: mark.perryman@cbpel.com
  Education: CA
  Background: Manager, PricewaterhouseCoopers
  Ted Bell, Partner
  e-mail: richard.lott@cbpel.com
  Education: CIMA
  Background: 3i Plc, Unilever
  Directorships: Aurigny Anglo Group, SP Systems
  Iain Slater, Partner
  Education: CA, BA(Maths);University of Warwick
  Background: Senior Manager, The Cooperative Bank; Manager, KPMG
  Directorships: Chance & Hunt, Capital Incentives
  Simon Wildig, Partner
  e-mail: simon.wildig@cbpel.com
  Education: CA, Degree in Accountancy & Finance(Kingston University)
  Background: Deloitte & Touche
  Directorships: ATC Holdings, Hillarys Blinds
  John Snook, Managing Director, Chairman
  e-mail: john.snook@cbpel.com
  Education: CA
  Background: 3i Plc; Cinven; Deloitte Haskins & Sells
  Directorships: Founder Director, senior partner,
  Nick MacNay, Partner
  e-mail: nick.macnay@cbpel.com
  Education: MA
  Background: Director, Rothschild Ventures; Investment Controller, 3i Plc
  Directorships: Corpack Ltd., Chessington Computer Services, Abbseal Ltd.
  Neil Murphy, Partner
  e-mail: neil.murphy@cbpel.com
  Education: Degree from the University of Birmingham
  Background: Manager, Norwich Union Venture Capital
  Directorships: quoted fund manager, private equity team manager
  Sean Dinnen, Partner
  e-mail: francesco.santinon@cbpel.com
  Education: BACC, ACA
  Background: Investment Manager, Clydesdale Bank Equity; Executive, RMD Corporate Finance; Manager, Price Waterhouse
  John Fisher, Investment Manager
  e-mail: john.fisher@cbpel.com
  Education: CA
  Background: Corporate Finance, NM Rothschild; Chartered Accountant, Arthur Andersen

2609 CM CAPITAL
Level 8
379 Queen Street
Brisbane
Queensland 4000
Australia
Phone: 61-738382888 Fax: 61-738311256
e-mail: admin@taluventures.com
web: www.cmcapital.com

Mission Statement: CM Capital is a pioneer of the Australian Venture Capital industry and is regarded as one of the market leaders. Our team combines management experience, industry knowledge, technology and financial expertise to help our portfolio companies build upon and transform great ideas into great companies. At CM Capital, we partner with the management teams of innovative companies to help create market leaders in their respective fields.
Average Investment: $500,000 - $8 million
Investment Criteria: Early-Stage
Industry Group Preference: Life Sciences, Telecommunications, Information Technology, Renewable Energy
Portfolio Companies: Alchemia, Dilthium Networks, Altiris Therapeutics, Pharmaxis, Phenomix, Xumii, CathRx, DSpace, Sunshine Heart, Mesaplexx, Mantara, AdGent, Piedmont Pharmaceuticals, Threat Metrix, Ingenero, Datacastle, BCode, Anteo Diagnostics, Osprey Medical, Universal Biosensors
Key Executives:
  Andy Jane, Managing Partner, Life Sciences
  Education: BSc, Electrical Engineering, Cornell

Venture Capital & Private Equity Firms / International Firms

University
Background: Co-Founder, Technology Concepts
Directorships: Dilthium Networks, Mantara, Ingenero, BCode

2610 COACH & CAPITAL
West Higgins Road 37
Stockholm SE-111
Sweden

Phone: 46-701800800
e-mail: anders@ingestrom.se
web: www.coachandcapital.se

Mission Statement: Coach & Capital is a venture company in Sweden focusing on investing in emerging growth companies in the commercialisation phase. We are very active in the companies we invest. For instance, in addition to active board work, we also have a dedicated Project Leader that works at least one day a week in the company we have invested.

Geographic Preference: Sweden
Founded: 2008
Investment Criteria: Growth-Stage
Industry Group Preference: Information Technology, Telecommunications, Internet, Media, Energy, Environment, Healthcare, Manufacturing
Portfolio Companies: Axiomatics, Biometron, ClimaCheck, Gardio, Idevio, Infrafone, Minimarketsimasys, uTales
Key Executives:
  Anders Ingeström, Partner
  Education: BSc, Economics
  Background: IBM; CEO, Data Routine

2611 COFINEP
26, rue André Pingat
Rheims 51100
France

Phone: 03-51308157 Fax: 33-26833554
web: www.cofinep.fr

Mission Statement: Actively seeking new investments.
Fund Size: Ffr70 million
Founded: 1991
Minimum Investment: Ffr1 million
Investment Criteria: Revenues of more than 3 million Euros
Industry Group Preference: All Sectors Considered
Portfolio Companies: Cedrepa, Champagne Gardet, Malteurop International SA, Sucreries de Berneuil
Key Executives:
  Hans de Breda, CEO
  Yves Besset, director of investment

2612 COLLER CAPITAL LIMITED
33 Cavendish Square
London W1G OTT
United Kingdom

Phone: 44-2076318500 Fax: 44-2076318555
e-mail: Jeremycoller@collercapital.com
web: www.collercapital.com

Mission Statement: Coller Capital is dedicated to the worldwide purchase of secondary interests in venture capital, buyout and mezzanine fund investments.

Geographic Preference: Worldwide
Fund Size: $3.5 Billion
Founded: 1990
Average Investment: $1 million to $1 billion
Investment Criteria: Application of a proven bottom-up valuation methodology, alternative investments held by institutions
Industry Group Preference: Telecommunications, Information Technology, Internet Technology, Technology, Communications
Portfolio Companies: NVP Brightstar, British Telecom, Lucent Technologies, National Westminster Bank, Shell Oil
Key Executives:
  Jeremy Coller, Chief Executive Officer
  e-mail: jordan@collercapital.com
  Background: Chief Executive, Hansing Associates, Europe; Managing Director, Equitable Capital Management Corporation (New York and London); Executive Vice President, International Division, Bayerische Hypotheken und Wechsel-Bank (Munich and New York); Executive Direc
  Jonathon Freeman, Partner
  e-mail: jeremy@collercapital.com
  Education: MA Philosophy from Sussex University. BSc (Hons) Management Sciences from Manchester School of Management, UMIST. Diplome Cours de Civilisation from Sorbonne University.
  Background: Venture Capital and Buyout Manager at ICI Pension Plan; Investment Analyst at Fidelity International. Attended Carmel College
  David Platter, Partner
  e-mail: groen@collercapital.com
  Education: MBA from École des Hautes Études Commerciales (Montreal). Canadian Chartered Accountant. Fluent in English and French.
  Background: Director, Private Equity, for Caisse de Dépot et Placement du Québec
  Stephen Bull, Partner
  e-mail: springett@collercapital.com
  Education: MBA, Stanford Graduate School of Business. Graduate of HEC Paris
  Background: Founder and Chief Executive of Crédit National Group's private equity arm, Financière Saint-Dominique (FSD), and deputy CEO of Crédit National, co-founder of Euro Private Equity Partners.

2613 COLONIAL FIRST STATE PRIVATE EQUITY
Reply Paid 27
Sydney 2000
Australia

Phone: 61-2293033000 Fax: 02-93033200
e-mail: contactus@colonialfirststate.com.au
web: www.colonialfirststate.com.au

Mission Statement: Formerly known as Hambro-Grantham Management, we are committed to funding high growth companies throughout Australia and New Zealand. Colonial First State Private has invested in over 70 companies and assisted them with the implementation of their growth plans.

Geographic Preference: Australia, New Zealand
Fund Size: $300 Million
Founded: 1988
Average Investment: $10 Million
Minimum Investment: $3 Million
Investment Criteria: Early Stage, Late Stage
Industry Group Preference: All Sectors Considered
Portfolio Companies: Agrilink Holdings, Amber Technology, AtCor Medical, Australian Kitchen Industries, Endeavour Healthcare, Integration Management, Mincom Limited, Penrice, Ruthinium Group, SG Fleet Services, Sigtec Pty, Space-Time Research, Speedscan, Technisyst
Key Executives:
  Brian Bissaker, Chief Executive Officer
  e-mail: privateequity@colonialfirststate.com.au
  Education: BE (Hons) MSci (Eng) MBA
  Background: Chief Engineer of the Commonwealth Bank of Australia
  Nicolette Rubinsztein, General Manager, Advocacy and Retirement
  e-mail: privateequity@colonialfirststate.com.au
  Education: Bachelor of Commerce (Honours) degree from the University of Cape Town
  Background: Price Waterhouse and director (and treasurer) of Australian Venture Capital Association Limited (AVCAL)

Venture Capital & Private Equity Firms / International Firms

Chris Stevens, General Manager Custom Solutions
e-mail: privateequity@colonialfirststate.com.au
Education: BSc from University of Sydney, with a major in Mathematics
Peter Chun, General Manager, Product and Investments
e-mail: privateequity@colonialfirststate.com.au
Education: BComm, M.App.Fin, MBA, CPA
Background: Worked with Australian National Industries Limited Group for 20 years.
Directorships: Group Secretary
Geoff Peck, General Manager, Marketing and Distribution
e-mail: privateequity@colonialfirststate.com.au
Education: B Acc, CA, ASIA
Background: Tom had over 5 years experience in Corporate Recovery with Arthur Andersen
Scott Durbin, General Manager, Strategy
e-mail: privateequity@colonialfirststate.com.au
Education: BComm, CA
Background: Seven years experience at PricewaterhouseCoopers

2614 COMMERCE ASSET VENTURES Sdn Bhd
No. 6, Commerce House
Damansara Heights
Kuala Lumpur 50490
Malaysia

Phone: 60-327325577 Fax: 60-327321343
e-mail: enquiry@commerce-ventures.com.my
web: www.commerce-ventures.com.my

Mission Statement: Consistently generates superior returns by infusing value inputs and growth capital into outstanding business opportunities.

Geographic Preference: Malaysia
Fund Size: $80 Million
Founded: 1980
Average Investment: $23 Million
Minimum Investment: $6.6 Million
Investment Criteria: Business Start-Ups, Small and Medium-Sized Enterprises
Industry Group Preference: Information Technology, Communications, Life Sciences
Portfolio Companies: Dbix Systems, Insyncro, Nasioncom, Nexusedge Technologies, Radiant Range, Vector Holding, Good Way Rubber Industries, Malaysia Steel Works, Flex-P Industries

2615 COMMERZ BETEILIGUNGSGESELLSCHAFT
Commerzbank Ag
Frankfurt 60261
Germany

Phone: 49-6913620 Fax: 49-69285389
e-mail: info@commerzbank.com
web: www.commerzbank.com

Mission Statement: Maintains an on-going flow of communication with investors for successful outcomes.

Geographic Preference: Germany, Asia, USA
Fund Size: $500 Billion
Founded: 1940
Investment Criteria: Seed, Startup, First-Stage, Second-Stage, Mezzanine, Expansion And Development, Mbo, Management Buy-In, Lbo
Industry Group Preference: All Sectors Considered

Key Executives:
Frank Annuscheit, Chief Operating Officer
Martin Blessing, Chairman

2616 COMPAGNIE FINANCIERE E DE ROTHSCHILD BANQUE
47 rue Du Faubourg St. Honor
Cedex 08
Paris 75401
France

Phone: 33-140172525 Fax: 33-040172402
web: www.edmond-de-rothschild.fr

Mission Statement: Actively seeking new investments.

Geographic Preference: France, Europe, America, Japan
Fund Size: $357 Million
Average Investment: $89 Million
Minimum Investment: $60 Million
Investment Criteria: High-Growth, Pre-Ipo.
Industry Group Preference: Infrastructure, Applications Software & Services, Multimedia, Information Technology, Telecommunications, E-Commerce & Manufacturing, Manufacturing, Electronic Technology, Food & Beverage, Distribution, Tourism, Media, Environment Products & Services, Life Sciences, Medical
Portfolio Companies: Ceraver Osteal, Hybrigenics, Actelion, Seche/Tredi, Le Figaro, Oenalliance, Sensas, Plasticos, Gespac, Avenir Finance, Tradingcom Europe, Groupe Eurilogic, Make Music, Brainpower, Kaidara.

Key Executives:
Joel Warschawski, President/CEO
Victor Sasson, Vice Chairman

2617 COMPANHIA RIOGRANDENSE DE PARTICIPACOES
Soledad Avenue, 550 - Set 1001
8th Floor
Porto Alegre 90010 230
Brazil

Phone: 55-5132110777 Fax: 55-5132110777
e-mail: crp@crp.com.br
web: www.crp.com.br

Mission Statement: Manages venture capital and private equity funds at all stages.

Geographic Preference: Brazil, South America
Founded: 1981
Investment Criteria: Growth Oriented Companies
Industry Group Preference: Technology
Portfolio Companies: 3Di, Ag2, Apyon, Aquamundi, Brasilmobile, Chronos/Checkforte, Conectt, Digilab, Fk-Biotecnologia, Fulano, Gens, Grupos, Gesplan, Hotelbar.Com, Impacto, Nano Endoluminal, Plugar, Ponfac, Teikon, Uni5.Com, 3Di, Ag2, Apyon.

Key Executives:
Clovis Benoni Meurer, Managing Partner and CEO
Ricardo Hingel, Director

2618 CONCEPT FINANCIAL SERVICES
Level 10, 365 Little Collins Street
Melbourne 3000
Australia

Phone: 61-386760581 Fax: 61-386760589

Mission Statement: Direct investor using proprietary funds building shareholder wealth and value.

Geographic Preference: Australia
Fund Size: $100 million
Founded: 1991
Average Investment: $10 million
Minimum Investment: $1 million
Investment Criteria: Development & Growth Capital for companies at various stages of maturation
Industry Group Preference: All Sectors Considered

Key Executives:
Marcus H. Rose, Founder and Principal
e-mail: mhr@concept.net.au

Education: MBA, FFin, AREI, FAICD
Background: Equity Capital and Property Markets, Henty Corporation.
Directorships: Various

2619 CONCORD VENTURES
85 Medinat Hayehudim St.
4th Floor
PO Box 4011
Harzelia 46140
Israel

Phone: 972-99602020 **Fax:** 972-99602022
e-mail: office@concordventures.com

Mission Statement: Invests in early and later-stage companies.
Geographic Preference: Europe, North America, Israel
Fund Size: $260 Million
Founded: 1995
Average Investment: $4.5 Million
Minimum Investment: $100,000
Investment Criteria: Privately-held companies with leading edge technologies that satisfy needs in large and growing markets
Industry Group Preference: Communications, Computer Related, Information Technology, Internet Technology, Life Sciences, Medical & Health Related, Communications, Telecommunications, Applications Software & Services, Internet Technology, Medical, Semiconductors, Software, Infrastructure

Key Executives:
  Yair Safrai, General Partner
  e-mail: avi@concordventures.com
  Education: B.Sc. in Electrical Engineering from the Technion Institute of Technology and a M.Sc. in Business Management from the Boston/Ben Gurion joint program.
  Background: Founded and served as CEO of Seabridge Ltd., Senior Director at ECI Telecom
  Directorships: Focuses on the Data and Telecommunications sector.
  Matty Karp, Managing Partner
  e-mail: matty@concordventures.com
  Education: B.Sc. cum laude in Electrical Engineering from the Technion Institute of Technology and is a graduate of the Harvard Business School Advanced Management Program.
  Background: CEO of the Nitzanim Venture Fund and CEO of Kardan Technologies, Matty spent fifteen years at Elbit Computers Ltd. Matty served as jet fighter pilot in the Israeli Air Force.
  Yaron Rosenboim, General Partner and CFO
  e-mail: shai@concordventures.com
  Education: B.Sc. in Computer Science from the University of Maryland and an MBA in marketing and financial management from the University of Maryland
  Background: President & CEO of Emblaze Systems, Vice President at Comverse Technology, Co-founder and Vice President of Coni Communication
  Directorships: Focuses on information technology with a specialization in wireless and cellular networks.

2620 CONNECT VENTURES
Unit 11, Zeus House
16-30 Provost Street
London N1 7NG
United Kingdom

web: www.connectventures.co.uk

Mission Statement: Connect Ventures is a venture capital firm investing in early stage Internet and mobile businesses. We're based in London and invest throughout Europe. We take a hands-on approach to investing by helping founders grow their startups into companies and provide our expertise on product, marketing, and financing strategy. As a small and focused fund, we are able to move quickly and give our portfolio companies the time and attention they deserve.
Geographic Preference: Europe
Average Investment: £200,000 - 1 million
Investment Criteria: Seed-Stage, Early-Stage
Industry Group Preference: Mobile, Internet, Digital Media & Marketing
Portfolio Companies: Citymapper, Ondango, Secret Sales, Space Ape Games, Teleportd, Urli.st, YourGrind

Key Executives:
  Pietro Bezza, Managing Partner
  Background: Founder, Neo Network
  Bill Earner, Managing Partner
  Education: BS, Engineering, Harvey Mudd College; MBA, London Business School
  Background: Investment Manager, Amadeus Capital Partners
  Sitar Teli, Managing Partner
  Education: Mechanical Engineering & Economics, Duke University
  Background: Investment Manager, Doughty Hanson Technology Ventures; Jefferies

2621 CONOR VENTURE PARTNERS OY
Innopoli 2
Tekniikantie 14
FI-02150 Espoo
Finland

Fax: +358 9 812 7305
e-mail: jari@conor.vc
web: www.conor.vc

Mission Statement: Our mission is to spot the brightest enabling technologies and help in turning them into global winners. We believe in building businesses that grow and succeed as leaders in their categories. We value niche solutions for a specific gloval market over more general offerings with limited geographical reach. Our approach is best suited for ambitious entrepreneurs with a global mindset. As opposed to building references in neighborhoods close by, we will push you to go directly to the ideal customers, wherever in the world they are.
Geographic Preference: Nordic, Baltic
Founded: 2005
Minimum Investment: $500,000
Investment Criteria: Early Stage
Industry Group Preference: ICT, Electronics, Embedded Systems, New Materials, Optics
Portfolio Companies: Aito Technologies, AnaCatum, BehavioSec, Crystalsol, Eniram, Fits.me, Imbera Electronics, Neo Technology, Omegawave, Plexpress, Scint-X, Scoopshot, Sensinode, Sticky, Supponor Systems, TactoTek

Other Locations:
  Birger Jarlsgatan 2
  SE-114 34 Stockholm
  Sweden

Key Executives:
  Jari Mieskonen, Managing Partner
  +358 50 563 6992
  e-mail: jari@conor.vc
  Background: Founding Partner, Eqvitec Partners; Investment Director, Sitra
  Manu Mäkelä, Partner
  +358 400 442 873
  e-mail: manu@conor.vc
  Background: Investment Director, Holtron Ventures; Investment Director, Eqvitec Partners
  Jarkko Penttilä, Partner
  +358 50 516 6420
  e-mail: jarkko@conor.vc
  Background: Partner, Eqvitec; Manager, Ericsson Business Innovations
  Chris Barchak, Partner
  +44 7852 333 965

Venture Capital & Private Equity Firms / International Firms

e-mail: chris@conor.vc
Background: Principal, Fidelity Growth Partners Europe; Associate, Index Ventures

2622 CONTINENTAL VENTURE CAPITAL LIMITED
Level 42, Suncorp Place, 259 George Street
Sydney 2000
Australia

Phone: 61-290878000 Fax: 61-290878088
e-mail: cvc@cvc.com.au
web: www.cvc.com.au

Mission Statement: Seeks investment opportunities in predominantly established, profitable, high growth companies across all industry sectors.

Geographic Preference: Australia
Fund Size: $130 Million
Founded: 1984
Average Investment: $1 Million - $5 Million
Minimum Investment: $.5 Million
Investment Criteria: Funding at all stages and for all sectors
Industry Group Preference: Renewable Energy, Biotechnology, Medical & Health Related, Property Management, Information Technology, Technology
Portfolio Companies: CVC Sustainable, CVC Private Equity

Key Executives:
Jason Ters, Non-Executive Director
Education: Bachelor of Commerce from the University of New South Wales.
Background: He was General Manager of Pacific Communications Holdings Limited from January 1997 until May 1998AND With Tetley Medical Limited.As managing director of an ASX listed environmental waste processing company
Directorships: Chief Executive Officer of CVC Limited and he is also a Director of Greens Foods Limited, Pro-Pac Group Limited, CVC Sustainable Investments Limited and CVC Investment Manager
Alexander Beard, Chief Executive Officer
Education: Bachelor of Commerce in Accountancy and Master of Commerce in Accounting and Financial Management (UNSW);
Background: Worked Chartered Accountant for Greenwood Challoner.Established Gould Ralph and Company in 1976
Directorships: Chairman of the listed public company Macarthur National Limited

2623 CONVEXA Tyveholmen AS
Tjuvholmen Alle 19
Oslo N-0252
Norway

Phone: 47-22-39-8900
e-mail: post@convexa.com
web: www.convexa.no

Mission Statement: Convexa is a leading Norwegian venture capital company investing in technology companies in various areas. We invest in early-stage/growth technology companies that promise to deliver high growth and exceptional returns. We seek companies which have developed breakthrough technologies. Convexa focuses on accelerating these technology companies to international markets. We bring first-class competence and high energy level in combining broad strategic and deep operational insights, business development skills, private and public financing and exit capabilities, and a broad network to talented entrepreneurs in growth companies. We strive to be a superior partner to build leading companies.

Geographic Preference: United States, Europe
Founded: 2000
Investment Criteria: Early-Stage, Growth Stage

Industry Group Preference: Technology, Consumer Internet, Enabling Software, Cloud Computing, Wireless, Telecommunications, Oil & Gas, Materials Technology
Portfolio Companies: Confluence Solar, Innova Light, Solar Implant Techn9logies, Wirescan, Nordic Energy Services, Wellbore Solutions, Brogea, OnTime Networks, Axxessit, Metamerge, Apptix, Consorte, TeleComputing

2624 CORE PACIFIC - YAMAICHI CAPITAL LIMITED Core Pacific Securities Company Ltd
36th Floor, Cosco Tower
Grand Millennium Plaza
183 Queen's Road
Central
Hong Kong

Phone: 852-21663888 Fax: 852-29180409
e-mail: info@cpy.com.hk
web: www.cpy.com.hk

Mission Statement: Provides a broad range of investment banking services to the region

Geographic Preference: Beijing, Los Angeles, Shanghai, Shenzhen, Taipei
Fund Size: $128 Million
Founded: 1992
Industry Group Preference: Corporate Services, Technology, Communications, Biotechnology, Industrial Services, Media
Portfolio Companies: Core Pacific Group, Yuanta Financial Group, Chang Hwa Bank, Nanjing Sample Technology Co. Ltd., Sjtu Sunway Software Industry Ltd., Technologies Co. Ltd., Shaanxi Northwest New Technology Industry Co. Ltd., Powerleader Science & Technology Ltd.

Key Executives:
Mr. Shen Qingjing, Chairman
Education: Graduated from National Chung-Hsing University, Master of Science from University of Southern California U.S.A., Doctor degree in University of La Verne, MBA..
Background: Director of Global Securities Finance Corporation, Chung Hsing Bills Finance Company, Central Investment Holding Company & Jen Hwa Investment Holding Company throughout the years.
Mr. Chen Qisheng, Chief Executive Officer

2625 CORVINUS NEMZETKOZI BEFEKTETESI RT Corvinus International Investment Ltd.
Fehérvári út 24. IV/1
Budapest 1117
Hungary

Phone: 36-17890575 Fax: 36-17002627
e-mail: ps@ps.hu
web: www.siteset.hu

Mission Statement: Inests in Hungarian companies abroad and equipped to ensure sufficient financial resources for its partners' investment projects.

Geographic Preference: Hungary
Founded: 1997
Average Investment: $0.28 Million
Minimum Investment: $0.10 Million
Investment Criteria: Facilitates foreign investments by creating, acquiring and developing ventures abroad
Industry Group Preference: All Sectors Considered

Key Executives:
Zoltán Lex, Chairman
e-mail: info@corvinus.hu
Viktor Katona, Director

Venture Capital & Private Equity Firms / International Firms

2626 COVENT INDUSTRIAL CAPITAL INVESTMENT COMPANY
27 Maros U
Budapest H-1122
Hungary

Phone: 36-13552493 Fax: 36-12022381

Mission Statement: Focuses on the rehabilitation of industrial real estate and park development.
Geographic Preference: Hungry
Fund Size: $2.9 Million
Founded: 1993
Investment Criteria: Early Stage, Turnaround
Industry Group Preference: Real Estate, Property Management, Marketing, Legal, Industrial Services
Portfolio Companies: Bicske-M1 Industrial Park And Logistic Centre, Ozd Industrial Park, Vivien Mineral Water And Beverage Company Ltd.
Key Executives:
  János Antal Bolyky, Chief Executive Officer
  Györgyi Bereczkei, Head of Secretariat

2627 CRB INVERBIO
Almagro 1
1 Dcha
Madrid 28010
Spain

Phone: 34-914467897 Fax: 34-917021018
e-mail: info@crbinverbio.com
web: www.crbinverbio.com

Mission Statement: Cross Road Biotech Inversiones Biotecnologicas is a venture capital management firm. CRB Inverbio manages venture capital firms that invest in the development of seed stage companies in life sciences that address unmet medical needs and have the potential to grow into successful businesses. To that end, the company selects innovative projects led by prestigious scientists and entrepreneurs, providing financing, management support and strategic advice.
Geographic Preference: Spain
Investment Criteria: Seed Stage
Industry Group Preference: Life Sciences, Biotechnology
Key Executives:
  Enrique Castellon, President
  Education: Universidad Complutense de Madrid
  Background: Secretary of State, Spanish Ministry of Health & Consumer Affairs; Executive President, Spanish Drug Agency; CEO, Galician Health Service

2628 CREANDUM
Jakobsbergsgatan 18
Stockholm 103 86
Sweden

Phone: +46 8 524 636 30
web: www.creandum.com

Mission Statement: We help our investments with recruiting, advisory boards, office spaces and all sorts of great leads to help them build and grow their businesses. Our network covers the globe, which leaves us with the possibility of helping our investments with pretty much everything.
Industry Group Preference: Consumer Hardware, Consumer Software, Hardware, Software
Portfolio Companies: PlayRaven, Vivino, Spotify, Brisk.io, Autobutler, Edgeware, Appear TV, 13th Lab, Xeneta, Aito Technologies, Itslearning, Cint, Wrapp, Linas Matkasse, VideoPlaza, Nonstop Games, Jays, Tripbirds, iZettle, JustBook, TrustWeaver, Xtract, Norstel, Mitrionics, IPtronics

Other Locations:
470 Ramona St.
Palo Alto, CA 94301
Key Executives:
  Erik Olofsson, Investment Team
  e-mail: erik.olofsson@creandum.com
  Education: M.S.c, Industrial Engineering, Linkoping Institute of Technology; MBA, Harvard Business School
  Background: CEO, Fakturino; Founder, Klipster
  Lasse Pilgaard, Investment Team
  Education: M.S.c, Economics, Aarhus University
  Joel Eriksson Enquist, Investment Team
  e-mail: joel.eriksson@creandum.com
  Education: M.S.c, Industrial Engineering, Chalmers School of Entrepreneurship
  Daniel Blomquist, Investment Team
  e-mail: daniel.blomquist@creandum.com
  Education: M.S.c, Industrial Engineering and Management, Linkoping Institute of Technology; MBA, Stockholm School of Economics

2629 CREATHOR VENTURE
Marienbader Platz 1
Bad Hamburg 61348
Germany

Phone: 49-6172139720 Fax: 49-61721397229
web: www.creathor.de

Mission Statement: We are looking for entrepreneurs who address new markets and have the potential to turn their company into a global market leader. Decisiveness and speed of building your business is important to us. We invest in all venture capital situations, with our primary focus on seed and startup phases. As a lead investor we support our portfolio companies through active mentoring during all stages of development, including further financing rounds as well as trade sales or IPOs. We utilize our experience at building companies and developing them on an international scale. We also tap into our global industry, scientific and financial networks for the benefit of our portfolio companies.
Geographic Preference: Europe
Fund Size: 150 million Euro
Founded: 1984
Average Investment: 10 million Euro
Investment Criteria: Seed-Stage, Startup
Industry Group Preference: High Technology, Telecommunications, Information Technology, Internet, Media, Life Sciences, Nanotechnology, New Materials, Electronics, Clean Technology
Portfolio Companies: Accovion, Alrise Biosystems, Caprotec, Cevec, Cloud Control, Cube Biotech, Donato, Dedendo, Hojoki, ITN Nanovation, Insited, Joiz, Kigo, Mobiles Republic, Net Biscuits, Phenex, Purmeo, Room Beats, Shopgate, Sirion Biotech, Sivdon Diagnostics, Sofialys, Stylefruits.de, Tellja, Viewster, Wired Minds, Zadego, Zimory
Key Executives:
  Gert Kohler, Chief Executive Officer
  Education: Master degree in Mathematics, Physics, Operational Research & Business Administration, PhD, Mathematics
  Background: Managing Director, Herbert Quandt Group; Founder, Technologieholding

2630 CRESCENDO VENTURE MANAGEMENT LLC
600 Hansen Way
Mayfair
Palo Alto, CA 94304

Phone: 001-6504701200 Fax: 001-6504701201
e-mail: investorservices@crescendoventures.com
web: www.crescendoventures.com

Venture Capital & Private Equity Firms / International Firms

Mission Statement: The mission of being the best venture partner for emerging communication and enterprise infrastructure companies.
Geographic Preference: Europe, America
Founded: 1993
Investment Criteria: Early-stage funding and growth resources to high-potential companies.
Industry Group Preference: Software, Communications, Computer Related, Electronic Technology
Portfolio Companies: airBand Communications, Arteris, bDNA, Broadsoft, Cognima, Compellent Technologies, CoreOptics, Dust Networks, eSilicon Corporation, Lumenaré Networks.

Key Executives:
David Spreng, Managing General Partner
e-mail: dspreng@crescendoventures.com
Education: Graduate from University of Minnesota with a degree in Accounting
Background: IAI Ventures, Investment Advisers, Inc., Salomon Brothers, Dain Bosworth,
John Borchers, General Partner

2631 CROSBY ASSET MANAGEMENT
Unit 502, 5th Floor, AXA Centre
151 Gloucestor Road
Wan Chai
Hong Kong

Phone: 85-234762700 **Fax:** 852-21690008
web: www.crosbycapitallimited.com

Mission Statement: A leading independent investment banking and asset management firm in Asia.
Geographic Preference: Asia, Middle East, Europe
Fund Size: $600 Million
Founded: 2007
Investment Criteria: Expansion & Development
Industry Group Preference: Telecommunications, Natural Resources, Oil & Gas, Imports/Exports

Key Executives:
Clive Ng Cheang Neng, Chairman and Executive Director
e-mail: info@crosby.com
Background: British Foreign Service and Treasury, Chairman of Lloyds Bank Group, Worked with Hong Kong Government (Securities & Futures Commission), Nomura Asia Holdings, Techpacific Capital Ltd, International Securities Consultancy Ltd.
Liu Guang He, Executive Director

2632 CROSBY CAPITAL LIMITED
Unit 502, 5th Floor, AXA Centre
151 Gloucestor Road
Wan Chai
Hong Kong

Phone: 852-34762700 **Fax:** 852-21690008
web: www.crosbycapitallimited.com

Mission Statement: Asia's premier independent corporate finance and investment banking firm.
Geographic Preference: Hong Kong
Fund Size: $350 Million
Founded: 2007
Average Investment: $24 Million
Investment Criteria: Private equity firms, buy-out funds and corporate and institutional investors
Industry Group Preference: Banking

Key Executives:
Clive Ng Cheang Neng, Chairman and Executive Director
Background: Managing Director of Nomura International Plc, member of Nomura's European Board of Directors, Credit Suisse First Boston in London as its Managing Director of convertible Eurobonds at Yamaichi International (Europe) Ltd

2633 CSL INVESTMENT & FINANCE
Somkid Place, 6 Soi Somkid
Bangkok 10330
Thailand

Phone: 66-2-650-3172-4 **Fax:** 66-2-650-3175
web: www.csl.cc

Mission Statement: Advisors in Asia for venture capital, project finance, real estate investment funds, energy finance and privatization.

Key Executives:
Jonathan Price, Chief Executive Officer
66-265031724

2634 CVC ASIA PACIFIC LIMITED CVC Capital Partners
Suite 901-3, ICBC Tower
Citibank Plaza ICBI Tower
3 Garden Road
Central
Hong Kong

Phone: 852-35186360 **Fax:** 852-35186380

Mission Statement: CVC Asia Pacific is an investment and advisory company focusing on buy-out opportunities in the Asia Pacific Region.
Geographic Preference: Asia Pacific region
Fund Size: $50 Billion
Founded: 1999
Investment Criteria: Buy-outs
Industry Group Preference: Manufacturing, Construction, Food & Beverage, Chemicals, Automotive
Portfolio Companies: Pacific Brands, Haitai Confectionery and Foods

Key Executives:
Srdjan Dangubic, Investment Director, Pan Asia Team
Education: Bachelors from Monash University, Business Degree from the University of Newcastle, Australia, MBA from Stanford University
Background: Inchcape Plc, Fosters Brewing Group and Elders Investments, McKinsey & Company,
William Ho, Managing Director

2635 CVC CAPITAL PARTNERS LTD
111 Strand
London WC2R 0AG
United Kingdom

Phone: 44-2074204200 **Fax:** 44-2074204231
web: www.cvc.com

Mission Statement: An independent investment and advisory company dedicated to European Private Equity.
Geographic Preference: United Kingdom, Asia, Western Europe
Fund Size: $18 Billion
Founded: 1981
Average Investment: $28 Billion
Minimum Investment: $180 Million
Investment Criteria: Focuses on companies in market-leading positions, with strong, motivated management teams
Industry Group Preference: Construction, Manufacturing, Food & Beverage, Chemicals, Automotive
Portfolio Companies: Acordis, Amatek, BSN Glasspack, Bols Royal Distilleries, Cartiere del Garda, Colomer Group, Dorna Promocion del Deporte, Dutton-Forshaw, Hozelock, Invensys Sealing Systems, Kappa Packaging, Parisa Group, Synstar International, Wavin, William Hill

Key Executives:
Jonathan Feuer, Managing Partner - Co-Head of UK Investments

Venture Capital & Private Equity Firms / International Firms

e-mail: info@cvceurope.com
Education: BA Degree in Business Administration from Yonsei University in Korea.
Background: McKinsey & Company in Seoul.
Rob Lucas, Managing Partner - Co-Head of UK Investments
e-mail: cvc@cvcltd.com.au
Education: CA
Background: Solution 6 Holdings Limited and Star City Holdings Limited, Mobile Innovations Limited, G-Tek Limited,
Richard Blackburn, Director
e-mail: info@cvceurope.com
Education: Degree in English from Pennsylvania State University, Masters in International Management, American Graduate School of International Management
Background: VP/Credit Officer/Operations Head, Citibank AG, Foreign Service Officer, US State Department
Julia Agafonova Director, Fund Administration
e-mail: info@cvceurope.com
Education: MA, Economics, Columbia University, LLM, University of Utrecht, Holland
Background: Citicorp Corporate Finance
Nick Archer Partner, Fund Administration
e-mail: info@cvceurope.com
Education: Commercial Engineering, Catholic University of Louvain, AMP from Insead.
Background: BBL in Brussels, investment banking department
Marc Boughton, Managing Partner
e-mail: info@cvceurope.com
Education: BA, Middlebury College
Background: Citibank Mezzanine Finance
Graham Brooke, Managing Director
e-mail: info@cvceurope.com
Education: Masters Degree in Economics, Erasmus University, Rotterdam, CA
Background: CVC's European Business.
Directorships: Chief Investment Officer
Tony Clamp, Director
e-mail: info@cvceurope.com
Education: MBA, New York University
Background: Steniel Manufacturing, Asia Printers Group, and Yellow Pages Singapore. Previously, Mr. King headed Citicorp's Taiwan.
Calum Conway, Legal Counsel
e-mail: info@cvceurope.com
Education: BA in Economics, University of Stirling, Scotland
Background: Citigroup, M.D. of Citigroup China Investment Management Limited
Benjamin Edgar, Managing Director, London
e-mail: info@cvceurope.com
Education: BA from Duke University, MBA, University of California, Los Angeles
Background: Citicorp Investment Management Group; Citibank Mezzanine Finance Group
Iain Parham, Managing Partner, London
e-mail: info@cvceurope.com
Education: Degree in Economics, Manchester University, CA
Background: CIN Venture Managers, City Office of 3i Plc.
Donald Mackenzie, Co-Founder and Co-Chairman
e-mail: info@cvceurope.com
Education: LLB, University of Dundee, Scotland, CA
Background: Investment Director, 3i Plc, Deloitte Haskins & Sells
Alex Fotakidis, Senior Managing Director
e-mail: info@cvceurope.com
Education: MBA, Stockholm School of Economics
Background: Senior Partner of BPEP Internationa, Chairman of MphasiS BFL Limitedco
Sebastian K☐nne, Investment Director
e-mail: info@cvceurope.com
Education: PhD in Economics from University of Vienna
Background: CEO, Helarb Management SA; B Metzler Seel Sohn & Company; Co-Headed, M&A and Corporate Finance

2636 CVC INVESTMENT MANAGERS LIMITED
259 George Street
AAP Centre
Level 42
Sydney NSW 2000
Australia

Phone: 61-290878000 Fax: 61-290878088
e-mail: lmacklin@cvc.com.au
web: www.cvc.com.au

Mission Statement: CVC Limited is one of the pioneering venture capital firms in Australia and has evolved to be a significant player in the private equity market.

Geographic Preference: Australia
Founded: 1984
Average Investment: $10 Million
Minimum Investment: $1 Million
Investment Criteria: Start-up through expansion, mezzanine, mature.
Industry Group Preference: Environmental Protection, Bio Materials, Environment Products & Services, Transportation, Energy, Packaging
Portfolio Companies: PRO-PAC Packaging, Wind Corporation Australia, Traffic Technologies, Soilwise, Plantic Technologies, Biodiesel Producers.

2637 CYBERAGENT VENTURES
6-1 Shinjuku Sumitomo Building 25F
Shinjuku-ku, Nishi 2-chome
Minato-ku
Tokyo 163-0225
Japan

Phone: 81-359095536 Fax: 81-3-5772-1233
web: www.cyberagentventures.com

Mission Statement: Our main aim is to be a specialist in the internet-mobile business fields and find/develop start-up companies that are expected to prosper further. We play a role as a partner of a start-up company to which we invest money. We not only provide money but also support its development and management providing management know-hows necessary for the company to succeed.

Geographic Preference: China, Taiwan, Vietnam, Indonesia, United States
Fund Size: 360 million yen
Founded: 2006
Investment Criteria: Early-Stage
Industry Group Preference: Internet
Portfolio Companies: Revolver, Piece of Cake, A-Star, Tunnel, Best Teacher, Imonomi, CrowdWorks, Qrunch, Zawatt, Kaditt, Retty, FrogApps, Samurai International, Mind Palette Co., ONEofTHEM, Insight Plus, GCLOUD, KAYAC, Bank of Innovation, Fringe81, Sparcyz, Realworld.co, PhotoCreate, SANSAN, Valuedesign, Fillmore Advisory, Smile Maker, Pankaku

Key Executives:
Soichi Tajima, President
Education: Osaka University
Background: Unoh, Synergy Marketing, Full Speed, CROOZ, VECTOR

2638 CYBERSTARTS
Mikhmoret, HaMerkaz
Israel

web: cyberstarts.com

Mission Statement: Aims to support entrepreneurs who are focused on identifying and solving cybersecurity problems.

Fund Size: $50 Million

Investment Criteria: Cybersecurity
Industry Group Preference: Cybersecurity
Key Executives:
Gili Raanan, Founder/General Partner
Education: BA, Computer Science, Tel Aviv University; MBA, Recanati School, Tel Aviv University
Background: Sanctum; AppScan; NLayers; Sequoia Capital Israel

2639 CZECH VENTURE PARTNERS SRO K+
Venture Partners B.V.
Opletalova 41/1683
Praha 113 32
Czech Republic
Phone: 420-556701900 Fax: 420-556709123
web: cvp.czechtrade.us

Mission Statement: Czech Venture Partners is an investment advisory company that manages venture capital funds in the Czech Republic.
Geographic Preference: Czech Republic
Fund Size: $12.67 Million
Founded: 1999
Average Investment: $ 2.26 Million
Minimum Investment: $ 0.95 Million
Investment Criteria: Private Small and Medium-sized enterprises
Industry Group Preference: Manufacturing, Services
Portfolio Companies: Health and Fitness Central Europe (HFCE), Finance New Europe, AMTEX Radiátory

2640 DAHER CAPITAL
Arab Bank Building, 2nd Flor
Riad el Solh Street
Beirut Central District
Lebanon
web: www.dahercapital.com

Mission Statement: Daher Capital is a Beirut-based family office that was founded and is led by Michel Daher, a veteran entrepreneur with over 30 years of experience across several sectors including financial services, manufacturing, distribution and agriculture.
Founded: 2003
Industry Group Preference: Financial Services, Manufacturing, Distribution, Agriculture
Portfolio Companies: Big Frame. Bonds.com, Browz, Burstly, Chownow, DataSift, Digital Air Strike, Divshot, Eagle Crest Energy Company, FXCM, Grubwithus, Maker, Master, Master Capital Group, Momentfeed, Poppins, SteelHouse, Stonegate Mortgage, Text+, Tradesy, TrueCar, Victor, YieldMetrics
Key Executives:
Michel Draher, Founder
Background: Founder, Master Global Assets
Directorships: Victor IB Holdings

2641 DAIMLERCHRYSLER VENTURE GmbH
DaimlerChrysler AG
Mercedesstrasse 137
Stuttgart 70327
Germany
Phone: 49-711170 Fax: 49-7111722244
e-mail: dialog@daimler.com
web: www.daimler.com

Mission Statement: Actively seeking new investments.
Geographic Preference: Germany, USA
Fund Size: $42.87 Billion
Investment Criteria: Early Stage, Expansion & Development Capital, Seed Capital, Start-up Capital, Bridge
Industry Group Preference: Communications, Electronic Technology, High Technology, Internet Technology, Information Technology, Transportation
Key Executives:
Dieter Zetsche, Chairman
Background: Board Member of Mercedes-Benz, EUCLID Inc., Daimler-Benz AG, Daimler-Benz Aerospace AG.
Dr. Christine Hohmann-Dennhardt, Integrity and Legal Affairs

2642 DANSK KAPITALANLAEG A/S
Havnegade 39
PO Box 1080
Copenhagen K 1058
Denmark
Phone: 45-77993250 Fax: 45-33369444

Mission Statement: Actively seeking new investments.
Geographic Preference: Denmark
Fund Size: $240 Million
Founded: 1984
Average Investment: EUR 5-35 million
Investment Criteria: Start-up, Expansion and Development, Long-term Capital Growth, MBO, Replacement, Turnaround, Restructuring
Portfolio Companies: 7-Technologies, A2SEA, ACADIA Pharmaceuticals, Inc., Accent Equity 2003 Ltd, Active Sportswear International, Agramkow Fluid Systems, Arpida AG, Baltic Rim Fund Ltd., Bison, CAT Forsknings-og Teknologipark
Key Executives:
Jesper Johansen, Partner
Lars Dybkjær, Partner
Arne J Gillin, Vice President
e-mail: dankap@dankap.dk
Education: Master of Science, Copenhagen Commercial College
Background: Revision/KPMG C.Jespersen, Vølund A/S., Display Systems Biotech A/S, Innovision A/S.
Peter B Kristensen, Investment Manager
e-mail: dankap@dankap.dk
Background: KPMG C.Jespersen, Combio A/S, Sophion Bioscience A/S, Structural Bioinformatics, Inc., Torsana Diabetes Diagnostics A/S.

2643 DB CAPITAL PARTNERS (ASIA)
Deutsche Bank AG
Taunusanlage 12
Frankfurt am Main 60325
Germany
Phone: 49-6991000 Fax: 49-6991034225
web: www.db.com

Mission Statement: A private equity investment group of Deutsche Bank which targets growth capital investments and buyouts in technology, telecommunications and new media, as well as consumer products and industrial companies.
Geographic Preference: Asia Pacific region, Central and Eastern Europe, and Latin America
Fund Size: $1.5 billion
Investment Criteria: Buy-outs
Industry Group Preference: Telecommunications, Technology, Consumer Products, Industrial Services
Portfolio Companies: Displaytech, eTime Capital, Exult, GlobalSight, iLumin Corporation, Paradigm4, PC On Call
Key Executives:
J☐rgen Fitschen, Co-Chairman
Stefan Krause, Chief Financial Officer

Venture Capital & Private Equity Firms / International Firms

2644 DEFI GESTION SA Banque Cantonale Vaudoise
Bd de Grancy 1
Lausanne CH-1006
Switzerland
Phone: 41-216143444 Fax: 41-216143445

Mission Statement: Focuses on financing start-up companies within Initiative Capital SA.
Geographic Preference: Europe, France, Italy, Germany, Switzerland
Fund Size: CHF 115 million
Founded: 1990
Investment Criteria: Seed, Start-up, Expansion, Buyout.
Industry Group Preference: Electronic Technology, Services, Logistics, Automotive, Transportation, Distribution
Portfolio Companies: France Hélices SA, Bartech System Corp, Financière Fouquet II, Came Automatismes, Actar International SA, Groupe Emera SA, Vanguard A.G., Stradeblu Srl, Financière C.T. (Captain Tortue).

Key Executives:
  Mohammed Diab, Managing Director and Partner
  e-mail: mdiab@definvest.com
  Education: Engineer EPFL, MBA Laussane University
  Background: Private Equity
  Claude Suard, CFO and Partner

2645 DELTA PARTNERS Delta Partners FZ-LLC
Media One, Level 29
PO Box 502428
Dubai Media City
India
Phone: 971-43692999 Fax: 971-43688408
e-mail: info@deltapartnersgroup.com
web: www.deltapartnersgroup.com

Mission Statement: Delta Partners is the leading Management Advisory and Investment Firm specialized in Telecoms, Media, and Technology within the Middle East, Africa, Eastern Europe, Emerging Asia and Latin America. Through our different businesses lines, we partner with C-level clients within telecom operators, vendors, and other TMT players to help them address their most challenging strategic issues in a fast-growing and liberalizing market environment.
Geographic Preference: Middle East, Africa, Eastern Europe, Asia, Latin America
Average Investment: $25 - $75 million
Investment Criteria: Growth-Stage
Industry Group Preference: Telecommunications, Media
Portfolio Companies: Aricent, Armenian Datacom Company, Karoui&Karoui World, Mobiserve, Vigin Connect, Vox Spectrum

Key Executives:
  Javier Alvarez, Managing Partner
  Education: BBA, BS, Psychology, MBA, IESE Business School
  Background: Senior Principal, DiamondCluster

2646 DELTA VENTURES LIMITED
PO Box 163
PO Box 4033
Kibutz Glil Yam 46905
Israel
Phone: 972-99517755 Fax: 972-99517799
web: www.delta-ventures.com

Mission Statement: The fund investment focus on information technology that provide business solutions, internet infrastructure, and telecommunications.
Fund Size: $65 Million
Founded: 1999
Average Investment: $1-$3 million
Minimum Investment: $1 million
Investment Criteria: Seed, First or Second round
Industry Group Preference: Communications, Data Communications, Wireless Technologies, Information Technology, Internet Technology, Medical Devices, Software
Portfolio Companies: Appilog, BroadLight, Chiaro Networks, ClickFox, E4X, G.I. View, Medigus, MonaLiza, OpTun's, Provigent, Resolute

Key Executives:
  Mark Chais, Managing Partner & Co-Founder
  e-mail: ofer@delta-ventures.com
  Education: BA, Business Administration & Economics, Haifa University
  Background: Combat Pilot, Israeli Air Force; President, JACADA; Management, Western Systems
  Ben Harel, Managing Partner & Co-Founder
  e-mail: ben@delta-ventures.com
  Education: BSc, Chemistry & Biology, Louisanna College; MBA, Management, Keller Graduate School
  Background: Founder, Interlogic; CEO, Konami
  Directorships: TDNet; Provigent; Resolute; MonaLiza Medical

2647 DEMETER PARTNERS
7-9 Rue de la Boetie
75008 Paris
France
Phone: +33 1 43 12 53 33 Fax: +33 1 43 12 53 30
e-mail: contact@demeter-partners.com
web: demeter-partners.com/en

Mission Statement: Demeter Partners positions itself as the largest Private Equity managemetn company devoted to "green" investments in Europe. Because of its sector positioning, it takes into account the concept of Sustainable Development within its investments and this for all the funds it manages. It selects companies based on the filter sector of eco-energy and environmental industries, companies whose business is to improve the protection of the environment, to save energy and to reduce greenhouse gas emissions.
Geographic Preference: Europe, France
Founded: 2005
Investment Criteria: Expansion Capital
Industry Group Preference: Eco-Industries, Eco-Energies, Energy Efficiency, Renewal Energy, Site Remediation, Water, Waste & Recycling

Other Locations:
  C/ Jose Abascal 52 2izda
  28003 Madrid
  Spain
  Phone: +34 915 639 704 Fax: +34 915 619 506

  Kurfurstendamm 58
  10707 Berlin
  Germany
  Phone: +49 30 890 68 296-8 Fax: +49 30 890 68 296-1

Key Executives:
  Sophie Paturle-Guesnerot, Partner
  Education: Masters, Political Science, Insitut d'Etudes Politiques de Paris
  Stephane Villecroze, Partner
  Education: Charter Engineer, Ecole Polytechnique and Ecole des Ponts et Chaussees
  Lionel Cormier, Partner

2648 DERBYSHIRE FIRST INVESTMENTS LIMITED
Bridge House, Riverside Village, Hady Hill
Chesterfield
Derbyshire S41 0DT
United Kingdom
Phone: 44-1246207390 Fax: 44-1246221080

Venture Capital & Private Equity Firms / International Firms

Mission Statement: DFI has undertaken economic development and inward investment promotional activity for Derbyshire County Council.
Geographic Preference: East Midlands, Derbyshire
Fund Size: $4 Million
Founded: 1987
Average Investment: £50,000 to £250,000
Minimum Investment: $0.09 Million
Investment Criteria: Invests in Start-up Businesses with Established Profitability and Good Growth Prospects
Industry Group Preference: All Sectors Considered
Portfolio Companies: Advanced Composite Group, Bespoke Furniture Ltd., Cobb Slater Ltd., Peter Geeson Ltd.

Key Executives:
David Bookbinder, Chairman
e-mail: info@dfil.co.uk
Background: China Britain Investments Limited
Melvyn Faulkner, Director

2649 DEUTSCHE ASSET & WEALTH MANAGEMENT
Elsa-Brändström-Str. 10-12
Cologne 50668
Germany

Phone: 49-8954908580 Fax: 49-895-49085845
e-mail: dbpe-info@db.com
web: www.dbpe.com

Mission Statement: As a fund-of-funds manager, provides individuals and institutional investors access to the highest performing partnerships in the private equity sector.
Geographic Preference: USA, Europe
Founded: 1991
Investment Criteria: All Stages
Industry Group Preference: All Sectors Considered
Portfolio Companies: TA Associates Battery, Seven Rosen, Bqteicg, USPT

Key Executives:
Ferdinand Dalhuisen, Director, Europe Head Cologne
Education: Studied Business Administration at European Business School in Oestrich-Winkel, London and Paris
Background: Norddeutsche Landesbank, Matuschka GmbH
Directorships: CO-Founder
Andreas Schmidt, Managing Director, Global Head
Education: Law and Economics in Munich and Lausanne
Background: Partner Matuschka GmbH .Co-Founder TVM Techno Venture Management, Deutsche Entwicklungs Gesellschaft (DEG) and Munich Reinsurance Company
Directorships: CO-Founder

2650 DEUTSCHE ASSET MANAGEMENT (AUSTRALIA) LIMITED Deutsche Bank AG
Deutsche Bank Place
Level 16
Sydney 2000
Australia

Phone: 800-034-402 Fax: 61-28-258-1600
Toll-Free: 1800-034402
e-mail: client.services@ironbarkam.com
web: www.deawm.com

Mission Statement: Deutsche Asset Management is one of the world's largest fund managers.
Geographic Preference: Global
Fund Size: $722 Billion
Founded: 1974
Investment Criteria: Expansion and Development, Mezzanine and Bridge
Industry Group Preference: All Sectors Considered, Global Equities, Global Insurance Solutions
Portfolio Companies: BHP Billiton, Westpac Banking, ANZ Banking Corp, Commonwealth Bank, National Australia Bank, Woolworths, Rio Tinto, Orica, St George Bank, Coles Myer

Key Executives:
Michele Faissola, Head of Deutsche Asset & Wealth Management
Education: B.E.(Honours) in Chemical Engineering from the University of Sydney and from the University of Melbourne with a Masters of Business Administration.
Background: AIDC Limited, Optus, Statewide Roads and Wyuna Water, Australian Pacific Technology Limited.

2651 DEUTSCHE BETEILIGUNGS AG
Börsenstraäe 1
Frankfurt 60313
Germany

Phone: 49-699578701 Fax: 49-6995787199
web: www.deutsche-beteiligung.de

Mission Statement: Deutsche Beteiligungs AG is a highly experienced private equity company.
Geographic Preference: Austria, Eastern Europe, France, Germany, Switzerland, USA
Fund Size: s1.3 Billion
Founded: 1965
Average Investment: $180 Million
Minimum Investment: $60 Million
Investment Criteria: Invests in companies with a positive earnings position and potential to build additional value
Industry Group Preference: Automotive, Machinery, Printing, Industrial Services, Technology, Construction, Media, Packaging, Logistics
Portfolio Companies: Bauer AG, Clyde Bergemann Group, Coveright Surfaces GmbH, Harvest Partners III L.P., Harvest Partners IV L.P., Hochtemperatur Engineering GmbH, Homag Group AG, Otto Sauer Achsenfabrik GmbH, Preh GmbH, Quartus Capital Partners

Key Executives:
Andrew Richards, Chairman
e-mail: welcome@deutsche-beteiligung.de
Education: Studied business administration and economics at the Johann Wolfgang Goethe-University of Frankfurt/Main.
Background: 14 years of experience in private equity and corporate finance.
Jochen Baumann, Senior Vice President
Livio Zanotelli, Investment Manager
e-mail: welcome@deutsche-beteiligung.de
Education: Law in Hamburg and Lausanne
Background: Experience in Private Equity and Investment Banking, Finance Director for a major German retail chain.
Reinhard Loffler, Member Board of Management
e-mail: welcome@deutsche-beteiligung.de
Education: Studied business administration and engineering at the University of Karlsruhe.
Background: Filitz-Metzler Group, Papst Motoren GmbH & Company, St. Georgen, Wfg Deutsche Geseilischaft

2652 DFC LTD
Torrent d'en Vidalet 55, L3
Barcelona 08024
Spain

Phone: 34 657 96 65 34
e-mail: fwc-lot6@bcn.thedfcgroup.com
web: www.thedfcgroup.com

Mission Statement: Actively seeking new investments in medium-sized private companies.
Geographic Preference: Europe, Americas, Asia, Africa
Founded: 1980
Investment Criteria: Expansion and Development, Mezzanine and Bridge

Industry Group Preference: Information Technology, Pensions, Financial Services, Corporate Services, Processing, Insurance

Key Executives:
José Luis Mombrú, Group Managing Partner
e-mail: barcelona@thedfcgroup.com
Education: Univ. of Barcelona; Harvard Business School
Background: European Investment Bank, Commercial Banking and Development Finance Sector., EIB,

2653 DFJ ESPRIT
14 Buckingham Gate
London SW1E 6LB
United Kingdom

Phone: 44-20-7931-8800 **Fax:** 44-20-7931-8866

Mission Statement: At DFJ Esprit we believe that good venture capital begins with good judgement and good relationships. Our partners have a track record of helping entrepreneurs to make their companies successful. In today's world the best businesses have global ambitions from day one and the best venture funds have the networks to support those ambitions. DFJ Esprit is a member of the Draper Fisher Jurvetson Global Network, the largest venture capital network in the world with 140 investment professionals and over 600 portfolio companies.

Geographic Preference: Nordics, Germany, France, United Kingdom, Ireland, Spain
Average Investment: $500,000 - $15 million
Investment Criteria: Early-Stage, Later-Stage
Industry Group Preference: Electronics, Software, Internet, Medical Technology, Mobile
Portfolio Companies: Achica, Airweb, Alphamosaic, ApaTech, Arieso, Avantium, Aveillant, AwoX, Biotie Therapies, Bitbar, BIW, BlackSpider Technologies, Bookham Technology, Bottomline Technologies, Buy.at, Cambridge Positioning Systems, Cambridge Silicon Radio, CamSemi, Cast, Cerillion Technologies, Clearswift, CloudApps, Connectivity, Conversocial, Datahug, DiBcom, Digital Route, Displaydata, DisplayLink, DNA Research, Enteraction TV, European Telecommunications & Technology, EVE, FillFactory, Formscape Group, Foviance Group, Garlik, Graze, GreenPeak Technologies, Healthcare Brands International, Horizon Discovery, Icera, Imagine Communications, Intense, Ipanema, Kiadis, Kiala, KVS, Lagan, Light Blue Optics, Lime Microsystems, LOVEFiLM, Lyst, Message Pad, Metalysis, Microcosm Communications, MindMatrics, Mobile Commerce, Mobile Travel Technologies, Mobile2Win, Mobixell Networks, MXData, NeoPhotonics, Neteconomy, Netonomy, Netronome, Neul, Nimbus Partners, Nordnav Technologies, OneAccess, OverSi Networks, Oxford BioMedica, Oxford Immunotec, PacketExchange, Phyworks, Polatis, PortWise, Powerlase, Psytechnics, Pulmagen, Qosmos, Radium One, Redkite Financial Markets, Road Angel, Rock Mobile Corp, Silecs, Speech Recognition, SportPursuit, StrikeAd, SVOX, Tagsys RFID, Taptu, The Cloud, The Listening Co., Trace One, Tribold, Virata Corp, VirtualLogix, WAYN, Webify Solutions, Xaar, Xitec Software, Xmos, Zeus Technology

Other Locations:
Building 1010
Cambourne Business Park
Cambourne
Cambridge CB23 6DP
United Kingdom
Phone: 11-1223-307-770 **Fax:** 44-1223-307-771

Key Executives:
Simon Cook, CEO
Education: University of Manchester Institute of Science & Technology
Background: Cazenove Private Equity; Partner, Elderstreet Investments; Director, 3i

2654 DIGITAL SKY TECHNOLOGIES
Hong Kong

e-mail: info@dst-global.com

Portfolio Companies: Virool, MemSQL, Klarna, Airbnb, Spotify, Facebook, Groupon, Nival, Zynga, Forticom

2655 DIRECT CAPITAL PRIVATE EQUITY LIMITED
Level 6, 2 Kitchener Street
Aukland
New Zealand

Phone: 64-93072562 **Fax:** 64-93072349
web: www.directcapital.co.nz

Mission Statement: Actively seeking new investments.
Fund Size: $141 Million
Founded: 1994
Average Investment: $7.1 Million
Minimum Investment: $.07 Million
Investment Criteria: Seed, Early, Expansion
Industry Group Preference: Education, Information Technology, Healthcare, Industrial Services, Life Sciences, Entertainment, Financial Services, Business to Business, Food & Beverage, Manufacturing, Retailing, Processing
Portfolio Companies: Airwork, Blue Star (Acquired By Us Office Products), Communicado (Now Screentime Communicado), Eftpos New Zealand, Ezibuy, Genesis (Gen), Image Centre, Moore, Moore Gallagher, Nobil, Noel Leeming, Open Networks, Pacificflight Catering, Palliser Estate, Pc Dir

Key Executives:
Ross George, LLB, Managing Director
e-mail: ross.george@directcapital.co.nz
Directorships: Directorships :Blue Star, Nobilo Wines, Pacific Flight Catering, EMS, Communicado and Robinson Industries.
Mark Hutton, BCom, Director

2656 DIRIGEANTS ET INVESTISSEURS
31 rue Des Poissonniers
Neuilly-Sur-Seine F-92200
France

Phone: 33-141920292 **Fax:** 33-146410025
web: www.di-groupe.com

Mission Statement: Invests in companies at all stages to help them become profitable

Geographic Preference: Europe
Industry Group Preference: Management

Key Executives:
Martial Papineau, Président
e-mail: martial.papineau@di-groupe.com

2657 DISCOUNT INVESTMENT CORPORATION LIMITED
3 Azrieli Center, 44th floor
Tel Aviv 6702301
Israel

Phone: 972-36075888 **Fax:** 972-36075889
e-mail: Investor.Relations@dic.co.il
web: www.dic.co.il

Mission Statement: As one of Israel's most prominent investment companies for the past four decades, DIC has taken a substantial part in the major development of the Israel economy.

Geographic Preference: Israel
Founded: 1961
Industry Group Preference: All Sectors Considered
Portfolio Companies: Cellcon, Net Vision, Elron, Scitex,

Key Executives:
Ami Erel, President & Chief Executive Officer
e-mail: oren.lieder@dic.co.il

Venture Capital & Private Equity Firms / International Firms

Education: Bachelor of Arts, University of Haifa.
Background: Elco Holdings, BEZEQ
Directorships: Board Member, Israeli enterprises.
Michel Dahan, Acting General Manager, Vice President & Chief Financial Officer
e-mail: Investor.Relations@dic.co.il
Education: Bachelors of science degree in electrical engineering from the Technion.
Background: The Israel Telecommunication Corp., Israel's Association of Electronics & Information Industries, ForSoft Ltd. & Formula Computer Technologies Ltd.
Directorships: Scitex Corporation Ltd. (Chairman).

2658 DJF DRAGONFUND CHINA
Unit 3102, Wheelock Square
No. 1717 West Nanjing Road
Shanghai 200040
China

Phone: 86-21-6280-0580 Fax: 86-21-6280-0585
e-mail: info@dfjdragon.com
web: www.dfjdragon.com

Mission Statement: Established in March of 2006, DFJ DragonFund is a leading venture capital firm in the People's Republic of China. It is the China affiliated fund of the internationally recognized venture capital firm Draper Fisher Jurvetson (www.dfj.com). As a joint venture between DFJ and DragonVenture, DFJ DragonFund leverages an unparalleled track record of experiences, knowledge, and successes in venture capitals both internationally and domestically. At DFJ DragonFund, we focus on China-centric early-stage companies in the technology market. We work closely with them in developing their business strategies as well as providing necessary operating guidance from time to time.

Geographic Preference: China
Founded: 2006
Investment Criteria: Early-Stage
Industry Group Preference: Technology
Portfolio Companies: AltoBeam, Crystechcoating, Donson, DraTek Technologies, EDDA Technology, FastWeb, Fountain Medical Development, GD Interactive, GridNt, Hudong, Jing Jin Electric, Luxul, Miartech, Mobim Technologies, Splashtop, Senodia Technologies, StreamOcean, Synacast, TongCard Holdings, Viewhigh Technologies, Vital Therapies, YeePay

Other Locations:
Unit 818, SOHO Building
Zhongguancun
Beijing 100080
China
Phone: 86-10-8286-8228 Fax: 86-10-8286-8205

2882 Sand Hill Road
Suite 150
Menlo Park, CA 94025
Phone: 650-233-9000 Fax: 650-233-9233

Key Executives:
Larry Guanxin Li, Founding Managing Director
Education: PhD, Applied Mechanics, Shanghai Jiaotong University
Background: Co-Founder, Managing Director, SHVC-Shanghai DJ Venture; Managing Director, Shanghai VC

2659 DN CAPITAL
2 Queen Anne's Gate Buildings
Dartmouth Street
London SW1H 9BP
United Kingdom

Phone: 44-02073401600 Fax: 44-02073401601
e-mail: info@dncapital.com
web: www.dncapital.com

Mission Statement: DN Capital's objective is to identify, invest in and actively support leading digital media, e-commerce, software and mobile applications companies on a global basis. The investment professionals at DN Capital bring more than 50 years of early stage and growth equity experience to their investments, and work with portfolio companies to guide their growth through the various stages of development. We help portfolio companies by leveraging our extensive global network of managers, investors, and intermediaries who are actively involved with DN Capital's portfolio companies.

Investment Criteria: Early-Stage, Growth-Stage
Industry Group Preference: Digital Media & Marketing, E-Commerce & Manufacturing, Software, Mobile
Portfolio Companies: Shazam, Apsmart, AirSense Wireless, Mobile Roadie, Just Book, Digital Chocolate, Windeln.de, Mister Spex,

Other Locations:
228 Hamilton Avenue
3rd Floor
Palo Alto, CA 94301
Phone: 650-7985424

Key Executives:
Nenad Marovac, Founder/CEO/Managing Partner
Education: BS, Business Administration, San Diego State University; MBA, Harvard Business School
Background: Partner, Advent International

2660 DOTCORP PRIVATE EQUITY FUND
125 Avenue du X Septembre
L-2551
Luxembourg

e-mail: info@dotcorp.lu

Mission Statement: At Dotcorp Private Equity we are entrepreneurs who dedicate our experience and expertise to growing companies and mentoring founding CEOs.

Geographic Preference: Europe, Israel
Founded: 2007
Investment Criteria: All Stages
Industry Group Preference: All Sectors Considered
Portfolio Companies: Deezer, Mythings, Primavista, Interplay, Covertix, Lot18mimesis Republic, Restopolitan, IFrameApps, Guidespromos.Com, My Social Book, Step-In

Key Executives:
Steve Rosenblum, Co-Founder
Education: La Sorbonne; BA, Economics, Concordia University
Background: Co-Founder, Pixmania.Com; Co-Founder, The Kase
Jean-Emile Rosenblum, Co-Founder
Background: Co-Founder, Pixmaxia.Com; Co-Founder, The Kase

2661 DOUBLE IMPACT BUSINESS ADVISORY
12th Floor, Empire Tower
Bangkok 10120
Thailand

Phone: 66-0226701100 Fax: 66-0226701101

Mission Statement: A well established advisory group assisting businesses present in Thailand and their activities in Asia and around the world.

Industry Group Preference: Manufacturing, Retailing, Financial Services, Media, Publishing

Key Executives:
Bruce Darrington, Managing Director
Rob Hurenkamp, Deputy Managing Director

Venture Capital & Private Equity Firms / International Firms

2662 DOUGHTY HANSON & CO.
45 Pall Mall
London SW1Y 5JG
United Kingdom

Phone: 44-20-7663-9300
e-mail: info@doughtyhanson.com
web: www.doughtyhanson.com

Mission Statement: We invest in ambitious entrepreneurs and help them build industry leading businesses in the mobile technology, internet software and cleantech sectors.

Geographic Preference: Europe
Industry Group Preference: Mobile Communications Devices, Internet Technology, Clean Technology
Portfolio Companies: Actionality, Alphamosaic, Adaptive Mobile, Everbridge, Forth Dimension Displays, Garlik, Gomez, Handmade, MBAPolymers, Mega Zebra, Mobango, Nscaled, Orchestria, Plazes, RainStar, Secretsales, Eguana Technologies, Soundcloud, Sube, SDLtridion, Ubidyne

Key Executives:
Nigel Grierson, Co-Head, Technology Ventures
Background: Group Director, Intel Capital; AT&T
George Powlick, Co-Head, Technology Ventures
Education: BS, Materials Science & Engineering, University of California, Berkeley; MBA, Anderson School of Business
Background: Intel Corporation

2663 DPIXEL
Via Filippo Turati 38
20121 Milan
Italy

e-mail: info@dpixel.it
web: www.dpixel.it

Mission Statement: We are a venture capital firm, we are looking for entrepreneurs who want to change the world.

Geographic Preference: Italy
Investment Criteria: Seed Stage
Industry Group Preference: Internet
Portfolio Companies: Mangatar, Eco4Cloud, Affare Del Giorno, Sardex.net, Ciceroos, CrowdEngineering, Cortilla, Iubenda, SmartRM, Sounday, Farman

Key Executives:
Gianluca Dettori, Partner & Chairman
Education: University of Turin
Background: Manager, Italia Online (Olivetti); General Manager, Lycos Bertelsmann; Founder, Vitaminic; Head of Mergers & Acquisitions, Buongiorno Group
Antonio Concolino, Partner & CEO
Education: Business Engineering, University of Calabria
Background: Process Analyst, Andersen Consulting; Consultant, IT Sistem at University "La Sapienza" in Rome; Italian Regional Telecommunication Operator at Lombardiacom Spa; Chief Financial Officer and Financial Controller, Elitel Telcom Spa

2664 DR NEUHAUS TECHNO NORD GmbH
30 Jungfernstieg
Hamburg 20354
Germany

Phone: 49-403552820 Fax: 49-403-5528239
e-mail: info@drneuhaus.de
web: www.drneuhaus.de

Mission Statement: Actively seeking new investments.
Geographic Preference: Germany, German speaking countries
Fund Size: $62 Million
Founded: 1998
Average Investment: $2.1 Million
Minimum Investment: $0.6 Million
Investment Criteria: Seed, Startup, Expansion
Industry Group Preference: Information Technology, Software, Telecommunications, Internet Technology
Portfolio Companies: 7d Software GmbH & Co., Agentscape, Blau Mobilfunk GmbH, ePrint Factory GmbH, EUTEX European Telco Exchange, Exit Games GmbH, Gentleware, Infitel International N.V., Intenium GmbH, Newtention Extended Networks GmbH, Micro Technology

Key Executives:
Gottfried Neuhaus, Managing Partner
Education: MBA
Matthias Grychta, Managing Partner
Education: Electrical engineering in Argentina, PhD in computer science at the Technical University in Berlin.

2665 DRAPER ESPRIT
20 Garrick Street
London WC2E 9BT
United Kingdom

Phone: 44 (0)20 7931 8800
e-mail: info@draperesprit.com
web: draperesprit.com

Mission Statement: Draper Esprit invests into visionary and growing companies, primarily focused on innovative technologies. As one of the largest VC firms in Europe, Draper takes on projects on a long-term and multi-stage basis.

Fund Size: $1 billion
Founded: 2006
Industry Group Preference: Technology
Portfolio Companies: Apatech, Areso, Aveillant, Bitbar, Black Spider Technologies, Bright Computing, Buyat, CPS, CamSemi, Clavis Insight, Clear Swift, Cloud Apps, Clue, KCom, Conversocial, Crate, Crowdcube.com, Data Hug, DiBcom, Display Data, DisplayLink, Episode 1, GTT, Eve, Fill Factory, Fluidic Analytics, Foviance, Garlik, GetBulb, Graphcore, Graze, Green Peak, Healthcare Brands International, Horizon, Icera, Intense, Ipanema, Kiadis Pharma, KVS, Lagan, Lifesum, Light Blue Optics, Lime Microsystems, LoveFilm.com, Lyst, M-Files, Metalysis, Mobile Commerce, Movidius, Moviepilot, MTT, Fiserv., Netronome, Neul, TIBC, Oxford Immunotec, Packetexchange, Perkbox, Phyworks, Pod Point, Polatis, PremFina, Psytechnics, Push Doctor, QOSMOS, Raven Pack, Red Kite, Resolver, Seedcamp, Sport Pursuit, Tails.com, Taptu, The Cloud, Serco, Transferwise, Trust Pilot, Unbound, Verve, Xmos, Zeus

Other Locations:
O'Connell Bridge House
8th Floor
D'Olier Street
Dublin D02 RR99
Ireland
Phone: 353 (0)1 881 8792

Building 1010
Cambourne Business Park
Cambourne
Cambridge CB23 6DP
United Kingdom
Phone: 44 (0)1223 307 770

Key Executives:
Simon Cook, Chief Executive Officer
Education: University of Manchester Institute of Science & Technology
Background: Partner, Cazenove Private Equity; Partner, Elderstreet Investments
Directorships: Investment Director, 3i Technology Europe
Stuart Chapman, Chief Operating Officer
Education: Loughborough University
Background: Partner, 3i Ventures
Directorships: Board Member, Loughborough School of Business and Economics

Venture Capital & Private Equity Firms / International Firms

2666 DTA CAPITAL PARTNERS S/B
24A, Jalan Datuk Sulaiman
Taman Tun Drive Ismail
Kuala Lumpur 60000
Malaysia

Phone: 60-377222560 Fax: 60-377222570
e-mail: dtav@dtacapital.com
web: www.dtacapital.com

Fund Size: $16.3 Million
Founded: 1996
Average Investment: $1.08 Million
Industry Group Preference: Financial Services

Key Executives:
Dali Sardar, Chief Executive Officer
e-mail: dali@dtacapital.com
Directorships: Chairman
KC Tan, Chief Operating Officer
e-mail: naim@dtacapital.com
Background: Ex-Citicorp; Citibank
Directorships: Deputy Chairman

2667 DUKE STREET CAPITAL Duke Street
Nations House
103 Wigmore Street
London W1U 1QS
United Kingdom

Phone: 44-02076638500 Fax: 44-02076638501
e-mail: mail@dukestreet.com
web: www.dukestreetcapital.com

Mission Statement: Duke Street Capital is an independent private equity company which principally invests in established, mid-market UK and French businesses.

Geographic Preference: United Kingdom, Western Europe
Fund Size: $2.4 Billion
Founded: 1988
Average Investment: Euro 300 Million
Investment Criteria: Mid stage
Industry Group Preference: Business to Business, Retailing, Healthcare, Leisure, Financial Services, Outsourcing & Efficiency, Consumer Services
Portfolio Companies: Xafinity, Waste link, Leisure link, Navimo, Accantia, Marie Brizard, Focus, Groupe Proclif, Affinity Healthcare, Thornbury Nursing Services, Paragon, Cremascoli Ortho, Cox Insurance

Key Executives:
Peter Taylor, Managing Partner
Education: BSc. (Hons) from Durham University.
Background: County Bank,
Paul Adams, Investment Manager
Education: graduate of Ecole Supérieure des Sciences Commerciales
Background: Smith Barney in New York City
Elaine Fullerton, General Counsel
Education: graduate of Institut Commercial de Nancy,
Background: Donaldson Lufkin & Jenrette in London, Credit Suisse
Emmanuel Logan-Moll, Investment Executive
Education: BBA from Stockholm University & MSc in Engineering Physics and Financial Mathematics from the Royal Institute of Technology, Stockholm.
Background: AB Segulah
Christian Fellowes, Investment Executive
Education: MBA from Havard University
Background: Rhône Capital, Donaldson, Lufkin & Jenrette,
Jean Garbois, Operating Partner
Education: Graduate from Loughborough University of Technology & Chartered Accountant
Background: Cannons Group Plc. & NatWest Equity Partners
Crispin Goldsmith, Investment Director
Education: BA in economics from Duke University and a Masters in business administration from Harvard University.
Background: Celfin & Morgan Stanley
Johanna Waterous, Operating Partner
Education: Modern Languages degree from Durham University.
Charlie Troup, Partner
Education: Degree in economics from Durham University.
Background: Bankers Trust's leveraged buyout groups
Directorships: He is an Associate of the Institute of Investment Management & Research. He was Chairman of the British Venture Capital Association 2001-2002.
Ben Long, Investment Director
Education: Graduate from Bocconi University, Milan.
Background: Merrill Lynch - Advisor

2668 DUNEDIN CAPITAL PARTNERS LIMITED
Saltire Court
20 Castle Terrace
Edinburgh EH1 2EN
United Kingdom

Phone: 44-1312256699 Fax: 20-7292-2110
e-mail: info@dunedin.com
web: www.dunedin.com

Mission Statement: Dunedin Capital Partners provides equity finance for management buy-outs and management buy-ins with a transaction size of $10 million - $50 million.

Geographic Preference: United Kingdom
Fund Size: $531 Million
Founded: 1983
Average Investment: $38 Million
Minimum Investment: $5.3 Million
Investment Criteria: All stages
Industry Group Preference: Construction, Consumer Products, Financial Services, Healthcare, Leisure, Media, Manufacturing, Services, Building Materials & Services, Consumer Services
Portfolio Companies: CET, Practice Plan Group Ltd., Zenith Vehicle Contracts Ltd., New Horizons, Celtic Inns, Total Fitness, ABI (UK) Ltd., Supreme Imports, Simply Smart Group, Home & Legacy, Hickson & Welch, Jessops Ltd., Gardner Aerospace, Caledonian Building Systems Ltd.

Key Executives:
Simon Miller, Chairman
e-mail: brian.scouler@dunedin.com
Education: Graduate from Glasgow University and CA.
Background: Royal Bank Development Capital & Charterhouse Development Capital Limited.
Nicol Fraser, Director
e-mail: nicol.fraser@dunedin.com
Background: Bridgepoint Capital & Scott Oswald,
Ross Marshall, Managing Director
e-mail: ross.marshall@dunedin.com
Education: BCom from Edinburgh University and chartered accountant
Background: Price Waterhouse, 3i, UK private equity
Dougal Bennett, Partner
e-mail: dougal.bennett@dunedin.com
Education: Graduate in biochemistry Edinburgh University
Background: OSS Group & Gardner Aerospace,
Shaun Middleton, Managing Partner
e-mail: shaun.middleton@dunedin.com
Education: Graduate from University of Witwatersrand and Chartered Accountant
Background: ABI

2669 DUTCH GROUP
Soestdijkerstraatweg 27 B
Hilversum 1213 VR
Netherlands

Phone: 31-205038070 Fax: 31-0205038071
web: www.dutch.com

Venture Capital & Private Equity Firms / International Firms

Mission Statement: Focuses on temporary management solutions.
Geographic Preference: Netherlands, Israel, Belgium, England
Founded: 1984
Key Executives:
Anda Van Liere, Business Professional
e-mail: mail@ws-transition.com
Background: Dutch management consultancy
Directorships: Non-executive board member and chairman

2670 DVC DEUTSCHE VENTURE CAPITAL
Munich
Germany

Phone: +49 89 452 352-352 **Fax:** +49 89 452 352-110

Geographic Preference: Europe
Fund Size: $300 million Euro
Founded: 1998
Average Investment: $1 - $10 million Euro
Industry Group Preference: Information Technology, Telecommunications, Semiconductor, Industrial Technology, Life Sciences, Medical Technology

2671 E-CAPITAL MANAGEMENT
Tervurenlaan 273 - 1150
1150 Brussels
Brussels 1030
Belgium

Phone: 32-26422000 **Fax:** 32-26422009
e-mail: info@e-capital.be
web: www.e-capital.be

Mission Statement: E-Capital is an investment fund dedicated to the funding and/or the take-over (MBO, MBI) of small and mid-sized unquoted companies.
Geographic Preference: Belgium
Fund Size: $95 Million
Founded: 1999
Average Investment: $2.4 Million
Minimum Investment: $1.2 Million
Investment Criteria: Start-up and Growth-stage
Industry Group Preference: All Sectors Considered
Portfolio Companies: Biocode-Hycel, Gevaert Bandweverij, Globe, Guillaume-Teco, Kapitol, Splen, Unibioscreen & Zetes

Key Executives:
Jerome Lamfalussy, Investment Partner
Yves Trouveroy, Investment Partner

2672 E.BRICKS DIGITAL
Avenida República do Libano, 1214
Vila Nova Conceiçao
Sao Paulo 04502-001
Brazil

Phone: 21-30500750
web: www.ebricksdigital.com.br

Mission Statement: e.Bricks invests in companies that are in a stage of rapid growth, with excellence and entrepreneurs operating in markets with great growth potential. There are three main sectors: e-commerce segmented, mobile and digital media and technology. At the heart of the strategy are the technology and scalability of business.

Founded: 2012
Investment Criteria: Growth-Stage
Industry Group Preference: E-Commerce & Manufacturing, Mobile, Digital Media & Marketing, Technology

Key Executives:
Fabio Bruggioni, Chief Executive Officer
Background: Vice President, Telefonica Group

2673 EARLYBIRD
Maximilianstr. 14
Munchen 80539
Germany

Phone: 49-892907020 **Fax:** 49-8929070222
web: www.earlybird.com

Mission Statement: Adds value to our portfolio companies through active support – serving as a sparring partner in decision making processes.

Geographic Preference: Germany, Switzerland, Austria, Netherlands, UK, USA, Italy, France
Fund Size: 430 millin Euros
Founded: 1997
Average Investment: 3 million Euros
Minimum Investment: 1 million Euros
Investment Criteria: Early stage, Startup, Expansion
Industry Group Preference: Online Consumer Services, Internet, Cloud-Based IT Services, Information Technology, Software, Communication Technology, Clean Technology, Medical Technology
Portfolio Companies: Alantos Pharmaceuticals, Asyntis Gmbh, Biovalve, Europroteome AG, Graviton, Hemoteq Gmbh, IQ Labs, Identify Sotware, Intime Software, Internetwork AG/Q Inc

Other Locations:
Maximilianstr. 14
Munchen 80539
Germany
Phone: 49-892907020 **Fax:** 49-8929070222

Key Executives:
Hendrick Brandis, Co-Founder and Partner
04-0432-9410
e-mail: nagel@earlybird.com
Education: Dipl.Wi-Ing., Technical University of Hamburg; PhD in Management from St. Gallen University, Switzerland.
Background: Co-Founder & Managing Partner, SMB Industrieholding Wildau GmbH; DH Industriholding Hohenthurm; Consultant, McKinsey & Company
Directorships: Crowdpark, BridgeCo, Lumics, madvertise, Smava, Yoom
Christian Nagel, Partner
089-290-7020
e-mail: brandis@earlybird.com
Education: Dipl.-Ing, PhD, Aerospace Engineering, Technical University of Munich
Background: Co-Founder, GMM; Project Manager, EADS; Partner, McKinsey & Company
Directorships: B2X Care Solutions, conject, nfton, Mikini Media, Music Network
Roland Manger, Partner
089-290-7020
e-mail: manger@earlybird.com
Education: Dipl.Wi-Ing, University of Karlshuhe; MBA, Georgetown University
Background: Co-Founder & Marketing Director, Cybernet AG; Director, Business Development, Ditec AG; Principal, Gemini Consulting
Directorships: OneShield, Scoreloop
Rolf Mathies, Partner
04-043-294-10
e-mail: mathies@earlybird.com
Education: Dipl.-Kfm. degree (MBA equivalent) specializing in information science from the University of Hamburg
Background: Co-Founder & Managing Partner, ConAction AG; Consultant, Bain & Company
Directorships: azeti Networks, Hemoteq, enTRUST & TITLE
Ciarán O'Leary, Partner
e-mail: jung@earlybird.com
Education: PhD, and Dipl.- Biol. (MS equivalent) from the Ludwig-Maximilians-University in Munich.
Thom Rasche, Partner

Venture Capital & Private Equity Firms / International Firms

Wolfgang Siebold, Partner
Heiko Thiel, Head of Finance

2674 EAST FUND MANAGEMENT GmbH
GiroCredit
Somolickeho 1/b
Bratislava SK- 81105
Slovakia

Phone: 43-152-22285 Fax: 43-152-22285
e-mail: office@hkkpartners.com
web: www.eastfund.com

Mission Statement: EFM and its holding company HKK Partners is a Central European based private Equity Investor with operations in Vienna, Prague, Bratislava and Bucharest.
Geographic Preference: Europe, Austria
Fund Size: $50 Million
Founded: 1994
Investment Criteria: All stages
Industry Group Preference: Media, Food & Beverage, Automotive, Logistics, Chemicals, Financial Services, Information Technology, Distribution
Portfolio Companies: Mec.com, Sky Europe, X Radio Express, Bohemia Prints, Seibold, Komptech Farwicks, Steiger, Tovarnity, Sigus Slovakia, Monopoly Media, Terapia

Key Executives:
Roland Haas, Managing Partner
Education: Degree in Economics from Vienna University.
Background: Slovak Post Privatisation Fund & Investment Bank Austria's Research department
Mark Kaltenbacher, Managing Director
Education: BA in Economics from the University of California and an MBA in Finance from Columbia Business School
Background: Merrill Lynch

2675 EASTLABS
75 Zhylianska Street
4th Floor
Kyiv
Ukraine

Phone: 44 377 74 79
e-mail: info@eastlabs.co
web: www.eastlabs.co

Mission Statement: Eastlabs looks for talented teams with ideas that have the potential to change the world. We feel that just as important as having an innovative idea that can shake the internet/mobile space, is to have a team determined to execution excellence. We are open to acception teams from any international location as long as they meet our selction criteria.
Average Investment: $20, 000
Investment Criteria: Start-Up
Industry Group Preference: Internet, Mobile, Digital Media & Marketing

Key Executives:
Eveline Buchatskiy, Managing Partner
Education: BS, Chemical Engineering, UC Berkeley; Master of Engineering, SUNY Buffalo; MBA, INSEAD
Background: CEO, Ekonomika; CEO, APCT; Engineering Associate, Praxair
Ken Leaver, Managing Partner
Education: BS, Cornell University; MBA, IESE Business School in Barcelona, Spain
Background: CEO, Groupon Ukraine; Co-Founder, uGift; Executive, Visa Inc; Senior Manager, Strategy Partners

2676 EC1 CAPITAL LTD
Rainmaking Loft
International House
1 St Katharine's Way
E1W 1UN London
United Kingdom

e-mail: info@ec1capital.com
web: www.ec1capital.com

Mission Statement: We provide capital, expertise and connections for web based tech startups that provides a firm footing to further develop the technology.
Geographic Preference: London, Dublin, Edinburgh
Founded: 2012
Minimum Investment: £50,000
Investment Criteria: Seed Stage, Early Stage
Industry Group Preference: Web Applications & Services, Mobile
Portfolio Companies: CitySocializer, TRULY, User Replay, HANDS HQ, SmartTrade, Toothpick, Hybrid Cluster, SimpleTax, Unifyo, CultureLabel, Glean.in, Highgate Labs, Lifecake, HouseBites, Retronaut

Key Executives:
Julian Carter, Co-Founder & Managin Director
Directorships: Lifecake, Highgate Labs, Glean.in, Culture Label, Unifyo, Truly, User Replay, CitySocializer
Badr AlSabban, Co-Founder & Director

2677 ECAPITAL ENTREPRENEURIAL PARTNERS AG
Hafenweg 24
Münster 48155
Germany

Phone: 49 0251-7037670 Fax: 49 0251-70376722
e-mail: info@ecapital.de
web: www.ecapital.de

Mission Statement: eCAPITAL is a venture capital firm that provides early to growth stage funding to technology companies in the fields of software & information technology, cybersecurity, industry 4.0, new materials and cleantech. Founded in 1999, eCAPITAL has a history of leveraging relationships and supporting entrepreneurs determined to build companies with lasting significance. Partnering with eCAPITAL means joining a unique network of entrepreneurs, business leaders, operators, investors and scientists.
Geographic Preference: Germany, Europe
Fund Size: $200 million
Founded: 1999
Average Investment: $3 million
Minimum Investment: $0.5 million
Investment Criteria: Early-Stage, Later-Stage
Industry Group Preference: Information Technology, Software, Cybersecurity, New Materials, Industry, Cleantech, Semiconductor
Portfolio Companies: 4JET Technologies, BrandMaker GmbH, CNM Technologies, CREPAPER GmbH, Cysal, Evodos, Ferroelectric Memory GmbH, Greenergetic, Heliatek, INMATEC Technologies GmbH, Jedox, Milk the Sun, Open-Xchange, Perora GmbH, Prolupin GmbH, Rhebo GmbH, RIPS Technologies, saperatec, Smarthouse, Smart Hydro Power, Sonnen GmbH, Subitec, temicon GmbH, THEVA Dünnschichttechnik GmbH, Variowell Development, Videantis GmbH, VMRay GmbH

Key Executives:
Dr. Paul-Josef Patt, Managing Partner/CEO
e-mail: patt@ecapital.de
Education: University of Tubingen
Background: Roland Berger & Partner; Kaufhof Holding AG; MBI Ernstings
Michael Mayer, Managing Partner
0251 703767 0
e-mail: m.mayer@ecapital.de
Education: University of Konstanz

Background: Founder, Technostart GmbH; Fraunhofer Institute; Transmedia Verlag GmbH & Co
Willi Mannheims, Managing Partner
e-mail: w.mannheims@ecapital.de
Education: Queen's College, UK; Henley Management College, UK; MBA, University of Houston
Background: Fond Dasa/Daimler Chrysler; CUBIS AG; Secunet AG; Escrypt GmbH

2678 ECI VENTURES
Brettenham House
Lancaster Place
London WC2E 7EN
United Kingdom

Phone: 44-2076061000 **Fax:** 44-2072405050

Mission Statement: ECI provides capital for UK unquoted and smaller quoted companies including finance for various transactions.

Geographic Preference: United Kingdom
Fund Size: $887 Million
Founded: 1976
Average Investment: $97.5 Million
Minimum Investment: $17.75 Million
Investment Criteria: MBO, MBI, Institutional Buy-Out, Expansion, Acquisition, Turnarounds, Refinancing. No Early-Stage
Industry Group Preference: All Sectors Considered, Chemicals, Distribution, Information Technology, Manufacturing, Outsourcing & Efficiency, Communications, Transportation, Financial Services, Publishing
Key Executives:
  Sean Whelan, member of the investment committee
  Education: Degree in Material Science and metallurgy from Cambridge University.
  Background: PriceWaterhouseCoopers where he gained an ACA and spent a period in business regeneration, effectively acting as FD to various struggling companies
  Tim Raffle, Dierctor
  Education: Graduated from Cambridge University and qualified with KPMG.
  Stephen Dawson, Non-Executive Director
  Background: ECI, business management experience at Sema, Logica, Reuters and as managing director of a start-up company. A director of the computer and electronics division at British Technology Group.
  Directorships: MD.
  Janet Brooks, Manager, Investor Relations/Marketing
  Education: Graduated from Cambridge University and has a MBA from INSEAD.
  Background: member of the BVCA's Investor Relations Committee and was a member of the EVCA's Investor Relations Committee from 1999 to 2004, She was previously an investment manager at fund-of-funds group VenCap International.
  Steve Tudge, Director
  Education: Graduating from Warwick University in management sciences.
  Background: PriceWaterhouseCoopers, gaining an ACA and specialising in advising small and medium sized businesses
  Ken Landsberg, Director
  Education: Graduated in computer sciences from Bristol University and qualified as an accountant with Deloitte & Touche in 1983.
  Background: service sector investments and has held board seats at Highway Emergency Services, Guardian iT, Hoseasons and Data Entry International. & director Enviros and Omnipack.

2679 ECONA AG
Wöhlert street 12/13
3rd Inner Court
Berlin 10115
Germany

Phone: 49-309210640 **Fax:** 49-3092106431
web: www.econa.com

Mission Statement: Actively seeking new investments in Internet based companies

Geographic Preference: Berlin
Founded: 1999
Investment Criteria: MBI, MBO
Industry Group Preference: Internet Technology, Media
Key Executives:
  Bernd Hardes, Founder Partner
  Education: MA
  Background: Banker; Management Consultant in the range strategy and marketing
  Daniel Engelbarts, Managing Director

2680 ECUS PRIVATE EQUITY Ecus Private Equity/AXA Capital Chile
Magdalena 140, 5th Floor
Las Condes
Santiago 7550104
Chile

Phone: 56-2-25772200 **Fax:** 56-2-25772222
e-mail: desk@ecuscapital.com
web: www.ecuscapital.com

Average Investment: $3 Million - $6Million

2681 EDBI Pte LTD.
250 North Bridge Road
#28-00 Raffles City Tower
179101
Singapore

Phone: 65-6832-6832 **Fax:** 65-6832-6838
e-mail: infoHQ@ebdi.com
web: www.edbi.com

Mission Statement: Investing since 1991, EDBI is a Singapore-based global investor in select high growth technology sectors ranging from Information & Communication Technology (ICT), Emerging Technology (ET), Healthcare (HC), and other strategic industries. As a value creating investor, EDBI assists companies achieve their ambitious goals by leveraging our broad network, resources and expertise. With our patient capital, EDBI supports companies seeking to grow in Asia and globally through Singapore.

Geographic Preference: US, Europe, Asia
Founded: 1991
Investment Criteria: Growth & Late Stage
Industry Group Preference: Healthcare Information Technology, Medical Devices, Therapeutics, Information Technology, Communication Technology, Consumer Internet, SaaS, Cloud Computing, Telecommunications, Infrastructure
Portfolio Companies: Adamas Pharmaceuticals, Addex Pharmaceuticals, Ambiq Micro, Appier, Artisan Pharma, Bitmain, Bright Machines, Byte Dance, Carousell, Chevron Phillips, Codexis, Connexions Asia, CounterTack, Coursera, Cyclacel Pharmaceuticals, DocuSign, Druva, Enginge Biosciences, Five Prime Therapeutics, FORMA Therapeutics, GoBalto, Green Wave Systems, Hedvig, Idenix, Iflix, I-Mab Biopharma, Inviragen, Ironwood, Ivantis, Joby Aviation, KaloBios Pharmaceuticals, Kalpsys, Klook, Knewton, Leqee, Livongo, LogRhythm, Lonza Biologics, LucasFilm Animation, Maccine, Magic Leap, Mdaq, Meiban, MerLion Pharma, MetricStream, Moderna, NanoFilm, Patientsafe, Moka, OakNorth, Paxata, Pear Therapeutics, Perlegen, Pindrop, Puppet, QTVascular, Ramp, Rapid Micro Biosystems, Renovis, Retail Next, Revance Therapeutics, Rotimatic, S*Bio, Savioke, Shape, Singapore Suzhou

Venture Capital & Private Equity Firms / International Firms

Township Development, Sotera Wireless, Sprinklr, Taulia, Tessa Therapeutics, Vanda, Vobile, WalkMe, Welltok

Other Locations:
250A, Twin Dolphin Drive
Redwood City, CA 94065-1402
Phone: 650-591-9102 **Fax:** 650-591-1328

Key Executives:
Swee Yeok Chu, Chief Executive Officer/President
Background: CEO, Bio*One Capital; Singapore Economic Development Board
Directorships: Merlion Pharmaceuticals, Singapore Suzhou Township Development, Alexandra Health Endowment Fund

2682 EDEN VENTURES
14 Golden Square
London W1F 9JF
United Kingdom

Phone: 44-0-22077583440
e-mail: info@edenventures.co.uk
web: www.edenventures.co.uk

Mission Statement: Eden Venture's background is that of serial entrepreneurs with a strong seed investment track record. We offer our portfolio companies considerable operational management expertise in creating businesses of lasting value. Eden's investment strategy is to provide early stage funding (seed and Series A). However, we also reserve allocation within our funds to follow our successful investments through their lifetime, meaning that entrepreneurs can focus on getting on with business knowing they have a strong investment partner by their side.

Investment Criteria: Early-Stage
Industry Group Preference: Telecommunications, Software, Enterprise Software, SaaS, Digital Media & Marketing, E-Commerce & Manufacturing, Internet, Social Media, Gaming, Mobile
Portfolio Companies: Borro, Reevoo, The Filter, We7, BaseKit, UberVU, Greenman Gaming, Lookk, What's In My Handbag, VoiceVault, Acunu, Doccom, Huddle, Tru, Zemanta, Brightpearl, New Voice Media, AFrame, Response Tap, Ontology, Tribold, Voss, Evolved Intelligence

Other Locations:
1 Widcombe Crescent
Bath BA2 6AH
United Kingdom
Phone: 44-0-1225-472950

Key Executives:
Mark Caroe, Partner
Background: Finance Director, Apertio; CFO, Paragon Software

2683 EIRCOM ENTERPRISE FUND LIMITED
1 Heuston South Quarter
St. John's Road
Dublin 8
Ireland

Phone: 353-167-14444 **Fax:** 353-16797253
web: www.eir.ie

Mission Statement: Actively seeking new investments.
Geographic Preference: Ireland
Minimum Investment: $45, 500
Investment Criteria: Seed Capital, Start-Up Capital, Early Stage
Industry Group Preference: Communications

Key Executives:
Cathal Magee, Managing Director
Alfie Kane, Group Chief Executive

2684 ELAIA PARTNERS
54 rue de Ponthieu
Paris 75008
France

Phone: 33-176749250 **Fax:** 33-176749260
e-mail: contact@elaia.com
web: www.elaia.com

Mission Statement: An independent private equity boutique focused on Digital Economy. Our belief is twofold: digital economy-related technologies are increasingly driving innovation growth in every key sectors and our focus in this sector will keep us among the leading experts in this domain.

Fund Size: $45 Million
Founded: 2002
Industry Group Preference: Information Technology, Financial Services, Enterprise Software
Portfolio Companies: Agnito, Allmyapps, Climpact, Criteo, Digital Healthcare, ePawn, Goom Radio, Mirakl, Orchestra Networks, Scoop.it, Sensorly, Sigfox, Total Immersion, Wyplay, Ykone

Key Executives:
Philippe Gire, Partner
Education: Ecole Polytechnique
Background: Accenture, Valeo Ventures

2685 ELECTRA PARTNERS ASIA LIMITED SFC of Hong Kong
18/F, 8 Queen's Road
1 Connaught Place
Central
Hong Kong

Phone: 852-25308700 **Fax:** 852-25305525
web: www.electra-asia.com

Mission Statement: Concentrates on established but high growth international companies based in Asia.

Geographic Preference: Asia
Founded: 1995
Investment Criteria: Growth Capital, Significant Minority Shareholdings
Industry Group Preference: Cable, Internet Technology, Construction, Outsourcing & Efficiency, Ancillary Services, Chemicals, Storage, Packaging, Processing, Software Services, Optical Technology, Manufacturing, Tourism, Media
Portfolio Companies: Aksh Optifibre Ltd. (India), Asia Travelmart Ltd. (Malaysia), Convansys Inc (Us/India), Locus Corporation (Korea), Meghmani Organics Ltd. (India), Moser Baer India Ltd. (India), Spi Technologies Inc, Zensar Technologies Ltd

Key Executives:
John Levack, Managing Director
e-mail: info@electra-asia.com
Education: Degree in business administration from Bath University in the UK.
Background: Electra, 3i Pic in Asia and Europe
Jessica Mak, Associate

2686 ELECTRA PARTNERS EUROPE
Paternoster House
65n St Paul's Churchyard
London EC4M 8AB
United Kingdom

Phone: 44-2072144200 **Fax:** 44-2072144201
e-mail: info@electrapartners.com

Mission Statement: Actively seeking new investments.

Geographic Preference: France, Belgium, Switzerland
Fund Size: £450 million
Average Investment: Euro 3 Billion
Minimum Investment: Ffr150 million
Investment Criteria: MBO, MBI, Replacement

Venture Capital & Private Equity Firms / International Firms

Industry Group Preference: Financial Services, Healthcare, Industrial Services, Services, Consumer Services
Portfolio Companies: CPI, Covenant Healthcare, Global Solutions, KSM Castings, UK Support Services, Urbium
Key Executives:
    Shakira Adigun-Boaye, Investment Associate
    Education: Lyon Business School
    Background: VP, Europe@Web; Investment Director, Fonds Partnaires (Lazard Freres & Cie); Arthur Andersen
    Nicholas Board, Marketing Executive
    Education: Ecole Polytechnique; Ecole Nationale des Ponts
    Background: Principal, Apax; BNP Paribas; Arthur Andersen
    Alex Cooper-Evans, Investment Partner & Head of Investor Relations
    Education: BS, Queen's University
    Background: Director, Prudential Venture Managers; Corporate Finance, Coopers & Lybrand; Chartered Accountant
    Philip Dyke, Partner
    Education: BS Civil Engineering, University of London; MBA, Cranfield Business School
    Background: VP, Citibank Leveraged Buyout Department
    Alex Fortescue, Chief Investment Partner
    Education: Chemistry degree, Nottingham University
    Background: Managing Director, L&G Ventures GmbH; Investment Manager, 3i; Chemist, BP Chemicals

2687 ELEVEN
4 Gurko Street
2nd floor
Sofia 1000
Bulgaria

Phone: +35 9886852881
web: www.eleven.bg

Mission Statement: Eleven is a EUR 12 million venture fund that provides financing to early-stage startups using an incremental investment approach alongside iterative development - thereby, starting with many small experiments, filter out failures, and invest in successes.

Fund Size: EUR 12 million
Founded: 2012
Average Investment: 150,000 Euro
Investment Criteria: Seed-Stage, Early-Stage
Portfolio Companies: KeenSkim, Fh, Filement, Meister Plus, Olympix, Lakoteka, SoccerScout.com, VetCloud, Sponsia, Squee, Unioncy, Sensika, Eventyard, Playground Energy, SoundVamp
Key Executives:
    Daniel Tomov, Partner
    Dilyan Dimitrov, Partner
    Ivo Simov, Partner
    Jonathan Bradford, Mentor-in-chief

2688 EM WARBURG, PINCUS & COMPANY INTERNATIONAL
Almack House
28 King Street, St. James's
London SW1Y 6QW
United Kingdom

Phone: 44-2073060306 **Fax:** 44-2073210881
e-mail: info@warburgpincus.com
web: www.warburgpincus.com

Mission Statement: Actively seeking new investments.
Geographic Preference: United Kingdom, Central Europe, Western Europe
Fund Size: $40 Billion
Founded: 1966
Average Investment: $25 Million
Minimum Investment: $8.85 Million
Investment Criteria: Early Stage, Expansion And Development, Secondary Purchase/Replacement Capital, Rescue/Turnaround, MBO, MBI
Industry Group Preference: Technology, Consumer Services, Education, Communications, Energy, Financial Services, Real Estate, Information Technology, Business to Business, Industrial Services, Natural Resources
Portfolio Companies: Asia Ec, Campsystems, Cobalt, Globalspec, Gt Nexus, Mach, Rmi, Workscape, Ugs, Iss, Vodlee, Aicent, Fibernet, Lssi, Bharti Enterprise, Neustar, Mbi, Jarden, Knoll, Polypore, Transdigm, The Neiman Marcus Group, Ambuja Cement, Northpole, Karsen, 4Gl, Aspen
Key Executives:
    Charles R. Kaye, Co-Chief Executive Officer
    e-mail: cjoung@warburgpincus.com
    Education: A.B. in physics from Dartmouth College and an M.B.A. with High Distinction from the Amos Tuck School of Business, where he was an Edward Tuck Scholar.
    Background: head of the Americas Natural Resources Group (Energy and Power practice) in the Investment Banking Division of Goldman, Sachs & Co
    Joseph P. Landy, Co-Chief Executive Officer
    e-mail: sarenare@warburgpincus.com
    Education: B.A. in political science magna cum laude from the University of Pennsylvania.
    Background: attorney in the Corporate and Finance department
    Michael Clancy, Managing Director
    Education: B.A. in economics from Yale University and an M.B.A. from the Stanford University Graduate School of Business.
    Background: engagement manager with McKinsey & Company and was Executive Vice President of InfoUSA
    Directorships: Director.
    Steve Coates, Managing Director
    e-mail: scoates@warburgpincus.com
    Education: M.A. in Politics, Philosophy and Economics from Oxford University and is a Chartered Accountant.
    Background: a corporate finance director for Arthur Andersen & Co.& 3i

2689 EM WARBURG, PINCUS & COMPANY JAPAN
Hibiya Marine Bldg., 8th Floor
Cjoupda-ku
Tokyo 100-0006
Japan

Phone: 81-355216830 **Fax:** 81-355210066
web: www.warburgpincus.com

Mission Statement: Invests in worldwide opportunities, actively seeking new investments
Geographic Preference: Worldwide
Fund Size: $8 Billion
Founded: 1966
Average Investment: $40 Billion
Investment Criteria: Early stage, growth and late stage
Industry Group Preference: Business to Business, Communications, Consumer Services, Education, Energy, Financial Services, Healthcare, Life Sciences, Information Technology, Media, Real Estate, Technology, Industrial Services, Natural Resources
Portfolio Companies: AsiaEC.com, CAMP Systems, Cobalt, GlobalSpec, GT Nexus, InfoGenesis, Institutional Shareholder Services, Inc., MACH, Manugistics, AsiaInfo & Aicent
Key Executives:
    Charles R. Kaye, Co-President
    Education: B.S.E. from Princeton University
    Background: Oliver , Wyman & Co. & IMPEX
    Directorships: Director, UL Systems & Director, Resolution Property plc

Venture Capital & Private Equity Firms / International Firms

Joseph P. Landy, Co-President

2690 ENDEAVOUR CAPITAL PTY LIMITED
Endeavour Capital
Level 1, 432 Kent Street
Sydney 2000
Australia

Phone: 61-0280969222 Fax: 61-0280969229
e-mail: pw@endeavourcapital.com.au
web: www.endeavourcapital.com.au

Mission Statement: Independent corporate advisory firm, focusing exclusively on smaller and mid-market companies.

Geographic Preference: Australia, New Zealand
Founded: 1998

Key Executives:
Peter Wallace, Founder & Managing Director
e-mail: pw@endeavourcapital.com.au
Background: Investment Director, Hambro-Grantham
Directorships: Ambertech Limited; The Executive Connection Pty Ltd.; Carte Blanche Australia Pty Limited

2691 ENERGY VENTURES
Kongsgaardbakken 1
Stavanger 4005
Norway

Phone: 47 51 84 12 95

Mission Statement: Energy Ventures is an independent venture capital firm dedicated to new upstream oil and gas technologies. From the initial investment to the exit, we take a hands-on approach. By truly partnering with our portfolio companies, we ensure the most effective use of capital and talent. Our method is proven by our record: since Energy Ventures' creation in 2002 we have reviewed more than 2500 deals, made thirty-two investments and successfully exited twelve companies.

Geographic Preference: North Sea, North America
Fund Size: $750 million
Average Investment: $5 - $35 million
Industry Group Preference: Oil & Gas, Energy
Portfolio Companies: Acoustic Zoom, ARKeX, Foster Findlay Associates, Fotech Solutions, Ingrain, Wireless Seismic, 2TD, Abrado Welbore Services, Cubility, Deep Casing Tools, Energy Drilling, IWC, Meta, Oxane Materials, READ Cased Hole, Ziebel, Zilift, DeepFlex, Energreen, HalfWave, OsComp Systems, PanGeo Subsea, Produced Water Absorbents, Reality Mobile, Sigma Offshore

Other Locations:
10777 Westheimer
Suite 1175
Houston, TX 77042
Phone: 281-768-6721 Fax: 281-768-6726

Key Executives:
Jim Sledzik, Senior Partner

2692 ENNOVENT
Neubaugasse 11/14
4910 Ried im Innkreis
Vienna 1070
Austria

Phone: 43-1236585920 Fax: 43-1236585921
e-mail: office@ennovent.com
web: www.ennovent.com

Mission Statement: Ennovent is a venture catalyst that accelerates innovations for sustainability at the base of the economic pyramid. We work with a global network of entrepreneurs, investors and experts to discover, finance and scale up the best innovations.

Geographic Preference: India
Industry Group Preference: Energy, Food & Beverage, Water, Healthcare, Education

2693 ENSO VENTURES
10-11 Park Place
London SW1A 1LP
United Kingdom

Phone: 020-71484499
e-mail: info@ensoventures.com

Mission Statement: CLS Capital is a private investment and project management company that specializes in making highly selective equity investments in US and European biomedical companies with potential for capitalizing on technology transfer and product development in Russia and the CIS.

Geographic Preference: United States, Europe
Industry Group Preference: Healthcare, Life Sciences, Biomedical
Portfolio Companies: Novelos Therapeutics, Egalet, Seres Health

Other Locations:
747 3rd Avenue
2nd Floor
New York, NY 10017
Phone: 1-646-6960056

Key Executives:
Andrey Kozlov, Partner
Education: BS, Economics, St. Petersburg State University; MBA, Booth School of Business
Background: HSBC Investment Global Banking

2694 ENSPIRE CAPITAL PTE LTD
317 Outram Road
#B1-07 Holida Inn Atrium
169075
Singapore

Phone: +65 6349 0836 Fax: +65 6234 0532
e-mail: admin@enspire-capital.com
web: www.enspire-capital.com

Mission Statement: Our investment philosophy is to identify entrepreneurs with vision, innovative technology, and a strong sense of commitment. In addition to providing companies with venture capital, we also assume an active role in offering strategic advice to, and sharing our management expertise, experiences, and business connections with our portfolio companies.

Geographic Preference: United States West Coast, China, Taiwan, Hong Kong, Singapore
Minimum Investment: $1 million
Investment Criteria: Various Stages
Industry Group Preference: Technology, Media, Telecommunications, Internet
Portfolio Companies: A10 Networks, Amplus Communication Pte Ltd, ArrowSpan, Create Electronic Optical Co, Cipherium Systems Co, Dnium Pte Ltd, DynaScan Technology Corp, Egis Technology, Emine Software, Ether Optronics Inc, FocalTech Sytems, Genie Network Resource Management Inc, Global Communication Semiconductors, Hoodinn Interactive Limited, MBA Polymers, Pixelmetrix Corporation, Solapoint, Transcast Media, Voltafield Technology,

Key Executives:
Chay Kwong Soon, Founder & Chairman
Education: BSc, Physics, National University of Singapore
Background: Co-Founder and President, Creative Technology Ltd
Dr. Lung Yeh, Managing Director
Education: BSEE, Communication Engineering, National Chiao-Tung University, Hsin-Chu, Taiwan; PhD, Electrical and Computer Engineering, University of Wisconsin - Madison
Background: Senior Vice President of Marketing, Sales and Operation, Centrality Communications; Co-Founder and Presdient and CEO, Pico Communications; Vice President of the Internet and Communication Division at

Creative Labs; Founder, ShareVision Technology; Apple Computer; Verizon; Eastman Kodak

2695 ENTERPRISE EQUITY (NI) LTD
78A Dublin Road
Belfast BT2 7HP
United Kingdom

Phone: 44-2890242500 Fax: 44-2890242487

Mission Statement: Enterprise Equity backs growth orientated companies at various stages of their development.
Geographic Preference: Northern Ireland, Ireland
Fund Size: $12.4 Million
Founded: 1987
Average Investment: $1.06 Million
Minimum Investment: $445, 000
Investment Criteria: Start-up, Other early stage, Expansion and Development, Secondary purchase/replacement capital, Rescue/turnaround, MBO, MBI
Industry Group Preference: Biotechnology, Medical & Health Related, Chemicals, Materials Technology, Energy, Construction, Building Materials & Services, Industrial Services, Manufacturing, Transportation, Communications, Information Technology, Computer Hardware & Software, Internet Technology, Electronic Technology
Portfolio Companies: Balcas Ltd, Bluechip Technologies Holdings Ltd, EZ-DSP Ltd, FIN Engineering Group Ltd, Gendel Ltd, Toughglass Holdings Ltd, TriVirix

Key Executives:
Aidan Langan, Chief Executive Officer
e-mail: info@eeni.com
Education: Doctor of Public Administration
Background: Gaeltarra Éireann
Brian Cummings, Director
e-mail: bob@eeni.com
Education: Chartered Accountant
Background: Non-Executive Director, Board Member

2696 ENTERPRISE EQUITY IRELAND LIMITED
Dublin Road
Teagasc Building
Dundalk, Co. Louth
Ireland

Phone: 353-429333167 Fax: 353-429334857
e-mail: info@enterpriseequity.ie
web: www.enterpriseequity.ie

Mission Statement: Commercial providers of Venture Capital to new and expanding business .
Geographic Preference: Ireland
Fund Size: $53 Million
Founded: 1987
Average Investment: $1.5 Million
Minimum Investment: $10.7 Million
Investment Criteria: Expansion - development, Seed, Small buyout (£m equity), Start-up
Portfolio Companies: International Test Technologies, Datacare Software Group, Ansamed Ltd, Iontas Ltd, Merenda Limited, Avenue Ltd, Duolog Ltd, Duolog Ltd, Aimware Limited, Swift Fine Foods Limited, SigmaX Limited, Celtrak Ltd, Neutekbio Ltd, AMT3D Limited.

Key Executives:
Conor O'Connor, Managing Partner
e-mail: info@enterpriseequity.ie
Education: A Chartered Accountant he completed his training with PriceWaterhouseCoopers in Dublin
Background: Chairman of the Irish Venture Capital Association as well as representing Ireland on the Board of the European Venture Capital Association (EVCA)
Directorships: Director
Rory Hynes, Partner
Background: Civil Service; Gaeltarra Eireann; Udaras na Gaeltachta

Tom Shinkwin, Partner
Education: Bachelor of Commerce degree; MBA
Background: Expreience: construction , engineering, corporate finance, management, property, banking
Directorships: Strategic Equity Partners

2697 ENTERPRISE INVESTORS
Warsaw Financial Center, Emilii Plater 53
Warsaw 00-113
Poland

Phone: 48-224588500 Fax: 48-224588555
e-mail: info@ei.com.pl
web: www.ei.com.pl

Mission Statement: Actively seeking new investments.
Geographic Preference: Poland, Central and Eastern Europe
Fund Size: $2 billion
Founded: 1990
Average Investment: $28.8 Million
Investment Criteria: Start-up, buyouts, restructuring, strategic joint ventures, expansion financing for fast-growing companies, equity increase followed by flotation on the stock exchange, privatization with management s
Industry Group Preference: Computer Related, Financial Services, Industrial Equipment, Manufacturing, Telecommunications, Industrial Services
Portfolio Companies: AB SA, Wroclaw, DGS SA, Wloclawek, Agros Nova Sp. z o.o., Warsaw, Artima SA, Romania, Gamet Sp. z o.o., Torun, Kruk SA, Wroclaw, Magellan Sp. z o.o., Lódz, Medycyna Rodzinna SA, Warsaw

Key Executives:
Robert Faris, Chairman
e-mail: info@ei.com.pl
Background: Director Corporate Development, Amoco Chemical/Standard Oil, Indiana; President/General Partner, Alan Patricof Associates
Directorships: CEO
Jacek Siwicki, President
e-mail: info@ei.com.pl
Background: Polish Deputy Minister of Privatization and as adviser to the International Finance Corporation. Mr. Siwicki focuses on privatization
Michael Rusiecki, Managing Partner
e-mail: info@ei.com.pl
Background: Director at the Polish Ministry of Privatization, negotiated transactions with International Paper, ABB, Philips,
Robert Manz, Managing Partner
e-mail: info@ei.com.pl
Background: Financial Analyst, Dillon, Read and Co. Inc.
Dariusz Pronczuk, Managing Partner
e-mail: info@ei.com.pl
Background: Financial Analyst, Multicraft and PDG Partners; Vice President, Hejka Michna Inc.
Tod Kersten, Portfolio Manager
e-mail: info@ei.com.pl
Background: Polish-American Enterprise Fund, Finance and a Director at the investment bank
Stanislaw Knaflewski, Portfolio Manager
e-mail: info@ei.com.pl
Background: he worked for The Boston Consulting Group in Warsaw and Paris

2698 ENTERPRISE VENTURE LIMITED
23 Berkeley Square
London W1J 6HE
United Kingdom

Phone: 0845-0948886 Fax: 0845-0948887
e-mail: mail@equityventures.co.uk
web: www.evgroup.uk.com

Mission Statement: Actively seeking new investments.
Geographic Preference: United Kingdom
Fund Size: $35.4 Million

Venture Capital & Private Equity Firms / International Firms

Average Investment: Euro 100 Million
Minimum Investment: $88, 500 Million
Investment Criteria: Expansion and Development, Refinancing bank debt, Secondary purchase/replacement capital, MBO, MBI, Mezzanine
Industry Group Preference: All Sectors Considered
Portfolio Companies: Acrohone Ltd., Jackson Vending Ltd.

Key Executives:

Valerie Andrew, Investment Executive
e-mail: david@equityventures.co.uk
Education: London School of Economics with a BSc Honours degree in Economics and International Relations, Masters degree in Business Analysis at Lancaster Universit
Background: Price Waterhouse, Ernst & Young

Ian Atkinson, Investment Manager
e-mail: robert@equityventures.co.uk
Education: University of Oxford , Honours in Politics Philosophy and Economics, Institute of Business Administration in Fontainbleau(MBA)
Background: First National Bank of Boston in London , Hoare Govett,

2699 ENTERPRISE VENTURES LIMITED
Preston Technology Management Centre
Marsh Lane
Preston PR1 8UQ
United Kingdom

Phone: 0845-0948886 **Fax:** 0845-0948887
e-mail: richard.bamford@enterprise-ventures.co.uk
web: www.evgroup.uk.com

Mission Statement: Actively seeking new investments.

Geographic Preference: United Kingdom
Fund Size: $79.7 Million
Founded: 1941
Average Investment: $0.62 Million
Minimum Investment: $0.04 Million
Investment Criteria: Seed, Start-up, Other early stage, Expansion and Development, Rescue/turnaround, MBO, MBI
Industry Group Preference: All Sectors Considered
Portfolio Companies: RisingStars Growth Fund, Lancashire Rosebud Fund, Coalfields Enterprise Fund, eXML, Femeda Ltd, Bio Futures PLC, Avanticare, Specialist Heating Components Ltd, Cliq Designs Ltd, Transport Models, Farmhouse Fare Ltd

Key Executives:

Richard Bamford, Executive Chairman
Education: MA, Solicitor
Background: Chaired the BVCA Legal & Technical Committee for several years

Jonathan Diggines, Chief Executive
Education: ACIB
Background: Richard has been a leading private equity practitioner for some twenty years, and is highly experienced in all aspects of private equity,

Lisa Ward, Investment Manager
Education: ACIB
Background: He was previously a Senior Corporate Lending Manager for a major UK bank.
Directorships: Senior Corporate Lending Manager

Mark Wyatt, Investment Manager
Education: MBA, BA (Hons)
Background: Spent five years with 3i plc as an early stage technology investor in its Northern Investor team. He has considerable experience in undertaking, managing and exiting venture capital investments from start-ups to MBOs/MBIs in a variety of industrial sectors.

Julian Viggars, Head of Technology Investment
Education: BSc, ACA
Background: Director of BioProjects International, an AIM-listed early stage technology fund. Julian has particular expertise in the healthcare sector.

John Charles, Investment Director
Education: ACIB
Background: Previously held a number of senior positions in corporate banking, including North West Regional Commercial Banking Director for a major high street bank

John Simpson, Finance Director
Education: MA, FCA
Background: Head of UK Corporate Finance at strategy consultants, Arthur D Little.
Directorships: Senior Investment Manager

Melanie Lowe, Fund Administrator
Education: BSc, ACA
Background: Chartered Accountant with a broad range of financial experience at main board level in both listed and private equity backed companies

2700 ENTREE CAPITAL
124 Baker Street
London W1U 6TY
United Kingdom

web: www.entreecap.com

Mission Statement: Entree Capital provides multi-stage funding for innovative seed, early and growth companies all over the world. Entree Capital was founded by entrepreneurs with a track record of having successfully invested and exited many businesses on five continents in the past two decades. Our offices are located in London and Tel Aviv, yet we make investments in most countries.

Geographic Preference: Worldwide
Investment Criteria: Seed-Stage, Early-Stage, Growth Stage
Industry Group Preference: Enterprise Software, Consumer Internet, High Technology, Business Products & Services, Real Estate, Medical Devices
Portfolio Companies: Cura Software, Intec Telecom Systems, JustEnough Software, CQS, Coupang, Internet Sports Marketing, DragonPlay, Connected Backup, UltraDNS, Maestro Commerce, 365Media, Independent Commercial, Harvest Automation, Concillium, Automated Fuel Systems Group, Bandit Vehicle Security, Mondial Risk Management, Brightside, Insight Technologies Network Academy, IOCORE, Zenprop, Virtual Ports

2701 ENTREPRENEURS FUND
3rd Floor, Standbrook House
2-5 Old Bond Street
London W1S 4PD
United Kingdom

Phone: 44-02073551011 **Fax:** 44-02073556199
e-mail: info@entrepreneursfund.com
web: www.entrepreneursfund.com

Mission Statement: There is nothing average about us or our partners. We believe our attitude and experience represent a major opportunity to companies. Simply, we allow them to overcome any restrictions to their growth objectives more quickly and more easily. And importantly we do that together. By using the global presence of our group parent to strengthen the potential and status of young companies. By networking companies together. By playing an active role in our investments. New sectors offer new opportunities and different dynamics. We actively seek out these challenges.

Geographic Preference: Worldwide
Investment Criteria: Early-Stage
Industry Group Preference: Life Sciences, Clean Technology
Portfolio Companies: CPT, Cytoo, D3O, Evolva, Exosect, Fits.me, FutureE, General Fusion, Lifeline Scientific, N-Tec, OptiNose, Prosonix, ProtAffin, Real Eyes, Sequana Medical, T2Cure, Technolas, The New Motion, VasoPharm, Xeros

Key Executives:

Klass de Boer, Managing Partner
Education: MSc, Physics; MBA, INSEAD

Venture Capital & Private Equity Firms / International Firms

Background: Vanenburg Group; Consultant, McKinsey & Company

2702 EPISODE 1 PARTNERS
Kingsbourne House
229-231 High Holborn
London WC1 V7DA
United Kingdom

Phone: 44-02074864841 Fax: 44-02079357963
e-mail: info@episode1.com
web: www.episode1.com

Mission Statement: Takes an active role in helping to build the businesses we invest in

Geographic Preference: United Kingdom
Founded: 1942
Investment Criteria: early stage investments in technology and information services
Industry Group Preference: Internet Technology, Banking
Portfolio Companies: Commerce Decisions, Magicalia, Moreover Technologies, Natural Motion, Shazam, Wall Street Transcript, Betfair.com, Online Partners, Openharbor.com, Clovis, FriendsAbroad.com, Video Island

Key Executives:
Adrian Lloyd, Partner
Simon Murdoch, Co-founder
Education: BA in Physics and a PhD in Computer Science and Expert Systems
Background: Vice President Europe of Amazon.com. Managing Director of a UK-based software house, Triptych Systems.
Directorships: Vice President

2703 EQT PARTNERS AB
Hovslagargatan 3, PO Box 16409
Stockholm SE-111 48
Sweden

Phone: 46-850655300 Fax: 46-850655319
web: www.eqt.se

Mission Statement: Actively seeking new investments in Nordic medium-sized companies as investment adviser to EQT Scandinavian I and II, EQT Danmark and EQT Finland.

Geographic Preference: Denmark, Finland, Germany, Norway, Sweden
Founded: 1995
Average Investment: Euro 11 Billion
Investment Criteria: have significant potential for top-line and earnings growth, can retain or attract high-quality management, have well-defined realization alternatives.
Industry Group Preference: Chemicals, Consumer Services, Consumer Products, Industrial Equipment, Telecommunications, Materials Technology, Retailing, Industrial Services, Carriers
Portfolio Companies: AG Kühnle Kopp & Kausch, Aleris AB, BHS Getriebe GmbH, Brandtex Group A/S, Carl Zeiss Vision GmbH, Contex A/S, Eldon Holding AB, Metall Technologie Holding GmbH

Key Executives:
Johan Bygge, Chief Operating Officer
e-mail: juha.lindfors@eqt.fi
Education: graduated with a M.Sc. (Econ.) from the Helsinki School of Economics in 1994
Background: Cultor Group in investor relations, and with Strategic Analysis & Management Inc., a management consulting firm
Marcus Brennecke, Partner
e-mail: marcus.brennecke@eqt.de
Education: Graduated from the University of St. Gallen, Switzerland
Background: Managing Partner and entrepreneurial investor at German private equity company SMB, Founder/CEO of a tv-sport rights company.
Directorships: Entrepreneurial investor

Caspar Callerström, Director
e-mail: caspar.callerstrom@eqt.se
Education: M.Sc. at the Stockholm School of Economics with two majors (Financial Economics, and International Business).
Bjorn Hoi Jensen, Director
e-mail: bjorn.jensen@eqt.de
Education: Graduated from Copenhagen University with a Master of Science in Economics in 1985
Background: 10 years in investment banking and private equity in London and Copenhagen, with amongst others Citibank, SDS and Enskilda Securities
Hakan Johansson, Director
e-mail: hakan.johansson@eqt.se
Education: Graduate of the University of Gothenburg with majors in Accounting and Finance.
Background: Volvo Group Finance in Amsterdam, Electrolux, Senior Vice President and Head of Mergers and Acquisitions at Electrolux.
Thomas Von Koch, Director
e-mail: thomas.vonkoch@eqt.se
Education: Graduated from the Stockholm School of Economics in 1992 with two majors (Financial Economics and Accounting & Finance
Background: Investor AB, director of the boards of Com Hem AB, Plantasjen ASA, VTI Technologies and Duni AB.
Jan Stahlberg, Director
e-mail: jan.stahlberg@eqt.se
Education: Graduated from the Stockholm School of Economics in 1985 with two majors (Economic Analysis and Accounting & Finance).
Background: Ovako Steel as Senior Vice President of Finance and member of the Executive Management
Vesa Koskinen, Partner
e-mail: vesa.koskinen@eqt.fi
Education: MSc degree with a major in Finance in the Helsinki School of Economics.
Background: JPMorgan and Metso Corporation

2704 EQUINET VENTURE PARTNERS AG
97 Graefstrasse
Frankfurt 60487
Germany

Phone: 49-69589970 Fax: 49-695-8997299
e-mail: info@equinet-ag.de
web: www.equinet-ag.de

Mission Statement: Equinet Venture Partners AG is the VC specialist of Equinet AG, an investment bank focused on rapidly growing technology companies.

Geographic Preference: Germany
Fund Size: $18 Million
Founded: 1999
Investment Criteria: Expansion - development, Seed, Start-up, Other early stage
Industry Group Preference: Information Technology, Life Sciences, High Technology
Portfolio Companies: Phenex Pharmaceuticals AG, Nova Ratio AG, Mobotix, Sysgo, iTAC, Geneart, Nanogate Technologies, Euroimmun, Eisfeld Datentechnik, Ihr Partner Software, Newtron

Key Executives:
Lutz Weiler, CEO
e-mail: lutz.weiler@equinet-ag.de
Background: IPO transactions and was responsonsible for the bank's leading position, member of the Primary Market Advisory Committee
Anita Prattki, CFO
e-mail: goetz.gollan@equinet-ag.de
Background: Mid-caps in particular on IPOs, pre IPO financing, M&As and stock option schemes.
Prof. Dr. Andreas Wiedemann, Chairman of the Supervisory Board
e-mail: farsin.yadegardjam@equinet-ag.de

Venture Capital & Private Equity Firms / International Firms

2705 EQUISTONE
Condor House, St Paul's Churchyard
Canary Wharf
London EC4M 8AL
United Kingdom

Phone: 44-02075129900 Fax: 44-2076535301ÿ
e-mail: rob.myers@equistonepe.com
web: www.barcap.com

Mission Statement: Invests as a strategic partner alongside management teams, working together to build and realise shareholder value.
Geographic Preference: United Kingdom, France, Germany, Italy
Fund Size: $1.97 Billion
Average Investment: $164 Million
Minimum Investment: $30 Million
Investment Criteria: Expansion and Development, Refinancing bank debt, Secondary purchase/replacement capital, MBO, MBI, Institutional BO, Leveraged Build Up, Public-to-Private
Industry Group Preference: Engineering, Automotive, Consumer Services, Transportation, Healthcare, Household Goods, Construction, Retailing, Financial Services, Chemicals, Food & Beverage, Electronic Technology, Oil & Gas, Tourism, Logistics
Portfolio Companies: Médi-Partenaires, Laho Equipement, Jack Wolfskin, Kurt Geiger, Maisons du Monde, Neumayer Tekfor, CEME Group, Alstom Power Conversion

Key Executives:
  Eric Bommensath, Co-Chief Executive, Corporate and Investment Banking
  e-mail: brian.blakemore@barcap.com
  Background: Investor Relations Director at Midlands
  Tom King, Co-Chief Executive, Corporate and Investment Banking
  e-mail: paul.goodson@barcap.com
  Background: Director in 3i transaction team
  Directorships: Board Member, Special Director
  Justin Bull, Chief Operating Officer, Corporate and Investment Banking
  e-mail: olvier.jennings@barcap.com
  Background: Head of Infrastructure in Bank of America, PPP/PFI sectors, Director in Price Waterhouse
  Lee Guy, Co-Chief Risk Officer
  e-mail: mark.taylor@barcap.com
  Background: Chartered Accountant at Price Waterhouse
  Directorships: Non-Executive Director

2706 EQUITY PARTNERS PTY LIMITED
Level 12, 201 Kent Street
Sydney 2000
Australia

Phone: 61-282985100 Fax: 61-282985150

Mission Statement: Actively seeking new investments
Geographic Preference: Australia, New Zealand, South Africa, Asia, United Kingdom
Fund Size: $350 million
Founded: 1995
Investment Criteria: Global Expansion, MBO, Acquisitions
Industry Group Preference: Technology, Management, Enterprise Services
Portfolio Companies: BOSS (Business Operations & Software Solutions), TOWER Software Engineering, Energetics, Snowball Group Limited, Yambay Technologies Pty Limited, Protocom Development Systems Pty Limited, Portland Orthopaedics Pty Limited, Agrilink Holdings Pty Limited, Imm

Key Executives:
  Quentin Jones BA Ll.B, Partner
  e-mail: kim.durack@equitypartners.com.au
  Education: Bachelor of Science in Biochemistry, a Bachelor of Arts in Economics and Journalism, a Post Graduate Certificate in Technology Management, and is completing an MBA at MGSM
  Background: Sale and marketing arms of two blue-chip pharmaceutical companies, Hoffman La-Roche and Schering Plough
  Rajeev Dhawan BCom, CA, MBA, Partner
  e-mail: peterbj@equitypartners.com.au
  Education: BCom (Hons) CA(SA)
  Background: Manufacturing, health care and other service delivery businesses
  Greg Wang BCom, CA, MBA, Associate Director
  e-mail: rgregson@equitypartners.com.au
  Education: BSc (Hons I) PhD MBA
  Background: Telecommunications, on-line business, software and hardware systems, health care services, biotechnology, energy, and other services

2707 EQVITEC PARTNERS OY
8 Fabianinkatu
PO Box 65
Helsinki 00131
Finland

Phone: 358-5066563 Fax: 358-207-809801
e-mail: jukka.makinen@eqvitec.com

Mission Statement: Actively seeking new investments.
Geographic Preference: Denmark, Estonia, Finland, Lithuania, Norway, Sweden
Fund Size: $360 Million
Founded: 1998
Investment Criteria: Early-Stage, Expansion and Development Capital, Mezzanine, Startup Capital, Buyout and Buyin
Industry Group Preference: Communications, Computer Related, Electronic Technology, Industrial Products, Industrial Services, Chemicals, Materials Technology
Portfolio Companies: AffectoGenimap Group Oyj, Aidox Oy, Anilinker Oy, Codenomicon Oy, Codetoys Oy, DynaRoad Oy, Envox Group AB (publ.), Fastrax Oy, Fox Technologies, Inc, FRENDS Technology Oy, Navicore Ltd, Oy 4Pharma Ltd, Samstock Oy, Sanako Corporation, Saraware Oy, Selmic Oy, SEVEN

Key Executives:
  Jukka Mäkinen, Managing Partner
  Background: Vice Chairman, Finnish Venture Capital Association, Director in, SITRA
  Directorships: Managing Director, CEO
  Juha Mikkola, Senior Partner

2708 ESPIRITO SANTO VENTURES
Rue Alexandre Herculano
38, 5 piso
Lisboa 1250-011
Portugal

Phone: 351-213106490 Fax: 351-213106425
web: www.es-ventures.com

Mission Statement: Espirito Santo Ventures is a venture capital firm of Espirito Santo Group, focused on technology based companies and innovative business projects with high-growth potential.
Fund Size: 200 million Euros
Founded: 2000
Average Investment: 1 - 10 million Euros
Industry Group Preference: Clean Technology, Healthcare, Information Technology
Portfolio Companies: A123 Systems, Advanced Cyclone Systems, Altraverda, AquaSpy, Banco Best, Chipidea, Clarity Payment Solutions, Contact, Coreworks, Global Active, IOSIL Energy, MagPower, Malo Clinic, Megamedia, Milcom Technologies, Multiwave, Nanosolar, Novabase, Nutrigreen, Oceanlinx, Opthalmopharma, OutSystems, Petra Solar, Prepaid Capital, Prepaid Media, SafetyPay, Spectrum Bridge,

Sousacamp, Super Bac, TxVia, UltraCell, Vortal, Watson Brown, Ydreams

Key Executives:
Joaquim Servulo Rodriques, Chief Executive Officer and Executive Director
Education: BSc, MSc, Electrotechnical Engineering, IST; MBA, INSEAD
Background: Assistant Professor, IST; Research Project Leader, INSEC; General Manager, Direct Channels Department, BES; CEO, CrediFlash SA
Pedro Ribeiro Santos, Executive Director, Chief Financial Officer
Education: BSc, Economics, UCP
Background: Investment Banking, CISF; Sociedada Independente de Servicios Financeiros; BPI
Jose Guerreiro de Sousa, Principal
Education: BSc, Electrotechnical Engineering & Computers, UCP
Background: Researcher, INESC; Assistant Professor, ISEG; Novabase SA; BES Group
Pedro Ribeiro Santos, Principal
Education: BSc, Physics Engineering, IST; MBA & MSc, Economics, UNL
Background: Researcher, Physics, University of Oxford; Accenture
Duarte Mineiro, Principal
Education: BSc, Management & Industrial Engineering, IST; MBA, Tuck School of Business, Dartmouth College
Background: Boston Consulting Group

2709 ETHOS PRIVATE EQUITY LIMITED: SA
PO Box 9773
Johannesburg 2000
South Africa

Phone: 27-113287400 Fax: 27-113287410
e-mail: cwilkinson@ethos.co.za
web: www.ethos.co.za

Mission Statement: Participates in the development and financing of companies within the university college sphere.

Geographic Preference: South Africa
Fund Size: $0.46 Million
Founded: 1998
Average Investment: $78, 000
Minimum Investment: $15, 500
Investment Criteria: Seed
Portfolio Companies: C-Takt AB, Cellectricom AB, Elektron AB, Eutech Medical AB, Framespot AB, Geositian AB, LightUp Technologies AB, Medeikonos AB, MicVac AB, Nanofactory Instruments AB, Q-Sense AB, Radiaus Innova AB, Sauiba Sensors AB

Key Executives:
Bill Ashmore, Partner
e-mail: aroux@ethos.co.za
Education: B.com (University of Withwatersand)
Background: More than 20 yrs experience ininvestment banking.
Directorships: Serves on the Dunlop Board
Andre Roux, Deputy Chairman

2710 EURAZEO
32 rue de Monceau
Paris 75008
France

Phone: 33-144150111 Fax: 33147668441
e-mail: Eurazeo_investor_relations@eurazeo.com

Mission Statement: Formerly Gaz-et-Eaux. An investment company unlike conventional holding companies, it is highly proactive and forward-looking; actively seeks new investment opportunities and works to enhance the value of those already in its portfolio.

Geographic Preference: Europe
Minimum Investment: $1, 000, 000 EURO
Investment Criteria: LBO, Expansion & Development Capital, Replacement Capital
Industry Group Preference: Communications, Consumer Services, Electronic Technology, Information Technology, Industrial Services, Internet Technology, Multimedia
Portfolio Companies: Distacom, Eutelsat, Fraikin, Rexel, Sandinvest, Terreal

Key Executives:
Patrick Sayer, Chairman
Education: Ecole Polytechnique; Ecole des Mines
Background: Managing Director, Lazard Freres et Cie
Directorships: Fraikin, Ipsos, Eutelsat
Bruno Keller, Chief Operating Officer
Education: Ecole Polytechnique
Background: Technical Project Manager, French Ministry of Defense
Virginie Morgon, Chief Operating Officer
Education: HEC, Paris
Background: JP Morgan
Philippe Audouin, Chief Financial Officer
Education: Ecole Polytechnique

2711 EUROFUND LP
87 Hayarkon Street
Tel Aviv 63432
Israel

Phone: 972-35202555 Fax: 972-35270041
e-mail: info@eurofund.co.il

Mission Statement: Eurofund and Eurofund 2000 are venture capital funds with a strongly defined identity and distinct areas of operation. They were established in alliance with powerful strategic partners who are industry leaders in the global marketplace. Eurofund 2000 still is open to new investments.

Geographic Preference: Israel
Fund Size: $ 72 Million
Investment Criteria: Early Stage
Industry Group Preference: Telecommunications, Microelectronics, Information Technology, Internet Technology, Security
Portfolio Companies: ART Advanced Recognition Technologies, BeInSync, ColorChip, CyOptics, Eldat, Exactium, Foxcom, Hotbar.com, Idanit, MobileAccess Networks, Passave Technologies, Radwin, Schema, Silicon Value, TEVET Process Control Technologies, Verisity

Key Executives:
Michael Federmann, Chairman
Education: BA Economics, Hebrew University
Directorships: Chairman/CEO, Federmann Enterprises; Elbit Systems; Dan Hotels Corp
Aharon Beth-Halachmi, Managing Partner
e-mail: betha@eurofund.co.il
Education: BSEE, Technion Institute of Technology, Israel; MS Computer Science, Naval Postgraduate School, Monterey
Background: Head R&D/Chief of Defense, Israeli Airforce; Director/General, Ministry of Defense; President, TAHAL; President, Federman Enterprises-Industries & Technology
Ron Hiram, Managing Partner
Education: MBA, Columbia University
Background: CEO/VP/Managing Director, Lehman Brothers; Managing Director, Soros Fund Management; TeleSoft Partners
Directorships: Comverse Technology, Ulticom, Systems Management ARTS, Hotbar.com, Tevet Process Control Technologies, ART Advanced Recognition Technologies
Moshe Price, Venture Partner
Education: BSEE, MS Management Sciences, West Coast University
Background: R&D Director, Tadiran Telecommunications
Directorships: Passave Technologies, Colorchip, Eldat Communication

Venture Capital & Private Equity Firms / International Firms

Tzvika Kerner, CFO
e-mail: tzvika@eurofund.co.il
Education: BA Economics/Accountancy, Master degree Business Management, Hebrew University
Background: Federmann Group; Tadiran Communication

2712 EUROMEZZANINE CONSEIL
11 rue Scribe
Paris 75009
France

Phone: 33-153302330 Fax: 33-153302340
web: www.euromezzanine.com

Mission Statement: Actively seeking new projects.
Geographic Preference: European Countries
Fund Size: $38.81 Million
Founded: 2000
Average Investment: $2.75 Million
Minimum Investment: $0.27 Million
Investment Criteria: Mezzanine, Growth/Development Capital, Large Buyout/in, Replacement, Public-to-Private
Industry Group Preference: All Sectors Considered
Portfolio Companies: Alain Afflelou, Autodis, Ccmx, Cnn, Daher Lhotellier, Fianciere Felix, Hoffiges, Laho Equipment, Oberthur Smart Cards

Key Executives:
Thierry Raiff, President
e-mail: louis.vaillant@euromezzanine.com
Education: Institut d'Etudes Politiques
Background: Financiere BFCE, Director, LBO Investment, Ciclad, Director, LBO Investment, Credit Lyonnais, Vice President, Structured Finance
Ajit Jayaratnam, Associate Director
e-mail: guy.fabritius@euromezzanine.com
Education: HEC
Background: BNP Private Equity, Director, LBO & Mezzanine Investment, IRDI Director, Investment, Protex, Vice President, Administration & Finance

2713 EUROPEAN ACQUISITION CAPITAL LIMITED
14 Floral Street
London WC2E 9DH
United Kingdom

Phone: 44-2074208800 Fax: 44-2074208827
e-mail: info@milestone-capital.com

Mission Statement: EAC is a well-established and respected player in the European buy-in, buy-out and development capital sectors.
Geographic Preference: United Kingdom, Austria, Belgium, Denmark, Finland, France, Germany
Fund Size: $473.4 Million
Founded: 1991
Average Investment: Euro 454 Million
Minimum Investment: $5.9 Million
Investment Criteria: Start-up, development, turnaround, MBO, MBI
Industry Group Preference: All Sectors Considered
Portfolio Companies: The Eton Group Ltd, MW Group Ltd, IX Europe PLC, Renaissance BV, 5 à Sec BV, ADP Dental Company Ltd, Groupe d'Emballages Souples

Key Executives:
Bill Robinson, Managing Partner
Philip Conboy, Partner

2714 EUROPEAN FOUNDERS FUND
e-mail: businessplan@europeanfounders.com
web: www.europeanfounders.com

Mission Statement: We are intimately familiar with every stage of establishing a successful company: raising money, getting started, building and growing an organization into a very large business and realizing significant value for all stakeholders through a definition of exit strategies.
Investment Criteria: Early-Stage, Later-Stage
Industry Group Preference: Internet, Software, Wireless, Technology
Portfolio Companies: Facebook, HomeAway, Linkedin, Nasza-Klasa, Sport1

Key Executives:
Alexander Samwer, Partner
Background: Founder, Alando.de; Founder, Jamba! AG; Managing Director, Ebay

2715 EUROPEAN INVESTMENT FUND
15 avenue J.F. Kennedy
L-2968
Luxembourg

Phone: 352-24851 Fax: 352-248581200
e-mail: info@eif.org
web: www.eif.org

Mission Statement: An European institution committed to support the creation, growth and development of Small and Medium-sized Enterprises.
Geographic Preference: Europe
Fund Size: $3.06 Billion
Founded: 1994
Investment Criteria: Early Stage, Development and Expansion, Preferably Technology Oriented
Industry Group Preference: Technology, Information Technology, Biotechnology
Portfolio Companies: E-Capital, Euroventures III, UBF Mittelstandfinanzierungs AG, Genesis Private Equity Fund, SEEFT Ventures

Key Executives:
Dario Scannapieco, Chairman
Richard Pelly, Chief Executive
Francis Carpenter, CEO
Jean-Philippe Burcklen, Head of Division, Venture Capital Operations1
Marjut Santoni, Chief Executive
Dr. Matthias Ummenhofer, Deputy Head of Venture Capital Operations 2

2716 EUROVENTURES CAPITAL
Mártonhegyi út 61/A
Budapest H-1124
Hungary

Phone: 36-13097900 Fax: 36-13194762
e-mail: office@euroventures.hu
web: www.euroventures.hu

Mission Statement: Euroventures is one of the longest-established and leading independent private equity firms in Central Europe.
Geographic Preference: Hungary
Fund Size: $79 Million
Founded: 1989
Average Investment: $3.3 Million
Minimum Investment: $0.6 Million
Investment Criteria: Early-stage, expansion/development, smaller buyouts
Industry Group Preference: Information Technology, Industrial Services, Consumer Services, Media, Logistics, Transportation, Food & Beverage, Automotive, Processing
Portfolio Companies: Alfa, AP Aqua, Avonmore Pásztó, Enigma Software, Euronet

Key Executives:
András Geszti, Founder
Péter Tánczos, Investment Analyst

Venture Capital & Private Equity Firms / International Firms

2717 EVERGREEN VENTURE PARTNERS
25 Habarzel Street
Tel Aviv 69710
Israel

Phone: 972-37108282 Fax: 372-37108210
e-mail: info@evergreen.co.il

Mission Statement: Evergreen was established in 1987 by Jacob Burak as one of Israel's first Venture Capital firms, and has grown into a leader, generating successful exits with tangible rewards for investors and entrepreneurs.

Geographic Preference: Israel
Fund Size: $700 million
Founded: 1987
Investment Criteria: Early-Stage
Industry Group Preference: Communications, Internet, Media, Software, Healthcare
Portfolio Companies: Activiews, Amimon, AniBoom, Aquarius Technologies, CorAssist, eAsic, Flash Networks, Inneractive, Nephera, NiTi Surgical Solutions, Notal Vision, N-Trig, Optimal Test, Peer Medical, PeerApp, Pentalum, Pontis, Precede, Pythagoras, QualiSystems, Siklu, Siverge, Taboola, Varonis

Key Executives:
  Boaz Dinte, General Partner
  e-mail: bdinte@evergreen.co.il
  Background: Corporate Business Development Manager, M-Systems; Senior Consultant, POC
  Directorships: N-Trig, Pontis, Pythagoras Solar, Qualisystems

2718 EXCELSIOR CAPITAL ASIA
Units 1208-1209, Level 12
Core F, Cyberport 3
100 Cyberport Road

Hong Kong

Phone: 852-22309800 Fax: 852-22309898
e-mail: businessplans@excelcapasia.com
web: www.excelsiorcapitalasia.com

Mission Statement: Excelsior Capital Asia is an independent Asian-based direct investment firm which invests in companies throughout the Asian region.

Geographic Preference: China, Hong Kong, Taiwan, Korea
Fund Size: $324 million
Founded: 1998
Average Investment: $15 - $50 million
Investment Criteria: Acquisitions, Growth Capital
Industry Group Preference: Media, Consumer Products, Manufacturing
Portfolio Companies: CKH Food & Health Limited, CJ HelloVision Co., Ganzhou Dingsheng Water Technological Co., Lida Holdings Limited, Quanzhou Jinhua Edible Oil Co., SBM Co.

Other Locations:
  9th Floor, 27 Yeouinaru-ro
  Yeongdeungpo-gu
  Seoul 07321
  South Korea
  Phone: 82-220881288 Fax: 82-220881387

Key Executives:
  Gary Lawrence, Managing Partner
  e-mail: gary.lawrence@excelcapasia.com
  Education: BA, Yale University; MA, University of Oxford; LLB, McGill University
  Background: Managing Director, Merchant Banking Group, Lehman Brothers; Managing Director, Tiger Management; Mergers & Acquisitions Department, Goldman Sachs; Attorney, White & Case
  Directorships: CJ HelloVision, Tony Wear Fashion Co., Sanlih E-Television, Tainan Enterprises, Zest Health Clubs, Downer EDI, DC Chemical, Nation Multimedia Group

  Junghyung Cho, Partner
  e-mail: junghyung.cho@excelcapasia.com
  Education: Seoul National University; MBA, Kellogg School of Management, Northwestern University
  Background: Direct Investment Specialist, Merrill Lynch; Lehman Brothers; Bank of Korea

  Thomas Frick, Partner
  e-mail: thomas.frick@excelcapasia.com
  Education: Kenyon College; CFA
  Background: Founding Director, Odyssey Venture Group; Lehman Brothers

  Michael Kent, Partner
  e-mail: michael.kent@excelcapasia.com
  Education: BA, Australian National University; MBA, University of New South Wales
  Background: Consultant, Peregrine Direct Investments; Finance Director, Adelaide Steamship Company Group
  Directorships: Ganzhou Dingsheng Water Technology Co.

  Seungki Min, Partner
  e-mail: seungki.min@excelcapasia.com
  Education: BA, Business Administration, MA, Financial Engineering, Korea University
  Background: Senior Managing Director, Keystone Private Equity Korea; CEO, HTC Asset Management; Senior Managing Director, Hyundai Securities; Senior Managing Director/CIO, Heungkuk Financial Group

  John Yang, Partner
  e-mail: john.yang@excelcapasia.com
  Education: BA, University of Toronto; CFA
  Background: Investment Director, PrimePartners Asset Management Group; Equity Analyst, Cazenove Asia Limited; PricewaterhouseCoopers; Ernst & Young
  Directorships: Quanzhou Jinhua Edible Oil, China King-Highway, Gazhou Dingsheng Water, Sunrex Technology

  Kihong Ryu, Managing Director
  e-mail: kihong.ryu@excelcapasia.com
  Education: BA, Business Administration, Yonsei University
  Background: Managing Director, Keystone Private Equity Korea; Hyundai Securities; Heungkuk Life Insurance

  Albert Chung, Principal
  e-mail: albert.chung@excelcapasia.com
  Education: BS, Computer Engineering, National Chiao Tung University; MBA, National Central University
  Background: Senior Manager, Corporate Finance Advisory Group, KPMG

  Dicken Chiu, Principal
  e-mail: dicken.chiu@excelcapasia.com
  Education: Imperial College of Science, Technology and Medicine, London
  Background: Business Development Manager, Dairy Farm; Manager, Ernst & Young; MTR Corporation

  James Yu, Senior Associate
  e-mail: james.yu@excelcapasia.com
  Education: BS, Economics, Duke University; MS, Finance, Imperial College of Science, Technology and Medicine, London; CFA
  Background: Senior Associate, Corporate Financial Advisory Group, Deloitte & Touche

2719 EXPIBEL BV
8C Arsenalsgatan
Stockholm 103 32
Sweden

Phone: 46-86142000 Fax: 46-86142150
e-mail: Stefan.Stern@investorab.com
web: www.investorab.com

Mission Statement: Investor contributes to the development of its holdings and focuses on the special circumstances and potential of each individual holding in order to contribute to healthy long-term value of

Geographic Preference: Northern Europe, USA, Asia
Fund Size: $1.8 Billion

Venture Capital & Private Equity Firms / International Firms

Founded: 1916
Average Investment: $26.5 Million
Minimum Investment: $3 Million
Investment Criteria: Expansion and Development Capital
Industry Group Preference: Technology, Engineering, Healthcare, Financial Services
Portfolio Companies: Aerocrine, Affibody, Amkor Technology, Inc, Apollo International, Applied Sensor, Asia Renal Care Ltd, Atrica Axcan Pharma, AxioMed, Biotage, BMI Asia Inc, Cameron Health, Carmel Pharma, Cavidi Tech AB, Cellectricon, CHF Solutions, Endo Vasix, Epigenesis

Key Executives:
 Stefan Stern, Head of Corp. Relations and Communications
 Education: M.Sc. in Engineering(Royal Institute of Technology, Stockholm), M.B.A.(INSEAD)
 Magnus Dalhammar, Head of Investor Relations

2720 EXPLORADOR CAPITAL MANAGEMENT
Rua Fidencio Ramos 101
Suite 61
Villa Olimpia
Sao Paulo 04551-010
Brazil

Phone: 55-11-4064-5300
e-mail: contact@explorador.net
web: www.explorador.net

Mission Statement: Our investment objective is to preserve capital under different market environments, while seeking to achieve above average returns on a risk-adjusted basis.

Geographic Preference: Latin America
Fund Size: $60 million
Founded: 1995
Average Investment: $4 million
Minimum Investment: $500,000

Key Executives:
 Andrew H Cummins, President & CIO
 e-mail: andy@explorador.net
 Education: MBA, Corporate Strategy/Finance, Harvard Business School; BS, University of California, LA
 Background: Management, Emerging Markets Management; JMB Realty Corporation
 Fernando Jasnis, Portfolio Manager
 Education: Industrial Engineering Degree, Instituto Tecnologico de Buenos Aires (ITBA); MBA, University of California, Berkeley
 Background: Citigroup, Buenos Aires
 Daniel Delabio, Portfolio Manger
 Education: Bachelor's Degree, Business Administration, FGV-Brazil
 Background: Dimaio Ahmad Capital

2721 FENNO MANAGEMENT OY
Toppelundintie 5 B 10
Espoo 2170
Finland

Phone: 358-400706072

Mission Statement: Specializing in generating value growth in the mid size companies. Fenno Management typically seeks acquisition and investment cases where there is need for strategic re-thinking, re-positioning, add on acquisitions or other clear growth strategies.

Fund Size: EUR 83 million
Average Investment: EUR 1 Million - 25 million
Investment Criteria: Re-positioning, add on acquisitions or other clear growth strategies.

Key Executives:
 Aaro Cantell, Managing Partner

2722 FERD CAPITAL
Strandveien 50
PO Box 34
Lysaker N-1324
Norway

Phone: 47-67-10-80-00 Fax: 47-67-10-80-01
e-mail: post@ferd.no
web: www.ferd.no

Mission Statement: Ferd is a family-owned Norwegian industrial and financial group that is an active and long-term owner of strong companies with international potential and carries out financial activities through investments in a broad range of asset classes. Ferd Capital is an active and long-term investor in privately held and listed companies. This means that Ferd Capital assesses when to invest or sell its investments, as well as working actively with the companies in which it invests for the duration of its ownership in order to ensure the best possible value creation. Ferd Capital carries out its role as an active investor through collaboration with the management of its portfolio companies.

Geographic Preference: Nordic Countries
Fund Size: NOK 7 billion
Average Investment: NOK 100-1, 000 million
Investment Criteria: Development Stage, Expansion Stage
Portfolio Companies: Aibel, Elopak, Interwell, Mestergruppen, Servi Group, Swix Sport, Telecomputing, Arkex, CFEngine, Eniram, Napatech, Vensafe, Wimp

Key Executives:
 Peter Sunde, Investment Director/Co-Head
 67-10-80-69
 e-mail: jps@ferd.no
 Education: MSc, Norwegian School of Management; CFA
 Background: Senior Vice President, Telenor ASA; Vice President, Saga Petroleum
 Directorships: TeleComputing, Mestergruppen
 Morten Borge, Investment Director/Co-Head
 67-10-80-86
 e-mail: mb@ferd.no
 Education: MSc, Norwegian School of Management; CPA
 Background: CFO, Interwell; Audit & Transactions, PricewaterhouseCoopers
 Directorships: Aibel, Interwell, Servi Group, Gladiator GT
 Trond Solberg, Investment Director/Co-Head
 67-10-80-39
 e-mail: ts@ferd.no
 Education: MSc, Norwegian School of Management; CEFA
 Background: Project Leader, Norway Post; Analyst, Ferd Invest; Analyst, Accenture
 Directorships: Elopak, Swix

2723 FERRANTI LIMITED
43 Rosary Gardens
London SW7 4NQ
United Kingdom

Phone: 44-02078351325 Fax: 44-02072448387
e-mail: mike@ferranti.com
web: www.ferranti.com

Mission Statement: Provides firms with the business support and investment

Geographic Preference: United Kingdom, USA
Fund Size: $7.08 Million
Founded: 1982
Average Investment: $ 0.8 Million
Minimum Investment: $0.04 Million
Investment Criteria: Seed, Start-up, Other early stage, Expansion and Development, Bridge finance, Refinancing bank debt, Secondary purchase/replacement capital, Rescue/turnaround, MBO, MBI
Industry Group Preference: Communications, Information Technology, Energy, Internet Technology, Industrial Equipment, Electronic Technology, Computer Hardware &

Software, Engineering, Pharmaceuticals, Financial Services, Industrial Services
Portfolio Companies: Ziani's, Post Impressions, Update Software, Plasmanet, Marlin, SSI, Carlton Corporate Finance, Chelford Group PLC
Key Executives:
  Howard Flight, Chairman
  e-mail: jane.weyman@ferranti.co.uk
  Background: over twenty years experience in banking and has worked for N.M. Rothschild and NatWest Bank in establishing a new merchant bank - Rothschild Intercontinental, which was later acquired by American Express.Mrs Weyman also worked for Banque de Paris et des P
  Directorships: finance controller
  Adrian De Ferranti, Managing Director
  e-mail: adrian@ferranti.co.uk
  Education: Degree in Engineering
  Background: Chairman of Technology and a Treasurer of the Conservative Party from 1991 to 2004., experience spans all aspects of corporate finance from venture capital and private equity through to M&A and public floatations.
  Michael Campbell, Director
  e-mail: mike.campbell@ferranti.co.uk
  Education: Degree in Electronic Engineering and an MBA.
  Background: Over fifteen years of international business consulting experience in the technology sector.
  Directorships: He is also a regular guest lecturer at Warwick University.

2724 FIDELITY GROWTH PARTNERS ASIA
Unit 2207, 22nd Floor, Tower 2
China Central Plaza
No. 79 Jianguo Road, Chaoyang District
Beijing 100025
China

Phone: 86-1065989336 **Fax:** 86-1065989335
e-mail: fgpa@fil.com

Mission Statement: Fidelity Growth Partners Asia (previously named Fidelity Asia Ventures) is the venture capital and private equity arm of Fidelity focused on investing in Greater China. We help companies accelerate growth by providing them with Fidelity's proprietary capital, expertise and access to global resources.
Geographic Preference: Asia
Average Investment: $5 - $30 million
Investment Criteria: Early-Stage, Growth-Stage
Industry Group Preference: Technology, Media, Telecommunications, Healthcare, Education, Logistics, Financial Services, Consumer Products
Portfolio Companies: Alibaba, Asianinfo, CDP, Crystal CG, Datou, Dianji, Hurray, Huaxun Technology, iSoftstone, Linktone, MFG.com, Mineloader, Netqin, UiTV, Wisers, Xunlei, Asia Renal Care, Hile Bio-pharma, Pharmanex, NovaMed, TCT, Wuxi AppTec
Key Executives:
  Daniel Auerbach, Managing Partner/Senior Managing Director
  Education: BA, Dartmouth College; MBA, Harvard Business School
  Background: Partner, Arral & Partners Ltd; Analyst, Fidelity Investments
  Directorships: Dianji Technology Holdings, MFG, CDP

2725 FIDELITY GROWTH PARTNERS EUROPE
25 Cannon Street
London EC4M 5TA
United Kingdom

Phone: 011-442070745610

Mission Statement: A venture capital firm that invests where it can make a difference, creating real, long term value.
Geographic Preference: Europe
Founded: 1969
Industry Group Preference: Technology, Software, Cloud Computing, Data Services, Energy Efficiency, Healthcare Information Technology
Portfolio Companies: Asset Control, Curam Software, Neverfail, Newbay, QUMAS, Seatwave,
Key Executives:
  Simon Clark, Managing Partner
  Education: MA, Politics, Philosophy & Economics, Wadham College, Oxford
  Background: Chief Financial Officer & General Manager, International, TheStreet.com; Reuters; Chartered Accountant, Pricewaterhouse
  Davor Hebel, Partner
  Education: BS, Angelo State University; MS, Information Systems Management, Carnegie Mellon University; MBA, Harvard Business School
  Background: Co-Founder, Experia; McKinsey & Company
  Florian Oettinger, Senior Associate
  Education: BA, Jurisprudence, St Edmund Hall, Oxford
  Background: Partner, DFJEspirit
  Directorships: FirstMe Limited

2726 FINADVANCE
Le Derby, 570, avenue du Club Hippique
Aix eu Provence 13090
France

Phone: 33-0442529130 **Fax:** 33-0442529139

Mission Statement: Private equity funds management.
Geographic Preference: France
Fund Size: $26 Million
Founded: 1988
Average Investment: $1.83 Million
Investment Criteria: Takes minority holding in new or recently created companies.
Industry Group Preference: Electronic Technology, Telecommunications, Software
Portfolio Companies: Metrix Systems, SEA, Infobjects, VRTV Studios

2727 FINAM GLOBAL
Nastasinsky Pereulok, 7, Bld. 2
Moscow 127006
Russia

Phone: 7-495-796-9388
e-mail: invest@finamglobal.com

Mission Statement: FINAM Global creates Private Equity funds and makes Direct Investments focused on growth capital and buy-outs in the global TMT sector. FINAM Global operates within FINAM Group, a leading Russian brokerage and asset management firm. FINAM Global is one of the largest and most successful investment funds in the TMT sector in Russia.
Geographic Preference: Russia
Average Investment: $1 - $50 million
Industry Group Preference: Technology
Portfolio Companies: Badoo, Shape.AG, Moneymail, MGid

2728 FINANCE WALES
Oakleigh House
Park Place
Cardiff CF10 3DQ
Wales

Phone: 0800-5874140 **Fax:** 029-20338101
e-mail: info@financewales.co.uk
web: www.financewales.com

Venture Capital & Private Equity Firms / International Firms

Mission Statement: Finance Wales makes commercial investments in Wales-based businesses with the potential to grow.
Geographic Preference: Wales
Founded: 2009
Average Investment: £50,000 - 1 million
Investment Criteria: Seed-Stage, Growth-Stage
Industry Group Preference: Technology
Portfolio Companies: Mesura, Asalus, Cymtec, Haemair, AssayMetrics, Q Chip, Calon Cardio, GeoVS, Acutas Medical, Orthos
Key Executives:
  Sian Lloyd Jones, Chief Executive
  Education: Somerville College
  Background: Chief Executive, Development Board for Rural Wales

2729 FINANCIERE DE BRIENNE FCPR
48 rue de Lisbonne
Paris 75008
France

Phone: 01 58 56 25 62 Fax: 01 58 56 25 63
web: www.bpifrance.fr

Mission Statement: Actively seeking new investments, specializing in aeronautics and defense industries
Geographic Preference: France
Fund Size: $122 Million
Founded: 1993
Minimum Investment: $3.6 Million
Investment Criteria: Early-stage, Expansion, Development
Industry Group Preference: Aerospace, Defense and Government, Computer Related, Software, Electronic Technology, Industrial Equipment
Key Executives:
  Yves Michot, Chairman & managing Director
  Jean-Pierre Rochard, Chairman & managing Director

2730 FINLOMBARDA SpA
2 Piazza Belgioso
Milan 20121
Italy

Phone: 39-027-60441 Fax: 39-027-80819
web: www.finlombarda.it/

Mission Statement: Finlombarda operates in the Region of Lombardy's local and economic planning to implement regional and local economic and social development.
Geographic Preference: Europe
Founded: 1971
Investment Criteria: Startup, Early-Stage, Expansion, Development, Bridge
Industry Group Preference: Consumer Services, Energy, Manufacturing, Industrial Equipment, Consumer Products
Key Executives:
  Marisa Bedoni, President

2731 FINNISH INDUSTRY INVESTMENT LIMITED
Mannerheimintie 14 A (9th floor)
PO Box 685
Helsinki 00101
Finland

Phone: 358-96803680 Fax: 358-96121680
e-mail: juha.marjosola@industryinvestment.com
web: www.industryinvestment.com

Mission Statement: Actively seeking new investments.
Geographic Preference: Finland
Fund Size: $395 Million
Founded: 1995
Average Investment: $100 million
Investment Criteria: Seed and growth stage enterprises together with private investors.
Industry Group Preference: All Sectors Considered
Portfolio Companies: MB Equity Fund Ky, Forenvia Venture I Ky, Telecomia Venture I Ky, Profita Fund I Ky, Fenno Rahasto Ky, MB Equity Fund II Ky, Wedeco Seed Fund I Ky Kb , Jutron Oy
Key Executives:
  Juha Marjosola, President & CEO
  e-mail: juha.marjosola@industryinvestment.com
  Anne Tamminen, Executive Assistant

2732 FINNVERA PLC
8 Etelesplanadi
PO Box 1010
Helsinki 00130
Finland

Phone: 358-2046011 Fax: 358-204607220
web: www.finnvera.fi

Mission Statement: Specialised financing company owned by the State of Finland, Finnvera plc provides services to supplement the Finnish financial market. Finnvera's task is to promote the development of enterprise, regions and the exports of Finnish companies.
Geographic Preference: Finland, Europe
Fund Size: $1.2 Million
Founded: 1999
Minimum Investment: $0.2 Million
Investment Criteria: Early Stage, Expansion and Development Capital, Privatisation, Start-up Capital, Buyout and Buyin
Industry Group Preference: Communications, Biotechnology
Key Executives:
  Pauli Heikkilä, Chief Executive Officer
  e-mail: kalle.korhonen@finnvera.fi
  Education: M.Sc. (Tech.)
  Background: Finnish Industry Investment Ltd(Board member), SME Foundation(Board member)
  Mr Topi Vesteri, Executive Vice President, Export Financing
  e-mail: Pekka.Laajanen@finnvera.fi
  Education: L.L.M.
  Background: Fide Ltd (Vice Chairman), Ministry of Finance (Governmental Counsellor, Director of Legislative Affairs)

2733 FIR CAPITAL PARTNERS
Praca Carlos Chagas, 49
7 Andar
ZIP: 30170-020
Belo Horizonte MG
Brazil

Phone: 55 31 3074 0020 Fax: 55 31 3074 0015
web: www.fircapital.com

Mission Statement: Achieve extraordinary profits in partnership with exceptional entrepreneurs and companies, following the Principle for Responsible Investment.
Geographic Preference: Brazil
Founded: 1999
Investment Criteria: Emerging
Portfolio Companies: Akwan, Biobras, Minar
  Andre Capistrano Emrich

2734 FIRST CORPORATE PTY LIMITED
Level 9, 105 St. George Terrace
Perth 6000
Australia

Phone: 61-892260326 Fax: 61-892260327
web: www.firstgroup.com.au

Mission Statement: Corporate advisory group specializing in transitioning private companies to public listed status. Also coordinates private equity funding for growth orientated companies in Asia / Pacific.
Geographic Preference: Asia Pacific, Australia
Founded: 1996
Investment Criteria: Mezzanine/pre-IPO stage projects, SME
Key Executives:
  Jeffrey C Broun, Director
  e-mail: jbroun@firstgroup.com.au
  Education: CA, ACA, BA
  Background: ERG Limited, Mayne Nickless, Guardian Royal Exchange Limited
  Kent B Burwash, Director
  e-mail: mslater@firstgroup.com.au
  Education: Fellow of the Institute of Chartered Accountants in Australia
  Background: Chartered Accountant, M&A, Governance
  Directorships: ERG Limited, Mayne Nickless, Guardian Royal Exchange Limited

2735 FIRST INVESTMENT CORPORATION LIMITED
Level 20. 300 Queen Street.
Brisbane City 2067
Australia
Phone: 07-30235089 Fax: 61-284488101
e-mail: peter.janssen@corporatefirst.com.au

Mission Statement: Provides investment banking and fund management services.

2736 FIRST ISRAEL MEZZANINE INVESTORS LIMITED
Electra Tower
98 Yigal Alon St
Tel Aviv 67891
Israel
Phone: 972-35652244 Fax: 972-35652245
e-mail: sec@fimi.co.il
web: www.fimi.co.il

Mission Statement: Actively seeking new investments.
Geographic Preference: Israel
Fund Size: $215 Million
Founded: 1996
Investment Criteria: Leveraged Buy-Outs (LBOs), Management Buy-Outs (MBOs), Growth Capital Financing
Industry Group Preference: Computer Hardware & Software, Consumer Services, Communications, Automotive, Plastics, Textiles, Metals, Water, Food & Beverage, Electronic Technology
Portfolio Companies: Tadir-Gan, Tadiran Com Ltd., Tedea, Mer Group, Elco-Brandt Group, Lipman, R.H. Electronics, Medtechnica, Formula Systems, Ginegar Plastic Products Ltd, TAT Technologies Ltd.
Key Executives:
  Ishay Davidi, Founder & Chief Executive Officer
  e-mail: ishay@fimi.co.il
  Background: Tikvah Fund (CEO)
  Gillon Beck, Senior Partner

2737 FLANDERS' FOREIGN INVESTMENT OFFICE
Koning Albert-II laan 37
Brussels 1030
Belgium
Phone: 32-25048871 Fax: 32-25048870
e-mail: invest@fitagency.be
web: www.investinflanders.be

Mission Statement: Provides confidential advice free of charge on all aspects of investing in the Flanders region of Belgium.
Geographic Preference: Flanders
Fund Size: $136 Million
Founded: 2005
Industry Group Preference: Automotive, Information Technology, Life Sciences, Logistics, Chemicals, Food & Beverage, Electronic Technology, Telecommunications, Transportation
Key Executives:
  Lucas Huybrechts, Account Manager
  e-mail: invest@fitagency.be
  Education: Bachelor's degree in business economics, Master's degree in law
  Background: Financial & Administrative Director(Commercial Advice center; Ghent)
  Rita Saeys, Director Business Development

2738 FONDINVEST CAPITAL
33 rue de La Baume
Paris 75008
France
Phone: 33-158364800 Fax: 33-1-5836-4828
e-mail: mailbox@fondinvest.com
web: www.fondinvest.com

Mission Statement: Invests in new funds in Europe; acquires secondary interests in funds worldwide; has invested in over 210 private equity funds.
Geographic Preference: USA, Europe, Asia
Founded: 1994
Key Executives:
  Charles Soulignac, Managing Partner
  33-1-5836-4800
  e-mail: c.soulignac@fondinvest.com
  Education: Engineer (INSA), MBA (CPA; Paris)
  Background: CDC Participations, BRED, Maynard, ex EVCA Board of Directors
  Emmanuel Roubinowitz, Partner
  Catherine Lewis La Torre, Partner

2739 FORBION CAPITAL PARTNERS
Goolmeer 2-35
DC Naarden 1411
Netherlands
Phone: 31-0-35-699-3000 Fax: 31-0-35-699-3001
e-mail: info@forbion.com
web: www.forbion.com

Mission Statement: At Forbion Capital Partners we invest in Life Sciences and Biomedical Technology companies developing world-class drugs and technologies, with a clear focus on product development. The Forbion team is specialized in the evaluation of late stage preclinical / early stage clinical development programs. We focus on companies that have innovative technologies and drug development programs with unique advantages over current treatments. Furthermore, we invest in medical device companies with a special focus on interventional devices in cardiology, gastroenterology and pulmonology that are close to market approval.
Fund Size: 450 million euro
Founded: 2006
Investment Criteria: Early-Stage
Industry Group Preference: Life Sciences, Biotechnology, Medical Devices
Portfolio Companies: Abiomed, ACADIA Pharmaceuticals, Inc., Accelerated Technologies, Acorda Therapeutics, Alantos Pharmaceuticals, Allecra Therapeutics, Amakem, Am-Pharma, Amt, Ardana, Argen-X, Argos Therapeutics, Ario Pharma, Bioceros, Biovex, Bluebird Bio, Borean Pharma, Cardoz, Cell Based Delivery, Cellnovo, Circulite, Crucell, Curetis, Cytheris, Dezima Pharma, Exosome Diagnostics, Flowmedica, Fovea, Galapagos, Gho Holding, Gicare Pharma, Glycart, Hookipa Biotech, Impella

Venture Capital & Private Equity Firms / International Firms

Cardiosystems, Insmed, Jari Pharmaceuticals, Mitralign, Ness, Neutec Pharma, Novogi, Oxyrane, Pangenetics, Pathway Medical Technologies, Pieris, Pneumrx, Promedior, Pulmagen Therapeutics, Rhein Biotech, Santaris Pharma, Transave, Unique, X-Cell Medical, Xention

Other Locations:
Maximillanstrasse 36
Munchen 80539
Germany
Phone: 49-89-41-6161-950 **Fax:** 49-89-41-6161-959

Key Executives:
G-J Mulder MD, General Partner
e-mail: greet-jan.mulder@forbion.com
Education: MD, University of Utrecht
Background: ABN AMRO Capital Life Sciences; Resident, Obstetrics & Cynecology, University Medical Center, Utrecht
Directorships: Exosome Diagnostics, Promedior, Ario Pharma
Sander Slootweg, Managing Partner
e-mail: sander.slootweg@forbion.com
Education: Business & Financial Economics, Free University of Amsterdam; Business Administration, Nijenrode University
Background: Co-Founder, ABN AMRO Capital Life Sciences
Directorships: Dezima Pharma, Xention Discovery, Ario Pharma, Pulmagen Therapeutics, Oxyrane, UniQure
Holger Reighinger, General Partner
e-mail: holger.reighinger@forbion.com
Education: PhD, Biochemistry, Max-Planck Institute of Biophyciscs; BS, Molecular Biology, University of Heidelberg & University of Munich
Background: Product Development, Biometra; Investment Manager, Technologieholding VC; Director, 3i Group
Directorships: Curetis, Allecra Therapeutics

2740 FORESIGHT VENTURE PARTNERS
The Shard
32 London Bridge Street
London SE1 6PQ
United Kingdom
Phone: +44 (0) 20 3667 8100
e-mail: info@foresightgroup.eu
web: www.foresightgroup.eu

Mission Statement: Foresight strives to generate increasing dividends and capital appreciation for its investors over the long term.

Industry Group Preference: Solar Infrastructure, Biomass, Energy
Portfolio Companies: Birmingham BioPower, Wharfedale Hospital, Stobhill Hosptial, Lochgilphead Hospital, Bishop Auckland Hospital, Staffordshire Schools, Sandwell Schools, Stirling Schools, Drumglass High School

2741 FORMULA VENTURES LIMITED Formula Group
11 Galgalei Haplada, PO Box 2062
Herzliya 46120
Israel
Phone: 972-99601800 **Fax:** 972-99601818
web: www.formulaventures.com

Mission Statement: Formula Ventures was founded as the successor fund for Argotec, a Formula Group company. Formula Ventures manages two venture funds – FV-I and FV-II.

Geographic Preference: Israel
Founded: 1998
Investment Criteria: Seed-stage ventures, First round funding, Later stage investments.
Industry Group Preference: Data Communications, Telecommunications, Internet Technology, Enterprise Services, Storage, Semiconductors, Media, Infrastructure, Software
Portfolio Companies: Civcom Inc., Commil Ltd., Composit Ltd., Radiotel Ltd., Radlan Ltd., Radview Software Ltd., Demantra Ltd., Maincontrol, Earnix, Identify, Magink, Nanomagnetics Ltd., Transtech control, Phonetic Systems Ltd.

Key Executives:
Shai Beilis, Managing Partner
e-mail: shai@formulaventures.com
Education: B.Sc. In Mathematics and Economics(Hebrew University), M.Sc. in Computer Science (Weizmann Institute of Science in Rehovot)
Background: Argotec Ltd(CEO), Crystal Systems Solutions(Chairman), Wiztec Solutions(Chairman), Clal Computers and Technology (CEO), Yael Software and Services Ltd(CEO)
Directorships: Chairman
Nir Linchevski, Partner

2742 FORUM TECHNOLOGIES VENTURE CAPITAL COMPANY Forum Group
34 Jerusalem St.
Raanana 43501
Israel
Phone: 972-97754646 **Fax:** 972-97601551

Mission Statement: Forum Technologies is designed to offer investors a unique opportunity to benefit from the success of Israeli Start-ups in the HighTechnology sector.

Geographic Preference: Israel
Founded: 1993
Investment Criteria: Startup Companies
Industry Group Preference: High Technology, Cable
Portfolio Companies: Manov, Shacham, ContentWise, VersaMed

Key Executives:
Amit Segal, President
e-mail: amir@forum-group.com
Education: BA in Economics, MBA in Finance and Management of Financial Institutions(Tel-Aviv University)
Background: Dun & Bradstreet(Senior Analyst), The Israel General Bank(Head of Marketing and International Relations), The Maritime Bank of Israel Ltd(Managing Director & CEO),
Ami Segal, President

2743 FORWARD PARTNERS
Floor 2, Centro 3
19 Mandela Street
Camden NW1 0DU
England
web: www.forwardpartners.com

Mission Statement: We blend investment with access to a specialist team of experts who work full time with entrepreneurs and founders.

Portfolio Companies: Appear[Here], BlikBook, Captalis, Driftrock, Hailo, Hubbub, Loyalty Bay, Makers Academy, Somo, Squawka, Top10, Unbound, Wool And The Gang, Zopa

Key Executives:
Carlos Vilhena, Senior Developer
Chris O'Sullivan, Senior Developer
Dharmesh Raithatha, Head of Product
Ed Davidson, Strategic Marketer
Emma Gresko, Operations Manager
Emma Patricios, Senior Front-End Developer

2744 FOUNDATION CAPITAL LIMITED
Minshull House, 67 Wellington Road North
Stockport SK4 2LP
United Kingdom

e-mail: info@foundation-capital.com

Mission Statement: Operates an open ended fund which aims to support the commercialisation of exceptional entrepreneurial business ideas in return for an equity stake.

Geographic Preference: United Kingdom, Scandinavia
Average Investment: £20K and £100k
Investment Criteria: Early to growth stage investments, start-up capital and/or sales marketing expansion capital
Industry Group Preference: Consumer Products, Wholesale, Imports/Exports, Hotels, Consumer Services, Retailing, Construction

Key Executives:
Kai Rothoff Svendsen, Board Director & Chairman
Background: Tradifood A/S, H.I.K Football APS(Board Director), AV Center CPH. A/S; ALFA HOTEL Holding (France)- (Board Director)

2745 FOUR SEASONS VENTURE CAPITAL
Vika Atrium/Munkedamsveien 45F
Munkedamsveien 45F
PO Box 1216 Vika
Oslo NO-0250
Norway

Phone: 47-24137000 Fax: 47-24137001
web: www.verdanecapital.com

Mission Statement: Actively seeking new investments. Invests in the primary venture capital market as well as the secondary direct market. Entrepreneurs are assisted in building outstanding companies through a wealth of investment experience and a global network. Four Seasons Venture currently has six active funds.

Geographic Preference: Sweden, Norway, Finland
Fund Size: $415 Million
Founded: 1985
Average Investment: $3 Million
Investment Criteria: All Stages
Industry Group Preference: All Sectors Considered
Portfolio Companies: Abeo, Active 24 ASA, Advertising.com, Affitech, Ahhaaa!, AquaGen, Axlon International, Banqsoft, Biosensor, Biotec Pharmacon, Bozoka.com Sweden, Brendmoe & Kirkestuen, Chipcon, Coding Technologies, Colibria, Conoptica, DebiTech, Direct 2 Internet, Dynapel Systems, Elprint, Evolving Systems, Exie AS, Fact Based Communication Ltd, Fjord Marin, Genomar, Global Name Registry, Ikivo, Keytouch Corporation, Maritech International, Markland Technologies, Metronor, Minox Technology, Mobilaris, Nordisk Terapi, Odim, Omnia, Optinel Systems, PortWise, Prenax Global, Procaptura, Read ASA, ResLab Holding, Reslink, Scali, Scanbio, Scanrope, Scanvacc, Seabed Geophysical, Sicom, Spring Consulting, talk2me, Telitas US, Tertio Service Management Systems, Tordivel, TradeDoubler, Troux Technologies, TwoWay Media, Vector International, Viz Risk Management, Voss of Norway

Key Executives:
Bjarne K. Lie, Co-Founder & COO
Education: Masters of Economics, BI-Norwegian School of Management; MBA, INSEAD
Background: McKinsey & Company; Sales/Support Manager, Guru Software
Birger Nergaard, Founder
Education: BS Finance, St. John's University; MBA, INSEAD
Background: Senior Associate, Braxton Associates; Management Consultant, Deloitte Consulting

2746 FOURIERTRANSFORM
Sveavagen 17, 10th Floor
Stockholm SE-111 57
Sweden

Phone: 46-841040600 Fax: 46-8-410-40-640
web: www.fouriertransform.se

Mission Statement: Fouriertransform is a state-owned venture capital company tasked with strengthening the Swedish automotive cluster's international competitiveness on a commercial basis. The mission includes taking an active role as an owner in order to help to ensure the structured and successful commercialization and continued growth of the portfolio companies. Fouriertransform contributes expertise by placing qualified representatives on the boards of all the companies in which it holds an interest.

Geographic Preference: Sweden
Fund Size: SEK 3 billion
Industry Group Preference: Automotive, Transportation
Portfolio Companies: Alelion Batteries, Applied Nano Surfaces Sweden, ArcCore, CeDe Group, EELCEE, El-Forest, Jobro Platkomponenter, LeanNova Engineering, Max Truck, Norstel, Pelagicore, Powercell Sweden, Smart Eye, TitanX, Vicura

Key Executives:
Per Nordberg, CEO
e-mail: per.nordberg@fouriertransform.se

2747 FRANKLIN TEMPLETON INVESTMENT
Indiabulls Finance Centre, Tower 2, 12th Floo
Elphinstone Road
Mumbai 400013
India

Phone: 91-56325820 Fax: 91-22810923
Toll-Free: 1800-4254255
e-mail: service@templeton.com
web: www.franklintempletonindia.com

Mission Statement: Actively seeking new investments.

Geographic Preference: India
Fund Size: $3.62 Billion
Founded: 1947
Investment Criteria: Equity, Second Stage, Expansion

Key Executives:
Jennifer J. Bolt, Executive Vice President - Operations & Technology
Vijay C. Advani, Executive Vice President - Global Advisor Services

2748 FRESHWATER VENTURE PARTNERS
Laan van Niftarlake 54
Utrecht Tienhoven 3612 BT
Netherlands

Phone: 31-653935800 Fax: 31-346282613

Mission Statement: Established as a venture capital firm focused on software. It's goal is to provide startups with private equity financing, support them in developing winning visions and strategies and help them execute with operational excellence.

Minimum Investment: $200,000
Investment Criteria: Early Stage, Start-up
Industry Group Preference: Computer Hardware & Software, Internet Technology

2749 FRIULIA SpA
Via Locchi 19
Trieste 34123
Italy

Phone: 39-04031971 Fax: 39-040-3197400
e-mail: mail@friulia.it
web: www.friulia.it

Venture Capital & Private Equity Firms / International Firms

Mission Statement: Developing the economy of the Friulia-Venezia Giulia region in Northeastern Italy.
Fund Size: $278 Million
Founded: 1967
Average Investment: $950,000
Minimum Investment: $60, 000
Industry Group Preference: Chemicals, Industrial Products, Electronic Technology, Retailing, Distribution
Key Executives:
  Sara Spogliarich, General Secretariat and Communication
  e-mail: augusto.antonucci@friulia.it
  Daniela Ziraldo, Human Resources
  e-mail: federico.marescotti@friulia.it
  Dear Mark, Finance and Control Manager
  e-mail: michele.degrassi@friulia.it

2750 FRONTLINE VENTURES
17 Rosebery Ave.
London EC1R4SP
United Kingdom

e-mail: info@frontline.vc
web: www.frontline.vc

Mission Statement: Frontline Ventures invest in ambitious seed-stage B2B companies in Europe. We are a pioneering early stage venture capital firm, believing in ideas, and investing in passion. We offer capital, mentorship when needed and a network of people that will assist the Founder in building their company. We spend time working with companies to win reference customers, make key hires, and develop the strategy for gaining access to commercial partners. With our backing, Founders can focus on customer discovery and development from the outset and get to proof of performance within months, not years.
Geographic Preference: Europe
Fund Size: Fund I 50m Euro (2013); Fund II 60m Euro (2016)
Founded: 2012
Average Investment: 200k - 1m Euro
Minimum Investment: 200k Euro
Investment Criteria: Pre-Seed, Seed
Industry Group Preference: Business to Business, Enterprise, Machine Learning
Portfolio Companies: BrightFlag, Currencyfair, James, Logentrics, Qstream, Signal AI, Verve
Other Locations:
  26-28 Lombard St. E
  Dublin 2
  Ireland
Key Executives:
  Shay Garvey, Partner
  Education: BSc, University College Dublin; MEng, University of New Brunswick; MBA, Harvard Business School
  Directorships: Qstream, Roomex, Linked Finance, AQMetrics, TravelNest, Finbourne
  Will Prendergast, Partner
  Education: Chemical Engineering Degree, University College Dublin
  Background: Partner, NCB Venture Capital; Consultant, Accenture UK
  William McQuillan, Partner
  Background: Co-Founder and CEO, Osmoda.com; Founding Employee, Ondra Partner

2751 FSE GROUP
Riverside House, 4 Meadows Business Park
Station Approach
Blackwater
Camberley, Surrey GU17 9AB
United Kingdom

Phone: 01276-608510 Fax: 02176-608539
e-mail: fundingenquiries@thefsegroup.com
web: www.thefesgroup.com

Mission Statement: The FSE Group invests in small and medium-sized enterprises (SMEs) that have the potential for significant growth. We understand the funding challenges facing emerging and mid-sized companies looking to expand, and we provide funds and support, including mentors where appropriate, to help bridge the funding gap. A newer area of focus is that of Social Impact Funding, where we are working alongside experienced partners to finance social enterprises and communities.
Geographic Preference: United Kingdom
Investment Criteria: Small & Mediuim Enterprises
Industry Group Preference: Social Enterprises, Renewable Energy
Portfolio Companies: Bowman Power Group, BritishEco, Datasift, DevelopIP, Duvas Technologies, Imaginatik Limited, Omega Ingredients, ParcelGenie, Plum Baby, Quotient Diagnostics, Redd & Whyte, Solution Builders Limited, Stokes Sauces, TeraView Limited, TBD Fusion, ToxiMet, UltraSoc Technologies, VerdEng Connectors
Key Executives:
  Robert Spencer, Chairman
  Background: Founder, Regional Venture Capital Funds
  Kevan Jones, CEO
  01276-608527
  e-mail: kevan.jones@thefsegroup.com
  Education: MBA, Warwick Business School
  Background: Group Sales & Marketing Director, Ultimate Finance Group
  Directorships: NatWest

2752 FUEL CAPITAL
Unit 721
Cyberport 1
100 Cyberport Road

Hong Kong

e-mail: inquiry@fuelcapitalpartners.com
web: www.fuelcapitalpartners.com

Mission Statement: Founded in 2009 by industry veterans. Collectively, the founding team has over 40 collective years of leading investments at top-tier, China-focused venture capital and private equity funds, including Intel Capital, Walden International, AIG, and First Eastern, invested and managed a portfolio of approximately US$1 billion and have over 70 exits , including more than 40 IPOs in various stock exchanges around the world.
Geographic Preference: China
Founded: 2009
Investment Criteria: Early-Growth Stage
Industry Group Preference: Clean Technology, Healthcare, Environment
Portfolio Companies: United Imaging Healthcare, DSM Green Power, PowerGenix, Waveguider Optical Telecom Technology, ZBest Technology Company
Other Locations:
  Suite 36B
  118 Zihun Road
  Shanghai 200051
  China

  Suite 1218-1219, Caohu Building
  1 Yongchangjing Avenue
  Xiangcheng Economic Development Zone

Suzhou, Jiangsu Province 215144
China

Key Executives:
Cadol Cheung, Founding Partner
Education: Engineering Degree, Hong Kong Polytechnic; MBA, Chinese University of Hong Kong
Background: Intel Capital

2753 FULL CIRCLE INVESTMENTS
Nassima Tower, Level 2, Office 205
Sheikh Zayed Road
Dubai
United Arab Emirates

Phone: 9714-3516122 Fax: 9714-3516123
e-mail: admin@fullcircleinvest.com
web: www.fullcircleinvest.com

Mission Statement: Full Circle Investments combines strategy consulting, corporate finance and execution capabilities to deliver integrated strategic, operational and financial solutions to corporate clients and investment groups.

Geographic Preference: Middle East
Founded: 2006
Industry Group Preference: Financial Services, Energy, Technology, Healthcare, Real Estate, Food & Beverage

Key Executives:
Ghassan Medawar, Founding Partner, Managing Director
Education: BS, Economics, Wesleyan University; Law Degree, University of London
Background: ING Barings; ABN Ambro
Laya Medawar, Partner
Education: Chemistry, Oxford University; MBA, INSEAD
Background: Consulting, Bain & Company; Greig Fester
Nessrine Salah, Director
Education: BS, Business Administration, American University, Cairo
Background: Consultant, McKinsey & Company; Sernior Associate, Korn Ferry International
Richard Maddison, Venture Partner
Education: MBA, INSEAD
Background: Wireline Engineer, Schlumberger; Chief Analyst, ARCO; Robert Flemings; Bankers Trust; Deutsche Bank
Claudio Gonzalez, Venture Partner
Education: Bachelor's Degree in Economics, London School of Economics
Background: West Merchant Bank; Scotiabank Sudamericano; Director, Latin American Sales, ABN Ambro

2754 FUTURE VENTURE CAPITAL COMPANY LIMITED
4th Floor Karasuma-Chuo Building
659 Tearaimizu-cho, Nishikikoji-agaru Karasuma-dori
Nakagyo-ku
Kyoto 604-8152
Japan

Phone: 81-752572511 Fax: 81-752111601
web: www.fvc.co.jp

Mission Statement: Actively seeking new investments.

Key Executives:
Keiji Imajo, President & Chief Executive Officer
Tomohisa Suzuki, Director

2755 G & H KAPITAL PARTNER AG
Schwarzenbergplatz 16
Vienna 1010
Austria

Phone: 43-1502200 Fax: 43-150220249
e-mail: mail@gutmann.at
web: www.gutmann.at

Geographic Preference: Austria, Central and Eastern Europe, Germany, Latin America
Fund Size: $15.3 Billion
Founded: 1922
Minimum Investment: $2.4 Million
Investment Criteria: Buyout & Buyin

Key Executives:
Alexander Kahane, Chairman
Matthias Albert, Partner

2756 GALILEO II
109, boulevard Haussmann
Paris 75008
France

Phone: 33-153594500 Fax: 33-153599200
web: www.galileo.fr

Mission Statement: Actively seeking new investments.

Founded: 1989
Average Investment: $1.82 Million
Minimum Investment: $1.2 Million
Investment Criteria: Startup, Early Stage; Expansion—Development
Industry Group Preference: Communications, Internet Technology, Telecommunications, Computer Related
Portfolio Companies: Alapage.com, Business_Doc, Canal Web, Consodata, Icm, Influe, Netgem, Pictoris, Protraining

Key Executives:
Yoann Le Berrigaud, Co-founder and Marketing Director
e-mail: jflichy@galileo.fr
Education: Engineering and Economics degrees, Ecole Centrale de Lyon
Background: Co-Founder of Galileo Partners, 1989; M&A and Investment Specialist with Corporate Finance Department of CIC Bank
François Duliège, Partner

2757 GAON ASSET MANAGEMENT
Gaon House, 6 Kaufman Street, 14th Floor
Tel Aviv 68012
Israel

Phone: 972-037954100 Fax: 972-037954103
e-mail: info@gaon.com
web: www.gaon.com

Mission Statement: Initiates and promotes investments in various areas in Israel and abroad.

Geographic Preference: Israel
Founded: 1998
Investment Criteria: All stages considered.
Industry Group Preference: Financial Services, Agribusiness, Retailing, Wholesale

Key Executives:
Moshe Gaon, Chairman
e-mail: info@gaon.com
Education: M.B.A.and L.L.B.
Background: Legal Counselor in Koor Industries Legal Department.
Directorships: Member of the Board of Companies.
Avi Hochman, Chief Executive Officer

Venture Capital & Private Equity Firms / International Firms

2758 GE ASIA PACIFIC CAPITAL TECHNOLOGY FUND
Building 7A, 6th Floor
Sector 25A, DLF Cyber City, Phase III
3A Charter Road
Gurgaon, Haryana 122002
India

Phone: 91-1244808000 Fax: 852-2530-5527
Toll-Free: 1800-4334480
e-mail: ashok@geapctechfund.com
web: www.gecapital.in

Mission Statement: A joint venture between GE and Asia Pacific Capital Group. Flexible as to size and range of investment.
Geographic Preference: China, India
Founded: 1992
Average Investment: $3-100 million
Industry Group Preference: Technology, Life Sciences, Consumer Products, Infrastructure
Key Executives:
  Anish Shah, President and CEO
  Education: BE Mechanical Engineering, MS University, India; MS Industrial Engineering, Stanford University
  Background: Strategy Consultant, Deloitte & Touche; CEO/Regional President, WR Grace; President, PPG Industries (Pittsburgh Plate Galss)
  Neeta Mukherji, SVP & Business Head
  Education: AB Government, Harvard University; JD, Columbia University School of Law
  Background: Co-Founder, Asia Pacific Capital Ltd; US State Department; Adjunct Professor, Saigon Law School; Coudent Brothers; Founding Partner, ChinaVest
  Satyanarayanan Eluri, Business Leader, Healthcare Financial Services
  Education: PGDM, Indian Institute of Management
  Background: VP Finance Sponsors Group, Kotak Investment Banking; GE Equity India; GE Structured Finance
  Raghuveer Kurada, Business Leader, Energy Financial Services
  Education: BS Economics, Wharton School; MA, Fletcher School of Law & Diplomacy (Tufts University)
  Background: Global Strategy Grp, Elan Pharmaceuticals; VP, Prudential Asia Mezzanine Fund; Founding Principal, NetFuel Ventures; Cap Gemini; Ernst & Young; Lend Lease; Air Touch International
  Directorships: One Ummah
  Anand Trivedi, Business Leader, Private Equity
  Education: Bachelor of Law, Fu-Jen University; JD, Columbia University School of Law
  Background: VP Investment Banking, Morgan Stanly Dean Witter
  Directorships: International Bank of Taipei; FWU-Sheng Investment Co
  Raghuveer Kurada, Business Leader, Energy Financial Services
  Education: BS Finance/Economics, California State University; CPA
  Background: Head Audit Division, CPA firm

2759 GE CAPITAL SERVICES INDIA LIMITED
Building 7A, 6th Floor, Sector 25A
DLF Cyber City, Phase III
Gurgaon 122002
India

Phone: 91-1244808000 Fax: 91-124-2358044
Toll-Free: 1800-4334480

Mission Statement: Provides access to the financial tools and services vital to businesses and individuals.
Key Executives:
  Anish Shah, President and CEO
  Ashish Sharma, Business Leader, Corporate Accounts Group

2760 GE EQUITY EUROPE
Clarges House
London NV
United Kingdom

Phone: 207-3026310 Fax: 207-3026810

Geographic Preference: United Kingdom, Central Europe, Western Europe
Fund Size: $310 Million
Average Investment: $10 Million
Minimum Investment: $1 Million
Investment Criteria: Early Stage, Expansion, Replacement Capital, MBO, MBI
Industry Group Preference: Data Communications, Computer Related, Financial Services, Consumer Services, Consumer Products
Portfolio Companies: Cell Networks, Cell Ventures, Group Trade, Intrinsic, Media Surface, SM Logistics, TravelPrice
Key Executives:
  Frank Ertl, Chief Financial Officer
  Ed Hrvatin, Chief Marketing Officer

2761 GEMINI ISRAEL VENTURE FUNDS LIMITED
9 Hamenotim Street
Herzliya Pituach 46725
Israel

Phone: 972-99719111 Fax: 972-99584842
e-mail: info@gemini.co.il
web: www.gemini.co.il

Mission Statement: A pioneer in Israel's venture capital industry, Gemini provides start-up financing and expert guidance to help talented entrepreneurs build successful companies.
Geographic Preference: Israel
Fund Size: $700 Million
Founded: 1993
Average Investment: $150 Million
Minimum Investment: $5 Million
Investment Criteria: Early stage, start up
Industry Group Preference: Telecommunications, Data Communications, Internet Technology, Semiconductors, Medical, Infrastructure, Technology
Portfolio Companies: D-Pharm, Mellanox, Diligent TechnologiesAllot, Atrica, Celletra, Ceragon Networks, Commil ltd, IXI Mobile Inc, Olista Software Corporation, Ornet Data Communication, Outsmart Ltd, Radnet Ltd, Riverhead Networks Inc, Schema Ltd, Starhome, Tdsoft
Key Executives:
  Ed Mlavsky, Founding Partner & Chairman
  e-mail: info@gemini.co.il
  Education: Bachelor of Science & MBA
  Background: Managing Partner of Gemini Funds, Vice President, Marketing of DSP Group.
  Directorships: Board Member of Adimos Inc & IXI Mobile Inc.
  Yossi Sela, Managing Partner

2762 GENERAL ATLANTIC PARTNERS
Suite 5815, 58/F, Two IFC, 8 Finance Street
International Finance Tower
Central, Hong Kong
China

Phone: 852-36022600 Fax: 852-36022611
e-mail: vfeng@gapartners.com
web: www.generalatlantic.com

Venture Capital & Private Equity Firms / International Firms

Mission Statement: For over 25 years, General Atlantic has provided equity financing to private and public companies globally.
Geographic Preference: Worldwide
Fund Size: $17 Billion
Founded: 1980
Average Investment: $75 Million - $400 Million
Minimum Investment: $25 Million
Industry Group Preference: Information Technology, Outsourcing & Efficiency, Communications
Portfolio Companies: A-Max, abaxx, aI METRIX, Altair engineering, Archipelago, Compugroup, computershare, Criticalpath, DiceInc, Digital China, eOne Globe, Genpact, Healthvison, Hewitt, insightexpress, IHSInc, Intec, IPValue, iSoft, Organosys, Lenovo, LHS
Key Executives:
  Steven A. Denning, Chairman
  Education: Degree in Economics, MBA.
  Background: Senior Associate, Technology Crossover Ventures, Senior Business Analyst, McKinsey & Company.

2763 GENERAL ENTERPRISE MANAGEMENT SERVICES
805 Citibank Tower, 3 Garden Road
Central
Hong Kong

Phone: 852-28380093 Fax: 852-28380292
e-mail: contact@gems.com.hk
web: www.gems.com.hk

Mission Statement: General Enterprise Management Services Limited (GEMS) is a private equity fund management group that manages the GEMS Funds (GEMS I, II and III) - these in turn make direct investments in the Asia Pacific region.
Geographic Preference: China, Japan, Thiland, Hong Kong, Singapore, South Korea
Fund Size: $600 Million
Founded: 1998
Average Investment: $15 Million
Minimum Investment: $10 Million
Investment Criteria: Invests in well-managed and well-positioned companies in need of equity for strategic growth, acquisitions, market expansion or balance sheet restructuring
Industry Group Preference: Energy, Electronic Technology, Transportation, Telecommunications, Software, Financial Services, Retailing, Real Estate, Natural Resources, Media
Portfolio Companies: Cape Energy, CNOOC, Compass, Crescendo, E-mice, eBANK, Eutech, Grace, Hi-Tech Wealth, IP Flex, NatSteel, Newlife, Sino-Forest, Taejin, The Executive Centre, Trisara, Yozan
Key Executives:
  Simon Murray, Executive Chairman
  e-mail: contact@gems.com.hk
  Education: Bachelor of Arts degree in Economics
  Background: Vice President of Morgan's Capital Markets Group in Hong Kong.
  David Van Oppen, Senior Partner
  e-mail: contact@gems.com.hk
  Education: Master of Arts degree.
  Background: Vice President of Lazard Asia Investment Management.

2764 GENERICS GROUP LIMITED Generics Group
Harston Mill
Harston
Cambridge CB22 7GG
United Kingdom

Phone: 44-1223875200 Fax: 44-1223875201
e-mail: info@sagentia.com
web: www.sagentia.com

Mission Statement: The Generics Group (Generics) is a leading integrated technology consulting, development and investment organisation.
Geographic Preference: Worldwide
Founded: 1987
Industry Group Preference: Engineering, Telecommunications, Medical, Physical Sciences, Materials Technology, Electronic Technology, Management, Life Sciences, Energy
Key Executives:
  Dr Alistair Brown, Executive Director, Sales & Marketing
  Background: PricewaterhouseCoopers, based in Stockholm, Sweden.
  Martin Frost, Group Managing Director
  Background: GEC-Marconi, where he served as Financial Controller.
  Directorships: Board of Scientific Generics and several of the Group's spin-out companies.
  Gordon Edge, Non-Executive Director
  Background: Founding members of Cambridge Consultants Ltd & founder of PA Technology.

2765 GENES GMBH VENTURE SERVICES
Koelner Strasse 27
PO Box 560
Frechen D-50226
Germany

Phone: 49-2234955460 Fax: 49-2234955464
web: www.genes-ventures.de

Mission Statement: Focuses on transnational deals and pre-IPO investments by divesting existing funds and setting up new international venture capital funds.
Geographic Preference: Germany
Fund Size: $72.5 Million
Founded: 1978
Average Investment: $3.6 Million
Industry Group Preference: Technology
Key Executives:
  Klaus Nathusius, General Partner
  Kfm Lutz Nathusius, Partner
  e-mail: service@genes-ventures.de
  Dr. Detlev Geiss, Sr Partner
  e-mail: service@genes-ventures.de
  Andy Klose, Partner
  e-mail: service@genes-ventures.de

2766 GENESIS PARTNERS
11 HaMenofim Street
Ackerstein Towers
Building B, 4th Floor
Herzliya Pituach NV
Israel

Phone: 972- 99729000 Fax: 972-99729001
e-mail: innovation@genesispartners.com

Mission Statement: Genesis Partners is one of Israel's largest and most experienced venture capital firms.
Geographic Preference: Israel
Fund Size: $600 Million
Founded: 1996
Average Investment: $3.5 Million
Minimum Investment: $2 Million
Investment Criteria: All Stages
Industry Group Preference: Communications, Wireless Technologies, Storage, Internet Technology, Infrastructure Software, Hardware, Enterprise Software, Internet Applications and Services, Digital Media & Marketing, Consumer Services, Mobile Services
Portfolio Companies: Airsphere, Allot, Cloverleaf, Colbar, Commprize, Comsys, Comview, Elcom, Filesx, Foxcom Wireless, Fundtech, G Connect, Gonet, Harmonycom, Healinx, AG Associates, Agentics Inc., Appilog Inc.,

Venture Capital & Private Equity Firms / International Firms

Audiocodes Ltd., Butterfly VLSI, Ltd., Celtro Inc., Clicksoftwar

Key Executives:
Dr. Eyal Kishon, Founder & Managing Partner
e-mail: eyal@genesisvp.com
Education: PhD, Computer Science, Robotics, New York University; BA, Computer Science, Technion, Haifa
Background: Associate Director, Polaris Fund; Chief Technology Officer, Yozma Venture Capital; Research Positions, IBM Research Center, At&T's Bell Laboratories
Eddy Shaler, Managing Partner
e-mail: eddy@genesisvp.com
Education: MS in Information Systems, BA in Statistics, Tel Aviv University
Background: Oscar Gruss and Son Inc.; Co-Founded, Mofet Israel Technology Fund; Large Systems Expert and Account Executive, IBM (Israel); Large Strategic Planner, IBM (United Kingdon)
Directorships: CEO
Yair Shoham, General Partner
e-mail: yair@genesisvp.com
Education: JD, Loyola University School of Law; BA, Haifa University, Israel
Background: VP Business Development, Butterfly; Partner, Goldfarb, Levy, Eran & Company
Gary Gannot, General Partner
e-mail: gary@genesisvp.com
Education: BSc in Computer Engineering, Technion - Israel Institute of Technology
Background: Co-Founder and Chief Operating Officer, Healink Corporation; Vice President of Engineering, Exemplar Logic; Project Leader, Intel

2767 GENEZIS CAPITAL TECHNOLOGY
Bld 2-11
Ugreshskaja Str.
Moscow 115088
Russia

Phone: 7-495-225-58-09
e-mail: info@geneziscap.com
web: www.geneziscap.com

Mission Statement: We seek creative, smart and entrepreneurial spirited people whose ambition is to grow businesses and tap new markets. We prefer long-term investments of 3-7 years.
Geographic Preference: Russia, CIS, United States, Europe, Asia
Minimum Investment: $25, 000
Investment Criteria: Seed, Venture, Growth
Portfolio Companies: Fleecs, Martmania, B-152, System Heat, Aknol
Key Executives:
Maxim Shekhovtsov, Chairman, Managing Partner
Background: Co-Founder, TexDrive; Founder and Head of Venture Capital Division, Allianz SE; Advisor, RTI-Systems
Denis Burlakov, Managing Partner
Background: Founder, Front Line Capital
Directorships: AGIC Group

2768 GESTION DE CAPITAL RIESGO DEL PAIS VASCO
Alameda de Urquijo, 36 4TH Floor Plaza Bizkai
Bilbao 48011
Spain

Phone: 34-944037000 Fax: 34-944-037056
e-mail: info@spri.es
web: www.spri.es

Mission Statement: Actively seeking new investments. Acts on behalf of third parties, managing venture capital companies and funds. It was founded by the Basque Government in order to promote and develop activities relating to venture capital in Basque Country.
Geographic Preference: Basque
Fund Size: $155 Million
Founded: 1985
Minimum Investment: $8.4 Million
Industry Group Preference: All Sectors Considered
Key Executives:
Alexander Arriola Lizarriturri, Director-General
Background: Vice Secretary, Information Society
Directorships: Shanghai Municipal People
Alexander Arriola Lizarriturri, Director-General

2769 GET2VOLUME ACCELERATOR
67 Ayer Rajah Crescent Unit 03-20/22
Singapore 139950
Singapore

Phone: +65 6777 9750 Fax: +65 6777 9750
e-mail: info@g2vaccelerator.com
web: www.g2vaccelerator.com

Mission Statement: We believe that the right eco-system of capital, connections, and capabilities is critical to successfully growing a technology company in Singapore. At Get2Volume, our approach is to work alongside entrepreneurs as a part of their team. We bring the capital capabilities and connections to complement the entrepreneurial team. Our deep experience in successfully growing and exiting enterprise and microelectronics centric companies allows us to complement the companies that we work with, enabling faster growth. We believe these companies are global from day one. This means that we bring global capabilities to address focused growth needs. We leverage these capabilities across our portfolio of companies to improve the efficiency.
Geographic Preference: Singapore
Industry Group Preference: Technology
Portfolio Companies: Silicon Cloud, Mobicart, Eco Consumer Services, Tabsquare, gridComm, Sprooki, Plunify, Semitech Semiconductor, ConnectedHealth, DarbeeVision, Novelics
Key Executives:
Mike Holt, Managing Partner

2770 GILDE INVESTMENT FUNDS
Herculesplein 104
3584 AA Utrecht
Utrecht 3508 AB
Netherlands

Phone: 31-882202600 Fax: 31-882202601
e-mail: info@gilde.nl
web: www.gilde.com

Mission Statement: Actively seeking new investments.
Geographic Preference: Europe, USA, Israel
Fund Size: $240.5 Million
Founded: 1982
Average Investment: $75 - $600 million
Minimum Investment: $120, 000
Investment Criteria: Start-up, First stage and Growth stage.
Industry Group Preference: Communications, Computer Related, Software, Electronic Technology, Mobile Communications Devices
Portfolio Companies: AtoBe, Cambridge Broadband, Application Networks, Augeo, Carmen Systems, Covast, Cyco Software, I-Logix, JobPartners, Mondosoft, Tridion, Truston, WebCollage and HSCG.
Key Executives:
Gerhard Nordemann, Managing Partner
Education: Masters Degree in business economics .
Background: Private equity .
Remko Jager, Managing Partner
Boudewijn T Molenaar, Managing Director
Education: Graduated with a degree in electronic

engineering.
Background: ABN AMRO's private equity.
Directorships: Executive board member.
Ferry de Vries, Investment Director
Education: Business administration and business financing
Background: Rabobank International.

2771 GIMV GIMV
Karel Oomsstraat 37
Antwerp 2018
Belgium

Phone: 32-32902100 Fax: 32-32902105
e-mail: info@gimv.be
web: www.gimv.com

Mission Statement: Supports the economic development of the Kempen region

Geographic Preference: Europe
Fund Size: $1.19 Billion
Founded: 1980
Minimum Investment: $3 Million
Investment Criteria: Seed, Startup, Early-Stage
Industry Group Preference: Biotechnology, Communications, Electronic Technology, Energy, Industrial Equipment, Medical & Health Related
Portfolio Companies: 3mensio, Ablynx, AGY Therapeutics, Alfacam, Ambit, Arcomet, Arrow Therapeutics, Astex Therapeutics, Avalon Pharmaceuticals, Barco New

Key Executives:
Koen Dejonckheere, CEO
e-mail: receptie@gimv.be
Education: Degree in applied economics from the University of Antwerp
Dirk Boogmans, General Counsel - Executive Vice President
e-mail: receptie@gimv.be
Education: Degree in Applied Economics-State University of Ghent.
Background: Barco, various other non-quoted companies.

2772 GIMV NV
37 Karel Oomsstraat
Antwerp 2018
Belgium

Phone: 32-32902100 Fax: 32-32384193
e-mail: info@gimv.com
web: www.gimv.com

Mission Statement: GIMV is the only prominent investment company in Flanders specialised in private equity i.e. investing in the equity of unlisted companies.

Geographic Preference: Europe
Fund Size: $643 Million
Founded: 1980
Average Investment: $2.1 Billion
Minimum Investment: $3 Million
Investment Criteria: All Stages
Industry Group Preference: All Sectors Considered
Portfolio Companies: Cril Telecom Software, Interwise, Intuwave, Mediornet, ORMvision, Telenet, Voxtron, Ablynx, AGY Therapeutics, Ambit, Arrow Therapeutics, CareX, Crop Design, Tops Foods, Mondi Foods, EBT, UFO, Westerlund Group

Key Executives:
Koen Dejonckheere, Chief Executive Officer
e-mail: receptie@gimv.be
Education: Master Degree.
Background: PricewaterhouseCoopers in Brussel.

2773 GIZA VENTURE CAPITAL
Ramat Aviv Tower
12th Floor, 40 Einstein St.
PO Box 17672
Tel Aviv 61175
Israel

Phone: 972-36402323 Fax: 972-36402319
e-mail: zholtzman@gizavc.com
web: www.giza.co.il

Mission Statement: Giza has investment professionals with a wealth of expertise and experience in Communication, Information Technology, Enterprise Software and Life Sciences. The Fund has the highest ratio of professionals to capital managed of any VC fund based in Israel.

Geographic Preference: Israel, USA, Singapore
Fund Size: $500 Million
Founded: 1992
Average Investment: $500,000
Minimum Investment: $300,000
Investment Criteria: Early-stage
Industry Group Preference: Communications, Information Technology, Enterprise Services, Life Sciences, Software, Semiconductors, Internet/Mobile/Media
Portfolio Companies: Advasense, Altair Semiconductor, Butterfly, Envara, Flash Networks, Horizon Semiconductors, Iamba, Libit, Lucid, Mysitcom Ltd, Oplus Technologies, Resolute Networks, Smart Link Ltd, Surf Communication Solutions, Telegate, Telrad Conneqy, TMT Coaxial Network

Key Executives:
Ori Kirshner, Managing Partner
e-mail: zholtzman@gizavc.com
Education: BA, Hebrew University; MBA, Tel Aviv University
Background: Executive VP, Leumi & Co Investment Bankers; Lehman Brothers; Advisor to: Scitex, Elscint, Koor, Discount Investment Corporation, Poalim Investments, Bezeq; Founding Member, Israel Venture Association
Zvi Schechter, Co-Founder/Managing Director
e-mail: zvi@gizavc.com
Education: BS, Technion; MBA, Tel Aviv University
Background: Leumi & Co Investment Bankers; Financial Advisor to major Israeli banks
Ezer Soref, Managing Director
e-mail: esoref@gizavc.com
Education: BA Management and Economics, MA Economics, Tel Aviv University
Background: Corporate Research, Franklin Mint Corporation
Tal Mizrahi, CFO
Education: MBA, MD, Tel Aviv University; postdoctoral, Columbia University
Background: Vice Chairman, Abarbanel Hospital; Head Residency Training, Tel Aviv University Medicine;
Directorships: Chief Editor, Israeli National Board Examination
Zeev Holtzman, Chairman & Founder
e-mail: zholtzman@gizavc.com
Education: MBA in Finance, from Columbia University
Background: Former Executive VP at Leumi & Co. Investment Bankers and worked at Lehman Brothers in New York
Directorships: founder
Eyal Niv, Managing Director USA
Education: BA in Economics from The Hebrew University of Jerusalem
Background: Bynet; Iscar; Economist, Giyo International

Venture Capital & Private Equity Firms / International Firms

2774 GLOBAL EQUITY PARTNERS BETEILIGUNGS-MANAGEMENT
Mariahilfer Strasse 1/Getreidemarkt 17
Vienna 1060
Austria

Phone: 43-15818390 Fax: 43-18517611
e-mail: office@gep.at
web: www.gep.at

Mission Statement: Global equity partner is an internationally operating investment company head-quartered in Vienna.

Geographic Preference: Austria, Germany, Switzerland
Fund Size: $550 Billion
Founded: 1998
Average Investment: $6.6 Million
Minimum Investment: $1.20 Million
Investment Criteria: Seed and start up, expansion
Industry Group Preference: Biotechnology, Communications, Computer Related, Industrial Products, Industrial Services, Manufacturing
Portfolio Companies: Integriertes Resource Management, ABATEC Electronics AG, Ray Sono AG, VennWorks LLC, WS Beteiligungs AG, PaysafeCard.com, Wertkarten AG, Goldbach Media, Stage1 Beteiligungs Invest, Indian Dreams, BET and WIN.com

Key Executives:
  Michael Tojner, Founder/ CEO
  Education: Master's in Business Administration
  Background: Creditanstalt, WKBG, Teleperformance, and Siemens.
  Herbert Herdlicka, Management Board
  Education: Master's degree .
  Background: Private Customer Department at Deutsche Bank Capital.

2775 GLOBAL FINANCE
7 Fragoklissas Str, 15125
Global Finance SA
Athens 15125
Greece

Phone: 30-2108124500 Fax: 30-2108055430
e-mail: office@globalfinance.gr
web: www.globalfinance.gr

Mission Statement: Global Finance takes a proactive role in backing exceptional entrepreneurs and managers, providing growth capital to companies with a potential for significant expansion. Global Finance has offices in Greece, Romania and Bulgaria.

Geographic Preference: Europe, Russia
Fund Size: $300 Million
Founded: 1991
Investment Criteria: Expansion.
Industry Group Preference: Manufacturing, Information Technology, Retailing, Media, Telecommunications, Services
Portfolio Companies: Baring Hellenic Ventures SA (BHV), Euromerchant Balkan Fund (EBF), Goody's, Chipita, Germanos, Jumbo, Dodoni, Yioula, Nikas, NetMed, United Milk Company, Sicomed, Temenos, Corporation Dermoaesthetica (Spain), Mobiltel .

Key Executives:
  George Gondicas, Non-Executive Director
  Education: BA in Economic And Business Sciences, MBA.
  Angelos Plakopitas, Managing Partner
  Education: MS, MBA, INSEAD.
  Background: General Manager, Shelman (wood products company); 14 years experience in corporate banking with Citibank and Hellenic Industrial Development Bank.
  Theodore Klakidis, Partner
  Education: MSc in Mathematics, MPP in International Trade and Finance.

2776 GLOBAL LIFE SCIENCE VENTURES GmbH
Tal 26
Munchen D - 80331
Germany

Phone: 49-892881510 Fax: 49-8928815130
e-mail: mailbox@glsv-vc.com
web: www.glsv-vc.com

Mission Statement: Global Life Science Ventures (GLSV) is a leading, independent venture capital fund focusing exclusively on the life sciences.

Geographic Preference: Western Europe, USA
Fund Size: 200 Million Euros
Founded: 1996
Average Investment: 5 million Euros
Minimum Investment: 1 million Euros
Investment Criteria: Early Stage and Later stage.
Industry Group Preference: Biotechnology, Life Sciences, Medical Technology, Pharmaceuticals
Portfolio Companies: Pieris AG, Santaris A/S, IMI AG, Agendia B/V, Horizon Pharma, Nabriva Therapeutics AG, Zalicas Inc., Neurogesx Inc., Glycart AG, Intercell AG, Cyberkinetics Inc., Cytos Biotechnology AG, DeveloGen AG, Sequenom Inc., Memory Inc., Exelixis Pharmaceuticals Inc., Artemis Pharmaceuticals GmbH, Coley Pharmaceutical Group, MBT Ag

Other Locations:
  Postplatz 1
  PO Box 626
  Zug 6301
  Switzerland
  Phone: 41-4172719 40 Fax: 41-41-727-1945

Key Executives:
  Dr. Hans A Kuepper, Partner
  e-mail: ha.kuepper@glsv-vc.com
  Education: PhD, Biochemistry
  Background: Senior management positions in research and R&D managment with biotech and pharm companies, technology assessment, and corporate M&A
  Dr. Peter H Reinisch, Partner
  e-mail: p.reinisch@glsv-vc.com
  Education: PhD, Business & Engineering
  Background: Senior management positions in the life science industry and in particular for the strategic coordination and business development of diagnostics worldwide
  Dipl.-Kfm Hanns-Peter Weiss, Partner
  Education: MBA
  Background: Senior management positions in private equity and venture capital firms investing across a range of industries in Europe and the USA, and in particular the life sciences

2777 GLOBAL MARITIME VENTURES BERHAD
Leve 15, Menara Bank Pembangunan
Jalan Sultan Ismail
Level 11
Kuala Lumpur 50250
Malaysia

Phone: 60-326-988231 Fax: 60-326-940860
web: www.gmv.com.my

Mission Statement: Global Maritime Ventures Berhad (GMV) is a marine venture capital investment holding company.

Geographic Preference: Malaysia
Fund Size: RM500 million
Founded: 1993
Industry Group Preference: Marine Services

Key Executives:
  En. Ahmad Sharifuddin bin Abdul Kadir, Chief Executive Officer
  En. Abdul Karim bin Ismail, Chief Operating Officer

Venture Capital & Private Equity Firms / International Firms

2778 GLOBAL TECHNOLOGY VENTURES
#23/2 Coffee Day Square
Vittal Mallya Road
Suite 23/2
Bangalore 560 001
India

Phone: 91-8040012345
e-mail: info@gtvltd.com

Mission Statement: Global Technology Ventures Ltd. (GTV) is a venture capital firm specializing in early stage, start up, and late stage financing. The firm typically invests in the technology sector, and seeks to invest in companies located in India, with a specific focus on Bangalore.

Key Executives:
V.G. Siddhartha, Managing Partner

2779 GLOBAL VENTURES MANAGEMENT LIMITED
2-6 Granville Road, Suite 1508, Tsimshatsui
Kowloon
Hong Kong

Phone: 852-27241223 **Fax:** 852-27224373
web: www.galliance.com

Mission Statement: Asia's first venture investment bank.
Geographic Preference: Japan, Hong Kong, British Virgin Islands
Founded: 1994
Portfolio Companies: Pacific Mandarin Assets Ltd., Spellacy Universal Ltd., Infinity Finance Ltd.

Key Executives:
C.J. Wilson, Group Managing Director
Education: Bachelors Degree in Economics from University of Wisconsin and a Masters Degree from Harvard University School of Business Administration.
Background: Banker and venture finance specialist.
Directorships: Co-head of international M&A for Asahi Bank in Japan.
Roger W Mills, Executive Managing Director

2780 GMT COMMUNICATIONS PARTNERS LLP
21 Gloucester Place
London W1U 8HR
United Kingdom

Phone: 44-2072929333
e-mail: tim.green@gmtpartners.com
web: www.gmtpartners.com

Mission Statement: GMT Communications Partners LLP is an independent private equity firm focused on investments in European content, communications infrastructure and tech-enabled services in Europe.
Geographic Preference: United Kingdom, Continental Europe
Fund Size: 542 million Euros
Founded: 1993
Average Investment: 25-30 million Euros
Minimum Investment: 10 million Euros
Investment Criteria: Later stage
Industry Group Preference: Communications, Software Services, Internet Technology, Telecommunications, Media, Computer Related

Key Executives:
Timothy S. Green, Managing Partner
e-mail: tim.green@gmtpartners.com
Education: MSc, Sloan Fellow, London Business School; ACA
Background: Partner, Baring Communications Equity; Partner, Baring Private Equity Partners; Chartered Accountant; KPMG
Directorships: TES Media
Ashley Long, Partner
e-mail: ashley.long@gmtpartners.com
Education: BA, Univ. of Kent
Background: Triton Private Equity
Directorships: Primesight
Vikram Krishna, Partner
e-mail: vikram.krishna@gmtpartners.com
Education: BA, Univ. of Oxford
Background: PricewaterhouseCoopers
Directorships: MeetingZone; Primesight

2781 GOBI PARTNERS
Building 7, Zhangjiang Innovation Park
399 Keyuan Road
Shanghai 201203, PRC
China

Phone: 86-2151601618 **Fax:** 86-2152929730
web: www.gobivc.com

2782 GOGIN CAPITAL COMPANY LIMITED
71 Shirakata honmachi, Matsue shi
Shimane 690-0061
Japan

Phone: 81-852-28-7170 **Fax:** 81-852-28-7177
web: www.gogin.co.jp

Fund Size: 54, 259 one million Yen

Key Executives:
Makoto Kose, President

2783 GOLDMAN SACHS INTERNATIONAL UK
133 Fleet Street
Peterborough Court
London EC4A 2BB
United Kingdom

Phone: 44-1717741000 **Fax:** 44-2077-741181
web: www.goldmansachs.com

Mission Statement: Actively seeking new investments.
Geographic Preference: United Kingdom, Europe
Founded: 1995
Investment Criteria: Early stage to Expansion
Industry Group Preference: All Sectors Considered
Portfolio Companies: Alliance Hotelerie, Diamond Cable, GCR Holdings Ltd, Pears Portfolio, Stirling Cooke Browne, Suez Portfolio

Key Executives:
Lloyd C. Blankfein, Chairman & Chief Executive Officer
Gary D. Cohn, President & Co-Chief Operating Officer

2784 GORILLA VENTURES
Aleksanterinkatu 15 B
0100 Helsinki
Finland

web: www.gorillaventures.fi

Mission Statement: Gorilla Ventures is a business accelerator which helps entrepreneurs realize their dreams by making seed investments and participating in the operationsal running of the company - whether strategy and customer development, go-to-market execution or globalization.

Investment Criteria: Seed

Other Locations:
Väinä Linnan aukio 15
33210 Tampere
Finland

Key Executives:
Petri Lehmuskoski
e-mail: petri.lehmuskoski@gorillaventures.fi
Risto Rautakorpi
e-mail: risto.rautakorpi@gorillaventures.fi
Reijo Syrjalainen
e-mail: reijo.syrjalainen@gorillaventures.fi
Timo Tiihonen
e-mail: timo.tiihonen@gorillaventures.fi

Venture Capital & Private Equity Firms / International Firms

2785 GRANITE VENTURE CAPITAL CORPORATION
One Bush Street
Suite 1350
San Francisco, California 94104
South Korea

Phone: 415-5917700 Fax: 415-5917720
web: www.granitevc.com

Mission Statement: Actively seeking investments.

Fund Size: $625 Million
Founded: 1998
Industry Group Preference: Software, Industrial Services
Portfolio Companies: Sibley & Associates, General Donlee, King-Reed & Associates, Vignette

Key Executives:
Chris Mckay, Managing Director

2786 GRANVILLE BAIRD CAPITAL PARTNERS
Mint House, 77 Mansell Street
London E1 8AF
United Kingdom

Phone: 44-2076678400 Fax: 44-2076678481
e-mail: mproudlock@bcpe.co.uk
web: www.bairdcapital.com

Mission Statement: Actively seeking new investments. The European private equity arm of Robert W Baird & Co.

Geographic Preference: United Kingdom, Germany, Spain
Fund Size: $789 Million
Founded: 1971
Average Investment: £10 Million and £50 Million
Minimum Investment: $1.2 Million
Investment Criteria: MBO, MBI, Buy and Build, Growth Capital
Industry Group Preference: Business to Business, Healthcare, Industrial Equipment
Portfolio Companies: Alukon, Amann, Armor Group, Balzac Coffee, Berkenhoff, Capital Consulting, Castlecare, Cerillion, Controlex, Eisenworld, ETC, Hahl, Mentor, MI International, Mobile.de, Nobis, Public Recruitment Group, SSB, Team BS, TSL, Ultralase, Vistorm, Westfalia

Key Executives:
James Benfield, Managing Director
Background: County Bank; Chartered Accountant, Ernst & Young; GKN
Andrew Ferguson, Managing Director
Background: Chartered Accountant, KPMG; Grant Thornton; NatWest Ventures
David Barrass, Operating Partner
Education: BBA
Background: Founder/Managing Director, M&A consultancy; Angermann Consulting
Simon Havers, Director
Education: MBA
Background: ABN AMRO Capital; Planning/Rollout, BBC World Service Television; Strategy Consultant
Directorships: ArmorGroup; Cerillion

2787 GRAPHITE CAPITAL MANAGEMENT LTD
Berkeley Square House
Berkeley Square
London W1J 6BQ
United Kingdom

Phone: 44-2078255300 Fax: 44-2078255399
e-mail: info@graphitecapital.com
web: www.graphitecapital.com

Mission Statement: Graphite Capital has been a private equity investor since 1981 as F&C Ventures and became independent in 2001. Emphasis is put on rapid decision-making and deliverability for quality management teams with strong track records.

Geographic Preference: United Kingdom, Western Europe
Fund Size: £1.5 billion
Founded: 1981
Average Investment: £200 million
Minimum Investment: $3.5 Million
Industry Group Preference: Retailing, Consumer Services, Leisure, Property Management, Services, Distribution, Manufacturing, Financial Services, Healthcare, Consumer Products
Portfolio Companies: Alliance Medical, Aktrion, Applied Energy, Avery Haelth, Business Advirory Service, Clearminster, Clinovia, Computacenter, Denison, Denplan, Dewhurst/Angloarch, Equanet, Game, Go Plant, Golden Tulip, Hiscox, Huntress, JTF, Jane Norman, Kingsclear, Leading Edge Labels, Leaderflush, London & Henley, MMS, Maplin, Ottakar's, PIFC, PSD Group, Paperchase, Ridgmont, SBJ, Salt Union, Sealine, Sharelink, Sodastream, Stalwart, Streamline, Tesla, U Pol, Vardon, Wagamama

Key Executives:
Emma Osborne, Partner
Education: Oxford University; MBA, INSEAD
Background: McKinsey & Co; Bell & Howell Ltd
Rod Richards, Managing Partner
Education: Oxford University
Background: Hill Samuel Development Capital; Management Consultant, LEK
Andrew Gray, Partner
Education: Stirling University; MBA, Warwick Business School
Background: Morgan Grenfell Development Capital
Markus Golser, Partner
Education: Business degree, HEC Paris; MBA with distinction, Oxford University
Background: Morgan Grenfell Development Capital
Jeremy Gough, Partner
Education: Oxford University
Background: Director, Morgan Grenfell Development Capital; 3i; Close Brothers
John O'Neill, Investment Manager
Education: Business/Accounting degrees, University College, Dublin
Background: Finance Advisor, Hawkpoint Partners; antfactory; Chartered Accountant, Deloitte & Touche
Jenny Michelman, Investment Director
Education: Oxford University; MBA, Open Business School
Background: J Henry Schroder & Co Ltd; Manager International Distribution Center, Pitney Bowes; Development Manager, Boral UK
Mike Tilbury, Investment Director
Education: Nottingham University
Background: Deutsche Bank; NatWest Securities; NatWest Ventures
Mike Innes, Investment Director
Education: St Andrews University; MBA, London School of Business
Background: Integrated Finance Team, Bank of Scotland; Solicitor, Clifford Chance; Founder, internet-based legal recruitment consultancy
Mark Hudson, Investment Director
Education: Modern History degree, Oxford University; MBA, INSEAD
Background: Management Consultant, OC&C Strategy Consultants; East Africa Operations, Tilda Rice; Founder, internet software company
Anne Hoffmann, Investment Manager
Education: Queen's University; MBA, JL Kellogg Graduate School
Background: Strategy Consultant, McKinsey & Co; PPM Ventures

2788 GRAZIA EQUITY
Breitscheidstrasse 10
Stuttgart 70174
Germany

Phone: 49-711-90-710-90 Fax: 49-711-90-710-988
e-mail: info@grazia.com
web: www.grazia.com

Mission Statement: Grazia Equity, based in Stuttgart and Munich, is one of Europe's top names in venture capital. Grazia specializes in start-up or early-stage financing for innovative companies with market-changing potential and opportunities for superior returns. Our successful track record and expanding global network now enable us to fund selected start-ups elsewhere in Europe as well as in the US.

Geographic Preference: Europe, United States
Founded: 200
Portfolio Companies: 4-Antibody, Adconion, B2X Care Solutions, BeStylish, Delivery Agent, Immatics, Mister Spex, Moviepilot, Mysportgroup, Quantenna, Starboard, SiTime, Statista, StyleTread, Urbanara

Key Executives:
Jochen Kluppel, Partner
Background: McKinsey & Company
Directorships: Adconion, Moviepilot, Mister Spex, MySportGroup, Urbanara, Statista, Immatics

2789 GREE VENTURES
Roppongi Hills, Mori Tower
6-10-1 Roppongi
Minato-ku
Tokyo
Japan

e-mail: info@greeventures.com
web: www.greeventures.com

Mission Statement: At GREE Ventures, we leverage our successful experiences with Japan's fastest growing enterprises and the resulting industry know-how in addition to our exclusive network to invest in and support start-ups in the field of Internet and mobile services.

Geographic Preference: Southeast Asia
Founded: 2011
Average Investment: 30 million yen to 100 million
Investment Criteria: Early-Stage
Industry Group Preference: Internet, Mobile, E-Commerce & Manufacturing, Advertising, Social Media
Portfolio Companies: Aucfan, PT Pricearea Andalan Prestasi, Star Festival, Geniee, PT Bukalapak.com, Retty.com, PT Berrybenka, Luxola

Key Executives:
Naoki Aoyagi, Managing Partner
Education: BS, Policy Management, Keio University
Background: Deutsche Bank

2790 GRESHAM PRIVATE EQUITY LIMITED
Level 17, 167 Macquarie Street
Sydney 2000
Australia

Phone: 61-292215133 Fax: 61-292216814
e-mail: GPE@gresham.com.au
web: www.gresham.com.au

Mission Statement: Actively seeking new investments.

Geographic Preference: Australia, Europe, America, Asia, Africa
Fund Size: $200 Million
Founded: 1985
Average Investment: $11.16 Million to $14.8 Million
Minimum Investment: $7.4 Million
Investment Criteria: MBO, MBI and Development Capital. Generally Later Stage Deals in Established Companies
Industry Group Preference: Corporate Advisory, Private Equity, Property Development, Asset Finance
Portfolio Companies: Norcos

Key Executives:
David Feetham, Deputy Chairman
Directorships: Electronic Banking Solutions
Antony Breuer, Director
61-292215133
Fax: 61-292239072
Directorships: Norcos, Eurogestion, Raywood, Electronic Banking Solutions
Charles Graham, Managing Director
61-292215133
Fax: 61-292239072
Directorships: Eroc
Bruce McLennan, Head of Advisory and Managing Director
61-292215133
Fax: 61-29223-9072
Directorships: Raywood, Electronic Banking Solutions
Chris Stephenson, Chief Financial Officer

2791 GRUPO BISA
Recongquista 1166
11th Floor
Buenos Aires 1003
Argentina

Phone: 54-1143133830 Fax: 54-1143139030
web: www.grupobisa.com

Mission Statement: To make capital gains for investors as an active investor whose management skills contribute to create value in portfolio companies.

Fund Size: $150 Million
Founded: 1992
Average Investment: $15 Million
Minimum Investment: $5 Million
Investment Criteria: First Stage, Acquisitions, Recapitalizations, Special Situations, Consolidations, Privatization
Industry Group Preference: Broadcasting, Business to Business, Consumer Services, Entertainment, Financial Services, Food Services, Manufacturing, Retailing, Telecommunications, Wholesale, Cable, Radio, Distribution

Key Executives:
Nichollas Wollak, Director, Partner
Education: AB, Harvard University
Background: VP, Private Placement Department of Drexel Burnham Lambert, Executive Director, Invercapital

2792 GSR VENTURES
5620, China World Trade Center Tower III
No. 1 Jianguomenval Street
Chaoyang District
Beijing 100004
China

Phone: 86-10-5706-9898 Fax: 86-10-5706-9899
web: www.gsrventures.com

Mission Statement: GSR Ventures is a venture capital fund that invests primarily in early and growth stage technology companies with substantial operations in China.

Geographic Preference: China
Fund Size: $1 billion
Industry Group Preference: Semiconductors, Internet, Wireless, Green Technology

Other Locations:
245 Lytton Avenue
Suite 350
Palo Alto, CA 94301
Phone: 650-331-7300 Fax: 650-331-7301

Golden Sand River (Hong Kong) Limited

18 Harbour Road
Wanchai

Venture Capital & Private Equity Firms / International Firms

Hong Kong
Phone: 852-2201-6300 **Fax:** 852-2877-9833
Key Executives:
  James Ding, Managing Director
  e-mail: ding@gsrventures.com
  Education: BS, Chemistry, Peking University; MS, Information Science, UCLA; Haas Business School
  Background: Co-Founder, AsiaInfo-Linkage
  Directorships: BORQS, China Rainbow, NQ Mobile

2793 GUANGDONG TECHNOLOGY VENTURE CAPITAL COMPANY
13F. Hi-Tech R&D Center, 100 Mid Xianlie Rd
Guangzhou
China
Phone: 020-87683662 **Fax:** 020-87684955
Geographic Preference: Guangdong Province, China
Fund Size: 1.2 billion RMB
Founded: 1998
Investment Criteria: Expansion Stage
Industry Group Preference: Electronic Technology, Physical Sciences, Medical, Bioengineering, Environmental Protection, Materials Technology, Optical Technology
Portfolio Companies: Zhuhai Yueke Tsinghua Electronic Ceramics, Guangdong Hongtu Technology, Guangdong Ronsen Super Micro-wire, Shenzhen Sunlord Electronics, Shenzhen Yinboda Telecommunication Technology, Haikou Qili Pharmaceutical, Shenzhen WuZhouLong Motors, Shenzhen Green Materials Hi-tech

2794 GUIDANT EUROPE SA
Green Square, Lambroekstraat 5D
Culliganlaan 2B
Diegem 1831
Belgium
Phone: 32-24167011 **Fax:** 32-27141665
web: www.bostonscientific.com
Mission Statement: Investing in new medical technologies.
Geographic Preference: Europe
Fund Size: $47.3 Billion
Founded: 1979
Average Investment: $895 million
Minimum Investment: $3.8áBillion
Investment Criteria: Design and development of cardiovascular medical products
Industry Group Preference: Medical & Health Related
Portfolio Companies: Johnson and johnson
Key Executives:
  Michael F. Mahoney, President and Chief Executive Officer
  Kevin Ballinger, Senior Vice President and Global President

2795 GUJARAT STATE FERTILIZERS COMPANY LIMITED
PO Fertilizernagar
Vadodara 391 750
India
Phone: 91-2652242451 **Fax:** 91-2652240966
e-mail: info@gsfcltd.com
web: www.gsfclimited.com
Mission Statement: Actively seeking new investments.
Geographic Preference: India
Fund Size: $11 Million
Founded: 1962
Key Executives:
  Dr. Varesh Sinha, IAS, Chairman
  Dr. Hasmukh Adhia, IAS, Director

2796 HALDER BETEILIGUNGSBERATUNG GmbH
Bockenheimer Landstraáe 98-100
Frankfurt am Main 60323
Germany
Phone: 49- 692425330 **Fax:** 49-69236866
e-mail: mail@halder.eu
web: www.halder.eu
Mission Statement: Invests private equity in mature, profitable and well-managed mid to large-size companies.
Geographic Preference: Germany, Penelopes
Fund Size: $1.32 Billion
Founded: 1991
Average Investment: $8.4 Million
Minimum Investment: $15.2 Million
Investment Criteria: MBO, Management Buy-In, Expansion and Development
Industry Group Preference: Industrial Equipment, Manufacturing, Industrial Services
Portfolio Companies: FMA France, Deka-Brushes
Key Executives:
  Paul De Ridder, Partner
  e-mail: mail@halder-d.com
  Education: MBA, Business Administration
  Background: Private Equity
  Michael Wahl, Partner
  e-mail: mail@halder-d.com
  Background: Private Equity, Corporate Finance
  Susanne Quint, Managing Director, Partner
  e-mail: mail@halder-d.com
  Education: Degree, Business Administration
  Background: Private Equity(Halder)_
  Michael Wahl, Managing Partner
  e-mail: mail@halder-d.com
  Education: Degree, Business Administration
  Background: Private equity and Investment Banking

2797 HALDER HOLDINGS BV
Bockenheimer Landstraáe 98-100
Frankfurt am Main 60323
Germany
Phone: 49- 692425330 **Fax:** 49-69236866
e-mail: mail@halder.eu
web: www.halder.eu
Mission Statement: Invests private equity in mature, profitable and well managed companies mid to large-size companies.
Geographic Preference: Belgium, Europe, Germany, Netherlands
Founded: 1983
Minimum Investment: $150 Million
Investment Criteria: Expansion and Development, MBO, Management Buy-In, Bridge, Replacement
Industry Group Preference: Consumer Services, Industrial Equipment, Transportation, Industrial Services
Portfolio Companies: Arma Beheer BV, Badenia Bettcomfort GmbH & Company KG, Benefood NV, Bopack NV, Care4Data NV, Control Systems BV, Essanelle Hair Group AG, Euretco NV, FCS, Gealean Holding GmbH, Geka-brush GmbH, Goffin NV, Happich Fahzeug-und Industrieteile GmbH
Key Executives:
  Thomas Fotteler, Partner
  e-mail: mail@halder-d.com
  Background: 14 years private equity experience (Halder)
  Tanja Kilb, Office Manager
  e-mail: info@halder.nl
  Background: Risk capital (Halder, Oranje-Nassau Groep), Auditing (KPMG and Ernst & Young)
  Magdalena Kijak, Office Manager
  e-mail: info@halder.nl
  Background: Private equity, Management Consultancy , Marketing and Sales

Venture Capital & Private Equity Firms / International Firms

2798 HALLIM VENTURE CAPITAL
Kangnam-Gu Nonhyun-Dong 237-11
Dong Gang
Nam Gu
Seoul 135-010
South Korea

Phone: 82-2-511-6100 Fax: 82-2-511-6108

Geographic Preference: Korea
Founded: 1998
Industry Group Preference: Internet Technology, Biotechnology, Information Technology, Machinery
Portfolio Companies: Charm Engineering, Comware, Daewon Special Wire Co, ECtelecom, Integrant Technologies, JS Digitech, MEDIAI Co, PSIA, Sung Industrial, Tae-san Techno, Teltron Telecommunications & Electronics

Key Executives:
Kim Kwang, Chief Executive Officer
Education: BA Economics, MA Public Administration, Seoul National University; MS Finance, London Business School
Background: Assistant Planning Manager, Hansol Paper; President/CEO, Asia M&A Corp; President/CEO, A-One Venture Capital; Author; Director, Pan-Pacific Trading
Jung Dong Soo, Executive Director
Education: BBA, University of Korea
Background: Kookmin Venture Capital; Doobon Corp; Aztec Venture Capital Corp
Dong Soo Jung, Executive Director
Education: BA Chemical Engineering, Seoul National University; MBA, University of Washington
Background: Handysoft Corp; Deloitte Tohmatsu Japan; HP Consulting Corp; SUDO Pharm Corp
Jung Hoon Lee, General Manager
Education: BA Economics, Kyunghee University
Background: KICPA; Sinhan Accounting firm; AI Investment Management

2799 HAMBRO CAPITAL MANAGEMENT LTD
Ground Floor, Ryder Court, 14 Ryder Street
London SW1Y 6QB
United Kingdom

Phone: 44-2077475678 Fax: 44-2077-475647
e-mail: info@johcm.co.uk
web: www.johcm.co.uk

Mission Statement: JO Hambro's private equity funds invest in companies that are not listed on the stockmarket. Investments usually involve focused management by the team or fund managers and held for tww through five years before sale. The three funds are: Trident Private Equity Fund; Trident Private equity Fund II; and Leisure & Media VCT plc.

Fund Size: Euro 8.4 Billion
Industry Group Preference: Leisure, Media

Key Executives:
Jamie Hambro, Chairman
Background: Fund Manager, Kleinwort Benson; Citibank; Managing Director, Smith New Court Europe; Senior Fund Manager, Rowe Price Fleming International
Directorships: Northern Rock plc
Nichola Pease, Chief Executive
020-77475601
e-mail: slockyear@johcm.co.uk
Background: Samual Montagu Limited; Montagu Investment Management Limited; Director, Invesco MIM
Directorships: NASCIT; American Opportunity Trust
Gavin Rochussen, Chief Executive Officer
020-77475602
e-mail: jbrade@johcm.co.uk
Education: Science, Oxford University
Background: Diplomatic Officer, Foreign & Commonwealth Office
Maarten Hemsley, Fund Manager
020-77475604
e-mail: mhemsley@johcm.co.uk
Background: Founder, Bryanston Management Ltd; President/CFO of several companies
Directorships: Sterling Construction Company

2800 HAMON INVESTMENT GROUP
3510 - 3515 Jardine House, 1 Connaught Place
Central
Hong Kong

Phone: 852-25264268 Fax: 852-25267277
e-mail: enquiry@hamon.com.hk
web: www.hamon.com.hk

Mission Statement: Hamon Group is an independent asset management firm specializing in investing in the shares of regional Asian companies and emerging blue chip growth companies.

Geographic Preference: Hong Kong, China, South Korea, Taiwan, Singapore, Thailand, Malaysia
Founded: 1989

Key Executives:
Hugh Simon, Chief Executive Officer
e-mail: enquiry@hamon.com.hk
Background: he worked for Schroders in London, Australia and Hong Kong for five years. He has over 20 years of experience in Asian regional investments.
Raymond Chan, Managing Director & Chief Investment Officer

2801 HANNOVER FINANZ GmbH
Gunther-Wagner-Allee 13
Hanover 30177
Germany

Phone: 49-511280070 Fax: 49-5112800737
e-mail: mail@hannoverfinanz.de
web: www.hannoverfinanz.de

Mission Statement: Actively seeking new investments in growing companies, both for its own account and on behalf of five funds under its management.

Fund Size: $449 Million
Founded: 1979
Average Investment: $4.9 Million
Minimum Investment: $1.2 Million
Investment Criteria: Later Stage, Development, Buyout, Pre-IPO, Replacement
Industry Group Preference: Engineering, Service Industries, Telecommunications, Manufacturing, Financial Services, Media
Portfolio Companies: AIXTRON Semiconductor Technologie, Alt United Garment Service, AWECO, Biologische Analysensystem, BAG Med, BIG, Peter Butz, Commerz, Back-und Kondit, Display Design & Instore Marketing, Dittmers Korrosionsschutz, Wandel und Gotermann Management Holding, HL Leasing, Hanseatische Verlags-Beteiligung, Markant Sdwest Handel, Mecoswiss, Mechanische Componenten, MobilCom Holding

Key Executives:
Andreas Schober, Chief Executive Officer
Education: MBA
Johannes Voss, Investment Manager
Education: MSEE
Steffen Frenzel, Investment Manager
Education: Diploma-Kfm

Venture Capital & Private Equity Firms / International Firms

2802 HANSUTTAM FINANCE LIMITED
H-57, Connaught Circus
1st Floor
Suite 11-57
New Delhi 110001
India

Phone: 91-1123320876 Fax: 91-1123353944
e-mail: hfl@hansuttam.com
web: www.hansuttam.com

Mission Statement: A leading investment banking company headquartered in New Delhi

Geographic Preference: Malaysia, Singapore, Dubai, Turkey, UK, Israel
Founded: 1986
Investment Criteria: Sponsors, developers, investors, contractors, service companies, operators, financial institutions, governments
Industry Group Preference: All Sectors Considered

Key Executives:
Dipti Chopra, Chairman
e-mail: hfl@hansuttam.com
Background: PHDCCI, FICCI, ASSOCHAM
Shyam Kishore, Executive Director

2803 HANWHA VC CORPORATION
Hanwha Bldg., 15F # 1 Changgyo-Dong
Kangnam-Gu
Seoul NV
South Korea

Phone: 82-272-92836 Fax: 82-272-91447
web: www.hanwha.co.kr

Mission Statement: Actively seeking new investments.
Fund Size: $87.7 Billion
Founded: 1952
Industry Group Preference: Biotechnology

2804 HASSO PLATTNER VENTURES
PO Box 90 02 62
Potsdam D-14438
Germany

Phone: 49-033197992101 Fax: 49-033197992130
e-mail: info@hp-ventures.com
web: www.hp-ventures.com

Mission Statement: Our mission, instilled by our main investor, Prof. Dr. h.c. Hasso Plattner, founder and chairman of software giant SAP, is to support and inspire young software and IT entrepreneurs in the successful transformation of their ideas into sustainable and viable products and companies, in Germany and abroad.

Geographic Preference: Germany, Israel, Europe
Fund Size: 150 million Euro
Founded: 2005
Average Investment: 250,000 - 10 million Euro
Industry Group Preference: Information Technology, Software
Portfolio Companies: Monoqi, SponsorPay, ReBuy.de, Collax, Ujam, GoEuro, Panaya, D-Labs, Facton, Smeet, Senzari, Opensynergy, Dreamlines.de, Vioso, Diablo Technologies, Inchron, Kenesto, Vasco.de, My Heritage

Key Executives:
Yaron Valler, Managing Partner
Education: MBA, Tel Aviv University
Background: ProSeed Capital Fund, Eurofund, Inventech

2805 HASTINGS FUNDS MANAGEMENT PTY LIMITED
Level 27, 35 Collins Street
Melbourne 3000
Australia

Phone: 61-386503600 Fax: 61-386503701

Mission Statement: Activelty seeking new investments.
Geographic Preference: Australia
Fund Size: A$7.2 Billion
Founded: 1994
Portfolio Companies: Integrated Packaging Group, Acme Fine Furniture Natra Group, Craigcare Group, MCS Property Group.

Key Executives:
Andrew Day, CEO
e-mail: hfm@hfm.com.au
Education: Masters in Applied Statistics and a Masters in Mathematics from Oxford University.
Background: Cargill's
Colin Atkin, Executive Director
e-mail: hfm@hfm.com.au
Education: BCom, ACA
Background: Director of the private equity group

2806 HBM PARTNERS
Bundesplatz 1
2454 West Bay Road
Zug CH-6300
Switzerland

Phone: 41-438887171 Fax: 41-438887172
e-mail: lesieur@hbmcayman.com
web: www.hbmpartners.com

Mission Statement: HBM Partners is among the global leaders in healthcare-focused investing. HBM focuses on development stage, growth and buy-out financings of private companies as well as investments in public companies. HBM Partners advises HBM Healthcare Investments AG, HBM BioCapital and further specialized private-equity and public-equity funds. HBM has a complementary team of experienced professionals to source, analyze, execute and exit investments in the pharma/biotech, medical devices and diagnostics industries. We have been an active contributor to value creation in our portfolio companies, generating over 40 trade sales and IPOs since inception.

Fund Size: $800 million
Investment Criteria: Development Stage, Growth-Stage, Buyout
Industry Group Preference: Healthcare, Pharmaceuticals, Biotechnology, Medical Devices, Diagnostics
Portfolio Companies: Barofold, Cathay Industrial Biotech, Delenex, Enanta, Koltan Pharmaceuticals, Lux Biosciences, Nabriva, Nereus, Odyssey Thera, Opththotech, Paratek, Probiodrug, PTC, Symphony Evolution

Key Executives:
Andreas Wicki, CEO
Education: MSc, PhD, Chemistry & Biochemistry, University of Berne
Background: Co-Owner/CEO, ANAWA Holding, Clinserve

2807 HEALTHCAP Odlander, Fredrikson & Co AB
Strandvagen 5B
Stockholm SE-114 51
Sweden

Phone: 46-84425850 Fax: 46-84425879
e-mail: bjorn.odlander@ofco.se
web: www.healthcap.se

Mission Statement: HealthCap is a family of multi-stage venture capital funds, investing globally in life sciences, with the Odlander Fredrikson Group as their exclusive investments advisor. With committed capital exceeding 800 million Euros, HealthCap is one of the largest specialized providers of venture capital within life sciences in Europe.

Geographic Preference: Worldwide
Investment Criteria: Early State, Later Stage
Industry Group Preference: Life Sciences, Pharmaceuticals, Biotechnology, Medical Technology
Portfolio Companies: Aerocrine AB, Affibody AB, Alba Therapeutics, Algeta AS, Apoxis SA, Benechill Inc.,

BioStratum, Biotage AB, Bonesupport AB, Cardoz AB, Cebix, Cerenis Therapeutics, ChemoCentryx, Creative Peptides Sweden AB, Evotec, FerroKin Biosciences, Five Prime, Genzion BioSciences, IDEA AG, Immune Targeting Systems, Inion Ltd., LTB4 Sweden AB, Lumavita AG, MIPS AB, NeuroNova AB, Nexstim Ov, Nucleonics Inc., Odyssey Thera Inc., Oncos Therapeutics Ltd., Optuvt AB, Orexo AB, OxThera AB, PTC Therapeutics, PulmonX Corp., Renovis Inc., Sopherion Therapeutics Inc., SpineVision SA, Technolas Perfect Vision GmbH, Tengion Inc., TopoTarget A/S, Trigen Ltd., Ultrazonix DNT AB

Other Locations:
Odlander Fredrikson SA
18 Avenue D'Ouchy
Lausanne CH-1066
Switzerland
Phone: 41-21-614-3500 **Fax:** 41-21-601-5544

Key Executives:
Bjorn Odlander MD, Founding Partner
e-mail: bjorn.odlander@ofco.se
Education: PhD, Medical Chemistry
Background: Head, ABB Aros Health Care Equity Research Team

Peder Fredrikson, Founding Partner
e-mail: peder.fredrikson@healthcap.ch
Education: BSc, University of Lund
Background: Corporate Finance, ABB Aros; Managing Director, Dillon Read & Co., Inc.; Managing Director, Prudential-Bache Capital Funding

Staffan Lindstrand, Partner
e-mail: staffan.lindstrand@ofco.se
Education: MSc, Engineering, Royal Institute of Technology, Sweden
Background: Vice President, Aros Securities

Anki Forsberg, Partner
e-mail: anki.forsberg@ofco.se
Education: LLM, University of Helsinki; MBA, University of Uppsala
Background: Chief Administrative Officer, Odlander Fredrikson; President, Skandigen AB; Vice President, Industriforvaltnings AB Skandigen

Per Samuelsson, Partner
e-mail: per.samuelsson@ofco.se
Education: MSc, Engineering, Institute of Technology, Linkoping
Background: Director, Aros Securities

Johan Christenson, Partner
e-mail: johan.christenson@ofco.se
Education: MD, Karolinsak Institute
Background: SEB Foretagsinvest; Project Director, Astra Pain Control; Project Director, AstraZeneca

Marten Steen MD, Partner
e-mail: marten.steen@healthcap.eu
Education: BSc, Business Administration, Lund University School of Economics & Management; MD, Lund University; PhD, Clinical Chemistry
Background: Merck Serno

Jacob Gunterberg, Partner
e-mail: jacob.gunterberg@ofco.se
Education: MSc, Business Administration & Economics, University of Lund; University of St. Gallen
Background: Hjalmarsson & Gunterberg Corporate Finance; ABB Aros; Aros Securities

Eugen Steiner, Partner
e-mail: steiner.eugen@gmail.com
Background: CEO, Creative Peptides; CEO, Affibody AB; CEO, Calab Medical AB; CEO, Eurona Medical AB; CEO, Melacure Therapeutics AB; CEO, PyroSequencing AB; CEO, Visual Bioinformatics

Carl-Johan Dalsgaard, Partner
e-mail: carl-johan.dalsgaard@ofco.se
Education: PhD, Neurobiology, Harvard Medical School
Background: CEO, Biolipox AB; CEO, CePeP AB; CEO, Biofactor Therapeutics AB; CEO, Biocrine AB; VP Preclinical Research, Astra Pain Control AB

2808 HELIANT VENTURES
7/F, Kin On Commercial Building
49-51 Jervois Street
Sheng Wan
Hong Kong

Mission Statement: A Hong Kong based venture capital fund providing end-to-end support to its portfolio companies, leveraging its Asia/Australia relationships.

Geographic Preference: Asia, Australia
Investment Criteria: Early-Stage, Late-Stage
Industry Group Preference: Technology

Key Executives:
Ben Weiss, Managing Partner
Education: BCom, LLB, University of New South Whales; CFA; Sydney College of Law
Background: Salomon Smith Barney, Macquarie Bank, Shinsei Bank, AXA, CLSa, Baker & McKenzie

2809 HELION VENTURE PARTNERS, LLC
International Management (Mauritius) Ltd
Les Cascades Building
Edith Cavell Street
Port Louis
Mauritius

Phone: 230-212-9800 **Fax:** 230-212-9833
e-mail: contact.helion@gmail.com
web: www.helionvc.com

Mission Statement: Our mission is "Partnering with entrepreneurs to build world-class companies." We believe that companies are fundamentally built from inside, but as Board members we play an active role. Typically we help companies in making strategic choices in building and organization that can execute on strategy. We have access to world-class executives that we can bring to our portfolio companies. We also help in building a high quality Board of Directors/Advisors. We also team with the management and provide operational value in the area of finance, HR, technology, marketing and operations. In helping manage rapid growth, we participate in future rounds of financing in syndication with other venture partners.

Geographic Preference: India
Fund Size: $605 million
Investment Criteria: Early - mid Stage
Industry Group Preference: Clean Technology, Consumer Services, Education, Enterprise Software, Healthcare, Internet, Media, Mobile, Outsourcing & Efficiency, Technology-Enabled Products
Portfolio Companies: Azure Power, Brand Calculus, Qwikcilver, Hummingbird, YLG, Mast Kalandar, GTT, Attano, Vienova, Seclore, NetAmbit, IndiaHomes, Shubham, Eye-q, LifeCell, Jivox, Komli Media, TaxiForSure, MySmartPrice, ShopClues, 9.9 Media, GETiT, Ngpay, Kirusa, GupShup, Amba, Anantara, Hurix Systems, Mindworks, UnitedLex, Zmanda

Other Locations:
Helion Advisors Private Limited

Marathalli - Sarjapur Outer Ring Road
Bangalore 560 103
Karnataka
India
Phone: +91 80 4018 3333 **Fax:** +91 80 4018 3456

Helion Advisors Private Limited

Vatika Towers, Sector 54
Gurgaon 122 002
Haryana
India
Phone: +91 124 461 5333 **Fax:** +91 124 461 5345

Key Executives:
Ashish Gupta, Senior Managing Director, Co-Founder
Education: BA, Indian Institute Of Technology Kanpur; Ph.D, Computer Science, Stanford University

Background: Co-Founder, Tavant Technologies; Co-Founder, Junglee; Woodside Fund; Oracle Corporation, IBM
Directorships: Baboye.com, Dhingana, InfoEdge, Jivox, Kirusa, Komli, MySmartPrice.com, Pubmatic, SMSGupshup
Sanjeev Aggarwal, Senior Managing Director, Co-Founder
Education: Bachelors degree in Electrical Engineering; MBA
Background: Founder & CEO, Daksh; Motorola India; Digital Equipment Corporation; CEO 3COM India
Directorships: IndiaHomes, Azure Power, Amba Research, Eye-Q, ShopClues
Sandeep Fakun, Member Board of Directors
Dourvesh Kumar (Vikas) Chumun, Member Board of Director

2810 HELIX INVESTMENTS
Corner St. Georges and de Chazel Streets
Port Louis
Mauritius

Phone: 230-2036600
web: www.helix-investments.com

Founded: 2007
Average Investment: $5-20 million

2811 HELMET CAPITAL FUND MANAGEMENT OY
Fredrikinkatu 48 A, 11th floor
Helsinki 00100
Finland

Phone: 358-96869220 Fax: 358-968692241
e-mail: info@helmetcapital.fi
web: www.helmetcapital.fi

Mission Statement: Helmet specializes in ownership arrangements and development of non-listed growth companies.
Geographic Preference: Finland
Fund Size: $24, 2 Million
Founded: 1995
Investment Criteria: Early Stage, Mid-Stage
Industry Group Preference: Biotechnology, Metals, Electronic Technology, Information Technology, Electronic Technology, Retailing
Key Executives:
 Seppo Ahonen, Founding Partner
 e-mail: pauli@helmetcapital.fi
 Education: MSc, (Eng.), MBA
 Background: Fortum Oyj & Tamro Group
 Kalevi Puonti, Founding Partner

2812 HENDERSON PRIVATE CAPITAL
201 Bishopsgate
London EC2M 3AE
United Kingdom

Phone: 44-2078181818 Fax: 44-2078181819
web: www.henderson.com

Mission Statement: Henderson is a leading investor in a new and constantly growing area of the European infrastructure market — operational stakes in Private Finance Initiative (PFI) projects.
Geographic Preference: Europe, Asia Pacific
Fund Size: Euro 64, 825 Million
Founded: 1934
Industry Group Preference: Waste & Recycling, Education, Health Related, Leisure, Publishing
Portfolio Companies: Baydrive Limited, Boat International Publications, Leisure Link Holdings Limited, Redecam Group SpA, Vacant Property Security Limited, Homann Chilled Foods

Key Executives:
 Andrew Formica, Chief Executive
 e-mail: paul.woodbury@henderson.com
 Education: BA (Hons) in Politics and Economics
 Background: Member of Institute of Transport and Logistics
 Roger Thompson, Chief Financial Officer
 e-mail: roger.greville@henderson.com
 Education: Bachelor of Agricultural Economics & Master of Commerce (Economics)
 Directorships: Chairman of the Investment Committee.
 Phillip Apel, Head of Fixed Income
 e-mail: rahul.bhargava@henderson.com
 Education: Bachelor of Science (Economics) from the University of Calcutta and an MBA from the Australian Graduate School of Management.
 Background: Ion Global
 Lesley Cairney, Chief Operating Officer
 e-mail: matteo.perale@henderson.com
 Education: MBA from Columbia University, a master degree in international business from HEC in Paris and has a summa cum laude degree in economics from Bocconi in Milan.
 Background: Palamon Capital Partners, Warburg Pincus & McKinsey & Co
 Jacqui Irvine, General Counsel
 e-mail: guy.pigache@henderson.com
 Education: BSc Honours degree in Maths and Physics from Kings College, London.
 Background: HSBC
 Graham Kitchen, Head of Equities
 e-mail: steven.proctor@henderson.com
 Education: Chartered Management Accountant & Economics Degree from St. Andrews University.
 Background: Sumitomo Mitsui Banking Corporation

2813 HENQ
Herengracht 124-128
1015 BT Amsterdam
Netherlands

Phone: +31 10 452 1346
e-mail: info@henq.nl
web: www.henq.nl

Mission Statement: henQ helps its companies to build a strong international network, access high-level expertise and distribution power, attract the right people to grow the company, set ambitious goals and stick to them, apply a lean methodology for efficient growth, and maintain focus. henQ's founders have a considerable experience in both business and investing, and know how to make companies grow. Through their extensive network, they can also hook up entrepreneurs with other valuable people.
Geographic Preference: The Netherlands
Investment Criteria: Startup
Industry Group Preference: E-Commerce & Manufacturing, Mobile, Analytics & Analytical Instruments, Software Development
Portfolio Companies: Campalyst, CWR Mobility, IS enterprise, Libersy, Mads, Mendix, Monolith, Myngle, PlayToTV, Seedcamp, SEOshop, Studytube, Videostrip, Wakoopa, Xite
Key Executives:
 Herman Hintzen, Co-Founder
 Background: Founder, Arpa Systems; Co-Founder, Great Idea Factory
 Coen van Duiven, Co-Founder
 Background: Unilever Investement Group

2814 HG CAPITAL
2 More London Riverside
Minerva House
3rd Floor
London SE1 2AP
United Kingdom

Phone: 44-2070897888 Fax: 44-2070897999
e-mail: info@hgcapital.com
web: www.hgcapital.net

Mission Statement: Hg Capital is the successor to Mercury Private Equity (founded 1985). The staff of MPE aquired the business from Merrill Lynch and renamed the company. It has funds under management of 1.4 billion euro and services over 200 institutional clients and manag

Geographic Preference: United Kingdom, Western Europe, Ireland, Germany, Benelux
Fund Size: $42.48 Billion
Founded: 2000
Average Investment: $177 Million
Minimum Investment: $70 Million
Investment Criteria: Expansion, Leveraged Buy-Out, Public-to-Private, Turnarounds, Divisions, Business Assets
Industry Group Preference: All Sectors Considered, Health Related, Consumer Services, Media, Leisure, Industrial Services, Technology, Renewable Energy, Consumer Products
Portfolio Companies: Addison Software, Alizyme, Allegro, Axiom, Ballygowan, Barracuda, Belfast International Airport, Bertram, Boosey & Hawkes, Braitrim, BrightReasons, Britt Allcroft Group, Burns e-Commerce Solutions, Castlebeck, Checkpoint, CityFlyer Express, Clarion Events

Key Executives:

Martin Block, Director
e-mail: frances.jacob@hgcapital.net
Education: Engineering degree, Durham University
Background: Production Engineer, 3i plc

Stephen Bough, Director, Finance
2070897982
e-mail: stephen.bough@hgcapital.net
Education: Stephen qualified as an accountant while at Prudential Assurance Company where he spent ten years.
Background: Accountant, Prudential Assurance Company

James Bath, Portfolio Management Team
2070897962
e-mail: lindsay.dibden@hgcapital.net
Education: Aeronautical Engineering, Imperial College
Background: Corporate Finance, Coopers & Lybrand

Tom Murley, Head Renewable Energy Team
e-mail: tom.murley@hgcapital.net
Background: Co-Head Renewable Energy Team, Allianz Private Equity; EIF Group; Corporate Lawyer

Martin Block, Portfolio Management Team
2070897950
e-mail: ian.armitage@hgcapital.net
Education: Politics, Philosophy, Economics, Oxford University
Background: 3i plc
Directorships: Chairman, Investor Relations Committee of the British Venture Capital Association; Orbiscom; ClinPhone; Comnitel; Profiad

Lisa Stone, Portfolio Management
2070897960
e-mail: lisa.stone@hgcapital.net
Education: Human Sciences, Oxford University
Background: Director Strategy/Business Planning, LucasVarity; Management Consultant, Kalchas; Management Consultant, Bain & Co
Directorships: IRIS Software; Remploy; Newchurch; Match; Tunstall; Profiad; Trados

Nic Humphries, Managing Partner
2070897987
e-mail: nic.humphries@hgcapital.net
Education: First Class degree Electronic Engineering; IEEE; National Engineering Council Scholar
Background: General Partner, Geocapital Partners; Telecom/IT Team Head, Barclay Private Equity; 3i plc
Directorships: Axiom; IRIS Software; Rolfe & Nolan; Xyratex

Rob de Laszlo, Renewable Energy Team
2070897892
Education: BA, MBA, London School of Business
Background: Strategy Consultant, Braxton Associates
Directorships: The Sanctuary Spa

Saad Islam, Renewable Energy Team
2070897940
Education: Psychology, Durham University
Background: Leveraged Finance, Bankers Trust; Chartered Accountant, Coopers & Lybrand; Corporate Finance, Charterhouse Bank

2815 HIGH-TECH GRUENDERFONDS
Schlegelstrasse 2
Bonn 53113
Germany

Phone: 0228-82300100 Fax: 0228-82300050
web: www.high-tech-gruenderfonds.de

Mission Statement: Since 2005, High-Tech Grunderfonds has been financing young technology companies on attractive terms and actively supporting their management teams with a strong network and entrepreneurial expertise. We are focused on investing in early stage companies in life science, materials science, and information technology. In our first 5 years we financed approximately 250 companies from the high-tech sector and successfully set them on their way.

Geographic Preference: Germany
Fund Size: 301 million Euro
Founded: 2005
Investment Criteria: Early-Stage
Industry Group Preference: Life Sciences, Materials Technology, Information Technology, Clean Technology, Consumer Products, Nanotechnology
Portfolio Companies: AdvanceCOR, Advanova, Algiax, Altruja, Amedo, Amedrix, Antispameurope, Audiocure, Autoaid, Autoloader, Anvendeo Designwelt, Avidal, AyoxxA, Babla, Baimos Technologies, Base Case Management, Biametrics, BioRob, Bohner-EH, Bomedus, Bubbles & Beyond, C-Lecta, C2Call, CA Customer Alliance, Capical, CargoGuard, Caterna, ChromoTek, Cliqloc, Collinor Software, Commercetools, Compositence, Conceptboard, Confovis, Contros, ConWeaver, Corrmoran, CorTec, Crealytics, Crossvertise, Cryotherpeutics, CrystAI-N, Cubical, Cuculus, Cumulocity, CureFab, Cysal, Deal United, Dilitronics, Divolution, DJTunes.com, DRDx, E-Senza Technologies, EBS Technologies, EcoIntense, eGym, Enercast, Enexion, Entellios, Evocatal, ExCentos, Eyefactive, Eyesight&Vision, Ezeep, FamPlus, Fiagon, Fidlock, Fos4x, Fruux, FTAPI SecuTransfer, Futalis, Galantos Pharma, GameGenetics, GeneQuine, Gestigon, Gfnmediber, Gilupi, Gimahot, GME, GrandCentrix, H.C. Carbon, Hapila, Heliatek, Hematris Wound Care, HiperScan, HMC+, HR New Media, Humangride, Humedics, IBK Bioanalytik, ILIAS-Medical, Immunservice, Implandata Opthalmic Products, InnoCyte, InnoMotix, Intana Bioscience, Intermed, IQ Evolution, JeNaCell, JenAffin, JobLeads, Keyrocket, Klmeta, Kiwigrid, KonTEM, Krohnert Infotecs, LaTherm, Lenimed, Limata, Lipocalyx, Livedome, Locr, Lophius Biosciences, Luceo Technologies, Luphos, M2p-Labs, Maxment, Mbm Systems, Medovent, MeinProspekt, MicroNet Automation, Microstim, MimoOn, MinCell, Mister Spex, Mivenion, ML-C,

Key Executives:

Alexander von Frankenberg, Managing Director
e-mail: a.frankenberg@high-tech-gruenderfonds.de
Education: Business Economics, University of Manheim; MBA, University of Texas, Austin
Background: Andersen Consulting, Siements Management Consulting, Siemens Technology Accelerator

Venture Capital & Private Equity Firms / International Firms

2816 HIGHGROWTH
Tuset, 20-24, 4 5
Barcelona 08006
Spain

Phone: 34-933630386 Fax: 34-932183333

Mission Statement: Highgrowth is an independent financial company that invests in innovative companies with growth potential, providing them with support, advice and guidance, through two clearly differentiated business lines: management of venture capital funds aimed at companies in their initial launch phases, business consulting and training of entrepreneurs.

Key Executives:
Ferran Lemus, President/Partner
Education: Economics, Barcelona University; MA, European Studies, Reading University
Background: Banco de Vizcaya, Argentaria/Banco Exterior

2817 HIKARI TSUSHIN CAPITAL
1-16-15 Toshima-ku, Minami-Ikebukuro
Tokyo 171-0021
Japan

Phone: 81-359513718 Fax: 81-359513709
e-mail: info@po.hikari.co.jp
web: www.hikari.co.jp

Mission Statement: Hikari Tsushin has taken a leadership role in investing in the ever-changing world of communications and technology

Geographic Preference: Japan
Founded: 1988
Industry Group Preference: Internet Technology, Information Technology, Telecommunications
Portfolio Companies: Estore, Edge, MTI, Goodwill Group, Global Media Online, KBOS, SOTEC, Digital Arts, Nexus, Prime System, Emachines

Key Executives:
Shigeta Yasumitsu, Chairman & Chief Executive Officer
e-mail: info@po.hikari.co.jp
Takeshi Tamamura, President & Chief Operating Officer

2818 HILKO UK LTD/VALCO CAPITAL PARTNERS
80 New Bond Street
London W1S 1SB
United Kingdom

Phone: 44-02073172050 Fax: 44-02073172051
e-mail: info@hilcouk.com

Mission Statement: Hilco is uniquely positioned to evaluate, recommend and implement the best course of action. We do this successfully because we are an independent, objective team with unique skills and substantial experience. We have been involved in many of the most notable retail restructuring projects in the last five years in the UK and continental Europe.

Geographic Preference: United Kingdom, Europe
Investment Criteria: Retail Acquisitions, Mergers, Divestitures, Restructurings, Asset Disposition
Industry Group Preference: Retailing

Key Executives:
Paul McGowan, Principal and Senior Directors
Background: KPMG; Operations Director, Jacqmar Plc; Leslie Fay Ltd
Andrew Pepper, Principal and Senior Directors
Background: Partner, Kroll & BDO; KMPG; PwC
Howard Gunn, European Chief Financial Officer
Background: Accountant, Peat Marwick Mitchell & Co; Finance Director, CHS Electronics Plc
Mark O'Neill, Investment Analyst
Background: Vice President, Lesco; Roses Discount Stores; Target Stores; Macy's Department Store
Chris Emmott, Investment Director
Henry Foster, Investment Director
Steven Pell, Investment Director
Background: Strategy Consultant, Kalchas Group; CRO Team, NTL

2819 HOLLAND VENTURE BV
Franz Zieglerstraat 24
Amsterdam 1087 HN
Netherlands

Phone: 31-203119411 Fax: 31-206973326
e-mail: info@hollandventure.com
web: www.hollandventure.com

Mission Statement: Holland Venture is an independent private equity fund located in Amsterdam. Since 1981 Holland Venture has realized the growth potential of many of its investments and has proven to be a trustworthy partner.

Geographic Preference: Netherlands
Fund Size: $216 Million
Founded: 1981
Industry Group Preference: Business to Business, Medical, Security
Portfolio Companies: Sunday's Nederland BV, Brinkhof Group International NV, SigValue Technologies Inc., Bwise BV, Decell, Mr.Ted Ltd. Macaw BV, INS SA, Royal Mosa BV & Freecom Technologies BV

Key Executives:
Rolf Deves, managing director
e-mail: info@hollandventure.com
Hubert Verbeek, Managing Partner
e-mail: info@hollandventure.com
Ewout Prins, Managing Partner
e-mail: info@hollandventure.com

2820 HOLTZBRINCK VENTURES
Kaiserstrasse 14b
Munich 80801
Germany

Phone: 49-892060770 Fax: 49-8920607742
web: www.holtzbrinck-ventures.com

Mission Statement: Being one of the most successful venture capital firms, we have been supporting founders in developing their Internet companies for over a decade. During this time, we as a team have financed over 100 companies. We seek founders who share our passion for growth and innovation and who want to achieve excellence working as a team.

Founded: 2000
Average Investment: 250,000 - 5 million Euro
Investment Criteria: Early-Stage
Industry Group Preference: Internet
Portfolio Companies: Zalando, Dafiti, Wooga, Westwing, eDarling, Game Duell, Experteer, GlossyBox, Adscale, Lamoda, Home 24, 21Diamonds, Delivery Hero, Auctionata, BerryAvenue, Hello Fresh, DaWanda, Fashion for Home, Pippa Jean, Kiveda, Lazada, Linio, Namshi, Mindmatics, MeinAuto.de, Outfittery, YepDoc, MusicPlayr, DropGifts, BillPay, Payleven, Paymill, Ozon.ru, Goodbeans, Semasio, HitFox Group, Autoda, Care.com, Studitemps, Stylight, Seatwave, Lecturio, Classmarkets, Cafe Press, TrustYou, Kissnofrog, InterNations, VirtualNights, Rumble Media, Proximic, Restaurant-Kritik.de, Gute TV Laune, Newtron, Deutsche Startups, Innofact

Key Executives:
Sven Achter, General Partner
e-mail: sven.achter@holtzbrinck.net
Education: Masters, Information Technology, Technical University of Munich
Background: Consultant, Hewlett Packard

Venture Capital & Private Equity Firms / International Firms

2821 HONGKONG LAND INFRASTRUCTURE LIMITED
8th Floor, One Exchange Square
Central
Hong Kong

Phone: 852-28428428 **Fax:** 852-28459226
e-mail: gpobox@hkland.com
web: www.hkland.com

Mission Statement: Actively seeking new investments.
Geographic Preference: Hongkong, Singapore, Vietnam, China
Founded: 1889
Key Executives:
Simon Keswick, Chairman
e-mail: gpobox@hkland.com
Background: Jardine Matheson group,
Directorships: Chairman of Jardine Matheson Limited, and managing director of Dairy Farm International Holdings, Jardine Matheson Holdings, Jardine Strategic Holdings and Mandarin Oriental I
Y.K. Pang, Chief Executive

2822 HORIZONS VENTURES
Hong Kong

e-mail: general@horizonsventures.com
web: www.horizonsventures.com

Mission Statement: Horizons Ventures is Hong Kong based venture capital firm, focused on technology and disruptive ideas.
Geographic Preference: Hong Kong
Founded: 2006
Industry Group Preference: Hardware, Electronics, Artificial Intelligence, Financial Services, Mobile, Digital Media & Marketing, Social Media, Analytics & Analytical Instruments, Security, Data & Analytics
Portfolio Companies: Affdex, Aniways, Bitcase, Bitpay, Bitstrips, Core Photonics, Cortica, Crosswire, Deepmind, Desti, Everything.me, Facebook, Filip, Fixmo, Friendsurance, Genetic Finance, Ginger, Guardtime, Hampton Creek, Hola!, How.do, HzO, Interaxon, Invi, Kaiima, Kuato, Lock8, Magisto, Medial Cancer Screening, MeMed, Meteo-Logic, Misfit, Mishor, Nanoleaf, NanoSpun, NBA.com China, Nipendo, Onavo, Preen.me, Rubikloud, Secondmarket, Shine, Siri, Skype, Spotify, Stevie, Summly, Tempo, Traity, Trap!T, Union Mobile Pay, Waze, Wibbitz, Zoom
Key Executives:
Li Ka-Shing, Founder/Chairman

2823 HORIZONTE VENTURE MANAGEMENT GmbH
c/o Regus Opera
Kärntner Ring 5-7
Wien A-1010
Austria

Phone: 43-15335601 **Fax:** 43-153356014
e-mail: office@horizonte.at
web: www.horizonte.at

Mission Statement: Actively seeking investments in small and medium-sized enterprises which have the potential to achieve internationally important market positions
Geographic Preference: Austria, Central European countries
Fund Size: $8.4 Million
Founded: 1985
Average Investment: $1.2 Million
Minimum Investment: $600, 000
Investment Criteria: Start-up
Industry Group Preference: Biotechnology, Information Technology
Portfolio Companies: Rudjer Boskovic Institute, Splonum, Styrotherm
Key Executives:
Martin Wodak, Managing Partner
Education: Physics at the Technical University in Vienna and obtained a doctorate in physics (Ph.D.) from the University of Pennsylvania, Philadelphia
Background: Dr. Krejs worked in the area of financing of technical innovations in Vienna (Innova, FGG
Directorships: participated in TVM-Techno Venture Management's start-up.
Alfred Matzka, Managing Partner
e-mail: dansco@horizonte.at
Education: Doctorate in business administration from the Wirtschaftsuniversität Wien
Background: Worked at the Austrian Ministry of Trade and subsequently as a consultant to small and medium sized companies
Directorships: After three years with an accounting and auditing firm he joined FGG in 1981 and led FGG's division for risk financing and turn-around management. Dr. Matzka joined Horizonte
Dr. Matej Penca, Managing Partner
e-mail: dansco@horizonte.at
Education: Ph.D. in chemistry of the University of Ljubljana and wrote his doctoral thesis on Decision Algorithms for Chemical Information Systems.
Background: Was an associate professor at the University of Ljubljana, and a Visiting Fellow at the US National Institutes of Health (NIH) design of IR search medule for the Chemical Information System (CIS) run by NIH and the Environmental Protection Agency (EPA).
Directorships: He later was director of the Informatics Department at SMELT global project management, Ljubljana and Counsellor to the Ministry of Science and Technology in the Government of

2824 HOSEO VENTURE CAPITAL
1603-54 Seocho-dong
Kangnam Telpia Building
13th Floor
Seoul 137-070
South Korea

Phone: 82-234-878400 **Fax:** 82-234-878500

Mission Statement: Actively seeking new investments.
Geographic Preference: South Korea
Fund Size: $69 Million
Founded: 2000
Investment Criteria: Early-stage and growth companies
Industry Group Preference: Telecommunications, Information Technology
Portfolio Companies: Uju Electronics, D-gate Semiconductor, CJ Entertainment, Innostream, Bellwave, MC Technology, Chips & Media, Gravity

2825 HOXTON VENTURES
1 Fore St.
London EC2Y 9DT
United Kingdom

e-mail: businessplans@hoxton.vc
web: www.hoxtonventures.com

Mission Statement: Hoxton Ventures partners with founders in early stage technology who are seeking to invent new market categories or transform existing ones.
Geographic Preference: United Kingdom, United States, India
Investment Criteria: Early-Stage
Industry Group Preference: Technology, Software, Internet, Mobile
Portfolio Companies: Adazza, Algomi, Babylon, Behavox, DarkTrace, Deliveroo, Mainframe, Optimo Route, Raptor Supplies, Super Awesome, Tourradar, Vitesse, Yieldify

Venture Capital & Private Equity Firms / International Firms

Key Executives:
  Hussein Kanji, Partner
  Education: Stanford University; MBA, London Business School
  Directorships: POPxo, bd4travel, Darktrace, TourRadar, Babylon, Behavox, Yieldify
  Rob Kniaz, Partner
  Education: Stanford University; BS, University of Maryland
  Directorships: Deliveroo, Raptor Supplies, Babylon

2826 HRL MORRISON & COMPANY LIMITED
Level 19, 1 Eagle Street, Waterfront Place
Brisbane
Queensland 4001
Australia

Phone: 61-733600295 Fax: 61-732200855
e-mail: info@hrlmorrison.com.au
web: www.hrlmorrison.com

Mission Statement: Actively seeking new investments.
Geographic Preference: Australia, New Zealand, Europe
Fund Size: $5 Billion
Founded: 1988
Industry Group Preference: Infrastructure, Energy, Aviation
Key Executives:
  Rob Morrison, Chairman
  Steven Fitzgerald, Executive Director Airports Group

2827 HSBC VENTURES UK LIMITED
78 St. James Street
London SW1A 1JB
United Kingdom

Phone: 44-2078605000 Fax: 44-2078605001
web: www.hsbcprivatebank.com

Mission Statement: Invests in British companies that are at least three years old and which offer potential for growth.
Geographic Preference: United Kingdom
Founded: 1853
Average Investment: $26.59 Million
Minimum Investment: $3.55 Million
Investment Criteria: Expansion and Development, Refinancing bank debt, Secondary purchase/replacement capital, MBO, MBI
Industry Group Preference: All Sectors Considered
Portfolio Companies: Comcen Computer Supplies Ltd, Connaught Group Ltd, Lady In Leisure Ltd, Reward Group Ltd, VFG Plc
Key Executives:
  Stephen K Green, Chairman
  Peter Widmer, Vice Chairman
  Paul Chambers, Director
  Tom Chaloner, Director
  Mike Barstow, Investment Manager
  Derek King, Investment Manager

2828 HUMMINGBIRD VENTURES
Hangar 26/27
Rijinkaai 98
Antwerp 2000
Belgium

Phone: 32-32923710
e-mail: info@hummingbird-ventures.com
web: www.hummingbirdventures.com

Mission Statement: Hummingbird Ventures is a venture capital fund for high-growth digital media and software companies. In addition to funding, Hummingbird Ventures leverages its extensive operational experience and worldwide network to actively help startups accelerate their growth.
Geographic Preference: Europe, Turkey, Middle East
Founded: 2000
Average Investment: 500,000 - 2 million Euros
Investment Criteria: Early-Stage
Industry Group Preference: Digital Media & Marketing, Software
Portfolio Companies: Amplidata, Avinity, CicekSepeti, Clear2Pay, CVWarehouse, Cybersports, Dacentec/Awingu, DataCenter Technologies, Dedigate, Digitouch, IS/Pins, iQu, Peak Games, PeopleCube, Q-layer, MarkaVIP, Ractivity, Shutl, Wakoopa
Other Locations:
  2nd Floor, White Bear Yard
  144A Clerkenwell Road
  London EC1R 5DF
  United Kingdom

  Esentepe Mah. Atom Sokak
  King Plaza 18, 6th Floor
  Levent
  Istanbul
  Turkey
Key Executives:
  Barend Van den Brande, Managing Partner
  e-mail: barend@hummingbird-ventures.com
  Education: MS, Economics, University of Louvain, Belgium
  Background: President, Benelux Tech Tour; Co-Founder, SwiftTouch
  Directorships: Clear2Pay, MMO Life, Wakoopa, Travel Intelligence Group, Cybersports, Shutl

2829 HV HOLTZBRINCK VENTURES
Kaiserstrasse 14b
Munich 80801
Germany

Phone: 49-89-20-60-770 Fax: 49-89-20-60-7742
e-mail: information@holtzbrinck.net
web: www.holtzbrinck-ventures.com

Mission Statement: Being one of the most successful venture capital firms, we have been supporting founders in developing their Internet companies for over a decade. During this time, we as a team have financed over 100 companies. We seek founders who share our passion for growth and innovation and who want to achieve excellence working as a team.
Investment Criteria: Seed Stage, Early-Stage
Industry Group Preference: Internet
Portfolio Companies: Zalando, Dafiti, Wooga, Westwing, eDarling, Game Duell, Experteer, GlossyBox, Lamoda, Home24, 21Diamonds, Delivery Hero, Aucionata, Outfittery, Hello Fresh, DaWanda, Fashion for Home, Pippa Jean, Kiveda, Paymill, Jabong, Lazada, Linio, Namshi, Flixbus, JetLore, Depop, HitFox Group, Mindmatics, MeinAuto, Springlane, Wonga, BillPay, Payleven, Ozon.ru, Goodbeans, Semasio, Care.com, L'ArcoBaleno, Studitemps, Stylight, Seatwave, Lecturi, Classmarkets, Cupo Nation, Trust You, Kiss No Frog, Smartlaw, InterNations, Virtual Nights, GlamLoop, Locafox, Funanga, MusicPlayr, BerryAvenue, Rumble Media, Proximic, Gute TV Laune, Newtron, Deutsche Startups, Innofact AG, Restaurant Kritic
Key Executives:
  Sven Achter, General Partner
  e-mail: sven.achter@holtzbrinck.net
  Education: Master Degree, Information Techology, Technical University of Munich
  Background: Immobileenscout, Hewlett-Packard

2830 HYUNDAI VENTURE INVESTMENT CORPORATION
National Information Society Agency Bldg.
4th Floor
Seoul
South Korea

Phone: 82-27288990 Fax: 82-27288999
e-mail: webmaster@hvic.co.kr
web: www.hvic.co.kr

Venture Capital & Private Equity Firms / International Firms

Mission Statement: HVIC partners with companies who have innovative technology but weak finances and management.
Geographic Preference: South Korea
Fund Size: $39.6 Million
Founded: 1997
Investment Criteria: Small-stage and Mid-stage
Industry Group Preference: Information Technology, Biotechnology, Software, Internet Technology
Portfolio Companies: Dusan Co. LTD, Daum Communications corp, DB and SOFT, Ecoin Co Ltd, Em Teck, Econex, Gracel, GaeaSoft. ICO Inc. & Imas Co Ltd.
Key Executives:
  Mong-il Chung, Chairman & Chief Executive Officer
  e-mail: webmaster@hvic.co.kr
  Education: Graduates Business Administration dept. of Yonsei University
  Background: Daewoo Corp. & Hyundai International Merchant Bank
  Jong-Sung Lee, Adviser
  e-mail: webmaster@hvic.co.kr
  Education: Graduates Bae-jae High School & MBA from George Washington University in U.S.A
  Background: Hyundai International Merchant Bank & Hyundai Capital

2831 I-PACIFIC PARTNERS
6rd Floor, Hyundai Intellex Bldg
Samsung Dong Gang
Nam Gu
Seoul 135-832
Korea

Phone: 82-234-465861 Fax: 82-234-465864

Mission Statement: Invests in promising new ventures and provides hand-on management support. Manages three funds.
Fund Size: 46.5 Million
Founded: 2000
Industry Group Preference: Wireless Technologies, Telecommunications, Software, Electronic Technology, Media
Key Executives:
  Youngmin Yune, President & Chief Executive Officer
  Jerry Shim, Director

2832 IBB BETEILIGUNGSGESELLSCHAFT MBH
Bundesallee 210
10719 Berlin
Germany

Phone: +49 30 2125 3201 Fax: +49 30 2125 3202
e-mail: venture@ibb-bet.de
web: www.ibb-bet.de

Mission Statement: IBB Beteiligungsgesellschaft mbH provides venture capitalfor young Berlin-based technology-oriented companies and companies from the creative industries. We were founded in 1997 as a 100% subsidiary of Investitionsbank Berlin to support Berlin-based small and medium-sized enterprises. Since 1997, syndicates involving IBB Beteiligungsgesellschaft mbH have provided Berlin-based companies with more than 1, 430 m EUR.
Geographic Preference: Berlin
Fund Size: 100 Mio. EUR
Founded: 1997
Average Investment: 500 KEUR
Minimum Investment: 200 KEUR
Investment Criteria: Equity
Industry Group Preference: Creative Industries, Information Technology, Communication Technology, Life Sciences, Industrial Technology
Portfolio Companies: 21sportsgroup, ALRISE, Blinks Labs, blogfoster, CareerFoundry, Content Flow, CrossEngage, Crowd Guru, dailyme TV, Dalia Research, Dentolo, DiaMonTech, EMC (Emmy), Eternygen, Fairr.De, flexperto, Fliit, German Auto Labs, Getsurance, Hey Group, High-Mobility, Humedics, JobUFO, labfolder, Learnfield (Skoove), Lesson Nine (Babbel), LLS Internet (loopline), Lumenaza, Lunchio, machtfit, Media4Care, Meetrics, Myelo, MyGall, MYMORIA, Natural Dental Implants, Neonga, NursIT, Omeicos, ONO Labs, Outfittery, Paper and Tea, PictureTree, Qinous, R3 Communications, Realbest, Remerge, Selfapy, Seniovo, Smart Host, Sofatutor, Softgames, Spark Networks, Spontaneous Order, Store2be, SuitePad, Tausendkind, Thermondo, Travelcircus, Ubitricity, Vetevo, Viasto, Websitebutler, Wunderflats
Key Executives:
  Roger Bendisch, Managing Director
  Marco Zeller, Managing Director

2833 IBK CAPITAL CORPORATION Industrial Bank of Korea
702-22 Yoksam-dong
Seoul NV
South Korea

Phone: 82-25543131 Fax: 82-25683533
web: www.ibk.co.kr

Mission Statement: Focuses on promoting growth among Korea's small and medium-sized enterprises (SMEs).
Geographic Preference: Korea
Founded: 1961
Investment Criteria: Small and medium-sized enterprises (SMEs

2834 IBRIDGE CAPITAL CORPORATION
Stanley Street
5th & 17th Floor, Malahon Centre
Central
Hong Kong

Phone: 852-25263280 Fax: 852-25267299

Mission Statement: iBridge Capital Group is a pan-Asian group of companies with two principal business areas providing professional services to established businesses as well as young, growing companies.
Geographic Preference: Asia

2835 IBUSINESS CORPORATION
12/F Cheung Kong Center, 2 Queen's Road
Central
Hong Kong

Phone: 852-21263333 Fax: 852-21211111
web: www.ibusiness-hk.com

Mission Statement: iBusiness Corporation Limited invests in and builds profitable e-commerce, m-commerce, Internet and software technology infrastructure businesses.
Geographic Preference: Asia
Fund Size: $250 Billion
Investment Criteria: Start up and Eastablished companies
Portfolio Companies: AMTD, Excel Technology, mReferral
Key Executives:
  Victor Li, Deputy Chairman & Managing Director
  e-mail: contact@ibusiness-hk.com
  Directorships: Executive Director, CEO - iBusiness Corporation Ltd.
  Edmond Ip, Executive Director

2836 ICAN ISRAEL-CANNABIS.COM
Hauman 5
Beit Shemesh
Israel

Phone: 972-545-604843
e-mail: info@israel-cannabis.com
web: www.israel-cannabis.com

Mission Statement: An Israel-based accelerator and incubator firm dedicated to the global medical cannabis inudstry.
Fund Size: $3.1M

Venture Capital & Private Equity Firms / International Firms

Founded: 2015
Investment Criteria: Seed
Industry Group Preference: Cannabis, Healthcare, Biotech
Portfolio Companies: Cannabis Mercantile Trading Exchange, Yom Chai, CannRx Technology Inc., Cannabinit

Key Executives:
   Saul Kaye, Founer/CEO
   Education: BSc, Pharmacy, Curtin University of Technology; BPharm, University of Sydney
   Background: Founer, Pharma Shaul Pharmacy; Founder/Investor, Start Up Beit Shemesh; Co-Founder, CannaTech
   Reavis Daniel Moore, Managing Director
   Education: BS, Education, Ohio State University; MS, Human Services, Southern Illinois University Edwardsville
   Background: CEO/Founder, MBC Networks; Sr. Advisor, Higher Octave Music; Founder, CannabisReal; Partner, Deep Green Agency; Co-Founder, Earthdance Global
   Directorships: Chairman, Cannabics Pharmaceuticals Inc; YouLicense; iAlbums
   David Yahid, Director of Marketing
   Education: BA, Marketing, Yeshiva University
   Background: Marketing Manager, Applause; Sr. Marketing Consultant, Aquakef; Founder/Marketing Manager, Mobilized Marketing; Director of Marketing, Steven Land; CMO, Guiderr; Founder, Yahid Consulting; Consultant, Penguin Strategies; Co-Director, Startup Grind; Founder/Business Development, Sparkly

2837 ICF VENTURES PVT LTD
No. 205, Krishnaji, 3rd main, Defence Colony
Bangalore 560 038
India

Phone: 91-8051269191 **Fax:** 91-8051269393

Mission Statement: ICF Ventures has been founded US and European institutional investors and individuals with global contacts and experience in building highly innovative companies.

Geographic Preference: India
Fund Size: $16.51 Million
Founded: 2001
Average Investment: $1.65 Million
Minimum Investment: $1.1 Million
Investment Criteria: Start-up, Early Stage/Growth and Development/Expansion
Industry Group Preference: Computer Hardware & Software, Information Technology, Consumer Products, Biotechnology, Consumer Services, Media
Portfolio Companies: Linc Software, MatexNet, Sasken, Explocity, Gangagen

Key Executives:
   Robin Farkas, Chairman
   Background: Lazard Freres & Co, Citibank.
   Directorships: Managing Partner
   Vijay Angadi, Managing Partner

2838 IDG CAPITAL PARTNERS
6th Floor, Tower A
COFCO Plaza
8 Jianguomennei Avenue
Beijing 100005
China

Phone: 86-10-6526-2400 **Fax:** 86-10-6526-0700
e-mail: idgvc@idgvc.com.cn
web: www.idgvc.com

Mission Statement: IDG Capital Partners is a China-focused investment firm with over US$2.5B capital under management. With in-depth understanding of local market, we invest in high quality companies with long-term growth potential. We continuously dedicate ourselves to the growth of great Chinese companies.

Geographic Preference: China
Average Investment: $1 - $100 million
Investment Criteria: All Stages
Industry Group Preference: Consumer Products, Franchising, Internet, Wireless, New Media, Education, Healthcare, New Energy, Advanced Manufacturing
Portfolio Companies: Allyes Information Technology, Bus Online, DAC, Shanghai Framedia Advertisement, Impression-Show, Media China Corp, Mei Ah Entertainment, Ocean Butterflies, Wuzhen Tourism Development, Yadii

Other Locations:
Room 1105, Aetna Tower
No 107 Zunyi Road
Shanghai 200051
China
Phone: 86-21-6237-5408 **Fax:** 86-21-6237-5409

Rm 2506, South Tower, Poly
International Plaza, No. 1, East
Pazhoudadao, Haizhu District
Guangzhou 510308
China
Phone: 86-20-8412-0357 **Fax:** 86-20-8412-0490

Room 29018, Jinzhoughuan Business Bldg
No. 3037 Jintian Road
Futian District
Zhenzhen 518048
China
Phone: 86-75-8280-5462 **Fax:** 86-755-8280-5475

Unit 5505, 55th Floor, The Center
99 Queen's Road
Central
Hong Kong
Phone: 852-2529-1016 **Fax:** 852-2529-1619

2839 IDG TECHNOLOGY VENTURE INVESTMENT
6 Floor, Tower A, COFCO Plaza
8 Jianguomennei Ave
Jianguomem Nei Dajie
Beijing 100005
China

Phone: 86-1065262400 **Fax:** 86-1065260700
e-mail: idgvc@idgvc.com.cn
web: www.idgvc.com

Mission Statement: Provides venture capital to high tech start-up companies developing products or services in market sectors with the greatest potential for rapid growth.

Geographic Preference: China
Fund Size: $200 Million
Founded: 1992
Average Investment: $1 Million - $100 Million
Minimum Investment: $500,000
Investment Criteria: Start up
Industry Group Preference: High Technology, Internet Technology, Information Services, Software, Telecommunications, Networking, Biotechnology, Life Sciences, New Energy, Healthcare

Key Executives:
   Alexandre Quirici, Partners
   e-mail: idgvc@idgvc.com.cn
   Education: BS - China Science and Technology University, Ph.D. in fiber optics-Rutgers University.
   Directorships: General Partner

Venture Capital & Private Equity Firms / International Firms

2840 IDG VENTURES INDIA International Financial Services Limited
IFS Court
Twenty-Eight, Cybercity
Ebene
Mauritius

Phone: 230-4673000 Fax: 230-4674000
e-mail: contact@idgvcindia.com

Mission Statement: We offer years of experience in helping build world-class companies by leveraging the IDG Ventures India team and IDG global platform.

Industry Group Preference: Internet, Mobile, Software, SaaS, Enterprise Services, Medical Devices

Portfolio Companies: 3DSoc, Agile Financial Technologies, Apalya Technologies, Aujas Netowks, ConnectM, eShakti.com, Brainbees Technologies, Forus Health, iCreate Software, iProf Learning Solutions, iViZ Techno Solutions, Kreeda Games, Manthan Software Services, Myntra.com, Ozone Media Solutions, Perfint Healthcare, Sourcebits Technologies, Valyoo Technologies, vServe Digital Services, Zivame.com

Key Executives:
Sudhir Sethi, Founder/Chairman/Managing Director
Education: BTech, Engineering, MBA, FMS, Delhi
Background: Walden International India
Directorships: Aujas, ConnectM, iProf, iViZ, Manthan, Mynthra, Perfint, 3DSoC

2841 IDG-ACCEL
8 Jianguomennei Avenue
6th Floor, Tower A
COFCO Plaza
Beijing 100005
China

Phone: 86-10-6526-2400 Fax: 86-10-6526-0700
e-mail: idgvc@idgvc.com.cn

Portfolio Companies: 21ViaNet, 265.com, 39.net, 5173.com, 51edu.com, Tiange Technology, JiuDing China, Baidu, Baofeng.com, Colorme Info, Ctrip, China Finance Online, Ketai, Kkeye, L99, HiChina, Net Movie, Poco, Shenzhoufu.com, Sohu, SouFun, QQ, Toudou.com, Xunlei, Yesky, Yoka, Zhongsou, 798 Entertainment, 3G, A8 Music Group, App Annie, Archermind Technology, Hook Mobile, Ilink, Longcheer Holdings Limited, Beijing Yangpuweiye Technology Development, Simlife, Techfaith Wireless, Tengwu, Gbits Network Technology, Fuzhou Skyunion Digital, Linekong, Netdragon, G10 Entertainment Korea, Amlogic, Baud Data Communications, Shenzhen Guanri Telecom, Memsic, RDA Microelectronics, Royole, Sun & Sea, VeriSilicon, Bonson Inormation Technology, CAXA Technology, Double Bridge Technology, Shanghai Hintsoft Software, Shenzhen Kingdee Software, Shenzhen Kingsky, Longshine Information Technology, Mapbar, MobilePeak Systems, Goodview International, Superdata Technology, Supresoft, Sursen, Tongtech, Zhizhen Node, Tiantian Online, Emay, Great Wall, Kong.net, Longmaster Information & Technology, MIG, Beijing MMIM Technologies, Guangdong Fendhua High-Tech, Sate, Shanghai Superrfid Electronics Technology, Bosideng, Competitor Sports Technology, Doright Fashion, EVE NY, Tiannong, Shin Kong International, Chamate, Mansion Hotel, Home Inns, Hanting Inns & Hotels, Secoo, Wumart Group, Dangdang, Didatuan, Eachnet, iHaveU, SinoBnet, Vancl, Yeecare, 51edu, ChinaEdu, Elite Education Media Group, New Channel, Tarena International

Other Locations:
No. 107 Zunyi Road
Aetna Tower
Room 1105
Shanghai 200051
China
Phone: 86-21-6237-5408 Fax: 86-21-6237-5899

No. 1 East Pazhoudadao
Poly International Plaza
Room 2506-2508, South Tower, Haizhu District
Guangzhou 510308
China
Phone: 86-20-8412-0357 Fax: 86-20-8412-0490

No. 3037 Jintian Road
Jinzhounghuan Business Building, Room 2901B
Futian District
Shenzhen 518048
China
Phone: 86-755-8280-5462 Fax: 86-755-8280-5475

99 Queen's Road
The Center, Unit 5505, 55th Floor
Central
Hong Kong
China
Phone: 852-2529-1016 Fax: 852-2529-1619

Key Executives:
Suyang Zhang, Partner
Education: Bachelor's Electronics Engineering, Shanghai University; EMBA China Europe International Business School
Background: Central Programming Coordination Manager, Shanghai Bell; Deputy Director, Shanghai Factory 520 of Minister of Poster and Telecommunications; General Manager, Hainan Vantone Group
Dongliang Liu, Venture Partner
Education: Tsinghua University
Background: Senior Research Fellow, Development Research Center of the State Department of China; CitiBank New York
Drake Yu, Venture Partner
Education: MBA Cheung Kong Graduate School of Business; Jianxi University of Chinese Medicine
Background: Sinotrust Managerial Consulting Company; Jiangzhong Pharmaceutical Co., Ltd.
Quan Zhou, Managing Director
Education: Bachelor's China Science and Technology University; Master's Chinese Academy of Science; PhD Fiber Optics Rutgers University

2842 IDINVEST PARTNERS
117, avenue des Champs Elysees
Paris 75008
France

Phone: 33 0 1 58 18 56 56 Fax: 33 0 1 58 18 56 89
web: www.idinvest.com

Mission Statement: A private equity and venture capital firm that invests in small to medium sized European companies through venture and growth capital, private debt, and dedicated portfolios and funds.

Geographic Preference: Europe
Fund Size: $8.1 Billion
Founded: 1997
Investment Criteria: Small Sized, Medium Sized, European
Industry Group Preference: Internet Technology, All Sectors Considered
Portfolio Companies: 1000mercis, 21Buttons, Acces, Acta Groupe, Actility, Adocia, AlVest, Ammeraal Beltech, Amplitude, AMTrust, Appart City, Appsfire, Asarina, AS International Group, Assystem, Audisoft, Automic, Aveni, Averys, Axelliance, Back Werk, Bequam, bGroupe Berkem, Bimedia, Biogroup LCD, Biotie Therapies, Blink Biomedical, BreezoMeter, Boxtal, byTourexcel, Campanda, Cardiologs, Cast, CCM Benchmark, Cerelia, Clustree, Chereau, Colisee, Cooptalis, Concours Mania Groupe, Corti, Criteo, Curse, Dailymotion, Delpharm, Domainiac, Domain Therapeutics, Drive For Me, Dunlop, Dupont, Dynacure, EDH Groupe des Ecoles, Eolite, ER, Erytech, Euro Part, European Homes,

Venture Capital & Private Equity Firms / International Firms

Europe Snacks, Exxelia Magnetics, Famoco, Frichti, Genticel, GHD, Grand Cru, Grand Frais, Groupe Bertrand, Groupe Bio7, Groupe Segex, Grupo Terratest, Habx, Halex, Hensoldt, Homeperf, House of HR, Iberchem, Inseec, Integragen, Italmatch Chemicals, J&S, Kantox, Keesing, KEP Technologies, Kether, Kiala, Konecta, Lea, Leosphere, Lima Corporate, LSR Group, Lumapps, M2i, MAINtag, Maisons Babeau-Seguin, MDX Health, Median, Meetic, Meilleire Gestion, Meilleurmobile.com, Megadyne, Memora, Mentum, Minoryx, Mix.com, Molotov.tv, Mondo Minerals, MP Hygiene, NETASQ, Nexway, Neurala, NG Data, Nosto, October, Okko Hotels, OneAccess, ONXEO, Orbility, Organica, Ornikar, OxThera, Ouicar, Papernest, Parella, PathoQuest, Pharmacie Lafayette, Planday, Platform.sh, Plumble, Pretty Simple, Prosensa, Proxiserve, Pure People, Quadrimex, R2P, Reworld Media

Other Locations:
An der Welle 4
Frankfurt 60322
Amsterdam

22F Jing An Kerry Centre Tower 3
1228 Yan An Zhong Road
Shanghai 200040
China

Key Executives:
Christophe Baviere, CEO/Managing Partner
Education: MBA, University of Ottawa; ESLSCA
Background: AGF-Allianz Group; Caisse des Depots et Consignations; BNP Paribas
Directorships: President, Private Equity Commission, AFG
Benoist Grossmann, Managing Partner
Education: MBA, Institut d'Etudes Politiques; PhD, Universite de Paris VI
Background: Partner, Viventures; Investment Manager, La Financiere de Brienne; EDF; NASA; Thompson-CSF Optronique
Directorships: Criteo, Dailymotion, Deezer, Meetic
Matthieu Baret, Managing Partner
Education: CENTRALE-SUPELEC; MS, Electrical Engineering, Georgia Tech; MBA, INSEAD
Background: VP, Italtel; Europatweb; Cap Gemini Telecom; Bouygues Telecom
Directorships: Private Equity Steering Committee, UNPRI
Nicolas Chaudron, Managing Partner
Education: MBA, Wharton School, University of Pennsylvania; MBA, College des Ingenieurs; PhD, Mathematics, University of Paris VI; Peking University
Background: Europatweb
Francois Lacoste, Managing Partner
Education: MS, Banking/Finance, Paris-Dauphine University
Background: Fortis Bank; Banque Worms
Christophe Simon, Managing Partner
Education: MS, Corporate Finance/Financial Engineering, University of Paris-Dauphine
Background: Ernst & Young

2843 IFE CONSEIL (INTERMEDIATE FINANCE EUROPE)
41 George V Avenue
Paris 75008
France

Phone: 33-156520240 Fax: 33-147200694
web: www.ifemezzanine.com

Mission Statement: IFE Conseil is the investment adviser of IFE Fund (Intermediate Finance Europe Fund), a fund dedicated to mezzanine financing in continental Europe
Geographic Preference: Europe
Fund Size: $ 200 Million
Founded: 1999
Average Investment: $ 10 Million
Minimum Investment: $ 5 Million

Investment Criteria: Mezzanine, LBO, MBO and companies with experienced management team, and strong growth perspectives
Industry Group Preference: All Sectors Considered
Portfolio Companies: Global Garden Products, Fraikin, Center Parcs, BB Hotels, Eau Ecarlate, Gautier, CFP Flexible Packaging, Oberthur Card Systems, Allen Afflelou

Key Executives:
Michel Dupont, Chairman
e-mail: info@ifeconseil.com
Education: Graduate of ESC Rouen, with a major in Finance.
Background: Analyst with Société Générale's Asset Recovery Management department, Paribas' M&A team.
Directorships: No other Position held in the company
Jean-Pascal Ley, Director Associate
e-mail: info@ifeconseil.com
Education: A French business school and MBA graduate
Background: In charge of Acquistion Finance, Banque du Phénix, principal of Phénix Mezzanine
Directorships: No other Position held in the company
Christian Quets, Head of Management Control
e-mail: info@ifeconseil.com
Education: A graduate of HEC and of the Harvard Business School.
Background: Suez Group—- commercial and investment banking.
Julien Drie, Investment Director
e-mail: info@ifeconseil.com
Education: A graduate of IEP Paris, INSEAD, and the Harvard Business School.
Background: CII and then Olivetti —— Strategy and Planning department, Director in Management Consulting, notably with Hay and Solving International, Downer & Co., a US-based M&A boutique, as Director.
Directorships: No other Position held in the company

2844 IGLOBE PARTNERS
11 Biopolis Way
Helios #09-03
Singapore 138867
Singapore

Phone: +65 6478 9716 Fax: +65 6478 9717
e-mail: contact@iglobepartners.com
web: www.iglobepartners.com

Mission Statement: Seek global investment opportunities in high growth companies and assist these companies in their globalization strategy and ensure best of breed corporate governance practices, transparency and risk management in order to achieve superior returns for our investors.

Geographic Preference: United States, Europe, Asia
Founded: 1999
Industry Group Preference: Wireless Technologies, Mobile Apps, Digital Media & Marketing, Clean Technology, Next Generation Materials, Semiconductors, IT/BIO Convergence
Portfolio Companies: 3PAR, Aicent, Anacle, ASK, Celestry, Fortemedia, IntruGuard, Kilopass, Lypanosys Limited, Matterport, Projectpartner, Shop Your World, Silicon Blue, Sparky Animation, StarMaker Interactive, Telenav, uBlox, Unity Technologies, VeriSilicon, VKorus Pte Ltd, Wise Giant Enterprise, Xumii, Zephyr Technology

Other Locations:
5201 Great America Parkway
Suite 320
Santa Clara, CA 95054
Phone: 408-982-2126 Fax: 408-982-2129

Unit 16
43D Apollo Drive
Mairangi Bay, Auckland 0632
New Zealand
Phone: +64 9 915 3401 Fax: +64 9 968 8431

Key Executives:
Philip Yeo, Chairman

Soo Boon Koh, Founder & Managing Partner
Michel Birnbaum, Partner
Joyce Ng, Partner

2845 IGNITE JAPAN KK Ignite Group
1F Place Canada
7-3-37 Akasaka
Minato-ku
Tokyo 107-0052
Japan

Phone: 81-368947680 Fax: 81-368947701
web: www.ignite.co.jp

Mission Statement: Ignite has been very successful in operating IT industry focused venture investment activities.
Geographic Preference: US, Japan, Asia
Fund Size: $20 Billion
Founded: 2000
Industry Group Preference: Software, Communications, Internet Technology, Computer Related, Printing, Graphic Arts
Portfolio Companies: Acca Networks, atmarkIT, Wine in style, Natural Communications, Realcom, E-Supportlink ltd, Axiom, Virtualex, Sitecare, Ariel Networks, Pacific Design, Fibest.
Key Executives:
Natsuaki Sasaki, President
e-mail: contact@ignite.co.jp
Education: B.A.-Economics from Hitotsubashi University, MBA - Columbia Business School.
Background: Lehman Brothers Tokyo, Pangaea Wireless.
Hiroaki Yano, President

2846 ILE-DE-FRANCE
66 Sartrouville Road
3 Technological Park of Maples
Pecq Cedex 78232
France

Phone: 33-130156400 Fax: 33-130156409

Mission Statement: IDFD intervenes in own capital stocks and clean quasi-bottoms: ordinary actions or of priority, convertible, good obligations of subscription and actions.
Geographic Preference: France
Fund Size: $16.8 Million
Founded: 1995
Average Investment: $370, 000
Minimum Investment: $180, 000
Investment Criteria: MBOs
Industry Group Preference: Industrial Products, Technology, Services
Portfolio Companies: Abaxia, Hello Machines, Adventuer Ventures, Carlipa Systems, Square Gourmet, Coralog, DG Industries, Delia Systems, Deltamed, Multi-Media Digilab, E-printing Company, Euro Services Laboratory, Exentive F.B. Technology, GO Albert Group, Epsitech Group

2847 IMI.VC
Bolshaya Tulskaya, 44
Moscow 115191
Russia

Phone: 7495-9582862
e-mail: au@imi.vc
web: www.imi.vc

Mission Statement: IMI.VC is an investment company funding innovative mobile applications that are able to change the market and behavior of mobile device users.
Industry Group Preference: Internet, Mobile
Portfolio Companies: Game Insight, NARR8, Farminers Startup Academy, Social Insight, WeHeartPics, Planner5D, Monosnap, App in the Air, BeatTheBushes, Gipis, Inflow, Kloudpics, Cookwizme, Dish.fm, IPQ2, FreeBrie, My-apps, Cute Town, Kula, CoFoundit, Prognolic, Woodla

Key Executives:
Igor Matsanyuk, Founder

2848 IMM INVESTMENT CORP HCI Private Equity Fund
110 Sokong-Dong
Chung-Gu
4F Hanwa Building
Seoul 100-755
South Korea

Phone: 82-027330540 Fax: 82-027331942
web: www.imm.co.kr

Fund Size: $200 million
Founded: 1999
Investment Criteria: Recapitalizations, Consolidations, Buyout
Portfolio Companies: 12Soft, AD Technology, ALBA 1, Allm, Altrium CNI, ArtLab, Bellwave, CD Networks, CD Park, CJ Entertainemnt, Cy World, D&F Solution, Daekyung Machinery & Engineering, Doum & Nanum, Dream Execution, EMLSI, enCross Partners, Enium, Ensiz Technology, Epivalley, Etoos, FCI, Funkyfunky, Geomind, Greek and Roman mythology, Green Cross Biotech, Hannetware, IHQ, Independence, Innochip Technology, Intvnet, Jinu, KING&I, Korea OTC, Lets, MLT, Magiceyes, Mediaflex, Modemore, Namotech, Nanum Technologies, Naviya Entertainment, Needs Entertainment, Ness Display, Net TV, Netinbiz, Next Instrument, Ninza Turtle, Nongshim, Peptron, Pipax Environment, Polimedia, Possmedia, SK Sinsegi Telecom, Sanyang Electronics, Secure Soft, Sysdaq, Taeyang 3C, Teradian, Thinkware, Xemi Interactive, Zen Holdings
Key Executives:
Dong Woo Chang, Chief Executive Officer
Jae Mo Jeon, Chief Executive Officer

2849 IMPERIAL INNOVATIONS
52 Princes Gate
Exhibition Road
London SW7 2PG
United Kingdom

Phone: 44-02075814949
e-mail: info@imperialinnovations.co.uk
web: www.imperialinnovations.co.uk

Mission Statement: Imperial Innovations builds and invests in technology and healthcare businesses based on research from the UK's four leading universities: Imperial College London, Cambridge, Oxford and University College London.
Geographic Preference: United Kingdom
Founded: 1986
Investment Criteria: All Stages
Industry Group Preference: Healthcare, Technology
Portfolio Companies: Circassia, Veryan, PsiOxus Therapeutics, Cell Medica, PolyTherics, Oxford Immunotec, Stanmore Implants, TopiVert, Abingdon Health, Autifony Therapeutics, Mission Therapeutics, Ixico, Nexeon, Cortexica Vision Systems, Plaxica, Evo Electric, Process Systems Enterprise, Permasense, FeatureSpace, Acunu, Econic Technologies, Fractal
Key Executives:
Russ Cummings, Chief Executive Officer
Education: MA, Chemistry, Oxford University
Background: Montech, Signet Group, Bank of Nova Scotia, Shell Chemicals Limited
Directorships: Plaxica, Evo Electric, Thiakls

Venture Capital & Private Equity Firms / International Firms

2850 INDASIA FUND ADVISORS PVT LTD
3, Scheherazade, Justice Vyas Road, Colaba
Justice Vyas Road
Colaba
Mumbai 400 005
India

Phone: 91-2222881301 Fax: 91-2222830376
e-mail: info@indasiafund.com
web: www.indasiafund.com

Mission Statement: Provides advisory services for mergers and acquisitions, joint ventures and strategic alliances, business development, and corporate finance matters to both domestic and multi-national corporations.
Geographic Preference: Worldwide
Founded: 1998
Average Investment: $25 million
Minimum Investment: $15 million
Investment Criteria: Growth, Development/Expansion, MBO, Joint Ventures
Industry Group Preference: Information Technology, Biotechnology, Media, Computer Hardware & Software, Pharmaceuticals, Information Technology, Distribution, Communications, Life Sciences, Logistics, Oil & Gas
Portfolio Companies: Associated Container Terminals Ltd, Enable M, ARSS Infrastructure Ltd, Innova B2B Logistics
Key Executives:
  Pradip Shah, Founder/Chairman
  Education: MBA (Harvard Business School), Bachelor of Commerce (Sydenham College)
  Background: Housing Development Finance Corporation, Asian Development Bank, World Bank, Reserve Bank of India, Credit Rating and Information Services of India Limited

2851 INDEX VENTURES
3 Burlington Gardens
London W1S 3EP
United Kingdom

Phone: 44 20 7154 2020 Fax: 44 20 7154 2021
web: www.indexventures.com

Mission Statement: Index Ventures network has invested in 160 consumer and enterprise technology companies in 24 countries.
Geographic Preference: Europe, Israel, USA
Founded: 1996
Average Investment: $100,000 to $2 million
Investment Criteria: Seed to Growth
Industry Group Preference: Infrastructure, Entertainment, Business Products & Services, Fintech, Retail, Consumer & Leisure
Portfolio Companies: BlaBlaCar, Criteo, Dropbox, Etsy, Flipboard, Funding Circle, Hortonworks, King, Lookout, Nasty Gal, Pure Storage, SoundCloud, Squarespace, Supercell
Key Executives:
  Neil Rimer, Co-Founder
  e-mail: anete@indexventures.com
  Education: Stanford University
  Background: Montgomery Securities; Index Securities
  Damir Becirovic, Principle
  Education: BS, Business Admin., University of Southern California
  Background: Goldman Sachs; Coatue; Activision Blizzard; Apple; Flextronics
  Directorships: Glossier, Hollar

2852 INDIAN DIRECT EQUITY ADVISORS PVT LTD
1007, Raheja Centre, Nariman Point
Mumbai 400 021
India

Phone: 91-2222041140 Fax: 91-222818156
web: www.ideaequity.com

Mission Statement: The company approaches high risk investments with the philosophy of identifying promoters and ideas which can scale up significantly in a short period.
Geographic Preference: India
Fund Size: $34 Million
Founded: 1999
Average Investment: $2.3 Million
Minimum Investment: $1 Million
Investment Criteria: Mezzanine to High-Growth Companies
Industry Group Preference: Media, Building Materials & Services, Communications, Services, Software, Textiles, Entertainment
Portfolio Companies: Alok Textile Industries Limited, BrainGEM L.L.C, Delta Innovative Enterprises Limited, Drish Shoes Limited, Ecoboard Industries Limited, New World Application, Secure Meters Limited, Sun Earth Ceramics Limited, Time Packaging Limited, United Studios Ltd
Key Executives:
  Sanjaya Kulkarni, Managing Director
  Education: Engineering Degree from IIT Bombay, MBA - IIM Ahmedabad.
  Background: Citibank N.A.'s Merchant Banking department, 20th Century Leasing Corporation.
  Nimesh Grover, Vice President

2853 INDUFIN
Research Park
Interveuvenlaan 1515-D1
Heverlee 3001
Belgium

Phone: 32-016393040 Fax: 32-016393049
e-mail: evelyne.ackermans@indufin.be
web: www.indufin.be

Mission Statement: Indufin is a Private Equity investment company (not a fund) with the long term commitment of its shareholders. We provide capital and know-how to support (international) growth, buy-outs and buy-ins. We invest in medium-sized companies in Belgium and Luxembourg and have a selected approach towards investment opportunities in neighbouring countries. Talented and passionate people are key to the success of an enterprise. We partner with entrepreneurs and entrepreneurial managers based on a shared vision of the future and a relationship of trust. We are an active shareholder focused on strategic opportunities and value creation. We are not a substitute for management and do not interfere in day-to-day decisions.
Geographic Preference: Belgium, Luxembourg
Founded: 2001
Average Investment: 3 - 15 million Euro
Investment Criteria: Growth Financing, Buy-Outs, Buy-Ins
Portfolio Companies: All-Tag Security, Alphamin, Bartech, Herbalgem, Kyotec Group, Preflexibel, Rowies, SecureLink
Key Executives:
  Guy Wygaerts, Partner
  e-mail: guy.wygaerts@indufin.be
  Education: Commercial Engineer, KU Leuven; INSEAD
  Background: Managing Partner, Andersen Consulting; Deloitte
  Directorships: Rowies, SecureLink

2854 INDUSTRI KAPITAL SVENSKA AB
4 Birger Jarlsgatan
Stockholm 11434
Sweden

Phone: 46-086789500 Fax: 46-086780336
web: www.industrikapital.com

Mission Statement: Industri Kapital strives to build lasting value in businesses by effecting fundamental performance improvement.
Geographic Preference: Sweden, Finland, Norway, Denmark, Benelux countries, France, Germany

Venture Capital & Private Equity Firms / International Firms

Fund Size: $4.8 Billion
Founded: 1989
Investment Criteria: Mid sized companies.
Industry Group Preference: Manufacturing, Services, Retailing, Food & Beverage, Processing, Building Materials & Services, Media, Wholesale, Distribution
Portfolio Companies: Addum, Amas, Crisplant Industries, Guldfynd Holding, Hjem Is Europa, Idesta, Lithells, Nobia, Nyge Aero, Nyge Aero, Idesta, Bonna Sabla, Tradeka Ltd., Kid Interiør, The SIA Group, Myresjöhus, Idex, Ekstrem Lavpris, CEVA Santé Animale, Welzorg, Gardena
Key Executives:
  Kristian Carlsson Kemppinen, Partner
  e-mail: bjorn.saven@industrikapital.com
  Education: Degree - Stockholm School of Economics, MBA - Harvard Business School
  Background: Esselte Group in Sweden, the UK and the US.
  Directorships: CEO
  Helena Stjernholm, Partner, Sweden
  e-mail: kim.wahl@industrikapital.com
  Education: University of San Diego, MBA - Harvard Business School.
  Background: Corporate Finance Department at Goldman Sachs in New York and in London.
  Helena Stjernholm, Partner, Benelux
  e-mail: kristiaan.nieuwenburg@industrikapital.com
  Education: M.Sc.(Chem Eng)-Delft University of Technology, MBA-Harvard Business School.
  Background: Investment banking at Lehman Brothers in London.
  Erik Ingemarsson, Director, Swedish
  e-mail: detlef.dinsel@industrikapital.com
  Education: MBA-INSEAD, MSc.- Mechanical Engineering from the Technical University of Munich.
  Background: Bain & Company, Schmidlin division of Hilti AG, Liechtenstein.
  Carl Jakobsson, Associate
  e-mail: samir.kamal@industrikapital.com
  Education: BSc.-Electrical & Electronic Engineering(Imperial College, University of London), MSc. in Business Administration and Economics(Stockholm School of Economics).
  Background: Investment Banking Division of Carnegie.
  Daniel Mogerud, Director, Manager Operations
  e-mail: gustav.ohman@industrikapital.com
  Education: MSc.(Econ)-Financial Economics and Business Administration(Stockholm School of Economics), with a major in Finance from Ecole des Hautes Etudes Commerciales (HEC) in Paris.
  Background: Corporate Finance Department of Enskilda in Stockholm
  Directorships: CEO (Region West-Benelux, France, Denmark/Norway)
  Christoffer Zilliacus, Director
  e-mail: michael.rosenlew@industrikapital.com
  Education: MSc.(Econ)-Corporate Finance and Accounting from Swedish School of Economics, Business Administration
  Background: Amer Group
  Directorships: CEO (Region East- Sweden, Finland, Germany)
  Kristian Larsen, Deputy Director
  e-mail: erik.larsson@industrikapital.com
  Education: MSc. in Economics and Business Administration(Stockholm School of Economics), CEMS Masters from Universität zu Köln, MBA from Harvard Business School.
  Thomas Ramsay, Partner, Finland
  e-mail: thomas.ramsay@industrikapital.com
  Education: MSc.(Econ)Major in Accounting from the Swedish School of Economics and Business Administration in Helsinki.
  Background: Corporate Finance Department of Salomon Brothers in London.

  Anders Peterson, Associate Director
  e-mail: anders.petersson@industrikapital.com
  Education: MSc. in Economics and Business Administration from the University of Uppsala.
  Background: Investment Banking Division of JP Morgan.

2855 INDUSTRIAL DEVELOPMENT BANK OF INDIA
IDBI Tower, WTC Complex, Cuffe Parade, Colaba
Mumbai 400005
India
Phone: 91-2266937000 **Fax:** 91-2222181294
Toll-Free: 1800-2001947
e-mail: customercare@idbi.co.in
web: www.idbi.com

Mission Statement: Actively seeking new investments.
Fund Size: $29.6 Billion
Founded: 1964
Investment Criteria: Expansion, diversification and modernisation of existing projects.
Key Executives:
  M. S. Raghavan, Chairman & Managing Director
  e-mail: vp.shetty@idbi.co.in
  B. K. Batra, Deputy Managing Director

2856 INDUSTRIALIZATION FUND FOR DEVELOPING COUNTRIE
Fredericiagade 27
Copenhagen K 1310
Denmark
Phone: 45-33637500 **Fax:** 45-33637599
e-mail: ifu@ifu.dk
web: www.ifu.dk

Mission Statement: IFU offers capital and advice to joint venture enterprises in developing countries.
Geographic Preference: Nordic countries, Europe, Beijing, Johannesburg, New Delhi, Cape Town,
Average Investment: $12.01 Million
Portfolio Companies: The Investment Fund For Central and Eastern Europe, The Investment Fund for Emerging Markets
Key Executives:
  Tommy Thomsen, Manging Director
  e-mail: ifu@ifu.dk
  Torben Huss, Deputy Managing Director
  e-mail: ifu@ifu.dk
  Alex Unsgaard, Senior Investment Manager
  e-mail: ifu@ifu.dk
  Anders Nellemose, Senior Investment Manager
  e-mail: ifu@ifu.dk

2857 INDUSTRIEBANK LIOF NV
Boschstraat 76, 6211 AX
PO Box 1310
Maastricht 6201 BH
Netherlands
Phone: 31-433280280 **Fax:** 31-433-280200
web: www.liof.com

Mission Statement: Actively seeking new investments
Fund Size: $460, 000
Founded: 1975
Minimum Investment: $48, 000
Industry Group Preference: Communications, Consumer Services, Electronic Technology, Pollution, Industrial Equipment, Medical & Health Related, Life Sciences, Automotive, Mobile Communications Devices, Consumer Products, Data Communications
Key Executives:
  Mark Koppers, Project Manager Logistics, Agro-Food
  Jacques Mikx, Director Foreign Investments

2858 INDUSTRIFONDEN
Vasagatan 11, Box 1163
Stockholm SE - 111 91
Sweden

Phone: 46-858791900 Fax: 46-858791950
web: www.industrifonden.se

Mission Statement: Industrifonden provides development capital, competence and networks for Swedish growth companies; offer various types of financing, both loans for specific projects and equity capital.

Geographic Preference: Sweden
Fund Size: $458 Million
Founded: 1979
Minimum Investment: $0.13 Million
Investment Criteria: Early stage, Start-up, medium sized enterprises
Industry Group Preference: Biotechnology, Computer Related, Semiconductors, Electronic Technology, Industrial Equipment, Industrial Services, Medical, Healthcare
Portfolio Companies: Småföretagsinvest, Emano, Investa Företagskapital, CIMON Medical, Malmöhus Invest, Lunova, KTH Seed Capital, Lumitec, SRK, Uminova Invest, Iteksa Venture.

Key Executives:
  Charlotte Brogren Karlberg, Chairman
  e-mail: lennart.samuelsson @industrifonden.se
  Education: B.Sc. in business administration
  Anders Schelin, Investment Manager Technology
  e-mail: claes.de.neergaard @industrifonden.se
  Education: M Sc in Economics ans Business Administration

2859 INDUSTRIO VENTURES
Via Ora del Garda, 97
Trento 38121
Italy

e-mail: info@industrio.co
web: www.industrio.co

Mission Statement: Industrio transforms teams into companies, and prototypes into products.

Geographic Preference: Italy
Average Investment: 50,000 euro
Investment Criteria: Early-Stage, Seed-Stage
Industry Group Preference: Technology, Medical Devices
Portfolio Companies: Meccatronicore, Melixa, Sinphoniq

Key Executives:
  Jari Ognibeni, CEO/Co-Founder
  e-mail: jo@industrio.com
  Alfredo Maglione, President/Co-Founder
  Background: President, Optio Group
  Directorships: Trentino Sviluppo
  Alberto Gasperi, Co-Founder
  Education: Chartered Accountant
  Background: Founder & President, CSI
  Alessio Romani, Co-Founder
  Background: Plant Manager, Zobele Group

2860 INFINITY VENTURE PARTNERS
Japan

web: www.infinityventures.com

Mission Statement: At Infinity Venture Partners, we strive to create venture companies with infinite possibilities. We bridge JAPAN - the second largest global economy and CHINA - the world's growth engine, to support the birth of new ventures. Infinity Venture Partners is a unique venture capital firm which combines industry platform with venture capital financing. Infinity Venture Partners not only provides venture capital, but also brings the vast network of experienced, international partners. We strive to maximize the value of young ventures with our strategic support. Furthermore, strategic investors in the IVP fund bring opportunities in business and technology partnerships and thus accelerate growth of our portfolio companies.

Geographic Preference: Japan, China
Founded: 2007
Investment Criteria: Early-Stage
Industry Group Preference: Internet, Mobile
Portfolio Companies: Groupon Japan, JMTY, Mlab, Muse & Co., The One Of Them, Rekoo Japan, Smart Education, App Annie, Daguu, Goyoo Networks, Jihua.fm, Mobcent, Moyo Game, Order With Me, Yeahka, DeNA China, DragonsMeet, Rekoo

Key Executives:
  Akio Tanaka, Co-Founder/Managing Partner
  Education: Master's Degree, University of British Columbia
  Background: Head of Venture Investments, Adobe; CTO, Macromedia Japan
  Hirofumi Ono, Co-Founder/Managing Partner
  Education: BS, Biological Science, MS, Molecular Biology, University of Tokyo
  Background: Co-Founder/COO, CA Mobile
  Masashi Kobayashi, Co-Founder/Managing Partner
  Education: BS, Naval Architecture & Ocean Engineering, University of Tokyo
  Background: Partner, Globis Capital Partners
  Directorships: RecycleOne, Interactive Brains, Interscope, Ariel Networks, VirtualeX

2861 INFOCOMM INVESTMENTS
10 Pasir Panjang Road #10-01
Mapletree Business City
117438
Singapore

Phone: 65-62110888
e-mail: info@infocomminvestments.com
web: www.infocomminvestments.com

Mission Statement: Infocomm Investments is the VC arm of Singapore's Infocomm Development Authority. As an investment fund, our main objective is to invest in innovative technology companies that complement our vision of building a competitive IT landscape in Singapore.

Geographic Preference: Singapore
Fund Size: $200 million
Industry Group Preference: Information Technology
Portfolio Companies: Moonshoot, JustCommodity, Bubble Motion, GuardTime, Data Security Systems Solutions, Sconce, Quid, Game Ventures, Twilo, Mobilewalla

Other Locations:
3 Twin Dolphin Drive
Suite 260
Redwood City, CA 94065
Phone: 650-5931716

Unit 1, Level 3
Explorer Block, International Tech Park
Whitefield Road
Bangalore 560 066
India
Phone: 91-8051156400

1038 Nanjing West Road
Westgate Tower 18-01
Shanghai 200041
China
Phone: 86-2162178822

Key Executives:
  Lee Kheng Nam, Chairman
  Education: BS, MS, Doctorate, Electrical Engineering, MIT

Background: Senior Sales & Business Development Executive, Ancentuate; Reputation Technologies; Consultant, Boston Consulting Group

2862 INGENIOUS VENTURES
15 Golden Square
London W1F 9JG
United Kingdom

Phone: 44-02073194000 Fax: 44-02073194001
e-mail: generalenquiries@ingeniousmedia.co.uk

Mission Statement: We invest in media and entertainment companies. The finance and expertise we provide helps them keep growing. Our understanding of both the media and private equity sectors means we speak fluently to investors and media owners alike. We are active investors. Our deep knowledge of the media and entertainment industries adds significant value to the companies we invest in.

Geographic Preference: United Kingdom
Founded: 1998
Average Investment: £2 million
Investment Criteria: Expansion-Stage, MBO
Industry Group Preference: Music, Marketing, Television, Gaming, Entertainment, Media
Portfolio Companies: Digital Theatre, Property Network, Casabu, Whizz Kid Entertainment, DRG Limited, Brand Events Holdings, BrandRapport Group, Review Centre Limited

Key Executives:
Patrick Bradley, CEO/Director
e-mail: patrick.bradley@ingeniousmedia.co.uk
Education: King's College, Worcester College, Oxford University
Background: Lawyer

2863 INITIAL CAPITAL
Avenida Paulista
Sao Paulo 2073
Brazil

e-mail: hello@initial.vc
web: www.initial.vc

Mission Statement: Initial Capital is a firm, not a fund. This means we have neither limited partners, nor an investment committee taking part in our decision making process. Being focused on early-stage startups, our sweet-spot is the $100K-300K range, however, we do have the flexibility to invest higher amounts.

Geographic Preference: Brazil, Israel
Average Investment: $100,000 - $300,000
Investment Criteria: Early-Stage
Industry Group Preference: Internet, Business Products & Services
Portfolio Companies: Soluto, Glambox, Enprego Ligado, Samba Ads, Startupi.com.br, Pitzi, Evoz, Wibbitz, Shine, Parallel Universe, POSE

Other Locations:
Ehad Ha'am 72
Tel Aviv
Israel

Key Executives:
Roi Carthy, Managing Partner
e-mail: roi@initial.vc
Background: Zend Technologies, Head of Products, Soluto

2864 INNOFINANCE OY
Westendintie 99-101 A 28
Espoo 02160
Finland

Phone: 358-207-43-2500 Fax: 358-207-43-2501
e-mail: office@innofinance.fi

Mission Statement: A venture capital company that invests in small and medium sized Finnish companies. Actively seeking new investments.

Fund Size: $1.1 Million
Founded: 1997
Average Investment: $40,800
Minimum Investment: $10,200
Investment Criteria: Early Stage
Industry Group Preference: Electronic Technology, Security, Biotechnology, Energy, Chemicals, Consumer Services, Medical, Industrial Equipment, Industrial Services
Portfolio Companies: ABR Innova Oy, Absolute Engery, Acusto Oy, Addoz, B-Band, Bevesys Oy, Book-It Oy, Ch5 Finland Oy, Codetoys Oy, CWP Coloured Wood Products Oy, Delsitech, Deveinfo Oy, Eagle Filter, Ellibs Oy, Emillion Oy, Euroelektro International Oy, Futurice Oy, Granula, Greenvironment Oy, Group Intelligentia Oy, Heeros Systems Oy, Homesoft Oy, Hydrox Pipeline Oy, Ima Engineering, Imagetalk Oy, Karhu Sporting Goods, Kuusama Design Oy, Labgas Instrument Company, Liekki Oy, Mandrel Oy, On-Motion Oy, Openbit Oy, Oy Plusdial Ab, Oy Stinghorn, Oy Wireless Media Finland, Prewise Group Oy, Primet Oy, Remote Analysis, R.Rouvari Oy, Staselog Oy, Suomen Kuitulava Suvisoft Oy, Suomen Teollisuusosa Oy, Taipale Telematics, Viope Solutions Oy, Voxpoint Technologies Oy

Key Executives:
Martti Hintikka, President and CEO, Partner
358-400-302-081
e-mail: martti.hintikka@innofinance.fi
Juha Turunen, Investment Director, Partner

2865 INNOGEST CAPITAL
Via A. Locatelli 2
Milano 20124
Italy

Phone: 39 011 5091411 Fax: 39 011 590488
e-mail: info@innogest.it
web: www.innogestcapital.com

Mission Statement: A leading Italian seed- and early-stage venture capital fund with offices in Turin, Geneva and San Francisco.

Geographic Preference: Italy, Europe, USA
Fund Size: 200 million Euro
Founded: 2006
Average Investment: 200,000 - 2 million Euro
Investment Criteria: Seed-Stage, Early-Stage
Industry Group Preference: Healthcare, Fintech, Foodtech, Fashion/Lifestyle, Digital Health
Portfolio Companies: Cornerjob, GreenBone Ortho, Empatica, MedLumics, Diet to go, Digital Magics, Anaconda, CV Lab, BetaGlue Technologies, Supermercato24, Newronika, Sardex, Armadio Verde, D-Eye, Prestiamoci, Pi-Cardia, Angiodroid, Drexcode, Thron, Atricath, 40 South Energy, Agroils, Cuebiq, Beintoo, MBooster, Erydel

Key Executives:
Claudio Giuliano, Founder and Managing Partner
Education: MS, Politecnico di Torino; MBA, INSEAD
Background: The Carlyle Group, Bain & Company, Hewlett Packard

2866 INNOVACOM SA
23 rue Royale
Paris 75008
France

Phone: 33-144941500 Fax: 33-144941515
e-mail: info@innovacom.com
web: www.innovacom.com

Mission Statement: Works with the most promising entrepreneurs whose ideas improve the ability of telecom carriers to deliver services.

Geographic Preference: France and Europe
Founded: 1988

Venture Capital & Private Equity Firms / International Firms

Average Investment: $500,000 - $10 million
Investment Criteria: Expansion and Development Capital, Early Stage, Startup Capital
Industry Group Preference: Materials Technology, Telecommunications, Software, Enterprise Services, Content, Components & IoT, Computer Hardware & Software
Portfolio Companies: CyOptics, Defacto, Heptagon, HighWave, IFOTEC, Innova Card, Actelis, Aperto Networks, Astellia, Atrica, Avilinks, Danger, Appium, Active Circle, Air2Web, Assima, Envivio, FrontCall, Groupe SQLI, Highdeal, Kabira, Kimotion.
Key Executives:
 Denis Champenois, Chairman
 Education: Graduate of the French business school HEC and the École Nationale Supérieure des Postes et Télécommunications
 Background: Boards of directors of many communications companies in France and Europe (Editions Glénat, Algety, Madrid Film), etc.
 Jerome Lecoeur, CEO

2867 INNOVATION CAPITAL
57 Avenue Franklin Delano Roosevelt
Paris 75008
France

Phone: 33-1-40-76-99-00 Fax: 33-1-45-61-24-78
e-mail: businessplan@innovationcapital.fr
web: www.innovationcapital.fr

Mission Statement: Founded in 1996, Innovation Capital is an international venture capital firm with its head office in Paris and a local presence in the Silicon Valley. With over 415 M Euro currently under management, our focus is on venture investments at both the early and late stage, in two sectors: information technologies and life sciences.
Founded: 1996
Investment Criteria: Early-Stage, Later Stage
Industry Group Preference: Information Technology, Life Sciences, Telecommunications, Biotechnology
Portfolio Companies: 6 Wind, Anevia, Expway, Maeglin, One Access, Ask, Citilog, Crocus, EI Technologies, Linedata Services, Micropole Univers, Roctool, RSI, Stantum, Teem Photonics, TES, FAB Pharma, Genoway, Integragen, Scynexis, Txcell, Zealand Pharma, DMS, Kuros Biosurgery, Orthopaedic Synergy, Therodiag, Tronic's Micro Systems
Key Executives:
 Valery Huot, Managing Partner
 Education: MS, Electrical Engineering, Stanford University; Ecole Polytechnique, Paris
 Background: Co-Leader, Fund of Fund Team, Caisse des Depotss; SME Financing Office, French Treasury; French Defense Procurement Agency; Telstra
 Directorships: Expway, Anevia, Ask, 6 Wind, Stantum
 Franck Noiret, General Partner
 Education: Sciences-Po Paris; Masters in Corporate Finance, Paris-Dauphine University; MBA, Wharton School
 Background: Director, Apax Partners; Principal Banker, EBRD
 Directorships: Ei Technologies, Genoway, Maeglin, Tronic's
 Michel Desbard, Venture Partner
 Background: Financial Auditor, Thomson Group; Financial Controller, Fairchild Semiconductor; COO, Matra-Harris
 Directorships: Crocus Technology, One Access, Teem Photonics, TES Electronics Solutions
 Bertrand Limoges, Partner
 Education: Sciences-Po Paris, HEC School of Management
 Background: Viventures
 Chantal Parpex, President/Managing Partner
 Education: MD, Faculte de Medecine de Paris; International Program of General Management, INSEAD/CEDEP
 Background: Founder/Managing Partner, Bioam Gestion; Rhone-Poulenc Rorer Group; Medical Director, Synthelabo
 Directorships: IntegraGen
 Florian Reinaud, Partner
 Education: BA, Physiology, Oxford University; MD, Imperial College London
 Background: CFO, DBV Technologies; Apax Partners; Equity Analyst, Schroder Salomon Smith Barney/Citigroup
 Directorships: FAB Pharma, Orthopaedic Synergy, Zealand Pharma

2868 INNOVATION CAPITAL LIMITED
Suite 401, 35 Lime St
Sydney 2000
Australia

Phone: 61-282966000 Fax: 61-282966066
web: www.innovationcapital.net

Mission Statement: Innovation Capital focuses on Australian technology intensive businesses.
Geographic Preference: Australia, US
Fund Size: $100 Million
Investment Criteria: Seed, Early
Industry Group Preference: Wireless Technologies, Energy, Medical & Health Related, Biopharmaceuticals, Management, Environmental Protection, Media, Telecommunications, Information Technology, Engineering, Clean Technology, Biotechnology
Portfolio Companies: ActiveSky, cap-XX, Enterix, QRxPharma, Neuromonics, Micromet.
Key Executives:
 Michael A Quinn, Managing Partner
 e-mail: michaelquinn@innovationcapital.net
 Education: Harvard University MBA University of Western Australia Bachelor of SciencePhysics and Applied Mathematics; Bachelor of Science BEc MBA
 Background: Chief Executive Officer of Phoenix Scientific Industries Limited; Co-founded Memtec; active director of ResMed Inc
 Directorships: QRxPharma Pty Ltd Board Member Warren Centre for Advanced Engineering at Sydney University Board Member (past); ATP Innovations Pty Ltd Chair of NSW Enterprise Workshop and
 Robert Frater, Chief Technology Officer

2869 INNOVATIONSKAPITAL
1 Kungsportsplatsen
Gothenburg SE-411 10
Sweden

Phone: 46-31609190 Fax: 46-31609199
e-mail: info@innkap.se
web: www.innkap.se

Mission Statement: To invest in start-up and early stage private companies in the Nordic region. The investment strategy is directed towards companies in the Information Sciences and Healthcare industry sectors, with special emphasis on the commercial development of leading
Geographic Preference: Sweden, Denmark, Finland, Norway
Fund Size: $323 Million
Founded: 1994
Average Investment: $1.27 Million
Minimum Investment: $0.12 Million
Investment Criteria: Startup, Early Stage, Expansion/development, Seed
Industry Group Preference: Information Technology, Health Related, Hardware, Software, Telecommunications
Portfolio Companies: Altitun, Appgate, Bioinvent, Carmen Systems, Comlase, Cureon, Firedoor, Formex, Heptagon,

Mathcore, Medeikonos, Mitra, Nassko, Plexus, Radians Innova, Samba Sensors, Simtra Aerotech Spotfire

Key Executives:
Staffan Ingeborn, Managing Investment Director
e-mail: info@innkap.se
Education: MSc in European Accounting and Finance from an Erasmus Programme, MSc in Business Administration and Economics from the University of Göteborg
Background: Managing Director of Healthcare Division, SCA M'lnlycke; Technical Director and Executive Vice President, SCA M'lnlycke Group
Gunnar Fernström, Investment Director
e-mail: info@innkap.se
Education: MBA certificate from the University of North Carolina. He holds an Executive MBA from Stockholm School of Economics, an MSc in Business Administration and Economics from the University of Gothenburg and has studied engineerin
Gabriella Ohldin, Chief Financial Officer
e-mail: info@innkap.se

2870 INTEGRATED TECHNOLOGIES LIMITED
Viking House
Ellingham Way
Ashford, Kent TN23 6NF
United Kingdom

Phone: 44-1233638383 Fax: 44-1233639401
web: www.itl.co.uk

Mission Statement: A joint ownership by Israel Aircraft Industries (IAI) and a $1.6 billion conglomerate comprised of Israeli & US entrepreneurs, bankers and industrialists.

Geographic Preference: Germany, Europe, Israel, North America

2871 INTELLIGENT CAPITAL SDN BHD
18-2, Jalan 1/76C, Desa Pandan
Kuala Lumpur 55100
Malaysia

Phone: 60-392-816588 Fax: 60-3-9281-6598
web: www.intelligentvc.com

Fund Size: $16 Million
Founded: 2000
Average Investment: $3 Million
Minimum Investment: 500000
Investment Criteria: Focus on companies that can protect their margin or that have excellent management
Industry Group Preference: High Technology

2872 INTER-ASIA VENTURE MANAGEMENT LIMITED
141 Des Voeux Road
510, China Insurance Group Building,
Central
Hong Kong

Phone: 852-25285717 Fax: 85225279704
e-mail: iavm@iavmhk.com
web: www.iavmhk.com

Geographic Preference: America, Africa, Asia Pacific
Fund Size: $ 60 million
Founded: 1972
Average Investment: $ 8 Million
Minimum Investment: $ 1 million
Investment Criteria: Start-up, Early Stage
Industry Group Preference: Food & Beverage, Software, Environmental Protection, Logistics, Distribution, Healthcare, Health Related, Information Technology, Alternative Energy, Processing
Portfolio Companies: ACL Wireless, Asia Foods, Asia Renal Care, China Veg, Contech, Exsequor, Heart Center, IKEA, Jump, McDonald's, New Horizons, PNE/Ecogas, Ross Systems, Solarex Photovaltaic, Temenos

Key Executives:
Lewis P. Rutherfurd, Co-founder & Managing Partner
Education: BA East Asian Studies, Princeton University; MBA, Harvard Business School
Background: Governor/VP, American Chamber of Commerce in Hong Kong; Chairman, Honk Kong Venture Capital Association
Louis S. K. Wong, Executive Director
Education: Lingnan University
Background: Senior Accountant, Thomas Lee C Kuen & Co
Bolormaa Luvsandorj, Partner, Ulaanbaator
Education: MBA, Harvard Business School
Background: Director: Hong Kong Sheraton Hotel & Shopping Mall, IKEA, Five Pillars Indonesia Office Park, McDonald's of Singapore; US Navy Underwater Demolition Team; US Navy SEAL Team 2
Cyril Fung, Co-founder & Chairman
Education: BBA, University of Missouri
Background: Senior VP/CFO, GE Asia Pacific Capital Technology Fund; Finance/Administrative Manager, Sumitomo Metal Group; CPA

2873 INTER-RISCO: SOCIEDADE DE CAPITAL DE RISCO
284 rua Tenente Valadim
OPorto 4100-476
Portugal

Phone: 351-226073111 Fax: 351-226006488
web: www.bancobpi.pt

Mission Statement: Invests in Expansion, Development, Small buyout, Minority Equity opportunities.

Geographic Preference: Portugal
Industry Group Preference: All Sectors Considered

2874 INTERMEDIATE CAPITAL GROUP PLC
100 St Paul's Churchyard
Juxon House
London EC4M 8BU
United Kingdom

Phone: 44-02032017700 Fax: 44-02072482536
e-mail: terri.jasper@icgplc.com
web: www.icgplc.com

Mission Statement: Actively seeking new investments.

Geographic Preference: France, Germany, Italy, Netherlands, Spain, United Kingdom
Fund Size: Euro 12.1 Billion
Founded: 1989
Average Investment: $8 Million
Minimum Investment: $2 Million
Investment Criteria: Bridge, Expansion, Management Buy-In, Management Buy-Out, Refinancing Bank Debt, Secondary Purchase and Replacement Capital, Mezzanine
Industry Group Preference: Consumer Products, Insurance, Manufacturing, Information Technology, Textiles, Biotechnology, Aviation
Portfolio Companies: Acova, Cartiere del Garda, Calvet, Coal Products, Convenience Food Systems, Electrokoppar, Elmville, Great Western Holdings, MTL, Thomson Directories, Unipart Rail Holdings

Key Executives:
Christophe Evain, Managing Director and CEO
Education: University of Hamburg
Background: Citibank for five years in Frankfurt and New York and three years for Bankgesellschaft Berlin/Landesbank Berlin
Philip Keller, Managing Director and Chief Financial Officer
Education: Graduate from Oxford University & qualified as a chartered accountant.
Background: for Price Waterhouse for seven years

Venture Capital & Private Equity Firms / International Firms

Andreas Klein, Associate Director - Credit Fund Management
Education: MBA from the London Business School
Background: he worked for Chemical Bank for seven years
Andreas Mondovits, Senior Managing Director
Education: MBA, Univ. of Southern California
Background: UBS Global Asset Management
Alan Carey, Associate Director - CFM Administration
Background: Williams & Glyns, Chemical Bank & Specialist Finance Group
Chris Connelly, Director of Operations
Education: Oxford University and subsequently qualified as a chartered accountant
Background: he worked for Coopers & Lybrand for seven years
Benoit Durteste, Managing Director and Head of European Mezzanine
Education: MBA from Heriot-Watt University Business School, graduate of Napier University and subsequently qualified as a Certified Accountant
Background: he worked for The Royal Bank of Scotland for two years
Alex Hone, Associate Director - Mezzanine Funds Administration
Education: Vrije University
Background: he worked for the private equity firm HAL Investments in the Netherlands for four year
Amalia Formoso, Associate - Marketing and Client Relations
e-mail: james.davis@icgplc.co.uk
Education: Graduate from Oxford University & C.A.
Background: Deloitte & Touche
Ian Stanlake, Financial Controller
Education: graduate of Copenhagen Business School and has an MBA from the European School of Management
Background: he worked as a strategy consultant for Braxton Associates for three years

2875 INTERNATIONAL PRIVATE EQUITY SERVICES LIMITED Guernsey
1, Royal Plaza, Royal Avenue
St Peter Port
Channel Islands
Guernsey GY1 2HL
United Kingdom

Phone: 44-1481713843 **Fax:** 44-1481715219
web: www.ipes.com

Mission Statement: Independent provider offering services for private equity and venture capital funds and their related vehicles
Geographic Preference: United Kingdom
Fund Size: $50 Billion
Founded: 1998
Key Executives:
Andrew Whittaker, Managing Director, Guernsey
e-mail: ipesgsy@aol.com
Education: Qualified banker and a Chartered Director.
Background: 25 years administration, investment and management experience working with major international finance institutions in the offshore industry.
Directorships: founder
Sharon Alvarez, Director, Guernsey

2876 INVEMAX
ul. M. Reja 13/15
81-874 Sopot
Poland

e-mail: info@invemax.com
web: www.invemax.com

Mission Statement: The thing that a fresh idea needs the most is acceleration. Ideas should be constantly tested, modified and validated asap. Our specialty is seed investing. Beyond financial support we provided contact with the most important startup hot-spots in the world.
Investment Criteria: Seed
Portfolio Companies: 3HACK.PL, Startup Weekend Trojmiasto, ElimiDateapp.com, Coinbase, TeleportMe

2877 INVENTURE PARTNERS
Novinsky Boulevard 31, Office 8-20B
Floor 8
Moscow 123242
Russia

Phone: 7 495 641 3635 **Fax:** 7 495 641 3866
e-mail: info@inventurepartners.com
web: www.inventurepartners.com

Mission Statement: We are solely focused on investing in the equity of young technology companies in Russia. We seek investments with unique value propositions. We generally seek a representation on the board of the companies we invest in, as we believe we can make a valuable contribution in the strategic decision making process.
Geographic Preference: Russia
Investment Criteria: Early Stage
Industry Group Preference: Internet, Mobile, Software, E-Commerce & Manufacturing
Portfolio Companies: GetTaxi, Fogg, OnlineTours, Starcard, GetGoing, Smarfin, Happlink
Key Executives:
Sergey Azatyan, Managing Partner
Anton Inshutin, Managing Partner

2878 INVEST EQUITY MANAGEMENT CONSULTING GmbH
Garnisongasse 7/Top 22
Vienna 1090
Austria

Phone: 43-15320551 **Fax:** 43-15320551
e-mail: office@investequity.at
web: www.investequity.at

Mission Statement: INVEST EQUITY enjoys an excellent reputation as an active and reliable investor in unlisted companies with the focus on growth companies and mid-market buy-outs and is a strong local partner for both international investors and private equity players alike.
Geographic Preference: Czech Republic and Slovakia
Fund Size: $110 Million
Founded: 1998
Average Investment: $1.5 Million
Minimum Investment: $800, 000
Investment Criteria: Seed, start-up, expansion, pre-IPO, buy-out
Industry Group Preference: Industrial Products, Industrial Services, Manufacturing
Portfolio Companies: Chemson, Infoniqa, Kolbe-Coloco, LMF, Logim, Steudle, Strohal
Key Executives:
Jörgen Hausberger, Managing Partner
Education: Graduate engineer from Vienna University of Technology
Background: 15 year experience in PE/VC market, having previously worked in the area of corporate finance at Investkredit Bank AG and also for many years in the Austrian industry

2879 INVESTMENT AB BURE
Dawson Street 6
Stockholm 114 34
Sweden

Phone: 08-6140020 **Fax:** 08-6140038
e-mail: info@bure.se
web: www.bure.se

Mission Statement: Focuses on long-term ownership of unlisted companies with strong and stable earnings.

Geographic Preference: Sweden
Founded: 1993
Industry Group Preference: Communications, Computer Related, Medical & Health Related, Industrial Services
Portfolio Companies: Appelberg, Carl Bro, Celemi, Citat, Cygate, Mercuri International, Retea, Systeam, Textilia, Vittra Utbildning, Mitra Medical, Kreatel

Key Executives:
Patrik Tigerschiöld, Chairman
e-mail: info@bure.se
Agneta Schein, Director secretary

2880 INVESTMENT FUND FOR CENTRAL & EASTERN EUROPE
Fredericiagade 27
Copenhagen K 1310
Denmark

Phone: 45-33637500 Fax: 45-33637599

Mission Statement: IFU participates as a partner in the joint ventures through committing equity capital and/or loans and through board membership.

Geographic Preference: Central, Eastern Europe
Founded: 1967
Average Investment: $1.5 Million
Minimum Investment: $100,000
Investment Criteria: Invests in profitable companies with Danish base
Industry Group Preference: Pharmaceuticals, Transportation, Chemicals, Beverages, Wood Industries, Construction, Consumer Products, Research & Development
Portfolio Companies: Camsavon, Aldaph, Camtainer, NOBRA, CITB, SAM, Sedan, Danilait, Dilaz, El Rayan Danfarm, EPL, African Lakes Ethiopia, Muk Air, Pako Bay, Volta Arkil

Key Executives:
Tommy Thomsen, Managing Director
Torben Huss, Deputy Managing Director

2881 INVESTOR AB
8C Aresenalsgatan
Stockholm SE-103 32
Sweden

Phone: 46-86141800 Fax: 46-86141809
e-mail: info@investorab.com
web: www.investorab.com

Mission Statement: The group focuses on being an active, value-added investor in technology and healthcare companies in North America and Europe.

Geographic Preference: China, South Korea
Fund Size: $1.8 Billion
Founded: 1916
Average Investment: $26.5 Million
Minimum Investment: $0.63 Million
Investment Criteria: Expansion stage companies with customers and revenue, buy-out and co-control deals, branded consumer goods and services, manufacturing business for outsourcing and export markets
Industry Group Preference: Healthcare, Information Technology, Communications, Manufacturing
Portfolio Companies: Aerocrine, Affibody, Amkor Technology, Inc., Apollo International, Applied Sensor, Asia Renal Care Ltd, Atrica, Axcan Pharma, Biotage, Cameron Health, Cavidi Tech AB, CHF Solutions, EDT Learning, eSilicon Corporation, Excosoft, Gyros, Info Talk, JP Mobil

Key Executives:
Jacob Wallenberg, Chairman
e-mail: info@investorab.com
Education: B.Sc. Economics and M.B.A., Wharton School, University of Pennsylvania
Background: President and CEO, SEB, Head of Enskilda Division, Advisor to the President and CEO, SEB, Executive Vice President and CFO, Investor
Henry E Gooss, Managing Director
e-mail: info@investorab.com
Education: M.B.A. in Investments, New York University and B.A. in Economics, Rutgers University
Background: Director of Mainstream Data, Inc. and Telegea, Inc
Börje Ekholm, President and CEO
e-mail: info@investorab.com
Education: M.Sc. in Engineering, Royal Institute of Technology, Stockholm
Background: President, CEO and Chairman AB Electrolux, Chairman Saab-Scania AB, Member of the Board The Federation of Swedish Industries
Sune Carlsson, Vice Chairman
e-mail: info@investorab.com
Education: M.Sc. in Mechanical Engineering, Chalmers University of Technology, Gothenburg
Background: Executive Vice President, ASEA AB and ABB Ltd, President and CEO, SKF
Susanne Ekblom, Chief Financial Officer
e-mail: info@investorab.com
Education: D.Sc. (Econ.), Helsinki School of Economics
Background: Economist and Head of Office, Bank of Finland, Director General, Economics Department, Finnish Ministry of Finance
Susanna Sjödin, Communications Officer
e-mail: info@investorab.com
Education: M.Sc. in Business Administration and Economics, Stockholm School of Economics, M.B.A., Massachusetts Institute of Technology
Background: Managing Director and member of Management Group, Portfolio Manager Öhman Fondkommission
Gunnar Brock, Director
e-mail: info@investorab.com
Education: Sc.D. in Applied Biochemistry, Royal Institute of Technology, Stockholm
Background: President and CEO, AB Marabou and Astra AB
O. Griffith Sexton, Director
e-mail: info@investorab.com
Education: M.B.A., Stanford University Graduate School of Business and B.S.E., Princeton University
Background: Advisory Director, Morgan Stanley, Managing Director, Morgan Stanley
Marcus Wallenberg, Director
e-mail: info@investorab.com
Education: M.Sc. in Engineering, Royal Institute of Technology, Stockholm and The Management Development Institute (IMEDE), Lausanne
Background: CEO and Chairman, Ericsson, CEO, SEB

2882 INVEXCEL PATRIMONIO
Claudio Coelle 78
Madrid 28001
Spain

Phone: 34-915783676 Fax: 34-914319303
e-mail: info@invexcel.com
web: www.invexcel.com

Mission Statement: Excel Partners is an active investor in all companies in which it holds a stake, supporting its shareholders and managers with all our resources and ability in the design of the most appropriate strategy to be implemented by the company.

Geographic Preference: Europe, Latin America, Iberian Peninsula
Fund Size: $100 Million
Founded: 1991
Average Investment: $30 Million
Minimum Investment: $ 2 Million

Venture Capital & Private Equity Firms / International Firms

Investment Criteria: Management buy-outs, buy-ins, buy-and-build, reorganizations and spin-offs, divestments, expansions, joint-ventures
Industry Group Preference: Software, Consumer Products, Information Technology, Distribution, Industrial Services, Electronic Technology, Telecommunications, Components & IoT
Portfolio Companies: Gas Gas, PrintOne, Real Musical, Rotographik, Unitronics
Key Executives:
  José María López de Letona, Partner
  Ramón Menéndez de Luarca, Partner
  Background: Three Cities Research Fund
  Ramon Menendez de Luarca, Partner
  Education: Degree in Economic Science and Business(Pontifical University of Comillas - ICADE), MBA in Industrial Management (Carnegie Mellon University; Pittsburgh, USA) ,
  Background: Arthur D. Little, Boston Consulting Group
  Directorships: Principal

2883 IP GROUP
24 Cornhill
London EC3V 3ND
United Kingdom

Phone: 44-2074440050 Fax: 44-2079296415
web: www.ipgroupplc.com

Mission Statement: IP Group is a leading UK intellectual property commercialisation company, developing technology innovations primarily from its research intensive partner universities. The Group offers far more than traditional venture capital, providing its companies with access to business building expertise, networks, recruitment and business support.
Founded: 2001
Investment Criteria: Early-Stage to Later-Stage
Industry Group Preference: Energy, Renewable Energy, Medical Devices, Pharmaceuticals, Biotechnology, Information Technology, Communications, Chemicals, Advanced Materials
Portfolio Companies: Activiomics, Actual Experience, Amaethon, Arkivum, Asalus, Avacta, Azellon, Capsant, CCapture, Ceres Power, Ch4e, Chamelic, Crysalin, Durham Graphene, DyeCat, Emdot, Empiricom, Encos, Evocutis, FrontierIP, Gusion, Getech, Glythera, Green Chemicals, Icona, Iuka, Inhibox, IQur, Karus Therapeutics, Mode Diagnositics, Modern Water, Nanotecture, Overlay Media, Oxford Advanced Surfaces, Oxford Catalysts, Nanopore, Oxford RF Sensors, Oxtox, Oxyntix, Perpetuum, Pharminax, Photopharmica, Plexus, Polar Oled, Progenteq, Proximagen, Retroscreen Virology, Revolymer, RDR, RSI, Seren, Stratophase, Structure Vision, Surrey Nanosystems, Sustainable Resource Solutions, Synairgen, Tissue Regenix, Tracsis, Xeros
Key Executives:
  Alan Aubrey, Chief Executive Officer
  Education: BA, Economics, University of Leeds; MBA, University of Bradford
  Background: Joint Founder, Chief Executive, Techtran Group; KPMG

2884 IPBM Group IDI
18 Matignon Avenue
Paris 75008
France

Phone: 33-155-278000 Fax: 33-140170444

Mission Statement: Actively seeking new investments.
Geographic Preference: Asia, Eastern Europe
Fund Size: $396 Million
Founded: 1970
Average Investment: $9.60 Million
Minimum Investment: $1.2 Million
Investment Criteria: Small-stage and Mid-stage
Industry Group Preference: All Sectors Considered

2885 IPG GROUP
24 Cornhill
Warwick Court
London ECV3 3ND
United Kingdom

Phone: 44-02074440050 Fax: 44-02079296415
e-mail: hatt@toptechnology.co.uk
web: www.ipgroupplc.com

Mission Statement: Top Technology Ventures is a UK-based venture capital company which specialises in providing equity funding for early stage technology based growth companies.
Geographic Preference: United Kingdom
Fund Size: $74 Million
Founded: 1986
Average Investment: Euro 49 Million
Minimum Investment: $708, 000
Investment Criteria: Start-up, Other early stage, Expansion and Development
Industry Group Preference: Medical & Health Related, Communications, Information Technology, Computer Hardware & Software, Internet Technology
Portfolio Companies: nCipher, Focus Solutions Group, IP2IPO Group, Wire-e Limited, Commerce Decisions Ltd, One clickHR, Metapack Ltd, Webabcus Ltd, Infoucs Health Ltd, AP Benson Ltd, ANT, Nanotecture Ltd, Arieso Ltd, Netronome Systems Ltd, Oxford Immunotec Ltd
Key Executives:
  Alan Aubrey, Chief Executive Officer
  Mike Townend, Chief Investment Officer

2886 IPOSCOPE NV/SA
19 Jan van Boendalelaan, Tervuren
Brussels 3080
Belgium

Phone: 32-27672500 Fax: 32-27682994
e-mail: e.hallmann@iposcope.com
web: www.iposcope.com

Mission Statement: Global advisory for high growth companies on private equity and going public regardless of the clients geographic origins.
Industry Group Preference: Information Technology, Software, Life Sciences

2887 IRDI MIDI-PYRENEES
18 Dupuy Place
BP 808
Cedex 6
Toulouse 31080
France

Phone: 33-581317320 Fax: 33-581317339
e-mail: contact@irdi.fr
web: www.irdi.fr

Mission Statement: Actively seeking new investments.
Fund Size: $66.3 Million
Minimum Investment: $36, 000
Industry Group Preference: Industrial Equipment, Industrial Services
Key Executives:
  Thierry Letailleur, President
  Dorothée Watine, Investment Manager

2888 IRIS CAPITAL
62 rue Pierre Charron
Paris 75008
France

Phone: 33-145627373 Fax: 33-145627370
e-mail: c.micoski@iriscapital.com
web: www.iriscapital.com

Mission Statement: A pan-European venture and development capital fund specializing in media and entertainment, communications and IT.
Geographic Preference: Europe, North America, Asia
Founded: 1986
Average Investment: $1.2 Million -$24 Million
Minimum Investment: $0.6 Million
Investment Criteria: Early Stage, Expansion and Development Capital
Industry Group Preference: Communications, Media, Information Technology, Entertainment
Portfolio Companies: 1-2-3.TV, Abry, Acapela Group, Alphanim, Altitude, Altitude, American Greetings Interactive, Apach Network, Atrica, Canal Guyane, Cirpack, Cityneo, DataDirect Networks, E-Net, Editions Montparnasse, Elitel, Everbee, Exception Wild Bunch, Fast Booking
Key Executives:
   Antoine Garrigues, Managing Partner
   e-mail: c.blanche@iriscapital.com
   Education: Institut Superieur du Commerce de Paris
   Background: PricewaterhouseCoopers Luxembourg
   Pierre de Fouquet, Managing Partner
   e-mail: p.defouquet@iriscapital.com
   Education: Graduate PhD in Economics .
   Background: Strategic Planning at CDC.
   Denis Barrier, Partner
   e-mail: a.garrigues@iriscapital.com
   Education: Graduate of the French Ecole Polytechnique and Ecole des Ponts et Chaussees engineering schools
   Background: The Director of International Affairs and Development for Dassault A.T.

2889 ISIS EP LLP F & C
2nd Floor, 100 Wood Street
London EC2V 7AN
United Kingdom
Phone: 44-2075065600 Fax: 44-2075065665
e-mail: leanne.metcalfe@isisep.com

Mission Statement: Centered on helping entrepreneurial management teams achieve substantial capital gain.
Geographic Preference: United Kingdom, Germany, Netherlands
Fund Size: £1.2 Billion
Founded: 1995
Average Investment: $8.8 Million
Minimum Investment: $3.5 Million
Industry Group Preference: Business to Business, Media, Consumer Services, Technology, Financial Services, Healthcare, Education, Communications
Key Executives:
   James Bagan, Operating Partner

2890 ISOURCE GESTION
23 Avenue D'Iena
Paris 75116
France
Phone: 33-0-1-4501-4646 Fax: 33-0-1-4501-4660
e-mail: info@isourcevc.com
web: www.isourcevc.com

Mission Statement: These past few years, a certain number of capital risk players, including entrepreneur funds, have reinforced the market's capacity to initiate new start-ups. As a result, young companies have emerged with force, often with promising futures. But once their first goals are accomplished i.e. finalizing a product or completing a team, these enterprises must raise consequent funds during the 1st round. It is these companies, still in the early phase of development and that require significant funds (0.5 to 5 million euros), that iSource specializes in assisting. It is this momentum that capital investment players hesitate over and which iSource believes is the best time for creating value, therefore establishing a market opportunity.
Geographic Preference: France, Western Europe
Average Investment: 0.5 to 5 million euros
Investment Criteria: Early-Stage, First Round
Industry Group Preference: Business Software, Technology, Telecommunications, Internet, Embedded Systems, Managed Services, Green Technology, Information Technology, Software
Portfolio Companies: BeamExpress, Captain Dash, Commpario, Cyanide, DarQroom, Digital Media Solutions, E-Blink, EdXact, Expway, eYeka, Fluoptics, IDS, IJenko, IMinent, Jetchange.fr, LeddarTech, Link Care Services, Metablo, Movea, Rhapso, Sequans Communicatinos, Smartesting, Total Immersion
Key Executives:
   Didier Moret, Managing Partner
   Education: Centrale Paris Engineering School
   Directorships: Captain Dash, Compario, IDS, JeChange.fr, LeddarTech, Link Care Services, Rhapso, Smartesting

2891 ISRAEL CLEANTECH VENTURES
Hakfar Hayorok Youth Village
Ramat Hasharon 47800
Israel
Phone: 972-36446611 Fax: 972-36493737
web: www.israelcleantech.com

Mission Statement: Israel Cleantech Ventures is the leading venture capital fund focused on backing Israel's emerging clean technology companies. We are dedicated to providing value added growth capital to exceptional entrepreneurs building Israel's energy, water and environmental technology leaders. Our geographical focus and market leadership enable us to take advantage of Israel's prominence as an innovative market leader in energy, water and agricultural technologies, as well as ancillary cleantech sectors including energy efficiency, smart-grid/communications, green IT, power electronics and capital equipment.
Geographic Preference: Israel
Founded: 2006
Industry Group Preference: Clean Technology, Energy, Water, Agriculture, Energy Efficiency, Power
Portfolio Companies: AcousticEye, Aqwise, Better Place, Cellera, Emefcy, FRX Polymers, Metrolight, Panoramic Power, Pythagoras, Scodix, Tigo Energy
Key Executives:
   Jack Levy, Partner
   Education: BA, Harvard College; JD, Columbia Law School
   Background: Vice President & General Counsel, Register.com

2892 IT VENTURES LIMITED Digital Heritage Publishing Ltd.
29 Floor, EGL Tower, 83 Hung To Road
Kwun Tong
Kowloon
Hong Kong
Phone: 852-23023011 Fax: 852-27308686
web: www.itventuresltd.com

Mission Statement: Actively seeking new investments.
Fund Size: $700 Million
Founded: 1995
Industry Group Preference: Information Technology
Key Executives:
   Gabriel Chi Ming Yu, Founder & Chairman

Venture Capital & Private Equity Firms / International Firms

2893 IT-PARTNERS NV
105 H. Henneaulaan
Zaventem 1930
Belgium

Phone: 32-27251838 Fax: 32-27214435

Mission Statement: Invests in companies in the ICT sector.
Geographic Preference: Belgium, USA, Netherlands
Fund Size: $79.4 Million
Founded: 1997
Investment Criteria: Early-stage, 2nd Round, Expansion.
Industry Group Preference: Information Technology, Telecommunications, Security
Portfolio Companies: Captor N.V., Coware Inc., EDS Docdata B.V., Encore Media Systems B.V., Fillfactory N.V., Hypertrust N.V., Lenel Systems International, Inc., Septentrio N.V., Target Compiler Technologies N.V.

Key Executives:
Paul Verdurme, Investment Manager
e-mail: info@it-partners.be
Education: Master degree in electronics and applied mathametics.
Background: GTE Sylyania.
Stefaan Nicolay, Investment Manager
e-mail: info@it-partners.be
Education: Master degree in electronics.
Background: General Banking.

2894 ITC VENTURES
Centro Empresarial Mourisco
Praia de Botafogo
Cep 22250-040
Brazil

Phone: 55-2193115200
web: www.itcventures.com

Mission Statement: ITC Ventures focuses exclusively on internet related businesses in Latin America in their early stages of business models and financing
Geographic Preference: Brazil, Latin America, US, Europe
Fund Size: $200,000
Founded: 1999
Average Investment: $450,000
Minimum Investment: $700, 000
Investment Criteria: Medium sized international companies
Industry Group Preference: Internet Technology, Technology, Media, Financial Services

Key Executives:
Indio Brasileiro Guerra Neto, General Partner
e-mail: ben@itcventures.com
Education: Graduated from Washington University, graduate of the University of Nebraska, College of Law.
Background: KPMG International in Santiago de Chile.
Ben Hormel Harris, Corporate Development Officer

2895 IXORA VENTURES
Ixora Ventures Pvt. Ltd.
Suite No. 28
The Lodhi Hotel, Lodhi Road
New Delhi 110003
India

Phone: 91-1124362424

Mission Statement: Ixora's strategy follows one of sector focused investing, looking for opportunities where capital, experience and insight can release the potential of businesses and lead to significant growth. The firm attempts to grow businesses by acting as a catalyst for change and we have established clear processes to maximize the value of each member of our portfolio.
Geographic Preference: ASEAN Region, India
Investment Criteria: Seed-Stage, Early-Stage
Industry Group Preference: Technology, Healthcare, Education, Aerospace, Defense and Government
Portfolio Companies: Learnpedia, AlmaConnect, Warranty Asia

Key Executives:
Sunder Mulchandani, General Partner
Background: Managing Director, Argus Systems Private Limted

2896 J-SEED VENTURES INCORPORATED
Isshin Building 9F
2-11-7 Yaesu
Chuo-ku
Tokyo 104-0028
Japan

Phone: 81-345205424 Fax: 81-362038466
e-mail: info@j-seed.com
web: www.j-seed.com

Mission Statement: International provider of management and technology consulting services and solutions.
Geographic Preference: Worldwide
Fund Size: 52.6 Million Yen
Founded: 2000
Industry Group Preference: Management, Technology

Key Executives:
C. Jeffrey Char, President & Chief Executive Officer

2897 JAFCO COMPANY LIMITED JAPAN
Otemachi First Square, West Tower 11F
1-5-1 Otemachi, Chiyoda-ku
Tokyo 100-0004
Japan

Phone: 81-352237536 Fax: 81-352237561
e-mail: info@jafco.co.jp
web: www.jafco.co.jp

Mission Statement: Focuses on venture capital and buyout investment and management of related funds
Geographic Preference: Japan, USA, Asia, Europe
Fund Size: $3 Billion
Founded: 1973
Average Investment: $3 Million
Minimum Investment: $.19 Million
Investment Criteria: Companies with long term profitablity and sustainable growth potential.
Industry Group Preference: Electronic Technology, Software, Information Technology, Restaurants, Medical, Manufacturing, Distribution, Retailing

Key Executives:
Shinichi Fuki, President & Chief Executive Officer
e-mail: info@jafco.co.jp
Directorships: CEO
Hiroshi Yamada, Executive Managing Director

2898 JAPAN ASIA INVESTMENT COMPANY LIMITED
Seiko Takebashi-Kyodo Building
3-11 Kandanishiki-cho, Chiyoda-ku
Tokyo 101-8570
Japan

Phone: 81-335048518 Fax: 81-335048511
web: www.jaic-vc.co.jp

Mission Statement: Independent venture capital company that invests in unlisted venture companies .
Geographic Preference: Japan
Founded: 1981
Industry Group Preference: Biotechnology, Medical, Computer Hardware & Software, Medical Devices, Information Technology, Internet Technology
Portfolio Companies: Inter Co., Ltd., Tay Two Co., Ltd., Nihon Eslead Corp, PC Depot Corp, MediaPlex, Inc, Procomp Informatics, Handsman Co., Ltd, Bell-Park Co.,

Ltd, Taiwan Cellular Corp, Design EXchange Co., Ltd, Nihon Trim Co., Ltd, Nextware Ltd., Prime Network Inc.

Key Executives:
Toyoji Tatsuoka, President & Chief Executive Officer
Directorships: CEO
Yoshiki Sasaki, Senior Managing Directors

2899 JAVELIN INVESTMENTS
Guang Cheng Yuan, Building 16, Suite 21A
Haidian District
Beijing 100088
China

Phone: 86-1062381066 Fax: 86-1062355459

Mission Statement: Full service investment company that invests in high-growth private sector companies in China.

Geographic Preference: China, Beijing, Shanghai, Dallas, Hong Kong
Average Investment: $5.5 Million
Minimum Investment: $1 Million
Investment Criteria: High-technology start-up companies and foreign investors including investment banks, private equity funds, venture capital companies.
Industry Group Preference: Wireless Technologies, Electronic Technology, Information Technology, Computer Related, Biotechnology, Industrial Equipment, Petrochemicals, Food & Beverage, Packaging, Consumer Products, Automotive, Telecommunications, Chemicals

2900 JC TECHNOLOGIES LTD
21 Havaad Haleumi Street
PO Box 16031
Jerusalem 91160
Israel

Phone: 972-2751123 Fax: 972-2751195

Mission Statement: Cultivates promising technology-based businesses by providing excellent conditions for business success.

Geographic Preference: Jerusalem
Industry Group Preference: Optical Technology, Microelectronics, Medical, Instrumentation, Electronic Technology, Software, Applied Mathematics

2901 JERUSALEM VENTURE PARTNERS
24 Hebron Road
Jerusalem 93542
Israel

Phone: 972-26409000 Fax: 972-26409001
e-mail: info@jvpvc.com
web: www.jvpvc.com

Mission Statement: Venture capital fund with a unique international network; focuses on building technology-based market leaders in the areas of enterprise software and media technologies, semiconductors and innovative materials and communications and networking.

Geographic Preference: North America, Europe, Israel and Asia
Fund Size: $680 Million
Founded: 1993
Investment Criteria: Early-stage technology companies in the Enterprise Software & Media Technologies, Semiconductors & Innovative Materials and Communications & Networking sectors.
Industry Group Preference: Components & IoT, Innovative Products & Services, Enterprise Services, Media, Communications, Networking, Semiconductors, Software
Portfolio Companies: Celltick Software Technologies, Chromatis Networks, Cogent Communications, ComSong Interactive Technologies, CyOptics, First Access, Fundtech, Geophysical, InLight Communications, Kerenix, Macada, MysticCom, Native Networks, Netro Corporation, Nuvisio

Key Executives:
Erel N. Margalit, Founder & Managing Partner
e-mail: info@jvpvc.com
Education: MBA from Columbia Business School, BS from Tel Aviv University.
Background: McKinsey & Company in London.
Gadi Tirosh, General Partner
Haim Kopans, Partner and CTO
e-mail: info@jvpvc.com
Education: BS in International Economics and Finance from Georgetown University.
Background: JVP's Israel office in 1996 as an analyst, President of the Stern Group.
Kobi Rozengarten, General Partner
Education: BS in Electrical Engineering from University of Cape Town, MBA from INSEAD.
Background: GE Capital in London, MAC Consulting Group.

2902 JTP CORPORATION
1-30-20, Kaminoge, Setagaya-ku
Yoga, Setagaya-ku
Tokyo 158-0097
Japan

Phone: 81-364322337 Fax: 81-364322338
e-mail: jtmerge@gmail.com
web: www.transaction.co.jp

Mission Statement: Advisors specializing in complex transactions: mergers and acquisitions, spin-offs, strategic alliances, and joint ventures.

Geographic Preference: Japan

Key Executives:
Nicholas E Benes, Founder & President
e-mail: nbenes@transaction.co.jp
Education: BA in Political Science from Stanford University, MBA and law degree (JD) from UCLA.
Background: Senior Managing Director in The Kamakura Corporation, Vice President at JP Morgan.

2903 JUMPSEED VENTURES
PICO Jerusalem
2 Poalei Tzedek
4th Fllor
Talpiot, Jerusalem
Israel

Mission Statement: If a portfolio company wants us to take a more active, day-to-day role, we are available to work hand in hand with the founder(s), executing the company's business development and marketing strategy as active members of the team. Portfolio companies can, but are not required to, choose from a range of levels of hands-on support.

Geographic Preference: Israel
Average Investment: $50,000 - $150,000
Investment Criteria: Early-Stage
Industry Group Preference: Internet

Key Executives:
Ben Wiener, Managing Partner
Education: BA, Economics, Yeshiva University; JD, Columbia Law School
Background: Vice President, IDT Corp.; Corporate Lawyer; Clerk, Israel Supreme Court

2904 JUNGLE VENTURES
306 Tanglin Road
Phoenix Park Office Campus
247973
Singapore

Phone: 65-64239516 Fax: 65-64239516
e-mail: amit@jungle-ventures.com
web: www.jungle-ventures.com

Venture Capital & Private Equity Firms / International Firms

Mission Statement: Jungle Ventures is a SIngapore native global venture capital firm that provides early stage investments and business building infrastructure to startups.
Geographic Preference: Singapore, India, South East Asia
Investment Criteria: Early-Stage
Portfolio Companies: Cinemacraft, Doc Doc, eBus.TV, Ekstop.com, Mobikon, One Animation, Sconce Solutions, Travelmob

Key Executives:
  Peng T Ong, Fund Advisor
  Background: Partner, GSR Ventures; President, Interwoven
  Directorships: Singapore Telecommunications

2905 KAEDAN INVESTMENTS
6 Wallenberg Street
PO Box 13169
Ramat Hachayal
Tel Aviv 61131
Israel

Phone: 972-77-234-8890 Fax: 972-77-234-8880
e-mail: contact@kaedan.com
web: www.kaedan.com

Mission Statement: Kaedan Capital is a private investment firm engaged in seed to early stage ventures in focus areas of Internet, Mobile applications & services, Digital Media, On Demand Software (Saas), and Digital Marketing & Advertising. We view active investment involvement as our guideline in creating value. Therefore, one of Kaedan's team members, with the required skill set and ability to add value to the specific investment, will assume an active role in the invested company's board. Our strategy and motivation are well aligned with those of the entrepreneurs in which we invest, exemplified by taking a long investment horizon and participating in follow on investments when needed.
Geographic Preference: Israel
Investment Criteria: Early-Stage
Industry Group Preference: Internet, Mobile Apps, Digital Media & Marketing, Software, SaaS, Digital Marketing, Advertising, Consumer Products
Portfolio Companies: Playtika, 5minMedia, Tvinci, Somoto, Jelly Button, Bizzabo, Visualead, JoyTunes, Adience, Flayvr, Baligam, ONE, WhiteSmoke, YCD Multimedia, Mobile 1

Key Executives:
  Yair Hamburger, Chairman
  Education: BA, Economics & Social Sciences, Hebrew University
  Background: Chairman, Harel Insurance Investments
  Ron Tamir, Founder/Managing Partner
  Education: LLB, Tel Aviv University; MBA, Kellogg School of Management
  Directorships: Tvinci, Citynet
  Ofer Lazovski, Director
  Education: BSc, Computer Science, Technion
  Background: Co-Founder, 888.com
  Directorships: 5min
  Ziv Yanous, Director
  Background: Founder, Hydepark.co.il; Founding Team, eToro

2906 KALORI GROUP INVESTMENTS
131 Macquarie Street
Level 14
Sydney 2000
Australia

Phone: 61293864646 Fax: 61-29-386-4420
e-mail: cwitt@kalorigroup.com

Mission Statement: Develops and invests in young technology-intensive businesses. A single dedicated team takes a project from inception to implementation.
Founded: 1998
Investment Criteria: Early Stage
Industry Group Preference: Technology, Information Technology, Telecommunications, Software, Internet Technology, Medical Devices, Infrastructure, Retail, Consumer & Leisure, Oil & Gas, Fashion, Hospitality, Medical Technology
Portfolio Companies: Health Communications Network Limited
Key Executives:
  Christopher Witt, Partner
  e-mail: cwitt@kalorigroup.com
  Education: BS Industrial Engineering/Economics, Northwestern University; MBA, Kellogg Graduate School of Management
  Background: GM Radio Producst Group, Motorola; Telstra; Ameritech Corp; Professor, DePaul University
  David Wright, Partner

2907 KARDAN LTD
154 Menachem Begin Road
Tel Aviv Yafo 64921
Israel

Phone: 972-36083444 Fax: 972-36083434
e-mail: info@kardan.nl
web: www.kardan.com

Key Executives:
  Peter Sheldon, Chairman
  Background: Israeli Defense Forces
  Directorships: Tahal, Aeronautics Defense Systems

2908 KBL FOUNDER SA
2, boulevard Emmanuel Servais
L-2535
Luxembourg

Phone: 325-4730251 Fax: 352-479-773900
e-mail: luxembourg@puilaetco.com
web: www.kbl.lu

Mission Statement: Actively seeking new investments
Geographic Preference: Europe, Germany
Fund Size: $30 Billion
Founded: 1949
Investment Criteria: Start-up, Expansion and Development
Industry Group Preference: Biotechnology, Communications, Computer Related, Software, Electronic Technology, Energy, Medical & Health Related
Key Executives:
  Jan Huyghebaert, Chairman
  e-mail: info@kbl-bank.com
  Education: Degree in Accounting and Fiscal studies and post graduate degree in computer.
  Background: CEO of Krefima NV and Concentra NV.
  George Nasra, Vice-Chairman
  e-mail: info@kbl-bank.com
  Education: Degree in Civil Engineering from University of Louvania, and MBA from University of Chicago.
  Background: Generale Bank,

2909 KERNEL CAPITAL
Rubicon Centre
Rossa Avenue
Bishoptown
Cork
Ireland

Phone: 353-0214928974
e-mail: boi_seedfund@kernelcapital.ie
web: www.kernelcapital.ie

Mission Statement: Kernel Capital is one of Ireland's largest and most active venture capital funds. The firm has a portfolio of investee companies across, technology, life science and general industry.
Founded: 2002
Average Investment: 100,000 - 5 million Euro

Industry Group Preference: Technology, Life Sciences
Portfolio Companies: AES, AGI, Alimentary Health, BioAtlantis, Biocroi, Biosensia, Brightwork, ChipSensors, Crescent Diagnostics, DecaWave, Deerac Fluidics, Diabetica, Ely Medical Group, Farran Technology, Feedhenry, H2HCare, Hybrid Energy, Ikon Semiconductor, InishTech, Intune Networks, Medicom Medical, Merrion, Mini Storage Self Storage Center, MPStor, NeoSurgical, Nova Science, Novate, Opsona Therapeutics, Quanta Fluid Solutions, Qumas, Radisens Diagnostics, Resourcekraft, Service Frame, Smart Telecom, Sonru, Straatum, Stokes Bio, Teamer, Wavebreak Media, Xention, Zolk

Key Executives:
Ger Goold, Partner
Education: BComm, University College Cork
Background: KPMG

2910 KFW-BANKENGRUPPE
5-9 Palmengartenstasse
Frankfurt 60325
Germany

Phone: 49-6974310 Fax: 49- 6974312944
e-mail: info@kfw.de
web: www.kfw.de

Mission Statement: Focuses on improving the economy, society and ecology in Germany, Europe and the world over.
Geographic Preference: Worldwide
Fund Size: $395 Billion
Founded: 1948
Investment Criteria: SMEs, in home finance or housing modernization.

Key Executives:
Günther Bräunig, Managing Director
e-mail: peter.fleischer@kfw.de
Education: Studies in Economics at the University of Münster; 1981 Doctorate in political science
Background: Chairman of the Managing Board of DtA
Dr Ulrich Schröder, Chief Executive Officer (CEO)
e-mail: hans.riech@kfw.de
Education: Bank training, Graduation form Bankfachwirt
Background: Credit Secretariat of Dresdner Bank AG, Export Finance Department of KfW, Chief Export Finance Department, Special Export Finance Department.

2911 KIBO VENTURES
Suero de Qunones, 34-36
3 planta
Madrid 28002
Spain

e-mail: info@kiboventures.com
web: www.kiboventures.com

Mission Statement: Kibo Ventures invest in exceptional digital companies led by great teams and entrepreneurs. We invest in their earlier stages and look for exponential growth.
Average Investment: 250,000 - 750,000 Euro
Investment Criteria: Early-Stage
Industry Group Preference: E-Commerce & Manufacturing, Internet, Digital Media & Marketing
Portfolio Companies: PromocionesFarma.com, Nonabox, Ludei, Mimub, Blink, Jobandtalent, Stop&Walk, SinDelantal.com, Mediasmart, Visualnet, Super Truper, Smarty Content, Colingo, Ducksboard

Key Executives:
Aquilino Pena, Founding Partner
Education: MBA, Harvard Business School; Law & Business Administration, ICADE
Background: CEO, MediaEdge
Directorships: BaseKit, Acierto, Matrix, Bodeboca, PayCo, Virtual Contenidos, Alice

2912 KIZOO TECHNOLOGY CAPITAL
Amaliebadstrasse 41
Karlsruhe D-76227
Germany

e-mail: ventures@kizoo.com
web: www.kizoo.com

Mission Statement: KIZOO helps young start-up teams grow. We provide seed and early stage financing with a focus on SaaS, Internet & Mobile Services and Social Applications. Apart from our financial resources, we are happy to share our longtime experience in development, marketing and product management in those markets.
Investment Criteria: Early-Stage
Industry Group Preference: SaaS, Internet, Mobile, Social Applications
Portfolio Companies: Hijoki, Takyca, Mambu, Babbel, Umbono, Reposito, MegaZebra, Keebitz, Advertory, CatchApp

Key Executives:
Michael Greve, Managing Partner
Background: Founder, Flug.de; Founder, Lastminute.de
Matthias Hornberger, Chief Financial Officer

2913 KK RESEARCH/KK SWISS VALUE INVESTOR
Forsterstreet 30
CH-8044
Zurich CH-8044
Switzerland

Phone: 41-12679020 Fax: 41-1-267-9025
e-mail: kern@kkresearch.com
web: www.kkresearch.com

Mission Statement: Invests in a limited number of companies with above average prospects for long term growth.
Geographic Preference: Switzerland
Founded: 1986
Investment Criteria: Small - Medium sized companies
Industry Group Preference: All Sectors Considered
Portfolio Companies: Advanced Digital Broadcast, Also, Amazys, Arpida, Ascom, Austriàmicrosystems, Barry Callebaut, Batigroup, Berna Biotech, Charles Voegele, Clariant, Converium, Dottikon, Dufry, Ems Chemie, Esmertec, Interroll, Mobimo, Oridion, OZ Holding, Panalpina, Quadrant, Saia Burgess, Saurer, Speedel, Wachstum, Winterthur Technologie

2914 KLEINWORT CAPITAL LIMITED
10 Slingsby Place
St. Martin's Courtyard
London WC2E 9AB
United Kingdom

Phone: 44-02076328200 Fax: 44-02076328201
web: www.augustequity.com

Mission Statement: Kleinwort Benson Development Capital leads private equity investments in medium sized growth companies.
Geographic Preference: United Kingdom, Ireland, Continental Europe
Fund Size: $402 Million
Founded: 1980
Average Investment: $ 17 Million
Minimum Investment: $ 8.85 Million
Investment Criteria: Expansion and Development, Refinancing Bank Department, Secondry Purchase/Replacement Capital, MBO, MBI, Medium sized companies
Industry Group Preference: Media, Manufacturing, Healthcare, Technology, Media
Portfolio Companies: Sona Group, Intermad, Discovery Group, Video Arts, Hat Tricks Group, Kangol, Rayner Foods, Hale Hamilton, Securistyle, Vivista Holdings

Venture Capital & Private Equity Firms / International Firms

Key Executives:
Richard Green, Chairman
e-mail: richard.green@Dresdner-bank.com
Background: the Chairman of the British Venture Capital Association.
Directorships: Octopus Publishing Group, Tractiv, Hale Hamilton
Ian Grant, Partner
e-mail: andrew.hartley@Dresdner-bank.com
Education: MBA, City University Business School
Background: Worked in a finance company as a credit analyst, Kleinwort Benson Development Capital in 1995
Directorships: Eye Clinic, Kangel, TBP Group, Octopus Publishing Group
Aatif Hassan, Partner
e-mail: anoosha.livani@Dresdner-bank.com
Education: BA Arabic and Middle Eastern Studies, Durham University
Background: Marketing Assistant, American Express
Tim Clarke, Partner
e-mail: tim.clarke@Dresdner-bank.com
Education: BA Economics, University of Kent; Member, The Institute of Chartered Accountants in England and Wales
Background: Merchant bank, Kleinwort Benson

2915 KOREA FIRST VENTURE CAPITAL CORPORATION
8F, Shinil bldg., 64-5 2ka, Chungmu-ro, Chung
Seoul 100-012
Korea

Phone: 82-27757302 Fax: 82-27757305
web: www.kfvc.co.kr

Mission Statement: Invests in core potential venture capital companies in all stages.

Geographic Preference: China, USA
Fund Size: $48 Million
Founded: 1990
Investment Criteria: Core Potential Venture Companies
Industry Group Preference: Information Technology, Environmental Protection, Manufacturing, Semiconductors, Internet Technology, Electronic Technology
Portfolio Companies: Hunger Computer, Natia, UBK, Sewon Telecom, Gold Bank Communications, Goldbook, Netian, Darks Club, Mimoatec Co. Ltd, Bit Computer, Moatech, Ed Laboratory, Humax, CTI Semiconductor, M.K Electron Co. Ltd, Prochips Inc., E&B Technology Co., GenoProt Ltd
Key Executives:
Joong-Hyun Shin, chairman
Young-Pan Hur, President & Chief Executive Officer

2916 KOREA INVESTMENT CORPORATION
100 State Tower Namsan-dong, Jung-gu
17, 18 toegyero floor
Seoul 100-768
South Korea

Phone: 82-221791000 Fax: 82-221-791065
e-mail: info_kic@kic.go.kr
web: www.kic.go.kr

Founded: 1986
Key Executives:
Serck-Joo Hong, President & Chief Executive Officer
Je Yeong Park, Chief Operating Officer

2917 KOREA TECHNOLOGY & BANKING (KTB) NETWORK CORP
Securities Building
23-3 Yeongdeungpo-gu
Seoul 150-709
South Korea

Phone: 82-0234662000 Fax: 82-0221842050
e-mail: webmaster@ktb.co.kr
web: www.ktb.co.kr

Mission Statement: KTBnetwork provides clients with financial support through direct capital investments plus a variety of services to help maximize corporate value.

Geographic Preference: China, Taiwan, South Korea, India, Southeast Asia
Fund Size: $230 Million
Founded: 1981
Average Investment: $30 Million
Investment Criteria: From startups to SMEs, MBOs or LBOs
Industry Group Preference: Aerospace, Defense and Government, Wireless Technologies, Broadband
Portfolio Companies: Airespace, Inc., Berkana Wireless, Inc., BitFone, GPE II LP., Inphi Corporation, Novera Optics, OnePath Networks, Polaris Networks, Terawave Communications

Key Executives:
Won Ju, Chairman
e-mail: webmaster@ktb.co.kr
Education: Yonsei University, Business Administration, BA, University of Missouri, MBA
Background: CEO, Korea M&A Corporation, CEO, The Will-bes Co. (formerly Kunja Industrials Co.)
Han-Sup Kim, President & Chief Executive Officer

2918 KUBOTA CORPORATION
1-2-47 Shikitsu-higashi, Naniwa-ku
Osaka 556-8601
Japan

Phone: 06-6648-2111 Fax: 06-6648-3862
web: www.kubota.co.jp

Fund Size: $ 6.8 Billion
Founded: 1890
Industry Group Preference: Agriculture, Cement Roofing, Metals, Construction
Portfolio Companies: Mycogen
Key Executives:
Ekihon Yasuo, Chairman of the Board and Chief Executive Officer
Tetsuji Tomita, Representative Director and Executive Vice President

2919 LAKESTAR
Zurich
Switzerland

web: www.lakestar.com

Mission Statement: A venture capital firm that invests in outstanding entrepreneurs worldwide.

Portfolio Companies: Skype, Spotify, Klarna, Facebook, Airbnb, KupiVIP, Markafoni, Algomi Ltd., Harry's, Angie's List, Maker Studios, Confide, GoEuro, Taulia, Lookback, Teralytics, Nu3
Key Executives:
Klaus Hommels, Founder
Education: PhD Finance, University of Fribourg; MBA University of Fribourg
Background: Venture Partner, Benchmark Capital; Freenet

Venture Capital & Private Equity Firms / International Firms

2920 LANDSBANKI VENTURES
Austurstraeti 11
Reykjavik 155
Iceland

Phone: 354-410-4000
e-mail: info@landsbanki.is
web: www.landsbankinn.com

Mission Statement: Actively seeking new investments.
Geographic Preference: Europe, North America, Iceland, Scandinavia
Fund Size: $11.75 Billion
Minimum Investment: $100,000
Investment Criteria: Expansion and Development Capital, Mezzanine, Buyout and Buyin
Industry Group Preference: Communications, Computer Related, Industrial Equipment, Industrial Services, High Technology, Computer Related, Software

Key Executives:
  Bjorn Sigurdsson, Correspondent Banking
  Sigurður Erlingsson, Correspondent Banking

2921 LANTA DIGITAL VENTURES
Barcelona
Spain

e-mail: investors@lantacapital.com
web: www.lantacapital.com

Mission Statement: Lanta Digital Ventures is a Barcelona-based early stage venture capital fund focused in investing in innovative Spanish and European Startups with high potential growth.
Geographic Preference: Spain, Europe
Founded: 2015
Average Investment: 300, 000 EUR
Investment Criteria: Seed, Early Stage
Industry Group Preference: Digital Media & Marketing, Mobile, Internet

Key Executives:
  Angel Garcia, Founding Partner
  Education: MBA, Stanford University

2922 LAUNCHPAD VENTURES
Knowledge House
6, Kasturirangan Road, Alwarpet
Chennai
Chennai 600 018
India

Phone: 91-44-3912-3456
web: www.launchpadventures.com

Mission Statement: Launchpad Ventures seeks to partner with entrepreneurs to build admirable companies and looks forward to a facilitating role in companies we invest in. We are not afraid of investing in pre-revenue companies and often provide a company's first outside capital. Though we are primarily seed-stage investors, we also engage with companies which are currently not realizing their full value potential. As a group, we are well connected with potential customers, service providers, partners and future sources of funding. Our members come from a variety of backgrounds and profiles, including former bureaucrats, technology experts, finance and other domain experts.
Founded: 2004
Investment Criteria: Early-Stage
Industry Group Preference: Energy, Technology, Food & Beverage, Education, Marketing
Portfolio Companies: I-Food Chains, Launchpad Global Consulting, Language Labs, DTX Studios, Uniq Investigation & Security Services

Key Executives:
  Sriram Venkatasubramanian, Founder
  Background: HCL, EAP Global

2923 LBBW VENTURE CAPITAL
King street
10C
Stuttgart D-70173
Germany

Phone: 49-71130589200 Fax: 49-711305892099
web: www.lbbw-venture.de

Mission Statement: We see ourselves as a partner who provides the economic framework for the growth of promising ideas and business models. Moreover, we stand with our extensive network and a lot of technical know-how at any time to advise you.
Investment Criteria: Startup, Expansion-Stage, Pre-IPO
Industry Group Preference: Information Technology, Software, Telecommunications, Innovative Products & Services, Life Sciences
Portfolio Companies: Biametrics, Bubbles & Beyond, CargoGuard, CheckMobile, Conceptboard, CorTec, Crealytics, Fludicon, Oxid Esales, Phenex Pharmaceuticals, Technolas,

2924 LBO FRANCE
148 University Street
Paris 75007
France

Phone: 33-140627767 Fax: 33-140627555
e-mail: radia.guria@lbofrance.com
web: www.lbofrance.com

Mission Statement: Seeks out leveraged buyout transactions in which it can acquire a majority stake.
Geographic Preference: France
Fund Size: 1 Billion Euros
Founded: 1985
Average Investment: 10 Million - 2, 500 Million Euros
Minimum Investment: Negotiable
Investment Criteria: Market leaders with growth potential, Subsidiaries of major groups or family-owned companies
Industry Group Preference: All Sectors Considered

Key Executives:
  Robert Daussun, Président
  e-mail: elizabeth.oreilly@lbofrance.com
  Education: MA economics HEC
  Background: Worked for four years at Arthur Anderson
  Pascal Oddo, Chairman of the Supervisory Board
  e-mail: elizabeth.oreilly@lbofrance.com
  Education: Engineering degree Telecom paris, DESS postgraduate degree in bussiness and tax law
  Background: specialized in M&A and Taxation at international law firm freshfields.

2925 LEAD ANGELS
A-102, Neelam Center
S K Ahire Marg, Worli
Mumbai 400030
India

Phone: 022 65660023
e-mail: info@leadangels.in
web: www.leadangels.in

Mission Statement: The founding team at Lead Angels originally from IIT Bombay and its members include entrepreneurs who have built successful companies, angel investors who have invested in multiple startups, academics who have nurtured innovation and entrepreneurship and consultants who have been advisors to high growth companies.
Geographic Preference: India
Investment Criteria: Seed-Stage, Early-Stage

Key Executives:
  Atul Pradhan, Director
  Background: Founder, Transfolign Consulting; KPMG India; Managing Partner, KPMG Consulting

Venture Capital & Private Equity Firms / International Firms

2926 LEGAL AND GENERAL VENTURES LIMITED
One Coleman Street
London EC2R 5AA
United Kingdom

Phone: 44-2031242900 Fax: 44-2031242546
e-mail: enquiries@ventures.landg.com

Mission Statement: LGV is a well established provider of private equity in the UK and has professionally managed funds on behalf of external investors.

Geographic Preference: United Kingdom, Ireland
Fund Size: $325 Million
Founded: 1986
Average Investment: $1.6 Billion
Minimum Investment: $ 35.4 Million
Investment Criteria: Expansion, MBO, Management Buy-In, Secondary Purchase, Replacement Capital, Infrastructure Project Financing
Industry Group Preference: Communications, Consumer Services, Industrial Equipment, Food & Beverage, Medical & Health Related, Consumer Products
Portfolio Companies: Air Energi, Novus Leisure, ABI, Amber Taverns, Snow+Rock, The Liberation Group, South Lakeland Parks, IDH, Classic Hospitals, Verna Group, Tragus, Kingfield Health, Club Company, LGC, Vue Cinemas, Jeyes, Unique Pub Company, Craegmoor, Bourne Leisure

Key Executives:
Zoe Clements, Director
James Dawes, Finance Director
e-mail: enquiries@ventures.landg.com
Education: Qualified as a Chartered Accountant
Background: 3i plc, where he spent six years, specialising in venture capital and project finance
Michael Mowlem, Managing Director
e-mail: enquiries@ventures.landg.com
Background: Hambros Bank-corporate finance division

2927 LEGEND CAPITAL
10F, Tower A
Reycom Infotech Park
No. 2 Kexueyuan South Road, Zhongguancun
Haidian District, Beijing 100190
China

Phone: 86-10-6250-8000 Fax: 86-10-6250-9100
e-mail: master@legendcapital.com.cn

Mission Statement: The core business of Legend Capital is early-stage Venture Capital and expansion-stage Growth Capital investment.

Investment Criteria: Early-Stage, Expansion Stage
Industry Group Preference: Healthcare, Clean Technology, Advanced Manufacturing, Consumer Products
Portfolio Companies: ASP, AutoNavi, Auto Radio, Access Medical, Berkana, Boloni, BitAuto, Bonck Education, Beauty in Fashion, BOC International Limited, Bonovo, Berrygenomics, BYJC, Chongqing Broadband, Covics, China SpeedNet, Chipsbank, China Search, CDIM, Cub Digital, Crystal CG, Chongqing New Standard, Cybrid, Careray, Car King, CCID, Calsys, ChinaInvent, Digital China Jinxin, Dianji, Dooland, Urachip, DENOVO, Eyang Holdings, Eedoo, Evercare, Evergreen Group, Fullhan, Fengkai Machinery, Ftuan, Golden Eye, BGE, HolyTax, Hiconics, Happy Elements, Huicheng Pectechnology, Hichain, HDR, iFLYTEK, ITS, innogreen, Oyo, Jolimark Holdings, Kaitone, Kawin Technology, Lakala, Life Express, Live By Touch, Luxin Evotech, Leepet, Linglong Tire, Lihua Group, LocoJoy, McAobao, Amcare, Mosh, Minsheng Energy, MobCrete, New Vision, Norel Systems, New China Life, Nouriz, Oak Pacific Interactive, Pod Inn, OPDA, Photonic Bridges, Precom, Phylion Battery, Power Genius, Parade, Pharmaron, PEAK Sports, PPA, PBA, Rock Mobile, Renren, Reach Surgical, Rye Studio, RenRui, Spreadtrum, Shanghai Huahong, Surekam, Sinocom, 7234, Sling Media, SolarFun, Sunshine Paper, Saturday Shoes, Sihe Wood, Sate Auto, ShopEx, Shenzhen Yuton, Suzhou Anjie Technology, Selavo Machinery, 16fun, Sportica, 7Gege, Tianya, Tengchuang, 21cake, Tianji New Materials, Tanyuan Tech, TeChen, Tongbanjie, Universe Media, Universal Education, Unicell, UStar, VanceInfo, VeriSilicon, Virtuos, Viscap, Wep, Watch Data, Weiyun, Wuxi Lead Auto Equipment

Key Executives:
Zhu Linan, Founder/CEO
Education: MSEE, Shanghai Jiaotong University
Background: General Manager, Shenzhen Legend Computer
Directorships: Saturday Shoes, Peak Sports

2928 LEONIA MB GROUP/MB FUNDS
1 Boulevarde A
Helsinki 00100
Finland

Phone: 358-9131011 Fax: 358-913101310
web: www.mbfunds.fi

Mission Statement: Invests in buy-outs and privatizations to build transactions and expansion capital.

Geographic Preference: US
Fund Size: $240 Million
Founded: 1992
Average Investment: $132 Million
Minimum Investment: $28 Million
Investment Criteria: Expansion, Buyout, Bridge, Buy-outs, Privatizations, buy and build transactions and expansion capital.
Industry Group Preference: Machinery, Technology, Confectionery, Healthcare, Electronic Technology, Plastics, Components & IoT
Portfolio Companies: Makua Foods Oy, Parmaco Oy, Suomen Transval Oy

Key Executives:
Juhani Suomela, Chairman of the board
e-mail: juhani.suomela@leonia.fi
Education: MSc Econ
Background: Vice President of the Mortgage Bank of Finland Ltd and President of MB Corporate Bank
Directorships: President
Matti Mertsola, Partner
e-mail: matti.mertsola@leonia.fi
Education: Msc, Tech, CEFA
Background: Director at MB Corporate Bank

2929 LETA CAPITAL
Derebenevskaya Naberezhnaya 7
Building 9
Moscow 115114
Russia

Phone: 7(495)-797-26-94
e-mail: info@leta.vc

Mission Statement: We believe that enthusiastic entrepreneurs are able to present the world with new values. The aim of our fund is to support innovative IT startup companies at their seed or early growth stage.

Minimum Investment: $400, 000
Investment Criteria: Seed, Early Growth
Industry Group Preference: Information Technology
Portfolio Companies: Wakie, MSU Business Incubator, Displair, RedHelper, Hamstersoft, rollApp, RoboCV, Geeklist, iBinom, 365Scores, bright box

Key Executives:
Sergey Toporov, Principal
e-mail: stoporov@leta.ru
Education: Ural State University
Alex Chachava, Managing Partner
e-mail: alex@leta.ru
Education: Moscow National University

Venture Capital & Private Equity Firms / International Firms

2930 LIFE SCIENCES PARTNERS BV
Johannes Vermeerplein 9
Amsterdam 1071 DV
Netherlands

Phone: 31-206645500 **Fax:** 31-206768810
web: www.lspvc.com

Mission Statement: A leading European venture capital fund, providing private equity capital to early stage life sciences companies.

Geographic Preference: Netherlands, Europe, America
Fund Size: $204 Million
Founded: 1996
Average Investment: $87 Million
Minimum Investment: $500,000
Investment Criteria: Early Stage, Expansion and Development Capital, Startup
Industry Group Preference: Life Sciences, Medical & Health Related, IT Services, Industrial Services, Food & Beverage, Bio Materials
Portfolio Companies: Illuminoss, Ventaleon, Rotation Medical, Atlas Genetics, Mint Solutions, Mendor, Merus, Sequana Medical, Curetis, Harvest Automation, Cobalt, IBI Biosensors, Seahorse Bioscience, ActoGeniX, Pronota, EyeSense, Vitromics, ISTO, Kiadis Pharma

Key Executives:
Martijn Kleijwegt, managing partner
e-mail: rkuijten@lspvc.com
Education: MBA degree from INSEAD in Fontainebleau, France ., PhD studies at the University of Pennsylvania in the area of oncology,
Background: Worked at McKinsey & Company for eight years as a senior consultant and co-leader of the European Pharmaceuticals and Health Care Practice.
Directorships: he directed multiple teams of client executives on strategic and organizational assignments in Amsterdam , Brussels and Zurich
René Kuijten, general partner
e-mail: mkleijwegt@lspvc.com
Education: Masters degree in economics at Amsterdam University .
Background: He has gained extensive experience in all aspects of biotech venture capital. On behalf of LSP, Martijn served on the supervisory board of Crucell (NL)
Directorships: He served on the supervisory board of, amongst others, Rhein Biotech (G, NL), Qiagen (G) and Quadrant (UK). In 1998, Martijn co-founded the first Life Sciences Partners fund,
Joachim Rothe, Managing Partner
e-mail: jrothe@lspvc.com
Education: Masters degree in Biochemistry from the Free University in Berlin , and he earned his PhD degree from the University of Freiburg in Germany
Background: Was at McKinsey & Company where he worked as an engagement manager on assignments in the chemical and pharmaceutical industries
Directorships: as a scientist with Hoffmann-La Roche in Basel , Switzerland , and at the Imperial Cancer Research Fund in London , Joachim focused on molecular immunology and genomics.
Fouad Azzam, Partner
e-mail: tschwarz@lspvc.com
Education: Masters degree in pharmacy from the University of Utrecht .
Background: Interpharm, one of the largest pharmaceutical wholesalers in the Netherlands
Directorships: Tom played an important role at the start of BioPartner, a Dutch government agency supporting starting biotech companies in the Netherlands , and participated in the superviso
John de Koning, Partner
e-mail: mwegter@lspvc.com
Education: Masters degree in business economics from the Erasmus University of Rotterdam.
Background: ING Barings Investment Banking in Amsterdam and São Paulo , where he worked as a senior analyst on Global Risk Management
Directorships: served as the assistant to a member of the executive committee, with worldwide responsibility for risk management.

2931 LIFE.SREDA
Varshavskoye Shosse, 9-1 B
Moscow
Russia

web: www.lifesreda.com

Mission Statement: Life.SREDA is a venture capital firm focusing on mobile and online fintech startups.

Investment Criteria: Any Stage
Industry Group Preference: Finanical Mobile, Internet Applications and Services
Portfolio Companies: SumUp, Scorista, Settle, Anthemis Gropu, Fidor Russia, Simple, Instabank, LifePAD, LifePay, Moven, My-Apps, MyWishBoard,

Key Executives:
Vladislav Solodkiy, CEO, Managing Partner
Alexander Ivanov, CFO, Partner

2932 LINK TECHNOLOGIES LIMITED
3 Mallard Way
Strathclyde Business Park
Bellshill ML4 3BF
Scotland

Phone: 44-1698849911 **Fax:** 44-1698849922
web: www.linktech.co.uk

Mission Statement: To provide the unique link between scientists working in biological research, and the chemical tools and technologies that they require.

Geographic Preference: Scotland
Founded: 1989
Investment Criteria: All Stages
Industry Group Preference: Pharmaceuticals, Biotechnology, Global Industries, Diagnostics, Life Sciences

Key Executives:
Michael J. McLean, Ph.D., , Chairman
e-mail: support@linktech.co.uk
Background: Investment executive in the venture capital industryt
Dr Mike Gray, Managing Director

2933 LION SELECTION GROUP LIMITED
Level 4/15 Queen Street
Melbourne 3000
Australia

Phone: 61-396148008 **Fax:** 61-396148009
web: www.lionselection.com.au

Mission Statement: Lion Selection Group Limited is a publicly listed resource investment company, providing patient equity capital to carefully selected Small and Medium Enterprises (SME's).

Geographic Preference: Australia, Africa, South East Asia
Fund Size: $100 Million
Founded: 1997
Average Investment: $12.5 Million
Minimum Investment: $5 Million
Investment Criteria: Small and Medium Enterprises
Industry Group Preference: Mining
Portfolio Companies: Doray Minerals, Rum Jungle Resources, Auricup Resources, Roxgold, Toro Gold, Kasbah Resources, One Asia Resources, Asian Mineral Resources, Sihayo Gold, Manas Resources

Key Executives:
Peter Maloney, Chairman
e-mail: lionselection@lsg.com.au
Education: BComm, MBA (Roch)

Background: senior executive-WMC Limited, FH Faulding & Co
Directorships: CFO
Chris Melloy, Non-Executive Director
e-mail: lionselection@lsg.com.au
Education: MSc, DIC, BSc (Eng), ARSM, FIMMM
Background: Chief Executive Officer of Lihir Gold Limited
Barry Sullivan, Non Executive Director
e-mail: lionselection@lsg.com.au
Education: BEc (Hons)
Background: Chief Financial Officer and Company Secretary of Acacia

2934 LIONBIRD
HaBarzel 25
Tel Aviv 69710
Israel

Phone: 972-35333885 Fax: 972-35333995
e-mail: jonathan@lionbird.com
web: www.lionbird.com

Mission Statement: By harnessing cloud computing and crowd networking, companies are revolutionizing certain offline markets in ways never previously imagined. These technologies open endless opportunities to meaningfully improve healthcare delivery, retail processes and enterprise collaboration. LionBird invests in young companies capable of making it happen.
Average Investment: $200,000 - $500,000
Investment Criteria: Early-Stage
Industry Group Preference: Cloud Computing, Mobile, Internet
Portfolio Companies: Bento, Sweetch, amSTATZ, Tyto, PhysiHome, Genome Compiler, KitCheck, physIQ, Telesofia, Fundbox, CartCrunch, Ovuline, Marqueta, ShopClues
Other Locations:
708 Church Street
Suite 252
Evanston, IL 60201
Phone: 847-7212171 Fax: 847-3489161
Key Executives:
Ed Michael, Managing Partner
Education: BA, Politics & Government, JD, Indiana University
Background: EVP, Diagnostic Products, Abbott Laboratories

2935 LLOYDS DEVELOPMENT CAPITAL LIMITED
One Vine Street
London W1J 0AH
United Kingdom

Phone: 44-02077583680 Fax: 44-02077583681
e-mail: churley@ldc.co.uk
web: www.ldc.co.uk

Mission Statement: We are private equity specialists with a 30 year history of supporting management buy-outs, equity release (cash out), development (DevCap) and acquisition finance transactions. With a current portfolio of 60+ businesses valued in excess of £2billion LDC's experience in the private equity arena is well known.
Geographic Preference: United Kingdom
Founded: 2000
Average Investment: £2 - 100 million
Investment Criteria: Management Buyouts, Equity Release, DevCap, Acquisition Finance
Industry Group Preference: Clean Technology, Renewable Energy, Construction, Financial Services, Healthcare, Industrial Services, Retailing, Travel & Leisure
Portfolio Companies: Waterfall Services, United House Developments, One Two Four, Capital Economics, Eley Group, Adler and Allen, Clifford Thames, Anite Travel, Stroma, Ministry of Cake, Connect Managed Servies, Prism Medical UK, CEL Procurement, Imagine Nation, Bluestone, Nexinto, The Property Software, Joules, Twofour Group, Express Engineering, The Training Room, Equiom, uSwitch, Angus Fire, Rimor, Node4, D&D London, NRS Healthcare, New World Trading, Validus IVC, Ramco Oil Services, Fever Tree, ATG Access, Blue Rubicon, MAMA & Company, Keoghs, Forest Holidays, Dale Power Solutions, Metronet, BigHand, Ocean Outdoor, Bifold Group, Showcard Print, Airline Services, Corporate Trael International, Best Kids (YeeHoo Baby World), Pertemps Network Group, Benson Group, PDJ Group, Kirona, Evander Group, Scottish Equity Partners, learndirect, WRG, Angel Springs, Original Additions, Driver Hire, UK2, A-Gas, OnApp, musicMagpie.co.uk, Kee Safety, The ComplEAT Food Group, United Legal Services, Easynet & MDNX, Mountain Warehouse, AIM Aviation, Antler, Exceed Midlands Advantage Fund, Unite House, Matrix, Vysionics, Integrated Dental Holdings, Marussia F1 Team, Avelo, Orion Media, The Independent Group, Cranswick Pet and Aquatics (Tropical Marine Center), Nuclear Engineering Services, Quantum Pharmaceuticals, Snell, Porterbrook, CNEI, Zenith-Leaerive, Eve, kidsunlimited, United Living Group, Davies Group, Omega Red, JCC, GVA, The Pallet Network, VSG, Direct Group, Epi-V, Kimberly Access Limited, British Salt,

Key Executives:
Darryl Eales, Chief Executive Officer
Candida Morley, Chief Operating Officer
e-mail: deales@ldc.co.uk
Education: Chartered Accountant
Background: Ran the Birmingham office from 1994 to 1999, became Regional Managing Director for the Midlands
Directorships: North in 1999 and was appointed Managing Director in January 2003.
Jonathan Caswell, Investment Director
e-mail: jandrew@ldc.co.uk
Education: Graduated from Durham University with an honours degree in Molecular Biology and Biochemistry Jonathan
Background: Price Waterhouse in the UK and Australia and at Arcadia Group, the high street fashion retailer
Directorships: Jonathan was a founder member of PwC's Operations and Post Deal Services team where he specialised in working closely with private equity backed management teams to implement
Jane Gilbert, Investment Director
e-mail: mdraper@ldc.co.uk
Background: ten years with PricewaterhouseCoopers,
Directorships: Grant became Regional Director for the North in August 2003 and became Head of New Business in August 2004 where he is now responsible for all new investment activity national
Daniel Sasaki, Marketing Director
e-mail: rpendleton@ldc.co.uk
Background: Previous new business and marketing roles were held with Lloyds Bowmaker (Corporate, Consumer, and Home Improvement Division) during an eleven-year term.
Directorships: Rob specialises in B2B and B2C financial services marketing.
Waqqas Ahmad, Investment Director
e-mail: aleach@ldc.co.uk
Education: Andy is a mathematics graduate of Oxford University, After qualifying as a Chartered Accountant with Coopers & Lybrand
Background: Andy joined Byvest, an Australian based private equity fund.
Directorships: he spent 10 years with 3i in Manchester. After two years with Montagu Capital Andy joined LDC in September 2004.
Gordon Hague, Investment Director
Background: Following six successful years with County he moved to LDC in 1990.

Directorships: Over the last four years he has specialised on working with portfolio companies.
Andrew McMurray, Portfolio Director
e-mail: amcmurray@ldc.co.uk
Education: Having completed a Law Degree at Kings College London, Andrew qualified as a Chartered Accountant with Ernst and Whinney
Background: He joined Hill Samuel in 1986
Directorships: and has specialised in portfolio work since 1991.
John Harper, Investment Director
e-mail: cmorley@ldc.co.uk
Education: Law Degree from Oxford and a Masters Degree in Small Business,
Background: Extensive experience in investment banking / M&A (with Barings), venture capital (at 3i)
Directorships: corporate development within a large plc (Harrisons & Crosfield)

2936 LMBO FINANCE
5 rue de Castiglione
Paris 75001
France

Phone: 33-171732020 **Fax:** 33-171732021
e-mail: lmbo@lmbo.com
web: www.lmbo.com

Mission Statement: By using resources that are varied and often well-spread, human, economic and financial, an LMBO amounts to the re-creation of a firm.

Geographic Preference: France
Fund Size: $240 Million
Founded: 1986
Average Investment: $132 Million
Minimum Investment: $24 Million
Investment Criteria: Mid market firms
Industry Group Preference: Retailing, Industrial Services, Telecommunications, Electronic Technology
Portfolio Companies: Groupe Caillé, Ora VéHicules Electriques, Technocer

Key Executives:
  Gerard Favarel, President
  e-mail: f.desmarest@lmbo.com
  Mary Kim Bennett, Secretary General
  Yvan Favarel, Investor
  e-mail: a.riss@lmbo.com
  Pierre Favarel, Compliance Officer and Internal Control
  e-mail: nc.macleod@lmbo.com
  Gérard Favarel, President
  Directorships: Chairmain

2937 LOMBARD/APIC (HK) LIMITED
Room 2202, 22/F
Tower 1, Lippo Centre
Queensway 89
Hong Kong

Phone: 852-28787388 **Fax:** 852-28787288
e-mail: info@lombardinvestments.com
web: www.lombardinvestments.com

Mission Statement: Lombard invests private equity capital in competitive enterprises needing financing for expansion or to complete financial restructuring.

Geographic Preference: San Francisco, Hong Kong, Bangkok
Founded: 1985
Average Investment: $25 Million
Minimum Investment: $10 Million
Investment Criteria: All Stages
Industry Group Preference: All Sectors Considered
Portfolio Companies: Asia Books Company, Asiasoft Corporation, Career Choices, Inc., Centara Hotels and Resorts, Central Pattana, Dakota, Minnesota & Eastern Railroad, Easy Buy, Fu Sheng Industrial, Good Morning Shinhan Securities, Hansol Gyoyook Company, Kantana Group, Krungthep Land, KSNET, Inc., MC Group PLC, Mega Lifesciences, Mermaid Maritime, Nok Airlines, Overseas Dragon China, Pruska Real Estate, Robinson Department Store, S. Pack & Print, San Shing Fastech Corporation, S&P Syndicate, SNC Former, Somboon Advance Technology, The Medical Cit, TICON Industrial, Trinity Watthana, Viet - UC Group

Key Executives:
  Kanchit Bunajinda, Director
  e-mail: tsmith@lombardinvestments.com
  Education: Mr. Smith graduated cum laude from Harvard College (A.B. 1975).
  Background: CEO and CFO of ACI, Inc.
  Directorships: Managing Director
  Anita Chik, Director

2938 LOOL VENTURES
Tushiya 2
4th Floor
Tel Aviv
Israel

e-mail: info@lool.vc
web: www.lool.vc

Mission Statement: Investor in early-stage startups based in Tel Aviv.

Geographic Preference: Israel
Industry Group Preference: Internet, Digital Media & Marketing, Social Media
Portfolio Companies: Zooz, Wibbitz, LawGeex, Brodmann17, MarketMan, MediSafe, Talenya, DBmaestro, Farm Dog, KIDOZ, SiteAware, Sensibo, ClipCall, MyPermissions, Mabaya

Key Executives:
  Avichay Nissenbaum, General Partner
  e-mail: avichay@lool.vc
  Yaniv Golan, General Partner
  e-mail: yaniv@lool.vc

2939 LOUGH SHORE INVESTMENTS
47 A Botanic Avenue
Belfast BT7 1JL
Northern Ireland

Phone: 0044-2890438510 **Fax:** 0044-2890436651
web: www.loughshore.co

Mission Statement: Our mission is to invest in high potential management teams and partner with them to build great businesses. Our goal is to bring ten great companies to exit or IPO by 2025.

Geographic Preference: Ireland
Portfolio Companies: Geopii, The Shore, World Desk, Converser, SendbyBag, Profeshion

Key Executives:
  Danny Moore, Founder
  Background: COO, NYSE Euronext Trading; COO/CEO, Wombat Financial Software

2940 LRM - INVESTERINGSMAATSCHAPPIJ VOOR LIMBURG
555 Kempische Steenweg
Hasselt 3500
Belgium

Phone: 33-11246801 **Fax:** 32-011246850
e-mail: info@lrm.be
web: www.lrm.be

Mission Statement: LRM provides private equity to industrial and service companies which located in Limburg Province of Belgium. Further, LRM is also involved in Real Estate financing.

Geographic Preference: Belgium

Venture Capital & Private Equity Firms / International Firms

Fund Size: $360 Million
Founded: 1994
Average Investment: $6 Million
Minimum Investment: $0.12 Milliom
Investment Criteria: All size companies, Minority shareholding, Start-up capital, Growth capital, MBO, MBI, Spin offs, Project financing
Industry Group Preference: Real Estate, Pharmaceuticals, Security, Carpet Yarn, Software, Biotechnology
Portfolio Companies: Cegeka, C-Mine Crib, Comm-Art International, Corda Campus, D Square, Doxis Lighting Factory, Elan Languages, Excico, Jordens DC, Ledlite, Maris Group, NASCOM, Niceberg Studios, Ontoforce, Pearlchain.net, Right Brain, Rmoni Wireless, Soulco, Sparkcentral, Thalento, TopSportLab, Zappware, 3DD Pharma, Amakem, Apitope, Arcarios, Bioville, Bocasa, Complix, FF Pharmaceuticals, Promethera, SEPS Pharma, Ter Hulst, Therasolve, Tigenix, 4HAMCOGEN, Bio Gas Bree, Bis-Technics 2000, Bruno Invest, Capricorn, Epigan, Fish2BE, HCJ, KEY/VISYS, Limburg Gas, Limburg Win (D) T, Limburgs Klimaatfonds, Machiels Building Solutions, Minerva, Punch Powertrain, Restore, Ridley - Race Productions, Visiomatics, Vivixtum, Zonnecentrale Limburg, Cavale Steel Company, Different Hotels Group, Fremach Groep, Kristalpark III, MCGZ, Quinsis, Scana Noliko, Value Retail, Alro, Blue Line Logistics, Bosmans Graphics, Brouwerij Martens, Cobelguard CIT, Connect Group, D2E Capital, Diresco, Ducatt, ETG, Spaas Kaarsen, VCST, Veldeman Group

Key Executives:
  Hugo Leroi, Chairman
  Jean Claude Van Red, Vice President

2941 MACMILLAN DIGITAL EDUCATION
The MacMillan Building
4 Crinan St.
London N1 9XW
United Kingdom

Phone: 44-20-7418-5581
web: www.digital-education.com

Mission Statement: Launched in January 2012 by one of the world's leading educational publishers, Macmillan Digital Education captures opportunities in the consumer online education markets. A corporate venture capital investor and incubator, we are technology and service driven to make learning more effective and fun whilst embracing our user centric business understanding.

Geographic Preference: Global
Founded: 2012
Investment Criteria: Early-Stage
Industry Group Preference: Online Education
Portfolio Companies: Mobile Teacher, MacTrac, Maths Doctor, tutoria, EnglishUp, Easyaula, Veduca

Key Executives:
  Matthias Ick, Managing Director
  Sebastian Peck, Finance Director

2942 MACQUARIE DIRECT INVESTMENT LIMITED
50 Martin Place
Sydney 2000
Australia

Phone: 61-282323333
web: www.macquarie.com.au

Mission Statement: Macquarie Bank is a pre-eminent provider of investment banking and financial services.

Geographic Preference: Australia, New Zealand
Fund Size: $29.7 Billion
Founded: 1969
Average Investment: $22 Million
Minimum Investment: $7 Million
Investment Criteria: Expansion, Mezzanine Debit, Mezzanine Funding, Management Buyout, Leveraged Buyout, Recapitalization
Industry Group Preference: Broadcasting, Communications Equipment, Computer Hardware & Software, Electronic Technology, Energy, Food & Beverage, Components & IoT, Internet Technology, Manufacturing, Medical, Publishing, Retailing, Telecommunications, Wholesale, Cable
Portfolio Companies: Neverfail Water, Crevet Limited, Broadcast Media Group, Millers Self Storage, Hermes Precisa Australia, Millers Fashion Group, Com Tech Communications, Tower Technology, Volante, JB Hi Fi, Staging Connections, InvoCare, Repco, The Reject Shop

Key Executives:
  David S Clarke, Chairman
  e-mail: mdi@macquarie.com
  Education: BEcon Hons (Syd), MBA (Harvard), Hon DScEcon Sydney
  Background: Chairman of McGuigan Simeon Wines Limited, the Wine Committee of the Royal Agricultural Society of New South Wales, the Sydney Advisory Board of the Salvation Army and the Opera Australia Capital Fund, Member of the Investment Advisory Committee of the Australian Olympic Foundation, Royal Agricultur
  Directorships: Honorary life member of the Financial Markets Foundation for Children, Committee member of the NIDA Stage II Project and Governor of the Australian Ireland Fund and Vice Presi
  Allan E Moss, Managing Director
  e-mail: Roblee@Macquarie.Com
  Education: BS (Cornell), MBA (Harvard)
  Background: Macquarie Bank with 3 years investing bank funds, Experienced in structured finance, capital raisings and acquisitions and disposals, Appointed head of Macquarie Direct Investments and Director of Surf Hardware, Ringwood, Club Hotels, FNS and Helmsman Funds Management.
  Mark R G Johnson, Executive Deputy Chairman
  e-mail: mdi@macquarie.com
  Education: B Com (Hons) (Rhodes), CA
  Background: Joined Macquarie Financial Operations Division in 2003 and Macquarie Direct Investment in 2004, Extensive experience in general management, accounting and financial control.
  John G Allpass, Chairman of Board Audit & Compliance Committee
  e-mail: Riyna.Denett@Macquarie.Com
  Education: B Bus (UTS), MBA-Exec (AGSM), CA, ASIA
  Background: Joined Macquarie Financial Operations Division in 2000 and Macquarie Direct Investment in 2001, Extensive experience working in accounting and financial control roles,
  Directorships: Former Chief Financial Officer of Macquarie Direct Investment.

2943 MAGMA VENTURE PARTNERS
22 Rothschild Boulevard
25th Floor
Tel Aviv 6688218
Israel

Phone: 972-36967285 Fax: 972-36955960
e-mail: info@magmavc.com
web: www.magmavc.com

Mission Statement: Magma Venture Partners invests in early stage communication, semiconductor, internet and media companies and helps to build these companies to target global markets and create industry leading success stories. Our approach is based on an unrelenting commitment to quality and innovation and the courage to invest in ideas at their early stages. We concentrate on the fields we know best, seeking the brightest ventures in communication, semiconductors, internet and media. The fund invests in opportunities that have the potential to define and shape the industry. Our approach is

Venture Capital & Private Equity Firms / International Firms

active, integrative, and dynamic. We provide our portfolio companies with the contact networks, resources, advice, and tools needed to succeed.

Geographic Preference: Israel
Investment Criteria: Early-Stage
Industry Group Preference: Communications, Semiconductors, Internet, Media
Portfolio Companies: Applitools, Appreciate, AppsFlyer, Argus, Autotalks, CloudEndure, Core Photonics, DesignArt Networks, Forty Cloud, GreenSQL, Guesty, Hola!, Magisto, Nipendo, Oliver Solution, Onavo, Phonetic Systems, PhotoMania, Provigent, Sentrix, TabTale, Teridion, Trivnet, Valens Semiconductor, Waze, Wintegra, WireX, Xplenty

Key Executives:
  Modi Rosen, Co-Founder/Managing Partner
  e-mail: modi@magmavc.com
  Background: Monitor Company, Shaldor Ltd
  Directorships: Amdocs, Provigent, Crescendo Networks, Hola!, Nipendo

2944 MAKERS FUND
Hong Kong
China

web: www.makersfund.com

Mission Statement: Dedicated to supporting businesses in the area of interactive entertainment.

Geographic Preference: Global, United States, China, Europe
Fund Size: $180 Million
Founded: 2018
Average Investment: $1,000,000 - $10,000,000
Minimum Investment: $1 Million
Investment Criteria: Series A, Seed
Industry Group Preference: Gaming, Entertainment
Portfolio Companies: Active8, Bossa Studios UK, Facet, FRVR, Genvid, Klang, Medal Playlabs, Popdog, Superdata, Teacher Gaming, Tiny Build, TSM, Typhoon Studios

Key Executives:
  Jay Chi, Founding Partner
  Education: BA, Stanford University
  Background: McKinsey & Company; Kowloon Nights
  Michael Cheung, Partner
  Education: BEng, University of Warwick
  Background: Brynleigh Tech; dunnhumby; McKinsey & Company; Tencent
  Directorships: Klang Games

2945 MARATHON VENTURE CAPITAL FUND LIMITED
85 Medinat Hayehudim Street
Herzlia 46766
Israel

Phone: 972-99602010 Fax: 972-99569081
web: www.marathonvc.com

Mission Statement: To finance Israeli Hi-Tech companies engaged in the development of highly innovative technologies based on firm patents.

Geographic Preference: Israel
Fund Size: $22 Million
Founded: 1993
Average Investment: $4 Million.
Minimum Investment: $2 Million
Investment Criteria: Seed, Start-up, First Stage
Industry Group Preference: Communications, Electronic Technology, Industrial Services, Medical Devices, Biotechnology, Artificial Intelligence, Software, Components & IoT
Portfolio Companies: Nanomotion Ltd., Optibase Ltd., Arel Communication and Software Ltd., Pegasus Technologies Ltd., Margan Business Development Ltd., Qronus Interactive Ltd., IRLan Ltd, Aisys Ltd., Bioview Ltd, Polygene Ltd, Optinex Inc, Metabogal Ltd.

2946 MARCEAU INVESTISSEMENTS
France

Phone: +44 (0) 20 7881 2990 Fax: +44 (0) 7866 030 464
e-mail: stasmichael@mergers-alliance.com
web: www.mergers-alliance.com

Mission Statement: Marceau Finance offers specialist advice covering strategy, corporate finance and negotiations.

Geographic Preference: France
Founded: 1987
Investment Criteria: Development, Restructuring
Industry Group Preference: Telecommunications, Information Technology, Electronic Technology, Construction, Engineering, Food & Beverage, Building Materials & Services

Key Executives:
  Patrick Atzel, Senior Advisor
  Background: CEO of Compagnie Générale d'Electricite, Principal Secretary of various French Ministers in France.
  Nicolas Balon, Director

2947 MATI-HIGH-TECH
11 HaTassia Street
Ra'anana 4366107
Israel

Phone: 972-97602716 Fax: 972-97602245
e-mail: efrat@startup.org.il
web: www.matiran.org.il

Geographic Preference: Israel
Founded: 1994

2948 MATURO KAPITAL
Leirvollen 23
Skein 3736
Norway

Phone: 47-35505550 Fax: 47-35505555
web: www.maturo.no

Mission Statement: Invests in companies with unique a technology or which operates in business areas with rapid growth.

Geographic Preference: Nordic Region
Fund Size: NOK 330 millioin
Industry Group Preference: Energy, Environment

Key Executives:
  Leif Svarstad, Managing Partner
  47-3550-5551
  e-mail: leif.svarstad@maturo.no

2949 MAYBAN VENTURES
100 Jalan Tun Perak
Menara Maybank
26th Floor
Kuala Lumpur 50050
Malaysia

Phone: 60-320322188 Fax: 60-320312188

Mission Statement: Mayban Ventures manages several private equity funds which invest in companies at all stages.

Geographic Preference: Malaysia
Founded: 1993
Average Investment: $4.1 Million
Minimum Investment: $0.26 Million
Investment Criteria: Start-ups, Mezzanines, Pre-IPOs, and Specific purpose business.
Portfolio Companies: Picarda Holdings Sdn. Bhd, Proprietary Fund,

Venture Capital & Private Equity Firms / International Firms

2950 MEDICAL RESEARCH COMMERCIALIZATION FUND
Level 9
278 Collins Street
Melbourne VIC 3000
Australia
Phone: 61-396570700 Fax: 61-396570777
e-mail: info@mrcf.com.au
web: www.mrcf.com.au

Mission Statement: The Medical Research Commercialisation Fund provides dedicated, investment funding to support the commercialisation of early-stage medical research discoveries that originate from its member institutes. The collaborative nature of the MRCF seeks to foster best practice in the commercialisation of medical innovations.

Founded: 2007
Investment Criteria: Early-Stage
Industry Group Preference: Healthcare, Medical Technology
Portfolio Companies: Auspherix, Fibrotech Therapeutics, GI-Therapies, Global Kinetics, Helmedix, miReven, OccuRx, Osprey Medical, Otifex, PolyActiva, Protego Medical, Q-Sera, University of South Australia - The Mawson Institute, Vaxxas, Verva Pharmaceuticals

Key Executives:
Alan Stockdale, Chairman
Background: Treasurer & Minister for IT & Multimedia; Investment Banker, Macquarie Bank

2951 MEDRA CAPITAL
60/2 Melita Street
Valetta VLT 1122
Malta
e-mail: info@medracapital.com
web: www.medracapital.com

Mission Statement: We are a private investment company providing seed and Series A funding for start-ups. As well as backing in-house ventures under our own direction, we are particularly interested in opportunities in technology, manufacturing, robotics, renewable energy, and sustainability, where our team's expertise adds most value.

Founded: 2013
Investment Criteria: Seed-Stage, Series A
Industry Group Preference: Technology, Manufacturing, Robotics, Software, Renewable Energy
Portfolio Companies: Appvance, Boatbound, Evvnt, Incrediblue, Knowledge Transmission, Mover, PocketFM, Sailogy, Scaled Networks, Sugru, Vantage Power

2952 MEKONG CAPITAL
Capital Place, 8th Floor
6 Thai Van Lung St.
District 1
Ho Chi Minh City
Vietnam
Phone: 84-88273161 Fax: 84-88273162
e-mail: info@mekongcapital.com
web: www.mekongcapital.com

Mission Statement: A private equity investment company that specializes in investing in the leading private companies in Vietnam.

Geographic Preference: Vietnam, Cambodia, Laos
Fund Size: $168.5 Million
Founded: 2001
Average Investment: $1.2 Million
Minimum Investment: $1 Million
Investment Criteria: Expansion, Restructuring, MBO
Industry Group Preference: Consumer Products, Retailing, Distribution
Portfolio Companies: Phu Nhuan Jewelry, Mobile World, Asia Chemical Corporation, FPT Corporation, Nam Long Investment Corporation, Intresco, Vietnam Australia International School, An Giang Plant Protection, Traphaco, Minh Hoang Garment

Key Executives:
Chris Freund, Partner
e-mail: info@mekongcapital.com
Education: Latin School of Chicago; BS Psychology, University of California, Santa Cruz
Background: VP/Portfolio Manager, Templeton Asset Management, Investment Research, Harris Associates, Consultant, Templeton Vietnam
Chad Ovel, Partner
Education: Dr. Economic Sciences & Capital Markets Theory, Vienna University of Economics, Vienna
Background: Executive Director, Templeton Asset Management in Singapore; Portfolio Manager, BIDV-Vietnam Partners Investment Management

2953 MERCAPITAL SA
Padilla 17
1 Edificio 14
28223 Pozuelo de Alarcon
Madrid 28006
Spain
Phone: 34-915578000 Fax: 34-913-449191

Mission Statement: Actively seeking new investments
Geographic Preference: Spain
Fund Size: $2 Million
Founded: 1982
Average Investment: 25 and 150 million
Minimum Investment: $36,000
Investment Criteria: Iberion Buyouts, LBO, MBO, MBI, Buy-And-Builds, Growth Capital Transactions, Middle Market
Industry Group Preference: All Sectors Considered
Portfolio Companies: ADL Technology, Blinker, Bodegas Lan, Broadnet, Cesa, Grupo Abaco Menorquin Yachts, Holmes Place, Jofel, KA International Group, Lasem, MSC Wellness Experts, Occidental Hotels Allegro Resorts, Piaggio/Derbi Record, Quiron Hospital Group, Recoletos, Saprogal, System, USP Hospitales, Xfera, Ydilo

Key Executives:
Gonzalo de Rivera, CEO
e-mail: mzurita@mercapital.com
Education: Degree Law & Business Studies, ICADE; MBA with Honors, INSEAD
Background: Project Director, MexCapital
Directorships: Wellness Experts; Bodegas Lan; Grupo Logistico Santos
Federico Pastor, Chairman
e-mail: cbg@mercapital.com
Education: MBA, INSEAD; Degree Business & Economics, Universidad Pontificia Comillas (ICADE)
Background: Graduate Trainee, Airbus Industrie, Peugeot & Ernst & Young
Directorships: Quiron; Hospiten

2954 MERIFIN CAPITAL
Place Flagey 18
Brussels B-1050
Belgium
Phone: 32-26462580 Fax: 32-26463036
e-mail: enquiries@merifin.com
web: www.merifin.com

Mission Statement: Actively seeking new investments as a private international investment group.
Geographic Preference: Brussels, Geneva, New York
Founded: 1980
Investment Criteria: Early-Stage, Expansion and Development, Management Buyout, Management Buyin, Turn-Around and Restructuring
Industry Group Preference: All Sectors Considered

Key Executives:
Simona Heidempergher, Director
e-mail: enquiries@merifin.com

2955 MERRILL LYNCH (ASIA PACIFIC) LIMITED Merrill Lynch Group
15/F Citibank Tower, 3 Garden Road
Central
Hong Kong

Phone: 85-225363888 Fax: 85-225363789

Mission Statement: Leading financial management and advisory company.

Geographic Preference: Worldwide
Fund Size: $1.6 Trillion
Founded: 1914
Investment Criteria: Expansion, Restructuring, MBO
Industry Group Preference: Consumer Products, Electronic Technology, Information Technology, Leisure, Media, Medical, Retailing, Wholesale, Telecommunications, Transportation, Distribution, Consumer Services, Entertainment

Key Executives:
John A Thain, Chairman & Chief Executive Officer
Education: Juris Doctor degree from Yale Law School, Bachelor of Arts degree, summa cum laude, in economics from Colgate University.
Background: co-head of the Global Financial Institutions Group, Global Investment Banking, Served as a Financial Advisor to Leading Banking.
Rosemary Berkery, Vice Chairman & General Counsel
Education: Master's of Business Administration with Finance from Harvard University, Graduate of Kettering University
Background: Merrill Lynch's U.S. Private Client group, General Motors Corporation in New York and Madrid,
Directorships: Chairman of the Board, Chief Executive Officer
Ahmass Fakahany, Vice Chairman
Education: Bachelor of Science degree from Boston University School of Management and an M.B.A from Columbia University.
Background: Served as senior vice president and finance director, Global Chief Financial Officer and Chief Administrative Officer for the Corporate and Institutional Client Group .
Directorships: Chief Administrative Officer

2956 MEZZANINE MANAGEMENT LIMITED Mezzanine Management UK Ltd.
One Strand
1-3 Strand
London WC2N 5HR
United Kingdom

Phone: 44-2070242200 Fax: 44-2070242201
e-mail: info@mezzanine-management.co.uk
web: www.mmlcapital.com

Mission Statement: Actively seeking new investments

Geographic Preference: USA, Europe
Fund Size: $1 Billion
Founded: 1988
Average Investment: $10 million and $50 million
Minimum Investment: $10 Million
Investment Criteria: Expansion and Development, Refinancing bank debt, Secondary purchase/replacement capital, MBO, MBI, Institutional BO, Leveraged Build Up
Industry Group Preference: Aerospace, Defense and Government, Petrochemicals, Industrial Equipment, Media, Engineering
Portfolio Companies: Apache, Arena Group, Argyle Security, ATA Groiup, Carre Blanc, Clyde Bergemann, Coventya, EIC, FrontierMedEx, GlobeOp, Hawkpoint, IAC, Instant, Lomond, Nactis, Optionis Group, PAR, Precision, Regard, Tournus, TNT, Vanguard Healthcare, VIP Cinema Seating, Vulcanic, WSH, XServ, Yonkers

Key Executives:
Rory Brooks, Founding Partner
e-mail: info@mezzanine-management.co.uk
Education: Bachelor's degree from the University of Michigan and an MBA degree in Finance from the University of Pittsburgh.
Background: Toronto-Dominion Bank and Held numerous commercial and merchant banking positions in the United States and the United Kingdom.Much of his career has been spent as a cash flow lender and equity provider analyzing and arranging financings in New York and Lo
Edward Baker, Investment Manager
e-mail: info@mezzanine-management.co.uk
Education: Bachelor's degree in Management from the University of Manchester Institute of Science and Technology
Background: Bank of Boston , Director of BPC, Ferembal, Sicli, Century Inns, Eurofarad and Polestar.
Gemma Chivers, Investor Relation Manager
e-mail: info@mezzanine-management.co.uk
Education: Masters of Science in International Banking and Finance from Herriot Watt University in Edinburgh.
Background: Bank of Scotland , Director of Hallmark
Robert Devonshire, Investment Manager
e-mail: info@mezzanine-management.co.uk
Education: BA and MA from Cambridge University
Background: Private Equity Investor.in US and Europe.
Parag Gandesha, Chief Operating Officer
e-mail: info@mezzanine-management.co.uk
Education: Parag has a BSc in Accounting and Finance and an MBA in International Management and is ACCA qualified.
Background: Finance Director of Cdb Web Tech Group, BC Partners

2957 MIDINVEST LIMITED
Kauppakatu 31 C
Jyväskylä 40100
Finland

Phone: +358 50 539 9378
web: www.midinvest.fi

Mission Statement: Midinvest Management Oy is a venture capital company which manages seven regional venture capital funds.

Geographic Preference: Finland
Fund Size: $70 Million
Founded: 2000
Average Investment: $1.83 Million
Minimum Investment: $42, 000
Investment Criteria: Startup, Expansion, MBO/MBI, Seed
Industry Group Preference: Software, Manufacturing, Education, Healthcare
Portfolio Companies: A-Lab Oy, C2 SmartLight Oy, Flaaming Oy, Inka Oy, Intelle Innovations, Kilosoft Oy, Kotidata, Metcase Consulting Oy, Paytrail Oyj, Pisla Oy, Polarmatic Oy, Soikea Solutions Oy, Stafix Oy, Valttori Oy

Key Executives:
Jukka-Pekka Nikula, Managing Director

2958 MIDVEN
Cavendish House
39-41 Waterloo St.
Birmingham B2 5PP
United Kingdom

Phone: 0121-7101990 Fax: 0121-7101999
e-mail: enquiries@midven.com
web: www.midven.co.uk

Mission Statement: Midven is an owner managed, entrepreneurial, venture capital company located in the heart of Birmingham. We have been successfully investing in dynamic,

Venture Capital & Private Equity Firms / International Firms

small and medium sized businesses since we started in 1990 when six Midlands based entrepreneurs established the business.
Geographic Preference: Midlands
Founded: 1990
Average Investment: £1 million
Investment Criteria: Early-Stage
Industry Group Preference: Biotechnology, Environment, Digital Media & Marketing, Software, Hardware, Consumer Services, Manufacturing, Engineering
Portfolio Companies: 21Net, Abgentis, AccurIC, Activ8, Admedo, AerisTech, Aitua, Allinea, Amalyst, Amba Defence, Anaxsys, Anvil Semiconductors, Ardentia, BeGo, Big Button, BioSyntha, Breaking Free, Caperfly, Caption Data, Cellcentric, Cellfacts, Cipher Surgical, Claresys, Clearview, Cobalt Light Systems, Complyserv, Concurrent Thinking, Connexica, Consero Consulting, Contego Fraud, Corso UK, CPA, Craft Dragon, Crescendo Biologics, Crowd Technologies, Cytox, Diamond Software, Diverse World, Dynamic Change, E-Motion Ventures, Eagle Genomics, Edudo, Edududes Ltd., Etive Technologies, Everyclick, Fertility Focus, Foodient T/A Whisk, Formolgy, Fubar Radio, Gemba Solutions, GeoScience International, H4-Global, Health2works, I-Solutions Global, Igloo Education, Igloo Vision, Infinity CCS, Inscentinel, Ionic Polymer Solutions, Isys Interactive, Kallik, Keit, Kobus Services, L3 Technology, Learning Labs, Lontra, LumeJet, Meals & Media, Microbial Solutions, Microvisk, Midland Industrial Glass, Minivator, MVI Technology, Netmania, Novacta, Occam Systems, Orbital Optics, Orthogem, Oxsensis, P2i, Perfectus Biomed, Phasor Solutions, Phoenix Health & Safety, Playmob, Portal Entertainment, Prism Network, Procarta Biosystems, ProKyma, Prolojik, Quantum Compliance, SALT, Scriptswitch, Silver Lining Solutions, Simworx, Soshi Games, Sparcana, Spectral Edge, Speed Plastics, Talecom, Tokamak Energy, TR Fleet, Uni2 Hold Tight, WalkinWifi, Warwick Audio Technologies, Webmoco, Your Vets
Key Executives:
Tony Stott, Chief Executive Officer
0121-710-1990
Education: Economics & Politics, Manchester University
Background: Principal, HSBC Enterprise & Exceed Funds; Deloitte & Touche

2959 MINI VENTURES
Pakistan

e-mail: info@miniventures.com

Mission Statement: Mini Ventures is a seed fund for small sized ventures aiming to fund, mentor and help launch start-ups to create an entrepreneur-friendly eco-system in the Pakistan market.
Geographic Preference: Pakistan
Investment Criteria: Seed-Stage
Key Executives:
Faizan Laghari, Founding Partner
Education: Business & Information Technology Degree, Curtin University of Technology
Background: Founder, Suite401; Founder, Textualy; Founder, Viaduct

2960 MIRAE ASSET VENTURE ACCELERATOR
Mirae Asset Group
28/F Seoul Finance Center
84, Taepyungro 1-ka, Chung-ku
Seoul 100-768
South Korea

Phone: +82 2 3707 0400
web: www.miraeasset.com

Mission Statement: Mainly supports companies in the initial stages of business set-ups.
Geographic Preference: Asia, Korea
Fund Size: 53.85 Billionÿ
Founded: 1999
Investment Criteria: Small & medium-sized enterprises and venture start-ups.
Industry Group Preference: Multimedia, Internet Technology, Bioengineering, Information Technology, Security
Portfolio Companies: Softmax, Fi-on, Tmax soft, Geni Tech, J-Tell, Alpha vision tech, Dinalit System, Wow Tv, Tel-loin, Dae-in-lnfo sys, Hitech, Al-F-Hitech, Han net, Hans bio med.
Key Executives:
Hyeon Joo Park, Chairman
Background: Research Head of Mirae Asset Securities

2961 MITSUBISHI UFJ CAPITAL
1-7-17 Nihonbashi, Chuo-Ku
Tokyo 103-0027
Japan

Phone: 81-0-3-5205-8581 Fax: 81-0-3-3273-5570
web: www.mucap.co.jp/english

Mission Statement: Formed by the merger of Diamond Capital and UFJ Capital, Mitsubishi UFJ Capital have financed more than 1,000 companies, more than 290 of which have gone public.
Fund Size: 2.95 billion Yen
Founded: 2005
Industry Group Preference: Healthcare, Biotechnology, Information Technology, Electronics, High Technology
Portfolio Companies: Sucampo Pharmaceuticals, Affymax, OPKO Health, FivePrime Therapeutics, MacroGenics, FibroGen, Acologix, Acucela, BrainCells, Aveo, Inotek, iPerian, KaloBios, Cardiac Dimensions, AnGesMG, TransGenic, MediBic, MEDINET, Shin Nippon Biomedical Laboratories, Takara Bio, MediciNova, GNI, R-Tech Ueno, NanoCarrier, TMRC, GreenPeptide, Perseus Proteomics, CanBas, Y's Therapeutics, UMN Pharma, Dynavec, D.Western Therapeutics, Japan Tissue Engineering, CellSeed, ReproCELL, Carna Biosciences, Big Matrix Research Institute, MC Laboratory, ReqMed Company
Key Executives:
Kei Andoh, President

2962 MITSUI SUMITOMO INSURANCE VENTURE CAPITAL CO
Yaesu Nagoya Bldg 3F
Yaesu 2-2-10
Chuo-Ku, Toky 104-0028
Japan

Phone: 81 3 3279 3672 Fax: 81 3 3242 3068
web: www.msivc.co.jp

Mission Statement: Our mission is to contribute to the technological advance and service enhancement that helps our society be sustainable. This is also our significance of existence as a venture capital which continues to be essential in our society. For the past two decades, we have supported a number of venture companies go public through investing into and connecting them to the right partners to realize their potential value. We support entrepreneurs according to the stages of their development. We offer entrepreneurs broad support such as leadership and entrepreneurship education in university as well as providing capital, management skills and networks to help early-stage R&D and commercialization.
Geographic Preference: Asia
Founded: 1990
Investment Criteria: Later Stage, Early Stage, Middle Stage, Start-Up
Industry Group Preference: Real Estate, Construction, Financial Services, Consumer Products, Web Applications & Services, Biotechnology, Healthcare, Electronics, Semiconductors, Telecommunications, Energy, Environment, Sustainability

Key Executives:
Hitoshi Igarashi, President

2963 MMC VENTURES
2 Kensington Square
London W8 5EP
United Kingdom

Phone: 020-79382220 Fax: 020-79382259
e-mail: jennifer.newall@mmcventures.com

Mission Statement: MMC invests in early stage, high growth companies. We give our investors access to a professionally managed fund, investing growth equity in dynamic young companies in the UK.

Geographic Preference: United Kingdom
Founded: 2000
Investment Criteria: Early-Stage
Industry Group Preference: Business Products & Services, Digital Media & Marketing, Consumer Internet, Healthcare, Financial Services, Clean Technology, E-Commerce & Manufacturing
Portfolio Companies: AlexandAlexa, Appear Here, Base79, Bottica.com, Breathing Buildings, Brightpearl, Creativity Software, Gousto, iJento, Immedia, Interactive Investor, Invenias, Knowledgemill, LoveHomeSwap, Masabi, MBA & Company, MoneyExpery, MUBI, Neoss, NewVoiceMedia, Obillex, OneClick HR, Pact, PayasUgym, Reevoo, SafeGuard, Small World, Somo Global, The Practice, TotalMobile, Tyres on the Drive, VC-Net, WeDo, Wool and the Gang

Key Executives:
Bruce Macfarlane, Managing Partner
e-mail: bruce.macfarlane@mmcventures.com
Education: BA, English, Leeds University
Background: Managing Director, Merrill Lynch; Securities Lawyer, Skadden Arps
Directorships: Neoss, Interactive Investor, Breathing Buildings

2964 MMT MILLENNIUM MATERIALS TECHNOLOGIES FUND LP
6 Kaufman St, Beit Gibor
14th Floor
Tel Aviv 68012
Israel

Phone: 972-35167674 Fax: 972-35167301
web: www.mmtfund.com

Mission Statement: Actively seeking new investments.
Geographic Preference: Israel
Fund Size: $40 Million
Founded: 1998
Investment Criteria: Early Stage
Industry Group Preference: Microelectronics, Pharmaceuticals, Biotechnology, Communications, Nanotechnology, Technology, Bio Materials, Energy
Portfolio Companies: Cima Nanotech, Cymbet Corp, Enzymotec, Glycominds Ltd, MeMPile Ltd, Nanolayers, Power Paper Ltd, Real-time Radiography Ltd, Sol-Gel Ltd, Triton BioSystems.

Key Executives:
Zwi Vromen, Senior Partner
e-mail: info@mmtfund.com
Education: Bachelor's degree in Social Sciences
Background: Astra Technological Investments Ltd
Nir Belzer, Senior Partner
e-mail: info@mmtfund.com
Education: MBA, Bachelor's degree in Mathematics and computers
Background: Business Development Manager at IDBH, Director of Marketing and Business Development at Globes.
Didi Kalaydzhiev, Public and Investor Relations
e-mail: info@mmtfund.com
Education: B.Sc. degree in Chemical Engineering and business diploma from the Hebrew University of Jerusalem.
Background: Vice President of Business Development at Koor Chemicals, a Director on the Board of Tambour Ltd., Agan Chemicals Ltd., as well as the Joint Managing Director of Plantex and Ikapharm and General Manager of SBRC Ltd
Oren Gafri, Senior Partner
e-mail: info@mmtfund.com
Education: B.Sc. and M.Sc. studies in Materials & Process Engineering at Ben-Gurion University.and Business Administration for Engineers program at the Hebrew University of Jerusalem
Background: CEO of Pulsar Welding Ltd, General Manager of Chemitas Ltd.and executive of the Israeli Aircraft Industries Ltd (IAI)
Dr. Ram Vromen, Partner
e-mail: info@mmtfund.com
Education: PhD in History , LLB in law and a BA in history
Background: Portfolio manager of the First IsraTech Fund, Partner in the law firm of Bach, Arad, Scharf & Co.

2965 MOBILE INTERNET CAPITAL
Jowa Akasaka 1-chome Building, 8th Floor
1-11-28 Akasaka
Minato-ku
Tokyo 107-0052
Japan

web: www.mickk.com

Mission Statement: Mobile Internet Capital Inc. is a corporate VC specializing in Japan-based mobile and internet technologies.

Geographic Preference: Japan
Fund Size: 100 Million Yen
Founded: 1999
Investment Criteria: Technology, contents and services for mobile communications, the internet and related fields
Industry Group Preference: Wireless Technologies, Internet Technology
Portfolio Companies: Shanon, Monstar Lab, ReNet Japan Group, StreetAcademy, MINKABU, Music Securities, S-cubism Holdings, Techpoint, Tattva, SUVACO, Ruby Groupe, Skeed, FLENS, Accounting SaaS Japan Co., CredoRax, Remote Co., SAN Home Entertainment, WEIC, Showcase-TV, Ricmedia, sMedio, GainSpan, REAL SAMURAI, GoNet Systems, Jin-Magic, Audyssey Laboratories, Explay-Japan, Innofidei Corporation, Agile Media Network, Chelsio Communications, HEROZ, Mlog, Centrix, Net-Marketing Corporation, eflow, Japan Carlife Assist, C2cube

Key Executives:
Hidemiÿ Horseback, President, Chief Executive Officer
e-mail: micinfo@mickk.com
Education: Masters in engineering
Background: Sharp Corporation , Intel Japan as vice-president
Directorships: CEO, CIO
Takeshi Inada, Director, Investment Officer

2966 MOMENTUM FUNDS MANAGEMENT PTY LIMITED
Level 1, 230 Balaclava Rd, Caulfield
Melbourne 3162
Australia

Phone: 61-395089333 Fax: 61-395089343
e-mail: mail@momentumvc.com.au
web: www.momentumvc.com.au

Venture Capital & Private Equity Firms / International Firms

Mission Statement: Invests in companies with high growth potential based on the commercialisation of Australian research and development.
Geographic Preference: Australia
Fund Size: $30 Million
Founded: 1999
Investment Criteria: High tech, Early stage
Industry Group Preference: Electronic Technology, Biotechnology, Biosciences, Manufacturing, Software, Communications
Portfolio Companies: EnGene IC, Benthic Geotech, Panviva, CR-X, Petrecycle, Retriever Communications, Biovend, Briter Electronics, Cerylid, DSP Holdings, Juswin Technologies
Key Executives:
   John Thompson, Chairperson
   Education: B.Comm, Melbourne University; MBA, Melbourne Business School
   Background: Arthur Andersen
   Directorships: Panviva Ltd., Benthic Geotech Ltd.
   Martha Cleary, Director
   Education: B.Sc (Summa Cum Laude) in Physics from University College Dublin & Ph.D in astronomy from ANU, Canberra
   Background: Marketing and sales manager of the new ICIA diagnostics & Director of Client Operations at Dendrite International
   Directorships: Director of Justwin Technologies Inc
   Ron Finkel, Principal and Executive Director
   e-mail: mail@momentumvc.com.au
   Education: Bachelor of Business

2967 MONASHEES CAPITAL
R. Samuel Morse
74 CJ 39
Sao Paulo 04576-060
Brazil

Phone: +55 11 5501 2032
e-mail: contact@monashees.com.br
web: www.monashees.com.br

Mission Statement: Monashees Capital is a venture capital firm that partners with outstanding entrepreneurs to build great companies. They have a long-term approach and a business model that is tailored to the Brazilian environment.
Geographic Preference: Brazil
Portfolio Companies: Algentis, Baby.com.br, Bidu.com.br, Boo-Box, Buzzerd.com, Dabee, Elo7, Getninjas, Keepcon, Madeira Madeira, Medicinia, Mind Lab, Olook, Oppa, Peixeurbano, Pet Love, Playlore, VivaReal

2968 MONTAGU PRIVATE EQUITY LIMITED
2 More London Riverside
Vinters Place
London SE1 2AP
United Kingdom

Phone: 44-02073369955 **Fax:** 44-02073369961
e-mail: investment@montagu.com
web: www.montagu.com

Mission Statement: Montagu is a leading private equity advisors.
Geographic Preference: UK, France, Germany, Poland, Nordic Region
Fund Size: Euro 2.5 Billion
Founded: 1968
Average Investment: $152 Million
Minimum Investment: $35 Million
Investment Criteria: Secondary purchase/replacement capital, MBO, MBI, Institutional BO, Leveraged Build Up
Industry Group Preference: Environment, Industrial Products, Business Products & Services, Industrial Services, Chemicals, Consumer Products, Consumer Retail, Consumer Services, Energy
Portfolio Companies: Visma, Arkopharma, Nemera, DORC, CliniSys, University of Law, St-Hubert, BSN Medical, Euromedic International, Maplin Electronics
Key Executives:
   Jason Gatenby, CEO
   e-mail: chris.masterson@montagu.com
   Education: Psychology at University College & MBA from Manchester Business School
   Chris Masterson, Chairman
   Simon Pooler, Director
   e-mail: vince.obrien@montaguequity.com
   Education: Graduate in Modern History & Chartered Accountant
   Background: Coopers & Lybrand
   Directorships: Chairman of the British Venture Capital Association

2969 MORNINGSIDE VENTURES
e-mail: enquiries@morningside.com
web: www.morningside.com

Mission Statement: Morningside Group was founded in 1986, by the Chan family of Hong Kong to make private equity and venture capital investments. The group is managed by investment professionals who are entrepreneurial, have deep industry knowledge and are effective in the local environment in which they operate. In addition to its investment activitites, Morningside Group is strongly committed to social responsibility.
Founded: 1986
Portfolio Companies: Alpha Therm, ANZ, CrestMarc, Dakota Bodies, Magnatech, PressPass, Southland Log Homes, The Tile Shop, Clearn Membranes, Combined Solar, Green Biologics, ZinniaTek, Advanced Cell Diagnostics, BioScale, Cancer Targeting Systems, Heuresis, Insilixa, RapidScan, Cognoa, Excera, Glysure, Knoa, Vioptix, Converd, HD Biosciences, HumanZyme, KBI, Kindstar, Microscreen, Origene, PHC, Synermore, Aduro, Apellis, Argo, Atea, Atreaon, CellCentric, Chimerix, CVI, Edison, Envisia, Genocea, Liquidia, Matatu, Matriavax, MicuRx, Nucana, OrienGene, Oxyrane, Pinteon, Procarta, Stealth Peptides, Sunbio, Synchroneuron, Vaccine Tech, Building For Good, China Homerun, CO Everywhere, Forensic Logic, Hailo, Idibon, NPIC, One Smart, Phoenix New Media, Proximiant, Skycredit, TTPOD, VoiceBox, Xiaomi
Key Executives:
   Richard Liu, Managing Director
   Education: B.A. Beijing University of Science and Technology; MBA China Europe International Business School

2970 MOUNTAIN PARTNERS
Unterer Leihof
Fuhrstrasse 12
Waedenswil CH-8820
Switzerland

Phone: 41-447838030 **Fax:** 41-447838040
e-mail: contact@mountain.partners
web: www.mountain-partners.ch

Mission Statement: We are a global investment holding headquartered in Switzerland with currently more than 100 corporate investments. Our shareholders and co-investors benefit from our long-time experience in the 'value creation' and the management of our strong portfolio. We are close to our affiliated companies - with the help of our unique network and thanks to intensive support. An active role is important to us. Globally operating divisions cover our strategic business areas. Through this worldwide interaction, we also promote technology transfer into emerging markets. It is our aim to create real 'value add' for all of our stakeholders.
Geographic Preference: Switzerland
Industry Group Preference: Clean Technology, Information Technology, Financial Services

Portfolio Companies: Bab.La, Biocell, Bio Gate, Crealytics, Customer Alliance, Datapine, ePetWorld GmbH, Exasol, FCF Fox Corporate Finance, GEPPERT, Global Group, Grunspar, GVO, Hetan Technologies, Identive Group, ITEMBASE, Lashou, LOCR, xishiwang.com, Mixxt, Motionet AG, MovingImage24, Pearfection, Rebuy, ReigoHelden, SCHUTZKLICK, Secusmart, Shirtinator, Sinosol AG, Smart Loyalty, Torqeedo, URBANARA, Ushi.cn, VIPSTORE, yasni

Key Executives:
Jens-Jurgen Bockel, Chairman
Background: Henkel, Bahlsen, Werhaha-Group, Schickdanz-Holding; COO/CFO, Tengelmann Group
Directorships: CDU Wirtschaftsrat

2971 MVC CORPORATION
No. 3 No. 7 Nihon Keizai Shimbun headquarters
Chiyoda-ku
Tokyo 100-0004
Japan

Phone: 81-0332853124 **Fax:** 81-0332859156

Mission Statement: Provides early-stage venture capital to various types of technology firms.

Geographic Preference: US, China, Korea, Japan
Fund Size: $35 Million
Founded: 1984
Average Investment: $5.5 Million
Minimum Investment: $500,000
Investment Criteria: Early-Stage
Industry Group Preference: Information Technology, Healthcare, Consumer Services

Key Executives:
Kenichi Kimura, President & Chief Executive Officer
Education: MBA from the University of Chicago
Background: Nippon Venture Capital Corporation
Masashi Kiyomine, Investment Director

2972 MVM LIFE SCIENCE PARTNERS
6 Henrietta Street
London WC2E 8PU
United Kingdom

Phone: 44-02075577500 **Fax:** 44-02075577501
e-mail: hh@mvm.com
web: www.mvmlifescience.com

Mission Statement: MVM's approach focuses on the risk and return characteristics of an investment rather than those criteria that are often used to define investments (e.g. sector, therapeutic area, stage of asset development). Hence, MVM invests in both early stage and late stage companies, platforms and products, discovery and development, devices and drugs.

Geographic Preference: Europe, Israel, United States
Fund Size: $500 million
Founded: 1997
Investment Criteria: Early-Stage, Later-Stage
Industry Group Preference: Biopharmaceuticals, Diagnostics, Drug Delivery, Gene Therapy, Healthcare Information Technology, Medical Devices, Life Sciences, Healthcare
Portfolio Companies: eZono AG, Patient Connect Service Limited, Horizon Discovery Limited, AccuVein, Lombard Medical Technologies, Vascular Pathways, Solx, Cheetah Medical Holdings, Tarsa Therapeutics, Alliance Pharma, Vantia Limited, Heptares Therapeutics, Cara Therapeutics, Zention Limited, Pulmagen Therapeutics, Wilson Therapeutics

Other Locations:
Old City Hall
45 School Street
Boston, MA 02108
Phone: 617-3832101 **Fax:** 617-3832106

Key Executives:
Stephen Reeders, Founder
e-mail: sr@mvm.com
Education: Cambridge University; MD, Oxford University
Background: Saunders Karp & Megrue
Directorships: Beacon Endoscopic, Biomedix, Cara Therapeutics, Cheetah Medical, Pulmagen Therapeutics

2973 NANYANG VENTURES PTY LIMITED
Level 5 NAB House, 255 George Street
Sydney 2000
Australia

Phone: 61-292474866 **Fax:** 61-292411087
web: www.nanyang.com.au

Mission Statement: To provide outstanding returns to investors by subscribing equity into mainly private companies that have the potential to develop into substantial, listable corporations.

Geographic Preference: Australia
Fund Size: $150 Million
Founded: 1996
Average Investment: $3 Million
Minimum Investment: $2 Million
Investment Criteria: MBO, MBI
Industry Group Preference: All Sectors Considered

2974 NAPKN VENTURES
Brazil

web: www.napkn.co

Mission Statement: Napkn Ventures invests in outstanding entrepreneurs who want to change the world.

Portfolio Companies: Dabee, 2Mundos, Everwrite, Conta Azul

Key Executives:
Luciano Tavares, Partner
e-mail: luciano@napkn.co
Education: BS, Business Administration, Fundacao Getulio Vargas; MS, Financial Engineering, Escola Politecnica da Universidade de Sao Paulo
Background: VP, Equity Derivatives, Merrill Lynch

2975 NARANYA VENTURES
Lazaro Cardenas 2400 Pte
Garza Garcia
Nuevo Leon CP 66260
Mexico

Phone: 52-81-8044-4500

Mission Statement: Naranya Ventures is a seed capital fund for mobile tech startups. We fund teams in their early stages that are looking for distribution and monetisation platforms in emerging markets with business models that solve meaningful problems and we help them with strategic advice, business development, financing, distribution, marketing and M&A at inflection points throughout their life.

Geographic Preference: Latin America
Investment Criteria: Seed-Stage, Early-Stage
Industry Group Preference: Mobile
Portfolio Companies: Cotton Tracks, Oja.la, Bit Pagos, PingStamp, Hostspot, Kuona, String, Cine+, AlmaBox, Flipter, Twitt2go, Tic, Compro Pago, Cre Apps

Key Executives:
Arturo Galvan, Founding Partner
e-mail: arturo.galvan@naranya.com
Pablo Salazar, Managing Partner/Director
e-mail: pablo.salazar@naranya.com
Education: BS, Marketing, MS, Entrepreneurship, London Business School

Background: Co-Founder, Latinstocks.com; Partner, IGNIA
Sergio Romo, Managing Partner
e-mail: sergio.romo@naranya.com
Background: Co-Founder, Miorden.com; Co-Founder, Ploombox.com
Jonathan Lewy, Managing Partner
e-mail: jonathan.lewy@naranya.com
Background: Co-Founder, Wise Media Group; Drake Finance; Co-Founder, Investomex

2976 NATWEST VENTURES LIMITED
Fenchurch Exchange, 8 Fenchurch Place
London EC3M 4TE
United Kingdom

Phone: 44-1713743000 Fax: 44-1713743572
web: www.natwest.com

Mission Statement: Supplying private equity across a broad range of sectors as part of the NatWest Group

Fund Size: $1 Billion
Founded: 1969
Average Investment: $7 Million
Minimum Investment: $1 Million
Industry Group Preference: All Sectors Considered
Portfolio Companies: Abec Group, Alperton Ford & Truck, Artcraft, Charrington Fuels, Bodegas Campo Burgo, El Rancho, Financiere Orefi, Graphics Arts Equipment, Mercury Taverns, Porter Lancastrian, Rusts of Cromer, DBS Nationwide, Expocolour, Gibbons Refractories, Groupe Soloc, Industrias Y Fundiciones Iglesias, John Barker Group, Magnus, Morris Homes, PKL Group, Pelham Homes, Peterhouse Group, Robison and Davidson, Rodgers Plant Hire, Thomas Steelwork, Trevi Holdings, Victor Homes Charco 99, France Portes, Hill Leigh Group, Wade Building Services, Chemical Express, Chemical Manufacturing and Refining, HRP Refrigerants, Solrec, Sterling Technology, Victrex

2977 NAUSICAA VENTURES
Axisparc Business Center
Rue Fond Cattelain 2/1.2
Mont-Saint-Guibert B-1435
Belgium

Phone: 32-010485020 Fax: 32-010485021
Toll-Free: 21
web: www.nausicaa-ventures.be

Mission Statement: Nausicaa Ventures is an early stage investment fund organisation focused on investment rounds between EUR 1 and 4 million. Nausicaa Ventures was created in 2009 by bringing together 35 private investors and selected institutional investors, such as the European Investment Fund or ING Bank, under the management of an experienced investment team. The target size of Nausicaa Ventures is upwards of EUR 20 million. Nausicaa Ventures combines the best of institutional venture capital groups and individual investors. It aims to cover the equity gap faced by most, promising early stage companies on their path towards profitable growth.

Geographic Preference: Belgium
Average Investment: 1 - 4 million Euro
Investment Criteria: Early-Stage, Early Growth-Stage
Industry Group Preference: Information Technology, Communications, Medical Technology, Clean Technology, High Technology

Key Executives:
Bart Luyten, General Partner
Education: Applied Economics, University of Antwerp
Background: Parter, Privast Capital Partners; Director, Partners@Venture

2978 NAUTA CAPITAL
Avda. Diagonal, 593 7th Floor
Barcelona 08014
Spain

Phone: 34-93-503-5900
e-mail: info@nautacapital.com
web: www.nautacapital.com

Mission Statement: Nauta Capital, founded in 2004 with presence in Barcelona (Spain), Boston (USA) and London (UK), is a Venture Capital firm specialized in early stage disruptive technology companies having a special focus on 3 segments: wireless/mobility, enterprise software/security, and ecommerce/internet. Nauta seeks to invest in companies that have developed highly disruptive technologies or business models, have strong potential to grow and a clear strategy to develop international markets. Nauta partners with highly committed and solvent executive teams in Europe and the USA.

Geographic Preference: Europe, United States
Fund Size: £170 million
Founded: 2004
Investment Criteria: Early-Stage
Industry Group Preference: Wireless Technologies, Mobile, Enterprise Software, Internet, E-Commerce & Manufacturing, Security
Portfolio Companies: Abiquo, Agnitio, AirSense, BaseKit, Brandwatch, CarrierIQ, Eyeview, Fizzback, Fractus, GCM, Nubera, Groupalia, Handmade, iJento, In Crowd, Jitterbug, Marfeel, Mobileaware, Mysportgroup, Privalia, Scytl, Socialpoint, Taptap, Yuilop

Other Locations:
200 High Street
Third Floor
Boston, MA 02110
Phone: 617-986-5060

42-44 Grosvenor Gardens
London SW1W 0EB
United Kingdom
Phone: 44-0-203-553-5757

Key Executives:
Dominic Endicott, General Partner
Education: BS, Economics, London School of Economics; MBA, MIT Sloan School of Management
Background: TMT Practice, Diamond Cluster International; Booz Allen

2979 NBC CAPITAL PTY LIMITED
493 Ipswich Road
Level 1
Annerley Qld 4103
Australia

Phone: 61-732339200 Fax: 61-732339223
e-mail: info@nbccapital.com.au

Mission Statement: Equity capital for growing companies.

Fund Size: $100 Million
Founded: 1999
Average Investment: $5 Million
Minimum Investment: $2 Million
Investment Criteria: High Growth Sectors
Industry Group Preference: Manufacturing, Agribusiness, Health Related, Food & Beverage, Technology

Key Executives:
Bruce Scott, Managing Director
Education: Bachelor of Commerce
Background: Pioneer's Chief Executive Officer, Trinity Consolidated Group Limited, Northern Business Consultants
Bernard Stapleton, Director

Venture Capital & Private Equity Firms / International Firms

2980 NEO TECHNOLOGY VENTURES
Australia

Mission Statement: Neo's investment model and expertise is based on identifying innovative and sustainable technology-based businesses through which it can help passionate entrepreneurs create the next market leaders.

Geographic Preference: Australia
Average Investment: Up to $5 million
Investment Criteria: Early And Expansion Stage
Industry Group Preference: Internet, Digital Media & Marketing, Communications, Clean Technology
Portfolio Companies: Open Kernel Labs, Genbook, SigNav, RPO

Key Executives:
Brett Morris, General Partner
+61 414 918 600
e-mail: brett.morris@ntfund.com
Education: BSc, University of Auckland
Marc Woodward, General Partner
+61 439 980 299
e-mail: marc.woodward@ntfund.com
Education: Georgetown University

2981 NEOMARKKA OYJ Neomarkka
Niinistönkatu 8 to 12
Helsinki 05800
Finland

Phone: 358-207-209190 Fax: 358-968446531
e-mail: info@neoindustrial.fi

Mission Statement: Invests in industrial companies with long term potential.

Geographic Preference: Finland
Fund Size: $115 Million
Founded: 1987
Average Investment: $6.62 Million
Minimum Investment: $1.2 Million
Investment Criteria: Synergic Industrial Investments
Industry Group Preference: Cable
Portfolio Companies: Aspocomp Group Oyj, Atria Yhtymä Oyj, Finnair Oyj, Finnlines Oyj, Fortum Oyj, HK Ruokatalo Oyj, Huhtamäki Oyj, Kemira Oyj, Kemira GrowHow Oyj, Kesko Oyj, M-Real Oyj, Okmetic Oyj, Osuuspankkien Keskuspankki Oyj, Olvi Oyj, Outokumpu Oyj, Pohjola-Yhtymä Oyj, Raisio Yhtymä Oyj, Rautaruukki Oyj, Stora Enso Oyj, Tecnomen Oyj, UPM-Kymmene Oyj

Key Executives:
Markku E. Rentto, Chairman
Education: Master of Science (Econ.)
Background: Kaupthing New York, Managing Director, Kaupthing Bank hf., Dep. CEO, Kaupthing hf., Dep. CEO
Directorships: CEO
Sari Tulander, Chief Financial Officer
Education: Master of Science (Econ.)
Background: Kaupthing Bank hf., Managing Director and CEO, Kaupthing hf., Deputy Managing Director
Directorships: Director

2982 NEOTENY COMPANY LIMITED
3F Plaza Mikado, 2-14-5 Akasaka Minato-ku
Tokyo 107-0052
Japan

Phone: 81-355492270 Fax: 81-355492271
e-mail: jito@neoteny.com
web: www.neoteny.com

Mission Statement: Invests in developing and supporting information technology-based businesses.

Geographic Preference: Silicon Valley, Japan
Fund Size: $86, 200
Founded: 2000
Investment Criteria: Early Stage, Seed
Industry Group Preference: Communications, Networking, Enabling Technology, Electronic Technology, Technology
Portfolio Companies: 3Dsolve, BeatCraft, Inc., Blockline, Inc. (e-Colle), BrainSellers.com, Contents Japan, Generation Create, fyto, IP Infusion Inc., Mediaprobe Inc., Neoteny Venture Development, Six Apart

Key Executives:
Joichi Ito, Chief Executive Officer & Founder
e-mail: jito@neoteny.com
Education: B.A. in Economics, MBA (Harvard Business School)
Background: Managing Director and Branch Manager of the Tokyo office of Goldman, Sachs & Co.
Jun Makihara, Chairman

2983 NESBIC INVESTMENT FUND II
Rozenburglaan 3
3503 RM
PO Box 8530
Groningen 9727 DL
Netherlands

Phone: 31-502110100 Fax: 31-502110119

Mission Statement: Value added Venture Capital Investors enabling, supporting and accelerating growth.

Geographic Preference: Europe, North America, South America
Fund Size: $144 Million
Founded: 1997
Average Investment: $14.4 Milllion
Minimum Investment: $2.4 Million
Investment Criteria: Invests in companies with Well Balanced Management Team, Predictable Cash Flow, Pan European Growth Opportunities, Realistic Business Plan, Springboard Position in their Market Segment
Industry Group Preference: Food & Beverage, Business to Business, Publishing, Media, Logistics, Healthcare
Portfolio Companies: Boekhandels Groep Nederland Holding BV, Boemer BV, Fair Information Services BV, Incotec Holding BV, JSI NV, Koninklijke Swets and Zeitlinger BV

Key Executives:
Robert Wilhelm, Managing Partner
Education: Master Degree, Economics, University of Amsterdam
Background: Over five years of international venture capital experience at Atlas Venture in Amsterdam and Boston.
Directorships: Senior Executive Mergers & Acquisitions of the pan European telecommunications joint venture Unisource NV for four years
Willem Van Vark, Chief Financial Officer
Education: SPD degree next to a degree as Auditor for small and medium-sized business companies (AA).
Background: Financial controller at Amev
Directorships: Certified Public Auditor (CPA)

2984 NETROVE ASIA SDN BHD
140 One Pacific Place, Floor 17th, Unit 1703-
Sukhumvit Rd
Klongteoy
Bangkok 10110
Thailand

Phone: 60-380231360 Fax: 60-380231361
e-mail: ideas@netrove.com
web: www.netrove.com

Mission Statement: Generating net value through sharing.

Geographic Preference: Asia
Fund Size: $17 Million
Founded: 1999
Average Investment: $500,000
Minimum Investment: $100,000
Investment Criteria: Start-up, Growth

Venture Capital & Private Equity Firms / International Firms

Industry Group Preference: Semiconductors, Agriculture, Biotechnology, Web Applications & Services
Portfolio Companies: Corpmart.com, MnEBay, V2 Technology, Deltaknot
Key Executives:
Teh Kim Seng, Chairman
Education: Graduated, Electrical and Electronics Engineering, MIS degree.
Background: NCR, AT&T and Bell Lab.
Bryan Chung, Partner
Education: L.L.B, L.L.M.
Background: Clarion Capital.

2985 NEUHAUS PARTNERS
Jungfernsteig 30
Hamburg 20354
Germany

Phone: 49-40-355-2820 Fax: 49-40-355-28239
web: www.neuhauspartners.com

Mission Statement: Founded in 1998, Neuhaus Partners is headquartered in the heart of Hamburg. The team is composed of 10 individuals who are mostly IT specialists with successful careers in the industry. Dr. Gottfried Neuhaus (Managing Partner) developed his hardware and software company into one of Germany's most successful telecommunications companies in the 1980's and 1990's. Dr. Neuhaus Computer KGaA produced a number of pioneering products in the field of data telecommunications.

Geographic Preference: European Union
Fund Size: 126 million euro
Founded: 1998
Industry Group Preference: High Technology, Information Technology, Hardware, Software, Infrastructure, Laser, Photonics, Microsystems, Telecommunications, Multimedia
Portfolio Companies: Antispameurope, Apprupt, Charismathics, Content Fleet, Exit Games, HR New Media, INTENIUM, Kaboa, MAZ Germany, MyHeritage, Next Kraftwerke, Propertybase, Searchmetrics, Smava, Sofatronic, Tellja, Testroom, Tolingo

Key Executives:
Gottfried Neuhaus, Managing Partner
Education: PhD
Background: Founder, Neuhaus Computer

2986 NEW MODEL VENTURE CAPITAL
58 Davies St.
London W1K 5JF
United Kingdom

Phone: 44-020-3538-5274
e-mail: info@newmodel.vc
web: newmodel.vc

Mission Statement: New Model Venture Capital is a team of experienced private equity and venture capital professionals who offer investors a pragmatic approach to venture capital, private equity, and corporate finance.

Portfolio Companies: EyeQuant, Live Better With, MOGO BankConnect, Property Detective, Radara, Wazoku, Xenomorph

Key Executives:
James King, Managing Director
Mark Hanington, Managing Director
Education: University of Leeds
Background: Managing Director, Fig
Robin McIlvenny, Managing Director
Background: Deutsche Bank; Security Pacific National Bank; Creditanstalt; JP Morgan
David Marshall, Managing Director

2987 NEW WORLD INFRASTRUCTURE LIMITED
17/F, New world tower, 18 Queens Road
Tower II
Central
Hong Kong

Phone: 852-21310600 Fax: 852-21310611
e-mail: nwsnews@nwsh.com.hk

Mission Statement: Committed to taking an instrumental role in incubating china dotcom companies.

Geographic Preference: Hong Kong
Fund Size: $2.4 Billion
Founded: 1995
Industry Group Preference: Infrastructure, Energy, Cargo Handling, Water

Key Executives:
Zheng Jiachun, Chairman
Background: Marriott international Inc.
Tsang Yam Pui, Executive Director

2988 NEWABLE VENTURES
140 Aldersgate Street
6th Floor
London EC1A 4HY
United Kingdom

e-mail: privateinvesting@newable.co.uk
web: www.newable.co.uk/private-investing

Mission Statement: The Fund targets the funding gap that exists for companies which have de-risked their technology, developed traction with customers and now seek funding to scale their commercial operations. The Fund aims to provide investors with a diversified portfolio of 7-10 Qualifying Companies.

Geographic Preference: United Kingdom
Fund Size: £2 Million
Founded: 1982
Average Investment: £250,000
Minimum Investment: £50,000
Investment Criteria: Early-Stage, Growth, Pre-Series A
Industry Group Preference: Space Technology, Downstream Technologies, Electronics, Automation, Medical Technology, Life Sciences
Portfolio Companies: BluWireless Technology, Contact Engine, Sphere Fluidics, Rezatec, Hummingbird Technologies, Jellagen, Hopster, Oxtex, City Pantry, Benivo

Key Executives:
Alex Sleigh
Education: MA, Economics/Modern History, University of St. Andrews; MA, General Management, Vlerick Ghent Management School, Belgium
Background: Investor In Residence, King's College
Anthony Clarke
Background: Co-Founder/Director, Seraphim Capital VC Fund; Co-Founder/Chair, UK Business Angel Association; President Emeritus, European Business Angel Network; Chartered Accountant/Chartered Secretary, Deloitte Haskins & Sells

2989 NEWMARGIN VENTURE CAPITAL
Villa 11, Radisson Plaza, 78 Xing Guo Road
Shanghai 200052
China

Phone: 86-2162138000 Fax: 86-2162123900
e-mail: info@newmargin.com
web: www.newmargin.com

Mission Statement: Mission is to support China's emerging entrepreneurs to build world-class companies.

Geographic Preference: China
Fund Size: $120 Million
Founded: 1999
Average Investment: $1-$5 Million

Minimum Investment: $1 Million
Investment Criteria: Early Stage Investments
Industry Group Preference: Information Technology, Healthcare, Biotechnology, Environment Products & Services, Materials Technology
Portfolio Companies: Asiainfo, CNC, Chinalliances, E-Future, Geong, Infosec, Lanjing Technology, M&W, One Wave, Rongshu.com, Roxus, Shanghai Mining Software Company, Sinofusion

Key Executives:
Feng Tao, Founder & CEO
e-mail: info@newmargin.com
Zhou Shuiwen, Managing Partner

2990 NEXIT VENTURES OY
Kaisaniemenkatu 2 b
Helsinki Fl-00100
Finland

Phone: 358 9 6818 910
e-mail: info@nexitventures.com
web: www.nexitventures.com

Mission Statement: Venture capital firm focused on mobile and wireless innovation.
Geographic Preference: Nordics, U.S. West Coast
Founded: 1999
Investment Criteria: Start-up, Growth
Industry Group Preference: Mobile, Wireless
Portfolio Companies: Bitfone, Futuremark, Hantro, HDmessaging, Hybrid Graphics, Mobile 365, Octoshape, Rightware, SkyPilot

Other Locations:
Nexit Ventures Inc.

14th Floor
San Francisco, CA 94105
Phone: 408-725-8400

Key Executives:
Michel Wendell, General Partner
e-mail: michel.wendell@nexitventures.com
Background: Cadence Design Systems
Artturi Tarjanne, General Partner
e-mail: artturi.tarjanne@nexitventures.com
Background: Solid Information Technology; AT Consulting
Pekka Salonoja, General Partner
e-mail: pekka.salonoja@nexitventures.com
Education: Helsinki University of Technology
Background: Nokia; Startupfactory
Sami Karppinen, Investment Director
e-mail: sami.karppinen@nexitventures.com
Education: Helsinki University of Technology
Risto Yli-Tainio, Chief Financial Officer
e-mail: risto.yli-tainio@nexitventures.com
Education: University of Vaasa
Background: Sitra; Sonera Corp.; SmartTrust

2991 NEXTEC DEVELOPMENT CAPITAL LIMITED
Suite 4, Level 10
66 Hunter Street
Sydney 2000
Australia

Phone: 61-292378600 **Fax:** 61-29-237-8690
e-mail: richard.gibson@nextec.com.au
web: www.nextec.com.au

Mission Statement: Specializes in providing strategic capital and independent corporate advice for growth orientated companies.
Geographic Preference: Australia
Founded: 1996
Industry Group Preference: Media, Information Technology, Healthcare, Entertainment, High Value Added Manufacturing, Retail, Consumer & Leisure, Financial Services, Healthcare

Key Executives:
Richard Gibson, Managing Director
e-mail: mail@nextec.com.au
Neil Bourne, Managing Director

2992 NEXUS VENTURE PARTNERS Nexus India Capital Advisors Pvt Ltd
G-2 Sarjan Plaza
100, Dr. Annie Besant Road
Worli
Mumbai 400018
India

Phone: 91-2266260000 **Fax:** 91-2266260001
web: www.nexusvp.com

Mission Statement: Nexus Venture Partners is India's leading Venture Capital fund. NVP invest in early and early growth stage companies across sectors in India and US. They are a team of successful entrepreneurs with extensive investing and operating experience, who love to get their hands dirty. They understand the unique challenges faced by entrepreneurs and know that it takes teamwork and exceptional execution capability for a company to succeed. Their partner companies have access to the entire Nexus team in India and Silicon Valley for help in recruiting talent, forging new alliances, opening doors to new customers, shaping strategy and connecting with best-of-breed executives, advisors, co-investors and board members.

Geographic Preference: India, United States
Average Investment: Up to $10 million
Investment Criteria: Early-Stage, Early Growth-Stage
Industry Group Preference: Internet, Media, Technology, Agriculture, Consumer Services, Consumer Products, Business Products & Services
Portfolio Companies: Altruist, Armor5, Aryaka, BSB, Cloud.com, CloudByte, Craftsvilla.com, Datagres, Dimdim, D.Light, Druva, Eka, EyeQ, Genwi, Gluster, GreyWater, Helpshift, ISFC, Kaltura, Kirusa, Komli, Map My India, MChek, Mistral, Netmagic, OLX, Prana, Pubmatic, Salorix, ScaleARc, Sedemac, ShopClues.com, Snapdeal.com, Sohan Lal Commodity, Suminter India Organics, Talent Sprint, Unicon, Unmetric, Vdopia, What's On India

Other Locations:
Nexus India Capital Advisors Pvt Ltd
Suite 1001, 10th Floor, Tower B, RMZ Millenia
No. 1&2, Murphy Road, Close to Ulsoor Lake
Bangalore 560 008
India
Phone: 91-8049456600

2200 Sand Hill Road
Suite 230
Menlo Park, CA 94025
Phone: 650-2330700

Key Executives:
Naren Gupta, Co-Founder
e-mail: naren@nexusvp.com
Education: BTech, Indian Institute of Technology; MS, California Institute of Technology; PhD, Stanford University
Background: Co-Founder, Integrated Systems
Directorships: Red Hat, Tibco

Venture Capital & Private Equity Firms / International Firms

2993 NHN INVESTMENT
7th FL, KT&G Tower
416 Yeongdong-daero
Gangnam-gu
Seoul 135-549
Korea

Phone: 82-221364500
web: www.nhninv.com

Mission Statement: Provides investment, loan, management as well as technological guidance to new technology enterprises and venture businesses.

Industry Group Preference: Internet, Mobile, Gaming, Information Technology, Communications, Internet, Semiconductors, Medical Devices

Portfolio Companies: LTC, Dongwoon Anatech, M-Biz Global, Mekics Co., Dym Co., Nanoom Tech, Glosil, Smart Ace, Nepes Display, ATO Solution Co., Kostek Systems, SPM, Wonil Co., Saehwa IMC, Caffe Bene, Vessel Co., Solueta Co., DCG Systems, UGint, Doobic, Rekoo

Key Executives:
Jong-Seung Lee, Executive Director
Background: CEO, Korea Investment Partners

2994 NIELSEN INNOVATE FUND
PO Box 3113
15 Halamish St
Northern Industrial Park
Caesarea 30889
Israel

Phone: 972-722-700-790 Fax: 927-722-700-791
e-mail: info@nif.co.il
web: www.nielseninnovate.com

Mission Statement: Nielsen Innovate is an early stage technological incubator licensed by the Chief Scientist of Israel. It operates as an incubator and investment fund.

Geographic Preference: Israel
Founded: 2013
Investment Criteria: Early Stage
Industry Group Preference: Market Research, Consumer Behavior, Data & Analytics, Marketing, Big Data, Social Services, Mobile, New Media
Portfolio Companies: eDealya, Zollo, Revuze, Evolita, Adstrix, cValue, Mobilibuy

Key Executives:
Esther Barak-Landes, CEO
e-mail: esther@nif.co.il
Education: LL.b, Tel Aviv University; MBA, IDC Business School
Background: CEO, Partam Hightech; Founding Partner, Israel-Angels; Senior Business Development Executive, Cash U Mobile Technologies; Corporate Attorney, Kantor, Elhanni, Tal and Co
Dov Yarkoni, VP Business Development
e-mail: dov@nif.co.il
Education: Bachelor of Technology, Engineering and Management, Shenkar
Background: SVP, Business Development and Sales, Matomy Media Group; VP, Client Services, Amadesa; Director of Consumer Division, Deltathree

2995 NIF VENTURES COMPANY LIMITED
1-2-1, Kyobashi
Daiwa Yaesu Building Chuo-ku
5th Floor
Tokyo 104-0031
Japan

Phone: 81-352011570 Fax: 81-352011518
web: www.nif.co.jp

Mission Statement: Committed to developing worldwide opportunities for both investors and entrepreneurs.

Geographic Preference: Tokyo

Fund Size: 10 Million Yen
Founded: 2006

2996 NIPPON TECHNOLOGY VENTURE PARTNERS LIMITED
Ekimae Bldg. 4th Floor, 4-1-1
Todoroki, Setagaya-ku
Tokyo 158-0082
Japan

Phone: 81-357581311 Fax: 81-357581322
web: www.ntvp.com

Mission Statement: Invests in independent innovative individuals and institutions with incubating new businesses with international cooperation and investment incentives.

Geographic Preference: Japan
Fund Size: 14 Billion Yen
Founded: 1998
Investment Criteria: Venture Finance, Management Consultation
Industry Group Preference: Information Technology, Financial Services, Management, Marketing

Key Executives:
Kazutaka Muraguchi, Representative Director
Education: Bachelor in Economics from Keio University
Background: Investment Manager in JAFCO.
Directorships: Founder.

2997 NISSAY CAPITAL
No. 4 No. 8 Nissei Nagata-cho Building
8th Floor
Nagatacho, Chiyoda-ku
Tokyo 100-0014
Japan

Phone: 03-35016644 Fax: 03-35016640
web: www.nissay-cap.co.jp

Mission Statement: Responds to a wide range of on-stage capital policy. Makes a wide range of investment capital policy stance based on the medium-and long-term investment, an eye to the post-listing from the startup.

Fund Size: 3 billion yen
Founded: 1991
Portfolio Companies: Nippon Dry-Chemical, Morpho, Pharmaceutical SymBio, Berg Earth, Double-Scope, Chiome Bioscience, Startflyer, Tee Life

2998 NOMURA PHASE4 VENTURES LTD
Nomura House
1 St Martins-le-Grand
London EC1A 4NP
United Kingdom

Phone: 44-20-7521-2386 Fax: 44-20-7521-1291
web: www.nomura.com

Mission Statement: To provide a premium rate of return for investors by creating, identifying and investing in development stage healthcare companies.

Geographic Preference: United States, Europe
Average Investment: $10 - $25 million
Industry Group Preference: Healthcare, Pharmaceuticals, Medical Devices
Portfolio Companies: ACADIA Pharmaceuticals, Inc., Albrieo, Altus Pharamceuticals, Arakis, Ark Therapeutics, ARYx Therapeutics, Atani, Avant Immunotherapeutics, Cerimon Pharmaceuticals, Chroma Therapeutics, Contec Medical, DeveloGen, DrugAbuse Sciences, Idenix, Immgenics, Intercell, Morphochem, Nabriva Therapeutics, OmniSonics Medical Technologies, OncoMed Pharmaceuticals, Paratek Pharmaceuticals, Pharmion, Phenomix, Proteolix, Sequenom, Targacept, Viacell, Weston Medical, Zosano Pharma

Key Executives:
  Koji Nagai, Group CEO
  Education: PhD & BSc, Birmingham University; University of California, Berkeley
  Background: Investment Manager, Rothschild Asset Management
  Directorships: Albireo, Cerimon, Indenix, Nabriva, OncoMed
  Atsushi Yoshikawa, President and Group COO
  Education: LLB, Hull University
  Background: Corporate Lawyer, Freshfield
  Naveed Siddiqi, Partner
  Education: Medical Degree, Guy's Hospital, London
  Background: EFG Group

2999 NORDIC CAPITAL
4A Stureplan
Stockholm SE-11435
Sweden

Phone: 46-84405050 Fax: 46-86117998
web: www.nordiccapital.se

Mission Statement: Actively seeking new investments.
Geographic Preference: Denmark, Finland, Norway, Sweden, Continental Europe
Fund Size: $0.19 Billion
Founded: 1989
Average Investment: $6.35 - 82.6 Million
Minimum Investment: $63, 500 - $0.5 Million
Investment Criteria: Focuses on companies with predictable cash-flows, strong market positions, turnarounds and development capital situations with a view to create long-term value rather than current profits
Industry Group Preference: All Sectors Considered
Portfolio Companies: Elmo-Calf, Eosex, Gislaved Folic, Hilding Anders, Molnlycke Health Care, Nycomed Pharma, Wilson Logistics Group
Key Executives:
  Mark Bulmer, Partner and Head of Banking
  e-mail: cathrine.siwers@nordiccapital.com
  Education: M. Sc. in Business Administration and Economics .
  Background: Sifo Research International.
  Jonas Agnblad, Partner
  e-mail: robert.andreen@nordiccapital.se
  Education: MSc, PhD in Industrial Management.
  Background: SKF, Svenska Handelsebanken.
  Bo Soderberg, Partner
  e-mail: bo.soderberg@nordiccapital.se
  Education: MSc in Economics.
  Background: Industrivarden AB, Spira Invest, Forreningsbanken.
  Robert Andreen, Partner
  e-mail: christian.dyvig@nordiccapital.se
  Education: LLM and MBA (Hons).
  Background: Department at Morgan Stanley .
  Anders Hultin, Partner
  e-mail: lars.spongberg@nordiccapital.se
  Education: MSc in Economics.
  Background: Electrolux Group, Svenska Handelsbanken, Svenska Finans International, AB Handel & Industri, Autoliv Group, Spectra Physics.
  Fredrik Näslund, Partner
  e-mail: kent.stevens.larsen@nordiccapital.se
  Education: MBA, INSEAD; MS, Engineering.
  Background: McKinsey & Company.
  Ulf Rosberg, Senior Adviser
  e-mail: ulf.rosberg@nordiccapital.se
  Education: MSc in Economics , Major in Finance.
  Background: Corporate Finance at Enskilda Fondkommission, Leirndorfer Bernhardtson Westerberg & Partners.
  Peter Hansson, Partner
  e-mail: peter.hansson@nordiccapital.se

  Education: MSc in Economics .
  Background: Merrill Lynch in London.
  Joakim Karlsson, Managing Partner
  e-mail: joakim.karlsson@nordiccapital.se
  Education: MS, Economics, Graduate Business School.
  Background: JP Morgan in London, Swedish Embassy in Moscow.
  Kristoffer Melinder, Managing Partner
  e-mail: kristoffer.melinder@nordiccapital.se
  Education: MSc in Economics and The University of Cologne.
  Background: JP Morgan in London, UN-Officer Bosnia.
  Morgan Olsson, Partner
  e-mail: morgan.olsson@nordiccapital.se
  Education: M.Sc.. Business Administration
  Background: Svetab, Svenska Handelsbanken.
  Toni Weitzberg, Partner
  e-mail: felix.bjorklund@nordiccapital.se
  Education: M.Sc. in Economics and Business Administration .
  Background: Fazer Group.
  Kim Gulstad, Principal
  e-mail: kim.gulstad@nordiccapital.com
  Education: M.Sc. in Applied Economics and Finance and a B.Sc. in Economics and Business Administration .
  Background: Investment Banking Division at Goldman Sachs in London.

3000 NORDIC MEZZANINE LIMITED
Mikonkatu 4 B
4th Floor
Helsinki 00100
Finland

Phone: 358-96840640 Fax: 358-968406410
e-mail: vesa.suurmunn@nordicmezzanine.com
web: www.nordicmezzanine.com

Mission Statement: Nordic Mezzanine provides mezzanine financing for buyouts, growth and capital restructuring.
Geographic Preference: Nordic Countries, Germany, Austria, Switzerland, the Netherlands, Belg
Fund Size: EUR 480 million
Founded: 1998
Average Investment: EUR 10 to 40 million
Minimum Investment: $6 Million
Investment Criteria: Buyouts, Buyins, Growth Capital
Industry Group Preference: All Sectors Considered
Portfolio Companies: Dyno Nobel A, Nycomed Pharma, Frigoscandia, pParoc, Dynapac, Global Garden Products, Jamo, Dometic, ANI Printing Inks
Key Executives:
  Vesa Surmunne, CEO
  e-mail: pekka.hietaniemi@nordicmezzanine.com
  Education: MSC, MBA.
  Background: Hambro European Ventures, MB Corporate Finanace, Postidankki Limited.
  Pekka Hietaniemi, Executive Director
  e-mail: pekkasunila@compuserve.com
  Education: MSC, MBA.
  Background: Hambro European Ventures, MB Corporate Finance, Control Data.

3001 NORTH WEST FUND
The Maltings
98, Wilderspool Causeway
Warrington WA4 6PU
United Kingdom

Phone: 01925-418232
web: www.thenorthwestfund.co.uk

Mission Statement: The North West Fund provides debt and equity finance from £50,000 to £2 million to small and medium

Venture Capital & Private Equity Firms / International Firms

sized businesses based in, or relocating to, the North West of England to start, develop and grow.
Geographic Preference: North West United Kingdom
Founded: 1982
Average Investment: £50,000 to £2 million
Investment Criteria: Early-Stage, Start-Up
Industry Group Preference: Technology
Portfolio Companies: Compliance Control, BiOxyDyn, SenseLogix Limited, Molplex, Redtree People, Dot Medical
Key Executives:
   Malcolm Edge, Chairman NWBF
   Background: Vice Chairman, KPMG UK

3002 NORTHERN ENTERPRISE LIMITED
11 Waterloo Square
Newcastle upon Tyne
Gateshead NE1 4DP
United Kingdom
Phone: 44-8451111850 Fax: 44-8451111853
e-mail: enquiries@nel.co.uk
web: www.nel.co.uk

Mission Statement: Independent fund management organization that provides risk funding to growth businesses that are based in the North East Region.
Geographic Preference: United Kingdom
Fund Size: £90 Million
Founded: 1989
Average Investment: $0.31 Million
Minimum Investment: $0.04 Million
Investment Criteria: Seed, Start-up, Early Stage, Expansion and Development, MBO, MBI, Mezzanine
Industry Group Preference: Biotechnology, Chemicals, Industrial Services, Industrial Equipment, Consumer Services, Energy, Environment Products & Services, Leisure, Medical & Health Related, Electronic Technology, Manufacturing, Service Industries, Transportation, Materials Technology
Portfolio Companies: Non Linear Dynamics Ltd, Orchard Information Systems Ltd, Visitech International Ltd, Torque Tension Systems Ltd, Appleyards Plastics Ltd.
Key Executives:
   Barrie Hensby, Chief Executive
   e-mail: enquires@nel.co.uk
   Background: Northern Enterprise Limited
   Chris Parker, Investment Executive
   e-mail: enquires@nel.co.uk

3003 NORTHSTAR VENTURES
Maybrook House, 5th Floor
27-35 Grainger Street
Newcastle upon Tyne NE1 5JE
United Kingdom
Phone: 44-0191-229-2770
web: www.northstarventures.co.uk

Mission Statement: Based in Newcastle, Northstar is a venture capital firm with over £80m under management. Northstar has been inspiring local entrepreneurs with financial backing and the expertise of a highly experienced team since 2004, investing in over 200 pioneering, high potential enterprises.
Geographic Preference: North East UK
Fund Size: £80 million
Founded: 2004
Investment Criteria: Early-Stage
Industry Group Preference: Biotechnology, Technology, Television, Film, Digital Media & Marketing, Music, Gaming, Healthcare, Energy, Environment
Portfolio Companies: Orangebus, Screenreach, Aframe, Low Carbon Lighting, Car 2 U, The Wood Heating Company, Mylearnadfriend, Applied Graphene Materials, Audacious, Biomass CHP, Komodo, Socialrel8

Key Executives:
   Ian Richards, Director
   0191-229-2778
   e-mail: ian.richards@northstarventures.co.uk
   Background: 3i, National Westminster Bank
   Alasdair Greig, Director
   0191-229-2775
   e-mail: alasdair.greig@northstarventures.co.uk
   Education: BA, Heriot Watt University; MBA, Ashridge
   Background: The Cambridge Gateway Fund; Emerging Markets Credit Risk, CIBC World Markets

3004 NORTHZONE
Master Samuelsgatan 42, 16 tr
Box 7257
Stockholm 103 89
Sweden
Phone: 46-8-599-05-880
e-mail: info@northzone.com
web: www.northzone.com

Mission Statement: Northzone is a technology investment partnership. Over the past 17 years we have been chosen by some of Europe's most exceptional entrepreneurs as a long-term partner for growth. We have thus far invested in over 75 companies, injecting some 200 years of collective operational and investment experience into businesses that truly make a difference.
Geographic Preference: Nordics, United States, Europe
Founded: 1996
Investment Criteria: Early-Stage, Expansion-Stage
Industry Group Preference: Digital Media & Marketing, Media, E-Commerce & Manufacturing, Energy Efficiency, Cloud Computing
Portfolio Companies: Appear Networks, Artfinder, Avito, Asetek, Billian, Bilguiden, BraveNew Talent, ChapDrive, Climatewell, Colibria, Doubletwist, Edvantage Group, Energy Micro, Envox, EPiServer, EProspects, Fox Technologies, Fotango Ltd, Funcom, Global Name Registry, Hugin, Ibistic, Imbera, Innotech Solar, Intility, IZettle, Jasper, Lastminute, Mamut, Massmarket, MCP, Naptech, Nevion, NextGenTel, Nimsoft, Norstel, NYX Security, Photonyx, P1.CN, Playdo, PortIT, PriceRunner, Reisefeber, ReVolt Technology, Silex Microsystems, Soundrop, Spaceape Games, Spotify, Stepstone, Sticky, Supponor, Testfreaks, The Online Backup Company, Tinde, Tobii, Trolltech, Trustpilot, VideoPlaza, VisualDNA, Widespace, X5 Music Group, Xcerion

Other Locations:
   Bygdoy Alle 2
   Pb. 573 Sentrum
   Oslo 0105
   Norway
   Phone: 47-22-12-5010

   Strandvejen 100, 4th Floor
   Hellerup 2900
   Denmark
   Phone: 45-70-222-475

Key Executives:
   Tellef Thorleifsson, Co-Founder
   Education: MSc, Business Adminstration, Norwegian School of Economics, MSc, Economics, London School of Economics
   Background: Founder, Western Bulk Shipping
   Directorships: Innotech Solar, Online Backup Company, Chapdrive, Silex

Venture Capital & Private Equity Firms / International Firms

3005 NOTION CAPITAL
8a Ledbury Mews North
London W11 2AF
United Kingdom

Phone: 44-08454989393
e-mail: info@notioncapital.com
web: www.notioncapital.com

Mission Statement: Notion is an entrepreneur-backed venture capital firm focused on Cloud Computing and Software-as-a-Service. We have a unique approach to investing that is founded on entrepreneurial empathy and a laser focus on a market that we know very well.

Geographic Preference: United Kingdom
Industry Group Preference: Cloud Computing, SaaS
Portfolio Companies: Brightpearl, Concentra, eSellerProf, New Voice Media, Norland Technology, Selfnet, Shutl, Star, The Currency Cloud, Tradeshift, Zattikka

Other Locations:
Suite 101
Eagle Tower
Montpellier Drive, Cheltenham
Gloucestershire GL50 1TA
United Kingdom
Phone: 44-1-845-498-9393

Key Executives:
Stephen Chandler, Managing Partner
Education: University of Exeter
Background: Deloitte, UBS Investment Bank
Directorships: SelfNet, Star, Tradeshift

3006 NOVO A/S
Tuborg Havnevej 19
Hellerup Dk-2900
Denmark

Phone: 45-35276500 Fax: 45-35276510
e-mail: ventures@novo.dk
web: www.novo.dk

Mission Statement: An active and independent company in its support of biotech ventures. The aspiration is to bring together the best of both worlds: industry insight and network from our pharma/biotech inheritance combined with a venture capital mindset that focuses on results and value creation.

Geographic Preference: Denmark, Europe, North America
Founded: 1999
Average Investment: 1 - 15 million Euro
Investment Criteria: Startups, Seed Stage, IPO, Public Companies
Industry Group Preference: Biotechnology, Life Sciences, Medical Devices
Portfolio Companies: 7TM Pharma, Alios BioPharma, AlloCure, Altheos, Amira Pharmaceuticals, AnaptysBio, Asante Solutions, BioMimetic Therapeutics, Cell Biosciences, Celltrix, Cytochroma, f-star GmbH, Funxional Therapeutics, Inogen, LifeCycle Pharma, Light Sciences Oncology, Logical Therapeutics, Lux Biosciences, MediQuest Therapeutics, Metabolex, NeoMend, NeuroTherapeutics Pharma, Nuevolution, Ophthotech Corporation, Otonomy, PTC Therapeutics, Reata Pharmaceuticals, Santaris Pharma, Symphogen, Synosia Therapeutics, Tarsa Therapeutics, Tobira Therapeutics, Vantia Therapeutics, Xenon Pharmaceuticals

Other Locations:
Novo Ventures US
1700 Owens Street
Suite 450
San Francisco, CA 94158

Key Executives:
Henrik Gürtler, Chief Executive Officer
Directorships: 7TM Pharma, PTC Therapeutics, Santaris Pharma, Arpida
Peter Bisgaard, Partner
Education: MSc, Technical University of Denmark
Background: General Consultant, McKinsey & Co.
Directorships: Altheos, Asante Solutions, Light Science Oncology, Otonomy
Kim L Dueholm, Partner
Education: MSc, Chemistry & Business Administration, Odense University; PhD, Organic Chemistry, University of Copenhagen
Background: Principal Scientific Analyst, Novo Nordisk A/S
Directorships: f-star GmbH, Neurokey
Thomas Dyrberg, Senior Partner
Education: DMSc, MD, University of Copenhagen
Background: Hagedorn Research Institute; Scripps Research Institute; International Clinical Project Manager, Novo Nordisk A/S
Directorships: AlloCure, LifeCycle Pharma, Lux Biosciences, Ophthotech Corporation
Martin W Edwards, Senior Partner
Background: CEO, ReNeuron Holdings; VP, Head of Drug Development, Novo Nordisk A/S; VP, Pharmacology & Medical Affairs, ZymoGenetics; Senior VP, Medical Affairs, Novo Nordisk
Directorships: Funxional Therapeutics, Logical Therapeutics, Tarsa Therapeutics
Heath Lukatch, Partner
Education: BA, Biochemistry, University of California, Berkeley; PhD, Neurosciences, Stanford University
Background: Managing Director, Piper Jaffray Ventures; SightLine Partners; Bench Scientist, Cetus Chiron & Roche Bioscience; McKinsey & Co.; Founder & CEO, AutoMate Scientific
Directorships: Synosia, Amira, Anaptys, Inogen, Neurtherapeutics
Peter Moldt, Partner
Education: PhD, Medicinal Chemistry, Royal Danish School of Pharmacy
Background: Co-Founder, Curalogic; COO, 7TM Pharma; Clinical Drug Development, NeuroSearch
Directorships: Cytochroma
Jack B Nielsen, Partner
Background: R&D Strategy, Novozymes A/S
Directorships: Alios BioPharma, Cell Biosciences, MediQuest Therapeutics, NewMend, Reata Pharmaceuticals, Tobira Therapeutics

3007 NUTEK (NARINGS- OCH TEKNIKUTVECKLINGSVERKET) NUTEK
Götgatan 74
Stockholm 11786
Sweden

Phone: 46-086819100 Fax: 46-488196826
e-mail: tillvaxtverket@tillvaxtverket.se
web: www.tillvaxtverket.se

Mission Statement: Actively seeking new investments

Geographic Preference: Sweden
Investment Criteria: Seed
Industry Group Preference: Manufacturing, Financial Services, Business to Business

Key Executives:
Lars Nyberg, Director & politikområdesansvarig
Sune Halvarsson, Director-General

3008 NVM PRIVATE EQUITY LIMITED
Rotterdam House
116 Quayside
Newcastle-Upon-Tyne NE1 3DY
United Kingdom

Phone: 44-1912446000 Fax: 44-1912446001
web: www.nvm.co.uk

Mission Statement: nVM is independently owned with 25 years experience of investing in UK businesses. Our executives live and work on the ground in regional business communities across the UK. NVM manages over £170 million of funds and is

Venture Capital & Private Equity Firms / International Firms

a generalist investor specializing in making equity investments in UK unquoted companies. We are focused on making equity investments of between £2 million and £10 million.

Geographic Preference: United Kingdom
Fund Size: Euro 170 million
Founded: 1984
Average Investment: Euro 5 Million
Minimum Investment: Euro 2 Million
Investment Criteria: Expansion and Development, MBO, MBI, Public-to-Private, Purchase of quoted shares
Portfolio Companies: Longhurst Group, DMN Installations, Keith Prowse, Stainton Metals, TJ Brent, John Laing Partnership, Omnico Plastics, I G Doors, Pivotal Laboratories

Other Locations:
Forbury Court
12 Forbury Road
Reading RG1 1SB
United Kingdom
Phone: 44-01189517000 **Fax:** 44-01189517001

82 King Street
301 Deansgate
Manchester M2 4WQ
United Kingdom
Phone: 44-01619358419

Key Executives:
Mark R Dixon, CEO
0118-951-7000
e-mail: new@nvm.co.uk
Education: MBA, Cranfield
Background: Officer in the Royal Navy for ten years, he held line management positions with Shell UK and International Paints before becoming general manager of Tremco Limited, the specialist construction products subsidiary of B F Goodrich Inc. He joined Northern I
Directorships: Northern 3 VCT PLC

James Arrowsmith, Investment Team
0118-951-7000
Education: Banking & Finance, Loughborough University
Background: HSBC London; 3i
Directorships: Northern 3 VCT PLC

Chris Mellor, Investment Team
0191-244-6000
e-mail: new@nvm.co.uk
Education: FCA MSI, Physics, chartered accountant with Spicer & Pegler
Background: Chartered accountant with Spicer & Pegler; Northern Investors Company PLC

Norman Yarrow, Investment Team
0162-081-0428
Education: BCom, Edinburgh University; Chartered Accountant, Thomson McLintock
Background: Investment Management; Advisor, Turcan Connell; Non-Executive Director, Dunedin Smaller Companies Investment Trust PLC

Alastair Conn, Investment Team
e-mail: new@nvm.co.uk
Education: Philosophy, politics and economics.
Background: Price Waterhouse in Newcastle

Clive Austin, Investment Manager
0845-272-7023
Education: Read Applied Physics, Durham University; MBA, Warwick University
Background: Consulting, Accenture; 3i; Catapult Venture Managers

Mauro Biagioni, Investment Manager
0191-244-6025
Education: Chartered Accountant, KPMG

Peter Hodson, Investment Manager
0845-272-7014
Education: Read Mechanical Engineering, University of Exeter
Background: BMW Group; 3i

3009 OCTOPUS INVESTMENTS
33 Holborn
London EC1N 2HT
United Kingdom

Toll-Free: 800-316-2295
web: www.octopusinvestments.com

Mission Statement: The Ventures team at Octopus finds and supports talented individuals and exceptional businesses. We're straight-talking, human investors who back people, rather than specific sectors. We look for opportunities that are capable of creating, transforming or dominating an industry.

Portfolio Companies: 21Net, AdBrain, Affectiv, Aframe, Amplience, Artesian, BehavioSec, Vowman, Box-It, Calastone, CertiVox, Coal, Conversocial, CSL DualCom, e-Therapeutics, ECNlive, Ecrebo, Elliptic, Evi, GetLenses.co.uk, Graze.com, Iovox, ITM Power, Kabbee, KeTech, Lovefilm.com, Luther Pendragon, Mailcloud, Metrasens, Mi-Pay, Michelson Diagnostics, Phasor Solutions, Plum, Progility, Property Partners, Rangespan, Reading Room, Secret Escapes, Seedcamp, Semafone, Shopa, SmartKem, Sofar Sounds, StreetHub, Surrey Nanosystems, SwifyKey, Swoon Editions, T4 Media Group, Tails.com, The Faction Collective, The History Press, The Kendal Group, TrialReach, Tristar, Ultra SoC Technologies, UniPlaces, Vega-Chi, YPlan, Zoopla Property Group, Zynstra

Key Executives:
Alan Wallace, Senior Investment Director
Education: BA, Economics, Liverpool University; PhD, Business Administration, University of Manchester
Background: Managing Director, Cambridge Nutrition, Dairy Crest, Premier Brands

3010 OJAS VENTURE PARTNERS
#772, 3rd Floor, 80ft
Peripheral Road
4th Block Koramangala
Bangalore 560 034
India

Phone: +91 80 4061 0300 **Fax:** +91 80 4142 5476
e-mail: pingus@ojasventures.com

Mission Statement: Ojas Venture Parners is a US $35 Million, India-focused early stage venture capital financing & investing firm investing in technology based businesses and other businesses that use technology in innovative ways to create high growth business opportunities. Typically, from our first fund corpus of US $35 Million, we make an initial investment of US $250,000 to US $1.5 Million and follow that by participating in subsequent rounds up to a maximum of US $3 Million per company over the life of the company.

Geographic Preference: India
Fund Size: $35 million
Investment Criteria: Early Stage
Industry Group Preference: Mobile Apps, Telecommunications, Embedded Software, Web Applications & Services, Consumer Internet, Low Capex Semiconductor, Enterprise Software, Technology-Enabled Business
Portfolio Companies: Tyfone, Ziva Software, Mango Technologies, Vizury, CoCubes.Com, Radiowalla, BrizzTV, Telibrahma, RiverSilica, Insieve, Cbazaar

Key Executives:
Dr. Rajesh Srivathsa, Managing Partner
e-mail: rajesh@ojasventures.com
Education: BT, National Institute Of Technology Karnataka at Suratkal; MS, University of Texas at Austin; Ph.D, University of Illinois at Urbana-Champaign
Background: Mobile Terminals Business Unit (MTBU), Aricent, Inc; CTO, Emuzed

Pavan Krishnamurthy, Partner
e-mail: pavan@ojasventures.com
Education: BS, Mathematics, Economics, & Statistics
Background: Nadathur Holdings; SRW Advisors;

Syndicated Research Group; Ernst & Young; Price Waterhouse
Gautam Balijepalli, Partner
e-mail: gautam@ojasventures.com
Education: BT, Indian Institute of Technology, Madras; MBA, London Business School
Background: Nomura; Business Development, Sun Microsystems
Raghu Batta, Partner
e-mail: raghu@ojasventures.com
Education: BE, Manipal Institute of Technology; MBA, Baruch College
Background: VantagePoint Venture Partners; Madge Networks; Bay Networks; Assured Access; Alcatel; CopperCom

3011 OMNES CAPITAL
37-41 rue de Rocher
Paris 75008
France

Phone: 33-0180487900 **Fax:** 33-0142934855
web: www.omnescapital.com

Mission Statement: Omnes Capital, a leading name in private equity, is directly involved in financing the economy by providing companies with the equity needed to expand. It thus helps to drive growth, innovation and job creation. We play the role of an active shareholder, working with the managers of the companies in which we invest and sharing with them a single commercial and strategic vision of how best to pursue their expansion plans. As the leading equity investor in French SMEs, Omnes Capital works on a daily basis to support 160 businesses and infrastructure projects.
Investment Criteria: All Stages
Industry Group Preference: Energy, Life Sciences, Renewable Energy
Portfolio Companies: ACCO, AEMI, AT Internet, Abakus Solar, Abcia, Adamence, Adictiz, Amakem, Ameos, Annonay Productions France, Arcarios, Ariane Systems, Armatis, Bailtrand, CMR Group, COIFF'Idis, CPC, CaméRus, Cellnovo, Compin Group, Complix, Conexia Energy, Confortvisuel.com, Cooltech Applications, Cytheris, Daltys, Delete, Deny all, Diam, EA Pharma, ERA Biotech, Edagora, Elettrostudio Energia, Elettrostudio Energia Infrastructure, Enterome, Eptica, Eratome, European Games Group, ExaProtect, Exclusive Networks, Exosun, EyeTechCare, Fine Sounds Group, FlexGen, Fondis Electronic, France Géothermie, Futures, Gerard Darel, Gecko Biomedical, Greenbureau, Groupe BPS, Groupe Eyssautier, Groupe Hermés-Métal Yudigar, Roupe Pommier, Groupe Unafinance, HTI, Heidrich, Hermés Métal, Ikaros Solar, Ividence, Keldelice, Labco, Les Fréres Blanc, Lyonnaise de Garantie, METabolic EXporer, MONCLER, Medisse, Minimax Viking Group, Mister Bell, Multitec, Neoen Netzoptiker, Nomios, Novate Medical, Numericable, Opsona Therapeutics, Orexo, Oxatis, PanGenetics, Pixium, Pomme de Pain, Porcher Industries, Poste Imo, Poxel, Prodealcenter, Progexia, Qualtera, R&R Ice Cream, RAC, Regency Entertainment, SCT Telecom, SEVE, SIMP, SLG Recycling, SVP, Sateco, Scality, Solar Energies, Solar Participations, SpineGuard, Splendia, Stentys, SuperSonic Imagine, Temis, Tennis Point, Themis, Tiama, Titanobel, Tronic's Micro Systems, TrustYou, Trusted Shops, Turtle Entertainment GmbH, Urbasolar, Valorem, Visiware, Vivalto Santé, Weole Ene
Key Executives:
Fabien Prevost, Chairman
Education: Civil Engineering, Ecole Polytechnique, Ecole National des Ponts et Chaussees; MEng, University of California, Berkeley
Background: Boston Consulting Group
Directorships: AFIC

3012 ONO PHARMACEUTICALS COMPANY LIMITED
8-2, Kyutaromachi 1-chome, Chuo-ku
Chuo-ku
Osaka 541-8564
Japan

Phone: 81-0662635670
web: www.ono.co.jp

Mission Statement: Actively seeking new investments.
Geographic Preference: Japan
Fund Size: $17, 358 Million YEn
Founded: 1717
Industry Group Preference: Medical & Health Related
Key Executives:
Gyo Sagara, President, Representative Director and CEO

3013 OYSTER INVEST
Denmark

Phone: +45 25 68 00 00

Mission Statement: Oyster Invest is a Danish based investment firm, dedicated to tech and startups with a global perspective. We bring entrepreneur expertise to all stages from angel investment to pre IPO, Our portfolio currently consists of a variety of companies engaged in both software, hardware and mobile.
Investment Criteria: Start-Up
Industry Group Preference: Technology, Software, Hardware, Mobile
Portfolio Companies: Meedor, Responsfabrikken, BlueTown, Axcess, A-Solutions
Key Executives:
Peter Warnoe, Owner

3014 OneVentures
Suite 13.02
179 Elizabeth St.
Sydney NSW 2000
Australia

Phone: +62 2 8205 7379
e-mail: admin@one-ventures.com
web: www.one-ventures.com.au

Mission Statement: OneVentures is one of Australia's leading venture capital firms, with over $320M in funds under management. The OneVentures Team applies their years of experience, expertise, operational and executional excellence to accelerate the growth of OneVentures portfolio companies and launch them into global markets. Our Investment Team has helped create 5 Nasdaq and 3 ASX listed companies, and realised returns to investors of over $1 billion.
Geographic Preference: Australia
Fund Size: $330 million
Founded: 2010
Minimum Investment: $1.5 million
Investment Criteria: Seed, Start Up, Early Expansion
Industry Group Preference: Telecommunications, Information Technology, New Media, Clean Technology, Life Sciences, Healthcare, SaaS
Portfolio Companies: 8i, BiVACOR, Blade Therapeutics, Clinical Genomics, Employment Hero, Find-Me Technologies, Hatchtech, Madorra, OVO Mobile, Paragen Bio, Prota Therapeutics, Smart Sparrow, Vaxxas
Other Locations:
The Precint, Level 2
315 Brunswick St.
Fortitude Valley QLD 4006
Australia

C/O FB Rice
Level 14
90 Collins St.

Melbourne VIC 3000
Australia

Key Executives:
Dr. Michelle Deaker, Managing Partner and Executive Director
Education: BS, University of Sydney; MS, University of Sydney; PhD, Applied Science, University of Canberra
Background: Founder, E Com Industries
Directorships: 8i, Smart Sparrow, Incoming Media, Employment Hero
Dr. Paul Kelly, General Partner & Executive Director
Education: MBBS, MD, University of New South Wales; FRACP
Background: CEO, Medcenter Holdings Inc; President and CEO, Orchid Cellmark; CEO, Gemini Genomics; Researcher and Physician at St. Vincent's Hospital, Sydney, Australia; Research Physician, Garvan Institute for Medical Research, Co-Founder, MEARS Technologies; Co-Founder, AgaMatrix
Directorships: Vaxxas, Clinical Genomics, Find-Me Technologies, Hatchtech, Agamatrix, Garvan Institute of Medical Research
Anne-Marie Birkill, General Partner & Executive Director
Education: BSc, Flinders University; MBA, The University of Queensland; FIML; GAICD
Background: CEO, i.lab Incubator; UniQuest
Directorships: Find-Me Technologies, Madorra, Paragen Bio, Creative Enterprises Australia, Advance Queensland Business Development Fund, AVCAL

3015 PAC-LINK MANAGEMENT CORP.
13Fl. 2. Tun Hwa South Road, Sec.2
Taipei
Taiwan

Phone: +866-2-2755-5000 **Fax:** +866-2-2755-2000
web: www.paclinkventure.com

Mission Statement: Pac-Link seeks to invest in companies in which our unique resources and insights can generate significant gains for all shareholders. We work closely with company managers to minimize risks, maximize opportunities, and help build rapidly growing businesses in Asia and North America. Pac-Link connects the best of emerging companies with the best business relationships to achieve maximum growth potential.

Geographic Preference: Asia, North America
Fund Size: $370 million
Founded: 1998
Industry Group Preference: Automotive, Semiconductors, Electronics, Communications, Optical, Software, Information Technology, Life Sciences

Other Locations:
1301 Shoreway Road
Ste 160
Belmont, CA 94002
Phone: 650-857-0686

Key Executives:
Allen Hsu
Education: BS, Managemnt Science, Chiao Tung University in Taiwan; MBA, Cheng-Chi University in Taiwan
Background: Current Vice Executive Officer, Yulon Group Headquarters
Directorships: Altek Technology Corp, Taiwan Mask Corp, Century-Myson Semiconductor Corp
Ming Hsu, President
Education: BS, Communication Engineering, Chiao Tung University in Taiwan; MS, Computer and Electrical Engineering, North Carolina State University in Raleigh
Background: Founder and President, Elite Group Computer Systems; Founder, APAQ
Bill Shelander, Managing Director
Education: BS, Systems Engineering, Georgia Institute of Technology; MSE, Chemical Engineering, West Virginia College of Graduate Studies; MBA, Stanford University
Background: Chairmand and CEO, Micronics Computers; Co-President, JAFCO America Ventures Inc; National Product Manager, Liquid Air Corporation; Systems Engineer, Union Carbide
Directorships: Wavesat, CrossFiber, GlobalLocate, BrightPlanet

3016 PACIFIC EQUITY PARTNERS PTY LIMITED
Level 31, 126 Phillip Street
Sydney 2000
Australia

Phone: 61-282382600
web: www.pep.com.au

Mission Statement: focusing on buyouts and late stage expansion capital
Geographic Preference: Australia, New Zealand
Fund Size: $2.5 Billion
Founded: 1998
Average Investment: $500 Million
Minimum Investment: $6 Million
Investment Criteria: Buy-outs, Late Stage, Expansions
Industry Group Preference: All Sectors Considered
Portfolio Companies: Spotless, Energy Developments, American Stock Transfer & Trust Company, Veda, Xtralis, Link Market Services

Key Executives:
Rickard Gardell, Managing Director
e-mail: information@pep.com.au
Education: Rickard received a BSc/MSc from the Stockholm School of Economics where he was awarded Carl Liljevalchs Scholar and an IMP Scholar attending McGill University Graduate School of Management.
Background: Founder PE, Director of Bain & Company
Directorships: Board of Link MS Group & A&R Whitcoulls
Cameron Blanks, Managing Director

3017 PAI MANAGEMENT
232, rue de Rivoli
Paris 75054
France

Phone: 33-143166300 **Fax:** 33-143166389
e-mail: pai.paris@paipartners.com
web: www.paimanagement.com

Mission Statement: PAI Management operates PAI LBO Fund, future funds to be created and Paribas direct investments (Paribas Affaires Industrielles) on a contractual basis.

Geographic Preference: Europe
Fund Size: $4.3 billion
Founded: 1994
Average Investment: $100 and $300 million
Minimum Investment: $5 Million
Investment Criteria: Mid-sized companies with High Growth, LBO
Industry Group Preference: Media, Communications, Telecommunications, Information Technology, Agribusiness, Pharmaceuticals, Chemicals, Distribution, Engineering, Energy
Portfolio Companies: Custom Sensors & Technologies, DomusVi, EMG, Labeyrie Fine Foods, VPS, R&R Ice Cream, ADB Airfield Solutions, IPH, Marcolin, Kiloutou, Swissport, The Nuance Group, Hunkemoller, Cerba European Lab, Zella, Atos, Kaufman & Broad, Perstorp, Global Closure Systems, Grupo Cortefiel

Key Executives:
Christopher Afors, Investment Director
e-mail: cvarin@cobepa.be
Education: Diploma, Institut d'Etudes Politiques; MBA, Wharton Graduate School of Business; PhD, Business Administration

Venture Capital & Private Equity Firms / International Firms

Background: Paribas-New York, Hong Kong, Singapore; COBEPA
Lionel Zinsou, Partner
Education: Graduate, Ecole des Hautes Etudes Commerciales; Graduate, Ecole Nationale d'Administration
Background: Jean-Marie began his career in the Budget Department of French Ministry of Finance where he was Adviser to the Minister of Finance.
Directorships: Head of Finance Department.
Pauline Ammeux, Investment Officer
Education: Graduate, Ecole des Hautes Etudes Commerciales
Background: Banque Paribas; PAI
Francesco Capurro, Investment Director
Education: Graduate, Institut d'Etudes Politiques; Masters, Economics and Management
Background: Paribas; PAI
Edward Chandler, Partner
Education: Graduate, CPA, Stanford Business School
Background: A.B. Volvo; PAI
Directorships: Chairman and Chief Executive Officer

3018 PAMA GROUP
Hong Kong

Phone: 852-97403373
e-mail: robert@pama.hk
web: www.pama.hk

Mission Statement: Utilizes experience and established working relationships in regional markets to make and support investments.
Geographic Preference: Asia Pacific Region
Fund Size: $500 Million
Average Investment: $30 Million
Minimum Investment: $10 Million
Investment Criteria: Development, Expansion, Buy-In/Buy-Out
Key Executives:
  Robert Suen, CEO
  Education: Brigham Young University; Harvard Graduate School of Business Administration
  Background: General Mills; Continental Grain Company; Richina Group; Asia Access Investment Company
  Timothy CM Chia, President
  Education: Fairleigh Dickinson University
  Background: American International Assurance Company Limited
  Cliff L Cheung, Chief Investment Officer/Managing Director
  Education: University of Hong Kong
  Background: Hamburgische Landesbank
  Tan Yong-Nang, Managing Director
  Education: Cambridge University
  Background: Hamburgische Landesbank

3019 PARKWALK ADVISORS
University House
11-13 Lower Grosvenor Place
London SW1W 0EX
United Kingdom

Phone: 44-2077592285
e-mail: enquiries@parkwalkadvisors.com
web: www.parkwalkadvisors.com

Mission Statement: Parkwalk is a truly independent investment management firm seeking to generate significant capital gains through venture capital investing, enhanced by the attractive tax relief provided by the Enterprise Investment Scheme. Parkwalk is dedicated to providing clients with access to some of the most exciting deal-flow emanating from British R&D intensive institutions and Universities. Parkwalk invests in, and raises capital for, innovative UK technology companies. Parkwalk portfolio companies all have deeply-embedded IP and commercial potential, and range from early stage seed capital, through development and commercial capital to AIM-listed investments.
Geographic Preference: United Kingdom
Founded: 2009
Industry Group Preference: Technology, Internet, Information Technology, Communications, Life Sciences, Clean Technology, Electronics, Semiconductors, Chemicals, Advanced Materials, Medical Technology, Energy, Renewable Power
Portfolio Companies: Fluidic Analytics, TheySay, Salunda, Nandi Proteins, Fuel 3D, Perpetuum, Brainomix, Oxtex, RoadMap, Tracsis, Jukedeck, Vocal IQ, Revise, AQDOT, Symetrica, Omega Diagnostics, Microsaic Systems, Horizon Discovery, Tangentix, Sphere Fluidics, DefiniGEN, Clean Air Power, YASA Motors, Inotec AMD, Cambridge CMOS Sensors, Arkivum, Mode DX, Arvia Technology, Surrey Nanosystems, Reinnervate, Lime Microsystems, Xeros, First Light Fusion, OxfordPV, Revolymer, Acal Energy, Eykona Technolgies

Other Locations:
Atenas 2
Pozuelo de Alarcon
Madrid 28224
Spain
Phone: 34-91-709-1130

Key Executives:
  Alastair Kilgour, CIO
  44-20-7759-2290
  e-mail: akilgour@parkwalkavdisors.com

3020 PARTNERS GROUP
57 Zugerstrasse
Baar 6341
Switzerland

Phone: 41-417846000 Fax: 41-417846001
web: www.partnersgroup.ch

Mission Statement: Partners Group is a Private Equity Asset Manager that invests worldwide, both directly in portfolio companies and as a Limited Partner in more than 2000 Partnerships managed by some of the most renowned Private Equity Managers. We put our extensive multi-
Geographic Preference: Europe, North America, Israel, Asia, Latin America
Fund Size: $8.4 Billion
Founded: 1996
Average Investment: $1.2 Billion
Minimum Investment: $5 Million
Investment Criteria: Invests in companies with Strong Leadership and Growth Potential
Industry Group Preference: All Sectors Considered
Key Executives:
  Alfred Gantner, Co-Founder and Executive Chairman
  Education: He holds a degree from the Swiss Banking School, Zurich, Switzerland.
  Background: Partners Group in the private equity team with responsibilities in buyout partnerships selection and was a member of the private equity investment committee.
  Directorships: Prior to joining Partners Group, Mr. Trommsdorff headed the asset management division at the Cantonal Bank of Zug and worked as a trader and investment manager at the Industri
  Dr. Cyrill Wipfli, Chief Financial Officer
  Education: He holds a degree in business administration from the University of Zurich, Switzerland.
  Background: Was a member of the executive board of Bank Hofmann.
  Directorships: he headed Credit Suisse Private Banking in Germany after assignments at Credit Suisse in Zurich and in the private banking department of Credit Suisse in New York.
  Jurg Wenger, Chief Operating Officer and Head Resources
  Education: He holds a master's degree in business

administration from the University of St. Gallen (HSG), Switzerland
Background: Has held various private equity investment management positions at Partners Group and was instrumental in building Partners Group's portfolio of venture capital investments in Europe and the USA.
Directorships: Prior to joining Partners Group, Mr. Gysler worked for UBS Warburg (now UBS Investment Bank) in Zurich, where he advised institutional clients regarding equities, derivatives

Urs Wietlisbach, Co-Founder and Executive Member
Education: He holds a master's degree in business administration from the University of St. Gallen (HSG), Switzerland.
Directorships: He is a member of the private equity investment committee

Christoph Rubeli, Co-Chief Executive Officer and Head Private Equity Directs
Education: He holds an MBA degree from INSEAD, Paris, and a master's degree in industrial engineering from the Swiss Federal Institute of Technology (ETH), Zurich, Switzerland
Background: Was Head of the Private Equity Investment Management business group, where he was responsible for the firm's private equity partnership, direct and secondary investment activities.
Directorships: Prior to joining Partners Group, Mr. Rubeli spent 11 years at UBS, ultimately as a Singapore-based manager for Southeast Asia, with responsibility for all business units in th

Claude Angeloz, Co-Head Private Real Estate
Education: He holds a master's degree in business administration from the University of St. Gallen (HSG), Switzerland.
Background: Headed the firm's structuring business unit, where he was responsible for developing and structuring Partners Group's private equity transactions and products.
Directorships: Prior to joining Partners Group, Mr. Angéloz spent seven years with Credit Suisse Financial Products in Zurich and London and served as a Director with responsibility for Swis

Dr. Stephan Schali, Head Private Equity
Education: He holds an MBA degree from the University of Chicago and a doctorate and master's degree in business administration from the University of St. Gallen (HSG), Switzerland.
Background: He started in primary partnership investments before assuming responsibility for Partners Group's global secondaries business.
Directorships: Prior to joining Partners Group, Mr. Schäli worked for UBS, where he was a business and management associate with assignments in the firm's branch performance analysis and str

Walter Keller, Private Equity
Education: He holds a degree in economics and business administration from the Zurich University of Applied Sciences, and is a Certified Public Accountant (CPA).
Background: Significant experience in investment origination, valuation, execution and monitoring.
Directorships: Prior to joining Partners Group, Mr. Keller was a member of the transaction group at PriceWaterhouseCoopers with responsibilities in the field of IPOs, mergers & acquisitions

3021 PASSION CAPITAL
White Bear Yard
144a Clerkenwell Road
2nd Floor
London EC1R 5DF
United Kingdom

web: www.passioncapital.com

Mission Statement: We invest in ambitious entrepreneurs who have global ambition for their early stage digital media and technology startups.
Investment Criteria: Early-Stage
Industry Group Preference: Digital Media & Marketing, Technology
Portfolio Companies: Adzuna, Birdback, CarThrottle, Coinfloor, Digital Shadows, DueDil, DueGo, EyeM, Flattr, Future Ad Labs, GoCardless, GoSquared, Lazook, Limejump, Loopcam, Lulu, Mixlr, Narrative, On Device Research, OpenSignal, Pusher, Sho My Homework, Smarkets, Swipe, Thread, Toothpick, Tray.io, Trucktrack, ViCampo, WeDo, Wine In Black, WireWax, Zesty

Key Executives:
    Eileen Burbidge, Founding Partner
    Education: BS, Computer Science, University of Illinois at Urbana-Champaign
    Background: Apple; Sun Microsystems; Skype; PalmSource; Yahoo!
    Directorships: Chair, Tech City UK; Special Envoy, FinTech; Tech Ambassador, Mayor of London's Office

3022 PATHENA
Edificio Peninsula, sala 506
Praça do Bom Sucesso, Nø131
4150-456 Porto
Portugal

Phone: +351 225 430 707
e-mail: info@pathena.com
web: www.pathena.com

Mission Statement: Pathena is a specialized investment firm focused on boosting the success of Information Technology companies.
Investment Criteria: Late Early Stage, Growth Phase
Industry Group Preference: Information Technology, Applied Science, Digital Convergence
Portfolio Companies: Cardmobil, Exago, iMobileMagic, iM3MDICAL, NMusic, Stemmatters, Vortal, MedChronic, i2s

Key Executives:
    Antonio Murta, Managing Partner and Co-Founder
    e-mail: antonio.murta@pathena.com
    Education: Minho University; University of Porto
    Background: Corporate Information Officer, Sonae Distribuicao; Founder and CEO, Enabler; VP of Retail Services, Wipro; Founder, Mobicomp; Founder, ITPeers; Founder, Profimetrics; Founder, QuiiQ; Founder, Cardmobili

    Jorge Brás, Managing Partner and Co-Founder
    e-mail: jorge.bras@pathena.com
    Education: University of Minho
    Background: Co-Founder and COO, Enabler; General Manager-Head of Delivery, Wipro; IT Director, Sonae Retail

3023 PENTECH VENTURES
One Alfred Place
London WC1E 7EB
United Kingdom

Phone: 44-2031287473
e-mail: info@pentechvc.com
web: www.pentechvc.com

Mission Statement: We invest in technology companies, including Internet, social media, e-commerce, digital media, mobile, SaaS, enterprise software, telecom software, and embedded applications companies. We are not prescriptive on quantum or stage, but rather focus on the opportunity, and whether there is a smart, passionate and energetic entrepreneurial team that possesses the determination to build a globally successful business.

Average Investment: £500,000 - 4 million
Investment Criteria: All Stages

Industry Group Preference: Internet, Social Media, E-Commerce & Manufacturing, Digital Media & Marketing, Mobile, SaaS, Telecommunications
Portfolio Companies: Acunu, CertiVox, Critical Blue, FanDuel, Flightman, Maxymiser, Nutmeg, Outplay Entertainment, SecretSales, Semetric/Musicmetric, Struq
Other Locations:
39 Melville Street
Edinburgh EH3 7JF
United Kingdom
Phone: 44-1312408280
Key Executives:
Craig Anderson, Partner
e-mail: craig@pentechvc.com
Background: Chartered Accountant, Arthur Andersen; Group Financial Controller, Kwik-Fit; CFO/COO, Voxar

3024 PERMIRA Permira Advisers LLP
80 Pall Mall
London SW1Y 5ES
United Kingdom
Phone: 44-2076321000 **Fax:** 44-2079303185
web: www.permira.com

Mission Statement: Offering a fresh approach to private equity with eighteen funds.
Geographic Preference: Worldwide
Fund Size: 11 billion euro
Founded: 1985
Average Investment: 50 million - 5 billion euro
Minimum Investment: 50 million euro
Investment Criteria: LBO, LBI, Turnarounds, Growth Buyouts, Acquisitions, Public to private transactions
Industry Group Preference: Business to Business, Chemicals, Consumer Products, Healthcare, Industrial Services, Technology, Industrial Equipment
Portfolio Companies: Akindo Sushiro, Ancestry.com, Rysta LifeScience, Asia Broadcast Satellite, Atrium Innovations, BakerCorp, CABB, Cortefiel, Creganna-Tactx Medical, Dr. Martens, Freescale, Genesys, Hugo Boss, iglo Group, Intelligrated, Just Retirement, LegalZoom, Maxeda DIY Group, MESA and Asteral, Metalogix, Netafim, New Look, OdigeO, Pharmaq, Saga (Acromas), Sisal, TeamViewer, Telepizza, Tilney Bestinvest
Other Locations:
Permira Beteiligungsberatung GmBH
Bockenheimer Landstrasse 33
Frankfurt am Main 60325
Germany
Phone: 49-699714660 **Fax:** 49-6997146699

Plaza del Marques de Salamanca, 10
Primero Izquierda
Madrid 28006
Spain
Phone: 34-914182499 **Fax:** 34-914261193

320 Park Avenue
33rd Floor
New York, NY 10022-4690
Phone: 212-3867480 **Fax:** 212-3867481

Permira Associati SpA
Via San Paolo 10
Milan 20121
Italy
Phone: 39-0276004740 **Fax:** 39-0276004706

Permira Advisers KB
Birger Jarlsgatan 12
Stockholm 114 34
Sweden
Phone: 46-850312200 **Fax:** 46-850312299

Permira Advisers KK
Akasaka Intercity Building 3F
1-11-44 Akasaka
Minato-ku, Tokyo 107-0052
Japan
Phone: 81-0362302051 **Fax:** 81-0362302052
Key Executives:
Kurt Björklund, Co-Managing Partner
212-386-7480
Fax: 212-386-7481
e-mail: allen.haight@permira.com
Education: BBA, Washington & Lee University; MBA, University of Virginia
Background: KPMG; Chemical Bank
Guido Paolo Gamucci, Chairman
39 02 76 00 47 40
Fax: 39 02 76 00 47 06
e-mail: guido.gamucci@permira.com
Education: Mechanical Engineering degree, University of Rome, Italy; MBA, INSEAD, France
Background: Founding Partner/Managing Director, UBS Capital, Italy; Deputy Head Investment Banking, Citicorp
Veronica Eng, Partner/Operating Committee
44 207 632 1000
Fax: 44 207 497 2174
e-mail: veronica.eng@permira.com
Education: BBA, University of Singapore
Background: Head Corporate Finance, Schroder Investment Bank, Singapore
Gianluca Andena, Partner
39 02 76 00 47 40
Fax: 39 02 76 00 47 06
e-mail: gianluca.andena@permira.com
Education: BBA, Bocconi University
Background: Sales/Marketing, Pirelli Group
Paolo Colonna, Partner
39 02 76 00 47 40
e-mail: paolo.colonna@permira.com
Education: Chemical Engineering degree, Politecnico di Torino; MBA, Harvard Business School
Background: Co-Founder, several small MBOs; VP Planning/Marketing, Italsider; McKinsey & Company, Chigao and Milan
Mike Garland, Partner
44 207 632 1000
e-mail: mike.garland@permira.com
Education: Mechanical Engineering degree, University of Southampton, England; Chartered Accountant
Background: Finance Director, Williams Holdings; Price Waterhouse, London
Paul Armstrong, Principal
46 8 503 122 00
e-mail: kurt.bjorklund@permira.com
Education: Economics degree, Swedish School of Economics and Business Administration, Finland; MBA, INSEAD; Graduate studies, Rensselaer Polytechnic Institute
Background: Boston Consulting Group, Stockholm; IT reseller, Finland
Philip Bassett, Partner
44 207 632 1000
e-mail: philip.bassett@permira.com
Education: Classics degree, Oxford University; Chartered Accountant
Background: Fundraising/Investor Communications, Schroder Ventures
Martin Clarke, Partner
44 207 632 1000
e-mail: martin.clarke@permira.com
Education: MA, PhD History, Cambridge University
Background: Senior Director, PPMV
Fidel Baptista, Organisational Professional
44 207 632 1000
e-mail: guy.davies@permira.com
Education: BS Economics, London School of Economics; Chartered Accountant
Background: Price Waterhouse

Venture Capital & Private Equity Firms / International Firms

Audinga Besusparyte, Investment Professional
49 69 97 14 66 0
Education: BBA, Frankfurt University; Programme for Management Development, Harvard Business School
Background: Audit/Corporate Finance, Arthur Andersen, Frankfurt
Robert Van Goethem, Partner
33 1 40 73 85 00
Education: BBA, University of Louvain-la-Neuve, Belgium; Law degree, Universities of Louvain and Antwerp; MBA, University of Chicago
Background: Director, Salomon Barney, London; Leveraged Finance, Citibank, London; Chase Manhattan Bank, NY
Uwe Kolb, Partner
49 69 97 14 66 0
e-mail: uwe.kolb@permira.com
Education: MBA, Saarbrucken University
Background: Managing Partner, PwC Transaction Services, Germany

3025 PHENOMEN VENTURES
Russia

web: www.linkedin.com/company/3258746

Mission Statement: Phenomen Ventures is a venture capital investment firm focused on internet and tech phenomenons.

Industry Group Preference: Internet, Technology

3026 PHILLIP MUTUAL BERHAD
B-2-7, Megan Avenue II
12, Jalan Yap Kwan Seng
Kuala Lumpur 50450
Malaysia

Phone: 603-27830300 Fax: 603-27113036
e-mail: phillipmutual@poems.com.my
web: www.phillipmutual.com

Mission Statement: The Malaysian unit trust management company of the Phillip Capital Group. It is approved by the Securities Commission to carry out unit trust management business.

Founded: 2002
Key Executives:
En. Mohd Fadzli Bin Mohd Anas, Chief Executive Officer

3027 PHOENIX EQUITY PARTNERS LIMITED
25 Bedford Street
London WC2E 9ES
United Kingdom

Phone: 44-02074346999 Fax: 44-02030041496
e-mail: enquiries@phoenix-equity.com
web: www.phoenix-equity.com

Mission Statement: Formerly known as DLJ European Private Equity Limited, an independent provider of equity financing for UK, middle-market management buy-outs, buy-ins and expansion capital transactions.

Geographic Preference: United Kingdom
Fund Size: $619 Million
Founded: 2001
Average Investment: $88 Million
Minimum Investment: $1.7 Million
Investment Criteria: Buy-outs and Buy-ins, Expansion
Industry Group Preference: Transportation, Logistics, Consumer Services, Leisure, Retailing, Education, Healthcare, Industrial Services, Media
Portfolio Companies: Andrew Page, Ashtead Technology, Busaba Eathai, CloserStill, Edif Group, Global Navigation Solutions, Just Childcare, Karma Communications Group, Key Retirement, LK Bennett, Musto, Palletways, Porthaven Care Homes, Radley, Riviera Travel, Signum Technology, The Gym, Vivid Toy Group

Key Executives:
Sandy Muirhead, Managing Partner
Hugh Lenon, Chairman
020-74346987
e-mail: hugh.lenon@phoenix-equity.com
Background: Chartered Accountant, Touche Ross
Directorships: Palletways

3028 PHOSPHAGENICS
11 Duerdin Street
Clayton VIC 3168
Australia

Phone: 1300 354-942 Fax: 61-0395651151

Mission Statement: Phosphagenics is a pharmaceutical and neutraceutical comapny with a diversified portfolio of technologies encompassing drug delivery, drug enhancement, and active ingredients for dietary supplements, functional foods and personal care products.

Geographic Preference: Worldwide
Founded: 1993
Industry Group Preference: Plastics, Biotechnology
Key Executives:
Harry Rosen, President & Chief Executive Officer
e-mail: info@phosphagenics.com
Education: B.A. Psychology, LLB
Background: Attorney for 10 years, specializing in taxation and corporate law and Founders of Betatene Ltd and Denehurst Ltd , Vice-President, Corporate Development. President of Henkel Corporation
Jonathan Addison, Chairman and Independent Director
e-mail: info@phosphagenics.com
Education: BVsc, MVPM
Background: Director of, the Mackinnon Project at the University of Melbourne
Directorships: Non-executive Director of Ridley Corporation Ltd, Animal Health Australia Ltd, Primesafe, the Australian Sheep Industry Cooperative Research Centre and the Zoological Parks an
Sandra Webb, Independent Director
e-mail: info@phosphagenics.com
Education: BSc. (Hons), & PhD
Background: Asia/Pacific Director in charge of the Nutrition and Health Division of Cognis, Managing Director of Betatene
Directorships: Managing Director of Betatene
Don Clarke, Independent Director
e-mail: info@phosphagenics.com
Education: BS, MD, FACP, FRACP
Background: Director of the Macfarlane Burnet Institute for Medical Research
Directorships: Managing Director of Advanced Diagnostic Concepts Ltd, a consulting physician at the Alfred and Austin Hospitals, a non-executive Director of GBS Venture Partners Ltd and Mana
Stuart James, Independent Director
e-mail: info@phosphagenics.com
Education: BSc (Hons) PhD
Background: Dr Ogru conducted research at Monash University's Department of Biochemistry and Molecular Biology for Metabolic Pharmaceuticals Limited

3029 PINEHURST ADVISORS
Tokyo
Japan

e-mail: info@pinehurstadvisors.com
web: www.pinehurstadvisors.com

Mission Statement: Pinehurst Advisors is an early stage angel/seed fund management company with an investment focus in the internet media, mobile, and ecommerce space.

Founded: 2010
Investment Criteria: Seed Stage, Early-Stage

Industry Group Preference: Internet, Media, Mobile, E-Commerce & Manufacturing
Portfolio Companies: Cacafly, Cubie, Replaid, East District, Goodlife, Bosslady, e27, Viscovery, Gamelet, QLL, Cycle Taiwan, WritePath
Key Executives:
Mark Hsu, Partner
Background: Co-Founder, Sinanet; Co-Founder, KKBox; Co-Founder & Partner, TMIÆHolding
Kevin Chen, Partner
Background: COO, Laureate China; Managing Director, Ingram Micro Hong Kong; Head of M&A, Ingram Micro Asia
Munetaka Takahashi, Partner
Background: Managing Director, Hedgecafe.com; CFO, GABA Corp.

3030 PITANGO VENTURE CAPITAL
11 HaMenofim St. Building B
Herzliya 46725
Israel
Phone: 972-99718100 Fax: 972-99718102
e-mail: pitango@pitango.com
web: www.pitango.com

Mission Statement: Israel's largest venture capital firm and a lead investor in seed, early stage and expansion stage companies.
Geographic Preference: Israel
Fund Size: $1.3 Billion
Founded: 1993
Average Investment: $50 Million
Investment Criteria: Seed, Early-Stage, Expansion-Stage
Industry Group Preference: Communications, Software, Infrastructure, Wireless Technologies, Networking, Storage, Medical & Health Related, Semiconductors, Internet Technology, Mobile Communications Devices, Clean Technology
Other Locations:
Pitango Silicon Valley
540 Cowper St.
Suite 200
Palo Alto, CA 94301
Phone: 1-6503222201 Fax: 1-6504731347
Key Executives:
Rami Kalish, Managing General Partner & Co-Founder
Education: B.Sc. in Industrial Engineering and Information Science from the Technion Institute of Technology
Background: Garnered rich managerial experience at high-technology firms in the U.S., Europe and Israel. He previously held sales and marketing positions at IBM and senior executive roles at Orbotech
Directorships: Serves on the Board of Directors of Surf, CTI2, ForeScout, Comsys, and VCON (La Nouveau Marche).
Nechemia (Chemi) J Peres, Managing General Partner & Co-Founder
Education: MBA degree and a Bachelor of Science degree in Industrial Engineering & Management from Tel Aviv University
Background: Founded and managed the Mofet Israel Technology Fund, VP Marketing and Business Development at Decision Systems Israel (DSI), and a Senior Consultant to Israel Aircraft Industries (IAI). Mr. Peres served as a pilot in the Israeli Air Force for 10 years.
Directorships: Board of Dir: Olive Software; Provident; Speedbit; Voltaire; Precede Technologies. Founder & Chairman of IVA (Israel Venture Assoc.); serves on the Board of MOIT Seed Fund.
Aaron Mankovski, General Managing Partner
e-mail: aaron.m@pitango.com
Education: B.Sc. in Computer Science and Statistics from Tel Aviv University
Background: Co-founded Eucalyptus Ventures, and served as Managing Director; 16 years of experience in Executive Management (CEO, Sales and Marketing) in the high-technology sector in Israel and abroad he served as Corporate Vice President of Orbotech Ltd.
Directorships: Serves on the Board of Directors of Optimal-Test, Precede Technologies, Kilopass Technology Inc.; Compass-EOS; Kaminario and Jinko Solar in China
Isaac Hillel, General Managing Partner
e-mail: isaac.h@pitango.com
Education: B.Sc. in Electrical Engineering from Tel Aviv University and an M.B.A. from the Anderson School of Management at UCLA
Background: Executive Vice President at NEC Computers International, Board member of nine subsidiaries of NEC, a member of NEC's Executive Committee, and Chairman of its Worldwide Internet Strategy Committee; Casio PhoneMate.
Directorships: Serves on the Board of Directors of: AeroScout; 51 Global Ecommerce (formerly E4X); Winbuyer; Techtium; Celeno Communications; Discretix
Rami Beracha, General Managing Partner
e-mail: rami.b@pitango.com
Education: J.D. from Tel Aviv University, L.L.M. from Fordham University, NY, and M.B.A. from INSEAD, France
Background: Practiced law in New York at the corporate financing department of Fried, Frank, Harris, Shriver and Jacobson, a leading Wall Street law firm.
Directorships: Currently serves on the Board of Directors of Annobit; Convergin; dbMotion; Fixya; MobileAccess Newrworks; mySupermarket; Optier; Neebula
Zeev Binman, General Partner & Chief Financial Officer
Education: BA, Economics, MBA, Finance, Tel Aviv University
Background: Vice President, Finance, PazGas; Vice President, Finance, Fibronics International USA; referent for the defense industries in the Budget Department of the Israel Ministry of Finance
Directorships: Galil Medical

3031 PITON CAPITAL
Venture House
5th Floor
27-29 Glasshouse Street
London W1B 5DF
United Kingdom
Phone: 44-2074080451
e-mail: info@pitoncap.com
web: www.pitoncap.com

Mission Statement: Choosing network economics as the focus of our investments means that we contribute the most valuable part of our knowledge and experience to the right businesses. And this lets us continually learn and improve our input to the companies we invest in.
Industry Group Preference: Internet, E-Commerce & Manufacturing
Portfolio Companies: Watchfinder & Co., Quandoo, BundleTech, JamesEdition, Videdressing, 3Scale, MBA & Company, BullionVault, DaWanda, FanDuel, DocPlanner
Key Executives:
Andrin Bachmann, Managing Director
e-mail: andrin.bachmann@pitoncap.com
Education: MSc, Computer Science, Swiss Federal Institute of Technology
Background: Co-Founder, Glocalnet; Partner, M/C Venture Partners

Venture Capital & Private Equity Firms / International Firms

3032 PLUS VENTURES
A 283, 1st Floor
Defence Colony
New Delhi 110024
India

Phone: 91-1141012350 **Fax:** 91-1141654689
web: www.plusventures.com

Mission Statement: Plus Ventures is an early-stage venture capital investment firm. We look to invest in extraordinary entrepreneurs and support them to build great teams that create superior companies. Plus Ventures investments are primarily focused on technology enabled products and services in sectors like Internet, Mobile, Education and Consumer Services.

Geographic Preference: India
Average Investment: $500,000 - $3 million
Investment Criteria: Early-Stage
Industry Group Preference: Technology-Enabled Services, Internet, Mobile, Education, Consumer Services
Portfolio Companies: Gridstone Research, Accela Media, Info Pro Solutions

Other Locations:
1000, Route 9 North
Suite 102
Woodbridge, NJ 07095
Phone: 732-8959432

Key Executives:
Vivek Bansal, Founder/Managing Director
Education: Engineering Degree, MS University, India; MS, Computer Science, Kansas State University
Background: EVP/General Manager, GlobespanVirata

3033 PMV
Oude Graanmarkt 63
Brussels 1000
Belgium

Phone: 02-229-5230 **Fax:** 02-229-5231
e-mail: seed@pmv.eu
web: www.pmv.eu

Mission Statement: PMV provides risk capital to innovative starters and young companies in their initial growth phase. Through its sub-offer of risk capital in this phase, PMV plays a key catalytic role. At the same time, PMV mainly considers those businesses that can demonstrate a major potential for creating added value for their stakeholders in Flanders. In this sense, PMV wants to help create the future motors of Flemish prosperity.

Geographic Preference: Belgium
Investment Criteria: Seed Stage, Early-Stage
Industry Group Preference: Clean Technology, Information Technology, Life Sciences, Real Estate, Infrastructure, Renewable Energy
Portfolio Companies: 2Rivers/Yesplan, Absynthe Minded, AescAp Venture, Agrosavfe, Alvey, Amakem Therapeutics, Aminolabs, Any Media, Apitope, Arcarios, Arendsoog, Arkavund Media, Ark-Angels Fund, ARKimedes, Asia Pacific Carbon Fund, Baby Belle, Baekeland Fonds, Bedrijvencentrum Waasland, Belwind, Big Bang Ventures, Biocartis, Biofer, Biotech Fonds Vlaanderren, Boma International, Bout'chou, Bumba, Cafe Costume, Caliopa, Capital-E, Cartagenia, Choupettes, Citymesh, Clear2Pay, Cmosis, Complix, Dacentec, De Boelekes, Deborah Centrum, De Kleine Kikker, De Kleine Wereld, Deme Blue Energy, Den Berenboot, De Toverboom, De Zebra, Dink, Dou-Dou, Drie Pees, Dsquare, Ducatt, Duimelotje, Eastvillage, Eco Projects, Electrawinds, Engeltjes & Bengeltjes, Ensamblage, Esaturnus, Excico Group, Exuvis, Ffpharma, Fien En Mile, Filoukes, Flanders' Drive, Formac Pharmaceuticals, Fringilunch, GDM Electronics, Gigarant, Ginsenga, Goednavond, Grenslandhallen, Het Engeltje, High Wind, Ikaros Solar Fund, Iparc, ISPC, Intineris, Judas Theatreproducteies, Kabron, KBC Arkiv, Kelst, Kids Garden, Kids Kitchen, Kmofin Arkiv, La Luna, Larian Publishing, Layerwise, LRM, Madoc, Ma Maison Fleur, Michael Verheyden, Moeke, Morthier Catering, Multiplicom, Newtec, Niceberg Studios, NMDG Engineering, Novovil, Office Baroque Gallery, Okapi Sciences, Vof Clemence & Juliette, V2W Fun4kids, Waarborgeheer

Key Executives:
Clair Ysebaert, Chairman

3034 POD INVESTMENT
Grev Turegatan 19
Stockholm 114 38
Sweden

Phone: 46-854506460 **Fax:** 46-854506469
e-mail: info@podinvestment.com
web: www.podinvestment.se

Mission Statement: We aim to build the next generation of internationally successful Nordic growth companies. We invest in companies with turnovers from 5 to 50 million Euros. As owners we add value by actively providing competence and capital.

Founded: 2000
Portfolio Companies: Adra Match, Birdstep, op5, STING Capital, Transmode

3035 POINT NINE CAPITAL
Germany

e-mail: info@pointninecap.com
web: www.pointninecap.com

Mission Statement: Like all good angel investors, we are a friendly source of capital with lots of additional value-add. We strive to become your mentors, someone who you can trust and who you're happy to call in good AND in bad times. At the same time you benefit from our ability to invest much larger amounts of capital, as well as the extensive expertise and network of all of our partners.

Geographic Preference: Europe, Germany, Poland
Average Investment: 100,000 - 500,000 Euro
Investment Criteria: Early-Stage
Industry Group Preference: Internet, SaaS, E-Commerce & Manufacturing, Mobile
Portfolio Companies: 15Five, Algolia, Bitbond, Brainly, Ciband, Clio, Combatant Gentlement, Contactually, Contentful, CouchSurfing, DaWanda, Delivery Hero, DigitaleSeiten, Docplanner.com, ePetWorld GmbH, Gengo, Handshake, Hipclub, inFakt, Infogr.am, Jobber, Kekemeke, Kreditech, Lieferheld, Mambu, Mention, Mister Spex, Mobilike, Oferteo.pl, Pomocni.pl, Positionly, PurMeo, Risk Methods, Roomorama, Scondoo, ShiftPlanning, Spinnakr, SponsorPay, StyleSeat, Typeform, Unbounce, Userfox, Vend, Westwing, Wirkaufens, Xeneta

Key Executives:
Pawel Chudzinski, Co-Founder/Managing Partner
Education: Leipzig Graduate School of Management
Background: Co-Founder, Team Europe; Associate, Greenhill & Co.

3036 POLYTECH VENTURES
Ecole Polytechnique Federale de Lausanne
Innovation Park
Batiment E
Ecublens CH-1015
Switzerland

Phone: 41-0-21-693-9210
e-mail: gdubray@polytechventures.ch
web: www.polytechventures.ch

Mission Statement: An early stage VC firm based in Switzerland with a strong international focus.

Geographic Preference: Switzerland
Founded: 2008
Investment Criteria: Early-Stage

Industry Group Preference: Information Technology, Digital Media & Marketing, Healthcare Information Technology
Portfolio Companies: Beam Express, Lotaris, Netguardians, Abionic, Slyde, Typesafe, Bugbuster, Paper.li, Seevibes
Key Executives:
Alexandre Cadosch, Chairman
e-mail: acadosch@eurofin.ch
Education: Hospitality Mangement, Ecole Hoteliere de Lausanne
Background: Vice President, Gestar SA; Tradition Financial Services

3037 POLYTECHNOS VENTURE PARTNERS GmbH
12 Promenadeplatz
Munich 80333
Germany

Phone: 49-0892422620 Fax: 49-08924226221

Mission Statement: PolyTechnos Venture-Partners is a leading independent European venture capital firm based in Munich, Germany, with a track record of building world class technology companies.

Geographic Preference: Europe
Fund Size: $240 Million
Founded: 1998
Average Investment: EUR 5 - 15 Million
Minimum Investment: $6 Million
Investment Criteria: Early to Expansion Stage
Industry Group Preference: Information Technology, Communications, Microelectronics, Life Sciences
Portfolio Companies: Cappella, IMI Intelligent Medical Implants AG, ColorChip, DBD Deutsche Breitband Dienste GmbH, Innolume GmbH, Media Lario Technologies, Nanotron Technologies GmbH, Panoratio Database Images, Power Paper, Vaioptic

Key Executives:
Tonio Barlage, Partner
Education: MBA, PhD Physics
Background: Monsanto, Product development manager at Zeneca, Senior research scientist at ICI Advanced Materials division
Knut Heitmann, Partner
e-mail: knut.heitmann@polytechnos.com
Education: Degree in electrical engineering from the Technical University of Darmstadt.
Background: Siemens, Proctor & Gamble, Baring, Managing director of Freiberger Compound Materials, Director of the technology monitoring division,
Dirk Kanngiesser, Founder, Managing Partner (IT)
Education: Electrical engineering from the Technical University of Dortmund, Germany, and his MBA from the University of Michigan.
Background: McKinsey, Bosch, Quandt, venture capital,
Directorships: Partner of Baring Private Equity Partners,
Dan Maher, Partner
Education: MBA from the Heriot-Watt University in Edinburgh, a graduate of the Harvard Graduate Business School's Advanced Management Program, a degree from the Basel School of Business & Economics.
Background: Monsanto, EuropaBio and the U.S.-China business council,
Dr. Lee Schalop, Partner
e-mail: eric.achtmann@polytechnos.com
Education: B.S. in mechanical engineering, M.S. in aeronautics & astronautics from MIT, post-graduate degree from the Von Karman Institute for Fluid Dynamics, Belgium, He received his MBA from the MIT.
Background: MS, MBA, McKinsey & Co., BMW, Daimler-Benz Aerospace, and McDonnell-Douglas, Petrotech International
Directorships: Board member or observer

3038 POND VENTURES
Grand Prix House
102-104 Sheen Road
Richmond
Surrey TW9 1UF
United Kingdom

Phone: 44-0-20-8940-1001

Mission Statement: Our team in Silicon Valley, London & Israel is dedicated to building technology into global success stories. We focus on investing in ideas which start in any of our geographies, but whose success is destined to be Worldwide.

Geographic Preference: United States, Europe, Israel
Investment Criteria: Early-Stage
Industry Group Preference: Energy, Water, New Media, Software, Consumer Products, Consumer Services
Portfolio Companies: 4Home, LiveRail, Broadway Networks, Gigle Networks, Nanotech Semiconductor, Microcosm Commnications, Transitive, PicoChip, ACCO, Mekanist, Swapit, Emefcy

Other Locations:
2033 Gateway Place
Suite 600
San Jose, CA 95110
Phone: 408-467-3806

Ackerstein Towers
Building B, 5th Floor
11, Hamenofim Street
Herzliya Pituach 46120
Israel
Phone: 972-2-971-6010

Key Executives:
Richard Irving, Co-Founder
e-mail: richard@pondventures.com
Education: BSc, MSc, Electrical Engineering, Manchester University
Background: Technical Staff, Bell Labs; Strategic Marketing Manager, AMD
Directorships: Acco Semiconductor, Emefcy
Charles Irving, Co-Founder
Education: Kingston University
Background: Glencore

3039 PORTUGAL CAPITAL VENTURES
Institutional Headquarters
Av. Dr. Antuens Guimaraes, 103
Porto 4100-079
Portugal

Phone: 351-226-165-390 Fax: 351-226-102-089
e-mail: contact@portugalventures.pt
web: www.portugalventures.pt

Mission Statement: We aim to improve the competitiveness of the Portuguese economy by investing in cutting edge industries and technologies.

Geographic Preference: Portugal
Fund Size: 600 million euros
Investment Criteria: All Stages
Industry Group Preference: Industrial, Energy, Tourism, Transportation, Technology, Life Sciences, Creative Industries
Portfolio Companies: A. Silva & Silva, Abyssal, ACH BRITO & CIA, AJP Motos, Aldeia da Pedralva - Empreend. Turisticos, Alert Life Sciences Computing, Anusbisnetworks, Aptoide, Arlant, BERD, Biomode, Biosurfit, Biotrend - Inovacao e Engenharia Em Biotecnologia, BParts, C-Side, Catari, Chic by Choice, Coimbra Genomics, Critical Links, DuritCast, EDIGMA.com, Eneida, Epedal, Exponor Digital, Friday, Frissul, G3P, GenePreDiT, GebIBET, GetSocial, Girissima, Gleam, Greenfiber Tech, Grupo Salvador Caetano, Grupo Visabeira, Guestcentric Systems, iM3dical, JScrambler, Just in Time Tourist, Kinematix, Liquid Data Intelligence, Longevity, Luzitin, Lymphact, Magnomics, Marope Algarve, Marriott Praia D'El Rey, ME 3I,

MediaOmics, Medical Port, Moneris, Muzzley, Desenvolvimento de Colucoes Digitais, MyChild, New Coffee Co. II, Nutri Ventures, Oasis Atlantico - Hotelaria e Turismo, Omniflow, Outsystems, Parkalgar, Passworks, Pastceram, Perceive 3D, Pestana Berlin, PETsys Electronics, Pharma 73, Process'ware, Quinta da Marinha Leisure, SABE Online, Sagrotel - Sociedade Imobiliaria, Science4You, Serafim Silva - Atividades Hoteleiras, SGGHM - Soc. Geral Gestao Hoteis de Mocambique, ShiftForward, Shopitur, Skaphandrus, Somelos Tecidos, SPPTH, Steambolico, Taifas, Thelial Technologies, Travel Store, Treat U, TTR - Transactional Track Record, Tuizzi, Vista Alegre Atlantis, Whizztek, Windplus, Wizdee, Wizi to Find, Xhockware, Xtourmaker, youbeQ, Zaask

Key Executives:
  Jose Franca, Chairman and CEO
  Education: PhD, Imperial College of Science, Technology and Medicine; Degree in Electrical Engineering from the Technical University of Lisbon
  Background: Professor, Technical University of Lisbon; CEO and Chairman, CHIPIDEA; State Secretary for Education, Portugal; Director, MIPS Technologies
  Luis Filipe Lopes, Deputy CEO

3040 PRACTICA CAPITAL
Naurgarduko Street 3
Vilnius LT-03231
Lithuania

Phone: 370-5-260-3159
e-mail: info@practica.lt
web: www.practica.lt

Mission Statement: Practica Capital manages seed and venture capital funds established under JEREMIE initiative. The funds invest in early-stage development of high-potential business ideas (seed, startup) and expansion of established businesses in Lithuania.

Geographic Preference: Lithuania
Fund Size: 6 million Euro
Founded: 2011
Average Investment: 300, 000 - 3 million Euro
Investment Criteria: Early-Stage
Portfolio Companies: Fast Goods Groups UAB, Tokia.It, MCT, TVC, Mano daktaras, TrackDuck, adtarget.me, CGTrader.Om, Cheap Data Communications, Trustribe, Trafi, Kurgyvenu.It, Dragdis, Mobassurance, ImpressPages, AdDuplex, GAUDRE, Gifty, TransferGo, TransferGo, Benjamin River Productions, Celi APS, Startup.Lt

Key Executives:
  Anatoly Faktorovicius
  370-699-28-655
  e-mail: antolijus@practica.lt

3041 PREVIZ VENTURES
Ackerstein Towers
Building D, 10th Floor
12 Abba Eban Ave.
Herzeliya 46725
Israel

Phone: 972-99720467 Fax: 972-99520732
web: www.previzv.com

Mission Statement: Previz Ventures is a venture capital fund with an existing portfolio of investments in innovative technology companies addressing critical challenges primarily in the medical sector, with secondary focus on the information & communications technologies (ICT) sector. The fund invests in early stage firms, post proof of concept, at initial or approaching commercial stage, targeting large underserved markets with scalable solutions. The fund targets primarily Israeli based companies given the attractiveness of the technology and innovation landscape and the unique market access of the fund's management team.

Geographic Preference: Israel
Investment Criteria: Early-Stage
Industry Group Preference: Medical Devices, Information Technology, Communications, Mobile, Education, Security
Portfolio Companies: ReWalk, LunGuard, Clear-Cut Medical, Real Imaging, Profility, CellRox, Giraffic

Key Executives:
  Dan Baruchi, Managing Partner
  Education: BA, Economics, Haifa University; MBA, Tel-Aviv University
  Background: Senior Partner, Monitor Group

3042 PRIME TECHNOLOGY VENTURES NV
Museumplein 5A
PO Box 51129, 1007 EC
Amsterdam 1071 DJ
Netherlands

Phone: 31-202050820 Fax: 31-202050819
e-mail: info@ptv.com

Mission Statement: Leading early stage venture capital firm.
Geographic Preference: Europe
Fund Size: $144 Million
Founded: 1999
Average Investment: Euro5 - 15 Million
Minimum Investment: $600, 500
Investment Criteria: Expansion, Development, Seed, Start-up, Other early stage, Small buyout
Industry Group Preference: Communications, Computer Related, Electronic Technology, Internet Technology, Telecommunications, Semiconductors, E-Commerce & Manufacturing, Digital Media & Marketing, Software, Mobile
Portfolio Companies: 3mensio Medical Imaging, AppLift, Bright Computing, Cint, Civolution, Codenomicon, Buddy, Eutechnyx, Genkey, Global Collect, Greetz, Human Inference, Intrinsic ID, Ipida, Layar, Liquavista, MarkaVIP, MarketXS, Mendix, Nedstat, Pairingo, Pulsic, Q-GO, SAAS, Service2Media, Silicon Hive, Takeaway.com, Tridion, ZeroLight, Watermark Inc.

Other Locations:
  Wellington House
  East Road
  Cambridge CB1 1BH
  United Kingdom
  Phone: 44-1223-451-007 Fax: 44-1223-451-100

Key Executives:
  Monish Suri, General Partner
  e-mail: info@ptv.com
  Education: Bachelor degree in Computer Engineering, MBA degree from Rotterdam School of Management and J.L. Kellogg Graduate School of Management.
  Background: Held various commercial management positions with Baan Company(Channel Management director, Business Development director and International Marketing Manager).
  Directorships: Serves on the board of Codenomicon and Navicore as a board observer with MarketXS.
  Jelto Kromwijk Smits, General Partner
  e-mail: info@ptv.com
  Education: B.Sc. and M.Sc. degrees in Physics from the University of Helsinki.
  Background: Chairman of Solid (Finnish company).
  Sake Bosch, Founder/Managing Partner
  e-mail: sake@primeventures.com
  Education: BA, Management Science, MSc, Business Administration
  Background: Senior Principal, Holland Ventures
  Directorships: 3mensio Medical Imaging, Civolution, MarkaVIP, MarketXS, Nedstat, Service2Media, SaaSPlaza, Tridion, Watermark

3043 PRINCIPIA SGR
Via Pietro Mascagnia
n.20
Milan 20122
Italy

Phone: 39-0236589750 Fax: 39-0236589779
e-mail: info@principiasgr.it
web: www.principiasgr.it

Mission Statement: Thanks to the institutional connections and a management with a history of success in business innovation, Principia SGR is one of the largest of the Italian venture capital, both for longevity and experience of its team for both the relevance of assets under management.

Geographic Preference: Italy
Founded: 2002
Investment Criteria: All Stages
Industry Group Preference: Internet, Mobile, E-Commerce & Manufacturing, Digital Media & Marketing, Entertainment
Portfolio Companies: Tacati, Eximia, Neodata Group, MoneyFarm, Bibutek, Bangbite, DoveConviene, Games Are Social, Altilia, Docebo, Emediamarketing, 4w MarketPlace, ITSworld Sicilia, Weekend Company, PharmaEste, JUSP, X2 TV, im3D Clinic South, Vivocha, Ciceroos, Zoorate, Simplicissius Book Farm, D-Share, Applix, CrowdEngineering, Sounday, Eco4Cloud, Rhysto, Banza, EOS SpA, Citynews, 6sicuro

Key Executives:
Roberto Mazzei, Chief Executive Chairman

3044 PRIVATE EQUITY PARTNERS SPA
Via degli Omenoni, 2
Milano 20121
Italy

Phone: 39-28052171 Fax: 39-28052321
e-mail: info@privateequitypartners.com
web: www.privateequitypartners.com

Mission Statement: Developed a unique experience and expertise in Italy as a fund manager in Eastern Europe.

Geographic Preference: Eastern Europe
Fund Size: $240 Million
Founded: 1989
Average Investment: $18 Million
Minimum Investment: $6 Million
Investment Criteria: Expansion, Buy-outs
Industry Group Preference: Pharmaceuticals, Medical, Ceramic Tiles, Food Services, Automotive, Household Goods, Software, Electronic Technology, Furniture, Logistics

Key Executives:
Fabio Lorenzo Sattin, Presidente & Chairman
e-mail: info@privateequitypartners.com
Giovanni Campolo, Amministratore Delegato & Managing Director
e-mail: info@privateequitypartners.com
Directorships: Founding Partner
Alessandra Stea, Investment Manager
e-mail: info@privateequitypartners.com
Directorships: Founding Partner
Pier Paolo Quaranta, Investment Manager
e-mail: info@privateequitypartners.com
Directorships: Chairman
Leonardo Bruzzichesi, Partner
e-mail: info@privateequitypartners.com

3045 PROCURITAS PARTNERS KB
Linnegatan 9-11
Stockholm SE-114 47
Sweden

Phone: 46-850614300 Fax: 46-850614344

Mission Statement: One of the leading private equity houses in Scandinavia.

Geographic Preference: Denmark, Sweden
Fund Size: $0.37 Billion
Founded: 1986
Average Investment: $75 Million
Minimum Investment: $32.1 Million
Investment Criteria: MBO's, Buyouts
Industry Group Preference: Manufacturing, Telecommunications, Data Communications, Electronic Technology, Water, Waste & Recycling, Education, Concrete, Logistics
Portfolio Companies: Global Scanning, Pierce, Farma Holding, Gram Equipment, Team Olivia, Oral Care, Osby Glas, Perimter Protection Group, Sonas, Wermland Paper AB, Expan, Lekolar, Ariterm, Disa Holding, Zone Holding, North Trade, KGH Customs Services

Key Executives:
Michael Ahlstrom, Founder and Partner
e-mail: andersen@procuritas.se
Education: MSc in Business Administration from the Business School in Aarhus.
Background: JPMorgan.
His Wikse, Managing Partner
e-mail: karlander@procuritas.se
Education: MSc in Economics and Business Administration from the Stockholm School of Economics.
Background: Board member of the private equity companies Företagskapital AB (1989-92) and Atle AB (1992-95).
Mattias Feiff, Partner
Education: MBA in Finance and International Business from the Stern School of Business at New York University and a BSc in Economics from Copenhagen Business School.
Background: NSG Logistics AB, Sandå Projekt AB, Axenti A/S, Expan Holding A/S and Thermia Holding AB.
Directorships: Senior Partner.
Björn Lindberg, Partner
e-mail: toyberg@procuritas.se
Education: MSc in Economics from Copenhagen Business School.
Background: Started his professional career with Procuritas In 1993.
Johan Conradsson, Investment Manager
e-mail: wiske@procuritas.se
Education: MBA from INSEAD and an MSc in Engineering Physics from the University of Uppsala.
Background: Vice President of ABB.
Directorships: Partner of Procuritas since 1998.
Daniel Schuss, Investment Manager
e-mail: rignell@procuritas.se
Education: MSc in Engineering Physics from the Royal Institute of Technology in Stockholm and an MSc in Finance and Business Administration from Stockholm School of Economics.
Background: Consultant at Andersen Consulting Strategic Services and at SIAR-Bossard.
Directorships: Partner

3046 PROFOUNDERS CAPITAL
3 Cadogan Gate
Chelsea
London SW1X 0AS
United Kingdom

Phone: 44-02077666900
e-mail: rogan@profounderscapital.com
web: www.profounderscapital.com

Mission Statement: Our aim is to invest in and support new businesses with capital plus proactive advice and expertise. We believe that the combination of dynamic new entrepreneurs and PROfounders' experience leads to a strong base for new ventures to flourish. Our goal is to create long-term value and promote entrepreneurism.

Geographic Preference: Europe
Average Investment: £500,000 - 2.5 million

Investment Criteria: Early-Stage
Industry Group Preference: Digital Media & Marketing, Technology
Portfolio Companies: Cursogram, Small Giant Games, Compass, Festicket, Splash, Younity, busuu, GetYourGuide, easyCar, Lulu, Leap Motion, 9flats, onefinestay, CitySocializer, Mangahigh, Made.com
Key Executives:
Rogan Angelini-Hurll, Partner
e-mail: rogan@profounderscapital.com
Background: Pan European Media Research Team, Citi; Salomon Brothers; Spectrum Strategy Consultants

3047 PROJECT A VENTURE GmBH & CO. KG
Julie-Wolfthorn-Straáe 1
Berlin 10115
Germany

Phone: 49-30-340-606-300 Fax: 49-30-340-606-399
e-mail: info@project-a.com
web: www.project-a.com/en

Mission Statement: Project A Ventures is a company builder focusing on Internet, Advertising Technology and Mobile. With our experts' operational know-how and our financial support, we help start-ups to build up competence in key areas such as IT, Performance Marketing, Business Intelligence and Organization Building, and thus contribute to their sustainable success. Our experts, based in Berlin and Sao Paulo, are among the best in their field and have been involved in building more than 50 market leading companies worldwide within the last 15 years.
Geographic Preference: Worldwide
Investment Criteria: Seed, Growth
Industry Group Preference: Internet, Advertising Technology, Mobile
Portfolio Companies: 42matters, Catawiki, Contorion, ESV Digital, Evino, Eyeota, Glow, Intelipost, Kouchzauber, Kyto, Loopline Systems, Metrigo, MiNodes, Natue, nu3, Procompra, Saatchi Art, Semasio, Spryker, Tictail, Tirendo, uberall, Wine in Black, Worldremit, ZenMate

Other Locations:
Project A Ventures Latam

775 cj 133
Sao Paulo
Brazil
Phone: 55-11-4872-8008
Olivier Raussin, Managing Director
Key Executives:
Dr. Florian Heinemann, Co-Founder and Managing Director
Education: MBA, WHU Koblenz
Background: Managing Director, Rocket Internet; Co-Founder and Managing Director, JustBooks/AbeBooks; Co-Head, Online Marketing Department, Jamba!

3048 PROMETHEAN INVESTMENTS LLP
5 Old Balley
2nd Floor
London EC4M 7BA
United Kingdom

Phone: +44 20 7426 2590
web: www.prometheaninvestments.com

Mission Statement: Promethean Investments LLP is a special situations principal investment firm founded in 2005. We are an independent partnership providing innovative capital solutions in the UK lower mid-market.
Geographic Preference: United Kingdom
Founded: 2005
Investment Criteria: Special Situations

Other Locations:
1 Hill Street
3rd Floor
Edinburgh EH2 3JP
United Kingdom
Key Executives:
Sir Peter Burt, Partner

3049 PROMETHYAN LABS
Portfolio Companies: Jabbit, BabaBoo, Prelert, Rivermuse
156 Blackfriars Road
London SE1 8EN
United Kingdom

3050 PROSEED
85 Yehuda Halevi Street
Tel Aviv 65796
Israel

Phone: 972-3-566-1284 Fax: 972-3-566-1285
e-mail: admin@proseed.co.il

Mission Statement: ProSeed, solidly positioned on the Israeli Venture Capital map since April 2000, has recently taken major steps in establishing itself in the forefront of the VC market, providing funding as well as hands-on managerial assistance and analytical support to capable technology-based enterprises.
Geographic Preference: Israel
Founded: 2000
Investment Criteria: Seed-Stage, Early-Stage
Industry Group Preference: Renewable Energy, Computer Hardware & Software, Healthcare
Portfolio Companies: PerfAction, EarlySense, Argo Medical Technologies, Gene Grafts, Regentis Biomaterials, Medic Vision, CorrelSense, VibeSec, Genieo, DataEssence, Attunity, Tehuti Networks, DigiFlex, Capital Nature
Key Executives:
Shai Levy, CEO
e-mail: shai@proseed.co.il
Education: BS, Accounting, Tel Aviv University
Background: CFO/CIO, Tahari Family; Director, Financial Reporting, Deutsch
Adina Makover, Life Science Director
e-mail: adina@proseed.co.il
Education: PhD, Life Sciences, Columbia University; MBA, Bar-Ilan University
Background: Post Doctoral Fellow, Weizmann Institute

3051 PROVENTURE AG
7101 Executive Center Drive
Suite 200
Brentwood, TN 37027

Phone: 615-3770909 Fax: 615-3776921
e-mail: info@proventure.com
web: www.proventure.com

Mission Statement: The Proventure companies are advisers to private equity fund-of-funds.
Geographic Preference: Europe
Fund Size: $ 215 Million
Founded: 1999
Average Investment: $5.4 Million
Minimum Investment: $2.4 Million
Investment Criteria: Seed, start-up, early stage or expansion financings.
Industry Group Preference: All Sectors Considered

3052 PT BHAKTI INVESTAMA TBK
MNC Tower 16th Floor
Jl. Kebon Sirih Kav 17-19
Jakarta Pusat 10340
Indonesia

Phone: 62-213922949 Fax: 62-213910454
Toll-Free: 01-8001262626

Mission Statement: Striving to become one of the largest and most successful investment banks in Indonesia.

Geographic Preference: Indonesia
Founded: 1989
Industry Group Preference: Electronic Components, Services, Logistics, Distribution, Cellular Service & Products
Portfolio Companies: Global Mediacom, Media Nusantara Citra, MNC Sky Vision, Infokom Elektrindo, MNC Kapital Indonesia, MNC Securities, MNC Asset Management, MNC Finance, MNC Life Assurance, MNC Asuransi Indonesia, MNC Bank, MNC Land, MNC Energy, Global Transport Services

Key Executives:
Hary Djaja, Director
Darma Putra, Director

3053 PT BNI NOMURA JAFCO MANAJEMEN VENTURA
Alexandra House
6th Floor
18 Chater Road
Central 10210
Hong Kong

Phone: 65-62246383 Fax: 65-62213690
e-mail: enquiry_hongkong@jafcoasia.com
web: www.jafcoasia.com

Mission Statement: Actively seeking new investments.

Fund Size: $100 Million
Founded: 1990
Portfolio Companies: Mobilewalla, Unmetric, Bubble Motion, Customer XPs Software Private Limited, Vriti Infocom, Consilium Software, Data Security Systems Solutions, Mozat, Si2 Microsystems, Apnapaisa Private, Tessolve Solutions, Mistral Solutions, Consistel, Microquai Techno, Avega Systems, Vignani Technologis, Microland Limited, RPO, Run Service, Dilithium Networks, Inzign Private, Merlion Pharmaceuticals, R&B Technology Holding Corporation, ShowWorld Holding, ByPay Information, Shezhen Shenzinlong Industry, Boqii, Lumi Holdings, IHAVEU.com, China Synthetic Mica Technology, Meize Energy Industries Holding Limited, M2 Holdings Limited, Athieva, UltiZen Games, Modjoy, JD Holding, Synerchip, Greatville Limited, iPeer Multimedia International, eHi Car Services, OptoTrace Technologies, Amsky Technology, Tarena, R & V, Global Market Group, First Point Holdings, hiu! Media, 51 Deco, Medsphere International Holding, Heguang International, Palm Commerce Holdings, Ether Optronics, GolferPass, LDK Solar, JRD Communication, Sungy Mobile, Tudou, Ambow Education Holding, Madhouse, Cgen Diital Media Company Limited, Leadtone Limited, Cash River, Canadia Solar, Agape Package Manufacturing, Arkmicro Technologies, BCD Semiconductor, China Wireless, Fiberxon, HiSoft Technology International, InterChina Network Software, Photonic Bridges Holdings, Pollex Mobile, China GrenTech Holdings Limited, Egis Tecnology, Gamemage Interactive, DSM-AGI Corporation, Sunlux Energy, Grandsys Technologies & Service

Key Executives:
Richard Uichel Joung, Chief Investment Officer & Managing Director

3054 PUILAETCO PRIVATE BANKERS KBL
Group
46 Herrmann Debroux Avenue
Brussels 1160
Belgium

Phone: 32-26794511 Fax: 32-26794622
e-mail: private.banking@puilaetcodewaay.be

Mission Statement: Provides specialised services in asset management, investment funds, estate planning; specialises in active European equity management

Geographic Preference: Worldwide
Founded: 1868
Investment Criteria: Long Term, Bottom-up, Global approach

Key Executives:
Jacques Peters, President
Bettina Leysen, Administrator

3055 PWC
113-119 The Terrace
Wellington
New Zealand

Phone: 64-44627000 Fax: 64-44627001
Toll-Free: 0800 229 229
web: www.pwc.co.nz/lombard-finance/

Mission Statement: The Lombard Group of Companies is a New Zealand owned and operated financier providing an innovative approach to finance and investment options for its clients throughout New Zealand.

Geographic Preference: New Zealand
Founded: 1989
Minimum Investment: $1, 000
Investment Criteria: Performance and risk management, Mortgage Backed Property, Unsecured Lending
Industry Group Preference: Machinery, Financial Services, Consumer Services, Property Management

Key Executives:
Jonathan Freeman, Chairman
Background: General manager with a Brierley owned subsidiary
Directorships: Director
Bruce Hassall, Chief Executive Officer and Senior Partner

3056 QBIC FUND
Gaston Crommelaan 8
Gent 9050
Belgium

web: www.qbic.be

Mission Statement: Qbic Fund seeks to invest in spin-off companies of the universities of Ghent, Brussels and Antwerp, leveraging the creativity of more than 8.500 researchers. This strategic alliance provides a sufficient level of critical mass to set up a sizeable, professionally managed fund. The fund mainly targets life sciences, new materials, cleantech and ICT start-ups.

Geographic Preference: Belgium
Investment Criteria: Seed-Stage, Early-Stage, Spin-Offs
Industry Group Preference: Life Sciences, New Materials, Clean Technology, Information Technology, Communications
Portfolio Companies: AgroSavfe, Multiplicom, Track4C, CoScale, PharmaFluidics, Biogazelle

Key Executives:
Marc Zabeau, Founder/Managing Partner
Education: MSc, Zoology, PhD, Genetics, University of Ghent
Background: Plant Genetic Systems, KeyGene
Directorships: Trinean, Calicopa

3057 QIMING VENTURE PARTNERS
Room 3906
Jinmao Tower
88 Century Boulevard
Shanghai 200121
China

Phone: +86 21 6101 6522 Fax: +86 21 6101 6512
web: www.qimingventures.com

Venture Capital & Private Equity Firms / International Firms

Mission Statement: We believe in helping companies succeed and we are committed to supporting them as they become sector leaders in China. With a portfolio featuring over 70 investments, Qiming captures market opportunities, choosing promising enterprises with great growth potential, undervalued enterprises, and high-tech enterprises with independent innovation technologies. Our entrepreneurs benefit from access to our portfolio of companies and our global network. While striving to be the investor of choice, Qiming also works closely with other leading venture capital firms in China to deliver the investor value that growing Chinese companies require.

Geographic Preference: China
Fund Size: $1.1 Billion
Founded: 2006
Investment Criteria: Early stage, Growth stage
Industry Group Preference: Information Technology, Consumer, Retail, Consumer & Leisure, Healthcare, Clean Technology

   Qiming Shaghai Office

   Shanghai 200121
   China
   Phone: +86 21 6101 6522 **Fax:** +86 21 6101 6512

   Qiming Beijing Office

   Jianguomenwai Street
   Beijing 100004
   China
   Phone: +86 10 5961 1188 **Fax:** +86 10 5961 1288

   Qiming Suzhou Office

   Suzhou Industrial Park
   Jiangsu
   China
   Phone: +86 21 6588 3308

   Qiming Development HK Limited

   Queens Road East
   Hong Kong
   Phone: +852 2855 6901

3058 QUADRAN GESTION Deutsche Beteiligungs AG
Börsenstraáe 1
Frankfurt 60313
Germany
Phone: 49-699578701 **Fax:** 49-6995787199
web: www.deutsche-beteiligung.de

Mission Statement: Actively seeking new investments.
Founded: 1965
Investment Criteria: MBO, Mid-market segment
Industry Group Preference: Automotive, Machinery, Printing, Construction
Portfolio Companies: Broetje-Automation GmbH Wiefelstede, Clyde-Bergemann-Gruppe Wesel/Glasgow/Delaware, DNS:NET Internet Service GmbH, FDG-Gruppe, Formel D GmbH, Grohmann GmbH Prum, Heytex Bramsche GmbH Bramsche, inexio Informationstechnologie und Telekommunikation KGaA, JCK KG, Plant Systems & Services PSS GmbH, Romanoco-Gruppe Karlsruhe, Schulerhilfe Gelsenkirchen, Spheros GmbH, Stephan Machinery GmbH, Unser Heimatbacker Holding GmbH

Key Executives:
   Torsten Grede, Chief Executive Officer

3059 QUANTUM WAVE FUND
Tsvetnoy Bulvar, 11, Building 6
6th Floor
Moscow 127051
Russia
Phone: 404-537-2055

Mission Statement: Quantum Wave Fund is a venture capital firm focused on seeking out early stage private companies with breakthrough quantum technology. Our mission is to help these companies capitalize on their opportunities and provide a platform fo our investors to participate in the quantum technology wave.

Investment Criteria: Early Stage
Industry Group Preference: Security, Telecommunications, Military, Data Storage, Data Mining, Microprocessors, Microcontrollers, New Materials, Physical Sciences
Portfolio Companies: Centice, Clifton, ID Quantique, Nano-Meta Technologies, Lunera Lighting

Other Locations:
   4105 Peachtree-Dunwoody Road NE
   Atlanta, GA 30342
   Phone: 678-999-4474

Key Executives:
   Serguie Kouzmine, Managing and Founding Partner, Board Member
   e-mail: sk@qwcap.com
   Education: Master's Degree in Physics from Novosibirsk State University and PhD in Physics from Institute of Nuclear Physics in Russia. Degree in Business Administration from the University of Chicago Business School
   Background: Founder, Nonolet; CEO, Ritzio Entertainment Group; General Partner, Solution Fund
   Directorships: Nano-Meta Technologies, Inc
   Frank Creer, Partner, Managing Director West Coast
   e-mail: fc@qwcap.com
   Education: Degree in Finance and Entrepreneurship from the University of Utah
   Background: Founding Member, Stevens Wood Consulting Group; Co-Founder, Wasatch Venture Fund; Founder and Managing Director, Zone Venture Fund
   Directorships: Lunera Lighting Inc, Centice Corp

3060 QUEST FOR GROWTH
Lei 19, Box 3
Leuven B-3000
Belgium
Phone: 32-0-16-28-41-28 **Fax:** 32-0-16-28-41-29
e-mail: quest@questforgrowth.com
web: www.questforgrowth.com

Mission Statement: Quest for Growth is a Privak that focuses on European growth companies covering a diversity of sectors. Quest for Growth focuses on European technology-based growth companies in sectors such as life sciences, information technology, software, semiconductors, telecom, electronics, new materials and special situations in other growth sectors.

Geographic Preference: Europe
Fund Size: 112 million euro
Investment Criteria: Growth Stage
Industry Group Preference: Life Sciences, Information Technology, Software, Semiconductors, Telecommunications, Electronics, New Materials
Portfolio Companies: Init Innovation, Nemetschek, SAP, USU Software, EVS Broadcast Equipment, LEM Holding, TKH Group, Tomra Systems, Melexis, Fresenius, Gerresheimer, Nexus, Pharmagest Interactive, Sartorius, UDH Healthcare, Andritz, Arcadis, Bertrandt, Centrotec, Kendrion, Nibe, Saft Groupe, Schaltbau Holding, FMC, Umicore, Aliaxis, Anteryon, Capricorn Cleantech Co-Investments, Idea AG, Kiadis Pharma, Magwel, Mapper Lithography, Prosonix

Key Executives:
Rene Avonts, Chairman

3061 QUESTER CAPITAL MANAGEMENT LIMITED
5 St John's Lane
London EC1M 4BH
United Kingdom

Phone: 44-2081230665 Fax: 44-2078-517770
e-mail: enquiries@sparkventures.com
web: www.sparkventures.com

Mission Statement: Quester invests in the UK's best technology to create great companies. As well as capital, we bring a wealth of experience of developing high growth companies in a variety of technologies from early stage through IPO or trade sale.

Geographic Preference: UK, Western Europe
Fund Size: $380 Million
Founded: 1984
Average Investment: Euro 165 Million
Minimum Investment: $1.32 Million
Investment Criteria: Focuses on Start-ups and early stage companies seeking to raise their first or second round of venture capital, MBO, MBI
Industry Group Preference: Healthcare, Nanotechnology, Education, Electronic Technology, Security, Biotechnology, Software, Leisure, Media, Life Sciences, Communications, Environment Products & Services
Portfolio Companies: Academia, Antenova, Aspex Semiconductor, Celoxica Holdings, Cluster Seven, DEM Solutions, Firebox.com, Gambling Compliance, Haemostatix, IMImobile, Kobalt Music, Mind Candy, MyDeco, Nototehighstreet.com, OpenX, Oxford Immunotec, Perpetuum, Xention, Xtera Communications

3062 RABO BLACK EARTH Eagle Venture Partners
Str. Arbat street, 10
13-3 Building One
Moscow 119002
Russia

Phone: 7495-6204885 Fax: 7495-6204886
e-mail: info@evp.ru

Mission Statement: Actively seeking new investments.
Geographic Preference: Central and Eastern Europe
Fund Size: $31.7 Million
Founded: 1996
Investment Criteria: Early stage, Small and Medium Enterprises
Industry Group Preference: Confectionery, Cement Roofing, Construction, Beverages, Cosmetics, Ice Cream, Agribusiness, Telecommunications
Portfolio Companies: Polypack, Stroidetal, BEZRK, Kodotel, Lipetski Khladokombinat , Izorok , Tamak, TAKF, Kreker

Key Executives:
Yang Devingart, Managing Director
e-mail: valery@evp.ru
Casper Heijsteeg, Managing Director

3063 RAFAEL DEVELOPMENT CORPORATION (RDC) LIMITED
The Triangle Tower
42nd Floor
Tel Aviv 67023
Israel

Phone: 972-36075500 Fax: 972-36075529
e-mail: info@rdc.co.il
web: www.rdc.co.il

Mission Statement: Focuses on generating new businesses by applying the core technologies of RAFAEL.
Geographic Preference: Israel
Fund Size: $150 Million
Founded: 1993
Investment Criteria: Companies from inception to maturity
Industry Group Preference: Aerospace, Defense and Security, Information Technology, Software, Communications, Medical Devices, Advanced Weapons Systems, Electronic Technology
Portfolio Companies: Given Imaging, Galil Medical, Medingo, Starling, SELA, 3DV, Sync-Rx, Kyma, Smart Wave

Key Executives:
Avishai Friedman, President & Chief Executive Officer
e-mail: rbaron@rdc.co.il
Hezi Nahum, Vice President Business Development

3064 RED DOT VENTURES
Singapore

Phone: 65-63249730 Fax: 65-63241637
e-mail: contact@reddotventures.com
web: www.reddotventures.com

Mission Statement: Established in 2011, Red Dot Ventures is a seed-stage venture capital firm focused on Singapore-based high-tech startups in areas including ICT, Interactive Digital Media, MedTech, Nanotech, CleanTech, and Engineering.
Geographic Preference: Singapore
Founded: 2011
Investment Criteria: Early-Stage
Industry Group Preference: High Technology, Digital Media & Marketing, Medical Technology, Nanotechnology, Clean Technology, Engineering
Portfolio Companies: iCarsclub, Ascenz, aSpecial, The Stakeholder Company, Paywhere, Daylight Studios, Pirate3D, GCoreLab, Digify, Gnosis Analytics, Ractiv, I3 Precision, Pytheas, Intuitive Creations, Protag, Socialwalk, Taamkru, Algo Access

Key Executives:
Leslie Loh, Managing Director
Education: BComm, Finance, Saint Mary's University
Background: Founder/Chairman/CEO, System Access
Directorships: SPRING Singapore

3065 REED ELSEVIER VENTURES
1-3 Strand
London WC2N 5JR
United Kingdom

Phone: 44-20-7166-5500 Fax: 44-20-7166-5799
e-mail: london@reedelsevier.com
web: www.reedelsevier.com/aboutus/ventures/pages/home.aspx

Mission Statement: Founded in 2000, Reed Elsevier Ventures is a venture capital firm with offices in London and San Francisco. We are backed by one of the world's most successful media and information companies, Reed Elsevier. Our mission is to invest in entrepreneurs and management teams that have the vision to build great companies. We take an active role in the development of our companies and help our entrepreneurs to build value via our extensive network of industry contacts & business relationships.

Geographic Preference: United States, Europe, Israel
Investment Criteria: All Stages
Industry Group Preference: Internet, Media, Technology, New Media, Mobile, Big Data, Healthcare Information Technology, Software

Key Executives:
Luke Smith, Investment Analyst
e-mail: luke.smith@reedelsevierventures.com

Venture Capital & Private Equity Firms / International Firms

3066 REGENT PACIFIC PRIVATE EQUITY LIMITED Regent Pacific Group Ltd.
8th Floor, Henley Building
5 Queen's Road Central
Central
Hong Kong

Phone: 852-25146111 Fax: 852- 28104792
e-mail: info@regentpac.com
web: www.regentpac.com

Mission Statement: Actively seeking new investments.

Geographic Preference: Asia Pacific Region

Key Executives:
James Mellon, Non-Executive Co-Chairman
Stephen Roland Dattels, Non-Executive Co-Chairman

3067 REITEN & CO STRATEGIC INVESTMENTS AS Reiten & Company
Haakon VIIs gt. 1, 3rd floor
Oslo 0161
Norway

Phone: 47-23113700 Fax: 47-23113721
e-mail: post@reitenco.no
web: www.reitenco.no

Mission Statement: A leading Nordic Investment and Advisory firm specializing in private equity and corporate advisory.

Geographic Preference: Denmark, Finland, Norway, Sweden
Fund Size: $264 Million
Founded: 1992
Average Investment: EUR 10 and 40 Million
Minimum Investment: $12 Million
Investment Criteria: Expansion and Development Capital, Buyout and Buyin
Industry Group Preference: Computer Related, Medical & Health Related, Energy, Consumer Services, Financial Services, Real Estate, Business to Business, Industrial Services, Insurance
Portfolio Companies: Data Respons, Webstep, Grilstad, Con-Fom, Brubakken, Malthus, QuestBack, NEAS, Competentia

Key Executives:
Narve Reiten, Founding Partner
e-mail: an@reitenco.no
Education: Masters of Science degree in Mathematics(Norwegian University of Science and Technology)
Background: Bearingpoint(Adviser), Sensonor(R&D group)
Kathryn M. Baker, Partner
e-mail: nr@reitenco.no
Education: Master of Business and Economics degree(Norwegian School of Management), CFA(Norwegian School of Economics and Business Administration)
Background: I.M. Skaugen(M&A, Project development)
Terje Bakken, Partner
Education: Toronto
Background: ON
Brath Brath Ingero, Partner
e-mail: bbi@reitenco.no
Education: Degree in Economics(University of Oslo)
Background: The Norwegian Association of Masters of Science in Business(Visiting Lecturer)
Morten Viksoy, Partner
e-mail: mv@reitenco.no
Education: Master of Business and Economics degree(Norwegian School of Economics and Business Administration)
Background: Telenor Broadcast(Project Director), McKinsey & Co(Management Consultant)
John M. Bjerkan, Partner & CFO
e-mail: jmb@reitenco.no
Education: MBA, Master of Business and Economics(Norwegian School of Management)
Background: Telenor(Project Manager), PA Consulting Group(Research Analyst)

3068 RENAISSANCE PARTNERS
44 Lowicka
Warszawa 02-551
Poland

Phone: 48-228488777 Fax: 48-228568935
web: www.rp.com.pl

Mission Statement: Renaissance Partners is the management company of the European Renaissance Capital venture capital funds. The mission is to seek and analyze potential investment opportunities, finance projects through purchase of shares and contribute to increasing the values.

Geographic Preference: Poland, Czech Republic, Solvakia, USA
Fund Size: $39.5 Million
Founded: 1994
Average Investment: $1 Million
Minimum Investment: $0.5 Million
Industry Group Preference: Broadcasting, Global Industries, Communications, Energy
Portfolio Companies: Bielsko Business Center, Pirios, Solgaz, Slovpack Bratislava, Ticketstream

Key Executives:
Peter Bardadin, Partner
Education: Graduated(Czech Technical University), Diploma from postgraduate studies(Sloan School of Management, MIT)
Background: Bank of America, Victor Computers, Tandem Computers(Executive position)
Marlena Czyzewska, Office Manager
Witold Grabowski, 9 Canton Road
Education: Kowloon
Background: National and Pennsylvania Labor Relations Boards
Radoslaw Czyrko, Partner
Education: Graduated(Agricultural University), Financial management (Georgetown University, USA)
Background: Czech-American Enterprise Fund(Investment Officer)

3069 REVO CAPITAL
Barbaros Mh. Halk Cd. Kardelen Sok.
Palladium Tower Kat:9
Ofis:36 Atasehir
Istanbul 34357
Turkey

Phone: 90-212-327-2184
web: www.revo.vc

Mission Statement: A venture capital fund investing in truly innovative, seed & early-stage B2B or B2C technology ventures in Turkey.

Geographic Preference: Turkey
Investment Criteria: Early-Stage, Seed-Stage
Industry Group Preference: Business to Business, Technology, Cloud Computing, Internet, E-Commerce & Manufacturing, Gaming
Portfolio Companies: Fit Solutions, SkyAtlas, 8digits, Parasut, Onedio

Key Executives:
Ozcan Tahincioglu, General Partner
Background: Chairman/CEO, Tahincioglu Holding; Chairman, Endeavor Turkey; Chairman, Kent Gida

Venture Capital & Private Equity Firms / International Firms

3070 RFC AMBRIAN RFC Group Ltd.
L14, 19-31 Pitt Street
Sydney NSW 2000
Australia

Phone: 61-292500000 Fax: 61-292500001
web: www.rfcambrian.com

Mission Statement: Resource Finance Corporation is a merchant and investment bank; provides world leading expertise in mining and other areas of specialised finance to private and public sector corporations, banks, institutional investors and government.

Geographic Preference: Australia, Canada, North America, South America, South Africa
Fund Size: $3.95 Million
Founded: 1985
Investment Criteria: Early Stage project development capital for natural resources and mining industry related projects and technology
Industry Group Preference: Mining, Oil & Gas

3071 RHB - H&F MANAGEMENT COMPANY SDN BHD RHB Capital
Level 5, Tower One, RHB Centre
Kuala Lumpur 50400
Malaysia

Phone: 60-392-802536 Fax: 60-321427573
e-mail: enquiry@rhb.com.my
web: www.rhb.com.my

Mission Statement: Actively seeking new investments.
Geographic Preference: Malaysia
Fund Size: $3.57 Million
Founded: 1997
Industry Group Preference: Consumer Services, Commercial Services, Corporate Services, Banking, Consumer Products

Key Executives:
Chay Wai Leong, Managing Director
Roslan Haji Tik, Senior Vice President

3072 RHODIUM
91 Medinat Hayehudium
St. Herteliya
Pituach 46140

Phone: 972-9-960-6900 Fax: 972-9-960-6910
web: www.rhodium.co.il

Mission Statement: Rhodium invests in early-stage ventures in Israel, New York, and Silicon Valley. We focus on identifying and partnering with the very best and most promising entrepreneurs and innovators with a view to building disruptive, world-changing companies.

Geographic Preference: Israel, New York, California
Investment Criteria: Early-Stage
Portfolio Companies: Switch, Outbrain, Zooz, Face.com, Yotpo, HopStop, Rounds, Captain Up, Compass, SambaAds, Chosen, Green SQL

Other Locations:
535 Madison Avenue
New York, NY 10022

Key Executives:
Daniel Recanati, Founder/CEO
Education: BA, LLB, Interdisciplinary Center, Herzliya
Directorships: Face.com, Hopstop, YieldMo, ZooZ, GreenSQL, Yotpo, Rounds.com
Yaron Kniajer, Managing Director
Education: MBA, London Business School; CPA
Background: Investment Banking, Lehman Brothers; CFO, Mediagate
Directorships: Rounds.com, GreenSQL, Yotpo, CaptainUp, Face.com

3073 RICHINA CAPITAL PARTNERS LIMITED
56 Jiang Xi Zhong Road
Shanghai 200002
China

Phone: 86-216-323-1200 Fax: 86-216-323-1511

Mission Statement: A China-centric investment firm with high ethics, performance and acumen.

Geographic Preference: China, New Zealand
Fund Size: $150 Million
Founded: 1993
Industry Group Preference: Real Estate, Financial Services, Manufacturing

3074 RMB VENTURES LIMITED RMB Australia
Level 13, 60 Castlereagh Street
Sydney NSW 2000
Australia

Phone: 61-292566200 Fax: 61-292566290
web: www.rmb.com.au

Mission Statement: Provides financing and strategic support for management buyouts and expansion capital as medium to long term investors.

Geographic Preference: Australia, New Zealand
Fund Size: $300 Million
Founded: 1988
Minimum Investment: $10 Million
Investment Criteria: MBOs, MBIs, IBOs
Industry Group Preference: All Sectors Considered

Key Executives:
Mark Habner, Director
Education: B.COM, LLB (Hons), MM (Kellogg), ASA
Background: Booz Allen and Hamilton

3075 ROAD KING INFRASTRUCTURE LIMITED
Suite 501, 5th Floor, Tower 6
9 Canton Road, Tsimshatsui
Kowloon
Hong Kong

web: www.roadking.com.hk

Mission Statement: Road King Infrastructure Limited is a leading Hong Kong publicly listed company with its core business in the investment, development, operation and management of toll roads and bridges in China.

Geographic Preference: China
Investment Criteria: Propert development
Industry Group Preference: Transportation, Bridges

Key Executives:
William Zen Wei Pao, Chairman
Education: Bachelor of Science degree in Physics & Master of Business Administration degree
Background: Member and a fellow member of Hong Kong Institution of Highways and Transportation
Ko Yuk Bing, Managing Director & Chief Executive Officer

3076 ROCHE VENTURE FUND F. Hoffman-La Roche AG
Grenzacherstrasse 124
Basel CH-4070
Switzerland

Phone: +41 61-688 1111 Fax: +41 61-691-9391
web: www.venturefund.roche.com

Mission Statement: The Roche Venture Fund is a committed long-term stable investor with sufficient money reserved for follow-on financing rounds. As part of a multinational healthcare company, the Roche Venture Fund has access to considerable expertise both internally and externally. We

Venture Capital & Private Equity Firms / International Firms

co-invest with leading venture funds, including other corporate venture funds, on a regular basis.

Geographic Preference: Europe, North America, Pacific Region
Fund Size: CHF 500 million
Founded: 2002
Average Investment: CHF 1-5 million
Investment Criteria: Series B
Industry Group Preference: Life Sciences
Portfolio Companies: 23andMe, Afferent Pharmaceuticals, Aileron Therapeutics, Alios BioPharma, Allakos, Ambit Biosciences, Ambrx, Biodesy, Conatus Pharmaceuticals, Curetis, CytomX Therapeutics, Epic Sciences, Foundation Medicine, Horizon, LTO, Maclogix, Mission Therapeutics, Opsona Therapeutics, Proacta, Senseonics, Stratos, Symphogen, TiGenix, Xenon

Key Executives:
Severin Schwan, Chief Executive Officer

3077 ROTHSCHILD AUSTRALIA - ARROW PRIVATE EQUITY Rothschild Group
Level 21, No. 120 Collins Street
Melbourne 3000
Australia

Phone: 61-396564600 **Fax:** 61-396564700
web: www.rothschild.com

Mission Statement: Rothschild provides leading financial advice and services to organisations worldwide.

Geographic Preference: Australia
Fund Size: 1 Billion AUD
Founded: 1992
Industry Group Preference: Manufacturing, Global Financial Advisory, Wealth Management & Trust, Merchant Banking, Institutional Asset Management, Specialist Financial Businesses

Key Executives:
Baron David de Rothschild, Chairman
Nigel Higgins, Chief Executive Officer

3078 RU-NET VENTURES
B.Ovchinnikovsky per., 16,
4th Floor, Office 402
Moscow 115184
Russian Federation

Phone: +7(495)797-97-63

Mission Statement: Driven by a passionate, principled and expert senior team, ru-Net's approach to investment is long term. Aiming not just to invest in, but also to partner with its target companies, ru-Net works to share knowledge, build capacity and develop expertise to help company teams achieve their growth ambitions. Combined with strict investment criteria, clear strategies and demonstrable investment goals, this approach is enabling ru-Net to shape a successful future for some of the world's most exciting technology companies.

Geographic Preference: United States, Europe, Russia, Southeast Asia
Founded: 1999
Investment Criteria: Early-stage, Energy, E-Commerce & Manufacturing, Outsourcing & Efficiency

Other Locations:
RTP Ventures

25th Floor
New York, NY 10022

Key Executives:
Leonid Boguslavsky, Chairman of the Board
Oleg Sundukov, Vice-President, IT Business
Maria Krayukhina, Director, Internet and IT Business
Galina Chifina, Investment Director
Alexander Pavlov, Investment Director

3079 RUNA CAPITAL
Russian Federation

Phone: 7-4959849703
e-mail: info@runacap.com
web: www.runacap.com

Mission Statement: Runa Capital is a technology-focused venture capital firm whose investments have created or incubated companies with more than US$10 billion in assets. It was established to seek growth opportunities in the rapidly growing areas of the tech sector, with specific focus on cloud computing and other hosted services, virtualization and mobile applications. The key execution point is to select promising teams and drive and support them in the global marketplace, turning them into international champions.

Fund Size: $135 million
Industry Group Preference: Cloud Computing, Internet, Software, Mobile
Portfolio Companies: Gninx, Ecwid, LinguaLeo, Acumatica, Jelastic, Jopa, Cellrox, B2B Center, Dhebhuk, Profi.ru

Key Executives:
Serguei Beloussov, Founder/Senior Partner
Education: BS, Physics, MS, Electrical Engineering, PhD, Computer Science, Moscow Institute of Physics & Technology
Background: Venture Partner, Almaz Capital; Founder, Parallels; Founder, Acumatica
Directorships: Acumatica

3080 RUSSELL INVESTMENT MANAGEMENT LIMITED
Level 29
135 King Street
Sydney NSW 2000
Australia

Phone: 02-92295111 **Fax:** 02-92214505
web: www.russell.com

Mission Statement: A global investment services firm, providing investment management, advisory and diversified funds to clients.

Geographic Preference: Australia, Canada, China, Spain, Finland, Hong Kong, US, Malaysia, UK
Fund Size: $3.2 Trillion
Founded: 1936
Industry Group Preference: All Sectors Considered

Key Executives:
Alan Schoenheimer, Managing Director
e-mail: info@russell.com
Education: B.Sc., Mathematics, M.Sc., Mathematics, Ph.D., Business Administration
Background: Professor in the Accounting and Finance Department at the University of Auckland; professor at the Australian Graduate School of Management; faculty member in the Statistics and Econometrics group at the Graduate School of Business, University of Chicago;
Directorships: Board of Trustees of the National Provident Fund, Boards of a number of companies in the financial sector in Auckland
Linda Elkins, Managing Director

3081 S-REFIT GmbH & COMPANY KG
15 Sedanstrasse
Regensburg 93055
Germany

Phone: 49-941695560 **Fax:** 49-9416955611
e-mail: info@s-refit.de
web: www.s-refit.de

Mission Statement: Actively seeking new investments.

Founded: 1990
Key Executives:
Walter Paulus-Rohmer, Chairman
Peter Terhart, CEO

Venture Capital & Private Equity Firms / International Firms

3082 SABIC VENTURES
Europa Boulevard 1
PO Box 5151
Sittard 6130 PD
Netherlands

Phone: 31-0-46-722-2479
e-mail: ventures@sabic.com
web: www.sabic.com/ventures

Mission Statement: SABIC Ventures is a wholly-owned subsidiary of SABIC that is focused on providing seed and early stage venture capital financing to innovative companies in the fund's sectors of interest on a global scale. We aim to invest in outstanding entrepreneurial teams who dare to challenge the status quo in their respective industries and who are seeking to build extraordinary businesses that can support SABIC's innovation and growth strategy. We seek to invest and co-invest with a broad network of VC partners, angel investors or investment groups that specialize in our targeted investment markets and geographies. Through collaborative innovation, we can leverage SABIC's global footprint and turn our strategic insights into market impact.

Geographic Preference: Middle East, North America, Europe, India, China
Average Investment: $2 - $20 million
Investment Criteria: Seed-Stage, Early-Stage, Later-Stage
Industry Group Preference: Advanced Materials, Alternative Energy, Renewable Energy, Clean Technology

Key Executives:
Hans Kolnaar, Managing Director

3083 SAFFRON HILL VENTURES
4/5 Park Place
London SW1A 1LP
United Kingdom

Phone: 44-02076938300
e-mail: contact@saffronhill.com
web: www.saffronhill.com

Mission Statement: Saffron Hill works with entrepreneurs and partners to transform disruptive ideas into world class companies.

Geographic Preference: Europe
Founded: 2000
Average Investment: £500,000 to £2 million
Investment Criteria: Seed Capital to Later-Stage Growth Equity
Industry Group Preference: Technology, Media, Clean Technology
Portfolio Companies: Agilyx, Coyuchi, Entuity, Flogit4u, Faceware, Image Metrics, InfraTrac, Optasia Medical, Tagsys Rfid

Key Executives:
Ranjeet Bhatia, Co-founder
e-mail: rbhatia@saffronhill.com
Education: BA, Environmental Science, Occidental College; MBA, UCLA Anderson School of Business; MA, International Relations & Economics, Johns Hopkins University School of Advanced International Studies
Background: Advisor, Loot Ltd.; Advisor, Lord Rothschild; Booz-Allen & Hailton; Dynacorp-Meridian
Shawn Luetchens, Co-founder
e-mail: sluetchens@saffronhill.com
Education: BS, Physical Sciences, University of Nebraska; MBA, Kellogg Graduate School of Management
Background: Principal, Tribune Ventures; Senior Project Manager, US Environmental Protechtion Agency

3084 SAIF PARTNERS
Suites 2516-2520
Two Pacific Place
88 Queensway

Hong Kong

Phone: 852-2918-2200 **Fax:** 852-2234-9116
web: www.sbaif.com

Mission Statement: SAIF Partners is a leading private equity firm that provides growth capital to companies in Asia.

Geographic Preference: Asia
Fund Size: $3.5 billion
Founded: 2001
Average Investment: $10 million - $100 million
Investment Criteria: Early-Stage, Growth Stage
Industry Group Preference: Information Technology, Internet, Mobile, Consumer Products, Consumer Services, Healthcare, Clean Technology, Education, Agriculture, Financial Services, Manufacturing
Portfolio Companies: Xiamen Orient Wanli Stone, Acorn International, Advision Media Holdings, Alchip Technologies, Appotronics, ATA, Beijing Hua Yu Network Technology Development, Beijing Jingeng Clean Energy, Beijing Lepro Seva Da Technologiy Development, Beijing Rising Technology Co., Beijing Ryzur Exiom Medical Investment Co., Beijing Yize Jianyuan Technology Co., Best Elite International, Biosensors International Group, Bona Film Group, Bros Catering, Careland International, ChannelSoft Holdings, China Broad Media Corp, China Digital TV Holding Co.

Other Locations:
18F Tower C, Central Intl Trade Center
6a Jianguomenwai Avenue
Chao Yang District
Beijing 100022
China
Phone: 86-10-6563-0202 **Fax:** 86-10-6563-0252

Villa +16, Shanghai Hong Qiao State Hotel
1591 Hong Qiao Road
Shanghai 200336
China
Phone: 86-21-6295-2768 **Fax:** 86-21-6295-2783

Unit 511, 5th Floor
Time Tower, MG Road
Gurgaon
Haryana 122002
India
Phone: 91-98-6646-1770 **Fax:** 91-22-6645-9581

Key Executives:
Andrew Y. Yan, Managing Partner
Education: BS, Engineering, Nanjing Aeronautic Institute; MA, Sociology, Peking University; MA, International Political Economy, Princeton University
Background: Managing Director, Emerging Markets Partnership; Director, Sprint International Corporation

3085 SAINT-GOBAIN NOVA EXTERNAL VENTURING
Les Miroirs
18, avenue d'Alsace
Courbevoie 92400
France

web: www.saint-gobain.com

Mission Statement: NOVA External Venturing is the Saint-Gobain unit dedicated to developing strategic partnerships between the Group and star-up companies all over the world.

Geographic Preference: United States, Europe, Asia
Investment Criteria: Early-Stage
Industry Group Preference: Energy, Environment, Construction

Venture Capital & Private Equity Firms / International Firms

3086 SALFORD CAPITAL PARTNERS
Bulevar Mihajla Pupina 115 G
Belgrade 11070
Yugoslavia

Phone: 381-11-2222-500 Fax: 381-11-2222-533

Mission Statement: A private equity firm investing primarily in developing markets.
Geographic Preference: Former Soviet Union, Central & Eastern Europe
Founded: 2001
Portfolio Companies: Adjara Hotel, Bambi/Banat, Borjomi, IDS/Morshinkaya, Imlek Group, Knjaz Milos, Standard Bank, Subotica, Telenet, United States Embassy Residential Community
Other Locations:
Salford Investment Limited
2-Ya Magistrinaya Street
8a, 4th Floor
Moscow 123290
Russia
Phone: 7-495-787-5314 Fax: 7-495-787-5316

Salford Old Georgia
44 Leselidze Street
Tbilisi 0105
Georgia
Phone: 995-32-505-400 Fax: 995-32-505-406

Salford (UK) Ltd
78 Pall Mall
London SW1Y 5ES
United Kingdom
Phone: 44-20-3178-4850 Fax: 44-20-3178-4851

3087 SAMBRINVEST SA
Avenue Georges Lema, tre, 62
Aéropole
Gosselies 6041
Belgium

Phone: 32-71259494 Fax: 32-71259499
e-mail: sambrinvest@sambrinvest.be
web: www.sambrinvest.be

Mission Statement: SAMBRINVEST and its subsidiaries is a source of venture capital to support the development of SME in the Charleroi and Thuin districts.
Founded: 1985
Investment Criteria: Start-up, Development stage, Transfer of ownership.
Industry Group Preference: Aviation, Building Materials & Services, Pharmaceuticals, Electronic Technology, Environment Products & Services, Food Services, Metals, Manufacturing, Wholesale, Services, Printing, Glass, Wood Industries
Key Executives:
Guy Paeau, President
Education: Engineering
Denis Tillier, Partner

3088 SAMOS INVESTMENTS
22 Charing Cross Road
London WC2H 0HS
United Kingdom

Phone: 44-0-2076322520
e-mail: contact@samos.uk.com

Mission Statement: Samos Investments is a private equity investor with a focus on high-growth European businesses. Samos takes a proactive approach with its portfolio companies, working alongside many of the US and Europe's top venture funds, family offices and private investors.
Geographic Preference: Europe
Industry Group Preference: Financial Services, Retailing, Clean Technology, Energy, Natural Resources, Transportation, Medical Technology, Digital Media & Marketing, E-Commerce & Manufacturing
Portfolio Companies: 3legs, Betfair, Business of Fashion, BytePlay, Carwow, Charlotte Tilbury, Cointerra, Coniq, Clenarm, Goal.com, Gridpoint, Ironstone Resources, Insightra Medical, Kabbee, Kincora Group, LDC, Nuji, Ocado, Second Home, Senhouse Capital, Seedcamp, Small World, Vouchedfor, WTG
Key Executives:
Charles Cecil, Chairman

3089 SAMSUNG VENTURE INVESTMENT CORPORATION Samsung Electronics
06620 Samsung Electronics 29F
Seocho-Daero 74-Gil
Seocho-Gu
Seoul
Korea

Phone: 02 2255-0299
web: www.samsungventure.co.kr

Mission Statement: Samsung Electronics (SEC) seeks to form strategic partnerships with start-ups are growing companies engaged in the development of new technologies.
Fund Size: $340 Billion
Founded: 1999
Average Investment: $10.2 Million
Minimum Investment: $500,000
Investment Criteria: Start-Up, Growth Capital
Industry Group Preference: Internet Technology, Information Technology, Semiconductors, Medical, Biotechnology, Telecommunication, Software, Bioengineering
Portfolio Companies: Cool Dry, Delta ID, HIMS, Kateeva, Kngine, Maluuba, MasterImage 3D, Mecatronix, Mindmeld, Mixaroo(Boxfish), nLight, Novasentis, nuTonomy, Philoptics, Power By Proxy, Scientific Magnetics, TeraView, YuMe
Other Locations:
2440 Sand Hill Road
Suite 302
Menlo Park, CA 94025

260 Franklin Street
Suite 510
Boston, MA 02110

Plot No. 2A
Sector 127
NOIDA
Utter Pradesh
India

Lidabashi Grand Bloom Sakura Terrace
2-10-2 Fujimi
Chiyoda-ku
Tokyo 102-0071
Japan

18F TaiYangGong Plaza
12A TaiYangGong Middle Road
Chaoyang District
Beijing
China

Crane Building 3F
22 Lavington Street
London SE1 0NX
England

1st Floor
Holland Building
Europark
Yakum
Israel

Key Executives:
Yongbae Jeon, President/CEO
Background: Samsung Fire & Marine Insurance; Samsung Future Strategic Office; Samsung Electronics; Samsung

President's Office Tream 2; Samsung Corporate Restructuring Office; Samsung Life Insurance

3090 SAUDI ARAMCO ENERGY VENTURES
9/F Al-Midra Tower
Dhahran 31311
Saudi Arabia

Mission Statement: Saudi Aramco Energy Ventures is the corporate venturing subsidiary of Saudi Aramco, the Saudi Arabian national oil company. Established in 2012 as a wholly-owned subsidiary of Saudi Aramco, our mission is to invest globally into start-up and high growth companies with technologies of strategic importance to Saudi Aramco and to accelerate their development and their deployment in the Kingdom.

Geographic Preference: Worldwide
Founded: 2012
Average Investment: $1 to $30 million
Investment Criteria: Seed Stage, Growth Venture Capital
Industry Group Preference: Oil & Gas, Renewable Energy, Energy Efficiency, Water
Portfolio Companies: Utildata, AnTech, inflow Control, Novomer, Rive Technology, Sekal, Zilift, Siluria, Wearable Intelligence

Other Locations:
Aramco Energy Ventures

Houston, TX 77096-1799
Phone: 713-432-5422
Cory Steffek

Key Executives:
Caroline Slind Svae
47-97-00-82-11
e-mail: caroline.svae@energycapital.no

3091 SB CHINA VENTURE CAPITAL
15A-C, HuaMin Empire Plaza
728 YanAn Road (West)
Suite 15 A-C
Shanghai 200050
China

Phone: 86-2152534888
e-mail: contact@sbcvc.com

Mission Statement: Actively seeking new investments in the China marketplace.
Geographic Preference: Shanghai
Founded: 2000
Industry Group Preference: TMT, Clean Technology, Healthcare, Consumer Retail, Advanced Manufacturing, New Materials
Portfolio Companies: Alibaba, Taobao, Focus Media, PPTV, OCJ, GDS, Linkage, Tianpin, Etrans, Easou, Hairun, Suninfo, Yooli, Edai.com, Shenwu, DKT, NYF, SRET, Hi-Tech, ECOSO, Jiangli, Di'an, EDAN, EYES, BGI, Panther, NANOMED, KingYee, Precise, Goodbaby, DMTG, Loncin, Deyu Agri, Glory, Jiahua, Yifang

3092 SBRC INVESTMENT CONSULTATION LIMITED
3 Daniel Frisch Street
Tel Aviv 64731
Israel

Phone: 972-36950666 **Fax:** 972-36950222
e-mail: Daniela.f@cukierman.co.il
web: www.cukierman.co.il

Mission Statement: The firm provides a full scope of European focused investment banking activities, including corporate finance, equity investment, strategic consulting and alliances, as well as capital market services to Israeli and European companies.

Geographic Preference: Europe
Fund Size: Euro 3.5 Billion
Founded: 1993
Average Investment: $2 Million
Minimum Investment: $1 Million
Investment Criteria: European focused investment banking activities, including corporate finance, equity investment, strategic consulting and alliances
Industry Group Preference: Telecommunications, Software, Medical Devices, Multimedia
Portfolio Companies: Tufin, Cyren, Dori Media, MobilEye, Harmon.ie, Omrix, Lamina Technologies, Miba Plast, Dot Hill, Better Online Solutions, PowerD, Orex Technologies

Key Executives:
Edouard Cukierman, Chairman
e-mail: info@cukierman.co.il
Education: BA from Tel-Aviv University in Accounting and Economics, Licence in CPA
Background: Corporate Finance Consultant at Ernst & Young, Israel
Haggai Ravid, Chief Executive Officer
e-mail: info@cukierman.co.il
Education: B.Sc from the Technion - Israel Institute of Technology, MBA - INSEAD(Fontainebleau, France).
Background: Citec-Environment and Services in Paris, Lamina Technologies.

3093 SCALE INVESTORS
Level 4
167 Flinders Lane
Melbourne VIC 3000
Australia

Phone: 61-3-9653-5314 **Fax:** 61-432-324-324
web: www.scaleinvestors.com.au

Mission Statement: Scale helps investors and entrepreneurial women to connect, invest and succeed. Scale is a female focused angel investor network. We were founded in Melbourne in March 2013 inspired by the US based organization Golden Seeds. Our founding members are women, but we welcome and include men who share our vision of maximizing returns by supporting early stage businesses that value gender diverse leadership.

Founded: 2013
Average Investment: $50,000 - $500,000
Investment Criteria: Female Founder; Early-Stage

Key Executives:
Susan Oliver, Founding Chairman
Directorships: Fusion Retail Brands, CNPR, Coffey International

3094 SCOTTISH ENTERPRISE
Atrium Court
50 Waterloo Street
Glasgow G2 6HQ
United Kingdom

Phone: 0845-6078787
e-mail: enquiries@scotent.co.uk
web: www.scottish-enterprise.com

Mission Statement: Actively seeking new investments in emerging growth companies in Scotland.
Geographic Preference: Scotland
Fund Size: $25 Million
Founded: 1982
Investment Criteria: Start-up
Industry Group Preference: Education, Aerospace, Defense and Government, Chemicals, Energy, Telecommunications, Optical Technology, Multimedia, Industrial Services

Key Executives:
Anne MacColl, Chief Executive
Education: BSc, CA
Background: Corporate Finance, Venture Capital
Directorships: Bathgate Investment Fund Ltd, Edinburgh Technology Fund

Venture Capital & Private Equity Firms / International Firms

Paul Lewis, Managing Director Operations - Sectors, Commercialisation and Inv

3095 SCOTTISH EQUITY PARTNERS
17 Blythswood Square
Glasgow G2 4AD
United Kingdom

Phone: 44-01412734000
web: www.sep.co.uk

Mission Statement: A leading venture capital and growth equity investor focused on the UK and other European countries. As well as investing in early stage companies, we invest in more established companies looking to build scale and momentum. All of the companies we partner with have the potential to build and strong and defensible competitive position in the global marketplace.

Geographic Preference: United Kingdom, Europe
Fund Size: Euro 200 Million
Founded: 1991
Investment Criteria: Early-Stage, Growth-Stage
Industry Group Preference: Information Technology, Energy, Healthcare, Life Sciences, Clean Technology, Digital Media & Marketing
Portfolio Companies: Anesco, Arakis Aridhia, Arkex, Atlantech, Biovation, BioVex, CamSemi, Carloan 4U, Clavis Insight, Cmed, Control Circle, Craneware, CSR, Cyberhawk, Cyclacel, Daysoft.com, Deep Casting Tools, Exco inTouch, Fotech Solutions, Gai Energy, Gigle Networks, Green Highland, Hetras, Indigo Vision, Indigo Pipelines, IntelligentReach, IP Access, Klala, Matches, Metaforic, Mister Spex, MTEM, Nallatech, Orbital, Picophip, Rhetorical, Searchspace, Silent, Skyscanner, Smarter Grid Solutions, SocialBro, Solar Century, Stentys, Sumerian, Tideway, TotallyMoney.com, Tryzens Group, Vital Energi, Virtensys, Voxar, Wayn, Wolfson, Workshare, Zeus, Zinwave

Other Locations:
29 St. George Street
London W1S 2FA
United Kingdom
Phone: 44-02077585900 Fax: 44-02077585901

Key Executives:
Adrian Pike, Founder and CEO
44-0-20-7758-5938
e-mail: contact_richard@sep.co.uk
Calum Paterson, Co-Founder, Managing Partner
44-0-20-7758-5930
e-mail: contact_calum@sep.co.uk
Background: Ernst & Young
Directorships: Skyscanner, Daysoft UV, Sumerian
Andrew Davison, Partner
44-0-20-7758-5938
e-mail: contact_andrewd@sep.co.uk
Directorships: IP Access, Kiala, Surfkitchen, Zeus
Brian Kerr, Partner
44-0-20-7758-5938
e-mail: contact_brian@sep.co.uk
Directorships: Cmed, Stensys
Gary Le Sueur, Partner
44-0-20-7758-5938
e-mail: contact_gary@sep.co.uk
Fearghal O Riordain, Partner
44-0-20-7758-5930
e-mail: contact_fearghal@sep.co.uk
Education: MEng Sc, BE, Electrical Engineering, National University of Ireland; MBA, INSEAD
Background: Founding Principal & Partner, Accel Partners; Ericsson
Directorships: Clavis Technology, Powervation
Stuart Paterson, Partner
44-0-20-7758-5938
e-mail: contact_stuart@sep.co.uk
Education: Venture Capital Executive Program, Harvard Business School
Directorships: Control Circle, Elonics, PicoChip, Virtensys, Gigle Networks
Jan Rutherford, Partner
44-0-20-7758-5930
e-mail: contact_jan@sep.co.uk
Background: Life Science team, Dresdner Kleinwort Capital
Directorships: Sosei, BioVex, Cmed
David Sneddon, Partner
44-0-20-7758-5938
e-mail: contact_david@sep.co.uk
Directorships: ARKeX, Atraverda, Deep Casingtools, Fotech
Gordon Beveridge, Principal
44-0-20-7758-5930
e-mail: contact_gordon@sep.co.uk
Background: Corporate Finance, Ernst & Young
Directorships: CamSemi
Andrew Buchan, General Counsel
44-0-20-7758-5938
e-mail: contact_andrewb@sep.co.uk
Education: Glasgow University
Background: Private Practice, Maclay Murray & Spens
Mark Gracey, Principal
44-0-20-7758-5930
e-mail: contact_mark@sep.co.uk
Background: European Director, Sensory Networks
Directorships: Zinwave
Fraser McLatchie, Associate
44-0-20-7758-5938
e-mail: contact_fraser@sep.co.uk
Education: MA, Social Science, University of Glasgow

3096 SEAYA VENTURES
Plaza de la Independencia 2, 3º Izda
Madrid 28001
Spain

Phone: 34-911-10-86-97
e-mail: info@seayaventures.com
web: www.seayaventures.com

Mission Statement: Seaya Ventures seeks to transform early and growth stage companies into category leaders. We look for innovative businesses that require growth or expansion capital and can build a lasting value. At Seaya we understand what being an entrepreneur means. We empower outstanding teams and businesses and help them navigate the path from early and growth stages into rapid growth and sustainable profitability with a focus on expansion in Latin America.

Geographic Preference: Spain
Investment Criteria: Early Stage, Growth Stage
Industry Group Preference: Computer Related, Consumer Internet, Consumer Mobile Media, Consumer Software, Internet Technology
Portfolio Companies: Plenum Media, Restalo, Sin Delental, Ticketea.com, Cabify

Key Executives:
Beatriz Gonzalez, Founder and Managing Partner
Education: Business Degree from CUNEF; MBA, Columbia Business School
Background: Head of Private Equity Program In Telefonica's Pension Fund; Darby Overseas Investments; Excel Partners; Equity Research Department, Morgan Stanley
Michael Kleindl, Founder and Managing Partner
Education: Oestrich-Winkel
Background: Co-Founder and CEO, AdLINK Internet Media AG
Directorships: Hi Media S.A.

Venture Capital & Private Equity Firms / International Firms

3097 SEB VENTURE CAPITAL
Sweden

Phone: +4687639110
e-mail: press@seb.se
web: www.sebgroup.com

Mission Statement: SEB Venture Capital creates opportunities for entrepreneurs and innovators to build and develop successful companies. Our goal is sustainable, long-term value creation.

Fund Size: SEK 2.4 billion
Founded: 1995
Average Investment: SEK 20 - 80 million
Industry Group Preference: Life Sciences, Technology

3098 SEED CAPITAL LIMITED
Magdalen Centre, Oxford Science Park
Oxford Science Park
Oxford OX4 4GA
United Kingdom

Phone: 44-1865784466 Fax: 44-1865784430
e-mail: lucius@oxfordtechnology.com
web: www.oxfordtechnology.com

Mission Statement: Actively seeking new investments in early-stage technology companies in and around Oxford.

Geographic Preference: United Kingdom
Fund Size: $40 Million
Founded: 1983
Average Investment: Euro 2, 000, 000
Minimum Investment: $0.08 Million
Investment Criteria: Seed, Start-up, Other Early Stage
Industry Group Preference: Biotechnology, Medical & Health Related, Chemicals, Industrial Equipment, Instrumentation, Energy, Natural Resources, Genetic Engineering, Industrial Products, Medical & Health Related, Materials Technology
Portfolio Companies: Run 3D, BioMoti, Combat Medical, Message Missile, Ibexis Technologies, Lightpoint Medical, Metal Powders & Process, Powder OLEDs, Abgentis, Designer Carbon Materials, Sasets, Sime Diagnostics, BioCote, Dataflow, DHA, Equitalk, Getmapping, MET, Scancell, Select Technology, Valid Information Systems, Arecor, Commerce Decisions, DHA, ImmunoBiology, Inaplex, Insense, MET, OC Robotics, Orthogem, Oxis Energy, Plasma Antennas, Select Technology, Telegesis, Allinea Software, BioAnaLab, Concurrent Thinking, Glide Pharma, Invro, Ixaris, Metal Nanopowders, Promic, Superhard Materials, Warwick Effect Polymers, Bluewater Bio International, Dexela, Diamond Hard Surfaces, Dynamic Extractions Historic Futures, Imagineer Systems, Impact Applications, Meciria, MirriAd, Naked Objects, Novacta Biosystems, OxTox, Pharma Engineering, Select Technology

Key Executives:
Lucius Cary, Founder and Managing Director
Education: Degree in Cell and Molecular Biology, D.Phil in Biochemistry from Oxford University.
Background: Astra Zeneca, British Biotech subsidiary.
Jackson John, Chairman
Education: Degree in engineering and economics- Oxford University, MBA-Harvard Business School, was an engineering apprentice at the Atomic Energy Research Establishment, Harwell.
Background: Venture Capital Report.
Directorships: Founder

3099 SEEDCAMP
4-5 Bonhill Street
Shoreditch
London EC2A 4BX
United Kingdom

e-mail: info@seedcamp.com
web: seedcamp.com

Mission Statement: Seedcamp believes investing at the earliest stage is the best approach to building a successful company.

Geographic Preference: United Kingdom, EU
Fund Size: $1 billion
Founded: 2007
Portfolio Companies: Bunker Ex, Creative Labs, SeedLegals, CyberSmart, Heresy, Fraugster, The Engineering Company, Stupeflix, Gyant, Cuvva, Labstep, 9fin, Stowga, VChain, Legit Patents, Beagle, Wevat, Telleroo, Ai Build, Sunlight, Clause, Libryo, Viz.ai, Pollen, Weengs, TheWaveVR, Grocer, ThirdEye, CRU Kafe, Trail, Reposit, Thriva, Oratio, Juro, Splash, ActionBar, YodelTalk, Vinterior, KareInn, CharlieHR, ThingThing, SwiftShift, Repositive, Open Sensors, Propoly, Nevercode, Wefox, Cardlife, Buuldcon, Beeline, Authentiq, Alterest, Curve, Edgefolio, Pointy, Revolut, MagicTab, Data Smoothie, Pleo, Wombo, Evercontact, Land Insight, Hitch, Captini, GetAgent, Adventures, MyRecovery, Acasa, Spoke, Traderion, Talkpush, Trussle, UiPath, Priori Data, WealthKernel, Cymmetria, Monese, Rialto, Rienfer, Oinky, Kasko, Intelliment Security, Findify, Hubble, HOKO, MarcoPolo Learning, Queueco, JOBDOH, Twine, Car Quids, Lateral, Divido, Podo Labs, Cronofy, BranchTrack, Property Partner, EMoov, Wriggle, Shoprocket, Homeshift, Voyage Control, Teleport, FarmHopping, BridgeU, Oradian, Reedsy, Tanaza, GoWorkaBit, Interact.io, We Are Colony, Elliptic, Formisimo, Lodgify, Krak, Satago, Popcorn Metrics, BorrowMyDoggy, Winnow, Stamplay, ShareLaTeX, Saberr, Revision App, Apperio, Hype!, Ctrlio, Fishbrain, TruckTrack, Countly, Line-Up, Minubo, Maily, Codeship, SimpleTax, Codacy, Hole19, CrowdProcess, Poq, TRDATA, Rawstream, Try.com, Traity, Antavo, Sayduck, 24symbols, Audiense, Qminder, Blossom, Totems, Transferwise, Farmeron

Key Executives:
Reshma Sohoni, Co-Founder/Manager Partner
Carlos Eduardo Espinal, Managing Partner
Background: Doughty Hanson Technology Ventures, Advanced Communications Technologies Group of The New York Stock Exchange, PKI Developer, Cybertrust/Baltimore Technologies
Tom Wilson, Investment Partner
Background: King & Wood Mallesons
Sia Houchangnia, Investment Partner
Education: MSc, International Management, ESADE Business School

3100 SEEDFUND
3 Turf Estate
Shakti Mills Lane
Off. Dr. E. Moses Road, Mahalaxmi
Mumbai 400 011
India

Phone: +91 22 2490
e-mail: info@seedfund.in
web: www.seedfund.in

Mission Statement: SeedFund identifies market disrupters in different industries and backs them early to promote stable growth.

Portfolio Companies: Afaqs!, AxisRooms, Browntape, CarWale, Cumbak, DailyObjects, Done By None, EduSports, Fetise, Frontier Markets, Healthizen, Heckyl, Innoz, Ixsight, Jeevanti, Jeeves, Level10 Comics, Lifeblob, Technium Labs, My Dentist, Nearify, Nevales, Printo, RedBus, Rupeetalk, Sportskeeda, ThinkLabs, Uhuroo, Vaatsalya, ViralMint, Voonik, V Resorts

Venture Capital & Private Equity Firms / International Firms

3101 SENETAS CORPORATION LIMITED
Senatas Group
312 Kings Way
South Melbourne VIC 3205
Australia

Phone: 61-398684555 Fax: 61-398214899
e-mail: security@senetas.com
web: www.senetas.com

Mission Statement: Provides world-leading encryption products, the ability to tailor and implement whole-organisation security solutions, and innovative Enterprise Information Professional Services.

Geographic Preference: Australia, New Zealand, United Kingdom
Founded: 1999
Key Executives:
Francis W. Galbally, Non-Executive Chairman
e-mail: enquiries@senetas.com
Background: Finance Express Home Loans Pty Ltd, Barrister and Solicitor of the High Court of Australia and Supreme Courts of Victoria and New South Wales.
Directorships: Chairman
Lachlan Given, Director

3102 SERGE PUN & ASSOCIATES (MYANMAR) LIMITED
380 Bogyoke Aung San Street, Pebedan Township
10th Floor, FMI Centre
Yangon
Myanmar

Phone: 95-1240363 Fax: 95-1246881
web: www.spa-myanmar.com

Mission Statement: Actively seeking new investments.
Geographic Preference: Myanmar, Thailand, Hongkong
Founded: 1991
Industry Group Preference: Financial Services, Real Estate, Automotive, Healthcare
Key Executives:
Serge Pun, Chairman
e-mail: mail@spa.com.mm
Education: Doctorate in Business Administration.
Martin Pun, Non-executive Vice Chairman

3103 SEVEN SPIRES INVESTMENTS
33c Davenant Road
Oxford OX2 8BU
United Kingdom

Phone: 44-0-1865-302-909 Fax: 44-0-7966-892-335
web: www.sevenspires.co.uk

Mission Statement: Seven Spires Investments Ltd. (SSIL) is a private, off-shore investment company. SSIL was established in 2003 and invests around £5 million annually across the existing portfolio and new investments. We are actively seeking new investment opportunities in high-tech companies in the United Kingdom. We look for excellent management, defensible Intellectual Property, a well characterized route to market and global scalability to an expected market capitalization in excess of $100m.

Geographic Preference: United Kingdom
Founded: 2003
Investment Criteria: All States
Industry Group Preference: High Technology, Automotive, Energy
Key Executives:
Ian Page, Managing Partner
Background: Reader in Computation, Programming Research Group, University of Oxford; Founder, Celonica Ltd; Visiting Professor, Imperial College & Cass Business School

Edward McCabe, Managing Partner
Background: Investment Management

3104 SEVENTURE PARTNERS
5-7 rue de Monttessuy
Paris 75340
France

Phone: 33-0158192270 Fax: 33-0158192280
e-mail: contact@seventure.fr
web: www.seventure.fr

Mission Statement: Seventure Partners finance innovation and participate in the entrepreneurial adventure alongside our entrepreneurs. We share their passion to succeed. As an active partner of French and European technology firms with strong growth potential, we finance the development of innovative companies in two areas: Information and Communication Technology (ICT) and Life Sciences (LS).

Geographic Preference: Europe
Fund Size: 600 million Euro
Founded: 1997
Industry Group Preference: Information Technology, Communications, Life Sciences
Portfolio Companies: Airtag, Anevia, Anyware, Balyo, EBlink, Ipdia, Microwave Vision, Mootwin, MReadBooks, Netasq, Nexess, Parrot, Presto Engineering, Scaleo Chip, Scentys, Silkan, Swapcom, Transatel, Volubill, Web Geo Services, Xiring, Alsyon Technologies, Arlettie, AssurOne, Caledrra, Conject, DailyCall, DSO Interactive, Easyvoyage, Efficity, Emailvision, Eodom, Footways, FromAtoB.com, Hi Media, imusic-school, IsCool, Kayentis, L4 Epsilon, LeGuide.com, Maximiles, MinuteBuzz, MLstate, Myobis, Navabi, Netino, Plinga, Praditus, PrestaShop, Recommerce Solutions, Retailo, Santessima, Sidetrade, SoFactory, SquareClock, Studitemps, TalentSoft, Testbirds, Tigerlily, Tradoria, Vistaprint, W4, WebInterpret, Acarix, Advanced Accelerator Applications, arGEN-X, BiancaMed, BioAlliance Pharma, Biomatlante, BioPhytis, Corwave, Domain Therapeutics, Endocontrol, Enterome, Fluxome Sciences, Global Bioenergies, Humedics, Impeto Medical, Implanet, Ipsogen, Kebony, LNC, Lucane Pharma, MaaT Pharma, Mainstay Medical, Mauna Kea Technologies, MDX Health, Metabolic Explorer, Middle Peak Medical, Mint Solutions, Nanobiotix, Noxxon, Nutrionix, OPi, Personal Medsystems, Phosphonics, Pixium Vision, Polaar, Polaris, ProTip, Quanta, Santaris Pharma, Syntaxin, Txcell, Vivostat

Key Executives:
Isabelle de Cremoux, CEO/Managing Partner
Education: Ecole Centrale, Paris
Background: Arthur Andersen, Pfizer, Fournier

3105 SHANGHAI INFORMATION INVESTMENT INCORPORATED
32nd floor, BEA Finance Tower
66 Huayuan Shiqiao Road
Lujiazui Financial Trade Zone, Pudong New Area
Shanghai 200120
China

Phone: 86-2133831700 Fax: 86-2133831724
web: www.sii.com.cn

Mission Statement: Makes strategic and exemplary investment in the city's major information projects; provides substantial coordinating efforts among different sectors and entities.

Geographic Preference: China
Founded: 1997
Industry Group Preference: Telecommunications, Internet Technology, Infrastructure, E-Commerce & Manufacturing, Services, Banking, Enabling Technology
Key Executives:
Yadong Liu, Chairman

3106 SHANNON COMMERCIAL PROPERTIES
Shannon Commercial Properties
2nd Floor
Arrivals Building, Shannon Airport
Shannon
Ireland

Phone: +353 (0)61 710000 Fax: +353 (0)61 712859
web: www.shannonproperty.ie

Mission Statement: Pioneers Regional Development for the technical knowledge era.
Geographic Preference: Ireland
Founded: 1959
Investment Criteria: Seed, Start-up, Management Buyin, MBO, Expansion and Development, Early Stage
Industry Group Preference: Biotechnology, Communications, Computer Related, Software, Electronic Technology, Medical & Health Related
Key Executives:
  Kevin Thompstone, Chief Executive
  Sean Fitzgibbon, Corporate Development Director
  John King, Director(Heritage & Tourism)
  Eugene Brennan, Director(Knowledge Enterprise)
  Martin McKeogh, Director(Spatial Development)

3107 SHAW KWEI AND PARTNERS
1601 Euro Trade Centre
13 Connaught Road
Central
Hong Kong

Phone: 852-31628479 Fax: 852-31628499
e-mail: info@shawkwei.com
web: www.shawkwei.com

Mission Statement: Invests in later-stage private companies.
Geographic Preference: Asia, Taiwan, China, Singapore, USA
Founded: 1999
Investment Criteria: Growth Capital, MBO, Buyouts
Industry Group Preference: Technology, Electronic Technology, Manufacturing, Food & Beverage, Medical & Health Related, Transportation, Materials Technology
Key Executives:
  Kyle Shaw, Managing Director
  e-mail: info@shawkwei.com
  Education: Diplomas in Production Engineering and Management Studies from Hong Kong Polytechnic
  Background: Flextronics International , National Semiconductor (HK) Ltd., GTE Sylvania Far East Ltd. and NCR (Mfg.) Hong Kong Ltd.
  Tsui Sung Lam (S.L), Managing Director
  e-mail: info@shawkwei.com
  Education: BS Commerce, University of Virginia; MBA, Wharton School
  Background: Flextronics International (Singapore), China Fangda Group (China), Suga International (Hong Kong), Abest Communication Corp. (Taiwan), SNP Leefung Holdings Ltd. (Hong Kong), B & B Natural Products Ltd. (Hong Kong), the University of Virginia Alumni Assoc

3108 SHENZHEN INTERNATIONAL HOLDINGS LIMITED
Rooms 2205-08, 22/F., Greenfield Tower
Concordia Plaza, No. 1 Science Museum Road
Tsimshatsui East
Kowloon NV
Hong Kong

Phone: 852-23660268 Fax: 852-27395123
e-mail: info@szihl.com
web: www.szihl.com

Mission Statement: Focuses on the provision of total logistics and transportation ancillary services, as well as investment, operation and management of related assets and projects.
Geographic Preference: Hong Kong, Bermuda
Key Executives:
  Gao Lei, Chairman
  Education: Bachelor's degree in engineering from Wuhan University of Technology
  Background: Shenzhen Expressway Company Limited
  Directorships: Chief Executive
  Li Jing Qi, Chief Executive Officer

3109 SIEMENS VENTURE CAPITAL
Otto-Hahn-Ring 6
Munich 81739
Germany

Phone: 49-8963633585 Fax: 49-8963634884
web: finance.siemens.com

Mission Statement: Venture Capital team takes a hands-on approach to investments in all stages.
Geographic Preference: Europe, North America, Israel
Founded: 1999
Investment Criteria: First Class Management Team and Businessplan
Industry Group Preference: Communications, Information Technology, Industrial Equipment, Medical & Health Related
Portfolio Companies: Agilliance Group, Agility Communications, Air2Web Asera, Alvarion, Apptitude, Band of Angels, BeamReach Networks, Blue Pumpkin Software, Caly Networks, Cambridge Positioning Systems Limited, Cambridge Silicon Radio, Carmel Ventures, Chiaro Networks
Key Executives:
  Michael Aust, Senior Investment Associate
  e-mail: eugene.yeh@siemens.com
  Education: dual Bachelor's degrees in Molecular and Cell Biology and Business Administration, University of California
  Background: Financial analyst at ChevronTexaco.
  Eric Bielke, Senior Investment Associate
  e-mail: thomas.kolbinger@seimens.com
  Education: MBA
  Background: Corporate Strategy & Development
  Doris Blasel, Managing Partner Siemens Global Innovation Partners
  Education: Doctorate, University of Stuttgart
  Background: President of the Medical Engineering Group (now: Medical Solutions) , Siemens Ltd. Bombay, India, Managing Director
  Eric Emmons, Investment Partner Venture Capital
  Education: Young Managers Programme, INSEAD Fontainebleau
  Background: Member of the Group Executive Management of the Automation and Drives Group
  Jackie Hoffmann, Investment Partner
  e-mail: jackie.hoffmann@siemens.com
  Education: University of California, Bachelor's in Mathematics, MBA UC Berkeley's Haas School of Business
  Background: Intel.
  Dr. Andrew Jay, Investment Partner Venture Capital
  Education: Bachelor of Science degree in Computer Engineering, MBA from Southern Methodist University
  Background: Director, Service Evolution within the Chief Technology Office of seimens
  Madeline Song, Investment Partner
  e-mail: madeline.song@siemens.com
  Education: Bachelor's degree in Chemical Engineering, and a Master of Business Administration.
  Background: Managing Director of First Group Holding, Ltd
  Kathrin Fox, Executive Assistant
  e-mail: kathrin.fox@siemens.com
  Education: studied languages

Venture Capital & Private Equity Firms / International Firms

Background: administrative and executive Assistant in U.S.A., Italy and Luxembourg.
Mike Majors, Investment Partner Venture Capital
e-mail: alexander.rietz@siemens.com
Education: MBA (Dipl.-Kfm.) in finance from the Johann Wolfgang Goethe-University
Background: South African electricity monopolist Eskom, Junior Investment Manager for a Venture Capital firm in Cape Town
Gerd Goette, Partner
e-mail: gerd.goette@siemens.com
Education: masters degree in electrical engineering (Dipl. Ing.) from Technische Hochschule Darmstadt, Germany
Background: Investment Partner of Mustang Ventures,
Svetoslav Simeonov, Head of Accounting & Controlling
Background: Luis held a variety of managerial jobs in research and development as well as product line management at the Siemens Carrier Division in Florida
Joyce E. Jordan, Executive Assistant
Education: Physics Diploma from Technical University Munich (TUM).
Background: Rohde und Schwarz, BMW, EADS Astrium and Siemens Venture Capital.

3110 SIF TRANSYLVANIA
2, Nicolae Iorga Street
Brasov 500057
Romania

Phone: 0268 419 460 Fax: 0268 473 215
e-mail: siftransilvania@siftransilvania.ro
web: www.transif.ro

Geographic Preference: Romania
Fund Size: $81.9 Billion
Founded: 1996
Average Investment: $5 Million
Minimum Investment: $50,000
Industry Group Preference: Chemicals, Financial Services, Tourism, Machinery, Agribusiness, Transportation, Food & Beverage, Banking
Key Executives:
  Ec. Razvan Gavaneanu, President of the Supervisory Board
  Education: Accounting
  Background: Economist; Director, PRESCON Group Brasov
  Ec. Stefan Szabo, Vice President of the Supervisory Board
  e-mail: marketing@transif.ro
  Education: Ph.D. in economics (business management)
  Directorships: General Manager
  Constantin Fratila, Member of the Supervisory Board
  e-mail: marketing@transif.ro
  Education: Economics
  Ec. Gheorghe Lutac, Member of the Supervisory Board
  e-mail: transif@transif.ro

3111 SIGNATURE CAPITAL LLC
76 Merrion Square
Dublin 2
Ireland

Phone: 353-16690700 Fax: 353-16760694
e-mail: info@signaturecapital.com
web: www.signaturecapital.com

Mission Statement: A results-oriented venture capital firm that leverages its insight, wisdom and proven track record to allow breakthrough technology-based startup businesses to reach their full potential.

Founded: 1997
Investment Criteria: Early, Seed
Industry Group Preference: Biotechnology, Communications, Electronic Technology, Information Technology, Software, Internet, Telecommunications, Semiconductors, Healthcare

Other Locations:
Savignyplatz 9-10
Berlin 10623
Germany
Phone: 49-3031804920 Fax: 49-30318049211

Berkely Square House
Berkely Square
London W1J 6BD
United Kingdom
Phone: 44-2078871517

Key Executives:
  Ciaran McNamara, Co-Founder/Managing Director
  Education: University College of Dublin
  Enda Woods, Co-Founder/Director
  Education: University of California, Davis

3112 SINGTEL INNOV8
71 Ayer Rajah Crescent
#02-22
139951
Singapore

Phone: 65-68384686 Fax: 65-68728456
e-mail: newsroom@singtel.com
web: innov8.singtel.com

Mission Statement: SingTel Innov8, a wholly-owned subsidiary of the SingTel Group, is a corporate venture capital fund, with its own set of decision making, approval and funding processes. Innov8 focuses its investments on technologies and solutions that lead to quantum changes in network capabilities, next generation devices, digital content services and enablers to enhance customer experience. It works closely with the ecosystem of leading innovators, developers, government agencies, R&D and capital providers to bring cutting-edge technologies and solutions to the various markets the SingTel Group operates in.

Geographic Preference: Asia Pacific, Africa
Fund Size: S$200 million
Average Investment: S$100,000 - S$30 million
Investment Criteria: All Stages
Industry Group Preference: Internet, Digital Media & Marketing
Portfolio Companies: Ninja Blocks, Bitglass, Pokkt, DemystData, TheNeura, Arista Networks, MobileIron, Maker Studios, Fab, Kai Square, Tempo.AI, TubeMogul, Net Power & Light, Yodo1, ShopSpot, Flocations, Everything.me, Vuclip, Venuemob, 121cast, Qvivo, Moment.me, General Moile, Jasper Wireless, Nexage, Ruckus Wireless, InGameAd, Le Kan, Sodacard, Bubble Motion, Massive Impact, Baynote, 2359 Media

Other Locations:
Shanghai Times Square
Unite 1210
93 Huai Hai Zhong Road
Shanghai 200021
China
Phone: 86-2161371258

100 Marine Parkway
Suite 450
Redwood City, CA 94065

Key Executives:
  Edgar Hardless, Chief Executive Officer
  Education: BSc, Business Administration, University of Bath
  Background: VP, Strategic Investments, SingTel; British Telecommunications

Venture Capital & Private Equity Firms / International Firms

3113 SLOVAK AMERICAN ENTERPRISE FUND
58 Obchodna
PO Box 100
Bratislava 810 00
Slovakia

Phone: 421-257100200 Fax: 421-252731323
web: www.saef.sk

Mission Statement: Actively seeking new investments.
Geographic Preference: Slovakia, Czech Republic
Founded: 1991
Average Investment: $2.2 Million
Minimum Investment: $500,000
Investment Criteria: Expansion - development, Other early stage, Small buyout, Start-up
Industry Group Preference: All Sectors Considered
Portfolio Companies: Profesia, Gotive, MäsospiÜ, Slovlepex, Novomanip, Rabbit Farm, Esox s.r.o., Ameta s.r.o., ZIN s.r.o., Leader Gasket of Slovakia s.r.o., Gamma spol. s r.o., Bee-keeping Dedinský.

Key Executives:
Martina Rosková, President
e-mail: chren@saef.sk
Education: MBA, Old Dominion University
Background: Investment Banking
Mary Hurajová, Director General, Stock Exchange
e-mail: graic@saef.sk
Education: Master Degree in Engineering
Background: Venture Capital
Directorships: Member of Boards in investee companies

3114 SMAC PARTNERS
Germany

web: www.smacpartners.com

Geographic Preference: Germany, Western Europe
Founded: 2001
Investment Criteria: Management Buyouts, Single and portfolio secondary direct transactions, Merger between two companies with additional operational funding needs, Distressed situations
Industry Group Preference: Technology, Telecommunications
Portfolio Companies: Actelis, Alchip, Exit Games, Flash Networks, nLight, Olive Software, Rock Mobile

Key Executives:
Dr. Dietrich Ulmer, Managing Partner and Co-Founder
Education: Technical University (RWTH) of Aachen; PHd, Sociology, Konstanz University
Background: CEO and President, Siemens Acceleration; Chief Strategist, O2 Germany
Oliver Kolbe, Managing Partner and Co-Founder
Education: University of Applied Sciences in Munich, Germany
Background: CFO, Simens Acceleration; Vice President Strategy and Marketing BA, Siemens Mobile

3115 SMART BUSINESS CONSULTING
85 Medinat Hayehudim Street
Herzliya Pituach 46851
Israel

Phone: 972-99710710 Fax: 972-99710711
web: www.smartandbetter.co.il

Mission Statement: Focuses on the high-tech market, with an Israeli emphasis, especially by partnering with start-ups, and using our global network to bring Israeli technology to the world.
Geographic Preference: Israel, USA, Europe
Fund Size: $500 Million
Founded: 1997
Investment Criteria: Start-up
Industry Group Preference: Wireless Technologies, Communications, Internet Technology, Enterprise Services, Infrastructure, Software
Portfolio Companies: Interwise, XOR Technologies, Pl-x, Vidius, BIS, Odimo, SpeedBit, Mobile Access, Memscap, Flash Networks, Prominence Networks

3116 SOCIALATOM VENTURES
Bogata
Columbia

web: www.socialatomventures.com

Mission Statement: An international team of entrepreneurs, investors and business professionals that invests in and partners with high-technology companies offering global solutions across the Americas. Our unique founder-centric services provide both capital and in-depth services across the entrepreneurial life cycle.
Geographic Preference: Latin America
Founded: 2005
Investment Criteria: Early-Stage
Industry Group Preference: High Technology
Portfolio Companies: Micarga.com, Gone App, Mortgage Hippo, Replica Labs, Socrex, PulsoSocial, Seahorse App, Agora, Viajala, Ustraap, Oppten, Genuisly, CodeRise, Authy, Entryless, Cambly, AllTheRooms, Play Vox, Oja.la, Bankity, Donortap, LetsLunch, Streem

Key Executives:
Andres Barreto, Managing Partner
Hernando Barreto, Managing Partner

3117 SOCIEDAD REGIONAL DE PROMOCION DEL PRINCIPADO
Parque Tecnologico de Asturias
Llanera 33428
Spain

Phone: 34-985980096 Fax: 34-985980222
e-mail: srp@srp.es
web: www.srp.es

Mission Statement: Its objective is the promotion of investments in the region, participating in the share capital in societies to constitute or already existing by means of the capital risk modality. Actively seeking new investments
Fund Size: $21.9 Million
Founded: 1984
Industry Group Preference: All Sectors Considered

Key Executives:
Víctor M. González Marroquín, President
María Callejón Fornieles, Vice President

3118 SOFTBANK VENTURES KOREA
Kyobo Tower
13th Floor, A-Wing
Seocho-Dong, Seocho-Gu
Seoul 1302-22
Korea

Phone: 02-34849000 Fax: 02-34849010
web: www.softbank.co.kr

Mission Statement: Goes beyond a mere financial investor, Softbank Ventures, aids in the creation and development of each company's value as a strategic partner.
Industry Group Preference: Internet, Mobile, Entertainment, Education
Portfolio Companies: Naldo, Aiara, Buzzbil, Chinada, Classting, Clipcomm, Cocone, Dadam Game, Doobic, Dramafever, Ender's Fund, Enermont, Enswers, FXGear, Smartots, Gretech, GSM, Healcerion, HelloNature, ID INCU, IMX, Infomark, ini3, IntelRa, Knowre, KNS, Korbit, LeisureQ, Mangoplate, Microsoftware, Mirageworks, MOS, NBIZ, Ngine, nPlatform, PenAndFree, Pishoniac, Phychips, Megaphone TV, Playnery, Pulsus, Qualson, RadioPulse, R-Square, Redmart, Seworks, Snaps, Standard Networks,

Strong Hold, Systran, TeraSquare, Tokopedia, Jandi, TVU, Uway, Vaimi, Value Creators & Company, TVU Pack, Wave3Studio, Xavis

Key Executives:
  Greg Moon, CEO/President
  Education: BA, Spanish Literature, Korea University; MBA, Drexel University
  Background: Business Development, Trigen Computers; Associate, Softbank Technology Ventures; CEO, Softbank Commerce Korea; Co-CEO, KeyEast

3119 SOLID VENTURES
1001 LH Amsterdam
Amsterdam 1001 LH
Netherlands

Phone: 31-655-32-58-73
e-mail: info@solidventures.nl
web: www.solidventures.nl

Mission Statement: Solid Ventures invests in young, innovative and fast growing companies in the Netherlands.
Geographic Preference: The Netherlands
Industry Group Preference: Internet, Telecommunications, Software, Digital Media & Marketing
Portfolio Companies: SoldPrint Europe, Sixpack Mobile Applications, Scense, Boostermedia, BackupAgent B.V., Immidio, Mirror 42, Respectance B.V., 24access Solutions B.V., Avinity Systems B.V.

Key Executives:
  Floris van Alkemade, Partner
  Herman DeLatte, Partner
  Robert Wilhelm, Partner

3120 SONY EUROPE
Kemperplatz 1
Berlin 10785
Germany

Phone: 49-30585812345 Fax: 49-1805252587
e-mail: support.l@eu.sony.com
web: www.sony.de

Founded: 1946
Minimum Investment: $ 1000000 EURO
Investment Criteria: Early Stage, Expansion and Development Capital, Seed Capital, Startup Capital
Industry Group Preference: Communications, Computer Related, Electronic Technology, Financial Services, Internet Technology, Insurance, Real Estate

Key Executives:
  Howard Stringer, Chairman and CEO

3121 SOVEREIGN CAPITAL
25 Victoria Street
London SW1H 0EX
United Kingdom

Phone: 44-2073408800 Fax: 44-2073408811
e-mail: info@sovereigncapital.co.uk
web: www.sovereigncapital.co.uk

Mission Statement: Formerly Nash, Sells & Partners.
Geographic Preference: United Kingdom
Fund Size: $794 Million
Founded: 1988
Average Investment: $3.5-17.6 Million
Investment Criteria: MBO, MBI, Development Capital, Refinancing, Restructuring, IBO, Acquisitions
Industry Group Preference: Leisure, Healthcare, Waste & Recycling, Education, Corporate Services, Environment Products & Services
Portfolio Companies: 8 Solutions, Alcumus Group, Axis Group Integrated Services, Cordium

Key Executives:
  Andrew Hayden, Managing Partner
  Education: BS Medical Applications, University of London
  Background: Commercial Director, Industrial MBI
  Monica Bergvall, Investment Manager
  Education: BA History, Cambridge University
  Background: Director, Gresham Trust

3122 SPARK VENTURES
5 St. John's Lane
London EC1M 4BH
United Kingdom

Phone: (0)20 8123 0665
e-mail: enquirie@sparkventures.com
web: www.sparkventures.com

Mission Statement: SPARK Ventures is a leading European early stage venture capital company. Across a range of funds, we invest in the UK's best technology to create great companies with world class potential.
Geographic Preference: Europe
Investment Criteria: Early-Stage
Industry Group Preference: Technology
Portfolio Companies: Academia, Aspex Semiconductor, DEM Solutions, Firebox.com, Gambling Compliance, IMImobile, Kobalt Music, Mind Candy, MyDeco, Notonthehighstreet.com, OpenX

Key Executives:
  Charles Berry, Non-Executive Director
  Education: C.A.(KPMG)
  Background: Carnegie Group, Union Bank of Switzerland, the Bank of Tokyo-Mitsubishi, London
  Andrew Carruthers, Director
  Education: CA..(Moore Stephens)
  Background: 3i plc, Investment Trust plc(non-executive director)
  Directorships: Co-founder
  Helen Sinclair, Non-Executive Director
  Education: C.A., MA in Economics(Cambridge University)
  Background: Advent Venture Partners(Finance Director), Coopers & Lybrand(Accountancy), Laurence Prust(Corporate Finance)

3123 SPINUP VENTURE
Ozerkovskaya Nab.
50/1 Office 512
Moscow 1150504
Russia

Phone: +7 916 665 71 48
e-mail: info@spinupper.com
web: www.spinupventure.com

Mission Statement: SpinUp Venture has been founded by professionals with vast experience in business consultancy, corporate banking, project management and executive search. We offer a hands-on and pragmatic approach to commercialization of new concepts, expanding the potential of original ideas and providing a sound platform to build a link between the talents, innovators and traditional venture capital.
Geographic Preference: Russia, Asia, United States, Europe
Investment Criteria: Early-Stage
Industry Group Preference: Internet, Mobile, Robotics, Alternative Energy, Clean Technology, New Materials, Nanotechnology, Biomedical, High Technology
Portfolio Companies: JFDI.Asia, HaxAsia, Displair

Key Executives:
  Sergey Gorokhov, General Director/Partner
  e-mail: sgorokhov@spinupper.com
  Education: MBA, Open University Business School

3124 SRIJAN CAPITAL
Sri Sai Complex, 1st Floor
Pampa Extension
Hebbal Kempapura
Bangalore 24
India

e-mail: ravi@srijancapital.com
web: www.srijancapital.com

Mission Statement: Srijan provides seed stage investments to technology startups. We target start-ups that are based out of India, or have India as a target market.
Geographic Preference: India
Investment Criteria: Early-Stage
Industry Group Preference: E-Commerce & Manufacturing, SaaS, Mobile, Social Media, Consumer Internet
Portfolio Companies: Explara, Tokitaki, Mech Mocha, Venturesity, CollateBox, CouponRani, AllConnect, Mediaspan, BuildLinks, Visionair

Key Executives:
Ravi Trivedi, Founder
Education: MS, Computer Science, Indian Institute of Technology; MBA, Fuqua School of Business
Background: Principal, Southeast Interactive Technology Funds; Equity Analyst, Bank of America

3125 SRIW SA SRIW Group
13 Destenay Avenue
Liege 4000
Belgium

Phone: 32-42219811 Fax: 32-42219999
e-mail: info@sriw.be
web: www.sriw.be/en/

Mission Statement: Actively seeking new investments.
Industry Group Preference: Metals, Chemicals, Agribusiness, Wood Industries, Tourism, Services, Construction, Glass, Paper, Printing, Publishing
Portfolio Companies: Barthel Pauls, Comes Bois, Spacebel, Ateliers Jean Del'Cour, Cortigroupe, Bodymat, Belga-Films, Trendy Foods Finances, Briqueteries de Ploegsteert, Coprosain, ISIS, Grandes Distilleries de Charleroi, Equilis, Cap Energie II, Lampiris, TPF, Istar Medical, Cardio 3 Biosciences, Euroscreen, Icarus, Ronveaux

Key Executives:
Jean-Claude Dehovre, Chairman
Bernard Marchand, Vice Chairman

3126 SSE VENTURES
200 Dunkeld Road
Perth PH1 3AQ
United Kingdom

Phone: 44-0-1738-456-253
e-mail: ventures@sse.com

Mission Statement: SSE Ventures was established to develop and grow SSE's portfolio of investments in small and medium-sized businesses offering renewable, sustainable and energy efficiency products and services. The team is interested in products and services which support current activities within the SSE group or which we expect to play key roles in the future.
Geographic Preference: United Kingdom, Ireland, Europe, United States, Asia
Industry Group Preference: Energy, Energy Efficiency
Portfolio Companies: Aquamarine Power, BiFab, Wind Towers Ltd, ONZO, SSE Rogerstone, IE CHP, Intelligent Energy, Logan Energy, Premium Power

Key Executives:
Alistair Phillips-Davies, Chief Executive

3127 STAGEONE VENTURES
89 Medinat HaYehudim Street
Building E, 11th Floor
Herzliya Pituach
Israel

Phone: 972-3-649-4000 Fax: 972-3-649-5000
e-mail: info@stageonevc.com
web: www.stageonevc.com

Mission Statement: StageOne Ventures provides financing and professional guidance to early-stage companies in order to help building exceptional enterprises. We invest primarily in early stage companies in the fields of Software, Communications, Internet and Media, The fund is committed to providing its portfolio companies with top value creation through the technological and financial strength of its team. By acting in synergy with the dominant trends in IT & Telecommunications, StageOne invests in start-ups whose exceptional technologies address market leaders' true needs.
Geographic Preference: Israel
Fund Size: $50 million
Investment Criteria: Early-Stage
Industry Group Preference: Software, Communications, Internet, Media
Portfolio Companies: AVANAN, cVidya Networks

Key Executives:
Yuval Cohen, Managing Partner
Education: LLB, MBA, Hebrew University
Background: General Partner, Israel Infinity Fund; Vice President, ISAL
Directorships: Traffix Systems, Trivnet, Guardium, Radwiz, Oridion Medical, Lab-One Innovations, cVidya Networks, Oversi Networks

3128 STAR VENTURES
Maximilianstr. 35a
Munich D-80539
Germany

e-mail: info@star-ventures.de
web: www.star-ventures.com

Mission Statement: Invests in private, emerging and later-stage companies.
Geographic Preference: Israel, USA
Fund Size: $1 Billion
Founded: 1992
Investment Criteria: Seed, start-up and late stage investments.
Industry Group Preference: Telecommunications, Enterprise Services, Wireless Technologies, Life Sciences
Portfolio Companies: Accord, Acopia Networks, AeroScout, Airspan, Aigotec, Alvarion, Answersoft, Applied Science Fiction, Armon, Aspect, Advanced Vision Technology, Be, Benchmarq Microelectronics, BigBand Networks, Bioline Rx, Brix Networks, Broadbus, Broadlight, C-Port, Cadent, Capstone, Cedar Point Communications, Celerica, Celletra, Ceragon Networks, Ciena, CigniTens, Creo Products, Cube Optics AG, cVidya, Decalog B.V., Decru, EFI Electronics for Imaging, Entrisphere, EveryDay Health, Evotec NeuroSciences GmbH, EZchip, Fuego Tech, Fundtech, GENBAND, Geotek, Groove Mobile, Identity Software, iloxx GmbH, Imedia, Intercell AG, Jacada, Kabira, PPU Maconomy, maincontrol, Mangrove, Medical Present Value, MediGene AG, Mercado, Mintera, NextNet Wireless, Nicecom, Nur, Odin, Omnia Communications, Onex Communications, OraMetrix, OrSense, OSHAP, Paradigm, Precise Software Solutions, Procognia, RADCOM, RAScom, RF Micro Devices, RiT, Sequenom, Sheer Networks, Siano, Sipera, Softcom, Summit, Technomatix, Proxim Wireless, Topio, TranSwitch, Trivnet, UltraCom, UPTI, Vidyo, Viryanet, Vizrt, Wayport, Xignal, Xtera

Other Locations:
Ackerstein Towers Bldg. C
10 Abba Eben Avenue

Venture Capital & Private Equity Firms / International Firms

PO Box 12600
Herzelia Pituach 4672528
Israel
Phone: 972-97662226 **Fax:** 972-97662227

Two Galleria Tower
13455 Noel Road
Suite 1670
Dallas, TX 75240
Phone: 972-776-1516 **Fax:** 972-702-1103

Key Executives:
Dr. Meir Barel, Managing Partner
e-mail: jb@star-ventures.com
Education: MS, University of Texas; BS, Texas A&M University
Background: Director of Strategic Investments for Intel Capital, Founder, CEO and President of AnswerSoft, Davox as VP Marketing, VP Marketing of NetBoost Corporation
Amit Barel, Investment Manager
e-mail: BAR@star-ventures.com
Education: Dr. Barel holds a Master's Degree and a Doctorate Degree (Dr.-Ing.) in Electrical Engineering from the Department of Data Communication at the Technical University in Aachen, Germany.
Background: Investment Manager & Managing Partner of TVM - Techno Venture Management GmbH & Co. KG
Petra Pornin, Assistant to Managing Partner
Education: Mr. Maher graduated Cum Laude with a Masters Degree in Electrical Engineering and Physics from the University of Illinois in 1969.
Background: Member of the Board of Directors for Siemens Information and Communication Networks Group from 1997 - 2002. Founded and chaired Mustang Ventures; President - Access; Director of Marketing for worldwide product planning within the Public Communication Netw
Directorships: Investment Manager

3129 STARFISH VENTURES
Level 1
120 Jolimont Road
East Melbourne VIC 3002
Australia

Phone: 61-3-9654-2121
e-mail: admin@starfishvc.com
web: www.starfishvc.com

Mission Statement: Starfish Ventures partners with talented entrepreneurs to build successful innovative global technology companies. Their team's proven expertise in venture capital investing, entrepreneurship and technology gives the firm the skills to navigate the challenges of seeding, building and managing high growth technology businesses from an Australian base.

Geographic Preference: Australia
Fund Size: AU $400 million
Founded: 2001
Average Investment: $1 - $5 million
Investment Criteria: All Stages
Industry Group Preference: Information Technology, Life Sciences
Portfolio Companies: Aktano, Armaron Bio, Audinate, Bubble Gum, DesignCrowd, dorsaVi, ImpediMed, MetaCDN, Mimetica, MuriGen Therapeutics, Myriax, Nitro Software, Protagonist

Key Executives:
John Dyson, Investment Principal
Education: BS, Monash University, Graduate Diploma, Finance & Investment, Securities Institute of Australia; MBA, RMIT University
Background: General Manager, JAFCO Investment; Schroders, Nomura Securities, KPMG, ANZ McCaughan
Directorships: Aruspex, Atmail, Audinate, Ausra, Distra, Holly Australia, Icix, Myriax, Quickcomm, Space-Time Research, Xelor, Zoom Systems
Michael Panaccio, Investment Principal
Education: BS, PhD, Medicine, University of Melbourne; MBA, RMIT University
Background: Investment Manager, JAFCO Investment; Head of the Department of Microbiology, Victorian Institute of Animal Science
Directorships: DorsaVi, Energy Response, Impedimed, Murigen, Neuprotect, Ofidium

3130 STARPHARMA POOLED DEVELOPMENT LIMITED
4-6 Southampton Crescent
Abbotsford 3067
Australia

Phone: 61-385322700 **Fax:** 61-395105955
e-mail: info@starpharma.com
web: www.starpharma.com

Mission Statement: An ASX listed company developed to invest in both pharmaceutical and non-pharmaceutical applications of dendrimer nanotechnology.

Geographic Preference: Australia
Founded: 1996
Industry Group Preference: Drug Delivery, Agrochemicals

Key Executives:
Peter T Bartels AO, FAISM, FRS, Chairman & Non-Executive Director
e-mail: john.raff@starpharma.com
Education: John Raff received a Ph.D. from Melbourne University in 1982 for molecular biology studies on cell recognition systems, under the supervision of Professor Adrienne Clarke
Background: General Manager of the Biomolecular Research Institute
Directorships: Executive Director
Jackie Fairley, BSc, BVSc (Hons), MBA, Chief Executive Officer

3131 STATE STREET GLOBAL ADVISORS
68th Floor, Two International Finance Centre
Hong Kong
China

Phone: 852-21030288 **Fax:** 852-21030200
web: www.ssga.com

Mission Statement: Established in Asia to service clients and develop new institutional business.

Geographic Preference: Worldwide
Fund Size: $1.4 Trillion
Founded: 1990

Key Executives:
Bernard P. Reilly, Global Head of Strategy
Education: BA Economics and Agricultural Economics, University of Exeter
Background: Private Client Portfolio Manager, KBIM; Research Team, KBIM UK; Senior Asian Fund Manager, KBIM
Scott F. Powers, President and CEO

3132 STATOIL TECHNOLOGY INVEST
Norway

web: innovate.statoil.com

Mission Statement: Statoil engages in projects with entrepreneurs and industrial companies in order to help new and emerging technologies reach the market. We have a particular focus on the development and commercialisation phases of new technology. This includes detailed product development, prototyping, testing and verification, and market planning. Our contribution to a project can include technical expertise, defining user requirements, project supervision, pilot tests, establishing networks, business/commercial advice, and financial support.

Geographic Preference: Norway
Investment Criteria: Seed-Stage, Early-Stage
Industry Group Preference: Oil & Gas, Energy
Portfolio Companies: AGR Enhanced Drilling Systems, Aptomar AS, Fisbones AS, Octio AS, Resman AS, Sekal AS, Silixa Ltd., TracID AS, Verdande Technology AS, Coreteq Systems, Ecotone AS, Gravitude AS, Hybond AS, Lux Assure, Neodrill AS, Numascale AS, Robotic Drilling Systems AS, Sofitech AS, TechInvent AS

3133 STEAMBOAT VENTURES
Unit 1002-1005
One Corporate Avenue
222 Hu Bin Road
Shanghai 200021
China

Phone: 86 (21) 2308 1800 **Fax:** 86 (21) 2308 1999
web: www.steamboatvc.com

Mission Statement: To help young companies successfully face the challenges of becoming leaders in their markets.

Geographic Preference: United States, China
Founded: 2000
Average Investment: $2 - $15 million
Investment Criteria: Early-Stage, Mid-Stage
Industry Group Preference: Technology, Digital Media & Marketing, Consumer Products
Portfolio Companies: 51Fanli.com, 56.com, Bokecc, Cocoa China, FunPlus, GoPro, Gridsum, Netmovie, Shangpin, Troodon, UUSee, Youxigu, Yoyi, YY.com

20/F Wellable Commercial Building
513 Hennessy Road, Causeway Bay
Hong Kong SAR
China
Phone: 852-35119276 **Fax:** 852-35119002

801 North Brand Boulevard
Suite 665
Glendale, CA 91203
Phone: 818-858-1890 **Fax:** 818-696-2686

Key Executives:
John Ball, Founder & Managing Director
e-mail: john.ball@steamboatvc.com
Education: BA, Biological Sciences, Tufts University; MBA, Harvard Business School
Background: Corporate Development Group, Walt Disney Company; Burr Egan Deleage & Co.
Directorships: RazorGator, Beijing NetMovie
Liping Fan, Chief Financial Officer
e-mail: liping.fan@steamboatvc.com
Education: MS, Accounting, MBA, Finance, Binghamton University
Background: CFO, RWI Ventures; Senior Financial Analyst, Merck & Company; Senior Associate, PricewaterhouseCoopers
Directorships: VCBC

3134 STEELHOUSE VENTURES
Sundgauer Strasse 105c
Berlin 14169
Germany

Phone: 49-030221608199

Mission Statement: Steelhouse Ventures Limited has been established to bring capital and expertise to new business start-ups in the areas of energy, telecommunications and advanced technology.

Geographic Preference: Europe
Average Investment: £500,000
Investment Criteria: Early-Stage
Industry Group Preference: Energy, Technology

Key Executives:
Peter Bryant, Founding Partner
e-mail: peter@steelhouse-ventures.com

3135 STEPSTONE
57-59 St James's Street
London SW1A 1LD
United Kingdom

Phone: 44 0 207 647 7550 **Fax:** 44 0 207 647 7599
web: www.stepstoneglobal.com

Mission Statement: A dedicated purchaser of secondary private equity interests and advises funds in excess of $700 million. The team has the capacity to manage deals in a broad range of sizes worldwide.

Geographic Preference: Europe, United States, Middle East, Far East
Founded: 2000
Investment Criteria: Discreet liquidity solutions, buyout, growth, mezzanine: Corporations, Financial Institutions, Family Offices

Key Executives:
Marleen Groen, Senior Advisor
e-mail: groen@greenparkcapital.co.uk
Education: BA, MA, Leiden University; MBA, Rotterdam School of Management
Zifri Baharudin, Performance Monitoring Manager
e-mail: jordan@greenparkcapital.co.uk
Education: MBA, Leicester Business School
Background: Strategic Acquisitions, international real estate company; Business Analyst, US family office
John Bohill, Senior Advisor
e-mail: french@greenparkcapital.co.uk
Education: BS, University of Southampton
Background: Chartered Accountant, KPMG
Nicole Chadwick, Executive Assistant
e-mail: topley@greenparkcapital.co.uk
Education: BS Biochemistry, Imperial College; MBA, INSEAD
Background: Partner, early stage venture capital fund; CSFB

3136 STIC VENTURES CORPORATION LIMITED
10 Fl. MSA Bldg., 12, Teheran-ro 78-gil
Gangnam-gu
Seoul 135-840
South Korea

Phone: 82-234047800 **Fax:** 82-234535188
web: www.stic.co.kr

Mission Statement: Actively seeking new investments.

Geographic Preference: South Korea, USA, Hong Kong, China
Fund Size: $333 Million
Founded: 1999
Average Investment: $2 Million
Minimum Investment: $500,000
Investment Criteria: Early-stage
Industry Group Preference: Information Technology
Portfolio Companies: LIG, CSL, Yusin, Daesung Eltec, Songwoo, Orion Technology, Wooyang HC, TacBright, Hyundai Oil Terminal, Posco Energy, RFHIC, Innorex Technologies, New Focus Auto, SaehWa, AccessBio, Soulbrain, Shinsung Solar Energy, Hy-Lok, MDS Technology, JNTC, TIB, JEL Hydraulics, YG, Medytox, Golfzon, Kona International, Genic, Vieworks, Sapphire Technology

Key Executives:
Yong Hwan Do, Founder and Chairman
e-mail: log@stic.co.kr
Education: BA. Business Administration from Yeungnam University and completed MBA course at Seoul National

Venture Capital & Private Equity Firms / International Firms

University.
Background: Dongsuh Securities
Byung Won Choi, Founding Member / Executive Partner & CEO
e-mail: log@stic.co.kr
Education: BSEE from Sogang University
Background: Samsung Electronics

3137 STRAND HANSON LIMITED
26 Mount Row
Mayfair
London W1K 3SQ
United Kingdom

Phone: 44-02074093494 Fax: 44-02074091761
e-mail: mail@strandhanson.co.uk
web: www.strandhanson.co.uk

Mission Statement: Provides financial advice to public and private UK corporates, private equity houses and qualified investors.

Geographic Preference: Europe
Founded: 1993
Investment Criteria: Mbos, Mbis
Industry Group Preference: Technology, E-Commerce & Manufacturing, Financial Services, Telecommunications, Biotechnology
Portfolio Companies: Education Overseas Ltd, European Investor Services, Federated Foods, Newsletter Publishing

Key Executives:
Simon Raggett, Chief Executive
e-mail: simonraggett@strandhanson.co.uk
Background: Grieg Middleton & Co
Hon. Robert Hanson, Chairman
e-mail: roberthanson@strandhanson.co.uk
Education: Oxford University
Background: Associate Director, NM Rothschild & Sons
Rory Murphy, Director
e-mail: rorymurphy@strandhanson.co.uk
Background: Accountant, KPMG; Grieg Middleton & Co; Charterhouse Securities Limited
James Harris, Director
e-mail: jamesharris@strandhanson.co.uk
Background: Robert Fleming Securities; SG Securities; Arbuthnot Securities
Stuart Faulkner, Director
e-mail: stuartfaulkner@strandhanson.co.uk
Education: St. Anne's College, Oxford University
Background: Investment Banking, Barclays de Zoete Wedd; Merrill Lynch
Matthew Chandler, Director of Corporate Finance
e-mail: matthewchandler@strandhanson.co.uk
Education: BS, Bath University
Background: Capita Corporate Finance Ltd
Angela Hallett, Director of Corporate Finance
e-mail: angelapeace@strandhanson.co.uk
Education: BA & BC, University of Melbourne
Background: Accountant, Arthur Andersen
Richard Tulloch, Director of Corporate Finance
e-mail: richardtulloch@strandhanson.co.uk
Education: Bristol University
Background: Corporate Finance, ING Barings; Arbuthnot Securities
Warren Pearce, Managing Director, Strand Hanson South Africa
e-mail: warrenpearce@strandhanson.co.uk
Education: Business Science, University of Cape Town
Richard Evans, Chief Operating Officer and Compliance Director
e-mail: paulcocker@strandhanson.co.uk
Background: Day Investment Banking; Deloitte London
James Spinney, Director of Corporate Finance
e-mail: jamesspinney@strandhanson.co.uk
Education: Durham University
Background: Accountant, Pricewaterhousecoopers; Corporate Finance, Earnst & Young

Andrew Emmott, Director of Corporate Finance
e-mail: davidaltberg@strandhanson.co.uk
Background: Corporate Dept, Rosenblatt Solicitor
Naiem Hussain, Director - Strand Ventures
e-mail: liambuswell@strandhanson.co.uk
Education: University of Warwick
Background: Investment Banking, Merrill Lynch; Inenco Group
James Bellman, Analyst
e-mail: rorychichester@strandhanson.co.uk
Background: Kandahar Real Estate; Carphone Warehouse
Scott McGregor, Analyst
e-mail: williambarkes@strandhanson.co.uk
Education: Newcastle University
Background: Killik & Co Stockbrokers; Evolution Securities; Daniel Stewart; St Helen's Capital
Simon Wharmby, Non-Executive Director
e-mail: simonwharmby@strandhanson.co.uk
Education: University of East Anglia
Background: Corporate Stockbroker, Sheppards, Charles Stanley, Corporate Synergy

3138 SUMMIT BRIDGE CAPITAL
No. 7 East Third Ring Middle Road
Chaoyang District
Beijing 100020
China

Phone: +86 (10) 5979 7669 Fax: +86 (10) 6804 3607
web: www.summitbridgecapital.com

Mission Statement: Summit Bridge Capital is a growth technology fund co-managed by Atlantic Bridge Capital and WestSummit Capital. The Fund targets fast growing technology companies with a presence or strategic interest in Ireland and China.

Geographic Preference: Ireland, China
Fund Size: $100 million
Industry Group Preference: Technology, Software, Semiconductors, Cloud Computing, Big Data, Clean Technology, Food & Beverage, Medical Technology, Agriculture, Financial Services
Portfolio Companies: Accuris, Fieldaware

3139 SUNEVISION HOLDINGS LIMITED
52/F, Sun Hung Kai Centre
30 Harbour Road
Wanchai
Hong Kong

Fax: 852-25115388
e-mail: enquiry@sunevision.com
web: www.sunevision.com

Mission Statement: SUNeVision is the first company in China and Asia to integrate and leverage the entire Internet value chain to achieve critical mass with significant economies of scale.

Geographic Preference: China, Asia
Founded: 1972
Investment Criteria: Start-up
Industry Group Preference: Technology, Internet Technology

Other Locations:
37/F, Shanghai Central Plaza
381 Huai Hai Zhong Road
Shanghai 200020
China
Phone: 86-21-6391-5123 Fax: 86-21-6391-5868

Room 1117, 11/f, Office Tower 2, Sun Dong An
Sun Dong An Plaza
138 Wang Fu Jing Da Jie
Beijing
China
Phone: 86-10-6528-1822 Fax: 86-10-6528-1823

Key Executives:
Ping Luen, Chairman

3140 SUNSTONE CAPITAL
Lautrupsgade 7
5th Floor
Copenhagen 2100
Denmark

Phone: 45-20126000 Fax: 45-39209898
web: www.sunstone.eu

Mission Statement: Headquartered in Copenhagen, Sunstone Capital is an early-stage Life Science and Technology venture capital company investing in European start-up companies with strong potential to achieve global success in their markets. Since our establishment in 2007, we have built a strong portfolio currently totaling 50 companies and have completed several successful trade sales and IPOs.

Geographic Preference: Europe
Fund Size: 700 million Euro
Founded: 2007
Investment Criteria: Early-Stage
Industry Group Preference: Life Sciences, Technology
Portfolio Companies: Acarix, Adenium Biotech, Alligator Bioscience, Amen, Anergis, Asante, Asetek, Atonomics, Biomonitor, Booztgroup, Cloud Made, Contrast, Egalet, Evolva, F2G, FBC Device, FlatFrog, Folicum, Freespree, Galecto Biotech, Gidsy, Imix, Ipt, Issuu, Jenavalve, Jurag Separation, Layar, MakieLab, Microtask, Neotechnology, Nsgene, Nuevolution, OrphaZyme, Paymill, Podio, Preview Networks, Prezi, Rovsing Dynamics, Santaris Pharma, Symphogen, Trunk Archive, Vaximm, Vivostat, Zealand Pharma, Zymenex

Other Locations:
1370 Willow Road
2nd Floor
Menlo Park, CA 94025
Phone: 650-5871518

Angelholmsvagen 28
Bastad 26931
Sweden
Phone: 46-431311740

Key Executives:
Jimmy Fussing Nielsen, Co-Founder/Managing Partner
45-27-12-8221

3141 SUPREMUM CAPITAL
10 Haymarket
London SW1Y 4BP
United Kingdom

Phone: 44-2071291061
web: www.supremum-capital.com

Mission Statement: Supremum Capital Partners have a broad and diversified investment mandate focused on VC investments in Cleantech, Internet & Digital as well as Innovative Technology sectors. Within those broad sectors we tend to prefer companies that offer a unique solution to real customer issues as well as products that offer a distinct and defensible technology advantage.

Geographic Preference: Europe, Israel, Russia
Average Investment: $500,000 - $10 million
Industry Group Preference: Clean Technology, Internet, Digital Media & Marketing, Technology
Portfolio Companies: Inplat, Atosho, CTRL, MRGK, Webbankir, Domfinans

Other Locations:
Donskaya str. 29/9, build. 1
Moscow 119049
Russia
Phone: 7-4955024780

Key Executives:
Ilya Belyaev, Co-Founder
Background: JP Morgan, Barclays Capital, VEB Capital

3142 SVI VEN CAPITAL
1 Raffles Place
#18-03 One Raffles Place
048616
Singapore

Phone: 65-6536-6123 Fax: 65-6536-6983

Mission Statement: SBI Ven Capital is a Singapore-based, leading private equity firm that invests in growth capital opportunities across Asia. We have a proven track record of partnering with growth-stage companies and assembling critical resources needed to grow businesses in Asia. Our investment team combines financial acumen, industry insight and operational expertise to enhance the value of the companies we invest in.

Geographic Preference: Asia
Investment Criteria: Growth-Stage
Portfolio Companies: Greenlots, Liqvid, HNB, Commercial Bank of Ceylon, Panviva

3143 SWISSCOM
Alte Tiefenaustrasse 6
Worblaufen 3048
Switzerland

web: www.swisscom.ch

Mission Statement: Swisscom Ventures seeks to acquire minority stakes in companies that operate in promising markets for information, communication and entertainment technologies. We invest in innovative areas that are strategic for Swisscom, in terms of revenue increase, quality improvements and cost reductions. As a value-creating investor, Swisscom is able to provide companies with the technical know-how and strategic experience of an established telecommunications provider.

Geographic Preference: Switzerland
Founded: 1852
Industry Group Preference: Telecommunications, Communications
Portfolio Companies: Amplidata, Asoka, ASSIA, Connect.me, Glass2Energy, I-Concerts, Matrixx, MVP, MyStrom, Piston Cloud Computing, Poken, Quantenna, Softbank Broadband Fund, Swiss VC/PE Investment, Vilant Systems, Firecomms, Kyte, LiberoVision, Sequans

Key Executives:
Hansueli Loosli, Chairman of the Board of Directors
Education: PhD, University of Saarland
Background: Google; Director Product Management & Engineering, YouTube

3144 SYDNEY SEED FUND
Level 2, 60 Clarence Street
Sydney NSW 2000
Australia

web: www.sydneyseedfund.com.au

Mission Statement: The Sydney Seed Fund is an early stage investment fund managed by experienced entrepreneurs looking to invest in Australia's most passionate tech founders.

Geographic Preference: Australia
Founded: 2013
Average Investment: $100,000
Investment Criteria: Early-Stage
Industry Group Preference: Technology
Portfolio Companies: Qwilr, CeeQTM, Rate Us, GoFar

Key Executives:
Benjamin Chong, Co-Director
Education: BComm, University of New South Wales

Venture Capital & Private Equity Firms / International Firms

3145 SYNERGO SGR
Via Campo Lodigiano, 3
Milan 20122
Italy

Phone: +39 02 859111 Fax: +39 02 72094122
e-mail: welcome@synergosgr.it

Mission Statement: Specializes in partnering with ambitious entrepreneurs in order to increase the value of their companies.

Average Investment: 35 million
Minimum Investment: 20 million
Portfolio Companies: Air Italy, allSystem, Arquati, Bozzetto Group, Building Energy, Cobra, Cast Futura, Cartonplast Group, Ducati, Glutinatus, E-Motion, IPC, Kinetika, Mediacontech, Redecam Group, Trei, Tecnowind Group, Unopiu, Valvitalia, V2, Waste Italia, Motovario, Fin Tyre, Lediberg, Riri, Roenest Group, Byte, Kiian Group, Optissimo, Selènia, Vending System, Teckal, Cemengal, TMCI Padovan, Raccortubi Group, Colony Sardegna

3146 T-VENTURE HOLDINGS GmbH Deutsche Telecom
156 Gotenstrasse
Bonn 53175
Germany

Phone: 49-228308480 Fax: 49-22830848819
web: www.t-venture.de

Mission Statement: T-Venture invests in the seed and early stages of growth and expansion of companies in the TIMES market.

Geographic Preference: Europe, USA, Asia
Founded: 1997
Average Investment: EUR0.5 - EUR10 million
Minimum Investment: $0.6 Million
Investment Criteria: Start-up
Industry Group Preference: Information Technology, Communications, Telecommunications, Wireless Technologies
Portfolio Companies: BelAir Networks, Bol.com, CoreMedia, Danger, Flarion Technologies, Flash Networks, Gamigo, High-Tech Grunderfonds, Kineto Wireless, MessageVine, MindMatics & Mobile Commerce

Key Executives:
Patrick Meisberger, Managing Director and Fund Manager Digital Services
Katharina Hollender, Managing Director / CFO

3147 TAISHAN CAPITAL CORPORATION
2906, Central International Trade Center
6A Jianguomenwai Avenue
Chao Yang District
Beijing 100022
China

Phone: 86-1058693440 Fax: 86-1084193495
e-mail: investbank@taishancapital.com
web: www.taishancapital.com

Mission Statement: Focuses on investment banking, primarily corporate finance, mergers and acquisitions, and project finance; works closely with some of the world's leading investment banks, direct investment funds, and accounting and legal firms.

Geographic Preference: United States, Europe, China & Hong Kong
Fund Size: $10 Million.
Founded: 1998
Investment Criteria: Small and Mid-Stage
Industry Group Preference: All Sectors Considered

Key Executives:
Po-Wen Huang, Chairman and CEO

3148 TALIS CAPITAL
Unit 4 Rowan Court
56 High Street
Wimbledon
London SW19 5EE
United Kingdom

Phone: 44-02035426260 Fax: 44-02089447264
web: www.taliscapital.com

Mission Statement: As a multi family office, Talis Capital offers a differentiated approach to traditional technology venture firms. We offer a flexible approach in deal structuring with long term and hands on support to management teams. We look to create long term value by not only providing capital, but with our networks, contacts, sector experience and on-going commitment to the management team.

Industry Group Preference: Digital Media & Marketing
Portfolio Companies: Navmii Holdings, FuelQuest, Iwoca, Queremos/WeDemand

Key Executives:
Bob Finch, Co-Founder
Background: Co-Founder, Finch Investments
Directorships: The Vitol Group

3149 TAMAR TECHNOLOGY VENTURES LIMITED
Okeanos
50 Ramat Yam
Herzliya Pituach 46851
Israel

Phone: 972-99543555 Fax: 972-99543423

Mission Statement: Tamar Ventures, a venture capital partnership headquartered in Israel, invests in Israeli technology companies in Israel.

Geographic Preference: Europe, USA, Israel
Founded: 1998
Investment Criteria: All stages consider
Industry Group Preference: Technology, Communication Technology, Software, Networks, Optical Networks and Components, Wireless Technologies
Portfolio Companies: Allot Communication Ltd., Cergaon Networks Ltd, RADVision, Ex Libris Ltd., Hotbar.com, Edge Medical Devices Ltd, Lenslet Ltd., Silicon Value Ltd, Wisair Inc.

Key Executives:
Zohar Gilon, Managing Partner
e-mail: zohar@tamarventures.com
Education: MBA from Tel Aviv University
Background: W.S.P. Capital Holdings,
Thomas I. Unterberg, General Partner

3150 TAMIR FISHMAN VENTURES
38 Habarzel St
Tel Aviv 69710
Israel

Phone: 972-36849333 Fax: 972-36853393
web: www.tamirfishman.com

Mission Statement: The Tamir Fishman Group is Israel's leading and fastest growing full-service financial group.

Geographic Preference: Israel
Fund Size: $275 Million
Founded: 1997
Average Investment: $6.5 Million
Minimum Investment: $3 Million
Investment Criteria: Early Stage, Seed, Late Stage
Industry Group Preference: Communications, Software, Internet Technology, Life Sciences
Portfolio Companies: Sagitta, Nova, Disksites, Voltaire, MindGuard, Allot Comm, Expand Network, Native Networks, Celight & Blade fusion

Venture Capital & Private Equity Firms / International Firms

Key Executives:
Eldad Tamir, President & Joint Chief Executive Officer
Education: B.A. in Economics and an M.B.A. in Finance from Tel Aviv University.
Background: Evergreen Group & Clal Financing & Investment
Ilan Yanoshevsky, VP Finance

3151 TANK STREAM VENTURES
Level 10, 17-19 Bridge Street
Sydney NSW 2000
Australia

Phone: 61-2-9247-2232
e-mail: info@tankstream.vc
web: www.tankstream.vc

Mission Statement: Tank Stream Ventures is a technology focused fund investing in the brightest Australian early-stage startups.

Geographic Preference: Australia
Investment Criteria: Early-Stage
Industry Group Preference: Technology, Mobile, E-Commerce & Manufacturing, Software
Portfolio Companies: GoCatch, Spring.me, Pocketbook

Key Executives:
Jonathan Lui, Director/Founding Member
Background: Co-Founder/COO, Airtasker; Executive, IBM

3152 TARGET PARTNERS
Kardinal-Faulhaber-Strasse 10
Munich 80333
Germany

Phone: 49 (89)2070490 Fax: 49 (89)2070499
e-mail: info@targetpartners.de
web: www.targetpartners.de

Mission Statement: Target Partners invests in young technology companies in Germany, Austria and Switzerland.

Geographic Preference: Germany, Austria, Switzerland
Fund Size: 300 million Euro
Founded: 1999
Average Investment: 1 - 4 million Euro
Minimum Investment: 1 million Euro
Investment Criteria: Early-Stage
Industry Group Preference: Software, SaaS, Mobile, Green Technology, E-Commerce & Manufacturing, Internet
Portfolio Companies: Abusix, adjust, adsquare, ArangoDB, Datapath.io, Dedrone, Doo, Finanzchef24, German Auto Labs, Gpredictive, Instana, Locanis, Mercateo, NavVis, Quobyte, Scanbot (by Doo), Senic, Sicoya, Simplaex, So1, Suitpad, Swarm 64, tado§, Theva, TIS

Key Executives:
Kurt Muller, Partner
Education: Northwestern University; MBA, University of Chicago
Directorships: Mercateo AG, tadoø, ArangoDB, Adjust, NavVis, Theva DÜNnschichttechnik
Waldemar Jantz, Partner
Directorships: Finanzchef24, Gpredictive, Locanis, Sicoya, Abusix, Quobyte, Dedrone
Dr. Berthold von Freyberg, Partner
e-mail: berthold@targetpartners.de
Education: Diploma, Doctorate, Physics, ETH; MBA, INSEAD
Background: Investment Manager, TVM Capital; Office Product Division, Microsoft
Directorships: German Auto Labs, Simplaex, So1, SuitePad, Treasury Intelligence Solutions, Instana
Dr. Michael Munnix, Partner
Education: Technical University of Berlin; PhD, University of Duisberg-Essen
Directorships: Adsquare, Datapath.io, Swarm64

3153 TAT CAPITAL PARTNERS LTD.
Sonnhalde 2
PO Box
Oberrohrdorf CH-5452
Switzerland

Phone: 41-628323262 Fax: 41-56-485-8985
web: www.tat.ch

Mission Statement: TAT capital partners is a sector focused transatlantic venture firm investing in early stage and established companies in U.S. and Europe.

Geographic Preference: Worldwide, United States, West Coast
Fund Size: $100 million
Average Investment: $1 million
Investment Criteria: Early Stage, Expansions, Seed
Industry Group Preference: Biotechnology, Communications, Electronic Technology, Manufacturing, Medical
Portfolio Companies: Actano Ltd, Applied Spectral Imaging, Applied Sensor AB, Colibrys Ltd, Diamedica Ltd, EndoArt Ltd, Inovise Medical Inc, Medizinaltechnik Ltd, Media-Streams.Com, Nextek Inc, nLine Systems Corp, Sunlight Ltd, Unitive, Vertis Neuroscience Inc, Xemics Ltd

Other Locations:
Pletterjiweg Oost 1
Ara Hill Top Building
PO Box 6085
Curacao
Netherlands
Phone: 599-97323200 Fax: 599-9723232

Key Executives:
Dr. Thomas Egolf, Managing Director, Partner
e-mail: mputney@tat.ch
Mark Putney, Partner
e-mail: tegolf@tat.ch
Education: PhD Chemistry, MBA, University of Zurich
Background: Managing Director, Cellpack; Chairman/CEO, Zevatech
Johan Ekman, Partner
e-mail: jekman@tat.ch
Education: Masters Engineering Physics, Chalmers University of Technology; Masters Electrical Engineering, Swiss Federal Institute; Graduated, Business Information, IBO
Background: Management, Erni & Company AG; Consultant, Datex; Invent Management AB;
Rolf Haegler, Managing Director/Partner
e-mail: rhaegler@tat.ch
Background: Head of Sales, Ruegge Medical AG; Co-Owner/Managing Director, Schiller Ltd

3154 TECH TOUR
Place Flagey 7/7
Brussels 1050
Belgium

Phone: 32-26446580 Fax: 32-26446581
e-mail: info@e-unlimited.com
web: www.e-unlimited.com

Mission Statement: Profiles Europe's best technology companies through research, events and consulting.

Geographic Preference: Belgium
Fund Size: $200 Million
Founded: 1998

Key Executives:
Piet Serrure, Chairman
William Stevens, Chief Executive Officer

Venture Capital & Private Equity Firms / International Firms

3155 TECHNOLOGY PARK MALAYSIA CORPORATION SDN BHD
Level 5, Enterprise 4
Lebuhraya Puchong
Sg Besi
Kuala Lumpur 57000
Malaysia

Phone: 60-389982020 Fax: 60-389982110
e-mail: info@tpm.com.my
web: www.tpm.com.my

Mission Statement: Actively seeking new investments.
Geographic Preference: Worldwide
Founded: 1996
Investment Criteria: Various Stages
Industry Group Preference: Engineering, Biotechnology, Marketing, Communications, Property Management, Information Technology, Publishing
Portfolio Companies: Novozymes Malaysia Sdn Bhd, CCM Pharma Sdn Bhd, TT dotCom Sdn Bhd, Momentum Technologies Sdn Bhd, BERNAMA Systems And Solutions Advisor Sdn Bhd, MyStudyWeb Sdn Bhd, Intralink Concept Sdn Bhd, Datascan Berhad, Pilot Multimedia (M) Sdn Bhd

Key Executives:
YBhg Dato' Hj. Mohd Azman Hj. Shahidin, President and Chief Executive Officer
YB Dato' Nasarudin Hashim, Chairman

3156 TECNET
Niederosterreichring 2
Haus B
St. Polten 3100
Austria

Phone: 43-2742900019300 Fax: 43-2742900019319
web: www.tecnet.co.at

Mission Statement: Tecnet equity is a very experienced and open-minded contact for high technology firms in Lower Austria. Highly skilled in the fields of technology, and capital, engineering and business administration, our team provides a wide array of services for technology companies in Lower Austria. tecnet equity supports projects as they develop from innovative ideas to economically successful business ventures. tecnet's activities have created a strong economic stimulus for Lower Austria as a business location for technology companies.

Geographic Preference: Lower Austria
Fund Size: 38.3 million Euro
Average Investment: 300, 000 - 3 million Euro
Investment Criteria: Seed-Stage, Startup, Early-Stage, Expansion Stage
Industry Group Preference: Technology
Portfolio Companies: Anagnostics Bioanalysis, Indoo.rs, Kinamu Business Solutions, NxtControl, SeaLife Pharma, Sipwise, Visocon, Wikitude

Key Executives:
Georg Bartmann, Chairman

3157 TEKINVEST KK
3-17-14 Higashi 7F
Shibuya-ku
Tokyo 150-0011
Japan

Phone: 81-354669222
e-mail: info@tekinvest.com

Mission Statement: Actively seeking new investments.
Geographic Preference: Tokyo, North America
Fund Size: $10 Million
Founded: 1990
Investment Criteria: Direct Representation Service, Restructuring, Negotiating, Fundraising
Industry Group Preference: Information Technology, Banking, Distribution

Portfolio Companies: Mixx Entertainment Inc, Watchfire, XaQti Corporation, Vitesse Semiconductor Corporation
Key Executives:
Ray Klein, President
Education: Fluent speaker of English and a native speaker of Japanese. He graduated with a degree in Management and Economy from Hosei University
Background: General Manager, OEM and channel management strategy
Masahiro Kano, Executive Director

3158 TEKNOINVEST MANAGEMENT
Stranden 1A
Oslo 250
Norway

Phone: 47-22979000 Fax: 47-22979001

Mission Statement: Provides investors with attractive venture capital returns by assisting outstanding people building excellent companies based on innovative technologies.
Geographic Preference: Scandinavia, USA
Fund Size: $70 Million
Founded: 1984
Average Investment: NOK 5-50 million
Minimum Investment: $100,000
Investment Criteria: Seed, Start-up, First Stage, Second Stage
Industry Group Preference: Information Technology, Communications, Life Sciences, Medical & Health Related, Electronic Technology
Portfolio Companies: Affitech, AKVASmart, Angiogenix, BioForm

Key Executives:
Rune Dybesland, Chief Financial Officer Oslo - Norway
Education: M.Sc. degree in Computer Engineering(Norwegian Institute of Technology), MBA from INSEAD
Background: McKinsey & Co, Scandinavian companies, R&D strategy
Dr. Steinar J. Engelsen, Partner
Education: M.Sc. degree in Control Engineering from The Norwegian Institute of Technology
Background: Tandberg AS, AT Kearney, Norcontrol, The Norwegian Venture Capital Association, (EVCA),
Directorships: Partner Oslo - Norway
Andreas Mollatt, Partner
Education: M.Sc. degree in Economics and Business Administration,
Background: Amersham, Strategic Planning and Development, Thyssen Industrie AG,

3159 TELECOM VENTURE GROUP LIMITED
Unit A, 8th Floor, World Trust Tower
50 Stanley Street
Suite 4903
Central
Hong Kong

Phone: 852-21472080 Fax: 852-21473320

Mission Statement: International private equity firm that originates and structures transactions, and acts as a principal investor in companies involved in the Communications, Media, and Technology industries.
Geographic Preference: Asia Pacific
Fund Size: $600 Million
Industry Group Preference: Communications, Media, Technology
Portfolio Companies: Harbour Networks, Hanaro Telecom, PowerTel, Japan Telecom, Saehan Enertech, Neighborhood Cable, Request Broadband, Initech, 90East, SpeedCast, TransACT, inter-touch, Haansoft, Suntel, Usha Martin, BPL Communications, WorldxChange, PowerTel, Spectrum Network Systems, BayanT

Key Executives:
  Varun Bery, Managing Director & Co-Founder
  e-mail: contact@tvglp.com
  Education: Yale University Bachelor of Arts, summa cum laude, Harvard Business School MBA
  Background: AIFAL, Hanaro Telecom Inc, Newbridge Capital Korean Ltd.
  Directorships: Co-Founder
  John Troy, Managing Director & Co-Founder

3160 TELEFONICA VENTURES
20 Air Street
London W1B 5DN
United Kingdom

web: www.telefonica.com

Mission Statement: With offices in London, Silicon Valley and Madrid, Telefonica Ventures aims to maximise the VC portfolio value within the Telefonica Group, enhance Telefonica's relationship with start-ups and identify tomorrow's opportunities.

Geographic Preference: Europe, United States, Israel
Investment Criteria: Early-Stage, Mid-Stage, Late-Stage
Industry Group Preference: Technology, Communications, Digital Media & Marketing, Financial Services, Advertising, Cloud Computing, Healthcare, Security
Portfolio Companies: Amobee, Assia, Kit Digital, Eventful, Quantenna, Joyent, Boku

Other Locations:
  200 Evelyn Avenue
  Suite 120
  Mountain View, CA 94041

  Avenida das Nacoes Unidas 12901
  Torre Norte, 36th Floor
  Sao Paulo 04578-000 SP
  Brazil

  Rua Martiniano de Carvalho, 851
  Sao Paulo 01321-001 SP
  Brazil

  Distrito Telefonica
  Ronda de la Comunicadcion s/n
  Madrid 28050
  Spain

  Hadidhar 17
  Raanana
  Tel Aviv
  Israel

Key Executives:
  Matthew Key, Chief Executive Officer
  Education: Birmingham University
  Background: Chairman & CEO, Telefonica Europe; CEO O2 UK

3161 TENGELMANN VENTURES
Wissollstrasse 5-43
Mulheim an der Ruhr 45478
Germany

Phone: 49-0-208-5830 Fax: 49-0-208-583-2148
web: www.tev.de

Mission Statement: Since 2009, the Tengelmann Group's e-commerce strategy has involved investing in fast-growing, innovative e-commerce and internet companies. Indeed, since late 2009 Tengelmann-Ventures GmbH, a 100% subsidiary of the Tegelmann Group, has acquired shares in young, dynamic companies under the motto 'Funding your ideas'. Today, the company is already among the most important start-up companies in Germany. The focus of these investments is on e-commerce and social commerce concepts, market places, as well as on internet and web 2.0 technologies. Moreover, Tengelmann-Ventures GmbH not only offers financing expertise for start-ups, but also and management know-how and a useful infrastructure.

Founded: 2009
Investment Criteria: Seed-Stage, Early-Stage
Industry Group Preference: E-Commerce & Manufacturing, Social Media, Internet
Portfolio Companies: Baby-Mart.de, Brands4Friends, Canimix, Coffee Circle, Dafiti, Deal United, Delivery Hero, EKomi, Fab Furnish, High-Tech Grunderfonds, HitFox, Jumia, Lamoda, Lazada, Lieferheld, Linio, Mac IT Solutions, Mebelorama, Neonga, Olivenoel, Otto Gourmet, Selektessen, Stylight, Sum Up, Supreme, The Iconic, Trademob, Vinogusta, Zalando, Zalora, Zando, Zanui, Zitra

3162 TEUZA MANAGEMENT & DEVELOPMENT LTD
PO Box 25266
Haifa 31250
Israel

Phone: 972-48728788 Fax: 972-48729393
web: www.teuzafund.com

Mission Statement: To manage venture capital and to invest venture capital in Israel and abroad and also co-invest with the funds managed by it.

Geographic Preference: Israel
Fund Size: $300 Million
Founded: 1992
Average Investment: $500,000 -$4 million
Minimum Investment: $500,000
Investment Criteria: Start-up, Second Stage, Early Stage
Industry Group Preference: Telecommunications, Internet Technology, Biotechnology, Healthcare, Semiconductors, Software
Portfolio Companies: Botlex, Celtronix, Diagnostic Technology, Foxborn NMR, NESS, Nova, Oramir, Sagantea

Key Executives:
  Avi Kerbs, Chief Executive Officer
  Prof. Moshe Arens, Chairman

3163 TFG CAPITAL AG
Mainstra, 16
Marl 45768
Germany

Phone: 49-236597800 Fax: 49-236-5978033

Mission Statement: Actively seeking new investments.

Geographic Preference: Germany
Fund Size: $173 Million
Founded: 1994
Investment Criteria: Innovation, Management, IPO, Trade Sale
Industry Group Preference: Software, Biotechnology, Electronic Technology, Technology
Portfolio Companies: Eclerot and Ziegler AG, Oar AG, Power Automation AG, Viction AG

Key Executives:
  Detlef Geldmacher, Investment Manager
  Education: Banking background and is a business management graduate
  Background: Manager of a financial research institute
  Mechthild Oblӓnder, Office Manager
  Background: Commercial employee in TFG

3164 THE ABRAAJ GROUP
1 Grafton Street
Sureste de Multiplaza Edificio
London W1S 4FE
United Kingdom

Phone: 44-02035401500 Fax: 44-02035401501

Mission Statement: The Abraaj Capital Group is a leading private equity manager investing in global growth markets. Founded in 2002 by Arif Naqvi, the group has raised over $8

billion and distributed $3.5 billion to investors. Employing over 300 people, the group has 33 offices spread across 7 regional hubs in Bogota, Dubai, Istanbul, London, Mumbai, Nairobi and Singapore.
Geographic Preference: Panama, Costa Rica, Nicaragua, Guatemala
Fund Size: $7.5 Billion
Average Investment: $10 Million - $100 Million
Industry Group Preference: Technology, Healthcare, Education, Community Engagement
Portfolio Companies: Viking, Saham Finances, Kuwait Energy, Network International, Karachi Electric Supply Company, Mediaquest, Man Infraconstruction, Ramky Infrastructure, ECI Engineering & Construction, Numarine

Other Locations:
510 Madison Avenue
Sureste de Multiplaza Edificio
New York, NY
Phone: 10022 **Fax:** 506 2015033

Key Executives:
Arif Naqvi, Group Chief Executive
Education: London School of Economics
Background: Arthur Andersen, American Express Bank, Olayan Group, Cupola Group
Ahmed Badreldin, Regional Managing Partner
Education: BA, Political Science, California at Berkeley; MBA, Golden Gate University
Background: Bank of America; Provident Group Ltd
Ashish Dave, Partner
Education: MA, Economics & Industrial Engineering, Texas Tech University
Background: Privatization Manager, El Salvador Government; Finance Senior Consultant, KPMG Consulting
Hanjaya Limanto, Partner
Education: MBA, National University; BA, Universidad Autonoma CentroAmerica
Background: Privatization Manager, El Salvador Government; Finance Senior Consultant, KPMG Consulting
Sev Vettivetpillai, Partner
Education: MB, Wharton School; MA, International Studies, University of Pennsylvania; BA, Economics, University of California at Berkeley
Background: Provident Group Ltd

3165 THE MORPHEUS
India

e-mail: neo@themorpheus.com
web: www.themorpheus.com

Mission Statement: The Morpheus was started without any set agenda. It was simply for the joy of growing ourselves by working with smart young entrepreneurs & contributing to the eco-system. Today, The Morpheus is a 6 year old project that is made up of a strong community of 160+ entrepreneurs called the morpheusgang, who provide non-stop support to each other.
Geographic Preference: India
Founded: 2008
Investment Criteria: Startups
Portfolio Companies: CloudEngine, Dwll.in, MathHarbor, MotrPart, MyCodeSchool, Padhaaro, Pocket Science
Key Executives:
Sameer Guglani
Education: BE, Electrical Engineering, Thapar University
Background: Co-Founder, Madhouse Media; Vice President, Corporate Strategy, Seventymm
Nandini Hirianniah
Education: MS, Communications, Bangalore University; Bachelors in Journalism, Mount Carmel College, Bangalore
Background: Co-Founder, Madhouse Media
Sarvjeet Ahuja
e-mail: sa@themorpheus.com

Education: IIT Roorkee
Background: Microsoft; HP; PPI; Times of India; Shell

3166 THOMPROPERTIES OY
Fredrikinkatu 51-53 B
Helsinki 00100
Finland

Phone: 358-9681661 **Fax:** 358-968166205
e-mail: Pekka.Soikkeli@thominvest.fi
web: www.thominvest.fi

Mission Statement: Actively seeking new investments.
Geographic Preference: Finland
Fund Size: $30 Million
Founded: 1911
Average Investment: $1.2 Million
Minimum Investment: $0.6 Million
Investment Criteria: Equity, Expansion Capital
Industry Group Preference: Real Estate, Financial Services, Banking, Information Technology, Environment Products & Services

Key Executives:
Pekka Soikkeli, Chief Executive Officer
e-mail: juha.jouhki@thominvest.fi
Mats Söderström, Chief Investment Officer

3167 THOMSON-CSF VENTURES
45 rue de Villiers
Neuilly-sur-Seine Cedex 92526
France

Phone: 33-157778000 **Fax:** 33-144-889969
web: www.thalesgroup.com

Mission Statement: Actively seeking new investments.
Geographic Preference: Europe, USA
Fund Size: $13 Million
Founded: 1968
Average Investment: $8.6 million
Minimum Investment: $500,000
Investment Criteria: Expansion, Turnaround, Buyin
Industry Group Preference: Communications, Computer Related, Software, Consumer Services, Components & IoT, Electronic Technology, Consumer Products

Key Executives:
Jean-Bernard Lévy, Chairman and Chief Executive Officer
Bruno Bézard, Managing Director

3168 THROUNARFELAG ISLANDS PLC
Sudurlandsbraut 22
Reykjavik IS - 00108
Iceland

Phone: 354-568-8266 **Fax:** 354-568-0191
e-mail: andri.tf@skyggnir.is

Mission Statement: Actively seeking new investments, specializing in high-technology industries
Geographic Preference: Europe, Iceland
Minimum Investment: EUR50,000
Investment Criteria: Expansion & Development, MBO, MBI, Turnaround & Restructing, Replacement, Bridge, Mezzanine
Industry Group Preference: Transportation, Communications, Computer Related, Computer Hardware & Software, Electronic Technology, Industrial Equipment, Information Technology, Medical & Health Related

Key Executives:
David Gudmundsson, Investment Manager

3169 TIANGUIS LIMITED
5 Edwardes Place
London W8 6LR
United Kingdom

Phone: 44-2076037788 Fax: 807-7625734
e-mail: info@tianguis-ltd.com
web: www.tianguis-ltd.com

Mission Statement: Focuses on developing companies in the chemical industry.
Geographic Preference: Global
Founded: 1985
Investment Criteria: Mid market buyout;Small buyout;Turnaround - restructuring
Industry Group Preference: Chemicals, Allied Process Industries
Portfolio Companies: Calpulli Inc, European Colour plc, Finnish Chemicals, Brunner Mond, Magadi Soda, Penrice Soda Products, EuroChlor, CEFIC

Key Executives:
Steve Smith, Chairman
e-mail: info@tianguis-ltd.com
Education: Case Institute of Technology Davidson College
Background: Europe Independent Director; Chairman of European Colour plc; Managing Director and Chief Executive Officer of Erikem Luxembourg SA & Finnish Chemicals Oy; Managing Director and Chief Executive Officer of the Australian based Penrice Group & the Brunner
Directorships: President Pochteca Corporation United States; Director Calpulli Inc (USA); member of the Society of the Chemical Industry (SCI) and the American Chemical Society (ACS); on the

3170 TLCOM CAPITAL
188 Hammersmith Road
London W6 7DJ
United Kingdom

Phone: 44-0-208-23770-70 Fax: 44-0-208-23770-79
e-mail: info@tlcom.co.uk
web: www.tlcom.co.uk

Mission Statement: TLcom is dedicated to the success of entrepreneurs and investors. Success in technology ventures is created by teams of exceptional people working inside and around a company, focused on delivering on an ambitious, market driven business vision. We look for entrepreneurs with the ability to identify an innovative solution to a relevant need, and the humility to recognize the need to align multiple contributions in order to achieve tangible results. TLcom works for the success of the entrepreneur by providing, in addition to finance, deep company building expertise based on the experience and breadth of skills within our team.

Geographic Preference: Europe, Israel, Sub-Saharan Africa
Fund Size: 200 million Euro
Founded: 1999
Industry Group Preference: Telecommunications, Media, Technology
Portfolio Companies: Axerra, Beintoo, Cognima, CommProve, Eblana Photonics, Iobox, IXI Mobile, Media Lano, Movirtu, Netscalibur Limited, Noos, Packetfront, Runcom, Sphera, TheBlogTgv, Topica, Upstream, Userfarm, Xtempus, Xypoint

Other Locations:
1st Floor, Chaka Place
Argwings Kodhek Road
Nairobi
Kenya
Phone: 254-731-955-922

Key Executives:
Maurizio Caio, Founder/Managing Partner
Education: Business Adminitration, Bocconi Unveristy & New York University; MBA, Stanford University
Background: Founding Partner, Bain & Company
Directorships: Movirtu, PacketFront, TheBlogTV, Medial Lario, Topica

3171 TMG CAPITAL PARTNERS
Rua Joaquim Floriano, 72, CJ 93
Sao Paulo, SP 04534-000
Brazil

Phone: 55-1130795055 Fax: 55-1140645056
e-mail: tmg_capital@tmg.com.br
web: www.tmg.com.br

Mission Statement: To increase the value of investee companies through the injection of capital, modern management practices and scale in order to attain international levels of performance.
Fund Size: $100 Million
Founded: 1997
Average Investment: $15 Million
Minimum Investment: $5 million
Investment Criteria: Consolidation and Expansion of Medium Sized Companies in Segments that are still Fragmented
Industry Group Preference: Healthcare, Education, Food & Beverage, Information Technology, Telecommunications, Media, Cosmetics
Portfolio Companies: Cade (Dental Care), Clidec, Conductor (Credit Card Processing), Multiacao (Call Center), Odontoprev, Softway, Unident

Key Executives:
Luiz Francisco Novelli Viana, President & CEO
Peter André Dias, Investment

3172 TMI
11F-1, No. 159, Sec.1
Keelung Rd., Xinyi Dist.
Taipei 11070
Taiwan

Phone: 888-2-2769-1698

Mission Statement: Founded in 2012, TMI is a Taiwan-based company that looks to make early stage investments and also to incubate promising entrepreneurs. We are looking for entrepreneurs who want to tackle a global market. Through our assembled network of seasoned professionals, serial entrepreneurs and institutional investors from across the globe, we can allow a start-up to "soft land" in any major market. We are eager to work with entrepreneurs/start-ups looking at the Mobile, Internet and eCommerce spaces.

Geographic Preference: Taiwan
Founded: 2012
Average Investment: $100,000 - $300, 000
Investment Criteria: Early-Stage
Industry Group Preference: Mobile, Internet, E-Commerce & Manufacturing
Portfolio Companies: Eumakh, KPop Stage, Re.mu, Roam & Wander, Citiesocial, Driving Curve, Codementor, 4Free WiFi, Swivi, 886 Food, Puman, Pagineer

Key Executives:
Lucas Wang, Chief Executive Officer / Partner
e-mail: lucas.wange@tmi.vc
Education: BA, Finance, National Taiwan University in Taiwan; MBA, National Sun Yat-Sen University
Background: Partner, WI Harper; Investment Manager, Corporate Venture Department, Microelectronics Technology
Kevin Ho, Chief Investment Officer / Partner
e-mail: kevin.ho@tmi.vc
Education: MS, Opto-Electronics Science Research, National Central University; BS, Physics, Chung Yuan Christian University in Taiwan
Background: Vice President, ITIC; ITRI USA

Venture Capital & Private Equity Firms / International Firms

3173 TOKIO MARINE CAPITAL COMPANY LIMITED
Tokio Marine Nichido Building Shinkan 6F
1-2-1, Marunouchi
Chiyoda-ku
Tokyo 100-0005
Japan
Phone: 81-352233516 Fax: 81-352233547
Mission Statement: Actively seeking new investments through partnering with companies in all stages, including sustained growth, business restructuring, and succession.
Geographic Preference: Japan
Fund Size: 400 million yen
Founded: 1991
Investment Criteria: Established companies located or having core operation in Japan that exhibit stable future cash flows will be targeted. Seed stage/early stage
Industry Group Preference: Information Technology
Portfolio Companies: Xymax, Angel food Systems, Sportsplex Japan, Weathernews Inc, Vehicle Trasportation Service, Intellasset, Japan Medical Data Centre, Business Service Corporatiom, Wanbishi Archives, Sweet Garden, Benex
Key Executives:
  Hideaki Fukazawa, President and Managing Partner
  e-mail: sasaki@tmcap.co.jp
  Koji Sasaki, General Partner

3174 TONG YANG VENTURE CAPITAL CORPORATION Tong Yang Cement Corporation
19/F., High-Living Bldg, 890-16 Daechi-Dong
Seoul 135-280
Korea
Phone: 82-25610056 Fax: 82-25619191
web: www.tyvc.co.kr
Mission Statement: Tong Yang, as the largest merchant bank of Korea, is devoting all its energies for development and globalization of Korean financial market.Its affiliate is Tong Yang Venture Capital for establishing a cohesive marketing system which is exclusive of Tong.
Geographic Preference: South Korea
Fund Size: $1.69 Billion
Founded: 1989
Average Investment: $1 Million
Minimum Investment: $0.5 Million
Investment Criteria: All Stages
Industry Group Preference: Information Technology, Biotechnology
Portfolio Companies: Tatron, M.S Solutions
Key Executives:
  Jae Hyun Hyun, Chairman
  SeungIk Jang, Chief Executive Officer

3175 TPA CORPORATE FINANCE CONSULTING GMBH Horwath International
62-64 Praterstrasse
Vienna 1020
Austria
Phone: 43-1588350 Fax: 43-158835500
e-mail: webmail@tpa-horwath.com
Mission Statement: Actively seeking new investments.
Geographic Preference: Austria
Founded: 2000
Investment Criteria: small and medium-sized enterprises (SMEs), associations, foundations, and individuals.
Industry Group Preference: Biotechnology, Winegrowing & Agriculture, Waste & Recycling, Transportation, Trade, Real Estate, Non-profit & Public Authorities, Hotel, Tourism & Leisure, Manufacturing, Information Technology & Media, Banking, Insurance, Financial Services, Energy, Pharmaceuticals
Key Executives:
  Klaus Bauer-Mitterlehner, Partner
  e-mail: janeba-hirtl.emilie@tpawt.com
  Helene Bovenkamp, Partner
  e-mail: klaus.bauer-mitterlehner@tpa-horwath.com
  Education: Economist

3176 TRANS COSMOS INCORPORATED
3-25-18, Shibuya
Shibuya-ku
Tokyo 150-8530
Japan
Phone: 81-343631111 Fax: 81-343630111
e-mail: pressroom@trans-cosmos.co.jp
web: www.trans-cosmos.co.jp
Mission Statement: Actively seeking new investments.
Geographic Preference: Japan
Founded: 1985
Investment Criteria: Expansion, Mezzanine
Industry Group Preference: Information Technology, Software, Manufacturing, Machinery, Transportation
Key Executives:
  Hideaki Fukazawa, President
  Koji Funatsu, Chairman & Chief Executive Officer

3177 TRANSATLANTIC CAPITAL LTD
17 Devonshire Street
Suite 3
London W1N 2EY
United Kingdom
Phone: 44-2074361216 Fax: 44-2074361226
Mission Statement: Actively seeking new investments.
Geographic Preference: North America, Western Europe
Investment Criteria: Startup, Early-Stage, Development, Expansion
Industry Group Preference: Biotechnology, Environmental Protection, Medical
Portfolio Companies: Alliance Medical Ltd, Cardinal Medical Ltd, Ethical Pharmaceuticals Ltd, Micromed Technology

3178 TRANSYLVANIA FINANCIAL INVESTMENT COMPANY
2 Nicolae Iorga Street
Brasov 2200
Romania
Phone: 40-0268413752 Fax: 40-0268473215
e-mail: marketing@transif.ro
web: www.transif.ro
Mission Statement: Actively seeking new investments, using the latest state-of-the-art technology.
Geographic Preference: Romania
Fund Size: $819 Billion
Founded: 1996
Investment Criteria: Early Stage
Industry Group Preference: Chemicals, Financial Services, Machinery, Agribusiness, Building Materials & Services, Food & Beverage, Transportation
Portfolio Companies: Ludus, Upruc Tap-Sdv SA, Upruc Ctr SA, Marchim SA, Marasesti, IT-Pac Romania SA, Nitramonia SA, Rompetrol Rafinare SA, Constanta, Antibiotice, IASI, Armax Gaz SA
Key Executives:
  Floriean Firu, Member of the Supervisory Board
  e-mail: ffiru@transif.ro
  Education: Graduate, Economics, Doctor Economics
  Background: Financial Management

Venture Capital & Private Equity Firms / International Firms

Ec. Mihai Fercala, PhD, President of the Executive Board/Chief Executive Officer
e-mail: ctraian@transif.ro
Education: Graduate, Economics, Chartered Evaluator
Background: Macroeconomic analysis, valuations and audit
Ec. Ion Mihaila, Vice President of the Executive Board / Deputy C.E.O.
e-mail: pioan@transif.ro
Education: Graduate, Economics, Chartered Accountant
Background: Valuation and financial audit reports
Ec. Iulian Stan, PhD., Vice President of the Executive Board / Deputy C.E.O.
e-mail: paura@transif.ro
Education: Graduate, information Technology
Background: Co-ordination, development and maintenance of information and communication systems

3179 TRIANGLE VENTURE CAPITAL GROUP
Talstrasse 27e
Bensheim-Auerback D-64614
Germany

Phone: 49-6251-800-830 Fax: 49-6251-800-839
e-mail: triangle@triangle-venture.com
web: www.triangle-venture.com

Mission Statement: For more than 16 years Triangle has been focusing on research spin-offs to create outstanding and highly innovative companies.

Geographic Preference: Europe
Industry Group Preference: Technology, Information Technology, Medical Devices, Clean Technology
Portfolio Companies: FG Microtek, iOpener Media, IPCentury, iPharro Media, Takwak

Key Executives:
  Bernd Geiger, Managing General Partner/Founder
  e-mail: b.geiger@triangle-venture.com
  Education: PhD, Natural Science, University of Heidelberg

3180 TRIGENTA CAPITAL GmbH
Kreuzstraáe 34
Duesseldorf 40210
Germany

Phone: 49-211-86289-0 Fax: 49-211-86289-455

Geographic Preference: German-Speaking Europe
Fund Size: EUR 500 million
Founded: 1999
Minimum Investment: EUR 1 million
Investment Criteria: Invests small & medium-sized companies with annual sales volume of EUR 20-200 million, operatinal profitability and positive cash flows; Late-State Venture; Portfolio Transactions
Industry Group Preference: All Sectors Considered

Other Locations:
  Markgrafenstrasse 33
  Berlin 10117
  Germany

  Schiffgraben 13
  Hanover 30159
  Germany

Key Executives:
  Sybille Lutje, Chief Financial Officer
  Peter Folle, Managing Partner
  Dr. Anthony Bunker, Partner

3181 TRIGINITA CAPITAL
Kreuzstraáe 34
Triginta Capital GmbH
Dusseldorf 40210
Germany

Phone: 49-211862890 Fax: 49-21186289455
e-mail: info@triginta-capital.com
web: www.triginta-capital.com

Mission Statement: Actively accompanying the portfolio.

Geographic Preference: Europe
Founded: 1983
Minimum Investment: EUR 0.2 million
Investment Criteria: Seed, Startup, Early-Stage
Industry Group Preference: Information Technology, Telecommunications, Environment Products & Services, Communications, Life Sciences, Advanced Materials, Microelectronics
Portfolio Companies: Lenscare AG, TITUS AG, X VERLEIH, Analyticon Discovery GmbH, ATTO-TEC GmbH, Capsulation NanoScience AG, Chiracon GmbH, GenPat77 Pharmacogenetics AG, Getemed AG Medizin- und Informationstechnik, NOXXON Pharma AG, SEPIAtec GmbH, Zellwerk GmbH

Other Locations:
  Kreuzstrade 34
  Triginita Capital GmbH
  Dusseldorf 40210
  Germany
  Phone: 49-211-862890 Fax: 49-211-86289455

Key Executives:
  Sybille Lutje, Chief Financial Officer
  Peter Folle, Managing Partner
  Dr. Anthony Bunker, Partner
  Johannes Rabini, Managing Director
  Crsten Just, Authorized Officer

3182 TRINITY VENTURE CAPITAL TVC Holdings plc
Block 2A, Richview Office Park
Clonskeagh
Clonskeagh
Dublin 4
Ireland

Phone: 353-12057700 Fax: 353-12057701
e-mail: info@tvc.com
web: www.tvc.com

Mission Statement: Trinity Venture Capital provides equity capital for early stage and expanding private technology companies, particularly in Ireland.

Geographic Preference: Ireland
Fund Size: $195 Million
Founded: 1997
Average Investment: $4.8 Million
Minimum Investment: $1.2 Million
Investment Criteria: Early and Growth Stage Technology Companies
Industry Group Preference: Communications, Computer Related, Consumer Services, Electronic Technology, Industrial Services, Industrial Products, Computer Related, Software
Portfolio Companies: AePONA, APT, ChangingWorlds, CR2, Havok, Nova Science, Rococo Software, Valista

Venture Capital & Private Equity Firms / International Firms

3183 TRIVENTURES
6 Hahoshilm St
1st Floor
PO Box 12006
Herzliya 46722
Israel

Phone: 972-99721080
e-mail: info@triventures.net
web: www.triventures.net

Mission Statement: TriVentures brings together the best attributes of a venture fund and a device accelerator. We have a unique approach to venture investing. We leverage our first hand knowledge and an international blend of clinical, technical and strategic expertise to successfully identify, invent and integrate new medical technologies. Our partners have years of accumulative experience in the fields of medicine, engineering, venture investing, founding start-ups, and working with strategic partners.

Geographic Preference: Israel
Investment Criteria: Early-Stage
Industry Group Preference: Medical Technology
Portfolio Companies: Angioslide, Apica, Assis Medical, Cardiva Medical, MST, Orthspace, Pop Medical, VasoStar

Key Executives:
Michal Geva, Co-Foudner/Managing Partner
Background: BgyPass, AST, GI View

3184 TROIKA CAPITAL PARTNERS
4, Romanov Perelok
Moscow 125009
Russia

Phone: 495-258-0500 Fax: 495-258-0547

Mission Statement: Troika Dialog is one of the oldest and largest investment houses in the CIS. Throughout our 20-year history, we have consistently demonstrated market leadership in our core lines of business: capital markets, investment banking, asset management, alternative investments, and personal investments and finance. We are an integrated securities firm that aims to bring the best global solutions and world-class service to clients.

Founded: 1991
Industry Group Preference: High Technology, Information Technology, Internet, Alternative Energy, Clean Technology, New Materials, Electronics

Key Executives:
Peter Derby, Partner

3185 TSING CAPITAL
Unit B23-B, BUP
No.10 Jiuxianqiao RD
Beijing 100084
China

Phone: 86-1056815700 Fax: 86-1056815788
e-mail: info@tsingcapital.com
web: www.tsingcapital.com

Mission Statement: Established in 2001, Tsing Capital is the pioneering and leading cleantech venture capital firm in China. Through its China Environment Fund and Yiyun Cleantech Fund series, Tsing Capital works intimately with its portfolio companies across China in areas of renewable energy, energy efficiency, environmental protection, new materials, sustainable transportation, smart grids, sustainable agriculture and cleaner production.

Founded: 2001
Industry Group Preference: Clean Technology, Renewable Energy, Energy Efficiency, Environment, Transportation, Agriculture
Portfolio Companies: Enevate, CCTM, CPCEP, Polyvera, Jinfengyuan, Golsun, Convertergy, Miartech, EEMCO, Anpute, Baichuan, Hybolic, Renle, BBS, InvenLux, Qinyuan, Tonys Farm, EcoMade, Hong Bang, Haocen, Devotion New Energy, Sunpreme, Atieva, BGB, Neo-Neon, Nobao, SureAuto, Fengguang Bio-Fan, Sound Fuhua, Longmen, Top Gain, Net Power, CHC, ET Solar, China Sunergy, TGBS, Haiyuan Group, LDK, Giant Hemu, ESG, PowerU, Dong Jiang

Other Locations:
B2102, Dawning Center
500 Hongbaoshi Road
Shanghai 201103
China
Phone: 86-2160907180 Fax: 86-2160907181

Unit 2301, 23/F
New World Tower 1
16-18 Queen's Road Central
Central
Hong Kong
Phone: 852-36283859 Fax: 852-36283854

Key Executives:
Don Ye, Founding Managing Partner

3186 TTP VENTURES
Melbourn Science Park
Melbourn
Hertfordshire SG8 6EE
United Kingdom

Phone: 44-1763-262626 Fax: 44-1763-262265
web: www.ttpventures.com

Mission Statement: TTP Ventures is a member of TTP Group, a leading technology development and services company. Through our investment and incubation activities we have supported over 75 companies.

Fund Size: £34 million
Investment Criteria: Early-Stage
Industry Group Preference: Technology
Portfolio Companies: Alphamosaic, Argenta Discovery, Azuro, Cambridge Semiconductor, Element 14, Ocuity, Oxford Diffraction, Pulmagen Therapeutics, TeraView, ZBD

3187 TVM CAPITAL
Ottostrabe 4
Munich 80333
Germany

Phone: 49 (89) 998 992-0
web: www.tvm-capital.com

Mission Statement: Particularly focuses on Trans-Atlantic opportunities where detailed understanding of the private equity markets in both Europe and the United States provides investors with added flexibility and value.

Geographic Preference: North America, Europe
Fund Size: Funds Raised Under Management: $1 billion
Founded: 1983
Average Investment: $10 million
Minimum Investment: $500,000
Industry Group Preference: Information Technology, Life Sciences, Communications, Healthcare
Portfolio Companies: Aspireo Pharmaceuticals, Wilex AG, Albireo, Altor BioScience, Anchor Therapeutics, Argos Therapeutics, Biovertis, Bluebird Bio, Cerenis Therapeutics, Concert Pharmaceuticals, DIREVO Industrial Biotechnology, Enanta Pharmaceuticals, Evotec, FAAH Pharma, F-Star, GLWL Research, Horizon Pharma, Invendo Medical, Lxchelsis, Kaneq Bioscience, MediGene, Newron Pharmaceuticals, NOXXON Pharma, PRCL Research, Precision Therapeutics, Pridenta, Probiodrug, Proteon Therapeutics, Rapid Micro Biosystems, SelectX Pharmaceuticals, Spepharm Holding, Bourn Hall International, Cambridge Medical & Rehabilitation Center, Manzil Health Care Services, ProVita International Medical Center

Venture Capital & Private Equity Firms / International Firms

Other Locations:
TVM Capital GmbH
Maximillanstr, 35, Entrance C
Munich D-80539
Germany
Phone: 49-89-998-992-0

TVM Capital MENA Ltd.
DIFC Gate Village
Building 4, PO Box 113355
Dubai
United Arab Emirates

Key Executives:
Helmut Sch☐hsler, Managing Partner
Education: University of Vienna
Background: Investment Manager, Horizonte Venture Management
Directorships: SelectX Pharmaceuticals
Alexandra Goll, PhD, General Partner
Education: Freie Universitat Berlin; Phillips Universitat
Background: Roche Ltd
Directorships: Albireo; Biovertis AG; Cerenis Therapeutics
Hubert Birner, General Partner
Education: MBA, Harvard Business School; Ludwig-Maximilians University
Background: Head of Business Development, AstraZeneca; Consultant, McKinsey & Company's Healthcare and Pharmaceutical; Assistant Professor, Ludwig-Maximilians University
Directorships: Argos Therapeutics, Proteon Therapeutics, SpePharm Holding BV

3188 UCA UNTERNEHMER CONSULT AG
29 Stefan George Ring
Munich 81929
Germany

Phone: 49-899931940 **Fax:** 49-8999319444
e-mail: info@uca.de
web: www.uca.de

Mission Statement: U.C.A. provides equity capital to innovative and fast-growing companies while endeavouring to be more than just a money-lender.

Geographic Preference: Austria, France, Germany, Italy, Switzerland, United Kingdom
Founded: 1998
Investment Criteria: Small and mid-sized companies
Industry Group Preference: All Sectors Considered, Communications, Computer Related, Electronic Technology, Healthcare, Tourism, Biotechnology
Portfolio Companies: DeTeBe AG, aovo Touristik AG, MedLEARNING AG, My Blog Media GmbH, Sportnex GmbH

3189 UDD VENTURES
Av Las Condees 11287
3rd Floor Tower
Santiago
Chile

Phone: 56-223279266

Mission Statement: Promotes innovative ventures in early stages of development, through the continuous support of the entrepreneur, providing expertise, support tools, support, advice and links to relevant networks to create value, so that each project materialize his idea so successful. Our aspiration is to become the benchmark for value creation and support for enterprises generated in Chile, standing out for innovative businesses enhance high-impact social and economic development of the country.

Geographic Preference: Chile
Founded: 2010
Industry Group Preference: Environment, Healthcare

Key Executives:
Federico Valdes
Education: Civil Engineering, University of Chile; MS, Management, Stanford University

3190 UNILAZER VENTURES
75, Dr. Annie Besant Road
Nishuvi, 3rd Floor
Worli
Mumbai 400 018
India

Phone: 022-40983730 **Fax:** 022-40983722
e-mail: careers@unilazer.com

Mission Statement: Unilazer Ventures Ltd has morphed (originally called Unilazer Exports & Management Consultants Ltd) into a company spanning Treasure Operations on the one side, increasing Fixed Income and Debt Instruments to an active Equity Investor in the public markets space, to being active in the commodities market, to being a strategic investor in start ups, early stage and mature companies, to building an active business model in certain sectors.

Investment Criteria: Startup, Early-Stage
Portfolio Companies: Blume Ventures Fund, Himex Limited, INI Farms, Mera Career Guide, M.I.T.R.A, Oncontract.com, Valyoo Technologies

Key Executives:
Ronnie Screwvala, Founder/Advisor

3191 UNION BANK OF SWITZERLAND
45 Bahnhofstrasse
Zurich 8001
Switzerland

Phone: 41-44-234 11 11 **Fax:** 41-44-238 44 70
web: www.ubs.com

Mission Statement: Actively seeking new investments.

Geographic Preference: Switzerland, Europe, USA, Asia
Industry Group Preference: All Sectors Considered

Key Executives:
Marcel Ospel, Chairman
Stephan Haeringer, Executive Vice Chairman

3192 UNISON CAPITAL PARTNERS LP
The New Otani Garden Court 9F
4-1 Kioicho
Chiyoda-ku
Tokyo 102-0094
Japan

Phone: 81-335113901
web: www.unisoncap.com

Mission Statement: Our philosophy is to orchestrate all parties involved to work in unison to maximize corporate value.

Geographic Preference: Japan
Fund Size: 600 Billion Yen
Founded: 1998
Average Investment: $0.03 Billion
Minimum Investment: $0.02 Billion
Investment Criteria: Invests in Non-core or under-performing divisions or subsidiaries of large corporations
Industry Group Preference: Agriculture, Insurance, Real Estate, Media, Automotive, Retailing, Manufacturing
Portfolio Companies: Intelsat Holdings, ENOTECA, Minit Asia Pacific, Asahi Tec Corporation, Showa Yakuhin Kako, Nexcon, Dexerials

Key Executives:
John Ehara, Partner
Education: B.A. in Economics from Keio University and an M.B.A. from the Harvard Graduate School of Business Administration.

Venture Capital & Private Equity Firms / International Firms

Background: Director of Finance at NextCard and McKinsey and Goldman Sachs
Tatsuya Hayashi, Partner

3193 USHA MARTIN VENTURES LIMITED
2A Shakespeare Sarani
Mangal Kalash
Kolkata 700071
India

Phone: 91-3339800300 Fax: 91-3322829029
e-mail: contact@ushamartin.co.in
web: www.ushamartin.com

Mission Statement: Acts as a venture investor for expansion stage to consolidation stage equity financing.
Geographic Preference: India
Founded: 1961
Investment Criteria: expansion stage to consolidation stage
Industry Group Preference: Information Technology, Telecommunications, E-Commerce & Manufacturing, Media, Biotechnology

Key Executives:
  Prashant Jhawar, Chairman
  A. K. Somani, Chief Financial Officer and Company Secretary

3194 VAEKSTFONDEN
104A Stramdveaen
Hellerup 2900
Denmark

Phone: 45-35298600
e-mail: vf@vf.dk
web: www.vf.dk

Mission Statement: We provide funding to fast-growing Danish companies and act as a fund-of-funds investor in the private equity sector in the Nordic region.
Geographic Preference: Denmark
Fund Size: $360 Million
Founded: 1992
Average Investment: $8.05 Million
Minimum Investment: $16, 000
Investment Criteria: Invests in Small- and medium-size businesses
Industry Group Preference: Biotechnology, Communications, Computer Related, Industrial Equipment, High Technology, Medical & Health Related, Pollution
Portfolio Companies: Abeo, Adenium Biotech, Advalight, Agilic, Akustikken, AnyBody Technology, API Maintenance Systems, Aporta Digital, Asetek, Autolog Systems, Bennedikthegaard, Bennedsgaard, Billetto, Blackwood Seven, Blueprinter, Borg & Bigum, Brdr. Sommer, Capevo, Carta Finana, CBIT, Celco, Cetrea, Christiansopigens Sild, CodeSealer, Cost:bart, CrossEyes, Dao Aviation, Deli'en, Deskwolf, DITA Exchange, Drivr, EffiMat, Ellipse, Energy Cool, ExpreS2ion Biotechnologies, Falby Design, Falcon Social, FBC Device, Fiberline, Hanegal, HeSaLight, Hjem-IS, Holmris, Iconfinder, ipvision, Jens Jorgensen, Jydsk Aluminum Industrial, Jydsk Planteservice, Jorn Ditlevsen, LeanEco, Leon Hansen Maskinfabrik, LogPoint, Lyngsaa, Merus Audio, Microlytic, Microshade, Milling Hotels, MT MembraTec, Multimac, Murermester Jon Rasmussen, Nanovi, Nocopo, Observe Medical, Oosterhof Dairy, Operator Systems, PF Group, Plast Team, Reapplix, Regal, RushFiles, Rodvig Kro & Badehotel, Sigma Estimates, Skansogaard, SmartShare, Sorbisense, Sticks'n'Sushi, Sumisura, SwipBox, Symphogen, Saelvigbugtens Camping, Tantaline, TeesuVac, Teklatech, Tier1Asset, Tresu, Trustpilot, UNO Danmark, Vivino, Volt, VoresVilla, watAgame, Water for Life, WorldTicket, Ostergard, Aavangs Fiskehus

Key Executives:
  Peter Bruun, Communications

3195 VALUE PARTNERS LIMITED
9th Floor, Nexxus Building
41 Connaught Road
Suite 3301
Central 89
Hong Kong

Phone: 852-28809623 Fax: 852-25648487
e-mail: vpl@vp.com.hk
web: www.valuepartners.com.hk

Mission Statement: Actively seeking new investments.
Geographic Preference: Greater China region
Founded: 1993
Investment Criteria: Bottom Up Stocks, Fund Investment Company
Industry Group Preference: Banking

Key Executives:
  Chean Cheng Hye, Chief Investment Officer & Chairman
  Background: Founder-Morgan Grenfell group in Hong Kong and financial journalist with The Asian Wall Street Journal and Far Eastern Economic Review,
  Directorships: Chairman
  So Chun Ki Louis, Deputy Chairman and Co-Chief Investment Officer
  Education: Bachelor's degree in finance from the University of British Columbia and is a CFA charterholder.
  Background: Director-Manulife Asset Management (Hong Kong) Limited

3196 VCN GROUP INCORPORATED
Kazusaya Bldg. 5F, 1-8-1, Ebisu Nishi
Shibuya-ku
Tokyo 150-0021
Japan

Phone: 81-0354571650 Fax: 81-0354571658
e-mail: info@vcn.co.jp
web: www.vcn.co.jp

Mission Statement: VCN assists spirited entrepreneurs in the Japanese market place.
Geographic Preference: Japan
Founded: 1996
Investment Criteria: Early stage

Key Executives:
  Hiroyuki Shibata, Representative Director
  e-mail: info@vcn.co.jp
  Education: Graduated from the Social Science Department, Waseda University
  Background: Joined JAFCO Co., Ltd. (formerly Japan Associated Finance Co., Ltd.) in April 1985 and was assigned to a post in the Investment Evaluation Division, Investment Evaluation Department.
  Hajime Sugiura, Director
  e-mail: info@vcn.co.jp
  Education: Graduated from the Chemistry Division, Department of Science and Engineering, Waseda University.
  Background: NIF Ventures Co., Ltd. (NIF) (formerly Nippon Investment & Finance Co., Ltd.), Office of Director - Pan-Asia Air Lines Co., Ltd.
  Nobuyuki Hata, Non-executive Director
  e-mail: info@vcn.co.jp
  Education: Obtained a master's degree in economics from Waseda University.
  Background: Nomura Research Institute, Ltd. in March 1974 and was assigned to a post in the Corporate Research Department.professor in the Economics Department, Kokugakuin University in April, and then a professor of the university's Economics Department in April 199

Venture Capital & Private Equity Firms / International Firms

3197 VENCAP
King Charles House
Park End Street
Oxford OX1 1JD
United Kingdom

Phone: 44-1865799300 Fax: 44-1865799301
web: www.vencap.com

Mission Statement: Actively seeking new investments.
Geographic Preference: US, Europe, China and India
Fund Size: US$1.9 billion
Founded: 1987
Investment Criteria: All Stages
Key Executives:
Michelle Ashworth, Director of Fund Investments
e-mail: info@vencapintl.com
Education: B.Comm. from the University of Alberta and an MBA from Wharton
Background: Association of British Insurers as an economist and statistician
Tim Cruttenden, Chief Executive Officer
e-mail: info@vencapintl.com
Education: Chartered Accountant and a graduate of Cambridge University.
Background: Saatchi and Saatchi group
David Howells, Investment Manager
e-mail: info@vencapintl.com
Education: MBA with honours from the Anderson School at UCLA, a JD from UC Hastings College of Law, and a BA in Economics from UCLA.
Background: Executive Director in the Telecommunications Investment Banking Group at Bear, Stearns & Co

3198 VENISTA VENTURES
Erftstr. 19a
Cologne 50672
Germany

Phone: 49-0221933167700 Fax: 49-0221933167170
web: www.venista-ventures.com

Mission Statement: We are a Cologne, Germany-based mobile ventures group specializing in early-stage mobile entertainment and value products. We secure the seed-financing, technical expertise, marketing knowledge and international connectivity necessary to guide mobile media ideas from concept to market.
Geographic Preference: Germany
Investment Criteria: Early-Stage
Industry Group Preference: Communications, Marketing
Portfolio Companies: KissMyAds, Stylemarks, GTX Messaging, Spyke Media, Startupbootcamp, Secret Escapes, datapine, Need, Familonet, mjoy, Klash
Key Executives:
Olivier Wimmertoth, Owner
Christian Teichert, Owner

3199 VENTECH
47, Avenue de l'Opera
Paris 75002
France

Phone: 33-183798190 Fax: 33-183798200
e-mail: contact@ventechvc.com
web: www.ventech.fr

Mission Statement: Alongside the best entrepreneurs and managers, we fund ambitious companies seeking to create a major market break to generate quickly a leading position. Our industry expertise enables us to work closely with these projects in their product development and market creation.
Geographic Preference: Europe, China
Fund Size: 360 million Euro
Founded: 1998
Industry Group Preference: Information Technology, Digital Media & Marketing, Entertainment, Enterprise Software, Semiconductors, Infrastructure, Communications
Portfolio Companies: Adore Me, AnneLutfen.com, Altitude Telecom, Alapage.com, Arteris, AsGoodAsNew, Augure, Ateme, Ad Valem Technologies, Arkoon, Business & Decision, Blink, B-Process, Bonitasoft, Byecity.com, Believe, Calendra, Cyrano, Com6, Crocus Technology, Curse, Easou, Ekinops, Eyeka, Futureo, Genesys, Hassle.com, Internext, We Hostels, iBase, interCloud, Jimu Box, Jumei.com, K Mobile, Kai Yuan, Keopsys, Adikteev, myBlee, Musiwave, Meilleurtaux.com, Mamsy, Nineyu, Ogury, Orchestra, Oktogo, Picanova, Qarnot Computing, Qiandai.com, Racing-Live, SoJeans, Shopmium, Sinocampus, Secoo, Shenzhoufu, StickyADS.tv, TVSmiles, Trends for Friends Brands, Umanto.com, Virtools, Vestiaire Collective, Viadeo, Viva, Walkin, Withings, Wengo, Wise Media, Webedia, 21Diamonds, 3Guu.com, 51wan.com

Other Locations:
2140-05 Yintai Office Tower
Beijing Yintai Centre
No. 2 Jinaguomenwai Road, Chaoyang District
Beijing 100022
China
Phone: 86-10-8517-2122

Key Executives:
Alain Caffi, Founder/General Partner
Education: MS, University of Kansas
Background: Accor Group
Directorships: Omen, Webedia, Viadeo, Believe, Curse, Eyeka, WomenJournal

3200 VENTURE FUND ROTTERDAM BV Indofin Group
Westerkade 3
Rotterdam 3016 CL
Netherlands

Phone: 31-104144544 Fax: 31-104332879
e-mail: info@indofin.nl
web: www.indofin.nl

Mission Statement: Invests in strong, established, growing companies with excellent management, or in need of management support.
Geographic Preference: Europe, USA, Canada, Australia, Asia
Founded: 1968
Investment Criteria: Expansion and Development, MBO, Turnaround, Mezzanine, Bridge
Industry Group Preference: All Sectors Considered
Portfolio Companies: IHC Merwede Group, Technische Handelsmaatschappij Marchand-Andriessen N.V., HES Beheer, Net Display Systems, AND Automotive Navigation Data, Energia Zachod, Nordofin Resources, Vooruitgang Energie, DPW Van Stolk Holding, Mannesmann Plastics Machinery, Roosland

3201 VENTURE INVESTORS
Kremencova 17
Prague 1 110 00
Czech Republic

Phone: 420-224931600
e-mail: rm@vi.cz
web: www.ventureinvestors.cz

Mission Statement: Finds suitable solutions for the development of strong and growing companies in the Central and Eastern European region.
Geographic Preference: Europe, Czech Republic, Poland, Hungary, USA
Founded: 1999
Investment Criteria: Early-Stage, Expansion & Development Capital, Start-Up Capital, Buyout & Buyin

Venture Capital & Private Equity Firms / International Firms

Industry Group Preference: Communications, Computer Related, Biotechnology, Medical & Health Related, Consumer Services, Industrial Equipment, Financial Services, Real Estate, Insurance

Key Executives:
Michael Rostock, Founding Partner

3202 VENTUREAST
5B, Ramachandra Avenue, Seethammal
Colony, First Main Road, Alwarpet
Chennai 600 018
India

Phone: +91 44 2432 9864 Fax: +91 44 2432 9865
e-mail: info@ventureast.net
web: www.ventureast.net

Mission Statement: Ventures into new markets and provides cutting-edge ideas to help navigate the challenges of building a business related to India.

Geographic Preference: India
Investment Criteria: Seed Stage, Early Stage, Growth Stage
Industry Group Preference: Information Technology, Life Sciences, Healthcare, Clean Environment, Emerging Markets, Sectors & Technologies
Portfolio Companies: Atyati, Loyalty Rewardz, Sai Sudhir, Royalimages.in, Ad2pro, Goli, Bharat Light and Power (BLP), Central Parking Services, E2E Rail, Richcore, eYantra, Orca Systems, Si2, Vysr, Little Eye Labs, OneBreath, SmartRx, Stylecraze, Seclore, Vortex, Inopen, Mobien Technologies, Crederity, Desicrew, Intelizon Energy, Rope, Reviews 42, Polygenta, Sresta, Bioserve, Onconova Therapeutics, Evolva, Sapala, Elbit, iMedX, Naturol, Neurosynaptics, Mardil Medical, Melior Discovery, Comprehensive Prosthetics & Orthotics, Ocean Sparkle, Gland Pharma, EPI, Moschip, Itero Biopharmaceuticals, Dodla Dairy, Vibromech, Four Soft, VKS Farms

Key Executives:
Sarath Naru, Managing Partner
Ramesh Alur, General Partner
Raghuveer Mendu, General Partner
Bobba Venkatadri, General Partner

3203 VERITAS VENTURE PARTNERS
2A Hamelacha St., 3rd Floor
Ra'anana 43661
Israel

Phone: 972-99561621 Fax: 972-737146734
e-mail: info@veritasvc.com
web: www.veritasvc.com

Mission Statement: Actively seeking new investments.

Geographic Preference: USA, Israel
Founded: 1990
Investment Criteria: Invest primarily in technology-based companies at the seed and very early stages of their lives
Industry Group Preference: Genetic Engineering, Medical & Health Related, Enterprise Services, Networking, Software, Communications
Portfolio Companies: Polycom, Nuance, Asankya, Rumcom, Sandvine, Cisco Systems, fring, Gilat Satellite Networks, Trivnet, ClickFox, Guardium, IBM, WebLayers, Lumenis, UltraSPECT, Escape Rescuse Systems, Siemens AG, Sandisc

3204 VERSOVENTURES
Mikonkatu 6
Helsinki 00100
Finland

Phone: 358-505890520
e-mail: info@versoventures.com
web: www.versoventures.com

Mission Statement: VersoVentures is a new finance sector company that has developed a unique model for corporate spin-offs. The model offers a financially attractive way for corporations to enable new jobs to be created from non-strategic activities. Founded by Anssi Kariola in 2012, VersoVentures is currently investing into spin-offs via the first Verso Spin-off Fund, with first investments targeted in November 2012.

Geographic Preference: Finland
Founded: 2012
Investment Criteria: Spin-Offs
Portfolio Companies: Boftel Oy, Cumulocity GmbH, Dedicated Network Partners Oy, CloudStreet Oy, Atrinet Ltd.

Key Executives:
Ansii Karlota, Managing Partner

3205 VERTEX VENTURE CAPITAL
1 HaShikma Street
PO Box 89
Savyon 56530
Israel

Phone: 972-37378888 Fax: 972-37378889
e-mail: contact@vertexvc.com
web: www.vertexvc.com

Mission Statement: Actively seeking new investments.

Geographic Preference: Israel, UK, USA, Singapore, Japan
Fund Size: $600 Million
Founded: 1997
Average Investment: $10 Million
Minimum Investment: $1 Million
Investment Criteria: Invests in Israeli and Israel-related high tech companies, with significant and sustainable competitive advantages
Industry Group Preference: Digital Media & Marketing, Fixed & Mobile Broadband, Enterprise IT & Infrastructure, Green Technology
Portfolio Companies: Actelis Argus Cyber Security, Asocs, Aternity, ColorChip, Correlsense, Cyber-Ark, DigiFlex, Heptagon, InnoPath, Leadspace, Mediaboost, MoreCom, MultiPhy, Neuralitic, Perfecto Mobile, Sidense, Solar Edge, Vigilance Networks

Key Executives:
Yoram Oron, Founder & Managing Partner
e-mail: contact@vertexvc.com
Education: Degree in Electrical Engineering from Columbia University, New York, MBA program at Babson College, Massachusetts.
Background: Philips Electronics, President and CEO of MoreCom Inc
Ehud Levy, Managing Partner
Orit Einstein, Controller
e-mail: contact@vertexvc.com
Education: MA, Economics and Business Administration; BA Economics and Mathematics, Tel Aviv University
Background: President & CEO, Aryt Industries, Co-Founder, Geotek Communications, Co-Founder, President & CEO, Reshef Technologies, Co-Founder & Chairman, Telegate Ltd.
David Heller, Managing Partner
e-mail: contact@vertexvc.com
Education: LLB, Hebrew University; LLM, Kyoto University
Background: Partner, Yossi Avraham & Company, Wakabayashi & Watanabe, VP, Israel International Fund
Emanuel Timor, Managing Partner
e-mail: contact@vertexvc.com
Education: BA, LLB, Tel Aviv University
Background: Muscal, Shimonov, Barnea
Merav Shemesh, Controller
e-mail: contact@vertexvc.com
Education: B.Sc.in Electrical Engineering from the Technion - Israel Institute of Technology, MBA, cum laude, from Tel Aviv University.
Background: Partner at Formula Ventures, Vice President and Chief Technology Officer of the DSP Group

Ran Gartenberg, Managing Partner and CFO
e-mail: contact@vertexvc.com
Education: BA, Accounting & Economics, Tel Aviv University; MBA, New York University
Background: Business Development Manager, Israel Corporation, Supervising Auditor, Price Waterhouse Coopers
Paula Trostchansky, Office Administrator
e-mail: contact@vertexvc.com
Education: DEC, Commerce, Marianopolis College; BA, Political Science & International Relations, Hebrew University; MSc, Boston University
Background: Corporate Marketing & Communications, 3M
Iris Elkayam, Office Manager
e-mail: contact@vertexvc.com
Education: MBA from Tel-Aviv University, B.A in Economics and Management (cum laude) from the Technion - Israel Institute of Technology
Background: Investment banker in the Global Technology, Media and Telecom Group at JPMorgan Chase & Co

3206 VICKERS FINANCIAL GROUP
1 Maritime Square
#09-28 Harbourfront Centre
Singapore 0099253
Singapore

Phone: 65-6339-0338
web: www.vickersventure.com

Mission Statement: Vickers Capital Group is an investment house with offices in Shanghai and Singapore. The group manages 3 funds and proprietary capital. Founded in 2004 by Dr. Finian Tan, the Group seeks to create long term value for our investors by investing in and building a stable of great companies focused primarily on the Asia Pacific market.

Geographic Preference: Asia
Founded: 2004
Industry Group Preference: Technology, Media, Healthcare, Energy, Automotive, Education, Real Estate
Portfolio Companies: Sammumed, Jing-Jin Electric, CalUniversity, Asian Food Channel, UUCun, Tenfen, Matchmove, Sunfun (iPart), Lotaris, Mobinex, Cambridge, The Wellness Group, Spicy Horse, RTG Asia, M-Daq, Hillstone, LL Games, Roomorama, Cardvalue, Appletoon, Delivering Happiness Group/Daredu, Chinaway, Skyroam, Alo7, Lumina Looue, Affordable Luxury Network, Luminaire, Babeeta, Playpeli, Netpower, Vitamin Research, Benchmark

Key Executives:
Finian Tan, Chairman
Education: BSc, Engineering, University of Glasgow
Background: Partner & Managing Director, Draper Fisher Jurvetson Eplanet

3207 VIKING VENTURE
Nedre Bakklandet 77
Trondheim 7014
Norway

web: www.vikingventure.no

Geographic Preference: Norway, Nordic Countries
Fund Size: $200 million
Founded: 2001
Investment Criteria: Early-Stage
Industry Group Preference: Electronics, Software, Oil & Gas, Materials Technology, Clean Technology
Portfolio Companies: Enhanced Drilling, Evatic, ExproSoft, Gas Secure, MemfoACT, Meta, poLight, READ, Room Sketcher, Safetel, Signicat, Ziebel, Zilift, PetroStreamz, 4subsea, Eco Online

Key Executives:
Erik Hagen, Managing Partner
47-920-22-430
Education: MSc, Computer Science, NTH; MBA, INSEAD
Background: Partner, Arthur Andersen; CEO, Schibsted Nett; Marketing Director, NetCom ASA; Consultant, McKinsey & Company
Harald Jeremiassen, Partner
47-932-58-570
Education: MSc, Business & Administration, NHH; Owen Graduate School of Managment, Vanderbilt University
Jostein Vlk, Partner
47-922-22-392
Education: MSc, Business & Administration, Norwegian School of Management
Background: Business Manager, Lilleborg; Business Controller, Carlsberg Breweries;
Directorships: Safetel ASA, InvivoSense ASA, Iqua Oy, MyVR Technologies AS, Cinevation AS
Joar Welde, Partner
47-982-06-930
Education: BA, Business & Administration, Norwegian School of Management; MBA, University of Warwick
Background: Project Manager, Ernst & Young; Consultant, DnB Eiendom
Directorships: Aqualyng AS, Ziebel AS, Ecowat, Signicat AS
Eivind Bergsmyr, Partner
47-920-99-010
Education: MSc, Electronics Engineering, Norwegian University of Technology & Science; Norwegian School of Management
Background: CEO, Nacre AS; Siemens Telecom; Siemens Electrical Heating

3208 VINACAPITAL GROUP
17th Floor, Sun Wah Tower
115 Nguyen Hue, Dist. 1
Ho Chi Minh City
Vietnam

Phone: 84-88219930 **Fax:** 84-88219931
web: www.vinacapital.com

Mission Statement: Invests in all stages of business in the Vietnamese market place.

Geographic Preference: Vietnam, China, Cambodia, Laos
Fund Size: $1.6 Billion
Founded: 2003
Investment Criteria: Expansion capital; Mid-Stage
Industry Group Preference: Real Estate, Insurance, Beverages, Telecommunications, Media, Materials Technology, Infrastructure

Key Executives:
Dr. Jonathan Choi, Chairman
e-mail: info@vinacapital.com
Education: Holds a joint Masters degree in Engineering, Economics and Management from Oxford University
Background: Engagement Manager, McKinsey & Co; Founder, two Greenfield companies, China; Restructuring of state-owned enterprise, Pritzker family
Don Lam, CEO
e-mail: info@vinacapital.com
Education: BA Commerce and Political Science, University of Toronto
Background: Partner-in-Charge, PricewaterhouseCoopers; Deutsche Bank; Coopers & Lybrand

3209 VINCERA CAPITAL
17th Floor
105 Tun-Hwa S Road
Sec.2
Taipei, Taiwan 106
China

Phone: 886-227540168 **Fax:** 886-227540169
web: www.vinceracapital.com

Venture Capital & Private Equity Firms / International Firms

Mission Statement: A top tier private equity firm that sponsors growth capital in Greater China.
Geographic Preference: China
Fund Size: $230 Million
Founded: 1997
Average Investment: $2 - $20 million
Investment Criteria: Early, Expansion & Mezzanine
Industry Group Preference: Consumer Products, Industrial, Technology
Portfolio Companies: Advanced Ceramic X Corp, Alcor Micro, Alltop Tech, Amigo Technology, Ampire Co, Arima Computer Corp., Aten International, Celxpert Energy Corp., Chip Hope Co., Cincon Electronics, Compal Communications, Divio, Enable Semiconductor, Entergy Industrial, Etronic, Epox Computer, Firich Enterprises, Formosa Epitaxy, Galaxy Far East, Genaissance Pharmaceuticals, Global Mixed-Mode Technology, Himax Technologies, Hold Jinn Electronics, Honghua Group Limited, Hsin Yung Chien Co., IC Media, Jarllytec Co., KG Telecom, Largan Precision, Maxteck Technology, NAFACO, Nanya Technology, Palmax, Plotech, Polytronics, Rapidstream, Silicon Touch Technology, Uniscape, Verplex Systems, Worldwide Semicondctor, Xintec

Key Executives:
John S.C.Tang, Chairman
e-mail: sc.tang@vinceracapital.com
Education: MS, PhD, Economics, Takushoku University; BS, Accounting, Soochow University
Background: Chairman, Kuo Hua Life Insurance; President, Cathay Life Insurance
Richard S. H. Chen, Chairman & CEO
e-mail: richard.chen@vinceracapital.com
Education: MA, International Studies, University of Pennsylvania; MBA, Wharton School
Background: EVP, GFC Ltd; Huang & Chen Financial Services; Global Shearson Financial Services; Proctor & Gamble
Dr In-Chyuan Ho, Vice Chairman & CTO
e-mail: ic.ho@vinceracapital.com
Education: PhD, Electrical Engineering, National Cheng Kung University
Background: China Steel Corp; Ascentek Venture Capital Corp.; Vice President, Gains Investment Corp.
Benjamin MS Cheng, CIO
Education: BS, Control Engineering, National Chiao Tung University
Background: Investment Manager, Gains Investment Corp.; ABB Taiwan

3210 VINTAGE INVESTMENT PARTNERS
12 Abba Eban Avenue
Ackerstein Towers, Bldg D, 10th Floor
Herzilyah Pituach 46120
Israel

Phone: 972-99548464 Fax: 972-99541012

Mission Statement: With over $500 million under management, Vintage Investment Partners is the only combined secondary, co-invest and fund of funds manager focused on Israel. The management team combined has over 100 years experience with Israeli companies in both the private and public equity markets as well as long-standing relationships with top-tier Israeli funds and foreign investors.
Geographic Preference: Israel, Europe
Fund Size: $500 million
Key Executives:
Alan Feld, Founder/Managing Partner
Education: BA, Commerce & Finance, University of Toronto; MBA, York University
Background: General Partner, Israel Seed Partners, Vertex Ventures, Founding Chairman, StartUp Jerusalem

3211 VIOLA FINTECH
12 Abba Eban Avenue
Ackerstein Towers Bldg. D
Herzeliya 47625
Israel

Phone: 972 9 9720 400 Fax: 972 9 9720 401
e-mail: info@viola-group.com
web: www.viola-group.com

Mission Statement: Viola FinTech is a cross-stage venture fund that invests in financial institutions and startup projects focused on modernizing financial markets.
Geographic Preference: Israel, Europe, North America
Fund Size: $100 million
Founded: 2017
Average Investment: $3M-$7M
Investment Criteria: Startups
Industry Group Preference: Technology, Wealth & Asset Management, Finance, Commercial Real Estate, Insurance
Key Executives:
Daniel Tsiddon, Founder/General Partner
e-mail: danielt@violafintech.com
Background: Deputy CEO, Bank Leumi; Chairman, Leumi Partners; Professor, Economics, Berglas School, Tel Aviv University
Tomer Michaeli, General Partner
e-mail: tomerm@violafintech.com
Education: M.Eng, Biomedical Engineering, Israel's Institute of Technology; BSc, Physics, Mathematics & Chemistry, Hebrew University, Jerusalem; MBA, INSEAD
Background: Co-Founder/Chief Operating Officer, FUNDBOX; Principal, Viola Ventures; Israeli Defense Forces
Itzik Avidor, Partner
e-mail: itzika@viola-group.com
Education: BA, Accounding & Economics, MBA, Tel Aviv University
Background: Senior Audit Manager, Oshap & Technomatix; CFO, Viola Group;

3212 VIOLA VENTURES
12 Abba Eban Avenue
Ackerstein Towers, Building D
Hertzliya 4672530
Israel

Phone: 972 9 9720 400 Fax: 972 9 9720 401
e-mail: info@viola-group.com
web: www.viola-group.com

Mission Statement: A venture capital firm whose mission is to invest in early stage Israeli tech companies.
Geographic Preference: Israel
Fund Size: $2.8 Billion
Founded: 2000
Investment Criteria: Growth Stage, Early Stage, Israeli
Industry Group Preference: All Sectors Considered
Portfolio Companies: Cellwize, Clarizen, Cloudyn Code Fresh, Cooladata, Coppergate, CrediFi, Deep, Design Art Networks, ECI The Elastic Network, Ensilo, Ever Compliant, Exelate, Followap Telecommunications, Iron Source, Kampyle, Kontera, Lightricks, LiveU, Lucky Fish, Maapilim, Mov.ai, MultiPhy, Nice Actimize, Nsknox, Optimal, Origami Logic, Oversi, Pagaya, Pando Logic, Parallel, Payoneer, Perfecto, Peronetics, PlainID, Playbuzz, ProteanTecs, Puls, Redbend, Redis Labs, Reduxio, Samanage, Seebo, Skybox Security, Snapt, SPlacer, Sunday Sky, Tapingo, Taranis, Tradair, Utbrain, Vaya Vision, VM Ware Wanova, Worthy
Key Executives:
Shlomo Dovrat, Co-Founder/General Partner
Background: Oshap; Tecnomatix; ECI Telecom; Wanova; Redbend; eXeleate;
Avi Zeevi, Co-Founder/General Partner
Background: MINT Technologies; Oshap; Actimize

Directorships: Payoneer; SundaySky; Personetics; TradAir; Evercompliant; CrediFi; Pagaya; ParallelM; The Center for Educational Technology; Technion
Ronen Nir, General Partner
Education: BA, Economics/Middle-East History, Tel Aviv University; MSc, Technology Management, University of Maryland University College
Background: VP of Product Management, Verint Systems; Director of Product Management, ECtel; Israeli Defense Forces
Directorships: Samanage; ironSource; Perfecto Mobile; enSilo; Redis Labs; CodeFresh
Daniel Cohen, General Partner
Education: BA, Computer Science, Tel Aviv University; MBA, INSEAD
Background: Commtouch; Scitex; Gemini Israel Ventures
Directorships: Circle of Friends

3213 VIRGIN GREEN FUND
United Kingdom

Portfolio Companies: Gevo, Solyndra, Odersun, Metrolight, Wildcat Discovery Technologies, DuraTherm, Seven Seas, Quench USA, GreenRoad

Other Locations:
The Battleship Building
179 Harrow Road
London \W2 6NB
United Kingdom
Phone: 44-2073391500

Key Executives:
Evan Lovell, Partner
e-mail: evan.lovell@virgingreenfund.com
Education: University of Vermont
Background: Director, International Development, Culligan Water Technologies
Directorships: DuraTherm, Quench, Seven Seas Water
Shai Weiss, Partner
e-mail: shai.weiss@virgingreenfund.com
Education: MBA, Columbia University
Background: ntl:Telewest
Michael Odai, General Counsel & COO
e-mail: michael.odai@virgingreenfund.com
Education: BA, Economics, University of Rochester; JD, Albany Law School
Background: General Counsel, Virgin Money Australia
Mike Willis, Principal
e-mail: mike.willis@virgingreenfund.com
Education: BCom, Queen's University; MBA, INSEAD
Background: Virgin Management Limited; Bedford Capital

3214 VITAMINA K VENTURE CAPITAL
C/de La Botanica
Madrid 4 28028
Spain

Phone: 34-915613719
web: www.vitaminak.com

Mission Statement: Vitamin K is an SCR that invests in technology companies and internet in its early stages.

Average Investment: $200,000
Investment Criteria: Early-Stage
Industry Group Preference: Technology, Internet
Portfolio Companies: Otogami, Chicisimo, The Mad Video, Ludei, YPD Online, Promociones Farma, 8Fit, Mailtrack, Blinkfire, Cartodb, Icontainers, Selltag

Key Executives:
Rafael Garrido, Founder/CEO
Background: Co-Founder, Sequoias, Bubok, 737 Shaker, Kschool, Kaleidos, Experit, Mimub

3215 VITULUM VENTURES
Mediarena 7
Amsterdam 1114 BC
Netherlands

web: www.vitulumventures.com

Mission Statement: Vitulum Ventures BV is a Dutch micro VC based in Amsterdam. It was formed when 5 Dutch angel investors started to work together: Camiel Dobbelaar, Chang Ng, Erwin van der Veen, Jaap Visser and Ian Zein. We look for seed stage deals in promising internet/mobile startups. Our involvement is in the form of a mentoring shareholder.

Geographic Preference: The Netherlands
Average Investment: 50,000 - 100,000 Euro
Investment Criteria: Seed-Stage, Early-Stage
Industry Group Preference: Internet, Mobile
Portfolio Companies: Earlydoc, Human.co, Wercker, Karma, Nouncy, Gibbon

Key Executives:
Camile Dobbelaar, Partner

3216 VIVES
Chemin du Cyclotron 6
Louvain-la-Neuve B-1348
Belgium

Phone: 00-32010390021 **Fax:** 00-32010390029
e-mail: info@vivesfund.com
web: www.vivesfund.com

Mission Statement: Vives is a private seed capital that invests in high-technology companies. This multi-sectoral fund supports young companies in all technological sectors, with particular emphasis on eco-innovation projects. Vives invests in companies at all stages of maturity: seed, start-up and growth. The deal flow of Vives is ensured by UCL spin-offs as well as by technological start-ups located within a radius of 250km around Louvain-la-Neuve.

Geographic Preference: Belgium
Investment Criteria: All Stages
Industry Group Preference: High Technology
Portfolio Companies: Alterface, Cissoid, DELFMEM, GreenWatt, IntoPIX, Iteos, Keemotion, Novadip, Promethera, Viridaxis, Xylowatt

Key Executives:
Philippe Durieux, Chief Executive Officer
e-mail: p.durieux@sopartec.com
Education: Graduate Degree, Economics, Louvain-la-Neuve, Post-Graduate Degree, Finance, Hautes Etudes Commerciales Saint-Louis
Background: CEO, Sopartec SA; Senior Investment Manager, Dexia Private Equity

3217 VOLVO GROUP VENTURE CAPITAL
AB Volvo
Gothenburg SE-405 08
Sweden

Phone: 46-31-66-660000
web: www.volvogroup.com/venturecapital

Mission Statement: At Volvo Group Venture Capital, we dedicate ourselves to the success of each of our investments. We make the difference by contributing not only with capital but also with extensive investing experience coupled with the unique capabilities of the entire Volvo Group.

Industry Group Preference: Automotive, Consumer Electronics, Telecommunications

Other Locations:
425 Market Street
Suite 2200

San Francisco, CA 94105
Phone: 415-691-5835

Key Executives:
Olof Persson, President and CEO
e-mail: johan.m.carlsson@volvo.com

3218 VON BRAUN & SCHREIBER PRIVATE EQUITY PARTNERS
Ottostrasse 1
Munich 80333
Germany

Phone: 49-892869520 Fax: 49-8928695210
e-mail: private.equity@braunschreiber.com
web: www.braunschreiber.com

Mission Statement: Leading independent European fund of funds managers for private equity.

Geographic Preference: Europe, USA
Founded: 1999
Investment Criteria: Venture capital, Buyout, Distressed
Industry Group Preference: Administration and Accounting, Legal and Compliance

Other Locations:
150 South US Highway One
Suite 305
Jupiter, FL 33477

Key Executives:
Emmeram von Braun, Managing Directors
e-mail: Private.Equity@BraunSchreiber.com
Education: Law degree from University of Augsburg & Master's degree in business administration from the Academy in Villingen-Schwenningen (Germany).
Background: Allianz AG
Alexander C Binz, Managing Director
Emmeram von Braun, Managing Director
Timothy J Reynolds, Managing Director

3219 VONTOBEL PRIVATE EQUITY MANAGEMENT CAYMAN
Third Floor
22 Sackville Street
London W1S 3DN
United Kingdom

Phone: 44-2072558300 Fax: 44-2072558301
web: www.vontobel.com

Mission Statement: Focused on asset management in the Swiss private.

Fund Size: $57.7 billion
Founded: 1984
Investment Criteria: Early-Stage, Expansion & Development Capital, Mezzanine & Bridge Finance, Replacement Capital, Start-up Capital, Turnaround & Restructuring, Buyout & Buyin

Key Executives:
Herbert J. Scheidt, Chairman
Dominic Brenninkmeyer, Member of the Risk and Audit Committee

3220 VTB CAPITAL
10, Presnenskaya Emb.
Block C
Moscow 123317
Russia

Phone: 7-495-725-5540 Fax: 7-495-725-5538
web: www.vtbcapital-im.com

Mission Statement: VTB Capital venture business leads the way in the venture capital market in Russia and the CIS. Investing in Russian innovative cutting-edge technology is among VTB Capital's priorities.

Geographic Preference: Russia
Fund Size: $320 million
Founded: 2007
Investment Criteria: Early-Stage
Industry Group Preference: Information Technology, Internet, Digital Media & Marketing, E-Commerce & Manufacturing
Portfolio Companies: Breeze Tecnhologies, Fab.com, Avalanche Technology, SmS Tnzotherm, Rolith, Fast Lane Ventures, Eccentex, Oktogo.ru, AiHit, Grid Dynamics, MOBI.Money, Russian Navigation Technologies

Key Executives:
Tim McCarthy, Managing Director, Chief of Staff

3221 WALDEN ISRAEL VENTURE CAPITAL
13 Zarchin Street
Building C, 8th floor
Raanana
Israel

Phone: 972-99605565 Fax: 972-35214587
e-mail: office@walden.co.il

Mission Statement: To be the leading quality early-stage venture capital firm in Israel.

Geographic Preference: Global
Fund Size: $185 Million
Founded: 1993
Average Investment: $2.5 Million
Minimum Investment: $1 Million
Investment Criteria: Invests in First-Stage
Industry Group Preference: Communications, Internet Technology, Software, Healthcare, E-Commerce & Manufacturing, Infrastructure
Portfolio Companies: Abirnet, Axeda Systems, ClearForest, Enigma Information Systems, Ex Libris, Informative, Mercado Software, nLayers, Safend, Sanctum, SintecMedia, Universal Ad, Zend Technologies, Camero, CogniTens, EPOS, D-Pharm, Odin Technologies, Peptor, Actelis, Allot Communications, Amimon, CableMatrix, Colorchip, Mellanox Technologies, Narus, Ornet, Passave Technologies, Radcom, Schema, Siano, Terayon

Key Executives:
Shirley Zakar Menda, Administrative Assistant
e-mail: noga@walden.co.il
Education: Economics and psychology
Background: Consortium International and Koor Communications.
Eyal Kaplan, General Partner
e-mail: eyal@walden.co.il
Education: MBA at the Wharton School of Business
Background: Geotek Communications
Roni Hefetz, General Partner
e-mail: moty@walden.co.il
Education: B.Sc. degree in Electronic Engineering & MBA degree from Tel Aviv University
Background: Radcom & Elisra

3222 WATERLAND PRIVATE EQUITY INVESTMENT
Nieuwe's-Gravelandseweg 17
Bussum 1405 HK
Netherlands

Phone: 31-356941680 Fax: 31-356970972
e-mail: info@waterland.nu
web: www.waterland.nu

Mission Statement: Waterland is an independent private equity investment group that supports entrepreneurs in realizing their growth ambitions. With substantial financial resources and committed relevant expertise.

Geographic Preference: Belgium, Germany, Netherlands
Fund Size: $1.7 billion
Founded: 1999
Average Investment: $10 - $200 million
Minimum Investment: $12 Million

Investment Criteria: Buyout and Buyin, Expansion and Development Capital, Replacement Capital
Industry Group Preference: Consumer Services, Industrial Products, Industrial Services, Medical & Health Related, Outsourcing & Efficiency
Portfolio Companies: A-ROSA, Actuera, Aevitae, Attero, BioMCN, Brouwerij Bosteels, Casino Royal, Didix, Diversi Foods, FleetPro, Infra Group/Verbraeken, Interbest, Ipcom, JVH Gaming, Mauritsklinieken, Omega Pharma, Ranger Marketing, RHM Klinik und Pflegeheime, Sarens, SENIOcare, U-Center, VeluwseBron, VivaNeo

Key Executives:
Lex Douze, Principal

3223 WELLINGTON PARTNERS VENTURE CAPITAL GmbH
6 Theresienstr
Munich 80333
Germany

Phone: 49-892199410
e-mail: munich@wellington-partners.com
web: www.wellington.de

Mission Statement: To be a quality leader in the European early-stage venture capital industry.
Geographic Preference: Europe, US
Fund Size: $800 million
Founded: 1990
Average Investment: $15 million
Minimum Investment: $1.2 million
Investment Criteria: Focuses on Companies with Experienced Management Team, Large Market, and Strong Technology
Industry Group Preference: Medical Technology, Diagnostics, Therapeutics, Digital Media & Marketing, Resource Efficiency, Internet Technology
Portfolio Companies: ACG, Astaro, Cobion, Gardeners, Gten, Safe-id, Belenus, Collax, Covast, Meiosys, Nexwave, Reportive, SAF, SWYX, Voice Objects, WLAN, Enocean, Multiplex, Nawotec, WWNET, Immobilienscout24, Netmobile, Openbc, Truck24, Zopa, 1-2-3.TV, Alando, Ciao, Codetoys

Key Executives:
Rolf Christof Dienst, General Partner
e-mail: boehnke@wellington-partners.com
Education: Business Administration from the University of Essen
Background: J.P. Morgan, IBM
Bart Markus, General Partner
e-mail: dienst@wellington-partners.com
Education: Law degree from Ludwig-Maximilians University of Munich
Background: Munich-based Matuschka Group & Techno Venture Management

---

3224 WESTERN NIS ENTERPRISE FUND
4 Rayevskoho street
Kyiv 01042
Ukraine

Phone: 380-442475580 Fax: 380-2475589

Mission Statement: Investing in small and medium-sized enterprises operating in what are expected to be the fastest growing sectors in Ukraine, Moldova and Belarus, providing them with capital and the necessary management tools to evolve from entrepreneurial ventures into professionally managed companies. Arranging for experienced Western executives to work with local management in order to prepare and position them for growth, and seek to achieve long-term appreciation with a modest current return on its capital, which was initially provided by the United States government.
Geographic Preference: Ukraine, Moldova
Fund Size: $150 Million
Founded: 1995
Average Investment: $2.3 Million
Minimum Investment: $500,000
Investment Criteria: All sectors
Industry Group Preference: Agriculture, Communications, Construction, Ice Cream, Confectionery, Food & Beverage, Financial Services, Industrial Equipment, Management, Pharmaceuticals, Forestry, Fishing, Energy
Portfolio Companies: ProCredit Bank, AVK, International Mortgage Bank, Ecoprod, Glass Container Company (GCC), Troyanda, Shvydko, ProCredit Moldova, Vitanta-Intravest

Key Executives:
Natalie A. Jaresko, President and Chief Executive Officer
Education: B.A.Degree in International Business, Master's in Business Administration from New York University
Background: Philip Morris International, National Demographics
Directorships: Head of Marketing Department for Philip Morris Ukraine
Mark A. Iwashko, Executive Vice President and Chief Investment Officer
Education: Business Administration Degree at the Richard Ivey School of Business in London
Background: Coopers & Lybrand & Ashurst Technology Corporation Ltd
Lenna Koszarny, CA, Chief Financial and Administrative Officer
Education: MBA) from the Fisher Business School at Ohio State University
Background: BancOne Corporation
Directorships: Chairperson of the Finance and Investment Committee of the American Chamber of Commerce in Ukraine

---

3225 WESTSUMMIT CAPITAL
A-3805 Fortune Centre, No.7
East Third Ring Middle Road
Chaoyang District
Beijing 100020
China

Phone: 86-1059797669 Fax: 86-1058043607
web: www.westsummitcap.com

Mission Statement: WestSummit Capital is a China-based technology investment firm with deep local expertise in China and a global approach to creating market leaders. We are the first growth capital firm sponsored by the most prestigious financial institution in China focused on growth-stage technology companies operating between China and the rest of the world. Our senior partners collectively bring over 100 years of success as entrepreneurs, public company executives and investors of many leading technology companies in China and the United States. Through our offices in Beijing and Silicon Valley, we closely partner with our companies to realize the full potential of developing their businesses in China to become global industry leaders.

Geographic Preference: China, United States
Average Investment: $10 - $30 million
Industry Group Preference: Technology, New Media, Clean Technology, Consumer Services, Mobile, Software, Enabling Technology
Portfolio Companies: Accent, Anji-Micro, Couchbase, GigaDevice, Inside-Secure, Maginatics, Mirantis, NetBase, Nexenta, Shanghai-Haier-IC, SilkRoad, Tilera, Twitch, Union-Optech, Unity, VeriSilicon, YuMe

Other Locations:
720 University Avenue
Suite 100
Palo Alto, CA 94301
Phone: 650-847-1886 Fax: 650-887-1489

Key Executives:
Raymond Yang, Co-Founder/Managing Director
Education: BS, Tsinghua University; MS, Graduate

School of China
Background: Managing Partner, Navi Capital Partner; CEO, Linktone
Directorships: Unity Technologies

3226 WESTTECH VENTURES
Saarbuucker Strasse 36
Berlin 10405
Germany

Phone: 49 (0)30-21 430 6613 Fax: 49 (0)30-21 280 6660
e-mail: info@westtechventures.com
web: www.westtechventures.com

Mission Statement: Pre-seed and seed-stage venture capital firm in Berlin.

Geographic Preference: Germany
Founded: 2012
Minimum Investment: 25K EUR
Investment Criteria: Pre-Seed, Seed-Stage, Early-Stage
Industry Group Preference: Business to Business, Developer Tools, Enterprise Software, Media Technology, Education
Portfolio Companies: Applause, Book A Tiger, Cookies, Craftrad, Dalia, Dailyme, Delivery Hero, Edition F, Familonet, Fliit, Itembase, Knotable, Knotel, Marley Spoon, Remerge, Semknox, Sensorberg, Softgames, Startup Bootcamp, Styla, Tab, Talent Wunder, Testhub, Test Object, Ubeeko, Vertical Techmedia, Volocopter, Wunderdata

Key Executives:
Masoud Kamali, Founder & Managing Director
Background: Founder, S&S Media Group
Alexander Kolpin, Partner & Managing Director
Background: Founder, German Startups Group

3227 WHEB GROUP
2 Fitzhardinge Street
London W1H 6EE
United Kingdom

Phone: 44-0-20-3219-3441 Fax: 44-0-20-3219-3451
e-mail: info@whebgroup.com
web: www.whebgroup.com

Mission Statement: WHEB is a specialist investor focused on the opportunities created by the global transition to more sustainable, resource efficient and energy efficient economies.

Investment Criteria: SME
Industry Group Preference: Energy Efficiency, Energy Storage, Sustainable Materials, Renewable Energy, Waste & Recycling, Recycling, Water

Other Locations:
Maximillanstrasse 36
Munchen 80539
Germany
Phone: 49-89-122-2808-20 Fax: 49-89-122-2808-11

Key Executives:
James McNaught-Davis, Managing Partner
Education: MA, University of Cambridge; MBA, Wharton School
Background: General Partner, Advent; Partner, Warburg Pincus
Directorships: Watson Brown, Green Energy Group, PassivSystems, Petainer, WEMS
Jorg Sperling, Partner
Education: MS, Electrical Engineering, RWTH Aachen
Background: Venture Partner, Targe Partners; Global VP Sales, ZMD
Directorships: FriedolaTech Hoffmeister, PvXchange, SensorTran, Torqeed, VIA Optronics, UBC GmbH
Rob Wylie, Partner
Education: MA, PhD, University of Cambridge
Background: Agrochemical Business, Shell; Bioscience Unit, Rothschild; KPMG
Directorships: AquaSpy, EVAP, Exosect, Steritrox

Alexander Domin, Partner
Education: MSc, Biological Sciences, Stanford University; PhD, Chemical Engineering, University of Cambridge
Background: Boston Consulting Group; Founder, Enval Ltd.
Directorships: Resysta, Torqeedo, VIA Optronics, Hoffmeister

3228 WINE INVESTMENT FUND
15 Clifford Street
London W1S 4JY

Phone: 44-2070430885
web: www.wineinvestmentfund.com

Mission Statement: The International Wine Investment Fund was created for the purpose of holding wine investment assets, in particular.

Geographic Preference: Australia
Founded: 1989

Key Executives:
Andrew Della Casa, Director

3229 XANGE PRIVATE EQUITY
Maximillianstrasse 45
Munchen D-80538
Germany

Phone: 49-89381699730 Fax: 49-89381699739
web: www.xange.fr

Mission Statement: We invest in innovation in the broadest sense, focusing on sectors where we have developed truly specialized expertise. We look for inspiring projects. We invest in growth companies, innovative ideas and outstanding people.

Geographic Preference: France, Germany
Fund Size: 375 million Euro
Founded: 2004
Average Investment: 500,000 - 5 million Euro
Industry Group Preference: Direct Marketing, Business Products & Services, Logistics, Printing, Mobile, Clean Technology, Telecommunications, Internet, Software, Electronics
Portfolio Companies: A Little Market, A/B Tasty, ABC Cosmétique, Altaven, Assima, Ateme, Au Forum du Batiment, Believe, Clinique Développement, Conexance, Dolead Dynadmic, European Homes, Evaneos, Exoplatform, Expé, Fidor, Groupe IP, H-Log, Harvest, IDS, Intent Technologies, ITL Canis, Kayentis, KissKissBankBank, Kxen, La Ruche qui dit Oui!, Luneau Technology, Marcel & Fils, Mein Auto, Mister Spex, Mobiles Republick, Mysportgroup, Naskeo, Neolane, Nexway, Novawatt, Odoo, Orolia, Pactas, Pixways, PrestaShop, Pret a changer, PrivateLot, Provendi, Qeep, Royal Cactus, Sculpteo, SequoiaSoft, Shopmium, SideTrade, Sinequa, SmartAngels, Snadec, Sparkow, Sport Universal Process, Studitemps, Tag Commander, Technoflex, The Currency Cloud, Travador, TVH, Ucopia, VOSS, Webedia, Wedia, Woman Journal

Other Locations:
12 rue Tronchet
Paris 75008
France
Phone: 01-53430530 Fax: 01-53300225

44 place de la Republique
Lyon 69002
France
Phone: 04-37262530

Key Executives:
Herve Schricke, CEO
Education: Masters, International Law
Background: Managing Director, Financiere Natexis

Venture Capital & Private Equity Firms / International Firms

3230 XENIA VENTURE CAPITAL
Igal Alon 76
Tel Aviv
Israel

Phone: 972-9-957-5259 Fax: 972-2-625-70-83
e-mail: info@xenia.co.il
web: www.xenia.co.il

Mission Statement: Xenia Venture Capital is an investment company publicly traded in the Tel-Aviv Stock Exchange that operates a technological incubator, and is engaged in the initiation and build-up of high-technology start up companies in Israel, in the fields of Information Technology and Life Sciences Medical Devices.

Geographic Preference: Israel
Founded: 2004
Investment Criteria: Early-Stage
Industry Group Preference: Information Technology, Life Sciences, Medical Devices, High Technology
Portfolio Companies: ActiVein, Bio Protect, Ninox, Medi Tate, Neat Stitch, Ortho Space, PolyPid, Xenolith, Saguna, Superfish, Playcast, LiveTune, Arcos, Correlix, SafePeak, Samanage, IntuView, BandWD, VCortex

Key Executives:
Anat Segal, Chief Executive Officer
Education: BS, Economics & Management, MBA, Finance, LLB, Tel Aviv University
Background: Managing Director, Tamir Fishman & Co.; VP Investment Banking, Robertson Stephens/Evergreen

3231 XT INVESTMENTS
Ramat Aviv Tower
40 Einstein Street
PO Box 11
Tel Aviv 69102
Israel

Phone: 972-37456060 Fax: 972-37604650
e-mail: xtht@xtholdings.com
web: www.xtholdings.com

Mission Statement: XT Investments is a leading investor in technology-based companies. XT Investments portfolio is diversified; concentrating mainly around the fields of information technologies and healthcare, from early-stage to publicly-traded companies.

Founded: 1956
Investment Criteria: Early-Stage
Industry Group Preference: Information Technology, Healthcare
Portfolio Companies: Lumenis, Enzymotec, RayV, Angioslide, Checkmarx, Intratech Medical, NanoPass, MGVS, PainReform, EndoCross, NextNine, YouLicense, Applied Spectral Imaging, dPharm, CorAssist

Key Executives:
Yoav Doppelt, CEO, XT Investments
Education: BS, Economics, Technion-Israel Institute of Technology; MBA, Haifa University
Background: CEO, XT Hi-Tech
Directorships: Israel Corporation, Lumenis, TowerJazz, Enzymotec, MGVS, Yozma, RayV, Angioslide

3232 YASUDA AND PAMA LIMITED
Shinwa Building
5/F, 2-9-11, Toranomon
Minato-ku
Tokyo 105-0001
Japan

Phone: 81-335970051 Fax: 81-335970053
e-mail: ymc@yasudamakoto.com
web: www.yasudamakoto.com

Fund Size: $540 million
Key Executives:
Makoto Yasuda, Chief Executive

3233 YASUDA ENTERPRISE DEVELOPMENT COMPANY
Marumasu Kojimachi Bldg. 8F
3-3-8 Kojimachi
Chiyoda-ku
Tokyo 102-0083
Japan

Phone: 81-368117100 Fax: 81-352133405

Geographic Preference: Japan, United States
Fund Size: $400 Million
Investment Criteria: Start-up/Early stage, Expansion/Development stage
Industry Group Preference: Information Technology, Medical Devices, Biotechnology

Key Executives:
Yuji Kawakami, President
Masanori Ando, Senior Managing Director

3234 YFM GROUP
5th Floor
Valiant Building
14 South Parade
Leeds LS1 5QS
United Kingdom

Phone: 0113 244 1000
e-mail: info@yfmep.com
web: www.yfmgroup.co.uk

Mission Statement: Meeting the demand for risk capital, consultancy and property services from entrepreneurially led small companies.

Geographic Preference: United Kingdom
Fund Size: £310 Million
Founded: 1982
Average Investment: £500,000
Minimum Investment: £100,000
Investment Criteria: Early-Stage, Later-Stage, MBO, Management Buy-In, Secondary Buy-Outs, Startup
Industry Group Preference: Business Products & Services, Retail, Consumer & Leisure, Healthcare, Software, Telecommunications
Portfolio Companies: Macro Art, Deep Secure, Mangar International, GO Outdoors, Leengate Valves, GTK UK, Gill, Harvey Jones, Seven Technologies, Intelligent Office, Bagel Nash, Harris Hill, PowerOasis, RMS Group, Selima, Insider Technologies, Dryden Human Capital, Caterplus, Displanplan, Callstream, Cambridge Cognition, President Engineering, Nanoco, Pressure Technologies, DataLase, Gentronix, ImmunoBiology, Intamac, K3

Key Executives:
David Hall, Managing Director, YFM Private Equity
Andrew Marchant, Chairman

3235 YISSUM TECHNOLOGY TRANSFER
Hi-Tech Park, Edmond J. Safra Campus
Givat-Ram
PO Box 39135
Jerusalem 91390
Israel

Phone: 972-26586688 Fax: 972-26586689
e-mail: info@yissum.co.il
web: www.yissum.co.il

Mission Statement: Yissum Research Development Company of the Hebrew University of Jerusalem Ltd. Founded in 1964 to protect and commercialize the Hebrew University's intellectual property. Ranked among the top technology transfer companies, Yissum has registered over 7,000 patents covering 2,023 inventions; has licensed out 530 technologies and has spun-off 72 companies. Products that are based on Hebrew University technologies and were commercialized by Yissum generate today over $2 Billion in annual sales.

Geographic Preference: Israel

Venture Capital & Private Equity Firms / International Firms

Founded: 1964
Industry Group Preference: Agriculture, Chemicals, Advanced Materials, Clean Technology, Environment, Computer Related, Engineering, Food & Beverage, Life Sciences, Biotechnology, Electronics, Nanotechnology
Portfolio Companies: Angiob, Atox Bio, Bactusense, Beelogics, Biocancell Therapeutics, Biosensor Application AB, Breedit, Briefcam, Chiasma, Collplant, Danziger Innovations, Eggdetect, En Gibton, Ex Libris, Futuragene, HIL Applied Medical, HumanEyes Technologies, Intec Pharma, Jexys Pharmaceuticals, Kovax, Maimonidex RA, Medgenics, MELODEA, MobilEye, Morflora, Morria Biopharmaceuticals, Nanonics Imaging, NasVax, Novagali Pharma SA, Novel Therapeutic Technologies, Novotyr Therapeutics, Paulee Cleantec, Pepticom, Phenome Networks, Protein Laboratories Rehovot, Qlight Nanotech, Rav Galai, Real-Time Radiography, SCT Stem Cell Technology, Sensotrade, Sol-Gen, TheraVir, Tiltan Pharma, TreaTec21, Valentis
Key Executives:
  Yaacov Michlin, President/CEO
  Education: Bachelor of Law & Economics, Master of law, Bar-Ilan University; MBA, Technion Israel Institute of Technology
  Background: Partner, Tulchinsky Stern & Co. Law Offices

3236 YL VENTURES
PO Box 847
Grand Cayman KY1-1103
Cayman Islands

Phone: 415-3000039 **Fax:** 415-7237703
web: www.ylventures.com

Mission Statement: YL Ventures invests early in core technology software companies in and around the Internet space, and accelerates their evolution via value-added involvement and Silicon Valley-based business development. We then spearhead the exit process, with particular expertise in arranging strategic acquisitions by US-based corporations known to the firm.
Geographic Preference: Israel
Average Investment: $1M - $2M
Investment Criteria: Early-Stage
Industry Group Preference: Software, E-Commerce & Manufacturing, Infrastructure, Cloud Computing, Mobile Technology, Analytics & Analytical Instruments, Business Intelligence
Portfolio Companies: Hexadite, Seculert, BlazeMeter, FireLayers, Upstream Commerce, 6Scan
Other Locations:
  San Francisco, CA
  Phone: 415-300-0039 **Fax:** 415-723-7703

  Tel Aviv
  Israel
  Phone: 972-9971-6021 **Fax:** 972-9777-0119
Key Executives:
  Yoav Andrew Leitersdorf, Managing Partner
  Education: MBA, Columbia University
  Background: CEO/Co-Founder, Movota; Associate, DFJ Gotham Ventures
  Directorships: ClickTale, Seculert, Upstream Commerce, BlazeMeter

3237 YLR CAPITAL MARKETS LTD
16 Beit Hashoeva Lane
Tel Aviv 65814
Israel

Phone: 972-35667339 **Fax:** 972-35605818

Mission Statement: YLR enables its clients create the foundation for a strong business, and a strong future, through a comprehensive offering of investment banking services.
Geographic Preference: North America, Europe, Asia

Founded: 1990
Investment Criteria: Start-up, Development.
Industry Group Preference: Internet Technology, Telecommunications, Healthcare, Marketing, Retailing, High Technology

3238 YUUWA CAPITAL
Enterprise Unit 3, Suite 4, Office 7
9 De Laeter Way
Bently WA 6102
Australia

Phone: 61-400605960 **Fax:** 61-8-9355-5694
e-mail: matthew@yuuwa.com.au
web: www.yuuwa.com.au

Mission Statement: Yuuwa Capital is a $40M early-stage venture capital firm based in Perth, Western Australia. We are actively seeking outstanding investment opportunities where Yuuwa can provide both capital and expertise to help founders, management and early investors to turn good ideas into great companies.
Geographic Preference: Australia
Fund Size: $40 million
Average Investment: $1,000,000 to $5,000,000
Investment Criteria: Early-Stage
Industry Group Preference: Software, Life Sciences, Biotechnology, Communications, Clean Technology
Portfolio Companies: GordianTec, OzSonotek, Adalta, iCetana, Agworld, Filter Squad, Dealised
Key Executives:
  Liddy McCall, Managing Director
  Education: LLB, BJuris, BCom
  Background: Co-Founder, Tessitura Pty Ltd; Co-Founder, iCeutica Group; Associate Director, Macquarie Bank

3239 YVC - YOZMA MANAGEMENT & INVESTMENTS LIMITED
Ramat Aviv Tower
40 Einstein Street
Tel Aviv 69102
Israel

Phone: 972-36437766 **Fax:** 972-36437888
e-mail: keren@yozma.com
web: www.yozma.com

Geographic Preference: Israel
Fund Size: $170 Million
Founded: 1993
Average Investment: $1 million and $6 million
Minimum Investment: $1 Million
Investment Criteria: Primary focus on Early-Stage, High-Growth.
Industry Group Preference: Communications, Information Technology, Technology, Life Sciences
Portfolio Companies: Brighthaul (Israel) Ltd., Clariton, Hywire Ltd., KaiLight Photonics, KiloLambda, Paragon, Pegasus, Radiotel, Telegate, CardonetCommtouch, eShip-4U, E-SIM, Ligature, Maincontrol, NextNine, Security 7, Ubique, ASI, Biosense, Can-Fite BioPharma, Collgard, CorAssist, Discote
Key Executives:
  Orli Disi Ben-Zion, Chief Financial Officer
  Education: B.Sc. and M.Sc. in Chemistry and an MBA from the Hebrew University of Jerusalem.
  Background: Founder of Gemini, JPV, Nitzanim (Concord), Polaris, STAR and Walden Israel.
  Yoav Sebba, Partner

3240 ZERNIKE SEED FUND BV
Paterswoldseweg 802
Groningen 9728 BM
Netherlands

Phone: +31 (0)50 30 50 600 **Fax:** +31 (0)50 30 50 601

Venture Capital & Private Equity Firms / International Firms

Mission Statement: Actively seeking investments
Geographic Preference: Europe, Asia, North America
Fund Size: $150 million
Founded: 1992
Investment Criteria: Start-up , Development.
Industry Group Preference: Agriculture, Biotechnology, Computer Related, Forestry, Industrial Products, Medical & Health Related

3241 ZHENFUND
China World Trade Center
Tower 1
Jianguomenwai Dajie Beijing
Beijing 100004
China

e-mail: dream@zhenfund.com
web: www.zhenfund.com

Mission Statement: ZhenFund is a seed investment firm based in Beijing in collaboration with Sequoia Capital China.
Geographic Preference: United States, China
Founded: 2011
Industry Group Preference: TMT, IOT, Mobile Internet, Entertainment, Enterprise Software, O2O, E-Commerce, Education
Portfolio Companies: Jumei.com, LightInTheBox.com, Jiayuan.com, Zhaogang.com, Everstring, Miyabaobei, com, Nice, 51talk, Yongche.com, Melele, Ehang, Meicai.cn, KV Games, The ONE, Bobo, Jeepglint, Mobvoi, Super Evil Megacorp, NWay

Key Executives:
Bob Xu, Founder
Background: Co-Founder, New Oriental Education
Victor Wang, Co-Founder
Education: Foundation Fellow of Harris Manchester College, University of Oxford
Background: Co-Founder/VP/Chairman, New Oriental Education

3242 ZOUK VENTURES
100 Brompton Road
London SW3 1ER
United Kingdom

Phone: 44-2079473400 Fax: 44-2079473449
web: www.zouk.com

Mission Statement: To leverage our established position, networks and partnerships to optimize the value created through investment in the cleantech market.
Geographic Preference: Europe, Asia, Middle East, the Americas
Fund Size: Euro 400 Million
Founded: 2000
Investment Criteria: Development Stage, Operational Stage
Industry Group Preference: Clean Technology, Renewable Infrastructure, Renewable Energy, Resource Efficiency, Environmental Infrastructure
Portfolio Companies: Anesco, Nanotron Technologies, Orb, Ozz Electric, SiC Processing, Solarcentury, Trilliant, Va-Q-Tec, LightingScience, The Mobility House, Space-Ime Insight, iZettle

Key Executives:
Samer Salty, Founder and CEO
Education: BS, Electrical Engieering, California Polytechnic; MS, Management & Finance, MIT
Background: JP Morgan, Martin Lockheed, AT&T, Hughes Aircraft, US Federal Aviation Administration
Directorships: Orb Energy, Solarcentury
Erich Becker, Partner
Education: MS, Economics, University of Cologne, Germany; CEP, Institut d'Etudes Politeques, Paris
Background: JP Morgan, French Ministry of Finance, German Chamber of Commerce, Russia

Anthony Fox, Partner
Background: Chief Executive, Global Ecommerce, Kingfisher Plc; Managing Director, Kingfisher Asia Pacific Limited; CFO, Planning Sciences International/Gentia Software
Alois Flatz, Partner
Education: International Management, HEC; MBA, Vienna University of Economics; PhD, Business Administration, University of St. Gallen
Background: Partner, Head of Research, Sustainable Asset Management; Managing Partner, BTS Investment Advisors; Austrian Ministry of the Environment
Directorships: SiC Processing
Colin Campbell, Partner
Education: BSc, Chemical & Process Engineering
Background: CEO, Killingholme Power Group Ltd; VP, Corporate M&A, TXU Europe; Project Finance Manager, Mitsui Babcock; FCA, Coopers & Lybrand
Directorships: Enviromena Power Systems
Richard Pereira, CFO
Background: Ernst & Young; KPMG London

3243 ZURCHER KANTONALBANK
Stockerstrasse 33
Postfach 8010
Zurich 8010
Switzerland

Phone: 41-844-843823 Fax: 41-12928792
web: www.zkb.ch

Mission Statement: Actively seeking new investments
Geographic Preference: Switzerland
Founded: 1870
Investment Criteria: Expansion and Development, MBO
Industry Group Preference: All Sectors Considered
Key Executives:
Urs Oberholzer, Chairman
Liselotte Illi, Deputy-Chairman

3244 ZURMONT MADISON PRIVATE EQUITY
Eisengasse 15
PO Box 272
Zurich 8034
Switzerland

Phone: 41-0442675000 Fax: 41-0442675001
web: www.zurmontmadison.ch

Geographic Preference: Switzerland, Southern Germany, Austria
Founded: 2006
Investment Criteria: Buyout of established mid-market industrial and consumer goods companies. MBO/MBI, Corporate spin-offs, succession solutions.
Industry Group Preference: Industrial Products, Medical Devices, Machinery, Consumer Products, Logistics, Business Products & Services

Key Executives:
Guido Patroncini, Founding Partner
Werner Schnorf, Founding Partner & Chief Executive Officer
Dr. Björn Böckenförde, Founding Partner / CFO
Kurt Hitz, Partner
Andreas Ziegler, Partner / Investor Relations

Venture Capital & Private Equity Firms / International Firms

[Page is heavily faded/mirrored and largely illegible]

National & State Associations

Venture Capital & Private Equity Firms / National & State Associations

3245 AMERICAN INVESTMENT COUNCIL
799 9th Street NW
Suite 200
Washington, DC 20001

Phone: 202-465-7700
e-mail: info@investmentcouncil.org
web: www.investmentcouncil.org

Mission Statement: Advocacy organization develops and provides information on the private equity investment industry.

Founded: 2007
Portfolio Companies: Members: ACON Investments, Adams Street Partners, Altamont Capital Partners, Alvarez & Marsal Capital, Apollo Global Management, ArcLight Capital Partners, The Blackstone Group, Brookfield Asset Management, The Carlyle Group, CCMP Capital Advisors, Clearlake Capital Group, Crestview Partners, CVC Capital Partners, The Edgewater Funds, EnCap Investments, Energy Capital Partners, Genstar Capital, Goldman Sachs, GTCR, HarbourVest Partners, Hellman & Friedman, Investcorp International, The Jordan Company, Kelso & Company, Kline Hill Partners, Kohlberg Kravis Roberts & Co., KPS Capital Partners, Madison Dearborn Partners, New Mountain Capital, Pantheon Ventures, Providence Equity Partners, The Riverside Company, Silver Lake, SoftBank Group, Sterling Partners, TA Associates, Thoma Bravo, TPG, Vector Capital, Vestar Capital Partnrs, Welsh, Carson, Anderson & Stowe

Key Executives:
Drew Maloney, President & CEO
Background: Principal Liaison between the Treasury and Congress
Emily Schillinger, Senior Vice President, Public Affairs
Education: BA, Clemson University
Background: Communications Director, House Ways & Means Committee; Press Secretary, Speaker of the House John Boehner; Communications Director, Senator John Barrasso and the Senate Republican Policy Committee; Press Secretary, Department of Commerce; Asst. Press Secretary, White House

3246 AMERICAN SUSTAINABLE BUSINESS NETWORK
712 H Street NE
PMP 42
Washington, DC 20002

web: www.asbnetwork.org

Mission Statement: World's largest early-stage investing network, formerly known as Investors' Circle and Social Venture Network.

Geographic Preference: North America
Fund Size: $3 million
Founded: 1992
Average Investment: $250,000 - $500,000
Investment Criteria: Startup, Early-Stage
Industry Group Preference: Energy, Consumer Products, Agriculture, Healthcare, Biotechnology, Digital Media & Marketing, Software, Education, Health & Wellness
Portfolio Companies: Agora Fund, Alter Eco America, APDS, Aunt Bertha, Avancen, aWhere, AYZH, Big City Farms, Bioceptive, BlocPower, California Safe Soil, Cardinal Resources, Castlewood Surgical, Community Sourced Capital, CSRHub, DailyWorth.com, DR2, E3Bank, EcoTensil, Edthena, Emerge, Eniware, EnSolve Biosystems, Episencial, EV Connect, Farmland LP, First Light Hospitality, Food Matters Market, Genomic Expression, Goalbook, Gridtest, Grower's Secret, Indow Windows, Isidore Electronics Recycling, Jack and Jake's, Jail Education Solutions, Kickboard, KnipBio, LearnZillion, Listen Current, Locus Energy, Lomo Market, Mamma Chia, Medolac, MicroEnergy Credits, MovingWorlds, MPOWERD, Mytonomy, Natural Systems Utilities, Oliberte, OtoSense, Pact Apparel, Peepoople, Portapure, Querium, Relay Foods, Rezzcard, Rivertop Renewables, Runa, Scrible, Seal Innovation, Social Imprints, Sundolier, SunFunder, Sustainable Minds, Susty Party, Thread, Transparent Healthcare, United By Blue, Validic, VOZ, Wash Cycle Laundry, Waste Enterprisers, Zagster

Key Executives:
Isaac Graves, Chief Operating Officer
Background: Executive Director, Social Venture Circle

3247 ANGEL CAPITAL ASSOCIATION
10977 Granada Lane
Suite 103
Overland Park, KS 66211

Phone: 913-894-4700
web: www.angelcapitalassociation.org

Mission Statement: Professional development organization for angel investors with more than 14,000 members.

Key Executives:
Pat Gouhin, Chief Executive Officer
e-mail: pgouhin@angelcapitalassociation.org
Education: Aerospace Engineering, Ohio State University; MA, George Washington Unviersity; Certificate, Stanford University Graduate School of Business; Certificate, Wharton School
Background: Association Advisor; Executive Director & CEO, ISA; COO, AIAA; VP, Operations & Technology Transfer, National Institute of Aerospace
Directorships: Past Chair, Council of Engineering & Scientific Society Executives; Ctte. Member, The Center for Association Leadership
Sarah Dickey, Membership Director
e-mail: sdickey@angelcapitalassociation.org
Education: BA, Northwest Missouri State University; MA, Communication, May Business School, Texas A&M University
Background: VP, Research, Angel Resource Institute

3248 CALIFORNIA COAST VENTURE FORUM
800 Anacapa Street
Suite A
Santa Barbara, CA 93101

Phone: 805-495-6962
web: www.ccvf.org

Mission Statement: Non-profit organization promotes tech companies in California.

Geographic Preference: California
Founded: 1996
Investment Criteria: Emerging Growth, Later Stage
Industry Group Preference: Software & Internet, Technology, Mechanical Products, Retail, Restaurants & Distribution, Food & Beverage, Utilities & Farming
Portfolio Companies: ACQI, Apeel Sciences, Channel Wind, ECO Products, Foxy's Pash, Gramercy Beverage, Harvest, Hope20, Kaibae, Kiwa, Locali, LyfeStart International, Maker Labs, Mica Sense, Necessity LLC, Next, Ojai Energy Systems, Re-Leash, Seaters, Sierra Lifestyle, Slightly Nutty, SweetSpring Salmon, T4 Spatial, Teecinno, Waiakea, Wash-it

Key Executives:
Jerry Knotts, President & CEO
e-mail: jeknotts@ccvf.org
Education: BSEE, Pennsylvania State University; MBA, Auburn University; Defense Systems Management College; Industrial College of the Armed Forces; Air War College
Background: VP & General Manager, Defense Electronics Division, California Microwave; VP, American Nucleonics Corporation

Venture Capital & Private Equity Firms / National & State Associations

3249 CANADIAN VENTURE CAPITAL ASSOCIATION Canadian Venture Capital & Private Equity Association
372 Bay Street
Toronto, ON M5H 2W9
Canada

e-mail: info@cvca.ca
web: www.cvca.ca

Mission Statement: CVCA's mission is to help its members fuel the economy of the future by growing the businesses of today. They accomplish this by supporting and connecting the private capital industry with advocacy, research, and education. Please see www.cvca.ca for a complete list of member firms.

Founded: 1974
Industry Group Preference: Energy, Power, Hospitality, Healthcare, Life Sciences, Clean Technology, Media, Food & Beverage, Infrastructure, Consumer, Information Technology, Manufacturing, Industrial, Transportation, Business Products & Services
Portfolio Companies: 7 Gate Ventures, AIMCo, AIP Private Capital, Alberta Enterprise Corporation, Alberta Teachers' Retirement Fund, Atlas Partners LP, Amplitude Ventures, Anges Quebec Capital, Ardenton Capital Corporation, AVAC Ltd., Azimuth Capital Management, Azure Capital Partners, BC Tech Fund, BCF Ventures, BDC Capital, Bedford Capital Limited, Bioindustrial Innovation Canada, Birch Hill Equity Partners Management, BlueSky Equities, BMO Capital Partners, Bond Capital, Brightspark Ventures, British Columbia Investment Management Corporation, Brookfield Asset Management, CAI Capital Partners, Caisse de depot et placement du Quebec, Canada Pension Plan Investment Board, Canadian Business Growth Fund, Cathay Capital NA LLC, Cedarpoint Investments, Celtic House Venture Partners, CIBC Innovation Banking, CIC Capital Canada, CIC Capital Ventures, Clairvest Group, Clearspring Capital Partners, Coller Capital, Comerica Bank, CTI Life Sciences Fund, Cycle Capital Management, Dancap Family Investment Office, Dream Maker Ventures, EnerTech Capital, Espresso Capital, Evok Innovations, Export Development Canada, Extreme Venture Partners, FACIT, FirePower Debt GP, First Ascent Ventures, First West Capital, Fondaction, Fonds de soliderite FTQ, Framework Venture Partners, Freycinet Investments, Fulcrum Capital Partners, Genesys Capital Management, Georgian Partners, Globalive, Golden Ventures, Good News Ventures, GreenSoil Building Innovation Fund, Hamilton Lane, HarbourVest Partners, Headwater Equity

Key Executives:
Kim Furlong, CEO
Education: BA, American History, Mgill University; MA, Trade Policy & Global Finance, Norman Paterson School Of International Affairs, Carleton University
Background: Director, Federal Government Affairs, Amgen; VP, Federal Government Relations, Retail Council of Canada; Department of Foreign Affairs
Jon Jackson, Head, Communications
Education: Broadcasting, Fanshawe College; Public Relations, Seneca College of Applied Arts & Technology
Background: Producer, Bell Media; Producer, Corus Entertainment; Producer, Newcap Radio
Fil Varino, Head, Development & Member Engagement
Education: BSc, University Of Ottawa; Certificate, Fundraising Management, Humber College; Executive Boardroom Education Program, Institute of Corporate Directors
Background: RightBlue Labs; Social Profit Partners; The DMZ at Ryerson University; Causeway Work Centre, Salvation Army
David Kornacki, Associate, Research & Product
Education: BA & Certificate in Project Management, University of Toronto
Background: GSK

3250 COUNCIL FOR ENTREPRENEURIAL DEVELOPMENT
600 Park Offices Drive
Suite 100
Triangle Park, NC 27709

Phone: 919-549-7500
web: cednc.org

Mission Statement: To promote high growth companies in North Carolina by providing education and capital formation resources to entrepreneurs in a broad range of industries, including the life sciences, technology and services sectors.
Geographic Preference: North Carolina
Founded: 1984
Investment Criteria: High Growth, Startups, Growth Stage
Industry Group Preference: Advanced Manufacturing & Materials, Clean Technology, Green Technology, Life Sciences
Portfolio Companies: 10 for Humanity, 3DFS Power Solutions, 8 Rivers Capital, Abbey Road Consulting, Acorn Applications, Adamas Nanotechnologies, Affinergy, Agile Sciences, Airwavz Solutions, Akili Software, Align Global Consulting, All Elements, Alston & Bird, Altaravision, Atmospheric Plasma Solutions, Aura Life, Axial Exchange, Bagchi Law, BBVA Compass, BCombs, BDO, Bernard Robinson & Company, BioKier, BioMASON, BioResource International, Bioventus, Blue Gas Marine, Bridge Bank, Bright View Technologies, Bull City Forward, Business Ready Solutions, C10 Connect, CAI, Candlescience, Canopy, Capitol Broadcasting Company, Cary Street Partners, CDS Outsourcing, CertifiGroup, ChannelAdvisor, Charlotte Research Institute, Chimerix, Chubb Insurance Group, Cii Technology, Cisco Systems, Cityzen, CivaTech Oncology, Clark Nexsen, Clarkston Consulting, Clinipace Worldwide, Cloud Pharmaceuticals, Code A Site, Concentrx Pharmaceuticals, Cooley, Cornerstone Medical & Technology Financial, Creas Carolinas, CrossComm, Cushman & Wakefield, DecisionPoint, Deloitte LLP, Diagnosoft, Dignify Therapeutics, Diposta, Divvy Investments, DNA Group, Dude Solutions, Eco-Site, EG Gilero, EmployUs, Enzerna Biosciences, Ever EdTech, Expion, FabSource, Fennebresque, Fidelity Investments, Financial Directions Group, FLAG Therapeutics, FM:Systems, Forecast Health, Forge Communications, Fuentek, Full Scale Solutions, GlaxoSmithKline, Goldhat Advisors, Grant Thornton LLP, HireNetworks, HQ Raleigh, Hughes Pittman & Gupton LLP, Ici

Key Executives:
Kelly Rowell, President and CEO
Education: BA, Marketing, Small Business Management and Entrepreneurship

3251 FLORIDA VENTURE FORUM
707 W. Azeele Street
Tampa, FL 33606

Phone: 813-335-8116
web: www.flventure.org

Mission Statement: The Florida Venture Forum is a not-for-profit organization designed to provide financial advice and management assistance to entrepreneurs. The Forum organizes educational programs across the state that offer insight on a number of topics, including raising equity and debt capital, development, marketing, research and management. The goal of the Forum is to help drive the success of entrepreneurial enterprises.

Geographic Preference: Florida
Founded: 1984
Investment Criteria: Early Stage
Portfolio Companies: Aegis Business Credit, Agro Arms, Aim Above, Akerman LLP, Amzur Technologies, AON, AquaMelon Water, Arsenal Venture Partners, Auxadyne, AZZLY, Bairo, Ballast Point Ventures, Bank of America Merrill Lynch, BedaBox, Berger Singerman LLP, Bit Cauldron, Bridge Bank, Cambridge Solutions, CapitalSouth

Partners, CareAngel, CarePredict, CBIZ, Cherry Bekaert LLP, Citrix Systems, CliftonLarsonAllen, Concentric Equity Partners, CoTEch Ventures, Cross Fernandez & Riley, Crowe Horwath, DATIS HR Cloud, eNow, Enterprise Florida, Eonian Technology, Equastream, FFI Contracting Services, Florida Blue, Florida Funders, Florida Gulfshore Capital, Foley & Lardner LLP, Frontier Capital, Fulcrum Equity Partners, FVF, Grant Thornton LLP, Greenberg Traurig, Gretel, Harbert Management, Harbert Venture Partners, Harbor View Advisors, Hercules Technology Growth Capital, Hill Ward Henderson, Holland & Knight LLP, Hopkins Capital Group, Hub International, Hunter Business Law, Hyde Park Capital Partners, Hydrocore, iCare.com, InformedDNA, Innovatia Medical Systems, Insolu, Intrepid, Ioppolo Law Group, Johnson Biomedical Capital, Keiretsu, Key Associates, KynderMed, Laughlin & Associates, Lenley Holdings, LFE Capital, LifeNet Systems, Locke Lord LLP, LogZilla, Luma Sleep, MAJEC Ventures, MassInvestor, MedAffinity, Medical Tracking Solutions, My Senior Portal, Nawboi Technologies, New World Angels, Noro-Moseley Partners, Norstrem Associates, Nperspective, Oakstone Holdings, Ocean Current Energy, Offerdat, Oo

Key Executives:
Kevin Burgoyne, President & CEO
305-343-0617
e-mail: kevin@flventure.org
Education: BS, University of Florida; MBA, University of Chicago
Background: Walt Disney Company; PanAmSat; Global Crossing
Pat Schneider, Vice President
e-mail: pat@flventure.org
Education: BA, International Business, Florida International University
Background: Executive Assistant, The Florida Aquarium; Dominion Financial Group; Home Shopping Network

3252 GLOBAL PRIVATE CAPITAL ASSOCIATION
58 8th Avenue
Floor 18
New York, NY 10018

Phone: 646-315-6735
e-mail: membership@GPCapital.org
web: www.globalprivatecapital.org

Mission Statement: GCPA's mission is to promote and support private capital investment in emerging markets. Formerly known as the Emerging Markets Private Equity Association.

Geographic Preference: Emerging Markets
Portfolio Companies: Members: 17 Asset Management, 3TS Capital Partners, 57 Stars, AA Consulting & Associates, ABC TEST, Abu Dhabi Investment Authority, Accion, Actis, Adams Street Partners, Adansonia Management Services Limited, Adenia Partners, ADM Capital, Advanced Finance & Investment Group LLC, Affirma Capital, Africa50, African Capital Alliance, African Infrastructure Investment Managers Pty (Ltd.), AfricInvest, Aif Capital Ltd, Akin Gump Strauss Hauer & Feld LLP, Albright Capital Management LLC, Alloy Merchant Finance LP, Alothon Group, Alpha Associates, Alta Growth Capital, Alta Semper Capital, Amadeus Capital Partners, Amethis Finance, APS Investments, Aqua Capital, ARM-Harith Infrastructure Investments Ltd, Artha Partners, Asante Capital Group, Ascent Capital Partners, Ashburton Investments, Asia Alternatives Management, Asia Grown Capital Advisors (S) Pte Ltd, Asia Partners, Asian Development Bank, Asian Infrasturcture Investments Bank, ATP-PEP, Austral Capital Partners, Avanz Capital, AZB & Partners, Baker McKenzie, Baltoro Capital, Baring Private Equity Asia Ltd, Baring Vostok Capital Partners, Barnellan Equity Advice Ltd, Bill & Melinda Gates Foundation, BIO - Belgian Investment Company for Developing Countries, Blackpeak Group, BlueOrchard Finance, BluePeak Private Capital, Brookfield Asset Management, Bull Capital Partners Pte Ltd, Caisse de Depot et Placement du Quebec, CalPERS, CalSTRS, Cambridge Associates LLC, Capital Dynamics, Capria Ventures LLC, Cartica Management LLC,

Key Executives:
Cate Ambrose, Chief Executive Officer
Education: Universidad Compultense de Madrid; BA, Saint Lawrence University; MPA, Columbia University - School of International & Public Affairs
Background: President & CEO, LAVCA; Chief of Advocacy, Commission on Legal Empowerment of the Poor, UN Development Programme; Executive Director, Programmes, The Economist
Directorships: Youth INC NYC; Girls Write Now
Holly Radel, Managing Director, Institutional Relations
e-mail: HRadel@GPCapital.org
Education: BA, Rice Univ.; MA, Johns Hopkins Univ.
Background: World Affairs Council (Houston)
Jeff Schlapinski, Managing Director, Research
e-mail: JSchlapinski@GPCapital.org
Education: Beijing Center for Chinese Studies; BSFS, Georgetown University
Background: English Program Manager, Beijing Fermat Edu; Intern, True Run Media; Business Development Associate, News Distribution Network Inc.; Teaching Assistant, Georgetown University; Intern, Jeffrey J. Kimbell Associates
Julie Ruvolo, Managing Director, Venture Capital
646-315-6735
e-mail: JRuvolo@GPCapital.org
Education: BA, Stanford University
Background: Journalist, TechCrunch, Buzzfeed, GOOD Magazine, Advertising Age, atlanticCityLab.com and others
Directorships: LatinSF; Latin American Tech Growth Coalition

3253 HAWAII VENTURE CAPITAL ASSOCIATION
PO Box 4677
Honolulu, HI 96812

e-mail: admin@hvca.org
web: hvca.org

Mission Statement: The Hawaii Venture Capital Association seeks to promote entrepreneurial development and growth by serving as a platform for capital formation, network, education and entrepreneurship.

Geographic Preference: Hawaii
Founded: 1988

Key Executives:
Meli James, President
Education: BS, Cornell University
Background: Head, New Ventures, Sultan Ventures; Program Director & Entrepreneur in Residence, XLR8UH; Founder, HonNewTech; Founding Member, Startup Paradise

3254 HEALTHCARE PRIVATE EQUITY ASSOCIATION
2500 Williston Drive
Charlottesville, VA 22901

e-mail: info@hcpea.org
web: www.hcpea.org

Mission Statement: The Healthcare Private Equity Association's mission is to support and promote the healthcare private equity industry of the United States.

Founded: 2010
Industry Group Preference: Healthcare
Portfolio Companies: Members: A&M Capital Partners, Advent International, Apax Partners, Archimedes Health Investors, Ares Management LLC, Arsenal Capital Partners, Audax Private Equity, Bain Capital, Beecken Petty O'Keefe & Company, Blackstone Group, BlueMountain Capital, Brookfield Asset Management, Century Equity Partners, Chicago Pacific Founders, Cinven, Clayton Dubilier & Rice,

Venture Capital & Private Equity Firms / National & State Associations

Comvest Partners, Concord Health Partners, Court Square Capital Partners, The Cranemere Group, Cressey & Company, CVC Capital Partners, Deerfield Management, DW Healthcare Partners, EQT, EW Healthcare Partners, FFL Partners, Flexpoint Ford, Formation Capital, Frazier Healthcare Partners, General Atlantic, GI Partners, Granite Growth Health Partners, Harren Equity Partners, Harvest Partners, HealthEdge Investment Partners, Health Enterprise Partners, HealthInvest Equity Partners, HealthQuest Capital, Hellman & Friedman, Heritage Group, HIG Capital, Kelso & Company, KKR, Lee Equity Partners, Leonard Green & Partners, Linden Capital Partners, LLR Partners, Madison Dearborn Partners, Martis Capital, MBF Healthcare Partners, Morgan Stanley Capital Partners, Mubadala Investment Company, Nautic Partners, Oak HC/FT, OMERS Private Equity, Ontario Teachers' Pension Plan, PPC Partners, Revelstoke Capital Partners, The Riverside Company, Spindletop Capital, Summit Partners, Sverica Capital Management, SV Health Investors, TA Associates, Thomas H. Lee Partners, TPG, Varsity Healthcare Partners, Vesey Street Capital Partners,

Key Executives:
Melissa Gardiner, Executive Director
e-mail: mgardiner@hcpea.org
Leslie Thornbury, Director
e-mail: lthornbury@hcpea.org

3255 ILLINOIS VENTURE CAPITAL ASSOCIATION
27 N Wacker Drive
Suite 405
Chicago, IL 60606

web: www.illinoisvc.org

Mission Statement: The Illinois Venture Capital Association seeks to foster the development and growth of the venture capital and private equity industry in Illinois by offering member networking opportunities and educational programs in private equity.

Geographic Preference: Illinois
Founded: 2000
Investment Criteria: Early Stage to Buyout Stage
Portfolio Companies: Adams Street Partners LLC, Anderson Pacific Corporation, Arbor Investments, ARCH Venture Partners, Baird Capital, Beecken Petty O'Keefe & Company, BlueCross BlueShield Venture Partners, CapX Partners, Chicago Ventures, Chrysalis Ventures, CHS Capital LLC, Cressey & Company, Duchossois Capital Management, Dundee Venture Capital, Dunrath Capital, Financial Investments Corporation, First Analysis, Frontenac Company, Golder Investment Management LLC, GTCR LLC, Harrison Street Capital, HIG Capital, High Street Capital, Hyde Park Venture Partners, IllinoisVENTURES LLC, LaSalle Capital, Limerick Investments, Linden Capital Partners, Liquidity Ventures, Madison Dearborn Partners, MATH Venture Partners, Mercury Fund, Mesirow Financial Private Equity, Mid Oaks Investments LLC, MK Capital, Monroe Capital, Motorola Solutions Venture Capital, MVC Capital, New Enterprise Associates, NIN Ventures, Ninth Street Advisors, Northern Trust Private Equity, OCA Venture Partners, Origin Ventures, Paradigm Capital, Patriot Capital, PPM America Capital Partners, Prairie Capital, Pritzker Group, Prospect Partners LLC, RCP Advisors, Romar Partners, RoundTable Healthcare Partners, Sandbox Industries, Shore Capital Partners, Sterling Partners, Svoboda Capital Partners, The Edgewater Funds, Thoma Bravo, Tribune Company, Victory Park Capital, Vistria Group, Water Street Healthcare Partners, Waveland Investments, Wind Point Partners, Winona Capital Management LLC, WP Global Partners, Wynnchurch Capital, Zeb

Key Executives:
Maura O'Hara, Executive Director
e-mail: mohara@illinoisvc.org
Education: BA, Economics, University of Illinois, Urbana-Champaign; MBA, Kellogg School of Management, Northwestern University
Background: VP, Customer Strategies & Consumer Research, Sears Roebuck & Co.; Operational Planning, Helene Curtis; Investment Banking, Stevenson & Company

3256 INSTITUTIONAL LIMITED PARTNERS ASSOCIATION
1776 I Street NW
Suite 525
Washington, DC 20006

Phone: 416-941-9393 Fax: 416-941-9307
e-mail: info@ilpa.org
web: ilpa.org

Mission Statement: Global organization of institutional private equity investors including public pensions, corporate pensions, foundations and sovereign wealth funds.

Other Locations:
55 York Street
Suite 1200
Toronto, ON M5J 1R7
Canada
Phone: 416-941-9393 Fax: 416-941-9307

Key Executives:
Jennifer Choi, Acting CEO
e-mail: jchoi@ilpa.org
Education: BA, Augustana College; MA, Fletcher School, Tufts University
Background: Emerging Markets Private Equity Assoc.
Greg Durst, Managing Direcor, Corporate Development
647-325-2889
e-mail: gdurst@ilpa.org
Education: BS, Georgetown University; Certificate, New York University; MBA, Harvard Business School
Background: Co-Founder & Senior Advisor, The Imprint Group LLC; Head, Business Development & Launch COO, Marto Capital LLC; EVP & COO, Accommodations Plus International; Executive Director, Seabury Group; Principal, Horizon Equity Partners; Managing Director, Endeavor South Africa; Managing Director, Conscripti

3257 LONG ISLAND CAPITAL ALLIANCE
1111 Marcus Avenue
Lake Success, NY 11042

e-mail: info@licapital.org
web: www.licapital.org

Mission Statement: LICA connects investors with opportunities in the state of New York.

Geographic Preference: New York
Founded: 1984
Portfolio Companies: Abrams Fensterman, ActionCOACH, Ambrose, Applied Visions, Asset Enhancement Solutions LLC, BDO USA, The Berkman Law Firm, Blue Pixels Media, Breslow & Walker LLP, Broad Hollow Bioscience Park, Button Down Solutions LLC, Campolo Middleton & McCormick LLP, Capell Barnett Matalon & Schoenfeld, Chasella Capital Partners, Checks and Balances Bookkeeping, Collaborative Medical, CORE Interactive, Crystal & Company, Darrow Associates, EAA Inspection Services, Eagle Business Solutions, EisnerAmper LLP, Executive Strategies Group LLC, Farrell Fritz PC, Ferrera DeStefano & Caporusso, FranchiseKnowHow LLC, Fulwisdom Capital, Golden Seeds, Grassi & Co., GxG Management LLC, HJMT Communications LLC, Hoffman & Baron LLP, Insperity, iSine, Jaspan Schlesinger LLP, Jericho Capital Corp., Jove Equity Partners, JP Morgan Private Bank, Katz Sapper & Miller, Ken Taub, Kildare Capital, Marcum LLP, Northwood Ventures, NYIT, Oximeter Plus, Patient Innovations, Protegrity Advisors, Pryor Cashman LLP, Ringo, Riscica Associates, Rivkin Radler LLP, Ruskin Moscou

Faltischek, Soundview Advice, Stony Brook University, Trident Group, TriNet

Key Executives:
Michael Lane, Chairman
e-mail: mlane@licapital.com
Education: BA, University Of California, Los Angeles; MBA, Columbia Business School
Background: CEO, SteriLux Systems; President, Plum Logic; President, Real Content Media Group; President & CEO, Data Impact Inc.; General Manager & SVP, Bottomline Technologies; Managing Director, Pegasystems Inc.; Managing Director, Vitria Technology; CMO, Accenture
Directorships: Darrow Associates; Saint Matthew's Society; Broadlook Technologies; RingLead Inc.

3258 LOS ANGELES VENTURE ASSOCIATION
11301 Olympic Boulevard
Suite 376
Los Angeles, CA 90064

e-mail: info@lava.org
web: www.lava.org

Mission Statement: Learning and networking forum for Los Angeles entrepreneurs and investors.

Geographic Preference: Los Angeles
Founded: 1985
Portfolio Companies: Members: Applied Facts, Arizona Technology Enterprises, Bryant Stibel, Direct Health Delivery, Fine Line Services LLC, Fox Rothschild, Knobbe Martens, Knobbe Martens Olson & Bear, March Capital Partners, Moss Adams, Peate Institute for Entrepreneurs, Silver Regulatory Associates, Stubbs Alderton & Markiles LLP, Toronto Stock Exchange, Trade & Invest British Columbia, USC Stevens Center for Innovation

Key Executives:
Darren Eng, Executive Director
Education: BS, Yale University
Background: Executive Director, SoCal; Founder, The Sponsorship Group; CEO, Greenbelt Resources Corporation

3259 MICHIGAN VENTURE CAPITAL ASSOCIATION
6632 Telegraph Road
Suite 286
Bloomfield Hills, MI 48301

e-mail: info@michiganvca.org
web: michiganvca.org

Mission Statement: Association of the Michigan entrepreneurial and investment community.

Geographic Preference: Michigan
Founded: 2002
Portfolio Companies: 5AM Ventures, Allos Ventures, Amherst Fund, Ann Arbor Angels, Apjohn Ventures, Arbor Partners, Arboretum Ventures, Arsenal Venture Partners, Augment Ventures, Baird Capital, BELLE Michigan, Beringea, Capital Community Angels Investors, Chrysalis Ventures, Cultivian Sandbox, Detroit Innovate, Detroit Venture Partners, Dow Venture Capital, Draper Triangle Ventures, EDF Ventures, Flagship Ventures, Fletcher Spaght Ventures, Fontinalis Partners, GM Ventures, Grand Angels, Great Lakes Angels, Grosvenor Capital Management, Hopen Life Sciences Venture, Huron River Ventures, Hyde Park Venture Partners, IncWell, Invest Detroit, Invest Michigan, Ludlow Ventures, Mercury Fund, Michigan Accelerator Fund, Michigan Angel Fund, Michigan eLab, MK Capital, Muskegon Angels, North Coast Technology Investors, Northern Michigan Angels, Plymouth Ventures, Renaissance Venture Capital Fund, Resonant Venture Partners, River Cities Capital Funds, RPM Ventures, Start Garden, TGap Ventures, Three Leaf Ventures, Valenti Capital, Venture Investors, Wolverine Venture Fund

Key Executives:
Ara Topouzian, Executive Director
e-mail: Ara@MichiganVCA.org
Education: Marketing, Oakland Community College; BA, Wayne State University
Background: Musician; President & CEO, Troy Chamber of Commerce; Economic Development Director, City of Novi, Michigan; Owner, American Recording Productions; President, Farmington Chamber of Commerce
Directorships: Michigan Society of Association Executives; Michigan Council for Arts & Cultural Affairs; Creative Many Michigan; Troy Community Foundation
Angela Helfin, Associate Director
e-mail: Angela@MichiganVCA.org
Education: BA, Spring Arbor University; MBA, Liberty University
Background: Head Osoccer Coach, Ann Arbor Public Schools; Founder, Vaulted Foundations; Co-Founder & Executive Officer, Education for All; Business Development Strategist & HR Director, Employees Only; Director of Development, MI Association of Public Schools; Chief Academic Officer, K-12 School District
Directorships: Ann Arbor Public Schools; Early Childhood Initiatives; Northrock Church

3260 MID-ATLANTIC VENTURE ASSOCIATION
1400 K Street NW
Suite 1100
Washington, DC 20005

e-mail: mava@mava.org
web: mava.org

Mission Statement: Association serves the needs of innovators, venture capital and private equity in the Mid-Atlantic region.

Geographic Preference: Mid-Atlantic
Portfolio Companies: Investor Members: 3TS Capital Partners, ABS Capital Partners, Boulder Ventures, Camber Creek, CIT GAP Funds, Columbia Capital, Core Capital Partners, Fulcrum Equity Partners, Harbert Growth Partners, Inner Loop Capital, In-Q-Tel, JMI Equity, Kinetic Ventures, New Enterprise Associates, Osage Venture Partners, Paladin Capital Group, Revolution Growth, River Cities Capital Funds, Route 66 Ventures, Sands Capital Ventures, Squadra VC, TCP Venture Capital, TDF Ventures, Updata Partners, Vital Venture Capital

Key Executives:
Julia Spicer, Executive Director
Education: BA, Communications, University of North Carolina
Background: VP, Communications, Columbia Capital; President & COO, IntellEvents; GTE Corporation
Jason Waxberg, Senior Director, Strategic Services
Education: BA, Franklin & Marshall College; MBA, College of William & Mary
Background: Principal Consultant, Water's Edge Strategies; Founder, RoadFan; Founder & CEO, Receptive Mail; Strategic Markets Analyst, Holland & Knight LLP; Market Research Analyst, Waxberg Consulting Company

3261 MISSOURI VENTURE FORUM
St. Louis, MO 63141

web: www.mvfstl.org

Mission Statement: The Missouri Venture Forum is a non-profit organization designed to provide a means for entrepreneurs to grow their companies through networking, education, information exchange and access to financial resources.

Founded: 1985
Portfolio Companies: Sponsors: BDO, Carmody MacDonald, Danna McKitrick PC, Evans & Dixon, Greensfelder, Mueller Prost, Regional Growth Capital, Schmersahl Treloar & Co., St. Louis Arch Angels

Venture Capital & Private Equity Firms / National & State Associations

3262 NATIONAL VENTURE CAPITAL ASSOCIATION
25 Massachusetts Ave NW
Suite 730
Washington, DC 20001

Phone: 202-864-5920 Fax: 202-864-5930
web: nvca.org

Mission Statement: The National Venture Capital Association is a trade association that represents the venture capital community of the Unites States. The NVCA supports entrepreneurial activity by promoting policies that encourage innovation and investment, as well as providing data resources and professional services for its member firms.

Portfolio Companies: Industry Partners: Deloitte, Dentons, DLA Piper, Duff & Phelps, EY, First Republic Bank, Gunderson Dettmer, IHS Markit, KPMG, Latham & Watkins, Morgan Lewis, Morrison & Foerster, Nelson Mullins, Pacific Western Bank, Perkins Coie, Phoenix American Financial, PitchBook, Proskauer, Sensiba San Filippo, Shaerworks, Sidley Austin, Signature Bank, Sparkpr, SRS Acquiom, VMS Fund Administration, William Blair, WilmerHale, Wilson Sonsini Goodrich & Rosati, Withum

Other Locations:
214 Grant Avenue
Suite 325
San Francisco, CA 94108

Key Executives:
Bobby Franklin, President & CEO
202-864-5925
e-mail: bfranklin@nvca.org
Education: BSBA, Finance & Banking, University of Arkansas, Fayetteville
Background: EVP, CTIA The Wireless Association; VP, Federal Government Affairs, ALLTEL; Legislative Director, AESOP Enterprises

3263 NEW ENGLAND VENTURE CAPITAL ASSOCIATION

e-mail: info@newenglandvc.org
web: newenglandvc.org

Mission Statement: The New England Venture Capital Association's mission is to promote venture capital investing and strengthen the entrepreneurial community in New England. NEVCA seeks to accelerate the growth of new businesses, help build partnerships between entrepreneurs and investors, and support innovation-friendly public policies.

Geographic Preference: New England
Portfolio Companies: Members: Abingworth, Ascent Venture Partners, Atlas Venture, Battery Ventures, Bessemer Venture Partners, Boston Seed Capital, Breakthrough Energy Ventures, Broadview Ventures, Connecticut Innovations, Converge Venture Partners, CRV, Dell Technologies, Echo Health Ventures, F-Prime Capital, Flare Capital Partners, Flybridge Capital Partners, Founder Collective, G20 Ventures, General Catalyst Partners, Highland Capital Partners, In-Q-Tel, Infinite Road, Innospark Ventures, Innouvo, Johnson & Johnson Innovation, LaunchCapital, LRV Health, LS Polaris Innocation Fund, MassCEC, MassDevelopment, MassVentures, Matrix Partners, MPM Capital, New Enterprise Associates, NextView Ventures, Novartis Venture Fund, Oak HC/FT, Omega Funds One Way Ventures, Optum Ventures, Orion Equity Partners, Point Judith Capital, Polaris Partners, Pulse Ventures, RA Capital, Romulus Capital, Schooner Capital, SR One, SV Health Investors, Tectonic Ventures, The Engine, Third Rock Ventures, Tiger Iron Capital, Underscore, Venrock, Victress Capital, Vida Ventures, Will Ventures, XFactor Ventures, Zaffre Investments

Key Executives:
Jody Rose, President
Background: SVP, Corporate Development & Digital Strategy, Blueprint; Swirl Networks; Rue La La; MTV Networks; The Food Network; HGTV
Directorships: My Sister's Keeper
Ari Fine Glantz, Executive Director
Education: Vassar College

3264 PITTSBURGH VENTURE CAPITAL ASSOCIATION
700 Bursca Dr
Suite 706
Bridgeville, PA 15017

Phone: 412-228-5826 Fax: 412-228-5879
e-mail: information@thepvca.org
web: thepvca.org

Mission Statement: The Pittsburgh Venture Capital Association was formed in 1982 to promote venture capital investment and entrepreneurship in the western Pennsylvania region. The PVCA represents western Pennsylvania's private equity investors and advocates for the venture capital industry through various programs, including networking events and other promotional activities.

Geographic Preference: Western Pennsylvania
Founded: 1982
Portfolio Companies: Sponsors: Activate Venture Partners, Adams Capital Management, Baker Tilly, Birchmere Ventures, BlueTree Allied Angels, BNY Mellon Wealth Management, Buchanan Ingersol & Rooney, Burns Scalo Real Estate, Carnegie Mellon University, Cherin Law Offices, CliftonLarsonAllen, Cohen & Company, Cohen & Grigsby, Dinsmore, Donnelley Financial Solutions, Connelly-Boland and Associates, Draper Triangle, EY, Fox Rothschild, IdeaFoundry, Innovation Works, KPMG, Kuzneski Financial Group, Louis Plung & Company, The Lynch Law Group, Meyer Unkovic & Scott, Morgan Lewis, Pepper Hamilton, Pittsburgh Equity Partners, Pittsburgh Life Sciences Greenhouse, Pittsburgh Technology Council, Quaker Capital Investments, Reed Smith, Right Brain + Left Brain, Rivers Agile, Saul Ewing Arnstein & Lehr, Schnader Attorneys at Law, Sisterson, TJS Insurance Group, Tucker Arsenberg Attorneys, University of Pittsburgh Innovation Institute, UPMC Enterprises, West Allen Capital

Key Executives:
Mike Stubler, Chairman
Education: BBA, University of Notre Dame
Background: Vice President, CFO, International Cybernetics Corp.; CFO, Draper Triangle; Touche Ross & Company
Directorships: New Media, Ayalogic, Unitask, TOA Technologies, Landslide
Kelly Szejko, President
Education: University of Pittsburgh
Background: Founder, Tikes; Association for Corporate Growth (Pittsburgh Chapter)

3265 ROCKY MOUNTAIN VENTURE CAPITAL ASSOCIATION
798 Pope Drive
Erie, CO 80516

e-mail: info@rockymountainvca.com
web: www.rockymountainvca.com

Mission Statement: The Rocky Mountain Venture Capital Association is an association for venture capitalists and entrepreneurs in the Rocky Mountain region of the United States.

Geographic Preference: Rocky Mountain Region
Founded: 1999
Portfolio Companies: Members: 104 West, Access Venture Partners, Aegis Legal Consulting, Bigfoot Captial, Boulder Ventures, Bow River Capital, Break Trail Ventures, Bridge Bank, Bullish, Canal Partners, Carta, Catalyst Law Group, Catapult Growth, CCIG, CIBC, Cobre Capital, Colorado Technology Association, Cooley, Coplex, Cornerstone Fund

Services, Crawley Ventures LLC, Crowe UK LLP, Deloitte & Touche, Delta-V Partners, Epic Ventures, First Hill Partners, Foundry Group, Grayhawk Capital LLC, Greylock Partners, Holland & Hart, HSBC, Invest Southwest, Iron Gate Capital, Jones Lang LaSalle, Kickstart Seed Fund, KPMG, Liberty Global Ventures, Mercato Partners, Moreton and Company, Peak Ventures, Pelion Venture Partners, Perpetual Ventures, Point B Capital LLC, Rockies Venture Fund, RSM US, Signal Peak Ventures, Signature Bank NY, Silicon Valley Bank, SRS Acquiom, Stout Street Capital, Sun Mountain Capital, Tahoma Ventures, Tango/High Country Venture, Techstars Ventures, TenEighty, TMX, Trinity Capital Investment, UAVenture Capital, University of Denver, Upslope Capital Management

Key Executives:
Nanette Schunk, Executive Director
e-mail: nanette@rockymountainvca.com
Education: BA, German, Math, Rutgers University
Background: Principal, Strategic Solutions Marketing and Events; Chapter Manager, Entrepreneurs' Organization

3266 TECH UNITED
111 Town Square Place
Jersey City, NJ 07310

Phone: 732-456-5700
web: techunited.co

Mission Statement: TechUnited represents New Jersey's technology-related businesses. The NJTC supports its member companies by providing access to a variety of resources, including business development, education and networking opportunities. Formerly known as the New Jersey Tech Council.

Geographic Preference: New Jersey
Founded: 1996
Portfolio Companies: Members: DLA Piper, ECI Technology, Edison Partners, Eisner Amper, EPIC Insurance Brokers & Conultants, Ernst & Young, GHO Ventures, Grant Thornton, Kirusa, KPMG, Mercer County Community College, Morgan Lewis, Optima Global Solutions, Phone.com, PNC, Radiant Systems, Rowan University, Rutgers University, SPHERE Technology Solutions, Stevens Institute of Technology, Synchronoss Technologies, The Harris Agency, Tierpoint, Valley National Bank, Verizon, Wayside Technology Group, Yorktel

Key Executives:
Aaron Price, President & CEO
Background: Founder, Propelify; Founder, NJ Tech Meetup

3267 TEXAS VENTURE ASSOCIATION
PO Box 1131
Austin, TX 78767

web: www.texasventureassociation.org

Mission Statement: The Texas Venture Association is a non-profit association that represents venture capital firms in Texas. In addition to protecting venture capital firms from harmful legislation, the TxVA also provides information resources to its members and promotes the venture capital industry in both public and political environments.

Founded: 2004

3268 THE COLLABORATIVE
10 S 5th Street
Suite 415
Minneapolis, MN 55402

Phone: 612-338-3828
e-mail: info@collaborative.net
web: www.collaborative.net

Mission Statement: The Collaborative serves to support Minnesota's community of investors, entrepreneurs and innovators. The Collaborative works with a range of businesses and teams, including startups, CFOs and growth-company CEOs, angels, venture capitalists and veteran investors. The organization's goal is to assist building companies in Minnesota.

Geographic Preference: Minnesota
Founded: 1987
Portfolio Companies: 2020 Marketing, ABILITY Network, ABRA Auto Body, Advanced Circulatory Systems, Affinity Capital Management, American Medical Systems, Baker Tilly, Barnes & Thornburg, BFL Capital, Black Dog Investment, Cairn Ventures, Calabrio, Code 42 Software, Comerica Bank, Cresa, Datuit, DelaGet, Dorsey & Whitney, EarthClean, Electromed, EY, Field Solutions, Galil Medical, General Blood, Grant Thornton, HDH Advisors, HSIO Technologies, Infinite Graphics, Insignia Systems, JAMF Software, Jones Lang LaSalle, Key Investment, Kidblog, Lemhi Ventures, LFE Capital, Lifecore Biomedical, Medafor, MicroNet, MOCON, MRI Robotics, Nanocopoeia, Norwest Equity Partners, Oak Investment Partners, Osprey Medical, Preventice, ProfoundNano, Proto Labs, Qumu, Respicardia, RespirTech, Restaurant Technologies, ReUrban, SALO, Segetis, SetSight, Sport Ngin, SterilMed, Technology Village, TFF, Tornier, Twin Cities Business, UAS Laboratories, Venture Bank, Virteva, Vital Images, Winland Electronics, Wipfli, XRS, Zimmer Spine, Zivix

Key Executives:
Dan Carr, Founder

3269 UPSTATE CAPITAL ASSOCIATION OF NEW YORK
42 N Chestnut Street
Suite 101
New Paltz, NY 12561

Phone: 845-204-8090
e-mail: info@upstatecapital.org
web: www.upstatecapital.org

Mission Statement: Statewide network of investors and advisors helps to build businesses in Upstate New York.

Geographic Preference: Upstate New York
Founded: 2003

Key Executives:
Noa Simons, President & CEO
Education: BA, Politics, Brandeis University
Background: Founding Manager, Hudson Valley Startup Fund; Co-Founder, Community Compost Company; TianDi Growth Capital; Executive Director, Mary Ferrell Foundation

3270 VENTURE CAPITAL ASSOCIATION OF ALBERTA
AB
Canada

e-mail: hello@vacc.ca
web: www.vcaa.ca

Mission Statement: Focuses on the professional development of members of the VC industry in Alberta.

3271 VENTURE CLUB OF INDIANA
5211 Whipple Wood Court
Indianapolis, IN 46226

Phone: 317-926-2622
web: www.ventureclub.org

Mission Statement: The Venture Club of Indiana is a non-profit organization dedicated to assembling entrepreneurs and investors through networking opportunities and ensuring the success of emerging and established companies. The Venture Club provides programs, seminars, luncheons, and other networking and education resources for Indiana's professional community.

Founded: 1984

Venture Capital & Private Equity Firms / National & State Associations

3272 VENTURE CONNECTORS
462 S Fourth Street
Suite 2600
Louisville, KY 40202

e-mail: contact@ventureconnectors.org
web: www.ventureconnectors.org

Mission Statement: The Venture Connectors was established to advance business and commercial investment activities in the Kentuckiana area. The organization participates in monthly luncheon meetings and other entrepreneurial events with the goal of uniting entrepreneurs and investors.

Geographic Preference: Kentucky and Indiana
Founded: 1995

3273 WESTERN ASSOCIATION OF VENTURE CAPITALISTS

e-mail: membership@wavc.org
web: www.wavc.org

Mission Statement: The Western Association of Venture Capitalists is a non-profit venture capital organization dedicated to bringing venture capitalists together to socialize and network.

Geographic Preference: West Coast
Founded: 1969
Portfolio Companies: Members: Abingworth, Acacia Venture Partners, Accel Partners, Acuity Ventures, Alloy Ventures, Almaz Capital Partners, Altos Ventures, Asset Management Company, August Capital, Battery Ventures, Bay Partners, Benchmark Capital, BlueRun Ventures, Canaan Partners, Charter Life Sciences, Claremont Creek Ventures, Comerica, Costella Kirsch, DeNovo Ventures, Doll Capital Management, Draper Fisher Jurvetson, Draper Richards, El Dorado Ventures, Financial Technology Ventures, Focus Ventures, Foundation Capital, Fremont Ventures, Gabriel Venture Partners, Globespan Capital Partners, Glynn Capital Management, Highland Capital Partners, Horizon Partners, Hummer Winblad Venture Partners, Icon Ventures, IDG Ventures SF, Inman Investment Management, Institutional Venture Partners, InterWest Partners, Javelin Venture Partners, Khosla Ventures LLC, Kleiner Perkins Caufield Byers, Labrador Ventures, Lauder Partners, Legacy Venture, Levensohn Venture Partners, Lexington Partners, Lighthouse Capital Partners, Lightspeed Venture Partners, Longitude Capital, Matrix Partners, Mayfield Fund, MedVenture Associates, Menlo Ventures, Mission Ventures, Mohr Davidow Ventures, Montreaux Equity Partners, Morgenthaler Ventures, New Enterprise Associates, Norwest Venture Partners, Onset Ventures, Osprey Ventures, Partech International, Peninsula Ventures, Pinnacle Ventures, Pitango Venture Capital, Redpoint Ventures, Rembrandt Venture Partners, RockPort Capital Partners, SBV Venture Partners, Scale Venture

Key Executives:
  Ira Ehrenpreis, Co-President
  e-mail: ira@dblpartners.vc
  Education: BA, University of California, Los Angeles; JD, Stanford Law School; MBA, Stanford Graduate School of Business
  Background: Founder & Managing Partner, DBL Partners; Technology Partners
  Philip Sanderson, Managing Director
  Education: BA, Economics, Hamilton College; MBA, Harvard Business School
  Background: Managing Director, IDG Ventures; Chairman, VCNetwork; General Partner, WaldenVC; Associate, Robertson Stephens; Financial Analyst, Goldman Sachs

3274 WOMEN'S ASSOCIATION OF VENTURE & EQUITY INC.
10 Winton Farm Road
Newtown, CT 06470

Phone: 203-763-9255
Toll-Free: 855-928-3606
e-mail: wavecoordinator@gmail.com
web: women-wave.org

Mission Statement: Women's Association of Venture and Equity is a non-profit association that represents professional women in the venture capital and private equity industries. The organization offers a network of industry contacts with the goal of creating opportunities for its members.

Founded: 2003
Portfolio Companies: Sponsors: ACG New York, Association of Asiona American Investment Managers, CAIA Association, Kayo Conference Series, Mergers & Acquisitions
Key Executives:
  Julie Gionfriddo, President

A.B. Freeman School of Business
Daniel Finkelstein, 850

Aalborg University
Bo Ilsoe, 1331

Academy of Economic Studies
Raluca Florea, 335

Acadia University
Tyson Birchall, 2171

Adelphi University
John S Schnabel, 1377

Adrian College
Roger Goddu, 337

Aga Khan University
Zia Agha, 1974

Albert Einstein College
Carl Goldfischer, MD, 240
Doug Kelly MD, 87

Albion College
Eric V Bacon, 1136
William Y Campbell, 1429
Nicholas S. Christopher, 1097
Evonna Karchon, 985
Peter W Klein, 351
Edward S. Pentecost, 1460

Alfred University
Marlin Miller, 1347

Allegheny College
Michael S Bruno Jr, 1747
Sean Ward, 293

Ambassador College
W. Jack Kessler Jr., 496

American Graduate School of Mgmt
Lou Gerken, 826
Richard Harding, 1015
JJ Healy, 853
Robert Okun MIM, 1775
Phil Samper, 808
Arnold B Siemer, 607
Robert L. Zorich, 673

American International College
Joelle Marquis, 172

American University
Stephen S Beitler, 636
Joy E. Binford, 1348
John Brecker, 99
Amy Burr, 1039
Matt Cheney, 500
James Conlon, 361
Celia Daly, 395
Troy Dayton, 1810
Vin Fabiani, 941
Robert J Flanagan, 510
John K Giannuzzi, 1668
David Gladstone, 832
Michael P Hompesch, 633
Richard E Maybaum, 1138
Michelle McCarthy, 1928
Ian J Mount, 1277
Robert Raynard, 1953
Bob Shaw, 194
Robert Shaw, Jr., 161

American University of Beirut
Raymond Debbane, 1022

Amherst College
Michael Barach, 994
Samuel Bartlett, 458
Brian J Conway, 1778
Alex De Winter, 812
David Douglass, 605
Paul Ferris, 218
David A Fiorentino, 1053
Michael T. Fitzgerald, 523
John W. Flanigan, 463
Standish Fleming, 772
William E. Ford, 819
Paul Goodrich, 1162
Douglas C Grissom, 1160
H. Irving Grousbeck, 952
Gregory Grunberg, 1147
Paulus J Ingram, 2239
Jeff Jordan, 125
Robert Keith, 1830
Rich Lawson, 962
Steven A Leese, 1505
Glen Lewy, 957
Brent Nicklas, 1116
James Patchett, 1307
Chris Pike, 61
Jon D. Ralph, 786
Mark Rosen, 458
Lisa Schule, 838
Tim Shannon, 389
Rob Sherman, 315
George W. Siguler, 1681
John I Snow III, 1505
Andrew Snyder, 851
Jason Sowers, 2000
Christopher Spofford, 346
Peter Taft, 1266
Devin Talbott, 681
Richard Upton, 910
Barry Volpert, 560
Tyler Wick, 20
Nicolas D. Zerbib, 1746

Amherst University
Benjamin Santonelli, 598

Amos Tuck School of Business
Allan Chou, 1341

Amsterdam School of Economics
Deborah de Rooij, 2239

Anderson School of Management
Michael Banks, 875
Frank Brenninkmeyer, 1434
Mike Carlotti, 206
Adam Chesnoff, 1602
Grace Chui-Miller, 545
Richard R Crowell, 1906
Greg Ennis, 1430
Alan Foster, 1795
David C. Franklin, 954
Tammy Funasaki, 334
Randy Glein, 610
Philip Han, 1602
Derek Idemoto, 485
Don Jamieson, 377
Buck Jordan, 400
Brian Knitt, 469
Michael A. LaSalle, 1663
Arthur Levine, 1115
James McDermott, 1897
Dana Moraly, 504
Michael Morgan, 376
Brian R. Nelson, 874
Robin Nourmand, 228
Daniel E Pansing, 1210
Paula Robins, 127
Charles W. Roellig, 451
Mark Rosenbaum, 202
Stephen D. Royer, 1663
Chris Shipman, 429
Rick Shuart, 377
Ryan A Smiley, 1570
Shahan D Soghikian, 1411
Sharon Stevenson DVM, PhD, 1371
Anil Tammineedi, 127
Cleve Tzung, 206
Vishal Vasishth, 1363
Eric D Wedbush, 1970
William J. Wynperle, 1663

Andhra University
Pabhakar Reddy, 1284

Aquinas College
John M. Goense, 842

Arizona State University
Michael J Ahearn, 1861
Larry L. Aschebrook, 805
Jon W Bayless, 1661
David Baylor, 1912
Brian N Burns, 861
Daley Ervin, 678
Bart Faber, 194
Natalie Fleming Arora, 1760
Al Foreman, 1866
Gregory J Forrest, 767
Bill Harding, 1908
Paul D Kestler, 607
Steve Kirby, 300
Shannon Masjedi, 1400
Raj Pai, 838
Joseph Piper JD, 1007
Greg Robinson, 9
Scot E Swenberg, 480

Art Center College of Design
Adam Bruss, 267

Ashland University
Michael Butler, 1285
Kristy Campbell, 1556
Richard M. Ferrari, 599
Vince Owens, 891

Assumption College
Chris F. Corey, 1278
John Lawrence, 1150

Aston Business School
Ha Nguyen, 2183

Auburn University
Kevin D Cantrell, 1579
Billy L. Harbert, 285
Raymond J. Harbert, 907
Jerry Knotts, 3248
Jim Little, 1292
Charles R Martin, 112
Charles D. Miller, 907
Ron Sansom, 1576

Augsburg College
Kinney Johnson, 1656

Augustana College
Jennifer Choi, 3256
Blaine Crissman, 1481
Rafael Romero, 668

Australian National University
Nathan Campbell, 873
Richard Cawsey, 606
Jeremy Liew, 1125

College/University Index / Babson College

Babson College
Brady Bohrmann, 209
Braden M (Brady) Bohrmann, 1178
Glen R Bressner, 51, 1386
John Burns, 332, 1165
Yumin Choi, 224
Kevin Colleran, 1696
Dan Corcoran, 1176
Bob Davis, 938
Christopher W. Dick, 180
Michael J Dolce, 1160
Suzanne L Dwyer, 1176
Cory Eaves, 819
Brett Gordon, 912
Mark Jrolf, 929
Andrew H Kalnow, 90
Caitlyn MacDonald, 1108
Robert J. Maccini, 126
William F McKinley, 1429
James F Milbery, 470
Mike O'Malley, 993
Amanda Outerbridge, 912
Stacie Rader, 748
David B Ragins, 494
Roger Roche, 1025
Sam Thompson, 1488
Randall Ussery, 1985
Martha DiMatteo Vorlicek, 912
Scott Voss, 912
Karan Wadhera, 420
Paul Weinstein, 218
John D. White, 777
John Whorf, 1293
Herbert P. Wilkins, Jr., 1773
Caleb Winder, 704

Baldwin Wallace College
Will Lynn, 886
David Moll, 992
Jeff Morton, 47
Karen Tuleta, 1266

Ball State University
James L Smeltzer, 412

Bandung Institute of Technology
Helman Sitohang, 555

Bangalore University
Mark Fernandes, 1672

Bar Iian University
Iian Bunimovitz, 43

Barnard College
Laura Belle Sachar, 1741
Beth Seidenberg, 1079

Barry University
Ali Safiedine DPM, 1288

Baruch College
Walter Barandiaran, 162
Mark Berman, 1364
Iian Bunimovitz, 43
Steven Chrust, 450
Daniel Colon, Jr., 509
Matthew Croft, 1134
Warren H. Haber, 777
Robert E Kelly, 1741
Jay F Laudauer, 1883
Kathleen Thomas, 1037

Bates College
J Michael Chu, 1092
Patrick J Donnellan, 692
Gregory A. Ehret, 1448

Lori Lombardo, 684
Jennifer VanBelle, 811

Baylor College of Medicine
Billy Cohn, MD, 1622
Stephanie Kreml MD, 244
Philip Sanger MD, 1803

Baylor Law School
Kevin Green, 546

Baylor University
James G Benedict, 1075
Joe Cunningham MD, 1622
Jerry DeVries, 1803
Brenda D Gavin, 1510

Beedie School of Business
Leah Nguyen, 2144

Beijing Center for Chinese Studies
Jeff Schlapinski, 3252

Beijing Normal University
Ru-Guang Bal, 908

Beijing University
Ting Gootee, 659

Beirut University
Firas El Amine, 1021

Belmont University
Theresa Sexton, 495

Beloit College
Justin Benshoof, 376
Arthur Schneiderman, 837

Bemidji State University
Dan Hodgson, 1135

Ben Gurion University
Dror Berman, 1001
Gideon Soesman, 2136

Benares Hindu University
Vish Mishra, 504

Benedictine University
Richard P Earley, 636

Benjamin N. Cordozo School of Law
Alison Berman, 1402

Bentley College
Jason Caplain, 1712
Paul Flanagan, 1675
Kevin Gillis, 1814
Craig Gilmore, 417
Paul Homer, 1344
Edward J Keefe, 1157
Edward A Lafferty, 1626
Kelly Meldrum, CFA, 56
Marcus Ogawa, 1515
Bruce Tiedemann, 315
Richard Zannino, 435

Berea College
Mark Bolinger, 1068

Berkeley School of Law
David Baylor, 1912

Berkeley School of Public Health
Joel Finlayson, 2141

Berklee College of Music
Michael Godwin, 1550

Bernard Baruch College
Marta De La Cruz, 838

Berry College
Karen Houghton, 191

Bethany College
Dave Carlson, 686

Bethel College
Tim DeVries, 1345

Bilkent University
Murat Aktihanoglu, 685

Binghamtom University
Steven G Glenn, 1957

Binghamton University
Alberto Bianchinotti, 1217
Rich Levandov, 209
Richard W Levandov, 1178
David Rubin, 1206
Sean C. White, 1727

Birla Institute of Technology
Ajay Chopra, 1855
Vijay C Parikh, 837

Birmingham Southern College
Donald C. Harrison, 460

Bishop's University
Sasha Jacob, 2069
Sam Saintonge, 2282
Eric Schmadtke, 677

Bloomsburg University
Kimberly Kyle, 21
Vincent P. Menichelli, 52
Jordan Ormont, 1203

Boalt Hall School of Law
Anthony Patek, 256

Bob Jones University
Meredith Pflug, 216

Bocconi University
Luca Bassi, 223
Emilio S Pedroni, 734

Bogazici University
Santo Politi, 1718

Bombay University
Sandeep D Alva, 1377
Atul Kamra, 1690
Darshana Zaveri, 428

Booth School of Business
Sean Barrette, 470
Gale Bowman, 1023
Scott Brown, 654
Lauren K Bugay, 634
Brian F. Chambers, 1410
Ashish Chandarana, 1927
Joanne Chen, 773
Nicholas S. Christopher, 1097
Adam Cranford, 1292
Krisin Custar, 1049
Kaitlyn Doyle, 1023
Sean Doyle, 1613
Paul W. Drury, 1115
Mark Emery, 1049

College/University Index / Bowdoin College

Ryan Gembala, 1423
Nathan J Good, 1473
Michael Goy, 1267
John Grafer, 1625
Thomas R. Groh, 104
Anna Haghgooie, 1618
Matthew Hankins, 931
Jason Heltzer, 1385
Brent Hill, 1385
Charlie Hipwood, 1175
Timothy Huang, 1116
Andy Jones, 1172
Steve Klammer, 1369
Scott McConnell, 88
Sean M McNally, 1473
Drew Molinari, 578
Paul Purcell, 225
Pabhakar Reddy, 1284
Frank Reppenhagen, 531
Joseph R Rondinelli, 792
Douglas J. Rosenstein, 878
Ian Ross, 531
Konrad Salaber, 1990
Jay W Schemelter, 1578
Jason Sowers, 2000
Edwin Tan, 404
Guy Turner, 965
Kyle Veatch, 929
Ira Weiss, 965

Boston College
Rich Aldrich, 1149
David L. Anderson, 1759
Darrell W Austin, 204
Tate Bevis, 1044
Anik Bose, 252
Aaron Bright, 1435
John Burns, 332
Steve Burns, 1507
John Burton, 1888
James D. Carey, 1746
Mike Carlotti, 206
Matthew T. Carroll, 1979
Amit Chandra, 223
Andrew Chang, 1119
William C Connell, 934
Dan Corcoran, 1176
Chris J. Crosby, 1278
Paul D'Addario, 1403
Mark DeBlois, 362
Mark DeNino, 1830
Joe Del Guercio, 510
Kenneth M. Doyle, 899
Jere Doyle, 1675
Scott Feldmen, 1761
David Fialkow, 820
Andy Flaster, 1944
Christopher S. Gaffney, 862
Wayne P. Garrett, 65
Bill Geary, 749
Anthony Giannobile, 362
Brian Gorczynski, 1927
Mark Gordon, 2200
Marshall Griffin, 530
Brendyn T Grimaldi, 902
Marty Hernon, 315
Tim Heston, 258
Erika Highland, 832
Jason Hill, 1197
Charlie Hipwood, 1175
Mary T Hornby, 17
Lincoln Isetta, 1255
Raymond J Jeandron III, 1148
Thomas H Jennings, 1754
Matthew E Keis, 815
Charlie Kim, 1189
Paul LaViolette, 1631

Paul LaViolette, 1764
John Malloy, 299
TJ Maloney, 1131
Jack Manning, 312
Michael Marino, 203
Louis Marino, 822
Matthew McCooe, 532
John F McCormack, 1654
Ryan Milligan, 470
Eric C. Morgan, 1460
Albert A. Notini, 1300
Daniel Nova, 938
Tim O'Loughlin, 646
Frank J Pados Jr, 633
Mike Pellini, 1646
Joseph Pesce, 864
Barbara Piette, 1081
Brian Pryor, 1197
Jill C. Raker, 867
Jonathan M Rather, 1973
Michael Rawlings, 479
Kevin M. Rendino, 5
Andrew Riley, 1910
Bijan Sabet, 1718
Corey Schmid, 1659
Mary Shannon, 587
Mary M Shannon, 1178
Keith C Shaughnessy, 1225
Kyparissia Sirinakis, CPA, 690
Theodore J. Smith, 638
Jeb S Spencer, 1871
Geoffrey D. Spillane, 878
Brian Stansky, 1008
Kevin Starr, 1814
Greg Stupore, 13
Mark A. Tarini, 157
Lee J Tesconi, 1116
Mike Wong, 941
Steve Wood, 839
Caroline Yeager, 1023

Boston College Law School
James D. Carey, 1746
Joel Cutler, 820
Mary T Hornby, 17
Brian J. Knez, 424
James D. Leroux, 181
Christopher Mirabile, 1104
John P Shoemaker, 1234
Daniel Weintraub, 197

Boston College School of Management
Richard Joseph, 197

Boston University
Bruce Adams, 983
Matthew Ahern, 1081
Mitch Baruchowitz, 1208
Eric Berke, 2264
Bryan Biniak, 1497
Kevin Blank, 886
Chris Bodnar, 646
Mike Bologna, 865
Glen R Bressner, 51, 1386
Thomas E. Brew Jr., 65
Richard Burnes, 457
Keith Carlton, 891
Brian Cohen, 1305, 1309
Ira D Cohen, 1888
Evan Corley, 1413
Todd Dagres, 1718
Rick Defieux, 1691
Trung Q. Do, 1421
Gregory A. Ehret, 1448
Jamie E Elias, 1859
Dave Fachetti, 839

Sidney J Feltenstein, 1654
Adam E Fine, 1993
Hadley Ford, 970
Constance Freedman, 1246
A Leigh Fulmer, 647
Jonathan Glass, 1235
Brett Gordon, 912
Jeff Grammer, 2231
Shai Greenwald, 383
Mark G. Hilderbrand, 952
Eugene Hill, 1631
George R. Hutchinson, 1036
Masa Isono, 603
Angela Jackson, 1467
Linda Jacobson, 31
Jeffrey R. Jay, MD, 864
Debbie Johnson, 20
Thomas W Jones, 1875
James Jordon, 1452
Brandon M. Katz, 494
Ryan Keating, 1430
Ugur Kilic, 2069
John E Knutsen, 1160
Scott Kokones, 891
Peter Lamm, 722
Charles R Lax, 853
Renske Lynde, 7
Michael J Lyons, 1131
Robert MacInnis, 20
Ian B. MacTaggart, 360
Rebecca Norlander, 980
Albert A. Notini, 1300
Geoffrey S. Oblak, 180
Anne-Mari Paster, 1373
Gordon R Penman, 1922
Robert Raynard, 1953
Shari Redstone, 59
Manu Rekhi, 1017
Vin Ryan, 1630
Aydin Senkut, 720
Arjun Sethi, 1850
Chris Shipman, 429
Zubeen Shroff, 809
Joshua B. Siegel, 1599
R Adam Smith, 483
Gideon Soesman, 2136
Lou Volpe, 1084
Marc J Walfish, 1210
Paul Walsh, 371
Todd Warden, 910
James Westra, 61
Mike Wong, 941
Ron Wooten, 1349
Darshana Zaveri, 428
Jeffrey M. Zucker, 865

Boston University School of Law
Michael L. Gordon, 128
Randal A. Nardone, 769
Jonathan D. Salon, 245
Richard Taney, 1866

Bowdoin College
Tom Costin, 1393
Brendan Dickinson, 389
Patrick D. Dunn, 1498
Mike Farrell, 1720
Harry A George, 1704
Ryan Giles, 2267
Thomas Groves, 63
Peter Grua, 941
Jason P Hafler, 1621
Paul A Howard, 1198
Julie Jubeir, 409
Michael P McQueeney, 1753
Tom Needham, 1777
Henry W Newman, 1704

College/University Index / Bowling Green State University

Jake Odden, 19
Jared B Paquette, 362
Jeff Patterson, 518
Scott B. Perper, 1410
Peter R. Seaver, 140
Sheldon Stone, 1362
Joshua R. Weiner, 741
Tim Wilson, 176

Bowling Green State University
William Y Campbell, 1429
Kenneth Petrilla, 475
Maribeth Rahe, 768
Brad Seaman, 2206
Tom Shehab, 150

Bradeis School of Law
Tianpeng Wang, 2187

Bradford University
Steven Tang, 627
Timothy Watkins, 1904

Bradley University
Brent Hill, 1385
Nancy O'Leary, 1042
Robert Riemer, 177

Brandeis University
Nick Adams, 615
Mitch Baruchowitz, 1208
Stephen Berger, 1368
Kevin Gillis, 1814
Jonathan Ginns, 45
Matt Gorin, 535
Brian Hirsch, 1851
Beto Pallares, 169
Jeffry S. Pfeffer, 410
Bruce Pollack, 449
Noa Simons, 3269
Eric D. Starr, 410
Scott Tobin, 238

Bridgewater State College
Suzanne L Dwyer, 1176

Brigham Young University
Peter Bodine, 84
G Stephen Browning, 1655
Fraser Bullock, 1707
Gavin Christensen, 1074
John Clark, 1434
Gary Crittenden, 962
Matt Downs, 1618
Nick Efstratis, 689
Paul K. Erickson, 464
John Fife, 472
Stewart Gollmer, 1798
Sid Krommenhoek, 79
Tim Layton, 1707
Rand Lewis, 443
Legrand Lewis, 1707
Ryan Lucero, 785
Mark Ludwig, 1707
Robert Lund, 1004
John Mayfield, 79
Ron Mika, 1707
Allen Miner, 1757
Blake Modersitzki, 1428
Diogo Myrrha, 79
Chad Packard, 1428
Shane R. Peery, 464
Scott Petty, 1679
Robert Pothier, 1545
Andrew Ray, 2148
Trevor C Rich, 1151
Bryce Roberts, 1359
Colin Robinson, 472

Ryan Sanders, 1205
Sean Schickedanz, 499
Brian S Smith, 861
Scott L. Snow, 747
Luke Sorenson, 1707
Spencer Tall, 84
Tyler Thompson, 1645
Brandon Tidwell, 1679
Kenton S. Van Harten, 905
Kirk Whickman, 128
Brandon C. White, 458
Steve Young, 962
Dal Zemp, 1545

Brighton Polytechnic University
Stephen K Smith, 1178

Bringham Young University
Jeff Kearl, 1428
Ben Lambert, 1428

Bristol Polytechnic
Peter Van Cuylenburg, 556

Bristol University
Mark Emery, 1049
Stuart Gent, 223
Tom Hulme, 894
Duncan Priston, 242

Brooklyn College
Harry Edelson, 651
Irwin Federman, 1898

Brooklyn College Law School
Mark Berman, 1364
Steven E Berman, 1402
Jack Feiler, 1402
Steven M. Friedman, 687
Howard Goldstein, 1913

Brooklyn Law School
Andrew Sturner, 558

Brooklyn Polytechnic Institute
Stephen Einhorn, 403

Brown University
William F Aikman, 887
Norman W. Alpert, 1933
C Mark Arnold, 1532
Zaid Ashai, 1463
Mark Attanasio, 557
Marc C Bergschneider, 1738
Alison Berman, 1402
Elizabeth Q Betten, 1160
William Bianco, 1620
Eric D Bommer, 1654
Orlando Bravo, 1817
Robert M Brill, 1313
Jeff Brodlieb, 450
Bernie Buonanno, 1278
James J. Burke Jr., 1027
C.A. Burkhardt, 956
Phil Calian, 1965
Rich Caputo, 1049
Ashish Chandarana, 1927
David Chao, 597
Robert A. Comey, 1020
Glenn M. Creamer, 1498
Duncan Davidson, 361
Owen Davis, 1358
Michael Dearing, 914
Lister Delgado, 975
Jonathan E Dick, 1480
Brendan Dickinson, 389
Hythem T El-Nazer, 1778
Karim Faris, 894

Timothy J Flynn, 1113
Scott Friend, 224
Matt Garfunkle, 1413
Chris Girgenti, 1483
David Goldburg, 1208
Ross Goldstein, 609
Bob Goodman, 263
Habib Y Gorgi, 1278
Theresia Gouw, 182
Anthony P. Green, PhD, 249
Oliver Haarmaan, 2243
Geoff Harris, 757
Randy Haykin, 1390
Ned Hazen, 1122
Blair Hendrix, 223
Troy Henikoff, 1181
Eric Hjerpe, 1069
Spencer P Hoffman, 1151
Ben Holbrook, 1174
James Joaquin, 1363
G. Kent Kahle, 893
Steven E Karlson, 1994
Peter Keehn, 88
James T. Kiernan, 2080
Richard C Klaffky, 740
Lauren Kolodny, 182
James Kondo, 824
Nathaniel V Lentz, 1388
Felix Lo, 843
Hambleton Lord, 1104
Fern Mandelbaum, 1249, 1941
Saif Mansour, 334
Paul Margolis, 1150
Christopher Masto, 790
Samuel M Mencoff, 1160
Anthony Moretti, 355
Kevin A. Mundt, 1933
Brian R. Nelson, 874
Jonathan M. Nelson, 1498
Carl Nichols, 1390
Daniel S. O'Connell, 1933
Kenneth O'Keefe, 1933
Christian L. Oberbeck, 1624
Michael B Persky, 80
Robert Petty, 506
Geoffrey S. Raker, 1779
Patrick Rea, 395
Andy Sack, 776
Andrew Schiff, MD, 73
Mark Selcow, 548
Eric H. Sillman, 137
Brad Silverberg, 978
Lawrence B. Sorrel, 1779
Barry S. Sternlicht, 1742
Dickson Suit, 1025
Craig C. Taylor, 87
John Toomay, 1409
J Russell Triedman, 1133
James E Vandervelden, 1826
Timothy Wang, 1978
Donna Williamson, 454
Stoddard M Wilson, 1583
Tyler Wolfram, 1360
Naeem Zafar, 95
Alex Zisson, 1820
Alex von der Goltz, 313

Bryant College
Scott Voss, 912

Bryant University
Jim Barra, 1025
Matthew J Hurley, 1377
Daniel M Kortick, 1984
Christopher Quinn, CPA, 884
Jennifer Trzepacz, 1985
Walter Wiacek, 722

Bryn Mawr College
Karen Kerr, 812

Bucknell University
Mark Allsteadt, 404
Nathaniel P Bacon, 362
Michael Brooks, 1507
Frank Brown, 819
Richard E Caruso PhD, 1496
James Conlon, 361
Michael J. Dominguez, 1498
Richard B Emmitt, 1931
Daniel M Gill, 1686
Lisa Hagerman, 596
Lee C Hansen, 1214
Doug Hitchner, 1368
James Howland, 1256
Karen Kassouf, 439
Matt Kraus, 441
Mark Langer, 404
Robert Le Blanc, 2201
Jessica Livingston, 2011
James McLaughlin, 1131
Scott A Perricelli, 1140
F. Matthew Petronzio, 1873
Dennis G Prado, 1163
Brian Regan, 1720
John Reynolds, 1129
James LD Roser, 1590
Gerald Saltarelli, 654
John Sinnerberg, 578
Robert M. Williams Jr., 1041
Ryan Ziegler, 655

Butler University
Jorge Jaramillo, 1387
Sean McGould, 1123
Joseph P Schaffer, 1252

CalTech
Karen Gilmore, 489

Caleton University
Bernie Zeisig, 2187

California Institute of Technology
Dr Philippe H Adam, 188
Scott Chou, 808
Gil Elbaz, 1800
Ilya Fushman, 1079
Venky Ganesan, 1203
Bill Gross, 976
Dylan Hixon, 830
Wen Hsieh, 1079
Michael Hunkapiller, 87
Robert M Jaffe, 1708
JJ Kang, PhD, 519
Regis B Kelly PhD, 1238
Walter Kortschak, 1677
Dr. David Lee, 496
Janis Naeve, PhD, 113
Leo Polovets, 1760
Mike Ross, 1764
Michael Ross PhD, 1631
Micah Siegel, 2270

California Polytechnic State Univ.
Craig Chrisney, 976
Daniel L. Delaney, 989
Mark Lydon, 1009
Matthew McDonald, 230
Matthew T. Potter, 605
Carol Wong, 596

California State University
Bary Bailey, 559
Gil Beyda, 818
Eva Bjorseth, 1365
Bruce Cleveland, 1985
Gary Cuccio, 1795
John Earhart, 838
Doug Fahoury, 1024
Edward Hamati, 270
Kirby Harris, 232
R. Bryan Jadot, 928
Jim Johnson, 1917
Craig A.T. Jones, 1826
Leo Kim PhD, 217
Nellie Levchin, 1634
Claudia L. Llanos, 133
Jeff Low, 645
Sonja Markova, MBA, 229
William Miller, 127
Michelle Moreno, 630
Lori L. Murphree, 1369
Javier Noris, 1633
Lisa Riedmiller, 152, 1408
Rami Rostami, 1878
Mary Ann Sigler, 1455
Gordon Smythe, 2187
Kevin T. Walsh, 949

California State University, Chico
Nick Sturiale, 1661

California State University, LA
Ana Quintana, 278

California Western School of Law
Bruce Taub, 192

Caltech
Michael Ehlers, 144

Calvin College
Mike DeVries, 652

Cambridge University
Michael Chae, 280
Ashish Chandarana, 1927
Joel Finlayson, 2141
Wei Liu, 222
Amy Salzhauer McMarlin, 849

Campbell University
Michael S. Marr, 408

Canisius College
Brian D'Amico, 1753
Lindsay Karas, 1285

Cardozo School of Law
Sonia Gardner, 211
Jeffrey Schultz, 1282

Caregie Mellon University
Sreekar Gadde, 296

Carleton College
Brian Birk, 1756
Stephen Davis, 230
Craig Hanson, 1319
Laurence Lederer, 330
Matthew Strongin, 739
Alexander D Whittemore, 1754
Charles Yim, 641

Carleton University
Sean Brownlee, 2231
Patrick Edeburn, 855
Kim Furlong, 3249
Ryan Haughn, 2237
Deepak Kamra, 389
Richard R Kracum, 1990
Rob MacLellan, 2196
Pablo Srugo, 2187
Paul Weiss, 1923

Carlson School of Business
Darren Brathol, 1722

Carlson School of Management
Kathleen A Tune, 1820

Carnegie Mellon University
Joel P. Adams, 55
Robert C. Ammerman, 405
Roger D Bailey, 607
Jacques Benkowski PhD, 1898
Jonathan Berkowitz, 1813
Jeff Branman, 940
Philip L. Bronner, 1348
Paul Burke, 1813
Jason Cahill, 411
Babs Carryer, 1102
Tony M Chou, 1931
Patrick J Donnellan, 692
Edward R Engler, 1451
Geoff Entress, 1501
Michael Farah, 1132
Kim P. Goh, 957
Gregory T Hebrank MD, 1102
Peter Herz, 7
Larry Kaplan, 245
Jay Katarincic, 629
Vinod Khosla, 1073
Manu Kumar, 1054
Eric Kwan, 1142
Rich Lunak, 1003
J. Kenneth Moritz, 1749
Vince Owens, 891
Cindy Padnos, 980
Justin B. Petro, 1813
Randall E. Poliner, 132
Dava Ritchea, 1638
Maryanna Saenko, 803
Tom Shehab, 150
Avie Tevanian, 660
Stanley W Tucker, 1209
Dan Watkins, 1207
Robert B. Wetzel, 199
Young Yeo, 1866

Carroll School of Management
J.P. Sanday, 1203
Steve Wood, 839

Carroll University
Daniel J. Greifenkamp, 243

Carson Newman College
Dell Larcen, 886

Case Western Reserve University
Vijay Aggarwal, PhD, 1811
Cindy Babbit, 578
Mike Biddle, 2105
Asheem Chandna, 877
Tony M Chou, 1931
Jason R. Cornacchione, 1460
Leonard M Cosentino, 1286
Michael D'Agostino, 1435
Suzette Dutch, 1849
David Fries, 1908
Timothy Gosline, 1576
Brian Hersman, 1045
David Jargiello, 758
David Kabakoff, 924, 1700
Frank Linsalata, 1136
Will Lynn, 886
Joe Mandato, 599
Bassem A Mansour, 1548
John McIlwraith, 86

College/University Index / Catholic University of America

Ryan Meany, 653
Shailesh Mehta, 856
Ki Mixon, 1548
Jon Pastor, 301
Edward S. Pentecost, 1460
Arvind Purushotham, 488
Steven H Rosen, 1548
David Ryan, 1239
Richard Schwarz, 653
Rachid Sefrioui, 730
Karen Spilizewski, 1578
Robert Strother, 1286
Geoffrey B Thrope, 1286

Catholic University of America
Jorge Aguilo, 524
Manuel Jose Balbontin, 524
William Robbins, 1399
Thomas A Scully, 1973
Jim Walker, 56

Catholic University of Eichstaett
Martin Beck, 225

Cedarville University
Mark Horne, 1459

Central Connecticut State
Kristen Kosofsky, 928

Central Connecticut State Univ.
Alexander R Castaldi, 1043

Central Michigan University
Matthew Blevins, 505
Steven E Hall, 1128
Kevin Hofmann, 1580
Doug Neal, 657

Central Washington University
Steve Bailey, 785
Denny Weston, 755

Chapman University
Doug Francis, 665
Steve Nelson, 475

Chiao-Tung University
C.K. Cheng, 908

Chicago-Kent College of Law
Mary Capasso, 1471
Maurice Doyle, 60
Daniel Norr, 206

China Europe Int. Business School
Dennis Wu, 293

Christian Brothers University
Ryan Schuler, 178
Russ Williams, 15

Chuo University
Michio Fujimura, 185

City College of New York
Steven Kotler, 831

City University London
James D.C. Pitt, 1116
Tim Wright, 853

City University of New York
Ira D Cohen, 1888
Peter Kalkanis, 2231
Ralph Montana, 1961
I. Donald Rosuck, 1097
Anthony J Veith, 505

Jeanette M Welsh JD, 1794

City of London College
Neil J. Taylor, 324

Claremont Graduate University
José Blanco, 574
P Frank Limbaugh, 761

Claremont McKenna College
Michael Arrington, 565
Kevin Baker, 371
Sean Dempsey, 1219
Patrick Gallagher, 565
Russell J. Greenberg, 104
E David Hetz, 573
Jeffrey Johnson, 279
Jeffrey W. Johnson, 831
Randy Moser, 203
Scott I. Oakford, 903
George Roberts, 1086

Claremont Men's College
Michael Martin, 1957

Clark Atlanta University
H Bryan Britt, 1532

Clark University
Larry Bohn, 820
Dan Devorsetz, 949
Sonia Gardner, 211
Howard Goldstein, 1913
Bob Hurst, 560
Marc Lasry, 211
John Morris, 912
T Nathanael Shepherd, 1864
Steven Swain, 442

Clarkson University
Thomas J. Buono, 266

Clemson University
Matt Dunbar, 1925
Pat Duncan, 216
Thomas L Greer, 797
Stuart McWhorter, 497
Emily Schillinger, 3245
Lane W Wiggers, 165

Cleveland Marshall College of Law
Peter W Klein, 351
Arnold B Siemer, 607

Cleveland State University
Mark Sims, 2233

Colby College
Charles Beeler, 1525
Joel Cutler, 820
Michael D'Agostino, 1435
Michael L. Gordon, 128
Todd W. Halloran, 786
Matthew G Hamilton, 1754
Michael Henderson-Cohen, 850
Matt Lapides, 20
Alex Levental, 1025
Mike O'Malley, 993
Steve Rappaport, 1376
Glenn Rieger, 1316
Ned Scheetz, 139
Kevin Starr, 1814
Cal Wheaton, 21
Caleb Winder, 704

Colby-Sawyer College
Charlotte D. MacDonald, 952

Colgate University
Christopher J. Ackerman, 751
Will Adams, 92
Brion B Applegate, 1720
Matt Auster, 1600
John C. Bombara, 949
Lee E Bouyea, 789
Scott Brown, 654
Bob Chatham, 1695
Jean-Pierre L. Conte, 823
Brian Dovey, 622
James L. Elrod Jr., 1933
David Fialkow, 820
Charles Fleischmann, 1853
Andrew S. Gelfand, 358
Gary L Goldberg, 1627
Jonathan Grad, 902
Christopher Hooper, 1973
David W Jahns, 809
Christian B. Johnson, 786
William Johnston, 912
Elliott Jones, 170
Jamie Lane, 1869
David Lincoln, 658
Christopher W. Lynch, 180
Dave Marple, 1909
John Mazzarino, 465
Edward McNulty, 574
Christopher Mirabile, 1104
Thomas Murphy, 819
Ramzi M Musallam, 1927
Gordon G. Pan, 225
Jean-Pierre Paquin, 243
Jeffrey Reals, 1434
Tyler Reeder, 676
Jonathan D. Salon, 245
Graham Schena, 1266
Stefan L Shaffer, 1729
Mayank Singh, 448
Eric Von Stroh, 1145
Bruce Wesson, 809

College of Charleston
Richard Maclean, 793

College of Notre Dame
Nancy McCroskey, 185
Casey Tansey, 1898

College of Saint Elizabeth
John Guiliana DPM, 1288

College of St. Catherine
Ann Winblad, 959

College of William & Mary
Matthew P. Antaya, 989
Tom Benedetti, 291
Alexander E. Carles, 1972
James J Connors II, 1066
Ted Dintersmith, 457
Edmund J Feeley, 1138
Tim Komada, 601
D Scott Mackesy, 1973
Stacey McKittrick, 143
James B Murray Jr, 552
Lisbeth Poulos, 983
Craig Staub, 1368
James W. Tucker, 547
Jason Waxberg, 3260

College of William and Mary
Mark McFadden, 435
Scott Perkins, 1123

College of Wooster
David G. Arscott, 526

College/University Index / Columbia University

Tom Jones, 629
John Kneen, 247

College of the Holy Cross
Edward J Condon Jr, 1416
Kevin J. Curley, 1041
Bill Fitzgerald, 820
Thomas W Gorman, 1639
Michael Greene, 65
Daniel James, 1853
Jay Katarincic, 629
Jeffrey Keay, 912
Brian P Kelley, 1133
Robert J. Maccini, 126
Hank Mannix, 1066
Stephen Muniz, 1503
John J Murphy Jr, 1274

Colorado College
Nicholas B Binkley, 767
Alexander Ellis III, 1583
Dave Furneaux, 1084
Craig Hart, 211
Eric Hender, 16
Pete Hudson, 94
William E James, 1583
James McDermott, 1897
Eben S Moulton, 1639
Mike Slade, 1644
Lucius H. Taylor, 157
Timothy Thompson Black, 1007
Peter O. Wilde, 1498

Colorado School of Mines
David Becker, 1196
Ross Bhappu, 1551
Tom Glanville, 697

Colorado State University
Celia Daly, 395
Doug Fahoury, 1024
John Greff, 1656
Alan Howard, 1795
Brian Knitt, 469
Tracy Marshbanks, 733
John Ord, 543
Phil Parrott, 469
Timothy Reeser, 147
Ryan Williams, 543

Columbia Business School
Jeffrey S Barber, 1778
Jonathan P Barnes, 902
Luca Bassi, 223
Stacey Bishop, 1629
Timothy P Bradley, 1676
Michael S Bruno Jr, 1747
Jon Canarick, 1336
Michael Cardamone, 29
Mike Cardamone, 771
Russell Carson, 1973
Mark H Carter, 1778
Eli Casdin, 422
Jerome A Chazen, 462
David F Chazen, 462
Alan Chen, 377
Ben Choi, 1110
Trace Cohen, 1309
Jim Collis, 1641
Elizabeth Colonna, 921
Stephen B. Connor, 903
Chris F. Corey, 1278
Ben Dahl, 1679
Owen Davis, 1358
James T. Denton, 346
A. Sinclair Dunlop, 690
Roger Ehrenberg, 969
Hythem T El-Nazer, 1778
Derek Eve, 674
Dorian Faust, 886
Alex Ferrara, 263
Matthew W Finlay, 1230
James Frischling, 883
Chris Girgenti, 1483
Liron Gitig, 796
Michael Goldberg, 99
Tom Groos, 490
Stewart KP Gross, 1127
Mukul Gulati, 2017
Timothy T. Hall, 478
David Heidecorn, 1092
Michael Henderson-Cohen, 850
Daniel Hoffer, 207
Kevin M. Jackson, 878
Janet James, 1583
Teddy Kaplan, 1300
John Kim, 936
Matt Kinsey, 364
Roger Kitterman, 1421
John Kornreich, 1620
Michael Lane, 3257
Eric Lauerwald, 1027
Amy S Lazarus, 1729
Jean-Francois Le Ruyet, 1519
Jeffrey A. Lipsitz, 547
Scott MacLeod, 838
John F. MacMurray, 1624
Marc Magliacano, 1092
James Manges, 1853
Carol Mao, 802
Lenard Marcus, 655
Edward W Martin, 494
David Martirano, 1463
Peter C McWilliams PhD, 1619
Chip Meakem, 1851
Ezra Mehlman, 921
Frank Mora, 961
Malcolm C Nolen, 1676
Dennis O'Brien, 1135
Ting-Pau Oei, 644
Grant Palmer, 1853
Stephanie Palmeri, 1881
Douglas A Parker, 1230
Anil Patel, 504
Michael Patterson, 1913
Brian Peters, 936
Grant Pritchard, 1977
Jay Radtke, 1174
Marc Rappoport, 1304
Manu Rekhi, 1017
Anthony Ressler, 160
Jake Reynolds, 1787
Saul Richter, 1572
David S Rose, 1588
Devraj Roy, 1026
Laura Belle Sachar, 1741
Jason Santiago, 1751
Sandeep Sardana, 298
Douglas Schrier, 1543
Bob Schulz, 921
Lawrence R Simon, 505
Vic Singh, 680
Craig Slutzkin, 1297
Robert Smith, 1940
Joshua Sobeck, 13
Jose M. Sosa del Valle, 1116
Dickson Suit, 1025
Patrick Sullivan, 223
Neil S. Suslak, 325
Steven Swartzman, 367
Hans Swildens, 990
Bob Tamashunas, 1641
Andrew C. Taub, 1092
Owen G. Tharrington, 878
James W. Tucker, 547
Jordan Turkewitz, 2019
Emily Turner, 488
Mark F Vassallo, 1127
W Lambert Welling, 1199
Robert J. Wenzel, 73
Ryan Wierck, 854
Eric J. Wilkins, 1410
Keith Zadourian, 1026
Gerard von Dohlen, 346
Max von Zuben, 1984

Columbia College
Andrew Fink, 1846

Columbia Law School
Thomas A Alberg, 1162
Rashid Alvi, 916
Kevin J. Curley, 1041
Andrew Fink, 1846
Stephen Friedman, 1746
Neil Garfinkel, 782
Liron Gitig, 796
Gregory P Ho, 1733
Lauren B Leichtman, 1115
Arthur Levine, 1115
Michael Martin, 1957
Ivar W. Mitchell, 124
Anil Patel, 504
Jon Rattner, 194
Bob Shapiro, 571
Robert Shapiro, 1618
Stephen C. Sherrill, 357
Dick Spalding, 1063
Brandon Tidwell, 1679

Columbia Teachers College
Thomas H Kean, 1506

Columbia University
Kenneth S Abramowitz, 1325
Cate Ambrose, 3252
Ed Anderson, 1335
Mark Attanasio, 557
Stuart A. Auerbach, 119
Gerald T. Banks, 101
Jeffrey Barman, 1434
Robert J. Beckman, 1811
Michael Bego, 1080
Michael C Bellas, 264
James G Benedict, 1075
Jay Bernstein, 1089
Len Blavatnik, 33
Christopher D. Brady, 459
Jamie M Brodsky, 1577
Mike Brown Jr., 320
C.A. Burkhardt, 956
Kristina Burow, 154
Stephen E. Canter, 2017
Eli Casdin, 422
Mike Cataldo, 1146
Kevin Centofanti, 355
Duncan A Chapman, 1116
Robert Chefitz, 1329
Jonathan Y Chou, 699
Todd Clapp, 429
Gregory E. Clark, 949
Vanessa Colella, 488
John Connor, 20
Sally Corning, 1756
Usama Cortas, 1113
Stephen Davis, 230
Charles A. Davis, 1746
Steven DeCillis II, 63
Rick Defieux, 1691
James R. Deitzer, 358
David N Deutsch, 590

College/University Index / Columbia University Law School

Elias Dokas, 1231
Christopher M. Doody, 1746
George Doomany, 124
John Drew, 1787
Charles P. Durkin, Jr., 1624
Ron Eastman, 698
Dr. Edgar G Engleman, 1943
Dean E Fenton, 1738
Paul J Ferri, 1184
Roger S Fine, 1993
Ronald D Fisher, 1701
Steven Flyer, 196
Jean-Francois Formela, MD, 193
Joseph M Gantz, 1447
Andrew S. Gelfand, 358
Kim P. Goh, 957
Robert Goldberg, 538
Michelle Goldberg, 978
Edwin A Goodman, 51
Bob Goodman, 263
Habib Y Gorgi, 1278
Jorge Gross Jr, 1859
Peter Grua, 941
Oliver Guinness, 1258
Joshua L. Gutfreund, 496
Charles Gwirtsman, 1090
Seth L. Harrison, M.D., 144
Rob Hayes, 742
Michael Henderson-Cohen, 850
Charles Ho, 40
Ben Horowitz, 125
Joe Horowitz, 972
Timothy F Howe, 476
Peter Hsing, 1219
Mark Hsu, 897
Thomas S Huseby, 1640
Nikos Iatropoulos, 1055
Phil Jakeway, 1131
Don Jamieson, 377
J. Blair Jenkins, 464
Richard Johnson, 1228
Elliott Jones, 170
Habib Kairouz, 1561, 2231
Julius Kalcevich, 970
George C Kenney, 1667
Fred Kittler, 731
Richard C Klaffky, 740
Stephen Knight MD, 711
Henry R Kravis, 1086
Celine Kwok, 863
A. Rachel Laheny, 1900
Peter Lamm, 722
Mark Langer, 404
Douglas Leone, 1657
Anton Levy, 819
Jeanne Li, 127
Richard Lipkin, 644
Cherie Liu, 1391
James LoGerfo, 643
Paul Lucas, 2145
Megan Lundy, 1133
Patrick A. Maciariello, 525
Josh Makower, 1296
David Marquardt, 200
Matthew McCooe, 532
Doug McCormick, 1561
Edward McNulty, 574
Chip Meakem, 1084
Matt Miller, 1953
Sami Mnaymneh, 931
Bernard Moon, 1719
John Morris, 912
David Moszer, 1493
Eben S Moulton, 1639
Fayez S. Muhtadie, 1746
Shay Murphy, 1324
Christian L. Oberbeck, 1624

Arnie Oronsky, 1014
Carlo Padovano, 1376
Jim Pastoriza, 1784
James A. Pelusi, 214
Michael S Pfeffer, 1469
Cary Pfeffer MD, 1814
Brett L. Prager, 611
Thomas Queenan, 1445
Gary Ragusa, 411
Steve Rappaport, 1376
Robert F Raucci, 1313
Brian Rich, 429
Saul Richter, 1572
Marcos A Rodriguez, 1404
Jonathan D Root MD, 1898
David S Rose, 1305
Laura Belle Sachar, 1741
Rohan Saikia, 864
Jason Santiago, 1751
Jamie Schiff, 1344
Andrew Schiff, MD, 73
Daniel Schultz, 609
George J Schultze, 1632
Rick Shuart, 377
Stephan Siegel, 2263
Ian Sigalow, 876
Michal Silverberg, 1350
Ajit Singh, 176
R Adam Smith, 483
Stephen H Spahn, 1506
Edson W. Spencer Jr., 67
Donald Spero, 1298
Sheldon Stone, 1362
Béla Szigethy, 1576
John L. Teeger, 777
John Trbovich, 173
Robert Tucker, 404
Gayle L Veber, 1911
Martin Vogelbaum, 1561
John E Walvoord, 1699
Michael Weingarten, 1678
Joshua S. Weinstein, 406
Robert Weisskoff PhD, 711
Bruce Wesson, 809
Christoph Westphal, 1149
Bill Wiberg, 58
Alan Wilkinson, 63
Robert M. Williams Jr., 1041
Katherine Zamsky, 411
Gabriel de Alba, 2067
Gerard von Dohlen, 346

Columbia University Law School
Hiram A. Bingham, 589

Columbia University School of Law
Brian P. Friedman, 1036

Concordia University
Joe Canavan, 2193
Cam Di Prata, 2127
Michael Griffiths, 2162
Khalil Maalouf, 2282
Genevieve Morin, 2113
David Nault, 2172
Jerome Nycz, 2048
Daniel Pharand, 432
Karl Reckziegel, 2048
Zoya Shcuhpak, 2149
Amy Ssuto, 163

Connecticut College
Seth W Alvord, 740
Tim Armstrong, 135
Andrew P. Bonanno, 1085
Michael J Dubilier, 632
Will Manuel, 111

Connecticut State University
Steven F. Wood, 1018

Copenhagen Business School
Jan Leschly, 415

Copenhagen College of Pharmacy
Jan Leschly, 415

Copenhagen University
Christian Borcher, 414

Cornell College
Chris Christoffersen PhD, 1126

Cornell Law School
John C. Bombara, 949
David Castle, 330
C Deryl Couch, 1755
Steven Flyer, 196
James McLaughlin, 1131
Jonathan H. Owsley, 1092
Frank Schiff, 1231
Stefan L Shaffer, 1729
Andrew Spring, 1231
David J. Wermuth, 1746
Shari H. Wolkon, 1818

Cornell University
Neeraj Agrawal, 238
Eric Aguitar, MD, 73
Sandeep D Alva, 1377
Seth W Alvord, 740
Dr. Alf L. Andreassen, 1401
David Bainbridge, 1929
Dr John Baldeschwieler, 188
Dennis Baldwin, 332
John Balen, 389
Rajeev Batra, 1187
Eric Beckman, 333, 334
Michael Bego, 1080
Cécile Belaman, 223
Adam Bendell, 1833
Michael Biggee, 1852
Bluette N. Blinoff, 1801
Chris Bodnar, 646
David J Breazzano, 598
Frank W. Bruno, 453
Andrew M Bushell, 542
Andrew Byrd, Jr., 1872
Stephen E. Canter, 2017
J Michael Cline, 38
John Collins, 1753
Ed Colloton, 263
David D Croll, 1157
Tim DeVries, 1345
Karen Derr Gilbert, 796
Salil Deshpande, 224
Dan Devorsetz, 949
Omar Diaz, 630
Christopher W. Dick, 180
Jeffrey Diehl, 56
A. Barr Dolan, 460
Douglas M. Dunnan, 880
Park Durrett, 28
David Eichler, 1500
Stephen Einhorn, 403
Daniel Einhorn, 403
Neil Exter, 1814
Noel J Fenton, 1855
Paul J Ferri, 1184
Ari Fine, 149
Michael J Foster, 1560
Craig D Frances MD, 1754
Lizzie Francis, 345
Stephen Friedman, 1746
Michael Fulton MD, 946

College/University Index / Dartmouth College

Quin Garcia, 207, 208
Benjamin D. Geiger, 786
David S. Gellman, 804
Jason Gerlach, 1758
Jim Gilbert, 748
Gary L Goldberg, 1627
Allan R. Goldberg, PhD, 1811
Noah Goodhart, 1980
Jonah Goodhart, 1980
Michael D Goodman, 854
Alissa Grad, 848
Mitch Green, 2075
Tom Groos, 490
Oliver Guinness, 1258
Eugene Hahn, 1043
Ammar H. Hanafi, 87
Leonard M. Harlan, 425
Christopher R Hemmeter, 1808
Shar Heslam, 257
Geoff A. Hill, 1580
Eva Ho, 729
Stuart Holden, MD, 1492
Aaron Holiday, 12
Timothy Huang, 1116
Ron Hunt, 1297
Anwar Hussain, 1562
Meli James, 3253
Dave Johnson, 1009
Scott Johnson, 1290
Andy Jones, 1172
Thomas W Jones, 1875
Habib Kairouz, 1561, 2231
Jonathan Kalman, 1029
Krishnamurty Kambhampati, 507
Agha Khan, 1746
William J Kidd, 1075
Ruben J King-Shaw Jr, 1168
Craig B Klosk, 1984
Lester B. Knight, 1594
Michael Koby, 4
Peggy Koenig, 20
Peter Kolchinsky, 1522
Mehmet Kosematoglu, 253
Marlene R. Krauss, 1062
Jennifer Krusius, 518
Samir Kumar, 1158
Dr. Anja König, 1350
Jeremy D. Lack, 190
Gerry Langeler, 1392
Cliff Lardin, 434
Jenny Lee, 827
Douglas Leone, 1657
Quinn Li, 1511
Michael Lynch, 1200
E Peter Malekian, 1192
Randy Maslow, 970
Michael Matly, MD, 1251
W. Christian McCollum, 1113
Kevin M. McGovern, 1194
Chip Meakem, 1084, 1851
Tony Miller, 1111
Daniel H Miller, 1584
Matt Miller, 1953
Ravi Mohan, 1666
Michael E. Najjar, 547
Jerrold Newman, 1986
Yi-Jian Ngo, 85
Scott Nolan, 778
Peter J Nolan, 1113
Nickie Norris, 929
Dale S Okonow, 1963
Adele C. Oliva, 4, 1510
Douglas E. Onsi, 922
Peter B. Orthwein, Jr., 1730
Jeffrey P Parker, 853
Brian Peiser, 654
Lee Pillsbury, 1808
Benjamin M. Polk, 1927
Bob Proctor, 288
Phil Proujansky, 434
John Raguin, 711
Lee Rand, 1756
Stan J Reiss, 1184
Meredith L Rerisi, 17
Joseph R Robinson, 1230
Micah Rosenbloom, 774
Jonathan D Roth, 17
Bryon C Roth, 1592
Lawrence Rusoff, 1434
Bruce Sachs, 457
Doug Schillinger, 639
Sam Sezak, 291
Rajeev Shah, 1522
Saurabh Sharma, 1050
Bob Shaw, 194
Robert Shaw, Jr., 161
Thomas R Shepherd, 1864
Zachary Shulman, 434
Andrew Singer, 676
Craig Smith, 1471
Robert Smith, 1940
Donald Spero, 1298
Gregory Stento, 912
David Stern, 504
John Stobo, 21
Gordon Stofer, 466
Richard Stokes, 931
Brent Stone, 20
David Strasser, 1768
Roger A Strauch, 1584
Thorsten Suder, 404
Ilya Sukhar, 1184
Jason R. Tagler, 386
Juliet Tammenoms Bakker, 1147
Larry Tanenbaum, 2162
Jennifer Tegan, 434
Ralph Terkowitz, 21
Bill Trenchard, 742
Jordan Turkewitz, 2019
Guy Turner, 965
Christopher Turner, 1957
Jeff Valentine, 706
Andrew W Verhalen, 1184
Carter A. Ward, 157
Gus Warren, 1614
Jeffrey M. Webb, 989
Andrew J Weisenfeld, 1271
Victor Westerlind, 812
Bill Wiberg, 58
Gred Widroe, 1197
Charles A. Wiebe, 266
L John Wilkerson, 809
Matthew L Witte, 1171
Josh Wolfe, 1155
Shari H. Wolkon, 1818
Philip M Young, 1898
James W Young PhD, 11

Cornell University Medical College
Craig D Frances MD, 1754
Andrew Schiff, MD, 73

Cranfield School of Management, UK
Bill Kelsall, 682
Neil J. Taylor, 324

Creighton University
Mike Buttry, 466
Mark Hasebroock, 635
Jeanne Mariani Sullivan, 1741
S Edward Torres, 1128

Creighton University School of Law
Patrick J Duffy, 1276

Cumberland School of Law
Charles A Cox, 1148
John W. McCullough, 907

Curtin University, Australia
Bill Kelsall, 682

D'Amore-Mckim School of Business
Michael P. Murphy, 1589

Dalhousie University
Peter Bilodeau, 2117
Carl Burlock, 2106
Stephen Denton, 2242
Tom Eisenhauer, 2059
Joel Finlayson, 2141
Jody Forsyth, 2034
Daniel Lee, 2066
Alex MacBeath, 2157
Chris Moyer, 2208
Yann Robard, 2281
Brice Scheschuk, 2128
Michael Siltala, 2279
Jeff Van Steenbergen, 2044
Peter Williams, 2034

Daniels College of Business
Anders Bjork, 20

Darden School of Business
Wes Blackwell, 1635
Jonathan B. Blanco, 747
Douglas Burns, 552
Thomas A. Carver, 913
Gregory W. Cashman, 848
Randy Castleman, 552
C Taylor Cole Jr, 913
Terry Daniels, 1507
Christopher Delaney, 1027
Jonathan Ebinger, 299
S. Whitfield Edwards, 747
Sean Foote, 1093
Paul Johan, 227
Sean M. Kelley, 878
Robert Kibble, 1239
Joel Lanik, 793
Richard Maclean, 793
David M Maher, 355
Rajan Mehra, 504
Bob More, 94
William Powell, 2062
Jeffrey Schutz, 443
William B. Thompson, 783
Richard Upton, 910
Jonathan R Wallace, 1389
Russ Williams, 15

Dartmouth College
Brent Ahrens, 389
Reis L Alfond, 1883
Alexei Andreev, 208
Paul Asel, 1331
Richard Aube, 1447
Kathleen Bacon, 912
Michael Balmuth, 1764
Maren Thomas Bannon, 1030
Peter Barris, 1296
Andrew Beebe, 1363
Walter M (Jerry) Bird, 1175
Daniel L Black, 1984
Stephen Bloch, 389
Graham Brooks, 1
Mark Brooks, 1629
Brian J. Buenneke, 1413
Bill Burgess, 22
Jon Callaghan, 1862
Dana Callow, 315

College/University Index / David Eccles School of Business

William J Canestaro, 2007
Baron Carlson, 63
John R Carroll, 1754
Russell Carson, 1973
Eric Chin, 564
Allan Chou, 1341
William D Christ, 1778
Peter Chung, 1255
Doug Cole, 748
William E Conway Jr, 416
Everett R Cook, 1470
Marshall Cooper, 868
Jeffrey M Crowe, 1346
Benton Cummings, 1518
Sean L. Cunningham, 889
Diane M. Daych, 436
Gerard A Debiasi, 1075
Liam Donohue, 1
Dana Donovan, 632
Chris Egan, 61
Patrick Fallon, 28
Matt Fates, 180
Phil Ferneau, 311
Jim Feuille, 564
Michael Fisch, 111
Peter Fitzgerald, 1098
Walter C Florence, 792
Tony Florence, 1296
Andrew N. Ford, 906
Walter G. Freedman, 1097
Charlie Friedland, 824
Carolyn Galiette, 1025
Bob Geiman, 433
Steven Gillis, 154
Cliff Gilman, 71
Tom Goodrich, 582
Steven C. Graham, 851
Kenneth A. Graham, 1018
Jason Green, 666
Jonathan M Haas, 494
Beth Haas, 578
Kallie Hapgood, 878
John Henderson, 970
Ted Henderson, 1630
David Hodgson, 819
Alec Hufnagel, 1066
William S. Hughes, 1498
Jonathan E. Hunnicutt, 1979
Michael C. Jackson, 952
Jeff Jackson, 1808
Glenn Jacobson, 1853
Janet James, 1583
Ross M. Jones, 257
Daniel G. Jones, 1818
Scott A. Kehoe, 1018
Yoo Jin Kim, 1108
Rick Kimball, 1787
Thies O Kolln, 16
Mark Koulogeorge, 1242
Jeffrey Kovach, 172
Mike Krupka, 224
Farouk Ladha, 780
Stephen M LeSieur, 1720
Morgan Livermore, 824
Bernardo H. Llovera, 707
Phil Loughlin, 223
Chris Lund, 903
David Mace, 828
Ben Magnano, 785
Rick Magnuson, 828
David M Maher, 355
John Maldonado, 61
Andrew R. Mayer, 1779
Frederick Maynard, 912
Tim McAdam, 1787
Stephen McCormack, 523
Matt McIlwain, 1162

Roger McNamee, 660
Nate Mitchell, 824
Brendan M. Moore, 687
Erik Moore, 232
Chris Moore, 1537
John H. Moragne, 1852
Mark J Morrissette, 1334
Rick Moss, 256
Richard Nathan, 2160
Joseph M. Niehaus, 952
John Nies, 1044
Nate Niparko, 27
Scott O'Hare, 595
Jake Odden, 19
William Ogden, 1883
Sandy Osborne, 1066
Jonathan W Osgood CFA, 573
Bart D Osman, 1116
Bruce Ou, 884
John E. Palmer, 906
David J. Parker, 119
Victor E Parker, 1720
Marni F. Payne, 257
Tripp Peake, 1146
Doug Pepper, 1666
Dennis Phelps, 1006
Tony Pritzker, 1482
Tony Pritzker, 1483
Jake Reynolds, 1787
James T Rich, 815
Jeff Richards, 827
Matt Rightmire, 311
Ren Riley, 1361
Bryan Roberts, 1918
Greg Robinson, 9
Doug Roeder, 605
Jonathan D Root MD, 1898
Mike Ross, 1764
Michael Ross PhD, 1631
John G Rudge, 1116
Aaron Sack, 1256
John K. Saer Jr., 828
Enrique Salem, 224
Scott Sandell, 1296
Aaron Sandoski, 1347
Dan Sanner, 92
Hondo Sen, 190
Derek Senft, 2118, 2210, 2266
Scott Silverman, 69
David Silverman, 564
Stanley T. Smith, 1773
Mark Soane, 143
Stephen Socolof, 1304
Stephen H Spahn, 1506
Holden Spaht, 1817
John L Steffens, 1733
Josh Stein, 610
Scott Stuart, 1606
Eric Swanson, 893
Dave Tabors, 238
Bill Tarr, 1258
Robert M Tichio, 1577
Michael Triplett, 1005
Emily Turner, 488
Kapil Venkatachalam, 1787
Tom Washing, 1656
Daniel Weintraub, 197
Forest Wester, 1859
T.J. Whalen, 789
Edward J. Whelan, 257
Kirk Whickman, 128
Elizabeth C Williamson, 792
Robert D Winneg, 1295
Chris Winship, 796
Alfred S Woodworth Jr, 647
William J. Wynperle, 1663
Royce G. Yudkoff, 20

Keith Zadourian, 1026
Casper de Clercq, 1346

David Eccles School of Business
Brad Money, 874

Davidson College
Cathy Belk, 1051
Peter L. Clark, Jr., 418
Joe Cook III, 1261
William Dunbar, 540
Jacqueline Glynn, 840
Chris Holden, 552
Christopher N. Jones, 747
John Moore, 196
J Michael Schafer, 1299
Andrew J Schwab, 11
Gregg Smart, 722
Jennifer Steans, 531
Ben Wallace, 216

DeGroote School of Business
Colin Walker, 2083

DePaul University
Thomas S. Bagley, 1438
Denio R. Bolzan, 1438
David Carlson, 1539
Kevin Delaplane, 1883
C Michael Foster, 1232
Jeffrey Howard, 1613
J Allan Kayler, 1232
Eric Kutsenda, 1648
Matt Leinauer, 402
Timothy W Maloney, 17
Lee J. Monahan, 913
Michael E Moran, 351
Jeffry S. Pfeffer, 410
Robert Riemer, 177
Nick Rosa, 571
Nick Rosa, 1618
William H. Schaar, 948
Jim Schultz, 1380
John J. Starcevich, 1438
Ana M Winters, 1232

DePauw University
Steve A Cobb, 480
Thomas P. Cooper, MD, 137
David C. Coquillette, 1300
R Glen Mayfield, 1575
Peter Munson, 412
Luke Reese, 2000
Douglas Schrier, 1543
Michael L Smith, 412
John Tullis, 1868
Anthony J de Nicola, 1973

DeVry Institute of Technology
Wayne Cantwell, 556
Michael A Steinbeck, 1747

DeVry University
Michael Hara, 928

Defence System Management College
Thomas K Churbuck, 65

Defense Research Institute
Alexander Galitsky, 89

Dehli University
Alipt Sharma, 838

Delaware Law School
Jon Powell, 1660

College/University Index / Duquesne University

Delhi College of Engineering
Raman Khanna, 604

Delhi University
Promod Haque, 1346
Nitin Pachisia, 1887

Denison University
Jason Allen, 1175
Michael Bevan, 658
Maddie Callander, 310
John A Canning Jr, 1160
Eugene P. Conese Jr., 878
Charlie Gifford, 929
Timothy D. Johnson, 847
Suzanne Kriscunas, 1576
Kenneth Mabbs, 712
William C Mulligan, 1480
Ralph Schlosstein, 700
Jack Wyant, 290

Dickinson College
Henry J. Boye, 1818
W Ryan Davis, 1163
Jay Grossman, 20
John Paul Kirwin III, 165

Dominican College
Debra Guerin Beresini, 1015

Downing College
Jonathan Aberman, 120

Drake University
John C Aplin, 480
John Meilner, 341
Michael E Moran, 351
Stephen P Mullin, 630
Gordon Roth, 1592
Darren M Snyder, 1473

Drew University
Joseph T. Sobota, MD, 140
Jamie Weston, 1733

Drexel University
Mel Baiada, 233
David William Baum, 1737
Y.K. Chu, 1983
Michael Cohen, 1369
Harry D'Andrea, 1901
David Dorsey, 3
Alex Katz, 724
Charles Lewis, 261
Jesse Middleton, 756
Robert Migliorino, 1949
Richelle P. Parham, 386
Mike Pellini, 1646

Drury College
Joel Rommines, 1081

Dublin City University
Antoinette "Toni" Chaltiel, 1535

Duke Fuqua School of Business
Atul Kamra, 1690

Duke University
Matthew L. Altman, 167
Andrew J. Armstrong. Jr., 1727
Christopher Austen, 353
Chip Austin, 967
Merrick Axel, 559
Charles Ayres, 1853
Jeffrey Barnes, 273
Fouad Bashour, 479
Steven S Beckett, 1429
Cathy Belk, 1051
David Biesel, 1322
Mike Bingle, 1685
Dave Blivin, 550
Philip Borden, 809
Jan Bouten, 999
Larry Bradshaw, 696
Kenneth S. Bring, 257
Jamie M Brodsky, 1577
Steve Brotman, 91, 1682
Ben Browning, 1123
Thomas A. Burger Jr., 878
Doug Cameron, 739
John A Canning Jr, 1160
Roger Carolin, 1636
Jack Carsten, 950
Gillis C Cashman, 1157
Scott E. Chappell, 266
Robert Cioffi, 80
Christopher L Collins, 1066
Richard H Copans, 1160
Jeffrey Craver, 60
Todd Creech, 924
David Cummings, 191
Daniel Dickinson, 920
Andrew C. Dodson, 1419
Andy Donner, 1442
Dana Donovan, 632
Dennis Dougherty, 1013
Kenneth M. Doyle, 899
Matt Edgerton, 1066
Frederick W. Eubank II, 1410
Peter W Farner, 1804
Mark L Feidler, 1270
Josh Felser, 787
David Fishman, 1912
David C. Franklin, 954
Christopher J Garber, 1964
Ned Gilhuly, 1606
Cliff Gilman, 71
Jim Glasheen, 1788
Rob Go, 1322
Michael Gorman, 1728
Dave Gravano, 1976
Marshall Griffin, 530
Gregory Grunberg, 1147
Steve Gullans PhD, 704
Lawrence S. Hamelsky, 257
L. Watts Hamrick III, 1410
Felda Hardymon, 263
Tom Hawkins, 770
Jeff Haywood, 1720
R Trent Hickman, 1929
Grant Hill, 1433
Gerald Holtz, 1496
Davis Hostetter, 899
Joseph Huffsmith, 1376
Andrew Humphries, 914
Jeffrey M. Hurst, 523
Mudit Jain PhD, 1774
A. Bruce Johnston, 1778
Matt Jones, 1355
Azra Kanji, 20
Rishi Kapoor, 1021
Bruce Karsh, 1362
Aftab R. Kherani, MD, 73
David Kirkpatrick, 1691
Justin Klein, 1919
Garheng Kong, 924
Trent Kososki, 676
Larry Kubal, 1093
Tatsuya Kubo, 912
Joel Lanik, 793
Jeremy Levine, 263
Dan Levitan, 1186
Regan Li, 2077
Bill Luby, 1641
Bruce Luehrs, 1572
Joshua A. Lutzker, 257
Ian B. MacTaggart, 360
J Matthew Mackowski, 1794
Mike Marcantonio, 291
Norvell E Miller IV, 1711
Aaron Money, 790
Mitch Mumma, 1013
Peter M. Mundheim, 1746
Timothy M Murray, 470
Suzanne Niemeyer, 52
Stephen Pagliuca, 223
Grant Palmer, 1853
Travis Pearson, 828
Douglas S. Perry, 589
Steven F. Piaker, 436
David Pierson, 1776
Todd T Pietri, 51
JB Pritzker, 1482
J.B. Pritzker, 1483
Diana Propper de Callejon, 707
Steven G Raich, 1138
Michael Ramich, 793
Leigh Randall, 1834
Scott Raney, 1537
Ganesh B. Rao, 1818
Geoffrey Rehnert, 197
Pamela L. Reiland, 893
Scott A Reilly CFA, 1429
Meredith L Rerisi, 17
Bruce Roberts, 417
Carmichael Roberts, 1180
Alex Rogers, 912
Bruce Rogers, 1090
Jim Rorer, 1466
Jonathan D Roth, 17
Michael W Rubel, 1560
David M Rubenstein, 416
Peter M. Rubin, 192
Camille Samuels, 1918
Kenneth T Schiciano, 1778
Sean Schickedanz, 499
Adam Schimel, 242
Michael Schnabel, 449
Eric Schwartz, 425
Christian Schwartz, 1822
Jon Seeber, 1888
Ron Shah, 1751
Adam Sharkawy, 1180
Ben Sheridan, 292
Raleigh A. Shoemaker, Jr., 257
Benjamin M Spero, 1720
Adam Spivack, 520
W Brad Stephens, 286
Mark D. Taber, 862
Stephen C. Tardio, 956
Ted Wang, 553
Michael Weiss, 867
R Patrick Weston CFA, 216
Ken Widder, 1098
Jim Woody, 1098
James Zelter, 141
Bob Zipp, 115

Duke University Law School
William K. Richardson, 942

Duke University School of Medicine
John Kim, MD, 139

Dundee University
Paul Daccus, 1755

Duquesne University
Tom Eddy, 1031
Robert Swartz, 1208

College/University Index / Durham University

Robert A Theleen, 475

Durham University
Paul Clark, 1925

EAP European School of Management
Gabriel Caillaux, 819

ESADE Business School
Gina Domanig, 2101

ESADE University
Janie C. Bécque, 2114

ESC Nice
Maor Amar, 2143

Earlham College
J. Russell Chapman, 174
John May, 1303

Eastern Illinois University
Jeffrey Holdsberg, 376
Robert A Ingram, 918

Eastern Kentucky University
Brenda McDaniel, 1068
Jerry Rickett, 1068

Eastern Michigan University
David Breach, 1940

Eckerd College
Russ Wilson, 1859

Ecole Centrale de Paris
Philippe Amouyal, 1022
Stefan Goetz, 927

Ecole Nationale des Mines de Paris
John Piret, 1311

Ecole Polytechnique
Lionel Assant, 280
Claude Vachet, 2087

Ecole Speciale des Travaux Publics
Marcel Fournier, 425

Edinburgh University
Andrew Cleland, 520

Edith Cowan University
Simon Cresswell, 136

Eisenhower College
Allen F Grum, 1526

Elizabethtown College
James B Hoover, 588

Eller College of Management
Sean Doyle, 1613

Elmhurst College
Mary Capasso, 1471

Elon University
Ashton Newhall, 872

Embry-Riddle University
Steve Whitlock, 1725

Emerson College
Caitlyn MacDonald, 1108
Paul A Santinelli, 1335

Emery University
Neil A. Wizel, 741

Emory University
Cory S Anderson, 39
Craig Baker, 1573
Sean Banks, 1865
Stuart Barkoff, 838
Scott Bluestein, 928
Jeffrey B Bunder, 1133
Nathan R. Every, MD, MPH, 785
Doug Fisher, 825
Gardiner W Garrard III, 1865
Dave Gould, 1790
David Greenberg, 1045
Bahniman Hazarika, 860
Paul Johan, 227
Kim Kamdar, PhD, 622
Alan Kelley, 1691
Michael S. Marr, 408
Marc Michel, 527
Ashish H. Mistry, 285
Dave Munichiello, 894
W. Carter Neild, 1383
Grant A Patrick, 247
Mark Patricof, 1223
Douglas S. Perry, 589
Wendell Reilly, 1425
Charles Rim, 627
Cynthia Ringo, 596
Mark Swaine, 496
David E Thomas Jr, 1529

Emory University School of Law
David S. Gorton, 1779
Michael Hyatt, 1026
Arthur Rogers, 153

Erasmus University
Claudio Nessi, 1373
Joost F. Thesseling, 478
Fred van Beuningen, 2072

European University Brussels
Marc der Kinderen, 13
Jean-Edouard van Praet, 982

Exeter University
Dennis Atkinson, 691

FW Olin Graduate School of Business
Matthew Ahern, 1081
John Whorf, 1293

Fairfield University
Derek Blazensky, 414
Phil Cagnassola, 903
Mary Lincoln Campbell, 652
Gerard N. Casale, 1878
Scott Dupcak, 534
Kevin Gahwyler, 1282
Lorraine Hliboki, 1466
J. Ryan Kelly, 777
Joel Krikston, 1206
Paul LaViolette, 1631
Paul LaViolette, 1764
Christopher A Layden, 2014
John G Loverro, 1116
Owen G. Tharrington, 878
Gwen Weiss, 6

Fairleigh Dickinson University
Beth L. Bernstein, 687
James J. Dowling, 1036
Daniel Gulino, 1567
Tom Mac Mahon, 749

Fanshaw College
Jon Jackson, 3249

Federal Institute of Technology
Francois Helou, 189

Fergusson College
Sonali Vijayavargiya, 198
Devdutt Yellurkar, 457

Fisher College of Business
Mark Roehrenbeck, 1561

Fitchburg State College
John W Bullock, 1994

Fletcher School of Law & Diplomacy
Jennifer Choi, 3256
Chris Farmer, 1677
Steven Ritterbush, 1208

Florida Atlantic University
David Fries, 1908
Maynard Webb, 1969

Florida Institute of Technology
Edward C McCarthy, 1575

Florida International University
Ruben J King-Shaw Jr, 1168
Eric Manlunas, 1966
Pat Schneider, 3251

Florida State University
Nick Grabowski, 1665
Grant A Jackson, 551
Kenneth A. Minihan, 1401
Lawrence Mock, 1279

Fordham Graduate School of Business
Richard W. Gaenzle Jr., 831

Fordham University
Tarik Abbas, 1838
Geoffrey Baehr, 89
Jack Baron, 566
Michael V. Caso, 1589
Christopher Childres, 653
Winston J Churchill, 1636
Paul Clark, 1925
Robert A. Comey, 1020
John R Costantino, 1325
Ryan J. Faulkingham, 525
Jonathan Glass, 1235
Steven G Glenn, 1957
Luke Gosselin, 448
Gen. John M Keane, 1636
Thomas Keaveney, 60
Kevin Lynch, 433
Patricia Muoio, 1689
Daniel J. O'Brien, 1041
Scott Powers, 52
Joseph Saviano, 226
Bruce K. Taragin, 304
Jamie Weston, 1733
James W Young PhD, 11

Fordham University School of Law
Scott Birnbaum, 1533
Dave Butler, 1049
TJ Maloney, 1131
Robert B Nolan Jr, 902
Andrew Tananbaum, 566
Jeanette M Welsh JD, 1794
David Wolmer, 1115

College/University Index / Georgetown University

Foreign Trade University
Ha Nguyen, 2183

Foster School of Business
Noel de Turenne, 1250

Fox School of Business
Tyler Dautrich, 871
Timothy G. Fallon, 148
Dean Sciorillo, 677

Fox School of Business & Management
Charles Kerrigan, 1697

Franklin & Marshall College
Nancy C Floyd, 1355
Steven Hobman, 1316
Richard S Kollender, 1510
Dennison T Veru, 1402
Jason Waxberg, 3260
Matthew Young, 687

Franklin College
Matteo Volpi, 2068

Free University of Brussels
Alain Schreiber, MD, 1492

Freie Universität Berlin
Thomas Korte, 129

Fu-Jen Catholic University
Ronald Han, 909

Fuller Seminary
Phil Chen, 1477

Fuqua School of Business
Christopher Austen, 353
Nathaniel C Brinn, 1942
Ben Brooks, 1712
James D. Carey, 1746
Blaine Crissman, 1481
Jim Duda, 583
Josh Felser, 787
Jim Gunton, 1329
Mark W Kehaya, 1214
John Kim, MD, 139
Michael Miller, 445
Steven C Pierson, 1151
Ned Scheetz, 139
David Strasser, 1768
Paul Straub, 493
Tim Wilson, 176

Furman University
C Deryl Couch, 1755
Scott Hoch, 793

Gabelli School of Business
Michael V. Caso, 1589

Garvin School of International Mgmt
Michael J Dubilier, 632

General Assembly
Lauren Robinson, 2140

General Motors Institute
Thien-Ly Ngo, 528

Geneva College
John W Manzetti, 1452

George Brown College
Marat Mukhamedyarov, 2132

George Institute of Technology
AT Gimble, 191

George Mason School of Law
John Malloy, 299

George Mason University
Dave Armstrong, 773
E Peter Malekian, 1192
Thien-Ly Ngo, 528
Don Rainey, 881

George Washington University
Jonathan Aberman, 120
Charles Auster, 1600
Mel Billingsley PhD, 1120
Elon S Broms, 1101
Michael Brosgart, 1810
Kate Chhabra, 430
Evan DeCorte, 518
Kirk Fichtner, 1170
John Fletcher, 750
Sreekar Gadde, 296
Laura Gladstone, 832
Pat Gouhin, 3247
Bulbul Gupta, 1397
Ronald Han, 908, 909
Terry L. Jones, 1773
John Paul Kirwin III, 165
David Kivitz, 156
Randy Klueger, 540
Bob Kocher MD, 1918
Christopher A Layden, 2014
Mark Levine, 540
Cyril L. Meduna, 62
Jonathan Murray, 642
William Osborn, 522
Alex Radcliffe, 409
Ned J Renzi, 275
Michael S. Sarner, 406
Geoff Schneider, 433
Larry Schnurmacher, 1443
Jeffrey D Serkes, 1402
John W. Snow, 453
Oak Strawbridge, 880
Steven Swain, 442
Micah Tapman, 395
Peggy Wallace, 845
April Young, 928
Philip M Young, 1898

Georgetown University
John F Aiello, 1133
Roger Altman, 700
Joseph Baratta, 280
Jeffrey Bartoli, 449
Tom Benedetti, 291
Matt Bigge, 564
Tim Billings, 1507
Scott Birnbaum, 1533
Michael Brown, 238
Curtis L Buser, 416
Andrew Byrd, 1872
Janie C. Bé‹que, 2114
David J Cooney, 247
Mike Cooper, 1670
Sally Corning, 1756
Fred Craves, PhD, 240
Michael J Cromwell III, 1389
Vahe A Dombalagian, 1160
Donald J Donahue Jr, 692
Michael F. Donoghue, 1730
Liam Donohue, 1
Robb Doub, 1298
James B. Dougherty, MD, 158
Egon Durban, 1685
Eliot Durbin, 308
Greg Durst, 3256
Anne Dwane, 1935
Scott W Edwards, 1755
David Eichler, 1500
Robert Y Emmert, 1276
Beth Engel, 635
Steve Engelberg, 1618
William Ericson, 1247
Bill Ericson, 1985
Jonathan Farber, 1129
Robert M. Feerick, 948
Adam Fisher, 263
Robert J Flanagan, 510
Dave Flanagan, 1009
Jennifer Fonstad, 182
C Michael Foster, 1232
Elizabeth Galbut, 1703
Joseph V. Gallagher, 126
Rupert Gerard, 893
Antonio Gracias, 1904
Stephen X Graham, 563
Michael D. Granoff, 1466
Mark Grovic, 1298
Donald L Hawks III, 356
Chad Heath, 674
Rick Heitzmann, 744
Marty Hernon, 315
Phil Jakeway, 1131
Dan Janney, 94
Mike Jerstad, 1474
Christopher M. King, 878
Michael Kosty, 336
Chris Kryder, 749
Pete Labbat, 676
Maja Lapcevic, 488
Kyle Largent, 832
Christopher Lee, 832
Joshua M. Levinson, 848
Daniel C Lubin, 1523
John Lyman, 894
Salvatore A Massaro, 656
Michelle McCarthy, 1928
John C McNamara II, 1148
Andrew Montgomery, 1223
Cheryl Moss, 791
Paul F Murphy, 1654
Oleg Nodelman, 710
Robert B Nolan Jr, 902
Charles L Palmer, 1333
Douglas S. Perry, 589
Richard A. Petrocelli, 1624
Thomas Pryma, 63
Michael Psaros, 1089
Ben Rabinowitz, 117
Benjamin J. Ramundo, 167
Anthony Ressler, 160
Ellis F. Rinaldi, 1742
Andrew C. Romans, 1599
Jason Rottenberg, 173
Noah Roy, 867
Chris Sacca, 1153
Andrew Sachs, 1603
Andrew Salenbier, 36
Zita Saurel, 927
Jeff Schlapinski, 3252
David Schroder, 16
David R. Schroder, 1020
Robert Seidler, 1648
Sam Sezak, 291
Judd Sher, 927
Brian J Siegel, 896
Joshua B. Siegel, 1599
Matthew M Smith, 17
Tammi Smorynski, 1009
Joseph T. Sobota, MD, 140
Michael Sotirhos, 280
McLain Southworth, 564

1001

College/University Index / Georgetown University Law Center

Nicholas J Stanley, 1911
Caroline Stout, 710
Matthew Strottman, 983
Devin Talbott, 681
Bob Tamashunas, 1641
Andrew Tichenor, 291
C. Bowdoin Train, 880
Andy Weissman, 1884
Marshall C. White, 747
David C. Wodlinger, 167

Georgetown University Law Center
Zachary Bogue, 586
Paul Diaz, 559
Daniel K Flatley, 1178
Mark Jacobsen, 1359
Suzanne Niemeyer, 52
Steve Oetgen, 843
Lisa Schule, 838
Bruce Taub, 192
Annie S Terry, 1160

Georgia Institute of Technology
Chris Allen, 1404
Craig Baker, 1573
Gregory Bloom, 47
Lee Bryan, 530
Mark Buffington, 274
Brook Byers, 1079
Robert Coneybeer, 1666
Adam Cranford, 1292
Michael DeRosa, 658
Steven Denning, 819
David Dullum, 832
Tom Dyal, 1537
Dick Hunter, 595
Ariel Jaduszliwer, 327
Anthony V Lando, 39
John L Long Jr, 1843
Scott Marlette, 1696
John Paul Milciunas, 31
Said Mohammadioun, 1790
Randall E. Poliner, 132
James Robinson, III, 1597
Randy Scott, 924
W Thomas Smith Jr, 1865
Gregory A. White, 1818

Georgia State University
Michael L Bailey, 1487
Brian Cayce, 860
James S Douglass, 797
Said Mohammadioun, 1790
Matt Oguz, 1407
Todd T Pietri, 51
Cynthia Ringo, 596

Georgia Tech
Mark G Miller, 1196
Tom Noonan, 1790

Georgian College
Marat Mukhamedyarov, 2132

Gettysburg College
John C. Acker, 1730
John Willert, 404

Ghent University
Sigrid Van Bladel, 19

Glasgow University
A. Sinclair Dunlop, 690

Goizueta Business School
David W Averett, 1754
Jeff Black, 1433
Jeffrey Black, 1928

David Greenberg, 1045
Billy L. Harbert, 285
Rimas Kapeskas, 383
Tory Rooney, 357

Golden Gate University
Mark J Gill, 714
Richard Harding, 1015
Raman Khanna, 604
James A Kohlberg, 1085
Bill McDonagh, 1953
Kate Mitchell, 1629
Steven Peterson, 1845
Kenneth Petrilla, 475
Robin Praeger, 1930
Richard Stubblefield, 1122
Henry Wong, 613, 810

Goldey Beacom College
Anna May L Trala, 889

Gonzaga University
Sean Cunningham, 765
Bridget Storm, 1001

Graduate School of Mgmt, Koblenz
Boriz Wertz, 2272

Grand Valley State University
Mike DeVries, 652
Turner Novak, 814
Mark Olesnavage, 946

Graziadio School of Business & Mngm
Greg Bettinelli, 1890

Grenoble Institute of Technology
Ludovic André, 2082

Grinnell College
Siddharth Srivastava, 2183

Grove City College
Sean Ammirati, 275
Jennifer E. Parulo, 55

Gubkin State University
Marat Mukhamedyarov, 2132

Gujarat University
Gary Gauba, 575

Gustavus Adolphus College
Mik Gusenius, 466
George G. Hicks, 1909
Jeff Miller, 1413
Marcia L. Page, 1909

HAAS School of Business
Tim Heston, 258

HEC
Pierre-Olivier Lamoureux, 848

HEC - Paris
Ludovic André, 2082

HEC Lausanne
Robert Fenwick-Smith, 147

HEC Montreal
Marie-Claude Boisvert, 2076
Charles Emond, 2064
André Gauthier, 2252
Jean-Francois Le Ruyet, 1519
Philippe Leroux, 2251
Genevieve Morin, 2113

Claude Vachet, 2087

HEC Paris
Nicolas Massard, 20
Eamonn McConnell, 2160

Haas School of Business
Gavin Bates, 377
Jeffrey M. Calhoun, 1779
Gary Coover, 1614
Melissa Daniels, 1255
Keval Desai, 1014
Gary Dillabough, 1281
Andy Donner, 1442
John Dougery, 1017
Danny Jaffe, 127
Jed Katz, 1032
Carlos Kokron, 1511
Steve Kuo, 928
Brian D Martin, 1906
Jim Pettit, 1281
Arun Ramamoorthy, 1449
Manu Rekhi, 1017
Steve Schuman, 900
Kirill Sheynkman, 1598
Thorne Sparkman, 1695
Daniel K Turner III, 1251
Andrew Williamson PhD, 1442

Hahnemann University
Matthew Naythons MD, 164

Haifa University
Michal Silverberg, 1350

Hamilton College
Andrew D. Barous, 1300
Bob Delaney, 560
Richard T Dell'Aquila, 356
Edward I Dresner, 646
Donald R Kendall Jr, 1067
Kevin Kester, 1681
Robert Kuhling, 1379
Woody Marshall, 1787
Rob Morris, 1372
James O'Mara, 1986
Geoffrey S. Oblak, 180
Arthur Rogers, 153
Philip Sanderson, 3273
Jason Schwarz, 1989
Thomas W Scozzafava, 1642
Harry D Taylor, 1778
Baran Tekkora, 1577

Hampden-Sydney College
Matthew E Gormly III, 1984
Robert M. Stewart, 1730

Hampshire College
Jeff Davison, 993

Hampton University
Edwin Shirley, 715

Hanover College
Michael Miller, 445

Harding University
Michael Blue, 1484

Hartford University
Jerome Nycz, 2048

Hartwick College
Richard W. Gaenzle Jr., 831
Stephen Rossetter, 450

College/University Index / Harvard Business School

Harvard Business
AT Gimble, 191

Harvard Business School
Todd M. Abbrecht, 1818
Kenneth S Abramowitz, 1325
Andrew Abrams, 1302
Jenny Abramson, 1555
Robert W Ackerman, 1963
Charles E Adair, 539
Samantha A. Adams, 257
Ajay Agarwal, 224
Neeraj Agrawal, 238
Payal Agrawal Divakaran, 1
Garrick Ahn, 376
Adel A Alderbas, 1952
Dmitry Alimov, 795
Chris Allen, 1404
Zaid F Alsikafi, 1160
Mark M. Anderson, 889
Frank Angella, 884
Brion B Applegate, 1720
Joe Aragona, 205
Thomas W. Arenz, 917
David Aronoff, 756
Zaid Ashai, 1463
Lindsay Aspegren, 1337
Dennis Atkinson, 691
Stuart A. Auerbach, 119
Chip Austin, 967
Merrick Axel, 559
Charles F Baird Jr, 1336
John Baker, 226
Jeffrey L Balash, 529
Thomas J. Baldwin, 357
Perry O. Ballard, 751
Michael Balmuth, 1764
Michael Barach, 994
Paul Barber, 1045
Hayley Barna, 742
Gregory M Barr, 1686
Peter Barrett, 193
Thomas C. Barry, 2017
Upal Basu, 1331
Rajeev Batra, 1187
Len Batterson, 237
Richard Bauerly, 855
David William Baum, 1737
Dan Baum, 2236
Josh Bekenstein, 223
Michael A. Bell, 1818
Kent Bennett, 263
Scott Benson, 1315
Erik Benson, 1947
Michael S Berk, 1778
Chaz Bertrand, 332
Neal Bhadkamkar, 1249
Matt Bigge, 564
Peter Binas, 1630
Kate Bingham, 1631, 1764
Hubert Birner, 2268
Pete Blackshaw, 482
Len Blavatnik, 33
Rick Bolander, 657, 808
John Borchers, 556
David C. Bordeau, 257
Philip Borden, 809
Simita Bose, 1348
Leslie Bottorff, 812
Martin Brand, 280
Greg Brenneman, 435
Peter C Brockway, 351
Jeff Brodlieb, 450
Matthew Bronfman, 41
John Brooke, 353
Kenneth Brotman, 45
Sonya Brown, 1346
Terry Brubaker, 832
Kurt A. Brumme, 1419
Lee Bryan, 530
Charles A Bryan, 1424
Adam Bryant, 648
Roberto Buaron, 734
Bernie Buonanno, 1278
Bill Burgess, 22
David Burgstahler, 212
John Burke, 1485
James J. Burke Jr., 1027
Christopher M. Busby, 862
Jeffrey Bussgang, 756
Jon Callaghan, 1862
Joe Canavan, 2193
Sean Cantwell, 1944
Thomas J Caracciolo, 633
Paul Carbone, 1482
James C. Carlisle, 1818
Roger Carolin, 1636
Andrew Carragher, 639
Chris C Casciato, 1127
John K. Castle, 425
Todd C. Chaffee, 1006
Victor Chaltiel, 1535
James Cham, 287
J. Russell Chapman, 174
Drew Chen, 223
Jerry Chen, 877
Neil Chheda, 1585
Eric Chin, 564
Hoon Cho, 828
Arjun Chopra, 752
Tony Christianson, 466
Nelson Chu, 1076
Jeff Chung, 108
Young Chung, 582
Patrick Chung, 709
Tom Clark, 530
Ryan Clark, 823
Miles Clements, 27
J Michael Cline, 38
Ed Cluss, 1680
David Coats, 545
Steve A Cobb, 480
Jay Cohan, 1976
Ira D Cohen, 1888
David M Coit, 1334
Jeffrey J Collinson, 476
Stuart Collinson, 772
R. Craig Collister, 1594
Mark M Colodny, 1957
John Connaughton, 223
William C Connell, 934
Tim Connor, 1656
Wayne Cooper, 868
Dennis B Costello, 1849
McCall Cravens, 960
Andrew Crawford, 819
Glenn M. Creamer, 1498
Bryan Cressey, 559
Gary Crittenden, 962
David D Croll, 1157
Allan Crosbie, 2083
Chris J. Crosby, 1278
Matthew Cross, 2160
Bob Cummings, 1990
Chip Cureton, 893
James Currier, 1323
Daniel A D'Aniello, 416
Scott A. Dahnke, 1092
Anupam Dalal MD, 1063
Andy Dale, 1250
John E Dancewicz, 620
John G Danhakl, 1113
Roanne Daniels, 927
Stuart Davidson, 1093
Timothy C Davis, 789
Michael B. DeFlorio, 917
Mark DeNino, 1830
Thompson Dean, 212
Christopher J Dean, 1754
Michael Dearing, 914
Gerard A Debiasi, 1075
Michael W Dees, 1133
Joe Del Guercio, 510
Bob Delaney, 560
Thanasis Delistathis, 1290, 1485
Sasha Dichter, 54
Jorge Dickens, 45
Chun Ding, 474
Andrew C. Dodson, 1419
Elias Dokas, 1231
Adam B. Dolder, 864
Michael J. Dominguez, 1498
Mark Dorman, 674
Edith Dorsen, 2003
Brian Dovey, 622
Jere Doyle, 1675
Tim Draper, 627
Timothy Draper, 2020
William H Draper III, 628
Samuel L. Duboc, 2098
Kevin Dunwoodie, 1413
Greg Durst, 3256
Anne Dwane, 1935
Tom Eddy, 1031
Patrick Edeburn, 855
Donald J. Edwards, 751
Jamie E Elias, 1859
Michael G. Eliasek, 1493
Qian W. Elmore, 973
James L. Elrod Jr., 1933
Juan Enriquez, 704
Martin Escobari, 819
Neil Exter, 1814
Bruce F Failing, 80
Henrik Falktoft, 1518
Michael Farah, 1132
Michael J. Farello, 1092
Karim Faris, 894
Brad Farkas, 967
Jim Farrell, 371
Mike Farrell, 1720
Deborah A Farrington, 1741
Brandon Farwell, 709
Jesse Feldman, 238
Robert Fenwick-Smith, 147
John Fife, 472
Robert Finkel, 1481
David A Fiorentino, 1053
Mark L. First, 687
Michael T. Fitzgerald, 523
John W. Flanigan, 463
Raluca Florea, 335
Brian Flynn, 775
Tom Flynn, 1764
Norman A. Fogelsong, 1006
David I. Foley, 280
Todd Foley, 1268
Jennifer Fonstad, 182
Bob Forlenza, 1731
Frank Foster, 794
Frank H Foster, 830
Michael J. Fourticq Sr., 905
David Frankel, 774
Will Franklin, 1129
Robert Fraser, 203
Kris Fredrickson, 511
John F Freund, 1693
Scott Friend, 224
Dean Frost, 256
Eric T Fry, 1133
Max Gazor, 457

College/University Index / Harvard Business School

Bob Geiman, 433
Scott Gibaratz, 920
Jim Gilbert, 748
Steven J. Gilbert, 831
Marc A. Gineris, 986
Jonathan Ginns, 45
David Gladstone, 832
Rob Go, 1322
Roger Goddu, 337
David L Gold, 362
Marc Goldberg, 273
William J Golden, 1096
Andy Goldfarb, 839
Amir Goldman, 1761
Johnathan M Goldstein, 1778
Brian P Golson, 1419
Lawrence E. Golub, 848
Peter D Goodson, 632
Brian Gorczynski, 1927
Chris Gordon, 223
Benjamin Gordon, 383
Matt Gorin, 535
Maria Gotsch, 1422
Blake L. Gottesman, 257
Greg Gottesman, 1501
Drew Graham, 227
Christopher D. Graham, 1742
McComma Grayson III, 912
Michael Greeley, 749
Myles D Greenberg, 476
Michael Greene, 65
Phil Greer, 1382
Rick Grinnell, 713, 833
David Gross-Loh, 223
Jay Grossman, 20
H. Irving Grousbeck, 952
Harry Gruner, 1045
Alex Gruzen, 546
Arun Gupta, 518
Leo Guthart, 1834
Perry Ha, 627
Oliver Haarmaan, 2243
Thomas M. Hagerty, 1818
H H Haight, 163
Lawrence S. Hamelsky, 257
Mamoon Hamid, 1079
Philip Hammarskjold, 927
Leonard M. Harlan, 425
Steve Harrick, 1006
Hendrik J. Hartong III, 360
Hendrik J. Hartong, Jr., 360
Jay Hass, 1597
John Hawkins, 822
Frank J Hawley Jr, 1627
John G. Hayes, 862
Randy Haykin, 1390
Chip Hazard, 756
Ned Hazen, 1122
Robert P Healy, 470
Patrick Healy, 927
Donald B. Hebb, Jr., 21
Tom Hedrick, 1946
Rick Heitzmann, 744
Christopher R Hemmeter, 1808
Ted Henderson, 1630
Patrick Heron, 785
Brian Hersman, 1045
E David Hetz, 573
Tom Hickey, 1507
John B Higginbotham, 1717
Mark G. Hilderbrand, 952
Todd Hixon, 1290
James S. Hoch, 1779
Steve Hochberg, 179
Benjamin A Hochberg, 1108
Don Hofmann, 566
Jeffrey J Holland, 1639

David Horing, 111
Zachary Hornby, 489
Jim Hornthal, 194
Camilo E. Horvilleur, 931
Bob Howe, 8
Paul Hsiao, 399
Michael Hsieh, 799
Geoffrey C. Hsu, 1383
Eion Hu, 1049
Edward Huang, 280
William S. Hughes, 1498
Gregory Hulecki, 712
Tom Hulme, 894
Wende Hutton, 389
Tony Ignaczak, 1507
Robert M Jaffe, 1708
Thomas Janes, 1071
Jeffrey R. Jay, MD, 864
Mark Jennings, 822
Jeffrey Johnson, 279
Jeffrey W. Johnson, 831
Brent P Johnstone, 1513
Terry L. Jones, 1773
Reginald L. Jones III, 867
TJ Jubeir, 409
Roger B Kafker, 1778
Samantha Kaminsky, 553
Deepak Kamra, 389
Edward W Kane, 912
Thomas Kaneb, 2186
Julia Karol, 1963
Joseph R Katcha, 935
Samir Kaul, 1073
Patrick Keefe, 2063
Brian P Kelley, 1133
Peter Kellner, 1564
Thomas L. Kelly II, 463
William C. Kessinger, 1419
Trevor Kienzle, 545
Yoo Jin Kim, 1108
Chris Kitching, 936
Ronald J. Klammer, 1369
Stephan Klee, 2217
Adam Klein, 560
Michael I Klein, 1138
Lewis S. Klessel, 1300
Josh Klinefelter, 202
Steven B Klinsky, 1300
Ailliam Knoke, 916
Laurie G. Kolbeins, 1801
James Kondo, 824
Stephen Kraus, 263
Marlene R. Krauss, 1062
Dave Kreter, 828
Arvind Krishnamurthy, 1226
Jennifer Krusius, 518
Robert Kuhling, 1379
Ethan Kurzweil, 263
Farouk Ladha, 780
Christopher M Laitala, 1133
Kevin M. Lalande, 1622
Rachel Lam, 981
David Lane, 1379
Michael S Langdon, 792
Gregory G Lau, 1973
Tom Lavin, 1302
Rich Lawson, 962
Matthew Laycock, 202
Laurence Lederer, 330
Peter Lee, 231
Kewsong Lee, 416
Aileen Lee, 553
Peter Lee, 664
Chris Legg, 1488
Paul Lehman, 1026
Dan Levitan, 1186
Legrand Lewis, 1707

Rick Lewis, 1898
Frank Linsalata, 1136
Peter Lipson, 912
C. Malcolm Little, 167
Simon Lonergan, 248
Greg Long, 1169
Ian Loring, 223
Phil Loughlin, 223
Daniel C Lubin, 1523
Joshua A. Lutzker, 257
Christopher W. Lynch, 180
Joe Machado, 1266
Robert W Macleod, 1199
Paul Maeder, 938
John Maldonado, 61
Elliot Maluth, 931
Sulu Mamdani, 1766
Peter M. Manos, 167
John Mapes, 202
Mike Maples Jr., 752
Paul Margolis, 1150
Michael Marino, 203
Roger Marrero, 530
Kim Marvin, 110
Alex Mason, 419
Christopher Masto, 790
Michael Matly, MD, 1251
Alan Mattamana, 715
Gary S Matthews, 1256
Rob May, 1463
John A. (Tony) Mayer, 707
Steve McConahey, 1024
Douglas McCormick, 920
Burton McGillivray, 507
Terry McGuire, 1464
Dale McIvor, 1714
Jeffrey McKibben, 1368
Marc McManus, 491
John C McNamara II, 1148
Scott Meadow, 654
Seth Meisel, 280
Prakash A. Melwani, 280
Samuel M Mencoff, 1160
Frances Messano, 1315
Lloyd M. Metz, 973
Alex Meyer, 1385
Gerald A. Michaud, 949
Fred A Middleton, 1222, 1619
Constantine S. Mihas, 889
Ron Mika, 1707
Brian C Miller, 1132
W Scott Miller, 1152
Marlin Miller, 1347
Cory D. Mims, 973
Sami Mnaymneh, 931
Lee J. Monahan, 913
H. DuBose Montgomery, 1203
Michael C Morgan, 1848
Frederic H. Morris, 352
Mark J Morrissette, 1334
Allen S Moseley, 1332
David Motley, 301
Andre V. Moura, 1300
Terrence Mullen, 172
Corey Mulloy, 938
Jennifer M Mulloy, 1778
Kevin A. Mundt, 1933
Dave Munichiello, 894
Tom Murphy, 560
Dr. Campbell Murray, 1350
Sunil Nagaraj, 1879
Ajit Nedungadi, 1778
Jonathan M. Nelson, 1498
Joshua M. Nelson, 1818
Denis Newman, 1230
Ha Nguyen, 1724
Carl Nichols, 1390

College/University Index / Harvard College

Joseph M. Niehaus, 952
David W. Niemiec, 1624
John Nies, 1044
Charles E. Noell, 1045
A. Bilal Noor, 167
Daniel Nova, 938
Carl Novotny, 1922
Ben Nye, 224
Soren L. Oberg, 1818
Jonathan T. Oka, 751
Nnamdi Okike, 12
Meghan Otis, 1965
Stephen Pagliuca, 223
Eric Paley, 774
Gilbert S. Palter, 2098
Greg J. Pappas, 257
Scott G Pasquini, 1160
Jon Pastor, 301
Marni F. Payne, 257
Marshall Payne, 479
James A. Pelusi, 214
Kevin S Penn, 41
Kevin Penn, 111
Scott B. Perper, 1410
Justin J. Perreault, 523
William Perry, 992
Paul Peterson, 1990
Scott Petty, 1679
M Troy Phillips, 247
Joshua S. Phillips, 428
Charles G. Phillips, IV, 1624
Vincente Piedrahita, 1818
Barbara Piette, 1081
Randall E. Poliner, 132
Scott Pressly, 274
Diana Propper de Callejon, 707
Steven Puccinelli, 1360
Robert Puopolo, 688
Arvind Purushotham, 488
Mitchell Quain, 41
Jeffrey K. Quake, 741
William Quigley, 504
Ali Rahimtula, 568
Jill C. Raker, 867
Geoffrey S. Raker, 1779
Michael Ramich, 793
Lee Rand, 1756
Zeena Rao, 973
Ganesh B. Rao, 1818
Jason Reed, 1997
Corby Reese, 1769
Roland Reynolds, 990
Matt Rice, 227
Andrew Richards, 1769
Anders Richardson, 1403
William T. Richter, 453
Randy O. Rissman, 1112
Collin E. Roche, 889
Steven C Rodger, 692
Jesse Rogers, 96
Alex Rogers, 912
Rafael Romero, 668
Jonathan Roosevelt, 990
Jim Rorer, 1466
Rick Rosen, 931
Micah Rosenbloom, 774
Jason Rottenberg, 173
Joshua Ruch, 1561
Atul Rustgi, 36
Joseph A. Saldutti Jr., 878
Wayne Sales, 985
Anthony Salewski, 823
Maninder Saluja, 1518
David G. Samuel, 2056
Camille Samuels, 1918
Philip Sanderson, 3273
Julie Sandler, 1501

Aaron Sandoski, 1347
Carmen Scarpa, 1731
Doug Schillinger, 639
Cas Schneller, 790
Brian D. Schwartz, 931
Gerry Schwartz, 2201
Stephen A. Schwarzman, 280
Conner Searcy, 1858
Jon Seeber, 1888
Alan G. Sellery, 2156
Kristina Serafim, 1928
Rudina Seseri, 713, 833
Dana Settle, 876
Andrew Sheiner, 2030
Rob Sherman, 315
Jack Shields, 313
Raleigh A. Shoemaker, Jr., 257
John Siegel, 518
George W. Siguler, 1681
Eric H. Sillman, 137
George L Sing, 1096
Karl Slatoff, 2019
Alex Slusky, 1912
Robert J. Small, 257
Jed Smith, 430
Stephen K Smith, 1178
Scott L. Snow, 747
Christopher Sobecki, 1022
Edward P Sobol, 1973
James Socas, 1888
Erica S. Son, 167
Lawrence B. Sorrel, 1779
Holden Spaht, 1817
Mike Speiser, 1762
Jeb S Spencer, 1871
Scott M. Sperling, 1818
Samuel W. Spirn, 257
Scott Stanford, 44
Ira Starr, 1145
Christopher Staudt, 668
Martin Stein, 279
Gregory Stento, 912
James A. Stern, 576
Barry S. Sternlicht, 1742
Todd Stevens, 1545
Lawrence Stevenson, 2076
E Jack Stewart, 1922
Gordon Stofer, 466
Rick Stowe, 921
Christian R Strain, 1754
Ned Stringham, 8
Santi Subotovsky, 666
Somu Subramaniam, 1302
Matt Sullivan, 1425
Ryan Sweeney, 27
Jeff T. Swenson, 1818
Peter Taft, 1266
Dave Tamburri, 921
Tony Tamer, 931
Jo Tango, 1069
Thomas M Tarnowski, 1754
Jake Tarr Jr., 1076
Harry D Taylor, 1778
Jeffrey J Teschke, 1053
David Teten, 724
Michael G. Thonis, 458
Allen Thorpe, 927
Ethan Thurow, 371
Robert M Tichio, 1577
Paul E. Tierney Jr., 137
Andrew B. Tindel, 1410
Tony Tjan, 568
David Tolmie, 654
David B Tom, 1910
Graves Tompkins, 819
John Toomey Jr., 912
John Trbovich, 173

Victoria Treyger, 720
Mitch Truwit, 136
Tenno Tsai, 931
Jim Tullis, 1868
David Tunnell, 927
James Tybur, 1434
Matthew T. Vettel, 862
Tefan Vitorovic, 1934
Andrew Vogel, 2019
Barry Volpert, 560
James F Wade, 1157
Eliot Wadsworth II, 952
Peter Wagner, 1996
Rob Walsh, 1772
Mike Ward, 1517
Jermaine L. Warren, 973
Alex Washington, 1990
Frank Z Wei, 1957
John Weinberg, 700
Michael Weingarten, 1678
Gregory M Weinhoff MD, 476
Kent R. Weldon, 1818
Richard Wells, 1005
Scott Werry, 2030
Ted West, 775
Casey West, 1735
Forest Wester, 1859
Victor Westerlind, 812
Edward J. Whelan, 257
Gregory A. White, 1818
Peter O. Wilde, 1498
Mark N. Williamson, 371
Elizabeth C Williamson, 792
Andrew Wilson, 203
Peter Wilson, 912
Stoddard M Wilson, 1583
Rob Wolfson, 931
Marc Wolpow, 197
Raymond L.M. Wong, 1733
Willie E. Woods Jr., 973
Christopher G. Wright, 557
Ravi Yadav, 1314
Chris Yeh, 1959
Krishna Yeshwant, 894
Matt Yohe, 1266
Gwill York, 1122
Glenn A Youngkin, 416
Royce G. Yudkoff, 20
Guy Zaczepinski, 451
Jeff Zanarini, 931
Strauss Zelnick, 2019
Wan Li Zhu, 713
Eric Zinterhofer, 2243
Adriaan Zur Muhlen, 1488
Anthony J de Nicola, 1973
Carlo A. von Schroeter, 1979
Johan von der Goltz, 313

Harvard College
Samantha A. Adams, 257
Charles F Baird Jr, 1336
Ben Ball, 782
Michael S Berk, 1778
Darren M Black, 1754
Peter Brooke, 353
John Brooke, 353
John Caddedu, 582
Brian Cassidy, 560
Caley Castelein MD, 1063
Michael Chae, 280
Anna H. Chen, PhD, 785
Larry Cheng, 1944
Young Chung, 582
Patrick Chung, 709
Ryan Clark, 823
Robert Clark Jr, 362
Andy Dale, 1250

Michael W Dees, 1133
Paul Desmarais III, 2090, 2217
David Dominik, 843
Daniel K Doyle, 1772
Alex Earls, 886
Martin Escobari, 819
Jeffrey A. Ferrell, 190
Andy Fillat, 1106
Christopher Finn, 416
John Fisher, 610
William Fitzgerald, 1991
Kobie Fuller, 1890
Neil Garfinkel, 782
Andrew Garman, 1304
James Gellert, 1991
Michael Gellert, 1991
Michael Gladstone, 193
Andy Goldfarb, 839
David Golob, 782
David B. Golub, 848
Chris Gordon, 223
Nicholas Green, 1103
Leo Guthart, 1834
John Hamel, 568
Robert M. Hannon, 1826
Kenneth Hao, 1685
Benjamin A Hochberg, 1108
Matthew S. Holt, 1300
Bob Horne, 2021
Greg Huff, 702
Jason Hurd, 362
David W. Jaffin, 324
Thomas Janes, 1071
Brent P Johnstone, 1513
Peter Kagan, 1957
Roger Kitterman, 1421
Adam Klein, 560
Blake Kleinman, 927
Jon Kossow, 1346
Arvind Krishnamurthy, 1226
A. Rachel Laheny, 1900
Christopher M Laitala, 1133
Mitch Lasky, 251
Gregory G Lau, 1973
Kewsong Lee, 416
Thomas H Lee, 1108
Jeffrey Lee, 1340
Oliver Libby, 1689
Jonathan E. Lim, MD, 489
Robert D Lindsay, 1133
David Lippin, 1376
Michael H. Lustbader, 167
Sulu Mamdani, 1766
Benjamin Mao, 1085
Tom Mawhinney, 972
Kevin M. McCafferty, 428
Aevin M McCafferty, 1295
Scott McCormack, 1641
Burton McGillivray, 507
Ryan McNally, 429
Scott Meadow, 654
Frances Messano, 1315
Jonathan Miller, 59
Jeb Miller, 972
Lawrence G Miller, MD, 1198
Antonio Miranda, 1138
Lawrence Mock, 1279
John Moon, 1256
Andre V. Moura, 1300
Michael Mullany, 972
John J Nowaczyk, 1234
Ben Nye, 224
Soren L. Oberg, 1818
Joe Osnoss, 1685
Robert Porell, 813
Bill Reichert, 721
Jon Rezneck, 824

Anders Richardson, 1403
William L. Richter, 453
Jonathan Roosevelt, 990
Alex Rose, 560
Charles E. Ryan, 89
Anthony Salewski, 823
Greg Sands, 548
Bob Shapiro, 571
Robert Shapiro, 1618
Carlyle Singer, 54
Dick Spalding, 1063
Samuel W. Spirn, 257
Scott Stanford, 44
Jonathan A. Stein, 547
Howard Steyn, 1092
Laela Sturdy, 579
Sam Teller, 1103
Tony Tjan, 568
Catherine Ulrich, 744
Peter Wagner, 1996
Peter Wallace, 280
Albert Wenger, 1884
James Westra, 61
Kevin Zhang, 1889
Max von Zuben, 1984

Harvard Divinity School
Jason Allen, 1175

Harvard Graduate School
Anthony J. DiNovi, 1818
Steven E Karol, 1963
Peter Roshko, 318
Harold R. Werner, 922

Harvard Graduate School of Business
Jean-Pierre L. Conte, 823
Leslie M Corley, 1141
Steve Crihfield, 903
Paul J Finnegan, 1160
Brian Fitzgerald, 404
Fred Harman, 1361
Stephen Holmes, 1014
Vikrant Raina, 364
George Sarlo, 1953
R. Scott Schafler, 547
Brian E Stern, 1738
Steve Tomlin, 209
Nicolas D. Zerbib, 1746

Harvard Kennedy School
Jeremy G. Philips, 1718
Graves Tompkins, 819

Harvard Law School
Kevin Baker, 371
Jeffrey L Balash, 529
Andrew Banks, 20
Michael Barach, 994
John F. Barry III, 1493
Skip Baum, 1107
Michael S Berk, 1778
Jordan S. Bernstein, 478
William Bianco, 1620
Peter Binas, 1630
David Bonderman, 1837
Michael Borrus, 2010
Bruce C. Bruckmann, 357
Victor Budnick, 1025
Patrick Chung, 709
Scott C Collins, 1754
Ed Colloton, 263
Mark M Colodny, 1957
Bryan Cressey, 559
David Dominik, 843
Douglas M. Dunnan, 880
Bill Elkus, 504

Robert C Embry Jr, 18
Steve Engelberg, 1618
Alv Epstein, 1745
John F. Erhard, 157
Norman A. Fogelsong, 1006
Tully M. Friedman, 790
Francisco Garcia, 644
Steven J. Gilbert, 831
David Golden, 1558
Richard Goldstein, 64
Lawrence E. Golub, 848
Greg Gottesman, 1501
Donald B. Hebb, Jr., 21
Shar Heslam, 257
Jeff Hinck, 1525
David Hornik, 200
Richard M Horowitz, 1524
David Jegen, 711
Craig A.T. Jones, 1826
Michael S Kaye, 503
Justin Klein, 1919
Steven B Klinsky, 1300
Jeffrey T Leeds, 1109
Andrew McLaughlin, 937
Sami Mnaymneh, 931
Nnamdi Okike, 12
Travis Pearson, 828
Leigh Randall, 1834
Edward Reitler, 151
Murray E Rudin, 1579
John E Runnells, 1931
John H. Simpson, 346
Rick Smith, 562
Lawrence B. Sorrel, 1779
Thomas S Souleles, 1160
Yanev Suissa, 1689
Sanjay Swani, 1779
Matthew E. Swanson, 1567
Barry Volpert, 560
Marc Wolpow, 197
Strauss Zelnick, 2019

Harvard Medical School
Eric Aguitar, MD, 73
David Berry, 748
Kevin Bitterman, PhD, 193
Casey Cunningham, MD, 1622
James Eadie, MD, 1622
John F Freund, 1693
Sen. William H. Frist, MD, 559
David Grayzel, MD, 193
David Hirsch MD, PhD, 1147
Geoffrey C. Hsu, 1383
Marlene R. Krauss, 1062
Andrew Levin, 1522
Lawrence G Miller, MD, 1198
James Nelson MD, 1007
Dr. Boris Nikolic, 271
Kush M Parmar, MD, PhD, 11
David Schnell MD, 1495
David A Shaywitz, 1780
Robert Tepper, MD, 1814
Gregory M Weinhoff MD, 476
Christoph Westphal, 1149
Krishna Yeshwant, 894
Brett Zbar, 764

Harvard School of Business
Vahe A Dombalagian, 1160
Douglas C Grissom, 1160
David Mace, 828
Thomas S Souleles, 1160

Harvard University
Frank A. Adams, 881
Adzmel Adznan, 1453
William F Aikman, 887

College/University Index / Harvard University

Mohammed Alardhi, 1021
Thomas A Alberg, 1162
Dave Ament, 1419
David L Anderson, 1762
Matt Anderson, 1977
Dan Aquilano, 86
Joe Aragona, 205
Peter Arrowsmith, 1045
Jonathan Axelrod, 685
Roy Bahat, 287
John Baker, 226
Manuel Jose Balbontin, 524
Steven Baloff, 58
Jonathan P Barnes, 902
Doug Barry, 1649
Richard Bauerly, 855
David Becker, 1196
Gregory C. Belmont, 852
Hazem Ben-Gacem, 1021
R David Bergonia, 1333
Betsy Biemann, 440
Peter Binas, 1630
Jason Black, 1597
Peter Blacklow, 316
Stephen Bloch, 389
David J. Blumberg, 304
James J. Bochnowski, 605
Zachary Bogue, 586
Gaye Bok, 704
Ralph Booth, 762
Steve Bowsher, 983
Richard Bradlow, 2211
Sayles Braga, 80
Jim Breyer, 339
Bruce C. Bruckmann, 357
Ethan A. Budin, 751
Ian Bund, 1459
Sylvester Burley, 335
Richard Burnes, 457
Luke Burns, 180
Jeffrey Bussgang, 756
Thomas R Callahan, 1131
Joseph Carrabino, Jr., 63
J. Ryan Carroll, 458
Tom Cervantez, 31
Jeffrey T Chambers, 1778
John F Chappell, 1456
Jean-Marc Chapus, 557
Chris Cheever, 762
Anna H. Chen, PhD, 785
Julian Cheng, 1957
Michael Choe, 458
Iris Choi, 752
Ben Choi, 1110
Scott Chou, 657, 808
Peter Y Chung, 1754
John Clarke, 413
Hugh Cleland, 2234
James D Coady, 1654
Ross Cockrell, 696
Scott C Collins, 1754
Mark M Colodny, 1957
David Cowan, 263
Alan Crane, 1464
Catherine Crockett, 884
John Crumpler, 918
Gary Cuccio, 1795
Richard A D'Amore, 1335
Robert R. Davenport III, 343
Stuart Davidson, 1093
Kim G. Davis, 458
Ken DeAngelis, 205
Donald F. DeMuth, 611
Lawson DeVries, 881
Satish Dharmaraj, 1537
Anthony J. DiNovi, 1818
Sasha Dichter, 54

Jonathan E Dick, 1480
Jeffrey Diehl, 56
A. Barr Dolan, 460
Timothy Draper, 610
Ted Driscoll, PhD, 493
William Dunbar, 540
Philip Eliot, 1401
Stuart Ellman, 1597
Dr. Edgar G Engleman, 1943
Juan Enriquez, 704
Hugh D. Evans, 1927
Patrick Fallon, 28
Brad Farkas, 967
Andrew Farquharson, 984
Brian Feinstein, 263
Dean E Fenton, 1738
Mark Fernandes, 1672
Paul J Finnegan, 1160
Daniel T Fleming, 1575
Mark Follows, 2066
Frank Foster, 794
Frank H Foster, 830
Constance Freedman, 1246
Bradford M. Freeman, 786
Mason Freeman MD, 11
John F Freund, 1693
Samuel P Frieder, 1085
Alexander A. Friend, 791
Francisco Garcia, 644
Luis E Garcia Garcia de Brigard, 142
Bob Gay, 962
Aaron Gershenberg, 1766
Flip Gianos, 1014
Michael W Gibbons, 714
Douglas H. Gilbert, 611
Walter Gilbert, PhD, 273
Tehinder Gill, 514
Jim Glasheen, 1788
Charles E. Glew, Jr., 751
Kim P. Goh, 957
Marc Goldberg, 273
Michelle Goldberg, 978
David Golden, 1558
Greg S Goldfarb, 1754
Lawrence E. Golub, 848
James J Goodman, 815
Carl L. Gordon PhD, 1383
Michael Gorman, 1728
John Patrick Grayken, 1144
Bruns Grayson, 22
McComma Grayson III, 912
Jason Green, 666
Brad Greiwe, 728
Stewart KP Gross, 1127
Drew Guff, 1681
Eric Gulve PhD, 270
Sophie Hagerty, 849
William A. Hanna, 374
Felda Hardymon, 263
Drew Harman, 1014
Sam Hartwell, 204
John Hawkins, 822
Patrick Healy, 927
George J Henry, 1131
Scott Hilinski, 1278
Eva Ho, 729
Brian Hoesterey, 63
Daniel Hoffer, 207
Bob Hower, 58
Michael Hsieh, 799
Eion Hu, 1049
Dean Jacobson, 28
David Jaffe, 449
John Jaggers, 1661
Andrew S. Janower, 458
Michael Johnson, 60
John Johnston, 200

Nigel W Jones, 1875
John T. Kaden, 1282
Rebecca Kaden, 1884
Brian Kahn, 1937
JJ Kang, PhD, 519
Sharon Kedar, 1342
Pat Kenealy, 1566
James T. Kiernan, 2080
Philip Kim, 1131
John Kim, MD, 139
Charles F Kireker, 789
Jonathan I. Kislak, 132
Gil Kliman, 1014
Paul Klingenstein, 19
Robert B Knauss, 1957
Peter Kolchinsky, 1522
Mehmet Kosematoglu, 253
Roy Kosuge, 1773
Joshua Kushner, 1823
David Lane, 614
Lou Lange, MD, PhD, 183
Gerry Langeler, 1392
Andrew Laurence, 1937
Thong Q Le, 30
Troy LeMaile-Stovall, 1792
Lisa M. Lee, 1498
Eric J Lee, 1973
Steven A Leese, 1505
H Jeffrey Leonard, 838
Sam Lessin, 1696
Jimmy Levin, 1638
Ping Li, 27
Richard Lim, 1373
Alfred Lin, 1657
Jessica Lin, 2006
Gary Little, 399
Vernon Lobo, 2190
Rad Lovett, 1152
Jeff Low, 645
Vishal Lugani, 48
Michael J Lyons, 1131
Kenneth Mabbs, 712
William I MacDonald, 1107
Rob MacLellan, 2196
Nurzhas Makishev, 1330
Adam J Margolin, 1720
Dorothy Margolskee, 764
Arthur J Marks, 1901
James Marlas, 1883
Salvatore A Massaro, 656
Russ Mayerfeld, 88
Brendan McCafferty, 1295
Christopher McElhone, 2030
Thomas McKinley, 413
Kevin W McMurchy, 630
James E Meketa, 1201
Adrian Mendoza, 1202
David Michael, 134
David F Millet, 815
Charles Moldow, 773
John Moon, 1256
Scott Murphy, 60
Patricia Nakache, 1855
Kirk Nelson, 1919
James Nelson MD, 1007
Jennifer Keiser Neundorfer, 1030
Howard H Newman, 1447
David W. Niemiec, 1624
Tom Noonan, 1790
George D O'Neill, 1216
Nnamdi Okike, 12
Larry Orr, 1855
Mark Paris, 1896
Kush M Parmar, MD, PhD, 11
Robert Paulson, 66
Ezra Perlman, 782
Charles G. Phillips, IV, 1624

1007

College/University Index / Harvey Mudd College

Charles Phipps, 1661
Marguerite A Piret, 1311
John Piret, 1311
David B. Pittaway, 425
Mike Pongon, 1462
Will Porteous, 1597
Robert Puopolo, 688
Dennis Purcell, 73
Deborah Quazzo, 888
David P Quinlivan, 1608
Keith Rabois, 778
Eduardo Rallo, 327
Scott Raney, 1537
Bill Reichert, 810
Andrew Richards, 1769
Aaron Richmond, 674
James Riley, 2067
Steven Ritterbush, 1208
Bryan Roberts, 1918
James Robinson, 1597
James Robinson, III, 1597
Antonio Rodriguez, 1184
James LD Roser, 1590
Mike Ross, 1764
Michael Ross PhD, 1631
Steven J Rosston, 840
Michael Rubin, 1342
Amy Salzhauer McMarlin, 849
Jim Savage, 1150
Omar A Sawaf, 2012
Carmen Scarpa, 1731
Joseph L. Schocken, 349
Peter M. Schulte, 509
John Scull, 1713
Ben Sheridan, 292
Valerie J Sill, 637
Ed Sim, 308
John Simon, 1675
Andrew Singer, 676
Steven F. Skoler, 791
Alex Slusky, 1912
Robert A. Smith, 424
Thomas Smith, 1143
Stephen B Solomon MD, 573
Daniel Sonshine, 2264
Thorne Sparkman, 1695
Ronald P. Spogli, 786
Dimitri Steinberg, 775
Matthew E. Swanson, 1567
Steven R. Swartz, 925
Steven Swartzman, 367
Alan J Taetle, 1332
Gus Tai, 1855
Jim Tananbaum, 764
William N. Thorndike, 952
Clay B Thorp, 918
Ethan Thurow, 371
Esther Tian, 346
Keith Titan, 259
Dafina Toncheva, 1898
John Toomey Jr., 912
Timothy Tully, 1869
David Tunnell, 927
Adam Valkin, 820
Mark F Vassallo, 1127
Drew Volpe, 1486
John Vrionis, 1125
Robert Wadsworth, 912
Eliot Wadsworth II, 952
David Weiden, 1073
Sharon Weinbar, 1629
Ed Weinfurtner, 292
Gregory M Weinhoff MD, 476
Robert Weisskoff PhD, 711
Peter Wendell, 1672
Christoph Westphal, 1149
James N White, 1762

Greg Williams, 28
Edward C. Williams, III, 352
Kyle Winters, 2193
Daniel B. Wolfe, Ph.D, 5
Gordon H Woodward, 1085
Alfred S Woodworth Jr, 647
Gwill York, 1122
Brian D. Young, 687
Philip M Young, 1898
Janie Yu, 799
David Yuan, 1787
Kareem Zaki, 1823
Darshana Zaveri, 428

Harvey Mudd College
David A Krekel, 1399
Hodong Nam, 100
Jon Soberg, 1269

Haskayne School of Business
Jason Brooks, 2155
Allison M. Taylor, 2155
Jason White, 2159

Hastings College of Law
Tom Bevilacqua, 1908
Elliot B Evers, 1197

Haverford College
Phin Barnes, 742
Steven L. Begleiter, 751
Roger B Kafker, 1778
Brian C. McDaid, 1730
Dave Stubbs, 383

Heald Engineering
Bob Marshall, 1649

Hebrew University
Jonathan Klahr, 1761
Gideon Soesman, 2136

Hebrew University of Jerusalem
Hagai Barlev, 670

Helsinki University of Technology
Petri Vainno, MD, PhD, 698

Hendrix College
Todd McIntyre, 875

Henley Business School
Lorraine Audsley, 2106

Henley Management College
Dr. Markus Goebel, 1350
Charles Vaslet, 2101

Herbrew University of Jerusalem
Arie S. Belldegrun, 1934

Heriot-Watt University
Mark Bonnar, 1713
Alan MacIntosh, 50

Hillsdale College
John McIlwraith, 86

Hobart College
Jon Flint, 1464
David L Gold, 362
Daniel M Kortick, 1984
Terry McGuire, 1464
Benjamin M. Polk, 1927

Hofstra University
David Benyaminy, 196
Don Hofmann, 566

Michael P. Murphy, 1589
Joe Rubin, 151
John S Schnabel, 1377
Alyse Skidmore, 1336
Jermaine L. Warren, 973

Hollins College
Martha P.E. Arscott, 526

Holy Cross College
Christopher Colecchi, 350
John Dean, 942
Tom Flynn, 1764
Mary M Shannon, 1178

Hong Kong International Law School
Diana Saca, 682

Howard University
Cory D. Mims, 973
Laurence C. Morse PhD, 715
JoAnn H. Price, 715

Humber College
Fil Varino, 3249

Humboldt University
Rodger P Adams, 1911

Hunter College
Jeanette M Welsh JD, 1794

Huron University College
Matt Hall, 2081

IIT-Bombay
Shailesh Mehta, 856

INEAD
Andy Burgess, 2236

INSEAD
Nilanana Bhowmik, 536
Pavel Bogdanov, 89
Marie-Claude Boisvert, 2076
Roberto Buaron, 734
Eric Buatois, 252
Lionel Carnot, 240
Ilfryn Carstair, 1909
Andrew Cleland, 520
Ronan Cunningham, 1720
Paul Desmarais III, 2090, 2217
Sebastien Dhonte, 2075
Rutvik Doshi, 1017
Rupert Gerard, 893
David Gussarsky, 1125
Drew Harman, 1014
Francois Helou, 189
Carlos Heneine, 1518
Daniel Hullah, 812
Alan MacIntosh, 50
Marc Manasterski, 1518
Loudon Mclean Owen, 2191
Loudon Owen, 2147
James D.C. Pitt, 1116
Pal B Ristvedt, 1116
Subhanu Saxena, 1301
Corry J. Silbernagel, 2058
Andrew Sillitoe, 136
Raj Singh, 1039
Rick Stahl, 661
Alastair Tedford, 78
Merav Weinryb, 1511

Idaho State University
Hatch Graham, 185

College/University Index / Ivey Business School

Illinois Benedictine University
John M. Reher, 326

Illinois Institute of Technology
Bob Bode, 1026
Daniel Norr, 206
Marc Sokol, 754
Andrew A Thomas, 1747

Imeperial College London
Raj Singh, 1039

Imperial College
Nick Adams, 108
Pietro Dova, 2009

Imperial College London
Upal Basu, 1331
Will Honeybourne, 741
Mohit Kaushal MD, 19

Imperial College of Science
Oded Ben-Joseph PhD, 1389

Indian Institute of Management
Parag Dhol, 1017
Ashu Garg, 773
Vishal Gupta, 263
Amit Gupta, 506
Hemant Khatwani, 691
Samir Kumar, 1017

Indian Institute of Technology
Neal Bhadkamkar, 1249
Parag Dhol, 1017
Rutvik Doshi, 1017
Ashu Garg, 773
Ramneek Gupta, 488
Amit Gupta, 506
Kiran Hebbar, 1901
Uttam Jain, 190
Krishnamurty Kambhampati, 507
Rishi Kapoor, 1021
Vinod Khosla, 1073
Samir Kumar, 1017
Sundeep Peechu, 720
Arvind Purushotham, 488
Ramesh Radhakrishnan, 176
Arun Ramamoorthy, 1449
Kanwal Rekhi, 1017
Shrikant Sathe, 1913
Parag Saxena, 1913
Bipul Sinha, 1125
Amit Srivastava, 683
Somu Subramaniam, 1302

Indian School of Business
Aditya Arora, 838
Alipt Sharma, 838

Indiana State University
Brad Muse, 70

Indiana University
Farraz Abassi, 445
Jack K Ahrens II, 1804
Jeff Akers, 56
Laura Albrecht, 1169
Blake Austin, 1026
Roger D Bailey, 607
Brian Bastedo, 1582
David L. Belzer, 1493
Julie A Bender, 792
Julian L Carr, 247
John M. Carsello, 904
John Chambers, 1035
Chris Christoffersen PhD, 1126
Tony Conrad, 1862
Thomas P. Cooper, MD, 137
Curtis D Crocker, 1547
Omar Diaz, 630
John W Doerer, 1465
Scott Dorsey, 932
Rajat Duggal, 790
Christopher M. Eline, 904
Jim Farnsworth, 2044
Kathy Fields, 1045
Michael E Flannery, 634
Michael Gallagher, 931
Ting Gootee, 659
James B Hoover, 588
Sumeet Jaisinghani, 1602
David Jegen, 711
J Allan Kayler, 1232
Daniel Kessler, 578
Ted H. Kramer, 904
David Krane, 894
Suzanne Kriscunas, 1576
Jim Lim, 872
Rebecca Luse, 1297
Scott Lutzke, 445
Florence J. Mauchant, 956
Mark Maybell, 645
Bart A McLean, 1270
Dr Evan Melrose, 1725
Craig Overmyer, 947
Brent L Paris, 633
David E Pequet, 1160
Luke A. Phenicie, 904
Champ Raju, 1471
Andy Reed, 319
Douglas J. Rosenstein, 878
Shannon Rothschild, 1725
Stephen N Sangalis, 1487
Joseph P Schaffer, 1252
David K. Schaible, 1727
David R. Scholl, 189
Harpinder Singh, 1001
Brian S Smith, 861
Michael A Steinbeck, 1747
Jeff Thermond, 2010
Shoshana Vernick, 1745
William D. Waldrip, 672
Thomas D Weldon, 39
Stephen Wertheimer, 1949
Darell E Zink Jr, 412

Indiana University School of Law
James C. Snyder, 904

Indiana University of Pennsylvania
Tom Wallace, 754
Terry Williams, 1321

Indiana University, Bloomington
Angie Grimm, 971

Indiduan Institute of Technology
Nilanana Bhowmik, 536

Inst. for Management Development
Eric Rosenfeld, 794, 1384

Institut Commercial de Nancy
Florence J. Mauchant, 956

Institut d'Etudes Politiques
Gonzalo Cordova, 1913
W. Carter Neild, 1383
Joern Nikolay, 819

Institute of Actuaries
Mark Arnold, 78

International Inst. of Mgmt Dev.
Jui Tan, 299

International Space University
Andrew Ray, 2148

International Technical University
David Tsang, 46

International University of Monaco
Matt Turner, 114

Iona College
Maria F Costanzo, 1624
Peter Polimino, 104
R Peter Reiter, Jr, 1560

Iowa State University
Dan Broderick, 270
Frederick J Dotzler, 599
Spiros Liras, 144
Alan Marty, 1110
Vivek Mehra, 200
James A Severson PhD, 844
Paul Spieker, 737
Anil Tammineedi, 127

Isenberg School of Management
Jeffrey Mark, 509

Ithaca College
Alexander Cuomo, 1325
Damien A. Dovi, 266
Matt Kinsey, 364
Paul A. Scott, 272

Ivey Business School
Rob Barbara, 2063
Roger Chabra, 2231
Robert Cherun, 2042
Scott Clark, 2081
Ryan DeCaire, 2041
Stephen J. Dent, 2056
Bill Di Nardo, 2104
Cam Di Prata, 2127
Michael Duncan, 2083
Stuart M. Elman, 2212
Nicole Fich, 2211
J Kristofer Galashan, 1113
Darrick Geant, 334
Ryan Giles, 2267
Kerri Golden, 2146
Mark Gordon, 2200
Ewout Heersink, 2201
Blaine Hobson, 2280
Robbie Isenberg, 2075
Daniel Israelsohn, 2216
Donald Jackson, 2207
Dan Jacques, 2138
Scott Kaplanis, 2102
Stephan Klee, 2217
Michael Lay, 2200
Mark Lerohl, 2222
John Loh, 2056
Justin MacCormack, 2142
Kenneth MacKinnon, 2175
Ian Macdonell, 2083
Erik Mikkelsen, 2042
Anuj Ranjan, 2062
Gary Rubinoff, 2250
David G. Samuel, 2056
Russell Samuels, 2280
Pierre J. Schuurmans, 2056
Sunil Selby, 2265
Matt Shalhoub, 2134
Ray Sharma, 2107
Joseph Shlesinger, 2076

College/University Index / Ivey School of Business

Nathan Tam, 2041
Douglas B. Trussler, 277
Mac Van Wielingen, 2036
Michael Wagman, 2075

Ivey School of Business
Monica J. Holec, 1115

J. Reuben Clark Law School
Steve Young, 962

JL Kellogg School Of Management
Rebecca Lucia, CFA, 11

JW Goethe University
Ansbert K Gadicke MD, 1268

James E. Beasley School of Law
Richard Taney, 1866

James Madison University
Joseph F. Damico, 1594
Christopher D. Graham, 1742
Steve Guffey, 838
Paul Holland, 773
Mike Marcantonio, 291
Don Rainey, 881
Michael W Rubel, 1560
Michael S. Sarner, 406
Tige Savage, 1558
David A Stienes, 1140
Randall Ussery, 1985
Joshua Wilson, 851

Jawaharlal Nehru University
Eric Beckman, 334

Jefferson Medical College
Mike Pellini, 1646

John Carroll University
Carl E. Baldassarre, 1460
Anthony Nader, 1768
Arnold B Siemer, 607
Sean Ward, 293

John Hopkins School of Medicine
JH Bilenker, MD, 73

John Hopkins University
Charles Homcy, MD, 1814
Christoph Lengauer, PhD, 1814
Greg Raiten, 744
Shermaine Tilley, 2086

John Molson School of Business
Sam Ifergan, 2141

Johns Hopkins School of Medicine
Dorothy Margolskee, 764
Vance Vanier, 471
Damion Wicker, 1411

Johns Hopkins University
Garrick Ahn, 376
Jeffrey Aronson, 444
Stephen Auvil, 1792
John Avirett, 872
Jeffrey S Barber, 1778
Nicholas B Binkley, 767
Keith Carlton, 891
Matt Cheney, 500
Tom Clark, 530
Michael Ehlers, 144
Robert Finkel, 1481
James Flynn, 602
Elizabeth Galbut, 1703
Simeon J. George, 1734

Richard Gilmore, 829
Michael Goldberg, 340
Stewart Gollmer, 1798
Casey Gordon, 1341
David Hirsch MD, PhD, 1147
Michael C. Jackson, 952
Yan Ke, 1340
Dennis Lockhart, 1279
Edward B Marsh, MD, 1199
Chris Pacitti, 205
Mark Paris, 1896
Caroline Popper MD MPH, 244
Holly Radel, 3252
R. Scott Schafler, 547
John W. Snow, 453
Megan Sparks, 534
William H Taylor II, 1262
Tim Weglicki, 21
Daniel Yardley, 1424

Johnson Grad. School of Business
Karen Derr Gilbert, 796

Johnson Grad. School of Management
Sven K. Grasshoff, 1377

Jones Graduate School of Business
Stephanie Campbell, 953

Kalamazoo College
William J Oberholtzer, 935

Kansas State University
Dixon Doll, 597
Brian Lueger, 1057
Marshall D. Parker, 1057
Chris Traylor, 758

Karl Franzens University
Matthias G Allgaier, 1754

Kean University
Mark L. Benaquista, 1818

Keio University
George Hara, 603
Yasunori Kaneko MD, 1693
James Kondo, 824
Koji Osawa, 837
Terry Suzuki, 1387

Kelley School of Business
Michael Goy, 1267
Blair Greenberg, 336
Angie Grimm, 971
Mark Hollis, 445
Chris LaMothe, 659
Jill Margetts, 445

Kellogg School of Management
John F Ackerman, 412
Christopher J. Ackerman, 751
Will Adams, 92
Laura Albrecht, 1169
Alexandre Alvim, 838
Brad Armstrong, 1151
Robert M Austin, 989
Keith Bank, 1060,1061
Hagai Barlev, 670
Derek Beaty, 838
Julie A Bender, 792
Stephen A Bennett, 1748
Kent Berkley, 785
Brian Birk, 1756
George Bischof, 1213
Geoff Bland, 1970

Robert D Blank, 470
Jason Booma, 518
Karen Buckner, 1242
Brian J. Buenneke, 1413
Andrew M Bushell, 542
Kevin D Cantrell, 1579
Virginia Cargill, 80
John R Carroll, 1754
John M. Carsello, 904
Michael Castellarin, 2075
Chris Cathcart, 899
Cheryl Cheng, 299
Rob Chesney, 473
Sach Chitnis, 1050
Gavin Christensen, 1074
Matt Clary, 1964
Michael Cohn, 888
Richard H Copans, 1160
Kelly A. Cornelis, 1097
Chuck Cullen, 881
D Patrick Curran, 367
Joseph Cutts, 1382
Albert DaValle Jr., 1042
Robert E Davis, 1138
Jordan S Davis, 1523
Rob Day, 1732
Brian Demkowicz, 963
Sunny Dhillon, 1680
James Dimitri, 1927
Mishone B. Donelson, 949
Robert Dreier, 362
Jim Dugan, 1364
Justin C Dupere, 1964
Chris A. Durbin, 1933
Park Durrett, 28
Steven A. Elms, 73
Thomas Erickson, 739
Jeff Farrero, 470
David Fishman, 1912
Andy Fligel, 1009
Walter C Florence, 792
Andrew N. Ford, 906
Tod Francis, 1666
Peter B Franz, 753
Marc-Henri Galletti, 1147
Evan R Gallinson, 1210
Christopher J Garber, 1964
David S. Gellman, 804
Charlie Gifford, 929
Aziz Gilani, 1207
Stefan Goetz, 927
Miki Granski, 538
Blair Greenberg, 336
Carter Griffin, 1888
Tony Grover, 1596
Michael Gruber, 987
Michael C. Gruber, 1613
Andrew S Gustafson, 1686
Jonathan M Haas, 494
James N. Hallene, 410
Frederic Halley, 1319
Rob C Hart CFA, 1794
Tom Hawkins, 770
John Hennegan, 1670
Jay R. Henry, 1410
Deborah Hodges, 1231
John Hoesley, 1481
Beth Hoffman, 257
Brett P Holcomb, 1494
Ken Hooten, 531
Jim Huston, 1467
Grant A Jackson, 551
Jeff Jackson, 1808
David W Jahns, 809
Brian James, 491
Rich Jander, 1169
Stephen M. Johnson, 952

College/University Index / Leeds University

Gregory Jones, 654
Julie Jubeir, 409
Bill Kaczynski, 341
Joe Kaiser, 1205
Jonathan Kalman, 1029
Scott A. Kehoe, 1018
Ryan Kelley, 1670
Colton King, 1090
Demian Kircher, 1169
John Kneen, 247
Laird Koldyke, 2000
Adam Koopersmith, 1483
Ronald W Kuehl, 792
John Kuelper, 178
John LeMay, 293
Jenny Lee, 827
Mark Leigh, 953
Gigi Levy-Weiss, 1323
Rand Lewis, 443
Alex Lieberman, 491
Bernardo H. Llovera, 707
Bruce Luehrs, 1572
Peter N Magas, 247
Sumant Mandal, 1812
Bernard B Markey, 1280
Woody Marshall, 1787
Alfred M. Mattaliano, 1582
Erik E Maurer, 1494
Bret Maxwell, 1242
Matt McCall, 1483
Michael McCullough, 987
Steve McKay, 775
John Meilner, 341
Ryan Milligan, 470
William H. Miltenberger, 988
Gregory Moerschel, 247
Anthony J. Moore, 826
Jason B Moskowitz, 634
James Neary, 1957
Bradley C O'Dell, 1494
Maura O'Hara, 3255
John E. Palmer, 906
Gordon G. Pan, 225
Thomas Parkinson, 947, 979
Steven W. Parks, 1097
Jeff Patterson, 518
Brian Paul, 1798
Randy Paulson, 1368
Mike Peck, 1380
Gil Penchina, 1566
Scott A Perricelli, 1140
Peter S Pettit, 1270
Matthew W Raino, 1160
Champ Raju, 1471
Thomas R. Raterman, 805
Chris Redmond, 402
Jason Rosenberg, 1745
George Rossolatos, 2065
Sarah G Roth, 165
Laura M. Rubin, 1742
Lawrence Rusoff, 1434
Brent T Sacha, 1748
Neel Sarkar, 443
Adam Schimel, 242
David L. Schnadig, 547
Jodi Sherman Jahic, 83
Terrance M Shipp, 1210
Walker C. Simmons, 1410
James R Simons, 1728
Paul Smith, 834
Peter Sonsini, 1296
Andrew Souder, 1524
Jennifer Steans, 531
Roderick Stephan, 99
Gary Stevenson, 1190
Mark Strauch, 92
Nancy Sullivan, 979
Eric Swanson, 893
Mark D. Taber, 862
Pete Tedesco, 921
Brian C. Tilley, 611
Joseph Tou, 1705
Rob Veres, 1724
Sona Wang, 454
Michael Watts, 1132
Reeve B Waud, 1964
William Wick, 1939
J. Alberto Yepez, 1852
Ari M. Zur, 351

Kenan-Flagler Business School
Brad Armstrong, 1151
Charles A Cox, 1148
Benton Cummings, 1518
Stuart W Hawley, 1627
Dan Rua, 994
Krishnan Varier, 152
Thomas H. Westbrook, 747

Kennedy School of Government
Zaid Ashai, 1463
Catherine Crockett, 884
Edith Dorsen, 2003
Andrew Dunn, 1376
Dr. Campbell Murray, 1350
Juliet Tammenoms Bakker, 1147

Kent Business School
Oscar Alvarado, 1341

Kent State University
Timothy Gosline, 1576
Drew Molinari, 578
Joseph J. Zabik, 346

Kenyon College
Jeremy Bauman, 1303
Donald B. Hebb, Jr., 21
Brett P Holcomb, 1494
Karl Slatoff, 2019
John Tomes, 919

Kettering University
Gregory Hulecki, 712
Kristina Serafim, 1928
Matt Tsien, 821

King's College
Jonathan Klahr, 1761
Chuck Parente, 670
Alan Wilkinson, 63

Kingston Business School
Malcolm Moss, 254

Kingston University
Philip Cole, 1765

Knox College
Rajeev Dadoo, 1734
Joseph H Heinen, 847
Timothy F. Sutherland, 1229

Kogod School of Business
Paul Diaz, 559

Kolping College
Eckard Weber, MD, 622

Krannert Grad. School of Management
Ron Sansom, 1576

Kuwait University
Fawaz Al-Mubaraki, 1952

Kwantlen Polytechnic University
Norton Singhavon, 2095

Kyoto University
Shunichiro Matsumoto, PhD, 184

LMU University
Ahim Kandler, 761

La Salle University
Raymond Larkin, 573
Kevin Provost, 871
Dean Sciorillo, 677
Brian J Siegel, 896
Raymond F Weldon, 356

La Sorbonne
David Mes, 1370

LaSalle University
Robert Graham, 1431
Dean Sciorillo, 677

Lafayette College
Craig Bural, 1531
Bruce A Eatroff, 902
Stephen A. Hanna, 1747
Hendrik J. Hartong III, 360
Robert Hinaman, 47
Andrew Mitchell, 328
Gil Ozir, 2050
Craig Pisani, 170
Daniel R. Revers, 157
Edward F Sager Jr, 1204
Adam F. Stulberger, 1779

Lake Erie College
Stephen B Perry, 1136

Lake Forest College
Mark Headrick, 538
Matthew Roszak, 1683
Peter G. Schiff, 1344

Lakehead University
Jim Boyle, 994
Harry Jaako, 2091

Lauder Institute
Marcos A Rodriguez, 1404
Dalton Wright, 1074

Laval University
André Dallaire, 475
Jean-Philippe Lemay, 727
Andree-Lise Methot, 2087
Sophie Perreault, 2108
Charles Sirois, 163, 2252

Lawrence University
George L. Buzzy, 292
Andrew H Kalnow, 90
Steve Mech, 567
Scott D. Roeper, 719
Chris Whitcomb, 1369

Lebanese American University
Firas El Amine, 1021

Lee Business School
Matthew Neely, 1694

Leeds University
Andy Bayliffe, 144

College/University Index / Lehigh University

Lehigh University
William J. Amelio, 595
Stephen D. Aronson, 1580
Jack Baron, 566
Thomas A Berglund, 734
John Bolduc, 242
Steve Carpenter, 1120
Mike Carusi, 58, 1126
Kevin Clayton, 676
Diane M. Daych, 436
Ryan J. Faulkingham, 525
Stewart Fisher, 1090
Philip Fleck, 1347
Timothy T. Hall, 478
David Heidecorn, 1092
Kenneth J Heuer, 1075
Stephen Holmes, 1014
Bill Kirsch, 549
Josh Kuzon, 1531
Paul S. Levy, 1043
Paul Martino, 361
Vincent P. Menichelli, 52
Matthew Nicklin, 733
Greg J. Pappas, 257
David J Reuter, 1140
Mark R. Ross, 1369
Joseph Saviano, 226
Fredrick D. Schaufeld, 1768
Geoff Schneider, 433
Samuel L Schwerin, 1235
Mark Strauch, 92
Gordon T Wyatt, 39

Lehman College
Peter Kalkanis, 1561
Ruben Rodriguez, 363

Lenoir-Rhyne University
Kenneth B Lee, 918
Philip W Martin, 1609

Leonard N Stern School of Business
Joshua Ho-Walker, 1314

Lewis & Clark College
Mark Dorman, 674
Sam Thompson, 1488

Liberty University
Angela Helfin, 3259

Loma Linda University
Wes Ferrari, 976
Jim Woody, 1098

Lomonosov Moscow State University
Anna Batarina, 144

London Business School
Gerald T. Banks, 101
Stephan Bey, 2052
Ravi Bhaskaran, 760
Matthew Foy, 1734
Mona Kung, 2132
Matt Lee, 474
Kristopher Prakash, 1369
Norman Rokosh, 2267
Derek Senft, 2118, 2210
Tim Stubbs, 1755
Andrew Tarazid-Tarawali, 54
Erol Uzumeri, 2243
Jennifer VanBelle, 811
Matteo Volpi, 2068

London City University
Cécile Belaman, 223

London School of Economics
Jonathan Aberman, 120
James Appleyard, 2120
Rajay Bagaria, 1961
David Beecken, 247
Sven H. Borho, 1383
Justin Burden, 990
Paul D'Addario, 1403
Hythem T El-Nazer, 1778
William F Foote, 1586
Elizabeth Galbut, 1703
Ralf Gruss, 136
Charles Holt, 2153
Asad Jamal, 691
Arrun Kapoor, 1691
Serge LeVert-Chiasson, 2239
H Jeffrey Leonard, 838
Bernardo H. Llovera, 707
Lawrence Mock, 1279
Quinn Morgan, 448
Rory O'Driscoll, 1629
Will Porteous, 1597
Jason Reed, 1997
Ken Rotman, 2075
Siddharth Srivastava, 2183
Paul Strachman, 1533
James E Thomas, 1820

London University
Mark Arnold, 78
Carlos Heneine, 1518

Long Beach City College
Russ Aldrich, 892

Long Island University
Charlotte Chapanoff, 308
Kim P. Goh, 957
Steven Insalaco, 372
Joe Mandato, 599
Joseph B Rotberg, 1108
Jeffrey M. Sauerhoff, 179

Louisiana State University
Jerry DeVries, 1803
Marcia Haydel, 1434
D. Martin Phillips, 673
Steven L. Soignet, MD, 158
S Somasegar, 1162
Martin Sutter, 698
W. Anthony Toups, 60

Louisiana Tech University
Jarett Carson, 677
William D. Waldrip, 672

Lowell Technological Institute
Peter Barrett, 193

Loyola College
Stephen Auvil, 1792
Greg Barger, 1316
David Freschman, 151
Eileen O'Rourke, 18
Jim Zucco, 507

Loyola Law School
Lloyd Greif, 874
Craig Gunther, 281

Loyola Marymount University
Elmer Baldwin, 466
Tom Cervantez, 31
Jim Demetriades, 1055
Mark E Farrell, 1808
Ted Fourticq, 905
Monty Lapica, 515
Michael Steed, 1401
Briana J. Zelaya, 1905

Loyola University
Chuck Cullen, 881
Michael T Dieschbourg, 991
Jeff Griffor, 1122
Donald W. Hughes, 386
Stephen V King, 1473
Rick Kohr, 702
Rocco J. Martino, 1097
Omar Mejias, 62
William H. Miltenberger, 988
Annie Piotrowski, 237
Jeff Schechter, 1745
Michael Steed, 1401
Nancy Sullivan, 979
Eric Thompson, 872
Mary Tolan, 471
Kyle Welborn, 570

Université de Chambéry
Bernie Zeisig, 2187

Loyola University of Chicago
Jennifer Carolan, 1530
Tracy Killoren Chadwell, 6
David Knoch, 1026
Paul A. Scott, 272

Lubin School of Business
Alexander Cuomo, 1325

Ludwig Maximilian University
Hubert Birner, 2268
Dr. Markus Goebel, 1350

Lycoming College
Donald W. Hughes, 386

M. Katz Grad. School of Business
Michael Beauregard, 963

MIT
Shaun Abrahamson, 1896
Noubar Afeyan, 748
Payal Agrawal Divakaran, 1
Yuval Almog, 538
Jorge Amador, 110
David L Anderson, 1762
Vikram Bajaj, 764
Henry G. Baker, 226
Eric Baker, 2186
Daria Becker, 1493
Gregory C. Belmont, 852
Stephen Berenson, 748
David Berry, 748
James J. Bochnowski, 605
Teymour Boutros-Ghali, 1249
Hugo Braun, 1337
Josh Breinlinger, 1028
Luke Burns, 180
Mark Bye, 1256
Brian Byun, 1073
Doug Cameron, 739
John K. Castle, 425
Brownell Chalstrom, 210
James Cham, 287
Wesley Chan, 720
Pierre Chao, 681
Richard A. Charpie, 119
Nelson Chu, 1076
Joyce Chung, 810
Ed Cluss, 1680
Jay Cohan, 1976
Vanessa Colella, 488
Dennis R. Costello, 325
Will Cowen, 1146

Gregory S Czuba, 692
Jeff Davison, 993
Stephen P DeFalco, 1133
Tom Dennedy, 176
Brian Dixon, 661
Mishone B. Donelson, 949
Rami Elkhatib, 40
Bill Elkus, 504
David O Ellis, 656
Charles H Esserman, 1863
Saman Farid, 222
Brad Feld, 779, 1245, 1791
Andy Fillat, 1106
Todd Foley, 1268
Bill Ford, 762
Richard Fox, 975
Arthur L Fox, 1595
Richard H. Frank, 585
Ben Fu, 1319
Sameer Gandhi, 27
Shri Ganeshram, 788
Luis E Garcia Garcia de Brigard, 142
Shauntel Garvey, 1530
Max Gazor, 457
Jim Goldinger, 713
Johnathan M Goldstein, 1778
Carl L. Gordon PhD, 1383
Mark Gorenberg, 2018
Paul Grim, 693, 1757
Rick Grinnell, 713, 833
Alex Gruzen, 546
Greg Gunn, 490
Krishna K Gupta, 1585
Perry Ha, 627
Steven E Hall, 1128
Howard Hartenbaum, 200
Kamil Hassan, 856
William Heflin, 1076
David Hirsch MD, PhD, 1147
Janey Hoe, 485
Karen Hong, 1780
Larry Hootnick, 53
Jeff Horing, 1005
Paul Hsiao, 399
Maha Ibrahim, 389
Brian Jacobs, 666
Uttam Jain, 190
John W. Jarve, 1203
Sheena Jindal, 520
Gregory Johnson, 1490
Mark Jrolf, 929
Alex Khalin, 1928
Kevin J. Kinsella, 209
Dave Kowalick, 892
Chris Kryder, 749
Richard P Kuntz, 1667
Philippe Laffont, 511
Vijay Lathi, 1297
Patrick Latterell, 1098
Kenneth Lau, 448
Jay F Laudauer, 1883
Derek Leck, 110
Peter Lee, 231
Aileen Lee, 553
Peter Lee, 664
Sara Leggat, 1659
Douglas Leone, 1657
Andrew Levin, 1522
Nurzhas Makishev, 1330
Josh Makower, 1296
Jill Margetts, 445
Kim Marvin, 110
Scott Maxwell, 1381
Howard Mayson, 2044
John Mazzarino, 465
Mark McDowell, 50, 1100
Fred A Middleton, 1222, 1619
David S. Miller, 498
George M Milne, Jr. PhD, 1523
H. DuBose Montgomery, 1203
Amir Nashat, 1464
Jim Pastoriza, 1784
Tom Penn, 1275
Thomas A Penn, 1431
William Perry, 992
Mark Perutz, 596
John Piret, 1311
Serge Plotkin, 1382
Lisa Porter, 983
Tim Porter, 1162
Stan J Reiss, 1184
Raju Rishi, 1597
Scott M Rocklage PhD, 11
Alexander Rosen, 1566
Phil Samper, 808
Dave Samuel, 787
Dr. N. Darius Sankey, 2020
Neel Sarkar, 443
Zach E Schaumburg, 1220
Kenneth T Schiciano, 1778
Bob Schulz, 921
Shantnu Sharma, 107
David A Shaywitz, 1780
Ben Shih, 972
Mark A. Siegel, 1203
Ian Sigalow, 876
Jeff Silverman, 69
Peter Sinclair, 1106
Greg Somer, 693
Bart Stuck, 1678
Katie Szczepaniak Rice, 689
Jim Tananbaum, 764
Hemant Taneja, 820
Ralph Taylor-Smith, 812
Jim Tenkle, 1621
Yaniv Tepper, 127
Tyler Thompson, 1645
Michael G. Thonis, 458
Tomas Valis, 2070
Gayle L Veber, 1911
Jim Walker, 56
Robert Ward, 1213
David Waxman, 1800
David Weiden, 1073
Robert Weisskoff PhD, 711
Albert Wenger, 1884
Andy Wheeler, 894
Damion Wicker, 1411
Fred Wilson, 1884
Rich Wong, 27
David Yuan, 1537
Wan Li Zhu, 713
Geoffrey von Maltzahn, 748
Johan von der Goltz, 313
Alex von der Goltz, 313

MIT Sloan School of Management
Sim Blaustein, 259
Prashanth V. Boccasam, 1348
Gaye Bok, 704
Clara Brenner, 1895
Justin Butler, 648
Chris Davis, 813
Stephen P DeFalco, 1133
Pietro Dova, 2009
Rami Elkhatib, 1711
Karimah Es Sabar, 2221
Nikhil Garg, 1732
Jeffrey P Gerson, 854
Jim Goldinger, 713
Bob Greene, 535
Paul Grim, 693, 1757
Bradley C Harrison, 1635
Eric Hjerpe, 1069
Paul A Howard, 1198
Michael Huber, 1508
Scott Johnson, 1290
Daniel G. Jones, 1818
Amit Karp, 263
Ray Leach, 1051
Julie Lein, 1895
Stephen O. Marshall, 2098
Scott Maxwell, 1381
Bill McCullen, 1101
Preetish Nijhawan, 456
Zach Noorani, 773
Kola Olofinboba, 715
Mark Perutz, 596
Steve Rappaport, 1376
Andy Sack, 776
Graham Schena, 1266
Joel Serface, 256
Paul Spieker, 737
Brian Stansky, 1008
Philip N. Sussman, 1811
Sanjay Swani, 1779
Gus Tai, 1855
Peter Tertzakian, 2036
Lee J Tesconi, 1116
Jeff Williams, 1731
Donna Williamson, 454
Paul Wu, 875
George Zachary, 457
Mark A deLaar, 1754

MS University Baroda
Amit Shah, 176

Macalester College
Paul Batcheller, 1474
Beth Hoffman, 257
Michael Huber, 1508
Evis Hursever, 698
Seth Levine, 779
Seth Levine, 1245
John L Ritter, 740

Manchester Business School
John W. Littlechild, 922

Manchester University
John W. Littlechild, 922

Manhattan College
Tracie E. Ahern, 1448
Bob DeSena, 883
Sally A. DeVino, 1746
Brian J. Girvan, 180
Robert E Kelly, 1741
Anthony V Lando, 39
Jose Minaya, 1356
Philip N. Sussman, 1811

Manhattanville College
Christina Bushey, 1404
Paula G. McInerney, 302
Larry Reinharz, 2004
Thorsten Suder, 404

Mannheim University
Matthias G Allgaier, 1754

Marietta College
Dean Didato, 999

Marquette University
Joel Andryc, 1602
Phil D. Bronsteatter, 1438
Chad M. Cornell, 847
Jim Domach, 1174
Scott A. Finegan, 1438
Paul Kreie, 1232

College/University Index / Marriott School of Management

Lesya Kulchenko, 928
Mark McDonnell, 154
Greg Myers, 1174
Gregory J. Purcell, 148
Paul J. Raab, 719
Robert Shen, 897
David Trotter, 1999

Marriott School of Management
Ryan Lucero, 785

Marshall School of Business
Jerry Lotter, 665
Jason Schwarz, 1989
Gordon Smythe, 2187
Sean Stiefel, 1282
Keith Wasserman, 814

Marshall University
David Becker, 1196
Barry B Conrad, 988

Maryland Institute
Elizabeth Galbut, 1703
Nabeel Hyatt, 1718

Massachusettes Maritime Academy
John Whorf, 1293

Massachusetts College of Pharmacy
Argeris Karabelas, 415
Ronald P Thiboutot PhD, 1120

Mayo Clinic
Michael Matly, MD, 1251

Mays Business School
Ben Stanton, 893

McCombs School of Business
Randall Crowder, 1803
James Eadie, MD, 1622
Dwight Scott, 280
Ryan Shulz, 703
Shravan Thadani, 1858

McDaniel College
William J. Westervelt, Jr., 181

McDonough School Of Business
Matthew Ritchie, 47

McDonough School of Business
Cheryl Moss, 791

McGill University
Maor Amar, 2143
Dan Baum, 2236
Pierre Beauparlant, 2261
Justin Beber, 2062
Raghu Bharat, 2082
Andrew Bishop, 2052
Keith Bisson, 440
Cédric Bisson, 2259
Adam Breslin, 2211
David Brown, 1791
Jake Cassaday, 2228
Matthew Chapman, 2264
Liam Cheung, 2251
Dr Ronald Chwang, 974
Todd Clapp, 429
Thomas D'Halluin, 72
Marcus Daniels, 2140
Sebastien Dhonte, 2075
Andrea Drager, 218
Dr. Sheldon Elman, 2212
Luigi Fraquelli, 2127
Kim Furlong, 3249

Lee M. Grunberg, 2218
William A. Hanna, 374
Andrew Heintzman, 2153
Kyle Hickey, 2237
Sam Ifergan, 2141
Avak Kahvejian, 748
Julius Kalcevich, 970
Maha Katabi, 1700
Daniel H. Kosoy, MD, 189
Francois Lafortune, 2090
David Lawee, 579
Felix-Etienne Lebel, 2056
Dr. David Lee, 496
Shawn Lewis, 2266
Jonathan E. Lim, MD, 489
Simon Lockie, 2128
Andrew Lugsdin, 2119
Kenneth MacKinnon, 2175
Shunichiro Matsumoto, PhD, 184
Eamonn McConnell, 2160
Benn Mikula, 2080
Rick Ness, 2251
John Philp, 2121
Alireza Rahnema, 2025
Giorgio Riva, 2281
Lauren Robinson, 2140
Beni Rovinski, 2173
Zoya Shcuhpak, 2149
Andrew Sheiner, 2030
Pascal Tremblay, 2198
Mario Venditti, 2149
Morty White, 2008
Greg Williams, 582
Peter Wilson, 912
Christopher Winn, 2186
Ben Yoskovitz, 2140
Christian Zabbal, 1732

McIntire School of Commerce
Mark M. Anderson, 889
J.S. Gamble, 288
Teddy Kaplan, 1300
Jonathan R Wallace, 1389

McMaster University
Richard Betsalel, 2083
Jim Boyle, 994
Laurel C. Broten, 2197
Adam Felesky, 2217
Mark Hatfield, 1796
Bill Kostenko, 2050
Elaine Kunda, 2092
Damian Lamb, 2125
Joe Mattina, 2211
Michelle McBane, 2248
Robert S. McLeese, 2026
Sanjana Muthanna, 2178
Hamish Sutherland, 2147, 2279
Colin Walker, 2083

Medical College of Pennsylvania
Barbara J Dalton PhD, 1439

Medical College of Virginia
Vijay Aggarwal, PhD, 1811
Sandeep Naik, 819

Medical College of Wisconsin
Zia Agha, 1974

Meinders School Of Business
Craig Woodruff, 47

Memphis College of Art
Gary Backaus, 15

Mercer University
Roddy JH Clark, 1536

Merrimack College
James Jordon, 1452
Robert MacInnis, 20

Methodist University
Sami Sawaf, 2012

Meyers College
Gary Graham, 737

Miami University
Robert D Blank, 470
Michael Boniello, 1468
Andrew J Collins, 1754
Daniel Colon, Jr., 509
Jason R. Cornacchione, 1460
Todd Creech, 924
Bruce Downey, 1316
David A Gezon, 1232
Stephen R Haynes, 835
Rich Jander, 1169
Mark A Johnson, 1865
Gregory Jones, 654
John LeMay, 293
Brian Leonard, 653
Peter N Magas, 247
Frederic H Mayerson, 1955
Scott McConnell, 88
Ryan Meany, 653
Patrick Meenan, 175
Lisa Ondrula, 1049
Chris Orndorff, 1948
Steve G. Pattison, 1460
Susan Sheskey, 595
Paul Smith, 834
Nelson Teng, 460
Bob West, 203
Adriaan Zur Muhlen, 1488

Miami University of Ohio
Mike Gausling, 1386
Peter Mogk, 963
Daniel E Pansing, 1210

Michigan Law School
Duncan Davidson, 361

Michigan State University
Deepak Advani, 927
Aohn Cambier, 975
Robert DesMarais, 1769
Linda Fingerle, 652
Kelly Ford Buckley, 655
Jeff Frederick DPM, 1288
Tom Gores, 1455
Steve Grizzell, 1004
Michael Gross, 254
Justin Ishbia, 1670
Michael Janish, 1906
Ryan Kelley, 1670
Ted Lai, 974
Sumant Mandal, 1812
James Marasco, 1971
Dennis McCrary, 1413
Lake McGuire, 928
John Melstrom, 985
Terry Opdendyk, 1379
Blake Robins, 1154
Ian Ross, 531
Jay W Schemelter, 1578
Chris Sugden, 655
Christopher G. Wright, 557
Yipeng Zhao, 664

Michigan Technological University
Kanwal Rekhi, 1017
Wade Sheffer, 821

Middle Tennessee State University
Marshall Cole, 216

Middlebury College
Brandon Avrutin, 1554
Christopher D. Brady, 459
C. Andrew Brickman, 225
James W. Brush, MD, 785
Christopher PH Cheang, 1469
Schuyler Coppedge, 676
David N Deutsch, 590
Chun Ding, 474
James T Donelan, 1639
Christopher M. Doody, 1746
Alex Finkelstein, 1718
Michael D. Gregorich, 1746
Andrew S Gustafson, 1686
Parker Harris, 1610
Justin Harrison, 364
Ronald C Hess Jr, 1480
Eugene Hill, 1631
Jeremy Janson, 785
Robert Jenkins, 1470
Samantha Kaminsky, 553
Bill Maris, 1646
Brian W Michaud, 1138
Bob More, 94
Tyler Newton, 429
Jonathan H. Owsley, 1092
Keith W. Pennell, 611
Joe Powers, 1165
John G Rudge, 1116
Rick Scanlon, 1001
Kathleen Schoemaker, 622
Jeffrey Schutz, 443
Jed Smith, 430
Peter H Smith Jr, 1738
Joshua Sobeck, 13
Gus Taylor, 719
Robert Tucker, 404
Ted Virtue, 1231
Reeve B Waud, 1964
W Lambert Welling, 1199

Millikin University
Dennis Beard, 1380
Holly Kaczmarczyk, 1971

Minnesota State University
Jane Bortnem, 466

Minot State University
Curtis Armstrong, 2166

Mississippi College
Rebecca Irish, 1433

Missouri Univ. of Science & Tech.
Dennis F. Jaggi, 672
Brian Matthews, 570

Montana State University
Cairn G Cross, 789

Montclair State University
Thomas Girardi, 956
Gene Wolfson, 429

Monterey Institute of Int'l Studies
Wes Ferrari, 976

Montreal University
Laurence Rulleau, 2086

Moore School
Alex Doll, 1796

Moore School of Business
Amy Burr, 1039

Moore School of Engineering
Jeff Lieberman, 1005
Bret Pearlman, 660
Adam L Suttin, 1053

Morehead State University
David A Henderson, 1856

Morehouse College
Chris Allen, 1404
Qian W. Elmore, 973
Kirby Harris, 232
H Beecher Hicks, III, 1532
Aaron Holiday, 12
Ira L. Moreland, 973
David C Neverson, 1109
Alex Washington, 1990
Willie E. Woods Jr., 973

Morgan State University
R Randy Croxton, 1209
Timothy L Smoot, 1209
Stanley W Tucker, 1209
Anthony L Williams, 1209

Moritz College of Law
Eric Kaup, 940

Moscow Institute of Physics
Pavel Bogdanov, 89
Alexander Galitsky, 89

Moscow Institute of Steel and Alloy
Alexei Andreev, 207

Moscow State Technical University
Dmitry Grishin, 879

Moscow State University
Yuri Milner, 616

Moscow Steel And Alloys Institute
Alexei Andreev, 208

Mount Allison University
Malcolm Fraser, 2148
Zac McIsaac, 2182
Craig Noble, 2062
Annie Thériault, 2084

Mount Holyoke College
Nissa Bartalsky, 80
Maria Cirino, 1

Mount Saint Vincent University
Dawn House, 2148

Mount St. Mary College
Peter Ianello, 1364
Daniel Yardley, 1424

Muhlenberg College
Matthew Naythons MD, 164

Murdoch University
Mason Hills, 1551

NY Stern School of Business
Sam Barthelme, 1037

NYC Stern School of Business
Donald J Donahue Jr, 692

NYU School of Medicine
Josh Makower, 1296

NYU Stern School of Business
Tracie E. Ahern, 1448
Samy Ben Aissa, 1928
Sikandar Atiq, 2194
David Bainbridge, 1929
Christopher PH Cheang, 1469
Chris Chung, 883
John Daileader, 867
Harry DeMott, 1528
Bob Delaney, 560
Michael DiPiano, 1316
Brendan Dickinson, 389
Jeff Drazan, 260
Michael J Dubilier, 632
Tammy Funasaki, 334
Jeffrey M Goodrich, 934
Michael D. Gregorich, 1746
Matthew Hermann, 178
Kenneth J Heuer, 1075
Lorraine Hliboki, 1466
Matthew Kimble, 211
Eric R. Korsten, 330
Joel Krikston, 1206
Pierre-Olivier Lamoureux, 848
Peter A Lyons, 1109
Paula G. McInerney, 302
Thomas Murphy, 819
Shay Murphy, 1324
Alexandra Prima, 1807
John Raguin, 711
Bob Rees, 1740
Loren Schlachet, 1576
Mayank Singh, 448
Matt Smalley, 383
Eric D. Starr, 410
Scott Steele, 1044
Roy Thiele-Sardina, 936
Justin Topilow, 253
Christopher Turner, 1957
Anibal Wadih, 838
David J. Wermuth, 1746
Dal Zemp, 1545
Scott Zoellner, 63
Gabriel de Alba, 2067

Nanyang Technological University
Jui Tan, 299

Nasson College
Joe Mandato, 599

National Cheng Chi University
Ted Lai, 974

National Cheng Kung University
Y.K. Chu, 1983
Hsing Kung, 46
Robert Shen, 897
Ed Yang, 974

National Chiao Tung University
Sam Lee, 730
M.R. Lin, 908

National Sun Yat-Sen University
Lucas Wang, 521

National Taiwan University
Wu-Fu Chen, 46
T.C. Chou, 908
Christy Chou, 1924
William Chung, 897
Ta-Lin Hsu, 897
George J Lee, 118
M.R. Lin, 908
Woody Sing-Wood Yeh, 118
Kai Tsang, 1924

College/University Index / National Tsing Hua University

John Tzeng, 908
Lucas Wang, 521
Tzyy-Po Wang, 908

National Tsing Hua University
Dr. Frank Kung, 1943
Jackie Yang, 1840

National University
Josef Friedman, 1750

National University of Ireland
Robert W. Mulcare, 1300

National University of Singapore
Jixun Foo, 827
Evelyn Sun, 149

Natl. Tech. University of Athens
Niko Bonatsos, 820

Naval Postgraduate School
Steven Denning, 819
Kenneth A. Minihan, 1401

New College, Oxford
John Frankel, 724

New England College
Chris Mathieu, 949

New England School of Law
John Fitzgerald, 469
Stephen Muniz, 1503

New Hampshire College
Cairn G Cross, 789

New Jersey Institute of Technology
Charles E Larsen, 39

New Mexico State University
Larry Lujan, 1926

New York Law School
Eric Hatzimemos, 1689
Marc Lasry, 211

New York Medical College
Paul Eisenberg, 144
Lawrence Howard MD, 957

New York State University
Rod Ferguson, 1411

New York University
Krishna K Agrawal, 1133
John F Aiello, 1133
Jeffrey Aronson, 444
Rajay Bagaria, 1961
Stephen A Baker, 768
Scott Barry, 698
Nicolas Berggruen, 253
Brett Berson, 742
Barry Blattman, 2062
Timothy P Bradley, 1676
Clara Brenner, 1895
Jeffrey B Bunder, 1133
Robin Ellis Busch, 1729
Andrew Chang, 1119
Wayne Cohen, 1638
Charles Cohen, 1777
Ao Ann Corkran, 845
Michael Dempsey, 527
Gerry Doherty, 1277
Jeff Drazan, 260
Greg Durst, 3256
Andrew L. Dworkin, 1913

Harry Edelson, 651
Bart Faber, 194
Peter Feinstein, 273
Adam E Fine, 1993
Thomas Giannetti, 1116
Jay N. Goldberg, 957
Alan E Goldberg, 1133
Michael Gontar, 1951
Michael D Goodman, 854
Mark K Gormley, 1108
Arthur P. Gould, 174
Andrew G Gould, 174
Stephen A. Hanna, 1747
Charles Heilbronn, 1263
Bruce M. Hernandez, 1727
Ted Hirose, 1793
Eric Hixon, 830
Jerry Hobbs, 364
Charles B Hughes III, 644
David W. Jaffin, 324
Richard Johnson, 1228
Robert Johnston, 1048
Donald A Juricic, 1560
Arrun Kapoor, 1691
Anita K. Kerr, 243
Brian Kinsman, 362
Peter W Klein, 351
Michael I Klein, 1138
James A Kohlberg, 1085
Mike Kwatinetz, 218
Robert Le Blanc, 2201
Matt Lee, 474
William D. Lese, 325
Waiman Leung, 1992
Basil Livanos, 78
Eric J. Lomas, 956
Timothy W Maloney, 17
Michael Marocco, 1620
Lauren M Massey, 17
Mark McAndrews, 645
Thomas McKinley, 413
Ivar W. Mitchell, 124
Britton Murdoch, 1572
Nader Naini, 785
Joshua Nussbaum, 527
Arnie Oronsky, 1014
Gil Ozir, 2050
Raja M. Parvez, 1061
Paolo Parziale, 17
Emily Paxhia, 1468
Thomas B Pennell, 1432
Peter Petrillo, 854
Richard A. Petrocelli, 1624
Craig Pisani, 170
John Poindexter, 1034
Robert Porell, 813
Jonathan Pulitzer, 812
Steven G Raich, 1138
Marc Rappoport, 1304
Thomas G Rebar, 1636
R Peter Reiter, Jr, 1560
Christopher W Roser, 1590
Ken Rotman, 2075
Kathleen Schoemaker, 622
Dominique Semon, 1217
David Shainberg, 228
J. Frederick Simmons, 786
Robert J. Simon, 324
Edward J Siskin, 940
Alyse Skidmore, 1336
John I Snow III, 1505
Jason Stein, 1992
William H Stewart, 1280
Timothy F. Sutherland, 1229
David Tisch, 321
Robert Toan, 1951
Jon Trauben, 99

Michele Valenti, 1551
David Wachter, 1949
Katherine Watts, 1714
David Weiden, 1073
Wayne B Weisman, 1636
Sean C. White, 1727
Bill Winterer, 1419
Chris Xie, 2263

New York University Business School
Joshua L. Gutfreund, 496
Joseph P Landy, 1957
Steven J Taubman, 1910

New York University School of Law
Jonathan Aberman, 120
Lawrence S. Atinsky, 179
Mitchell Davidson, 1469
Roger S Fine, 1993
David Gershman, 1859
Greg Raiten, 744
David Robbins, 1846
David Rosenstein, 819
Richard L Sherman, 1636
Yves Sisteron, 1890
Donald Spencer, 1681
Adam F. Stulberger, 1779

New York University of Law
Dave Marple, 1909

Newberry College
Charlie Banks, 1925

Nicholls State University
Corey Callais, 375

Nicholls University
Harold Callais II, 375

Nijenrode School of Business
Marc der Kinderen, 13

North Carolina School of Law
Dan Rua, 994

North Carolina State University
Robert Hester, 1349
Michael Marshall, 899
Jaime McMillan, 393
William B. Thompson, 783
Vishal Vasishth, 1363
Ken Woody, 999

North Dakota State University
Doug Burgum, 175
James Burgum, 175
John G. Cosgriff, 1020
Steven D Kloos PhD, 1861
Vish Mishra, 504
Gerald F Schmidt, 539
Matthew T. Vettel, 862

North Park College
Thomas S. Bagley, 1438

Northeastern University
Nick Adams, 615
Jason Allen, 1175
Peter Barrett, 193
Adam Bryant, 648
Dennis P Cameron, 646
Thomas J Caracciolo, 633
Paul Ciriello, 713
Richard A D'Amore, 1335
Bob Davis, 938
Robin W Devereux, 1754
Jeffrey H. Goldstein, 312

College/University Index / Ohio State University

Frances N. Janis, 1466
Steve Klammer, 1369
Edward A Lafferty, 1626
Benjamin Marino, 1435
Edward C McCarthy, 1575
Gerald A. Michaud, 949
Michael P. Murphy, 1589
Ed Olkkola, 1785
James J Pallotta, 1527
Morgan Polotan, 818
Benjamin P Procter, 1963
David Ryan, 1239
Bruce C Ryan, 1710
Bruce Sachs, 457
Matt Saunders, 2109
Stuart Skinner, 319
Nina Stepanov, 29
Michael S Weissenburger, 598

Northeastern University, China
Lili Zhou, 542

Northern Arizona University
Brian Connors, 766
Jim Upchurch, 376, 377

Northern Illinois University
John I Abernethy, 636
Bob Flannery, 1539
Adrienne Foo, 1866
John McKearn PhD, 1578
Daniel Norr, 206
Nick Rosa, 571, 1618
Michael Siemplenski, 733

Northwest Missouri State University
Sarah Dickey, 3247

Northwestern Oklahoma State Univ.
H Lee Frost, 592

Northwestern University
Matthew S Ahearn, 1861
Aaron C. Aiken, 906
Jeff Akers, 56
Alexandre Alvim, 838
Ricardo Angel, 1453
C Mark Arnold, 1532
A Craig Asher, 1942
Robert M Austin, 989
Lee Bailey, 1897
Keith Bank, 1061
Peter Barris, 1296
Bret Batchelder, 465
James A. Beakey, 1278
Derek Beaty, 838
Maurey J Bell, 620
Kent Berkley, 785
Terrence Berland, 1078
John P. Birkelund, 1624
Charles Birnbaum, 263
Jason Booma, 518
Simita Bose, 1348
Dennis C Bottorff, 551
Duncan S. Bourne, 2008
Sonya Brown, 1346
John Buttrick, 1884
John M. Carsello, 904
Robert Chefitz, 1329
Cheryl Cheng, 299
Christopher Childres, 653
Chris Chung, 883
James D Coady, 1654
Philippe Collombel, 1418
Anthony B Davis, 1132
Robert E Davis, 1138
Robert DesMarais, 1769
Mishone B. Donelson, 949

Scott Dorsey, 932
Mark Downs, 1279
Jim Duda, 583
Jeff Eby, 2007
William Ericson, 1247
Bill Ericson, 1985
Rod Ferguson, 1411
Scott A. Finegan, 1438
Brian Flucht, 281
David I. Foley, 280
Andrew N. Ford, 906
Tod Francis, 1666
T. Bondurant French, 56
Michael Fulton MD, 946
Brian Gallagher, CFA, 1873
David A Gezon, 1232
Charlie Gifford, 929
Wade D Glisson, 1686
Stefan Goetz, 927
Rashmi Gopinath, 1158
James Gordon, 654
Alex Gregor, 1082
Michael C. Gruber, 1613
Jonathan M Haas, 494
Lee C Hansen, 1214
Promod Haque, 1346
John Harris, 1033
Robert A Heimann, 1575
John Henderson, 970
Troy Henikoff, 1181
Jeff Hinck, 1525
Summer Hinton, 2057
James Ho, 63
Jay Hoag, 1787
Beth Hoffman, 257
Stephen J Hoffman MD, 1693
W Joseph Imhoff, 1280
Robbie Isenberg, 2075
Scott Jacobson, 1162
Brian James, 491
Peter Jarman, MBA, 561
Timothy D. Johnson, 847
Stephen M. Johnson, 952
Kim Kamdar, PhD, 622
Nagraj Kashyap, 1158
Peter Keehn, 88
Laird Koldyke, 2000
Richard P Kuntz, 1667
Charles T Lake II, 1676
Jamie Lane, 1869
Joe Lawler, 1990
Mark Leigh, 953
Gigi Levy-Weiss, 1323
Jack R. Luderer, MD, 140
Mark T Lupa PhD, 933
Timothy J MacKenzie, 1210
Robert Maeder, 768
Dan Malven, 9
Joe Mandato, 599
Bret Maxwell, 1242
Matt McCall, 1483
Spence McCelland, 1332
Ryan R. McKenzie, 148
Jeff Miller, 1413
Gregory Moerschel, 247
David Moll, 992
Stephen Natali, 654
Kenneth O'Keefe, 247
Meghan Otis, 1965
John E. Palmer, 906
Charles L Palmer, 1333
Gordon G. Pan, 225
Greg Parekh, 1301
Thomas Parkinson, 947
Thomas Parkinson, 979
Don Parsons, 143
Tom Petzinger, 1102

Lee Pillsbury, 1808
Naomi Pilosof, 1203
Will Price, 1317
JB Pritzker, 1482
J.B. Pritzker, 1483
John M. Reher, 326
Douglas Rescho, 1095
Joseph R Rondinelli, 792
Jason Rosenberg, 1745
David Scalzo, 1078
Jim Schultz, 1380
Jon Soberg, 1269
Todd Solow, 1345
Michael Stark, 564
Roderick Stephan, 99
Chelsea Stoner, 238
David Stott, 1990
Nancy Sullivan, 979
Eric Swanson, 893
Jeff T. Swenson, 1818
Joseph Tou, 1705
Leda Trivinos, 748
Philip A Tuttle, 592
Ahmed Wahla, 1085
Mike Ward, 1517
Todd Warren, 619
Stephen Wertheimer, 1949
James N White, 1762
Ken Widder, 1098
Rob Wolfson, 931
Mark Wright, 290
Paul Wu, 875
Philip Yau, 828
Ari M. Zur, 351

Northwestern University Law School
Rob C Hart CFA, 1794
Kevin P Kenealey, 1174
Jason Rosenberg, 1745

Norwich University
David Orfao, 820

Nottingham University
Steven Tang, 627

Nova University
Dayakar Puskoor, 1284

Oakland Community College
Ara Topouzian, 3259

Oberlin College
Joe Apprendi, 1557
Billy Cohn, MD, 1622
Kevin M. Jackson, 878
Jim Petras, 642
Béla Szigethy, 1576

Occidental College
Eric Gulve PhD, 270
Steven Hartanto, 465
Chris Howard, 978

Odessa University
Ilya Nykin, 1490

Ohio Northern University
Charlie Kim, 1189

Ohio State University
Michael Butler, 1285
Dennis R. Costello, 325
Bruce Downey, 1316
Alv Epstein, 1745
Daniel T Fleming, 1575
Christopher Fountas, 173
Pat Gouhin, 3247

College/University Index / Ohio University

Colleen Greenrod, 293
Mark A Johnson, 1865
Lindsay Karas, 1285
Anthony M Lacenere, 991
Rich Langdale, 1285
Sam Lee, 730
Wally Lennox, 1465
Fayez S. Muhtadie, 1746
Jay D Pauley, 1754
Dan Phelps, 1612
David W. Pidwell, 87
Michael Price, 452
Eric A Reeves, 634
John M. Rice, 481
John M Rice PhD, 1849
David A. Sands, 1460
Omar A Sawaf, 2012
David R. Scholl, 189
Richard Schwarz, 653
Sharon Stevenson DVM, PhD, 1371
Robert Unkovic, 1102
John Willert, 404

Ohio University
Kristy Campbell, 1556
John P. Gilliam, 302
Jeff Griffor, 1122
H Randall Litten, 351
Seun Salami, 1356
Brian C. Tilley, 611

Ohio Wesleyan University
Darrell W Austin, 204
Charlie MacMillan, 642

Oklahoma Baptist University
Michael Hunkapiller, 87

Oklahoma Christian University
W Michael Partain, 592

Oklahoma City University
Tom Walker, 1556

Oklahoma State University
Dennis Dougherty, 1013
Richard Garman, 796
Michael D Long, 1270
Jason Reed, 1997
Carl D Thoma, 1817
James Thorp, 16
Anis Uzzaman, 721
Craig Woodruff, 47

Old Dominion University
Kevin Gibbs, 1208

Olin Business School
Stephen Broun, 402
Kevin Malone, 1109

Olin Graduate School of Business
David Q. Anderson, 119
Michael Harden, 177
Tom Needham, 1777

Olivet Nazarene University
Curtis D Crocker, 1547

Oregon State University
John Becker, 110
Wesley R. Edens, 769
Maurice Gunderson, 207, 208
Utkarsh Kanal, 201
Walter Kortschak, 1677
Ali Shadman, 1042
Ed Yang, 974

Osgoode Hall Law School
Bradley W. Ashley, 2218
Justin Beber, 2062
Daniel Brothman, 2216
Rocco DiPucchio, 2067
Carey Diamond, 2280
Jody Forsyth, 2034
Loudon Mclean Owen, 2191
Loudon Owen, 2147
Evan Siddal, 2029
Adam Szweras, 2117

Ottawa Heart Institute
Brad Bolzon, 1930

Oxford Said School of Business
Yanev Suissa, 1689

Oxford University
Kate Bingham, 1764
Trevor Burgess, 1129
William J Canestaro, 2007
Bennett Cohen, 1453
Bill Guttman, 1626
Whitney Haring-Smith, 134
Patrick Pichette, 2150
Subhanu Saxena, 1301
Andrew Scotland, 242
Tim Stubbs, 1755
Jonathan Victor, 228

PSG Tech
Anil Tammineedi, 127

Pace University
Roland V. Bernardon, 407
Alexander Cuomo, 1325
Pasquale DeAngelis, 1492
Gerry Doherty, 1277
Jason D Drattell, 1472
John Dugan, 1364
Thomas P (Todd) Gibbons, 306
Jack Iacovone, 1287
Shant Mardirossian, 1085
Steven J Morgenthal, 165
Jonathan M Rather, 1973
Stephen Rossetter, 450
Tony Shum, 38
Savitha Srinivasan, 971
Andrew H. Steuerman, 848
Gene Wolfson, 429
Richard Zannino, 435
Thomas de Jager, 119

Pacific Lutheran University
Erik Benson, 1947
Armen B Shanafelt, 1128

Pacific Union College
Clinton W. Walker, 496

Pacific University
Zachary C. Berk, 1062

Panthéon-Sorbonne University
Marcel Fournier, 425
Eric Hippeau, 1114
Karen Noel, 1418

Paris University of Medicine
Jean-Francois Formela, MD, 193

Paul Merage School of Business
Justin Hartfield, 665

Peking University
Shan Fu, 1943

Carol Mao, 802
Evelyn Sun, 149

Pennsylvania State University
Kevin Adamek, 754
Susan Adams, 22
Edward Anchel, 670
Jason S Barg, 1151
Bruce Booth, 193
John Burns, 1165
Steve Carpenter, 1120
Bryan Castillo, 43
Adam H Curtin, 1234
Joseph Cutts, 1382
Harry D'Andrea, 1901
Barbara J Dalton PhD, 1439
W Ryan Davis, 1163
J. Bradley Davis, 1565
Gary R DiLella, 1496
Michael DiPiano, 1316
James B. Dougherty, MD, 158
Greg Dracon, 1
Jerry Engel, 1249
Ken Fox, 1751
Mark Fruehan, 1244
John Gannon, 693, 1757
Eerik Giles, 1279
A. Bruce Johnston, 1778
Paul S. Kasper, 679
Jason Klein, 28
Jerry Knotts, 3248
Ira M Lubert, 1140, 1510
Michael Lynch, 1200
David J Machlica, 1166
Jim Marra, 293
Michael McMahon, 1050
James M Mead, 1523
Kirk Morgan, 52
Scott Nissenbaum, 249
Steven G Park, 617
Ned J Renzi, 275
John E Runnells, 1931
Santosh Sankar, 640
Peter D. Schreiber, 617
Steven J Taubman, 1910
Joseph Zanone, 582

Pepperdine University
Wilson Allen, 1977
Lisa Atia, 221
Warren Bergen, 2043
Greg Bettinelli, 1890
Dan Chiriaev, 866
Mark Fields, 93
Matt Fuller, 824
Joshua Mack, 503
Eric Manlunas, 1966
Bob Marshall, 1649
Jim Marshall, 1649
Chris Perry, 491
Dennis Podlesak, 622
Luke K. Stanton, 1694
Mark Swaine, 496

Pepperdine University School of Law
B Marc Averitt, 1371
Gerard N. Casale, 1878

Philadelphia University
RoseAnn B. Rosenthal, 249
Janet L. Stott, 1830

Philips International Institute
Ed Yang, 974

Pierce College
Michael Dunn, 694

College/University Index / Princeton University

Pitzer College
Shahan D Soghikian, 1411

Politecnico di Milano
Roberto Buaron, 734

Polytechnic Institute of Brooklyn
Ta-Lin Hsu, 897

Polytechnic Institute of New York
John R. Kline, 1300

Polytechnic University of New York
Paul J Ferri, 1184
Robert Humes, 1042

Pomona College
Steve Crihfield, 903
Marc A. Gineris, 986
Marcia Goodstein, 976
Wei Hopeman, 149
Kristin Johnson, 96
M. Scott Jones, 898
Loretta Little, 2007
Daniel I. Rubin, 87
Jodi Sherman Jahic, 83
Michael S Solomon, 1113
Christopher Staudt, 668
Brian Wheeler, 260

Portland State University
Steve Bailey, 785
David Dolezal, 1917
John Saefke, 1917
Corey Schmid, 1659

Princeton University
Andrew Adams, 1361
Joseph B. Alala III, 408
Brandon Allen, 1877
James G Andersen, 505
Robert Anderson, 796
Carl T Anderson, 840
Christopher Anderson, 1085
Merrick Andlinger, 124
Brian Ascher, 1918
Jeffrey L Balash, 529
Tom Barnds, 28
Redington Barrett III, 1435
John F. Barry III, 1493
Nikhil Basu Trivedi, 1666
Croom Beatty, 1203
Matthew M. Bennett, 1300
Betsy Biemann, 440
JH Bilenker, MD, 73
James G Binch, 1131
John P. Birkelund, 1624
Jim Blair, PhD, 622
David C. Bordeau, 257
Michael Borrus, 2010
Peter L. Briger Jr., 769
Graham Brooks, 1
Bob Brown, 1275
Steve Brownlie, 96
Terry Brubaker, 832
C.J. Brucato, 20
Andy Burgess, 2236
Kevin T. Callaghan, 257
James C. Carlisle, 1818
Randy Castleman, 552
David G Chandler, 470
Frank Chang, 757
Naynika Chaubey, 2105
Brian Cherry, 1360
Stephen Chiao, 1771
Hoon Cho, 828
David Coats, 545

Brooke B Coburn, 416
Michael M Cone, 632
Ryan Cotton, 223
James Currier, 1323
Ben Dahl, 1679
Harry DeMott, 1528
Matt DeNichilo, 676
Thanasis Delistathis, 1290, 1485
John D Diekman PhD, 11
Donald Dixon, 765
Donald R. Dixon, 1852
Charles P. Durkin, Jr., 1624
Rory Eakin, 484
Joshua C. Empson, 1498
John F. Erhard, 157
Christopher Erickson, 1822
Luke B Evnin, 1268
Robert Faber, 227
Jim Farrell, 371
Stephen A. Feinberg, 453
Brian Fitzgerald, 404
Bill Ford, 762
Charles C Freyer, 1636
Sen. William H. Frist, MD, 559
Marc-Henri Galletti, 1147
John Garcia, 63
Edward F. Glassmeyer, 1361
Michael Goldberg, 340
Allan R. Goldberg, PhD, 1811
Andrew Grapkowski, 101
Gerald Greenwald, 867
Phil Greer, 1382
Philip Hammarskjold, 927
Seth L. Harrison, M.D., 144
Jay Hass, 1597
Todd Hixon, 1290
Deborah Hodges, 1231
Adam Hopkins, 660
Jim Hornthal, 194
Charles B Hughes III, 644
John Hummer, 959
Krist Jake, 1538
John Johnston, 200
Robert Johnston, 1048
Greg Kats, 401
Thomas H Kean, 1506
Peter Kellner, 1564
Jay Kern, 1070
John Kilgallon, 223
Charles F Kireker, 789
Ilya Kirnos, 1677
Fred Kittler, 731
Joshua A. Klevens, 458
John Kole, 1146
Paul Koontz, 773
Dave Kreter, 828
Stephen M LeSieur, 1720
Anthony Lee, 100
Scott Lenet, 794
H Jeffrey Leonard, 838
Andrew Levin, 1522
Joshua Lewis, 1611
Richard Lipkin, 644
John F. MacMurray, 1624
Joe Machado, 1266
Paul Maeder, 938
Edward B Marsh, MD, 1199
Paul Martino, 361
Alan Mattamana, 715
Gary S Matthews, 1256
John A. (Tony) Mayer, 707
Peter C McWilliams PhD, 1619
Sameet Mehta, 856
Seth Meisel, 280
Christian T Miller, 699
Brian C Miller, 1132
Alison Minter, 1336

Chris Mitchell, 1720
Ryan Moore, 37
G. Mason Morfit, 1905
Laurence C. Morse PhD, 715
Robert W. Mulcare, 1300
Tom Murphy, 560
Nathan Myhrvold, 1010
Andriy Mykhaylovskyy, 728
Joshua M. Nelson, 1818
Kara Nortman, 1890
James D. O'Brien, 97
Standish O'Grady, 857
William Osborn, 522
Rob Palumbo, 28
Kush M Parmar, MD, PhD, 11
Scott G Pasquini, 1160
Heidi Patel, 1555
Vincente Piedrahita, 1818
Nic Poulos, 320
John L Pouschine, 1470
Robert S Powell Jr, 1277
Russell Pyne, 194
Deborah Quazzo, 888
David Ramsay, 415
Roland Reynolds, 990
John Richardson, 1279
Gordon Ritter, 666
Sarah Rogers, 840
Brett J Rome, 1339
Donald C. Roth, 671
Jared Ruger, 260
Juan Sabater, 1904
Jeff Samberg, 25
Eric Schmidt, 1001
Bryan Schreier, 1657
Keoni Schwartz, 96
Jim Shapiro, 1063
Brian Sheng, 788, 1810
Craig Sherman, 1213
Edwin Shirley, 715
John Siegel, 518
Steve Sloane, 1203
Bruce Smith, 417
Thomas S Souleles, 1160
Ira Starr, 1145
Wright Steenrod, 477
Dimitri Steinberg, 775
P Bart Stephens, 286
Marcus Stroud, 1877
Daniel Sugar, 1927
Sanjay Swani, 1779
William H Taylor II, 1262
Ralph Taylor-Smith, 812
Pete Tedesco, 921
Robert Tepper, MD, 1814
Graves Tompkins, 819
Jesse Treu, PhD, 622
Scott Ungerer, 677
Tom Vander Schaaff, 655
Jonathan Victor, 228
Patrick Wack, 1561
Bradaigh Wagner, 674
Brendan Wallace, 728
Trevor Watt, 927
Graham Weaver, 92
John Weinberg, 700
Peter Wendell, 1672
Harold R. Werner, 922
Ted West, 775
Andrew Wilson, 203
Frank Winslow, 1507
Shari H. Wolkon, 1818
Geoff Yang, 1537
Philip Yau, 828
Ben Yu, 1672

1019

College/University Index / Principia College

Principia College
Andy Reed, 319
Bob Rees, 1740

Pritzker School of Law
John Kuelper, 178

Punjab University
Vivek Mehra, 200

Purdue University
Mark Achler, 1181
Adel A Alderbas, 1952
Mike Asem, 1159
Sherman Atkinson, 1237
Brooke Beier, 1842
Thomas A Berglund, 734
Leslie Bottorff, 812
Eric J Bruun, 480
Jerome Camp, 388
Bob Curry, 1098
Albert DaValle Jr., 1042
Brian Demkowicz, 963
Rami Elkhatib, 40, 1711
Bill Elmore, 773
Ting Gootee, 659
Pramod Gosavi, 3
Brian Graves, 630
Tony Grover, 1596
Mamoon Hamid, 1079
Robert Humes, 1042
Nabeel Hyatt, 1718
Rouz Jazayeri, 431
Scott Lutzke, 445
Dan Malven, 9
Tracy Marshbanks, 733
Dean Nelson, 1606
Tim R. Palmer, 458
Tom Scholl, 1348
Paul Slaats, 1234
Brian R Smith, 1601
Christopher Sobecki, 1022
Scott M. Sperling, 1818
Sven Strohband, 1073
Scot E Swenberg, 480
Eric Terhorst, 733
Andrew A Thomas, 1747
John Tzeng, 908
J. William Uhrig, 1822
Thomas D Weldon, 39

Queen's University
David Adderley, 2070
Robin Axon, 2176
Trent Baker, 2022
Eric Baker, 2186
Rob Barbara, 2063
Gregory Baylin, 2200
Brent Belzberg, 2252, 2264
John Berton, 2126
Arif N. Bhalwani, 2214
J. Peter Blaney, 2145
Seth Boro, 1817
Robert Bramer, 2207
Nathan Brown, 1990
Michael Castellarin, 2075
Matthew Cross, 2160
Lauchlan Currie, 2036
Chad Danard, 2267
Marcus Daniels, 2140
Chris Davis, 813
James Dent, 2182
Shayn Diamond, 2280
Peter Dowse, 2156
Tom Eisenhauer, 2059
David Eisler, 2227
Michael Graham, 2199
Christopher Harris, 2142
Ewout Heersink, 2201
Kelly Holman, 2125
Thomas Kaneb, 2186
Thomas Kennedy, 2160
Larry LaKing, 2181
Damian Lamb, 2125
Paul Laufert, 2165
Lars Leckie, 959
Chris Legg, 1488
Michael List, 2135
Eddie Lucarelli, 2233
Paul Lucas, 2145
Alan Lysne, 2109
John B. MacIntyre, 2056
Ian Macdonell, 2083
Kevin McBride, 2031
Zac McIsaac, 2182
Cory Michalyshyn, 2070
Salil Munjal, 2283
Anthony Munk, 2201
Jeffrey N. Murphy, 2156
Mike Murray, 2209
Richard Osborn, 2225, 2256
Michael Overvelde, 2085
Christopher Payne, 919
John Philp, 2121
Sam Pollock, 2062
Paul Richardson, 2230
Art Robinson, 2171
George Rossolatos, 2065
Rob Rutledge, 823
Chris Seasons, 2036
Michael Siltala, 2279
Ray Simonson, 2271
Gregory Smith, 2151
Gregory J. Smith, 2158
Jamie Stiff, 2125
Jeremy Thompson, 2211
Robert Trudeau, 1787
Gregory G. Turnbull, 2068
David Unsworth, 2146
Mark Usher, 2074
Jeff Van Steenbergen, 2044
Ben Vaughan, 2062
John Veitch, 2076
Peter van der Velden, 2173
Carlo A. von Schroeter, 1979

Queen's University Belfast
Ruairi Grant, 1314
Mairead Lavery, 2106

Queens College
Michael Falk, 530
Richard Goldstein, 64
Harris Landgarten, 174
Brenda Marex, 1302
Howard Matlin, 1066
Jordan Odinsky, 882
Sylvia F. Rosen, 425
Craig Slutzkin, 1297

Queensland University of Technology
Rory Quinlan, 1520

Questrom School of Business
Jeffrey M. Zucker, 865

Quinnipiac University
Kevin Crowley, 532
Daniel Wagner, 532

Radford University
Randal J. Kirk, 1815

Rady School of Management
Niall A O'Donnell PhD, 1578

Randolph-Macon College
Benjamin Schapiro, 1517

Red McCombs School of Business
Wesley Gottesman, 328
Matthew J. Nordgren, 152
Charlie Plauche, 1601

Reed College
Venky Ganesan, 1203
Behzad Khosrowshahi, 2097
Heather Redman, 757
Charles L Schroeder, 1343

Regis University
Dan Aweida, 213
Scott Morris, CPA, 737

Reims Management School
David Espitallier, 730

Rensselaer Polytechnic Institute
Jim Collis, 1641
Bob Cummings, 1990
John Daileader, 867
Peter Fitzgerald, 1098
Mike Gausling, 1386
George C Kenney, 1667
Richard Kiley, 290
Cyril L. Meduna, 62
Dennis O'Brien, 1135
Justin J. Perreault, 523
Elias J. Sabo, 525
David R Schopp, 1747
Sean Sebastian, 275
Wade Sheffer, 821
David Shen, 591
Amit Srivastava, 683
Rick Stowe, 921
Patrick Sullivan, 223
Jason P Torres, 1168
Jesse Treu, PhD, 622
Mark Visser, 248
Chris Young, 1557

Rhodes College
Thomas Gieselmann, 641
David Lightburn, 191

Rice University
Cliff Atherton Jr., 893
Forest Baskett, 1296
Jay Benear, 639
Stephanie Campbell, 953
Tony Di Bona, 87
Jeff Eby, 2007
Grace Ge, 1203
Barton Goodwin, 577
John Jaggers, 1661
Michael Kane, 377
Sharon Kedar, 1342
Carl Novotny, 1922
Christopher O'Neill, 1946
Howard Park, 828
Amit A. Patel, 1393
Sam H. Pyne, 898
Holly Radel, 3252
Leighton Read, 329
J. Leighton Read, MD, 87
Pamela L. Reiland, 893
Beni Rovinski, 2173
Richard Simoni, 183
Thomas J Stephenson, 1926
Daniel Tompkins, 1354
Philip A Tuttle, 592
Aamir Virani, 780
Dan Watkins, 1207

Brent Williams, 899
Daniel B. Wolfe, Ph.D, 5
Glenn A Youngkin, 416

Richard Ivey School of Business
Matthew Cross, 2160

Richmont Graduate University
Karen Houghton, 191

Ricker College
Robert E Davoli, 1675

Roanoke College
Jake Tarr Jr., 1076

Robert H. Smith School of Business
Code Cubitt, 2187
Randy Guttman, 1045
Meghan M. McGee, 386

Rochester Institute of Technology
Scott Condron, 1988
Allen F Grum, 1526
Michael Stanek, 1044

Rockefeller University
Carl L. Gordon PhD, 1383

Rockhurst University
Kevin F. Mullane, 1020
Jared Poland, 367

Rockhust Jesuit University
Kevin Mullane, 16

Rollins College
Jennifer Dunham, 173

Rome Center for International Law
Bruce Rogers, 1090

Rose Polytechnic
Felda Hardymon, 263

Ross School of Business
Adrian Fortino, 1207
Anna Haghgooie, 1618
Dan Kidle, 150
Marcy Marshall, 150
Paul McCreadie, 150
Tige Savage, 1558
Christopher W Solomon, 1973
Ryan Waddington, 964

Rotman School of Management
Chris Anastasopoulos, 2097
Matthew Chapman, 2264
Tom Eisenhauer, 2059
Mona Kung, 2132
Larry Y. Liu, 2123
Jamie Stiff, 2125
Craig Strong, 2235
Kevin Talbot, 2228
Jim Taylor, 2115
Andrew Walton, 2156
Kyle Winters, 2193

Rowan University
Larry A Colangelo, 1230
Paul M Grassinger, 165

Royal Military College
Lawrence Stevenson, 2076

Rutgers Business School
Thomas Girardi, 956

Rutgers Grad. School of Business
Kevin P. Costello, 312

Rutgers Law School
Andrew M Bushell, 542
Gerry Doherty, 1277
Daniel Gulino, 1567
Randy Maslow, 970

Rutgers University
Mark L. Benaquista, 1818
Kevin Bitterman, PhD, 193
Donald F. DeMuth, 611
James T. Denton, 346
Richard B Emmitt, 1931
Mark Fields, 93
Nancy C Floyd, 1355
Glenn C Harrison, 1472
Sheldon Howell, 973
Mir Imran, 984
Murray Karp, CPA, 676
Roman Kikta, 1244
Jay Levy, 2016
Wayne Marino, 1751
Gerald A. Michaud, 949
Vineet Pruthi, 1131
Sandeep Sardana, 298
Thomas A Schlesinger, 247
George J Schultze, 1632
Nanette Schunk, 3265
Jeffrey T Stevenson, 1929
Tony Tamer, 931
Jim Thornton, 892
Keith Titan, 259
Jon Trauben, 99
Patrick J Welsh, 1973
Ravi Yadav, 1314
Tomer Yosef-Or, 20
David W. Young, 436

Ryerson University
David Henderson, 2282
Scott Monteith, 2189
Whitney Rockley, 2183
Michael Serruya, 2245
Joseph Shlesinger, 2076

Sacramento State University
Skip Glass, 773
Daniel K Turner III, 1251

Saint Bonaventure University
Kevin P. Fahey, 302

Saint Edward's University, Texas
Atif Abdulmalik, 153

Saint Edwards University
Rudy Garza, 807

Saint Joe's University
Scott Nissenbaum, 249

Saint John's University
Bob DeSena, 883
Kevin M. McGovern, 1194

Saint Joseph's University
Robert Graham, 1431

Saint Leo University
Krista Covey, 738

Saint Louis University
Joe Kaiser, 1205
Luke Sage, 1427
April Young, 928

Saint Mary's College
Joe Kell, 1310
Brad Triebsch, 574

Saint Mary's College of California
Steven Rea, 187

Saint Mary's University
Chris Moyer, 2208
Andrew Ray, 2148

Saint Michael's College
José Blanco, 574
Peter A Lyons, 1109

Saint Vincent College
Robert Swartz, 1208

Salem State College
John Fiato, 912
Elliot M. Katzman, 523

Salisbury University
Jeff Elburn, 1745

Salmon P Chase College
Jack Wyant, 290

Salve Regina University
R. Wade Aust, 77
Stephan C. Sloan, 126

Sam Houston State University
Matt Anderson, 1977
Brian Hawkins, 1977
Ron Norris, 1924

Samara State Aerospace University
Dmitry Alimov, 795

Samford University
Ted Alling, 640
Philip L Hodges, 1536
John W. McCullough, 907
R. Clayton McWhorter, 497

San Diego School of Law
David Stern, 504
Court R. Turner, J.D., 30

San Diego State University
Caroline Barberio, 1239
Christopher J Bower, 1398
Rich DeMartini, 560
Josef Friedman, 1750
Aaron M Gurewitz, 1592
Alex Kanayev, 2027
Steven Rea, 187
Tighe Reardon, 209
Bryon C Roth, 1592
Rick Slaughter, 1758
Court R. Turner, J.D., 30
Dino Vendetti, 766, 1659
Eric D Wedbush, 1970

San Francisco State University
Kirsi Fontenot, 952
Elizabeth Gamboa, 1299
Stacy Huynh, 152
Carolyn Ticknor, 994
James Vaughan, 237

San Jose State University
Ron Conway, 1763
Pauline Duffy, 1543
John E. Hall, 950
Lara Kwong, 998
Chris LeBlanc, 1795

College/University Index / Santa Barbara College of Law

Robert May, 990
Teresa McDaniel, 171
Christie Pitts, 221
Ven N. Reddy, 131
Rudy Ruano, 1976
Kirk Westbrook, 1015

Santa Barbara College of Law
Debra P Geiger, 830

Santa Clara University
George Arnold, 1081
Kevin Carter, 1763
Gianna Conci Orozco, 493
Gary Coover, 1614
Wayne Doiguchi, 217
Irwin Federman, 1898
Peter Fitzgerald, 1098
Tim Haley, 1537
John E. Hall, 950
Stephen Hyndman, 827
Hsing Kung, 46
Chris LeBlanc, 1795
Vivian Loh Nahmias, 840
Jim Marshall, 1649
Matthew McDonald, 230
Kirsten A. Mello, 1203
Matthew Miau, 908
Angela Nuttman, 773
Kevin Ober, 619
Chad Packard, 1428
Ken Pearlman, 1365
Brian Pokorny, 1763
Larry Randall, 94
Diana Saca, 682
Dana Stalder, 1184
Pete Thomas, 185
David Tsang, 46
Doug Tsui, 950
Robert L Underwood, 1333
David Wanek, 1976
Joseph Zanone, 582

Sarah Lawrence College
Carl Goldfischer, MD, 240

Schiller International University
Chris Xie, 2263

Schulich School of Business
John Albright, 2228
Bradley W. Ashley, 2218
Alex Baker, 2228
Justin Beber, 2062
Richard Betsalel, 2083
Andrew Bishop, 2052
Daniel Brothman, 2216
Roman S. Dubczak, 2073
Michael Graham, 2199
Lee M. Grunberg, 2218
Serge LeVert-Chiasson, 2239
Craig Noble, 2062
Alireza Rahnema, 2025
Gene Shkolnik, 2142
Alex Storcheus, 2117
Hamish Sutherland, 2147, 2279
Peter van der Velden, 2173

Seattle University
Steve Hooper, 978
Kent Johnson, 82
Joseph Piper JD, 1007
Mike Templeman, 892
Timothy Thompson Black, 1007

Seneca College
Jon Jackson, 3249

Seoul National University
Henry Chung, 627

Seton Hall University
Kenneth J. Kulaga, 725

Shanghai Jiao Tong University
Benson He, 897

Shanghai Jiotong University
Franklin Jiang, 2221

Shanghai University
Dennis Wu, 293
Eric Xu, 827

Sheffield Hallam University
Jonathan Tunnicliff, 1349

Sichuan MBA College
Jesson Chen, 2221

Sichuan University
Jesson Chen, 2221

Sienna College
Thomas J. Baldwin, 357
Thomas Iannarone, 280

Simmons College
Jean George, 58
Jean George, 1126

Simmons Grad. School of Management
Jennifer Trzepacz, 1985

Simon Fraser University
Gerry Bellerive, 2227
Dan Jacques, 2138
Gursh Kundan, 1002
Leah Nguyen, 2144
Caroline Sanche, 2249

Simon School of Business
Brennan Mulcahey, 352
Kyle Stanbro, 352

Skidmore College
Rob Adams, 1321
David Castle, 330
Nick MacShane, 1488
Emily Paxhia, 1468
Chris Young, 1557

Slippery Rock University
David Koegler, 1196

Sloan School of Management
Mike Bryant, 1082
Casey Gordon, 1341
Chris McLeod, 661

Smith College
Grace Ames, 1361
Deborah A Farrington, 1741
Joelle Kayden, 36
Michele Kinner, 1518
Jennifer Tegan, 434

Smith School of Business
Eddie Lucarelli, 2233

Sonoma State University
Greg Lyon, 648
Patrick Teixeira, 1397

South Dakota School of Mines
Richard H. Frank, 585
Terry Rock, 446

South Dakota State University
Tyler J Stowater, 300

Southeastern University
Krista Covey, 738

Southern Connecticut University
Kevin McGrath, 1287

Southern Illinois University
John Fletcher, 750
Herb Shear, 383
Jamie Wehrung, 178

Southern Methodist University
Rugger Burke, 1625
Jack Carsten, 950
A Baron Cass III, 367
Michael Coppola, 583
Jeff Davis, 47
Daniel Einhorn, 403
Marty Flanagan, 1019
Kevin Gabelein, 755
Lou Gerken, 826
Kevin Green, 546
Patrick Hamner, 1424
Bob Howe, 8
Peter Huff, 294
Neenah Jain, 1523
Brian Jolly, 960
Stuart Larkins, 473
Troy LeMaile-Stovall, 1792
Kevin L. Listen, 905
Jim Madden, 419
Clayton Main, 336
Charles R Martin, 112
Mark L Masinter, 1552
Felipe Mendoza, 166
David B. Miller, 673
Dennis E Murphree, 1273
Ryan K Nagim, 1148
James Outland, 1292
Alexandra Prima, 1807
Louis Rajczi, 770
Jason C. Schmidly, 418
Jim Schultz, 1380
Robert Shen, 897
Tim Storer, 8
Vik Thapar, 577
Paul A Yeoham, 1487
Jeff Zanarini, 931

Southwest Missouri State University
Richard Garman, 796
Joseph Zell, 881

Southwest University
Jesson Chen, 2221

Southwestern University
Victoria Dominguez-Edington, 447
Lauren B Leichtman, 1115
Alex Maleki, 976

Spelman College
Kateri Jones, 1773

Spring Arbor University
Angela Helfin, 3259

Spring Hill College
Stephanie Campbell, 953

College/University Index / Stanford Grad. School of Business

St. Andrews University
David O Ellis, 656
Ned Truslow, 1560

St. Anselm College
David H Donabedian, 1149
JJ Healy, 853

St. Bonaventure University
Bill Taranto, 1206
David J. Zatlukal, 1041

St. Catherine University
Ann Winblad, 959

St. Edward's University
Bob Goodman, 395

St. Francis Xavier University
Peter MacAskill, 2197
Paul Rowe, 2121
Jeff White, 2192

St. John Fisher College
Kyle Stanbro, 352

St. John's University
Richard Bauerly, 855
Scott L Becker, 1343
Buzz Benson, 1673
John Brecker, 99
Kenneth Burns, 1681
Tony Christianson, 466
Thomas P Fitzpatrick, 1654
John Guiliana DPM, 1288
Arnold J Hoegler, 1107
Steven Insalaco, 372
Joe Kaczorowski, 334
Michael Kenny, 1986
Ira D. Kleinman, 917
Emanuel Martinez, 870
Howard Matlin, 1066
Michael R McCarthy, 1276
Thomas E. McInerney, 302
John L. McInerney, 302
Dan Moorse, 920
Kevin Ober, 619
Paolo Parziale, 17
Sylvia F. Rosen, 425
Angela Santi, 34
Andrew H. Steuerman, 848
Brian Sullivan, 1992

St. Joseph's University
Kevin Clayton, 676
Timothy G. Fallon, 148
Chris Fralic, 742
Daisy Mellet, 1208
Adele C. Oliva, 4, 1510

St. Lawrence University
Cate Ambrose, 3252
Lee Bailey, 1897
Keith L. Crandell, 154
William Ford, 858
Chris Lund, 903
Carol Newell, 2230

St. Louis University
Stephen Broun, 402
Bill Conley, 383
Charles Resnick, 994
Steve M. Welborn, 2008

St. Mary's College
Gary Cuccio, 1795
George Schmitt, 1795

St. Mary's University
Matthew Towns, 2242

St. Norbert College
Thomas F Campion, 1210
John Connolly, 224
Jim Domach, 1174

St. Olaf College
Josh Baltzell, 1728
Thomas Erickson, 739
Mark Jacobsen, 1359
B. Kristine Johnson, 67
Tony Miller, 1111

St. Peter's College
Pasquale DeAngelis, 1492
Tom Mac Mahon, 749
Kenneth J Mathews, 384

Stanford Grad. School of Business
Krishna K Agrawal, 1133
Mark Allsteadt, 404
Matthew L. Altman, 167
William J. Amelio, 595
Steve Anderson, 234
Carl T Anderson, 840
Merrick Andlinger, 124
Paul Asel, 1331
Stephen E. Babson, 674
John Backus, 1290
Ben Ball, 782
Steven Baloff, 58
Zach Barasz, 305
Tom Barnds, 28
William Barnum, 337
Carrie Bates, 1849
Allen Beasley, 1537
William Beckett, 813
David Bell, 328
Dror Berman, 1001
Elizabeth Q Betten, 1160
Nikhil J. Bhat, 1933
David Biesel, 1322
Jeff Bird, 1762
Christian Borcher, 414
Seth Boro, 1817
Roelof Botha, 1657
Scott Brady, 1001
Orlando Bravo, 1817
Jeff Brody, 1537
Doug Burgum, 175
M Roy Burns, 1778
John Caddedu, 582
Kevin T. Callaghan, 257
Paul D Carbery, 792
Douglas C. Carlisle, 1203
Brian Cassidy, 560
Todd C. Chaffee, 1006
Leon Chen, PhD, 519
Robert Cherun, 2042
Helen Chiang, 111
Ian Chiu, 1393
Joyce Chung, 810
Peter Chung, 1255
Lisa Coca, 812
Dave Coglizer, 1978
Christopher L Collins, 1066
Tom Costin, 1393
Ryan Cotton, 223
Ryan Craig, 260
Jeffrey M Crowe, 1346
Natalie D Cryer, 381
Scott Darling, 604
Paul L Davies III, 381
Ben DeRosa, 110
Dipanjan (DJ) Deb, 782

Raymond Debbane, 1022
Steven Denning, 819
Donald R. Dixon, 1852
Alex Doll, 1796
Matt Downs, 1618
David Dullum, 832
Ira Ehrenpreis, 596
Ira M Ehrenpreis, 1788
Ira Ehrenpreis, 3273
Peter Ehrich, 559
Bill Elmore, 773
Brian Fearnow, 371
Noel J Fenton, 1855
Brett Fisher, 745
Skip Fleshman, 183
Pete Flint, 1323
John Fogelsong, 840
William E. Ford, 819
Gene Frantz, 579
Sameer Gandhi, 27
Brian Garrett, 562
Shauntel Garvey, 1530
Eric Gevada, 1109
Charles E. Glew, Jr., 751
David Glynn, 840
Ross Goldstein, 609
David Golob, 782
David B. Golub, 848
Tom Goodrich, 582
Michael N. Gray, 1498
Maurice Gunderson, 207
Maurice Gunderson, 208
Russell B Hall, 1110
Craig Hanson, 1319
Chris Harris, 790
David Hodgson, 819
Adam Hopkins, 660
Bob Horne, 2021
James Howland, 1256
Peter Huff, 294
Jay Huffard, 533
Victor Hwang, 990
Dean Jacobson, 28
Scott Jacobson, 1162
Kurt R Jaggers, 1778
Kristin Johnson, 96
James A Johnson, 1997
Ross M. Jones, 257
Leland Jones, 674
Nigel W Jones, 1875
Jeff Jordan, 125
Scott Jordon, 840
Steve Jurvetson, 803
Annie Kadavy, 1537
Yasunori Kaneko MD, 1693
Rimas Kapeskas, 383
Paul S. Kasper, 679
Joelle Kayden, 36
Karen Kenworthy, 1751
Vinod Khosla, 1073
Paul Klingenstein, 19
Lauren Kolodny, 182
Thomas Korte, 129
Mark Koulogeorge, 1242
Steven M Krausz, 1898
Larry Kubal, 1093
Patrick Latterell, 1098
Gary Lauder, 1099
Lars Leckie, 959
Nathaniel V Lentz, 1388
Mark Leschly, 1561
Ping Li, 27
Robert D Lindsay, 1133
Casey Lynch, 96
Paul Madera, 1213
Rick Magnuson, 828
Billy Maguy, 92

College/University Index / Stanford Grad. School of Education

Fern Mandelbaum, 1249
Nino Marakovic, 1623
Peter N. Masucci, 1300
George E Matelich, 1066
Tom Mawhinney, 972
Tim McAdam, 1787
Thomas McKinley, 413
Mark A. McLaughlin, 952
David Michael, 134
Antonio Miranda, 1138
Chris Moore, 1537
John H. Moragne, 1852
Arneek Multani, 1852
Matt Murphy, 1203
Andriy Mykhaylovskyy, 728
Patricia Nakache, 1855
Tom Newby, 1116
Brent Nicklas, 1116
Nate Niparko, 27
Vincent M Occhipinti, 2005
Larry Orr, 1855
Toshi Otani, 1840
Victor E Parker, 1720
Harsh Patel, 493
Amit A. Patel, 1393
Heidi Patel, 1555
Harsh Patel, 2001
Tory Patterson, 430
Tory Patterson, 1393
Sundeep Peechu, 720
Thomas A Penn, 1431
Carol Pereira, 96
Ezra Perlman, 782
Michael B Persky, 80
Michal Petrzela, 1127
Nick Pianim, 582
Chris A. Pierce, 1278
Naomi Pilosof, 1203
Scott Plumridge, 899
Tim Porter, 1162
Jason Pressman, 1666
David P Quinlivan, 1608
Erik Ragatz, 927
David Ramsay, 415
Alan H. Resnikoff, 1663
Barry D. Reynolds, 952
Robin Richards Donohoe, 628
Aaron Richmond, 674
Antonio Rodriguez, 1184
Sarah Rogers, 840
Alexander Rosen, 1566
Peter L Rottier, 1754
Jared Ruger, 260
John K. Saer Jr., 828
J.P. Sanday, 1203
Greg Sands, 548
Kenneth B Sawyer, 1608
Eric Schwartz, 425
Chris Scoggins, 1656
Tasha Seitz, 1042
Mark Selcow, 548
Jim Shapiro, 1063
Jason Shideler, 1160
Ben Shih, 972
Greg Shove, 1087
Mark A. Siegel, 1203
Peter Sinclair, 1106
Harpinder Singh, 1001
Mike Slade, 1644
Sam Smith-Eppsteiner, 1001
Mark Soane, 143
Katie Solomon, 823
McLain Southworth, 564
C Morris Stout, 1769
Paul Strachman, 1533
Laela Sturdy, 579
Timothy P Sullivan, 1160

William P. Sutter Jr., 947
John A Svoboda, 1767
Gus Taylor, 719
Nelson Teng, 460
Carl D Thoma, 1817
William N. Thorndike, 952
John Thornton, 205
Carolyn Ticknor, 994
Dafina Toncheva, 1898
Jason P Torres, 1168
Pavan Tripathi, 336
Richard C Tuttle, 1494
Tom Uhlman, 1304
Sigrid Van Bladel, 19
Sigrid Van Bladel, PhD, 19
Steve Vassallo, 773
John Walecka, 1537
Brendan Wallace, 728
Trevor Watt, 927
Graham Weaver, 92
Sharon Weinbar, 1629
Eric Weiner, 294
Eli Weiss, 823
Steve Westly, 1978
Dave Whorton, 1867
Timothy Wollaeger, 1619
Geoff Yang, 1537
David Yuan, 1787
TX Zhuo, 1059
Chris Zugaro, 1858
Casper de Clercq, 1346

Stanford Grad. School of Education
Shauntel Garvey, 1530
Amit A. Patel, 1393

Stanford Law School
Michael Arrington, 565
Stephen E. Babson, 674
William Barnum, 337
Orlando Bravo, 1817
Tom Dennedy, 176
Ira Ehrenpreis, 596
Ira M Ehrenpreis, 1788
Ira Ehrenpreis, 3273
Kathy Fields, 1045
Michael Johnson, 60
Geoffrey Rehnert, 197
John Roos, 824
Lisa Y. Roskens, 70
Alan E Salzman, 1908
David Smolen, 828
Peter Thiel, 778
Daniel Weiss, 127

Stanford Medical School
Jeff Bird, 1762
Thomas A Raffin MD, 1794

Stanford University
Jenny Abramson, 1555
Frank A. Adams, 881
Ajay Agarwal, 224
Daniel Agroskin, 1043
Robert Amen, 1912
Alexei Andreev, 207, 208
R. David Andrews, 886
George Arnold, 1081
Brian Ascher, 1918
A Craig Asher, 1942
Stephen E. Babson, 674
John Backus, 1290, 1785
Eric V Bacon, 1136
Darran A. Baird, 1746
Dado Banatao, 1781
Michael Banks, 875
Maren Thomas Bannon, 1030

Paul Barber, 1045
Jeffrey Barman, 1434
Jeffrey Barnes, 273
William Barnum, 337
Timothy A Barrows, 1184
Upal Basu, 1331
Carrie Bates, 1849
Stuart Baxter, 1576
Laura Baxter-Simmons, 1476
Allen Beasley, 1537
Nick Beim, 1918
David Bell, 328
Eric Benhamou, 252
Neal Bhadkamkar, 1249
George Bischof, 1213
Phil Black, 1862
Geoff Bland, 1970
David J. Blumberg, 304
Rick Blume, 704
Simon Boag, 985
Pavel Bogdanov, 89
Niko Bonatsos, 820
Steve Bowsher, 983
Phil Brady, 841
Sam Brasch, 1056
Jim Breyer, 339
Chris L Britt, 1171
Randall Brouckman, 1784
Gerry Brunk, 2173
Don Butler, 1821
Brook Byers, 1079
John Cable, 1729
Bandel L. Carano, 1361
Shawn T. Carolan, 1203
Jennifer Carolan, 1530
Chris G. Carter, 1326
Chris G Carter, 1328
Xavier Casanova, 775
Jane Castle, 211
Navin Chaddha, 1187
John Chaisson, 682
Jeffrey T Chambers, 1778
Connie Chan, 125
William Chan, 1142
David Chao, 597
Jerry Chen, 877
Alice Chen, PhD, 30
Leon Chen, PhD, 519
Cheryl Cheng, 299
Ian Chiu, 1393
Alan Chiu, 2010
Scott Chou, 657, 808
Peter Y Chung, 1754
John D Cochran, 1151
Fred Cohen, 1934
Brian J Conway, 1778
Wayne Cooper, 868
Everett Cox, 666
Scott Crabill, 1817
Ryan Craig, 260
David Cremin, 794
Todd R Crockett, 1778
Natalie D Cryer, 381
Ben Cukier, 442
Chip Cureton, 893
D Patrick Curran, 367
Rajeev Dadoo, 1734
Shivanandan A. Dalvie, 63
Natalie L Davies, 381
Paul L Davies III, 381
Jerel Davis, 1930
Casper de Clercq, 1346
Elisa del Gaudio, 40
Alex De Winter, 812
Dain F DeGroff, 1848
Kipp DeVeer, 159
Salil Deshpande, 224

College/University Index / Stanford University

Timothy Dick, 1740
John D Diekman PhD, 11
Ted Dintersmith, 457
Donald Dixon, 765
A. Barr Dolan, 460
Michael Dolbac, 812
David A. Donnini, 889
David Douglass, 605
Stephen M Dow, 1661
Ryan Drant, 1516
Timothy Draper, 610
Tim Draper, 627
Timothy Draper, 2020
Ted Driscoll, PhD, 493
Tim Dugan, 1962
Matt Dunbar, 1925
Tom Dyal, 1537
Randall Eason, 96
Barry Eggers, 1125
Steven A. Elms, 73
Greg Ennis, 1430
Patrick Enright, 1147
Charles H Esserman, 1863
Daniel Estes, PhD, 785
Neil Exter, 1814
Michael J. Farello, 1092
Brandon Farwell, 709
Brian Fearnow, 371
David S. Felman, 874
Peter Fenton, 251
Jim Feuille, 564
Michael Fisch, 111
Doug Fisher, 1014
Peter Fitzgerald, 1098
Morgan Flager, 1687
Jim Fleming, 518
Wade Flemons, 2210
Ryan Floyd, 1750
John Fogelsong, 840
Norman A. Fogelsong, 1006
Hadley Ford, 970
Alan Foster, 1795
Adam J. Fountain, 349
Clinton Foy, 562
Robert Fraser, 203
David Frazee, 1564
Bradford M. Freeman, 786
Tully M. Friedman, 790
Alexander A. Friend, 791
Leslie Frécon, 1117
Adam Fuller, 336
Ilya Fushman, 1079
Quin Garcia, 207, 208
Nikhil Garg, 1732
Andrew Garman, 1304
Brian Garrett, 562
Keith Geeslin, 782
Flip Gianos, 1014
Michael W Gibbons, 714
Ned Gilhuly, 1606
Richard Ginn, 549
John W. Glynn, 840
Jim Goetz, 1657
Jocelyn Goldfein, 2018
Daria Gonzalez, 895
Giles Goodhead, 868
Peter D Goodson, 632
Bing Gordon, 1079
Mark Gorenberg, 2018
Greg Gottesman, 1501
Pat Gouhin, 3247
Theresia Gouw, 182
David Grayzel, MD, 193
Madison F. Grose, 1742
Lauren Gross, 778
Jim Gunton, 1329
Ramneek Gupta, 488

Arun Gupta, 518
Arjun Gupta, 1795
Saar Gur, 457
James Halow, 371
Mamoon Hamid, 1079
Ammar H. Hanafi, 87
George Hara, 603
Eric Hardgrave, 53
Fred Harman, 1361
Chris Harris, 790
John Harris, 1033
Dr. Ryan A Harris, 1346
Randy Hawks, 493
Chip Hazard, 756
Robert Headley, 978
James Healy, 1700
Shahram Hejazi, 269
Peter Henry, 1647
Dr. Steve Herrod, 820
Mar Hershenson, 1426
Pete Higgins, 1644
Mark G. Hilderbrand, 952
Reid Hoffman, 877
Kirk Holland, 35
Jeffrey J Holland, 1639
Wei Hopeman, 149
Avshalom Horan, 340
Zachary Hornby, 489
David Hornik, 200
Andrew J. Howard, 1663
Jonathan Hsu, 1850
Tony Huie, 1677
John Hummer, 959
Andrew Humphries, 914
Thomas S Huseby, 1640
Wende Hutton, 389
Victor Hwang, 990
Maha Ibrahim, 389
Masazumi Ishii, 217
Brian Jacobs, 666
Asha Jadeja, 624
Wilfred Jaeger, 923
Kurt R Jaggers, 1778
Krist Jake, 1538
David Jargiello, 758
John W. Jarve, 1203
Peter T Jensen, 1720
Jared L. Johnson, 1417
James A Johnson, 1997
TJ Jubeir, 409
Steve Jurvetson, 803
Annie Kadavy, 1537
Rebecca Kaden, 1884
Julia Karol, 1963
Jonathan Kaskow, 294
Greg Kats, 401
Mohit Kaushal MD, 19
Guy Kawasaki, 810
Michael S Kaye, 503
Doug Kelly MD, 87
George C Kenney, 1667
William C. Kessinger, 1419
Asad Khaliq, 48
Jennifer W Kheng, 1116
Han Kim, 100
Doug Kimmelman, 676
Kirt Kirtland, 667
Chris Kitching, 936
Joshua A. Klevens, 458
Gil Kliman, 1014
Ailliam Knoke, 916
Garheng Kong, 924
Paul Koontz, 773
Steven M Krausz, 1898
Manu Kumar, 1054
Ethan Kurzweil, 263
Tim Kutzkey, PhD, 519

Eric Kwan, 1142
Francois Lafortune, 2090
Ann Lamont, 1361
Robert E. Larson, 24
Robert E Larson, 2005
Deval A Lashkari PhD, 1794
Vijay Lathi, 1297
Troy LeMaile-Stovall, 1792
Lars Leckie, 959
Anthony Lee, 100
Lisa M. Lee, 1498
Jess Lee, 1657
Julie Lein, 1895
Jean-Philippe Lemay, 727
Alda Leu Dennis, 995
William Lewis, 2020
Jeremy Liew, 1125
Jonathan E. Lim, MD, 489
Alfred Lin, 1657
David S Lobel, 1654
Dennis Lockhart, 1279
Greg Long, 790
Steve Loughlin, 27
Trevor R Loy, 758
Casey Lynch, 96
Paul Maeder, 938
David Magerman, 615
Billy Maguy, 92
Aditi Maliwal, 1890
Jules Maltz, 1006
Fern Mandelbaum, 1941
Peter M. Manos, 167
Mike Maples Jr., 752
Lenard Marcus, 655
Paul Mariani, 21
Scott Marlette, 1696
David Marquardt, 200
Alan Marty, 1110
Renee Masi, 272
Arun Mathew, 27
Erik E Maurer, 1494
Dirk McDermott, 98
Josh McFarland, 877
Ryan McIntyre, 779
Todd McIntyre, 875
Peter H McNerney, 1820
Sameet Mehta, 856
Richard Melmon, 361
Brian Melton, 1798
Thomas C Melzer, 1578
Lloyd M. Metz, 973
Ravi Mhatre, 1125
Sandy Miller, 1006
Daniel H Miller, 1584
Kate Mitchell, 1629
Ann Miura-Ko, 752
Andrew Moley, 1125
Geoffrey Moore, 1985
Brian Morfitt, 785
Michael C Morgan, 1848
Takeshi Mori, 841
Michael Mullany, 972
Jennifer M Mulloy, 1778
Hodong Nam, 100
Guido Neels, 698
Jennifer Keiser Neundorfer, 1030
Peter Nieh, 1125
Scott Nolan, 778
Zach Noorani, 773
Kara Nortman, 1890
Jacqueline Novogratz, 54
Scott O'Hare, 595
Christopher O'Neill, 1946
Vincent M Occhipinti, 2005
Selahattin Onen, 1407
Terry Opdendyk, 1379
Nick Orum, 886

College/University Index / State University of New York

Clare Ozawa, 1930
Raquel Palmer, 1089
James Patchett, 1307
Anthony Patek, 256
Anil Patel, 504
Jean-Marc Patouillaud, 1418
Marshall Payne, 479
Tom Penn, 1275
E. Kenneth Pentimonti, 1401
Doug Pepper, 1666
Carlos Perea, 970
David L Pesikoff, 1848
George Petracek, 194
Nancy Pfund, 596
David W. Pidwell, 87
Scott Platshon, 710
Will Porteous, 1597
Lisa Porter, 983
Russell Pyne, 194
Keith Rabois, 778
Thomas A Raffin MD, 1794
Erik Ragatz, 927
Heather Redman, 757
Bill Reichert, 721, 810
Alan H. Resnikoff, 1663
Matt Rightmire, 311
Paula Robins, 127
Antonio Rodriguez, 1184
Charles W. Roellig, 451
Jesse Rogers, 96
John Roos, 824
Susie Roos, 824
Rick Rosen, 931
Eric Rosenfeld, 794, 1384
Peter Roshko, 318
Steven J Rosston, 840
Stephen D. Royer, 1663
Rob Rutledge, 823
Julie Ruvolo, 3252
Jordan Ryan, 1562
Juan Sabater, 1904
Donald Sackman, 987
Neil Sadraranganey, 621
Kamil Saeid, 182
Jeff Samberg, 25
Scott Sandell, 1296
Julie Sandler, 1501
Kenneth B Sawyer, 1608
Kenneth T Schiciano, 1778
George Schmitt, 1795
Toni Schneider, 1862
David Schnell MD, 1495
Pierre J. Schuurmans, 2056
Kosha Shah, 1885
Nick Shalek, 1563
Bob Shaw, 194
David E. Shaw, 580
Robert Shaw, Jr., 161
David Shen, 591
Kirill Sheynkman, 1598
John F. Shoch, 87
Clara Sieg, 1558
Rob Siegel, 2010
David Silverman, 564
Bonny Simi, 1039
Richard Simoni, 183
James R Simons, 1728
Carlyle Singer, 54
Brian Singerman, 778
Steven F. Skoler, 791
Sarah Smith, 224
Sam Smith-Eppsteiner, 1001
David Smolen, 828
Ian Sobieski, PhD, 229
Edward P Sobol, 1973
Stephen Socolof, 1304
Katie Solomon, 823

Glenn Solomon, 827
Greg Somer, 693
Tyler Sosin, 1203
Pearson Spaght, 750
Ronald P. Spogli, 786
Jon Staenberg, 1736
Clancey Stahr, 841
Josh Stein, 610
Scott R. Stevens, 1410
Roger A Strauch, 1584
Sven Strohband, 1073
Scott Stuart, 1606
David Sze, 877
Napoleon Ta, 778
Tony Tamer, 931
Garry Tan, 995
Bryan Taylor, 61
Craig C. Taylor, 87
Eric Terhorst, 733
Peter Thiel, 418
Allen Thorpe, 927
Daniel Tompkins, 1354
James N. Topper, MD, PhD, 785
Tommy Tsai, 1142
Matt Tsien, 821
Jim Tullis, 1868
Hans Tung, 827
Richard C Tuttle, 1494
Louie Ucciferri, 916
Salman Ullah, 1219
Robert L Underwood, 1333
Petri Vainno, MD, PhD, 698
Vance Vanier, 471
Vince Vannelli, 1088
Thomas Vardell, 1341
Steve Vassallo, 773
Jonathan Victor, 228
Paul R. Vigano, 1041
Eric Vishria, 251
Tefan Vitorovic, 1934
Andy Vitus, 1629
John Von Schlegell, 674
John Vrionis, 1125
John Walecka, 1537
Hunter Walk, 944
Sona Wang, 454
Steve Waters, 1813
Allen A Weaver, 1440
Eckard Weber, MD, 622
Daniel Weiss, 127
Robert J. Wenzel, 73
Maurice Werdegar, 1976
Victor Westerlind, 812
Steve Westly, 1978
J.P. Whelan, 1070
Bill Wiberg, 58
William Wick, 1939
Melissa Widner, 1640
Tom Woiwode, 1930
Kirk Wolfe, 1242
Chris Yeh, 1959
Krishna Yeshwant, 894
Kwan Yoon, 299
Bill Youstra, 1087
Homan Yuen, 802
Lu Zang, 802
Dennis Zaslavsky, 1965
Stephanie Zhan, 1657
TX Zhuo, 729

State University of New York
Joel P. Adams, 55
Elliot Attie, 1853
Sid Banon, 462
Josh Bouk, 706
Kenneth Burns, 1681
Phil Carpenter III, 1026

Ryan Chan, 2244
William G. Connors, 1747
Jordan S Davis, 1523
Paul R DiBella, 539
Joe El Chami, 1026
Robert Frankel, 174
Steven G Glenn, 1957
Frances N. Janis, 1466
Peter Petrillo, 854
John Richardson, 2051

Stephen F. Austin State University
John T Harkrider, 1067
Dayakar Puskoor, 1284

Stephen M. Ross School of Business
John Yang, 328

Stetson University
Peter C Brockway, 351
Edward C McCarthy, 1575
Bruce Rogers, 1090
Steven D Singleton, 1261
Troy D Templeton, 1859

Stevens Institute of Technology
David Kronfeld, 1042
Steven J Morgenthal, 165
George L Sing, 1096

Stirling University
Bernie Zeisig, 2187

Stockholm School of Economics
Mats Lederhausen, 568

Stonehill College
Kevin P. Costello, 312

Stony Brook University
Shmuel Einav, PhD, 1811

Stuart School of Business
Bob Bode, 1026

Suffolk University
Charles E. Ball, 124
Bill Fitzgerald, 820
Peter A. Hunter, 214
Edward J Keefe, 1157
Senofer Mendoza, 1202
Mike O'Malley, 993

SUNY Albany
Paul Dibella, 770
Michael B Kaplan, 1138
Rocky Mountain, 595
Gene J Ostrow, 1529
Edward J Siskin, 940

SUNY Binghamton
Sean Barrette, 470
Ira D. Kleinman, 917
Lauren M Massey, 17
Devin Mathews, 470

SUNY Buffalo
Kevin Centofanti, 355
Paul Ciriello, 713
Chris Kryder, 749
George J Lee, 118
Michael G. Levine, 359
Daniel P Penberthy, 1526
Frank Reppenhagen, 531
Brian Rich, 429
Robert A. Spass, 407
Patrick Tan, 870
William E Watts, 1053

College/University Index / Trinity College

Margaret Whalen Brechtel, 1526

SUNY College of Arts & Sciences
John P. Truehart, 957

SUNY College of Technology
Jennifer Dunham, 173

SUNY Cortland
Brian G. Murphy, 1316

SUNY Fredonia
Dennis R. Costello, 325

SUNY Geneseo
Andy Roche, 1468

SUNY Oneonta
John Fitzgerald, 469
Calvin A Neider, 505

SUNY Oswego
Juli Marley, 293

SUNY Stony Brook
Ajay Chopra, 1855
Larry Kaplan, 245
Philip N. Sussman, 1811

Susquehanna University
Richard E Caruso PhD, 1496
William J Kennedy Jr, 1377

Swarthmore College
Bruce Adams, 983
Rob Day, 1732
Eric Elenko, 1503
Michel Glouchevitch, 1579
Roger C. Holstein, 1933
Darby Kopp, 910
Corey Mulloy, 938
Anthony J. Orazio, 1419

Swiss Federal Inst. of Technology
George Arnold, 1081

Sydeham College
Rajan Mehra, 504

Sydney Law School
Yanev Suissa, 1689

Syracuse University
Steven Barnes, 223
Steven E Berman, 1402
Michael Cardamone, 29
Mike Cardamone, 771
Jamie Choi, 1614
Brian Cohen, 1305, 1309
Trace Cohen, 1309
Daniel A D'Aniello, 416
Stephen P DeFalco, 1133
A. Sinclair Dunlop, 690
Luke Gosselin, 448
Roger Hurwitz, 1944
Michael Hyatt, 1026
Peter Hébert, 1155
William Johnston, 912
Charles R Martin, 112
John May, 1303
Jeffrey S McCormick, 1626
Doug K. Mellinger, 494
Michal Petrzela, 1127
Thomas Queenan, 1445
Michael Schattner, 1378
Chris Setaro, 1665
Ajit Singh, 176
Michael G. Thonis, 458

Taylor University
Donald A Krier, 2004

Technical University (Karlsruhe)
Ralf Gruss, 136

Technical University of Munich
Peter Johann PhD, 1325

Technion
Dan Avida, 1382
Jacques Benkowski PhD, 1898
Shmuel Einav, PhD, 1811
Miki Granski, 538
Amit Karp, 263
Itzik Parnafes, 238
Eyal Shaked, 538
Merav Weinryb, 1511

Technion Israel Institute of Tech
Elena Winefeld, 40

Tel Aviv University
Izhar Armony, 457
Adam Chesnoff, 1602
Yoni Chiefetz, 1125
Vered Digmy, 117
David Gussarsky, 1125
Mony Hassid, 1158
Eyal Miller, 1614
Shimrit Samuel, 117
Yafit Schwartz, 117
Eyal Shaked, 538
Shlomi Shiloni Shem Tov, 438
Michal Silverberg, 1350

Temple University
Steve Berman, 162
Michael F Daly, 1524
Tyler Dautrich, 871
Joseph Falkenstein, 1329
Saul A. Fox, 781
Anthony P. Green, PhD, 249
Karen Greene, 52
John Guiliana DPM, 1288
Fred Hosaisy, 1697
Edward L Kuntz, 1654
Scott Powers, 52
RoseAnn B. Rosenthal, 249
David Rubin, 1206
Dean Sciorillo, 677
Richard Taney, 1866
Tyrone Wilson, 1773

Temple University School of Law
Alex Katz, 724
Robert Keith, 1830

Tennessee Technological University
L Edward Wilson PE, 539

Tepper School of Business
Sreekar Gadde, 296
Ben T. Smith, IV, 31

Terry College of Business
Jennifer D Lackey, 1542

Texas A&M University
Kevin Brady, 1977
Gil Burciaga, 595
Clinton W. Bybee, 154
Sherman I Chu, 861
Scott Collier, 1857
Derrick K Collins, 1465
Joe Cunningham MD, 1622
Sarah Dickey, 3247
Heidi Hargrove, 703
Camilo E. Horvilleur, 931
William R. Lemmons, Jr., 672
David McWhorter, 427
Jeffrey R. Shannon, 547
Ben Stanton, 893
Matthew Van Alstyne, 1367
John White, 1273
Steve Whitlock, 1725
Bob Zipp, 115
Chris Zugaro, 1858

Texas Christian University
Roger D Bailey, 607
Blake Bonner, 1858
Brian Hoesterey, 63

Texas Tech University
Lynn Alexander, 1066
Paul W. Drury, 1115
Kirk Fichtner, 1170
Felipe Mendoza, 166
Gary R. Petersen, 673
Art Reidel, 950
Philip Sanger MD, 1803
Meg Taylor, 988

Thayer School, Dartmouth College
Terry McGuire, 1464

The Citadel
Tim Komada, 601
Wally Lennox, 1465

The Darden School
Gene Lockhart, 1240

Thomas Jefferson University
Brian K. Halak, PhD, 622

Thomas More College
Edwin T Robinson, 1575

Thunderbird School of Management
Dave Carlson, 686
Gina Domanig, 2101
Holly Kaczmarczyk, 1971
Mark Mullen, 309
Mark Mullen, 625
Lori L. Murphree, 1369
Andrew Ogawa, 1515
Robert A Theleen, 475
Andy Unanue, 196
Gijs FJ Van Thiel, 13
Blue VanDyke, 8
Tom Whiteaker, 915

Tilburg University
Ralph Hamers, 1880

Tohoku University
Koji Osawa, 837

Tokyo Institute of Technology
Anis Uzzaman, 721

Tokyo Metropolitan University
Anis Uzzaman, 721

Towson University
Mark Maloney, 1401

Trinity College
Jeff Barry, 1459
James A. Beakey, 1278
Todd Dagres, 1718
Robert M Golding, 2014
Kyle Griswold, 796

College/University Index / Trinity College Dublin

John Howard, 1026
Terry L. Jones, 1773
Tracy Killoren Chadwell, 6
Charles T Lake II, 1676
Ian Loring, 223
Bill Luby, 1641
Dan MacKeigan, 1731
Robert W Macleod, 1199
J Carter McNabb, 1575
Rick Moss, 256
Andy Newcomb, 1240
Logan V. O'Connor, 2014
Benjamin P Procter, 1963
Robert L. Rosner, 1933
Jamie Schiff, 1344
David L. Schnadig, 547
C. Bowdoin Train, 880
Timothy Walsh, 435
Mimi Wolfe Strouse, 38
Scott Zoellner, 63

Trinity College Dublin
Laela Sturdy, 579

Trinity College, Hartford
Chauncey Hamilton, 623

Trinity Law School
Jaime McMillan, 393

Trinity University
Cam McMartin, 446
Chris Scoggins, 1656
John Thornton, 205

Tsinghua University
C.K. Cheng, 908
Lixin Li, 1340
T Chester Wang, 46
Mingyao Wang, 521

Tuck School of Business
Rich Aldrich, 1149
Jim Andelman, 309, 1569
Charles Ayres, 1853
Kathleen Bacon, 912
Redington Barrett III, 1435
Marshall Bartlett, 745
Lee E Bouyea, 789
Thomas J. Buono, 266
John Cable, 1729
Mike Carusi, 58, 1126
Jennifer Chalmers Balbach, 1753
David G Chandler, 470
Brian Chee, 1464
Jim Conroy, 1372
Everett R Cook, 1470
Jeffrey G. Dishner, 1742
Dana Donovan, 632
Scott W Edwards, 1755
Robert Faber, 227
William Ford, 858
Walter G. Freedman, 1097
Thomas W Gorman, 1639
Kenneth A. Graham, 1018
Russell J. Greenberg, 104
Steve Halstedt, 443
John Henderson, 970
Bob Hower, 58
Luisa Hunnewell, 1986
Jonathan E. Hunnicutt, 1979
Sheena Jindal, 520
John Kilgallon, 223
Darby Kopp, 910
Jeffrey Kovach, 172
Nancy Lotane, 223
Chris Lund, 903
Devin Mathews, 470

Frederick Maynard, 912
Roger McNamee, 660
Michael P McQueeney, 1753
Jose Minaya, 1356
Rob Morris, 1372
Rick Moss, 256
John J Murphy Jr, 1274
Daniel P Neuwirth, 1506
Jerrold Newman, 1986
Jeffrey T Newton, 815
John O'Connor, 1131
Standish O'Grady, 857
Jonathan W Osgood CFA, 573
Bruce Ou, 884
Howard Park, 828
Jonathan Perl, 318
Jonathan Pressnell, 293
Bill Reiland, 1255
Daniel R. Revers, 157
Brett J Rome, 1339
Thomas R Shepherd, 1864
Frank V. Sica, 1779

Tuck University
Joe Powers, 1165
Nina Scheepers, 1165

Tufts University
Charles Auster, 1600
Sophie Bakalar, 514
Brad Bernstein, 796
Jeffrey M. Calhoun, 1779
Dana Callow, 315
Mitchell Davidson, 1469
Samuel L. Duboc, 2098
Stephen Eisenstein, 917
Rick Elfman, 1745
Bruce F Failing, 80
Chris Farmer, 1677
Matthew Hermann, 178
Mike Jerstad, 1474
Steven E Karol, 1963
Julia Karol, 1963
Jack W Lasersohn, 1931
James D. Leroux, 181
Nancy Lotane, 223
William I MacDonald, 1107
John Mandile, 1675
Stuart I Mathews, 1225
Yoni Meyer, 420
Matt Murphy, 1203
James Neary, 1957
Pierre Omidyar, 1374
Jonathan Perl, 318
Michael S Pfeffer, 1469
Nick Pianim, 582
Daniel Prawda, 838
Sam H. Pyne, 898
Shari Redstone, 59
Steven Ritterbush, 1208
Steve Romaniello, 1580
Ken Rotman, 2075
Tim Rotolo, 156
Charles L Schroeder, 1343
Nicholas Scola, 20
Andrew A. Silverman, 405
James A. Stern, 576
Richard Taney, 1866
Kathryn Taylor, 704
Lou Volpe, 1084
David Wachter, 1949
Paul Walsh, 371
Jeffrey M. Walters, 1097
Sebastian C. Widmann, 1134
Robert D Winneg, 1295
Daniel Zilberman, 1957
Kurt von Holzhausen, 346

Tulane Freeman School of Business
Marcia Haydel, 1434

Tulane University
Adit Abhyankar, 760
Cory S Anderson, 39
Mark Buffington, 274
Nicholas Callais, 375
Jarett Carson, 677
Urs Cete, 259
Wayne Cohen, 1638
Avantika Daing, 1458
Daniel Finkelstein, 850
Howard Glynn, 1208
Michael Goldberg, 99
Jeffrey M. Hurst, 523
Josh Klinefelter, 202
Omar Mejias, 62
J Peter Pierce Jr, 1450
Rick S Rees, 1148
Shannon Rothschild, 1725
David H. Rowe, 65
Bradley Sheftel, 1904
Joseph T. Sobota, MD, 140
Andrea Turner Moffitt, 1458

Tulane University Sch of Medicine
Gregory T Hebrank MD, 1102

Tulane University School of Law
Charles Booker, 60

Turku Institute of Technology
Anne-Mari Paster, 1373

U. of Illinois - Urbana/Champaign
Amitt Mahajan, 1477

U. of Pennsylvania School of Med.
Doug Fisher, 1014

UCLA Anderson School of Management
Gregory Bloom, 47

UCLA School of Law
Bob Brownell, 667

UIBE
Tianpeng Wang, 2187

UNC Business School
David Kirkpatrick, 1691

Union College
Dennis Baldwin, 332
David J Breazzano, 598
William F Case Jr, 505
John Cozzi, 63
David Gershman, 1859
Steve Gullans PhD, 704
Eric Lauerwald, 1027
Jeffrey A. Lipsitz, 547
Jeremy Lynch, 1853
Rob May, 1463
Ting-Pau Oei, 644

Union University
Richard D. Parsons, 981

United States Air Force Academy
Michael C Giese, 1193
Brian Hibblen, 1689

United States Military Academy
David Pierson, 1776

College/University Index / University of Calgary

United States Naval Academy
Wes Blackwell, 1635
Bill Lyons, 490

Univ. of Pittsburgh, School of Law
Michael Beauregard, 963

Univeristy College London
Matthew Foy, 1734

Univeristy of New South Wales
Matt Lee, 474

Univeristy of Wisconsin-Madison
Jacob Smith, 3

Univerity of Western Ontario
Larry LaKing, 2181

Universidad Compultense de Madrid
Cate Ambrose, 3252

Universidad de Bogota
Gina E. Molano, 1883

Universiry of Pennsylvania
Anne Bovaird Nevins, 1445

Universite de Paris
Charles Heilbronn, 1263

Universite de Sherbrooke
Charles Sirois, 163

Universite du Quebec a Montreal
Laurence Rulleau, 2086

University British Columbia
Matt Cunning, 2171

University College
Alastair Tedford, 78

University College Dublin
Ronan Cunningham, 1720
Mark E Farrell, 1808
John O'Connor, 1131
John O'Neill, 1115

University of Aberdeen
David Q. Anderson, 119

University of Akron
Ray Leach, 1051
John W Manzetti, 1452
Sheila Mutter, 1788
Michael Price, 452
Chad W Souvignier, 1546

University of Alabama
Charles E Adair, 539
Yuval Almog, 538
Jon W Bayless, 1661
Jeff Demond, 155
Neeraj Gupta, 456
Donald C. Harrison, 460
Stuart McWhorter, 497
Wanda R Morgan, 1270
Doug Sellers, 1536
Toni F. Sikes, 378
Miller Welborn, 461

University of Alaska
Jeff Fagnan, 37

University of Alberta
Shawn Abbott, 2150
Sikandar Atiq, 2194
Dan Barclay, 2057
Kevin Brown, 2036
Kerry Brown, 2116
Mike Cabigon, 2116
Tanya Causgrove, 2036
Code Cubitt, 2187
Jim Elliott, 2058
Craig Golinowski, 2159
Donald Jackson, 2207
Mark Lerohl, 2222
Francesco Mele, 2044
Mitch Putnam, 2022
Anuj Ranjan, 2062
Jim Taylor, 2115
Peter Tertzakian, 2036
Davis Vaitkunas, 2058
Jason White, 2159
Kristina Williams, 2028

University of Alexandria
Ossama Hassanein, 1310

University of Amsterdam
Paulus J Ingram, 2239
John R Jonge Poernik, 1134

University of Antwerp
Lode J Devlaminck, 637

University of Arizona
Dan Aquilano, 86
Joel Backman, 1213
Todd Belfer, 390
Ross Bhappu, 1551
Andrew Braccia, 27
Jerome Camp, 388
Abbie Celniker, 1814
Sherman I Chu, 861
Sean Doyle, 1613
Robert Dreier, 362
Skip Glass, 773
Bill Harding, 1908
Brian J. Knez, 424
Loretta Little, 2007
Loretta McCarthy, 845
Donald R. Parfet, 140
George Sarlo, 1953
Chad W Souvignier, 1546
Mike Speiser, 1762
Anthony J Veith, 505
Brian D Wallace, 35

University of Arkansas
Tyler A. Bozynski, 612
Jerome Camp, 388
Larry B. Carter, 612
Jeff Davis, 47
Bobby Franklin, 3262
Randy Hawks, 493
Joe T. Hays, 612
Ron Norris, 1924

University of Auckland
David Bell, 328

University of Baltimore
Frank A. Adams, 881
Stephen Auvil, 1792
Olleb Douglass, 1259
Kimberly Kyle, 21
William J. Westervelt, Jr., 181

University of Baltimore Law School
Steven B. Fader, 192
Peter M. Rubin, 192

University of Bangalore
Nupur Jalan, 838

University of Bath
David Atterbury, 912

University of Bayreuth
Sven H. Borho, 1383
Stephan Siegel, 2263

University of Behrain
Hisham Al Raee, 153

University of Bombay
Raj Pai, 838
Deepa Pakianathan, PhD, 605
Vineet Pruthi, 1131
Varsha Tagare, 1511

University of Boston
Khaled Jalanbo, 1902

University of Bradford
Daniel Docter, 604

University of Bridgeport
Ivar W. Mitchell, 124

University of Brighton
Suresh Patel, 2271

University of Bristol
Anthony W. Garton, 1116

University of British Columbia
Brian Begert, 2284
Rod Campbell, 2274
Alan Chiu, 2010
Charles Cook, 2091
Russ Cranswick, 1551
Harry Culham, 2073
David Eisler, 2227
Steve Faraone, 2209
Graham Flater, 2121
Ossama Hassanein, 1310
Andrew Haughian, 2205
Ashton Herriott, 368
Wilfred Jaeger, 923
Franklin Jiang, 2221
Shamsh Kassam, 2249
Moe Kermani, 2270
Simon Koch, 2138
Laurie G. Kolbeins, 1801
Sara Leggat, 1659
Wei Lin, 2168
Ward Mallabone, 2219
John McEwen, 2091
Tracey McVicar, 368
Arda M Minocherhomjee, 470
Jeffrey N. Murphy, 2156
Omkaram Nalamasu, Ph.D., 145
Richard Osborn, 2225, 2256
Norman Rokosh, 2267
Cooper Seeman, 2227
Corry J. Silbernagel, 2058
Akio Tanaka, 641
Natasha Tsai, 2061
Mike Walkinshaw, 2262
Kaley Wilson, 2221

University of Buffalo
Dorian Faust, 886

University of Calcutta
Aditya Arora, 838

University of Calgary
Dan Barclay, 2057
John Berton, 2126
Larry Birchall, 2171

College/University Index / University of California

Aaron Bunting, 2237
Dave Chapman, 2284
Lauchlan Currie, 2036
John Dielwart, 2036
Ryan Dunfield, 2237
Chris Erickson, 2205
Rebecca Giffen, 2028
Paul Godman, 2028
Barclay W. Hambrook, 2035
Jim Hardin, 2043
Chandra Henry, 2171
Adam Jenkins, 2085
Curtis Johansson, 368
Kel Johnston, 2159
Patrick Lor, 2204
Ward Mallabone, 2219
Sonny Mottahed, 2068
Dave Pearce, 2044
Whitney Rockley, 2183
Eric Schmadtke, 677
Martin Vetter, 2043
Imed Zine, 2234

University of California
Robert R. Ackerman, Jr., 84
Tom Banahan, 1798
Laura Baxter-Simmons, 1476
Walter Beinecke, 352
Pete Blackshaw, 482
Robert Blazej, PhD, 1238
Mike Brunell, 1369
John Burke, 1485
Justin Butler, 648
Jeff Carmody, 68
Michael Carney, 1890
Brownell Chalstrom, 210
Daniel Corry, 68
Fred Craves, PhD, 240
Todd R Crockett, 1778
Luke B Evnin, 1268
Brett Gibson, 995
Mark J Gill, 714
Chris Grant, 1056
Russell B Hall, 1110
Rob C Hart CFA, 1794
Justin Hartfield, 665
William Hopkins, 1368
Tamiko Hutchinson, 1009
Ray Jang, 1559
Leland Jones, 674
Tom Kastner, 1369
Hsing Kung, 46
Dr. Frank Kung, 1943
Anthony V Lando, 39
Michael Lane, 3257
Damian Langere, 814
Dr. Robert P Lee, 613
Will Lin, 765
Zack Lynch, 1033
Renske Lynde, 7
John Mapes, 202
David J Matlin, 1182
Dorian Merritt, 1798
Matt Moore, 92
Brian R. Nelson, 874
Niall A O'Donnell PhD, 1578
Robert Paulson, 66
Barry D. Reynolds, 952
George Roberts, 1086
Charles W. Roellig, 451
Anhishek Shukla, 930
Mark Silverman, 430
Nat Simmons, 1476
Michael Spector, 1941
Richard Stubblefield, 1122
Robert Swan, 1123
Paulette Taylor, 1619
David Titus, 1995
Arthur Trueger, 255
Christine Tsai, 10
Doug Tsui, 950
Brad Webb, PhD, 493
Gred Widroe, 1197
Kenny Zou, 2077

University of California, Berkeley
Roy Bahat, 287
Dr John Baldeschwieler, 188
Kirby Bartlett, 44
Tom Beerle, 260
Amy Belt Raimundo, 1056
Mark Benham, 441
Arthur Berliner, 1953
Tom Bevilacqua, 1908
Ravi Bhaskaran, 760
Richard C. Blum, 303
Michael Borrus, 2010
Jeff Branman, 940
David Brewer, 146
Jeff Brody, 1537
Bob Brownell, 667
Justin Burden, 990
Kristina Burow, 154
Douglas C. Carlisle, 1203
Clint Chao, 766
Paul Chau, 1983
Wu-Fu Chen, 46
Joanne Chen, 773
Alice Chen, PhD, 30
Leon Chen, PhD, 519
Jeff Chung, 108
William E Conway, 204
Anupam Dalal MD, 1063
John G Danhakl, 1113
Ben Dahl, 1679
Rahsaan Dean, 996
Alex De Winter, 812
Dipanjan (DJ) Deb, 782
Byron Deeter, 263
Michael Deleray, 346
John Dougery, 1017
Sean Doyle, 1009
Noah J. Doyle, 1032
Ken Ehrhart, 693
Ken Ehrhart, 1757
Nicolase El Baze, 1418
Elliot B Evers, 1197
Andrew Farquharson, 984
Mark Fernandes, 1672
Tami Flores, 232
Joe Floyd, 666
Gene Frantz, 579
Dean Frost, 256
Purvi Gandhi, 945
Jan Garfinkle, 150
Max Gazor, 457
Shomit Ghose, 1379
Nat Goldhaber, 493
Mark Grovic, 1298
Debra Guerin Beresini, 1015
H H Haight, 163
Steven J Hamerslag, 1871
Charles Hamilton, 1090
James Hardiman, 586
Gregory Harriman, 269
Richard Harroch, 1908
Kamil Hassan, 856
Rob Hayes, 742
David Haynes, 796
Charles Haythornthwaite, 2072
James Healy, 1700
Dave Herron, 499
Cliff Higgerson, 980
Michael Hodges, 185
Janey Hoe, 485
Paul Holland, 773
Karen Hong, 1780
Herbert H. Hooper, 119
Ta-Lin Hsu, 897
Jonathan Hsu, 1850
Derek Idemoto, 485
Ariel Jaduszliwer, 327
Danny Jaffe, 127
David Jargiello, 758
Andrew Jensen, 1063
Trevor Johnstone, 2118
Ellis Jones, 1961
Scott Jordon, 840
Brendan Kennedy, 1484
Rene Kern, 819
Eurie Kim, 763
Jason Krikorian, 597
Amit Kumar, 27
Tim Kutzkey, PhD, 519
Mark D. Kvamme, 631
Mike Kwatinetz, 218
Rachel Lam, 981
Leif Langensand, 130
Deval A Lashkari PhD, 1794
Rick Lewis, 1898
William Lewis, 2020
Darren Liccardo, 431
Anthony Lin, 1009
John Lyman, 894
Rebecca Lynn, 399
Jeff Marcus, 560
Larry Marcus, 1953
Jim Marver, 1908
Brendan Mathews, 1259
Nancy McCroskey, 185
Ron Meeusen, PhD, 571
Richard Melmon, 361
Frank Mendicino III, 35
Jonathan Mi, 343
Matthew Miau, 908
Timothy C Mills PhD, 1619
Antonis Mistras, CFA, 637
Dan Mitchell, 1656
Cameron Myhrvold, 978
Amir Nashat, 1464
Thomas Neustaetter, 1042
Jessica Ngo, 474
David Nguyen, 127
Vincent M Occhipinti, 2005
Mimo Ousseimi, 813
Tracy Pappas, 1774
Elizabeth Park, 785
Lisa Parks, 232
Anu Pathria, 545
Rob Pomeroy, 949
Barry Porter, 496
Robin Praeger, 1930
Steven Puccinelli, 1360
Will Quist, 1696
Roger J Quy PhD, 1788
Jill A. Raimondi, 952
Pal B Ristvedt, 1116
Scott M Rocklage PhD, 11
Dennis D Ryan, 764
Phil Samper, 808
Eric Schmidt, 1001
Jeffrey A. Schoenfeld, 243
Steve Schuman, 900
Armen B Shanafelt, 1128
Rob Shurtleff, 619
Rob Siegel, 2010
Peter Sonsini, 1296
Carsten Sorensen, 2210
Jared Stasik, 608
Jason Stein, 1822
Nick Sturiale, 1661

Trey Sykes, 1018
Nelson Teng, 460
Jim Tenkle, 1621
Yaniv Tepper, 127
Ralph Terkowitz, 21
Bryant J Tong, 1355
Leda Trivinos, 748
Christine Tsai, 10
Daniel Weiss, 127
Dave Whorton, 1867
Randy Williams, 1065
Karen Wilson, 1014
Jay Wintrob, 1362
Tim Woodward, 1355
Veronica Wu, 945
Tuff Yen, 1658
Peter Yi, 972
Homan Yuen, 802
Shelley Zhuang, 3
Leo de Luna, 1158

University of California, Davis
Amira Atallah, 691
Dave Coglizer, 1978
Skip Fleshman, 183
Edward Hamati, 270
John E Hamer PhD, 844
Matt Jones, 1355
Rick Lewis, 1898
Thomas E Mallett, 103
Joncarlo Mark, 1894
Michael Marquez, 1254
Scott Maxwell, 1381
Craig Muir, 1814
Richard Pardoe, 468
Mark Poff, 1769
Ben T. Smith, IV, 31
Sharon Stevenson DVM, PhD, 1371
Steven J Taubman, 1910
Tiffine Wang, 1269
Scott D. Winship, 893

University of California, Irvine
Timothy Dick, 1740
Trung Q. Do, 1421
Shahi Ghanem, 1983
Bruce Hallett, 1237
Michelle Kincanon, 127
Robert G McNeil PhD, 1619
Amit Shah, 176

University of California, LA
Fred Anderson, 660
Jim Armstrong, 504
Cristy Barnes, 1122
Gregory Bloom, 47
Greg Brackett, 376
Brett Brewer, 562
Chris L Britt, 1171
Brad J. Brutocao, 786
Don Butler, 1821
Lou Caballero, 277
Justin Camp, 388
Mike Carlotti, 206
Romeo Cerutti, 555
Walter Chung, 334
John D Cochran, 1151
Gill Cogan, 1382
Topher Conway, 1763
Karen Derr Gilbert, 796
Wayne Doiguchi, 217
Ned Doubleday, 1156
Sean Doyle, 1009
Adam Draper, 310
Jesse Draper, 901
Brian Draves, 1796
Barry Eggers, 1125
Ira Ehrenpreis, 596
Ira M Ehrenpreis, 1788
Ira Ehrenpreis, 3273
David S. Felman, 874
James Fitzgerald, 1899
Standish Fleming, 772
Natalie Fonseca Licciardi, 1836
Kris Fredrickson, 511
Leslie Frécon, 1117
Jim Gauer, 1408
Richard Ginn, 549
Kirsten Green, 763
Lloyd Greif, 874
Richard G. Grey, 942
Madison F. Grose, 1742
Alejandro Guerrero, 49
Craig Gunther, 281
Pamela Hagenah, 1008
Bruce Hallett, 1237
Philip Han, 1602
Richard Harroch, 1908
Travis Haynes, 228
Eric D. Heglie, 989
Ben Horowitz, 125
Mark Hsu, 897
Tamiko Hutchinson, 1009
John S. Hwang, 786
Scott Irwin, 1543
Dan Janney, 94
Buck Jordan, 400
Jed Katz, 1032
Guy Kawasaki, 810
Bill Kirsch, 549
Walter Kortschak, 1677
Christopher Lane, 1090
Larry Lasky, PhD, 519
Alda Leu Dennis, 995
Kevin L. Listen, 905
Gary Little, 399
Christopher Lucas, 278
Susan Mason, 83
Manan Mehta, 1887
Dana Moraly, 504
Nathan Myhrvold, 1010
David Nagel, PhD, 770
Thomas Neustaetter, 1042
Carey Ng, 1222
Robin Nourmand, 228
Mimo Ousseimi, 813
Arrie Park, 927
Stuart Peterson, 177
T.M. Ravi, 1812
Marc Reich, 1025
Mark Rosenbaum, 202
Peter Seidler, 1648
Robert Seidler, 1648
Steve Simonian, 84
Tammi Smorynski, 1009
Pavan Tripathi, 336
Cleve Tzung, 206
Patrick J Welsh, 1973
Tim Woodward, 1355
Kevin Yamashita, 260

University of California, Riverside
Andrea Caoile, 496
Amy L. Laforteza, 952
Ken Pearlman, 1365

University of California, SB
Keval Desai, 1014
Richard G. Grey, 942
Alex Maleki, 976
Andrew Ogawa, 1515
William K. Richardson, 942
Hans Swildens, 990
Kevin Thau, 1718
Robert L. Zorich, 673

University of California, SC
Richard R Crowell, 1906
Scott Darling, 604

University of California, SF
Caley Castelein MD, 1063
Douglas Crawford PhD, 1238
Anupam Dalal MD, 1063
Mason Freeman MD, 11
Dr. Ryan A Harris, 1346
Russell Hirsch MD, PhD, 1495
Philip Sanger MD, 1803

University of California, San Diego
Jim Adler, 1836
Ashvin Bachireddy, 824
Abbie Celniker, 1814
Andy Chen, 511
Phil Chen, 1477
Grace Chui-Miller, 545
Paul Conley, 1401
Eric Elenko, 1503
David V. Goeddel PhD, PhD, 519
Gregory Harriman, 269
Doug Kelly MD, 87
Michelle Kincanon, 127
Robert G. Leupold, 24
Peter Lipson, 912
Joncarlo Mark, 1894
Dan Mytels, 1612
Carey Ng, 1222
Eduardo Rallo, 327
Whitney Sales, 29
Mike Scanlin, 2187
Laura Siegal, 47
Leo Spiegel, 1239
John Stobo, 21
Mark Suster, 1890
Yipeng Zhao, 664
Geoffrey von Maltzahn, 748

University of Cambridge
Andrew Abrams, 1302
Houman Ashrafian, 1764
Oded Ben-Joseph PhD, 1389
Niko Bonatsos, 820
Teymour Boutros-Ghali, 1249
Roger Byford, 301
Lincoln E Frank, 1506
Walter Gilbert, PhD, 273
Giles Goodhead, 868
Jason P Hafler, 1621
Inès Holzbaur, 2031
David Hornik, 200
Mark W Kehaya, 1214
Dean M Kline, 1431
John Leibovitz, 518
Tim Lemmon, 135
Simon Lonergan, 248
Mike Majors, 587
Peter C McWilliams PhD, 1619
Prakash A. Melwani, 280
Lawrence G Miller, MD, 1198
Anthony J. Moore, 826
Nathan Myhrvold, 1010
Khaled Nasr, 1014
Howard H Newman, 1447
Deep Shah, 782
Andrew Williamson PhD, 1442
Robbie Woodman, 1780

University of Campinas
Anderson Thees, 641

University of Cape Town
Shaun Abrahamson, 1896

College/University Index / University of Chattanooga

Roelof Botha, 1657
Joel R. Jacks, 509
Karen Meidlinger, 1200
Wayne Platt, 1369
Ryan Pollock, 1024
Steven Rostowsky, 2067
Andy Vitus, 1629
Andrew Walton, 2156

University of Chattanooga
Michael L Bailey, 1487

University of Chicago
Roger Altman, 700
Matt Anderson, 1977
Bernard Aronson, 45
Michael E. Aspinwall, 436
J.P. Bauman, 98
Eric Becker, 1745
David Beecken, 247
Robert M Belke, 1151
Mark Benham, 441
Stephen Berger, 1368
Marc C Bergschneider, 1738
Ravi Bhaskaran, 760
Mark Bounds, 319
Duncan S. Bourne, 2008
Richard Brekka, 1643
Nathan Brown, 1990
Lauren K Bugay, 634
Karla J Bullard, 1160
Kevin Burgoyne, 3251
Kristina Burow, 154
Scott Button, 1923
Clinton W. Bybee, 154
Philip A. Canfield, 889
Paul Carbone, 1482
Eric Carlborg, 200
Bill Carson, 957
Joanne Chen, 773
David Christopher, 1424
David Christopher, 1425
Derrick K Collins, 1465
John Compall, 491
John Connor, 20
William E Conway Jr, 416
Keith L. Crandell, 154
Adam Cranford, 1292
Krisin Custar, 1049
C Bryan Daniels, 1473
Anthony B Davis, 1132
Daniel L. Delaney, 989
Daniel Dickinson, 920
Frederick J Dotzler, 599
Sean Doyle, 1613
Steven M Dresner, 630
Tim Dugan, 1962
Douglas M. Dunnan, 880
Jon Edelson, MD, 179
Rick Elfman, 1745
Mark Emery, 1049
David S. Evans, 834
Hugh D. Evans, 1927
Timothy P Fay, 1639
Robert M. Feerick, 948
Robert J Fitzsimmons, 934
Marcel Fournier, 425
Steven M. Friedman, 687
John Gannon, 693
John Gannon, 1757
Rommel Garcia, 1169
John Gardner, 1331
Matthew N Garff, 1755
Daniel M Gill, 1686
Paul D. Ginsberg, 1580
John M. Goense, 842
Stewart Gollmer, 1798

Charles Gonzalez, 78
Stephen X Graham, 563
Terrence M. Graunke, 1095
Brian Graves, 630
Daniel J. Greifenkamp, 243
Greg Gunn, 490
Victor Gutwein, 1159
James Hardiman, 586
Bill Harlan, 1481
Russell Hirsch MD, PhD, 1495
Paul E Hoffman, 630
Joseph Huffsmith, 1376
Mike Jerstad, 1474
David M Jones, 1210
Peter Kagan, 1957
Louis W Kenter, 1494
Jay Kern, 1070
Karen Kerr, 812
Daniel Kessler, 578
Quintin Kevin, 56
Christopher T Killackey, 1473
John Kim, 936
Rick Kimball, 1787
Daniel Kimerling, 600
Stephen V King, 1473
John R. Kline, 1300
Eric D Kogan, 494
Richard S Kollender, 1510
Thies O Kolln, 16
Richard R Kracum, 1990
Paul Kreie, 1232
Tom Lane, 676
Pat Lanigan, 1873
David Lawee, 579
Derek Leck, 110
John Lee, 1719
Kyle Lefkoff, 318
Karthee Madasamy, 1243
James Mahoney, 963
Howard Marks, 1362
James Marlas, 1883
Tracy Marshbanks, 733
Kevin M. McCafferty, 428
Aevin M McCafferty, 1295
Scott McConnell, 88
Charles P McCusker, 1424
Ryan R. McKenzie, 148
Michael W. Miller, 528
Peter Mogk, 963
Drew Molinari, 578
Ira L. Moreland, 973
William C Mulligan, 1480
Timothy M Murray, 470
Ramzi M Musallam, 1927
Koichiro Nakamura, 1716
W. Carter Neild, 1383
Robert T. Nelsen, 154
Dean Nelson, 1606
Lawrence Neubauer, 1518
Matthew Nicklin, 733
Kenneth O'Keefe, 247
William J Oberholtzer, 935
Chris Orndorff, 1948
Peter Pacelli, 1082
Raj Pai, 838
Tim R. Palmer, 458
Jared B Paquette, 362
Brent L Paris, 633
Grant A Patrick, 247
Steve G. Pattison, 1460
Laura Pearl, 454
James N Perry, Jr, 1160
Stuart Peterson, 177
Dan Phelps, 1612
Luke A. Phenicie, 904
Greg Phillips, 346
Mike Pongon, 1462

Clark Prickett, 1123
Tony Pritzker, 1482
Tony Pritzker, 1483
Gregory J. Purcell, 148
Paul J. Raab, 719
Damon Rawie, 60
Scott Rogan, 676
Douglas J. Rosenstein, 878
Donald C. Roth, 671
David M Rubenstein, 416
Donald Sackman, 987
Zachary Sadek, 1419
Michael J. Salamon, 2056
William H. Schaar, 948
Jay W Schemelter, 1578
Peter G. Schiff, 1344
Thomas A Schlesinger, 247
David Seldin, 134
David Shapiro, 1089
Saurabh Sharma, 1050
Woody Sing-Wood Yeh, 118
Paul Slaats, 1234
Robert Smith, 367
Byron Smith, 1261
Darren M Snyder, 1473
Nicholas Somers, 1765
Vipul B. Soni, 360
Martin Stein, 279
Chelsea Stoner, 238
Mark Suster, 1890
Terry Suzuki, 1387
Scot E Swenberg, 480
Katie Szczepaniak Rice, 689
Andrew A Thomas, 1747
Nikhil Thukral, 1092
Mary Tolan, 471
John Tomes, 919
Bradley Tusk, 1870
J. William Uhrig, 1822
Scott VanHoy, 1109
John Vrionis, 1125
Bonnie K Wachtel, 1950
Timothy Walsh, 435
Jeffrey M. Webb, 989
Jason Wilson, 1493
Ana M Winters, 1232
James D Witherington Jr, 1735
Robert Womsley, 1962
Ford Worthy, 1414
Benjamin W Yarborough, 1210
Paul G. Yovovich, 1095

University of Chicago Law School
Stephen D. Aronson, 1580
Adam Bendell, 1833
Antonio Gracias, 1904
Glen Lewy, 957
Lee M Mitchell, 1817
J Russell Triedman, 1133
J.P. Whelan, 1070
Adrian van Schie, 230

University of Cincinnati
Stephen A Baker, 768
Prashanth V. Boccasam, 1348
Laura Dotson, 1067
Thomas J Fogarty MD, 667
John Gardner, 1331
Jim Goetz, 1657
Hendrik J. Hartong, Jr., 360
Dan McKinney, 1321
Edwin T Robinson, 1575
Brian R Smith, 1601

University of Cologne
Nicolase El Baze, 1418

College/University Index / University of Houston

University of Colorado
Seth Berman, 1760
Christopher J Bower, 1398
Ryan Broshar, 1179
Chad Byers, 1760
Will Cowen, 1146
Dave Flanagan, 1009
Dietz Fry, 674
Debra P Geiger, 830
Jessica Geran, 638
David V. Goeddel PhD, PhD, 519
Jeffrey H. Goldstein, 312
Sven K. Grasshoff, 1377
Stephen J Hoffman MD, 1693
Andrew Hopping, 1853
Pete Hudson, 94
Kevin Kester, 1681
Rand Lewis, 443
Jeffrey D Lovell, 1151
Hans Lundin, 1007
Jiong Ma, 325
Susan Mason, 83
Loretta McCarthy, 845
Timothy C Mills PhD, 1619
Dave Morin, 1696
Scott Morris, CPA, 737
Phil Parrott, 469
Patten Pettway, 1573
Daniel Pfeffer, 81
Joseph Piper JD, 1007
Peter Rosenberg, 1208
Christopher W Roser, 1590
Stuart L Rudick, 1236
Stephen N Sangalis, 1487
Scott Savitz, 587
Zach E Schaumburg, 1220
Frank Schiff, 1231
Terrance M Shipp, 1210
Frank Simon, 174
Napoleon Ta, 778
Ryan Williams, 543

University of Columbia
Bennett Cohen, 1453
Avantika Daing, 1458
Deborah Jackson, 1458
Khaled Jalanbo, 1902
Andrea Turner Moffitt, 1458

University of Connecticut
David L. Anderson, 1759
Greg Barger, 1316
Jim Barra, 1025
Nissa Bartalsky, 80
Derek Blazensky, 414
Nick Bologna, 646
Gregory E. Clark, 949
Al Foreman, 1866
Heidi M. Goldstein, 104
Rimas Kapeskas, 383
Peter Longo, 532
Deborah Magid, 971
Pauline Murphy, 532
Randal A. Nardone, 769
Calvin A Neider, 505
Dennis O'Brien, 886
Enrico Picozza, 941
Marc Reich, 1025
Marc Riiska, 1866
John L Ritter, 740
Robert Rodin, 1579
Mathias Rumilly, 505
Guy M. Russo, 389
Tim Shannon, 389
James Sidwa, 404
Michael S Weissenburger, 598

University of Costa Rica
Jorge Amador, 110

University of Dallas
Matthew J. Nordgren, 152
Brad Seaman, 2206

University of Dayton
Brent Ahrens, 389
Anthony M Lacenere, 991
Bassem A Mansour, 1548
Peter J Muth, 1749
Rick Ruffolo, 80
Steve Schuman, 900
Judd Sher, 927
Mike Venerable, 481
Daniel Wagner, 532

University of Delaware
Nathaniel C Brinn, 1942
Daryl B Brown, 637
Jeff Davidson, 467
Robert Di Geronimo, 1435
David Freschman, 151
Michael Kelley, 151
Bart A McLean, 1270
Diane Messick, 993
Dennis Purcell, 73
David Rowley, 467
Eileen Sivolella, 61
David L. Warnock, 386

University of Delhi
Anik Bose, 252
Bahniman Hazarika, 860

University of Denver
Ed Anderson, 1335
Anders Bjork, 20
Mark K Gormley, 1108
Gregory L. Greenberg, 104
John Greff, 1656
Carolina B Hensley, 1487
Mark C Masur, 1684
James Minnick, 1151
Mark Mullen, 309, 625
Selahattin Onen, 1407
John Ord, 543
Christopher Quinn, CPA, 884
Tina Saxton, 472
Alex Suh, 374
Mike West, 469

University of Denver College of Law
Bluette N. Blinoff, 1801

University of Dundee
Niall A O'Donnell PhD, 1578

University of Durham
Michael Lee, 1776

University of East Anglia
Brian E Stern, 1738

University of Edinburgh
Regis B Kelly PhD, 1238
Thomas Kennedy, 2160

University of Florida
Jim Adler, 1836
Andrew Banks, 20
Scott Brady, 1001
Kevin Burgoyne, 3251
Kevin J Calhoun, 1755
Wu-Fu Chen, 46
Gonzalo Cordova, 1913

Seth Ellis, 1433
Randy Glein, 610
Michael B Goldberg, 1066
Melissa Guzy, 149
David Hellier, 260
Thomas O Holland Jr, 1424
Kevin J. May, 949
John Morgan, 1433
Scott Pressly, 274
Jonathan D Root MD, 1898
Dan Rua, 994
Bryan Simpson Jr., 830
Greg Stewart, 2135
Mark Zittman, 1866

University of Fribourg
Romeo Cerutti, 555

University of Geneva
Lionel Carnot, 240
Otello Stampacchia, 1373

University of Georgia
Jon Birdsong, 191
Brian Cayce, 860
Scott E. Chappell, 266
Charles A Cox, 1148
Doug Fisher, 825
Ryan Gembala, 1423
David Griest, 1691
G Thomas Lackey, Jr, 1542
Michael A. Lonergan, 825
Melanie Martin, 770
Jeffrey S Muir, 797
Shahzad Pirvani, 2021
Marcus Smith, 1815

University of Ghent
Sigrid Van Bladel, PhD, 19

University of Glasgow
James B. Walker, 555

University of Gothenburg
Lars Ekman, 1700

University of Guelph
Paul Eldridge, 2121
Christopher A. Johnson, 2085
Allan Johnston PhD, 1775
Justin MacCormack, 2142
Evan Siddal, 2029

University of Guyana
Purnesh Seegopaul, 2205

University of Haifa
Gurion De Zwirek, 2245

University of Hartford
Brett Finkelstein, 1443
Douglas H. Leighton, 638
Peter Longo, 532

University of Hawaii
Richard D. Parsons, 981
Steven Ritterbush, 1208
Darell E Zink Jr, 412

University of Houston
Joseph L Harberg, 1552
James K. Lam, 898
Jeffrey Sheldon, 487
Martin Sutter, 698
Jim P. Wise, 898
Timothy Zappala, 172

University of Hull, UK
Hisham Al Raee, 153

University of Idaho
Carol Eckert, 785

University of Illinois
Collin Abert, 1095
Daniel K. Alport, 1582
Jonathan H Alt, 542
Ricardo Angel, 1453
Derek Beaty, 838
Paul Bragiel, 1477
Karla J Bullard, 1160
Eric Carlborg, 200
Barrett D. Carlson, 410
David Carlson, 1539
Shawn T. Carolan, 1203
Aaron D. Cohen, 889
John Compall, 491
David J Cooney, 247
Leslie M Corley, 1141
Bob Curry, 1098
John Dugenske, 88
Donald J. Edwards, 751
Jeff Farrero, 470
Rod Ferguson, 1411
Michael E Flannery, 634
Jacques V Galante, 1109
David Gervase, 531
Wade D Glisson, 1686
Charles Gonzalez, 78
Nathan J Good, 1473
James N. Hallene, 410
Laurence Hayward, 987
William Heflin, 1076
Kristina Heinze, 470
John Hennegan, 1670
Rob Herb, 1629
Cliff Higgerson, 980
John Hoesley, 1481
Ken Hooten, 531
Brian James, 491
Eric Keen, 551
Louis W Kenter, 1494
Quintin Kevin, 56
Christopher T Killackey, 1473
Matthew Kimble, 211
Stephen V King, 1473
John R. Kline, 1300
Eric Kutsenda, 1648
Mark Leigh, 953
Max Levchin, 1634
Christin Leybold, 641
Jay Lichter, PhD, 209
Timothy J MacKenzie, 1210
Jeanne Mariani Sullivan, 1741
Mark Maybell, 645
Russ Mayerfeld, 88
Sean M McNally, 1473
Alex Meyer, 1385
Constantine S. Mihas, 889
Michael W. Miller, 528
Tony Miller, 1111
Peter Misek, 2119
Dan Mitchell, 1656
Michelle Moreno, 630
Scott Mygind, 834
James J. Norton, 1438
Maura O'Hara, 3255
Steve Oetgen, 843
Bob Paluck, 446
Mike Parilla, 1169
Harsh Patel, 493, 2001
Chris Perry, 491
William Petty Jr, 247
Devin Quarles, 850
Douglas Rescho, 1095
Rick Schell, 1379
Stewart Schuster, 1354
Jeffrey R. Shannon, 547
Tom W Siegel, 1667
Michael Siemplenski, 733
Rick Smith, 562
Sajid A. Sohail, 95
Christopher R Stalcup, 472
John A. Strom, 898
Jeanne M. Sullivan, 1810
Stephen C. Tardio, 956
Steven Taslitz, 1745
Annie S Terry, 1160
Nikhil Thukral, 1092
Kai Tsang, 1924
Jana Vazé, 1341
Sriram Venkataraman, 212
Steve Vivian, 1481
Michelle A Waldusky, 634

University of Illinois, Urbana
Marc Andreessen, 125
Bruce N. Barron, 1385
Dennis Beard, 1380
Krisin Custar, 1049
Michael Hills, 1077
Bill Kaczynski, 341
Steven N. Miller, 1385
Mike Parilla, 1169
Laura Pearl, 454
Sundeep Peechu, 720

University of Indiana
Chris LaMothe, 659

University of Iowa
Kenneth D. Anderson, 123
George Anson, 912
John C Aplin, 480
Bob Bode, 1026
Mark Bounds, 319
James H. Cavanaugh, PhD, 922
Cory Eaves, 819
Jodi Hubler, 1111
Kinney Johnson, 1656
Utkarsh Kanal, 201
Jason Lettmann, 1126
Peter N. Masucci, 1300
Michael McCullough, 987
Greg Myers, 1174
Paul Peterson, 1990
Michael H. Reynoldson, 1020
Sarah Rogers, 840
Carol Sands Langensand, 130
Susan Simko, 1474

University of Johannesburg
Neil Ruthven, 778

University of Kansas
Chris Abshire, 721
David Burgstahler, 212
Fred Coulson, 746
Patrick Healy, 367
Leo Kim, PhD, 217
Kendall Mohler, PhD, 30
Brett A Parr, 402
Mike Peck, 1380
David B. Pittaway, 425
Robert Smith, 367
David Wanek, 1976

University of Keele
Roger J Quy PhD, 1788

University of Kent
John Garcia, 63

University of Kentucky
Christopher McCleary, 290
Jerry D. Wethington, 1574

University of King's College
Tom Eisenhauer, 2059

University of La Laguna
Manuel Lopez-Figueroa, 240

University of Las Palmas
Manuel Lopez-Figueroa, 240

University of Law at Lyon
Yves Sisteron, 1890

University of Leeds
Charles Vaslet, 2101

University of Lethbridge
Art Robinson, 2171

University of Leuven
Guido Neels, 698

University of Liverpool
Karen Meidlinger, 1200
Jonathan Tunnicliff, 1349

University of London
Richard E Caruso PhD, 1496
Karimah Es Sabar, 2221
Ivan Gergel, 1301
Karim Gillani, 2172
Richard Harris, 2118
Donald O'Shea, 572
Ash Patel, 1254
Tom Rand, 2037
John Televantos, 172
Jim Woody, 1098

University of Louisville
Charles W Beckman, 958
Mike Biddle, 2105
Robert Nardelli, 668
Jerry D. Wethington, 1574

University of Lund
Mark T Lupa PhD, 933

University of Maine
John Burns, 1165
Michael A. Foisy, 904
Jean George, 58
Jean George, 1126
Edward J Keefe, 1157
Steve Salmon, 1098
Judd Sher, 927
Jason Syversen, 2

University of Manchester
Eric Xu, 827

University of Manitoba
David Cheadle, 2068
Candy Dong, 2226
Marcus Enns, 2071
Larry Evans, 2022
Albert D. Friesen, 2071
Kel Johnston, 2159
James Kinley, 2071
Gerry Schwartz, 2201
Rod Senft, 2118, 2206, 2210
John Zaplatynsky, 2210

University of Mannheim
Thomas Korte, 129

University of Maryland
G. Woodrow Adkins, 719
Rajeev Batra, 1187
Hope Brown, 379
Jerome Camp, 388
Steve DeAngelo, 1810
Scott Dupcak, 534
Adam Feinstein, 1932
Arthur L Fox, 1595
Mukul Gulati, 2017
Randy Guttman, 1045
Kiran Hebbar, 1901
Marty Hernon, 315
David Hirsch, 527
Larry Hootnick, 53
Greg Huff, 702
Samir Kaul, 1073
Wayne D Kimmel, 1660
Howard Kra, 192
Meghan M. McGee, 386
Dale McIvor, 1714
Jon Powell, 1660
Jason Pressman, 1666
Steven H Rosen, 1548
Rob Runett, 1259
Jeff Schechter, 1745
Curtis Schickner, 534
Mike Schuh, 773
Shounok Sinha, 534
Jack Slye, 1140
Joseph Statter, 702
Bruce Taub, 192
Katie Vasilescu, 838
Lane W Wiggers, 165
Herbert P. Wilkins, Jr., 1773
Bill Youstra, 1087
Natty Zola, 1179

University of Maryland College Park
Arjun Sethi, 1850
Megan Sparks, 534

University of Massachusetts
Dave Andonian, 581
Mark M Andrew, 1116
Stacey Bauer, 809
Larry Bohn, 820
Christopher Colecchi, 350
David H Donabedian, 1149
Dave Fachetti, 839
Arnie Freedman, 1389
Rick Gallagher, 1488
Steve Grizzell, 1004
Ralf Gruss, 136
Paul A Howard, 1198
John Hunt, 20
Jeff Low, 645
David J Machlica, 1166
Benjamin Marino, 1435
Ed Olkkola, 1785
James J Pallotta, 1527
Gil Penchina, 1566
Ellis F. Rinaldi, 1742
Michael Rubin, 1342
Scott Sandler, 1384
Paul L. Schaye, 467
Alyse Skidmore, 1336
Prabakar Sundarrajan, 504
Edward C. Williams, III, 352

University of Massachussetts
Senofer Mendoza, 1202

University of Melbourne
Simon Cresswell, 136

University of Memphis
Wally Rose, 15
Cynthia S Sheridan, 244
Burton B Weil, 1921

University of Mexico
David Wanek, 1976

University of Miami
Cindy Babbit, 578
Todd Boren, 558
Scott Broder, 997
Christopher Fountas, 173
Adam Kalish, 1155
James Niedel, 1297
J. Travis Prichett, 907
Beth Seidenberg, 1079
John Tullis, 1868
Andy Unanue, 196
Robert A. Vigoda, 428

University of Miami School of Law
Paul R DiBella, 539
Paul Dibella, 770

University of Michigan
John F Ackerman, 412
Rob Adams, 1321
Jim Adox, 1923
Lynn Alexander, 1066
David Armstrong, 198
Eric Arnson, 1386
David G. Arscott, 526
Perry O. Ballard, 751
Michael Beauregard, 963
Michael C Bellas, 264
Steven T. Berg, 424
Brian S. Berkin, 1779
Casey Berman, 380
Jay Bernstein, 1089
Stacey Bishop, 1629
William Blake III, 254
Barry Blattman, 2062
David Bohnett, 231
Rick Bolander, 657, 808
David Breach, 1940
Randall Brouckman, 1784
Paul Brown, 657
Ben Browning, 1123
Karen Buckner, 1242
Mary Lincoln Campbell, 652
Jon Canarick, 1336
Eric Ceresnie, 919
Roger Chen, 1687
David Christopher, 1424, 1425
Wayee Chu, 1530
Brian M Clark, 1157
Josh Cohen, 490
Jake Cohen, 608
Michael Cohn, 888
R. Craig Collister, 1594
Bradley E. Cooper, 407
Marshall Cooper, 868
Kevin Costantino, 869
Kelli Cullinane, 1110
Brian Dixon, 661
John W Doerer, 1465
Dixon Doll, 597
James Eadie, MD, 1622
Roger Ehrenberg, 969
Steve Engelberg, 1618
Gary C Epstein, 940
Daniel Estes, PhD, 785
David S. Evans, 834
Lawrence Fang, 1986
Karim Faris, 894
Peter W Farner, 1804
Edmund J Feeley, 1138
Matthew S. Feldman, 494
Linda Fingerle, 652
James Flynn, 602
Adrian Fortino, 1207
Evan R Gallinson, 1210
Michael Godwin, 1550
Mitch Green, 2075
Alex Gregor, 1082
Tony Grover, 1596
Bulbul Gupta, 1397
Robert A. Hamwee, 1300
Matthew Hankins, 931
Robert A Heimann, 1575
Jason Heltzer, 1385
Dave Herron, 499
Jay Hoag, 1787
Steve Hochberg, 179
Seth H Hollander, 1085
Sheldon Howell, 973
James A Illikman CFA, 1429
Anurag Jain, 1436
Michael Jandernoa, 946
David Kaplan, 160
Gabe Karp, 608
Samir Kaul, 1073
Brad Keywell, 1121
Dan Kidle, 150
Demian Kircher, 1169
Steven B Klinsky, 1300
Scott Kokones, 891
Ted H. Kramer, 904
Brian Kwait, 1368
Karle E LaPeer PE CFA, 1429
Michael S Langdon, 792
John Leckrone, 57
Jason Lettmann, 1126
Nan Li, 1363
Roy Y. Liu, 928
Karthee Madasamy, 1243
Kent Madsen, 689
Arthur J Marks, 1901
Joelle Marquis, 172
Marcy Marshall, 150
Richard McClain, 935
Stephen McCormack, 523
Dennis McCrary, 1413
Paul McCreadie, 150
Lake McGuire, 928
Dale McIvor, 1714
Cam McMartin, 446
Jason Mendelson, 779
Ravi Mohan, 1666
Jake Moilanen, 1658
Steven Moore, 337
Jay Moorin, 1492
Mark Mullen, 625
Jonathan Murray, 642
P Sherrill Neff, 1510
Michael Ozechov, 544
Cindy Padnos, 980
Donald R. Parfet, 140
Vijay C Parikh, 837
John Park, 413
Don Parsons, 143
James A Parsons, 1560
Anthony Patek, 256
Brian Peiser, 654
Kenneth R Pelowski, 1449
Brian Peters, 936
Timothy Petersen, 150
Jim Petras, 642
Laura Petterle, 762
J. Travis Prichett, 907
Matthew W Raino, 1160
Louis Rajczi, 770
Arun Ramamoorthy, 1449

College/University Index / University of Michigan Law School

Milton K Reeder, 32
Eric A Reeves, 634
Randy O. Rissman, 1112
Sanford Robertson, 782
Eric Y Rogoff, 1377
Charlie Rothstein, 254
Atul Rustgi, 36
Ali Safiedine DPM, 1288
Neal G Sahney, 792
Gerald Saltarelli, 654
Maninder Saluja, 1518
Martin A. Sarafa, 451
Robert H Savoie, 1449
J Michael Schafer, 1299
Greg Schulte, 891
Jeffrey Schultz, 1282
Evan Schwartzberg, 1367
David Shapiro, 1089
Kevin Shin, 883
M.G. Siegler, 894
Mark Sims, 2233
Michael C Skaff, 1651
David S. Slackman, 956
Roman Sobachevskiy, 895
Todd Solow, 1345
Michael Stark, 564
Jared Stasik, 608
William Staudt, 668
Scott Steele, 1044
Jason Stoffer, 1186
Kathryn J Stokel, 17
David Stott, 1990
Ben Sun, 1479
Alan J Taetle, 1332
Andrew Tananbaum, 566
Andrew C. Taub, 1092
Jim Tenkle, 1621
Keith Titan, 259
James N. Topper, MD, PhD, 785
Peter Torenberg, 1935
S Edward Torres, 1128
Joseph Tou, 1705
Jason Townsend, 1550
Brent Traidman, 721
Jonathon Triest, 1154
Matt Turner, 114
Amherst Turner, 114
Paul R. Vigano, 1041
Ryan Waddington, 964
Marc Weiser, 1596
Morty White, 2008
Evan Wildstein, 1085
Kirk Wolfe, 1242
David Wolmer, 1115
Austin Wright, 362
Victor L Wu, 1116
Dr. Lan Xeuzhao, 235
Anthony W Zambelli, 1651
Dennis Zaslavsky, 1965
Toby Zhang, 474
Brett deMarrais, 1154

University of Michigan Law School
Paul Arnold, 1770
Geoff Entress, 1501
Steven Florsheim, 1891
David Frazee, 1564
Robert B Knauss, 1957
John Kole, 1146
Eric Lefkofsky, 1121
Frederic H Mayerson, 1955
Douglas E. Onsi, 922
Luke Reese, 2000
Tom Washing, 1656

University of Minnesota
Bruce Anderson, 1973
Josh Baltzell, 1728
Greg Baszucki, 775
Scott L Becker, 1343
Justin Benshoof, 376
Greg Benson, 962
Darren Brathol, 1722
Ryan Broshar, 1179
Todd C. Chaffee, 1006
Daniel Docter, 604
Robin Dowdle, 67
Mark Gorenberg, 2018
Mik Gusenius, 466
Charles M. Hall, PhD, 140
Chad Johnson, 466
Kevin P Kenealey, 1174
Steve LaPorte, 1379
Christopher S Meldrum, 844
Vish Mishra, 504
Michael Moe, 888
Andrea R Nelson, 1722
Marcia L. Page, 1909
Constance Paiement, 739
Randy Paulson, 1368
Greg Reichow, 648
Judy Romlin, 1233
Peter L Rottier, 1754
Gerald F Schmidt, 539
Jeffrey Sheldon, 487
Robert J. Simon, 324
William H Spell, 1722
David Spreng, 556
Kathleen A Tune, 1820
Naeem Zafar, 95

University of Minnesota Law School
George G. Hicks, 1909
Michael A.G. Korengold, 679

University of Minnesota Med. School
Ronald J. Shebuski, PhD, 140

University of Mississippi
Bill Ellison, 1000
Charlie Plauche, 1601
Bryan M. Wethington, 1574

University of Missouri
Dmitry Alimov, 795
Erik Allison, 1694
Charlie Bolten, 270
Andy Butler, 367
Robert Ehrhart, 223
Brenda D Gavin, 1510
Rebecca Lynn, 399
Rod MacDonald, 595
Hank Plain, 1126
Douglas Reed MD, 918
Ted Roth, 1592
Gary Stevenson, 1190
Steve M. Welborn, 2008
Bill Witzofsky, 402
Jackie Yang, 1840
Shelley Zhuang, 3

University of Missouri Rolla
Sean Foote, 1093

University of Montana
John Connors, 978
David Dillman, 1556
Richard Harding, 1015

University of Montreal
Cédric Bisson, 2259
Philippe Leroux, 2251
Andree-Lise Methot, 2087
Riadh Zine, 2234

University of Mumbai
Keval Desai, 1014
Rashmi Gopinath, 1158
Vivek Ladsariya, 1689
Sandeep Naik, 819
Ashwini Sahasrabudhe, 860
Mathew Veedon, 1714

University of Mysore
Nagraj Kashyap, 1158

University of Nebraska
Eric M. Ball, 109
Barry Dunaway, 109
Thomas M Galvin, 943
Vinod Gupta, 701
David Guthrie, 109
Mark Hasebroock, 635
Steven King Neff, 997
George Krauss, 70
Richard L Sherman, 1636
Eli L. Thomssen, 140
Michael Yanney, 70

University of Neuchatel
Dominique Semon, 1217

University of Nevada
Thomas Bell, 515
Lucius H. Taylor, 157

University of Nevada Las Vegas
Matthew Neely, 1694

University of New Brunswick
Joe Allen, 675
Karl Reckziegel, 2048
Laura Richard, 2192

University of New Hampshire
Janice Borque, 928
Roland DuBois, 2189
Julie Eiermann, 912
Michael A. Foisy, 904
Lawrence Howard MD, 957
Michele Kinner, 1518
Robert Kirby, 843
Augustine Lawlor, 922
John H. Turner, 1979
Mike Tyrrell, 1918
Michael Van Vleck, 858
Timothy Zappala, 172

University of New Mexico
Ron J McPhee, 1926
Carlos Perea, 970
Chris Traylor, 758

University of New Orleans
Steven L. Soignet, MD, 158

University of New South Wales
Matthew Leibowitz, 2216
Jeremy G. Philips, 1718
Purnesh Seegopaul, 2205

University of New York
Charles Cohen, 1777

University of Newcastle
Jonathan Tunnicliff, 1349

University of North Carolina
Lee Ainslie, 1185
Bret Batchelder, 465
Matt Becker, 703
Scott Benson, 1315

College/University Index / University of Oregon

Philip E Berney, 1066
Jeffrey Black, 1928
Jonathan B. Blanco, 747
Kenneth S. Bring, 257
Ben Brooks, 1712
Charles A Bryan, 1424
Walter W. Buckley III, 52
Christopher M. Busby, 862
Aohn Cambier, 975
Melissa Daniels, 1255
Tom Darden, 465
Lister Delgado, 975
David H Donabedian, 1149
Bruce B. Dunnan, 880
David Dupree, 899
S. Whitfield Edwards, 747
Charles Elliott, 656
Mike Elliott, 1332
Robert C. Eubanks Jr., 783
Alston Gardner, 797
Gardiner W Garrard III, 1865
Robert Girardi, 212
Brian P Golson, 1419
Michael N. Gray, 1498
Carter Griffin, 1888
Lisa Hagerman, 596
Seth Harward, 793
Stuart W Hawley, 1627
Frank J Hawley Jr, 1627
H Beecher Hicks, III, 1532
Ian A.W. Howes, 30
Herbert W Jackson, 1544
Ray Jang, 1559
Kevin B Jessup, 1609
David Jones, 1712
Victor Kats, 178
Greg Kats, 401
W. Brent Kulman, 747
Matthew Laycock, 202
Kenneth B Lee, 918
Steve Lerner, 1100
Michael Marquez, 1254
Michael S. Marr, 408
Tom McDermott, 656
Nannette McNally, 63
Robert J. McParland, 1830
Elizabeth Merritt, 465
Erik O. Morris, 1580
Allen S Moseley, 1332
Sunil Nagaraj, 1879
Tom Newby, 1116
Frank T Nickell, 1066
Charles E. Noell, 1045
Julie Ocko, 912
George A Parker, 1107
John Powell, 1008
Robert S Powell Jr, 1277
Steve Rakes, 1711
Robin Richards Donohoe, 628
Matthew Ritchie, 47
David Rosenstein, 819
Lloyd R. Sams, 266
Nelson Schwab III, 418
Dwight Scott, 280
John W Shearburn, 1957
Bryan Simpson Jr., 830
Bradley Sloan, 1516
Tom Smith, 1628
Julia Spicer, 3260
William Starling, 1774
Scott R. Stevens, 1410
James Stevenson, 21
Kathleen Thomas, 1037
Clay B Thorp, 918
Andrew A. Tisdale, 1498
David G Townsend, 747
Tom Uhlman, 1304
Scott VanHoy, 1109
Krishnan Varier, 152
Anita Watkins, 1559
Scott Werry, 2030
Thomas H. Westbrook, 747
Eric J. Wilkins, 1410
Adrian Wilson, 1844
Ron Wooten, 1349
Ford Worthy, 1414
Phil Yates, 336

University of North Dakota
Bill Marcil, Jr., 817
Douglas E Mark, 1343
Lauris Molbert, 175
Scott A Reilly CFA, 1429
Paul Unruh, 1795

University of North Texas
Tex Sekhon, 1170

University of Northern Colorado
Dan Aweida, 213
James P. Kelley, 1933

University of Northern Iowa
Joseph Galligan, 767
Dave Latzke, 466
Paul Rhines, 16

University of Notre Dame
Brian Bastedo, 1582
John M Baumer, 1113
R David Bergonia, 1333
Terrence Berland, 1078
Mark Birschbach, 1645
Christopher J Blum, 620
Gale Bowman, 1023
Jason T. Brass, 847
Frank Brenninkmeyer, 1434
Lauren K Bugay, 634
Dave Butler, 1049
Sean Cantwell, 1944
Bill Carson, 957
Charles Cascarilla, CFA, 1119
Edward A. Chestnut, 1498
Richard Conklin, 733
Kelly A. Cornelis, 1097
Catherine Crockett, 884
Dino Cusumano CFA, 110
Scott A. Dahnke, 1092
Christopher J Dean, 1754
Kevin Delaplane, 1883
Michael Denvir, 1049
Joe Dimberio, 1873
Maurice Doyle, 60
Kaitlyn Doyle, 1023
Kevin Dunwoodie, 1413
Chris A. Durbin, 1933
Richard P Earley, 636
Beth Engel, 635
Geoff Entress, 1501
Daniel K Flatley, 1178
Brian Flynn, 775
Shawn Foley, 211
Clinton Foy, 562
Brian Gallagher, CFA, 1873
Chris Geneser, 491
Eric Gevada, 1109
John W. Glynn, 840
David Glynn, 840
William J Golden, 1096
John Grafer, 1625
Doug Groh, 481
Brad Gurasich, 427
Thomas M. Hagerty, 1818
Bill Harlan, 1481
John A. Hatherly, 2008
Tom Hedrick, 1946
Bobby Helmedag, 1559
Jim Hunt, 288
Matthew A. Janchar, 257
David M Jones, 1210
James P. Kelley, 1933
Colton King, 1090
David J. Koo, 1594
Ronald W Kuehl, 792
Timothy Kuehl, 1345
Michael A. LaSalle, 1663
Pat Lanigan, 1873
Ian Larkin, 1169
Joe Linnen, 1049
Greg Long, 1169
Patrick A. Maciariello, 525
Ben Magnano, 785
Wayne Marino, 1751
Rocco J. Martino, 1097
Alfred M. Mattaliano, 1582
Tom McCloskey, 543
Bill McDonagh, 1953
Jack McGlinn, 408
Steve McKay, 775
Andrew McLellan, 1961
Ed Mello, 577
Arthur Monaghan, 855
Jason B Moskowitz, 634
Terrence Mullen, 172
David Neighbors, 1964
Michael E. Nugent, 1582
Karl Peterson, 1837
M Troy Phillips, 247
Don Pierce, 1670
Jonathan Pressnell, 293
Paul Purcell, 225
Chris Redmond, 402
Cas Schneller, 790
John W Sherman, 598
Andrew Souder, 1524
Luke K. Stanton, 1694
Roderick Stephan, 99
Matthew Strottman, 983
Mike Stubler, 629
Mike Stubler, 3264
David Sutherland, 1229
Ryan Sweeney, 27
Dave Thomas, 843
Paul E. Tierney Jr., 137
James F Wade, 1157
Kent R. Weldon, 1818
Jason Wilson, 1493
David Wurzer, 532
Caroline Yeager, 1023
Douglas Zych, 1049

University of Nottingham
Gavin Bates, 377

University of Oklahoma
Jon W Bayless, 1661
Jay Benear, 639
Barry M Davis, 592
Brian Grigsby, 546
S Kim Hatfield, 554
Scott Meacham, 968
Rick Nagel, 47
John Scull, 1713
Blake Trippet, 1224
Tom Walker, 1556
Ben West, 38

University of Oregon
Rodger P Adams, 1911
Ashley Cravens, 1881
Rocky Dixon, 674

College/University Index / University of Otago

Angela Jackson, 1467
John R Nelson, 1667
John Saefke, 1917
T Chester Wang, 46

University of Otago
Adrian van Schie, 230

University of Ottawa
Anne-Marie Bourgeois, 677
Stephanie Butt Thibodeau, 2106
Elizabeth Douville, 2031
Matt Golden, 2130, 2131
Charles Holt, 2153
Mona Kung, 2132
Michelle McBane, 2248
Neil Ryan, 1868
Eric Schmadtke, 677
Fil Varino, 3249

University of Oxford
Shiri Ailons, 1776
George E. Aitken-Davies, 97
Houman Ashrafian, 1764
Roy Bahat, 287
Andrew Banks, 20
Nick Beim, 1918
Kate Bingham, 1631
Bruce Booth, 193
Martin Brand, 280
Winston J Churchill, 1636
Stuart Collinson, 772
Sunny Dhillon, 1680
Andrew Dunn, 1376
Spencer Fleischer, 790
Pete Flint, 1323
Matthew Foy, 1734
Keith Geeslin, 782
David B. Golub, 848
Bruns Grayson, 22
Richard Harris, 2118
Ryan Hemingway, 689
Kyle Hickey, 2237
Reid Hoffman, 877
Daniel Hullah, 812
Patrick Keefe, 2063
Robert Kibble, 1239
Paul Kusserow, 958
Jeremy D. Lack, 190
Thong Q Le, 30
Kathryn Leaf, 1413
Jeffrey T Leeds, 1109
Matthew Leibowitz, 2216
Joshua Lewis, 1611
James Marlas, 1883
Niall A O'Donnell PhD, 1578
Ryan Pollock, 1024
Laura Richard, 2192
Ned Scheetz, 139
Andrew Sillitoe, 136
Scott Silverman, 69
John Simon, 1675
Stephen H Spahn, 1506
Michael Thorson, 2002
Salman Ullah, 1219
Mark N. Williamson, 371
Robbie Woodman, 1780

University of the Pacific
Rick Blume, 704

University of Paris
Philippe Collombel, 1418
Elliot B Evers, 1197
Laurent D. Hermouet, 190

Universié Paris Dauphine
Carine Magescas, 129

Université Paris Descartes
Jeff Clavier, 1881

University of Pavia
Claudio Nessi, 1373
Otello Stampacchia, 1373

University of Pennsylvania
Mike Ackrell, 43
Deepak Advani, 927
Sandip Agarwala, 1147
Rahul Aggarwal, 337
William F Aikman, 887
Izhar Armony, 457
Jon Auerbach, 457
Keith Bank, 1061
Josh Baumgarten, 128
David Bell, 328
Larry Benaroya, 250
Jordan S. Bernstein, 478
Charles Birnbaum, 263
Jim Blair, PhD, 622
Sam Brasch, 1056
Philip L. Bronner, 1348
Bob Brown, 1275
Frank W. Bruno, 453
Thomas A. Burger Jr., 878
Barbara Burns, 63
Tara Butler, MD, 178
Justin Camp, 388
David F Chazen, 462
Ray Cheng, 1235
Iris Choi, 752
Yee-Ping Chu, 277
Chris Chung, 883
Andrew B. Cohen, 513
Doug Cole, 748
Stephen B. Connor, 903
David C. Coquillette, 1300
Chad M. Cornell, 847
Ben Cukier, 442
Rahman D'Argenio, 676
Nicholas Daraviras, 1036
Tyler Dautrich, 871
Ken DeAngelis, 205
Ben DeRosa, 110
John Dean, 942
Peter Detkin, 1010
Randolph C Domolky, 1137
Ted Driscoll, PhD, 493
Andrew L. Dworkin, 1913
Loren Easton, 111
Yaron Eitan, 1636
Joe El Chami, 1026
Donald J Elmer, 1399
Nathan R. Every, MD, MPH, 785
Jonas Fajgenbaum, 1022
Mark E Farrell, 1808
Stacy Feld, 1046
Stacy Feld, 1442
Alex Ferrara, 263
Beth Ferreira, 744
Jason Fiedler, 1533
Stewart Fisher, 1090
Jason Fisherman, 1777
Robert J Fitzsimmons, 934
Andy Flaster, 1944
Philip Fleck, 1347
Kerri Ford, 1600
Saul A. Fox, 781
Robert A Fox, 1524
Lincoln E Frank, 1506
Brian P. Friedman, 1036
J.S. Gamble, 288
Joseph M Gantz, 1447
Jan Garfinkle, 150
Wesley H.R. Gaus, 509
Simeon J. George, 1734
Jeffrey P Gerson, 854
Liron Gitig, 796
Newton Glassman, 2067
Amir Goldman, 1761
Jeffrey M Goodrich, 934
Dave Gould, 1790
Michael D. Granoff, 1466
Jonathan Gray, 280
Myles D Greenberg, 476
James H. Greene III, 952
Michael Gruber, 987
Michael C. Gruber, 1613
Sarah Guo, 877
Beth Haas, 578
Christopher J. Hadley, 257
Brian K. Halak, PhD, 622
Hadley Harris, 680
David W Harris, 1710
Brooke Hayes, 156
Eric D. Heglie, 989
Andrew Hertzmark, 822
Justin Heyman, 838
Ryan Hinkle, 1005
Mitchell L Hollin, 1140
Laura C. Holson, 1300
David Horing, 111
Jeff Horing, 1005
Richard M Horowitz, 1524
Davis Hostetter, 899
Lee Hower, 1322
Luisa Hunnewell, 1986
Evis Hursever, 698
David Istock, 297
Joel R. Jacks, 509
Matthew Jacobson, 1100
Uttam Jain, 190
Amish Jani, 744
Craig N. Johnson, 836
Stephen M. Johnson, 952
Rick Jones, 269
Christopher N. Jones, 747
G. Kent Kahle, 893
Edward W Kane, 912
Jonathan D. Kelly, 407
Rene Kern, 819
Christopher M. King, 878
Ronald J. Klammer, 1369
Karin Klein, 287
Scott Kleinman, 141
Lewis S. Klessel, 1300
Gil Kliman, 1014
Eric D Kogan, 494
David P Kollock, 836
Michael Kopelman, 655
John Kornreich, 1620
Eric R. Korsten, 330
Krzysztof A. Kowal, CFA, 637
Leon Kuan, 745
Monish Kundra, 518
Gary Lauder, 1099
Christopher Lawler, 851
Seth J Lehr, 1140
Jonathan Lehr, 2006
John Leibovitz, 518
Tim Lemmon, 135
Ben Lerer, 1114
Paul S. Levy, 1043
Regan Li, 2077
Jeff Lieberman, 1005
Ben Lin, 863
David Lincoln, 658
Paul Lisiak, 1226
Angus C Littlejohn Jr., 1138
Alexander Lloyd, 31
John Loftus, 52
Lori Lombardo, 684

Peter Macdonald, 277
Kent Madsen, 689
David Magerman, 615
Deborah Magid, 971
Stephen A. Magida, 124
Marc Magliacano, 1092
Vishal Mahadevia, 1957
Mohamad Makhzoumi, 1296
Scott M. Marimow, 1498
Howard Marks, 1362
Edward W Martin, 494
Arun Mathew, 27
Stephen McClean, 172
Andrew McCormack, 1899
Bill McKee Jr., 851
Marc McMorris, 419
Nihal Mehta, 680
Dr Evan Melrose, 1725
Mark Menell, 1418
Alex Millar, 297
Charles D. Miller, 907
Jeff Monat, 1208
Erik Moore, 232
Michael Morgan, 376
Christina Morin, 851
J. Kenneth Moritz, 1749
Michael B. Morrissey, 1018
Mira Muhtadie, 41
Peter M. Mundheim, 1746
Britton Murdoch, 1572
Nader Naini, 785
Michael E. Najjar, 547
Vas Natarajan, 27
Robert Newbold, 851
Jason Ostheimer, 59
Frank J Pados Jr, 633
Satya Patel, 944
Bret Pearlman, 660
Thomas A Penn, 1431
Thomas B Pennell, 1432
James N Perry, Jr, 1160
Joseph Pesce, 864
Robert W Petit, 1216
Cary Pfeffer MD, 1814
J Peter Pierce, 1450
Barry Porter, 496
Brett L. Prager, 611
David G Proctor, 1234
Mitchell Quain, 41
David B Ragins, 494
Daniel Raynor, 162
Josh Resnick, 1522
Jon Rezneck, 824
Jason Rhodes, 193
Charles Rim, 627
Gregory A. Robbins, 848
Eric Roberts, 1900
Marcos A Rodriguez, 1404
Mark Rosenbaum, 202
Bennett Rosenthal, 160
Howard D Ross, 1140
Adam Rothenberg, 321
Judson Samuels, 929
Jim Sanger, 1643
Martin A. Sarafa, 451
Loren Schlachet, 1576
Ted Schlein, 1079
Adam Schwartz, 128
Scott Schwartz, 491
Brian D. Schwartz, 931
Andrew M. Schwartz, 1115
Jonathan Seiffer, 1113
David Seldin, 134
Aydin Senkut, 720
John Seung, 799
John P Shoemaker, 1234
Brian J Siegel, 896

Mark Sims, 2233
Vic Singh, 680
John Sinnerberg, 578
Geoffrey W. Smith, 179
David Stark, 882
Rob Stavis, 263
Keith Stimson, 886
Matt Sullivan, 1425
Adam L Suttin, 1053
Dov Szapiro, 558
Edwin Tan, 404
Dharmesh Thakker, 238
David Tisch, 321
Bradley Tusk, 1870
Cleve Tzung, 206
Richard J Ulevitch PhD, 11
Marc A Utay, 494
Michael Van Vleck, 858
David Wassong, 1314
Ellen Weber, 1581
Wayne B Weisman, 1636
Richard Wells, 1005
John D. White, 777
Tyler Wolfram, 1360
Dalton Wright, 1074
Benjamin W Yarborough, 1210
Tim Young, 680
Guy Zaczepinski, 451
Howard S. Zeprun, 1852
Toby Zhang, 474
Eric Zinterhofer, 2243
Andy Ziolkowski, 571
Ari M. Zur, 351
Charles H van Horne, 17

University of Peshawar
Raja M. Parvez, 1061

University of Phoenix
Chris Cooper, 1428
Gerald A. Michaud, 949
Christie Pitts, 221

University of Pittsburgh
Mel Billingsley PhD, 1120
Joseph P. Campolo, 148
Gerald S Casilli, 1543
James R. Deitzer, 358
Mark Downs, 1279
Jay Katarincic, 629
Rich Lunak, 1003
Jim Marra, 293
Mark G Miller, 1196
J. Kenneth Moritz, 1749
David Motley, 301
Peter J Muth, 1749
Dennis G Prado, 1163
Jonathan Pressnell, 293
Ned J Renzi, 275
John Richardson, 1279
Stephen G Robinson, 1451
Ralph Schlosstein, 700
Kelly Szejko, 3264
John Tippins, 1749
Anthony L Tomasello, 991
Ryan Walsh, 752

University of Portsmouth
Larry Y. Liu, 2123

University of Pretoria
Thomas de Jager, 119

University of Prince Edward Island
Alex MacBeath, 2157

University of Puget Sound
Robert T. Nelsen, 154

University of Pune
Jana Vazé, 1341

Université du Québec, Montréal
Patrick Pichette, 2150

University of Quebec
Anne-Marie Bourgeois, 677

University of Queensland
Ilfryn Carstair, 1909
Bob Christiansen, 1713

University of Reading
Lorraine Audsley, 2106

University of Redlands
Lou Gerken, 826
Carolyn Ticknor, 994

University of Regina
Harold Huber, 2160
Franklin Jiang, 2221
Dean Popil, 2166

University of Rhode Island
Michael Ashton, 20
Dave Barrett, 1464
Paul Caliento, 505
James S Gladney, 1118
Richard J Harrington, 568
David Martirano, 1463
Morgan Pahxia, 1468
Matt Pierson, 2
Brian St. Jean, 20
John S Struck, 1956

University of Richmond
John Borchers, 556
Jeffrey Craver, 60
Clark F. Davis, 1565
Neil Q. Gabriele, 302
Mary Gay, 170
Kyle Grace, 902
Thomas B. Hoyt, 988
Christopher Lawler, 851
Bradley C O'Dell, 1494
William Powell, 2062
Clark Prickett, 1123
David E Thomas Jr, 1529
Andrew Tichenor, 291
Michael Walden, 1553, 1980

University of Rochester
Robert W. Bruml, 358
Sach Chitnis, 1050
George Doomany, 124
David Drahms, 1388
Jim Dugan, 1364
Jeff Fagnan, 37
Karen Greene, 52
Bruce Greenwald, 64
Abigail Hunter-Syed, 1105
Gregg E. Johnson, 266
Lou Lange, MD, PhD, 183
Rohit Makharia, 821
Richard E Maybaum, 1138
John Moore, 196
Brennan Mulcahey, 352
Dennis O'Brien, 1135
Steven F. Piaker, 436
Murray E Rudin, 1579
Dr. N. Darius Sankey, 2020
Neil S. Suslak, 325
Jeffrey J Teschke, 1053
Avie Tevanian, 660
Tom Uhlman, 1304

College/University Index / University of Salford

Robert A. Vigoda, 428
Nicole Vitullo, 622

University of Salford
Karimah Es Sabar, 2221

University of San Diego
Glenn Argenbright, 1509
Sean Banks, 1865
Greg Bettinelli, 1890
Kevin R Green, 1856
Shelley Lyford, 1974
Jason Stein, 1822
Brent Weinstein, 1885

University of San Francisco
Kirby Bartlett, 44
Jackie Berterretche, 857
David Brewer, 146
Alexander Fries, 650
Mark E. Pearson, 131
Aaron White, 1941
J. Alberto Yepez, 1852

University of Santa Clara
Brent Jones, 1341
Dennis D Ryan, 764

University of Saskatchewan
Warren Bergen, 2043
Ryan Crawford, 2159
Michael Hoffort, 2108
Harold Huber, 2160
Steven Leakos, 2115
E. Craig Lothian, 2166
Mick MacBean, 2267
Dion Madsen, 1442
Mark Poelzer, 2034
Richard Prytula, 2254
Tyler Stuart, 2134
Todd Tessier, 2270

University of Scranton
James Caccavo, 1744
Eugene Galantini, 1643
Howard Kaufman, 1641
Thomas G Rebar, 1636

University of Sheffield
David Q. Anderson, 119
Howard Mayson, 2044
Andy McLoughlin, 1881

University of Sherbrooke
Sophie Forest, 2060
Pierre FréChette, 1594
Charles Sirois, 2252
Pascal Tremblay, 2198

University of Singapore
Jenny Hsui, 475

University of the South
David Beecken, 247
Charles M. Hall, PhD, 140
W Scott Miller, 1152

University of South Carolina
Jeremy Bauman, 1303
Nilanana Bhowmik, 536
Frank X Dalton, 539
Frank X Dalton, 797
David M Faris, 1609
Martin P. Gilmore, 747
Chris Heivly, 194
Mark Rostick, 1009
R Patrick Weston CFA, 216

University of South Dakota
Sandy Horst, 300
Steve Kirby, 300
Nikole Mulder, 300
Dave O'Hara, 175
Susan Simko, 1474

University of South Florida
Marc Blumenthal, 754
Richard M. Ferrari, 599
Stephen M. Krupa, 1500
Tyler Lasher, 1512
Christian Lassonde, 2143
Michael A. Novielli, 638
Josh Richardson, 1147
Steven D Singleton, 1261
Joe Volpe, 1206

University of Southampton
Charles Haythornthwaite, 2072
Philip Roeper, 1272

University of Southern California
Amir Akhavan, 1037
David Aronoff, 756
B Marc Averitt, 1371
Eric Baroyan, 110
Brian Begert, 2284
Marc Benioff, 1610
Nilanjana Bhowmik, 1150
David Bohnett, 231
Richard Brekka, 1643
James W. Brush, MD, 785
Alan Chen, 377
Jai Choi, 1418
Dr Ronald Chwang, 974
Everett Cox, 666
William M. Custer, 572
Feng Deng, 1340
Patrick J Duffy, 1276
Leonard C Ferrington, 1754
Brian Flucht, 281
Gregory J Forrest, 767
Jeff Fox, 911
Kris Fredrickson, 511
Tammy Funasaki, 334
Thomas O Gephart, 1920
Randy Glein, 610
David Glickman, 1548
Michael F. Gooch, 905
Lloyd Greif, 874
Craig Gunther, 281
Desmond Henry, 1858
William Hopkins, 1368
Greg Howorth, 377
Henry Huey, 173
Jerry Ilhuyn Cho, 691
Martin Irani, 905
W. Jack Kessler Jr., 496
Jeff Klemens, 1606
Brian Knitt, 469
David Lane, 614
David Lane, 1379
Huan Le, 954
J Christopher Lewis, 1579
Jerry Lotter, 665
Jeffrey D Lovell, 1151
Christopher Lucas, 278
Peter Macdonald, 277
Adrian Mendoza, 1202
Matthew Mundy, 2233
Janis Naeve, PhD, 113
Preetish Nijhawan, 456
Eric Pakravan, 121
Kristopher Prakash, 1369
Grant Pritchard, 1977
William Quigley, 504
Stephen P. Rader, 496
Susie Roos, 824
Jason Schwarz, 1989
James Shen, 1511
Mary Ann Sigler, 1455
Rick Slaughter, 1758
William Starling, 1774
Sean Stiefel, 1282
Timothy P Sullivan, 1160
Pocket Sun, 1703
Rob Ukropina, 278
Samit Varma, 133
Joshua S. Weinstein, 406
Brent Weinstein, 1885
William Woodward, 133
Simon Yu, 394

University of Southern Illinois
Kevin Swan, 1962

University of Southern Indiana
Mark Hollis, 445

University of Southern Maine
Michael Marocco, 1620

University of Southern Mississippi
Shane McCarthy, CPA, 679

University of St. Andrews
Christopher J Mairs, 1109

University of St. Cyril
Sonja Markova, MBA, 229

University of St. Francis
Mike Bryant, 1082

University of St. Gallen
Markus Moor, 2101
Mathias Schilling, 641
Kyle Winters, 2193

University of St. Thomas
Jason T. Brass, 847
Chuck Gorman, 466
Stephanie McCoy, 1525
Constance Paiement, 739
Steve Polski, 1135
James W Rikkers, 1722
Steve Schwen, 1728
Dave Stassen, 1728
Ann Winblad, 959

University of Stirling
James B. Walker, 555

University of Sussex
Mark T Lupa PhD, 933
David R Skok, 1184

University of Sydney
Ian Bund, 1459
Amber Caska, 1370
Ash Fontana, 2018
David Scaysbrook, 1520

University of Tennessee
Jim Baker, 1573
Mike Brookshire, 1573
Joe Cook Jr, 1261
Vinse Davidson, 1785
Joelle Fox, 678
Wilma Jordan, 1037
Dell Larcen, 886
Blake Lewis, 1573
Christy Shaffer PhD, 918
Burton B Weil, 1921

University of Texas
Farraz Abassi, 445
Wilson Allen, 1977
Jorge Amador, 110
Jay I Applebaum, 1997
Cliff Atherton Jr., 893
Charles W Beckman, 958
Stephen A Bennett, 1748
Craig A. Bondy, 889
Larry Bradshaw, 696
Daryl B Brown, 637
Duncan Butler, 443
Philip A. Canfield, 889
Chris G. Carter, 1326
Mike Chambers, 366
Ross Cockrell, 696
Scott Collier, 1857
Keith L. Crandell, 154
Jon D'Andrea, 1977
Jason M. DeLorenzo, 673
Bowen S. Diehl, 406
Victoria Dominguez-Edington, 447
David Druley, 382
Sean Ebert, 98
Randy Eisenman, 1625
Michael J. Fourticq Sr., 905
Will Franklin, 1129
Matt Fuller, 824
Rudy Garza, 807
Brenda D Gavin, 1510
Scott Gibaratz, 920
Aziz Gilani, 1207
Patrick Hamner, 1424
Joseph L Harberg, 1552
Thomas M. Hargrove, 893
Charles Ho, 40
David Hull, 443
Mark Jennings, 822
Nagraj Kashyap, 1158
Jonathan Kaskow, 294
Charles R Kaye, 1957
Douglas M. Kelley, 406
Bill Kennedy, 807
Laura J Kilcrease, 1857
Huan Le, 954
John L Long Jr, 1843
Richard McClain, 935
Kip McClanahan, 1687
Dr Robert McDonald, 1725
David McWhorter, 427
Jake Moilanen, 1658
David Moross, 717
Rocky Mountain, 595
Robert Newbold, 851
Ron Nixon, 427
Beto Pallares, 169
Jonathan Pearce, 294
Charlie Plauche, 1601
J. Leighton Read, MD, 87
Gary D. Reaves, 741
Scott Rogan, 676
Ryan Sanders, 1205
Tony Schell, 696
Dwight Scott, 280
Mike Sherman, 1190
Jason Shideler, 1160
Jonathan K. Shulkin, 1904
Kevin Spain, 666
Bryan Stolle, 1985
Douglas E. Swanson Jr., 673
Dharmesh Thakker, 238
Ned Truslow, 1560
Elias "Lee" Urbina, 595
Frank Z Wei, 1957
Eric Weiner, 294
Brent Williams, 899
Leo de Luna, 1158

University of Texas Health Science
Tony Di Bona, 87
Kendall Mohler, PhD, 30

University of Texas School of Law
M. Scott Jones, 898
John White, 1273

University of Texas Southwestern
Casey Cunningham, MD, 1622

University of Texas at Austin
Matthew Bryant, 558
Chris G Carter, 1328
Matt Hawkins, 558
Matthew J. Nordgren, 152
Krishnan Varier, 152
James Yang, 13

University of Texas, Arlington
Paul A Yeoham, 1487

University of Texas, Austin
Jim Armstrong, 504
Mark Austin, 1977
Jeff Baker, 703
Forest Baskett, 1296
Alan J. Blackburn, 893
Arjun Chopra, 752
Rob Cohen, 1024
Vinse Davidson, 1785
Lister Delgado, 975
Michael J. Fourticq Jr., 905
Chase Fraser, 784
Brad Gurasich, 427
Dr. Steve Herrod, 820
Bob Inman, 1130
Tom Inman, 1130
Brian Jolly, 960
J. Chris Jones, 898
Stephanie Kreml MD, 244
Colt Leudde, 893
Clark Lipscomb, 543
Brian J. Lobo, 893
Christopher Manning, 1853
Roger Marrero, 530
Jim McBride, 294
J.D. McCulloch, 517
Yatin Mundkur, 176
Robert Norris, 427
Ryan Pollock, 1024
Philip Sanger MD, 1803
Bruce W Schnitzer, 1956
Michael T Segrest, 1684
Joel Serface, 256
Cynthia S Sheridan, 244
Ryan Shulz, 703
Thomas J Stephenson, 1926
Kenneth G. Walter Jr., 905

University of Texas, Dallas
Chuck Butler, 1409
Timothy P Fay, 1639
Arlan Harris, 1244
Vik Thapar, 577

University of Tokyo
Masazumi Ishii, 217
Kenichi Kimura, 1241
Kazunori Maruyama, PhD, 184
Takeshi Mori, 841

University of Toledo
Carmen Evola, 279
Roger Goddu, 337
Edward Kinsey, 1077
H Randall Litten, 351
John W. Snow, 453
Bryan J. Toth, 761

University of Toronto
Bert Amato, 2130
Chris Anastasopoulos, 2097
James Appleyard, 2120
Robin Axon, 2176
Rajiv Bakshi, 2177
Imran Bashir, 2107
Jeff Belford, 2267
Brent Belzberg, 2252, 2264
Jason Berenstein, 2093
Simon Boag, 985
Brad Bolzon, 1930
Jake Cassaday, 2228
George H. Cholakis, 2026
Allan Crosbie, 2083
Gurion De Zwirek, 2245
Sara Defina, 2146
Michael Dixon, 2261
Roman S. Dubczak, 2073
Paul Eldridge, 2121
Chris Erickson, 2205
Gavin Foo, 2196
Karim Gillani, 2172
Newton Glassman, 2067
Alan Greenberg, 2136
Barclay W. Hambrook, 2035
Patrick W.A. Handreke, 2246
Sabrina Hao, 2102
Andrew Haughian, 2205
Michael Hollend, 2264
Sasha Jacob, 2069
David Kornacki, 3249
Mona Kung, 2132
Matthew B. Kunica, 2056
Anthony Lacavera, 2128
René Lajous, 381
Matthew Leibowitz, 2216
Simon Lockie, 2128
Luc Marengere, 2268
Mohan Markandaier, 2132
Barry Markowsky, 2145
Loudon Mclean Owen, 2191
Arda M Minocherhomjee, 470
Matthew Mundy, 2233
Salil Munjal, 2283
Raj Natarajan, 2023
Richard Nathan, 2160
Rob Normandeau, 2242
Loudon Owen, 2147
Gilbert S. Palter, 2098
Donna Parr, 2084
Larry Porcellato, 292
Jim Probert, 2076
Prathna Ramesh, 2178
Tom Rand, 2037
Craig Rankine, 2264
Paul Richardson, 2230
James Riley, 2067
Jamie Rosenblatt, 2130
Jeffrey Rosenthal, 2142
Michael J. Salamon, 2056
Jody Schnarr, 2111
Sachin Shah, 2062
Ameet Shah, 2130, 2131
Brad Silverberg, 978
Daniel Sonshine, 2264
Greg Stewart, 2135
Shermaine Tilley, 2086
Angela Tran, 2272
Gregory G. Turnbull, 2068
Erol Uzumeri, 2243
Tomas Valis, 2070
Stuart Waugh, 2196
Bruce Yang, 2185

College/University Index / University of Toulouse

University of Toulouse
Pierre Lamond, 648

University of Tsukuba
Shunichiro Matsumoto, PhD, 184

University of Tulsa
Julian L Carr, 247
Kyle Largent, 832

University of Twente
Menno Derks, 2239
Alain le Loux, 550

University of Ulm Medical School
Eckard Weber, MD, 622

University of Ulster
Ruairi Grant, 1314

University of Utah
Paul Arnold, 1770
Michael Ballard, 146
José Blanco, 574
Peter Bodine, 84
Chris Cooper, 1428
Frank M. Creer, 2020
Kamran Elahian, 837
Doug Folsom, 8
Matthew N Garff, 1755
Bob Gay, 962
Paul Goodrich, 1162
Steve Grizzell, 1004
J. Blair Jenkins, 464
Len Jordan, 1162
Sid Krommenhoek, 79
Luke Mau, 228
Christopher S Meldrum, 844
Brad Money, 874
John Neis, 1923
Jonathan M Ruga, 1655
Lance Ruud, 639
Alex Soffe, 1074
Todd Stevens, 1545
Ned Stringham, 8
Pete Thomas, 185
Matthew Van Alstyne, 1367
Greg Warnock, 1205
Henry Wong, 613, 810
Dalton Wright, 1074
Scott F Young, 1655

University of Vermont
David Aronoff, 756
Eric Berke, 2264
Robert Cioffi, 80
Jackson Craig, 242
Timothy C Davis, 789
Charles A. Davis, 1746
Robb Doub, 1298
Konstantine Drakonakis, 1101
Sarah Fay, 833
Bruce M. Hernandez, 1727
Amy S Lazarus, 1729
Jeffrey T Newton, 815
Evan Nisselson, 1105
David Pann, 1379
Andrew C. Romans, 1599
Joseph Scharfenberger, 435
Todd Warden, 910
Steve Wood, 839
Caroline L. Young, 904

University of Victoria
Jill Earthy, 2144
David Mortimer, 2144
Steve Romanyshyn, 2203

Kalen Stewart, 2269

University of Virginia
Lee Ainslie, 1185
Amir Akhavan, 1037
Frank Angella, 884
Martha P.E. Arscott, 526
Robert M Austin, 989
Mike Avon, 21
Tiki Barber, 883
Melissa Barry, 929
Kent Bennett, 263
Douglas Berman, 931
A.G.W. Biddle III, 1348
Wes Blackwell, 1635
Jonathan B. Blanco, 747
John Bolduc, 242
Gerry Brunk, 2173
Lee Buck, 289
Lee Buck, 1100
Frank K Bynum, Jr, 1066
Thomas A. Carver, 913
Gregory W. Cashman, 848
John H Chadwick, 495
Miles Clements, 27
Phil Clough, 21
C Taylor Cole Jr, 913
Elizabeth Colonna, 921
Robert Coneybeer, 1666
Paul Conley, 1401
John Connaughton, 223
James J Connors II, 1066
Jim Conroy, 1372
Mike Crothers, 703
Roanne Daniels, 927
Terry Daniels, 1507
Thompson Dean, 212
Christopher Delaney, 1027
Douglas Diamond, 694
Michael F. Donoghue, 1730
Steve Dutton, 1066
David A. Eagle, 360
Jonathan Ebinger, 299
Tom Eddy, 1031
S. Whitfield Edwards, 747
David Eichler, 1500
Michael G. Eliasek, 1493
Chad Ellis, 41
Jeffrey W Ferguson, 416
Andy Fligel, 1009
Jason Gabriel, 1776
David Gladstone, 832
Tom Glanville, 697
John W. Glynn, 840
Jacqueline Glynn, 840
Michael B Goldberg, 1066
Wesley Gottesman, 328
Andrew Grapkowski, 101
Bruns Grayson, 22
Kirk B Griswold, 165
Kevin T. Hammond, 1043
George J Henry, 1131
Tom Hickey, 1507
Paul Holland, 773
Thomas B. Hoyt, 988
William L Hudson, 1332
Charles B Hughes III, 644
Scott Irwin, 1543
Gregg E. Johnson, 266
Thad Jones, 1507
David Jones, 1712
Teddy Kaplan, 1300
Bruce Karsh, 1362
Sean M. Kelley, 878
Robert Kibble, 1239
Trevor Kienzle, 545
Randal J. Kirk, 1815

Randal Klein, 211
Jason Krikorian, 597
Doug Kuribayashi, 1478
Chris Lanning, 819
Mitch Lasky, 251
Anton Levy, 819
Peter Lipson, 912
C. Malcolm Little, 167
Gene Lockhart, 1240
Frank J Loverro, 1066
John G Loverro, 1116
Laura L. Lukaczyk, 210
David M Maher, 355
Brendan Mathews, 1259
George McCabe, 913
Glenn McGonnigle, 1790
Chris McKay, 857
Sandy Miller, 1006
Church M Moore, 1066
Christina Morin, 851
John E. Morningstar, 1972
David Moszer, 1493
James B Murray Jr, 552
A. Bilal Noor, 167
Christopher B. Norton, 408
Jacqueline Novogratz, 54
Cody Nystrom, 1691
Julie Ocko, 912
William Ogden, 1883
Michael J Orend, 1579
Tim R. Palmer, 458
Shaneel D. Patel, 1041
Robert Paull, 1155
Peter S Pettit, 1270
Kurt Pilecki, 277
Robert Pollak, 1763
John Powell, 1008
Brian Powers, 927
Alex Radcliffe, 409
Ramesh Radhakrishnan, 176
Matt Rice, 227
Josh Richardson, 1147
Steven C Rodger, 692
Arthur C. Roselle, 1410
Frank Rotman, 1504
Brent T Sacha, 1748
Andrew Salenbier, 36
Judson Samuels, 929
Michael Schattner, 1378
Barbara Schilberg, 269
Thomas A Scully, 1973
Peter Seidler, 1648
Timothy D Sheehan, 247
Walker C. Simmons, 1410
John W. Snow, 453
James Socas, 1888
Esteban Sosnik, 1530
Paul Straub, 493
Richard D Tadler, 1778
William B. Thompson, 783
David Tolmie, 654
Mary Traer CPA, 912
John Tullis, 1868
James Tybur, 1434
Robbert Vorhoff, 819
Bonnie K Wachtel, 1950
Robert Wadsworth, 912
Ted Wang, 553
Scott Warren, 1234
Alexander D Whittemore, 1754
Russ Williams, 15
Greg Williams, 28
Aaron P Wolfe, 1755
Caroline L. Young, 904

University of Virginia Law School
Timothy P Agnew, 1178

College/University Index / University of Wisconsin, Oshkosh

Jon Flint, 1464
Gordon R Penman, 1922

University of Wales
Terry Matthews, 2276
Stu Phillips, 241

University of Warwick
Gautam Banerjee, 280
Makhtar Diop, 1012
Ian A.W. Howes, 30
Shahzad Pirvani, 2021

University of Washington
Steve Anderson, 234
David L. Belzer, 1493
EJ Blanchfield, 1462
Brad Bodden, 2002
David Bonderman, 1837
William J Canestaro, 2007
Matt Clary, 1964
Bryan Cressey, 559
Neal Dempsey, 241
Derek Eve, 674
Nathan R. Every, MD, MPH, 785
Clinton Foy, 562
Alan D. Frazier, 785
Kevin Gabelein, 755
Brad Gillespie, 969
Tom Gonser, 1659
Nick Hanauer, 1644
Scott Hardman, 82
Kirk Holland, 35
Chris Howard, 978
Simon James, 696
Kent Johnson, 82
Brendan Kennedy, 1484
Bob Kocher MD, 1918
David A Krekel, 1399
James LoGerfo, 643
Wendy Lung, 971
Elliot Maluth, 931
Alex Mason, 419
Pete McCormick, 1186
Geoffrey Moore, 1985
Mike Pongon, 1462
Michael H. Reynoldson, 1020
Johnathan Roberts, 978
Joseph L. Schocken, 349
Stewart Schuster, 1354
Dana Settle, 876
Steven Stull, 60
Paulette Taylor, 1619
Mike Templeman, 892
Victoria Treyger, 720
Dino Vendetti, 766
Dino Vendetti, 1659
Katherine Watts, 1714
Denny Weston, 755
Melissa Widner, 1640
Jen Wolf, 995
Noel de Turenne, 1250

University of Waterloo
Andrew Abouchar, 2253
Steve Balaban, 2185
Bharat Choudhary, 2279
Patrick Chung, 2245
Bonnie Foley-Wong, 2215
Devon Galloway, 2122
Karim Gillani, 2172
Paul Godman, 2028
Chris Govan, 2201
Duncan Hill, 2176
Daryl Hodges, 2033
Randall Howard, 2271
Tim Jackson, 2253
Arif Janmohamed, 1125
Ken Kember, 2106
Kevin Kimsa, 2240
Larry LaKing, 2181
Paul Langill, 2029
Mike Lazaridis, 2220
Vernon Lobo, 2190
Lisa Low, 2081
A.J. (Sandy) Marshall, 2054
Mike McCauley, 2122
Vihangi Mehta, 2178
Kevin Negus, 388
Karamdeep Nijjar, 2150
Chamath Palihapitiya, 1698
Anu Pathria, 545
Tom Rand, 2037
Neil Sadraranganey, 621
Ray Simonson, 2271
George So, 2151, 2158

University of Western Australia
Mason Hills, 1551
James McClements, 1551
Ben Yu, 1672

University of Western Ontario
David Adderley, 2070
Christopher J Albinson, 1411
Geoff Beattie, 2228
Brian Boulanger, 2036
Richard Bradlow, 2211
Laurel C. Broten, 2197
Andrew Carragher, 639
Roger Chabra, 2231
Dave Chapman, 2284
Aubrey Dan, 2088
Christopher Darby, 983
Carey Diamond, 2280
Shayn Diamond, 2280
John Eckert, 2191
Ron Farmer, 2190
Wade Flemons, 2210
Rob Gavin, 2281
Craig Golinowski, 2159
Jordan Goodman, 2041
Bruce Hodge, 2210
Michael Hollend, 2264
Wally Hunter, 677
Christian Lassonde, 2143
David Lawee, 579
Jeff Lucassen, 2196
Stephen O. Marshall, 2098
Jeff McAllister, 2059
Murray McCaig, 2037
Robert S. McLeese, 2026
John McMullen, 2167
Minhas Mohamed, 2188
Jim Nieuwenburg, 2044
Karamdeep Nijjar, 2150
Rob Normandeau, 2242
Jeff Parr, 2075
Richard Prytula, 2254
John Richardson, 2051
David Roff, 2128
Jamie Rosenblatt, 2130
Gary Rubinoff, 2250
Peter Samson, 2156
Russell Samuels, 2280
Peter Schwartz, 2165
Alan G. Sellery, 2156
Allison M. Taylor, 2155
Robert Trudeau, 1787
Douglas B. Trussler, 277
Jeff Wigle, 2045

University of Westminster
Adam Kalish, 1155

University of Windsor
Doug Fregin, 2220
James C. Johnson, 2246
Jeff Lucassen, 2196
Tristan Velez, 929

University of Winsconsin-Madison
Stuart Holden, MD, 1492

University of Wisconsin
Andrew B Albert, 1767
David J. Anderson, 463
Lawrence S. Atinsky, 179
Robert M Belke, 1151
Darren Brathol, 1722
Scott Button, 1923
Brian F. Chambers, 1410
Jerome A Chazen, 462
Mark Flower, 1964
Jason Gerlach, 1758
Eric M Gordon, 1693
Adam S. Gruber, 687
Christopher J. Hadley, 257
John A. Hatherly, 2008
Eric Hender, 16
Steven D Kloos PhD, 1861
Steve LaPorte, 1379
Laura L. Lukaczyk, 210
Steve McConahey, 1024
Steve Mech, 567
John Neis, 1923
John R Nelson, 1667
Timothy Petersen, 150
Margaret Riley, 1913
George Roberts, 1381
Arthur Schneiderman, 837
David R. Schroder, 1020
David Schroder, 16
Ronald J. Shebuski, PhD, 140
Sarah Smith, 224
Michael Steinberg, 1531
Paul A Stone JD, 11
John Streur, 379
John H. Underwood, 1438
Ryan Waddington, 964
David L. Warnock, 386
Michael Yanney, 70

University of Wisconsin, Eau Claire
Chad W Souvignier, 1546

University of Wisconsin, Madison
Andy Boszhardt, 863
Thomas F Campion, 1210
Robert DeBruin, 1291
Christopher Erickson, 1822
David Gitter, 1291
Charlie Goff, 1291
Saar Gur, 457
Kent C Haeger, 935
Joseph R Katcha, 935
Bernard Moon, 1719
Judy M. Owen, 378
John Philosophos, 863
Andrew Sandler, 1620
Toni F. Sikes, 378
Tom Smith, 1174
Vipul B. Soni, 360
Varsha Tagare, 1511
Roy Thiele-Sardina, 936
Terrence R Wall, 584
Linda Watchmaker, 538
Paul Weiss, 1923
Leon R Wilkosz, 584

University of Wisconsin, Oshkosh
Charlie Goff, 1291

1043

Steve Predayna, 1291

University of Wisconsin-Madison
Tyler Matlock, 1769

University of Witwatersrand
Grant Behrman, 248
Spencer Fleischer, 790
Sven M Jacobson, 663
David S Lobel, 1654
Caroline Popper MD MPH, 244
John L. Teeger, 777

University of Wyoming
Frank Mendicino II, 35

University of York
Nick Morriss, 838

University of Zagreb
Kresimir Letinic MD PhD, 644
Dr. Boris Nikolic, 271

Uppsala University
Kristina Williams, 2028

US Air Force Academy
Tom Dennedy, 176
Paul Madera, 1213

US Airforce Institute of Technology
Brian Hibblen, 1689

US Coast Guard Academy
Hans Lundin, 1007

US Military Academy
David W Averett, 1754
Chris C Casciato, 1127
Brian Chee, 1464
Phil Clough, 21
Randall Crowder, 1803
John Drew, 1787
Russell B Hall, 1110
Bradley C Harrison, 1635
Robert P Healy, 470
Han Kim, 100
Douglas McCormick, 920
Paul F Murphy, 1654
Dave Tamburri, 921
Michael Thorson, 2002
Mark A deLaar, 1754

US Naval Academy
Ted Alexander, 1239
Ted Ardell, 1788
Thomas W. Arenz, 917
Sean Banks, 1865
Dennis B Costello, 1849
David Jones, 1712
Jeffrey R. Shannon, 547
Timothy P Sullivan, 1160
Michael Taylor, 912
Samit Varma, 133
Robert N. Verratti, 1830

Utah State University
José Blanco, 574
Ryan Hemingway, 689
L John Wilkerson, 809

Valdosta State University
Thomas M Tarnowski, 1754

Valparaiso University
Steven W. Parks, 1097
Ben A Schnakenberg, 934

Vanderbilt Law School
Mark L Feidler, 1270
Stacy Feld, 1046
Stacy Feld, 1442

Vanderbilt School of Engineering
Brian Harrison, 1470

Vanderbilt University
Charles E Adair, 539
Jeff Barry, 1459
Michael Berolzheimer, 246
Erik W. Bloom, 842
Charles Booker, 60
Dennis C Bottorff, 551
Brandon B. Boze, 1905
Andrew Byrd, 1872
Andrew Byrd, Jr., 1872
Mark H Carter, 1778
Mike Collett, 1491
McCall Cravens, 960
Bowen S. Diehl, 406
James Dimitri, 1927
Craig Driscoll, 938
Ted Fourticq, 905
Diane Fraiman, 1947
Bryan C. Frederickson, 893
Neil Q. Gabriele, 302
John Gaffney, 366
Katie H Gambill, 551
David S. Gorton, 1779
Gregory T Hebrank MD, 1102
Patrick Hendy, 518
Chris Hollod, 14
Justin Ishbia, 1670
Adam Jackson, 775
Dave Johnson, 1009
Mark Jones, 1573
Stephen A. Lasher, 893
Joshua M. Levinson, 848
Spence McCelland, 1332
Marc McManus, 491
J Carter McNabb, 1575
Eben S Moulton, 1639
Ian J Mount, 1277
Thiago Olson, 678
R Wilson Orr III, 1735
Ross Perot, Jr., 1436
F. Matthew Petronzio, 1873
Joshua S. Phillips, 428
Jay Radtke, 1174
Jon Rattner, 194
Wendell Reilly, 1425
Andrew Roche, 491
Ian Rountree, 398
Conner Searcy, 1858
John W Shearburn, 1957
Dave Stevenson, 1206
David Stinnett, 1858
Tim Storer, 8
C Morris Stout, 1769
William Timmerman III, 851
Andrew B. Tindel, 1410
John Tippins, 1749
Andrew A. Tisdale, 1498
William Tomai, 449
Rurik G Vandevenne, 1575
John Vincent, 1557
Ben Wallace, 216
Burton B Weil, 1921
Patrick F Whelan, 1427
Jay Wilkins, 917
Hunter Witherington, 1735
James D Witherington Jr, 1735
Robert Womsley, 1962
Mark Wright, 290
J.D. Wright, 491

Darell E Zink Jr, 412

Vassar College
Timothy P Agnew, 1178
Stuart Barkoff, 838
Caterina Fake, 2013
Ari Fine Glantz, 3263
Jeffrey Goldstein, 927
Michael A.G. Korengold, 679
Kyle Lefkoff, 318
Paul Lehman, 1026
Mitch Truwit, 136
Hunter Walk, 944

Villanova University
Daniel H Bathon Jr, 1994
Matthew M. Bennett, 1300
Steve Berman, 162
Joseph P. Campolo, 148
Matthew A Cook, 1075
Steven DeCillis II, 63
Gary R DiLella, 1496
Chris Fralic, 742
Christopher G Hanssens, 699
Joseph Heinmiller, 851
Gerald Holtz, 1496
Thomas Iannarone, 280
Donald A Juricic, 1560
Karen Kassouf, 439
Ronald J. Klammer, 1369
George Krautzel, 1240
Marc Lederman, 1316
John Loftus, 52
James Mahoney, 963
Bernard B Markey, 1280
Paul Mehring, 34
Robert P Moran, 1456
Stephanie Palmeri, 1881
John Park, 413
Steven Peterson, 1845
Philip Siuta, 532
Andrew Souder, 1524
William H Stewart, 1280
Steven Swain, 442
Daniel Terpak, 467
Sean M Traynor, 1973
Christine Vogt, 78
Robert Walsh, 700
Raymond F Weldon, 356

Villanova University School of Law
John Buttrick, 1884
Paul D'Addario, 1403
Anne-Marie Shelley, 38

Virginia Commonwealth University
Brenda Bracken, 860
Casey Jones, 206

Virginia Military Institute
Casey West, 1735

Virginia Polytechnic Institute
Nelson Chu, 1076
Jonathan Ebinger, 299
Steve Fredrick, 881
Tim Guleri, 1672
John B Higginbotham, 1717
William H. Kucheman, 272
Zach Malone, 629
Charles P McCusker, 1424
Steven C Pierson, 1151
Shrikant Sathe, 1913
Ian Sobieski, PhD, 229
Stuart Vyule, 1573
Pete Zippelius, 1113

College/University Index / West Chester University

Virginia State University
William H. Kucheman, 272

Virginia Tech
Dave Armstrong, 773
Raman Khanna, 604

Vrije Universiteit
Paulus J Ingram, 2239
Wal van Lierop, 2072

Vrunel University
Donald O'Shea, 572

W.P. Carey School of Business
Al Foreman, 1866
Kyle Hufford, 230

WHU Otto Beisheim School of Mgmt
Joern Nikolay, 819

WM Penn University
Gordon Roth, 1592

Wabash College
C Bryan Daniels, 1473
James C. Snyder, 904

Wagner College
Steven Leischner, 943

Wake Forest University
Joseph B. Alala III, 408
Kurt E. Bolin, 1746
John Bradley, 1349
Sean Britain, 242
M. Hunt Broyhill, 408
Chris Cathcart, 899
Matthew S Crawford, 1502
Adam B. Dolder, 864
David Dupree, 899
Frederick W. Eubank II, 1410
Thomas P (Todd) Gibbons, 306
R. Scott Glass, Jr., 1410
Todd A Goergen, 1587
Matthew E Gormly III, 1984
Thomas L Greer, 797
G. Thomas Hough, 1419
Chris Julich, 696
Sean M. Kelley, 878
Brian Melton, 1798
Deepa Pakianathan, PhD, 605
George A Parker, 1107
Scott Plumridge, 899
Christopher W Solomon, 1973
Robert M. Stewart, 1730
David I Wahrhaftig, 1066
Felix J Wong, 753

Walsh College
David Armstrong, 198

Waseda University
Masayuki Fuji, 1716
Shinya Imai, 1241
Masa Isono, 603
Tatsuya Kubo, 912
Tak Miyata, 1637
Koichiro Nakamura, 1716

Washburn University
Greg Brenneman, 435
R Clayton Funk, 1197
Ted Roth, 1592

Washington & Jefferson College
David Glickman, 1548

Richard J Ulevitch PhD, 11

Washington & Lee University
Douglas Burns, 552
M Roy Burns, 1778
Brian Castleberry, 293
William D Christ, 1778
Andrew Crawford, 819
Louis Dubuque, 60
Bruce B. Dunnan, 880
Bob Forlenza, 1731
Blair Garrou, 1207
Michael Harden, 177
Cliff Holekamp, 570
John W. McCullough, 907
Noah F. Rhodes III, 864
Lloyd R. Sams, 266
Thomas R Shepherd, 1864
Bennett Thompson, 1090
Thomas R Wall, IV, 1066
Michael Watts, 1132
Matt Yohe, 1266

Washington College
Tim Connor, 1656

Washington College of Law
James Conlon, 361

Washington State University
Roy C. Carriker, PhD, 836
Arjun Gupta, 1795
Ronald S Howell, 2007
Karin Lagerlund, 912
Michael Mayer, 1251
Ted Nark, 1090
John R Nelson, 1667
Bridget Storm, 1001
Martin Tan, 153

Washington University
Andrew B Albert, 1767
Stuart Bassin, 1603
Andrew P. Bonanno, 1085
Aaron Bright, 1435
Steve Brotman, 91
Steve Brotman, 1682
Brian Clevinger, 1490
Mike Collett, 1491
Jeff Fox, 911
Sherri Haskell, 391
Jorge Jaramillo, 1387
John Kuelper, 178
Mark Levin, 1814
Philip Lewis, 797
Jim Lim, 872
Lisa Nelson, 1158
Brett A Parr, 402
Teddy Shalon, 1490
Dave Stevenson, 1206
Andrew Sturner, 558
Phyllis Whiteley, 1985

Washington University School of Law
Lee Bailey, 1897
Jonathan Goldstein, 60

Washington University, St. Louis
Len Batterson, 237
Jeffrey Craver, 60
Jeremy Degenhart, 60
Louis Dubuque, 60
Gaurav Garg, 1996
Cliff Holekamp, 570
Quinn Li, 1511
Ted Maidenberg, 1850
Ezra Mehlman, 921
Rick Ruffolo, 80

Konrad Salaber, 1990
Ryan Schuler, 178
Nicholas Somers, 1765

Wayne State University
Bob Flannery, 1539
Gerald Greenwald, 867
Gabe Karp, 608
Ali Safiedine DPM, 1288
Tom Shehab, 150
Ara Topouzian, 3259

Weatherhead School
Brian Hersman, 1045

Weatherhead School of Management
Anthony Nader, 1768

Weber State University
Mark C Masur, 1684
Scott Stenberg, 1004

Webster University
Sherri Haskell, 391
Matt Turner, 114
Gijs FJ Van Thiel, 13

Weizmann Institute of Science
Yoni Chiefetz, 1125

Wellesley College
Daria Becker, 1493
Virginia Cargill, 80
Alisa Frederick, 377
Maria Gotsch, 1422
Melissa Guzy, 149
Maia Heymann, 536
Tasha Seitz, 1042
Rudina Seseri, 713
Rudina Seseri, 833
Valerie J Sill, 637

Wenzhou University
Chris Xie, 2263

Wesleyan University
Gregory M Barr, 1686
Scott Barry, 698
Alex Benik, 238
Brad Burnham, 1884
Stuart Ellman, 1597
Jesse Feldman, 238
James Frischling, 883
Aaron Gershenberg, 1766
Nicholas Iovino, 834
Paul Kusserow, 958
Tom Lavin, 1302
Christian Lawless, 537
Frederick Maynard, 912
Lee M Mitchell, 1817
P Sherrill Neff, 1510
Michael Patterson, 1913
Damon Rawie, 60
Ted Roth, 1592
Rick Segal, 1554
Frank V. Sica, 1779
Donald Spencer, 1681
Andrew Vogel, 2019
Andy Weissman, 1884
Strauss Zelnick, 2019
TX Zhuo, 729, 1059

West Chester University
Jason M Cunningham, 165
Chris Heivly, 194
Steven Hobman, 1316

College/University Index / West Point

West Point
James M. Bannantine, 192

West Virginia University
Patrick A Bond, 1262
John Chambers, 1035
Karen Evans, 1689
Gary Gauba, 575
John K Giannuzzi, 1668
J Rudy Henley, 1262
Jay R. Henry, 1410
Marvin W Ritchie, 1311

Western Illinois University
Robert Nardelli, 668
Dennis Podlesak, 622
Warren Weiss, 773

Western Kentucky University
Thomas C. Fitzgerald, 363
Gen. John M Keane, 1636
Jerry D. Wethington, 1574

Western Maryland College
Steven B. Fader, 192
David I Wahrhaftig, 1066
Jim Zucco, 507

Western Michigan University
Jim Farnsworth, 2044
Tom Kurtz, 1424
Luke Sage, 1427
Eli L. Thomssen, 140

Western New England College
Joelle Marquis, 172

Western New England University
Sean O'Keefe, 1961

Western University
Jill Earthy, 2144
Darrick Geant, 334
Ed Giacomelli, 2083
Dave Harris Kolada, 2136
Ian Macdonell, 2083
Mark McQueen, 2074
Lisa Melchior, 2273
Shay Nulman, 2168
Aaron Serruya, 2245
Mark Usher, 2074

Western Washington University
Donald J Elmer, 1399

Westminster College
Jeffrey Howard, 1613

Westmont College
Lou Caballero, 277

Wharton School
Todd M. Abbrecht, 1818
Mike Ackrell, 43
Dr Philippe H Adam, 188
Deepak Advani, 927
Sandip Agarwala, 1147
Rahul Aggarwal, 337
Daniel Agroskin, 1043
Zaid F Alsikafi, 1160
Robert Amen, 1912
Jim Andelman, 309, 1569
James G Andersen, 505
Izhar Armony, 457
Keith Bank, 1060, 1061
James M. Bannantine, 192
Jason S Barg, 1151

Phin Barnes, 742
John M Baumer, 1113
Josh Baumgarten, 128
Charles Beeler, 1525
Grant Behrman, 248
Michael A. Bell, 1818
Steven T. Berg, 424
Thomas A Berglund, 734
Brian S. Berkin, 1779
Douglas Berman, 931
Robert A Bernstein, 1109
Michael Bevan, 658
Nikhil J. Bhat, 1933
James G Binch, 1131
Charles Birnbaum, 263
Anders Bjork, 20
Darren M Black, 1754
Alan J. Blackburn, 893
Erik W. Bloom, 842
Kurt E. Bolin, 1746
Anne Bovaird Nevins, 1445
Henry J. Boye, 1818
Sam Brasch, 1056
Adam Breslin, 2211
Peter L. Briger Jr., 769
Philip L. Bronner, 1348
Mark Brooks, 1629
Kenneth Brotman, 45
Bob Brown, 1275
Robert W. Bruml, 358
Mike Brunell, 1369
Frank W. Bruno, 453
Thomas A. Burger Jr., 878
Steve Burns, 1507
Tara Butler, MD, 178
William F Case Jr, 505
A Baron Cass III, 367
John H Chadwick, 495
Roger Chen, 1687
Ray Cheng, 1235
Brian Cherry, 1360
Stephen Chiao, 1771
Kyce Chihi, 196
Iris Choi, 752
Jonathan Y Chou, 699
T.C. Chou, 908
Yee-Ping Chu, 277
John Clarke, 413
Lisa Coca, 812
Michael Cohen, 1369
Robert Coneybeer, 1666
Richard Conklin, 733
Stephen B. Connor, 903
Schuyler Coppedge, 676
David C. Coquillette, 1300
John Cozzi, 63
Sean L. Cunningham, 889
Rajeev Dadoo, 1734
Nicholas Daraviras, 1036
Ken DeAngelis, 205
Michael B. DeFlorio, 917
Dain F DeGroff, 1848
Michael DeRosa, 658
John Dean, 942
Feng Deng, 1340
Karl D Dillon, 943
Jeffrey G. Dishner, 1742
Michael Dolbac, 812
Alex Doll, 1796
Edith Dorsen, 2003
Greg Dracon, 1
David Drahms, 1388
Steven M Dresner, 630
Russell S Dritz, 1506
Justin C Dupere, 1964
Suzette Dutch, 1849
Shomik Dutta, 937

David A. Eagle, 360
Loren Easton, 111
Bruce A Eatroff, 902
Peter Ehrich, 559
Stephen Eisenstein, 917
Yaron Eitan, 1650
Joe El Chami, 1026
Martin Eltrich III, 63
Jerry Engel, 1249
Patrick Enright, 1147
Mark E Epstein, 1271
Jonas Fajgenbaum, 1022
Beth Ferreira, 744
Robert J Fioretti, 717
Mark L. First, 687
Doug Fisher, 1014
Jason Fisherman, 1777
John Fletcher, 750
Joe Floyd, 666
Kerri Ford, 1600
Peter B Franz, 753
Brian P. Friedman, 1036
W Robert Friedman Jr, 630
Eric T Fry, 1133
Michael Gallagher, 931
J.S. Gamble, 288
John Garcia, 63
Kirt Gardner, 1880
Wesley H.R. Gaus, 509
Simeon J. George, 1734
Steven J. Gilbert, 831
Robert Girardi, 212
Liron Gitig, 796
R. Scott Glass, Jr., 1410
Pramod Gosavi, 3
Pat Gouhin, 3247
Jonathan Gray, 280
Bob Greene, 535
Charles S. Grigg, 418
Kirk B Griswold, 165
Jorge Gross Jr, 1859
David Gross-Loh, 223
Aflalo Guimaraes, 1022
Sarah Guo, 877
Beth Haas, 578
Christopher J. Hadley, 257
Eugene Hahn, 1043
Robert M. Hannon, 1826
Christopher G Hanssens, 699
Hadley Harris, 680
Donald L Hawks III, 356
Brooke Hayes, 156
Joe T. Hays, 612
Kiran Hebbar, 1901
Eric D. Heglie, 989
Eric Hender, 16
Andrew Hertzmark, 822
Justin Heyman, 838
R Trent Hickman, 1929
Ryan Hinkle, 1005
Summer Hinton, 2057
Andrew B. Hochman, 1594
Spencer P Hoffman, 1151
Mitchell L Hollin, 1140
Laura C. Holson, 1300
Michael P Hompesch, 633
Osuke Honda, 597
Steve Hooper, 978
David Horing, 111
Jeff Horing, 1005
Mark Horne, 1459
Joe Horowitz, 972
Fred Hosaisy, 1697
Davis Hostetter, 899
Lee Hower, 1322
Peter Hsing, 1219
Ron Hunt, 1297

College/University Index / Wharton School

Bob Hurst, 560
Roger Hurwitz, 1944
Tony Ignaczak, 1507
David Istock, 297
Joel R. Jacks, 509
Matthew Jacobson, 1100
Ariel Jaduszliwer, 327
David Jaffe, 449
Mudit Jain PhD, 1774
Amish Jani, 744
Arif Janmohamed, 1125
Andrew S. Janower, 458
Peter T Jensen, 1720
Craig N. Johnson, 836
Stephen M. Johnson, 952
Christopher N. Jones, 747
John R Jonge Poernik, 1134
G. Kent Kahle, 893
Victor Kats, 178
Jonathan D. Kelly, 407
Rene Kern, 819
Eurie Kim, 763
Doug Kimmelman, 676
Christopher M. King, 878
Jason Klein, 28
Randal Klein, 211
Karin Klein, 287
Gentry S Klein, 1138
Scott Kleinman, 141
Lewis S. Klessel, 1300
Michael Koby, 4
Peggy Koenig, 20
Eric D Kogan, 494
David P Kollock, 836
Tim Komada, 601
Adam Koopersmith, 1483
Michael Kopelman, 655
Josh Kopelman, 742
David Kronfeld, 1042
Rodger R Krouse, 1755
Alex T. Krueger, 741
Stephen M. Krupa, 1500
Leon Kuan, 745
Timothy Kuehl, 1345
W. Brent Kulman, 747
C Todd Kumble, 1729
Monish Kundra, 518
Brian Kwait, 1368
Pete Labbat, 676
René Lajous, 381
Joseph P Landy, 1957
Curtis S Lane, 1271
Gary Lauder, 1099
Christopher Lawler, 851
Marc J Leder, 1755
Marc Lederman, 1316
Jeffrey Lee, 1340
Seth J Lehr, 1140
Tim Lemmon, 135
Scott Lenet, 794
Chris Leong, 162
Jeff Lieberman, 1005
Ben Lin, 863
Alexander Lloyd, 31
Scott Lopano, 678
Mark Ludwig, 1707
Melanie C Lyren, 165
Kenneth Mabbs, 712
Peter Macdonald, 277
J Matthew Mackowski, 1794
Kent Madsen, 689
Stephen A. Magida, 124
Marc Magliacano, 1092
Nurzhas Makishev, 1330
Christopher Manning, 1853
Scott M. Marimow, 1498
Howard Marks, 1362

Renee Masi, 272
David J Matlin, 1182
Andrew R. Mayer, 1779
Howard Mayson, 2044
John McCarty, 1425
Stephen McClean, 172
Tom McCloskey, 543
W. Christian McCollum, 1113
Dr Robert McDonald, 1725
Bill McKee Jr., 851
Jeffrey McKibben, 1368
John McKinley, 1100
Marc McMorris, 419
Kevin W McMurchy, 630
Dr Evan Melrose, 1725
Mark Menell, 1418
David Mes, 1370
Marc Michel, 527
Alex Millar, 297
Christian T Miller, 699
Yuri Milner, 616
Cory Moelis, 882
Charles Moldow, 773
Andrew Moley, 1125
Jeff Monat, 1208
Greg Mondre, 1685
Mario Montoya, 1992
Erik Moore, 232
Frank Mora, 961
Christina Morin, 851
John E. Morningstar, 1972
Michael B. Morrissey, 1018
Randy Moser, 203
Mira Muhtadie, 41
Arneek Multani, 1852
Dennis E Murphree, 1273
Vijay Nagappan, 1227
Ryan K Nagim, 1148
Sandeep Naik, 819
Michael E. Najjar, 547
David C Neverson, 1109
Robert Newbold, 851
Henry W Newman, 1704
Ha Nguyen, 1724
Matthew W Norton, 1160
Brian O'Malley, 763
Ben Orthlieb, 1370
Jason Ostheimer, 59
David B Outcalt, 1116
Jean-Pierre Paquin, 243
Deven Parekh, 1005
David J. Parker, 119
Keval Patel, 931
Brian Paul, 1798
Jay D Pauley, 1754
Christopher Payne, 919
Bret Pearlman, 660
Kevin S Penn, 41
Kevin Penn, 111
Joseph Pesce, 864
Robert W Petit, 1216
Patten Pettway, 1573
Cary Pfeffer MD, 1814
Wayne Platt, 1369
Dennis Podlesak, 622
Santo Politi, 1718
Barry Porter, 496
Brett L. Prager, 611
David G Proctor, 1234
Travis Putnam, 1281
Thomas Queenan, 1445
David B Ragins, 494
Rashad Rahman, 357
Zeena Rao, 973
Daniel Raynor, 162
Douglas Reed MD, 918
Eric Reiter, 337

Josh Resnick, 1522
Peter Restler, 368
Jon Rezneck, 824
Jason Rhodes, 193
Trevor C Rich, 1151
Glenn Rieger, 1316
Marvin W Ritchie, 1311
Gregory A. Robbins, 848
David Robbins, 1846
Joseph R Robinson, 1230
Frank J. Rodriguez, 1043
Marcos A Rodriguez, 1404
Alex Rose, 560
Mark Rosenbaum, 202
Bennett Rosenthal, 160
Eric L. Rosenzweig, 1746
Robert L. Rosner, 1933
John M. Roth, 786
Marc Rowan, 141
Laura M. Rubin, 1742
Neil Ryan, 1868
Aaron Sack, 1256
Neal G Sahney, 792
Judson Samuels, 929
Martin A. Sarafa, 451
Shrikant Sathe, 1913
Parag Saxena, 1913
Scott Schleifer, 1828
Ben A Schnakenberg, 934
Jeffrey A. Schoenfeld, 243
Richard R Schreiber, 617
Amanda Schutzbank, 121
Nelson Schwab III, 418
Scott Schwartz, 491
Andrew M. Schwartz, 1115
Christian Schwartz, 1822
Samuel L Schwerin, 1235
Stacey D. Seltzer, 73
Aydin Senkut, 720
Ned Sherwood, 2021
Zubeen Shroff, 809
Lawrence R Simon, 505
Mark Sims, 2233
Bipul Sinha, 1125
John Sinnerberg, 578
Jack Slye, 1140
Gregg Smart, 722
Ryan A Smiley, 1570
Andrew Snyder, 851
Jon Soberg, 1269
Erica S. Son, 167
Luke Sorenson, 1707
Kevin Spain, 666
Andrew Spring, 1231
Amit Srivastava, 683
Rob Stavis, 263
Howard Steyn, 1092
Keith Stimson, 886
Jason Stoffer, 1186
Kathryn J Stokel, 17
Dave Stubbs, 383
Daniel Sugar, 1927
Trey Sykes, 1018
Dov Szapiro, 558
Karim A. Tabet, 1498
Richard D Tadler, 1778
Lucius H. Taylor, 157
Michael Taylor, 912
Dharmesh Thakker, 238
James E Thomas, 1820
Shawn Thompson, 1369
Rick Thompson, 1680
James Thorp, 16
William Tomai, 449
Sean M Traynor, 1973
David W. Truetzel, 199
Daniel G. Tully, 97

College/University Index / Wheaton College

John H. Turner, 1979
Marc A Utay, 494
Michael Van Vleck, 858
Sriram Venkataraman, 212
Bradaigh Wagner, 674
Alyse Wagner, 1113
David Wassong, 1314
Allen A Weaver, 1440
Ellen Weber, 1581
Tim Weglicki, 21
Andrew J Weisenfeld, 1271
Richard Wells, 1005
Cal Wheaton, 21
Patrick F Whelan, 1427
John D. White, 777
Damion Wicker, 1411
Ryan Wierck, 854
Richard J. Williams, 1979
Fred Wilson, 1884
Tyler Wolfram, 1360
Marc Wolpow, 197
Emil Woods, 1119
Dalton Wright, 1074
Victor L Wu, 1116
John Yang, 328
Cene Yoon, 336
Guy Zaczepinski, 451
Philip Zaorski, 785
Howard S. Zeprun, 1852
Toby Zhang, 474
Daniel Zilberman, 1957
Andy Ziolkowski, 571
Ari M. Zur, 351

Wheaton College
Kate Castle, 1555
Dean M Kline, 1431
Tom Lane, 676
Kathleen Schoemaker, 622

Whitman College
Bill Burkoth, 1439
Karl D Dillon, 943

Whittemore School of Business
Michael A. Foisy, 904

Whittier College
Fred Anderson, 660

Widener University
Donald E. Stewart, 1727

Widener University School of Law
Wayne D Kimmel, 1660

Wilfrid Laurier University
Robert Antoniades, 2146
Steve Balaban, 2185
Stephan Bey, 2052
Justin Catalano, 2110
Greg Collings, 2121
Adrianna Czornyj, 2212
Stephen J. Dent, 2056
Vipon Ghai, 2177
Michael Gubbels, 2281
Sasha Jacob, 2069
Mark Kennedy, 2023
Martin Kent, 2160
Omar Khalifa, 2110
Stephan Klee, 2217
Tom Lunan, 2051
Christopher McElhone, 2030
Annie Thériault, 2084
Matthew Towns, 2242
John Travaglini, 2023
David Unsworth, 2146

William Mitchell College of Law
Scott L Becker, 1343
Mark Headrick, 538

William Paterson University
Jennifer Cerminaro, 170

William Woods University
Erik Allison, 1694

Williams College
Timothy A Barrows, 1184
Andrew Brennan, 503
Matthew Bronfman, 41
Kurt A. Brumme, 1419
Ed Cahill, 941
Charles P Coleman III, 1828
Charlie Crawford, 477
Christopher Delaney, 1027
Shomik Dutta, 937
Ron Eastman, 698
Michael R. Eisenson, 458
Robert C Embry Jr, 18
Kirt Gardner, 1880
Douglas H. Gilbert, 611
Steven Gillis, 154
Steven C. Graham, 851
Michael Greeley, 749
Matt Harris, 224
John G. Hayes, 862
Brian Higgins, 1049
James S. Hoch, 1779
Reginald L. Jones III, 867
Robert Manning, 1600
Nino Marakovic, 1623
Jim Marver, 1908
Matt McCall, 1483
Daniel P Neuwirth, 1506
Bruce Ou, 884
David B Outcalt, 1116
Todd G. Owens, 346
James A Parsons, 1560
Tory Patterson, 430
Tory Patterson, 1393
David L Pesikoff, 1848
Timothy Petersen, 150
Adam Piatkowski, 851
Jeffrey K. Quake, 741
Josh Resnick, 1522
Collin E. Roche, 889
Sarah G Roth, 165
Chris Seitz, 704
J. Frederick Simmons, 786
John H. Simpson, 346
Geoffrey W. Smith, 179
Jonathan Sokoloff, 1113
Edson W. Spencer Jr., 67
John A Svoboda, 1767
Brad Svrluga, 1479
Chris Sweeney, 1962
Martha Tracey, 554
Tenno Tsai, 931
Robert Ward, 1213
Wilson S Warren, 1116
Kara Weber, 345
Bill Winterer, 1419

Winona State University
Carl Nelson, 920

Wittenberg University
Anthony Eames, 379
Ki Mixon, 1548

Wofford College
Thomas H. Westbrook, 747

Woodrow Wilson School
Robert W. Mulcare, 1300

Woodrow Wilson School, Princeton
Thanasis Delistathis, 1290
Michael A. Kumin, 862
John Locke, 27
Lawrence Neubauer, 1518
Edwin Shirley, 715

Worcester Polytechnic Institute
Michael E. Aspinwall, 436
Adam Bryant, 648
Steve Halstedt, 443
Jiong Ma, 325
John Mandile, 1675
Bob Mason, 1489
Bill McCullen, 1101
Sean Sebastian, 275
Jack Shields, 313
Jason Syversen, 2
Zhi Tan PhD, 1340
Steve Vassallo, 773

Wright State University
Deepak Advani, 927

Xavier University
Larry A Colangelo, 1230
Thomas J Fogarty MD, 667
Betsy Hoover, 937

Xi'an Jiaotong University
Evelyn Sun, 149

Yale College
Michael E Donovan, 1973
Gregory P Ho, 1733
Roger McNamee, 660
Brian T Regan, 1973
Raymond L.M. Wong, 1733

Yale Law School
Robert S Adelson, 1388
Eric Beckman, 333, 334
Michael Chae, 280
Winston J Churchill, 1636
Tom Darden, 465
Rajat Duggal, 790
Charles C Freyer, 1636
John H Friedman, 644
David Jones, Jr., 477
John T. Kaden, 1282
Peter Kellner, 1564
Jack W Lasersohn, 1931
John Leibovitz, 518
Phillip C Molner, 1480
Arrie Park, 927
Matt Turck, 744

Yale School Management
Brendan Kennedy, 1484

Yale School of Management
Rob Bettigole, 661
Michael Blue, 1484
Elon S Broms, 1101
Victor Budnick, 1025
Chris Cheever, 762
Alexander Ellis III, 1583
Craig Hart, 211
John Howard, 1026
Ellis Jones, 1961
Stephen Knight MD, 711
Nancy Pfund, 596
Peter M. Schulte, 509
Anderson Thees, 641

Tuff Yen, 1658

Yale School of Medicine
Mel Billingsley PhD, 1120
Stephen Knight MD, 711
Stephen B Solomon MD, 573
Robert J. Wenzel, 73

Yale University
Robert W Ackerman, 1963
Robert S Adelson, 1388
Timothy B. Armstrong, 1580
Lindsay Aspegren, 1337
Thomas C. Barry, 2017
Marshall Bartlett, 745
Anna Batarina, 144
Skip Baum, 1107
Eric Beckman, 334
Josh Bekenstein, 223
Michael C Bellas, 264
Amy Belt Raimundo, 1056
Rob Bettigole, 661
Evren Bilimer, 1022
Hiram A. Bingham, 589
Timothy P Bradley, 1676
Chris Brady, Jr., 459
Hugo Braun, 1337
Victor Budnick, 1025
Nick Burger, 2021
Ed Cahill, 941
Paul D Carbery, 792
Jane Castle, 211
Dorothy Jean Chang, 1119
Neil Chheda, 1585
Helen Chiang, 111
Matt Cohler, 251
David M Coit, 1334
Jeffrey J Collinson, 476
Michael M Cone, 632
William E Conway, 204
Matthew A Cook, 1075
Michael J Cromwell III, 1389
Shivanandan A. Dalvie, 63
John E Dancewicz, 620
Kipp DeVeer, 159
Chris DeVore, 776
David A. Donnini, 889
Ned Doubleday, 1156
Chris Douvos, 71
Konstantine Drakonakis, 1101
William H Draper III, 628
John Earhart, 838
Jon Edelson, MD, 179
Michael R. Eisenson, 458
Darren Eng, 3258
Matt Fates, 180
Benjamin Felt, 1022
Matthew W Finlay, 1230
Brett Fisher, 745
Jason Fisherman, 1777
F. Barron Fletcher III, 1417
Steven Florsheim, 1891
William F Foote, 1586
Molly Fowler, 623
John H Friedman, 644
Christopher Gaughan, 1689
Jonathan Goldstein, 60
Jeffrey Goldstein, 927
Noah Goodhart, 1980
Edwin A Goodman, 51
Benjamin Gordon, 383
Bing Gordon, 1079
Andrew G Gould, 174
Myles D Greenberg, 476
Matt Greenfield, 1554
David Griest, 1691
Charles S. Grigg, 418
Peter S.H. Grubstein, 1324
Harry Gruner, 1045
Aflalo Guimaraes, 1022
David Hanson, 1156
Whitney Haring-Smith, 134
Steve Harrick, 1006
Sam Hartwell, 204
Dylan Hixon, 830
Edward Huang, 280
Jay Huffard, 533
Frederick J Iseman, 478
David Jones, Jr., 477
David Kabakoff, 924, 1700
John T. Kaden, 1282
Tom Kastner, 1369
Eric Kaup, 940
James P. Kelley, 1933
Thomas L. Kelly II, 463
Karen Kenworthy, 1751
Brian Kinsman, 362
James Kondo, 824
Andrew Korn, 1606
Daniel H. Kosoy, MD, 189
Stephen Kraus, 263
C Todd Kumble, 1729
Vivek Ladsariya, 1689
Augustine Lawlor, 922
Roger Lee, 238
Jeffrey T Leeds, 1109
Kresimir Letinic MD PhD, 644
Daniel Levine, 27
Scott MacLeod, 838
Jules Maltz, 1006
James Manges, 1853
Mark McAndrews, 645
Niall McComiskey, 867
Andrew McLaughlin, 937
Chris McLeod, 661
Peter H McNerney, 1820
Jonathan W Meeks, 1778
George M Milne, Jr. PhD, 1523
Lou Mischianti, 1372
Ann Miura-Ko, 752
Phillip C Molner, 1480
Frederic H. Morris, 352
Patricia Muoio, 1689
Ajit Nedungadi, 1778
Denis Newman, 1230
Malcolm C Nolen, 1676
Daniel S. O'Connell, 1933
Matt Ocko, 586
Jonathan T. Oka, 751
Peter Pacelli, 1082
Douglas A Parker, 1230
Tripp Peake, 1146
Chris A. Pierce, 1278
Brian Powers, 927
Jack W. Qian, 1300
Vikrant Raina, 364
Corby Reese, 1769
Bill Reiland, 1255
Jason Rhodes, 193
Rosemary Ripley, 1324
John L Ritter, 740
David S Rose, 1305, 1588
Mark Rosen, 458
Devraj Roy, 1026
Will Sale, 1765
Stephen A. Schwarzman, 280
Stacey D. Seltzer, 73
Nick Shalek, 1563
J. Louis Sharpe, 63
Anne-Marie Shelley, 38
Stephen C. Sherrill, 357
Robert J. Small, 257
John Spinale, 1033
Jerry Sprole, 1107
Rick Stahl, 661
William Staudt, 668
E Jack Stewart, 1922
Christian R Strain, 1754
Yanev Suissa, 1689
William P. Sutter Jr., 947
David Sze, 877
Jim Tananbaum, 764
Jo Tango, 1069
David Teten, 724
Jeff Thermond, 2010
Steve Tomlin, 209
Justin Topilow, 253
Martha Tracey, 554
Kyle Veatch, 929
Mathew Veedon, 1714
Rob Walsh, 1772
Eli Weiss, 823
David J. Wermuth, 1746
Jeff Williams, 1731
Richard J. Williams, 1979
Timothy Wollaeger, 1619
Veronica Wu, 945
Brett Zbar, 764
Peter Ziebelman, 1406
Shivon Zilis, 287

Yeshiva University
Alan E Goldberg, 1133
Bruce K. Taragin, 304

Yonsei University
Jamie Choi, 1614

York University
Daniel Brothman, 2216
George H. Cholakis, 2026
Kim Coote, 2280
Kim Davis, 2273
Stephen Foote, 2196
Matt Golden, 2130, 2131
Michael Griffiths, 2162
Mark Hatfield, 1796
Alex Kanayev, 2027
Mark Kennedy, 2023
Lisa Melchior, 2273
Shay Nulman, 2168
Donna Parr, 2084
Jeffrey Rosenthal, 2142
Alex Storcheus, 2117
Hamish Sutherland, 2147, 2279
Adam Szweras, 2117
Kevin Talbot, 2228
Ken Teslia, 2107

Zhejiang University
Erica Yu, 827

Zicklin School of Business
Marta De La Cruz, 838

Executive Name Index

A

Abassi, Farraz, 445
Abbas, Tarik, 1838
Abbott, Shawn, 2150
Abbrecht, Todd M., 1818
Abdulmalik, Atif, 153
Abele, Chris, 567
Aberman, Jonathan, 120
Abernethy, John I, 636
Abert, Collin, 1095
Abhyankar, Adit, 760
Abouchar, Andrew, 2253, 2262
Abrahamson, Shaun, 1896
Abram, Joshua, 541
Abramowitz, Kenneth S, 1325
Abrams, Andrew, 1302
Abramson, Jenny, 1555
Abshagen, Jonathan, 885
Abshire, Chris, 721
Achler, Mark, 1181
Acker, John C., 1730
Ackerley, Christopher, 42
Ackerley, Ted, 42
Ackerley Cleworth, Kim, 42
Ackerman, John F, 412
Ackerman, Christopher J., 751
Ackerman, Robert W, 1963
Ackerman, Jr., Robert R., 84
Ackrell, Mike, 43
Adair, Charles E, 539
Adam, Dr Philippe H, 188
Adamek, Kevin, 754
Adams, Susan, 22
Adams, Joel P., 55
Adams, Will, 92
Adams, Nick, 108
Adams, Samantha A., 257
Adams, Nick, 615
Adams, Frank A., 881
Adams, Bruce, 983
Adams, Rob, 1321
Adams, Andrew, 1361
Adams, Rodger P, 1911
Adderley, David, 2070
Addiego, Joe, 93
Adelman, Robert, 1916
Adelson, Robert S, 1388
Adkins, G. Woodrow, 719
Adler, Jason, 850
Adler, Jim, 1836
Adomait, Natalie, 2062
Adox, Jim, 1923
Advani, Deepak, 927
Adznan, Adzmel, 1453
Afeyan, Noubar, 748
Agarwal, Ajay, 224
Agarwala, Sandip, 1147
Aggarwal, Rahul, 337
Aggarwal, PhD, Vijay, 1811
Agha, Zia, 1974
Agnew, Timothy P, 1178
Agrawal, Neeraj, 238
Agrawal, Krishna K, 1133
Agrawal Divakaran, Payal, 1
Agroskin, Daniel, 1043
Aguilo, Jorge, 524
Aguitar, MD, Eric, 73
Aharwal, Shradha, 732
Ahearn, Michael J, 1861
Ahearn, Matthew S, 1861
Ahern, Matthew, 1081
Ahern, Tracie E., 1448
Ahn, Garrick, 376
Ahrens, Brent, 389
Ahrens II, Jack K, 1804
Aiello, John F, 1133
Aiken, Aaron C., 906
Aikman, William F, 887
Ailons, Shiri, 1776
Ainslie, Lee, 1185
Ainsworth, Ian, 2107
Aissa, Samy Ben, 1928
Aitken-Davies, George E., 97
Akers, Jeff, 56
Akers, Roger, 74
Akhavan, Amir, 1037
Aktihanoglu, Murat, 685
Al-Mubaraki, Fawaz, 1952
Alala III, Joseph B., 408
Alardhi, Mohammed, 1021
Alberg, Thomas A, 1162
Albert, Andrew B, 1767
Albinson, Christopher J, 1411
Albrecht, Laura, 1169
Albright, John, 2228
Alderbas, Adel A, 1952
Aldrich, Russ, 892
Aldrich, Rich, 1149
Alexander, Lynn, 1066
Alexander, Ted, 1239
Alfond, Reis L, 1883
Ali, Lori, 1499
Aliber, Bill, 1499
Alimov, Dmitry, 795
Allan, Rob, 682
Allen, Christopher, 76
Allen, Joe, 675
Allen, Nancy S, 718
Allen, Jason, 1175
Allen, Chris, 1404
Allen, Brandon, 1877
Allen, Wilson, 1977
Allgaier, Matthias G, 1754
Alling, Ted, 640
Allison, Erik, 1694
Allsteadt, Mark, 404
Almany, MD, Steven L., 272
Almog, Yuval, 538
Alpert, Norman W., 1933
Alport, Daniel K., 1582
Alsikafi, Zaid F, 1160
Alsop, Stewart, 93
Alt, Jonathan H, 542
Altman, Matthew L., 167
Altman, Roger, 700
Altug, Okan, 2069
Alva, Sandeep D, 1377
Alvarado, Oscar, 1341
Alvi, Rashid, 916
Alvim, Alexandre, 838
Alvord, Seth W, 740
Amador, Jorge, 110
Amar, Maor, 2143
Amato, Bert, 2130
Ambrose, Cate, 3252
Amelio, William J., 595
Amen, Robert, 1912
Ament, Dave, 1419
Ames, Grace, 1361
Amidi, Rahim, 116
Amidi, Saeed, 116
Ammerman, Robert C., 405
Ammirati, Sean, 275
Amouyal, Philippe, 1022
Anastasopoulos, Chris, 2097
Anchel, Edward, 670
Andelman, Jim, 309, 1569
Andersen, James G, 505
Anderson, Cory S, 39
Anderson, David Q., 119
Anderson, Kenneth D., 123
Anderson, Steve, 234
Anderson, David J., 463
Anderson, Fred, 660
Anderson, Robert, 796
Anderson, Carl T, 840
Anderson, Mark M., 889
Anderson, Christopher, 1085
Anderson, Ed, 1335
Anderson, David L., 1759
Anderson, David L, 1762
Anderson, Edward R., 1860
Anderson, Bruce, 1973
Anderson, Matt, 1977
Andlinger, Merrick, 124
Andonian, Dave, 581
Andreassen, Dr. Alf L., 1401
Andreessen, Marc, 125
Andreev, Alexei, 207, 208
Andreola, Paul, 2061
Andrew, Mark M, 1116
Andrews, R. David, 886
Andrews, Lawrence D, 1177
Andrianopoulos, Alex, 1055
Andryc, Joel, 1602
André, Ludovic, 2082
Angel, Ricardo, 1453
Angell, Suzanne, 422
Angella, Frank, 884
Anson, George, 912
Antalich, Alejandro, 2055
Antaya, Matthew P., 989
Antoniades, Robert, 2146
Aplin, John C, 480
Applebaum, Jay I, 1997
Applegate, Brion B, 1720
Appleyard, James, 2120
Apprendi, Joe, 1557
Aquilano, Dan, 86
Aragona, Joe, 205
Ardell, Ted, 1788
Arenz, Thomas W., 917
Argenbright, Glenn, 1509
Armony, Izhar, 457
Armstrong, Tim, 135
Armstrong, David, 198
Armstrong, Jim, 390, 504
Armstrong, Dave, 773
Armstrong, Brad, 1151
Armstrong, Lance, 1318
Armstrong, Timothy B., 1580
Armstrong, Curtis, 2166
Armstrong. Jr., Andrew J., 1727
Arnold, Mark, 78
Arnold, George, 1081
Arnold, C Mark, 1532
Arnold, Paul, 1770
Arnson, Eric, 1386
Aronoff, David, 756
Aronson, Bernard, 45
Aronson, Jeffrey, 444
Aronson, Neal K., 1580
Aronson, Stephen D., 1580
Arora, Aditya, 838
Arrington, Michael, 565
Arrowsmith, Peter, 1045
Arroyo, Damian, 1122
Arscott, David G., 526
Arscott, Martha P.E., 526
Arsenault, Chris, 2150
Arzubi, Luis, 1781
Aschebrook, Larry L., 805
Ascher, Brian, 1918
Asel, Paul, 1331
Asem, Mike, 1159
Ashai, Zaid, 1463
Asher, A Craig, 1942
Ashley, Bradley W., 2218
Ashrafian, Houman, 1631, 1764
Ashton, Michael, 20
Aspegren, Lindsay, 1337
Aspinwall, Michael E., 436
Assant, Lionel, 280
Atallah, Amira, 691
Atherton Jr., Cliff, 893
Atia, Lisa, 221
Atinsky, Lawrence S., 179
Atiq, Sikandar, 2194
Atkinson, Dax, 426
Atkinson, Dennis, 691
Atkinson, Fraser, 695
Atkinson, Sherman, 1237
Attanasio, Mark, 557
Atterbury, David, 912
Attie, Elliot, 1853
Aube, Richard, 1447
Audsley, Lorraine, 2106
Auer-Welsbach, Christoph, 971
Auerbach, Stuart A., 119
Auerbach, Jon, 457
Aust, R. Wade, 77
Austen, Christopher, 353
Auster, Charles, 1600
Auster, Matt, 1600
Austin, Darrell W, 204
Austin, Chip, 967
Austin, Robert M, 989
Austin, Blake, 1026
Austin, Mark, 1977
Auvil, Stephen, 1792
Averett, David W, 1754
Averitt, B Marc, 1371
Avida, Dan, 1382
Avirett, John, 872
Avnur, Zafrira, 2221
Avon, Mike, 21
Avrutin, Brandon, 1554
Aweida, Jesse, 213
Aweida, Dan, 213
Axel, Merrick, 559
Axelrod, Jonathan, 685
Axon, Robin, 2176
Ayres, Charles, 1853

B

Babbit, Cindy, 578
Babson, Stephen E., 674
Bachireddy, Ashvin, 824
Backaus, Gary, 15
Backman, Joel, 1213
Backus, John, 1290, 1485
Bacon, Nathaniel P, 362
Bacon, Kathleen, 912
Bacon, Eric V, 1136
Baehr, Geoffrey, 89
Bagaria, Rajay, 1961
Bagley, Thomas S., 1438
Bahat, Roy, 287
Baiada, Mel, 233
Bailey, Bary, 559
Bailey, Roger D, 607
Bailey, Steve, 785
Bailey, Michael L, 1487
Bailey, Lee, 1897
Bainbridge, David, 1929
Baird, Darran A., 1746
Baird Jr, Charles F, 1336
Bajaj, Vikram, 764
Bakalar, Sophie, 514
Baker, John, 226
Baker, Henry G., 226
Baker, Kevin, 371
Baker, Jeff, 703
Baker, Stephen A, 768
Baker, Jim, 1573
Baker, Craig, 1573
Baker, Trent, 2022
Baker, Eric, 2186

Executive Name Index

Baker, Alex, 2228
Bakshi, Rajiv, 2177
Bal, Ru-Guang, 908
Balaban, Steve, 2185
Balash, Jeffrey L, 529
Balbontin, Manuel Jose, 524
Baldassarre, Carl E., 1460
Baldeschwieler, Dr John, 188
Baldwin, Dennis, 332
Baldwin, Thomas J., 357
Baldwin, Elmer, 466
Balen, John, 389
Ball, Eric M., 109
Ball, Charles E., 124
Ball, Ben, 782
Ballard, Michael, 146
Ballard, Perry O., 751
Ballenegger, Kenneth, 1396
Balmuth, Michael, 1631, 1764
Baloff, Steven, 58
Balter, Dave, 316
Baltzell, Josh, 1728
Banahan, Tom, 1798
Banatao, Dado, 1781
Banerjee, Gautam, 280
Bank, Keith, 1060
Bank, Keith, 1061
Banks, Andrew, 20
Banks, Gerald T., 101
Banks, Michael, 875
Banks, Sean, 1865
Banks, Charlie, 1925
Bannantine, James M., 192
Bannon, Maren Thomas, 1030
Banon, Sid, 462
Bao Bean, William, 1709
Baptiste, Stonly, 1896
Barach, Michael, 994
Barandiaran, Walter, 162
Barasz, Zach, 305
Baratta, Joseph, 280
Barbara, Rob, 2063
Barber, Tiki, 883
Barber, Paul, 1045
Barber, Jeffrey S, 1778
Barberio, Caroline, 1239
Barclay, Dan, 2057
Barg, Jason S, 1151
Barger, Greg, 1316
Barker, CFA, Karey, 561
Barkoff, Stuart, 838
Barlev, Hagai, 670
Barman, Jeffrey, 1434
Barna, Hayley, 742
Barnds, Tom, 28
Barnes, Steven, 223
Barnes, Jeffrey, 273
Barnes, Phin, 742
Barnes, Jonathan P, 902
Barnes, Cristy, 1122
Barnum, William, 337
Baron, Jack, 566
Barous, Andrew D., 1300
Baroyan, Eric, 110
Barr, David, 825
Barr, Gregory M, 1686
Barra, Jim, 1025
Barrelet, Blaise, 122
Barrett, Peter, 193
Barrett, Ross P., 365
Barrett, Dave, 1464
Barrett III, Redington, 1435
Barrette, Sean, 470
Barris, Peter, 1296
Barron, Bruce N., 1385
Barrows, Timothy A, 1184
Barry, Scott, 698

Barry, Melissa, 929
Barry, Jeff, 1459
Barry, Doug, 1649
Barry, Thomas C., 2017
Barry III, John F., 1493
Bartalsky, Nissa, 80
Barthelme, Sam, 1037
Bartlett, Kirby, 44
Bartlett, Samuel, 458
Bartlett, Marshall, 745
Bartol, Stopher, 732
Bartoli, Jeffrey, 449
Baruchowitz, Mitch, 1208
Bashir, Imran, 2107
Bashour, Fouad, 479
Baskett, Forest, 1296
Bassi, Luca, 223
Bassin, Stuart, 1603
Bastedo, Brian, 1582
Basu, Upal, 1331
Basu Trivedi, Nikhil, 1666
Baszucki, Greg, 775
Batarina, Anna, 144
Batchelder, Bret, 465
Batcheller, Paul, 1474
Bates, Gavin, 377
Bates, Carrie, 1849
Bathon Jr, Daniel H, 1994
Batra, Rajeev, 1187
Batterson, Len, 237
Bauer, Stacey, 809
Bauerly, Richard, 855
Baum, Skip, 1107
Baum, David William, 1737
Baum, Dan, 2236
Bauman, J.P., 98
Bauman, Jeremy, 1303
Baumann, Gabor (Gabe), 1351
Baumer, John M, 1113
Baumgarten, Josh, 128
Baxter, Stuart, 1576
Baxter-Simmons, Laura, 1476
Bayless, Jon W, 1661
Bayliffe, Andy, 144
Baylin, Gregory, 2200
Baylor, David, 1912
Beakey, James A., 1278
Beard, Dennis, 1380
Beasley, Allen, 1537
Beaton, Kirk M., 1116
Beattie, Randy, 2213
Beattie, Geoff, 2228
Beatty, Croom, 1203
Beaty, Derek, 838
Beauparlant, Pierre, 2261
Beauregard, Michael, 963
Beber, Justin, 2062
Beck, Martin, 225
Becker, John, 110
Becker, Matt, 703
Becker, David, 1196
Becker, Scott L, 1343
Becker, Daria, 1493
Becker, Eric, 1745
Becker, Doug, 1745
Beckett, William, 813
Beckett, Steven S, 1429
Beckman, Eric, 333, 334
Beckman, Charles W, 958
Beckman, Robert J., 1811
Beebe, Andrew, 1363
Beecken, David, 247
Beeler, Charles, 1525
Beerle, Tom, 260
Begert, Brian, 2284
Begleiter, Steven L., 751
Bego, Michael, 1080

Behm, Denny, 173
Behrman, Grant, 248
Beier, Brooke, 1842
Beim, Nick, 1918
Beinecke, Walter, 352
Beitler, Stephen S, 636
Bekenstein, Josh, 223
Belaman, Cécile, 223
Belfer, Todd, 390
Belford, Jeff, 2267
Belk, Cathy, 1051
Belke, Robert M, 1151
Bell, David, 328
Bell, Thomas, 515
Bell, Maurey J, 620
Bell, Michael A., 1818
Bell, Jr., Thomas D., 1220
Bellas, Michael C, 264
Bellas, Robin, 1257
Belldegrun, Arie S., 1934
Bellerive, Gerry, 2227
Belmont, Gregory C., 852
Belt Raimundo, Amy, 1056
Beltramini, Enrico, 1283
Belzberg, Brent, 2252
Belzberg, Brent, 2264
Belzer, David L., 1493
Ben-Gacem, Hazem, 1021
Ben-Joseph PhD, Oded, 1389
Benaquista, Mark L., 1818
Benaroya, Larry, 250
Bendele, Jenner, 725
Bendell, Adam, 1833
Bender, Julie A, 792
Benear, Jay, 639
Benedetti, Tom, 291
Benedict, James G, 1075
Benham, Mark, 441
Benhamou, Eric, 252
Benik, Alex, 238
Benioff, Marc, 1610
Benkowski PhD, Jacques, 1898
Bennett, Kent, 263
Bennett, Matthew M., 1300
Bennett, Stephen A, 1748
Bennett, Cathy, 2238
Benshoof, Justin, 376
Benson, Greg, 962
Benson, Scott, 1315
Benson, Buzz, 1673
Benson, Erik, 1947
Benyaminy, David, 196
Berenson, Stephen, 748
Berenstein, Jason, 2093
Berg, Steven T., 424
Berge, David, 1882
Bergen, Warren, 2043
Berger, Stephen, 1368
Berggruen, Nicolas, 253
Berglund, Thomas A, 734
Bergner, Richard F., 695
Bergonia, R David, 1333
Bergschneider, Marc C, 1738
Berk, Zachary C., 1062
Berk, Michael S, 1778
Berke, Eric, 2264
Berkin, Brian S., 1779
Berkley, Kent, 785
Berkowitz, Barak, 256
Berkowitz, Jonathan, 1813
Berland, Terrence, 1078
Berliner, Arthur, 1953
Berman, Steve, 162
Berman, Jeffrey, 380
Berman, Casey, 380
Berman, Douglas, 931
Berman, Dror, 1001

Berman, Mark, 1364
Berman, Alison, 1402
Berman, Steven E, 1402
Berman, Seth, 1760
Bernardon, Roland V., 407
Berney, Philip E, 1066
Bernier, Jacques, 2259
Bernstein, Jordan S., 478
Bernstein, Beth L., 687
Bernstein, Brad, 796
Bernstein, Jay, 1089
Bernstein, Robert A, 1109
Berolzheimer, Michael, 246
Berry, David, 748
Berson, Brett, 742
Berterretche, Jackie, 857
Berton, John, 2126
Bertrand, Chaz, 332
Besthoff, Skip, 1499
Betsalel, Richard, 2083
Betten, Elizabeth Q, 1160
Bettigole, Rob, 661
Bettinelli, Greg, 1890
Bevan, Michael, 658
Bevilacqua, Tom, 1908
Bevis, Tate, 1044
Bey, Stephan, 2052
Beyda, Gil, 818
Bhadkamkar, Neal, 1249
Bhalwani, Arif N., 2214
Bhappu, Ross, 1551
Bharat, Raghu, 2082
Bhaskaran, Ravi, 760
Bhat, Nikhil J., 1933
Bhowmik, Nilanana, 536, 1150
Bianchinotti, Alberto, 1217
Bianco, William, 1620
Bice, William F, 1926
Biddle, Mike, 2105
Biddle III, A.G.W., 1348
Biemann, Betsy, 440
Biesel, David, 1322
Bigge, Matt, 564
Biggee, Michael, 1852
Bilenker, MD, JH, 73
Bilimer, Evren, 1022
Billings, Tim, 1507
Billingsley PhD, Mel, 1120
Bilodeau, Peter, 2117
Binas, Peter, 1630
Binch, James G, 1131
Binford, Joy E., 1348
Bingham, Hiram A., 589
Bingham, Kate, 1631, 1764
Bingle, Mike, 1685
Biniak, Bryan, 1497
Binkley, Nicholas B, 767
Birchall, Larry, 2171
Birchall, Tyson, 2171
Bird, Walter M (Jerry), 1175
Bird, Jeff, 1762
Birdsong, Jon, 191
Birk, Brian, 1756
Birkelund, John P., 1624
Birnbaum, Charles, 263
Birnbaum, Scott, 1533
Birner, Hubert, 2268
Birschbach, Mark, 1645
Bischof, George, 1213
Bishop, Stacey, 1629
Bishop, Andrew, 2052
Bisson, Keith, 440
Bisson, Cédric, 2259
Biswas, Samir, 2033
Bitterman, PhD, Kevin, 193
Bjork, Anders, 20
Bjorseth, Eva, 1365

Executive Name Index

Black, Jeff, 1433
Black, Jason, 1597
Black, Darren M, 1754
Black, Phil, 1862
Black, Jeffrey, 1928
Black, Daniel L, 1984
Black, Richard, 2112
Blackburn, Alan J., 893
Blacklow, Peter, 316
Blackshaw, Pete, 482
Blackwell, Wes, 1635
Blair, PhD, Jim, 622
Blake III, William, 254
Blanchfield, EJ, 1462
Blanco, José, 574
Blanco, Jonathan B., 747
Bland, Geoff, 1970
Blaney, J. Peter, 2145
Blank, Robert D, 470
Blank, Kevin, 886
Blanton, Darren, 517
Blaszkiewicz, David, 743
Blattman, Barry, 2062
Blaustein, Sim, 259
Blavatnik, Len, 33
Blazej, PhD, Robert, 1238
Blazensky, Derek, 414
Blevins, Matthew, 505
Blidner, Jeff, 2062
Blinoff, Bluette N., 1801
Blivin, Dave, 550
Bloch, Stephen, 389
Bloom, Gregory, 47
Bloom, Erik W., 842
Blue, Michael, 1484
Bluestein, Scott, 928
Blum, Richard C., 303
Blum, Christopher J, 620
Blumberg, David J., 304
Blume, Rick, 704
Blumenthal, Marc, 754
Boag, Simon, 985
Boboff, Peter, 1841
Boccasam, Prashanth V., 1348
Bochnowski, James J., 605
Bodden, Brad, 2002
Bode, Bob, 1026
Bodine, Peter, 84
Bodnar, Chris, 646
Bogdanov, Pavel, 89
Bogue, Zachary, 586
Bohn, Larry, 820
Bohnett, David, 231
Bohrmann, Brady, 209
Bohrmann, Braden M (Brady), 1178
Boisvert, Marie-Claude, 2076
Bok, Gaye, 704
Bok, Scott L., 869
Bolander, Rick, 657
Bolander, Rick, 808
Bolduc, John, 242
Bolin, Kurt E., 1746
Bolinger, Mark, 1068
Bologna, Nick, 646
Bologna, Mike, 865
Bolten, Charlie, 270
Bolzan, Denio R., 1438
Bolzon, Brad, 1930
Bombara, John C., 949
Bommer, Eric D, 1654
Bonanno, Andrew P., 1085
Bonatsos, Niko, 820
Bond, Patrick A, 1262
Bonderman, David, 1837
Bondy, Craig A., 889
Boniello, Michael, 1468

Bonnar, Mark, 1713
Bonner, Blake, 1858
Booker, Charles, 60
Booma, Jason, 518
Booth, Bruce, 193
Booth, Ralph, 762
Borcher, Christian, 414
Borchers, John, 556
Bordeau, David C., 257
Borden, Philip, 809
Boren, Todd, 558
Borhanu, Nabil, 859
Borho, Sven H., 1383
Boro, Seth, 1817
Borque, Janice, 928
Borrus, Michael, 2010
Borsum, Christina, 370
Bortnem, Jane, 466
Bose, Anik, 252
Bose, Simita, 1348
Boswell, Patrick, 1802
Boszhardt, Andy, 863
Botha, Roelof, 1657
Bottorff, Dennis C, 551
Bottorff, Leslie, 812
Bouk, Josh, 706
Boulanger, Brian, 2036
Bounds, Mark, 319
Bourgeois, Anne-Marie, 677
Bourne, Duncan S., 2008
Bourque, Donna, 2148
Bouten, Jan, 999
Boutros-Ghali, Teymour, 1249
Bouyea, Lee E, 789
Bovaird Nevins, Anne, 1445
Bower, Christopher J, 1398
Bowman, Gale, 1023
Bowman, Tim, 2049
Bowsher, Steve, 983
Boye, Henry J., 1818
Boyle, Jim, 994
Boze, Brandon B., 1905
Bozynski, Tyler A., 612
Braccia, Andrew, 27
Bracken, Brenda, 860
Brackett, Greg, 376
Bradley, John, 1349
Bradley, Timothy P, 1676
Bradlow, Richard, 2211
Bradshaw, Larry, 696
Brady, Christopher D., 459
Brady, Phil, 841
Brady, Scott, 1001
Brady, Kevin, 1977
Brady, Jr., Chris, 459
Braga, Sayles, 80
Bragiel, Paul, 1477
Bragiel, Paul, 1783
Brake, Jr., Patrick E., 2154
Bramer, Robert, 2207
Branchflower, Michael, 2197
Brand, Martin, 280
Brand, Hanan, 544
Brandon, Cheryl, 2275
Branman, Jeff, 940
Brasch, Sam, 1056
Brass, Jason T., 847
Brathol, Darren, 1722
Braun, Jeff, 256
Braun, Hugo, 1337
Bravo, Orlando, 1817
Breach, David, 1940
Breazzano, David J, 598
Brecker, John, 99
Breinlinger, Josh, 1028
Brekka, Richard, 1643
Brennan, Andrew, 503

Brenneman, Greg, 435
Brenner, Clara, 1895
Brenninkmeyer, Frank, 1434
Breslin, Adam, 2211
Bressner, Glen R, 51
Bressner, Glen R, 1386
Brew Jr., Thomas E., 65
Brewer, David, 146
Brewer, Brett, 562
Breyer, Jim, 339
Bricault, Paul, 121
Brickman, C. Andrew, 225
Briger Jr., Peter L., 769
Bright, Aaron, 1435
Brill, Robert M, 1313
Bring, Kenneth S., 257
Brinn, Nathaniel C, 1942
Britain, Sean, 242
Britt, Chris L, 1171
Britt, H Bryan, 1532
Brockway, Peter C, 351
Broder, Scott, 997
Broderick, Dan, 270
Broderick, Shawn, 1709
Brodlieb, Jeff, 450
Brodsky, Jamie M, 1577
Brody, Jeff, 1537
Broeker, Alexander C, 1843
Broms, Elon S, 1101
Bronfman, Matthew, 41
Bronfman Jr, Edgar, 38
Bronner, Philip L., 1348
Bronson, Po, 1709
Bronsteatter, Phil D., 1438
Brooke, Peter, 353
Brooke, John, 353
Brooks, Graham, 1
Brooks, Michael, 1507
Brooks, Mark, 1629
Brooks, Ben, 1712
Brooks, Jason, 2155
Brookshire, Mike, 1573
Brosgart, Michael, 1810
Broshar, Ryan, 1179
Broten, Laurel C., 2197
Brothman, Daniel, 2216
Brotman, Kenneth, 45
Brotman, Steve, 91
Brotman, Steve, 1682
Brouckman, Randall, 1784
Broun, Stephen, 402
Brown, Michael, 238
Brown, Hope, 379
Brown, Thomas P., 387
Brown, Daryl B, 637
Brown, Scott, 654
Brown, Paul, 657
Brown, Jeffrey J., 767
Brown, Frank, 819
Brown, Bob, 1275
Brown, Sonya, 1346
Brown, Richard A, 1456
Brown, David, 1791
Brown, Paul, 1886
Brown, Nathan, 1990
Brown, Kevin, 2036
Brown, Andrew, 2046
Brown, Kerry, 2116
Brown Jr., Mike, 320
Brownell, Bob, 667
Browning, Ben, 1123
Browning, G Stephen, 1655
Brownlee, Sean, 2231
Brownlie, Steve, 96
Broyhill, M. Hunt, 408
Brubaker, Terry, 832
Brucato, C.J., 20

Bruckmann, Bruce C., 357
Bruml, Robert W., 358
Brumme, Kurt A., 1419
Brunell, Mike, 1369
Brunk, Gerry, 2173
Bruno, Frank W., 453
Bruno Jr, Michael S, 1747
Brush, MD, James W., 785
Bruss, Adam, 267
Brutocao, Brad J., 786
Bruun, Eric J, 480
Bryan, Lee, 530
Bryan, Charles A, 1424
Bryan, Scott, 2104
Bryant, Matthew, 558
Bryant, Adam, 648
Bryant, Mike, 1082
Buaron, Roberto, 734
Buatois, Eric, 252
Bubnack, Tim, 961
Buchanan, Doug, 2133
Buck, Lee, 289
Buck, Lee, 1100
Buckley III, Walter W., 52
Buckner, Karen, 1242
Budin, Ethan A., 751
Budnick, Victor, 1025
Buehler, Dr Kai, 1509
Buenneke, Brian J., 1413
Buffington, Mark, 274, 1412
Bugay, Lauren K., 634
Bukovinsky, Eric, 2283
Bullard, Karla J, 1160
Bullock, Fraser, 1707
Bullock, John W, 1994
Bund, Ian, 1459
Bunder, Jeffrey B, 1133
Bundy, Brock, 2274
Bunimovitz, Iian, 43
Bunting, Aaron, 2237
Buonanno, Bernie, 1278
Buono, Thomas J., 266
Bural, Craig, 1531
Burch, John R., 497
Burch, John, 718
Burciaga, Gil, 595
Burden, Justin, 990
Burger, Nick, 2021
Burger Jr., Thomas A., 878
Burgess, Bill, 22
Burgess, Trevor, 1129
Burgess, Andy, 2236
Burgoyne, Kevin, 3251
Burgstahler, David, 212
Burgum, Doug, 175
Burgum, James, 175
Burke, John, 1485
Burke, Rugger, 1625
Burke, Paul, 1813
Burke Jr., James J., 1027
Burkhardt, C.A., 956
Burkle, Ron, 14, 2015
Burkoth, Bill, 1439
Burley, Sylvester, 335
Burlock, Carl, 2106
Burnes, Richard, 457
Burnham, Brad, 1884
Burns, Barbara, 63
Burns, Luke, 180
Burns, John, 332
Burns, Douglas, 552
Burns, Brian N, 861
Burns, John, 1165
Burns, Steve, 1507
Burns, Kenneth, 1681
Burns, M Roy, 1778
Burow, Kristina, 154

Executive Name Index

Burr, Amy, 1039
Burstein, Daniel L, 1235
Burton, John, 1888
Busby, Christopher M., 862
Busch, Robin Ellis, 1729
Buser, Curtis L, 416
Bushell, Andrew M, 542
Bushey, Christina, 1404
Bussgang, Jeffrey, 756
Buten, Matthew, 764
Butler, Andy, 367
Butler, Duncan, 443
Butler, Justin, 648
Butler, Dave, 1049
Butler, Michael, 1285
Butler, Chuck, 1409
Butler, Don, 1821
Butler, MD, Tara, 178
Butt Thibodeau, Stephanie, 2106
Button, Scott, 1923
Buttrick, John, 1884
Buttry, Mike, 466
Buzzy, George L., 292
Bybee, Clinton W., 154
Bye, Mark, 1256
Byers, Brook, 1079
Byers, Chad, 1760
Byford, Roger, 301
Bynum, Jr, Frank K, 1066
Byrd, Andrew, 1872
Byrd, Jr., Andrew, 1872
Byun, Brian, 1073

C

Caballero, Lou, 277
Cabigon, Mike, 2116
Cable, John, 1729
Caccavo, James, 1744
Cacioppo, Lu, 2050
Caddedu, John, 582
Cagnassola, Phil, 903
Cahill, Jason, 411
Cahill, Ed, 941
Caillaux, Gabriel, 819
Caldbeck, Ryan, 484
Calhoun, Kevin J, 1755
Calhoun, Jeffrey M., 1779
Calian, Phil, 1965
Caliento, Paul, 505
Callaghan, Kevin T., 257
Callaghan, Jon, 1862
Callahan, Thomas R, 1131
Callahan PhD, Jerry, 946
Callais, Corey, 375
Callais, Nicholas, 375
Callais II, Harold, 375
Callander, Maddie, 310
Callow, Dana, 315
Cambier, Aohn, 975
Cameron, Dennis P, 646
Cameron, Doug, 739
Camp, Justin, 388
Camp, Jerome, 388
Camp, Gregory T., 1312
Campbell, Mary Lincoln, 652
Campbell, Alex, 732
Campbell, Nathan, 873
Campbell, Stephanie, 953
Campbell, William Y, 1429
Campbell, Kristy, 1556
Campbell, Stephen, 2081
Campbell, Rod, 2274
Campion, Thomas F, 1210
Campolo, Joseph P., 148
Canarick, Jon, 1336
Canavan, Joe, 2193
Canestaro, William J, 2007

Canfield, Philip A., 889
Canning Jr, John A, 1160
Cannon, MD, Louis, 272
Canter, Stephen E., 2017
Cantrell, Kevin D, 1579
Cantwell, Wayne, 556
Cantwell, Sean, 1944
Canty, Ed, 229
Caoile, Andrea, 496
Capasso, Mary, 1471
Caplain, Jason, 1712
Caputo, Rich, 1049
Caracciolo, Thomas J, 633
Carano, Bandel L., 1361
Carbery, Paul D, 792
Carbone, Paul, 1482
Cardamone, Michael, 29
Cardamone, Mike, 771
Carey, James D., 1746
Cargill, Virginia, 80
Carlborg, Eric, 200
Carles, Alexander E., 1972
Carlisle, Douglas C., 1203
Carlisle, James C., 1818
Carlotti, Mike, 206
Carlson, Baron, 63
Carlson, Barrett D., 410
Carlson, Dave, 686
Carlson, David, 1539
Carlson, Mark, 2043
Carlton, Keith, 891
Carmody, Jeff, 68
Carney, Michael, 1890
Carnot, Lionel, 240
Carolan, Shawn T., 1203
Carolan, Jennifer, 1530
Carolin, Roger, 1636
Caron, Richard, 2278
Caron, Don, 2278
Carpenter, Steve, 1120
Carpenter III, Phil, 1026
Carr, Julian L, 247
Carr, Dan, 3268
Carra, Phillip C., 140
Carrabino, Jr., Joseph, 63
Carragher, Andrew, 639
Carriker, PhD, Roy C., 836
Carroll, J. Ryan, 458
Carroll, John R, 1754
Carroll, Matthew T., 1979
Carryer, Babs, 1102
Carsello, John M., 904
Carson, Jarett, 677
Carson, Bill, 957
Carson, Russell, 1973
Carstair, Ilfryn, 1909
Carsten, Jack, 950
Carter, Larry B., 612
Carter, Chris G., 1326, 1328
Carter, Kevin, 1763
Carter, Mark H, 1778
Carusi, Mike, 58
Carusi, Mike, 1126
Caruso PhD, Richard E, 1496
Carver, Thomas A., 913
Casabona, Mario, 421
Casale, Gerard N., 1878
Casanova, Xavier, 775
Cascarilla, CFA, Charles, 1119
Casciato, Chris C, 1127
Casdin, Eli, 422
Case Jr, William F, 505
Cashman, Gregory W., 848
Cashman, Gillis F, 1157
Casilli, Gerald S, 1543
Caska, Amber, 1370
Casnocha, Ben, 1935

Caso, Michael V., 1589
Cass III, A Baron, 367
Cassaday, Jake, 2228
Cassidy, Brian, 560
Cassidy, Karen, 1420
Castaldi, Alexander R, 1043
Castelein MD, Caley, 1063
Castellarin, Michael, 2075
Castillo, Bryan, 43
Castle, Jane, 211
Castle, John S., 330
Castle, David, 330
Castle, John K., 425
Castle, Kate, 1555
Castleberry, Brian, 293
Castleman, Randy, 552
Castro, Ramphis, 1633
Catalano, Justin, 2110
Cataldo, Mike, 1146
Cathcart, Chris, 899
Cato, Jo, 432
Cato MD PhD, Allen, 432
Causgrove, Tanya, 2036
Cavanaugh, PhD, James H., 922
Cawsey, Richard, 606
Cayce, Brian, 860
Cegelski, Mike, 2204
Celniker, Abbie, 1814
Centofanti, Kevin, 355
Ceresnie, Eric, 919
Cerminaro, Jennifer, 170
Cerra, Italo, 2053
Cerrudo, Shirley, 1354
Cerutti, Romeo, 555
Cervantez, Tom, 31
Cete, Urs, 259
Chabra, Roger, 2231
Chaddha, Navin, 1187
Chadwick, John H, 495
Chae, Michael, 280
Chaffee, Todd C., 1006
Chaisson, John, 682
Chait, Jon, 581
Chalmers Balbach, Jennifer, 1753
Chalstrom, Brownell, 210
Chaltiel, Victor, 1535
Chaltiel, Antoinette "Toni", 1535
Cham, James, 287
Chamberlain, Alex, 2153
Chambers, Mike, 366
Chambers, John, 1035
Chambers, Brian F., 1410
Chambers, Jeffrey T, 1778
Chan, Connie, 125
Chan, Wesley, 720
Chan, William, 1142
Chan, Ryan, 2244
Chandarana, Ashish, 1927
Chandler, David G, 470
Chandna, Asheem, 877
Chandra, Amit, 223
Chang, Frank, 757
Chang, Andrew, 1119
Chang, Dorothy Jean, 1119
Chao, David, 597
Chao, Pierre, 681
Chao, Clint, 766
Chapanoff, Charlotte, 308
Chapman, J. Russell, 174
Chapman, Duncan A, 1116
Chapman, Tim, 2099
Chapman, Matthew, 2264
Chapman, Dave, 2284
Chappell, Scott E., 266
Chappell, John F, 1456
Chapus, Jean-Marc, 557
Charpie, Richard A., 119

Chatham, Bob, 1695
Chau, Paul, 1983
Chaubey, Naynika, 2105
Chazen, Jerome A, 462
Chazen, David F, 462
Cheadle, David, 2068
Cheang, Christopher PH, 1469
Chee, Brian, 1464
Cheever, Chris, 762
Chefitz, Robert, 1329
Chen, Wu-Fu, 46
Chen, Drew, 223
Chen, Alan, 377
Chen, Andy, 511
Chen, Joanne, 773
Chen, Jerry, 877
Chen, Jesse, 1183
Chen, Phil, 1477
Chen, Roger, 1687
Chen, Jesson, 2221
Chen, PhD, Alice, 30
Chen, PhD, Leon, 519
Chen, PhD, Anna H., 785
Cheney, Matt, 500
Cheng, Cheryl, 299
Cheng, C.K., 908
Cheng, Ray, 1235
Cheng, Larry, 1944
Cheng, Julian, 1957
Cherkashin, Pavel, 895
Cherry, Brian, 1360
Chertok, Doug, 581
Cherun, Robert, 2042
Chesney, Rob, 473
Chesnoff, Adam, 1602
Chesse, Jean Pierre, 284
Chessick, Cary, 732
Chestnut, Edward A., 1498
Chestnut, Edward, 1499
Cheung, Gordon, 2102
Cheung, Liam, 2251
Chhabra, Kate, 430
Chheda, Neil, 1585
Chiang, Helen, 111
Chiao, Stephen, 1771
Chiarelli, Paul, 2276
Chiefetz, Yoni, 1125
Chihi, Kyce, 196
Childres, Christopher, 653
Childress, Stacey, 1315
Chin, Eric, 564
Chintamaneni, Prasad, 1300
Chiriaev, Dan, 866
Chitnis, Sach, 1050
Chiu, Ian, 1393
Chiu, Alan, 2010
Cho, Hoon, 828
Choe, Michael, 458
Choi, Yumin, 224
Choi, Iris, 752
Choi, Ben, 1110
Choi, Jai, 1418
Choi, Jamie, 1614
Choi, Jennifer, 3256
Cholakis, George H., 2026
Chong, Simon, 2126
Chopra, Arjun, 752
Chopra, Ajay, 1855
Chou, Scott, 657
Chou, Jonathan Y, 699
Chou, Scott, 808
Chou, T.C., 908
Chou, Allan, 1341
Chou, Christy, 1924
Chou, Tony M, 1931
Choudhary, Bharat, 2279
Chrisney, Craig, 976

Executive Name Index

Chrisoffersen, Ralph E, 1257
Christ, William D, 1778
Christensen, Gavin, 1074
Christiansen, Bob, 1713
Christianson, Tony, 466
Christianson, MBA, Tyler, 561
Christoffersen PhD, Chris, 1126
Christopher, Nicholas S., 1097
Christopher, David, 1424
Christopher, David, 1425
Chrust, Steven, 450
Chu, Yee-Ping, 277
Chu, Sherman I, 861
Chu, Nelson, 1076
Chu, J Michael, 1092
Chu, Wayee, 1530
Chu, Y.K., 1983
Chuang, Connie, 1183
Chui-Miller, Grace, 545
Chung, Jeff, 108
Chung, Walter, 334
Chung, Young, 582
Chung, Henry, 627
Chung, Patrick, 709
Chung, Joyce, 810
Chung, Chris, 883
Chung, William, 897
Chung, Peter, 1255
Chung, Patrick, 1283
Chung, Peter Y, 1754
Chung, Patrick, 2245
Churbuck, Thomas K, 65
Churchill, Winston J, 1636
Chwang, Dr Ronald, 974
Cioffi, Robert, 80
Ciriello, Paul, 713
Cirino, Maria, 1
Claassen, Robert, 387
Clancy, John, 1499
Clapp, Todd, 429
Clark, Tom, 530
Clark, Ryan, 823
Clark, Gregory E., 949
Clark, Brian M, 1157
Clark, John, 1434
Clark, Roddy JH, 1536
Clark, Paul, 1925
Clark, Scott, 2081
Clark Jr, Robert, 362
Clark, Jr., Peter L., 418
Clarke, John, 413
Clary, Matt, 1964
Clavier, Jeff, 1702
Clavier, Jeff, 1881
Clayton, Kevin, 676
Cleland, Andrew, 520
Cleland, Hugh, 2234
Clements, Miles, 27
Cleveland, Bruce, 1985
Clevinger, Brian, 1490
Cline, J Michael, 38
Clough, Phil, 21
Cloyd, Malcolm, 188
Cluss, Ed, 1680
Coady, James D, 1654
Coats, David, 545
Cobb, Steve A, 480
Coburn, Brooke B, 416
Coburn, Chris, 1421
Coca, Lisa, 812
Cochran, John D, 1151
Cochrane, Greg, 2274
Cockrell, Ross, 696
Cogan, Gill, 1382
Coglizer, Dave, 1978
Cohan, Jay, 1976
Cohen, Josh, 490

Cohen, Andrew B., 513
Cohen, Jake, 608
Cohen, Aaron D., 889
Cohen, Rob, 1024
Cohen, Brian, 1305
Cohen, Brian, 1309
Cohen, Trace, 1309
Cohen, Michael, 1369
Cohen, Bennett, 1453
Cohen, Wayne, 1638
Cohen, Charles, 1777
Cohen, David, 1791
Cohen, Ira D, 1888
Cohen, Fred, 1934
Cohen, Matt, 2232
Cohler, Matt, 251
Cohn, Michael, 888
Cohn, MD, Billy, 1622
Coit, David M, 1334
Colangelo, Larry A, 1230
Cole, Marshall, 216
Cole, Doug, 748
Cole, Philip, 1765
Cole, James A, 1995
Cole Jr, C Taylor, 913
Colecchi, Christopher, 350
Colella, Vanessa, 488
Coleman III, Charles P, 1828
Colleran, Kevin, 1696
Collett, Mike, 1491
Collier, Cesar, 1681
Collier, Scott, 1857
Collings, Greg, 2121
Collins, Matthew, 501
Collins, Christopher L, 1066
Collins, Derrick K, 1465
Collins, John, 1753
Collins, Andrew J, 1754
Collins, Scott C, 1754
Collinson, Jeffrey J, 476
Collinson, Stuart, 772
Collis, Jim, 1641
Collister, R. Craig, 1594
Collombel, Philippe, 1418
Colloton, Ed, 263
Colmenares, Alan, 1783
Colodny, Mark M, 1957
Colon, Jr., Daniel, 509
Colonna, Elizabeth, 921
Comey, Robert A., 1020
Compall, John, 491
Conacher, Lionel, 1318
Conci Orozco, Gianna, 493
Condon Jr, Edward J, 1416
Condron, Scott, 1988
Cone, Michael M, 632
Conese Jr., Eugene P., 878
Coneybeer, Robert, 1666
Conklin, Richard, 733
Conley, Bill, 383
Conley, Paul, 1401
Conlon, James, 361
Connaughton, John, 223
Connell, William C, 934
Connelly, Patrick, 106
Connolly, John, 224
Connor, John, 20
Connor, Stephen B., 903
Connor, Tim, 1656
Connors, Brian, 766
Connors, John, 978
Connors, Tim, 1454
Connors, William G., 1747
Connors II, James J, 1066
Conrad, Barry B, 988
Conrad, Tony, 1862
Conrado, Eduardo, 1260

Conroy, Jim, 1372
Conte, Jean-Pierre L., 823
Conti, Vincent S, 1523
Conway, William E, 204
Conway, Ron, 1763
Conway, Topher, 1763
Conway, Brian J, 1778
Conway Jr, William E, 416
Cook, Matthew A, 1075
Cook, Everett R, 1470
Cook, Charles, 2091
Cook III, Joe, 1261
Cook Jr, Joe, 1261
Cooney, David J, 247
Cooper, Bradley E., 407
Cooper, Wayne, 868
Cooper, Marshall, 868
Cooper, Chris, 1428
Cooper, Mike, 1670
Cooper, MD, Thomas P., 137
Coote, Kim, 2280
Coover, Gary, 1614
Copans, Richard H, 1160
Copeland, Gene, 1839
Coppedge, Schuyler, 676
Coppinger, Liam, 2177
Coppola, Michael, 583
Coquillette, David C., 1300
Corcoran, Dan, 1176
Cordova, Gonzalo, 1913
Corey, Chris F., 1278
Corkran, Ao Ann, 845
Corley, Leslie M, 1141
Corley, Evan, 1413
Cormier, Guy, 2089
Cornacchione, Jason R., 1460
Cornelis, Kelly A., 1097
Cornell, Chad M., 847
Corning, Sally, 1756
Corry, Daniel, 68
Cortas, Usama, 1113
Corzine, Nicola, 229
Cosentino, Leonard M, 1286
Cosgriff, John G., 1020
Costantino, Kevin, 869
Costantino, John R, 1325
Costanzo, Maria F, 1624
Costello, Kevin P., 312
Costello, Dennis R., 325
Costello, Dennis B, 1849
Costin, Tom, 1393
Cote, Diane, 2184
Cotton, Ryan, 223
Couch, C Deryl, 1755
Coughran, Bill, 1657
Coulson, Fred, 746
Cournoyer, JS, 2224
Couture, Luc, 2259
Coveny, Amy, 1509
Covey, Krista, 738
Cowan, David, 263
Cowen, Will, 1146
Cox, Everett, 666
Cox, Charles A, 1148
Cozzi, John, 63
Crabill, Scott, 1817
Craig, Jackson, 242
Craig, Ryan, 260
Cramer, Yeon, 271
Crandell, Keith L., 154
Crane, Alan, 1464
Cranford, Adam, 1292
Cranswick, Russ, 1551
Crasto, Anil L, 1828
Cravens, McCall, 960
Cravens, Ashley, 1881
Craver, Jeffrey, 60

Craves, PhD, Fred, 240
Crawford, Charlie, 477
Crawford, Andrew, 819
Crawford, Matthew S, 1502
Crawford, Ryan, 2159
Crawford PhD, Douglas, 1238
Creamer, Glenn M., 1498
Creasey, Fred, 2246
Creech, Todd, 924
Creer, Frank M., 2020
Cremin, David, 794
Cressey, Bryan, 559
Cresswell, Simon, 136
Crihfield, Steve, 903
Crisalis, Robert, 1802
Crissman, Blaine, 1481
Crittenden, Gary, 962
Crocker, Curtis D, 1547
Crockett, Catherine, 884
Crockett, Todd R, 1778
Croft, Matthew, 1134
Croll, David D, 1157
Cromwell III, Michael J, 1389
Cronkey, Damon, 2010
Crosbie, Allan, 2083
Crosby, Chris J., 1278
Cross, Cairn G, 789
Cross, Matthew, 2160
Cross, Stacey, 2260
Crothers, Mike, 703
Crouthamel, Jamie, 732
Crowder, Randall, 1803
Crowe, Jeffrey M, 1346
Crowell, Bill, 93
Crowell, Richard R, 1906
Crowley, Kevin, 532
Croxon, Bruce, 2235
Croxton, R Randy, 1209
Crumpler, John, 918
Crussel, David, 790
Cruz, Brandon, 732
Cryer, Natalie D, 381
Cubitt, Code, 2187
Cuccio, Gary, 1795
Cukier, Ben, 442
Culham, Harry, 2073
Cullen, Chuck, 881
Cullinane, Kelli, 1110
Cummings, David, 191
Cummings, Benton, 1518
Cummings, Bob, 1990
Cunning, Matt, 2171
Cunningham, Jason M, 165
Cunningham, Sean, 765
Cunningham, Sean L., 889
Cunningham, Ronan, 1782
Cunningham MD, Joe, 1622
Cunningham, MD, Casey, 1622
Cuomo, Alexander, 1325
Cureton, Chip, 893
Curley, Kevin J., 1041
Curran, D Patrick, 367
Currie, Lauchlan, 2036
Currier, James, 1323
Curry, Bob, 1098
Curry, Michael, 2153
Curtin, Adam H, 1234
Custar, Krisin, 1049
Custer, William M., 572
Cusumano CFA, Dino, 110
Cutler, Joel, 820
Cutts, Joseph, 1382
Czarny, Samuel, 253
Czornyj, Adrianna, 2212
Czuba, Gregory S, 692

Executive Name Index

D

D'Addario, Paul, 1403
D'Argenio, Rahman, 676
Daccus, Paul, 1755
Dadoo, Rajeev, 1734
D'Agostino, Michael, 1435
Dagres, Todd, 1718
Dahl, Ben, 1679
Dahnke, Scott A., 1092
Daileader, John, 867
Daing, Avantika, 1458
Dalal MD, Anupam, 1063
Dale, Andy, 1250
Dallaire, André, 475
Dalton, Frank X, 539, 797
Dalton PhD, Barbara J, 1439
Dalvey, David, 344
Dalvie, Shivanandan A., 63
Daly, Celia, 395
Daly, Michael F, 1524
D'Amico, Brian, 1753
Damico, Joseph F., 1594
D'Amore, Richard A, 1335
Dan, Aubrey, 2088
Danard, Chad, 2267
Dancewicz, John E, 620
D'Andrea, Harry, 1901
D'Andrea, Jon, 1977
Danhakl, John G, 1113
Dani, Nick, 626
D'Aniello, Daniel A, 416
Daniels, Roanne, 927
Daniels, Melissa, 1255
Daniels, C Bryan, 1473
Daniels, Terry, 1507
Daniels, Marcus, 2140
Daraviras, Nicholas, 1036
Darby, Christopher, 983
Darden, Tom, 465
Darling, Scott, 604
Dautrich, Tyler, 871
DaValle Jr., Albert, 1042
Davenport III, Robert R., 343
Davidson, Duncan, 361
Davidson, Jeff, 467
Davidson, Stuart, 1093
Davidson, Mitchell, 1469
Davidson, Vinse, 1785
Davies, Natalie L, 381
Davies, Rhiannon, 2238
Davies III, Paul L, 381
Davis, Jeff, 47
Davis, Stephen, 230
Davis, Kim G., 458
Davis, Barry M, 592
Davis, Allan, 640
Davis, Timothy C, 789
Davis, Chris, 813
Davis, Bob, 938
Davis, Anthony B, 1132
Davis, Robert E, 1138
Davis, W Ryan, 1163
Davis, Owen, 1358
Davis, Jordan S, 1523
Davis, J. Bradley, 1565
Davis, Clark F., 1565
Davis, Charles A., 1746
Davis, Anthony, 1845
Davis, Jerel, 1930
Davis, Kim, 2273
Davison, Jeff, 993
Davoli, Robert E, 1675
Day, Rob, 1732
Day, Marcus, 2062
Dayal, Munish, 2062
Daych, Diane M., 436
Dayton, Troy, 1810

de Alba, Gabriel, 2067
Dean, Thompson, 212
Dean, John, 942
Dean, Rahsaan, 996
Dean, John C, 1740
Dean, Christopher J, 1754
DeAngelis, Ken, 205
DeAngelis, Pasquale, 1492
DeAngelo, Steve, 1810
Dearing, Michael, 914
Deb, Dipanjan (DJ), 782
Debbane, Raymond, 1022
Debiasi, Gerard A, 1075
DeBlois, Mark, 362
DeBruin, Robert, 1291
DeCaire, Ryan, 2041
Dechet, Rainer, 1265
DeCillis II, Steven, 63
de Clercq, Casper, 1346
DeCorte, Evan, 518
Dedes Gallagher, Marina, 1936
Deeb, George, 732
Dees, Michael W, 1133
Deeter, Byron, 263
DeFalco, Stephen P, 1133
Defieux, Rick, 1691
Defina, Sara, 2146
DeFlorio, Michael B., 917
Degenhart, Jeremy, 60
DeGroff, Dain F, 1848
Degroot, Seth, 344
Deitzer, James R., 358
de Jager, Thomas, 119
deLaar, Mark A, 1754
De La Cruz, Marta, 838
Delaney, Bob, 560
Delaney, Daniel L., 989
Delaney, Christopher, 1027
Delaplane, Kevin, 1883
Deleray, Michael, 346
Delgado, Lister, 975
del Gaudio, Elisa, 40
Del Guercio, Joe, 510
Delistathis, Thanasis, 1290, 1485
Dell'Aquila, Richard T, 356
Dellenbach, Hans, 2101
DeLorenzo, Jason M., 673
DeLuca, Dino, 2267
de Luna, Leo, 1158
deMarrais, Brett, 1154
DeMartini, Rich, 560
Demetriades, Jim, 1055
Demkowicz, Brian, 963
Demond, Jeff, 155
DeMott, Harry, 1528
Dempsey, Neal, 241
Dempsey, Michael, 527
Dempsey, Sean, 1219
DeMuth, Donald F., 611
Deng, Feng, 1340
DeNichilo, Matt, 676
de Nicola, Anthony J, 1973
DeNino, Mark, 1830
Dennedy, Tom, 176
Denning, Steven, 819
Denos, Kenneth I., 695
Dent, Stephen J., 2056
Dent, James, 2182
Denton, James T., 346
Denton, Stephen, 2242
Denvir, Michael, 1049
Derks, Menno, 2239
Derr Gilbert, Karen, 796
Dershem, Dan, 1759
de Rooij, Deborah, 2239
DeRosa, Ben, 110
DeRosa, Michael, 658

der Kinderen, Marc, 13
DeRubertis, Jamie J., 302
Desai, Keval, 1014
DeSena, Bob, 883
Deshpande, Salil, 224
DesMarais, Robert, 1769
Des Pallieres, Bertrand, 695
Desmarais III, Paul, 2090, 2217
Detkin, Peter, 1010
Deutsch, David N, 590
de Turenne, Noel, 1250
DeVeer, Kipp, 159
Devereux, Robin W, 1754
DeVino, Sally A., 1746
Devita, Andrea, 374
Devitte, Jesse, 311
Devlaminck, Lode J, 637
DeVore, Chris, 776
Devorsetz, Dan, 949
DeVos, Rick, 1739
DeVries, Mike, 652
DeVries, Lawson, 881
DeVries, Tim, 1345
DeVries, Jerry, 1803
De Winter, Alex, 812
De Zwirek, Gurion, 2245
D'Halluin, Thomas, 72
Dhami, Narinder, 2179
Dharmaraj, Satish, 1537
Dhillon, Sunny, 1680
Dhol, Parag, 1017
Dhonte, Sebastien, 2075
Di Bona, Tony, 87
Di Geronimo, Robert, 1435
Di Nardo, Bill, 2104
Di Prata, Cam, 2127
DiBella, Paul R, 539
DiLella, Gary R, 1496
DiNovi, Anthony J., 1818
DiPiano, Michael, 1316
DiPucchio, Rocco, 2067
Diallo, Vincent, 1011
Diamond, Douglas, 694
Diamond, Carey, 2280
Diamond, Shayn, 2280
Diaz, Paul, 559
Diaz, Omar, 630
Dibella, Paul, 770
Dichter, Sasha, 54
Dick, Christopher W., 180
Dick, Jonathan E, 1480
Dick, Timothy, 1740
Dickens, Jorge, 45
Dickey, Sarah, 3247
Dickinson, Brendan, 389
Dickinson, Daniel, 920
Dickinson, Arlene, 2093
Didato, Dean, 999
Diehl, Jeffrey, 56
Diehl, Bowen S., 406
Diekman PhD, John D, 11
Dielwart, John, 2036
Dieschbourg, Michael T, 991
Digmy, Vered, 117
Dillabough, Gary, 1281
Dillman, David, 1556
Dillon, Karl D, 943
Dimberio, Joe, 1873
Dimitri, James, 1927
Ding, Chun, 474
Dintersmith, Ted, 457
Diop, Makhtar, 1012
Dishner, Jeffrey G., 1742
Dixon, Brian, 661
Dixon, Rocky, 674
Dixon, Donald, 765
Dixon, Donald R., 1852

Dixon, Michael, 2261
Dlugos, Andrea, 2002
Do, Trung Q., 1421
Dobbin, Mark, 2161
Docter, Daniel, 604
Dodson, Andrew C., 1419
Doerer, John W, 1465
Doherty, Gerry, 1277
Doiguchi, Wayne, 217
Dokas, Elias, 1231
Dolan, A. Barr, 460
Dolbac, Michael, 812
Dolce, Michael J, 1160
Dolder, Adam B., 864
Dolezal, David, 1917
Doll, Dixon, 597
Doll, Alex, 1796
Domach, Jim, 1174
Domanig, Gina, 2101
Dombalagian, Vahe A, 1160
Dominguez, Michael J., 1498
Dominguez-Edington, Victoria, 447
Dominik, David, 843
Domolky, Randolph C, 1137
Donabedian, David H, 1149
Donaghy, Brian, 347
Donahue Jr, Donald J, 692
Donatelli, Mark, 2051
Donelan, James T, 1639
Donelson, Mishone B., 949
Doner, Chris, 256
Dong, Candy, 2226
Donnellan, Patrick J, 692
Donner, Andy, 1442
Donnini, David A., 889
Donoghue, Michael F., 1730
Donohue, Liam, 1
Donovan, Dana, 632
Donovan, Michael E, 1973
Doody, Christopher M., 1746
Dooley, John, 1031
Doomany, George, 124
Dorman, Mark, 674
Dorsen, Edith, 2003
Dorsey, David, 3
Dorsey, Scott, 932
Doshi, Rutvik, 1017
Dotson, Laura, 1067
Dotzler, Frederick J, 599
Doub, Robb, 1298
Doubleday, Ned, 1156
Dougery, John, 1017
Dougherty, Dennis, 1013
Dougherty, MD, James B., 158
Douglass, David, 605
Douglass, James S, 797
Douglass, Olleb, 1259
Douville, Elizabeth, 2031
Douvos, Chris, 71
Dova, Pietro, 2009
Dovey, Brian, 622
Dovi, Damien A., 266
Dow, Stephen M, 1661
Dowdle, Robin, 67
Dowling, James J., 1036
Downey, Bruce, 1316
Downs, Mark, 1279
Downs, Matt, 1618
Dowse, Peter, 2156
Dowty, Scott, 206
Doyle, Maurice, 60
Doyle, Kenneth M., 899
Doyle, Sean, 1009
Doyle, Kaitlyn, 1023
Doyle, Noah J., 1032
Doyle, Sean, 1613
Doyle, Jere, 1675

Executive Name Index

Doyle, Daniel K, 1772
Dracon, Greg, 1
Drager, Andrea, 218
Drahms, David, 1388
Drakonakis, Konstantine, 1101
Drant, Ryan, 1516
Draper, Adam, 310
Draper, Timothy, 610
Draper, Tim, 627
Draper, Jesse, 901
Draper, Timothy, 2020
Draper III, William H, 628
Drattell, Jason D, 1472
Draves, Brian, 1796
Drazan, Jeff, 260
Drechsel, Dan, 1412
Dreier, Robert, 362
Dresner, Steven M, 630
Dresner, Edward I, 646
Drew, John, 1787
Drewlo, Norm, 2249
Dreyfuss, Andy, 1446
Driscoll, Craig, 938
Driscoll, PhD, Ted, 493
Dritz, Russell S, 1506
Drokova, Masha, 594
Druley, David, 382
Drury, Paul W., 1115
DuBois, Roland, 2189
Dubczak, Roman S., 2073
Dubilier, Michael J, 632
Duboc, Samuel L., 2098
Dubuque, Louis, 60
Duda, Jim, 583
Duffy, Patrick J, 1276
Duffy, Pauline, 1543
Dugan, Jim, 1364
Dugan, John, 1364
Dugan, Tim, 1962
Dugenske, John, 88
Duggal, Rajat, 790
Duguid, Rob, 2213
Dullum, David, 832
Dunaway, Barry, 109
Dunbar, William, 540
Dunbar, Matt, 1925
Duncan, Pat, 216
Duncan, Michael, 2083
Dunfield, Ryan, 2237
Dunham, Jennifer, 173
Dunlap, Kevin, 373
Dunlop, A. Sinclair, 690
Dunlop, Scott, 2078
Dunn, Michael, 694
Dunn, Andrew, 1376
Dunn, Patrick D., 1498
Dunn, Andy, 1534
Dunnan, Bruce B., 880
Dunnan, Douglas M., 880
Dunwoodie, Kevin, 1413
Dupcak, Scott, 534
Dupere, Justin C, 1964
Dupree, David, 899
Durban, Egon, 1685
Durbin, Eliot, 308
Durbin, Chris A., 1933
Durkin, Jr., Charles P., 1624
Durrett, Park, 28
Durst, Greg, 3256
Dutch, Suzette, 1849
Dutta, Shomik, 937
Dutton, Steve, 1066
Dutton, Joseph, 1961
Dwane, Anne, 1935
Dworkin, Andrew L., 1913
Dwyer, Suzanne L, 1176
Dyal, Tom, 1537

E

Eadie, MD, James, 1622
Eagle, David A., 360
Eakin, Rory, 484
Eames, Anthony, 379
Earhart, John, 838
Earley, Richard P, 636
Earls, Alex, 886
Earthy, Jill, 2144
Eason, Randall, 96
Eastburn Jr., John S., 1087
Eastman, Ron, 698
Easton, Loren, 111
Eatroff, Bruce A, 902
Eaves, Cory, 819
Ebersweiler, Cyril, 1709
Ebert, Sean, 98
Ebinger, Jonathan, 299
Eby, Doug, 1375
Eby, Jeff, 2007
Eckert, Carol, 785
Eckert, John, 2191, 2235
Eddy, Tom, 1031
Edeburn, Patrick, 855
Edelson, Harry, 651
Edelson, MD, Jon, 179
Edens, Wesley R., 769
Edgerton, Matt, 1066
Edwards, S. Whitfield, 747
Edwards, Donald J., 751
Edwards, Scott W, 1755
Efstratis, Nick, 689
Egan, Chris, 61
Egan, Michael, 2274
Eggers, Barry, 1125
Ehlers, Michael, 144
Ehrenberg, Roger, 969
Ehrenpreis, Ira, 596, 3273
Ehrenpreis, Ira M, 1788
Ehret, Gregory A., 1448
Ehrhart, Robert, 223
Ehrhart, Ken, 693
Ehrhart, Ken, 1757
Ehrich, Peter, 559
Eichler, David, 1500
Eiermann, Julie, 912
Einav, PhD, Shmuel, 1811
Einhorn, Stephen, 403
Einhorn, Daniel, 403
Eisenberg, Paul, 144
Eisenberg, Dave, 1534
Eisenberg, Jonathan, 1845
Eisenhauer, Tom, 2059
Eisenman, Randy, 1625
Eisenson, Michael R., 458
Eisenstein, Stephen, 917
Eisler, David, 2227
Eitan, Yaron, 1636, 1650
Ekman, Lars, 1700
El Amine, Firas, 1021
El Baze, Nicolase, 1418
El Chami, Joe, 1026
El-Nazer, Hythem T, 1778
Elahian, Kamran, 837
Elbaz, Gil, 1800
Elburn, Jeff, 1745
Eldridge, Paul, 2121
Elenko, Eric, 1503
Elfman, Rick, 1745
Elgner, Claude, 2099
Elgner, Roger, 2099
Elias, Jamie E, 1859
Eliasek, Michael G., 1493
Eline, Christopher M., 904
Eliot, Philip, 1401
Elishis, Isser, 2275
Elkhatib, Rami, 40, 1711

Elkus, Bill, 504
Elliott, Charles, 656
Elliott, Mike, 1332
Elliott, Jim, 2058
Elliott, William, 2100
Ellis, Chad, 41
Ellis, David O, 656
Ellis, Seth, 1433
Ellis, Jonathan, 1617
Ellis III, Alexander, 1583
Ellison, Bill, 1000
Ellman, Stuart, 1597
Elman, Dr. Sheldon, 2212
Elman, Stuart M., 2212
Elmer, Donald J, 1399
Elmore, Bill, 773
Elmore, Qian W., 973
Elms, Steven A., 73
Elrod Jr., James L., 1933
Eltrich III, Martin, 63
Embry Jr, Robert C, 18
Emery, Mark, 1049
Emmert, Robert Y, 1276
Emmitt, Richard B, 1931
Emond, Charles, 2064
Empson, Joshua C., 1498
Emry, Deric, 872
Eng, Darren, 3258
Engel, Beth, 635
Engel, Jerry, 1249
Engelberg, Steve, 1618
Engelhardt, Philip, 1441
Engestrom, Jyri, 2013
Engle, Bridget E, 306
Engleman, Dr. Edgar G, 1943
Engler, Edward R, 1451
Enjoji, Kay, 1793
Ennis, Greg, 1430
Enns, Marcus, 2071
Enright, Patrick, 1147
Enriquez, Juan, 704
Entress, Geoff, 1501
Epstein, Gary C, 940
Epstein, Mark E, 1271
Epstein, Alv, 1745
Erhard, John F., 157
Erickson, Paul K., 464
Erickson, Thomas, 739
Erickson, Christopher, 1822
Erickson, Chris, 2205
Ericson, William, 1247
Ericson, Bill, 1985
Ervin, Daley, 678
Es Sabar, Karimah, 2221
Escobar, Sergio, 2047
Escobari, Martin, 819
Espitallier, David, 730
Esserman, Charles H, 1863
Essex, Rick, 1499
Estes, PhD, Daniel, 785
Eubank II, Frederick W., 1410
Eubanks Jr., Robert C., 783
Evans, David S., 834
Evans, Karen, 1689
Evans, Hugh D., 1927
Evans, Larry, 2022
Eve, Derek, 674
Evers, Elliot B, 1197
Every, MD, MPH, Nathan R., 785
Evnin, Luke B, 1268
Evola, Carmen, 279
Exshaw, Christian, 2073
Exter, Neil, 1814

F

Faber, Bart, 194
Faber, Robert, 227

Fabiani, Vin, 941
Fachetti, Dave, 839
Fade, Richard, 978
Fader, Steven B., 192
Fagnan, Jeff, 37
Fahey, Kevin P., 302
Fahoury, Doug, 1024
Failing, Bruce F, 80
Fajgenbaum, Jonas, 1022
Fake, Caterina, 2013
Falk, Michael, 530
Falk, Thomas, 1557
Falkenstein, Joseph, 1329
Falktoft, Henrik, 1518
Fallon, Patrick, 28
Fallon, Timothy G., 148
Fang, Lawrence, 1986
Farah, Michael, 1132
Faraone, Steve, 2209
Farber, Jonathan, 1129
Farello, Michael J., 1092
Farid, Saman, 222
Faris, Karim, 894
Faris, David M, 1609
Farkas, Brad, 967
Farmer, Chris, 1677
Farmer, Ron, 2190
Farner, Peter W, 1804
Farnsworth, Jim, 2044
Farquhar, Sharon, 2100
Farquharson, Andrew, 984
Farrar, James, 2244
Farrell, Jim, 371
Farrell, Mike, 1720
Farrell, Mark E, 1808
Farrero, Jeff, 470
Farrington, Deborah A, 1741
Farsht, Steve, 732
Farwell, Brandon, 709
Fassnacht, Michael, 732
Fates, Matt, 180
Faulkingham, Ryan J., 525
Faust, Dorian, 886
Fawcett, David, 2102
Fay, Sarah, 833
Fay, Timothy P, 1639
Fearnow, Brian, 371
Federman, Irwin, 1898
Feeley, Edmund J, 1138
Feeney, Gordon, 2274
Feerick, Robert M., 948
Feidler, Mark L, 1270
Feiler, Jack, 1402
Feinberg, Stephen A., 453
Feinstein, Brian, 263
Feinstein, Peter, 273
Feinstein, Adam, 1932
Feld, Brad, 779, 1245, 1791
Feld, Stacy, 1046, 1442
Feldman, Jesse, 238
Feldman, Matthew S., 494
Feldmen, Scott, 1761
Felesky, Adam, 2217
Felman, David S., 874
Felser, Josh, 787
Felt, Benjamin, 1022
Feltenstein, Sidney J, 1654
Fenton, Peter, 251
Fenton, Dean E, 1738
Fenton, Noel J, 1855
Fenwick-Smith, Robert, 147
Ferguson, Jeffrey W, 416
Ferguson, Rod, 1411
Fernandes, Mark, 1672
Fernandez, Jason, 1509
Ferneau, Phil, 311
Ferrara, Alex, 263

Executive Name Index

Ferrari, Richard M., 599
Ferrari, Wes, 976
Ferrari, Marco, 1499
Ferreira, Beth, 744
Ferrell, Jeffrey A., 190
Ferri, Paul J, 1184
Ferrington, Leonard C, 1754
Ferris, Paul, 218
Feuille, Jim, 564
Fialkow, David, 820
Fiato, John, 912
Fich, Nicole, 2211
Fichtner, Kirk, 1170
Fiedler, Jason, 1533
Fields, Mark, 93
Fields, Kathy, 1045
Fife, John, 472
Filipowski, Andrew "Flip", 1683
Fillat, Andy, 1106
Finch, Lawrence G, 1674
Fine, Ari, 149
Fine, Adam E, 1993
Fine, Roger S, 1993
Fine Glantz, Ari, 3263
Finegan, Scott A., 1438
Fingerle, Linda, 652
Fink, Andrew, 1846
Finkel, Robert, 1481
Finkelstein, Daniel, 850
Finkelstein, Brett, 1443
Finkelstein, Alex, 1718
Finkelstein, Kenny, 2164
Finlay, Matthew W, 1230
Finlayson, Joel, 2141
Finn, Christopher, 416
Finnegan, Paul J, 1160
Fiorentino, David A, 1053
Fioretti, Robert J, 717
First, Mark L., 687
Fisch, Michael, 111
Fisher, Adam, 263
Fisher, Bob, 495
Fisher, John, 610
Fisher, Brett, 745
Fisher, Doug, 825, 1014
Fisher, Stewart, 1090
Fisher, Mark, 1191
Fisher, Ronald D, 1701
Fisherman, Jason, 1777
Fishman, David, 1912
Fitzgerald, Thomas C., 363
Fitzgerald, Brian, 404
Fitzgerald, John, 469
Fitzgerald, Michael T., 523
Fitzgerald, Bill, 820
Fitzgerald, Peter, 1098
Fitzgerald, James, 1899
Fitzgerald, William, 1991
Fitzpatrick, Thomas P, 1654
Fitzsimmons, Robert J, 934
Flager, Morgan, 1687
Flanagan, Robert J, 510
Flanagan, Dave, 1009
Flanagan, Marty, 1019
Flanagan, Paul, 1675
Flanigan, John W., 463
Flannery, Michael E, 634
Flannery, Bob, 1539
Flaster, Andy, 1944
Flater, Graham, 2121
Flatley, Daniel K, 1178
Flatt, Bruce, 2062
Fleck, Philip, 1347
Fleischer, Spencer, 790
Fleischmann, Charles, 1853
Fleming, Jim, 518
Fleming, Standish, 772

Fleming, Daniel T, 1575
Fleming Arora, Natalie, 1760
Flemons, Wade, 2210
Fleshman, Skip, 183
Fletcher, John, 750
Fletcher III, F. Barron, 1417
Flickinger, Mark, 1412
Fligel, Andy, 1009
Flint, Pete, 1323
Flint, Jon, 1464
Florea, Raluca, 335
Florence, Walter C, 792
Florence, Tony, 1296
Flores, Tami, 232
Florsheim, Steven, 1891
Florsheim, Riley, 1892
Flower, Mark, 1964
Floyd, Joe, 666
Floyd, Nancy C, 1355
Floyd, Ryan, 1750
Flucht, Brian, 281
Flyer, Steven, 196
Flynn, James, 602
Flynn, Brian, 775
Flynn, Timothy J, 1113
Flynn, Tom, 1631
Flynn, Tom, 1764
Fogarty MD, Thomas J, 667
Fogel, Lawrence M, 761
Fogelsong, John, 840
Fogelsong, Norman A., 1006
Foisy, Michael A., 904
Foisy, Jacques, 2198
Foley, Shawn, 211
Foley, David I., 280
Foley, Todd, 1268
Foley-Wong, Bonnie, 2215
Folk, M. Holly, 140
Follows, Mark, 2066
Folsom, Doug, 8
Fonseca Licciardi, Natalie, 1836
Fonstad, Jennifer, 182
Fontana, Ash, 2018
Fontenot, Kirsi, 952
Foo, Jixun, 827
Foo, Adrienne, 1866
Foo, Gavin, 2196
Foote, Sean, 1093
Foote, William F, 1586
Foote, Stephen, 2196
Ford, Bill, 762
Ford, William E., 819
Ford, William, 858
Ford, Andrew N., 906
Ford, Hadley, 970
Ford, Kerri, 1600
Ford Buckley, Kelly, 655
Foreman, Al, 1866
Forest, Sophie, 2060
Forlenza, Bob, 1731
Formela, MD, Jean-Francois, 193
Forrest, Gregory J, 767
Forrest, Brady, 939
Forsyth, Jody, 2034
Fortino, Adrian, 1207
Foster, Frank, 794
Foster, Frank H, 830
Foster, C Michael, 1232
Foster, Michael J, 1560
Foster, Alan, 1795
Fountain, Adam J., 349
Fountas, Christopher, 173
Fournier, Marcel, 425
Fourticq, Ted, 905
Fourticq Jr., Michael J., 905
Fourticq Sr., Michael J., 905
Fowler, Molly, 623

Fox, Joelle, 678
Fox, Saul A., 781
Fox, Jeff, 911
Fox, Richard, 975
Fox, Robert A, 1524
Fox, Arthur L, 1595
Fox, Ken, 1751
Foy, Clinton, 562
Foy, Matthew, 1734
Fraiman, Diane, 1947
Fralic, Chris, 742
Frances MD, Craig D, 1754
Francis, Lizzie, 345
Francis, Doug, 665
Francis, Tod, 1666
Frank, Richard H., 585
Frank, Bill, 1285
Frank, Lincoln E, 1506
Frankel, Robert, 174
Frankel, John, 724
Frankel, David, 774
Franklin, David C., 954
Franklin, Will, 1129
Franklin, Bobby, 3262
Frantz, Gene, 579
Franz, Peter B, 753
Fraquelli, Luigi, 2127
Fraser, Robert, 203
Fraser, Chase, 784
Fraser, Malcolm, 2148
Frazee, David, 1564
Frazier, Alan D., 785
Frederick, Alisa, 377
Frederick DPM, Jeff, 1288
Frederickson, Bryan C., 893
Fredrick, Steve, 881
Fredrickson, Kris, 511
Freedman, Walter G., 1097
Freedman, Constance, 1246
Freedman, Arnie, 1389
Freeman, Bradford M., 786
Freeman MD, Mason, 11
Fregin, Doug, 2220
Freisinger, John, 1789
French, T. Bondurant, 56
French, Douglas D., 1622
Freschman, David, 151
Freund, John F, 1693
Freyer, Charles C, 1636
Frieder, Samuel P, 1085
Friedland, Charlie, 824
Friedman, John H, 644
Friedman, Steven M., 687
Friedman, Tully M., 790
Friedman, Brian P., 1036
Friedman, Stephen, 1746
Friedman, Josef, 1750
Friedman Jr, W Robert, 630
Friend, Scott, 224
Friend, Alexander A., 791
Fries, Alexander, 650
Fries, David, 1908
Friesen, Albert D., 2071
Frischling, James, 883
Frist, MD, Sen. William H., 559
Frost, Dean, 256
Frost, H Lee, 592
Fruchan, Mark, 1244
Fry, Dietz, 674
Fry, Eric T, 1133
FréChette, Pierre, 1594
Frécon, Leslie, 1117
Fu, Ben, 1319
Fu, Shan, 1943
Fuji, Masayuki, 1716
Fujimura, Michio, 185
Fulgoni, Gian, 732

Fuller, Adam, 336
Fuller, Matt, 824
Fuller, Kobie, 1890
Fulmer, A Leigh, 647
Fulton MD, Michael, 946
Funasaki, Tammy, 334
Funcannon, Bill, 1392
Funk, Andy J., 800
Funk, R Clayton, 1197
Furlong, Kim, 3249
Furneaux, Dave, 1084
Fushman, Ilya, 1079

G
Gabelein, Kevin, 755
Gabriel, Jason, 1776
Gabriele, Neil Q., 302
Gadde, Sreekar, 296
Gadicke MD, Ansbert K, 1268
Gaenzle Jr., Richard W., 831
Gaffney, John, 366
Gaffney, Christopher S., 862
Gahwyler, Kevin, 1282
Galante, Jacques V, 1109
Galantini, Eugene, 1643
Galashan, J Kristofer, 1113
Galbut, Elizabeth, 1703
Galiette, Carolyn, 1025
Galitsky, Alexander, 89
Gallagher, Joseph V., 126
Gallagher, Patrick, 565
Gallagher, Michael, 931
Gallagher, Rick, 1488
Gallagher, CFA, Brian, 1873
Galletti, Marc-Henri, 1147
Galligan, Joseph, 767
Gallinson, Evan R, 1210
Galloway, Devon, 2122
Galvin, Thomas M, 943
Gambill, Katie H, 551
Gamble, J.S., 288
Gamboa, Elizabeth, 1299
Gandhi, Sameer, 27
Gandhi, Koonal, 253
Gandhi, Purvi, 945
Ganesan, Venky, 1203
Ganeshram, Shri, 788
Ganguly, Raj, 219
Gannon, John, 693
Gannon, John, 1757
Gantz, Joseph M, 1447
Garbe, Michael, 2232
Garber, Christopher J, 1964
Garcia, John, 63
Garcia, Quin, 207
Garcia, Quin, 208
Garcia, Francisco, 644
Garcia, Rommel, 1169
Garcia de Brigard, Luis E Garcia, 142
Gardiner, Melissa, 3254
Gardner, Sonia, 211
Gardner, David, 512
Gardner, Alston, 797
Gardner, John, 1331
Gardner, JD, 1375
Gardner, Kirt, 1880
Garff, Matthew N, 1755
Garfinkel, Neil, 782
Garfinkle, Jan, 150
Garfunkle, Matt, 1413
Garg, Ashu, 773
Garg, Nikhil, 1732
Garg, Gaurav, 1996
Garman, Richard, 796
Garman, Andrew, 1304
Garner, Jason, 554
Garrard III, Gardiner W, 1865

Executive Name Index

Garrett, Wayne P., 65
Garrett, Brian, 562
Garrou, Blair, 1207
Garton, Anthony W., 1116
Garvey, Shauntel, 1530
Garza, Rudy, 807
Gauba, Gary, 575
Gauer, Jim, 1408
Gaughan, Christopher, 1689
Gaus, Wesley H.R., 509
Gausling, Mike, 1386
Gauthier, André, 2252
Gavin, Brenda D, 1510
Gavin, Rob, 2281
Gay, Mary, 170
Gay, Bob, 962
Gazor, Max, 457
Ge, Grace, 1203
Geant, Darrick, 334
Geary, Bill, 749
Geeslin, Keith, 782
Gehringer, Ryan, 866
Geiger, Benjamin D., 786
Geiger, Debra P, 830
Geiman, Bob, 433
Gelfand, Andrew S., 358
Geliebter, David M, 663
Gelinas, Simon, 2045
Gellert, James, 1991
Gellert, Michael, 1991
Gellman, David S., 804
Gembala, Ryan, 1423
Geneser, Chris, 491
Gent, Stuart, 223
George, Jean, 58
George, Jean, 1126
George, Harry A, 1704
George, Simeon J., 1734
Gephart, Thomas O, 1920
Geran, Jessica, 638
Gerard, Rupert, 893
Gerber, Scott, 816
Gergel, Ivan, 1301
Gerken, Lou, 826
Gerlach, Jason, 1758
Gerry, Peter, 1771
Gershenberg, Aaron, 1766
Gershman, David, 1859
Gerson, Jeffrey P, 854
Gervase, David, 531
Gevada, Eric, 1109
Gezon, David A, 1232
Ghaffary, Mike, 399
Ghai, Vipon, 2177
Ghanem, Shahi, 1983
Ghori, Mansoor, 1653
Ghose, Shomit, 1379
Giacomelli, Ed, 2083
Giannetti, Thomas, 1116
Giannobile, Anthony, 362
Giannuzzi, John K, 1668
Gianos, Flip, 1014
Gibaratz, Scott, 920
Gibbons, Thomas P (Todd), 306
Gibbons, Michael W, 714
Gibbs, Kevin, 1208
Gibson, Brett, 995
Gideon, Austin, 746
Giese, Michael C, 1193
Gieselmann, Thomas, 641
Giffen, Rebecca, 2028
Gifford, Charlie, 929
Gilani, Aziz, 1207
Gilbert, Dan, 608
Gilbert, Douglas H., 611
Gilbert, Jim, 748
Gilbert, Steven J., 831

Gilbert, Daryl, 2159
Gilbert, PhD, Walter, 273
Giles, Eerik, 1279
Giles, Ryan, 2267
Gilhuly, Ned, 1606
Gill, Tehinder, 514
Gill, Mark J, 714
Gill, Daniel M, 1686
Gillani, Karim, 2172
Gillespie, Brad, 969
Gilliam, John P., 302
Gillis, Steven, 154
Gillis, Kevin, 1814
Gilman, Cliff, 71
Gilmore, Craig, 417
Gilmore, Karen, 489
Gilmore, Martin P., 747
Gilmore, Richard, 829
Gimble, AT, 191
Gineris, Marc A., 986
Ginn, Richard, 549
Ginns, Jonathan, 45
Ginsberg, Paul D., 1580
Gionfriddo, Julie, 3274
Girardi, Robert, 212
Girardi, Thomas, 956
Girgenti, Chris, 1483
Girvan, Brian J., 180
Gitig, Liron, 796
Gitter, David, 1291
Gladney, James S, 1118
Gladstone, Michael, 193
Gladstone, David, 832
Gladstone, Laura, 832
Glanville, Tom, 697
Glasheen, Jim, 1788
Glass, Skip, 773
Glass, Jonathan, 1235
Glass, Jr., R. Scott, 1410
Glassman, Newton, 2067
Glassmeyer, Edward F., 1361
Glein, Randy, 610
Glenn, Steven G, 1957
Glew, Jr., Charles E., 751
Glickman, David, 1548
Glisson, Wade D, 1686
Glouchevitch, Michel, 1579
Glynn, John W., 840
Glynn, Jacqueline, 840
Glynn, David, 840
Glynn, Howard, 1208
Go, Rob, 1322
Goddu, Roger, 337
Godman, Paul, 2028
Godwin, Michael, 1550
Goebel, Dr. Markus, 1350
Goeddel PhD, PhD, David V., 519
Goense, John M., 842
Goergen, Todd A, 1587
Goetz, Stefan, 927
Goetz, Jim, 1657
Goff, Charlie, 1291
Goggin, Peter, 164
Goh, Kim P., 957
Gold, David L, 362
Gold, Robert, 1568
Goldberg, Michael, 99, 430
Goldberg, Marc, 273
Goldberg, Robert, 538
Goldberg, Jay N., 957
Goldberg, Michelle, 978
Goldberg, Michael B, 1066
Goldberg, Alan E, 1133
Goldberg, Gary L, 1627
Goldberg, PhD, Allan R., 1811
Goldburg, David, 1208
Golden, William J, 1096

Golden, David, 1558
Golden, Matt, 2130, 2131
Golden, Kerri, 2146
Goldenberg, Adam, 562
Goldenberg, Axel, 2069
Goldfarb, Andy, 839
Goldfarb, Greg S, 1754
Goldfein, Jocelyn, 2018
Goldfischer, MD, Carl, 240
Goldhaber, Nat, 493
Golding, Robert M, 2014
Goldinger, Jim, 713
Goldman, Amir, 1761
Goldsmith, Barry M, 1888
Goldstein, Jonathan, 60
Goldstein, Richard, 64
Goldstein, Heidi M., 104
Goldstein, Jeffrey H., 312
Goldstein, Ross, 609
Goldstein, Jeffrey, 927
Goldstein, Daniel, 1001
Goldstein, Johnathan M, 1778
Goldstein, Howard, 1913
Golinowski, Craig, 2159
Gollmer, Stewart, 1798
Golob, David, 782
Golson, Brian P, 1419
Golub, Lawrence E., 848
Golub, David B., 848
Gonser, Tom, 1659
Gontar, Michael, 1951
Gonzalez, Charles, 78
Gonzalez, Daria, 895
Gooch, Michael F., 905
Good, Nathan J, 1473
Goodhart, Noah, 1980
Goodhart, Jonah, 1980
Goodhead, Giles, 868
Goodman, Edwin A, 51
Goodman, Bob, 263, 395
Goodman, James J, 815
Goodman, Michael D, 854
Goodman, Corey, 1916
Goodman, Jordan, 2041
Goodrich, Tom, 582
Goodrich, Jeffrey M, 934
Goodrich, Paul, 1162
Goodson, Peter D, 632
Goodstein, Marcia, 976
Goodwin, Barton, 577
Gootee, Ting, 659
Gopinath, Rashmi, 1158
Gorczynski, Brian, 1927
Gordon, Michael L., 128
Gordon, Chris, 223
Gordon, Benjamin, 383
Gordon, James, 654
Gordon, Brett, 912
Gordon, Bing, 1079
Gordon, Casey, 1341
Gordon, Eric M, 1693
Gordon, Jonathan, 1737
Gordon, Mark, 2200
Gordon PhD, Carl L., 1383
Gore, Arun, 860
Gorenberg, Mark, 2018
Gores, Tom, 1455
Gorgi, Habib Y, 1278
Gorin, Matt, 535
Gorman, Chuck, 466
Gorman, Thomas W, 1639
Gorman, Michael, 1728
Gormley, Mark K, 1108
Gormly III, Matthew E, 1984
Gorton, David S., 1779
Gosavi, Pramod, 3
Gosline, Timothy, 1576

Gosselin, Luke, 448
Gotsch, Maria, 1422
Gottesman, Blake L., 257
Gottesman, Wesley, 328
Gottesman, Greg, 1501
Gouhin, Pat, 3247
Gould, Arthur P., 174
Gould, Andrew G, 174
Gould, Dave, 1790
Gouw, Theresia, 48
Gouw, Theresia, 182
Govan, Chris, 2201
Goy, Michael, 1267
Grabowski, Nick, 1665
Grace, Kyle, 902
Gracias, Antonio, 1904
Grad, Alissa, 848
Grad, Jonathan, 902
Grafer, John, 1625
Graham, Hatch, 185
Graham, Drew, 227
Graham, Stephen X, 563
Graham, Gary, 737
Graham, Steven C., 851
Graham, Kenneth A., 1018
Graham, Robert, 1431
Graham, Christopher D., 1742
Graham, Michael, 2199
Graig, Les, 1317
Grammer, Jeff, 2231
Granoff, Michael D., 1466
Granski, Miki, 538
Grant, Chris, 1056
Grant, Ruairi, 1314
Grapkowski, Andrew, 101
Grasshoff, Sven K., 1377
Grassinger, Paul M, 165
Graunke, Terrence M., 1095
Gravano, Dave, 1976
Graves, Brian, 630
Graves, Isaac, 3246
Gray, Jonathan, 280
Gray, Michael N., 1498
Grayken, John Patrick, 1144
Grayson, Bruns, 22
Grayson III, McComma, 912
Grayzel, MD, David, 193
Greeley, Michael, 749
Green, Kevin, 546
Green, Jason, 666
Green, Kirsten, 763
Green, Nicholas, 1103
Green, Kevin R, 1856
Green, Mitch, 2075
Green, PhD, Anthony P., 249
Greenberg, Russell J., 104
Greenberg, Gregory L., 104
Greenberg, Blair, 336
Greenberg, Myles D, 476
Greenberg, David, 1045
Greenberg, Alan, 2136
Greene, Karen, 52
Greene, Michael, 65
Greene, Bob, 535
Greene III, James H., 952
Greenfield, Matt, 1554
Greenhill, Robert F., 869
Greenrod, Colleen, 293
Greenwald, Bruce, 64
Greenwald, Shai, 383
Greenwald, Gerald, 867
Greer, Thomas L, 797
Greer, Phil, 1382
Greff, John, 1656
Gregor, Alex, 1082
Gregorich, Michael D., 1746
Greif, Lloyd, 874

Executive Name Index

Greifenkamp, Daniel J., 243
Greiwe, Brad, 728
Grenfall, Steven J, 1605
Gretsch, Greg, 1028
Grey, Richard G., 942
Griest, David, 1691
Griffin, Marshall, 530
Griffin, Carter, 1888
Griffiths, Michael, 2162
Griffor, Jeff, 1122
Grigg, Charles S., 418
Grigsby, Brian, 546
Grim, Paul, 693
Grim, Paul, 1757
Grimaldi, Brendyn T, 902
Grimm, Angie, 971
Grinnell, Rick, 713
Grinnell, Rick, 833
Grishin, Dmitry, 879
Grissom, Douglas C, 1160
Griswold, Kirk B, 165
Griswold, Kyle, 796
Grizzell, Steve, 1004
Groh, Thomas R., 104
Groh, Doug, 481
Groh, Christian, 1484
Groos, Tom, 490
Gros, Florent, 1350
Grose, Madison F., 1742
Gross, Michael, 254
Gross, Lauren, 778
Gross, Bill, 976
Gross, Stewart KP, 1127
Gross Jr, Jorge, 1859
Gross-Loh, David, 223
Grossman, Jay, 20
Grousbeck, H. Irving, 952
Grover, Tony, 1596
Groves, Thomas, 63
Grovic, Mark, 1298
Grua, Peter, 941
Gruber, Adam S., 687
Gruber, Michael, 987
Gruber, Michael C., 1613
Grubstein, Peter S.H., 1324
Gruenberg, Paul, 155
Grum, Allen F, 1526
Grunberg, Gregory, 1147
Grunberg, Lee M., 2218
Gruner, Harry, 1045
Gruss, Ralf, 136
Gruzen, Alex, 546
Gubbay, David, 717
Gubbels, Michael, 2281
Guerin Beresini, Debra, 1015
Guerrero, Alejandro, 49
Guff, Drew, 1681
Guffey, Steve, 838
Guiliana DPM, John, 1288
Guimaraes, Aflalo, 1022
Guinness, Oliver, 1258
Gulati, Mukul, 2017
Guldin, Andreas, 669
Guleri, Tim, 1672
Gulino, Daniel, 1567
Gullans PhD, Steve, 704
Gulve PhD, Eric, 270
Gunderson, Maurice, 207
Gunderson, Maurice, 208
Gunn, Greg, 490
Gunther, Craig, 281
Gunton, Jim, 1329
Guo, Sarah, 877
Gupta, Vishal, 263
Gupta, Neeraj, 456
Gupta, Ramneek, 488
Gupta, Amit, 506

Gupta, Arun, 518
Gupta, Vinod, 701
Gupta, Bulbul, 1397
Gupta, Krishna K, 1585
Gupta, Arjun, 1795
Gupta, Shyam, 2283
Gupta, Sophie, 2283
Gur, Saar, 457
Gurasich, Brad, 427
Gurewitz, Aaron M, 1592
Gusenius, Mik, 466
Gussarsky, David, 1125
Gustafson, Andrew S, 1686
Gutfreund, Joshua L., 496
Guthart, Leo, 1834
Guthrie, David, 109
Guttman, Randy, 1045
Guttman, Bill, 1626
Guttman, William, 1799
Gutwein, Victor, 1159
Guzman, Arlene, 394
Guzy, Melissa, 149
Gwirtsman, Charles, 1090

H

Ha, Perry, 627
Haarmaan, Oliver, 2243
Haas, Jonathan M, 494
Haas, Beth, 578
Haber, Warren H., 777
Hadley, Christopher J., 257
Haeger, Kent C, 935
Hafler, Jason P, 1621
Hagenah, Pamela, 1008
Hagerman, Lisa, 596
Hagerty, Sophie, 849
Hagerty, Thomas M., 1818
Haghgooie, Anna, 1618
Hahn, Eugene, 1043
Haight, H H, 163
Hairston, Tanaha, 1824
Halak, PhD, Brian K., 622
Haley, Tim, 1537
Hall, Timothy T., 478
Hall, John E., 950
Hall, Russell B, 1110
Hall, Steven E, 1128
Hall, Matt, 2081, 2180
Hall, PhD, Charles M., 140
Hallene, James N., 410
Hallett, Bruce, 1237
Halley, Frederic, 1319
Halloran, Todd W., 786
Halow, James, 371
Halstedt, Steve, 443
Hamamci, Ruchan, 2069
Hamati, Edward, 270
Hambrook, Barclay W., 2035
Hamel, John, 568
Hamelsky, Lawrence S., 257
Hamer PhD, John E, 844
Hamers, Ralph, 1880
Hamerslag, Steven J, 1871
Hamid, Mamoon, 1079
Hamilton, Arlan, 221
Hamilton, Chauncey, 623
Hamilton, Charles, 1090
Hamilton, Matthew G, 1754
Hammarskjold, Philip, 927
Hammer, Michael Christoph, 305
Hammer, John R, 1444
Hammond, Kevin T., 1043
Hamner, Patrick, 1424
Hamrick III, L. Watts, 1410
Hamwee, Robert A., 1300
Han, Ronald, 908, 909
Han, Philip, 1602

Hanafi, Ammar H., 87
Hanauer, Nick, 1644
Handreke, Patrick W.A., 2246
Hankins, Matthew, 931
Hankinson, Henry W., 695
Hanna, William A., 374
Hanna, Stephen A., 1747
Hannon, Robert M., 1826
Hansen, Lee C, 1214
Hanson, David, 1156
Hanson, Craig, 1319
Hanssens, Christopher G, 699
Hao, Kenneth, 1685
Hao, Sabrina, 2102
Hapgood, Kallie, 878
Haque, Promod, 1346
Hara, George, 603
Hara, Michael, 928
Harberg, Joseph L, 1552
Harbert, Billy L., 285
Harbert, Raymond J., 907
Harden, Michael, 177
Hardgrave, Eric, 53
Hardiman, James, 586
Hardin, Jim, 2043
Harding, Richard, 1015
Harding, Bill, 1908
Hardman, Scott, 82
Hardy, John A., 695
Hardy, Roger, 2137
Hardymon, Felda, 263
Hargrove, Heidi, 703
Hargrove, Thomas M., 893
Haring-Smith, Whitney, 134
Harjes, Richard, 1317
Harkrider, John T, 1067
Harlan, Leonard M., 425
Harlan, Jason, 726
Harlan, Bill, 1481
Harman, Drew, 1014
Harman, Fred, 1361
Harrick, Steve, 1006
Harriman, Gregory, 269
Harrington, Richard J, 568
Harrington, John, 1375
Harris, Matt, 224
Harris, Kirby, 232
Harris, Hadley, 680
Harris, Geoff, 757
Harris, Chris, 790
Harris, John, 1033
Harris, Arlan, 1244
Harris, Dr. Ryan A, 1346
Harris, Parker, 1610
Harris, David W, 1710
Harris, Richard, 2118
Harris, Christopher, 2142
Harrison, Justin, 364
Harrison, Donald C., 460
Harrison, Brian, 1470
Harrison, Glenn C, 1472
Harrison, Bradley C, 1635
Harrison, Nancy, 2032
Harrison, M.D., Seth L., 144
Harroch, Richard, 1908
Hart, Craig, 211
Hart CFA, Rob C, 1794
Hartanto, Steven, 465
Hartenbaum, Howard, 200
Hartfield, Justin, 665
Hartong III, Hendrik J., 360
Hartong, Jr., Hendrik J., 360
Hartwell, Sam, 204
Harward, Seth, 793
Hasebroock, Mark, 635
Haskell, Sherri, 391
Hass, Jay, 1597

Hass, David, 2049
Hassan, Kamil, 856
Hassanein, Ossama, 1310
Hassid, Mony, 1158
Hatch, Chad, 276
Hatfield, S Kim, 554
Hatfield, Mark, 1796
Hatherly, John A., 2008
Hatzimemos, Eric, 1689
Haub, Christian W.E., 669
Haug, Andreas, 641
Haughian, Andrew, 2205
Haughn, Ryan, 2237
Hawkins, Matt, 558
Hawkins, Tom, 770
Hawkins, John, 822
Hawkins, Brian, 1977
Hawks, Randy, 493
Hawks III, Donald L, 356
Hawley, Stuart W, 1627
Hawley Jr, Frank J, 1627
Haydel, Marcia, 1434
Hayes, Brooke, 156
Hayes, David, 322
Hayes, Rob, 742
Hayes, John G., 862
Haykin, Randy, 1390
Haynes, Travis, 228
Haynes, David, 796
Haynes, Stephen R, 835
Hays, Joe T., 612
Haythornthwaite, Charles, 2072
Hayward, Laurence, 987
Haywood, Jeff, 1720
Hazard, Chip, 756
Hazarika, Bahniman, 860
Hazen, Ned, 1122
He, Benson, 897
Headley, Robert, 978
Headrick, Mark, 538
Healy, Christian, 367
Healy, Robert P, 470
Healy, JJ, 853
Healy, Patrick, 927
Healy, James, 1700
Heath, Chad, 674
Hebb, Jr., Donald B., 21
Hebbar, Kiran, 1901
Hebrank MD, Gregory T, 1102
Hedrick, Tom, 1946
Heersink, Ewout, 2201
Heflin, William, 1076
Heglie, Eric D., 989
Heidecorn, David, 1092
Heilbronn, Charles, 1263
Heimann, Robert A, 1575
Heinen, Joseph H, 847
Heinmiller, Joseph, 851
Heintzman, Andrew, 2153
Heinze, Kristina, 470
Heitzmann, Rick, 744
Heivly, Chris, 194
Hejazi, Shahram, 269
Helbing, Scott C., 595
Helfin, Angela, 3259
Hellier, David, 260
Helmedag, Bobby, 1559
Helou, Francois, 189
Heltzer, Jason, 1385
Hemingway, Ryan, 689
Hemmeter, Christopher R, 1808
Hemmig, Raymond C, 1552
Hender, Eric, 16
Henderson, John, 970
Henderson, Ted, 1630
Henderson, David A, 1856
Henderson, David, 2282

Executive Name Index

Henderson-Cohen, Michael, 850
Hendrix, Blair, 223
Hendy, Patrick, 518
Heneine, Carlos, 1518
Henikoff, Troy, 1181
Henley, J Rudy, 1262
Hennegan, John, 1670
Hennessy, James, 2275
Henrickson, Stuart, 2226
Henry, George J, 1131
Henry, Jay R., 1410
Henry, Peter, 1647
Henry, Desmond, 1858
Henry, Chandra, 2171
Henshall, Laing, 2168
Hensley, Carolina B, 1487
Hera, Jonathan, 2179
Herb, Rob, 1629
Hermann, Matthew, 178
Hermouet, Laurent D., 190
Hernandez, Bruce M., 1727
Hernon, Marty, 315
Heron, Patrick, 785
Herriott, Ashton, 368
Herrod, Dr. Steve, 820
Herron, Dave, 499
Hershenson, Mar, 1426
Hersman, Brian, 1045
Herthel, Christopher, 501
Hertzmark, Andrew, 822
Herz, Peter, 7
Heslam, Shar, 257
Hess, David, 1845
Hess Jr, Ronald C, 1480
Hester, Robert, 1349
Heston, Tim, 258
Hetu, Daniel, 2173
Hetz, E David, 573
Heuer, Kenneth J, 1075
Heyman, Justin, 838
Heymann, Maia, 536
Hibblen, Brian, 1689
Hickey, Tom, 1507
Hickey, Kyle, 2237
Hickman, R Trent, 1929
Hicks, George G., 1909
Hicks, III, H Beecher, 1532
Higgen, Uwe, 305
Higgerson, Cliff, 980
Higginbotham, John B, 1717
Higgins, Ron, 942
Higgins, Brian, 1049
Higgins, Pete, 1644
Highland, Erika, 832
Hildebrandt, Joseph P, 584
Hilderbrand, Mark G., 952
Hilinski, Scott, 1278
Hill, Jason, 1197
Hill, Brent, 1385
Hill, Grant, 1433
Hill, Geoff A., 1580
Hill, Eugene, 1631
Hill, Duncan, 2176
Hills, Michael, 1077
Hills, Mason, 1551
Hinaman, Robert, 47
Hinck, Jeff, 1525
Hinkle, Ryan, 1005
Hinton, Summer, 2057
Hippeau, Eric, 1114
Hipwood, Charlie, 1175
Hirose, Ted, 1793
Hirsch, David, 527
Hirsch, Brian, 1851
Hirsch MD, PhD, David, 1147
Hirsch MD, PhD, Russell, 1495
Hirshland, Mike, 1549

Hitchner, Doug, 1368
Hixon, Dylan, 830
Hixon, Eric, 830
Hixon, Todd, 1290
Hjerpe, Eric, 1069
Hliboki, Lorraine, 1466
Hnatiuk, Steve, 2169
Ho, Charles, 40
Ho, James, 63
Ho, Eva, 729
Ho, Gregory P, 1733
Ho, Derrick, 2180
Ho-Walker, Joshua, 1314
Hoag, Jay, 1787
Hobbs, Jerry, 364
Hobman, Steven, 1316
Hobson, Blaine, 2280
Hoch, Scott, 793
Hoch, James S., 1779
Hochberg, Steve, 179
Hochberg, Benjamin A, 1108
Hochman, Andrew B., 1594
Hodge, Bruce, 2210
Hodges, Michael, 185
Hodges, Deborah, 1231
Hodges, Philip L, 1536
Hodges, Daryl, 2033
Hodgson, David, 819
Hodgson, Dan, 1135
Hoe, Janey, 485
Hoegler, Arnold J, 1107
Hoehn-Saric, Christopher, 1745
Hoesley, John, 1481
Hoesterey, Brian, 63
Hoffer, Daniel, 207
Hoffman, Beth, 257
Hoffman, Paul E, 630
Hoffman, Reid, 877
Hoffman, Spencer P, 1151
Hoffman MD, Stephen J, 1693
Hoffort, Michael, 2108
Hofmann, Don, 566
Hofmann, Kevin, 1580
Hogan, Brian, 2078
Holbrook, Ben, 1174
Holcomb, Brett P, 1494
Holcomb, Charles, 1839
Holden, Chris, 552
Holden, MD, Stuart, 1492
Holdsberg, Jeffrey, 376
Holec, Monica J., 1115
Holekamp, Cliff, 570
Holiday, Aaron, 12
Holland, Kirk, 35
Holland, Paul, 773
Holland, Jeffrey J, 1639
Holland Jr, Thomas O, 1424
Hollander, Seth H, 1085
Hollend, Michael, 2264
Hollin, Mitchell L, 1140
Hollis, Mark, 445
Hollod, Chris, 14
Holman, Kelly, 2125
Holmes, Stephen, 1014
Holson, Laura C., 1300
Holstein, Roger C., 1933
Holt, Matthew S., 1300
Holt, Charles, 2153
Holtz, Gerald, 1496
Holzbaur, Inès, 2031
Homcy, MD, Charles, 1814
Homer, Paul, 1344
Hompesch, Michael P, 633
Honda, Osuke, 597
Honeybourne, Will, 741
Hong, Karen, 1780
Hooper, Herbert H., 119

Hooper, Steve, 978
Hooper, Christopher, 1973
Hooten, Ken, 531
Hootnick, Larry, 53
Hoover, James B, 588
Hoover, Betsy, 937
Hopeman, Wei, 149
Hopkins, Adam, 660
Hopkins, William, 1368
Hopping, Andrew, 1853
Horan, Avshalom, 340
Horing, David, 111
Horing, Jeff, 1005
Hornby, Mary T, 17
Hornby, Zachary, 489
Horne, Mark, 1459
Horne, Bob, 2021
Hornik, David, 200
Hornthal, Jim, 194
Horowitz, Ben, 125
Horowitz, Joe, 972
Horowitz, Richard M, 1524
Horst, Sandy, 300
Horvilleur, Camilo E., 931
Hosaisy, Fred, 1697
Hostetter, Davis, 899
Hough, G. Thomas, 1419
Houghton, Karen, 191
House, Dawn, 2148
Howard, Chris, 978
Howard, John, 1026
Howard, Paul A, 1198
Howard, Matthew D, 1346
Howard, Newton, 1394
Howard, Jeffrey, 1613
Howard, Andrew J., 1663
Howard, Alan, 1795
Howard, Randall, 2271
Howard MD, Lawrence, 957
Howe, Bob, 8
Howe, Timothy F, 476
Howe, Timothy, 923
Howell, Sheldon, 973
Howell, Ronald S, 2007
Hower, Bob, 58
Hower, Lee, 1322
Howes, Ian A.W., 30
Howland, James, 1256
Howorth, Greg, 377
Hoyt, Thomas B., 988
Hsiao, Paul, 399
Hsieh, Michael, 799
Hsieh, Wen, 1079
Hsieh, Tony, 1914
Hsing, Peter, 1219
Hsu, Ta-Lin, 897
Hsu, Mark, 897
Hsu, Geoffrey C., 1383
Hsu, William, 1783
Hsu, Jonathan, 1850
Hsui, Jenny, 475
Hu, Eion, 1049
Huang, Edward, 280
Huang, Timothy, 1116
Huang PhD, He, 1340
Huber, Michael, 1508
Huber, Harold, 2160
Hubler, Jodi, 1111
Hudson, Pete, 94
Hudson, L'Sheryl D, 695
Hudson, William L, 1332
Hudson, Charles, 1475
Huey, Henry, 173
Huff, Peter, 294
Huff, Greg, 702
Huffard, Jay, 533
Hufford, Kyle, 230

Huffsmith, Joseph, 1376
Hufnagel, Alec, 1066
Hughes, Donald W., 386
Hughes, William S., 1498
Hughes, Edward, 1499
Hughes III, Charles B, 644
Huie, Tony, 1677
Hulecki, Gregory, 712
Hull, David, 443
Hullah, Daniel, 812
Hullet, JK, 1094
Hulme, Tom, 894
Humes, Robert, 1042
Hummer, John, 959
Humphries, Andrew, 914
Hunkapiller, Michael, 87
Hunnewell, Luisa, 1986
Hunnicutt, Jonathan E., 1979
Hunt, John, 20
Hunt, Jim, 288
Hunt, Ron, 1297
Hunter, Peter A., 214
Hunter, Dick, 595
Hunter, Wally, 677
Hunter-Syed, Abigail, 1105
Hurd, Jason, 362
Hurley, Matthew J, 1377
Hursever, Evis, 698
Hurst, Jeffrey M., 523
Hurst, Bob, 560
Hurwitz, Roger, 1944
Huseby, Thomas S, 1640
Hussain, Anwar, 1562
Huston, Jim, 1467
Hutcheson, Zenas, 1525
Hutchins, Will, 2103
Hutchinson, Tamiko, 1009
Hutchinson, George R., 1036
Hutton, Wende, 389
Huynh, Stacy, 152
Hwang, John S., 786
Hwang, Victor, 990
Hyatt, Michael, 1026
Hyatt, Nabeel, 1718
Hyndman, Stephen, 827

I

Iacovone, Jack, 1287
Iaffaldano, Paul, 274, 1412
Ianello, Peter, 1364
Iannarone, Thomas, 280
Iatropoulos, Nikos, 1055
Ibrahim, Maha, 389
Idemoto, Derek, 485
Ifergan, Sam, 2141
Ignaczak, Tony, 1507
Ilhuyn Cho, Jerry, 691
Illikman CFA, James A, 1429
Ilsoe, Bo, 1331
Imai, Shinya, 1241
Imhoff, W Joseph, 1280
Imran, Mir, 984
Ingram, Robert A, 918
Ingram, Paulus J, 2239
Inman, Bob, 1130
Inman, Tom, 1130
Insalaco, Steven, 372
Iovino, Nicholas, 834
Irani, Martin, 905
Irish, Rebecca, 1433
Irvin, Thomas J., 890
Irwin, Scott, 1543
Irwin, Brenda, 2229
Isaacson, Mark, 1539
Iseman, Frederick J, 478
Isenberg, Robbie, 2075
Isetta, Lincoln, 1255

Executive Name Index

Ishbia, Justin, 1670
Ishii, Masazumi, 217
Isono, Masa, 603
Israelsohn, Daniel, 2216
Israely, Gal, 438
Issa, Natalie, 594
Istock, David, 297

J

Jaako, Harry, 2091
Jacks, Joel R., 509
Jackson, Grant A, 551
Jackson, Adam, 775
Jackson, Kevin M., 878
Jackson, Michael C., 952
Jackson, Deborah, 1458
Jackson, Angela, 1467
Jackson, Herbert W, 1544
Jackson, Jeff, 1808
Jackson, Donald, 2207
Jackson, Tim, 2253
Jackson, Ron, 2267
Jackson, Jon, 3249
Jacob, Sasha, 2069
Jacobs, Brian, 666
Jacobsen, Mark, 1359
Jacobson, Dean, 28
Jacobson, Linda, 31
Jacobson, Sven M, 663
Jacobson, Matthew, 1100
Jacobson, Scott, 1162
Jacobson, Glenn, 1853
Jacobson, Lorne, 2267
Jacques, Dan, 2138
Jadeja, Asha, 624
Jadot, R. Bryan, 928
Jaduszliwer, Ariel, 327
Jaeger, Wilfred, 923
Jaffe, Danny, 127
Jaffe, David, 449
Jaffe, Robert M, 1708
Jaffin, David W., 324
Jaggers, John, 1661
Jaggers, Kurt R, 1778
Jaggi, Dennis F., 672
Jahns, David W, 809
Jain, Uttam, 190
Jain, Anurag, 1436
Jain, Neenah, 1523
Jain PhD, Mudit, 1774
Jaisinghani, Sumeet, 1602
Jake, Krist, 1538
Jakeway, Phil, 1131
Jalan, Nupur, 838
Jalanbo, Khaled, 1902
Jamal, Asad, 691
James, Brian, 491
James, Simon, 696
James, William E, 1583
James, Janet, 1583
James, Daniel, 1853
James, Jamie, 2136
James, Meli, 3253
Jamieson, Don, 377
Janchar, Matthew A., 257
Jander, Rich, 1169
Jandernoa, Michael, 946
Janes, Thomas, 1071
Jang, Ray, 1559
Jani, Amish, 744
Janis, Frances N., 1466
Janish, Michael, 1906
Janmohamed, Arif, 1125
Janney, Dan, 94
Janower, Andrew S., 458
Janson, Jeremy, 785
Jaramillo, Jorge, 1387

Jargiello, David, 758
Jarman, MBA, Peter, 561
Jarve, John W., 1203
Jay, MD, Jeffrey R., 864
Jazayeri, Rouz, 431
Jeandron III, Raymond J, 1148
Jegen, David, 711
Jenkins, J. Blair, 464
Jenkins, Robert, 1470
Jenkins, Adam, 2085
Jennings, Mark, 822
Jennings, Thomas H, 1754
Jensen, Andrew, 1063
Jensen, Peter T, 1720
Jerstad, Mike, 1474
Jesselson, Michael, 1038
Jessup, Kevin B, 1609
Jiang, Franklin, 2221
Jin, Will, 2103
Jindal, Sheena, 520
Jivraj, Alkarim, 2103
Joaquin, James, 1363
Johan, Paul, 227
Johann PhD, Peter, 1325
Johansson, Curtis, 368
Johns, Brad, 2283
Johnson, Debbie, 20
Johnson, Michael, 60
Johnson, B. Kristine, 67
Johnson, Kent, 82
Johnson, Kristin, 96
Johnson, Gregg E., 266
Johnson, Jeffrey, 279
Johnson, Chad, 466
Johnson, Christian B., 786
Johnson, Jeffrey W., 831
Johnson, Craig N., 836
Johnson, Timothy D., 847
Johnson, Stephen M., 952
Johnson, Dave, 1009
Johnson, Ken, 1064
Johnson, Richard, 1228
Johnson, Scott, 1290
Johnson, Jared L., 1417
Johnson, Gregory, 1490
Johnson, Kinney, 1656
Johnson, Mark A, 1865
Johnson, Jim, 1917
Johnson, James A, 1997
Johnson, Christopher A., 2085
Johnson, James C., 2246
Johnston, John, 200
Johnston, William, 912
Johnston, Robert, 1048
Johnston, A. Bruce, 1778
Johnston, Kel, 2159
Johnston PhD, Allan, 1775
Johnstone, Brent P, 1513
Johnstone, Trevor, 2118
Jolly, Brian, 960
Jones, Elliott, 170
Jones, Casey, 206
Jones, Charles S., 245
Jones, Ross M., 257
Jones, Rick, 269
Jones, Tom, 629
Jones, Gregory, 654
Jones, Leland, 674
Jones, Christopher N., 747
Jones, J. Chris, 898
Jones, M. Scott, 898
Jones, Andy, 1172
Jones, David M, 1210
Jones, Brent, 1341
Jones, Matt, 1355
Jones, Thad, 1507
Jones, Mark, 1573

Jones, David, 1712
Jones, Terry L., 1773
Jones, Kateri, 1773
Jones, Daniel G., 1818
Jones, Craig A.T., 1826
Jones, Thomas W, 1875
Jones, Nigel W, 1875
Jones, Ellis, 1961
Jones III, Reginald L., 867
Jones, Jr., David, 477
Jonge Poernik, John R, 1134
Jordan, Jeff, 125
Jordan, Buck, 400
Jordan, Wilma, 1037
Jordan, Len, 1162
Jordon, Scott, 840
Jordon, James, 1452
Joseph, Richard, 197
Jrolf, Mark, 929
Jubeir, TJ, 409
Jubeir, Julie, 409
Judge, Paul, 1412
Julich, Chris, 696
Jung, Edward, 1010
Juricic, Donald A, 1560
Jurvetson, Steve, 803

K

Kabakoff, David, 924, 1700
Kabbes, Scott R, 247
Kaczmarczyk, Holly, 1971
Kaczorowski, Joe, 334
Kaczynski, Bill, 341
Kadavy, Annie, 1537
Kaden, John T., 1282
Kaden, Rebecca, 1884
Kafker, Roger B, 1778
Kagan, Peter, 1957
Kahle, G. Kent, 893
Kahn, Brian, 1937
Kahvejian, Avak, 748
Kairouz, Habib, 1561
Kairouz, Habib, 2231
Kaiser, Joe, 1205
Kalcevich, Julius, 970
Kalish, Adam, 1155
Kalkanis, Peter, 1561, 2231
Kalman, Jonathan, 1029
Kalnow, Andrew H, 90
Kambhampati, Krishnamurty, 507
Kamdar, PhD, Kim, 622
Kaminsky, Samantha, 553
Kamra, Deepak, 389
Kamra, Atul, 1690
Kanal, Utkarsh, 201
Kanayev, Alex, 2027
Kandler, Ahim, 761
Kane, Michael, 377
Kane, Edward W, 912
Kaneb, Thomas, 2186
Kaneko MD, Yasunori, 1693
Kang, PhD, JJ, 519
Kanji, Azra, 20
Kapeskas, Rimas, 383
Kaplan, David, 160
Kaplan, Larry, 245
Kaplan, Michael B, 1138
Kaplan, Teddy, 1300
Kaplanis, Scott, 2102
Kapoor, Rishi, 1021
Kapoor, Arrun, 1691
Kapor, Mitchell, 1058
Kapor Klein, Freada, 1058
Karabelas, Argeris, 415
Karas, Lindsay, 1285
Karchon, Evonna, 985
Karlson, Steven E, 1994

Karol, Steven E, 1963
Karol, Julia, 1963
Karp, Amit, 263
Karp, Gabe, 608
Karp, CPA, Murray, 676
Karsh, Bruce, 1362
Kashyap, Nagraj, 1158
Kaskow, Jonathan, 294
Kasper, Paul S., 679
Kassam, Shamsh, 2249
Kassouf, Karen, 439
Kastner, Tom, 1369
Katabi, Maha, 1700
Katarincic, Jay, 629
Katcha, Joseph R, 935
Kats, Victor, 178
Kats, Greg, 401
Katz, Brandon M., 494
Katz, Rami, 705
Katz, Alex, 724
Katz, Harold, 896
Katz, David A, 896
Katz, Jed, 1032
Katzman, Elliot M., 523
Kaufman, Howard, 1641
Kaul, Samir, 1073
Kaup, Eric, 940
Kaushal MD, Mohit, 19
Kawasaki, Guy, 810
Kayden, Joelle, 36
Kaye, Michael S, 503
Kaye, Charles R, 1957
Kayler, J Allan, 1232
Ke, Yan, 1340
Kean, Thomas H, 1506
Keane, Gen. John M, 1636
Keane, Patrick, 2078
Kearl, Jeff, 1428
Keating, Ryan, 1430
Keaveney, Thomas, 60
Keay, Jeffrey, 912
Kedar, Sharon, 1342
Keefe, Edward J, 1157
Keefe, Patrick, 2063
Keehn, Peter, 88
Keen, Eric, 551
Kehaya, Mark W, 1214
Kehoe, Scott A., 1018
Keis, Matthew E, 815
Keith, Robert, 1830
Kell, Joe, 1310
Kelley, Michael, 151
Kelley, Douglas M., 406
Kelley, Sean M., 878
Kelley, Brian P, 1133
Kelley, Ryan, 1670
Kelley, Alan, 1691
Kelley, James P., 1933
Kellner, Peter, 1564
Kelly, Jonathan D., 407
Kelly, J. Ryan, 777
Kelly, Robert E, 1741
Kelly II, Thomas L., 463
Kelly MD, Doug, 87
Kelly PhD, Regis B, 1238
Kelsall, Bill, 682
Kelsey, Beth, 549
Kember, Ken, 2106
Kendall Jr, Donald R, 1067
Kenealey, Kevin P, 1174
Kenealy, Pat, 1566
Kennedy, Danny, 370
Kennedy, Charles, 385
Kennedy, Bill, 807
Kennedy, Keith, 1192
Kennedy, Brendan, 1484
Kennedy, Mark, 2023

Executive Name Index

Kennedy, Thomas, 2160
Kennedy Jr, William J, 1377
Kenney, George C, 1667
Kenny, Michael, 1986
Kent, Chelsea, 1103
Kent, Martin, 2160
Kenter, Louis W, 1494
Kenworthy, Karen, 1751
Kermani, Moe, 2270
Kern, Rene, 819
Kern, Jay, 1070
Kerr, Anita K., 243
Kerr, Karen, 812
Kerrigan, Charles, 1697
Kershisnik, Thomas, 746
Kertzman, Mitchell, 959
Kessinger, William C., 1419
Kessler, Daniel, 578
Kessler Jr., W. Jack, 496
Kester, Kevin, 1681
Kestler, Paul D, 607
Kevin, Quintin, 56
Kewalramani, Kabir, 253
Keywell, Brad, 1121
Keziah, Sanford, 1094
Khalifa, Omar, 2110
Khalin, Alex, 1928
Khaliq, Asad, 48
Khan, Agha, 1746
Khanna, Raman, 604
Khatwani, Hemant, 691
Kheng, Jennifer W, 1116
Kherani, MD, Aftab R., 73
Khosla, Vinod, 1073
Khosrowshahi, Behzad, 2097
Kibble, Robert, 1239
Kidd, William J, 1075
Kidle, Dan, 150
Kienzle, Trevor, 545
Kiernan, James T., 2080
Kikta, Roman, 1244
Kilar, Jason, 1829
Kilcrease, Laura J, 1857
Kiley, Richard, 290
Kilgallon, John, 223
Kilic, Ugur, 2069
Killackey, Christopher T, 1473
Killoren Chadwell, Tracy, 6
Kim, Han, 100
Kim, Andrew, 235
Kim, Eurie, 763
Kim, John, 936
Kim, Yoo Jin, 1108
Kim, Philip, 1131
Kim, Charlie, 1189
Kim, David, 1692
Kim PhD, Leo, 217
Kim, MD, John, 139
Kimball, Rick, 1787
Kimble, Matthew, 211
Kimerling, Daniel, 600
Kimmel, Wayne D, 1660
Kimmelman, Doug, 676
Kimsa, Kevin, 2240
Kimura, Kenichi, 1241
Kimzey, Jackie, 1661
Kincanon, Michelle, 127
King, Matthew, 497
King, Matthew A, 718
King, Christopher M., 878
King, Colton, 1090
King, Stephen V, 1473
King III, Madding, 387
King Neff, Steven, 997
King-Shaw Jr, Ruben J, 1168
Kingston, Brian, 2062
Kinley, James, 2071

Kinner, Michele, 1518
Kinsella, Kevin J., 209
Kinsey, Matt, 364
Kinsey, Edward, 1077
Kinsman, Brian, 362
Kirby, Steve, 300
Kirby, Robert, 843
Kircher, Demian, 1169
Kireker, Charles F, 789
Kirk, Randal J., 1815
Kirkpatrick, David, 1691
Kirnos, Ilya, 1677
Kirsch, Bill, 549
Kirtland, Kirt, 667
Kirwin III, John Paul, 165
Kislak, Jonathan I., 132
Kitchens, Ron, 1715
Kitching, Chris, 936
Kitterman, Roger, 1421
Kittler, Fred, 731
Kivitz, David, 156
Klaffky, Richard C, 740
Klahr, Jonathan, 1761
Klammer, Ronald J., 1369
Klammer, Steve, 1369
Klapper, Paul, 508
Klapper, Brad, 508
Klar, Larry, 2039
Klass, Daniel, 2163
Klee, Stephan, 2217
Klein, Jason, 28
Klein, Randal, 211
Klein, Karin, 287
Klein, Peter W, 351
Klein, Adam, 560
Klein, Terry, 595
Klein, Michael I, 1138
Klein, Gentry S, 1138
Klein, Justin, 1919
Kleinhandler, Mitchell, 615
Kleinman, Scott, 141
Kleinman, Ira D., 917
Kleinman, Blake, 927
Klemens, Jeff, 1606
Klessel, Lewis S., 1300
Klevens, Joshua A., 458
Kliman, Gil, 1014
Kline, John R., 1300
Kline, Dean M, 1431
Klinefelter, Josh, 202
Klingenstein, Paul, 19
Klinsky, Steven B, 1300
Kloos PhD, Steven D, 1861
Klosk, Craig B, 1984
Klueger, Randy, 540
Knapp, Hans, 2283
Knauss, Robert, 695
Knauss, Robert B, 1957
Kneen, John, 247
Knez, Brian J., 424
Knight, Lester B., 1594
Knight MD, Stephen, 711
Knitt, Brian, 469
Knoch, David, 1026
Knoke, Ailliam, 916
Knotts, Jerry, 3248
Knox, Dave, 1936
Knox, Elliott, 2049
Knudsen, Todd, 1412
Knutsen, John E, 1160
Koby, Michael, 4
Koch, Simon, 2138
Kocher MD, Bob, 1918
Kodde, Pieter, 1131
Koegler, David, 1196
Koenig, Peggy, 20
Koenig, Robert, 2004

Kogan, Eric D, 494
Kohlberg, James A, 1085
Kohlberg, James A., 1087
Kohr, Rick, 702
Kokones, Scott, 891
Kokron, Carlos, 1511
Kolada, Dave Harris, 2136
Kolbeins, Laurie G., 1801
Kolchinsky, Peter, 1522
Koldyke, Laird, 2000
Kole, John, 1146
Kollender, Richard S, 1510
Kolln, Thies O, 16
Kollock, David P, 836
Kolodny, Lauren, 48
Kolodny, Lauren, 182
Komada, Tim, 601
Kometz, MD, Avi, 179
Kondo, James, 824
Kong, Garheng, 924
Koo, David J., 1594
Kook, Grant J., 2129, 2277
Koontz, Paul, 773
Koopersmith, Adam, 1483
Kopelman, Michael, 655
Kopelman, Josh, 742
Kopp, Darby, 910
Kopp, Tim, 965
Korengold, Michael A.G., 679
Korn, Andrew, 1606
Kornacki, David, 3249
Kornreich, John, 1620
Korsten, Eric R., 330
Korte, Thomas, 129
Kortick, Daniel M, 1984
Kortschak, Walter, 1677
Kosematoglu, Mehmet, 253
Kosofsky, Kristen, 928
Kososki, Trent, 676
Kosoy, MD, Daniel H., 189
Kossow, Jon, 1346
Kostenko, Bill, 2050
Kosty, Michael, 336
Kosuge, Roy, 1773
Kotler, Steven, 831
Koulogeorge, Mark, 1242
Kovach, Jeffrey, 172
Kowal, CFA, Krzysztof A., 637
Kowalick, Dave, 892
Kra, Howard, 192
Kracum, Richard R, 1990
Kramer, Ted H., 904
Krane, David, 894
Kraus, Stephen, 263
Kraus, Matt, 441
Krauss, George, 70
Krauss, Marlene R., 1062
Krausz, Steven M, 1898
Krautzel, George, 1240
Kravis, Henry R, 1086
Kraynak, Mark, 48
Kreie, Paul, 1232
Krekel, David A, 1399
Kreml MD, Stephanie, 244
Krenn, Mike, 1615
Kreter, Dave, 828
Krier, Donald A, 2004
Krikorian, Jason, 597
Krikston, Joel, 1206
Kriscunas, Suzanne, 1576
Krishnamurthy, Arvind, 1226
Krnic, Sinisa, 1499
Krommenhoek, Sid, 79
Kronfeld, David, 1042
Kropp, JB, 1936
Krouse, Rodger R, 1755
Krueger, Alex T., 741

Krupa, Stephen M., 1500
Krupka, Mike, 224
Krusius, Jennifer, 518
Kryder, Chris, 749
Kuan, Leon, 745
Kubal, Larry, 1093
Kubo, Tatsuya, 912
Kucheman, William H., 272
Kuczinski, Anthony J, 1272
Kuegler, Tom, 1959
Kuehl, Ronald W, 792
Kuehl, Timothy, 1345
Kuelper, John, 178
Kuhling, Robert, 1379
Kulaga, Kenneth J., 725
Kulchenko, Lesya, 928
Kulman, W. Brent, 747
Kumar, Amit, 27
Kumar, Samir, 1017, 1158
Kumar, Manu, 1054
Kumble, C Todd, 1729
Kumin, Michael A., 862
Kunda, Elaine, 2092
Kundan, Gursh, 1002
Kundra, Monish, 518
Kung, Hsing, 46
Kung, Dr. Frank, 1943
Kung, Mona, 2132
Kunica, Matthew B., 2056
Kuntz, Edward L, 1654
Kuntz, Richard P, 1667
Kuo, Steve, 928
Kuribayashi, Doug, 1478
Kurshat, Marcus, 501
Kurtz, Tom, 1424
Kurtzman, Gary J, 1605
Kurzweil, Ethan, 263
Kushner, Joshua, 1823
Kusserow, Paul, 958
Kutcher, Ashton, 14
Kutsenda, Eric, 1648
Kutzkey, PhD, Tim, 519
Kuzon, Josh, 1531
Kvamme, Mark D., 631
Kwait, Brian, 1368
Kwan, Eric, 1142
Kwatinetz, Mike, 218
Kwok, Celine, 863
Kwong, Lara, 998
Kyle, Kimberly, 21

L

LaKing, Larry, 2181
LaMothe, Chris, 659
LaPeer PE CFA, Karle E, 1429
LaPorte, Steve, 1379
LaSalle, Michael A., 1663
LaSorda, Tom, 985
LaViolette, Paul, 1631, 1764
Labbat, Pete, 676
Lacavera, Anthony, 2128
Lacenere, Anthony M, 991
Lack, Jeremy D., 190
Lackey, Jennifer D, 1542
Lackey, Jr, G Thomas, 1542
Ladha, Farouk, 780
Ladsariya, Vivek, 1689
Lafayette, Justin, 2126
Lafferty, Edward A, 1626
Laffont, Philippe, 511
Laforteza, Amy L., 952
Lafortune, Francois, 2090
Lagerlund, Karin, 912
Laheny, A. Rachel, 1900
Lai, Ted, 974
Laitala, Christopher M, 1133
Lajous, René, 381

Executive Name Index

Lake II, Charles T, 1676
Lalande, Kevin M., 1622
Lam, James K., 898
Lam, Rachel, 981
Lamb, Damian, 2125
Lambert, Ben, 1428
Lamm, Peter, 722
Lamond, Pierre, 648
Lamont, Ann, 1361
Lamoureux, Pierre-Olivier, 848
Landgarten, Harris, 174
Lando, Anthony V, 39
Landy, Joseph P, 1957
Lane, David, 614
Lane, Tom, 676
Lane, Christopher, 1090
Lane, Curtis S, 1271
Lane, David, 1379
Lane, Jamie, 1869
Lane, Michael, 3257
Langdale, Rich, 1285
Langdon, Michael S, 792
Lange, MD, PhD, Lou, 183
Langeler, Gerry, 1392
Langensand, Leif, 130
Langer, Mark, 404
Langere, Damian, 814
Langill, Paul, 2029
Lanier, Cam, 1076
Lanigan, Pat, 1873
Lanik, Joel, 793
Lanning, Chris, 819
Lapcevic, Maja, 488
Lapica, Monty, 515
Lapides, Matt, 20
Larcen, Dell, 886
Lardin, Cliff, 434
Large, Barry, 640
Largent, Kyle, 832
Larkin, Raymond, 573
Larkin, Ian, 1169
Larkins, Stuart, 473
Larsen, Charles E, 39
Larson, Robert E., 24, 2005
Lasala, Carolyne, 849
Lasersohn, Jack W, 1931
Lasher, Stephen A., 893
Lasher, Stuart G, 1512
Lasher, Tyler, 1512
Lashkari PhD, Deval A, 1794
Lasky, Mitch, 251
Lasky, PhD, Larry, 519
Lasry, Marc, 211
Lassonde, Christian, 2143
Lathi, Vijay, 1297
Latterell, Patrick, 1098
Latzke, Dave, 466
Lau, Kenneth, 448
Lau, Gregory G, 1973
Lau, Sandra, 2029
Laudauer, Jay F, 1883
Lauder, Gary, 1099
Lauerwald, Eric, 1027
Laufert, Paul, 2165
Laurence, Andrew, 1937
Lavery, Mairead, 2106
Lavin, Tom, 1302
Lawee, David, 579
Lawler, Christopher, 851
Lawler, Joe, 1990
Lawless, Christian, 537
Lawlor, Augustine, 922
Lawrence, John, 1150
Lawrence, Charlotte, 1499
Lawrence, J Eric, 1552
Lawry, Richard V, 656
Lawson, Rich, 962

Lawson, Brian, 2062
Lawson-Johnston II, Peter O., 890
Lax, Charles R, 853
Lay, Michael, 2200
Laycock, Matthew, 202
Layden, Christopher A, 2014
Layton, Tim, 1707
Lazaridis, Mike, 2220
Lazarus, Amy S, 1729
Lazzer, Enio, 2103
Le, Thong Q, 30
Le, Huan, 954
Le Blanc, Robert, 2201
le Loux, Alain, 550
Le Ruyet, Jean-Francois, 1519
LeBlanc, Chris, 1795
LeMaile-Stovall, Troy, 1792
LeMay, John, 293
LeSieur, Stephen M, 1720
LeVert-Chiasson, Serge, 2239
Leach, Ray, 1051
Leaf, Kathryn, 1413
Leakos, Steven, 2115
Lebel, Felix-Etienne, 2056
Leck, Derek, 110
Leckie, Lars, 959
Leckrone, John, 57
Leder, Marc J, 1755
Lederer, Laurence, 330
Lederhausen, Mats, 568
Lederman, Marc, 1316
Lee, Nancy, 93
Lee, Anthony, 100
Lee, George J, 118
Lee, Peter, 231
Lee, Roger, 238
Lee, Kewsong, 416
Lee, Matt, 474
Lee, Dr. David, 496
Lee, Aileen, 553
Lee, Dr. Robert P, 613
Lee, Peter, 664
Lee, Sam, 730
Lee, Jenny, 827
Lee, Christopher, 832
Lee, Kenneth B, 918
Lee, Thomas H, 1108
Lee, Jeffrey, 1340
Lee, Lisa M., 1498
Lee, Lisa, 1499
Lee, David, 1653
Lee, Jess, 1657
Lee, John, 1719
Lee, Michael, 1776
Lee, Eric J, 1973
Lee, Daniel, 2066
Lee, V. Paul, 2270
Leeds, Jeffrey T, 1109
Leese, Steven A, 1505
Lefkoff, Kyle, 318
Lefkofsky, Eric, 1121
Legault, Eric, 2259
Legg, Chris, 1488
Leggat, Sara, 1659
Lehman, Paul, 1026
Lehr, Seth J, 1140
Lehr, Jonathan, 2006
Leibovitz, Hila, 438
Leibovitz, John, 518
Leibowitz, Matthew, 2216
Leichtman, Lauren B, 1115
Leigh, Mark, 953
Leighton, Douglas H., 638
Leiher, Edina, 78
Leiman, James, 1338
Lein, Julie, 1895
Leinauer, Matt, 402

Leischner, Steven, 943
Lemay, Jean-Philippe, 727
Lemmer, Johan, 2121
Lemmon, Tim, 135
Lemmons, Jr., William R., 672
Lenet, Scott, 794
Lengauer, PhD, Christoph, 1814
Lennox, Wally, 1465
Lentz, Nathaniel V, 1388
Leonard, Brian, 653
Leonard, H Jeffrey, 838
Leone, Douglas, 1657
Leong, Chris, 162
Leprince, Jean-Francois, 2086
Lerer, Kenneth, 1114
Lerer, Ben, 1114
Lerner, Steve, 1100
Lerohl, Mark, 2222
Leroux, James D., 181
Leroux, Philippe, 2251
Leschly, Jan, 415
Leschly, Mark, 1561
Lese, William D., 325
Lessin, Sam, 1696
Letinic MD PhD, Kresimir, 644
Lettmann, Jason, 1126, 1257
Leu Dennis, Alda, 995
Leudde, Colt, 893
Leung, Waiman, 1992
Leupold, Robert G., 24
Levandov, Rich, 209
Levandov, Richard W, 1178
Levchin, Max, 1634
Levchin, Nellie, 1634
Levental, Alex, 1025
Levin, Andrew, 1522
Levin, Jimmy, 1638
Levin, Mark, 1814
Levine, Daniel, 27
Levine, Jeremy, 263
Levine, Michael G., 359
Levine, Mark, 540
Levine, Seth, 779
Levine, Arthur, 1115
Levine, Seth, 1245
Levinson, Joshua M., 848
Levitan, Dan, 1186
Levy, Anton, 819
Levy, Paul S., 1043
Levy, Jay, 2016
Levy-Weiss, Gigi, 1323
Lew, Jacob J, 1133
Lewis, Charles, 261
Lewis, Rand, 443
Lewis, Philip, 797
Lewis, Blake, 1573
Lewis, J Christopher, 1579
Lewis, Joshua, 1611
Lewis, Legrand, 1707
Lewis, Rick, 1898
Lewis, William, 2020
Lewis, Shawn, 2266
Lewis II, Alan D., 1016
Lewy, Glen, 957
Leybold, Christin, 641
Li, Ping, 27
Li, Jeanne, 127
Li, Lixin, 1340
Li, Nan, 1363
Li, Quinn, 1511
Li, Regan, 2077
Liao, Sophie, 1396
Liao, Bill, 1709
Libby, Oliver, 1689
Liccardo, Darren, 431
Lichter, PhD, Jay, 209
Lieberman, Alex, 491

Lieberman, Jeff, 1005
Liew, Jeremy, 1125
Liff, M Steven, 1755
Lightburn, David, 191
Lim, Jim, 872
Lim, Richard, 1373
Lim, MD, Jonathan E., 489
Limbaugh, P Frank, 761
Lin, Will, 765
Lin, Ben, 863
Lin, M.R., 908
Lin, Anthony, 1009
Lin, Alfred, 1657
Lin, Jessica, 2006
Lin, Wei, 2168
Lincoln, David, 658
Lindner, Andrew, 793
Lindsay, Robert D, 1133
Linn, Jaff, 1183
Linnen, Joe, 1049
Linsalata, Frank, 1136
Lipkin, Richard, 644
Lippin, David, 1376
Lipscomb, Clark, 543
Lipsitz, Jeffrey A., 547
Lipson, Peter, 912
Liras, Spiros, 144
Lisiak, Paul, 1226
List, Michael, 2135
Listen, Kevin L., 905
Litten, H Randall, 351
Little, C. Malcolm, 167
Little, Gary, 399
Little, Jim, 1292
Little, Loretta, 2007
Littlechild, John W., 922
Littlejohn Jr., Angus C, 1138
Liu, Wei, 222
Liu, Roy Y., 928
Liu, Cherie, 1391
Liu, Larry Y., 2123
Livanos, Basil, 78
Livermore, Morgan, 824
Livingston, Jessica, 2011
Llanos, Claudia L., 133
Llovera, Bernardo H., 707
Lloyd, Alexander, 31
Lo, Felix, 843
LoGerfo, James, 643
Lobel, David S, 1654
Lobo, Brian J., 893
Lobo, Vernon, 2190
Locke, John, 27
Lockhart, Gene, 1240
Lockhart, Dennis, 1279
Lockie, Simon, 2128
Loftus, John, 52
Loh, John, 2056
Loh Nahmias, Vivian, 840
Loiacono, John, 185
Lomas, Eric J., 956
Lombardo, Lori, 684
Lonergan, Simon, 248
Lonergan, Michael A., 825
Long, Greg, 790
Long, Greg, 1169
Long, Michael D, 1270
Long Jr, John L, 1843
Longo, Peter, 532
Lopano, Scott, 678
Lopes, Luiz, 2062
Lopez, Alberto, 765
Lopez-Figueroa, Manuel, 240
Lor, Patrick, 2204
Lord, Hambleton, 1104
Lorenzen, Lee, 103
Loring, Ian, 223

Executive Name Index

Lotane, Nancy, 223
Lothian, E. Craig, 2166
Lotter, Jerry, 665
Loughlin, Steve, 27
Loughlin, Phil, 223
Louie, Gilman, 93
Lovell, Jeffrey D, 1151
Loverro, Frank J, 1066
Loverro, John G, 1116
Lovett, Rad, 1152
Low, Jeff, 645
Low, Lisa, 2081
Loy, Trevor R, 758
Loy, A. Thomas, 1224
Lubert, Ira M, 1140, 1510
Lubin, Daniel C, 1523
Luby, Bill, 1641
Lucarelli, Eddie, 2233
Lucas, Christopher, 278
Lucas, Paul, 2145
Lucassen, Jeff, 2196
Lucero, Ryan, 785
Lucia, CFA, Rebecca, 11
Lucke, Joe, 2169
Luderer, MD, Jack R., 140
Ludwig, Mark, 1707
Lueger, Brian, 1057
Luehrs, Bruce, 1572
Lugani, Vishal, 48
Lugsdin, Andrew, 2119
Lujan, Larry, 1926
Lukaczyk, Laura L., 210
Lunak, Rich, 1003
Lunan, Tom, 2051
Lund, Chris, 903
Lund, Robert, 1004
Lundin, Hans, 1007
Lundy, Megan, 1133
Lung, Wendy, 971
Lupa PhD, Mark T, 933
Luse, Rebecca, 1297
Lustbader, Michael H., 167
Lutzke, Scott, 445
Lutzker, Joshua A., 257
Ly, Eric, 662
Lydon, Mark, 1009
Lyford, Shelley, 1974
Lyman, John, 894
Lynch, Casey, 96
Lynch, Christopher W., 180
Lynch, Kevin, 433
Lynch, Zack, 1033
Lynch, Michael, 1200
Lynch, Jeremy, 1853
Lynde, Renske, 7
Lynn, Rebecca, 399
Lynn, Will, 886
Lyon, Greg, 648
Lyons, Bill, 490
Lyons, Peter A, 1109
Lyons, Michael J, 1131
Lyren, Melanie C, 165
Lysne, Alan, 2109

M

Ma, Jiong, 325
Maalouf, Khalil, 2282
Mabbs, Kenneth, 712
Mac Mahon, Tom, 749
MacAskill, Peter, 2197
MacBean, Mick, 2267
MacBeath, Alex, 2157
MacCormack, Justin, 2142
MacDonald, Rod, 595
MacDonald, Charlotte D., 952
MacDonald, William I, 1107
MacDonald, Caitlyn, 1108
MacDonald, Bill, 2068
MacDonald, Scott, 2183
MacInnis, Robert, 20
MacIntosh, Alan, 50
MacIntosh, Alan, 2224
MacIntyre, John B., 2056
MacKeigan, Dan, 1731
MacKenzie, Timothy J, 1210
MacKinnon, Kenneth, 2175
MacLellan, Rob, 2196
MacLeod, Scott, 838
MacMillan, Charlie, 642
MacMurray, John F., 1624
MacShane, Nick, 1488
MacTaggart, Ian B., 360
Maccini, Robert J., 126
Macdonald, Peter, 277
Macdonell, Ian, 2083
Mace, David, 828
Machado, Joe, 1266
Machlica, David J, 1166
Maciariello, Patrick A., 525
Mack, Joshua, 503
Mackesy, D Scott, 1973
Mackley, Anna, 1938
Mackowski, J Matthew, 1794
Maclean, Richard, 793
Macleod, Robert W, 1199
Madasamy, Karthee, 1243
Madden, Jim, 419
Madera, Paul, 1213
Madon, Cyrus, 2062
Madsen, Kent, 689
Madsen, Dion, 1442, 2032
Maeder, Robert, 768
Maeder, Paul, 938
Magas, Peter N, 247
Magerman, David, 615
Magescas, Carine, 129
Magid, Deborah, 971
Magida, Stephen A., 124
Magliacano, Marc, 1092
Magnano, Ben, 785
Magnuson, Rick, 828
Maguy, Billy, 92
Mahadevia, Vishal, 1957
Mahajan, Amitt, 1477
Maher, David M, 355
Mahesh, Shripriya, 1724
Mahoney, James, 963
Maidenberg, Ted, 1850
Main, Clayton, 336
Mairs, Christopher J, 1109
Majors, Mike, 587
Makharia, Rohit, 821
Makhzoumi, Mohamad, 1296
Makishev, Nurzhas, 1330
Makower, Josh, 1296
Maldonado, John, 61
Maldonado, Alejandro, 142
Maleki, Alex, 976
Malekian, E Peter, 1192
Maliwal, Aditi, 1890
Malka, Meyer, 1563
Mallabone, Ward, 2219
Mallett, Thomas E, 103
Mallios, Demetrios, 1016
Malloy, John, 299
Malone, Zach, 629
Malone, Kevin, 1109
Maloney, Timothy W, 17
Maloney, TJ, 1131
Maloney, Mark, 1401
Maloney, Drew, 3245
Maltz, Jules, 1006
Maluth, Elliot, 931
Malven, Dan, 9
Mamdani, Sulu, 1766
Manasterski, Marc, 1518
Mandal, Sumant, 1812
Mandato, Joe, 599
Mandelbaum, Fern, 1249, 1941
Mandile, John, 1675
Mandl, Ryan, 746
Manges, James, 1853
Manlunas, Eric, 1966
Manning, Jack, 312
Manning, Robert, 1600
Manning, Christopher, 1853
Mannix, Hank, 1066
Manos, Peter M., 167
Mansour, Saif, 334
Mansour, Bassem A, 1548
Manuel, Will, 111
Manzetti, John W, 1452
Mao, Carol, 802
Mao, Benjamin, 1085
Mapes, John, 202
Maples Jr., Mike, 752
Marakovic, Nino, 1623
Marasco, James, 1971
Marcantonio, Mike, 291
Marcil, Jr., Bill, 817
Marcoux, Jean-Francois, 1982
Marcus, Jeff, 560
Marcus, Lenard, 655
Marcus, Adam, 1499
Marcus, Larry, 1953
Mardirossian, Shant, 1085
Marengere, Luc, 2268
Mareuse, Aldo, 1499
Marex, Brenda, 1302
Margetts, Jill, 445
Margolin, Adam J, 1720
Margolis, Paul, 1150
Margolskee, Dorothy, 764
Mariani, Paul, 21
Mariani Sullivan, Jeanne, 1741
Mariel, Serafin, 363
Marimow, Scott M., 1498
Marini, Giacomo, 1352
Marino, Michael, 203
Marino, Louis, 822
Marino, Benjamin, 1435
Marino, Wayne, 1751
Marion, Guillaume, 2090
Maris, Bill, 1646
Mark, Jeffrey, 509
Mark, Douglas E, 1343
Mark, Joncarlo, 1894
Markandaier, Mohan, 2132
Markey, Bernard B, 1280
Markova, MBA, Sonja, 229
Markowsky, Barry, 2145
Marks, Howard, 1362
Marks, Arthur J, 1901
Marlas, James, 1883
Marlette, Scott, 1696
Marley, Juli, 293
Marocco, Michael, 1620
Marple, Dave, 1909
Marquardt, David, 200
Marquez, Michael, 1254
Marquis, Joelle, 172
Marquis, John, 1499
Marr, Michael S., 408
Marra, Jim, 293
Marrero, Roger, 530
Marschmeyer, Carsten, 1173
Marsh, MD, Edward B, 1199
Marshall, Marcy, 150
Marshall, Michael, 899
Marshall, Bob, 1649
Marshall, Jim, 1649
Marshall, Woody, 1787
Marshall, A.J. (Sandy), 2054
Marshall, Stephen O., 2098
Marshbanks, Tracy, 733
Martin, Charles R, 112
Martin, Edward W, 494
Martin, Tim, 542
Martin, Melanie, 770
Martin, Philip W, 1609
Martin, Michael, 1780
Martin, Brian D, 1906
Martin, Michael, 1957
Martineau-Fortin, Eric, 1982
Martinez, Ignacio, 748
Martinez, Emanuel, 870
Martino, Paul, 361
Martino, Rocco J., 1097
Martirano, David, 1463
Marty, Alan, 1110
Maruyama, PhD, Kazunori, 184
Marver, Jim, 1908
Marvin, Kim, 110
Masi, Renee, 272
Masinter, Mark L, 1552
Masjedi, Shannon, 1400
Maslow, Randy, 970
Mason, Susan, 83
Mason, Alex, 419
Mason, Bob, 1489
Massard, Nicolas, 20
Massaro, Salvatore A, 656
Massey, Lauren M, 17
Masto, Christopher, 790
Masucci, Peter N., 1300
Masur, Mark C, 1684
Matelich, George E, 1066
Mathew, Arun, 27
Mathews, Kenneth J, 384
Mathews, Devin, 470
Mathews, Stuart I, 1225
Mathews, Brendan, 1259
Mathieu, Chris, 949
Matlin, Howard, 1066
Matlin, David J, 1182
Matlock, Tyler, 1769
Matly, MD, Michael, 1251
Matsumoto, PhD, Shunichiro, 184
Mattaliano, Alfred M., 1582
Mattamana, Alan, 715
Matthews, Brian, 570
Matthews, Gary S, 1256
Matthews, Terry, 2276
Mattina, Joe, 2211
Mau, Luke, 228
Mauchant, Florence J., 956
Maurer, Erik E, 1494
Mawani, Shafeen, 2260
Mawhinney, Tom, 972
Maxwell, Bret, 1242
Maxwell, Scott, 1381
May, Kevin J., 949
May, Robert, 990
May, John, 1303
May, Rob, 1463
Maybaum, Richard E, 1138
Maybell, Mark, 645
Mayer, John A. (Tony), 707
Mayer, Michael, 1251
Mayer, Andrew R., 1779
Mayerfeld, Russ, 88
Mayerson, Frederic H, 1955
Mayfield, John, 79
Mayfield, R Glen, 1575
Maynard, Frederick, 912
Mayson, Howard, 2044
Mayton, Jennifer, 1938
Mazzarino, John, 465

Executive Name Index

Mazzullo, Theresa B, 705
McAdam, Tim, 1787
McAllister, Jeff, 2059
McAndrews, Mark, 645
McBane, Michelle, 2248
McBride, Jim, 294
McBride, Kevin, 2031
McCabe, George, 913
McCafferty, Kevin M., 428
McCafferty, Aevin M, 1295
McCafferty, Brendan, 1295
McCaig, Murray, 2037
McCall, Matt, 1483
McCann, Stephen, 1709
McCarthy, Loretta, 845
McCarthy, Michael R, 1276
McCarthy, Edward C, 1575
McCarthy, Michelle, 1928
McCarthy, CPA, Shane, 679
McCarty, John, 1425
McCarty, Bob, 1789
McCauley, Mike, 2122
McCelland, Spence, 1332
McClain, Richard, 935
McClanahan, Kip, 1687
McClean, Stephen, 172
McCleary, Christopher, 290
McClements, James, 1551
McCloskey, Tom, 543
McCollum, W. Christian, 1113
McComiskey, Niall, 867
McConahey, Steve, 1024
McConnell, Scott, 88
McConnell, Eamonn, 2160
McConoughey, Jim, 926
McCooe, Matthew, 532
McCormack, Stephen, 523
McCormack, Scott, 1641
McCormack, John F, 1654
McCormack, Andrew, 1899
McCormick, Douglas, 920
McCormick, Pete, 1186
McCormick, Doug, 1561
McCormick, Jeffrey S, 1626
McCoy, Stephanie, 1525
McCrary, Dennis, 1413
McCreadie, Paul, 150
McCrimmon, Daniel, 2115
McCroskey, Nancy, 185
McCullagh, Mahala, 2257
McCullen, Bill, 1101
McCulloch, J.D., 517
McCullough, John W., 907
McCullough, Michael, 987
McCusker, Charles P, 1424
McDaid, Brian C., 1730
McDaniel, Teresa, 171
McDaniel, Brenda, 1068
McDermott, Dirk, 98
McDermott, Tom, 656
McDermott, James, 1897
McDonagh, Bill, 1953
McDonald, Matthew, 230
McDonald, Dr Robert, 1725
McDonald, Robert, 1936
McDonald, Deborah, 2274
McDonnell, Mark, 154
McDowell, Mark, 50, 1100
McElhone, Christopher, 2030
McEwen, John, 2091
McFadden, Mark, 435
McFarland, Josh, 877
McGee, Meghan M., 386
McGillivray, Burton, 507
McGlinn, Jack, 408
McGonnigle, Glenn, 1790
McGould, Sean, 1123

McGovern, Kevin M., 1194
McGowan Sr, Gene, 1195
McGrath, Kevin, 1287
McGuire, Lake, 928
McGuire, Terry, 1464
McIlwain, Matt, 1162
McIlwraith, John, 86
McInerney, Thomas E., 302
McInerney, Paula G., 302
McInerney, John L., 302
McIntyre, Ryan, 779
McIntyre, Todd, 875
McIsaac, Zac, 2182
McIvor, Dale, 1714
McKay, Samuel, 215
McKay, Steve, 775
McKay, Chris, 857
McKearn PhD, John, 1578
McKee Jr., Bill, 851
McKenna, Joe, 2161
McKenzie, Ryan R., 148
McKibben, Jeffrey, 1368
McKiernan, Erika, 1665
McKinley, Thomas, 413
McKinley, John, 1100
McKinley, William F, 1429
McKinney, Dan, 1321
McKittrick, Stacey, 143
McLaughlin, Andrew, 937
McLaughlin, Mark A., 952
McLaughlin, James, 1131
McLean, Bart A, 1270
McLeese, Robert S., 2026
McLellan, Andrew, 1961
McLemore, Don, 495
McLeod, Chris, 661
McLoughlin, Tim, 512
McLoughlin, Andy, 1881
McMahon, Michael, 1050
McMahon, Jack, 2275
McManus, Marc, 491
McMartin, Cam, 446
McMillan, Jaime, 393
McMorris, Marc, 419
McMullen, John, 2167
McMurchy, Kevin W, 630
McNabb, J Carter, 1575
McNally, Nannette, 63
McNally, Ryan, 429
McNally, Sean M, 1473
McNamara II, John C, 1148
McNamee, Roger, 660
McNeil PhD, Robert G, 1619
McNerney, Peter H, 1820
McNulty, Edward, 574
McParland, Robert J., 1830
McPhee, Ron J, 1926
McQueen, Mark, 2074
McQueeney, Michael P, 1753
McVicar, Tracey, 368
McWhorter, David, 427
McWhorter, Stuart, 497
McWhorter, R. Clayton, 497
McWilliams PhD, Peter C, 1619
Mclean, Dave, 1661
Mclean Owen, Loudon, 2191
Meacham, Scott, 968
Mead, James M, 1523
Meadow, Scott, 654
Meakem, Chip, 1084
Meakem, Chip, 1851
Meakpeace, Mark, 1988
Meany, Ryan, 653
Mech, Steve, 567
Meduna, Cyril L., 62
Meehan, Frank, 1719
Meeks, Jonathan W, 1778

Meenan, Patrick, 175
Meeusen, PhD, Ron, 571
Mehlman, Ezra, 921
Mehra, Vivek, 200
Mehra, Rajan, 504
Mehring, Paul, 34
Mehta, Nihal, 680
Mehta, Shailesh, 856
Mehta, Sameet, 856
Mehta, Manan, 1887
Mehta, Vihangi, 2178
Meidlinger, Karen, 1200
Meilner, John, 341
Meisel, Seth, 280
Mejias, Omar, 62
Meketa, James E, 1201
Melchior, Lisa, 2273
Meldrum, Christopher S, 844
Meldrum, CFA, Kelly, 56
Mele, Francesco, 2044
Mellet, Daisy, 1208
Mellinger, Doug K., 494
Mello, Ed, 577
Mello, Kirsten A., 1203
Melmon, Richard, 361
Melohn, Joseph, 708
Melohn, Ryan, 708
Melrose, Dr Evan, 1725
Melstrom, John, 985
Melton, Brian, 1798
Melwani, Prakash A., 280
Melzer, Thomas C, 1578
Mencoff, Samuel M, 1160
Mendelson, Alan, 215
Mendelson, Jason, 779
Mendez, David, 849
Mendicino II, Frank, 35
Mendicino III, Frank, 35
Mendoza, Felipe, 166
Mendoza, Adrian, 1202
Mendoza, Senofer, 1202
Menell, Mark, 1418
Menichelli, Vincent P., 52
Merritt, Elizabeth, 465
Merritt, Dorian, 1798
Mes, David, 1370
Messano, Frances, 1315
Messick, Diane, 993
Methot, Andree-Lise, 2087
Metz, Lloyd M., 973
Meyer, Yoni, 420
Meyer, Alex, 1385
Mhatre, Ravi, 1125
Mi, Jonathan, 343
Miau, Matthew, 908
Michael, David, 134
Michalyshyn, Cory, 2070
Michaud, Gerald A., 949
Michaud, Brian W, 1138
Michel, Marc, 527
Middleton, Jesse, 756
Middleton, Fred A, 1222, 1619
Miele, Perry, 2050
Migliorino, Robert, 1949
Mihas, Constantine S., 889
Mika, Ron, 1707
Mikkelsen, Erik, 2042
Mikula, Benn, 2080
Milbery, James F, 470
Milciunas, John Paul, 31
Millar, Alex, 297
Miller, Jonathan, 59
Miller, William, 127
Miller, Michael, 445
Miller, David S., 498
Miller, Michael W., 528
Miller, David B., 673

Miller, Christian T, 699
Miller, Charles D., 907
Miller, Jeb, 972
Miller, Sandy, 1006
Miller, Tony, 1111
Miller, Brian C, 1132
Miller, W Scott, 1152
Miller, Mark G, 1196
Miller, Steve, 1231
Miller, Marlin, 1347
Miller, Steven N., 1385
Miller, Jeff, 1413
Miller, Daniel H, 1584
Miller, Eyal, 1614
Miller, Matt, 1953
Miller IV, Norvell E, 1711
Miller, MD, Lawrence G, 1198
Millet, David F, 815
Milligan, Ryan, 470
Mills PhD, Timothy C, 1619
Milne, Jr. PhD, George M, 1523
Milner, Yuri, 616
Miltenberger, William H., 988
Mimran, Joe, 2127
Mims, Cory D., 973
Minaya, Jose, 1356
Miner, Allen, 1757
Minerd, B. Scott, 890
Minihan, Kenneth A., 1401
Minnick, James, 1151
Minocherhomjee, Arda M, 470
Minter, Alison, 1336
Mirabile, Christopher, 1104
Miranda, Antonio, 1138
Mischianti, Lou, 1372
Misek, Peter, 2119
Mishra, Vish, 504
Mistras, CFA, Antonis, 637
Mistry, Ashish H., 285
Mitchell, Ivar W., 124
Mitchell, Andrew, 328
Mitchell, Nate, 824
Mitchell, Kate, 1629
Mitchell, Dan, 1656
Mitchell, Chris, 1720
Mitchell, Lee M, 1817
Miura-Ko, Ann, 752
Mixon, Ki, 1548
Miyata, Tak, 1637
Mnaymneh, Sami, 931
Moan, Gerry, 1697
Mock, Lawrence, 1279
Modersitzki, Blake, 1428
Modica, Pino N, 1456
Moe, Michael, 888
Moelis, Cory, 882
Moerschel, Gregory, 247
Mogk, Peter, 963
Mohamed, Minhas, 2188
Mohammadioun, Said, 1790
Mohan, Ravi, 1666
Mohler, PhD, Kendall, 30
Moilanen, Jake, 1658
Molano, Gina E., 1883
Molbert, Lauris, 175
Moldow, Charles, 773
Moley, Andrew, 1125
Molinari, Drew, 578
Moll, David, 992
Molner, Phillip C, 1480
Monaghan, Arthur, 855
Monahan, Lee J., 913
Monat, Jeff, 1853
Moncrief, Ray, 1215
Mondre, Greg, 1685
Money, Aaron, 790
Money, Brad, 874

Executive Name Index

Montana, Ralph, 1961
Monteith, Scott, 2189
Montgomery, H. DuBose, 1203
Montgomery, Andrew, 1223
Montoya, Mario, 1992
Moon, John, 1256
Moon, Bernard, 1719
Moor, Markus, 2101
Moore, Ryan, 37
Moore, Matt, 92
Moore, John, 196
Moore, Erik, 232
Moore, Steven, 337
Moore, Brendan M., 687
Moore, Anthony J., 826
Moore, Church M, 1066
Moore, Terry, 1253
Moore, Chris, 1537
Moore, Paul, 1739
Moore, Geoffrey, 1985
Moorin, Jay, 1492
Moorse, Dan, 920
Mora, Frank, 961
Moragne, John H., 1852
Moraly, Dana, 504
Moran, Michael E, 351
Moran, Robert P, 1456
More, Bob, 94
Moreland, Ira L., 973
Moreno, Michelle, 630
Moretti, Anthony, 355
Morfit, G. Mason, 1905
Morfitt, Brian, 785
Morgan, Kirk, 52
Morgan, Howard, 219
Morgan, Jonathan, 256
Morgan, Michael, 376
Morgan, Quinn, 448
Morgan, Wanda R, 1270
Morgan, John, 1433
Morgan, Eric C., 1460
Morgan, Michael C, 1848
Morgenthal, Steven J, 165
Mori, Takeshi, 841
Morin, Christina, 851
Morin, Dave, 1696
Morin, Mike, 1739
Morin, Genevieve, 2113
Moritz, Michael, 1657
Moritz, J. Kenneth, 1749
Morningstar, John E., 1972
Moross, David, 717
Morris, Frederic H., 352
Morris, John, 912
Morris, Rob, 1372
Morris, Nigel, 1504
Morris, Erik O., 1580
Morris, CPA, Scott, 737
Morriss, Nick, 838
Morrissette, Mark J, 1334
Morrissey, Michael B., 1018
Morrow, David, 1802
Morse PhD, Laurence C., 715
Mortimer, David, 2144
Morton, Jeff, 47
Moseley, Allen S, 1332
Moser, Randy, 203
Moskowitz, Jason B, 634
Mosman, Matt, 1428
Moss, Malcolm, 254
Moss, Rick, 256
Moss, Cheryl, 791
Mossler, Fred, 1914
Moszer, David, 1493
Motley, David, 301
Mott, Catherine, 296, 301
Mottahed, Sonny, 2068

Moulton, Eben S, 1639
Mount, Ian J, 1277
Mountain, Rocky, 595
Moura, Andre V., 1300
Moyer, Chris, 2208
Muhtadie, Mira, 41
Muhtadie, Fayez S., 1746
Muir, Jeffrey S, 797
Muir, Craig, 1814
Mukhamedyarov, Marat, 2132
Mulcahey, Brennan, 352
Mulcare, Robert W., 1300
Mulder, Nikole, 300
Mullane, Kevin, 16
Mullane, Kevin F., 1020
Mullany, Michael, 972
Mullen, Terrence, 172
Mullen, Mark, 309
Mullen, Mark, 625
Mullen, Dave, 2139
Mulligan, William C, 1480
Mullin, Stephen P, 630
Mulloy, Corey, 938
Mulloy, Jennifer M, 1778
Multani, Arneek, 1852
Mumma, Mitch, 1013
Munakata, PhD, Ryosuke, 184
Mundheim, Peter M., 1746
Mundkur, Yatin, 176
Mundt, Kevin A., 1933
Mundy, Matthew, 2233
Munichiello, Dave, 894
Muniz, Stephen, 1503
Munjal, Salil, 2283
Munk, Anthony, 2201
Munson, Peter, 412
Muoio, Patricia, 1689
Murdoch, Britton, 1572
Murphree, Dennis E, 1273
Murphree, Lori L., 1369
Murphy, Scott, 60
Murphy, Pauline, 532
Murphy, Tom, 560
Murphy, Thomas, 819
Murphy, Matt, 1203
Murphy, Brian G., 1316
Murphy, Shay, 1324
Murphy, Michael P., 1589
Murphy, Paul F, 1654
Murphy, Jeffrey N., 2156
Murphy Jr, John J, 1274
Murray, Timothy M, 470
Murray, Alan, 541
Murray, Jonathan, 629, 642
Murray, Dr. Campbell, 1350
Murray, Arthur G, 1883
Murray, Mike, 2209
Murray Jr, James B, 552
Murray-Tateishi, Sheila, 2049
Musallam, Ramzi M, 1927
Muse, Brad, 70
Muth, Peter J, 1749
Muthanna, Sanjana, 2178
Mutter, Sheila, 1788
Myers, Greg, 1174
Mygind, Scott, 834
Myhrvold, Cameron, 978
Myhrvold, Nathan, 1010
Mykhaylovskyy, Andriy, 728
Myrrha, Diogo, 79
Mytels, Dan, 1612

N

Nader, Anthony, 1768
Naeve, PhD, Janis, 113
Nagappan, Vijay, 1227
Nagaraj, Sunil, 1879

Nagel, Rick, 47
Nagel, PhD, David, 770
Nagim, Ryan K, 1148
Nahumi, Dror, 1346
Naik, Sandeep, 819
Naimi, Ramtin, 23
Naini, Nader, 785
Najjar, Michael E., 547
Nakache, Patricia, 1855
Nakamura, Koichiro, 1716
Nalamasu, Ph.D., Omkaram, 145
Nam, Hodong, 100
Nankivell, Alison, 2048
Narayan, Sridhar, 838
Nardelli, Robert, 668
Nardone, Randal A., 769
Nark, Ted, 1090
Nashat, Amir, 1464
Nasr, Khaled, 1014
Natali, Stephen, 654
Natarajan, Vas, 27
Natarajan, Raj, 2023
Nathan, Richard, 2160
Nault, David, 2172
Naythons MD, Matthew, 164
Neal, Doug, 657
Neal, Maria, 996
Neary, James, 1957
Nechiti, Ionel V., 1002
Nedungadi, Ajit, 1778
Needham, Tom, 1777
Neels, Guido, 698
Neely, Matthew, 1694
Neff, P Sherrill, 1510
Negus, Kevin, 388
Neider, Calvin A, 505
Neighbors, David, 1964
Neild, W. Carter, 1383
Neis, John, 1923
Neldner, Derek, 2223
Nelsen, Robert T., 154
Nelson, Steve, 475
Nelson, Brian R., 874
Nelson, Carl, 920
Nelson, Lisa, 1158
Nelson, Jonathan M., 1498
Nelson, Dean, 1606
Nelson, John R, 1667
Nelson, Andrea R, 1722
Nelson, Joshua M., 1818
Nelson, Kirk, 1919
Nelson MD, James, 1007
Ness, Rick, 2251
Nessi, Claudio, 1373
Netravali, Dr. Arun, 1375
Neubauer, Lawrence, 1518
Neundorfer, Jennifer Keiser, 1030
Neustaetter, Thomas, 1042
Neuwirth, Daniel P, 1506
Neverson, David C, 1109
New, Marcus, 2154
Newbold, Robert, 851
Newby, Tom, 1116
Newcomb, Andy, 1240
Newell, Carol, 2230
Newhall, Ashton, 872
Newman, Bruce, 684
Newman, Denis, 1230
Newman, Howard H, 1447
Newman, Henry W, 1704
Newman, Jerrold, 1986
Newton, Tyler, 429
Newton, Jeffrey T, 815
Ng, Carey, 1222
Ngo, Yi-Jian, 85
Ngo, Jessica, 474
Ngo, Thien-Ly, 528

Nguyen, David, 127
Nguyen, Ha, 1724
Nguyen, Leah, 2144
Nguyen, Ha, 2183
Nichols, Carl, 1390
Nickell, Frank T, 1066
Nicklas, Brent, 1116
Nicklin, Matthew, 733
Niedel, James, 1297
Nieh, Peter, 1125
Niehaus, Joseph M., 952
Niemeyer, Suzanne, 52
Niemiec, David W., 1624
Nies, John, 1044
Nieuwenburg, Jim, 2044
Nijhawan, Preetish, 456
Nijjar, Karamdeep, 2150
Nikolay, Joern, 819
Nikolic, Dr. Boris, 271
Niparko, Nate, 27
Nisselson, Evan, 1105
Nissenbaum, Scott, 249
Nixon, Ron, 427
Noble, Craig, 2062
Nodelman, Oleg, 710
Nodine, Ralph, 1164
Noel, Karen, 1418
Noell, Charles E., 1045
Nof, Jordan, 1870
Nolan, Scott, 778
Nolan, Peter J, 1113
Nolan Jr, Robert B, 902
Nolen, Malcolm C, 1676
Nolet, Marie-Hélène, 2089
Noonan, Tom, 1790
Noor, A. Bilal, 167
Noorani, Zach, 773
Nordgren, Matthew J., 152
Noris, Javier, 1633
Norlander, Rebecca, 980
Normandeau, Rob, 2242
Noronha, Austin, 1706
Norr, Daniel, 206
Norreri, Federica, 162
Norris, Robert, 427
Norris, Nickie, 929
Norris, Ron, 1924
Nortman, Kara, 1890
Norton, Christopher B., 408
Norton, Matthew W, 1160
Norton, James J., 1438
Notini, Albert A., 1300
Nourmand, Robin, 228
Nova, Daniel, 938
Novak, Turner, 814
Novak, Jr., E. Rogers, 1348
Novielli, Michael A., 638
Novogratz, Jacqueline, 54
Novotny, Carl, 1922
Novotny, Chad, 1922
Nowaczyk, John J, 1234
Noy, Oded, 121
Nozad, Pejman, 1426
Nugent, Michael E., 1582
Nulman, Shay, 2168
Nussbaum, Joshua, 527
Nuttman, Angela, 773
Nycz, Jerome, 2048
Nye, Ben, 224
Nykin, Ilya, 1490
Nystrom, Cody, 1691

O

O'Brien, James D., 97
O'Brien, William, 662
O'Brien, Dennis, 886
O'Brien, Daniel J., 1041

Executive Name Index

O'Brien, Dennis, 1135
O'Connell, Daniel S., 1933
O'Connor, John, 1131
O'Connor, Logan V., 2014
O'Dell, Bradley C, 1494
O'Donnell, Charlie, 354
O'Donnell PhD, Niall A, 1578
O'Driscoll, Rory, 1629
O'Grady, Standish, 857
O'Hara, Dave, 175
O'Hara, Maura, 3255
O'Hare, Scott, 595
O'Keefe, Kenneth, 247
O'Keefe, Kenneth, 1933
O'Keefe, Sean, 1961
O'Leary, Nancy, 1042
O'Loughlin, Tim, 646
O'Malley, Brian, 763
O'Malley, Mike, 993
O'Mara, James, 1986
O'Neill, John, 1115
O'Neill, George D, 1216
O'Neill, Christopher, 1946
O'Rourke, Eileen, 18
O'Shaughnessy, Patrick, 344
O'Shea, Donald, 572
O'Sullivan, Michael P, 1456
O'Sullivan, Sean, 1709
Oakford, Scott I., 903
Ober, Kevin, 619
Oberbeck, Christian L., 1624
Oberg, Soren L., 1818
Oberholtzer, William J, 935
Oblak, Geoffrey S., 180
Occhipinti, Vincent M, 2005
Ocko, Matt, 586
Ocko, Julie, 912
Odden, Jake, 19
Odinsky, Jordan, 882
Oei, Ting-Pau, 644
Oetgen, Steve, 843
Ogawa, Andrew, 1515
Ogawa, Marcus, 1515
Ogden, William, 1883
Ogince, Michoel, 1992
Ogorek, Gregory, 2141
Oguz, Matt, 1407
Oka, Jonathan T., 751
Okike, Nnamdi, 12
Okonow, Dale S, 1963
Okun MIM, Robert, 1775
Olah, Amy, 2074
Olesnavage, Mark, 946
Oliva, Adele C., 4
Oliva, Adele C, 1510
Olkkola, Ed, 1785
Olofinboba, Kola, 715
Olsen, Chris, 631
Olson, Thiago, 678
Omidyar, Pierre, 1374
Ondrula, Lisa, 1049
Onen, Selahattin, 1407
Onofrio, Joe, 746
Onsi, Douglas E., 922
Opdendyk, Terry, 1379
Orazio, Anthony J., 1419
Ord, John, 543
Orend, Michael J, 1579
Orfao, David, 820
Ormont, Jordan, 1203
Orndorff, Chris, 1948
Oronsky, Arnie, 1014
Orr, Larry, 1855
Orr III, R Wilson, 1735
Orthlieb, Ben, 1370
Orthwein, Jr., Peter B., 1730
Orum, Nick, 886

Osawa, Koji, 837
Osawa, Shoichi, 1706
Osborn, William, 522
Osborn, Richard, 2225, 2256
Osborne, John, 849
Osborne, Sandy, 1066
Oseary, Guy, 14
Osgood CFA, Jonathan W, 573
Osman, Bart D, 1116
Osnoss, Joe, 1685
Ostheimer, Jason, 59
Ostrow, Gene J, 1529
Otani, Toshi, 1840
Otis, Meghan, 1965
Ou, Bruce, 884
Ousseimi, Mimo, 813
Outcalt, David B, 1116
Outerbridge, Amanda, 912
Outland, James, 1292
Overmyer, Craig, 947
Overvelde, Michael, 2085
Owen, Judy M., 378
Owen, Loudon, 2147
Owens, Todd G., 346
Owens, Vince, 891
Owsley, Jonathan H., 1092
Owusu, George Y, 1167
Oxaal, John, 1661
Ozawa, Clare, 1930
Ozechov, Michael, 544
Ozir, Gil, 2050

P

Pacelli, Peter, 1082
Pachisia, Nitin, 1887
Pacitti, Chris, 205
Packard, Chad, 1428
Padnos, Cindy, 980
Pados Jr, Frank J, 633
Padovano, Carlo, 1376
Page, Marcia L., 1909
Pagliuca, Stephen, 223
Pahxia, Morgan, 1468
Pai, Raj, 838
Paiement, Constance, 739
Pakianathan, PhD, Deepa, 605
Pakravan, Eric, 121
Paley, Eric, 774
Palihapitiya, Chamath, 1698
Pallares, Beto, 169
Pallotta, James J, 1527
Palm IV, Dr. Peter J, 1405
Palmer, Tim R., 458
Palmer, John E., 906
Palmer, Raquel, 1089
Palmer, Charles L, 1333
Palmer, Grant, 1853
Palmeri, Stephanie, 1702, 1881
Palter, Gilbert S., 2098
Paluck, Bob, 446
Palumbo, Rob, 28
Pan, Gordon G., 225
Pann, David, 1379
Pansing, Daniel E, 1210
Pappas, Greg J., 257
Pappas, Tracy, 1774
Paquette, Jared B, 362
Paquin, Jean-Pierre, 243
Pardoe, Richard, 468
Parekh, Deven, 1005
Parekh, Greg, 1301
Parente, Chuck, 670
Parfet, Donald R., 140
Parham, Richelle P., 386
Parikh, Vijay C, 837
Parilla, Mike, 1169
Paris, Brent L, 633

Paris, Mark, 1896
Pariseau, Jean-Francois, 2032
Park, John, 413
Park, Steven G, 617
Park, Elizabeth, 785
Park, Howard, 828
Park, Arrie, 927
Park, Min H., 1692
Parker, David J., 119
Parker, Jeffrey P, 853
Parker, Marshall D., 1057
Parker, George A, 1107
Parker, Douglas A, 1230
Parker, Victor E, 1720
Parkinson, Thomas, 947, 979
Parks, Lisa, 232
Parks, Steven W., 1097
Parmar, MD, PhD, Kush M, 11
Parnafes, Itzik, 238
Parr, Brett A, 402
Parr, Jeff, 2075
Parr, Donna, 2084
Parra, Ro, 595
Parrott, Phil, 469
Parsons, Don, 143
Parsons, Richard D., 981
Parsons, James A, 1560
Partain, W Michael, 592
Partlow, Ann, 643
Parulo, Jennifer E., 55
Parvez, Raja M., 1061
Parziale, Paolo, 17
Pascucci III, Vic, 1121
Pasquini, Scott G, 1160
Paster, Anne-Mari, 1373
Pastor, Jon, 301
Pastor, Ken, 2086
Pastoriza, Jim, 1784
Patchett, James, 1307
Patek, Anthony, 256
Patel, Harsh, 493
Patel, Anil, 504
Patel, Keval, 931
Patel, Satya, 944
Patel, Shaneel D., 1041
Patel, Ash, 1254
Patel, Amit A., 1393
Patel, Heidi, 1555
Patel, Harsh, 2001
Patel, Suresh, 2271
Pathria, Anu, 545
Patouillaud, Jean-Marc, 1418
Patrick, Grant A, 247
Patricof, Alan, 876
Patricof, Mark, 1223
Patterson, Tory, 430
Patterson, Jeff, 518
Patterson, Tory, 1393
Patterson, Michael, 1913
Pattison, Steve G., 1460
Patton, Blake, 678
Paul, Brian, 1798
Pauley, Jay D, 1754
Paull, Robert, 1155
Paulos, Joey, 515
Paulson, Robert, 66
Paulson, Randy, 1368
Paxhia, Emily, 1468
Paymaster, Kunal, 1673
Payne, Marni F., 257
Payne, Marshall, 479
Payne, Christopher, 919
Peake, Tripp, 1146
Pearce, Jonathan, 294
Pearce, Dave, 2044
Pearl, Laura, 454
Pearlman, Bret, 660

Pearlman, Ken, 1365
Pearson, Mark E., 131
Pearson, Travis, 828
Pearson, Lori, 2062
Peck, Mike, 1380
Pecorini, Domenico, 355
Pedroni, Emilio S, 734
Peechu, Sundeep, 720
Peel, Doug, 2162
Peery, Shane R., 464
Pehl, Mikel, 1335
Peiser, Brian, 654
Pellini, Mike, 1646
Pelowski, Kenneth R, 1449
Pelusi, James A., 214
Penberthy, Daniel P, 1526
Penchina, Gil, 1566
Penman, Gordon R, 1922
Penn, Kevin S, 41
Penn, Kevin, 111
Penn, Tom, 1275
Penn, Thomas A, 1431
Pennell, Keith W., 611
Pennell, Thomas B, 1432
Pentecost, Edward S., 1460
Pentimonti, E. Kenneth, 1401
Pepper, Doug, 1666
Pequet, David E, 1160
Perea, Carlos, 970
Pereira, Carol, 96
Perkins, Scott, 1123
Perl, Jonathan, 318
Perlman, Ezra, 782
Perot, Jr., Ross, 1436
Perper, Scott B., 1410
Perreault, Justin J., 523
Perreault, Sophie, 2108
Perricelli, Scott A, 1140
Perrier, Jean-Damien, 956
Perry, Chris, 491
Perry, Douglas S., 589
Perry, William, 992
Perry, Stephen B, 1136
Perry, Jr, James N, 1160
Persky, Michael B, 80
Perutz, Mark, 596
Pesce, Joseph, 864
Pesikoff, David L, 1848
Peters, Brian, 936
Petersen, Timothy, 150
Petersen, Gary R., 673
Peterson, Stuart, 177
Peterson, Tom, 1525
Peterson, Karl, 1837
Peterson, Steven, 1845
Peterson, Paul, 1990
Petit, Robert W, 1216
Petracek, George, 194
Petras, Jim, 642
Petrilla, Kenneth, 475
Petrillo, Peter, 854
Petro, Justin B, 1813
Petrocelli, Richard A., 1624
Petronzio, F. Matthew, 1873
Petrzela, Michal, 1127
Petterle, Laura, 762
Pettit, Peter S, 1270
Pettit, Jim, 1281
Pettway, Patten, 1573
Petty, Robert, 506
Petty, Scott, 1679
Petty Jr, William, 247
Petzinger, Tom, 1102
Peyron, Mat, 1370
Pfeffer, Daniel, 81
Pfeffer, Jeffry S., 410
Pfeffer, Michael S, 1469

Executive Name Index

Pfeffer MD, Cary, 1814
Pflug, Meredith, 216
Pfund, Nancy, 596
Pharand, Daniel, 432
Phelps, Dennis, 1006
Phelps, Dan, 1612
Phenicie, Luke A., 904
Philips, Jeremy G., 1718
Phillips, Stu, 241
Phillips, M Troy, 247
Phillips, Greg, 346
Phillips, Joshua S., 428
Phillips, D. Martin, 673
Phillips, IV, Charles G., 1624
Philosophos, John, 863
Philp, John, 2121
Phipps, Charles, 1661
Piaker, Steven F., 436
Pianim, Nick, 582
Piatkowski, Adam, 851
Pichette, Patrick, 2150
Picozza, Enrico, 941
Pidwell, David W., 87
Piedrahita, Vincente, 1818
Pierce, Chris A., 1278
Pierce, J Peter, 1450
Pierce, Don, 1670
Pierce Jr, J Peter, 1450
Pierson, Matt, 2
Pierson, Steven C, 1151
Pierson, David, 1776
Pietri, Todd T, 51
Piette, Barbara, 1081
Pike, Chris, 61
Pilecki, Kurt, 277
Pillsbury, Lee, 1808
Pilosof, Naomi, 1203
Piotrowski, Annie, 237
Piper JD, Joseph, 1007
Piret, Marguerite A, 1311
Piret, John, 1311
Pirvani, Shahzad, 2021
Pisani, Craig, 170
Pitt, James D.C., 1116
Pittaway, David B., 425
Pittman, Sherri, 369
Pitts, Christie, 221
Plain, Hank, 1126
Plain, Hank, 1257
Platshon, Scott, 710
Platt, Wayne, 1369
Plauche, Charlie, 1601
Plotkin, Serge, 1382
Plumridge, Scott, 899
Podlesak, Dennis, 622
Poelzer, Mark, 2034
Poff, Mark, 1769
Poindexter, John, 1034
Pokorny, Brian, 1763
Poland, Jared, 367
Policy, Dan, 996
Polimino, Peter, 104
Poliner, Randall E., 132
Politi, Santo, 1718
Polk, Benjamin M., 1927
Pollack, Bruce, 449
Pollak, Robert, 1763
Pollard, Chip, 1499
Pollock, Ryan, 1024
Pollock, Sam, 2062
Polotan, Morgan, 818
Polovets, Leo, 1760
Polski, Steve, 1135
Pomeroy, Rob, 949
Pongon, Mike, 1462
Popil, Dean, 2166
Popper MD MPH, Caroline, 244

Porcellato, Larry, 292
Porell, Robert, 813
Porteous, Will, 1597
Porter, Barry, 496
Porter, Lisa, 983
Porter, Tim, 1162
Pothier, Robert, 1545
Potter, Matthew T., 605
Poulos, Nic, 320
Poulos, Lisbeth, 983
Pouschine, John L, 1470
Powell, John, 1008
Powell, Jon, 1660
Powell, William, 2062
Powell Jr, Robert S, 1277
Powers, Scott, 52
Powers, Brian, 927
Powers, Joe, 1165
Prado, Dennis G, 1163
Praeger, Robin, 1930
Prager, Brett L., 611
Prakash, Kristopher, 1369
Prawda, Daniel, 838
Predayna, Steve, 1291
Pressly, Scott, 274
Pressman, Jason, 1666
Pressnell, Jonathan, 293
Price, Michael, 452
Price, JoAnn H., 715
Price, Will, 1317
Price, Aaron, 3266
Prichett, J. Travis, 907
Prickett, Clark, 1123
Pries, Gerhard, 2239
Prima, Alexandra, 1807
Priston, Duncan, 242
Pritchard, Grant, 1977
Pritzker, JB, 1482, 1483
Pritzker, Tony, 1482, 1483
Probert, Jim, 2076
Procter, Benjamin P, 1963
Proctor, Bob, 288
Proctor, David G, 1234
Propper de Callejon, Diana, 707
Proujansky, Phil, 434
Provost, Kevin, 871
Pruthi, Vineet, 1131
Pryma, Thomas, 63
Pryor, Brian, 1197
Prytula, Richard, 2254
Psaros, Michael, 1089
Puccinelli, Steven, 1360
Puglia, Marc, 1499
Pulitzer, Jonathan, 812
Puopolo, Robert, 688
Purcell, Dennis, 73
Purcell, Gregory J., 148
Purcell, Paul, 225
Purushotham, Arvind, 488
Puskoor, Dayakar, 1284
Putnam, Travis, 1281
Putnam, Mitch, 2022
Pyne, Russell, 194
Pyne, Sam H., 898

Q

Qian, Jack W., 1300
Quain, Mitchell, 41
Quake, Jeffrey K., 741
Quarles, Devin, 850
Quay, Ulrich, 305
Quazzo, Deborah, 888
Queenan, Thomas, 1445
Quigley, William, 504
Quinlan, Rory, 1520
Quinlivan, David P, 1608
Quinn, CPA, Christopher, 884

Quintana, Ana, 278
Quist, Will, 1696
Quy PhD, Roger J, 1788

R

Raab, Paul J., 719
Rabinowitz, Ben, 117
Rabois, Keith, 778
Radbod, Antony, 156
Radcliffe, Alex, 409
Radel, Holly, 3252
Rader, Stephen P., 496
Rader, Stacie, 748
Radhakrishnan, Ramesh, 176
Radtke, Jay, 1174
Rae, Katie, 1489
Raee, Hisham Al, 153
Raffin MD, Thomas A, 1794
Ragatz, Erik, 927
Ragins, David B, 494
Raguin, John, 711
Ragusa, Gary, 411
Rahe, Maribeth, 768
Rahimtula, Ali, 568
Rahman, Rashad, 357
Rahnema, Alireza, 2025
Raich, Steven G, 1138
Railhac, Romain, 1499
Raimondi, Jill A., 952
Raina, Vikrant, 364
Rainey, Don, 881
Raino, Matthew W, 1160
Raiten, Greg, 744
Rajczi, Louis, 770
Raju, Champ, 1471
Rajwani, Suraj, 626
Raker, Jill C., 867
Raker, Geoffrey S., 1779
Rakes, Steve, 1711
Rallo, Eduardo, 327
Ralls, Rawleigh, 1094
Ralph, Jon D., 786
Ramamoorthy, Arun, 1449
Ramesh, Prathna, 2178
Ramich, Michael, 793
Rammal, Danny, 1499
Ramsay, David, 415
Ramundo, Benjamin J., 167
Rand, Lee, 1756
Rand, Tom, 2037
Randall, Larry, 94
Randall, Leigh, 1834
Raney, Scott, 1537
Ranjan, Anuj, 2062
Rankine, Craig, 2264
Rao, Zeena, 973
Rao, Ganesh B., 1818
Rappaport, Steve, 1376
Rappoport, Marc, 1304
Raterman, Thomas R., 805
Rather, Jonathan M, 1973
Rattner, Jon, 194
Raucci, Robert F, 1313
Ravi, T.M., 1812
Rawie, Damon, 60
Rawlings, Michael, 479
Ray, Andrew, 2148
Raynard, Robert, 1953
Raynor, Daniel, 162
Rea, Steven, 187
Rea, Patrick, 395
Read, Leighton, 329
Read, MD, J. Leighton, 87
Reals, Jeffrey, 1434
Reardon, Tighe, 209
Reardon, Tom, 1499
Reaves, Gary D., 741

Rebar, Thomas G, 1636
Reckziegel, Karl, 2048
Reddon, Phil, 2081
Reddy, Ven N., 131
Reddy, Pabhakar, 1284
Redlitz, Chris, 1841
Redman, Heather, 757
Redmond, Chris, 402
Redstone, Shari, 59
Reed, Andy, 319
Reed, Jason, 1997
Reed, Marty, 2105
Reed MD, Douglas, 918
Reeder, Milton K, 32
Reeder, Tyler, 676
Rees, Rick S, 1148
Rees, Bob, 1740
Reese, Corby, 1769
Reese, Luke, 2000
Reeser, Timothy, 147
Reeves, Eric A, 634
Regan, Brian, 1720
Regan, Brian T, 1973
Reher, John M., 326
Rehnert, Geoffrey, 197
Reich, Marc, 1025
Reichert, Bill, 721, 810
Reichow, Greg, 648
Reid, Richard, 2039
Reidel, Art, 950
Reiland, Pamela L., 893
Reiland, Bill, 1255
Reilly, Wendell, 1425
Reilly CFA, Scott A, 1429
Reinharz, Larry, 2004
Reiniger, Carissa, 816
Reininger, Barbara, 561
Reiss, Stan J, 1184
Reiter, Eric, 337
Reiter, Jr, R Peter, 1560
Reitler, Edward, 151
Rekhi, Kanwal, 1017
Rekhi, Manu, 1017
Rendino, Kevin M., 5
Renna, James, 1168
Renzi, Ned J, 275
Reppenhagen, Frank, 531
Rerisi, Meredith L, 17
Rescho, Douglas, 1095
Resnick, Charles, 994
Resnick, Josh, 1522
Resnikoff, Alan H., 1663
Ressler, Anthony, 160
Restler, Peter, 368
Reuter, David J, 1140
Revers, Daniel R., 157
Reynolds, Barry D., 952
Reynolds, Roland, 990
Reynolds, John, 1129
Reynolds, Jake, 1787
Reynoldson, Michael H., 1020
Rezneck, Jon, 824
Rhines, Paul, 16
Rhodes, Jason, 193
Rhodes III, Noah F., 864
Rice, Matt, 227
Rice, John M., 481
Rice PhD, John M, 1849
Rich, Brian, 429
Rich, James T, 815
Rich, Trevor C, 1151
Rich, Laurie M., 1802
Richard, Laura, 2192
Richards, Jeff, 827
Richards, Andrew, 1769
Richards Donohoe, Robin, 628
Richardson, William K., 942

Executive Name Index

Richardson, Josh, 1147
Richardson, John, 1279
Richardson, Anders, 1403
Richardson, John, 2051
Richardson, Paul, 2230
Richmond, Aaron, 674
Richter, William L., 453
Richter, Saul, 1572
Rickett, Jerry, 1068
Riedmiller, Lisa, 152, 1408
Rieger, Glenn, 1316
Riemer, Robert, 177
Rightmire, Matt, 311
Riiska, Marc, 1866
Rikkers, James W, 1722
Riley, Ren, 1361
Riley, Andrew, 1910
Riley, Margaret, 1913
Riley, James, 2067
Rim, Charles, 627
Rimas, Tony, 784
Rinaldi, Ellis F., 1742
Ring, Jonathan, 1653
Ringo, Cynthia, 596
Ripley, Rosemary, 1324
Rishi, Raju, 1597
Rissman, Randy O., 1112
Ristvedt, Pal B, 1116
Ritchea, Dava, 1638
Ritchie, Matthew, 47
Ritchie, Marvin W, 1311
Ritter, Gordon, 666
Ritter, John L, 740
Ritterbush, Steven, 1208
Riva, Giorgio, 2281
Robard, Yann, 2281
Robbins, Gregory A., 848
Robbins, William, 1399
Robbins, David, 1846
Roberson, Bruce, 1755
Roberts, Bruce, 417
Roberts, Johnathan, 978
Roberts, George, 1086
Roberts, Carmichael, 1180
Roberts, Bryce, 1359
Roberts, George, 1381
Roberts, Eric, 1900
Roberts, Bryan, 1918
Roberts, Peter, 2249
Robertson, Sanford, 782
Robins, Paula, 127
Robins, Blake, 1154
Robinson, Greg, 9
Robinson, Colin, 472
Robinson, Joseph R, 1230
Robinson, Stephen G, 1451
Robinson, Edwin T, 1575
Robinson, James, 1597
Robinson, Lauren, 2140
Robinson, Art, 2171
Robinson, Samuel, 2217
Robinson, III, James, 1597
Rocco, Melissa, 106
Roche, Andrew, 491
Roche, Collin E., 889
Roche, Roger, 1025
Roche, Andy, 1468
Rock, Terry, 446
Rocklage PhD, Scott M, 11
Rockley, Whitney, 2183
Rodger, Steven C, 692
Rodin, Robert, 1579
Rodriguez, Ruben, 363
Rodriguez, Frank J., 1043
Rodriguez, Antonio, 1184
Rodriguez, Marcos A, 1404
Rodriguez Jr., Harold J., 869

Roe, Wayne, 984
Roeder, Doug, 605
Roehrenbeck, Mark, 1561
Roellig, Charles W., 451
Roeper, Scott D., 719
Roeper, Philip, 1272
Roeshkin, Nikolai, 662
Roff, David, 2128
Rogan, Scott, 676
Rogers, Jesse, 96
Rogers, Arthur, 153
Rogers, Sarah, 840
Rogers, Alex, 912
Rogers, Bruce, 1090
Rogoff, Eric Y, 1377
Rokosh, Norman, 2267
Romaniello, Steve, 1580
Romans, Andrew C., 1599
Romanyshyn, Steve, 2203
Rome, Brett J, 1339
Romero, Rafael, 668
Romlin, Judy, 1233
Rommines, Joel, 1081
Rondinelli, Joseph R, 792
Rooney, Tory, 357
Roos, John, 824
Roos, Susie, 824
Roosevelt, Jonathan, 990
Root MD, Jonathan D, 1898
Rorer, Jim, 1466
Rosa, Nick, 571, 1618
Rose, Wally, 15
Rose, Alex, 560
Rose, David S, 1305
Rose, David S, 1588
Rose, Jody, 3263
Roselle, Arthur C., 1410
Rosen, Sylvia F., 425
Rosen, Mark, 458
Rosen, Rick, 931
Rosen, Steven H, 1548
Rosen, Alexander, 1566
Rosen Wildstein, Amy, 307
Rosenbaum, Mark, 202
Rosenberg, Peter, 1208
Rosenberg, Jason, 1745
Rosenblatt, Jamie, 2130
Rosenbloom, Micah, 774
Rosenfeld, Eric, 794, 1384
Rosenfield, Andrew M,, 890
Rosenstein, David, 819
Rosenstein, Douglas J., 878
Rosenthal, Bennett, 160
Rosenthal, RoseAnn B., 249
Rosenthal, Jeffrey, 2142
Rosenzweig, William, 1442
Rosenzweig, Eric L., 1746
Roser, Christopher W, 1590
Roser, James LD, 1590
Roshko, Peter, 318
Roskens, Lisa Y., 70
Rosner, Robert L., 1933
Ross, Ian, 531
Ross, Howard D, 1140
Ross, Mark R., 1369
Ross, Mike, 1764
Ross PhD, Michael, 1631
Rossetter, Stephen, 450
Rossolatos, George, 2065
Rosston, Steven J, 840
Rostami, Rami, 1878
Rostick, Mark, 1009
Rostowsky, Steven, 2067
Rosuck, I. Donald, 1097
Roszak, Matthew, 1683
Rotberg, Joseph B, 1108
Roth, Jonathan D, 17

Roth, Sarah G, 165
Roth, Donald C., 671
Roth, John M., 786
Roth, Bryon C, 1592
Roth, Gordon, 1592
Roth, Ted, 1592
Rothenberg, Adam, 321
Rothschild, Shannon, 1725
Rothstein, Charlie, 254
Rotman, Frank, 1504
Rotman, Ken, 2075
Rotolo, Tim, 156
Rottenberg, Jason, 173
Rottier, Peter L, 1754
Rountree, Ian, 398
Rovinski, Beni, 2173
Rowan, Marc, 141
Rowe, David H., 65
Rowe, Paul, 2121
Rowell, Kelly, 3250
Rowley, David, 467
Rowntree, David, 2139
Roy, Noah, 867
Roy, Devraj, 1026
Royer, Stephen D., 1663
Rua, Dan, 994
Ruano, Rudy, 1976
Rubel, Michael W, 1560
Rubenstein, David M, 416
Rubin, Daniel I., 87
Rubin, Joe, 151
Rubin, Peter M., 192
Rubin, David, 1206
Rubin, Michael, 1342
Rubin, Laura M., 1742
Rubinoff, Gary, 2250
Ruch, Joshua, 1561
Rudge, John G, 1116
Rudick, Stuart L, 1236
Rudin, Murray E, 1579
Ruffolo, Rick, 80
Ruga, Jonathan M, 1655
Ruger, Jared, 260
Rulleau, Laurence, 2086
Rumilly, Mathias, 505
Runett, Rob, 1259
Runnells, John E, 1931
Rusoff, Lawrence, 1434
Russo, Guy M., 389
Rustgi, Atul, 36
Ruston, Derek, 2104
Ruthven, Neil, 778
Rutledge, Rob, 823
Ruud, Lance, 639
Ruvolo, Julie, 3252
Ryan, Charles E., 89
Ryan, Dennis D, 764
Ryan, David, 1239
Ryan, Jordan, 1562
Ryan, Vin, 1630
Ryan, Bruce C, 1710
Ryan, Neil, 1868

S

Saban, Haim, 1602
Sabater, Juan, 1904
Sabet, Bijan, 1718
Sabo, Elias J., 525
Saca, Diana, 682
Sacca, Chris, 1153
Sacha, Brent T, 1748
Sachar, Laura Belle, 1741
Sachs, Bruce, 457
Sachs, Andrew, 1603
Sack, Andy, 776
Sack, Aaron, 1256
Sackman, Donald, 987

Sadek, Zachary, 1419
Sadraranganey, Neil, 621
Saefke, John, 1917
Saeid, Kamil, 182
Saenko, Maryanna, 803
Saer Jr., John K., 828
Safiedine DPM, Ali, 1288
Sage, Luke, 1427
Sager Jr, Edward F, 1204
Sagisi, Patrick, 26
Sahasrabudhe, Ashwini, 860
Sahney, Neal G, 792
Saifee, Moiz, 545
Saikia, Rohan, 864
Saintonge, Sam, 2282
Salaber, Konrad, 1990
Salami, Seun, 1356
Salamon, Michael J., 2056
Saldutti Jr., Joseph A., 878
Sale, Will, 1765
Salem, Enrique, 224
Salenbier, Andrew, 36
Sales, Whitney, 29
Sales, Wayne, 985
Salewski, Anthony, 823
Salmon, Steve, 1098
Salon, Jonathan D., 245
Saltarelli, Gerald, 654
Saluja, Maninder, 1518
Salvino, Mike, 419
Salzhauer McMarlin, Amy, 849
Salzman, Alan E, 1908
Samberg, Jeff, 25
Samper, Phil, 808
Sams, Lloyd R., 266
Samson, Peter, 2156
Samuel, Shimrit, 117
Samuel, Dave, 787
Samuel, David G., 2056
Samuels, Judson, 929
Samuels, Camille, 1918
Samuels, Russell, 2280
Sanche, Caroline, 2249
Sanday, J.P., 1203
Sandell, Scott, 1296
Sanders, Ryan, 1205
Sanderson, Philip, 3273
Sandler, Scott, 1384
Sandler, Julie, 1501
Sandler, Andrew, 1620
Sandoski, Aaron, 1347
Sands, Greg, 548
Sands, David A., 1460
Sands Langensand, Carol, 130
Sangalis, Stephen N, 1487
Sanger, Jim, 1643
Sanger MD, Philip, 1803
Sankar, Santosh, 640
Sankey, Dr. N. Darius, 2020
Sanner, Dan, 92
Sansom, Ron, 1576
Santi, Angela, 34
Santiago, Jason, 1751
Santinelli, Paul A, 1335
Santonelli, Benjamin, 598
Sarafa, Martin A., 451
Sardana, Sandeep, 298
Sarkar, Neel, 443
Sarlo, George, 1953
Sarner, Michael S., 406
Sartre, Joseph, 1011
Sathe, Shrikant, 1913
Sato, Tak, 1269
Sauerhoff, Jeffrey M., 179
Saunders, Matt, 2109
Saurel, Zita, 927
Sauvé, Jean-François, 2080

Executive Name Index

Savage, Jim, 1150
Savage, Tige, 1558
Saverin, Eduardo, 219
Saviano, Joseph, 226
Saville, B Hagen, 1192
Savitz, Scott, 587
Savoie, Robert H, 1449
Sawaf, Omar A, 2012
Sawaf, Sami, 2012
Sawyer, Kenneth B, 1608
Saxena, Subhanu, 1301
Saxena, Parag, 1913
Saxton, Tina, 472
Scalzo, David, 1078
Scanlin, Mike, 2187
Scanlon, Rick, 1001
Scarpa, Carmen, 1731
Scaysbrook, David, 1520
Schaar, William H., 948
Schafer, J Michael, 1299
Schaffer, Joseph P, 1252
Schafler, R. Scott, 547
Schaible, David K., 1727
Schapiro, Benjamin, 1517
Scharfenberger, Joseph, 435
Schattner, Michael, 1378
Schaufeld, Fredrick D., 1768
Schaumburg, Zach E, 1220
Schaye, Paul L., 467
Schechter, Jeff, 1745
Scheepers, Nina, 1165
Scheetz, Ned, 139
Scheinfeld, Larry, 2016
Schell, Tony, 696
Schell, Rick, 1379
Schellenberg, David A., 2139
Schemelter, Jay W, 1578
Schena, Graham, 1266
Scheschuk, Brice, 2128
Schiciano, Kenneth T, 1778
Schickedanz, Sean, 499
Schickner, Curtis, 534
Schiff, Frank, 1231
Schiff, Jamie, 1344
Schiff, Peter G., 1344
Schiff, MD, Andrew, 73
Schifino Jr, William J, 1512
Schilberg, Barbara, 269
Schilling, Mathias, 641
Schillinger, Doug, 639
Schillinger, Emily, 3245
Schimel, Adam, 242
Schlachet, Loren, 1576
Schlapinski, Jeff, 3252
Schleifer, Scott, 1828
Schlein, Ted, 1079
Schlesinger, Thomas A, 247
Schlosstein, Ralph, 700
Schmadtke, Eric, 677
Schmid, Corey, 1659
Schmidly, Jason C., 418
Schmidt, Gerald F, 539
Schmidt, Eric, 1001
Schmitt, George, 1795
Schnabel, Michael, 449
Schnabel, John S, 1377
Schnadig, David L., 547
Schnakenberg, Ben A, 934
Schnarr, Jody, 2111
Schneider, Geoff, 433
Schneider, Stephanie, 746
Schneider, Toni, 1862
Schneider, Pat, 3251
Schneiderman, Arthur, 837
Schnell MD, David, 1495
Schneller, Cas, 790
Schnitzer, Bruce W, 1956

Schnurmacher, Larry, 1443
Schock, Paul, 276
Schocken, Joseph L., 349
Schoemaker, Kathleen, 622
Schoenfeld, Jeffrey A., 243
Schoettler, Jason, 373
Scholl, David R., 189
Scholl, Tom, 1348
Schopp, David R, 1747
Schraith, Jim, 794
Schreiber, Richard R, 617
Schreiber, Peter D., 617
Schreiber, MD, Alain, 1492
Schreier, Bryan, 1657
Schreier, W Terrence, 1839
Schrier, Douglas, 1543
Schroder, David, 16
Schroder, David R., 1020
Schroder, Marc, 1173
Schroeder, Charles L, 1343
Schuh, Mike, 773
Schule, Lisa, 838
Schuler, Ryan, 178
Schulte, Peter M., 509
Schulte, Greg, 891
Schultz, Daniel, 609
Schultz, Jeffrey, 1282
Schultz, Jim, 1380
Schultz, Chris, 1945
Schultze, George J, 1632
Schulz, Bob, 921
Schuman, Steve, 900
Schunk, Nanette, 3265
Schuster, Stewart, 1354
Schutz, Jeffrey, 443
Schutzbank, Amanda, 121
Schuurmans, Pierre J., 2056
Schwab, Andrew J, 11
Schwab III, Nelson, 418
Schwartz, Keoni, 96
Schwartz, Yafit, 117
Schwartz, Adam, 128
Schwartz, Eric, 425
Schwartz, Scott, 491
Schwartz, Alan D., 890
Schwartz, Brian D., 931
Schwartz, Andrew M., 1115
Schwartz, Christian, 1822
Schwartz, Hagi, 1976
Schwartz, Peter, 2165
Schwartz, Gerry, 2201
Schwartzberg, Evan, 1367
Schwarz, Richard, 653
Schwarz, Jason, 1989
Schwarzman, Stephen A., 280
Schwen, Steve, 1728
Schwerin, Samuel L, 1235
Sciorillo, Dean, 677
Scoggins, Chris, 1656
Scola, Nicholas, 20
Scotland, Andrew, 242
Scott, Paul A., 272
Scott, Dwight, 280
Scott, Randy, 924
Scozzafava, Thomas W, 1642
Scull, John, 1713
Scully, Thomas A, 1973
Scully, Rob, 2177
Seaman, Brad, 2206
Searcy, Conner, 1858
Seasons, Chris, 2036
Seaver, Peter R., 140
Sebastian, Sean, 275
Seeber, Jon, 1888
Seegopaul, Purnesh, 2205
Seeman, Cooper, 2227
Sefrioui, Rachid, 730

Segal, Rick, 1554
Segrest, Michael T, 1684
Seidenberg, Beth, 1079
Seidler, Peter, 1648
Seidler, Robert, 1648
Seiffer, Jonathan, 1113
Seitz, Chris, 704
Seitz, Tasha, 1042
Sekhon, Tex, 1170
Selby, Sunil, 2265
Selcow, Mark, 548
Seldin, David, 134
Sellers, Doug, 1536
Sellery, Alan G., 2156
Seltzer, Stacey D., 73
Semon, Dominique, 1217
Sen, Hondo, 190
Senft, Rod, 2118
Senft, Derek, 2118
Senft, Rod, 2206
Senft, Derek, 2210
Senft, Rod, 2210
Senft, Derek, 2266
Senkut, Aydin, 720
Serafim, Kristina, 1928
Serena, Ottavio, 1131
Serface, Joel, 256
Serkes, Jeffrey D, 1402
Serruya, Michael, 2245
Serruya, Aaron, 2245
Serruya, Simon, 2245
Seseri, Rudina, 713, 833
Setaro, Chris, 1665
Sethi, Arjun, 1850
Settle, Dana, 876
Seung, John, 799
Severson PhD, James A, 844
Sexton, Theresa, 495
Seymour, Tim, 1662
Sezak, Sam, 291
Shackelford, Tom, 1825
Shadman, Ali, 1042
Shaffer, Stefan L, 1729
Shaffer PhD, Christy, 918
Shah, Amit, 176
Shah, Deep, 782
Shah, Niren, 1346
Shah, Rajeev, 1522
Shah, Ron, 1751
Shah, Kosha, 1885
Shah, Sachin, 2062
Shah, Ameet, 2130, 2131
Shainberg, David, 228
Shaked, Eyal, 538
Shalek, Nick, 1563
Shalhoub, Matt, 2134
Shalon, Teddy, 1490
Shanafelt, Armen B, 1128
Shankar, Shubhang, 1776
Shannon, Tim, 389
Shannon, Jeffrey R., 547
Shannon, Mary, 587
Shannon, Mary M, 1178
Shapansky, Kerry, 2274
Shapiro, Craig, 514
Shapiro, Bob, 571
Shapiro, Jim, 1063
Shapiro, David, 1089
Shapiro, Robert, 1618
Sharkawy, Adam, 1180
Sharma, Shantnu, 107
Sharma, Alipt, 838
Sharma, Saurabh, 1050
Sharma, Ray, 2107
Sharpe, J. Louis, 63
Shaughnessy, Keith C, 1225
Shaw, Bob, 194

Shaw, David E., 580
Shaw, Jr., Robert, 161
Shaywitz, David A, 1780
Shcuhpak, Zoya, 2149
Shear, Herb, 383
Shearburn, John W, 1957
Shebuski, PhD, Ronald J., 140
Sheehan, Timothy D, 247
Sheffer, Wade, 821
Sheftel, Bradley, 1904
Shehab, Tom, 150
Sheiner, Andrew, 2030
Sheldon, Jeffrey, 487
Shelley, Anne-Marie, 38
Shen, David, 591
Shen, Robert, 897
Shen, Dave, 1101
Shen, James, 1511
Sheng, Brian, 788, 1810
Shepherd, T Nathanael, 1864
Shepherd, Thomas R, 1864
Sher, Judd, 927
Sheridan, Cynthia S, 244
Sheridan, Ben, 292
Sherman, Rob, 315
Sherman, John W, 598
Sherman, Mike, 1190
Sherman, Craig, 1213
Sherman, Richard L, 1636
Sherman Jahic, Jodi, 83
Sherrill, Stephen C., 357
Sherwood, Ned, 2021
Sheskey, Susan, 595
Sheynkman, Kirill, 1598
Shideler, Jason, 1160
Shields, Jack, 313
Shih, Ben, 972
Shiloni Shem Tov, Shlomi, 438
Shim, Brian, 422
Shin, Kevin, 883
Shipman, Chris, 429
Shipp, Terrance M, 1210
Shiriam, Ram, 1669
Shirley, Edwin, 715
Shkolnik, Gene, 2142
Shlesinger, Joseph, 2076
Shoch, John F., 87
Shoemaker, John P, 1234
Shoemaker, Jr., Raleigh A., 257
Shoham, Amnon, 438
Shove, Greg, 1087
Shroff, Zubeen, 809
Shuart, Rick, 377
Shuchman, Salem, 684
Shukla, Anhishek, 930
Shulkin, Jonathan K., 1904
Shulman, Zachary, 434
Shulz, Ryan, 703
Shum, Tony, 38
Shurtleff, Rob, 619
Sica, Frank V., 1779
Siddal, Evan, 2029
Sidwa, James, 404
Sieg, Clara, 1558
Siegal, Laura, 47
Siegel, John, 518
Siegel, Brian J, 896
Siegel, Mark A., 1203
Siegel, Joshua B., 1599
Siegel, Tom W, 1667
Siegel, Rob, 2010
Siegel, Stephan, 2263
Siegel, Micah, 2270
Siegler, M.G., 894
Siemer, Arnold B, 607
Siemplenski, Michael, 733
Sigalow, Ian, 876

Executive Name Index

Sigler, Mary Ann, 1455
Siguler, George W., 1681
Sikes, Toni F., 378
Sikkens, Hans, 1754
Silbernagel, Corry J., 2058
Sill, Valerie J., 637
Sillitoe, Andrew, 136
Sillman, Eric H., 137
Siltala, Michael, 2279
Silton, Michael, 49
Silverberg, Brad, 978
Silverberg, Michal, 1350
Silverman, Scott, 69
Silverman, Jeff, 69
Silverman, Andrew A., 405
Silverman, Mark, 430
Silverman, David, 564
Sim, Ed, 308
Simi, Bonny, 1039
Simko, Susan, 1474
Simmons, J. Frederick, 786
Simmons, Walker C., 1410
Simmons, Nat, 1476
Simon, Frank, 174
Simon, Robert J., 324
Simon, Lawrence R., 505
Simon, John, 1675
Simoni, Richard, 183
Simonian, Steve, 84
Simons, James R, 1728
Simons, Noa, 3269
Simonson, Ray, 2271
Simpson, John H., 346
Simpson, Todd, 2150
Simpson, Merv, 2274
Simpson Jr., Bryan, 830
Sims, Mark, 2233
Sinclair, Peter, 1106
Sinclair, Craig, 2099
Sing, George L, 1096
Sing-Wood Yeh, Woody, 118
Singer, Carlyle, 54
Singer, Andrew, 676
Singerman, Brian, 778
Singh, Ajit, 176
Singh, Mayank, 448
Singh, Vic, 680
Singh, Harpinder, 1001
Singh, Raj, 1039
Singhavon, Norton, 2095
Singleton, Steven D, 1261
Sinha, Shounok, 534
Sinha, Bipul, 1125
Sinnerberg, John, 578
Sirinakis, CPA, Kyparissia, 690
Sirois, Charles, 163
Sirois, Charles, 2252
Sirois, Francois-Charles, 2255
Sirois, Charles, 2255
Sirois, Denis M., 2255
Siskin, Edward J, 940
Sisteron, Yves, 1890
Sitohang, Helman, 555
Siuta, Philip, 532
Sivolella, Eileen, 61
Skaff, Michael C, 1651
Skapinker, Mark, 2060
Skarinka, Bill, 1499
Skidmore, Alyse, 1336
Skinner, Stuart, 319
Skok, David R, 1184
Skoler, Steven F., 791
Slaats, Paul, 1234
Slackman, David S., 956
Slade, Mike, 1644
Slatoff, Karl, 2019
Slaughter, Rick, 1758

Sloan, Stephan C., 126
Sloan, Bradley, 1516
Sloane, Steve, 1203
Slodowitz, Mitchell, 419
Slusky, Alex, 1912
Slutzkin, Craig, 1297
Slye, Jack, 1140
Small, Robert J., 257
Smalley, Matt, 383
Smardon, Dave, 2053
Smart, Gregg, 722
Smeltzer, James L, 412
Smiga, Brian, 91
Smiley, Ryan A, 1570
Smith, Jacob, 3
Smith, Matthew M, 17
Smith, Geoffrey W., 179
Smith, Sarah, 224
Smith, Robert, 367
Smith, Michael L, 412
Smith, Bruce, 417
Smith, Robert A., 424
Smith, Jed, 430
Smith, R Adam, 483
Smith, Rick, 562
Smith, Theodore J., 638
Smith, Paul, 834
Smith, Brian S, 861
Smith, Adrian, 978
Smith, Thomas, 1143
Smith, Tom, 1174
Smith, Stephen K, 1178
Smith, Byron, 1261
Smith, Jed, 1393
Smith, Craig, 1471
Smith, Brian R, 1601
Smith, Tom, 1628
Smith, Stanley T., 1773
Smith, Paul G, 1797
Smith, Marcus, 1815
Smith, Vinny, 1831
Smith, Robert, 1940
Smith, Bill, 2040
Smith, Gregory, 2151
Smith, Gregory J., 2158
Smith Jr, Peter H, 1738
Smith Jr, W Thomas, 1865
Smith, IV, Ben T., 31
Smith-Eppsteiner, Sam, 1001
Smith-Maxwell, Andrew, 726
Smolen, David, 828
Smoot, Timothy L, 1209
Smorynski, Tammi, 1009
Smulowitz, Warren, 2069
Smythe, Gordon, 2187
Snow, John W., 453
Snow, Scott L., 747
Snow III, John I, 1505
Snyder, Pete, 618
Snyder, Andrew, 851
Snyder, James C., 904
Snyder, Darren M, 1473
So, George, 2151, 2158
So, Susan, 2202
Soane, Mark, 143
Sobachevskiy, Roman, 895
Sobeck, Joshua, 13
Sobecki, Christopher, 1022
Soberg, Jon, 1269
Sobieski, PhD, Ian, 229
Sobiloff, Peter, 1005
Sobol, Edward P, 1973
Sobota, MD, Joseph T., 140
Socas, James, 1888
Socolof, Stephen, 1304
Soesman, Gideon, 2136
Soffe, Alex, 1074

Soghikian, Shahan D, 1411
Sohail, Sajid A., 95
Soignet, MD, Steven L., 158
Sokol, Marc, 754
Sokol, Marc, 1042
Sokoloff, Jonathan, 1113
Solomon, Katie, 823
Solomon, Glenn, 827
Solomon, Michael S, 1113
Solomon, David, 1212
Solomon, Christopher W, 1973
Solomon, Joel, 2230
Solomon MD, Stephen B, 573
Solow, Mark G, 566
Solow, Todd, 1345
Solvik, Pete, 1028
Somasegar, S, 1162
Somer, Greg, 693
Somers, Nicholas, 1765
Son, Erica S., 167
Soni, Vipul B., 360
Sonshine, Daniel, 2264
Sonsini, Peter, 1296
Sorensen, Carsten, 2210
Sorenson, Luke, 1707
Sorrel, Lawrence B., 1779
Sosa del Valle, Jose M., 1116
Sosin, Tyler, 1203
Sosnik, Esteban, 1530
Sotirhos, Michael, 280
Souder, Andrew, 1524
Souleles, Thomas S, 1160
Southworth, McLain, 564
Souvignier, Chad W, 1546
Sowers, Jason, 2000
Spaght, Pearson, 750
Spahn, Stephen H, 1506
Spaht, Holden, 1817
Spain, Kevin, 666
Spalding, Dick, 1063
Sparkman, Thorne, 1695
Sparks, Megan, 534
Spass, Robert A., 407
Spector, Michael, 1941
Speiser, Mike, 1762
Spell, William H, 1722
Spencer, Donald, 1681
Spencer, Jeb S, 1871
Spencer Jr., Edson W., 67
Sperling, Scott M., 1818
Spero, Donald, 1298
Spero, Benjamin M, 1720
Spicer, Julia, 3260
Spiegel, Leo, 1239
Spieker, Paul, 737
Spilizewski, Karen, 1578
Spillane, Geoffrey D., 878
Spinale, John, 1033
Spirn, Samuel W., 257
Spivack, Adam, 520
Splinter, Patricia, 1908
Spofford, Christopher, 346
Spogli, Ronald P., 786
Spreng, David, 556
Spring, Andrew, 1231
Sprole, Jerry, 1107
Srinivasan, Savitha, 971
Sripadam, Kumar, 1827
Srivastava, Amit, 683
Srivastava, Siddharth, 2183
Srugo, Pablo, 2187
Ssuto, Amy, 163
St. Jean, Brian, 20
Stack MD, Richard, 1774
Staenberg, Jon, 1736
Stahl, Rick, 661
Stahr, Clancey, 841

Stalcup, Christopher R, 472
Stalder, Dana, 1184
Stampacchia, Otello, 1373
Stanbro, Kyle, 352
Stancik Boyce, Maureen, 849
Stanek, Michael, 1044
Stanford, Scott, 44
Stanley, Nicholas J, 1911
Stansky, Brian, 1008
Stanton, Ben, 893
Stanton, Luke K., 1694
Starcevich, John J., 1438
Stark, Michael, 564
Stark, David, 882
Starling, William, 1774
Starr, Eric D., 410
Starr, Ira, 1145
Starr, Kevin, 1814
Stasik, Jared, 608
Stassen, Dave, 1728
Stata, Nicole M., 316
Statter, Joseph, 702
Staub, Craig, 1368
Staudt, William, 668
Staudt, Christopher, 668
Stavis, Rob, 263
Steans, Jennifer, 531
Steed, Michael, 1401
Steele, Scott, 1044
Steenrod, Wright, 477
Stefanski, Bob, 657
Steffens, John L, 1733
Stein, Martin, 279
Stein, Jonathan A., 547
Stein, Josh, 610
Stein, Christian, 1499
Stein, Jason, 1822, 1992
Steinbeck, Michael A, 1747
Steinberg, Dimitri, 775
Steinberg, Michael, 1531
Stenberg, Scott, 1004
Stento, Gregory, 912
Stepanov, Nina, 29
Stephan, Roderick, 99
Stephens, W Brad, 286
Stephens, P Bart, 286
Stephenson, Thomas J, 1926
Stern, David, 504
Stern, James A., 576
Stern, Brian E, 1738
Stern, Ronald N, 2249
Sternlicht, Barry S., 1742
Steuerman, Andrew H., 848
Stevens, Scott R., 1410
Stevens, Todd, 1545
Stevens, Mike, 2040
Stevens, John, 2040
Stevenson, James, 21
Stevenson, Gary, 1190
Stevenson, Dave, 1206
Stevenson, Jeffrey T, 1929
Stevenson, Lawrence, 2076
Stevenson DVM, PhD, Sharon, 1371
Stewart, William H, 1280
Stewart, Donald E., 1727
Stewart, Robert M., 1730
Stewart, E Jack, 1922
Stewart, Andy, 1988
Stewart, Greg, 2135
Stewart, Kalen, 2269
Steyn, Howard, 1092
Stiefel, Sean, 1282
Stienes, David A, 1140
Stiff, Jamie, 2125
Stimson, Keith, 886
Stinnett, David, 1858
Stobo, John, 21

Executive Name Index

Stofer, Gordon, 466
Stoffer, Jason, 1186
Stokel, Kathryn J, 17
Stokes, Richard, 931
Stokes, John, 2224
Stolle, Bryan, 1985
Stone, Brent, 20
Stone, Sheldon, 1362
Stone, Matt, 1499
Stone JD, Paul A, 11
Stoner, Chelsea, 238
Storcheus, Alex, 2117
Storer, Tim, 8
Storm, Bridget, 1001
Stott, Janet L., 1830
Stott, David, 1990
Stout, Caroline, 710
Stout, C Morris, 1769
Stowater, Tyler J, 300
Stowe, Rick, 921
Strachman, Paul, 1533
Strain, Christian R, 1754
Strasser, David, 1768
Straub, Paul, 493
Strauch, Mark, 92
Strauch, Roger A, 1584
Strawbridge, Oak, 880
Streur, John, 379
Strickberger, Neal, 1647
Stringham, Ned, 8
Strohband, Sven, 1073
Strom, John A., 898
Strong, Melanie, 1318
Strong, Craig, 2235
Strongin, Matthew, 739
Strother, Robert, 1286
Strottman, Matthew, 983
Stroud, Marcus, 1877
Struck, John S, 1956
Stuart, Scott, 1606
Stuart, Tyler, 2134
Stubblefield, Richard, 1122
Stubbs, Dave, 383
Stubbs, Tim, 1755
Stubler, Mike, 629
Stubler, Mike, 3264
Stuck, Bart, 1678
Stulberger, Adam F., 1779
Stull, Steven, 60
Stupore, Greg, 13
Sturdy, Laela, 579
Sturiale, Nick, 1661
Sturner, Andrew, 558
Sturtevant, Reed, 1489
Subotovsky, Santi, 666
Subramaniam, Somu, 1302
Suder, Thorsten, 404
Sugar, Daniel, 1927
Sugarman, Mark, 1227
Sugden, Chris, 655
Suh, Alex, 374
Suissa, Yanev, 1689
Suit, Dickson, 1025
Sukhar, Ilya, 1184
Sullivan, Patrick, 223
Sullivan, Nancy, 979
Sullivan, Timothy P, 1160
Sullivan, Matt, 1425
Sullivan, Jeanne M., 1810
Sullivan, Brian, 1992
Sun, Evelyn, 149
Sun, Ben, 1479
Sun, Pocket, 1703
Sundarrajan, Prabakar, 504
Suri, Saurabh, 455
Susan, Lior, 648
Suslak, Neil S., 325

Sussman, Philip N., 1811
Suster, Mark, 1890
Sutherland, Timothy F., 1229
Sutherland, David, 1229
Sutherland, Hamish, 2147, 2279
Sutter, Martin, 698
Sutter Jr., William P., 947
Suttin, Adam L, 1053
Sutton, Lynda, 432
Sutton, Howard, 2258
Suzuki, Terry, 1387
Svennilson, Peter, 519
Svoboda, John A, 1767
Svrluga, Brad, 1479
Swain, Steven, 442
Swaine, Mark, 496
Swan, Robert, 1123
Swan, Kevin, 1962
Swani, Sanjay, 1779
Swanson, Eric, 893
Swanson, Matthew E., 1567
Swanson Jr., Douglas E., 673
Swartz, Steven R., 925
Swartz, Robert, 1208
Swartzman, Steven, 367
Sweeney, Ryan, 27
Sweeney, Malcolm, 1486
Sweeney, Chris, 1962
Swenberg, Scot E, 480
Swenson, Jeff T., 1818
Swildens, Hans, 990
Sykes, Trey, 1018
Syversen, Jason, 2
Szapiro, Dov, 558
Szczepaniak Rice, Katie, 689
Sze, David, 877
Szejko, Kelly, 3264
Szigethy, Béla, 1576
Szweras, Adam, 2117

T

Ta, Napoleon, 778
Taber, Mark D., 862
Tabet, Karim A., 1498
Tabors, Dave, 238
Tadler, Richard D, 1778
Taetle, Alan J, 1332
Taft, Peter, 1266
Tagare, Varsha, 1511
Tagler, Jason R., 386
Tai, Gus, 1855
Talalla, Dominic, 2265
Talbot, Kevin, 2228
Talbott, Devin, 681
Tall, Spencer, 84
Tam, Nathan, 2041
Tamashunas, Bob, 1641
Tamburri, Dave, 921
Tamer, Tony, 931
Tammenoms Bakker, Juliet, 1147
Tammineedi, Anil, 127
Tan, Martin, 153
Tan, Jui, 299
Tan, Edwin, 404
Tan, Patrick, 870
Tan, Garry, 995
Tan PhD, Zhi, 1340
Tanaka, Akio, 641
Tananbaum, Andrew, 566
Tananbaum, Jim, 764
Taneja, Hemant, 820
Tanenbaum, Larry, 2162
Taney, Richard, 1866
Tang, Steven, 627
Tango, Jo, 1069
Tannas, Scott, 2260
Tannenbaum, Jeff, 299

Tansey, Casey, 1898
Tapman, Micah, 395
Taragin, Bruce K., 304
Taranto, Bill, 1206
Tarazid-Tarawali, Andrew, 54
Tardio, Stephen C., 956
Tarini, Mark A., 157
Tarnowski, Thomas M, 1754
Tarr, Bill, 1258
Tarr Jr., Jake, 1076
Taslitz, Steven, 1745
Taub, Bruce, 192
Taub, Andrew C., 1092
Taubman, Steven J, 1910
Taylor, Bryan, 61
Taylor, Craig C., 87
Taylor, Lucius H., 157
Taylor, Neil J., 324
Taylor, Kathryn, 704
Taylor, Gus, 719
Taylor, Michael, 912
Taylor, Meg, 988
Taylor, Paulette, 1619
Taylor, Harry D, 1778
Taylor, Jonathon W, 1802
Taylor, Jim, 2115
Taylor, Allison M., 2155
Taylor II, William H, 1262
Taylor-Smith, Ralph, 812
Tedesco, Pete, 921
Tedford, Alastair, 78
Teeger, John L., 777
Tegan, Jennifer, 434
Teixeira, Patrick, 1397
Tekkora, Baran, 1577
Televantos, John, 172
Teller, Sam, 1103
Templeman, Mike, 892
Templeton, Troy D, 1859
Teng, Nelson, 460
Tenkle, Jim, 1621
Tepper, Yaniv, 127
Tepper, MD, Robert, 1814
Terhorst, Eric, 733
Terkowitz, Ralph, 21
Terpak, Daniel, 467
Terry, Annie S, 1160
Tertzakian, Peter, 2036
Teschke, Jeffrey J, 1053
Tesconi, Lee J, 1116
Teslia, Ken, 2107
Tessier, Todd, 2270
Teten, David, 724
Tevanian, Avie, 660
Thadani, Shravan, 1858
Thakker, Dharmesh, 238
Thapar, Vik, 577
Tharrington, Owen G., 878
Thau, Kevin, 1718
Thees, Anderson, 641
Theleen, Robert A, 475
Thermond, Jeff, 2010
Thesseling, Joost F., 478
Thiboutot PhD, Ronald P, 1120
Thiel, Peter, 778
Thiele-Sardina, Roy, 936
Thoma, Carl D, 1817
Thomas, Pete, 185
Thomas, Harry, 254
Thomas, Dave, 843
Thomas, Kathleen, 1037
Thomas, Andrew A, 1747
Thomas, James E, 1820
Thomas Jr, David E, 1529
Thompson, William B., 783
Thompson, Eric, 872
Thompson, Bennett, 1090

Thompson, Shawn, 1369
Thompson, Sam, 1488
Thompson, Tyler, 1645
Thompson, Rick, 1680
Thompson, Jeremy, 2211
Thompson Black, Timothy, 1007
Thompson PhD, James, 885
Thomssen, Eli L., 140
Thonis, Michael G., 458
Thornbury, Leslie, 3254
Thorndike, William N., 952
Thornton, John, 205
Thornton, Jim, 892
Thorp, James, 16
Thorp, Clay B, 918
Thorpe, Allen, 927
Thorson, Michael, 2002
Thrope, Geoffrey B, 1286
Thukral, Nikhil, 1092
Thurow, Ethan, 371
Thériault, Annie, 2084
Tian, Esther, 346
Tichenor, Andrew, 291
Tichio, Robert M, 1577
Ticknor, Carolyn, 994
Tidwell, Brandon, 1679
Tiedemann, Bruce, 315
Tierney Jr., Paul E., 137
Tilley, Brian C., 611
Tilley, Shermaine, 2086
Timmerman III, William, 851
Tindel, Andrew B., 1410
Tippins, John, 1749
Tisch, David, 321
Tisdale, Andrew A., 1498
Titan, Keith, 259
Titus, David, 1995
Tjan, Tony, 568
To, Kilin, 1771
Toan, Robert, 1951
Tobin, Scott, 238
Toby, Elias, 2088
Tolan, Mary, 471
Tolle, Steve, 941
Tolmie, David, 654
Tom, David B, 1910
Tomai, William, 449
Tomasello, Anthony L, 991
Tomes, John, 919
Tomlin, Steve, 209
Tompkins, Graves, 819
Tompkins, Daniel, 1354
Toncheva, Dafina, 1898
Tong, Bryant J, 1355
Toomay, John, 1409
Toomey Jr., John, 912
Topilow, Justin, 253
Topouzian, Ara, 3259
Topper, MD, PhD, James N., 785
Torenberg, Peter, 1935
Torres, S Edward, 1128
Torres, Jason P, 1168
Torres Picon, Pedro, 1521
Toth, Bryan J., 761
Tou, Joseph, 1705
Toups, W. Anthony, 60
Towns, Matthew, 2242
Townsend, David G, 747
Townsend, Jason, 1550
Tracey, Martha, 554
Traer CPA, Mary, 912
Traidman, Brent, 721
Train, C. Bowdoin, 880
Trala, Anna May L, 889
Tran, Angela, 2272
Trang, John, 2212
Traub, Michael, 1835

Executive Name Index

Trauben, Jon, 99
Travaglini, John, 2023
Travers, Chris, 1534
Traylor, Chris, 758
Traynor, Sean M, 1973
Trbovich, John, 173
Tremblay, Pascal, 2198
Trenchard, Bill, 742
Trenk, Steve, 1139
Treu, PhD, Jesse, 622
Treyger, Victoria, 720
Triebsch, Brad, 574
Triedman, J Russell, 1133
Triest, Jonathon, 1154
Tripathi, Pavan, 336
Triplett, Michael, 1005
Trippet, Blake, 1224
Trivinos, Leda, 748
Trochu, Jean-Louis, 1825
Troost, Peter, 1499
Troppe, Asher, 1845
Trotter, David, 1999
Trudeau, Robert, 1787
Trueger, Arthur, 255
Truehart, John P., 957
Truetzel, David W., 199
Truslow, Ned, 1560
Trussler, Douglas B., 277
Truwit, Mitch, 136
Trzcinka, Terry, 1975
Trzepacz, Jennifer, 1985
Tsai, Christine, 10
Tsai, Tenno, 931
Tsai, Tommy, 1142
Tsai, Natasha, 2061
Tsang, David, 46
Tsang, Kai, 1924
Tsien, Matt, 821
Tsui, Doug, 950
Tucker, Robert, 404
Tucker, James W., 547
Tucker, Stanley W, 1209
Tucker, Jeff S, 1220
Tuleta, Karen, 1266
Tullis, Jim, 1868
Tullis, John, 1868
Tully, Daniel G., 97
Tully, Timothy, 1869
Tune, Kathleen A, 1820
Tung, Hans, 827
Tunnell, David, 927
Tunnicliff, Jonathan, 1349
Turck, Matt, 744
Turkewitz, Jordan, 2019
Turnbull, Gregory G., 2068
Turner, Matt, 114
Turner, Amherst, 114
Turner, Emily, 488
Turner, Guy, 965
Turner, Duncan, 1709
Turner, Patrick N.W., 1929
Turner, Christopher, 1957
Turner, John H., 1979
Turner III, Daniel K, 1251
Turner Moffitt, Andrea, 1458
Turner, J.D., Court R., 30
Turowsky, Jason, 106
Tusk, Bradley, 1870
Tuttle, Philip A, 592
Tuttle, Richard C, 1494
Twiford, J. Rainer, 387
Tybur, James, 1434
Tylee, Greg, 2244
Tyrrell, Mike, 1918
Tzeng, John, 908
Tzung, Cleve, 206

U

Ucciferri, Louie, 916
Uhlman, Tom, 1304
Uhrig, J. William, 1822
Ukropina, Rob, 278
Ulevitch PhD, Richard J, 11
Ullah, Salman, 1219
Ulrich, Catherine, 744
Unanue, Andy, 196
Underwood, Robert L, 1333
Underwood, John H., 1438
Ungerer, Scott, 677
Unkovic, Robert, 1102
Unruh, Paul, 1795
Unsworth, David, 2146
Unterberger, Steve, 419
Upchurch, Jim, 376, 377
Upton, Richard, 910
Urbina, Elias "Lee", 595
Uribe, Juan, 142
Usher, Mark, 2074
Usman, Nassim, 1257
Ussery, Randall, 1985
Utay, Marc A, 494
Uzumeri, Erol, 2243
Uzzaman, Anis, 721

V

Vachet, Claude, 2087
Vainno, MD, PhD, Petri, 698
Vaitkunas, Davis, 2058
Vaknin, Motti, 438
Valenti, Michele, 1551
Valentine, Jeff, 706
Valis, Tomas, 2070
Valkin, Adam, 820
Van Alstyne, Matthew, 1367
van Beuningen, Fred, 2072
Van Bladel, Sigrid, 19
Van Bladel, PhD, Sigrid, 19
Van Cuylenburg, Peter, 556
van der Velden, Peter, 2173
Van Harten, Kenton S., 905
van Horne, Charles H, 17
van Lierop, Wal, 2072
Van Marken, Tony, 2112
van Praet, Jean-Edouard, 982
van Schie, Adrian, 230
Van Steenbergen, Jeff, 2044
Van Thiel, Gijs FJ, 13
Van Vleck, Michael, 858
Van Wielingen, Mac, 2036
VanBelle, Jennifer, 811
VanDyke, Blue, 8
VanHoy, Scott, 1109
Vandaele, Christophe, 1907
Vander Schaaff, Tom, 655
Vanderbeck, Sunny, 1625
Vanderhoofven, Grady, 1215
Vandervelden, James E, 1826
Vandevenne, Rurik G, 1575
Vanier, Vance, 471
Vannelli, Vince, 1088
Vardell, Thomas, 1341
Vardhana, Anarghya, 1186
Varier, Krishnan, 152
Varino, Fil, 3249
Varma, Samit, 133
Varshneya, Rajeev, 281
Vasilescu, Katie, 838
Vasishth, Vishal, 1363
Vaslet, Charles, 2101
Vassallo, Steve, 773
Vassallo, Mark F, 1127
Vaughan, James, 237
Vaughan, Ben, 2062
Vazé, Jana, 1341

Veale, Stuart, 254
Veatch, Kyle, 929
Veber, Gayle L, 1911
Veedon, Mathew, 1714
Veitch, John, 2076
Veith, Anthony J, 505
Velazquez, Louis, 725
Velez, Tristan, 929
Vendetti, Dino, 766, 1659
Venditti, Mario, 2149
Venerable, Mike, 481
Venkatachalam, Kapil, 1787
Venkataraman, Sriram, 212
Vere Nicoll, Neville, 543
Veres, Rob, 1724
Verhalen, Andrew W, 1184
Vermylen Jr, Paul A, 1072
Vernal, Mike, 1657
Vernick, Shoshana, 1745
Vernudachi, Charles, 1499
Verratti, Robert N., 1830
Veru, Dennison T, 1402
Vettel, Matthew T., 862
Vetter, Martin, 2043
Victor, Jonathan, 228
Victor, Skip, 228
Vigano, Paul R., 1041
Vigoda, Robert A., 428
Vijayavargiya, Sonali, 198
Vincent, John, 1557
Virani, Aamir, 780
Virtue, Ted, 1231
Vishria, Eric, 251
Visser, Mark, 248
Vitorovic, Tefan, 1934
Vitullo, Nicole, 622
Vitus, Andy, 1629
Vivaldi, Nicole, 2112
Vivian, Steve, 1481
Vogel, Andrew, 2019
Vogelbaum, Martin, 1561
Vogt, Christine, 78
Vohooshi, Amir, 2025
Volftsun, Lev, 1960
Volpe, Lou, 1084
Volpe, Joe, 1206
Volpe, Drew, 1486
Volpert, Barry, 560
Volpi, Matteo, 2068
von der Goltz, Johan, 313
von der Goltz, Alex, 313
von Dohlen, Gerard, 346
von Holzhausen, Kurt, 346
von Maltzahn, Geoffrey, 748
von Schroeter, Carlo A, 1979
Von Schlegell, John, 674
Von Stroh, Eric, 1145
von Zuben, Max, 1984
Vorhoff, Robbert, 819
Vorlicek, Martha DiMatteo, 912
Voss, Scott, 912
Vrionis, John, 1125
Vyule, Stuart, 1573

W

Wachtel, Bonnie K, 1950
Wachter, David, 1949
Wack, Patrick, 1561
Waddington, Ryan, 964
Wade, James F, 1157
Wadhera, Karan, 420
Wadih, Anibal, 838
Wadsworth, Robert, 912
Wadsworth II, Eliot, 952
Wagman, Michael, 2075
Wagner, Daniel, 532
Wagner, Bradaigh, 674

Wagner, Alyse, 1113
Wagner, Peter, 1996
Wahla, Ahmed, 1085
Wahrhaftig, David I, 1066
Walden, Michael, 1553, 1554
Waldrip, William D., 672
Waldusky, Michelle A, 634
Walecka, John, 1537
Walfish, Marc J, 1210
Walk, Hunter, 944
Walker, Jim, 56
Walker, Clinton W., 496
Walker, James B., 555
Walker, Tom, 1556
Walker, Colin, 2083
Walkinshaw, Mike, 2262
Wall, Terrence R, 584
Wall, IV, Thomas R, 1066
Wallace, Brian D, 35
Wallace, Ben, 216
Wallace, Peter, 280
Wallace, Brendan, 728
Wallace, Tom, 754
Wallace, Peggy, 845
Wallace, Jonathan R, 1389
Walrath, Michael, 1980
Walsh, Paul, 371
Walsh, Timothy, 435
Walsh, Robert, 700
Walsh, Ryan, 752
Walsh, Kevin T., 949
Walsh, Rob, 1772
Walter, Tobi, 512
Walter, Mark R., 890
Walter Jr., Kenneth G., 905
Walters, Jeffrey M., 1097
Walton, Andrew, 2156
Walvoord, John E, 1699
Wanek, David, 1976
Wang, T Chester, 46
Wang, Sona, 454
Wang, Mingyao, 521
Wang, Lucas, 521
Wang, Ted, 553
Wang, Tzyy-Po, 908
Wang, Xiao, 998
Wang, Tiffine, 1269
Wang, Ryan, 1391
Wang, Timothy, 1978
Wang, Tianpeng, 2187
Ward, Carter A., 157
Ward, Sean, 293
Ward, Robert, 1213
Ward, Mike, 1517
Ward, J.R. Kingsley, 2274
Warden, Todd, 910
Ware, Matt, 1164
Ware, Zach, 1914
Warnock, David L., 386
Warnock, Greg, 1205
Warren, Todd, 619
Warren, Jermaine L., 973
Warren, Wilson S, 1116
Warren, Scott, 1234
Warren, Gus, 1614
Washing, Tom, 1656
Washington, Alex, 1990
Washington, Kyle, 2079
Wasserman, Keith, 814
Wassong, David, 1314
Watchmaker, Linda, 538
Waters, Steve, 1813
Watkins, Dan, 1207
Watkins, Anita, 1559
Watkins, Timothy, 1904
Watt, Trevor, 927
Watts, William E, 1053

Executive Name Index

Watts, Michael, 1132
Watts, Katherine, 1714
Waud, Reeve B, 1964
Waugh, Stuart, 2196
Waxberg, Jason, 3260
Waxman, David, 1800
Weaver, Graham, 92
Weaver, Allen A, 1440
Webb, Jeffrey M., 989
Webb, Maynard, 1969
Webb, PhD, Brad, 493
Weber, Kara, 345
Weber, Tony R., 1326
Weber, Ellen, 1581
Weber, Paul, 2202
Weber, MD, Eckard, 622
Wedbush, Eric D, 1970
Weglicki, Tim, 21
Wehrung, Jamie, 178
Wei, Frank Z, 1957
Weiden, David, 1073
Weil, Burton B, 1921
Weinbar, Sharon, 1629
Weinberg, John, 700
Weiner, Eric, 294
Weiner, Joshua R., 741
Weinfurtner, Ed, 292
Weingarten, Michael, 1678
Weinhoff MD, Gregory M, 476
Weinryb, Merav, 1511
Weinstein, Paul, 218
Weinstein, Joshua S., 406
Weinstein, Brent, 1885
Weintraub, Daniel, 197
Weisenfeld, Andrew J, 1271
Weiser, Marc, 1596
Weisman, Wayne B, 1636
Weiss, Gwen, 6
Weiss, Daniel, 127
Weiss, Warren, 773
Weiss, Eli, 823
Weiss, Michael, 867
Weiss, Ira, 965
Weiss, Paul, 1923
Weissenburger, Michael S, 598
Weisskoff PhD, Robert, 711
Weissman, Andy, 1884
Welborn, Miller, 461
Welborn, Kyle, 570
Welborn, Steve M., 2008
Weldon, Thomas D, 39
Weldon, Raymond F, 356
Weldon, Norman, 1420
Weldon, Kent R., 1818
Welling, W Lambert, 1199
Wells, Richard, 1005
Wells, James, 1653
Wells, Richard, 2275
Welsh, Patrick J, 1973
Welsh JD, Jeanette M, 1794
Wendell, Peter, 1672
Wenger, Albert, 1884
Wenzel, Robert J., 73
Werdegar, Maurice, 1976
Wermuth, David J., 1746
Werner, Harold R., 922
Werry, Scott, 2030
Wertheimer, Stephen, 1949
Wertz, Boriz, 2272
Wesson, Bruce, 809
West, Ben, 38
West, Bob, 203
West, Mike, 469
West, Ted, 775
West, Casey, 1735
Westbrook, Thomas H., 747
Westbrook, Kirk, 1015

Wester, Forest, 1859
Westerlind, Victor, 812
Westervelt, Jr., William J., 181
Westly, Steve, 1978
Weston, Denny, 755
Weston, Jamie, 1733
Weston CFA, R Patrick, 216
Westphal, Christoph, 1149
Westra, James, 61
Wethington, Jerry D., 1574
Wethington, Bryan M., 1574
Wetzel, Robert B., 199
Whalen, T.J., 789
Whalen Brechtel, Margaret, 1526
Wheaton, Cal, 21
Wheeler, Brian, 260
Wheeler, Andy, 894
Whelan, Edward J., 257
Whelan, J.P., 1070
Whelan, Patrick F, 1427
Whickman, Kirk, 128
Whims, Jim, 93
Whitcomb, Chris, 1369
White, Brandon C., 458
White, Marshall C., 747
White, John D., 777
White, John, 1273
White, Sean C., 1727
White, James N, 1762
White, Gregory A., 1818
White, Aaron, 1941
White, Morty, 2008
White, Jason, 2159
White, Jeff, 2192
Whiteaker, Tom, 915
Whiteaker, Thomas, 971
Whiteley, Phyllis, 1985
Whitlock, Steve, 1725
Whittemore, Alexander D, 1754
Whorf, John, 1293
Whorton, Dave, 1867
Wiacek, Walter, 722
Wiberg, Bill, 58
Wick, Tyler, 20
Wick, Sam, 1885
Wick, William, 1939
Wicker, Damion, 1411
Wickham, Phil, 1716
Widder, Ken, 1098
Widmann, Sebastian C., 1134
Widner, Melissa, 1640
Widroe, Gred, 1197
Wiebe, Charles A., 266
Wierck, Ryan, 854
Wiggers, Lane W, 165
Wigle, Jeff, 2045
Wilcox, Harry, 748
Wild, Jason, 1052
Wilde, Peter O., 1498
Wilder, Lawrence, 1938
Wildstein, Evan, 1085
Wilkerson, L John, 809
Wilkins, Jay, 917
Wilkins, Eric J., 1410
Wilkins, Jr., Herbert P., 1773
Wilkinson, Alan, 63
Wilkosz, Leon R, 584
Willert, John, 404
Williams, Russ, 15
Williams, Greg, 28
Williams, Brayton, 310
Williams, Ryan, 543
Williams, Greg, 582
Williams, Brent, 899
Williams, Randy, 1065
Williams, Anthony L, 1209
Williams, Terry, 1321

Williams, Ev, 1363
Williams, Jeff, 1731
Williams, Richard J., 1979
Williams, Kristina, 2028
Williams, Peter, 2034
Williams, Tom, 2161
Williams Jr., Robert M., 1041
Williams, III, Edward C., 352
Williamson, Mark N., 371
Williamson, Donna, 454
Williamson, Elizabeth C, 792
Williamson, Glenn, 1289
Williamson PhD, Andrew, 1442
Wilson, Tim, 176
Wilson, Andrew, 203
Wilson, Brent, 464
Wilson, Joshua, 851
Wilson, Peter, 912
Wilson, Karen, 1014
Wilson, Jason, 1493
Wilson, Stoddard M, 1583
Wilson, Tyrone, 1773
Wilson, Adrian, 1844
Wilson, Russ, 1859
Wilson, Fred, 1884
Wilson, Kaley, 2221
Wilson PE, L Edward, 539
Wiltse, Jeannette, 2228
Winblad, Ann, 959
Winblad, Ann, 959
Winder, Caleb, 704
Winefeld, Elena, 40
Winklevoss, Tyler, 1998
Winklevoss, Cameron, 1998
Winn, Christopher, 2186
Winneg, Robert D, 1295
Winship, Chris, 796
Winship, Scott D., 893
Winslow, Frank, 1507
Winterer, Bill, 1419
Winterroth, Seth, 648
Winters, Ana M, 1232
Winters, Kyle, 2193
Wintrob, Jay, 1362
Wirt, Richard, 1394
Wise, Jim P., 898
Witherington, Hunter, 1735
Witherington Jr, James D, 1735
Witte, Curt, 336
Witte, Matthew L, 1171
Witzofsky, Bill, 402
Wizel, Neil A., 741
Wodlinger, David C., 167
Woiwode, Tom, 1930
Wojtowicz, Jean, 385
Wolf, Michael, 283
Wolf, Jen, 995
Wolfe, Josh, 1155
Wolfe, Kirk, 1242
Wolfe, Aaron P, 1755
Wolfe Strouse, Mimi, 38
Wolfe, Ph.D, Daniel B., 5
Wolfond, Henry, 2046
Wolfram, Tyler, 1360
Wolfson, Gene, 429
Wolfson, Rob, 931
Wolin, Harry, 107
Wolkon, Shari H., 1818
Wollaeger, Timothy, 1619
Wolmer, David, 1115
Wolpow, Marc, 197
Womsley, Robert, 1962
Wong, Rich, 27
Wong, Carol, 596
Wong, Henry, 613
Wong, Felix J, 753
Wong, Henry, 810

Wong, Mike, 941
Wong, Raymond L.M., 1733
Wood, Steve, 839
Wood, Steven F., 1018
Wood, Bob, 2002
Woodman, Robbie, 1780
Woodruff, Craig, 47
Woods, Emil, 1119
Woods Jr., Willie E., 973
Woodward, William, 133
Woodward, Gordon H, 1085
Woodward, Tim, 1355
Woodworth Jr, Alfred S, 647
Woody, Ken, 999
Woody, Jim, 1098
Wooten, Ron, 1349
Worthy, Ford, 1414
Wright, Mark, 290
Wright, Austin, 362
Wright, J.D., 491
Wright, Christopher G., 557
Wright, Tim, 853
Wright, Dalton, 1074
Wrinch, Colin, 2154
Wu, Dennis, 293
Wu, Paul, 875
Wu, Veronica, 945
Wu, Victor L, 1116
Wu, David, 1186
Wu, Tony, 1340
Wurzer, David, 532
Wyant, Jack, 290
Wyatt, Gordon T, 39
Wynperle, William J., 1663

X

Xeuzhao, Dr. Lan, 235
Xie, Chris, 2263
Xu, Peter, 662
Xu, Eric, 827

Y

Yadav, Ravi, 1314
Yamashita, Kevin, 260
Yang, James, 13
Yang, John, 328
Yang, Hai, 437
Yang, Ed, 974
Yang, Geoff, 1537
Yang, Jackie, 1840
Yang, Bruce, 2185
Yanney, Michael, 70
Yarborough, Benjamin W, 1210
Yardley, Daniel, 1424
Yates, Phil, 336
Yau, Philip, 828
Yeager, Caroline, 1023
Yeh, Chris, 1959
Yellurkar, Devdutt, 457
Yen, Tuff, 1658
Yeo, Young, 1866
Yeoham, Paul A, 1487
Yepez, J. Alberto, 1852
Yeshwant, Krishna, 894
Yi, Peter, 972
Yim, Charles, 641
Yoder, Lacey, 1824
Yohe, Matt, 1266
Yoon, Kwan, 299
Yoon, Cene, 336
York, Gwill, 1122
Yosef-Or, Tomer, 20
Yoskovitz, Ben, 2140
Young, John, 155
Young, David W., 436
Young, Tim, 680
Young, Brian D., 687

Executive Name Index

Young, Matthew, 687
Young, Caroline L., 904
Young, April, 928
Young, Steve, 962
Young, Chris, 1557
Young, Scott F, 1655
Young, Philip M, 1898
Young, Will, 1914
Young, Sarah, 2238
Young PhD, James W, 11
Youngkin, Glenn A, 416
Youstra, Bill, 1087
Yovovich, Paul G., 1095
Yu, Simon, 394
Yu, Janie, 799
Yu, Erica, 827
Yu, Ben, 1672
Yuan, David, 1537
Yuan, David, 1787
Yudkoff, Royce G., 20
Yuen, Homan, 802

Z

Zabbal, Christian, 1732
Zabik, Joseph J., 346
Zachary, George, 457
Zacuto, Adam, 451
Zaczepinski, Guy, 451
Zadourian, Keith, 1026
Zafar, Naeem, 95
Zaki, Kareem, 1823
Zambelli, Anthony W, 1651
Zamsky, Katherine, 411
Zanarini, Jeff, 931
Zang, Lu, 802
Zannino, Richard, 435
Zanone, Joseph, 582
Zaorski, Philip, 785
Zaplatynsky, John, 2210
Zappala, Timothy, 172
Zaslavsky, Dennis, 1965
Zatlukal, David J., 1041
Zaveri, Darshana, 428
Zbar, Brett, 764
Zeisig, Bernie, 2187

Zelaya, Briana J., 1905
Zell, Joseph, 881
Zelnick, Strauss, 2019
Zelter, James, 141
Zemp, Dal, 1545
Zeprun, Howard S., 1852
Zerbib, Nicolas D., 1746
Zhan, Stephanie, 1657
Zhang, Toby, 474
Zhang, Kevin, 1889
Zhao, Yipeng, 664
Zhou, Lili, 542
Zhou, Sha, 1391
Zhu, Wan Li, 713
Zhuang, Shelley, 3
Zhuo, TX, 729
Zhuo, TX, 1059
Ziebelman, Peter, 1406
Ziegler, Ryan, 655
Zilberman, Daniel, 1957
Zilis, Shivon, 287
Zine, Riadh, 2234
Zine, Imed, 2234

Zink Jr, Darell E, 412
Zinterhofer, Eric, 2243
Ziolkowski, Andy, 571
Zipp, Bob, 115
Zippelius, Pete, 1113
Zisson, Alex, 1820
Zittman, Mark, 1866
Zoellner, Scott, 63
Zohar, Daphne, 1503
Zola, Natty, 1179
Zolfaghari, Paul, 419
Zorich, Robert L., 673
Zou, Kenny, 2077
Zucco, Jim, 507
Zucker, Jeffrey M., 865
Zugaro, Chris, 1858
Zur, Ari M., 351
Zur Muhlen, Adriaan, 1488
Zurek, Andrea, 2009
Zych, Douglas, 1049

Geographic Index

Amsterdam
IDINVEST PARTNERS, 2842

Argentina
ACONCAGUA VENTURES, 2326
ALANTRA, 77
AXVENTURES, 2461
COMPASS GROUP, 524
GRUPO BISA, 2791

Australia
ACCEDE CAPITAL, 2315
ACRUX LIMITED, 2327
ACUMEN VENTURES, 2333
ADVANCE PROPERTY FUND, 2338
AMWIN MANAGEMENT PTY LIMITED, 2390
ANACACIA CAPITAL, 2391
ARCHER CAPITAL, 2411
ARES MANAGEMENT LLC, 160
AUSTRALIAN ETHICAL INVESTMENT LIMITED, 2447
BAIN CAPITAL PRIVATE EQUITY, 223
BLACKBIRD VENTURES, 2511
BLACKSTONE PRIVATE EQUITY GROUP, 280
BLUE COVE VENTURES, 2514
BRANDON CAPITAL PARTNERS, 2527
BROOKFIELD ASSET MANAGEMENT, 2062
CARLYLE GROUP, 416
CATALYST INVESTMENT MANAGERS PTY LIMITED PPM Capital, 2564
CISCO INVESTMENTS, 485
CLEANTECH VENTURES, 2604
CM CAPITAL, 2609
COLONIAL FIRST STATE PRIVATE EQUITY, 2613
CONCEPT FINANCIAL SERVICES, 2618
CONTINENTAL VENTURE CAPITAL LIMITED, 2622
CVC INVESTMENT MANAGERS LIMITED, 2636
DEUTSCHE ASSET MANAGEMENT (AUSTRALIA) LIMITED Deutsche Bank AG, 2650
ENDEAVOUR CAPITAL PTY LIMITED Endeavour Capital, 2690
ENTER VENTURES, 682
EQUITY PARTNERS PTY LIMITED, 2706
FIRST CORPORATE PTY LIMITED, 2734
FIRST INVESTMENT CORPORATION LIMITED, 2735
FORTRESS INVESTMENT GROUP LLC, 769
GREENHILL SAVP, 869
GRESHAM PRIVATE EQUITY LIMITED, 2790
HASTINGS FUNDS MANAGEMENT PTY LIMITED, 2805
HRL MORRISON & COMPANY LIMITED, 2826
INNOVATION CAPITAL LIMITED, 2868
JEGI CAPITAL, 1037
KALORI GROUP INVESTMENTS, 2906
KOHLBERG KRAVIS ROBERTS & COMPANY, 1086
LION SELECTION GROUP LIMITED, 2933
MACQUARIE DIRECT INVESTMENT LIMITED, 2942
MEDICAL RESEARCH COMMERCIALIZATION FUND, 2950
MOMENTUM FUNDS MANAGEMENT PTY LIMITED, 2966
NANYANG VENTURES PTY LIMITED, 2973
NBC CAPITAL PTY LIMITED, 2979
NEO TECHNOLOGY VENTURES, 2980
NEXTEC DEVELOPMENT CAPITAL LIMITED, 2991
NORTHLEAF CAPITAL PARTNERS, 2196
OneVentures, 3014
PACIFIC EQUITY PARTNERS PTY LIMITED, 3016
PHOSPHAGENICS, 3028
QUINBROOK INFRASTRUCTURE PARTNERS, 1520
RESOURCE CAPITAL FUNDS, 1551
RFC AMBRIAN RFC Group Ltd., 3070
RIVERSIDE COMPANY, 1576
RMB VENTURES LIMITED RMB Australia, 3074
ROTHSCHILD AUSTRALIA - ARROW PRIVATE EQUITY Rothschild Group, 3077
RUSSELL INVESTMENT MANAGEMENT LIMITED, 3080
SCALE INVESTORS, 3093
SENETAS CORPORATION LIMITED Senatas Group, 3101
SOUTHERN CROSS VENTURE PARTNERS, 1713
STARFISH VENTURES, 3129
STARPHARMA POOLED DEVELOPMENT LIMITED, 3130
SYDNEY SEED FUND, 3144
TANK STREAM VENTURES, 3151
TPG CAPITAL, 1837
YUUWA CAPITAL, 3238

Austria
3TS CAPITAL PARTNERS, 2301
ALANTRA, 77
ANDLINGER & COMPANY INC, 124
DARBY OVERSEAS INVESTMENTS LTD, 585
ENNOVENT, 2692
G & H KAPITAL PARTNER AG, 2755
GLOBAL EQUITY PARTNERS BETEILIGUNGS-MANAGEMENT, 2774
HORIZONTE VENTURE MANAGEMENT GmbH, 2823
INVEST EQUITY MANAGEMENT CONSULTING GmbH, 2878
TECNET, 3156
TPA CORPORATE FINANCE CONSULTING GMBH Horwarth International, 3175

Bahrain
ARCAPITA INC, 153
INVESTCORP, 1021

Bavaria
BAYERN KAPITAL, 2486

Belgium
3M UNITEK, 2299
ACKERMANS & VAN HAAREN, 2324
ALLEGRO INVESTMENT FUND, 2358
ANDLINGER & COMPANY INC, 124
AON RISK SOLUTIONS Aon Corporation, 2405
ARKAFUND MEDIA & ICT, 2417
BAEKELAND FUNDS, 2467
CAPRICORN VENTURE PARTNERS NV, 2554
E-CAPITAL MANAGEMENT, 2671
FLANDERS' FOREIGN INVESTMENT OFFICE, 2737
GIMV GIMV, 2771
GIMV NV, 2772
GUIDANT EUROPE SA, 2794
HUMMINGBIRD VENTURES, 2828
INDUFIN, 2853
IPOSCOPE NV/SA, 2886
IT-PARTNERS NV, 2893
LRM - INVESTERINGSMAATSCHAPPIJ VOOR LIMBURG, 2940
MERIFIN CAPITAL, 2954
NAUSICAA VENTURES, 2977
NEW RHEIN HEALTHCARE INVESTORS, 1301
PMV, 3033
PUILAETCO PRIVATE BANKERS KBL Group, 3054
QBIC FUND, 3056
QUEST FOR GROWTH, 3060
RIVERSIDE COMPANY, 1576
SAMBRINVEST SA, 3087
SRIW SA SRIW Group, 3125
TECH TOUR, 3154
VIVES, 3216

Bermuda
ATILA VENTURES, 2433
D.E. SHAW & CO. LP, 580
LONE STAR FUNDS, 1144
WAFRA INC, 1952

Brazil
ACELERADORA, 2323
ACON INVESTMENTS, 45
AEM CAPITAL, 2341
ASTELLA INVESTMENTS, 2429
ATOMICO, 2437
BR OPPORTUNITIES, 2524
BROOKFIELD ASSET MANAGEMENT, 2062
BRZTECH, 2536
CARLYLE GROUP, 416
COMPANHIA RIOGRANDENSE DE PARTICIPACOES, 2617

Geographic Index

DARBY OVERSEAS INVESTMENTS LTD, 585
E.BRICKS DIGITAL, 2672
E.VENTURES, 641
EVERCORE CAPITAL PARTNERS, 700
EXPLORADOR CAPITAL MANAGEMENT, 2720
FIR CAPITAL PARTNERS, 2733
GENERAL ATLANTIC PARTNERS, 819
INITIAL CAPITAL, 2863
ITC VENTURES, 2894
MONASHEES CAPITAL, 2967
NAPKN VENTURES, 2974
PLEXUS VENTURES, 1456
PROJECT A VENTURE GmBH & CO. KG Project A Ventures Latam, 3047
QUALCOMM VENTURES, 1511
SIGULER GUFF & COMPANY, 1681
TELEFONICA VENTURES, 3160
TMG CAPITAL PARTNERS, 3171
WARBURG PINCUS LLC, 1957

Bulgaria

AXXESS CAPITAL, 2462
ELEVEN, 2687

Canada

FOUNDATION EQUITY CORPORATION, 2116
RELENTLESS PURSUIT PARTNERS, 2229
SANDPIPER VENTURES, 2238

AB

32 DEGREES CAPITAL, 2022
500 STARTUPS CANADA, 2024
ALBERTA ENTERPRISE, 2028
ALBERTA INVESTMENT MANAGEMENT CORP., 2029
ANNAPOLIS CAPITAL, 2034
APECTEC, 2035
ARC FINANCIAL, 2036
AVAC, 2043
AZIMUTH CAPITAL MANAGEMENT, 2044
AZURE CAPITAL PARTNERS, 218
CBI2 CAPITAL, 2068
CLARITY CAPITAL, 2602
CROWN CAPITAL PARTNERS, 2085
DISTRICT VENTURES CAPITAL, 2093
ENERTECH CAPITAL, 677
FORAGE CAPITAL PARTNERS, 2115
GREEN ACRE CAPITAL, 2134
INTRINSIC VENTURE CAPITAL, 2152
INVICO CAPITAL CORPORATION, 2155
JOG CAPITAL, 2159
KENSINGTON CAPITAL PARTNERS, 2160
LIONHART CAPITAL LTD, 2170
LONGBOW CAPITAL, 2171
MCROCK CAPITAL, 2183
NEXT EQUITIES, 2194
PANACHE VENTURES, 2204
PRIVITI CAPITAL, 2219
REGIMEN PARTNERS, 2227
RELAY VENTURES, 2228
RENEWABLETECH VENTURES, 1545
SAF GROUP, 2237
THE WESTERN INVESTMENT COMPANY OF CANADA, 2260
TRIWEST, 2267
VENTURE CAPITAL ASSOCIATION OF ALBERTA, 3270
WESTERN AMERICA CAPITAL GROUP, 2278
YALETOWN VENTURE PARTNERS, 2283

BC

7 GATE VENTURES, 2025
AMPLITUDE, 2032
ARDENTON, 2038
BOND CAPITAL, 2058
BRISIO INNOVATIONS INC., 2061
CAI CAPITAL PARTNERS, 368
CHRYSALIX, 2072
CM PARTNERS, 2077
COPPERLION CAPITAL, 2079

DISCOVERY CAPITAL, 2091
DOVENTI CAPITAL, 2095
EQUUS TOTAL RETURN, 695
EVOK INNOVATIONS, 2105
FOUNDERS GROUP OF FOOD COMPANIES, 2118
FRAMEWORK VENTURE PARTNERS, 2119
FULCRUM CAPITAL PARTNERS, 2121
HARDY CAPITAL PARTNERS, 2137
HEADWATER EQUITY PARTNERS, 2138
HIGHLAND WEST CAPITAL, 2139
HIGHLINE BETA, 2140
INBC INVESTMENT CORP, 2144
INVESTX, 2154
KENSINGTON CAPITAL PARTNERS, 2160
LIGHTHEART MANAGEMENT PARTNERS, 2168
LIGHTHOUSE EQUITY PARTNERS, 2169
LUMIRA CAPITAL, 2173
PANACHE VENTURES, 2204
PANGAEA VENTURES LTD, 2205
PARALLEL49 EQUITY, 2206
PENDER WEST CAPITAL PARTNERS, 2210
PIQUE VENTURES, 2215
QUARK VENTURE, 2221
RECAPHEALTH VENTURES, 2225
REGIMEN PARTNERS, 2227
RENEWAL FUNDS, 2230
SAF GROUP, 2237
SCALEUP VENTURES, 2240
SECOND CITY REAL ESTATE, 2244
STERN PARTNERS, 2249
TELUS VENTURES, 2256
TENX VENTURES, 2257
TIMIA CAPITAL, 2262
TOP RENERGY INC., 2263
TRICOR PACIFIC CAPITAL, 2266
VANCITY CAPITAL, 2269
VANEDGE CAPITAL PARTNERS, 2270
VERSANT VENTURES, 1930
VERSION ONE VENTURES, 2272
VRG CAPITAL, 2274
YALETOWN VENTURE PARTNERS, 2283
YELLOW POINT EQUITY PARTNERS, 2284

MB

CENTRESTONE VENTURES, 2071
RED LEAF CAPITAL, 2226

NB

ENERGIA VENTURES, 675
NEW BRUNSWICK INNOVATION FOUNDATION, 2192

NL

KILLICK CAPITAL, 2161
PELORUS VENTURE CAPITAL, 2208

NS

BIOENTERPRISE, 2053
BUILD VENTURES, 2063
INNOVACORP, 2148
NOVA SCOTIA BUSINESS INC., 2197
SEAFORT CAPITAL, 2242
TECHNOCAP, 2254

ON

4FRONT CAPITAL PARTNERS, 2023
ACCESS CAPITAL CORPORATION, 2026
AIP PRIVATE CAPITAL, 2027
ALBERTA INVESTMENT MANAGEMENT CORP, 2029
ALTAS PARTNERS, 2030
AMPLITUDE, 2032
ANCIENT STRAINS, 2033
ARCTERN VENTURES, 2037
ARDENTON, 2038
ARGOSY PARTNERS, 2039
ARVA LIMITED, 2040
ASHBRIDGE PARTNERS, 2041
AUXO MANAGEMENT, 2042

Geographic Index

BANYAN CAPITAL PARTNERS, 2045
BAYSHORE CAPITAL, 2046
BEDFORD CAPITAL, 2049
BERINGER CAPITAL, 2050
BEST FUNDS, 2051
BINGLEY CAPITAL, 2052
BIOENTERPRISE, 2053
BIOINDUSTRIAL INNOVATION CANADA, 2054
BIOMINDS LABS INC., 2055
BIRCH HILL EQUITY PARTNERS, 2056
BMO CAPITAL MARKETS, 2057
BONNEFIELD FINANCIAL, 2059
BRIGHTSPARK VENTURES, 2060
BROOKFIELD ASSET MANAGEMENT, 2062
CANADIAN BUSINESS GROWTH FUND, 2065
CANADIAN VENTURE CAPITAL ASSOCIATION Canadian Venture Capital & Private Equity Association, 3249
CARPEDIA INTERNATIONAL, 2066
CATALYST CAPITAL GROUP, 2067
CCEI, 2069
CELTIC HOUSE VENTURE PARTNERS, 2070
CIBC CAPITAL MARKETS, 2073
CIBC INNOVATION BANKING, 2074
CLAIRVEST GROUP, 2075
CLEARSPRING CAPITAL PARTNERS, 2076
COBALT CAPITAL, 2078
COVINGTON CAPITAL CORP., 2081
CREDIT MUTUEL EQUITY, 2082
CROSBIE & COMPANY, 2083
CROSS-BORDER IMPACT VENTURES, 2084
CROWN CAPITAL PARTNERS, 2085
CYCLE CAPITAL MANAGEMENT, 2087
DANCAP PRIVATE EQUITY, 2088
DIAGRAM VENTURES, 2090
DISRUPTION VENTURES, 2092
DMZ VENTURES, 2094
DREAM MAKER VENTURES, 2096
DRI CAPITAL, 2097
DW HEALTHCARE PARTNERS, 639
EDGESTONE CAPITAL PARTNERS, 2098
ELGNER GROUP INVESTMENTS, 2099
ELNOS, 2100
EMERALD TECHNOLOGY VENTURES, 2101
ENERTECH CAPITAL, 677
EPIC CAPITAL MANAGEMENT, 2102
ESPRESSO CAPITAL, 2103
EVENTI CAPITAL PARTNERS, 2104
EVERCORE CAPITAL PARTNERS, 700
EXPORT DEVELOPMENT CANADA, 2106
EXTREME VENTURE PARTNERS, 2107
FASTBREAK VENTURES, 2109
FENGATE, 2110
FIBERNETICS VENTURES, 2111
FIRST ASCENT VENTURES, 2112
FOUNDATION MARKETS, 2117
FRAMEWORK VENTURE PARTNERS, 2119
FREYCINET INVESTMENTS, 2120
FULCRUM CAPITAL PARTNERS, 2121
GARAGECAPITAL, 2122
GCI CAPITAL, 2123
GENESIS CAPITAL CORPORATION, 2124
GENESYS CAPITAL, 2125
GEORGIAN PARTNERS, 2126
GIBRALTAR & COMPANY, 2127
GLOBALIVE, 2128
GOLDEN VENTURE PARTNERS, 2130
GOLDEN VENTURES, 2131
GOOD NEWS VENTURES, 2132
GRANITE PARTNERS, 2133
GREEN ACRE CAPITAL, 2134
GREENHILL SAVP, 869
GREENSKY CAPITAL INC, 2135
GREENSOIL INVESTMENTS, 2136
HARBOURVEST PARTNERS LLC, 912
HIGHLINE BETA, 2140
HILCO BRANDS, 940
IANTHUS CAPITAL MANAGEMENT, 970

IGAN PARTNERS, 2141
IMPERIAL CAPITAL, 2142
IMPRESSION VENTURES, 2143
INDURAN VENTURES INC., 2145
INFORMATION VENTURE PARTNERS, 2146
INITIATIVE CAPITAL LIMITED, 2147
INOVIA CAPITAL, 2150
INSTARAGF, 2151
INSTITUTIONAL LIMITED PARTNERS ASSOCIATION, 3256
INVESTECO, 2153
IRONBRIDGE EQUITY PARTNERS, 2156
InstarAGF, 2158
KENSINGTON CAPITAL PARTNERS, 2160
KILMER CAPITAL PARTNERS, 2162
KLASS CAPITAL, 2163
KNIGHT'S BRIDGE CAPITAL PARTNERS, 2164
LAURENCE CAPITAL, 2165
LUGE CAPITAL, 2172
LUMIRA VENTURES, 2174
MANTELLA VENTURE PARTNERS, 2176
MANULIFE CAPITAL, 2177
MAPLE LEAF ANGELS, 2178
MARIGOLD CAPITAL, 2179
MARKET SQUARE EQUITY PARTNERS, 2180
MARS INVESTMENT ACCELERATOR FUND, 2181
MCCAIN CAPITAL PARTNERS, 2182
MCROCK CAPITAL, 2183
MINK CAPITAL, 2185
MISTRAL VENTURE PARTNERS, 2187
MMV CAPITAL PARTNERS, 2188
MONTECO STRATEGIC CAPITAL, 2189
MOSAIC CAPITAL PARTNERS, 2190
McLEAN WATSON CAPITAL, 2191
NEXT CANADA, 2193
NIAGARA BUSINESS & INNOVATION FUND, 2195
NORTHLEAF CAPITAL PARTNERS, 2196
NOVACAP, 2198
OMERS PRIVATE EQUITY, 2199
ONCAP, 2200
ONEX PARTNERS, 2201
ONPOINT VENTURES, 2202
ONTARIO CAPITAL GROWTH CORPORATION, 2203
PANACHE VENTURES, 2204
PARKVIEW CAPITAL PARTNERS, 2207
PELOTON CAPITAL MANAGEMENT, 2209
PENFUND, 2211
PERSISTENCE CAPITAL PARTNERS, 2212
PINNACLE MERCHANT CAPITAL, 2214
PLAZA VENTURES, 2216
PORTAG3 VENTURES, 2217
PRIVEQ CAPITAL FUNDS, 2218
QUANTUM VALLEY INVESTMENTS, 2220
RADAR CAPITAL, 2222
RBC CAPITAL MARKETS, 2223
REAL VENTURES, 2224
REGIMEN PARTNERS, 2227
RELAY VENTURES, 2228
RESOURCE CAPITAL FUNDS, 1551
RIPPLE VENTURES, 2232
RIV CAPITAL, 2233
ROADMAP CAPITAL INC., 2234
ROUND 13 CAPITAL, 2235
RUSSELL SQUARE PARTNERS, 2236
SAIL VENTURE PARTNERS, 1607
SARONA ASSET MANAGEMENT, 2239
SCALEUP VENTURES, 2240
SCOTIABANK PRIVATE EQUITY, 2241
SEARCHLIGHT, 2243
SERRUYA PRIVATE EQUITY, 2245
SIGNAL HILL EQUITY PARTNERS, 2246
SKYPOINT CAPITAL, 2247
STANDUP VENTURES, 2248
SUMMERHILL VENTURE PARTNERS, 2250
SWANDER PACE CAPITAL, 1769
TECH CAPITAL PARTNERS, 2253
TERA CAPITAL CORPORATION, 2258
TORQUEST PARTNERS, 2264

Geographic Index

TRELLIS CAPITAL CORPORATION, 2265
TRU MANAGEMENT, 1860
VERDEXUS, 2271
VERSANT VENTURES, 1930
VERTU CAPITAL, 2273
VRG CAPITAL, 2274
WATERTON GLOBAL RESOURCE MANAGEMENT, 2275
WELLS FARGO CAPITAL FINANCE, 1971
WESLEY CLOVER, 2276
WHITECAP VENTURE PARTNERS, 2280
WHITEHORSE LIQUIDITY PARTNERS, 2281
WHITE SHEEP CORP, 2279
WYNNCHURCH CAPITAL, 2008
XPV WATER PARTNERS, 2282
YALETOWN VENTURE PARTNERS, 2283

PE
ISLAND CAPITAL PARTNERS, 2157

QC
AMORCHEM, 2031
AMPLITUDE, 2032
ARGO GLOBAL CAPITAL, 163
BCF VENTURES, 2047
BDC CAPITAL, 2048
BRIGHTSPARK VENTURES, 2060
CAISSE DE DEPOT ET PLACEMENT DU QUEBEC, 2064
CATO BIOVENTURES, 432
CLEARSPRING CAPITAL PARTNERS, 2076
CORDIANT CAPITAL, 2080
CREDIT MUTUEL EQUITY, 2082
CTI LIFE SCIENCES, 2086
CYCLE CAPITAL MANAGEMENT, 2087
DESJARDINS CAPITAL, 2089
DIAGRAM VENTURES, 2090
ENERTECH CAPITAL, 677
ENTREPIA VENTURES, 683
FIRST ASCENT VENTURES, 2112
FONDACTION, 2113
FONDS DE SOLIDARITE FTQ, 2114
HIGHLINE BETA, 2140
INNOVOBOT, 2149
INOVIA CAPITAL, 2150
LGC CAPITAL, 2167
LONE STAR FUNDS, 1144
LUGE CAPITAL, 2172
LUMIRA CAPITAL, 2173
MACKINNON, BENNETT & CO., 2175
MEDTEQ+, 2184
MIRALTA, 2186
NORTHLEAF CAPITAL PARTNERS, 2196
NOVACAP, 2198
PANACHE VENTURES, 2204
PERSISTENCE CAPITAL PARTNERS, 2212
PROQUEST INVESTMENTS, 1492
REAL VENTURES, 2224
RHO CANADA VENTURES, 2231
RHO VENTURES, 1561
SANDERLING VENTURES, 1619
SOFINNOVA VENTURES, 1700
SPRING LANE CAPITAL, 1732
TACTICO, 2251
TANDEM EXPANSION FUND, 2252
TELESYSTEM, 2255
TERALYS CAPITAL, 2259
THERILIA, 2261
TVM LIFE SCIENCE MANAGEMENT, 2268
WHITE STAR CAPITAL, 1982
YALETOWN VENTURE PARTNERS, 2283

SK
FARM CREDIT CANADA, 2108
GOLDEN OPPORTUNITIES FUND, 2129
LEX CAPITAL MANAGEMENT, 2166
PFM CAPITAL, 2213
WESTCAP, 2277

Cayman Islands
BBH CAPITAL PARTNERS, 243
CEDRUS INVESTMENTS, 2572
YL VENTURES, 3236

Channel Islands
ACCENT EQUITY PARTNERS, 2317

Chile
AUSTRAL CAPITAL PARTNERS, 2446
AXON PARTNERS GROUP, 2460
COMPASS GROUP, 524
ECUS PRIVATE EQUITY Ecus Private Equity/AXA Capital Chile, 2680
LEXINGTON PARTNERS, 1116
RESOURCE CAPITAL FUNDS, 1551
UDD VENTURES, 3189

China
ADAMS STREET PARTNERS, LLC Adams Street Partners (Beijing) Co., Ltd., 56
ADVENT INTERNATIONAL CORPORATION, 61
ALANTRA, 77
ALOE PRIVATE EQUITY, 2364
ALPINVEST GmbH, 2369
ALPINVEST PARTNERS B.V., 2371
AMALFI CAPITAL MANAGEMENT, 2379
AMERICAN SECURITIES LLC, 111
ANT FINANCIAL, 2396
APAX PARTNERS, 136
ARES MANAGEMENT LLC, 160
ASIAN STRATEGIC INVESTMENTS CORPORATION, 2426
ASIAVEST PARTNERS, 2427
ASTER CAPITAL, 2430
ATOMICO, 2437
AUTHOSIS VENTURES, 2448
BAIDU VENTURES, 222
BAIN CAPITAL PRIVATE EQUITY, 223
BBH CAPITAL PARTNERS, 243
BEIJING HIGH TECHNOLOGY INVESTMENT COMPANY, 2490
BEIJING VENTURE CAPITAL COMPANY LIMITED, 2491
BLACKSTONE PRIVATE EQUITY GROUP, 280
BLUE POINT CAPITAL PARTNERS, 293
BLUERUN VENTURES, 299
BROADLINE PRINCIPAL CAPITAL, 2533
BROOKFIELD ASSET MANAGEMENT, 2062
CANTON VENTURE CAPITAL COMPANY LIMITED, 2548
CAPITAL TODAY, 2551
CARLYLE GROUP, 416
CATHAYA CAPITAL, 2567
CDH INVESTMENTS, 2570
CEYUAN, 2575
CHENGWEI VENTURES, 2581
CHINA ISRAEL VALUE CAPITAL, 2584
CHINA VEST LIMITED, 2587
CHINA WALDEN MANAGEMENT LIMITED Walden Group, 2588
CHINAVEST, 475
CID GROUP, 2594
CISCO INVESTMENTS, 485
CYCLE CAPITAL MANAGEMENT, 2087
D.E. SHAW & CO. LP, 580
DCM, 597
DEERFIELD MANAGEMENT, 602
DJF DRAGONFUND CHINA, 2658
DUTCHESS CAPITAL, 638
E.VENTURES, 641
EPLANET CAPITAL, 691
FIDELITY GROWTH PARTNERS ASIA, 2724
FORTRESS INVESTMENT GROUP LLC, 769
FUEL CAPITAL, 2752
GCI CAPITAL, 2123
GENERAL ATLANTIC PARTNERS, 819, 2762
GGV CAPITAL, 827
GOBI PARTNERS, 2781
GREENHILL SAVP, 869
GSR VENTURES, 2792
GUANGDONG TECHNOLOGY VENTURE CAPITAL COMPANY, 2793

Geographic Index

H&Q ASIA PACIFIC, 897
HARBOURVEST PARTNERS LLC, 912
IDG CAPITAL PARTNERS, 2838
IDG TECHNOLOGY VENTURE INVESTMENT, 2839
IDG-ACCEL, 2841
IDINVEST PARTNERS, 2842
INFOCOMM INVESTMENTS, 2861
JAVELIN INVESTMENTS, 2899
KLEINER PERKINS, 1079
KOHLBERG KRAVIS ROBERTS & COMPANY, 1086
LEGEND CAPITAL, 2927
LIGHTSPEED VENTURE PARTNERS, 1125
MAKERS FUND, 2944
MITSUI GLOBAL INVESTMENT, 1241
MOUSSE PARTNERS, 1263
NEWMARGIN VENTURE CAPITAL, 2989
NGP CAPITAL, 1327
NORTHERN LIGHT VENTURE CAPITAL, 1340
OAKTREE CAPITAL MANAGEMENT LLC, 1362
ORBIMED HEALTHCARE FUND MANAGEMENT, 1383
PFINGSTEN PARTNERS LLC, 1438
QIMING VENTURE PARTNERS Qiming Suzhou Office, 3057
QUALCOMM VENTURES, 1511
QUARK VENTURE, 2221
REDPOINT VENTURES, 1537
RICHINA CAPITAL PARTNERS LIMITED, 3073
RIVERSIDE COMPANY, 1576
SAIF PARTNERS, 3084
SAMSUNG VENTURE INVESTMENT CORPORATION, 3089
SB CHINA VENTURE CAPITAL, 3091
SCULPTOR CAPITAL MANAGEMENT Sculptor Overseas Investment Fund Management Co., Ltd., 1638
SEQUOIA CAPITAL, 1657
SHANGHAI INFORMATION INVESTMENT INCORPORATED, 3105
SIGULER GUFF & COMPANY, 1681
SINGTEL INNOV8, 3112
SOSV, 1709
STATE STREET GLOBAL ADVISORS, 3131
STEAMBOAT VENTURES, 3133
SUMMIT BRIDGE CAPITAL, 3138
SUN CAPITAL PARTNERS, 1755
SUNEVISION HOLDINGS LIMITED, 3139
TAISHAN CAPITAL CORPORATION, 3147
TALLWOOD VENTURE CAPITAL, 1781
TPG CAPITAL, 1837
TRANSLINK CAPITAL, 1840
TSING CAPITAL, 3185
VANTAGEPOINT CAPITAL PARTNERS, 1908
VENTECH, 3199
VENTURE TECH ALLIANCE, 1924
VINCERA CAPITAL, 3209
VIVO CAPITAL, 1943
WALL STREET VENTURE CAPITAL, 1954
WARBURG PINCUS LLC, 1957
WESTSUMMIT CAPITAL, 3225
WI HARPER GROUP, 1983
WILSHIRE PRIVATE MARKETS, 1988
ZHENFUND, 3241

Colombia
ACON INVESTMENTS, 45
ACUMEN, 54
ADVENT INTERNATIONAL CORPORATION, 61
COMPASS GROUP, 524
DARBY OVERSEAS INVESTMENTS LTD, 585
HARBOURVEST PARTNERS LLC, 912
SOCIALATOM VENTURES, 3116

Costa Rica
ROOT CAPITAL, 1586

Czech Republic
3TS CAPITAL PARTNERS, 2301
ARX, 2420
CZECH VENTURE PARTNERS SRO K+ Venture Partners B.V., 2639
VENTURE INVESTORS, 3201

Denmark
ATP PRIVATE EQUITY PARTNERS, 2438
DANSK KAPITALANLAEG A/S, 2642
INDUSTRIALIZATION FUND FOR DEVELOPING COUNTRIE, 2856
INVESTMENT FUND FOR CENTRAL & EASTERN EUROPE, 2880
NORTHZONE, 3004
NOVO A/S, 3006
OYSTER INVEST, 3013
SUNSTONE CAPITAL, 3140
VAEKSTFONDEN, 3194

Dubai
ARES MANAGEMENT LLC, 160

England
AEA INVESTORS, 63
AON MERGERS & ACQUISITIONS GROUP, 2404
FORWARD PARTNERS, 2743
LONE STAR FUNDS, 1144
NEW RHEIN HEALTHCARE INVESTORS, 1301
RIVERSTONE, 1577
SAMSUNG VENTURE INVESTMENT CORPORATION, 3089
VALIA, 1902
WAFRA INC, 1952

Estonia
AMBIENT SOUND INVESTMENTS, 2382
BALTCAP MANAGEMENT LTD, 2471

Finland
ABOA VENTURE MANAGEMENT OY, 2310
AURA CAPITAL OY Auratum Group, 2442
BIO FUND MANAGEMENT OY, 2503
BUTZOW NORDIA ADVOCATES LTD, 2543
CAPMAN CAPITAL MANAGEMENT OY, 2553
CLEANTECH INVEST, 2603
CONOR VENTURE PARTNERS OY, 2621
EQVITEC PARTNERS OY, 2707
FENNO MANAGEMENT OY, 2721
FINNISH INDUSTRY INVESTMENT LIMITED, 2731
FINNVERA PLC, 2732
GORILLA VENTURES, 2784
HELMET CAPITAL FUND MANAGEMENT OY, 2811
INNOFINANCE OY, 2864
LEONIA MB GROUP/MB FUNDS, 2928
MIDINVEST LIMITED, 2957
NEOMARKKA OYJ Neomarkka, 2981
NEXIT VENTURES OY, 2990
NOKIA GROWTH PARTNERS, 1331
NORDIC MEZZANINE LIMITED, 3000
THOMPROPERTIES OY, 3166
VERSOVENTURES, 3204

France
21 PARTNERS, 2285
360 CAPITAL PARTNERS 360 Capital Management SA, 2288
3I GESTION SA 3i Group, 2294
3T CAPITAL, 2300
3i GROUP PLC, 2303
ABM AMRO CAPITAL FRANCE ABN AMRO Group, 2309
ACTIVA CAPITAL, 2330
ACTOMEZZ Groupama Private Equity SA, 2332
ADVENT INTERNATIONAL CORPORATION, 61
AGF PRIVATE EQUITY Allianz Group, 2346
ALANTRA, 77
ALIVE IDEAS, 2357
ALLIANCE ENTREPRENDRE, 2360
ALOE PRIVATE EQUITY, 2364
ALPHA BETEILIGUNGSBERATUNG GmbH, 2367
ALTO INVEST, 2375
ALVEN CAPITAL, 2377
ANVAR, 2400
ARCIS GROUP, 2412
ARES MANAGEMENT LLC, 160
ASTER CAPITAL, 2430
ATRIA CAPITAL PARTENAIRES, 2439

Geographic Index

AURIGA PARTNERS, 2444
AVENIR TOURISME, 2450
AXA INVESTMENT MANAGERS PRIVATE EQUITY EUROPE, 2457
BANEXI VENTURES PARTNERS, 2472
BARCLAYS PRIVATE EQUITY FRANCE, 2476
BAYSIDE CAPITAL H.I.G. European Capital Partners SAS, 242
BLACKFIN CAPITAL PARTNERS, 2512
BLACKSTONE PRIVATE EQUITY GROUP, 280
BUTLER CAPITAL PARTNERS FRANCE, 2542
CARLYLE GROUP, 416
CIC FINANCE CIC Group, 2592
CICLAD, 2593
CITA GESTION, 2598
COFINEP, 2611
COMPAGNIE FINANCIERE E DE ROTHSCHILD BANQUE, 2616
CREDIT MUTUEL EQUITY, 2082
DEMETER PARTNERS, 2647
DIRIGEANTS ET INVESTISSEURS, 2656
ELAIA PARTNERS, 2684
EURAZEO, 2710
EUROMEZZANINE CONSEIL, 2712
FINADVANCE, 2726
FINANCIERE DE BRIENNE FCPR, 2729
FONDINVEST CAPITAL, 2738
GALILEO II, 2756
HARBERT MANAGEMENT CORPORATION, 907
IDINVEST PARTNERS, 2842
IFE CONSEIL (INTERMEDIATE FINANCE EUROPE), 2843
ILE-DE-FRANCE, 2846
INNOVACOM SA, 2866
INNOVATION CAPITAL, 2867
INVUS GROUP, 1022
IPBM Group IDI, 2884
IRDI MIDI-PYRENEES, 2887
IRIS CAPITAL, 2888
ISOURCE GESTION, 2890
KOHLBERG KRAVIS ROBERTS & COMPANY, 1086
L CATTERTON PARTNERS, 1092
LBO FRANCE, 2924
LMBO FINANCE, 2936
LONE STAR FUNDS, 1144
MARCEAU INVESTISSEMENTS, 2946
NEXT WORLD CAPITAL, 1319
OAKTREE CAPITAL MANAGEMENT LLC, 1362
OMNES CAPITAL, 3011
PAI MANAGEMENT, 3017
PARTECH INTERNATIONAL, 1418
SAINT-GOBAIN NOVA EXTERNAL VENTURING, 3085
SANOFI-GENZYME BIOVENTURES, 1621
SEVENTURE PARTNERS, 3104
THOMSON-CSF VENTURES, 3167
VENTECH, 3199
WHITE STAR CAPITAL, 1982
XANGE PRIVATE EQUITY, 3229

Georgia
SALFORD CAPITAL PARTNERS, 3086

Germany
3I DEUTSCHLAND GESELLSCHAFT FUR 3i Group, 2291
3I GERMANY GmbH 3i Group, 2293
3I TEUPSCHLAND GmbH 3i Group, 2297
3i GROUP PLC, 2303
ACCERA AG, 2319
ADAMS STREET PARTNERS, LLC Adams Street (Europe) GmbH, 56
ADASTRA, 2335
ADVENT INTERNATIONAL CORPORATION, 61
AEA INVESTORS, 63
ALANTRA, 77
ALLIANZ CAPITAL PARTNERS GmbH, 2362
AMMER PARTNERS, 2385
AON JAUCH & HUBENER GmbH Aon Corporation, 2403
APAX PARTNERS, 136
APOLLO GLOBAL MANAGEMENT, 141
ARES MANAGEMENT LLC, 160
ASTUTIA VENTURES, 2432
AURELIA PRIVATE EQUITY, 2443

B-TO-V PARTNERS, 2466
BAIN CAPITAL PRIVATE EQUITY, 223
BASF VENTURE CAPITAL, 2483
BAY BG BAVARIAN VENTURE CAPITAL CORP, 2485
BAYSIDE CAPITAL H.I.G. European Capital Partners GmbH, 242
BERENBERG PRIVATE CAPITAL, 2493
BERLIN TECHNOLOGIE, 2494
BM-T BETEILIGUNGS MANAGEMENT THURINGEN GmbH, 2518
BMP AKTIENGESELLSCHAFT BMP Venture Capital, 2519
BOEHRINGER INGELHEIM VENTURE FUND, 2521
BONVENTURE, 2522
BRIDGEPOINT CAPITAL GmbH, 2528
CAPITON AG, 2552
CARLYLE GROUP, 416
CATAGONIA CAPITAL, 2560
CINCO CAPITAL, 2595
CIPIO PARTNERS, 2597
CLIFFORD CHANCE PUNDER, 2605
CLOSE BROTHERS EQUITY MARKETS Close Brothers Group, 2607
COMMERZ BETEILIGUNGSGESELLSCHAFT, 2615
CREATHOR VENTURE, 2629
CREDIT MUTUEL EQUITY, 2082
DAIMLERCHRYSLER VENTURE GmbH DaimlerChrysler AG, 2641
DB CAPITAL PARTNERS (ASIA), 2643
DEMETER PARTNERS, 2647
DEUTSCHE ASSET & WEALTH MANAGEMENT, 2649
DEUTSCHE BETEILIGUNGS AG, 2651
DR NEUHAUS TECHNO NORD GmbH, 2664
DVC DEUTSCHE VENTURE CAPITAL, 2670
E.VENTURES, 641
EARLYBIRD, 2673
ECAPITAL ENTREPRENEURIAL PARTNERS AG, 2677
ECONA AG, 2679
EQUINET VENTURE PARTNERS AG, 2704
EVERCORE CAPITAL PARTNERS, 700
FIELDSTONE PRIVATE CAPITAL GROUP, 726
FORBION CAPITAL PARTNERS, 2739
FORTRESS INVESTMENT GROUP LLC, 769
GENERAL ATLANTIC PARTNERS, 819
GENES GMBH VENTURE SERVICES, 2765
GLOBAL LIFE SCIENCE VENTURES GmbH, 2776
GRAZIA EQUITY, 2788
GREENHILL SAVP, 869
HALDER BETEILIGUNGSBERATUNG GmbH, 2796
HALDER HOLDINGS BV, 2797
HANNOVER FINANZ GmbH, 2801
HASSO PLATTNER VENTURES, 2804
HIGH-TECH GRUENDERFONDS, 2815
HOLTZBRINCK VENTURES, 2820
HV HOLTZBRINCK VENTURES, 2829
IBB BETEILIGUNGSGESELLSCHAFT MBH, 2832
KFW-BANKENGRUPPE, 2910
KIZOO TECHNOLOGY CAPITAL, 2912
KPS CAPITAL PARTNERS, 1089
LBBW VENTURE CAPITAL, 2923
LONE STAR FUNDS, 1144
NEUHAUS PARTNERS, 2985
NGN CAPITAL, 1325
OAKTREE CAPITAL MANAGEMENT LLC, 1362
ONE EQUITY PARTNERS, 1376
PARTECH INTERNATIONAL, 1418
PERMIRA, 3024
PERSEUS FUNDS, 1437
PLEXUS VENTURES, 1456
POINT NINE CAPITAL, 3035
POLYTECHNOS VENTURE PARTNERS GmbH, 3037
PROJECT A VENTURE GmbH & CO. KG, 3047
QUADRAN GESTION Deutsche Beteiligungs AG, 3058
RIVERSIDE COMPANY, 1576
S-REFIT GmbH & COMPANY KG, 3081
SAMSUNG NEXT, 1614
SIEMENS VENTURE CAPITAL, 3109
SIGNATURE CAPITAL LLC, 3111
SMAC PARTNERS, 3114
SONY EUROPE, 3120
STAR VENTURES, 3128
STEELHOUSE VENTURES, 3134

1082

Geographic Index

T-VENTURE HOLDINGS GmbH Deutsche Telecom, 3146
TARGET PARTNERS, 3152
TENGELMANN VENTURES, 3161
TFG CAPITAL AG, 3163
TRIANGLE VENTURE CAPITAL GROUP, 3179
TRIGENTA CAPITAL GmbH, 3180
TRIGINITA CAPITAL, 3181
TVM CAPITAL, 3187
UCA UNTERNEHMER CONSULT AG, 3188
VENISTA VENTURES, 3198
VON BRAUN & SCHREIBER PRIVATE EQUITY PARTNERS, 3218
WELLINGTON PARTNERS VENTURE CAPITAL GmbH, 3223
WESTTECH VENTURES, 3226
WHEB GROUP, 3227
XANGE PRIVATE EQUITY, 3229

Ghana

MANSA CAPITAL, 1167

Greece

ALANTRA, 77
ALPHA BANK, 2366
GLOBAL FINANCE, 2775

Hong Kong

ANGELO, GORDON & CO., 128
ANGLO CHINESE INVESTMENT COMPANY LIMITED, 2394
APOLLO GLOBAL MANAGEMENT, 141
AQUITAINE INVESTMENT ADVISORS LIMITED, 2409
ARGO GLOBAL CAPITAL, 163
ASIAN INFRASTRUCTURE FUND ADVISERS LIMITED AIF Capital, 2425
BARING PRIVATE EQUITY PARTNERS ASIA, 2479
BASF VENTURE CAPITAL, 2483
BIGFOOT VENTURES, 2502
BLACKSTONE PRIVATE EQUITY GROUP, 280
BOCI DIRECT INVESTMENT MANAGEMENT LIMITED Bank of China, 2520
CARLYLE ASIA INVESTMENT ADVISORS LIMITED Carlyle Group, 2556
CHASE CAPITAL PARTNERS, 2579
CHEUNG KONG INFRASTRUCTURE HOLDINGS LIMITED, 2582
CHINA MERCHANTS CHINA INVESTMENT MANAGEMENT, 2585, 2586
CHINAVEST, 475
CLEARWATER CAPITAL PARTNERS, 506
COATUE MANAGEMENT, 511
CORE PACIFIC - YAMAICHI CAPITAL LIMITED Core Pacific Securities Company Ltd, 2624
CROSBY ASSET MANAGEMENT, 2631
CROSBY CAPITAL LIMITED, 2632
CVC ASIA PACIFIC LIMITED CVC Capital Partners, 2634
D.E. SHAW & CO. LP, 580
DARBY OVERSEAS INVESTMENTS LTD, 585
DIGITAL SKY TECHNOLOGIES, 2654
ELECTRA PARTNERS ASIA LIMITED SFC of Hong Kong, 2685
EVERCORE CAPITAL PARTNERS, 700
EXCELSIOR CAPITAL ASIA, 2718
FUEL CAPITAL, 2752
GENERAL ATLANTIC PARTNERS, 819
GENERAL ENTERPRISE MANAGEMENT SERVICES, 2763
GLOBAL VENTURES MANAGEMENT LIMITED, 2779
GSR VENTURES Golden Sand River (Hong Kong) Limited, 2792
H&Q ASIA PACIFIC, 897
HAMON INVESTMENT GROUP, 2800
HARBOURVEST PARTNERS LLC, 912
HELIANT VENTURES, 2808
HONGKONG LAND INFRASTRUCTURE LIMITED, 2821
HORIZONS VENTURES, 2822
IBRIDGE CAPITAL CORPORATION, 2834
IBUSINESS CORPORATION, 2835
IDG CAPITAL PARTNERS, 2838
INTER-ASIA VENTURE MANAGEMENT LIMITED, 2872
INVUS GROUP, 1022
IT VENTURES LIMITED Digital Heritage Publishing Ltd., 2892
KOHLBERG KRAVIS ROBERTS & COMPANY, 1086
LEXINGTON PARTNERS, 1116
LIGHTHOUSE PARTNERS, 1123
LOMBARD INVESTMENTS, 1143
LOMBARD/APIC (HK) LIMITED, 2937
LONE STAR FUNDS, 1144
MERRILL LYNCH (ASIA PACIFIC) LIMITED Merrill Lynch Group, 2955
NEW WORLD INFRASTRUCTURE LIMITED, 2987
NORTHERN LIGHT VENTURE CAPITAL, 1340
PAMA GROUP, 3018
PANTHEON VENTURES (US) LP, 1413
POMONA CAPITAL, 1466
PT BNI NOMURA JAFCO MANAJEMEN VENTURA, 3053
QIMING VENTURE PARTNERS Qiming Development HK Limited, 3057
REGENT PACIFIC PRIVATE EQUITY LIMITED Regent Pacific Group Ltd., 3066
ROAD KING INFRASTRUCTURE LIMITED, 3075
ROTH CAPITAL PARTNERS, 1592
SAIF PARTNERS, 3084
SCULPTOR CAPITAL MANAGEMENT Sculptor Capital Management Hong Kong Limited, 1638
SHAW KWEI AND PARTNERS, 3107
SHENZHEN INTERNATIONAL HOLDINGS LIMITED, 3108
SIGULER GUFF & COMPANY, 1681
SILVER LAKE, 1685
SUNEVISION HOLDINGS LIMITED, 3139
TA ASSOCIATES, 1778
TELECOM VENTURE GROUP LIMITED, 3159
TSING CAPITAL, 3185
VALUE PARTNERS LIMITED, 3195
WARBURG PINCUS LLC, 1957
WHITE STAR CAPITAL, 1982

Hungary

ACME LABS, 2325
CORVINUS NEMZETKOZI BEFEKTETESI RT Corvinus International Investment Ltd., 2625
COVENT INDUSTRIAL CAPITAL INVESTMENT COMPANY, 2626
DARBY OVERSEAS INVESTMENTS LTD, 585
EUROVENTURES CAPITAL, 2716

Iceland

LANDSBANKI VENTURES, 2920
THROUNARFELAG ISLANDS PLC, 3168

India

3i GROUP PLC, 2303
AAVISHKAAR, 2305
ACCEL, 27
ACUMEN, 54
ADVENT INTERNATIONAL CORPORATION, 61
ALOE PRIVATE EQUITY, 2364
ANZ GRINDLAYS 31 INVESTMENT SERVICES LIMITED, 2401
APAX PARTNERS, 136
APIDC-VENTURE CAPITAL LIMITED, 2407
APOLLO GLOBAL MANAGEMENT, 141
AVIGO CAPITAL, 2451
BAIN CAPITAL PRIVATE EQUITY, 223
BARING PRIVATE EQUITY PARTNERS INDIA, 2481
BESSEMER VENTURE PARTNERS, 263
BLACKSTONE PRIVATE EQUITY GROUP, 280
BLUESHIFT INTERNET VENTURES Blueshift, 2516
BLUME VENTURES, 2517
BROOKFIELD ASSET MANAGEMENT, 2062
CAPITAL 18, 2549
CARLYLE GROUP, 416
CISCO INVESTMENTS, 485
DARBY OVERSEAS INVESTMENTS LTD, 585
DELTA PARTNERS Delta Partners FZ-LLC, 2645
FIELDSTONE PRIVATE CAPITAL GROUP, 726
FRANKLIN TEMPLETON INVESTMENT, 2747
GE ASIA PACIFIC CAPITAL TECHNOLOGY FUND, 2758
GE CAPITAL SERVICES INDIA LIMITED, 2759
GENERAL ATLANTIC PARTNERS, 819
GLOBAL ENVIRONMENT FUND, 838
GLOBAL TECHNOLOGY VENTURES, 2778
GRAY GHOST VENTURES, 860
GUJARAT STATE FERTILIZERS COMPANY LIMITED, 2795
HANSUTTAM FINANCE LIMITED, 2802

Geographic Index

HELION VENTURE PARTNERS, LLC Helion Advisors Private Limited, 2809
ICF VENTURES PVT LTD, 2837
INDASIA FUND ADVISORS PVT LTD, 2850
INDIAN DIRECT EQUITY ADVISORS PVT LTD, 2852
INDUSTRIAL DEVELOPMENT BANK OF INDIA, 2855
INFOCOMM INVESTMENTS, 2861
INVENTUS, 1017
IXORA VENTURES, 2895
KOHLBERG KRAVIS ROBERTS & COMPANY, 1086
LAUNCHPAD VENTURES, 2922
LEAD ANGELS, 2925
LIGHTSPEED VENTURE PARTNERS, 1125
NAYA VENTURES, 1284
NEXUS VENTURE PARTNERS, 2992
NORWEST VENTURE PARTNERS, 1346
OJAS VENTURE PARTNERS, 3010
OMIDYAR NETWORK, 1374
ORBIMED HEALTHCARE FUND MANAGEMENT, 1383
PFINGSTEN PARTNERS LLC, 1438
PLUS VENTURES, 3032
QUALCOMM VENTURES, 1511
SAIF PARTNERS, 3084
SAMSUNG VENTURE INVESTMENT CORPORATION, 3089
SEEDFUND, 3100
SEQUOIA CAPITAL Sequoia Capital India Advisors Pvt. Ltd., 1657
SIGULER GUFF & COMPANY, 1681
SRIJAN CAPITAL, 3124
TA ASSOCIATES, 1778
THE MORPHEUS, 3165
TPG CAPITAL, 1837
UNILAZER VENTURES, 3190
USHA MARTIN VENTURES LIMITED, 3193
VENTUREAST, 3202
WARBURG PINCUS LLC, 1957
ZEPHYR MANAGEMENT LP, 2017

Indonesia
CARLYLE GROUP, 416
PT BHAKTI INVESTAMA TBK, 3052

Ireland
ACT VENTURE CAPITAL LIMITED, 2328
AIB SEED CAPITAL FUND Dublin Business Innovation Centre, 2347
ALANTRA, 77
ATLANTIC BRIDGE, 2434
BBH CAPITAL PARTNERS, 243
BLOOM EQUITY, 2513
CAMPUS COMPANIES VENTURE CAPITAL FUND, 2545
CARLYLE GROUP, 416
CLARENDON FUND MANAGERS, 2601
DRAPER ESPRIT, 2665
EIRCOM ENTERPRISE FUND LIMITED, 2683
ENTERPRISE EQUITY IRELAND LIMITED, 2696
FRONTLINE VENTURES, 2750
GUGGENHEIM PARTNERS, 890
INTELLECTUAL VENTURES, 1010
KERNEL CAPITAL, 2909
LIGHTSTONE VENTURES, 1126
SHANNON COMMERCIAL PROPERTIES, 3106
SIGNATURE CAPITAL LLC, 3111
SOSV, 1709
TRINITY VENTURE CAPITAL TVC Holdings plc, 3182

Israel
ACCELMED, 2316
AFTERDOX, 2344
AGATE MEDICAL INVESTMENTS, 2345
AMANET TECHNOLOGIES LIMITED, 2381
APAX PARTNERS, 136
AQUAGRO FUND, 2408
ASTER CAPITAL, 2430
AURUM VENTURES MKI, 2445
AVIV VENTURE CAPITAL, 2453
BATTERY VENTURES, 238
BLUMBERG CAPITAL, 304
BRIDGE INVESTMENT FUND, 340

BRM SEED, 2532
CARMEL VENTURES, 2557
CATALYST FUND LP, 2562
CEDAR (ISRAEL) FINANCIAL ADVISORS LIMITED Cedar Fund, 2571
CHALLENGE FUNDS - ETGAR LP, 2576
CHINA ISRAEL VALUE CAPITAL, 2584
CISCO INVESTMENTS, 485
CLAL ELECTRONICS INDUSTRIES LIMITED, 2600
CONCORD VENTURES, 2619
CYBERSTARTS, 2638
DELTA VENTURES LIMITED, 2646
DISCOUNT INVESTMENT CORPORATION LIMITED, 2657
EUROFUND LP, 2711
EVERGREEN VENTURE PARTNERS, 2717
FIRST ISRAEL MEZZANINE INVESTORS LIMITED, 2736
FORMULA VENTURES LIMITED Formula Group, 2741
FORUM TECHNOLOGIES VENTURE CAPITAL COMPANY Forum Group, 2742
GAON ASSET MANAGEMENT, 2757
GEMINI ISRAEL VENTURE FUNDS LIMITED, 2761
GENESIS PARTNERS, 2766
GIZA VENTURE CAPITAL, 2773
ICAN ISRAEL-CANNABIS.COM, 2836
INITIAL CAPITAL, 2863
INNOVATION ENDEAVORS, 1001
ISRAEL CLEANTECH VENTURES, 2891
JC TECHNOLOGIES LTD, 2900
JERUSALEM VENTURE PARTNERS, 2901
JUMPSEED VENTURES, 2903
KAEDAN INVESTMENTS, 2905
KARDAN LTD, 2907
LIGHTSPEED VENTURE PARTNERS, 1125
LIONBIRD, 2934
LOOL VENTURES, 2938
MAGMA VENTURE PARTNERS, 2943
MARATHON VENTURE CAPITAL FUND LIMITED, 2945
MATI-HIGH-TECH, 2947
MITSUI GLOBAL INVESTMENT, 1241
MMT MILLENNIUM MATERIALS TECHNOLOGIES FUND LP, 2964
NIELSEN INNOVATE FUND, 2994
NORWEST VENTURE PARTNERS, 1346
ORBIMED HEALTHCARE FUND MANAGEMENT, 1383
PITANGO VENTURE CAPITAL, 3030
POND VENTURES, 3038
PREVIZ VENTURES, 3041
PROSEED, 3050
QUALCOMM VENTURES, 1511
RAFAEL DEVELOPMENT CORPORATION (RDC) LIMITED, 3063
SAMSUNG NEXT, 1614
SAMSUNG VENTURE INVESTMENT CORPORATION, 3089
SBRC INVESTMENT CONSULTATION LIMITED, 3092
SEQUOIA CAPITAL, 1657
SMART BUSINESS CONSULTING, 3115
SONY INNOVATION FUND, 1705
STAGEONE VENTURES, 3127
STAR VENTURES, 3128
TAMAR TECHNOLOGY VENTURES LIMITED, 3149
TAMIR FISHMAN VENTURES, 3150
TELEFONICA VENTURES, 3160
TEUZA MANAGEMENT & DEVELOPMENT LTD, 3162
TRIVENTURES, 3183
VERITAS VENTURE PARTNERS, 3203
VERIZON VENTURES, 1928
VERTEX VENTURE CAPITAL, 3205
VINTAGE INVESTMENT PARTNERS, 3210
VIOLA FINTECH, 3211
VIOLA VENTURES, 3212
WALDEN ISRAEL VENTURE CAPITAL, 3221
XENIA VENTURE CAPITAL, 3230
XT INVESTMENTS, 3231
YISSUM TECHNOLOGY TRANSFER, 3235
YL VENTURES, 3236
YLR CAPITAL MARKETS LTD, 3237
YVC - YOZMA MANAGEMENT & INVESTMENTS LIMITED, 3239

Isreal
HARBOURVEST PARTNERS LLC, 912

Geographic Index

NFX, 1323

Italy
21 PARTNERS, 2285
360 CAPITAL PARTNERS, 2288
ALANTRA, 77
ALICE VENTURES SRL, 2356
AMBIENTA ENVIRONMENTAL ASSETS, 2383
ANGELAB VENTURES, 2393
ANGELO, GORDON & CO., 128
ANNAPURNA VENTURES, 2395
ARGOS SODITIC SPAIN, 2415
BAYSIDE CAPITAL Ih.I.G. European Capital Partners Italy S.r.I., 242
BERRIER CAPITAL, 2495
CARLYLE GROUP, 416
DPIXEL, 2663
FINLOMBARDA SpA, 2730
FRIULIA SpA, 2749
INDUSTRIO VENTURES, 2859
INNOGEST CAPITAL, 2865
PERMIRA, 3024
PLEXUS VENTURES, 1456
PRINCIPIA SGR, 3043
PRIVATE EQUITY PARTNERS SPA, 3044
SYNERGO SGR, 3145

Japan
ADAMS STREET PARTNERS, LLC Adams Street Partners Japan G.K., 56
ADVANTAGE PARTNERS, 2339
ANGELO, GORDON & CO., 128
APAX GLOBIS PARTNERS & COMPANY Globis Capital Partners/Apax, 2406
ASAHI BANK INVESTMENT COMPANY LIMITED, 2421
ASAHI LIFE CAPITAL COMPANY LIMITED, 2422
ATOMICO, 2437
AZCA, 217
B DASH VENTURES, 2465
BAIN CAPITAL PRIVATE EQUITY, 223
BASF VENTURE CAPITAL, 2483
BBH CAPITAL PARTNERS, 243
BLACKSTONE PRIVATE EQUITY GROUP, 280
CARLYLE GROUP, 416
CYBERAGENT VENTURES, 2637
DCM, 597
E.VENTURES, 641
EM WARBURG, PINCUS & COMPANY JAPAN, 2689
ENTREPIA VENTURES, 683
EPIDAREX CAPITAL, 690
FORTRESS INVESTMENT GROUP LLC, 769
FUTURE VENTURE CAPITAL COMPANY LIMITED, 2754
GLOBAL CATALYST PARTNERS, 837
GOGIN CAPITAL COMPANY LIMITED, 2782
GREE VENTURES, 2789
GREENHILL SAVP, 869
GUGGENHEIM PARTNERS, 890
HARBOURVEST PARTNERS LLC, 912
HIKARI TSUSHIN CAPITAL, 2817
IGNITE JAPAN KK Ignite Group, 2845
INFINITY VENTURE PARTNERS, 2860
J-SEED VENTURES INCORPORATED, 2896
JAFCO COMPANY LIMITED JAPAN, 2897
JAPAN ASIA INVESTMENT COMPANY LIMITED, 2898
JTP CORPORATION, 2902
KOHLBERG KRAVIS ROBERTS & COMPANY, 1086
KUBOTA CORPORATION, 2918
LIGHTHOUSE PARTNERS, 1123
LONE STAR FUNDS, 1144
MITSUBISHI UFJ CAPITAL, 2961
MITSUI GLOBAL INVESTMENT, 1241
MITSUI SUMITOMO INSURANCE VENTURE CAPITAL CO, 2962
MOBILE INTERNET CAPITAL, 2965
MVC CORPORATION, 2971
NEOTENY COMPANY LIMITED, 2982
NIF VENTURES COMPANY LIMITED, 2995
NIPPON TECHNOLOGY VENTURE PARTNERS LIMITED, 2996
NISSAY CAPITAL, 2997
OAKTREE CAPITAL MANAGEMENT LLC, 1362
ONO PHARMACEUTICALS COMPANY LIMITED, 3012
PERMIRA, 3024
PINEHURST ADVISORS, 3029
PLEXUS VENTURES, 1456
SAMSUNG VENTURE INVESTMENT CORPORATION, 3089
SIGULER GUFF & COMPANY, 1681
SONY INNOVATION FUND, 1705
SOZO VENTURES, 1716
SUNBRIDGE PARTNERS, 1757
TEKINVEST KK, 3157
TEL VENTURE CAPITAL, 1793
TOKIO MARINE CAPITAL COMPANY LIMITED, 3173
TRANS COSMOS INCORPORATED, 3176
TRANSLINK CAPITAL, 1840
UNISON CAPITAL PARTNERS LP, 3192
VCN GROUP INCORPORATED, 3196
WHITE STAR CAPITAL, 1982
YASUDA AND PAMA LIMITED, 3232
YASUDA ENTERPRISE DEVELOPMENT COMPANY, 3233

Kenya
ACUMEN, 54
ROOT CAPITAL, 1586
TLCOM CAPITAL, 3170

Korea
ACE VENTURE CAPITAL LIMITED, 2322
ALTOS VENTURES, 100
ANGELO, GORDON & CO., 128
BLACKSTONE PRIVATE EQUITY GROUP, 280
BLUERUN VENTURES, 299
CARLYLE GROUP, 416
DARBY OVERSEAS INVESTMENTS LTD, 585
H&Q ASIA PACIFIC, 897
I-PACIFIC PARTNERS, 2831
KOHLBERG KRAVIS ROBERTS & COMPANY, 1086
KOREA FIRST VENTURE CAPITAL CORPORATION, 2915
NHN INVESTMENT, 2993
OAKTREE CAPITAL MANAGEMENT LLC, 1362
SAMSUNG NEXT, 1614
SAMSUNG VENTURE INVESTMENT CORPORATION Samsung Electronics, 3089
SOFTBANK VENTURES KOREA, 3118
TONG YANG VENTURE CAPITAL CORPORATION Tong Yang Cement Corporation, 3174
TPG CAPITAL, 1837
TRANSLINK CAPITAL, 1840

Kuwait
WAFRA INC, 1952

Lebanon
BERYTECH FUND, 2497
DAHER CAPITAL, 2640

Lithuania
PRACTICA CAPITAL, 3040

Luxembourg
ANTHEMIS GROUP, 2398
APOLLO GLOBAL MANAGEMENT, 141
ARES MANAGEMENT LLC, 160
BBH CAPITAL PARTNERS, 243
CARLYLE GROUP, 416
CASTLELAKE, 426
DOTCORP PRIVATE EQUITY FUND, 2660
EUROPEAN INVESTMENT FUND, 2715
KBL FOUNDER SA, 2908
L CATTERTON PARTNERS, 1092
OAKTREE CAPITAL MANAGEMENT LLC, 1362
RIVERSIDE COMPANY, 1576
STARWOOD CAPITAL GROUP LLC, 1742
SUMMIT PARTNERS, 1754
TPG CAPITAL, 1837
TRILANTIC CAPITAL PARTNERS, 1853

Geographic Index

Malaysia
AMANAH VENTURES SDN BHD, 2380
CELADON CAPITAL GROUP, 2573
COMMERCE ASSET VENTURES Sdn Bhd, 2614
DTA CAPITAL PARTNERS S/B, 2666
FIELDSTONE PRIVATE CAPITAL GROUP, 726
GLOBAL MARITIME VENTURES BERHAD, 2777
INTELLIGENT CAPITAL SDN BHD, 2871
MAYBAN VENTURES, 2949
PHILLIP MUTUAL BERHAD, 3026
RHB - H&F MANAGEMENT COMPANY SDN BHD RHB Capital, 3071
TECHNOLOGY PARK MALAYSIA CORPORATION SDN BHD, 3155

Malta
MEDRA CAPITAL, 2951

Mauritius
ADLEVO CAPITAL CIM Fund Services, 2337
AVIGO CAPITAL, 2451
BASIL PARTNERS Kross Border Trust Services Limited, 2484
CHRYSALIS CAPITAL ChrysCapital, 2590
CHRYSCAPITAL MANAGEMENT COMPANIES ChrysCapital, 2591
HELION VENTURE PARTNERS, LLC International Management (Mauritius) Ltd, 2809
HELIX INVESTMENTS, 2810
IDG VENTURES INDIA International Financial Services Limited, 2840

Mexico
ACON INVESTMENTS, 45
ADVENT INTERNATIONAL CORPORATION, 61
ALTA GROWTH CAPITAL, 2373
ALTA VENTURES MEXICO, 2374
COMPASS GROUP, 524
DARBY OVERSEAS INVESTMENTS LTD, 585
EVERCORE CAPITAL PARTNERS, 700
GENERAL ATLANTIC PARTNERS, 819
NARANYA VENTURES, 2975
NORTHGATE, 1341
RIVERSTONE, 1577
ROOT CAPITAL, 1586

Myanmar
SERGE PUN & ASSOCIATES (MYANMAR) LIMITED, 3102

Netherlands
3i GROUP PLC, 2303
AAC CAPITAL PARTNERS, 2304
AESCAP VENTURE, 2342
ALANTRA, 77
ALPINVEST HOLDING NV Alpinvest, 2370
ALPINVEST PARTNERS B.V., 2371
AMPERSAND CAPITAL PARTNERS, 119
ANGELO, GORDON & CO., 128
ANTERRA CAPITAL, 2397
BENCIS CAPITAL PARTNERS, 2492
BIOGENERATION VENTURES, 2505
BRABANTSE ONTWIKKELINGSMIJ NV (BOM), 2525
BROOKLYN VENTURES, 2534
CARLYLE GROUP, 416
COTTONWOOD TECHNOLOGY FUND, 550
DUTCH GROUP, 2669
FORBION CAPITAL PARTNERS, 2739
FRESHWATER VENTURE PARTNERS, 2748
GENERAL ATLANTIC PARTNERS, 819
GILDE INVESTMENT FUNDS, 2770
HENQ, 2813
HOLLAND VENTURE BV, 2819
INDUSTRIEBANK LIOF NV, 2857
LIFE SCIENCES PARTNERS BV, 2930
NESBIC INVESTMENT FUND II, 2983
OAKTREE CAPITAL MANAGEMENT LLC, 1362
ONE EQUITY PARTNERS, 1376
PRIME TECHNOLOGY VENTURES NV, 3042
SABIC VENTURES, 3082
SOLID VENTURES, 3119
TAT CAPITAL PARTNERS LTD., 3153
VENTURE FUND ROTTERDAM BV Indofin Group, 3200
VITULUM VENTURES, 3215
WATERLAND PRIVATE EQUITY INVESTMENT, 3222
WILSHIRE PRIVATE MARKETS, 1988
ZERNIKE SEED FUND BV, 3240

New Zealand
AMP PRIVATE CAPITAL NEW ZEALAND LIMITED AMP Capital, 2387
ANZ PRIVATE EQUITY Private Equity Media, 2402
BIOPACIFIC VENTURES, 2507
BT FUNDS MANAGEMENT LIMITED, 2537
DIRECT CAPITAL PRIVATE EQUITY LIMITED, 2655
IGLOBE PARTNERS, 2844
PWC, 3055
THE CHANNEL GROUP Pacific Channel Ltd., 1811

Northern Ireland
AMICUS CAPITAL PARTNERS, 2384
LOUGH SHORE INVESTMENTS, 2939

Norway
ALLIANCE VENTURE, 2361
BIRK VENTURE, 2510
CONVEXA Tyveholmen AS, 2623
ENERGY VENTURES, 2691
FERD CAPITAL, 2722
FOUR SEASONS VENTURE CAPITAL, 2745
MATURO KAPITAL, 2948
NORTHZONE, 3004
REITEN & CO STRATEGIC INVESTMENTS AS Reiten & Company, 3067
STATOIL TECHNOLOGY INVEST, 3132
TEKNOINVEST MANAGEMENT, 3158
VIKING VENTURE, 3207

Pakistan
ACUMEN, 54
MINI VENTURES, 2959

Panama
CANALIS CAPITAL, 2546

Peru
CARLYLE GROUP, 416
COMPASS GROUP, 524

Philippines
AB CAPITAL & INVESTMENT CORPORATION The Phinma Group, 2306

Poland
21 PARTNERS, 2285
3TS CAPITAL PARTNERS, 2301
ABRIS CAPITAL, 2311
BARING CORILIUS PRIVATE EQUITY, 2478
BBH CAPITAL PARTNERS, 243
DARBY OVERSEAS INVESTMENTS LTD, 585
ENTERPRISE INVESTORS, 2697
INVEMAX, 2876
PLEXUS VENTURES, 1456
RENAISSANCE PARTNERS, 3068

Portugal
AITEC, 2349
ALANTRA, 77
ESPIRITO SANTO VENTURES, 2708
INTER-RISCO: SOCIEDADE DE CAPITAL DE RISCO, 2873
PATHENA, 3022
PORTUGAL CAPITAL VENTURES Institutional Headquarters, 3039

Qatar
INVESTCORP, 1021

Geographic Index

Republic of Korea
ADAMS STREET PARTNERS, LLC Adams Street Partners, LLC (Korea Branch), 56

Romania
3TS CAPITAL PARTNERS, 2301
AXXESS CAPITAL, 2462
SIF TRANSYLVANIA, 3110
TRANSYLVANIA FINANCIAL INVESTMENT COMPANY, 3178

Russia
ABRT VENTURE FUND, 2312
ADD VENTURE, 2336
AIP PRIVATE CAPITAL, 2027
ALFA CAPITAL Alfa Group, 2355
ASTOR CAPITAL GROUP, 2431
AWAY REALTY, 2456
BARING VOSTOK CAPITAL PARTNERS, 2482
BIOPROCESS CAPITAL PARTNERS, 2508
BRIGHT CAPITAL, 2531
BURAN VENTURE CAPITAL, 2540
FINAM GLOBAL, 2727
GENEZIS CAPITAL TECHNOLOGY, 2767
IMI.VC, 2847
INVENTURE PARTNERS, 2877
LETA CAPITAL, 2929
LIFE.SREDA, 2931
PHENOMEN VENTURES, 3025
QUANTUM WAVE FUND, 3059
RABO BLACK EARTH Eagle Venture Partners, 3062
SALFORD CAPITAL PARTNERS, 3086
SPINUP VENTURE, 3123
SUPREMUM CAPITAL, 3141
TROIKA CAPITAL PARTNERS, 3184
VTB CAPITAL, 3220

Russian Federation
RU-NET VENTURES, 3078
RUNA CAPITAL, 3079

Saudi Arabia
INVESTCORP, 1021
SAUDI ARAMCO ENERGY VENTURES, 3090

Scotland
LINK TECHNOLOGIES LIMITED, 2932

Senegal
PARTECH INTERNATIONAL, 1418

Shanghai
AEA INVESTORS, 63

Singapore
3I ASIA PACIFIC 3i Group, 2289
3i GROUP PLC, 2303
ADAMS STREET PARTNERS, LLC Adams Street Partners Singapore Pte. Ltd., 56
AFC MERCHANT BANK, 2343
APOLLO GLOBAL MANAGEMENT, 141
ARCAPITA INC, 153
AZIONE CAPITAL, 2464
B CAPITAL GROUP, 219
BAF SPECTRUM, 2468
BIO*ONE CAPITAL EDMI, 2504
BIOVEDA CAPITAL, 2509
BLACKSTONE PRIVATE EQUITY GROUP, 280
CARLYLE GROUP, 416
CISCO INVESTMENTS, 485
EDBI Pte LTD., 2681
EMERALD TECHNOLOGY VENTURES, 2101
ENSPIRE CAPITAL PTE LTD, 2694
EVERCORE CAPITAL PARTNERS, 700
GENERAL ATLANTIC PARTNERS, 819
GET2VOLUME ACCELERATOR, 2769
IGLOBE PARTNERS, 2844
INFOCOMM INVESTMENTS, 2861
JUNGLE VENTURES, 2904
L CATTERTON PARTNERS, 1092
LIGHTSTONE VENTURES, 1126
LONE STAR FUNDS, 1144
OAKTREE CAPITAL MANAGEMENT LLC, 1362
OMERS PRIVATE EQUITY, 2199
PLATINUM EQUITY, 1455
RED DOT VENTURES, 3064
RIVERSIDE COMPANY, 1576
SEQUOIA CAPITAL Sequoia Capital India Advisors, 1657
SINGTEL INNOV8, 3112
SVI VEN CAPITAL, 3142
VARDE PARTNERS, 1909
VICKERS FINANCIAL GROUP, 3206
WARBURG PINCUS LLC, 1957
WILSHIRE PRIVATE MARKETS, 1988

Slovakia
DARBY OVERSEAS INVESTMENTS LTD, 585
EAST FUND MANAGEMENT GmbH GiroCredit, 2674
SLOVAK AMERICAN ENTERPRISE FUND, 3113

South Africa
CLARITY CAPITAL, 2602
ETHOS PRIVATE EQUITY LIMITED: SA, 2709
FIELDSTONE PRIVATE CAPITAL GROUP, 726

South Korea
AIP PRIVATE CAPITAL, 2027
AJU CAPITAL COMPANY, 2350
AMOREPACIFIC VENTURES, 2386
DRAPER ATHENA, 627
EXCELSIOR CAPITAL ASIA, 2718
GRANITE VENTURE CAPITAL CORPORATION, 2785
HALLIM VENTURE CAPITAL, 2798
HANWHA VC CORPORATION, 2803
HARBOURVEST PARTNERS LLC, 912
HOSEO VENTURE CAPITAL, 2824
HYUNDAI VENTURE INVESTMENT CORPORATION, 2830
IBK CAPITAL CORPORATION Industrial Bank of Korea, 2833
IMM INVESTMENT CORP HCI Private Equity Fund, 2848
KOREA INVESTMENT CORPORATION, 2916
KOREA TECHNOLOGY & BANKING (KTB) NETWORK CORP, 2917
MIRAE ASSET VENTURE ACCELERATOR Mirae Asset Group, 2960
SIGULER GUFF & COMPANY, 1681
STIC VENTURES CORPORATION LIMITED, 3136

Spain
3I SPAIN 3i Group, 2296
3i GROUP PLC, 2303
ACTIVE VENTURE PARTNERS, 2331
ADARA VENTURE PARTNERS, 2334
ADVENT INTERNATIONAL CORPORATION, 61
ALANTRA, 77
AXIS PARTICIPATIONES EMPRESARIALES, 2458
AXON PARTNERS GROUP, 2460
BARCELONA EMPREN, 2474
BARING PRIVATE EQUITY PARTNERS ESPANA SA, 2480
BAYSIDE CAPITAL H.I.G. European Capital Partners Spain, S.L.U., 242
BIG SUR VENTURES, 2501
BULLNET, 2539
CAIXA CAPITAL RISC, 2544
CARLYLE GROUP, 416
CATALANA D'INICIATIVES CR SA, 2561
CRB INVERBIO, 2627
DEMETER PARTNERS, 2647
DFC LTD, 2652
EVERCORE CAPITAL PARTNERS, 700
GESTION DE CAPITAL RIESGO DEL PAIS VASCO, 2768
HARBERT MANAGEMENT CORPORATION, 907
HIGHGROWTH, 2816
INVEXCEL PATRIMONIO, 2882
KIBO VENTURES, 2911
LANTA DIGITAL VENTURES, 2921

1087

Geographic Index

LONE STAR FUNDS, 1144
MERCAPITAL SA, 2953
NAUTA CAPITAL, 2978
PARKWALK ADVISORS, 3019
PERMIRA, 3024
RIVERSIDE COMPANY, 1576
SEAYA VENTURES, 3096
SOCIEDAD REGIONAL DE PROMOCION DEL PRINCIPADO, 3117
TELEFONICA VENTURES, 3160
VITAMINA K VENTURE CAPITAL, 3214

Sri Lanka
ZEPHYR MANAGEMENT LP, 2017

Sweden
3i GROUP PLC, 2303
ALANTRA, 77
ALMI FORETAGSPARTNER AB, 2363
ALTOR EQUITY PARTNERS, 2376
ARES MANAGEMENT LLC, 160
ATOMICO, 2437
AUGMENTA, 2440
COACH & CAPITAL, 2610
CONOR VENTURE PARTNERS OY, 2621
CREANDUM, 2628
EQT PARTNERS AB, 2703
EXPIBEL BV, 2719
FOURIERTRANSFORM, 2746
GREENHILL SAVP, 869
HEALTHCAP Odlander, Fredrikson & Co AB, 2807
INDUSTRI KAPITAL SVENSKA AB, 2854
INDUSTRIFONDEN, 2858
INNOVATIONSKAPITAL, 2869
INVESTMENT AB BURE, 2879
INVESTOR AB, 2881
NORDIC CAPITAL, 2999
NORTHZONE, 3004
NUTEK (NARINGS- OCH TEKNIKUTVECKLINGSVERKET) NUTEK, 3007
PERMIRA, 3024
POD INVESTMENT, 3034
PROCURITAS PARTNERS KB, 3045
RIVERSIDE COMPANY, 1576
SEB VENTURE CAPITAL, 3097
SUNSTONE CAPITAL, 3140
VOLVO GROUP VENTURE CAPITAL, 3217

Switzerland
21 PARTNERS, 2285
3W VENTURES Latour & Zuberbuhler GmbH, 2302
ABB TECHNOLOGY VENTURES, 2307
ACE & COMPANY, 2321
ALPHA ASSOCIATES, 2365
ALPHAMUNDI GROUP LTD, 2368
ANTHEMIS GROUP, 2398
ARAVIS VENTURES, 2410
ARGOS SODITIC SA, 2414
ARMADA INVESTMENT GROUP, 2418
ATLANTIC VENTURES, 2435
B-TO-V PARTNERS, 2466
BANK J VONTOBEL COMPANY AG, 2473
BB BIOTECH VENTURES, 2487
BBH CAPITAL PARTNERS, 243
BIOMED PARTNERS, 2506
CAPVIS EQUITY PARTNERS, 2555
CENTRALWAY, 2574
CREDIT MUTUEL EQUITY, 2082
DEFI GESTION SA Banque Cantonale Vaudoise, 2644
ECOSYSTEM VENTURES, 650
EMERALD TECHNOLOGY VENTURES, 2101
GLOBAL LIFE SCIENCE VENTURES GmbH, 2776
HBM PARTNERS, 2806
HEALTHCAP, 2807
KK RESEARCH/KK SWISS VALUE INVESTOR, 2913
LAKESTAR, 2919
MOUNTAIN PARTNERS, 2970
NOKIA GROWTH PARTNERS, 1331
NOVARTIS VENTURE FUNDS, 1350
PARTNERS GROUP, 3020
PLEXUS VENTURES, 1456
POLYTECH VENTURES, 3036
ROCHE VENTURE FUND F. Hoffman-La Roche AG, 3076
SWISSCOM, 3143
TAT CAPITAL PARTNERS LTD., 3153
UNION BANK OF SWITZERLAND, 3191
VERSANT VENTURES, 1930
ZURCHER KANTONALBANK, 3243
ZURMONT MADISON PRIVATE EQUITY, 3244

Taiwan
CHINA DEVELOPMENT INDUSTRIAL BANK CDFH, 2583
H&Q ASIA PACIFIC, 897
HARBINGER VENTURE MANAGEMENT, 908
PAC-LINK MANAGEMENT CORP., 3015
SOSV, 1709
STAGE 1 VENTURES, 1737
TMI, 3172
VIVO CAPITAL, 1943
WI HARPER GROUP, 1983

Thailand
CSL INVESTMENT & FINANCE, 2633
DOUBLE IMPACT BUSINESS ADVISORY, 2661
NETROVE ASIA SDN BHD, 2984

The Netherlands
RIVERSTONE, 1577
SARONA ASSET MANAGEMENT, 2239
STARWOOD CAPITAL GROUP LLC, 1742

Turkey
212 CAPITAL PARTNERS, 2286
3TS CAPITAL PARTNERS, 2301
AKSOY INTERNET VENTURES, 2351
ASLANOBA CAPITAL, 2428
DARBY OVERSEAS INVESTMENTS LTD, 585
HUMMINGBIRD VENTURES, 2828
REVO CAPITAL, 3069

Ukraine
BULL VENTURES, 2538
EASTLABS, 2675
WESTERN NIS ENTERPRISE FUND, 3224

United Arab Emirates
ABU DHABI INVESTMENT AUTHORITY, 2313
AIP PRIVATE CAPITAL, 2027
BLACKSTONE PRIVATE EQUITY GROUP, 280
BROOKFIELD ASSET MANAGEMENT, 2062
CARLYLE GROUP, 416
FULL CIRCLE INVESTMENTS, 2753
GUGGENHEIM PARTNERS, 890
KOHLBERG KRAVIS ROBERTS & COMPANY, 1086
TVM CAPITAL, 3187

United Kingdom
350 INVESTMENT PARTNERS, 2287
3I AUSTRIA BETEILGUNG GmbH 3i Group, 2290
3I EUROPE PLC 3i Group, 2292
3I ITALY 3i Group, 2295
3I UK 3i Group, 2298
3i GROUP PLC, 2303
ABINGWORTH MANAGEMENT LIMITED, 2308
ACACIA CAPITAL PARTNERS, 2314
ACCEL, 27
ACCEL-KKR LLC, 28
ACCENTURE TECHNOLOGY VENTURES, 2318
ACORN GROWTH COMPANIES, 47
ACTIS, 2329
ACUMEN, 54
ADAMS STREET PARTNERS, LLC Adams Street Partners UK LLP, 56
ADVENT INTERNATIONAL CORPORATION, 61
ADVENT VENTURE PARTNERS, 2340

Geographic Index

ALANTRA, 77
ALBEMARLE PRIVATE EQUITY LIMITED, 2352
ALBERTA INVESTMENT MANAGEMENT CORP., 2029
ALCHEMY PARTNERS, 2353
ALCUIN CAPITAL PARTNERS LLP, 2354
ALLELE FUNDS, 2359
ALLSTATE INVESTMENTS LLC, 88
ALOE PRIVATE EQUITY, 2364
ALTA BERKELEY ASSOCIATES, 2372
AMADEUS CAPITAL PARTNERS LIMITED, 2378
AMPEZZO PARTNERS, 2388
AMPHION CAPITAL PARTNERS, 2389
ANGEL COFUND, 2392
ANGELO, GORDON & CO., 128
ANTHEMIS GROUP, 2398
ANTRAK CAPITAL, 2399
APAX PARTNERS, 136
APOLLO GLOBAL MANAGEMENT, 141
APPLE TREE PARTNERS, 144
ARCAPITA INC, 153
ARDENTON, 2038
ARES MANAGEMENT LLC, 160
ARGAN CAPITAL, 2413
ARGUS CAPITAL LTD, 2416
ARTS ALLIANCE, 2419
ASCENSION VENTURES, 2423
ASCLEPIOS BIORESEARCH, 2424
ATLANTIC BRIDGE, 2434
ATOMICO, 2437
AUGMENTUM CAPITAL, 2441
AVANTI CAPITAL, 2449
AVISTA PARTNERS, 2452
AVLAR BIOVENTURES, 2454
AVONMORE DEVELOPMENTS, 2455
AXM VENTURE CAPITAL, 2459
AZINI CAPITAL PARTNERS, 2463
BAIN CAPITAL PRIVATE EQUITY, 223
BAIRD CAPITAL PARTNERS, 225
BALDERTON CAPITAL, 2469
BALLPARK VENTURES, 2470
BARCLAYS LEVERAGED FINANCE, 2475
BARCLAYS VENTURES Barclays, 2477
BARING PRIVATE EQUITY PARTNERS INDIA, 2481
BATTERY VENTURES, 238
BAYSIDE CAPITAL H.I.G. European Capital Partners LLP, 242
BBH CAPITAL PARTNERS, 243
BC PARTNERS LIMITED, 2488
BERINGEA, 254
BERTI INVESTMENTS, 2496
BESTPORT VENTURES, 2498
BIG SOCIETY CAPITAL, 2500
BLACKSTONE PRIVATE EQUITY GROUP, 280
BLUEGEM CAPITAL PARTNERS, 2515
BOTTS & COMPANY LIMITED, 2523
BRAINSPARK PLC, 2526
BRIDGEPOINT CAPITAL LIMITED, 2529
BRIDGES VENTURES, 2530
BROOKFIELD ASSET MANAGEMENT, 2062
BRYAN GARNIER & COMPANY, 2535
BUSINESS GROWTH FUND, 2541
CANDOVER, 2547
CAPITAL INTERNATIONAL Capital Group Companies, 2550
CARLYLE GROUP, 416
CASS ENTREPRENEURSHIP FUND Cass Business School, 2558
CASTLELAKE, 426
CASTROL INNOVENTURES, 2559
CATALYST FUND MANAGEMENT & RESEARCH LIMITED, 2563
CATALYST VENTURE PARTNERS, 2565
CATAPULT VENTURE MANAGERS, 2566
CAZENOVE PRIVATE EQUITY Cazenove Capital, 2568
CDC CAPITAL PARTNER CDC Group, 2569
CENTRALWAY, 2574
CHARLOTTE STREET CAPITAL, 2577
CHARTERHOUSE CAPITAL PARTNERS I Charterhouse, 2578
CHELSFIELD PARTNERS, 2580
CHORD CAPITAL, 2589
CINVEN LIMITED, 2596
CISCO INVESTMENTS, 485
CITI VENTURES, 488
CITY OF LONDON INVESTMENT GROUP PLC, 2599
CLARITY CAPITAL, 2602
CLIMATE CHANGE CAPITAL, 2606
CLOSE BROTHERS PRIVATE EQUITY Close Brothers Group, 2608
COLLER CAPITAL LIMITED, 2612
CONNECT VENTURES, 2620
CVC CAPITAL PARTNERS LTD, 2635
D.E. SHAW & CO. LP, 580
DERBYSHIRE FIRST INVESTMENTS LIMITED, 2648
DFJ ESPRIT, 2653
DN CAPITAL, 2659
DOUGHTY HANSON & CO., 2662
DRAPER ESPRIT, 2665
DUKE STREET CAPITAL Duke Street, 2667
DUNEDIN CAPITAL PARTNERS LIMITED, 2668
DUTCHESS CAPITAL, 638
EC1 CAPITAL LTD, 2676
ECI VENTURES, 2678
EDEN VENTURES, 2682
ELECTRA PARTNERS EUROPE, 2686
EM WARBURG, PINCUS & COMPANY INTERNATIONAL, 2688
ENSO VENTURES, 2693
ENTERPRISE EQUITY (NI) LTD, 2695
ENTERPRISE VENTURE LIMITED, 2698
ENTERPRISE VENTURES LIMITED, 2699
ENTREE CAPITAL, 2700
ENTREPRENEURS FUND, 2701
EPIDAREX CAPITAL, 690
EPISODE 1 PARTNERS, 2702
EPLANET CAPITAL, 691
EQUISTONE, 2705
ESSEX WOODLANDS HEALTH VENTURES LLC, 698
EUROPEAN ACQUISITION CAPITAL LIMITED, 2713
EVERCORE CAPITAL PARTNERS, 700
F-PRIME CAPITAL PARTNERS, 711
FERRANTI LIMITED, 2723
FIDELITY GROWTH PARTNERS EUROPE, 2725
FIELDSTONE PRIVATE CAPITAL GROUP, 726
FISHER LYNCH CAPITAL, 745
FORESIGHT VENTURE PARTNERS, 2740
FORTRESS INVESTMENT GROUP LLC, 769
FOUNDATION CAPITAL LIMITED, 2744
FRANCISCO PARTNERS, 782
FRONTLINE VENTURES, 2750
FSE GROUP, 2751
GE EQUITY EUROPE, 2760
GENERAL ATLANTIC PARTNERS, 819
GENERICS GROUP LIMITED Generics Group, 2764
GMT COMMUNICATIONS PARTNERS LLP, 2780
GOLDMAN SACHS INTERNATIONAL UK, 2783
GRANVILLE BAIRD CAPITAL PARTNERS, 2786
GRAPHITE CAPITAL MANAGEMENT LTD, 2787
GREENHILL SAVP, 869
GUGGENHEIM PARTNERS, 890
HAMBRO CAPITAL MANAGEMENT LTD, 2799
HARBERT MANAGEMENT CORPORATION, 907
HARBOURVEST PARTNERS LLC, 912
HELLMAN & FRIEDMAN LLC, 927
HENDERSON PRIVATE CAPITAL, 2812
HG CAPITAL, 2814
HIG CAPITAL HIG European Capital Partners LLP, 931
HILCO BRANDS, 940
HILKO UK LTD/VALCO CAPITAL PARTNERS, 2818
HOXTON VENTURES, 2825
HSBC VENTURES UK LIMITED, 2827
HUMMINGBIRD VENTURES, 2828
IMPERIAL INNOVATIONS, 2849
INDEX VENTURES, 2851
INDUSTRY VENTURES, 990
INGENIOUS VENTURES, 2862
INOVIA CAPITAL, 2150
INTEGRATED TECHNOLOGIES LIMITED, 2870
INTERMEDIATE CAPITAL GROUP PLC, 2874
INTERNATIONAL PRIVATE EQUITY SERVICES LIMITED Guernsey, 2875

Geographic Index

INVESTCORP, 1021
INVUS GROUP, 1022
IP GROUP, 2883
IPG GROUP, 2885
ISIS EP LLP F & C, 2889
JEGI CAPITAL, 1037
KLEINWORT CAPITAL LIMITED, 2914
KOHLBERG KRAVIS ROBERTS & COMPANY, 1086
LEGAL AND GENERAL VENTURES LIMITED, 2926
LEXINGTON PARTNERS, 1116
LIGHTHOUSE PARTNERS, 1123
LIGHTSPEED VENTURE PARTNER, 1124
LLOYDS DEVELOPMENT CAPITAL LIMITED, 2935
MACMILLAN DIGITAL EDUCATION, 2941
MEZZANINE MANAGEMENT LIMITED Mezzanine Management UK Ltd., 2956
MIDVEN, 2958
MMC VENTURES, 2963
MONTAGU PRIVATE EQUITY LIMITED, 2968
MVM LIFE SCIENCE PARTNERS, 2972
NATWEST VENTURES LIMITED, 2976
NAUTA CAPITAL, 2978
NEW MODEL VENTURE CAPITAL, 2986
NEWABLE VENTURES, 2988
NEXT WORLD CAPITAL, 1319
NOMURA PHASE4 VENTURES LTD, 2998
NORTH WEST FUND, 3001
NORTHERN ENTERPRISE LIMITED, 3002
NORTHLEAF CAPITAL PARTNERS, 2196
NORTHSTAR VENTURES, 3003
NOTION CAPITAL, 3005
NVM PRIVATE EQUITY LIMITED, 3008
OAKTREE CAPITAL MANAGEMENT LLC, 1362
OCTOPUS INVESTMENTS, 3009
OMERS PRIVATE EQUITY, 2199
OMIDYAR NETWORK, 1374
ONEX PARTNERS, 2201
PALADIN CAPITAL GROUP, 1401
PANTHEON VENTURES (US) LP, 1413
PARKWALK ADVISORS, 3019
PASSION CAPITAL, 3021
PENTECH VENTURES, 3023
PERMIRA Permira Advisers LLP, 3024
PHOENIX EQUITY PARTNERS LIMITED, 3027
PITON CAPITAL, 3031
PLATINUM EQUITY, 1455
PLEXUS VENTURES, 1456
POMONA CAPITAL, 1466
POND VENTURES, 3038
PRIME TECHNOLOGY VENTURES NV, 3042
PROFOUNDERS CAPITAL, 3046
PROMETHEAN INVESTMENTS LLP, 3048
PROMETHYAN LABS, 3049
PROVIDENCE EQUITY PARTNERS, 1498
PSG, 1499
QUESTER CAPITAL MANAGEMENT LIMITED, 3061
QUINBROOK INFRASTRUCTURE PARTNERS, 1520
REED ELSEVIER VENTURES, 3065
RESOURCE CAPITAL FUNDS, 1551
RIVERSIDE COMPANY, 1576
SAFFRON HILL VENTURES, 3083
SALFORD CAPITAL PARTNERS, 3086
SAMOS INVESTMENTS, 3088
SCHRODER VENTURES HEALTH INVESTORS, 1631
SCOTTISH ENTERPRISE, 3094
SCOTTISH EQUITY PARTNERS, 3095
SCULPTOR CAPITAL MANAGEMENT Sculptor Capital Management Europe Limited, 1638
SEARCHLIGHT, 2243
SEED CAPITAL LIMITED, 3098
SEEDCAMP, 3099
SEVEN SPIRES INVESTMENTS, 3103
SIGNATURE CAPITAL LLC, 3111
SIGULER GUFF & COMPANY, 1681
SILVER LAKE, 1685
SOVEREIGN CAPITAL, 3121
SPARK VENTURES, 3122
SR ONE LTD, 1734
SSE VENTURES, 3126
STARWOOD CAPITAL GROUP LLC, 1742
STEPSTONE, 3135
STRAND HANSON LIMITED, 3137
SUMMIT PARTNERS, 1754
SUN CAPITAL PARTNERS, 1755
SUPREMUM CAPITAL, 3141
SV HEALTH INVESTORS, 1764
TA ASSOCIATES, 1778
TALIS CAPITAL, 3148
TECHNOLOGY CROSSOVER VENTURES, 1787
TELEFONICA VENTURES, 3160
THE ABRAAJ GROUP, 3164
TIANGUIS LIMITED, 3169
TLCOM CAPITAL, 3170
TPG CAPITAL, 1837
TRANSATLANTIC CAPITAL LTD, 3177
TREVI HEALTH CAPITAL, 1846
TRILANTIC CAPITAL PARTNERS, 1853
TTP VENTURES, 3186
VARDE PARTNERS, 1909
VENCAP, 3197
VIRGIN GREEN FUND, 3213
VONTOBEL PRIVATE EQUITY MANAGEMENT CAYMAN, 3219
WARBURG PINCUS LLC, 1957
WHEB GROUP, 3227
WHITE STAR CAPITAL, 1982
WILSHIRE PRIVATE MARKETS, 1988
YFM GROUP, 3234
ZOUK VENTURES, 3242

United States

Alabama
ADVANTAGE CAPITAL PARTNERS, 60
C&G CAPITAL PARTNERS, 366
CAMP ONE VENTURES, 387
HARBERT MANAGEMENT CORPORATION, 907
MURPHREE VENTURE PARTNERS, 1273
NEW CAPITAL PARTNERS, 1292
REDMONT VENTURE PARTNERS, 1536
STONEHENGE GROWTH CAPITAL, 1748

Arizona
ACACIA CAPITAL, 24
BILTMORE VENTURES, 267
C3 CAPITAL PARTNERS LP, 367
CANAL PARTNERS, 390
CLEAR SKY CAPITAL, 501
FINAVENTURES, 730
FOGEL INTERNATIONAL, 761
GRAYHAWK CAPITAL, 861
HYPUR VENTURES, 966
LIZADA CAPITAL LLC, 1139
NEST VENTURES, 1289
PANGAEA VENTURES LTD, 2205
RESEARCH CORPORATION TECHNOLOGIES, 1546
SOURCE CAPITAL GROUP, 1710
THUNDERBIRD ANGEL NETWORK, 1824
TRU MANAGEMENT, 1860
TRUE NORTH VENTURE PARTNERS, 1861
VALLEY VENTURES LP, 1903
WELLS FARGO CAPITAL FINANCE, 1971

Arkansas
DIAMOND STATE VENTURES LP, 612

California
11.2 CAPITAL, 3
1ST COURSE CAPITAL, 7
500 STARTUPS, 10
5AM VENTURES, 11
7 GATE VENTURES, 2025
A-GRADE INVESTMENTS, 14
ABERDARE VENTURES, 19
ABINGWORTH MANAGEMENT LIMITED, 2308

Geographic Index

ABS CAPITAL PARTNERS, 21
ABSTRACT VENTURES, 23
ACACIA CAPITAL, 24
ACARIO INNOVATION, 26
ACCEL, 27
ACCEL-KKR LLC, 28
ACCELEPRISE, 29
ACCELERATOR LIFE SCIENCE PARTNERS, 30
ACCELERATOR VENTURES, 31
ACCENT CAPITAL PARTNERS LLC, 32
ACERO CAPITAL, 40
ACKRELL CAPITAL, 43
ACME CAPITAL, 44
ACON INVESTMENTS, 45
ACORN CAMPUS VENTURES, 46
ACREW CAPITAL, 48
ACT ONE VENTURES, 49
ACUITY VENTURES LLC, 53
ADAMS STREET PARTNERS, LLC Adams Street Partners, Inc., 56
ADOBE VENTURES LP, 57
ADVANCED TECHNOLOGY VENTURES, 58
ADVANTAGE CAPITAL PARTNERS, 60
AGILITY CAPITAL LLC, 68
AHOY CAPITAL, 71
AIRBUS VENTURES, 72
AKERS CAPITAL LLC, 74
ALACRITY VENTURES, 76
ALIGNED PARTNERS, 83
ALLEGIS CYBER CAPITAL, 84
ALLOY VENTURES, 87
ALMAZ CAPITAL, 89
ALPINE INVESTORS, 92
ALSOP LOUIE PARTNERS, 93
ALTAIR VENTURES, 95
ALTAMONT CAPITAL PARTNERS, 96
ALTOS VENTURES, 100
ALTURA VENTURES LLC, 103
AMD VENTURES, 107
AME CLOUD VENTURES, 108
AMGEN VENTURES, 113
AMICUS CAPITAL, 115
AMIDZAD PARTNERS, 116
AMKEY VENTURES, 118
AMPLIFY, 121
ANALYTICS VENTURES, 122
ANDREESSEN HOROWITZ, 125
ANGELENO GROUP, 127
ANGELO, GORDON & CO., 128
ANGELS' FORUM LLC, 130
ANNEX VENTURES, 131
ANTHEM VENTURE PARTNERS, 133
ANZU PARTNERS, 134
AOL VENTURES, 135
APHELION CAPITAL, 139
APOLLO GLOBAL MANAGEMENT, 141
APPLIED MATERIALS VENTURES, 145
ARAGON VENTURES, 146
ARCADIAN FUND, 152
ARCH VENTURE PARTNERS, 154
ARCHYTAS VENTURES, 156
ARES MANAGEMENT LLC, 160
ARGONAUT VENTURES, 164
ARROWHEAD INVESTMENT MANAGEMENT, 170
ARSENAL VENTURE PARTNERS, 173
ARTIMAN VENTURES, 176
ARTIS VENTURES, 177
ASIAVEST PARTNERS, 2427
ASPECT VENTURES, 182
ASSET MANAGEMENT VENTURES, 183
ASTELLAS VENTURE MANAGEMENT, 184
ATA VENTURES, 185
ATEL CAPITAL GROUP, 186
ATHENAEUM FUND, 188
ATRIUM CAPITAL, 194
AUDAX GROUP, 197
AUGUST CAPITAL, 200
AURORA CAPITAL GROUP, 202
AUTO TECH VENTURES, 207
AUTOTECH VENTURES, 208
AVALON VENTURES, 209
AZCA, 217
AZURE CAPITAL PARTNERS, 218
B CAPITAL GROUP, 219
BACKSTAGE CAPITAL, 221
BAIDU VENTURES, 222
BAIN CAPITAL VENTURES, 224
BALMORAL FUNDS, 228
BAND OF ANGELS LLC, 229
BANNEKER PARTNERS, 230
BARODA VENTURES, 231
BASE VENTURES, 232
BASF VENTURE CAPITAL, 2483
BASIS SET VENTURES, 235
BATTERY VENTURES, 238
BAY CITY CAPITAL LLC, 240
BAY PARTNERS, 241
BEE PARTNERS, 246
BENCHMARK, 251
BENHAMOU GLOBAL VENTURES, 252
BERGGRUEN HOLDINGS, 253
BERKELEY VC INTERNATIONAL LLC, 255
BERKELEY VENTURES, 256
BERTRAM CAPITAL, 260
BESSEMER VENTURE PARTNERS, 263
BI WALDEN MANAGEMENT SDN Walden International, 2499
BINARY CAPITAL, 268
BISON CAPITAL ASSET MANAGEMENT LLC, 277
BLACK DIAMOND VENTURES, 278
BLACKSTONE PRIVATE EQUITY GROUP, 280
BLADE VENTURES, 281
BLOCKCHAIN CAPITAL, 286
BLOOMBERG BETA, 287
BLUE SKY CAPITAL, 295
BLUEFISH VENTURES, 297
BLUEPOINTE VENTURES, 298
BLUERUN VENTURES, 299
BLUM CAPITAL PARTNERS, 303
BLUMBERG CAPITAL, 304
BMW I VENTURES, 305
BONFIRE VENTURES, 309
BOOST VC, 310
BRAIN TRUST ACCELERATOR FUND, 326
BRAINSTORM VENTURES, 327
BRANDON CAPITAL GROUP, 329
BREAKWATER INVESTMENTS, 333
BREAKWATER MANAGEMENT, 334
BRENTWOOD ASSOCIATES, 337
BREYER CAPITAL, 339
BRIDGESCALE PARTNERS, 342
BRIGHT CAPITAL, 2531
BRIGHTPATH CAPITAL PARTNERS, 343
BRILLIANT VENTURES, 345
BROADHAVEN CAPITAL PARTNERS, 346
BULLPEN CAPITAL, 361
BUNKER HILL CAPITAL, 362
CALCEF CLEAN ENERGY FUND, 370
CALERA CAPITAL, 371
CALIBRATE VENTURES, 373
CALIFORNIA COAST VENTURE FORUM, 3248
CALIFORNIA TECHNOLOGY VENTURES, 374
CALTIUS EQUITY PARTNERS, 376
CALTIUS STRUCTURED CAPITAL, 377
CAMP ONE VENTURES, 387
CAMP VENTURES, 388
CANAAN PARTNERS, 389
CANNA ANGELS LLC, 391
CANNABIS CAPITAL, 392
CANNABIS STRATEGIC VENTURES, 394
CANTOS VENTURES, 398
CANVAS VENTURES, 399
CANYON CREEK CAPITAL, 400
CAPX PARTNERS, 410
CARDINAL VENTURE CAPITAL, 414
CARLYLE GROUP, 416

Geographic Index

CARRICK CAPITAL PARTNERS, 419
CASA VERDE CAPITAL, 420
CATAMOUNT VENTURES LP, 430
CATAPULT VENTURES, 431
CATO BIOVENTURES, 432
CELERITY PARTNERS, 441
CENTANA GROWTH PARTNERS, 442
CENTRE PARTNERS MANAGEMENT LLC, 449
CENTURY PARK CAPITAL PARTNERS, 451
CEO VENTURES, 452
CERRACAP VENTURES, 455
CERVIN VENTURES, 456
CHARLES RIVER VENTURES, 457
CHARTER LIFE SCIENCES, 460
CHICAGO PACIFIC FOUNDERS, 471
CHINAROCK CAPITAL MANAGEMENT VENTURES, 474
CHINAVEST, 475
CIPIO PARTNERS, 2597
CIRCLEUP, 484
CISCO INVESTMENTS, 485
CITI VENTURES, 488
CITY HILL VENTURES, 489
CLAREMONT CREEK VENTURES, 493
CLARITY PARTNERS, 496
CLEAN PACIFIC VENTURES, 499
CLEANPATH VENTURES, 500
CLEARLAKE CAPITAL, 502
CLEARLIGHT PARTNERS, 503
CLEARSTONE VENTURE PARTNERS, 504
CLEARVIEW CAPITAL, 505
CLYDESDALE VENTURES, 508
COATUE MANAGEMENT, 511
COLUMN GROUP, 519
COMCAST VENTURES, 520
COMET LABS, 521
COMPASS GROUP MANAGEMENT LLC, 525
COMPASS TECHNOLOGY PARTNERS LP, 526
COMSTOCK CAPITAL PARTNERS LLC, 529
CONSOR CAPITAL, 533
CORNERSTONE CAPITAL HOLDINGS, 542
CORNERSTONE HOLDINGS, 543
CORRELATION VENTURES, 545
COSTANOA VENTURE CAPITAL, 548
COSTELLA KIRSCH, 549
COWBOY VENTURES, 553
CREANDUM, 2628
CRESCENDO VENTURE MANAGEMENT LLC, 2630
CRESCENDO VENTURES, 556
CRESCENT CAPITAL GROUP LP, 557
CROSSCUT VENTURES, 562
CROSSLINK CAPITAL, 564
CRUNCHFUND, 565
CUTLASS CAPITAL LLC, 573
CVF CAPITAL PARTNERS, 574
CXO FUND, 575
D.E. SHAW & CO. LP, 580
DAG VENTURES, 582
DATA COLLECTIVE, 586
DBL PARTNERS, 596
DCM, 597
DE NOVO VENTURES, 599
DECIENS CAPITAL, 600
DEEP FORK CAPITAL, 601
DEFTA PARTNERS, 603
DFJ VENTURE CAPITAL, 610
DIAMOND TECHVENTURES, 613
DIAMONDHEAD VENTURES, 614
DJF DRAGONFUND CHINA, 2658
DN CAPITAL, 2659
DOCOMO INNOVATIONS, 621
DOMAIN ASSOCIATES LLC, 622
DOT EDU VENTURES, 624
DOUBLE M PARTNERS, 625
DOUBLEROCK VENTURE CAPITAL, 626
DRAPER ATHENA, 627
DRAPER RICHARDS KAPLAN FOUNDATION, 628
E.VENTURES, 641

ECLIPSE VENTURES, 648
ECOSYSTEM VENTURES, 650
EDBI Pte LTD., 2681
ELAB VENTURES, 657
ELEVATION PARTNERS, 660
ELYSIUM VENTURE CAPITAL, 662
EMBARK VENTURES, 664
EMERALD OCEAN CAPITAL, 665
EMERGENCE CAPITAL PARTNERS, 666
EMERGENT MEDICAL PARTNERS, 667
ENDEAVOUR CAPITAL, 674
ENERGY CAPITAL PARTNERS, 676
ENERTECH CAPITAL, 677
ENIAC VENTURES, 680
ENTER VENTURES, 682
EPLANET CAPITAL, 691
ESPRESSO CAPITAL, 2103
EVERCORE CAPITAL PARTNERS, 700
EXPERIMENT FUND, 709
EcoR1 CAPITAL, 710
FAIRMONT CAPITAL, 714
FAIRVIEW CAPITAL PARTNERS, 715
FALCON FUND, 716
FELICIS VENTURES, 720
FENOX VENTURE CAPITAL, 721
FIFTH WALL, 728
FIKA VENTURES, 729
FINAVENTURES, 730
FIRELAKE CAPITAL, 731
FIRST ASCENT VENTURES, 2112
FIRST ROUND CAPITAL, 742
FISHER LYNCH CAPITAL, 745
FLOODGATE FUND, 752
FOCUS VENTURES, 759
FOG CITY CAPITAL, 760
FORERUNNER VENTURES, 763
FORESITE CAPITAL, 764
FORGEPOINT CAPITAL, 765
FORMATIVE VENTURES, 766
FORREST BINKLEY & BROWN, 767
FORTRESS INVESTMENT GROUP LLC, 769
FORTÉ VENTURES, 770
FORUM VENTURES, 771
FORWARD VENTURES, 772
FOUNDATION CAPITAL, 773
FOUNDER PARTNERS, 775
FOUNDERS FUND, 778
FOUR RIVERS GROUP, 780
FOX PAINE & COMPANY LLC, 781
FRANCISCO PARTNERS, 782
FRAZIER HEALTHCARE VENTURES, 785
FREEMAN SPOGLI & CO., 786
FRESH VC, 788
FRIEDMAN, FLEISCHER & LOWE LLC, 790
FRONTIER VENTURE CAPITAL, 794
FRONTIER VENTURES, 795
FTV CAPITAL, 796
FUNDERS CLUB, 798
FUNG CAPITAL USA, 799
FUNK VENTURES, 800
FUSE CAPITAL, 801
FUSION FUND, 802
FUTURE VENTURES, 803
GABRIEL VENTURE PARTNERS, 808
GARAGE TECHNOLOGY VENTURES, 810
GCI CAPITAL, 2123
GE VENTURES, 812
GENERAL ATLANTIC PARTNERS, 819
GENERAL CATALYST PARTNERS, 820
GENERATION PARTNERS, 822
GENSTAR CAPITAL LP, 823
GEODESIC CAPITAL, 824
GERKEN CAPITAL ASSOCIATES, 826
GGV CAPITAL, 827
GI PARTNERS, 828
GIDEON HIXON FUND, 830
GLADSTONE CAPITAL, 832

Geographic Index

GLOBAL CATALYST PARTNERS, 837
GLOBALIVE, 2128
GLOBESPAN CAPITAL PARTNERS, 839
GLYNN CAPITAL MANAGEMENT, 840
GOAHEAD VENTURES, 841
GOLDEN GATE CAPITAL, 843
GOLUB CAPITAL, 848
GRANITE HILL CAPITAL PARTNERS, LLC, 856
GRANITE VENTURES, 857
GRAPHENE VENTURES, 859
GREENHILL SAVP, 869
GREENSPRING ASSOCIATES, 872
GREIF & COMPANY, 874
GREY SKY VENTURE PARTNERS, 875
GREYCROFT PARTNERS, 876
GREYLOCK PARTNERS, 877
GRISHIN ROBOTICS, 879
GRYPHON INVESTORS, 886
GSR VENTURES, 2792
GSV VENTURES, 888
GUGGENHEIM PARTNERS, 890
GV, 894
GVA CAPITAL, 895
H&Q ASIA PACIFIC, 897
HALLEY VENTURE PARTNERS, 900
HANCOCK PARK ASSOCIATES, 905
HANOVER PARTNERS, 906
HARBERT MANAGEMENT CORPORATION, 907
HARBINGER VENTURE MANAGEMENT, 908
HARRISON METAL, 914
HARVARD CAPITAL GROUP, 916
HEALTHQUEST CAPITAL, 924
HELLMAN & FRIEDMAN LLC, 927
HERCULES TECHNOLOGY GROWTH CAPITAL, INC, 928
HEWLETT PACKARD ENTERPRISE, 930
HIG CAPITAL, 931
HIGHBAR PARTNERS, 936
HIGHLAND CAPITAL PARTNERS, 938
HIGHWAY1, 939
HOMEBREW MANAGEMENT, 944
HONE CAPITAL, 945
HORIZON TECHNOLOGY FINANCE, 949
HORIZON VENTURES LLC, 950
HOULIHAN LOKEY, 951
HOUSATONIC PARTNERS, 952
HUMMER WINBLAD VENTURE PARTNERS, 959
HUNTINGTON CAPITAL, 961
HUNTSMAN GAY GLOBAL CAPITAL, 962
ICON VENTURES, 972
ID VENTURES AMERICA LLC, 974
IDEALAB, 976
IGLOBE PARTNERS, 2844
IGNITION PARTNERS, 978
ILLUMINATE VENTURES, 980
IN-Q-TEL, 983
INCUBE VENTURES, 984
INDEX VENTURES, 2851
INDUSTRIAL GROWTH PARTNERS, 989
INDUSTRY VENTURES, 990
INFOCOMM INVESTMENTS, 2861
INITIALIZED CAPITAL, 995
INITIO GROUP, 996
INNOSPRING, 998
INNOVATION ENDEAVORS, 1001
INOVIA CAPITAL, 2150
INSTITUTIONAL VENTURE PARTNERS, 1006
INTEGRAL CAPITAL PARTNERS, 1008
INTEL CAPITAL, 1009
INTELLECTUAL VENTURES, 1010
INTERWEST PARTNERS, 1014
INVENCOR, 1015
INVENT, 1016
INVENTUS, 1017
JACKSON SQUARE VENTURES, 1028
JAVELIN VENTURE PARTNERS, 1032
JAZZ VENTURE PARTNERS, 1033
JC2 VENTURES, 1035

JETBLUE TECHNOLOGY VENTURES, 1039
JF SHEA VENTURES, 1040
JMI EQUITY FUND LP, 1045
K9 VENTURES, 1054
KAIROS VENTURES, 1055
KAISER PERMANENTE VENTURES, 1056
KARLIN VENTURES, 1059
KEARNY VENTURE PARTNERS, 1063
KEIRETSU FORUM, 1065
KERN WHELAN CAPITAL, 1070
KHOSLA VENTURES, 1073
KINSEY HILLS GROUP, 1077
KLEINER PERKINS, 1079
KODIAK CAPITAL, 1083
KOHLBERG KRAVIS ROBERTS & COMPANY, 1086
KOHLBERG VENTURES, 1087
KPG VENTURES, 1088
KTB VENTURES, 1091
LATTERELL VENTURE PARTNERS, 1098
LAUNCHPAD LA, 1103
LEAPFROG VENTURES, 1106
LEASING TECHNOLOGIES INTERNATIONAL INC., 1107
LEGACY VENTURE, 1110
LEONARD GREEN & PARTNERS LP, 1113
LEVINE LEICHTMAN CAPITAL PARTNERS, 1115
LEXINGTON PARTNERS, 1116
LIGHTHOUSE CAPITAL PARTNERS, 1122
LIGHTSPEED VENTURE PARTNERS, 1125
LIGHTSTONE VENTURES, 1126
LOCUS VENTURES, 1142
LOMBARD INVESTMENTS, 1143
LONGITUDE CAPITAL, 1147
LOS ANGELES VENTURE ASSOCIATION, 3258
LOVELL MINNICK PARTNERS LLC, 1151
LOWERCASE CAPITAL, 1153
LUX CAPITAL, 1155
M12, 1158
MARWIT CAPITAL LLC, 1171
MASCHMEYER GROUP VENTURES, 1173
MATON VENTURE, 1183
MATRIX PARTNERS, 1184
MAVERICK VENTURES, 1185
MAYFIELD FUND, 1187
MEDIA VENTURE PARTNERS, 1197
MENLO VENTURES, 1203
MERITECH CAPITAL PARTNERS, 1213
MERITURN PARTNERS, 1214
MERUS CAPITAL, 1219
MESA VERDE PARTNERS, 1222
MHS CAPITAL, 1227
MINDFULL INVESTORS, 1236
MIRAMAR VENTURE PARTNERS, 1237
MISSION BAY CAPITAL, 1238
MISSION VENTURES, 1239
MITSUI GLOBAL INVESTMENT, 1241
MOBILE FOUNDATION VENTURES, 1243
MOHR-DAVIDOW VENTURES, 1247
MONITOR VENTURES, 1249
MONTREUX EQUITY PARTNERS, 1251
MOORE VENTURE PARTNERS, 1253
MORGENTHALER VENTURES, 1257
MOTIV PARTNERS, 1258
MPM CAPITAL, 1268
MS&AD VENTURES, 1269
NATIONAL VENTURE CAPITAL ASSOCIATION, 3262
NAVITAS CAPITAL, 1281
NAXURI CAPITAL, 1283
NEEDHAM CAPITAL PARTNERS, 1287
NEW ENTERPRISE ASSOCIATES, 1296
NEW LEAF VENTURE PARTNERS, 1297
NEWBURY VENTURES, 1310
NEWSCHOOLS VENTURE FUND, 1315
NEXIT VENTURES OY Nexit Ventures Inc., 2990
NEXT WORLD CAPITAL, 1319
NEXUS VENTURE PARTNERS, 2992
NFX, 1323
NGEN PARTNERS, 1324

Geographic Index

NGP CAPITAL, 1327
NORTHERN LIGHT VENTURE CAPITAL, 1340
NORTHGATE, 1341
NORTHLEAF CAPITAL PARTNERS, 2196
NORWEST VENTURE PARTNERS, 1346
NOVENTI VENTURES, 1352
NOVO A/S, 3006
NOVUS VENTURES LP, 1354
NTH POWER TECHNOLOGIES, 1355
NVIDIA INCEPTION, 1357
O'REILLY ALPHATECH VENTURES, 1359
OAK HILL CAPITAL PARTNERS, 1360
OAK INVESTMENT PARTNERS, 1361
OAKTREE CAPITAL MANAGEMENT LLC, 1362
OBVIOUS VENTURES, 1363
OCEANSHORE VENTURES, 1365
OCTANe, 1366
ODYSSEY INVESTMENT PARTNERS, 1368
OEM CAPITAL, 1369
OFF THE GRID VENTURES, 1370
OKAPI VENTURE CAPITAL, 1371
OMIDYAR NETWORK, 1374
ONSET VENTURES, 1379
OPUS CAPITAL, 1382
ORBIMED HEALTHCARE FUND MANAGEMENT, 1383
OUTLOOK VENTURES, 1390
OUTPOST CAPITAL, 1391
OWL VENTURES, 1393
OXFORD BIOSCIENCE PARTNERS, 1395
OYSTER VENTURES, 1396
PAC-LINK MANAGEMENT CORP., 3015
PACIFIC COMMUNITY VENTURES, 1397
PACIFIC VENTURES GROUP, 1400
PALADIN CAPITAL GROUP, 1401
PALISADES VENTURES, 1403
PALO ALTO VENTURE PARTNERS, 1406
PALO ALTO VENTURE SCIENCE, 1407
PALOMAR VENTURES, 1408
PANORAMA CAPITAL, 1411
PANTHEON VENTURES (US) LP, 1413
PARTECH INTERNATIONAL, 1418
PARTHENON CAPITAL, 1419
PATHBREAKER VENTURES, 1423
PEAR VC, 1426
PEGASUS CAPITAL GROUP, 1427
PENINSULA VENTURES, 1430
PHILQUO VENTURES, 1441
PHYSIC VENTURES, 1442
PINNACLE VENTURES, 1449
PITANGO VENTURE CAPITAL, 3030
PIVA, 1453
PIVOTNORTH CAPITAL, 1454
PLATINUM EQUITY, 1455
PLEXUS VENTURES, 1456
PLUG AND PLAY VENTURES, 1457
POLARIS VENTURE PARTNERS, 1464
POND VENTURES, 3038
POSEIDON ASSET MANAGEMENT, 1468
PRECURSOR VENTURES, 1475
PRELUDE VENTURES, 1476
PRESIDIO VENTURES, 1478
PRITZKER GROUP PRIVATE CAPITAL, 1482
PRITZKER GROUP VENTURE CAPITAL, 1483
PROQUEST INVESTMENTS, 1492
PROSPECT VENTURE PARTNERS, 1495
PSILOS GROUP, 1500
QUALCOMM VENTURES, 1511
QUEST VENTURE PARTNERS, 1515
QUESTA CAPITAL, 1516
RALLY VENTURES, 1525
REACH CAPITAL, 1530
REDPOINT VENTURES, 1537
REDWOOD CAPITAL CORPORATION, 1538
REEFI CAPITAL, 1540
RELAY VENTURES, 2228
REMBRANDT VENTURE PARTNERS, 1543
RESOLUTE.VC, 1549
RHO VENTURES, 1561
RHYTHM VENTURE CAPITAL, 1562
RIBBIT CAPITAL, 1563
RIDGE VENTURES, 1566
RINCON VENTURE PARTNERS, 1569
RIVERSIDE COMPANY, 1576
RIVERSTONE, 1577
RLH EQUITY PARTNERS, 1579
RODA GROUP, 1584
ROSEWOOD CAPITAL, 1591
ROTH CAPITAL PARTNERS, 1592
RUBICON VENTURE CAPITAL, 1599
SACRAMENTO ANGELS, 1604
SAGEVIEW CAPITAL, 1606
SAIL VENTURE PARTNERS, 1607
SALESFORCE VENTURES, 1610
SALT CREEK CAPITAL, 1612
SAMSUNG NEXT, 1614
SAMSUNG VENTURE INVESTMENT CORPORATION, 3089
SAN DIEGO VENTURE GROUP, 1615
SAND HILL ANGELS, 1616
SANDBOX INDUSTRIES, 1618
SANDERLING VENTURES, 1619
SAPPHIRE VENTURES, 1623
SCALE VENTURE PARTNERS, 1629
SCIFI VC, 1634
SCRUM VENTURES, 1637
SEACOAST CAPITAL CORPORATION, 1639
SEED MILESTONE FUND, 1647
SEIDLER EQUITY PARTNERS, 1648
SELBY VENTURE PARTNERS, 1649
SHAMROCK CAPITAL ADVISORS, 1663
SHAMROCK HOLDINGS, 1664
SHARESPOST, 1665
SHASTA VENTURES, 1666
SHEPHERD VENTURES, 1667
SHERPALO VENTURES, 1669
SIERRA VENTURES, 1672
SIGNAL FIRE, 1677
SIGNIA VENTURE PARTNERS, 1680
SILVER LAKE, 1685
SINGTEL INNOV8, 3112
SJF VENTURES, 1691
SK TELECOM VENTURES, 1692
SKYLINE VENTURES, 1693
SKYTREE CAPITAL PARTNERS, 1694
SLOW VENTURES, 1696
SOFINNOVA VENTURES, 1700
SOFTBANK CAPITAL, 1701
SOFTTECH VC, 1702
SONY INNOVATION FUND, 1705
SONY STRATEGIC TECHNOLOGY PARTNERSHIPS, 1706
SORRENTO VENTURES, 1708
SOSV, 1709
SOURCE CAPITAL GROUP, 1710
SOUTHERN CROSS VENTURE PARTNERS, 1713
SOZO VENTURES, 1716
SPARK CAPITAL, 1718
SPARKLABS GLOBAL VENTURES, 1719
SPECTRUM EQUITY INVESTORS LP, 1720
SPERO VENTURES, 1724
SR ONE LTD, 1734
STAGE 1 VENTURES, 1737
STARTUP CAPITAL VENTURES, 1740
STARWOOD CAPITAL GROUP LLC, 1742
STEAMBOAT VENTURES, 3133
STEELPOINT CAPITAL PARTNERS, 1744
STORM VENTURES, 1750
SUMMIT PARTNERS, 1754
SUN CAPITAL PARTNERS, 1755
SUNBRIDGE PARTNERS, 1757
SUNRISE CAPITAL PARTNERS, 1758
SUNSTONE CAPITAL, 3140
SUSA VENTURES, 1760
SUTTER HILL VENTURES, 1762
SV ANGEL, 1763
SVB CAPITAL, 1766

Geographic Index

SWANDER PACE CAPITAL, 1769
SWITCH VENTURES, 1770
SYCAMORE VENTURES, 1771
SYNERGY LIFE SCIENCE PARTNERS, 1774
SYNERGY VENTURES, 1775
TA ASSOCIATES, 1778
TAKEDA VENTURES, 1780
TALLWOOD VENTURE CAPITAL, 1781
TAYRONA VENTURES, 1783
TECH COAST ANGELS, 1786
TECHNOLOGY CROSSOVER VENTURES, 1787
TECHNOLOGY PARTNERS, 1788
TEL VENTURE CAPITAL, 1793
TELEFONICA VENTURES, 3160
TELEGRAPH HILL PARTNERS, 1794
TELESOFT PARTNERS, 1795
TEN ELEVEN VENTURES, 1796
TENAYA CAPITAL, 1798
TENONETEN VENTURES, 1800
THAYER VENTURES, 1808
THE ALCHEMIST ACCELERATOR, 1809
THE ARCVIEW GROUP, 1810
THE HIVE, 1812
THIRD ROCK VENTURES, 1814
THIRD SECURITY, 1815
THOMA BRAVO LLC, 1817
THOMAS WEISEL VENTURE PARTNERS, 1819
THOMAS, MCNERNEY & PARTNERS, 1820
THOMVEST VENTURES, 1821
TOBA CAPITAL, 1831
TONIIC, 1833
TOYOTA AI VENTURES, 1836
TPG CAPITAL, 1837
TRANSLINK CAPITAL, 1840
TRANSMEDIA CAPITAL, 1841
TRIANGLE PEAK PARTNERS, 1848
TRIBE CAPITAL, 1850
TRIDENT CAPITAL, 1852
TRINITY VENTURES, 1855
TRUE VENTURES, 1862
TSG CONSUMER PARTNERS, 1863
TUGBOAT VENTURES, 1867
TVC CAPITAL, 1871
TYLT LAB, 1878
UBIQUITY VENTURES, 1879
UNCORK CAPITAL, 1881
UNITED TALENT AGENCY VENTURES, 1885
UNSHACKLED VENTURES, 1887
UPFRONT VENTURES, 1890
UPWELLING CAPITAL GROUP, 1894
URBAN US, 1896
US RENEWABLES GROUP, 1897
US VENTURE PARTNERS, 1898
VALIA, 1902
VALUEACT CAPITAL, 1905
VANCE STREET CAPITAL, 1906
VANTAGEPOINT CAPITAL PARTNERS, 1908
VCFA GROUP, 1910
VECTOR CAPITAL, 1912
VENBIO, 1916
VENROCK ASSOCIATES, 1918
VENTANA CAPITAL MANAGEMENT LP, 1920
VENTURE TECH ALLIANCE, 1924
VERIZON VENTURES, 1928
VERSANT VENTURES, 1930
VERTICAL GROUP, 1931
VILLAGE GLOBAL, 1935
VISTA EQUITY PARTNERS, 1940
VISTA VENTURE PARTNERS, 1941
VIVO CAPITAL, 1943
VOLVO GROUP VENTURE CAPITAL, 3217
VOYAGER CAPITAL, 1947
WALDEN VENTURE CAPITAL, 1953
WARBURG PINCUS LLC, 1957
WASABI VENTURES, 1959
WAVEMAKER PARTNERS, 1966
WAVEPOINT VENTURES, 1967
WEDBUSH CAPITAL PARTNERS, 1970
WELLS FARGO CAPITAL FINANCE, 1971
WELSH, CARSON, ANDERSON & STOWE, 1973
WEST HEALTH INVESTMENT FUND, 1974
WESTERN STATES INVESTMENT GROUP, 1975
WESTERN TECHNOLOGY INVESTMENT, 1976
WESTLY GROUP, 1978
WESTSUMMIT CAPITAL, 3225
WI HARPER GROUP, 1983
WILDCAT VENTURE PARTNERS, 1985
WILSHIRE PRIVATE MARKETS, 1988
WINDWARD VENTURES, 1995
WING VENTURE PARTNERS, 1996
WIREFRAME VENTURES, 2001
WOMEN'S VENTURE CAPITAL FUND, 2003
WOODSIDE FUND, 2005
WYNNCHURCH CAPITAL, 2008
XSEED CAPITAL MANAGEMENT, 2010
Y COMBINATOR, 2011
YES VC, 2013
YL VENTURES, 3236
YUCAIPA COMPANIES, 2015
ZETTA VENTURE PARTNERS, 2018
ZONE VENTURES, 2020

Colorado
ACCESS VENTURE PARTNERS LLC, 35
ALTA PARTNERS, 94
ALTIRA GROUP LLC, 98
APPIAN VENTURES, 143
ARAVAIPA VENTURES, 147
AWEIDA VENTURE PARTNERS, 213
BOULDER VENTURES LTD, 318
CANNABIS CAPITAL GROWTH, 393
CANOPY BOULDER, 395
CENTENNIAL VENTURES, 443
CHB CAPITAL PARTNERS, 463
CHEYENNE CAPITAL, 469
CORNERSTONE HOLDINGS, 543
CRAWLEY VENTURES, 554
ENDEAVOUR CAPITAL, 674
FIRST CAPITAL VENTURE, 736
FOUNDRY GROUP, 779
FRASER MCCOMBS CAPITAL, 784
GREEN LION PARTNERS, 865
GROTECH VENTURES, 881
GROWTH FUND PRIVATE EQUITY, 885
HIGH COUNTRY VENTURE, 933
INFIELD CAPITAL, 992
IRON GATE CAPITAL, 1024
KRG CAPITAL PARTNERS, 1090
LACUNA GAP CAPITAL, 1094
LYNWOOD CAPITAL PARTNERS, 1156
MEDIA VENTURE PARTNERS, 1197
MERITAGE FUNDS, 1212
MOBIUS VENTURE CAPITAL, 1245
PARTISAN MANAGEMENT GROUP, 1420
POINT B CAPITAL, 1462
PROGRESS EQUITY PARTNERS, 1487
RESOURCE CAPITAL FUNDS, 1551
ROCKY MOUNTAIN VENTURE CAPITAL ASSOCIATION, 3265
ROSER VENTURES LLC, 1590
SEQUEL VENTURE PARTNERS, 1656
STONEHENGE GROWTH CAPITAL, 1748
TECHSTARS, 1791
TEN ELEVEN VENTURES, 1796
TICONDEROGA PRIVATE EQUITY, 1826
TRANSITION PARTNERS LTD, 1839
VESTAR CAPITAL PARTNERS, 1933
WELLS FARGO CAPITAL FINANCE, 1971
WILSHIRE PRIVATE MARKETS, 1988

Connecticut
1843 CAPITAL, 6
ACCESS MEDICAL VENTURES, 2320
ADVANTAGE CAPITAL PARTNERS, 60
AEA INVESTORS, 63

Geographic Index

ALERION PARTNERS, 80
ALTPOINT CAPITAL, 101
ALTUS CAPITAL PARTNERS, 104
ARROWHEAD INVESTMENT MANAGEMENT, 170
AXIOM VENTURE PARTNERS, 215
BLUFF POINT ASSOCIATES, 302
BROOKSIDE EQUITY PARTNERS LLC, 356
BRYNWOOD PARTNERS, 360
CANAAN PARTNERS, 389
CAPITAL PARTNERS, 404
CAVA CAPITAL, 433
CCP EQUITY PARTNERS, 436
CENTRIPETAL CAPITAL PARTNERS, 450
CHL MEDICAL PARTNERS, 476
CLEARVIEW CAPITAL, 505
CLEARWATER CAPITAL PARTNERS, 506
CLOQUET CAPITAL PARTNERS, 507
COHEN PRIVATE VENTURES, 513
COMPASS GROUP MANAGEMENT LLC, 525
CONNECTICUT INNOVATIONS, 532
DAVENPORT RESOURCES LLC, 589
DAWNTREADER VENTURES, 593
DUBILIER & COMPANY, 632
EASTVEN VENTURE PARTNERS, 645
ELM STREET VENTURES, 661
EMIL CAPITAL PARTNERS, 669
EQUINOX CAPITAL, 692
EXPANSION CAPITAL PARTNERS, 707
FAIRVIEW CAPITAL PARTNERS, 715
FERRER FREEMAN & COMPANY LLC, 723
FIRST NEW ENGLAND CAPITAL LP, 740
FIRST RESERVE, 741
FORTRESS INVESTMENT GROUP LLC, 769
GALEN PARTNERS, 809
GE CAPITAL, 811
GENERAL ATLANTIC PARTNERS, 819
GENERATION PARTNERS, 822
GILBERT GLOBAL EQUITY PARTNERS, 831
GREAT POINT PARTNERS, 864
GREENHAVEN PARTNERS, 868
GRIDIRON CAPITAL, 878
HAMILTON ROBINSON CAPITAL PARTNERS, 903
HARTFORD VENTURES, 915
HEALTHINVEST EQUITY PARTNERS, 923
HEARTLAND INDUSTRIAL PARTNERS, 926
HERCULES TECHNOLOGY GROWTH CAPITAL, INC, 928
HORIZON TECHNOLOGY FINANCE, 949
IRONWOOD CAPITAL, 1025
JH WHITNEY & COMPANY, 1041
JORDAN COMPANY, 1049
KIDD & COMPANY, 1075
KLINE HILL PARTNERS, 1080
L CATTERTON PARTNERS, 1092
LAUNCHCAPITAL, 1101
LEASING TECHNOLOGIES INTERNATIONAL INC., 1107
LIBERTY CAPITAL PARTNERS, 1118
LIME ROCK PARTNERS, 1129
LITTLEJOHN & COMPANY LLC, 1138
LONGITUDE CAPITAL, 1147
NGN CAPITAL, 1325
NORTH CASTLE PARTNERS, 1336
OAK HILL CAPITAL PARTNERS, 1360
OAK INVESTMENT PARTNERS, 1361
OAKTREE CAPITAL MANAGEMENT LLC, 1362
OEM CAPITAL, 1369
OLYMPUS PARTNERS, 1372
PALLADIUM EQUITY PARTNERS, 1404
PERFORMANCE EQUITY MANAGEMENT, LLC, 1434
PLATINUM EQUITY, 1455
RFE INVESTMENT PARTNERS, 1560
ROPART ASSET MANAGEMENT, 1587
SAGEVIEW CAPITAL, 1606
SAUGATUCK CAPITAL COMPANY, 1627
SIGNAL LAKE, 1678
SOURCE CAPITAL GROUP, 1710
SOUTHPORT PARTNERS, 1714
SPENCER TRASK VENTURES, 1723
SPINNAKER CAPITAL PARTNERS, 1726
STARBOARD CAPITAL PARTNERS, 1738
STONE POINT CAPITAL LLC, 1746
SV INVESTMENT PARTNERS, 1765
THOMAS, MCNERNEY & PARTNERS, 1820
TULLIS HEALTH INVESTORS, 1868
TWJ CAPITAL, 1875
VITAL FINANCIAL LLC, 1942
WARWICK GROUP, 1958
WOMEN'S ASSOCIATION OF VENTURE & EQUITY INC., 3274
WOODBRIDGE GROUP, 2004

Delaware
BBH CAPITAL PARTNERS, 243
DUPONT CAPITAL, 637
INFLECTION POINT VENTURES, 993
SMARTINVEST VENTURES, 1697

District of Columbia
ACCOLADE PARTNERS, 36
ACON INVESTMENTS, 45
ACORN GROWTH COMPANIES, 47
ACTA CAPITAL, 50
ADVANTAGE CAPITAL PARTNERS, 60
AMERICAN INVESTMENT COUNCIL, 3245
AMERICAN SUSTAINABLE BUSINESS NETWORK, 3246
ANZU PARTNERS, 134
CALVERT INVESTMENT MANAGEMENT, 379
CAPITAL E, 401
CARLYLE GROUP, 416
CM EQUITY PARTNERS, 509
CORE CAPITAL PARTNERS, 540
DARBY OVERSEAS INVESTMENTS LTD, 585
EMP GLOBAL, 671
EVERCORE CAPITAL PARTNERS, 700
GRANTHAM CAPITAL, 858
GROSVENOR FUNDS, 880
HALIFAX GROUP LLC, 899
HCI EQUITY PARTNERS, 920
INSTITUTIONAL LIMITED PARTNERS ASSOCIATION, 3256
INTERNATIONAL FINANCE CORPORATION (IFC), 1012
MID-ATLANTIC VENTURE ASSOCIATION, 3260
NATIONAL VENTURE CAPITAL ASSOCIATION, 3262
OMIDYAR NETWORK, 1374
OXANTIUM VENTURES, 1394
PALADIN CAPITAL GROUP, 1401
QUESTA CAPITAL, 1516
REVOLUTION LLC, 1558
RISE OF THE REST, 1571
STARWOOD CAPITAL GROUP LLC, 1742
TPG CAPITAL, 1837
UPDATA VENTURE PARTNERS, 1888
WACHTEL & CO. INC, 1950

Florida
ACCUITIVE MEDICAL VENTURES LLC, 39
ADVANTAGE CAPITAL PARTNERS, 60
AEROEQUITY, 65
ANDLINGER & COMPANY INC, 124
ANTARES CAPITAL CORPORATION, 132
ANZU PARTNERS, 134
ARSENAL VENTURE PARTNERS, 173
ATHENIAN VENTURE PARTNERS, 189
AXON PARTNERS GROUP, 2460
BALLAST POINT VENTURES, 227
BAYSIDE CAPITAL, 242
BIGFOOT VENTURES, 2502
BLAST FUNDING, 282
BOLDSTART VENTURES, 308
BROCKWAY MORAN & PARTNERS, 351
CAMBRIDGE CAPITAL, 383
CAPITALA, 408
CARPEDIA INTERNATIONAL, 2066
COMVEST PARTNERS, 530
DARBY OVERSEAS INVESTMENTS LTD, 585
DRESNER COMPANIES, 630
DUBIN CLARK & COMPANY, 633

Geographic Index

ENERGY CAPITAL PARTNERS, 676
ENERTECH CAPITAL, 677
EVERCORE CAPITAL PARTNERS, 700
FLORIDA CAPITAL PARTNERS, 753
FLORIDA VENTURE FORUM, 3251
FULCRUM EQUITY PARTNERS, 797
HIG CAPITAL, 931
HORIZON PARTNERS, LTD, 948
INFLEXION PARTNERS, 994
KIRENAGA, 1078
LFE CAPITAL, 1117
LIBERTY CAPITAL PARTNERS, 1118
LIGHTHOUSE PARTNERS, 1123
LM CAPITAL SECURITIES, 1141
LONE STAR FUNDS, 1144
NORTH AMERICAN FUND, 1333
NORWEST EQUITY PARTNERS, 1345
PALISADE CAPITAL MANAGEMENT, 1402
PARTISAN MANAGEMENT GROUP, 1420
PENTA MEZZANINE FUND, 1433
PHYTO PARTNERS, 1443
PROQUEST INVESTMENTS, 1492
QUANTUM CAPITAL PARTNERS, 1512
SOURCE CAPITAL GROUP, 1710
STARWOOD CAPITAL GROUP LLC, 1742
STERLING PARTNERS, 1745
STONE POINT CAPITAL LLC, 1746
STONEHENGE GROWTH CAPITAL, 1748
SUN CAPITAL PARTNERS, 1755
THIRD SECURITY, 1815
TRIVEST PARTNERS, 1859
TULLIS HEALTH INVESTORS, 1868
VINTAGE CAPITAL MANAGEMENT, 1937
VON BRAUN & SCHREIBER PRIVATE EQUITY PARTNERS, 3218
WELLS FARGO CAPITAL FINANCE, 1971
WESTLAKE SECURITIES, 1977

Georgia
ACCEL-KKR LLC, 28
ACCUITIVE MEDICAL VENTURES LLC, 39
ARCAPITA INC, 153
ARES CAPITAL CORPORATION, 159
ARES MANAGEMENT LLC, 160
BIP CAPITAL, 274
BLH VENTURE PARTNERS, 285
CAPITALA, 408
CEDAR VENTURES LLC, 439
CEO VENTURES, 452
CORDOVA VENTURES, 539
EGL HOLDINGS, 656
ENGAGE VENTURES, 678
EQUITY SOUTH, 694
FORTRESS INVESTMENT GROUP LLC, 769
FORTÉ VENTURES, 770
FULCRUM EQUITY PARTNERS, 797
GEORGIA OAK PARTNERS, 825
GRAY GHOST VENTURES, 860
GUGGENHEIM PARTNERS, 890
HARBERT MANAGEMENT CORPORATION, 907
HIG CAPITAL, 931
ICV PARTNERS, 973
INVESCO PRIVATE CAPITAL, 1019
KINETIC VENTURES, 1076
MESA CAPITAL PARTNERS, 1220
MSOUTH EQUITY PARTNERS, 1270
NAVIGATION CAPITAL PARTNERS, 1279
NORO-MOSELEY PARTNERS, 1332
PANORAMIC VENTURES, 1412
PEACHTREE EQUITY PARTNERS, 1425
QUANTUM WAVE FUND, 3059
RED CLAY CAPITAL HOLDINGS, 1532
RELATIVITY CAPITAL, 1542
RIVER CAPITAL, 1574
ROARK CAPITAL GROUP, 1580
STARWOOD CAPITAL GROUP LLC, 1742
TECHOPERATORS, 1790
TTV CAPITAL, 1865

UPS STRATEGIC ENTERPRISE FUND, 1893
WELLS FARGO CAPITAL FINANCE, 1971

Hawaii
HAWAII VENTURE CAPITAL ASSOCIATION, 3253
HMS HAWAII MANAGEMENT, 942
SOURCE CAPITAL GROUP, 1710
STARTUP CAPITAL VENTURES, 1740

Idaho
RENEWABLETECH VENTURES, 1545

Illinois
ADAMS STREET PARTNERS, LLC, 56
ADVANTAGE CAPITAL PARTNERS, 60
AGMAN PARTNERS, 69
ALLSTATE INVESTMENTS LLC, 88
ALPHA CAPITAL PARTNERS, 90
ALTUS CAPITAL PARTNERS, 104
AMITI VENTURES, 117
ANDERSON PACIFIC CORPORATION, 123
ANGELO, GORDON & CO., 128
APEX VENTURE PARTNERS, 138
ARBOR INVESTMENTS, 148
ARCH VENTURE PARTNERS, 154
ARES MANAGEMENT LLC, 160
BAIRD CAPITAL PARTNERS, 225
BAXTER VENTURES, 239
BAYSIDE CAPITAL, 242
BBH CAPITAL PARTNERS, 243
BEECKEN PETTY O'KEEFE & COMPANY, 247
BOUNDS EQUITY PARTNERS, 319
BRIDGE STREET CAPITAL, 341
BROADHAVEN CAPITAL PARTNERS, 346
CAPX PARTNERS, 410
CERES VENTURE FUND, 454
CHICAGO GROWTH PARTNERS, 470
CHICAGO PACIFIC FOUNDERS, 471
CHICAGO VENTURE PARTNERS LP, 472
CHICAGO VENTURES, 473
CIVC PARTNERS, 491
COMVEST PARTNERS, 530
CONCENTRIC EQUITY PARTNERS Financial Investments Corporation, 531
CRESSEY & COMPANY LP, 559
CULTIVIAN SANDBOX VENTURES, 571
CYPRIUM PARTNERS, 578
DN PARTNERS LLC, 620
DRESNER COMPANIES, 630
DUCHOSSOIS CAPITAL MANAGEMENT, 634
DUNRATH CAPITAL, 636
EDGEWATER FUNDS, 654
EVERCORE CAPITAL PARTNERS, 700
FIRST ANALYSIS, 733
FLEXPOINT FORD LLC, 751
FRASER MCCOMBS CAPITAL, 784
FRONTENAC COMPANY, 792
G SQUARED, 805
GLADSTONE CAPITAL, 832
GLENCOE CAPITAL, 834
GOENSE & COMPANY LLC, 842
GOLUB CAPITAL, 848
GREENHILL SAVP, 869
GTCR, 889
GUGGENHEIM PARTNERS, 890
HAWTHORN EQUITY PARTNERS, 919
HCI EQUITY PARTNERS, 920
HERCULES TECHNOLOGY GROWTH CAPITAL, INC, 928
HIG CAPITAL, 931
HIGH STREET CAPITAL, 935
HIGHER GROUND LABS, 937
HILCO BRANDS, 940
HOPEWELL VENTURES, 947
HYDE PARK VENTURE PARTNERS, 965
ILLINOIS VENTURE CAPITAL ASSOCIATION, 3255
ILLINOIS VENTURES, 979
INDEPENDENCE EQUITY, 987

Geographic Index

IRISH ANGELS, 1023
JK&B CAPITAL, 1042
JORDAN COMPANY, 1049
JUMP CAPITAL LLC, 1050
KB PARTNERS, 1060
KB PARTNERS LLC, 1061
KNOX CAPITAL, 1082
LAKE CAPITAL, 1095
LASALLE CAPITAL GROUP, 1097
LEO CAPITAL HOLDINGS, LLC, 1112
LIGHTBANK, 1121
LIGHTHOUSE PARTNERS, 1123
LINDEN LLC, 1132
LIONBIRD, 2934
M25 GROUP, 1159
MADISON DEARBORN PARTNERS, 1160
MARANON CAPITAL, 1169
MATH VENTURE PARTNERS, 1181
MERIT CAPITAL PARTNERS, 1210
MIDWEST MEZZANINE FUNDS, 1232
MK CAPITAL, 1242
MODERNE VENTURES, 1246
MOTOROLA SOLUTIONS VENTURE CAPITAL, 1260
MPG EQUITY PARTNERS, 1267
NEEDHAM CAPITAL PARTNERS, 1287
NEWSPRING CAPITAL, 1316
NORTH AMERICAN FUND, 1333
NORTHLEAF CAPITAL PARTNERS, 2196
OCA VENTURES, 1364
ONE EQUITY PARTNERS, 1376
OPEN PRAIRIE VENTURES, 1380
ORIGIN VENTURES, 1385
PARADIGM CAPITAL LTD, 1416
PARALLEL49 EQUITY, 2206
PATRIOT CAPITAL, 1424
PFINGSTEN PARTNERS LLC, 1438
PGIM PRIVATE CAPITAL, 1440
POLESTAR CAPITAL, 1465
PPM AMERICA CAPITAL PARTNERS, 1471
PRAIRIE CAPITAL, 1473
PRISM CAPITAL, 1481
PRITZKER GROUP PRIVATE CAPITAL, 1482
PRITZKER GROUP VENTURE CAPITAL, 1483
PROMUS VENTURES, 1491
PROSPECT PARTNERS LLC, 1494
REDWOOD CAPITAL GROUP, 1539
RLH EQUITY PARTNERS, 1579
ROCK ISLAND CAPITAL, 1582
ROTH CAPITAL PARTNERS, 1592
ROUNDTABLE HEALTHCARE PARTNERS, 1594
SALVEO CAPITAL, 1613
SANDALPHON CAPITAL, 1617
SANDBOX INDUSTRIES, 1618
SECOND CENTURY VENTURES, 1645
SHORE CAPITAL PARTNERS, 1670
SILKROAD EQUITY, 1683
SILVER OAK SERVICES PARTNERS, 1686
STARWOOD CAPITAL GROUP LLC, 1742
STATELINE ANGELS, 1743
STERLING PARTNERS, 1745
SVOBODA CAPITAL PARTNERS, 1767
THOMA BRAVO LLC, 1817
TRUE NORTH VENTURE PARTNERS, 1861
TWIN BRIDGE CAPITAL PARTNERS, 1873
UBS GLOBAL ASSET MANAGEMENT, 1880
UPHEAVAL INVESTMENTS, 1892
VALOR EQUITY PARTNERS, 1904
VISTA EQUITY PARTNERS, 1940
WALL STREET VENTURE CAPITAL, 1954
WATER STREET HEALTHCARE PARTNERS, 1962
WAUD CAPITAL PARTNERS LLC, 1964
WAVELAND INVESTMENTS LLC, 1965
WELLS FARGO CAPITAL FINANCE, 1971
WILSHIRE PRIVATE MARKETS, 1988
WIND POINT PARTNERS, 1990
WINONA CAPITAL MANAGEMENT, 2000
WYNNCHURCH CAPITAL, 2008

Indiana
ALLOS VENTURES, 86
CAMBRIDGE VENTURES LP, 385
CARDINAL EQUITY PARTNERS, 412
CARLYLE GROUP, 416
CENTERFIELD CAPITAL PARTNERS, 445
CID CAPITAL, 480
ELEVATE VENTURES, 659
HAMMOND, KENNEDY, WHITNEY & COMPANY, 904
HIGH ALPHA, 932
HYDE PARK VENTURE PARTNERS, 965
LILLY VENTURES, 1128
MONUMENT ADVISORS, 1252
TRASK INNOVATIONS FUND Purdue Research Foundation, 1842
TRIATHLON MEDICAL VENTURES, 1849
VENTURE CLUB OF INDIANA, 3271

Iowa
AAVIN PRIVATE EQUITY, 16
BROADHORN CAPITAL, 347
INVESTAMERICA VENTURE GROUP, 1020
PALMS & COMPANY, 1405

Kansas
ANGEL CAPITAL ASSOCIATION, 3247
D.E. SHAW & CO. LP, 580
KANSAS VENTURE CAPITAL, 1057

Kentucky
CHRYSALIS VENTURES, 477
HUMANA VENTURES, 958
KENTUCKY HIGHLANDS INVESTMENT CORPORATION, 1068
MERITUS VENTURES, 1215
SOURCE CAPITAL GROUP, 1710
TRIATHLON MEDICAL VENTURES, 1849
VENTURE CONNECTORS, 3272

Louisiana
ADVANTAGE CAPITAL PARTNERS, 60
BVM CAPITAL, 365
CALLAIS CAPITAL MANAGEMENT, 375
ENHANCED CAPITAL, 679
INNOVATION CATALYST, 1000
LONGUEVUE CAPITAL LLC, 1148
SAIL VENTURE PARTNERS, 1607
STONEHENGE GROWTH CAPITAL, 1748
VOODOO VENTURES, LLC, 1945
WESTLAKE SECURITIES, 1977

Maine
CEI VENTURES, 440
MAINE VENTURE FUND, 1165
NORTH ATLANTIC CAPITAL CORPORATION, 1334

Maryland
ABELL FOUNDATION VENTURES, 18
ABS CAPITAL PARTNERS, 21
ALLEGIS CYBER CAPITAL, 84
APOLLO GLOBAL MANAGEMENT, 141
ARES MANAGEMENT LLC, 160
ARLINGTON CAPITAL PARTNERS, 167
ASHBY POINT CAPITAL, 181
ATLANTIC CAPITAL GROUP, 192
BOULDER VENTURES LTD, 318
CAMBER CREEK, 380
CAMDEN PARTNERS HOLDINGS LLC, 386
CAPITOL PARTNERS, 409
CATO BIOVENTURES, 432
CNF INVESTMENTS Clark Enterprises, Inc., 510
DFW CAPITAL PARTNERS, 611
ENLIGHTENMENT CAPITAL, 681
EPIDAREX CAPITAL, 690
EVERGREEN ADVISORS, 702
GIC GROUP, 829
GLOBAL ENVIRONMENT FUND, 838
GREENSPRING ASSOCIATES, 872
GROTECH VENTURES, 881

Geographic Index

GUGGENHEIM PARTNERS, 890
HERCULES TECHNOLOGY GROWTH CAPITAL, INC, 928
JMI EQUITY FUND LP, 1045
KINETIC VENTURES, 1076
MARYLAND VENTURE FUND, 1172
MERIDIAN MANAGEMENT GROUP, 1209
NEW ENTERPRISE ASSOCIATES, 1296
NEW MARKETS VENTURE PARTNERS, 1298
NEWSPRING CAPITAL, 1316
NEXTGEN ANGELS, 1320
NORTHPOND VENTURES, 1342
NOVAK BIDDLE VENTURE PARTNERS, 1348
PATRIOT CAPITAL, 1424
QUESTMARK PARTNERS LP, 1517
SAVANO CAPITAL PARTNERS, 1628
SPRING CAPITAL PARTNERS LP, 1730
STERLING PARTNERS, 1745
SYNCOM VENTURE PARTNERS, 1773
TDF, 1784
TEDCO, 1792
TEXADA CAPITAL CORPORATION, 1801
TWJ CAPITAL, 1875
VITAL FINANCIAL LLC, 1942

Massachusetts

.406 VENTURES, 1
5AM VENTURES, 11
ABINGWORTH MANAGEMENT LIMITED, 2308
ABRY PARTNERS, 20
ABS VENTURES, 22
ACCESS BRIDGE-GAP VENTURES, 33
ACCOMPLICE, 37
ADAMS STREET PARTNERS, LLC, 56
ADVANCED TECHNOLOGY VENTURES, 58
ADVANCIT CAPITAL, 59
ADVENT INTERNATIONAL CORPORATION, 61
ALANTRA, 77
AMPERSAND CAPITAL PARTNERS, 119
ANZU PARTNERS, 134
APPLE TREE PARTNERS, 144
ARCLIGHT CAPITAL PARTNERS, 157
ARGO GLOBAL CAPITAL, 163
ASCENT VENTURE PARTNERS, 180
ATLAS VENTURE, 193
ATLAS VENTURE: FRANCE, 2436
AUDAX GROUP, 197
AVALON VENTURES, 209
AXIA CAPITAL, 214
AZCA, 217
BAIN CAPITAL PRIVATE EQUITY, 223
BAIN CAPITAL VENTURES, 224
BATTERY VENTURES, 238
BBH CAPITAL PARTNERS, 243
BERKSHIRE PARTNERS LLC, 257
BERWIND PRIVATE EQUITY, 262
BESSEMER VENTURE PARTNERS, 263
BIOVENTURES INVESTORS, 273
BLACKSTONE PRIVATE EQUITY GROUP, 280
BOREALIS VENTURES, 311
BOSTON CAPITAL, 312
BOSTON CAPITAL VENTURES, 313
BOSTON GLOBAL VENTURES, LLC, 314
BOSTON MILLENNIA PARTNERS, 315
BOSTON SEED CAPITAL, 316
BOSTON UNIVERSITY - TECHNOLOGY DEVELOPMENT, 317
BREAKAWAY VENTURES, 332
BROADVIEW VENTURES, 350
BROOK VENTURE FUND, 352
BROOKE PRIVATE EQUITY ASSOCIATES, 353
BUNKER HILL CAPITAL, 362
BV INVESTMENT PARTNERS, 364
CALERA CAPITAL, 371
CAMBRIDGE ASSOCIATES, 382
CAPITAL RESOURCE PARTNERS, 405
CAPX PARTNERS, 410
CASTANEA PARTNERS, 424
CATALYST HEALTH VENTURES, 428
CATO BIOVENTURES, 432
CEDAR FUND, 438
CHARLES RIVER VENTURES, 457
CHARLESBANK CAPITAL PARTNERS, 458
CLEAN ENERGY VENTURE GROUP, 498
COLUMBIA CAPITAL, 518
COMMONS CAPITAL, 522
COMMONWEALTH CAPITAL VENTURES LP, 523
CONVERGE VENTURE PARTNERS, 536
CRESCENT CAPITAL GROUP LP, 557
CUE BALL GROUP, 568
CUTLASS CAPITAL LLC, 573
D.E. SHAW & CO. LP, 580
DACE VENTURES, 581
DATA POINT CAPITAL, 587
DDJ CAPITAL MANAGEMENT, 598
DUBIN CLARK & COMPANY, 633
DUTCHESS CAPITAL, 638
EASTWARD CAPITAL PARTNERS, 646
ECHELON VENTURES, 647
EVERCORE CAPITAL PARTNERS, 700
EXCEL VENTURE MANAGEMENT, 704
EXPERIMENT FUND, 709
F-PRIME CAPITAL PARTNERS, 711
FA TECHNOLOGY VENTURES, 712
FAIRHAVEN CAPITAL, 713
FISHER LYNCH CAPITAL, 745
FLAGSHIP PIONEERING, 748
FLARE CAPITAL PARTNERS, 749
FLETCHER SPAGHT VENTURES, 750
FLYBRIDGE CAPITAL PARTNERS, 756
GE VENTURES, 812
GEMINI INVESTORS, 815
GEN Y CAPITAL PARTNERS Young Entrepreneur Council, 816
GENERAL CATALYST PARTNERS, 820
GLOBESPAN CAPITAL PARTNERS, 839
GOOD GROWTH CAPITAL, 849
GRANDBANKS CAPITAL, 853
GREAT HILL PARTNERS LLC, 862
GREYLOCK PARTNERS, 877
GROVE STREET ADVISORS LLC, 884
GRYPHON MANAGEMENT COMPANY, 887
GUGGENHEIM PARTNERS, 890
GUIDE MEDICAL VENTURES, 891
GV, 894
HARBOURVEST PARTNERS LLC, 912
HEALTHCARE VENTURES LLC, 922
HERCULES TECHNOLOGY GROWTH CAPITAL, INC, 928
HERITAGE PARTNERS, 929
HIG CAPITAL, 931
HIGHLAND CAPITAL PARTNERS, 938
HLM VENTURE PARTNERS, 941
HOUSATONIC PARTNERS, 952
IN-Q-TEL, 983
INVUS GROUP, 1022
JARVINIAN VENTURES, 1031
JEGI CAPITAL, 1037
JMH CAPITAL, 1044
JW CHILDS ASSOCIATES, 1053
KEPHA PARTNERS, 1069
KERRY CAPITAL ADVISORS, 1071
KNIGHTSBRIDGE ADVISERS, 1081
KODIAK VENTURE PARTNERS, 1084
LAUNCHCAPITAL, 1101
LAUNCHPAD VENTURE GROUP, 1104
LEASING TECHNOLOGIES INTERNATIONAL INC., 1107
LEXINGTON PARTNERS, 1116
LIGHTHOUSE CAPITAL PARTNERS, 1122
LIGHTSTONE VENTURES, 1126
LONG RIVER VENTURES, 1146
LONGWOOD FUND, 1149
LONGWORTH VENTURE PARTNERS, 1150
LUMIRA CAPITAL, 2173
M/C PARTNERS, 1157
MADISON PARKER CAPITAL, 1161
MANSA EQUITY PARTNERS, 1168
MASS VENTURES, 1175

Geographic Index

MASSACHUSETTS CAPITAL RESOURCE COMPANY, 1176
MASSACHUSETTS GROWTH CAPITAL CORPORATION, 1177
MASTHEAD VENTURE PARTNERS, 1178
MATERIAL IMPACT, 1180
MATRIX PARTNERS, 1184
MEDIA VENTURE PARTNERS, 1197
MEDIPHASE VENTURE PARTNERS, 1198
MEKETA INVESTMENT GROUP, 1201
MENDOZA VENTURES, 1202
METAPOINT PARTNERS, 1225
MONITOR CLIPPER PARTNERS, 1248
MPE PARTNERS, 1266
MPM CAPITAL, 1268
MVM LIFE SCIENCE PARTNERS, 2972
McCARTHY CAPITAL, 1276
NAUTA CAPITAL, 2978
NEEDHAM CAPITAL PARTNERS, 1287
NEW ATLANTIC VENTURES, 1290
NEW ENGLAND BUSINESS EXCHANGE, 1294
NEW ENGLAND CAPITAL PARTNERS, 1295
NEWBURY, PIRET & COMPANY, 1311
NEXTVIEW VENTURES, 1322
NKM CAPITAL, 1330
NORTH BRIDGE VENTURE PARTNERS, 1335
NORTH HILL VENTURES, 1339
NORTHPOND VENTURES, 1342
NORWICH VENTURES, 1347
NOVARTIS VENTURE FUNDS, 1350
OMEGA FUNDS, 1373
ONEX FALCON, 1377
ONEX PARTNERS, 2201
OPENVIEW VENTURE PARTNERS, 1381
OUTCOME CAPITAL, 1389
OXFORD BIOSCIENCE PARTNERS, 1395
PAR CAPITAL MANAGEMENT, 1415
PARTHENON CAPITAL, 1419
PARTNERS HEALTHCARE RESEARCH VENTURES, 1421
PERMAL CAPITAL MANAGEMENT, 1435
PLATINUM EQUITY, 1455
POINT JUDITH CAPITAL, 1463
POLARIS VENTURE PARTNERS, 1464
PROCYON VENTURES, 1486
PROGRESS VENTURES, 1488
PROJECT 11 VENTURES, 1489
PSG, 1499
PURETECH VENTURES, 1503
QUABBIN CAPITAL, 1505
QUARRY CAPITAL MANAGEMENT, 1513
RA CAPITAL MANAGEMENT, 1522
RAPTOR GROUP, 1527
ROCKPORT CAPITAL, 1583
ROMULUS CAPITAL, 1585
ROOT CAPITAL, 1586
ROTH CAPITAL PARTNERS, 1592
ROUGH DRAFT VENTURES, 1593
ROYALTY CAPITAL MANAGEMENT, 1595
SAMSUNG VENTURE INVESTMENT CORPORATION, 3089
SANOFI-GENZYME BIOVENTURES, 1621
SATURN PARTNERS, 1626
SCHOONER CAPITAL LLC, 1630
SCHRODER VENTURES HEALTH INVESTORS, 1631
SEACOAST CAPITAL CORPORATION, 1639
SIGMA PRIME VENTURES, 1675
SIGNAL LAKE, 1678
SIGULER GUFF & COMPANY, 1681
SOFTBANK CAPITAL, 1701
SOLSTICE CAPITAL LP, 1704
SOURCE CAPITAL GROUP, 1710
SPARK CAPITAL, 1718
SPECTRUM EQUITY INVESTORS LP, 1720
SPRING LAKE EQUITY PARTNERS, 1731
SPRING LANE CAPITAL, 1732
STAGE 1 VENTURES, 1737
SUMMIT PARTNERS, 1754
SUPPLY CHAIN VENTURES, 1759
SV HEALTH INVESTORS, 1764
SYMMETRIC CAPITAL, 1772
SYNTHESIS CAPITAL, 1777
TA ASSOCIATES, 1778
TEN ELEVEN VENTURES, 1796
THIRD ROCK VENTURES, 1814
THOMAS H LEE PARTNERS, 1818
TICONDEROGA PRIVATE EQUITY, 1826
TSG EQUITY PARTNERS, 1864
TULLY & HOLLAND, 1869
VELOCITY EQUITY PARTNERS LLC, 1915
VENROCK ASSOCIATES, 1918
VENTURE CAPITAL FUND OF NEW ENGLAND, 1922
VIDA VENTURES, 1934
VINTAGE CAPITAL MANAGEMENT, 1937
VOLITION CAPITAL, 1944
WALL STREET VENTURE CAPITAL, 1954
WATERMILL GROUP, 1963
WELLS FARGO CAPITAL FINANCE, 1971
WESTVIEW CAPITAL PARTNERS, 1979
WINDSPEED VENTURES, 1994

Michigan
AMHERST FUND, 114
APJOHN GROUP LLC, 140
ARBORETUM VENTURES, 150
ARSENAL VENTURE PARTNERS, 173
AUGMENT VENTURES, 198
BERINGEA, 254
BIOSTAR VENTURES, 272
BLACKFORD CAPITAL LLC, 279
BRIDGE STREET CAPITAL, 341
DETROIT VENTURE PARTNERS, 608
DRAPER TRIANGLE VENTURES, 629
EDF VENTURES, 652
ELAB VENTURES, 657
FIRST STEP FUND, 743
FONTINALIS PARTNERS, 762
GELT VC, 814
GENERAL MOTORS VENTURES, 821
GLENCOE CAPITAL, 834
HOPEN LIFE SCIENCE VENTURES, 946
HURON CAPITAL PARTNERS LLC, 963
HURON RIVER VENTURES, 964
INCWELL VENTURE CAPITAL, 985
LIBERTY CAPITAL PARTNERS, 1118
LONG POINT CAPITAL, 1145
LUDLOW VENTURES, 1154
MERCURY FUND, 1207
MICHIGAN VENTURE CAPITAL ASSOCIATION, 3259
MK CAPITAL, 1242
NEMO CAPITAL PARTNERS, 1288
NORTH COAST TECHNOLOGY INVESTORS LP, 1337
PENINSULA CAPITAL PARTNERS LLC, 1429
PLYMOUTH MANAGEMENT COMPANY 555 Briarwood Circle, 1459
RESONANT VENTURE PARTNERS, 1550
RPM VENTURES, 1596
SENECA PARTNERS, 1652
SOUTHWEST MICHIGAN FIRST LIFE SCIENCE FUND Southwest Michigan First, 1715
TGAP VENTURES, 1804
VENTURE INVESTORS LLC, 1923

Minnesota
AFFINITY CAPITAL MANAGEMENT, 67
ARTHUR VENTURES, 175
BRIGHTSTONE VENTURE CAPITAL, 344
CASTLELAKE, 426
CHERRY TREE COMPANIES, 466
EVERCORE CAPITAL PARTNERS, 700
FIRST GREEN PARTNERS, 739
GOLDNER HAWN, 847
GRANITE EQUITY PARTNERS, 855
INVESTAMERICA VENTURE GROUP, 1020
LEMHI VENTURES, 1111
LFE CAPITAL, 1117
MATCHSTICK VENTURES, 1179
MILESTONE GROWTH FUND, 1233
NDI MEDICAL, 1286

Geographic Index

NEEDHAM CAPITAL PARTNERS, 1287
NORTHSTAR CAPITAL, 1343
NORWEST EQUITY PARTNERS, 1345
RALLY VENTURES, 1525
SIGHTLINE PARTNERS, 1673
SPELL CAPITAL PARTNERS LLC, 1722
SPLIT ROCK PARTNERS, 1728
THE COLLABORATIVE, 3268
THOMAS, MCNERNEY & PARTNERS, 1820
TRIPLETREE LLC, 1856
VARDE PARTNERS, 1909
VENSANA CAPITAL, 1919
WAYZATA INVESTMENT PARTNERS, 1968
WELLS FARGO CAPITAL FINANCE, 1971

Mississippi
ADVANTAGE CAPITAL PARTNERS, 60
GLASSWING VENTURES, 833
STONEHENGE GROWTH CAPITAL, 1748

Missouri
ADVANTAGE CAPITAL PARTNERS, 60
ASCENSION HEALTH VENTURES LLC, 178
AUGURY CAPITAL PARTNERS, 199
BIOGENERATOR, 270
C3 CAPITAL PARTNERS LP, 367
CAPITAL FOR BUSINESS, INC, 402
CULTIVATION CAPITAL, 570
EVERCORE CAPITAL PARTNERS, 700
FIVE ELMS CAPITAL, 746
GUGGENHEIM PARTNERS, 890
HARBOUR GROUP, 911
INVESTAMERICA VENTURE GROUP, 1020
MEDIA VENTURE PARTNERS, 1197
MISSOURI VENTURE FORUM, 3261
PROLOG VENTURES, 1490
PSG, 1499
RIVERVEST VENTURE PARTNERS, 1578
SIXTHIRTY, 1690
STONEHENGE GROWTH CAPITAL, 1748

Montana
NEXT FRONTIER CAPITAL, 1317

Nebraska
AGMAN PARTNERS, 69
AGRIBUSINESS MANAGEMENT COMPANY, 70
AMERICA FIRST INVESTMENT ADVISORS, 109
DUNDEE VENTURE CAPITAL, 635
EVEREST GROUP, 701
McCARTHY CAPITAL, 1276
TENASKA CAPITAL MANAGEMENT, 1797

Nevada
ADVANTAGE CAPITAL PARTNERS, 60
AUSTRALIS CAPITAL, 206
COLOMA VENTURES, 515
JOHNSTON ASSOCIATES, 1048
REDHILLS VENTURES, 1535
SIERRA ANGELS, 1671
SKYTREE CAPITAL PARTNERS, 1694
VEGAS TECHFUND, 1914

New Hampshire
10X VENTURE PARTNERS, 2
ADVANTAGE CAPITAL PARTNERS, 60
ARETE CORPORATION, 161
BOREALIS VENTURES, 311
ECOAST ANGEL NETWORK, 649
HARBOR LIGHT CAPITAL PARTNERS, 910

New Jersey
180 DEGREE CAPITAL, 5
BASECAMP VENTURES, 233
BBH CAPITAL PARTNERS, 243
CAMBRIDGE CAPITAL CORPORATION, 384
CARDINAL PARTNERS, 413
CARE CAPITAL, 415
CASABONA VENTURES, 421
CRYSTAL RIDGE PARTNERS, 566
D.E. SHAW & CO. LP, 580
DFW CAPITAL PARTNERS, 611
DOMAIN ASSOCIATES LLC, 622
EDELSON TECHNOLOGY PARTNERS, 651
EDISON PARTNERS, 655
ENERGY CAPITAL PARTNERS, 676
ENTREPIA VENTURES, 683
FRIEND SKOLER & COMPANY LLC, 791
JOHNSON & JOHNSON INNOVATION, 1047
JOHNSTON ASSOCIATES, 1048
MERCK GLOBAL HEALTH INNOVATION FUND, 1206
MIDMARK CAPITAL LP, 1230
MUNICH REINSURANCE AMERICA, INC, 1272
NASSAU CAPITAL, 1277
NAVIGATOR PARTNERS LLC, 1280
NEW VENTURE PARTNERS, 1304
NEW YORK LIFE CAPITAL PARTNERS, 1308
NJTC VENTURE FUND, 1329
NOVITAS CAPITAL, 1353
OMNICAPITAL GROUP, 1375
ONEX PARTNERS, 2201
OSAGE PARTNERS, 1388
PALISADE CAPITAL MANAGEMENT, 1402
PLUS VENTURES, 3032
RIDGEWOOD CAPITAL, 1567
SCP PARTNERS, 1636
SELWAY CAPITAL, 1650
SOSV, 1709
SOURCE CAPITAL GROUP, 1710
SWANDER PACE CAPITAL, 1769
SYCAMORE VENTURES, 1771
TECH UNITED, 3266
VERIZON VENTURES, 1928
VERTICAL GROUP, 1931
WILSHIRE PRIVATE MARKETS, 1988
YORK STREET CAPITAL PARTNERS LLC, 2014

New Mexico
ARROWHEAD INNOVATION FUND, 169
COTTONWOOD TECHNOLOGY FUND, 550
FLYWHEEL VENTURES, 758
NEW MEXICO COMMUNITY CAPITAL, 1299
PSILOS GROUP, 1500
SUN MOUNTAIN CAPITAL, 1756
TECHNOLOGY VENTURES CORPORATION, 1789
VERGE FUND, 1926

New York
3i GROUP PLC, 2303
747 CAPITAL, 13
ABBOTT CAPITAL MANAGEMENT LLC, 17
ACADIA WOODS PARTNERS, 25
ACCELERATOR LIFE SCIENCE PARTNERS, 30
ACCESS CAPITAL, 34
ACCRETIVE LLC, 38
ACI CAPITAL, 41
ACTIVATE VENTURE PARTNERS, 51
ACUMEN, 54
ADAMS STREET PARTNERS, LLC Adams Street Partners, Inc., 56
ADVANCIT CAPITAL, 59
ADVANTAGE CAPITAL PARTNERS, 60
ADVENT INTERNATIONAL CORPORATION, 61
AEA INVESTORS, 63
AEP CAPITAL LLC, 64
AISLING CAPITAL, 73
ALBION INVESTORS LLC, 78
ALEUTIAN CAPITAL PARTNERS, 81
ALPHA VENTURE PARTNERS, 91
ALPINVEST PARTNERS B.V. AlpInvest U.S. Holdings, LLC, 2371
ALTARIS CAPITAL PARTNERS, 97
ALTITUDE INVESTMENT MANAGEMENT, LLC, 99
AMERICAN INDUSTRIAL PARTNERS, 110
AMERICAN SECURITIES LLC, 111
ANDLINGER & COMPANY INC, 124
ANGELO, GORDON & CO., 128

Geographic Index

ANGELPAD, 129
ANTHEMIS GROUP, 2398
AOL VENTURES, 135
APAX PARTNERS, 136
APERTURE VENTURE PARTNERS, 137
APOLLO GLOBAL MANAGEMENT, 141
APPLE TREE PARTNERS, 144
ARBOR INVESTMENTS, 148
ARC ANGEL FUND, 151
ARCHTOP VENTURES, 155
ARCUS VENTURES, 158
ARES MANAGEMENT LLC, 160
ARGENTUM GROUP, 162
ARSENAL CAPITAL PARTNERS, 172
ARTHUR P GOULD & COMPANY, 174
ASCENT BIOMEDICAL VENTURES, 179
ATHYRIUM CAPITAL MANAGEMENT, 190
ATYPICAL VENTURES, 195
AUA PRIVATE EQUITY PARTNERS, 196
AUDAX GROUP, 197
AVENUE CAPITAL GROUP, 211
AVISTA CAPITAL PARTNERS, 212
AXXESS CAPITAL, 2462
B CAPITAL GROUP, 219
BABSON CAPITAL MANAGEMENT LLC, 220
BAIN CAPITAL PRIVATE EQUITY, 223
BAIN CAPITAL VENTURES, 224
BAKER CAPITAL, 226
BATTERY VENTURES, 238
BAYSIDE CAPITAL, 242
BBH CAPITAL PARTNERS, 243
BEDFORD FUNDING, 245
BEHRMAN CAPITAL, 248
BERINGER CAPITAL, 2050
BERTELSMANN DIGITAL MEDIA INVESTMENTS, 259
BESSEMER VENTURE PARTNERS, 263
BISON CAPITAL ASSET MANAGEMENT LLC, 277
BLACKSTONE PRIVATE EQUITY GROUP, 280
BLEU CAPITAL, 284
BLOOMBERG BETA, 287
BMO CAPITAL MARKETS, 2057
BNY MELLON CAPITAL MARKETS, 306
BOLDCAP VENTURES LLC, 307
BOWERY CAPITAL, 320
BOXGROUP, 321
BR VENTURE FUND, 323
BRADFORD EQUITIES MANAGEMENT LLC, 324
BRAEMAR ENERGY VENTURES, 325
BRAND FOUNDRY VENTURES, 328
BRANFORD CASTLE, 330
BREGAL ENERGY, 335
BREGAL SAGEMOUNT, 336
BRERA CAPITAL PARTNERS, 338
BROADHAVEN CAPITAL PARTNERS, 346
BROOKFIELD ASSET MANAGEMENT, 2062
BROOKLYN BRIDGE VENTURES, 354
BROOKS HOUGHTON & COMPANY, 355
BRUCKMANN, ROSSER, SHERRILL & COMPANY, 357
BUSINESS CONSORTIUM FUND, 363
CAI CAPITAL PARTNERS, 368
CALGARY ENTERPRISES, 372
CAMBER CREEK, 380
CANAAN PARTNERS, 389
CANROCK VENTURES, 396
CANTOR VENTURES, 397
CAPITAL Z PARTNERS, 407
CAPX PARTNERS, 410
CARBON VENTURES, 411
CARLYLE GROUP, 416
CASDIN CAPITAL, 422
CASTLE HARLAN, 425
CASTLELAKE, 426
CATALYST INVESTORS, 429
CAYUGA VENTURE FUND, 434
CCMP CAPITAL, 435
CENTANA GROWTH PARTNERS, 442
CENTERBRIDGE PARTNERS, 444

CENTRE LANE PARTNERS, 448
CENTRE PARTNERS MANAGEMENT LLC, 449
CERBERUS CAPITAL MANAGEMENT, 453
CHARLESBANK CAPITAL PARTNERS, 458
CHART VENTURE PARTNERS, 459
CHAZEN CAPITAL PARTNERS, 462
CHESTNUT HILL PARTNERS, 467
CI CAPITAL PARTNERS, 478
CIRCLE PEAK CAPITAL, 483
CIT GROUP, 486
CITI VENTURES, 488
CITY LIGHT CAPITAL, 490
CLARION CAPITAL PARTNERS LLC, 494
CM EQUITY PARTNERS, 509
COATUE MANAGEMENT, 511
COMCAST VENTURES, 520
COMPASS GROUP, 524
COMPOUND, 527
CONTOUR VENTURE PARTNERS, 535
CONVERSION CAPITAL, 537
CORIOLIS VENTURES, 541
CORNERSTONE VENTURE PARTNERS, 544
CORRELATION VENTURES, 545
CORTEC GROUP, 547
CREDIT MUTUEL EQUITY, 2082
CREDIT SUISSE PRIVATE EQUITY Credit Suisse Group, 555
CRESCENT CAPITAL GROUP LP, 557
CRESTVIEW PARTNERS, 560
CULTIVATE CAPITAL, 569
CYPRIUM PARTNERS, 578
D.E. SHAW & CO. LP The D.E. Shaw Group, 580
DAUPHIN CAPITAL PARTNERS, 588
DAVID N DEUTSCH & COMPANY LLC, 590
DEERFIELD MANAGEMENT, 602
DFJ GOTHAM VENTURES, 609
DIFFERENTIAL VENTURES, 615
DRESNER COMPANIES, 630
DUTCHESS CAPITAL, 638
EARTHRISE CAPITAL, 643
EASTON CAPITAL INVESTMENT GROUP, 644
EMIGRANT CAPITAL, 668
EMINENT CAPITAL PARTNERS, 670
ENERGY CAPITAL PARTNERS, 676
ENHANCED CAPITAL, 679
ENSO VENTURES, 2693
ENTREPRENEURS ROUNDTABLE ACCELERATOR, 685
EOS PARTNERS LP, 687
EPIC PARTNERS, 688
ESSEX WOODLANDS HEALTH VENTURES LLC, 698
EVERCORE CAPITAL PARTNERS, 700
EXCELL PARTNERS, INC., 705
EXIUM PARTNERS, 706
EXPANSION VENTURE CAPITAL, 708
FALCONHEAD CAPITAL, 717
FF VENTURE CAPITAL, 724
FGA PARTNERS, 725
FIELDSTONE PRIVATE CAPITAL GROUP, 726
FIERA CAPITAL, 727
FIRST ATLANTIC CAPITAL LTD., 734
FIRST ROUND CAPITAL, 742
FIRSTMARK CAPITAL, 744
FLEXPOINT FORD LLC, 751
FLYBRIDGE CAPITAL PARTNERS, 756
FORESITE CAPITAL, 764
FORTRESS INVESTMENT GROUP LLC, 769
FOUNDER COLLECTIVE, 774
FOUNDERS EQUITY, 777
FREEMAN SPOGLI & CO., 786
FTV CAPITAL, 796
FdG ASSOCIATES LP, 804
GEFINOR CAPITAL, 813
GENACAST VENTURES, 818
GENERAL ATLANTIC PARTNERS, 819
GENERAL CATALYST PARTNERS, 820
GILBERT GLOBAL EQUITY PARTNERS, 831
GLADSTONE CAPITAL, 832
GLOBAL PRIVATE CAPITAL ASSOCIATION, 3252

Geographic Index

GLOBALIVE, 2128
GOLDEN SEEDS, 845
GOLDMAN SACHS INVESTMENT PARTNERS, 846
GOLUB CAPITAL, 848
GOTHAM GREEN PARTNERS, 850
GRAND CENTRAL HOLDINGS, 852
GRANITE BRIDGE PARTNERS, 854
GREAT OAKS VENTURE CAPITAL, 863
GREENBRIAR EQUITY GROUP LLC, 867
GREENHILL SAVP, 869
GREENHILLS VENTURES, LLC, 870
GREYCROFT PARTNERS, 876
GROVE GROUP MANAGEMENT, 883
GUGGENHEIM PARTNERS, 890
GV, 894
HALYARD CAPITAL, 902
HAMMOND, KENNEDY, WHITNEY & COMPANY, 904
HARBERT MANAGEMENT CORPORATION, 907
HARVEST PARTNERS, 917
HEALTH ENTERPRISE PARTNERS, 921
HEARST VENTURES, 925
HELLMAN & FRIEDMAN LLC, 927
HERCULES TECHNOLOGY GROWTH CAPITAL, INC, 928
HIG CAPITAL, 931
HIGH ROAD CAPITAL PARTNERS, 934
HIGHLAND CAPITAL PARTNERS, 938
HOLDING CAPITAL GROUP, 943
HQ CAPITAL, 955
HT CAPITAL ADVISORS LLC, 956
HUDSON VENTURE PARTNERS, 957
I-HATCH VENTURES LLC, 967
IA VENTURES, 969
IANTHUS CAPITAL MANAGEMENT, 970
IBM VENTURE CAPITAL GROUP, 971
ICV PARTNERS, 973
IDG CAPITAL, 977
IMAGINATION CAPITAL, 981
IMPLEMENT CAPITAL, 982
INNOVATION ENDEAVORS, 1001
INSIGHT VENTURE PARTNERS, 1005
INTERLACE VENTURES, 1011
INVESTCORP, 1021
INVESTX, 2154
INVUS GROUP, 1022
IRVING PLACE CAPITAL, 1026
J. BURKE CAPITAL PARTNERS, 1027
JEFFERIES CAPITAL PARTNERS, 1036
JEGI CAPITAL The Jordan Edminston Group, Inc., 1037
JESSELSON CAPITAL CORPORATION, 1038
JLL PARTNERS, 1043
JORDAN COMPANY, 1049
JUMP CAPITAL LLC, 1050
JW ASSET MANAGEMENT, 1052
KBL HEALTHCARE VENTURES, 1062
KELSO & COMPANY, 1066
KESTREL ENERGY PARTNERS, 1072
KIRENAGA, 1078
KOHLBERG & COMPANY LLC, 1085
KOHLBERG KRAVIS ROBERTS & COMPANY, 1086
KPS CAPITAL PARTNERS, 1089
L CATTERTON PARTNERS, 1092
LAUNCHCAPITAL, 1101
LDV CAPITAL, 1105
LEE EQUITY PARTNERS, 1108
LEEDS EQUITY PARTNERS, 1109
LERER HIPPEAU VENTURES, 1114
LEXINGTON PARTNERS, 1116
LIBERTY CITY VENTURES, 1119
LIGHTHOUSE PARTNERS, 1123
LIGHTYEAR CAPITAL, 1127
LINCOLNSHIRE MANAGEMENT, 1131
LINDSAY GOLDBERG, 1133
LINLEY CAPITAL, 1134
LONE STAR FUNDS, 1144
LONG ISLAND CAPITAL ALLIANCE, 3257
LONG POINT CAPITAL, 1145
LONGUEVUE CAPITAL LLC, 1148
LOVELL MINNICK PARTNERS LLC, 1151
LUX CAPITAL, 1155
MANHATTAN INVESTMENT PARTNERS, 1166
MATLINPATTERSON, 1182
MBF CAPITAL CORPORATION, 1191
MCGOVERN CAPITAL, 1194
MERIDA CAPITAL PARTNERS, 1208
MERIWETHER CAPITAL CORPORATION, 1216
MERLIN NEXUS, 1217
MERRILL LYNCH VENTURE CAPITAL, 1218
MESA GLOBAL, 1221
MESA+, 1223
METROPOLITAN PARTNERS GROUP, 1226
MIDOCEAN PARTNERS, 1231
MILLENIUM TECHNOLOGY VALUE PARTNERS, 1235
MOUSSE PARTNERS, 1263
MTS HEALTH INVESTORS, 1271
MURPHY & PARTNERS FUND LP, 1274
NAVY CAPITAL, 1282
NEEDHAM CAPITAL PARTNERS, 1287
NEW ENTERPRISE ASSOCIATES, 1296
NEW LEAF VENTURE PARTNERS, 1297
NEW MOUNTAIN CAPITAL, 1300
NEW SCIENCE VENTURES, 1302
NEW YORK ANGELS, 1305
NEW YORK CITY ENTREPRENEURIAL FUND New York City Economic Development Corporation, 1306
NEW YORK VENTURE PARTNERS, 1309
NEWFIELD CAPITAL, 1312
NEWLIGHT MANAGEMENT, 1313
NEWLIGHT PARTNERS, 1314
NEWSPRING CAPITAL, 1316
NGEN PARTNERS, 1324
NORTHLEAF CAPITAL PARTNERS, 2196
NORTHWOOD VENTURES, 1344
NOVELTEK CAPITAL CORPORATION, 1351
NUVEEN, 1356
NYC SEED, 1358
OAK HILL CAPITAL PARTNERS, 1360
OAKTREE CAPITAL MANAGEMENT LLC, 1362
ODEON CAPITAL PARTNERS, 1367
ODYSSEY INVESTMENT PARTNERS, 1368
OMERS PRIVATE EQUITY, 2199
ONCAP, 2200
ONE EQUITY PARTNERS, 1376
ONEX PARTNERS, 2201
ONONDAGA VENTURE CAPITAL FUND, 1378
ORBIMED HEALTHCARE FUND MANAGEMENT, 1383
PALADIN CAPITAL GROUP, 1401
PALLADIUM EQUITY PARTNERS, 1404
PANTHEON VENTURES (US) LP, 1413
PARTNERSHIP FUND FOR NEW YORK CITY, 1422
PENNELL VENTURE PARTNERS LLC, 1432
PERMAL CAPITAL MANAGEMENT, 1435
PERMIRA, 3024
PERSEUS FUNDS, 1437
PFIZER VENTURE INVESTMENTS, 1439
PINE BROOK ROAD PARTNERS, 1447
PINEBRIDGE INVESTMENTS, 1448
PLATINUM EQUITY, 1455
PLUM ALLEY, 1458
POLARIS VENTURE PARTNERS, 1464
POMONA CAPITAL, 1466
POST CAPITAL PARTNERS, 1469
POUSCHINE COOK CAPITAL MANAGEMENT LLC, 1470
PRAESIDIAN CAPITAL, 1472
PRIMARY VENTURE PARTNERS, 1479
PROGRESS VENTURES, 1488
PROSPECT CAPITAL CORPORATION, 1493
PROVIDENCE EQUITY PARTNERS, 1498
PSILOS GROUP, 1500
QUAD PARTNERS, 1506
QUADRANGLE GROUP, 1508
QUILVEST CAPITAL PARTNERS, 1518
QUOTIDIAN VENTURES, 1521
RADIUS VENTURES, 1523
RAND CAPITAL CORPORATION, 1526

Geographic Index

RAPTOR GROUP, 1527
RECIPROCAL VENTURES, 1531
RED SEA VENTURES, 1533
RELATIVITY CAPITAL, 1542
RESOURCE CAPITAL FUNDS, 1551
RETHINK COMMUNITY, 1553
RETHINK EDUCATION, 1554
RETHINK IMPACT, 1555
REVEL PARTNERS, 1557
RHO VENTURES, 1561
RHODIUM, 3072
RHYTHM VENTURE CAPITAL, 1562
RICHMOND GLOBAL, 1564
RIVERSIDE COMPANY, 1576
RIVERSTONE, 1577
ROARK CAPITAL GROUP, 1580
ROSE TECH VENTURES, 1588
ROSECLIFF VENTURES, 1589
ROTH CAPITAL PARTNERS, 1592
RRE VENTURES, 1597
RTP VENTURES, 1598
RU-NET VENTURES RTP Ventures, 3078
RUBICON VENTURE CAPITAL, 1599
RUNTIDE CAPITAL, 1600
SALMON RIVER CAPITAL, 1611
SAMSUNG NEXT, 1614
SANDLER CAPITAL MANAGEMENT, 1620
SARATOGA PARTNERS, 1624
SARONA ASSET MANAGEMENT, 2239
SCHULTZE ASSET MANAGEMENT, 1632
SCOUT VENTURES, 1635
SCULPTOR CAPITAL MANAGEMENT, 1638
SEAPORT CAPITAL, 1641
SEARCHLIGHT, 2243
SEAWAY VALLEY CAPITAL CORPORATION, 1642
SECOND ALPHA, 1643
SENTINEL CAPITAL PARTNERS, 1654
SEYMOUR ASSET MANAGEMENT, 1662
SIGNAL EQUITY PARTNERS, 1676
SIGULER GUFF & COMPANY, 1681
SILICON ALLEY VENTURE PARTNERS, 1682
SILVER LAKE, 1685
SJF VENTURES, 1691
SOFTBANK CAPITAL, 1701
SOGAL VENTURES, 1703
SOSV, 1709
SOURCE CAPITAL GROUP, 1710
SPARK CAPITAL, 1718
SPENCER TRASK VENTURES, 1723
SPIRE CAPITAL PARTNERS, 1727
SPP CAPITAL, 1729
SPRING MOUNTAIN CAPITAL, 1733
STARVEST PARTNERS, 1741
STONE POINT CAPITAL LLC, 1746
STONEBRIDGE PARTNERS, 1747
STONEHENGE GROWTH CAPITAL, 1748
STRIPES GROUP, 1751
SUMMER STREET CAPITAL PARTNERS, 1753
SUN CAPITAL PARTNERS, 1755
SWAN & LEGEND VENTURES, 1768
SYCAMORE VENTURES, 1771
TAILWIND CAPITAL, 1779
TECHNOLOGY CROSSOVER VENTURES, 1787
TH LEE PUTNAM VENTURES, 1806
THAYER STREET PARTNERS, 1807
THE ABRAAJ GROUP, 3164
THE CHANNEL GROUP, 1811
THREE CITIES RESEARCH, 1822
THRIVE CAPITAL, 1823
TIGER GLOBAL MANAGEMENT, 1828
TIME WARNER INVESTMENT CORPORATION, 1829
TOPSPIN PARTNERS, 1834
TPG CAPITAL, 1837
TRANSCENDENT CAPITAL, 1838
TRESS CAPITAL LLC, 1845
TREVI HEALTH CAPITAL, 1846
TRIBECA VENTURE PARTNERS, 1851
TRILANTIC CAPITAL PARTNERS, 1853
TSG CONSUMER PARTNERS, 1863
TUATARA CAPITAL, 1866
TUSK VENTURES, 1870
TWO SIGMA VENTURES, 1876
UNION CAPITAL CORPORATION, 1883
UNION SQUARE VENTURES, 1884
UNITED TALENT AGENCY VENTURES, 1885
UPSTATE CAPITAL ASSOCIATION OF NEW YORK, 3269
URBAN US, 1896
US RENEWABLES GROUP, 1897
VALAR VENTURES, 1899
VALENCE LIFE SCIENCES, 1900
VALIA, 1902
VARDE PARTNERS, 1909
VCFA GROUP, 1910
VEDANTA CAPITAL LP, 1913
VENBIO, 1916
VENROCK ASSOCIATES, 1918
VERITAS CAPITAL FUND LP, 1927
VERIZON VENTURES, 1928
VERONIS SUHLER STEVENSON, 1929
VERSANT VENTURES, 1930
VESEY STREET CAPITAL PARTNERS LLC, 1932
VESTAR CAPITAL PARTNERS, 1933
VISION CAPITAL, 1939
VISTA EQUITY PARTNERS, 1940
W CAPITAL PARTNERS, 1949
WAFRA CAPITAL PARTNERS INC, 1951
WAFRA INC, 1952
WALL STREET VENTURE CAPITAL, 1954
WAND PARTNERS, 1956
WARBURG PINCUS LLC, 1957
WASSERSTEIN & CO., 1961
WELLS FARGO CAPITAL FINANCE, 1971
WELLSPRING CAPITAL MANAGEMENT LLC, 1972
WELSH, CARSON, ANDERSON & STOWE, 1973
WGI GROUP, 1980
WHEATLEY PARTNERS, 1981
WHITE STAR CAPITAL, 1982
WICKS GROUP OF COMPANIES, LLC, 1984
WILLOWRIDGE PARTNERS, 1986
WINDCREST PARTNERS, 1991
WINDFORCE VENTURES, LLC, 1992
WINDHAM VENTURE PARTNERS, 1993
WORK-BENCH, 2006
ZELKOVA VENTURES, 2016
ZEPHYR MANAGEMENT LP, 2017
ZM CAPITAL, 2019
ZS FUND LP, 2021

North Carolina
BBH CAPITAL PARTNERS, 243
BLUE BRIGHT VENTURES, 289
BLUE POINT CAPITAL PARTNERS, 293
CAPITALA, 408
CAROLINA FINANCIAL GROUP, 417
CAROUSEL CAPITAL, 418
CATO BIOVENTURES, 432
CHEROKEE INVESTMENT PARTNERS, 465
COUNCIL FOR ENTREPRENEURIAL DEVELOPMENT, 3250
FIRST FLIGHT VENTURE CENTER, 738
FIVE POINTS CAPITAL, 747
FRANKLIN STREET EQUITY PARTNERS, 783
FRONTIER CAPITAL, 793
GOLDEN PINE VENTURES, 844
GOLUB CAPITAL, 848
HALIFAX GROUP LLC, 899
HATTERAS VENTURE PARTNERS, 918
IDEA FUND PARTNERS, 975
INTERSOUTH PARTNERS, 1013
MERITURN PARTNERS, 1214
NDI MEDICAL, 1286
NOVAQUEST CAPITAL MANAGEMENT, 1349
PAMLICO CAPITAL, 1410
PAPPAS VENTURES, 1414
PIEDMONT ANGEL NETWORK, 1446

Geographic Index

REX HEALTH VENTURES, 1559
RIVER CITIES CAPITAL FUNDS, 1575
SALEM INVESTMENT PARTNERS, 1609
SJF VENTURES, 1691
SOUTHEAST INTERACTIVE TECHNOLOGY FUNDS, 1711
SOUTHERN CAPITOL VENTURES, 1712
SUNBRIDGE PARTNERS, 1757
SYNGENTA VENTURES, 1776
TRELYS FUNDS, 1844
TRIANGLE ANGEL PARTNERS, 1847
WELLS FARGO CAPITAL FINANCE, 1971
WILMINGTON INVESTOR NETWORK, 1987

North Dakota
ARTHUR VENTURES, 175
GEN7 INVESTMENTS, 817
INVESTAMERICA VENTURE GROUP, 1020
LINN GROVE VENTURES, 1135
NORTH DAKOTA DEVELOPMENT FUND, 1338
NORTHSTAR CAPITAL, 1343

Ohio
ALLOS VENTURES, 86
ARBORETUM VENTURES, 150
ARSENAL VENTURE PARTNERS, 173
ATHENIAN VENTURE PARTNERS, 189
AUSTIN CAPITAL PARTNERS LP, 204
BEVERAGE MARKETING CORPORATION, 264
BLUE CHIP VENTURE COMPANY, 290
BLUE POINT CAPITAL PARTNERS, 293
BRIDGE INVESTMENT FUND, 340
BRUML CAPITAL CORPORATION, 358
CASE TECHNOLOGY VENTURES Case Western Reserve University, 423
CHARTER LIFE SCIENCES, 460
CINCYTECH, 481
CINTRIFUSE, 482
CUSTER CAPITAL, 572
CYPRIUM PARTNERS, 578
DESCO CAPITAL, 607
DRAPER TRIANGLE VENTURES, 629
DRIVE CAPITAL, 631
EARLY STAGE PARTNERS, 642
EDGEWATER CAPITAL PARTNERS, 653
EQUITEK CAPITAL, 693
FORT WASHINGTON CAPITAL PARTNERS GROUP, 768
GLENGARY LLC, 835
HOPEN LIFE SCIENCE VENTURES, 946
JANE VC, 1030
JUMPSTART INC, 1051
LINSALATA CAPITAL PARTNERS, 1136
MPE PARTNERS, 1266
NCT VENTURES, 1285
NDI MEDICAL, 1286
PNC ERIEVIEW CAPITAL, 1460
PRIMUS CAPITAL, 1480
QUEEN CITY ANGELS, 1514
RESERVOIR VENTURE PARTNERS, 1547
RESILIENCE CAPITAL PARTNERS, 1548
REV1 VENTURES, 1556
RIVER CITIES CAPITAL FUNDS, 1575
RIVERSIDE COMPANY, 1576
RIVERVEST VENTURE PARTNERS, 1578
STONEHENGE GROWTH CAPITAL, 1748
SUNBRIDGE PARTNERS, 1757
TRIATHLON MEDICAL VENTURES, 1849
WALNUT GROUP, 1955

Oklahoma
ACORN GROWTH COMPANIES, 47
DAVIS, TUTTLE VENTURE PARTNERS LP, 592
ENCAP FLATROCK MIDSTREAM, 672
I2E, 968
KNIGHTSBRIDGE ADVISERS, 1081
METAFUND, 1224
REGENT PRIVATE CAPITAL, 1541

Oregon
ENDEAVOUR CAPITAL, 674
HANOVER PARTNERS, 906
OREGON ANGEL FUND, 1384
OVP VENTURE PARTNERS, 1392
PORTLAND SEED FUND, 1467
SEVEN PEAKS VENTURES, 1659
VEBER PARTNERS LLC, 1911
VENCORE CAPITAL, 1917
VOYAGER CAPITAL, 1947
WELLS FARGO CAPITAL FINANCE, 1971

Pennsylvania
1315 CAPITAL, 4
ACTIVATE VENTURE PARTNERS, 51
ACTUA, 52
ADAMS CAPITAL MANAGEMENT, 55
ARGOSY CAPITAL, 165
AUGUSTUS VENTURES, 201
BBH CAPITAL PARTNERS, 243
BEN FRANKLIN TECHNOLOGY PARTNERS, 249
BERWIND CORPORATION, 261
BIOADVANCE, 269
BIRCHMERE VENTURES, 275
BLUE TREE ALLIED ANGELS, 296
BLUETREE VENTURE FUND, 301
COMCAST VENTURES, 520
CORNERSTONE CAPITAL HOLDINGS, 542
DIMELING SCHREIBER & PARK, 617
DRAPER TRIANGLE VENTURES, 629
ELEMENT PARTNERS, 658
ENERTECH CAPITAL, 677
ENTREPRENEUR PARTNERS, 684
EUREKA GROWTH CAPITAL, 699
FIRST ROUND CAPITAL, 742
GENACAST VENTURES, 818
GLENTHORNE CAPITAL, 836
GRAHAM PARTNERS, 851
GREENHOUSE VENTURES, 871
H KATZ CAPITAL GROUP, 896
INETWORKS ADVISORS LLC, 991
INNOVATION WORKS, 1003
INVERNESS GRAHAM INVESTMENTS, 1018
JAGUAR CAPITAL PARTNERS, 1029
LANCET CAPITAL, 1096
LAUNCHCYTE, 1102
LIFE SCIENCES GREENHOUSE OF CENTRAL PA, 1120
LLR PARTNERS INC, 1140
LOVELL MINNICK PARTNERS LLC, 1151
MAIN STREET CAPITAL HOLDINGS LLC, 1163
MEAKEM/BECKER VENTURE CAPITAL, 1196
MEIDLINGER PARTNERS, 1200
MENTOR CAPITAL PARTNERS LTD, 1204
MILESTONE PARTNERS, 1234
MISSIONOG, 1240
MVP CAPITAL PARTNERS, 1275
NEW RHEIN HEALTHCARE INVESTORS, 1301
NEWSPRING CAPITAL, 1316
NEXTSTAGE CAPITAL, 1321
NORWICH VENTURES, 1347
ORIGINATE VENTURES, 1386
OSAGE PARTNERS, 1388
PENN VENTURE PARTNERS, 1431
PI CAPITAL GROUP LLC, 1444
PIDC PHILADELPHIA, 1445
PIONEER CAPITAL, 1450
PITTSBURGH EQUITY PARTNERS, 1451
PITTSBURGH LIFE SCIENCES GREENHOUSE, 1452
PITTSBURGH VENTURE CAPITAL ASSOCIATION, 3264
PLEXUS VENTURES, 1456
PNC RIVERARCH CAPITAL, 1461
PROVCO GROUP, 1496
QUAKER BIOVENTURES, 1510
RAF INDUSTRIES, 1524
RITTENHOUSE VENTURES, 1572
ROBIN HOOD VENTURES, 1581
SAFEGUARD SCIENTIFICS, 1605

Geographic Index

SCP PARTNERS, 1636
SEVENTYSIX CAPITAL, 1660
SPIRE CAPITAL PARTNERS, 1727
SPRING CAPITAL PARTNERS LP, 1730
SR ONE LTD, 1734
STONEWOOD CAPITAL MANAGEMENT, 1749
SUSQUEHANNA GROWTH EQUITY, 1761
THINKTIV VENTURES, 1813
TL VENTURES, 1830
WELLS FARGO CAPITAL FINANCE, 1971
WILSHIRE PRIVATE MARKETS, 1988

Rhode Island
ANGEL STREET CAPITAL, 126
FENWAY PARTNERS, 722
NAUTIC PARTNERS, 1278
PROVIDENCE EQUITY PARTNERS, 1498
SLATER TECHNOLOGY FUND, 1695

South Carolina
AZALEA CAPITAL, 216
BATTELLE VENTURES, 236
CULTIVATION CAPITAL, 570
GOOD GROWTH CAPITAL, 849
VENTURESOUTH, 1925

South Dakota
BIRD DOG EQUITY PARTNERS, 276
BLUESTEM CAPITAL COMPANY, 300
MCGOWAN CAPITAL GROUP, 1195
PRAIRIEGOLD VENTURE PARTNERS, 1474

Tennessee
AM VENTURES, 15
BBH CAPITAL PARTNERS, 243
CHATTANOOGA RENAISSANCE FUND, 461
CLARITAS CAPITAL, 495
CLAYTON ASSOCIATES, 497
COUNCIL CAPITAL, 551
CRESSEY & COMPANY LP, 559
DYNAMO VC, 640
FCA VENTURE PARTNERS, 718
HARBERT MANAGEMENT CORPORATION, 907
INNOVA MEMPHIS, 999
MB VENTURE PARTNERS, 1190
MERITUS VENTURES, 1215
MOUNTAIN GROUP CAPITAL, 1261
PROVENTURE AG, 3051
RED CLAY CAPITAL HOLDINGS, 1532
RIVER ASSOCIATES INVESTMENTS LLC, 1573
SSM PARTNERS, 1735
TENNESSEE COMMUNITY VENTURES, 1799
TVV CAPITAL, 1872
VENTURE ASSOCIATES PARTNERS LLC, 1921

Texas
ADVANTAGE CAPITAL PARTNERS, 60
AM VENTURES, 105
AMBERJACK CAPITAL PARTNERS, 106
AMERIMARK CAPITAL CORPORATION, 112
APOLLO GLOBAL MANAGEMENT, 141
ARDENTON, 2038
ARISTOS VENTURES, 166
ARROWPATH VENTURE PARTNERS, 171
AUSTIN VENTURES, 205
BCM TECHNOLOGIES, 244
BLUE SAGE CAPITAL, 294
BP ALTERNATIVE ENERGY VENTURES, 322
BRAND FOUNDRY VENTURES, 328
CAMBRIA GROUP, 381
CAPITAL SOUTHWEST CORPORATION, 406
CASTLELAKE, 426
CATALYST GROUP, 427
CCMP CAPITAL, 435
CENTERPOINT VENTURE PARTNERS, 446
CENTRAL TEXAS ANGEL NETWORK, 447
CHEVRON TECHNOLOGY VENTURES, 468
CIC PARTNERS, 479
CITARETX INVESTMENT PARTNERS, 487
COLT VENTURES, 517
CORSA VENTURES, 546
CRESCO CAPITAL PARTNERS, 558
CYPRESS GROWTH CAPITAL, 577
DALLAS VENTURE PARTNERS, 583
DAVIS, TUTTLE VENTURE PARTNERS LP, 592
ENCAP FLATROCK MIDSTREAM, 672
ENCAP INVESTMENTS LP, 673
ENERGY CAPITAL PARTNERS, 676
ENERGY VENTURES, 2691
EQUUS TOTAL RETURN, 695
ESCALATE CAPITAL PARTNERS, 696
ESCHELON ENERGY PARTNERS, 697
ESSEX WOODLANDS HEALTH VENTURES LLC, 698
EVERCORE CAPITAL PARTNERS, 700
EVOLVE CAPITAL, 703
FENGATE, 2110
FIRST CAPITAL GROUP, 735
FIRST RESERVE, 741
FORTRESS INVESTMENT GROUP LLC, 769
FRASER MCCOMBS CAPITAL, 784
G-51 CAPITAL LLC, 806
GENERATION PARTNERS, 822
GIDEON HIXON FUND, 830
GREENHILL SAVP, 869
GUGGENHEIM PARTNERS, 890
GULFSTAR GROUP, 893
HADDINGTON VENTURES LLC, 898
HALIFAX GROUP LLC, 899
HANCOCK PARK ASSOCIATES, 905
HARBERT MANAGEMENT CORPORATION, 907
HIG CAPITAL, 931
HOLDING CAPITAL GROUP, 943
HOUSTON ANGEL NETWORK, 953
HOUSTON HEALTH VENTURES, 954
HUNT INVESTMENT GROUP, 960
INCYTE VENTURES, 986
INDEPENDENT BANKERS CAPITAL FUND, 988
INNOVATION PLATFORM CAPITAL, 1002
JB POINDEXTER & COMPANY, 1034
KENMONT CAPITAL PARTNERS, 1067
KOHLBERG KRAVIS ROBERTS & COMPANY, 1086
LIME ROCK PARTNERS, 1129
LIMESTONE VENTURES, 1130
LONE STAR FUNDS, 1144
MANSA CAPITAL, 1167
MARKPOINT VENTURE PARTNERS, 1170
MERCURY FUND, 1207
MERIT ENERGY COMPANY, 1211
MOBILITY VENTURES, 1244
MURPHREE VENTURE PARTNERS, 1273
NAYA VENTURES, 1284
NEW CAPITAL PARTNERS, 1292
NGP, 1326
NGP ENERGY CAPITAL, 1328
ORIX, 1387
PALOMINO CAPITAL, 1409
PARALLEL INVESTMENT PARTNERS, 1417
PARTHENON CAPITAL, 1419
PEROT JAIN, 1436
PROGRESS EQUITY PARTNERS, 1487
PTV SCIENCES, 1502
QUAKE CAPITAL PARTNERS, 1509
QUINBROOK INFRASTRUCTURE PARTNERS, 1520
RETAIL & RESTAURANT GROWTH CAPITAL LP, 1552
RIDGEWOOD ENERGY, 1568
RIVERSIDE COMPANY, 1576
RIVERSTONE, 1577
S3 VENTURES, 1601
SANTE VENTURES, 1622
SATORI CAPITAL, 1625
SAUDI ARAMCO ENERGY VENTURES Aramco Energy Ventures, 3090
SENTIENT VENTURES, 1653
SEVIN ROSEN FUNDS, 1661
SIGULER GUFF & COMPANY, 1681

Geographic Index

SILVER CREEK VENTURES, 1684
SILVERTON PARTNERS, 1687
SOCIAL SECTOR VENTURES, 1699
SPINDLETOP CAPITAL, 1725
STAR VENTURES, 3128
STONEHENGE GROWTH CAPITAL, 1748
TEAKWOOD CAPITAL, 1785
TEXAS EMERGING TECHNOLOGY FUND, 1802
TEXAS VENTURE ASSOCIATION, 3267
TEXO VENTURES, 1803
TGF MANAGEMENT, 1805
THINKTIV VENTURES, 1813
TI VENTURE CAPITAL Texas Instruments Incorporated, 1825
TPG CAPITAL, 1837
TRELLIS PARTNERS, 1843
TRIANGLE PEAK PARTNERS, 1848
TRITON VENTURES, 1857
TRIVE CAPITAL, 1858
TXV PARTNERS, 1877
VISTA EQUITY PARTNERS, 1940
VORTEX PARTNERS, 1946
WAFRA INC, 1952
WARBURG PINCUS LLC, 1957
WELLS FARGO CAPITAL FINANCE, 1971
WESTLAKE SECURITIES, 1977
WINGATE PARTNERS, 1997
YELLOWSTONE CAPITAL, 2012

Utah
42 VENTURES, 8
ALBUM VC, 79
ALTA VENTURES MEXICO, 2374
CHEROKEE & WALKER, 464
CROSS CREEK ADVISORS, 561
DW HEALTHCARE PARTNERS, 639
EPIC VENTURES, 689
INNOVENTURES CAPITAL PARTNERS, 1004
KICKSTART SEED FUND, 1074
LONGUEVUE CAPITAL LLC, 1148
MCG CAPITAL MANAGEMENT, 1193
MERCATO PARTNERS, 1205
ORIGIN VENTURES, 1385
PELION VENTURE PARTNERS, 1428
RENEWABLETECH VENTURES, 1545
SENTRY FINANCIAL CORPORATION, 1655
SIGNAL PEAK VENTURES, 1679
SORENSON CAPITAL, 1707
UNIVERSITY VENTURE FUND, 1886

Vermont
FRESHTRACKS CAPITAL, 789
UNDERDOG VENTURES, 1882

Virginia
ALTRIA VENTURES, 102
AMPLIFIER VENTURE PARTNERS, 120
AVANSIS VENTURES, 210
BIA DIGITAL PARTNERS LP, 266
BLU VENTURE INVESTORS, 288
BLUE HERON CAPITAL, 291
COLUMBIA CAPITAL, 518
COURT SQUARE VENTURES, 552
CROSSHILL FINANCIAL GROUP, 563
DISRUPTOR CAPITAL, 618
EVERGREEN ADVISORS, 702
GLADSTONE CAPITAL, 832
GREEN TOWER CAPITAL, 866
GROTECH VENTURES, 881
HARBERT MANAGEMENT CORPORATION, 907
HARREN EQUITY PARTNERS, 913
HEALTHCARE PRIVATE EQUITY ASSOCIATION, 3254
HORIZON TECHNOLOGY FINANCE, 949
IN-Q-TEL, 983
INDUSTRY VENTURES, 990
LIQUID CAPITAL GROUP, 1137
MCG CAPITAL CORPORATION, 1192
MIDDLEBURG CAPITAL DEVELOPMENT, 1229
MOTLEY FOOL VENTURES, 1259
NEW ATLANTIC VENTURES, 1290
NEW VANTAGE GROUP, 1303
OUTCOME CAPITAL, 1389
PRO-RATA OPPORTUNITY FUND, 1485
QUAD-C MANAGEMENT, 1507
RENAISSANCE VENTURES, 1544
RIDGE CAPITAL PARTNERS LLC, 1565
SAIL VENTURE PARTNERS, 1607
SAVANO CAPITAL PARTNERS, 1628
SINEWAVE VENTURES, 1689
SWAN & LEGEND VENTURES, 1768
THIRD SECURITY, 1815
VALHALLA PARTNERS, 1901
VENSANA CAPITAL, 1919
VENTANA CAPITAL MANAGEMENT LP, 1920
VIRGINIA SMALL BUSINESS FINANCING AUTHORITY, 1938
WASHINGTON CAPITAL VENTURES, 1960
WELLS FARGO CAPITAL FINANCE, 1971

Washington
ACCELERATOR LIFE SCIENCE PARTNERS, 30
ACKERLEY PARTNERS LLC, 42
ALEXANDER HUTTON, 82
ALLIANCE OF ANGELS, 85
ARCH VENTURE PARTNERS, 154
BENAROYA COMPANIES, 250
BIOMATICS CAPITAL, 271
BLUE POINT CAPITAL PARTNERS, 293
BROADMARK CAPITAL, 348
DIVERGENT VENTURES, 619
ENDEAVOUR CAPITAL, 674
FLUKE VENTURE PARTNERS, 755
FLYING FISH, 757
FOUNDER'S CO-OP, 776
FRAZIER HEALTHCARE VENTURES, 785
GREY SKY VENTURE PARTNERS, 875
GUIDE VENTURES, 892
HOLDING CAPITAL GROUP, 943
IGNITION PARTNERS, 978
INTEGRA VENTURES, 1007
INTELLECTUAL VENTURES, 1010
INVESTAMERICA VENTURE GROUP, 1020
LAUNCHBOX DIGITAL, 1100
MADRONA VENTURE GROUP, 1162
MONTLAKE CAPITAL, 1250
NAYA VENTURES, 1284
OVP VENTURE PARTNERS, 1392
PACIFIC HORIZON VENTURES, 1399
PALMS & COMPANY, 1405
POINT B CAPITAL, 1462
PRIVATEER HOLDINGS, 1484
PSL VENTURES, 1501
SEAPOINT VENTURES, 1640
SECOND AVENUE PARTNERS, 1644
SPEKTRA CAPITAL, 1721
STAENBERG VENTURE PARTNERS, 1736
TIE ANGELS GROUP SEATTLE, 1827
TRILOGY PARTNERSHIP, 1854
VENTURE TECH ALLIANCE, 1924
VOYAGER CAPITAL, 1947
WELLS FARGO CAPITAL FINANCE, 1971
WRF CAPITAL, 2007

West Virginia
MOUNTAINEER CAPITAL, 1262

Wisconsin
4490 VENTURES, 9
BAIRD CAPITAL PARTNERS, 225
CALUMET VENTURE FUND, 378
CAPITAL MIDWEST FUND, 403
CSA PARTNERS, 567
DANEVEST TECH FUND ADVISORS, 584
FCF PARTNERS LP, 719
HORIZON PARTNERS, LTD, 948
KEGONSA CAPITAL PARTNERS, 1064

Geographic Index

MASON WELLS, 1174
NEW CAPITAL FUND, 1291
STONEHENGE GROWTH CAPITAL, 1748
VENTURE INVESTORS LLC, 1923
WINNEBAGO SEED FUND, 1999
WISCONSIN INVESTMENT PARTNERS, 2002

Wyoming
AEROSTAR CAPITAL LLC, 66
ALTA PARTNERS, 94

Vietnam
MEKONG CAPITAL, 2952

VINACAPITAL GROUP, 3208

Wales
FINANCE WALES, 2728

Yugoslavia
SALFORD CAPITAL PARTNERS, 3086

Zimbabwe
CLARITY CAPITAL, 2602

Industry Preference Index / Advertising

3D Technology
PANACHE VENTURES, 2204

AD Tech
BERTELSMANN DIGITAL MEDIA INVESTMENTS, 259

AI
ANGELPAD, 129
BOOST VC, 310
DAY ONE VENTURES, 594
ENERTECH CAPITAL, 677
FLORIDA FUNDERS, 754
NAYA VENTURES, 1284
PANACHE VENTURES, 2204
YES VC, 2013

API
ANGELPAD, 129

Accessbility
CANTOS VENTURES, 398

Accessories
BREAKAWAY VENTURES, 332

Ad Tech
500 STARTUPS, 10

AdTech
QUAKE CAPITAL PARTNERS, 1509

Administration and Accounting
AUSTRALIAN ETHICAL INVESTMENT LIMITED, 2447
VON BRAUN & SCHREIBER PRIVATE EQUITY PARTNERS, 3218

Administrative Automation
HEALTH ENTERPRISE PARTNERS, 921

Advance Polymers
MOUNTAINEER CAPITAL, 1262

Advanced Data Compression Technologies
SONY STRATEGIC TECHNOLOGY PARTNERSHIPS, 1706

Advanced Energy
ARTIS VENTURES, 177

Advanced Manufacturing
ALLOS VENTURES, 86
AMANAH VENTURES SDN BHD, 2380
ELEVATE VENTURES, 659
FIRST STEP FUND, 743
GE VENTURES, 812
IDG CAPITAL PARTNERS, 2838
LEGEND CAPITAL, 2927
SB CHINA VENTURE CAPITAL, 3091

Advanced Manufacturing & Materials
ARCTERN VENTURES, 2037
COUNCIL FOR ENTREPRENEURIAL DEVELOPMENT, 3250

Advanced Marine Applications
CONNECTICUT INNOVATIONS, 532

Advanced Materials
AMHERST FUND, 114
ANGELENO GROUP, 127
ARCH VENTURE PARTNERS, 154
BIRCHMERE VENTURES, 275
BRIGHT CAPITAL, 2531
CHEVRON TECHNOLOGY VENTURES, 468
CHORD CAPITAL, 2589
CLEAN PACIFIC VENTURES, 499
CONNECTICUT INNOVATIONS, 532
DOMAIN ASSOCIATES LLC, 622
ELEMENT PARTNERS, 658
EMERALD TECHNOLOGY VENTURES, 2101
EXPANSION CAPITAL PARTNERS, 707
GENERAL MOTORS VENTURES, 821
INNOVATION WORKS, 1003
IP GROUP, 2883
MADISON PARKER CAPITAL, 1161
MARS INVESTMENT ACCELERATOR FUND, 2181
NGEN PARTNERS, 1324
OXANTIUM VENTURES, 1394
PANGAEA VENTURES LTD, 2205
PARKWALK ADVISORS, 3019
PI CAPITAL GROUP LLC, 1444
PRESIDIO VENTURES, 1478
REV1 VENTURES, 1556
ROCKPORT CAPITAL, 1583
SABIC VENTURES, 3082
SATURN PARTNERS, 1626
SEVIN ROSEN FUNDS, 1661
SILVERTON PARTNERS, 1687
SOUTHERN CROSS VENTURE PARTNERS, 1713
TANDEM EXPANSION FUND, 2252
TECHNOLOGY PARTNERS, 1788
TENNESSEE COMMUNITY VENTURES, 1799
TRELLIS CAPITAL CORPORATION, 2265
TRIGINITA CAPITAL, 3181
TRITON VENTURES, 1857
WRF CAPITAL, 2007
YISSUM TECHNOLOGY TRANSFER, 3235

Advanced Technologies
B-TO-V PARTNERS, 2466
DISCOVERY CAPITAL, 2091

Advanced Weapons Systems
RAFAEL DEVELOPMENT CORPORATION (RDC) LIMITED, 3063

Advertising
ABU DHABI INVESTMENT AUTHORITY, 2313
AEP CAPITAL LLC, 64
AFTERDOX, 2344
ALLSTATE INVESTMENTS LLC, 88
ANGELPAD, 129
ARCHTOP VENTURES, 155
ARTS ALLIANCE, 2419
ATRIUM CAPITAL, 194
AZURE CAPITAL PARTNERS, 218
BUTLER CAPITAL PARTNERS FRANCE, 2542
CITA GESTION, 2598
COMCAST VENTURES, 520
FAIRHAVEN CAPITAL, 713
FIVE ELMS CAPITAL, 746
GREAT OAKS VENTURE CAPITAL, 863
GREE VENTURES, 2789
GREYCROFT PARTNERS, 876
HARBOURVEST PARTNERS LLC, 912
HUDSON VENTURE PARTNERS, 957
INVENTUS, 1017
KAEDAN INVESTMENTS, 2905
KHOSLA VENTURES, 1073
KOHLBERG VENTURES, 1087
M/C PARTNERS, 1157
MADRONA VENTURE GROUP, 1162
MESA+, 1223
MHS CAPITAL, 1227
NEW ATLANTIC VENTURES, 1290
QUOTIDIAN VENTURES, 1521
RAPTOR GROUP, 1527
SPARK CAPITAL, 1718
STAGE 1 VENTURES, 1737
TELEFONICA VENTURES, 3160
TIME WARNER INVESTMENT CORPORATION, 1829
TRANSMEDIA CAPITAL, 1841
TRIBECA VENTURE PARTNERS, 1851
TUGBOAT VENTURES, 1867
UNION CAPITAL CORPORATION, 1883
VERIZON VENTURES, 1928
WASABI VENTURES, 1959
WICKS GROUP OF COMPANIES, LLC, 1984
ZM CAPITAL, 2019

Industry Preference Index / Advertising Technology

Advertising Technology
FOUNDER COLLECTIVE, 774
PROJECT A VENTURE GmBH & CO. KG, 3047
RUBICON VENTURE CAPITAL, 1599
SCOUT VENTURES, 1635
VENROCK ASSOCIATES, 1918

Aerospace
BLUE POINT CAPITAL PARTNERS, 293
CATAPULT VENTURES, 431
CM EQUITY PARTNERS, 509
CORNERSTONE CAPITAL HOLDINGS, 542
HAMMOND, KENNEDY, WHITNEY & COMPANY, 904
HANCOCK PARK ASSOCIATES, 905
KILLICK CAPITAL, 2161

Aerospace Defense
BLAST FUNDING, 282

Aerospace and Defence
BRANFORD CASTLE, 330
GREIF & COMPANY, 874

Aerospace and Defense
IBM VENTURE CAPITAL GROUP, 971

Aerospace, Defense and Government
ACORN GROWTH COMPANIES, 47
AEROEQUITY, 65
AEROSTAR CAPITAL LLC, 66
ALANTRA, 77
ALEUTIAN CAPITAL PARTNERS, 81
AMERICAN SECURITIES LLC, 111
ANDLINGER & COMPANY INC, 124
ARES MANAGEMENT LLC, 160
ARLINGTON CAPITAL PARTNERS, 167
AURORA CAPITAL GROUP, 202
AZALEA CAPITAL, 216
CAI CAPITAL PARTNERS, 368
CAPITAL FOR BUSINESS, INC, 402
CAPITAL SOUTHWEST CORPORATION, 406
CARLYLE ASIA INVESTMENT ADVISORS LIMITED Carlyle Group, 2556
CARLYLE GROUP, 416
CELERITY PARTNERS, 441
CERBERUS CAPITAL MANAGEMENT, 453
CHART VENTURE PARTNERS, 459
CI CAPITAL PARTNERS, 478
CIT GROUP, 486
CLEARLAKE CAPITAL, 502
COLORADO MILE HIGH FUND, 516
COMSPACE, 528
CONNECTICUT INNOVATIONS, 532
COTTONWOOD TECHNOLOGY FUND, 550
DUBIN CLARK & COMPANY, 633
DUNRATH CAPITAL, 636
ENLIGHTENMENT CAPITAL, 681
FALCON FUND, 716
FINANCIERE DE BRIENNE FCPR, 2729
FIRST ATLANTIC CAPITAL LTD., 734
FIRST NEW ENGLAND CAPITAL LP, 740
FOUNDERS FUND, 778
GOLUB CAPITAL, 848
GREENBRIAR EQUITY GROUP LLC, 867
HARREN EQUITY PARTNERS, 913
HCI EQUITY PARTNERS, 920
HERITAGE PARTNERS, 929
HIG CAPITAL, 931
IRONWOOD CAPITAL, 1025
IXORA VENTURES, 2895
JLL PARTNERS, 1043
JORDAN COMPANY, 1049
KOREA TECHNOLOGY & BANKING (KTB) NETWORK CORP, 2917
LEVINE LEICHTMAN CAPITAL PARTNERS, 1115
LINLEY CAPITAL, 1134
MEZZANINE MANAGEMENT LIMITED Mezzanine Management UK Ltd., 2956

NEW BRUNSWICK INNOVATION FOUNDATION, 2192
NOVA SCOTIA BUSINESS INC., 2197
ODYSSEY INVESTMENT PARTNERS, 1368
ONEX PARTNERS, 2201
OUTCOME CAPITAL, 1389
PARKVIEW CAPITAL PARTNERS, 2207
PIDC PHILADELPHIA, 1445
SCOTTISH ENTERPRISE, 3094
SCP PARTNERS, 1636
SENTINEL CAPITAL PARTNERS, 1654
SPACEVEST, 1717
VANCE STREET CAPITAL, 1906
VENTANA CAPITAL MANAGEMENT LP, 1920
VENTURE ASSOCIATES PARTNERS LLC, 1921
VERITAS CAPITAL FUND LP, 1927
WALNUT GROUP, 1955
WELLSPRING CAPITAL MANAGEMENT LLC, 1972

Aerospace, Defense and Security
RAFAEL DEVELOPMENT CORPORATION (RDC) LIMITED, 3063

Affordable Housing
ENHANCED CAPITAL, 679

Aftermarket Products
CAPITAL PARTNERS, 404

AgTech
FORAGE CAPITAL PARTNERS, 2115
QUAKE CAPITAL PARTNERS, 1509

Agribusiness
AMERICA FIRST INVESTMENT ADVISORS, 109
BAY CITY CAPITAL LLC, 240
CATALYST INVESTMENT MANAGERS PTY LIMITED PPM Capital, 2564
GAON ASSET MANAGEMENT, 2757
GIC GROUP, 829
INTERNATIONAL FINANCE CORPORATION (IFC), 1012
NBC CAPITAL PTY LIMITED, 2979
PAI MANAGEMENT, 3017
PENN VENTURE PARTNERS, 1431
RABO BLACK EARTH Eagle Venture Partners, 3062
SIF TRANSYLVANIA, 3110
SRIW SA SRIW Group, 3125
TRANSYLVANIA FINANCIAL INVESTMENT COMPANY, 3178

Agricultural Technologies
AVAC, 2043
BIOENTERPRISE, 2053
FIRST GREEN PARTNERS, 739

Agriculture
1ST COURSE CAPITAL, 7
AAVISHKAAR, 2305
ACUMEN, 54
AGRIBUSINESS MANAGEMENT COMPANY, 70
ALBEMARLE PRIVATE EQUITY LIMITED, 2352
ALPHAMUNDI GROUP LTD, 2368
AMERICAN SECURITIES LLC, 111
AMERICAN SUSTAINABLE BUSINESS NETWORK, 3246
ANTERRA CAPITAL, 2397
AQUAGRO FUND, 2408
ARROWHEAD INNOVATION FUND, 169
ARTHUR VENTURES, 175
BASF VENTURE CAPITAL, 2483
BIO FUND MANAGEMENT OY, 2503
BIOGENERATOR, 270
BLUESTEM CAPITAL COMPANY, 300
BOND CAPITAL, 2058
BONNEFIELD FINANCIAL, 2059
CANNA ANGELS LLC, 391
CARBON VENTURES, 411
CHINA MERCHANTS CHINA DIRECT INVESTMENTS LTD., 2585
CHRYSALIX, 2072
CLEAN PACIFIC VENTURES, 499
CREDIT MUTUEL EQUITY, 2082
CULTIVIAN SANDBOX VENTURES, 571

Industry Preference Index / All Sectors Considered

DAHER CAPITAL, 2640
EMP GLOBAL, 671
EXCEL VENTURE MANAGEMENT, 704
FARM CREDIT CANADA, 2108
FORAGE CAPITAL PARTNERS, 2115
FOX PAINE & COMPANY LLC, 781
GRANITE EQUITY PARTNERS, 855
GROVE STREET ADVISORS LLC, 884
HALLEY VENTURE PARTNERS, 900
HURON RIVER VENTURES, 964
IANTHUS CAPITAL MANAGEMENT, 970
INNOVA MEMPHIS, 999
ISRAEL CLEANTECH VENTURES, 2891
KHOSLA VENTURES, 1073
KODIAK CAPITAL, 1083
KUBOTA CORPORATION, 2918
LINN GROVE VENTURES, 1135
M25 GROUP, 1159
MERITURN PARTNERS, 1214
NAVY CAPITAL, 1282
NETROVE ASIA SDN BHD, 2984
NEXUS VENTURE PARTNERS Nexus India Capital Advisors Pvt Ltd, 2992
OBVIOUS VENTURES, 1363
PALMS & COMPANY, 1405
PANGAEA VENTURES LTD, 2205
PFM CAPITAL, 2213
ROOT CAPITAL, 1586
SAIF PARTNERS, 3084
SEAWAY VALLEY CAPITAL CORPORATION, 1642
SKYTREE CAPITAL PARTNERS, 1694
SOUTHERN CROSS VENTURE PARTNERS, 1713
SUMMIT BRIDGE CAPITAL, 3138
TRUE NORTH VENTURE PARTNERS, 1861
TSING CAPITAL, 3185
UNISON CAPITAL PARTNERS LP, 3192
US VENTURE PARTNERS, 1898
WESTCAP, 2277
WESTERN NIS ENTERPRISE FUND, 3224
YISSUM TECHNOLOGY TRANSFER, 3235
ZERNIKE SEED FUND BV, 3240

Agriculture Technologies
JC2 VENTURES, 1035

Agrochemicals
STARPHARMA POOLED DEVELOPMENT LIMITED, 3130

Air Transportation
CLIFFORD CHANCE PUNDER, 2605

Airlines
THAYER VENTURES, 1808

All Sectors Considered
21 PARTNERS, 2285
3I UK 3i Group, 2298
ABM AMRO CAPITAL FRANCE ABN AMRO Group, 2309
ACKERMANS & VAN HAAREN, 2324
ADVANTAGE PARTNERS, 2339
AGMAN PARTNERS, 69
ALCHEMY PARTNERS, 2353
ALLIANCE ENTREPRENDRE, 2360
ALLIANZ CAPITAL PARTNERS GmbH, 2362
ALMI FORETAGSPARTNER AB, 2363
ALPHA BANK, 2366
ALPHA BETEILIGUNGSBERATUNG GmbH, 2367
ARCIS GROUP, 2412
ARES CAPITAL CORPORATION, 159
ARX, 2420
AVONMORE DEVELOPMENTS, 2455
BACKSTAGE CAPITAL, 221
BARCLAYS LEVERAGED FINANCE, 2475
BERENBERG PRIVATE CAPITAL, 2493
BM-T BETEILIGUNGS MANAGEMENT THURINGEN GmbH, 2518
BRABANTSE ONTWIKKELINGSMIJ NV (BOM), 2525
BROOKS HOUGHTON & COMPANY, 355
CALGARY ENTERPRISES, 372
CATALANA D'INICIATIVES CR SA, 2561
CAYUGA VENTURE FUND, 434
CHARTERHOUSE CAPITAL PARTNERS I Charterhouse, 2578
CICLAD, 2593
CLAIRVEST GROUP, 2075
COFINEP, 2611
COLONIAL FIRST STATE PRIVATE EQUITY, 2613
COMMERZ BETEILIGUNGSGESELLSCHAFT, 2615
CONCEPT FINANCIAL SERVICES, 2618
CORVINUS NEMZETKOZI BEFEKTETESI RT Corvinus International Investment Ltd., 2625
CRESCENT CAPITAL GROUP LP, 557
D.E. SHAW & CO. LP The D.E. Shaw Group, 580
DERBYSHIRE FIRST INVESTMENTS LIMITED, 2648
DEUTSCHE ASSET & WEALTH MANAGEMENT, 2649
DEUTSCHE ASSET MANAGEMENT (AUSTRALIA) LIMITED Deutsche Bank AG, 2650
DISCOUNT INVESTMENT CORPORATION LIMITED, 2657
DOTCORP PRIVATE EQUITY FUND, 2660
E-CAPITAL MANAGEMENT, 2671
ECI VENTURES, 2678
ENTERPRISE VENTURE LIMITED, 2698
ENTERPRISE VENTURES LIMITED, 2699
EUROMEZZANINE CONSEIL, 2712
EUROPEAN ACQUISITION CAPITAL LIMITED, 2713
FAIRVIEW CAPITAL PARTNERS, 715
FINNISH INDUSTRY INVESTMENT LIMITED, 2731
FOGEL INTERNATIONAL, 761
FONDS DE SOLIDARITE FTQ, 2114
FOUR SEASONS VENTURE CAPITAL, 2745
GESTION DE CAPITAL RIESGO DEL PAIS VASCO, 2768
GIMV NV, 2772
GOLDEN VENTURES, 2131
GOLDMAN SACHS INTERNATIONAL UK, 2783
H&Q ASIA PACIFIC, 897
HANSUTTAM FINANCE LIMITED, 2802
HG CAPITAL, 2814
HSBC VENTURES UK LIMITED, 2827
IDINVEST PARTNERS, 2842
IFE CONSEIL (INTERMEDIATE FINANCE EUROPE), 2843
INTER-RISCO: SOCIEDADE DE CAPITAL DE RISCO, 2873
IPBM Group IDI, 2884
JANE VC, 1030
KK RESEARCH/KK SWISS VALUE INVESTOR, 2913
LBO FRANCE, 2924
LIGHTHOUSE PARTNERS, 1123
LOMBARD/APIC (HK) LIMITED, 2937
MAINE VENTURE FUND, 1165
MANSA CAPITAL, 1167
MERCAPITAL SA, 2953
MERIFIN CAPITAL, 2954
MILESTONE GROWTH FUND, 1233
NANYANG VENTURES PTY LIMITED, 2973
NATWEST VENTURES LIMITED, 2976
NEW VANTAGE GROUP, 1303
NORDIC CAPITAL, 2999
NORDIC MEZZANINE LIMITED, 3000
OAKTREE CAPITAL MANAGEMENT LLC, 1362
OREGON ANGEL FUND, 1384
PACIFIC EQUITY PARTNERS PTY LIMITED, 3016
PARTNERS GROUP, 3020
PENTA MEZZANINE FUND, 1433
PERFORMANCE EQUITY MANAGEMENT, LLC, 1434
PGIM PRIVATE CAPITAL, 1440
PINEBRIDGE INVESTMENTS, 1448
PROSPECT CAPITAL CORPORATION, 1493
PROVENTURE AG, 3051
QUEEN CITY ANGELS, 1514
RICHMOND GLOBAL, 1564
RMB VENTURES LIMITED RMB Australia, 3074
RUSSELL INVESTMENT MANAGEMENT LIMITED, 3080
SLOVAK AMERICAN ENTERPRISE FUND, 3113
SOCIEDAD REGIONAL DE PROMOCION DEL PRINCIPADO, 3117
SPRING MOUNTAIN CAPITAL, 1733
TAISHAN CAPITAL CORPORATION, 3147
TRELYS FUNDS, 1844

Industry Preference Index / Allied Process Industries

TRIGENTA CAPITAL GmbH, 3180
TWIN BRIDGE CAPITAL PARTNERS, 1873
UCA UNTERNEHMER CONSULT AG, 3188
UNION BANK OF SWITZERLAND, 3191
UPWELLING CAPITAL GROUP, 1894
VENTURE FUND ROTTERDAM BV Indofin Group, 3200
VIOLA VENTURES, 3212
WILSHIRE PRIVATE MARKETS, 1988
ZURCHER KANTONALBANK, 3243

Allied Process Industries
TIANGUIS LIMITED, 3169

Alternative Energy
ACI CAPITAL, 41
ANGELENO GROUP, 127
BERGGRUEN HOLDINGS, 253
BP ALTERNATIVE ENERGY VENTURES, 322
BREAKWATER INVESTMENTS, 333
CHEVRON TECHNOLOGY VENTURES, 468
CNF INVESTMENTS Clark Enterprises, Inc., 510
CROSSLINK CAPITAL, 564
EASTWARD CAPITAL PARTNERS, 646
FIRST RESERVE, 741
FRONTIER VENTURE CAPITAL, 794
INFIELD CAPITAL, 992
INTER-ASIA VENTURE MANAGEMENT LIMITED, 2872
NGEN PARTNERS, 1324
PALADIN CAPITAL GROUP, 1401
SABIC VENTURES, 3082
SOLSTICE CAPITAL LP, 1704
SPINUP VENTURE, 3123
TRELLIS CAPITAL CORPORATION, 2265
TRIANGLE PEAK PARTNERS, 1848
TROIKA CAPITAL PARTNERS, 3184

Alternative Power
ECHELON VENTURES, 647

Analysis
M12, 1158

Analytics
AMD VENTURES, 107
DENALI VENTURE PARTNERS, 606
FIRST ASCENT VENTURES, 2112
LIGHTSPEED VENTURE PARTNERS, 1125

Analytics & Analytical Instruments
AUGMENT VENTURES, 198
CHICAGO VENTURES, 473
GE VENTURES, 812
HENQ, 2813
HORIZONS VENTURES, 2822
JMH CAPITAL, 1044
PROCYON VENTURES, 1486
PROGRESS VENTURES, 1488
YL VENTURES, 3236

Ancillary Services
ELECTRA PARTNERS ASIA LIMITED SFC of Hong Kong, 2685
ENTER VENTURES, 682

Animal Health
BIOGENERATOR, 270
CULTIVIAN SANDBOX VENTURES, 571

Apparel
BREAKAWAY VENTURES, 332
BREAKWATER MANAGEMENT, 334
CERBERUS CAPITAL MANAGEMENT, 453
HOLDING CAPITAL GROUP, 943
KILMER CAPITAL PARTNERS, 2162

Apparel & Footwear
BLUE POINT CAPITAL PARTNERS, 293

Application Software
GRANITE VENTURES, 857
MOTIV PARTNERS, 1258

Applications
ANALYTICS VENTURES, 122
COATUE MANAGEMENT, 511
FIFTH WALL, 728
FOUNDER PARTNERS, 775
FUSION FUND, 802
GEODESIC CAPITAL, 824
GOOD NEWS VENTURES, 2132
INDUSTRY VENTURES, 990
JK&B CAPITAL, 1042
LOCUS VENTURES, 1142
NEW YORK VENTURE PARTNERS, 1309
NKM CAPITAL, 1330
OWL VENTURES, 1393
REACH CAPITAL, 1530
SIGNAL FIRE, 1677
SLOW VENTURES, 1696
SPERO VENTURES, 1724
SWITCH VENTURES, 1770
TEN ELEVEN VENTURES, 1796
UNCORK CAPITAL, 1881
YES VC, 2013

Applications Software & Services
APEX VENTURE PARTNERS, 138
ASSET MANAGEMENT VENTURES, 183
AUSTIN VENTURES, 205
AZURE CAPITAL PARTNERS, 218
BAKER CAPITAL, 226
BOREALIS VENTURES, 311
CHICAGO VENTURE PARTNERS LP, 472
COMCAST VENTURES, 520
COMPAGNIE FINANCIERE E DE ROTHSCHILD BANQUE, 2616
CONCORD VENTURES, 2619
CONNECTICUT INNOVATIONS, 532
FINAVENTURES, 730
FIRSTMARK CAPITAL, 744
GENERAL CATALYST PARTNERS, 820
HUMMER WINBLAD VENTURE PARTNERS, 959
INSIGHT VENTURE PARTNERS, 1005
LONGWORTH VENTURE PARTNERS, 1150
REMBRANDT VENTURE PARTNERS, 1543
SPACEVEST, 1717

Applied Mathematics
JC TECHNOLOGIES LTD, 2900

Applied Science
PATHENA, 3022

Applied Technology
GLENGARY LLC, 835
SYMMETRIC CAPITAL, 1772

Aritificial Intelligence
INTEL CAPITAL, 1009

Artificial Intelligence
11.2 CAPITAL, 3
42 VENTURES, 8
645 VENTURES, 12
ACREW CAPITAL, 48
AMPLIFY, 121
ANALYTICS VENTURES, 122
BAIDU VENTURES, 222
BASIS SET VENTURES, 235
BLUEPOINTE VENTURES, 298
BMW I VENTURES, 305
BOLDSTART VENTURES, 308
BREYER CAPITAL, 339
BRIGHTSPARK VENTURES, 2060
CARBON VENTURES, 411
CATAPULT VENTURES, 431

Industry Preference Index / Autonomous Driving

CHINAROCK CAPITAL MANAGEMENT VENTURES, 474
CHRYSALIX, 2072
COATUE MANAGEMENT, 511
COMET LABS, 521
ECLIPSE VENTURES, 648
ELYSIUM VENTURE CAPITAL, 662
FIFTH WALL, 728
FIKA VENTURES, 729
FIRST ASCENT VENTURES, 2112
FLYING FISH, 757
FREYCINET INVESTMENTS, 2120
FUSION FUND, 802
FUTURE VENTURES, 803
GEORGIAN PARTNERS, 2126
GLASSWING VENTURES, 833
GLOBALIVE, 2128
GOLDEN VENTURE PARTNERS, 2130
GOOD GROWTH CAPITAL, 849
GOOD NEWS VENTURES, 2132
GROUND UP VENTURES, 882
GV, 894
GVA CAPITAL, 895
HORIZONS VENTURES, 2822
IGAN PARTNERS, 2141
INOVIA CAPITAL, 2150
INTERLACE VENTURES, 1011
LDV CAPITAL, 1105
LOCUS VENTURES, 1142
LUGE CAPITAL, 2172
M12, 1158
MANTELLA VENTURE PARTNERS, 2176
MAPLE LEAF ANGELS, 2178
MARATHON VENTURE CAPITAL FUND LIMITED, 2945
MISTRAL VENTURE PARTNERS, 2187
MOBILE FOUNDATION VENTURES, 1243
MOTLEY FOOL VENTURES, 1259
NEW YORK VENTURE PARTNERS, 1309
NEXT CANADA, 2193
NKM CAPITAL, 1330
OUTPOST CAPITAL, 1391
PATHBREAKER VENTURES, 1423
PLAZA VENTURES, 2216
PORTAG3 VENTURES, 2217
QUAKE CAPITAL PARTNERS, 1509
QUALCOMM VENTURES, 1511
RBC CAPITAL MARKETS, 2223
SAMSUNG NEXT, 1614
SCIENCEVEST, 1633
SMARTINVEST VENTURES, 1697
SONY INNOVATION FUND, 1705
SPERO VENTURES, 1724
SUSA VENTURES, 1760
TEN ELEVEN VENTURES, 1796
THE HIVE, 1812
TOYOTA AI VENTURES, 1836
UBIQUITY VENTURES, 1879
UNCORK CAPITAL, 1881
VANEDGE CAPITAL PARTNERS, 2270
VERIZON VENTURES, 1928
WILDCAT VENTURE PARTNERS, 1985
YALETOWN VENTURE PARTNERS, 2283
ZETTA VENTURE PARTNERS, 2018

Arts
URBAN INNOVATION FUND, 1895

Asset Finance
GRESHAM PRIVATE EQUITY LIMITED, 2790

Asset Management
AMANAH VENTURES SDN BHD, 2380
CHRYSALIX, 2072
DAVIS, TUTTLE VENTURE PARTNERS LP, 592
HARBOURVEST PARTNERS LLC, 912
JW CHILDS ASSOCIATES, 1053

Assisted Living
CAMBRIDGE CAPITAL CORPORATION, 384

Audio & Video Distribution
SONY STRATEGIC TECHNOLOGY PARTNERSHIPS, 1706

Automation
ACME CAPITAL, 44
AMPLIFY, 121
AXIA CAPITAL, 214
BM-T BETEILIGUNGS MANAGEMENT THURINGEN GmbH, 2518
CATAPULT VENTURES, 431
ENERTECH CAPITAL, 677
FIKA VENTURES, 729
GROUND UP VENTURES, 882
MS&AD VENTURES, 1269
NEWABLE VENTURES, 2988
RTP VENTURES, 1598

Automotive
ALANTRA, 77
ATP PRIVATE EQUITY PARTNERS, 2438
AVIV VENTURE CAPITAL, 2453
BALTCAP MANAGEMENT LTD, 2471
BARING PRIVATE EQUITY PARTNERS ESPANA SA, 2480
BC PARTNERS LIMITED, 2488
BRIDGEPOINT CAPITAL GmbH, 2528
BRIDGEPOINT CAPITAL LIMITED, 2529
CAPVIS EQUITY PARTNERS, 2555
CARLYLE ASIA INVESTMENT ADVISORS LIMITED Carlyle Group, 2556
CARLYLE GROUP, 416
CERBERUS CAPITAL MANAGEMENT, 453
CHINA DEVELOPMENT INDUSTRIAL BANK CDFH, 2583
CLIFFORD CHANCE PUNDER, 2605
CVC ASIA PACIFIC LIMITED CVC Capital Partners, 2634
CVC CAPITAL PARTNERS LTD, 2635
DEFI GESTION SA Banque Cantonale Vaudoise, 2644
DEUTSCHE BETEILIGUNGS AG, 2651
EAST FUND MANAGEMENT GmbH GiroCredit, 2674
ECLIPSE VENTURES, 648
ELGNER GROUP INVESTMENTS, 2099
EQUISTONE, 2705
EUROVENTURES CAPITAL, 2716
FIRST ISRAEL MEZZANINE INVESTORS LIMITED, 2736
FLANDERS' FOREIGN INVESTMENT OFFICE, 2737
FOURIERTRANSFORM, 2746
FRASER MCCOMBS CAPITAL, 784
GENERAL MOTORS VENTURES, 821
HAMMOND, KENNEDY, WHITNEY & COMPANY, 904
HCI EQUITY PARTNERS, 920
IBM VENTURE CAPITAL GROUP, 971
INDUSTRIEBANK LIOF NV, 2857
JAVELIN INVESTMENTS, 2899
JORDAN COMPANY, 1049
LINSALATA CAPITAL PARTNERS, 1136
LITTLEJOHN & COMPANY LLC, 1138
M12, 1158
MOBILE FOUNDATION VENTURES, 1243
NAVIGATION CAPITAL PARTNERS, 1279
PAC-LINK MANAGEMENT CORP., 3015
PRIVATE EQUITY PARTNERS SPA, 3044
PROSPECT PARTNERS LLC, 1494
QUADRAN GESTION Deutsche Beteiligungs AG, 3058
QUALCOMM VENTURES, 1511
RESILIENCE CAPITAL PARTNERS, 1548
SERGE PUN & ASSOCIATES (MYANMAR) LIMITED, 3102
SEVEN SPIRES INVESTMENTS, 3103
STARBOARD CAPITAL PARTNERS, 1738
SUN CAPITAL PARTNERS, 1755
UNISON CAPITAL PARTNERS LP, 3192
VICKERS FINANCIAL GROUP, 3206
VOLVO GROUP VENTURE CAPITAL, 3217

Autonomous Driving
BMW I VENTURES, 305

Industry Preference Index / Autonomous Mobility

Autonomous Mobility
TOYOTA AI VENTURES, 1836

Autonomous Vehicles
INTEL CAPITAL, 1009

Aviation
COPPERLION CAPITAL, 2079
GE CAPITAL, 811
HRL MORRISON & COMPANY LIMITED, 2826
INTERMEDIATE CAPITAL GROUP PLC, 2874
JETBLUE TECHNOLOGY VENTURES, 1039
MVP CAPITAL PARTNERS, 1275
SAMBRINVEST SA, 3087

Aviation Services
ARGOSY CAPITAL, 165

B2B
ENTREPRENEURS ROUNDTABLE ACCELERATOR, 685
GCI CAPITAL, 2123
GENACAST VENTURES, 818
GOOD NEWS VENTURES, 2132
MISTRAL VENTURE PARTNERS, 2187
NAYA VENTURES, 1284
NEWLIGHT PARTNERS, 1314
RED CLAY CAPITAL HOLDINGS, 1532

B2B Services
ARGOSY CAPITAL, 165

B2B Software
FOUNDATION EQUITY CORPORATION, 2116

B2C
ANGELPAD, 129
ENTREPRENEURS ROUNDTABLE ACCELERATOR, 685

Banking
BARING PRIVATE EQUITY PARTNERS INDIA, 2481
CAMBRIDGE CAPITAL CORPORATION, 384
CHINA MERCHANTS CHINA DIRECT INVESTMENTS LTD., 2585
COLLABORATIVE FUND, 514
CROSBY CAPITAL LIMITED, 2632
EPISODE 1 PARTNERS, 2702
IBM VENTURE CAPITAL GROUP, 971
PORTAG3 VENTURES, 2217
RHB - H&F MANAGEMENT COMPANY SDN BHD RHB Capital, 3071
SHANGHAI INFORMATION INVESTMENT INCORPORATED, 3105
SIF TRANSYLVANIA, 3110
TEKINVEST KK, 3157
THOMPROPERTIES OY, 3166
TPA CORPORATE FINANCE CONSULTING GMBH Horwarth International, 3175
VALUE PARTNERS LIMITED, 3195

Beauty & Personal Care
TSG CONSUMER PARTNERS, 1863

Behavioral Health
HEALTH ENTERPRISE PARTNERS, 921

Behavioral Management
FIRST ANALYSIS, 733

Beverages
BEVERAGE MARKETING CORPORATION, 264
BRIDGEPOINT CAPITAL GmbH, 2528
BRIDGEPOINT CAPITAL LIMITED, 2529
CLIFFORD CHANCE PUNDER, 2605
INVESTMENT FUND FOR CENTRAL & EASTERN EUROPE, 2880
RABO BLACK EARTH Eagle Venture Partners, 3062
VINACAPITAL GROUP, 3208

Big Data
42 VENTURES, 8
ARCHTOP VENTURES, 155
AUGMENT VENTURES, 198
BLUEPOINTE VENTURES, 298
CORNERSTONE VENTURE PARTNERS, 544
CORSA VENTURES, 546
DRAPER ATHENA, 627
FIRST ASCENT VENTURES, 2112
G SQUARED, 805
GOOD NEWS VENTURES, 2132
GREEN TOWER CAPITAL, 866
GVA CAPITAL, 895
IMAGINATION CAPITAL, 981
INTEL CAPITAL, 1009
KHOSLA VENTURES, 1073
LIGHTSPEED VENTURE PARTNERS, 1125
M12, 1158
MIDDLEBURG CAPITAL DEVELOPMENT, 1229
MOBILE FOUNDATION VENTURES, 1243
NAYA VENTURES, 1284
NIELSEN INNOVATE FUND, 2994
O'REILLY ALPHATECH VENTURES, 1359
PROCYON VENTURES, 1486
REED ELSEVIER VENTURES, 3065
RTP VENTURES, 1598
RUBICON VENTURE CAPITAL, 1599
SINEWAVE VENTURES, 1689
SUMMIT BRIDGE CAPITAL, 3138
SUSA VENTURES, 1760

Big Data & Analytics
CISCO INVESTMENTS, 485
NFX, 1323
WORK-BENCH, 2006

Bio Materials
CVC INVESTMENT MANAGERS LIMITED, 2636
LATTERELL VENTURE PARTNERS, 1098
LIFE SCIENCES PARTNERS BV, 2930
MMT MILLENNIUM MATERIALS TECHNOLOGIES FUND LP, 2964

Biochemicals & Biomaterials
BIOINDUSTRIAL INNOVATION CANADA, 2054

Bioenergy
BIOINDUSTRIAL INNOVATION CANADA, 2054

Bioengineering
GUANGDONG TECHNOLOGY VENTURE CAPITAL COMPANY, 2793
MIRAE ASSET VENTURE ACCELERATOR Mirae Asset Group, 2960
SAMSUNG VENTURE INVESTMENT CORPORATION Samsung Electronics, 3089

Biofuel
BIOINDUSTRIAL INNOVATION CANADA, 2054

Biofuels
US RENEWABLES GROUP, 1897
VENROCK ASSOCIATES, 1918

Bioinformatics
ALLOY VENTURES, 87
CALUMET VENTURE FUND, 378
LANCET CAPITAL, 1096
NEW VENTURE PARTNERS, 1304
SAND HILL ANGELS, 1616

Biologicals
THE CHANNEL GROUP, 1811

Biomass
FORESIGHT VENTURE PARTNERS, 2740

Biomedical
BAY CITY CAPITAL LLC, 240
ENSO VENTURES, 2693
GOLDEN PINE VENTURES, 844
SPINUP VENTURE, 3123
WRF CAPITAL, 2007

Industry Preference Index / Biotechnology

Biometrics
ALTAIR VENTURES, 95
CHORD CAPITAL, 2589

Biopharmaceutical
5AM VENTURES, 11

Biopharmaceuticals
ABERDARE VENTURES, 19
ADAMS STREET PARTNERS, LLC, 56
ALTA PARTNERS, 94
APERTURE VENTURE PARTNERS, 137
APJOHN GROUP LLC, 140
ARCUS VENTURES, 158
ASCENT BIOMEDICAL VENTURES, 179
AUGURY CAPITAL PARTNERS, 199
BAY CITY CAPITAL LLC, 240
CALIFORNIA TECHNOLOGY VENTURES, 374
CARDINAL PARTNERS, 413
CATALYST FUND LP, 2562
CTI LIFE SCIENCES, 2086
DOMAIN ASSOCIATES LLC, 622
DRI CAPITAL, 2097
F-PRIME CAPITAL PARTNERS, 711
FLARE CAPITAL PARTNERS, 749
FORWARD VENTURES, 772
FRAZIER HEALTHCARE VENTURES, 785
HATTERAS VENTURE PARTNERS, 918
HEALTHCARE VENTURES LLC, 922
INNOVATION CAPITAL LIMITED, 2868
KBL HEALTHCARE VENTURES, 1062
LANCET CAPITAL, 1096
LIGHTSTONE VENTURES, 1126
LUMIRA VENTURES, 2174
MBF CAPITAL CORPORATION, 1191
MEDIPHASE VENTURE PARTNERS, 1198
MONTREUX EQUITY PARTNERS, 1251
MORGAN STANLEY EXPANSION CAPITAL, 1255
MVM LIFE SCIENCE PARTNERS, 2972
NEW ENTERPRISE ASSOCIATES, 1296
NEW LEAF VENTURE PARTNERS, 1297
NOVAQUEST CAPITAL MANAGEMENT, 1349
PAPPAS VENTURES, 1414
PROSPECT VENTURE PARTNERS, 1495
QUAKER BIOVENTURES, 1510
REX HEALTH VENTURES, 1559
RHO VENTURES, 1561
ROBIN HOOD VENTURES, 1581
SPINDLETOP CAPITAL, 1725
SYNTHESIS CAPITAL, 1777
TAKEDA VENTURES, 1780
TREVI HEALTH CAPITAL, 1846
TRIATHLON MEDICAL VENTURES, 1849
VENROCK ASSOCIATES, 1918
VENTANA CAPITAL MANAGEMENT LP, 1920

Biopolymers
NOVARTIS VENTURE FUNDS, 1350

Biosciences
CINCYTECH, 481
COTTONWOOD TECHNOLOGY FUND, 550
GIDEON HIXON FUND, 830
HALLEY VENTURE PARTNERS, 900
LIFE SCIENCES GREENHOUSE OF CENTRAL PA, 1120
MOMENTUM FUNDS MANAGEMENT PTY LIMITED, 2966

Biotech
AMORCHEM, 2031
ARROWHEAD INNOVATION FUND, 169
BIOMINDS LABS INC., 2055
CANNA ANGELS LLC, 391
FIRST CAPITAL VENTURE, 736
ICAN ISRAEL-CANNABIS.COM, 2836
KODIAK CAPITAL, 1083

Biotechnology
5AM VENTURES, 11
ABELL FOUNDATION VENTURES, 18
ABINGWORTH MANAGEMENT LIMITED, 2308
ACADIA WOODS PARTNERS, 25
ACCELERATOR LIFE SCIENCE PARTNERS, 30
ACE VENTURE CAPITAL LIMITED, 2322
ACRUX LIMITED, 2327
ADVENT VENTURE PARTNERS, 2340
AISLING CAPITAL, 73
ALBEMARLE PRIVATE EQUITY LIMITED, 2352
ALFA CAPITAL Alfa Group, 2355
ALTA BERKELEY ASSOCIATES, 2372
ALTA PARTNERS, 94
ALTRIA VENTURES, 102
AMANAH VENTURES SDN BHD, 2380
AMERICAN SUSTAINABLE BUSINESS NETWORK, 3246
AMGEN VENTURES, 113
AMKEY VENTURES, 118
AMPERSAND CAPITAL PARTNERS, 119
ANDLINGER & COMPANY INC, 124
ANNEX VENTURES, 131
ANTHEM VENTURE PARTNERS, 133
APERTURE VENTURE PARTNERS, 137
APPLE TREE PARTNERS, 144
ARBORETUM VENTURES, 150
ASTELLAS VENTURE MANAGEMENT, 184
ATHENAEUM FUND, 188
ATHYRIUM CAPITAL MANAGEMENT, 190
AUSTRALIAN ETHICAL INVESTMENT LIMITED, 2447
AVALON VENTURES, 209
AXIOM VENTURE PARTNERS, 215
AXVENTURES, 2461
AZCA, 217
BAND OF ANGELS LLC, 229
BARCELONA EMPREN, 2474
BASF VENTURE CAPITAL, 2483
BATTERSON VENTURE CAPITAL LLC, 237
BCM TECHNOLOGIES, 244
BEZOS EXPEDITIONS, 265
BIO FUND MANAGEMENT OY, 2503
BIOMED PARTNERS, 2506
BIOPACIFIC VENTURES, 2507
BIOPROCESS CAPITAL PARTNERS, 2508
BLACK DIAMOND VENTURES, 278
BOULDER VENTURES LTD, 318
BRIGHTSTONE VENTURE CAPITAL, 344
BROOK VENTURE FUND, 352
CAMBRIDGE CAPITAL CORPORATION, 384
CAMPUS COMPANIES VENTURE CAPITAL FUND, 2545
CAPRICORN VENTURE PARTNERS NV, 2554
CARE CAPITAL, 415
CATO BIOVENTURES, 432
CEDRUS INVESTMENTS, 2572
CEI VENTURES, 440
CELADON CAPITAL GROUP, 2573
CHALLENGE FUNDS - ETGAR LP, 2576
CHEVRON TECHNOLOGY VENTURES, 468
CHINA DEVELOPMENT INDUSTRIAL BANK CDFH, 2583
CHL MEDICAL PARTNERS, 476
CITA GESTION, 2598
CLARENDON FUND MANAGERS, 2601
COLT VENTURES, 517
COLUMN GROUP, 519
CONNECTICUT INNOVATIONS, 532
CONTINENTAL VENTURE CAPITAL LIMITED, 2622
CORDOVA VENTURES, 539
CORE PACIFIC - YAMAICHI CAPITAL LIMITED Core Pacific Securities Company Ltd, 2624
CRB INVERBIO, 2627
DELPHI VENTURES, 605
EDGEWATER FUNDS, 654
ENTERPRISE EQUITY (NI) LTD, 2695
ESSEX WOODLANDS HEALTH VENTURES LLC, 698
EUROPEAN INVESTMENT FUND, 2715
EXPANSION VENTURE CAPITAL, 708
EcoR1 CAPITAL, 710

Industry Preference Index / Biotechnology

FARM CREDIT CANADA, 2108
FINNVERA PLC, 2732
FLETCHER SPAGHT VENTURES, 750
FORBION CAPITAL PARTNERS, 2739
FOUNDERS FUND, 778
FRONTIER VENTURE CAPITAL, 794
GENESYS CAPITAL, 2125
GIC GROUP, 829
GIDEON HIXON FUND, 830
GIMV GIMV, 2771
GLOBAL EQUITY PARTNERS BETEILIGUNGS-MANAGEMENT, 2774
GLOBAL LIFE SCIENCE VENTURES GmbH, 2776
GOLDEN PINE VENTURES, 844
GRYPHON MANAGEMENT COMPANY, 887
HALLIM VENTURE CAPITAL, 2798
HANWHA VC CORPORATION, 2803
HARBOURVEST PARTNERS LLC, 912
HBM PARTNERS, 2806
HEALTH ENTERPRISE PARTNERS, 921
HEALTHCAP Odlander, Fredrikson & Co AB, 2807
HELMET CAPITAL FUND MANAGEMENT OY, 2811
HIGH COUNTRY VENTURE, 933
HMS HAWAII MANAGEMENT, 942
HORIZONTE VENTURE MANAGEMENT GmbH, 2823
HYUNDAI VENTURE INVESTMENT CORPORATION, 2830
ICF VENTURES PVT LTD, 2837
IDG TECHNOLOGY VENTURE INVESTMENT, 2839
INDASIA FUND ADVISORS PVT LTD, 2850
INDURAN VENTURES INC., 2145
INDUSTRIFONDEN, 2858
INITIATIVE CAPITAL LIMITED, 2147
INNOFINANCE OY, 2864
INNOVA MEMPHIS, 999
INNOVATION CAPITAL, 2867
INNOVATION CAPITAL LIMITED, 2868
INNOVATION WORKS, 1003
INTERMEDIATE CAPITAL GROUP PLC, 2874
INTERSOUTH PARTNERS, 1013
INVUS GROUP, 1022
IP GROUP, 2883
JAPAN ASIA INVESTMENT COMPANY LIMITED, 2898
JAVELIN INVESTMENTS, 2899
JF SHEA VENTURES, 1040
JOHNSON & JOHNSON INNOVATION, 1047
JOHNSTON ASSOCIATES, 1048
KBL FOUNDER SA, 2908
KEGONSA CAPITAL PARTNERS, 1064
KLEINER PERKINS, 1079
LATTERELL VENTURE PARTNERS, 1098
LEASING TECHNOLOGIES INTERNATIONAL INC., 1107
LIGHTSTONE VENTURES, 1126
LILLY VENTURES, 1128
LINK TECHNOLOGIES LIMITED, 2932
LONGITUDE CAPITAL, 1147
LRM - INVESTERINGSMAATSCHAPPIJ VOOR LIMBURG, 2940
MAINE ANGELS, 1164
MARATHON VENTURE CAPITAL FUND LIMITED, 2945
MAYFIELD FUND, 1187
MB VENTURE PARTNERS, 1190
MIDVEN, 2958
MISSION BAY CAPITAL, 1238
MITSUBISHI UFJ CAPITAL, 2961
MITSUI SUMITOMO INSURANCE VENTURE CAPITAL CO, 2962
MMT MILLENNIUM MATERIALS TECHNOLOGIES FUND LP, 2964
MOMENTUM FUNDS MANAGEMENT PTY LIMITED, 2966
MORGENTHALER VENTURES, 1257
MPM CAPITAL, 1268
NEST VENTURES, 1289
NETROVE ASIA SDN BHD, 2984
NEW SCIENCE VENTURES, 1302
NEW YORK CITY ENTREPRENEURIAL FUND New York City Economic Development Corporation, 1306
NEW YORK LIFE CAPITAL PARTNERS, 1308
NEWMARGIN VENTURE CAPITAL, 2989
NGN CAPITAL, 1325
NORTHERN ENTERPRISE LIMITED, 3002
NORTHSTAR VENTURES, 3003
NOVELTEK CAPITAL CORPORATION, 1351
NOVO A/S, 3006
OKAPI VENTURE CAPITAL, 1371
OMEGA FUNDS, 1373
OPEN PRAIRIE VENTURES, 1380
OXFORD BIOSCIENCE PARTNERS, 1395
PAPPAS VENTURES, 1414
PENN VENTURE PARTNERS, 1431
PHOSPHAGENICS, 3028
PIDC PHILADELPHIA, 1445
PITTSBURGH LIFE SCIENCES GREENHOUSE, 1452
PLEXUS VENTURES, 1456
PRAIRIEGOLD VENTURE PARTNERS, 1474
PTV SCIENCES, 1502
QUARK VENTURE, 2221
QUESTER CAPITAL MANAGEMENT LIMITED, 3061
RESEARCH CORPORATION TECHNOLOGIES, 1546
RHO VENTURES, 1561
SAMSUNG VENTURE INVESTMENT CORPORATION Samsung Electronics, 3089
SANDERLING VENTURES, 1619
SANOFI-GENZYME BIOVENTURES, 1621
SATURN PARTNERS, 1626
SCALE VENTURE PARTNERS, 1629
SCHRODER VENTURES HEALTH INVESTORS, 1631
SCIENCEVEST, 1633
SEED CAPITAL LIMITED, 3098
SHANNON COMMERCIAL PROPERTIES, 3106
SIGNATURE CAPITAL LLC, 3111
SKYLINE VENTURES, 1693
SORRENTO VENTURES, 1708
SR ONE LTD, 1734
STARBOARD CAPITAL PARTNERS, 1738
STATELINE ANGELS, 1743
STRAND HANSON LIMITED, 3137
SUTTER HILL VENTURES, 1762
SV HEALTH INVESTORS, 1764
SVB CAPITAL, 1766
SYCAMORE VENTURES, 1771
SYNTHESIS CAPITAL, 1777
TAT CAPITAL PARTNERS LTD., 3153
TECH COAST ANGELS, 1786
TECHNOLOGY PARK MALAYSIA CORPORATION SDN BHD, 3155
TERA CAPITAL CORPORATION, 2258
TEUZA MANAGEMENT & DEVELOPMENT LTD, 3162
TFG CAPITAL AG, 3163
THE CHANNEL GROUP, 1811
THOMAS, MCNERNEY & PARTNERS, 1820
TL VENTURES, 1830
TONG YANG VENTURE CAPITAL CORPORATION Tong Yang Cement Corporation, 3174
TPA CORPORATE FINANCE CONSULTING GMBH Horwarth International, 3175
TRANSATLANTIC CAPITAL LTD, 3177
TRANSITION PARTNERS LTD, 1839
TRELYS FUNDS, 1844
TULLIS HEALTH INVESTORS, 1868
TWIN CITIES ANGELS, 1874
UCA UNTERNEHMER CONSULT AG, 3188
USHA MARTIN VENTURES LIMITED, 3193
VAEKSTFONDEN, 3194
VEDANTA CAPITAL LP, 1913
VENTANA CAPITAL MANAGEMENT LP, 1920
VENTURE INVESTORS, 3201
VERSANT VENTURES, 1930
VERTICAL GROUP, 1931
VIDA VENTURES, 1934
VIVO CAPITAL, 1943
WESTERN TECHNOLOGY INVESTMENT, 1976
WI HARPER GROUP, 1983
WILMINGTON INVESTOR NETWORK, 1987
WOODSIDE FUND, 2005
WRF CAPITAL, 2007
YASUDA ENTERPRISE DEVELOPMENT COMPANY, 3233
YISSUM TECHNOLOGY TRANSFER, 3235
YUUWA CAPITAL, 3238
ZERNIKE SEED FUND BV, 3240

Industry Preference Index / Business Process Outsourcing

Biotherapeutics
SHEPHERD VENTURES, 1667

Bitcoin
500 STARTUPS, 10

Blockchain
AMPLIFY, 121
CHINAROCK CAPITAL MANAGEMENT VENTURES, 474
CHRYSALIX, 2072
DIAGRAM VENTURES, 2090
ELYSIUM VENTURE CAPITAL, 662
FGA PARTNERS, 725
FUTURE VENTURES, 803
LUGE CAPITAL, 2172
MISTRAL VENTURE PARTNERS, 2187
OUTPOST CAPITAL, 1391
OYSTER VENTURES, 1396
PANACHE VENTURES, 2204
QUAKE CAPITAL PARTNERS, 1509
SAMSUNG NEXT, 1614
SCIENCEVEST, 1633
SIGNIA VENTURE PARTNERS, 1680
THE HIVE, 1812

Blockchain/cryptocurrencies
ALTPOINT CAPITAL, 101

Branded Goods
BARING VOSTOK CAPITAL PARTNERS, 2482
BRYAN GARNIER & COMPANY, 2535
CHENGWEI VENTURES, 2581
CLEARVIEW CAPITAL, 505
EMIGRANT CAPITAL, 668
RAPTOR GROUP, 1527

Bridges
ROAD KING INFRASTRUCTURE LIMITED, 3075

Broadband
ALLEGIS CYBER CAPITAL, 84
AZURE CAPITAL PARTNERS, 218
BRAINSTORM VENTURES, 327
CENTENNIAL VENTURES, 443
CLARITY PARTNERS, 496
COLUMBIA CAPITAL, 518
COMCAST VENTURES, 520
FIRST ANALYSIS, 733
I-HATCH VENTURES LLC, 967
KOREA TECHNOLOGY & BANKING (KTB) NETWORK CORP, 2917
NORO-MOSELEY PARTNERS, 1332
PALOMAR VENTURES, 1408
SCALE VENTURE PARTNERS, 1629
SEAPOINT VENTURES, 1640
SIGNAL LAKE, 1678
WI HARPER GROUP, 1983

Broadcasting
ABU DHABI INVESTMENT AUTHORITY, 2313
AEP CAPITAL LLC, 64
ALLSTATE INVESTMENTS LLC, 88
GRUPO BISA, 2791
MACQUARIE DIRECT INVESTMENT LIMITED, 2942
MANHATTAN INVESTMENT PARTNERS, 1166
MCG CAPITAL CORPORATION, 1192
MEDIA VENTURE PARTNERS, 1197
NORTHWOOD VENTURES, 1344
RAPTOR GROUP, 1527
RENAISSANCE PARTNERS, 3068
SYCAMORE VENTURES, 1771
TIME WARNER INVESTMENT CORPORATION, 1829
VENTURE CAPITAL FUND OF NEW ENGLAND, 1922
WICKS GROUP OF COMPANIES, LLC, 1984

Brokering
AMANAH VENTURES SDN BHD, 2380
CHINA MERCHANTS CHINA DIRECT INVESTMENTS LTD., 2585

Building Innovation
GREENSOIL INVESTMENTS, 2136

Building Materials & Resources
SCOTIABANK PRIVATE EQUITY, 2241

Building Materials & Services
ALTUS CAPITAL PARTNERS, 104
AUDAX GROUP, 197
BOUNDS EQUITY PARTNERS, 319
CALERA CAPITAL, 371
CERBERUS CAPITAL MANAGEMENT, 453
DESCO CAPITAL, 607
DUBIN CLARK & COMPANY, 633
DUNEDIN CAPITAL PARTNERS LIMITED, 2668
ENTERPRISE EQUITY (NI) LTD, 2695
GEORGIA OAK PARTNERS, 825
GRAHAM PARTNERS, 851
HIG CAPITAL, 931
INDIAN DIRECT EQUITY ADVISORS PVT LTD, 2852
INDUSTRI KAPITAL SVENSKA AB, 2854
JLL PARTNERS, 1043
JMH CAPITAL, 1044
JORDAN COMPANY, 1049
KOHLBERG & COMPANY LLC, 1085
LINSALATA CAPITAL PARTNERS, 1136
MARCEAU INVESTISSEMENTS, 2946
NAVIGATION CAPITAL PARTNERS, 1279
NAVITAS CAPITAL, 1281
PALOMINO CAPITAL, 1409
SAMBRINVEST SA, 3087
STARBOARD CAPITAL PARTNERS, 1738
STONEBRIDGE PARTNERS, 1747
TRANSYLVANIA FINANCIAL INVESTMENT COMPANY, 3178
WATERMILL GROUP, 1963
XPV WATER PARTNERS, 2282

Building Products
SIGNAL HILL EQUITY PARTNERS, 2246

Building Sciences
FIFTH WALL, 728

Business
GOLDMAN SACHS INVESTMENT PARTNERS, 846

Business & Commercial Services
FIVE POINTS CAPITAL, 747

Business & Consumer Services
IMPERIAL CAPITAL, 2142
SIGNAL HILL EQUITY PARTNERS, 2246

Business & Financial Services
ADVENT INTERNATIONAL CORPORATION, 61
SPRING LAKE EQUITY PARTNERS, 1731

Business Aircraft
CIT GROUP, 486

Business Consulting
CANNA ANGELS LLC, 391

Business Intelligence
YL VENTURES, 3236

Business Model Innovation
ACME CAPITAL, 44

Business Outsourcing
LAKE CAPITAL, 1095
NORO-MOSELEY PARTNERS, 1332
TH LEE PUTNAM VENTURES, 1806

Business Process Outsourcing
CARRICK CAPITAL PARTNERS, 419

Industry Preference Index / Business Products & Services

Business Products & Services
3I EUROPE PLC 3i Group, 2292
3I GESTION SA 3i Group, 2294
3I ITALY 3i Group, 2295
3TS CAPITAL PARTNERS 3i Group plc, 2301
3i GROUP PLC, 2303
ABRY PARTNERS, 20
ABS CAPITAL PARTNERS, 21
ACI CAPITAL, 41
ACTIVA CAPITAL, 2330
ADAMS STREET PARTNERS, LLC, 56
ADLEVO CAPITAL CIM Fund Services, 2337
ADVANTAGE CAPITAL PARTNERS, 60
AEP CAPITAL LLC, 64
AIP PRIVATE CAPITAL, 2027
ALANTRA, 77
ALBION INVESTORS LLC, 78
ALERION PARTNERS, 80
ALEUTIAN CAPITAL PARTNERS, 81
ALTAMONT CAPITAL PARTNERS, 96
ANGELO, GORDON & CO., 128
APEX VENTURE PARTNERS, 138
APOLLO GLOBAL MANAGEMENT, 141
ARC ANGEL FUND, 151
ARCAPITA INC, 153
ARES MANAGEMENT LLC, 160
ARLINGTON CAPITAL PARTNERS, 167
ARROWHEAD INVESTMENT MANAGEMENT, 170
ASTELLA INVESTMENTS, 2429
AUA PRIVATE EQUITY PARTNERS, 196
AUDAX GROUP, 197
AUGUST CAPITAL, 200
AUSTIN VENTURES, 205
AZALEA CAPITAL, 216
BALMORAL FUNDS, 228
BANNEKER PARTNERS, 230
BBH CAPITAL PARTNERS, 243
BERKSHIRE PARTNERS LLC, 257
BERTRAM CAPITAL, 260
BESTPORT VENTURES, 2498
BEZOS EXPEDITIONS, 265
BIA DIGITAL PARTNERS LP, 266
BIP CAPITAL, 274
BLACKFORD CAPITAL LLC, 279
BLACKSTONE PRIVATE EQUITY GROUP, 280
BLAZER VENTURES, 283
BLUE POINT CAPITAL PARTNERS, 293
BLUEGEM CAPITAL PARTNERS, 2515
BLUESTEM CAPITAL COMPANY, 300
BOUNDS EQUITY PARTNERS, 319
BOWERY CAPITAL, 320
BRAZOS PRIVATE EQUITY PARTNERS, 331
BREAKWATER INVESTMENTS, 333
BREGAL SAGEMOUNT, 336
BRIDGE STREET CAPITAL, 341
BRIDGESCALE PARTNERS, 342
BRIGHTPATH CAPITAL PARTNERS, 343
BRYAN GARNIER & COMPANY, 2535
BRYNWOOD PARTNERS, 360
BUNKER HILL CAPITAL, 362
BUSINESS GROWTH FUND, 2541
CAI CAPITAL PARTNERS, 368
CALERA CAPITAL, 371
CALTIUS EQUITY PARTNERS, 376
CALTIUS STRUCTURED CAPITAL, 377
CALUMET VENTURE FUND, 378
CAMBRIA GROUP, 381
CAMDEN PARTNERS HOLDINGS LLC, 386
CANADIAN VENTURE CAPITAL ASSOCIATION Canadian Venture Capital & Private Equity Association, 3249
CAPITALA, 408
CARLYLE GROUP, 416
CAROUSEL CAPITAL, 418
CARPEDIA INTERNATIONAL, 2066
CATALYST INVESTORS, 429
CENTRE PARTNERS MANAGEMENT LLC, 449
CERES VENTURE FUND, 454

CHEYENNE CAPITAL, 469
CHICAGO GROWTH PARTNERS, 470
CHRYSALIS CAPITAL ChrysCapital, 2590
CI CAPITAL PARTNERS, 478
CIVC PARTNERS, 491
CLARION CAPITAL PARTNERS LLC, 494
CLARITY PARTNERS, 496
CLEARLAKE CAPITAL, 502
CLEARLIGHT PARTNERS, 503
CLEARSPRING CAPITAL PARTNERS, 2076
COLORADO MILE HIGH FUND, 516
CONCENTRIC EQUITY PARTNERS Financial Investments Corporation, 531
CONTOUR VENTURE PARTNERS, 535
CORRELATION VENTURES, 545
CSA PARTNERS, 567
CUE BALL GROUP, 568
CUSTER CAPITAL, 572
CYPRESS GROWTH CAPITAL, 577
DESJARDINS CAPITAL, 2089
DIAMOND STATE VENTURES LP, 612
EDGESTONE CAPITAL PARTNERS, 2098
EMINENT CAPITAL PARTNERS, 670
ENDEAVOUR CAPITAL, 674
ENTREE CAPITAL, 2700
EPIC VENTURES, 689
EUREKA GROWTH CAPITAL, 699
FIRST NEW ENGLAND CAPITAL LP, 740
FIVE ELMS CAPITAL, 746
FOG CITY CAPITAL, 760
FRANCISCO PARTNERS, 782
FRIEND SKOLER & COMPANY LLC, 791
FRONTENAC COMPANY, 792
FRONTIER CAPITAL, 793
FTV CAPITAL, 796
GENERAL ATLANTIC PARTNERS, 819
GENERATION PARTNERS, 822
GEORGIA OAK PARTNERS, 825
GLADSTONE CAPITAL, 832
GLENGARY LLC, 835
GLYNN CAPITAL MANAGEMENT, 840
GOENSE & COMPANY LLC, 842
GOLDNER HAWN, 847
GRAHAM PARTNERS, 851
GRANITE PARTNERS, 2133
GRYPHON INVESTORS, 886
GULFSTAR GROUP, 893
HALYARD CAPITAL, 902
HAMILTON ROBINSON CAPITAL PARTNERS, 903
HARBOUR GROUP, 911
HARREN EQUITY PARTNERS, 913
HARVEST PARTNERS, 917
HELLMAN & FRIEDMAN LLC, 927
HERITAGE PARTNERS, 929
HIG CAPITAL, 931
HORIZON VENTURES LLC, 950
HOUSATONIC PARTNERS, 952
HURON CAPITAL PARTNERS LLC, 963
ICV PARTNERS, 973
IMPLEMENT CAPITAL, 982
INDEX VENTURES, 2851
INITIAL CAPITAL, 2863
INVERNESS GRAHAM INVESTMENTS, 1018
IRISH ANGELS, 1023
IRONBRIDGE EQUITY PARTNERS, 2156
IRONWOOD CAPITAL, 1025
J. BURKE CAPITAL PARTNERS, 1027
JH WHITNEY & COMPANY, 1041
JLL PARTNERS, 1043
JMH CAPITAL, 1044
JMI EQUITY FUND LP, 1045
KERRY CAPITAL ADVISORS, 1071
KOHLBERG & COMPANY LLC, 1085
KPS CAPITAL PARTNERS, 1089
KRG CAPITAL PARTNERS, 1090
LASALLE CAPITAL GROUP, 1097
LEE EQUITY PARTNERS, 1108

Industry Preference Index / Business Services

LEEDS EQUITY PARTNERS, 1109
LEONARD GREEN & PARTNERS LP, 1113
LFE CAPITAL, 1117
LINLEY CAPITAL, 1134
LLR PARTNERS INC, 1140
LONG POINT CAPITAL, 1145
LONG RIVER VENTURES, 1146
LOVELL MINNICK PARTNERS LLC, 1151
LOVETT MILLER & COMPANY, 1152
LYNWOOD CAPITAL PARTNERS, 1156
MADISON PARKER CAPITAL, 1161
MADRONA VENTURE GROUP, 1162
MARANON CAPITAL, 1169
MARWIT CAPITAL LLC, 1171
MASON WELLS, 1174
MCG CAPITAL CORPORATION, 1192
MENTOR CAPITAL PARTNERS LTD, 1204
MIDDLEBURG CAPITAL DEVELOPMENT, 1229
MIDOCEAN PARTNERS, 1231
MIDWEST MEZZANINE FUNDS, 1232
MISSIONOG, 1240
MMC VENTURES, 2963
MONTAGU PRIVATE EQUITY LIMITED, 2968
MONTLAKE CAPITAL, 1250
MOUNTAIN GROUP CAPITAL, 1261
MPG EQUITY PARTNERS, 1267
MSOUTH EQUITY PARTNERS, 1270
MURPHY & PARTNERS FUND LP, 1274
MVP CAPITAL PARTNERS, 1275
NAUTIC PARTNERS, 1278
NAVIGATION CAPITAL PARTNERS, 1279
NEW CAPITAL PARTNERS, 1292
NEW ENGLAND CAPITAL PARTNERS, 1295
NEW MEXICO COMMUNITY CAPITAL, 1299
NEW MOUNTAIN CAPITAL, 1300
NEWSPRING CAPITAL, 1316
NEXUS VENTURE PARTNERS Nexus India Capital Advisors Pvt Ltd, 2992
NORTH AMERICAN FUND, 1333
NORTH ATLANTIC CAPITAL CORPORATION, 1334
NORTHSTAR CAPITAL, 1343
NORWEST VENTURE PARTNERS, 1346
OAK HILL CAPITAL PARTNERS, 1360
ODYSSEY INVESTMENT PARTNERS, 1368
OSAGE PARTNERS, 1388
PALLADIUM EQUITY PARTNERS, 1404
PALOMINO CAPITAL, 1409
PAMLICO CAPITAL, 1410
PARALLEL49 EQUITY, 2206
PARKVIEW CAPITAL PARTNERS, 2207
PARTHENON CAPITAL, 1419
PEACHTREE EQUITY PARTNERS, 1425
PENN VENTURE PARTNERS, 1431
PFINGSTEN PARTNERS LLC, 1438
PIVOTNORTH CAPITAL, 1454
PNC RIVERARCH CAPITAL, 1461
POLARIS VENTURE PARTNERS, 1464
POST CAPITAL PARTNERS, 1469
POUSCHINE COOK CAPITAL MANAGEMENT LLC, 1470
PRAIRIE CAPITAL, 1473
PRIVEQ CAPITAL FUNDS, 2218
QUARRY CAPITAL MANAGEMENT, 1513
RBC CAPITAL MARKETS, 2223
REDMONT VENTURE PARTNERS, 1536
RIDGE CAPITAL PARTNERS LLC, 1565
RIVER ASSOCIATES INVESTMENTS LLC, 1573
RIVER CAPITAL, 1574
RLH EQUITY PARTNERS, 1579
ROARK CAPITAL GROUP, 1580
ROBIN HOOD VENTURES, 1581
ROCK ISLAND CAPITAL, 1582
ROPART ASSET MANAGEMENT, 1587
ROTH CAPITAL PARTNERS, 1592
SALEM INVESTMENT PARTNERS, 1609
SALT CREEK CAPITAL, 1612
SATORI CAPITAL, 1625
SEACOAST CAPITAL CORPORATION, 1639
SEAPORT CAPITAL, 1641
SENTINEL CAPITAL PARTNERS, 1654
SIGMA PARTNERS, 1674
SILVER OAK SERVICES PARTNERS, 1686
SJF VENTURES, 1691
SOUTHEAST INTERACTIVE TECHNOLOGY FUNDS, 1711
SPECTRUM EQUITY INVESTORS LP, 1720
SPIRE CAPITAL PARTNERS, 1727
SPLIT ROCK PARTNERS, 1728
SSM PARTNERS, 1735
STAENBERG VENTURE PARTNERS, 1736
STATELINE ANGELS, 1743
STERLING PARTNERS, 1745
STONEHENGE GROWTH CAPITAL, 1748
STONEWOOD CAPITAL MANAGEMENT, 1749
SUMMIT PARTNERS, 1754
SUN CAPITAL PARTNERS, 1755
SUNBRIDGE PARTNERS, 1757
SV INVESTMENT PARTNERS, 1765
SVOBODA CAPITAL PARTNERS, 1767
SYMMETRIC CAPITAL, 1772
TA ASSOCIATES, 1778
TAILWIND CAPITAL, 1779
TENNESSEE COMMUNITY VENTURES, 1799
THAYER STREET PARTNERS, 1807
THOMA BRAVO LLC, 1817
THOMAS H LEE PARTNERS, 1818
TL VENTURES, 1830
TOBA CAPITAL, 1831
TORQUEST PARTNERS, 2264
TRIDENT CAPITAL, 1852
TRILANTIC CAPITAL PARTNERS, 1853
TRIVEST PARTNERS, 1859
TRIWEST, 2267
TWJ CAPITAL, 1875
UNION CAPITAL CORPORATION, 1883
UPDATA VENTURE PARTNERS, 1888
VALOR EQUITY PARTNERS, 1904
VEBER PARTNERS LLC, 1911
VENCORE CAPITAL, 1917
VERONIS SUHLER STEVENSON, 1929
VORTEX PARTNERS, 1946
WALNUT GROUP, 1955
WARBURG PINCUS LLC, 1957
WATERMILL GROUP, 1963
WAVELAND INVESTMENTS LLC, 1965
WELSH, CARSON, ANDERSON & STOWE, 1973
WESTERN AMERICA CAPITAL GROUP, 2278
WESTLAKE SECURITIES, 1977
WESTVIEW CAPITAL PARTNERS, 1979
WHEATLEY PARTNERS, 1981
WOODBRIDGE GROUP, 2004
WYNNCHURCH CAPITAL, 2008
XANGE PRIVATE EQUITY, 3229
YELLOW POINT EQUITY PARTNERS, 2284
YFM GROUP, 3234
ZURMONT MADISON PRIVATE EQUITY, 3244

Business Services

ALPINE INVESTORS, 92
BISON CAPITAL ASSET MANAGEMENT LLC, 277
BLUE HERON CAPITAL, 291
BOSTON MILLENNIA PARTNERS, 315
BRANFORD CASTLE, 330
BV INVESTMENT PARTNERS, 364
CAPITAL RESOURCE PARTNERS, 405
CENTURY PARK CAPITAL PARTNERS, 451
CVF CAPITAL PARTNERS, 574
EPIC PARTNERS, 688
FISHER LYNCH CAPITAL, 745
GRANTHAM CAPITAL, 858
HAWTHORN EQUITY PARTNERS, 919
HUNTSMAN GAY GLOBAL CAPITAL, 962
PENDER WEST CAPITAL PARTNERS, 2210
PENFUND, 2211
RIVERSIDE COMPANY, 1576
SAGEVIEW CAPITAL, 1606

Industry Preference Index / Business Software

W CAPITAL PARTNERS, 1949

Business Software
BENHAMOU GLOBAL VENTURES, 252
ISOURCE GESTION, 2890
SILICON ALLEY VENTURE PARTNERS, 1682

Business Technology
RALLY VENTURES, 1525
WING VENTURE PARTNERS, 1996

Business to Business
ABU DHABI INVESTMENT AUTHORITY, 2313
ACCENTURE TECHNOLOGY VENTURES, 2318
ACTUA, 52
ADAMS STREET PARTNERS, LLC, 56
AEA INVESTORS, 63
ALEXANDER HUTTON, 82
ARGOSY CAPITAL, 165
ARLINGTON CAPITAL PARTNERS, 167
ARSENAL CAPITAL PARTNERS, 172
ARTIMAN VENTURES, 176
BAIRD CAPITAL PARTNERS, 225
BARCLAYS VENTURES Barclays, 2477
BEE PARTNERS, 246
BLU VENTURE INVESTORS, 288
BMP AKTIENGESELLSCHAFT BMP Venture Capital, 2519
BONFIRE VENTURES, 309
BOSTON CAPITAL VENTURES, 313
BOSTON SEED CAPITAL, 316
BRENTWOOD ASSOCIATES, 337
BRUML CAPITAL CORPORATION, 358
C3 CAPITAL PARTNERS LP, 367
CAPITAL MIDWEST FUND, 403
CAPITAL PARTNERS, 404
CARLYLE ASIA INVESTMENT ADVISORS LIMITED Carlyle Group, 2556
CATALYST INVESTMENT MANAGERS PTY LIMITED PPM Capital, 2564
CCP EQUITY PARTNERS, 436
CEI VENTURES, 440
CENTERFIELD CAPITAL PARTNERS, 445
CEO VENTURES, 452
CERVIN VENTURES, 456
CHICAGO VENTURES, 473
CHRYSALIS CAPITAL ChrysCapital, 2590
CHRYSCAPITAL MANAGEMENT COMPANIES ChrysCapital, 2591
CINVEN LIMITED, 2596
CLOSE BROTHERS PRIVATE EQUITY Close Brothers Group, 2608
CORTEC GROUP, 547
CRYSTAL RIDGE PARTNERS, 566
DAVID N DEUTSCH & COMPANY LLC, 590
DFW CAPITAL PARTNERS, 611
DIAMONDHEAD VENTURES, 614
DIRECT CAPITAL PRIVATE EQUITY LIMITED, 2655
DUKE STREET CAPITAL Duke Street, 2667
EDGEWATER FUNDS, 654
EM WARBURG, PINCUS & COMPANY INTERNATIONAL, 2688
EM WARBURG, PINCUS & COMPANY JAPAN, 2689
EMIGRANT CAPITAL, 668
ENTER VENTURES, 682
ENTREPRENEUR PARTNERS, 684
ENTREPRENEURS ROUNDTABLE ACCELERATOR, 685
EOS PARTNERS LP, 687
EVERGREEN ADVISORS, 702
FGA PARTNERS, 725
FLOODGATE FUND, 752
FLORIDA CAPITAL PARTNERS, 753
FOUNDER COLLECTIVE, 774
FOUNDERS EQUITY, 777
FRANKLIN STREET EQUITY PARTNERS, 783
FRIEDMAN, FLEISCHER & LOWE LLC, 790
FRONTLINE VENTURES, 2750
FdG ASSOCIATES LP, 804
G-51 CAPITAL LLC, 806
GEMINI INVESTORS, 815
GENACAST VENTURES, 818
GENERATION PARTNERS, 822
GILBERT GLOBAL EQUITY PARTNERS, 831
GLENCOE CAPITAL, 834
GRANVILLE BAIRD CAPITAL PARTNERS, 2786
GRAYHAWK CAPITAL, 861
GREAT HILL PARTNERS LLC, 862
GROTECH VENTURES, 881
GRUPO BISA, 2791
GTCR, 889
HAMILTON ROBINSON CAPITAL PARTNERS, 903
HOLLAND VENTURE BV, 2819
HORIZON PARTNERS, LTD, 948
HUMMER WINBLAD VENTURE PARTNERS, 959
HYDE PARK VENTURE PARTNERS, 965
IRON GATE CAPITAL, 1024
ISIS EP LLP F & C, 2889
LIGHTBANK, 1121
LINSALATA CAPITAL PARTNERS, 1136
LOMBARD INVESTMENTS, 1143
LONGWORTH VENTURE PARTNERS, 1150
MERIT CAPITAL PARTNERS, 1210
MURPHREE VENTURE PARTNERS, 1273
NAYA VENTURES, 1284
NESBIC INVESTMENT FUND II, 2983
NEW MOUNTAIN CAPITAL, 1300
NEWBURY, PIRET & COMPANY, 1311
NEWLIGHT MANAGEMENT, 1313
NORTH DAKOTA DEVELOPMENT FUND, 1338
NORWEST EQUITY PARTNERS, 1345
NTH POWER TECHNOLOGIES, 1355
NUTEK (NARINGS- OCH TEKNIKUTVECKLINGSVERKET) NUTEK, 3007
ODEON CAPITAL PARTNERS, 1367
OLYMPUS PARTNERS, 1372
ORIGIN VENTURES, 1385
OUTLOOK VENTURES, 1390
PALOMAR VENTURES, 1408
PARADIGM CAPITAL LTD, 1416
PARALLEL INVESTMENT PARTNERS, 1417
PENNELL VENTURE PARTNERS LLC, 1432
PERMIRA Permira Advisers LLP, 3024
PRIMUS CAPITAL, 1480
PROGRESS VENTURES, 1488
QUANTUM CAPITAL PARTNERS, 1512
REITEN & CO STRATEGIC INVESTMENTS AS Reiten & Company, 3067
REVO CAPITAL, 3069
SCHOONER CAPITAL LLC, 1630
SEAPORT CAPITAL, 1641
SHASTA VENTURES, 1666
SOFTBANK CAPITAL, 1701
SPRING CAPITAL PARTNERS LP, 1730
STARVEST PARTNERS, 1741
STRIPES GROUP, 1751
TECHOPERATORS, 1790
VOYAGER CAPITAL, 1947
WALL STREET VENTURE CAPITAL, 1954
WEDBUSH CAPITAL PARTNERS, 1970
WESTTECH VENTURES, 3226
WICKS GROUP OF COMPANIES, LLC, 1984
WIND POINT PARTNERS, 1990
WINGATE PARTNERS, 1997
ZS FUND LP, 2021

Business to Consumer
ENTREPRENEURS ROUNDTABLE ACCELERATOR, 685

Cable
ALLSTATE INVESTMENTS LLC, 88
ANDERSON PACIFIC CORPORATION, 123
ELECTRA PARTNERS ASIA LIMITED SFC of Hong Kong, 2685
FORUM TECHNOLOGIES VENTURE CAPITAL COMPANY Forum Group, 2742
GRUPO BISA, 2791
MACQUARIE DIRECT INVESTMENT LIMITED, 2942
NEOMARKKA OYJ Neomarkka, 2981
SPACEVEST, 1717

Industry Preference Index / Chemicals

TIME WARNER INVESTMENT CORPORATION, 1829
VENTURE CAPITAL FUND OF NEW ENGLAND, 1922
WICKS GROUP OF COMPANIES, LLC, 1984

Cannabis
ACKRELL CAPITAL, 43
ALTITUDE INVESTMENT MANAGEMENT, LLC, 99
ANCIENT STRAINS, 2033
ARCADIAN FUND, 152
ARCHYTAS VENTURES, 156
AUSTRALIS CAPITAL, 206
BASE VENTURES, 232
BLAST FUNDING, 282
BREAKWATER MANAGEMENT, 334
CANALIS CAPITAL, 2546
CANNA ANGELS LLC, 391
CANNABIS CAPITAL, 392
CANNABIS CAPITAL GROWTH, 393
CANNABIS STRATEGIC VENTURES, 394
CANOPY BOULDER, 395
CASA VERDE CAPITAL, 420
CBIý CAPITAL, 2068
CJV CAPITAL, 492
CRESCO CAPITAL PARTNERS, 558
CULTIVATE CAPITAL, 569
DOVENTI CAPITAL, 2095
DUTCHESS CAPITAL, 638
EMERALD OCEAN CAPITAL, 665
FIRST CAPITAL VENTURE, 736
FOUNDATION MARKETS, 2117
FRESH VC, 788
GOLDEN OPPORTUNITIES FUND, 2129
GOTHAM GREEN PARTNERS, 850
GREEN ACRE CAPITAL, 2134
GREEN LION PARTNERS, 865
GREEN TOWER CAPITAL, 866
GREENHOUSE VENTURES, 871
GROVE GROUP MANAGEMENT, 883
HALLEY VENTURE PARTNERS, 900
HOUSTON HEALTH VENTURES, 954
HYPUR VENTURES, 966
IANTHUS CAPITAL MANAGEMENT, 970
ICAN ISRAEL-CANNABIS.COM, 2836
INITIATIVE CAPITAL LIMITED, 2147
JW ASSET MANAGEMENT, 1052
KODIAK CAPITAL, 1083
LGC CAPITAL, 2167
LIZADA CAPITAL LLC, 1139
MCGOVERN CAPITAL, 1194
MERIDA CAPITAL PARTNERS, 1208
NAVY CAPITAL, 1282
PHYTO PARTNERS, 1443
POSEIDON ASSET MANAGEMENT, 1468
PRIVATEER HOLDINGS, 1484
REEFI CAPITAL, 1540
RIV CAPITAL, 2233
SALVEO CAPITAL, 1613
SERRUYA PRIVATE EQUITY, 2245
SKYTREE CAPITAL PARTNERS, 1694
SLOW VENTURES, 1696
TENX VENTURES, 2257
THE ARCVIEW GROUP, 1810
TRESS CAPITAL LLC, 1845
TUATARA CAPITAL, 1866
WHITE SHEEP CORP, 2279

Capital Equipment
ELGNER GROUP INVESTMENTS, 2099
FCF PARTNERS LP, 719

Capital Goods
NEW MOUNTAIN CAPITAL, 1300
RESILIENCE CAPITAL PARTNERS, 1548

Capital Markets
INFORMATION VENTURE PARTNERS, 2146

Carbon Management
BP ALTERNATIVE ENERGY VENTURES, 322

Cargo Handling
NEW WORLD INFRASTRUCTURE LIMITED, 2987

Carpet Yarn
LRM - INVESTERINGSMAATSCHAPPIJ VOOR LIMBURG, 2940

Carriers
ANDERSON PACIFIC CORPORATION, 123
EQT PARTNERS AB, 2703

Cellular Communications
QUAKE CAPITAL PARTNERS, 1509

Cellular Service & Products
ANDERSON PACIFIC CORPORATION, 123
PT BHAKTI INVESTAMA TBK, 3052

Cement Roofing
KUBOTA CORPORATION, 2918
RABO BLACK EARTH Eagle Venture Partners, 3062

Ceramic Tiles
PRIVATE EQUITY PARTNERS SPA, 3044

Chemicals
3I TEUPSCHLAND GmbH 3i Group, 2297
ACTIS, 2329
AEA INVESTORS, 63
AKERS CAPITAL LLC, 74
ALBEMARLE PRIVATE EQUITY LIMITED, 2352
ALLSTATE INVESTMENTS LLC, 88
AMADEUS CAPITAL PARTNERS LIMITED, 2378
AMPERSAND CAPITAL PARTNERS, 119
ANDLINGER & COMPANY INC, 124
APOLLO GLOBAL MANAGEMENT, 141
APPLE TREE PARTNERS, 144
ARROWHEAD INVESTMENT MANAGEMENT, 170
ATHENAEUM FUND, 188
ATRIUM CAPITAL, 194
AUSTIN CAPITAL PARTNERS LP, 204
AVENUE CAPITAL GROUP, 211
AZCA, 217
BASF VENTURE CAPITAL, 2483
BIO FUND MANAGEMENT OY, 2503
BLUE POINT CAPITAL PARTNERS, 293
BRANFORD CASTLE, 330
BRIDGEPOINT CAPITAL GmbH, 2528
BRIDGEPOINT CAPITAL LIMITED, 2529
BROOK VENTURE FUND, 352
BRUML CAPITAL CORPORATION, 358
C3 CAPITAL PARTNERS LP, 367
CANDOVER, 2547
CAPVIS EQUITY PARTNERS, 2555
CENTURY PARK CAPITAL PARTNERS, 451
CLIFFORD CHANCE PUNDER, 2605
CVC ASIA PACIFIC LIMITED CVC Capital Partners, 2634
CVC CAPITAL PARTNERS LTD, 2635
DAVID N DEUTSCH & COMPANY LLC, 590
EAST FUND MANAGEMENT GmbH GiroCredit, 2674
ECI VENTURES, 2678
EDGEWATER CAPITAL PARTNERS, 653
ELECTRA PARTNERS ASIA LIMITED SFC of Hong Kong, 2685
ELEMENT PARTNERS, 658
EMIGRANT CAPITAL, 668
ENTERPRISE EQUITY (NI) LTD, 2695
EQT PARTNERS AB, 2703
EQUISTONE, 2705
EQVITEC PARTNERS OY, 2707
FIRST ANALYSIS, 733
FLANDERS' FOREIGN INVESTMENT OFFICE, 2737
FRIULIA SpA, 2749
GLENCOE CAPITAL, 834
GLENTHORNE CAPITAL, 836
INNOFINANCE OY, 2864

Industry Preference Index / Chemicals & Advanced Materials

INTERNATIONAL FINANCE CORPORATION (IFC), 1012
INVESTMENT FUND FOR CENTRAL & EASTERN EUROPE, 2880
IP GROUP, 2883
JAVELIN INVESTMENTS, 2899
KELSO & COMPANY, 1066
KHOSLA VENTURES, 1073
KOHLBERG KRAVIS ROBERTS & COMPANY, 1086
LITTLEJOHN & COMPANY LLC, 1138
LOMBARD INVESTMENTS, 1143
MERITURN PARTNERS, 1214
MONTAGU PRIVATE EQUITY LIMITED, 2968
NORTHERN ENTERPRISE LIMITED, 3002
ONE EQUITY PARTNERS, 1376
PAI MANAGEMENT, 3017
PARKWALK ADVISORS, 3019
PERMIRA Permira Advisers LLP, 3024
RESILIENCE CAPITAL PARTNERS, 1548
SCOTTISH ENTERPRISE, 3094
SEED CAPITAL LIMITED, 3098
SIF TRANSYLVANIA, 3110
SPELL CAPITAL PARTNERS LLC, 1722
SRIW SA SRIW Group, 3125
TIANGUIS LIMITED, 3169
TORQUEST PARTNERS, 2264
TRANSYLVANIA FINANCIAL INVESTMENT COMPANY, 3178
WATERMILL GROUP, 1963
YISSUM TECHNOLOGY TRANSFER, 3235

Chemicals & Advanced Materials
CHRYSALIX, 2072

Chemistry
TELEGRAPH HILL PARTNERS, 1794

Child Care
OWL VENTURES, 1393

Childcare
NEXT EQUITIES, 2194

Children
COLLABORATIVE FUND, 514

Civic Technology
DECIENS CAPITAL, 600

Clean Energy
ALTRIA VENTURES, 102
ARCTERN VENTURES, 2037
BERKELEY VENTURES, 256
BMW I VENTURES, 305
BRIGHTPATH CAPITAL PARTNERS, 343
EARTHRISE CAPITAL, 643
ENERTECH CAPITAL, 677
GENERAL CATALYST PARTNERS, 820
MACKINNON, BENNETT & CO., 2175
SIERRA ANGELS, 1671
TERA CAPITAL CORPORATION, 2258
TOP RENERGY INC., 2263

Clean Environment
VENTUREAST, 3202

Clean Tech
GOOD GROWTH CAPITAL, 849

Clean Technology
350 INVESTMENT PARTNERS, 2287
360 CAPITAL PARTNERS 360 Capital Management SA, 2288
3TS CAPITAL PARTNERS 3i Group plc, 2301
ABB TECHNOLOGY VENTURES, 2307
ACCESS VENTURE PARTNERS LLC, 35
ACERO CAPITAL, 40
ACME LABS, 2325
ACTIVE VENTURE PARTNERS, 2331
ADAMS STREET PARTNERS, LLC, 56
ADARA VENTURE PARTNERS, 2334
ADVANCED TECHNOLOGY VENTURES, 58
ADVANTAGE CAPITAL PARTNERS, 60
AIP PRIVATE CAPITAL, 2027
ALBERTA ENTERPRISE, 2028
ALLIANCE OF ANGELS, 85
ALLOY VENTURES, 87
AMMER PARTNERS, 2385
AMPLIFIER VENTURE PARTNERS, 120
ANDLINGER & COMPANY INC, 124
ANGELS' FORUM LLC, 130
APEX VENTURE PARTNERS, 138
AQUAGRO FUND, 2408
ARAVAIPA VENTURES, 147
ARCH VENTURE PARTNERS, 154
ASTER CAPITAL, 2430
AURUM VENTURES MKI, 2445
AVIV VENTURE CAPITAL, 2453
AXVENTURES, 2461
BATTERY VENTURES, 238
BERINGEA, 254
BERTI INVESTMENTS, 2496
BEST FUNDS, 2051
BEZOS EXPEDITIONS, 265
BIG SUR VENTURES, 2501
BIRCHMERE VENTURES, 275
BLACK DIAMOND VENTURES, 278
BP ALTERNATIVE ENERGY VENTURES, 322
BRIGHTSTONE VENTURE CAPITAL, 344
BUSINESS GROWTH FUND, 2541
CALCEF CLEAN ENERGY FUND, 370
CANADIAN VENTURE CAPITAL ASSOCIATION Canadian Venture Capital & Private Equity Association, 3249
CATHAYA CAPITAL, 2567
CDH INVESTMENTS, 2570
CEDAR FUND, 438
CEDRUS INVESTMENTS, 2572
CELADON CAPITAL GROUP, 2573
CHINA ISRAEL VALUE CAPITAL, 2584
CLEAN ENERGY VENTURE GROUP, 498
CLEAN PACIFIC VENTURES, 499
CLEANTECH INVEST, 2603
CLEANTECH VENTURES, 2604
CLIMATE CHANGE CAPITAL, 2606
COLORADO MILE HIGH FUND, 516
CONNECTICUT INNOVATIONS, 532
CORRELATION VENTURES, 545
COTTONWOOD TECHNOLOGY FUND, 550
COUNCIL FOR ENTREPRENEURIAL DEVELOPMENT, 3250
CREATHOR VENTURE, 2629
CYCLE CAPITAL MANAGEMENT, 2087
DALLAS VENTURE PARTNERS, 583
DAVENPORT RESOURCES LLC, 589
DBL PARTNERS, 596
DOUGHTY HANSON & CO., 2662
DRAPER ATHENA, 627
DYNAMO VC, 640
EARLY STAGE PARTNERS, 642
EARLYBIRD, 2673
EASTWARD CAPITAL PARTNERS, 646
ECOSYSTEM VENTURES, 650
ELEMENT PARTNERS, 658
EMERALD TECHNOLOGY VENTURES, 2101
ENTREPRENEURS FUND, 2701
EPIC VENTURES, 689
ESPIRITO SANTO VENTURES, 2708
EVOK INNOVATIONS, 2105
EXPANSION CAPITAL PARTNERS, 707
FIRST ANALYSIS, 733
FIRST STEP FUND, 743
FLYWHEEL VENTURES, 758
FOUNDATION CAPITAL, 773
FUEL CAPITAL, 2752
FUNK VENTURES, 800
GABRIEL VENTURE PARTNERS, 808
GARAGE TECHNOLOGY VENTURES, 810
GENERAL MOTORS VENTURES, 821
GLOBESPAN CAPITAL PARTNERS, 839
GRAY GHOST VENTURES, 860

Industry Preference Index / Cloud Computing

HARBOR LIGHT CAPITAL PARTNERS, 910
HELION VENTURE PARTNERS, LLC International Management (Mauritius) Ltd, 2809
HERCULES TECHNOLOGY GROWTH CAPITAL, INC, 928
HIGH COUNTRY VENTURE, 933
HIGH-TECH GRUENDERFONDS, 2815
HORIZON TECHNOLOGY FINANCE, 949
ICON VENTURES, 972
IDEALAB, 976
IGLOBE PARTNERS, 2844
ILLINOIS VENTURES, 979
INBC INVESTMENT CORP, 2144
INCWELL VENTURE CAPITAL, 985
INDEPENDENCE EQUITY, 987
INETWORKS ADVISORS LLC, 991
INFIELD CAPITAL, 992
INLAND TECHSTART FUND, 997
INNOVATION CAPITAL LIMITED, 2868
ISRAEL CLEANTECH VENTURES, 2891
KEIRETSU FORUM, 1065
KINETIC VENTURES, 1076
KOHLBERG VENTURES, 1087
LEGEND CAPITAL, 2927
LINLEY CAPITAL, 1134
LLOYDS DEVELOPMENT CAPITAL LIMITED, 2935
LONG RIVER VENTURES, 1146
MAINE ANGELS, 1164
MARS INVESTMENT ACCELERATOR FUND, 2181
MASS VENTURES, 1175
MATRIX PARTNERS, 1184
MINDFULL INVESTORS, 1236
MMC VENTURES, 2963
MMV CAPITAL PARTNERS, 2188
MOHR-DAVIDOW VENTURES, 1247
MOTIV PARTNERS, 1258
MOUNTAIN PARTNERS, 2970
NAUSICAA VENTURES, 2977
NAVITAS CAPITAL, 1281
NEEDHAM CAPITAL PARTNERS, 1287
NEO TECHNOLOGY VENTURES, 2980
NEW VENTURE PARTNERS, 1304
NGEN PARTNERS, 1324
NORTHERN LIGHT VENTURE CAPITAL, 1340
NOVA SCOTIA BUSINESS INC., 2197
NOVENTI VENTURES, 1352
ONTARIO CAPITAL GROWTH CORPORATION, 2203
OneVentures, 3014
PANGAEA VENTURES LTD, 2205
PARKWALK ADVISORS, 3019
PARTNERSHIP FUND FOR NEW YORK CITY, 1422
PINNACLE VENTURES, 1449
PITANGO VENTURE CAPITAL, 3030
PMV, 3033
POINT JUDITH CAPITAL, 1463
PRAIRIEGOLD VENTURE PARTNERS, 1474
PRESIDIO VENTURES, 1478
QBIC FUND, 3056
QIMING VENTURE PARTNERS, 3057
RED DOT VENTURES, 3064
RENEWABLETECH VENTURES, 1545
RESERVOIR VENTURE PARTNERS, 1547
ROADMAP CAPITAL INC., 2234
ROCKPORT CAPITAL, 1583
ROTH CAPITAL PARTNERS, 1592
SABIC VENTURES, 3082
SAFFRON HILL VENTURES, 3083
SAIF PARTNERS, 3084
SAIL VENTURE PARTNERS, 1607
SAMOS INVESTMENTS, 3088
SAND HILL ANGELS, 1616
SB CHINA VENTURE CAPITAL, 3091
SCOTTISH EQUITY PARTNERS, 3095
SEQUEL VENTURE PARTNERS, 1656
SIGMA PARTNERS, 1674
SJF VENTURES, 1691
SOLSTICE CAPITAL LP, 1704
SPINUP VENTURE, 3123

SUMMIT BRIDGE CAPITAL, 3138
SUNBRIDGE PARTNERS, 1757
SUPREMUM CAPITAL, 3141
SVB CAPITAL, 1766
TANDEM EXPANSION FUND, 2252
TAO VENTURE CAPITAL PARTNERS, 1782
TECH COAST ANGELS, 1786
TECHNOLOGY PARTNERS, 1788
TENAYA CAPITAL, 1798
TERALYS CAPITAL, 2259
TIE ANGELS GROUP SEATTLE, 1827
TRELLIS CAPITAL CORPORATION, 2265
TRIANGLE VENTURE CAPITAL GROUP, 3179
TROIKA CAPITAL PARTNERS, 3184
TSING CAPITAL, 3185
TYLT LAB, 1878
VANTAGEPOINT CAPITAL PARTNERS, 1908
VENTURE INVESTORS LLC, 1923
VERGE FUND, 1926
VIKING VENTURE, 3207
WAVEPOINT VENTURES, 1967
WESTLY GROUP, 1978
WESTSUMMIT CAPITAL, 3225
WI HARPER GROUP, 1983
XANGE PRIVATE EQUITY, 3229
XSEED CAPITAL MANAGEMENT, 2010
YALETOWN VENTURE PARTNERS, 2283
YISSUM TECHNOLOGY TRANSFER, 3235
YUUWA CAPITAL, 3238
ZOUK VENTURES, 3242

Clean Transportation
ANGELENO GROUP, 127

Cleantech
ECAPITAL ENTREPRENEURIAL PARTNERS AG, 2677
PANACHE VENTURES, 2204

Clinical Development
BALTCAP MANAGEMENT LTD, 2471

Clinical Research
FIRST ANALYSIS, 733

Cloud
CORNERSTONE VENTURE PARTNERS, 544
WILDCAT VENTURE PARTNERS, 1985

Cloud Computing
10X VENTURE PARTNERS, 2
212 CAPITAL PARTNERS, 2286
42 VENTURES, 8
ACCESS VENTURE PARTNERS LLC, 35
ACUMEN VENTURES, 2333
AMITI VENTURES, 117
ARTIS VENTURES, 177
ATLANTIC BRIDGE, 2434
AUGMENT VENTURES, 198
AZURE CAPITAL PARTNERS, 218
BASECAMP VENTURES, 233
BENCHMARK, 251
BESSEMER VENTURE PARTNERS, 263
BEST FUNDS, 2051
BIG SUR VENTURES, 2501
BREGAL SAGEMOUNT, 336
BRIGHTSTONE VENTURE CAPITAL, 344
CAMP ONE VENTURES, 387
CATALYST INVESTORS, 429
CHARLES RIVER VENTURES, 457
CONVERGE VENTURE PARTNERS, 536
CONVEXA Tyveholmen AS, 2623
CORSA VENTURES, 546
DATA COLLECTIVE, 586
DELL VENTURES, 604
DENALI VENTURE PARTNERS, 606
DIVERGENT VENTURES, 619
DOUBLEROCK VENTURE CAPITAL, 626
EDBI Pte LTD., 2681

Industry Preference Index / Cloud Data

EMERGENCE CAPITAL PARTNERS, 666
FIDELITY GROWTH PARTNERS EUROPE, 2725
FIRST ASCENT VENTURES, 2112
FLYING FISH, 757
FOUNDATION CAPITAL, 773
G SQUARED, 805
GEORGIAN PARTNERS, 2126
GGV CAPITAL, 827
GOOD GROWTH CAPITAL, 849
GRAYHAWK CAPITAL, 861
GREAT OAKS VENTURE CAPITAL, 863
GROVE STREET ADVISORS LLC, 884
HUMMER WINBLAD VENTURE PARTNERS, 959
ICON VENTURES, 972
ID VENTURES AMERICA LLC, 974
INLAND TECHSTART FUND, 997
IRISH ANGELS, 1023
LIONBIRD, 2934
MERCURY FUND, 1207
NAYA VENTURES, 1284
NEW ENTERPRISE ASSOCIATES, 1296
NORTHZONE, 3004
NOTION CAPITAL, 3005
REVO CAPITAL, 3069
RTP VENTURES, 1598
RUBICON VENTURE CAPITAL, 1599
RUNA CAPITAL, 3079
RUNTIDE CAPITAL, 1600
SALESFORCE VENTURES, 1610
SEVEN PEAKS VENTURES, 1659
SIGMA PRIME VENTURES, 1675
SINEWAVE VENTURES, 1689
SPARK CAPITAL, 1718
SUMMERHILL VENTURE PARTNERS, 2250
SUMMIT BRIDGE CAPITAL, 3138
SUNBRIDGE PARTNERS, 1757
TECHOPERATORS, 1790
TELEFONICA VENTURES, 3160
UPFRONT VENTURES, 1890
VALAR VENTURES, 1899
VANEDGE CAPITAL PARTNERS, 2270
WESLEY CLOVER, 2276
WING VENTURE PARTNERS, 1996
YL VENTURES, 3236

Cloud Data
BLUEPOINTE VENTURES, 298

Cloud Infrastructure
BENHAMOU GLOBAL VENTURES, 252
CROSSLINK CAPITAL, 564
INTEL CAPITAL, 1009
M12, 1158
RESONANT VENTURE PARTNERS, 1550

Cloud Native Infrastructure
WORK-BENCH, 2006

Cloud Software
GREENHILLS VENTURES, LLC, 870

Cloud Technologies
GVA CAPITAL, 895

Cloud-Based IT Services
COSTANOA VENTURE CAPITAL, 548
EARLYBIRD, 2673
WALDEN VENTURE CAPITAL, 1953

Cloud/SaaS
GOOD NEWS VENTURES, 2132

Coal Processes
MOUNTAINEER CAPITAL, 1262

Coding
RUSSELL SQUARE PARTNERS, 2236

Commerce
AMPLIFY, 121
BRILLIANT VENTURES, 345
CITI VENTURES, 488
FIRSTMARK CAPITAL, 744
INTERLACE VENTURES, 1011
LIBERTY CITY VENTURES, 1119
RUBICON VENTURE CAPITAL, 1599
VERIZON VENTURES, 1928

Commerce and Trade
DYNAMO VC, 640

Commercial & Industrial
CIT GROUP, 486

Commercial Air
CIT GROUP, 486

Commercial Contracts
BUTZOW NORDIA ADVOCATES LTD, 2543

Commercial Real Estate
SECOND CITY REAL ESTATE, 2244
VIOLA FINTECH, 3211

Commercial Services
BRUCKMANN, ROSSER, SHERRILL & COMPANY, 357
CERBERUS CAPITAL MANAGEMENT, 453
CHEROKEE INVESTMENT PARTNERS, 465
FRONTENAC COMPANY, 792
ICV PARTNERS, 973
MPE PARTNERS, 1266
RHB - H&F MANAGEMENT COMPANY SDN BHD RHB Capital, 3071
UNION CAPITAL CORPORATION, 1883

Commercial Software
NFX, 1323

Commercial Transportation
LIONHART CAPITAL LTD, 2170

Commodities
APOLLO GLOBAL MANAGEMENT, 141
SAF GROUP, 2237

Communication
W CAPITAL PARTNERS, 1949

Communication Technology
AMPLIFIER VENTURE PARTNERS, 120
AUTHOSIS VENTURES, 2448
COLUMBIA CAPITAL, 518
COMMONWEALTH CAPITAL VENTURES LP, 523
EARLYBIRD, 2673
EDBI Pte LTD., 2681
HARBERT MANAGEMENT CORPORATION, 907
IBB BETEILIGUNGSGESELLSCHAFT MBH, 2832
MASTHEAD VENTURE PARTNERS, 1178
MORGAN STANLEY EXPANSION CAPITAL, 1255
MOUNTAINEER CAPITAL, 1262
SARONA ASSET MANAGEMENT, 2239
SUMMIT PARTNERS, 1754
TAMAR TECHNOLOGY VENTURES LIMITED, 3149
TGAP VENTURES, 1804
THIRD SECURITY, 1815
TRELYS FUNDS, 1844

Communications
212 CAPITAL PARTNERS, 2286
3I AUSTRIA BETEILGUNG GmbH 3i Group, 2290
3I DEUTSCHLAND GESELLSCHAFT FUR 3i Group, 2291
3I GERMANY GmbH 3i Group, 2293
3I TEUPSCHLAND GmbH 3i Group, 2297
3T CAPITAL, 2300
ABRY PARTNERS, 20
ABS CAPITAL PARTNERS, 21

Industry Preference Index / Communications

ABS VENTURES, 22
ABU DHABI INVESTMENT AUTHORITY, 2313
ACKERLEY PARTNERS LLC, 42
ACONCAGUA VENTURES, 2326
ACT VENTURE CAPITAL LIMITED, 2328
ACTIVE VENTURE PARTNERS, 2331
ADAMS STREET PARTNERS, LLC, 56
ADOBE VENTURES LP, 57
ADVANTAGE CAPITAL PARTNERS, 60
ADVENT VENTURE PARTNERS, 2340
AEP CAPITAL LLC, 64
AEROSTAR CAPITAL LLC, 66
ALBEMARLE PRIVATE EQUITY LIMITED, 2352
ALICE VENTURES SRL, 2356
ALMAZ CAPITAL, 89
ALPHA CAPITAL PARTNERS, 90
ALTA VENTURES MEXICO, 2374
ALTPOINT CAPITAL, 101
AMADEUS CAPITAL PARTNERS LIMITED, 2378
AMBIENT SOUND INVESTMENTS, 2382
AMERIMARK CAPITAL CORPORATION, 112
AMMER PARTNERS, 2385
ANDERSON PACIFIC CORPORATION, 123
ARGO GLOBAL CAPITAL, 163
ARVA LIMITED, 2040
ASCENT VENTURE PARTNERS, 180
ATHENIAN VENTURE PARTNERS, 189
ATLAS VENTURE, 193
AUGUST CAPITAL, 200
AURELIA PRIVATE EQUITY, 2443
AVISTA CAPITAL PARTNERS, 212
AXIOM VENTURE PARTNERS, 215
BALDERTON CAPITAL, 2469
BALLAST POINT VENTURES, 227
BARING PRIVATE EQUITY PARTNERS INDIA, 2481
BATTERSON VENTURE CAPITAL LLC, 237
BATTERY VENTURES, 238
BBH CAPITAL PARTNERS, 243
BENHAMOU GLOBAL VENTURES, 252
BERKELEY VC INTERNATIONAL LLC, 255
BERKSHIRE PARTNERS LLC, 257
BI WALDEN MANAGEMENT SDN Walden International, 2499
BIGFOOT VENTURES, 2502
BLUE CHIP VENTURE COMPANY, 290
BOTTS & COMPANY LIMITED, 2523
BOULDER VENTURES LTD, 318
BRAINSPARK PLC, 2526
BRIDGESCALE PARTNERS, 342
BRM SEED, 2532
BROADMARK CAPITAL, 348
BURAN VENTURE CAPITAL, 2540
CALIFORNIA TECHNOLOGY VENTURES, 374
CAMP VENTURES, 388
CAMPUS COMPANIES VENTURE CAPITAL FUND, 2545
CANDOVER, 2547
CAPITAL FOR BUSINESS, INC, 402
CAPMAN CAPITAL MANAGEMENT OY, 2553
CARMEL VENTURES, 2557
CASABONA VENTURES, 421
CAZENOVE PRIVATE EQUITY Cazenove Capital, 2568
CEDAR (ISRAEL) FINANCIAL ADVISORS LIMITED Cedar Fund, 2571
CEDAR FUND, 438
CELTIC HOUSE VENTURE PARTNERS, 2070
CENTERPOINT VENTURE PARTNERS, 446
CHALLENGE FUNDS - ETGAR LP, 2576
CHARLES RIVER VENTURES, 457
CHARLESBANK CAPITAL PARTNERS, 458
CHENGWEI VENTURES, 2581
CHEVRON TECHNOLOGY VENTURES, 468
CHINA WALDEN MANAGEMENT LIMITED Walden Group, 2588
CIBC CAPITAL MARKETS, 2073
CIC FINANCE CIC Group, 2592
CIT GROUP, 486
CIVC PARTNERS, 491
CLAL ELECTRONICS INDUSTRIES LIMITED, 2600
CLARENDON FUND MANAGERS, 2601
CLARITY PARTNERS, 496

CLEARLAKE CAPITAL, 502
CLOQUET CAPITAL PARTNERS, 507
COLLER CAPITAL LIMITED, 2612
COLORADO MILE HIGH FUND, 516
COLUMBIA CAPITAL, 518
COMCAST VENTURES, 520
COMMERCE ASSET VENTURES Sdn Bhd, 2614
COMMONWEALTH CAPITAL VENTURES LP, 523
COMPASS TECHNOLOGY PARTNERS LP, 526
CONCORD VENTURES, 2619
CONSTELLATION TECHNOLOGY VENTURES, 534
CORAL GROUP, 538
CORDOVA VENTURES, 539
CORE CAPITAL PARTNERS, 540
CORE PACIFIC - YAMAICHI CAPITAL LIMITED Core Pacific Securities Company Ltd, 2624
COURT SQUARE VENTURES, 552
CRESCENDO VENTURE MANAGEMENT LLC, 2630
CRESCENDO VENTURES, 556
DAIMLERCHRYSLER VENTURE GmbH DaimlerChrysler AG, 2641
DAVID N DEUTSCH & COMPANY LLC, 590
DEFTA PARTNERS, 603
DELTA VENTURES LIMITED, 2646
DISCOVERY CAPITAL, 2091
DOCOMO INNOVATIONS, 621
DOUBLE M PARTNERS, 625
DRAPER RICHARDS KAPLAN FOUNDATION, 628
DRESNER COMPANIES, 630
DUCHOSSOIS CAPITAL MANAGEMENT, 634
E.VENTURES, 641
EASTVEN VENTURE PARTNERS, 645
EASTWARD CAPITAL PARTNERS, 646
ECHELON VENTURES, 647
ECI VENTURES, 2678
ECLIPSE VENTURES, 648
EDISON PARTNERS, 655
EGL HOLDINGS, 656
EIRCOM ENTERPRISE FUND LIMITED, 2683
EM WARBURG, PINCUS & COMPANY INTERNATIONAL, 2688
EM WARBURG, PINCUS & COMPANY JAPAN, 2689
ENTERPRISE EQUITY (NI) LTD, 2695
EPIC VENTURES, 689
EQUINOX CAPITAL, 692
EQVITEC PARTNERS OY, 2707
EURAZEO, 2710
EVERCORE CAPITAL PARTNERS, 700
EVERGREEN VENTURE PARTNERS, 2717
FERRANTI LIMITED, 2723
FINNVERA PLC, 2732
FIRST ISRAEL MEZZANINE INVESTORS LIMITED, 2736
FIRSTMARK CAPITAL, 744
FISHER LYNCH CAPITAL, 745
FOCUS VENTURES, 759
FONTINALIS PARTNERS, 762
FORMATIVE VENTURES, 766
FORREST BINKLEY & BROWN, 767
FRANCISCO PARTNERS, 782
FUSE CAPITAL, 801
GABRIEL VENTURE PARTNERS, 808
GALILEO II, 2756
GENERAL ATLANTIC PARTNERS, 2762
GENERATION PARTNERS, 822
GENESIS PARTNERS, 2766
GILDE INVESTMENT FUNDS, 2770
GIMV GIMV, 2771
GIZA VENTURE CAPITAL, 2773
GLADSTONE CAPITAL, 832
GLOBAL EQUITY PARTNERS BETEILIGUNGS-MANAGEMENT, 2774
GLOBESPAN CAPITAL PARTNERS, 839
GMT COMMUNICATIONS PARTNERS LLP, 2780
GRANITE EQUITY PARTNERS, 855
GREAT HILL PARTNERS LLC, 862
GREENSPRING ASSOCIATES, 872
GROTECH VENTURES, 881
GTCR, 889
GUGGENHEIM PARTNERS, 890
HALYARD CAPITAL, 902

Industry Preference Index / Communications

HARBINGER VENTURE MANAGEMENT, 908
HELLMAN & FRIEDMAN LLC, 927
HIGHLAND CAPITAL PARTNERS, 938
HORIZON VENTURES LLC, 950
HOUSATONIC PARTNERS, 952
HUDSON VENTURE PARTNERS, 957
HUMANA VENTURES, 958
I-HATCH VENTURES LLC, 967
ICON VENTURES, 972
ID VENTURES AMERICA LLC, 974
IDEALAB, 976
IGNITE JAPAN KK Ignite Group, 2845
INDASIA FUND ADVISORS PVT LTD, 2850
INDIAN DIRECT EQUITY ADVISORS PVT LTD, 2852
INDUSTRIEBANK LIOF NV, 2857
INDUSTRY VENTURES, 990
INETWORKS ADVISORS LLC, 991
INFLEXION PARTNERS, 994
INSTITUTIONAL VENTURE PARTNERS, 1006
INTERNATIONAL FINANCE CORPORATION (IFC), 1012
INTERSOUTH PARTNERS, 1013
INVENTUS, 1017
INVESCO PRIVATE CAPITAL, 1019
INVESTMENT AB BURE, 2879
INVESTOR AB, 2881
IP GROUP, 2883
IPG GROUP, 2885
IRIS CAPITAL, 2888
ISIS EP LLP F & C, 2889
JEGI CAPITAL The Jordan Edminston Group, Inc., 1037
JERUSALEM VENTURE PARTNERS, 2901
KB PARTNERS LLC, 1061
KBL FOUNDER SA, 2908
KELSO & COMPANY, 1066
KILMER CAPITAL PARTNERS, 2162
KINETIC VENTURES, 1076
KLEINER PERKINS, 1079
KNIGHTSBRIDGE ADVISERS, 1081
KODIAK VENTURE PARTNERS, 1084
KOHLBERG KRAVIS ROBERTS & COMPANY, 1086
LABRADOR VENTURES, 1093
LANDSBANKI VENTURES, 2920
LEAPFROG VENTURES, 1106
LEGAL AND GENERAL VENTURES LIMITED, 2926
LIQUID CAPITAL GROUP, 1137
LOVETT MILLER & COMPANY, 1152
M/C PARTNERS, 1157
M12, 1158
MADISON DEARBORN PARTNERS, 1160
MAGMA VENTURE PARTNERS, 2943
MANHATTAN INVESTMENT PARTNERS, 1166
MARATHON VENTURE CAPITAL FUND LIMITED, 2945
MARS INVESTMENT ACCELERATOR FUND, 2181
MARYLAND VENTURE FUND, 1172
MASSACHUSETTS CAPITAL RESOURCE COMPANY, 1176
MASSACHUSETTS GROWTH CAPITAL CORPORATION, 1177
MATRIX PARTNERS, 1184
MAYFIELD FUND, 1187
MCG CAPITAL CORPORATION, 1192
MCGOVERN CAPITAL, 1194
MEDIA VENTURE PARTNERS, 1197
MENLO VENTURES, 1203
MERIDIAN MANAGEMENT GROUP, 1209
MERITECH CAPITAL PARTNERS, 1213
METROPOLITAN PARTNERS GROUP, 1226
MILLENIUM TECHNOLOGY VALUE PARTNERS, 1235
MISSION VENTURES, 1239
MMT MILLENNIUM MATERIALS TECHNOLOGIES FUND LP, 2964
MMV CAPITAL PARTNERS, 2188
MOBIUS VENTURE CAPITAL, 1245
MOHR-DAVIDOW VENTURES, 1247
MOMENTUM FUNDS MANAGEMENT PTY LIMITED, 2966
MONITOR VENTURES, 1249
MOTOROLA SOLUTIONS VENTURE CAPITAL, 1260
McLEAN WATSON CAPITAL, 2191
NAUSICAA VENTURES, 2977
NAUTIC PARTNERS, 1278

NEEDHAM CAPITAL PARTNERS, 1287
NEO TECHNOLOGY VENTURES, 2980
NEOTENY COMPANY LIMITED, 2982
NEST VENTURES, 1289
NEW MOUNTAIN CAPITAL, 1300
NEW VENTURE PARTNERS, 1304
NEW YORK LIFE CAPITAL PARTNERS, 1308
NEWLIGHT MANAGEMENT, 1313
NHN INVESTMENT, 2993
NORTH BRIDGE VENTURE PARTNERS, 1335
NOVAK BIDDLE VENTURE PARTNERS, 1348
OEM CAPITAL, 1369
ONTARIO CAPITAL GROWTH CORPORATION, 2203
OPUS CAPITAL, 1382
OUTCOME CAPITAL, 1389
OVP VENTURE PARTNERS, 1392
PAC-LINK MANAGEMENT CORP., 3015
PAI MANAGEMENT, 3017
PALISADES VENTURES, 1403
PAMLICO CAPITAL, 1410
PANTHEON VENTURES (US) LP, 1413
PARKWALK ADVISORS, 3019
PARTECH INTERNATIONAL, 1418
PARTNERSHIP FUND FOR NEW YORK CITY, 1422
PEACHTREE EQUITY PARTNERS, 1425
PELION VENTURE PARTNERS, 1428
PERMAL CAPITAL MANAGEMENT, 1435
PIDC PHILADELPHIA, 1445
PITANGO VENTURE CAPITAL, 3030
POLESTAR CAPITAL, 1465
POLYTECHNOS VENTURE PARTNERS GmbH, 3037
POMONA CAPITAL, 1466
PREVIZ VENTURES, 3041
PRIME TECHNOLOGY VENTURES NV, 3042
PRIMUS CAPITAL, 1480
PROGRESS EQUITY PARTNERS, 1487
PROVCO GROUP, 1496
PROVENANCE VENTURES, 1497
QBIC FUND, 3056
QUADRANGLE GROUP, 1508
QUANTUM VALLEY INVESTMENTS, 2220
QUESTER CAPITAL MANAGEMENT LIMITED, 3061
RAFAEL DEVELOPMENT CORPORATION (RDC) LIMITED, 3063
RAND CAPITAL CORPORATION, 1526
REDPOINT VENTURES, 1537
REMBRANDT VENTURE PARTNERS, 1543
RENAISSANCE PARTNERS, 3068
RHO VENTURES, 1561
RIDGEWOOD CAPITAL, 1567
ROSER VENTURES LLC, 1590
ROYALTY CAPITAL MANAGEMENT, 1595
RRE VENTURES, 1597
RUNTIDE CAPITAL, 1600
SABAN CAPITAL GROUP, 1602
SAINTS CAPITAL, 1608
SALEM INVESTMENT PARTNERS, 1609
SAND HILL ANGELS, 1616
SANDLER CAPITAL MANAGEMENT, 1620
SARATOGA PARTNERS, 1624
SCHOONER CAPITAL LLC, 1630
SCP PARTNERS, 1636
SEACOAST CAPITAL CORPORATION, 1639
SEAPOINT VENTURES, 1640
SEAPORT CAPITAL, 1641
SELBY VENTURE PARTNERS, 1649
SERAPH GROUP, 1658
SEVENTURE PARTNERS, 3104
SEVIN ROSEN FUNDS, 1661
SHAMROCK CAPITAL ADVISORS, 1663
SHANNON COMMERCIAL PROPERTIES, 3106
SIEMENS VENTURE CAPITAL, 3109
SIERRA ANGELS, 1671
SIERRA VENTURES, 1672
SIGMA PARTNERS, 1674
SIGNAL EQUITY PARTNERS, 1676
SIGNAL PEAK VENTURES, 1679
SIGNATURE CAPITAL LLC, 3111

Industry Preference Index / Computer Hardware & Software

SILVER CREEK VENTURES, 1684
SMART BUSINESS CONSULTING, 3115
SONY EUROPE, 3120
SORRENTO VENTURES, 1708
SOURCE CAPITAL GROUP, 1710
SOUTHPORT PARTNERS, 1714
SPECTRUM EQUITY INVESTORS LP, 1720
SPIRE CAPITAL PARTNERS, 1727
SPRING CAPITAL PARTNERS LP, 1730
STAENBERG VENTURE PARTNERS, 1736
STAGEONE VENTURES, 3127
STAR VENTURES, 3128
SUMMIT PARTNERS, 1754
SUN CAPITAL PARTNERS, 1755
SVB CAPITAL, 1766
SWISSCOM, 3143
T-VENTURE HOLDINGS GmbH Deutsche Telekom, 3146
TAMIR FISHMAN VENTURES, 3150
TAT CAPITAL PARTNERS LTD., 3153
TDF, 1784
TECH CAPITAL PARTNERS, 2253
TECHNOLOGY PARK MALAYSIA CORPORATION SDN BHD, 3155
TEKNOINVEST MANAGEMENT, 3158
TELECOM VENTURE GROUP LIMITED, 3159
TELEFONICA VENTURES, 3160
TELESOFT PARTNERS, 1795
TENAYA CAPITAL, 1798
THOMSON-CSF VENTURES, 3167
THROUNARFELAG ISLANDS PLC, 3168
TL VENTURES, 1830
TRIGINITA CAPITAL, 3181
TRILOGY PARTNERSHIP, 1854
TRINITY VENTURE CAPITAL TVC Holdings plc, 3182
TRINITY VENTURES, 1855
TRITON VENTURES, 1857
TRU MANAGEMENT, 1860
TSG EQUITY PARTNERS, 1864
TVM CAPITAL, 3187
UCA UNTERNEHMER CONSULT AG, 3188
UNITED TALENT AGENCY VENTURES, 1885
US VENTURE PARTNERS, 1898
VAEKSTFONDEN, 3194
VALLEY VENTURES LP, 1903
VELOCITY EQUITY PARTNERS LLC, 1915
VENISTA VENTURES, 3198
VENTECH, 3199
VENTURE CAPITAL FUND OF NEW ENGLAND, 1922
VENTURE INVESTORS, 3201
VERITAS VENTURE PARTNERS, 3203
VERONIS SUHLER STEVENSON, 1929
VESTAR CAPITAL PARTNERS, 1933
VISION CAPITAL, 1939
WALDEN ISRAEL VENTURE CAPITAL, 3221
WALNUT GROUP, 1955
WARBURG PINCUS LLC, 1957
WASHINGTON CAPITAL VENTURES, 1960
WASSERSTEIN & CO., 1961
WELLS FARGO CAPITAL FINANCE, 1971
WESTERN NIS ENTERPRISE FUND, 3224
WESTERN STATES INVESTMENT GROUP, 1975
WESTERN TECHNOLOGY INVESTMENT, 1976
WESTLAKE SECURITIES, 1977
WHEATLEY PARTNERS, 1981
WHITECAP VENTURE PARTNERS, 2280
WICKS GROUP OF COMPANIES, LLC, 1984
WINDSPEED VENTURES, 1994
YELLOW POINT EQUITY PARTNERS, 2284
YUUWA CAPITAL, 3238
YVC - YOZMA MANAGEMENT & INVESTMENTS LIMITED, 3239
ZONE VENTURES, 2020

Communications Equipment
ACORN CAMPUS VENTURES, 46
ALEXANDER HUTTON, 82
ALLSTATE INVESTMENTS LLC, 88
AMPERSAND CAPITAL PARTNERS, 119
ANDLINGER & COMPANY INC, 124
ANTHEM VENTURE PARTNERS, 133
APPLIED MATERIALS VENTURES, 145
ARTIMAN VENTURES, 176
ATHENAEUM FUND, 188
AVALON VENTURES, 209
BAKER CAPITAL, 226
HARBERT MANAGEMENT CORPORATION, 907
MACQUARIE DIRECT INVESTMENT LIMITED, 2942

Communications Software
DOT EDU VENTURES, 624
MOBIUS VENTURE CAPITAL, 1245

Community Engagement
THE ABRAAJ GROUP, 3164

Company Law
BUTZOW NORDIA ADVOCATES LTD, 2543

Compliance/Traning/Certification
ENTREPRENEUR PARTNERS, 684

Components & IoT
500 STARTUPS, 10
ADAMS STREET PARTNERS, LLC, 56
ALTA BERKELEY ASSOCIATES, 2372
ATLAS VENTURE: FRANCE, 2436
BARING PRIVATE EQUITY PARTNERS INDIA, 2481
BAY PARTNERS, 241
BLUERUN VENTURES, 299
BRM SEED, 2532
CRESCENDO VENTURES, 556
FINAVENTURES, 730
FRANCISCO PARTNERS, 782
INNOVACOM SA, 2866
INSTITUTIONAL VENTURE PARTNERS, 1006
INVEXCEL PATRIMONIO, 2882
JERUSALEM VENTURE PARTNERS, 2901
LEONIA MB GROUP/MB FUNDS, 2928
MACQUARIE DIRECT INVESTMENT LIMITED, 2942
MARATHON VENTURE CAPITAL FUND LIMITED, 2945
MOBIUS VENTURE CAPITAL, 1245
SEQUOIA CAPITAL, 1657
SPACEVEST, 1717
THOMSON-CSF VENTURES, 3167
VENTURE ASSOCIATES PARTNERS LLC, 1921

Computer Hardware & Software
AB CAPITAL & INVESTMENT CORPORATION The Phinma Group, 2306
ABU DHABI INVESTMENT AUTHORITY, 2313
ACCESS VENTURE PARTNERS LLC, 35
ADAMS STREET PARTNERS, LLC, 56
AKERS CAPITAL LLC, 74
ALEXANDER HUTTON, 82
AMBIENT SOUND INVESTMENTS, 2382
AMPERSAND CAPITAL PARTNERS, 119
ANDLINGER & COMPANY INC, 124
ANTHEM VENTURE PARTNERS, 133
APPIAN VENTURES, 143
APPLIED MATERIALS VENTURES, 145
ARROWPATH VENTURE PARTNERS, 171
ARTIMAN VENTURES, 176
ASSET MANAGEMENT VENTURES, 183
ATHENAEUM FUND, 188
AUSTIN VENTURES, 205
AVALON VENTURES, 209
CAMBRIDGE CAPITAL CORPORATION, 384
ENTERPRISE EQUITY (NI) LTD, 2695
FERRANTI LIMITED, 2723
FIRST ISRAEL MEZZANINE INVESTORS LIMITED, 2736
FRESHWATER VENTURE PARTNERS, 2748
HARBINGER VENTURE MANAGEMENT, 908
ICF VENTURES PVT LTD, 2837
IDG CAPITAL, 977
INDASIA FUND ADVISORS PVT LTD, 2850
INNOVACOM SA, 2866
IPG GROUP, 2885

Industry Preference Index / Computer Related

JAPAN ASIA INVESTMENT COMPANY LIMITED, 2898
KB PARTNERS LLC, 1061
MACQUARIE DIRECT INVESTMENT LIMITED, 2942
MENLO VENTURES, 1203
MVP CAPITAL PARTNERS, 1275
PENN VENTURE PARTNERS, 1431
PROSEED, 3050
RHO VENTURES, 1561
THROUNARFELAG ISLANDS PLC, 3168
TIME WARNER INVESTMENT CORPORATION, 1829

Computer Related
3I AUSTRIA BETEILGUNG GmbH 3i Group, 2290
3I TEUPSCHLAND GmbH 3i Group, 2297
ABU DHABI INVESTMENT AUTHORITY, 2313
AITEC, 2349
ALBEMARLE PRIVATE EQUITY LIMITED, 2352
AMANET TECHNOLOGIES LIMITED, 2381
AUGUST CAPITAL, 200
BARING PRIVATE EQUITY PARTNERS INDIA, 2481
BATTERSON VENTURE CAPITAL LLC, 237
BERKELEY VC INTERNATIONAL LLC, 255
BRIDGEPOINT CAPITAL GmbH, 2528
BRIDGEPOINT CAPITAL LIMITED, 2529
CANDOVER, 2547
CAZENOVE PRIVATE EQUITY Cazenove Capital, 2568
CHICAGO VENTURE PARTNERS LP, 472
CLEARSTONE VENTURE PARTNERS, 504
COMPASS TECHNOLOGY PARTNERS LP, 526
CONCORD VENTURES, 2619
CRESCENDO VENTURE MANAGEMENT LLC, 2630
DAVID N DEUTSCH & COMPANY LLC, 590
DRESNER COMPANIES, 630
ENTERPRISE INVESTORS, 2697
EQVITEC PARTNERS OY, 2707
FINANCIERE DE BRIENNE FCPR, 2729
FORREST BINKLEY & BROWN, 767
GALILEO II, 2756
GE EQUITY EUROPE, 2760
GILDE INVESTMENT FUNDS, 2770
GLOBAL EQUITY PARTNERS BETEILIGUNGS-MANAGEMENT, 2774
GMT COMMUNICATIONS PARTNERS LLP, 2780
HUMANA VENTURES, 958
ID VENTURES AMERICA LLC, 974
IGNITE JAPAN KK Ignite Group, 2845
INDUSTRIFONDEN, 2858
INVESTMENT AB BURE, 2879
JAVELIN INVESTMENTS, 2899
KBL FOUNDER SA, 2908
KLEINER PERKINS, 1079
KNIGHTSBRIDGE ADVISERS, 1081
LANDSBANKI VENTURES, 2920
LANDSBANKI VENTURES, 2920
LEAPFROG VENTURES, 1106
MANHATTAN INVESTMENT PARTNERS, 1166
MASSACHUSETTS CAPITAL RESOURCE COMPANY, 1176
MASSACHUSETTS GROWTH CAPITAL CORPORATION, 1177
MAYFIELD FUND, 1187
MEDIA VENTURE PARTNERS, 1197
MERIDIAN MANAGEMENT GROUP, 1209
NEEDHAM CAPITAL PARTNERS, 1287
NEW YORK LIFE CAPITAL PARTNERS, 1308
NORTH ATLANTIC CAPITAL CORPORATION, 1334
NOVAK BIDDLE VENTURE PARTNERS, 1348
OEM CAPITAL, 1369
PALO ALTO VENTURE PARTNERS, 1406
PERMAL CAPITAL MANAGEMENT, 1435
PIDC PHILADELPHIA, 1445
POLESTAR CAPITAL, 1465
POMONA CAPITAL, 1466
PRIME TECHNOLOGY VENTURES NV, 3042
PROVCO GROUP, 1496
RAF INDUSTRIES, 1524
REITEN & CO STRATEGIC INVESTMENTS AS Reiten & Company, 3067
ROYALTY CAPITAL MANAGEMENT, 1595
SEACOAST CAPITAL CORPORATION, 1639
SEAYA VENTURES, 3096
SEQUEL VENTURE PARTNERS, 1656
SHANNON COMMERCIAL PROPERTIES, 3106
SIERRA VENTURES, 1672
SIGMA PARTNERS, 1674
SILVER CREEK VENTURES, 1684
SONY EUROPE, 3120
SOURCE CAPITAL GROUP, 1710
SOUTHPORT PARTNERS, 1714
STARBOARD CAPITAL PARTNERS, 1738
SUTTER HILL VENTURES, 1762
TECHNOCAP, 2254
THOMSON-CSF VENTURES, 3167
THROUNARFELAG ISLANDS PLC, 3168
TRANSITION PARTNERS LTD, 1839
TRINITY VENTURE CAPITAL TVC Holdings plc, 3182
UCA UNTERNEHMER CONSULT AG, 3188
VAEKSTFONDEN, 3194
VENCORE CAPITAL, 1917
VENTURE CAPITAL FUND OF NEW ENGLAND, 1922
VENTURE INVESTORS, 3201
VISION CAPITAL, 1939
WASSERSTEIN & CO., 1961
WESTERN STATES INVESTMENT GROUP, 1975
WESTERN TECHNOLOGY INVESTMENT, 1976
YISSUM TECHNOLOGY TRANSFER, 3235
ZERNIKE SEED FUND BV, 3240

Computer Software
CAMP VENTURES, 388

Computers & Peripherals
BEZOS EXPEDITIONS, 265
STATELINE ANGELS, 1743

Computing
MOBILE FOUNDATION VENTURES, 1243
SIERRA ANGELS, 1671

Concrete
PROCURITAS PARTNERS KB, 3045

Confectionery
LEONIA MB GROUP/MB FUNDS, 2928
RABO BLACK EARTH Eagle Venture Partners, 3062
WESTERN NIS ENTERPRISE FUND, 3224

Connected Mobility
CISCO INVESTMENTS, 485

Conservation
AUSTRALIAN ETHICAL INVESTMENT LIMITED, 2447
BIG SOCIETY CAPITAL, 2500
SENTRY FINANCIAL CORPORATION, 1655
UNDERDOG VENTURES, 1882

Construction
ARVA LIMITED, 2040
ASTOR CAPITAL GROUP, 2431
AVENUE CAPITAL GROUP, 211
BARING PRIVATE EQUITY PARTNERS ESPANA SA, 2480
CATAPULT VENTURES, 431
CHRYSALIX, 2072
CLIFFORD CHANCE PUNDER, 2605
COPPERLION CAPITAL, 2079
CVC ASIA PACIFIC LIMITED CVC Capital Partners, 2634
CVC CAPITAL PARTNERS LTD, 2635
DAVID N DEUTSCH & COMPANY LLC, 590
DEUTSCHE BETEILIGUNGS AG, 2651
DUBIN CLARK & COMPANY, 633
DUNEDIN CAPITAL PARTNERS LIMITED, 2668
ELECTRA PARTNERS ASIA LIMITED SFC of Hong Kong, 2685
ENTERPRISE EQUITY (NI) LTD, 2695
EQUISTONE, 2705
FOUNDATION CAPITAL LIMITED, 2744
FdG ASSOCIATES LP, 804
GENESIS CAPITAL CORPORATION, 2124
GOLDEN OPPORTUNITIES FUND, 2129

Industry Preference Index / Consumer Internet

INVESTMENT FUND FOR CENTRAL & EASTERN EUROPE, 2880
KUBOTA CORPORATION, 2918
LIONHART CAPITAL LTD, 2170
LLOYDS DEVELOPMENT CAPITAL LIMITED, 2935
MARCEAU INVESTISSEMENTS, 2946
MITSUI SUMITOMO INSURANCE VENTURE CAPITAL CO, 2962
PALMS & COMPANY, 1405
QUADRAN GESTION Deutsche Beteiligungs AG, 3058
RABO BLACK EARTH Eagle Venture Partners, 3062
SAINT-GOBAIN NOVA EXTERNAL VENTURING, 3085
SRIW SA SRIW Group, 3125
STARBOARD CAPITAL PARTNERS, 1738
TGF MANAGEMENT, 1805
WESTERN AMERICA CAPITAL GROUP, 2278
WESTERN NIS ENTERPRISE FUND, 3224

Consumer
1843 CAPITAL, 6
3I EUROPE PLC 3i Group, 2292
3I ITALY 3i Group, 2295
645 VENTURES, 12
ACCEL, 27
ACON INVESTMENTS, 45
ACREW CAPITAL, 48
AMPLIFY, 121
APAX PARTNERS, 136
BESSEMER VENTURE PARTNERS, 263
BINGLEY CAPITAL, 2052
BRAND FOUNDRY VENTURES, 328
BRANFORD CASTLE, 330
BROOKE PRIVATE EQUITY ASSOCIATES, 353
CANADIAN VENTURE CAPITAL ASSOCIATION Canadian Venture Capital & Private Equity Association, 3249
CEDRUS INVESTMENTS, 2572
EDELSON TECHNOLOGY PARTNERS, 651
FIFTH WALL, 728
FIRST ROUND CAPITAL, 742
FOUNDER COLLECTIVE, 774
GENERAL CATALYST PARTNERS, 820
GOLDMAN SACHS INVESTMENT PARTNERS, 846
GOOD GROWTH CAPITAL, 849
GROUND UP VENTURES, 882
HALOGEN VENTURES, 901
INTERLACE VENTURES, 1011
JACKSON SQUARE VENTURES, 1028
KEIRETSU FORUM, 1065
KHOSLA VENTURES, 1073
LDV CAPITAL, 1105
LEE EQUITY PARTNERS, 1108
LERER HIPPEAU VENTURES, 1114
LIGHTSPEED VENTURE PARTNERS, 1125
LINLEY CAPITAL, 1134
MERCATO PARTNERS, 1205
MIDOCEAN PARTNERS, 1231
NEW ATLANTIC VENTURES, 1290
NKM CAPITAL, 1330
ORIGINATE VENTURES, 1386
PENFUND, 2211
PRITZKER GROUP VENTURE CAPITAL, 1483
QIMING VENTURE PARTNERS, 3057
RECIPROCAL VENTURES, 1531
RISE OF THE REST, 1571
RIVERSIDE COMPANY, 1576
RUSSELL SQUARE PARTNERS, 2236
SAINTS CAPITAL, 1608
SOCIAL CAPITAL, 1698
SPERO VENTURES, 1724
SUSA VENTURES, 1760
TA ASSOCIATES, 1778
THOMAS H LEE PARTNERS, 1818
TIGER GLOBAL MANAGEMENT, 1828
TXV PARTNERS, 1877
VALUEACT CAPITAL, 1905
W CAPITAL PARTNERS, 1949

Consumer Behavior
NIELSEN INNOVATE FUND, 2994

Consumer Brands
SWAN & LEGEND VENTURES, 1768

Consumer Commercial
500 STARTUPS, 10

Consumer Electronics
CATAPULT VENTURES, 431
CHINA ISRAEL VALUE CAPITAL, 2584
INNOVATION WORKS, 1003
TYLT LAB, 1878
VOLVO GROUP VENTURE CAPITAL, 3217

Consumer Finance
KAPOR CAPITAL, 1058

Consumer Goods
ACKRELL CAPITAL, 43
BASE VENTURES, 232
BLAST FUNDING, 282
BUSINESS GROWTH FUND, 2541
CIT GROUP, 486
CREDIT MUTUEL EQUITY, 2082
DUTCHESS CAPITAL, 638

Consumer Goods & Services
SARONA ASSET MANAGEMENT, 2239

Consumer Hardware
CREANDUM, 2628

Consumer Internet
A-GRADE INVESTMENTS, 14
AM VENTURES, 15
ACCESS VENTURE PARTNERS LLC, 35
ACTIVE VENTURE PARTNERS, 2331
ADAMS STREET PARTNERS, LLC, 56
AKSOY INTERNET VENTURES, 2351
ANNAPURNA VENTURES, 2395
AOL VENTURES, 135
ASPECT VENTURES, 182
ATA VENTURES, 185
ATLANTIC VENTURES, 2435
ATOMICO, 2437
BAF SPECTRUM, 2468
BALDERTON CAPITAL, 2469
BARODA VENTURES, 231
BASELINE VENTURES, 234
BLACKBIRD VENTURES, 2511
BLH VENTURE PARTNERS, 285
BLUMBERG CAPITAL, 304
BOSTON SEED CAPITAL, 316
BRIDGESCALE PARTNERS, 342
BRIGHTSTONE VENTURE CAPITAL, 344
BULLPEN CAPITAL, 361
CATAMOUNT VENTURES LP, 430
CHARLES RIVER VENTURES, 457
CLYDESDALE VENTURES, 508
CONVEXA Tyveholmen AS, 2623
CROSSLINK CAPITAL, 564
DCM, 597
DEEP FORK CAPITAL, 601
DOUBLEROCK VENTURE CAPITAL, 626
EDBI Pte LTD., 2681
ENTREE CAPITAL, 2700
FELICIS VENTURES, 720
FENOX VENTURE CAPITAL, 721
FLOODGATE FUND, 752
GENACAST VENTURES, 818
GV, 894
ICON VENTURES, 972
INSIGHT VENTURE PARTNERS, 1005
INTEL CAPITAL, 1009
INVENTUS, 1017
KPG VENTURES, 1088
LIGHTBANK, 1121
MADRONA VENTURE GROUP, 1162

Industry Preference Index / Consumer Marketing

MANTELLA VENTURE PARTNERS, 2176
MATRIX PARTNERS, 1184
MERITECH CAPITAL PARTNERS, 1213
MMC VENTURES, 2963
MORADO VENTURE PARTNERS, 1254
NOVAK BIDDLE VENTURE PARTNERS, 1348
OJAS VENTURE PARTNERS, 3010
OMIDYAR NETWORK, 1374
OUTLOOK VENTURES, 1390
PRESIDIO VENTURES, 1478
RUBICON VENTURE CAPITAL, 1599
SCOUT VENTURES, 1635
SEAYA VENTURES, 3096
SERAPH GROUP, 1658
SHERPALO VENTURES, 1669
SILVERTON PARTNERS, 1687
SOFTTECH VC, 1702
SPARKLABS GLOBAL VENTURES, 1719
SRIJAN CAPITAL, 3124
STRIPES GROUP, 1751
SV ANGEL, 1763
TENAYA CAPITAL, 1798
TENAYA CAPITAL, 1798
TUGBOAT VENTURES, 1867
VALAR VENTURES, 1899
VERSION ONE VENTURES, 2272
VILLAGE GLOBAL, 1935
VINE ST VENTURES, 1936
XG VENTURES, 2009

Consumer Marketing
DACE VENTURES, 581

Consumer Marketplace
HYDE PARK VENTURE PARTNERS, 965

Consumer Media
ACTIVE VENTURE PARTNERS, 2331

Consumer Medicine
HEALTHQUEST CAPITAL, 924
TECHNOLOGY PARTNERS, 1788

Consumer Mobile Media
SEAYA VENTURES, 3096

Consumer Networks
DUNDEE VENTURE CAPITAL, 635

Consumer Products
3I GESTION SA 3i Group, 2294
3M UNITEK, 2299
3i GROUP PLC, 2303
ACE & COMPANY, 2321
ACI CAPITAL, 41
ACTIVA CAPITAL, 2330
AEA INVESTORS, 63
ALANTRA, 77
ALBION INVESTORS LLC, 78
ALERION PARTNERS, 80
ALEUTIAN CAPITAL PARTNERS, 81
ALLIANCE OF ANGELS, 85
ALPHA CAPITAL PARTNERS, 90
ALTAIR VENTURES, 95
AMERICAN SECURITIES LLC, 111
AMERICAN SUSTAINABLE BUSINESS NETWORK, 3246
ANGELO, GORDON & CO., 128
ANGELS' FORUM LLC, 130
APOLLO GLOBAL MANAGEMENT, 141
ARCAPITA INC, 153
ARES MANAGEMENT LLC, 160
ARROWHEAD INVESTMENT MANAGEMENT, 170
ASIAVEST PARTNERS, 2427
ATRIA CAPITAL PARTENAIRES, 2439
AUA PRIVATE EQUITY PARTNERS, 196
AUDAX GROUP, 197
AVANTI CAPITAL, 2449
AVISTA CAPITAL PARTNERS, 212

AWAY REALTY, 2456
AZALEA CAPITAL, 216
BALMORAL FUNDS, 228
BARING PRIVATE EQUITY PARTNERS INDIA, 2481
BAY BG BAVARIAN VENTURE CAPITAL CORP, 2485
BBH CAPITAL PARTNERS, 243
BERKSHIRE PARTNERS LLC, 257
BERTRAM CAPITAL, 260
BEZOS EXPEDITIONS, 265
BLACKSTONE PRIVATE EQUITY GROUP, 280
BLUEGEM CAPITAL PARTNERS, 2515
BOND CAPITAL, 2058
BRAZOS PRIVATE EQUITY PARTNERS, 331
BREAKAWAY VENTURES, 332
BREAKWATER INVESTMENTS, 333
BREAKWATER MANAGEMENT, 334
BRENTWOOD ASSOCIATES, 337
BRIDGE STREET CAPITAL, 341
BROCKWAY MORAN & PARTNERS, 351
BRUCKMANN, ROSSER, SHERRILL & COMPANY, 357
BRYNWOOD PARTNERS, 360
BUNKER HILL CAPITAL, 362
CAI CAPITAL PARTNERS, 368
CALERA CAPITAL, 371
CALTIUS EQUITY PARTNERS, 376
CALTIUS STRUCTURED CAPITAL, 377
CAMBRIA GROUP, 381
CAPITAL TODAY, 2551
CAPITALA, 408
CAPX PARTNERS, 410
CARDINAL EQUITY PARTNERS, 412
CARLYLE GROUP, 416
CAROUSEL CAPITAL, 418
CASTANEA PARTNERS, 424
CASTLE HARLAN, 425
CATALYST GROUP, 427
CCMP CAPITAL, 435
CEDAR VENTURES LLC, 439
CEI VENTURES, 440
CELERITY PARTNERS, 441
CENTERFIELD CAPITAL PARTNERS, 445
CENTRAL TEXAS ANGEL NETWORK, 447
CENTRE PARTNERS MANAGEMENT LLC, 449
CENTURY PARK CAPITAL PARTNERS, 451
CERBERUS CAPITAL MANAGEMENT, 453
CHARLESBANK CAPITAL PARTNERS, 458
CHAZEN CAPITAL PARTNERS, 462
CHENGWEI VENTURES, 2581
CHEYENNE CAPITAL, 469
CHICAGO VENTURE PARTNERS LP, 472
CHRYSALIS CAPITAL ChrysCapital, 2590
CID CAPITAL, 480
CIRCLE PEAK CAPITAL, 483
CIRCLEUP, 484
CLARION CAPITAL PARTNERS LLC, 494
CLEARLAKE CAPITAL, 502
CLEARLIGHT PARTNERS, 503
CLEARSPRING CAPITAL PARTNERS, 2076
CLYDESDALE VENTURES, 508
COMCAST VENTURES, 520
COMSTOCK CAPITAL PARTNERS LLC, 529
COMVEST PARTNERS, 530
CRYSTAL RIDGE PARTNERS, 566
CYPRESS GROUP, 576
DANCAP PRIVATE EQUITY, 2088
DANEVEST TECH FUND ADVISORS, 584
DARBY OVERSEAS INVESTMENTS LTD, 585
DB CAPITAL PARTNERS (ASIA), 2643
DENALI VENTURE PARTNERS, 606
DESCO CAPITAL, 607
DIAMOND STATE VENTURES LP, 612
DISTRICT VENTURES CAPITAL, 2093
DRESNER COMPANIES, 630
DRIVE CAPITAL, 631
DUBILIER & COMPANY, 632
DUNEDIN CAPITAL PARTNERS LIMITED, 2668
EMIGRANT CAPITAL, 668

Industry Preference Index / Consumer Products

EMIL CAPITAL PARTNERS, 669
EMINENT CAPITAL PARTNERS, 670
ENDEAVOUR CAPITAL, 674
EOS PARTNERS LP, 687
EQT PARTNERS AB, 2703
EQUUS TOTAL RETURN, 695
EUREKA GROWTH CAPITAL, 699
EXCELSIOR CAPITAL ASIA, 2718
FAIRHAVEN CAPITAL, 713
FENWAY PARTNERS, 722
FIDELITY GROWTH PARTNERS ASIA, 2724
FINLOMBARDA SpA, 2730
FIRST ATLANTIC CAPITAL LTD., 734
FIRST STEP FUND, 743
FLORIDA CAPITAL PARTNERS, 753
FLUKE VENTURE PARTNERS, 755
FORREST BINKLEY & BROWN, 767
FOUNDATION CAPITAL, 773
FOUNDATION CAPITAL LIMITED, 2744
FOUNDERS EQUITY, 777
FOX PAINE & COMPANY LLC, 781
FRESH VC, 788
FRIEDMAN, FLEISCHER & LOWE LLC, 790
FRIEND SKOLER & COMPANY LLC, 791
FRONTENAC COMPANY, 792
FULCRUM CAPITAL PARTNERS, 2121
FUNG CAPITAL USA, 799
FdG ASSOCIATES LP, 804
GABRIEL VENTURE PARTNERS, 808
GE ASIA PACIFIC CAPITAL TECHNOLOGY FUND, 2758
GE CAPITAL, 811
GE EQUITY EUROPE, 2760
GEFINOR CAPITAL, 813
GEMINI INVESTORS, 815
GENERAL ATLANTIC PARTNERS, 819
GEORGIA OAK PARTNERS, 825
GIBRALTAR & COMPANY, 2127
GLADSTONE CAPITAL, 832
GLENCOE CAPITAL, 834
GOLDEN GATE CAPITAL, 843
GOLDEN SEEDS, 845
GOLDNER HAWN, 847
GOLUB CAPITAL, 848
GRANITE BRIDGE PARTNERS, 854
GRAPHITE CAPITAL MANAGEMENT LTD, 2787
GRAYHAWK CAPITAL, 861
GREAT OAKS VENTURE CAPITAL, 863
GREIF & COMPANY, 874
GROTECH VENTURES, 881
GRYPHON INVESTORS, 886
GULFSTAR GROUP, 893
HALIFAX GROUP LLC, 899
HARBOURVEST PARTNERS LLC, 912
HARREN EQUITY PARTNERS, 913
HARVEST PARTNERS, 917
HERITAGE PARTNERS, 929
HG CAPITAL, 2814
HIG CAPITAL, 931
HIGH-TECH GRUENDERFONDS, 2815
HIGHLAND CAPITAL PARTNERS, 938
HILCO BRANDS, 940
HORIZON PARTNERS, LTD, 948
HUNTSMAN GAY GLOBAL CAPITAL, 962
HURON CAPITAL PARTNERS LLC, 963
ICF VENTURES PVT LTD, 2837
ICV PARTNERS, 973
IDG CAPITAL PARTNERS, 2838
INCWELL VENTURE CAPITAL, 985
INDUSTRIEBANK LIOF NV, 2857
INTERMEDIATE CAPITAL GROUP PLC, 2874
INVESTMENT FUND FOR CENTRAL & EASTERN EUROPE, 2880
INVEXCEL PATRIMONIO, 2882
INVUS GROUP, 1022
IRONBRIDGE EQUITY PARTNERS, 2156
IRONWOOD CAPITAL, 1025
IRVING PLACE CAPITAL, 1026
JAVELIN INVESTMENTS, 2899

JEFFERIES CAPITAL PARTNERS, 1036
JH WHITNEY & COMPANY, 1041
JOHNSON & JOHNSON INNOVATION, 1047
JORDAN COMPANY, 1049
JW CHILDS ASSOCIATES, 1053
KAEDAN INVESTMENTS, 2905
KARLIN VENTURES, 1059
KB PARTNERS, 1060
KENSINGTON CAPITAL PARTNERS, 2160
KERRY CAPITAL ADVISORS, 1071
KIDD & COMPANY, 1075
KILMER CAPITAL PARTNERS, 2162
KNIGHT'S BRIDGE CAPITAL PARTNERS, 2164
KOHLBERG & COMPANY LLC, 1085
KOHLBERG KRAVIS ROBERTS & COMPANY, 1086
KOHLBERG VENTURES, 1087
L CATTERTON PARTNERS, 1092
LAUNCHCAPITAL, 1101
LEGAL AND GENERAL VENTURES LIMITED, 2926
LEGEND CAPITAL, 2927
LEONARD GREEN & PARTNERS LP, 1113
LEVINE LEICHTMAN CAPITAL PARTNERS, 1115
LFE CAPITAL, 1117
LIGHTBANK, 1121
LITTLEJOHN & COMPANY LLC, 1138
LIZADA CAPITAL LLC, 1139
LM CAPITAL SECURITIES, 1141
LUDLOW VENTURES, 1154
MADISON DEARBORN PARTNERS, 1160
MADISON PARKER CAPITAL, 1161
MAINE ANGELS, 1164
MANHATTAN INVESTMENT PARTNERS, 1166
MARANON CAPITAL, 1169
MASSACHUSETTS CAPITAL RESOURCE COMPANY, 1176
MCG CAPITAL CORPORATION, 1192
MEDIA VENTURE PARTNERS, 1197
MEKONG CAPITAL, 2952
MERITURN PARTNERS, 1214
MERRILL LYNCH (ASIA PACIFIC) LIMITED Merrill Lynch Group, 2955
MHS CAPITAL, 1227
MIDWEST MEZZANINE FUNDS, 1232
MINDFULL INVESTORS, 1236
MITSUI SUMITOMO INSURANCE VENTURE CAPITAL CO, 2962
MONITOR VENTURES, 1249
MONTAGU PRIVATE EQUITY LIMITED, 2968
MONTLAKE CAPITAL, 1250
MVP CAPITAL PARTNERS, 1275
NAVY CAPITAL, 1282
NEW ENGLAND CAPITAL PARTNERS, 1295
NEW MEXICO COMMUNITY CAPITAL, 1299
NEW MOUNTAIN CAPITAL, 1300
NEWFIELD CAPITAL, 1312
NEXUS VENTURE PARTNERS Nexus India Capital Advisors Pvt Ltd, 2992
NORTH AMERICAN FUND, 1333
NORTH CASTLE PARTNERS, 1336
NORTHERN LIGHT VENTURE CAPITAL, 1340
NORWEST EQUITY PARTNERS, 1345
NORWEST VENTURE PARTNERS, 1346
OAK INVESTMENT PARTNERS, 1361
PALLADIUM EQUITY PARTNERS, 1404
PAMLICO CAPITAL, 1410
PANTHEON VENTURES (US) LP, 1413
PARALLEL INVESTMENT PARTNERS, 1417
PARALLEL49 EQUITY, 2206
PARTHENON CAPITAL, 1419
PEACHTREE EQUITY PARTNERS, 1425
PENINSULA CAPITAL PARTNERS LLC, 1429
PERMAL CAPITAL MANAGEMENT, 1435
PERMIRA Permira Advisers LLP, 3024
PHILQUO VENTURES, 1441
PHYSIC VENTURES, 1442
POND VENTURES, 3038
POST CAPITAL PARTNERS, 1469
POUSCHINE COOK CAPITAL MANAGEMENT LLC, 1470
PRAIRIE CAPITAL, 1473
PROSPECT PARTNERS LLC, 1494

Industry Preference Index / Consumer Products & Services

PROVCO GROUP, 1496
RAF INDUSTRIES, 1524
RAYMOND JAMES CAPITAL, 1529
RBC CAPITAL MARKETS, 2223
REDWOOD CAPITAL CORPORATION, 1538
RHB - H&F MANAGEMENT COMPANY SDN BHD RHB Capital, 3071
RIDGE CAPITAL PARTNERS LLC, 1565
ROBIN HOOD VENTURES, 1581
ROPART ASSET MANAGEMENT, 1587
ROSEWOOD CAPITAL, 1591
ROTH CAPITAL PARTNERS, 1592
ROYALTY CAPITAL MANAGEMENT, 1595
RRE VENTURES, 1597
SAIF PARTNERS, 3084
SALEM INVESTMENT PARTNERS, 1609
SATORI CAPITAL, 1625
SEACOAST CAPITAL CORPORATION, 1639
SEAWAY VALLEY CAPITAL CORPORATION, 1642
SENTINEL CAPITAL PARTNERS, 1654
SERAPH GROUP, 1658
SORRENTO VENTURES, 1708
SOURCE CAPITAL GROUP, 1710
STARBOARD CAPITAL PARTNERS, 1738
STATELINE ANGELS, 1743
STEAMBOAT VENTURES, 3133
STRIPES GROUP, 1751
SUMMIT PARTNERS, 1754
SVOBODA CAPITAL PARTNERS, 1767
SWANDER PACE CAPITAL, 1769
SYMMETRIC CAPITAL, 1772
TECH COAST ANGELS, 1786
TGF MANAGEMENT, 1805
TH LEE PUTNAM VENTURES, 1806
THOMA BRAVO LLC, 1817
THOMSON-CSF VENTURES, 3167
TORQUEST PARTNERS, 2264
TRIVEST PARTNERS, 1859
TSG CONSUMER PARTNERS, 1863
TULLY & HOLLAND, 1869
TYLT LAB, 1878
UNDERDOG VENTURES, 1882
UNIVERSITY VENTURE FUND, 1886
US VENTURE PARTNERS, 1898
VALOR EQUITY PARTNERS, 1904
VENCORE CAPITAL, 1917
VERITAS CAPITAL FUND LP, 1927
VESTAR CAPITAL PARTNERS, 1933
VINCERA CAPITAL, 3209
WALNUT GROUP, 1955
WASSERSTEIN & CO., 1961
WEDBUSH CAPITAL PARTNERS, 1970
WESTLAKE SECURITIES, 1977
WESTVIEW CAPITAL PARTNERS, 1979
WINONA CAPITAL MANAGEMENT, 2000
WOODBRIDGE GROUP, 2004
YORK STREET CAPITAL PARTNERS LLC, 2014
ZS FUND LP, 2021
ZURMONT MADISON PRIVATE EQUITY, 3244

Consumer Products & Services
ALTAMONT CAPITAL PARTNERS, 96
BALLAST POINT VENTURES, 227
CAPITAL RESOURCE PARTNERS, 405
INNOSPRING, 998
SCOTIABANK PRIVATE EQUITY, 2241

Consumer Retail
MONTAGU PRIVATE EQUITY LIMITED, 2968
SB CHINA VENTURE CAPITAL, 3091
VEBER PARTNERS LLC, 1911

Consumer Services
3i GROUP PLC, 2303
AB CAPITAL & INVESTMENT CORPORATION The Phinma Group, 2306
ABU DHABI INVESTMENT AUTHORITY, 2313
ACCENTURE TECHNOLOGY VENTURES, 2318

ACCESS CAPITAL, 34
ACE & COMPANY, 2321
ADLEVO CAPITAL CIM Fund Services, 2337
AEP CAPITAL LLC, 64
ALBEMARLE PRIVATE EQUITY LIMITED, 2352
ALLIANCE OF ANGELS, 85
ALPHA CAPITAL PARTNERS, 90
ALTA VENTURES MEXICO, 2374
AMBIENT SOUND INVESTMENTS, 2382
AMERIMARK CAPITAL CORPORATION, 112
AMMER PARTNERS, 2385
ANDREESSEN HOROWITZ, 125
APEX VENTURE PARTNERS, 138
ARTHUR P GOULD & COMPANY, 174
AUA PRIVATE EQUITY PARTNERS, 196
AVISTA CAPITAL PARTNERS, 212
BALDERTON CAPITAL, 2469
BARING PRIVATE EQUITY PARTNERS INDIA, 2481
BAY PARTNERS, 241
BBH CAPITAL PARTNERS, 243
BENAROYA COMPANIES, 250
BERKELEY VC INTERNATIONAL LLC, 255
BERTRAM CAPITAL, 260
BLAZER VENTURES, 283
BREGAL SAGEMOUNT, 336
BRENTWOOD ASSOCIATES, 337
BRIDGEPOINT CAPITAL GmbH, 2528
BRIDGEPOINT CAPITAL LIMITED, 2529
BRUCKMANN, ROSSER, SHERRILL & COMPANY, 357
CAI CAPITAL PARTNERS, 368
CALTIUS EQUITY PARTNERS, 376
CALTIUS STRUCTURED CAPITAL, 377
CAMBRIA GROUP, 381
CANYON CREEK CAPITAL, 400
CARLYLE ASIA INVESTMENT ADVISORS LIMITED Carlyle Group, 2556
CAROUSEL CAPITAL, 418
CARPEDIA INTERNATIONAL, 2066
CASTLE HARLAN, 425
CATALYST INVESTORS, 429
CENTRAL TEXAS ANGEL NETWORK, 447
CHASE CAPITAL PARTNERS, 2579
CHAZEN CAPITAL PARTNERS, 462
CHEYENNE CAPITAL, 469
CHICAGO GROWTH PARTNERS, 470
CHINA WALDEN MANAGEMENT LIMITED Walden Group, 2588
CHINAVEST, 475
CI CAPITAL PARTNERS, 478
CINVEN LIMITED, 2596
CIVC PARTNERS, 491
CLEARLAKE CAPITAL, 502
CLEARLIGHT PARTNERS, 503
CLOSE BROTHERS PRIVATE EQUITY Close Brothers Group, 2608
CONCENTRIC EQUITY PARTNERS Financial Investments Corporation, 531
CORRELATION VENTURES, 545
DANCAP PRIVATE EQUITY, 2088
DANEVEST TECH FUND ADVISORS, 584
DAVID N DEUTSCH & COMPANY LLC, 590
DIAMOND STATE VENTURES LP, 612
DOUBLEROCK VENTURE CAPITAL, 626
DRIVE CAPITAL, 631
DUKE STREET CAPITAL Duke Street, 2667
DUNEDIN CAPITAL PARTNERS LIMITED, 2668
EDGESTONE CAPITAL PARTNERS, 2098
EDGEWATER FUNDS, 654
ELECTRA PARTNERS EUROPE, 2686
EM WARBURG, PINCUS & COMPANY INTERNATIONAL, 2688
EM WARBURG, PINCUS & COMPANY JAPAN, 2689
EMERGENCE CAPITAL PARTNERS, 666
EMIGRANT CAPITAL, 668
EOS PARTNERS LP, 687
EPIC VENTURES, 689
EQT PARTNERS AB, 2703
EQUISTONE, 2705
EURAZEO, 2710
EUREKA GROWTH CAPITAL, 699

Industry Preference Index / Consumer, Retail & Dining

EUROVENTURES CAPITAL, 2716
EVERGREEN ADVISORS, 702
FALCONHEAD CAPITAL, 717
FINLOMBARDA SpA, 2730
FIRST ISRAEL MEZZANINE INVESTORS LIMITED, 2736
FIRST NEW ENGLAND CAPITAL LP, 740
FIVE ELMS CAPITAL, 746
FLUKE VENTURE PARTNERS, 755
FOCUS VENTURES, 759
FORREST BINKLEY & BROWN, 767
FOUNDATION CAPITAL, 773
FOUNDATION CAPITAL LIMITED, 2744
FOUNDERS EQUITY, 777
FdG ASSOCIATES LP, 804
GE EQUITY EUROPE, 2760
GEMINI INVESTORS, 815
GENESIS PARTNERS, 2766
GEORGIA OAK PARTNERS, 825
GILBERT GLOBAL EQUITY PARTNERS, 831
GOLDNER HAWN, 847
GOLUB CAPITAL, 848
GRAPHITE CAPITAL MANAGEMENT LTD, 2787
GREAT HILL PARTNERS LLC, 862
GRUPO BISA, 2791
GRYPHON INVESTORS, 886
GULFSTAR GROUP, 893
H KATZ CAPITAL GROUP, 896
HALDER HOLDINGS BV, 2797
HALIFAX GROUP LLC, 899
HELION VENTURE PARTNERS, LLC International Management (Mauritius) Ltd, 2809
HG CAPITAL, 2814
HILCO BRANDS, 940
HUMANA VENTURES, 958
HUMMER WINBLAD VENTURE PARTNERS, 959
HURON CAPITAL PARTNERS LLC, 963
IA VENTURES, 969
ICF VENTURES PVT LTD, 2837
ICV PARTNERS, 973
INDUSTRIEBANK LIOF NV, 2857
INNOFINANCE OY, 2864
INVUS GROUP, 1022
IRONBRIDGE EQUITY PARTNERS, 2156
IRVING PLACE CAPITAL, 1026
ISIS EP LLP F & C, 2889
J. BURKE CAPITAL PARTNERS, 1027
KELSO & COMPANY, 1066
L CATTERTON PARTNERS, 1092
LEGAL AND GENERAL VENTURES LIMITED, 2926
LEONARD GREEN & PARTNERS LP, 1113
LFE CAPITAL, 1117
LLR PARTNERS INC, 1140
LOVETT MILLER & COMPANY, 1152
MADISON DEARBORN PARTNERS, 1160
MADRONA VENTURE GROUP, 1162
MARANON CAPITAL, 1169
MAVERON LLC, 1186
MAYFIELD FUND, 1187
MERRILL LYNCH (ASIA PACIFIC) LIMITED Merrill Lynch Group, 2955
MIDDLEBURG CAPITAL DEVELOPMENT, 1229
MIDVEN, 2958
MINDFULL INVESTORS, 1236
MOBIUS VENTURE CAPITAL, 1245
MONTAGU PRIVATE EQUITY LIMITED, 2968
MOUNTAIN GROUP CAPITAL, 1261
MPG EQUITY PARTNERS, 1267
MVC CORPORATION, 2971
NEEDHAM CAPITAL PARTNERS, 1287
NEW MEXICO COMMUNITY CAPITAL, 1299
NEWFIELD CAPITAL, 1312
NEXUS VENTURE PARTNERS Nexus India Capital Advisors Pvt Ltd, 2992
NORTH CASTLE PARTNERS, 1336
NORTH DAKOTA DEVELOPMENT FUND, 1338
NORTHERN ENTERPRISE LIMITED, 3002
NORTHERN LIGHT VENTURE CAPITAL, 1340
NORTHWOOD VENTURES, 1344
NORWEST EQUITY PARTNERS, 1345
NOVELTEK CAPITAL CORPORATION, 1351
NTH POWER TECHNOLOGIES, 1355
PARALLEL49 EQUITY, 2206
PARTHENON CAPITAL, 1419
PEACHTREE EQUITY PARTNERS, 1425
PHILQUO VENTURES, 1441
PHOENIX EQUITY PARTNERS LIMITED, 3027
PIVOTNORTH CAPITAL, 1454
PLUS VENTURES, 3032
POLARIS VENTURE PARTNERS, 1464
POLESTAR CAPITAL, 1465
POMONA CAPITAL, 1466
POND VENTURES, 3038
POUSCHINE COOK CAPITAL MANAGEMENT LLC, 1470
PWC, 3055
QUESTMARK PARTNERS LP, 1517
REITEN & CO STRATEGIC INVESTMENTS AS Reiten & Company, 3067
REVEL PARTNERS, 1557
RHB - H&F MANAGEMENT COMPANY SDN BHD RHB Capital, 3071
ROARK CAPITAL GROUP, 1580
ROSEWOOD CAPITAL, 1591
SAIF PARTNERS, 3084
SAINTS CAPITAL, 1608
SCHOONER CAPITAL LLC, 1630
SENTINEL CAPITAL PARTNERS, 1654
SHASTA VENTURES, 1666
SIERRA VENTURES, 1672
SILVER OAK SERVICES PARTNERS, 1686
SPLIT ROCK PARTNERS, 1728
SSM PARTNERS, 1735
STAENBERG VENTURE PARTNERS, 1736
SWANDER PACE CAPITAL, 1769
TAO VENTURE CAPITAL PARTNERS, 1782
THOMSON-CSF VENTURES, 3167
TRIDENT CAPITAL, 1852
TRILANTIC CAPITAL PARTNERS, 1853
TRINITY VENTURE CAPITAL TVC Holdings plc, 3182
TSG EQUITY PARTNERS, 1864
UNIVERSITY VENTURE FUND, 1886
UPFRONT VENTURES, 1890
VENTURE INVESTORS, 3201
VESTAR CAPITAL PARTNERS, 1933
VISION CAPITAL, 1939
WALNUT GROUP, 1955
WASSERSTEIN & CO., 1961
WATERLAND PRIVATE EQUITY INVESTMENT, 3222
WAVELAND INVESTMENTS LLC, 1965
WELLSPRING CAPITAL MANAGEMENT LLC, 1972
WESTLAKE SECURITIES, 1977
WESTSUMMIT CAPITAL, 3225
WIND POINT PARTNERS, 1990
WINGATE PARTNERS, 1997
WINONA CAPITAL MANAGEMENT, 2000

Consumer Software
ABRT VENTURE FUND, 2312
CREANDUM, 2628
SEAYA VENTURES, 3096
SEVEN PEAKS VENTURES, 1659

Consumer Tech
ELYSIUM VENTURE CAPITAL, 662

Consumer Technology
FLYBRIDGE CAPITAL PARTNERS, 756
LEAPFROG VENTURES, 1106
LEO CAPITAL HOLDINGS, LLC, 1112
NEW ENTERPRISE ASSOCIATES, 1296
PALO ALTO VENTURE SCIENCE, 1407
SIERRA VENTURES, 1672
VENROCK ASSOCIATES, 1918

Consumer, Retail & Dining
BAIN CAPITAL PRIVATE EQUITY, 223

Industry Preference Index / Consumer/Retail

Consumer/Retail
TPG CAPITAL, 1837

Content
BLOOMBERG BETA, 287
INNOVACOM SA, 2866

Contracting
CATALYST INVESTMENT MANAGERS PTY LIMITED PPM Capital, 2564

Conventional Energy
RIVERSTONE, 1577

Convergent Technologies
LINSALATA CAPITAL PARTNERS, 1136

Copper
SPACEVEST, 1717

Core Financial Applications
INFORMATION VENTURE PARTNERS, 2146

Corporate Advisory
GRESHAM PRIVATE EQUITY LIMITED, 2790

Corporate Insolvency
BUTZOW NORDIA ADVOCATES LTD, 2543

Corporate Services
CORE PACIFIC - YAMAICHI CAPITAL LIMITED Core Pacific Securities Company Ltd, 2624
DAVIS, TUTTLE VENTURE PARTNERS LP, 592
DFC LTD, 2652
ENTER VENTURES, 682
RHB - H&F MANAGEMENT COMPANY SDN BHD RHB Capital, 3071
SOVEREIGN CAPITAL, 3121

Cosmetics
BIOPACIFIC VENTURES, 2507
RABO BLACK EARTH Eagle Venture Partners, 3062
TMG CAPITAL PARTNERS, 3171

Cost-Effective Medicine
TECHNOLOGY PARTNERS, 1788

Cosumer Products
HAMMOND, KENNEDY, WHITNEY & COMPANY, 904

Creative Industries
ASCENSION VENTURES, 2423
CLARITY CAPITAL, 2602
IBB BETEILIGUNGSGESELLSCHAFT MBH, 2832
PORTUGAL CAPITAL VENTURES Institutional Headquarters, 3039

Cryptocurrency
DIAGRAM VENTURES, 2090
SAMSUNG NEXT, 1614

Culture and Media
CHINA MERCHANTS CHINA DIRECT INVESTMENTS LTD., 2585

Cyber Insurance
GROUND UP VENTURES, 882

Cyber Security
11.2 CAPITAL, 3
BENHAMOU GLOBAL VENTURES, 252
BESSEMER VENTURE PARTNERS, 263
BOLDSTART VENTURES, 308
COLUMBIA CAPITAL, 518
ENERTECH CAPITAL, 677
MARYLAND VENTURE FUND, 1172
MS&AD VENTURES, 1269
PANACHE VENTURES, 2204
QUAKE CAPITAL PARTNERS, 1509
TEN ELEVEN VENTURES, 1796
VANEDGE CAPITAL PARTNERS, 2270

VERDEXUS, 2271

Cybersecurity
.406 VENTURES, 1
CYBERSTARTS, 2638
ECAPITAL ENTREPRENEURIAL PARTNERS AG, 2677
FGA PARTNERS, 725
GENACAST VENTURES, 818
GLASSWING VENTURES, 833
GV, 894
SINEWAVE VENTURES, 1689

DNA
IN-Q-TEL, 983

Data
ANGELPAD, 129
BRILLIANT VENTURES, 345
CAMP VENTURES, 388
FIKA VENTURES, 729
INNOVATION ENDEAVORS, 1001
PORTAG3 VENTURES, 2217

Data & Analytics
ACCESS VENTURE PARTNERS LLC, 35
AME CLOUD VENTURES, 108
CROSSLINK CAPITAL, 564
DOT EDU VENTURES, 624
DYNAMO VC, 640
EXTREME VENTURE PARTNERS, 2107
FIRSTMARK CAPITAL, 744
GERKEN CAPITAL ASSOCIATES, 826
HORIZONS VENTURES, 2822
MISSIONOG, 1240
NIELSEN INNOVATE FUND, 2994
PROGRESS VENTURES, 1488
SCIFI VC, 1634
SIGNAL FIRE, 1677
VERIZON VENTURES, 1928
WING VENTURE PARTNERS, 1996

Data & Cloud
.406 VENTURES, 1

Data Analysis
BAIDU VENTURES, 222
CANOPY BOULDER, 395
UNCORK CAPITAL, 1881

Data Analytics
11.2 CAPITAL, 3
BOLDSTART VENTURES, 308
BREYER CAPITAL, 339
CHRYSALIX, 2072
CITI VENTURES, 488
DELL VENTURES, 604
HALYARD CAPITAL, 902
MOBILE FOUNDATION VENTURES, 1243
MOTIV PARTNERS, 1258
PHYTO PARTNERS, 1443
RUNTIDE CAPITAL, 1600
SAMSUNG NEXT, 1614
TOYOTA AI VENTURES, 1836

Data Center
MK CAPITAL, 1242
QUALCOMM VENTURES, 1511
SPRING LAKE EQUITY PARTNERS, 1731

Data Centre
CISCO INVESTMENTS, 485

Data Communications
ALTA BERKELEY ASSOCIATES, 2372
BENAROYA COMPANIES, 250
COMCAST VENTURES, 520
DELTA VENTURES LIMITED, 2646
FORMULA VENTURES LIMITED Formula Group, 2741

Industry Preference Index / Diagnostics

FOUNDATION CAPITAL, 773
GE EQUITY EUROPE, 2760
GEMINI ISRAEL VENTURE FUNDS LIMITED, 2761
HARBOURVEST PARTNERS LLC, 912
IN-Q-TEL, 983
INDUSTRIEBANK LIOF NV, 2857
INSTITUTIONAL VENTURE PARTNERS, 1006
NEWBURY VENTURES, 1310
PROCURITAS PARTNERS KB, 3045
WINDWARD VENTURES, 1995

Data Infrastructure
DENALI VENTURE PARTNERS, 606

Data Management
GROUND UP VENTURES, 882
INITIATIVE CAPITAL LIMITED, 2147

Data Mangement
MS&AD VENTURES, 1269

Data Mining
GVA CAPITAL, 895
QUANTUM WAVE FUND, 3059

Data Science
GOOD GROWTH CAPITAL, 849

Data Security
ACCESS VENTURE PARTNERS LLC, 35
HEALTH ENTERPRISE PARTNERS, 921
LUGE CAPITAL, 2172
SIGNIA VENTURE PARTNERS, 1680

Data Services
BLOOMBERG BETA, 287
EDGESTONE CAPITAL PARTNERS, 2098
EVERCORE CAPITAL PARTNERS, 700
FIDELITY GROWTH PARTNERS EUROPE, 2725
IN-Q-TEL, 983
MENLO VENTURES, 1203
TELUS VENTURES, 2256

Data Storage
ACCEL-KKR LLC, 28
ALMAZ CAPITAL, 89
AMD VENTURES, 107
ARTIS VENTURES, 177
AWEIDA VENTURE PARTNERS, 213
BOULDER VENTURES LTD, 318
BRIGHTSTONE VENTURE CAPITAL, 344
DATA COLLECTIVE, 586
DELL VENTURES, 604
DIVERGENT VENTURES, 619
FAIRHAVEN CAPITAL, 713
FOUNDATION CAPITAL, 773
MIRAMAR VENTURE PARTNERS, 1237
QUANTUM WAVE FUND, 3059
SIGMA PARTNERS, 1674
US VENTURE PARTNERS, 1898

Data Technology
BASE VENTURES, 232
SOZO VENTURES, 1716

Data-Defined Security
WORK-BENCH, 2006

Data-driven marketplaces
ALTPOINT CAPITAL, 101

Database Services
ASSET MANAGEMENT VENTURES, 183
CELERITY PARTNERS, 441
DOT EDU VENTURES, 624
EVERGREEN ADVISORS, 702
MVP CAPITAL PARTNERS, 1275
TEXADA CAPITAL CORPORATION, 1801

Debt Management
3I AUSTRIA BETEILGUNG GmbH 3i Group, 2290

Deep Learning
PATHBREAKER VENTURES, 1423

Deep Tech
CXO FUND, 575

Deep Technology
COMET LABS, 521

Defense
CM EQUITY PARTNERS, 509
CORNERSTONE CAPITAL HOLDINGS, 542

Defense & Aerospace
BEHRMAN CAPITAL, 248

Design
500 STARTUPS, 10
645 VENTURES, 12

Developer Platforms
BESSEMER VENTURE PARTNERS, 263

Developer Tools
WESTTECH VENTURES, 3226

Diagnostic & Drug Discovery Platforms
ARCH VENTURE PARTNERS, 154

Diagnostics
ALLOS VENTURES, 86
ASCLEPIOS BIORESEARCH, 2424
ATHYRIUM CAPITAL MANAGEMENT, 190
AVLAR BIOVENTURES, 2454
AZCA, 217
BAY CITY CAPITAL LLC, 240
BIOADVANCE, 269
BIOGENERATION VENTURES, 2505
BIOGENERATOR, 270
BIOMED PARTNERS, 2506
BIOVENTURES INVESTORS, 273
BLADE VENTURES, 281
BROADVIEW VENTURES, 350
CAPITAL FOR BUSINESS, INC, 402
CATALYST HEALTH VENTURES, 428
CENTRESTONE VENTURES, 2071
CHL MEDICAL PARTNERS, 476
DOMAIN ASSOCIATES LLC, 622
EASTON CAPITAL INVESTMENT GROUP, 644
ELM STREET VENTURES, 661
EXCEL VENTURE MANAGEMENT, 704
FIRST ANALYSIS, 733
FLARE CAPITAL PARTNERS, 749
FLETCHER SPAGHT VENTURES, 750
FORESITE CAPITAL, 764
HATTERAS VENTURE PARTNERS, 918
HBM PARTNERS, 2806
HEALTHQUEST CAPITAL, 924
HLM VENTURE PARTNERS, 941
HOPEN LIFE SCIENCE VENTURES, 946
IDEA FUND PARTNERS, 975
INETWORKS ADVISORS LLC, 991
INNOVA MEMPHIS, 999
JOHNSON & JOHNSON INNOVATION, 1047
KAISER PERMANENTE VENTURES, 1056
KB PARTNERS LLC, 1061
LANCET CAPITAL, 1096
LATTERELL VENTURE PARTNERS, 1098
LAUNCHPAD VENTURE GROUP, 1104
LINK TECHNOLOGIES LIMITED, 2932
LONG RIVER VENTURES, 1146
LONGITUDE CAPITAL, 1147
MAINE ANGELS, 1164
MARYLAND VENTURE FUND, 1172

Industry Preference Index / Digital Business Services

MERCK GLOBAL HEALTH INNOVATION FUND, 1206
MESA VERDE PARTNERS, 1222
MOUNTAIN GROUP CAPITAL, 1261
MVM LIFE SCIENCE PARTNERS, 2972
NEW LEAF VENTURE PARTNERS, 1297
NOVARTIS VENTURE FUNDS, 1350
OKAPI VENTURE CAPITAL, 1371
ONSET VENTURES, 1379
PARTNERS HEALTHCARE RESEARCH VENTURES, 1421
PFIZER VENTURE INVESTMENTS, 1439
PITTSBURGH LIFE SCIENCES GREENHOUSE, 1452
PTV SCIENCES, 1502
PURETECH VENTURES, 1503
RA CAPITAL MANAGEMENT, 1522
ROBIN HOOD VENTURES, 1581
SAND HILL ANGELS, 1616
SCP PARTNERS, 1636
SHEPHERD VENTURES, 1667
SIGNAL PEAK VENTURES, 1679
SPINDLETOP CAPITAL, 1725
TEXO VENTURES, 1803
THE CHANNEL GROUP, 1811
THIRD ROCK VENTURES, 1814
THOMAS, MCNERNEY & PARTNERS, 1820
TWIN CITIES ANGELS, 1874
VALLEY VENTURES LP, 1903
VENROCK ASSOCIATES, 1918
WATER STREET HEALTHCARE PARTNERS, 1962
WELLINGTON PARTNERS VENTURE CAPITAL GmbH, 3223

Digital Business Services
SYNCOM VENTURE PARTNERS, 1773

Digital Cars
BMW I VENTURES, 305

Digital Commerce
SWAN & LEGEND VENTURES, 1768

Digital Content
PIQUE VENTURES, 2215

Digital Convergence
PATHENA, 3022

Digital Health
BREYER CAPITAL, 339
CANVAS VENTURES, 399
CROSSLINK CAPITAL, 564
GCI CAPITAL, 2123
HEALTHQUEST CAPITAL, 924
INNOGEST CAPITAL, 2865
QUALCOMM VENTURES, 1511
SAMSUNG NEXT, 1614
SV HEALTH INVESTORS, 1764
VILLAGE GLOBAL, 1935
WILDCAT VENTURE PARTNERS, 1985
WINDHAM VENTURE PARTNERS, 1993

Digital Health Technology
SEVEN PEAKS VENTURES, 1659

Digital Infrastructure
NEWLIGHT PARTNERS, 1314

Digital Learning
REACH CAPITAL, 1530

Digital Marketing
CROSSLINK CAPITAL, 564
KAEDAN INVESTMENTS, 2905
RUNTIDE CAPITAL, 1600

Digital Media
ACKRELL CAPITAL, 43
CAVA CAPITAL, 433
IA VENTURES, 969
IMAGINATION CAPITAL, 981

JUMPSTART INC, 1051
LERER HIPPEAU VENTURES, 1114
PANACHE VENTURES, 2204
PLAZA VENTURES, 2216
RUNTIDE CAPITAL, 1600
SAFEGUARD SCIENTIFICS, 1605
SLOW VENTURES, 1696
VANEDGE CAPITAL PARTNERS, 2270

Digital Media & Marketing
.406 VENTURES, 1
212 CAPITAL PARTNERS, 2286
ABRY PARTNERS, 20
ACCESS VENTURE PARTNERS LLC, 35
ACME LABS, 2325
ADOBE VENTURES LP, 57
ALMAZ CAPITAL, 89
AMERICAN SUSTAINABLE BUSINESS NETWORK, 3246
ANGEL STREET CAPITAL, 126
ANNAPURNA VENTURES, 2395
ANTRAK CAPITAL, 2399
APAX GLOBIS PARTNERS & COMPANY Globis Capital Partners/Apax, 2406
ARC ANGEL FUND, 151
ARKAFUND MEDIA & ICT, 2417
ASCENSION VENTURES, 2423
ASTUTIA VENTURES, 2432
AVISTA PARTNERS, 2452
AZIONE CAPITAL, 2464
AZURE CAPITAL PARTNERS, 218
BAF SPECTRUM, 2468
BARODA VENTURES, 231
BASELINE VENTURES, 234
BATTERY VENTURES, 238
BERTELSMANN DIGITAL MEDIA INVESTMENTS, 259
BI WALDEN MANAGEMENT SDN Walden International, 2499
BIG SUR VENTURES, 2501
BLUERUN VENTURES, 299
BLUMBERG CAPITAL, 304
BRIDGESCALE PARTNERS, 342
BRIGHTSTONE VENTURE CAPITAL, 344
BURAN VENTURE CAPITAL, 2540
CAMPUS COMPANIES VENTURE CAPITAL FUND, 2545
CARDINAL VENTURE CAPITAL, 414
CATALYST INVESTORS, 429
CINCYTECH, 481
COLOMA VENTURES, 515
COMMONWEALTH CAPITAL VENTURES LP, 523
COMPOUND, 527
CONNECT VENTURES, 2620
CONSTELLATION TECHNOLOGY VENTURES, 534
CONTOUR VENTURE PARTNERS, 535
CONVERGE VENTURE PARTNERS, 536
CORE CAPITAL PARTNERS, 540
CUE BALL GROUP, 568
DACE VENTURES, 581
DAWNTREADER VENTURES, 593
DEEP FORK CAPITAL, 601
DETROIT VENTURE PARTNERS, 608
DFJ GOTHAM VENTURES, 609
DN CAPITAL, 2659
E.BRICKS DIGITAL, 2672
EASTLABS, 2675
EDEN VENTURES, 2682
ELEVATION PARTNERS, 660
EMERGENCE CAPITAL PARTNERS, 666
ESPRESSO CAPITAL, 2103
EVERGREEN ADVISORS, 702
FAIRHAVEN CAPITAL, 713
FIRESTARTER FUND, 732
FORTÉ VENTURES, 770
FUSE CAPITAL, 801
GENACAST VENTURES, 818
GENESIS PARTNERS, 2766
GEORGIAN PARTNERS, 2126
GGV CAPITAL, 827
GLYNN CAPITAL MANAGEMENT, 840

Industry Preference Index / Distribution

GREYCROFT PARTNERS, 876
GROTECH VENTURES, 881
GUGGENHEIM PARTNERS, 890
HARBOUR GROUP, 911
HELLMAN & FRIEDMAN LLC, 927
HIGHLAND CAPITAL PARTNERS, 938
HORIZONS VENTURES, 2822
HUMMINGBIRD VENTURES, 2828
ICON VENTURES, 972
IDEALAB, 976
IGLOBE PARTNERS, 2844
INBC INVESTMENT CORP, 2144
INSTITUTIONAL VENTURE PARTNERS, 1006
INTEL CAPITAL, 1009
INTERSOUTH PARTNERS, 1013
INVENTUS, 1017
JAVELIN VENTURE PARTNERS, 1032
KAEDAN INVESTMENTS, 2905
KARLIN VENTURES, 1059
KIBO VENTURES, 2911
KODIAK VENTURE PARTNERS, 1084
KOHLBERG VENTURES, 1087
KTB VENTURES, 1091
LABRADOR VENTURES, 1093
LANTA DIGITAL VENTURES, 2921
LONGWORTH VENTURE PARTNERS, 1150
LOOL VENTURES, 2938
MADRONA VENTURE GROUP, 1162
MASS VENTURES, 1175
MERCURY FUND, 1207
MERITECH CAPITAL PARTNERS, 1213
MESA GLOBAL, 1221
MESA+, 1223
MHS CAPITAL, 1227
MIDVEN, 2958
MILLENIUM TECHNOLOGY VALUE PARTNERS, 1235
MK CAPITAL, 1242
MMC VENTURES, 2963
MOTOROLA SOLUTIONS VENTURE CAPITAL, 1260
NEO TECHNOLOGY VENTURES, 2980
NEST VENTURES, 1289
NORO-MOSELEY PARTNERS, 1332
NORTH BRIDGE VENTURE PARTNERS, 1335
NORTHSTAR VENTURES, 3003
NORTHZONE, 3004
ONTARIO CAPITAL GROWTH CORPORATION, 2203
OPENVIEW VENTURE PARTNERS, 1381
PARTECH INTERNATIONAL, 1418
PASSION CAPITAL, 3021
PELION VENTURE PARTNERS, 1428
PENTECH VENTURES, 3023
PINNACLE MERCHANT CAPITAL, 2214
PIQUE VENTURES, 2215
POLARIS VENTURE PARTNERS, 1464
POLYTECH VENTURES, 3036
PRIME TECHNOLOGY VENTURES NV, 3042
PRINCIPIA SGR, 3043
PROFOUNDERS CAPITAL, 3046
PROVENANCE VENTURES, 1497
QUOTIDIAN VENTURES, 1521
RAPTOR GROUP, 1527
REAL VENTURES, 2224
RED DOT VENTURES, 3064
RELAY VENTURES, 2228
REVEL PARTNERS, 1557
SAMOS INVESTMENTS, 3088
SCOTTISH EQUITY PARTNERS, 3095
SELBY VENTURE PARTNERS, 1649
SINGTEL INNOV8, 3112
SK TELECOM VENTURES, 1692
SOFTBANK CAPITAL, 1701
SOLID VENTURES, 3119
SOUTHERN CAPITOL VENTURES, 1712
SOUTHERN CROSS VENTURE PARTNERS, 1713
SPECTRUM EQUITY INVESTORS LP, 1720
SPRING LAKE EQUITY PARTNERS, 1731
STEAMBOAT VENTURES, 3133

SUMMERHILL VENTURE PARTNERS, 2250
SUNBRIDGE PARTNERS, 1757
SUPREMUM CAPITAL, 3141
TALIS CAPITAL, 3148
TELEFONICA VENTURES, 3160
TELESYSTEM, 2255
TELUS VENTURES, 2256
TENNESSEE COMMUNITY VENTURES, 1799
THINKTIV VENTURES, 1813
TRANSMEDIA CAPITAL, 1841
TRIBECA VENTURE PARTNERS, 1851
TRIDENT CAPITAL, 1852
TRUE VENTURES, 1862
UPFRONT VENTURES, 1890
VALHALLA PARTNERS, 1901
VANTAGEPOINT CAPITAL PARTNERS, 1908
VENTANA CAPITAL MANAGEMENT LP, 1920
VENTECH, 3199
VERTEX VENTURE CAPITAL, 3205
VOYAGER CAPITAL, 1947
VTB CAPITAL, 3220
WALDEN VENTURE CAPITAL, 1953
WELLINGTON PARTNERS VENTURE CAPITAL GmbH, 3223
WESLEY CLOVER, 2276
WI HARPER GROUP, 1983
WOMEN'S VENTURE CAPITAL FUND, 2003
XG VENTURES, 2009

Digital Media Delivery
AMITI VENTURES, 117

Digital Networks
ENERTECH CAPITAL, 677

Digital Rights Management
LIQUID CAPITAL GROUP, 1137
SONY STRATEGIC TECHNOLOGY PARTNERSHIPS, 1706

Digital Security
LIQUID CAPITAL GROUP, 1137

Digital Services
FLYWHEEL VENTURES, 758

Digital Technology
DISRUPTION VENTURES, 2092

Digital Transformation
IGNITION PARTNERS, 978

Direct Marketing
AUDAX GROUP, 197
BREGAL SAGEMOUNT, 336
BRENTWOOD ASSOCIATES, 337
ENTREPRENEUR PARTNERS, 684
FREEMAN SPOGLI & CO., 786
LINSALATA CAPITAL PARTNERS, 1136
STERLING PARTNERS, 1745
TEXADA CAPITAL CORPORATION, 1801
UNION CAPITAL CORPORATION, 1883
VENTURE CAPITAL FUND OF NEW ENGLAND, 1922
XANGE PRIVATE EQUITY, 3229
ZM CAPITAL, 2019

Display Technologies
SONY STRATEGIC TECHNOLOGY PARTNERSHIPS, 1706

Distributed Electricity
VENROCK ASSOCIATES, 1918

Distribution
3I TEUPSCHLAND GmbH 3i Group, 2297
AAVIN PRIVATE EQUITY, 16
ACCESS CAPITAL, 34
ACTIVA CAPITAL, 2330
AEA INVESTORS, 63
AGRIBUSINESS MANAGEMENT COMPANY, 70
ALEUTIAN CAPITAL PARTNERS, 81

Industry Preference Index / Distribution

ALLSTATE INVESTMENTS LLC, 88
ALTIRA GROUP LLC, 98
AMERIMARK CAPITAL CORPORATION, 112
APOLLO GLOBAL MANAGEMENT, 141
ARGOSY CAPITAL, 165
ARTHUR P GOULD & COMPANY, 174
ASTOR CAPITAL GROUP, 2431
AUDAX GROUP, 197
AUGUST CAPITAL, 200
AURORA CAPITAL GROUP, 202
AZALEA CAPITAL, 216
BARING PRIVATE EQUITY PARTNERS INDIA, 2481
BBH CAPITAL PARTNERS, 243
BERKELEY VC INTERNATIONAL LLC, 255
BISON CAPITAL ASSET MANAGEMENT LLC, 277
BLACKFORD CAPITAL LLC, 279
BLUE POINT CAPITAL PARTNERS, 293
BLUE SAGE CAPITAL, 294
BLUEGEM CAPITAL PARTNERS, 2515
BOND CAPITAL, 2058
BOUNDS EQUITY PARTNERS, 319
BRADFORD EQUITIES MANAGEMENT LLC, 324
BRANDON CAPITAL GROUP, 329
BRANFORD CASTLE, 330
BRAZOS PRIVATE EQUITY PARTNERS, 331
BRENTWOOD ASSOCIATES, 337
BRIDGE STREET CAPITAL, 341
BROOKSIDE EQUITY PARTNERS LLC, 356
BRUML CAPITAL CORPORATION, 358
BUTLER CAPITAL PARTNERS FRANCE, 2542
C3 CAPITAL PARTNERS LP, 367
CAMBRIDGE CAPITAL, 383
CAMBRIDGE CAPITAL CORPORATION, 384
CAPITAL FOR BUSINESS, INC, 402
CAPITAL PARTNERS, 404
CARDINAL EQUITY PARTNERS, 412
CARPEDIA INTERNATIONAL, 2066
CASTLE HARLAN, 425
CATALYST GROUP, 427
CATALYST INVESTMENT MANAGERS PTY LIMITED PPM Capital, 2564
CENTERFIELD CAPITAL PARTNERS, 445
CERBERUS CAPITAL MANAGEMENT, 453
CHARLESBANK CAPITAL PARTNERS, 458
CHB CAPITAL PARTNERS, 463
CI CAPITAL PARTNERS, 478
CID CAPITAL, 480
CLEARLIGHT PARTNERS, 503
COMPAGNIE FINANCIERE E DE ROTHSCHILD BANQUE, 2616
COMPASS GROUP MANAGEMENT LLC, 525
COMSTOCK CAPITAL PARTNERS LLC, 529
CORTEC GROUP, 547
COVINGTON CAPITAL CORP., 2081
CRYSTAL RIDGE PARTNERS, 566
CUSTER CAPITAL, 572
CYPRIUM PARTNERS, 578
DAHER CAPITAL, 2640
DEFI GESTION SA Banque Cantonale Vaudoise, 2644
DESCO CAPITAL, 607
DN PARTNERS LLC, 620
DRESNER COMPANIES, 630
EAST FUND MANAGEMENT GmbH GiroCredit, 2674
ECI VENTURES, 2678
EDGEWATER CAPITAL PARTNERS, 653
ELGNER GROUP INVESTMENTS, 2099
EMIGRANT CAPITAL, 668
EMIL CAPITAL PARTNERS, 669
EMINENT CAPITAL PARTNERS, 670
EQUITY SOUTH, 694
EQUUS TOTAL RETURN, 695
FAIRMONT CAPITAL, 714
FCF PARTNERS LP, 719
FENWAY PARTNERS, 722
FIRST NEW ENGLAND CAPITAL LP, 740
FLORIDA CAPITAL PARTNERS, 753
FREEMAN SPOGLI & CO., 786
FRIEND SKOLER & COMPANY LLC, 791

FRIULIA SpA, 2749
FdG ASSOCIATES LP, 804
GEMINI INVESTORS, 815
GLADSTONE CAPITAL, 832
GOLDNER HAWN, 847
GOLUB CAPITAL, 848
GRANITE EQUITY PARTNERS, 855
GRANTHAM CAPITAL, 858
GRAPHITE CAPITAL MANAGEMENT LTD, 2787
GREENBRIAR EQUITY GROUP LLC, 867
GRUPO BISA, 2791
GTCR, 889
HALIFAX GROUP LLC, 899
HAMILTON ROBINSON CAPITAL PARTNERS, 903
HAMMOND, KENNEDY, WHITNEY & COMPANY, 904
HARBOUR GROUP, 911
HARREN EQUITY PARTNERS, 913
HARVEST PARTNERS, 917
HCI EQUITY PARTNERS, 920
HERITAGE PARTNERS, 929
HIG CAPITAL, 931
HIGH ROAD CAPITAL PARTNERS, 934
HIGH STREET CAPITAL, 935
HOLDING CAPITAL GROUP, 943
HORIZON PARTNERS, LTD, 948
HUMANA VENTURES, 958
INDASIA FUND ADVISORS PVT LTD, 2850
INDEPENDENT BANKERS CAPITAL FUND, 988
INDUSTRI KAPITAL SVENSKA AB, 2854
INTER-ASIA VENTURE MANAGEMENT LIMITED, 2872
INVESTAMERICA VENTURE GROUP, 1020
INVEXCEL PATRIMONIO, 2882
IRONBRIDGE EQUITY PARTNERS, 2156
IRONWOOD CAPITAL, 1025
JAFCO COMPANY LIMITED JAPAN, 2897
JEFFERIES CAPITAL PARTNERS, 1036
KERRY CAPITAL ADVISORS, 1071
KOHLBERG VENTURES, 1087
LEE EQUITY PARTNERS, 1108
LEONARD GREEN & PARTNERS LP, 1113
LINCOLNSHIRE MANAGEMENT, 1131
LINSALATA CAPITAL PARTNERS, 1136
LITTLEJOHN & COMPANY LLC, 1138
LM CAPITAL SECURITIES, 1141
LOMBARD INVESTMENTS, 1143
LONG POINT CAPITAL, 1145
LYNWOOD CAPITAL PARTNERS, 1156
MAIN STREET CAPITAL HOLDINGS LLC, 1163
MARANON CAPITAL, 1169
MARWIT CAPITAL LLC, 1171
MEKONG CAPITAL, 2952
MENTOR CAPITAL PARTNERS LTD, 1204
MERIT CAPITAL PARTNERS, 1210
MERITURN PARTNERS, 1214
MERIWETHER CAPITAL CORPORATION, 1216
MERRILL LYNCH (ASIA PACIFIC) LIMITED Merrill Lynch Group, 2955
MHS CAPITAL, 1227
MIDMARK CAPITAL LP, 1230
MIDWEST MEZZANINE FUNDS, 1232
MILESTONE PARTNERS, 1234
MONUMENT ADVISORS, 1252
MSOUTH EQUITY PARTNERS, 1270
MVP CAPITAL PARTNERS, 1275
NAVIGATION CAPITAL PARTNERS, 1279
NEW ENGLAND CAPITAL PARTNERS, 1295
NORTH AMERICAN FUND, 1333
NORTH BRIDGE VENTURE PARTNERS, 1335
NORTHSTAR CAPITAL, 1343
NORWEST EQUITY PARTNERS, 1345
NTH POWER TECHNOLOGIES, 1355
OAK HILL CAPITAL PARTNERS, 1360
ODEON CAPITAL PARTNERS, 1367
PAI MANAGEMENT, 3017
PALOMINO CAPITAL, 1409
PAMLICO CAPITAL, 1410
PARALLEL49 EQUITY, 2206
PARTHENON CAPITAL, 1419

Industry Preference Index / Drug Delivery Technology

PEGASUS CAPITAL GROUP, 1427
PENINSULA CAPITAL PARTNERS LLC, 1429
PENN VENTURE PARTNERS, 1431
PERMAL CAPITAL MANAGEMENT, 1435
PFINGSTEN PARTNERS LLC, 1438
PNC ERIEVIEW CAPITAL, 1460
PNC RIVERARCH CAPITAL, 1461
PRIVEQ CAPITAL FUNDS, 2218
PROVCO GROUP, 1496
PT BHAKTI INVESTAMA TBK, 3052
QUAD-C MANAGEMENT, 1507
QUARRY CAPITAL MANAGEMENT, 1513
RESILIENCE CAPITAL PARTNERS, 1548
RFE INVESTMENT PARTNERS, 1560
RIDGE CAPITAL PARTNERS LLC, 1565
RIVER ASSOCIATES INVESTMENTS LLC, 1573
RIVER CAPITAL, 1574
ROCK ISLAND CAPITAL, 1582
SALEM INVESTMENT PARTNERS, 1609
SALT CREEK CAPITAL, 1612
SARATOGA PARTNERS, 1624
SEACOAST CAPITAL CORPORATION, 1639
SEAFORT CAPITAL, 2242
SEIDLER EQUITY PARTNERS, 1648
SENTRY FINANCIAL CORPORATION, 1655
SORRENTO VENTURES, 1708
SOURCE CAPITAL GROUP, 1710
STARBOARD CAPITAL PARTNERS, 1738
STATELINE ANGELS, 1743
STERLING PARTNERS, 1745
STERN PARTNERS, 2249
STONEHENGE GROWTH CAPITAL, 1748
STONEWOOD CAPITAL MANAGEMENT, 1749
SUN CAPITAL PARTNERS, 1755
SVOBODA CAPITAL PARTNERS, 1767
TEKINVEST KK, 3157
TGF MANAGEMENT, 1805
TH LEE PUTNAM VENTURES, 1806
THREE CITIES RESEARCH, 1822
TRIWEST, 2267
TSG CONSUMER PARTNERS, 1863
TULLY & HOLLAND, 1869
TVV CAPITAL, 1872
UNION CAPITAL CORPORATION, 1883
UPFRONT VENTURES, 1890
VEBER PARTNERS LLC, 1911
VISION CAPITAL, 1939
WAND PARTNERS, 1956
WARWICK GROUP, 1958
WATERMILL GROUP, 1963
WAUD CAPITAL PARTNERS LLC, 1964
WAVELAND INVESTMENTS LLC, 1965
WELLS FARGO CAPITAL FINANCE, 1971
WELLSPRING CAPITAL MANAGEMENT LLC, 1972
WESTERN AMERICA CAPITAL GROUP, 2278
WESTLAKE SECURITIES, 1977
WESTVIEW CAPITAL PARTNERS, 1979
WINGATE PARTNERS, 1997
WOODBRIDGE GROUP, 2004
WYNNCHURCH CAPITAL, 2008
ZS FUND LP, 2021

Distribution & Logistics
FULCRUM CAPITAL PARTNERS, 2121

Distribution Services
RED CLAY CAPITAL HOLDINGS, 1532

Distribution and Logistics
CVF CAPITAL PARTNERS, 574

Diversified
3I SPAIN 3i Group, 2296
ABU DHABI INVESTMENT AUTHORITY, 2313
ACCENT EQUITY PARTNERS, 2317
ADVENT-MORRO EQUITY PARTNERS, 62
AFC MERCHANT BANK, 2343

ALABAMA FUTURES FUND, 75
ALLSTATE INVESTMENTS LLC, 88
ANDLINGER & COMPANY INC, 124
ANTARES CAPITAL CORPORATION, 132
ANTHEM VENTURE PARTNERS, 133
ARMADA INVESTMENT GROUP, 2418
ATLANTIC CAPITAL GROUP, 192
AVENUE CAPITAL GROUP, 211
BANYAN CAPITAL PARTNERS, 2045
BAYSIDE CAPITAL, 242
BLUM CAPITAL PARTNERS, 303
BROADLINE PRINCIPAL CAPITAL, 2533
BUSINESS CONSORTIUM FUND, 363
C&G CAPITAL PARTNERS, 366
CAMBRIDGE ASSOCIATES, 382
CAMBRIDGE VENTURES LP, 385
CENTRE LANE PARTNERS, 448
CHATTANOOGA RENAISSANCE FUND, 461
COBALT CAPITAL, 2078
COFOUNDERS CAPITAL, 512
COMPASS GROUP MANAGEMENT LLC, 525
DAVID N DEUTSCH & COMPANY LLC, 590
DUPONT CAPITAL, 637
ENGAGE VENTURES, 678
FIERA CAPITAL, 727
FORT WASHINGTON CAPITAL PARTNERS GROUP, 768
GELT VC, 814
GEN7 INVESTMENTS, 817
HONE CAPITAL, 945
INNOVATION CATALYST, 1000
INVESTCORP, 1021
KANSAS VENTURE CAPITAL, 1057
KENMONT CAPITAL PARTNERS, 1067
LEXINGTON PARTNERS, 1116
LONE STAR FUNDS, 1144
MCGOWAN CAPITAL GROUP, 1195
MERRILL LYNCH VENTURE CAPITAL, 1218
MONITOR CLIPPER PARTNERS, 1248
NAVIGATOR PARTNERS LLC, 1280
NUVEEN, 1356
ONEX FALCON, 1377
PANORAMIC VENTURES, 1412
PORTLAND SEED FUND, 1467
PPM AMERICA CAPITAL PARTNERS, 1471
RELATIVITY CAPITAL, 1542
RIVER CITIES CAPITAL FUNDS, 1575
SACHS CAPITAL, 1603
SAUGATUCK CAPITAL COMPANY, 1627
SHARESPOST, 1665
SIGULER GUFF & COMPANY, 1681
SOSV, 1709
START GARDEN, 1739
SUN MOUNTAIN CAPITAL, 1756
TRIVE CAPITAL, 1858
UNSHACKLED VENTURES, 1887
WILLOWRIDGE PARTNERS, 1986
WINNEBAGO SEED FUND, 1999
ZEPHYR MANAGEMENT LP, 2017

Downstream Technologies
NEWABLE VENTURES, 2988

Drones & 3D
FRONTIER VENTURES, 795

Drug Delivery
ARCUS VENTURES, 158
MVM LIFE SCIENCE PARTNERS, 2972
NOVARTIS VENTURE FUNDS, 1350
ONSET VENTURES, 1379
PARTISAN MANAGEMENT GROUP, 1420
PFIZER VENTURE INVESTMENTS, 1439
SIGNAL PEAK VENTURES, 1679
STARPHARMA POOLED DEVELOPMENT LIMITED, 3130

Drug Delivery Technology
5AM VENTURES, 11

Industry Preference Index / Drug Development

Drug Development
AMHERST FUND, 114
APPLE TREE PARTNERS, 144
ATLAS VENTURE: FRANCE, 2436
BIRCHMERE VENTURES, 275
BRANDON CAPITAL PARTNERS, 2527
CHL MEDICAL PARTNERS, 476
DRI CAPITAL, 2097
EcoR1 CAPITAL, 710
INTEGRA VENTURES, 1007
JOHNSTON ASSOCIATES, 1048
KBL HEALTHCARE VENTURES, 1062
MBF CAPITAL CORPORATION, 1191
MESA VERDE PARTNERS, 1222
ORBIMED HEALTHCARE FUND MANAGEMENT, 1383
PAPPAS VENTURES, 1414
RA CAPITAL MANAGEMENT, 1522
STONEWOOD CAPITAL MANAGEMENT, 1749
US VENTURE PARTNERS, 1898

Drug Discovery
ECHELON VENTURES, 647

E-Commerce
ALPHA VENTURE PARTNERS, 91
AMPLIFY, 121
BERTELSMANN DIGITAL MEDIA INVESTMENTS, 259
BLUE POINT CAPITAL PARTNERS, 293
CREDIT MUTUEL EQUITY, 2082
ENTREPRENEURS ROUNDTABLE ACCELERATOR, 685
PANACHE VENTURES, 2204
RUNTIDE CAPITAL, 1600
SIGNIA VENTURE PARTNERS, 1680
ZHENFUND, 3241

E-Commerce & Manufacturing
360 CAPITAL PARTNERS 360 Capital Management SA, 2288
ACCESS VENTURE PARTNERS LLC, 35
ACTUA, 52
ACUMEN VENTURES, 2333
ADASTRA, 2335
ALBUM VC, 79
ALMAZ CAPITAL, 89
AMADEUS CAPITAL PARTNERS LIMITED, 2378
ANGELS' FORUM LLC, 130
ANNAPURNA VENTURES, 2395
ARCHTOP VENTURES, 155
ASLANOBA CAPITAL, 2428
ATILA VENTURES, 2433
AUGMENTUM CAPITAL, 2441
AUTHOSIS VENTURES, 2448
AZURE CAPITAL PARTNERS, 218
BAIRD CAPITAL PARTNERS, 225
BALDERTON CAPITAL, 2469
BARODA VENTURES, 231
BLACKBIRD VENTURES, 2511
BLH VENTURE PARTNERS, 285
BOXGROUP, 321
BRAINSTORM VENTURES, 327
BREAKAWAY VENTURES, 332
BULL VENTURES, 2538
BURAN VENTURE CAPITAL, 2540
CALUMET VENTURE FUND, 378
CATALYST INVESTORS, 429
CAVA CAPITAL, 433
CHARLES RIVER VENTURES, 457
CHICAGO VENTURE PARTNERS LP, 472
CLEARSTONE VENTURE PARTNERS, 504
COMCAST VENTURES, 520
COMPAGNIE FINANCIERE E DE ROTHSCHILD BANQUE, 2616
COMPOUND, 527
DATA POINT CAPITAL, 587
DEEP FORK CAPITAL, 601
DETROIT VENTURE PARTNERS, 608
DFJ GOTHAM VENTURES, 609
DN CAPITAL, 2659
DUBILIER & COMPANY, 632
DUNDEE VENTURE CAPITAL, 635
E.BRICKS DIGITAL, 2672
ECOAST ANGEL NETWORK, 649
EDEN VENTURES, 2682
EDISON PARTNERS, 655
EMIL CAPITAL PARTNERS, 669
EPLANET CAPITAL, 691
EXPANSION VENTURE CAPITAL, 708
FELICIS VENTURES, 720
FIRESTARTER FUND, 732
FIVE ELMS CAPITAL, 746
FORTÉ VENTURES, 770
FOUNDER COLLECTIVE, 774
FRIEND SKOLER & COMPANY LLC, 791
FUNG CAPITAL USA, 799
GENACAST VENTURES, 818
GOLDEN SEEDS, 845
GREAT OAKS VENTURE CAPITAL, 863
GREE VENTURES, 2789
GREYCROFT PARTNERS, 876
HENQ, 2813
IDEALAB, 976
IDG CAPITAL, 977
INFLECTION POINT VENTURES, 993
INLAND TECHSTART FUND, 997
INSIGHT VENTURE PARTNERS, 1005
INVENTURE PARTNERS, 2877
INVENTUS, 1017
INVESCO PRIVATE CAPITAL, 1019
JMI EQUITY FUND LP, 1045
KIBO VENTURES, 2911
LAUNCHPAD VENTURE GROUP, 1104
LEASING TECHNOLOGIES INTERNATIONAL INC., 1107
LIGHTSPEED VENTURE PARTNERS, 1125
LIQUID CAPITAL GROUP, 1137
M25 GROUP, 1159
MAYFIELD FUND, 1187
MESA+, 1223
MHS CAPITAL, 1227
MISSION VENTURES, 1239
MMC VENTURES, 2963
MORADO VENTURE PARTNERS, 1254
MURPHREE VENTURE PARTNERS, 1273
NAUTA CAPITAL, 2978
NEW ATLANTIC VENTURES, 1290
NEWLIGHT MANAGEMENT, 1313
NORTHZONE, 3004
OAK INVESTMENT PARTNERS, 1361
PALO ALTO VENTURE SCIENCE, 1407
PAMLICO CAPITAL, 1410
PARTECH INTERNATIONAL, 1418
PENTECH VENTURES, 3023
PINEHURST ADVISORS, 3029
PITON CAPITAL, 3031
POINT NINE CAPITAL, 3035
PRIMARY VENTURE PARTNERS, 1479
PRIME TECHNOLOGY VENTURES NV, 3042
PRINCIPIA SGR, 3043
QUESTMARK PARTNERS LP, 1517
QUOTIDIAN VENTURES, 1521
RAPTOR GROUP, 1527
REVO CAPITAL, 3069
REVOLUTION LLC, 1558
ROUGH DRAFT VENTURES, 1593
RTP VENTURES, 1598
RU-NET VENTURES, 3078
SAMOS INVESTMENTS, 3088
SATORI CAPITAL, 1625
SATURN PARTNERS, 1626
SHANGHAI INFORMATION INVESTMENT INCORPORATED, 3105
SHASTA VENTURES, 1666
SILICON ALLEY VENTURE PARTNERS, 1682
SOFTBANK CAPITAL, 1701
SORRENTO VENTURES, 1708
SOUTHERN CAPITOL VENTURES, 1712
SRIJAN CAPITAL, 3124
STARBOARD CAPITAL PARTNERS, 1738

STRAND HANSON LIMITED, 3137
SUSQUEHANNA GROWTH EQUITY, 1761
SV ANGEL, 1763
SYCAMORE VENTURES, 1771
TANK STREAM VENTURES, 3151
TARGET PARTNERS, 3152
TENGELMANN VENTURES, 3161
TENNESSEE COMMUNITY VENTURES, 1799
TEXADA CAPITAL CORPORATION, 1801
THINKTIV VENTURES, 1813
TMI, 3172
TRIBECA VENTURE PARTNERS, 1851
TRINITY VENTURES, 1855
TRUE VENTURES, 1862
USHA MARTIN VENTURES LIMITED, 3193
VEDANTA CAPITAL LP, 1913
VENTURE CAPITAL FUND OF NEW ENGLAND, 1922
VERSION ONE VENTURES, 2272
VTB CAPITAL, 3220
WALDEN ISRAEL VENTURE CAPITAL, 3221
WASABI VENTURES, 1959
WESTERN STATES INVESTMENT GROUP, 1975
WHITE STAR CAPITAL, 1982
WI HARPER GROUP, 1983
YL VENTURES, 3236

E-Mobility
BMW I VENTURES, 305

Earth Sciences
HMS HAWAII MANAGEMENT, 942

Eco-Energies
DEMETER PARTNERS, 2647

Eco-Industries
DEMETER PARTNERS, 2647

Ecommerce
DUTCHESS CAPITAL, 638

Economics
NCT VENTURES, 1285

EdTech
WILDCAT VENTURE PARTNERS, 1985

Education
AAVISHKAAR, 2305
ABRY PARTNERS, 20
ABS CAPITAL PARTNERS, 21
ACCRETIVE LLC, 38
ACUMEN, 54
ALLSTATE INVESTMENTS LLC, 88
ALPHAMUNDI GROUP LTD, 2368
AMERICAN SUSTAINABLE BUSINESS NETWORK, 3246
ANTHEM VENTURE PARTNERS, 133
APPIAN EDUCATION VENTURES, 142
ARCHTOP VENTURES, 155
ARLINGTON CAPITAL PARTNERS, 167
ASTELLA INVESTMENTS, 2429
AUDAX GROUP, 197
AUSTRALIAN ETHICAL INVESTMENT LIMITED, 2447
AZURE CAPITAL PARTNERS, 218
BARCLAYS VENTURES Barclays, 2477
BARING PRIVATE EQUITY PARTNERS INDIA, 2481
BEZOS EXPEDITIONS, 265
BIA DIGITAL PARTNERS LP, 266
BIG SOCIETY CAPITAL, 2500
BIGFOOT VENTURES, 2502
BONVENTURE, 2522
BREGAL SAGEMOUNT, 336
BRENTWOOD ASSOCIATES, 337
BRIGHTPATH CAPITAL PARTNERS, 343
CALUMET VENTURE FUND, 378
CALVERT INVESTMENT MANAGEMENT, 379
CAMBRIA GROUP, 381
CAMDEN PARTNERS HOLDINGS LLC, 386
CAMPUS COMPANIES VENTURE CAPITAL FUND, 2545
CAPITAL FOR BUSINESS, INC, 402
CAPITAL PARTNERS, 404
CARBON VENTURES, 411
CASTANEA PARTNERS, 424
CATALYST INVESTMENT MANAGERS PTY LIMITED PPM Capital, 2564
CATALYST INVESTORS, 429
CDH INVESTMENTS, 2570
CENTERFIELD CAPITAL PARTNERS, 445
CHARLESBANK CAPITAL PARTNERS, 458
CHENGWEI VENTURES, 2581
CHICAGO GROWTH PARTNERS, 470
CID CAPITAL, 480
CITY LIGHT CAPITAL, 490
CIVC PARTNERS, 491
CLEARLIGHT PARTNERS, 503
COMMONS CAPITAL, 522
COMVEST PARTNERS, 530
DAY ONE VENTURES, 594
DECIENS CAPITAL, 600
DIRECT CAPITAL PRIVATE EQUITY LIMITED, 2655
EM WARBURG, PINCUS & COMPANY INTERNATIONAL, 2688
EM WARBURG, PINCUS & COMPANY JAPAN, 2689
EMIGRANT CAPITAL, 668
ENDEAVOUR CAPITAL, 674
ENNOVENT, 2692
EPIC PARTNERS, 688
EXPANSION VENTURE CAPITAL, 708
FELICIS VENTURES, 720
FIDELITY GROWTH PARTNERS ASIA, 2724
FIRSTMARK CAPITAL, 744
FRIEDMAN, FLEISCHER & LOWE LLC, 790
GEMINI INVESTORS, 815
GREAT OAKS VENTURE CAPITAL, 863
GRYPHON INVESTORS, 886
GSV VENTURES, 888
HELION VENTURE PARTNERS, LLC International Management (Mauritius) Ltd, 2809
HENDERSON PRIVATE CAPITAL, 2812
HERITAGE PARTNERS, 929
HIG CAPITAL, 931
HOULIHAN LOKEY, 951
IBM VENTURE CAPITAL GROUP, 971
IDG CAPITAL PARTNERS, 2838
INNOVATION PLATFORM CAPITAL, 1002
INSIGHT VENTURE PARTNERS, 1005
INTERNATIONAL FINANCE CORPORATION (IFC), 1012
INVENTUS, 1017
IRONWOOD CAPITAL, 1025
ISIS EP LLP F & C, 2889
IXORA VENTURES, 2895
J. BURKE CAPITAL PARTNERS, 1027
JEFFERIES CAPITAL PARTNERS, 1036
JLL PARTNERS, 1043
JORDAN COMPANY, 1049
KAPOR CAPITAL, 1058
KARLIN VENTURES, 1059
KHOSLA VENTURES, 1073
KOHLBERG KRAVIS ROBERTS & COMPANY, 1086
LAUNCHPAD VENTURES, 2922
LEASING TECHNOLOGIES INTERNATIONAL INC., 1107
LEEDS EQUITY PARTNERS, 1109
LLR PARTNERS INC, 1140
LOMBARD INVESTMENTS, 1143
M25 GROUP, 1159
MAYFIELD FUND, 1187
MCG CAPITAL CORPORATION, 1192
MHS CAPITAL, 1227
MIDINVEST LIMITED, 2957
MIDWEST MEZZANINE FUNDS, 1232
MURPHY & PARTNERS FUND LP, 1274
NEW MARKETS VENTURE PARTNERS, 1298
NEW MOUNTAIN CAPITAL, 1300
NEWSCHOOLS VENTURE FUND, 1315
NORTH AMERICAN FUND, 1333
NORTHSTAR CAPITAL, 1343

Industry Preference Index / Education Technology

NOVAK BIDDLE VENTURE PARTNERS, 1348
OBVIOUS VENTURES, 1363
OCA VENTURES, 1364
OWL VENTURES, 1393
PARALLEL INVESTMENT PARTNERS, 1417
PARALLEL49 EQUITY, 2206
PARKVIEW CAPITAL PARTNERS, 2207
PEACHTREE EQUITY PARTNERS, 1425
PENN VENTURE PARTNERS, 1431
PHOENIX EQUITY PARTNERS LIMITED, 3027
PLUS VENTURES, 3032
POLESTAR CAPITAL, 1465
POUSCHINE COOK CAPITAL MANAGEMENT LLC, 1470
PRAIRIE CAPITAL, 1473
PREVIZ VENTURES, 3041
PRIMUS CAPITAL, 1480
PROCURITAS PARTNERS KB, 3045
PROSPECT PARTNERS LLC, 1494
QUAD PARTNERS, 1506
QUESTER CAPITAL MANAGEMENT LIMITED, 3061
REACH CAPITAL, 1530
RETHINK COMMUNITY, 1553
RETHINK EDUCATION, 1554
REVOLUTION LLC, 1558
RISE OF THE REST, 1571
RIVERSIDE COMPANY, 1576
SAIF PARTNERS, 3084
SALMON RIVER CAPITAL, 1611
SARONA ASSET MANAGEMENT, 2239
SCHOONER CAPITAL LLC, 1630
SCOTTISH ENTERPRISE, 3094
SEIDLER EQUITY PARTNERS, 1648
SINEWAVE VENTURES, 1689
SOCIAL CAPITAL, 1698
SOFTBANK VENTURES KOREA, 3118
SOLSTICE CAPITAL LP, 1704
SOUTHPORT PARTNERS, 1714
SOVEREIGN CAPITAL, 3121
SPIRE CAPITAL PARTNERS, 1727
STERLING PARTNERS, 1745
SUMMER STREET CAPITAL PARTNERS, 1753
SUMMIT PARTNERS, 1754
SUTTER HILL VENTURES, 1762
THE ABRAAJ GROUP, 3164
THOMA BRAVO LLC, 1817
TIE ANGELS GROUP SEATTLE, 1827
TMG CAPITAL PARTNERS, 3171
TONIIC, 1833
TOP RENERGY INC., 2263
URBAN INNOVATION FUND, 1895
VALAR VENTURES, 1899
VALHALLA PARTNERS, 1901
VERONIS SUHLER STEVENSON, 1929
VICKERS FINANCIAL GROUP, 3206
WESTTECH VENTURES, 3226
WHEATLEY PARTNERS, 1981
WICKS GROUP OF COMPANIES, LLC, 1984
WILDCAT VENTURE PARTNERS, 1985
ZHENFUND, 3241

Education Technology
MK CAPITAL, 1242
MOUNTAINEER CAPITAL, 1262
PALO ALTO VENTURE SCIENCE, 1407

Educational Technologies
APPIAN EDUCATION VENTURES, 142

Efficient Transport
AUSTRALIAN ETHICAL INVESTMENT LIMITED, 2447

Electric Power
ALTIRA GROUP LLC, 98

Electric Transmission
ENERGY CAPITAL PARTNERS, 676

Electrical Distribution
HT CAPITAL ADVISORS LLC, 956

Electronic Components
3I TEUPSCHLAND GmbH 3i Group, 2297
AKERS CAPITAL LLC, 74
ALEXANDER HUTTON, 82
ALLSTATE INVESTMENTS LLC, 88
AMPERSAND CAPITAL PARTNERS, 119
ANDLINGER & COMPANY INC, 124
ANTHEM VENTURE PARTNERS, 133
ARCH VENTURE PARTNERS, 154
ARTHUR P GOULD & COMPANY, 174
AUGUST CAPITAL, 200
AUSTIN VENTURES, 205
BERKELEY VC INTERNATIONAL LLC, 255
CAPITAL FOR BUSINESS, INC, 402
DEFTA PARTNERS, 603
DRAPER RICHARDS KAPLAN FOUNDATION, 628
DRESNER COMPANIES, 630
KLEINER PERKINS, 1079
MANHATTAN INVESTMENT PARTNERS, 1166
MASSACHUSETTS CAPITAL RESOURCE COMPANY, 1176
MASSACHUSETTS GROWTH CAPITAL CORPORATION, 1177
MAYFIELD FUND, 1187
MOTOROLA SOLUTIONS VENTURE CAPITAL, 1260
NORTH BRIDGE VENTURE PARTNERS, 1335
NOVAK BIDDLE VENTURE PARTNERS, 1348
OEM CAPITAL, 1369
PARTECH INTERNATIONAL, 1418
PERMAL CAPITAL MANAGEMENT, 1435
PIDC PHILADELPHIA, 1445
POLESTAR CAPITAL, 1465
PROVCO GROUP, 1496
PT BHAKTI INVESTAMA TBK, 3052
RAF INDUSTRIES, 1524
ROYALTY CAPITAL MANAGEMENT, 1595
SEACOAST CAPITAL CORPORATION, 1639
SILVER CREEK VENTURES, 1684
SOURCE CAPITAL GROUP, 1710
SOUTHPORT PARTNERS, 1714
VALLEY VENTURES LP, 1903
VISION CAPITAL, 1939
WESTERN STATES INVESTMENT GROUP, 1975
WESTERN TECHNOLOGY INVESTMENT, 1976
WINGATE PARTNERS, 1997

Electronic Technology
3I AUSTRIA BETEILGUNG GmbH 3i Group, 2290
3I DEUTSCHLAND GESELLSCHAFT FUR 3i Group, 2291
3I GERMANY GmbH 3i Group, 2293
ABOA VENTURE MANAGEMENT OY, 2310
ABU DHABI INVESTMENT AUTHORITY, 2313
ACE VENTURE CAPITAL LIMITED, 2322
ADVENT VENTURE PARTNERS, 2340
AITEC, 2349
AJU CAPITAL COMPANY, 2350
ALTAIR VENTURES, 95
AMADEUS CAPITAL PARTNERS LIMITED, 2378
AMANET TECHNOLOGIES LIMITED, 2381
AMWIN MANAGEMENT PTY LIMITED, 2390
AXA INVESTMENT MANAGERS PRIVATE EQUITY EUROPE, 2457
BALTCAP MANAGEMENT LTD, 2471
BANEXI VENTURES PARTNERS, 2472
BARING PRIVATE EQUITY PARTNERS INDIA, 2481
BI WALDEN MANAGEMENT SDN Walden International, 2499
BROOK VENTURE FUND, 352
CAPRICORN VENTURE PARTNERS NV, 2554
CAPVIS EQUITY PARTNERS, 2555
CAZENOVE PRIVATE EQUITY Cazenove Capital, 2568
CHINA DEVELOPMENT INDUSTRIAL BANK CDFH, 2583
CHINA WALDEN MANAGEMENT LIMITED Walden Group, 2588
CLAL ELECTRONICS INDUSTRIES LIMITED, 2600
COMPAGNIE FINANCIERE E DE ROTHSCHILD BANQUE, 2616
CRESCENDO VENTURE MANAGEMENT LLC, 2630
DAIMLERCHRYSLER VENTURE GmbH DaimlerChrysler AG, 2641
DEFI GESTION SA Banque Cantonale Vaudoise, 2644

Industry Preference Index / Enabling Technology

EDISON PARTNERS, 655
ENTERPRISE EQUITY (NI) LTD, 2695
EQUISTONE, 2705
EQVITEC PARTNERS OY, 2707
EURAZEO, 2710
FERRANTI LIMITED, 2723
FINADVANCE, 2726
FINANCIERE DE BRIENNE FCPR, 2729
FIRST ISRAEL MEZZANINE INVESTORS LIMITED, 2736
FLANDERS' FOREIGN INVESTMENT OFFICE, 2737
FRIULIA SpA, 2749
GENERAL ENTERPRISE MANAGEMENT SERVICES, 2763
GENERICS GROUP LIMITED Generics Group, 2764
GILDE INVESTMENT FUNDS, 2770
GIMV GIMV, 2771
GLYNN CAPITAL MANAGEMENT, 840
GUANGDONG TECHNOLOGY VENTURE CAPITAL COMPANY, 2793
HELMET CAPITAL FUND MANAGEMENT OY, 2811
HT CAPITAL ADVISORS LLC, 956
I-PACIFIC PARTNERS, 2831
ID VENTURES AMERICA LLC, 974
INDUSTRIEBANK LIOF NV, 2857
INDUSTRIFONDEN, 2858
INNOFINANCE OY, 2864
INVEXCEL PATRIMONIO, 2882
JAFCO COMPANY LIMITED JAPAN, 2897
JAVELIN INVESTMENTS, 2899
JC TECHNOLOGIES LTD, 2900
KBL FOUNDER SA, 2908
KOREA FIRST VENTURE CAPITAL CORPORATION, 2915
LEONIA MB GROUP/MB FUNDS, 2928
LMBO FINANCE, 2936
MACQUARIE DIRECT INVESTMENT LIMITED, 2942
MARATHON VENTURE CAPITAL FUND LIMITED, 2945
MARCEAU INVESTISSEMENTS, 2946
MERRILL LYNCH (ASIA PACIFIC) LIMITED Merrill Lynch Group, 2955
MOMENTUM FUNDS MANAGEMENT PTY LIMITED, 2966
NEOTENY COMPANY LIMITED, 2982
NEW YORK LIFE CAPITAL PARTNERS, 1308
NORTHERN ENTERPRISE LIMITED, 3002
PRIME TECHNOLOGY VENTURES NV, 3042
PRIVATE EQUITY PARTNERS SPA, 3044
PROCURITAS PARTNERS KB, 3045
QUESTER CAPITAL MANAGEMENT LIMITED, 3061
RAFAEL DEVELOPMENT CORPORATION (RDC) LIMITED, 3063
RHO VENTURES, 1561
ROSER VENTURES LLC, 1590
SAMBRINVEST SA, 3087
SELBY VENTURE PARTNERS, 1649
SEQUOIA CAPITAL, 1657
SHANNON COMMERCIAL PROPERTIES, 3106
SHAW KWEI AND PARTNERS, 3107
SIERRA VENTURES, 1672
SIGMA PARTNERS, 1674
SIGNATURE CAPITAL LLC, 3111
SONY EUROPE, 3120
SOURCE CAPITAL GROUP, 1710
STARBOARD CAPITAL PARTNERS, 1738
STARVEST PARTNERS, 1741
SVB CAPITAL, 1766
TAT CAPITAL PARTNERS LTD., 3153
TECH CAPITAL PARTNERS, 2253
TECHNOCAP, 2254
TEKNOINVEST MANAGEMENT, 3158
TFG CAPITAL AG, 3163
THOMSON-CSF VENTURES, 3167
THROUNARFELAG ISLANDS PLC, 3168
TRINITY VENTURE CAPITAL TVC Holdings plc, 3182
TRU MANAGEMENT, 1860
TSG EQUITY PARTNERS, 1864
UCA UNTERNEHMER CONSULT AG, 3188
VALLEY VENTURES LP, 1903
VENTURE ASSOCIATES PARTNERS LLC, 1921
VENTURE CAPITAL FUND OF NEW ENGLAND, 1922
VERITAS CAPITAL FUND LP, 1927
WESTERN STATES INVESTMENT GROUP, 1975
WINDWARD VENTURES, 1995
WINGATE PARTNERS, 1997
WOODSIDE FUND, 2005

Electronics
3M UNITEK, 2299
ALBERTA ENTERPRISE, 2028
ATILA VENTURES, 2433
BEZOS EXPEDITIONS, 265
BM-T BETEILIGUNGS MANAGEMENT THURINGEN GmbH, 2518
BUSINESS GROWTH FUND, 2541
CALIFORNIA TECHNOLOGY VENTURES, 374
CASABONA VENTURES, 421
CONOR VENTURE PARTNERS OY, 2621
CREATHOR VENTURE, 2629
DFJ ESPRIT, 2653
EPLANET CAPITAL, 691
FLORIDA FUNDERS, 754
FREESTYLE, 787
GOLDEN GATE CAPITAL, 843
GOOD GROWTH CAPITAL, 849
HORIZON PARTNERS, LTD, 948
HORIZONS VENTURES, 2822
IBM VENTURE CAPITAL GROUP, 971
KILMER CAPITAL PARTNERS, 2162
MITSUBISHI UFJ CAPITAL, 2961
MITSUI SUMITOMO INSURANCE VENTURE CAPITAL CO, 2962
NEW ENTERPRISE ASSOCIATES, 1296
NEWABLE VENTURES, 2988
PAC-LINK MANAGEMENT CORP., 3015
PANGAEA VENTURES LTD, 2205
PARKWALK ADVISORS, 3019
QUEST FOR GROWTH, 3060
SIGMA PARTNERS, 1674
SORRENTO VENTURES, 1708
STATELINE ANGELS, 1743
TEL VENTURE CAPITAL, 1793
TENAYA CAPITAL, 1798
TROIKA CAPITAL PARTNERS, 3184
VERGE FUND, 1926
VIKING VENTURE, 3207
XANGE PRIVATE EQUITY, 3229
YISSUM TECHNOLOGY TRANSFER, 3235

Embedded Software
OJAS VENTURE PARTNERS, 3010

Embedded Systems
CONOR VENTURE PARTNERS OY, 2621
ISOURCE GESTION, 2890

Emerging Markets, Sectors & Technologies
M12, 1158
QUILVEST CAPITAL PARTNERS, 1518
TEXAS EMERGING TECHNOLOGY FUND, 1802
TI VENTURE CAPITAL Texas Instruments Incorporated, 1825
VENTURE TECH ALLIANCE, 1924
VENTUREAST, 3202

Emerging Media
CHINAROCK CAPITAL MANAGEMENT VENTURES, 474

Emerging Technology
NAYA VENTURES, 1284
PRITZKER GROUP VENTURE CAPITAL, 1483

Emissions Control
ANGELENO GROUP, 127

Enabling Software
CONVEXA Tyveholmen AS, 2623

Enabling Technology
ALLEGIS CYBER CAPITAL, 84
BRAINSTORM VENTURES, 327
CORE CAPITAL PARTNERS, 540
EASTVEN VENTURE PARTNERS, 645
FUNG CAPITAL USA, 799
I-HATCH VENTURES LLC, 967

Industry Preference Index / Energy

KOHLBERG VENTURES, 1087
MADISON PARKER CAPITAL, 1161
MILLENIUM TECHNOLOGY VALUE PARTNERS, 1235
NEOTENY COMPANY LIMITED, 2982
NEWSPRING CAPITAL, 1316
OXANTIUM VENTURES, 1394
PHYSIC VENTURES, 1442
SHANGHAI INFORMATION INVESTMENT INCORPORATED, 3105
WESTSUMMIT CAPITAL, 3225

Energy
3M UNITEK, 2299
3TS CAPITAL PARTNERS 3i Group plc, 2301
3i GROUP PLC, 2303
AAVISHKAAR, 2305
ABB TECHNOLOGY VENTURES, 2307
ABELL FOUNDATION VENTURES, 18
ACCERA AG, 2319
ACERO CAPITAL, 40
ACKRELL CAPITAL, 43
ACON INVESTMENTS, 45
ACTIS, 2329
ACUMEN, 54
ADVANTAGE CAPITAL PARTNERS, 60
AEM CAPITAL, 2341
ALBEMARLE PRIVATE EQUITY LIMITED, 2352
ALBERTA ENTERPRISE, 2028
ALLOY VENTURES, 87
ALTIRA GROUP LLC, 98
AMBIENTA ENVIRONMENTAL ASSETS, 2383
AMERICAN SUSTAINABLE BUSINESS NETWORK, 3246
ANDLINGER & COMPANY INC, 124
ANGELENO GROUP, 127
ANNAPOLIS CAPITAL, 2034
ARC FINANCIAL, 2036
ARCAPITA INC, 153
ARCLIGHT CAPITAL PARTNERS, 157
ARES MANAGEMENT LLC, 160
ARROWHEAD INNOVATION FUND, 169
ARTHUR P GOULD & COMPANY, 174
ARTHUR VENTURES, 175
ARTIS VENTURES, 177
ASSET MANAGEMENT VENTURES, 183
ASTER CAPITAL, 2430
ATRIUM CAPITAL, 194
AUDAX GROUP, 197
AUGMENT VENTURES, 198
AURORA CAPITAL GROUP, 202
AUSTRALIAN ETHICAL INVESTMENT LIMITED, 2447
AVENUE CAPITAL GROUP, 211
AVISTA CAPITAL PARTNERS, 212
AWAY REALTY, 2456
AZALEA CAPITAL, 216
AZIMUTH CAPITAL MANAGEMENT, 2044
AZIONE CAPITAL, 2464
BAIN CAPITAL PRIVATE EQUITY, 223
BARING PRIVATE EQUITY PARTNERS INDIA, 2481
BARING VOSTOK CAPITAL PARTNERS, 2482
BASF VENTURE CAPITAL, 2483
BATTELLE VENTURES, 236
BEIJING HIGH TECHNOLOGY INVESTMENT COMPANY, 2490
BERKSHIRE PARTNERS LLC, 257
BERTI INVESTMENTS, 2496
BLACKSTONE PRIVATE EQUITY GROUP, 280
BLAST FUNDING, 282
BLUE SAGE CAPITAL, 294
BLUESTEM CAPITAL COMPANY, 300
BOCI DIRECT INVESTMENT MANAGEMENT LIMITED Bank of China, 2520
BP ALTERNATIVE ENERGY VENTURES, 322
BRAEMAR ENERGY VENTURES, 325
BRANFORD CASTLE, 330
BREAKWATER INVESTMENTS, 333
BREGAL ENERGY, 335
BRIGHT CAPITAL, 2531
BRIGHTSTONE VENTURE CAPITAL, 344
C3 CAPITAL PARTNERS LP, 367

CAI CAPITAL PARTNERS, 368
CALCEF CLEAN ENERGY FUND, 370
CALVERT INVESTMENT MANAGEMENT, 379
CANADIAN VENTURE CAPITAL ASSOCIATION Canadian Venture Capital & Private Equity Association, 3249
CAPITAL FOR BUSINESS, INC, 402
CAPITAL SOUTHWEST CORPORATION, 406
CAPITALA, 408
CAPITOL PARTNERS, 409
CAPRICORN VENTURE PARTNERS NV, 2554
CAPX PARTNERS, 410
CARBON VENTURES, 411
CARLYLE GROUP, 416
CASTLE HARLAN, 425
CATALYST GROUP, 427
CEDAR VENTURES LLC, 439
CEDRUS INVESTMENTS, 2572
CEI VENTURES, 440
CHARLESBANK CAPITAL PARTNERS, 458
CHEVRON TECHNOLOGY VENTURES, 468
CHEYENNE CAPITAL, 469
CHICAGO VENTURE PARTNERS LP, 472
CHORD CAPITAL, 2589
CIBC CAPITAL MARKETS, 2073
CIC PARTNERS, 479
CIT GROUP, 486
CITY LIGHT CAPITAL, 490
CLARITY CAPITAL, 2602
CLEAN ENERGY VENTURE GROUP, 498
CLEAN PACIFIC VENTURES, 499
CLEARLAKE CAPITAL, 502
CLIFFORD CHANCE PUNDER, 2605
COACH & CAPITAL, 2610
COLORADO MILE HIGH FUND, 516
COMMONS CAPITAL, 522
CONNECTICUT INNOVATIONS, 532
CREDIT MUTUEL EQUITY, 2082
CRESTVIEW PARTNERS, 560
CVC INVESTMENT MANAGERS LIMITED, 2636
DAG VENTURES, 582
DARBY OVERSEAS INVESTMENTS LTD, 585
DAVENPORT RESOURCES LLC, 589
DISCOVERY CAPITAL, 2091
DUBIN CLARK & COMPANY, 633
DYNAMO VC, 640
EARTHRISE CAPITAL, 643
ECOSYSTEM VENTURES, 650
EDGESTONE CAPITAL PARTNERS, 2098
ELEMENT PARTNERS, 658
EM WARBURG, PINCUS & COMPANY INTERNATIONAL, 2688
EM WARBURG, PINCUS & COMPANY JAPAN, 2689
EMERALD TECHNOLOGY VENTURES, 2101
ENCAP FLATROCK MIDSTREAM, 672
ENERGY VENTURES, 2691
ENNOVENT, 2692
ENTERPRISE EQUITY (NI) LTD, 2695
EOS PARTNERS LP, 687
ESCHELON ENERGY PARTNERS, 697
EXCEL VENTURE MANAGEMENT, 704
EXPANSION CAPITAL PARTNERS, 707
EXPANSION VENTURE CAPITAL, 708
EXPERIMENT FUND, 709
EXPORT DEVELOPMENT CANADA, 2106
FERRANTI LIMITED, 2723
FIELDSTONE PRIVATE CAPITAL GROUP, 726
FINLOMBARDA SpA, 2730
FIRELAKE CAPITAL, 731
FIRST ANALYSIS, 733
FIRST RESERVE, 741
FISHER LYNCH CAPITAL, 745
FORESIGHT VENTURE PARTNERS, 2740
FORTRESS INVESTMENT GROUP LLC, 769
FOUNDERS FUND, 778
FOX PAINE & COMPANY LLC, 781
FULL CIRCLE INVESTMENTS, 2753
GE CAPITAL, 811
GE VENTURES, 812

Industry Preference Index / Energy

GENERAL ENTERPRISE MANAGEMENT SERVICES, 2763
GENERICS GROUP LIMITED Generics Group, 2764
GIMV GIMV, 2771
GOOD GROWTH CAPITAL, 849
GROVE STREET ADVISORS LLC, 884
GRYPHON MANAGEMENT COMPANY, 887
GULFSTAR GROUP, 893
HADDINGTON VENTURES LLC, 898
HAMILTON ROBINSON CAPITAL PARTNERS, 903
HAMMOND, KENNEDY, WHITNEY & COMPANY, 904
HELLMAN & FRIEDMAN LLC, 927
HIG CAPITAL, 931
HOPEWELL VENTURES, 947
HRL MORRISON & COMPANY LIMITED, 2826
HUMANA VENTURES, 958
HURON RIVER VENTURES, 964
IBM VENTURE CAPITAL GROUP, 971
IN-Q-TEL, 983
INETWORKS ADVISORS LLC, 991
INLAND TECHSTART FUND, 997
INNOFINANCE OY, 2864
INNOVATION CAPITAL LIMITED, 2868
INNOVATION PLATFORM CAPITAL, 1002
INNOVATION WORKS, 1003
INSIGHT VENTURE PARTNERS, 1005
INVICO CAPITAL CORPORATION, 2155
IP GROUP, 2883
IRON GATE CAPITAL, 1024
ISRAEL CLEANTECH VENTURES, 2891
JEFFERIES CAPITAL PARTNERS, 1036
JOG CAPITAL, 2159
JORDAN COMPANY, 1049
KAIROS VENTURES, 1055
KBL FOUNDER SA, 2908
KENSINGTON CAPITAL PARTNERS, 2160
KERRY CAPITAL ADVISORS, 1071
KESTREL ENERGY PARTNERS, 1072
KOHLBERG KRAVIS ROBERTS & COMPANY, 1086
KRG CAPITAL PARTNERS, 1090
LAUNCHPAD VENTURES, 2922
LEX CAPITAL MANAGEMENT, 2166
LIME ROCK PARTNERS, 1129
LINLEY CAPITAL, 1134
LOMBARD INVESTMENTS, 1143
LONGBOW CAPITAL, 2171
LUX CAPITAL, 1155
MACQUARIE DIRECT INVESTMENT LIMITED, 2942
MADISON DEARBORN PARTNERS, 1160
MANHATTAN INVESTMENT PARTNERS, 1166
MASS VENTURES, 1175
MATRIX PARTNERS, 1184
MATURO KAPITAL, 2948
MERIT ENERGY COMPANY, 1211
MERITURN PARTNERS, 1214
MHS CAPITAL, 1227
MITSUI SUMITOMO INSURANCE VENTURE CAPITAL CO, 2962
MMT MILLENNIUM MATERIALS TECHNOLOGIES FUND LP, 2964
MONTAGU PRIVATE EQUITY LIMITED, 2968
MURPHREE VENTURE PARTNERS, 1273
NEST VENTURES, 1289
NEW BRUNSWICK INNOVATION FOUNDATION, 2192
NEW MEXICO COMMUNITY CAPITAL, 1299
NEW MOUNTAIN CAPITAL, 1300
NEW WORLD INFRASTRUCTURE LIMITED, 2987
NEWLIGHT PARTNERS, 1314
NGP ENERGY CAPITAL, 1328
NORTHERN ENTERPRISE LIMITED, 3002
NORTHSTAR VENTURES, 3003
NOVELTEK CAPITAL CORPORATION, 1351
NTH POWER TECHNOLOGIES, 1355
OAK INVESTMENT PARTNERS, 1361
OBVIOUS VENTURES, 1363
ODYSSEY INVESTMENT PARTNERS, 1368
OMERS PRIVATE EQUITY, 2199
OMNES CAPITAL, 3011
ONE EQUITY PARTNERS, 1376
PAI MANAGEMENT, 3017

PAMLICO CAPITAL, 1410
PANACHE VENTURES, 2204
PANGAEA VENTURES LTD, 2205
PANTHEON VENTURES (US) LP, 1413
PARALLEL INVESTMENT PARTNERS, 1417
PARKVIEW CAPITAL PARTNERS, 2207
PARKWALK ADVISORS, 3019
PARTECH INTERNATIONAL, 1418
PENN VENTURE PARTNERS, 1431
PFM CAPITAL, 2213
PIDC PHILADELPHIA, 1445
PINE BROOK ROAD PARTNERS, 1447
POND VENTURES, 3038
PORTUGAL CAPITAL VENTURES Institutional Headquarters, 3039
PRAIRIEGOLD VENTURE PARTNERS, 1474
PRITZKER GROUP VENTURE CAPITAL, 1483
PRIVITI CAPITAL, 2219
QUAKE CAPITAL PARTNERS, 1509
RAYMOND JAMES CAPITAL, 1529
REITEN & CO STRATEGIC INVESTMENTS AS Reiten & Company, 3067
RENAISSANCE PARTNERS, 3068
RESOURCE CAPITAL FUNDS, 1551
RIDGEWOOD CAPITAL, 1567
RIDGEWOOD ENERGY, 1568
ROBIN HOOD VENTURES, 1581
ROCKPORT CAPITAL, 1583
ROYALTY CAPITAL MANAGEMENT, 1595
RPM VENTURES, 1596
RU-NET VENTURES, 3078
SAF GROUP, 2237
SAIL VENTURE PARTNERS, 1607
SAINT-GOBAIN NOVA EXTERNAL VENTURING, 3085
SAMOS INVESTMENTS, 3088
SARATOGA PARTNERS, 1624
SARONA ASSET MANAGEMENT, 2239
SCOTTISH ENTERPRISE, 3094
SCOTTISH EQUITY PARTNERS, 3095
SEED CAPITAL LIMITED, 3098
SENTRY FINANCIAL CORPORATION, 1655
SEQUOIA CAPITAL, 1657
SEVEN SPIRES INVESTMENTS, 3103
SEVIN ROSEN FUNDS, 1661
SILKROAD EQUITY, 1683
SKYTREE CAPITAL PARTNERS, 1694
SOURCE CAPITAL GROUP, 1710
SOUTHERN CROSS VENTURE PARTNERS, 1713
SPRING LANE CAPITAL, 1732
SSE VENTURES, 3126
STARBOARD CAPITAL PARTNERS, 1738
STATELINE ANGELS, 1743
STATOIL TECHNOLOGY INVEST, 3132
STEELHOUSE VENTURES, 3134
SUMMIT PARTNERS, 1754
TECHNOCAP, 2254
TELESOFT PARTNERS, 1795
TENASKA CAPITAL MANAGEMENT, 1797
TPA CORPORATE FINANCE CONSULTING GMBH Horwarth International, 3175
TRIANGLE PEAK PARTNERS, 1848
TRUE NORTH VENTURE PARTNERS, 1861
URBAN INNOVATION FUND, 1895
URBAN US, 1896
US RENEWABLES GROUP, 1897
US VENTURE PARTNERS, 1898
VALUEACT CAPITAL, 1905
VANTAGEPOINT CAPITAL PARTNERS, 1908
VENROCK ASSOCIATES, 1918
VENTANA CAPITAL MANAGEMENT LP, 1920
VICKERS FINANCIAL GROUP, 3206
WAND PARTNERS, 1956
WARBURG PINCUS LLC, 1957
WASABI VENTURES, 1959
WESTERN NIS ENTERPRISE FUND, 3224
WOODSIDE FUND, 2005
WYNNCHURCH CAPITAL, 2008
YELLOW POINT EQUITY PARTNERS, 2284

Industry Preference Index / Energy Efficiency

Energy Efficiency
ANGELENO GROUP, 127
ARAVAIPA VENTURES, 147
BRIGHT CAPITAL, 2531
CALCEF CLEAN ENERGY FUND, 370
CHORD CAPITAL, 2589
CLAREMONT CREEK VENTURES, 493
CLEAN PACIFIC VENTURES, 499
CLIMATE CHANGE CAPITAL, 2606
DEMETER PARTNERS, 2647
EARTHRISE CAPITAL, 643
EPLANET CAPITAL, 691
FIDELITY GROWTH PARTNERS EUROPE, 2725
GLOBAL ENVIRONMENT FUND, 838
ID VENTURES AMERICA LLC, 974
ISRAEL CLEANTECH VENTURES, 2891
KOHLBERG VENTURES, 1087
NGEN PARTNERS, 1324
NORTHZONE, 3004
RENEWABLETECH VENTURES, 1545
SAUDI ARAMCO ENERGY VENTURES, 3090
SSE VENTURES, 3126
TSING CAPITAL, 3185
VANTAGEPOINT CAPITAL PARTNERS, 1908
WHEB GROUP, 3227

Energy Equipment & Services
ENERGY CAPITAL PARTNERS, 676

Energy Infrastructure
ENCAP FLATROCK MIDSTREAM, 672

Energy Management
TI VENTURE CAPITAL Texas Instruments Incorporated, 1825

Energy Products
DESCO CAPITAL, 607

Energy Services
BAY PARTNERS, 241
BREGAL ENERGY, 335
FOUNDATION EQUITY CORPORATION, 2116
GENESIS CAPITAL CORPORATION, 2124
GLADSTONE CAPITAL, 832
HARREN EQUITY PARTNERS, 913
SALT CREEK CAPITAL, 1612
TRILANTIC CAPITAL PARTNERS, 1853
VALOR EQUITY PARTNERS, 1904
WESTLAKE SECURITIES, 1977

Energy Storage
ARCTERN VENTURES, 2037
AUTO TECH VENTURES, 207
CLEAN PACIFIC VENTURES, 499
EARTHRISE CAPITAL, 643
NGEN PARTNERS, 1324
OCEANSHORE VENTURES, 1365
TEL VENTURE CAPITAL, 1793
WHEB GROUP, 3227

Energy Technology
.406 VENTURES, 1
FA TECHNOLOGY VENTURES, 712
FLYBRIDGE CAPITAL PARTNERS, 756
FLYWHEEL VENTURES, 758
HOUSTON ANGEL NETWORK, 953
MAYFIELD FUND, 1187
McLEAN WATSON CAPITAL, 2191
NTH POWER TECHNOLOGIES, 1355
RIDGEWOOD CAPITAL, 1567
TANDEM EXPANSION FUND, 2252
TECHNOLOGY PARTNERS, 1788
YELLOWSTONE CAPITAL, 2012

Energy and Resources
CHINA MERCHANTS CHINA DIRECT INVESTMENTS LTD., 2585

Engineered Materials
ARGOSY CAPITAL, 165

Engineered Products
CENTURY PARK CAPITAL PARTNERS, 451

Engineering
360 CAPITAL PARTNERS 360 Capital Management SA, 2288
3I ASIA PACIFIC 3i Group, 2289
ABOA VENTURE MANAGEMENT OY, 2310
ACCESS CAPITAL CORPORATION, 2026
ARROWHEAD INNOVATION FUND, 169
ATYPICAL VENTURES, 195
BARING PRIVATE EQUITY PARTNERS ESPANA SA, 2480
BM-T BETEILIGUNGS MANAGEMENT THURINGEN GmbH, 2518
COPPERLION CAPITAL, 2079
CREDIT MUTUEL EQUITY, 2082
EQUISTONE, 2705
EXPIBEL BV, 2719
EXPORT DEVELOPMENT CANADA, 2106
FERRANTI LIMITED, 2723
GENERICS GROUP LIMITED Generics Group, 2764
HANNOVER FINANZ GmbH, 2801
INNOVATION CAPITAL LIMITED, 2868
INNOVATION ENDEAVORS, 1001
KAIROS VENTURES, 1055
KB PARTNERS LLC, 1061
LIME ROCK PARTNERS, 1129
MARCEAU INVESTISSEMENTS, 2946
MEZZANINE MANAGEMENT LIMITED Mezzanine Management UK Ltd., 2956
MIDVEN, 2958
PAI MANAGEMENT, 3017
RED DOT VENTURES, 3064
TECHNOLOGY PARK MALAYSIA CORPORATION SDN BHD, 3155
YISSUM TECHNOLOGY TRANSFER, 3235

Enterprise
FIRST ROUND CAPITAL, 742
FRONTLINE VENTURES, 2750
INTEL CAPITAL, 1009
JACKSON SQUARE VENTURES, 1028
KHOSLA VENTURES, 1073
LIGHTSPEED VENTURE PARTNERS, 1125
QUALCOMM VENTURES, 1511
SOCIAL CAPITAL, 1698
W CAPITAL PARTNERS, 1949

Enterprise & Consumer
FRONTIER VENTURES, 795

Enterprise Applications
CATAMOUNT VENTURES LP, 430
EDISON PARTNERS, 655
FELICIS VENTURES, 720
GABRIEL VENTURE PARTNERS, 808
MOBIUS VENTURE CAPITAL, 1245
OSAGE PARTNERS, 1388
SALESFORCE VENTURES, 1610
SHEPHERD VENTURES, 1667
STORM VENTURES, 1750
SUMMERHILL VENTURE PARTNERS, 2250

Enterprise Blockchain
RIPPLE VENTURES, 2232

Enterprise Cloud
SOZO VENTURES, 1716

Enterprise IT
CITI VENTURES, 488

Enterprise IT & Infrastructure
VERTEX VENTURE CAPITAL, 3205

Enterprise Mobility
BENHAMOU GLOBAL VENTURES, 252

Industry Preference Index / Entertainment

NEW ENTERPRISE ASSOCIATES, 1296

Enterprise Services
ACCEL-KKR LLC, 28
ADOBE VENTURES LP, 57
ALLEGIS CYBER CAPITAL, 84
ANGELS' FORUM LLC, 130
APEX VENTURE PARTNERS, 138
ASCENT VENTURE PARTNERS, 180
AUSTIN VENTURES, 205
BLUE CHIP VENTURE COMPANY, 290
BLUMBERG CAPITAL, 304
CATALYST FUND LP, 2562
CEDAR (ISRAEL) FINANCIAL ADVISORS LIMITED Cedar Fund, 2571
CEDAR FUND, 438
CHENGWEI VENTURES, 2581
CONSTELLATION TECHNOLOGY VENTURES, 534
DENALI VENTURE PARTNERS, 606
EQUITY PARTNERS PTY LIMITED, 2706
EVERCORE CAPITAL PARTNERS, 700
FORMULA VENTURES LIMITED Formula Group, 2741
GIZA VENTURE CAPITAL, 2773
GROTECH VENTURES, 881
IDG CAPITAL, 977
IDG VENTURES INDIA International Financial Services Limited, 2840
INNOVACOM SA, 2866
JERUSALEM VENTURE PARTNERS, 2901
LONGWORTH VENTURE PARTNERS, 1150
OAK INVESTMENT PARTNERS, 1361
ODEON CAPITAL PARTNERS, 1367
PALO ALTO VENTURE PARTNERS, 1406
REDPOINT VENTURES, 1537
SCALE VENTURE PARTNERS, 1629
SMART BUSINESS CONSULTING, 3115
SPACEVEST, 1717
STAR VENTURES, 3128
STARVEST PARTNERS, 1741
TRITON VENTURES, 1857
UPDATA VENTURE PARTNERS, 1888
VERITAS VENTURE PARTNERS, 3203
VOYAGER CAPITAL, 1947

Enterprise Software
ACTIVE VENTURE PARTNERS, 2331
ACUMEN VENTURES, 2333
ALMAZ CAPITAL, 89
AMBIENT SOUND INVESTMENTS, 2382
AMPLIFIER VENTURE PARTNERS, 120
ANDREESSEN HOROWITZ, 125
ANNAPURNA VENTURES, 2395
ARCHTOP VENTURES, 155
ARTHUR VENTURES, 175
ASPECT VENTURES, 182
ATA VENTURES, 185
AVANSIS VENTURES, 210
AXIA CAPITAL, 214
BAY PARTNERS, 241
BLH VENTURE PARTNERS, 285
BLUEFISH VENTURES, 297
BLUERUN VENTURES, 299
BOSTON CAPITAL VENTURES, 313
BRAINSTORM VENTURES, 327
BREGAL SAGEMOUNT, 336
BRIGHTSTONE VENTURE CAPITAL, 344
BULLPEN CAPITAL, 361
CEDAR FUND, 438
CINCYTECH, 481
COMCAST VENTURES, 520
CORRELATION VENTURES, 545
CRESCENDO VENTURES, 556
DOT EDU VENTURES, 624
EDEN VENTURES, 2682
EGL HOLDINGS, 656
ELAIA PARTNERS, 2684
ENTREE CAPITAL, 2700
EPIC VENTURES, 689
F-PRIME CAPITAL PARTNERS, 711
FA TECHNOLOGY VENTURES, 712
FGA PARTNERS, 725
FLOODGATE FUND, 752
GENESIS PARTNERS, 2766
GEORGIAN PARTNERS, 2126
GV, 894
HELION VENTURE PARTNERS, LLC International Management (Mauritius) Ltd, 2809
HUDSON VENTURE PARTNERS, 957
HUMMER WINBLAD VENTURE PARTNERS, 959
INCWELL VENTURE CAPITAL, 985
INNOVATION WORKS, 1003
INSTITUTIONAL VENTURE PARTNERS, 1006
IRISH ANGELS, 1023
KLASS CAPITAL, 2163
LERER HIPPEAU VENTURES, 1114
MATRIX PARTNERS, 1184
MENLO VENTURES, 1203
MERITECH CAPITAL PARTNERS, 1213
MHS CAPITAL, 1227
MISSION VENTURES, 1239
MISSIONOG, 1240
MORGAN STANLEY EXPANSION CAPITAL, 1255
MORGENTHALER VENTURES, 1257
NAUTA CAPITAL, 2978
NOVUS VENTURES LP, 1354
OJAS VENTURE PARTNERS, 3010
OPUS CAPITAL, 1382
PLAZA VENTURES, 2216
PRITZKER GROUP VENTURE CAPITAL, 1483
RALLY VENTURES, 1525
RELAY VENTURES, 2228
RIPPLE VENTURES, 2232
RRE VENTURES, 1597
SALESFORCE VENTURES, 1610
SERAPH GROUP, 1658
SIGMA PARTNERS, 1674
SIGNAL PEAK VENTURES, 1679
SILVERTON PARTNERS, 1687
SORRENTO VENTURES, 1708
SOUTHEAST INTERACTIVE TECHNOLOGY FUNDS, 1711
SPARKLABS GLOBAL VENTURES, 1719
SPLIT ROCK PARTNERS, 1728
SUNBRIDGE PARTNERS, 1757
SV ANGEL, 1763
TICONDEROGA PRIVATE EQUITY, 1826
TRIDENT CAPITAL, 1852
TRUE VENTURES, 1862
TUGBOAT VENTURES, 1867
TXV PARTNERS, 1877
VALAR VENTURES, 1899
VELOCITY EQUITY PARTNERS LLC, 1915
VENTECH, 3199
WESTTECH VENTURES, 3226
WOODSIDE FUND, 2005
ZHENFUND, 3241

Enterprise Tech
OFF THE GRID VENTURES, 1370

Enterprise Technology
CLYDESDALE VENTURES, 508
COLUMBIA CAPITAL, 518
JUMP CAPITAL LLC, 1050

Entertainment
360 CAPITAL PARTNERS 360 Capital Management SA, 2288
645 VENTURES, 12
ABRY PARTNERS, 20
ABU DHABI INVESTMENT AUTHORITY, 2313
ACKERLEY PARTNERS LLC, 42
ACKRELL CAPITAL, 43
ADVANCIT CAPITAL, 59
AEP CAPITAL LLC, 64
ARCHTOP VENTURES, 155
BASE VENTURES, 232
BERINGEA, 254

1147

Industry Preference Index / Environment

BIA DIGITAL PARTNERS LP, 266
BIGFOOT VENTURES, 2502
BOTTS & COMPANY LIMITED, 2523
BREAKAWAY VENTURES, 332
BREAKWATER MANAGEMENT, 334
BREYER CAPITAL, 339
CANDOVER, 2547
CATALYST INVESTMENT MANAGERS PTY LIMITED PPM Capital, 2564
CEI VENTURES, 440
CIT GROUP, 486
COMSTOCK CAPITAL PARTNERS LLC, 529
DETROIT VENTURE PARTNERS, 608
DIRECT CAPITAL PRIVATE EQUITY LIMITED, 2655
DYNAMO VC, 640
ELEVATION PARTNERS, 660
FALCONHEAD CAPITAL, 717
FIRSTMARK CAPITAL, 744
GEODESIC CAPITAL, 824
GREIF & COMPANY, 874
GRUPO BISA, 2791
IDEALAB, 976
INDEX VENTURES, 2851
INDIAN DIRECT EQUITY ADVISORS PVT LTD, 2852
INGENIOUS VENTURES, 2862
INLAND TECHSTART FUND, 997
INTEL CAPITAL, 1009
IRIS CAPITAL, 2888
KILMER CAPITAL PARTNERS, 2162
LEO CAPITAL HOLDINGS, LLC, 1112
LEVINE LEICHTMAN CAPITAL PARTNERS, 1115
LOMBARD INVESTMENTS, 1143
MAKERS FUND, 2944
MANHATTAN INVESTMENT PARTNERS, 1166
MARS INVESTMENT ACCELERATOR FUND, 2181
MARWIT CAPITAL LLC, 1171
MCG CAPITAL CORPORATION, 1192
MERRILL LYNCH (ASIA PACIFIC) LIMITED Merrill Lynch Group, 2955
MOTOROLA SOLUTIONS VENTURE CAPITAL, 1260
NEW ATLANTIC VENTURES, 1290
NEXTEC DEVELOPMENT CAPITAL LIMITED, 2991
NFX, 1323
ONEX PARTNERS, 2201
PARTNERSHIP FUND FOR NEW YORK CITY, 1422
PRINCIPIA SGR, 3043
PROVIDENCE EQUITY PARTNERS, 1498
QUOTIDIAN VENTURES, 1521
RAPTOR GROUP, 1527
RISE OF THE REST, 1571
ROBIN HOOD VENTURES, 1581
SABAN CAPITAL GROUP, 1602
SANDLER CAPITAL MANAGEMENT, 1620
SCOUT VENTURES, 1635
SENTRY FINANCIAL CORPORATION, 1655
SHAMROCK CAPITAL ADVISORS, 1663
SIGNAL FIRE, 1677
SOFTBANK VENTURES KOREA, 3118
SONY INNOVATION FUND, 1705
SPECTRUM EQUITY INVESTORS LP, 1720
SUMMIT PARTNERS, 1754
TELESYSTEM, 2255
TORNANTE COMPANY, 1835
TYLT LAB, 1878
UNITED TALENT AGENCY VENTURES, 1885
VENTECH, 3199
VERIZON VENTURES, 1928
WALNUT GROUP, 1955
WESLEY CLOVER, 2276
ZHENFUND, 3241

Environment
1ST COURSE CAPITAL, 7
3TS CAPITAL PARTNERS 3i Group plc, 2301
AMBERJACK CAPITAL PARTNERS, 106
AMBIENTA ENVIRONMENTAL ASSETS, 2383
AMERICAN SECURITIES LLC, 111
ASTER CAPITAL, 2430
BATTELLE VENTURES, 236
BIG SOCIETY CAPITAL, 2500
BROOKSIDE EQUITY PARTNERS LLC, 356
CALVERT INVESTMENT MANAGEMENT, 379
CASABONA VENTURES, 421
CATAMOUNT VENTURES LP, 430
CHORD CAPITAL, 2589
CITY LIGHT CAPITAL, 490
COACH & CAPITAL, 2610
COMMONS CAPITAL, 522
CULTIVIAN SANDBOX VENTURES, 571
DISCOVERY CAPITAL, 2091
EARTHRISE CAPITAL, 643
EDELSON TECHNOLOGY PARTNERS, 651
FUEL CAPITAL, 2752
INETWORKS ADVISORS LLC, 991
MATURO KAPITAL, 2948
MIDVEN, 2958
MINDFULL INVESTORS, 1236
MITSUI SUMITOMO INSURANCE VENTURE CAPITAL CO, 2962
MONTAGU PRIVATE EQUITY LIMITED, 2968
NEW MEXICO COMMUNITY CAPITAL, 1299
NGEN PARTNERS, 1324
NORTHSTAR VENTURES, 3003
SAINT-GOBAIN NOVA EXTERNAL VENTURING, 3085
SOUTHERN CROSS VENTURE PARTNERS, 1713
SPRING LANE CAPITAL, 1732
TONIIC, 1833
TSING CAPITAL, 3185
UDD VENTURES, 3189
UNDERDOG VENTURES, 1882
VANCITY CAPITAL, 2269
WOMEN'S VENTURE CAPITAL FUND, 2003
YISSUM TECHNOLOGY TRANSFER, 3235

Environment Products & Services
APEX VENTURE PARTNERS, 138
ASSET MANAGEMENT VENTURES, 183
AUDAX GROUP, 197
CAPRICORN VENTURE PARTNERS NV, 2554
COMPAGNIE FINANCIERE E DE ROTHSCHILD BANQUE, 2616
CONNECTICUT INNOVATIONS, 532
CVC INVESTMENT MANAGERS LIMITED, 2636
FOUNDERS EQUITY, 777
GLOBAL ENVIRONMENT FUND, 838
GRYPHON MANAGEMENT COMPANY, 887
IRONWOOD CAPITAL, 1025
J. BURKE CAPITAL PARTNERS, 1027
MAYFIELD FUND, 1187
NEWMARGIN VENTURE CAPITAL, 2989
NORTHERN ENTERPRISE LIMITED, 3002
PACIFIC COMMUNITY VENTURES, 1397
PARTECH INTERNATIONAL, 1418
PIDC PHILADELPHIA, 1445
POUSCHINE COOK CAPITAL MANAGEMENT LLC, 1470
QUESTER CAPITAL MANAGEMENT LIMITED, 3061
ROARK CAPITAL GROUP, 1580
SAMBRINVEST SA, 3087
SOLSTICE CAPITAL LP, 1704
SOVEREIGN CAPITAL, 3121
SUMMER STREET CAPITAL PARTNERS, 1753
TELESYSTEM, 2255
THOMPROPERTIES OY, 3166
TRIGINITA CAPITAL, 3181

Environmental
COPPERLION CAPITAL, 2079

Environmental & Waste Management
GENESIS CAPITAL CORPORATION, 2124

Environmental Controls
ELEMENT PARTNERS, 658

Environmental Infrastructure
ENERGY CAPITAL PARTNERS, 676
ZOUK VENTURES, 3242

Industry Preference Index / Financial Services

Environmental Protection
ANDLINGER & COMPANY INC, 124
BEIJING HIGH TECHNOLOGY INVESTMENT COMPANY, 2490
BEIJING VENTURE CAPITAL COMPANY LIMITED, 2491
CVC INVESTMENT MANAGERS LIMITED, 2636
GUANGDONG TECHNOLOGY VENTURE CAPITAL COMPANY, 2793
INNOVATION CAPITAL LIMITED, 2868
INTER-ASIA VENTURE MANAGEMENT LIMITED, 2872
KOREA FIRST VENTURE CAPITAL CORPORATION, 2915
TECHNOCAP, 2254
TRANSATLANTIC CAPITAL LTD, 3177
VENTANA CAPITAL MANAGEMENT LP, 1920
WATERMILL GROUP, 1963

Environmental Science
MOUNTAINEER CAPITAL, 1262

Environmental Services
BLUE POINT CAPITAL PARTNERS, 293

Environmental Technology
NEW BRUNSWICK INNOVATION FOUNDATION, 2192
PENN VENTURE PARTNERS, 1431

Equipment
ABU DHABI INVESTMENT AUTHORITY, 2313
AEROSTAR CAPITAL LLC, 66
BAY PARTNERS, 241
CHICAGO VENTURE PARTNERS LP, 472
LEVINE LEICHTMAN CAPITAL PARTNERS, 1115
LIBERTY CAPITAL PARTNERS, 1118
MASSACHUSETTS CAPITAL RESOURCE COMPANY, 1176
MASSACHUSETTS GROWTH CAPITAL CORPORATION, 1177
POMONA CAPITAL, 1466
RAF INDUSTRIES, 1524
SPACEVEST, 1717

Esports
FIRST CAPITAL VENTURE, 736
IMAGINATION CAPITAL, 981
MCGOVERN CAPITAL, 1194

Ethnic Products & Services
PACIFIC COMMUNITY VENTURES, 1397

Fabless IC
AUTHOSIS VENTURES, 2448

Facial Analysis
NEXT EQUITIES, 2194

Family Tech and Education
500 STARTUPS, 10

Family-Owned
AZALEA CAPITAL, 216

Farming
ANTERRA CAPITAL, 2397
BONNEFIELD FINANCIAL, 2059
CREDIT MUTUEL EQUITY, 2082

Fashion
KALORI GROUP INVESTMENTS, 2906
M25 GROUP, 1159
NAXURI CAPITAL, 1283
PIQUE VENTURES, 2215
TYLT LAB, 1878

Fashion/Lifestyle
INNOGEST CAPITAL, 2865

Federal Services
CM EQUITY PARTNERS, 509

Film
ABU DHABI INVESTMENT AUTHORITY, 2313
ARTS ALLIANCE, 2419
NORTHSTAR VENTURES, 3003

FinTech
CORNERSTONE VENTURE PARTNERS, 544
MS&AD VENTURES, 1269
RECIPROCAL VENTURES, 1531
WILDCAT VENTURE PARTNERS, 1985

Finance
ABSTRACT VENTURES, 23
CANTOS VENTURES, 398
CULTIVATE CAPITAL, 569
GOOD NEWS VENTURES, 2132
GROUND UP VENTURES, 882
INNOVATION PLATFORM CAPITAL, 1002
M25 GROUP, 1159
MOTIV PARTNERS, 1258
SCOTIABANK PRIVATE EQUITY, 2241
SINEWAVE VENTURES, 1689
THE HIVE, 1812
URBAN US, 1896
VALUEACT CAPITAL, 1905
VIOLA FINTECH, 3211

Finances
MEKETA INVESTMENT GROUP, 1201

Financial
ANT FINANCIAL, 2396
GERKEN CAPITAL ASSOCIATES, 826
KEIRETSU FORUM, 1065
LAKE CAPITAL, 1095

Financial Data Applications
INFORMATION VENTURE PARTNERS, 2146

Financial Security & Crime Prevention
INFORMATION VENTURE PARTNERS, 2146

Financial Services
360 CAPITAL PARTNERS 360 Capital Management SA, 2288
3I GESTION SA 3i Group, 2294
3TS CAPITAL PARTNERS 3i Group plc, 2301
3i GROUP PLC, 2303
ABU DHABI INVESTMENT AUTHORITY, 2313
ACCESS CAPITAL CORPORATION, 2026
ACE & COMPANY, 2321
ACI CAPITAL, 41
ACME LABS, 2325
ACON INVESTMENTS, 45
ACTIS, 2329
ADVANTAGE CAPITAL PARTNERS, 60
AIG INVESTMENT CORPORATION (ASIA) LIMITED, 2348
AIP PRIVATE CAPITAL, 2027
ALBEMARLE PRIVATE EQUITY LIMITED, 2352
ALLSTATE INVESTMENTS LLC, 88
ALPHA CAPITAL PARTNERS, 90
ALTAMONT CAPITAL PARTNERS, 96
AMANET TECHNOLOGIES LIMITED, 2381
ANGELO, GORDON & CO., 128
ANTHEMIS GROUP, 2398
APOLLO GLOBAL MANAGEMENT, 141
ARSENAL CAPITAL PARTNERS, 172
ASHBY POINT CAPITAL, 181
ASIAN INFRASTRUCTURE FUND ADVISERS LIMITED AIF Capital, 2425
ASTELLA INVESTMENTS, 2429
ASTOR CAPITAL GROUP, 2431
AUGURY CAPITAL PARTNERS, 199
AUSTIN VENTURES, 205
AUSTRALIAN ETHICAL INVESTMENT LIMITED, 2447
AWAY REALTY, 2456
AZURE CAPITAL PARTNERS, 218
BAIN CAPITAL PRIVATE EQUITY, 223
BALDERTON CAPITAL, 2469
BARCLAYS VENTURES Barclays, 2477
BARING PRIVATE EQUITY PARTNERS INDIA, 2481
BATTERY VENTURES, 238

Industry Preference Index / Financial Services

BAYSHORE CAPITAL, 2046
BERGGRUEN HOLDINGS, 253
BESSEMER VENTURE PARTNERS, 263
BEST FUNDS, 2051
BEZOS EXPEDITIONS, 265
BLACKFIN CAPITAL PARTNERS, 2512
BLACKSTONE PRIVATE EQUITY GROUP, 280
BMP AKTIENGESELLSCHAFT BMP Venture Capital, 2519
BOND CAPITAL, 2058
BOTTS & COMPANY LIMITED, 2523
BRAZOS PRIVATE EQUITY PARTNERS, 331
BREAKWATER INVESTMENTS, 333
BREGAL SAGEMOUNT, 336
BRERA CAPITAL PARTNERS, 338
BRIDGEPOINT CAPITAL GmbH, 2528
BRIDGEPOINT CAPITAL LIMITED, 2529
BROADHAVEN CAPITAL PARTNERS, 346
BROOKSIDE EQUITY PARTNERS LLC, 356
BUTZOW NORDIA ADVOCATES LTD, 2543
CAI CAPITAL PARTNERS, 368
CALERA CAPITAL, 371
CAMBRIDGE CAPITAL CORPORATION, 384
CAMDEN PARTNERS HOLDINGS LLC, 386
CANDOVER, 2547
CAPITAL Z PARTNERS, 407
CARDINAL EQUITY PARTNERS, 412
CARDINAL VENTURE CAPITAL, 414
CARLYLE GROUP, 416
CATALYST FUND MANAGEMENT & RESEARCH LIMITED, 2563
CATALYST INVESTMENT MANAGERS PTY LIMITED PPM Capital, 2564
CCP EQUITY PARTNERS, 436
CEI VENTURES, 440
CENTERFIELD CAPITAL PARTNERS, 445
CENTRE PARTNERS MANAGEMENT LLC, 449
CERBERUS CAPITAL MANAGEMENT, 453
CHARLESBANK CAPITAL PARTNERS, 458
CHASE CAPITAL PARTNERS, 2579
CHEYENNE CAPITAL, 469
CHINA MERCHANTS CHINA DIRECT INVESTMENTS LTD., 2585
CHINA MERCHANTS CHINA INVESTMENT MANAGEMENT, 2586
CHINA VEST LIMITED, 2587
CHRYSALIS CAPITAL ChrysCapital, 2590
CHRYSCAPITAL MANAGEMENT COMPANIES ChrysCapital, 2591
CIBC CAPITAL MARKETS, 2073
CINCO CAPITAL, 2595
CIRCLE PEAK CAPITAL, 483
CITI VENTURES, 488
CIVC PARTNERS, 491
CLEARLIGHT PARTNERS, 503
CLIFFORD CHANCE PUNDER, 2605
CLYDESDALE VENTURES, 508
COLT VENTURES, 517
COMSTOCK CAPITAL PARTNERS LLC, 529
COMVEST PARTNERS, 530
CONCENTRIC EQUITY PARTNERS Financial Investments Corporation, 531
CONTOUR VENTURE PARTNERS, 535
CONVERSION CAPITAL, 537
CORDOVA VENTURES, 539
CRAWLEY VENTURES, 554
CRESTVIEW PARTNERS, 560
DAHER CAPITAL, 2640
DARBY OVERSEAS INVESTMENTS LTD, 585
DAVID N DEUTSCH & COMPANY LLC, 590
DAVIS, TUTTLE VENTURE PARTNERS LP, 592
DECIENS CAPITAL, 600
DFC LTD, 2652
DIAGRAM VENTURES, 2090
DIRECT CAPITAL PRIVATE EQUITY LIMITED, 2655
DOUBLE IMPACT BUSINESS ADVISORY, 2661
DTA CAPITAL PARTNERS S/B, 2666
DUKE STREET CAPITAL Duke Street, 2667
DUNEDIN CAPITAL PARTNERS LIMITED, 2668
EAST FUND MANAGEMENT GmbH GiroCredit, 2674
ECI VENTURES, 2678
EDISON PARTNERS, 655

ELAIA PARTNERS, 2684
ELECTRA PARTNERS EUROPE, 2686
EM WARBURG, PINCUS & COMPANY INTERNATIONAL, 2688
EM WARBURG, PINCUS & COMPANY JAPAN, 2689
EMIGRANT CAPITAL, 668
ENIAC VENTURES, 680
ENTER VENTURES, 682
ENTERPRISE INVESTORS, 2697
EQUISTONE, 2705
EVERGREEN ADVISORS, 702
EXPIBEL BV, 2719
FAIRHAVEN CAPITAL, 713
FCF PARTNERS LP, 719
FELICIS VENTURES, 720
FERRANTI LIMITED, 2723
FIDELITY GROWTH PARTNERS ASIA, 2724
FIELDSTONE PRIVATE CAPITAL GROUP, 726
FISHER LYNCH CAPITAL, 745
FIVE ELMS CAPITAL, 746
FLEXPOINT FORD LLC, 751
FORTRESS INVESTMENT GROUP LLC, 769
FOX PAINE & COMPANY LLC, 781
FRIEDMAN, FLEISCHER & LOWE LLC, 790
FTV CAPITAL, 796
FULL CIRCLE INVESTMENTS, 2753
FdG ASSOCIATES LP, 804
GAON ASSET MANAGEMENT, 2757
GE CAPITAL, 811
GE EQUITY EUROPE, 2760
GEFINOR CAPITAL, 813
GENERAL ATLANTIC PARTNERS, 819
GENERAL ENTERPRISE MANAGEMENT SERVICES, 2763
GENSTAR CAPITAL LP, 823
GIC GROUP, 829
GLENCOE CAPITAL, 834
GLENTHORNE CAPITAL, 836
GOLDEN GATE CAPITAL, 843
GOLDEN SEEDS, 845
GRAND CENTRAL HOLDINGS, 852
GRANDBANKS CAPITAL, 853
GRANITE HILL CAPITAL PARTNERS, LLC, 856
GRAPHITE CAPITAL MANAGEMENT LTD, 2787
GRAYHAWK CAPITAL, 861
GREIF & COMPANY, 874
GRUPO BISA, 2791
GTCR, 889
GULFSTAR GROUP, 893
H KATZ CAPITAL GROUP, 896
HALIFAX GROUP LLC, 899
HANNOVER FINANZ GmbH, 2801
HARBOURVEST PARTNERS LLC, 912
HELLMAN & FRIEDMAN LLC, 927
HIGHLAND WEST CAPITAL, 2139
HOLDING CAPITAL GROUP, 943
HORIZON PARTNERS, LTD, 948
HORIZONS VENTURES, 2822
HOULIHAN LOKEY, 951
HUDSON VENTURE PARTNERS, 957
HUNTSMAN GAY GLOBAL CAPITAL, 962
IANTHUS CAPITAL MANAGEMENT, 970
IMPLEMENT CAPITAL, 982
INSIGHT VENTURE PARTNERS, 1005
INTERNATIONAL FINANCE CORPORATION (IFC), 1012
INVENTUS, 1017
ISIS EP LLP F & C, 2889
ITC VENTURES, 2894
J. BURKE CAPITAL PARTNERS, 1027
JAGUAR CAPITAL PARTNERS, 1029
JEFFERIES CAPITAL PARTNERS, 1036
JLL PARTNERS, 1043
JORDAN COMPANY, 1049
JUMP CAPITAL LLC, 1050
KARLIN VENTURES, 1059
KENSINGTON CAPITAL PARTNERS, 2160
KHOSLA VENTURES, 1073
KOHLBERG & COMPANY LLC, 1085
KOHLBERG KRAVIS ROBERTS & COMPANY, 1086

Industry Preference Index / Fintech

KRG CAPITAL PARTNERS, 1090
LAUNCHPAD VENTURE GROUP, 1104
LAURENCE CAPITAL, 2165
LEE EQUITY PARTNERS, 1108
LEONARD GREEN & PARTNERS LP, 1113
LEVINE LEICHTMAN CAPITAL PARTNERS, 1115
LIBERTY CAPITAL PARTNERS, 1118
LIGHTYEAR CAPITAL, 1127
LINLEY CAPITAL, 1134
LLOYDS DEVELOPMENT CAPITAL LIMITED, 2935
LLR PARTNERS INC, 1140
LOMBARD INVESTMENTS, 1143
LOVELL MINNICK PARTNERS LLC, 1151
LOVETT MILLER & COMPANY, 1152
MADISON DEARBORN PARTNERS, 1160
MAINE ANGELS, 1164
MANULIFE CAPITAL, 2177
MENTOR CAPITAL PARTNERS LTD, 1204
MERITURN PARTNERS, 1214
MHS CAPITAL, 1227
MISSIONOG, 1240
MITSUI SUMITOMO INSURANCE VENTURE CAPITAL CO, 2962
MMC VENTURES, 2963
MONTLAKE CAPITAL, 1250
MOUNTAIN PARTNERS, 2970
NAVIGATION CAPITAL PARTNERS, 1279
NEEDHAM CAPITAL PARTNERS, 1287
NEW CAPITAL PARTNERS, 1292
NEW MOUNTAIN CAPITAL, 1300
NEWFIELD CAPITAL, 1312
NEXTEC DEVELOPMENT CAPITAL LIMITED, 2991
NIPPON TECHNOLOGY VENTURE PARTNERS LIMITED, 2996
NORO-MOSELEY PARTNERS, 1332
NORTH AMERICAN FUND, 1333
NORTH ATLANTIC CAPITAL CORPORATION, 1334
NORTHSTAR CAPITAL, 1343
NORTHWOOD VENTURES, 1344
NORWEST EQUITY PARTNERS, 1345
NORWEST VENTURE PARTNERS, 1346
NOVA SCOTIA BUSINESS INC., 2197
NUTEK (NARINGS- OCH TEKNIKUTVECKLINGSVERKET) NUTEK, 3007
OAK HILL CAPITAL PARTNERS, 1360
OAK INVESTMENT PARTNERS, 1361
OCA VENTURES, 1364
OLYMPUS PARTNERS, 1372
OUTCOME CAPITAL, 1389
PALLADIUM EQUITY PARTNERS, 1404
PAMLICO CAPITAL, 1410
PARALLEL49 EQUITY, 2206
PARKVIEW CAPITAL PARTNERS, 2207
PARTHENON CAPITAL, 1419
PEACHTREE EQUITY PARTNERS, 1425
PINE BROOK ROAD PARTNERS, 1447
POST CAPITAL PARTNERS, 1469
POUSCHINE COOK CAPITAL MANAGEMENT LLC, 1470
PRAIRIE CAPITAL, 1473
PWC, 3055
QUANTUM CAPITAL PARTNERS, 1512
RAYMOND JAMES CAPITAL, 1529
REDMONT VENTURE PARTNERS, 1536
REITEN & CO STRATEGIC INVESTMENTS AS Reiten & Company, 3067
REVOLUTION LLC, 1558
RIBBIT CAPITAL, 1563
RICHINA CAPITAL PARTNERS LIMITED, 3073
RISE OF THE REST, 1571
RITTENHOUSE VENTURES, 1572
ROBIN HOOD VENTURES, 1581
ROPART ASSET MANAGEMENT, 1587
ROSEWOOD CAPITAL, 1591
ROUGH DRAFT VENTURES, 1593
RRE VENTURES, 1597
SAFEGUARD SCIENTIFICS, 1605
SAGEVIEW CAPITAL, 1606
SAIF PARTNERS, 3084
SAMOS INVESTMENTS, 3088
SARATOGA PARTNERS, 1624
SARONA ASSET MANAGEMENT, 2239
SATORI CAPITAL, 1625
SCP PARTNERS, 1636
SENTRY FINANCIAL CORPORATION, 1655
SEQUOIA CAPITAL, 1657
SERGE PUN & ASSOCIATES (MYANMAR) LIMITED, 3102
SIERRA VENTURES, 1672
SIF TRANSYLVANIA, 3110
SIXTHIRTY, 1690
SOCIAL CAPITAL, 1698
SONY EUROPE, 3120
SOURCE CAPITAL GROUP, 1710
SOUTHPORT PARTNERS, 1714
STATELINE ANGELS, 1743
STONE POINT CAPITAL LLC, 1746
STRAND HANSON LIMITED, 3137
SUMMIT BRIDGE CAPITAL, 3138
SUMMIT PARTNERS, 1754
SUN CAPITAL PARTNERS, 1755
SUSQUEHANNA GROWTH EQUITY, 1761
SYCAMORE VENTURES, 1771
SYMMETRIC CAPITAL, 1772
TA ASSOCIATES, 1778
TACTICO, 2251
TELEFONICA VENTURES, 3160
TERA CAPITAL CORPORATION, 2258
TH LEE PUTNAM VENTURES, 1806
THAYER STREET PARTNERS, 1807
THOMA BRAVO LLC, 1817
THOMAS H LEE PARTNERS, 1818
THOMPROPERTIES OY, 3166
TORQUEST PARTNERS, 2264
TPA CORPORATE FINANCE CONSULTING GMBH Horwarth International, 3175
TRANSITION PARTNERS LTD, 1839
TRANSYLVANIA FINANCIAL INVESTMENT COMPANY, 3178
TRIBECA VENTURE PARTNERS, 1851
TRILANTIC CAPITAL PARTNERS, 1853
TTV CAPITAL, 1865
UPDATA VENTURE PARTNERS, 1888
UPFRONT VENTURES, 1890
URBAN INNOVATION FUND, 1895
VALLEY VENTURES LP, 1903
VARDE PARTNERS, 1909
VEDANTA CAPITAL LP, 1913
VENTURE INVESTORS, 3201
VESTAR CAPITAL PARTNERS, 1933
VISION CAPITAL, 1939
VITAL FINANCIAL LLC, 1942
VRG CAPITAL, 2274
WAND PARTNERS, 1956
WARBURG PINCUS LLC, 1957
WAVELAND INVESTMENTS LLC, 1965
WELLSPRING CAPITAL MANAGEMENT LLC, 1972
WESTERN NIS ENTERPRISE FUND, 3224
WESTLAKE SECURITIES, 1977
YELLOW POINT EQUITY PARTNERS, 2284

Financial Technology
CHINAROCK CAPITAL MANAGEMENT VENTURES, 474

Finanical Mobile
LIFE.SREDA, 2931

Fintech
.406 VENTURES, 1
ADAMS STREET PARTNERS, LLC, 56
ALTPOINT CAPITAL, 101
BAIN CAPITAL VENTURES, 224
BLUFF POINT ASSOCIATES, 302
BOXGROUP, 321
BREYER CAPITAL, 339
CAMP ONE VENTURES, 387
CANVAS VENTURES, 399
COMVEST PARTNERS, 530
CORRELATION VENTURES, 545

Industry Preference Index / Fishing

CROSSLINK CAPITAL, 564
CXO FUND, 575
DAY ONE VENTURES, 594
DECIENS CAPITAL, 600
DFJ GOTHAM VENTURES, 609
DISRUPTION VENTURES, 2092
DRAPER ATHENA, 627
EDISON PARTNERS, 655
ELYSIUM VENTURE CAPITAL, 662
ENTREPRENEURS ROUNDTABLE ACCELERATOR, 685
F-PRIME CAPITAL PARTNERS, 711
FINAVENTURES, 730
FIRST ROUND CAPITAL, 742
FIRSTMARK CAPITAL, 744
FLORIDA FUNDERS, 754
FORTÉ VENTURES, 770
GENERAL CATALYST PARTNERS, 820
GOLDEN VENTURE PARTNERS, 2130
GOOD GROWTH CAPITAL, 849
GRANDBANKS CAPITAL, 853
GREAT HILL PARTNERS LLC, 862
GVA CAPITAL, 895
HARDY CAPITAL PARTNERS, 2137
IMPRESSION VENTURES, 2143
INDEX VENTURES, 2851
INNOGEST CAPITAL, 2865
LIGHTSPEED VENTURE PARTNERS, 1125
LUGE CAPITAL, 2172
MILLENIUM TECHNOLOGY VALUE PARTNERS, 1235
MOTLEY FOOL VENTURES, 1259
NORO-MOSELEY PARTNERS, 1332
NORTH HILL VENTURES, 1339
OBVIOUS VENTURES, 1363
OFF THE GRID VENTURES, 1370
OYSTER VENTURES, 1396
PANACHE VENTURES, 2204
PORTAG3 VENTURES, 2217
RITTENHOUSE VENTURES, 1572
RUBICON VENTURE CAPITAL, 1599
SALMON RIVER CAPITAL, 1611
SATURN PARTNERS, 1626
SIGNIA VENTURE PARTNERS, 1680
SONY INNOVATION FUND, 1705
SOZO VENTURES, 1716
TACTICO, 2251
TECHNOLOGY CROSSOVER VENTURES, 1787
TENX VENTURES, 2257
URBAN US, 1896
VILLAGE GLOBAL, 1935
W CAPITAL PARTNERS, 1949
WIREFRAME VENTURES, 2001

Fishing
BIO FUND MANAGEMENT OY, 2503
FARM CREDIT CANADA, 2108
WESTERN NIS ENTERPRISE FUND, 3224

Fitness
SIGNIA VENTURE PARTNERS, 1680
STEELPOINT CAPITAL PARTNERS, 1744

Fixed & Mobile Broadband
VERTEX VENTURE CAPITAL, 3205

Flexible Packaging
SUN CAPITAL PARTNERS, 1755

Food
FORAGE CAPITAL PARTNERS, 2115
FOUNDERS GROUP OF FOOD COMPANIES, 2118
RISE OF THE REST, 1571

Food & Agriculture
GLOBAL ENVIRONMENT FUND, 838

Food & Beverage
1ST COURSE CAPITAL, 7
AGRIBUSINESS MANAGEMENT COMPANY, 70

ALANTRA, 77
AMERICA FIRST INVESTMENT ADVISORS, 109
AMHERST FUND, 114
ARBOR INVESTMENTS, 148
AUDAX GROUP, 197
AUSTRALIAN ETHICAL INVESTMENT LIMITED, 2447
BALTCAP MANAGEMENT LTD, 2471
BASE VENTURES, 232
BENCIS CAPITAL PARTNERS, 2492
BEZOS EXPEDITIONS, 265
BIO FUND MANAGEMENT OY, 2503
BIOGENERATION VENTURES, 2505
BIOPACIFIC VENTURES, 2507
BOND CAPITAL, 2058
BOULDER VENTURES LTD, 318
BREAKWATER MANAGEMENT, 334
BRIGHTPATH CAPITAL PARTNERS, 343
BROOKSIDE EQUITY PARTNERS LLC, 356
BRYNWOOD PARTNERS, 360
CALIFORNIA COAST VENTURE FORUM, 3248
CANADIAN VENTURE CAPITAL ASSOCIATION Canadian Venture Capital & Private Equity Association, 3249
CAPITAL FOR BUSINESS, INC, 402
CAPITAL PARTNERS, 404
CARPEDIA INTERNATIONAL, 2066
CATALYST INVESTMENT MANAGERS PTY LIMITED PPM Capital, 2564
CEDAR VENTURES LLC, 439
CENTERFIELD CAPITAL PARTNERS, 445
CENTRAL TEXAS ANGEL NETWORK, 447
CENTRE PARTNERS MANAGEMENT LLC, 449
CHARLESBANK CAPITAL PARTNERS, 458
CIC PARTNERS, 479
CID CAPITAL, 480
CLARENDON FUND MANAGERS, 2601
CLYDESDALE VENTURES, 508
COMPAGNIE FINANCIERE E DE ROTHSCHILD BANQUE, 2616
CULTIVIAN SANDBOX VENTURES, 571
CVC ASIA PACIFIC LIMITED CVC Capital Partners, 2634
CVC CAPITAL PARTNERS LTD, 2635
DAVID N DEUTSCH & COMPANY LLC, 590
DIRECT CAPITAL PRIVATE EQUITY LIMITED, 2655
EAST FUND MANAGEMENT GmbH GiroCredit, 2674
ENDEAVOUR CAPITAL, 674
ENNOVENT, 2692
EQUISTONE, 2705
EUROVENTURES CAPITAL, 2716
FALCONHEAD CAPITAL, 717
FARM CREDIT CANADA, 2108
FCF PARTNERS LP, 719
FIRST ATLANTIC CAPITAL LTD., 734
FIRST ISRAEL MEZZANINE INVESTORS LIMITED, 2736
FLANDERS' FOREIGN INVESTMENT OFFICE, 2737
FOUNDATION MARKETS, 2117
FOUNDERS EQUITY, 777
FRONTENAC COMPANY, 792
FULL CIRCLE INVESTMENTS, 2753
GLENCOE CAPITAL, 834
GOLDNER HAWN, 847
H KATZ CAPITAL GROUP, 896
HERITAGE PARTNERS, 929
HIG CAPITAL, 931
HORIZON PARTNERS, LTD, 948
HT CAPITAL ADVISORS LLC, 956
ICV PARTNERS, 973
INDUSTRI KAPITAL SVENSKA AB, 2854
INTER-ASIA VENTURE MANAGEMENT LIMITED, 2872
INVUS GROUP, 1022
J. BURKE CAPITAL PARTNERS, 1027
JAVELIN INVESTMENTS, 2899
KILMER CAPITAL PARTNERS, 2162
KOHLBERG VENTURES, 1087
L CATTERTON PARTNERS, 1092
LASALLE CAPITAL GROUP, 1097
LAUNCHPAD VENTURES, 2922
LEGAL AND GENERAL VENTURES LIMITED, 2926
LEVINE LEICHTMAN CAPITAL PARTNERS, 1115

Industry Preference Index / Gaming

LIBERTY CAPITAL PARTNERS, 1118
LIFE SCIENCES PARTNERS BV, 2930
LITTLEJOHN & COMPANY LLC, 1138
LYNWOOD CAPITAL PARTNERS, 1156
M25 GROUP, 1159
MACQUARIE DIRECT INVESTMENT LIMITED, 2942
MAIN STREET CAPITAL HOLDINGS LLC, 1163
MARCEAU INVESTISSEMENTS, 2946
MCGOVERN CAPITAL, 1194
MIDWEST MEZZANINE FUNDS, 1232
NAVIGATION CAPITAL PARTNERS, 1279
NBC CAPITAL PTY LIMITED, 2979
NESBIC INVESTMENT FUND II, 2983
NEW BRUNSWICK INNOVATION FOUNDATION, 2192
NEW MEXICO COMMUNITY CAPITAL, 1299
NORTH AMERICAN FUND, 1333
ONE EQUITY PARTNERS, 1376
PARALLEL49 EQUITY, 2206
PARTHENON CAPITAL, 1419
PENINSULA CAPITAL PARTNERS LLC, 1429
PNC ERIEVIEW CAPITAL, 1460
PROGRESS EQUITY PARTNERS, 1487
PROSPECT PARTNERS LLC, 1494
ROOT CAPITAL, 1586
SERRUYA PRIVATE EQUITY, 2245
SHAW KWEI AND PARTNERS, 3107
SHERBROOKE CAPITAL, 1668
SIF TRANSYLVANIA, 3110
SPRING LANE CAPITAL, 1732
SUMMIT BRIDGE CAPITAL, 3138
SUN CAPITAL PARTNERS, 1755
SWANDER PACE CAPITAL, 1769
TENNESSEE COMMUNITY VENTURES, 1799
TGF MANAGEMENT, 1805
TMG CAPITAL PARTNERS, 3171
TORQUEST PARTNERS, 2264
TRANSYLVANIA FINANCIAL INVESTMENT COMPANY, 3178
TSG CONSUMER PARTNERS, 1863
TULLY & HOLLAND, 1869
TVV CAPITAL, 1872
UNDERDOG VENTURES, 1882
UNION CAPITAL CORPORATION, 1883
WAND PARTNERS, 1956
WELLSPRING CAPITAL MANAGEMENT LLC, 1972
WESTERN NIS ENTERPRISE FUND, 3224
WHITECAP VENTURE PARTNERS, 2280
XPV WATER PARTNERS, 2282
YELLOWSTONE CAPITAL, 2012
YISSUM TECHNOLOGY TRANSFER, 3235
YORK STREET CAPITAL PARTNERS LLC, 2014

Food & Beverage Related
PACIFIC VENTURES GROUP, 1400

Food & Consumer Products
SIGNAL HILL EQUITY PARTNERS, 2246

Food Products & Services
CALERA CAPITAL, 371

Food Safety
CULTIVIAN SANDBOX VENTURES, 571

Food Services
1ST COURSE CAPITAL, 7
ABU DHABI INVESTMENT AUTHORITY, 2313
AGRIBUSINESS MANAGEMENT COMPANY, 70
ATP PRIVATE EQUITY PARTNERS, 2438
BERINGEA, 254
CLIFFORD CHANCE PUNDER, 2605
FCF PARTNERS LP, 719
FOUNDERS EQUITY, 777
GOLUB CAPITAL, 848
GRUPO BISA, 2791
HOLDING CAPITAL GROUP, 943
JMH CAPITAL, 1044
MOTIV PARTNERS, 1258

PALLADIUM EQUITY PARTNERS, 1404
PRIVATE EQUITY PARTNERS SPA, 3044
SAMBRINVEST SA, 3087
SENTINEL CAPITAL PARTNERS, 1654
SWANDER PACE CAPITAL, 1769

Food Tech & Digital Healthcare
500 STARTUPS, 10

Food Technology
1ST COURSE CAPITAL, 7
CXO FUND, 575

Food and Beverage
GREIF & COMPANY, 874

Foodtech
ARCTERN VENTURES, 2037
INNOGEST CAPITAL, 2865

Footwear
BREAKAWAY VENTURES, 332

Forensic Science
MOUNTAINEER CAPITAL, 1262

Forestry
BIO FUND MANAGEMENT OY, 2503
FARM CREDIT CANADA, 2108
GLOBAL ENVIRONMENT FUND, 838
LIONHART CAPITAL LTD, 2170
MERITURN PARTNERS, 1214
SOURCE CAPITAL GROUP, 1710
WESTERN NIS ENTERPRISE FUND, 3224
ZERNIKE SEED FUND BV, 3240

Franchising
ARGOSY CAPITAL, 165
BIP CAPITAL, 274
CAPITAL PARTNERS, 404
FOUNDERS EQUITY, 777
H KATZ CAPITAL GROUP, 896
IDG CAPITAL PARTNERS, 2838
LEVINE LEICHTMAN CAPITAL PARTNERS, 1115
SALT CREEK CAPITAL, 1612
SENTINEL CAPITAL PARTNERS, 1654
WOODBRIDGE GROUP, 2004

Frontier
SOCIAL CAPITAL, 1698

Fund Management
CAPMAN CAPITAL MANAGEMENT OY, 2553

Fundraising
CAPMAN CAPITAL MANAGEMENT OY, 2553

Furniture
PRIVATE EQUITY PARTNERS SPA, 3044

Gaming
3W VENTURES Latour & Zuberbuhler GmbH, 2302
ARCHTOP VENTURES, 155
AZURE CAPITAL PARTNERS, 218
BERKELEY VENTURES, 256
BERTELSMANN DIGITAL MEDIA INVESTMENTS, 259
BEZOS EXPEDITIONS, 265
BLAST FUNDING, 282
CLARENDON FUND MANAGERS, 2601
COLOMA VENTURES, 515
DALLAS VENTURE PARTNERS, 583
DATA POINT CAPITAL, 587
EDEN VENTURES, 2682
EPLANET CAPITAL, 691
FELICIS VENTURES, 720
FIRSTMARK CAPITAL, 744
GENACAST VENTURES, 818
GGV CAPITAL, 827

1153

Industry Preference Index / Gene Therapy

GREAT OAKS VENTURE CAPITAL, 863
GREYCROFT PARTNERS, 876
INGENIOUS VENTURES, 2862
INLAND TECHSTART FUND, 997
INSIGHT VENTURE PARTNERS, 1005
MAKERS FUND, 2944
NHN INVESTMENT, 2993
NORTHSTAR VENTURES, 3003
NOVA SCOTIA BUSINESS INC., 2197
RAPTOR GROUP, 1527
REVO CAPITAL, 3069
ROTH CAPITAL PARTNERS, 1592
SEIDLER EQUITY PARTNERS, 1648
SILKROAD EQUITY, 1683
SONY INNOVATION FUND, 1705
SV ANGEL, 1763
THAYER VENTURES, 1808
TRUE VENTURES, 1862
WASABI VENTURES, 1959
WHITE STAR CAPITAL, 1982
XG VENTURES, 2009

Gene Therapy
MVM LIFE SCIENCE PARTNERS, 2972

General Industrial
3I EUROPE PLC 3i Group, 2292

Genetic Engineering
AMPHION CAPITAL PARTNERS, 2389
ARTHUR P GOULD & COMPANY, 174
MASSACHUSETTS CAPITAL RESOURCE COMPANY, 1176
MASSACHUSETTS GROWTH CAPITAL CORPORATION, 1177
NORTH BRIDGE VENTURE PARTNERS, 1335
PERMAL CAPITAL MANAGEMENT, 1435
PLEXUS VENTURES, 1456
PROVCO GROUP, 1496
ROYALTY CAPITAL MANAGEMENT, 1595
SEED CAPITAL LIMITED, 3098
SEQUEL VENTURE PARTNERS, 1656
SOURCE CAPITAL GROUP, 1710
VERITAS VENTURE PARTNERS, 3203
WASSERSTEIN & CO., 1961
WESTERN TECHNOLOGY INVESTMENT, 1976

Genomics
APPLE TREE PARTNERS, 144
CHL MEDICAL PARTNERS, 476
HEALTH ENTERPRISE PARTNERS, 921
OXFORD BIOSCIENCE PARTNERS, 1395
SPENCER TRASK VENTURES, 1723

Genomics & Bioinformatics
ARCH VENTURE PARTNERS, 154

Glass
SAMBRINVEST SA, 3087
SRIW SA SRIW Group, 3125

Global Equities
DEUTSCHE ASSET MANAGEMENT (AUSTRALIA) LIMITED Deutsche Bank AG, 2650

Global Financial Advisory
ROTHSCHILD AUSTRALIA - ARROW PRIVATE EQUITY Rothschild Group, 3077

Global Industries
CENTENNIAL VENTURES, 443
GREENBRIAR EQUITY GROUP LLC, 867
LINK TECHNOLOGIES LIMITED, 2932
RENAISSANCE PARTNERS, 3068
UBS GLOBAL ASSET MANAGEMENT, 1880

Global Insurance Solutions
DEUTSCHE ASSET MANAGEMENT (AUSTRALIA) LIMITED Deutsche Bank AG, 2650

Global Supply Chains
FIRELAKE CAPITAL, 731

Golf
KB PARTNERS, 1060

GovTech
URBAN US, 1896

Government
CI CAPITAL PARTNERS, 478
ENLIGHTENMENT CAPITAL, 681
INSIGHT VENTURE PARTNERS, 1005
MOTOROLA SOLUTIONS VENTURE CAPITAL, 1260
NAVIGATION CAPITAL PARTNERS, 1279
OMIDYAR NETWORK, 1374
OUTCOME CAPITAL, 1389
PEACHTREE EQUITY PARTNERS, 1425

Government Services
GLADSTONE CAPITAL, 832
RLH EQUITY PARTNERS, 1579

Graphic Arts
CAMBRIDGE CAPITAL CORPORATION, 384
CLAL ELECTRONICS INDUSTRIES LIMITED, 2600
IGNITE JAPAN KK Ignite Group, 2845
MAYFLY CAPITAL, 1188

Graphics
INSIGHT VENTURE PARTNERS, 1005

Green Building
CAPITAL E, 401
ROCKPORT CAPITAL, 1583

Green Energy
EPLANET CAPITAL, 691

Green Tech
GOOD GROWTH CAPITAL, 849

Green Technology
10X VENTURE PARTNERS, 2
COUNCIL FOR ENTREPRENEURIAL DEVELOPMENT, 3250
EARTHRISE CAPITAL, 643
GSR VENTURES, 2792
INFIELD CAPITAL, 992
ISOURCE GESTION, 2890
KLEINER PERKINS, 1079
NGEN PARTNERS, 1324
SCIENCEVEST, 1633
SIERRA ANGELS, 1671
TARGET PARTNERS, 3152
VERTEX VENTURE CAPITAL, 3205
ZELKOVA VENTURES, 2016

Ground Transportation
AUTOTECH VENTURES, 208

Group Finances
CAPMAN CAPITAL MANAGEMENT OY, 2553

HOA Financing
BLAST FUNDING, 282

Handicrafts
AAVISHKAAR, 2305

Hardware
ACCEL-KKR LLC, 28
ACME CAPITAL, 44
ACT VENTURE CAPITAL LIMITED, 2328
AUSTIN VENTURES, 205
BAY PARTNERS, 241
CAZENOVE PRIVATE EQUITY Cazenove Capital, 2568
CIBC CAPITAL MARKETS, 2073
CREANDUM, 2628

Industry Preference Index / Healthcare

ECHELON VENTURES, 647
FIRST ROUND CAPITAL, 742
FIRSTMARK CAPITAL, 744
FLOODGATE FUND, 752
FRANCISCO PARTNERS, 782
G-51 CAPITAL LLC, 806
GENESIS PARTNERS, 2766
HARBOURVEST PARTNERS LLC, 912
HIGHWAY1, 939
HORIZONS VENTURES, 2822
ID VENTURES AMERICA LLC, 974
INNOVATIONSKAPITAL, 2869
LEASING TECHNOLOGIES INTERNATIONAL INC., 1107
MASS VENTURES, 1175
MCROCK CAPITAL, 2183
MIDVEN, 2958
NEUHAUS PARTNERS, 2985
NEW VENTURE PARTNERS, 1304
OXANTIUM VENTURES, 1394
OYSTER INVEST, 3013
SELBY VENTURE PARTNERS, 1649
STORM VENTURES, 1750
SVB CAPITAL, 1766
SWANDER PACE CAPITAL, 1769

Hardware Technology
McLEAN WATSON CAPITAL, 2191

Hardwood Products
MOUNTAINEER CAPITAL, 1262

Hazardous Waste
VENTANA CAPITAL MANAGEMENT LP, 1920

Healtcare
CANTOS VENTURES, 398

Health
CREDIT MUTUEL EQUITY, 2082
INTEL CAPITAL, 1009
KHOSLA VENTURES, 1073
M25 GROUP, 1159
PANGAEA VENTURES LTD, 2205
REVOLUTION LLC, 1558
SECTION 32, 1646
SIGNIA VENTURE PARTNERS, 1680
URBAN INNOVATION FUND, 1895
VIVO CAPITAL, 1943

Health & Wellness
645 VENTURES, 12
AMERICAN SUSTAINABLE BUSINESS NETWORK, 3246
AMOREPACIFIC VENTURES, 2386
AMPLIFY, 121
ARCHTOP VENTURES, 155
BASE VENTURES, 232
BREAKWATER MANAGEMENT, 334
BRIGHTPATH CAPITAL PARTNERS, 343
CLYDESDALE VENTURES, 508
FUNK VENTURES, 800
HMS HAWAII MANAGEMENT, 942
KODIAK CAPITAL, 1083
MCGOVERN CAPITAL, 1194
NEW YORK VENTURE PARTNERS, 1309
SONY INNOVATION FUND, 1705
SPERO VENTURES, 1724
STEELPOINT CAPITAL PARTNERS, 1744
THE HIVE, 1812

Health Care
CXO FUND, 575
SILICON ALLEY VENTURE PARTNERS, 1682

Health IT
BIOADVANCE, 269

Health Related
3M UNITEK, 2299

ACCUITIVE MEDICAL VENTURES LLC, 39
AFFINITY CAPITAL MANAGEMENT, 67
AGATE MEDICAL INVESTMENTS, 2345
ALFA CAPITAL Alfa Group, 2355
ALLOY VENTURES, 87
ALPHA CAPITAL PARTNERS, 90
AMPERSAND CAPITAL PARTNERS, 119
AMWIN MANAGEMENT PTY LIMITED, 2390
ANTHEM VENTURE PARTNERS, 133
BATTELLE VENTURES, 236
BOULDER VENTURES LTD, 318
BRENTWOOD ASSOCIATES, 337
CALVERT INVESTMENT MANAGEMENT, 379
CHL MEDICAL PARTNERS, 476
FOUNDER COLLECTIVE, 774
GTCR, 889
GULFSTAR GROUP, 893
HALIFAX GROUP LLC, 899
HENDERSON PRIVATE CAPITAL, 2812
HG CAPITAL, 2814
INNOVATIONSKAPITAL, 2869
INTER-ASIA VENTURE MANAGEMENT LIMITED, 2872
LEASING TECHNOLOGIES INTERNATIONAL INC., 1107
NBC CAPITAL PTY LIMITED, 2979
NORTH ATLANTIC CAPITAL CORPORATION, 1334
NORTHWOOD VENTURES, 1344
PACIFIC COMMUNITY VENTURES, 1397
PACIFIC HORIZON VENTURES, 1399
PAPPAS VENTURES, 1414
PROSPECT PARTNERS LLC, 1494
SENTRY FINANCIAL CORPORATION, 1655
SEQUEL VENTURE PARTNERS, 1656
SWANDER PACE CAPITAL, 1769
TECHNOCAP, 2254
US VENTURE PARTNERS, 1898

Health Science
QUARK VENTURE, 2221

Health Tech
GOOD GROWTH CAPITAL, 849

Health Technology
CROSS-BORDER IMPACT VENTURES, 2084
RELENTLESS PURSUIT PARTNERS, 2229

Healthcare
11.2 CAPITAL, 3
3I ASIA PACIFIC 3i Group, 2289
3I DEUTSCHLAND GESELLSCHAFT FUR 3i Group, 2291
3I EUROPE PLC 3i Group, 2292
3I GERMANY GmbH 3i Group, 2293
3I GESTION SA 3i Group, 2294
3I ITALY 3i Group, 2295
3I TEUPSCHLAND GmbH 3i Group, 2297
3W VENTURES Latour & Zuberbuhler GmbH, 2302
3i GROUP PLC, 2303
5AM VENTURES, 11
AAVIN PRIVATE EQUITY, 16
AAVISHKAAR, 2305
ABELL FOUNDATION VENTURES, 18
ABERDARE VENTURES, 19
ABS CAPITAL PARTNERS, 21
ABS VENTURES, 22
ABSTRACT VENTURES, 23
ACCELERATOR LIFE SCIENCE PARTNERS, 30
ACCOLADE PARTNERS, 36
ACCRETIVE LLC, 38
ACI CAPITAL, 41
ACKRELL CAPITAL, 43
ACREW CAPITAL, 48
ACTIVA CAPITAL, 2330
ACUMEN, 54
ADAMS STREET PARTNERS, LLC, 56
ADVANCED TECHNOLOGY VENTURES, 58
ADVENT INTERNATIONAL CORPORATION, 61
AESCAP VENTURE, 2342

Industry Preference Index / Healthcare

AFFINITY CAPITAL MANAGEMENT, 67
AGATE MEDICAL INVESTMENTS, 2345
AISLING CAPITAL, 73
ALANTRA, 77
ALEXANDER HUTTON, 82
ALLELE FUNDS, 2359
ALTA VENTURES MEXICO, 2374
ALTAMONT CAPITAL PARTNERS, 96
ALTARIS CAPITAL PARTNERS, 97
ALTAS PARTNERS, 2030
AMBIENT SOUND INVESTMENTS, 2382
AMERICAN SUSTAINABLE BUSINESS NETWORK, 3246
AMICUS CAPITAL PARTNERS, 2384
AMPERSAND CAPITAL PARTNERS, 119
ANGELO, GORDON & CO., 128
ANGELPAD, 129
APAX GLOBIS PARTNERS & COMPANY Globis Capital Partners/Apax, 2406
APAX PARTNERS, 136
APERTURE VENTURE PARTNERS, 137
APHELION CAPITAL, 139
APJOHN GROUP LLC, 140
APPLE TREE PARTNERS, 144
ARBORETUM VENTURES, 150
ARCAPITA INC, 153
ARCUS VENTURES, 158
ARES MANAGEMENT LLC, 160
ARGENTUM GROUP, 162
ARLINGTON CAPITAL PARTNERS, 167
ARROWHEAD INVESTMENT MANAGEMENT, 170
ARSENAL CAPITAL PARTNERS, 172
ARTHUR VENTURES, 175
ARTIS VENTURES, 177
ASCENSION HEALTH VENTURES LLC, 178
ASSET MANAGEMENT VENTURES, 183
ASTELLA INVESTMENTS, 2429
ATHYRIUM CAPITAL MANAGEMENT, 190
ATP PRIVATE EQUITY PARTNERS, 2438
ATRIA CAPITAL PARTENAIRES, 2439
AURORA CAPITAL GROUP, 202
AUSTRALIAN ETHICAL INVESTMENT LIMITED, 2447
AVENUE CAPITAL GROUP, 211
AVISTA CAPITAL PARTNERS, 212
AVLAR BIOVENTURES, 2454
AZALEA CAPITAL, 216
AZCA, 217
BAIN CAPITAL PRIVATE EQUITY, 223
BAIN CAPITAL VENTURES, 224
BAIRD CAPITAL PARTNERS, 225
BALLAST POINT VENTURES, 227
BARCLAYS VENTURES Barclays, 2477
BARING PRIVATE EQUITY PARTNERS INDIA, 2481
BAXTER VENTURES, 239
BB BIOTECH VENTURES, 2487
BBH CAPITAL PARTNERS, 243
BC PARTNERS LIMITED, 2488
BEECKEN PETTY O'KEEFE & COMPANY, 247
BERINGEA, 254
BERTRAM CAPITAL, 260
BESSEMER VENTURE PARTNERS, 263
BESTPORT VENTURES, 2498
BIOGENERATION VENTURES, 2505
BIOMED PARTNERS, 2506
BIOVEDA CAPITAL, 2509
BIOVENTURES INVESTORS, 273
BIP CAPITAL, 274
BISON CAPITAL ASSET MANAGEMENT LLC, 277
BLACKSTONE PRIVATE EQUITY GROUP, 280
BLUE CHIP VENTURE COMPANY, 290
BLUE HERON CAPITAL, 291
BLUE POINT CAPITAL PARTNERS, 293
BLUE SAGE CAPITAL, 294
BLUESTEM CAPITAL COMPANY, 300
BOEHRINGER INGELHEIM VENTURE FUND, 2521
BOLDCAP VENTURES LLC, 307
BOND CAPITAL, 2058
BOSTON MILLENNIA PARTNERS, 315

BRAIN TRUST ACCELERATOR FUND, 326
BRAZOS PRIVATE EQUITY PARTNERS, 331
BREAKWATER INVESTMENTS, 333
BREGAL SAGEMOUNT, 336
BRERA CAPITAL PARTNERS, 338
BRIDGE STREET CAPITAL, 341
BRIDGEPOINT CAPITAL GmbH, 2528
BRIDGEPOINT CAPITAL LIMITED, 2529
BRISIO INNOVATIONS INC., 2061
BROADMARK CAPITAL, 348
BROADVIEW VENTURES, 350
BROOKE PRIVATE EQUITY ASSOCIATES, 353
BRUCKMANN, ROSSER, SHERRILL & COMPANY, 357
BRYAN GARNIER & COMPANY, 2535
BRYANT PARK VENTURES, 359
BULLNET, 2539
BUSINESS GROWTH FUND, 2541
CAI CAPITAL PARTNERS, 368
CALERA CAPITAL, 371
CALTIUS STRUCTURED CAPITAL, 377
CALUMET VENTURE FUND, 378
CAMBRIDGE CAPITAL CORPORATION, 384
CAMDEN PARTNERS HOLDINGS LLC, 386
CANAAN PARTNERS, 389
CANADIAN VENTURE CAPITAL ASSOCIATION Canadian Venture Capital & Private Equity Association, 3249
CAPITALA, 408
CAPITOL PARTNERS, 409
CAPRICORN VENTURE PARTNERS NV, 2554
CAPX PARTNERS, 410
CARDINAL EQUITY PARTNERS, 412
CARDINAL PARTNERS, 413
CARLYLE ASIA INVESTMENT ADVISORS LIMITED Carlyle Group, 2556
CARLYLE GROUP, 416
CASDIN CAPITAL, 422
CATALYST HEALTH VENTURES, 428
CATALYST INVESTMENT MANAGERS PTY LIMITED PPM Capital, 2564
CATAPULT VENTURES, 431
CATHAYA CAPITAL, 2567
CCMP CAPITAL, 435
CCP EQUITY PARTNERS, 436
CDH INVESTMENTS, 2570
CEI VENTURES, 440
CELADON CAPITAL GROUP, 2573
CELERITY PARTNERS, 441
CENTERFIELD CAPITAL PARTNERS, 445
CENTRAL TEXAS ANGEL NETWORK, 447
CENTRE PARTNERS MANAGEMENT LLC, 449
CERBERUS CAPITAL MANAGEMENT, 453
CERES VENTURE FUND, 454
CHALLENGE FUNDS - ETGAR LP, 2576
CHARLESBANK CAPITAL PARTNERS, 458
CHASE CAPITAL PARTNERS, 2579
CHENGWEI VENTURES, 2581
CHICAGO GROWTH PARTNERS, 470
CHICAGO PACIFIC FOUNDERS, 471
CHINA ISRAEL VALUE CAPITAL, 2584
CHINA VEST LIMITED, 2587
CHINAVEST, 475
CHL MEDICAL PARTNERS, 476
CHRYSALIS CAPITAL ChrysCapital, 2590
CHRYSALIS VENTURES, 477
CHRYSCAPITAL MANAGEMENT COMPANIES ChrysCapital, 2591
CIBC CAPITAL MARKETS, 2073
CINVEN LIMITED, 2596
CIT GROUP, 486
CITY HILL VENTURES, 489
CLAREMONT CREEK VENTURES, 493
CLARITAS CAPITAL, 495
CLAYTON ASSOCIATES, 497
CLEARLAKE CAPITAL, 502
CLEARSPRING CAPITAL PARTNERS, 2076
CLIFFORD CHANCE PUNDER, 2605
COACH & CAPITAL, 2610
COLLABORATIVE FUND, 514

Industry Preference Index / Healthcare

COMMONS CAPITAL, 522
COMVEST PARTNERS, 530
CORAL GROUP, 538
CORDOVA VENTURES, 539
CORRELATION VENTURES, 545
COUNCIL CAPITAL, 551
COVINGTON CAPITAL CORP., 2081
CRESSEY & COMPANY LP, 559
CRESTVIEW PARTNERS, 560
CROSS-BORDER IMPACT VENTURES, 2084
CRYSTAL RIDGE PARTNERS, 566
CUSTER CAPITAL, 572
CUTLASS CAPITAL LLC, 573
CVF CAPITAL PARTNERS, 574
DANCAP PRIVATE EQUITY, 2088
DARBY OVERSEAS INVESTMENTS LTD, 585
DAUPHIN CAPITAL PARTNERS, 588
DAY ONE VENTURES, 594
DE NOVO VENTURES, 599
DEERFIELD MANAGEMENT, 602
DIAGRAM VENTURES, 2090
DIRECT CAPITAL PRIVATE EQUITY LIMITED, 2655
DRI CAPITAL, 2097
DRIVE CAPITAL, 631
DUKE STREET CAPITAL Duke Street, 2667
DUNEDIN CAPITAL PARTNERS LIMITED, 2668
DW HEALTHCARE PARTNERS, 639
EARLY STAGE PARTNERS, 642
EASTON CAPITAL INVESTMENT GROUP, 644
EASTWARD CAPITAL PARTNERS, 646
ECOAST ANGEL NETWORK, 649
EDF VENTURES, 652
EGL HOLDINGS, 656
ELECTRA PARTNERS EUROPE, 2686
EM WARBURG, PINCUS & COMPANY JAPAN, 2689
EMBARK HEALTHCARE, 663
EMERGENT MEDICAL PARTNERS, 667
EMIGRANT CAPITAL, 668
ENNOVENT, 2692
ENSO VENTURES, 2693
EPIC CAPITAL MANAGEMENT, 2102
EPLANET CAPITAL, 691
EQUINOX CAPITAL, 692
EQUISTONE, 2705
ESCALATE CAPITAL PARTNERS, 696
ESPIRITO SANTO VENTURES, 2708
ESSEX WOODLANDS HEALTH VENTURES LLC, 698
EVERGREEN VENTURE PARTNERS, 2717
EVOLVE CAPITAL, 703
EXCEL VENTURE MANAGEMENT, 704
EXPERIMENT FUND, 709
EXPIBEL BV, 2719
FCA VENTURE PARTNERS, 718
FELICIS VENTURES, 720
FERRER FREEMAN & COMPANY LLC, 723
FIDELITY GROWTH PARTNERS ASIA, 2724
FIRST ANALYSIS, 733
FIRST CAPITAL VENTURE, 736
FIRST NEW ENGLAND CAPITAL LP, 740
FIRST ROUND CAPITAL, 742
FIRSTMARK CAPITAL, 744
FISHER LYNCH CAPITAL, 745
FLAGSHIP PIONEERING, 748
FLETCHER SPAGHT VENTURES, 750
FLEXPOINT FORD LLC, 751
FLUKE VENTURE PARTNERS, 755
FORESITE CAPITAL, 764
FORTRESS INVESTMENT GROUP LLC, 769
FORWARD VENTURES, 772
FOUNDERS EQUITY, 777
FOUNDERS FUND, 778
FRAZIER HEALTHCARE VENTURES, 785
FRESH VC, 788
FRIEDMAN, FLEISCHER & LOWE LLC, 790
FRONTENAC COMPANY, 792
FUEL CAPITAL, 2752
FULCRUM EQUITY PARTNERS, 797
FULL CIRCLE INVESTMENTS, 2753
FUSION FUND, 802
GALEN PARTNERS, 809
GE CAPITAL, 811
GE VENTURES, 812
GEMINI INVESTORS, 815
GENERAL ATLANTIC PARTNERS, 819
GENESYS CAPITAL, 2125
GLENGARY LLC, 835
GLOBALIVE, 2128
GOLDEN OPPORTUNITIES FUND, 2129
GOLUB CAPITAL, 848
GOOD NEWS VENTURES, 2132
GRANVILLE BAIRD CAPITAL PARTNERS, 2786
GRAPHITE CAPITAL MANAGEMENT LTD, 2787
GREAT HILL PARTNERS LLC, 862
GREAT POINT PARTNERS, 864
GREENSPRING ASSOCIATES, 872
GREIF & COMPANY, 874
GREY SKY VENTURE PARTNERS, 875
GROSVENOR FUNDS, 880
GROTECH VENTURES, 881
GROVE STREET ADVISORS LLC, 884
GRYPHON INVESTORS, 886
GV, 894
H KATZ CAPITAL GROUP, 896
HALYARD CAPITAL, 902
HARBERT MANAGEMENT CORPORATION, 907
HARBOR LIGHT CAPITAL PARTNERS, 910
HARBOURVEST PARTNERS LLC, 912
HBM PARTNERS, 2806
HEALTH ENTERPRISE PARTNERS, 921
HEALTHCARE PRIVATE EQUITY ASSOCIATION, 3254
HEALTHCARE VENTURES LLC, 922
HELION VENTURE PARTNERS, LLC International Management (Mauritius) Ltd, 2809
HELLMAN & FRIEDMAN LLC, 927
HERITAGE PARTNERS, 929
HIG CAPITAL, 931
HIGH ROAD CAPITAL PARTNERS, 934
HIGHLAND CAPITAL PARTNERS, 938
HOPEWELL VENTURES, 947
HORIZON TECHNOLOGY FINANCE, 949
HOULIHAN LOKEY, 951
HOUSTON HEALTH VENTURES, 954
HT CAPITAL ADVISORS LLC, 956
HUMANA VENTURES, 958
HUNTSMAN GAY GLOBAL CAPITAL, 962
HURON CAPITAL PARTNERS LLC, 963
IA VENTURES, 969
IANTHUS CAPITAL MANAGEMENT, 970
IBM VENTURE CAPITAL GROUP, 971
ICAN ISRAEL-CANNABIS.COM, 2836
ICV PARTNERS, 973
IDG CAPITAL, 977
IDG CAPITAL PARTNERS, 2838
IDG TECHNOLOGY VENTURE INVESTMENT, 2839
IMPERIAL CAPITAL, 2142
IMPERIAL INNOVATIONS, 2849
INCWELL VENTURE CAPITAL, 985
INDUSTRIFONDEN, 2858
INETWORKS ADVISORS LLC, 991
INLAND TECHSTART FUND, 997
INNOGEST CAPITAL, 2865
INNOVA MEMPHIS, 999
INNOVATION PLATFORM CAPITAL, 1002
INSIGHT VENTURE PARTNERS, 1005
INTER-ASIA VENTURE MANAGEMENT LIMITED, 2872
INTERNATIONAL FINANCE CORPORATION (IFC), 1012
INTERWEST PARTNERS, 1014
INVENTUS, 1017
INVESTOR AB, 2881
IRISH ANGELS, 1023
IRON GATE CAPITAL, 1024
IRONWOOD CAPITAL, 1025
ISIS EP LLP F & C, 2889
IXORA VENTURES, 2895

Industry Preference Index / Healthcare

J. BURKE CAPITAL PARTNERS, 1027
JEFFERIES CAPITAL PARTNERS, 1036
JH WHITNEY & COMPANY, 1041
JLL PARTNERS, 1043
JOHNSTON ASSOCIATES, 1048
JORDAN COMPANY, 1049
JUMPSTART INC, 1051
JW ASSET MANAGEMENT, 1052
JW CHILDS ASSOCIATES, 1053
KAISER PERMANENTE VENTURES, 1056
KAPOR CAPITAL, 1058
KARLIN VENTURES, 1059
KEARNY VENTURE PARTNERS, 1063
KEIRETSU FORUM, 1065
KELSO & COMPANY, 1066
KENSINGTON CAPITAL PARTNERS, 2160
KERRY CAPITAL ADVISORS, 1071
KILMER CAPITAL PARTNERS, 2162
KLEINWORT CAPITAL LIMITED, 2914
KOHLBERG KRAVIS ROBERTS & COMPANY, 1086
KRG CAPITAL PARTNERS, 1090
KTB VENTURES, 1091
LAKE CAPITAL, 1095
LATTERELL VENTURE PARTNERS, 1098
LAUNCHCAPITAL, 1101
LAUNCHPAD VENTURE GROUP, 1104
LEGEND CAPITAL, 2927
LEMHI VENTURES, 1111
LEONARD GREEN & PARTNERS LP, 1113
LEONIA MB GROUP/MB FUNDS, 2928
LEVINE LEICHTMAN CAPITAL PARTNERS, 1115
LFE CAPITAL, 1117
LINDEN LLC, 1132
LITTLEJOHN & COMPANY LLC, 1138
LLOYDS DEVELOPMENT CAPITAL LIMITED, 2935
LOMBARD INVESTMENTS, 1143
LONGWOOD FUND, 1149
LOVETT MILLER & COMPANY, 1152
LUX CAPITAL, 1155
MADISON DEARBORN PARTNERS, 1160
MANSA EQUITY PARTNERS, 1168
MARS INVESTMENT ACCELERATOR FUND, 2181
MARWIT CAPITAL LLC, 1171
MASSACHUSETTS CAPITAL RESOURCE COMPANY, 1176
MCG CAPITAL CORPORATION, 1192
MEDICAL RESEARCH COMMERCIALIZATION FUND, 2950
MEDIPHASE VENTURE PARTNERS, 1198
MEKETA INVESTMENT GROUP, 1201
MENTOR CAPITAL PARTNERS LTD, 1204
MERCK GLOBAL HEALTH INNOVATION FUND, 1206
MERIDIAN MANAGEMENT GROUP, 1209
MERLIN NEXUS, 1217
MIDATLANTIC FUND, 1228
MIDINVEST LIMITED, 2957
MISSION BAY CAPITAL, 1238
MITSUBISHI UFJ CAPITAL, 2961
MITSUI SUMITOMO INSURANCE VENTURE CAPITAL CO, 2962
MMC VENTURES, 2963
MONTLAKE CAPITAL, 1250
MONTREUX EQUITY PARTNERS, 1251
MORGAN STANLEY EXPANSION CAPITAL, 1255
MOTIV PARTNERS, 1258
MOTOROLA SOLUTIONS VENTURE CAPITAL, 1260
MPG EQUITY PARTNERS, 1267
MPM CAPITAL, 1268
MS&AD VENTURES, 1269
MURPHY & PARTNERS FUND LP, 1274
MVC CORPORATION, 2971
MVM LIFE SCIENCE PARTNERS, 2972
NAUTIC PARTNERS, 1278
NAVY CAPITAL, 1282
NEMO CAPITAL PARTNERS, 1288
NESBIC INVESTMENT FUND II, 2983
NEW MARKETS VENTURE PARTNERS, 1298
NEW MOUNTAIN CAPITAL, 1300
NEWBURY, PIRET & COMPANY, 1311
NEWLIGHT PARTNERS, 1314

NEWMARGIN VENTURE CAPITAL, 2989
NEWSPRING CAPITAL, 1316
NEXTEC DEVELOPMENT CAPITAL LIMITED, 2991
NFX, 1323
NGN CAPITAL, 1325
NOMURA PHASE4 VENTURES LTD, 2998
NORO-MOSELEY PARTNERS, 1332
NORTH BRIDGE VENTURE PARTNERS, 1335
NORTHERN LIGHT VENTURE CAPITAL, 1340
NORTHSTAR CAPITAL, 1343
NORTHSTAR VENTURES, 3003
NORWEST EQUITY PARTNERS, 1345
NORWEST VENTURE PARTNERS, 1346
NOVARTIS VENTURE FUNDS, 1350
NOVELTEK CAPITAL CORPORATION, 1351
OAK HILL CAPITAL PARTNERS, 1360
OAK INVESTMENT PARTNERS, 1361
OBVIOUS VENTURES, 1363
OLYMPUS PARTNERS, 1372
OMEGA FUNDS, 1373
ONE EQUITY PARTNERS, 1376
ONEX PARTNERS, 2201
ORIGINATE VENTURES, 1386
OUTCOME CAPITAL, 1389
OWL VENTURES, 1393
OneVentures, 3014
PALLADIUM EQUITY PARTNERS, 1404
PAMLICO CAPITAL, 1410
PANACHE VENTURES, 2204
PANTHEON VENTURES (US) LP, 1413
PARALLEL INVESTMENT PARTNERS, 1417
PARALLEL49 EQUITY, 2206
PARTHENON CAPITAL, 1419
PARTNERS HEALTHCARE RESEARCH VENTURES, 1421
PARTNERSHIP FUND FOR NEW YORK CITY, 1422
PEACHTREE EQUITY PARTNERS, 1425
PENFUND, 2211
PERMIRA Permira Advisers LLP, 3024
PERSISTENCE CAPITAL PARTNERS, 2212
PFIZER VENTURE INVESTMENTS, 1439
PHOENIX EQUITY PARTNERS LIMITED, 3027
PINNACLE VENTURES, 1449
PNC ERIEVIEW CAPITAL, 1460
POLARIS VENTURE PARTNERS, 1464
PRIMUS CAPITAL, 1480
PRISM CAPITAL, 1481
PRITZKER GROUP PRIVATE CAPITAL, 1482
PRITZKER GROUP VENTURE CAPITAL, 1483
PROGRESS EQUITY PARTNERS, 1487
PROQUEST INVESTMENTS, 1492
PROSEED, 3050
PSILOS GROUP, 1500
PTV SCIENCES, 1502
QIMING VENTURE PARTNERS, 3057
QUAKER BIOVENTURES, 1510
QUARRY CAPITAL MANAGEMENT, 1513
QUESTER CAPITAL MANAGEMENT LIMITED, 3061
QUESTMARK PARTNERS LP, 1517
RA CAPITAL MANAGEMENT, 1522
RADIUS VENTURES, 1523
RAND CAPITAL CORPORATION, 1526
RAYMOND JAMES CAPITAL, 1529
RECAPHEALTH VENTURES, 2225
REDHILLS VENTURES, 1535
REDMONT VENTURE PARTNERS, 1536
RESERVOIR VENTURE PARTNERS, 1547
RETHINK COMMUNITY, 1553
RHO VENTURES, 1561
RISE OF THE REST, 1571
RIVERSIDE COMPANY, 1576
RLH EQUITY PARTNERS, 1579
ROADMAP CAPITAL INC., 2234
ROBIN HOOD VENTURES, 1581
ROTH CAPITAL PARTNERS, 1592
ROUNDTABLE HEALTHCARE PARTNERS, 1594
SAFEGUARD SCIENTIFICS, 1605
SAIF PARTNERS, 3084

Industry Preference Index / Healthcare Information Technology

SAINTS CAPITAL, 1608
SARONA ASSET MANAGEMENT, 2239
SB CHINA VENTURE CAPITAL, 3091
SCALE VENTURE PARTNERS, 1629
SCOTTISH EQUITY PARTNERS, 3095
SEQUEL VENTURE PARTNERS, 1656
SERGE PUN & ASSOCIATES (MYANMAR) LIMITED, 3102
SEVENTYSIX CAPITAL, 1660
SEVIN ROSEN FUNDS, 1661
SHERBROOKE CAPITAL, 1668
SHORE CAPITAL PARTNERS, 1670
SIERRA ANGELS, 1671
SIGHTLINE PARTNERS, 1673
SIGNATURE CAPITAL LLC, 3111
SILKROAD EQUITY, 1683
SKYLINE VENTURES, 1693
SKYTREE CAPITAL PARTNERS, 1694
SOCIAL CAPITAL, 1698
SORRENTO VENTURES, 1708
SOVEREIGN CAPITAL, 3121
SPENCER TRASK VENTURES, 1723
SPLIT ROCK PARTNERS, 1728
STARBOARD CAPITAL PARTNERS, 1738
STERLING PARTNERS, 1745
STONEHENGE GROWTH CAPITAL, 1748
STONEWOOD CAPITAL MANAGEMENT, 1749
SUMMER STREET CAPITAL PARTNERS, 1753
SUMMIT PARTNERS, 1754
SUN CAPITAL PARTNERS, 1755
SV HEALTH INVESTORS, 1764
SYCAMORE VENTURES, 1771
TA ASSOCIATES, 1778
TAILWIND CAPITAL, 1779
TAKEDA VENTURES, 1780
TEL VENTURE CAPITAL, 1793
TELEFONICA VENTURES, 3160
TELEGRAPH HILL PARTNERS, 1794
TELESYSTEM, 2255
TEUZA MANAGEMENT & DEVELOPMENT LTD, 3162
TEXO VENTURES, 1803
THE ABRAAJ GROUP, 3164
THOMA BRAVO LLC, 1817
THOMAS H LEE PARTNERS, 1818
THOMAS, MCNERNEY & PARTNERS, 1820
TIE ANGELS GROUP SEATTLE, 1827
TMG CAPITAL PARTNERS, 3171
TONIIC, 1833
TOP RENERGY INC., 2263
TPG CAPITAL, 1837
TREVI HEALTH CAPITAL, 1846
TRIATHLON MEDICAL VENTURES, 1849
TRIPLETREE LLC, 1856
TULLIS HEALTH INVESTORS, 1868
TVM CAPITAL, 3187
TXV PARTNERS, 1877
TYLT LAB, 1878
UCA UNTERNEHMER CONSULT AG, 3188
UDD VENTURES, 3189
UNIVERSITY VENTURE FUND, 1886
UPDATA VENTURE PARTNERS, 1888
VALOR EQUITY PARTNERS, 1904
VALUEACT CAPITAL, 1905
VANTAGEPOINT CAPITAL PARTNERS, 1908
VEBER PARTNERS LLC, 1911
VENROCK ASSOCIATES, 1918
VENTURE INVESTORS LLC, 1923
VENTUREAST, 3202
VERSANT VENTURES, 1930
VERTICAL GROUP, 1931
VESTAR CAPITAL PARTNERS, 1933
VICKERS FINANCIAL GROUP, 3206
VIDA VENTURES, 1934
VRG CAPITAL, 2274
W CAPITAL PARTNERS, 1949
WALDEN ISRAEL VENTURE CAPITAL, 3221
WARBURG PINCUS LLC, 1957
WATER STREET HEALTHCARE PARTNERS, 1962
WELLS FARGO CAPITAL FINANCE, 1971
WELSH, CARSON, ANDERSON & STOWE, 1973
WEST HEALTH INVESTMENT FUND, 1974
WESTCAP, 2277
WESTERN TECHNOLOGY INVESTMENT, 1976
WESTLAKE SECURITIES, 1977
WHEATLEY PARTNERS, 1981
WHITECAP VENTURE PARTNERS, 2280
WI HARPER GROUP, 1983
WIND POINT PARTNERS, 1990
WINDHAM VENTURE PARTNERS, 1993
WIREFRAME VENTURES, 2001
WRF CAPITAL, 2007
XT INVESTMENTS, 3231
YELLOW POINT EQUITY PARTNERS, 2284
YELLOWSTONE CAPITAL, 2012
YFM GROUP, 3234
YLR CAPITAL MARKETS LTD, 3237
YORK STREET CAPITAL PARTNERS LLC, 2014

Healthcare Devices
NEW ENTERPRISE ASSOCIATES, 1296

Healthcare IT
BEDFORD FUNDING, 245
BIOGENERATOR, 270

Healthcare Information Technology
.406 VENTURES, 1
ALTARIS CAPITAL PARTNERS, 97
APERTURE VENTURE PARTNERS, 137
ARC ANGEL FUND, 151
ASCENSION HEALTH VENTURES LLC, 178
ASCENT BIOMEDICAL VENTURES, 179
ASPECT VENTURES, 182
AZURE CAPITAL PARTNERS, 218
BIO*ONE CAPITAL EDMI, 2504
BIOVENTURES INVESTORS, 273
BREGAL SAGEMOUNT, 336
BRIGHTSTONE VENTURE CAPITAL, 344
BROOK VENTURE FUND, 352
CARDINAL PARTNERS, 413
CATALYST INVESTORS, 429
CEDAR VENTURES LLC, 439
CHICAGO VENTURES, 473
CINCYTECH, 481
COUNCIL CAPITAL, 551
DEFTA PARTNERS, 603
DISCOVERY CAPITAL, 2091
DOMAIN ASSOCIATES LLC, 622
EASTON CAPITAL INVESTMENT GROUP, 644
EDBI Pte LTD., 2681
EDISON PARTNERS, 655
ELM STREET VENTURES, 661
F-PRIME CAPITAL PARTNERS, 711
FIDELITY GROWTH PARTNERS EUROPE, 2725
FLETCHER SPAGHT VENTURES, 750
FLYBRIDGE CAPITAL PARTNERS, 756
FRANCISCO PARTNERS, 782
GALEN PARTNERS, 809
GENERATION PARTNERS, 822
GRAND CENTRAL HOLDINGS, 852
GRAYHAWK CAPITAL, 861
GREAT POINT PARTNERS, 864
HATTERAS VENTURE PARTNERS, 918
HLM VENTURE PARTNERS, 941
HOPEN LIFE SCIENCE VENTURES, 946
HORIZON VENTURES LLC, 950
HOUSTON ANGEL NETWORK, 953
HUMANA VENTURES, 958
IGAN PARTNERS, 2141
INETWORKS ADVISORS LLC, 991
JAVELIN VENTURE PARTNERS, 1032
JMI EQUITY FUND LP, 1045
JUMP CAPITAL LLC, 1050
KAISER PERMANENTE VENTURES, 1056
KODIAK VENTURE PARTNERS, 1084

1159

Industry Preference Index / Healthcare Innovation

LONG RIVER VENTURES, 1146
MARYLAND VENTURE FUND, 1172
MASS VENTURES, 1175
MESA VERDE PARTNERS, 1222
MOBIUS VENTURE CAPITAL, 1245
MORGAN STANLEY EXPANSION CAPITAL, 1255
MVM LIFE SCIENCE PARTNERS, 2972
NEMO CAPITAL PARTNERS, 1288
NEW CAPITAL PARTNERS, 1292
OAK INVESTMENT PARTNERS, 1361
OKAPI VENTURE CAPITAL, 1371
ONSET VENTURES, 1379
OSAGE PARTNERS, 1388
PALO ALTO VENTURE SCIENCE, 1407
PFIZER VENTURE INVESTMENTS, 1439
PITTSBURGH LIFE SCIENCES GREENHOUSE, 1452
POINT JUDITH CAPITAL, 1463
POLYTECH VENTURES, 3036
PSILOS GROUP, 1500
REED ELSEVIER VENTURES, 3065
REX HEALTH VENTURES, 1559
RITTENHOUSE VENTURES, 1572
SALMON RIVER CAPITAL, 1611
SANTE VENTURES, 1622
SCHRODER VENTURES HEALTH INVESTORS, 1631
SENECA PARTNERS, 1652
SENTRY FINANCIAL CORPORATION, 1655
SHEPHERD VENTURES, 1667
SOUTHERN CAPITOL VENTURES, 1712
SPINDLETOP CAPITAL, 1725
SPRING LAKE EQUITY PARTNERS, 1731
SYNTHESIS CAPITAL, 1777
TEXO VENTURES, 1803
VENROCK ASSOCIATES, 1918
VERSANT VENTURES, 1930
WASABI VENTURES, 1959
WEST HEALTH INVESTMENT FUND, 1974
WHEATLEY PARTNERS, 1981

Healthcare Innovation
SANOFI-GENZYME BIOVENTURES, 1621

Healthcare Services
3TS CAPITAL PARTNERS 3i Group plc, 2301
ABRY PARTNERS, 20
ACON INVESTMENTS, 45
ALTARIS CAPITAL PARTNERS, 97
ARBORETUM VENTURES, 150
ARLINGTON CAPITAL PARTNERS, 167
ASCENT BIOMEDICAL VENTURES, 179
ATHYRIUM CAPITAL MANAGEMENT, 190
BEHRMAN CAPITAL, 248
BEZOS EXPEDITIONS, 265
BIOGENERATOR, 270
BLUE CHIP VENTURE COMPANY, 290
BOUNDS EQUITY PARTNERS, 319
BRANFORD CASTLE, 330
CAPITAL RESOURCE PARTNERS, 405
CAROUSEL CAPITAL, 418
CENTERFIELD CAPITAL PARTNERS, 445
CHICAGO GROWTH PARTNERS, 470
CIC PARTNERS, 479
CID CAPITAL, 480
CLARION CAPITAL PARTNERS LLC, 494
CLEARLIGHT PARTNERS, 503
CONCENTRIC EQUITY PARTNERS Financial Investments Corporation, 531
COUNCIL CAPITAL, 551
CRESSEY & COMPANY LP, 559
CUTLASS CAPITAL LLC, 573
DAUPHIN CAPITAL PARTNERS, 588
DBL PARTNERS, 596
DELPHI VENTURES, 605
DFW CAPITAL PARTNERS, 611
DIAMOND STATE VENTURES LP, 612
DUBIN CLARK & COMPANY, 633
EASTON CAPITAL INVESTMENT GROUP, 644
ELM STREET VENTURES, 661
EOS PARTNERS LP, 687
EPIC PARTNERS, 688
ESSEX WOODLANDS HEALTH VENTURES LLC, 698
EUREKA GROWTH CAPITAL, 699
EVERGREEN ADVISORS, 702
FIVE POINTS CAPITAL, 747
FLARE CAPITAL PARTNERS, 749
FORESITE CAPITAL, 764
GENERATION PARTNERS, 822
GENSTAR CAPITAL LP, 823
GLADSTONE CAPITAL, 832
GOLUB CAPITAL, 848
GRANTHAM CAPITAL, 858
GREAT POINT PARTNERS, 864
HARREN EQUITY PARTNERS, 913
HARVEST PARTNERS, 917
HERITAGE PARTNERS, 929
HIGH STREET CAPITAL, 935
HLM VENTURE PARTNERS, 941
HUMANA VENTURES, 958
INETWORKS ADVISORS LLC, 991
INTEGRA VENTURES, 1007
KAISER PERMANENTE VENTURES, 1056
KBL HEALTHCARE VENTURES, 1062
KOHLBERG & COMPANY LLC, 1085
LEE EQUITY PARTNERS, 1108
LLR PARTNERS INC, 1140
LOVETT MILLER & COMPANY, 1152
MARANON CAPITAL, 1169
MBF CAPITAL CORPORATION, 1191
MIDATLANTIC FUND, 1228
MORGAN STANLEY EXPANSION CAPITAL, 1255
MOUNTAIN GROUP CAPITAL, 1261
MTS HEALTH INVESTORS, 1271
MVP CAPITAL PARTNERS, 1275
NAVIGATION CAPITAL PARTNERS, 1279
NEW CAPITAL PARTNERS, 1292
NEW ENTERPRISE ASSOCIATES, 1296
NEWSPRING CAPITAL, 1316
NORO-MOSELEY PARTNERS, 1332
ODEON CAPITAL PARTNERS, 1367
OKAPI VENTURE CAPITAL, 1371
OSAGE PARTNERS, 1388
POST CAPITAL PARTNERS, 1469
POUSCHINE COOK CAPITAL MANAGEMENT LLC, 1470
PSILOS GROUP, 1500
QUAKER BIOVENTURES, 1510
REX HEALTH VENTURES, 1559
ROPART ASSET MANAGEMENT, 1587
SALEM INVESTMENT PARTNERS, 1609
SANTE VENTURES, 1622
SCHRODER VENTURES HEALTH INVESTORS, 1631
SENECA PARTNERS, 1652
SENTINEL CAPITAL PARTNERS, 1654
SEQUOIA CAPITAL, 1657
SILVER OAK SERVICES PARTNERS, 1686
SPINDLETOP CAPITAL, 1725
SSM PARTNERS, 1735
SYMMETRIC CAPITAL, 1772
SYNTHESIS CAPITAL, 1777
TELEGRAPH HILL PARTNERS, 1794
TICONDEROGA PRIVATE EQUITY, 1826
TREVI HEALTH CAPITAL, 1846
VEDANTA CAPITAL LP, 1913
VERSANT VENTURES, 1930
VESEY STREET CAPITAL PARTNERS LLC, 1932
WATER STREET HEALTHCARE PARTNERS, 1962
WESTVIEW CAPITAL PARTNERS, 1979

Healthcare Tech
ARROWHEAD INNOVATION FUND, 169

Healthcare Technology
BIOMATICS CAPITAL, 271
BLUFF POINT ASSOCIATES, 302
CAPITAL MIDWEST FUND, 403

GREENHILLS VENTURES, LLC, 870
RIPPLE VENTURES, 2232
SOZO VENTURES, 1716

Healthy Active Lifestyle
CAVA CAPITAL, 433

Heating
ATP PRIVATE EQUITY PARTNERS, 2438
BARING PRIVATE EQUITY PARTNERS ESPANA SA, 2480
BC PARTNERS LIMITED, 2488

High Performance Computing
ARCH VENTURE PARTNERS, 154

High Technology
ACONCAGUA VENTURES, 2326
ALACRITY VENTURES, 76
AMMER PARTNERS, 2385
ANNEX VENTURES, 131
ARAGON VENTURES, 146
AURA CAPITAL OY Auratum Group, 2442
AXIOM VENTURE PARTNERS, 215
AZINI CAPITAL PARTNERS, 2463
BAEKELAND FUNDS, 2467
BATTERSON VENTURE CAPITAL LLC, 237
BAY BG BAVARIAN VENTURE CAPITAL CORP, 2485
BAYERN KAPITAL, 2486
BIOPROCESS CAPITAL PARTNERS, 2508
BUSINESS GROWTH FUND, 2541
CDH INVESTMENTS, 2570
CONNECTICUT INNOVATIONS, 532
CREATHOR VENTURE, 2629
DAIMLERCHRYSLER VENTURE GmbH DaimlerChrysler AG, 2641
ENTREE CAPITAL, 2700
EPIC VENTURES, 689
EQUINET VENTURE PARTNERS AG, 2704
ESPRESSO CAPITAL, 2103
EXCELL PARTNERS, INC., 705
FIRST STEP FUND, 743
FORUM TECHNOLOGIES VENTURE CAPITAL COMPANY Forum Group, 2742
IDG TECHNOLOGY VENTURE INVESTMENT, 2839
INTELLIGENT CAPITAL SDN BHD, 2871
INVESTAMERICA VENTURE GROUP, 1020
KLEINER PERKINS, 1079
LANDSBANKI VENTURES, 2920
LAUNCHPAD VENTURE GROUP, 1104
LIMESTONE VENTURES, 1130
MITSUBISHI UFJ CAPITAL, 2961
MURPHREE VENTURE PARTNERS, 1273
NAUSICAA VENTURES, 2977
NEUHAUS PARTNERS, 2985
NEW YORK LIFE CAPITAL PARTNERS, 1308
PIDC PHILADELPHIA, 1445
RED DOT VENTURES, 3064
RODA GROUP, 1584
SECOND AVENUE PARTNERS, 1644
SEVEN SPIRES INVESTMENTS, 3103
SIERRA VENTURES, 1672
SOCIALATOM VENTURES, 3116
SPINUP VENTURE, 3123
SUTTER HILL VENTURES, 1762
TRIANGLE ANGEL PARTNERS, 1847
TROIKA CAPITAL PARTNERS, 3184
TWO SIGMA VENTURES, 1876
VAEKSTFONDEN, 3194
VENTANA CAPITAL MANAGEMENT LP, 1920
VENTURE CAPITAL FUND OF NEW ENGLAND, 1922
VISION CAPITAL, 1939
VIVES, 3216
WASHINGTON CAPITAL VENTURES, 1960
XENIA VENTURE CAPITAL, 3230
YLR CAPITAL MARKETS LTD, 3237

High Value Added Manufacturing
NEXTEC DEVELOPMENT CAPITAL LIMITED, 2991

Home Improvement
CARDINAL EQUITY PARTNERS, 412

Homeland Security
BRYANT PARK VENTURES, 359
CHART VENTURE PARTNERS, 459
MAIN STREET CAPITAL HOLDINGS LLC, 1163
OUTCOME CAPITAL, 1389
PALADIN CAPITAL GROUP, 1401

Horticulture
CARDINAL EQUITY PARTNERS, 412

Hospitality
CANADIAN VENTURE CAPITAL ASSOCIATION Canadian Venture Capital & Private Equity Association, 3249
FRESH VC, 788
GEODESIC CAPITAL, 824
GOLDEN OPPORTUNITIES FUND, 2129
KALORI GROUP INVESTMENTS, 2906
RAPTOR GROUP, 1527
RISE OF THE REST, 1571
THAYER VENTURES, 1808
WESTCAP, 2277

Hospitality & Travel
REVOLUTION LLC, 1558

Hospitals
BC PARTNERS LIMITED, 2488
QUANTUM CAPITAL PARTNERS, 1512

Hotel, Tourism & Leisure
TPA CORPORATE FINANCE CONSULTING GMBH Horwarth International, 3175

Hotels
CARPEDIA INTERNATIONAL, 2066
FOUNDATION CAPITAL LIMITED, 2744
STARWOOD CAPITAL GROUP LLC, 1742

Household Goods
CLIFFORD CHANCE PUNDER, 2605
EQUISTONE, 2705
PRIVATE EQUITY PARTNERS SPA, 3044
PROSPECT PARTNERS LLC, 1494
UNION CAPITAL CORPORATION, 1883

Housing
ACUMEN, 54
RETHINK COMMUNITY, 1553
TONIIC, 1833
URBAN INNOVATION FUND, 1895

Human Capital Consulting
AON RISK SOLUTIONS Aon Corporation, 2405

Human Resource Technology
RUBICON VENTURE CAPITAL, 1599

Human Resources
CAPMAN CAPITAL MANAGEMENT OY, 2553
GSV VENTURES, 888

Human Therapeutics
BIOVENTURES INVESTORS, 273

Human Wellness
FREYCINET INVESTMENTS, 2120

Human-Computer Interaction
BLOOMBERG BETA, 287

ICT
CONOR VENTURE PARTNERS OY, 2621

IOT
ZHENFUND, 3241

Industry Preference Index / IP Services

IP Services
CROSSLINK CAPITAL, 564

IT
ARROWHEAD INNOVATION FUND, 169
CREDIT MUTUEL EQUITY, 2082

IT & Managed Services
CALTIUS EQUITY PARTNERS, 376

IT & Software
TOP RENERGY INC., 2263

IT Consulting
ACCESS CAPITAL, 34

IT Cyber Risk
HALYARD CAPITAL, 902

IT Enabled Services
ACCEL-KKR LLC, 28

IT Infrastructure
AMITI VENTURES, 117
DIAMONDHEAD VENTURES, 614
ENTREPIA VENTURES, 683
NORWEST VENTURE PARTNERS, 1346
PROCYON VENTURES, 1486

IT Security
NEWBURY VENTURES, 1310

IT Services
BEDFORD FUNDING, 245
BEZOS EXPEDITIONS, 265
CROSS CREEK ADVISORS, 561
LIFE SCIENCES PARTNERS BV, 2930
MAINE ANGELS, 1164

IT-Intensive Life Science Applications
MASTHEAD VENTURE PARTNERS, 1178

IT/BIO Convergence
IGLOBE PARTNERS, 2844

Ice Cream
RABO BLACK EARTH Eagle Venture Partners, 3062
WESTERN NIS ENTERPRISE FUND, 3224

Image-Recognition
SONY STRATEGIC TECHNOLOGY PARTNERSHIPS, 1706

Imports/Exports
CROSBY ASSET MANAGEMENT, 2631
EMINENT CAPITAL PARTNERS, 670
FOUNDATION CAPITAL LIMITED, 2744

Industrial
3I ITALY 3i Group, 2295
3M UNITEK, 2299
ACON INVESTMENTS, 45
ADVENT INTERNATIONAL CORPORATION, 61
ALTAS PARTNERS, 2030
AMERICAN SECURITIES LLC, 111
APOLLO GLOBAL MANAGEMENT, 141
AURORA CAPITAL GROUP, 202
BAIN CAPITAL PRIVATE EQUITY, 223
BERTRAM CAPITAL, 260
BEZOS EXPEDITIONS, 265
BINGLEY CAPITAL, 2052
BLACKSTONE PRIVATE EQUITY GROUP, 280
BRANFORD CASTLE, 330
BROOKE PRIVATE EQUITY ASSOCIATES, 353
BROOKSIDE EQUITY PARTNERS LLC, 356
CANADIAN VENTURE CAPITAL ASSOCIATION Canadian Venture Capital & Private Equity Association, 3249
CARLYLE GROUP, 416
CCMP CAPITAL, 435

CENTRAL TEXAS ANGEL NETWORK, 447
CID CAPITAL, 480
CRESTVIEW PARTNERS, 560
DARBY OVERSEAS INVESTMENTS LTD, 585
ECOSYSTEM VENTURES, 650
FOX PAINE & COMPANY LLC, 781
FRANCISCO PARTNERS, 782
HARREN EQUITY PARTNERS, 913
JLL PARTNERS, 1043
KRG CAPITAL PARTNERS, 1090
LAUNCHPAD VENTURE GROUP, 1104
LINLEY CAPITAL, 1134
MASS VENTURES, 1175
MPE PARTNERS, 1266
PORTUGAL CAPITAL VENTURES Institutional Headquarters, 3039
PRAIRIEGOLD VENTURE PARTNERS, 1474
SAINTS CAPITAL, 1608
TECH COAST ANGELS, 1786
TIGER GLOBAL MANAGEMENT, 1828
VINCERA CAPITAL, 3209
WESTVIEW CAPITAL PARTNERS, 1979

Industrial Distribution
ALPHA CAPITAL PARTNERS, 90
HCI EQUITY PARTNERS, 920

Industrial Electronics
ARGOSY CAPITAL, 165

Industrial Equipment
3I TEUPSCHLAND GmbH 3i Group, 2297
ACCESS CAPITAL, 34
ALLSTATE INVESTMENTS LLC, 88
AMERIMARK CAPITAL CORPORATION, 112
AMPERSAND CAPITAL PARTNERS, 119
ANDLINGER & COMPANY INC, 124
ARTHUR P GOULD & COMPANY, 174
AUSTIN CAPITAL PARTNERS LP, 204
AVENUE CAPITAL GROUP, 211
AXIA CAPITAL, 214
BERKELEY VC INTERNATIONAL LLC, 255
BLUE SAGE CAPITAL, 294
BRADFORD EQUITIES MANAGEMENT LLC, 324
BRUCKMANN, ROSSER, SHERRILL & COMPANY, 357
BRUML CAPITAL CORPORATION, 358
CAPITAL FOR BUSINESS, INC, 402
CARDINAL EQUITY PARTNERS, 412
CORDOVA VENTURES, 539
DAVID N DEUTSCH & COMPANY LLC, 590
DRESNER COMPANIES, 630
ENTERPRISE INVESTORS, 2697
EQT PARTNERS AB, 2703
EQUUS TOTAL RETURN, 695
EXPORT DEVELOPMENT CANADA, 2106
FERRANTI LIMITED, 2723
FINANCIERE DE BRIENNE FCPR, 2729
FINLOMBARDA SpA, 2730
FIRST RESERVE, 741
FLORIDA CAPITAL PARTNERS, 753
GE CAPITAL, 811
GENERAL CATALYST PARTNERS, 820
GIMV GIMV, 2771
GLENCOE CAPITAL, 834
GRAHAM PARTNERS, 851
GRANVILLE BAIRD CAPITAL PARTNERS, 2786
HALDER BETEILIGUNGSBERATUNG GmbH, 2796
HALDER HOLDINGS BV, 2797
HAMILTON ROBINSON CAPITAL PARTNERS, 903
HCI EQUITY PARTNERS, 920
HEARTLAND INDUSTRIAL PARTNERS, 926
HT CAPITAL ADVISORS LLC, 956
HUMANA VENTURES, 958
ICV PARTNERS, 973
INDUSTRIEBANK LIOF NV, 2857
INDUSTRIFONDEN, 2858
INNOFINANCE OY, 2864
IRDI MIDI-PYRENEES, 2887

Industry Preference Index / Industrial Services

JAVELIN INVESTMENTS, 2899
JB POINDEXTER & COMPANY, 1034
LANDSBANKI VENTURES, 2920
LEGAL AND GENERAL VENTURES LIMITED, 2926
LITTLEJOHN & COMPANY LLC, 1138
LM CAPITAL SECURITIES, 1141
LOMBARD INVESTMENTS, 1143
MANHATTAN INVESTMENT PARTNERS, 1166
MASSACHUSETTS CAPITAL RESOURCE COMPANY, 1176
MASSACHUSETTS GROWTH CAPITAL CORPORATION, 1177
MERIT ENERGY COMPANY, 1211
METAPOINT PARTNERS, 1225
MEZZANINE MANAGEMENT LIMITED Mezzanine Management UK Ltd., 2956
NORTHERN ENTERPRISE LIMITED, 3002
PARTECH INTERNATIONAL, 1418
PERMAL CAPITAL MANAGEMENT, 1435
PERMIRA Permira Advisers LLP, 3024
PLEXUS VENTURES, 1456
RAF INDUSTRIES, 1524
ROYALTY CAPITAL MANAGEMENT, 1595
SARATOGA PARTNERS, 1624
SEACOAST CAPITAL CORPORATION, 1639
SEED CAPITAL LIMITED, 3098
SIEMENS VENTURE CAPITAL, 3109
SKYLINE VENTURES, 1693
SOURCE CAPITAL GROUP, 1710
STARBOARD CAPITAL PARTNERS, 1738
STARWOOD CAPITAL GROUP LLC, 1742
THREE CITIES RESEARCH, 1822
THROUNARFELAG ISLANDS PLC, 3168
TSG CONSUMER PARTNERS, 1863
VAEKSTFONDEN, 3194
VALLEY VENTURES LP, 1903
VENTURE CAPITAL FUND OF NEW ENGLAND, 1922
VENTURE INVESTORS, 3201
WESTERN NIS ENTERPRISE FUND, 3224
WINGATE PARTNERS, 1997
ZS FUND LP, 2021

Industrial Goods
SCOTIABANK PRIVATE EQUITY, 2241

Industrial Manufacturing
ARROWHEAD INVESTMENT MANAGEMENT, 170
BRIDGE STREET CAPITAL, 341
CALERA CAPITAL, 371
CATAPULT VENTURES, 431
COMVEST PARTNERS, 530
INCWELL VENTURE CAPITAL, 985
ODYSSEY INVESTMENT PARTNERS, 1368
REDMONT VENTURE PARTNERS, 1536
SENTINEL CAPITAL PARTNERS, 1654
YELLOWSTONE CAPITAL, 2012

Industrial Products
3I GESTION SA 3i Group, 2294
AAVIN PRIVATE EQUITY, 16
ALBEMARLE PRIVATE EQUITY LIMITED, 2352
ANGELS' FORUM LLC, 130
BLUE POINT CAPITAL PARTNERS, 293
BROCKWAY MORAN & PARTNERS, 351
BUNKER HILL CAPITAL, 362
CAMBRIA GROUP, 381
CENTRE PARTNERS MANAGEMENT LLC, 449
DESCO CAPITAL, 607
ECOAST ANGEL NETWORK, 649
EMINENT CAPITAL PARTNERS, 670
EQVITEC PARTNERS OY, 2707
FRIULIA SpA, 2749
GLOBAL EQUITY PARTNERS BETEILIGUNGS-MANAGEMENT, 2774
GOLDNER HAWN, 847
HARBOUR GROUP, 911
HELLMAN & FRIEDMAN LLC, 927
HERITAGE PARTNERS, 929
ILE-DE-FRANCE, 2846
INVEST EQUITY MANAGEMENT CONSULTING GmbH, 2878

IRVING PLACE CAPITAL, 1026
JORDAN COMPANY, 1049
MONTAGU PRIVATE EQUITY LIMITED, 2968
NCT VENTURES, 1285
ONEX PARTNERS, 2201
SEED CAPITAL LIMITED, 3098
SERAPH GROUP, 1658
SUMMIT PARTNERS, 1754
SYMMETRIC CAPITAL, 1772
TRELLIS CAPITAL CORPORATION, 2265
TRINITY VENTURE CAPITAL TVC Holdings plc, 3182
VALOR EQUITY PARTNERS, 1904
VELOCITY EQUITY PARTNERS LLC, 1915
WATERLAND PRIVATE EQUITY INVESTMENT, 3222
ZERNIKE SEED FUND BV, 3240
ZURMONT MADISON PRIVATE EQUITY, 3244

Industrial Services
360 CAPITAL PARTNERS 360 Capital Management SA, 2288
3i GROUP PLC, 2303
ALBEMARLE PRIVATE EQUITY LIMITED, 2352
ALTAMONT CAPITAL PARTNERS, 96
AMANAH VENTURES SDN BHD, 2380
AMERICAN INDUSTRIAL PARTNERS, 110
AMICUS CAPITAL PARTNERS, 2384
ARGOSY CAPITAL, 165
ATP PRIVATE EQUITY PARTNERS, 2438
ATRIA CAPITAL PARTENAIRES, 2439
AVISTA CAPITAL PARTNERS, 212
BAIRD CAPITAL PARTNERS, 225
BARING PRIVATE EQUITY PARTNERS INDIA, 2481
BAY BG BAVARIAN VENTURE CAPITAL CORP, 2485
BOTTS & COMPANY LIMITED, 2523
BRUCKMANN, ROSSER, SHERRILL & COMPANY, 357
CALTIUS EQUITY PARTNERS, 376
CARLYLE ASIA INVESTMENT ADVISORS LIMITED Carlyle Group, 2556
CATALYST INVESTMENT MANAGERS PTY LIMITED PPM Capital, 2564
CEI VENTURES, 440
CENTERPOINT VENTURE PARTNERS, 446
CHALLENGE FUNDS - ETGAR LP, 2576
CHEROKEE INVESTMENT PARTNERS, 465
CHICAGO GROWTH PARTNERS, 470
CIC FINANCE CIC Group, 2592
CINVEN LIMITED, 2596
CIVC PARTNERS, 491
CLEARLAKE CAPITAL, 502
CORE PACIFIC - YAMAICHI CAPITAL LIMITED Core Pacific Securities Company Ltd, 2624
CORNERSTONE CAPITAL HOLDINGS, 542
COVENT INDUSTRIAL CAPITAL INVESTMENT COMPANY, 2626
DB CAPITAL PARTNERS (ASIA), 2643
DEUTSCHE BETEILIGUNGS AG, 2651
DFW CAPITAL PARTNERS, 611
DIRECT CAPITAL PRIVATE EQUITY LIMITED, 2655
ELECTRA PARTNERS EUROPE, 2686
ELGNER GROUP INVESTMENTS, 2099
EM WARBURG, PINCUS & COMPANY INTERNATIONAL, 2688
EM WARBURG, PINCUS & COMPANY JAPAN, 2689
ENTERPRISE EQUITY (NI) LTD, 2695
ENTERPRISE INVESTORS, 2697
EQT PARTNERS AB, 2703
EQVITEC PARTNERS OY, 2707
EURAZEO, 2710
EUROVENTURES CAPITAL, 2716
EVOLVE CAPITAL, 703
FERRANTI LIMITED, 2723
FIVE POINTS CAPITAL, 747
FRIEND SKOLER & COMPANY LLC, 791
GENESIS CAPITAL CORPORATION, 2124
GILBERT GLOBAL EQUITY PARTNERS, 831
GLOBAL EQUITY PARTNERS BETEILIGUNGS-MANAGEMENT, 2774
GOLDEN GATE CAPITAL, 843
GRANITE VENTURE CAPITAL CORPORATION, 2785
GRYPHON MANAGEMENT COMPANY, 887
HALDER BETEILIGUNGSBERATUNG GmbH, 2796

Industry Preference Index / Industrial Technology

HALDER HOLDINGS BV, 2797
HAMMOND, KENNEDY, WHITNEY & COMPANY, 904
HARVEST PARTNERS, 917
HCI EQUITY PARTNERS, 920
HEARTLAND INDUSTRIAL PARTNERS, 926
HG CAPITAL, 2814
HUNTSMAN GAY GLOBAL CAPITAL, 962
INDUSTRIFONDEN, 2858
INNOFINANCE OY, 2864
INVEST EQUITY MANAGEMENT CONSULTING GmbH, 2878
INVESTMENT AB BURE, 2879
INVEXCEL PATRIMONIO, 2882
IRDI MIDI-PYRENEES, 2887
KB PARTNERS LLC, 1061
KENSINGTON CAPITAL PARTNERS, 2160
KIDD & COMPANY, 1075
LANDSBANKI VENTURES, 2920
LIFE SCIENCES PARTNERS BV, 2930
LLOYDS DEVELOPMENT CAPITAL LIMITED, 2935
LMBO FINANCE, 2936
MARATHON VENTURE CAPITAL FUND LIMITED, 2945
MIDMARK CAPITAL LP, 1230
MIDOCEAN PARTNERS, 1231
MIDWEST MEZZANINE FUNDS, 1232
MONTAGU PRIVATE EQUITY LIMITED, 2968
MONUMENT ADVISORS, 1252
NORTHERN ENTERPRISE LIMITED, 3002
NORWEST EQUITY PARTNERS, 1345
PAMLICO CAPITAL, 1410
PENINSULA CAPITAL PARTNERS LLC, 1429
PERMIRA Permira Advisers LLP, 3024
PHOENIX EQUITY PARTNERS LIMITED, 3027
POMONA CAPITAL, 1466
PRAIRIE CAPITAL, 1473
RAND CAPITAL CORPORATION, 1526
REITEN & CO STRATEGIC INVESTMENTS AS Reiten & Company, 3067
RIVER ASSOCIATES INVESTMENTS LLC, 1573
SCOTTISH ENTERPRISE, 3094
STONEBRIDGE PARTNERS, 1747
TELESYSTEM, 2255
TGF MANAGEMENT, 1805
TRINITY VENTURE CAPITAL TVC Holdings plc, 3182
TVV CAPITAL, 1872
VISION CAPITAL, 1939
WAND PARTNERS, 1956
WATERLAND PRIVATE EQUITY INVESTMENT, 3222
WELLSPRING CAPITAL MANAGEMENT LLC, 1972
WIND POINT PARTNERS, 1990
WOODSIDE FUND, 2005
WRF CAPITAL, 2007
WYNNCHURCH CAPITAL, 2008
YORK STREET CAPITAL PARTNERS LLC, 2014

Industrial Technology
ARCAPITA INC, 153
BATTERY VENTURES, 238
CAPITAL SOUTHWEST CORPORATION, 406
CHICAGO GROWTH PARTNERS, 470
DVC DEUTSCHE VENTURE CAPITAL, 2670
EARLY STAGE PARTNERS, 642
FORTÉ VENTURES, 770
GENSTAR CAPITAL LP, 823
IBB BETEILIGUNGSGESELLSCHAFT MBH, 2832
INCWELL VENTURE CAPITAL, 985
MENTOR CAPITAL PARTNERS LTD, 1204
RIPPLE VENTURES, 2232

Industrials
NEXT EQUITIES, 2194
TERA CAPITAL CORPORATION, 2258
TPG CAPITAL, 1837

Industry
645 VENTURES, 12
AMBERJACK CAPITAL PARTNERS, 106
BRISIO INNOVATIONS INC., 2061

CREDIT MUTUEL EQUITY, 2082
ECAPITAL ENTREPRENEURIAL PARTNERS AG, 2677
FUSION FUND, 802
HIGHLAND WEST CAPITAL, 2139
InstarAGF, 2158
JETBLUE TECHNOLOGY VENTURES, 1039
NOVACAP, 2198
PFM CAPITAL, 2213
RETHINK COMMUNITY, 1553
SONY INNOVATION FUND, 1705
SUPPLY CHAIN VENTURES, 1759
SUSA VENTURES, 1760
THE HIVE, 1812
URBAN US, 1896
VALUEACT CAPITAL, 1905
W CAPITAL PARTNERS, 1949

Industry Applications
COMET LABS, 521

Industry Software
BESSEMER VENTURE PARTNERS, 263

Info Technology
GREEN TOWER CAPITAL, 866

Information
HUNTSMAN GAY GLOBAL CAPITAL, 962

Information Services
.406 VENTURES, 1
ABRY PARTNERS, 20
BIA DIGITAL PARTNERS LP, 266
BLUESTEM CAPITAL COMPANY, 300
BULLNET, 2539
CAVA CAPITAL, 433
CHARLES RIVER VENTURES, 457
CITY LIGHT CAPITAL, 490
EMERGENCE CAPITAL PARTNERS, 666
FRONTIER VENTURE CAPITAL, 794
IDG TECHNOLOGY VENTURE INVESTMENT, 2839
LEEDS EQUITY PARTNERS, 1109
NORTH ATLANTIC CAPITAL CORPORATION, 1334
POMONA CAPITAL, 1466
PROVIDENCE EQUITY PARTNERS, 1498
QUADRANGLE GROUP, 1508
SALEM INVESTMENT PARTNERS, 1609
SEAPORT CAPITAL, 1641
SILICON ALLEY VENTURE PARTNERS, 1682
SPIRE CAPITAL PARTNERS, 1727
SUMMIT PARTNERS, 1754
TELEGRAPH HILL PARTNERS, 1794
THOMAS H LEE PARTNERS, 1818
TRIDENT CAPITAL, 1852
VOLITION CAPITAL, 1944
WESTLAKE SECURITIES, 1977

Information Technology
360 CAPITAL PARTNERS 360 Capital Management SA, 2288
3I ASIA PACIFIC 3i Group, 2289
3I DEUTSCHLAND GESELLSCHAFT FUR 3i Group, 2291
3I GERMANY GmbH 3i Group, 2293
3I TEUPSCHLAND GmbH 3i Group, 2297
3T CAPITAL, 2300
3TS CAPITAL PARTNERS 3i Group plc, 2301
3W VENTURES Latour & Zuberbuhler GmbH, 2302
AAVIN PRIVATE EQUITY, 16
ABS CAPITAL PARTNERS, 21
ABS VENTURES, 22
ACCEL-KKR LLC, 28
ACCUITIVE MEDICAL VENTURES LLC, 39
ACE VENTURE CAPITAL LIMITED, 2322
ACERO CAPITAL, 40
ACTIS, 2329
ACTIVA CAPITAL, 2330
ADAMS CAPITAL MANAGEMENT, 55
ADASTRA, 2335
ADVANCED TECHNOLOGY VENTURES, 58

Industry Preference Index / Information Technology

ADVANTAGE CAPITAL PARTNERS, 60
AEP CAPITAL LLC, 64
AFTERDOX, 2344
AIP PRIVATE CAPITAL, 2027
AJU CAPITAL COMPANY, 2350
ALEUTIAN CAPITAL PARTNERS, 81
ALICE VENTURES SRL, 2356
ALIGNED PARTNERS, 83
ALLIANCE OF ANGELS, 85
ALLIANCE VENTURE, 2361
ALLOY VENTURES, 87
ALPHA CAPITAL PARTNERS, 90
ALPHA VENTURE PARTNERS, 91
ALSOP LOUIE PARTNERS, 93
ALTA PARTNERS, 94
ALTIRA GROUP LLC, 98
ALVEN CAPITAL, 2377
AMICUS CAPITAL, 115
AMIDZAD PARTNERS, 116
AMITI VENTURES, 117
AMPERSAND CAPITAL PARTNERS, 119
ANDREESSEN HOROWITZ, 125
ANTHEM VENTURE PARTNERS, 133
APAX GLOBIS PARTNERS & COMPANY Globis Capital Partners/Apax, 2406
APEX VENTURE PARTNERS, 138
APJOHN GROUP LLC, 140
ARBORETUM VENTURES, 150
ARC ANGEL FUND, 151
ARCAPITA INC, 153
ARLINGTON CAPITAL PARTNERS, 167
ARTHUR VENTURES, 175
ASAHI BANK INVESTMENT COMPANY LIMITED, 2421
ASCENSION HEALTH VENTURES LLC, 178
ASCENT VENTURE PARTNERS, 180
ASIAVEST PARTNERS, 2427
ASSET MANAGEMENT VENTURES, 183
ATA VENTURES, 185
ATHENIAN VENTURE PARTNERS, 189
ATILA VENTURES, 2433
ATLANTIC BRIDGE, 2434
ATLAS VENTURE, 193
ATRIA CAPITAL PARTENAIRES, 2439
AUGURY CAPITAL PARTNERS, 199
AUGUST CAPITAL, 200
AURELIA PRIVATE EQUITY, 2443
AURIGA PARTNERS, 2444
AUSTRALIAN ETHICAL INVESTMENT LIMITED, 2447
AUTHOSIS VENTURES, 2448
AVALON VENTURES, 209
AXA INVESTMENT MANAGERS PRIVATE EQUITY EUROPE, 2457
AXIOM VENTURE PARTNERS, 215
AZCA, 217
BAF SPECTRUM, 2468
BALTCAP MANAGEMENT LTD, 2471
BANEXI VENTURES PARTNERS, 2472
BARING PRIVATE EQUITY PARTNERS INDIA, 2481
BASIL PARTNERS Kross Border Trust Services Limited, 2484
BAYSHORE CAPITAL, 2046
BCM TECHNOLOGIES, 244
BEIJING HIGH TECHNOLOGY INVESTMENT COMPANY, 2490
BEIJING VENTURE CAPITAL COMPANY LIMITED, 2491
BERINGEA, 254
BI WALDEN MANAGEMENT SDN Walden International, 2499
BIG SUR VENTURES, 2501
BLUE CHIP VENTURE COMPANY, 290
BLUERUN VENTURES, 299
BLUESHIFT INTERNET VENTURES Blueshift, 2516
BLUETREE VENTURE FUND, 301
BLUMBERG CAPITAL, 304
BM-T BETEILIGUNGS MANAGEMENT THURINGEN GmbH, 2518
BOLDSTART VENTURES, 308
BOSTON MILLENNIA PARTNERS, 315
BOSTON UNIVERSITY - TECHNOLOGY DEVELOPMENT, 317
BOULDER VENTURES LTD, 318
BRAINSPARK PLC, 2526
BREAKWATER INVESTMENTS, 333

BRIDGESCALE PARTNERS, 342
BRIGHTSPARK VENTURES, 2060
BROADMARK CAPITAL, 348
BROOK VENTURE FUND, 352
BUTLER CAPITAL PARTNERS FRANCE, 2542
BV INVESTMENT PARTNERS, 364
CALIFORNIA TECHNOLOGY VENTURES, 374
CANADIAN VENTURE CAPITAL ASSOCIATION Canadian Venture Capital & Private Equity Association, 3249
CANDOVER, 2547
CAPITAL MIDWEST FUND, 403
CAPITOL PARTNERS, 409
CAPMAN CAPITAL MANAGEMENT OY, 2553
CASABONA VENTURES, 421
CASE TECHNOLOGY VENTURES Case Western Reserve University, 423
CATALYST FUND LP, 2562
CATALYST INVESTMENT MANAGERS PTY LIMITED PPM Capital, 2564
CATAMOUNT VENTURES LP, 430
CAZENOVE PRIVATE EQUITY Cazenove Capital, 2568
CDH INVESTMENTS, 2570
CEI VENTURES, 440
CELERITY PARTNERS, 441
CELTIC HOUSE VENTURE PARTNERS, 2070
CENTERFIELD CAPITAL PARTNERS, 445
CERES VENTURE FUND, 454
CEYUAN, 2575
CHARLES RIVER VENTURES, 457
CHEVRON TECHNOLOGY VENTURES, 468
CHICAGO VENTURE PARTNERS LP, 472
CHINA ISRAEL VALUE CAPITAL, 2584
CHINA MERCHANTS CHINA DIRECT INVESTMENTS LTD., 2585
CHINA VEST LIMITED, 2587
CHINA WALDEN MANAGEMENT LIMITED Walden Group, 2588
CHINAVEST, 475
CHRYSALIS CAPITAL ChrysCapital, 2590
CHRYSCAPITAL MANAGEMENT COMPANIES ChrysCapital, 2591
CISCO INVESTMENTS, 485
CLAREMONT CREEK VENTURES, 493
CLARITY PARTNERS, 496
CLIFFORD CHANCE PUNDER, 2605
CM CAPITAL, 2609
COACH & CAPITAL, 2610
COATUE MANAGEMENT, 511
COLLER CAPITAL LIMITED, 2612
COLORADO MILE HIGH FUND, 516
COLUMBIA CAPITAL, 518
COMMERCE ASSET VENTURES Sdn Bhd, 2614
COMPAGNIE FINANCIERE E DE ROTHSCHILD BANQUE, 2616
COMPASS TECHNOLOGY PARTNERS LP, 526
COMSPACE, 528
COMVEST PARTNERS, 530
CONCORD VENTURES, 2619
CONNECTICUT INNOVATIONS, 532
CONSTELLATION TECHNOLOGY VENTURES, 534
CONTINENTAL VENTURE CAPITAL LIMITED, 2622
CONTOUR VENTURE PARTNERS, 535
CONVERGE VENTURE PARTNERS, 536
CORAL GROUP, 538
CORDOVA VENTURES, 539
CORE CAPITAL PARTNERS, 540
CORRELATION VENTURES, 545
CORSA VENTURES, 546
COTTONWOOD TECHNOLOGY FUND, 550
COURT SQUARE VENTURES, 552
COVINGTON CAPITAL CORP., 2081
CREATHOR VENTURE, 2629
CRESSEY & COMPANY LP, 559
DAG VENTURES, 582
DAIMLERCHRYSLER VENTURE GmbH DaimlerChrysler AG, 2641
DANEVEST TECH FUND ADVISORS, 584
DARBY OVERSEAS INVESTMENTS LTD, 585
DBL PARTNERS, 596
DEFTA PARTNERS, 603
DELTA VENTURES LIMITED, 2646
DESJARDINS CAPITAL, 2089
DFC LTD, 2652

Industry Preference Index / Information Technology

DFJ GOTHAM VENTURES, 609
DIRECT CAPITAL PRIVATE EQUITY LIMITED, 2655
DISCOVERY CAPITAL, 2091
DOMAIN ASSOCIATES LLC, 622
DR NEUHAUS TECHNO NORD GmbH, 2664
DRAPER RICHARDS KAPLAN FOUNDATION, 628
DUBILIER & COMPANY, 632
DUCHOSSOIS CAPITAL MANAGEMENT, 634
DVC DEUTSCHE VENTURE CAPITAL, 2670
E.VENTURES, 641
EARLY STAGE PARTNERS, 642
EARLYBIRD, 2673
EAST FUND MANAGEMENT GmbH GiroCredit, 2674
EASTVEN VENTURE PARTNERS, 645
EASTWARD CAPITAL PARTNERS, 646
ECAPITAL ENTREPRENEURIAL PARTNERS AG, 2677
ECI VENTURES, 2678
EDBI Pte LTD., 2681
EDF VENTURES, 652
EDGESTONE CAPITAL PARTNERS, 2098
EDGEWATER FUNDS, 654
EDISON PARTNERS, 655
EGL HOLDINGS, 656
ELAIA PARTNERS, 2684
ELEVATE VENTURES, 659
ELGNER GROUP INVESTMENTS, 2099
EM WARBURG, PINCUS & COMPANY INTERNATIONAL, 2688
EM WARBURG, PINCUS & COMPANY JAPAN, 2689
ENTERPRISE EQUITY (NI) LTD, 2695
ENTREPIA VENTURES, 683
EQUINET VENTURE PARTNERS AG, 2704
ESPIRITO SANTO VENTURES, 2708
ESSEX WOODLANDS HEALTH VENTURES LLC, 698
EURAZEO, 2710
EUROFUND LP, 2711
EUROPEAN INVESTMENT FUND, 2715
EUROVENTURES CAPITAL, 2716
EVERGREEN ADVISORS, 702
EXCEL VENTURE MANAGEMENT, 704
EXPERIMENT FUND, 709
EXPORT DEVELOPMENT CANADA, 2106
FCA VENTURE PARTNERS, 718
FERRANTI LIMITED, 2723
FIFTH WALL, 728
FIRST ANALYSIS, 733
FIRST FLIGHT VENTURE CENTER, 738
FIVE ELMS CAPITAL, 746
FLANDERS' FOREIGN INVESTMENT OFFICE, 2737
FLYBRIDGE CAPITAL PARTNERS, 756
FORTÉ VENTURES, 770
FOUNDATION CAPITAL, 773
FOUNDRY GROUP, 779
FULCRUM EQUITY PARTNERS, 797
FUTURE VENTURES, 803
GCI CAPITAL, 2123
GE CAPITAL, 811
GENERAL ATLANTIC PARTNERS, 819, 2762
GENERATION PARTNERS, 822
GEORGIAN PARTNERS, 2126
GIZA VENTURE CAPITAL, 2773
GLENGARY LLC, 835
GLOBAL FINANCE, 2775
GLOBESPAN CAPITAL PARTNERS, 839
GOLDEN GATE CAPITAL, 843
GRAY GHOST VENTURES, 860
GREAT HILL PARTNERS LLC, 862
GREENHILL SAVP, 869
GREENSPRING ASSOCIATES, 872
GROSVENOR FUNDS, 880
GROTECH VENTURES, 881
GTCR, 889
GULFSTAR GROUP, 893
HALIFAX GROUP LLC, 899
HALLIM VENTURE CAPITAL, 2798
HALYARD CAPITAL, 902
HARBERT MANAGEMENT CORPORATION, 907
HASSO PLATTNER VENTURES, 2804

HELLMAN & FRIEDMAN LLC, 927
HELMET CAPITAL FUND MANAGEMENT OY, 2811
HIG CAPITAL, 931
HIGH-TECH GRUENDERFONDS, 2815
HIGHLAND CAPITAL PARTNERS, 938
HIKARI TSUSHIN CAPITAL, 2817
HOPEWELL VENTURES, 947
HORIZON TECHNOLOGY FINANCE, 949
HORIZONTE VENTURE MANAGEMENT GmbH, 2823
HOSEO VENTURE CAPITAL, 2824
HOUSTON ANGEL NETWORK, 953
HOUSTON HEALTH VENTURES, 954
HUDSON VENTURE PARTNERS, 957
HYUNDAI VENTURE INVESTMENT CORPORATION, 2830
IBB BETEILIGUNGSGESELLSCHAFT MBH, 2832
ICF VENTURES PVT LTD, 2837
ID VENTURES AMERICA LLC, 974
IDEA FUND PARTNERS, 975
IDG CAPITAL, 977
IGNITION PARTNERS, 978
ILLINOIS VENTURES, 979
ILLUMINATE VENTURES, 980
IN-Q-TEL, 983
INBC INVESTMENT CORP, 2144
INCWELL VENTURE CAPITAL, 985
INDASIA FUND ADVISORS PVT LTD, 2850
INETWORKS ADVISORS LLC, 991
INFLECTION POINT VENTURES, 993
INFOCOMM INVESTMENTS, 2861
INNOVATION CAPITAL, 2867
INNOVATION CAPITAL LIMITED, 2868
INNOVATION WORKS, 1003
INNOVATIONSKAPITAL, 2869
INNOVENTURES CAPITAL PARTNERS, 1004
INSTITUTIONAL VENTURE PARTNERS, 1006
INTEGRAL CAPITAL PARTNERS, 1008
INTER-ASIA VENTURE MANAGEMENT LIMITED, 2872
INTERMEDIATE CAPITAL GROUP PLC, 2874
INTERNATIONAL FINANCE CORPORATION (IFC), 1012
INTERSOUTH PARTNERS, 1013
INTERWEST PARTNERS, 1014
INVESCO PRIVATE CAPITAL, 1019
INVESTOR AB, 2881
INVEXCEL PATRIMONIO, 2882
IP GROUP, 2883
IPG GROUP, 2885
IPOSCOPE NV/SA, 2886
IRIS CAPITAL, 2888
ISOURCE GESTION, 2890
IT VENTURES LIMITED Digital Heritage Publishing Ltd., 2892
IT-PARTNERS NV, 2893
JAFCO COMPANY LIMITED JAPAN, 2897
JAPAN ASIA INVESTMENT COMPANY LIMITED, 2898
JAVELIN INVESTMENTS, 2899
JEGI CAPITAL The Jordan Edminston Group, Inc., 1037
JK&B CAPITAL, 1042
KAISER PERMANENTE VENTURES, 1056
KALORI GROUP INVESTMENTS, 2906
KAPOR CAPITAL, 1058
KB PARTNERS LLC, 1061
KBL HEALTHCARE VENTURES, 1062
KENSINGTON CAPITAL PARTNERS, 2160
KINETIC VENTURES, 1076
KLEINER PERKINS, 1079
KODIAK VENTURE PARTNERS, 1084
KOREA FIRST VENTURE CAPITAL CORPORATION, 2915
KTB VENTURES, 1091
LABRADOR VENTURES, 1093
LAUDER PARTNERS LLC, 1099
LAUNCHPAD VENTURE GROUP, 1104
LBBW VENTURE CAPITAL, 2923
LEAPFROG VENTURES, 1106
LETA CAPITAL, 2929
LIQUID CAPITAL GROUP, 1137
LIZADA CAPITAL LLC, 1139
LLR PARTNERS INC, 1140
LOCUS VENTURES, 1142

Industry Preference Index / Information Technology

LONG RIVER VENTURES, 1146
LOVETT MILLER & COMPANY, 1152
MANTELLA VENTURE PARTNERS, 2176
MARCEAU INVESTISSEMENTS, 2946
MARS INVESTMENT ACCELERATOR FUND, 2181
MASON WELLS, 1174
MBF CAPITAL CORPORATION, 1191
MCG CAPITAL CORPORATION, 1192
MEAKEM/BECKER VENTURE CAPITAL, 1196
MENLO VENTURES, 1203
MENTOR CAPITAL PARTNERS LTD, 1204
MERITECH CAPITAL PARTNERS, 1213
MERRILL LYNCH (ASIA PACIFIC) LIMITED Merrill Lynch Group, 2955
MIDDLEBURG CAPITAL DEVELOPMENT, 1229
MIRAE ASSET VENTURE ACCELERATOR Mirae Asset Group, 2960
MIRAMAR VENTURE PARTNERS, 1237
MITSUBISHI UFJ CAPITAL, 2961
MOHR-DAVIDOW VENTURES, 1247
MORGAN STANLEY EXPANSION CAPITAL, 1255
MORGENTHALER VENTURES, 1257
MOSAIC CAPITAL PARTNERS, 2190
MOTLEY FOOL VENTURES, 1259
MOTOROLA SOLUTIONS VENTURE CAPITAL, 1260
MOUNTAIN PARTNERS, 2970
MOUNTAINEER CAPITAL, 1262
MPG EQUITY PARTNERS, 1267
MVC CORPORATION, 2971
McLEAN WATSON CAPITAL, 2191
NAUSICAA VENTURES, 2977
NEEDHAM CAPITAL PARTNERS, 1287
NEUHAUS PARTNERS, 2985
NEW BRUNSWICK INNOVATION FOUNDATION, 2192
NEW CAPITAL FUND, 1291
NEW MARKETS VENTURE PARTNERS, 1298
NEW SCIENCE VENTURES, 1302
NEWBURY VENTURES, 1310
NEWMARGIN VENTURE CAPITAL, 2989
NEWSPRING CAPITAL, 1316
NEXTEC DEVELOPMENT CAPITAL LIMITED, 2991
NHN INVESTMENT, 2993
NIPPON TECHNOLOGY VENTURE PARTNERS LIMITED, 2996
NORO-MOSELEY PARTNERS, 1332
NORTH DAKOTA DEVELOPMENT FUND, 1338
NORWEST VENTURE PARTNERS, 1346
NOVAK BIDDLE VENTURE PARTNERS, 1348
NOVELTEK CAPITAL CORPORATION, 1351
NOVUS VENTURES LP, 1354
NTH POWER TECHNOLOGIES, 1355
OAK INVESTMENT PARTNERS, 1361
OEM CAPITAL, 1369
OKAPI VENTURE CAPITAL, 1371
ONSET VENTURES, 1379
ONTARIO CAPITAL GROWTH CORPORATION, 2203
ORIGINATE VENTURES, 1386
OSAGE PARTNERS, 1388
OUTLOOK VENTURES, 1390
OXANTIUM VENTURES, 1394
OneVentures, 3014
PAC-LINK MANAGEMENT CORP., 3015
PAI MANAGEMENT, 3017
PALISADES VENTURES, 1403
PALO ALTO VENTURE PARTNERS, 1406
PAMLICO CAPITAL, 1410
PANTHEON VENTURES (US) LP, 1413
PARKWALK ADVISORS, 3019
PARTECH INTERNATIONAL, 1418
PARTNERSHIP FUND FOR NEW YORK CITY, 1422
PATHENA, 3022
PELION VENTURE PARTNERS, 1428
PENNELL VENTURE PARTNERS LLC, 1432
PI CAPITAL GROUP LLC, 1444
PINNACLE MERCHANT CAPITAL, 2214
PINNACLE VENTURES, 1449
PITTSBURGH EQUITY PARTNERS, 1451
PMV, 3033
POLARIS VENTURE PARTNERS, 1464
POLESTAR CAPITAL, 1465
POLYTECH VENTURES, 3036
POLYTECHNOS VENTURE PARTNERS GmbH, 3037
PREVIZ VENTURES, 3041
PRIMARY VENTURE PARTNERS, 1479
PRISM CAPITAL, 1481
PROSPECT PARTNERS LLC, 1494
QBIC FUND, 3056
QED INVESTORS, 1504
QIMING VENTURE PARTNERS, 3057
QUANTUM VALLEY INVESTMENTS, 2220
QUEST FOR GROWTH, 3060
RAFAEL DEVELOPMENT CORPORATION (RDC) LIMITED, 3063
RBC CAPITAL MARKETS, 2223
REDMONT VENTURE PARTNERS, 1536
RENEWABLETECH VENTURES, 1545
RESERVOIR VENTURE PARTNERS, 1547
RESONANT VENTURE PARTNERS, 1550
REV1 VENTURES, 1556
RHO VENTURES, 1561
ROADMAP CAPITAL INC., 2234
ROBIN HOOD VENTURES, 1581
ROSER VENTURES LLC, 1590
RRE VENTURES, 1597
SAIF PARTNERS, 3084
SALMON RIVER CAPITAL, 1611
SAMSUNG VENTURE INVESTMENT CORPORATION Samsung Electronics, 3089
SAND HILL ANGELS, 1616
SAPPHIRE VENTURES, 1623
SATORI CAPITAL, 1625
SATURN PARTNERS, 1626
SCOTTISH EQUITY PARTNERS, 3095
SCP PARTNERS, 1636
SELBY VENTURE PARTNERS, 1649
SELWAY CAPITAL, 1650
SEQUEL VENTURE PARTNERS, 1656
SERAPH GROUP, 1658
SEVENTURE PARTNERS, 3104
SHEPHERD VENTURES, 1667
SIEMENS VENTURE CAPITAL, 3109
SIERRA VENTURES, 1672
SIGNAL PEAK VENTURES, 1679
SIGNATURE CAPITAL LLC, 3111
SILVER CREEK VENTURES, 1684
SLATER TECHNOLOGY FUND, 1695
SOFINNOVA VENTURES, 1700
SOLSTICE CAPITAL LP, 1704
SOUTHEAST INTERACTIVE TECHNOLOGY FUNDS, 1711
SPECTRUM EQUITY INVESTORS LP, 1720
SPENCER TRASK VENTURES, 1723
SPLIT ROCK PARTNERS, 1728
STAR VENTURES, 3128
STARFISH VENTURES, 3129
STATELINE ANGELS, 1743
STIC VENTURES CORPORATION LIMITED, 3136
STORM VENTURES, 1750
SUNBRIDGE PARTNERS, 1757
SV ANGEL, 1763
SVB CAPITAL, 1766
T-VENTURE HOLDINGS GmbH Deutsche Telecom, 3146
TANDEM EXPANSION FUND, 2252
TAO VENTURE CAPITAL PARTNERS, 1782
TECH CAPITAL PARTNERS, 2253
TECH COAST ANGELS, 1786
TECHNOLOGY CROSSOVER VENTURES, 1787
TECHNOLOGY PARK MALAYSIA CORPORATION SDN BHD, 3155
TEKINVEST KK, 3157
TEKNOINVEST MANAGEMENT, 3158
TELESOFT PARTNERS, 1795
TENAYA CAPITAL, 1798
TERALYS CAPITAL, 2259
THOMAS WEISEL VENTURE PARTNERS, 1819
THOMPROPERTIES OY, 3166
THROUNARFELAG ISLANDS PLC, 3168
TL VENTURES, 1830
TMG CAPITAL PARTNERS, 3171
TOBA CAPITAL, 1831

Industry Preference Index / Information Technology & Media

TOKIO MARINE CAPITAL COMPANY LIMITED, 3173
TONG YANG VENTURE CAPITAL CORPORATION Tong Yang Cement Corporation, 3174
TRANS COSMOS INCORPORATED, 3176
TRELYS FUNDS, 1844
TRIANGLE VENTURE CAPITAL GROUP, 3179
TRIDENT CAPITAL, 1852
TRIGINITA CAPITAL, 3181
TRITON VENTURES, 1857
TROIKA CAPITAL PARTNERS, 3184
TRU MANAGEMENT, 1860
TSG EQUITY PARTNERS, 1864
TTV CAPITAL, 1865
TULLIS HEALTH INVESTORS, 1868
TVM CAPITAL, 3187
TWIN CITIES ANGELS, 1874
UNCORK CAPITAL, 1881
UPDATA VENTURE PARTNERS, 1888
USHA MARTIN VENTURES LIMITED, 3193
VALHALLA PARTNERS, 1901
VALLEY VENTURES LP, 1903
VALUEACT CAPITAL, 1905
VANTAGEPOINT CAPITAL PARTNERS, 1908
VEDANTA CAPITAL LP, 1913
VELOCITY EQUITY PARTNERS LLC, 1915
VENTECH, 3199
VENTURE CAPITAL FUND OF NEW ENGLAND, 1922
VENTUREAST, 3202
VERDEXUS, 2271
VERIZON VENTURES, 1928
VRG CAPITAL, 2274
VTB CAPITAL, 3220
WARBURG PINCUS LLC, 1957
WAVEPOINT VENTURES, 1967
WEBB INVESTMENT NETWORK, 1969
WELSH, CARSON, ANDERSON & STOWE, 1973
WESLEY CLOVER, 2276
WESTVIEW CAPITAL PARTNERS, 1979
WHEATLEY PARTNERS, 1981
WHITECAP VENTURE PARTNERS, 2280
WICKS GROUP OF COMPANIES, LLC, 1984
WING VENTURE PARTNERS, 1996
WRF CAPITAL, 2007
XENIA VENTURE CAPITAL, 3230
XSEED CAPITAL MANAGEMENT, 2010
XT INVESTMENTS, 3231
YALETOWN VENTURE PARTNERS, 2283
YASUDA ENTERPRISE DEVELOPMENT COMPANY, 3233
YVC - YOZMA MANAGEMENT & INVESTMENTS LIMITED, 3239
ZONE VENTURES, 2020

Information Technology & Media
TPA CORPORATE FINANCE CONSULTING GMBH Horwarth International, 3175

Information and Technology
FLYING FISH, 757

Infrastructure
3I AUSTRIA BETEILGUNG GmbH 3i Group, 2290
3i GROUP PLC, 2303
645 VENTURES, 12
ACCEL, 27
ACCEL-KKR LLC, 28
ACCENTURE TECHNOLOGY VENTURES, 2318
ACCESS VENTURE PARTNERS LLC, 35
ACI CAPITAL, 41
ACME CAPITAL, 44
ACUMEN VENTURES, 2333
ADLEVO CAPITAL CIM Fund Services, 2337
ADOBE VENTURES LP, 57
AEM CAPITAL, 2341
AGF PRIVATE EQUITY Allianz Group, 2346
ALBERTA INVESTMENT MANAGEMENT CORP., 2029
ALLEGIS CYBER CAPITAL, 84
ALTAIR VENTURES, 95
ALTUS CAPITAL PARTNERS, 104

AMBERJACK CAPITAL PARTNERS, 106
AMWIN MANAGEMENT PTY LIMITED, 2390
APEX VENTURE PARTNERS, 138
ARC FINANCIAL, 2036
ATLANTIC BRIDGE, 2434
AXIOM VENTURE PARTNERS, 215
AZIMUTH CAPITAL MANAGEMENT, 2044
BARING PRIVATE EQUITY PARTNERS INDIA, 2481
BATTERY VENTURES, 238
BENAROYA COMPANIES, 250
BESSEMER VENTURE PARTNERS, 263
BLUMBERG CAPITAL, 304
BOCI DIRECT INVESTMENT MANAGEMENT LIMITED Bank of China, 2520
BOSTON CAPITAL VENTURES, 313
BRIDGESCALE PARTNERS, 342
BROOKFIELD ASSET MANAGEMENT, 2062
CAI CAPITAL PARTNERS, 368
CANADIAN VENTURE CAPITAL ASSOCIATION Canadian Venture Capital & Private Equity Association, 3249
CAPITOL PARTNERS, 409
CARLYLE GROUP, 416
CEDAR (ISRAEL) FINANCIAL ADVISORS LIMITED Cedar Fund, 2571
CEDAR FUND, 438
CELTIC HOUSE VENTURE PARTNERS, 2070
CENTENNIAL VENTURES, 443
CENTERPOINT VENTURE PARTNERS, 446
CHARLES RIVER VENTURES, 457
CHEUNG KONG INFRASTRUCTURE HOLDINGS LIMITED, 2582
CHINA MERCHANTS CHINA INVESTMENT MANAGEMENT, 2586
CHRYSALIS CAPITAL ChrysCapital, 2590
CISCO INVESTMENTS, 485
CLEARSTONE VENTURE PARTNERS, 504
COLORADO MILE HIGH FUND, 516
COLT VENTURES, 517
COMCAST VENTURES, 520
COMPAGNIE FINANCIERE E DE ROTHSCHILD BANQUE, 2616
CONCORD VENTURES, 2619
CORE CAPITAL PARTNERS, 540
CRESCENDO VENTURES, 556
DAVENPORT RESOURCES LLC, 589
DAWNTREADER VENTURES, 593
DFJ GOTHAM VENTURES, 609
DUBIN CLARK & COMPANY, 633
DUNRATH CAPITAL, 636
EASTVEN VENTURE PARTNERS, 645
EDBI Pte LTD., 2681
EDGESTONE CAPITAL PARTNERS, 2098
EMP GLOBAL, 671
FIELDSTONE PRIVATE CAPITAL GROUP, 726
FIRST ANALYSIS, 733
FIRSTMARK CAPITAL, 744
FORMATIVE VENTURES, 766
FORMULA VENTURES LIMITED Formula Group, 2741
FORTRESS INVESTMENT GROUP LLC, 769
GABRIEL VENTURE PARTNERS, 808
GE ASIA PACIFIC CAPITAL TECHNOLOGY FUND, 2758
GEMINI ISRAEL VENTURE FUNDS LIMITED, 2761
GENERAL CATALYST PARTNERS, 820
GILBERT GLOBAL EQUITY PARTNERS, 831
GOLDEN OPPORTUNITIES FUND, 2129
GOOD NEWS VENTURES, 2132
GRANDBANKS CAPITAL, 853
GRANTHAM CAPITAL, 858
GREYCROFT PARTNERS, 876
GROTECH VENTURES, 881
GUIDE VENTURES, 892
GULFSTAR GROUP, 893
HAMMOND, KENNEDY, WHITNEY & COMPANY, 904
HARBINGER VENTURE MANAGEMENT, 908
HIG CAPITAL, 931
HRL MORRISON & COMPANY LIMITED, 2826
HUDSON VENTURE PARTNERS, 957
HUMMER WINBLAD VENTURE PARTNERS, 959
IDG CAPITAL, 977
IGNITION PARTNERS, 978
IN-Q-TEL, 983

Industry Preference Index / Insurance

INDEX VENTURES, 2851
INNOVATION PLATFORM CAPITAL, 1002
INSIGHT VENTURE PARTNERS, 1005
INTERNATIONAL FINANCE CORPORATION (IFC), 1012
INVESCO PRIVATE CAPITAL, 1019
JEGI CAPITAL The Jordan Edminston Group, Inc., 1037
JK&B CAPITAL, 1042
KALORI GROUP INVESTMENTS, 2906
KB PARTNERS LLC, 1061
KOHLBERG KRAVIS ROBERTS & COMPANY, 1086
KRG CAPITAL PARTNERS, 1090
LIGHTSPEED VENTURE PARTNERS, 1125
LONGBOW CAPITAL, 2171
LONGWORTH VENTURE PARTNERS, 1150
M/C PARTNERS, 1157
MADRONA VENTURE GROUP, 1162
MARWIT CAPITAL LLC, 1171
MEDIA VENTURE PARTNERS, 1197
MENLO VENTURES, 1203
MERITECH CAPITAL PARTNERS, 1213
METROPOLITAN PARTNERS GROUP, 1226
MILLENIUM TECHNOLOGY VALUE PARTNERS, 1235
MISSION VENTURES, 1239
MOBIUS VENTURE CAPITAL, 1245
MOHR-DAVIDOW VENTURES, 1247
MORGAN STANLEY EXPANSION CAPITAL, 1255
MVP CAPITAL PARTNERS, 1275
NAVIGATION CAPITAL PARTNERS, 1279
NEEDHAM CAPITAL PARTNERS, 1287
NEUHAUS PARTNERS, 2985
NEW MOUNTAIN CAPITAL, 1300
NEW WORLD INFRASTRUCTURE LIMITED, 2987
NEWLIGHT MANAGEMENT, 1313
NORTH BRIDGE VENTURE PARTNERS, 1335
NOVUS VENTURES LP, 1354
OAK INVESTMENT PARTNERS, 1361
OMERS PRIVATE EQUITY, 2199
OPUS CAPITAL, 1382
OUTLOOK VENTURES, 1390
PALOMAR VENTURES, 1408
PELION VENTURE PARTNERS, 1428
PENINSULA VENTURES, 1430
PHYTO PARTNERS, 1443
PITANGO VENTURE CAPITAL, 3030
PMV, 3033
QUAKE CAPITAL PARTNERS, 1509
RECIPROCAL VENTURES, 1531
RED CLAY CAPITAL HOLDINGS, 1532
REDPOINT VENTURES, 1537
REMBRANDT VENTURE PARTNERS, 1543
RPM VENTURES, 1596
S3 VENTURES, 1601
SEAFORT CAPITAL, 2242
SEVIN ROSEN FUNDS, 1661
SHANGHAI INFORMATION INVESTMENT INCORPORATED, 3105
SHASTA VENTURES, 1666
SHEPHERD VENTURES, 1667
SIGNAL LAKE, 1678
SINEWAVE VENTURES, 1689
SMART BUSINESS CONSULTING, 3115
SOFTTECH VC, 1702
SONY STRATEGIC TECHNOLOGY PARTNERSHIPS, 1706
SOUTHEAST INTERACTIVE TECHNOLOGY FUNDS, 1711
SPARK CAPITAL, 1718
STONEBRIDGE PARTNERS, 1747
TECH CAPITAL PARTNERS, 2253
TECHNOLOGY CROSSOVER VENTURES, 1787
TIE ANGELS GROUP SEATTLE, 1827
TOBA CAPITAL, 1831
TRELLIS CAPITAL CORPORATION, 2265
TRUE VENTURES, 1862
UPHEAVAL INVESTMENTS, 1892
URBAN US, 1896
VALHALLA PARTNERS, 1901
VALOR EQUITY PARTNERS, 1904
VARDE PARTNERS, 1909
VELOCITY EQUITY PARTNERS LLC, 1915
VENTECH, 3199
VERIZON VENTURES, 1928
VINACAPITAL GROUP, 3208
VOLITION CAPITAL, 1944
VOYAGER CAPITAL, 1947
WALDEN ISRAEL VENTURE CAPITAL, 3221
WALDEN VENTURE CAPITAL, 1953
WESTCAP, 2277
WINDWARD VENTURES, 1995
WRF CAPITAL, 2007
YES VC, 2013
YL VENTURES, 3236

Infrastructure Services
HAWTHORN EQUITY PARTNERS, 919
MARKET SQUARE EQUITY PARTNERS, 2180

Infrastructure Software
BAIN CAPITAL VENTURES, 224
BRM SEED, 2532
FLYWHEEL VENTURES, 758
GENESIS PARTNERS, 2766
MOBIUS VENTURE CAPITAL, 1245
ONSET VENTURES, 1379

Infrastructure Technology
CORIOLIS VENTURES, 541

Innovation
CIBC INNOVATION BANKING, 2074
GOLDEN OPPORTUNITIES FUND, 2129
VANCITY CAPITAL, 2269
WESTCAP, 2277

Innovative Products & Services
JERUSALEM VENTURE PARTNERS, 2901
LBBW VENTURE CAPITAL, 2923

Innovative Technology
CELADON CAPITAL GROUP, 2573

Institutional Asset Management
ROTHSCHILD AUSTRALIA - ARROW PRIVATE EQUITY Rothschild Group, 3077

Instrumentation
AXIA CAPITAL, 214
CHL MEDICAL PARTNERS, 476
COMMONWEALTH CAPITAL VENTURES LP, 523
DOMAIN ASSOCIATES LLC, 622
JC TECHNOLOGIES LTD, 2900
LATTERELL VENTURE PARTNERS, 1098
MASSACHUSETTS CAPITAL RESOURCE COMPANY, 1176
MASSACHUSETTS GROWTH CAPITAL CORPORATION, 1177
NOVAK BIDDLE VENTURE PARTNERS, 1348
POLESTAR CAPITAL, 1465
PROVCO GROUP, 1496
RAF INDUSTRIES, 1524
SEED CAPITAL LIMITED, 3098
SILVER CREEK VENTURES, 1684
SOUTHPORT PARTNERS, 1714
TECHNOCAP, 2254
VISION CAPITAL, 1939
WESTERN TECHNOLOGY INVESTMENT, 1976
ZS FUND LP, 2021

Insurance
ABSTRACT VENTURES, 23
AIG INVESTMENT CORPORATION (ASIA) LIMITED, 2348
AMANET TECHNOLOGIES LIMITED, 2381
ARGOS SODITIC SA, 2414
ATRIA CAPITAL PARTENAIRES, 2439
CCP EQUITY PARTNERS, 436
CHINA MERCHANTS CHINA DIRECT INVESTMENTS LTD., 2585
CIVC PARTNERS, 491
CLIFFORD CHANCE PUNDER, 2605
DFC LTD, 2652
DIAGRAM VENTURES, 2090

Industry Preference Index / Insurance Brokerage

FOX PAINE & COMPANY LLC, 781
GE CAPITAL, 811
HARDY CAPITAL PARTNERS, 2137
HELLMAN & FRIEDMAN LLC, 927
IBM VENTURE CAPITAL GROUP, 971
INTERMEDIATE CAPITAL GROUP PLC, 2874
JORDAN COMPANY, 1049
LUGE CAPITAL, 2172
MS&AD VENTURES, 1269
MUNICH REINSURANCE AMERICA, INC, 1272
NEW CAPITAL PARTNERS, 1292
NEWLIGHT PARTNERS, 1314
ODYSSEY INVESTMENT PARTNERS, 1368
PORTAG3 VENTURES, 2217
REITEN & CO STRATEGIC INVESTMENTS AS Reiten & Company, 3067
ROBIN HOOD VENTURES, 1581
SONY EUROPE, 3120
SOUTHPORT PARTNERS, 1714
STONE POINT CAPITAL LLC, 1746
THAYER STREET PARTNERS, 1807
THE HIVE, 1812
TPA CORPORATE FINANCE CONSULTING GMBH Horwarth International, 3175
UNISON CAPITAL PARTNERS LP, 3192
VENTURE INVESTORS, 3201
VINACAPITAL GROUP, 3208
VIOLA FINTECH, 3211
VISION CAPITAL, 1939
VRG CAPITAL, 2274
WAND PARTNERS, 1956
WELLSPRING CAPITAL MANAGEMENT LLC, 1972
WESTLAKE SECURITIES, 1977
ZS FUND LP, 2021

Insurance Brokerage
AON RISK SOLUTIONS Aon Corporation, 2405

Integrated Health Solutions
SANOFI-GENZYME BIOVENTURES, 1621

Interactive Media
SPARK CAPITAL, 1718

International/Emerging Markets
500 STARTUPS, 10

Internet
.406 VENTURES, 1
10X VENTURE PARTNERS, 2
212 CAPITAL PARTNERS, 2286
360 CAPITAL PARTNERS 360 Capital Management SA, 2288
ABRT VENTURE FUND, 2312
ACCEL-KKR LLC, 28
ACONCAGUA VENTURES, 2326
ACORN CAMPUS VENTURES, 46
ACTUA, 52
ACUITY VENTURES LLC, 53
ACUMEN VENTURES, 2333
ADASTRA, 2335
ADD VENTURE, 2336
AFTERDOX, 2344
ALACRITY VENTURES, 76
ALBERTA ENTERPRISE, 2028
ALMAZ CAPITAL, 89
ALTA VENTURES MEXICO, 2374
ALTOS VENTURES, 100
ALVEN CAPITAL, 2377
AMBIENT SOUND INVESTMENTS, 2382
AMPEZZO PARTNERS, 2388
ANTHEM VENTURE PARTNERS, 133
ANTRAK CAPITAL, 2399
ARC ANGEL FUND, 151
ARGONAUT VENTURES, 164
ARKAFUND MEDIA & ICT, 2417
ARTIS VENTURES, 177
ASTUTIA VENTURES, 2432

AUSTIN VENTURES, 205
AUTHOSIS VENTURES, 2448
B-TO-V PARTNERS, 2466
BAF SPECTRUM, 2468
BAND OF ANGELS LLC, 229
BANNEKER PARTNERS, 230
BERKELEY VENTURES, 256
BIG SUR VENTURES, 2501
BILTMORE VENTURES, 267
BLACKBIRD VENTURES, 2511
BLUE CHIP VENTURE COMPANY, 290
BLUE COVE VENTURES, 2514
BLUEFISH VENTURES, 297
BLUERUN VENTURES, 299
BOREALIS VENTURES, 311
BOSTON SEED CAPITAL, 316
BREGAL SAGEMOUNT, 336
CALIFORNIA TECHNOLOGY VENTURES, 374
CAPITAL TODAY, 2551
CARMEL VENTURES, 2557
CATAGONIA CAPITAL, 2560
CATALYST INVESTORS, 429
CENTRAL TEXAS ANGEL NETWORK, 447
CENTRALWAY, 2574
CEYUAN, 2575
CLEARSTONE VENTURE PARTNERS, 504
COACH & CAPITAL, 2610
COLOMA VENTURES, 515
COMMONWEALTH CAPITAL VENTURES LP, 523
CONNECT VENTURES, 2620
CONTOUR VENTURE PARTNERS, 535
CONVERGE VENTURE PARTNERS, 536
CREATHOR VENTURE, 2629
CROSS CREEK ADVISORS, 561
CXO FUND, 575
CYBERAGENT VENTURES, 2637
DATA COLLECTIVE, 586
DATA POINT CAPITAL, 587
DAVID SHEN VENTURES, 591
DAWNTREADER VENTURES, 593
DETROIT VENTURE PARTNERS, 608
DFJ ESPRIT, 2653
DOUBLE M PARTNERS, 625
DPIXEL, 2663
EARLYBIRD, 2673
EASTLABS, 2675
EDELSON TECHNOLOGY PARTNERS, 651
EDEN VENTURES, 2682
ENSPIRE CAPITAL PTE LTD, 2694
EPLANET CAPITAL, 691
EUROPEAN FOUNDERS FUND, 2714
EVERGREEN ADVISORS, 702
EVERGREEN VENTURE PARTNERS, 2717
EXPANSION VENTURE CAPITAL, 708
FF VENTURE CAPITAL, 724
FIVE ELMS CAPITAL, 746
FOCUS VENTURES, 759
FORMATIVE VENTURES, 766
FORTÉ VENTURES, 770
FOUNDER PARTNERS, 775
FOUNDER'S CO-OP, 776
FOUNDERS FUND, 778
FOUNDRY GROUP, 779
FRANCISCO PARTNERS, 782
FUNG CAPITAL USA, 799
GENERAL CATALYST PARTNERS, 820
GEORGIAN PARTNERS, 2126
GGV CAPITAL, 827
GLOBESPAN CAPITAL PARTNERS, 839
GLYNN CAPITAL MANAGEMENT, 840
GREE VENTURES, 2789
GROTECH VENTURES, 881
GSR VENTURES, 2792
HARBINGER VENTURE MANAGEMENT, 908
HELION VENTURE PARTNERS, LLC International Management (Mauritius) Ltd, 2809
HELLMAN & FRIEDMAN LLC, 927

Industry Preference Index / Internet Applications and Services

HIGH COUNTRY VENTURE, 933
HIGHLAND CAPITAL PARTNERS, 938
HOLTZBRINCK VENTURES, 2820
HOXTON VENTURES, 2825
HUDSON VENTURE PARTNERS, 957
HUMMER WINBLAD VENTURE PARTNERS, 959
HV HOLTZBRINCK VENTURES, 2829
IDEALAB, 976
IDG CAPITAL PARTNERS, 2838
IDG VENTURES INDIA International Financial Services Limited, 2840
IGAN PARTNERS, 2141
ILLUMINATE VENTURES, 980
IMI.VC, 2847
INFINITY VENTURE PARTNERS, 2860
INITIAL CAPITAL, 2863
INLAND TECHSTART FUND, 997
INSTITUTIONAL VENTURE PARTNERS, 1006
INTERSOUTH PARTNERS, 1013
INVENTURE PARTNERS, 2877
IRISH ANGELS, 1023
ISOURCE GESTION, 2890
JAVELIN VENTURE PARTNERS, 1032
JC2 VENTURES, 1035
JMI EQUITY FUND LP, 1045
JUMPSEED VENTURES, 2903
KAEDAN INVESTMENTS, 2905
KEGONSA CAPITAL PARTNERS, 1064
KIBO VENTURES, 2911
KIZOO TECHNOLOGY CAPITAL, 2912
KNIGHT'S BRIDGE CAPITAL PARTNERS, 2164
KODIAK VENTURE PARTNERS, 1084
LANTA DIGITAL VENTURES, 2921
LAUDER PARTNERS LLC, 1099
LAUNCHCAPITAL, 1101
LAUNCHPAD VENTURE GROUP, 1104
LEO CAPITAL HOLDINGS, LLC, 1112
LIONBIRD, 2934
LONG RIVER VENTURES, 1146
LONGWORTH VENTURE PARTNERS, 1150
LOOL VENTURES, 2938
MAGMA VENTURE PARTNERS, 2943
MAINE ANGELS, 1164
MASS VENTURES, 1175
MERCURY FUND, 1207
MILLENIUM TECHNOLOGY VALUE PARTNERS, 1235
MIRAMAR VENTURE PARTNERS, 1237
MOBILITY VENTURES, 1244
MORADO VENTURE PARTNERS, 1254
MORGENTHALER VENTURES, 1257
NAUTA CAPITAL, 2978
NEO TECHNOLOGY VENTURES, 2980
NEXT WORLD CAPITAL, 1319
NEXTVIEW VENTURES, 1322
NEXUS VENTURE PARTNERS Nexus India Capital Advisors Pvt Ltd, 2992
NHN INVESTMENT, 2993
NORWEST VENTURE PARTNERS, 1346
O'REILLY ALPHATECH VENTURES, 1359
OAK INVESTMENT PARTNERS, 1361
OKAPI VENTURE CAPITAL, 1371
OPENVIEW VENTURE PARTNERS, 1381
OPUS CAPITAL, 1382
ORIGINATE VENTURES, 1386
OSAGE PARTNERS, 1388
OUTCOME CAPITAL, 1389
OUTLOOK VENTURES, 1390
PARKWALK ADVISORS, 3019
PARTECH INTERNATIONAL, 1418
PELION VENTURE PARTNERS, 1428
PENTECH VENTURES, 3023
PHENOMEN VENTURES, 3025
PI CAPITAL GROUP LLC, 1444
PINEHURST ADVISORS, 3029
PINNACLE MERCHANT CAPITAL, 2214
PITON CAPITAL, 3031
PLUS VENTURES, 3032
POINT JUDITH CAPITAL, 1463

POINT NINE CAPITAL, 3035
PRINCIPIA SGR, 3043
PROJECT A VENTURE GmBH & CO. KG, 3047
REAL VENTURES, 2224
REED ELSEVIER VENTURES, 3065
REMBRANDT VENTURE PARTNERS, 1543
REVEL PARTNERS, 1557
REVO CAPITAL, 3069
RINCON VENTURE PARTNERS, 1569
RUNA CAPITAL, 3079
SAIF PARTNERS, 3084
SAINTS CAPITAL, 1608
SELBY VENTURE PARTNERS, 1649
SENTRY FINANCIAL CORPORATION, 1655
SEQUOIA CAPITAL, 1657
SEVIN ROSEN FUNDS, 1661
SHASTA VENTURES, 1666
SIGMA PARTNERS, 1674
SIGNAL PEAK VENTURES, 1679
SIGNATURE CAPITAL LLC, 3111
SINGTEL INNOV8, 3112
SK TELECOM VENTURES, 1692
SOFTBANK VENTURES KOREA, 3118
SOLID VENTURES, 3119
SORRENTO VENTURES, 1708
SOUTHERN CROSS VENTURE PARTNERS, 1713
SPECTRUM EQUITY INVESTORS LP, 1720
SPINUP VENTURE, 3123
SPLIT ROCK PARTNERS, 1728
STAGE 1 VENTURES, 1737
STAGEONE VENTURES, 3127
SUMMIT PARTNERS, 1754
SUPREMUM CAPITAL, 3141
SUSQUEHANNA GROWTH EQUITY, 1761
SVB CAPITAL, 1766
TAO VENTURE CAPITAL PARTNERS, 1782
TARGET PARTNERS, 3152
TECH COAST ANGELS, 1786
TECHNOLOGY CROSSOVER VENTURES, 1787
TELESYSTEM, 2255
TENGELMANN VENTURES, 3161
THINKTIV VENTURES, 1813
THRIVE CAPITAL, 1823
TIE ANGELS GROUP SEATTLE, 1827
TIGER GLOBAL MANAGEMENT, 1828
TMI, 3172
TOBA CAPITAL, 1831
TROIKA CAPITAL PARTNERS, 3184
TRUE VENTURES, 1862
TUGBOAT VENTURES, 1867
UNION SQUARE VENTURES, 1884
UNIVERSITY VENTURE FUND, 1886
UPDATA VENTURE PARTNERS, 1888
VALAR VENTURES, 1899
VANTAGEPOINT CAPITAL PARTNERS, 1908
VINE ST VENTURES, 1936
VISION CAPITAL, 1939
VITAMINA K VENTURE CAPITAL, 3214
VITULUM VENTURES, 3215
VOLITION CAPITAL, 1944
VTB CAPITAL, 3220
WGI GROUP, 1980
WINDSPEED VENTURES, 1994
WRF CAPITAL, 2007
XANGE PRIVATE EQUITY, 3229
YES VC, 2013
ZELKOVA VENTURES, 2016

Internet Advertising
CORIOLIS VENTURES, 541
TRUE VENTURES, 1862

Internet Applications and Services
GENESIS PARTNERS, 2766
LIFE.SREDA, 2931

Industry Preference Index / Internet Communications

Internet Communications
TRUE VENTURES, 1862

Internet Infrastructure
BASECAMP VENTURES, 233
BLUEFISH VENTURES, 297
COLUMBIA CAPITAL, 518
INNOVATION WORKS, 1003
MASTHEAD VENTURE PARTNERS, 1178
TGAP VENTURES, 1804

Internet Infrastructure Services
EVENTI CAPITAL PARTNERS, 2104

Internet Technology
ABELL FOUNDATION VENTURES, 18
ACCEL-KKR LLC, 28
ACCESS VENTURE PARTNERS LLC, 35
ACE VENTURE CAPITAL LIMITED, 2322
ACT VENTURE CAPITAL LIMITED, 2328
ADOBE VENTURES LP, 57
AEP CAPITAL LLC, 64
AKERS CAPITAL LLC, 74
ALEXANDER HUTTON, 82
ALICE VENTURES SRL, 2356
ALLEGIS CYBER CAPITAL, 84
ALTAIR VENTURES, 95
AMADEUS CAPITAL PARTNERS LIMITED, 2378
AMWIN MANAGEMENT PTY LIMITED, 2390
ANDERSON PACIFIC CORPORATION, 123
ANGELS' FORUM LLC, 130
ARGO GLOBAL CAPITAL, 163
ARROWPATH VENTURE PARTNERS, 171
ATHENIAN VENTURE PARTNERS, 189
ATRIUM CAPITAL, 194
AURA CAPITAL OY Auratum Group, 2442
AUSTIN VENTURES, 205
AVANSIS VENTURES, 210
AXA INVESTMENT MANAGERS PRIVATE EQUITY EUROPE, 2457
BAIRD CAPITAL PARTNERS, 225
BARCELONA EMPREN, 2474
BASECAMP VENTURES, 233
BOULDER VENTURES LTD, 318
CANAL PARTNERS, 390
CAPITOL PARTNERS, 409
CAPRICORN VENTURE PARTNERS NV, 2554
CAZENOVE PRIVATE EQUITY Cazenove Capital, 2568
CEDAR (ISRAEL) FINANCIAL ADVISORS LIMITED Cedar Fund, 2571
CEDAR FUND, 438
CENTENNIAL VENTURES, 443
CHALLENGE FUNDS - ETGAR LP, 2576
CHICAGO VENTURE PARTNERS LP, 472
COLLER CAPITAL LIMITED, 2612
COMMONWEALTH CAPITAL VENTURES LP, 523
CONCORD VENTURES, 2619
CORE CAPITAL PARTNERS, 540
DAIMLERCHRYSLER VENTURE GmbH DaimlerChrysler AG, 2641
DELTA VENTURES LIMITED, 2646
DIAMONDHEAD VENTURES, 614
DOUGHTY HANSON & CO., 2662
DR NEUHAUS TECHNO NORD GmbH, 2664
DRAPER RICHARDS KAPLAN FOUNDATION, 628
ECONA AG, 2679
EDGESTONE CAPITAL PARTNERS, 2098
EDISON PARTNERS, 655
ELECTRA PARTNERS ASIA LIMITED SFC of Hong Kong, 2685
ENTERPRISE EQUITY (NI) LTD, 2695
EPIC VENTURES, 689
EPISODE 1 PARTNERS, 2702
EURAZEO, 2710
EUROFUND LP, 2711
EVERCORE CAPITAL PARTNERS, 700
FERRANTI LIMITED, 2723
FORMULA VENTURES LIMITED Formula Group, 2741
FOUNDATION CAPITAL, 773
FRESHWATER VENTURE PARTNERS, 2748
GALILEO II, 2756

GEMINI ISRAEL VENTURE FUNDS LIMITED, 2761
GENESIS PARTNERS, 2766
GILBERT GLOBAL EQUITY PARTNERS, 831
GMT COMMUNICATIONS PARTNERS LLP, 2780
GRANDBANKS CAPITAL, 853
GRAYHAWK CAPITAL, 861
GREENHILL SAVP, 869
HALLIM VENTURE CAPITAL, 2798
HIKARI TSUSHIN CAPITAL, 2817
HYUNDAI VENTURE INVESTMENT CORPORATION, 2830
ID VENTURES AMERICA LLC, 974
IDG CAPITAL, 977
IDG TECHNOLOGY VENTURE INVESTMENT, 2839
IDINVEST PARTNERS, 2842
IGNITE JAPAN KK Ignite Group, 2845
IN-Q-TEL, 983
IPG GROUP, 2885
ITC VENTURES, 2894
JAPAN ASIA INVESTMENT COMPANY LIMITED, 2898
JK&B CAPITAL, 1042
KALORI GROUP INVESTMENTS, 2906
KB PARTNERS LLC, 1061
KINETIC VENTURES, 1076
KNIGHTSBRIDGE ADVISERS, 1081
KOREA FIRST VENTURE CAPITAL CORPORATION, 2915
LEASING TECHNOLOGIES INTERNATIONAL INC., 1107
MACQUARIE DIRECT INVESTMENT LIMITED, 2942
MADRONA VENTURE GROUP, 1162
MANHATTAN INVESTMENT PARTNERS, 1166
MASSACHUSETTS CAPITAL RESOURCE COMPANY, 1176
MASSACHUSETTS GROWTH CAPITAL CORPORATION, 1177
MASTHEAD VENTURE PARTNERS, 1178
MATRIX PARTNERS, 1184
MAYFIELD FUND, 1187
MENLO VENTURES, 1203
MERITECH CAPITAL PARTNERS, 1213
METROPOLITAN PARTNERS GROUP, 1226
MIRAE ASSET VENTURE ACCELERATOR Mirae Asset Group, 2960
MISSION VENTURES, 1239
MOBILE INTERNET CAPITAL, 2965
MOSAIC CAPITAL PARTNERS, 2190
NEW YORK CITY ENTREPRENEURIAL FUND New York City Economic Development Corporation, 1306
NEWBURY VENTURES, 1310
NEWLIGHT MANAGEMENT, 1313
NORTH ATLANTIC CAPITAL CORPORATION, 1334
NORTHWOOD VENTURES, 1344
NOVAK BIDDLE VENTURE PARTNERS, 1348
PITANGO VENTURE CAPITAL, 3030
PRIME TECHNOLOGY VENTURES NV, 3042
REDPOINT VENTURES, 1537
RHO VENTURES, 1561
RRE VENTURES, 1597
SAMSUNG VENTURE INVESTMENT CORPORATION Samsung Electronics, 3089
SEAYA VENTURES, 3096
SEQUEL VENTURE PARTNERS, 1656
SHANGHAI INFORMATION INVESTMENT INCORPORATED, 3105
SIERRA VENTURES, 1672
SMART BUSINESS CONSULTING, 3115
SONY EUROPE, 3120
SONY STRATEGIC TECHNOLOGY PARTNERSHIPS, 1706
SORRENTO VENTURES, 1708
SOUTHPORT PARTNERS, 1714
STAGE 1 VENTURES, 1737
SUNEVISION HOLDINGS LIMITED, 3139
SYCAMORE VENTURES, 1771
TAMIR FISHMAN VENTURES, 3150
TELUS VENTURES, 2256
TEUZA MANAGEMENT & DEVELOPMENT LTD, 3162
TIME WARNER INVESTMENT CORPORATION, 1829
TWJ CAPITAL, 1875
UNION SQUARE VENTURES, 1884
US VENTURE PARTNERS, 1898
VOYAGER CAPITAL, 1947
WALDEN ISRAEL VENTURE CAPITAL, 3221
WASSERSTEIN & CO., 1961

Industry Preference Index / Life Sciences

WELLINGTON PARTNERS VENTURE CAPITAL GmbH, 3223
WESTERN STATES INVESTMENT GROUP, 1975
WESTERN TECHNOLOGY INVESTMENT, 1976
WINDWARD VENTURES, 1995
YLR CAPITAL MARKETS LTD, 3237

Internet of Things
CHRYSALIX, 2072
EXTREME VENTURE PARTNERS, 2107
GOOD NEWS VENTURES, 2132

Internet-Enabled Hardware
CATALYST INVESTORS, 429

Internet/Mobile/Media
GIZA VENTURE CAPITAL, 2773

Internet/Web Services
BEZOS EXPEDITIONS, 265

Invention
INTELLECTUAL VENTURES, 1010

Investment Analysis and Research
AUSTRALIAN ETHICAL INVESTMENT LIMITED, 2447

Investor Relations
CAPMAN CAPITAL MANAGEMENT OY, 2553

IoT
CISCO INVESTMENTS, 485
CORNERSTONE VENTURE PARTNERS, 544
FLORIDA FUNDERS, 754
FOUNDER PARTNERS, 775
FREESTYLE, 787
GOOD GROWTH CAPITAL, 849
GRISHIN ROBOTICS, 879
INTEL CAPITAL, 1009
INVESTX, 2154
MS&AD VENTURES, 1269
PANACHE VENTURES, 2204
QUALCOMM VENTURES, 1511
SAMSUNG NEXT, 1614
SONY INNOVATION FUND, 1705
SOZO VENTURES, 1716
SWITCH VENTURES, 1770
WILDCAT VENTURE PARTNERS, 1985

Labour Law
BUTZOW NORDIA ADVOCATES LTD, 2543

Language Processing
CARBON VENTURES, 411
PATHBREAKER VENTURES, 1423

Laser
NEUHAUS PARTNERS, 2985

Law Enforcement
BRYANT PARK VENTURES, 359

Legal
COVENT INDUSTRIAL CAPITAL INVESTMENT COMPANY, 2626
M25 GROUP, 1159

Legal and Compliance
CAPMAN CAPITAL MANAGEMENT OY, 2553
VON BRAUN & SCHREIBER PRIVATE EQUITY PARTNERS, 3218

Leisure
3I ASIA PACIFIC 3i Group, 2289
ACTIS, 2329
APOLLO GLOBAL MANAGEMENT, 141
AVANTI CAPITAL, 2449
BARCLAYS VENTURES Barclays, 2477
BENCIS CAPITAL PARTNERS, 2492
BOTTS & COMPANY LIMITED, 2523
CANDOVER, 2547
CINVEN LIMITED, 2596
CLOSE BROTHERS PRIVATE EQUITY Close Brothers Group, 2608
CLYDESDALE VENTURES, 508
DUKE STREET CAPITAL Duke Street, 2667
DUNEDIN CAPITAL PARTNERS LIMITED, 2668
FALCONHEAD CAPITAL, 717
GRAPHITE CAPITAL MANAGEMENT LTD, 2787
HAMBRO CAPITAL MANAGEMENT LTD, 2799
HENDERSON PRIVATE CAPITAL, 2812
HG CAPITAL, 2814
MERRILL LYNCH (ASIA PACIFIC) LIMITED Merrill Lynch Group, 2955
NORTHERN ENTERPRISE LIMITED, 3002
PHOENIX EQUITY PARTNERS LIMITED, 3027
PROSPECT PARTNERS LLC, 1494
QUESTER CAPITAL MANAGEMENT LIMITED, 3061
SCHOONER CAPITAL LLC, 1630
SOVEREIGN CAPITAL, 3121
SWANDER PACE CAPITAL, 1769
WESLEY CLOVER, 2276

Leisure & Hospitality
BUSINESS GROWTH FUND, 2541

License Communications
SYNCOM VENTURE PARTNERS, 1773

Life Science
EMBARK VENTURES, 664

Life Sciences
3I TEUPSCHLAND GmbH 3i Group, 2297
5AM VENTURES, 11
ABINGWORTH MANAGEMENT LIMITED, 2308
ABOA VENTURE MANAGEMENT OY, 2310
ACCELERATOR LIFE SCIENCE PARTNERS, 30
ACCELMED, 2316
ACME LABS, 2325
ACORN CAMPUS VENTURES, 46
ACT VENTURE CAPITAL LIMITED, 2328
ADAMS STREET PARTNERS, LLC, 56
ADVANTAGE CAPITAL PARTNERS, 60
AGF PRIVATE EQUITY Allianz Group, 2346
AISLING CAPITAL, 73
ALBERTA ENTERPRISE, 2028
ALICE VENTURES SRL, 2356
ALLIANCE OF ANGELS, 85
ALLOY VENTURES, 87
ALPINVEST GmbH, 2369
ALPINVEST HOLDING NV Alpinvest, 2370
ALTA PARTNERS, 94
AMANET TECHNOLOGIES LIMITED, 2381
AMBIENT SOUND INVESTMENTS, 2382
AMGEN VENTURES, 113
AMIDZAD PARTNERS, 116
AMORCHEM, 2031
AMPHION CAPITAL PARTNERS, 2389
ANGELAB VENTURES, 2393
APPLE TREE PARTNERS, 144
ARAVIS VENTURES, 2410
ARBORETUM VENTURES, 150
ASCLEPIOS BIORESEARCH, 2424
ATHENIAN VENTURE PARTNERS, 189
ATLAS VENTURE, 193
ATLAS VENTURE: FRANCE, 2436
AUGURY CAPITAL PARTNERS, 199
AURELIA PRIVATE EQUITY, 2443
AURIGA PARTNERS, 2444
AURUM VENTURES MKI, 2445
AUSTRAL CAPITAL PARTNERS, 2446
AVALON VENTURES, 209
AWEIDA VENTURE PARTNERS, 213
AZCA, 217
BAIRD CAPITAL PARTNERS, 225
BAND OF ANGELS LLC, 229
BANEXI VENTURES PARTNERS, 2472
BATTELLE VENTURES, 236
BAY BG BAVARIAN VENTURE CAPITAL CORP, 2485

Industry Preference Index / Life Sciences

BAY CITY CAPITAL LLC, 240
BCM TECHNOLOGIES, 244
BEIJING HIGH TECHNOLOGY INVESTMENT COMPANY, 2490
BIOMED PARTNERS, 2506
BIOPACIFIC VENTURES, 2507
BIOVEDA CAPITAL, 2509
BIOVENTURES INVESTORS, 273
BIRK VENTURE, 2510
BLADE VENTURES, 281
BM-T BETEILIGUNGS MANAGEMENT THURINGEN GmbH, 2518
BMP AKTIENGESELLSCHAFT BMP Venture Capital, 2519
BOEHRINGER INGELHEIM VENTURE FUND, 2521
BOSTON UNIVERSITY - TECHNOLOGY DEVELOPMENT, 317
BOULDER VENTURES LTD, 318
BRAIN TRUST ACCELERATOR FUND, 326
BRANDON CAPITAL PARTNERS, 2527
BRIGHTSTONE VENTURE CAPITAL, 344
BROADMARK CAPITAL, 348
BROADVIEW VENTURES, 350
BRYAN GARNIER & COMPANY, 2535
BUSINESS GROWTH FUND, 2541
CALIFORNIA TECHNOLOGY VENTURES, 374
CANADIAN VENTURE CAPITAL ASSOCIATION Canadian Venture Capital & Private Equity Association, 3249
CAPITAL MIDWEST FUND, 403
CAPMAN CAPITAL MANAGEMENT OY, 2553
CARDINAL PARTNERS, 413
CARE CAPITAL, 415
CASDIN CAPITAL, 422
CASE TECHNOLOGY VENTURES Case Western Reserve University, 423
CATALYST HEALTH VENTURES, 428
CATALYST INVESTMENT MANAGERS PTY LIMITED PPM Capital, 2564
CATO BIOVENTURES, 432
CEDAR VENTURES LLC, 439
CELERITY PARTNERS, 441
CENTRESTONE VENTURES, 2071
CHARTER LIFE SCIENCES, 460
CHASE CAPITAL PARTNERS, 2579
CLARITY CAPITAL, 2602
CM CAPITAL, 2609
CNF INVESTMENTS Clark Enterprises, Inc., 510
COLUMN GROUP, 519
COMMERCE ASSET VENTURES Sdn Bhd, 2614
COMPAGNIE FINANCIERE E DE ROTHSCHILD BANQUE, 2616
CONCORD VENTURES, 2619
CORAL GROUP, 538
CORDOVA VENTURES, 539
CORRELATION VENTURES, 545
COUNCIL FOR ENTREPRENEURIAL DEVELOPMENT, 3250
CRB INVERBIO, 2627
CREATHOR VENTURE, 2629
CROSS CREEK ADVISORS, 561
CTI LIFE SCIENCES, 2086
CULTIVATION CAPITAL, 570
DAG VENTURES, 582
DANEVEST TECH FUND ADVISORS, 584
DE NOVO VENTURES, 599
DIRECT CAPITAL PRIVATE EQUITY LIMITED, 2655
DISCOVERY CAPITAL, 2091
DOMAIN ASSOCIATES LLC, 622
DVC DEUTSCHE VENTURE CAPITAL, 2670
EASTON CAPITAL INVESTMENT GROUP, 644
EDELSON TECHNOLOGY PARTNERS, 651
ELEVATE VENTURES, 659
ELM STREET VENTURES, 661
EM WARBURG, PINCUS & COMPANY JAPAN, 2689
EMERALD OCEAN CAPITAL, 665
EMERGENT MEDICAL PARTNERS, 667
ENSO VENTURES, 2693
ENTREPRENEURS FUND, 2701
EPIC VENTURES, 689
EPIDAREX CAPITAL, 690
EQUINET VENTURE PARTNERS AG, 2704
ESSEX WOODLANDS HEALTH VENTURES LLC, 698
EVOLVE CAPITAL, 703
EXCEL VENTURE MANAGEMENT, 704

FARM CREDIT CANADA, 2108
FIRST FLIGHT VENTURE CENTER, 738
FIRST STEP FUND, 743
FLAGSHIP PIONEERING, 748
FLANDERS' FOREIGN INVESTMENT OFFICE, 2737
FLETCHER SPAGHT VENTURES, 750
FORBION CAPITAL PARTNERS, 2739
FORWARD VENTURES, 772
FRAZIER HEALTHCARE VENTURES, 785
GE ASIA PACIFIC CAPITAL TECHNOLOGY FUND, 2758
GENERICS GROUP LIMITED Generics Group, 2764
GENESYS CAPITAL, 2125
GENSTAR CAPITAL LP, 823
GIZA VENTURE CAPITAL, 2773
GLENTHORNE CAPITAL, 836
GLOBAL LIFE SCIENCE VENTURES GmbH, 2776
GOLDEN PINE VENTURES, 844
GOLDEN SEEDS, 845
GRANITE HILL CAPITAL PARTNERS, LLC, 856
GREAT POINT PARTNERS, 864
GREENSPRING ASSOCIATES, 872
GROVE STREET ADVISORS LLC, 884
GUIDE VENTURES, 892
GV, 894
HATTERAS VENTURE PARTNERS, 918
HEALTHCAP Odlander, Fredrikson & Co AB, 2807
HEALTHCARE VENTURES LLC, 922
HERCULES TECHNOLOGY GROWTH CAPITAL, INC, 928
HIGH COUNTRY VENTURE, 933
HIGH-TECH GRUENDERFONDS, 2815
HOPEN LIFE SCIENCE VENTURES, 946
HOPEWELL VENTURES, 947
HORIZON TECHNOLOGY FINANCE, 949
HOUSTON ANGEL NETWORK, 953
IBB BETEILIGUNGSGESELLSCHAFT MBH, 2832
IDG TECHNOLOGY VENTURE INVESTMENT, 2839
ILLINOIS VENTURES, 979
INBC INVESTMENT CORP, 2144
INCUBE VENTURES, 984
INDASIA FUND ADVISORS PVT LTD, 2850
INDUSTRIEBANK LIOF NV, 2857
INFLEXION PARTNERS, 994
INNOVATION CAPITAL, 2867
INNOVATION WORKS, 1003
INOVIA CAPITAL, 2150
INTEGRA VENTURES, 1007
INTEGRAL CAPITAL PARTNERS, 1008
INTERSOUTH PARTNERS, 1013
INVESCO PRIVATE CAPITAL, 1019
IPOSCOPE NV/SA, 2886
JUMPSTART INC, 1051
KERNEL CAPITAL, 2909
KLEINER PERKINS, 1079
KRG CAPITAL PARTNERS, 1090
LAUNCHCYTE, 1102
LAUNCHPAD VENTURE GROUP, 1104
LBBW VENTURE CAPITAL, 2923
LEASING TECHNOLOGIES INTERNATIONAL INC., 1107
LIFE SCIENCES GREENHOUSE OF CENTRAL PA, 1120
LIFE SCIENCES PARTNERS BV, 2930
LIGHTHOUSE CAPITAL PARTNERS, 1122
LIGHTSTONE VENTURES, 1126
LINDEN LLC, 1132
LINK TECHNOLOGIES LIMITED, 2932
LINN GROVE VENTURES, 1135
LONGITUDE CAPITAL, 1147
LUMIRA VENTURES, 2174
LUX CAPITAL, 1155
MANULIFE CAPITAL, 2177
MARS INVESTMENT ACCELERATOR FUND, 2181
MARYLAND VENTURE FUND, 1172
MAYFIELD FUND, 1187
MB VENTURE PARTNERS, 1190
MEAKEM/BECKER VENTURE CAPITAL, 1196
MEDIPHASE VENTURE PARTNERS, 1198
MERCURY FUND, 1207
MERITURN PARTNERS, 1214

Industry Preference Index / Logistics

MERLIN NEXUS, 1217
MESA VERDE PARTNERS, 1222
MMV CAPITAL PARTNERS, 2188
MOHR-DAVIDOW VENTURES, 1247
MONTREUX EQUITY PARTNERS, 1251
MORGENTHALER VENTURES, 1257
MOUNTAIN GROUP CAPITAL, 1261
MURPHREE VENTURE PARTNERS, 1273
MVM LIFE SCIENCE PARTNERS, 2972
MVP CAPITAL PARTNERS, 1275
NEW BRUNSWICK INNOVATION FOUNDATION, 2192
NEW CAPITAL FUND, 1291
NEW SCIENCE VENTURES, 1302
NEWABLE VENTURES, 2988
NOVA SCOTIA BUSINESS INC., 2197
NOVARTIS VENTURE FUNDS, 1350
NOVO A/S, 3006
OKAPI VENTURE CAPITAL, 1371
OMNES CAPITAL, 3011
ONTARIO CAPITAL GROWTH CORPORATION, 2203
ORBIMED HEALTHCARE FUND MANAGEMENT, 1383
OUTCOME CAPITAL, 1389
OVP VENTURE PARTNERS, 1392
OXFORD BIOSCIENCE PARTNERS, 1395
OneVentures, 3014
PAC-LINK MANAGEMENT CORP., 3015
PACIFIC HORIZON VENTURES, 1399
PANORAMA CAPITAL, 1411
PAPPAS VENTURES, 1414
PARKWALK ADVISORS, 3019
PARTNERS HEALTHCARE RESEARCH VENTURES, 1421
PENN VENTURE PARTNERS, 1431
PFIZER VENTURE INVESTMENTS, 1439
PI CAPITAL GROUP LLC, 1444
PIEDMONT ANGEL NETWORK, 1446
PITTSBURGH EQUITY PARTNERS, 1451
PITTSBURGH LIFE SCIENCES GREENHOUSE, 1452
PMV, 3033
POLARIS VENTURE PARTNERS, 1464
POLYTECHNOS VENTURE PARTNERS GmbH, 3037
PORTUGAL CAPITAL VENTURES Institutional Headquarters, 3039
PRAIRIEGOLD VENTURE PARTNERS, 1474
PROLOG VENTURES, 1490
PTV SCIENCES, 1502
QBIC FUND, 3056
QUAKER BIOVENTURES, 1510
QUEST FOR GROWTH, 3060
QUESTER CAPITAL MANAGEMENT LIMITED, 3061
RA CAPITAL MANAGEMENT, 1522
RBC CAPITAL MARKETS, 2223
RENEWABLETECH VENTURES, 1545
RESEARCH CORPORATION TECHNOLOGIES, 1546
RIVERVEST VENTURE PARTNERS, 1578
ROADMAP CAPITAL INC., 2234
ROCHE VENTURE FUND F. Hoffman-La Roche AG, 3076
SAND HILL ANGELS, 1616
SANOFI-GENZYME BIOVENTURES, 1621
SANTE VENTURES, 1622
SCHRODER VENTURES HEALTH INVESTORS, 1631
SCOTTISH EQUITY PARTNERS, 3095
SCP PARTNERS, 1636
SEB VENTURE CAPITAL, 3097
SERAPH GROUP, 1658
SEVENTURE PARTNERS, 3104
SEVIN ROSEN FUNDS, 1661
SHEPHERD VENTURES, 1667
SIGNAL PEAK VENTURES, 1679
SLATER TECHNOLOGY FUND, 1695
SOFINNOVA VENTURES, 1700
SOLSTICE CAPITAL LP, 1704
SOUTHWEST MICHIGAN FIRST LIFE SCIENCE FUND Southwest Michigan First, 1715
SPENCER TRASK VENTURES, 1723
SPINDLETOP CAPITAL, 1725
SPLIT ROCK PARTNERS, 1728
STAR VENTURES, 3128
STARFISH VENTURES, 3129
STONEHENGE GROWTH CAPITAL, 1748
SUMMIT PARTNERS, 1754
SUNSTONE CAPITAL, 3140
SVB CAPITAL, 1766
SYNERGY LIFE SCIENCE PARTNERS, 1774
TAMIR FISHMAN VENTURES, 3150
TANDEM EXPANSION FUND, 2252
TECH COAST ANGELS, 1786
TECHNOLOGY PARTNERS, 1788
TEKNOINVEST MANAGEMENT, 3158
TEL VENTURE CAPITAL, 1793
TELEGRAPH HILL PARTNERS, 1794
TERALYS CAPITAL, 2259
TGAP VENTURES, 1804
THE CHANNEL GROUP, 1811
THIRD ROCK VENTURES, 1814
THIRD SECURITY, 1815
THOMAS, MCNERNEY & PARTNERS, 1820
TRASK INNOVATIONS FUND Purdue Research Foundation, 1842
TRELYS FUNDS, 1844
TRIANGLE ANGEL PARTNERS, 1847
TRIATHLON MEDICAL VENTURES, 1849
TRIGINITA CAPITAL, 3181
TULLIS HEALTH INVESTORS, 1868
TVM CAPITAL, 3187
US VENTURE PARTNERS, 1898
VALENCE LIFE SCIENCES, 1900
VALLEY VENTURES LP, 1903
VEDANTA CAPITAL LP, 1913
VENBIO, 1916
VENCORE CAPITAL, 1917
VENTUREAST, 3202
WATER STREET HEALTHCARE PARTNERS, 1962
WESTERN TECHNOLOGY INVESTMENT, 1976
WHEATLEY PARTNERS, 1981
WISCONSIN INVESTMENT PARTNERS, 2002
XENIA VENTURE CAPITAL, 3230
XSEED CAPITAL MANAGEMENT, 2010
YELLOWSTONE CAPITAL, 2012
YISSUM TECHNOLOGY TRANSFER, 3235
YUUWA CAPITAL, 3238
YVC - YOZMA MANAGEMENT & INVESTMENTS LIMITED, 3239

Lifestyle & Recreation
BEZOS EXPEDITIONS, 265
FUNK VENTURES, 800

Light Manufacturing
CARDINAL EQUITY PARTNERS, 412
CI CAPITAL PARTNERS, 478
EMINENT CAPITAL PARTNERS, 670
GRANTHAM CAPITAL, 858
SARONA ASSET MANAGEMENT, 2239

Lighting
CROSSLINK CAPITAL, 564

Litigation
BUTZOW NORDIA ADVOCATES LTD, 2543

Lodging
THAYER VENTURES, 1808

Logistics
ACI CAPITAL, 41
ACTIS, 2329
ALANTRA, 77
ALEUTIAN CAPITAL PARTNERS, 81
ANGELENO GROUP, 127
AURORA CAPITAL GROUP, 202
BARCLAYS VENTURES Barclays, 2477
BISON CAPITAL ASSET MANAGEMENT LLC, 277
BRIDGE STREET CAPITAL, 341
BULL VENTURES, 2538
BUTLER CAPITAL PARTNERS FRANCE, 2542
CAMBRIDGE CAPITAL, 383
CANTOS VENTURES, 398
CHINA VEST LIMITED, 2587

Industry Preference Index / Low Capex Semiconductor

CHINAVEST, 475
CHRYSALIX, 2072
CLOSE BROTHERS PRIVATE EQUITY Close Brothers Group, 2608
CREDIT MUTUEL EQUITY, 2082
DEFI GESTION SA Banque Cantonale Vaudoise, 2644
DEUTSCHE BETEILIGUNGS AG, 2651
EAST FUND MANAGEMENT GmbH GiroCredit, 2674
ENDEAVOUR CAPITAL, 674
ENTREPRENEURS ROUNDTABLE ACCELERATOR, 685
EOS PARTNERS LP, 687
EQUISTONE, 2705
EUROVENTURES CAPITAL, 2716
FENWAY PARTNERS, 722
FIDELITY GROWTH PARTNERS ASIA, 2724
FLANDERS' FOREIGN INVESTMENT OFFICE, 2737
FOUNDERS EQUITY, 777
FdG ASSOCIATES LP, 804
GE CAPITAL, 811
GEORGIA OAK PARTNERS, 825
GRANTHAM CAPITAL, 858
GREENBRIAR EQUITY GROUP LLC, 867
GULFSTAR GROUP, 893
HALIFAX GROUP LLC, 899
HARBOUR GROUP, 911
HCI EQUITY PARTNERS, 920
HIGH STREET CAPITAL, 935
INDASIA FUND ADVISORS PVT LTD, 2850
INTER-ASIA VENTURE MANAGEMENT LIMITED, 2872
JEFFERIES CAPITAL PARTNERS, 1036
KERRY CAPITAL ADVISORS, 1071
LEE EQUITY PARTNERS, 1108
M25 GROUP, 1159
MERIT CAPITAL PARTNERS, 1210
NAVIGATION CAPITAL PARTNERS, 1279
NCT VENTURES, 1285
NESBIC INVESTMENT FUND II, 2983
NEW MOUNTAIN CAPITAL, 1300
NORO-MOSELEY PARTNERS, 1332
PARADIGM CAPITAL LTD, 1416
PARALLEL49 EQUITY, 2206
PARTHENON CAPITAL, 1419
PENDER WEST CAPITAL PARTNERS, 2210
PHOENIX EQUITY PARTNERS LIMITED, 3027
POST CAPITAL PARTNERS, 1469
PRIVATE EQUITY PARTNERS SPA, 3044
PROCURITAS PARTNERS KB, 3045
PT BHAKTI INVESTAMA TBK, 3052
QUAKE CAPITAL PARTNERS, 1509
SALT CREEK CAPITAL, 1612
SARONA ASSET MANAGEMENT, 2239
SONY INNOVATION FUND, 1705
TH LEE PUTNAM VENTURES, 1806
VRG CAPITAL, 2274
WESTLAKE SECURITIES, 1977
WESTVIEW CAPITAL PARTNERS, 1979
WOODBRIDGE GROUP, 2004
WYNNCHURCH CAPITAL, 2008
XANGE PRIVATE EQUITY, 3229
ZURMONT MADISON PRIVATE EQUITY, 3244

Low Capex Semiconductor
OJAS VENTURE PARTNERS, 3010

Low Carbon and Renewable Energy Infrastructure
QUINBROOK INFRASTRUCTURE PARTNERS, 1520

Low Technology
PEGASUS CAPITAL GROUP, 1427
ROSER VENTURES LLC, 1590

Low-Capital Intensity Manufacturing
PACIFIC COMMUNITY VENTURES, 1397

Low-Tech Manufacturing
BLACKFORD CAPITAL LLC, 279

Loyalty
CHICAGO VENTURES, 473

Luxury Goods
EMINENT CAPITAL PARTNERS, 670

Luxury/Lifestyle
AVISTA PARTNERS, 2452

Machine Intelligence
FRONTIER VENTURES, 795

Machine Learning
AMD VENTURES, 107
ANALYTICS VENTURES, 122
CARBON VENTURES, 411
CHINAROCK CAPITAL MANAGEMENT VENTURES, 474
CITI VENTURES, 488
COMET LABS, 521
DELL VENTURES, 604
DRAPER ATHENA, 627
FIRST ASCENT VENTURES, 2112
FLYING FISH, 757
FRONTLINE VENTURES, 2750
GOOD GROWTH CAPITAL, 849
GREEN TOWER CAPITAL, 866
IGNITION PARTNERS, 978
IMAGINATION CAPITAL, 981
LDV CAPITAL, 1105
M12, 1158
PATHBREAKER VENTURES, 1423
QUAKE CAPITAL PARTNERS, 1509
UBIQUITY VENTURES, 1879
WILDCAT VENTURE PARTNERS, 1985

Machinery
BALTCAP MANAGEMENT LTD, 2471
CHINA VEST LIMITED, 2587
CORNERSTONE CAPITAL HOLDINGS, 542
DEUTSCHE BETEILIGUNGS AG, 2651
HALLIM VENTURE CAPITAL, 2798
JB POINDEXTER & COMPANY, 1034
LEONIA MB GROUP/MB FUNDS, 2928
PALMS & COMPANY, 1405
PWC, 3055
QUADRAN GESTION Deutsche Beteiligungs AG, 3058
SIF TRANSYLVANIA, 3110
TRANS COSMOS INCORPORATED, 3176
TRANSYLVANIA FINANCIAL INVESTMENT COMPANY, 3178
ZURMONT MADISON PRIVATE EQUITY, 3244

Managed Services
ISOURCE GESTION, 2890

Management
ACCENTURE TECHNOLOGY VENTURES, 2318
CHINA MERCHANTS CHINA DIRECT INVESTMENTS LTD., 2585
DIRIGEANTS ET INVESTISSEURS, 2656
ENTER VENTURES, 682
EQUITY PARTNERS PTY LIMITED, 2706
GENERICS GROUP LIMITED Generics Group, 2764
INNOVATION CAPITAL LIMITED, 2868
J-SEED VENTURES INCORPORATED, 2896
NIPPON TECHNOLOGY VENTURE PARTNERS LIMITED, 2996
WESTERN NIS ENTERPRISE FUND, 3224

Management Buyouts
WESTCAP, 2277

Manufacturing
3I ASIA PACIFIC 3i Group, 2289
AAVIN PRIVATE EQUITY, 16
ACI CAPITAL, 41
ACTIS, 2329
ADVANTAGE CAPITAL PARTNERS, 60
AEA INVESTORS, 63
ALBERTA ENTERPRISE, 2028
ALEUTIAN CAPITAL PARTNERS, 81
ALEXANDER HUTTON, 82
ALLSTATE INVESTMENTS LLC, 88

Industry Preference Index / Manufacturing

ALPHA CAPITAL PARTNERS, 90
AMERICAN INDUSTRIAL PARTNERS, 110
AMERIMARK CAPITAL CORPORATION, 112
AMHERST FUND, 114
AMPERSAND CAPITAL PARTNERS, 119
AMWIN MANAGEMENT PTY LIMITED, 2390
ANDLINGER & COMPANY INC, 124
APOLLO GLOBAL MANAGEMENT, 141
ARES MANAGEMENT LLC, 160
ARGENTUM GROUP, 162
ARGOSY CAPITAL, 165
ARLINGTON CAPITAL PARTNERS, 167
ARSENAL CAPITAL PARTNERS, 172
ARVA LIMITED, 2040
ASHBRIDGE PARTNERS, 2041
ASIAN INFRASTRUCTURE FUND ADVISERS LIMITED AIF Capital, 2425
ASIAVEST PARTNERS, 2427
ASTOR CAPITAL GROUP, 2431
AURORA CAPITAL GROUP, 202
AUSTIN CAPITAL PARTNERS LP, 204
AVENUE CAPITAL GROUP, 211
AZALEA CAPITAL, 216
BALMORAL FUNDS, 228
BARCLAYS VENTURES Barclays, 2477
BENAROYA COMPANIES, 250
BENCIS CAPITAL PARTNERS, 2492
BERINGEA, 254
BERKSHIRE PARTNERS LLC, 257
BLUE POINT CAPITAL PARTNERS, 293
BLUE SAGE CAPITAL, 294
BLUESTEM CAPITAL COMPANY, 300
BOCI DIRECT INVESTMENT MANAGEMENT LIMITED Bank of China, 2520
BOND CAPITAL, 2058
BOUNDS EQUITY PARTNERS, 319
BRADFORD EQUITIES MANAGEMENT LLC, 324
BRANDON CAPITAL GROUP, 329
BRAZOS PRIVATE EQUITY PARTNERS, 331
BREAKWATER INVESTMENTS, 333
BRIDGEPOINT CAPITAL GmbH, 2528
BRIDGEPOINT CAPITAL LIMITED, 2529
BRIGHTPATH CAPITAL PARTNERS, 343
BROOKSIDE EQUITY PARTNERS LLC, 356
BRUML CAPITAL CORPORATION, 358
BRYNWOOD PARTNERS, 360
C3 CAPITAL PARTNERS LP, 367
CAI CAPITAL PARTNERS, 368
CAMBRIA GROUP, 381
CAMBRIDGE CAPITAL, 383
CAMBRIDGE CAPITAL CORPORATION, 384
CANADIAN VENTURE CAPITAL ASSOCIATION Canadian Venture Capital & Private Equity Association, 3249
CANDOVER, 2547
CAPITAL FOR BUSINESS, INC, 402
CAPITAL MIDWEST FUND, 403
CAPITAL PARTNERS, 404
CAPX PARTNERS, 410
CARBON VENTURES, 411
CARPEDIA INTERNATIONAL, 2066
CASTLE HARLAN, 425
CATALYST GROUP, 427
CATALYST INVESTMENT MANAGERS PTY LIMITED PPM Capital, 2564
CELADON CAPITAL GROUP, 2573
CELERITY PARTNERS, 441
CENTERFIELD CAPITAL PARTNERS, 445
CERBERUS CAPITAL MANAGEMENT, 453
CHARLESBANK CAPITAL PARTNERS, 458
CHENGWEI VENTURES, 2581
CHEROKEE INVESTMENT PARTNERS, 465
CHEYENNE CAPITAL, 469
CHINA MERCHANTS CHINA DIRECT INVESTMENTS LTD., 2585
CHINA MERCHANTS CHINA INVESTMENT MANAGEMENT, 2586
CHINAVEST, 475
CHRYSALIS CAPITAL ChrysCapital, 2590
CHRYSALIX, 2072
CIBC CAPITAL MARKETS, 2073
CID CAPITAL, 480
CLEARLIGHT PARTNERS, 503
CLEARSPRING CAPITAL PARTNERS, 2076
CLEARVIEW CAPITAL, 505
CLOSE BROTHERS PRIVATE EQUITY Close Brothers Group, 2608
COACH & CAPITAL, 2610
COLORADO MILE HIGH FUND, 516
COMPAGNIE FINANCIERE E DE ROTHSCHILD BANQUE, 2616
COMPASS GROUP MANAGEMENT LLC, 525
CORNERSTONE CAPITAL HOLDINGS, 542
CORTEC GROUP, 547
COVINGTON CAPITAL CORP., 2081
CRAWLEY VENTURES, 554
CRYSTAL RIDGE PARTNERS, 566
CUSTER CAPITAL, 572
CVC ASIA PACIFIC LIMITED CVC Capital Partners, 2634
CVC CAPITAL PARTNERS LTD, 2635
CVF CAPITAL PARTNERS, 574
CYPRESS GROUP, 576
CYPRIUM PARTNERS, 578
CZECH VENTURE PARTNERS SRO K+ Venture Partners B.V., 2639
DAHER CAPITAL, 2640
DANCAP PRIVATE EQUITY, 2088
DAVID N DEUTSCH & COMPANY LLC, 590
DESCO CAPITAL, 607
DESJARDINS CAPITAL, 2089
DIAMOND STATE VENTURES LP, 612
DIMELING SCHREIBER & PARK, 617
DIRECT CAPITAL PRIVATE EQUITY LIMITED, 2655
DN PARTNERS LLC, 620
DOUBLE IMPACT BUSINESS ADVISORY, 2661
DUBIN CLARK & COMPANY, 633
DUNEDIN CAPITAL PARTNERS LIMITED, 2668
EARLY STAGE PARTNERS, 642
ECI VENTURES, 2678
ECLIPSE VENTURES, 648
EDGESTONE CAPITAL PARTNERS, 2098
EDGEWATER CAPITAL PARTNERS, 653
ELECTRA PARTNERS ASIA LIMITED SFC of Hong Kong, 2685
ELEMENT PARTNERS, 658
ELGNER GROUP INVESTMENTS, 2099
EMBARK VENTURES, 664
EMIGRANT CAPITAL, 668
ENDEAVOUR CAPITAL, 674
ENTERPRISE EQUITY (NI) LTD, 2695
ENTERPRISE INVESTORS, 2697
EQUITY SOUTH, 694
EUREKA GROWTH CAPITAL, 699
EXCELSIOR CAPITAL ASIA, 2718
EXPANSION CAPITAL PARTNERS, 707
EXPORT DEVELOPMENT CANADA, 2106
FAIRMONT CAPITAL, 714
FCF PARTNERS LP, 719
FINLOMBARDA SpA, 2730
FIRST NEW ENGLAND CAPITAL LP, 740
FLORIDA CAPITAL PARTNERS, 753
FOUNDATION EQUITY CORPORATION, 2116
FOUNDERS EQUITY, 777
FRIEND SKOLER & COMPANY LLC, 791
FULCRUM CAPITAL PARTNERS, 2121
FdG ASSOCIATES LP, 804
GEFINOR CAPITAL, 813
GEMINI INVESTORS, 815
GENESIS CAPITAL CORPORATION, 2124
GEORGIA OAK PARTNERS, 825
GLADSTONE CAPITAL, 832
GLENTHORNE CAPITAL, 836
GLOBAL EQUITY PARTNERS BETEILIGUNGS-MANAGEMENT, 2774
GLOBAL FINANCE, 2775
GOLDNER HAWN, 847
GOLUB CAPITAL, 848
GOOD GROWTH CAPITAL, 849
GRAHAM PARTNERS, 851
GRANITE BRIDGE PARTNERS, 854
GRANITE EQUITY PARTNERS, 855
GRANITE PARTNERS, 2133

1177

Industry Preference Index / Manufacturing

GRAPHITE CAPITAL MANAGEMENT LTD, 2787
GREIF & COMPANY, 874
GRIDIRON CAPITAL, 878
GRUPO BISA, 2791
GRYPHON INVESTORS, 886
GULFSTAR GROUP, 893
HALDER BETEILIGUNGSBERATUNG GmbH, 2796
HALIFAX GROUP LLC, 899
HAMILTON ROBINSON CAPITAL PARTNERS, 903
HAMMOND, KENNEDY, WHITNEY & COMPANY, 904
HANCOCK PARK ASSOCIATES, 905
HANNOVER FINANZ GmbH, 2801
HANOVER PARTNERS, 906
HARBOUR GROUP, 911
HARREN EQUITY PARTNERS, 913
HARVEST PARTNERS, 917
HEADWATER EQUITY PARTNERS, 2138
HERITAGE PARTNERS, 929
HIG CAPITAL, 931
HIGH ROAD CAPITAL PARTNERS, 934
HIGHLAND WEST CAPITAL, 2139
HOLDING CAPITAL GROUP, 943
HOPEWELL VENTURES, 947
HORIZON PARTNERS, LTD, 948
HOULIHAN LOKEY, 951
HT CAPITAL ADVISORS LLC, 956
HURON CAPITAL PARTNERS LLC, 963
HURON RIVER VENTURES, 964
IBM VENTURE CAPITAL GROUP, 971
ICV PARTNERS, 973
INDEPENDENT BANKERS CAPITAL FUND, 988
INDUSTRI KAPITAL SVENSKA AB, 2854
INDUSTRIAL GROWTH PARTNERS, 989
INNOVENTURES CAPITAL PARTNERS, 1004
INTERMEDIATE CAPITAL GROUP PLC, 2874
INVERNESS GRAHAM INVESTMENTS, 1018
INVEST EQUITY MANAGEMENT CONSULTING GmbH, 2878
INVESTAMERICA VENTURE GROUP, 1020
INVESTOR AB, 2881
IRISH ANGELS, 1023
IRONBRIDGE EQUITY PARTNERS, 2156
IRONWOOD CAPITAL, 1025
InstarAGF, 2158
J. BURKE CAPITAL PARTNERS, 1027
JAFCO COMPANY LIMITED JAPAN, 2897
JEFFERIES CAPITAL PARTNERS, 1036
KEGONSA CAPITAL PARTNERS, 1064
KELSO & COMPANY, 1066
KENSINGTON CAPITAL PARTNERS, 2160
KENTUCKY HIGHLANDS INVESTMENT CORPORATION, 1068
KERRY CAPITAL ADVISORS, 1071
KLEINWORT CAPITAL LIMITED, 2914
KOHLBERG & COMPANY LLC, 1085
KOREA FIRST VENTURE CAPITAL CORPORATION, 2915
KPS CAPITAL PARTNERS, 1089
LINLEY CAPITAL, 1134
LLR PARTNERS INC, 1140
LOMBARD INVESTMENTS, 1143
LONG POINT CAPITAL, 1145
LYNWOOD CAPITAL PARTNERS, 1156
M25 GROUP, 1159
MACQUARIE DIRECT INVESTMENT LIMITED, 2942
MADISON DEARBORN PARTNERS, 1160
MADISON PARKER CAPITAL, 1161
MAIN STREET CAPITAL HOLDINGS LLC, 1163
MANULIFE CAPITAL, 2177
MARANON CAPITAL, 1169
MARWIT CAPITAL LLC, 1171
MASSACHUSETTS CAPITAL RESOURCE COMPANY, 1176
MCROCK CAPITAL, 2183
MEDRA CAPITAL, 2951
MERIT CAPITAL PARTNERS, 1210
MERITURN PARTNERS, 1214
MERITUS VENTURES, 1215
MERIWETHER CAPITAL CORPORATION, 1216
MESA CAPITAL PARTNERS, 1220
METAPOINT PARTNERS, 1225

MIDDLEBURG CAPITAL DEVELOPMENT, 1229
MIDINVEST LIMITED, 2957
MIDMARK CAPITAL LP, 1230
MIDVEN, 2958
MIDWEST MEZZANINE FUNDS, 1232
MILESTONE PARTNERS, 1234
MOMENTUM FUNDS MANAGEMENT PTY LIMITED, 2966
MPE PARTNERS, 1266
MSOUTH EQUITY PARTNERS, 1270
NAUTIC PARTNERS, 1278
NAVIGATION CAPITAL PARTNERS, 1279
NBC CAPITAL PTY LIMITED, 2979
NEW BRUNSWICK INNOVATION FOUNDATION, 2192
NEW ENGLAND CAPITAL PARTNERS, 1295
NEW MEXICO COMMUNITY CAPITAL, 1299
NEWBURY, PIRET & COMPANY, 1311
NORTH AMERICAN FUND, 1333
NORTH DAKOTA DEVELOPMENT FUND, 1338
NORTHERN ENTERPRISE LIMITED, 3002
NORTHERN LIGHT VENTURE CAPITAL, 1340
NORTHSTAR CAPITAL, 1343
NORTHWOOD VENTURES, 1344
NORWEST EQUITY PARTNERS, 1345
NOVA SCOTIA BUSINESS INC., 2197
NUTEK (NARINGS- OCH TEKNIKUTVECKLINGSVERKET) NUTEK, 3007
ODEON CAPITAL PARTNERS, 1367
ONE EQUITY PARTNERS, 1376
PALLADIUM EQUITY PARTNERS, 1404
PAMLICO CAPITAL, 1410
PANTHEON VENTURES (US) LP, 1413
PARALLEL49 EQUITY, 2206
PARKVIEW CAPITAL PARTNERS, 2207
PARTHENON CAPITAL, 1419
PEACHTREE EQUITY PARTNERS, 1425
PEGASUS CAPITAL GROUP, 1427
PENN VENTURE PARTNERS, 1431
PFINGSTEN PARTNERS LLC, 1438
PNC ERIEVIEW CAPITAL, 1460
PNC RIVERARCH CAPITAL, 1461
POST CAPITAL PARTNERS, 1469
POUSCHINE COOK CAPITAL MANAGEMENT LLC, 1470
PRISM CAPITAL, 1481
PRITZKER GROUP PRIVATE CAPITAL, 1482
PROCURITAS PARTNERS KB, 3045
QUAD-C MANAGEMENT, 1507
QUAKE CAPITAL PARTNERS, 1509
QUANTUM CAPITAL PARTNERS, 1512
QUARRY CAPITAL MANAGEMENT, 1513
RAF INDUSTRIES, 1524
RAYMOND JAMES CAPITAL, 1529
RBC CAPITAL MARKETS, 2223
RED CLAY CAPITAL HOLDINGS, 1532
RESILIENCE CAPITAL PARTNERS, 1548
RFE INVESTMENT PARTNERS, 1560
RICHINA CAPITAL PARTNERS LIMITED, 3073
RISE OF THE REST, 1571
RIVER ASSOCIATES INVESTMENTS LLC, 1573
RIVER CAPITAL, 1574
RIVERSIDE COMPANY, 1576
ROBIN HOOD VENTURES, 1581
ROCK ISLAND CAPITAL, 1582
ROSER VENTURES LLC, 1590
ROTHSCHILD AUSTRALIA - ARROW PRIVATE EQUITY Rothschild Group, 3077
RPM VENTURES, 1596
SAIF PARTNERS, 3084
SALEM INVESTMENT PARTNERS, 1609
SAMBRINVEST SA, 3087
SATORI CAPITAL, 1625
SCOTIABANK PRIVATE EQUITY, 2241
SEACOAST CAPITAL CORPORATION, 1639
SEAFORT CAPITAL, 2242
SEAWAY VALLEY CAPITAL CORPORATION, 1642
SELBY VENTURE PARTNERS, 1649
SHAW KWEI AND PARTNERS, 3107
SONY INNOVATION FUND, 1705

Industry Preference Index / Marketplaces

SPELL CAPITAL PARTNERS LLC, 1722
SPLIT ROCK PARTNERS, 1728
STARBOARD CAPITAL PARTNERS, 1738
STERLING PARTNERS, 1745
STERN PARTNERS, 2249
STONEHENGE GROWTH CAPITAL, 1748
STONEWOOD CAPITAL MANAGEMENT, 1749
SUN CAPITAL PARTNERS, 1755
SUPPLY CHAIN VENTURES, 1759
TAT CAPITAL PARTNERS LTD., 3153
TENNESSEE COMMUNITY VENTURES, 1799
TGF MANAGEMENT, 1805
THREE CITIES RESEARCH, 1822
TOP RENERGY INC., 2263
TORQUEST PARTNERS, 2264
TPA CORPORATE FINANCE CONSULTING GMBH Horwarth International, 3175
TRANS COSMOS INCORPORATED, 3176
TRELLIS CAPITAL CORPORATION, 2265
TRIWEST, 2267
TSG EQUITY PARTNERS, 1864
UNION CAPITAL CORPORATION, 1883
UNISON CAPITAL PARTNERS LP, 3192
VALOR EQUITY PARTNERS, 1904
VANCE STREET CAPITAL, 1906
VEBER PARTNERS LLC, 1911
VELOCITY EQUITY PARTNERS LLC, 1915
VERITAS CAPITAL FUND LP, 1927
WALNUT GROUP, 1955
WARWICK GROUP, 1958
WATERMILL GROUP, 1963
WAUD CAPITAL PARTNERS LLC, 1964
WAVELAND INVESTMENTS LLC, 1965
WEDBUSH CAPITAL PARTNERS, 1970
WELLS FARGO CAPITAL FINANCE, 1971
WESTERN AMERICA CAPITAL GROUP, 2278
WESTLAKE SECURITIES, 1977
WESTVIEW CAPITAL PARTNERS, 1979
WINGATE PARTNERS, 1997
WOODBRIDGE GROUP, 2004
YELLOW POINT EQUITY PARTNERS, 2284
YORK STREET CAPITAL PARTNERS LLC, 2014
ZONE VENTURES, 2020

Manufacturing & Distribution
INNOVATION PLATFORM CAPITAL, 1002
PENDER WEST CAPITAL PARTNERS, 2210

MarTech
TACTICO, 2251

Marine
BRANFORD CASTLE, 330

Marine Services
GLOBAL MARITIME VENTURES BERHAD, 2777
PROSPECT PARTNERS LLC, 1494

Marine Transportation
COPPERLION CAPITAL, 2079

Maritime
CIT GROUP, 486

Maritime Industry
AZIONE CAPITAL, 2464

Market Research
NIELSEN INNOVATE FUND, 2994

Marketing
3TS CAPITAL PARTNERS 3i Group plc, 2301
ACCENTURE TECHNOLOGY VENTURES, 2318
ACTUA, 52
ALERION PARTNERS, 80
AMANET TECHNOLOGIES LIMITED, 2381
ANGELPAD, 129
BLUE CHIP VENTURE COMPANY, 290

BMP AKTIENGESELLSCHAFT BMP Venture Capital, 2519
BOSTON CAPITAL VENTURES, 313
BRENTWOOD ASSOCIATES, 337
BRILLIANT VENTURES, 345
BULL VENTURES, 2538
BUTLER CAPITAL PARTNERS FRANCE, 2542
CASTANEA PARTNERS, 424
CAVA CAPITAL, 433
CELERITY PARTNERS, 441
CINCO CAPITAL, 2595
CINCYTECH, 481
CITI VENTURES, 488
COVENT INDUSTRIAL CAPITAL INVESTMENT COMPANY, 2626
DACE VENTURES, 581
DUBILIER & COMPANY, 632
EDISON PARTNERS, 655
ENTREPRENEURS ROUNDTABLE ACCELERATOR, 685
EVERGREEN ADVISORS, 702
FOG CITY CAPITAL, 760
FOUNDERS EQUITY, 777
FRIEDMAN, FLEISCHER & LOWE LLC, 790
GGV CAPITAL, 827
GREYCROFT PARTNERS, 876
HALYARD CAPITAL, 902
HELLMAN & FRIEDMAN LLC, 927
HUDSON VENTURE PARTNERS, 957
INGENIOUS VENTURES, 2862
INSIGHT VENTURE PARTNERS, 1005
JEGI CAPITAL The Jordan Edminston Group, Inc., 1037
JUMP CAPITAL LLC, 1050
L CATTERTON PARTNERS, 1092
LAKE CAPITAL, 1095
LAUNCHPAD VENTURES, 2922
M25 GROUP, 1159
MHS CAPITAL, 1227
NCT VENTURES, 1285
NIELSEN INNOVATE FUND, 2994
NIPPON TECHNOLOGY VENTURE PARTNERS LIMITED, 2996
NORTH HILL VENTURES, 1339
PARKVIEW CAPITAL PARTNERS, 2207
PENN VENTURE PARTNERS, 1431
PROGRESS EQUITY PARTNERS, 1487
SAF GROUP, 2237
SCALE VENTURE PARTNERS, 1629
SHASTA VENTURES, 1666
STAGE 1 VENTURES, 1737
SUPPLY CHAIN VENTURES, 1759
TECHNOLOGY PARK MALAYSIA CORPORATION SDN BHD, 3155
TRANSMEDIA CAPITAL, 1841
UNION CAPITAL CORPORATION, 1883
UPFRONT VENTURES, 1890
VENISTA VENTURES, 3198
VERONIS SUHLER STEVENSON, 1929
YLR CAPITAL MARKETS LTD, 3237
ZM CAPITAL, 2019

Marketing Technology
BAIN CAPITAL VENTURES, 224
DETROIT VENTURE PARTNERS, 608
PANACHE VENTURES, 2204
PROGRESS VENTURES, 1488

Marketing/Sales Services
VRG CAPITAL, 2274

Marketplace
MISTRAL VENTURE PARTNERS, 2187
OYSTER VENTURES, 1396
RISE OF THE REST, 1571

Marketplace/On-Demand Services
CHICAGO VENTURES, 473

Marketplaces
BESSEMER VENTURE PARTNERS, 263
BOXGROUP, 321
CANVAS VENTURES, 399

Industry Preference Index / Material Handling

DECIENS CAPITAL, 600
GOOD NEWS VENTURES, 2132
JACKSON SQUARE VENTURES, 1028
ORIGIN VENTURES, 1385
REVOLUTION LLC, 1558
RUBICON VENTURE CAPITAL, 1599

Material Handling
ALANTRA, 77

Material Science
EMBARK VENTURES, 664
INDEPENDENCE EQUITY, 987

Materials
M25 GROUP, 1159

Materials Technology
ALBEMARLE PRIVATE EQUITY LIMITED, 2352
AMPLIFIER VENTURE PARTNERS, 120
ATHENAEUM FUND, 188
ATRIUM CAPITAL, 194
AUSTIN CAPITAL PARTNERS LP, 204
AVENUE CAPITAL GROUP, 211
AZINI CAPITAL PARTNERS, 2463
BATTERSON VENTURE CAPITAL LLC, 237
BEIJING VENTURE CAPITAL COMPANY LIMITED, 2491
BRIDGEPOINT CAPITAL GmbH, 2528
BRIDGEPOINT CAPITAL LIMITED, 2529
CANDOVER, 2547
CONVEXA Tyveholmen AS, 2623
ENTERPRISE EQUITY (NI) LTD, 2695
EQT PARTNERS AB, 2703
EQVITEC PARTNERS OY, 2707
FAIRHAVEN CAPITAL, 713
FIRELAKE CAPITAL, 731
GARAGE TECHNOLOGY VENTURES, 810
GENERICS GROUP LIMITED Generics Group, 2764
GUANGDONG TECHNOLOGY VENTURE CAPITAL COMPANY, 2793
HIGH-TECH GRUENDERFONDS, 2815
IDEA FUND PARTNERS, 975
INNOVACOM SA, 2866
LOMBARD INVESTMENTS, 1143
MASON WELLS, 1174
NEWMARGIN VENTURE CAPITAL, 2989
NORTH ATLANTIC CAPITAL CORPORATION, 1334
NORTHERN ENTERPRISE LIMITED, 3002
OKAPI VENTURE CAPITAL, 1371
RPM VENTURES, 1596
SEED CAPITAL LIMITED, 3098
SHAW KWEI AND PARTNERS, 3107
VIKING VENTURE, 3207
VINACAPITAL GROUP, 3208

Mechanical Products
CALIFORNIA COAST VENTURE FORUM, 3248

Media
360 CAPITAL PARTNERS 360 Capital Management SA, 2288
3TS CAPITAL PARTNERS 3i Group plc, 2301
3i GROUP PLC, 2303
ABRY PARTNERS, 20
ABS CAPITAL PARTNERS, 21
ACCEL, 27
ACI CAPITAL, 41
ACKERLEY PARTNERS LLC, 42
ACON INVESTMENTS, 45
ACTIVA CAPITAL, 2330
ADOBE VENTURES LP, 57
ADVANCIT CAPITAL, 59
AEP CAPITAL LLC, 64
ALBERTA ENTERPRISE, 2028
ALERION PARTNERS, 80
ALLIANCE VENTURE, 2361
ALVEN CAPITAL, 2377
AMERICAN SECURITIES LLC, 111
AMICUS CAPITAL PARTNERS, 2384
ANDERSON PACIFIC CORPORATION, 123

APOLLO GLOBAL MANAGEMENT, 141
ARCHTOP VENTURES, 155
ARKAFUND MEDIA & ICT, 2417
ARLINGTON CAPITAL PARTNERS, 167
AUA PRIVATE EQUITY PARTNERS, 196
AUDAX GROUP, 197
AURA CAPITAL OY Auratum Group, 2442
AVISTA CAPITAL PARTNERS, 212
AWAY REALTY, 2456
BALDERTON CAPITAL, 2469
BALLPARK VENTURES, 2470
BARCELONA EMPREN, 2474
BARCLAYS VENTURES Barclays, 2477
BARING PRIVATE EQUITY PARTNERS ESPANA SA, 2480
BARING PRIVATE EQUITY PARTNERS INDIA, 2481
BARING VOSTOK CAPITAL PARTNERS, 2482
BATTERY VENTURES, 238
BENCIS CAPITAL PARTNERS, 2492
BERINGEA, 254
BIA DIGITAL PARTNERS LP, 266
BLACKSTONE PRIVATE EQUITY GROUP, 280
BLADE VENTURES, 281
BLUE CHIP VENTURE COMPANY, 290
BLUE SAGE CAPITAL, 294
BLUERUN VENTURES, 299
BM-T BETEILIGUNGS MANAGEMENT THURINGEN GmbH, 2518
BOTTS & COMPANY LIMITED, 2523
BRAZOS PRIVATE EQUITY PARTNERS, 331
BREAKWATER MANAGEMENT, 334
BRIDGEPOINT CAPITAL GmbH, 2528
BRIDGEPOINT CAPITAL LIMITED, 2529
BRILLIANT VENTURES, 345
BRYAN GARNIER & COMPANY, 2535
BULL VENTURES, 2538
BULLNET, 2539
CANADIAN VENTURE CAPITAL ASSOCIATION Canadian Venture Capital & Private Equity Association, 3249
CANDOVER, 2547
CANYON CREEK CAPITAL, 400
CARLYLE ASIA INVESTMENT ADVISORS LIMITED Carlyle Group, 2556
CARMEL VENTURES, 2557
CATALYST GROUP, 427
CAZENOVE PRIVATE EQUITY Cazenove Capital, 2568
CEDRUS INVESTMENTS, 2572
CEI VENTURES, 440
CENTENNIAL VENTURES, 443
CENTRE PARTNERS MANAGEMENT LLC, 449
CHALLENGE FUNDS - ETGAR LP, 2576
CHARLESBANK CAPITAL PARTNERS, 458
CHASE CAPITAL PARTNERS, 2579
CHENGWEI VENTURES, 2581
CHEYENNE CAPITAL, 469
CHICAGO VENTURE PARTNERS LP, 472
CHINA VEST LIMITED, 2587
CHINAVEST, 475
CIC FINANCE CIC Group, 2592
CINCO CAPITAL, 2595
CITA GESTION, 2598
CIVC PARTNERS, 491
CLARITY PARTNERS, 496
CLEARLAKE CAPITAL, 502
CLIFFORD CHANCE PUNDER, 2605
COACH & CAPITAL, 2610
COLUMBIA CAPITAL, 518
COMCAST VENTURES, 520
COMPAGNIE FINANCIERE E DE ROTHSCHILD BANQUE, 2616
COMSTOCK CAPITAL PARTNERS LLC, 529
CONSTELLATION TECHNOLOGY VENTURES, 534
CORAL GROUP, 538
CORE PACIFIC - YAMAICHI CAPITAL LIMITED Core Pacific Securities Company Ltd, 2624
COURT SQUARE VENTURES, 552
CREATHOR VENTURE, 2629
CREDIT MUTUEL EQUITY, 2082
CRESTVIEW PARTNERS, 560
CYPRESS GROUP, 576

1180

Industry Preference Index / Media

DELTA PARTNERS Delta Partners FZ-LLC, 2645
DEUTSCHE BETEILIGUNGS AG, 2651
DOUBLE IMPACT BUSINESS ADVISORY, 2661
DOUBLE M PARTNERS, 625
DUBILIER & COMPANY, 632
DUNEDIN CAPITAL PARTNERS LIMITED, 2668
E.VENTURES, 641
EAST FUND MANAGEMENT GmbH GiroCredit, 2674
ECONA AG, 2679
ELECTRA PARTNERS ASIA LIMITED SFC of Hong Kong, 2685
ELEVATION PARTNERS, 660
EM WARBURG, PINCUS & COMPANY JAPAN, 2689
ENSPIRE CAPITAL PTE LTD, 2694
ENTREPRENEURS ROUNDTABLE ACCELERATOR, 685
EOS PARTNERS LP, 687
EUROVENTURES CAPITAL, 2716
EVERGREEN VENTURE PARTNERS, 2717
EXCELSIOR CAPITAL ASIA, 2718
FALCONHEAD CAPITAL, 717
FELICIS VENTURES, 720
FIDELITY GROWTH PARTNERS ASIA, 2724
FISHER LYNCH CAPITAL, 745
FOG CITY CAPITAL, 760
FORMULA VENTURES LIMITED Formula Group, 2741
FRIEDMAN, FLEISCHER & LOWE LLC, 790
GE CAPITAL, 811
GENERAL ENTERPRISE MANAGEMENT SERVICES, 2763
GENERATION PARTNERS, 822
GEODESIC CAPITAL, 824
GLADSTONE CAPITAL, 832
GLENCOE CAPITAL, 834
GLOBAL FINANCE, 2775
GLOBALIVE, 2128
GMT COMMUNICATIONS PARTNERS LLP, 2780
GOLDEN GATE CAPITAL, 843
GOLUB CAPITAL, 848
GRANDBANKS CAPITAL, 853
GRANITE EQUITY PARTNERS, 855
GREAT HILL PARTNERS LLC, 862
GREENHAVEN PARTNERS, 868
GREIF & COMPANY, 874
GTCR, 889
H KATZ CAPITAL GROUP, 896
HAMBRO CAPITAL MANAGEMENT LTD, 2799
HANNOVER FINANZ GmbH, 2801
HARBOURVEST PARTNERS LLC, 912
HAWTHORN EQUITY PARTNERS, 919
HEARST VENTURES, 925
HELION VENTURE PARTNERS, LLC International Management (Mauritius) Ltd, 2809
HELLMAN & FRIEDMAN LLC, 927
HG CAPITAL, 2814
HIG CAPITAL, 931
HIGH ROAD CAPITAL PARTNERS, 934
HOPEWELL VENTURES, 947
HOUSATONIC PARTNERS, 952
HUDSON VENTURE PARTNERS, 957
I-PACIFIC PARTNERS, 2831
ICF VENTURES PVT LTD, 2837
INDASIA FUND ADVISORS PVT LTD, 2850
INDIAN DIRECT EQUITY ADVISORS PVT LTD, 2852
INDUSTRI KAPITAL SVENSKA AB, 2854
INGENIOUS VENTURES, 2862
INLAND TECHSTART FUND, 997
INNOVATION CAPITAL LIMITED, 2868
INSIGHT VENTURE PARTNERS, 1005
INVENTUS, 1017
IRIS CAPITAL, 2888
ISIS EP LLP F & C, 2889
ITC VENTURES, 2894
JAGUAR CAPITAL PARTNERS, 1029
JEFFERIES CAPITAL PARTNERS, 1036
JEGI CAPITAL The Jordan Edminston Group, Inc., 1037
JERUSALEM VENTURE PARTNERS, 2901
KELSO & COMPANY, 1066
KENSINGTON CAPITAL PARTNERS, 2160
KERRY CAPITAL ADVISORS, 1071
KILMER CAPITAL PARTNERS, 2162
KLEINWORT CAPITAL LIMITED, 2914
KOHLBERG KRAVIS ROBERTS & COMPANY, 1086
L CATTERTON PARTNERS, 1092
LAUNCHPAD VENTURE GROUP, 1104
LEE EQUITY PARTNERS, 1108
LEONARD GREEN & PARTNERS LP, 1113
LIBERTY CITY VENTURES, 1119
LIGHTSPEED VENTURE PARTNERS, 1125
LOMBARD INVESTMENTS, 1143
LONG RIVER VENTURES, 1146
M/C PARTNERS, 1157
M25 GROUP, 1159
MADISON DEARBORN PARTNERS, 1160
MAGMA VENTURE PARTNERS, 2943
MAINE ANGELS, 1164
MAYFIELD FUND, 1187
MCG CAPITAL CORPORATION, 1192
MCGOVERN CAPITAL, 1194
MERRILL LYNCH (ASIA PACIFIC) LIMITED Merrill Lynch Group, 2955
MEZZANINE MANAGEMENT LIMITED Mezzanine Management UK Ltd., 2956
MURPHY & PARTNERS FUND LP, 1274
MVP CAPITAL PARTNERS, 1275
NAVIGATION CAPITAL PARTNERS, 1279
NESBIC INVESTMENT FUND II, 2983
NEW MOUNTAIN CAPITAL, 1300
NEW YORK ANGELS, 1305
NEWFIELD CAPITAL, 1312
NEXTEC DEVELOPMENT CAPITAL LIMITED, 2991
NEXUS VENTURE PARTNERS Nexus India Capital Advisors Pvt Ltd, 2992
NORTHERN LIGHT VENTURE CAPITAL, 1340
NORTHZONE, 3004
OAK HILL CAPITAL PARTNERS, 1360
ONE EQUITY PARTNERS, 1376
ONTARIO CAPITAL GROWTH CORPORATION, 2203
PAI MANAGEMENT, 3017
PALISADES VENTURES, 1403
PALLADIUM EQUITY PARTNERS, 1404
PAMLICO CAPITAL, 1410
PARTNERSHIP FUND FOR NEW YORK CITY, 1422
PEACHTREE EQUITY PARTNERS, 1425
PENN VENTURE PARTNERS, 1431
PHOENIX EQUITY PARTNERS LIMITED, 3027
PINEHURST ADVISORS, 3029
POMONA CAPITAL, 1466
POST CAPITAL PARTNERS, 1469
POUSCHINE COOK CAPITAL MANAGEMENT LLC, 1470
PRESIDIO VENTURES, 1478
PROVENANCE VENTURES, 1497
PROVIDENCE EQUITY PARTNERS, 1498
QUADRANGLE GROUP, 1508
QUESTER CAPITAL MANAGEMENT LIMITED, 3061
RAPTOR GROUP, 1527
REED ELSEVIER VENTURES, 3065
ROTH CAPITAL PARTNERS, 1592
RRE VENTURES, 1597
SABAN CAPITAL GROUP, 1602
SAFFRON HILL VENTURES, 3083
SALEM INVESTMENT PARTNERS, 1609
SANDLER CAPITAL MANAGEMENT, 1620
SCALE VENTURE PARTNERS, 1629
SCOUT VENTURES, 1635
SCP PARTNERS, 1636
SEAPORT CAPITAL, 1641
SECOND ALPHA, 1643
SEVIN ROSEN FUNDS, 1661
SHAMROCK CAPITAL ADVISORS, 1663
SIGNAL EQUITY PARTNERS, 1676
SOFTBANK CAPITAL, 1701
SOUTHEAST INTERACTIVE TECHNOLOGY FUNDS, 1711
SPECTRUM EQUITY INVESTORS LP, 1720
SPENCER TRASK VENTURES, 1723
SPIRE CAPITAL PARTNERS, 1727
STAGEONE VENTURES, 3127
STONEWOOD CAPITAL MANAGEMENT, 1749

Industry Preference Index / Media & Entertainment

SUMMIT PARTNERS, 1754
SUN CAPITAL PARTNERS, 1755
SUPPLY CHAIN VENTURES, 1759
SYCAMORE VENTURES, 1771
TAO VENTURE CAPITAL PARTNERS, 1782
TDF, 1784
TECH COAST ANGELS, 1786
TELECOM VENTURE GROUP LIMITED, 3159
TELESYSTEM, 2255
THAYER STREET PARTNERS, 1807
THIRD WAVE DIGITAL, 1816
THOMAS H LEE PARTNERS, 1818
THRIVE CAPITAL, 1823
TIGER GLOBAL MANAGEMENT, 1828
TLCOM CAPITAL, 3170
TMG CAPITAL PARTNERS, 3171
TORNANTE COMPANY, 1835
TRUE VENTURES, 1862
UNISON CAPITAL PARTNERS LP, 3192
UNITED TALENT AGENCY VENTURES, 1885
USHA MARTIN VENTURES LIMITED, 3193
VENCORE CAPITAL, 1917
VENROCK ASSOCIATES, 1918
VERIZON VENTURES, 1928
VERONIS SUHLER STEVENSON, 1929
VESTAR CAPITAL PARTNERS, 1933
VICKERS FINANCIAL GROUP, 3206
VINACAPITAL GROUP, 3208
W CAPITAL PARTNERS, 1949
WALNUT GROUP, 1955
WARBURG PINCUS LLC, 1957
WASABI VENTURES, 1959
WASSERSTEIN & CO., 1961
WESTVIEW CAPITAL PARTNERS, 1979
WICKS GROUP OF COMPANIES, LLC, 1984
WINDSPEED VENTURES, 1994
ZELKOVA VENTURES, 2016
ZM CAPITAL, 2019
ZONE VENTURES, 2020

Media & Entertainment
CLARION CAPITAL PARTNERS LLC, 494
KRG CAPITAL PARTNERS, 1090
SILKROAD EQUITY, 1683

Media & Telecommunications
ACCESS BRIDGE-GAP VENTURES, 33
BRANFORD CASTLE, 330
MIDOCEAN PARTNERS, 1231
TPG CAPITAL, 1837

Media Distribution
BLOOMBERG BETA, 287

Media Technology
PROGRESS VENTURES, 1488
RIPPLE VENTURES, 2232
RUBICON VENTURE CAPITAL, 1599
WESTTECH VENTURES, 3226

Medical
ABINGWORTH MANAGEMENT LIMITED, 2308
ALICE VENTURES SRL, 2356
ALTA PARTNERS, 94
AMPERSAND CAPITAL PARTNERS, 119
AMWIN MANAGEMENT PTY LIMITED, 2390
ANTHEM VENTURE PARTNERS, 133
APJOHN GROUP LLC, 140
CAPRICORN VENTURE PARTNERS NV, 2554
COMPAGNIE FINANCIERE E DE ROTHSCHILD BANQUE, 2616
CONCORD VENTURES, 2619
CORAL GROUP, 538
DEFTA PARTNERS, 603
GEMINI ISRAEL VENTURE FUNDS LIMITED, 2761
GENERICS GROUP LIMITED Generics Group, 2764
GLENTHORNE CAPITAL, 836
GUANGDONG TECHNOLOGY VENTURE CAPITAL COMPANY, 2793
HOLLAND VENTURE BV, 2819
INDUSTRIFONDEN, 2858
INNOFINANCE OY, 2864
JAFCO COMPANY LIMITED JAPAN, 2897
JAPAN ASIA INVESTMENT COMPANY LIMITED, 2898
JC TECHNOLOGIES LTD, 2900
MACQUARIE DIRECT INVESTMENT LIMITED, 2942
MANHATTAN INVESTMENT PARTNERS, 1166
MERRILL LYNCH (ASIA PACIFIC) LIMITED Merrill Lynch Group, 2955
PLEXUS VENTURES, 1456
PRIVATE EQUITY PARTNERS SPA, 3044
SAMSUNG VENTURE INVESTMENT CORPORATION Samsung Electronics, 3089
SKYLINE VENTURES, 1693
SVB CAPITAL, 1766
TAT CAPITAL PARTNERS LTD., 3153
TRANSATLANTIC CAPITAL LTD, 3177
WAVEPOINT VENTURES, 1967

Medical & Health Related
ACCESS CAPITAL, 34
ALBEMARLE PRIVATE EQUITY LIMITED, 2352
AMADEUS CAPITAL PARTNERS LIMITED, 2378
ARBORETUM VENTURES, 150
ARTHUR P GOULD & COMPANY, 174
ASCENSION HEALTH VENTURES LLC, 178
AURIGA PARTNERS, 2444
BARING PRIVATE EQUITY PARTNERS ESPANA SA, 2480
BARING PRIVATE EQUITY PARTNERS INDIA, 2481
BATTERSON VENTURE CAPITAL LLC, 237
BEECKEN PETTY O'KEEFE & COMPANY, 247
BERKELEY VC INTERNATIONAL LLC, 255
BIO FUND MANAGEMENT OY, 2503
CIC FINANCE CIC Group, 2592
CID CAPITAL, 480
CONCORD VENTURES, 2619
CONTINENTAL VENTURE CAPITAL LIMITED, 2622
DE NOVO VENTURES, 599
DELPHI VENTURES, 605
DRESNER COMPANIES, 630
ENTERPRISE EQUITY (NI) LTD, 2695
EQUUS TOTAL RETURN, 695
FERRER FREEMAN & COMPANY LLC, 723
GEFINOR CAPITAL, 813
GIMV GIMV, 2771
GLYNN CAPITAL MANAGEMENT, 840
GUIDANT EUROPE SA, 2794
HUMANA VENTURES, 958
INDUSTRIEBANK LIOF NV, 2857
INNOVATION CAPITAL LIMITED, 2868
INVESTMENT AB BURE, 2879
IPG GROUP, 2885
KBL FOUNDER SA, 2908
KLEINER PERKINS, 1079
KNIGHTSBRIDGE ADVISERS, 1081
LEGAL AND GENERAL VENTURES LIMITED, 2926
LIFE SCIENCES PARTNERS BV, 2930
LM CAPITAL SECURITIES, 1141
MASSACHUSETTS CAPITAL RESOURCE COMPANY, 1176
MASSACHUSETTS GROWTH CAPITAL CORPORATION, 1177
MAYFIELD FUND, 1187
NEW YORK LIFE CAPITAL PARTNERS, 1308
NORTHERN ENTERPRISE LIMITED, 3002
ONO PHARMACEUTICALS COMPANY LIMITED, 3012
PAMLICO CAPITAL, 1410
PARTECH INTERNATIONAL, 1418
PERMAL CAPITAL MANAGEMENT, 1435
PIDC PHILADELPHIA, 1445
PITANGO VENTURE CAPITAL, 3030
POMONA CAPITAL, 1466
PROVCO GROUP, 1496
RAF INDUSTRIES, 1524
REITEN & CO STRATEGIC INVESTMENTS AS Reiten & Company, 3067
ROYALTY CAPITAL MANAGEMENT, 1595
SANDERLING VENTURES, 1619
SEACOAST CAPITAL CORPORATION, 1639

1182

Industry Preference Index / Medical Devices

SEED CAPITAL LIMITED, 3098
SHANNON COMMERCIAL PROPERTIES, 3106
SHAW KWEI AND PARTNERS, 3107
SIEMENS VENTURE CAPITAL, 3109
SKYLINE VENTURES, 1693
SOURCE CAPITAL GROUP, 1710
SOUTHPORT PARTNERS, 1714
SR ONE LTD, 1734
SUTTER HILL VENTURES, 1762
TEKNOINVEST MANAGEMENT, 3158
THROUNARFELAG ISLANDS PLC, 3168
TRANSITION PARTNERS LTD, 1839
TULLY & HOLLAND, 1869
VAEKSTFONDEN, 3194
VALLEY VENTURES LP, 1903
VENTANA CAPITAL MANAGEMENT LP, 1920
VENTURE INVESTORS, 3201
VERITAS VENTURE PARTNERS, 3203
WASSERSTEIN & CO., 1961
WATERLAND PRIVATE EQUITY INVESTMENT, 3222
WESTERN STATES INVESTMENT GROUP, 1975
WESTERN TECHNOLOGY INVESTMENT, 1976
WOODSIDE FUND, 2005
ZERNIKE SEED FUND BV, 3240
ZS FUND LP, 2021

Medical Devices
AAVIN PRIVATE EQUITY, 16
ABELL FOUNDATION VENTURES, 18
ABERDARE VENTURES, 19
ACCELMED, 2316
ACCESS MEDICAL VENTURES, 2320
ACCUITIVE MEDICAL VENTURES LLC, 39
ACONCAGUA VENTURES, 2326
ADAMS STREET PARTNERS, LLC, 56
ADVENT VENTURE PARTNERS, 2340
AESCAP VENTURE, 2342
AFFINITY CAPITAL MANAGEMENT, 67
AGATE MEDICAL INVESTMENTS, 2345
ALBERTA ENTERPRISE, 2028
ALEUTIAN CAPITAL PARTNERS, 81
ALFA CAPITAL Alfa Group, 2355
ALLOS VENTURES, 86
ALTARIS CAPITAL PARTNERS, 97
AMHERST FUND, 114
AMKEY VENTURES, 118
AMPERSAND CAPITAL PARTNERS, 119
ANDLINGER & COMPANY INC, 124
ANGELS' FORUM LLC, 130
ANNEX VENTURES, 131
APERTURE VENTURE PARTNERS, 137
APJOHN GROUP LLC, 140
ARBORETUM VENTURES, 150
ARCH VENTURE PARTNERS, 154
ASCENSION HEALTH VENTURES LLC, 178
ASCENT BIOMEDICAL VENTURES, 179
ATHYRIUM CAPITAL MANAGEMENT, 190
ATLAS VENTURE: FRANCE, 2436
AUGURY CAPITAL PARTNERS, 199
AUSTIN CAPITAL PARTNERS LP, 204
AVIV VENTURE CAPITAL, 2453
AVLAR BIOVENTURES, 2454
AZCA, 217
BAY CITY CAPITAL LLC, 240
BB BIOTECH VENTURES, 2487
BCM TECHNOLOGIES, 244
BEECKEN PETTY O'KEEFE & COMPANY, 247
BIOADVANCE, 269
BIOGENERATION VENTURES, 2505
BIOGENERATOR, 270
BIOSTAR VENTURES, 272
BIOVENTURES INVESTORS, 273
BIRCHMERE VENTURES, 275
BLACK DIAMOND VENTURES, 278
BLADE VENTURES, 281
BRANDON CAPITAL PARTNERS, 2527
BREAKWATER INVESTMENTS, 333
BRIDGE INVESTMENT FUND, 340
BRIGHTSTONE VENTURE CAPITAL, 344
BROADVIEW VENTURES, 350
BROOK VENTURE FUND, 352
CALIFORNIA TECHNOLOGY VENTURES, 374
CAPITAL FOR BUSINESS, INC, 402
CARDINAL PARTNERS, 413
CATALYST FUND LP, 2562
CATALYST HEALTH VENTURES, 428
CEDAR VENTURES LLC, 439
CENTRESTONE VENTURES, 2071
CHALLENGE FUNDS - ETGAR LP, 2576
CHINA DEVELOPMENT INDUSTRIAL BANK CDFH, 2583
CHL MEDICAL PARTNERS, 476
CIBC CAPITAL MARKETS, 2073
CID CAPITAL, 480
CITARETX INVESTMENT PARTNERS, 487
CLARENDON FUND MANAGERS, 2601
COMPASS TECHNOLOGY PARTNERS LP, 526
CONNECTICUT INNOVATIONS, 532
CUTLASS CAPITAL LLC, 573
DE NOVO VENTURES, 599
DEFTA PARTNERS, 603
DELPHI VENTURES, 605
DELTA VENTURES LIMITED, 2646
DOMAIN ASSOCIATES LLC, 622
EASTON CAPITAL INVESTMENT GROUP, 644
ECHELON VENTURES, 647
EDBI Pte LTD., 2681
EGL HOLDINGS, 656
ELM STREET VENTURES, 661
EMERGENT MEDICAL PARTNERS, 667
ENTREE CAPITAL, 2700
ESCALATE CAPITAL PARTNERS, 696
ESSEX WOODLANDS HEALTH VENTURES LLC, 698
EVENTI CAPITAL PARTNERS, 2104
EVERGREEN ADVISORS, 702
EXCEL VENTURE MANAGEMENT, 704
F-PRIME CAPITAL PARTNERS, 711
FCF PARTNERS LP, 719
FIRST ANALYSIS, 733
FLARE CAPITAL PARTNERS, 749
FLETCHER SPAGHT VENTURES, 750
FORBION CAPITAL PARTNERS, 2739
FORESITE CAPITAL, 764
FORWARD VENTURES, 772
FRAZIER HEALTHCARE VENTURES, 785
FUNK VENTURES, 800
GALEN PARTNERS, 809
GRANTHAM CAPITAL, 858
GREAT POINT PARTNERS, 864
GREENHILLS VENTURES, LLC, 870
GUIDE MEDICAL VENTURES, 891
HAMMOND, KENNEDY, WHITNEY & COMPANY, 904
HATTERAS VENTURE PARTNERS, 918
HBM PARTNERS, 2806
HEALTHQUEST CAPITAL, 924
HIGH COUNTRY VENTURE, 933
HLM VENTURE PARTNERS, 941
HOPEN LIFE SCIENCE VENTURES, 946
HOPEWELL VENTURES, 947
ID VENTURES AMERICA LLC, 974
IDEA FUND PARTNERS, 975
IDG VENTURES INDIA International Financial Services Limited, 2840
INCUBE VENTURES, 984
INDUSTRIO VENTURES, 2859
INETWORKS ADVISORS LLC, 991
INLAND TECHSTART FUND, 997
INNOVA MEMPHIS, 999
INNOVATION WORKS, 1003
INTEGRA VENTURES, 1007
INVUS GROUP, 1022
IP GROUP, 2883
JAPAN ASIA INVESTMENT COMPANY LIMITED, 2898
JF SHEA VENTURES, 1040
JMH CAPITAL, 1044
JOHNSON & JOHNSON INNOVATION, 1047

1183

Industry Preference Index / Medical Devices & Implants

KAISER PERMANENTE VENTURES, 1056
KALORI GROUP INVESTMENTS, 2906
KB PARTNERS LLC, 1061
KBL HEALTHCARE VENTURES, 1062
KEARNY VENTURE PARTNERS, 1063
KEGONSA CAPITAL PARTNERS, 1064
LANCET CAPITAL, 1096
LATTERELL VENTURE PARTNERS, 1098
LAUNCHPAD VENTURE GROUP, 1104
LFE CAPITAL, 1117
LIGHTSTONE VENTURES, 1126
LONG RIVER VENTURES, 1146
LONGITUDE CAPITAL, 1147
LOVETT MILLER & COMPANY, 1152
MARATHON VENTURE CAPITAL FUND LIMITED, 2945
MARYLAND VENTURE FUND, 1172
MASS VENTURES, 1175
MB VENTURE PARTNERS, 1190
MBF CAPITAL CORPORATION, 1191
MERITECH CAPITAL PARTNERS, 1213
MESA VERDE PARTNERS, 1222
MONTREUX EQUITY PARTNERS, 1251
MORGENTHALER VENTURES, 1257
MOUNTAIN GROUP CAPITAL, 1261
MOUNTAINEER CAPITAL, 1262
MPM CAPITAL, 1268
MTS HEALTH INVESTORS, 1271
MURPHREE VENTURE PARTNERS, 1273
MVM LIFE SCIENCE PARTNERS, 2972
NDI MEDICAL, 1286
NEEDHAM CAPITAL PARTNERS, 1287
NEW LEAF VENTURE PARTNERS, 1297
NEW SCIENCE VENTURES, 1302
NEWSPRING CAPITAL, 1316
NGN CAPITAL, 1325
NHN INVESTMENT, 2993
NOMURA PHASE4 VENTURES LTD, 2998
NORWICH VENTURES, 1347
NOVO A/S, 3006
OKAPI VENTURE CAPITAL, 1371
OMEGA FUNDS, 1373
ONSET VENTURES, 1379
ORBIMED HEALTHCARE FUND MANAGEMENT, 1383
ORIGINATE VENTURES, 1386
OXFORD BIOSCIENCE PARTNERS, 1395
PAPPAS VENTURES, 1414
PARTISAN MANAGEMENT GROUP, 1420
PARTNERS HEALTHCARE RESEARCH VENTURES, 1421
PELION VENTURE PARTNERS, 1428
PITTSBURGH LIFE SCIENCES GREENHOUSE, 1452
PREVIZ VENTURES, 3041
PROSPECT VENTURE PARTNERS, 1495
PTV SCIENCES, 1502
PURETECH VENTURES, 1503
QUAKER BIOVENTURES, 1510
QUESTMARK PARTNERS LP, 1517
RA CAPITAL MANAGEMENT, 1522
RAFAEL DEVELOPMENT CORPORATION (RDC) LIMITED, 3063
RESEARCH CORPORATION TECHNOLOGIES, 1546
REX HEALTH VENTURES, 1559
RHO VENTURES, 1561
ROBIN HOOD VENTURES, 1581
ROUNDTABLE HEALTHCARE PARTNERS, 1594
SAND HILL ANGELS, 1616
SBRC INVESTMENT CONSULTATION LIMITED, 3092
SCALE VENTURE PARTNERS, 1629
SCHRODER VENTURES HEALTH INVESTORS, 1631
SCP PARTNERS, 1636
SENECA PARTNERS, 1652
SHEPHERD VENTURES, 1667
SHERBROOKE CAPITAL, 1668
SIGHTLINE PARTNERS, 1673
SIGNAL PEAK VENTURES, 1679
SKYLINE VENTURES, 1693
SORRENTO VENTURES, 1708
SPINDLETOP CAPITAL, 1725
SPLIT ROCK PARTNERS, 1728
STATELINE ANGELS, 1743
SV HEALTH INVESTORS, 1764
SYNERGY LIFE SCIENCE PARTNERS, 1774
SYNERGY VENTURES, 1775
SYNTHESIS CAPITAL, 1777
TELEGRAPH HILL PARTNERS, 1794
TEXO VENTURES, 1803
THE CHANNEL GROUP, 1811
THIRD ROCK VENTURES, 1814
THOMAS, MCNERNEY & PARTNERS, 1820
TI VENTURE CAPITAL Texas Instruments Incorporated, 1825
TIE ANGELS GROUP SEATTLE, 1827
TREVI HEALTH CAPITAL, 1846
TRIANGLE VENTURE CAPITAL GROUP, 3179
TRIATHLON MEDICAL VENTURES, 1849
TULLIS HEALTH INVESTORS, 1868
TWIN CITIES ANGELS, 1874
US VENTURE PARTNERS, 1898
VEDANTA CAPITAL LP, 1913
VENROCK ASSOCIATES, 1918
VERSANT VENTURES, 1930
VERTICAL GROUP, 1931
WESTERN TECHNOLOGY INVESTMENT, 1976
WHEATLEY PARTNERS, 1981
WILMINGTON INVESTOR NETWORK, 1987
WINDWARD VENTURES, 1995
XENIA VENTURE CAPITAL, 3230
YASUDA ENTERPRISE DEVELOPMENT COMPANY, 3233
ZURMONT MADISON PRIVATE EQUITY, 3244

Medical Devices & Implants
NOVARTIS VENTURE FUNDS, 1350

Medical Devices and Equipment
PRAIRIEGOLD VENTURE PARTNERS, 1474

Medical Equipment
SECTION 32, 1646

Medical Imaging
LDV CAPITAL, 1105

Medical Products
ROUNDTABLE HEALTHCARE PARTNERS, 1594
SEIDLER EQUITY PARTNERS, 1648
VANCE STREET CAPITAL, 1906

Medical Products & Services
CENTURY PARK CAPITAL PARTNERS, 451
NORTH AMERICAN FUND, 1333
WATER STREET HEALTHCARE PARTNERS, 1962

Medical Research
SECTION 32, 1646

Medical Supply
HOUSTON HEALTH VENTURES, 954

Medical Technology
10X VENTURE PARTNERS, 2
360 CAPITAL PARTNERS 360 Capital Management SA, 2288
ABS VENTURES, 22
ACCUITIVE MEDICAL VENTURES LLC, 39
AGATE MEDICAL INVESTMENTS, 2345
BANEXI VENTURES PARTNERS, 2472
BIOMED PARTNERS, 2506
BIOSTAR VENTURES, 272
BLUETREE VENTURE FUND, 301
CASABONA VENTURES, 421
CHORD CAPITAL, 2589
DFJ ESPRIT, 2653
DVC DEUTSCHE VENTURE CAPITAL, 2670
EARLYBIRD, 2673
EPLANET CAPITAL, 691
ESSEX WOODLANDS HEALTH VENTURES LLC, 698
F-PRIME CAPITAL PARTNERS, 711
GLOBAL LIFE SCIENCE VENTURES GmbH, 2776
GREY SKY VENTURE PARTNERS, 875

Industry Preference Index / Mobile

HEALTHCAP, 2807
HEALTHCAP Odlander, Fredrikson & Co AB, 2807
HLM VENTURE PARTNERS, 941
INTERSOUTH PARTNERS, 1013
KALORI GROUP INVESTMENTS, 2906
MEDICAL RESEARCH COMMERCIALIZATION FUND, 2950
MPM CAPITAL, 1268
NAUSICAA VENTURES, 2977
NEMO CAPITAL PARTNERS, 1288
NEWABLE VENTURES, 2988
ONSET VENTURES, 1379
PARKWALK ADVISORS, 3019
PSILOS GROUP, 1500
RED DOT VENTURES, 3064
REV1 VENTURES, 1556
SAMOS INVESTMENTS, 3088
SANTE VENTURES, 1622
SIGHTLINE PARTNERS, 1673
STAENBERG VENTURE PARTNERS, 1736
SUMMIT BRIDGE CAPITAL, 3138
SYNTHESIS CAPITAL, 1777
TRIVENTURES, 3183
TWIN CITIES ANGELS, 1874
VENBIO, 1916
WELLINGTON PARTNERS VENTURE CAPITAL GmbH, 3223
WHITECAP VENTURE PARTNERS, 2280
WINDHAM VENTURE PARTNERS, 1993

Medicine
ANALYTICS VENTURES, 122
EMERGENT MEDICAL PARTNERS, 667

Merchant Banking
ROTHSCHILD AUSTRALIA - ARROW PRIVATE EQUITY Rothschild Group, 3077

Metals
ABOA VENTURE MANAGEMENT OY, 2310
BRUML CAPITAL CORPORATION, 358
FIRST ISRAEL MEZZANINE INVESTORS LIMITED, 2736
HELMET CAPITAL FUND MANAGEMENT OY, 2811
IBM VENTURE CAPITAL GROUP, 971
JB POINDEXTER & COMPANY, 1034
JORDAN COMPANY, 1049
KUBOTA CORPORATION, 2918
MERITURN PARTNERS, 1214
RESILIENCE CAPITAL PARTNERS, 1548
RESOURCE CAPITAL FUNDS, 1551
SAMBRINVEST SA, 3087
SPELL CAPITAL PARTNERS LLC, 1722
SRIW SA SRIW Group, 3125
WATERMILL GROUP, 1963
WATERTON GLOBAL RESOURCE MANAGEMENT, 2275

Metals & Mining
CHRYSALIX, 2072
SAF GROUP, 2237

Microcontrollers
QUANTUM WAVE FUND, 3059

Microelectronics
180 DEGREE CAPITAL, 5
CORE CAPITAL PARTNERS, 540
EUROFUND LP, 2711
JC TECHNOLOGIES LTD, 2900
MMT MILLENNIUM MATERIALS TECHNOLOGIES FUND LP, 2964
POLYTECHNOS VENTURE PARTNERS GmbH, 3037
TRIGINITA CAPITAL, 3181
VALLEY VENTURES LP, 1903

Microfinance
ALPHAMUNDI GROUP LTD, 2368
GRAY GHOST VENTURES, 860

Microprocessors
QUANTUM WAVE FUND, 3059

Microsystems
NEUHAUS PARTNERS, 2985

Midstream
BREGAL ENERGY, 335

Midstream Growth
HADDINGTON VENTURES LLC, 898

Midstream Oil & Gas
ENERGY CAPITAL PARTNERS, 676

Military
ALTUS CAPITAL PARTNERS, 104
CELERITY PARTNERS, 441
QUANTUM WAVE FUND, 3059

Minerals
CLARITY CAPITAL, 2602
RESOURCE CAPITAL FUNDS, 1551

Mining
CIBC CAPITAL MARKETS, 2073
COPPERLION CAPITAL, 2079
GE CAPITAL, 811
INTERNATIONAL FINANCE CORPORATION (IFC), 1012
LIME ROCK PARTNERS, 1129
LION SELECTION GROUP LIMITED, 2933
LIONHART CAPITAL LTD, 2170
MERITURN PARTNERS, 1214
PALMS & COMPANY, 1405
RESOURCE CAPITAL FUNDS, 1551
RFC AMBRIAN RFC Group Ltd., 3070
SOUTHERN CROSS VENTURE PARTNERS, 1713
WATERTON GLOBAL RESOURCE MANAGEMENT, 2275

Mobile
10X VENTURE PARTNERS, 2
42 VENTURES, 8
ACCEL, 27
ACUMEN VENTURES, 2333
ALBUM VC, 79
ALLIANCE VENTURE, 2361
ALPHA VENTURE PARTNERS, 91
ALTOS VENTURES, 100
AMHERST FUND, 114
ANGELPAD, 129
ANNAPURNA VENTURES, 2395
ANTRAK CAPITAL, 2399
ARC ANGEL FUND, 151
ARCHTOP VENTURES, 155
ASLANOBA CAPITAL, 2428
ASPECT VENTURES, 182
AZURE CAPITAL PARTNERS, 218
B-TO-V PARTNERS, 2466
BAF SPECTRUM, 2468
BALLPARK VENTURES, 2470
BARODA VENTURES, 231
BENCHMARK, 251
BERKELEY VENTURES, 256
BESSEMER VENTURE PARTNERS, 263
BIRCHMERE VENTURES, 275
BLACKBIRD VENTURES, 2511
BLUMBERG CAPITAL, 304
BRIGHTSPARK VENTURES, 2060
BRIGHTSTONE VENTURE CAPITAL, 344
CARMEL VENTURES, 2557
CATAGONIA CAPITAL, 2560
CATALYST INVESTORS, 429
CAVA CAPITAL, 433
CENTRAL TEXAS ANGEL NETWORK, 447
CLEARSTONE VENTURE PARTNERS, 504
COLOMA VENTURES, 515
CONNECT VENTURES, 2620
CONVERGE VENTURE PARTNERS, 536
CORSA VENTURES, 546
DATA POINT CAPITAL, 587

Industry Preference Index / Mobile & Internet

DCM, 597
DFJ ESPRIT, 2653
DFJ GOTHAM VENTURES, 609
DN CAPITAL, 2659
DOUBLEROCK VENTURE CAPITAL, 626
E.BRICKS DIGITAL, 2672
EASTLABS, 2675
EC1 CAPITAL LTD, 2676
EDEN VENTURES, 2682
ENIAC VENTURES, 680
ESCALATE CAPITAL PARTNERS, 696
EXTREME VENTURE PARTNERS, 2107
FAIRHAVEN CAPITAL, 713
FELICIS VENTURES, 720
FINAVENTURES, 730
FIRST ASCENT VENTURES, 2112
FIRSTMARK CAPITAL, 744
FOUNDER COLLECTIVE, 774
FOUNDER PARTNERS, 775
FOUNDER'S CO-OP, 776
GABRIEL VENTURE PARTNERS, 808
GENACAST VENTURES, 818
GGV CAPITAL, 827
GOLDEN VENTURE PARTNERS, 2130
GOOD NEWS VENTURES, 2132
GRAYHAWK CAPITAL, 861
GREAT OAKS VENTURE CAPITAL, 863
GREE VENTURES, 2789
HELION VENTURE PARTNERS, LLC International Management (Mauritius) Ltd, 2809
HENQ, 2813
HORIZONS VENTURES, 2822
HOXTON VENTURES, 2825
ICON VENTURES, 972
IDG VENTURES INDIA International Financial Services Limited, 2840
IMI.VC, 2847
INFINITY VENTURE PARTNERS, 2860
INLAND TECHSTART FUND, 997
INNOVATION WORKS, 1003
INSTITUTIONAL VENTURE PARTNERS, 1006
INVENTURE PARTNERS, 2877
INVENTUS, 1017
IRISH ANGELS, 1023
KIZOO TECHNOLOGY CAPITAL, 2912
LANTA DIGITAL VENTURES, 2921
LAUNCHCAPITAL, 1101
LAUNCHPAD VENTURE GROUP, 1104
LIONBIRD, 2934
MASS VENTURES, 1175
MERCURY FUND, 1207
MHS CAPITAL, 1227
MOBILITY VENTURES, 1244
MORADO VENTURE PARTNERS, 1254
NARANYA VENTURES, 2975
NAUTA CAPITAL, 2978
NAYA VENTURES, 1284
NEW ATLANTIC VENTURES, 1290
NEXIT VENTURES OY, 2990
NEXIT VENTURES OY Nexit Ventures Inc., 2990
NEXT WORLD CAPITAL, 1319
NEXTGEN ANGELS, 1320
NHN INVESTMENT, 2993
NIELSEN INNOVATE FUND, 2994
O'REILLY ALPHATECH VENTURES, 1359
OMIDYAR NETWORK, 1374
OYSTER INVEST, 3013
PALO ALTO VENTURE SCIENCE, 1407
PENTECH VENTURES, 3023
PINEHURST ADVISORS, 3029
PLUS VENTURES, 3032
POINT NINE CAPITAL, 3035
PREVIZ VENTURES, 3041
PRIME TECHNOLOGY VENTURES NV, 3042
PRINCIPIA SGR, 3043
PROGRESS VENTURES, 1488
PROJECT A VENTURE GmBH & CO. KG, 3047
QUALCOMM VENTURES, 1511
QUOTIDIAN VENTURES, 1521
REAL VENTURES, 2224
REED ELSEVIER VENTURES, 3065
RELAY VENTURES, 2228
RRE VENTURES, 1597
RUNA CAPITAL, 3079
SAIF PARTNERS, 3084
SCOUT VENTURES, 1635
SCRUM VENTURES, 1637
SEQUOIA CAPITAL, 1657
SERAPH GROUP, 1658
SIERRA ANGELS, 1671
SIGMA PRIME VENTURES, 1675
SILICON ALLEY VENTURE PARTNERS, 1682
SILVERTON PARTNERS, 1687
SK TELECOM VENTURES, 1692
SOFTBANK VENTURES KOREA, 3118
SOFTTECH VC, 1702
SOUTHERN CAPITOL VENTURES, 1712
SPARK CAPITAL, 1718
SPINUP VENTURE, 3123
SPRING LAKE EQUITY PARTNERS, 1731
SRIJAN CAPITAL, 3124
STAGE 1 VENTURES, 1737
TANK STREAM VENTURES, 3151
TARGET PARTNERS, 3152
THIRD WAVE DIGITAL, 1816
TIE ANGELS GROUP SEATTLE, 1827
TMI, 3172
TRIBECA VENTURE PARTNERS, 1851
VERDEXUS, 2271
VERSION ONE VENTURES, 2272
VINE ST VENTURES, 1936
VITULUM VENTURES, 3215
WASABI VENTURES, 1959
WESLEY CLOVER, 2276
WESTSUMMIT CAPITAL, 3225
WHITE STAR CAPITAL, 1982
WOMEN'S VENTURE CAPITAL FUND, 2003
XANGE PRIVATE EQUITY, 3229
XG VENTURES, 2009

Mobile & Internet
BURAN VENTURE CAPITAL, 2540
MENLO VENTURES, 1203

Mobile & Tablet
500 STARTUPS, 10

Mobile Apps
BLACK DIAMOND VENTURES, 278
CAMP VENTURES, 388
DALLAS VENTURE PARTNERS, 583
EONCAPITAL, 686
IGLOBE PARTNERS, 2844
INVENTUS, 1017
KAEDAN INVESTMENTS, 2905
OJAS VENTURE PARTNERS, 3010
RHO CANADA VENTURES, 2231
SALESFORCE VENTURES, 1610
SERAPH GROUP, 1658
SPEKTRA CAPITAL, 1721
UPFRONT VENTURES, 1890

Mobile Broadband
MOTOROLA SOLUTIONS VENTURE CAPITAL, 1260

Mobile Commerce
OCA VENTURES, 1364

Mobile Communications Devices
AURA CAPITAL OY Auratum Group, 2442
AZIONE CAPITAL, 2464
BLUERUN VENTURES, 299
DOUGHTY HANSON & CO., 2662
GILDE INVESTMENT FUNDS, 2770
IDG CAPITAL, 977
INDUSTRIEBANK LIOF NV, 2857

Industry Preference Index / Natural Resources

JAVELIN VENTURE PARTNERS, 1032
PITANGO VENTURE CAPITAL, 3030
REDPOINT VENTURES, 1537
SALESFORCE VENTURES, 1610
SPENCER TRASK VENTURES, 1723

Mobile Computing
ALTA VENTURES MEXICO, 2374
LIQUID CAPITAL GROUP, 1137
SHEPHERD VENTURES, 1667
SIGMA PARTNERS, 1674
SIGNAL PEAK VENTURES, 1679
WING VENTURE PARTNERS, 1996

Mobile Data Services
I-HATCH VENTURES LLC, 967

Mobile Energy Transmission
INFIELD CAPITAL, 992

Mobile Enterprise
IGNITION PARTNERS, 978

Mobile Entertainment
TRUE VENTURES, 1862

Mobile Infrastructure
UPFRONT VENTURES, 1890

Mobile Internet
ZHENFUND, 3241

Mobile Media
BOREALIS VENTURES, 311
GRANDBANKS CAPITAL, 853

Mobile Services
ADARA VENTURE PARTNERS, 2334
DACE VENTURES, 581
GENESIS PARTNERS, 2766
RUNTIDE CAPITAL, 1600
TRUE VENTURES, 1862

Mobile Software
GREENHILLS VENTURES, LLC, 870

Mobile Technology
AMITI VENTURES, 117
AUTHOSIS VENTURES, 2448
BRIDGESCALE PARTNERS, 342
CALUMET VENTURE FUND, 378
GLOBESPAN CAPITAL PARTNERS, 839
GV, 894
MIDATLANTIC FUND, 1228
NGP CAPITAL, 1327
PLAZA VENTURES, 2216
POINT JUDITH CAPITAL, 1463
RELAY VENTURES, 2228
TRUE VENTURES, 1862
WINDFORCE VENTURES, LLC, 1992
YL VENTURES, 3236

Mobility
ABRT VENTURE FUND, 2312
ARCTERN VENTURES, 2037
ASTER CAPITAL, 2430
BOLDSTART VENTURES, 308
CAMP ONE VENTURES, 387
CARDINAL VENTURE CAPITAL, 414
CASTROL INNOVENTURES, 2559
CLAREMONT CREEK VENTURES, 493
DELL VENTURES, 604
ENTREPIA VENTURES, 683
FORTÉ VENTURES, 770
G SQUARED, 805
GREYCROFT PARTNERS, 876
HURON RIVER VENTURES, 964
INTEL CAPITAL, 1009
MOBILE FOUNDATION VENTURES, 1243
MS&AD VENTURES, 1269
OBVIOUS VENTURES, 1363
ONSET VENTURES, 1379
RUBICON VENTURE CAPITAL, 1599
SAMSUNG NEXT, 1614
SEIDLER EQUITY PARTNERS, 1648
SONY INNOVATION FUND, 1705
SUMMERHILL VENTURE PARTNERS, 2250
URBAN US, 1896
WILDCAT VENTURE PARTNERS, 1985

Mortgages
VARDE PARTNERS, 1909

Multimedia
AMD VENTURES, 107
CALIFORNIA TECHNOLOGY VENTURES, 374
COMPAGNIE FINANCIERE E DE ROTHSCHILD BANQUE, 2616
ENTREPIA VENTURES, 683
EURAZEO, 2710
MIRAE ASSET VENTURE ACCELERATOR Mirae Asset Group, 2960
NEUHAUS PARTNERS, 2985
SBRC INVESTMENT CONSULTATION LIMITED, 3092
SCOTTISH ENTERPRISE, 3094
SYNCOM VENTURE PARTNERS, 1773

Music
INGENIOUS VENTURES, 2862
NORTHSTAR VENTURES, 3003
RAPTOR GROUP, 1527
SECTION 32, 1646
ZM CAPITAL, 2019

Nano- and Microtechnologies
ARCH VENTURE PARTNERS, 154

Nanotechnology
180 DEGREE CAPITAL, 5
ASSET MANAGEMENT VENTURES, 183
BASF VENTURE CAPITAL, 2483
CEDRUS INVESTMENTS, 2572
CORE CAPITAL PARTNERS, 540
COTTONWOOD TECHNOLOGY FUND, 550
CREATHOR VENTURE, 2629
FRONTIER VENTURE CAPITAL, 794
HIGH-TECH GRUENDERFONDS, 2815
LUX CAPITAL, 1155
MAINE ANGELS, 1164
MMT MILLENNIUM MATERIALS TECHNOLOGIES FUND LP, 2964
NEW VENTURE PARTNERS, 1304
OXANTIUM VENTURES, 1394
PELION VENTURE PARTNERS, 1428
QUESTER CAPITAL MANAGEMENT LIMITED, 3061
RED DOT VENTURES, 3064
SOUTHERN CROSS VENTURE PARTNERS, 1713
SPINUP VENTURE, 3123
YISSUM TECHNOLOGY TRANSFER, 3235

Natural Gas
APECTEC, 2035
ENCAP FLATROCK MIDSTREAM, 672
HADDINGTON VENTURES LLC, 898
MOUNTAINEER CAPITAL, 1262
NGP ENERGY CAPITAL, 1328
PRIVITI CAPITAL, 2219

Natural Resources
ARTHUR P GOULD & COMPANY, 174
ATRIUM CAPITAL, 194
AVENUE CAPITAL GROUP, 211
BARING PRIVATE EQUITY PARTNERS INDIA, 2481
CEDRUS INVESTMENTS, 2572
CROSBY ASSET MANAGEMENT, 2631
EM WARBURG, PINCUS & COMPANY INTERNATIONAL, 2688
EM WARBURG, PINCUS & COMPANY JAPAN, 2689
EMP GLOBAL, 671
FIELDSTONE PRIVATE CAPITAL GROUP, 726

Industry Preference Index / Natural Resources & Chemicals

FOUNDATION MARKETS, 2117
GENERAL ENTERPRISE MANAGEMENT SERVICES, 2763
HUMANA VENTURES, 958
LYNWOOD CAPITAL PARTNERS, 1156
MIDDLEBURG CAPITAL DEVELOPMENT, 1229
NEW BRUNSWICK INNOVATION FOUNDATION, 2192
PIDC PHILADELPHIA, 1445
ROYALTY CAPITAL MANAGEMENT, 1595
SAMOS INVESTMENTS, 3088
SARATOGA PARTNERS, 1624
SEED CAPITAL LIMITED, 3098
SOURCE CAPITAL GROUP, 1710
STARBOARD CAPITAL PARTNERS, 1738
SUN CAPITAL PARTNERS, 1755
TERA CAPITAL CORPORATION, 2258
WAND PARTNERS, 1956
WOODSIDE FUND, 2005

Natural Resources & Chemicals
ACCESS BRIDGE-GAP VENTURES, 33

Network Infrastructure
FAIRHAVEN CAPITAL, 713
INNOVATION WORKS, 1003
SEAPOINT VENTURES, 1640

Network Infrastructure & Security
ADAMS CAPITAL MANAGEMENT, 55
ARCH VENTURE PARTNERS, 154
DYNAMO VC, 640
FIRST ANALYSIS, 733
STAENBERG VENTURE PARTNERS, 1736

Network Technology
FUSION FUND, 802

Networking
ACORN CAMPUS VENTURES, 46
ADOBE VENTURES LP, 57
AKERS CAPITAL LLC, 74
ALEXANDER HUTTON, 82
ALTAIR VENTURES, 95
AMADEUS CAPITAL PARTNERS LIMITED, 2378
AMBIENT SOUND INVESTMENTS, 2382
ANGELS' FORUM LLC, 130
ANTHEM VENTURE PARTNERS, 133
ARROWPATH VENTURE PARTNERS, 171
ARTIS VENTURES, 177
ASCENT VENTURE PARTNERS, 180
ASSET MANAGEMENT VENTURES, 183
ATHENAEUM FUND, 188
AVALON VENTURES, 209
AZURE CAPITAL PARTNERS, 218
BAND OF ANGELS LLC, 229
BATTERY VENTURES, 238
BENHAMOU GLOBAL VENTURES, 252
BLUMBERG CAPITAL, 304
CEDAR (ISRAEL) FINANCIAL ADVISORS LIMITED Cedar Fund, 2571
CEDAR FUND, 438
CEI VENTURES, 440
CELTIC HOUSE VENTURE PARTNERS, 2070
CHEVRON TECHNOLOGY VENTURES, 468
CHICAGO VENTURE PARTNERS LP, 472
COMCAST VENTURES, 520
CORE CAPITAL PARTNERS, 540
DALLAS VENTURE PARTNERS, 583
DELL VENTURES, 604
DUCHOSSOIS CAPITAL MANAGEMENT, 634
EASTVEN VENTURE PARTNERS, 645
ECLIPSE VENTURES, 648
FOUNDATION CAPITAL, 773
GILBERT GLOBAL EQUITY PARTNERS, 831
GOOD NEWS VENTURES, 2132
HARBINGER VENTURE MANAGEMENT, 908
IDG TECHNOLOGY VENTURE INVESTMENT, 2839
JERUSALEM VENTURE PARTNERS, 2901
LIQUID CAPITAL GROUP, 1137
MADRONA VENTURE GROUP, 1162
MATRIX PARTNERS, 1184
MBF CAPITAL CORPORATION, 1191
MENLO VENTURES, 1203
MILLENIUM TECHNOLOGY VALUE PARTNERS, 1235
MIRAMAR VENTURE PARTNERS, 1237
MONITOR VENTURES, 1249
MOTOROLA SOLUTIONS VENTURE CAPITAL, 1260
NEOTENY COMPANY LIMITED, 2982
NEW VENTURE PARTNERS, 1304
O'REILLY ALPHATECH VENTURES, 1359
PELION VENTURE PARTNERS, 1428
PENN VENTURE PARTNERS, 1431
PITANGO VENTURE CAPITAL, 3030
PROCYON VENTURES, 1486
SAND HILL ANGELS, 1616
SCALE VENTURE PARTNERS, 1629
SHEPHERD VENTURES, 1667
SIGNAL LAKE, 1678
SIGNAL PEAK VENTURES, 1679
SILICON ALLEY VENTURE PARTNERS, 1682
SINEWAVE VENTURES, 1689
SOFTBANK CAPITAL, 1701
SPACEVEST, 1717
STATELINE ANGELS, 1743
STORM VENTURES, 1750
SYCAMORE VENTURES, 1771
TELUS VENTURES, 2256
TI VENTURE CAPITAL Texas Instruments Incorporated, 1825
TIME WARNER INVESTMENT CORPORATION, 1829
TL VENTURES, 1830
VERITAS VENTURE PARTNERS, 3203
VERIZON VENTURES, 1928
WASHINGTON CAPITAL VENTURES, 1960
WESLEY CLOVER, 2276
WHEATLEY PARTNERS, 1981
WOODSIDE FUND, 2005
ZONE VENTURES, 2020

Networking & Equipment
ZM CAPITAL, 2019

Networks
CALUMET VENTURE FUND, 378
TAMAR TECHNOLOGY VENTURES LIMITED, 3149

Networks and Communities
BLOOMBERG BETA, 287

Neural Networks
GVA CAPITAL, 895

Neurotechnology
TECHNOLOGY PARTNERS, 1788

New Age Media
G SQUARED, 805

New Energy
COTTONWOOD TECHNOLOGY FUND, 550
IDG CAPITAL PARTNERS, 2838
IDG TECHNOLOGY VENTURE INVESTMENT, 2839
RHO VENTURES, 1561

New Enterprise
CANVAS VENTURES, 399

New Materials
360 CAPITAL PARTNERS 360 Capital Management SA, 2288
CONOR VENTURE PARTNERS OY, 2621
CREATHOR VENTURE, 2629
ECAPITAL ENTREPRENEURIAL PARTNERS AG, 2677
QBIC FUND, 3056
QUANTUM WAVE FUND, 3059
QUEST FOR GROWTH, 3060
SB CHINA VENTURE CAPITAL, 3091
SPINUP VENTURE, 3123
TROIKA CAPITAL PARTNERS, 3184

Industry Preference Index / Oil & Gas

New Media
3W VENTURES Latour & Zuberbuhler GmbH, 2302
ABRT VENTURE FUND, 2312
ACCESS VENTURE PARTNERS LLC, 35
ACKERLEY PARTNERS LLC, 42
AMPLIFIER VENTURE PARTNERS, 120
ANGELAB VENTURES, 2393
ANTHEM VENTURE PARTNERS, 133
ARTIS VENTURES, 177
AUSTIN VENTURES, 205
AVANSIS VENTURES, 210
BIG SUR VENTURES, 2501
BIGFOOT VENTURES, 2502
CORIOLIS VENTURES, 541
GENERAL CATALYST PARTNERS, 820
IDG CAPITAL, 977
IDG CAPITAL PARTNERS, 2838
KNIGHT'S BRIDGE CAPITAL PARTNERS, 2164
LAUNCHBOX DIGITAL, 1100
NEW ATLANTIC VENTURES, 1290
NIELSEN INNOVATE FUND, 2994
ONSET VENTURES, 1379
OUTCOME CAPITAL, 1389
OneVentures, 3014
POND VENTURES, 3038
REED ELSEVIER VENTURES, 3065
REMBRANDT VENTURE PARTNERS, 1543
RHO CANADA VENTURES, 2231
RHO VENTURES, 1561
VERDEXUS, 2271
WESTSUMMIT CAPITAL, 3225

New Organizational Models
BLOOMBERG BETA, 287

New Service Models
RUBICON VENTURE CAPITAL, 1599

New Technology
ARCHTOP VENTURES, 155

New Therapeutics & Platforms
NOVARTIS VENTURE FUNDS, 1350

Next Generation Computing
ENTREPIA VENTURES, 683

Next Generation Materials
IGLOBE PARTNERS, 2844

Next Generation Software
.406 VENTURES, 1

Niche Manufacturing
AUDAX GROUP, 197
BBH CAPITAL PARTNERS, 243
CELERITY PARTNERS, 441
CHB CAPITAL PARTNERS, 463
FCF PARTNERS LP, 719
FIVE POINTS CAPITAL, 747
GEORGIA OAK PARTNERS, 825
GOLDNER HAWN, 847
HIGH STREET CAPITAL, 935
JH WHITNEY & COMPANY, 1041
JMH CAPITAL, 1044
LINCOLNSHIRE MANAGEMENT, 1131
MAIN STREET CAPITAL HOLDINGS LLC, 1163
MIDOCEAN PARTNERS, 1231
MONUMENT ADVISORS, 1252
MPG EQUITY PARTNERS, 1267
MVP CAPITAL PARTNERS, 1275
NEW CAPITAL FUND, 1291
PALOMINO CAPITAL, 1409
PRAIRIE CAPITAL, 1473
PRIVEQ CAPITAL FUNDS, 2218
RIDGE CAPITAL PARTNERS LLC, 1565
STONEBRIDGE PARTNERS, 1747
SUMMER STREET CAPITAL PARTNERS, 1753
TRIVEST PARTNERS, 1859
TVV CAPITAL, 1872
WYNNCHURCH CAPITAL, 2008

Non-profit & Public Authorities
TPA CORPORATE FINANCE CONSULTING GMBH Horwarth International, 3175

Nontechnology
INFIELD CAPITAL, 992

Nutraceuticals
FARM CREDIT CANADA, 2108
MOUNTAIN GROUP CAPITAL, 1261

Nutrition
1ST COURSE CAPITAL, 7
BAY CITY CAPITAL LLC, 240
BIOGENERATOR, 270
BIOPACIFIC VENTURES, 2507
BOULDER VENTURES LTD, 318
NORTH CASTLE PARTNERS, 1336

O2O
ZHENFUND, 3241

Office Imaging & Technology
CIT GROUP, 486

Oil & Gas
32 DEGREES CAPITAL, 2022
3I ASIA PACIFIC 3i Group, 2289
AEM CAPITAL, 2341
AIP PRIVATE CAPITAL, 2027
ALFA CAPITAL Alfa Group, 2355
ALTIRA GROUP LLC, 98
AMANET TECHNOLOGIES LIMITED, 2381
ANNAPOLIS CAPITAL, 2034
APECTEC, 2035
ARC FINANCIAL, 2036
ARCLIGHT CAPITAL PARTNERS, 157
ASTOR CAPITAL GROUP, 2431
AZIMUTH CAPITAL MANAGEMENT, 2044
BARING VOSTOK CAPITAL PARTNERS, 2482
BASF VENTURE CAPITAL, 2483
BLAST FUNDING, 282
CHENGWEI VENTURES, 2581
CHEVRON TECHNOLOGY VENTURES, 468
CHRYSALIX, 2072
CIBC CAPITAL MARKETS, 2073
CNF INVESTMENTS Clark Enterprises, Inc., 510
COLT VENTURES, 517
CONVEXA Tyveholmen AS, 2623
CROSBY ASSET MANAGEMENT, 2631
ENCAP FLATROCK MIDSTREAM, 672
ENCAP INVESTMENTS LP, 673
ENERGY VENTURES, 2691
EQUISTONE, 2705
ESCHELON ENERGY PARTNERS, 697
FIRST RESERVE, 741
FOX PAINE & COMPANY LLC, 781
HUNT INVESTMENT GROUP, 960
IBM VENTURE CAPITAL GROUP, 971
INDASIA FUND ADVISORS PVT LTD, 2850
INTERNATIONAL FINANCE CORPORATION (IFC), 1012
JOG CAPITAL, 2159
KALORI GROUP INVESTMENTS, 2906
KESTREL ENERGY PARTNERS, 1072
LEX CAPITAL MANAGEMENT, 2166
LIME ROCK PARTNERS, 1129
LIONHART CAPITAL LTD, 2170
LONGBOW CAPITAL, 2171
MANULIFE CAPITAL, 2177
MCROCK CAPITAL, 2183
MERIT ENERGY COMPANY, 1211
NGP, 1326
NGP ENERGY CAPITAL, 1328

Industry Preference Index / Oil & Gas Services

PALMS & COMPANY, 1405
PRIVITI CAPITAL, 2219
RBC CAPITAL MARKETS, 2223
RFC AMBRIAN RFC Group Ltd., 3070
RIDGEWOOD CAPITAL, 1567
SAUDI ARAMCO ENERGY VENTURES, 3090
SOURCE CAPITAL GROUP, 1710
STATOIL TECHNOLOGY INVEST, 3132
VIKING VENTURE, 3207
WESTERN AMERICA CAPITAL GROUP, 2278
WESTLAKE SECURITIES, 1977
XPV WATER PARTNERS, 2282

Oil & Gas Services
BOND CAPITAL, 2058

Oil and Gas
BRANFORD CASTLE, 330

Oilfield Services
ARC FINANCIAL, 2036
LONGBOW CAPITAL, 2171

Oncology
SANOFI-GENZYME BIOVENTURES, 1621

Online Advertising
GENACAST VENTURES, 818
PROGRESS VENTURES, 1488
SPECTRUM EQUITY INVESTORS LP, 1720

Online Applications
SPARK CAPITAL, 1718

Online Consumer Services
EARLYBIRD, 2673

Online Content
ALEXANDER HUTTON, 82
ANTHEM VENTURE PARTNERS, 133
BATTERY VENTURES, 238
ID VENTURES AMERICA LLC, 974
PALO ALTO VENTURE PARTNERS, 1406

Online Education
MACMILLAN DIGITAL EDUCATION, 2941

Online Marketing
ARTS ALLIANCE, 2419

Online Marketplaces
MISTRAL VENTURE PARTNERS, 2187

Online Media
SALMON RIVER CAPITAL, 1611

Online Publishing
TRUE VENTURES, 1862

Online Services
NEW ATLANTIC VENTURES, 1290

Online To Offline Offerings
DECIENS CAPITAL, 600

Online Video
500 STARTUPS, 10

Open Source
.406 VENTURES, 1
AZURE CAPITAL PARTNERS, 218
SUNBRIDGE PARTNERS, 1757

Optical
HARDY CAPITAL PARTNERS, 2137
PAC-LINK MANAGEMENT CORP., 3015

Optical Networks and Components
TAMAR TECHNOLOGY VENTURES LIMITED, 3149

Optical Technology
BANEXI VENTURES PARTNERS, 2472
BROOK VENTURE FUND, 352
CORE CAPITAL PARTNERS, 540
DEFTA PARTNERS, 603
ELECTRA PARTNERS ASIA LIMITED SFC of Hong Kong, 2685
GILBERT GLOBAL EQUITY PARTNERS, 831
GUANGDONG TECHNOLOGY VENTURE CAPITAL COMPANY, 2793
JC TECHNOLOGIES LTD, 2900
NOVAK BIDDLE VENTURE PARTNERS, 1348
SCALE VENTURE PARTNERS, 1629
SCOTTISH ENTERPRISE, 3094
SPACEVEST, 1717
SPENCER TRASK VENTURES, 1723
WI HARPER GROUP, 1983

Optics
CONOR VENTURE PARTNERS OY, 2621
CRAWLEY VENTURES, 554

Optics & Photonics
ARCH VENTURE PARTNERS, 154

Other Energy Related Assets
ENERGY CAPITAL PARTNERS, 676

Outsourced Solutions
HALYARD CAPITAL, 902

Outsourcing & Efficiency
ARGENTUM GROUP, 162
ARLINGTON CAPITAL PARTNERS, 167
BRERA CAPITAL PARTNERS, 338
BRYAN GARNIER & COMPANY, 2535
BUSINESS GROWTH FUND, 2541
CELERITY PARTNERS, 441
CHRYSALIS CAPITAL ChrysCapital, 2590
CHRYSCAPITAL MANAGEMENT COMPANIES ChrysCapital, 2591
COMSTOCK CAPITAL PARTNERS LLC, 529
DUKE STREET CAPITAL Duke Street, 2667
ECI VENTURES, 2678
ELECTRA PARTNERS ASIA LIMITED SFC of Hong Kong, 2685
FCF PARTNERS LP, 719
FIRST ANALYSIS, 733
FIVE ELMS CAPITAL, 746
FOUNDERS EQUITY, 777
GENERAL ATLANTIC PARTNERS, 2762
GENERATION PARTNERS, 822
HAMILTON ROBINSON CAPITAL PARTNERS, 903
HELION VENTURE PARTNERS, LLC International Management (Mauritius) Ltd, 2809
HIGH STREET CAPITAL, 935
MTS HEALTH INVESTORS, 1271
NTH POWER TECHNOLOGIES, 1355
OAK INVESTMENT PARTNERS, 1361
ODEON CAPITAL PARTNERS, 1367
RITTENHOUSE VENTURES, 1572
ROSEWOOD CAPITAL, 1591
RU-NET VENTURES, 3078
SENTRY FINANCIAL CORPORATION, 1655
SEQUOIA CAPITAL, 1657
TEXADA CAPITAL CORPORATION, 1801
TGF MANAGEMENT, 1805
UPDATA VENTURE PARTNERS, 1888
WATERLAND PRIVATE EQUITY INVESTMENT, 3222

Packaging
ALTRIA VENTURES, 102
AMERICA FIRST INVESTMENT ADVISORS, 109
AMERICAN SECURITIES LLC, 111
APOLLO GLOBAL MANAGEMENT, 141
ARROWHEAD INVESTMENT MANAGEMENT, 170
ASHBRIDGE PARTNERS, 2041
CAMBRIDGE CAPITAL, 383

CVC INVESTMENT MANAGERS LIMITED, 2636
DEUTSCHE BETEILIGUNGS AG, 2651
ELECTRA PARTNERS ASIA LIMITED SFC of Hong Kong, 2685
FCF PARTNERS LP, 719
GEORGIA OAK PARTNERS, 825
GLENTHORNE CAPITAL, 836
GRAHAM PARTNERS, 851
HORIZON PARTNERS, LTD, 948
IRVING PLACE CAPITAL, 1026
JAVELIN INVESTMENTS, 2899
JORDAN COMPANY, 1049
MASON WELLS, 1174
MERITURN PARTNERS, 1214
PENDER WEST CAPITAL PARTNERS, 2210
PROSPECT PARTNERS LLC, 1494
RESILIENCE CAPITAL PARTNERS, 1548

Paper
AMERICAN SECURITIES LLC, 111
CERBERUS CAPITAL MANAGEMENT, 453
FCF PARTNERS LP, 719
MERITURN PARTNERS, 1214
SRIW SA SRIW Group, 3125

Parenting
CANTOS VENTURES, 398

Patient Safety
HEALTH ENTERPRISE PARTNERS, 921

Payment Services
ASHBY POINT CAPITAL, 181

Payments & Financial Services
500 STARTUPS, 10
CHICAGO VENTURES, 473
INFORMATION VENTURE PARTNERS, 2146
MISSIONOG, 1240

Pensions
ARGOS SODITIC SA, 2414
DFC LTD, 2652

Peripherals
STATELINE ANGELS, 1743

Personal Care
ASHBRIDGE PARTNERS, 2041

Personal Finance
PORTAG3 VENTURES, 2217

Pet Products
HERITAGE PARTNERS, 929

Petrochemicals
GRYPHON MANAGEMENT COMPANY, 887
JAVELIN INVESTMENTS, 2899
MEZZANINE MANAGEMENT LIMITED Mezzanine Management UK Ltd., 2956

Pharma Data
HEALTH ENTERPRISE PARTNERS, 921

Pharmaceutical
EMBARK HEALTHCARE, 663

Pharmaceutical Services
PFIZER VENTURE INVESTMENTS, 1439

Pharmaceuticals
3TS CAPITAL PARTNERS 3i Group plc, 2301
ACRUX LIMITED, 2327
ACTIVA CAPITAL, 2330
ALBERTA ENTERPRISE, 2028
ALFA CAPITAL Alfa Group, 2355
ALTARIS CAPITAL PARTNERS, 97
AMANAH VENTURES SDN BHD, 2380
AMANET TECHNOLOGIES LIMITED, 2381
AMGEN VENTURES, 113
AMKEY VENTURES, 118
AMORCHEM, 2031
AMPERSAND CAPITAL PARTNERS, 119
AMPHION CAPITAL PARTNERS, 2389
ANDLINGER & COMPANY INC, 124
ANTHEM VENTURE PARTNERS, 133
APJOHN GROUP LLC, 140
APPLE TREE PARTNERS, 144
ARBORETUM VENTURES, 150
ARCH VENTURE PARTNERS, 154
ASCLEPIOS BIORESEARCH, 2424
ASTELLAS VENTURE MANAGEMENT, 184
ATHENAEUM FUND, 188
ATHYRIUM CAPITAL MANAGEMENT, 190
AVALON VENTURES, 209
AZCA, 217
BAXTER VENTURES, 239
BAY CITY CAPITAL LLC, 240
BIOMED PARTNERS, 2506
BIOMINDS LABS INC., 2055
BIOPACIFIC VENTURES, 2507
BIOPROCESS CAPITAL PARTNERS, 2508
BIOVEDA CAPITAL, 2509
BLACKSTONE PRIVATE EQUITY GROUP, 280
BOEHRINGER INGELHEIM VENTURE FUND, 2521
CARDINAL EQUITY PARTNERS, 412
CARE CAPITAL, 415
CATO BIOVENTURES, 432
CHL MEDICAL PARTNERS, 476
CIBC CAPITAL MARKETS, 2073
CITA GESTION, 2598
CLIFFORD CHANCE PUNDER, 2605
COLLABORATIVE FUND, 514
COLUMN GROUP, 519
DOMAIN ASSOCIATES LLC, 622
EDGEWATER CAPITAL PARTNERS, 653
EDISON PARTNERS, 655
ESSEX WOODLANDS HEALTH VENTURES LLC, 698
FERRANTI LIMITED, 2723
FIRST ANALYSIS, 733
FLAGSHIP PIONEERING, 748
FORWARD VENTURES, 772
GALEN PARTNERS, 809
GLOBAL LIFE SCIENCE VENTURES GmbH, 2776
GREAT POINT PARTNERS, 864
HBM PARTNERS, 2806
HEALTHCAP, 2807
HEALTHCAP Odlander, Fredrikson & Co AB, 2807
INCUBE VENTURES, 984
INDASIA FUND ADVISORS PVT LTD, 2850
INDUSTRY VENTURES, 990
INETWORKS ADVISORS LLC, 991
INTERSOUTH PARTNERS, 1013
INVESTMENT FUND FOR CENTRAL & EASTERN EUROPE, 2880
IP GROUP, 2883
JK&B CAPITAL, 1042
JOHNSON & JOHNSON INNOVATION, 1047
JOHNSTON ASSOCIATES, 1048
JW ASSET MANAGEMENT, 1052
KEARNY VENTURE PARTNERS, 1063
KEGONSA CAPITAL PARTNERS, 1064
KODIAK CAPITAL, 1083
LATTERELL VENTURE PARTNERS, 1098
LILLY VENTURES, 1128
LINK TECHNOLOGIES LIMITED, 2932
LONGITUDE CAPITAL, 1147
LONGWOOD FUND, 1149
LRM - INVESTERINGSMAATSCHAPPIJ VOOR LIMBURG, 2940
LUMIRA VENTURES, 2174
MANHATTAN INVESTMENT PARTNERS, 1166
MMT MILLENNIUM MATERIALS TECHNOLOGIES FUND LP, 2964
MPM CAPITAL, 1268
NEW SCIENCE VENTURES, 1302
NEWSPRING CAPITAL, 1316
NOMURA PHASE4 VENTURES LTD, 2998

Industry Preference Index / Photonics

PAI MANAGEMENT, 3017
PALMS & COMPANY, 1405
PARTNERS HEALTHCARE RESEARCH VENTURES, 1421
PRIVATE EQUITY PARTNERS SPA, 3044
PROGRESS EQUITY PARTNERS, 1487
PTV SCIENCES, 1502
RITTENHOUSE VENTURES, 1572
ROUNDTABLE HEALTHCARE PARTNERS, 1594
SAMBRINVEST SA, 3087
SAND HILL ANGELS, 1616
SANDERLING VENTURES, 1619
SCHRODER VENTURES HEALTH INVESTORS, 1631
SCP PARTNERS, 1636
SOFINNOVA VENTURES, 1700
SPINDLETOP CAPITAL, 1725
TAKEDA VENTURES, 1780
THE CHANNEL GROUP, 1811
THOMAS, MCNERNEY & PARTNERS, 1820
TPA CORPORATE FINANCE CONSULTING GMBH Horwarth International, 3175
TRANSITION PARTNERS LTD, 1839
TULLIS HEALTH INVESTORS, 1868
TWIN CITIES ANGELS, 1874
VALLEY VENTURES LP, 1903
VERSANT VENTURES, 1930
WATER STREET HEALTHCARE PARTNERS, 1962
WESTERN NIS ENTERPRISE FUND, 3224

Photonics
CONNECTICUT INNOVATIONS, 532
LDV CAPITAL, 1105
MURPHREE VENTURE PARTNERS, 1273
NEUHAUS PARTNERS, 2985
TECH CAPITAL PARTNERS, 2253

Physical Sciences
CASE TECHNOLOGY VENTURES Case Western Reserve University, 423
GENERICS GROUP LIMITED Generics Group, 2764
GUANGDONG TECHNOLOGY VENTURE CAPITAL COMPANY, 2793
ILLINOIS VENTURES, 979
QUANTUM WAVE FUND, 3059

Plastics
BASF VENTURE CAPITAL, 2483
BROOKSIDE EQUITY PARTNERS LLC, 356
C3 CAPITAL PARTNERS LP, 367
CAPITAL FOR BUSINESS, INC, 402
DESCO CAPITAL, 607
EMIGRANT CAPITAL, 668
FIRST ATLANTIC CAPITAL LTD., 734
FIRST ISRAEL MEZZANINE INVESTORS LIMITED, 2736
GRAHAM PARTNERS, 851
HORIZON PARTNERS, LTD, 948
LEONIA MB GROUP/MB FUNDS, 2928
LINSALATA CAPITAL PARTNERS, 1136
LITTLEJOHN & COMPANY LLC, 1138
MCG CAPITAL CORPORATION, 1192
PHOSPHAGENICS, 3028
RESILIENCE CAPITAL PARTNERS, 1548
SPELL CAPITAL PARTNERS LLC, 1722
TGAP VENTURES, 1804
VENTURE ASSOCIATES PARTNERS LLC, 1921

Platform As A Service
SPEKTRA CAPITAL, 1721

Pollution
HT CAPITAL ADVISORS LLC, 956
INDUSTRIEBANK LIOF NV, 2857
NGEN PARTNERS, 1324
VAEKSTFONDEN, 3194
VENTANA CAPITAL MANAGEMENT LP, 1920

Power
AMERICAN SECURITIES LLC, 111
CANADIAN VENTURE CAPITAL ASSOCIATION Canadian Venture Capital & Private Equity Association, 3249
CARLYLE GROUP, 416

CIBC CAPITAL MARKETS, 2073
CLIMATE CHANGE CAPITAL, 2606
ISRAEL CLEANTECH VENTURES, 2891
KOHLBERG VENTURES, 1087
MCROCK CAPITAL, 2183
OXANTIUM VENTURES, 1394

Power Generation
ARC FINANCIAL, 2036
ENERGY CAPITAL PARTNERS, 676
HCI EQUITY PARTNERS, 920
US RENEWABLES GROUP, 1897

Power Infrastructure
ANGELENO GROUP, 127

Power Management
TI VENTURE CAPITAL Texas Instruments Incorporated, 1825

Power Storage
HADDINGTON VENTURES LLC, 898

Power Technologies
ACCESS CAPITAL CORPORATION, 2026
ALTIRA GROUP LLC, 98
ARCLIGHT CAPITAL PARTNERS, 157
BLUEFISH VENTURES, 297
CHEUNG KONG INFRASTRUCTURE HOLDINGS LIMITED, 2582
CHEVRON TECHNOLOGY VENTURES, 468
EMP GLOBAL, 671
NEW MOUNTAIN CAPITAL, 1300
NTH POWER TECHNOLOGIES, 1355
WYNNCHURCH CAPITAL, 2008

Predictive Medicine Technology
FLARE CAPITAL PARTNERS, 749

Premium Consumer Products
SJF VENTURES, 1691

Preventative Health and Services
SINEWAVE VENTURES, 1689

Prevention
JOHNSON & JOHNSON INNOVATION, 1047

Printing
ACCESS CAPITAL, 34
AVIV VENTURE CAPITAL, 2453
DEUTSCHE BETEILIGUNGS AG, 2651
IGNITE JAPAN KK Ignite Group, 2845
MASON WELLS, 1174
MAYFLY CAPITAL, 1188
QUADRAN GESTION Deutsche Beteiligungs AG, 3058
SAMBRINVEST SA, 3087
SRIW SA SRIW Group, 3125
UNION CAPITAL CORPORATION, 1883
XANGE PRIVATE EQUITY, 3229

Private Education
BOND CAPITAL, 2058

Private Equity
3I AUSTRIA BETEILGUNG GmbH 3i Group, 2290
747 CAPITAL, 13
BROOKFIELD ASSET MANAGEMENT, 2062
BUTZOW NORDIA ADVOCATES LTD, 2543
CHINA VEST LIMITED, 2587
COHEN PRIVATE VENTURES, 513
GRESHAM PRIVATE EQUITY LIMITED, 2790

Process Controls
DESCO CAPITAL, 607

Processing
DFC LTD, 2652
DIRECT CAPITAL PRIVATE EQUITY LIMITED, 2655
ELECTRA PARTNERS ASIA LIMITED SFC of Hong Kong, 2685

Industry Preference Index / Real Estate

EUROVENTURES CAPITAL, 2716
ICV PARTNERS, 973
INDUSTRI KAPITAL SVENSKA AB, 2854
INTER-ASIA VENTURE MANAGEMENT LIMITED, 2872
LEVINE LEICHTMAN CAPITAL PARTNERS, 1115
LITTLEJOHN & COMPANY LLC, 1138
LLR PARTNERS INC, 1140
MERITURN PARTNERS, 1214
NORTH DAKOTA DEVELOPMENT FUND, 1338

Productivity
M12, 1158

Products & Technology
CAPITAL RESOURCE PARTNERS, 405

Professional Services
MOBIUS VENTURE CAPITAL, 1245

Property Development
BOSTON CAPITAL, 312
GRESHAM PRIVATE EQUITY LIMITED, 2790

Property Management
AMANAH VENTURES SDN BHD, 2380
CHEROKEE INVESTMENT PARTNERS, 465
CONTINENTAL VENTURE CAPITAL LIMITED, 2622
COVENT INDUSTRIAL CAPITAL INVESTMENT COMPANY, 2626
GRAPHITE CAPITAL MANAGEMENT LTD, 2787
PWC, 3055
REDWOOD CAPITAL GROUP, 1539
STARWOOD CAPITAL GROUP LLC, 1742
TECHNOLOGY PARK MALAYSIA CORPORATION SDN BHD, 3155

Property Transactions
BUTZOW NORDIA ADVOCATES LTD, 2543

Proprietary Industrial Products & Services
CAPITAL RESOURCE PARTNERS, 405

Proprietary Products
WARWICK GROUP, 1958

Pub Tech
BERTELSMANN DIGITAL MEDIA INVESTMENTS, 259

Public Health & Safety
URBAN US, 1896

Publishers
ENTREPRENEUR PARTNERS, 684

Publishing
ADOBE VENTURES LP, 57
AEP CAPITAL LLC, 64
ALLSTATE INVESTMENTS LLC, 88
APPIAN EDUCATION VENTURES, 142
ARCHTOP VENTURES, 155
ATRIUM CAPITAL, 194
BC PARTNERS LIMITED, 2488
BMP AKTIENGESELLSCHAFT BMP Venture Capital, 2519
BROOK VENTURE FUND, 352
BRUML CAPITAL CORPORATION, 358
BUTLER CAPITAL PARTNERS FRANCE, 2542
CARDINAL EQUITY PARTNERS, 412
CASTANEA PARTNERS, 424
DAVID N DEUTSCH & COMPANY LLC, 590
DOUBLE IMPACT BUSINESS ADVISORY, 2661
DUBILIER & COMPANY, 632
ECI VENTURES, 2678
GREENHAVEN PARTNERS, 868
HENDERSON PRIVATE CAPITAL, 2812
JEGI CAPITAL The Jordan Edminston Group, Inc., 1037
KERRY CAPITAL ADVISORS, 1071
MACQUARIE DIRECT INVESTMENT LIMITED, 2942
MEDIA VENTURE PARTNERS, 1197
MERITURN PARTNERS, 1214
MVP CAPITAL PARTNERS, 1275
NESBIC INVESTMENT FUND II, 2983
POST CAPITAL PARTNERS, 1469
QUOTIDIAN VENTURES, 1521
SARATOGA PARTNERS, 1624
SOUTHPORT PARTNERS, 1714
SRIW SA SRIW Group, 3125
TECHNOLOGY PARK MALAYSIA CORPORATION SDN BHD, 3155
THREE CITIES RESEARCH, 1822
TIME WARNER INVESTMENT CORPORATION, 1829
WESTVIEW CAPITAL PARTNERS, 1979
WICKS GROUP OF COMPANIES, LLC, 1984
ZM CAPITAL, 2019

Publishing & Printing
STERN PARTNERS, 2249

Quantum
DAY ONE VENTURES, 594

Quantum Computing
FUTURE VENTURES, 803

Radio
ALLSTATE INVESTMENTS LLC, 88
BREAKWATER MANAGEMENT, 334
GRUPO BISA, 2791
LEVINE LEICHTMAN CAPITAL PARTNERS, 1115
MEDIA VENTURE PARTNERS, 1197
TIME WARNER INVESTMENT CORPORATION, 1829
VENTURE CAPITAL FUND OF NEW ENGLAND, 1922
WICKS GROUP OF COMPANIES, LLC, 1984

Rail
CIT GROUP, 486

Rail Transportation
COPPERLION CAPITAL, 2079

Railroad Services
SEIDLER EQUITY PARTNERS, 1648

Reagent Suppliers
TELEGRAPH HILL PARTNERS, 1794
THE CHANNEL GROUP, 1811

Real Estate
ACACIA CAPITAL, 24
ACCESS BRIDGE-GAP VENTURES, 33
ACKRELL CAPITAL, 43
ALBERTA INVESTMENT MANAGEMENT CORP., 2029
ASTOR CAPITAL GROUP, 2431
ATLANTIC CAPITAL GROUP, 192
AVENUE CAPITAL GROUP, 211
BARING PRIVATE EQUITY PARTNERS INDIA, 2481
BAYSHORE CAPITAL, 2046
BERGGRUEN HOLDINGS, 253
BLUE SKY CAPITAL, 295
BLUESTEM CAPITAL COMPANY, 300
BOCI DIRECT INVESTMENT MANAGEMENT LIMITED Bank of China, 2520
BOSTON CAPITAL, 312
BROOKFIELD ASSET MANAGEMENT, 2062
CAMBER CREEK, 380
CANTOS VENTURES, 398
CAPMAN CAPITAL MANAGEMENT OY, 2553
CARLYLE ASIA INVESTMENT ADVISORS LIMITED Carlyle Group, 2556
CATALYST FUND LP, 2562
CERBERUS CAPITAL MANAGEMENT, 453
CHALLENGE FUNDS - ETGAR LP, 2576
CHELSFIELD PARTNERS, 2580
CHEROKEE INVESTMENT PARTNERS, 465
CHINA MERCHANTS CHINA INVESTMENT MANAGEMENT, 2586
CIBC CAPITAL MARKETS, 2073
CLARITAS CAPITAL, 495
CLEAR SKY CAPITAL, 501
COHEN PRIVATE VENTURES, 513
CORDOVA VENTURES, 539

Industry Preference Index / Real Estate Rehabilitation

COVENT INDUSTRIAL CAPITAL INVESTMENT COMPANY, 2626
CREDIT MUTUEL EQUITY, 2082
CREDIT SUISSE PRIVATE EQUITY Credit Suisse Group, 555
DAVID N DEUTSCH & COMPANY LLC, 590
ELGNER GROUP INVESTMENTS, 2099
EM WARBURG, PINCUS & COMPANY INTERNATIONAL, 2688
EM WARBURG, PINCUS & COMPANY JAPAN, 2689
ENTREE CAPITAL, 2700
ENTREPRENEURS ROUNDTABLE ACCELERATOR, 685
FGA PARTNERS, 725
FIFTH WALL, 728
FULL CIRCLE INVESTMENTS, 2753
GE CAPITAL, 811
GENERAL ENTERPRISE MANAGEMENT SERVICES, 2763
GLOBALIVE, 2128
GREIF & COMPANY, 874
H KATZ CAPITAL GROUP, 896
HARDY CAPITAL PARTNERS, 2137
HQ CAPITAL, 955
HUNT INVESTMENT GROUP, 960
INITIO GROUP, 996
INVICO CAPITAL CORPORATION, 2155
IRON GATE CAPITAL, 1024
KB PARTNERS, 1060
KEIRETSU FORUM, 1065
LAURENCE CAPITAL, 2165
LEVINE LEICHTMAN CAPITAL PARTNERS, 1115
LRM - INVESTERINGSMAATSCHAPPIJ VOOR LIMBURG, 2940
MANHATTAN INVESTMENT PARTNERS, 1166
MANULIFE CAPITAL, 2177
MITSUI SUMITOMO INSURANCE VENTURE CAPITAL CO, 2962
NEWFIELD CAPITAL, 1312
NEXT EQUITIES, 2194
PLAZA VENTURES, 2216
PMV, 3033
QUILVEST CAPITAL PARTNERS, 1518
REDWOOD CAPITAL GROUP, 1539
REEFI CAPITAL, 1540
REITEN & CO STRATEGIC INVESTMENTS AS Reiten & Company, 3067
RICHINA CAPITAL PARTNERS LIMITED, 3073
ROBIN HOOD VENTURES, 1581
SCULPTOR CAPITAL MANAGEMENT, 1638
SEAWAY VALLEY CAPITAL CORPORATION, 1642
SECOND CENTURY VENTURES, 1645
SERGE PUN & ASSOCIATES (MYANMAR) LIMITED, 3102
SILKROAD EQUITY, 1683
SONY EUROPE, 3120
STARBOARD CAPITAL PARTNERS, 1738
STARWOOD CAPITAL GROUP LLC, 1742
THOMPROPERTIES OY, 3166
TPA CORPORATE FINANCE CONSULTING GMBH Horwarth International, 3175
UNISON CAPITAL PARTNERS LP, 3192
URBAN US, 1896
VARDE PARTNERS, 1909
VENTURE INVESTORS, 3201
VICKERS FINANCIAL GROUP, 3206
VINACAPITAL GROUP, 3208
WAFRA INC, 1952
WALNUT GROUP, 1955
WELLS FARGO CAPITAL FINANCE, 1971
WESLEY CLOVER, 2276

Real Estate Rehabilitation
ENHANCED CAPITAL, 679

Real Estate Tech
TACTICO, 2251

Real Estate Technology
ALBUM VC, 79

Real-Time Data
.406 VENTURES, 1

Reconfigurable Processors
SONY STRATEGIC TECHNOLOGY PARTNERSHIPS, 1706

Recreation
URBAN INNOVATION FUND, 1895

Recreational Vehicles
CARDINAL EQUITY PARTNERS, 412

Recycling
ALTRIA VENTURES, 102
AUSTRALIAN ETHICAL INVESTMENT LIMITED, 2447
AUTO TECH VENTURES, 207
CAMBRIDGE CAPITAL, 383
PENDER WEST CAPITAL PARTNERS, 2210
WHEB GROUP, 3227

Recycling Systems
AZCA, 217

Renewable Energy
ACCERA AG, 2319
ALPHAMUNDI GROUP LTD, 2368
ALTIRA GROUP LLC, 98
AMBIENTA ENVIRONMENTAL ASSETS, 2383
ANGELENO GROUP, 127
ARAVAIPA VENTURES, 147
ARAVIS VENTURES, 2410
BERTI INVESTMENTS, 2496
BP ALTERNATIVE ENERGY VENTURES, 322
BREGAL ENERGY, 335
BRIGHT CAPITAL, 2531
BUSINESS GROWTH FUND, 2541
CALCEF CLEAN ENERGY FUND, 370
CAPITAL E, 401
CASABONA VENTURES, 421
CHORD CAPITAL, 2589
CLARENDON FUND MANAGERS, 2601
CLEAN PACIFIC VENTURES, 499
CLEANPATH VENTURES, 500
CM CAPITAL, 2609
CONNECTICUT INNOVATIONS, 532
CONTINENTAL VENTURE CAPITAL LIMITED, 2622
CYCLE CAPITAL MANAGEMENT, 2087
DAVENPORT RESOURCES LLC, 589
EARTHRISE CAPITAL, 643
ENHANCED CAPITAL, 679
FIRST RESERVE, 741
FSE GROUP, 2751
GLOBAL ENVIRONMENT FUND, 838
HERCULES TECHNOLOGY GROWTH CAPITAL, INC, 928
HG CAPITAL, 2814
INVESTECO, 2153
IP GROUP, 2883
LLOYDS DEVELOPMENT CAPITAL LIMITED, 2935
MEDRA CAPITAL, 2951
MINDFULL INVESTORS, 1236
OMNES CAPITAL, 3011
PMV, 3033
PROSEED, 3050
RENEWABLETECH VENTURES, 1545
RIDGEWOOD CAPITAL, 1567
RIVERSTONE, 1577
SABIC VENTURES, 3082
SAUDI ARAMCO ENERGY VENTURES, 3090
SPRING LANE CAPITAL, 1732
TEL VENTURE CAPITAL, 1793
TSING CAPITAL, 3185
URBAN INNOVATION FUND, 1895
US RENEWABLES GROUP, 1897
WHEB GROUP, 3227
ZOUK VENTURES, 3242

Renewable Energy & Environment
BRYAN GARNIER & COMPANY, 2535

Industry Preference Index / Retail, Consumer & Leisure

Renewable Infrastructure
ZOUK VENTURES, 3242

Renewable Power
BROOKFIELD ASSET MANAGEMENT, 2062
PARKWALK ADVISORS, 3019

Renewable Resources
AGRIBUSINESS MANAGEMENT COMPANY, 70
COLORADO MILE HIGH FUND, 516
MARWIT CAPITAL LLC, 1171

Renewal Energy
DEMETER PARTNERS, 2647

Research
CANNA ANGELS LLC, 391
NCT VENTURES, 1285

Research & Development
AWAY REALTY, 2456
BIOMINDS LABS INC., 2055
CHEROKEE INVESTMENT PARTNERS, 465
INVESTMENT FUND FOR CENTRAL & EASTERN EUROPE, 2880
LATTERELL VENTURE PARTNERS, 1098
OXFORD BIOSCIENCE PARTNERS, 1395
VENTANA CAPITAL MANAGEMENT LP, 1920

Research Provider
CHINA VEST LIMITED, 2587

Research Services
BIOGENERATOR, 270

Research Tools
BIOADVANCE, 269
BIOGENERATOR, 270

Resource Efficiency
ROCKPORT CAPITAL, 1583
WELLINGTON PARTNERS VENTURE CAPITAL GmbH, 3223
ZOUK VENTURES, 3242

Resource Productivity Technologies
INVESTECO, 2153

Resource Services
SIGNAL HILL EQUITY PARTNERS, 2246

Resource Use & Efficiency
ARCTERN VENTURES, 2037

Resources
WESTCAP, 2277

Restaurants
AMERICAN SECURITIES LLC, 111
AMHERST FUND, 114
BRANFORD CASTLE, 330
BRUCKMANN, ROSSER, SHERRILL & COMPANY, 357
CARPEDIA INTERNATIONAL, 2066
CIC PARTNERS, 479
CIT GROUP, 486
CLIFFORD CHANCE PUNDER, 2605
CLYDESDALE VENTURES, 508
FAIRMONT CAPITAL, 714
FREEMAN SPOGLI & CO., 786
GEORGIA OAK PARTNERS, 825
GOLDEN GATE CAPITAL, 843
GOLUB CAPITAL, 848
HARREN EQUITY PARTNERS, 913
JAFCO COMPANY LIMITED JAPAN, 2897
JEFFERIES CAPITAL PARTNERS, 1036
L CATTERTON PARTNERS, 1092
MADISON PARKER CAPITAL, 1161
POUSCHINE COOK CAPITAL MANAGEMENT LLC, 1470
RBC CAPITAL MARKETS, 2223

RETAIL & RESTAURANT GROWTH CAPITAL LP, 1552
ROBIN HOOD VENTURES, 1581
ROSEWOOD CAPITAL, 1591
SEAWAY VALLEY CAPITAL CORPORATION, 1642
SUN CAPITAL PARTNERS, 1755
SWAN & LEGEND VENTURES, 1768
THAYER VENTURES, 1808
TSG CONSUMER PARTNERS, 1863
WALNUT GROUP, 1955
WELLS FARGO CAPITAL FINANCE, 1971

Restructuring
BUTZOW NORDIA ADVOCATES LTD, 2543

Retail
645 VENTURES, 12
ACREW CAPITAL, 48
BRAND FOUNDRY VENTURES, 328
BROOKE PRIVATE EQUITY ASSOCIATES, 353
FIFTH WALL, 728
GROUND UP VENTURES, 882
IBM VENTURE CAPITAL GROUP, 971
INTERLACE VENTURES, 1011
LDV CAPITAL, 1105
NFX, 1323
RIVERSIDE COMPANY, 1576
SERRUYA PRIVATE EQUITY, 2245
STERN PARTNERS, 2249
W CAPITAL PARTNERS, 1949

Retail Services
SWAN & LEGEND VENTURES, 1768

Retail, Consumer & Leisure
3TS CAPITAL PARTNERS 3i Group plc, 2301
AAVIN PRIVATE EQUITY, 16
ACON INVESTMENTS, 45
ADVENT INTERNATIONAL CORPORATION, 61
ALANTRA, 77
ALBUM VC, 79
ALPINE INVESTORS, 92
AMICUS CAPITAL PARTNERS, 2384
AMMER PARTNERS, 2385
APOLLO GLOBAL MANAGEMENT, 141
ASTOR CAPITAL GROUP, 2431
AVANTI CAPITAL, 2449
BALLPARK VENTURES, 2470
BALMORAL FUNDS, 228
BENCIS CAPITAL PARTNERS, 2492
BLACKSTONE PRIVATE EQUITY GROUP, 280
BLUEGEM CAPITAL PARTNERS, 2515
BLUESTEM CAPITAL COMPANY, 300
BREAKAWAY VENTURES, 332
BUSINESS GROWTH FUND, 2541
CAMBRIA GROUP, 381
CAPITAL TODAY, 2551
CARLYLE GROUP, 416
CIC PARTNERS, 479
CIT GROUP, 486
DENALI VENTURE PARTNERS, 606
GRANITE HILL CAPITAL PARTNERS, LLC, 856
HOLDING CAPITAL GROUP, 943
INDEX VENTURES, 2851
IRON GATE CAPITAL, 1024
IRVING PLACE CAPITAL, 1026
J. BURKE CAPITAL PARTNERS, 1027
KALORI GROUP INVESTMENTS, 2906
KOHLBERG KRAVIS ROBERTS & COMPANY, 1086
KRG CAPITAL PARTNERS, 1090
LEE EQUITY PARTNERS, 1108
LEONARD GREEN & PARTNERS LP, 1113
LINLEY CAPITAL, 1134
MAINE ANGELS, 1164
MARWIT CAPITAL LLC, 1171
NAXURI CAPITAL, 1283
NEXTEC DEVELOPMENT CAPITAL LIMITED, 2991
PALLADIUM EQUITY PARTNERS, 1404

Industry Preference Index / Retail, Restaurants & Distribution

POUSCHINE COOK CAPITAL MANAGEMENT LLC, 1470
QIMING VENTURE PARTNERS, 3057
RBC CAPITAL MARKETS, 2223
ROSEWOOD CAPITAL, 1591
SAINTS CAPITAL, 1608
SIGNAL FIRE, 1677
TECH COAST ANGELS, 1786
TH LEE PUTNAM VENTURES, 1806
TULLY & HOLLAND, 1869
VEDANTA CAPITAL LP, 1913
WALNUT GROUP, 1955
WESTVIEW CAPITAL PARTNERS, 1979
YFM GROUP, 3234

Retail, Restaurants & Distribution
CALIFORNIA COAST VENTURE FORUM, 3248

Retail, Restaurants & Franchising
ALTAMONT CAPITAL PARTNERS, 96

Retailing
ALANTRA, 77
AMANAH VENTURES SDN BHD, 2380
ANGELO, GORDON & CO., 128
APAX GLOBIS PARTNERS & COMPANY Globis Capital Partners/Apax, 2406
APEX VENTURE PARTNERS, 138
ARSENAL CAPITAL PARTNERS, 172
ATRIA CAPITAL PARTENAIRES, 2439
AVENUE CAPITAL GROUP, 211
BARCLAYS VENTURES Barclays, 2477
BAY BG BAVARIAN VENTURE CAPITAL CORP, 2485
BERINGEA, 254
BERKSHIRE PARTNERS LLC, 257
BOSTON CAPITAL VENTURES, 313
BOULDER VENTURES LTD, 318
BRADFORD EQUITIES MANAGEMENT LLC, 324
BREAKWATER INVESTMENTS, 333
BRUCKMANN, ROSSER, SHERRILL & COMPANY, 357
BRUML CAPITAL CORPORATION, 358
BRYAN GARNIER & COMPANY, 2535
CARLYLE ASIA INVESTMENT ADVISORS LIMITED Carlyle Group, 2556
CARPEDIA INTERNATIONAL, 2066
CATALYST INVESTMENT MANAGERS PTY LIMITED PPM Capital, 2564
CENTRE PARTNERS MANAGEMENT LLC, 449
CIC FINANCE CIC Group, 2592
CINVEN LIMITED, 2596
COMPASS GROUP MANAGEMENT LLC, 525
DAVID N DEUTSCH & COMPANY LLC, 590
DIRECT CAPITAL PRIVATE EQUITY LIMITED, 2655
DOUBLE IMPACT BUSINESS ADVISORY, 2661
DUKE STREET CAPITAL Duke Street, 2667
EMP GLOBAL, 671
ENTREPRENEUR PARTNERS, 684
EQT PARTNERS AB, 2703
EQUISTONE, 2705
FAIRMONT CAPITAL, 714
FENOX VENTURE CAPITAL, 721
FOUNDATION CAPITAL LIMITED, 2744
FREEMAN SPOGLI & CO., 786
FRIEND SKOLER & COMPANY LLC, 791
FRIULIA SpA, 2749
FUNG CAPITAL USA, 799
FdG ASSOCIATES LP, 804
GAON ASSET MANAGEMENT, 2757
GE CAPITAL, 811
GENERAL ENTERPRISE MANAGEMENT SERVICES, 2763
GLOBAL FINANCE, 2775
GOLDEN GATE CAPITAL, 843
GOLUB CAPITAL, 848
GRAPHITE CAPITAL MANAGEMENT LTD, 2787
GREIF & COMPANY, 874
GRUPO BISA, 2791
HANCOCK PARK ASSOCIATES, 905
HELMET CAPITAL FUND MANAGEMENT OY, 2811
HILCO BRANDS, 940
HILKO UK LTD/VALCO CAPITAL PARTNERS, 2818
HORIZON PARTNERS, LTD, 948
HOULIHAN LOKEY, 951
HUMMER WINBLAD VENTURE PARTNERS, 959
INDUSTRI KAPITAL SVENSKA AB, 2854
IRISH ANGELS, 1023
JAFCO COMPANY LIMITED JAPAN, 2897
JH WHITNEY & COMPANY, 1041
JW CHILDS ASSOCIATES, 1053
KELSO & COMPANY, 1066
KENSINGTON CAPITAL PARTNERS, 2160
KNIGHT'S BRIDGE CAPITAL PARTNERS, 2164
L CATTERTON PARTNERS, 1092
LLOYDS DEVELOPMENT CAPITAL LIMITED, 2935
LLR PARTNERS INC, 1140
LMBO FINANCE, 2936
LOMBARD INVESTMENTS, 1143
LOVETT MILLER & COMPANY, 1152
MACQUARIE DIRECT INVESTMENT LIMITED, 2942
MADISON PARKER CAPITAL, 1161
MANULIFE CAPITAL, 2177
MEKONG CAPITAL, 2952
MERRILL LYNCH (ASIA PACIFIC) LIMITED Merrill Lynch Group, 2955
MIDMARK CAPITAL LP, 1230
MONTLAKE CAPITAL, 1250
MVP CAPITAL PARTNERS, 1275
NEEDHAM CAPITAL PARTNERS, 1287
NORTH ATLANTIC CAPITAL CORPORATION, 1334
NORTHWOOD VENTURES, 1344
OAK INVESTMENT PARTNERS, 1361
PARTNERSHIP FUND FOR NEW YORK CITY, 1422
PENINSULA CAPITAL PARTNERS LLC, 1429
PHOENIX EQUITY PARTNERS LIMITED, 3027
QUANTUM CAPITAL PARTNERS, 1512
QUARRY CAPITAL MANAGEMENT, 1513
RESILIENCE CAPITAL PARTNERS, 1548
RETAIL & RESTAURANT GROWTH CAPITAL LP, 1552
SAMOS INVESTMENTS, 3088
SORRENTO VENTURES, 1708
SPLIT ROCK PARTNERS, 1728
STATELINE ANGELS, 1743
SUN CAPITAL PARTNERS, 1755
SWANDER PACE CAPITAL, 1769
TENNESSEE COMMUNITY VENTURES, 1799
THREE CITIES RESEARCH, 1822
UNISON CAPITAL PARTNERS LP, 3192
UPFRONT VENTURES, 1890
WELLS FARGO CAPITAL FINANCE, 1971
YLR CAPITAL MARKETS LTD, 3237
ZS FUND LP, 2021

Risk Management
AON RISK SOLUTIONS Aon Corporation, 2405

Robotic Systems
CHRYSALIX, 2072

Robotics
11.2 CAPITAL, 3
360 CAPITAL PARTNERS 360 Capital Management SA, 2288
ABSTRACT VENTURES, 23
AXIA CAPITAL, 214
BOOST VC, 310
CARBON VENTURES, 411
COMET LABS, 521
DRAPER ATHENA, 627
DYNAMO VC, 640
EMBARK VENTURES, 664
FA TECHNOLOGY VENTURES, 712
FRONTIER VENTURES, 795
FUTURE VENTURES, 803
GOLDEN VENTURE PARTNERS, 2130
GRISHIN ROBOTICS, 879
GV, 894
INNOVATION WORKS, 1003
KHOSLA VENTURES, 1073

Industry Preference Index / SaaS

LDV CAPITAL, 1105
MASS VENTURES, 1175
MEDRA CAPITAL, 2951
OUTPOST CAPITAL, 1391
PATHBREAKER VENTURES, 1423
QUAKE CAPITAL PARTNERS, 1509
SAMSUNG NEXT, 1614
SCIENCEVEST, 1633
SECTION 32, 1646
SONY INNOVATION FUND, 1705
SPINUP VENTURE, 3123
SUPPLY CHAIN VENTURES, 1759
TENX VENTURES, 2257
TOYOTA AI VENTURES, 1836
TRELLIS CAPITAL CORPORATION, 2265
UNCORK CAPITAL, 1881

Robots
CATAPULT VENTURES, 431

Rubber
DESCO CAPITAL, 607

Rural Innovations
AAVISHKAAR, 2305

SMB Productivity & Cloud Services
500 STARTUPS, 10

SaaS
10X VENTURE PARTNERS, 2
42 VENTURES, 8
ABRT VENTURE FUND, 2312
ACCEL, 27
ACCELEPRISE, 29
ACCESS VENTURE PARTNERS LLC, 35
ACTUA, 52
ADAMS STREET PARTNERS, LLC, 56
ADD VENTURE, 2336
ALBUM VC, 79
ALPHA VENTURE PARTNERS, 91
ALTA VENTURES MEXICO, 2374
AMPLIFY, 121
ANTRAK CAPITAL, 2399
ASCENT VENTURE PARTNERS, 180
ASLANOBA CAPITAL, 2428
ASPECT VENTURES, 182
AUGMENT VENTURES, 198
AZURE CAPITAL PARTNERS, 218
BANNEKER PARTNERS, 230
BARODA VENTURES, 231
BAY PARTNERS, 241
BENHAMOU GLOBAL VENTURES, 252
BEST FUNDS, 2051
BIP CAPITAL, 274
BIRCHMERE VENTURES, 275
BLACKBIRD VENTURES, 2511
BLUMBERG CAPITAL, 304
BOLDSTART VENTURES, 308
BOSTON SEED CAPITAL, 316
BOXGROUP, 321
BREGAL SAGEMOUNT, 336
BURAN VENTURE CAPITAL, 2540
CALUMET VENTURE FUND, 378
CAMP ONE VENTURES, 387
CANAL PARTNERS, 390
CARDINAL VENTURE CAPITAL, 414
CARMEL VENTURES, 2557
CARRICK CAPITAL PARTNERS, 419
CATALYST INVESTORS, 429
CEDAR FUND, 438
CELTIC HOUSE VENTURE PARTNERS, 2070
CEO VENTURES, 452
CHARLES RIVER VENTURES, 457
CISCO INVESTMENTS, 485
CLYDESDALE VENTURES, 508
CONVERGE VENTURE PARTNERS, 536
CYPRESS GROWTH CAPITAL, 577
DUNDEE VENTURE CAPITAL, 635
EDBI Pte LTD., 2681
EDEN VENTURES, 2682
EMERGENCE CAPITAL PARTNERS, 666
EONCAPITAL, 686
EVENTI CAPITAL PARTNERS, 2104
FAIRHAVEN CAPITAL, 713
FELICIS VENTURES, 720
FIRESTARTER FUND, 732
FIVE ELMS CAPITAL, 746
FLORIDA FUNDERS, 754
FORUM VENTURES, 771
GCI CAPITAL, 2123
GENACAST VENTURES, 818
GLASSWING VENTURES, 833
GOLDEN VENTURE PARTNERS, 2130
GREAT OAKS VENTURE CAPITAL, 863
GREYCROFT PARTNERS, 876
HUMMER WINBLAD VENTURE PARTNERS, 959
IDG VENTURES INDIA International Financial Services Limited, 2840
ILLUMINATE VENTURES, 980
INFORMATION VENTURE PARTNERS, 2146
INVENTUS, 1017
JACKSON SQUARE VENTURES, 1028
KAEDAN INVESTMENTS, 2905
KIZOO TECHNOLOGY CAPITAL, 2912
KLASS CAPITAL, 2163
LIGHTHOUSE EQUITY PARTNERS, 2169
LIGHTSPEED VENTURE PARTNERS, 1125
LOVETT MILLER & COMPANY, 1152
M12, 1158
MERCURY FUND, 1207
MERITECH CAPITAL PARTNERS, 1213
MHS CAPITAL, 1227
MIRAMAR VENTURE PARTNERS, 1237
MORADO VENTURE PARTNERS, 1254
NAYA VENTURES, 1284
NEW ATLANTIC VENTURES, 1290
NEW ENTERPRISE ASSOCIATES, 1296
NEXTGEN ANGELS, 1320
NOTION CAPITAL, 3005
ORIGIN VENTURES, 1385
OSAGE PARTNERS, 1388
OYSTER VENTURES, 1396
OneVentures, 3014
PANACHE VENTURES, 2204
PENTECH VENTURES, 3023
POINT NINE CAPITAL, 3035
PRIMARY VENTURE PARTNERS, 1479
PROCYON VENTURES, 1486
QUAKE CAPITAL PARTNERS, 1509
REAL VENTURES, 2224
RELAY VENTURES, 2228
RIDGE VENTURES, 1566
RTP VENTURES, 1598
RUBICON VENTURE CAPITAL, 1599
SIGMA PARTNERS, 1674
SIGMA PRIME VENTURES, 1675
SIGNIA VENTURE PARTNERS, 1680
SINEWAVE VENTURES, 1689
SPEKTRA CAPITAL, 1721
SRIJAN CAPITAL, 3124
STAGE 1 VENTURES, 1737
STRIPES GROUP, 1751
SUNBRIDGE PARTNERS, 1757
SUSQUEHANNA GROWTH EQUITY, 1761
TAO VENTURE CAPITAL PARTNERS, 1782
TARGET PARTNERS, 3152
THINKTIV VENTURES, 1813
TICONDEROGA PRIVATE EQUITY, 1826
TRIDENT CAPITAL, 1852
TRUE VENTURES, 1862
TUGBOAT VENTURES, 1867
UPFRONT VENTURES, 1890
VALHALLA PARTNERS, 1901
VANEDGE CAPITAL PARTNERS, 2270

Industry Preference Index / SaaS & Data Services

VERGE FUND, 1926
VERSION ONE VENTURES, 2272
VILLAGE GLOBAL, 1935
VOLITION CAPITAL, 1944
WESLEY CLOVER, 2276
WILDCAT VENTURE PARTNERS, 1985
ZELKOVA VENTURES, 2016

SaaS & Data Services
BAIN CAPITAL VENTURES, 224

SaaS Businesses
TACTICO, 2251

Safety
ALTRIA VENTURES, 102

Safety and Graphics
3M UNITEK, 2299

Safety, Testing & Inspection
BLUE POINT CAPITAL PARTNERS, 293

Sales & Marketing SaaS
CHICAGO VENTURES, 473

Sales and Marketing
AUSTRALIAN ETHICAL INVESTMENT LIMITED, 2447

Sanitation
AAVISHKAAR, 2305

Satellite Communications
ANDERSON PACIFIC CORPORATION, 123
APOLLO GLOBAL MANAGEMENT, 141
SPACEVEST, 1717

Satellite Imaging
LDV CAPITAL, 1105

Seafood
ARTHUR P GOULD & COMPANY, 174

Security
10X VENTURE PARTNERS, 2
645 VENTURES, 12
ACCEL, 27
ACTIVE VENTURE PARTNERS, 2331
ALEUTIAN CAPITAL PARTNERS, 81
ALTA VENTURES MEXICO, 2374
ALTAIR VENTURES, 95
AMD VENTURES, 107
AMMER PARTNERS, 2385
AMPLIFIER VENTURE PARTNERS, 120
AUXO MANAGEMENT, 2042
AVIV VENTURE CAPITAL, 2453
AZURE CAPITAL PARTNERS, 218
BALDERTON CAPITAL, 2469
BATTELLE VENTURES, 236
BLAST FUNDING, 282
BLUMBERG CAPITAL, 304
CELERITY PARTNERS, 441
CHART VENTURE PARTNERS, 459
CID CAPITAL, 480
CISCO INVESTMENTS, 485
CITI VENTURES, 488
CITY LIGHT CAPITAL, 490
CLAREMONT CREEK VENTURES, 493
DELL VENTURES, 604
DRAPER ATHENA, 627
DUNRATH CAPITAL, 636
EMBARK VENTURES, 664
ENLIGHTENMENT CAPITAL, 681
EUROFUND LP, 2711
FAIRHAVEN CAPITAL, 713
FOUNDERS EQUITY, 777
FRANCISCO PARTNERS, 782
GOOD NEWS VENTURES, 2132

GRANDBANKS CAPITAL, 853
GRAYHAWK CAPITAL, 861
GULFSTAR GROUP, 893
HOLLAND VENTURE BV, 2819
HORIZONS VENTURES, 2822
ICON VENTURES, 972
IDEALAB, 976
IGNITION PARTNERS, 978
IN-Q-TEL, 983
INNOFINANCE OY, 2864
INTEL CAPITAL, 1009
IT-PARTNERS NV, 2893
JACKSON SQUARE VENTURES, 1028
JC2 VENTURES, 1035
LDV CAPITAL, 1105
LEVINE LEICHTMAN CAPITAL PARTNERS, 1115
LIGHTSPEED VENTURE PARTNERS, 1125
LRM - INVESTERINGSMAATSCHAPPIJ VOOR LIMBURG, 2940
M12, 1158
MENLO VENTURES, 1203
MIRAE ASSET VENTURE ACCELERATOR Mirae Asset Group, 2960
MOTOROLA SOLUTIONS VENTURE CAPITAL, 1260
MS&AD VENTURES, 1269
NAUTA CAPITAL, 2978
NORO-MOSELEY PARTNERS, 1332
NOVA SCOTIA BUSINESS INC., 2197
NOVAK BIDDLE VENTURE PARTNERS, 1348
PALADIN CAPITAL GROUP, 1401
PREVIZ VENTURES, 3041
QUANTUM WAVE FUND, 3059
QUESTER CAPITAL MANAGEMENT LIMITED, 3061
SAMSUNG NEXT, 1614
SCP PARTNERS, 1636
SIGNAL PEAK VENTURES, 1679
SONY INNOVATION FUND, 1705
SOUTHERN CROSS VENTURE PARTNERS, 1713
STAGE 1 VENTURES, 1737
STORM VENTURES, 1750
TAO VENTURE CAPITAL PARTNERS, 1782
TELEFONICA VENTURES, 3160
VERIZON VENTURES, 1928
WALNUT GROUP, 1955
WESTERN TECHNOLOGY INVESTMENT, 1976
WINDSPEED VENTURES, 1994
YES VC, 2013

Seed
WAVEMAKER PARTNERS, 1966

Select Retail
RIVER ASSOCIATES INVESTMENTS LLC, 1573

Self-Driving Cars
DAY ONE VENTURES, 594

Semiconductor
CISCO INVESTMENTS, 485
DVC DEUTSCHE VENTURE CAPITAL, 2670
ECAPITAL ENTREPRENEURIAL PARTNERS AG, 2677
ECLIPSE VENTURES, 648

Semiconductor Manufacturing
ECHELON VENTURES, 647

Semiconductors
3I DEUTSCHLAND GESELLSCHAFT FUR 3i Group, 2291
3I GERMANY GmbH 3i Group, 2293
ACCESS VENTURE PARTNERS LLC, 35
ACE VENTURE CAPITAL LIMITED, 2322
ACKRELL CAPITAL, 43
ACORN CAMPUS VENTURES, 46
ADAMS CAPITAL MANAGEMENT, 55
ADARA VENTURE PARTNERS, 2334
ALICE VENTURES SRL, 2356
ALLIANCE VENTURE, 2361
ALTA BERKELEY ASSOCIATES, 2372
ALTAIR VENTURES, 95
AMBIENT SOUND INVESTMENTS, 2382

Industry Preference Index / Service Industries

AMWIN MANAGEMENT PTY LIMITED, 2390
APPLIED MATERIALS VENTURES, 145
ARCH VENTURE PARTNERS, 154
ARTIS VENTURES, 177
ASIAVEST PARTNERS, 2427
ASSET MANAGEMENT VENTURES, 183
ATLANTIC BRIDGE, 2434
AUSTIN VENTURES, 205
AUTO TECH VENTURES, 207
BALDERTON CAPITAL, 2469
BAND OF ANGELS LLC, 229
BANEXI VENTURES PARTNERS, 2472
BATTERY VENTURES, 238
BAY PARTNERS, 241
BI WALDEN MANAGEMENT SDN Walden International, 2499
BIRCHMERE VENTURES, 275
BLACK DIAMOND VENTURES, 278
BLUERUN VENTURES, 299
CALIFORNIA TECHNOLOGY VENTURES, 374
CAMP VENTURES, 388
CARMEL VENTURES, 2557
CENTERPOINT VENTURE PARTNERS, 446
CHALLENGE FUNDS - ETGAR LP, 2576
CHINA DEVELOPMENT INDUSTRIAL BANK CDFH, 2583
CHINA WALDEN MANAGEMENT LIMITED Walden Group, 2588
CID GROUP, 2594
CLAL ELECTRONICS INDUSTRIES LIMITED, 2600
CONCORD VENTURES, 2619
CORE CAPITAL PARTNERS, 540
DRAPER ATHENA, 627
DUCHOSSOIS CAPITAL MANAGEMENT, 634
EASTVEN VENTURE PARTNERS, 645
EMBARK VENTURES, 664
EPLANET CAPITAL, 691
FAIRHAVEN CAPITAL, 713
FINAVENTURES, 730
FOCUS VENTURES, 759
FORMATIVE VENTURES, 766
FORMULA VENTURES LIMITED Formula Group, 2741
FOUNDATION CAPITAL, 773
FRANCISCO PARTNERS, 782
GEFINOR CAPITAL, 813
GEMINI ISRAEL VENTURE FUNDS LIMITED, 2761
GIZA VENTURE CAPITAL, 2773
GOLDEN GATE CAPITAL, 843
GRAYHAWK CAPITAL, 861
GSR VENTURES, 2792
GUGGENHEIM PARTNERS, 890
HARBERT MANAGEMENT CORPORATION, 907
HARBINGER VENTURE MANAGEMENT, 908
ID VENTURES AMERICA LLC, 974
IGLOBE PARTNERS, 2844
INDUSTRIFONDEN, 2858
INTEL CAPITAL, 1009
INTERSOUTH PARTNERS, 1013
JERUSALEM VENTURE PARTNERS, 2901
JF SHEA VENTURES, 1040
JK&B CAPITAL, 1042
KB PARTNERS LLC, 1061
KHOSLA VENTURES, 1073
KODIAK VENTURE PARTNERS, 1084
KOREA FIRST VENTURE CAPITAL CORPORATION, 2915
LABRADOR VENTURES, 1093
MAGMA VENTURE PARTNERS, 2943
MATRIX PARTNERS, 1184
MBF CAPITAL CORPORATION, 1191
MENLO VENTURES, 1203
MERITECH CAPITAL PARTNERS, 1213
MIRAMAR VENTURE PARTNERS, 1237
MITSUI SUMITOMO INSURANCE VENTURE CAPITAL CO, 2962
MOHR-DAVIDOW VENTURES, 1247
MORGAN STANLEY EXPANSION CAPITAL, 1255
MURPHREE VENTURE PARTNERS, 1273
NEEDHAM CAPITAL PARTNERS, 1287
NETROVE ASIA SDN BHD, 2984
NEW VENTURE PARTNERS, 1304
NEWLIGHT MANAGEMENT, 1313
NHN INVESTMENT, 2993
NOVUS VENTURES LP, 1354
OKAPI VENTURE CAPITAL, 1371
OPUS CAPITAL, 1382
PAC-LINK MANAGEMENT CORP., 3015
PARKWALK ADVISORS, 3019
PI CAPITAL GROUP LLC, 1444
PITANGO VENTURE CAPITAL, 3030
PRESIDIO VENTURES, 1478
PRIME TECHNOLOGY VENTURES NV, 3042
QUEST FOR GROWTH, 3060
RIDGEWOOD CAPITAL, 1567
RPM VENTURES, 1596
SAINTS CAPITAL, 1608
SAMSUNG VENTURE INVESTMENT CORPORATION Samsung Electronics, 3089
SAND HILL ANGELS, 1616
SCALE VENTURE PARTNERS, 1629
SELBY VENTURE PARTNERS, 1649
SHASTA VENTURES, 1666
SIERRA VENTURES, 1672
SIGMA PARTNERS, 1674
SIGNATURE CAPITAL LLC, 3111
SILVERTON PARTNERS, 1687
SOUTHERN CROSS VENTURE PARTNERS, 1713
STATELINE ANGELS, 1743
STORM VENTURES, 1750
SUMMIT BRIDGE CAPITAL, 3138
SUMMIT PARTNERS, 1754
SUNBRIDGE PARTNERS, 1757
SYCAMORE VENTURES, 1771
TALLWOOD VENTURE CAPITAL, 1781
TECH CAPITAL PARTNERS, 2253
TEL VENTURE CAPITAL, 1793
TENAYA CAPITAL, 1798
TEUZA MANAGEMENT & DEVELOPMENT LTD, 3162
TI VENTURE CAPITAL Texas Instruments Incorporated, 1825
TRELLIS CAPITAL CORPORATION, 2265
US VENTURE PARTNERS, 1898
VENCORE CAPITAL, 1917
VENTECH, 3199
VENTURE TECH ALLIANCE, 1924
W CAPITAL PARTNERS, 1949
WESTERN TECHNOLOGY INVESTMENT, 1976
WESTLAKE SECURITIES, 1977
WINDWARD VENTURES, 1995
WOODSIDE FUND, 2005
XPV WATER PARTNERS, 2282

Semiconductors & Materials
RHO CANADA VENTURES, 2231

Semis/Coretech
CROSSLINK CAPITAL, 564

Sensors
AXIA CAPITAL, 214

Service Industries
ALLEGIS CYBER CAPITAL, 84
AMERIMARK CAPITAL CORPORATION, 112
BLUE SAGE CAPITAL, 294
CARDINAL EQUITY PARTNERS, 412
CARDINAL PARTNERS, 413
EDGEWATER FUNDS, 654
GLADSTONE CAPITAL, 832
GRANITE EQUITY PARTNERS, 855
HANNOVER FINANZ GmbH, 2801
HANOVER PARTNERS, 906
INVESTAMERICA VENTURE GROUP, 1020
KOHLBERG & COMPANY LLC, 1085
MIDMARK CAPITAL LP, 1230
NORTHERN ENTERPRISE LIMITED, 3002
NORTHWOOD VENTURES, 1344
QUANTUM CAPITAL PARTNERS, 1512
SIERRA VENTURES, 1672
SPLIT ROCK PARTNERS, 1728

Industry Preference Index / Services

THREE CITIES RESEARCH, 1822

Services
AAVIN PRIVATE EQUITY, 16
ACE VENTURE CAPITAL LIMITED, 2322
ALTAS PARTNERS, 2030
APAX PARTNERS, 136
BAKER CAPITAL, 226
BARING VOSTOK CAPITAL PARTNERS, 2482
BRANDON CAPITAL GROUP, 329
BRAZOS PRIVATE EQUITY PARTNERS, 331
BRIDGEPOINT CAPITAL GmbH, 2528
BRIDGEPOINT CAPITAL LIMITED, 2529
BRISIO INNOVATIONS INC., 2061
BROCKWAY MORAN & PARTNERS, 351
CATALYST GROUP, 427
CELADON CAPITAL GROUP, 2573
COMPASS GROUP MANAGEMENT LLC, 525
CZECH VENTURE PARTNERS SRO K+ Venture Partners B.V., 2639
DEFI GESTION SA Banque Cantonale Vaudoise, 2644
DIMELING SCHREIBER & PARK, 617
DN PARTNERS LLC, 620
DUNEDIN CAPITAL PARTNERS LIMITED, 2668
EDGEWATER FUNDS, 654
ELECTRA PARTNERS EUROPE, 2686
EQUITY SOUTH, 694
FAIRMONT CAPITAL, 714
FLORIDA CAPITAL PARTNERS, 753
FRIEND SKOLER & COMPANY LLC, 791
FULCRUM CAPITAL PARTNERS, 2121
GEFINOR CAPITAL, 813
GLOBAL FINANCE, 2775
GRANITE BRIDGE PARTNERS, 854
GRAPHITE CAPITAL MANAGEMENT LTD, 2787
GRIDIRON CAPITAL, 878
HARBERT MANAGEMENT CORPORATION, 907
HIGH ROAD CAPITAL PARTNERS, 934
ILE-DE-FRANCE, 2846
INDIAN DIRECT EQUITY ADVISORS PVT LTD, 2852
INDUSTRI KAPITAL SVENSKA AB, 2854
IRON GATE CAPITAL, 1024
MARWIT CAPITAL LLC, 1171
MESA CAPITAL PARTNERS, 1220
MILESTONE PARTNERS, 1234
NEWLIGHT MANAGEMENT, 1313
NORWEST VENTURE PARTNERS, 1346
PANTHEON VENTURES (US) LP, 1413
PNC ERIEVIEW CAPITAL, 1460
PRISM CAPITAL, 1481
PRITZKER GROUP PRIVATE CAPITAL, 1482
PT BHAKTI INVESTAMA TBK, 3052
QUAD-C MANAGEMENT, 1507
RESONANT VENTURE PARTNERS, 1550
RETAIL & RESTAURANT GROWTH CAPITAL LP, 1552
RFE INVESTMENT PARTNERS, 1560
SAMBRINVEST SA, 3087
SHANGHAI INFORMATION INVESTMENT INCORPORATED, 3105
SOUTHEAST INTERACTIVE TECHNOLOGY FUNDS, 1711
SRIW SA SRIW Group, 3125
STERN PARTNERS, 2249
TECH COAST ANGELS, 1786
WARWICK GROUP, 1958
WAUD CAPITAL PARTNERS LLC, 1964

Silicon-Related Technologies
COMPASS TECHNOLOGY PARTNERS LP, 526

Site Remediation
DEMETER PARTNERS, 2647

Skincare
MCGOVERN CAPITAL, 1194

Smart Buildings
CATAPULT VENTURES, 431

Smart Cities
CHINAROCK CAPITAL MANAGEMENT VENTURES, 474

MACKINNON, BENNETT & CO., 2175

Social
LIGHTSPEED VENTURE PARTNERS, 1125

Social Applications
KIZOO TECHNOLOGY CAPITAL, 2912

Social Determinants
HEALTH ENTERPRISE PARTNERS, 921

Social Enterprises
BIG SOCIETY CAPITAL, 2500
FSE GROUP, 2751
IRISH ANGELS, 1023

Social Impact
VANCITY CAPITAL, 2269

Social Media
10X VENTURE PARTNERS, 2
ARCHTOP VENTURES, 155
BENCHMARK, 251
BIRCHMERE VENTURES, 275
BLACKBIRD VENTURES, 2511
BLUERUN VENTURES, 299
BLUMBERG CAPITAL, 304
BREYER CAPITAL, 339
BULLPEN CAPITAL, 361
CAMP ONE VENTURES, 387
CAVA CAPITAL, 433
CLEARSTONE VENTURE PARTNERS, 504
COLOMA VENTURES, 515
CORSA VENTURES, 546
DATA POINT CAPITAL, 587
DETROIT VENTURE PARTNERS, 608
EDEN VENTURES, 2682
EMERGENCE CAPITAL PARTNERS, 666
G SQUARED, 805
GOLDEN SEEDS, 845
GREAT OAKS VENTURE CAPITAL, 863
GREE VENTURES, 2789
HORIZONS VENTURES, 2822
INLAND TECHSTART FUND, 997
INVESTX, 2154
JC2 VENTURES, 1035
LAUNCHPAD VENTURE GROUP, 1104
LIGHTBANK, 1121
LOOL VENTURES, 2938
M25 GROUP, 1159
MHS CAPITAL, 1227
MOTOROLA SOLUTIONS VENTURE CAPITAL, 1260
NFX, 1323
PANACHE VENTURES, 2204
PENTECH VENTURES, 3023
QUAKE CAPITAL PARTNERS, 1509
RAPTOR GROUP, 1527
REVEL PARTNERS, 1557
SOFTTECH VC, 1702
SPARK CAPITAL, 1718
SRIJAN CAPITAL, 3124
SUMMERHILL VENTURE PARTNERS, 2250
SV ANGEL, 1763
TECHOPERATORS, 1790
TENGELMANN VENTURES, 3161
THINKTIV VENTURES, 1813
TOP RENERGY INC., 2263
TRIDENT CAPITAL, 1852
VENROCK ASSOCIATES, 1918
WASABI VENTURES, 1959
WHITE STAR CAPITAL, 1982
WINDFORCE VENTURES, LLC, 1992
WOMEN'S VENTURE CAPITAL FUND, 2003
XG VENTURES, 2009

Social Services
BONVENTURE, 2522
NIELSEN INNOVATE FUND, 2994

Industry Preference Index / Software

RUBICON VENTURE CAPITAL, 1599

Software

212 CAPITAL PARTNERS, 2286
3I AUSTRIA BETEILGUNG GmbH 3i Group, 2290
3I DEUTSCHLAND GESELLSCHAFT FUR 3i Group, 2291
3I GERMANY GmbH 3i Group, 2293
3TS CAPITAL PARTNERS 3i Group plc, 2301
42 VENTURES, 8
4490 VENTURES, 9
AM VENTURES, 15
AAVIN PRIVATE EQUITY, 16
ABELL FOUNDATION VENTURES, 18
ABRT VENTURE FUND, 2312
ABS VENTURES, 22
ABSTRACT VENTURES, 23
ACCEL-KKR LLC, 28
ACCELEPRISE, 29
ACCESS CAPITAL, 34
ACKRELL CAPITAL, 43
ACONCAGUA VENTURES, 2326
ACT ONE VENTURES, 49
ACT VENTURE CAPITAL LIMITED, 2328
ACUITY VENTURES LLC, 53
ACUMEN VENTURES, 2333
ADVENT VENTURE PARTNERS, 2340
AFTERDOX, 2344
AGF PRIVATE EQUITY Allianz Group, 2346
AITEC, 2349
ALBERTA ENTERPRISE, 2028
ALLEGIS CYBER CAPITAL, 84
ALLIANCE VENTURE, 2361
ALLOS VENTURES, 86
ALPHA VENTURE PARTNERS, 91
ALPINE INVESTORS, 92
ALTOS VENTURES, 100
AMD VENTURES, 107
AMERICAN SUSTAINABLE BUSINESS NETWORK, 3246
AMPLIFIER VENTURE PARTNERS, 120
AMPLIFY, 121
ANALYTICS VENTURES, 122
ANGELS' FORUM LLC, 130
APAX GLOBIS PARTNERS & COMPANY Globis Capital Partners/Apax, 2406
APEX VENTURE PARTNERS, 138
ARC ANGEL FUND, 151
ASCENT VENTURE PARTNERS, 180
ATLAS VENTURE: FRANCE, 2436
ATRIUM CAPITAL, 194
AUGMENT VENTURES, 198
AURA CAPITAL OY Auratum Group, 2442
AURORA CAPITAL GROUP, 202
AUTHOSIS VENTURES, 2448
AVANSIS VENTURES, 210
AWEIDA VENTURE PARTNERS, 213
AXA INVESTMENT MANAGERS PRIVATE EQUITY EUROPE, 2457
AXIOM VENTURE PARTNERS, 215
AXVENTURES, 2461
AZINI CAPITAL PARTNERS, 2463
BALDERTON CAPITAL, 2469
BALLAST POINT VENTURES, 227
BAND OF ANGELS LLC, 229
BANNEKER PARTNERS, 230
BARCELONA EMPREN, 2474
BATTERY VENTURES, 238
BERKELEY VENTURES, 256
BEST FUNDS, 2051
BI WALDEN MANAGEMENT SDN Walden International, 2499
BLACKBIRD VENTURES, 2511
BLAST FUNDING, 282
BLU VENTURE INVESTORS, 288
BLUESHIFT INTERNET VENTURES Blueshift, 2516
BLUETREE VENTURE FUND, 301
BLUMBERG CAPITAL, 304
BMP AKTIENGESELLSCHAFT BMP Venture Capital, 2519
BOLDSTART VENTURES, 308
BONFIRE VENTURES, 309
BOSTON CAPITAL VENTURES, 313
BREGAL SAGEMOUNT, 336
BRIDGEPOINT CAPITAL GmbH, 2528
BRIDGEPOINT CAPITAL LIMITED, 2529
BRIGHTSPARK VENTURES, 2060
BUSINESS GROWTH FUND, 2541
CALUMET VENTURE FUND, 378
CAMBER CREEK, 380
CAMPUS COMPANIES VENTURE CAPITAL FUND, 2545
CANAL PARTNERS, 390
CANDOVER, 2547
CANROCK VENTURES, 396
CARDINAL VENTURE CAPITAL, 414
CARMEL VENTURES, 2557
CATALYST FUND LP, 2562
CAZENOVE PRIVATE EQUITY Cazenove Capital, 2568
CEDAR (ISRAEL) FINANCIAL ADVISORS LIMITED Cedar Fund, 2571
CEI VENTURES, 440
CENTENNIAL VENTURES, 443
CENTRAL TEXAS ANGEL NETWORK, 447
CERVIN VENTURES, 456
CHALLENGE FUNDS - ETGAR LP, 2576
CHARLES RIVER VENTURES, 457
CHAZEN CAPITAL PARTNERS, 462
CHENGWEI VENTURES, 2581
CHICAGO VENTURE PARTNERS LP, 472
CHINA WALDEN MANAGEMENT LIMITED Walden Group, 2588
CIBC CAPITAL MARKETS, 2073
CIBC INNOVATION BANKING, 2074
CLOQUET CAPITAL PARTNERS, 507
COATUE MANAGEMENT, 511
COLOMA VENTURES, 515
COLUMBIA CAPITAL, 518
COMVEST PARTNERS, 530
CONCORD VENTURES, 2619
CONTOUR VENTURE PARTNERS, 535
CONVERGE VENTURE PARTNERS, 536
CORAL GROUP, 538
CRAWLEY VENTURES, 554
CREANDUM, 2628
CREDIT MUTUEL EQUITY, 2082
CRESCENDO VENTURE MANAGEMENT LLC, 2630
CRESCENDO VENTURES, 556
CROSSLINK CAPITAL, 564
CSA PARTNERS, 567
CXO FUND, 575
CYPRESS GROWTH CAPITAL, 577
DAG VENTURES, 582
DALLAS VENTURE PARTNERS, 583
DATA COLLECTIVE, 586
DAWNTREADER VENTURES, 593
DEFTA PARTNERS, 603
DELL VENTURES, 604
DELTA VENTURES LIMITED, 2646
DETROIT VENTURE PARTNERS, 608
DFJ ESPRIT, 2653
DFJ VENTURE CAPITAL, 610
DIAGRAM VENTURES, 2090
DN CAPITAL, 2659
DOUBLEROCK VENTURE CAPITAL, 626
DR NEUHAUS TECHNO NORD GmbH, 2664
DRAPER ATHENA, 627
DRAPER RICHARDS KAPLAN FOUNDATION, 628
DUCHOSSOIS CAPITAL MANAGEMENT, 634
DYNAMO VC, 640
EARLYBIRD, 2673
EASTVEN VENTURE PARTNERS, 645
ECAPITAL ENTREPRENEURIAL PARTNERS AG, 2677
ECHELON VENTURES, 647
EDELSON TECHNOLOGY PARTNERS, 651
EDEN VENTURES, 2682
EDGESTONE CAPITAL PARTNERS, 2098
EDGEWATER FUNDS, 654
EDISON PARTNERS, 655
ELEVATION PARTNERS, 660
EQUITY SOUTH, 694
ESCALATE CAPITAL PARTNERS, 696

Industry Preference Index / Software

EUROPEAN FOUNDERS FUND, 2714
EVERCORE CAPITAL PARTNERS, 700
EVERGREEN VENTURE PARTNERS, 2717
FALCON FUND, 716
FENOX VENTURE CAPITAL, 721
FF VENTURE CAPITAL, 724
FIDELITY GROWTH PARTNERS EUROPE, 2725
FIFTH WALL, 728
FINADVANCE, 2726
FINANCIERE DE BRIENNE FCPR, 2729
FINAVENTURES, 730
FISHER LYNCH CAPITAL, 745
FLOODGATE FUND, 752
FLORIDA FUNDERS, 754
FLYWHEEL VENTURES, 758
FOCUS VENTURES, 759
FOG CITY CAPITAL, 760
FORMULA VENTURES LIMITED Formula Group, 2741
FOUNDATION CAPITAL, 773
FOUNDER PARTNERS, 775
FOUNDERS FUND, 778
FOUNDRY GROUP, 779
FRANCISCO PARTNERS, 782
FREESTYLE, 787
FRONTIER VENTURE CAPITAL, 794
FTV CAPITAL, 796
FUSION FUND, 802
G-51 CAPITAL LLC, 806
GABRIEL VENTURE PARTNERS, 808
GARAGE TECHNOLOGY VENTURES, 810
GE VENTURES, 812
GEFINOR CAPITAL, 813
GENACAST VENTURES, 818
GENERAL CATALYST PARTNERS, 820
GENERAL ENTERPRISE MANAGEMENT SERVICES, 2763
GENSTAR CAPITAL LP, 823
GGV CAPITAL, 827
GILDE INVESTMENT FUNDS, 2770
GIZA VENTURE CAPITAL, 2773
GLOBESPAN CAPITAL PARTNERS, 839
GLYNN CAPITAL MANAGEMENT, 840
GOLDEN GATE CAPITAL, 843
GOOD GROWTH CAPITAL, 849
GRANDBANKS CAPITAL, 853
GRANITE VENTURE CAPITAL CORPORATION, 2785
GRAYHAWK CAPITAL, 861
GREAT HILL PARTNERS LLC, 862
GREENHAVEN PARTNERS, 868
GREENHILL SAVP, 869
GREYLOCK PARTNERS, 877
GRISHIN ROBOTICS, 879
GROTECH VENTURES, 881
GROUND UP VENTURES, 882
GUGGENHEIM PARTNERS, 890
GULFSTAR GROUP, 893
GV, 894
HARBERT MANAGEMENT CORPORATION, 907
HARBINGER VENTURE MANAGEMENT, 908
HARBOURVEST PARTNERS LLC, 912
HASSO PLATTNER VENTURES, 2804
HELLMAN & FRIEDMAN LLC, 927
HIGH COUNTRY VENTURE, 933
HORIZON VENTURES LLC, 950
HOXTON VENTURES, 2825
HUDSON VENTURE PARTNERS, 957
HUMMER WINBLAD VENTURE PARTNERS, 959
HUMMINGBIRD VENTURES, 2828
HUNTSMAN GAY GLOBAL CAPITAL, 962
HYUNDAI VENTURE INVESTMENT CORPORATION, 2830
I-PACIFIC PARTNERS, 2831
IA VENTURES, 969
ICON VENTURES, 972
ID VENTURES AMERICA LLC, 974
IDEA FUND PARTNERS, 975
IDEALAB, 976
IDG TECHNOLOGY VENTURE INVESTMENT, 2839
IDG VENTURES INDIA International Financial Services Limited, 2840
IGAN PARTNERS, 2141
IGNITE JAPAN KK Ignite Group, 2845
IGNITION PARTNERS, 978
INCWELL VENTURE CAPITAL, 985
INDIAN DIRECT EQUITY ADVISORS PVT LTD, 2852
INETWORKS ADVISORS LLC, 991
INFLEXION PARTNERS, 994
INITIALIZED CAPITAL, 995
INLAND TECHSTART FUND, 997
INNOSPRING, 998
INNOVACOM SA, 2866
INNOVATION WORKS, 1003
INNOVATIONSKAPITAL, 2869
INSTITUTIONAL VENTURE PARTNERS, 1006
INTEL CAPITAL, 1009
INTER-ASIA VENTURE MANAGEMENT LIMITED, 2872
INTERSOUTH PARTNERS, 1013
INVENTURE PARTNERS, 2877
INVENTUS, 1017
INVEXCEL PATRIMONIO, 2882
INVUS GROUP, 1022
IPOSCOPE NV/SA, 2886
IRISH ANGELS, 1023
ISOURCE GESTION, 2890
JAFCO COMPANY LIMITED JAPAN, 2897
JC TECHNOLOGIES LTD, 2900
JERUSALEM VENTURE PARTNERS, 2901
JF SHEA VENTURES, 1040
JK&B CAPITAL, 1042
JMI EQUITY FUND LP, 1045
JUMPSTART INC, 1051
KAEDAN INVESTMENTS, 2905
KALORI GROUP INVESTMENTS, 2906
KBL FOUNDER SA, 2908
KERRY CAPITAL ADVISORS, 1071
KLASS CAPITAL, 2163
KODIAK VENTURE PARTNERS, 1084
LABRADOR VENTURES, 1093
LANDSBANKI VENTURES, 2920
LAUNCHCAPITAL, 1101
LAUNCHPAD VENTURE GROUP, 1104
LBBW VENTURE CAPITAL, 2923
LEAPFROG VENTURES, 1106
LEASING TECHNOLOGIES INTERNATIONAL INC., 1107
LEVINE LEICHTMAN CAPITAL PARTNERS, 1115
LIBERTY CAPITAL PARTNERS, 1118
LLR PARTNERS INC, 1140
LOCUS VENTURES, 1142
LONG RIVER VENTURES, 1146
LOVETT MILLER & COMPANY, 1152
LRM - INVESTERINGSMAATSCHAPPIJ VOOR LIMBURG, 2940
M/C PARTNERS, 1157
M25 GROUP, 1159
MAINE ANGELS, 1164
MANTELLA VENTURE PARTNERS, 2176
MARATHON VENTURE CAPITAL FUND LIMITED, 2945
MARYLAND VENTURE FUND, 1172
MASON WELLS, 1174
MASSACHUSETTS CAPITAL RESOURCE COMPANY, 1176
MASTHEAD VENTURE PARTNERS, 1178
MAYFIELD FUND, 1187
MBF CAPITAL CORPORATION, 1191
MCROCK CAPITAL, 2183
MEDRA CAPITAL, 2951
MERCURY FUND, 1207
MERITUS VENTURES, 1215
MERUS CAPITAL, 1219
METROPOLITAN PARTNERS GROUP, 1226
MIDINVEST LIMITED, 2957
MIDVEN, 2958
MILLENIUM TECHNOLOGY VALUE PARTNERS, 1235
MISSION VENTURES, 1239
MISSIONOG, 1240
MISTRAL VENTURE PARTNERS, 2187
MK CAPITAL, 1242
MMV CAPITAL PARTNERS, 2188
MOHR-DAVIDOW VENTURES, 1247

Industry Preference Index / Software

MOMENTUM FUNDS MANAGEMENT PTY LIMITED, 2966
MONITOR VENTURES, 1249
MOUNTAINEER CAPITAL, 1262
NAVITAS CAPITAL, 1281
NEEDHAM CAPITAL PARTNERS, 1287
NEST VENTURES, 1289
NEUHAUS PARTNERS, 2985
NEW ATLANTIC VENTURES, 1290
NEW MOUNTAIN CAPITAL, 1300
NEW VENTURE PARTNERS, 1304
NEW YORK CITY ENTREPRENEURIAL FUND New York City Economic Development Corporation, 1306
NEW YORK LIFE CAPITAL PARTNERS, 1308
NEW YORK VENTURE PARTNERS, 1309
NEWLIGHT MANAGEMENT, 1313
NEXT WORLD CAPITAL, 1319
NFX, 1323
NKM CAPITAL, 1330
NORTH ATLANTIC CAPITAL CORPORATION, 1334
NORTH BRIDGE VENTURE PARTNERS, 1335
NORWEST VENTURE PARTNERS, 1346
NOVAK BIDDLE VENTURE PARTNERS, 1348
NYC SEED, 1358
OAK INVESTMENT PARTNERS, 1361
OKAPI VENTURE CAPITAL, 1371
OLYMPUS PARTNERS, 1372
OPENVIEW VENTURE PARTNERS, 1381
OPUS CAPITAL, 1382
OSAGE PARTNERS, 1388
OVP VENTURE PARTNERS, 1392
OWL VENTURES, 1393
OXANTIUM VENTURES, 1394
OYSTER INVEST, 3013
PAC-LINK MANAGEMENT CORP., 3015
PALISADES VENTURES, 1403
PALO ALTO VENTURE PARTNERS, 1406
PALOMAR VENTURES, 1408
PARTECH INTERNATIONAL, 1418
PELION VENTURE PARTNERS, 1428
PENINSULA VENTURES, 1430
PENN VENTURE PARTNERS, 1431
PENNELL VENTURE PARTNERS LLC, 1432
PI CAPITAL GROUP LLC, 1444
PIEDMONT ANGEL NETWORK, 1446
PINNACLE MERCHANT CAPITAL, 2214
PITANGO VENTURE CAPITAL, 3030
POND VENTURES, 3038
PRESIDIO VENTURES, 1478
PRIME TECHNOLOGY VENTURES NV, 3042
PRIVATE EQUITY PARTNERS SPA, 3044
PROJECT 11 VENTURES, 1489
PROMUS VENTURES, 1491
PSG, 1499
QUEST FOR GROWTH, 3060
QUESTER CAPITAL MANAGEMENT LIMITED, 3061
QUESTMARK PARTNERS LP, 1517
RAFAEL DEVELOPMENT CORPORATION (RDC) LIMITED, 3063
REACH CAPITAL, 1530
RECIPROCAL VENTURES, 1531
REDPOINT VENTURES, 1537
REED ELSEVIER VENTURES, 3065
RESONANT VENTURE PARTNERS, 1550
REVEL PARTNERS, 1557
RIDGE VENTURES, 1566
RIDGEWOOD CAPITAL, 1567
RISE OF THE REST, 1571
ROPART ASSET MANAGEMENT, 1587
ROSER VENTURES LLC, 1590
ROUGH DRAFT VENTURES, 1593
RPM VENTURES, 1596
RRE VENTURES, 1597
RUNA CAPITAL, 3079
S3 VENTURES, 1601
SAINTS CAPITAL, 1608
SAMSUNG VENTURE INVESTMENT CORPORATION Samsung Electronics, 3089
SAND HILL ANGELS, 1616
SANDBOX INDUSTRIES, 1618
SATORI CAPITAL, 1625
SBRC INVESTMENT CONSULTATION LIMITED, 3092
SCALE VENTURE PARTNERS, 1629
SELBY VENTURE PARTNERS, 1649
SEQUOIA CAPITAL, 1657
SEVIN ROSEN FUNDS, 1661
SHANNON COMMERCIAL PROPERTIES, 3106
SHASTA VENTURES, 1666
SHEPHERD VENTURES, 1667
SIERRA ANGELS, 1671
SIERRA VENTURES, 1672
SIGMA PARTNERS, 1674
SIGNATURE CAPITAL LLC, 3111
SMART BUSINESS CONSULTING, 3115
SMARTINVEST VENTURES, 1697
SOLID VENTURES, 3119
SOUTHEAST INTERACTIVE TECHNOLOGY FUNDS, 1711
SOUTHERN CAPITOL VENTURES, 1712
SPACEVEST, 1717
SPECTRUM EQUITY INVESTORS LP, 1720
SPENCER TRASK VENTURES, 1723
SPERO VENTURES, 1724
SPLIT ROCK PARTNERS, 1728
SPRING LAKE EQUITY PARTNERS, 1731
STAENBERG VENTURE PARTNERS, 1736
STAGEONE VENTURES, 3127
STARTUP CAPITAL VENTURES, 1740
STARVEST PARTNERS, 1741
STATELINE ANGELS, 1743
STORM VENTURES, 1750
SUMMIT BRIDGE CAPITAL, 3138
SVB CAPITAL, 1766
SWITCH VENTURES, 1770
SYCAMORE VENTURES, 1771
SYMMETRIC CAPITAL, 1772
TAMAR TECHNOLOGY VENTURES LIMITED, 3149
TAMIR FISHMAN VENTURES, 3150
TANK STREAM VENTURES, 3151
TARGET PARTNERS, 3152
TEAKWOOD CAPITAL, 1785
TECH COAST ANGELS, 1786
TECHNOCAP, 2254
TECHNOLOGY CROSSOVER VENTURES, 1787
TELESOFT PARTNERS, 1795
TELESYSTEM, 2255
TEN ELEVEN VENTURES, 1796
TENAYA CAPITAL, 1798
TENX VENTURES, 2257
TEUZA MANAGEMENT & DEVELOPMENT LTD, 3162
TFG CAPITAL AG, 3163
TGAP VENTURES, 1804
THOMA BRAVO LLC, 1817
THOMSON-CSF VENTURES, 3167
TIE ANGELS GROUP SEATTLE, 1827
TL VENTURES, 1830
TRANS COSMOS INCORPORATED, 3176
TRANSITION PARTNERS LTD, 1839
TRIBECA VENTURE PARTNERS, 1851
TRINITY VENTURE CAPITAL TVC Holdings plc, 3182
TRINITY VENTURES, 1855
TRITON VENTURES, 1857
TRU MANAGEMENT, 1860
TRUE VENTURES, 1862
TSG EQUITY PARTNERS, 1864
TVC CAPITAL, 1871
UNCORK CAPITAL, 1881
UPDATA VENTURE PARTNERS, 1888
US VENTURE PARTNERS, 1898
VALAR VENTURES, 1899
VALLEY VENTURES LP, 1903
VELOCITY EQUITY PARTNERS LLC, 1915
VENCORE CAPITAL, 1917
VENTURE CAPITAL FUND OF NEW ENGLAND, 1922
VERDEXUS, 2271
VERITAS VENTURE PARTNERS, 3203
VERIZON VENTURES, 1928

Industry Preference Index / Software & IT

VIKING VENTURE, 3207
VISION CAPITAL, 1939
VITAL FINANCIAL LLC, 1942
VORTEX PARTNERS, 1946
VOYAGER CAPITAL, 1947
W CAPITAL PARTNERS, 1949
WALDEN ISRAEL VENTURE CAPITAL, 3221
WALDEN VENTURE CAPITAL, 1953
WESTERN AMERICA CAPITAL GROUP, 2278
WESTLAKE SECURITIES, 1977
WESTSUMMIT CAPITAL, 3225
WESTVIEW CAPITAL PARTNERS, 1979
WHEATLEY PARTNERS, 1981
WILDCAT VENTURE PARTNERS, 1985
WINDWARD VENTURES, 1995
WOODBRIDGE GROUP, 2004
WOODSIDE FUND, 2005
WRF CAPITAL, 2007
XANGE PRIVATE EQUITY, 3229
YFM GROUP, 3234
YL VENTURES, 3236
YUUWA CAPITAL, 3238
ZM CAPITAL, 2019
ZONE VENTURES, 2020

Software & IT
RIVERSIDE COMPANY, 1576

Software & Information Services
CAPITAL RESOURCE PARTNERS, 405

Software & Internet
CALIFORNIA COAST VENTURE FORUM, 3248
TRIBE CAPITAL, 1850

Software & Services
DCM, 597
REVOLUTION LLC, 1558

Software (incl. SaaS)
RHO CANADA VENTURES, 2231

Software Development
HENQ, 2813

Software Services
3I ASIA PACIFIC 3i Group, 2289
ADARA VENTURE PARTNERS, 2334
ALTA BERKELEY ASSOCIATES, 2372
ARGENTUM GROUP, 162
CENTERPOINT VENTURE PARTNERS, 446
CHRYSALIS CAPITAL ChrysCapital, 2590
CHRYSCAPITAL MANAGEMENT COMPANIES ChrysCapital, 2591
CITA GESTION, 2598
COMMONWEALTH CAPITAL VENTURES LP, 523
ELECTRA PARTNERS ASIA LIMITED SFC of Hong Kong, 2685
GMT COMMUNICATIONS PARTNERS LLP, 2780
GRANDBANKS CAPITAL, 853
INSIGHT VENTURE PARTNERS, 1005
MADRONA VENTURE GROUP, 1162
McLEAN WATSON CAPITAL, 2191
SOUTHERN CROSS VENTURE PARTNERS, 1713

Software Systems
CALIFORNIA TECHNOLOGY VENTURES, 374

Solar Energy
ANGELENO GROUP, 127
AZCA, 217
ENERTECH CAPITAL, 677

Solar Infrastructure
FORESIGHT VENTURE PARTNERS, 2740

Space
11.2 CAPITAL, 3
CORNERSTONE CAPITAL HOLDINGS, 542
KHOSLA VENTURES, 1073

Space Tech
GOOD GROWTH CAPITAL, 849

Space Technology
BESSEMER VENTURE PARTNERS, 263
BOOST VC, 310
FRONTIER VENTURES, 795
GOOD NEWS VENTURES, 2132
NEWABLE VENTURES, 2988

Specialist Financial Businesses
ROTHSCHILD AUSTRALIA - ARROW PRIVATE EQUITY Rothschild Group, 3077

Specialized Services
CLEARVIEW CAPITAL, 505

Specialty Chemicals
AMERICAN SECURITIES LLC, 111
BROOKSIDE EQUITY PARTNERS LLC, 356
CAPITAL FOR BUSINESS, INC, 402
CAPITAL SOUTHWEST CORPORATION, 406
CENTERFIELD CAPITAL PARTNERS, 445
FCF PARTNERS LP, 719
GLADSTONE CAPITAL, 832
GRYPHON MANAGEMENT COMPANY, 887
HERITAGE PARTNERS, 929
HIG CAPITAL, 931
HORIZON PARTNERS, LTD, 948
JMH CAPITAL, 1044
MOUNTAINEER CAPITAL, 1262
POUSCHINE COOK CAPITAL MANAGEMENT LLC, 1470

Specialty Consumer
HAWTHORN EQUITY PARTNERS, 919

Specialty Consumer Brands
CUE BALL GROUP, 568

Specialty Consumer Products
GRIDIRON CAPITAL, 878
PARALLEL INVESTMENT PARTNERS, 1417

Specialty Distribution
VALOR EQUITY PARTNERS, 1904
WATER STREET HEALTHCARE PARTNERS, 1962

Specialty Finance
BIP CAPITAL, 274
CLARION CAPITAL PARTNERS LLC, 494
SALT CREEK CAPITAL, 1612
WELLS FARGO CAPITAL FINANCE, 1971

Specialty Food Products
PACIFIC COMMUNITY VENTURES, 1397

Specialty Healthcare
ALLOS VENTURES, 86

Specialty Lending
NEWLIGHT PARTNERS, 1314

Specialty Manufacturing
ALBION INVESTORS LLC, 78
CALTIUS STRUCTURED CAPITAL, 377
GLADSTONE CAPITAL, 832
NEWSPRING CAPITAL, 1316
SIGNAL HILL EQUITY PARTNERS, 2246
STONEBRIDGE PARTNERS, 1747
TGAP VENTURES, 1804

Specialty Manufacturing & Distribution
BEHRMAN CAPITAL, 248

Specialty Packaging
STONEBRIDGE PARTNERS, 1747

Industry Preference Index / Technology

Specialty Retail
BUNKER HILL CAPITAL, 362
CASTANEA PARTNERS, 424
CLARION CAPITAL PARTNERS LLC, 494
GRYPHON INVESTORS, 886
HARVEST PARTNERS, 917
INVUS GROUP, 1022
SEIDLER EQUITY PARTNERS, 1648
TWJ CAPITAL, 1875

Specialty Servaces
LAKE CAPITAL, 1095

Specialty Services
PEGASUS CAPITAL GROUP, 1427

Specialty Staffing
CALTIUS STRUCTURED CAPITAL, 377

Speech and Natural Language
FLYING FISH, 757

Sports
ACKRELL CAPITAL, 43
BREAKAWAY VENTURES, 332
DETROIT VENTURE PARTNERS, 608
FALCONHEAD CAPITAL, 717
INTEL CAPITAL, 1009
KB PARTNERS, 1060
PROSPECT PARTNERS LLC, 1494
RAPTOR GROUP, 1527
SWANDER PACE CAPITAL, 1769
UNITED TALENT AGENCY VENTURES, 1885

Sports, Media & Entertainment
REVOLUTION LLC, 1558

Staffing
ACCESS CAPITAL, 34

Stem Cell Therapy
SPENCER TRASK VENTURES, 1723

Storage
ELECTRA PARTNERS ASIA LIMITED SFC of Hong Kong, 2685
EVERCORE CAPITAL PARTNERS, 700
FORMULA VENTURES LIMITED Formula Group, 2741
GENESIS PARTNERS, 2766
GOOD NEWS VENTURES, 2132
GRANDBANKS CAPITAL, 853
JACKSON SQUARE VENTURES, 1028
KHOSLA VENTURES, 1073
NEW VENTURE PARTNERS, 1304
NTH POWER TECHNOLOGIES, 1355
OAK INVESTMENT PARTNERS, 1361
PITANGO VENTURE CAPITAL, 3030
REDPOINT VENTURES, 1537

Storage & Computing
MENLO VENTURES, 1203

Storage Networking
ACCEL-KKR LLC, 28

Stored Energy
INFIELD CAPITAL, 992

Superannuation
AUSTRALIAN ETHICAL INVESTMENT LIMITED, 2447

Supply Chain Management
ODYSSEY INVESTMENT PARTNERS, 1368
TOP RENERGY INC., 2263

Supply Chain Technology
CAMBRIDGE CAPITAL, 383

Sustainability
ALTRIA VENTURES, 102
CULTIVIAN SANDBOX VENTURES, 571
DBL PARTNERS, 596
FLAGSHIP PIONEERING, 748
GRANITE HILL CAPITAL PARTNERS, LLC, 856
MINDFULL INVESTORS, 1236
MITSUI SUMITOMO INSURANCE VENTURE CAPITAL CO, 2962
PANGAEA VENTURES LTD, 2205
SJF VENTURES, 1691
SPRING LANE CAPITAL, 1732
URBAN INNOVATION FUND, 1895

Sustainable Energy
ATLANTA VENTURES, 191
CASTROL INNOVENTURES, 2559
KHOSLA VENTURES, 1073

Sustainable Food and Agriculture
INVESTECO, 2153

Sustainable Living
PHYSIC VENTURES, 1442

Sustainable Materials
WHEB GROUP, 3227

Sustainable Products
COLLABORATIVE FUND, 514

Sustainable Technologies
SELBY VENTURE PARTNERS, 1649

Sustainable Transportation
FUTURE VENTURES, 803

Systems & Hardware
GABRIEL VENTURE PARTNERS, 808
NORWEST VENTURE PARTNERS, 1346

Systems & Peripherals
GLOBESPAN CAPITAL PARTNERS, 839

Systems & Software
MASS VENTURES, 1175

TMT
3I GESTION SA 3i Group, 2294
SB CHINA VENTURE CAPITAL, 3091
ZHENFUND, 3241

Tech Enabled Services
ACTIVE VENTURE PARTNERS, 2331

Tech Services
CALTIUS STRUCTURED CAPITAL, 377

Tech-Enabled Business Services
BLUE HERON CAPITAL, 291

Technologies
NORTHGATE, 1341

Technology
.406 VENTURES, 1
1843 CAPITAL, 6
212 CAPITAL PARTNERS, 2286
3TS CAPITAL PARTNERS 3i Group plc, 2301
3i GROUP PLC, 2303
645 VENTURES, 12
A-GRADE INVESTMENTS, 14
AAVISHKAAR, 2305
ACACIA CAPITAL PARTNERS, 2314
ACADIA WOODS PARTNERS, 25
ACCEDE CAPITAL, 2315
ACCEL-KKR LLC, 28
ACCELEPRISE, 29
ACCELERATOR VENTURES, 31

Industry Preference Index / Technology

ACCENTURE TECHNOLOGY VENTURES, 2318
ACCESS VENTURE PARTNERS LLC, 35
ACCOLADE PARTNERS, 36
ACCOMPLICE, 37
ACE & COMPANY, 2321
ACKRELL CAPITAL, 43
ACREW CAPITAL, 48
ACT ONE VENTURES, 49
ACTIVE VENTURE PARTNERS, 2331
ADAMS CAPITAL MANAGEMENT, 55
ADAMS STREET PARTNERS, LLC, 56
ADVANCIT CAPITAL, 59
ALBUM VC, 79
ALLEGRO INVESTMENT FUND, 2358
ALLELE FUNDS, 2359
ALLIANCE VENTURE, 2361
ALMAZ CAPITAL, 89
ALPINVEST GmbH, 2369
ALPINVEST HOLDING NV Alpinvest, 2370
ALTA BERKELEY ASSOCIATES, 2372
ALTA PARTNERS, 94
ALTOS VENTURES, 100
AMANET TECHNOLOGIES LIMITED, 2381
AME CLOUD VENTURES, 108
AMICUS CAPITAL PARTNERS, 2384
AMPHION CAPITAL PARTNERS, 2389
ANALYTICS VENTURES, 122
ANT FINANCIAL, 2396
APAX GLOBIS PARTNERS & COMPANY Globis Capital Partners/Apax, 2406
ARAVAIPA VENTURES, 147
ARBOR VENTURES, 149
ARGENTUM GROUP, 162
ARMADA INVESTMENT GROUP, 2418
ARTHUR P GOULD & COMPANY, 174
ASCENT VENTURE PARTNERS, 180
ASTELLA INVESTMENTS, 2429
ATLANTA VENTURES, 191
ATLANTIC VENTURES, 2435
ATLAS VENTURE: FRANCE, 2436
ATOMICO, 2437
AUDAX GROUP, 197
AUGMENTUM CAPITAL, 2441
AUSTRAL CAPITAL PARTNERS, 2446
AUTO TECH VENTURES, 207
AVAC, 2043
AWAY REALTY, 2456
AXVENTURES, 2461
AZINI CAPITAL PARTNERS, 2463
BALLPARK VENTURES, 2470
BARCLAYS VENTURES Barclays, 2477
BARING VOSTOK CAPITAL PARTNERS, 2482
BASE VENTURES, 232
BASECAMP VENTURES, 233
BATTELLE VENTURES, 236
BATTERY VENTURES, 238
BC PARTNERS LIMITED, 2488
BDC CAPITAL, 2048
BEN FRANKLIN TECHNOLOGY PARTNERS, 249
BERINGER CAPITAL, 2050
BERLIN TECHNOLOGIE, 2494
BERTRAM CAPITAL, 260
BESTPORT VENTURES, 2498
BIGFOOT VENTURES, 2502
BIP CAPITAL, 274
BIRCHMERE VENTURES, 275
BISON CAPITAL ASSET MANAGEMENT LLC, 277
BLACK DIAMOND VENTURES, 278
BLACKSTONE PRIVATE EQUITY GROUP, 280
BLAST FUNDING, 282
BLOOM EQUITY, 2513
BLU VENTURE INVESTORS, 288
BLUE BRIGHT VENTURES, 289
BLUE HERON CAPITAL, 291
BLUEFISH VENTURES, 297
BLUETREE VENTURE FUND, 301
BLUMBERG CAPITAL, 304

BLUME VENTURES, 2517
BMP AKTIENGESELLSCHAFT BMP Venture Capital, 2519
BOLDCAP VENTURES LLC, 307
BOOST VC, 310
BOREALIS VENTURES, 311
BOSTON CAPITAL VENTURES, 313
BOSTON GLOBAL VENTURES, LLC, 314
BRADFORD EQUITIES MANAGEMENT LLC, 324
BRIGHTSTONE VENTURE CAPITAL, 344
BRILLIANT VENTURES, 345
BRISIO INNOVATIONS INC., 2061
BROADHAVEN CAPITAL PARTNERS, 346
BROADHORN CAPITAL, 347
BROOKLYN BRIDGE VENTURES, 354
BRUML CAPITAL CORPORATION, 358
BRYANT PARK VENTURES, 359
BUILD VENTURES, 2063
CALIFORNIA COAST VENTURE FORUM, 3248
CAMP ONE VENTURES, 387
CAMP VENTURES, 388
CANAAN PARTNERS, 389
CANOPY BOULDER, 395
CANROCK VENTURES, 396
CANYON CREEK CAPITAL, 400
CAPMAN CAPITAL MANAGEMENT OY, 2553
CAPX PARTNERS, 410
CARBON VENTURES, 411
CARDINAL VENTURE CAPITAL, 414
CARLYLE ASIA INVESTMENT ADVISORS LIMITED Carlyle Group, 2556
CARLYLE GROUP, 416
CASABONA VENTURES, 421
CASTROL INNOVENTURES, 2559
CAVA CAPITAL, 433
CEDAR VENTURES LLC, 439
CEO VENTURES, 452
CERBERUS CAPITAL MANAGEMENT, 453
CHARLOTTE STREET CAPITAL, 2577
CHASE CAPITAL PARTNERS, 2579
CHAZEN CAPITAL PARTNERS, 462
CHEVRON TECHNOLOGY VENTURES, 468
CHRYSALIS VENTURES, 477
CIBC CAPITAL MARKETS, 2073
CIBC INNOVATION BANKING, 2074
CINCO CAPITAL, 2595
CINTRIFUSE, 482
CLARITAS CAPITAL, 495
CLAYTON ASSOCIATES, 497
CLEARLAKE CAPITAL, 502
CLEARSPRING CAPITAL PARTNERS, 2076
CNF INVESTMENTS Clark Enterprises, Inc., 510
COATUE MANAGEMENT, 511
COLLABORATIVE FUND, 514
COLLER CAPITAL LIMITED, 2612
COLT VENTURES, 517
COMPANHIA RIOGRANDENSE DE PARTICIPACOES, 2617
COMPOUND, 527
CONTINENTAL VENTURE CAPITAL LIMITED, 2622
CONTOUR VENTURE PARTNERS, 535
CONVERSION CAPITAL, 537
CONVEXA Tyveholmen AS, 2623
CORE PACIFIC - YAMAICHI CAPITAL LIMITED Core Pacific Securities Company Ltd, 2624
COSTELLA KIRSCH, 549
COTTONWOOD TECHNOLOGY FUND, 550
COWBOY VENTURES, 553
CRUNCHFUND, 565
CULTIVATION CAPITAL, 570
CULTIVIAN SANDBOX VENTURES, 571
CUSTER CAPITAL, 572
CXO FUND, 575
CapitalG, 579
DANCAP PRIVATE EQUITY, 2088
DANEVEST TECH FUND ADVISORS, 584
DAVENPORT RESOURCES LLC, 589
DAVID N DEUTSCH & COMPANY LLC, 590
DAYLIGHT PARTNERS, 595

Industry Preference Index / Technology

DB CAPITAL PARTNERS (ASIA), 2643
DE NOVO VENTURES, 599
DEFTA PARTNERS, 603
DEUTSCHE BETEILIGUNGS AG, 2651
DFJ VENTURE CAPITAL, 610
DIAMOND TECHVENTURES, 613
DISCOVERY CAPITAL, 2091
DISRUPTOR CAPITAL, 618
DJF DRAGONFUND CHINA, 2658
DRAPER ESPRIT, 2665
DRAPER TRIANGLE VENTURES, 629
DRESNER COMPANIES, 630
DRIVE CAPITAL, 631
DUCHOSSOIS CAPITAL MANAGEMENT, 634
DUNDEE VENTURE CAPITAL, 635
DUTCHESS CAPITAL, 638
E.BRICKS DIGITAL, 2672
EASTVEN VENTURE PARTNERS, 645
ECOAST ANGEL NETWORK, 649
ECOSYSTEM VENTURES, 650
EDELSON TECHNOLOGY PARTNERS, 651
EDGEWATER CAPITAL PARTNERS, 653
EGL HOLDINGS, 656
EM WARBURG, PINCUS & COMPANY INTERNATIONAL, 2688
EM WARBURG, PINCUS & COMPANY JAPAN, 2689
EMERALD OCEAN CAPITAL, 665
EMIGRANT CAPITAL, 668
ENERTECH CAPITAL, 677
ENSPIRE CAPITAL PTE LTD, 2694
ENTREPIA VENTURES, 683
EQUITEK CAPITAL, 693
EQUITY PARTNERS PTY LIMITED, 2706
EUROPEAN FOUNDERS FUND, 2714
EUROPEAN INVESTMENT FUND, 2715
EVERCORE CAPITAL PARTNERS, 700
EXPERIMENT FUND, 709
EXPIBEL BV, 2719
FA TECHNOLOGY VENTURES, 712
FAIRHAVEN CAPITAL, 713
FCA VENTURE PARTNERS, 718
FGA PARTNERS, 725
FIDELITY GROWTH PARTNERS ASIA, 2724
FIDELITY GROWTH PARTNERS EUROPE, 2725
FIKA VENTURES, 729
FINAM GLOBAL, 2727
FINANCE WALES, 2728
FIRST CAPITAL VENTURE, 736
FIRST FLIGHT VENTURE CENTER, 738
FIRST NEW ENGLAND CAPITAL LP, 740
FISHER LYNCH CAPITAL, 745
FLAGSHIP PIONEERING, 748
FLORIDA FUNDERS, 754
FLUKE VENTURE PARTNERS, 755
FOCUS VENTURES, 759
FOG CITY CAPITAL, 760
FORREST BINKLEY & BROWN, 767
FOUNDATION MARKETS, 2117
FOUNDER PARTNERS, 775
FRANKLIN STREET EQUITY PARTNERS, 783
FREESTYLE, 787
FRESH VC, 788
FRESHTRACKS CAPITAL, 789
FREYCINET INVESTMENTS, 2120
FRONTENAC COMPANY, 792
FTV CAPITAL, 796
FULCRUM EQUITY PARTNERS, 797
FULL CIRCLE INVESTMENTS, 2753
GABRIEL VENTURE PARTNERS, 808
GARAGE TECHNOLOGY VENTURES, 810
GE ASIA PACIFIC CAPITAL TECHNOLOGY FUND, 2758
GEMINI INVESTORS, 815
GEMINI ISRAEL VENTURE FUNDS LIMITED, 2761
GENACAST VENTURES, 818
GENES GMBH VENTURE SERVICES, 2765
GEODESIC CAPITAL, 824
GET2VOLUME ACCELERATOR, 2769
GLASSWING VENTURES, 833

GLOBAL CATALYST PARTNERS, 837
GOLDEN OPPORTUNITIES FUND, 2129
GOLDEN SEEDS, 845
GOLDEN VENTURE PARTNERS, 2130
GOLDMAN SACHS INVESTMENT PARTNERS, 846
GRANITE HILL CAPITAL PARTNERS, LLC, 856
GRANITE VENTURES, 857
GREENSPRING ASSOCIATES, 872
GREIF & COMPANY, 874
GRISHIN ROBOTICS, 879
GROTECH VENTURES, 881
GROVE STREET ADVISORS LLC, 884
GSV VENTURES, 888
GUGGENHEIM PARTNERS, 890
GULFSTAR GROUP, 893
HALLEY VENTURE PARTNERS, 900
HALOGEN VENTURES, 901
HARBERT MANAGEMENT CORPORATION, 907
HARBOR LIGHT CAPITAL PARTNERS, 910
HARBOURVEST PARTNERS LLC, 912
HARRISON METAL, 914
HAWTHORN EQUITY PARTNERS, 919
HEARST VENTURES, 925
HELIANT VENTURES, 2808
HELLMAN & FRIEDMAN LLC, 927
HERCULES TECHNOLOGY GROWTH CAPITAL, INC, 928
HG CAPITAL, 2814
HIGH COUNTRY VENTURE, 933
HIGHER GROUND LABS, 937
HOPEWELL VENTURES, 947
HORIZON TECHNOLOGY FINANCE, 949
HORIZON VENTURES LLC, 950
HOUSTON HEALTH VENTURES, 954
HOXTON VENTURES, 2825
HUDSON VENTURE PARTNERS, 957
HYPUR VENTURES, 966
I-HATCH VENTURES LLC, 967
IBM VENTURE CAPITAL GROUP, 971
IDEALAB, 976
ILE-DE-FRANCE, 2846
IMPERIAL INNOVATIONS, 2849
INDUSTRIO VENTURES, 2859
INDUSTRY VENTURES, 990
INITIATIVE CAPITAL LIMITED, 2147
INNOSPRING, 998
INNOVA MEMPHIS, 999
INNOVACORP, 2148
INNOVATION ENDEAVORS, 1001
INNOVATION PLATFORM CAPITAL, 1002
INNOVATION WORKS, 1003
INOVIA CAPITAL, 2150
INSTITUTIONAL VENTURE PARTNERS, 1006
INTERLACE VENTURES, 1011
INVENT, 1016
INVESTX, 2154
ISIS EP LLP F & C, 2889
ISOURCE GESTION, 2890
ITC VENTURES, 2894
IXORA VENTURES, 2895
J-SEED VENTURES INCORPORATED, 2896
JAGUAR CAPITAL PARTNERS, 1029
JAVELIN VENTURE PARTNERS, 1032
JC2 VENTURES, 1035
JETBLUE TECHNOLOGY VENTURES, 1039
K9 VENTURES, 1054
KALORI GROUP INVESTMENTS, 2906
KEIRETSU FORUM, 1065
KENSINGTON CAPITAL PARTNERS, 2160
KEPHA PARTNERS, 1069
KERNEL CAPITAL, 2909
KERRY CAPITAL ADVISORS, 1071
KILLICK CAPITAL, 2161
KILMER CAPITAL PARTNERS, 2162
KLEINWORT CAPITAL LIMITED, 2914
KOHLBERG KRAVIS ROBERTS & COMPANY, 1086
KPG VENTURES, 1088
LAKE CAPITAL, 1095

Industry Preference Index / Technology

LASALLE CAPITAL GROUP, 1097
LAUDER PARTNERS LLC, 1099
LAUNCHBOX DIGITAL, 1100
LAUNCHCAPITAL, 1101
LAUNCHPAD LA, 1103
LAUNCHPAD VENTURES, 2922
LAURENCE CAPITAL, 2165
LDV CAPITAL, 1105
LEO CAPITAL HOLDINGS, LLC, 1112
LEONIA MB GROUP/MB FUNDS, 2928
LERER HIPPEAU VENTURES, 1114
LIBERTY CITY VENTURES, 1119
LIGHTHOUSE CAPITAL PARTNERS, 1122
LIGHTHOUSE EQUITY PARTNERS, 2169
LINLEY CAPITAL, 1134
LOVETT MILLER & COMPANY, 1152
LUDLOW VENTURES, 1154
LUX CAPITAL, 1155
M/C PARTNERS, 1157
MADRONA VENTURE GROUP, 1162
MAPLE LEAF ANGELS, 2178
MARYLAND VENTURE FUND, 1172
MASSACHUSETTS CAPITAL RESOURCE COMPANY, 1176
MATCHSTICK VENTURES, 1179
MATH VENTURE PARTNERS, 1181
MATON VENTURE, 1183
MCG CAPITAL CORPORATION, 1192
MCGOVERN CAPITAL, 1194
MEDIA VENTURE PARTNERS, 1197
MEDRA CAPITAL, 2951
MERCATO PARTNERS, 1205
MERITUS VENTURES, 1215
METROPOLITAN PARTNERS GROUP, 1226
MIRALTA, 2186
MISSION VENTURES, 1239
MISSIONOG, 1240
MMT MILLENNIUM MATERIALS TECHNOLOGIES FUND LP, 2964
MMV CAPITAL PARTNERS, 2188
MONTLAKE CAPITAL, 1250
MOTIV PARTNERS, 1258
MOUNTAIN GROUP CAPITAL, 1261
MOUNTAINEER CAPITAL, 1262
MOZART VENTURE PARTNERS, 1264
MS&AD VENTURES, 1269
NAVY CAPITAL, 1282
NBC CAPITAL PTY LIMITED, 2979
NEEDHAM CAPITAL PARTNERS, 1287
NEOTENY COMPANY LIMITED, 2982
NEW ATLANTIC VENTURES, 1290
NEW YORK ANGELS, 1305
NEW YORK VENTURE PARTNERS, 1309
NEWBURY VENTURES, 1310
NEWBURY, PIRET & COMPANY, 1311
NEXT FRONTIER CAPITAL, 1317
NEXTSTAGE CAPITAL, 1321
NEXUS VENTURE PARTNERS Nexus India Capital Advisors Pvt Ltd, 2992
NFX, 1323
NKM CAPITAL, 1330
NORO-MOSELEY PARTNERS, 1332
NORTH WEST FUND, 3001
NORTHERN LIGHT VENTURE CAPITAL, 1340
NORTHSTAR VENTURES, 3003
NORWEST EQUITY PARTNERS, 1345
NOVENTI VENTURES, 1352
NYC SEED, 1358
OAK HILL CAPITAL PARTNERS, 1360
OCA VENTURES, 1364
OCEANSHORE VENTURES, 1365
ONE EQUITY PARTNERS, 1376
OPEN PRAIRIE VENTURES, 1380
OPENVIEW VENTURE PARTNERS, 1381
OPUS CAPITAL, 1382
ORIGIN VENTURES, 1385
OUTCOME CAPITAL, 1389
OUTPOST CAPITAL, 1391
OWL VENTURES, 1393

OYSTER INVEST, 3013
PALADIN CAPITAL GROUP, 1401
PALOMAR VENTURES, 1408
PANORAMA CAPITAL, 1411
PAPPAS VENTURES, 1414
PARKWALK ADVISORS, 3019
PASSION CAPITAL, 3021
PENINSULA VENTURES, 1430
PERMIRA Permira Advisers LLP, 3024
PHENOMEN VENTURES, 3025
PHYTO PARTNERS, 1443
PI CAPITAL GROUP LLC, 1444
PIEDMONT ANGEL NETWORK, 1446
POLARIS VENTURE PARTNERS, 1464
PORTUGAL CAPITAL VENTURES Institutional Headquarters, 3039
PRAIRIEGOLD VENTURE PARTNERS, 1474
PRITZKER GROUP VENTURE CAPITAL, 1483
PROFOUNDERS CAPITAL, 3046
PROJECT 11 VENTURES, 1489
PSG, 1499
PSL VENTURES, 1501
QUANTUM CAPITAL PARTNERS, 1512
RAND CAPITAL CORPORATION, 1526
RAPTOR GROUP, 1527
RBC CAPITAL MARKETS, 2223
REACH CAPITAL, 1530
RECIPROCAL VENTURES, 1531
RED SEA VENTURES, 1533
REED ELSEVIER VENTURES, 3065
REMBRANDT VENTURE PARTNERS, 1543
RETHINK IMPACT, 1555
REVO CAPITAL, 3069
RIDGE VENTURES, 1566
RITTENHOUSE VENTURES, 1572
RIVERSIDE COMPANY, 1576
ROADMAP CAPITAL INC., 2234
ROPART ASSET MANAGEMENT, 1587
ROTH CAPITAL PARTNERS, 1592
RPM VENTURES, 1596
RUSSELL SQUARE PARTNERS, 2236
S3 VENTURES, 1601
SAFEGUARD SCIENTIFICS, 1605
SAFFRON HILL VENTURES, 3083
SAGEVIEW CAPITAL, 1606
SAINTS CAPITAL, 1608
SCALE VENTURE PARTNERS, 1629
SCALEUP VENTURES, 2240
SCIFI VC, 1634
SCOTIABANK PRIVATE EQUITY, 2241
SEAPORT CAPITAL, 1641
SEAWAY VALLEY CAPITAL CORPORATION, 1642
SEB VENTURE CAPITAL, 3097
SECOND ALPHA, 1643
SECTION 32, 1646
SEQUEL VENTURE PARTNERS, 1656
SEVEN PEAKS VENTURES, 1659
SEVENTYSIX CAPITAL, 1660
SEVIN ROSEN FUNDS, 1661
SHAW KWEI AND PARTNERS, 3107
SIERRA ANGELS, 1671
SIGNAL EQUITY PARTNERS, 1676
SIGNAL FIRE, 1677
SILKROAD EQUITY, 1683
SILVER LAKE, 1685
SINEWAVE VENTURES, 1689
SKYTREE CAPITAL PARTNERS, 1694
SLOW VENTURES, 1696
SMAC PARTNERS, 3114
SMARTINVEST VENTURES, 1697
SONY INNOVATION FUND, 1705
SORRENTO VENTURES, 1708
SOUTHEAST INTERACTIVE TECHNOLOGY FUNDS, 1711
SPARK VENTURES, 3122
SPERO VENTURES, 1724
SPRING CAPITAL PARTNERS LP, 1730
STEAMBOAT VENTURES, 3133
STEELHOUSE VENTURES, 3134

Industry Preference Index / Technology-Enabled Services

STERLING PARTNERS, 1745
STONEHENGE GROWTH CAPITAL, 1748
STONEWOOD CAPITAL MANAGEMENT, 1749
STRAND HANSON LIMITED, 3137
SUMMIT BRIDGE CAPITAL, 3138
SUN CAPITAL PARTNERS, 1755
SUNEVISION HOLDINGS LIMITED, 3139
SUNSTONE CAPITAL, 3140
SUPREMUM CAPITAL, 3141
SUSA VENTURES, 1760
SWITCH VENTURES, 1770
SYDNEY SEED FUND, 3144
TA ASSOCIATES, 1778
TACTICO, 2251
TAMAR TECHNOLOGY VENTURES LIMITED, 3149
TANK STREAM VENTURES, 3151
TAYRONA VENTURES, 1783
TDF, 1784
TECH CAPITAL PARTNERS, 2253
TECH COAST ANGELS, 1786
TECHNOCAP, 2254
TECHNOLOGY VENTURES CORPORATION, 1789
TECHOPERATORS, 1790
TECNET, 3156
TELECOM VENTURE GROUP LIMITED, 3159
TELEFONICA VENTURES, 3160
TELESOFT PARTNERS, 1795
TEN ELEVEN VENTURES, 1796
TENONETEN VENTURES, 1800
TFG CAPITAL AG, 3163
TH LEE PUTNAM VENTURES, 1806
THAYER STREET PARTNERS, 1807
THE ABRAAJ GROUP, 3164
THE ALCHEMIST ACCELERATOR, 1809
THOMA BRAVO LLC, 1817
TIGER GLOBAL MANAGEMENT, 1828
TLCOM CAPITAL, 3170
TOMORROW VENTURES, 1832
TOP RENERGY INC., 2263
TPG CAPITAL, 1837
TRANSCENDENT CAPITAL, 1838
TRANSLINK CAPITAL, 1840
TRASK INNOVATIONS FUND Purdue Research Foundation, 1842
TRELLIS CAPITAL CORPORATION, 2265
TRIANGLE PEAK PARTNERS, 1848
TRIANGLE VENTURE CAPITAL GROUP, 3179
TRILOGY PARTNERSHIP, 1854
TRIPLETREE LLC, 1856
TTP VENTURES, 3186
TWO SIGMA VENTURES, 1876
TYLT LAB, 1878
UNITED TALENT AGENCY VENTURES, 1885
UNIVERSITY VENTURE FUND, 1886
UPHEAVAL INVESTMENTS, 1892
VANTAGEPOINT CAPITAL PARTNERS, 1908
VEBER PARTNERS LLC, 1911
VECTOR CAPITAL, 1912
VENROCK ASSOCIATES, 1918
VENTANA CAPITAL MANAGEMENT LP, 1920
VENTURE INVESTORS LLC, 1923
VERGE FUND, 1926
VERIZON VENTURES, 1928
VERTICAL GROUP, 1931
VICKERS FINANCIAL GROUP, 3206
VINCERA CAPITAL, 3209
VIOLA FINTECH, 3211
VITAL FINANCIAL LLC, 1942
VITAMINA K VENTURE CAPITAL, 3214
WACHTEL & CO. INC, 1950
WASABI VENTURES, 1959
WASHINGTON CAPITAL VENTURES, 1960
WAVEMAKER PARTNERS, 1966
WELLS FARGO CAPITAL FINANCE, 1971
WESTSUMMIT CAPITAL, 3225
WI HARPER GROUP, 1983
WILDCAT VENTURE PARTNERS, 1985
WILMINGTON INVESTOR NETWORK, 1987
WIREFRAME VENTURES, 2001
WISCONSIN INVESTMENT PARTNERS, 2002
YELLOW POINT EQUITY PARTNERS, 2284
YES VC, 2013
YVC - YOZMA MANAGEMENT & INVESTMENTS LIMITED, 3239
ZETTA VENTURE PARTNERS, 2018
ZONE VENTURES, 2020

Technology & Telecommunications
APAX PARTNERS, 136

Technology Platforms
BLOOMBERG BETA, 287

Technology, Media & Telecommunications
ADVENT INTERNATIONAL CORPORATION, 61
BAIN CAPITAL PRIVATE EQUITY, 223
BRYAN GARNIER & COMPANY, 2535
NOVACAP, 2198

Technology-Enabled Business
ALLOS VENTURES, 86
NORWEST VENTURE PARTNERS, 1346
OJAS VENTURE PARTNERS, 3010
VOLITION CAPITAL, 1944

Technology-Enabled Businesses
ACTIVATE VENTURE PARTNERS, 51
SILVER LAKE, 1685
SSM PARTNERS, 1735

Technology-Enabled Products
HELION VENTURE PARTNERS, LLC International Management (Mauritius) Ltd, 2809
TENNESSEE COMMUNITY VENTURES, 1799

Technology-Enabled Services
.406 VENTURES, 1
1843 CAPITAL, 6
4490 VENTURES, 9
ABS VENTURES, 22
ACERO CAPITAL, 40
ACUMEN VENTURES, 2333
ALTIRA GROUP LLC, 98
ARC ANGEL FUND, 151
ARTS ALLIANCE, 2419
AURORA CAPITAL GROUP, 202
BALLAST POINT VENTURES, 227
BERLIN TECHNOLOGIE, 2494
BIG SUR VENTURES, 2501
BLH VENTURE PARTNERS, 285
BLUME VENTURES, 2517
CHICAGO GROWTH PARTNERS, 470
CINCYTECH, 481
CONCENTRIC EQUITY PARTNERS Financial Investments Corporation, 531
CORE CAPITAL PARTNERS, 540
CYPRESS GROWTH CAPITAL, 577
DAWNTREADER VENTURES, 593
DRIVE CAPITAL, 631
EMERGENCE CAPITAL PARTNERS, 666
ESCALATE CAPITAL PARTNERS, 696
GREENSPRING ASSOCIATES, 872
HEALTHQUEST CAPITAL, 924
INVENTUS, 1017
MADISON DEARBORN PARTNERS, 1160
MERITAGE FUNDS, 1212
NEW ENTERPRISE ASSOCIATES, 1296
NORO-MOSELEY PARTNERS, 1332
NORTH ATLANTIC CAPITAL CORPORATION, 1334
OPENVIEW VENTURE PARTNERS, 1381
PARTHENON CAPITAL, 1419
PLUS VENTURES, 3032
RITTENHOUSE VENTURES, 1572
SANDBOX INDUSTRIES, 1618
SIGMA PRIME VENTURES, 1675
SILVERTON PARTNERS, 1687
TEAKWOOD CAPITAL, 1785

Industry Preference Index / Technology-Enabled Software

TEXO VENTURES, 1803
THAYER STREET PARTNERS, 1807

Technology-Enabled Software
BREGAL SAGEMOUNT, 336
TECHOPERATORS, 1790

Telecommunication
AZCA, 217
SAMSUNG VENTURE INVESTMENT CORPORATION Samsung Electronics, 3089

Telecommunications
360 CAPITAL PARTNERS 360 Capital Management SA, 2288
3I ASIA PACIFIC 3i Group, 2289
3TS CAPITAL PARTNERS 3i Group plc, 2301
3W VENTURES Latour & Zuberbuhler GmbH, 2302
3i GROUP PLC, 2303
AB CAPITAL & INVESTMENT CORPORATION The Phinma Group, 2306
ABELL FOUNDATION VENTURES, 18
ACCESS VENTURE PARTNERS LLC, 35
ACE VENTURE CAPITAL LIMITED, 2322
ACON INVESTMENTS, 45
ACORN CAMPUS VENTURES, 46
ACTIS, 2329
ADAMS CAPITAL MANAGEMENT, 55
ADARA VENTURE PARTNERS, 2334
ADASTRA, 2335
AEP CAPITAL LLC, 64
AEROSTAR CAPITAL LLC, 66
AFTERDOX, 2344
AGF PRIVATE EQUITY Allianz Group, 2346
AKERS CAPITAL LLC, 74
ALEXANDER HUTTON, 82
ALFA CAPITAL Alfa Group, 2355
AMANET TECHNOLOGIES LIMITED, 2381
ANDERSON PACIFIC CORPORATION, 123
ANDLINGER & COMPANY INC, 124
ANTHEM VENTURE PARTNERS, 133
APEX VENTURE PARTNERS, 138
ARROWPATH VENTURE PARTNERS, 171
ARTIS VENTURES, 177
ARVA LIMITED, 2040
ASSET MANAGEMENT VENTURES, 183
ATHENAEUM FUND, 188
ATILA VENTURES, 2433
AURA CAPITAL OY Auratum Group, 2442
AUSTRALIAN ETHICAL INVESTMENT LIMITED, 2447
AVALON VENTURES, 209
AVANSIS VENTURES, 210
AVENUE CAPITAL GROUP, 211
AWAY REALTY, 2456
AXA INVESTMENT MANAGERS PRIVATE EQUITY EUROPE, 2457
BAIRD CAPITAL PARTNERS, 225
BALTCAP MANAGEMENT LTD, 2471
BAND OF ANGELS LLC, 229
BARCELONA EMPREN, 2474
BARCLAYS VENTURES Barclays, 2477
BARING PRIVATE EQUITY PARTNERS INDIA, 2481
BARING VOSTOK CAPITAL PARTNERS, 2482
BATTERY VENTURES, 238
BENAROYA COMPANIES, 250
BIA DIGITAL PARTNERS LP, 266
BLACK DIAMOND VENTURES, 278
BLACKSTONE PRIVATE EQUITY GROUP, 280
BMP AKTIENGESELLSCHAFT BMP Venture Capital, 2519
BOSTON CAPITAL VENTURES, 313
BRAZOS PRIVATE EQUITY PARTNERS, 331
BREAKWATER INVESTMENTS, 333
BRERA CAPITAL PARTNERS, 338
BULLNET, 2539
CALIFORNIA TECHNOLOGY VENTURES, 374
CAPITOL PARTNERS, 409
CARLYLE ASIA INVESTMENT ADVISORS LIMITED Carlyle Group, 2556
CARLYLE GROUP, 416

CATALYST FUND LP, 2562
CATALYST GROUP, 427
CEDAR (ISRAEL) FINANCIAL ADVISORS LIMITED Cedar Fund, 2571
CEDAR FUND, 438
CENTERFIELD CAPITAL PARTNERS, 445
CENTRAL TEXAS ANGEL NETWORK, 447
CHASE CAPITAL PARTNERS, 2579
CHICAGO VENTURE PARTNERS LP, 472
CHINA DEVELOPMENT INDUSTRIAL BANK CDFH, 2583
CHINAVEST, 475
CIBC CAPITAL MARKETS, 2073
CID GROUP, 2594
CINCO CAPITAL, 2595
CIVC PARTNERS, 491
CM CAPITAL, 2609
CNF INVESTMENTS Clark Enterprises, Inc., 510
COACH & CAPITAL, 2610
COLLER CAPITAL LIMITED, 2612
COMPAGNIE FINANCIERE E DE ROTHSCHILD BANQUE, 2616
COMSPACE, 528
CONCORD VENTURES, 2619
CONVEXA Tyveholmen AS, 2623
CORDOVA VENTURES, 539
CREATHOR VENTURE, 2629
CROSBY ASSET MANAGEMENT, 2631
CVF CAPITAL PARTNERS, 574
DARBY OVERSEAS INVESTMENTS LTD, 585
DB CAPITAL PARTNERS (ASIA), 2643
DELTA PARTNERS Delta Partners FZ-LLC, 2645
DESJARDINS CAPITAL, 2089
DOCOMO INNOVATIONS, 621
DR NEUHAUS TECHNO NORD GmbH, 2664
DRAPER RICHARDS KAPLAN FOUNDATION, 628
DVC DEUTSCHE VENTURE CAPITAL, 2670
EDBI Pte LTD., 2681
EDELSON TECHNOLOGY PARTNERS, 651
EDEN VENTURES, 2682
EDGESTONE CAPITAL PARTNERS, 2098
EMP GLOBAL, 671
ENSPIRE CAPITAL PTE LTD, 2694
ENTERPRISE INVESTORS, 2697
EPLANET CAPITAL, 691
EQT PARTNERS AB, 2703
EUROFUND LP, 2711
EXPORT DEVELOPMENT CANADA, 2106
FALCON FUND, 716
FIBERNETICS VENTURES, 2111
FIDELITY GROWTH PARTNERS ASIA, 2724
FIELDSTONE PRIVATE CAPITAL GROUP, 726
FINADVANCE, 2726
FLANDERS' FOREIGN INVESTMENT OFFICE, 2737
FORMULA VENTURES LIMITED Formula Group, 2741
FOUNDATION CAPITAL, 773
GALILEO II, 2756
GE CAPITAL, 811
GEFINOR CAPITAL, 813
GEMINI ISRAEL VENTURE FUNDS LIMITED, 2761
GENERAL ENTERPRISE MANAGEMENT SERVICES, 2763
GENERICS GROUP LIMITED Generics Group, 2764
GILBERT GLOBAL EQUITY PARTNERS, 831
GLOBAL FINANCE, 2775
GLOBALIVE, 2128
GMT COMMUNICATIONS PARTNERS LLP, 2780
GRAYHAWK CAPITAL, 861
GREENHILL SAVP, 869
GRUPO BISA, 2791
GTCR, 889
HALIFAX GROUP LLC, 899
HANNOVER FINANZ GmbH, 2801
HARBOURVEST PARTNERS LLC, 912
HIKARI TSUSHIN CAPITAL, 2817
HMS HAWAII MANAGEMENT, 942
HOSEO VENTURE CAPITAL, 2824
I-PACIFIC PARTNERS, 2831
IDG TECHNOLOGY VENTURE INVESTMENT, 2839
INCYTE VENTURES, 986
INFLECTION POINT VENTURES, 993

Industry Preference Index / Therapeutics

INLAND TECHSTART FUND, 997
INNOVACOM SA, 2866
INNOVATION CAPITAL, 2867
INNOVATION CAPITAL LIMITED, 2868
INNOVATIONSKAPITAL, 2869
INSIGHT VENTURE PARTNERS, 1005
INVEXCEL PATRIMONIO, 2882
ISOURCE GESTION, 2890
IT-PARTNERS NV, 2893
JAGUAR CAPITAL PARTNERS, 1029
JAVELIN INVESTMENTS, 2899
JEFFERIES CAPITAL PARTNERS, 1036
JK&B CAPITAL, 1042
JORDAN COMPANY, 1049
KALORI GROUP INVESTMENTS, 2906
KB PARTNERS LLC, 1061
KENSINGTON CAPITAL PARTNERS, 2160
LBBW VENTURE CAPITAL, 2923
LEASING TECHNOLOGIES INTERNATIONAL INC., 1107
LEVINE LEICHTMAN CAPITAL PARTNERS, 1115
LMBO FINANCE, 2936
LONG RIVER VENTURES, 1146
LOVETT MILLER & COMPANY, 1152
MACQUARIE DIRECT INVESTMENT LIMITED, 2942
MADISON DEARBORN PARTNERS, 1160
MARCEAU INVESTISSEMENTS, 2946
MAYFIELD FUND, 1187
MBF CAPITAL CORPORATION, 1191
MERRILL LYNCH (ASIA PACIFIC) LIMITED Merrill Lynch Group, 2955
MITSUI SUMITOMO INSURANCE VENTURE CAPITAL CO, 2962
MOTOROLA SOLUTIONS VENTURE CAPITAL, 1260
MURPHREE VENTURE PARTNERS, 1273
NEEDHAM CAPITAL PARTNERS, 1287
NEUHAUS PARTNERS, 2985
NEW YORK CITY ENTREPRENEURIAL FUND New York City Economic Development Corporation, 1306
NEWBURY VENTURES, 1310
NEWFIELD CAPITAL, 1312
NORTH ATLANTIC CAPITAL CORPORATION, 1334
NORTHERN LIGHT VENTURE CAPITAL, 1340
NORTHWOOD VENTURES, 1344
NOVELTEK CAPITAL CORPORATION, 1351
OAK HILL CAPITAL PARTNERS, 1360
OAK INVESTMENT PARTNERS, 1361
OJAS VENTURE PARTNERS, 3010
OneVentures, 3014
PAI MANAGEMENT, 3017
PALOMAR VENTURES, 1408
PANACHE VENTURES, 2204
PENN VENTURE PARTNERS, 1431
PENTECH VENTURES, 3023
PI CAPITAL GROUP LLC, 1444
PNC RIVERARCH CAPITAL, 1461
PRIME TECHNOLOGY VENTURES NV, 3042
PRITZKER GROUP VENTURE CAPITAL, 1483
PROCURITAS PARTNERS KB, 3045
PROVIDENCE EQUITY PARTNERS, 1498
QUANTUM WAVE FUND, 3059
QUEST FOR GROWTH, 3060
RABO BLACK EARTH Eagle Venture Partners, 3062
RBC CAPITAL MARKETS, 2223
RHO VENTURES, 1561
SATORI CAPITAL, 1625
SBRC INVESTMENT CONSULTATION LIMITED, 3092
SCOTTISH ENTERPRISE, 3094
SCP PARTNERS, 1636
SECOND ALPHA, 1643
SELWAY CAPITAL, 1650
SEQUEL VENTURE PARTNERS, 1656
SHANGHAI INFORMATION INVESTMENT INCORPORATED, 3105
SIGNAL LAKE, 1678
SIGNATURE CAPITAL LLC, 3111
SKYPOINT CAPITAL, 2247
SMAC PARTNERS, 3114
SOLID VENTURES, 3119
SOUTHEAST INTERACTIVE TECHNOLOGY FUNDS, 1711
SOUTHERN CROSS VENTURE PARTNERS, 1713

SPENCER TRASK VENTURES, 1723
STAR VENTURES, 3128
STRAND HANSON LIMITED, 3137
SWISSCOM, 3143
SYCAMORE VENTURES, 1771
T-VENTURE HOLDINGS GmbH Deutsche Telecom, 3146
TAILWIND CAPITAL, 1779
TECH CAPITAL PARTNERS, 2253
TECHNOCAP, 2254
TELUS VENTURES, 2256
TEUZA MANAGEMENT & DEVELOPMENT LTD, 3162
TIGER GLOBAL MANAGEMENT, 1828
TIME WARNER INVESTMENT CORPORATION, 1829
TLCOM, 3170
TMG CAPITAL PARTNERS, 3171
TRIGINITA CAPITAL, 3181
TVV CAPITAL, 1872
TWJ CAPITAL, 1875
TYLT LAB, 1878
USHA MARTIN VENTURES LIMITED, 3193
VENCORE CAPITAL, 1917
VENTANA CAPITAL MANAGEMENT LP, 1920
VERITAS CAPITAL FUND LP, 1927
VINACAPITAL GROUP, 3208
VOLVO GROUP VENTURE CAPITAL, 3217
WESLEY CLOVER, 2276
WINDWARD VENTURES, 1995
WOODSIDE FUND, 2005
XANGE PRIVATE EQUITY, 3229
YFM GROUP, 3234
YLR CAPITAL MARKETS LTD, 3237

Telecommunications & Media
IBM VENTURE CAPITAL GROUP, 971

Television
INGENIOUS VENTURES, 2862
MEDIA VENTURE PARTNERS, 1197
NORTHSTAR VENTURES, 3003

Test & Measurement
HCI EQUITY PARTNERS, 920
HERITAGE PARTNERS, 929

Textiles
CAPVIS EQUITY PARTNERS, 2555
CHINA VEST LIMITED, 2587
CITA GESTION, 2598
FIRST ISRAEL MEZZANINE INVESTORS LIMITED, 2736
INDIAN DIRECT EQUITY ADVISORS PVT LTD, 2852
INTERMEDIATE CAPITAL GROUP PLC, 2874
LITTLEJOHN & COMPANY LLC, 1138

Therapeutics
ABERDARE VENTURES, 19
AISLING CAPITAL, 73
AMGEN VENTURES, 113
ASTELLAS VENTURE MANAGEMENT, 184
BIOADVANCE, 269
BIOGENERATION VENTURES, 2505
BIOGENERATOR, 270
BRAIN TRUST ACCELERATOR FUND, 326
BROADVIEW VENTURES, 350
CENTRESTONE VENTURES, 2071
EASTON CAPITAL INVESTMENT GROUP, 644
EDBI Pte LTD., 2681
ELM STREET VENTURES, 661
EcoR1 CAPITAL, 710
F-PRIME CAPITAL PARTNERS, 711
FLAGSHIP PIONEERING, 748
FORESITE CAPITAL, 764
HOPEN LIFE SCIENCE VENTURES, 946
JOHNSTON ASSOCIATES, 1048
KAISER PERMANENTE VENTURES, 1056
LANCET CAPITAL, 1096
LIGHTSTONE VENTURES, 1126
LONGWOOD FUND, 1149

Industry Preference Index / Tools

LUMIRA VENTURES, 2174
MAINE ANGELS, 1164
NEW SCIENCE VENTURES, 1302
OMEGA FUNDS, 1373
OXFORD BIOSCIENCE PARTNERS, 1395
PFIZER VENTURE INVESTMENTS, 1439
PITTSBURGH LIFE SCIENCES GREENHOUSE, 1452
PURETECH VENTURES, 1503
RESEARCH CORPORATION TECHNOLOGIES, 1546
SANDERLING VENTURES, 1619
SOFINNOVA VENTURES, 1700
SYNERGY LIFE SCIENCE PARTNERS, 1774
THIRD ROCK VENTURES, 1814
VENBIO, 1916
VENTANA CAPITAL MANAGEMENT LP, 1920
WELLINGTON PARTNERS VENTURE CAPITAL GmbH, 3223

Tools
ASSET MANAGEMENT VENTURES, 183
ATLAS VENTURE: FRANCE, 2436

Tourism
ACTIS, 2329
AMANET TECHNOLOGIES LIMITED, 2381
AVENIR TOURISME, 2450
BUSINESS GROWTH FUND, 2541
CLOSE BROTHERS PRIVATE EQUITY Close Brothers Group, 2608
COMPAGNIE FINANCIERE E DE ROTHSCHILD BANQUE, 2616
ELECTRA PARTNERS ASIA LIMITED SFC of Hong Kong, 2685
EQUISTONE, 2705
NEW MEXICO COMMUNITY CAPITAL, 1299
PARTNERSHIP FUND FOR NEW YORK CITY, 1422
PORTUGAL CAPITAL VENTURES Institutional Headquarters, 3039
SIF TRANSYLVANIA, 3110
SRIW SA SRIW Group, 3125
UCA UNTERNEHMER CONSULT AG, 3188
UNION CAPITAL CORPORATION, 1883

Toxic Materials Handling
MOUNTAINEER CAPITAL, 1262

Toys
BALTCAP MANAGEMENT LTD, 2471

Trade
TPA CORPORATE FINANCE CONSULTING GMBH Horwarth International, 3175

Training
CASTANEA PARTNERS, 424
EPIC PARTNERS, 688
LEEDS EQUITY PARTNERS, 1109
SCHOONER CAPITAL LLC, 1630

Transaction Processing
CARRICK CAPITAL PARTNERS, 419
VEDANTA CAPITAL LP, 1913

Transformational Businesses
RUBICON VENTURE CAPITAL, 1599

Transmission
BREGAL ENERGY, 335

Transportation
3I ASIA PACIFIC 3i Group, 2289
ACCESS CAPITAL, 34
ACI CAPITAL, 41
ACTIS, 2329
AIP PRIVATE CAPITAL, 2027
ALEUTIAN CAPITAL PARTNERS, 81
ALEXANDER HUTTON, 82
APOLLO GLOBAL MANAGEMENT, 141
ASTER CAPITAL, 2430
ASTOR CAPITAL GROUP, 2431
ATP PRIVATE EQUITY PARTNERS, 2438
AURORA CAPITAL GROUP, 202
AUTO TECH VENTURES, 207
AUTOTECH VENTURES, 208
AVENUE CAPITAL GROUP, 211
BERKSHIRE PARTNERS LLC, 257
BLAST FUNDING, 282
BLUE POINT CAPITAL PARTNERS, 293
BOCI DIRECT INVESTMENT MANAGEMENT LIMITED Bank of China, 2520
BOND CAPITAL, 2058
BOSTON CAPITAL VENTURES, 313
CAMBRIA GROUP, 381
CAMBRIDGE CAPITAL, 383
CANADIAN VENTURE CAPITAL ASSOCIATION Canadian Venture Capital & Private Equity Association, 3249
CARBON VENTURES, 411
CARLYLE ASIA INVESTMENT ADVISORS LIMITED Carlyle Group, 2556
CARLYLE GROUP, 416
CARPEDIA INTERNATIONAL, 2066
CATALYST INVESTMENT MANAGERS PTY LIMITED PPM Capital, 2564
CERBERUS CAPITAL MANAGEMENT, 453
CHRYSALIX, 2072
CLIMATE CHANGE CAPITAL, 2606
CLOSE BROTHERS PRIVATE EQUITY Close Brothers Group, 2608
COLLABORATIVE FUND, 514
COMVEST PARTNERS, 530
CREDIT MUTUEL EQUITY, 2082
CVC INVESTMENT MANAGERS LIMITED, 2636
DAIMLERCHRYSLER VENTURE GmbH DaimlerChrysler AG, 2641
DEFI GESTION SA Banque Cantonale Vaudoise, 2644
DUBIN CLARK & COMPANY, 633
ECI VENTURES, 2678
ELGNER GROUP INVESTMENTS, 2099
EMP GLOBAL, 671
ENDEAVOUR CAPITAL, 674
ENERTECH CAPITAL, 677
ENTERPRISE EQUITY (NI) LTD, 2695
EOS PARTNERS LP, 687
EQUISTONE, 2705
EUROVENTURES CAPITAL, 2716
EXPANSION CAPITAL PARTNERS, 707
EXPORT DEVELOPMENT CANADA, 2106
FENWAY PARTNERS, 722
FIELDSTONE PRIVATE CAPITAL GROUP, 726
FLANDERS' FOREIGN INVESTMENT OFFICE, 2737
FONTINALIS PARTNERS, 762
FORTRESS INVESTMENT GROUP LLC, 769
FOURIERTRANSFORM, 2746
FRASER MCCOMBS CAPITAL, 784
FdG ASSOCIATES LP, 804
GE CAPITAL, 811
GENERAL ENTERPRISE MANAGEMENT SERVICES, 2763
GENERAL MOTORS VENTURES, 821
GEORGIA OAK PARTNERS, 825
GLADSTONE CAPITAL, 832
GLENTHORNE CAPITAL, 836
GOLDNER HAWN, 847
GRAHAM PARTNERS, 851
GRAND CENTRAL HOLDINGS, 852
GRANTHAM CAPITAL, 858
GREENBRIAR EQUITY GROUP LLC, 867
GULFSTAR GROUP, 893
GV, 894
HALDER HOLDINGS BV, 2797
HALIFAX GROUP LLC, 899
HARREN EQUITY PARTNERS, 913
HCI EQUITY PARTNERS, 920
HIG CAPITAL, 931
IBM VENTURE CAPITAL GROUP, 971
INFIELD CAPITAL, 992
INVESTMENT FUND FOR CENTRAL & EASTERN EUROPE, 2880
JB POINDEXTER & COMPANY, 1034
JEFFERIES CAPITAL PARTNERS, 1036
JORDAN COMPANY, 1049
KELSO & COMPANY, 1066
KHOSLA VENTURES, 1073
KPS CAPITAL PARTNERS, 1089

1212

MACKINNON, BENNETT & CO., 2175
MCROCK CAPITAL, 2183
MERRILL LYNCH (ASIA PACIFIC) LIMITED Merrill Lynch Group, 2955
NAVIGATION CAPITAL PARTNERS, 1279
NORTHERN ENTERPRISE LIMITED, 3002
NOVELTEK CAPITAL CORPORATION, 1351
OMERS PRIVATE EQUITY, 2199
PARKVIEW CAPITAL PARTNERS, 2207
PENDER WEST CAPITAL PARTNERS, 2210
PHOENIX EQUITY PARTNERS LIMITED, 3027
PORTUGAL CAPITAL VENTURES Institutional Headquarters, 3039
POST CAPITAL PARTNERS, 1469
RED CLAY CAPITAL HOLDINGS, 1532
RESILIENCE CAPITAL PARTNERS, 1548
REVOLUTION LLC, 1558
RISE OF THE REST, 1571
ROAD KING INFRASTRUCTURE LIMITED, 3075
ROCKPORT CAPITAL, 1583
SAMOS INVESTMENTS, 3088
SARONA ASSET MANAGEMENT, 2239
SHAW KWEI AND PARTNERS, 3107
SIF TRANSYLVANIA, 3110
SIGNIA VENTURE PARTNERS, 1680
SOUTHPORT PARTNERS, 1714
SUN CAPITAL PARTNERS, 1755
THROUNARFELAG ISLANDS PLC, 3168
TPA CORPORATE FINANCE CONSULTING GMBH Horwarth International, 3175
TRANS COSMOS INCORPORATED, 3176
TRANSYLVANIA FINANCIAL INVESTMENT COMPANY, 3178
TSING CAPITAL, 3185
URBAN INNOVATION FUND, 1895
URBAN US, 1896
WATERMILL GROUP, 1963
WELLS FARGO CAPITAL FINANCE, 1971
WYNNCHURCH CAPITAL, 2008

Transportation Solutions
INVESTECO, 2153

Transportation and Infrastructure
BRANFORD CASTLE, 330

Travel
DYNAMO VC, 640
NFX, 1323
RISE OF THE REST, 1571

Travel & Leisure
ARCHTOP VENTURES, 155
BLACKSTONE PRIVATE EQUITY GROUP, 280
LLOYDS DEVELOPMENT CAPITAL LIMITED, 2935
ONE EQUITY PARTNERS, 1376
RAPTOR GROUP, 1527

Travel/Leisure
TPG CAPITAL, 1837

Underground Hydrocarbon Storage
HADDINGTON VENTURES LLC, 898

Utilities
AWAY REALTY, 2456
CHEUNG KONG INFRASTRUCTURE HOLDINGS LIMITED, 2582
NTH POWER TECHNOLOGIES, 1355

Utilities & Electric Power
CHRYSALIX, 2072

Utilities & Farming
CALIFORNIA COAST VENTURE FORUM, 3248

Vaccines
SANOFI-GENZYME BIOVENTURES, 1621

Value-Added Distribution
ALBION INVESTORS LLC, 78
ARROWHEAD INVESTMENT MANAGEMENT, 170
BALMORAL FUNDS, 228
CID CAPITAL, 480
FIVE POINTS CAPITAL, 747
JMH CAPITAL, 1044
MPG EQUITY PARTNERS, 1267

Vehicle Technology
VENROCK ASSOCIATES, 1918

Venture Capital
INDUSTRY VENTURES, 990

Vertical
OYSTER VENTURES, 1396

Veterinary Medicine
TWIN CITIES ANGELS, 1874

Video Gaming
ALBUM VC, 79
SONY STRATEGIC TECHNOLOGY PARTNERSHIPS, 1706

Video Industry
TECH CAPITAL PARTNERS, 2253

Video Surveillance
AUXO MANAGEMENT, 2042

Virtual Reality
AMPLIFY, 121
BLUEPOINTE VENTURES, 298
BOLDSTART VENTURES, 308
BRIGHTSTONE VENTURE CAPITAL, 344
LDV CAPITAL, 1105
OUTPOST CAPITAL, 1391
PATHBREAKER VENTURES, 1423
QUAKE CAPITAL PARTNERS, 1509
SAMSUNG NEXT, 1614
SIGNIA VENTURE PARTNERS, 1680
SONY INNOVATION FUND, 1705
SUSA VENTURES, 1760
VERIZON VENTURES, 1928

Virtual Reality & Augmented Reality
AMD VENTURES, 107
BERTELSMANN DIGITAL MEDIA INVESTMENTS, 259
BOOST VC, 310
DAY ONE VENTURES, 594
FINAVENTURES, 730
FRONTIER VENTURES, 795
PRESENCE CAPITAL, 1477

Virtualization
ATLANTIC BRIDGE, 2434
NEW ENTERPRISE ASSOCIATES, 1296
STORM VENTURES, 1750

Vocational Training
APPIAN EDUCATION VENTURES, 142

Waste & Recycling
AMBIENTA ENVIRONMENTAL ASSETS, 2383
ANGELENO GROUP, 127
AUDAX GROUP, 197
CLARENDON FUND MANAGERS, 2601
CLIMATE CHANGE CAPITAL, 2606
DEMETER PARTNERS, 2647
GEMINI INVESTORS, 815
HENDERSON PRIVATE CAPITAL, 2812
NORTH ATLANTIC CAPITAL CORPORATION, 1334
PARALLEL49 EQUITY, 2206
PROCURITAS PARTNERS KB, 3045
SOVEREIGN CAPITAL, 3121
SPRING LANE CAPITAL, 1732
STRUCTURE CAPITAL, 1752
TPA CORPORATE FINANCE CONSULTING GMBH Horwarth International, 3175
TRUE NORTH VENTURE PARTNERS, 1861

Industry Preference Index / Waste & Resources

WHEB GROUP, 3227
WOODBRIDGE GROUP, 2004

Waste & Resources
ENERTECH CAPITAL, 677

Waste Management
CARBON VENTURES, 411

Waste Water Treatment
AZCA, 217

Water
AAVISHKAAR, 2305
ACUMEN, 54
ALTRIA VENTURES, 102
AQUAGRO FUND, 2408
AUDAX GROUP, 197
CLEAN PACIFIC VENTURES, 499
CLIMATE CHANGE CAPITAL, 2606
CULTIVIAN SANDBOX VENTURES, 571
DEMETER PARTNERS, 2647
EARTHRISE CAPITAL, 643
ELEMENT PARTNERS, 658
EMERALD TECHNOLOGY VENTURES, 2101
EMP GLOBAL, 671
ENNOVENT, 2692
EXPANSION CAPITAL PARTNERS, 707
FIRELAKE CAPITAL, 731
FIRST ISRAEL MEZZANINE INVESTORS LIMITED, 2736
FLYWHEEL VENTURES, 758
FREYCINET INVESTMENTS, 2120
ISRAEL CLEANTECH VENTURES, 2891
MCROCK CAPITAL, 2183
MEIDLINGER PARTNERS, 1200
NEW WORLD INFRASTRUCTURE LIMITED, 2987
POND VENTURES, 3038
PROCURITAS PARTNERS KB, 3045
SAIL VENTURE PARTNERS, 1607
SAUDI ARAMCO ENERGY VENTURES, 3090
SOUTHERN CROSS VENTURE PARTNERS, 1713
SPRING LANE CAPITAL, 1732
TEL VENTURE CAPITAL, 1793
TRUE NORTH VENTURE PARTNERS, 1861
WASSERSTEIN & CO., 1961
WHEB GROUP, 3227
XPV WATER PARTNERS, 2282

Water Purification
ALTUS CAPITAL PARTNERS, 104

Water Technologies
INVESTECO, 2153

Water Technology
ARROWHEAD INNOVATION FUND, 169
TECHNOLOGY PARTNERS, 1788

Water Treatment
CARDINAL EQUITY PARTNERS, 412

Wealth
PORTAG3 VENTURES, 2217

Wealth & Asset Management
LUGE CAPITAL, 2172
VIOLA FINTECH, 3211

Wealth Management & Trust
ROTHSCHILD AUSTRALIA - ARROW PRIVATE EQUITY Rothschild Group, 3077

Web Applications & Services
ARTHUR VENTURES, 175
BAND OF ANGELS LLC, 229
DALLAS VENTURE PARTNERS, 583
EC1 CAPITAL LTD, 2676
ENTREPIA VENTURES, 683
KLASS CAPITAL, 2163
MITSUI SUMITOMO INSURANCE VENTURE CAPITAL CO, 2962
NETROVE ASIA SDN BHD, 2984
OJAS VENTURE PARTNERS, 3010

Web Infrastructure
.406 VENTURES, 1

Web Platforms
SPARK CAPITAL, 1718

Web Related
NEXTGEN ANGELS, 1320

Web Services
SERAPH GROUP, 1658

Web-Enabled Services
SJF VENTURES, 1691
US VENTURE PARTNERS, 1898

Web/Mobile Applications
Y COMBINATOR, 2011

Wellness
APHELION CAPITAL, 139
BIG SOCIETY CAPITAL, 2500
FALCONHEAD CAPITAL, 717
JOHNSON & JOHNSON INNOVATION, 1047
OBVIOUS VENTURES, 1363
SWAN & LEGEND VENTURES, 1768
WIREFRAME VENTURES, 2001

Wholesale
ALLSTATE INVESTMENTS LLC, 88
BAY BG BAVARIAN VENTURE CAPITAL CORP, 2485
BENCIS CAPITAL PARTNERS, 2492
BOND CAPITAL, 2058
BRUML CAPITAL CORPORATION, 358
CINCO CAPITAL, 2595
FOUNDATION CAPITAL LIMITED, 2744
GAON ASSET MANAGEMENT, 2757
GRUPO BISA, 2791
GULFSTAR GROUP, 893
INDUSTRI KAPITAL SVENSKA AB, 2854
LOMBARD INVESTMENTS, 1143
MACQUARIE DIRECT INVESTMENT LIMITED, 2942
MERRILL LYNCH (ASIA PACIFIC) LIMITED Merrill Lynch Group, 2955
NORTH ATLANTIC CAPITAL CORPORATION, 1334
QUANTUM CAPITAL PARTNERS, 1512
SAMBRINVEST SA, 3087
WELLS FARGO CAPITAL FINANCE, 1971

Wholesale Distribution
AUSTIN CAPITAL PARTNERS LP, 204

Wind Power
ABB TECHNOLOGY VENTURES, 2307
BP ALTERNATIVE ENERGY VENTURES, 322

Winegrowing & Agriculture
TPA CORPORATE FINANCE CONSULTING GMBH Horwarth International, 3175

Wireless
10X VENTURE PARTNERS, 2
ACTIVE VENTURE PARTNERS, 2331
APOLLO GLOBAL MANAGEMENT, 141
ARCH VENTURE PARTNERS, 154
CALUMET VENTURE FUND, 378
CARMEL VENTURES, 2557
CATALYST INVESTORS, 429
CEYUAN, 2575
CID GROUP, 2594
COLUMBIA CAPITAL, 518
COMMONWEALTH CAPITAL VENTURES LP, 523
CONVEXA Tyveholmen AS, 2623
DIAMOND TECHVENTURES, 613

DOUBLEROCK VENTURE CAPITAL, 626
EPLANET CAPITAL, 691
ESCALATE CAPITAL PARTNERS, 696
EUROPEAN FOUNDERS FUND, 2714
FIRST ANALYSIS, 733
FORMATIVE VENTURES, 766
GSR VENTURES, 2792
GUGGENHEIM PARTNERS, 890
IDG CAPITAL PARTNERS, 2838
JARVINIAN VENTURES, 1031
KODIAK VENTURE PARTNERS, 1084
LAUNCHPAD VENTURE GROUP, 1104
LEAPFROG VENTURES, 1106
LEO CAPITAL HOLDINGS, LLC, 1112
MOBILITY VENTURES, 1244
NEXIT VENTURES OY, 2990
NEXIT VENTURES OY Nexit Ventures Inc., 2990
NORTHWOOD VENTURES, 1344
OKAPI VENTURE CAPITAL, 1371
OPUS CAPITAL, 1382
OXANTIUM VENTURES, 1394
PELION VENTURE PARTNERS, 1428
REMBRANDT VENTURE PARTNERS, 1543
SEAPOINT VENTURES, 1640
SHEPHERD VENTURES, 1667
STORM VENTURES, 1750
SUNBRIDGE PARTNERS, 1757
TELESOFT PARTNERS, 1795

Wireless Applications
BLUEFISH VENTURES, 297

Wireless Architectures
TI VENTURE CAPITAL Texas Instruments Incorporated, 1825

Wireless Communications
DOT EDU VENTURES, 624

Wireless Infrastructure
RHO CANADA VENTURES, 2231

Wireless Services
GRANDBANKS CAPITAL, 853

Wireless Software
GREENHILLS VENTURES, LLC, 870

Wireless Systems
CROSSLINK CAPITAL, 564

Wireless Technologies
ACCENTURE TECHNOLOGY VENTURES, 2318
ACORN CAMPUS VENTURES, 46
ACTA CAPITAL, 50
AKERS CAPITAL LLC, 74
ALLEGIS CYBER CAPITAL, 84
ARGO GLOBAL CAPITAL, 163
ASIAVEST PARTNERS, 2427
ATA VENTURES, 185
ATLANTIC BRIDGE, 2434
ATRIUM CAPITAL, 194
AUTHOSIS VENTURES, 2448
AVALON VENTURES, 209
AVANSIS VENTURES, 210
AZIONE CAPITAL, 2464
BAY PARTNERS, 241
BLUMBERG CAPITAL, 304
BRIGHTSPARK VENTURES, 2060
CEDAR (ISRAEL) FINANCIAL ADVISORS LIMITED Cedar Fund, 2571
CEDAR FUND, 438
CHINA DEVELOPMENT INDUSTRIAL BANK CDFH, 2583
CLARITY PARTNERS, 496
COMSPACE, 528
CRAWLEY VENTURES, 554
DELTA VENTURES LIMITED, 2646
DOCOMO INNOVATIONS, 621
FCA VENTURE PARTNERS, 718
GABRIEL VENTURE PARTNERS, 808
GENESIS PARTNERS, 2766
GRANDBANKS CAPITAL, 853
GROSVENOR FUNDS, 880
GUIDE VENTURES, 892
HARBINGER VENTURE MANAGEMENT, 908
HORIZON VENTURES LLC, 950
I-PACIFIC PARTNERS, 2831
IDG CAPITAL, 977
IGLOBE PARTNERS, 2844
INNOVATION CAPITAL LIMITED, 2868
JAVELIN INVESTMENTS, 2899
KOREA TECHNOLOGY & BANKING (KTB) NETWORK CORP, 2917
M/C PARTNERS, 1157
MADRONA VENTURE GROUP, 1162
MANTELLA VENTURE PARTNERS, 2176
MATRIX PARTNERS, 1184
MEDIA VENTURE PARTNERS, 1197
MERITECH CAPITAL PARTNERS, 1213
MOBILE INTERNET CAPITAL, 2965
MOTOROLA SOLUTIONS VENTURE CAPITAL, 1260
NAUTA CAPITAL, 2978
NEST VENTURES, 1289
NEWBURY VENTURES, 1310
NORTHERN LIGHT VENTURE CAPITAL, 1340
PITANGO VENTURE CAPITAL, 3030
REAL VENTURES, 2224
REDPOINT VENTURES, 1537
RIDGEWOOD CAPITAL, 1567
RPM VENTURES, 1596
SELBY VENTURE PARTNERS, 1649
SHASTA VENTURES, 1666
SIGMA PARTNERS, 1674
SKYPOINT CAPITAL, 2247
SMART BUSINESS CONSULTING, 3115
SONY STRATEGIC TECHNOLOGY PARTNERSHIPS, 1706
STAR VENTURES, 3128
T-VENTURE HOLDINGS GmbH Deutsche Telecom, 3146
TAMAR TECHNOLOGY VENTURES LIMITED, 3149
TECH CAPITAL PARTNERS, 2253
TELUS VENTURES, 2256
TI VENTURE CAPITAL Texas Instruments Incorporated, 1825
TRILOGY PARTNERSHIP, 1854
US VENTURE PARTNERS, 1898
VELOCITY EQUITY PARTNERS LLC, 1915
VENCORE CAPITAL, 1917
VENTANA CAPITAL MANAGEMENT LP, 1920
VOYAGER CAPITAL, 1947
WESTERN TECHNOLOGY INVESTMENT, 1976
WI HARPER GROUP, 1983
ZONE VENTURES, 2020

Wood Industries
INVESTMENT FUND FOR CENTRAL & EASTERN EUROPE, 2880
SAMBRINVEST SA, 3087
SRIW SA SRIW Group, 3125
WATERMILL GROUP, 1963

Workforce Development
URBAN US, 1896

Portfolio Companies Index

A

A & A Manufacturing Company, 197
A Head For Profits, 495
A la Carte Delivery, 1509
A Little Market, 3229
A Place for Mom, 1957
A Stucki Company, 1507
A Touch of Country Magic, 1609
A&A Trading, 2108
A&B American Style, 623
A&B Electronics, 440
A&D Environmental Services, 445, 1343
A&G Pharmaceutical, 1172
A&R Logistics, 1174
A&W, 2264
A+ Network, 1754
A-D Technologies, 197
A-Gas, 1086, 2935
A-Lab Oy, 2957
A-Life Medical, 1708
A-Max, 2762
A-ROSA, 3222
A-SaaS, 149, 1610
A-Solutions, 3013
A-Star, 2637
A-TEK, 509
A., 2435
A. & D. Prevost, 2089
A. & L. Pinard, 2114
A. Silva & Silva, 3039
A.A. Kachtan, 2381
A.R.E. Accessories, 566
A.S. Group, 2346
A.S. Nettoyage, 2114
A.S.T. Soldering Technologies, 2381
A.T.L.A.S. Aeronautique, 2089
A.V. Gauge & Fixture, 2156
A/B Tasty, 3229
A10 Capital, 931
A10 Networks, 908, 1754, 2694
A123 Systems, 173, 1161, 1335, 2708
A2 Biotherapeutics, 1934
A2M, 2205
A2SEA, 2642
A4 Health Systems, 1410
A5, 367
A8 Music Group, 2841
AA Asphalting, 1250
AA Audience, 10
AA Consulting & Associates, 3252
AAA Slaes & Engineering, 1424
AAB Smart Tools LLC, 911
AAC Acoustic, 1762, 2581
AAC Holdings Inc., 406
AAC Technologies, 827
Aaccredited Home Lenders, 407
AAD, 1350
AaDya, 12
AAG Energy Limited, 1957
AAMP of America, 197, 973
Aaptiv, 1005, 1426, 1770
Aardvark, 200, 234
AardvarQ, 1003
Aarohi Communications, 1795
Aaron Industries, 747
Aarowhead, 1045
Aarrowcast, 1041
Aarusha Homes, 54
Aasaan Jobs, 1017
AAT, 2413
Aavangs Fiskehus, 3194
Aavishkaar, 485
Aavya Health, 1618
AB SA, 2697
Abacas Insights, 1
Abaco PR, 62

Abaco Systems, 1927
Abacus, 12, 263, 894
Abacus Group LLC, 1979
Abacus.AI, 1669
Abacusnext, 1499
Abaka, 2398
Abakus Solar, 3011
Abasco Energy Technologies, 1577
ABATEC Electronics AG, 2774
Abaton.com, 958
Abaxia, 2846
abaxx, 2762
ABB Optical Group, 1300
Abbey Healthcare Staffing, 1071
Abbey Post, 1101
Abbey Road Consulting, 3250
Abbeypost, 10
ABC Cosmétique, 3229
Abc Environnement, 2114
abc Financial, 1344
ABC Home Medical Supply, 639
ABC Industries, 330, 441, 480
ABC Laboratories, 441
ABC Learning Centres Ltd, 2447
ABC Supply, 61
ABC TEST, 3252
Abcd, 2439
AbCelex Technologies, 571
AbCellera, 1669
Abcia, 3011
Abe's Market, 2557
Abec Group, 2976
Abeja, 1610
AbelConn, 165
AbelConn Holdings, 1560
Abengoa, 741
Abeo, 1419, 2745, 3194
Aberdeen Group, 523, 902
Abertis, 388, 2371
Abgentis, 2958, 3098
ABI, 2926
ABI (UK) Ltd., 2668
Abide Therapeutics, 413
Abierto Networks, 1164, 1165
Ability, 912, 1360
ABILITY Network, 224, 1754, 3268
Ability One, 1132
AbilTo, 941
Abingdon Health, 2849
AbioGenix, 1618
Abiomed, 2739
Abionic, 3036
Abipa Canada, 2114
Abiquo, 2978
Abirnet, 3221
ABK Biomedical, 1987, 2148
Abl, 742, 1393, 1530, 1554
ABL Technic, 1939
Ablathion Frontiers, 1976
Ablative Solutions, 272
Able, 708
Able Health, 863
Able Home Health, 409
Able Lending, 545
Able Planet, 60
AbleTo, 1
Ablexis, 374, 1439, 1814
Ablynx, 94, 2308, 2771, 2772
ABM Industris Inc., 874
AbMart, 1340
Abode Healthcare, 785
Abodo, 9, 635
AboGen, 1164
Abom, 1065
Abotic, 2522
Abound, 10
About.com, 597, 1107

About.me, 361, 779, 787, 894, 1702, 1862
AboutOne, 845
ABPathFinder, 635
ABR Innova Oy, 2864
Abra, 149, 310, 742, 927, 1114, 1223, 1469
ABRA Auto Body, 3268
ABRA Auto Body & Glass, 1404
Abrado Welbore Services, 2691
Abrams Fensterman, 3257
Abravax, 1509
Abre. Action Streamer, 481
ABRH, 1971
Abridean, 2188
Abridge, 1884
Abrigo, 28
Abrisa Industrial Glass, 1460
Abrisa Technologies, 851
Abrisud, 2330, 2332, 2439
Abrium, 2542
Abrizio, 1976
Abry, 2888
Abryx, 389
ABS Capital Partners, 3260
ABS Materials Inc., 5, 1051
AbSci, 1384, 2007
Absolute Commerce, 1695
Absolute Dental, 247
Absolute Dental Management, 159
Absolute Engery, 2864
Absolutely Custom Group, 1494
Absorbent Technologies, 1917
Abstract, 553, 742, 2272
Absynthe Minded, 3033
ABT Molecular Imaging, 1013
ABT Molecular Imaging Evermind, 1261
ABTL, 1498
Abu Dhabi Investment Authority, 3252
Abundant Robotics, 521, 894
Abusix, 3152
Abuzz Technologies, 1704
AbVitro, 1622
Abyssal, 3039
Abzena, 1973
AC Busines Media, 1722
AC Label, 668
AC Lordi, 470
AC&A, 65
ACA Compliance Group, 1300
Acacia, 523, 1184
Acacia Communications, 1754
Acacia Venture Partners, 1762, 3273
AcaciaPharma, 711
AcadeMedia, 1498
Academia, 3061, 3122
Academia.edu, 1718, 1862
Academic Management Services, 1754, 1772
Academic Management Systems, 1334
Academic Merit, 1164
Academic Partnerships, 1005
Academy for Urban School Leadership, 1315
Academy Sports + Outdoors, 1086
Acadia Healthcare, 1964
ACADIA Pharmaceuticals, 1395, 1456, 2642, 2739, 2998
Acal Energy, 194, 2287, 3019
Acalvia, 894
Acalvio, 27, 978, 2231
Acapela Group, 2888
Acapella, 517
Acarix, 3104, 3140
ACAS Equity Holdings Corporation, 159
ACAS Real Estate Holdings Corporation, 159
Acasa, 3099
ACB (India), 1957
ACC Systems, 1666
Acca Networks, 2845
Accantia, 2667

1217

Portfolio Companies Index

Accedian Networks, 1754
Accel, 36
Accel Entertainment, 2075
Accel Graphics, 35
Accel Growth Fund, 624
Accel IX Strategic Partners, 624
Accel KKR, 36
Accel Partners, 3273
Accel Semiconductor Corporation, 2588
Accela, 20, 257, 336, 1479
Accela Media, 3032
Accela Technology, 1757
Accelecare Holdings, 1631
Accelecare Wound Centers, 224
Accelera, 1718
Accelerant Holdings, 96
Acceleron, 1126
Accelerate Fund, 2028
Accelerate Learning, 1393
Accelerated Companies, 1417
Accelerated Networks, 1379
Accelerated Oil Technologies, 1086
Accelerated Orthopedic Technologies, 661, 679
Accelerated Rehabilitation Centers, 886
Accelerated Technologies, 2739
Acceleration Systems, 1065
Accelerator, 5
Accelerator Corporation, 1047, 2007
Accelergy, 1355, 1788
Accelero Pharma, 58
Acceleron, 1126
Acceleron Pharma, 209, 263, 748, 764, 928, 1464, 1762, 1918
Accella, 172
Accellent, 212, 223, 1090
Accello, 1273
Accellos, 443
Accelops, 185, 1237, 1898
Accent, 1781, 3225
Accent Energy, 41
Accent Equity 2003 Ltd, 2642
Accent Ood Services, 1686
Accent Therapeutics, 710
AccentCare, 61, 1360
AccentHealth, 1157
Acceo Solutions, 2089, 2114
Accept Software, 1741
Acceptd, 1556
Acces, 2842
Acces 360, 1750
Access, 257, 828, 897, 952, 1706
Access Cash, 1256
Access Closer, 990
Access Closure, 1379, 1449
Access Health, 51
Access Information Management, 20, 1754
Access Insurance, 96
Access Intelligence, 1929
Access Medical, 2927
Access MediQuip, 1962
Access Physicians, 921
Access Point Financial, 1746
Access Spectrum LLC, 1508
Access Sports Media, 518, 1239
Access Technology Ventures, 33
Access Venture Partners, 3265
Access360, 1976
AccessBio, 3136
AccessData, 1643, 1707
AccessESP, 1129
AccessLine, 808
AccessOne, 793
Accessories Marketing Inc., 791, 1460
Accio Energy, 743, 1550
Accion, 108, 3252
Accion Systems, 1696
Acciona Energia Internacional, 1086
Accipiter, 1013, 1711, 2218

Accipiter Systems, 1003
Accium Biosciences, 85, 2007
Acclara, 97
Acclarent, 1213
Acclaris, 1852, 1888, 2188
Acclivity Health Solutions, 1412
ACCO, 3011, 3038
Acco, 773, 1418
ACCO Material Handling Solutions, 1086
Accolade, 38, 125, 419, 520, 561, 696, 1162
Accolo, 549
Accomodations Plus Technologies, 159
Accompany, 553
Accompany Beta, 978
Accomplice, 69
Accord, 3128
Accord Networks, 58
Accordant Health Systems, 1013
Account Now, 861
Accountabil IT, 1979
Accounting SaaS Japan Co., 2965
AccountNow, 1852
AccountsIQ, 2347
Accoustical Material Services, 1507
Accovion, 2629
Accredible, 1058
Accredo Health, 1973
Accreon, 1168
Accretive Commerce, 38
Accretive Health, 38, 178
Accriva Diagnostics, 240, 1957
Accrue, 10
Accruent, 823, 1778, 1976
ACCT Holdings, 1729
Accu Metrics, 949
Accubuilt, 1401
Accucam Machining, 2121
Accudyne Industries, 416
Acculis, 623
Acculynk, 1361
Accume Partners, 225
Accumen, 38
Accumeter Labs, 1294
Accumetrics, 1061, 1578, 1794
Accupac, 931, 1041
Accuracy Microsensors, 1378
Accurate, 952
Accurate Component Sales, 934, 1343
Accurate Group, 1240
Accurate Group Holdings, 21, 1192
Accurate Metal Fabrications, 1377
Accuratus Lab Services, 119
AccuRev, 523, 1915
Accuri, 748
Accuri Cytometers, 1976
AccurIC, 2958
Accuride Corporation, 560, 1138
Accuris, 2434, 3138
Accuro, 1622, 1973
Accuronix, 270
Accuscore, 1786
AccuSource Solutions, 988
AccuSpec Electronics, 1163
Accutest Laboratories, 654
Accutrainee, 2558
Accuvally Inc., 1511
AccuVein, 263, 949, 2972
AccuWater, 447
ACE Cash Express, 1043
ACE Cogeneration, 157
Ace Gathering Holdings LLC, 406
Ace Learning, 1554
Ace Metrix, 1106, 1408
ACE*COMM, 870
ace2three.com, 2075
Aceable, 752, 1606, 1985
Acelero Learning, 1025

AcelRx Pharmaceuticals, 928, 1449, 1693
Acema Importations, 2089
AceMetrix, 959
Acention Digital, 623
Acer, 897, 2427
Acer Group, 1771
Acerta, 1158, 2122
Acerta Pharma, 785
Acertus, 1779
Aces, 101
ACES Quality Management, 1292
Acesion, 350
Acessa Health Inc., 159
Acessozero, 2323
Acetelion, 193
Aceva, 1976
ACG, 912, 3223
ACG Materials, 931
ACH BRITO & CIA, 3039
Achaogen, 11, 154, 622, 764, 1918
Achates Power, 1583, 1848
Acheogen, 785
Achica, 2653
Achieve 3000, 1005
Achieve3000, 1329
AchieveIt, 274
Achievelt, 1412
Achievement Preparatory Academy, 1315
Achievers, 853
Achillion, 532, 1414, 1510, 2436
Achillion Pharmaceuticals, 622, 1062, 1492, 1777
Achronix, 1302
Achronix Semiconductor, 683, 928
ACI, 1045, 2083
Aci Brands, 2121
Acier Fastech, 2114
Acier Majeau, 2089, 2114
Aciex Therapeutics, 240
Acino, 212
ACIS, 376
Acision, 2434
ACIST Medical Systems, 1410
Acivilate, 1412
Acko, 27
ACL, 1346
ACL Airshop, 216
ACL Wireless, 2872
Aclara, 119, 1755
Aclara Biosciences, 1414
Aclaris Therapeutics, 73, 137, 711, 764, 1522, 1700, 1943
Aclima, 1698
Aclime, 1555
ACM Research Corporation, 1771
ACME Cryogenics, 832, 851
Acme Fine Furniture Natra Group, 2805
Acme Finishing Company, 1609
Acme Packet, 58
Acme Technologies, 548
ACMI, 781
Acodec, 70
Acologix, 2961
Acompli, 1537
Aconex, 606, 782
Aconite, 752, 1391
Acopia, 27
Acopia Networks, 457, 3128
Acorda, 957
Acorda Therapeutics, 772, 1007, 1271, 2739
Acordis, 2635
Acorn, 101
Acorn Applications, 3250
Acorn International, 3084
Acorn Systems, 205
Acorns, 641, 863, 1181, 1744
Acosta, 416

Portfolio Companies Index

Acoustic Sensing Technology, 2287
Acoustic Technologies, 1875
Acoustic Zoom, 2691
AcousticEye, 2891
Acova, 2874
ACPI, 110
ACQI, 3248
Acquia, 36, 1335, 1674, 1675, 1728, 1798, 1949
Acquired.io, 662, 895
Acquisio, 2114
ACR Capital Holdings, 2292, 2303
ACR Electronics, 1333
ACR Group, 1049
ACRA Control, 2328
Acre Trader, 1557
Acreage Holdings, 393
Acres Cultivation & Cannabis, 558
Acrisure, 20, 823, 912, 1929
Acro Vape, 395
Acrobatiq, 629, 925
Acrodea, 57
Acrodyne Communications, 1313
Acrohone Ltd., 2698
Acromedia Inc., 624
AcroMetrix, 1794
Acronis, 89, 1235, 2312
Acrotec, 1518
Acrow Bridge, 632
AcryMed, 755
ACS, 2384
Acsis, 1608
ACT Biotech, 1325
ACT Lighting Inc., 578
Act On, 1898
Act!, 655
Act-On, 1787
Act-On Software, 1855, 1947
Acta, 1021
Acta Groupe, 2842
Acta Technology, 759
Acta Vascular Systems, 870
ActaCell, 145
Actano Ltd, 3153
Actar International SA, 2644
Actel, 58, 217
Actelioln, 2598
Actelion, 2598, 2616
Actelis, 185, 1976, 2866, 3114, 3221
Actelis Argus Cyber Security, 3205
Actelis Networks, 56, 837, 1608, 2499, 2556
Acteon, 1086, 2309
Actex, 1345
ACTi, 908
Actiance, 1042, 1629, 1762
Actifio, 58, 125, 1335, 1628, 1787
Actility, 485, 2842
Actimis, 1241
Actimize, 796
Actinobac Biomed, 1055
Action, 1753, 2303
Action Carting, 1025
Action For Children, 2530
Action Labs Inc., 467
Action Mecanique, 2089
Action Target, 633, 815
Action X, 1701, 2130
Actional Corporation, 200
Actionality, 2662
ActionBar, 3099
ActionCOACH, 3257
Actiondesk, 798
Actionfigure, 2262
ActionIQ, 320, 744, 1657
ActionSprout, 1384
ActionX, 1928, 2131
Actis, 3252
ACTIV Financial Systems, 263

Activ Surgical, 1705
Activ8, 2958
Activa Resources, 479
Activaero, 2506
Activamt, 927
Activant, 1045
Activate Capital Ltd., 1086
Activate Healthcare, 1271
Activate Networks, 704
Active 24 ASA, 2745
Active Aero Group Holdings Inc., 867
Active Campaign, 2074
Active Circle, 2866
Active Control eXperts, 1704
Active Endpoints, 1335, 2436
Active Industrial Solutions, 2207
Active Interest Media, 1990
Active Live Scientific, 1786
Active Mind Technology, 50, 1254
Active Minerals International, 1210
Active Network, 22, 205, 457, 1483, 1782, 1994
Active Optical MEMS, 1352
Active Power, 205, 446, 1561
Active Reactor Company, 2604
Active Semiconductors, 1649
Active Software, 759, 1976
Active Sportswear International, 2642
Active State, 2074
Active Voice, 1754
Active-Semi, 1649, 1798
Active.com, 1061, 1335, 1782
Active8, 2944
ActiveCard., 2535
Actived, 1925
Activehours, 1563
ActiVein, 3230
Actively Learn, 191
ActiveProspect, 746
ActiveSky, 2868
ActiveStyle, 1576
Activiews, 2717
Activiomics, 2883
Activity Hero, 1017
ActivityHero, 10
Actix, 1754
ACTO, 2107, 2132, 2181
Acto, 2178, 2204
ActoGeniX, 2342, 2467, 2930
ActOn, 1346
Acton Pharmaceuticals, 1228
Actona, 2453
Actown-Electrocoil, 1333
ACTR (GeoStrut), 1545
Actual Experience, 2883
ActualMeds, 1759
Actuate, 27, 1247
Actuera, 3222
Acturis, 1754
Actus Corporation, 2339
ACTV8me, 300
Acucela, 2961
AcuFocus, 39, 416, 1086, 1631, 1764, 1976, 2556
Acuity, 2051
Acuity Ventures, 3273
Acumatica, 89, 3079
Acumen, 285
Acumen Brands, 819
Acumentrics, 468, 498
Acumentrics Holding Corporation, 410
Acunote, 2321
Acunu, 2682, 2849, 3023
Acura Pharmaceuticals Inc., 809
Acurex, 1772
Acusphere, 1976
Acusto Oy, 2864
AcuStream, 1024

Acutas Medical, 2728
AcuteLogic Corporation, 2406
Acutus, 1383
Acutus Medical, 812
Acylin Therapeutics, 154, 2007
Ad Hawk Microsystems, 1009
Ad Lightning, 757
Ad Mass, 546
AD PathLabs, 767
AD Technology, 2848
Ad Valem Technologies, 3199
Ad Venture Interactive, 167
AD-Tech Plastic Systems, 467
Ad.ly, 876
Ad2pro, 3202
Ada, 2094, 2122
ADA Carbon Solutions, 676
Ada Support, 2272
AdAdapted, 114
Adagene, 711
Adalta, 3238
Adam Aircraft, 1949
Adam Software, 2417
Adama Materials, 1740
Adamas, 1247
Adamas Nanotechnologies, 3250
Adamas Pharmaceuticals, 582, 2504, 2681
Adamation, 1465
Adamence, 3011
Adams Brush Manufacturing, 1294
Adams Capital Management, 3264
Adams Childrenswear, 2528, 2529
Adams Harris, 56
Adams Pharma, 1341
Adams Publishing Group, 406
Adams Respiratory Therapeutics, 73
Adams Street Partners, 3245, 3252, 3255
Adande Refrigeration, 2298
Adansonia Management Services Limited, 3252
Adao Global, 988
Adap.TV, 263, 1537, 1718
Adapsyn Bioscience, 2125
Adapt Media, 1305
Adapt-N, 434
AdaptaMat, 2442
Adaptify, 1013
Adaptimmune, 711, 764, 1383
Adaptive, 421
Adaptive Biotechnologies, 764
Adaptive Blue, 267
Adaptive Computing, 689, 1731
Adaptive Insights, 414, 1045, 1379, 2146
Adaptive Mobile, 1009, 2662
Adaptive Ozone Solutions, 1839
Adaptive Planning, 1249, 1976
AdaptivEnergy, 983
Adaptix, 226, 1600
Adaptly, 696, 1114, 1829, 1901
Adapx, 85, 983, 1392, 1401, 1428
ADAR IT, 1242
Adara, 234, 1379, 1517, 1808
Adara Media, 200, 1257
Adare Pharmaceuticals, 1837
Adarza, 270, 705
Adarza BioSystems, 570
Adavium Medical, 150, 1918
Adaytum, 1728, 2073
Adazza, 2825
ADB Airfield Solutions, 3017
AdBm Technologies, 447
AdBrain, 3009
AdBrite, 549, 1241
Adcade, 863, 1521, 1635
Adchemy, 200, 624
ADCO Global, 202
ADCO Group, 136
Adco Products Inc, 836

Portfolio Companies Index

Adco Technologies, 836
Adconion, 2788
Adconion Media Group, 2595
ADD, 2334
Add, 641
Addapptation, 2
Addenda Capital, 2114
Addepar, 304, 724, 1904
AddEvent, 775
Addex Pharmaceuticals, 2504, 2681
Addex Therapeutics, 1271
ADDI, 1935
Addiction Campuses of America, 797
Addiko Bank, 61
Addison Group, 1368
Addison Lee Group, 416
Addison McKee, 78
Addison Software, 2814
Additech, 949
Addoz, 2864
Addressable, 1423
Addressograph-Bartizan, 1749
AddSecure, 20
Addstructure, 1179
AddThis, 1006, 1348, 1504, 1561
Addum, 2854
AdDuplex, 3040
Addus Healthcare, 687
Addvocate, 626
Addy, 1998
ADECN, 1354
Adelard Soucy, 2114
AdelaVoice, 1737
Adeliade Bank Ltd, 2447
Adelior, 2598
Adello Biologics, 403
Adelphic, 290, 1184
Aden & Anais, 1648, 1769
Adenia Partners, 3252
Adenios, 323
Adenium Biotech, 3140, 3194
Adenosine Therapeutics LLC, 186
Adenovir Pharma, 2440
Adeo Health Science, 1522
Adept, 564
Adept Plastic Finishing, 920
Adeptra, 22, 2340
Adeptus Health, 1745
Aderant Holdings, 782, 1160
Adernant, 1493
AdEspresso, 10, 1914
Adesso, 2285
Adesso Systems, 2556
Adesto, 56
Adesto Technologies, 5, 145, 154, 185, 186
ADF Restaurant Group, 159
AdFin, 397
Adforce, 194, 1406, 1976
ADG, 225
AdGent, 2609
adglow, 1982
Adgrok, 2321
AdHawk, 1179, 1705
AdHawk Microsystems, 2060
Adheron Therapeutics, 113
Adhersis, 2592
Adhezion Biomedical, 1386
Adiana, 772, 928
Adicet Bio, 1350
Adictiz, 3011
Adience, 2905
Adient Medical, 350, 953, 954
ADiFY, 1918
Adify, 1898
Adikteev, 3199
Adimab, 311, 1383, 1464, 1631, 1764
Adina, 1397

Adistry, 395
Aditazz, 176
Adjara Hotel, 3086
adjust, 3152
Adkeeper, 1718
Adknowledge, 1045, 1327, 1478, 1787
Adku, 1862
ADL Technology, 2953
Adler and Allen, 2935
Adler Hot Oil Service, 1722
Adlucent, 1813
Adludio, 2469
Adly, 1890, 1966
ADM Capital, 3252
Adma Biologics Inc., 73
AdMarvel, 1244
Admbit, 73
Admedo, 2958
Admeld, 1718
Admiral, 275
AdmitHub, 1530, 1554, 2228
Admittance Technologies, 447
Admitted.ly, 1521
Admittedly, 545
AdMob, 27, 582, 1341, 1657
AdMobius, 1750
Admovate, 775
AdNear, 389
Adnexus, 748, 1918
Adnexus Therapeutics, 193
Adobe Healthcare, 1779
Adobe Systems Inc., 1905
Adocia, 2842
Adolor Corporation, 94, 154
Adometry, 205, 1666
Adomic, 625, 1103, 1966
Adomo, 1976
AdOn Network, 1015
Adop, 100
Adore, 1766
Adore Me, 1535, 1890, 3199
AdoRx Therapeutics, 690
ADP Dental Company Ltd, 2713
ADP Primary Care, 2371
AdPay, 143
Adperfect, 2169
Adra Match, 3034
Adracare, 2141
Adraid, 10
Adreima, 336, 1964
AdRelevance, 892
Adrenaline, 377
Adria, 2384
Adrian, 58
Adrich, 1705
AdRise, 298
Adroit Digital, 289
AdRoll, 27, 773, 1219, 1976
Adroll, 752, 1006
Ads Native, 1379
ADS Technologies Inc., 467
Adscale, 2820
AdsNative, 623
Adspace Networks, 327, 597, 1955
Adspert, 259
adsquare, 3152
AdStage, 309, 625, 770, 787, 1310, 1928, 2009
AdStage.io, 10
Adstrix, 2994
ADstruc, 609, 1702
AdSwerve, 20
ADT CAPS Co., 416
ADT Security, 745
adtarget.me, 3040
Adthena, 2074
AdTheorent, 1928
AdTheos, 122

ADTI, 1755
Adtuitive, 1
Adult & Pediatric Dermatology, 1964
Adura Technologies, 1324, 1908
Aduro, 20, 2969
Adva-Net, 551
AdvaCare, 1754
Adval Tech, 77
Advalight, 3194
Advancce Health, 1754
Advance Auto Parts, 786
Advance Energy Partners, 673
Advance Engineered Products, 2156
Advance Group, 1971
Advance Health, 912
Advance ICU Care, 150
Advance Medical, 1754
Advance Technology Services, 467
AdvanceCOR, 2815
Advanced, 2020
Advanced Accelerator Applications, 3104
Advanced Accessory Systems, 441
Advanced Adnimal Diagnostics, 571
Advanced Analog Technology, 897
Advanced Analogic Technologies, 1183, 1771, 2594
Advanced Animal Diagnostics, 1013
Advanced AV, 815
Advanced Bio Development, 1092
Advanced BioCatalytics, 322
Advanced Biomarker, 1575
Advanced Biomarker Technologies, 1013
Advanced BioNutrition, 1172, 1668, 2101, 2483
Advanced Career Technologies, 790
Advanced Cath, 1018
Advanced Catheter Therapies, 461, 999
Advanced Cell Diagnostics, 1297, 1754, 2969
Advanced Ceramic X Corp, 3209
Advanced Circuits, 525
Advanced Circulatory Systems, 3268
Advanced Composite Group, 2648
Advanced Computer Systems, 2526
Advanced Cyclone Systems, 2708
Advanced Dermatology & Cosmetic Surgery, 197, 917
Advanced Diamond Technologies, 979, 987, 1743
Advanced Digital Broadcast, 2913
Advanced Digital Internet Corp., 189
Advanced Discovery, 1859
Advanced Disposal Services, 747
Advanced Drainage Systems, 257
Advanced Duplication Services, 1343, 1505
Advanced Electron Beams, 748
Advanced Equities Financial Corp., 138
Advanced Farm Technologies, 431
Advanced Fibre, 538
Advanced Fibre Communication, 1731
Advanced Finance & Investment Group LLC, 3252
Advanced H2O, 1210
Advanced ICU Care, 1852, 1976
Advanced Image Enhancement, 1695
Advanced Industrial Devices, 1582
Advanced Inquiry Systems, 145
Advanced Instruments Inc., 912
Advanced Interactive Systems, 2073
Advanced LEDs, 2392
Advanced Lighting Technologies Inc., 1624
Advanced M, 782
Advanced Material Process Corporation, 1337
Advanced Medical Personnel Services, 505
Advanced Metering Data Systems, 1148
Advanced Micro-Fabrication Equipment, 837
Advanced Microgrid Solutions, 596, 812
Advanced Network Solutions, 381, 679
Advanced Pain Management, 470

Portfolio Companies Index

Advanced Payment Solutions, 1852
Advanced Photonix, 983, 1920
Advanced Physical Therapy, 445
Advanced Power Electronics Corporation, 2594
Advanced Practice Strategies, 178, 1176
Advanced Processing and Imaging, 227
Advanced Recycling Systems, 1025
Advanced Scientifics, 1456
Advanced Sleep Medicine Services, 934
Advanced Solar Power, 1340
Advanced Solutions, 336
Advanced Structural Alloys, 961
Advanced Systems Automation, 897
Advanced Technology Healthcare Solutions, 1452
Advanced Technology Services, 1560
Advanced Technology Services UK Limited, 1979
Advanced Vision Technology, 3128
Advancell, 2474
AdvancePath, 549
Advancis Pharmaceutical Corp., 215
Advancis/Middle Brook, 1561
AdvanDx, 1206
Advano, 398, 1633
Advanova, 2815
Advanstar, 1929
Advanstar Communications, 927
Advanta, 781
Advantage, 2067
Advantage Home Health, 409
Advantage Home Telehealth, 705
Advantage Medical Electronics, 408
Advantage Sales & Marketing, 136, 1113
Advantaged Sintered Metals & Contact, 1210
Advantedge Healthcare Solutions, 777
Advantice Health, 1594
Advantmed, 277
Advantor Systems Corporation, 1276
Advarra, 1132
Advasense, 2773
Advekit, 121
Advent, 1966
Advent Aerospace Inc., 905
Advent International, 874, 3254
Advent Software, 1837
Adventa, 115
Adventr, 1509
Adventrx Pharmaceuticals, 1786
Adventuer Ventures, 2846
Adventure Gold, 2114
Adventure Sports Products, 1839
AdventureLink, 1917
Adventures, 3099
AdverCar, 389
Advertising.com, 881, 2745
Advertory, 2912
Adverum, 1930
Advidxchange, 912
Advion, 73, 1464
Advion BioSciences, 434, 1693
Advion Inc., 813
Advision Media Holdings, 3084
Advisor Group, 1127
Advocus, 1103
AdvoServ, 828
Advsir, 1317
Adway, 1509
Adways, 597
AdWeek, 2050
Adwerx, 881
Adwo, 1840
Adyen, 819
Adynxx, 622, 1271
Adzerk, 1847
Adzuna, 3021
AEB, 2436

AED-SICAD, 238
Aegea Medical, 87, 605
Aegerion Pharmaceuticals, 928, 1777
Aegis, 183, 952
Aegis AI, 623
Aegis Business Credit, 3251
Aegis Chemical Solutions, 106
Aegis Legal Consulting, 3265
Aegis Sciences Corporation, 20
Aegle Gear, 461
Aeglea Biotherapeutics, 1128, 1522
Aehr Text Systems, 1754
Aelin Therapeutics, 1350
Aeluros, 1241, 1976
Aemass, 310
AEMI, 3011
AEMT, 132
Aeolus Re, 1957
AEP Networks, 1178
AePONA, 2378, 3182
Aepona, 1464
Aera, 2126
Aera 1, 972
Aeration Industries, 855
Aereo, 744
Aereon, 1848
AerGen Leasing, 867
Aerial, 1009
Aerial Access Equipment, 408
Aerial Biopharma, 1559
Aerie Pharmaceuticals, 94, 764, 1700
Aerin Medical, 591, 1101
Aeris, 507
Aeris Communications, 549
AerisTech, 2958
Aernnova, 745
Aero, 827, 1969
Aero Communications, 1548
Aero Corporation, 1262
Aero Interiors Company, 228
Aero Mechanical Industries, 1299
Aero Products, 1021
Aero Systems Engineering, 445
Aero Thermal, 2287
Aero-Mark MRO, 1536
AeroCare, 1631, 1764
AeroCare Holdings, 723, 1271
Aerocrine, 2553, 2719, 2881
Aerocrine AB, 1383, 2807
Aerodesigns, 1464
Aeroflex, 843, 1927, 2451
AeroFS, 209
Aerofs, 2321
Aerogen, 1898, 1976
AeroGen-TEK, 542
Aeroglide Corporation, 525
Aerohive, 780, 1125, 1340
Aerohive Networks, 582, 1006
Aeromics, 350
Aeronics, 296
Aeroport International De Mont-Tremblant, 2114
Aeropost, 1335
AeroPrecision, 1368
AeroPRISE, 2374
AeroScout, 538, 1203, 1976, 3128
Aerosens, 754
Aerosol Services Company Inc., 874
Aerosol Servives Holdings Corp., 874
Aerospace Products International, 1548
Aerospares 2000, 47
Aerospike, 93
Aerostar Global Logistics, 445
Aerostructures Corporation, 2556
Aerothermal Group, 2530
Aerovance, 1325, 2487
Aerovox, 1294
Aerpio, 1383

Aerpio Therapeutics, 189, 481, 1063, 1849, 1923
AerSale Holdings, 1113
AERT, 931
Aeryon Labs, 1754
AES, 2909
AescAp Venture, 3033
Aesgen, 1976
AESSEAL, 2303
Aesynt, 782
AET, 1294
Aether Bio, 321
Aether Partners, 1170
AetherPal, 1304, 1463
Aethon, 178, 629, 1003, 1444, 1523, 1852
Aeva, 3, 1155
Aevere Systems, 1203
Aevitae, 3222
AEye, 1009, 1079
AF Global Corporation, 741
Afaqs!, 3100
Afara Websystems, 1976
AFC Enterprises, 786
Afero, 721
Affare Del Giorno, 2663
Affdex, 2822
Affectis Pharmaceuticals AG, 2342
Affectiv, 3009
Affectiva, 721, 1079, 1259
AffectoGenimap, 2553
AffectoGenimap Group Oyj, 2707
Affera, 1347
Afferent Pharmaceuticals, 622, 1297, 1414, 1814, 3076
Affibody, 2719, 2881
Affibody AB, 2807
Affiliated Power Services, 911
AffiliateShop, 1683
Affinaquest, 1699
Affinergy, 1813, 1987, 3250
Affinia Group Inc., 576
Affinimark Technologies, 1101
Affinio, 2063, 2235
Affinion Group, 819
AffiniPay, 862
Affinitiv, 1169
Affinity, 863, 1426
Affinity Capital Management, 3268
Affinity Dental Management, 1231
Affinity Engiens, 2448
Affinity Express, 928
Affinity Healthcare, 2667
Affinity Jobs, 1855
Affinity Lab, 679
Affinity Labs, 1323
Affinity Networks, 133
Affinity Neworks, 1966
Affinity Specialty Apparel, 1548
Affinity VideoNet, 928
Affinium Pharmaceuticals, 772
Affinnova, 748, 1668
Affinor Growers, 1083
Affirm, 125, 238, 827, 1073, 1125
Affirma Capital, 3252
Affirmed, 457, 1184, 1383
Affirmed Networks, 1125
Affirmify, 868
Affitech, 2745, 3158
Affomix Corp., 532
Affomix Corporation, 661
Affordable Care, 257
Affordable Interior Systems, 197, 352, 1971
Affordable Luxury Network, 3206
Affy Tapple, 341
Affymax, 263, 2961
Afina, 325
Afiniti Ventures, 1917
Afinity, 400

Portfolio Companies Index

Afinity Life Sciences, 2043
Afmedica, 140
Afram Plantation Limited, 838
AFrame, 2682
Aframe, 3003, 3009
Afraxis, 209
Afresh, 234, 1001
Africa Check, 1374
Africa50, 3252
African Capital Alliance, 3252
African Infrastructure Investment Managers Pty (Lt, 3252
African Lakes Ethiopia, 2880
African Leadership Academy, 1374
African Media Initiative, 1374
AfricInvest, 3252
AFS Technologies Inc., 20 162
After School, 553, 1614
AfterBOT, 477
AfterCollege, 758
Aftermarket Technology, 202
Aftermath, 20
AfterSteps, 1658
AG Associates, 2766
AG Data, 418
AG Global, 1577
AG Kings Holdings Inc., 406
AG Kühnle Kopp & Kausch, 2703
AG Semi, 128
Ag Trucking, 832
Ag2, 2617, 2617
Aga Khan Rural Support Program, 54
AGA Medical, 1973
Agada Bioscience, 2148
Against Gravity, 742, 1186, 1657
AgaMatrix, 723
Agami Systems, 928
Agape Package Manufacturing, 2581, 3053
Agari, 87, 238, 604, 742, 1346, 1629
Agarrius, 2595
Agate Logic, 46
AgBiome, 5, 154
AGC AeroComposites, 47
Ageia Technologies, 928
Agena Bioscience, 1794
Agena Technologies, 1921
Agence De Securite Mirado, 2089
Agencyport Software, 1818
AgencyQ, 60
Agendia B/V, 2776
AgenDx, 1023
AgenDx Biosciences, 659
Agent, 894, 1260
Agent Ace, 1848
Agent IQ, 1672
Agent Media Corporation, 1469
Agent Provocateur Limited, 2303
Agentase, 1003
AgentDesks, 129
Agentdesks, 998
Agentero, 708
Agentics Inc., 2766
AgentIQ, 1599
Agentiq, 474
Agentis, 2262
Agentology, 787
Agents Inspired, 2474
Agentscape, 2664
Agentum Technologies, 2442
Ageras, 1021
Agere, 205
AGF Group, 2114
Aggamin, 350
Aggregage, 1786
Aggregate Knowledge, 582, 773, 1407
Aggregated Knowledge, 361
AGI, 475, 2909

AGI Dermatics, 1846
Agile, 1247
Agile Financial Technologies, 2840
Agile Materials & Technologies Inc., 374
Agile Media Network, 2965
Agile Networks, 27
Agile Planet, 447
Agile Sciences, 3250
Agile Software, 27, 759, 1287, 1657
Agile Systems, 707, 2051
Agile Therapeutics, 73, 415, 1492, 1943
Agile Upstream, 98
AgileNano, 1786
Agilence, 857, 1321, 2188
Agilence Inc., 28
Agilex Fragrances, 1231
Agilic, 3194
Agilis, 1815
Agility, 907, 1049, 1235
Agility Communications Inc., 255
Agility Fuel Systems, 658
Agility Recovery, 1140
Agility Robotics, 1705
Agilix, 1679
Agilix Corporation, 2509
Agilliance Group, 3109
AgilOne, 1187, 1319, 1657, 1798
Agilone, 780
Agilux Labs, 119
Agilyx, 3083
Agios, 748
Agios Pharmaceuticals, 154, 1814
AGIS, 60, 1406, 1740
Agistics, 1976
AGL, 1350
Aglity Communications, 3109
AgLocal, 635
AGM Automotive, 1858
Agman Capital, 69
AgnioChem, 2188
Agnitio, 2978
Agnito, 2684
Agolo, 1158
Agora, 321, 3116
Agora Communication, 2114
Agora Fund, 3246
Agora.io, 827
Agoura Technologies, 1917
Agouron Pharmaceuticals, 1920
AGR Enhanced Drilling Systems, 3132
AGR Group, 2376
Agralogics, 1065
Agramkow Fluid Systems, 2642
AgraQuest, 307
Agreement Express, 793
Agreemint, 29
Agribiotics Inc., 2108
AgriDigital, 7
Agrileum, 1822
Agrilink Holdings, 2613
Agrilink Holdings Pty Limited, 2706
Agrilyst, 354, 527
Agrimetis, 1522
Agrinos, 1776
Agripharm, 2233
Agrisoma Biosciences, 2087
AgriSync, 999
Agritibi R.H., 2114
Agrivert, 2354
Agrivida, 571, 582, 805, 1474, 1478, 1776
Agro Arms, 3251
Agro-100 Ltee, 2114
Agro-Bio Controle, 2114
Agrocentre Belcan, 2114
AgroGeneration, 2364
Agroils, 2865
Agromillora, 1021

Agronomic Technology, 175
Agros Nova Sp. z o.o., 2697
AgroSavfe, 3056
Agrosavfe, 3033
Agrostar, 27
AGS, 874
AGS Health, 97
AgSmarts, 999
AgSolver, 583
AGTC, 1013, 1014, 1734
Aguamarina, 1073
Aguamur, 2480
AGV Logistica, 838
Agworld, 3238
AGY Holding Corporation, 1085
AGY Therapeutics, 2771, 2772
AH Harris, 792
AH Parallel Fund III-Q, 624
Aha, 1918
Aha!ogy, 481
AHAlife, 597
Ahalogy, 965, 1385
AHF Products, 110
Ahhaaa!, 2745
Ahlijasa, 721
Ahlsell, 2371
AHM, 167
AHP Billing, 352
Ahura Scientific, 154, 801, 885
ai, 810
Ai Build, 3099
AI Exchange, 1101
AI Fund, 877
aI METRIX, 2762
Aiara, 3118
Aibang.com, 1184
Aibel, 2722
Aicent, 1778, 1983, 2688, 2844
AiCO Technologies Co. Ltd, 2339
Aiconn Technology, 1924
AiCure, 225, 271, 1483
Aide, 2122
AidIn, 1534, 1585
Aidox Oy, 2707
Aiera, 756
Aif Capital Ltd, 3252
Aifi, 945
Aigotec, 3128
AiHit, 3220
Aikido, 2131
Aiko Biotechnology, 1165
Aikosolar, 977
Aileron, 1734
Aileron Solutions, 1826
Aileron Therapeutics, 704, 1128, 3076
Aim Above, 3251
AIM Aviation, 2935
AIM Health Group, 2051, 2142
AIM Software, 1973
Aim Technology, 2463
Aimbridge, 819
Aimbridge Hospitality, 61, 1108
AIMCo, 3249
Aimia Inc., 303
Aimmune Therapeutics, 764, 1147, 1522
AIMotive, 485
Aims, 289, 1383
AimSteady, 1509
Aimune Therapeutics, 73
Aimware Limited, 2696
Aingel, 1370
Ainsworth Lumber, 2062
Ainsworth Pet Nutrition, 1092
Aiotv, 2148
AIP Aerospace, 110
AIP Private Capital, 3249
aiPod, 976

Portfolio Companies Index

Aiptek International, 2594
AIQ, 125
Air Castle, 769
Air Chef, 1275
Air Energi, 2926
Air Italy, 3145
Air Lease Corp., 874
Air Lease Corporation, 160
Air Map, 1483
Air Media, 131
Air Medical Group Holdings, 223, 1275
Air Methods, 111
Air Monitor Corporation, 911
Air Movement Systems, 743
Air Serv, 1772
Air Tailor, 1179
Air Waves Inc., 367, 1344
Air-Inc, 1922
Air-sea Survival Equipment, 2353
Air2Web, 2866
Air2Web Asera, 3109
Aira, 150
Aira.io, 720, 1155
Airband, 20, 2188
Airband Communications Holdings, 556, 2630
Airbanq, 246
Airbase, 1935
Airbiquity, 85, 978, 1736
Airbnb, 44, 125, 265, 579, 680, 744, 778, 819, 820, 824, 827, 877, 1079, 1527, 1657, 1763, 1768
AirBoard, 310
Airborne 1, 1917
Airborne Entertainment, 1928
Airborne Intl., 2205
Airborne1, 1786
Airbud, 623
Airbug, 1125
Aircall, 2469
AirCell, 1483, 1771
AirClic, 767, 1045, 1304
Aircraft Fasteners, 952, 1493
Aircraft Technical Publishers, 1169
AircraftLogs, 1556
Aircuity, 1922
aire, 1982
Airespace, 1091, 1255, 1750, 2917
Airex Energy, 2087
Airfordable, 221
Airgo Networks, 27, 1976
AirHelp, 721, 1752, 2009
Airis Wellsite Services, 1129
Airlease, 2321
Airline Services, 2935
Airln Space, 2482
AirLogix, 958
Airmada, 623, 1489
AirMap, 820, 1511, 1698, 1705
Airmap, 222, 361, 521, 1155, 1158
Airnet Communications, 55
Airobotics, 299, 1158
Aironet, 215
AirPair, 10, 857
Airpax, 470
AirPlug, 1750, 1840
Airport Technology Center, 2556
Airpower Insurance, 267
AirPR, 545, 1247, 1610
AirSeed, 10
AirSense, 2978
AirSense Wireless, 2659
Airship, 1928
Airside, 881
Airsis, 1786
Airspace, 856, 1666
Airspace Link, 608
Airspace Technologies, 1511

Airspan, 1511, 1640, 3128
Airspan Networks, 1361, 1561, 1771
Airsphere, 2766
Airstone Labs, 1862
Airstream, 2107
AirStrip, 1657
Airstrip, 1511
Airswift, 1972
Airtable, 14, 321, 787, 945, 1696
Airtag, 3104
AirTight Networks, 1852, 2499
Airtime, 894, 1079, 1114, 1835
Airtreks, 508, 1538
Airvana, 1235, 2019
AirVine Scientific, 1099
AirVM, 2063
Airware, 125, 731, 1491
Airwatch, 27
Airwave, 894
Airwavz Solutions, 1410, 3250
Airway Services, 531
Airway Therapeutics, 481
Airweb, 2653
Airwide Solutions, 215, 1084, 1170
Airwork, 2655
Airworx Construction Equipment & Supply, 1057
Airxcel Holdings Inc., 357
AirXpanders, 545, 1490, 1943
Airy:3D, 474, 1009, 1983
Aisera, 1203, 1669
Aisle411, 570
Aisle50, 1385
Aislelabs, 1610, 2231, 2235
Aisys Ltd., 2945
AIT, 2201
AIT Bioscience, 659
AIT Worldwide Logistics, 1507
Aito Technologies, 2621, 2628
Aitua, 2958
Aiva Health, 49
AIXTRON Semiconductor Technologie, 2801
Aizon, 398
Ajax Health, 73, 1086
Ajax Health. Alcresta Therapeutics, 924
Ajax Intel, 999
Ajker Deal, 721
AJP Motos, 3039
AK Valley, 1703
Akadémos, 1087
Akamai, 226
Akamai Technology, 1107
Akamedia, 2375
Akari Therapeutics, 764, 1943
AkaRx, 1762
Akash Systems, 1073
Akebia Therapeutics, 189, 481, 1063, 1147, 1514, 1849, 1923
Akerman LLP, 3251
Akero, 1930
Akero Therapeutics, 144
Akeros Silicon, 1788
Akers Group, 2376
Akiban Technologies, 1335
Akibia, 523
Akido, 863
Akido Labs, 998
Akili Software, 3250
Akimbi, 1418
Akimbo Systems, 1976, 2020
Akin, 521, 1030
Akin Gump Strauss Hauer & Feld LLP, 3252
Akindo Sushiro Co., 2371, 3024
Akinova, 1269
Akiva Inc., 374, 1786
Akko, 1426
Aknol, 2767

Akonix Systems, 1408
Akonni Biosystems, 1172
Akorda, 1557
Akorri, 1335
Akouos, 11, 1350, 1522
Akoya, 1743
AKQA, 2073
Akqa, 782
Akros, 596
Akros Silicon, 1898
Aksh Optifibre Ltd. (India), 2685
Akshara Foundation, 1374
Aksys, 1762
Akta US LLC, 77
Aktana, 4, 1605, 2074
Aktano, 3129
Aktino, 1237, 1684, 1920
Aktis Oncology, 1934
AktiVax, 933
Aktive, 1892
Aktrion, 2787
Aktua, 444
Akubio, 2308
Akulaku, 149
Akustikken, 3194
AKVASmart, 3158
Akwan, 2733
Al Film, 33
AL Gulf Coast Terminals, 157
Al Nabil Food Industries, 416
Al Rajhi Capital, 153
AL Shore, 157
Al-F-Hitech, 2960
Alabama Theater, 1683
Alacritech Inc., 255, 1287
Aladdin, 1912
AlaFair, 1803
Alaffia Health, 2398
Alain Afflelou, 2712
Alamar Foods, 416
Alamito Minerals, 517
Alamo Drafthouse Cinema, 96
Alamosa Solar Generating Project, 416
Alan, 2217
Alando, 3223
Alantium, 2445
Alantos Pharmaceuticals, 2673, 2739
Alapage.com, 2756, 3199
Alarm.com, 21, 1787
Alarmguard Holdings, 1071
Alarts.com, 724
Alary, 2114
Alaska Airlines, 1971
Alaska Communications Systems, 781
Alasko, 1092
Alasko Foods Inc., 2115
Alate Partners, 2228
Alatest, 2466
Alation, 548, 972, 1800
Alauda.cn, 1009
Alauda.io, 2430
Alawar Entertainment, 89
AlayaCare, 2150, 2163, 2178, 2225
ALBA 1, 2848
Alba Therapeutics, 186, 1631, 2807
Albany Molecular Research, 1456
Albarelle, 2330
Albeo, 325
Albert, 10, 945, 2217
Albert Perron, 2089
Alberta Enterprise Corporation, 3249
Alberta Newsprint Company, 2249
Alberta Teachers' Retirement Fund, 3249
Albertville Quality Foods, 931
Albion Medical Holdings, 1529
Albireo, 3187
Albireo Energy, 963

1223

Portfolio Companies Index

Albridge Solutions, 215, 364, 957
Albrieo, 2998
Albright Capital Management LLC, 3252
AlbéA, 1755
ALC Concierge Service, 1587
Alcala Farma, 1777
Alcami, 1160
Alcentra, 2353
Alces, 222
Alces Technology, 35, 521
Alchemia, 2609
Alchemist Accelerator, 485, 812
Alchemista, 1489
Alchemy, 1370, 1576
Alchemy 43, 708, 763
Alchemy Semiconductor, 205
AlchemyAPI, 35
Alchimer, 2346
Alchip, 3114
Alchip Technologies, 3084
Alcholo Monitoring Systems, 1576
Alci, 2288
Alcide, 1009
ALCOM, 217
Alcon Computing, 1009
Alcontrol, 2547
Alcor Micro, 3209
Alcresta, 1814
Alcresta Therapeutic, 785
Alcumus Group, 3121
Alcyone Lifesciences, 910
Aldagen, 1013, 1446, 1844
Aldaph, 2880
Aldea Pharmaceuticals, 389
Aldeia da Pedralva - Empreend. Turisticos, 3039
Alder Biopharmaceuticals, 605, 764, 1661, 2007
Aldera, 21
Aldeyra Therapeutics, 622
Aldila Therapeutics, 710
Aldis, 236, 1273
Aldus, 755
Aleafia, 2245
Alector, 764, 894, 1238, 1383
Aledade, 271, 894, 1172
Aledadem Amino, 1918
Aledia, 325, 1009
Alegra AG, 2418
Alegus Technologies, 1127
Alektrona, 1695
Alelion Batteries, 2746
Alemite LLC, 911
Alentic Miscroscience, 2148
Alephd, 1418
AleraGroup, 823
Alere Medical, 1976
Alere Medical Inc., 573
Alereon, 443, 679, 1244
Alerion Biomedical, 1546
Aleris AB, 2703
Alert 360, 1754
Alert Labs, 2122
Alert Life Sciences Computing, 3039
Alert Logic, 35, 990, 1364, 1888, 1973
Alert1, 1854
Alertek, 1003
AlertEnterprise, 1382
AlertMe, 1908
AlertTech, 1813
Aleva, 2506
Aleva Neurotherpeutics, 2487
Alex & Von, 10
AlexandAlexa, 2963
Alexander Mann Solutions, 1300, 2199
Alexander Tank, 1433
Alexar Therapeutics, 1302
Alexion, 532
Alexis Biochemicals, 119

Alexis Bittar, 1863
Alexo Therapeutics, 1126
Alexza, 11
Alexza Molecular Delivery Corporation, 2308
Alexza Pharmaceuticals, 928
Alfa, 2716
Alfabet, 2369
Alfacam, 2771
AlfaLight, 652, 1923
Alfalight, 58, 154, 983
Alfred X Camera, 10
Alfresco, 27, 1187, 1235
Alfresco Software Alteryx, 1623
Alfy, 538
ALG USA Holdings, 1493
Algal Scientific, 743, 987
Algas Industries, 112
Algebra Ventures, 485
Algentis, 2967
Algeta, 2510
Algeta AS, 2807
Algety Telecom, 556
Algiax, 2815
Algo Access, 3064
Algolia, 10, 21, 1750, 3035
Algolux, 821, 2103
AlgometR, 421
Algomi, 2825
Algomi Ltd., 2919
AlgoPay, 10
Algopix, 1011
Algorand, 1884
Algorithmia, 601, 1162, 2006
Algorithmics, 2073
Ali Solutions, 138, 1865
ALI Technologies, 2091
Alianza, 861, 1074, 1430, 1679, 1886
Aliaxis, 3060
Alibaba, 827, 990, 2724, 3091
Alibaba Group, 805, 1235, 1685
Alibaba.com, 1680
Alibre, 200, 1561
Alibris, 1087
Alice, 12, 398, 1219
Alice.com, 584
Alien Technology, 56, 693, 950, 1561, 1757
Alien Vault, 1006, 1028
AlientVault, 827
AlienVault, 545, 1852, 2334
Aligence, 2430
Align, 336
Align Aerospace Holdings Inc., 867
Align Global Consulting, 3250
Align Technology, 1360
Alignable, 316, 1187, 1322, 1626
AlignAlytics, 1572
Aligned Carbon, 1616
Aligned Energy/Inertech, 1376
Aligned Telehealth, 1631
Aligned Teleheath, 1764
Alignment Healthcare, 819
Alignment Software, 950
Alignvest Management Corp., 2128
Aligos, 1930
Alimentary Health, 2909
Alimentation Coop Port-Cartier, 2114
Alimentation Francis Gravel, 2089
Alimentation L'epicier, 2114
Aliments Urbains, 2114
Alimera Sciences, 622, 1013, 1464, 1629, 1700, 1918
Alinea, 748
Alinea Pharma, 1631
Alinean, 1748
Alinta Energy, 1837
Alinta Ltd, 2447
Alion, 1927

Alios BioPharma, 3006, 3076
Alipay, 2396
ALIS, 1084
Alis, 154
Alitacare, 1085
Alithya, 2256
AliveCor, 1073, 1511
Alix Partners, 927
AlixPartners, 1021
Alizyme, 2814
Alkami, 1240, 1601
Alkar-RapidPak, 719
Alkira, 1079
Alku, 1979
All Aboard America!, 441, 815
All American Group, 931
All Around Roustabout, 410
All Def Digital, 59, 1816
All Elements, 3250
All Flex, 855
All Funds Bank, 927
All Gold Imports, 2227
All Island Media, 854
All Metro Health Care Services, 1278
All of It IT, 2440
All Safe, 1722
All Seasons Services, 1118
All Star Directories, 205
All States Ag Parts, 1169
All Tech/IESCO, 1343
All Traffic Data, 1641
All Traffic Solutions, 655
All Trails, 10
All Turtles, 820, 1610
All-Clad Holdings Inc., 494
All-State, 294
All-Tag Security, 2853
All3Media, 2528, 2529
All4, 1044
All4Staff, 1181
AllAboardToys, 686
AllAbout, 597
Allakos, 94, 1578, 3076
Allami Nyomda, 2478
Allant, 1231
Allay, 10, 129, 1770
Allbirds, 328, 708, 863, 1114, 1186, 1533, 1589
allbirds, 1696
Allbound, 390, 2074
AllBusiness, 1762
Allbusiness.com, 1908
Allcargo, 280
AllCloud, 1038
AllConnect, 696, 1355, 1711, 3124
AllDay, 10
AllDefDigital, 59
Allecra Therapeutics, 2739
Allegiance, 1543
Allegiance Hospice Group, 1631
Allegience Software, 352
Allego, 820
Allegra Direct Communications, 834
Allegro, 745, 912, 1335, 1912, 2814
Allegro Development Corp, 1731
Allegro Diagnostics, 428, 1084
Allegro Venture Partners, 1768
Allen Afflelou, 2843
Allen Edmonds, 337, 381
Allen Edmonds Shoe Corp., 847
Allen Foods Inc., 874
Allena Pharmaceutials, 1814
Allena Pharmaceuticals, 263, 785
Allergan, 1349
Allevi, 269
AlleWin Technologies, 1561
AllFacilities Energy Group, 1003
AllHeart, 791

Portfolio Companies Index

AllHere, 1554
Alliance, 1210
Alliance Boots, 2371
Alliance Boots plc, 416
Alliance Business Lending, 1514, 1971
Alliance Care, 409
Alliance Corp., 2156
Alliance Data Systems, 1973, 2371
Alliance Data Systems Corp., 1905
Alliance for Affordable Internet, 1374
Alliance for College-Ready Public Schools, 1315
Alliance Health, 689, 1205, 1442
Alliance Health Networks, 1947
Alliance Healthcare Services, 1271
Alliance Hotelerie, 2783
Alliance Laundry Systems LLC, 357
Alliance Medical, 2528, 2529, 2787
Alliance Medical Ltd, 3177
Alliance Pharma, 2972
Alliance Pharmaceutical, 1920
Alliance Sports Group, 406
Alliance Steel Service, 1722
Alliance Tire Company, 1971
AllianceCare, 405, 1631
Alliant, 912
Alliant Group, 1518
Alliant Insurance Services, 1133
Alliantgroup, 20
Allied 100 All Island Media, 1232
Allied Aerofoam Products, 1115
Allied Alloys, 1971
Allied Defense Group, 1493
Allied Glass Containers, 2608
Allied Reliability Group, 1438
Allied Resource Corporation, 1398
Allied S/A, 1376
Allied Technologies, 2364
Allied Vision Group Inc., 904
Allied Waste, 874
Alliedbarton Security, 886
AlliedPRA, 478
Alligator Bioscience, 3140
Allinea, 2958
Allinea Software, 3098
Allion Healthcare, 1377
Allison Marine, 1131
Allison Publications, 832
Allison Transmission Holdings Inc., 1905
Allituition, 1618
Allm, 2848
Allmyapps, 2684
Allocade, 603
Allocadia, 100, 980, 2150, 2257
Allocate, 1426, 2398
Allocation Specialists, 427
Allocine, 2598
AlloCure, 3006
Allogene Therapeutics, 1934
Allonnia LLC, 2105
Allopartis, 2010
Alloptic, 189
Allos Therapeutics, 73
Allos Ventures, 3259
Allosteros, 350
Allot, 2766
Allot Communication Ltd., 3149, 3150, 3221
Allovue, 1058, 1554
Alloy, 10, 36, 545, 680, 1203, 2019
Alloy Die Casting, 832
Alloy Merchant Finance LP, 3252
Alloy Ventures, 3273
AlloyCorp Mining, 1551
Allozyne, 154
Allpets.com, 2020
AllPoints, 1438
Allrecipes.com, 381
Allscripts, 263, 1255

Allsec Technologies, 416, 808
Allset, 125, 527
Allston Trading, 782
Allstream, 2067
allSystem, 3145
Alltec Global, 124
Alltech, 2570
ALLTELL, 1837
AllTheRooms, 1305, 1309, 3116
Alltop Tech, 3209
AllTrails, 129, 388, 1720
Alltricks.com, 1418
Alltrope Medical, 954
Alltrust Networks, 1389
Allume, 827
Allur Group Inc., 2061
Allure Security, 2018
Allure Security Technology, 833
Allure Systems, 1142
Allurion Technologies, 1585
Alluvium, 1155, 2006
Alluxio, 125
AllVirtuous, 10
Allvoices, 1908
AllWest Insurance Services, 2139, 2158
Allworx, 434, 1479
AllyAlign Health, 921
Allyes Information Technology, 2838
Allylix, 571, 1618, 1786, 2483
ALM Media, 1961
ALM Positioners, 1057
Alma, 720, 742
Alma Campus, 1346
AlmaBox, 2975
AlmaConnect, 2895
Almadtrac, 1452
Almalence, 1009
Almaz Capital, 485
Almaz Capital Partners, 3273
Alminder, 1867
Almond Systems, 1184
Almonde, 2073
Almotech, 2347
Alnara Pharmaceuticals, 263, 785, 1149, 1268, 1814
Alnylam, 2436
Alnylam Pharmaceuticals, 154, 193, 413
Alo, 2376
Alo7, 1511, 3206
AloDoketer, 721
Alogent, 238
ALOHA, 1998
Aloha, 669, 720, 742, 863, 938, 1666
Alok Textile Industries Limited, 2852
ALON and XL Associates, 1424
Alongside, 2123, 2192
Alooma, 1125
Alopa Networks, 1976
Alopexx Pharmaceuticals, 1421
AloStar Bank of Commerce, 1447, 1746
Alothon Group, 3252
Alpaca, 662
Alperton Ford & Truck, 2976
Alpex Pharma, 2487
Alpha, 564
Alpha & Omega Semiconductor, 908
Alpha Associates, 3252
Alpha Bay, 1679
Alpha Comm Enterprises, 1276
Alpha Draft, 121, 787, 1890
Alpha Foods, 814
Alpha Guardian, 1231
Alpha II, 1979
Alpha Imaging, 445
Alpha Innotech, 68
Alpha Media, 333, 334, 674
Alpha Networks, 2321, 2594

Alpha Outpost, 1154
Alpha Packaging, 1026
Alpha Ring, 1983
Alpha Sheets, 1489
Alpha Smart, 1754
Alpha Source Inc., 225
Alpha Therm, 2969
Alpha Vertex, 724
Alpha vision tech, 2960
Alphabet Energy Inc., 493
Alphabet Inc., 1669
Alphabeta Therapeutics, 946
Alphablock, 2257
AlphaBlox, 22, 990, 1008
Alphabox, 27
Alphabroder, 1138
AlphaDraft, 1566
Alphaeon, 1147
AlphaFlow, 10
AlphaICs, 2101
Alphamed, 1152
Alphamin, 2853
Alphamosaic, 2653, 2662, 3186
Alphanim, 2888
AlphaPoint, 1581
Alpharank, 10, 959
AlphaSense, 1001
AlphaStaff, 38
Alphatec, 1733
Alphatronix, 132
Alphion, 215, 1781
Alpin, 1317
Alpine Data Labs, 1239
Alpine Immune Sciences, 785
Alpine Oral Tech, 1073
Alpine Risk Services, 2354
Alps, 1151
Alreverie, 527
ALRISE, 2832
Alrise Biosystems, 2629
Alro, 2940
ALS Resolvion, 797
Alsalar, 1658
Alsay Inc., 988
Alsbridge, 1140
Alsentis, 1739
Alsid, 2288
Also, 2913
Also Energy, 2075
Alstom Power Conversion, 2705
Alston & Bird, 3250
Alsyon Technologies, 3104
Alt Bank, 2398
Alt School, 125, 234
Alt Tex, 2122
Alt United Garment Service, 2801
Alt12Apps, 1014
Alta Analog Inc., 131
Alta Devices, 200, 561, 582, 1478
Alta Growth Capital, 3252
Alta Rock Energy, 58
Alta Semper Capital, 3252
Altair engineering, 2762
Altair Global, 1276
Altair Semiconductor, 263, 2773
Altair Therapeutics, 1820
Altaire, 2095
Altamira, 518
Altamont Capital Partners, 3245
Altan China Co Ltd, 2490
Altaravision, 3250
AltaRock Energy, 1073
Altasciences Clinical Research, 2162
Altaven, 3229
Altead, 2439
Altec, 940
Altec Lansing, 1100

1225

Portfolio Companies Index

Altech Inspections, 1460
Altegra Health, 1419
Altegris, 823
Altegrity, 1498
Altela, 1926
Alteon Health, 785
Alteon Health LLC, 159
Alteon WebSystems, 759, 1091, 1379, 1684, 1762
Alter Eco America, 3246
Alter G, 493, 800, 1604, 1930
Altera, 388
Alterest, 3099
Alterface, 3216
AlterGeo, 89, 1009, 2336
Alteria Automation, 1509
Alterna, 1863
Alterna LLC, 97
Alternative, 1591
Alternative Biomedical Solutions, 448
Alternative Fuels Group, 993
Alternative Hose LLC, 1044
Alternative Solutions, 558
Alternative Technology Inc., 463
AlterPoint, 205, 1042, 1408
Alterra Power Corp., 1324
Alteryx, 1005, 1213, 1831
Altex Energy, 2044
Althea, 1786
Althea Technologies, 928, 1794
AltheaDx, 1794
Altheos, 3006
Altia, 2074
Altia Systems, 1009, 1284
Altice S.A., 416
Altieri Bakery, 1642
Altierre, 185, 186, 1976
Altierre Corporation, 1093
Altiga, 263
Altiga Networks, 523
Altilia, 3043
Altimate Medical, 855
Altiostar Networks, 485
Altiris, 1679, 2374
Altiris Therapeutics, 2609
Altiscale, 316, 1657
Altitude, 1637, 2009, 2888, 2888
Altitude Digital, 1205
Altitude Telecom, 3199
Altitun, 2869
AltiusEd, 1718
Alto, 121
Alto Pharmacy, 945, 1028
Alto Plastics, 2402
AltoBeam, 1898, 2658
AltoCom, 1754
Altopa Inc., 2279
Altor BioScience, 1619, 3187
Altor Networks, 582
Altos Ventures, 3273
Altostra, 1770
Altra, 405
Altraverda, 2589, 2708
Altrec, 961
Altria, 2605
Altrium CNI, 2848
Altruik, 609, 1305, 2016
Altruist, 2992
Altruja, 2815
AltSchool, 742, 778, 1534
AltspaceVR, 795, 1155
Altura Communication Solutions, 1686
Altura Medical, 58, 1297
Altus Assessments, 2074
Altus Pharmaceuticals, 2998
Altwork, 278
Alucid Technologies, 1219

Alukon, 2786
Alum.ni, 1467
Alumni Educational Solutions, 2156
Alumnify, 10, 461
Aluna, 849
Alung, 86
ALung Technologies, 296, 301, 1003, 1452
Alural Group, 2324
Alure, 652
Alutrans Canada, 2089
Alva, 2558
Alvarez & Marsal Capital, 3245
Alvarion, 2576, 3109, 3128
Alvarri, 1874
AlveolUs, 186
Alverix, 1304
AlVest, 2842
Alvey, 3033
Alvine, 1700
Alvine Pharmaceuticals, 748, 1014, 1411, 1495
Alvogen, 1138
Alwarebytes, 938
Always Hired, 1058
Always In Touch, 403
Always Market, 1244
Always Prepped, 1862
AlwaysOn, 1065
Alwaysprepped, 1533
AlwazPro, 999
AlyaaCare, 2074
Alyce, 2130, 2131
Alyotech Canada, 2089
Alzeca Biosciences, 447
Alzheimers Research & Treatment Center, 747
AM Conservation Group, 1859
AM Pharma, 2487
AM-BEO, 2340
Am-Pharma, 2739
AmacaThera, 2174
Amadesa, 2557
Amadeus, 2488, 2596
Amadeus Capital Partners, 3252
Amaethon, 2883
Amakem, 2739, 2940, 3011
Amakem Therapeutics, 3033
Amalfi Semiconductor, 597
Amalgamated Bean Coffee Trading Company, 585
Amalyst, 2958
Amann, 2786
Amann Girrbach AG, 1778
Amaranth Medical, 460
Amarillo Biosciences, 1839
Amarin, 1383, 1700, 1820
Amart All Sports, 2411
Amas, 2854
Amasten, 1101
Amatek, 2635
Amati, 1257
Amatis, 2136
Amaya Gaming Group, 2089
Amazon, 1867
Amazys, 2913
Amba, 2809
Amba Defence, 2958
Ambarella, 582, 1184, 1341
Ambassador, 175, 1154, 1179, 1739, 2016
Ambassador Theatre Group, 1498
Ambea AB, 1086
Amber Networks, 1750, 1976
Amber Road, 1888
Amber Taverns, 2926
Amber Technology, 2613
Amberdata, 959
AmberPoint, 564, 1762
Amberst Holdings, 1746
AmberWave, 1795

Ambience Healthcare, 10
Ambient, 1305
Ambient Air, 1729
Ambient Clinical Analytics, 300
Ambient Devices, 1588
Ambienta Biomasse, 2383
Ambion, 1794
Ambiq Micro, 205, 485, 964, 1207, 2681
Ambiqmicro, 1079
Ambit, 764, 2771, 2772
Ambit Biosciences, 209, 772, 1383, 1523, 3076
Ambition, 894, 1491
Ambition Solutions, 461
Ambow Education Holding, 2594, 3053
Ambra Health, 476
Ambric, 801
Ambrose, 3257
Ambrx, 11, 2410, 3076
Ambuja Cement, 2688
Ambulance Medilac, 2089
Ambulatory Services of America, 1133
Ambyint, 812, 1207
Ambys Medicines, 1780
AMC Entertainment, 223
Amc10, 325
Amcare, 2927
AMCC, 1657, 1924
AmCom, 1728
Amcor, 2381
AMCS, 1005
AMD Holdings, 751
Amdocs Ltd., 1973
AMEC, 241, 1014
Amec, 1125, 1511, 1537
Amecci, 2114
Ameda, 1169
Amedeo Capital Limited, 1447
Amedia, 33
Amedisys Resource Management Division, 409
Amedo, 2815
Amedrix, 2815
Amee, 1359
Amelia, 2065
Amen, 14, 3140
Amenity Analytics, 1009
Ameos, 3011
Amercable Inc., 989
AmerCareRoyal, 920
America Golf, 1755
America Isreal Cannabis Association, 865
America Latina Logistica, 838
America Rotor Company, 1536
America's PowerSports, 90, 1990
America's Thrift Stores, 92
Americam Physician Partners, 243
American & Efird LLC, 1089
American Academic Suppliers, 1438
American Achievement, 722
American Achievement Corporation, 1886
American Advisors Group, 790
American Alliance Dialysis Holdings, 973
American Apparel, 874
American Asphalt & Grading, 767
American Auto Auction Group, 225
American Axle & Manufacturing, 111
American Bath Group, 1275
American Beacon, 1066, 1837
American BioCare, 1425
American Broadband, 1493
American Candy, 1294
American Cannabis Company, 638
American Capital, 383
American Card Services, 1722
American Cellular Corporation, 822
American Clay, 1299
American Clinical Solutions, 408
American Community Newspapers, 1410, 1727

Portfolio Companies Index

American Consolidated Media, 377
American Construction Source, 502
American CyberSystems, 20
American Dental Partners, 1043
American Disposal Services, 1469
American Dryer Corporation, 1747
American Efficient, 499
American Endovascular, 1346
American Energy Partners, 1848
American Energy Permian Basin, 741
American Engineered Components, 847
American Exteriors, 408, 1487
American Federal Bank, 263
American Felt & Filter, 1294
American Freight, 1049
American Fuel Cell, 705
American Furniture Manufacturing, 467, 525
American Giant, 669
American Gilsonite, 1404, 1493
American Greetings Interactive, 2888
American Higher Educaion Development, 854
American Home/American Furniture Company, 905
American Honors, 510, 1298, 1784
American Hospice, 1576
American Huts, 165
American Independent Companies, 1956
American Industrial Machine, 16
American Industrial Partners, 1873
American Institute of Technology, 1377
American Internet Corp, 523
American Israeli Paper Mills2, 2600
American Leather, 165, 404
American Legal Fund, 267
American LegalNet, 1604
American Lighting Supply, 767
American Lock, 847
American Log Handlers, 679
American Made, 1626
American Marketing Industries Holdings Inc., 576
American Medical Systems, 3268
American Messaging Services, 986
American Millwork Corporation, 1524
American Mirrex, 836
American Nuts, 406
American Pipe & Plastics, 1627
American Piping Products, 654, 1427
American Prison Data Systems, 1554
American Products Co., 467
American Rec, 1755
American Renal, 444
American Renal Associates, 1140, 1410
American Reprographics Inc., 303
American Residential, 1372, 1973
American Residential Services, 458
American Resource Development, 673
American Roadprinting, 1003
American Roland Foods, 1933
American Scholar, 1748
American Screen Art, 694
American Seafoods LP, 449
American Signcrafters, 815
American Skiing Company, 1360
American Stencil, 467
American Stock Transfer & Trust Company, 1576, 3016
American Superconductor, 263
American Surgical Professionals, 864
American Threshold Industries, 1574
American Tire, 1021
American Tire Distributors Inc., 458, 867
American Traffic Solutions, 1949
American Wholesale, 56
AmeriCann, 1139
AmericasOne, 347
AmeriCast Technologies, 1089

Americo Manufacturing, 294
AmeriFile, 684
Amerifit Nutrition, 240
Amerigroup Real Solutions, 1762
Amerijet International, 931
AmeriMark, 408
Amerimed, 2373, 2374
AmeriPath, 1973
Ameriqual, 1138
AmeriQual Group LLC, 160
AmerisourceBergen Corporation, 357
AmeriSphere, 1276
Ameristop, 1955
Ameritox, 224, 1271, 1657, 1745, 1762
AMES, 1755, 1968
Ames Taping Tools, 202, 381
Ameta s.r.o., 3113
Amethis Finance, 3252
Ametros Financial Corp., 494
AMF, 654, 874
Amfora Packaging, 45
Amg, 1636
Amgen, 183
Amh Canada Ltee, 2114
AMHC Healthcare, 1065
Amherst Fund, 3259
Amherst Pierpont Securities, 819
AMI, 1760
AMI Holdings Inc., 1594
AMI Semiconductor, 782
Amiato, 586
Amicus, 785, 1358, 1374, 1479, 1521
Amicus Therapeutics, 1495, 1510, 1523
Amigo Insurance Holding Corporation, 1469
Amigo Technology, 3209
Amimon, 117, 438, 2717, 3221
Amino, 27, 48, 182, 321, 742, 894, 1323, 1884
Amino Technologies, 2463
Aminoagro, 1518
Aminolabs, 3033
Amionx, 1511
Amira, 1762
Amira Learning, 888, 1393
Amira Pharma, 1930
Amira Pharmaceuticals, 1495, 3006
Amitree, 27, 108, 945, 1254
Amixr.io, 10
Amkor Technology, 831, 1636, 2719, 2881
AML RightSource, 494
Amlogic, 977, 2841
Ammeraal Beltech, 2842
AMN Healthcare, 1372
Amnis, 85, 1007
Amobee, 3160
Amobee Media Systems, 27
Amonix, 56
Amor GmbH, 2303
Amorfix Life Sciences, 1839
Amorphology, 1055
Amour Vert, 669
Amourvert, 430
Amp Electrical Distribution Services, 658
AMP Robotics, 222, 521
AMP Therapeutics, 2521
Amp'd Mobile, 1561
AMPAC, 931
AMPAC Packaging, 1377
Ampad, 153
Ampaire, 1616
Ampathy, 1509
AMPAworks, 10
Amper, 59, 779
Amper Music, 354
Amperex Technology, 897
Amperion Cayman, 163
Amperity, 776, 1162
Ampersand, 125

Amphastar, 1949
Amphivena Therapeutics, 1268
Amphora, 468
Amphora Medical, 225, 711, 1147, 1874
Ampire Co, 3209
Ampla Pharmaceuticals, 1007, 1777
Ample, 10, 527, 945
Ample Communications, 1561, 1976
Ample Hills, 1114
Ample Hills Creamery, 354, 1533
Ample Medical, 1976
Ample Organics, 2134, 2279
Ampler, 69
Amplero, 978, 1610, 1985
Amplexor, 2554
Amplidata, 2828, 3143
Amplience, 3009
Amplified Technology Holdings, 632
Amplified Wind Solutions, 1051
Amplifinity, 629, 642
Amplifire, 1109
Amplify, 231, 400, 601, 641, 1966, 2398
Amplify Partners, 36
Amplify.ai, 548
Amplimed Corporation, 1903
Amplio Filtration Group, 2383
Amplion, 1659
AmpliPhi, 1815
Amplitude, 238, 251, 321, 1006, 1213, 1219, 1657, 1696, 1763, 2842
Amplitude Ventures, 3249
Amplity Health, 96
Amplus Communication Pte Ltd, 2694
Amply, 1363
Amplyx Pharmaceuticals, 845
AmpMe, 2024
Ampool, 456
Amprius, 1079, 1852, 1908
AmPro Mortgage Corporation, 592
Ampulse, 1976
AmQuip, 502
Amr Systems, 2474
AmRest, 1957
Amri, 912
AMRM, 18
Amromco Energy, 741
AmSafe Partners Inc., 867
Amsky Technology, 3053
AmSpec, 1372
amSTATZ, 1101, 2934
Amt, 2739
AMT3D Limited., 2696
AMTD, 2835
Amtec Precision Products, 1333
Amtech Corporation, 81
Amtek Auto, 1957
Amtex, 920
AMTEX Radiátory, 2639
Amtran, 2427
AMTrust, 2842
AMU Holdings, 1493
Amura, 2454
Amvonet, 1051
Amware Fulfillment LLC, 406
AmWINS Group, 1300
Amylin, 1657, 1762
Amynta Group, 1160
Amyris, 186
Amyris Biotechnologies, 582
Amzur Technologies, 3251
An Giang Plant Protection, 2952
AnaBios Corporation, 1065, 1786
AnaCatum, 2621
Anacle, 2468, 2844
Anaconda, 820, 2865
Anacor, 764, 949
Anacor Pharma, 1918

Portfolio Companies Index

Anacor Pharmaceuticals, 1561
Anadigm, 2436
Anadys, 2436
Anadys Pharmaceuticals, 1777
Anaergia, 2252
AnAerobics, 1378
Anaeropharma Science, 1241
Anafocus, 2539
Anafore, 2468
Anagin, 710
Anagnostics Bioanalysis, 3156
Anagram, 398
Anaheim, 851
AnaJet, 470
Analect Instruments, 189
AnalizaDX LLC, 1051
Analog Inference, 1243
Analogic, 97
Analogic Tech, 1183
Analogix, 597, 839
Analogix Semiconductor, 1976, 2005
Analyte Health, 1247, 1483
Analyte Media, 138
Analytical Space, 623, 756, 1330
Analyticon Discovery GmbH, 3181
Ananas, 395
Anandia Labs, 2134
Anant Raj, 263
Anantara, 2809
Anaplan, 511, 561, 857, 1213, 1666
Anaptys Bio, 785
Anaptys Biosciences, 209
AnaptysBio, 87, 3006
Anaqua, 1005
Anaren, 1927
Anark Corporation, 1273
Anasazi, 1255
Anaxsys, 2958
Ancera Corporation, 661
Ancestry, 1213, 1720
Ancestry.com, 56, 230, 564, 928, 990, 1679, 1949, 2371, 2374, 3024
Anchange Productions, 1441
Anchor, 27, 680, 894, 1049, 1724
Anchor BanCorp Wisconsin Inc., 407
Anchor Glass, 1968
Anchor Glass Container, 1089
Anchor Intelligence, 1042, 1976
Anchor Media Investors, 1360
Anchor Therapeutics, 922, 3187
Anchorage, 662
Ancient Mosaic Studios, 381
Ancile Solutions, 1169
Ancillary Advantage, 723
Ancora, 1886
AnD APT Inc., 1009
AND Automotive Navigation Data, 3200
Anda Tool and Fastener Ltd., 911
Andale, 1976
ANDalyze, 979, 1200
AnDAPT, 485
Andela, 79, 888, 894, 1610, 1719, 1760, 2140
Andera, 655, 1695
Anderson & Stowe, 3245
Anderson Aerospace, 1051
Anderson Group, 2089
Anderson Pacific Corporation, 3255
Andes Biotechnologies, 2446
Andia, 395
Andigilog, 1667, 1976
Andium, 411
Andjaro, 2469
Ando, 545
Andpad, 1610
Andre Potvin Cuisine/Salle De Bain, 2089
Andreessen Horowitz, 36
Andreessen Horowitz Fund II-A, 624

Andrena, 12
Andrew, 1304
Andrew Davidson & Company, 2188
Andrew Page, 3027
Andrew Technologies, 1329
Andrews International Holdings, 1275
Andrews International Inc., 467
Andritz, 3060
Androit, 133
Andromedia, 1042, 1566
Andromium, 10
Anduin Transactions, 10
Anduril, 820, 1716
Andy OS, 10
Andy Transport, 2114
Anello Photonics, 431
Anergis, 2506, 3140
Anesco, 3095, 3242
Anesiva, 215, 1777
Anessa, 2192
AneuRx, 1379
Anevia, 2867, 3104
AnexBusiness, 1376
Anfacto, 621
Angagio, 1346
Angaza, 1555, 1610
Angaza Design, 758
Angel food Systems, 3173
Angel Springs, 2935
Angela Bruderer, 2466
Angelini Group, 1456
Angelle, 1729
AngelList, 10, 37, 69, 232, 610, 650, 708, 752, 795, 894, 1058, 1079, 1154, 1491, 1696, 1841, 1998, 2228, 2272
AngelPad, 298
Anges Quebec Capital, 3249
AnGesMG, 2961
Angie's, 1668
Angie's List, 561, 641, 1122, 1481, 2919
Angiob, 3235
Angiocrine, 849
Angiodroid, 2865
AngioDynamics, 212
Angiogenix, 3158
AngioScore, 374, 990, 1428, 1500, 1794
Angioslide, 272, 2345, 3183, 3231
Angiosyn, 94
Angiotech, 1138
Angle, 820
Angle Technologies, 877
Angler Labs, 296
Anglian Group, 2353
Anglian Group Plc., 576
Anglian PLC, 2353
Anglo Suisse Offshore Partners, 157
Anglr, 1159
Angstrom, 1786, 2072
Angstrom Pharmaceuticals, 1704
Angstrom Power, 1908, 2144
Angstrom Publishing, 1194
Angury, 648
Angus Fire, 2935
ANI Pharmaceuticals, 733, 1275
ANI Printing Inks, 3000
Ani-Mat, 2114
AniBoom, 2717
Anika Therapeutics, 215
Anilinker Oy, 2707
Animal Adventure, 1722
Animal Health International, 458, 1113
Animal Supply Company, 899
AnimaPlus, 2212
Animart LLC, 847
Animated Dynamics Inc., 659
Animated Speech Corporation, 1671
Animex, 2553

Animon, 2571
Animoto, 1162, 1702, 1720
Anite Travel, 2935
Anitox, 1576
Aniways, 2822
Anji, 1340
Anji-Micro, 3225
Anju Software, 20, 1499
Anjuke.com, 1184
Ankasa, 545
Ankeena, 1855
Anker, 977
Anki, 125, 1876
Ankura, 1160
Anmestix, 326
Ann Arbor Angels, 3259
Ann Williams Group, 743
Ann's House of Nuts, 1372
Anna's Linens, 1591
AnneLutfen.com, 3199
Annexon Biosciences, 545, 1350
Annie's, 928
Annonay Productions France, 3011
Annovation Biopharma, 193, 1421
Annularspace, 2302
Anodyne, 352
Anokion, 1350, 1930
Anokiwave Inc., 813
Anomali, 820, 894, 1006, 1716
Anonymous Content, 1768
Anord Mardix, 260
Anova Data, 938
Anova Fertility & Reproductive Health, 2212
Anover.net, 1463
Anpute, 3185
Anquanbao, 1340
Ansa, 1561
Ansa Software, 209
Ansaar Management Company, 54
Ansamed Ltd, 2696
Ansaris, 1456
Ansaro, 888
Ansell Ltd, 2447
ANSIRA, 1090
Ansley at Roberts Lake, 1220
Ansley Commons, 1220
ANSR, 27
Answer IQ, 1162
AnswerDash, 1947, 2007
AnswerLogic, 1348
Answers, 1754, 1778
Answers Corporation, 136
Answers.com, 593, 1537
AnswerSoft, 205, 1561
Answersoft, 3128
Ansyr, 85
ANT, 2885
Ant Financial Cloud, 2396
Ant Fortune, 2396
Antares Holdings Limited, 1127
Antares Pharma, 1456, 2188
Antavo, 3099
AnTech, 3090
Anteis, 2487
Antengo, 1305
Antenna, 975, 1463, 1600
Antenna International, 1984
Antenna Software, 523, 1335, 1464
Antenna79, 1092
Antenova, 2463, 3061
Anteo Diagnostics, 2609
Anterios, 517
Antero Resources, 1957
Anteryon, 1511, 3060
Antheia, 1669
Anthemis Gropu, 2931

Portfolio Companies Index

Anthera Pharmaceuticals, 928, 1268, 1414, 1700, 1900, 1908
Anthony, 202
Anthony Machine, 988
Anthony's Coal Fired Pizza, 1092
Anthony's Pizza, 1518
Anthos, 36
Antibe Therapeutics, 2043
Antibiotice, 3178
Antig Technology Co, 2581
Antio Therapeutics, 2174
Antispameurope, 2815, 2985
Antiva Biosciences, 2174
Antler, 2935
Anton Capital Entertainment SCA, 1377
Antriabio, 240
AntVoice Group, 2377
Anudip Foundation, 1374
Anuluex Technologies, 1728
Anuncie La, 2323
Anusbisnetworks, 3039
Anutra Medical, 907
Anvato, 1305, 1394
Anvendeo Designwelt, 2815
Anvil, 748
Anvil Holdings, 357
Anvil International, 1779
Anvil Semiconductors, 2958
Any Media, 3033
Any Vision, 1511
Any.do, 304, 720
AnyBody Technology, 3194
Anycart, 1426
Anyka, 2427
AnyMeeting, 1786
Anymeeting, 400
Anyplace, 798
AnyPresence, 1076
Anypresence, 881
AnyRiver, 132
Anyroad, 10
Anyscale, 3, 1296
Anysource Media, 1321
AnyTime Access, 51
Anytime Fitness, 1580
Anyware, 3104
ANZ, 2969
ANZ Banking Corp, 2650
Anzamune, 2507
AOD Software, 1480
AOMS, 2060
AON, 3251
Aon3d, 1370, 2204
AOptix, 504, 1341, 1862
Aoptix Technologies, 582, 1949
Aorato, 27
AorTx Inc., 272
AOSP, 2570
aovo Touristik AG, 3188
AP Aqua, 2716
AP Benson Ltd, 2885
AP Technical Textiles, 2384
Ap+m, 1438
Apach Network, 2888
Apache, 1924, 2956
Apacheta Corporation, 1403
Apalya Technologies, 2840
Apama, 350
Apama Medical, 178
APANA, 1895
Aparium Hotel Group, 69
Apartment Data Services, 381, 1722
ApartmentJet, 296, 301
ApartmentList, 945, 1184
ApaTech, 2653, 2665
Apax CAES, 898
Apax Partners, 3254

APC Automotive Technologies, 917
Apcela, 495
Apcera, 586, 1862
APCOA, 1021
APCT, 1627
APDS, 3246
Apeel Science, 125
Apeel Sciences, 1786, 1890, 3248
Apeks, 2051
Apellis, 922, 2969
Apellis Pharma, 1943
Apellis Pharmaceuticals, 690
Apere, 1976
Aperia, 1604
Aperia Technologies, 198, 1671
Aperio, 587
Aperto Networks, 1042, 2866
Aperture, 531, 1723
Aperture Credentialing, 958
Apervita, 225, 812, 1181, 1483
Apesoft, 2544
Apex, 823
Apex Analytix, 418
Apex Companies, 1779
Apex Construction Systems, 1917
Apex Fund Services, 796
Apex Learning, 522, 1242
Apex Microtecnology, 1232
Apex Parks Group, 416, 654
Apex Revenue Technologies, 1979
Apex Service Partners, 92
Apex Towers, 543
Apex.AI, 1836
Apexian Pharmaceuticals, 659
APF - WFCF, 1971
APH Property Holdings, 1493
Apherma Corporation, 1183
Aphria, 393, 1139, 2245
API Healthcare, 782, 1971
API Heat Transfer, 197, 989
API Heat Transfer Inc., 1972
API Maintenance Systems, 3194
API Outsourcinv, 1117
API3, 1709
Apiary, 234
Apiary.io, 2009
Apica, 3183
Apidos CLO, 1493
Apigee, 241, 759, 1623
APIM Therapeutics, 2510
Apique, 1027
Apire Health, 1261
Apis Partners, 2398
Apitope, 2940, 3033
APJeT, 450
Apjohn Ventures, 3259
Apkudo, 1172
Apl Next Ed, 659
Aplix, 897
APMG, 2567
Apnapaisa Private, 3053
Apneon Inc., 573
ApoCell, 1754
Apogee, 843
Apogee IT Services, 291, 352
Apogee Translite, 1609
Apogen, 2007
ApoGen Biotechnologies, 30
Apogen Technologies, 167
Apolife, 743
Apollo, 2398
Apollo Computers, 1762
Apollo Endosurgery, 1502
Apollo Enterprise Solutions, 281
Apollo Fusion, 877
Apollo Global Management, 1271, 3245
Apollo International, 2719, 2881

Apollo MedFlight, 406
Apollo Medical Devices, 1051
Apollo Solar, 977
Aporeto, 1346
Aporta Digital, 3194
Apos, 2453
Apostrophe, 10
Apotek Hjartat, 2376
Apothecare, 505
Apothecare LLC, 1738
Apothecarry, 395
Apothecary Products, 1345
Apoxis SA, 2807
App Annie, 641, 977, 1006, 1657, 2841, 2860
App Central, 299
App in the Air, 2847
App Onboard, 10
App Press, 659
App.ic, 1515
App.io, 1637
App47, 1901
Appalachian Lighting Systems, 1003
AppAnnie, 876
Apparel Media Group, 1101, 1364
Appart City, 2842
AppAttach, 85, 1462, 2007
Appature, 776
AppBind, 10
Appbistro, 1658
Appboy, 31, 304, 488, 1525
AppBus, 51, 770
Appcast, 225, 1023
Appcelerator, 1187, 1478, 1543, 1750, 1840
AppCityLife, 758
Appconomy, 1862
Appcore, 347
Appcues, 1672
AppDetex, 1385
AppDirect, 779, 1741, 2150
AppDome, 1203
Appdome, 604
AppDynamics, 561, 819, 990, 1006, 1125
Appear Here, 728, 2963
Appear Networks, 3004
Appear TV, 2628
Appear [here], 2469
Appear[Here], 2743
Appelberg, 2879
Appen Butler Hill, 2391
Apperian, 263, 536, 1101, 1335
Apperio, 3099
Appetas, 1407
AppFirst, 744
Appfluent, 1888
Appfluent Technology, 1348
AppFog, 776
Appfog, 978
Appfolio, 641
Appfuel, 310
Appgate, 2869
Appglu, 1959
AppHero, 2130
Appia, 597, 1332, 1334, 1832, 1852, 1918
Appian, 1348
Appied Adhesives, 1232
Appier, 2681
Appili Therapeutics, 2148
Appilog, 438, 2646
Appilog Inc., 2571, 2766
Appinions, 323
Appionics Holdings, 1009
Appiphony, 1610
AppIQ, 58, 1335
Appirio, 819, 827, 1518, 1657
Appium, 2866
Applaud Medical, 1055, 1238
Applause, 1150, 1175, 1517, 1629, 3226

Portfolio Companies Index

Applauze, 10, 1058, 1862
Apple, 1657
Apple Computers, 1257
Apple Leisure Group, 1086
Apple Pie Capital, 387
Apple Toon, 1537
Apple Valley Waste, 1753
AppleBoard, 176
Applegate, 1769
ApplePie Capital, 1504
Appleseed's, 843
Appletoon, 3206
Appletree Institute for Education Innovation, 1315
Appletree.com, 794
Appleyards Plastics Ltd., 3002
Applicam, 2512
Application Networks, 58, 2770
Application Security, 1084, 1401
Applie Pie Capital, 787
Applied, 579, 927, 1045
Applied Adhesives, 847, 1767
Applied Aerospace Structures, 1921
Applied Biocode, 974
Applied Biomath, 2
Applied Biosystems, 183, 1898
Applied CleanTech, 1626
Applied Composites, 1921
Applied Consultants, 1278
Applied Energy, 2787
Applied Genetic Technologies, 1013
Applied Genetics, 1733
Applied Graphene Materials, 3003
Applied Impact Robotics, 2072
Applied Intuition, 125, 752, 1155, 1716, 1850
Applied Isotope Technologies, 1452
Applied Micro, 183, 1898
Applied MicroStructures, 526, 950
Applied Molded Products, 1921
Applied Molecular Evolution, 772
Applied Nano Surfaces Sweden, 2746
Applied Optoelectronics, 908, 1771
Applied Process, 935
Applied Proteomics, 622, 1948
Applied Science Fiction, 446, 1561, 1857, 3128
Applied Sensor, 2719, 2881
Applied Sensor AB, 3153
Applied Silver, 1867
Applied Solar Technologies, 263
Applied Spectral Imaging, 3153, 3231
Applied Systems, 223
Applied Visions, 3257
Applied Wave Research, 95, 885
Applieddata.net, 162
Applifier, 1227
AppLift, 3042
Applimation, 1408
Applitools, 1672, 2943
Applix, 2393, 3043
AppLovin, 1086, 1969
Apply, 321
Apply Board, 1051
Apply Financial, 1862
Apply Kit, 1959
ApplyBoard, 2024, 2122, 2123, 2130, 2131
AppMesh, 1014, 1784
AppNeta, 224, 1045
AppNexus, 541, 742, 1084, 1851, 1918
Appnexus, 1787
Appnique, 1284
Appnomic, 1346
Appnovation, 2065
Appolicious, 138
Apponboard, 1616
AppOrbit, 548
Apporbit, 1079
Apportable, 1254, 2321

Appotronics, 3084
Appplied Precision, 1794
AppRats, 10
Appreciate, 2943
Apprenda, 978, 1479
Apprente, 1423
Apprentice, 1483
Apprion, 468
Appriss, 224, 502, 912, 1005, 1045, 1346, 1991
Appro Healthcare, 1378
Appro Systems, 1772
Approach Software, 1337
Approva, 1348
Approvia, 2596
Approvisionnement Populaire, 2089
Apprupt, 2985
Apps Associates, 364
Apps.com, 1994
Appsamurai, 10
Appsbuilder, 2395
APPScomm, 1009
AppScotch, 89
Appsfire, 2842
AppsFlyer, 711, 2943
AppsFreedom, 861
Appshed, 2577
APPsolute Mobility, 2518
appssavvy, 1862
Appstores Inc., 650
AppStream, 1042
AppTap, 1290, 1773
Apptec Laboratory Services, 1820
Apptegy, 746, 2074
Apptentive, 85, 776, 861, 894, 1385, 2130, 2131
Apptera, 87
Appthority, 545, 1898, 1918
Appthwack, 1467
Apptient, 581
Apptimize, 548, 894, 1219, 2009
Apptio, 125, 485, 877, 1666
Apptis Holdings, 1300
Apptitude, 3109
Apptive, 447
Apptix, 2623
Apptonomy Mobile Technologies, 2148
Apptopia, 708
Appuri, 234
Appurify, 586
Appvance, 1032, 2951
Appy Couple, 724
AppZen, 10, 1537
APR Energy, 45, 1314
Aprea, 11, 1930
Aprecia Pharmaceuticals, 290
Aprecia Pharma, 1271
Apria Healthcare Group, 2371
Apricot Forest, 299
April, 100
Aprimo, 86, 1674, 1736
Aprio, 2262
aPriori, 1674, 1675
Apropos Technology, 154
APS Investments, 3252
Apsalar, 10, 545, 597, 776, 1254, 1821
APSE, 47
Apsmart, 2659
APT, 56, 3182
APT Pharmaceuticals, 1449, 1546
Aptalis Pharma, 1837
Aptanomics, 2346
AptDeco, 12, 863
Apteligent, 1629, 1666
Aptible, 788, 1155
Aptim, 1927
Aptinyx, 785, 1098, 1147, 2125
Aptis, 263, 1257
Aptitude Investment Management, 1133

Aptiv Solutions, 899, 1631
AptivIO, 1509
Apto, 1207
Aptoide, 641, 3039
Aptology, 540, 2018
Aptomar AS, 3132
Apton Biosystems Inc., 1073
Aptuit, 1973
Apture, 504
Aptus, 856
Aptus Endosystems, 1774, 1898
Apus, 1537
APW Yarn Technologies, 2384
APX, 1076, 1379, 2005
APX Labs, 1320, 1486, 1689
Apyon, 2617
AQDOT, 3019
Aqua, 48, 182, 1158
Aqua Capital, 3252
Aqua Mobile, 2460
Aqua Pharmaceuticals, 1594
Aqua Security, 1125
Aqua Systems, 412
Aqua-Flo LLC, 451
Aquaai, 221
AquaBlok, 1556
AquaBounty Technologies, 240
Aquabyte, 548, 2037
AquaChem, 1169
Aquacue, 499
AquaGen, 2745
AquAgro Lab, 2408
Aqualisa, 2608
Aqualitas, 1810, 2134, 2148
Aquamar Holdings, 963, 1612
Aquamarine Power, 2307, 3126
AquaMelon Water, 3251
Aquamiel Tequilla, 2117
AquaMost, 2002
Aquamundi, 2617
Aquantia, 116, 1125, 1924
Aquantia Corporation, 1449
aQuantive, 1640, 1947
Aquapharm BioDiscovery, 2342
Aquarelle.com, 2377
Aquaria Inc., 874
Aquarius Technologies, 2717
Aquasana, 679
AquaSprouts, 1509
AquaSpy, 571, 659, 2708
Aquaspy, 1618
Aquatic Informatics, 2282
AquaVenture Holdings, 658
AquaVentures Holdings LLC, 62
Aquea Scientific, 307
Aqueduct, 2007
Aqueduct Critical Care, 1065
Aquent, 1176, 1971
Aqueos, 988
Aquera, 1203, 1666, 1760
AqueSys, 39, 1561
Aquicore, 728, 1281
Aquilex, 1138
Aquilex Corporation, 917
Aquinox, 1439
Aquion, 1174
Aquion Energy, 58, 410, 773, 949, 1079
Aquion Water Treatment, 1964
Aquire, 245
Aquis, 1161
Aquto, 1184, 1335
Aqwise, 2891
AR Carton, 2317
Arabela Holding, 416
Arable, 398
Araccel, 2372
Arago, 1086

1230

Portfolio Companies Index

Aragon, 310
Aragon Pharmaceuticals, 73
Aragon Surgical, 240, 1008
Arakis, 2998
Arakis Aridhia, 3095
Aralez Pharmaceuticals, 1052
AraLight, 1304
Aramark, 435, 1818, 1957
Aramsco, 63, 1368
Arandell, 410, 1722
ArangoDB, 3152
Arann Healthcare, 2347
Aras, 649
Aras Corp., 812
Arasys Technologies, 1674
Aratana, 1618
Aratana Therapeutics, 209, 571, 1268
Aravo, 485
Aravo Solutions, 130, 327, 758
Arbe Robotics, 2288
Arbell Electronics, 2089
Arbinet, 186
ArBlast, 1456
ARBOC Specialty Vehicles, 931
Arbonne, 687
Arbor, 863
Arbor Investments, 3255
Arbor Networks, 652, 1125, 1478
Arbor Partners, 3259
Arbor Pharmaceuticals, 1086
Arbor/Hyperion, 1657
Arboretum Ventures, 3259
ArborMetrix, 150, 964, 1596
Arbortext, 1337
Arbovax, 1446, 1987
Arbutus Biopharma, 764, 1271
Arby's, 1580
Arby's Restaurant Group, 1971
ARC Center, 347
ARC Machines, 1171
Arc Terminals, 1848
ARC UAE Logistics II, 153
ARCA Biopharma, 318, 1271
ArcadeMonk, 2286
Arcadia, 321, 696, 812, 1616
Arcadia Biosciences, 2483
Arcadia Communications, 1070
Arcadia Data, 1009, 1187
Arcadia Healthcare Solutions, 723
Arcadia Power, 490
Arcadian Management, 1255
Arcadian Networks, 1029
Arcadis, 3060
Arcanvs, 1015
Arcapita International Luxury Residential Develope, 153
Arcapita Qatar Real Estate Investment I, 153
Arcapita US Residential Development II, 153
Arcapita US Residential Developmental III, 153
Arcapita Ventures I Limited, 153
Arcarios, 2467, 2505, 2940, 3011, 3033
Arcato Laboratories, 844
ArcCore, 2746
Arcellx, 1734
Arceo Analytics, 856
Arch, 521, 1049, 1219
Arch Aluminum and Glass, 1145
Arch Capital Group Ltd., 927
Arch Innotek, 270
ARCH Venture Partners, 2483, 3255
Arch Venture Partners, 990
ArcheMedX, 120
Archemix, 1561, 2436
Archemix Corp., 189
Archer, 1129
Archer Aviation, 1616
Archer Education, 1385
Archer Rppse, 1703
ArcherDX, 1149
Archermind, 977
Archermind Technology, 2841
Archetype Ventures Fund, 485
Archimede Technology Group, 1561
Archimedes Health Investors, 3254
Archimica, 73
Archipelago, 2762
Architizer, 1896
Archivas, 1335, 1704
Archive Systems, 655, 1329
ArchivesOne, 20, 952
Archon Woodworks, 1505
Archrock, 1666
Archstone Smith, 153
Archway Digital Solutions Inc, 2499
Archway Marketing Services, 1021, 1779
Arcion Therapeutics, 1014
ArcLight Capital Partners, 3245
Arcmail Technology, 60, 365
Arco, 2417
Arco Bodegas, 2528, 2529
Arcomet, 2771
Arcor Group, 1012
Arcoro, 1499
ARCOS, 1576
Arcos, 1576, 3230
Arcosa Inc., 1905
Arcot, 27, 57, 1379, 1913
Arcot Systems, 857
ArcSight, 1006, 1008, 1235, 1478
Arcsoft, 1731
Arctic, 173
Arctic Chiller Group, 2121
Arctic Glacier, 931, 1493
Arctic Oilfield Equipment, 1493
Arctic Wolf, 1125
ArcticDX, 2051
Arcturus BioCloud, 10
Arcus Biosciences, 73, 710, 764
Arcxis, 983
Ardais, 1096
Ardana, 2739
Ardelyx, 113, 764
Ardence, 405
Ardenham Energy, 2530
Ardent Health Services, 723, 1973
Ardent Hire Solutions, 2243
Ardent Services, 1148
ArdentCause, 743
Ardentia, 2958
Ardenton Capital Corporation, 3249
Ardeo Imaging, 2071
Arder Holdings, 1360
Ardian, 1728
Ardica Technologies, 1749
Ardmore Shipholding Ltd., 867
Ardonagh Group, 1160
Ardyne, 1129
Are You A Human, 608, 743
Area 1, 84, 553, 742
Area Wide Protective, 293
Area1, 1079
Arecor, 3098
Arel Communication and Software Ltd., 2945
Arena, 1045, 1414, 1629
Arena Group, 2956
Arena Gulf, 1129
Arena Solutions, 1976
Arendsoog, 3033
Ares Management LLC, 3254
Areso, 2665
Arevo, 1073
ARG, 2373
arGEN-X, 1383, 2505, 2739, 3104
Argent, 568
Argent (Ford Alloy Wheel Plant), 2402
Argenta Discovery, 3186
arGentis, 999
Argenx, 764
ArgNor Wireless Ventures BV, 163
Argo, 2969
Argo Group, 407
Argo Medical Technologies, 3050
Argo Tea, 333, 1955
Argo Tea Inc., 334
Argo-Tech Corporation, 867
ArgoMed, 1414
Argon Medical Devices, 1594
Argon Networks, 1335
Argos, 949
Argos Therapeutics, 1013, 1399, 2739, 3187
Argotec, 1990
Argus, 2943
ARGUS Software, 1127
Argyle Data, 40, 185, 1692
Argyle Security, 2956
Arhaus, 786
Aria, 604, 1014, 1464, 2277
Aria CV, 272, 350, 428
Aria Insights, 1155
Aria Systems, 224, 959, 1918
Ariad, 209, 772
Ariane Systems, 3011
Ariat, 337
Aricam, 2480
Aricent, 2645
Ariel Networks, 2845
Ariel Re, 1372
Arieso, 2287, 2653
Arieso Ltd, 2885
Arigo G360, 352
Arima Communications, 475
Arima Computer Corp., 3209
ARInsights, 2074
Ario Pharma, 1302, 2739
Ariosa Diagnostics, 1213, 1918
Aris Teleradiology, 864
Arisdyne, 468, 642
Arise, 38
Arisem, 2346
Arista, 27, 209, 1537
Arista MD, 545
Arista Networks, 990, 3112
Aristacom, 1561
AristaMD, 1
Ariston Global, 266, 1727
Aristos Logic, 1976, 2005
Aristotle Circle, 1305, 1561
Aristotle Corporation, 1169
Arit Optronics, 2381
Aritech, 1728
Ariterm, 3045
Arivale, 1186
ARIX Technologies, 2105
Arizona Center for Cancer Care, 1271
Arizona Nutritional Supplements, 674
Arizona Technology Enterprises, 3258
Ark, 457, 708, 1121, 1841
Ark Holding Company, 248
Ark Naturals, 216
Ark Therapeutics, 2998
Ark-Angels Fund, 3033
Ark-La-Tex Wireline Services, 1493
Arka, 10
Arkadium, 655
Arkados Group, 2027
Arkal Medical, 1820
Arkansas Automatic Sprinklers, 1215
Arkavund Media, 3033
ARKeX, 2691
Arkex, 2722, 3095
ARKimedes, 3033

Portfolio Companies Index

Arkin, 298
Arkis Biosciences, 999
Arkivum, 2883, 3019
ARKLATEX Energy Services, 913
Arkmicro Technologies, 3053
Arkoma Pipeline Partners, 157
Arkoon, 3199
Arkopharma, 2968
Arlant, 3039
Arlettie, 3104
ARM-Harith Infrastructure Investments Ltd, 3252
Arma Beheer BV, 2797
Armacell, 1021
Armada.ai, 640
Armadio Verde, 2865
ArmaGen, 1241
ArmaGen Technologies, 2521
Armand Agra, 2118
Armaron Bio, 3129
Armatis, 3011
Armatis-Laser Contact, 2330
Armax Gaz SA, 3178
Armeco, 2114
Armed Response Team, 1299
ArmedAngels, 2466
Armel Corporation, 2046
Armenia Tomato, 1012
Armenian Datacom Company, 2645
Armgo Pharma Inc., 73
ARMO Biosciences, 1383
Armoire, 901
Armon, 3128
Armonix, 1398
Armor Group, 2786
Armor Holding II, 1493
Armor Security, 1233
Armor5, 2992
Armored Things, 833, 1175, 2150
Armorize, 2382
ArmorText, 456
Armory, 232, 564, 1032, 1616
Armstrong, 1837
Armstrong Energy, 1797
Armstrong Flooring Inc., 1905
Armstrong Franklin, 1118
Armstrong World Industries Inc., 1905
Armtec Limited, 2062
Armune BioScience, 140
Arna Therapeutics, 2031
Arneg SPA, 77
Arnold Logistics, 1148
Arnold Magnetic Technologies, 197, 525
Arnott, 371
Aromyx, 626, 1219, 1716
Arosa+LivHome, 961
Arotech, 867
Arovia, 229
ARPAC, 607
Arpatia India Growth Capital I, 153
Arpeggio Biosciences, 798
Arpida, 2598, 2913
Arpida AG, 2642
Arquati, 3145
Arque, 2334
ArQule, 193, 1900
Arqule, 2436
Arradial, 317
Arradiance, 1237
Arraiy, 474, 1155
ArraVasc, 1241
Array, 337
Array BioPharma, 154, 318, 785, 1107, 1777
Array Health, 85, 776, 1332
Array Networks, 897
Array Power, 731
ArrayComm, 1706

Arrayent, 597
Arresto Biosciences, 1341
Arris, 1335
Arris Pharmaceutical, 263
Arriva Pharmaceuticals, 2073
Arrive, 254
Arrive BioVentures, 1559
Arrivo, 23
ARRM Holdings, 1493
Arro Corporation, 410
ArroHealth, 941
Arrow Material Handling Products, 402, 1057
Arrow Storage Products, 1968
Arrow Therapeutics, 193, 2771, 2772
Arrow Tru-Line, 1145, 1460
Arrow Tru-Line. Bar Louie, 1755
Arroweye, 225
ArrowEye Solutions, 56
Arrowhead, 1021
Arrowhead Brass Products, 376
Arrowhead Electrical Products, 1438
ArrowPass, 10
ArrowPath Venture Partners, 990
Arrowpoint, 27
ArrowPoint Communications, 1335
ArrowSpan, 2694
Arroyo, 597
Arroyo Video Solutions, 1976
Arsais, 1631
Arsanis, 1464, 1646, 1764
Arsanis Biosciences, 1383
Arsenal, 186
Arsenal Capital Partners, 1271, 3254
Arsenal Digital Studios, 1711
Arsenal Medical, 1013, 1335, 1464
Arsenal Venture Partners, 3251, 3259
Arsenic, 562
ARSS Infrastructure Ltd, 2850
Arstasis, 179
ART, 263
ART Advanced Recognition Technologies, 2711
Art For Everyday, 2039
ART Group, 585
Art of Click, 1966
Art Technology Group, 1731, 2601
Art.com, 1235, 1464, 1608, 1712, 1751
Art19, 259, 1885
Art2Wave, 1947
ArtCorgi, 10
Artcraft, 2976
Arteaus Therapeutics, 193
Artel Video, 317
Artel Video Systems, 457
Artemis, 6, 1074
Artemis Pharmaceuticals, 1777
Artemis Pharmaceuticals GmbH, 2776
Artemys, 321
Arteria Ai, 2131
Arteriocyte, 696
Arteriocyte Inc., 423
Arteriocyte Medical Systems, 639
Arteriors, 1345
Arteris, 556, 621, 2630, 3199
Arterys, 108, 183, 812, 1254, 1347
Artesian, 3009
Artfinder, 3004
Artful Home, 1643
ArtGo Holdings, 416
Artha Partners, 3252
Arthena, 773, 2398
Arthrosurface, 315
Arthus-Bertrand, 2593
Artic Wolf, 1537
Article, 2235
Articulinx, 1898
ArtiCure, 1013
Artie, 754

Artielle, 1619
Artifact Entertainment, 767
Artificial Muscle, 154, 1324
Artima SA, 2697
ArtimiCambridge Broadband, 2378
Artios, 1350, 1631, 1764
Artis Exploration, 2022
Artisan Components, 1898
Artisan Entertainment, 197
Artisan Partners, 927, 1762
Artisan Pharma, 1325, 2504, 2681
Artistic Holdings, 1145
Artisto Music, 2467
ArtistOnGo, 685
Artists Wanted, 1359
Artivest, 601, 1534, 1634, 2398
ArtLab, 2848
ARTMS, 2221
ARTONE Manufacturing, 78
Artrendex, 1073
Arts Alliance Media, 2419
Artsicl, 1521
Artspace, 389
ArtSquare, 999
Artsy, 321, 977, 1092, 1527
Artur'in, 1499
Artus Labs, 918
ArtusLabs, 1712
Aruba, 1657
Aruba Networks, 177, 759, 1855
ARUHI Corporation, 416
Arula Systems, 808
Arvegenix, 270, 570
Arvento, 1021
Arvia Technology, 3019
Arvinas, 11, 389, 1522
Arvinas Corporation, 661
Arvirago, 2539
Arweave, 1884
Arxan, 652, 1401
Arxan Technologies, 1778, 1784
Arxas Technologies, 1852
Arxis Capital Group, 560
ARXX, 1355
Arxx Building Products, 2188
ARXX ICF, 2051
Arxxus, 1610
Ary Therapeutics, 179
Aryaka, 1014, 1247, 1247, 1478, 1855, 2992
ARYX Therapeutics, 186
ARYx Therapeutics, 1122, 2998
Arzan, 1704
Arzeda Corp., 2007
ArzonSolar, 127
AS Groupe, 2346
AS International Group, 2842
AS Roma, 1527
ASA Events, 874
ASA Foodnesia, 1241
Asahi Tec Corporation, 3192
Asahi Tec/Trimas, 851
ASAlliances Biofuels, 1897
Asalus, 2728, 2883
Asana, 125, 251, 778, 1058
Asana Rebel, 641
Asankya, 983, 1658, 3203
Asante, 3140
Asante Capital Group, 3252
Asante Solutions, 599, 1820, 3006
Asap54, 641
Asarina, 2842
ASAY, 1703
Asbury Automotive Group, 786
ASC Signal, 1548
ASC Specialty Vehicle, 905
Ascade Telecom Software, 2553
Ascellus, 1

Portfolio Companies Index

Ascend Learning, 1498
Ascend Media, 1929
Ascend Wellness, 1468, 1613
Ascend.io, 27, 720
Ascendancy Healthcare, 240
Ascendant Advisors Group, 1505
Ascendant Spirits, 1786
Ascendas India Trust, 153
Ascendent Telecommunications, 767
Ascendify, 485, 812
Ascendis Pharma, 73, 764, 1522, 1700, 1943
Asceneuron, 1047, 1734
Ascension Insurance, 441, 1419
Ascension Orthopedics, 785
Ascensus, 823
Ascent 360, 35
Ascent Aviation Services Corporation, 1148
Ascent Bio-Nano Technologies, 738
Ascent Capital Partners, 3252
Ascent Energy, 1949
Ascent Healthcare Solutions, 1594, 1903
Ascent Pediatrics, 1071
Ascent Resources, 741
Ascent Venture Partners, 3263
Ascenta Therapeutics, 622, 1629, 1700, 1898
Ascenz, 3064
Ascom, 2913
Ascot Resources, 1551
Asempra, 186, 1898
Asentium Capital, 1948
Aseptia, 1691
Asera, 1008, 1976
Asetek, 3004, 3140, 3194
ASG, 92
ASG Security, 1419, 1964
ASG Technologies, 1138
AsGoodAsNew, 3199
Ash & Erie, 1023
Ash Access, 1420
ASH Technologies, 2328
Ashburton Investments, 3252
Ashby Industries, 911
Ashcroft Inc., 1089
Asher House Wellness, 394
Ashley Stewart, 502
Ashot Ashkelon (metal), 2381
Ashtead Technology, 3027
Ashtech, 1545
Ashvattha, 1172, 1616
Ashworth, 1745
ASI, 2576, 3239
Asia Alternatives Management, 3252
Asia Books, 1143
Asia Books Company, 2937
Asia Broadcast Satellite, 3024
Asia Chemical Corporation, 2952
Asia Ec, 2688
Asia Foods, 2872
Asia Grown Capital Advisors (S) Pte Ltd, 3252
Asia Info, 2581
Asia Opportunity Fund LP, 1012
Asia Pacific Carbon Fund, 3033
Asia Partners, 3252
Asia Renal Care, 2289, 2724, 2872
Asia Renal Care Ltd, 2719, 2881
Asia Satellite Telecom Holdings, 416
Asia Travelmart Ltd. (Malaysia), 2685
Asia Vital Components, 2594
AsiaEC.com, 2689
AsiaInfo, 475
Asiainfo, 2989
AsiaInfo & Aicent, 2689
Asiakastieto, 1021
Asian Development Bank, 3252
Asian Food Channel, 3206
Asian Genco, 819
Asian Health Alliance, 54

Asian Infrasturcture Investments Bank, 3252
Asian Mineral Resources, 2933
Asianinfo, 2724
Asiaray Media Group, 1092
Asiasoft, 1143
Asiasoft Corporation, 2937
AsiaTelco Technologies, 977
ASIMCO, 223
Asimov, 125
Asius Technologies, 1065
ASK, 2535, 2844
Ask, 1898, 2335, 2340, 2867
AskBio, 1934
Askey, 2427
AskMe, 990
Askola USA Corporation, 1976
AskWonder, 308
Ask|Net, 2335
ASLAN Pharmaceuticals, 2509
Asmacure, 2114
ASML, 1009
Asocs, 3205
Asoka, 1750, 3143
ASP, 1118, 2927
aSpecial, 3064
Aspect, 1912, 3128
Aspect Biosystems, 2205
Aspect Development, 1657
Aspect Medical Systems, 1762
Aspect Ratio, 1731
Aspect Software, 843, 1361
Aspect Ventures, 485
Aspective, 1021
Aspectrics, 1406
Aspen, 2688
Aspen Aerogels, 186, 770, 1583, 2483
Aspen Avionics, 857, 1299, 1679
Aspen Dental, 111
Aspen Dental Management, 160, 405, 1113
Aspen Education Group, 377
Aspen Energy Partners, 1326, 1328
Aspen Heigths, 1625
Aspen Insurance, 2547
Aspen Laser & Technologies, 1839
Aspen Marketing Group, 337
Aspen Marketing Services, 1090
Aspen Medical Products, 547
Aspen Midstream, 672
Aspen Pumps, 2303
Aspen Re, 1372
Aspen Surgical, 1594
Aspen Tech, 1176
Aspex Semiconductor, 3061, 3122
Aspinity, 296
Aspire Financial Services, 796
Aspire Food Group, 1035
Aspire Health, 94, 894
Aspire Home Care, 703
Aspire Medical, 1976
Aspire Public Schools, 1315
AspireIQ, 945, 959, 1426
Aspireo Pharmaceuticals, 3187
AspireU, 1315
Aspiring Minds, 1374
Aspirion, 274
Aspirion Health Resources, 1412
Asplundh Tree Expert Co., 836
Aspocomp Group Oyj, 2981
Asprevea Pharmaceuticals, 215, 2091
Assay Designs, 119
AssayMetrics, 2728
ASSE, 2353
Assemble, 10
Assembly, 570, 802, 1499, 1884
Assent, 2074, 2112
Asset Acceptance Capital Corp., 1507
Asset Allocation & Management Company, 1746

Asset Control, 2725
Asset Enhancement Solutions LLC, 3257
Asset International, 205
Asset Living, 1853
Asset Management Company, 3273
Asset Management Outsourcing, 189
Asset Matrix, 2051
AssetMark, 1151
AssetNation, 1727
ASSIA, 3143
Assia, 3160
Assicom, 2285
Assima, 2866, 3229
Assis Medical, 3183
Assistant Coach, 953
AssistGuide, 1015, 2448
Assistive Technologies, 1731
Associa, 1754
Associated Chemist Inc., 989
Associated Chemists, 1911
Associated Container Terminals Ltd, 2850
Associated Content, 1701
Associated Foods, 196
Associated Freezers Corporation, 2142
Associated Materials, 927, 1021, 1460
Associated Materials Inc., 917
Associated Partners, 1086
Association Financial Services, 1433
Association for Democratic Reforms, 1374
Association Member Benefits Advisors, 823
Association of Asiona American Investment Managers, 3274
Association of Certified Anti-Money Laundering Spe, 1957
Assure X Health, 86
Assured Risk Cover, 1017
AssuredPartners, 136
Assurely, 1635
AssureRx, 481, 1514
AssureRx Health, 493, 1556
Assurex Health, 561, 1657, 2001
AssurOne, 3104
Assystem, 2842
AST, 1779
Astadia, 1084, 1610, 1731
Astaro, 3223
Astech, 1772
Astellia, 2866
Aster Data, 624, 972, 1657
Aster Data Systems, 742, 1006
Asterand Bioscience, 922
Asteres, 1619
Astex Pharmaceuticals, 94, 990
Astex Therapeutics, 1777, 2771
Asthmatx, 1241, 1251
Astor Corporation, 202
Astound, 1812
Astound Inc., 2258
Astra Augmedix, 1616
Astral AR, 221
Astral Point Communications, 1976
Astranis, 108, 125, 321, 398, 720, 1155, 1330, 2122
AstraZeneca, 1456
Astro, 182, 708, 1537, 1998
Astro Electroplating, 1748
Astro Gaming, 1976
Astroboundary, 1848
AstroDigital, 895
Astrodyne Corporation, 197
Astronomer, 129, 481, 1672, 2001
Astroprint, 10
Astute Medical, 599, 622, 1268
Astute Networks, 1898
AsuraGen, 1206, 1502
Asuragen, 1794
Asure Software, 1118

Portfolio Companies Index

Asurion, 257, 952, 1498, 1854, 1973
Asurion Corporation, 1160
ASUSTek Computer, 1771
Asyntis Gmbh, 2673
AT Internet, 3011
At Last Software, 311
AT&T, 1100
At-Bay, 1073
ATA, 3084
ATA Groiup, 2956
Ataata, 1317
Atai Life Sciences, 803
Atakama Labs, 2446
Atani, 2998
Atara Bio, 113, 710
Atara Biotherapeutics, 582, 622
Atari, 1657
Atavium, 344, 881, 1385
Atbusiness, 2553
ATC, 2074
ATC Drivetrain, 560
AtCor Medical, 2613
Atea, 2969
Ateios, 849
Atelier D'Usinage Quenneville, 2114
Atelier Progun, 2114
Atelier Tangente, 2114
Ateliers Cfi Metal, 2089
Ateliers Jean Del'Cour, 3125
Atelka, 2162
Ateme, 3199, 3229
Atempo Group, 2522
Aten International, 3209
Aternity, 3205
ATG Access, 2935
ATG Rehab, 197
Atheer Labs, 1236
Athelas, 623, 1657, 1666, 2410
Athena, 1927
Athena Club, 568
athena Controls, 838
Athena Design, 2005
Athena Design Systems, 1976
Athena Diagnostics, 248
Athena Feminine Technologies, 1679
Athena Health, 182, 610
Athena Semiconductors, 1287
athenahealth, 827
Athenix, 315, 1013
AtheroGenics, 1399, 1619
AtheroMed, 1898, 1931
Atheros Communications, 200, 1478
Atherotech, 526, 990, 1287, 1536
Atherotech Diagnostics, 248
Athersys, 549, 1414, 1523, 1976
Athieva, 3053
Athilon Group Holdings Corp., 1127
Athleon, 85
Athletes' Performance, 405, 1464
Athletica Sport Systems, 2121
Athletico, 917
Athlon Holdings, 303
AtHoc, 56, 967
Athos, 1125, 1698
Athos Services Commemoratifs, 2114
ATI, 1460
ATI Physical Therapy, 1090
Atico Mining, 1551
Atieva, 3185
Atifon (Packaging prod.), 2381
Atipica, 1058
Atiti, 2263
Ativa Medical, 1874
Atlanta Cable Systems, 576
Atlanta Tech Village, 191
Atlantech, 3095
Atlantic Asset Management, 1151

Atlantic Beverage Company, 963, 1169
Atlantic Broadband, 20
Atlantic Broadband Group, 1360
Atlantic Capital Bancshares, 1746
Atlantic Cellular Company LP, 1624
Atlantic Diagnostic Laboratories, 165
Atlantic Horticulture, 2108
Atlantic Motor Labs, 2148
Atlantic Plywood, 1145
Atlantic Power Holdings, 157
Atlantic Wind Connection, 335
Atlantis Computing, 56, 1418, 1525, 1976
Atlantis Healthcare Group, 1493
Atlantium, 2430
Atlas, 310, 1103, 1530
Atlas 3D, 659
Atlas Aerospace, 416, 1707
Atlas Apps, 1786
Atlas Connectivity, 1582
Atlas Engineered Products, 2061
Atlas Genetics, 2487, 2930
Atlas Material Testing Solutions, 989
Atlas Obscura, 752
Atlas Organics, 1925
Atlas Partners LP, 3249
Atlas Venture, 69, 3263
Atlas Water, 352
Atlas-SSI, 2282
Atlassian Software, 27
Atlast Homewares Inc., 911
AtlasWatersystems, 649
AtlEn Opportunity, 1766
Atlice, 745
ATMA Software, 115
atmarkIT, 2845
ATMI, 532
Atmosera, 1641
Atmosphere Networks, 759
Atmospheric Plasma Solutions, 3250
ATMU, 416
Ato Bio, 1734
ATO Solution Co., 2993
AtoBe, 2770
Atom, 398, 2398
Atom Computing, 321, 1918
Atomation, 270
Atomic, 863, 2398
Atomicorp, 288
Atomos Nuclear and Space, 1892
Atomwise, 108
Aton Pharma, 73, 1733
Atonometrics, 447
Atonomics, 3140
Atop Holdings, 897
Atoptech, 46
Atos, 3017
Atosho, 3141
Atox Bio, 3235
ATP-PEP, 3252
Atrato, 213
Atreaon, 2969
Atreca, 710, 1238
Atrenta, 928, 1021
Atria, 1257
Atria Yhtymä Oyj, 2981
Atrica, 1042, 1976, 2576, 2761, 2866, 2881, 2888
Atrica Axcan Pharma, 2719
Atricath, 2865
Atricia, 252
AtriCure, 1898
ATRIN Pharmaceuticals, 1581
Atrinet Ltd., 3204
Atritech, 1820
Atritech Inc., 272
Atrium, 10, 125, 742, 820, 843, 945, 1028, 1666
Atrium Companies, 1460

Atrium Innovations, 2114, 3024
Atrium Underwriting Group, 1746
Atronix, 1343
ATRP Solutions, 1003, 1452
Atrributor, 1674
Atrua, 645
ATS Advanced Telematic Systems, 974
ATS Medical, 94
AtScale, 108, 1750
Atscale, 520
Atsu, 1162
ATT, 2427
AttachedApps, 1065, 1926
Attachmate, 782, 1045, 1817
Attachmate Group, 843
AttackIQ, 1511, 1610
Attainia, 1740
Attano, 2809
AtTask, 1381, 1608, 1707
Attena Neurosciences, 209
Attenda, 1157
Attendease, 2024, 2262
Attendo, 2528, 2529
Attends, 1089
Attenex, 1947
Attensa, 1947
Attensite Corporation, 1408
Attenti, 136, 782
Attentive, 1716
Attero, 3222
Attero Recycling, 856
Atticus, 729, 1426
Attitude.ai, 10
Attivio, 1361, 1813
ATTO-TEC GmbH, 3181
Attol, 2535
Attolight AG, 650
Attom Data Solutions, 1151
Attraction Media, 2089
Attributor, 115, 972, 1649
Attune, 1346, 1418, 1490
Attune Pharmaceuticals, 1522
Attune Technologies, 1511
Attunity, 3050
ATW, 1925
ATX Networks, 931, 1410
Atyati, 3202
Atyr Pharma, 1464
aTyr Pharma, 413, 622, 710
Atys, 2542
Atzuche, 925
Au Bon Pain Inc., 357
Au Financiers, 1957
Au Forum du Batiment, 3229
Auberge Et Spa Le Nordik, 2114
Auberge Relais Lac Cache, 2114
Auberge Resorts Collection, 427
Auburn Armature, 1424
Aucfan, 2789
Aucionata, 2829
AucSale, 1757
Auction Holdings, 523
Auction.com, 1746
Auctionata, 2820
Auctionpay, 143
Audacious, 3003
Audacy, 998
Audax Private Equity, 3254
Auden McKenzie, 1456
Audentes, 11, 73, 183, 764, 1522, 1930
Audentes Therapeutics, 1383, 1700
Audible, 259
Audible Reality, 2204
Audience, 1781, 1924, 1948
Audience Partners, 1504
Audience Science, 186, 1247
Audience.Ai, 9

1234

Portfolio Companies Index

AudienceFUEL, 1712
AudiencePoint, 461
AudienceScience, 624, 1187, 1644
Audiense, 3099
Audinate, 3129
Audio Network, 1751
Audio Precision, 238, 906
Audio Visual Services Corporation, 1066
Audiocodes Ltd., 2766
Audiocure, 2815
Audiodraft, 1491
AudioGo, 2354
AudioMicro, 1103
Audiomojo, 1917
Audiosocket, 250
AudioTalk Networks, 950
AudioVroom, 1305
Audisoft, 2842
AuditBoard, 49, 238
AuditFile, 10
AuditFile.com, 310
Auditude, 857, 1537
Audius, 820, 1079, 1125
Audm, 1770
Audyssey, 133
Audyssey Laboratories, 2965
Augement Therapy, 296
Augeo, 2770
Augeo FI, 1127
Augmate, 387, 705
AugMedix, 863
Augmedix, 94, 666
Augmenix, 178, 428
Augment, 1610
Augment Ventures, 3259
Augmented Pixels, 1812
Augmented Radar Imaging, 1557
Augmentix, 205
Augtera Networks, 48
Augur, 2141
Augure, 3199
Augury, 742, 1114, 1483
August, 553, 1186, 1521, 1561, 1702, 1998
August Capital, 36, 3273
August Capital Management V, 624
August Lock, 1254
Augusta Sportswear, 1066
Augusta Sportswear Group, 1507
Augusta Systems, 1474
Augustus Energy Partners II, 1129
Aujas Netowks, 2840
Auld Phillips, 2249
Aulera Autentication, 431
Aumet, 10
Aumni, 1317
Aunt Bertha, 3246
Auntie Anne's, 1580
Auntie Dolores, 1139
AUPU Group Holding Company, 585
Aura, 553, 1530, 1558
Aura Health Corp., 2117
Aura Life, 3250
Aura Light International AB, 2528, 2529
Auramicro, 1924
Auransa, 3, 1155
Aureon Labrotories, 2436
Auricup Resources, 2933
Aurigen, 1314, 2098
Aurigen Capital Limited, 1447
Aurinia, 1943
Aurinia Pharmaceuticals, 2174
Aurion Pro Solutions, 646
Aurionpro, 68
Auris, 1155, 1646
Auris Medica, 1700
Aurizon Mines Ltd, 2114
Aurizon Ultrasonics, 1291

Auro Robotics, 795
Aurochs Brewing, 296
AuroMira Energy, 2481
Auror Algae, 1352
Aurora, 877, 1426
Aurora Algae, 808, 1361
Aurora Biosciences Corp., 209
Aurora Cannabis, 206, 393, 2129
Aurora Diagnostics, 1090, 1754
Aurora Discovery, 1794
Aurora Flight Sciences, 681, 838
Aurora Flower Co., 558
Aurora Foods, 722
Aurora Labs, 708
Aurora Networks, 1478
Aurora Organic Dairy, 458
Aurora Products Group, 1085
Aurora SFC Systems, 139, 374
Aurora Solar, 728
Aurora Systems, 1021
AuroraNetics, 1084
Aurum, 1629
Aurum Software, 1255
Aurvista Gold Corporation, 2114
Ausenco, 1551
Aushon Biosystems, 1335
Auspex, 764, 1411
Auspex Pharmaceuticals, 1820
Auspherix, 2950
Auspion, 1055
Austal Ships, 2390
Austin Coctails, 296
Austin Entrepreneurs Foundation, 1653
Austin Fitness Group, 503
Austin Technology Incubator, 1653
Austral Capital Partners, 3252
Australian Central Credit Union, 2447
Australian Education, 2447
Australian Geographics, 2411
Australian Kitchen Industries, 2613
Australian Pipeline Trust, 2447
Australian Venue Co., 1086
Austri, 1340
Austriamicrosystems, 2913
Autekbio, 46
Auterion, 548
Auterra, 712, 789, 1479
Auth0, 776, 1054, 1213
AuthAir, 1
AuthenTec, 1313, 1748
Authentic Brands Group, 1113, 2164
Authentic8, 779, 1219
Authentica, 1335
Authentiq, 3099
Authentix, 416
Authntk, 1298
AuthO, 1467
Author Solutions, 260
Authorea, 724, 1155, 1305, 1309
Authoria, 245
Authority Brands, 136
AuthorityLabs, 92
Authy, 586, 1998, 3116
Auticon, 2251
Autifony, 1439, 1764
Autifony Therapeutics, 1631, 2849
Autinform GmbH, 2528, 2529
Autism Learning Partners, 864
AutismSees, 623
Autit, 640, 833
Auto Data Network, 1561
Auto Hauler Exchange, 2131
Auto Meter Products Inc., 911
Auto Radio, 597, 2927
Auto Trader Group, 136
Auto22, 2530
Autoaid, 2815

AutoAlert, 962
Autobar, 2371, 2578
Autobooks, 225, 608
Autobus Dionne, 2089
Autobus Dufresne, 2089
Autobus Lion, 2114
Autobutler, 2628
Autocam, 202
Autoda, 2560, 2820
Autodis, 2712
AutoDistribution, 2542
Autodistribution, 1021
Autoequip, 2480
AutoESL Design Technologies, 55
AutoFi, 10, 680, 1114
Autofi, 564
autoGraph, 1284, 1947, 2240
AutoGrid, 773, 1947
Autoland Inc., 449
Autoloader, 2815
Autolog Systems, 3194
Autology World, 2459
Automak Automotive Company, 1021
Automat, 520, 2228
Automatan LLC, 903
Automated Fuel Systems Group, 2700
Automated Insights, 552, 1364, 1388, 1901
Automated Systems Design, 445
Automatic, 115, 1862, 2398
Automatics, 1596
Automation Intellect, 512
AutomationHero, 222
AutomationQA, 2312
Automattic, 1005, 1153, 1464
Automic, 2842
Automile, 1005, 1610
Automobile Protection Coporation, 1746
Automotive Mastermind, 1045
Automsoft, 2314
AutoNavi, 2927
Autonet Mobile, 650, 1737
Autoniq, 784
Autonomic, 520, 1698
Autonomic Materials, 979, 987
Autonomic Technologies, 1014
Autonomix Medical Inc., 272
Autonomous Marine Systems Inc., 498
Autonomous Partners, 513, 1884
Autopay, 784
Autopilot, 1543, 1610, 1713
AutoServe1, 2189
AutoSource, 2201
AutoSource Motors, 2200
Autosplice, 1041, 1460
Autotalks, 117, 784, 1241, 2943
Autotask, 936, 1045
Autotask Corporation, 1334
Autotether, 679
Autotube, 2317
AutoVirt, 1674
Autowraptec, 447
Autumn Ai, 2131
Autumn Years at Newport Mesa, 961
Autumn Years at Ojai, 961
Auust Technology Corporation, 1287
Auvents W. Lecours, 2114
Auvik, 2070, 2231
Aux Money, 773
Auxadyne, 3251
Auxilium, 1728
Auxilum, 73
Auxmoney, 1418, 1884
Auxon, 308
AV Lab, 122
Av Smoot, 60
AVA, 2270
Ava, 623, 1114, 1323

1235

Portfolio Companies Index

Avaak, 1106
Avaamo, 3, 298, 1009, 1543, 1983
AVAC Ltd., 3249
Avacta, 2883
Avad Energy, 1326, 1328
Avadim Technologies Inc., 1925
Avago, 1685
Avail Media, 1678
Avail-TVN, 250
Availant, 313
Availink, 299, 780
Availity, 782
Avalanche Biotech, 1918
Avalanche Insights, 937
Avalanche Technology, 263, 949, 1821, 1948, 3220
Avalara, 175, 250, 1156, 1606
Avalent Technologies, 1771
Avalign Technologies, 167, 1132, 1594
Avalon, 782, 2129
Avalon Advisors, 416
Avalon Cable, 20
Avalon Pharmaceuticals, 2771
Avamar, 1125, 1255, 1976
AVANAN, 3127
Avancen, 3246
Avanex, 1657
Avangate, 2301
Avani Bio Energy, 54
Avanir, 764
Avanoo, 10
AvanStrate, 416
Avant, 819, 1385
Avant Credit, 36, 1504
Avant Healthcare Professionals, 1117
Avant Immunotherapeutics, 215, 2998
Avant!, 1762
AvantCredit, 1597
Avante Health Solutions, 654
Avantec Vascular, 1022
Avantech Testing Services, 1097
AvantGo, 57, 857, 1406
Avanti, 6
Avanti Marble & Granite, 1748
Avanticare, 2699
Avantis Medical Systems, 272, 1251
Avantium, 2370, 2653
Avantium BV, 2342
Avantium International B.V., 2568
Avanz Capital, 3252
Avanza, 2563
Avanza Laboratories, 73
Avanzar Medical, 1725
AVAST Software BV, 1754
Avatar Alliance, 34
Avatar International, 1576, 1929
AVATOUR, 10
Avaxia Biologics, 845, 1164, 1786
Avaya, 1685, 2371
Avaz, 1017
Aveanna Healthcare, 1041, 2211
Avec Lab, 1757
Avecia, 1021
Avecto, 1045
Avedro, 137, 311, 599, 647, 748, 924
Avega Systems, 3053
Avegant, 10, 1009
Aveillant, 2653, 2665
Aveksa, 457, 744, 796
Avelas Biosciences, 209
Avella Specialty Pharmacy, 1579
Avelo, 2935
Avena Foods, 2156
Avendus Capital, 1086
Aveni, 2842
Avenir Finance, 2616
Avent, 2578

Aventail, 759, 1235, 1855
Avention, 889
Aventium, 2430
Aventor Performance Materials Holdings, 1300
Aventura, 704, 941
Aventure, 2593
Avenue, 2262
Avenue A Razorfish, 1898
Avenue Ltd, 2696
Avenues: The World School, 1140
Aveo, 748, 2961
AVEO Pharmaceuticals, 263, 928, 1395, 1495
AvePoint, 1754
Aver, 812, 1285
Aver Inc., 631
Aver Informatics, 2002
Averail, 1750
Avere, 2073
Avere Systems, 1125, 1798
Averify, 583
Averna, 2252
Averon, 10, 1269
Avertec, 2472
Avery Haelth, 2787
Averys, 2842
Aveta, 128
Avetta, 1346, 1973
Avexegen, 1238
Avexis, 764, 1522, 1815
AVG Technologies, 56, 1778
Avgol (Plastics), 2381
AvhanaHealth, 1734
Avi Networks, 485, 877, 1203
Avi Networksm Barefoot Networks, 1125
AVI-SPL, 1685
AVIA, 1050, 1483
Avia Boisystems, 440
Aviacode, 793
Aviaion Inflatables, 1433
Aviary, 265, 1718
Aviate, 787
Aviation Partners, 2079
Aviation Technologies, 1368
Aviator, 2317
Aviatrix, 978
Avici Systems, 27, 1731
Avicin Therapeutics Ltd., 432
Avid, 94, 1762
Avid Radiopharmaceuticals, 1128
Avid Ratings, 9, 254
Avidal, 2815
AvidBots, 720, 827
Avidbots, 2024, 2130, 2131
Avidia, 113, 1693
Avidimer Therapeutics, 748, 1337
Avidity NanoMedicines, 710, 711
AvidXchange, 779, 1446
Avidyne, 938
Avila Therapeutics, 193
Avilinks, 2866
Avinity, 2828
Avinity Systems B.V., 3119
Avior Integrated Products, 2114
Aviron, 154
Avisare, 221
Avisena, 2188
Avision, 10
Aviso, 553, 742, 1629, 1666
Avist, 978
Avista, 1294
Avista Oil, 1230
Avista Pharma, 119
Avita Biomedical, 374
Avitas Systems, 812
Avitec, 2553
Avitide, 311, 1383, 1631, 1764
Avito, 27, 3004

Aviv REIT, 1133
Aviva Communications, 46
Avizent, 1090
Avizia, 288, 291, 924, 1320
Avjet Holding, 2089
AVK, 3224
AVM, 2354
AVMedical Dialysis Access Management, 2320
Avnera, 263, 582, 972
Avnera Corporation, 1449
AVO Carbon Holdings, 1230
Avocado, 234
Avocado Systems, 575
Avolent, 1561
Avolon Aerospace Limited, 1360
Avomeen, 935
Avonmore Pásztó, 2716
Avoxi, 227, 2074
Avrij, 2192
Avrio Capital, 2028
Avro Life Science, 1633, 1760, 2122
Avro Life Sciences, 664
AvroBio, 1631
Avrobio, 193, 1764
Avset, 2442
Avst, 1643
AVTEC, 1957
Avure Food Processing, 1234
Avvasi, 2253
Avvir, 1896
Avvo, 582, 978
AW Leil, 2242
Awake Chocolate, 2115
Awake Security, 877
AWAKENS, 1705
Awarables, 18
Aware Point, 209
Awareness, 1335
Awareness Technologies, 740
Awarepoint, 972, 1297, 1559
AWAS, 56
Away, 27, 520, 527, 763, 863
Away.com, 1483
Awayfind, 10
Awcloud, 1009
Awe.sm, 1890
AWECO, 2801
Awesomeness TV, 1242, 1483, 1885
aWhere, 147, 3246
AWL, 823
AwoX, 2653
AWS Convergence Technologies, 1424
AWT Labels & Packaging, 1174
AXA Stenman, 2492
Axalta Coating Systems, 416
Axcan Pharma, 73, 2029, 2881
Axcel Photonics, 1917
Axcella, 748
Axcess, 3013
AXCESS International Inc., 2389
Axcient, 1430, 1821
AXDRAFT, 798
Axeda, 1045, 2188
Axeda Systems, 3221
Axel, 2438
Axel Springer, 927
Axel Springer Digital Classifieds, 819
Axela, 2188
AxelaCare Holdings Inc., 917
Axelliance, 2842
Axent, 655
Axentra Corporation, 2051
Axerra, 3170
Axesnetwork Solutions, 2089
Axia Energy, 1326, 1328
Axial, 520, 655, 742, 1114, 1537, 1991
Axial BioTech, 186

Portfolio Companies Index

Axial Biotech, 1917
Axial Biotherapeutics, 1055, 1149
Axial Exchange, 389, 907, 1987, 3250
Axialog, 2457
AxiaMed, 921
AxieTech International Holdings, 416
Axikin Pharma, 1241
Axikin Pharmaceuticals, 1619
Axine, 1584
Axine Water Technologies, 2072
Axio, 427
Axio Biosolutions, 27
Axiom, 1411, 1830, 1898, 1924, 2378, 2568, 2814, 2845
Axiom CME, 1228
Axiom Global, 582
Axiom Law, 419
Axiom Legal, 628
Axiom Microdevices, 133, 1781
Axiom Space, 1616
Axioma, 1611, 1626
Axiomatics, 2610
AxioMed, 2719
AxioMed Spine, 642, 1190, 1547, 1820
AxioMx, 661, 1942
Axiomx, 532
Axion, 2340
Axion Power International, 643
Axios, 641, 1114
Axip Energy Services, 1837
Axipointe Inc., 303
Axis, 2132
Axis Capital Funding II, 1971
Axis Energy Services, 1129
Axis Group Integrated Services, 3121
AXIS Industrial Services, 1748
Axis Network Technology, 263
AxisPoint Health, 530
AxisRooms, 3100
AxisThree, 2601
Axitron, 1786
Axium Healthcare Pharmacy, 418
Axius, 1186
Axle, 2398
Axle Health, 1426
Axle.AI, 1509
AxleHire, 246, 648
Axlon International, 2745
AxoGen, 39, 186, 698
Axogen, 599
Axolotl, 1107
Axon AI, 288
Axoni, 125
Axonia Medical, 1380, 1715
Axonics Modulation Technologies, 1147
Axonify, 342, 1045
Axonize, 544
Axsol, 2518
Axsun Technologies, 1235, 1908
Axxana, 1478, 2557
Axxessit, 2623
Axxima, 2369
Aya, 2398
Ayalogic, 642, 1051
Ayannah, 1966
Ayar Labs, 1009
Ayasdi, 361, 488, 752, 812, 1006, 1079
Aydanaya, 2276
Aye, 579
Ayehu, 252
Ayla, 564
Ayla Networks, 485, 1691, 1947
Aylus Networks, 1184, 1335
Ayogo, 704
AyoxxA, 2815
AYTB, 1021
AYZH, 3246

Azahar Coffee, 54
Azaire Networks, 2005
Azalea, 1013
Azalea Health, 2074
Azaleos, 1644
AZB & Partners, 3252
Azellon, 2883
Azelon Pharmaceuticals, 1122
Azentic, 2089
Azerx, 1903
Azevan Pharmaceuticals, 179, 1120
Azimo, 641, 2398
Azimut Exploration, 2114
Azimuth, 1335
Azimuth Capital Management, 3249
Azimuth Systems, 1084
Azimuth Technology, 988, 1148
Azonic, 2051
Azorus, 2197
Azoti, 1285
Aztech Systems, 897
Aztek Networks, 881, 1784
Azuik, 1674
Azuki, 1069
Azul Systems, 1478
Azumio, 720
Azuqua, 610, 978, 1005
Azure Capital Partners, 990, 2028, 3249
Azure Films, 2565
Azure Power, 773, 2809
Azure Solutions, 1304
Azurity, 1349
Azuro, 1237, 1976, 3186
AZVIcode, 1712
AZZLY, 3251

B

B DNA, 1310
B Media, 543
B Media Group, 1641
B&B Hotels, 416
B&B Merger Corp., 1929
B&B Roadway Security Solutions, 963
B&C Foods Inc., 357
B&E Group, 1266
B&H Education, 20, 1506
B&W Quality Growers, 408
B+B SmartWorx, 851, 1018
B+H International LP, 2049
B+T Group, 832
B-152, 2767
B-Band, 2864
B-Dry, 832
B-Hive, 1918
B-Line, 843
B-Process, 3199
B-Sm@rk, 2513
B-Stock, 1720
B-Stock Solutions, 1761, 1862
B-Way Holding, 1160
B.B. Hobbs, 1691
B.E.T. - er Mix, 1210
B.M.B., 2114
B.R. Lee Industries Inc., 153
B12, 820
B12 Transportation Group, 1057
B2B Center, 3079
B2eMarkets, 2073
B2R Technologies, 2305
B2X, 1244
B2X Care Solutions, 2788
B8ta, 520, 680, 1011
b8ta, 728
BA Insight, 51, 1386
Ba&sh, 1092
BA-Insight, 1388
Baarb, 1509

Bab.La, 2970
BabaBoo, 3049
Babajob, 860
Babba Co., 1121
Babbaco, 1091, 1618
Babbel, 1327, 2912
Babeeta, 3206
Babelverse, 10
Babies, 1925
Babington, 2530
Babla, 2815
Babson CLO, 1493
Baby Belle, 3033
Baby Gourmet, 2043
Baby Plus, 659
Baby Quip, 1509
Baby Scripts, 1023
Baby-Mart.de, 3161
Baby.com.br, 1823, 2967
BabyCare, 2581
BabyCenter, 1855
Babycenter, 263, 1566
BabyEarth, 352
BabyJunk, 10
BabyList, 10, 1371
Babylon, 2825
Babyscript, 814
BabyTree, 1184
BabyUniverse, 928
Bac2 Ltd, 2455
Baccarat, 1092
Bacharach, 790
Bachman Information Systems, 1255
Back At You Media, 1645
Back in Motion, 2156
Back To Nature, 360
Back to the Roots, 1533, 2230
Back Werk, 2842
Back-und Kondit, 2801
Back9 Network, 874
Backlot Cars, 1385
BackOps, 586, 641, 1491
Backplane, 234, 1527
Backstage Capital, 2398
Backstop Solutions, 2074
Backtrace, 1525
Backtrace I/O, 1851
Backtype, 10, 787
BackupAgent B.V., 3119
Backupify, 209
BackWeb, 1855
Backyard Products, 445
Backyard Products LLC, 578
BACOM, 294
Bacrac Supply Company, 381
Bacterin, 1383
BacterioScan, 270
Bactusense, 3235
Badenia Bettcomfort GmbH & Company KG, 2797
Badgeville, 1014, 1525, 1855, 1969
Badoo, 2727
Baebies, 296, 1559
Baekeland Fonds, 3033
Baert, 2492
Bag Balm, 815
Bag Borrow or Steal, 1744
BAG Med, 2801
Bagcheck, 1254
Bagchi Law, 3250
BagDoom.com, 721
Bagel Nash, 3234
Bagnali Court, 2530
Bagrationi, 70
Bagwell Supply, 2041
Bahcesehir Schools, 416
Bahrain Bay, 153

1237

Portfolio Companies Index

Bai Du, 1088
BAI Global, 1294
Baichuan, 3185
Baidu, 610, 691, 2841
Baierl & Demmelhuber Innenausbau GmbH, 2485
Baihe, 1340, 1798
Baihe.com, 1187
Baike.com, 597
Bailey 44, 1346
Bailey International, 1438
Bailiwick, 1345
Bailtrand, 3011
Baimos Technologies, 2815
Bain Capital, 3254
Bainbridge, 153, 1176
Bainbridge Health, 269
BAInsight, 1401
Baird Capital, 3255, 3259
Bairo, 3251
Baixing, 1798
Baja Broadband, 1157
Bakcell, 1244
Baker & Taylor, 425
Baker Communications, 990
Baker Hughes Inc., 1905
Baker Manufacturing, 1582
Baker McKenzie, 3252
Baker Technologies, 152, 232, 1443, 1468, 1613, 1845
Baker Tilly, 3264, 3268
BakerCorp, 1127, 3024
Bakewise Brands, 1210
Bako, 119
Bakpax, 1363, 1393
Baku Coca-Cola Bottlers II, 1012
BAL, 2446
BalaDyne, 1337
Balance, 85, 387
Balance Bar, 360
Balance Re, 2398
Balance Therapeutics, 1247, 1414
Balance Water, 669
Balanced, 232
Balances M. Dodier, 2089
Balbix, 1035, 1187
Balboa Water Group, 1507
Balcas Ltd, 2695
BalconyTV, 876, 1464
Baldor Electric Co, 2447
Balena, 610, 812
Balenda, 182
Baligam, 2905
Balihoo, 1094, 1381
Balkrishna Industries, 2590, 2591
Ballard, 217
Ballard Leasing, 1496
Ballast Point Ventures, 3251
BallerTV, 79
Ballet Jewels, 791
Ballot Ready, 1159
BallotReady, 937
Ballston Plaza II, 2556
Bally Engineering, 357
Ballygowan, 2814
Balnea Erlebnisbäder GmbH & Co. Chieming/Obb, 2485
Balsa, 321
Baltic Rim Fund Ltd., 2642
Baltoro Capital, 3252
Balyo, 2288, 3104
Balzac Coffee, 2786
Balzac's Coffee, 2093
Bambecco, 1172, 1290
Bambeco, 21
Bambi/Banat, 3086
Bambino, 754

Bamboo HR, 1707
Bamboo Rose, 1276
Banana Boat, 1100
Banca FarmaFactoring, 444
Banca Romenesca, 2462
BancBoston Capital, 1294
Banco Best, 2708
Banco Indusval & Partners, 1957
BancWest Bancorp, 132
Band of Angels, 3109
Bandals, 743
Bandcamp, 1862
Bandit Vehicle Security, 2700
BandPage, 1247, 1566
Bandsintown, 50, 289
Bandura Systems, 288
Bandwagon, 221, 1309
Bandwango, 1317
BandWD, 3230
Bandwidth 10, 974
Banebys, 2331
Bang Er Medical, 711
Bangbite, 3043
Bangcle, 1537
Banjo, 299, 1914, 2469
Bank Invest, 2438
Bank of America Merrill Lynch, 3251
Bank of Innovation, 2637
Bank Of N.T. Butterfield & Son, 416
Bank of Qeensland, 2447
Bank of Western Australia, 2447
Bank United, 444
Bankers Systems, 847
BankFacil, 641
Bankier, 2519
Bankity, 3116
Bankons, 10
Bankrate, 132
Bankruptcy Management Solutions, 458
BankThai, 303
BankUnited, 1404
Banner Bank, 790
Banner Service Corp., 445
Banner Services Corporation, 445, 935, 1481
Banner Solutions, 1779
Bannerman, 788
Bannerman Resources, 1551
Banqsoft, 2745
Banshee Bungee, 85, 1786
Banshee Wines, 1737
Bansho, 2122
Banter, 2187
Banyan, 1074
Banyan Energy, 40
Banyan Technology, 1051
Banyan Water, 430, 568
Banza, 791, 1589, 3043
Banzai, 1616
Baobab, 59, 321, 520
Baobab Resources, 638
Baobab Studies, 1477
Baobab Studios, 474, 1614
Baobao, 827
Baofeng.com, 2841
Baoya Estates, 2478
Baozen, 846
Bar Harbor Biotechnology, 1165
Bar-Plate Manufacturing, 1524
Bara Energia do Brasil Petróleo e Gás, 1577
BARBRI, 1109
Barcalounger, 905
Barco New, 2771
Barcodes, 1368
Barcodes Inc., 547
Barcoo, 2435
Bard's Tale Beer, 1874
Bardy Diagnostics, 921, 2174

BardyDX, 1559
BardyDx, 178, 1631, 1764
Bare Escentuals, 170, 2014
Bare Snacks, 669, 1324
Barefoot Landing, 1683
Barefoot Networks, 125, 604, 1657
Barilla Draw, 517
Baring Hellenic Ventures SA (BHV), 2775
Baring Private Equity Asia Ltd, 3252
Baring Vostok Capital Partners, 3252
Barjan, 1438
Bark, 1059
Bark & Co., 1597
Bark Box, 1114
BarkBox, 1549
Barkbox, 1464
Barley, 2131
Barn & Willow, 10, 901
Barnacle Seafood, 1214
Barnellan Equity Advice Ltd, 3252
Barnes & Thornburg, 3268
BarNotes, 1945
Barnraiser, 328
Barofold, 318, 2806
BAROnova, 938, 1147, 1379, 1622, 2174
Barosense, 1414, 1886
Barra Energia, 741
Barracuda, 2578, 2814
Barracuda Networks, 56, 759, 782, 1657
Barrel Park Investments, 1370
Barried Therapeutics Inc., 73
BarrierSafe Solutions International, 654, 1132, 1368
BARRx, 928
Barrx Medical, 785, 1762
Barry Callebaut, 2913
Bartab, 650
Barteca, 819
Bartech, 2853
Bartech System Corp, 2644
Bartek, 2264
Barthel Pauls, 3125
Bartlett Holdings Inc., 917
Barton Nelson, 60
BarTrendr, 1065
Barvista Homes, 1748
BAS Broadcasting, 832
Base, 1364, 1597, 1698, 1724
Base 10 Group, 2210
Base Case Management, 2815
Base Culture, 669
BASE Engineering Inc., 911
BASE Entertainment, 496
Base Operations, 833, 849
Base Pair Biotechnologies, 2104
Base Venture, 1370
Base-2 Capital, 1364
Base79, 59, 2963
Basecamp, 265
Basecamp Fitness, 1580
Baseclick, 2483
Basefarm, 20
BaseKit, 2682, 2978
Baselane, 2090
Baselayer, 1483
Basepaws, 229
Basho, 1987
Basic 3C, 992
Basic-Fit, 2303
Basil, 2131
Basin Properties, 1129
Basis, 125, 597, 894, 1430
Basis Technology, 983
Basis.io, 1125
BASIX Group, 2305
Basix Krishi, 54
Bask, 21

Portfolio Companies Index

Basket Savings, 680
Basler, 2367
Basno, 1223
Basso, 2427
Batanga, 159, 1446, 1712, 1731
Bateel, 1092
Bathrooms.com, 2441
Batigroup, 2913
Batitech, 2089
Baton, 1531
Baton System, 93
Bats, 1720
BATS Global Markets, 1778
Batteries Plus Bulbs, 786, 1580
Batterii, 481
Battery Solutions, 445
Battery Streak, 49
Battery Ventures, 990, 3263, 3273
BattleBin, 461
Battlefly, 85
Battlefy, 121, 601
Bauble Bar, 876
BaubleBar, 27, 1114
Baublebar, 182, 520
BaubleBar Inc., 48
Baud Data Communications, 2841
Bauer AG, 2651
Bauer Marketplace, 2165
Bauer Performance Sports Ltd., 1085
Baurer, 2335
Bausch & Lomb, 1820, 1973
BAWAG, 1733
Baxano, 189, 1449
Baxano Surgical, 1063, 1495
Baxi Group, 2488
Baxter Group Ltd, 2447
Baxter International, 1271
Baxter Manufacturing, 1560
Bay Club, 1086
Bay Dynamics, 419, 520
Bay Labs Inc., 1073
Bay Microsystems, 983, 1287, 1608, 1649, 1949
Bay Partners, 3273
Bay State Physical Therapy, 371
Bay Tech, 1314
BayanT, 3159
Bayantel, 2425
Baydin, 1054
Baydon Solutions Ltd, 2545
Baydrive Limited, 2812
Bayhill Therapeutics, 1414, 1898
Baylor Home Care, 409
Baylor Home Infusion Therapy, 409
Baynes Electric Supply, 1176
Baynote, 624, 1042, 3112
Bayonne Energy Center, 157
BayPackets, 1795
Bayshore, 252
Bayshore Networks, 1614
Baystone Software, 538
Bayview Financial, 280, 842
Bayview Hospitality Group, 2039
Bayview Systems, 1465
Bazaar, 354
Bazaarvoice, 205, 742, 752, 819, 1813
BB Hotels, 2843
BBAM, 2201
BBE, 801
BBJ Rentals, 1169
BBN Technologies, 27, 523
BBox, 1660
BBOXX, 2175
BBS, 3185
BBVA Compass, 3250
BBy Inc., 1509
BC Decker Inc., 2088
BC Naturals, 2095

BC Partners VIII, 2438
BC Tech Fund, 3249
BC Technical, 1270
BC2Environmental Corp., 277
BC3 Technologies, 1509
BCD, 1918
BCD Semiconductor, 1537, 3053
BCF Ventures, 3249
BCG, 1316
Bci Broadband, 1518
BCI Burke, 899
BCode, 2609
BCombs, 3250
bContext, 1635
BCR Solid Solutions, 2282
BD Accuri, 114
BDC Capital, 3249
BDNA, 556, 1056, 1679, 2630
BDO, 3250
BDO USA, 3257
BDP International, 867
BDS, 1139
BDS Analytics, 99, 152, 395
BDTNDR, 395
Be, 200, 3128
Be Green Packaging, 1576
Be Jane, 1917
Be Power Tech, 748
Beach, 1086
BeachMint, 1121, 1235, 1855
Beacon, 2256
Beacon Analytical Systems, 440
Beacon Communications, 445
Beacon Fire & Safety, 952, 1397
Beacon Healthcare, 1786
Beacon Promotions, 319
Beaconhome, 863
Beagle, 3099
Beam, 10, 149, 631, 860, 1079, 1363, 2094
Beam Dental, 2126
Beam Express, 3036
Beam Impact, 345
Beam Messenger, 2107
Beamery, 129, 1158
BeamExpress, 2890
Beamr, 1001, 1928
BeamReach Networks, 255, 2499, 3109
Beanitos, 1092
Beanworks, 2215, 2262
Bear, 1554
Bear Down Brands, 333, 334
Bear Flag Robotics, 708
Bear Naked, 246
Bear Paw Energy, 898
Bearcom, 260
Bearence Management Group, 1276
BearingPoint, 790
Beast, 310
Beast Brands, 1616
Beat, 100
BeatBox, 1196
BeatCraft, 2982
BeatTheBushes, 2847
Beauceron Security, 2192
Beaudry & Theroux, 2089
Beautiful AI, 742, 1666
Beauty Bakerie, 12
Beauty Booke, 1305
Beauty Box 5, 447
Beauty First, 1552
Beauty in Fashion, 2927
BeautyCon, 901, 1816
Beautycounter, 1263, 1832
Beautylish, 1121
BeautyStat.com, 421
BeautyTouch, 985
Beaver Visitec, 1594

Beaver-Visitec International, 1837
BeavEx, 687
Bebe, 874
Bebestore, 2437
Bebop, 125
bebop, 1657
Beceem, 621, 1091, 1924
Beceem Communications, 837
Beceem Firetide, 1241
Becker Underwood Inc., 451
BeckerBs Healthcare, 1410
Beckett Corp., 467
Beckfield College, 1506
Beckon, 389, 1525, 1918
Becton, 1456
BedaBox, 3251
Bedford Capital Limited, 3249
Bedrijvencentrum Waasland, 3033
Bedrock, 980, 1768
Bedrock Analytics, 456
Bedrock Capital, 884
Bedrock Data, 1
Bee Free Honee, 1153
Bee-keeping Dedinský., 3113
Beecher Carlson, 205
Beecken Petty O'Keefe & Company, 3254, 3255
Beeem, 10
Beef 'O' Brady's, 1115
Beefeaters, 2142
Beefsteak, 1768
Beekeeper, 1614
BeeKeeper Labs, 2002
Beeline, 3099
Beeline Bikes, 10
Beelogics, 3235
Beeminder, 1467
Beenz, 813
Beepi, 1593
Beeswax, 779, 938
Befar Group, 2533
BeFree, 1107, 2005
Begin, 888
BeGo, 2958
Behalf, 1240
BehaveCare, 1993
Behavioral Health Group, 381, 792
Behavioral Interventions, 1507
Behavioral Signals, 1055
BehavioSec, 485, 2621, 3009
Behaviour Interactive, 2089
Behavioural Centers of America, 1132
Behavox, 2825
Behrens Manufacturing, 832
Bei Jing Lepro Seva, 2427
Beijing Amcare Women's & Children's Hospital, 1957
Beijing Capital Juda, 1086
Beijing Hua Yu Network Technology Development, 3084
Beijing Ibase Software Co Ltd, 2490
Beijing International Power Development & Investme, 2491
Beijing International Trust and Investment Co, 2491
Beijing Jingeng Clean Energy, 3084
Beijing King's Orient Hi-Tech Group Co Ltd, 2490
Beijing Lepro Seva Da Technologiy Development, 3084
Beijing Med-Pharm Co. Ltd., 2389, 2389
Beijing MMIM Technologies, 2841
Beijing Odyssey Chemicals, 2533
Beijing Phylion Battery Co Ltd, 2490
Beijing Rising Technology Co., 3084
Beijing Ryzur Exiom Medical Investment Co., 3084

Portfolio Companies Index

Beijing Tianyu Communications Equipment, 1957
Beijing UniSoc Technology Ltd., 1009
Beijing Yangpuweiye Technology Development, 2841
Beijing Yize Jianyuan Technology Co., 3084
BeInSync, 2453, 2711
Beintoo, 2865, 3170
BEL USA, 530
BelAir Networks, 2188, 3146
Belair Networks, 1411
Belazee, 721
Belcan, 65
Belden & Blake Corporation, 1577, 2556
Belenus, 3223
Belfast International Airport, 2814
Belga-Films, 3125
BeliefNet, 2188
Believe, 3199, 3229
Believeco, 2065
Belkin, 1772
Belkin International, 1754
Bell ActiMedia, 2073
Bell and Howell, 1979
Bell Automotive Products, 445, 1481
Bell Biosystems, 130, 1238
Bell Nursery Holdings, 1133
Bell Robotics, 1511
Bell Sports, 337
Bell'O International, 753
Bell-Park Co., 2898
Bella Pictures, 1917
BellaBeat, 721, 1491
BellBrook Labs, 2002
BELLE Michigan, 3259
Bellerophon, 11
Bellerophone Therapeutics, 1300
Bellgram, 10
Bellhops, 863, 1153
Bellicum, 764
Bellicum Pharmaceuticals, 1522
Bellisio Food LLC, 449
Bellisio Foods, 1377
Bellsystem24, 223
Bellwave, 2824, 2848
Bellwether Bio, 2007
Belly, 485, 1121
Belmont Meat Products, 1753, 2083
Belmont Technology, 1335
BeLocal, 2560
Beloola, 310
Belstar Investment, 2305
Belwater Capital Fund, 624
Belwind, 3033
Beme, 1125
BeMyEye, 2288
Benaissance, 1276
Benbria, 1928
Benbria Loop, 2276
Bench, 100, 535, 1114, 1479, 1521, 2150
Benchling, 125, 1203
Benchmark, 1071, 3206
Benchmark Capital, 3273
Benchmark Revenue Management, 1786
Benchmark Storage Innovations, 213
Benchmarq, 205
Benchmarq Microelectronics, 3128
BenchPrep, 1121, 1558
Benchprep, 1393
BenchSci, 2024, 2130, 2131, 2150
Bend, 1
Bendigo Bank Ltd, 2447
Bendon, 1026, 1984
BeneChill, 1325, 2807
Benefit, 1739
Benefit Express, 1140
Benefit Informatics, 551

Benefit Mall, 1255
Benefitfocus, 1361
BenefitMall, 205, 912, 958
Benefitter, 183
Benefix, 51
Benefood NV, 2797
Benefuel, 2054
Benestra, 912, 1157
BeneStream, 151, 1058
BeneSys, 935, 1576
Benetech, 470
Benetel, 2347
Benevis, 790, 1779
Benevis Practice Services, 1138
Benevity, 1045, 2074
Benex, 3173
Benihana, 128
Benivo, 2988
Benjamin River Productions, 3040
Benlowe Group Ltd, 2477
Bennedikthegaard, 3194
Bennedsgaard, 3194
Bennett Tool & Die Company, 402, 1057
Bennington Marine, 228
BenRevo, 10
Benson Group, 2935
Benson Hill Biosystems, 270, 570, 894, 1207
Bensussen Deutsch & Associates, 578
Bentek, 596
Bentek Corporation, 1397
Benten Bio Services, 1431
Benthic Geotech, 2966
Bentley Pharmaceuticals, 1456
Bentley Place, 1220
Bento, 10, 520, 2934
Bento for Business, 1240, 2398
Bentobox, 361
Benu, 1718, 1762
Benu Networks, 520, 1731
Benvenue, 599
Benvenue Medical, 622, 1788
Benzinga, 608, 1121, 2050
Bequam, 2842
Bera Outsmart, 2074
Bercomac Limitee, 2114
BERD, 3039
beRecruited, 1161
Berg Earth, 2997
Bergamotte, 2288
Bergen Medical Products, 296, 845
BerGenBio, 2510
Berger Singerman LLP, 3251
Berggi, 2334
Berggruen Car Rentals, 253
Bergteamet, 2317
Bering Media, 2253
Beringea, 3259
Beringer, 1837
Beringer Energy, 2036
Berkana, 2927
Berkana Wireless, 1237, 1750, 2917
Berkanna Wireless, 1091
Berkeley Capital Management, 1151
Berkeley Contract Packaging, 943
Berkeley Design Automation, 263, 1976, 2005
Berkeley Lights, 108, 278, 1657
Berkenhoff, 2786
Berkshire, 170
Berkshire Grey, 1073
Berlin Packaging, 1021, 1360
Berliner Verlag, 1929
Berna Biotech, 2913
BERNAMA Systems And Solutions Advisor Sdn Bhd, 3155
Bernard Robinson & Company, 3250
Berry, 851
Berry Aviation Inc., 47, 988

Berry Family Nurseries, 467
Berry Plastics, 141
BerryAvenue, 2820, 2829
Berrygenomics, 2927
Bertram, 2814
Bertrand Ducks, 2114
Bertrandt, 3060
Bertucci's Corporation, 1115
Beru AG, 2556
Beryllium, 815
Bespoke Furniture Ltd., 2648
Bespoke Global, 845
Bespoke Post, 12, 1635
Bessemer Venture Partners, 3263
Best Doctors, 243, 646, 1464, 1630
Best Elite International, 3084
Best Health, 1251
Best Kids (YeeHoo Baby World), 2935
Best Lawyers, 1115
Best Lighting Products, 854
Best Maid Cookie Co., 148
Best Teacher, 2637
Best Trash, 106
Best Version Media, 260
Best!, 655
Bestar, 2114, 2198
BeStylish, 2788
BET and WIN.com, 2774
Beta O2, 1608
Betable, 361, 1254, 1862
Betabrand, 779, 1254, 1359
BetaCat Pharmaceuticals, 1622
BetaGlue Technologies, 2865
Betaworks, 591, 641, 1009, 1114, 1597, 1701
Betfair.com, 2702, 3088
BeTheBeast.com, 1966
BeTrend, 1757
Bettcher Industries, 1266
Better, 1079
Better Bean, 1467
Better Finance, 1702
Better Life Medical, 711
Better Life Partners, 1
Better Life Technology LLC, 451
Better Mobile Security, 1305
Better Online Solutions, 3092
Better Place, 2891
Better Software Company, 2187
Better Than Cash Alliance, 1374
Better Things, 1965
Better Voicemail, 447
Better Walk, 1190
Better Workplace, 401
Better World, 2567
BetterBody Foods, 1004
BetterCloud, 27, 285, 641, 756, 876, 1235, 1851
BetterCompany, 299, 456, 1992
BetterDoctor, 10, 1223, 1702
Betterez, 1039
Betterfly, 473, 1121
BetterLesson, 938, 1298, 1315, 1393, 1530
Bettermarks, 2522
Betterment, 263, 488, 782, 1203, 1534, 2398
BetterUp, 564, 610, 787
Betterup, 1125, 2122
BetterView, 12, 527, 945
BetterView Marketplace, 10
BetterWalk, 999
Betterware, 2528, 2529
BetterWare de Mexico, 45
BetterWorks, 10, 545, 1079
BetweenMarkets, 205
Beverage House, 654
Beverage Innovations, 1194
Bevesys Oy, 2864
Bevi, 498, 623
BeVisible, 221

Portfolio Companies Index

Bevo Agro, 2045
Bevocal, 1898, 1976
BevSpot, 623
Beynd, 79
Beyond, 1752
Beyond 12, 1315
Beyond Games, 44, 708, 1121
Beyond Limits, 322
Beyond Meat, 514, 1079, 1099, 1363
Beyond Pricing, 361
Beyond The Rack, 1411, 2188
Beyond Trucks, 1426
Beyond View, 1423
BeyondCore, 1203
BeyondNow Technologies, 1839
BeyondTrust, 1927
BeyondTrust Software, 1971
BeyondView, 1477
BEZ Systems, 1915
Bezar, 354, 1223
BEZRK, 3062
BF Acquisitions Company LLC, 874
BFF GEMZ, 1618
BFG Supply, 2206
Bfinance, 225, 2556
BFL Capital, 3268
BFM, 2367
BFS Capital, 655
BGB, 3185
BGE, 2927
BGI, 1340, 3091
BGIS, 435
BGMedicine, 748
bGroupe Berkem, 2842
BH Cosmetics, 1231
Bharat Box Factory, 2451
Bharat Light and Power (BLP), 3202
Bharat Matrimony, 389
Bharat Serums and Vaccines, 1383
Bharti Enterprise, 2688
Bharti Infratel, 1086
Bharti Tele-Ventures, 2425
BHI Energy, 65
Bhoruka Power, 585
BHP Billiton, 2650
BHS Getriebe GmbH, 2703
BHS Specialty Chemical Products, 1733
BHS Specialty Chemicals, 1469
Bi Coastal Media, 670
Biametrics, 2815, 2923
BiancaMed, 3104
BianoGMP, 2518
Bias Power, 1743
Biba, 1014, 1855
Biba Apparels, 1957
BiblioMondo, 2254
Bibutek, 3043
Bicske-M1 Industrial Park And Logistic Centre, 2626
Bicycle Therapeutics, 184, 193, 1149, 1350, 1631, 1734, 1764
BID Group, 2139, 2158
Bid4assets, 327
Bidadoo Auctions, 85
BidClerk, 57, 857
Bidgely, 534, 1073, 2074, 2126
BidPal, 86, 1242
Bidtellect, 290
Bidu.com.br, 2967
Bielsko Business Center, 3068
Bien Cuit, 1422
Biex, 1255
BiFab, 3126
Bifold Group, 2935
BIG, 2801
Big, 125
Big 3 Precision Products, 1872

Big Bang Ventures, 3033
Big Box, 1186, 1391, 1666
Big Brain, 2131
Big Button, 2958
Big Cafe, 1091
Big City Farms, 3246
Big Fish Games, 1611
Big Frame, 133, 1483
Big Frame. Bonds.com, 2640
Big Heart Pet Brands, 1933
Big Issue Invest, 2500
Big Marble Farms, 2115
Big Matrix Research Institute, 2961
Big Night Entertainment Group, 638
Big River, 1051
Big Rock Sports LLC, 277
Big Sandy Equipment Company, 157
Big Sandy Peaker, 1797
Big Squid, 1074
Big Switch Networks, 604, 1009, 1257, 1537
Big Teams, 1768
BigBand Networks, 438, 457, 2571, 3128
BigBasket, 263
Bigbelly Solar, 1176
BigchainDB, 2398
Bigcommerce, 752, 820, 827, 1235, 1701, 1728, 1798
BIGcontrols, 10
BigDoor, 776
Biger Boat, 2020
Bigfinite, 10, 564
BigFix, 217, 971, 1213, 1649, 1728, 1949, 1976
Bigfoot Captial, 3265
Bigfoot Interactive, 957
Bigfoot Networks, 1335
BigFrame, 794, 1103
Bigger Pockets, 1276
Bigham Brothers, 1872
BigHand, 2935
BigHealth, 1056
BigID, 308, 520, 818, 2146
BigLeaf, 1384
BigMachines, 1045
BigMouth, 408, 480
BigPanda, 238, 840, 1187
Bigpoint GmbH, 1754, 1778
Bigscreen, 1477
BigStage, 1649
Bigstream, 1009
BigSwitch, 1073
Bijoux Terner, 153
BikeStation, 1786
Bil-Jax, 445
Bilguiden, 3004
Bilibili, 977
Bill & Melinda Gates Foundation, 3252
Bill Trust, 655
Bill.com, 200, 597, 666, 972, 1629, 1865
Bill4Time, 92
Billabong, 96
BillDesk, 504
Billeo, 185, 493
Billetto, 3194
BillGuard, 263
Billian, 3004
Billing Services Group, 20
BillingPlatform, 518
Billions Chemicals, 2533
BillionToOne, 10
BillMeLater, 218, 1890
BillPay, 2820, 2829
BilltoMobile, 1257
BillTrim, 10
Billtrust, 224
Billwerk, 1499
Bimedia, 2842
BINA, 1236

Binaris, 604, 1125
Binary Event Network, 346
Binary Fountain, 941
BinaryVR, 310
Bind, 1111
BIND Biosciences, 928, 1421
Bind Biosciences, 154, 748
Bind Therapeutics, 1464
Bindview, 1045
Bing Outdoor Media, 447
Bingdian, 1537
BingoBox, 827
BinOptics, 60, 434, 813, 1526
Binpress, 10, 1491, 1637
Binsentry, 2122
Binswanger Glass, 406
Binti, 321, 742, 1058, 1153
biNu, 1832
Binwise, 1600
BIO - Belgian Investment Company for Developing Co, 3252
Bio Agri Mix, 2056
Bio Futures PLC, 2699
Bio Gas Bree, 2940
Bio Gate, 2970
Bio Imagene, 178
Bio Protect, 3230
Bio Systems, 1064
Bio Theranostics, 924
Bio Trove, 428
Bio-Nobile Oy, 2310
Bio.Logis, 2560
Bioabsorable Therapeutics Inc., 272
BioAbsorbable Therapeutics, 1976
BIOAGE, 945
Bioage, 125, 1426
Bioage Labs, 720
BioAlliance Pharma, 2554, 3104
BioAmber, 1241
BioAnaLab, 3098
BioArray Solutions, 215, 1325
BioAstra Technologies, 2265
BioAtlantis, 2909
BioBeats, 680, 1614
Biobeats, 1527
BioBehavioral Diagnostics, 1421, 1661
Biobot Analytics, 1423
Biobras, 2733
Biocancell Therapeutics, 3235
Biocartis, 3033
Biocartis SA, 2342
Biocell, 2970
Biocept, 1287
Bioceptive, 3246
BioCeros, 2505
Bioceros, 2739
BioCision, 1546
Biocius Life Sciences, 428, 704
BioClinica, 119, 1043, 1962
Biocoat, 4
Biocode-Hycel, 2671
BioCollection, 623
BioConnect Systems, 711
BioConsortia, 1073
BioControl Limited, 1456
BioCore Holdings, 1631
BioCote, 3098
Biocroi, 2909
BioCryst Pharmaceuticals, 1920
Biodelivery Sciences, 764
Biodesy, 1439, 3076
BioDetego, 269
Biodiesel Producers., 2636
BioDigital, 354, 744
BioDuro, 61
Bioelectron, 1241
Bioenergy Development Company, 1314

Portfolio Companies Index

Bioenvision, 73
Bioerix SRL, 585
Biofer, 3033
Bioferma, 2480
BioFire Diagnostics, 190
BioForm, 3158
Bioform Medical, 1502
Bioformix, 1514
BioGanix, 2027
Biogazelle, 3056
Biogen Idec, 183
Biogenic Reagents, 695
Biognosys, 1776
Biogroup LCD, 2842
Biohaven, 532
Biohaven Pharma, 1943
BioHaven Pharmaceuticals, 73, 137, 764, 1522
BioHitech America, 1431
BioImagene, 2448
Bioindustrial Innovation Canada, 3249
Bioinvent, 2869
BioIQ, 924
BIOIVT, 172
Biokey, 118
BioKier, 350, 3250
BioLeap, 1510, 1776
Biolex, 1510
Biolex Therapeutics, 1013, 1844
Bioline Rx, 3128
BioLineRx, 1383
Biolinq, 875
Biolite, 54
Biologics, 1581
BiologicsMD, 953
Biologische Analysensystem, 2801
Biologos, 703
Biolonix, 2002
BioLumic, 2233
BiOM, 1675
Biomarin, 1268
BioMarker Strategies, 18
Biomarker.io, 10
BioMASON, 3250
Biomass CHP, 2601, 3003
Biomatlante, 3104
Biomatrica, 983, 1222
BioMCN, 3222
Biomedical Structures, 1772
Biomedican, 2279
Biomeme, 1581
BioMendics, 1051
Biomerix, 179
Biomet, 2371
Biometric Access Co., 192
Biometrix, 1976
Biometron, 2610
Biomimedica, 667
BioMimetic, 215
Biomimetic, 1190, 1502
BioMimetic Therapeutics, 3006
Biomode, 3039
Biomonitor, 3140
BioMoti, 3098
BioNano Genomics, 236, 622
BioNanovations, 999, 1190
Bionic Panda Games, 10
Bionic Sight, 1422
Bioniche Life Sciences, 2114
Bioniche Pharma, 1594
Bionova, 999
Bionumerik, 35
BioParadox, 599
BioPharmX, 1943
BioPhytis, 3104
Bioplexus, 532
Bioprocess H2O, 1695
Bioptigen, 296, 1446

BiOptix, 318
Bioreason, 1015
Bioreclamation, 1343
BioRegen, 711
BioReliance, 212
BioRelix, 661
Biorem, 707
BioRen, 240
Biorender, 798
Bioresearch, 225
BioResource International, 3250
BioRexis, 1510, 1868
BioRob, 2815
BioRx, 1772
BIOSAFE, 296, 1003
BioSafe, 1452
BioScale, 949, 1302, 1305, 2969
Bioscale, 1588
Bioscience, 2461
BioScrip, 1085
BioSeek, 240
Biosense, 3239
BioSensia, 2434
Biosensia, 2909
Biosensor, 2745
Biosensor Application AB, 3235
Biosensors International, 897
Biosensors International Group, 3084
Bioserve, 3202
BioSet, 652, 1190, 1298
BioSqueeze, 1317
BioStable Science & Engineering, 1622
Biostar, 1839
BioStorage Technologies, 1523
BioStratum, 2807
Biosurface Technologies, 1931
Biosurfit, 3039
BioSurplus, 1691
Biosyntech, 1414
BioSyntha, 2958
Biosynthetic Technologies, 322
Biota Technology, 2010
Biotage, 2719, 2881
Biotage AB, 2807
Biotec Pharmacon, 2745
Biotech Fonds Vlaanderren, 3033
Biotie, 1930
Biotie Therapies, 764, 2410, 2653, 2842
BioTie Therapies Oyj, 2310
Biotix, 723
Biotoscana, 698, 745
BioTrace Medical, 1371
BioTransplant, 1561
Biotrend - Inovacao e Engenharia Em Biotecnologia, 3039
Biotronic NeuroNetwork, 864
BioTrove, 647, 704
Biovalve, 2673
BioVascular, 2487
Biovation, 3095
Biovend, 2966
BioVentrix, 1794
Bioventus, 94, 119, 698, 1725, 3250
Biovertis, 3187
Biovest International, 1762
BioVex, 3095
Biovex, 1849, 2739
Bioview Ltd, 2945
BioVigilant, 236
Bioville, 2940
BioWare/Pandemic Studios, 660
BioWish Technologies, 1626
Bioworks, 1378
Biox, 2145
BIOX Corporation, 2108
BiOxyDyn, 3001
BiPar Sciences, 183, 1122, 1948

Birch Box, 27
Birch Hill Equity Partners Management, 3249
Birch Permian LLC, 159
Birch Telecom, 1929
BirchBox, 2377
Birchbox, 328, 520, 742, 763, 840, 1534
Birchmere Ventures, 3264
Bird, 27, 641, 1483, 1657, 2228
Bird Rock Bio, 11, 1734
Birdback, 3021
BirdBox, 686, 933
BirdDog Solutions, 952
BirdEye, 108
Birdi, 1058, 1703
Birdies, 763, 1346
Birdly, 2288
Birdstep, 3034
Birdstep Technology ASA, 163
Birmingham BioPower, 2740
Birst, 582
Birthday Express, 1674
BIS, 3115
Bis-Technics 2000, 2940
Biscayne Neurotherapeutics, 2221
BISCO Environmental, 1639
Biscotti, 1408
Bishop Auckland Hospital, 2740
Bishop Fox, 6
Bishop Rock Software, 508
BiSN, 322, 812
Bison, 2642
Bisuness Search Technologies, 683
BISYS Group, 1973
Bit Bliz, 1183
Bit Cauldron, 3251
Bit Computer, 2915
Bit Pagos, 2975
Bit.ly, 591, 1702
Bit9, 2436
Bitaksi, 2428
BitArmor Systems, 1003
BitAuto, 597, 2448, 2927
Bitband, 2453
BitBand Ltd, 2576
Bitbar, 1511, 2653, 2665
Bitbond, 3035
Bitboys Oy, 2310
Bitcasa, 1428
Bitcase, 2822
BitCentral, 990
Bitcoin, 125, 1998
BitDefender, 2462
BitDeli, 586
Bite, 344
Bite Squad, 336
Bitesize, 1370
Bitesnap, 724
Bitfone, 1091, 1352, 1994, 2917, 2990
Bitfusion, 1550, 2270
Bitglass, 1346, 3112
BitGo, 342, 1119, 1537
BitHeads, 2051
Bitium, 121, 309, 625, 1059, 1549
Bitly, 1058, 1359, 1597, 1720
Bitmain, 1125, 2681
Bitmaker, 2236
BitMEX, 1709
BitMinutes, 507
Bitmovin, 2437
Bitnet, 1969
Bitoya, 1698
Bitpay, 108, 720, 1203, 1597, 1865, 2822
Bitpipe, 1178
Bitproof.io, 310
Bitquick, 310
BitRefill, 310
Bitsbox, 758

Portfolio Companies Index

BitSight, 520, 523, 756, 839
BitSight Technologies, 827, 1203
Bitsqr, 1832
Bitstrips, 2822
BitTorrent, 582, 597, 1478
Bittware, 2601
BitVault, 1223
Bitvore Corporation, 1786
BitWall, 310
Bitwave Semiconductor, 1976
Bitwise, 1259
Bitwise Industries, 1530
BitYota, 1254, 1969
Bityota, 564
Bitzer Mobile, 40
BiVACOR, 3014
Bivio, 1684
Bivio Networks, 1976
BIW, 2653
Bix, 116, 1762, 1855
Bix Produce, 1169, 1345
Bix Produce Company, 1343
Biz360, 1976
Bizbuyer, 1786
BizBuyer.Com, 1255
Bizeebee, 10
Bizer, 1610
Bizible, 1227
BizLink Holdings, 1771
Bizly, 354, 708, 1039
Biznet Solutions, 2601
Bizo, 263, 564, 1918, 1948
Bizongo, 27
BizReach, 1610
BizTel One, 1603
Bizzabo, 1323, 2344, 2905
Bizzuka, 60
BJ's Wholesale Club, 1113, 1971
Bjb Education/Jade, 1518
Bjond, 629
BjondHealth, 946
bk Medical, 97
BKA Restoration, 842
bKash, 860
BKS Cable, 2301
Bkstg, 601, 1114
BL Healthcare, 1928
Bla-Bla.com, 957
Blaast, 2382
BlaBlaCar, 27, 1005, 2851, 2851
Black Bear Power, 157
Black Book Magazine, 462
Black Diamond, 1930
Black Diamond IT Services, 238
Black Diamond Therapeutics, 1296, 1522
Black Dog Investment, 3268
Black Duck, 1623, 1728
Black Duck Software, 759
Black Knight Financial Services, 1818
Black Letter Discovery, 1234
Black Mountain Sand, 1326, 1328
Black Point Petroleum, 157
Black Rock Systems, 1917
Black Sage, 47
Black Sand Technologies, 205, 1335
Black Sea Oil & Gas SRL, 416
Black Spider Technologies, 2665
Black Swan Energy, 1957
Blackarrow, 1187, 1464
Blackbaud, 927, 1045
Blackbeard Operating LLC, 1326, 1328
Blackbird Ventures, 485
Blackboard, 1348, 1360, 1498, 1949, 2556
BlackBook, 1635
Blackbuck, 27
BlackDuck, 696, 748
Blackeagle Energy Services, 607
Blacket, 823
BlackFog, 68
Blackfoot, 1976
BlackHawk Industrial, 331
BlackHorse Solutions, 1796
BlackJet, 232
Blackjewel, 1129
BlackLake Technology, 827
Blacklane Limiusines, 2466
BlackLine, 1685
BlackLogus, 1813
Blackmore, 1317, 1836
Blackmores Ltd, 2447
Blackpeak Group, 3252
Blacksmith Brands, 458
BlackSpider Technologies, 2568, 2653
Blackstone Group, 3254
BlackStratus, 1750
BlackThorn Therapeutics, 271, 894, 1207
BlackTies, 10
Blacktrace, 2006
Blackwave, 1674
Blackwood Seven, 3194
Blade, 85, 231, 820, 1114, 1268
Blade Games World Inc., 374
Blade Therapeutics, 3014
Bladelogic, 263, 1242
Blagden, 2353
Blair, 843
Blake & Pendleton, 1767
Blameless, 27
Blanc Labs, 2107
Blanclink, 2107
Blank Label, 1759
Blankpage AG, 2302
Blaschak Coal Corp., 406
Blaschak Coal Corporation, 1234
Blast, 108
Blast Motion, 108
Blast Movement Technologies, 1551
BlastPoint, 296
Blau Mobilfunk GmbH, 2664
Blausen Medical Communications, 953
Blavity, 10, 894
BLAZE, 49
Blaze Entertainment, 1976
Blaze Mobile, 256
Blaze Pizza, 337
Blaze Software, 308, 1255
Blaze.io, 316
BlazeMeter, 3236
Blazent, 936, 1953
BlazingDB, 1614
Bleach Group, 333
Bleach Group Inc., 334
Bleacher Report, 564
Blekko, 234, 1702, 1898, 1976
Blend, 537, 728, 877, 1125, 1719, 2009
Blend Financial, 10
Blend Labs, 1634
Blenderhouse, 1452
Blendid, 945
Blendoor, 221
Blendspace, 1315
Bleximo, 680
bLife, 1862
BlikBook, 2743
Blink, 520, 2470, 2911, 3199
Blink Biomedical, 2842
Blink Health, 321
Blink Twice, 1917
Blinker, 2953
Blinkfire, 3214
Blinkist, 641, 1005
Blinks Labs, 2832
BlinkTrade, 310
Blinkx, 43
BLiNQ, 2250
BLiNQ Networks, 1304
Blip.TV, 224, 2382
Blippy, 200, 1549
Blis, 254
Blismedia, 2470
Blispay, 744
Blisplay, 386
Bliss, 1092
Blissfully, 959
Blissmo, 10
Blitsy, 473, 510, 587, 732
Blitz, 562
Blitzen, 2122
BlitzESports, 59
Blivio, 2534
Bloc, 234, 1666
Block, 1114
Block 45, 2194
Block Cypher, 721, 773, 901
Block Renovation, 1363
Block Six Analytics, 59, 320, 1159
Blockable, 311, 1259, 1896
BlockApps, 149
Blockboard, 1058
Blockchain, 894, 1125
Blockchain Innovations Inc., 2117
BlockCypher, 10, 108
Blockcypher, 310, 857
Blockdaemon, 308, 520, 818
Blockline, 2982
BlockScore, 310, 1290
Blockspring, 125
Blockstack, 527, 623, 945, 1155, 1396, 1884, 2272
Blockstream, 108, 721, 1073, 1812
Blocktower Capital, 1884
BlockVigil, 10
Blocky, 1317
BlocPower, 1058, 1896, 3246
BlocWatch, 2187
blogfoster, 2832
BlogHer, 1918
Bloglovin', 1114, 1982
Blokable, 1058
Blood Monitoring Solutions, 999, 1190
Bloodbuy, 1813
Bloodhound, 10
Bloom, 1359, 2122
Bloom Automation, 395
Bloom Energy, 138, 186, 401, 582, 805, 1245, 1341, 1757
Bloom Farms, 1696
Bloom Health, 1271, 1618
Bloom Technologies, 1058
BloomAPI, 776, 1646
BloomBoard, 275
Bloomenergy, 1035
Bloomerang, 2074
Bloomfire, 205, 1684
Bloomin' Brands, 223
Bloomlife, 49
BloomNation, 473, 1718
BloomReach, 238
Bloomreach, 224, 1125, 1610
Bloomscape, 608, 1558
Bloomthat, 763
Bloomz, 545, 724
Blossom, 310, 1983, 3099
Bloud Tecnology Partners, 1596
Blount International, 111
Bloxr, 1428
Bloxroute Labs, 756
BLS Revecore, 2196
Blu Dot, 463
Blu Homes, 343
Blu Jay, 782

1243

Portfolio Companies Index

Blue 7 Communications, 131
Blue Acorn, 2050
Blue Agave Software, 1674
Blue Ant Media, 2127, 2228
Blue Apron, 742, 1751
Blue Ash Therapeutics, 481
Blue Belt Technologies, 1003
Blue Bird, 111
Blue Bottel Coffee, 1862
Blue Bottle, 1527
Blue Bottle Coffee, 514, 1142, 1696
Blue Bottle Coffee Co., 400
Blue Bottle Coffee Company, 1087
Blue Box Group, 1947
Blue Buffalo, 1022
Blue Calypso, 1244
Blue Capital, 722
Blue Cedar, 252
Blue Chip Partners Surgery Centers, 495
Blue Chip Surgery Centers Partners, 290
Blue Clean Gear, 849
Blue Cliff College, 1506
Blue Coat, 782, 1873, 1898
Blue Coat Systems, 1493, 1817
Blue Cod Technologies, 646, 655
Blue Danube Systems, 1657
Blue Dog Bakery, 381, 1250
Blue Dot Energy Services, 1148
Blue Fever, 901
Blue Gas Marine, 3250
Blue Heron, 1007
Blue Heron Paper Company, 1089
Blue Heron Technologies, 1917
Blue J, 2074
Blue J Legal, 2187, 2228
Blue Jeans Network, 27, 238
Blue Jeans Networks, 1996
Blue Lava Group, 1917
Blue Light, 461
Blue Line Logistics, 2940
Blue Line Protection Group, 966
Blue Lithium, 1953
Blue Lobster Software, 957
Blue Matador, 1074
Blue Medical, 227
Blue Medora, 1739
Blue Microphones, 1576
Blue Mountain Village, 2245
Blue Nile, 263, 1008, 1855
Blue Nile Bluevine, 1125
Blue Ocean Network, 2570
Blue Origin, 265
Blue Pillar, 86, 173, 493, 659, 677
Blue Pixels Media, 3257
Blue Point Capital Partners III(A) LP, 2088
Blue Pumpkin Software, 1649, 3109
Blue Pumpkin Software/Witness Systems, 1287
Blue Ribbon Baking Inc., 874
Blue Ribbon Dispatch, 1612
Blue Ridge Asphalt, 157
Blue Ridge ESOP Associates, 838
Blue Ridge Numerics, 838
Blue Ridge Paper Products Inc., 1089
Blue Ridge Pharmaceuticals, 1762
Blue River Technology, 1001
Blue Rock, 1930
Blue Rubicon, 2935
Blue Sky Research, 68
Blue Spark Technologies, 642, 1757
Blue Sprig Pediatrics, 1086
Blue Star (Acquired By Us Office Products), 2655
Blue Star Solutions, 1255
Blue Star Sports, 823
Blue Talon, 173
Blue Triangle, 1023
Blue Triangle Technologies, 288
Blue Vector Systems, 628
Blue Vision, 1477
Blue Wave, 1574
Blue Wire, 10
Blue Wolf Capital Fund II, 159
BlueAc, 1257
BlueArc, 468, 564
Bluearc, 2463
BlueArc Corporation, 561
BluEarth Renewables, 2036
Bluebank, 1009
Bluebeam Software, 1786
Blueberry, 1323
Blueberry Broadcasting, 1729
Bluebird, 897
Bluebird Bio, 154, 644, 1814, 2739, 3187
BlueBirdBio, 1522
Blueboard, 10
BlueBox, 1566
Bluebox Security, 1798
BlueCamroo, 1065
BlueCart, 7, 299
BlueCasa, 309
BlueCat Networks, 342, 1160, 1852
Bluecava, 1601
BlueCedar, 861
Bluechip Technologies, 2601
Bluechip Technologies Holdings Ltd, 2695
BlueConic, 1675
Bluecore, 720, 744, 776, 945, 2126
Bluecrew, 863
BlueCross BlueShield Venture Partners, 3255
Bluedata, 604, 978
Bluedot, 2131
Bluefield, 1887
Bluefields, 1914, 2470
Bluefin, 386
BlueFin Labs, 1537
Bluefin Labs, 1527, 1701
Bluefire Security Technologies, 1042
Bluefish Holdings LLC, 1822
Bluefly, 502, 1561
BlueFox, 234
Bluefox, 802
BlueFox.io, 1011
Bluegiga Technologies, 2442
BlueGill Technologies, 796, 1257
Bluegrass Dairy and Food, 1210
Bluegrass Dairy And Food Inc., 632
Bluegrass Materials Company, 1133
Bluehole Studio, 100
BlueJeans, 1346
BlueKai, 827, 1537, 1728, 1928
Bluekai, 641
BlueKat, 1449
Blueknight Energy Partners, 458
BlueLane, 1478
BlueLeaf, 1596, 2398
Bluelight, 1618
BlueLight Therapeutics, 11
BlueLine Grid, 1260
Bluemercury, 1022, 1603
BlueMountain Capital, 3254
Bluenog, 1316
Bluenose Analytics, 1698
BlueOrchard Finance, 3252
BluePay Processing, 1778
BluePay Processing Inc., 159
BluePeak Private Capital, 3252
Bluepoint Solutions, 1865
Blueprint, 2188
Blueprint Health, 1993
Blueprint Income, 623
Blueprint Medicines, 764, 1522, 1814
Blueprint Power, 728, 1896
Blueprint Registry, 1179
Blueprint Software Systems, 2252
Blueprint Ventures, 990
Blueprinter, 3194
BlueRoads, 1976
BlueRun Ventures, 3273
Bluerush, 2235
BlueShift, 1335, 2436
Blueshift, 863
BlueSky Equities, 3249
Bluesmart, 721, 1330
BlueSnap, 862, 1419
BlueSocket, 1976
Bluesocket, 318
Bluespace, 802
BlueSpace Software, 1130
BlueSpace Software Corp., 813
Bluespec, 1335, 2436
BlueSpire, 934
BlueStacks, 107, 978, 1009, 1478
Bluestacks, 1511
Bluestar Solutions, 1976
Bluestar.com, 79
BlueStem Brands, 408
Bluestem Brands, 224
Bluestone, 27, 2935
BlueStone Natural Resources, 1326
Bluestone Software, 55
BlueStrata Her, 570
Bluestreak, 1741
Bluestreak Technology, 683
Bluestreak Technology Inc., 683
BlueStripe, 1855, 1901
BlueTalon, 271
BlueTarp Financial, 440, 756, 1165, 1855
BlueTown, 3013
Bluetrain Mobile, 1101
BlueTrap Financial, 938
BlueTree Allied Angels, 3264
BlueVine, 488, 1158, 1203
BlueVine Capital, 545
Bluewater Bio International, 3098
BlueWhale, 1908
Bluewolf, 1579
BlueYield, 1504
Blujays Brand, 395
Blumberg Capital, 990
Blume Ventures Fund, 3190
Blurb, 133, 389, 928, 1608
Blutag, 49
Bluum, 421
BluVector, 1140
BluWireless Technology, 2988
BluWrap, 731, 2397
Blycos Biotechnologies, 830
Blyncsy, 1074
Blyth, 416
BMB Corp, 2339
BMC, 1086
Bmd, 2346
bMenu, 2361
BMI Asia, 2581
BMI Asia Inc, 2719
Bmi Canada, 2114
BML Pharmaceuticals, 132
BMM Compliance, 333, 334
BMO Capital Partners, 3249
BMS Reimbursement, 1239
BNI, 1410
BNI Video, 485
BNN Holdings, 1493
Bnocular, 344
BNX Systems, 2556
BNY Mellon Wealth Management, 3264
BOA Group, 63
Board Vantage, 773
Board Vitals, 795
BoardBookit, 296
BoardOnTrack, 1175

Portfolio Companies Index

BoardVantage, 241
BoarwalkTech, 1254
Boat International Publications, 2812
Boatbound, 10, 708, 1752, 2951
Boathouse Sports, 1668
Boats Group, 136
Boatsetter, 863
Boaz Energy LLC, 1328
Bob, 149
Bobbie, 7
Bobcat Gas Storage, 898
Bobo, 3241
BOC Edwards, 2371
BOC International Limited, 2927
Boca, 205
Boca Executive Beauty, 381
BOCADA, 892
Bocada, 1976
Bocasa, 2940
Bock & Clark, 935
Bodegas Campo Burgo, 2976
Bodegas Lan, 2953
Bodo, 802
Body & Labs, 744
Body and Mind, 206
Body Central, 1979
Body Evolution, 365
Body Media, 178
Body Phyx, 1051
BodyFX, 799
Bodymat, 3125
BodyMedia, 984
Bodymedia, 1626
Bodytech, 1092
Boekhandels Groep Nederland Holding BV, 2983
Boemer BV, 2983
Boftel Oy, 3204
Bogart Associates, 509
Bohemia Interactive Simulations, 1576
Bohemia Prints, 2674
Bohemian Guitars, 1752
Bohner-EH, 2815
Boingo Wireless, 186, 1241, 1744
Boisaco, 2089
Boise Cascade Company, 1160
Bojangles', 1049
Boka Sciences, 830
Bokecc, 3133
Boku, 125, 582, 1073, 3160
Bol.com, 3146
Bold, 2235
Bold Commerce, 2280
Bold Energy III, 673
BOLD Guidance, 1051
Bold Metrics, 546
Bold Threads, 773
Bolder Healthcare Solutions, 654
Bolder Industries, 147
BOLDstart Ventures, 990
Bolero, 2463
Boloco, 1161, 2000
Boloni, 2927
Bols Royal Distilleries, 2635
Bolstr, 1058
Bolstra, 86, 659
Bolt, 36, 485, 863, 879, 945, 949, 1418
Bolt Financial, 752
Bolt Insurance, 1643
Bolt Logistics, 2280
Bolt Threads, 778, 1001, 1238
Bolthouse Farms, 1160
Boly Media Communications, 46
Boma International, 3033
Bombardier, 2114
Bombardier Recreational Products, 223
Bombas, 862
BombBomb, 1645

BombFell, 591
Bombfell, 1585
Bomedus, 2815
Bomfell, 863
Bomgar, 782
BoMill, 1776
Bon Voyaging, 1309
Bon'App, 1618
Bona Film Group, 3084
Bonanza, 776, 1947
Bonck Education, 2927
Bond Capital, 3249
Bond Street, 279
Bondai, 10
BondDesk, 2371
Bonded Filter, 815
Bonded Holdings LLC, 64
Bonded Kayit Sistemleri AS, 253
Bonded Services Group, 1984
BondMart, 794
Bone Health Technologies, 849
Bonesupport AB, 2807
Bonfaire, 1121, 1855
Bonfire, 125, 564, 2122
Bonfire Wings, 953
Bongarde Holdings, 868
Bonitasoft, 3199
Bonmarché, 1755
Bonna Sabla, 2309, 2854
Bonne O, 2222
Bonneterie Richelieu, 2089
Bonotel, 416
Bonovo, 2927
Bonovo Orthopedics, 1383
Bonsai, 1158
Bonson Inormation Technology, 2841
Bonti, 517
Bonti Inc., 489
Bonusbox, 2435
Bonusly, 744, 1317
Boo-Box, 2967
Boohee, 1511
Book A Tiger, 3226
Book Jam, 100
Book-It Oy, 2864
Book. Stay. Go., 10
BookBub, 209, 1322
Booker, 881, 1050, 1784
Booker Software, 224, 646, 1942
BookFresh, 234
Bookham Technology, 2653
Booking Pal, 387
Bookly.co, 1074
Bookmarq, 10
BookMyShow, 27
BookNook, 1530, 1895
Bookyap, 1618
Boom, 310, 562, 795, 945, 981, 1121, 1330, 1597
Boom Entertainment, 830
Boom Fantasy, 623, 1599
Boom! Studios, 794, 1596
Boom.tV, 742
BoomBotix, 234, 549, 1953
Boomerage Commerce, 1666
Boomerang, 10
Boomerang Commerce, 1162
Boomerang's, 447, 953
Boomi, 249, 744
BoomTime, 1926
BoomTown, 387, 708, 787, 1761
BoomTrain, 10, 298
Boomz, 776
Boon, 10
Boon + Gable, 10, 562, 945, 1186
Boon Supply, 1363

Boone, 874
Boosey & Hawkes, 2814
booshaka, 795
Boost, 1119
Boost Biomes, 527
Boost CTR, 1969
Boost Insurance, 1346
Boost Juice Bars, 2541
Boost Media, 10, 238, 1032
Boostable, 10, 1254, 1637
Boosted, 795, 1696, 2150
Boosted Boards, 1073
Booster, 537, 708, 1162, 1186, 1925
Booster Fuels, 2272
Boostermedia, 3119
Boostr, 259
Boostsecurity.Io, 2131
BoostUp, 985
Bootlegger Clothing, 2249
Booya Fitness, 623
Booz Allen Hamilton, 416
Booztgroup, 3140
Bop.fm, 721
Bopack NV, 2797
Boqii, 846, 3053
Borchers, 1049
Borchers Americas Inc., 159
Border Construction Specialties, 1767
Border X Lab, 1079
Borderware, 2005
Boreal - Informations Strategiques, 2114
Boreal Drilling, 2114
Boreal Genomics, 983, 1063, 2144
Borean Pharma, 2410, 2739
Borer City Media, 1635
Borg & Bigum, 3194
Borjomi, 3086
Bormioli Rocco, 1939
Borqs, 1009, 1511
Borro, 389, 1504, 1563, 2441, 2682
Borrow, 1896
Borrowell, 1982, 2094, 2120, 2217
BorrowMyDoggy, 3099
Bortech, 649
Bos, 2562
Bosideng, 2841
Bosley's, 1580
Bosmans Graphics, 2940
BOSS, 846
BOSS (Business Operations & Software Solutions), 2706
Bossa Nova, 874
Bossa Nova Beverages Group, 1917
Bossa Nova Concepts, 1003
Bossa Studios, 2437
Bossa Studios UK, 2944
Bossanova, 1009
Bossard Metrics Inc., 911
Bosslady, 3029
Bostlnno, 316
Boston Biomedical, 1241
Boston Celtics, 1527
Boston Children's Hospital, 1271
Boston Color Graphics, 262
Boston Duck Tours, 1626
Boston Heart Diagnostics, 224
Boston Market, 1755
Boston Medical Technologies, 317
Boston Power, 1918
Boston Proper, 337
Boston Seed Capital, 3263
Boston Ship Repair, 617
Boston-Power, 808, 1361
Bot MD, 752
Botaneco, 2043
Botanical Labs, 1464
BotChain, 833

1245

Portfolio Companies Index

Botlex, 3162
Boto International, 2556
Botoanalytics, 10
BotSociety, 10
Bottica.com, 2963
Bottle Rock Power, 416, 1577
Bottle Rocket Power, 1897
Bottlenose, 1385, 1800, 1841
BottleRocket, 623
BottlesTonight, 10
Bottomline Technologies, 2653
Bottr, 10
Boudless, 779
Bouffard Sanitaire Et Acier Bouffard, 2089
Boulder, 742
Boulder Ionics, 1713
Boulder Scientific Company, 1507
Boulder Ventures, 990, 3260, 3265
Bouldin Creek Distillery, 447
Boulevard, 309
Bounce, 27
Bounce Exchange, 561, 1358, 1479
BounceExchange, 535
BounceX, 238, 2231
Bouncy, 310
Bound, 1385
Boundary, 1629
Boundless, 776, 1069, 1260, 1322, 1918, 2270
Boundless Mind, 1309
Boundless Network, 205, 1687, 1813
BountyJobs, 877, 1596
Bourgeois Guitars, 1165
Bourn Hall International, 3187
Bourne Leisure, 2547, 2926
Bout'chou, 3033
Boutique La Vie En Rose, 2114
Boutique Le Pentagone, 2089
Bouxtie, 130
Bow & Drape, 151, 1759, 1914
Bow River Capital, 3265
Bow Valley BBQ, 2093
Bowater Building Products Limited, 2298
Bowater Home Improvements Limited, 2298
Bowers & Wilkins, 108
Bowery, 380, 601, 708, 729, 742, 756, 820, 894, 1114, 1281, 1593
Bowery Farming, 827
Bowman Power Group, 2751
Bowstreet, 1255
Bowtech, 1345
Bowtie, 724
Box, 125, 263, 511, 610, 666, 791, 819, 1213, 1623, 1629, 1698
Box-It, 3009
Box.Net, 928
Boxbee, 1154
Boxbot, 176, 1426, 1836
BoxC, 173, 1998
BoxCast, 1051
Boxed, 108, 321, 680, 742, 827, 876
Boxed Wholesale, 601, 1680
Boxee, 1701, 1718
Boxer, 447, 1762
Boxer Cross, 526, 1287
Boxercraft, 1573
Boxever, 2513
Boxfish, 1284
BoxFox, 1159
Boxtal, 2842
Boyd Corp., 823
Boyd Industries, 1612
Bozoka.com Sweden, 2745
Bozzetto Group, 3145
BP Express, 367
BP3, 1813
BParts, 3039
BPL Communications, 3159

BPL Global, 1003, 1355
BPL Mobile Comunications, 1795
BPSC, 238
Bqteicg, 2649
Braavo, 321, 641
BRAC, 1374
Brace Industrial Gorup, 1745
BraceAbility, 1862
Bracket, 764, 1419
Bracket Computing, 84
BracNet, 603
Brad's Raw Foods, 249, 1589
Bradford Health Services, 449
Bradford Networks, 1888, 1994
Bradshaw Home, 2200
Bradshaw International, 2177
BradshawHome, 2201
Brady Enterprises, 815
Braeburn, 144, 212, 1522
Brahms, 2369
Braigo Labs, 624, 1009
Brain Corporation, 1511
Brain Sentry, 1305
Brain X, 1786
Brain.fm, 1696
Brainbees Technologies, 2840
BrainBits, 1267
BrainCells, 1414, 1788, 2961
BRAINcoBiopharma, 1456
BrainFx, 2141
BrainGEM L.L.C, 2852
Brainiac, 2288
Brainient, 2419
Brainlab, 1949
Brainly, 820, 3035
Brainomix, 3019
Brainpower, 2616
BrainRush, 304
Brainscape, 1635
BrainScope Company, 326, 1172
BrainSellers.com, 2982
BrainsGate, 2345
Brainshark, 1917
BrainSpec, 623
Brainstorm, 1074
Braintree, 27
BrainyWorks, 2339
Braitrim, 2814
Brakes Group, 223
Brami, 1114
Brammer Bio, 119
Brammo Motorsports, 2072
Branch, 49, 125, 309, 553, 608, 945, 976, 1142, 1162, 1179, 1296, 1614, 2398
branch, 1159
Branch Brook Holdings, 1769
Branch Messenger, 562
Branch Technology, 461
BranchOut, 43
Branchout, 1323
BranchTrack, 3099
Brand Affinity Technologies, 1237
Brand AI, 776
Brand Calculus, 2809
Brand Connections, 1929
Brand Connections LLC, 576
Brand Events Holdings, 2862
Brand Group Holdings, 416
Brand Networks, 63
Brand Shop, 2050
Brand Thunder, 1556
Brand Yourself, 1290
Brand.net, 759
Brandable, 1125
BrandAmerica, 1786
Brandbase Holdings Inc., 463
BrandBoards, 10

Brandcast, 545, 1666
Branded Online, 1024
BrandFX, 747, 1747
Branding Brand, 1005
Brandless, 44, 553, 894, 1537, 1696
Brandlive, 1384, 1467
BrandMaker GmbH, 2677
Brandmuscle, 1576
BrandRapport Group, 2862
Brands4Friends, 3161
Brandscreen, 1713
BrandsforFriends.com, 1418
Brandtex Group A/S, 2703
Brandtone, 1776
Brandwatch, 1606, 2398, 2978
BrandWeek, 2050
BrandYourself, 1309, 2016
Brant Instore Corp., 904
Brash Entertainment, 20
Brasilmobile, 2617
Brass Monkey, 1521
Brass Smith Innovations, 1115
Brasseler USA, 418
Brat, 1114
Brat TV, 321
Brava, 553
Bravanta, 68
Brave, 945
Brave Commerce, 2176
Brave Credit, 10
Brave Software, 23
Bravely, 354, 545
BraveNew Talent, 3004
Bravida, 223
Bravo Brio Restaurant Group Inc., 357
Bravo Health, 561, 785
Bravo Natural Resources LLC, 1326
Bravo Sierra, 321
Bravo Sports, 449, 1769
Bravo Target Safety, 2284
Bravo Wellness, 21
Brawler, 1848
Brawler Industries, 1779
Braxton Technologies, 928
Brayton Point Power, 676
Braze, 238, 361, 527, 561, 1213, 1566
Brazen, 1064
BRCK, 1896
BRD, 1119
BrdgAI, 803
Brdr. Sommer, 3194
Bread, 568, 1186, 1203, 1223
Breadless, 608
Break Trail Ventures, 3265
Break-Up Alert, 515
Breaker, 1966
Breaking Free, 2958
BreakingPoint Systems, 205
Breakthrough, 863, 1058, 1254, 1698
Breakthrough Energy Ventures, 3263
Breakup Goods, 1739
Breathe, 1079
Breathe for Change, 1530
Breathe Life, 2090
Breathe Technologies, 1775
BreatheAmerica Inc., 698
Breather, 894, 1203, 1597, 1696, 2140
Breathing Buildings, 2963
Breathometer, 1752
BRECIS Communications Corporation, 255
Breedit, 3235
Breen & Carolina Color, 172
Breethe, 18
Breeze Industrial Products Corp., 989
Breeze Tecnhologies, 3220
Breezeworks, 2010
BreezoMeter, 2842

Portfolio Companies Index

Breezy, 246, 680, 720, 1702
Breg, 698, 1962
Breguet, 1021
Breinify, 575
Breitenfeld, 1256
Brendmoe & Kirkestuen, 2745
Brenntaq, 223
Brentax Inc., 467
Brentwood Associates Private Equity IV LP, 2088
Brentwood Associates Private Equity V LP, 2088
Breslow & Walker LLP, 3257
Bresnan Broadband, 1508
Breveon, 1183
Brew Dr. Kombucha, 424
Brewpublik, 1589
Brewster, 863
BRG Sports, 722
BRG Sports Inc., 159
Bri-Chem Supply, 2278
Bri-Mar Manufacturing LLC, 906
Bricata, 655
Brick, 949
Brickell Biotech, 1402
Brickman Group, 2014
Brickstream, 646, 1247
Brickwood NYC, 1766
Brickwork, 59, 553, 763
Bride Story, 721
Bridea, 100
Brideside, 254
Bridg, 231, 400, 1966
Bridg. Brightfunnel, 1059
Bridge, 754, 1227, 1240
Bridge Bank, 3250, 3251, 3265
BRIDGE Energy Group, 1888
Bridge International Academies, 1073, 1374, 1554
Bridge International Academy, 1554
Bridge Semiconductor, 1003
Bridge2Solutions, 949
Bridgebio, 73
BridgeBio Pharma, 1086
Bridgefy, 985
BridgeLux, 549
Bridgelux, 597, 1908, 1924, 2072
Bridgepoint Education, 1957
Bridgepoint Medical, 1464
Bridgeport Tank Trucks, 197
Bridger, 1577
Bridger Energy Funding, 157
Bridges Ventures, 2500
Bridgespan, 1976
BridgeStream, 1465
BridgeU, 3099
BridgeUS, 10
BridgeWave Communications, 540, 1640
Bridgit, 2074, 2270
Bridj, 789, 1322
Brief, 101
BriefCam, 2453
Briefcam, 3235
Briefcase, 635
Brierley + Partners, 1762
Brigadier Oil & Gas, 673
Brigham Resources, 1447, 1957
Bright, 720, 742, 1760
bright box, 2929
Bright Cellars, 567, 1558
Bright Computing, 2665, 3042
Bright Edge, 1009
Bright Farms, 669
Bright Frams, 401
Bright Greens, 288
Bright Health, 561, 641, 1537
Bright Horizons, 223, 263, 1855
Bright Hub, 1013

Bright Light Systems, 797
Bright Machines, 648, 1155, 2681
Bright Now! Dental, 886
Bright Pattern, 456
Bright Peak, 1930
Bright Source, 322
Bright Tiger Technologies, 1335
Bright View Technologies, 3250
Bright.md, 1384, 1467, 1483, 1659
BrightBox, 2010
BrightBytes, 1005, 1315, 1554
BrightCloud, 1782
BrightContext, 1712
Brightcord Investment, 1771
Brightcove, 27, 925
Brightcrowd, 1323
Brightdoor, 975, 1389
BrightEdge, 238, 1005
Brightedge, 100, 980
Brighten, 121
Brighter, 1187, 1798
Brighter Dental, 1834
Brightex Industries, 585
BrightFarms, 429
Brightfarms, 1324
Brightfield, 1925
BrightFlag, 2750
BrightFunnel, 115
Brightfunnel, 564
Brighthaul (Israel) Ltd., 3239
BrightHeart, 377, 1140
BrightHouse, 1939
BrightInsights, 648
Brightleaf, 779
Brightmail, 27, 936
Brightmont Academy, 1242
BrightNest, 1364
Brighton Best International, 2594
Brightpearl, 2682, 2963, 3005
BrightPet Nutrition Group, 851
BrightReasons, 2814
BrightRoll, 56, 1088, 1319, 1629, 1852, 1862
Brightside, 520, 2700
Brightside Academy, 1140, 1691
BrightSource, 610
BrightSource Energy, 468, 596, 928, 1908
Brightspace, 780
Brightspark Ventures, 3249
BrightSpring, 2201
BrightStar, 1377
Brightstar Corp., 1133
Brightstorm, 1091
BrightTalk, 1335
BrightView, 1086
BrightVolt, 325
Brightware, 35
Brightwell Payments, 1279
Brightwheel, 564, 680, 827, 1153, 2130, 2131
Brightwork, 2909
Brill Street, 1364
Brill Street + Company, 454
Brille24, 2595
Brilliance Financial Technology, 654
Brilliant, 1058, 1142, 1698
Brilliant Bicycles, 328
Brilliant Telecommunications, 628
Brim, 97, 2143
Bringg, 1610
Bringhub, 400
BringIt, 1658
BringMeThat, 1521
BringShare, 1556
Brinkhof Group International NV, 2819
Brinks Home Security, 475
Brintons Carpets, 416
Brio Technology, 1731
Brion, 972

Brion Technologies, 1257, 1976
Briq, 680
Briqueteries de Ploegsteert, 3125
Brisbane Materials, 1713
brisbane Materials, 1304
Brisk.io, 2628
Bristol Compressors International Inc., 1089
Bristol Farms, 674, 874
Bristol Technology, 532
Brit + Co, 553, 1009, 1114, 1928
Brit Media, 1361
Britannia Pharmaceuticals Limited, 1456
Brite, 1346
Brite Health, 1887
Brite Semiconductor, 1014
Briter Electronics, 2966
British Columbia Investment Management Corporation, 3249
British Marine Holdings Ltd., 407
British Salt, 2935
British Telecom, 2612
BritishEco, 2751
Britt Allcroft Group, 2814
Brix Networks, 457, 3128
Brixton, 96
BrizzTV, 3010
Broad Daylight, 1976
Broad Hollow Bioscience Park, 3257
Broad Oak Energy II, 673
Broad River Power, 676
Broadband Access Systems, 1335
Broadband Communications, 1183
Broadband Services, 2073
Broadbase Software, 759, 1247
Broadbus, 3128
Broadbus Technologies, 457, 1449
Broadcast Electronics, 20
Broadcast Media Group, 2942
Broadcast Pix, 1164
Broadcast.com, 925
BroadcastAmerica.com, 440
Broadcasting Partners, 1145, 1929
Broadcom, 388
BroadHop, 318, 861, 1430
Broadhorn Farm, 347
BroadJump, 205
Broadlane, 1631
BroadLight, 2646
Broadlight, 218, 3128
BroadLogic, 200, 1561, 1829
Broadly, 779
Broadnet, 2953
Broadreach, 54
BroadRiver Communications, 538
Broadsoft, 263, 457, 556, 613, 881, 990, 1213, 2630
BroadSound, 908
BroadStar Energy, 679
Broadview Networks, 226
Broadview Networks Holdings, 1192
Broadview Ventures, 3263
BroadVision, 1762
Broadware Technologies, 1674
Broadway Networks, 3038
Broadway Roulette, 901
Broadxent Pte Ltd, 2499
Brocade, 936, 1125
Brocade Communications, 241, 1976
Brocase, 1247
Brock, 110
Broda Group, 2267
Broder Bros., 1493
Broder Brothers Co., 223
Broderbound, 564
Brodmann17, 1614, 2938
Broetje-Automation GmbH Wiefelstede, 3058
Brogea, 2623

Portfolio Companies Index

Brom compositions, 2381
Brome Financial Corporation, 2114
Bromium, 125, 978, 1009, 1125, 1213
Bromlum, 938
Bronco Manufacturing, 566
Bronco Midstream Holdings, 157
Broncus Technologies, 272, 1241, 1976
Brook Furniture Rental, 69
Brookdale Senior Living Inc., 407, 769
Brookfield Asset Management, 3245, 3249, 3252, 3254
Brookfield Real Estate & Relocation Services, 2062
Brookhaven Instruments, 238
Brooklin Concrete, 2156
Brooklinen, 623, 744
Brooks & Whittle Limited, 1560
Brooks Equipment Company, 248
Brooks Fiber Properties Inc., 1212
Brooks Instrument, 110
Brooks Service Group, 2353
Brooks24x7, 523
Brookside Mill CLO, 1493
Brookson, 1576
Brookstone, 217, 1971
Brookstreet, 2276
Brooktree Corporation, 1920
Bros Catering, 3084
Brouwerij Bosteels, 3222
Brouwerij Martens, 2940
Brown & Joseph, 1097
Brown Advisory, 510
Brown Industries, 16
Brown Integrated Logistics, 1279
Brown Jordan International, 1138
Browntape, 3100
Browserstack, 27
Browz, 2640
BRPH Architects-Engineers, 132
Brubakken, 3067
Bruce Foods Corporation, 77
Brud, 1657
Bruha, 2132
Bruin II, 1049
Brunner Mond, 3169
Bruno Invest, 2940
Bruno Saint Hilarie, 2330
Brunswick Bowling Products, 832
Brunton, 1100
Brushstrokes, 2067
Bruxie, 1092
Bruzd Foods, 623
Bryant & Stratton College, 1419
Bryant Stibel, 3258
Bryte, 1616
BryterCX, 180
BSB, 2992
BSI2000, 1839
BSL Wood Products, 2114
BSM, 45
BSM Wireless, 2051
BSN Glasspack, 2635
BSN Medical, 2968
BSO, 20
BT Imaging, 145
BT Wood, 2603
BTC Jam, 1563
BTCC, 1125
BTCJam, 10
bTendo, 2557
BTG, 20, 51
BTI Photonic Systems, 1084
BTI Studios, 416
BTI Systems, 224, 2188
BTM Company, 408
BTX Group, 1755
Bubble, 1074

Bubble Gum, 3129
Bubble Motion, 2861, 3053, 3112
Bubbles & Beyond, 2815, 2923
Bubbli, 200
Bubbly, 1408
Bubl, 985
Buchanan Ingersol & Rooney, 3264
Bucket, 10
Buckeye Cellulose Corporation, 1160
Buckeye Nutrition, 405
Buckeye Partners, 1577
Buckner Equipment Rental, 467
Buckzy, 2187
Bucyrus, 110
Budco, 834
Budding Enterprise Fund, 1139
Buddy, 85, 195, 1841, 3042
Buddy Media, 241, 827, 1006, 1701
BuddyTV, 85
Budget Propane, 2089
BudgIT, 1374
Budhire, 394
Budnitz Bicycles, 789
BudTender, 395
Bueda, 1003
Buenavision Cable TV, 874
Buf, 2122
Buffalo Coal, 1551
Buffalo Games, 1174
Buffalo Wild Wings, 1580
Buffer, 129, 232, 1643
Bug Labs, 552, 1718, 1928
Bugbuster, 3036
BugCrowd, 1401, 1418
Bugcrowd, 548, 1525, 1610
Bugsee, 1054
Bugsnag, 894
Bugukgangbyung Co., 585
build Ops, 882
Build Stream, 1896
Build-a-Bear Workshop, 1955
Buildable, 2131
BuildaBrand, 2558
BuildCraft Homes, 1711
BuildDirect, 1247
Builders FirstSource, 1043, 1957
Builders VC, 2028
BuildForge, 205
Building Connected, 564, 944, 1125
Building Energy, 1065, 3145
Building Engines, 1104
Building For Good, 2969
Building Material Distributors, 1971
Building Materials Holding Corporation, 1971
Building Products & Services Company, 1270
Building Robotics, 1534, 1978
Building Systems Design, 377
BuildingConnected, 246, 787, 945
BuildingDNA, 736
BuildingEngines, 380
BuildingIQ, 401, 1401, 2430
BuildLinks, 1711, 3124
BuillionVault.com, 2441
Built In, 1483
Built In Chicago, 635
Built in Menlo, 10
BUILT Robotics, 728
Built Robotics, 863, 1296
Built Technologies, 728
Builtr Labs, 311
Bujagali Hydropower Project, 280
BuldumBuldum.com, 2428
Bulitt, 2541
Bulk Handling Systems, 377
Bulk MRO, 1770
Bull Capital Partners Pte Ltd, 3252
Bull City Forward, 3250

Bull City Venture Partners, 485
Bull Moose Capital, 2267
Bulldog, 1813
Bulldog Group, 2051
Bulldog Solutions, 1735, 1748
Bulletin, 708, 721, 756, 901, 1079
Bulletin Intelligence, 632
Bullhorn, 823, 928, 1005, 1971
BullionVault, 3031
Bullish, 3265
Bullpen Capital, 298
BuluBox, 635
Bumba, 3033
Bumble Bee Foods LP, 449
Bumble Bee Seafoods, 874, 1873
Bumblebee, 1896
Bumblebee Spaces, 1836, 1895, 1935
Bump, 1079, 1907
Bunch, 2131
Bunchball, 857, 1848
BundleTech, 3031
Bundy Refrigeration, 1755
Bungalow, 623, 1073
Bunker, 520, 1724
Bunker Ex, 3099
Bunker's, 2374
Bunker's Group, 2373
Bunndle, 10, 1254
Bureau van Dijk, 2547
Burgaflex, 279
Burgaflex Holdings, 408
Burger King, 1837
Burke America Parts Group, 408
Burke Williams, 961
Burl Software, 1013
Burlington Coat Factory, 223
Burlywood, 25
Burn Manufacturing, 54
Burner, 10, 1800, 1918
Burning Glass, 1554
Burning Glass Technologies, 1499
Burns e-Commerce Solutions, 2814
Burns Scalo Real Estate, 3264
Burren Energy, 2482
Burrow, 328, 1581
Burrow Global, 988
Burst, 1813
Burstly, 309, 1701, 1890, 2640
BurstPoint Networks, 1994
Burtek Enterprises, 2008
Burton Flower & Garden, 1460
Burton Saw & Supply, 1438
Bus Online, 2838
Bus.com, 305, 1028, 2178
Busaba Eathai, 3027
Busbud, 1558, 2065, 2150, 2216
Buse Industries, 402
Bush Equities dba Cuddledown, 440
Bushel, 817
Bushnell, 2371
Business & Decision, 3199
Business Advisory Service, 2787
Business Backers, 1514, 1786
Business Computer News, 217
Business Connect China, 752
Business Engine, 1255, 1976
Business Exchange, 635
Business Infusions, 2043
Business Insider, 265, 1006, 1087, 1597
Business Intelligence Advisors, 1
Business Layers, 810
Business Materis, 2367
Business Monitor International, 1720
Business Networking International, 381
Business of Fashion, 3088
Business Ready Solutions, 3250
Business Search Technologies Corp., 683

Portfolio Companies Index

Business Service Corporatiom, 3173
Business Signatures, 115, 1867
Business.com, 1006, 1736
Businessland, 263
Businessolver, 1045
Business_Doc, 2756
Buster, 1533
Bustle, 820, 1698, 1829
Bustle Digital Group, 827
busuu, 3046
Butler, 1425
Butler Schein Animal Health, 1360
Butler's Pantry, 60
Butlr Technologies, 10
Buttercoin, 2574
Butterfield Fulcrum Group, 364
Butterfly, 389, 2773
Butterfly Fields, 2305
Butterfly VLSI, 2766
Button, 37, 1223, 1346
Button Down Solutions LLC, 3257
Button Inc., 1537
Buuldcon, 3099
Buy Back Booth, 2060
Buy.at, 2653
Buy.com, 502
Buyat, 2665
BuyerQuest, 733
Buyerquest, 162
Buyers Edge Platform, 336
BuyersEdge, 115
BuyerZone, 263, 523
BuyFi, 1635
BuyHappy, 495
Buyproperly, 2094
BuySafe, 881
Buysafe, 915
buySAFE, 540
Buysight, 1379
BuySquare, 256
Buytime Media, 496
Buzz Media, 928
Buzz Points, 527, 876
Buzz Referrals, 1618
Buzz Solutions, 1285
Buzzbil, 3118
Buzzerd.com, 2967
BuzzFeed, 125, 774, 819, 925, 1114, 1597, 1701
BuzzLogic, 1976
BuzzMedia, 759
Buzzparadise, 1518
Buzzsaw.com, 1255
Buzzstarter, 626, 1966
BVG India, 2303
BVRP, 2346
BW Landco LLC, 159
BW Manufacturing, 1609
BWGS, 1755
Bwise BV, 2819
BXM Holding Company, 1493
By Humankind, 321
ByAllAccounts, 523
Bybe, 1179
ByBox, 782, 2455
bydsign, 1757
Byecity.com, 3199
Byerly's, 847
Byggmax, 2376
BYJC, 2927
BYJU's, 1125
Byju's, 1393
Byliner, 209, 787
Bynder, 1005
BYNDL, 1065
Byndl, 1827
ByPay Information, 3053
Byram Healthcare, 781

Byram Holdings Inc., 573
Byrider, 96
Byrider Systems, 1493
Byte, 1477, 3145
Byte Cubed, 681
Byte Dance, 2681
Byte Foods, 173
ByteGain, 3
Bytegain, 1153
ByteGrid, 101
Bytelight, 758
ByteMobile, 163, 624, 645, 1852
BytePlay, 3088
Bytez, 10
byTourexcel, 2842

C

C And Co., 354
C MAC Microtechnology, 782
C&C Energia, 2036
C&D Technologies, 1089
C&J Energy Services, 819
C&K, 1163, 1755
C&M Corporation, 1963
C&V Portable, 2246
C&W Manufacturing and Sales, 1057
C-4 Analytics, 77, 364
C-Dilla, 2372
C-guys Inc, 2406
C-K Composites Co., 1749
C-Lecta, 2815
c-LEcta, 2518
C-Mine Crib, 2940
C-P Flexible Packaging, 734
C-Platform, 1340
C-Port, 263, 3128
C-Port Corporation, 317
C-Pro, 1771
C-sATS, 776
C-Side, 3039
C-Takt AB, 2709
C. Light Technologies, 623
C.B. Fleet Laboratories, 886
C.H.I. Overhead Doors, 170, 416
C.R.O.I., 2089
C.R.S/Vamic, 2089
C/R Energy Jade, 1577
C10 Connect, 3250
C1X, 149
C2 Micro, 2584
C2 Microsystems, 2557
C2 SmartLight Oy, 2957
C2 Therapeutics, 599, 1775
C2Call, 2815
C2cube, 2965
C2F, 731
C2FO, 488, 2250
C2RO, 2123
C3 Energy, 534, 1014, 1762
C3 IoT, 339
C3 Metrics, 1305
C3.ai, 1985
C3/CustomerContactChannels, 1746
C360, 296, 301
C360 Live, 1660
C4 Distro, 99
C7, 1679
C7 Data Centers, 1074, 1192
C8 Sciences, 1101
C9, 1014, 1187
CA Customer Alliance, 2815
Caarbon, 708, 1054, 1418
CaaScade, 1887
CaaStle, 1669
Caavo, 877, 925
Caavo Inc, 1099
Cabaletta Bio, 11

CABB, 3024
Cabela's, 435
Cabi, 1041
Cabify, 1534, 1998, 3096
Cabinet M, 845
CabinetM, 1104, 1759
Cable Management Ireland, 1929
Cable Sense, 2287
CableMatrix, 3221
CableOrganizer, 408
Cables Ben-Mor, 2089
Cabo Telecom, 45
Cabochon Aesthetics, 1495
Cabovisao, 2067
Cabrellis Pharmaceuticals, 772, 1578
Cacafly, 3029
Cacao De Colombia, 54
Cache IQ, 447
Cactus Commerce, 2089, 2114
Cadant, 1061
Cade (Dental Care), 3171
Cadena Bio, 748
Cadence, 1085, 1557, 1930
Cadence Aerospace, 167
Cadence Aerospace LLC, 159
Cadence Biomedical, 85
Cadence Capital Management, 1275
Cadence Pharmaceuticals, 240, 785, 1788, 2487
Cadent, 3128
Cadent Technologies, 1631
Cadent Therapeutics, 193
Cadforce, 309, 365, 1917
Cadia Networks, 1335
Cadient Group, 655
Cadiogen Sciences, 183
Cadmus, 681
Cadre, 125, 143, 820, 846, 1073, 1696
Cadre Technologies, 318
CadrioDx, 1414
Caelux Corporation, 1073
Caerphilly, 1340
CAES Development Company, 898
Caesars Entertainment, 141, 874, 2371
Cafe Communications, 1009
Cafe Costume, 3033
Cafe Enterprises, 1234
Cafe Express, 1552
Cafe Faro, 2114
Cafe Media, 938
Cafe Nero, 2354
Cafe Press, 2820
Cafe Rio, 786
Cafe X, 998
CafeMedia, 20
Cafepress, 1657
CafeX Communications, 485, 980
Caffe Bene, 2993
Caffeine, 125, 877
Cagenix, 999
CAI, 3250
CAI Capital Partners, 3249
CAIA Association, 3274
Caiman Energy II, 672
Cairn Ventures, 3268
Caisse de Depot et Placement du Quebec, 3249, 3252
Caithness Energy, 157
Cake, 79, 1074
Cake Financial, 234
Cake Marketing, 68
CakeHealth, 10
CakeStyle, 1618
Cal Pacific, 1997
Cala Health, 108, 1155
Calabrio, 1086, 1728, 3268
Caladrius Biosciences, 1271
CalAmp, 1239

Portfolio Companies Index

Calastone, 27, 3009
Calchan Holdings, 1297, 1631
CalciMedica, 1619, 1734
Caldan Therapeutics, 690
Caldwell & Gregory, 418
Calectro, 2593
Calednra, 3104
Caledonia Spirits, 789
Caledonian Building Systems Ltd., 2668
Caleel and Hayden, 1493
Calendly, 191, 985
Calendra, 3199
Calera, 928, 1073, 1561
Calero, 502
Calgary Scientific, 2043
Cali Bamboo, 934
Caliber Collision, 1113, 2199, 2211
Caliber Infosolutions, 1003, 1452
Calibra Medical, 785, 1013
Calibrium, 785
Calico Commerce, 1976
Calico Energy Services, 250, 1462
Calidora, 755
Calient Networks, 1795, 1976
Calient Technologies, 434, 1478
Calient Technologies Inc., 813
California Bank of Commerce, 508
California Check Cashing Stores, 843
California Comfort Corp., 911
California Cryobank, 1147
california Cryobank, 1349
California Cryobank Life Sciences, 828
California Gold Inc., 2117
California Linear Devices, 1920
California Manufacturing Enterprises, 874
California Medical Evaluators, 445
California Pizza Kitchen, 408, 843
California Pizza Kitchen Inc., 357, 406
California Power, 1968
California Safe Soil, 3246
California Trusframe, 2267
Caliopa, 2467, 3033
Caliper Life Sciences, 154, 154
Calista Technologies, 1125, 1976
Calistoga, 113, 785, 1098
Calistoga Pharma, 94
Calistoga Pharmaceuticals, 1449
Calithera, 1126, 1238
Calithera Biosciences, 58, 605, 1149, 1297, 1898
Calix, 218, 538, 773, 1008, 1076, 1728, 1795
Calix Networks, 1976
Calixa Therapeutics, 785
Call Connect, 538
Call My Name, 389
Call Rail, 285
Call-Net Enterprises Inc., 2067
Call2Action, 1699
Call9, 863, 1058
CallApp, 1761
Callaway Golf, 1898
Callbritannia, 2530
CallConnect Communications, 767
Callcredit Information Group, 889, 2371
Callery, 653
CallFire, 1255
CallGate, 627
Callia, 2131
Callidus, 1913
Callidus Capital Corporation, 2067
Callidus Software, 1379
Calligo, 1021
Calliper, 209
CallMiner, 983, 994, 1013, 1674, 1675
Callpod, 341, 341
CallRail, 390, 1606
CallRecall, 2517
Callserve, 2568

Callsign, 84
Callsign Inc, 27
Callstream, 3234
CallTime, 937
CallTower, 336
Calm, 1005
CalmImmune, 1522
CalmSea, 980
CalNet Technology Group, 381
Calo, 952
Calon Cardio, 2728
Calorics, 1464
Calosyn Pharma, 365, 1190
CalPeak Power, 416
CalPERS, 3252
Calpine Co., 2067
Calpine Corporation, 676
Calpulli Inc, 3169
Calsonic Kansei, 1086
Calstar, 1355
Calstar Products, 401, 1978
CalSTRS, 3252
Calsys, 2927
Caltex Resources, 1326, 1328
Calumet Energy, 1797
CalUniversity, 3206
Calupso Medical, 240
Calvert Education Serices, 510
Calvert Education Services, 1298
Calvert Healthcare Partners, 409
Calvet, 2874
Calvin Capital, 1086
Caly Networks, 3109
Calypso Medical Technologies, 1007, 1241, 1578, 2487
Calypso Technology, 1971
Calypte, 1917
Calypte Biomedical, 1788
Calypto, 972
Calypto Design Systems Inc., 1781
Calysta, 2205
Calytera, 2074
Calyx, 966, 1139, 1633
Calyx Therapeutics, 1414
Calyx Transportation Group, 2008
Cam-Trac Sag-Lac, 2089
Camber, 1300
Camber Creek, 3260
Cambium Learning Group, 1927, 1929
Cambium Networks, 1912
Cambly, 894, 1752, 3116
Cambria Security, 1042
Cambrian BioPharma, 803
Cambrian Genomics, 10, 1534, 1800, 1998
Cambrian Intelligence, 724
Cambridge, 3206
Cambridge Associates LLC, 3252
Cambridge Biotechnology, 2454
Cambridge Blockchain, 568, 1104
Cambridge Broadband, 2770
Cambridge Broadband Networks, 2334
Cambridge CMOS Sensors, 3019
Cambridge Cognition, 3234
Cambridge Display, 990
Cambridge Epigenetix, 894
Cambridge Heart, 1255
Cambridge International Inc., 989
Cambridge Major Laboratories, 167
Cambridge Medical & Rehabilitation Center, 3187
Cambridge Positioning Systems, 163, 2372, 2653
Cambridge Positioning Systems Limited, 3109
Cambridge Semiconductor, 3186
Cambridge Silicon Radio, 2378, 2653, 3109
Cambridge Solutions, 3251
Cambridge Sound Management, 832
Cambridge Wowo, 1511

CambridgeSoft, 655
Cambrios, 87, 186, 209, 1478
Cambrios Technology, 154, 983
Cambrooke Therapeutics, 809
Cambus Medical, 2347
Came Automatismes, 2644
CAMECA, 2556
Camelback Ventures Fellowship Program, 1315
Camelbak, 525
Camelot Education, 1576
Cameo, 680, 863, 1385, 1483
Cameo Communications, 2499
Camera IQ, 49, 1477, 1666
CameraIQ, 345
Camero, 3221
Cameron Health, 137, 1449, 1502, 1578, 1708, 1976, 2487, 2719, 2881
Cameron's Coffee & Distribution Co., 847
Camiant, 1335
Camile Products, 1337
Camillion Solutions, 2188
Camino Modular Systems, 1560
Camino Natural Resources, 1328
Camio, 752, 1105
Camiocam, 787
Camoplast Solideal, 2089, 2114
Camp, 1114
CAMP Systems, 889, 2689
CAMP Systems International, 364
Camp4, 11, 125
Campaign, 1154
Campaign Monitor, 1005, 2257
Campaignmonitor, 27
Campalyst, 2813
Campanda, 2466, 2842
Campania International, 1524
Campbell Grinder Company, 834
Campfire, 395
CampGroup, 376, 377
Camping World Holdings, 560
Campolo Middleton & McCormick LLP, 3257
Campsystems, 2688
Campus Book Rentals, 464
Campus Energy, 2056
Campus Explorer, 309, 1364, 1569
Campus Founders Fund, 1074
Campus Management, 1109
Campuslogic, 888
CampusTap, 638
Camras Vision, 738
Camsavon, 2880
CamSemi, 2287, 2653, 2665, 3095
CAMSIE Leasing, 1766
Camstar, 861
Camtainer, 2880
Camus Hydronics Ltd., 911
CaméRus, 3011
Can Art Aluminum Extrusion, 2196, 2264
Can Capial, 1504
CAN Capital, 1213, 1563
Can Capital, 27
Can-Do National Tape, 935, 1574
Can-Fite BioPharma, 1456, 3239
Canaan Partners, 3273
Canada Film Capital, 2210
Canada Metal (Pacific), 2156
Canada Metal Pacific, 330
Canada Moteurs Importations, 2114
Canada Pension Plan Investment Board, 3249
Canada Pooch Ltd., 357
Canadia Solar, 3053
Canadian Appliance Source, 2284
Canadian Bureau of Investigations & Adjustments, 2188
Canadian Business Growth Fund, 3249
Canadian Forestry Equipment, 2278
Canadian Helicopters, 2114

Portfolio Companies Index

Canadian National Stock Exchange, 2051
Canadian Northern Outfitters, 2161
Canal Guyane, 2888
Canal Partners, 3265
Canal Web, 2756
Canal+, 226, 1600
Canalyst, 2074, 2270
Canam, 110
Canamax Energy, 2022
Canapar, 2233
Canara, 518
Canary, 354, 1305, 1876
Canary Connect Inc., 1073
Canary Medical, 2221, 2229
CanAscen Group, 1866
CANBank, 2257
CanBas, 2961
CanBiocin, 2043
Canbriam Energy, 1957, 2036
Cancer Advances Inc., 432
Cancer Targeting Systems, 2969
CancerVax, 1976
Candela, 136, 1062
Candera, 189
Candex, 1227
Candid Co., 641
Candidate Labs, 321
Candis, 1125
Candlescience, 3250
Cando Rail Services, 2264
Candor Midstream, 672
Candy Club, 976
CandyClub, 562
Candyclub, 10
Candyking, 2317
CanEra Resources, 1577
Canes., 2556
CanGen, 463
CanGen Holdings, 1343
Canimix, 3161
CanImGuide, 2440
Canmec Group, 2089
Cann Trust Direct, 2088
Canna Zoning, 395
Cannabinit, 2836
Cannabis Big Data, 395, 2279
Cannabis Mercantile Trading Exchange, 2836
Cannabis Now, 1845
Cannabix Technologies, 2027
Cannactrl, 395
Cannalysis, 420
CannaPharmaRx, 1083
CannaRoyalty Corp., 1139
Cannasure, 966
CannaSys Inc., 1083
Canndescent, 99, 1208
Cannect Communications, 1839
Cannell Communications LP, 1624
Cannella Media, 1404
Cannella Response Television, 1929, 2019
Cannera Consulting, 2095
CannLabs, 1139
CannRx Technology Inc., 2836
CannTrust Holdings, 393
Canon Communications, 1929
Canopy, 512, 601, 689, 863, 975, 1184, 3250
Canopy at Belford Park, 1220
Canopy Biosciences, 270
Canopy Boulder, 1139
Canopy Labs, 1899, 2120
Canopy Servicing, 321
Canotic, 1501
Canpro Ingredients, 2277
Canstar Restorations, 2121
Cantaloip, 773
Cantaloupe Systems, 838
Cantex Pharmaceuticals, 622

Canto, 194
Canva, 720, 1184, 1666, 2511
Canvas, 380, 1381, 1388, 1575, 1816
Canvas Technology, 108
Canvaspop, 2070
Canvass, 2224
Canvia, 61
Canvs, 51, 1154, 1599
Canvs+, 1959
Canwest, 2067
Canyon Services Group, 2036
CAP (Children at Play) Toys, 1955
Cap Energie II, 3125
Cap Vert Finance, 2439
Cap Vert Finance SA, 416
cap-XX, 2868
Capa Finance, 2462
Capchase, 321
Cape, 1162
Cape Analytics, 1155
Cape By The Sea, 2114
Cape byron Power, 1520
Cape Clear, 2328
Cape Electrical Supply, 1767
Cape Energy, 2763
Cape Pine Investment Holdings, 838
Cape Productions, 2010
Capell Barnett Matalon & Schoenfeld, 3257
Capella, 278, 623, 766, 830
Capella Education, 1186
Capella Education Company, 1611
Capella Photonics, 1608
Capella Space, 108, 176, 1426
Caper, 798
Caperfly, 2958
Capevo, 3194
Capewell Aerial Systems, 165
Capewell Holdings, 1025
Capical, 2815
Capillary, 1346
Capillary Technologies, 1511
Capio, 246, 2371
Capio Exploration, 2036
Capitain D's, 1377
Capital, 803
Capital Bank Financial, 560
Capital Biochip Corporation, 2490
Capital Community Angels Investors, 3259
Capital Consulting, 2786
Capital Contractors Inc., 1404
Capital Drywall, 842
Capital Dynamics, 3252
Capital Economics, 2935
Capital Education Group, 1348
Capital Farm Credit, 15
Capital First Limited, 1957
Capital Nature, 3050
Capital Pawn, 406
Capital SLI Group, 1287
Capital Sports Holdings, 1377
Capital Sports Ventures, 1768
Capital Stream, 250, 1947
Capital Teaching Residency, 1315
Capital Tool & Design, 1507
Capital Vision Services, 2030
Capital-E, 3033
CapitaLand, 153
CapitalSource, 790, 1160, 1591
CapitalSouth Partners, 3251
Capitol Broadcasting Company, 3250
Caplinked, 10, 1959, 1966
Caplugs, 261
CapMAC, 1624
CapMAC Holdings, 1771
Capnamic Ventures, 485
Capnia, 1943, 2361
Cappella, 1241, 3037

Capria Ventures LLC, 3252
Capricoast, 27
Capricor, 350
Capricorn, 2940
Capricorn Cleantech Co-Investments, 3060
Caprion Proteomics, 470, 864
Capriza, 125, 457
CapRock Holdings, 20
Caprotec, 2629
Caps Visual Communications, 1883
Capsa Healthcare, 1115
Capsa Solutions, 1232
Capsalus, 708
Capsant, 2883
Capshare, 1074
Capsilon, 782
Capson, 1618
Capston Logistics, 1493
Capstone, 1049, 3128
Capstone Logistics, 858, 1270
Capstone Natural Resources II, 1129
Capstone Turbine, 1355
Capstone Turbine Corporation, 1561
Capsugel, 912
Capsule, 1045
Capsulution NanoScience AG, 3181
Captain Dash, 2890
Captain Ed's Lobster Trap, 1214
Captain Tortue Group, 1092
Captain Up, 3072
Captain401, 863
Captalis, 2743
Captek Softgel, 1473
Captini, 3099
Caption Data, 2958
Caption Health, 3
Captiv8, 1885
Captivate Network, 822
Captive Resources, 1108
Captor N.V., 2893
Captora, 224
Captricity, 37, 1058, 1698
Captronic Systems, 2460
Captura Software, 1731, 1947
Capture Education, 1556
Capture.io, 662
Capula, 2528, 2529
CapWay, 221
CapX Partners, 3255
Car 2 U, 3003
Car Dekho, 579
Car IQ, 229
Car King, 225, 2927
Car Quids, 3099
Car Wash Partners, 263
Car360, 1412
Cara Health, 1618
Cara Therapeutics, 179, 532, 1561, 2972
Cara Vita, 1007
Caralo Global, 1051
Caraustar, 1968
Caraustar Industries, 931
Caravan Health, 1929
Carbon, 305, 361, 812, 894, 1657
Carbon 38, 510, 1616
Carbon Black, 1, 37, 69, 938, 945, 1184, 1657
Carbon Cure, 2136
Carbon Design, 1184
Carbon Design Systems, 523
Carbon Health, 10, 1032, 1616
Carbon Media Group, 1242
Carbon Robotics, 1105, 1511
Carbon38, 901, 1998
Carbon60, 1157
Carbonated, 2130, 2131
CarbonCure, 2205
Carboncure, 2148

1251

Portfolio Companies Index

Carbonfire, 322
Carbonite, 564, 780, 1737, 1840
Carbonite Inc., 1203
Carbylan Biosurgery, 1014
Carbylan Therapeutics, 1943
Carchex, 192
Card, 121
Card Compliant, 1766
Card Establishment Services, 1973
Card Personalization Solutions, 670
Card.com, 133, 181, 1504, 1549, 1966
CarDash, 720
Cardax, 1007
Cardax Pharmaceuticals, 60, 1015, 1788
Cardconnect, 796
Cardeas Pharma, 209, 605, 2007
Cardenas, 1086
Cardero, 350
Cardeus Pharmaceuticals, 1241
CardFlick, 10
CardFlight, 724, 863, 1181
Cardia Access, 1874
Cardiac Dimensions, 137, 1014, 1464, 2174, 2961
Cardiac Insight, 2007
Cardiac Pathways, 1255
CardiaLen, 350
Cardialen, 270, 570, 1874
Cardiapex, 2316
CardiAQ, 1383
CardiAQ Valve, 350
CardiAQ Valve Technologies, 1930
Cardica, 561, 1762, 1976
Cardiff Software, 857
Cardikine, 2073
Cardinal Business Media Inc., 337
Cardinal Commerce, 835, 1480
Cardinal Gas Storage Partners, 676
Cardinal Medical Ltd, 3177
Cardinal Midstream III, 672
Cardinal Power Funding, 157
Cardinal Resources, 3246
Cardio 3 Biosciences, 3125
Cardio Dimensions, 150
Cardio Focus, 1976
Cardiocomm Solutions Inc, 2091
Cardiocore, 137
CardioCreate, 1786
CardioDX, 183, 1147, 1247
CardioDx, 582
Cardiodx, 2531
CardioFocus, 39, 317, 750, 1062, 1608, 1631, 1764
Cardiogram, 125
CardioInsight, 1051
CardioInsight Technologies Inc., 423
Cardiokine Biopharma, 73
CardioKinetix, 1116, 1411, 1898, 1917
Cardiokinetix, 1297
CardioKinetix Inc., 573
Cardiologs, 2842
Cardiome Pharma, 1395
CardioMEMS, 315, 749
Cardiomems, 137, 644
Cardiometrics, 85
CardioNet, 749, 1619
CardioNOW, 1976
CardioPhotonics, 1101
Cardiosolutions, 273
CardioSolv Ablation Technologies, 891
CardioSpectra, 517
Cardiovascular Systems, 1241
CardiOx, 1556
Cardiox, 642
Cardioxyl, 1383
Cardium, 532
Cardiva, 809

Cardiva Medical, 118, 908, 1502, 1771, 1976, 3183
Cardless, 1426
Cardlife, 3099
Cardlytics, 389, 1076, 1464, 1865
Cardmobil, 3022
Cardmunch, 10
CardonetCommtouch, 3239
Cardoz, 2739
Cardoz AB, 2807
Cardpool, 787, 863
CardScan, 523
CardSpring, 586
Cardspring, 27, 1254
CardStar, 50, 120, 1101, 1928
Carduus, 2530
Cardvalue, 3206
CardZee, 1683
Care, 1834
Care Concepts, 1839
Care Hospice, 1169
Care Hospice Inc., 159
Care Kinesis, 1386
Care Management Technologies, 476, 692
Care Services LLC, 1292
Care Thread, 1695
Care Wave, 875
Care Well Urgent Care, 545
Care.com, 561, 579, 1006, 1184, 1855, 2820, 2829
Care/of, 846
Care2, 1736
Care2.com, 381
Care4Data NV, 2797
CareAcademy, 221, 1554
CareAngel, 3251
Careanyware, 1152
CareCap, 1065
CareCentrix, 912, 1618, 1754, 1962
CareCloud, 56, 1009, 1346, 1798
CareCru, 2257
CareCycle Solutions, 988
Caredent, 1092
Caredox, 742
CareDx, 1008
Caredx, 1297
Careem, 91, 511
Career Choices, 1143, 2937
Career Education, 303
Career JSM, 2276
Career Now, 985
Career Point Infosystems, 585
CareerBuilder, 1406
CareerFoundry, 2832
Careerlist, 2122
Careerminds, 151
CareerStep, 747
CareerTu, 1142
Carefree, 444
CareFusion, 303
CareFx, 861
Carefx, 143, 1704
CareGain, 51, 993, 1313
Caregiver Inc., 551
Caregiver Services, 408, 1500
Carego, 2039
CareGuide, 2150, 2216
Careguide, 2122
CareHubs, 1618
CareIT, 999
Carekinesis, 1523
Careland International, 3084
Careline, 205
Carelulu, 10
Caremerge, 173, 812, 1005
CareMore Health, 435
Carena, 755

CareNet, 897
CareNexis, 512
CarePartners Plus, 269
CarePoint Health, 408
CarePoint Partners, 1964
CarePort, 234, 795
Careport Health, 316
CarePredict, 3251
Careray, 2927
CareSimply, 1618
CareSouth Health System, 409
CareSpot Express Healthcare, 1973
Carestack, 27
Carestream, 2201
Caresync, 907
Caretaker Medical, 1023
Careteam, 2215
CareWell Urgent Care, 476, 1846
CareWire, 1618
CareWise, 1399
CareWorx, 2216
CareX, 2772
Carex Health Brands, 1210
CareZone, 1363
Carezone, 430
Carfit, 252
Cargal, 2600
Cargo, 474, 608, 1011, 1550, 1589
Cargo Airport Services, 445, 1493
Cargo Airport Services USA, 973
Cargo Chief, 130
CargoGuard, 2815, 2923
Cargomatic, 1254, 1752, 1878, 1998
CargoSense, 1023, 1229
CargoTech, 1786
CargoX, 1511
CarHop, 92
Caribbean Restaurants, 425, 1360
Caribe, 1244
Caribeean Restaurants, 1507
Caribore Coffee, 153
Caribou Biosciences, 711, 1238
Caribou Wealth, 2122
CariHeal, 2316
Carillion, 952
Cariloop, 6
Caring Brands International, 899, 1115
Caring People, 467
Caring.com, 597, 1666, 1728
Caringo, 205, 1302
Caris Life Sciences, 1041
Carl Bro, 2879
Carl Data Solutions, 2027
Carl Zeiss Vision GmbH, 2703
Carlease, 1121
Carlile Bancshares, 1108, 1746
Carlipa Systems, 2846
carlisle Wide Plank Floors, 1044
Carloan 4U, 3095
Carlson Products, 1057
Carlton Corporate Finance, 2723
Carlyle Asia Partners III LP, 2088
Carmel Pharma, 2719
Carmel Ventures, 3109
Carmell Therapeutics, 296, 910, 1003, 1452
Carmen Systems, 2770, 2869
Carmera, 894, 1223
Carmichael Training Systems, 813
Carmody MacDonald, 3261
Carmot Therapeutics, 519
Carna Biosciences, 2961
Carnegie, 2376
Carnegie Fabrics, 371
Carnegie Mellon University, 3264
Carnegie Speech, 983, 1305
Carnegie Speech Company, 1003
Carnival Mobile, 320

Portfolio Companies Index

Carnot, 1522
Carolina Beverage Group LLP, 360
Carolina Skiff, 1526
Carolus Therapeutics, 209
Caroobi, 305
Carousel Capital, 1873
Carousell, 2681
CarPark, 2528, 2529
Carparts/ADN, 1561
Carpathia Hosting, 1727
CarPay, 121
Carpe, 1599
CarPrice, 89, 641
CarProof, 927
Carr Separations/Kendro Lab Products, 1107
Carre Blanc, 2956
Carrefour, 2605
Carrere Group, 2535
Carrick Therapeutics, 894
Carrier Access Corporation, 215
Carrier Energy Partners, 1577
Carrier IQ, 1247, 1478
Carriere Neigette, 2114
CarrierIQ, 457, 2978
Carroll Cuisine, 416
Carrosserie Pro 2010, 2114
Carrot, 221
Carrot Fertility, 708
Carrot Inc., 1073
Carrum Health, 1462, 1985
CARS, 1987
Carsabi, 586
Carsablanca, 2466
Carsala, 1101
Carsala Inc., 1093
CarServ, 1509
CARsgen Therapeutics, 1091
Carson, 3245
Carson Life, 567, 2002
CARSTAR, 1580
Carstar, 694
Carta, 1203, 1330, 1616, 1698, 1716, 1850, 2398, 3265
Carta Finana, 3194
Carta Healthcare, 1809
Carta Worldwide, 2161
Cartagenia, 3033
Cartasite, 277
Cartavi, 473, 732, 1364, 1462, 1483
CartCrunch, 2934
Cartegraph, 1410
Carter Haston JV, 1086
Carter's, 1021
Carter-Waters, 1210
Cartera Commerce, 530, 581, 1922
Cartes Networks, 291
Cartesis, 1418, 2340
Carthage Agricultural Company, 2321
Carthage Specialty Paperboard, 1424
CarThrottle, 3021
Cartica AI, 1836
Cartica Management LLC, 3252
Carticept Medical, 622
Cartier Resouces, 2114
Cartiere del Garda, 2635, 2874
CartiHeal, 2320
Cartiva, 94, 622, 1993
Carto, 27, 1610
Cartodb, 3214
Cartogram, 229, 1509
Cartonplast Group, 3145
CarTrade, 389
Cartrawler, 1005
Carvel, 1580
Carvoyant, 1737
CarWale, 3100
Carwoo, 304

Carwoo!, 2321
Carwow, 27, 2469, 3088
Cary Street Partners, 3250
Caryl Baker Visage, 2041
CAS Medical Systems, 1820
Casa, 527, 1114, 2530
Casa Madera, 334
Casa Systems, 1754
Casabella Holdings, 2021
Casabu, 2862
Casamba, 20
Casanov@, 2430
Casavant Brothers, 2114
Casavo, 2288
Cascade, 1608
Cascade Bancorp, 1113, 1127
Cascade Drilling LP, 668
Cascade Entertainment Group, 494
Cascade Pacific Pulp, 1968
Cascade Prodrug, 1384
Cascade Sensior Living, 1086
Cascade Windows, 96
Cascadia Windows & Doors, 2230
Casda Biomaterials, 223
Case Continuum, 1101
Case Logic, 1090
Case Status, 75, 1412
Case Text, 564
CaseCentral, 952, 1736
Casella, 2340
Casemaker, 1723
CaseNET, 1674
Casentric, 1051
Casero, 163
CaseStack, 304, 496, 1786
Casetext, 321, 1533, 1760
Cash Cycle Solutions, 266
Cash Management Solutions, 1343
Cash River, 3053
CashEdge, 2073
Cashie Commerce, 10, 1786
CashShield, 827
CashStar, 796, 1339
Casi, 988
Casimir Partners, 558
Casino Royal, 3222
Casino VR Poker, 310
Cask, 978
Casper, 545, 564, 1006, 1114, 1346, 1483, 1696
Caspida, 742, 1537
CAST, 2535
Cast, 2653, 2842
Cast & Crew, 20, 1685, 1929, 2019
Cast Futura, 3145
Cast Iron, 1913
CAST Software, 2039
Cast Steel Products, 2284
Cast.AI, 754
Cast21, 999
Castel Portfolio, 1086
Castell Oil Company, 1326
Castex Energy, 479
CastGrabber, 1003, 1444
Castify Networks, 2372
Castion Corp., 589
CastIron, 1798
Castle, 742
Castle Biosciences, 924, 1261, 1725
Castle Connolly, 852
Castle Networks, 263
Castle Pines Capital, 796
Castlebeck, 2814
Castlecare, 2786
Castlefield, 192
Castlerock, 1326
Castlerock Exploration, 1328
Castlewood Surgical, 3246

Castlight, 19
Castlight Health, 1898, 1918
Castro Cheese, 1404
CastStack, 810
Casual Living and Trigon Plastics, 165
Casugel, 2371
CAT Forsknings-og Teknologipark, 2642
Catabasis, 1126, 1631, 1764
Catabsis, 58
Catacel, 1051
Catalant, 812, 820
Catalent, 73
Catalia Health, 23, 802, 945
Catalina, 912, 927
Catalist, 1588
Catalliances, 2457
Catalog, 108, 398
Catalog DNA, 222
Catalog Technologies, 1423
Catalyst, 527, 796
Catalyst Biosciences, 922, 1126, 1546, 1700
Catalyst Clinical Research, 1349
Catalyst Law Group, 3265
Catalyst Oncology, 1917
Catalyst Orthosience, 1023
Catalyte, 1609
Catalytic, 308, 773, 1121, 1483
Catalytic Solutions, 1324, 1478
Catalyze.io, 473
Catamaran, 1750, 1795
Catamaran Communications, 1976
Catapult, 1326
Catapult Growth, 3265
Catapult Health, 921
Catapult Learning, 416, 1045
Catapult Services, 1328
CatapultX, 1509
Catari, 3039
Catastrophe Solutions International, 531
Catavolt, 497, 718, 1831
Catawiki, 27, 3047
Catch, 704, 882, 1658, 1895
Catchafire, 1058, 1555
CatchApp, 2912
Catchpoint Systems, 238
Catellus, 1837
Catena Networks, 255, 1257
Caterna, 2815
Caterplus, 3234
Cath Kidston, 1778
Cathay Capital NA LLC, 3249
Cathay Industrial Biotech, 2806
Cathbuddy, 623
Catherines, 1021
Catheter Connections, 139, 1074, 1886
Catheter Innovations, 1708
Catheter Robotics, 1375
CathRx, 2609
CathWorks, 2221
CathWorks Ltd., 272
Catlant, 938
Catlight Health, 1361
Catlin, 458, 576
Catlin Group Limited, 407
Catlin Westgen Group, 449
Cato Networks, 48, 182, 877
Cattle Care, 1142
Cattlog, 999
Cattron Group, 1560
Causera, 10
Causes, 116, 1976
Cava, 1768
Cavale Steel Company, 2940
Cavalia, 2089
Cavalier Fire Protection LLC, 1565
Cavalier Telephone, 747, 1157
Cavalry Investments, 1971

1253

Portfolio Companies Index

Cavario, 632
Cavendish Kinetics, 1511, 1781
Caveon, 1917
Cavidi Tech AB, 2719, 2881
Cavion, 1128, 1350
Cavium Networks, 614, 1543
Cawnetworks, 936
CAXA Technology, 2841
Cayenna Medical, 1728
Cayenne Medical, 750, 1190
Caymas Systems, 801
Caymas Systemts, 1976
Cazena, 125
CB News, 2598
CB Richard Ellis Services, 786
Cbana Labs, 979
cbanc Network, 56
Cbazaar, 1017, 3010
CBD Tech Ltd, 2576
Cbeyond, 56, 1160
Cbeyond Communications, 1908
Cbeyond Inc., 227
CBI (ARTE), 2600
CBI Health Group, 2199, 2211, 2284
Cbi Health Group, 2076
CBIT, 3194
CBIZ, 3251
CBR, 2596
CBRE Group, 303
CBRE Group Inc., 1905
CBS Payroll Services, 1772
CBT Technologies, 165
CBT Technology, 1560
CBx, 2141
Cc:Betty, 1658
CCA Floors & Interiors, 699
CCAM Biotherapeutics, 1383
CCapture, 2883
CCBN, 35
CCC, 1021
CCC Information Services, 61, 1113, 1837
CCD Holdings, 1278
CCELP Holding, 554
CCID, 2927
CCIG, 3265
cClearly, 1566
CCM Benchmark, 2842
CCM Hockey, 2056
CCM Pharma Sdn Bhd, 3155
CCMP Capital Advisors, 3245
Ccmx, 2712
Ccobox, 23
CCPI Holdings, 1493
CCS, 1965, 2029, 2073
CCS Medical, 1090
CCTM, 3185
CD Diagnostics Inc., 272
CD Dignostics, 1942
CD Networks, 2848
CD Park, 2848
CDC, 2367
CDG, 827, 2570
CDI Computer Dealers, 2083
CDIM, 2927
CDIm FMI, 65
CDM MAX LLC, 416
CDM Resource Management, 1577
CDNow, 881
CDP, 2724
CDS, 936
CDS Outsourcing, 3250
CDW, 1160, 1498
CDX, 1139
CE LA VI, 1092
CE Rental, 445
CE2 Carbon Capital, 676
Ceapro, 2043

Cebix, 1014, 1700, 1820, 2807
Cecilware, 740
CEDA, 2199
Cedar Capital, 796, 1140
Cedar Creek, 458
Cedar Electronics, 408
Cedar Gate Technologies, 889
Cedar Point Communications, 457, 759, 3128
CedarCrestone, 843, 2353
CedarPoint Communications, 186
Cedarpoint Investments, 3249
CeDe Group, 2746
Cedexis, 58
Cedip Infared Systems, 2375
Cedrepa, 2611
CEEK VR, 221
CeeQTM, 3144
CEFIC, 3169
Cegeka, 2940
Cegelec Holdings, 2578
CEGX, 1302, 1657
CEI Coastal Ventures III, 1164
Ceipal, 2187
CEL LEP, 931
CEL Polska, 528
CEL Procurement, 2935
Cel.ly, 1467
CelAccess, 447
Celarix, 205, 1008
Celaton, 2541
Celator Pharma, 1271
Celator Pharmaceuticals, 622, 1510, 1820, 1830, 1900
Celco, 3194
Celco Controls, 934
Celcore, 263
Celcuity, 344
Celebrate, 10
CelebrateExpress.com, 154
Celebration Restaurant Group, 1344
Celebrity Inc., 1090
Celect, 799
Celectis, 2346
Celemi, 2879
Celeno, 485
Celentail.ai, 998
Celequest, 1125
Celera, 748
Celerica, 3128
Celerion, 224, 1631
Celerion Holdings, 1271
Celeris AG, 2418
Celeritek, 1762
Celerity Pharmaceuticals, 1962
Celero Accelerated Commerce, 1140
Celery, 310
Celestial Semiconductor, 2499, 2588
Celestial Tiger Entertainment, 1602
Celestica, 2201
Celestite, 96
Celestry, 2844
Celetronix, 843
Celevity, 321
Celexion, 748
Celgen Biopharmaceutical Co., 2584
Celi APS, 3040
Celiant, 1304
Celight & Blade fusion, 3150
Celilo Group Media, 85
Celions, 27
Cell Based Delivery, 2739
Cell Biologics, 1091
Cell Biosciences, 3006
Cell Co., 57
Cell Design Labs, 1238
Cell Medica, 2849
Cell Microsystems, 738

Cell Networks, 2760
Cell Pathways, 1788
Cell Ventures, 2760
CellAccess, 263
Celladon, 1268, 1439, 1918
CellAegis, 350
Cellaegis Devices, 2086
Cellatope, 1510
CellBazaar, 860
CellCentric, 2958, 2969
Cellcon, 2657
Cellectar, 2002
Cellectar Biosciences, 1923
Cellective Therapeutics, 1013, 1098
Cellectricom AB, 2709
Cellectricon, 2719
CellEra, 2466
Cellera, 2891
CellerateRX, 427
Celleration, 1302, 1481, 1849, 1923
Celletra, 2761, 3128
Cellfacts, 2958
CellFE, 664
Cellfire, 1203, 1684, 1750, 1928, 1976
Cellfor, 365
CellGate, 1976
Cellicon, 317
Cellink, 1771
Cellit, 132
Cellity, 2466
CellMax Life, 176
Cellnovo, 2739, 3011
Cello Lighting, 229
Cellomics, 215
Cellotape, 956
CellPathways, 1399
CellRox, 3041
Cellrox, 3079
Cellscape, 1976
CellScope, 493
CellSeed, 2961
Celltick, 1352
Celltick Software Technologies, 2901
CellTrak, 1242
Celltrion Healthcare, 1376
Celltrix, 3006
Cellufuel, 2148
Cellular Line, 1092
Cellular Research, 11
CellularOne, 1157
Cellulosic Sugar Producers Co-Operative, 2054
Celluman, 1003
Cellwand Communications, 2165
Cellwize, 3212
Cellworks, 176
Celly, 1384
CellzDirect, 861, 990, 1704
Cellzdirect, 1903
Cellzone, 1777
Celo, 125, 2272
Celon Pharma, 1456
Celoxia, 2340
Celoxica, 2568
Celoxica Holdings, 3061
Celsense, 1102, 1452
Celsia Technologies, 994
Celsion Corp., 949
Celsius, 1194
Celsius Therapeutics, 894
Celsus Therapeutics, 1271
Celsys, 597
Celtaxsys, 622, 2174
Celtel, 263
Celtic House Venture Partners, 3249
Celtic Inns, 2668
Celtic Manor, 2276
Celtra, 713, 1701

Portfolio Companies Index

Celtra Technologies, 853
Celtrade, 2039
Celtrak Ltd, 2696
Celtro, 1561, 2571
Celtro Inc., 2766
Celtronix, 3162
Celtx, 2063, 2161
Celularity, 1646
Celunol, 1561
Celxpert Energy Corp., 3209
CEMA, 51
CEME, 1021
CEME Group, 2705
Cemengal, 3145
Cementos Balboa, 1086
Cempra, 73, 1510
Cempra Pharmaceuticals, 1013
Cems, 2427
Cencom Cable, 1212
Cendura, 564
Cendyn, 28
Cenega N.V., 2420
CeNeRx, 1414
CeNeS, 2454
Cengage, 2029
Cengage Learning, 136, 2243
Censia, 575
Censis, 1576
Census, 2122
Censys, 877, 894
Cent 17 CLO, 1493
Centage, 1871
Centagenetix, 317
Centah, 2103
Centara Hotels and Resorts, 1143, 2937
Centaur Communications, 1929
Centauri Health Solutions, 1631, 1764
Centennial Communications, 62, 1684
Centennial Healthcare Corporation, 1152
Centennial Resource Development LLC, 1328
Centennial Towers, 1160
Center For Discover & Adolescent Change, 874
Center for Financial Services Innovation, 1374
Center for Global Development, 1374
Center for Research and Teaching in Economics, 1374
Center for Vein Restoration, 547
Center on Democracy, 1374
Center Parcs, 280, 2843
Center Rock, 815
Center Square Investment Management, 1151
Center to Support Excellence in Teaching, 1315
CenterBeam, 759
Centerbeam, 549, 2463
Centerline Communications, 1344
Centerplate Inc., 1372
Centerpoint, 36
CenterPoint Ventures, 990
CenterPointe Behavioral Health, 921
CenterPost, 215
Centerre Healthcare, 1578
CenterRun, 1287
Centerrun, 564
CenterRun Software, 1657
CenterStone Technologies, 318, 554
Centessa, 1934
Centiba, 999
Centice, 1348, 3059
Centillium, 1091
Centillium Communications, 1898, 2499
Centor Software, 957
Centra, 1335
Centra Industries, 929
Centra Software, 523
Central Can Company, 620
Central Desktop, 928
Central Logic, 1205

Central Pacific Bank, 1740
Central Parking Services, 3202
Central Pattana, 1143, 2937
Central Power, 1582
Central Security Group, 1754
Central States Bus Sales, 402, 1057
Central Technology Services, 2227
Centrale Partners, 2535
Centrality Communications, 759, 908
CentralReach, 1005
Centrax, 77
Centre De Peinture L.B.G., 2114
Centre De Tri, 2089
Centre Des Congres De Sept-Œles, 2089
Centre Jardin Lac Pelletier, 2114
Centre Medical Le Mesnil, 2089
Centre Pacific Holdings LLC, 449
Centri, 1101
Centri Technology, 85
Centric, 2353
Centric Software, 313, 799, 1178, 1361
Centrify, 27, 621, 1028, 1187, 1674
CentriLogic, 1145
Centripetal, 1422
Centrix, 2965
Centrl, 568, 1499
Centro, 796
Centro Médico Teknon, 2488
Centron, 403
Centrotec, 3060
Centrue Financial Corporation, 407
Centrul Medical Unirea, 2301
Centrum Communic, 2499
Centurion Capital Group, 1151
Centurion Service Group, 4
Century 21. CRL, 874
Century Equity Partners, 3254
Century Fire Protection, 854
Century Graphics Corporation, 1507
Century Maintenance Supply, 786
Century Midstream, 741
Century Payments, 205
Century Resources, 1609
Century Wheel @ Rim, 1921
CENX, 561, 1928, 2187
Cenx, 597, 938
Cenzic, 58, 1042, 1247
Ceon Corporation, 255
Ceon Corporation/Convergys Corporation, 1287
Cephalon, 1456
Cepheid, 58, 388
Cepstral, 1003
Ceptaris, 1388
Ceptaris Therapeutics, 137
Ception Therapeutics, 137
Cequel Communications, 1508
Cequence Energy, 2036
Cequence Security, 1666
Cequent Pharmaceuticals, 1414
Cequint, 42, 554
CERAC, 719
Ceradis, 2397
Ceradyne, 1287
Ceragon Networks, 2761, 3128
Cerahelix, 1164, 1165
Ceramem, 1161
Ceramic/Apolo Group, 2414
Cerapedics, 1325, 1383
Ceraver Osteal, 2616
Cerba European Lab, 3017
Cerberian, 1679
Cerebra, 1408
Cerebral Assessment Systems, 705
Cerebras Systems, 648
Cerebri, 1158
Cerebro Tech Medical Systems, 953
Cerebrotech, 1261

Cerecor, 1268
Ceregene Inc., 374
Cerego, 327
Cerelia, 2842
Cerenicimo, 2303
Cerenis Therapeutics, 94, 1383, 2807, 3187
Cerensis Therapeutics, 652
Cerent, 1795, 1976
CEREP II Mezzanine Loan Partners LP, 2088
Ceres, 1395, 1957, 1976
Ceres Power, 2883
CereScan, 736
CeresImaging, 1005
Cereve, 1788
Cerexa, 785, 1251, 1414
Cergaon Networks Ltd, 3149
Ceridian, 1818, 1973, 2029
Ceridian Corp, 303
CeriFi, 1109
Cerillion, 2786
Cerillion Technologies, 2653
Cerimon Pharmaceuticals, 2998
Cerion, 325
Cerion Energy, 705
Cerity Partners, 1127
Cernostics, 1452
Ceroc, 881
Ceros, 510, 876, 1675, 1741
Certain Lending, 1935
Certara, 172, 1912
Certeon, 1674
Certes Networks, 1321
Certica, 352
Certicom, 1942
Certifacame.com, 2374
Certification Connect, 1000
Certificial, 512
Certified Recycling, 2206
Certified Safety, 920
Certified Security Solutions, 1459
CertifiedMail, 957
CertifiGroup, 3250
Certify, 1165
Certify Inc., 440
CertiPath, 554
Certiport, 1727
Certisign, 1009
CertiVox, 3009, 3023
Certn, 2204, 2276
Certona, 696
Certona Corp., 22
Certpoint, 957
Cerulean, 1155
Cerulean Pharma, 263, 1128, 1464
Cerulean Technology, 523
Cerus, 538
Cerus Endovascular, 1048
Cerved, 223
Cervelo Pharmaceuticals, 2487
CervilLenz, 1051
Cervo-Polygaz, 2089
Cerylid, 2966
Ceryx, 2104
CESA, 2528, 2529
Cesa, 2953
Cesar, 2542
Cesura, 1561
CET, 2668
Cetaccean Networks, 317
Cetacean Networks, 457
Cetera Financial Group, 1127
Ceterix, 11
Ceterix Orthopaedics, 1930
Cetero Research, 1090
Ceterus, 881
Cethar Vessels, 2481
Cetrea, 3194

Portfolio Companies Index

Cetrifuge Systems, 1348
CEVA Logistics, 141, 2371
CEVA Santé Animale, 2854
Cevec, 2629
CEYX Technologies, 1667
CF Stinson, 364
CFares, 810
CFEngine, 2722
CFGI, 751
CFM Religion Publishing Group, 1984
CFMG, 931
CFN, 2083
CFP Flexible Packaging, 2528, 2529, 2843
CFRC Water and Energy Solutions Inc., 1051
CFS Brands, 1049
CGCG, 908
Cgen, 1537
Cgen Diital Media Company Limited, 3053
CGI, 532, 748
CGI Pharmaceuticals, 1128, 1578, 1908
CGL Manufacturing Inc., 2160
Cgtrader, 1009
CGTrader.Om, 3040
Ch Group Limited Partnership, 2114
CH4 Energy, 1326, 1328
Ch4e, 2883
Ch5 Finland Oy, 2864
Cha Cha, 928
CHA Consulting, 1145, 1169
Chabert-Duval, 2414
ChaCha, 1561, 1908
Chacha, 265
Chai Labs, 1219
Chain, 10, 488, 1073, 1597
Chain Bureau, 2257
Chainalysis, 1716
CHAINalytics, 838
Chainsaw, 2133
Chair-Man Mills, 2133
Chairish, 775, 1359
Chairman Mom, 752
Chakshu Research, 1976
Chalk, 2178
Chalkable, 708
Chalkfly, 1739
ChalkTalk, 754
Challenge Post, 1588
Chamate, 1361, 2841
Chamberlain Gard, 467
Chamberlin Edmonds & Associates, 1852
Chameleon, 398
Chameleon Systems, 1976
Chamelic, 2883
Chamilia, 337
Champagne Gardet, 2611
Champion, 988
Champion Manufacturing, 1115
Champion Medical Technologies, 1050
Champion Petfoods LP, 2049
Champion Technologies Inc., 463
Champion Windows, 1754
Champions Oncolody, 1271
Champions Oncology, 238
Champlin Wind, 335
Champtek, 2427
Chancenwerk, 2522
Chancery Software, 2188
Chandler Industries, 1424
Chandler Signs, 406
Chandler/May, 167
Chang Hwa Bank, 2624
Changba, 299
Change Collective, 1322
Change Dynamix, 86
Change Healthcare, 927, 1241, 1332, 1618
Change Heroes, 2225
Change Research, 937

Change.org, 1363, 1374, 1555
ChangeCoin, 10
ChangePoint, 2051
Changetip, 1998
Changing Paradigms, 1955
ChangingWorlds, 3182
Chango, 527, 2176
Channel Advisor, 58
Channel Breeze, 299
Channel Control Marchants, 1086
Channel Insight, 1561
Channel Intelligence, 213
Channel IQ, 631
Channel Medsystems, 137, 1149
Channel Technologies Group, 832
Channel Technology, 35
Channel Wind, 3248
ChannelAdvisor, 1712, 3250
ChannelAdvisor Corporation, 1084
ChannelEyes, 320, 980
ChannelMeter, 10
ChanneLogics, 1711
ChannelSoft Holdings, 2588, 3084
Chantemor, 2592
ChanTest, 119, 1772
Chaoli, 827
Chaologix, 1987
Chaordix, 2283
CHAOSSEARCH, 1
ChaosSearch, 833
Chaoticom, 1084
Chaparral Energy, 435
Chaparral Network Storage, 189, 213
ChapDrive, 3004
Character Lab, 1315
Charcoal Group, 2165
Charcuterie L. Fortin Ltee, 2089
Chargbee, 1005
Charge Master, 305
Charge Point, 305, 1344
Chargeback, 1074, 1317
Chargebee, 27
ChargeItSpot, 1581
ChargePoint, 534, 1161, 1561, 1947
Chargepoint, 325
ChargePoint Inc., 159
Charger Oil & Gas, 157
Chargespot, 2122
Chargifi, 1009
Chariot, 474
Chariot Acquisition LLC, 159
Chariots Elevateurs Du Quebec, 2089
Charismathics, 2985
Charitweet, 1593
Charitygift, 1857
CharityStars, 2288
Charles Chocolates, 1658
Charles River, 212
Charles Voegele, 2913
Charleston Newspaper, 20
CharlestonPharma, 1925
Charli, 2283
CharlieHR, 3099
Charlotte Research Institute, 3250
Charlotte Russe Holdings Inc., 62
Charlotte Tilbury, 3088
Charlotte Tillbury, 1657
Charlotte's Web Holdings, 393
Charm Engineering, 2798
Charming Charlie, 905
Charrington Fuels, 2976
Chart Industries, 197
Chart.io, 209, 564
ChartBeat, 1153
Chartbeat, 610, 787, 1114, 1359, 1702
ChartBoost, 1692
Chartboost, 730, 1657, 1840, 2009

Chartcube, 1666
Charter Board Partners, 1315
Charter Brokerage, 172
Charter Communications, 560, 1948
Charter Life Sciences, 3273
Charter NEX Films, 1113, 1174
Chartio, 361, 863
Chartone, 1917
ChartSpan, 1412
Chartwell Healthcare, 112
ChartWise Medical Systems, 497, 718
Chase Pharmaceuticals, 326
Chasella Capital Partners, 3257
Chassis Breaks International, 1089
Chat Sports, 802
Chatalytic, 1323
ChatBlazer, 1683
ChatBook, 1610
Chatbooks, 1074
Chatdesk, 729, 1760
Chateau Bonne Entente, 2114
Chateau M.T., 2114
Chatfish, 1711
Chatfuel, 10
ChatGrid, 568
Chatgrid, 680
Chatham Technologies, 755, 1075
Chatitive, 1162
Chatkit, 2024, 2176
Chatlink, 2131
Chatmeter, 1499
Chatous, 2010
ChatQuery, 1509
Chatter, 2094, 2181
Chatter Research, 2024, 2107
Chatters, 2200, 2201
Chattr, 754
Chaumet, 1021
Chauvet, 547
CHC, 3185
CHC Helicopter Corporation, 741
CHC Solutions, 4
Che Behavioral Health Services, 96
Che101, 1125
Cheap Data Communications, 3040
Check, 780, 1257
Check Point, 1898
Check Point HR, 655
Check Point Software Technologies LTD., 775
Check24, 27
CheckAction, 1412
Checkbook, 310, 650
Checkers Drive-In Restaurants Inc., 1654, 1972
CheckiO, 1914
Checkmark, 1005
Checkmarx, 3231
CheckMobile, 2923
Checkpoint, 2814
CheckPoint HR, 2188
CheckPoint Pumps & Systems, 60
Checkpoint Surgical, 733, 1051, 1286
CheckR, 27
Checkr, 894, 1006, 2011
Checks and Balances Bookkeeping, 3257
Cheddar, 520, 570, 1125
Cheddar Up, 1074
Cheddar's Restaurants, 331
Cheddars, 1361
Cheese, 121
Cheetah, 648
Cheetah Digital, 1912
Cheetah Medical, 178
Cheetah Medical Holdings, 2972
Cheetah Technology, 752
Cheezburger, 209, 1701
Chef, 238, 488, 978, 1235
Chef Code Can, 610, 1629

Portfolio Companies Index

Chef'n, 480
Chef's Cut Real Jerky, 502
Chef's Plate, 669
ChefHero, 2130
Chefit, 2272
Chefsfeed, 177
Chegg, 582, 752, 773, 808, 990, 1235, 1449
Chelford Group PLC, 2723
Chelsea, 851
Chelsey Henry, 85
Chelsio Communications, 186, 950, 2965
Chemaid Laboratories, 1972
Chemco, 2114
ChemConnect, 990, 1255
ChemDAQ, 1452
Chemdex, 240
ChemDry, 225
Chemical Computing Group, 97
Chemical Express, 2976
Chemical Manufacturing and Refining, 2976
Chemical Week, 1929
Chemist Direct, 2437
ChemoCentryx, 2807
Chemogen, 440, 1165
ChemQuest chemicals, 653
Chemrec AB, 1908
Chemseco, 467
Chemson, 2878
Chemtura, 1138
Chengwei Capital, 1762
Cheniere, 280
Chenming Mold Industrial Corporation, 2594
Cheq, 238
Cheq Fm, 2089
Chequed.com, 1526
Chereau, 2842
Cheribundi, 434, 669
Cherin Law Offices, 3264
Chernin Group, 1498
Cherokee Partners, 157
Cherre, 1281
Cherry Bekaert LLP, 3251
Cherry Labs, 895
Cherry Road Technologies, 226
Cherrypick, 345
Cherwell, 1005
Cherwell Software, 1086
Chesapeake Energy, 1848
Chestnut Medical, 1775
Chevron Phillips, 2681
Chewse, 10, 779
Chewy.com, 872, 1944
CHF Solutions, 178, 2719, 2881
CHG Healthcare, 1495
CHG Healthcare Services, 160, 785, 1113
CHI, 790
CHI Overhead Doors, 1086, 1145
Chia, 125
Chiarezza, 2512
Chiaro Networks, 1561, 2646, 3109
Chiasma, 154, 1268, 3235
Chic by Choice, 3039
Chicago Deferred Exchange Company, 531, 1473
Chicago Miniature Lighting, 1858
Chicago Pacific Founders, 3254
Chicago Ventures, 3255
ChicagoLand Commissary, 943
Chicagoland Smile Group, 1670
Chicisimo, 3214
Chickapea Pasta, 2093
Chicken Kingdom, 70
Chicken Salad Chick, 337
Chicory, 1752
Chief, 756
Chief Executive Group, 868
Chieftain Sand and Proppant, 676, 1156
Child Development Schools, 834

Children & Teen Dental Group, 1270
Children's Cable Network, 1839
Children's Dental Health Associates, 611
Children's Discovery Center, 1255
Chill, 10
Chill Factor, 2530
Chimani, 1165
Chime, 182, 553, 564, 763, 944, 1023
Chime Bank, 1203
Chime Banking, 48
Chime Entertainment LLC, 508
Chimei Innolux, 897
Chimera Bioengineering, 130, 1055
Chimerix, 73, 94, 389, 1297, 1414, 1619, 2969, 3250
Chimerix Inc., 785
Chimeros, 794
China Agritech, 416
China Auto Rental, 1957
China Biologic Products, 1957
China Biologic Products Inc., 977
China Broad Media Corp, 3084
China Cablecom, 1029
China CYTS Tours Holding Co Ltd., 2491
China Digital TV Holding Co., 3084
China Dredging, 2584
China Finance Online, 2841
China Fire & Security Group, 223
China Fishery Group, 416
China Genetics Holdings, 374
China GrenTech Holdings Limited, 3053
China Homerun, 2969
China Int'l Capital Corp. Ltd., 1086
China Kidswant, 1957
China Materialia, 812
China Medicine, 1376
China Merchants Bank, 2585
China Merchants Bank Co. Ltd, 2586
China Merchants Plaza (Shanghai) Property C, 2586
China Merchants Securities Co. Ltd., 2585
China Motion Telecom International ltd, 2588
China Netcom, 2605
China Outfitters Holdings, 1086
China Rapid Finance, 1504
China Recycling Energy Group, 416
China Resources Cement Holdings Limited, 2394
China Search, 2927
China Senior Care, 1768
China SpeedNet, 2927
China Stem Cell, 1091
China Sunergy, 3185
China Synthetic Mica Technology, 3053
China Talent Group, 827
China Veg, 2872
China Wireless, 3053
Chinada, 3118
ChinaEdu, 263, 2841
ChinaInvent, 2927
Chinalliances, 2989
Chinatron Group Holdings, 163
Chinaway, 3206
Chinook Book, 1384
Chinook Energy, 2036
Chinook Therapeutics, 144
Chiome Bioscience, 2997
Chip and Pepper, 2245
Chip Express Corporation, 1255
Chip Hope Co., 3209
Chip X Corp (Chip Express), 1287
Chip-Man Technologies, 2442
Chipbond, 2427
ChipCare, 2178
Chipcon, 414, 2745
Chipidea, 2708
Chipita, 2775
Chipmore, 2427

Chipper, 10
Chips & Media, 1091, 2824
Chipsbank, 1009, 2927
ChipSensors, 2909
ChipX, 1908
Chiracon GmbH, 3181
Chirotouch, 1964
Chirpify, 1626, 1947
Chirpme, 304
Chisel, 1918
Chitter, 2122
Chloe & Isabel, 720
Chloe + Isabel, 1534, 1701
Chlorogen, 1536
Chlorophylle, 2089
CHMack, 1514
Chmerix Inc., 183
Chobani, 1837
Chobo Labs, 2009
Chockstone, 1917
Chocolat Jean-Talon, 2089
Choice, 1720
Choice Brands Adhesives, 1210
Choice Pet, 450
Cholestech, 1788
Cholestech Corp., 950
Chomp, 440
Chongqing Broadband, 2927
Chongqing New Standard, 2927
Chooch AI, 1616
Choose Energy, 1324
Choosy, 763
Chooze, 1810
Choozle, 863
Chopt, 1092
Chordiant Software, 1731
Choreo, 2051
Choridiant Software, 759
Chorum Technologies, 693, 1561
Chorus, 1537, 1716, 1885
Chorus Fitness, 779
Chorus.ai, 2126
Chosen, 3072
Chosen Security, 1
Choupettes, 3033
Chow Town, 365
Chowbotics, 779
Chowly, 1892
Chowly Inc., 1159
ChowNow, 309, 400, 429, 625, 1059, 1103, 1890
Chownow, 2640
Christ, 2303
Christiansopigens Sild, 3194
Christmas Tradition, 2088
Chroma Therapeutics, 928, 2998
Chromaflo Technologies, 111, 172
Chromalox, 435
ChromaTan, 296, 301
Chromatan, 1120
Chromatic Research, 1255, 1337
Chromatik, 231, 1103, 1491
Chromatin, 322, 979, 1442, 1923
Chromatis Networks, 2901
Chrome River, 733
Chromeriver, 162
Chromis Fiberoptics, 845, 1305, 1588
Chromium Graphics Inc., 874
ChromoTek, 2815
Chronic Health Metrics, 1452
Chronix Biomedical, 1474
Chrono, 11, 812
Chrono Therapeutics, 1238
Chrono.gg, 285
Chrono24, 1005
Chronocam, 2288
Chronogen, 2188
Chronometriq, 342

Portfolio Companies Index

Chronomics, 2398
Chronos Life Group, 1085
Chronos/Checkforte, 2617
Chrysalis, 263, 1257, 2051, 2073
Chrysalis Ventures, 3255, 3259
Chrysalix, 2028, 2483
Chrysalix Venture Capital, 990
Chrysler Holdings, 1733
CHS Capital LLC, 3255
CHT Group, 77
Chubb, 475
Chubb Insurance Group, 3250
Chubbies, 1114, 1566
Chukong Technologies, 827, 1340, 1511
Chumby, 1178, 1359
Chumby Industries, 1042
Chung's, 973
Chunyu, 299
Church Street Health Management, 153
Church's Chicken, 153, 790
Churchill Financial Group, 1372
Churchill Pharma, 1271
Churnzero, 881
Chushou TV, 827
Chute, 779, 787, 1898
ChyronHego, 1912
CI Medical Technologies, 97
Cianna Medical, 667
Ciao, 3223
Ciao Bella, 1668
Ciband, 3035
CIBC, 3265
CIBC Innovation Banking, 3249
Cibiem, 1631, 1764, 1814
Cibiem Inc., 272
CiBo, 748
CIBT, 20, 1085
CIBT Global, 197
CIC Capital Canada, 3249
CIC Capital Ventures, 3249
CIC Minerals, 479
CicekSepeti, 2828
Ciceroos, 2663, 3043
Ciclon Semiconductor, 1918
Cidade, 956
Cidara, 11
Cidara Therapeutics, 73, 785, 1522
CiDi, 222
Cido, 1772
CiDRA, 215, 1915
Cidra, 1608
Cielo, 28
Cielo24, 724
Ciena, 263, 1125, 1561, 1723, 3128
Ciespace, 154, 194
Ciespace Corporation, 1003
Cif Metal Ltd, 2089
CIFC, 458
CIG Logistics, 676
Cigital, 1140
Cignex, 2484
Cignifi, 1374
CigniTens, 3128
Cii Technology, 3250
Ciitizen, 125
Cima Nanotech, 2964
CIMB Group Holding, 303
CIMCON, 1104
CIMCON Lighting, 498
Ciment Blanc d'Algerie, 1012
CIMON Medical, 2858
CIMS, 2284
Cinario Ltd, 2545
Cinarra, 485
Cinarra Systems, 89
Cinchapi, 1423
Cinchy, 2074

Cincinnati Bell, 1360
Cinco Oil & Gas, 673
Cincon Electronics, 3209
CinCor, 11
Cindu International, 2324
Cine+, 2975
Cine-tal Systems, 1547
Cinedigm DC, 1493
Cinedigm Digital Cinema, 1230
Cinegif, 953
Cinelease, 197
Cinemacraft, 2904
Cinemagram, 1203
Cinemaki, 2437
Cinemark, 1160, 1508
Cinemark USA Inc., 576
Cinetopia, 1639
Cinnabon, 1580
Cinnafilm, 758
Cinnos, 2178
Cinova, 185
Cint, 2628, 3042
Cintel, 1091
Cinven, 3254
CIP Technologies, 2589
CiPerceptions, 2255
Cipher Surgical, 2958
Cipher Trace, 182
Cipher Trust, 1898
CipherCloud, 125
Ciphergen Biosystems, 1255, 1976
CipherHealth, 2074
Cipherium Systems Co, 2694
CipherOptics, 215, 1084, 1976
CipherTrace, 48
Ciqual Limited, 1832
CiraNova, 1976
CiRBA, 1674, 2188
Cirba, 1675
Circ Medtech, 54
CIRCA, 2000
Circa, 169, 626, 686, 721, 1154, 1521, 1635
Circa Corporation of America, 913
Circadian, 263
Circadiance, 1003, 1452
Circassia, 2849
Circet Groupe, 61
Circle, 339, 820, 977, 1184, 2228
Circle Back, 510
Circle Cardiovascular Imaging, 2116, 2283
Circle Ci, 1629
Circle Internet Financial, 1665
Circle Internet Financial Limited, 1361
Circle K, 1021
Circle Medical, 199
Circle of Moms, 1976
Circle Pharma, 1238
Circle Up, 1323
CircleBack, 881
CircleCI, 234, 586, 610
Circles, 925
CircleSt, 1103
CircleUp, 894, 1186, 1588
Circon Systems Corp, 2091
Circuit, 1896
Circuit World, 2083
CircuitHub, 894
CircuitMeter, 2037
Circuitronics, 832
Circularis, 398
Circulate, 361, 863
Circulite, 2739
CircusTrix, 1404
Ciris Energy, 1561
CirisEnergy, 325
Cirius Therapeutics, 785
Cirpack, 2888

Cirque Dreams, 196
Cirque Du Soleil, 1837
Cirquest, 999
Cirro, 1237, 1831
Cirro Secure, 1059, 2010
Cirrus, 153
Cirrus Logic, 564
Cirrusdata, 151
CirrusWorks, 1635
Cirtec Medical LLC, 451
Cirtemo, 1925
CIS, 47
CIS Secure Computing, 408
Cisco, 1100, 1657
Cisco Systems, 3203, 3250
Cision, 889
Cisse Cocoa, 845
Cissoid, 3216
CIT GAP Funds, 3260
Cita Neuro Pharmaceutical, 2188
Citadel, 962, 1125
Citadel Architectural Products, 1252
Citadel Communications, 20
Citadel Outsource Group, 1343
Citadel Plastics, 458
Citat, 2879
CITB, 2880
Citco, 819
Citco III, 1746
Citel Tech, 2340
Citelighter, 1305
Citiesocial, 3172
Citigroup Inc., 1905
Citilog, 2867
CitiPower I Pty Ltd, 2582
CitiusTech, 819
Citiva, 970
CitiXsys, 20
Citizant, 509
Citizen, 1058, 1155, 1657
Citizen Hex, 2272
Citra Health Solutions, 864
Citrine, 2010
Citrine Informatics, 108, 1001, 1254
Citrix Systems, 3251
Citron Hygiene, 2056
Citrus Lane, 234, 827, 1058, 1867
Cittio, 928
Citus Data, 361, 1073
CitusData, 586
City Barbeque, 786
City Bebe, 447
City Carting & Recycling, 60
City Carting Holding, 1025
City Center, 874
City Cloud International, 485
City Gear, 408
City Media, 1340
City Mortgage Corporation, 112
City on a Hill, 1315
City Pantry, 2988
City Place, 69
City Sports, 1971
City Ventures LLC, 160
City Wide Towing, 2246
Citybox, 827
CityFlyer Express, 2814
Cityfront Partners LLC, 123
CityGrowsm Contentplace, 1509
CityIndex, 782
Citymapper, 2469, 2620
CityMart, 1896
Citymesh, 3033
Cityneo, 2888
Citynews, 3043
CityNorth, 1968
Cityscan, 1385

Portfolio Companies Index

CityShop, 827
CitySmart, 1509
CitySocializer, 2676, 3046
CitySoft, 440, 1691
Cityspace, 2568
CitySquares, 649
Cityvoter, 581
Cityzen, 3250
CivaTech Oncology, 3250
CIVCO, 1090
Civcom Inc., 2741
Civic Eagle, 221, 937
Civic Partners, 1873
Civic Science, 1003
CivicConnect, 2127
CivicPlus, 364
CivicScience, 1290
Civil Maps, 108, 474
Civilized, 2233
Civis Analytics, 631, 1928
Civitas Learning, 205, 666, 720, 742, 752, 1298, 1554
Civitas Solutions, 1933
Civitas Therapeutics, 240, 389, 1522, 1700
Civitech, 937
Civolution, 3042
CJ Entertainemnt, 2848
CJ Entertainment, 2824
CJ Fallon, 1115
CJ Foods Inc., 1041
CJ HelloVision Co., 2718
CK Mechanical Plumbing & Heating, 679
CKE Restaurants, 1580
CKH Food & Health Limited, 2718
CKL Design Automation, 68
CL Educate, 856
Clad-Rex, 319
Cladwell, 1159
Claim Compass, 2132
Claim-Maps, 85
ClaimForce, 1385
Claire By 30 Seconds To Fly, 1039
Claire's, 141
Claire-Sprayway, 847
ClairMail, 972, 990, 1390
Clairsonic, 85
Clairvest Group, 3249
Clairvoyant Networks, 738
Clairvoyante, 1649, 1649
Clal Industries Ltd., 33
Clara, 23, 398, 623, 945, 1537
Clara Labs, 235
ClaraBridge, 318
Clarabridge, 820, 881, 907, 1013, 1628, 1754
Claranet, 20, 971
Claravine, 1317
Clare, 742
ClareMedica Health Partners, 247
Claremont, 1561
Claremont Creek Ventures, 3273
Claresys, 2958
Claret Medical, 644, 1126, 1622
Clari, 1657
Claria, 810
Clariant, 2913
Claricom Solutions, 1071
Clarifai, 894, 1105, 1155, 1203
Clarifi, 1511
Clarify, 1379
Clarify Health Solutions, 1086
Clarify Medical, 300
Clarigent Health, 481
Clario Medical, 1604
Clarion Brands, 1769
Clarion Events, 1929, 2371, 2814
Clarion Industries, 1404
Clarion Partners, 1127

Clariondoor, 175
ClariPhy, 990, 1379
Clariteam, 2314
Clariti, 2262
Claritics, 456
Clariton, 3239
Claritum, 2565
Clarity, 787
Clarity Health, 1335
Clarity Money, 23, 724, 1186
Clarity Payment Solutions, 2708
Clarity Solution Group, 1579
Clarity Visual Systems/Planar Systems, 1287
ClarityHealth, 85
Claritymoney, 488
Clarius, 2074
Clarivate Analytics, 2201
ClariVest Asset Management, 1151
Clarivoy, 1556
Clarizen, 582, 2557, 3212
Clark, 1071, 1125, 1554, 2217
Clark Brands, 1965
Clark Nexsen, 3250
Clarkston Consulting, 3250
Claros Diagnostics, 522
Claroty, 1001
Clarus, 1762
Clarus Glassboards, 260
Clarus Therapeutics, 1492, 1820
Clarus Ventures, 36
ClarVista Medical, 1993
ClasDojo, 1058
Class Box, 641
Class Dojo, 720, 1114, 1254
Class Technology, 1757
Classcraft, 2060
ClassDojo, 820, 888, 1315, 1530, 1666, 1677, 1702
ClassDoko, 1881
Classic Accessories, 480
Classic Chevy International, 911
Classic Events, 1748
Classic Hospitals, 2926
Classic Party Rentals, 952
Classic Specs, 816
Classic Sports Network, 1731
Classified Verticals, 1195
Classkick, 863, 1058, 1121
Classmarkets, 2820, 2829
Classmates, 931
Classmates Online, 154
ClassOne Group, 1609
ClassOwl, 194
ClassPass, 283, 298, 728, 820, 894, 1187, 1696
Classpass, 321, 1585
Classroom Connect, 337, 381
Classting, 3118
ClassTracks, 1703
ClassWallet, 337, 1315
Classwatch, 2565
Classy, 361, 1045, 1555, 1610
Clause, 3099
Clavert Education Services LLC, 386
Clavis Insight, 2665, 3095
Clay, 308, 321
Claymore Capital Management, 2051
Clayton Dubilier & Rice, 3254
Cleaire Advanced Emissions Control, 1733
Clean Air Partners, 2073
Clean Air Power, 3019
Clean Coal Technologies Inc., 1194
Clean Diesel Technologies, 1583, 2483
Clean Earth, 525, 1138
Clean Emission Fluids, 743
Clean Energy Fuels, 1113
Clean Fiber, 1104
Clean Power Finance, 499

Clean Power Finance Inc., 493
Clean Technology Solutions, 1607
Clean Water Works, 2180
Clean Well, 1978
Clean World Partners, 1604
Cleancut, 321
CleanFish, 1236
Cleanify, 232, 361, 650, 863, 1058
Cleanly, 1154
CleanScapes, 1691
CleanSlate, 924
Cleantech America, 508
Cleantech Group, 1607
CleanVolt Energy, 738
Clear Access, 281
Clear Align, 1305
Clear Blade, 546
Clear Catheter Systems, 1546
Clear Channel Communications, 223
Clear Choice, 1755
Clear Comfort, 147
Clear Contract, 1267
Clear Creek Midstream, 672
Clear Data, 749
Clear Flight Solutions, 550
Clear Flow Inc., 374
Clear Genetics, 527
Clear Labs, 720, 894, 1203
Clear NDA, 1267
Clear Object, 659
Clear Path Robotics, 812
Clear Scholar, 659
Clear Shape Technologies, 1898
Clear Slide, 1831
Clear Spring, 116
Clear Standards, 1076, 1348
Clear Story Data, 125
Clear Swift, 2665
Clear Technology, 1771
Clear Urban Energy, 1561
Clear Vascular Inc., 158
Clear Water, 225
Clear-Cut Medical, 3041
Clear-to-Send Electronics, 132
Clear2Pay, 2828, 3033
ClearAccess, 1384
ClearAccess IP, 613
ClearAccessIP, 810
Clearant, 1169
Clearas, 1317
ClearBalance, 128
ClearBanc, 2217
Clearbanc, 2130
Clearbit, 742, 2018
ClearBlade, 447
Clearblanc, 2150
Clearbrain, 1426
Clearbridge BioMedics, 2509
ClearCare, 238, 1947
ClearChoice Holdings LLC, 1092
Clearco, 1716, 2131
ClearCommerce, 205, 1947
ClearCount, 1452
ClearCount Medical Solutions, 1003
Clearcover, 1121
ClearCube, 205, 759
Clearcube, 1401
ClearDATA, 704, 941, 1346
ClearDATA Networks, 1206
ClearEdge, 380
ClearEdge 3D, 1446
ClearEdge Partners, 1462
ClearEdge Power, 145, 1087
ClearedIn, 1269
Clearent, 199, 646, 796
Clearent/FieldEdge, 61
Clearcon Fiber Networks, 632

1259

Portfolio Companies Index

Clearestate, 2090
CLEAResult, 819
Clearfit, 853
ClearFlame Engines, 1616
ClearFlow, 139, 1384
Clearfly Communications, 504
ClearForest, 3221
Clearforest, 22
ClearFuels Technology, 810, 810
ClearGov, 1175
ClearGraph, 863
ClearGuage, 194
ClearLab, 139
Clearlake Capital Group, 3245
ClearLaw AI, 1616
ClearLeap, 1332
Clearleap, 1761, 1855
Clearlink, 1410
Clearly.ca, 2137
ClearlySo, 2500
ClearMedical, 1007
ClearMedicare, 999
ClearMetal, 648
Clearmetal, 1001
Clearminster, 2787
ClearMotion, 1158, 1511
Clearn Membranes, 2969
ClearOrbit, 1857
Clearpath, 2150
ClearPath Diagnostics, 1670
Clearpath Robotics, 648, 1065, 2122, 2165
ClearPoint, 655
ClearPoint Metrics, 1042
Clearpool, 655
ClearRoad, 1896
ClearSaleing, 1556
Clearscope, 971
ClearServe, 1635
ClearSide, 1698
Clearside Biomedical, 918, 1261
ClearSky, 820, 938
Clearslide, 263
Clearspring Capital Partners, 3249
ClearStory, 1079
ClearStory Data, 582, 894
ClearStream, 979
Clearswift, 2378, 2653
Clearswift Corporation, 2568
Cleartrip, 582
Clearview, 2958
Clearview Capital Fund II LP, 2088
ClearVoice, 79
Clearwater, 97, 475, 1973
Clearwater Analytics, 1754
Clearwell, 1341, 1537
Clearwell Systems, 1657
Clearwire, 309, 597
Cleave, 11
Cleave Biosciences, 158, 184, 1383, 1898
Cleaver Brooks Inc., 1972
Cleaver-Brooks Inc., 911
Cledara, 2398
Clef, 1254
Clek Inc., 2081
Clementia, 710, 1383, 1522
Clementon Park Splash Worlld, 1991
Clenarm, 3088
Cleo, 92, 720, 763, 877, 2469
cleo fashions, 2249
Cleor, 2285
Cless Cosméticos, 1376
Clesse, 124
Clevamama, 2347
Cleveland HeartLab, 704, 835, 922, 1206
Cleveland Medical Polymers, 642
Clever, 752, 888, 894, 1058, 1125, 1657, 1702, 2011

CleverCoin, 310
Cleverly, 1412
Cleversafe, 237, 983, 1364, 1478, 1483
Cleversense, 1121
Cleverset, 85
Clevertap, 27
Clew, 2122
CLI Studios, 888
Clic, 2089
Click, 782
Click Diagnostics, 176
Click Energy, 127
Click.ai, 2094
Clickability, 2188
ClickAd, 2301
Clickatell, 582, 1657
Clickbooth, 406, 448
ClickDimensions, 28
Clicker, 972, 1537
ClickFox, 438, 928, 2571, 2646, 3203
ClickingHouse Pte Ltd, 2464
ClickPay, 51
Clickpay Services, 1386
Clickshare Service, 440
Clicksign, 641
Clicksoftwar, 2766
ClickSquared, 2188
Clicksquared Inc., 22
Clicktale, 1086
Clicktivated Video, 985
Clidec, 3171
Client Distribution Services, 1372
Client Outlook, 2181
Clientbook, 754
ClientSoft, 957
ClientSuccess, 79, 1659
Clifford Thames, 2935
Clifton, 2382, 3059
CliftonLarsonAllen, 3251, 3264
Climacell, 1039
ClimaCheck, 2610
Climastar, 2480
Climate Energy, 2606
Climatewell, 3004
Climatisation Mixair, 2089
Climax Portable Machine Tools, 989
Climos, 325
Climpact, 2684
Clinc, 631
Cline Driving Solutions, 747
Clinical Assessment Services, 2528, 2529
Clinical Genomics, 3014
Clinical Ink, 497, 718, 1349
Clinical Innovations, 1482, 1594
Clinical Logistics, 2148
Clinical Products, 1261
Clinical Research Investments, 1766
Clinical Research Laboratories LLC, 277
Clinical Sensors, 738
Clinical Supplies Management, 864
Clinicient, 429
Cliniconex, 2276
Clinipace Worldwide, 907, 918, 1255, 1407, 3250
Clinique D'Optometrie Vu, 2089
Clinique Développement, 3229
CliniSys, 2968
Clinitron, 1511
Clinkle, 689
Clinovia, 2787
Clinovo, 1065, 1604
Clinverse, 655, 918, 1942
CLIO, 1092
Clio, 2272, 3035
Clip, 972, 1240, 1521
Clip Industie, 238
Clipboard, 776

ClipCall, 1928, 2938
Clipcomm, 3118
Clipper Marine, 940
Cliptone, 1441
Cliq Designs Ltd, 2699
Cliqloc, 2815
CliQr, 773
CliqStudios, 862
Clique, 309
Clique Media, 625
Clique Media Group, 59, 641, 1114, 1223
Cliqz.com, 2595
Clir, 2037
Clix, 912
Clixtr, 116
CLK Design Automation, 1257
Cloakware, 713
Clobotics, 827, 1091
Clock Work, 1296
Clockwork Fox, 2161, 2208
Clockwork Solutions, 1785
Clondalkin, 1957
Close.io, 1718
ClosedLoop, 1
Closedloop Solutions, 1762
Closely, 115, 126, 686, 881
CloserStill, 3027
Closet Works, 1438
Closet world, 377
Clothes Horse, 535, 1358, 1479
Clothia, 283, 1335, 1521
Cloud Access, 1966
Cloud Agronomics, 198
Cloud Apps, 2665
Cloud Bees, 180
Cloud Business, 2558
Cloud Control, 2629
Cloud Cruiser, 1379, 1604, 1671, 1967
Cloud Elements, 881, 907, 1525
Cloud Elemts, 35
Cloud Genix, 1009
Cloud Health Technologies, 1629
Cloud Lending, 689
Cloud Made, 3140
Cloud MedX, 1155
Cloud Moment, 1125
Cloud Passage, 520, 545
Cloud Pharmaceuticals, 3250
Cloud Physics, 972
Cloud Simple, 1158
Cloud Technology Partners, 91, 1361, 1483
Cloud Temple, 971
Cloud.com, 1537, 2992
Cloud4Wi, 1382
Cloud66, 604
Cloud9, 1885
Cloud9 Analytics, 1106
Cloudability, 586, 779, 1467, 1791, 1855
Cloudamize, 1240
Cloudant, 209
CloudApps, 2653
CloudArena, 2428
CloudBeds, 570
CloudBees, 1184, 1928
Cloudbees, 1125
CloudBolt Software, 1005
CloudByte, 2992
CloudCheckr, 2187
CloudCherry, 485
CloudEndure, 604, 2943
CloudEngine, 3165
Cloudera, 27, 582, 840, 983, 1213
CloudFare, 1511
Cloudfiling, 603
CloudFlare, 872, 1428
Cloudflare, 579, 1884, 1918
CloudFX, 485

1260

Portfolio Companies Index

CloudGenix, 1187
cloudGuide SA, 650
CloudHealth Technologies, 1, 1213, 1675
CloudHelix, 1969
Cloudian, 1009
Cloudify, 1009
CloudIQ, 2530
Cloudkick, 209
CloudLanes, 1158
CloudLock, 438
Cloudmark, 31, 796, 978, 1327, 1478, 1754, 1976
Cloudmeter, 1196
Cloudnexa, 51
CloudOn, 773, 1543, 1698, 1840
CloudOne, 1459
CloudPassage, 780, 1213, 1666, 1716, 1798
CloudPay, 1561
CloudPhysics, 1079, 1187
Cloudreach, 1235
Cloudscaling, 1855
CloudSense, 1610, 1912
Cloudshare, 457
CloudShield, 1976
Cloudshield, 1401
CloudShield Technologies, 801
Cloudstitch, 1593
CloudStreet Oy, 3204
CloudSwitch, 523
CloudTags, 975
CloudVelocity, 1428
CloudVelox, 1187
CloudWave, 1979
Cloudwords, 1750
CloudX, 679
Cloudyn Code Fresh, 3212
Clourdera, 1310
Clove, 328
Clover, 85, 843, 945, 1254, 1762, 1985
Clover Health, 108, 742, 752, 894, 1657
Clover Imaging Group, 1345
Clover Letter, 901
Clover Tx, 398
Cloverhill Bakery, 1507
Cloverleaf, 2766
Clovis, 2702
Clovis Oncology, 19, 73, 94, 622, 785, 1439, 1930
Clowe & Cowan of El Paso, 1343
Cloyes, 1089
Cloze, 1322
CLP Resources, 470
CLS Holdings USA, 1282
Cls Info, 2089
CLT Research, 1294
Club Champion, 1060
Club Company, 2926
Club Staffing, 1372
Club W, 1966
ClubCorp Inc., 576
Clubessential, 238
Clubhosue, 1114
Clubhouse, 238, 354
ClubReady, 238
Clue, 2665
Clupedia, 1917
Cluster, 234
Cluster Seven, 3061
Clustree, 2842
Clustrix, 185, 936, 1898
Clutch, 1316, 1605, 1760
Clutter, 121, 728, 780, 894, 1032, 1657, 2437
Clyde Bergemann, 2956
Clyde Bergemann Group, 2651
Clyde Biosciences, 690
Clyde-Bergemann-Gruppe Wesel/Glasgow/Delaware, 3058

Clypd, 37, 316, 587, 787, 1841
clypd, 1851
CM Energy, 676
CMC, 386, 1388
CMC Biologics, 1248
Cmc Interconnect Technologies, 2162
CMD Bioscience, 679, 1101
Cmed, 3095
CMG, 568
CMG Health, 958
CMG Holdings, 1958
CMG Silhouette Sports Club, 2285
CMI, 2427
CMI Limited, 404
CMI-Dutchview, 2492
CML Group, 1294
CML Healthcare, 2225
CMOSIS, 1778
Cmosis, 3033
CMP Pharma, 97
CMP.LY, 1386
CMR Group, 3011
CMRA, 680
CMS, 170
CMS Management Solutions, 1573
Cmune, 597, 2437
CMW, 2427
CMWare, 1888
CNC, 2581, 2989
CNC Global, 791
CNCdata, 961
CNDAA, 1577
CNEI, 2935
CNEX Labs, 485, 1158, 1672
CNEXLabs, 604
CNK Telecom, 2425
CNM Technologies, 2677
Cnn, 2712
CNNH NeuroHealth, 551
CNOOC, 2763
CNote, 229
CNS Response, 1607
CNS Therapeutics, 1820
CNSX Markets, 2051
CO Everywhere, 2969
Co Star, 981
Co-Tech Copper Foil, 1771
co.don, 2369
CO2 GRO, 2054
Co3Systems, 915
Coach America, 722
CoachUP, 2
CoachUp, 332, 820
Coachup, 1463, 1791
CoActive Technologies, 1138
CoAdna Photonics, 974
Coagulex Inc., 487
Coagulo, 849
Coal, 3009
Coal Fire, 225
Coal Products, 2874
Coalescent Surgical, 1251, 1976
Coalfields Enterprise Fund, 2699
Coalfire Systems, 416
CoAlign Innovations, 87
Coalision, 2162
CoalTek, 325
Coapt Systems, 315
Coast Access, 624
Coast Appliances, 2267
Coast Composites, 445
Coast Crane, 197
Coast Gas Industries, 202
Coast of Maine, 1165
Coast of Maine Organic Products, 440
Coastal Carolina Clean Power, 1577
Coastal Carolina Clean Power LLC, 416

Coastal Community Bank, 1250
Coastal Companies, 1169, 1270
Coastal Credit, 1419
Coastal Drilling, 1410
Coastal Drilling Company, 1748
Coastal Sunbelt, 1270
Coastal Ventures, 1551
Coastal Waste & Recycling, 531
Coastal.com, 2137
Coates Hire, 416
Coating Excellence International, 1174
Cobalt, 310, 521, 775, 2688, 2689, 2930
Cobalt Boats, 1591
Cobalt International Energy, 416, 741, 1577
Cobalt Light Systems, 2958
Cobalt Networks, 200
Cobalt Office Park, 1968
Cobalt Robotics, 728, 1657, 1836
Cobalt Technologies, 1449, 1908
Cobalt.Io, 1809
Cobb Slater Ltd., 2648
Cobblestone Fayette, 1220
Cobblestone Golf Group, 381
Cobelguard CIT, 2940
Cobion, 3223
Cobli, 728
Cobotics, 1061
Cobra, 3145
Cobra Waire & Cable, 1210
Cobre Capital, 3265
Coca-Cola, 475, 2381
COCAT, 1487, 1748
Cockroach Labs, 744, 894, 1537, 2006
Cocoa China, 3133
Cocona, 713
Cocone, 3118
Coconft, 2122
Coconut Calendar, 2240
Coconut Software, 2074, 2146
CoCubes.Com, 3010
Cod Farmers, 2466
Coda, 108, 877, 1268
CODA Holdings, 1577
Coda Project Inc., 1073
Coda Signature, 736
CoDa Therapeutics, 622, 2507
Codacy, 3099
Coddle, 575
Code 42 Software, 3268
Code A Site, 3250
Code Climate, 1114, 1322, 1884
Code Combat, 721
Code Fights, 641
Code for America, 1374
Code Fresh, 1158
Code Green Networks, 241
Code42, 1045, 1643, 1728
Code42 Software, 27
Codeacademy, 320, 1359
Codecademy, 756, 1079, 1696, 1884
CodeCombat, 125
Codecov, 321
CodeEval, 256
Codefights, 545, 1223
Codegem, 2122
Codeherent, 2276
CodeHS, 1058, 1315, 1659
Codekingdoms, 1719
Codel Holding Company, 1494
Codementor, 3172
Codenomicon, 3042
Codenomicon Oy, 2707
CodeNow, 1315
Codenvy, 1831
CodeRed, 60
CodeRise, 3116
CodeRyte, 522, 1704, 1918

Portfolio Companies Index

CodeSealer, 3194
Codeship, 316, 711, 1675, 3099
Codesignal, 720
CodeSpark, 802, 976
Codespark, 1058
codeSpark, 1895
Codetoys, 3223
Codetoys Oy, 2707, 2864
Codeverse, 568
Codexis, 468, 2681
CODi, 1234
Codiak, 710, 748
Codice Software, 2539
Codigo Entertainment LLC, 62
Coding, 1125
Coding Technologies, 2745
Codiscope, 1140
Codon Devices, 748
Cody, 776, 1635
CoEdition, 328
coeo, 296
Cofactor Genomics, 108, 178, 270, 1203
COFCO Meat, 1086
Coferon, 918
Coffee Circle, 3161
Coffee Day Resorts, 1086
Coffee Meets Bagel, 597, 1121, 1983
Coffin Turbo Pump, 1275
Coficern/Sagem, 2592
CoFoundersLab, 1172
CoFoundit, 2847
Cogent Communications, 318, 2901
Cogent Healthcare, 1239, 1964
Cogent Midstream, 672
Cogentrix Power Management, 416
Cogiscan, 2089
Cogit.com, 1122
Cogito, 1610
Cognate Bioservices, 698
Cognet, 133
Cognetix, 1414
Cogni, 575
Cogniac, 207, 208
Cognical, 1851
Cognima, 2630, 3170
Cognio, 22, 1335
Cognita Schools, 1086
CogniTens, 3221
Cognition Therapeutics, 296, 845, 1003, 1452, 1786
Cognition Therapeutics Inc., 991
CognitionIP, 798
Cognitiv, 345
Cognitive Concepts, 1061
Cognitive Match, 2399
Cognitive Networks, 597
Cognitive Scale, 1009, 1158
Cognitive Toy Box, 1554
Cognitive Toybox, 623
CognitiveScale, 1346
Cognito, 2122
Cognivue Corporation, 2051, 2051
Cognoa, 2969
Cognoptix, 1104, 1164
Cogoport, 27
CogRx, 1305
CogX, 575
Cohda Wireless, 485
Cohealo, 1585, 1759
Cohen & Company, 3264
Cohen & Grigsby, 3264
Cohera Medical, 1003, 1070, 1086, 1452
Cohere Technologies, 108, 1125
Coherent, 183
Coherent Path, 308, 536, 853, 1675, 1737
Coherex Medical, 1679, 1886
Cohero Health, 269, 1614

Coherus BioSciences, 1086
Coherus Biosciences, 1128, 1522, 1700
Cohesity, 27, 177, 238, 485, 773, 894, 1255, 1511, 1657, 1716
Cohesive Network Systems, 1973
CohesiveFT, 1364
Cohn & Gregory, 988
Coi Pharmaceuticals, 209
COIFF'Idis, 3011
Coimbra Genomics, 3039
Coin, 1702
Coin Jar, 310
Coinage, 310
Coinapoly, 685
Coinbase, 48, 125, 238, 310, 621, 877, 1006, 1534, 1563, 1646, 1716, 1884, 2011, 2272, 2876
Coinbunble, 1770
CoinFlip, 1039
Coinfloor, 3021
Coinhako, 310
Coining of America, 1163
Coinjar, 2511
Coinmatch, 1949
Coinplug, 627
Coinprism, 310
Coinsetter, 1851
CoInspec, 1896
Coinstar, 250, 755, 755, 861
Cointerra, 3088
Coinut, 310
Cojoin, 1103
Coker Tire, 1026
Col-Met Spray Booths, 1748
CoLab, 798
CoLab Software, 2161
Colab Software, 2204
Colabot, 1812
CoLabs, 229
Colbar, 2766
Colby Pharmaceuticals, 1329
Cold Bore Technology, 2065
Cold Chain Technologies, 202
Cold Genesys, 1983
Cold PackSystem, 1893
Cold Spring Harbor Laboratory, 1271
ColdSpark, 1042
Coldwater Creek, 843
ColdWatt, 205
Coldwell Banker, 371
Cole Haan, 136
Cole Information, 352
Cole Real Estate Investments, 874
Cole Taylor Bank, 531
Cole-Parmer Instrument Company, 889
Coleman Swenson Booth, 990
Colerain RV, 1075
Coles Myer, 2650
Coletica, 2457
Coley, 2369
Coley Pharmaceutical Group, 1820, 2776
Colford Capital, 1248
Colgate Energy, 1326, 1328
Coliant Corporation, 743
Colibra, 238
Colibri, 623, 1507
Colibria, 2745, 3004
Colibrys Ltd, 3153
Colingo, 1254, 2911
Colisee, 912, 2842
CollabNet, 1140
CollabNet VersionOne, 1912
Collaborate.com, 1101
Collaborative Medical, 3257
Collaborative Practice Solutions, 1288
Collaborative Solutions, 1979
Collabornet, 1514

Collabrify, 1596
Collage, 2090, 2217
CollaGenex Pharmaceuticals, 73
Collanos AG, 650
Collarity, 1976
CollateBox, 3124
Collax, 2804, 3223
Collect, 310
Collect America, 1204
Collect Rx, 1292
Collectif, 395
Collection Papillon Gemme, 2089
Collections Marketing Center, 1386
Collective, 876
Collective Bias, 1888
Collective Health, 778, 863, 894, 1537
Collective Intellect, 143, 554, 881
Collective IP, 933
Collective Retreats, 321, 742, 1696
Collective Therapeutics, 772
CollectiveHealth, 1698
CollectiveIP, 686
Collectively, 1309
CollectiveMedical, 1079
CollectiveMedical Technologies, 1056
Collectors Universe, 1287
College Ave Student Loans, 520
College Enterprises/Blackboard, 1287
College Factual, 120
College of Natural Sciences Advisory Council, 1653
College Pharmaceuticals, 137
College Portfolio, 1813
Collegebacker, 1530
Collegenet, 1949
CollegeProwler.com, 1196
Collegiate Funding Services, 1127
Collegium, 315
Collegium Pharmaceutical, 710, 785, 1522, 1693
Coller Capital, 3249
Collgard, 3239
Collider, 461, 1130
Collider Media, 1813
Colligo, 2103
Collingwood Ethanol, 416
Collinor Software, 2815
Colloquis, 593
Collplant, 3235
COLO, 1630
Cologix, 518, 872
ColoHub LLC, 123
Colomer Group, 2635
Colonial Claims, 531
Colonial Pipeline Co., 1086
Colony Hardware, 63, 1779
Colony Sardegna, 3145
Color, 520, 764, 820, 1001, 1666
Color Genomics, 108, 721, 1073, 1677
Color Kinetics, 1287
Color Labs Enterprises, 961
Colorado Boxed Beef Company, 96
Colorado Technology Association, 3265
Colorbok, 1337
ColorChip, 2711, 3037, 3205
Colorchip, 3221
Colorcon, 261
Colorcraft Packaging, 836
Colore Science, 922, 1251
Coloredge, 1608
Colorescience, 4, 73, 622, 1149, 1728
Colormatrix, 197
Colorme Info, 2841
Colosceum, 2549
Colourlovers, 1254
Coloursmith, 2161
Colson Group, 1654
Colt CTX Resources, 517

1262

Portfolio Companies Index

Colt Mineral Interests, 517
Colt Unconventional Resources, 517
Colt WTX Resources, 517
Colter Energy, 2267
Colu Technologies, 321
Colubris Networks, 1784
CoLucid, 1414
CoLucid Pharma, 1271
CoLucid Pharmaceuticals, 622, 1849
Columbia Capital, 990, 3260
Columbia Green, 246
Columbia Green Techologies, 2283
Columbia Northwest, 296
Columbia Power Technologies, 1384
Columbus Manufacturing, 148
Columbus Recycling, 1859
Colusa Power Development, 157
com, 3241
Com 21, 759
Com Tech Communications, 2942
COM21, 1561
Com21, 1091
Com2Us, 1091
Com2uS, 1750
Com6, 3199
Comact Equipment, 2089
CoManage, 55
Comar, 851
Comark Building Systems, 331
Comark Services, 2249
Comat, 2451
ComAv, 574
Combat Gent, 1914
Combat Medical, 3098
Combat Networks, 2051
Combatant Gentleman, 1103
Combatant Gentlemen, 283, 876, 1227
Combatant Gentlement, 3035
CombiChem, 1708
Combichem, 772
Combinati, 229
CombinatoRx, 315
Combined Public Communications, 165
Combined Solar, 2969
Combined Systems, 416
Combinenet, 138
Combinent BioMedical Systems, 522
ComBrio, 993, 1922
comCables, 1839
Comcen Computer Supplies Ltd, 2827
Comcore Semiconductor, 767
Comedy.com, 1953
CoMentis, 460, 1619
Comergent, 1255
Comerica, 3273
Comerica Bank, 3249, 3268
Comes Bois, 3125
Comet Bio, 2054
Comet Ridge Resources, 1447
Comet Solutions, 189, 758
Comet Systems, 504, 957
Comfy, 493, 1158, 1281
Comgates, 2576
COMgroup International, 1839
Comic Rocket, 1467
Comilion, 1898
ComiXology, 1309
Comixology, 1588
Comlase, 2869
Comlinkdata, 92
Comm-Art International, 2940
Comm-Works Holdings, 1343
Comma, 125
Command Alkon, 1518
Command Audio, 1244, 1736
Command Health, 1027
Command Information, 1348, 1401

Command Security Corporation, 1839
CommandDot, 321
Commerce 5, 1898
Commerce Connect Media, 20
Commerce Decisions, 2702, 3098
Commerce Decisions Ltd, 2885
Commerce Guys, 2377
Commerce One, 759, 1042, 1255, 1561, 1976, 1983
Commercebear, 2122
CommerceSync, 387
Commercetools, 2432, 2815
Commercial Bank of Ceylon, 3142
Commercial Bearing Service, 2278
Commercial Credit, 1151
Commercial Defeasance, 1754
Commercial Financial Services, 112
Commercial Steel Trating Corporation, 920
Commercial Tribe, 35
Commercialware, 405
Commericial Advance, 874
Commericial Tribe, 881
Commerz, 2801
Commil ltd, 2761
Commil Ltd., 2741
Commit, 2122, 2442
CommitChange, 310
Committee to Protect Journalists, 1374
Commodity Blenders, 935
Common, 1153, 1186, 1346, 1696
Common Assets, 1813
Common Curriculum, 18
Common Networks, 648, 820, 1155
Common Resources III, 673, 1447
Common Sensing, 1511, 1621
CommonBond, 1698, 1851
CommonCents, 623
Commonfloor.com, 579
CommonTime, 2399
Commonwealth Bank, 2650
Commonwealth Business Media, 20, 1560
Commonwealth Chesapeake, 1797
Commonwealth Fusion Systems, 803
Commonwealth Network Technologies, 317
Commonwealth Sprague, 1294
Commonwealth Sprague Capacitor, 1753
Commpario, 2890
Commprize, 2766
CommProve, 3170
CommQuest, 250
Commrail, 1917
CommScope, 416
Commsoft, 1624
Communauto, 2175
Communicado (Now Screentime Communicado), 2655
Communication Science, 1535
Communications & Power Industries Inc., 576
Communications Products and Services, 1156
Communications Supply Corporation, 917
Communispace, 861
Community & Southern Bank, 1270
Community & Southern Bank Holdings, 1127
Community Broadcasters LLC, 1344
Community Cars, 679
Community Energy, 1691
Community First, 263
Community Health TV, 999
Community Home Health, 409
Community Investment Management, 1258
Community Investors, 1192
Community Links, 2530
Community Medicla Services, 505
Community of Science, 1603
Community Sift, 2150
Community Sourced Capital, 3246
Community Trust Financial Corp., 1447

Community Veterinary Partners, 547
CommunityBrands, 1005
CommunityOne Bancorp, 416
Communo, 2204
CommutAir, 1424
Commuter Advertising, 629
CommVerge Solutions, 1361, 1478, 2588
ComNet, 1140
Comoto Holdings, 1053
Compaas, 1058
Compact Particle Acceleration, 1380
Compact Particle Acceleration Corporation, 584
Compact Power Equipment Centers, 2162
Compagnie Européenne de Prestations Logistique, 153
Compal Communications, 3209
Companeo, 416
Companion, 1125
Company.com, 796
Compaq, 1561
Compaq Computer, 200
Comparably, 309, 520, 562, 564, 1153, 1890
Comparaonline.com, 1563
compare, 2353
CompareAsia, 846
Compas, 2437
CompAS Controls, 1444
Compass, 1, 846, 1006, 2763, 3046, 3072
Compass EOS, 1335
Compass Therapeutics, 271, 311, 894
Compass Water Solutions, 1275, 1280
Compassion-First Pet Hospitals, 1507
Compatible Systems, 318
Compbenefits, 1949
Compel, 874
Compellent Technologies, 556, 2630
Compellon, 1055
Compendium, 659
Compete, 470, 523, 928, 1728
Competentia, 3067
Competitive Power Ventures Holdings, 1957
Competitive Technology, 355
Competitor Group, 684
Competitor Sports Technology, 2841
Compex, 1964
Compin Group, 3011
Complete Genomics, 186, 1495
Complete Holdings Group, 1735
Complete Innovations, 1772
Completel, 1212
CompleteXrm, 1886
Complex Media, 27, 205
Complex Media Network, 1601
Complexa, 296, 1452
ComplexCare Solutions, 1957
Complexe Funeraire Ste-Bernadette, 2089
Complexe Sportif Interplus, 2089
Complia Health, 419
Compliance Assurance Corporation, 1003
Compliance Control, 3001
Complion, 254, 1051, 2074
Complix, 2940, 3011, 3033
Complix Alphabody Therapeutics, 2467
Comply 365, 631
Comply Advantage, 2469
ComplySci, 655
Complyserv, 2958
Compology, 1058, 1101
Component Sourcing International, 165
ComponentArt, 2051, 2051
CompoSecure, 1140
Composer, 2131
Composit Ltd., 2741
Composite Software, 624, 1408, 1798
Composite Systems, 504
Composite Technologies, 1275
Compositence, 2815

Portfolio Companies Index

Compound, 125, 298, 527, 1935
ComPower Systems, 2051
Compower Systems, 2051
Comprehend, 564, 644, 1125, 1521, 1657
Comprehensive Addiction Programs, 1275
Comprehensive Clinical Development, 476
Comprehensive NeuroScience, 692
Comprehensive Pharmacyservices, 178
Comprehensive Prosthetics & Orthotics, 3202
Compression Kinetics, 999, 1190
Compression Polymers Group, 467
Compressor Controls Corp., 467
Compro Pago, 2975
CompStak, 389
Compstak, 380, 708
Compucare, 1255
CompuCom Systems, 1818
CompuDyne Corporation, 502
Compugen, 1898
Compugroup, 2762
CompuLink, 2456
Compumotor, 263
Compund Therapeutics, 2436
CompUSA, 205
Compusearch, 167, 1045
Computable, 527, 1155, 1363
Computacenter, 2787
Computer Aided Services, 538
Computer Aided Technology, 491
Computer Generation Inc., 153
Computer Motion, 68
Computerized Electricity Systems, 2408
computershare, 2762
Computex Technology Solutions, 1279
Computility, 347
Computime, 60
CompuTrain Europe B.V, 2528, 2529
Compuware, 36
Compuware Corporation, 1817
ComRent, 838
ComRent InternationaldCLI, 2371
COMS Interactive, 1754
ComScore, 1679
Comscore, 27
Comscore Networks, 1006
ComSong Interactive Technologies, 2901
ComSpace, 1561
Comstellar, 496
Comstock Resources, 1086
Comstock Systems Corporation, 1013
Comsys, 1410, 2766
Comtempo Ceramic Tile, 470
Comverge, 931, 1355, 1583
Comvest Partners, 3254
Comview, 2766
Comware, 2798
Con-Fom, 3067
Conamix, 705
Conatus Pharmaceuticals, 240, 1268, 3076
Concent, 2528, 2529
Concentra, 559, 1255, 1973, 3005
Concentric, 1104
Concentric Educational Solutions, 1315
Concentric Equity Partners, 3251
Concentrx Pharmaceuticals, 3250
Concept 10 Inc., 624
Concept Mat, 2089
Concept Shopping, 1008
Concept Therapeutics, 1261
concept3D, 1094
Conceptboard, 2815, 2923
ConceptDrop, 1159
Conception Gsr, 2089
Conception Technology, 1839
Concepts Direct, 1839
Conceptua Math, 1065
Conceptus, 1379, 1908

Concerro, 137, 1056
Concert Industries, 2062
Concert Pharmaceuticals, 748, 1198, 1297, 1693, 3187
Concert Window, 1305
ConcertoHealth, 946
Concha, 398
Concierge Choice, 1588
Concierge Stat, 623
Concillium, 2700
Concord Communications, 317, 808
Concord Enviro, 838
Concord Foods, 148
Concord Health Partners, 3254
Concord Medical Service Co., 416
Concordia Coffee Company, 755
Concordia Fibers, 1695
Concours Mania Groupe, 2842
Concours Mold, 560
Concung, 1143
Concur, 1537
Concur Japan, 1757
Concur Technologies, 1006
Concurrent, 1543, 1862
Concurrent Electronic Design Automation, 1003
Concurrent Manufacturing, 228
Concurrent Real-Time, 238
Concurrent Thinking, 2958, 3098
Conditioned Air, 815
conditorei Coppenrath & Wiese GmbH & Co., 77
Condo Control Central, 2163
Condoit, 75
Condor Systems, 248
Conductor, 429, 646, 744, 1184
Conductor (Credit Card Processing), 3171
Conduit, 863, 1949, 2090
Conectt, 2617
Conelec, 1163
Conenza, 85
Conerstone, 724
ConertoHealth, 150
Conexance, 3229
Conexant, 843
Conexant Systems, 2005
ConexED, 1074
Conexia Energy, 3011
CoNextions, 273, 1074
Conexus Energy, 1326, 1328
Confer, 773, 1184
Confer Health, 1698
Confetti, 818
Confidant, 2074
Confide, 742, 894, 1114, 2919
Confident Cannabis, 361
Confident Financial Solutions, 784
Confie Seguros, 20
Configure8, 2131
ConfigureSoft, 1045
Confirm.io, 433, 2231
Confirma, 755, 1794, 1917, 1976
Confirma Software, 20
Conflucence Solar, 2623
Confluence Outdoor, 1041
Confluence Resources, 1326, 1328
Confluence Solar, 1365
Confluence Technologies, 1464
Confluences Life Sciences, 690
Confluent, 119, 251, 1657
Confluent Health, 654
Confluent Surgical, 178, 1449
Conforma Therapeutics, 772, 1578
Conformative, 205
Conformative Systems, 1449
ConforMIS, 1976
Confortvisuel.com, 3011
Confovis, 2815

Confuence Pharmaceuticals, 659
Conga, 1005, 1610
Congebec, 2089
Conger & Elsea, 1425
Congress Inns, 1405
Congressional Bank, 1603
Congruency, 2576
Congruex Holdings, 560
Coniq, 3088
Conject, 3104
ConjuGon, 2002
Conjur, 209
Connance, 1335
Connaught Group Ltd, 2827
Connect, 1629
Connect America Holdings, 1377
Connect Group, 2940
Connect Managed Servies, 2935
Connect Part, 2437
Connect Resource Services, 741
Connect South, 1255
Connect Towers, 1737
Connect-Air International, 557
Connect.me, 3143
ConnectBlue, 2430
Connected, 226, 857, 1704, 1741, 1855
Connected Backup, 2700
Connected Living Inc., 835
Connected Signals, 252, 1616, 1836
Connected2fiber, 180
ConnectedHealth, 2769
ConnectEDU, 1118
ConnectHQ, 1800
Connecticut Color, 324
Connecticut Innovations, 3263
Connectifier, 1103
Connectify, 983
Connection Brands, 1618
Connection Engine, 1762
ConnectiveRx, 764, 823
Connectivity, 1569, 1800, 2653
Connectivity Wireless, 1609
ConnectM, 2840
Connectria, 336
Connecture, 477, 782, 864, 1735, 1865
ConnectYourCare, 21
Connelly-Boland and Associates, 3264
Conner, 1855
Conner Perphirals, 1212
Connetbeam, 808
Connetics Corporation, 94
Connexica, 2958
Connexion Point, 1929
Connexions Asia, 2681
Connexity, 309
ConnexPay, 1412
Connextions, 1300
Connor Bros, 1460
Connotate, 1
ConnXus, 481
Conoisseur Communications, 20
Conoptica, 2745
Conor Medsystems, 137, 644
Conpoto, 1739
Conquer Mobile, 2148
Consecutive Capital, 752
Consejosano, 54
Consel On Call, 878
Conselytics, 863
Consensus, 79
Consensus Orthopedics, 333, 334
Consensus Point, 845
Consensys Imaging Services, 809
Consentry, 1913
Consero Consulting, 2958
Consero Global, 364
Consert, 1928

Portfolio Companies Index

Conserv, 1955
Conservis, 571
Consilient Health, 1456
Consilio & Advanced Discovery, 828
Consilium Software, 3053
Consistel, 3053
Consodata, 2756
Consol, 912
Consolidated Container Company, 223
Consolidated Energy Systems, 1545
Consolidated Equipment Group, 906
Consolidated Fire Protection, 376, 886
Consolidated Precision Products, 293, 1957
Consolidated Precision Products Corp., 167, 257
Consolidayed Precision Products Corp., 989
ConsoliDent, 1560
Consolitated Theatres, 20
Consoltex, 110
Consorte, 2623
Consorte Media, 1762
ConsortNT, 2457
Constant Contact, 523, 957, 1150, 1255, 1626
Constant Therapy, 1058
Constanta, 3178
Constantia Flexibles, 1376
Constella, 1410
Constellar, 1561
Constellation Pharma, 1918
Constellation Pharmaceuticals, 519, 1734, 1814
Constellation Services International, 716
Construct, 310
Construction Control, 2083
Construction L.F.G., 2089
Construction Labor Contractors, 467, 1686
Construction Leclerc Et Pelletier, 2089
Construction Software Technologies, 1826
Constructive Media, 931
Constructor, 2018, 2376
Constructor.io, 802
Consultative Group to Assist the Poor, 1374
Consulting Solutions, 531
Consumer Brands, 278
Consumer Media Network, 20
Consumer Physics, 669, 1073
ConsumerReview, 1649
Consumerunited, 1718
Consumr, 1223
Consure Medical, 27
Conta Azul, 2974
ContaAzul, 1563
Contac Services, 2085
Contact, 2708
Contact East, 1294
Contact Engine, 2988
Contact Solutions, 1335
Contactually, 316, 545, 881, 3035
Container Consultants & Systems, 2326
ContainerShip, 275
Contastic, 1486
Contec, 223
Contec Medical, 2998
Contech, 2872
Contech Engineered Solutions, 1138
Contego Fraud, 2958
Contego Fraud Solutions, 2558
Contego Medical, 918
Contego Services Group, 60
Contendo, 1798
Content Analytics, 89
Content Fleet, 2985
Content Flow, 2832
Content Raven, 649, 1104
Contentfly, 2122
Contentful, 820, 2469, 3035
Contently, 535, 724, 1028, 1121, 1358, 1675, 1791
Contents Japan, 2982

ContentWise, 2742
Contessa Premium Foods Inc., 467
Contex A/S, 2703
Contexo Media, 1929
Context Integration, 405
Context Logic, 1254
Context Media, 55
Contextin, 1718
ConteXtream, 1928
Contextream, 252
Continental, 929
Continental Airlines, 1837
Continental Business Credit, 1971
Continental Cablevision, 317
Continental Coal Ltd., 638
Continental Energy Systems LLC, 1133
Continental Fire & Safety, 952
Continental North Penn Technology, 874
Continental Services, 1582
Continental Structural Plastics, 479, 1343
Continental Warehousing, 1957
Continental Windpower, 1786
Contino, 518
Contintental Electronics Corp., 1927
Continuity, 28, 586, 1101
Continuity Control, 742, 1575
Continuous Computing, 1408
Continuous Computing Corp, 908
Continuum, 495, 552, 1754
Continuum Energy, 917
Continuum Photonics, 1042
ContinuumRx, 921, 1241, 1536
Contorion, 3047
Contour Aerospace, 874
Contour Energy Systems, 983, 1898
Contour Industries, 412
Contour Semiconductor, 713
Contract Land Staff, 1343
Contract Security, 1158
Contract Services Limited, 467
Contractor Quotes, 512
Contraline, 23
Contrast, 3140
Contrast Security, 40, 238, 820
Control Circle, 3095
Control Delivery Systems, 1255
Control Device, 1343
Control Devices LLC, 847
Control Systems BV, 2797
Control Works, 1917
Control4, 773, 1205, 1679, 1886
ControlCase, 1292
Controlex, 2786
Controlled Contamination Services, 703, 1424
Controlled Products, 505
Controls Southeast Inc., 989
ControlScan, 696, 907, 949, 1865
Controltec, 1786
Contros, 2815
Convansys Inc (Us/India), 2685
ConvaTec, 212, 416
Convene, 728
Convenience Food Systems, 2874
Convenient Power HK Limited, 1241
ConvenientMD, 381
Conventor, 1287
Conventus Orthopaedics, 300
Conventus Orthopaedics Inc., 272
Convera, 983
Convercent, 1561, 1623
Converd, 2969
Converge, 1614
Converge Venture Partners, 3263
Convergence Pharmaceuticals, 1297
ConvergeNet, 1795
Convergent, 1425
Convergent Dental, 332, 1146

ConvergeOne, 502
Convergex, 889
Convergint Technologies, 1090
Convergys Corp., 303
Converity, 773
Converium, 2913
Conversant, 1745
Converser, 2939
Conversica, 1499
Conversion Logic, 1114
ConversionLogic, 309, 562
Conversocial, 2653, 2665, 3009
Convert.com, 2374
Convertergy, 3185
Converting, 1174
Convertro, 263, 1227
Converus, 79, 1074
Convery Computer, 1014
Convex, 1561
Convey, 35, 325, 546
Convey Computer, 1561
Convey Health Solutions, 530
Convictional, 798, 1142, 2122
Convio, 56, 57, 186, 205, 857, 1543
CONVIVA, 1428
Conviva, 773, 827, 1608, 1829
Convo, 1257
Convox, 2122
Convoy, 265, 579, 877, 1533
ConWeaver, 2815
Cooby, 1426
Cooee, 2443
Cook & Boardman Group, 1138
Cook It, 2093
Cook Taste Eat, 304
Cookies, 3226
Cookin, 623
Cooking.com, 266, 504, 767
Cookitfor.us, 1618
Cookstr, 1305
Cookwizme, 2847
Cool Dry, 3089
Cool Energy, 976
Cool Gear International, 45, 1524
Cool Planet Energy Systems, 534, 894
Cooladata, 1610, 3212
Coolan, 1698
CoolBrands International, 2245
CoolChip Technolgies, 1914
CoolChip Technologies, 643, 985
Cooledge, 812, 2283
CoolEdge Lighting, 154, 2144
Coolerado, 262
Coolerado Corporation, 1733
Cooley, 3250, 3265
Coolfire Solutions, 1023
Coolibar, 1117
Cooliris, 621, 1978
CoolIT, 459
CoolIT Systems, 2043, 2150
Coolman Entertainment, 1091
CoolPlanet, 1335
Coolr, 1947
CoolSpotter, 1644
CoolTech, 18
Cooltech Applications, 3011
Cooper Equipment Rentals, 2242
Cooper-Standard Automotive Inc., 576
Cooperative De Travailleurs Actionnaire De Negotiu, 2089
Cooperative De Travailleurs Actionnaire De Tec, 2089
Cooperative Forestiere De Girardville, 2089
Cooperative Forestiere De L'Outaouais, 2089
Cooperative Funeraire De, 2089
Cooptalis, 2842
Coord, 1896

1265

Portfolio Companies Index

Coordinated Care Solutions, 1107
Copa90, 641
Copac, 418
Copado, 1005
Copan Systems, 205
Copano Energy, 1837, 1848
Copart Inc., 303
CoPatient, 1, 2225
Copia, 1330
Copient Health, 191
Copilot, 1890
CoPilot AI, 2074
Copiun, 1101, 1348
Coplex, 3265
Copper, 234, 894, 1086, 1346
Copper Key, 2020
Copper Mountain, 759, 1091, 1561, 1762
Copper Mountain Beverages, 1514
CopperEgg, 1813
CopperEye, 983
Copperfield Chimney Supply, 911
Coppergate, 3212
Coprocure, 771
Coprosain, 3125
Copysmith AI Inc., 1499
COR, 1762
Cor4 Oil, 1129
Cora Health Services, 886
Coradiant, 597, 1237
Coraid, 1076
Coral Eurobet, 2578
Coral Network, 1561
Coral Systems, 1399
Coral Therapeutics, 1631
Coralog, 2846
CorAssist, 2717, 3231, 3239
Corassist, 2445
CorasWorks, 1348
Coravin, 1993
Corbin Therapeutics Inc., 2031
Corbus Pharmaceuticals, 1164
Corcept Therapeutics, 1762, 1788
Corda Campus, 2940
Cordance, 85
Cordant, 1964
Cordata, 86, 481
Cordial, 1890
Cordium, 3121
Corduro, 894
Core, 1724
Core BTS, 1779
Core Business Technology Solutions, 777
Core Capital Partners, 3260
Core Commnications, 1603
CORE Diagnostics, 176
Core Innovation Capital, 1374
CORE Interactive, 3257
Core Line Pipe, 2022
Core OS, 2006
CORE Outdoor Power, 1626
Core Pacific Group, 2624
Core Pharma, 1594
Core Photonics, 2822, 2943
Core Security Technologies, 1255, 2326
Core Solutions, 1572, 1581
Core Tigo, 1672
CoreCare Systems, 1204
Coredial, 233, 1140
CoreHr, 1045
Corel, 1912
CoreLab, 119
CoreLab Partners, 56, 1631
Corelight, 27, 820
CoreLink Data Centers, 1157
CoreLogic, 303
CoreMedia, 3146
Coremetrics, 796, 1649, 1949

Corengi, 1618
Corensic, 2007
CoreObjects, 1408
CoreOptics, 556, 990, 2630
CoreOS, 2011
CorePharma Holdings, 1460
Corephotonics, 117
CorePower Yoga, 1092
CoreSpring, 1315
CoreStreet, 1888
Coretec, 2162
CoreTek, 55, 1042
Coretelligent, 1929
Coreteq Systems, 3132
CoreTrace, 1918
Coretronic, 2427
CoreValue Software, 226
Corevia Medical, 820
CoreView, 1005
Coreworks, 2708
Coreworx, 2103
Corex, 2562
Corfin Industries LLC, 248
Corgenix, 1839
Corgreen Technologies, 1083
Corhythm, 984
Corindus Vascular Robotics Inc., 272
Corio, 759
Coriolis Networks, 317
Cority, 1346, 2126
Cority Software Inc., 159
Corium, 139
Corix Group, 2045
Corixa, 772, 785, 1762
Cormetech, 676
Cormetrics, 27
Cormier Textile Products, 440
Corn. Van Loocke, 2324
Corneliani, 1021
Corner Bakery Cafe, 1580
Cornerjob, 641, 2865
Cornershop, 27, 1028
Cornerstone, 241
Cornerstone Automation Systems, 479
Cornerstone Brands, 1160
Cornerstone Chemical, 931
Cornerstone Chemical Company, 1138
Cornerstone Concrete, 464
Cornerstone Fund Services, 3265
Cornerstone Medical & Technology Financial, 3250
Cornerstone Natural Resources, 673
Cornerstone On Demand, 31
Cornerstone OnDemand, 263, 1213
Cornhusker Energy, 41
Cornice, 928
Cornice Corporation, 2073
Corona Labs, 1219
Corona Optical Systems, 1061
Coronado Curragh Pty., 971
Coronis, 2472
Coronis Health, 352
Coronis Systems, 2457
Corpak Medsystems, 1132
Corpmart.com, 2984
Corporate Trael International, 2935
Corporate Visions, 408
CorporateRewards, 1576
Corporation Dermoaesthetica (Spain), 2775
Corpus Medical, 119
Correct Care Solutions, 197, 889
CorrectNet, 2188
Corredge Networks, 1678
Correlated Magnetics Research, 1032
Correlia Biosystems, 2205
Correlix, 3230
CorrelSense, 3050

Correlsense, 3205
CorridorPharma, 1510
Corrigo, 115, 780, 1736, 1771
Corrmoran, 2815
Corrona, 864
Corsa, 2070
Corsa Technology, 2234
Corsair, 782
Corsair Communications, 1684
Corsica Innovations Inc., 492
Corsicana Mattress Company, 1145
Corso UK, 2958
CorSolutions Medical Corporation, 958
Cort, 357
CorTec, 2815, 2923
Cortefiel, 912, 3024
Cortene, 1099
Cortera, 238, 1832
Cortex, 9, 641, 1760
Cortex Pharmaceuticals, 979
Cortexica Vision Systems, 2849
Cortexyme, 1657, 1780
Corthera, 1900
Corti, 2842
Cortica, 1, 2822
Cortigroupe, 3125
Cortilla, 2663
Cortina, 87, 389, 597, 972
Cortina Systems, 1084, 1257, 1913
Corton Precision Optical Company, 1561
Corus Health Realty, 1603
Corus Pharma, 133, 1007
Corval Energy, 2022
Corvara, 2317
Corvas International, 1708, 1920
Corventis, 1247, 1502
Corvia Medical, 2174
Corvida Medical, 1065
Corvidia Therapeutics, 144
Corvil, 485, 1525, 2463
Corvita Corporation, 1379
Corvium, 571
Corvus, 1
Corvus Insurance, 1363
Corwave, 3104
CoScale, 3056
CoSchedule, 817
Cosemi Technologies, 1786
Cosential, 51
Cosentry, 1778
CoSine Communications, 759, 1795
Coskata, 58, 839, 1478
Cosm Care, 2141
Cosmetic Essence Innovations, 1138
Cosmic Cart, 635
Cosmosbay, 2346
Cosmosbay Vectis, 2346
Cosmotech, 2430
Cost:bart, 3194
Costanoa Venture Capital, 1762
Costco, 1100
Costco Wholesale, 874
Costella Kirsch, 3273
Costello, 659
CoStim, 1421
CoStim Pharmaceuticals, 193, 1268
Cota, 698
Cota Capital, 298
CoTap, 457
Cotap, 666
Cote Sud Invetissement, 2592
CoTEch Ventures, 3251
Cotendo, 1478
Cotera, 622
Cotherics, 785
Cotherix, 94
Cotiviti, 1927

Portfolio Companies Index

Cotopaxi, 328, 545, 728, 763, 1074, 1114, 2137
Cottan Cosmetic GmbH, 2485
Cotterlaz, 2309
Cotton Patch Cafe, 96
Cotton Tracks, 2975
Cottonwood Capital, 464
CoTweet, 234
Coty Inc., 745
COUB, 895
Couchbase, 27, 56, 621, 840, 978, 1187, 1335, 3225
CouchDB Relax, 1537
CouchSurfing, 820, 1203, 3035
Couchsurfing, 251, 1374
CouchUp, 587
Coulomb Technologies, 915
Council Oak Resources, 673
Counsel On Call, 495, 1169
Counsel Press, 832, 1194
Counselytics, 527
Counsyl, 778, 863
Countable, 937
Counterpane Internet Security, 263
CounterPath, 2276
CounterPoint Health Solutions, 974
CounterStorm, 1042, 1348
CounterTack, 173, 713, 1241, 2681
Countertop Foods, 121
Countly, 3099
Country Club Enterprises, 832
Country Fresh, 687
Country Pure Foods, 293, 620
Country Road Communications, 20
CountryBanc, 1372
Countryside Hospice, 935
Countryside Power Income Fund, 2067
Countrywide plc, 141
Coupa, 238, 299, 564, 1213, 1247, 1525
Coupang, 91, 100, 561, 774, 980, 1479, 2700
Coupling Wave Solutions, 2377
CouponRani, 3124
Coupons.com, 1848
CoupSmart, 1514
CoUrbanize, 311
Courier, 771
Courion, 1045, 1401, 1517
Course Hero, 116, 863, 888, 1186
Course Report, 1554
CourseHorse, 1305, 1309, 1358
Coursera, 805, 888, 1079, 1296, 1643, 2681
CourseStorm, 1165
Coursicle, 999
Court Buddy, 742
Court Square Capital Partners, 3254
Court Square Capital Partners III LP, 2088
Courtagen, 733
Courtagen Life Sciences, 910
CourtLink, 85
CourtTrax, 1227
Cova, 2129, 2262
Covacsis, 485
Covalent, 1426
Covalent Health, 929
Covariant, 222
Covariant AI, 3, 1614
Covario, 796, 1947
Covaro Networks, 446
Covast, 2770, 3223
Cove.tool, 1896
Covelight Systems, 1013
Covenant Care, 449
Covenant Healthcare, 2686
Covenant Review, 1109
Covenant Surgical Partners, 1086
Coventor, 815
CoVenture, 863
Coventya, 2956

Coveo, 2255
Coveo Solutions, 2252
Cover, 863, 1186, 1359, 1534, 1666, 1698, 1850
Cover FX, 1092
Cover My Test, 1172
Coverall, 973, 1493
Covercraft Industries LLC, 451
Coverfox, 27
CoverHound, 304, 361, 1597
Coverhound, 129
Coveright Surfaces GmbH, 2651
Coveright Surfaces Holding GmbH, 917
Coveris, 1755
Coverity, 454
CoverMyMeds, 782, 1051
Coveroo, 533, 1543
Covertix, 2660
CoverWallet, 773, 1884
Covestor, 241, 1718
Covics, 2927
covina Biomedical, 2148
CoWare, 1287
Coware Inc., 2893
Cox Insurance, 2667
Coxon, 2427
Coya, 641
Coyne Textile Services, 405
Coyote Logistics, 1957
Coyuchi, 549, 3083
Cozart, 2454
Cozi Group, 928
Cozy, 820, 894, 1659, 1698
Cozzini Bros, 197, 2056
Cozzini Bros., 159
CP Energy, 560
CP Media LLC, 670
CP Secure, 908
CP Well Testing, 1493
CPA, 2958
CPA Global, 745, 1113
CPC, 194, 3011
CPCEP, 3185
CPF Living Communities; Florida Elite Medical Grou, 471
CPG International, 63, 1041
CPG International Inc., 160
CPI, 170, 790, 2686
CPI Card Group, 2206
CPI International, 1927
CPI Luxury Group, 16
CPI. Crown Van Gelder, 124
CPL Industries, 1939
CPM Holdings, 831
CPO Commerce, 1843
CPower, 263, 707, 931
Cpower, 2430
CPS, 789, 2665
CPS Houston, 988
CPS Products Inc., 911
CPT, 2701
CPUsage, 1254
CPV Maryland Holding Company II, 159
CPV Wind Ventures, 157
CPX Lone Tree Hotel, 1024
CPX Security, 180
CQMS Razer, 110
CQS, 2700
Cquia, 1359
CQuotient, 224
CR Brands, 1548
CR Media Group, 2478
CR-X, 2966
CR2, 2328, 3182
CRA Continental Realty Advisors, 300
Crackle, 1323
Cradle Technologies, 928
Cradle Techologies, 1678

CradlePoint, 1205
Cradlepoint Technology, 1392
Craegmoor, 2926
Craft Dragon, 2958
Craft International, 517
Craft Media Network, 378
CraftArtEdu, 378
CraftMark Bakery, 479
Craftrad, 3226
Craftsmen Industries, 1481
Craftsvilla, 1125
Craftsvilla.com, 2992
Craftsy, 35, 1751
Craftyful, 1966
Craigcare Group, 2805
Crain Hot Old Services, 1057
Cramster.com, 1103
Crane & Co., 77, 1133
Crane 1, 1438
Crane Company, 836
Craneware, 3095
Cranial Technologies, 247
Cranite Systems, 1042
Cranium, 1186, 1867
Cranswick Pet and Aquatics (Tropical Marine Center, 2935
Crash, 1530
Crashlytics, 234
CrashMob, 1290
Crate, 2665
Crate.io, 2018
Crater, 229, 1323
Crave Labs, 1488
Crawfish Cogen, 157
Crawley Ventures LLC, 3265
Craxel, 856
Crayon, 234
CRB Innovations, 1561
CRC Health, 376, 377
CRC Health Group, 223
CRC Industries Inc., 261
CRCM Ventures, 485
Cre Apps, 2975
Creal, 2330
Crealta Pharmaceuticals, 889
Crealytics, 2815, 2923, 2970
Creas Carolinas, 3250
Creatcomm, 1511
Create Electronic Optical Co, 2694
Create&Learn, 888
Create1, 1589
Creation Holdings Inc., 159
Creation Technologies, 2073, 2076
Creative Artists Agency, 1837
Creative Circle, 1256
Creative Deign Systems, 627
Creative Forming, 1174
Creative Labs, 3099
Creative Live, 520, 720
Creative Market, 1150, 1658, 2024
Creative Mines, 851
Creative Multimedia, 755, 1399
Creative Peptides Sweden AB, 2807
Creative Solutions Group, 1294
CreativeDrive, 260
CreativeGig, 1959
CreativeLIVE, 1698, 2419
CreativeLive, 877
Creativelive, 888
creativeLIVE, 894
CreativeWorx, 1305
Creativity Software, 2963
Creator, 521, 894
CreatorDen, 2276
CREDANT Technologies, 556
Credant Technologies, 205, 990
Credence, 58

Portfolio Companies Index

Credence Resources, 2129
Credence Systems, 205, 1684
Credential, 2530
Credential Solutions, 337
Crederity, 3202
Credibly, 751
CrediFi, 238, 3212
Credit Benchmark, 2469
Credit Central, 1493
Credit Infonet Group, 1654
Credit Karma, 579, 720, 1504, 1761, 1949
Credit Key, 309
Credit Sesame, 387, 839, 1017, 1203
CreditCall Limited, 2498
CreditCards.com, 205
CreditEase, 977
CreditKarma, 1563
CreditSights, 712
CreditStacks, 1370
Credivalores, 45
Credly, 2074
Credo West, 517
CredoRax, 2965
Credorax, 304, 796
CredSimple, 320, 1479, 1993
CreekPath Systems, 1795
Creekstone Farms, 1755
Creganna, 97
Creganna-Tactx Medical, 3024
Crehana, 1554
Crelate Talent, 746
Cremascoli Ortho, 2667
Creme de la Creme, 64
Creme Mel, 931
Creo Products, 3128
CREPAPER GmbH, 2677
Cresa, 3268
Crescendo, 2122, 2763
Crescendo Biologics, 184, 1780, 2454, 2958
Crescendo Biosciences, 1247
Crescendo Biosciene, 1693
Crescendo Communications, 1855, 1898
Crescendo Networks, 2463
Crescendo Ventures, 990
Crescent, 418
Crescent City Schools, 1315
Crescent Diagnostics, 2909
Crescent Entertainment, 496
Crescent Sleep Products, 847
CrescentDx, 2347
Crescerance, 274
CRESecure, 1865
Cresilon, 623
Cressey & Company, 3254, 3255
Crestcom, 1280
Crestcom International, 1487
CrestMarc, 2969
Crestmark, 1220
Crestview Partners, 3245
Crestwood, 1848
Crestwood Midstream Partners, 280
Crete Energy, 1797
Crevet Limited, 2942
Crew, 48, 182, 877, 1101, 1657, 1724
Crexendo, 1587
CREXi, 787, 1059
Crexi, 231, 1028, 1114
CRFS Services, 935
CRG, 2107
CRH Healthcare, 786
CRI Worldwide, 119, 1631
Cribspot, 964
Cricket Health, 321, 742, 1323, 1659
Cril Telecom Software, 2346, 2772
CrimeReports, 205
Crimson Hexagon, 845, 863, 1441, 1588, 1759, 2016

Crimson Pipeline LP, 1326, 1328
Crimson Well Services Inc., 905
Crinetics, 11, 1522, 1930
Crioestaminal, 1576
Crisi Medical Systems, 1786
Crisp Media, 541, 1212
Crisplant Industries, 2854
Crispr, 1930
Crispr Therapeutics, 1296, 1734
Cristal Delivery, 2505
Criteo, 56, 263, 1701, 2684, 2842, 2851, 2851
Criteria Investment Partners LLC, 624
Criteria Labs, 1917
Criterion Brock, 1970
Critical Alert Systems, 1970
Critical Blue, 3023
Critical Links, 3039
Critical Media, 496
Critical Mention, 1305, 1588, 1682, 1748
Critical Path, 1247
Critical Perfusion, 1604
Critical Signal Technologies, 634, 636
Critical Solutions International, 1654, 1872
Critical Start, 336
CriticalFit, 452
Criticalpath, 2762
Critigen, 127, 843
Crius Energy, 127, 708
CRMnext, 1346
Crocodoc, 1585
Crocs, 280
Crocus, 2867
Crocus Technology, 3199
CrodFlower, 1515
Crom, 1270
Crompco Corp., 467
Crono, 1003
Cronofy, 945, 3099
Cronos, 1066
Crop Design, 2772
Croptimistic Technology Inc., 2115
Croptimize Inc., 395
Cropx, 1001
Crosman Acquisition Corporation, 767
Crosman Corporation, 1972
Cross, 494
Cross Fader, 1752
Cross Fernandez & Riley, 3251
Cross Mediaworks, 494, 520, 1108
Cross River, 125
Cross River Bank, 238
Cross Trees Medical, 179
Cross-Country Infrastructure Services Inc., 1368
Crossbar, 176, 545, 1079, 1340
Crossbeam, 742
Crossbeam Systems, 317, 457, 457, 523, 759, 1184, 1731
Crossboard Mobiel, 1597
Crossboard Mobil, 1290
Crossbow, 1401
Crossbow Technology, 381, 1257
CrossCHX, 631
CrossCom, 319
Crosscom National, 842
CrossComm, 3250
CrossEngage, 2832
CrossEyes, 3194
Crossfader, 721
CrossFiber, 173, 1304, 1713
Crossing Automation Inc., 1781
Crossing Rocks Energy, 1326
Crosslayer Networks, 1183
CrossLoop, 103
Crossman Corporation, 1493
Crossmark, 1957
Crossmatch, 782
CrossMedia Services, 162, 808

Crossover, 608
Crossplane Capital, 13
Crossrider, 1323
CrossRoads, 1190
Crossroads Systems, 205
Crosstown Traders, 843
Crosstown Traders Inc., 435
Crosstrees Medical, 1561
Crossvertise, 2815
Crossway Media Solutions, 2325
Crosswire, 2822
Crothall Healthcare, 1140
Crowd AI, 321
Crowd Architects, 2518
Crowd Compass, 85
Crowd Cow, 1162, 1186
Crowd Factory, 1750
Crowd Guru, 2832
Crowd Strike, 579
Crowd Supply, 1659
Crowd Technologies, 2958
CrowdAI, 108, 527, 1760
Crowdamp, 1125
Crowdanalytix, 27
Crowdbabble, 2094
Crowdbooster, 1515
Crowdcare, 2107
Crowdcast, 1323
CrowdCompass, 1384
CrowdComputing Systems, 876
Crowdcube, 2469
Crowdcube.com, 2665
Crowded, 151
CrowdEngineering, 2663, 3043
CrowdFlower, 263, 399, 787, 1054, 1855
CrowdHall, 1914
CrowdJustice, 742
Crowdly, 1104, 1305, 2016
Crowdpac, 545
CrowdProcess, 3099
CrowdRiff, 2127
CrowdRise, 1884, 1885
Crowdrise, 1121
CrowdStar, 949, 1829
Crowdster, 396
CrowdStreet, 1659
CrowdStrike, 27, 1371, 1957
CrowdTangle, 59, 1305
Crowdtap, 779, 1851
Crowdtest, 2323
Crowdtilt, 597
CrowdTwist, 686, 713, 1701, 1741
Crowdtwist, 1791
CrowdVision, 2392
CrowdWorks, 2637
Crowdz, 198
Crowe Horwath, 3251
Crowe Paradis Servicing Corp., 494
Crowe UK LLP, 3265
Crown Affair, 328
Crown Bioscience, 46, 1383
Crown Brands, 448
Crown Castle International, 1212
Crown Column, 418
Crown Fiberglass, 1921
Crown Group, 607
Crown Laboratories, 1251
Crown Pacific, 371
Crown Plastics, 60
Crown Products & Services, 1210
Crownit, 27
Crownpeak, 1028
CrownPeak Technology, 1674
CrownRock, 1129
CrownRock Minerals, 1129
CrownWheel Partners, 1147
CRS CraneSystems, 2227

Portfolio Companies Index

CRS Proppants, 687
CRS Reprocessing Services, 165
CRS Temporary Housing, 1169
CRT Midco, 1493
CRU Kafe, 3099
CRU-DataPort, 1911
Crucell, 193, 1777, 2370, 2739
CrucialTec, 1091
Cruise, 774, 945, 1330, 1680
Cruise Automation, 3
Crunch, 128
CrunchBase, 720
Crunchbase, 666, 1187, 1610, 2074
Crunchbutton, 788
Cruncher, 23
CrunchFund, 205
CrunchTime!, 238
Crunchvase, 553
Crunchyroll, 1918
Crushpath, 457
Crux Biomedical, 667, 928
Crux Ocm, 2131
Cruzar Medical, 428
CRV, 3263
Cryo-Cell, 1683
CryoCor, 186, 470, 1788
Cryocor, 561
Cryogen, 1788
Cryothermic Systems, 296, 1051, 1556
Cryotherpeutics, 2815
CryoVascular Systems, 1898
Crypt, 1114
Crypt TV, 59
CryptoKitties, 125, 527
CryptoMove, 1423
Cryptomove, 1698
CryptoNumerics, 3
Crysalin, 2883
CrystAI-N, 2815
Crystal, 275, 1610
Crystal & Company, 3257
Crystal CG, 2724, 2927
Crystal Decisions, 200
Crystal Dynamics, 132
Crystal Financial, 1314
Crystal IS, 1155
Crystal Jade, 1092
Crystal Optech, 2533
Crystal Orange Hotel Holdings, 416
Crystal Packaging, 1839
Crystal Semi, 1561
Crystal Semiconductor, 205
Crystal Semiconductor, 1684
Crystal Solar, 1365, 1793
Crystal-IS, 154
Crystalplex, 1102, 1452
Crystalsol, 2621
Crystaplex Corporation, 1003
Crystax, 2474
Crystechcoating, 2658
Crysteel Manufacturing, 620
CS Identity, 595, 953
CS Indemnity, 409
CSA Medical, 178, 291, 733, 891, 1013, 1298, 1631, 1764
CSA Service Solutions, 668
CSafe Global, 97
CSALC, 1340
CSAT Solutions, 368
CSC Media Group, 1929
CSDVRS, 1157, 1498
CSG Systems International, 1852
CSI Leasing, 458
CSID, 447
CSIdentity, 1021
CSK Auto, 1021
CSL, 3136

CSL DualCom, 3009
CSM Bakery Solutions, 408
CSP Business Media, 1424
CSP Holdings, 554
CSP II Destressed Opportunities Trust, 624
CSR, 2378, 3095
CSRHub, 3246
CST Images, 1839
CSTV, 42
CT Acquisition Corp., 1252
CT Therapeutics, 183
CTACCEL, 1009
CTEK Creator Group, 2376
CTERA, 485
Ctera, 1918
CTI Foods, 1138, 1818
CTI Life Sciences Fund, 3249
CTI Semiconductor, 2915
CTI Towers, 520
CTM Group Inc., 847
CTO.ai, 2283
Cto.Ai, 2204
CTP Hydrogen, 522
CTP Offshore-C Feeder Fund Ltd., 2088
Ctrip, 977, 2841
CTRL, 3141
CTRL-Labs, 894, 1155
Ctrlio, 3099
CTS, 1130
Cuadrilla Resources Holdings, 1577
Cub Digital, 2927
Cube, 586
Cube Biotech, 2629
Cube Optics, 1661
Cube Optics AG, 3128
Cube26, 1959
CubeTree, 1855
CubeWorks, 1009
Cubex, 961
Cubical, 2815
Cubie, 3029
Cubie Messenger, 2465
Cubility, 468, 2691
Cubist Pharmaceuticals, 413, 1456, 1777
Cuboh, 2132
Cubyn, 2288
Cuculus, 2815
Cudahy Tanning Co., 1214
Cue, 44, 1823
Cue & Co., 1086
Cuebiq, 151, 2865
Cuemath, 579
Cuff-Gard, 999
Cuff-Mate, 1190
Culcherd, 2093
Culinary Agents, 1223
Culinary Standards, 1333
Cullinan Oncology, 1268
Cultivian Sandbox, 3259
Culture Amp, 720
CultureIQ, 232, 1114, 1914
CultureiQ, 1483
CultureLabel, 2676
Culturelabel.com, 2577
CultureMob, 85
CulturVate, 2276
Culver's, 1580
Cumbak, 3100
Cumberland Consulting Group, 1779
Cumberland Therapy Services, 1670
Cumming Acquisition, 1460
Cumming Group, 1145, 1779
Cumulocity, 2815
Cumulocity GmbH, 3204
Cumulus, 125
Cumulus Media, 223, 560, 1818
Cumulus Networks, 238, 1657, 1996

Cunningham Lindsey, 1138
Cunningham Lindsey Group Limited, 1746
Cupo Nation, 2829
Cupoint, 2461
Cura Software, 2700
Curacity, 1557
Curacyte, 2369
Curagen, 532
Curai, 820
Curalate, 742
Curam Software, 2725
CuraSeal, 1993
Curaseal, 179
Curasen Therapeutics, 1147
Curaspan Health Group, 1176
Curative Orthopaedics, 623
Curb, 447
curbFlow, 1895
Curbide, 1800
Curbio, 1172
Curbo, 2176
Cure Match, 122
CureAtr, 1993
Cureatr, 51, 1422
Curebase, 709
Cureeo, 1618
CureFab, 2815
Curefab, 2466
Curefit, 27
Curejoy, 27
CureLauncher, 985
CureMint, 512
Cureo, 1051
Cureon, 2869
Curetis, 2506, 2739, 2930, 3076
Cureus, 493
Curie Co., 398
Curiosity, 1385
Curiosity.com, 1483
Curious AI Company, 2469
Curious.com, 1537
CurlMix, 221
Curo, 790
Curology, 44, 763
Curon Medical, 1379
Curoverse, 536, 918, 1463
Currency, 1151
Currency Capital, 408
Currency Cloud, 37
Currencycloud, 894, 2398
Currencyfair, 2750
Currensee, 1335
Current Analysis, 138
Current Media, 303
Current Motor Company, 743
Current TV, 1087
CurrentAnalysis, 993
Curriculet, 1315
Curriculum Associates, 257
Currie Medical, 1232
Currie Medical Specialties Inc., 1044
Curse, 827, 1702, 2842, 3199
Cursogram, 3046
CURT Manufacturing, 1438
Curtis Bay Energy, 1025
Curtis Bay Medical Waste Services, 1753
Curtis Industries Holdings, 1278
Curtis Papers Inc., 1089
Curtis Screw Company, 1971
Curvature, 1507
Curve, 3099
Curve Dental, 238
Curves, 1336
Curvo, 659
Cuseum, 802
Cushcraft Corporation, 692
Cushman & Wakefield, 1837, 2196, 3250

Portfolio Companies Index

Custom Composites, 1224
Custom Control Concepts, 1424
Custom Engineered Wheels Inc., 903
Custom Ink, 862, 1768
Custom Made, 1630
Custom Marketing, 402
Custom Molded Products, 753, 1461
Custom Profile, 279
Custom Sensors & Technologies, 416, 3017
Custom Steel Processing, 367
Custom Welding Services, 2278
Custom Wholesale Floors, 1216
Custom Window Systems, 1278
Custom Wood Products, 854
CustomAir, 368
CustomControl Concepts, 1707
Customer Alliance, 2970
Customer Matrix, 2430
Customer XPs Software Private Limited, 3053
Customer.io, 321, 1384, 1659, 2016
CustomerLink Systems Inc., 74
CustomMade, 1101, 1322
CustomVine, 1320
Custora, 773, 820, 1901
Cut, 520
Cute Metrix, 122
Cute Town, 2847
Cutera, 94
Cutex, 1424
CutisCare, 277
CutisPharma, 119
Cutler Repaving Inc., 1057
Cutters, 1131
Cutters Wireline Services, 1071
Cutting Edge Gamer, 447
Cuvva, 3099
Cuyana, 389
CV Finer Foods, 440
CV Holdings, 1425
CV Ingenuity, 1775
CV Ingenuity Corp., 272
CV Lab, 2865
CV Properties LLC, 1738
CV Therapeutics, 1777
CVA, 35
cValue, 2994
CVC Brasil Operadora e Agencia de Viagens S.A., 416
CVC Capital Partners, 3245, 3254
CVC Private Equity, 2622
CVC Sustainable, 2622
CVCI Growth Partnership II, 2088
CVE Technology Group Inc., 277
Cvent, 275, 1603
CVI, 2969
cVidya, 3128
cVidya Networks, 2557, 3127
CVRx, 22, 1063, 1993
CVS Sciences, 11
CVT, 2575
CVT Corp., 2087
CVT Therapeutics, 785
CVTCORP, 2255
CVWarehouse, 2828
CW Environmental, 2354
CW Financial Services, 769
CWC Well Services, 2062
CWK Network, 1955
CWP Coloured Wood Products Oy, 2864
CWR Mobility, 2813
Cx, 1832
CXO Systems, 1084
CxS Corporation, 416
Cy World, 2848
Cyalume, 172
Cyalume Technologies, 1424
Cyan, 218, 1076, 1784, 1798

Cyan Optics, 759
Cyanide, 2890
Cyanogen, 1511, 1537
Cyara, 872
Cybeats, 2178, 2232
Cyber Physical Systems, 1261
Cyber Rain, 68, 800, 1786
Cyber-Ark, 3205
Cyber-Care, 215
Cyber-Patrol, 1431
Cyber-Rain, 189
Cybera, 56, 495, 1730
CyberAlert, 124
CyberCore Technologies, 681, 1401
CyberGrants, 1964
CyberGRX, 84, 894, 1796
Cyberhawk, 3095
CyberHeart, 667
Cyberian Outpost, 532
Cyberinc, 252
Cyberis Group, 870
Cyberkinetics, 1695
Cyberkinetics Inc., 2776
Cybernetiq, 2178
Cyberpoint, 1730
Cyberrinc, 1032
CyberShift, 1140
CyberSmart, 3099
CyberSource, 1890
CyberSpa, 18
CyberSponse, 288
Cybersports, 2828
CyberX, 724, 1346
Cybex Computer Products Corporation, 1152
Cybrant, 556
Cybrary, 175, 288
Cybrid, 2131, 2927
CYC Fitness, 1589
Cyclacel, 3095
Cyclacel Pharmaceuticals, 2681
Cycle Capital Management, 3249
Cycle Gear Inc., 917
Cycle Taiwan, 3029
Cycleenergy, 2301
Cycleon, 2466
Cyclonaire Holding Corporation, 1494
Cyclone Commerce, 162
Cyclo<des, 2263
Cyco Software, 2770
Cycognito, 117
Cydan, 240, 1147, 1439
Cydas, 1610
Cydcor, 843
CyDex Pharmaceuticals, 1578
Cyence, 1006
Cyfe, 92
CyFir, 971
Cygate, 2879
CyGene Inc., 589
Cygent, 556
Cygilant, 1918
Cygnal, 205
Cygnal Technologies, 2051
Cygnus Hospitals, 711
Cygnus Solutions, 200
Cyient, 416
Cylacel Pharmaceuticals, 2504
Cylance, 488, 604, 713, 1005, 1073, 1086, 1796
Cylene Pharmaceuticals, 1241, 1546, 1619
Cylera, 1614
Cylex, 307, 379
CymaBay, 1930
CymaBay Therapeutics, 240, 764, 1908
Cymabay Therapeutics, 1918
Cymat, 2051, 2051
Cymax, 2137
Cymbet Corp, 2964

Cymbet Corporation, 186
Cymedica Orthopedics, 139
Cymer, 1920
Cymmetria, 44, 720, 3099
Cymphonix, 1205
Cymtec, 2728
Cynapsus, 73
Cynet, 1346
CYNGN, 125
Cynosure, 317
Cynvenio Biosystems, 133
CyOptics, 2711, 2866, 2901
Cyota, 263
CypherWorX, 705
Cyphort, 621, 773, 1184
CyPhy, 820
Cyphy, 1260
Cyphy Works, 720
Cypress, 1412, 1657
Cypress Cellular LP, 123
Cypress Communications, 153
Cypress Five Star, 2162
Cypress Semiconductor, 564, 1561
Cypress.io, 285
Cyrano, 3199
Cyras Systems, 1203, 1781
Cyren, 3092
CYRK, 799
CyrusOne, 20
Cysal, 2677, 2815
Cyteir Therapeutics, 1271, 1918
Cytheris, 2457, 2739, 3011
Cytimune Sciences, 1172
CytoAgents, 296
Cytochroma, 3006
Cytogel, 450
Cytogen Corp., 1048
Cytokinetics, 94
CytoLogix Corporation, 317
CytoMed, 1561
Cytomedix, 1172
CytomX Therapeutics, 389, 1814, 3076
Cytoo, 2701
CytoPherx, 139, 403, 642, 667, 1337, 1379
Cytos, 73
Cytos Biotechnology AG, 2776
Cytosolv, 1695
CytoSorbents, 1329
Cytosport, 1863
Cytovale, 222
Cytovance Biologics, 864
Cytovas, 269
Cytovia, 767
Cytoville, 711
Cytox, 2958
Cytrellis, 271
CYTYC, 58
Cytyc, 55
Cyvek, 532
CyVera, 1915
Cyvera, 304, 532
CYVision, 1009
Czech On Line, 2420
Cu□r, 1083

D

D Square, 2940
D&D London, 2935
D&F Solution, 2848
D&M Holdings, 223
D&S Community Services, 530
D&S Residential Services, 1424, 1487
D'Lisi Food Systems, 1748
D-Eye, 2865
D-gate Semiconductor, 2824
D-Labs, 2804
D-Link, 897

Portfolio Companies Index

D-Pharm, 2576, 2761, 3221
D-Share, 3043
D-Wave, 265
D-Wave Systems, 5
D.Light, 54, 2430, 2992
d.light, 860
D.Light Design, 794
D.light Design, 810
D.M. Robichaud, 2180
D.S. Brown, 445
D.Western Therapeutics, 2961
D1G1T, 2107
D1g1t, 2217
D2 Audio, 205
D2 Hawkeye, 352
D2Audio, 446
D2E Capital, 2940
D2Hawkeye, 1071
D2S, 582
D30, 254
D3O, 2701
D4C Dental Brands, 247
Dabbl, 89
dabble, 1159
Dabee, 2967, 2974
DAC, 2838
Dac, 2427
Dacentec, 3033
Dacentec/Awingu, 2828
Dachis Group, 205
Dacor, 874
Dadam Game, 3118
Daddies Board Shop, 1965
DadLabs, 595
Dae-in-lnfo sys, 2960
Daechun Greenwater, 585
Daekyung Machinery & Engineering, 2848
Daesan Energy, 585
Daesung Eltec, 3136
Daewon Special Wire Co, 2798
DAFCA, 1084, 1304
Dafiti, 2820, 2829, 3161
Dagne Dover, 623
Daguu, 2860
Daher Lhotellier, 2712
Dahlam Rose & Co., 1151
Dailey Grommet, 1101
DaileyCred, 894
Daily Harvest, 1125, 1599
Daily Juice, 447
Daily Secret, 641, 876
DailyBreak, 457
DailyBurn, 686
DailyCall, 3104
DailyLook, 1890
DailyMe, 1404
Dailyme, 3226
dailyme TV, 2832
Dailymotion, 1418, 2842
DailyObjects, 3100
DailyPay, 1643, 2112
DailyPerfect, 2382
DailyWOrth, 1832
DailyWorth, 609
DailyWorth.com, 3246
Dainese, 1021
DairyMart, 1071
Daisy Manufacturing Co., 357
Daisytek International, 470
Dakim, 809
Dakine, 96
Dakota, 2937
Dakota Arms, 381, 1917
Dakota Bodies, 2969
Dakota Minnesota & Eastern Railroad, 1143
Dakotaland Autoglass, 1195
Dakotaland Manufacturing, 300

Daktari, 1206
Daktari Diagnostics, 1347, 1421
Dal Bolognese Ristorante, 2393
Dalbo, 1071
Dalbo Holdings, 1131
Dalcor Pharmaceuticals, 2086
Dale Gas Partners, 479
Dale Power Solutions, 2935
Daleen Technologies, 1042
Dalet, 1991, 2346
Dali Wireless, 1302, 2448
Dali Wireless Systems, 1740
Dalia, 3226
Dalia Research, 2469, 2832
Dalie, 2593
Dalipal Pipe Company, 897
DalRybProm, 2482
Daltys, 2285, 3011
Dalus, 2374
Damac, 1826
Damac Products, 1473
Damar Aerosystems, 82
Damark International, 538
Damballa, 56, 304, 1014, 1401, 1408, 1674, 1675
Damon X Labs, 2107
Dan Howard Industries, 449
Dan-Loc, 165
Dan-Loc Bolt & Gasket, 1505
dan.com, 971
Dana, 444
Dana Hospitality, 2121
Dana-Farber Cancer Institute, 1271
Dancap Family Investment Office, 3249
DanceOn, 1103, 1816
DanChem, 653
Dancing Deer Baking, 845, 1025
Danco Machine, 832
Dandelion, 882
Dandelion Energy, 311, 514
Danforth Advisors LLC, 406
Dangdang, 2841
Dangdang.com, 597
Danger, 116, 614, 1006, 1213, 2866, 3146
Danger Inc, 186
Daniel's Jewelers, 1404
Danilait, 2880
Dank Business Systems Plc., 576
Danna McKitrick PC, 3261
Danone, 475
Dansk Erhvervsinvestering, 2438
Danskin, 799
Dantec Dynamics, 238
Dantom Systems Inc., 654
Dantz, 936, 1640
Dantz Development Corporation, 755
Danville, 1018
Danziger Innovations, 3235
Dao Aviation, 3194
Daojia, 1340
Dapper, 1918, 2272
Dapper Labs, 1614, 1884
Daptiv, 85
DARAG Group, 560
DarbeeVision, 2769
Darby Smart, 763, 1186
Darfon Electronics, 897
Dark, 308
Dark Cubed, 288
Dark Owl, 746
Dark Water Studios, 2601
Darks Club, 2915
Darkstore, 1935
DarkTrace, 1005, 2825
Darktrace, 1086, 1796
DarkVision Technologies, 2105
Darmiyan, 721
DarQroom, 2890

Darrow Associates, 3257
DART Aerospace, 867
Darwin, 1426
Darwin AI, 2132, 2150
DarwinAI, 1363
Darwinai, 2122
Darwinbox, 1125
Dash, 601, 623, 1305, 1896
Dash Hudson, 2063, 2148
Dash Navigation, 556
Dashbell, 1737
Dashbid, 450
DashBin, 1585
Dashboard Director, 868
Dashbot, 724, 1614
Dashdash, 27
Dasher, 1254
Dashlane, 263, 744, 1561
DashWire, 85
Dasient, 252
Data Allegro, 972
Data Analytics Media, 618
Data Council, 669
Data Direct, 843
Data Display Systems, 1609
Data Domain, 1762
Data Driven Delivery Systems, 1271
Data Fusion Technologies, 381
Data Gram, 1509
Data Hug, 2665
Data Iku, 744
Data Inventions, 481, 1285
Data Nerds, 779
Data Physics, 238
Data Plus Math, 520
Data Pop, 31
Data Respons, 3067
Data Return LLC, 1624
Data Robot, 1009
Data Role, 481
Data Science International, 561
Data Sciences, 1464
Data Sciences International, 67, 389
Data Security Systems Solutions, 2861, 3053
Data Smoothie, 3099
Data Synapse, 1682
Data TV Networks, 1061
Data Vision Resources, 583
Data.World, 752, 1614, 1666
DataBank, 654, 1767
DataBanq, 994
Databento, 849
Databetes, 623
Databox, 2122
Databricks, 125, 238, 824, 1296, 1763
DataCamp, 175, 1720
DataCandy, 2126
Datacare Software Group, 2696
Datacastle, 2609
DataCenter Technologies, 2828
Datacitics, 2601
Datacom Systems, 815
Datacoral, 1162, 1698
DataCore, 1005
DataCore Software, 1888
Datacraft Solutions, 1862
Datacy, 75
DataCycles, 526
DataDirect Networks, 2888
DataDog, 1213, 1381
Datadog, 535, 818, 1358, 1598
Datadog Inc., 969
DataEssence, 3050
Dataflow, 3098
DataFlyte, 461
Dataform, 1850
DataFox, 894

Portfolio Companies Index

DataGravity, 457
Datagres, 2992
Dataguise, 1614, 1831
Datahug, 2653
Dataiku, 238
Dataium, 784
DataKraft, 2347
DataLase, 3234
Datalase, 2483
Datalink, 826
DATAllegro, 55, 759, 1408, 1918
Datalogix, 548, 1006
Datalogue, 756
Datalot, 234, 1127
Datameer, 488, 1079, 1319, 1537
DataMentors, 20
Dataminr, 321, 537, 561, 601, 708, 840, 1006, 1918, 2154
DataMotion, 957
Datamyx, 902
DataNet Communications, 1508
Datanomix, 2
Datanyze, 894, 1566
DataOnline, 790
Datapath.io, 3152
Datapine, 2970
datapine, 3198
Datapipe, 20, 28, 1235
Datapoint, 585, 2353
DataPop, 309
Datapop, 1103, 1242, 1527, 1569
dataQorp, 1839
Dataquest, 1489
DataRobot, 37, 485, 945, 969
Datarobot, 1296
DataRPM, 1059
DataSage, 58
Datascan Berhad, 3155
DataScience, 562
Dataside, 1170
DataSift, 2640
Datasift, 2751
Datasnap.Io, 967
DataSource, 935, 1018
DataSphere, 978
DataSphere Technologies, 733
Datastax, 520, 561, 564, 1079, 1125, 1213, 1319, 1629
DataSynapse, 1748
Datatel, 1852
DataTorrent, 1254
DataTrak International, 215
Datavail, 260, 318, 429, 1212
Datavantage Corporation, 1624
Dataview Solutions, 1839
Dataware Technologies, 194
Datawire Communication Networks, 2073, 2188
DataXu, 37, 69, 756, 1203, 1821
Datec Coating Corporation, 2265
Datek Online, 62
Datera, 1073
DATEV eG, 971
Dathena Science, 1269
Datica, 175, 225
Datical, 205, 1207
Datiphy, 938
DATIS HR Cloud, 3251
Datometry, 604
Datorama, 438, 1001, 1125
Datos IO, 1125
Datou, 2724
Datran Media, 1908
Datrium, 1125
Datsphere Technologies, 1392
DATTUS, 1159
Dattus, 86, 567
Datuit, 3268

Daum Communications corp, 2830
Davalor, 279
Davco Restaurants LLC, 357
Dave, 1646
Dave & Buster's, 1360
Dave & Buster's Inc., 1972
Davenport Newberry Holdings, 1577
Daverci, 1384
DavexLabs, 376
David Energy, 321
David's Bridal, 1113
Davies Group, 962, 2935
Davis Standard, 2201
Davis-Standard, 2200
Davo Technologies, 1690
Davra Networks, 2347
DaWanda, 2820, 2829, 3031, 3035
DAX Solutions, 68
Dax Solutions, 1786
Daxko, 828, 1410
Daxsonics Ultrasound, 2148
Daxton, 2277
Day One Response, 845
Day4, 2072
Day4 Energy, 2091
Daya CNS, 270
Dayak, 1321
Dayforce, 342
Daylight, 2131, 2262, 2398
Daylight Forensic & Advisory, 796
Daylight Studios, 3064
DayNine, 1410
Days, 1534
Daysoft.com, 3095
Dayton Parts LLC, 63
Dayton Superior Corporation, 1368
Daz 3D, 518
Daz3D, 621
Daz3d, 1886
Dazel, 205
DB and SOFT, 2830
DB Networks, 488, 881, 1073
DBD Deutsche Breitband Dienste GmbH, 3037
Dbix Systems, 2614
DBmaestro, 2938
DBS Communications Inc., 654
DBS Nationwide, 2976
DBSH, 544
Dbvu, 2470
DC Devices, 1814
Dc Preparatory Academy, 1315
DC Public Charter School Board, 1315
DC Safety, 632
DC School Reform Now, 1315
DCG Systems, 2993
DCI Holdings, 722
DCL Medical Laboratories, 445
DCN Media Inc., 395
DCS Sanitation Management, 467
DCX, 1839
DDF, 1691
De Boelekes, 3033
De Kleine Kikker, 3033
De Kleine Wereld, 3033
De Novo Pharmaceuticals, 2454
De Toverboom, 3033
De Vecchi Group, 2414
De Zebra, 3033
De-Ice, 944
Dead Sea Industries (Chemicals), 2381
Deal United, 2815, 3161
Deal$ Nothing Over a Dollar, 1955
DealCloud, 570
DealCurrent, 1786
Dealer HQ, 784
Dealer Tire, 1133, 1778
Dealer-FX, 962

DealerHQ, 447
DealerSocket, 1213
Dealertrack Technologies, 1890
Dealflicks, 1599, 1966, 2009
Dealgenius.com, 940
Dealhub, 544
Dealised, 3238
Dealix, 775
Dealogic, 416
Dealsandyou.com, 1327
Dealsquare, 304
Dear Health, 1055
Dearborn Mid-West Conveyor Company, 77, 1377
Deb Shops, 1108
DebiTech, 2745
Debix, 1843
Deborah Centrum, 3033
Debut Bio, 398
Deca, 2437
Decalog, 2375
Decalog B.V., 3128
deCarta, 388, 414, 1245, 1692, 1840
Decartes Labs, 708
DecaWave, 2909
Decell, 2819
DeCell Technologies, 2148
Decibel Therapeutics, 894, 1734
Decide.com, 1186
DecImmune Therapeutics, 184
Deciphera, 1631, 1764
Deciphera Pharmaceuticals, 1839
Decision Dynamics, 2188
Decision Engines, 1812
Decision One, 1973
Decision Resources Inc., 364
DecisionNext, 130, 1525
DecisionPoint, 3250
DecisionView, 57
Decisive Farming, 2043, 2183
Decisyon, 949
Deck, 937
Declicmedia, 2357
DecImmune, 350
DecImmune Therapeutics, 922
DeCODE Genetics, 94
deCODE Genetics, 154, 193, 928, 1464, 1777
Decolar, 1657
Decolar.com, 819
Decru, 983, 3128
Dedenbear Products, 911
Dedendo, 2629
Dedicate Transport, 1424
Dedicated Computing, 1174
Dedicated Network Partners Oy, 3204
Dedicated Transport, 445
Dedigate, 2828
Dedrone, 720, 1035, 3152
Deduct, 1645
Dee Development Engineers, 416
Deel, 1716
Deem, 724, 1361, 1608
Deep, 1737, 3212
Deep Blue Medical Advances, 229
Deep Brain Innovations, 1286
Deep Breeze, 1636
Deep Casing Tools, 2691
Deep Casting Tools, 3095
Deep Domain, 85
Deep Eddy, 447
Deep Forest Media, 1812
Deep Genomics, 3, 803
Deep Genomics Inc., 1073
Deep Gulf Energy, 741
Deep Imaging, 1207
Deep Imaging Technologies, 953
Deep Lens, 1672

Portfolio Companies Index

Deep Motion, 474
Deep Secure, 3234
Deep Sentinal, 1666
Deep Sentinel, 1155
Deep Vein Medical Inc., 273
Deep Vision, 521
DeepBreeze, 2453
DeepCrawl, 746
Deepfield, 1550, 1596
DeepFlex, 468, 2691
DeepGram, 310
Deepgram, 527, 721, 1330
Deepgreen, 395
Deeplocal, 1003
DEEPMAP, 125
Deepmind, 2822
DeepNines Technologies, 593
Deepscale, 108, 207, 208
Deer Ridge Centre, 2165
Deerac Fluidics, 2909
Deerfield Management, 3254
Deerland, 1594
Deerpath Energy, 1583
Deeya Energy Inc, 186
Deezer, 2660
Defacto, 2866
DefenceStorm, 2074
Defense Mobile, 853
DefenseStorm, 2126
Defiance Stamping Company, 832
Define My Style, 1514
DefinedCrowd, 1705
Definiens AG, 2073
DefiniGEN, 3019
Definition 6, 1279
Definition6, 440
Definitive Healthcare, 61, 1720
Definity Health, 1908
Deflecto, 654
Defryus Inc., 2145
Defy, 1618
Defy Media, 21
Defy Trends, 1412
DEG, 1610
DegreeChamp, 623
Degreed, 79, 888, 1393, 1554
DEI Holdings, 458
Dejero, 2216
Dejero Labs, 2051
Dejima Inc., 990
Deka-Brushes, 2796
Dekko, 304, 591, 650
Dekko.co, 1101
Deko, 1240
Del Amo Diagnostic Center, 874
Del Monte, 2371
Del Monte Foods, 357, 1518
Del Real Foods, 1404
Del Taco, 458
Del Taco Holdings, 1113
Del.Icio.Us, 641
DelaGet, 3268
Delair, 1009
Delaware North, 15
Delco Corp., 1057
Delectable, 601
Delego, 2051
Delek Refining, 1971
Delenex, 2806
Delete, 3011
Delfigo Security, 1737
DELFMEM, 3216
Delfoi, 2442
Deli'en, 3194
Delia Systems, 2846
Delighted, 894
Delimex, 722

Delinea, 1903
Delinia, 193
Deliv, 964, 1596, 1855, 1890
DeliverCareRx, 80
Delivering Happiness Group/Daredu, 3206
Deliveroo, 820, 2825
Delivery Agent, 538, 759, 2788
Delivery Hero, 1005, 2820, 2829, 3035, 3161, 3226
Delivery-club.ru, 2336
Delivery.com, 397
DeliveryAgent, 186, 414, 1310
Dell, 55, 388, 1685
Dell Technologies, 3263
Dellwood, 1021
Deloitte, 971
Deloitte & Touche, 3265
Deloitte LLP, 3250
Delonex Energy, 1957
Delorio Foods, 1097
Delpharm, 2842
Delphi Behavioral Health Group, 406, 899
Delphia, 2130, 2131
Delphin Shipping, 1066
Delphinus, 254, 743
Delphinus Medical Technologies, 150, 946
Delphix, 238, 877, 972, 1125, 1754
Delpor, 1055
Delsey, 2413
Delsitech, 2864
DelStar Technologies, 1560
Delsys Pharmaceutical, 1561
Delta Career Education Corp., 886
Delta Data Software, 28
Delta ID, 3089
Delta Innovative Enterprises Limited, 2852
Delta Method, 641
Delta Rigging & Tools, 205
Delta Stream, 1296
Delta Systems, 1691
Delta-Q Technologies Corp., 2144
Delta-V Partners, 3265
DeltaBank, 2456
DeltaCredit, 2456
Deltak, 847
Deltaknot, 2984
DeltaLease-Far East, 2456
Deltamed, 2846
Deltanoid Pharmaceuticals, 1923, 2002
DeltaRail, 1939
Deltek, 1300, 1493, 1518, 1817
Deltona Corporation, 1405
Delve Networks, 85, 1093
DEM Solutions, 3061, 3122
Demand Base, 1629
Demand Media, 822, 1361, 1949
DemandBase, 1610, 1728, 1762
Demandbase, 57, 100, 548, 872, 1028, 1606, 1674
DemanderJustice.com, 1418
Demandforce, 752
DemandJump, 1412
DemandMedia, 133
DemandPoint, 1018, 1893
DemandQ, 534
DemandSage, 680
Demandtec, 627
Demandware, 1335
Demantra Ltd., 2576, 2741
DeMaT TransAsia, 2425
Dematic, 63
Demdex, 818, 1666
Deme Blue Energy, 3033
Demegen, 1749
Demegen Inc, 589
Demers Ambulances, 2076
DeMet's Candy Company, 360

Demex, 2398
Demilec, 1755
Demisto, 877
Democracy.com, 1813
Democrcy Prep Public School, 1315
Demodesk, 798
Demoflow, 1317
Demyst Data, 149
DemystData, 1240, 3112
DEN, 2549
Den Berenboot, 3033
DeNA China, 2860
Denali Therapeutics, 265, 271, 710, 711, 748
Denby, 940
Dendreon, 85, 1561, 1619
Dendrite, 655
Denion Pharmaceuticals, 1232
Denison, 2787
Dennis Conncer Sports, 1839
Denodo, 962
Denon & Marantz, 223
DeNovaMed, 2148
DENOVO, 2927
Denovo, 1009, 1157, 1340
Denovo Sciences, 743
DeNovo Ventures, 3273
Denplan, 2787
Densify, 2252
Densitas, 2148
Density, 1154, 1890
Dent Wizard, 878
Dental Care Alliance, 917, 1507
Dental Intelligence, 1499
:DentalPlans, 1576
Dental Services Group, 559, 654
Dental Technologies, 2045
Dentek, 1863
Dentem, 2107
Dentidesk, 1509
Dentigenix, 85
Dentistanbul, 838
Dentistry For Children, 1949
Dentolo, 2832
Dentons, 3262
Denver Biomedical, 197
Deny all, 3011
Deolan, 2357
DEOS, 532
Depict, 1527
Depop, 2469, 2829
Deposco, 1893
Deposit Solutions, 641
DepoTech, 1708
Dequingyuan, 838
Derby Jackpot, 361
DerbyJackpot, 1479
DerbySoft, 1340
Dering Hall, 608, 1114, 1701
Derive Systems, 838
Derksen Printers, 2249
Derma Sciences, 809, 1456
Dermaflage, 999
DermaRite, 1779
Dermatology Associates of Tyler, 1730
Dermatology Group, 1169
Dermira, 73, 240, 389, 764
Dermlink, 1618
DermTech International, 1786, 1975
Des-Case Corp., 989
Des-Case Corporation, 1438
Desalitech, 2408
Desantis, 2393
Descartes Labs, 545, 564, 571
Descartes Systems Group, 1759
Desch Plantpak, 1131
Descomplica, 1698
Descript, 125

1273

Portfolio Companies Index

Desenvolvimento de Colucoes Digitais, 3039
Desert Artisans, 2305
Deserve, 182
Deserve Cards, 48
Desi, 196
Desicrew, 3202
Design Art Networks, 3212
Design EXchange Co., 2898
Design Flux Technologies, 1051
Design Genie, 515
Design Ideas, 1971
Design Molded Plastics, 1872
Design Space, 1210
Design/Craft Fabric Holdings, 1278
DesignArt Networks, 2557, 2943
DesignBuddy, 1305
DesignCrowd, 3129
Designer Carbon Materials, 3098
Designer Protein, 1344
Designers House, 133
DesignMedix, 1384
DeskConnect, 1593
+Desk.com, 361
Deskera, 485
DeskForce, 544
Desktime, 1645
Desktone, 1701
Desktop Geneti, 1618
Desktop Metal, 305, 812, 894, 1155
Deskwolf, 3194
Desmos, 661, 894, 1058, 1530
Despegar, 27
Despegar.com, 1005
Despoke Post, 863
Desser Tire, 851
Desso, 2492
Desti, 2822
Destination Cinema, 1481
Destination Maternity, 1275, 1971
Destineer, 983
Destiny Pharma, 1456
Detacratic, 2103
DeTeBe AG, 3188
Detechtion Technologies, 658
Detectify, 1005
Detector Technology, 119
DeTelefoongids BV, 1929
Deter Magnetic Technologies, 1115
Determina, 1898
Detroit Innovate, 3259
detroit Labs, 608
Detroit Venture Partners, 3259
Deutsch-Dagan (Elect.), 2381
Deutsche Glasfaser, 1086
Deutsche Messe Interactive, 2560
Deutsche Rohstoff AG, 2483
Deutsche Startups, 2820, 2829
Dev/Con Detect, 999
Devas Multimedia, 518
Devax, 1898
Devax Inc., 272
Devcon, 843
DevCon Detect, 1370
Devcon Detect, 833
Deveinfo Oy, 2864
DeveloGen, 2998
DeveloGen AG, 2776
DevelopIP, 2751
Development and the Rule of Law, 1374
Devenson, 1610
Devergy, 54
Device Anywhere, 2188
Device Authority, 93
Device Fidelity, 583
Device Innovation Group, 918
Device Scape, 972
DeviceFidelity, 1261

Devicescape, 145
Devicescape Software, 200
DeviceVM, 1740
Devie Medical, 2518
DeVilbiss Healthcare, 1933
Devmynd, 1260
Devo, 1005
Devonway, 564
Devoted Health, 1363, 1918
Devotion New Energy, 3185
Devpost, 541, 1382
Devver, 1359
DeWayne's Quality Metal, 1609
Dewey's Bakery, 1609
Dewhurst/Angloarch, 2787
Dewpointx, 1001
Dex Media, 1973
Dex One, 1138
DexCom, 1728
Dexela, 3098
Dexerials, 3192
DexKo Global, 1089
Dext, 2074
Dexter + Chaney, 1410
Dexterra, 1674
Dextrys, 782
Deyu Agri, 3091
Dezima Pharma, 1302, 2505, 2739
Dezurik, 855
DF King World Wide, 20
DFA Capital Management, 1150
DFine, 1383, 1495, 1728
DFINITY, 125
Dfinity, 182
DFJ Venture Capital, 990
DFR, 1966
DFT Microsystems, 693, 2188
DG Industries, 2846
DG Power, 157
DG3, 172
DGAM, 2029
DGF, 2285
DGI Clinical, 2148
DGS Retail, 1582
DGS SA, 2697
DGSI, 238
DHA, 3098, 3098
Dharmacon, 318, 1794
Dhebhuk, 3079
DHI Group Inc., 1508
Dhingana, 1017
DHISCO, 931
DHL, 383
Dhrama, 398
Di'an, 3091
Dia & Co., 774, 945, 1114, 1186
Dia&Co, 1657
Diabetes Care Group, 1261, 1332
Diabetica, 2909
Diabetomics, 1384
Diablo Technologies, 1898, 2188, 2804
DiaDexus, 1629
diaDexus, 1561
Diagnosis One, 655
Diagnosoft, 3250
Diagnostek, 34
Diagnostic Imaging, 1972
Diagnostic Photonics, 979
Diagnostic Technology, 3162
Diagnotes, 659
Diagnovus, 1261
Diagram Ventures, 2122
Dialogic, 1021
DialogMuseum, 2522
DialogTech, 1385
Dialogue, 2090, 2112, 2217
Dialogue Marketing, 834

DialOnce, 252
Dialpad, 125, 720, 894, 1646, 2006
Diam, 3011
Diamanti, 610
Diamedica, 2071
Diamedica Ltd, 3153
Diameter Health, 51
Diametrics Medical, 1399
Diamond Assets LLC, 1438
Diamond Bank, 416
Diamond Cable, 2783
Diamond Contract Services, 961
Diamond Factory, 895
Diamond Foundry, 1363
Diamond Hard Surfaces, 3098
Diamond Innovations, 1138
Diamond Kinetics, 1660
Diamond Lane, 1684
Diamond Packaging, 1025
Diamond Rental, 952
Diamond S, 741
Diamond Software, 2958
Diamondback, 1493
Diamondback Drugs, 1779
DiaMonTech, 2832
Diamyd, 1003
Diandian Yangche, 827
Dianji, 2724, 2927
Dianon Systems Inc., 303
Dianping, 1125
Dianrong, 1340
Diapers.com, 263
Diasome, 1456, 1510
DiAthegen, 189
Diatomix, 1616
Diatos, 2346
Diatron Group, 1576
DiBcom, 2653, 2665
Dibs, 221
diCarta/Emptoris, 1287
Dice, 1982
DiceInc, 2762
Dicerna, 1522
Dicerna Pharmaceuticals, 622, 928, 1395, 1693
Dicerna Pharmeceuticals, 1734
Dick's Sporting Goods, 263, 1971
Dickinson, 279
Dickinson and Company, 1456
Dickinson Frozen Foods, 377, 1156
Dickinson Frozen Foods Inc., 451
Dickson Construction, 1707
DICOM Grid, 476
Dicom Grid, 389
Dicom Transportation Group, 1990
DicoverRx, 1255
Didatuan, 2841
Didera, 957
DiDi, 108
Didi, 44
Didi Chuxing, 827, 1099, 1184
Didix, 3222
Die Cuts With a View, 931
DIEL, 2607
Diesel Marine International Ltd, 2477
Diet to go, 2865
Diffbot, 720, 1969
Different Hotels Group, 2940
Differential Diagnostics, 1561
Diffinity Genomics, 705, 1101
Diffusion Pharma, 1271
Difinity Health, 94
Difter Entertainment, 1423
DiFusion Technologies, 447
Digabit, 758, 933
Digby, 595
Digex, 881
digg, 1982

Portfolio Companies Index

Digi-Prex, 1142
Digibonus, 2377
DigiCert, 1778
Digicert, 1464
Digicon Technologies, 721
Digidesign, 1762
DigiFlex, 3050, 3205
Digify, 3064
Digilab, 2617
Digilens, 93, 1705
Digimarc, 57, 857
DigiPath Inc., 1139
Digirad, 1619, 1708
Digit, 234, 820, 894
DIGIT Wireless, 1305
Digital Air Strike, 666, 1666, 1890, 2640
Digital Alloys, 1073
Digital Angel, 870
Digital Artists, 601
Digital Arts, 2817
Digital Assent, 285, 1412
Digital Bridges, 163
Digital Campaigns, 2020
Digital Capital Partners LLC, 123
Digital China, 2762
Digital China Jinxin, 2927
Digital Chocolate, 1390, 1762, 2581, 2659
Digital Claim, 1509
Digital Cognition Technologies, 564
Digital Compliance, 224
Digital Currency Group, 744, 1698
Digital Domain, 1377, 2257
Digital Envoy, 810
Digital Fortress, 902, 1212
Digital Founatin, 1706
Digital Fountain, 57, 810, 1184
Digital Fuel, 759, 2463
Digital Fuel Technologies, 1674
Digital Generation Systems, 538
Digital Genius, 527, 1114, 1610
Digital Golf Technologies, 1181
Digital Graphics, 532
Digital Guardian, 713, 1140
Digital H2O, 739
Digital Health Department, 1658
Digital Healthcare, 2684
Digital Island, 241, 1239, 1731
Digital Legends, 2539
Digital Life Technologies, 1164
Digital Lumens, 1327, 2430
Digital Magics, 2865
Digital Map Products, 1871
Digital Market, 1855
Digital Marketing Institute, 1720
Digital Media Agency, 406
Digital Media Professionals, 597
Digital Media Professionals Inc., 2406
Digital Media Solutions, 2075, 2890
Digital Medica Services, 445
Digital Music Network, 1674
Digital Objects, 1153
Digital Ocean, 410, 646, 1791
Digital Onboarding, 608
Digital Optics, 1013
Digital Orchid, 1667
Digital Payment Technologies, 2188
Digital Performance, 1569
Digital Pharmacist, 51
Digital Pickle, 1101
Digital Reality, 828
Digital Reasoning, 983, 1111, 1422
Digital Research, 1855
Digital River, 406
Digital Room, 1169
Digital Route, 163, 2653
Digital Royalty, 1914
Digital Shadows, 1796, 3021

Digital Signal, 949, 1348
Digital Signal Corporation, 1401
Digital Solid State Propulsion, 983
Digital Theatre, 2862
Digital Traffic Systems, 1587
Digital Virgo, 2285
DigitalBridge Communications, 266, 1348, 1401
DigitalED, 1499
DigitaleSeiten, 3035
DigitalFuel, 980, 1028
DigitalGenius, 594, 1153
DigitalOcean, 125, 969
Digitalpath.net, 100
DigitalPersona, 194
DigitalScirocco, 85
Digitalsmiths, 1
DigitalThink, 57, 857
Digitalwork, 138
Digitas, 927
Digitech, 1410
Digitouch, 2828
DigiTour, 1816
Digitrace/Sleepmed Inc., 1107
Digiturk, 1498
DigiTx Partners, 1268
Digium, 1184, 1798
Digium|Asterik, 60
Digmine, 624
Digney York Associates, 1210
Dignify Therapeutics, 738, 3250
DigyScores, 736
Dil Mil, 945
Dilaz, 2880
Diligence Labs, 705
Diligent, 502, 1005
Diligent Power Private, 1957
Diligent Robotics, 1423, 1879
Diligent TechnologiesAllot, 2761
Dilithium Networks, 2315, 3053
Dilitronics, 2815
DilMil, 624
Dilthium Networks, 2609
Dimdim, 2992
DIME, 254
Dimension IO, 310
Dimension Therapeutics, 711, 1271, 1383, 1522
Dimensional Dental, 1964
Dimensional Tools Inc., 911
DIMO Corp., 47
Dimora, 1049
Dinalit System, 2960
Dinamundo, 1862
Dinda, 1899
dinda, 720
Dine Market, 998
Dinghartinger Apfelstrudel Productions-UND Vertrie, 2485
Dinghy, 2469
Dink, 3033
Dinner Lab, 1000
Dino Lift Oy, 2310
DinoDirect, 1340
Dinoflex, 2210
Dinova, 793
Dinsmore, 3264
Diomed Holdings, 928
Diomet, 1837
Dionex, 1762
Dip Devices, 865
DipJar, 1489
Dipole Materials, 18
Diposta, 3250
Direct 2 Internet, 2745
Direct Buy, 1186
Direct Capital, 1971
Direct Chassis Link Inc., 1138
Direct Connect Lofistix, 963

Direct Flow, 1297
Direct Flow Medical, 749, 949, 1908
Direct General, 371, 1332
Direct Group, 2935
Direct Health Delivery, 3258
Direct Hit Technologies, 523
Direct Lending Investments, 1065
Direct Marketing Company, 2088
Direct Marketing Solutions, 445
Direct Medical Knowledge, 857
Direct Scale, 881
Direct Tavel, 1686
Direct Travel, 20
Direct Vet Marketing, 910
DirectBuy, 2073
DirectedAI, 2107
DirectedSensing, 1302
DirectEHR, 1288
DirectFlow Medical, 652
Directly, 548, 1158, 1614, 1831, 1862
DirectPath, 1169
Directr, 59, 316, 863
DirectScale, 1074, 1385
DirectVetMarketing, 1261
Directworks Inc., 159, 629
Diresco, 2940
DIREVO Industrial Biotechnology, 3187
Dirtt, 707
DIRTT Environmental Solutions, 1324
Dirtt Environmental Solutions, 138
Dirty Lemon, 232
Disa Holding, 3045
Disarm Therapeutics, 193
Disaster Kleenup International, 815
Discera, 549, 950
DisclosureNet, 2051
DISCO, 2126
Disco, 1017, 1074, 2122, 2131
Disconnect, 744, 938
Discord, 877, 1566
Discote, 3239
Discourse, 742
Discover Books, 1517
Discover Exploration, 416
Discover Video, 532
Discover.ly, 863
DiscoverMusic, 822
DiscoverOrg, 336
DiscoveRx, 1198, 1693
Discovery Data, 336
Discovery Education, 782
Discovery Foods, 790
Discovery Group, 2914
DiscoveryLabs, 1510
Disease Diagnostic Group, 1051
Disetronic, 2555
Dish.fm, 2847
Dishcarft, 1352
Dishcraft Robotics, 234, 742
Dishero, 1054
Disksites, 3150
Diskyver, 2276
Dispatch, 125, 853, 1610, 1823
Dispatch Goods, 7
Dispatch Health, 94
Dispatch Management Services, 132
Dispatch Tracking Solutions, 1786
Dispatch Transportation, 228
Dispatch.io, 2016
Dispatcher, 2010
Dispatchr, 752
Dispensarly, 395
DispenseSource, 767
DisperSol, 459
Dispersol Technologies, 25
Displair, 2929, 3123
Displanplan, 3234

Portfolio Companies Index

Display Data, 2665
Display Design & Instore Marketing, 2801
Display Link, 2469
Displaydata, 2653
DisplayLink, 582, 2653, 2665
DisplayPoints, 447
Displaytech, 1287, 2643
Disqo, 309
Disqus, 1335
Disrupt Beam, 1585
Disruption, 1521
Disruption Corporation, 1320
Disruptor Beam, 536, 894
Disston Precision, 1524
Distacom, 2710
Distant Lands Trading Co., 449
Distech Systems, 60
Distil Networks, 545, 724, 779, 975, 1791
Distocraft, 2553
Distractify, 59
Distribion, 8
Distribution International, 197
District of Columbia International School, 1315
DITA Exchange, 3194
Dittmers Korrosionsschutz, 2801
DITTO, 200
Ditto, 568, 1737
Diveo, 1212
Divergence, 571, 1490, 1618
Diversa Corp., 215
Diverse World, 2958
Diversi Foods, 3222
Diversified, 1270, 1779
Diversified Composites, 1921
Diversified Foodservice Supply, 1090
Diversified Graphics, 445
Diversified Human Resources, 376, 377
Diversified Machine Systems, 1487
Diversified Maintenance Systems, 792
Diversified Metal Engineering, 2076
Diversigen, 244
Diversio, 2131
DiversiTech, 935
Diverza, 2374
Divide, 308, 818, 1479
Divido, 3099
Divio, 3209
Divisions Maintenance Group, 377
DiVitas, 504
DiVitas Networks, 1122
Divolution, 2815
DivorseSecure, 999
Divshot, 309, 1103, 1569, 1800, 2640
Divvy, 48, 79, 1005
Divvy Cloud, 1499
Divvy Investments, 3250
DivvyCloud, 540, 1240
DivvyHQ, 635
DIVX, 414
DivX, 2020
Divx, 1983
Dixie Chemical Company, 834
Dixie Electric, 741
Dixie Elixirs, 638
Dixie Southern, 1748
DIY, 1079, 1718
DIYSEO, 595
Dizzion, 35, 545, 881
DJ Pharma, 470
DJI, 1079
DJO, 280, 2317
Djr Energy LLC, 1853
DJTunes.com, 2815
DJZ, 1223, 1549, 1752, 1862
DKT, 3091
DLA Piper, 3262
dlhBowles, 1266

DMA, 1576
Dmailer, 2375
DMC Stratex Networks, 2005
DMF Medical, 2148
DMN Installations, 3008
DMO Systems, 1898
DMS, 2867
DMT, 1606
DMTG, 3091
DMTI Spatial, 2188
DNA Diagnostics Center, 1271
DNA Group, 3250
DNA Research, 2653
DNA Response, 250, 554
DNANexus, 1702
DNAnexus, 493, 720, 742, 764, 894, 1054, 2001
DNAtrix Therapeutics, 1207
DNCA Finance SA, 1778
Dnium Pte Ltd, 2694
DNS Services, 1908
DNS:NET Internet Service GmbH, 3058
Doane Pet Care Enterprises Inc., 357
DOAR Communications, 1929
Dobie Media, 495
Dobler Metallbau GmbH, 2485
Doc AI, 521
Doc Authority, 724
Doc Doc, 2904
Docalytics, 567
Doccom, 2682
Docebo, 2163, 3043
Docker, 108, 251, 561, 877, 978, 1005, 1125, 1153, 1657, 1855, 2011
DocOnYou, 2460
Docphin, 1585
DocPlanner, 3031
Docplanner.com, 3035
Docracy, 1521
DocRun, 1549
DocSend, 553, 1114
Docsend, 1702
DocSynk, 1284
Doctor Evidence, 549
Doctor On Demand, 44, 894, 1511
Doctor on Demand, 91, 846, 1050, 1114, 1832, 1918
Doctor Wellington, 75
Doctor's Best, 1336
Doctor's Choice Home Care, 703
Doctors, 1509
DocTracker, 536
Doctrackr, 2357
Doctrakr, 1464
Docu Sign, 520
Docufide, 1786
Docufree, 1893
Docufree Corporation, 1152
DocuLynx, 1025
Document Depository Corp., 1581
Document Technologies, 416, 1507
DocuSign, 27, 85, 263, 488, 561, 604, 730, 840, 978, 1005, 1028, 1629, 1645, 1674, 2154, 2681
DocuWare, 1255
DocVerse, 234
Dodla Dairy, 3202
Dodoni, 2775
DOF Subsea, 741
Dog Parker, 901
Doggyloot, 1385, 1618
Dogswell, 874, 1863
DogVacay, 231
DogVacey, 773
Doit International, 458
Dojo Madness, 1812
Dolan Media Company, 20
Dolce Hotels & Resorts, 381

Dolead Dynadmic, 3229
Dolex, 56
DolEx Dollar Express Inc., 1404
Doll Capital Management, 3273
Dollar Express, 62
Dollar General Corporation, 2371
Dollar Shave Club, 125, 553, 763, 1483, 1666, 1787, 1918
Dollarama, 223
Dolls Kill, 545, 1186
Dolly, 1186, 2272
Dolphine Marine International, 1748
Dolphinsearch Inc., 374
Domaille Engineering, 402
Domain Elite Holdings, 622
Domain Surgical, 549, 1383
Domain Therapeutics, 2842, 3104
DomainHoldings, 1901
Domainiac, 2842
Domaininvest, 2417
Doman Surgical Inc., 272
Domdex, 1588
Dome Coffees, 2411
Dome9, 1382
DOmedia, 1285
DOmedic, 2256
Domenia Credit, 2462
Dometic, 2488, 3000
Domfinans, 3141
Domicile, 1162
Domidep, 2332
Dominion Diagnostics, 1695
Domino, 1101
Domino Data Lab, 1657, 1696, 2018
Domino's Pizza, 475
Domino's Pizza Japan, 223
Domio, 1599
Domio Health Audio, 2094
DOMO, 827, 1841
Domo, 265, 840, 877, 1006, 1205, 2018
Domo Retail, 2462
Domo Safety, 2302
Domo Technologies, 1428
Domus, 2354
Domuso, 594
Domuso Inc., 814
DomusVi, 3017
Donato, 2629
Donaza, 2344
Donde, 473
dondeEsta, 1737
Done By None, 3100
Done Right!, 200
Dong Jiang, 3185
Dongwoon Anatech, 2993
Donnadolce Service SRL, 2410
Donnelley Financial Solutions, 3264
DonorPath, 635
Donortap, 3116
Donseed, 2347
Donson, 2658
Donup, 1092
Donuts, 20, 205, 666, 696, 822, 1830
Doo, 3152
Doobic, 2993, 3118
Doodad, 1965
Dooland, 2927
Dooly, 321, 2204
dooly, 2240
DoorDash, 1073, 1079, 1657, 1665, 1763, 2011
Doordash, 1323, 1426
Doorr, 2132
Doorstat, 2194
Doorstead, 1142
Dopbox, 1657
DOPE Magazine, 966
Doppelganger, 186

Portfolio Companies Index

Dopplr.com, 2595
Dor, 2018
Dorado, 186, 1408, 1731
Dorado E&P, 673
Doray Minerals, 2933
DORC, 2968
Dori Media, 3092
Doright Fashion, 2841
Dorland Health, 1275
Dormeo, 646
Dorna Promocion del Deporte, 2635
Dorner Holding Corp., 159
dorsaVi, 3129
Dorsey & Whitney, 3268
Dorsey Schools, 815, 1506
DoSomething.org, 1374
Dot & Bo, 1254, 1361, 1855
dot Blockchain Music, 2024
Dot Health, 2107
Dot Hill, 3092
Dot Loop, 1855
Dot Medical, 3001
Dot Product, 1009
Dot Wireless, 133
DOTC United, 1125
DotCloud, 2321
Dotcom Therapy, 1292
DotDashPay, 521
Dote, 1125
dotFX, 1967
Dotgo, 689
DotNetNuke, 1428
Dotnetnuke, 200
Dotomi, 1898
Dotomi Direct Messaging, 1915
Dots, 720, 1993
Dotster, 226
Dottikon, 2913
Dou-Dou, 3033
Douban, 2575
Double Bridge Technology, 2841
Double Click, 927, 1045, 1125
Double Dutch, 31, 1101
Double E Company, 557
Double Fusion, 1829
Double Robotics, 879
DOUBLE Trade, 2535
Double-Scope, 2997
Double-Take Software, 1949
DoubleBeam, 387
DoubleDutch, 1086
Doubledutch, 361, 752, 1121
DoublePositive, 1389, 1712
Doubletwist, 3004
DoubleVerify, 304, 742, 818, 1006, 1045
Dough, 1121
Dough.com, 1787
Douglas Dynamics, 202
Douglas Products, 96
Douglas Steel Supply, 1971
Douguo, 827
Doum & Nanum, 2848
DoveConviene, 3043
Doveconviene/Shopfully, 2288
Dover Microsystems, 1511
Dovetail, 744
Dow Kokam, 1607
Dow Pharmaceutical Sciences, 1693
Dow Venture Capital, 3259
Dowley Security, 1273
Dowley Security Systems, 1748
Down, 310, 863
Downeast LNG, 1072
Downtyme, 1593
Doxel, 125, 1426
Doxim, 828
Doxim Inc., 159

Doximity, 610, 666, 1014, 1257
Doxis Lighting Factory, 2940
Doxo, 265, 1028, 1247
DOZ, 1752
Dozr, 2122
DPA Microphones, 1576
dPharm, 3231
DPI Specialty Foods, 148
DPM, 655
DPS Inc., 68
DPW Van Stolk Holding, 3200
DPx, 1043
Dr Lal PathLabs, 1778
Dr. Comfort, 1210
Dr. Dental, 20
Dr. Martens, 3024
Dr. On Demand, 1666
Dr. Wu, 1092
Dr.2, 1125
DR2, 3246
Draft, 59, 332, 650, 1890
Draft Day, 1121
Draft Kings, 316, 744
DraftKings, 37, 69, 827, 1537
Dragdis, 3040
Dragnet Solutions, 526, 794
Dragon Army, 191
Dragon Innovation, 1114
Dragonfly, 974, 2128
DragonPlay, 2700
DragonsMeet, 2860
DragonWave, 2051
Dragos Inc., 84
Drais, 1014, 1762
Drake Automotive, 963
Drake Equipment, 1612
Draker, 205, 789, 1101
DramaFever, 1242
Dramafever, 863, 3118
Draper Espirit, 990
Draper Fisher Jurvetson, 3273
Draper James, 763
Draper Richards, 3273
Draper Triangle, 3264
Draper Triangle Ventures, 3259
Draper's & Damon's, 843
DraTek Technologies, 2658
Drawbridge, 1079, 1086, 1657
Drawbridge Health, 812
Drawbridge Networks, 320, 1479
Dray Alliance, 49
Dray Now, 520
Drayer Physical Therapy Institute, 1132
DrayNow, 818
DRB Systems, 1473
DRDx, 2815
Dream Dinners, 508
Dream Execution, 2848
Dream Giveaway, 16
Dream Link Entertainment, 721
Dream Maker Ventures, 3249
Dream Square, 1340
Dreambox, 1393
DreameGGs, 802
DreamLine, 1266
Dreamlines, 101, 2432
Dreamlines.de, 2804
DreamLocal, 1165
DreamPayments, 2123
Dreams, 1755
Dreamscape, 1885
DreamWater, 2254
DreamWorks Animation SKG, 1948
Dremio, 485, 1125, 1346, 1537
Dresser, 1368, 1577
Dresser-Rand Group; Exterran Energy Corp., 1905

Drever Capital Management, 1065
Drew Foam Companies, 832
Drew Foam Companies Inc., 330
Drex-Chem Malaysia, 1576
Drexcode, 2865
Dreyfus-Corney, 679
DrFirst, 1628
DRG Limited, 2862
DRI Holdings Limited, 622
DribbleUp, 623
Drie Pees, 3033
Driessen Aerospace, 2370
Drift, 742, 820, 969, 1114, 1657
Drifter Entertainment, 1477
Drifting In Space, 2122
Driftrock, 2743
Driftwood Dairy Holding, 1171
DrillingInfo, 1005
Drillinginfo, 561, 1169
drillMap, 1583
Drimki, 2382
Drimmi, 2312
DRINKmaple, 789
Drip, 23, 354
Dripkit, 1509
Drish Shoes Limited, 2852
Drishtee, 54
Drishti, 125, 252, 1716
Drishyam AI, 29
Drive Factor, 1504
Drive For Me, 2842
Drive Motors, 361
Drive.ai, 827, 998
DriveAble Assessment Centres, 2116
Driveline Retail, 1095
Driven Brands, 170, 418, 1580
Driven Brands Inc., 917
Driven Inc., 406
Driven Performance Brands, 1232
DrivenBrands, 1873
Driver Hire, 2935
DriverSide, 915
Drivetime, 720
Drivetribe, 2437
Drivewyze, 666, 2150
Drivezy.com, 1760
Drivin, 1121
Driving Curve, 3172
Drivr, 3194
Drizly, 332, 433, 713
Drizzle, 2093
DRL, 1114
Drobo, 759, 1341, 1597, 1762
Drofika, 1509
Droice Labs, 623
Drone Base, 795, 1890
Drone Deploy, 129, 1629
Drone Racing League, 474, 925, 1155, 1816
DroneBase, 1483
Dronebase, 1884
DroneDeploy, 666, 1702, 1881
Dronen Consulting, 1252
DroneSeed, 1698, 1724
Drop, 221, 724, 1672, 1983, 2140, 2216, 2217
drop, 93, 1982
Drop.io, 609
Dropbox, 27, 116, 251, 457, 805, 840, 1006, 1763, 2011, 2851, 2851
DropCam, 241
Dropcam, 27, 1006, 1058
DropCountr, 1895
DropFire, 1737
DropGifts, 2820
Droplet, 1238
Droplr, 1467, 1659
Dropoff, 545
Dropout Labs, 308

1277

Portfolio Companies Index

DropThought, 2010
Drover, 322, 2272
Drug Emporium, 755
DrugAbuse Sciences, 2998
Drugstore.com, 925, 1008, 1186, 1867
Drum, 1985
Drumglass High School, 2740
Drummond Gold Limited, 1551
Drunc, 863
Druva, 604, 1657, 1798, 2681, 2992
Dry Soda, 845
Dry Soda Co., 85
Drybar, 424, 1580
Dryden Human Capital, 3234
DS Medical, 1964
DS Services, 560
DS-IQ, 1247
DSA/Phototech, 381
DSC, 1009
DSCI, 1276
dscout, 254
DSG, 1344
DSI Holding Company, 1460
DSI Renal, 785
DSL.Net, 759
DSM Green Power, 2752
DSM-AGI Corporation, 3053
DSO Interactive, 3104
DSP Concepts, 305
DSP Group, 263
DSP Group Inc, 2576
DSP Holdings, 2966
DSpace, 2609
Dsquare, 3033
DSST Public Schools, 1315
Dstillery, 433, 535, 541, 696, 1316, 1488, 1898, 1918
DSTLD, 121, 1966
DSTLD Premium Denim Co., 231
DSW Homes, 988
DTC Logistics, 674
DTE, 2072
Dtex Systems, 780, 1346
DTI Inc., 917
DTIQ, 364
DTl Transportation, 1425
DTLR Inc., 357
DTMS, 2291, 2293, 2297
DTN, 874, 1929
DTT Surveillance, 815, 1469
DTx, 132
DTX Studios, 2922
Du Pareil Au Meme, 2414
Dual Therapeutics, 1422
Dualtec, 2429
Duane Reade, 1360
Dub, 1773
Dubai Investment Park, 153
DuBois Chemicals, 202, 381
Dubois Chemicals, 2030
Dubset, 568
Dubsmash, 680, 1153, 2469
Ducati, 3145
Ducati Motor Holding Spa, 1837
Ducatt, 2940, 3033
Duchossois Capital Management, 3255
Duck Creek Technologies, 136
DuckDuckGo, 1884
Duckhorn, 828
Ducksboard, 2911
Duco, 1005
Dude Solutions, 502, 3250
DueDil, 3021
Duedil, 1361
DueGo, 3021
Duett AS, 28
Duetto, 238, 972, 1808

Duff & Phelps, 416, 1151, 1746, 3262
Dufry, 2913
Dugun.com, 2428
Duimelotje, 3033
Duke Realty, 1955
Dulce Vida, 447
Dumur Industries, 2156
Dunamu, 1511
Duncan Media Group, 508
Dundee Venture Capital, 3255
Dune, 2445
Dune Networks, 1898, 2372
Dunkin Brands, 223
Dunlop, 2842
Dunn Paper, 1169, 1214, 1997
Dunn Paper Inc., 406
Dunrath Capital, 3255
Dunwello, 1322
Duo, 824, 894, 1213
Duo Security, 1537, 1550, 1862
Duolingo, 579, 631, 1079, 1884
Duolog Ltd, 2696, 2696
Duoyuan, 838
Dupont, 2842
Durata, 73
Durata Therapeutics, 389, 1510, 1700, 1943
Duratap, 1768
DuraTherm, 3213
Duravant, 1368
Durcon, 1507
Durham Graphene, 2883
Durham Scientific Crystals Limited (DSC), 2389
DuritCast, 3039
Duropak, 1376
Dusan Co. LTD, 2830
Dust Identity, 1079
Dust Networks, 556, 983, 2630
Dustin, 2376
Dusty, 398
Dusty Robotics, 234
Dutch, 1778
Dutchie, 420
Dutton-Forshaw, 2635
Duvas Technologies, 2751
DVDO, 1750
DVN Holdings, 1771
DVS Sciences, 1247, 1439
DVT Corp., 153
DVTEL, 1650
Dvtel, 1636
DW Healthcare Partners, 3254
DWave, 610
Dwell, 1696
Dwellable, 1186
Dwelling, 2122
DwellWell, 2398
Dwll.in, 3165
DWOLLA, 125
Dwolla, 608, 779
DWT-Engineering Oy, 2310
Dx Biosciences, 794
DxUpClose, 845
DXY.com, 597
Dyadic, 488
Dyax, 764, 1096, 1561
Dydacomp, 1234
dYdX, 125
DyeCat, 2883
DYM, 1335
Dym Co., 2993
Dymant, 1418
DYN, 1335
Dyn, 311
Dyna Crane Services, 2129, 2277
Dynacare Kasper, 2076
Dynacast, 1949
Dynacure, 2842

Dynadec, 1118, 1695
DynaGen, 2197
DynaGrid Construction Group, 479
DynaIndustrial, 2129
Dynaindustrial, 2277
Dynamatic, 367
Dynament, 238
Dynamic Change, 2958
Dynamic Communicaties, 406
Dynamic Details, 441
Dynamic Extractions Historic Futures, 3098
Dynamic Industries, 416, 1577
Dynamic Medical Systems Inc., 874
Dynamic Mobile Data Systmes, 957
Dynamic Offshore Resources, 1577
Dynamic Organic Light, 1917
Dynamic Precision Group, 416
Dynamic Quest, 1727
Dynamic Signal, 485, 1158, 1543, 1918
Dynamic Sinal, 1829
Dynamic Systems, 920
Dynamic Yield, 1001
DynamicImaging, 405
DynamicOps, 1319
Dynamics, 55, 224
DynamicSignal, 1855
Dynamo, 782
DynaOptics, 1671
Dynaoptics, 1604
Dynapac, 3000
Dynapel Systems, 2745
Dynapower, 1438
DynaPump, 468
DynaRoad Oy, 2707
DynaScan Technology Corp, 2694
Dynasty, 742
Dynatect Manufacturing, 2303
Dynatherm Medical, 1619
Dynatrace, 241, 1817
Dynatrace Inc., 159
Dynavax, 772
Dynavax Corp., 215
Dynavax Technologies, 1619, 2509
Dynavec, 2961
DynCorp International, 1927
Dyne Therapeutics, 1934
Dynea Oy, 2371
Dynegy, 676
Dynepic, 849
Dynex Technologies, 119
Dynisco, 197
Dyno Holdings, 362
Dyno Nobel A, 3000
Dynogen, 1414, 2436
Dynogen Pharmaceuticals, 2308
Dynojet, 851, 1026
DynoSense, 1983
Dysonics, 1009

E

E 1023, 1527
E Band Communications, 209
E Ink, 925, 1704
E&B Technology Co., 2915
e+ Cancer Care, 1085
e+ CancerCare, 792
E-Band Communications, 928
E-Blink, 2890
E-Capital, 2715
E-Chromic Technologies, 120
E-Conolight, 1210
e-Courier Software, 92
E-Data Sift, 1629
e-Dialog, 523
E-Future, 2989
e-Glue, 438, 2571
e-Government Solutions, 1958

Portfolio Companies Index

e-infoda.com, 1839
e-Medical System, 1757
E-mice, 2763
E-Motion, 3145
E-Motion Medical Ltd., 2320
E-Motion Ventures, 2958
E-Net, 2888
E-One Moli, 1908
E-One Moli Energy, 2144
E-printing Company, 2846
e-Rewards, 1762, 1778
E-Scape Bio, 1350
E-Security, 58
e-Security, 1888
E-Senza Technologies, 2815
e-Sharing, 1957
E-SIM, 3239
E-Supportlink ltd, 2845
e-Therapeutics, 3009
E-Tran, 957
e-trees Japan Inc., 2406
E-Z Shipper Racks, 753
E.A.R.T.H., 1394
E.B. Bradey Co., 874
E.D. Smith & Sons, 2142
E.E. Stringer Funeral Homes, 112
E.L. Haynes Public Charter School, 1315
e.l.f. Cosmetics, 1863
E.Piphany, 1867
E/O Networks, 538
E14, 2378
e27, 3029
e2E Materials, 434
e2e Materials, 323
E2E Networks, 2517
E2E Rail, 3202
E2Open, 2074
E2open, 1005, 1042, 1913
e2Open, 561
E3Bank, 3246
E4 Health, 1168
E4X, 2646
E5 Systems Inc., 806
E8 Security, 84
e994, 2464
EA, 1383
EA Pharma, 3011
EAA Inspection Services, 3257
eAccess, 1771
Eachnet, 2841
EachScape, 535, 853
Eachscape, 1358
Eachwin Capital, 845
EACOM Timber, 1066
EAG Laboratories, 1368
Eagaveev, 310
Eager, 756
EagerPanda, 623
Eagle, 263
Eagle Battery, 412
Eagle Business Solutions, 3257
Eagle Crest Energy, 1890
Eagle Crest Energy Company, 2640
Eagle Energy Company of Oklahoma, 1577
Eagle Energy Exploration, 1577
Eagle Eye Analytics, 744
Eagle Filter, 2864
Eagle Foods, 1066
Eagle Genomics, 2958
Eagle Hardware & Garden, 755
Eagle Oil & Gas Co., 510
Eagle Pharmaceutical, 1492
Eagle Point Credit Management, 1746
Eagle Precision, 1057
Eagle Quest International, 1270
Eagle River Homes, 1459
Eagle Vision Pharmaceuticals, 269

EagleBurgmann, 2148
Eagleview, 502
EagleView Technologies, 1720
EAI-Vista, 1561
Earbits, 246
Eargo, 275, 564, 1186, 1533
EarLens, 1126
Earlens, 73, 1993
Earlydoc, 3215
EarlySense, 340, 3050
Earn, 1511
Earn Up, 387, 1058
Earn.com, 125
Earnest, 37, 309, 545, 561, 724, 1186, 1569
Earnest Research Company, 1388
Earnin, 125, 387, 720, 1184
Earnix, 2741
EarnUp, 600
Earnup, 54, 545
Earny, 520, 1187
Earshot, 275, 1462
Earth AI, 398
Earth Animal, 450
Earth Class Mail, 85
Earth Fare, 1360
Earth Networks, 1389, 1464
Earth Tech, 1524
EarthClean, 3268
EarthCube, 2288
Earthlink Network Inc., 1107
EarthLite, 330
EarthSense, 999
Ease, 310, 567
Ease Central, 601
Ease Entertainment Services, 277
Easecentral, 527, 787
eAsic, 949, 2717
EasilyDo, 1187, 1898
Easou, 3091, 3199
eAssist Global Solutions, 2073
East Balt Bakeries, 1376
East Club, 1966
East District, 3029
East Hampton Sandwich Co., 479
East Shore Aircraft, 1968
East West Manufacturing, 668
Eastern Broadcasting Company, 416
Eastern Elevator, 1405
EastMachinery, 1125
Easton Capital, 990
Easton-Bell Sports, 2014
EastPoint Sports, 319, 1174
Eastport Holdings, 408
Eastvillage, 3033
Easy Bike, 2430
Easy Buy, 1143, 2937
Easy Market, 1352
Easy Metrics, 1691
Easy Post, 894
Easyart.com, 2526
EasyAsk, 1674
Easyaula, 2941
easyCar, 3046
EasyCopay, 1305
Easyfinance.ru, 2336
EasyHealth, 2398
EasyLap, 1846
EASYLINK, 1771
Easynet & MDNX, 2935
Easynvest, 61
EasyPak, 851
EasyPost, 1223, 1669
Easypost, 2122
Easyship, 1599
EasyVote Solutions, 512
Easyvoyage, 3104
EAT Club, 742

Eat Club, 863, 1101
Eat Makhana, 623
Eat Street, 863
Eatalynet, 2288
Eatem Foods, 1460
Eatem Foods Co., 1136
Eatime Inc., 624
Eating Recovery Center, 435, 1108
Eaton Veterinary Pharmaceutical, 961
EatonTowers, 912
Eatsa, 1646
EatStreet, 9, 567, 987
Eau Ecarlate, 2414, 2843
Eave, 568
Eaze, 420, 788, 863, 1696, 1810
Eazytec, 1009
EB Brands, 1234
eBags, 990, 1787
eBANK, 2763
eBaoTech, 796
Ebara, 217
Ebates, 200, 389, 773
eBay, 251, 1186
Ebb, 1930
Ebb Tehrapeutics, 150
Ebb Therapeutics, 1086
Ebbu, 558, 1139, 1810
Ebel, 1021
eBenx, 1045
Eberle, 851
Eberly Design Inc., 331
eBest, 1183
EBI Life Sciences, 1923
Ebiquity, 1929
ebix.com, 538
Eblana Photonics, 3170
EbLens, 1053
EBlink, 2377, 3104
EBM Solutions, 1414
EBOOST, 1683
EBR Systems, 178, 1631, 1728, 1764
EBR Systems Inc., 605
eBrevia, 795
EBS Technologies, 2815
EBT, 2772
eBureau, 949, 1449, 1537, 1728, 1798
Ebury Partners, 2392
eBus.TV, 2904
EC Waste, 1469
ECA Medical Instruments, 1148
Ecamion, 2181
eCareOne.com, 409
Ecast, 759
Eccentex, 3220
Ecco Safety Group, 261
Eccrine Systems, 481
eCentria, 1255
ECG Management Consultants, 886
eChalk, 646, 2188
eChalk.com, 462
Echelon, 263, 1247
Echelon Aviation, 1493
Echelon Insights, 618
Echo, 549, 1982
Echo 360, 510, 552, 1636
Echo Active Learning, 634
Echo Health Ventures, 3263
Echo Nest, 523
Echo Pixel, 1009
Echo11, 656
Echo360, 1701, 1768
Echodyne, 1155, 1162, 2270
Echodyne Corp., 1010
Echogen Power Systems, 1051
Echolab, 670
EchoNous, 1086
Echopass, 389, 1390

Portfolio Companies Index

EchoPixel, 5
Echosec, 2262
EchoSign, 666, 1750
Echostar Corp., 303
Echoworx Corporation, 2051
Echtman Engineering Co., 2381
ECI, 1021, 2600
ECI Engineering & Construction, 3164
ECi Software Solutions, 136, 416
ECI Technology, 3266
ECI The Elastic Network, 3212
eCift, 2466
Eckler Industries, 911
Eckler's, 225
Eckler's Enterprises Inc., 451
Eclat, 1561
Eclectic Bars Limited, 2449
Eclerot and Ziegler AG, 3163
Eclipse, 1086
Eclipse Advantage, 1097
Eclipse Aviation, 693
Eclipse Resources, 673, 1848
Eclipse Therapeutics Inc., 489
Eclypsium, 1009, 1162, 1879
ECNlive, 3009
Eco Consumer Services, 2769
Eco Digitec, 2263
Eco Logic, 2051
Eco Online, 3207
ECO Products, 3248
Eco Projects, 3033
ECO Technologies, 2123
Eco-Dan, 2553
Eco-Site, 1270, 3250
Eco4Cloud, 2663, 3043
eCoast Marketing, 1298
EcoATM, 493, 1377, 1782
ecoATM, 186
Ecobee, 2196, 2253
ecobee, 2228
Ecoboard Holdings, 1748
Ecoboard Industries Limited, 2852
Ecobot, 512
EcoEnvelopes, 1874
EcoFactor, 493, 1583, 2430
Ecohaus, 1649
Ecoin Co Ltd, 2830
EcoIntense, 1255, 2815
EcoInteractive, 92
Ecolibrium Solar, 1556, 1987
Ecollege, 405
eCollege, 1483
EcoLogic, 186
Ecologic Brands, 343, 596
EcoLogicLiving, 2287
Ecom Food Industries, 2133
EcoMade, 3185
Ecometrica, 2496
eCommHub, 1675
eCommission, 1127
eCommission Financial Services, 1234
Ecomo, 1896
EcoMotors, 928
EconCore, 2358
Econex, 2830
Econic Technologies, 2849
Ecopackers, 2130
EcoPhos, 2554
EcoPlant, 252
Ecoprod, 3224
eCopy, 440
Ecore, 658
Ecoscape Solutions, 467
EcoScraps, 596, 1074
Ecosec, 2276
Ecosense, 748
Ecosense Lighting, 646

EcoSmart, 642
Ecosmart, 770
EcoSMART Technologies, 539, 1583
ECOSO, 3091
EcoSurg, 999, 1190
EcoSynthetic, 2054
ECOtality, 2307
EcoTensil, 3246
Ecotensil, 1604
Ecotone AS, 3132
Ecoult, 2604
Ecount, 1178
Ecova, 1100
Ecovacs Robotics, 977
Ecovation, 434
Ecovision Renewables, 2496
ECP/CH Industries, 747
Ecrebo, 3009
ECRM Holdings, 364
Ecron Acunova, 1383
ECS Environmental Solutions, 165
ECS Federal, 1133
ECS Learning Systems, 16
ECS Refining, 2021
ECS Tuning, 260
ECTel, 2600
ECtelecom, 2798
eCullet, 127
Ecutronic, 2334
ecVision, 799
Ecwid, 3079
Ed Laboratory, 2915
ED MAP, 1691
Ed Map, 1364
Ed., 1127
EDAC Technologies, 867
Edagora, 3011
Edai.com, 3091
Edaijia, 1125
EDAN, 3091
Edaris Health, 390, 1175
eDarling, 2820, 2829
eData Sift, 1890
eData Source, 1875
Edcamp Foundation, 1315
EdCast, 456, 1058, 1701
Edcentric, 1109
EDCO, 300, 364
Edcon, 223
EDDA Technology, 2658
Eddie Bauer, 843
Eddingpharm, 1383
Eddingpharm International Holdings Limited, 622
Eddy Packing, 1174
eDealya, 2994
Edelman Financial Services, 927
Edelweiss Financial Services, 416
Eden, 399, 520, 680, 728
Eden Geotech, 849
Eden Health, 12, 48, 328
Eden Park Illmination, 1596
Edenbridge, 1779
EdeniQ, 127, 186
Edeniq, 610, 1978
EdenPark Illumination, 979
Edenspace, 1776
Edesa Biotech, 2174
EDF Ventures, 3259
Edge, 2817
Edge Adhesives Holdings, 832
Edge Case Research, 296
Edge Compute, 802
Edge Connex, 520
Edge Fitness Clubs, 1345
Edge Intelligence, 108
Edge Makers, 209

Edge Medical Devices Ltd, 3149
Edge Technologies, 1609
Edge Trade, 655
Edgecase, 205, 535
EdgeCast, 309
EdgeConneX, 243, 1784
EdgeConnex, 1862
Edgeconnex, 1212
EdgeDB, 1426
Edgefolio, 3099
Edgemont, 1220
Edgen Corporation, 1748
Edgespring, 1125
Edgeware, 2628
Edgewater Markets, 796
Edgewater Networks, 646, 1408, 1525
EdgeWave, 185, 1871
EdgeWave Software, 68
Edgewise Networks, 1
Edgewood Partners Holdings, 416, 1746
Edgeworx, 1614
Edgile, 20
Edgwater Midstream, 672
Edgy Bees, 182
Edgybees, 1928
EDH Groupe des Ecoles, 2842
EDHC, 447
EDI, 858
Edible Arrangements, 1092
Edico Genome, 604
Edif Group, 3027
Edify, 1423
EDIGMA.com, 3039
Edimer, 1621, 1814
Edinburgh Molecular Imaging, 690
Edioma, 447, 595
Edison, 1187, 2969
Edison Agrosciences, 270
Edison Partners, 3266
Edisun Microgrids, 101, 976
Editas, 1814
Editas Medicine, 710, 748, 764, 1421
Edition F, 3226
Editions Montparnasse, 2888
Editions Oberthur, 2332
Editorially, 354
Edj Analytics, 477
Edlio, 1140
edly, 2187
Edmark Corporation, 1399
EDMC, 1498
Edmentum, 1493, 1817
Edmit, 1554
Edmodo, 1798
Edmund & Associates, 1140
EDN, 1786
edo Interactive, 1908
Edo Japan, 2284
edocs, 759, 2418
Edovo, 1058
EDR, 238, 532
eDreams, 597
eDreams Edusoft, 1017
edriving, 1169
EDS Docdata B.V., 2893
Edsby, 2074
EdSurge, 430, 1315, 2003
EDT Learning, 2881
Edtech Holdings, 364
Edthena, 3246
Edubridge, 54
Educate, 1745
Educate Online, 1745
Education Affiliates, 1043
Education Corporation of America, 1939
Education Dynamics, 902
Education Elements, 949, 1315, 1554, 1867

Portfolio Companies Index

Education Futures Group, 1494
Education Management Corporation, 1109, 2371
Education Networks of America, 1270
Education One D/B/A Penn Foster, 1377
Education Overseas Ltd, 3137
Education.com, 374, 1795
Educational Holdings LLC, 77
Educational Initiatives, 1348
Educents, 564, 601, 888, 1058
Educreations, 27, 1315
Edudo, 2958
Edududes Ltd., 2958
Edufii, 830, 1589, 1786
EduK, 720
EduK Group, 20, 1109
Edunav, 1382
EduSports, 3100
EDUSS, 688
Edvantage Group, 3004
Edvantage Group AS, 2361
Edward Don & Company, 745
Edward W. Brooke Charter School, 1315
Edwards Group, 435
Edwin, 659
Edwin Watts Golf, 170
Edwin Watts Golf Shops, 1972
EdXact, 2890
EDY International, 2462
Edyn, 721
ee4, 389
EEC Incorporated, 1209
Eedoo, 2927
Eefoof, 1786
EELCEE, 2746
EELF, 2462
Eemax, 1576
EEMCO, 3185
Eero, 108, 742, 863, 879, 1537, 1666, 1696
eEye Digital Security, 263
EFC International, 1507
Effective Measure, 1561, 1713
eFFECTOR, 1350, 1734
eFFECTOR Therapeutics, 184, 519, 1238, 1898
Efferent Labs, 705
Efficere, 1917
Efficient Finance, 389
Efficient Forms, 952
Efficient Networks, 861, 1408
EfficientFrontier, 1537
Efficity, 3104
EffiMat, 3194
Efflux Systems, 856
EFI, 57
EFI Electronics for Imaging, 3128
Eficia, 2430
EFileCabinet, 1679
eFileCabinet, 84
EFJohnson, 782
eflow, 2965
eFolder, 696
EFP Corp., 1034
Efreightsolutions, 28
EFront, 782
Eftia OSS Solutions, 163
Eftpos New Zealand, 2655
eFuneral, 1051
EG Gilero, 3250
eGain, 1603
eGain Communications, 1360
eGalax, 2594
Egalet, 2693, 3140
Egalet Corp., 193
EGAR Technology, 2456
EGB Investments, 2285
EGeen, 2382
Egenera, 205, 1084
eGenesis, 1073

eGenesis Bio, 271
Eggdetect, 3235
EggDrop, 1855
Eggrock, 1146
EGHC, 386
Egis Technology, 2694
Egis Tecnology, 3053
Egistec, 2427
eGistics, 1852
eGix, 445
Egnyte, 752, 894, 1079, 1464, 1684
eGO, 1695
egreetings.com, 1483
Egress, 2074
eGroups, 1629
Eguana Technologies, 2662
eGuardian, 1786
eGym, 2815
EHANG, 827
Ehang, 3241
eHarmony, 1235, 1787
Ehealth, 1125
eHealth Global Technologies, 1748
EHealth Technologies, 1206
eHealth Technologies, 51
eHedge AG, 2519
eHi Car Services, 3053
EI Technologies, 2867
EIC, 2956
Eichrom Technologies, 154
Eider, 2414
Eideticom, 2150
Eidex Education Analytics, 1739
Eidogen, 188
Eidos, 764, 1522
EidoSearch, 1549
Eigen Innovations, 2123, 2192
Eigen Technologies, 2398
Eiger, 1014, 1943
Eiger Biopharmaceuticals, 1522
Eight, 1073
8 Enterprises, 381
Eight O'Clock Coffee, 886
8 Rivers Capital, 3250
8 Security, 1812
8 Solutions, 3121
82 Labs, 10
860 South, 1220
886 Food, 3172
88Rising, 1816
89, 259, 310
89 Energy, 1326, 1328
89bio, 1147, 1522
8D World, 1718
8digits, 3069
8Fit, 3214
8I, 59
8i, 222, 795, 925, 1614, 1928, 3014
Eight Sleep, 788, 1330
Eight Spokes, 1101
8th Wall, 1666
8thBridge, 1852
8tracks, 1702
eInstruction, 470
eIQ Energy, 1324
Eisai, 1349, 1456
Eisenworld, 2786
Eisfeld Datentechnik, 2704
Eisner Amper, 3266
EisnerAmper LLP, 3257
eJamming, 1588
eJammingAudiiO, 1305
Ejara, 2398
Ejasent, 556
Eka, 2992
Eka Systems, 127, 1583
Ekahau, 949

Ekinops, 3199
Ekkia, 2439
eKnitting, 1538
Eko, 177, 1001, 1966
Eko Studio, 1614
EKomi, 3161
Ekona Power, 2105
EKOS, 263, 928, 1325
Ekos, 154, 178, 1788
Ekos Corporation, 1241
EkoStinger, 434, 705
EKR Therapeutics, 1140, 1268, 1510
Ekstop.com, 2904
Ekstrem Lavpris, 2854
Ektron Inc., 440
ekWateur, 2430
El Dorado Ventures, 3273
El Ganso, 1092
El Pharma, 1055
El Pollo Loco, 786
El Rancho, 2976
El Rayan Danfarm, 2880
El Super, 1723
El-Forest, 2746
EL-OP (Optics), 2381
ElaCarte, 591, 1121, 1585
Elan, 1456
Elan Languages, 2940
Elance, 759
Elance ODek, 1751
Elantec Semiconductors, 2372
Elara Caring, 1066
Elastagen, 2527
elastic, 251
Elastic Path, 1606, 2283
ElasticRun, 1346
Elasticsearch, 586
Elastifile, 238, 485, 1125
Elastix, 2334
Elastomeric Technologies, 51
Elatica, 1187
Elatifile, 604
Elation Health, 610, 1058
ElationEMR, 19
ELAXY, 2607
Elbi, 2381
Elbion, 2346
Elbit, 3202
Elcely Therapeutics, 1788
Elcelyx, 1126
Elco-Brandt Group, 2736
Elcom, 2766
Elcom Technologies, 2445
Eldat, 2711
Eldon Holding AB, 2703
Eldorado Bancshares. Ennis-Flint, 1372
Eldorado Stone, 851
Ele.me, 1184
Election, 36
Electra Bicycle Company, 376
Electra Vehicles, 1104
Electrawinds, 3033
Electric, 827
Electric AI, 320
Electric Cloud, 1187, 1543, 1597, 1898
Electric Imp, 1153, 1537
Electric Playhouse, 169
Electrical Components International, 1089
Electrical Source Holdings, 867
ElectrIQ Power, 2136
Electro Energy, 983
Electro-Motion Inc., 1612
Electro-Motive Diesel Inc., 867
Electro-Radiation Inc., 421
Electrochaea, 270
ElectroChemical Systems Inc., 738
ElectroCore, 644, 1206

Portfolio Companies Index

ElectroCraft, 1639
Electrokoppar, 2874
Electromed, 3268
Electron Beam Technologies, 324
Electron Database Company, 1051
Electronic, 2547
Electronic Arts, 840, 1657, 1787
Electronic Data Resources, 1748
Electronic Packaging Products Inc., 989
Electronic Systems Protection, 878
Electronics, 112
Electronics for Imaging, 303
Electrophotonics, 2258
Electrosteel Steels, 585
Electrovaya, 2051
Electrum Partners, 1139
Elegant Desserts, 196
Elegant Hotels Group, 1939
Elektron AB, 2709
Elektronabava, 971
Elektronik+Kabeltechnik Gmbh & Co., 2607
Eleme Medical, 652
Eleme Petrochemical, 2080
Elemedia, 1304
Element, 1009, 1158, 1269
Element 14, 3186
Element 5, 2291, 2293, 2297
Element AI, 2024
Element Analytics, 812, 2430
Element Data, 757
Element Energy, 493
Element Fleet Management Corp., 1905
Element Materials Technology, 2303
Element Petroleum, 157
Element Science, 1814
Element14, 263
Element451, 512
Elemental, 85
Elemental Technologies, 983, 1384, 1947
Elementary Robotics, 1836, 1879
ElementLabs, 707
Elements Behavioral Health, 785
Elements Casino, 2075
Elementum, 108, 812, 1125
Elemis, 1092
Elemtnal, 621
Elentec Semiconductor, 1898
Elephant Drive, 309, 1103
Elephant Oil & Gas, 1853
ElephantDrive, 1569, 1786
Eletrobras, 1733
Eletromidia, 931
Elettrostudio Energia, 3011
Elettrostudio Energia Infrastructure, 3011
Eleutian, 2382
Elevar Equity, 1374
Elevate, 680, 720, 1058, 1255, 1426, 1525, 1657
Elevate Accessories, 395
Elevate Credit, 1657, 1787
Elevate Digital, 60
Elevate K-12, 1023
Elevate Security, 548
Elevated, 754
Elevation Labs, 505
Elevation Partners, 42
Elevation Pharma, 1222
Elevation Resource Holdings, 1447
Elevator, 304
Eleven Biotherapeutics, 748, 1814
eleven-x, 2132
Elevian, 1099
Elevoc, 1511
Eley Group, 2935
Elgin Equipment Group, 197
Elgin Fastener Group, 197
Eli Research, 266
Eliason Corporation, 1234

Elicit, 724, 876
Eligo Bioscience, 1073
ElimiDateapp.com, 2876
eLink Communications, 528
Eliokem Materials & Concepts, 1138
Elira Therapeutics, 270
Elis II, 2488
Elit Teknoloji, 2301
Elite, 2480
Elite Advanced Laser Corporation, 2594
Elite Comfort Solutions, 172
Elite Daily, 1533, 1587
Elite Education Media Group, 2841
Elite One Source, 119
Elitel, 2888
Elitra, 1414
Elity Systems, 538, 957
ELIX Polymers, 1755
ELIXIA, 2376
Elixir, 1442
Elixir Pharmaceuticals, 928
Elixirs, 1139
Eliza Corporation, 1419
Elizabeth Arden, 1552
Ella Health, 476, 1464
Ellacoya, 2436
Ellen Tracy, 2164
Eller Media, 927
Ellery Homestyles, 1859
Ellevation, 1315, 1530, 1554
Ellevest, 535, 1610, 1634
Ellibs Oy, 2864
Ellie, 304, 1966
Ellie Mae, 116, 990
Elliegrid, 1509
Elliot, 320, 1760
Ellipse, 3194
Ellipse Technologies Inc., 272
Ellipsis Health, 1073
Elliptic, 3009, 3099
Ellis Communication Group, 1066
Ellison Bakery, 279, 531
Ello, 779, 789
Ellucian, 927, 1045, 1113, 1837
Ellumniate, 2188
Elm City Food Cooperative, 679
Elmira Pet Products, 2049
Elmo-Calf, 2999
Elmville, 2874
Elo Touch Solutions, 560
Elo7, 27, 1005, 2967
Eloan, 796
eLoan, 596
eLocal, 1140
Elogex, 722
Elona Bio Technologies, 1456
Elopak, 2722
Eloqua, 241, 263, 517, 1045
Eloqua Corp., 990
Eloquent, 1379
Eloquii, 901
eLoupes, 1009
Eloxx Pharmaceuticals, 2221
Elprint, 2745
Elron, 2657
Elroy Air, 431, 945, 1666
Elroy SPAC, 169
Elstar Therapeutics, 144
Elsy, 833
Eltek Group, 2376
Eltel Networks Oy, 2303
Elto.com, 2511
Elucent Medical, 225
Elucidate, 3
Elusys Therapeutics, 1456
Ely Medical Group, 2909
Elysium, 820, 1186

Elytra, 2358
EM Kinetics, 644
Em Teck, 2830
EM4, 226, 2188, 2553
Emachines, 2817
eMachines, 1561
Emageon, 178, 1536, 1622
Emagia, 1674
Emagine IT, 681
Emagix, 2148
Email Data Source, 1305, 1588
Emailage, 309, 720
Emailvision, 3104
Emano, 2858
EMarketer, 1751
Emarsys, 1912
Emay, 2841
Embarcadero Maritime, 1086
Embarcadero Technologies, 1817
Embark, 108, 305, 597, 787, 945, 1646
Embark General, 96
Embark Trucks, 1657, 2122
Embarke, 1491
Embedded Linux Technology Inc., 2406
Embedded Planet, 693
Ember, 2398
Ember Corporation, 983
Ember Resources, 468, 2062
Ember Technologies, 2604
Embera Neurotherapeutics, 365, 1065
EMBL Technology Fund, 2443
Emblem Corp., 393
Embodi, 1618
Embodied, 879, 1009, 1705, 1836
Embodied Intelligence, 1155
Embollic Protection, 1379
Embotics, 2074
embotics, 2258
Embrace, 680, 798
EMBrace Design, 999
Embrace Pet Insurance, 1051
Embrace.io, 231, 309, 321
Embrane, 1335, 1478
Embrella, 918
Embrella Cardiovascular Inc., 272
Embroker, 246
Emburse, 1426
EMC (Emmy), 2832
EmCasa, 623, 1426
Emcore, 1971
Emdeon, 280, 2371
Emdot, 2883
Emeco, 2411
EMED, 1772
eMed Technologies, 315
Emediamarketing, 3043
Emefcy, 2891, 3038
Emerald, 1414
Emerald BioAgricultre Corp., 90
Emerald Clean Power, 1577
Emerald Expositions, 2201
Emerald Media, 1086
Emerald Performance Materials, 111
Emerald Solutions, 1116, 1561
Emerald Textiles, 2196
Emerald Therapeutics, 778, 1630
Emeraude Chimie International, 2332
Emeraude International, 2332
Emerge, 2131, 3246
eMerge Americas, 754
Emergence BioEnergy, 860
Emergency Communications Network, 1576
Emergency Essentials, 1648
Emergent, 795, 894
Emergent Discovery, 1165
Emergent One, 708
Emergent Payments, 744

1282

Portfolio Companies Index

Emergent Respiratory Products, 1667
Emergent Trading, 472
Emerging Markets Communications, 20
Emerging Threats, 659
EmergingMed, 60
Emergo Therapeutics, 1559
Emeritus Corporation, 1624
Emerus, 1973
Emerus Hospital Partners LLC, 205
eMeter, 596, 1341
EMeter. Enernoc, 773
EMG, 3017
Emic, 2442
Emida, 1890
Emids, 225
Emids Experience Partnership, 551
Emillion Oy, 2864
eMindful, 1117
Emine Software, 2694
Emissary, 308, 894, 1223, 1322
EMIT Corporation, 487
Emitwise, 2037
Emjag Digital, 2393
EMLSI, 2848
Emmaus Life Science Inc., 68
Emme, 2372
Emme E2MS, 679
Emmerge, 1254
Emmersion, 1317
Emmes Corporation, 248
EMMI Solutions, 1480
Emnotion, 971
EMO Labs, 1922
emocha, 1703
emocha Mobile Health, 1058
EMoov, 3099
eMotion, 1191
Emotive Communications, 1348
Emovi, 2074
Empathica, 1045, 1707
Empathy, 1009
Empatica, 2865
Empaua, 1610
Emperative, 317
EMPG, 1169
Emphirix, 1184
Empire Brushes, 1955
Empire CLS, 874
Empire Generating, 676
Empire Global, 1083
Empire Petroleum Holdings, 1603
Empire Today, 1493
EmpirecLS Worldwide Chauffeured Services, 277
Empiricom, 2883
Empirix, 1798, 1817
Emplify, 86, 570
Employ Bridge, 1270
EmployBridge, 1256
Employease, 1152
Employee Channel, 545, 1247
Employer's Direct Insurance Company, 843
EmployerDirect, 1803
Employment Hero, 3014
Employment Staffinf, 495
EmployUs, 512, 3250
EMPO Corporation, 1233
Empolyease, 1406
Empow Networks, 180
Empower, 2314, 2568
Empower Energies, 821
Empower Interactive Group, 163
Empower RF Systems, 1754
Empowered, 1014, 2131
Empowered Careers, 857
empowertel, 1795
EmpowHR, 1412

Empresa Generadora de Electricidad Haina, 585
Empresas Verdes Argentina, 838
Empyr, 545, 1028
Empyrean, 495, 796
Emrgy, 1925
EMS, 1045
Ems Chemie, 2913
EMS Management & Consultants, 1343
Emsemble Therapeutics, 748
EMSI, 247
Emstone Engineering, 2440
Emtec, 1425
Emu Solutions, 288
Emu Technology, 1023, 1229
Emulate, 945
EN Engineering, 819, 1873
En Gibton, 3235
ENA, 1736
Enable Injections, 481, 1420
Enable M, 2850
Enable Semiconductor, 3209
Enanta, 1096, 2806
Enanta Pharmaceuticals, 990, 1777, 2371, 3187
EnAqua Solutions, 1487
Enara Networks, 1718
Enata Pharmaceuticals, 1395
Enbala, 677, 812, 1363, 2072
Enbrel, 2097
Encanto, 1041
Encanto Restaurants Inc., 917
Encap, 2361
EnCap Investments, 3245
Encelle, 1013
Enceptiv Energy, 301, 1451
Encentivenergy, 275
Encentuate, 200, 808
Encepta, 2276
Encino Energy, 1024
Encirq, 1354
Encoda Systems, 1727
Encoded Genomics, 94, 1918
Encoded Therapeutics, 1203
Encodia, 271
Encoding.com, 1843, 2016
EncoraTherapeutics, 849
Encore Capital Group Inc., 494
Encore Dermatology, 4, 698, 1147
Encore Fitness, 800
Encore Interactive, 2192
Encore Media Systems B.V., 2893
Encore Networks, 2276
Encore Paper, 470
EncoreAlert, 1320
EnCorps, 1315
Encos, 2883
Encover, 1674
enCross Partners, 2848
Encycle, 677, 2178, 2181
Encycle Therapeutics, 2181
End The Lix, 953
End2End, 22, 691, 2378
Endaga, 1058
Endame, 1079
Endear, 3
Endeavor, 745, 1859
Endeavor Robots, 167
Endeavor Schools, 1109
Endeavour, 1848, 2484
Endeavour Healthcare, 2613
Endeca, 263, 827
Endeca Technologies, 1798
Endeco, 2347
Ender's Fund, 3118
Endforce, 990
Endgame, 518, 1401, 1628, 1790
EndHub, 1645
Endicott Biofuels, 898

Endo Stim, 1622
Endo Vasix, 2719
Endo Via, 428
EndoArt Ltd, 3153
Endocardial Solutions, 1379
Endocare, 97
EndoChoice, 551, 1575, 1657
Endocontrol, 3104
EndoCross, 3231
Endocyte, 290, 1619, 1849
EndoGastric Solutions, 58, 389, 470, 1126, 1523
EndoInsight, 999
Endoinsight, 1190
Endologix, 698, 1268
EndoMedix, 1561
Endonetics, 1708
Endorsify, 1509
Endosense SA, 1325
Endoshape, 933
EndoSpan, 2316
EndoSphere, 1514, 1556
EndoStim, 1490
Endotex, 1379
Endotronix, 137, 273, 1051, 1631, 1764, 2174
EndPlay, 1908
Endres Processing, 1044
Endurance Energy, 1957
Endurance International, 1917
Endurance International Group, 197
Endurance Lift Holdings, 560
Endurance Specialty Holdings Ltd., 407
Endurance Specialty Insurance, 843
Endurance Wind Power, 2144
Enduro Resource Partners, 1577
Enduro Resource Partners II, 1577
EndWave, 1674
Endwave, 1257
Enecsys, 2606
Enefco, 1730
Enefco International, 165
Eneida, 3039
Ener-core, 1607
EnerAge, 1244
Enerbee, 2288
Enercast, 2815
Enercomp, 2603
Enercorp, 106
EnerG2, 731, 1392, 2007
Energate, 2087
Energetic Insurance, 498
Energetic Solutions, 595
Energetics, 2706
Energex, 658
Energia Zachod, 3200
Energreen, 2691
Energy Cache, 493
Energy Capital Partners, 3245
Energy Cool, 3194
Energy Credit Partners, 741
Energy Developments, 3016
Energy Distribution Partners, 531
Energy Drilling, 2691
Energy Financial and Physical, 554
Energy Fishing & Rental Services, 913
Energy Future Holdings, 2371
Energy Life One SRL, 2410
Energy Manufacturing, 1460
Energy Micro, 3004
Energy Network, 585
Energy Services Group, 28
Energy Solutions International, 1018
Energy Solutons, 1493
Energy Source, 858
Energy Source Partners, 679
Energy Storage Systmes, 1467
Energy Trade, 1520
EnergyCo. Holdings, 1270

1283

Portfolio Companies Index

EnergyHub, 43, 1442
Energyn Corporation, 2374
EnergySage, 498, 1104
EnergySolutions, 676, 1133
Energytics, 1813
Enerkem, 325, 1561, 1978, 2087
Enerkem Technologies, 186
Enermont, 3118
EnerNOC, 325
Enernoc, 610
Enerpulse, 1607
Enerqos, 2606
Enersciences, 60
Enersize, 2603
Enertech, 2200
EnerTech Capital, 3249
EnerTech Environmental, 1394
Enertia Software, 554
Enertiv, 728
EnerVault, 1241, 1365
Enervee, 1363
Enerworks, 2072
Enesco LLC, 228
eNeura, 386
eNeura Therapeutics, 18
Enevate, 186, 1239, 1478, 3185
EnEvolv, 571
Enexion, 2815
Enfield Logistics, 405
Enfora, 56, 1084
Enforcer eCoaching, 1051
Enfore, 108
Enforta, 263
Enfusen, 1051
Enfusion, 796
Engage, 1151
Engage Therapeutics, 2174
Engage2Excel, 878
Engage2Excell, 1169
Engage3, 278
Engagio, 742, 744
Engauge, 902
Engeltjes & Bengeltjes, 3033
Engendren Corporation, 1210
enGene, 2174
EnGene IC, 2966
Engility, 1086
Engine, 1095
Engine Bio, 222
Engine Efficiency, 325
Engine ML, 431
Engine Yard, 241, 582, 1478, 1917
Engineered Propulsion Systems, 1874
Engineering Ingegneria Informatica, 1376
Enginge Biosciences, 2681
Enginsight, 2518
English Bay Batter, 2162, 2177
English Boiler Tube, 1057
English Central, 894, 1692
English Color, 1979
English Ninjas, 2276
EnglishHelper, 1374
EnglishUp, 2941
Englobe, 2200, 2201
Engrade, 708, 1032, 1058, 1315, 1554
Enhanced Capital Partners, 1948
Enhanced Capital/Tree Line, 1746
Enhanced Drilling, 3207
Enhanced Energy Group, 1695
Enhatch, 752
enherent, 1561
Enigma, 520, 564, 708, 756, 1358, 2460
Enigma Information Systems, 3221
Enigma Software, 2716
Enigmatec, 2378
Eniram, 2621, 2722
Enium, 2848

Eniware, 3246
Enjovia, 2276
Enjoy, 805, 938, 1079
Enjoy Beer, 790
Enjoy Technology, 1361
Enkata, 549
Enkata Technologies, 138, 1604, 1674
Enki Technology, 145, 1583
Enlibrium, 545
Enlighten, 99, 1866
Enlightened, 1583
Enliken, 246
EnLink Geoenergy Services, 592
Enlink Midstream, 1328, 1837
Enlitic, 1659
Enlivant, 1837
Enliven Therapeutics, 11
Enlyton, 447
Enmass, 1561
Ennis-Flint, 331
eNNOV, 1991
Enocean, 2101, 3223
Enoflex, 2044
EnosiX, 1051
Enosix, 86
ENOTECA, 3192
Enotria, 2515
Enovix, 597, 1009, 1511, 1583, 1855
eNow, 3251
Enphase Energy, 145, 186, 241, 928, 949, 1583
Enpiorion, 928
Enplug, 976
Enpocket, 299
Enprecis, 336
Enprego Ligado, 2863
EnRoute, 85
EnrTech Capital, 2028
Ensamblage, 3033
Ensatus, 27
Ensemble Communications, 556
Ensemble Therapeutics, 154
Ensenda, 87
Ensenta, 2448
Enservio, 224, 1184
Ensighten, 130, 1005, 1944
Ensilo, 1125, 3212
Ensim, 759, 1379
Ensiz Technology, 2848
Enso Connect, 2176
Enso Relief, 108
EnSolve Biosystems, 3246
Ensoma, 11
Ensono, 458, 1157
Enspire DBS Therapy, 891
Enstar Group, 1746
Enstigo, 1786
EnStorage, 389
Enstream, 2256
Ensure Medical, 1098, 1898
Ensus, 416
Ensus Ethanol, 1577
Enswers, 3118
Ensyn, 2153
Ensyn Technologies, 2108
Entac Medical, 999
ENTACT, 1482, 1805
Entact, 205
Entangled Ventures, 1554
Entasis Therapeutics, 785
Entegra, 106
EntegraBlu, 1244
EnteGreat, 679
Entegreat, 1536
Entellios, 2815
Entellus Medical, 872, 1086, 1728
Entelo, 238, 545, 1666
Entelos, 318

Enter Crews, 2465
Entera, 556
Enteraction TV, 2653
Entercept Security Technologies, 614, 1042
Entergy Industrial, 3209
Enteric Medical Technologies, 1251
Enterix, 2868
EnterMedicare, 321
Enterome, 3011, 3104
EnteroMedics, 240, 460, 1379
Enterprise DB, 1840
Enterprise Electronics Corporation, 1927
Enterprise Florida, 3251
Enterprise Link, 35
Enterprise Macay, 2043
Enterprise Therapeutics, 690, 1350, 1930
EnterpriseDB, 457, 1234, 1901, 2188
Enterprises DB, 1316
Enterproid, 1358
Entertainment Cruises, 973, 1482
EnterVault, 1793
Entevo, 1348
Entevo Corp., 318
Enthentica, 169
Enthrill Distribution, 2043
Enthuse, 246
Entigral Systems, 1446, 1847
Entire Technology, 2594
Ento Bio, 1051
Entomo, 85, 1640
Entone, 538, 1629
Entone Technologies, 1408
Entorian Technologies, 205
Entouch, 2430
EnTouch Controls, 1691
Entrack, 984
Entrada, 11, 495, 696, 1268
Entrada Health, 718
Entrada Resources, 2044
Entrade, 990
Entrans International, 110
EntreMed, 2410
Entrepreneur First, 877
Entrigue Surgical, 137
ENTrique Surgical, 928
Entrisphere, 1908, 3128
Entropic, 759, 1928
Entropic Communications, 133, 730, 857, 1239
Entropix, 773
EntropySoft, 2377
Entryless, 3116
Entrypoint VR, 1614
Entuity, 3083
ENTvantage Diagnostics, 447
Enuma, 1054, 1058
Enuvis, 200
Enval, 2392
Envara, 2773
Enveil, 6
Enven Energy Corporation, 510
Envenio, 2070, 2123
Envera, 907
Enverus, 28
Envestnet, 138, 773, 1890
Envestra Limited, 2582
Envia Systems, 241
Enviance, 238
Enview, 564
Envirelation, 679
Enviro Vac, 1169
Envirocon, 2079
Envirogen, 1048
Environcom, 2364
Environics, 2104
Environment Furniture, 961
Environmental Express, 1461
Environmental Lighting Concepts, 1748

Portfolio Companies Index

Environmental Lights, 1438
Environmental Operating Solutions, 1200
Environmental Pest Service, 406
Environmental Pest Services, 531
Environmental Planning Group, 1276
Environmental Recovery Corporation, 1582
Environmental Support Solutions, 861
Environments@Work LLC, 649
EnvironWorks, 1071
EnviroScent, 80
EnviroSolutions, 1839
Envirosystems, 2177
Envis Corp, 1674
Envisagenics, 1158, 1162
Envisia, 389, 1414, 2969
Envisia Therapeutics, 1271
Envisics, 821
Envision, 886
Envision Healthcare, 1086
ENVision Mobile, 29
Envision Pharma Group, 899
EnvisionNet Computer Services, 440
EnvisionRX, 1837
Envista, 311, 1463
Enviva Holdings, 1577
Envivio, 556, 990, 1183, 2434, 2866
Envivo, 908
Envizi, 28
Envkey, 798
Envocore, 406, 611
Envoi, 2132
Envox, 3004
Envox Group AB (publ.), 2707
Envoy, 11, 125, 429, 490, 820, 1153, 1203
Envoy Networks, 523
Envy Modular Systems, 743
Enwoven, 101
ENXSuite, 1324
Enyvision, 1419
Enzen Global Solutions, 585
Enzerna Biosciences, 3250
Enzium, 269
Enzymedica, 1324
Enzymotec, 2964, 3231
Enzytech, 263
Eoconix, 1924
Eocycle, 2087
Eodom, 3104
Eoidio, 2553
Eolite, 2842
EOLO, 2243
Eolring Dynamic Cell Network, 2346
eOne Globe, 2762
Eonian Technology, 3251
eonMedia, 686
Eontec Limited, 2073
EoPlex Technologies, 628
EoPlex Technologies Inc., 1093
eOriginal, 1140
EOS, 322
Eos, 240
EOS Climate, 731
EOS Fitness Holdings LLC, 357
EOS SpA, 2342, 3043
Eosense, 2148
Eosex, 2999
EOSi, 2282
Eosi, 1618
EoStar, 1641
EP Canada Film Services, 2210
EP Energy, 33, 1577
Ep Minerals, 843
EP Sciences, 350
EPact, 2074
ePact, 2283
ePACT Network, 2215
ePact Network, 2092

ePanstwo Foundation, 1374
ePartners, 405, 1287
ePawn, 2684
EPD-visionk, 2505
Epedal, 3039
ePet World, 304
ePetWorld GmbH, 2970, 3035
EPharmix, 270
Ephesoft, 1205
EPI, 3202
Epi-V, 2935
Epic, 1530, 1969
Epic at Cub Run, 192
Epic Burger, 568
Epic Games, 1079, 1125
EPIC Insurance Brokers & Conultants, 3266
Epic Sciences, 158, 622, 1439, 3076
Epic Therapeutics, 263
Epic Ventures, 3265
Epic!, 1983
EpiCare, 403
EpiCept, 928
Epicor, 1086
Epicor Software, 1852
Epics, 981
EpiEP, 845, 1101
Epigan, 2940
Epigenesis, 2719
EpiGenesis Pharmaceuticals, 315
Epigenomics, 2291, 2293, 2297
Epigram, 58, 1247
Epiodyne, 1203, 1238
Epion, 993
Epion Health, 2074
Epiphany Dermatology, 478
Epiphany Solar Water Systems, 1003
Epiq, 917, 2199
Epirus, 11
Epirus Biopharmaceuticals, 1251
Episencial, 3246
Episensor, 2347
EPiServer, 3004
Episerver, 1005
Episode 1, 2665
Episodic, 857
EpiStar, 908
EpistoGraph, 2540
Epithany, 2007
Epitome Biosystems, 748
Epitomics, 118, 1771
EpiTop, 1340
Epivalley, 2848
EpiVax, 1695
EpiWorks, 1112
Epix, 263
EPIX Pharmaceuticals, 315
Epizyme, 113, 240, 764, 1268
EPL, 2880
EPO.com, 2563
Epocal, 2188
Epoch, 223
Epoch Biosciences, 240
Epoch Systems, 1091
Epocrates, 240, 610, 990, 1235
EPOS, 3221
Epox Computer, 3209
Epoxy, 59, 876, 1829, 1890
Epredix Campus Tele Video, 405
ePrint Factory GmbH, 2664
Eprise Corporation, 215
eprofessional GmbH, 2519
EPropertyData, 1645
EProspects, 3004
Epsagon, 1125
Epsilon, 743
Epsilon Power Holdings, 157
Epsitech Group, 2846

Eptam Plastics, 929
Eptica, 3011
Epuramat, 2531
EPV Solar, 2319
Epyon, 2072
EqcoLogic, 2358
Eqise, 2469
EQOS, 2340
EQT, 3254
Equal Media, 2437
Equal Opportunity Schools, 1315
Equality Specialities Inc., 1624
EqualLogic, 713, 759, 1028, 1674
Equallogic, 457
Equalum, 812
Equanet, 2787
Equastream, 3251
Equator, 116, 967
Equator Technologies, 1706, 2073
Eques, 1511
Equian, 864
Equibrand Holding Corporation, 1565
Equicare Health, 2283
Equidate, 1752
Equifax, 1905
eQuilibrium, 498
Equilis, 3125
Equinix, 564
Equinox, 300, 1092
Equinox Fitness, 1113
Equiom, 2935
Equip, 1
Equipboard, 1687
EquipmentShare, 863, 1616
Equipmentshare, 1396
EquipmentShare.co.nz, 1005
EquiPower Resources Corp., 676
Equipwell, 253
Equita GmbH & Co. Holdings, 77
Equitalk, 3098
Equitant, 38
Equitas, 389, 2305
Equity Broadcasting, 1771
Equity Trust, 2547
EquityLock Solutions, 1865
EquitySim, 79
Equityzen, 1101
Equivalent Data, 367
Equivest, 2607
Equus Energy, 695
Equus Media Development Company, 695
ER, 2842
ER Energy Group, 673
ER Experts, 842
Era, 318
ERA Biotech, 3011
Era-plantech, 2474
Eracom, 1561
EraGen, 1490
EraPlay, 2263
Eratech, 2039
Eratome, 3011
ERC midwest, 1582
ERC Wiping Products Inc., 467
Ercio, 1352
Ercom, 2377
eRecyclingCorps, 1324
eResearch Technology, 1140, 2371
Erewards, 1464
ERG, 1132
ERG Services, 585
Ergalis-Selpro-Plus RH, 2330
Ergis, 2420
Ergo Genesis, 988
Ergobaby, 525
ErgoGenesis, 1424
ergoTrade AG, 2519

1285

Portfolio Companies Index

ERI Solutions, 1727
Erickson, 1138
Eridan, 398
Eris Exchange, 711
Erlang Technology, 2448
ERM, 2199
ERMS Corporation, 2051
Erno Laszlo, 781
Ernst & Young, 3266
Eroom, 1949
eRoom Technology, 1335
Erplain, 2094
ERPLY, 720
Erply, 1537
ERT Systems, 743
Erthos, 2131
Eruditor Group, 1009
ErVaxx Limited, 1631
Erydel, 2865
Erytech, 2842
ES Robbins, 1971
(es) Corporation, 2465
ES-Plastic GmbH, 2485
Esanex, 1013, 1128
esanex, 1128
Esately, 85
Esaturnus, 3033
Escalade Energy, 157
Escalate, 843
Escape Rescue Systems, 3203
Escapia.com, 85
Escher Reality, 1477
Escient Pharmaceuticals, 11
ESCO Corporation, 674
Escorts Construction Equipment, 585
eSecLending, 1419
eSellerProf, 3005
Esentire, 655, 2146
eSentire, 2126
EServices, 1729
eServices, 1424, 1730
eSfot, 1839
ESG, 2303, 3185
eShakti.com, 2840
eShares, 708, 1054, 2009
eShip-4U, 3239
Esi Group SA, 2592
ESI Lighting, 1494
ESI Software, 1708
eSight, 2141, 2181
eSilicon, 430, 485
eSilicon Corporation, 2630, 2881
Esim Chemicals, 1755
Esionic, 1523
eSionic, 35, 689
Eska, 124, 1255
Esmalglass, 1021
Esmark, 1582
Esmertec, 2913
ESO, 28
ESO Solutions, 205, 447
Eso-Technologies, 584
Esoko, 54
eSolar, 976, 1361
eSolutions, 782, 1979
Esoterix Inc., 248
Esox s.r.o., 3113
ESP Pharma, 94
ESP Technologies, 2188
eSpark, 1242, 1315, 1483
eSpark Learning, 1530
Espaçolaser, 1092
Esper, 1423, 1879
Esperance, 1621
Esperance Pharmaceuticals, 60, 365, 1546
Esperanto Technologies, 521
Esperion Therapeutics, 73, 94, 183, 622

Espial Group, 2188
Esports, 1194
Esports Entertainment Group, 736
Esports One, 680
EsportsOne, 1509
Espresa, 564, 1566
Espressif, 1009
Espressive, 820
Espresso Capital, 3249
Espresso Logic, 1017
EspriGas, 551
Esprit Holidays Ltd, 2477
Esprit Pharma, 94
Esquire, 897
Esquire Bank, 708
ESS Inc., 2087, 2205
Ess Kay Finance, 1346
Essanelle Hair Group AG, 2797
Essence Group, 1618
EssenceHealthcare, 1079
Essent Group, 1314, 1447
Essentia, 424
Essential Cabinetry Group, 878
Essential Products, 1537
Essentialis, 1788, 1943
Essentialis Therapeutics, 772
Essention, 1644
Essess, 1486
Essex, 838
Essex WoodlandsFund, 958
Essner Manufacturing, 542
Est, 416
Establishment Labs, 895, 1052
EStarCom, 213
Estate Assist, 298
Estately, 1702
Estech, 1794
Estify, 121, 724, 1074, 1585
Estimize, 535, 1150
Estimote, 275, 1032
Estore, 2817
Estorian, 85, 318
Estrakon, 743
Estrohaze, 395
estudy Site, 441
eStyle, 2020
eSUB Construction Software, 1558
ESupply Systems, 784
Esurance, 1406
Esurg Corporation, 2073
ESV Digital, 3047
ET Solar, 3185
Etacts, 2321
EtaGen, 1073
Etam, 2598
Etanco, 2303
eTang, 1561
ETC, 34, 2786
Etcetera Edutainment, 1003
ETE Medical, 119
eTeamz, 1786
Eternygen, 690, 2832
ETF Securities, 796, 1235, 1761
ETG, 2940
Ethelo, 2225
Ether Optronics, 2570, 3053
Ether Optronics Inc, 2694
Ethereum, 125
Etherscan, 310
Etherstack, 983
Ethertronics, 1255, 1661
Ethex, 1285
Ethic, 398, 1058, 1895
Ethical Coffee Company, 2285
Ethical Pharmaceuticals Ltd, 3177
Ethical Property, 2500
Ethiochicken, 54

EthnicGrocer.Com, 1061
Ethoca, 1720
eThor, 2043
Ethos, 608, 894, 1657
Ethos Lending, 1073
ETI, 35, 124, 143
eTime Capital, 2643
Etive Technologies, 2958
ETix, 1712
Etohum, 2428
Etonenet, 1241
Etoos, 2848
Etoro, 1718
eToro, 2398
Etouch, 597
ETouches, 876
Etouches, 433
etouches, 162, 962
eToys.com, 263
Etrans, 3091
etrials, 1313
Etronic, 3209
Etronica, 1786
ETSA Utilities, 2582
ETSolar, 2575
Etsy, 27, 339, 840, 1884, 2851, 2851
ETT, 377
ETX, 654
EU Networks, 510
Eucalyptus, 641
Euclid, 2009
Euclises, 270
Euclises Pharmaceuticals Inc., 570
Eumakh, 3172
euNetworks, 518
Euphonix, 1379
EUR Systems Inc., 1624
Eureka II LP, 2088
Eureka Resources, 898
Eureka Therapeutics, 46
Eurekite, 550
Euretco NV, 2797
Euro Carter, 2376
Euro Part, 2842
Euro Services Laboratory, 2846
Euro-atomizado., 2480
EURO-DIESEL, 2303
EuroChlor, 3169
EuroDesign Cabinets, 1145
Euroelektro International Oy, 2864
EuroFem, 1776
Euroflow, 2565
Eurofresh Inc., 357
Euroimmun, 2704
Euromate, 2370
Euromedic, 838
Euromedic International, 2968
Euromerchant Balkan Fund (EBF), 2775
Euronet, 2716
Europe Apotheek, 2494
Europe Snacks, 2842
Europe Technologies, 2457
European Colour plc, 3169
European Directory Assistance, 2417
European Games Group, 3011
European Homes, 2439, 2842, 3229
European Investor Services, 3137
European Locomotive Leasing, 1086
European Secondary Development Fund IV LP, 2088
European Telecommunication Holding E.T.H. AG, 2519
European Telecommunications & Technology, 2568, 2653
European Wax Center, 331
Europroteome AG, 2673
Euroscreen, 3125

Portfolio Companies Index

Euroseas, 517
Eurospect Manufacturing Inc., 2098
Euroventures III, 2715
EUSA Pharma, 698, 1456
Eutech, 2763
Eutech Medical, 2553
Eutech Medical AB, 2709
Eutechnyx, 3042
Eutelsat, 2596, 2710
EUTEX European Telco Exchange, 2664
Euthymics Bioscience, 1923
EV Connect, 625, 1065, 3246
EV Energy Partners, 673
Eva, 310
Eva Airways, 2427
Evalve, 1728
Evalve Inc., 22, 573
Evander Group, 2935
evandtec, 1324
Evaneos, 3229
Evans, 371
Evans & Dixon, 3261
Evans & Sutherland, 2005
Evans and Sutherland, 1257
Evanston Capital Management, 1778
Evanta, 1109
Evariant, 921, 1125, 1610
Evatic, 3207
EVault, 551
Evault, 2051
EVCI Career Colleges, 530
Evco Research, 1691
EvConnect, 309
EVE, 2653
Eve, 2665, 2935
Eve Medical, 985
EVE NY, 2841
Eve Tab, 2107
Eve.com, 1125
Eved, 454, 1242, 1483
Evelo Bioscience, 894
Evelo Biosciences, 748
Even, 387, 1073, 1511
EVEN Financial, 711
Even Financial, 354, 1114
Evenflo Company Inc., 917
Event Farm, 1
Event Hi, 395
Event Photography Group, 1529
Event Rental Group, 2133
Event Zero, 1008
Eventbase, 1162
Eventbrite, 582, 1657, 1798
Eventful, 241, 3160
Eventovate, 2347
EventReviews.com, 1907
Events Core, 2464
Events.com, 1832, 1907
Eventup, 567, 1121
Eventus, 2074
Eventyard, 2687
eVenues, 1254
Evenus, 169
EVEO, 1239
Ever, 972, 2346, 2457
Ever Compliant, 149, 3212
Ever EdTech, 3250
Everalbum, 720
Everbank Financial Coporation, 1152
EverBank Financial Corporation, 1300
Everbee, 2346, 2888
Everbridge, 22, 646, 1643, 2662
Evercare, 2927
Everclaw, 1203
EverCommerce, 1499
Evercontact, 3099
Everdream, 1483, 1561

Everest Software, 318, 1888
Everex Systems, 1337
EverFi, 1554, 1832
Everfi, 265, 1555, 1949
Evergage, 58, 1463
Evergig, 1418
Evergreen, 874, 1138
Evergreen Group, 2927
Evergreen Holdings, 612
Evergreen Lodge, 1397
Evergreen Media Corporation, 576
Evergreen Services Group, 92
Evergreen Solar, 217, 1355, 1583, 1704
Evergreen Tank Solutions, 1368
Evergreen Transport, 1768
Everite Machine Products, 699
Everlance, 108
Everlane, 1073, 1114, 1186, 1696
Everlasting Wardrobe, 1509
Everlaw, 125, 1054, 1402
Everly, 461
Everly Well, 1703
Evernote, 108, 621, 840, 1213, 1254, 1257, 1610, 1657, 1696
Everplans, 1263, 1635
Everquote, 1628, 1643
Eversholt Leasing, 2547
Everside Health, 1296
Eversight, 666
Eversound, 2
Everspin, 689
Everspin Technologies, 1155, 1304, 1674
Everspring, 38, 419
Everstream, 1157
Everstring, 1125, 3241
EverTeam, 1418
EverTrue, 1483
Evertrue, 224, 316, 1534
EverWatch, 681
Everwise, 399, 780, 1657, 1969
Everwrite, 2974
Every Move, 85
Every Screen Media, 541
Everyaction, 1005
EverybodyFights, 332
Everyclick, 2958
EveryDay Health, 3128
Everyday Health, 773, 928, 1561, 1629
Everyday Learning, 154
Everyday Solutions, 748
Everykey, 985
EveryMove, 1618
Everymove, 1791
Everyone Counts, 68
EveryoneSocial, 1317
Everypath, 2073
EveryScape, 581, 1104, 1290
EveryScreen Media, 535
Everytable, 54, 1114
Everything, 2437
Everything Benefits, 175
Everything But The House, 872
Everything but the House, 641
Everything.me, 2822, 3112
eVestment, 1611
Evi, 3009
evian, 475
Evichat, 2094
EviCore Healthcare, 819
Evidation, 183, 812, 1555, 1631, 1764
Evident, 48, 285
Evident Software, 1321
Evident.io, 1862, 1918
Evidon, 1957
Evie, 742
Eviivo, 1021
Evikon, 2382

Evino, 3047
eVisit, 861, 1074
Evite, 200
EVO, 655
Evo Electric, 2849
EVO Payments International, 1160
Evocalize, 1162
Evocatal, 2815
Evoco Ltd., 2115
Evocutis, 2883
Evodos, 2677
Evogene, 2408
Evok Innovations, 3249
Evoke, 1098
Evoke Pharma, 622
Evoke Software Corp., 215
Evol Foods, 246, 1450
Evolable Asia, 721
Evolita, 2994
Evolution Equity, 485
Evolution Markets, 436
Evolution Midstream, 672
eVolution Networks, 812
Evolv, 827, 1125, 1908
Evolv Sports & Designs, 357
Evolv Technologies, 1010
Evolv Technology, 820, 1155
Evolva, 2410, 2506, 2701, 3140, 3202
Evolve, 1748
Evolve Energy, 1896
Evolve IP, 862
Evolved Intelligence, 2682
Evolved Meats, 2122
Evolving Systems, 2745
Evotec, 2807, 3187
Evotec NeuroSciences GmbH, 3128
Evox Therapeutics, 894
Evoz, 591, 2863
EVP EyeCare, 547
Evree, 2107, 2204
Evrest Broadband Networks, 317
Evriholder Products, 445
EVRS, 2565
Evrythng, 485
EVS Broadcast Equipment, 3060
Evvnt, 2951
EW Healthcare Partners, 3254
EwayTech, 2123
EWC, 551
eWise, 1865
EWT, 2101
Ex Libris, 843, 3221, 3235
Ex Libris Global Holdings, 1971
Ex Libris Ltd., 3149
EXA, 651
Exa Corporation, 313
Exabeam, 48, 182, 485, 972, 1125, 1346
Exablox, 597, 1898
Exacom, 1641
Exacq Technologies, 1061
Exact Imaging, 2141, 2174
Exact Media, 2231
Exact Target, 1629
Exactbid, 1720
Exactech, 1837
Exacter, 1285, 1556
Exactis.com, 318
Exactium, 2711
ExactTarget, 234, 561
EXACTUALS, 1865
Exadigm, 636
Exagen Diagnostics, 550, 689, 1222
Exago, 3022
Exagrid, 938
ExaGrid Systems, 1674, 1675, 1798
Exal Group, 1747
Exalt, 1014, 1855

1287

Portfolio Companies Index

Examination Management Services, 1271
Examity, 862
ExamSoft, 1720
ExamWorks, 1113
Exanet, 538
ExaProtect, 3011
Exari, 2074
Exaro Energy III, 1606
Exasol, 2970
Excaliard Pharmaceuticals, 1578
Excalibur Resources, 673
Excara, 1561
Exceed Midlands Advantage Fund, 2935
Excel Academy Charter Schools, 1315
Excel Engineering, 1582
Excel Fitness, 96
Excel Manufacturing, 1707
Excel Polymers, 41
Excel Technology, 2835
Excelan, 241
Excelcom, 2425
Excelerate Health Ventures, 738
Excelerate Labs, 1364
Excelero, 238, 1511
Excelitas Technologies, 1927
Excellere Capital Partners LP, 2088
excelleRx, 1140
Excelligence, 381, 1335
Excelligence Learning Corp., 337
excellRx, 1410
Excelsior Medical, 1460, 1594
ExCentos, 2815
Exception Wild Bunch, 2888
Excera, 2969
Excera Materials Group, 1337
Exchange Resources, 217
Exchange Solutions, 180, 1339, 1901, 2188
Exchangery, 1618
Excico, 2358, 2940
Excico Group, 3033
Excision Biotherapeutics, 177
Exclaim, 1771, 2188
Exclara, 1583, 1924
Exclusive Networks, 3011
Exco inTouch, 3095
EXCO Resources, 160
Exco Resources, 1086
Excosoft, 2881
ExecOnline, 1290, 1388
ExecThread, 1032
Executive Greetings Inc., 248
Executive Health Resources, 20, 1929, 1979
Executive Strategies Group LLC, 3257
Exegy, 1316
Exelate, 1316, 3212
eXelate, 1852, 2557
Exelis, 193
Exelixis, 1395, 1777
Exelixis Pharmaceuticals, 215
Exelixis Pharmaceuticals Inc., 2776
Exemplify, 1926
Exent, 485, 1829
Exentive F.B. Technology, 2846
Exergen, 1176
Exergyn, 1065
Exeter Finance Corporation, 1279
Exfm, 1718
Exhale, 337
Exie, 2304
Exie AS, 2745
Exigen, 759
Eximia, 3043
Eximias, 1510
Eximo Medical, 2316
Exinda, 872, 1381
Exini Diagnostics, 2440
Exist, 1966

eXist db, 1800
Exit Games, 2985, 3114
Exit Games GmbH, 2664
Exithera Pharmaceuticals, 1630
EXL Service, 796
Exl Services, 1360
ExLibris, 782
Exlinea, 2542
eXML, 2699
Exmplar, 1915
EXO, 1739
Exo Imaging, 1705
Exocor, 1627
Exodus, 808, 925
Exodus Communications, 241, 1042
ExoGenesis, 993, 1922
Exonhit, 2346
ExonHit Therapeutics, 1395
Exoplatform, 3229
Exoprise Systems, 713
EXOS, 21, 377
Exosect, 2701
Exosome Diagnostics, 158, 1325, 1421, 2739
Exosun, 3011
Exotec, 2288
Exotrail, 2288
Exp, 819
Expa, 1114
Expan, 3045
Expand Network, 3150
Expander, 2425
Expanding Orthopedics, 644, 1190, 1849
Expanse, 1760
Expansion Therapeutics, 11, 1079, 1350, 1522
Expect Labs, 1515, 1800
Expedi, 320
Expedock, 1426
Expel, 238, 1121
Expensable, 495
ExpenseBot, 1051
Expensify, 234, 1463, 1537
Expera Specialty Solutions, 1089
Experient, 1460
Experiment, 1876
Experiment 7, 1477
Expert Global Solutions, 1376
Expert Janitorial Services, 1424
Expert NJS, 1425
Expert Plan, 51, 162, 1275
Experteer, 2820, 2829
Experteer.dE, 641
ExpertFile, 2178
Experticity, 224, 1679
Experts Exchange, 1813
Expeto, 2187
Expeto Wireless, 2105
Expii, 863
Expion, 3250
Explara, 3124
Explay-Japan, 2965
Explocity, 2837
Explora Petroleum, 1957
Explore Schools, 1315
EXPLORER, 1159
ExplORer Surgical, 1633
Explorer Surgical, 139
Explorys, 749
Explorys Inc., 205
Explorys Medical, 1622
Expocolour, 2976
Exponential Entertainment, 1065, 1827
Exponor Digital, 3039
Exporo, 641
Export Development Canada, 3249
Exporta, 1426
Exposoft Solutions, 2188
ExpoTV, 1178

ExpreS2ion Biotechnologies, 3194
Express, 843
Express Energy Services, 874, 1138
Express Engineering, 2935
Express Food Group, 1143
Express KCS, 1626
Express Oil Change & Service Center, 418
Express Oil Change and Service Center, 170
Express Packaging, 920
Express Window Films, 815
ExpressCells, 1581
ExpressCoin, 1683
Expressions Furniture, 714
expresso, 1354
Expresso Education Limited, 2449
Expressor Software, 523
Expressor Software Corp, 1674
Expro, 2371
ExproSoft, 3207
Expway, 2867, 2890
Expé, 3229
ExSar Corporation, 1191
Exsequor, 2872
Extant Components, 1957
Extend, 1531
Extend Media, 1918
ExtendCredit, 1786
Extended Care Information Network, 654
Extended Stay America, 444
Extended Systems, 990
ExtendMedia, 1478
Extenet, 443
ExteNet Systems, 654, 1408
Extenet Systems, 1314
Extennet, 1661
Extensibility, 1013
Extensity, 1125, 1478
Exteria, 851
Enterprise, 205, 1857
Exterro, 1109
Extole, 1346, 1537, 1629, 1666, 1852
Extra Space Storage, 870
ExtraHop, 1162, 1213
ExtraHop Networks, 1787
Extranomical Tours, 1612
ExtraOrtho, 999
Extraprise, 523
Extreme DA, 116
Extreme Innovations, 2107
Extreme Networks, 1478, 1855
Extreme Packet Devices, 1084
Extreme Reach, 561, 1146, 1720
Extreme Venture Partners, 3249
ExtremeReach, 876
Extricity, 1912
Extricity Software, 759
Extrumed, 1018
Extrusion Dies Industries, 260
Exult, 38, 2643
Exuvis, 3033
Exvivo, 721
Exxcelia, 912
Exxelia Magnetics, 2842
Exym, 92
EY, 3262, 3264, 3268
Eyang Holdings, 2927
eYantra, 3202
Eye Care Centers Of America, 843
Eye Health America, 1140
Eye Q, 546
Eye Smart Technology, 1009
Eye-Fi, 1840
Eye-q, 2809
Eyebobs, 1345
eyeBrain Medical, 300
Eyebright Medical, 711
eyecandylab, 229

Portfolio Companies Index

Eyecare Partners, 790
EyeCare Services Partners, 917
EyeEm, 2435
Eyefactive, 2815
Eyeka, 3199
eYeka, 2890
Eyelation, 583
EyelCo, 1101
EyeM, 3021
Eyemart Expreess, 790
Eyeonics, 22
Eyeota, 3047
EyePoint Pharmaceuticals Inc., 698
EyeQ, 2992
EyeQuant, 2986
Eyequant, 2470
EYES, 3091
EyeSense, 2930
EyeSight Mobile Technologies, 1241
Eyesight&Vision, 2815
EyeSouth, 1169
Eyesquad, 2334
EyeTechCare, 3011
Eyevensys, 2221
Eyeview, 1125, 2978
Eyewitness News, 1929
Eyewitness Surveillance, 381, 1140
EyeWonder, 266
Eykona Technolgies, 3019
EYP Architecture & Design, 1145
Eyrus, 1259
EZ Apps, 1786
EZ Chip Technologies, 1042
EZ Lube, 874
EZ-DSP Ltd, 2695
Ez-Ways.Com, 852
EZ-WHEEL, 2288
ezboard, 1736
EzCater, 1005
ezCater, 1104, 1164
EZCertify.com, 1209
EZchip, 3128
Eze Software Group, 1837
EZE Trucking, 1481
Ezeep, 2815
Ezetap, 1698
Eziba, 1561
Ezibuy, 2655
Ezoic, 2469
Ezono, 2518
eZono AG, 2972
Ezra, 1105
EzRez Software, 2448
EZShield, 2098
EzTexting, 2074
eZuce, 1375

F

F&B Asias, 1630
F+W Media, 20
F-Prime Capital, 3263
F-Star, 1734, 3187
F-Star Alpha Limited, 193
f-Star GmBH, 2342
f-star GmbH, 3006
F.B. Leopold Company, 694
F.T. Silfies, 192
F/ELD, 2245
F2G, 73, 3140
F5, 1566
Faab-Fabicauto, 2332
FAAH Pharma, 3187
Fab, 621, 1187, 1441, 1598, 1702, 1823, 2437, 2466, 3112
Fab Furnish, 3161
FAB Pharma, 2867
Fab.com, 2016, 2595, 3220

Fabco Automotive, 2008
FabEnCo/BlueWater, 815
FabFitFun, 1823, 1890
FabHotels, 846, 1511
Fabl, 289
Fable, 1391
Fable Studio, 1666
Fabric, 1001, 1186, 1533
Fabric Genomics, 240
Fabrinet, 897
FabSource, 3250
Face U, 1125
Face.com, 3072
Facebook, 125, 339, 650, 660, 778, 840, 846, 990, 1213, 1235, 1787, 2654, 2714, 2822, 2919
Facebook Investment Fund LLC, 2595
Facecake, 2009
Faces Human Capital Management, 558
Facet, 2944
Facet Pricing, 870
FaceTime Communications, 1042
Faceware, 3083
FacilitySource, 1957
FACIT, 3249
Fact Based Communication Ltd, 2745
FactGem, 1285
Faction, 1212
Factivate, 512
Facton, 2804
Factor Trust, 1240
FactorTrust, 21
Factory Connection, 90
Factory Four, 18
Factory Logic, 55
FactSquared, 937
Factual, 101, 125, 976, 1237, 1608, 1890
Factual Beta, 720
Factury, 310
Faena Group, 33
Fafle Tech Labs, 2092
Fair, 44, 303, 305, 805, 1032, 1363
Fair Information Services BV, 2983
Fairchild Industrial Products Company, 557
FairClaims, 729
Fairclaims, 564
Faire, 763, 1073, 1125, 1657, 2130, 2131
Fairfield Collectibles, 1424
Fairfield Energy, 1577, 1957
Fairhaven Pharmaceuticals, 2125
Fairline Boats Holdings Ltd, 2298
FairLoan, 31
Fairly, 1323
Fairmarkit, 1175
Fairmont Hotels, 303
Fairmount Santrol, 111
Fairr.De, 2832
FairShake, 321
FairStreet, 1426
Fairway, 1231
Fairway America, 1065
Fairway Architectural Railing Solutions, 165
Fairway Biomed, 999
Fairway Energy, 898
Fairway Medical Technologies, 953
Fairway Outdoor, 889
Fairways Group (UK), 2298
Fairweather, 2245
Fairygodboss, 888
Faith Street, 1119
FaithStreet, 1521
Falanx AS, 2361
Falby Design, 3194
Falcon, 1021
Falcon Computing, 222, 1672
Falcon Gas Storage, 153
Falcon Genomics, 1452

Falcon Social, 3194
Falcon-Vision, 2478
Falconstor, 2427
Falkonry, 235, 2018
Fallbrook Technologies, 1324
Fallon Visual Products, 1131
Falls Fabricating, 1722
Falmac, 897
Falrion Technologies, 457
Fam, 1426
Fama, 121, 309
Fame and Partners, 744, 1890
FameBit, 1816, 2140
Famigo, 1687
Familia, 1588
Familia Dental, 899
Families for Excellent Schools, 1315
Familonet, 3198, 3226
Family Arc, 347
Family Care, 409
Family Home Health Services, 654, 1904
Family Plan, 1509
Family Tech, 481
FamilyID.com, 316
Familylink, 2374
FamilyMint, 743
Famo.us, 1032
Famoco, 2842
Famosa, 1755
Famoso, 2245
Famous, 1005, 1614
FamPlus, 2815
Fan AI, 474
Fan Duel, 520
Fan.tv, 1537
FanAI, 708, 1589
Fanaticall, 1832
Fanatics, 125, 1005, 1685
FanBank, 562
Fanbank, 387, 1531
FanBread, 121
Fanbread, 1966
FanBridge, 1702
Fanbridge, 1153
Fancred, 1914
Fancy, 820, 1527, 1533
Fancy Hands, 1114, 1464, 1549
Fandango, 38
Fandango Inc., 2394
Fandeavor, 1914
FanDuel, 872, 1086, 1663, 3023, 3031
Fanduel, 298, 361, 579
Fanfare, 759
FanFare Media Works, 20
FangDD, 1125
Fango, 1618
Fanhattan, 876
Fanimal, 1426
FanIQ, 1908
FanNation, 1644
Fannin Partners, 953
FanoFineFood, 2370
FanPlayr, 606
Fantasmo, 1105
Fantastic, 874
Fantasy Entertainment, 405
Fantasy Moguls, 1644
Fantasy Shopper, 2466
FantasySalesTeam, 447
Fantom, 2347, 2513
Fantrail, 595
Fantuan Delivery, 2123
FanTV, 641
FanXchange, 374, 2127, 2216
Fanzila, 304
FAOPEN, 1757
FAPS, 1639

1289

Portfolio Companies Index

Far Chemical Inc., 653
Far Niente, 828
Far Sounder, 1695
Faraday, 789, 1101, 2007
Farecast, 1449, 1762
FareChase, 22, 313
Farfaria, 1017
FarFetch, 641
Farfetch, 977
Farm Burger, 825
Farm Dog, 2938
Farm Fresh, 357
Farm Fresh Pet Foods, 2093
Farm Hill, 1119
Farm Market iD, 352
Farma Holding, 3045
Farman, 2663
Farmdrop, 2437
Farmeasy, 1511
FarmerBs Fridge, 1001
Farmeron, 1105, 1322, 1702, 3099
Farmers Business Network, 596, 894, 1079
Farmers Hope, 54
FarmHopping, 3099
Farmhouse Culture, 1384, 2230
Farmhouse Fare Ltd, 2699
Farmigo, 1668
Farminers Startup Academy, 2847
Farmland Keeper, 827
Farmland LP, 3246
FarmLogix, 507
FarmLogs, 608, 631, 743, 964, 965
FarmQA, 1135
FarmRaise, 1426
Farmshots, 1925
Farmstr, 1854
FarmWise, 235
Farmwise, 1809
Farnese Vini, 2285
Farralon Medical, 1917
Farran Technology, 2909
Farrell Fritz PC, 3257
Farther Farms, 623
Fashion and You, 1327
Fashion Cents, 791
Fashion for Home, 2820, 2829
Fashion One, 2502
Fashion Playres, 1101
Fashion Project, 1479, 1630
Fashionara, 1125
Fashionette, 2432
Fast, 8
Fast BioMedical, 659
Fast Booking, 2888
Fast Goods Groups UAB, 3040
Fast Lane Ventures, 3220
Fast Pace Urgent Care, 1670
Fast Pay Partners, 1971
Fast Sandwich LLC, 406
Fast Track Systems, 154
FastAsset, 649
Fastback Networks, 773, 857
FastCAP Systems, 1688
Fastcase, 1723
FastChannel, 42
Fastchip Inc., 255
FASTech Integration, 209, 317
Fasten, 89
Fasteners for Retail, 1460
Faster, 2413
Fastfox, 1125
Fastfrate, 722
Fastly, 238, 1566, 1716
FastMed Urgent Care, 20
FastPay, 488
Fastrax Oy, 2707
FastScale, 185

FASTSIGNS, 786
FASTSIGNS International, 1115
FastSoft, 68, 1237
Fastsoft, 194
FastSpring, 28, 381, 1826
FASTTAC, 1003, 1588
FastTrac, 1305
FastWeb, 2658
Fastyl, 1359
Fat Llama, 12
Fat Pipe, 1679
Fat Spaniel, 2072
Fat Spaniel Technologies, 145, 1398
Fatbrain.com/Barnesandnoble.com, 1287
Fate Therapeutics, 154, 1392, 1421, 1464, 1621, 1918
Fatherly, 259, 564, 863, 1114, 1885
FATHOM, 2282
Fathom, 863, 1724, 2256
Fathom Computing, 1423
FatWire, 1313
Fauna, 537, 548, 894
Faust Pharma, 2346
Faves, 1426
Favor, 310, 546, 1687
Favrille, 1287
Faxitron, 1018
FaxSav, 538
Fazoli's, 1755
FB Brands, 1232
FBC Device, 3140, 3194
FBGS, 2518
FBL Group LLC, 123
FBR & Co., 560
FC Holdings, 1043
FCA, 1481
FCA Packaging, 1473
FCF Fox Corporate Finance, 2970
FCI, 223, 2848
Fci, 1518
FCL Graphics, 620
FCS, 2797
FCV, 2465
FCX Performance, 1460
FCX Performance Inc., 917
FDG-Gruppe, 3058
FDH, 952
FDN Communications, 443
FE3 Medical, 130
Fe3 Medical, 984
Fearless, 310
Feasible, 2072
FeastFox, 623
Feastly, 310, 594, 1752, 1978
Feather, 999, 1079
Feature Labs, 756
FeatureSpace, 2849
febit, 983
Federal, 1090
Federated Foods, 3137
Federated Media Publishing, 318, 1411
Federated Sample, 1945
Federato, 1426
FedEx Ground, 16
Fedora, 1998
FedTax, 348
FeedBurner, 610, 1762
Feedhenry, 2909
Feedly, 1323
Feedtrail, 512
Feedvisor, 820
Feedzai, 488, 586
FeeFighters, 1364
Feefighters, 1618
Feel, 2398
Feeney Brothers Utility Services, 368
Feetz, 1073

FEEX, 304
Felins USA, 1252
Felix, 2065, 2176, 2280
Felix & Paul, 474
Felix & Paul Studios, 520
Felix Energy, 673
Fellow, 2122, 2150
Fellowship for Race and Equity in Education, 1315
Felt, 461
FEM, 1223
FEM Inc., 1032
Femco Machine, 1025
FEMCO Machine Co., 1627
Femeda Ltd, 2699
FemSelect, 1581
Femtosense, 2270
Fenavic, 2344
Feneral Paramterics, 1561
Fenergo, 1005
Fengguang Bio-Fan, 3185
Fengkai Machinery, 2927
Fenix Opportunity, 2046
Fennebresque, 3250
Fenno Rahasto Ky, 2731
FenSense, 1509
Fenwal, 1837
Fenway Summer, 387
Fenwick, 2592
Ferche Millwork, 1524
Ferfics, 2347
Fermata, 849
Fero Labs, 320
Ferrara Candy Company, 1092
Ferrara Fire Apparatus, 1210
Ferrell Companies, 1839
Ferrera DeStefano & Caporusso, 3257
Ferric Semiconductor, 1302
Ferring Pharmaceuticals, 1456
Ferris, 1890
Ferroelectric Memory GmbH, 2677
FerroKin Biosciences, 2807
Ferrosan Medical Devices, 2376
Fertility Focus, 2958
Fertiseeds, 2445
Festicket, 3046
Fetch, 863
Fetch Back, 527
Fetch Robotics, 1666
Fetch Technologies, 983
Fetcher, 1557
FetchNotes, 1739
Fetco Home Decor, 1230
Fetise, 3100
Fever Tree, 2935
FeVo, 1533
Fevo, 2231
Fewmo Tech Limited, 1241
FF Pharmaceuticals, 2940
FFC, 36
FFI Contracting Services, 3251
FFI Holdings Inc., 62
FFL Partners, 3254
FFO Home, 1755
Ffpharma, 3033
FG Microtek, 3179
FGA Media, 595
FGL, 1966
Fh, 2687
FI Info Net, 256
Fi Smart Dog Collar, 1309
Fi-on, 2960
fi360, 302
Fiagon, 2815
Fianciere Felix, 2712
Fiber By-Products, 254
Fiber Composites, 1232

Portfolio Companies Index

Fiber Optic Network Systems, 1257
Fiber-Line, 1025
Fiberex, 2194
FiberForge, 1839
Fiberight, 528
FibeRio, 1687
FibeRio Technology Corporation, 550
Fiberline, 3194
Fiberlink, 655
Fibernet, 2688
Fiberoptic Components, 214
Fibers, 2309
Fibersense Technology, 197
Fiberxon, 3053
FiberZone Networks, 1348
FiBest, 1757
Fibest., 2845
Fibocom Wireless, 1009
Fibroblast, 1618
Fibrocell Science, 1815
FibroGen, 764, 2961
Fibrotech, 2527
Fibrotech Therapeutics, 2950
Fictiv, 1009
Fiddlehead, 2063
Fiddlehead Technology, 2192
Fidelia Technology, 1994
Fidelica Microsystems, 1920
Fidelis, 993, 1058, 1359, 1463
Fidelis Education, 1348
Fidelis Insurance Holdings Limited, 560
Fidelis Security Systems, 1172, 1731
Fidelis SeniorCare, 938
Fidelis Seniorcare, 476
Fidelity Investments, 3250
Fidelity National Financial Inc., 1905
Fidelity National Financial Services, 1837
Fidelity Payment Services, 1169
Fidlock, 2815
Fido Labs, 1441
Fidor, 3229
Fidor Bank, 2398
Fidor Russia, 2931
Field Agent, 746
Field Day, 937
Field Lens, 1305, 1381
Field Solutions, 3268
FieldAware, 1381
Fieldaware, 3138
Fieldbrook Foods Corporation, 148
FieldCentrix, 194, 767, 1674, 1708
FieldCLIX, 685
FieldDay, 562
Fieldglass, 881, 1160, 1741
Fieldiens, 1358
FieldLens, 535, 1479, 1521, 1701
Fieldlens, 311
Fieldless Farms, 2115
FieldTest, 309
FieldView, 1691
FieldView Solutions, 1388
Fieldwire, 129
Fieldwood Energy, 1577
Fien En Mile, 3033
Fiesta Mart, 45
Fifth Creek Energy, 1326, 1328
FiftyOne, 56
Fight My Monster, 876
Fightcamp, 2204
Figma, 877, 1079
FIGS, 1527
Figs, 400, 1059, 1247
Figtagram, 1885
Figure, 234, 537
Figure 1, 1614, 2231, 2272
figure 1, 2181
Figure 8, 667

Figure 8 Wireless, 209
Figure Eight, 720, 1158, 1610
Figure1, 2094
Figure8 Surgical, 296
Fiix, 2122, 2126, 2165
Fiksu, 457
Filament, 221, 361, 564, 1550, 1614, 1928
Filament Brands Inc., 449
Filament Labs, 1596
Filco Carting, 1748
Filecoin, 125, 310, 1633, 1669
FileFacets, 2070, 2123
Filefacets, 2276
Fileforce, 1009
Filement, 2687
Filesx, 2766
FileTrek, 133, 2051
Filevine, 79
Filip, 2822
Fill Factory, 2665
Fillattice, 2414
Filld, 1032
FillFactory, 2653
Fillfactory N.V., 2893
Fillmore Advisory, 2637
Film Monkey, 2178
Film Track, 1005
FilmLoop, 810
Filmwerks LLC, 1641
Filoukes, 3033
Filson, 337, 381
Filter Easy, 173
Filter Minder, 1722
Filter Squad, 3238
FilterEasy, 975
FIMC, 952
FIN Engineering Group Ltd, 2695
Fin Robotics, 624
Fin Tyre, 3145
Finaeo, 2024, 2141
Final, 400, 1154
Finalcad, 2430
Finale, 1118
Finali Corporation, 318
FinalPrice, 89
Finalsite, 1720
Finance New Europe, 2639
Financelt, 1865
Financial Directions Group, 3250
Financial Engines, 759, 773, 840, 1360, 1949
Financial Guaranty Insurance Company, 576
Financial Guard, 464
Financial Health Services, 1470
Financial Investments Corporation, 3255
Financial Technology Ventures, 3273
FinancialContent, 241
FinancialForce, 1610
Financiere Orefi, 2976
Financière C.T. (Captain Tortue)., 2644
Financière Fouquet II, 2644
Finanical Engines, 796
Finanzcheck.De, 912
Finanzchef24, 3152
Finanzchek, 2466
Finastra, 745
FiNC, 721
Finch, 2074
Find-Me Technologies, 3014
Finderly, 1862
Findify, 3099
Findis, 1518, 2330
FindIt, 473, 965
Findit, 1593
FindMatic, 452
Findspace, 2216
Fine Line Services LLC, 3258
Fine Sounds Group, 3011

Fine Tubes, 1963
FineHeart, 350
FineLine Technologies, 470, 1848
Finery, 901
Finest City Broadcasting LLC, 20
Finetune, 1165
Finfox, 623
Fingi, 1065
Finicity, 608
Finisar, 2315
Finite Carbon, 1830
Finite State, 2018
Finix, 48
Finix Payments, 49, 944
Finjan, 252
Finjan Vital Security, 912
FinLeap, 1269
Finn AI, 6, 2283
Finn Corp, 1822
Finn Lamex Safety Glass Oy, 2310
Finn.ai, 757
Finnair Oyj, 2981
Finnish Chemicals, 3169
Finnlines Oyj, 2981
Fino, 1009
Finova Financial, 527
Finrise, 1323
Finsecur, 2457
FINsix, 1688, 1918
FINsix Corp., 498
Finsphere Corporation, 1247
Fintech, 2483
FinTech Innovation Lab, 535
Fintech Lab, 1561
Fintyre, 2515
Finxera, 234, 752, 773
Fios, 755, 1949, 2045
Fire & Life Safety America, 293, 747, 1090
Fire Apps, 978
Fire Door Solutions, 668
Fire Grill, 1171
Fire Rock, 679
FIRE Solutions, 1830
FIRE1, 1126
FireApps, 696, 1854
Firearms Training Systems Inc., 449
Firebase, 586, 708
Firebirds Restaurants, 128
Firebox.com, 3061, 3122
Firebrand Media, 2565
Firecomms, 3143
Firecraft Products, 2161
Firedoor, 2869
FireEye, 582, 780, 972, 983, 1657
Fireflies.Ai, 771
Firefly, 623, 1426
Firefly Energy, 1061
Firefly LED Lighting, 447
Firefly Solar Generators, 2496
Fireglass, 1125
Firehole Composites, 35
FireHUD, 623
FireKing Security Group, 1438
FireLayers, 3236
Fireman's Brew, 1065
Firemon, 1005
Firepoint, 390
Firepond, 2005
FirePower Debt GP, 3249
FireRein, 2054
FireRock, 60
Firesale, 395
Fireside Glamping, 679
Firestar Software Inc., 2389
Firestone Diamonds, 1551
Firetide, 538, 942
Fireweed Fund, 624

1291

Portfolio Companies Index

FireWheel Energy, 673
Firich Enterprises, 3209
Firm 58, 1335
Firm AS, 2073
Firm58, 1483
First, 975
First Access, 54, 2901
First Access Entertainment, 33
First Active Media, 2459
First Aid Shot Therapy, 1700
First Allied, 1151
First American Financial, 303
First American Payment Systems, 1133
First American Records Management, 952
First American Title Company of Marin, 874
First Analysis, 3255
First Ascent Ventures, 2074, 3249
First Asset Management, 2073
First Bancorp, 1818
First Bauxite, 1551
First Boulevard, 2398
First Crush, 705
First Data, 2371
First Data Corp., 1086
First Data Holdings, 1746
First Eagle Investment Management, 1778
First Equity, 1922
First Green Partners, 1957
First Health Group Corp., 303
First Hill Partners, 3265
First Insight, 55
First Insight Inc., 159
First Light Fusion, 3019
First Light Hospitality, 3246
First Marketing, 1772
First National Digital Currency, 2257
First Nickel, 1551
First Opinion, 720, 1491, 1637
First Orange Contact, 2442
First Point Holdings, 3053
First Quality, 475
First Republic Bank, 371, 828, 1657, 3262
First Source, 445
First Sun Capital, 1127
First Tower, 1493
First Utility, 1949
First Watch, 61
First Wave Products Group, 1526
First West Capital, 3249
First Western Financial, 554
First Wind Holdings, 1160
Firstbase, 771
FirstBest, 1316
FirstBest Systems, 646
FirstFuel, 238
FirstFuel Software, 1355, 1583
FirstLight HomeCare, 1280
FirstLight Power Enterprises, 676
Firstquote Masson Financial Services, 2563
FirstRain, 1361
FirstSense Software, 1335
Firth Rixon, 66
Firth Rixson, 1360
Fisbones AS, 3132
Fiscal Note, 895
Fiscalia Privada, 2446
FiscalNote, 12, 108, 537, 623, 788, 1616, 1998
Fischbein, 1493
Fischben, 1270
Fischer Block, 288
FISERV, 1973
Fiserv., 2665
Fish2BE, 2940
Fishbowl, 655, 696, 1901
Fishbrain, 3099
Fisher Scientific, 212
Fisher Unitech, 1169

Fisher/Unitech, 1576
Fisherman, 849
FishNet Security, 654
Fishtree, 1298
Fision, 770
Fisk, 858
FISOC, 595
Fispan, 2204
Fit & Fresh, 480
FIT Biotech Oyj, 2310
Fit Solutions, 3069
Fit XR, 1186
Fitamins, 394
Fitbit, 1623, 1701, 1702, 1862
Fitbod, 1426
Fitc&Color, 2428
FitLinxx, 1025, 2188
Fitmob, 708, 1323
fitmob, 1187
Fitn, 1786
Fitness Connection, 1580, 1979
Fitness First, 2596
Fitness Interactive Experience, 365
Fitness on Request, 1117
Fitnesskeeper, 1359
Fitnet, 1815
FitNexx, 999
Fitocracy, 680, 708, 1364, 1585
Fitorbit, 1718
Fitplan, 1114
Fits.me, 2621, 2701
FitStar, 59, 1223
Fitstar, 1855
Fitting Valve and Control Corporation, 112
Fitzroy, 1103
Five, 623
Five Across, 857
Five Apes, 1867
Five Below, 1140
Five Prime, 58, 2807
Five Prime Therapeutics, 596, 622, 2504, 2681
Five Star Finance, 1346
Five Star Food Service, 786, 912
Five Star Foods, 747
Five Star Franchising, 1004
Five Star Technologies, 468, 2188
Five Start Manufacturing, 1574
Five to Nine, 623, 1509
5 à Sec BV, 2713
5.11, 1778
500 Startups, 1966
500friends, 564, 799, 863, 1515, 1959
500px, 724
500V, 721
51 Deco, 3053
5173.com, 2841
51edu, 2841
51edu.com, 2841
51Fanli.com, 3133
51job, 597
51Talk, 597
51talk, 3241
51VR, 1125
51wan.com, 3199
55.1 Tactical, 525
555 Mansell, 1220
56.com, 57, 3133
57 Stars, 3252
58 Daojia, 1086
58.com, 597, 1957
Five9, 186
FiveAcross, 57
5AM Ventures, 3259
5asec, 1518
5i Medical, 1065
5iSciences, 281
5Medical Marketing, 1228

5miles, 977
5mina, 591
5minMedia, 1718, 2905
5Nine, 1005
FivePrime, 1930
FivePrime Therapeutics, 2961
Fiverr, 27, 263, 1121
FiveRun, 246
FiveRuns, 205
5Square Systems, 1976
FiveStar, 1257
FiveStars, 2011
Fivestars, 597, 1125
5th Element Tracking, 695
5to1, 801
5V Technologies, 1924
Fixed, 1219, 1752
Fixes 4 Kids, 1074
Fixmo, 1401, 1411, 2822
Fixya, 1187
Fizz, 1296
Fizzback, 2978
Fjord Marin, 2745
Fk-Biotecnologia, 2617
Fketchfab, 1418
Flaaming Oy, 2957
Flabeg, 1755
Flachsland Zukunftsshulen, 2522
Flaconi, 2432, 2466
FLAG Therapeutics, 3250
Flagship Pioneering, 884
Flagship Ventures, 3259
Flagstone Foods, 886
Flagstone Reinsurance Holdings Limited, 1127
Flair, 1896
Flamel Technologies FoldRx, 94
Flamingo Horticulture, 1755
Flanco International, 2420
Flanders' Drive, 3033
Flare Capital Partners, 3263
Flare Technologies, 623
Flaregames, 27
Flarion, 263, 1304
Flarion Technologies, 693, 3146
Flash Delivery, 925
Flash Networks, 117, 912, 1928, 2717, 2773, 3114, 3115, 3146
Flash Valet, 205
FlashBase, 593
Flashbox, 2122
FlashFoto, 53
Flashline, 55
FlashNetworks Ltd, 2576
Flashnotes, 1701, 1737
Flashpoint, 485, 2126
FlashSoft, 31, 361
Flashtalking, 1605, 1778
Flat Iron Energy Partners, 543
Flat Out of Heels, 221
Flat World, 1901
Flat World Knowledge, 1851
Flat-mx, 2398
FlatFrog, 3140
Flatiron, 863
Flatiron Health, 742
Flatiron School, 1823
Flatlay, 1509
Flatout Flatbread, 1336
Flatstack, 1945
Flattr, 3021
FlatWorld Knowledge, 1479
Flavor Infusion LLC, 77
Flavorl, 1755
Flavors Holdings, 408
Flayvr, 2905
Flect, 1610
Fleecs, 2767

Portfolio Companies Index

Fleet Complete, 1160
Fleet Hoster, 2262
Fleet One, 796, 1140
Fleet Worth Solutions, 162
FleetComplete, 2074
FleetCor, 60, 223
FleetCor Technologies, 1754
Fleetgistics Enterprises Inc., 911
FleetMatics, 1483
Fleetmatics, 1006, 1021
FleetMatics USA, 1971
Fleetops, 2132, 2204
FleetPride, 202, 381, 1021
FleetPride Inc., 337
Fleetpride Inc., 1837
FleetPro, 3222
Fleetsmith, 1203
Fleetwash, 1493
Fleetwood, 77
Fleksy, 680, 1079
FLENS, 2965
Fletcher Spaght Ventures, 3259
Fleux Pine, 1379
Flex, 1657
Flex Energy Solutions, 106
Flex Logix, 1155
Flex Logix Technologies, 648
Flex Pharma, 263, 1126, 1149
Flex Pharma Inc., 489
Flex-P Industries, 2614
Flexa, 976
Flexan, 1132
Flexday, 2137
FLEXE, 1644
Flexe, 1537
FlexEngage, 754
Flexential, 745, 828
Flexera Software, 1817
FlexGen, 2505, 3011
FlexGen Power Systems, 98, 812
Flexicath, 1452
Flexion, 11, 1930
Flexion Therapeutics, 1439
Flexitech, 1755
Flexiti Financial, 2128
Flexitive, 2137, 2240
Flexium Interconnect, 2594
FlexLight Networks, 538
FlexLogics, 624
FlexMinder, 2007
FlexNetworks, 2056
flexperto, 2832
FlexPharma, 545, 710
FlexPlay, 42
Flexpoint Ford, 3254
Flexport, 321, 720, 742, 778, 894, 945, 995, 1370, 1426, 1669, 1716, 1878, 1998
FlexRay, 1115
FlexReceipts, 126
FlexSpark, 999
Flexstar Technology, 197, 381
FlexTrip, 686
Flexuspine, 1931
Fliaz, 1848
Flickr, 1323
Fliggo, 1658
Flight Deck, 1051
Flight Office, 1065
Flight Options, 1548
Flight Training Acquisitions, 1131
Flight Trampoline Parks, 832
FlightCar, 827, 863, 1701
FlightCaster, 2321
Flightdocs, 162
Flightman, 3023
FlightWave Aero, 431, 814
Fliit, 2832, 3226

Flingo, 200
Flinks, 2172, 2204
Flinn Scientific Inc., 912
Flint, 1430, 1862
Flint Mobile, 1750
Flint Trading Inc., 747
Flip, 1125
Flipboard, 520, 827, 1005, 1079, 2851, 2851
Flipd, 2094
FlipGive, 2141
Flipgloss, 1103
Flipgrid, 175, 344
Flipkart, 27
Flipkart.com, 1948
Flipp, 1005
Flipside, 310
Flipter, 2975
FlipTop, 586
Fliptop, 1150, 1527
Fliptu, 1635
Flirtey, 1153, 1330, 1511
Flirtic, 89
Flixbus, 819, 2829
Flixel, 2107, 2176
Flixel Cinemagraph, 2192
FlixMaster, 686
Flixster, 1125, 1449
FlixWagon, 2344
Flo, 662, 2398, 2542
Float, 387, 2122, 2131
Floating Point Group, 623
Flocabulary, 1554
Flocations, 3112
Flock, 1426, 2398
FloDesign, 2483
Flogit4u, 3083
Flojos, 367
Flok, 1426
FloNetwork, 1771
Flood Data Services, 132
Floodgate, 205
Floop, 679
Floor & Decor, 786
Floor & Decor Outlets of America, 160, 1875
Floor & Décor, 1971
Floor & DéCor Outlets of America, 1627
Floored, 354, 876, 1534, 1597, 1876
FloQast, 121, 1005, 1831, 1966
Floravere, 328, 1770
Florence Healthcare, 246
Floreo, 1477
Florida Autism Center, 1670
Florida Bank, 227
Florida Bank Group, 1152
Florida Blue, 3251
Florida East Coast Industries, 769
Florida East Coast Railway, 769
Florida Food Products, 1231
Florida Funders, 3251
Florida Gulfshore Capital, 3251
Florida Marine Group, 1748
Florida Pallative Homecare, 409
Florimex Group, 2492
Flosonics Medical, 2125, 2141, 2181
FloSports, 259
FloType, 586
Flourish, 623
Flow, 763, 799, 816, 1635
Flow ++, 222
Flow Control Group, 260
Flow Control Solutions Inc., 159
Flow Dry Technology, 165
Flow Hub, 152, 1443
Flow Kana, 850, 1468, 1613
Flow Solutions, 1560
Flow State Media, 1719
Flow Traders BV, 1754

Flow-Dry, 1025
FlowBelow, 447
FlowCadia Inc., 785
FlowCardia, 1414
Flowchem, 172
Flowdock, 1566
FlowForward Medical, 1380
Flowhub, 99, 1810
Flowmedica, 2739
Flowonix Medical, 1375
Flowplay, 68, 1009, 2382
FlowTech Feuling, 679
Flowtown, 234, 1058
Flowtune, 623
Floyd, 254, 328
floyd, 608
FloydHub, 1614
FLRish, 558, 1139
FLS Transportation, 20
Flud, 1154
Fludicon, 2923
Fludrive, 405
Fluencr, 1914
Fluency Voice Technology, 2568
Fluensee, 979
Fluent Home, 336
Fluent.AI, 2178
Fluent.ai, 2024
FluentStream Technologies, 1499
Fluid, 545, 846, 881
Fluid Clarification, 2129, 2277
Fluid Delivery Solutions LLC, 1853
Fluid Screen, 198
Fluidic Analytics, 2665, 3019
Fluidigm, 561, 983, 1014
Fluidly, 2398
Fluidmesh Networks, 1965
Fluids Inc., 2283
Flume, 198
Flunt Industries, 1210
Fluoptics, 2890
Fluorous Technologies, 1003
Fluree, 9, 849
Flurry, 182, 311, 564, 610, 628, 742, 1014
Flutter, 1983
Flux, 311, 641, 894, 2398
FluxDrive, 85
Fluxion, 1238
Fluxion Biosciences, 493, 1084
Fluxome Sciences, 3104
Fluxus, 1418, 2346
Fluxx, 720
FLX Bio, 519, 894, 1079
Fly, 1533
Fly The Wave, 1165
Flybits, 2094, 2146, 2217, 2265
Flybridge Capital Partners, 3263
Flyby Media, 459
FlyCast, 296
Flycast, 263, 1728
FlyCleaners, 2016
Flyhomes, 1666
Flying Colours Corp., 929
Flynn Pharma, 1846
Flynn Restaurant Group, 2177
Flyp Technologies Inc., 2088
Flyr, 1039
Flyshot, 2094
FlyteComm, 1354
Flytrex, 252
Flywheel, 325, 1154
Flywheel Software, 1583
FlyWire, 316
Flywire, 711, 1186
FM Sylvan, 293
FM:Systems, 28, 3250
FMA France, 2796

1293

Portfolio Companies Index

FMC, 3060
FMH Aerospace, 989
FMI, 653
FMI International, 1090
FMP, 1101
FMS Advanced Systems Group, 983
FNB United, 1360
FNEX, 659
FNF Construction Inc., 1041
FNZ, 819
Foam Fabrications, 525
Foam Rubber Products, 1252
Foamix, 1943
Focal, 1399
Focal Point Data Risk, 902, 1345
Focal Point Pharmaceuticals, 1190
Focal Systems, 548, 2018
Focal Therapeutics, 667, 1371
FocalTech Sytems, 2694
Focus, 2667
FOCUS Brands, 1580
Focus Brands, 1493
Focus Diagnostics, 212
Focus Financial, 1464
Focus Financial Partners, 1086, 1754
Focus Genetics, 2507
Focus Media, 691, 1091, 2289, 3091
Focus Motion, 1637
Focus Solutions, 2463
Focus Solutions Group, 2885
Focus Ventures, 990, 3273
Focus:Trainr, 1103
Focused Health Solutions, 1132
FocusEdu.cn, 597
Fogbreak Software, 1674
Fogg, 2877
FogHorn, 604, 812, 1812
Foghorn Therapeutics, 748
FogLogic, 1666
Fogo De Chao, 1818
FogPharma, 894
Foko, 2187
Foldax, 1055
Foldax Inc., 272
Foley & Lardner LLP, 3251
Foley's, 2284
Folica, 1751
Folicum, 3140
FolioDynamix, 655
Foliot Furniture, 2198
Follica, 1464
Follow The Coin, 310
FollowAnalytics, 182, 1610, 2018
Followap Telecommunications, 3212
FollowMyCal, 1000
Folloze, 399, 456, 861
FON, 2437
Fon, 538
Fonality, 1227, 1235
Fondaction, 3249
Fondis Electronic, 3011
Fonds de soliderite FTQ, 3249
Fondu, 283, 680
Fonecta Oy, 1929
Foneric, 1511
Fongo, 2253
Fontainebleau, 874
Fontinalis Partners, 3259
Fontself.com, 2302
Food 4 Pets Canada, 2115
Food 52, 1114
Food Distributor, 1424
Food For All, 1896
Food Freshness Technology, 2397
Food Genius, 115, 473, 732, 1618, 1992
Food Matters Market, 3246
Food On The Table, 205

Food Should Taste Good, 1668
Food.ee, 85, 2283
Fooda, 1121, 1904
Foodbuzz, 311
Foodee, 2137
FoodGenius, 965
Foodient T/A Whisk, 2958
Foodini, 1618
FoodLogiQ, 2230
FoodMaster, 70
FoodMesh, 2215
foodpanda, 846
Foodspotting, 299
Foodware Group, 1372
Football For Good, 2120
Foothills Creamery, 2260
Foothold Technology, 92
Footnote, 1679
Footprint Retail Services, 470
Footways, 3104
For Days, 1011
For Us All, 773
Fora Financial, 1404
ForAtable.com, 2302
Foray, 562
Forbes, 660
Forbes Travel Guide, 285, 495, 1832
Forbius, 2174, 2181
Force, 1005
Force 10, 1898
Force 10 Networks, 1257
Force10, 564, 597, 1213, 1678
Force10 Networks, 199, 538, 1731
Forcepoint, 1116
Ford Models, 101
Ford Wholesale Co. Inc., 874
Forecast Health, 3250
ForeFlight, 1685
Forefront Dermatology, 2199, 2211
ForeFront Education, 377
Foreground, 1499
Forelinx, 814
Forendo Pharma, 1350
Forensic Logic, 2969
Forenvia Venture I Ky, 2731
ForeScout, 27, 48, 182, 561, 1213
ForeScout Technologies, 928
ForeSee, 1888
Foresee Results, 2188
Foreside, 1151
Foreside Company, 440
Foresight, 540, 1809
Foresight AI, 235
Foresight Diagnostics, 1426
Foresight Reserves, 1577, 1733
Forest Device, 623
Forest Holidays, 2935
Forest2Market, 643
Forethought, 1296, 1935
Forever, 1851
Forgame Holdings Limited, 1778
Forge, 623, 981, 1698
Forge Communications, 3250
Forge Energy, 673, 1447
Forge Global, 1396
Forged Metals, 66
ForgeRock, 27, 773, 1086
Forgerock, 1213
Foria, 638
Forkly, 686
Form Labs, 1001
Form Technologies, 110
FORMA Therapeutics, 2504, 2681
Forma Therapeutics, 186, 1128, 1350
Forma-Dis, 2285, 2332
Forma.Ai, 2131
Formac Pharmaceuticals, 2358, 3033

Formation Capital, 3254
Formation Data Systems, 1428
Formation Energy, 1133
Formation Systems, 22
Formative, 1554
Formel D GmbH, 3058
Formex, 2869
FormFactor, 1247
Formica Corporation, 1624
Formisimo, 3099
FormLabs, 779, 1101
Formlabs, 1058
Formolgy, 2958
Formosa Epitaxy, 2594, 3209
Formosa International, 2427
Formscape Group, 2653
Formspring, 234
Formspring.Me, 1464
Formstack, 1499
Formula 1, 927
Formula E, 1511
Formula Systems, 2736
Forno d'Asolo, 2285
Foro Energy, 468, 812, 1335
Forsake, 1688
ForSight Newco II, 1728
ForSight Vision 4, 1930
ForSight Vision 5, 1930
ForSight VISION4, 1126
ForSight VISIONS, 1126, 1788
Forst Point Power, 157
Fort Awesome, 709
Fort Dearborn Company, 1090
Fort Garry Brewing Co., 2129
Fort James, 263
Fort Scale, 1009
FORTE, 1660
FORTE Industrial Equipment Systems, 77
Forte Media, 1009
Forte Research Systems, 1291
Forte Tools, 1762
ForteBio, 1098
Fortegra Financial, 1754
Fortemedia, 2844
Forter, 3, 149, 1610, 1629
Forterro, 238
Forth Dimension Displays, 2662
Forthfield, 1473
Forticom, 2654
Fortify, 411, 1028
Fortify Software, 582, 1674
Fortinet, 597, 603, 990, 1213, 1478
Fortis Energy Services, 834
Fortius Financial, 464
Fortius Sport & Health, 2256
Fortress, 77, 520
Fortress Technologies, 421, 1091
FortressIQ, 308, 680
Fortum Oyj, 2981
Fortumo, 876, 1009
Fortune Cookie, 2526
Fortune Greek Gas Gathering and Processing, 335
Fortus Medical Inc., 344
Forty Cloud, 2943
Forty Seven, 1125
Forté, 1855
Forté Media, 621
FortéBio, 1268
Forum Pharmaceuticals, 711
Forus Health, 27, 2840
Forward, 742, 1073
Forward Health Group, 2002
Forward Networks, 125, 610
Forward Water Technologies, 2054
Fos4x, 2815
Foseco, 2596, 2596

Portfolio Companies Index

Fosen IKT, 971
Foss Manufacturing Company, 2008
Fossil Creek Resources, 673
Foster + Partners, 2292
Foster Findlay Associates, 2691
Fosun, 475
Fotango Ltd, 3004
Fotech, 322
Fotech Solutions, 2691, 3095
Fotokyte, 2288
Fotolia Holdings, 1778
Fotolog, 641
Fotoshkola, 2531
Fougera Pharmaceuticals, 990
Found Ocean, 2383
Foundation Capital, 990, 3273
Foundation Consumer Healthcare, 1066
Foundation DB, 1762
Foundation Medicine, 1814, 3076
Foundation Partners Group, 1745
Foundation Radiology Group, 477
Foundation Risk Partners Corp., 159
Foundation9, 782
Foundationworks, 1917
Founder Collective, 3263
Founder Sport Group, 435
Founder Suite, 724
FounderDating, 1058, 1702
FounderFuel, 50
Founders Advantage Capital, 2128
Foundry Group, 990, 3265
Foundry Networks, 597
Foundstone, 2045
Fount Therapeutics, 764
Fountain, 564, 1385, 1881
Fountain Medical Development, 2658
4 Energy, 2287
Four Eyes, 1966
Four Mine, 724
Four Seasons Health Care, 2353
Four Soft, 3202
Four Star Lighting Co., 467
Four Wheel Campers, 1612
4-Antibody, 2788
40 South Energy, 2865
410 Labs, 1862
410Labs, 1172
411.ca, 2216
41st Parameter, 972
42, 10, 1719
42 Floors, 263, 380, 1534
42 North Dental LLC, 159
420 Klean, 395
42matters, 3047
43Layers, 10
45M, 1335
480 Biomedical, 350, 1013, 1335, 1464
4AZA Bioscience, 2554
4C, 1050
4Charity.com, 1015
4doctor, 721
4Free WiFi, 3172
4Front, 1810
4Gas Holding B.V., 1577
4Gas Holding BV, 416
4Gl, 2688
4HAMCOGEN, 2940
4Home, 1928, 3038
4INFO, 1649
4info, 1241, 1948
4IQ, 252
4JET Technologies, 2677
4moms, 296, 424
FourPhase Systems, 263
Fourpost, 1760
FourQ, 632
4R Systems, 1806, 1864

4Refuel, 1066
FourSquare, 1341
Foursquare, 125, 1359, 1718, 1884
4subsea, 3207
4Tell, 1467
Fourth, 1005
4th Pass, 1021
Fourthwall Media, 1636
4w MarketPlace, 3043
4Wall Entertainment Inc., 1368
4Wheel Drive Hardware, 1438
Fove, 795
Fovea, 2308, 2739
Foviance, 2665
Foviance Group, 2653
Fox Head, 96
Fox Photo, 357, 1021
Fox Racing Shox, 525
Fox River Fiber, 931
Fox Rothschild, 3258, 3264
Fox Technologies, 2707, 3004
Fox Thermal Instruments Inc., 911
Foxborn NMR, 3162
Foxcom, 2711
Foxcom Wireless, 2766
Foxfire, 1691
FoxHollow Technology, 22
Foxlink, 897
Foxquilt Insurance, 2107
FoxTrot, 1114
Foxtrot, 728, 1759
Foxtrot Code, 86
Foxy's Pash, 3248
FP Newspapers, 2249
FPEE, 2439
FPG, 1493
FPMI Solutions, 1401
FPS Group, 302
FPT Corporation, 2952
FPX, 962
FR Midstream Holdings, 741
Fr8, 1370
FRA/Business Interactif, 2457
Fractal, 2849
Fractal Analytics, 136
Fractal Analytics Private Limited, 1778
Fractal Design, 857
Fractal Systems, 325, 1561
Fractus, 2474, 2978
Fractyl, 263, 820
Fractyl Laboratories, 622
Fragmob, 68, 1587
Fraikin, 2710, 2843
Frame, 1158
Frame Technology, 200
Frame.ai, 537, 744
Frame.io, 744, 1666, 1677
Framebridge, 1768
Framehawk, 545, 1848
FrameMax, 561
Framer, 1142
Framespot AB, 2709
Framework Venture Partners, 3249
France Champignon, 2542
France Géothermie, 3011
France Hélices SA, 2644
France Portes, 2976
Francesca's Collection, 435
Franchise, 1755
FranchiseKnowHow LLC, 3257
Francis Drilling Fluids, 832
Francising Works, 2500
Franco Signor, 364
Frank, 1530
Frank & Oak, 259, 1121, 2231, 2272
Frank Entertainment Group, 1639
Frank., 882

Franklin Energy, 20, 1085
Franklin Energy Services, 1460
Franlin Templeton Investments, 927
Frans Bonhomme, 2592
Franshion Properties, 1957
Frantic Films, 2188, 2218
Fraser River Pile & Dredge, 2267
FraudMetrix, 2430
FraudSciences, 1537
Fraudwall/Anchor Intelligence, 624
Fraugster, 3099
Frauscher Sensor Technology, 867
Frazier Healthcare Partners, 3254
Freak'n Genius, 1914, 1992
Freck, 234
Fred Sands, 874
Free, 1610
Free Awesome, 1635
Free Decision, 852
Free Flow Power, 262, 1897
Free Monee, 1762
Free Wheel, 773
FreeAgent, 1121
FreeBalance, 2254
Freebird, 820
FreeBorders, 440
Freeborders, 538
FreeBrie, 2847
Freedom Communication Technologies, 906
Freedom Group, 1971
Freedom Innovations, 1779, 1794
Freedom Medical, 1524
Freedom Meditech Inc., 1051
Freedom Mobile, 2245
Freedom Robotics, 1836
Freedom Scientific, 854
FreedomPay, 299, 540
FreedomPop, 597
Freee, 597, 641
FreeForm, 1566
Freeform, 31
FreeHand Surgical, 2589
Freelancers Union, 1422
Freeletics, 433
FreeLinc, 683, 683
FreeMarkets, 275, 1626
Freenome, 125, 183, 894, 1001, 1646
Freeosk, 254, 733
Freepath, 1604
Freepoint Commodities, 1746
FreeRange Games, 545, 1566
Freesbee, 2598
Freescale, 3024
Freespree, 3140
Freestyle Solutions, 1234
FreeTextbooks.Com, 1536
FreeWave Technologies, 1778
Freewebs, 116
FreeWill, 623
Freewill, 1426
Freight Farms, 1101
Freight Tiger, 1125
Freightliner, 153
Freightos, 812
FreightWaves, 1483
Fremach Groep, 2940
Fremont Ventures, 3273
French Founders, 1011
French Girls, 59, 787
FRENDS Technology Oy, 2707
Frenzoo, 1966, 2382
Fresca Mexican Foods, 1250
Fresenius, 3060
Fresh Choice, 1898
Fresh Dining, 1397
Fresh Dining Concepts, 408
Fresh Express, 874

Portfolio Companies Index

Fresh Food Concepts, 445
Fresh Nation, 1114
Fresh Origins, 1097
Fresh Squeeze, 1618
FreshBooks, 69, 1361, 2126, 2196
FreshDirect, 2073
Freshdirect, 1949
FreshGrade, 1315, 2228
Freshgrade, 1530
Freshly, 938, 1005, 1982
FreshMenu, 1125
Freshpak, 1755
Freshpet, 1231
FreshPlanet, 1566, 1702
FreshPlum, 586
Freshstone Brands, 2118
FreshTemp, 1635
Freshworks, 579
Fresno, 1698
Fresvii, 2465
Freudenberg, 77
Freycinet Investments, 3249
FRH Consumer Services, 1843
Frichti, 2842
FriCSo, 2453
Frictionless Commerce, 468
Friday, 3039
Friend.ly, 1323
Friend2friend, 327
FriendBuy, 876
Friendi, 691
Friendly's Garden Fresh Restaurant Corp., 1755
Friends & Allies Brewing, 447
Friends of Choice in Urban Schools, 1315
FriendsAbroad.com, 2702
Friendship Public Charter Schools, 1315
Friendsly, 1114
Friendsurance, 641, 2822
Frigoscandia, 3000
Frigotechnica, 2462
Fring, 1335
fring, 3203
Fringe81, 2637
Fringilunch, 3033
Frintit, 1618
Frissul, 3039
Fritz AI, 680
FrogApps, 2637
From the Ground Up, 502
FromAtoB.com, 3104
Front, 308, 610, 1657, 1696, 1698, 1702, 1850, 1881
Front Bridge, 1629
Front Desk, 1644
Front Porch Digital, 919
Front Range Biosciences, 99, 395, 900, 1443, 1613, 1616
Front Row, 1058
FrontBridge, 759
FrontCall, 2866
Frontdesk Connect, 999
Frontenac Company, 3255
Frontera Energy, 2067
Frontier Bank of Texas, 447
Frontier Capital, 3251
Frontier Car Group, 207, 208, 784
Frontier Drilling, 1577
Frontier Firewood, 1262
Frontier Markets, 54, 3100
Frontier Packaging, 832
Frontier Silicon, 2372, 2463
Frontier Spinning Mills, 111
Frontier Strategy Group, 1718
Frontier Ventures, 990
Frontier Waste Solutions, 294
FrontierIP, 2883
FrontierMedEx, 2956

FrontierVision Partners LP, 1372
Frontline Performance Group, 20
Frontline Selling, 1240
Frontrange, 782
FrontStream Payments, 1332, 1735
Frost Fighter, 2138
Frozen Specialties, 1769
FRS, 1361
Frubana, 1426
Fruition Partners, 1852
Fruux, 2815
FRVR, 2944
FRX Polymers, 2891
Fry's Electronics, 217
FSA Store, 51, 1386, 1463
FSB Global Holdings, 1133
FSI, 679
FSL 3D, 1753
Fsona Communications, 693
FSV Payment Systems, 227
FT Partner, 990
FTAPI SecuTransfer, 2815
FTE, 2607
FTL, 2565
FTRANS, 1851
Ftrans, 1865
Ftuan, 2927
FTV Capital, 990
Fu Sheng Industrial, 1143, 2937
Fubar Radio, 2958
Fubon Financial, 2427
Fuego, 1855
Fuego Tech, 3128
Fuel 3D, 3019
Fuel 50, 309
Fuel Powered, 1310
Fuel Systems, 331
Fuel Systems Solutions Inc., 277
FuelQuest, 2073, 3148
Fuentek, 3250
Fugoo, 68
Fugue, 540, 1172
Fuhu, 1255
Fuisz Media, 1223
Fuji Food Products, 800
Fuji Machinery Mfg. & Electronics Co. Ltd., 2339
Fulano, 2617
Fulcrum, 322, 1408, 2074
Fulcrum Bioenergy, 1608, 1897
Fulcrum Capital Partners, 3249
Fulcrum Composites, 1337
Fulcrum Equity Partners, 3251, 3260
Fulcrum Microsystems, 857
Fulcrum Technologies, 217
Fulcrum Therapeutics, 764
Fulham, 325
Full Circle, 85
Full Circle Feed, 705
Full Circle Insights, 1610
Full Circle Technologies, 1051
Full Contact, 933
Full Harvest, 571, 2001
Full Sail University, 1778
Full Scale Solutions, 3250
Full Spectrum, 1438
Full Vision, 112, 1057
FULLBEAUTY Brands, 136
Fullbeauty Brands, 458
Fullbridge, 1832
Fullcast.io, 553, 729
FullContact, 225, 686, 779, 1791, 2016
Fullerton, 377
Fullhan, 2927
FullScaleNANO, 1412
FullSeven Technologies, 1712
FullStory, 894

Fullstory, 1079, 1610
Fullterton Technology, 2594
FullTilt Solutions, 2188
Fultec Semiconductor, 556, 801
Fulwisdom Capital, 3257
Fun+, 1680
Fun-Life, 1757
Funanga, 2829
Funcom, 3004
Function of Beauty, 827, 1703
functionability, 2212
Functional Neuromodulation, 749, 2125
Fundacion Ciudadano Inteligente, 1374
Fundbox, 149, 265, 820, 1073, 2934
Fundera, 742, 1073, 1114, 1504
Funders Club, 1009
FundersClub, 720, 742, 1718
Funding Circle, 1563, 2851, 2851
Funding Gates, 568
Funding University, 600
Fundly, 1058, 1154, 1257, 1658
Fundrise, 380
Funds India, 773, 1017
Fundtech, 2766, 2901, 3128
FundThrough, 2240
FundWell, 1645
Fungible, 238, 1187
Funizen, 100
Funko, 45, 381
Funkyfunky, 2848
FunMobility, 1112
Funnel, 2469
Funnel Cake, 2265
Funny or Die, 582
Funny or Die (Sabse Technologies Inc.), 624
FunPlus, 3133
Funsherpa, 1959
Funxional Therapeutics, 3006
Funzio, 1566
Funzio G-Bits, 977
Fure Inventory, 1426
Furhat Robotics, 2469
Furie Operating Alaska, 676
Furnishare, 1114
Fusar Technologies, 421
Fuse, 518
Fuse Capital, 990
Fuse Energy, 673
Fuse.it, 1323
fusebill, 2240
Fusepoint, 1157
Fushe Kruje Cement, 1012
Fushion-IO, 1125
Fushun Cogen Power Plants, 2582
Fusient Media Ventures, 881
Fusio-Io, 1205
Fusion, 1109, 1481
Fusion Ads, 2464
Fusion Antibodies, 2601
Fusion Coolant, 743
Fusion Coolant Systems, 114
Fusion Education Group, 2000
Fusion Pharmaceuticals, 2125
Fusion Risk Management, 429
Fusion-io, 1213, 1478, 1848
Fusion.io, 125
Futalis, 2815
Futrli, 641
Futuragene, 3235
Future Ad Labs, 2470, 3021
Future Advisor, 863
Future Drinks, 2392
Future Family, 48, 182
Future Finance, 1504
Future Fuel, 1530
Future Is Now Schools, 1315
Future Point Systems, 1994

1296

Portfolio Companies Index

Future Publishing, 684
Future.Fit, 1877
FutureAdvisor, 399, 1058, 1657
Futuredontics, 568
FutureE, 2701
FutureFamily, 2150
Futuremark, 2990
FutureMark Group Manistique, 1963
FutureNet Group, 1459
Futureo, 3199
FuturePlay, 485
Futures, 3011
Futurestate IT, 2178
FutureStay, 1309
FutureTech Holdings, 1425
FutureTrade, 810
FutureVault, 309
Futurice Oy, 2864
Futuris, 502
Fuze Network, 600, 1074, 1184
Fuzhou Skyunion Digital, 2841
Fuzic, 86
Fuzz Pet Health, 680
Fuzzbuzz, 1760
FVF, 3251
FX Bridge, 1865
FXCM, 2640
FXGear, 3118
FXI Technologies, 2361
Fyber, 1327
Fyfe Group LLC, 277
Fynaz, 2016
Fyrfly, 1768
Fysical, 945
fyto, 2982

G

G Connect, 2766
G&H Orthodontics, 97, 654, 1576
G-Log, 759
G-Mode, 1757
G-TEC Natural Gas Systems, 1526
G.I. Group, 2121
G.I. View, 2646
G/O Media, 862
G1 Dynamics, 428
G1 Therapeutics, 918, 1261, 1522, 2174
G10 Entertainment Korea, 2841
G2 Crowd, 1483
G2 Microsystems, 2315
G2 Web Services, 1480
G20 Ventures, 3263
G2One, 241
G2X Energy, 1155, 1788
G3 Global Energy, 157
G3P, 3039
G5, 872, 1234, 1944
GA Communications, 408
GA Pack, 223
GAB Robins, 338
Gabbro, 225
Gabriel Logan, 1529
Gabriel Performance Products, 445, 653
Gabriel Venture Partners, 3273
GadgetSpace, 1711
Gadze Finance, 2131
Gadzoox Networks, 1379
GaeaSoft. ICO Inc. & Imas Co Ltd., 2830
Gaffey Healthcare, 97
GAGA, 1060
Gai Energy, 3095
Gaia Interative, 1006
Gaia Online, 1537, 1829
Gaiam, 874
GaiaTech, 1270
GaiaWorks, 1828
GaiaX, 1757

Gailileo Processing, 1205
Gain Capital, 655
GAIN Capital Group, 1908
Gain Capital Group, 1731
Gain Credit, 1247
GainFitness, 1014
Gainful, 623
GainSight, 224
Gainsight, 238, 485, 570, 1005, 1125, 1610, 1754
GainSpan, 388, 1304, 2965
Gainspan, 983
GainSpan Corp, 1674
Gala, 2596
Gala Biotech, 1923
Gala Group, 2547
Gala Therapeutics, 144
GalaGen, 1920
Galantos Pharma, 2815
Galapagos, 2370, 2739
Galatea, 310
Galaxy Desserts, 1397
Galaxy Far East, 3209
Galaxy II, 1493
Galaxy Tool Corporation, 832
Galbani, 2488
Gale Technologies, 1379
Galecto Biotech, 3140
Galera Therapeutics, 270, 545, 570, 1522
Galera Therapeutics Inc., 1350
Galey & Lord, 357
Galil Medical, 1820, 1931, 3063, 3268
Galileo, 1074
Galileo Global Education, 1498
Galileo Processing, 1917
Galileo Technology, 1125
Galleher, 1507
Galleon, 1126
Galleon Oil & Gas, 157
Gallery Watch, 1857
Galley, 2018
Gallo Holdings, 1929
Gallop, 2130, 2176
Galls, 458, 478
Galoob, 799
Galt Associates, 315
Galva Union, 2294
Galyan's Trading, 786
GamaLife, 136
Gamalon, 1, 720, 1009
Gambling Compliance, 3061, 3122
Gambol Pet Group, 1086
Game, 2787
Game Closure, 108
Game Duell, 2820, 2829
Game Equipment, 60
Game Insight, 2847
Game Mix, 1059
Game Plan, 1262
Game Plan Technologies, 1474
Game Ready, 800, 1584
Game Salad, 794, 876
Game Trust, 1875
Game Ventures, 2468, 2861
GameChanger, 548, 686, 1854, 2016
GameCo, 1032, 1309
GameDriver, 1412
GameFlip, 361, 1121
GameFly, 780, 1242, 1657, 1798
GameForge, 27
GameGenetics, 2815
Gamelayers, 1359
Gamelet, 3029
GameLogic, 928
Gamemage Interactive, 3053
GameMo, 2464
Gamer Sensei, 474, 1385
Gamersensei, 316

GamersFirst, 641
GamersFirt, 876
Games Are Social, 3043
Games Warehouse Ltd., 911
Games2Win.com, 504
GameSalad, 724, 1207
Gamet Sp. z o.o., 2697
Gametime, 894
GameTrust, 1682
Gamevice, 374
GameWisp, 1181
GAMFG Precision, 1174
Gamigo, 3146
Gamigo AG, 2519
Gamma Medica-Ideas, 405, 1500
Gamma Optical, 2594
Gamma spol. s r.o., 3113
Gammon, 2590, 2591
Gamo, 1518
Gamo Outdoor SL, 357
GAN Integrity, 655, 1240
GAN Systems, 2072
GaN Systems, 1583, 2087
Gan Systems, 305
Ganache Brands, 2118
Gander Mountain, 1971
Ganeden Biotech, 405
Ganesh Housing, 263
GangaGen, 186
Gangagen, 2837
Gangavaram Port, 1957
Gangwon Wind Power, 585
Ganjaboxes, 395
Ganji, 299, 1327
Ganni, 1092
Ganymede Games, 169
Ganzhou Dingsheng Water Technological Co., 2718
GAPbuster Worldwide, 733
Garage Technology Ventures, 990
Garantia Data, 224
Garapon, 1241
Garard Pasquier, 2593
Garbanzo Mediterranean Grill, 815
Gardein, 1863
Garden Fresh Holdings, 449
Garden Fresh Restaurant, 714, 1708
Garden Organics, 1786
Garden Ridge, 63
Gardena, 2854
Gardeners, 3223
Gardio, 2610
Gardner Aerospace, 2668
Gardner Denver, 1086
Gardner Denver Inc., 1905
Garena, 819
Garlik, 2653, 2662, 2665
Garneau Welding and Fabricating, 2278
Garner, 2051
Garretson Resolution Group, 917, 1438
Garrison Manufacturing, 1612
Gartmore, 927
Gartner, 263, 1210
Gartner Inc., 1905
Gary Platt Manufacturing, 1343
Gary's Tux Shops, 874
Gas Control Equipment, 2413
Gas Gas, 2882
Gas Secure, 3207
Gas Station TV, 254, 1377
GasBuddy, 1813
Gate Rocket, 1146
Gate5, 2435
GateGuru, 1635
Gatekeeper Innovation, 1810
Gatekeeper Innovation Inc., 1443
Gatekeeper Systems Inc., 904, 2061

Portfolio Companies Index

Gatekeepr Innovation, 1671
Gateway Casinos & Entertainment, 2067
Gateway EDI, 20
Gateway Healthcare, 1333
Gateway Rail Freight, 280
Gather, 1154
GatherUp, 92
Gatik, 1001
GATR Technologies, 983
Gatsby, 1426
GATX Logistics, 1360
GAUDRE, 3040
Gauge Insights, 623
Gauntlet, 742
Gauss Surgical, 1491, 1559
Gautier, 2843
Gavel & Gown, 2088
GawkBox, 1162
Gaze, 2013
Gazelle, 1442, 1583, 1918
GazelleLab, 1786
Gazillion, 784
gazillion, 1428
Gazillion Entertainment, 1361, 2321
Gazzang, 205, 1684
GB Auto Service Inc., 867
GB Foods, 912
Gbits Network Technology, 2841
GBT, 1522
GC Aesthetics, 1251, 1383
GC Partners Interational Ltd., 2088
GC-Rise Pharmaceutical, 1383
GCA Service Solutions, 1275
GCA Services Group, 1118
GCAN Insurance Company, 2073
GCL, 2570
GCLOUD, 2637
GCM, 2978
GCM Grosvenor, 927
GCM Grosvenor LS Power Equity Partners II, 2088
GCMW, 2482
GCommerce, 53, 68
GCoreLab, 3064
GCR Holdings Ltd, 2783
GCR Inc., 904
Gcrypt, 2392
GCS, 912
GCT, 621, 1983
GD Interactive, 2658
GDGT, 1718
GDI, 2056
GDM Electronics, 3033
GDS, 3091
GE Current, 110
Gealean Holding GmbH, 2797
Gearworks, 538
Geary LSF, 961
GebIBET, 3039
Gecko Biomedical, 3011
Gecko Robotics, 2122
GeckoCap, 1618
GED Integrated Solutions, 104
Gee Holdings, 962
Geeklist, 2929
Gehl, 217
Geisinger Health System, 971
GEKA GmbH, 2303
Geka-brush GmbH, 2797
Gekko Systems Pty Limited, 2390
Gelato Fiasco, 1164, 1165
Gelson's Market, 1837
Geltor, 571
Gem, 121, 231, 275, 527, 742, 976, 1223, 1608, 1966
Gem Mobile Treatment Services, 1745
Gem Shopping Network, 1755

Gema Diagnostics, 1337
Gemandforce, 1406
Gemba, 2192
Gemba Solutions, 2958
Gemcap Lending I, 1971
Gemcom, 1045
Gemcor II, 1526
Gemfire, 1924
Geminare, 2051
Gemini Equipment & Rents, 253
Gemini Solar and Battery Storage Project, 1520
Gemini Therapeutics, 193
Geminus, 1812
Geminx, 1900
Gemmus Pharma, 301, 1786, 1987
Gemphire Therapeutics, 403, 704
Gemstone Biotherapeutics, 18
GemTek, 908
Gemvara, 389
gen-E, 961
Gen.Video, 609
Gen3 Marketing, 1097
Genagro, 2321
Genaissance Pharmaceuticals, 532, 3209
Genalta Power, 2085
Genalyte, 493, 1073, 1793
Genasys, 2334
Genbad, 830
GENBAND, 1361, 1661, 3128
Genband, 540, 1076, 1376, 1608, 1843, 1913
Genbook, 2980
GENCO Distribution System Inc., 867
Gencove, 1724, 2272
Gendai Games, 1103
Gendel Ltd, 2695
Gene Grafts, 3050
Gene Logic, 1395
Geneart, 2704
Geneba Properties N.V., 2067
GeneCentric, 918
Genecis, 2123
Genedata, 1350
GenEdit, 1657
Geneoscopy, 623
Genepeeks, 949
GenePharm, 118
GenePreDiT, 3039
GeneQuine, 2815
Gener8tor, 567
Generac, 2029
Generac Power Systems, 435
General American, 1174
General Assembly, 265, 1006, 1186, 1527, 1554, 1914
General Atlantic, 3254
General Bandwidth, 1107
General Blood, 3268
General Catalyst, 36
General Catalyst Partners, 3263
General Compression, 1474, 1897
General Donlee, 2785
General Electric, 1294
General Finance Corp., 277
General Fusion, 265, 325, 2072, 2701
General Healthcare, 2596
General Healthcare Group, 2488
General Healthcare Group Limited, 136
General Moile, 3112
General Photonics, 730
General Products, 1230
General Sentiment, 396
General Tools & Instruments, 934
General Trailers, 1138
General Wireless, 163
GeneralRadar, 1079
Generate, 801
Generation Bio, 764

Generation Brands, 1507
Generation Capital Partners, 990
Generation Create, 2982
Generation Health, 1071
Generation5, 2188
GeneriCo, 270
Genesant Technologies Inc., 813
GeneSciences, 1055
Genesis, 1244
Genesis (Gen), 2655
Genesis Energy, 1086
Genesis Financial Solutions, 654, 674, 1389
Genesis Luxury, 1092
Genesis Media, 290
Genesis Networks, 1150, 1178
Genesis Offshore, 1748
Genesis Private Equity Fund, 2715
Genesis Worldwide Inc., 1089
GeneSpectrum, 1695
Genesys, 230, 927, 1787, 2371, 3024, 3199
Genesys Capital Management, 3249
Genetesis, 481
Genetic Finance, 2822
Genetic Therapy, 1395, 1561
Geneticure, 2001
GeneWeave, 2010
GeneWEAVE Inc., 493
Genewiz, 119
Genex, 1048
Genextropy, 1165
Gengo, 1009, 1058, 2437, 3035
Geni, 457
Geni Tech, 2960
Genia Photonics, 983
Geniachip, 1105
Genic, 3136
Genicon Inc., 440
Genie, 624
Genie Network Resource Management Inc, 2694
Geniee, 721, 2789
Genieo, 3050
Genies, 232, 527, 773, 863, 1114, 1186, 1296, 1533
Genius, 125, 601, 608, 721, 1114, 1701, 1841, 2011
Genius Genomatics, 1247
Genius Plaza, 1058
Genius Sports, 136
Genkey, 3042
Genmedica Therapeutics, 2424, 2544
Genoa, 200
Genoa Healthcare, 755, 2045
Genocea, 1734, 2969
Genocea Biosciences, 1464, 1693
GenoLogics, 1392
Genomar, 2745
Genomatica, 87, 610, 1908
Genome Compiler, 1323, 2934
Genome DX Biosciences, 225
Genome Medical, 812
Genome Profiling LLC, 5
GenomeDx, 1206
Genomenon, 1023
Genomera, 1101
Genomic Expression, 3246
Genomica, 154, 318
Genomics Collaborative, 748
Genomics Medicine Ireland, 894
Genomics PLC, 764
Genomind, 495
GenomOncology, 1051
Genopaver, 1815
GenoProt Ltd, 2915
Genoptix, 4, 119, 470
Genova Diagnostics, 1115
Genovique Specialties, 172
Genoway, 2867

Portfolio Companies Index

Genpact, 2762
Genpact Limited, 1360
GenPat77 Pharmacogenetics AG, 3181
GenPharm, 209
GenPrime, 85
GenPro, 1581
GenPro Profiling, 269
Gens, 2617
GenServe, 165
Genset S.A., 1395
Gensia Pharmaceuticals, 1708
GenSight, 1930
Genstar Capital, 3245
Gensyn Technologies, 642
Genta, 158, 1898
Gental Monster, 1092
Genticel, 2842
Gentis, 1414
Gentium, 1900
Gentle Monster, 977
Gentleware, 2664
Gentra Systems, 1117
Gentreo, 754
Gentronix, 3234
GenturaDx, 240
Genturi, 3
Genuisly, 3116
Genus, 1898
Genvault, 561
GenVec, 652, 1561
Genvec, 154
Genvid, 2944
Genwi, 1017, 1515, 2992
GenXcomm, 1009
Genzion BioSciences, 2807
Geo Mcquesten, 1294
Geo-Solutions, 1524
Geocea Biosciences, 1155
GeoCom TMS, 2188
GeoComm, 855
Geodelic Systems, 504
Geodex Communications, 838
GeoDigital, 677, 2101, 2153
Geodigital, 821
Geoforce, 2074
GeoIQ, 983
GeoiQ, 459
Geologic Systems LTD., 364
Geologistics, 383
Geoloqi, 1467, 1947
Geomagic, 1901
Geomagical, 1088
Geomind, 2848
Geong, 2989
GeoOrbital, 1104
Geopacific Resources, 1551
GeoPage, 85
Geophysical, 2901
Geophysical Research Company, 1224
Geopii, 2939
Georg Jensen, 1021
Georgian Partners, 485, 3249
GeoScience International, 2958
Geosemble, 983
Geosim Systems, 2526
Geosite, 1269
Geositian AB, 2709
Geospago, 1887
Geospiza, 85
Geostellar, 1172
Geotek, 855, 3128
GeoTix, 198
Geotrace Technologies, 1361
GeoVector, 388
GeoVera, 751
GeoVera Holdings Inc., 790
GeoVera Insurance, 927, 1292

GeoVideo Networks, 1304
GeoVS, 2728
Geoworks, 241
GEPPERT, 2970
Gerard Darel, 3011
Gerber Scientific, 1912
Gerber Technology, 110
German Auto Labs, 2832, 3152
Germanos, 2775
Germguardian, 835
Geroline, 2041
Geron Corporation, 1395
Geronimo Alloys, 815
Gerresheimer, 1021, 3060
Gerson Lehrman Group, 263
Gesco Group of Companies, 293
Gespac, 2616
Gesplan, 2617
Gestalt, 1140
Gestigon, 2815
GestureTek, 621
Gesundheit Foods, 558
Get AS, 1508
Get Back, 912
Get Fresh Kit, 1618
Get Point, 1533
GET Power, 2451
Get Real Health, 2256
Get Satisfaction, 1014, 1058, 1359, 1702
Getable, 1491
Getafive, 1618
GetAgent, 3099
Getaround, 14, 91, 325, 545, 1203, 1254, 1596, 1665, 1848
Getaway, 1092
GetBulb, 2665
Getech, 2883
Getemed AG Medizin- und Informationstechnik, 3181
GetFeedback, 1610
GetGlue, 1561
GetGOing, 586
GetGoing, 1121, 2877
Gethuman, 545
GetInsured.com, 263
Getinsured.com, 1418, 1855
GETiT, 2809
GetLenses.co.uk, 3009
Getmapping, 3098
Getmobile, 2595
Getninjas, 2967
GETPAID, 1888
GetRelevant, 1538
Getro, 1317
GetSocial, 3039
Getsurance, 2832
GetTaxi, 2877
GetThis, 1786
Getty Images, 927
Getwell Network, 1901
GetWellNetwork, 178, 634, 990, 1146, 1463, 1973
GetYourGuide, 238, 1086, 3046
Getyourguide, 1718
Gevaert Bandweverij, 2671
Gevity HR Inc., 1905
Gevo, 3213
GFarmalabs, 1139
GfK SE, 1086
Gfnmediber, 2815
GForce Group, 347
GFRC Cladding Systems, 832
Gfycat, 93
GGVS, 2484
GHD, 2842
GHN Online, 227
Gho Holding, 2739

GHO Ventures, 3266
Ghost, 1073
GHP Group, 2198
GHS Interactive, 1834
GI Dynamics, 622
Gi Dynamics, 58
GI Dynamics Inc., 573
GI Partners, 3254
GI Plastek, 832, 1730
GI Windows, 350
GI-Therapies, 2950
Giant, 1663
Giant Hemu, 3185
Giant Realm, 655
Giant Swarm, 321
Giant.AI, 1073
Gibbon, 3215
Gibbons Refractories, 2976
Gibraltar, 2128
Gibraltar Capital Holdings, 1625
Gibson Energy, 1577
Gicare Pharma, 2739
Gicram Groupe, 153
Gidsy, 2435, 3140
GIF, 2303
Gifnote, 1344
Gift Boogle, 738
Gift Certificate Center, 538
Gift Talk, 1511
Giftango, 1384
Giftbit, 787
Giftcard Zen, 1154
GiftCertificates.com, 1227
Giftcertificates.Com, 1636
Giftly, 234, 752, 1596
Giftspot, 85
Gifty, 3040
GIGA, 651
Giga Information Group, 1348
Giga Spaces, 796, 1009
Giga-Tronics, 1733
GigaComm, 1608
GigaDevice, 1340, 3225
GigaGen, 493
Gigamon, 938
GigaNet, 857
Gigante Central Wet-Mill, 54
Gigantor, 754
GigaOM, 1862
Gigarant, 3033
Gigared, 1636
GigaSpaces, 2532
GigaTrust, 192, 1608
Gigi Hill, 1855
Gigit, 1752
GigLabs, 1412
Gigle Networks, 3038, 3095
GigOptix, 1313
Gigoptix, 68
Gigster, 125, 720, 1537
Gigwalk, 31, 200, 1327, 1702
Gigya, 57, 510, 561, 582, 624, 742, 872, 1187
Giiant Pharma Inc., 2031
Gila, 1460
Gila Therapeutic, 350
Gilat Satellite Networks, 3203
Gilbarco Veeder-Root, 357
Gilchrist & Soames, 1769, 1873
Gild, 234, 839
Gilead Sciences Inc., 1203
Gill, 3234
Gill Mix Green, 1092
Gilt, 646
Gilt Groupe, 819, 1184, 1449, 1701, 1948
GILUPI, 2443
Gilupi, 2815
Gimahot, 2815

Portfolio Companies Index

Gimbal, 50
Gimlet Media, 1153
Gimme, 191
Gimmie, 1966
Ginegar Plastic Products Ltd, 2736
Giner.io, 1585
Ginger, 680, 2074, 2822
Ginger.io, 1056, 1058, 1073, 1101, 1862
Ginkgo Bioworks, 3, 720, 974, 1175
GinkgoTree, 1739
Ginni Designs, 1786
Ginsenga, 3033
Ginsey Holdings, 832
Giosis, 1361
Giphy, 820, 827, 840, 894, 1006, 1114, 1125, 1696
Gipis, 2847
Giraffic, 3041
Giraud International, 2542
Girissima, 3039
Girlboss, 1125
Girls Labs, 1703
GirlSense, 1112
GIS, 962
Giska, 827
Gislaved Folic, 2999
Gist, 1948
GitHub, 125, 1657
Github, 1006
GitLab, 894, 1073
Giuseppe Zanotti, 1092
Give & Go, 2211
Give & Go Prepared Foods Corp., 2162
Give More Media, 528
GiveCampus, 1703
GiveForward, 732, 1618
GiveGab, 434, 705
GiveLegacy, 1850
Given Imaging, 3063
Givit, 185
Gixo, 553, 877
Gizmo, 1959
Gizmo Beverages, 381
Gizmo5, 593
Gizwits, 1511
GKC Projects, 585
GL Education, 1115
GL Education Group, 1021
Glacier Bay Technology, 490
Gladiator Entertainment, 650
Gladius Pharmaceuticals, 1734, 2174
Gladly, 877, 1039
Gladly Software, 827
Glam Media, 56, 582, 876, 928, 1235
Glam.com, 1953
Glambot, 232
Glambox, 2863
GlamLoop, 2829
Glamour Sales Holding, 1241
GLAMSQUAD, 1701
Glamsquad, 1114
Gland Pharma, 3202
Glanola, 1737
Glass America, 777
Glass Container Company (GCC), 3224
Glass2Energy, 3143
Glassbreakers, 1058
Glassdoor, 251, 579, 582
Glassdoor.com, 1762
Glasshouse, 395
GlassHouse Technologies, 1084, 1674
GlassMasters Autoglass, 2260
Glassnetic Inc., 1644
Glassock Company, 747
GlassPoint, 1583, 1608
Glasspoint Solar, 1355
Glassybaby, 265

Glauconix, 705
Glaukos, 785, 1014, 1213, 1251, 1383, 1930
Glaukos Corporation, 622
GlaxoSmithKline, 1456, 3250
Glazer-Kennedy Insider's Circle, 1686
Gleam, 3039
Glean.in, 2676
Gleason, 1933
Gleason Research Associates, 681
Glenaden Shirts Limited, 2384
Glenmark Pharmaceuticals, 2329
Glenrose Instruments, 303
Glenveigh Medical, 461
Glide, 1203
Glide Pharma, 3098
Glidepath Power Solutions, 1520
Glider, 1467
Glidian, 1703
Glidr, 1768
Gliknik, 18
Glimmerglass, 145, 1379
Glimpse, 888
Glint, 263, 1213, 1666
Gliph, 310
Glitzi, 49
GLM, 377
GLM Industries, 2029
GLMX, 1762
glo AB, 1908
Global Active, 2708
Global Advanced Metals, 1551
Global Analytics, 564, 1106, 1504
Global Armour, 2384
Global Asset Alternatives, 1118
Global Atlantic Financial Group, 1447
Global Benefits Group Inc., 277
Global Bioenergies, 3104
Global Blood Therapeutics, 764, 1814
Global Blue, 1685, 2321
Global Brass and Copper Inc., 1089
Global Cash Access, 1731
Global Closure Systems, 3017
Global Collect, 3042
Global Communication Semiconductors, 2694
Global Communications, 730
Global Connection, 1234
Global Consumer Products, 1241
Global Custom Commerce, 1255
Global Eagle, 2243
Global Easy Water Products, 54
Global Education Learning Holdings, 1830
Global Employment Solutions, 1090, 1493
Global european Pharma, 1349
Global Exchange Services, 1561
Global Financial, 1151
Global Financial Technology, 1908
Global Forest Products, 838
Global Franchise Group, 1115, 2245
Global Garden Products, 2843, 3000
Global Geophysical Services, 1066
Global Graphics, 124
Global Group, 2970
Global Healthcare Exchange, 1817
Global ID Group, 1018, 1117
Global Indeminity Limited, 781
Global Integrity, 1374
Global Jet Capital, 65
Global Kinetics, 2527, 2950
Global Knowledge, 1169, 1231
Global Knowledge Network, 1973
Global Link Logistics, 1372
Global MailExpress, 56
Global Market Group, 3053
Global Market Insie, 1947
Global Material Exchange, 447
Global Media Online, 2817
Global Mediacom, 3052

Global Medical Isotope Systems, 1535
Global Medical Response, 1086
Global Mixed-Mode Technology, 2594, 3209
Global Name Registry, 2745, 3004
Global Navigation Solutions, 3027
Global Orthopaedic Technologies, 1576
Global Peersafe, 1125
Global Power Systems, 989
Global Radio, 528
Global Restoration Holdings, 333, 334
Global Savings Group, 641
Global Scanner, 827
Global Scanning, 3045
Global Signal, 769
Global Solutions, 2686
Global Sugar Art, 81
Global Sun Technology, 1771
Global Supply Chain Finance, 253
Global Talent Track, 485
Global Tel Link, 1927
Global Tel*Link, 111
Global Telecom & Technology, 266
Global Traffic Network, 889
Global Transport Services, 3052
Global Tranz, 1761
Global Tubing, 2036
Global Value Commerce, 1609, 1712
Global Vantedge, 2590, 2591
Global Voices, 1374
Global Wireless Unified Messaging, 870
Global Woods, 838
Global-e, 136
Global360, 1045
Globalblood Therapeutics, 73
GlobalCast, 1304
GlobalCollect, 1973
GlobaliD, 149
Globalive, 3249
GlobaliveXMG, 2128
GlobalMedic, 2254
GlobalOptions, 228
GlobalOutlook, 1284
GlobalServe, 957
Globalserve, 2188
GlobalSight, 2643
GlobalSIM, 2374
GlobalSim, 1679
GlobalSoft, 1678
GlobalSpec, 2689
Globalspec, 2688
GlobalTranz, 1498, 1944
GlobalView, 436
GlobalWide Media, 674
Globant, 796
Globe, 2671
Globe Sherpa, 1467
Globe Wirelss, 1754
Globecomm Systems, 1961
GlobeImmune, 56, 1126, 1128, 2007
Globeleq, 2329
GlobeOp, 2956
GlobeSherpa, 1384
Globesherpa, 85
Globespan Capital Partners, 3273
Globetouch, 1928
Globevestor, 310
Globoforce, 2469
Globys, 381, 1854
Glooko, 1614, 1698, 2126
gloProfessional, 1769
Glori Energy, 60, 1395
Glory, 3091
Glosil, 2993
Glossi, 133
Glossier, 763, 1006, 1114
GlossyBox, 2820, 2829
Gloucester Pharmaceuticals, 1495, 1561

Portfolio Companies Index

Glow, 125, 3047
Glow and Affirm, 1634
Glow Concept, 827
Glow Digital Media, 2455
GlowForge, 779
Glowing.io, 1142
Glowpoint, 696
GLS Companies, 1971
Glu, 1629
Glu Mobile, 827, 1449
GlucosAlarm, 999
GlucoVista, 724, 1733
Glue Networks, 130, 1604, 1671
Gluecode Software, 1408
Gluetech, 1509
Glunt Industries, 1210
Gluster, 2992
Glutinatus, 3145
GLWL Research, 3187
Glycart, 2739
Glycart AG, 2776
GlyciFi, 311
GlycoEra, 11
GlycoFi, 315
Glycomed, 1898
GlycoMimetics, 1502, 1621
Glycominds Ltd, 2964
GlycoProx, 310
Glyde, 457, 1596
Glympse, 978, 1284, 1478, 1928, 2009
Glynlyon, 1136
Glynn Capital Management, 3273
GlySens, 1993
Glysure, 2969
Glythera, 2883
GM Ventures, 3259
GMC Television Broadcasting, 1192
GME, 2815
GMedia, 1125
GMI, 796
GMIS, 263
GMZ Energy, 1241
GNAP, 792
+GNEO, 310
GNI, 2961
Gninx, 3079
Gnip, 742
Gnosis Analytics, 3064
GNS Healthcare, 323
Go, 1073
GO Albert Group, 2846
Go Daddy, 1086, 1787
Go Electric, 659
Go Fish, 307
Go Global Travel, 136
GO Outdoors, 2303, 3234
Go Plant, 2787
Go React, 746
Go Software, 1152
Go To Logistics, 920
Go Toast, 686
GO-JEK, 2270
Go-Jek, 1086
Go-Now, 421
Go2mo, 2300
GoAhead Software, 1947
Goal Zero, 1205, 1707
Goal.com, 263, 3088
Goalbook, 1315, 3246
GOAT, 1184
Goat, 742, 1890
GoBalto, 2681
goBalto, 1241, 1511, 2504
Gobble, 125, 720, 721, 1254
Gobbler, 1596
Gobee.Bike, 879
Gobi Partners, 485

Gobiquity Mobile Health, 1014
GoButler, 14
Goby, 328, 545, 1069, 1114, 1533, 1589, 2136
GoCardless, 27, 2321, 2469, 3021
GoCatch, 3151
GoChime, 686
GoCo, 1610
GoCoin, 1683
GoDaddy, 1685
Goddess Garden, 2230
GoDigital Networks, 538
GoDundMe, 1213
Goednavond, 3033
GoEuro, 238, 846, 1079, 2437, 2804, 2919
GoFar, 3144
Goffin NV, 2797
Goformz, 752
GoForward Inc., 1669
GoFundMe, 877
Gogo, 1340
Gogo Bot, 1323
GoGoGab, 1752
Gogotech, 381
GoGrab, 221
GoHealth, 1345
Goin, 2398
Going Green, 1065
Going Merry, 1426
GoingOn Networks Inc., 374, 2418
GoInstant, 234, 308
Gojee, 1014, 1058
Goji, 2398
Gokaldas Exports Limited, 280
Golazo, 2393
Gold Bank Communications, 2915
Gold Health Cre, 2129
Gold Lasso, 1172
Gold Medal Services, 1025
Gold Road Resources, 1551
Gold Standard Baking, 1169, 2206
Gold Star Foods, 425, 874
Gold's Gym, 464
Goldbach Media, 2774
Goldbely, 1009
Goldbook, 2915
Goldco, 1461
Golden Corral, 357
Golden Data, 1086
Golden Eye, 2927
Golden Gate, 36
Golden Gate Capital, 1762
Golden Harvest, 585
Golden Health Care, 2260, 2277
Golden Key, 1323
Golden Seeds, 3257
Golden State Overnight, 899
Golden State Towers, 1929
Golden State Vintners, 767
Golden Telecom, 2482
Golden Tulip, 2787
Golden Ventures, 3249
Golder Investment Management LLC, 3255
Goldhat Advisors, 3250
Golding Farms Foods Inc., 449
Goldleaf Financial Solutions, 1127
Goldman Sachs, 3245
Goldner Hawn, 1294
GoldStar, 1244
Goldwind, 1908
Golf In Corporation, 1405
GolferPass, 3053
GolfNet, 650
GolfNow, 267
Golfnow, 861
Golfzon, 3136
Goli, 3202
Goliath Solutions, 1955

Golinks, 798
GoInstant, 787
Golsun, 3185
GOME Electrical Appliances, 223
Gomez, 928, 2335, 2662
Gomez Inc., 22
Gone App, 3116
Gonet, 2766
GoNet Systems, 2965
GoNetworks, 252
Gong, 485
Gong.io, 1346
GoNoodle, 477
GoNoodle Inc., 813
Gonzo, 897
Good, 186, 209, 564, 1186, 1235, 1629, 1867
Good Boy Studies, 1509
Good Buy Gear, 1558, 2228
Good Company, 1509
Good Data, 711, 1009, 1359
Good Deal, 2544
Good Dog, 321
Good Eggs, 234, 251, 545, 1058, 1258, 1363, 1657, 1978
Good Good, 2131
Good Harbour Laboratories, 2189
Good Health Advertising, 1305
Good Health Natural Products, 1234
Good Morning Securities, 897
Good Morning Shinhan Securities, 1143, 2937
Good Natured, 2283
Good News Ventures, 3249
Good Readers, 1323
Good Shepherd Entertainment, 546
Good Start Genetics, 1383
Good Stock, 328
Good Technology, 281, 504, 610, 1255, 1361, 1543, 1626
Good Uncle, 742, 1114, 1483
Good Way Rubber Industries, 2614
Good Way Technologies, 1009
Good.co, 1719
Goodbaby, 3091
Goodbeans, 2820, 2829
Goodbelly, 669
Goodcover, 321
GoodData, 89, 125, 820, 1319, 1798, 1991
Goodeed, 1011
Gooder Foods, 7
Goodfair, 121
GoodGuide, 1442
Goodleap, 1296
Goodlife, 3029
GoodLife Fitness, 2177, 2211
Goodlux Technology, 1164
Goodman, 927
Goodmans, 1971
Goodpack, 1086
Goodpatch, 1610
Goodpath, 1770
Goodr, 901
Goodreads, 1800
GoodRx, 782, 1720, 1890
Goodship, 1484
Goodsie, 1322
Goodtime, 888
Goodview International, 2841
GoodWest Industries Inc., 1404
Goodwill Group, 2817
Goodworld, 387
Goodybag, 447
Goody's, 2775
Google, 1657, 1867
Goom Radio, 1418, 2684
Goop, 1125
Gooten, 724
Gopago, 1658

Portfolio Companies Index

Gopher Resource, 676
GoPresent, 452
GoPro, 1898, 3133
GoPuff, 91, 641
GordianTec, 3238
Gordmans, 1755
Gordon Murray Design, 1247
Gortz & Schiele, 2367
GoSecure, 1796
Goshi, 1618
Gospel, 1610
GoSpotCheck, 686, 1005
GoSquared, 2577, 3021
GossamerBio, 710
GoTenna, 354, 1884
goTenna, 1305, 1309
GotGame, 2178
Gotha Cosmetics, 912
Gotham Therapeutics, 1734, 1930
Gotive, 3113
Goto Software, 2294
GoToCall.com, 538
GoToMeeting, 308, 641
GoToMyPC, 593
GoTRIBE, 1509
Gotuit Media, 2436
GouKW, 1511
Gould & Lamb, 20
Gourmet Culinary Partners, 196
Gourmet Foods, 196
Gourmet Kitchen, 196
Gourmet Settings, 2039
Gousto, 2963
Government Brands, 1499
Govini, 1610
GoWorkaBit, 3099
GoWrench, 2132
Goyoo, 641
Goyoo Networks, 2860
GPA, 1767
GPA Acquisition Company, 1343
GPA Learn, 1412
GPC Biotech, 1777
GPE II LP., 2917
GPER G-1 Development Group, 169
Gpredictive, 3152
GPRS, 1169
GPS Insight, 336
GPS Trackit, 1018
GPSI Holdings, 717
GQ Life Sciences, 51
GR Energy Services Holdings, 1447
Gr8 People, 180
Grab, 827, 1125, 1665
Grab Media, 1150, 1701
Grab Networks, 1636
Grabango, 23, 521, 1566
Grabb-It, 1142
GrabCAD, 1791
GrabCad, 457, 1184
GrabGreen, 68
Grabr, 1323, 1677
Grace, 2763
Grace Hill, 1576
Grace THW Holdings, 897
Gracel, 2830
Gracenote, 263, 1994
Gracious Eloise, 845
Graco Supply & Integrated Services, 988
Gracon, 543
GracoRoberts, 509
Gradall, 1145
Grade Us, 92
GradeCheck, 743
Gradescope, 787, 888, 1054, 1530
GradeSlam, 275, 1530
Gradient, 87, 309, 625, 757

Gradient X, 231
GradLeaders, 367
GradSave, 975
Graduation Alliance, 205, 1298, 1679
Graduway, 1323
Graematter, 270
Graffiti Labs, 2009
Graham Waste, 16
GRAIL, 271, 1149
Grail, 265, 764, 894, 1484
Grain Bulk Handlers, 2329
Grain Communications Group, 1762
Grakon, 989
Grakon International Inc., 867
Gram, 395
Gram Equipment, 3045
Grameen America, 1422
Grameen Intel Social Business, 1009
Grameen Koota, 2305
Grameenphone, 2329
Gramercy Beverage, 3248
Gramex 2000, 585
Grammarly, 820, 1006, 1677, 1716
GrammaTech, 747
GrammaTech Inc., 406
Granada Learning Group, 1929
Grand Angels, 3259
Grand Cathay Securities, 2427
Grand Chip Microelectronics, 1009
Grand Circus, 608
Grand Cru, 1327, 2842
Grand Equipment, 279
Grand Frais, 2842
Grand Junction, 241, 1762
Grand Junction Networks, 200
Grand Peaks, 33
Grand Power Systems, 279
Grand Prairie Foods, 1195
Grand River Aseptic Manufacturing, 167
Grand Rounds, 877, 1918
Grand st., 1223
Grand-Hotel du Cap-Ferrat, 33
GrandCentrix, 2815
Grande, 443
Grande Cashe Coal, 2062
Grande Communications, 20, 205
Grandes Distilleries de Charleroi, 3125
Grandis, 145
Grandoil, 1340
Grandpoint, 371, 1231
Grandpoint Capital, 1746
Grands Vins De Girande, 2294
Grandsys Technologies & Service, 3053
Grandview Gallery, 480
Granicus, 1045
Granify, 1899, 2107, 2163
Granite & Marble Holdings Inc., 988
Granite City Food & Brewery, 479, 1195
Granite City Tool Company Inc., 911
Granite Growth Health Partners, 3254
Granite Seed Company, 1171
Granny's Kitchen Ltd., 467
GranQuartz, 988
GranQuartz Holdings LLC, 911
Grant Peaking Power, 157
Grant Thornton, 3266, 3268
Grant Thornton LLP, 3250, 3251
Grant Victor, 674
Grantium, 2051
Granula, 2864
Granular, 125, 720
GrapeviceLogic.com, 316
Grapevine, 1175
Graph Effect, 794
GraphAlchemist, 1467
Graphcore, 604, 773, 1657, 2437, 2665
Graphene Technologies, 1065

Graphenix Development, 705
Graphic Controls, 1753, 1979
Graphic.ly, 650
GraphicIQ, 1483
Graphics Arts Equipment, 2976
GraphIQ, 1079
Graphite Software, 2070, 2123
GraphPad Software, 1005
GraphScience, 1527
GraphSQL, 1254
Graphus, 288
Graphwear, 1238
Grass Valley, 782
Grass-Pass, 395
Grassi & Co., 3257
Grassroots, 99
Grassroots Greenhouse, 99
Grassroots Herbology, 99
Grassroots Unwired, 361, 1581
Grassroots Vermont, 970
GrassWire, 79
Gravie, 19, 344, 744, 812, 1728
Gravitant, 546, 1601
Graviton, 2673
Gravitude AS, 3132
Gravity, 200, 310, 1091, 1537, 1890, 2824
Gravity Oilfield Services Inc., 502
Gravwell, 1317
Gravy Analytics, 1731, 2074
Gravyty, 229, 1104
Gray Bug, 1172
Gray Energy Services, 449
Gray Line of Tennessee, 1532
Gray Peak Technologies, 1731
Gray Wolf Industrial, 458
GrayBug, 18
Graybug, 918
Grayhawk Capital LLC, 3265
Graylog, 641, 1207
GrayMatter LLC, 903
GraySpace Therapeutics Inc., 2145
Graze, 2653, 2665
Graze.com, 3009
Great Ajax, 751
Great Call, 552
Great Clips, 1560
Great Expressions Dental Centers, 197, 1580
Great Gate Network, 1361
Great HealthWorks, 1433
Great Jones, 564
Great Lakes Angels, 3259
Great Lakes Carbon, 110
Great Lakes Caring Home Health & Hospice, 1972
Great Lakes Dredge & Dock Corporation, 1160
Great Lakes Health Plan, 1251
Great Lakes Pharmaceuticals, 423, 460, 642, 946, 1051, 1556, 1923
Great Northwest Insurance Co., 494
Great Oakland Public Schools Leadership Center, 1315
Great Point Energy, 58
Great Point Power, 157
Great Point Ventures, 58
Great Wall, 2841
Great Western Holdings, 2874
Great Western Leasing & Sale, 165
Great Wolf Lodge, 444
GreatAmerica, 1410
GreatCall, 1744
Greatcall, 457
GreatHorn, 1, 724
Greatist, 752
GreatPoint Energy, 928, 1478
Greats, 1479
GreatSchools, 1315
Greatville Limited, 3053

Portfolio Companies Index

Greatwide Logistics, 722
Grede Casting, 1968
Greek and Roman mythology, 2848
Greeley Company, 902
Green & Tonic, 669
Green Bancorp, 1447
Green Bancorp Inc., 917
Green Bank, 790
Green Bio, 1340
Green Biologics, 2287, 2969
Green Bits, 420
Green Box, 597
Green Bureau, 2300
Green Chemicals, 2883
Green Compass, 367
Green Creative, 1210
Green Creative LLC, 911
Green Cross Biotech, 2848
Green Diamond Sand Products, 16
Green Distribution, 1433
Green Dot, 990, 1235, 1657, 1798, 1865, 1866, 1949
Green Earth Fuels, 1577
Green Energy Biofuels, 54
Green Fig, 1985
Green Flower, 99, 1443, 1810
Green Flower Media, 1139
Green For Life, 919
Green Highland, 3095
Green Light Auto Solutions, 464
Green Matters, 1114
Green Motion, 2565
Green Mountain Technology, 28
Green Organic Dutchman, 393
Green Pacific Biologicals, 2446
Green Patch, 1855
Green Peak, 2665
Green Power Labs, 2148
Green SQL, 3072
Green Tank Technologies, 420, 2134
Green Thumb Industries, 393, 558, 1139
Green Tree, 444
Green Wave Systems, 2681
Green Wizard, 401
Green Zebra Grocery, 1384
Green-Eye Technology, 2204
Greenberg Traurig, 3251
GreenBone Ortho, 2865
Greenbrook TMS, 4
Greenbureau, 3011
GreenCore, 2054
Greencore Group Plc, 77
Greenergetic, 2677
Greenergy, 838
Greenfiber Tech, 3039
GreenField Ethanol, 2088
Greenfield Global, 2056
Greenfield Midstream, 672
Greenfield Networks, 837
Greenfly, 1816
Greengate, 1324
GreenGoose, 1254, 2016
Greenhouse, 1305, 1549, 1698
Greenhouse Juice, 2233
Greenhouse.io, 720
Greenko, 838
Greenko Group Plc, 2364
GreenLancer, 1739
Greenleaf Biofuels, 60, 679
Greenleaf Book Group, 16
Greenlight, 2228
GreenLight Biosciences, 1084
Greenlight Guideline, 1616
Greenlight Technologies, 1750
Greenling, 115, 447, 953
Greenlots, 3142
Greenman Gaming, 2682

GreenMan Technologies, 1733
GreenMantra, 2037, 2181
GreenMantra Technologies, 2054
Greenmantra Technologies, 2087
Greenmountain, 1857
GreenPeak, 2358
GreenPeak Technologies, 2653
GreenPeptide, 2961
Greenphire, 744
Greenplum, 308, 593, 652, 957, 1213, 1239
GreenPrint, 191, 461
GreenQ, 1896
GreenRoad, 915, 3213
GreenScreens, 395
Greensfelder, 3261
Greensight Agronomics, 1633
GreenSky, 1504
Greenslate, 1929
GreenSoil Building Innovation Fund, 3249
Greenspark, 2398
GreenSQL, 2943
Greenstar Plant Products, 2249
GreenTec Bio-Pharmaceuticals, 2095
Greentech Innovation, 2495
GreenThrottle, 1855
Greenvironment Oy, 2864
GreenVolts, 2307
GreenWatt, 3216
GreenWave Systems, 1978
Greenway, 1410
Greenway Grameen, 54
GreenWorld Restoration, 447
Greenzie, 191
Greetz, 3042
Greg C. Rigamer & Associates, 467
Gregg Drilling & Testing, 2052
Gregor Diagnostics, 742
Gremlin, 1690
Gremlin Social, 570
Gremln, 1786
Grenadier Energy Partners II, 673
Grenslandhallen, 3033
Greo, 623, 752
GReply, 624
Gretech, 3118
Gretel, 3251
Greycells18, 2549
Greyline Instruments Inc., 911
Greylock Partners, 3265
Greylock XII Limted, 624
Greystripe, 1249
Greyter Water Systems, 2054
GreyWall Software, 679
GreyWater, 2992
Grid, 1254
Grid Dynamics, 252, 3220
Grid Expert, 2346
Grid Net, 485, 812
Gridants Inc., 624
GridApp Systems Inc., 813
GRIDbot, 447
Gridco Systems, 1335, 1583
gridComm, 2769
GridGain, 89, 1598
GridIron, 1855
Gridium, 1281
GridNet, 430
Gridnet, 325
GridNt, 2658
GridPlex, 1588
GridPlex Networks, 1305
GridPoint, 60
Gridpoint, 3088
Gridraster, 1887
Gridsmart Technologies, 1215
Gridspace, 795
Gridstone Research, 3032

Gridstore, 1379
Gridsum, 1327, 3133
Gridtential, 1584
Gridtest, 3246
Gries Deco, 2291, 2293, 2297
Grilstad, 3067
Grin, 798, 1666
Grin Scooters, 1142
Grind Networks, 1701
Griplock Systems, 377, 1612
Griswold, 1470
Griswold Home Care, 381
Griti, 1009
Gritston Oncology, 1930
Gritstone Oncology, 19, 240, 519, 785, 894
Gro, 285, 1412
GRO Biosciences, 1001
Gro-Well Brands, 410, 838
Grobo, 2122
Grocer, 3099
Grocery Outlet, 1493
Grocery Outlet Bargain Market, 927
Grocery Shopping Network, 1908
Grockit, 1008, 1315
Grohe, 1837
Grohmann GmbH Prum, 3058
Grokker, 182, 520, 545, 742, 1073
Grokr, 1898
GroLens, 29
Groome, 165
Groome Transportation, 547
Groove Biopharma, 154, 2007
Groove Mobile, 649, 1084, 3128
Groq, 1698, 2122
GroSocial, 1074
groSolar, 1691
Grosvenor Capital Management, 3259
Grouby, 2103
Ground Truth, 1006, 1158
GroundBase, 937
Groundhog Technologies, 897
GroundLink, 530
GroundMetrics, 1786
GroundWork, 1187, 1623
Groundwork, 389
Group Commerce, 2557
Group Dekko, 1460
Group Dekko Holdings Inc., 449
Group Intelligentia Oy, 2864
Group K Diagnostics, 269
Group Nine, 1114
Group Trade, 2760
Group Transportation Services, 920
Group Uriach, 77
Group14, 2007
Group360 Inc., 989
Group360 Worldwide, 60
GroupAero, 1424
Groupalia, 2544, 2978
Grouparoo, 680
Groupe Bertrand, 2842
Groupe Bio7, 2842
Groupe BPS, 3011
Groupe Caillé, 2936
Groupe Cyrus, 2512
Groupe d'Emballages Souples, 2713
Groupe De Presse Michel Hommell, 2592
Groupe Doucet, 2309
Groupe Emera SA, 2644
Groupe Eurilogic, 2616
Groupe Eyssautier, 3011
Groupe Hermés-Métal Yudigar, 3011
Groupe IP, 3229
Groupe Lucien Barriere, 2073
Groupe Moreau, 2008
Groupe Proclif, 2667
Groupe Rougnon, 2332

1303

Portfolio Companies Index

Groupe Segex, 2842
Groupe Soloc, 2976
Groupe SQLI, 2866
Groupe Unafinance, 3011
Groupement JV, 2357
Groupie, 2107
Groupize, 845, 1808
Grouply, 31, 1359
Groupmatics, 1051
GroupMe, 742, 1823
Groupon, 125, 641, 1186, 2654
Groupon Japan, 2860
GroupRaise, 1058
GroupSense, 288
Groupsense.io, 1023
Groupsite, 1966
Groupsite.com, 1172
Groupsize, 1104
Groupspaces, 2455
Grove, 720, 742, 1153, 1187, 1890
Grove Collaborative, 361, 945, 1346
Grove Labs, 623, 1593
Grover, 1614
GroveXR, 1426
Grovo, 51, 548, 1114, 1534, 1702
Grow, 1074
Grow Credit, 754
Grow Generation, 850, 1208
Grow Healthy, 558
Grow Journey, 1925
Grow Now, 156
Grow Progress, 937
GrowBLOX Science, 1139
Growcentia, 1139, 1810
Grower's Secret, 3246
Growers Holdings, 999
GrowGeneration, 1282
GrowHealthy, 970
GrowLab Ventures, 2144
Grownetics, 395, 1443, 1845
GrowSumo, 2120
Growth Networks, 1125
Growth Ventures Group, 347
GrowX, 232
GrubHub, 115, 582, 1112, 1125, 1385, 1751
Grubhub, 251, 1720
GrubHub Seamless, 1957
GrubMarket, 802, 827, 863, 2123
Grubwithus, 1969, 2640
Grun Style, 367
Grunspar, 2970
Grupo Abaco Menorquin Yachts, 2953
Grupo ARG, 2374
Grupo Corporativo Ono, 1508
Grupo Cortefiel, 3017
Grupo Phoenix, 1376
Grupo Sala, 45
Grupo Salvador Caetano, 3039
Grupo Terratest, 2842
Grupo TorreSur, 1498
Grupo Visabeira, 3039
Grupos, 2617
Gryphon Networks, 1772
Gryps, 1426
GRYT, 705
GSE Environmental, 1138
GSEI, 2371
GSI, 401, 444
GSI Group Inc., 77
GSI Health, 1572
GSM, 3118
GSMA Mobile for Development Intelligence, 1374
GSMA Mobile Money for the Unbanked, 1374
GSO, 1991
GST Holdings Ltd, 2289
GT Advanced Technologies, 127
GT Nexus, 799, 1957, 2073, 2689
Gt Nexus, 2688
GTar, 721
GTCR, 3245
GTCR LLC, 3255
Gten, 3223
GTESS Corporation, 1084
GTI, 2198
GTI Capital, 1241
GTI Capital Group, 1832
GTI Medivenures, 1832
GTK UK, 3234
GTP Operations, 1493
GTS, 263, 1157
GTS CE Holdings, 1361
GTT, 927, 2665, 2809
GTx, 73, 1190
GTX Messaging, 3198
GTxcel, 1302
Gu Sheng Tang, 711
Guadalupe Power, 1968
Guangdong Fendhua High-Tech, 2841
Guangdong Hongtu Technology, 2793
Guangdong Ronsen Super Micro-wire, 2793
Guangdong Yashii Group, 2533
Guardant, 1426
Guardant Health, 945, 1073, 1125, 1657
Guardent, 957
Guardhat, 608
Guardian, 54, 790
Guardian Analutics, 773
Guardian Analytics, 548, 1728, 1762, 1848
Guardian Capital Partners, 13
Guardian Compliance, 356
Guardian Pharmacy, 412
Guardian Technologies, 835
GuardianEdge, 414
GuardiCore, 238, 485, 604
Guardium, 438, 3203
Guardium Inc., 2571
Guardly, 2107
GuardTime, 2861
Guardtime, 2382, 2822
Guava Technologies, 928, 1007
GuavaPass, 1703
Guavus, 1517, 1840
Gucci, 1021
GUD, 1890
Guerilla RF, 1446
Guesser, 2272
Guestcentric Systems, 3039
Guesty, 2943
Guide, 1103
Guidebook, 1227
Guided Delivery Systems, 179
Guided Interventions, 1051
Guidehouse, 1927
Guideline, 709, 720, 1114
Guideline Research, 1294
Guidelines, 1828
Guidemark Health, 934
Guidepath Medical, 447
GuideSpark, 1213, 1566, 1750
Guidespromos.Com, 2660
Guidewire, 1898
Guidewire Software, 241
Guild, 553, 720, 1537, 1554, 1610, 1923
Guild Mortage Company, 1276
Guilded, 1760
Guildery, 553
Guillaume-Teco, 2671
Guitar Center, 223
Guldfynd Holding, 2854
Gulf American Land Corporation, 1405
Gulf Coast Coca-Cola Bottling Company, 1624
Gulf Coast Energy Resources, 1957
Gulf Coast LNG, 898
Gulf Coast Machine and Supply, 1493
Gulf Coast Shipyard Group, 1138
Gulf Cryo, 1021
Gulfstream, 1049
Gulfstream Services, 1748
Gulu Agricultural Development Company, 54
GumGum, 562, 742, 1255
Gumgum, 1103, 1890
Gummicube, 845
Gump's, 1953
Gumroad, 742
Gun, 310
Gunderson Dettmer, 3262
Guns & Oil Brewing, 447
Gunslinger Studios, 1816
Gunther International, 1191
GupShup, 1798, 2809
Gupshup, 457
Gupta Daniel, 395
Guru, 200, 744, 1610
GuruNet Corp., 810
Gushan Environmental, 1091
Gushcloud, 1966
Gusion, 2883
Gust, 1309, 1588
Gusto, 48, 108, 182, 561, 579, 666, 795, 820, 894, 945, 1079, 1426, 1610, 1634, 1669, 1696, 1763
GutCheck, 881, 1525
Gute TV Laune, 2820, 2829
Guvenrehberi, 2428
Guy & O'Neill Inc., 449
GV Meditech, 2305
GVA, 2935
GVK Power, 2425
GVO, 2970
GW Anglin Manufacturing, 2045
GW Pharmaceuticals, 393, 1139
gWallet, 56
GWC, 1511
Gweepi Medical, 1618
Gwynnie Bee, 381, 624, 949, 1768
Gwynnie Bee., 433
GxG Management LLC, 3257
GXS, 782
Gxs, 843
Gyant, 3099
Gyeonggi Expressway, 585
Gyft, 1059, 1585
Gymboree, 2243
Gymboree China, 223
Gymboree Corporation, 223
Gympact, 1549
Gympass, 641
Gymtrack, 1982
Gynesonics, 58, 545, 928, 1014, 2308
GynoPharma, 1561
Gyrodata, 733
Gyros, 2881
Gyros Protein, 119
Gyroscope, 788

H

H&E Equipment Services Inc., 357
H&S, 653
H-D Manufacturing, 1576
H-E Parts International, 792
H-Log, 3229
H.C. Berger Brewing Company, 1839
H.C. Carbon, 2815
H.J. Meyers & Co., 1839
H.M. Dunn AeroSystems Inc., 878
H2Gen, 2072
H2Gen Innovations, 379, 522
H2HCare, 2909
H2O Audio, 1786
H2Oil Energy, 560

Portfolio Companies Index

H2Scan, 1786
H2X, 1748
H3 Sportgear, 1234
H4-Global, 2958
H5, 1006, 1953
H5 Technologies, 2448
Haansoft, 3159
Haarslev Industries, 2376
HAAS Alert, 1285
Haas Alert, 1896
Haas School of Business, 217
Haawk, 309
Habana, 1009
Habana Labs, 238, 263
Haband, 843
Habit Analytics, 798
HabitAware, 221
Habiteo, 2430
Habito, 2437
Habx, 2842
Hachi, 1914
Hacker Automation, 2518
HackerOne, 251
HackHands, 998
Hackworks, 2107
Hadapt, 532, 679, 1101
Haemair, 2728
Haematologic Technologies, 653
Haemonetics Corp., 303
Haemostatix, 3061
Haggen, 530
Hahl, 2786
HAHT Commerce, 1711, 2073
Haht Commerce, 68
Haihong Hydraulic Science, 2533
Haikou Qili Pharmaceutical, 2793
Haiku Deck, 1854
Hail, 2437
Haila Technologies Inc., 2072
Hailify, 685
Hailo, 27, 1534, 2743, 2969
Hainan Airline, 897
Hainan Hailing Chemipharma Corporation, 1241
Hairun, 3091
Haitai Confectionery and Foods, 2634
Haitou, 998
Haitunjia, 827
Haiyuan Group, 3185
HAL Trust, 1496
Halathion, 1340
Halation Photonics, 145, 1241
HalCash North America, 181
Halcon Resouces, 673
Halcyon Loan Advisors, 1493
Hale and Hearty Soups, 408
Hale Hamilton, 2914
HALE.Life, 5
Halex, 2842
Halfpenny Technologies, 51, 1388, 1572, 1942
Halfpops, 1668
HalfWave, 2691
Halifax Biomedical, 2197
Halin, 2370
Halio, 11
Halite Energy Group, 589
Hall Research, 279
Hallcon, 2198
Hallcrest, 1438
Halliburton Co., 1905
Halo, 2530
Halo Branded Solutions, 525
Halo Business Intelligence, 1871
Halo Filters, 394
Halo Innovations, 1117
Halo Labs, 156, 269
Halo Neuro, 709
Halo Neuroscience, 568, 1155, 1702

Halogen Software, 1045
Halozyme, 1815
Halozyme Therapeutics, 517
Halp, 1317, 2094
HalSource, 1442
Halston, 940
Halter, 1879
Hamer LLC, 906
Hamilton Captive Management, 333, 334
Hamilton Insurance Group Ltd., 407
Hamilton Lane, 3249
Hamilton Robinson Captial Partners, 13
Hamilton State Bancshares, 1779
Hamilton State Bank, 128
Hammer & Chisel, 1829
Hammerhead Navigation, 1060
Hammerstone Corp., 2062
Hampton Creek, 2822
Hamster, 1757
Hamstersoft, 2929
Han net, 2960
HANA Micron, 897
Hanaro Telecom, 3159
Hancock's Wholesale Supply, 911
Hancor Inc., 357
Hand & Stone, 1115
Hand In Gag, 2522
Hand-In-Hand Home Health Care, 409
Handel Information Technologies Inc., 35
Handel's Ice Cream, 503
Handi Quilter, 906, 1886
Handle, 1186
Handle Financial, 752, 1058
Handmade, 2662, 2978
Handmark, 163, 311
Handminder, 999, 1190
HANDS HQ, 2676
HandShake, 1227
Handshake, 308, 666, 888, 1079, 1125, 1153, 1479, 1530, 1702, 1716, 3035
Handshake VR, 2265
Handsman Co., 2898
HandStands, 1859
Handwriting.io, 901
Handy Expert Home Services, 938
HandyLab, 652
Hanegal, 3194
Hangar Technology, 1155
Hangry, 2178
Hangtime, 1014, 1969
Hank's Maintenance, 2156
Hanley Wood, 20
Hanley Wood/Meyers Research, 1231
Hanley-Wood, 902, 1929
Hanleywood, 1138
Hanna Anderson, 1755
Hanna Andersson, 1092
Hannetware, 2848
Hannon Hill, 191
Hans Anders, 2371
Hans bio med., 2960
Hanseatische Verlags-Beteiligung, 2801
Hansen, 843
Hansen Engine, 830
Hansen Medical, 428, 599, 1495, 1693
Hanshow, 1125
Hansol Gyoyook Company, 1143, 2937
Hansons, 963
Hanting Inns & Hotels, 2841
Hantro, 2990
Hanweck, 162
Haocen, 3185
HaoDF, 2575
HaoDF.com, 597
HaoHaoZhu, 827
Hapara, 1315, 1554, 1867
Hapila, 2518, 2815

Happich Fahzeug-und Industrieteile GmbH, 2797
Happier, 1549, 1918
Happiest Babby, 894
Happiest Baby, 720, 1155, 1363
Happiest Minds, 389
Happify, 2466
Happist Minds, 1009
Happlink, 2877
Happy Cloud, 1038
Happy Elements, 597, 2927
Happy Floors, 1136
Happy Hour Creative, 355
Happy Joe's, 16
Happy Money, 2398
Happy Returns, 345, 1153, 1186, 1890
Happy Toy Machine, 1305
HappyCo, 1281
Happyview.fr, 2377
Hapten Sciences, 1190
HaptX, 1892
HapYak, 536
Hara, 1355
Hara Software, 759
Harbar, 1176
Harbert Growth Partners, 3260
Harbert Management, 3251
Harbert Venture Partners, 3251
Harbinger, 68
HARBO Technologies, 2105
Harbor, 125, 728
Harbor Community Bank, 912, 1066
Harbor Freight, 1971
Harbor View Advisors, 3251
Harborside Health Center, 1139, 1613
Harborside Healthcare, 1021
Harborside Inc., 2117
HarborTechnologies, 1165
Harbortouch Holdings of Delaware, 1493
Harbour, 1281
Harbour Antibodies, 193
Harbour Landing Village, 2213
Harbour Networks, 3159
Harbourgate Resort & Marina, 1683
HarbourVest Partners, 2367, 3245, 3249
Harbr, 2161, 2204
Harden Manufacturing, 1136, 1460
Hardent, 2074
HardMetrics, 1388
Hardmetrics, 1321
Hardware Resources, 911, 1460
Hardwear, 2604
Hargray Holdings, 1508
Haripur Power Project, 1012
Hark, 1537
Harley Marine Services, 1493
Harman International, 263
Harmar, 547
Harmless Harvest, 1263
Harmon.ie, 3092
Harmonic, 1898
Harmonic Inc., 950
Harmonix, 779, 1477
Harmonix Music Systems, 1176
Harmony Biosciences, 1943
Harmony Information Systems, 1888
Harmony Information Systems Inc., 1045
Harmony Toy, 1294
Harmonycom, 2766
Harness, 754, 1203
Harper Wilde, 345, 623
Harpoon, 1268
Harpoon Medical, 18, 690, 1172
HarQen, 403, 845, 2002
Harren Equity Partners, 3254
Harri, 400
Harrington Holdings Inc., 654
Harris Connect, 1984

Portfolio Companies Index

Harris Hill, 3234
Harris Research, 377
Harrison Metal, 36
Harrison Street Capital, 3255
Harron Communications LP, 364
Harry Winston, 722
Harry's, 321, 328, 938, 1022, 1534, 2919
Harry's Fresh Foods, 1163
Hart InterCivic, 931, 1857
Hart Systems, 1834
Hartmann, 494
Hartzell Manufacturing, 847
Harver, 1005
Harvery Automation, 1618
Harvest, 3229, 3248
Harvest Automation, 571, 1175, 2700, 2930
Harvest Cannabis Co., 558
Harvest Hill Beverage Company, 360
Harvest Labs, 623
Harvest Partners, 3254
Harvest Partners III L.P., 2651
Harvest Partners IV L.P., 2651
Harvest Power, 582
HarvestMark, 185
HarvestPort, 571
Harvey, 1698
Harvey Gulf, 1049
Harvey Jones, 3234
Harvey Tool, 1576
Hasec, 2518
Hashgo, 641, 876
HashiCorp, 827, 1187, 1537
Hashrabbit, 310
Hashtag Paid, 2120, 2132
Haskell Jewels, 943
Haskins Electric, 943
Hassle.com, 3199
Haste, 285
Hastings Holdings Corporation, 1560
Hat Tricks Group, 2914
Hatch Apps, 1030
Hatch Baby, 1153
Hatch Loyalty, 125
Hatchbuck, 570
Hatchtech, 3014
Hatfield & McCoy Whiskey, 1023
Hathway, 1498
Hatsize, 845, 2051
Hatteras Networks, 801
Haus, 328
Hausway, 2263
Haute Hijab, 221, 345, 568
Haute Hippie, 940
Hautelook, 1235
Hava Health, 1509
Havco Wood Products, 847
Haven, 564, 742, 945
Haven Behavioral, 497
Haven Behavioral Healthcare, 178, 243, 559
Havenly, 779, 1074
Haverfield, 838
Havok, 3182
Hawaii Biotech, 60, 942, 1007, 1015
Hawaiian Wireless Inc., 1624
Hawk Medical, 1973
Hawkeye Renewables, 1818, 1968
Hawkpoint, 2956
Hawkwood Energy, 1957
Hawthorne Effect, 1677
HaxAsia, 3123
Haxiot, 1244
Haydon Enterprises Inc., 911
Hayes Medical, 1771
Hayneedle, 1657
Haynes International, 1145
Haystack, 1169
Haystagg, 1959

Hayward, 435
Hayward Gordon, 658
Hazel, 685
Hazel Health, 1393
Hazelcast, 224
Hazinem, 2286
Hazinem Pirlanta, 2428
Hazy, 1158
HB Performance Systems Holdings, 1278
HB&G Building Products, 165
HB&G Building Products Inc., 851
HC Semitek, 977
Hc1.com, 659
HC360, 409
HCA, 223
HCBF Holding Company, 1746
HCCA International, 495
HCG Energy, 943
HCI Systems, 440
HCJ, 2940
HCOA Fitness, 1834
HCT Group, 2530
HCTec Partners, 495
HD Biosciences, 1439, 2969
HD Supply, 223
HD Vest, 1419
HD Vest Financial Services, 745, 1151
HDH Advisors, 3268
HDmessaging, 1122, 2990
HDR, 2927
HDT Global, 458, 1138
HDT Inc, 2581
HDVI, 207, 1121
Head Country, 832
Head Light, 1484
Headliner, 1682
Headnote, 1323
HeadOut, 1154
Headout, 2272
Headroom, 2122
Headsense, 812
Headset, 966, 1613, 1845, 2233
HeadSpace, 59
Headspace, 1720, 1763
HeadSpin, 894
Headspin, 1672
Headstrong, 897, 1973
Headwater Equity, 3249
Headway Technologies, 897, 1898
Heal, 1099
Heal.com, 164
Healcerion, 3118
Healhcare Financial Resources Inc., 952
Healint, 1966
Healinx, 2766
Healiqnics, 85
HealNow, 75
Healogics, 1629
Healogram, 1593
Health, 183
Health & Bliss, 999, 1190
Health & Safety Institute, 1169
Health Allies, 1561
Health and Fitness Central Europe (HFCE), 2639
Health AP, 863
Health at Home, 409
Health Cap, 2438
Health Carechain, 1917
Health Catalust, 1056
Health Catalyst, 689, 1346, 1657
Health Communications Network Limited, 2906
Health Credit Services, 796
Health Data Insights, 1535, 1890
Health Data Vision Inc., 1535, 1890
Health Diagnostic Laboratory, 1271
Health Dialog, 1, 1723
Health eFilings, 2002

Health Enterprise Partners, 3254
Health Essentials, 263
Health Extras Inc., 407
Health Fidelity, 460, 2074
Health Guru, 1146
Health Hero, 1509
Health Hero Network, 374, 1008
Health Information Designs, 477
Health Innovations Group, 2225
Health Integrated, 173, 1575, 1748, 2188
Health iPASS, 1267
Health iPass, 718
Health IQ, 125, 742, 773
Health Joy, 2074
Health Language, 1798
Health Market Science, 249, 655
Health Monitor Network, 1979
Health Monitoring Systems, 1003, 1452
Health Outcomes Sciences, 861
Health Outcomes Worldwide, 2148, 2197
Health Payment Systems, 376
Health QR, 2148
Health Reveal, 812
Health Sherpa, 1058
Health Systems Technologies, 1399
Health Watch Holdings, 1560
Health-E Commerce, 247
Health2works, 2958
HealthAllies, 504
HealthBridge, 9
Healthcall Optical Services, 2498
Healthcare Anywhere, 659
Healthcare Asset Network, 86
Healthcare Brands International, 2653, 2665
Healthcare Finance Group, 1140
Healthcare First, 1410
Healthcare Funding Corp., 1839
Healthcare Highways, 1622
Healthcare Interactive, 881
Healthcare Interative, 907
Healthcare Management Systems, 1460
Healthcare Recoveries, 958
Healthcare Solutions, 331, 1152
Healthcare Waste Solutions, 97
Healthcare.Com, 1643
HealthCareSolutions, 652
HealthcareSource, 782
HealthCatalyst, 1707
HealthChannels, 924
HealthClinicPlus, 1618
HealthComp Holdings, 92
HealthDelivery, 1618
HealthEdge, 1500
Healthedge, 949
HealthEdge Investment Partners, 3254
HealthEJourney, 2225
Healtheon-WebMD, 1107
HealthExpense, 1050
HealthFinch, 473
Healthfinch, 1364
Healthfuse, 1292
HealthFusion, 508
Healthgrades, 698, 912, 1933
Healthguru, 581
HealthHelp, 1007, 1271
HealthHiway, 877
Healthie, 275, 623
Healthify, 51, 54, 1058
Healthify Me, 1017
HealthifyMe, 1614
HealthiNation, 1242
HealthInvest Equity Partners, 3254
Healthium MedTech, 136
Healthizen, 3100
HealthKart, 1374
Healthland, 782
Healthline, 1056

Portfolio Companies Index

Healthline Networks, 1908
HealthLoop, 399, 1058, 1832
HealthLoop. Impinj, 1442
HealthMEDX, 1852
HealthMedX, 1720
HealthMyne, 9
HealthPlan, 377
HealthPlan Holdings, 1962
HealthPlanOne, 744, 876
Healthplus Corporation, 357
HealthPort, 20
HealthPrize Technologies, 1168
HealthQuest Capital, 3254
HealthQx, 921
Healthrageous, 1146, 1335
HealthSavings Administrators, 302
Healthscope, 1837
HealthSCOPE Benefits, 20
HealthScribe, 881
HealthSense, 1168
Healthsense, 1523
Healthshare Technology, 58
HealthSlate, 1644
HealthSnap, 754
Healthsnese, 1206
HealthSpot, 642
Healthspring, 1618, 1622
HealthSTAR, 931
HealthSun, 1404
HealthSynq, 1561
HealthTap, 1187
Healthtap, 1247
healthTap, 1867
HealthTeacher, 1735
HealthTech Holdings, 1460
HealthTell, 301, 1401, 1942
HealthTrans, 20
Healthtrax, 1025, 1753
Healthtrends Medical Investments, 2468
HealthTronics, 97
HealthTronics IT Solutions, 97
Healthvana, 231
Healthvison, 2762
HealthWarehouse.com, 1290
HealthWiz, 623
HealthWyse, 952
HealthX, 696, 1045
Healthy Directions, 41
Healthy Headie Lifestyle, 395, 1139
Healthy Pet, 377
Healthy Pets, 2093
Healthy Roots, 221
Healthy Roster, 1285
Healthy.io, 1614
HealthyOut, 1635
Healx, 2469
Heap, 1426
Hearland, 444
Hearsay, 1628
Hearsay Sustems, 1657
Hearsay Systems, 720
Heart & Paw, 1964
Heart Center, 2872
Heart Graffiti, 743
Heart This, 787
Heart to Heart Hospice, 1754
HeartBar, 1668
Heartbeat, 1, 1114
HeartFlow, 667, 1618, 1898
Hearthside Food Solutions, 458, 1933
Heartlab, 1118
Heartland, 1755
Heartland Automotive Services, 1507
Heartland Communications Group, 832
Heartland Dental Care, 1086
Heartland Payment Systems, 1140
Heartland Resources, 1786

Heartland Steel Products, 445
Heartsine Technologies, 2601
HeartStent, 1788
HeartThis, 1418
HeartVista, 1073
HeartWork, 234, 553
HeatGenie, 447, 1065
Heatwave Interactive, 1773
Heavybit, 1153
HeavyBit Industries, 586
Heckyl, 3100
Hedgeable, 1690
HedgeStreet, 928
Hedvig, 1363, 1862, 2398, 2681
Heemang Dream Haksa Co., 585
Heeros Systems Oy, 2864
Heffron Consulting, 606
Heguang International, 3053
Heidrich, 3011
Heineken, 475
Heinz, 475
Heleo, 520
Heliatek, 2483, 2677, 2815
Helicon Re, 654
Helicos, 2133
Helicos BioSciences Corp., 748
Helie Power, 322
Helinet Aviation Services LLC, 277
HelioCampus, 1410
Heliocentris Energiesysteme GmbH, 2519
Helion, 1762
Helios Coatings, 947
HelioVOlt, 1401
Heliovolt, 679
Helium, 398, 744, 894, 1101, 1703
Helium Systems, 1073
Helius, 1679
Helix, 610, 1079
Helix Sleep, 863
Helixis, 58, 1371
Hellas Direct, 2217
HellaWaller, 881
Hellman & Friedman, 3245, 3254
Hello ChuXing, 827
Hello Fresh, 1005, 2820, 2829
Hello Giggles, 795, 1816, 1885
Hello Machines, 2846
Hello People Ops, 395
Hello Tech, 545
Hello Vera, 724
HelloAva, 1703
HelloGiggles, 1483
HelloHome, 999
HelloNature, 3118
HelloSign, 894
Hellosign, 779, 1969
HelloSoft, 713, 1241
HelloTech, 121, 231, 562, 708, 976, 1059, 1162, 1890
HelloTechm Gyft, 400
HelloWallet, 1784
HelloWorld, 1092
Helly Hansen, 2376
Helly Hensen, 1021
Helmedix, 2950
Help, 1534
Help Around, 1993
Help At Home Inc., 1972
Help Scout, 779
Help Shift, 1009, 1158
Help Social, 546
Help Systems, 1728
Help/Systems, 197, 1754
Helpful, 2130, 2131
Helpr, 568
HelpSaude, 2429
HelpScout, 2016

HelpShift, 1610
Helpshift, 485, 1862, 2992
HelpSystems, 931
Helpsystems, 458
Helpwear, 2122
Helveta, 2287
Helvetic.com AG, 2418
Hem, 2437
Hema Source, 952
HemaSource, 851
Hematris Wound Care, 2443, 2815
Hemen Kiralik, 2286
Hemen Kiralikm, 2428
Hemisphere Media Group, 2243
Hemodynamic Therapeutics Inc., 432
Hemophelia Resources of America, 1772
Hemosense, 1949
Hemosphere, 667
Hemosphere Inc., 573
Hemoteq Gmbh, 2673
Hemp Business Journal, 395
Henan, 2582
HengFu Logistics, 1908
Hengxin Electric, 1340
HengZhi, 2466
Heniff Transporation Systems, 243
Heniff Transportation Systems LLC, 1372
Hennessy Capital Solutions, 355
Henniges Automotice Holdings, 2008
Hennings Automotive, 1138
Henry, 851
Henry Company, 111
Henry The Dentist, 328, 2194
Hensoldt, 1086, 2842
HEP Tech, 908
Hepaco, 418, 886
Hepregen, 236
Heptagon, 1327, 2866, 2869, 3205
Heptagon/AMS, 827
Heptares Therapeutics, 2972
Heptio, 1125
Hera Health Solutions, 999
Herald Media Holdings, 197
Herantis, 350
Herb, 361, 863, 1114
Herbal Magic, 2073
Herbalgem, 2853
Herbalife, 843
Herban Planet, 1139
Herbert, 2233
HerbPharm, 1250
Hercules, 804
Hercules Technology Growth Capital, 3251
HerdDogg, 999
Here, 1009
Heresy, 3099
Heritage Foodservice Group, 912
Heritage Group, 3254
Heritage Home Group, 1089
Heritage Inks International, 836
Heritage-Crystal Clean Inc., 357
Herld Media, 902
Hermes Precisa Australia, 2942
Hermois, 1678
Hermés Métal, 3011
Hero Digital, 478
Hero Investments, 223
Heroku, 234, 1537, 2011
HeroX, 490
HEROZ, 2965
Hertel Holding, 2324
Hertz, 1949
HES Beheer, 3200
HeSaLight, 3194
Hess Print Solutions Inc., 1972
Het Engeltje, 3033
Hetan Technologies, 2970

1307

Portfolio Companies Index

HeTexted, 1305, 1309
HeTian Hospital Management, 1086
Hetras, 3095
HETSCO, 1252
Hetworth Corp., 2088
Heureka Software, 1285
Heuresis, 2969
Hewitt, 2762
Hewlett-Packard, 1100
Hex Performance, 791
Hexadite, 1796, 3236
Hexagon Bio, 1669
HexaTech, 1013, 1661
Hexcel Corporation, 867
Hexion Specialty Chemicals, 141
Hey, 1718
Hey Group, 2832
Hey Orca!, 2208
HeyCater, 2288
Heyday, 728, 1114, 1589
Heyfair, 2518
Heymama, 1309
HeyMarket, 1566
Heyo, 1815
HeyOrca, 2161
Heysan, 2437
Heysta Energy, 1577
Heytex Bramsche GmbH Bramsche, 3058
HF2 SRL, 2410
HFFC, 263
HFSC Holdings, 767
HG Data, 309, 689
HGB, 1707
HGData, 1569
HGHI, 244
HGI Holdings, 1460
HH Ventures, 16
HHA eXchange, 1276
HHI Holdings LLC, 1089
Hi Bruno, 2288
Hi Corp., 597
Hi Fidelity Genetics, 738
Hi Media, 3104
Hi Technologies, 1511
Hi-G-Tek, 236
Hi-Grade Welding & Manufacturing, 402
Hi-Lo Automotive Inc., 1624
Hi-mart, 897
Hi-Media, 641
Hi-Rel Group, 1163
Hi-Tec Profiles, 2213
Hi-Tech, 3091
Hi-Tech Manufacturing, 1481
Hi-Tech Rubber Inc., 451
Hi-Tech Wealth, 2763
hi5 Networks, 928
Hiberna Corporation, 318
Hibernator, 2464
Hibernia Atlantic, 266
Hibernia Energy, 1326, 1328
Hichain, 2927
HiChina, 2841
Hickery Farms, 467
Hickory, 1554
Hickory Farms, 1755
Hickson & Welch, 2668
Hiconics, 2927
Hidden City, 42
Hidden Level, 1099
Hidrate Spark, 1703
Hidrotenecias, 45
HIG Capital, 3254, 3255
Higginbotham Insurance Agency, 1746
High Alpha, 666
High Beauty, 2233
High Branch Software, 655
High Brow Cat, 517

High Desert Power, 1797
High End Systems, 822
High Fidelity, 894, 1058, 1862
High Gear Media, 27, 582
High Ground Energy, 1447
High Ground Solutions, 1536
High Park, 1484
High Performance Building Systems, 1003
High Power Lithium, 691
High Pressure Equipment Company, 1961
High Q, 1255
High QA, 51
High Ridge Brands, 360
High Roads, 1084
High Sierra Energy Partners, 1057
High Street Capital, 3255
High Street Capital Partners, 558
High Street Insurance Partners, 963
High Technology Solutions, 1949
High Times, 152, 1139
High Wind, 3033
High-Mobility, 2832
High-Tech Grunderfonds, 3146, 3161
Highdeal, 2866
Highdef, 2466
Higher Education Partners, 1248
Higher Gear Group, 931
Higher Logic, 1045
Higher Power Nutrition, 1234
HigherNext, 1321
HigherOne, 1991
Highest Reward, 395
HighFive, 1125
Highfive, 820, 894
Highgate Hotels, 1853
Highgate Labs, 2676
HighGround, 1121
HighJump, 928, 1728
Highland Capital Partners, 3263, 3273
Highlands Bank, 517
Highlight, 610, 876
HighlightCam, 1054, 1515, 2321
Highlighter, 686
Highline, 2231, 2283
Highline Financial, 1727
Highline Media, 1727
Highline Wealth Management, 1603
Highmark Energy, 1326
HighPoint Solutions, 1140
HighRoads, 928, 2188
Highroads, 22
HighSpot, 1610
Highspot, 1162, 1666
Hightail, 36, 87, 666, 1028, 1661
Hightower, 1534, 1823
HighWave, 2866
Highwinds, 173
HighWire, 28
HIIG, 2371
Hijauan Bengkoka, 838
Hijoki, 2912
Hijro, 310, 562, 724
HijUp, 721
Hiku, 1254
HIL Applied Medical, 3235
Hilb Group, 20
Hilco Technologies, 815
Hilding Anders, 1021, 1086, 2999
Hile Bio-pharma, 2724
Hilite Industries, 1460
Hill & Valley, 483, 1481
Hill And Valley, 1518
Hill Country Holdings, 377
Hill Leigh Group, 2976
Hill Ward Henderson, 3251
Hillary's Group, 2608
Hillcrest, 646

Hillcrest Labs, 881
Hillier's, 940
Hillman Group, 1360
Hillsdale Furniture, 356
Hillsidecandy, 956
Hillstone, 1340, 3206
Hilton Worldwide, 874
Himadri, 223
himagine Solutions, 247
Himalayan Handmade Candles, 1609
HiMama, 2235
Himark Bogas, 2043
Himax Technologies, 3209
Himex Limited, 3190
HIMS, 337, 3089
Hims, 763
Hinge, 680, 863, 1534, 1666
Hinge Health, 3, 1005, 2437
Hingeto, 1058
HIP Digital, 876
Hip Digital, 1852
Hip Shot Dot, 1739
Hipbone, 950
Hipcamp, 1696
Hipclub, 3035
Hipdot, 1323
Hiperos, 1754
HiperScan, 2815
HipGeo, 1254
Hipmunk, 1006, 1327, 1361, 1808, 1969
Hipoges, 1086
Hippo, 23, 520, 720, 728, 1323
Hippo Insurance, 1099
Hippocrates Associates, 1839
HipSnip, 2392
Hipster, 1121
HipSwap, 876
HipVan, 1966
HiQ, 309, 625
Hiramatsu Inc., 2339
Hire An Esquire, 12
Hire Counsel & Mestel, 1145
Hire Dynamics, 1270
Hire IQ, 1790
Hire Vue, 1074
Hire.com, 205
HireArt, 720, 1014
Hired, 44, 520, 564, 863, 1672, 1702
HireMojo, 100
HireNetworks, 3250
Hireology, 225, 732, 1121
Hirequip Projex, 2411
HireRight, 597, 1728
HireVue, 857, 1657
HIRO, 438
Hirslanden Holdings, 2488
HIS, 2536
Hisarlar, 585
Hiscox, 2787
Hisoar Pharma, 2533
HiSoft Technology International, 691, 3053
Hispanic Yellow Pages, 20
Histogenics, 993, 1728
Histogenics Corporation, 315
Histogenics Hyperion Therapeutics, 1700
Histoire d'Or, 2367
Historic Futures, 2530
HistoRX, 352
HistoRx, 522
HistoSonics, 642, 750, 1804, 1923, 2174
Histosonics, 918
Hitachi Kokusai Electric, 1086
Hitch, 3099
HitCheck, 229
Hitech, 2960
HitecVision AS, 77

1308

Portfolio Companies Index

HitFix, 845, 1786
HitFox, 3161
HitFox Group, 2820, 2829
Hitmeister, 2466
HitRecord, 1616
HITS, 1113
hiu! Media, 3053
Hive, 129, 820
Hive II, 624
Hive9, 2074
HiveIO, 1525
HiveLive, 881
Hivemapper, 31
HiveUAV, 795
hiwire, 2020
Hixme, 1079
Hiya, 2469
Hjem Is Europa, 2854
Hjem-IS, 3194
HJMT Communications LLC, 3257
Hjr Asphalt, 2277
HK Ruokatalo Oyj, 2981
HL Leasing, 2801
HLine Digital Media, 1228
HLM, 36
HMC+, 2815
HMicro, 2010
HMP, 1761
HMR Foods, 2083
HMS Healthcare, 1090
HMT, 1779
HNA Group, 475
HNB, 3142
HNI Healthcare, 1622
HNW, 536, 593, 2188
Hoak Media Corporation, 443
Hobbico Inc., 578
Hobbs, 2298, 2303
Hobbs Bonded Fibers, 1025
Hobbs Rental Corporation, 367
Hobnob, 1346
Hobo Labs, 857, 1666
Hochtemperatur Engineering GmbH, 2651
Hockeystick, 2132
Hodges Ward Elliott, 1625
Hodges-Mace, 1746
Hodinkee, 752, 1153, 1760
Hodo, 475
Hodo Soy Beanery, 1101
Hoffiges, 2712
Hoffman & Baron LLP, 3257
Hoffman Media, 266, 1536
Hoffmaster Group, 170, 1460
Hoffmaster Group Inc., 1972
Hojoki, 2629
HOKO, 3099
Hokodo, 2398
Hoku Scientific, 810, 942
Hola, 1854
HOLA Home Furnishing, 1771
Hola!, 2822, 2943
Holaira, 58, 1126, 1728
Holberton, 1530
Holberton School, 108
Hold Jinn Electronics, 3209
Hole 19, 1982
Hole19, 3099
Holganix, 296, 1386
Holiday Enterainment, 2427
Holiday Inn Express, 2530
Holiday Retirement, 769
HolidayIQ, 27
Holland & Hart, 3265
Holland & Knight LLP, 3251
Holland Energy, 1797
Holland Services, 931
Hollander, 962

Hollander Sleep Products, 1654
Hollar, 520, 763, 1079, 1125, 1483
Holley, 1131
Hollinee, 319
Hollinger, 2067
Hollywood Tans, 41
Holman Boiler Works, 911
Holmes Place, 2953
Holmris, 3194
Holoclara, 1055
Hologram, 631
Holographix, 317
Holor, 1983
HolyTax, 2927
Homag Group AG, 2651
Homann Chilled Foods, 2812
Homax, 1372
Home & Legacy, 2668
Home 24, 2820
Home Appliances, 2391
Home Bistro, 1691
Home Care of St. Francis, 409
Home Chef, 68, 1092
Home Decor Holdings, 1460
Home Dialysis, 1957
Home Dialysis Plus, 1931
Home Director, 957
Home Health Holdings, 1424
Home Helpers, 1136
Home Inns, 2841
Home Inns & Hotel Management, 1771
Home Products International, 1955
Home Skinovations, 1846
Home Solutions, 1090
Home Town Cable, 20
Home.is, 1614
Home24, 2829
Home61, 594
HomeAway, 205, 1006, 1537, 1852, 2714
Homebase, 234, 553, 763, 1073
HomeBay, 773
HomeBistro Foods, 440
HomeCare, 1971
HomeCare.com, 1172, 1259
HomeCentric Healthcare, 1730
HomeCourt.ai, 1142
HomeEquity Bank, 2056
HomeGrocer.com, 85
Homegrown Natural Foods, 377
Homejoy, 1549
HomeLight, 361, 488, 894, 1203
Homelight, 564
HomeMe.ru, 2312
Homeperf, 2842
HOMEQ Corp., 2177
Homer, 354, 863, 1114, 1589
Homeroom, 1186
Homeschool, 1467
Homeshift, 3099
Homesnap, 1558
Homesoft Oy, 2864
HomeSphere, 1851
HomeSpotter, 344
HomeStars, 2103
Homestead Smart Health Plans, 4
Homestyle Selections, 2065
Homesuite, 623
HomeSun, 2496
Hometap, 820
Hometeam, 1155
HomeToGo, 1005
HomeTouch, 1618
Hometown Communications, 1574
Hometown Food Company, 360
Hometree, 2398
HomeVestors, 1115
Homewood Health, 2076

Homey, 999
Homie, 79, 608, 1074
Homigo, 2024
Homology Medicines, 11, 1934
Hone, 1530
Hone Comb, 1467
Honest Buildings, 311, 1247, 1281, 1583, 1978, 2136
Honest Networks, 728
Honest Tea, 192
Honey, 1154
Honey Smoked Fish, 1276
HoneyApps, 1867
Honeybee, 1760
Honeybee Health, 121
HoneyBook, 400, 1346
Honeybook, 1323
HoneyComb, 1065
Honeycomb.io, 641
Honeycommb, 1599
HoneyTree Films, 1164
Honeywell, 475
Hong Bang, 3185
Hong Kong Broadband Network, 2371
Hongchizhineng, 1125
HongHua Co., 1577
Honghua Group Limited, 3209
Hongkong Electric, 2582
Honk, 101, 309, 708, 1059, 1752, 1800
HONKON, 511
Honor, 125, 944, 1058, 1323, 1696
Honor Medical Staffing, 1609
Honors Holdings, 1053
Hoodinn Interactive Limited, 2694
Hoodline, 1426
Hoodong, 1340
Hooja, 508
Hook Logic, 224, 799
Hook Mobile, 50, 120, 2841
Hooked, 553, 1154
Hooked Media Group, 1898
Hookipa Biotech, 2739
Hookipa Biotech AG, 1780
Hookit, 1744
Hooks, 2317
Hoopla, 980, 1605, 1610, 1855
Hooters Restaurants, 1496
HootSuite, 27, 304, 925, 1235
Hootsuite, 1005, 2074, 2154
Hooven Heat Treating, 467
Hoover Group, 741
Hopdpddy, 1092
Hope, 937
Hope20, 3248
Hopen Life Sciences Venture, 3259
Hopkins, 2201, 2211
Hopkins Capital Group, 3251
Hopkins Manufacturing, 791, 1460, 2200
Hopper, 37, 2060
Hopscotch, 752, 1058, 1223, 1549
HopSkipDrive, 6, 744, 901, 1186, 1483, 1890
Hopster, 1291, 2988
HopStop, 3072
Hoptroff, 2398
Horizon, 2198, 2665, 3076
Horizon Blockchain Games, 2131
Horizon Cellular Group, 263
Horizon Development, 1955
Horizon Digital Enterprise, 1757
Horizon Discovery, 2653, 3019
Horizon Discovery Limited, 2972
Horizon Food Equipment Inc., 903
Horizon Mud Comapny, 1424
Horizon Organic, 543
Horizon Organic Dairy, 861
Horizon Packaging, 1229
Horizon Partners, 3273

1309

Portfolio Companies Index

Horizon Pharma, 190, 193, 1271, 1325, 1510, 1629, 1762, 2776, 3187
Horizon Robotics, 1009
Horizon Science, 2507
Horizon Semiconductors, 2773
Horizon Services, 1755
Horizon Systems, 1229
Horizon Therapeutics, 928
Horizon Ventures, 990
Hormos Medical Ltd Oy, 2310
Hornblower Holdings, 560
Hornet Group, 1748
Hornetsecurity, 1499
Horse Network, 316, 789
Horseburgh & Scott Co., 654
Horsehead, 1138
HorsePower, 1175
Hortex, 2413
Hortonworks, 251, 1798, 2851, 2851
Hospice Advantage Holdings, 1654
Hospice Link, 1332
Hospira, 1349
Hospital Corporation of America, 495
Hospital IQ, 1150
Hospital Therapy Services, 1839
Hospitalists Management Group LLC, 63
Hospitalists Now, 1725
Hospitality Associates, 1636
Hospitality Mints, 1136, 1460
Host Analytics, 58, 570, 646, 1319, 1741, 1852, 1912
Hosted Solutions, 20
Hostfully, 221, 2092
Hosting, 1410
Hostspot, 2975
Hostway, 1138, 1929
Hot Bread Kitchen, 1422
Hot Potato, 1823
Hot Rail/Conexant/Skyworks, 1287
Hot Topic, 1708
Hotbar.com, 22, 2711, 3149
HotChalk, 696, 888
Hotchalk, 1247
Hotel Booking Solutions, 564
Hotel El Convento, 62
Hotel Tonight, 48, 182, 763, 774, 1898
Hotel Urbano, 1005
Hotelbar.Com, 2617
Hotelogix, 27
HotelRunner, 2286
Hotelscene Limited, 2498
HotelTonight, 27, 238, 742, 827
HotJobs.com, 263
Hotjobs.com, 822
HotLink, 1106
Hotmail, 610
HotPads, 1196
HotRail, 1649
Hotrail, 35
HotSchedules, 227, 1076
Hotsip AB, 163
Hotspir Technologies Inc., 272
HotSpot Merchants, 2192
Hotspur Technologies, 1379
Hotswap, 1077
HotU, 1015
Hotwire.com, 1837
Houghton International Inc, 836
Houghton Mifflin Harcourt, 20
Houghton NYC, 221
Houlihan's Restaurants Inc., 847
House of Anita Dongre, 819
House of Blues, 1683
House of HR, 2842
House of Matriach, 1065
HouseBites, 2676
HouseCall, 641

Housecall Pro, 225
Housejoy, 1511
Houseparty, 520, 877, 1323, 1657, 1696, 1885
HouseTrip, 27
HouseValues, 470
Housing Development Finance Corporation, 2329
Houston Health Ventures, 953
Houston Medical Robotics Inc., 487
Houzz, 520, 827, 863, 1079, 1657
HOVER, 894
Hover, 89, 93
How About We, 1358
How.do, 2822
HowAboutWe.com, 724, 1227
Howcast, 42, 581, 1800
HowGood, 744, 863
HowStuffWorks, 1711
Hozelock, 2635
HPC Energy Services, 2022
HPR, 317
HPS Holding Company, 1278
HQ Medical Technology, 711
HQ Raleigh, 3250
HqO, 1281, 1483
HR New Media, 2815, 2985
HRA Pharma, 1456, 1576
HRI, 60, 798
HROI, 494
HRP Refrigerants, 2976
HSBC, 3265
HSE24, 1498
Hsin Yung Chien Co., 3209
HSIO Technologies, 3268
Hsiri Therapeutics, 269
HSS, 97, 377
HTBASE, 2132
HTG, 1734
HTG Molecular Diagnostics, 1704, 1903
HTI, 3011
HTI Technologies Holding Corporation, 1560
HTP, 1556
Hua Medicine, 154, 711, 1918
Huaqin, 1009
Huaxun Technology, 2724
Huaya Technology, 2581
Huayue Education, 136
HUB, 927
Hub International, 912, 2030, 3251
Hubb, 746, 1384
Hubba, 846, 2060, 2120, 2216
Hubbardton Forge, 362
Hubble, 744, 3099
Hubble Telemedical, 1190
Hubbli, 2094
Hubbub, 2743
HubCast, 523
Hubdoc, 2235
HubHaus, 820, 1698
HubPages, 1750
Hubspan, 1629, 1640, 2073, 2188
HubSpot, 457, 1184, 1657, 1798
Hubspot, 561, 1629
Hubster, 1896
Hubub, 510
HubX, 313
Huckleberry, 564, 641, 863, 1724
Huddle, 274, 972, 1184, 2682
Huddle House, 1507, 1654
Hudong, 2658
Hudson Baking Company, 148
Hudson Bay Company, 2062
Hudson Lock LLC, 1965
Hudson Medical Communications, 1228
Hudson Products, 2014
Hudson Products Corporation, 1577
Hudson Respiratory Care, 786

Huga Optotech, 1908
Hughes, 1232
Hughes Broadcasting Partners, 1929
Hughes Pittman & Gupton LLP, 3250
Hugin, 3004
Hugo Boss, 3024
Huhtamäki Oyj, 2981
Huicheng Pectechnology, 2927
Huiseoul, 183
Huiying Medical Technology, 1009
Huji, 2584
Hulafrog, 1527
Hullabalu, 863, 1119, 1635, 1719
Huma.ai, 802
Human Agency, 937
Human API, 125
Human Code, 205
Human Demand, 151
Human DX, 742
Human Dx, 1058
Human Eyes, 2532
Human Genome Science, 1561
Human Genome Sciences, 1395
Human Inference, 3042
Human Interest, 1760
Human Longevity Inc., 610
Human.co, 3215
Humana, 2413
HumanAPI, 129, 299
Humane, 398
HumanEyes Technologies, 3235
Humanfirst, 2204
Humanforce, 28
Humangride, 2815
Humanize, 316
Humanizing Autonomy, 2398
Humanoid, 1959
HumanZyme, 2969
Humax, 2915
Humble & Fume, 2134
Humble Bundle, 1657
Humble Dot, 1760
Humedica, 1206, 1335
Humedics, 2815, 2832, 3104
Humense, 1391
Humi, 2122
Humi HR, 2024
Humin, 1832
Humirel, 2472
Hummer Winblad Venture Partners, 3273
Hummingbird, 944, 2809
Hummingbird Technologies, 2988
Humon, 623
Hunch, 234, 263
Hungama.com, 1009
Hungarocamion Rt., 2420
Hunger Computer, 2915
Hungry, 1616
HUNGRY Marketplace, 1259
Hungry Root, 354, 564, 863, 1114, 1223
HungryRoot, 1125
Hunkemoller, 3017
Hunt Marcellus, 1066
Hunt Valve, 1169
Hunter Boot, 2243
Hunter Business Law, 3251
Hunter Defence Technologies, 248
Hunter Fan, 1231
Hunter Fan Holdings, 2371
Hunter's Specialties, 445
HuntForce, 635
Huntress, 2787
Huntress Labs, 288
Huntswood CTC Ltd, 2298
Huodongxing, 597
Hupnos, 229
Hurdle, 1

1310

Portfolio Companies Index

Hurix Systems, 2809
Huron, 1858
Huron Energy Corporation, 2036
Huron River Ventures, 3259
Hurray, 2724
Hurrier, 2140
Hurrikan Power, 157
Husk Power Systems, 54
Huskie Tools, 1343
Hustle, 773, 888, 894, 937, 1005, 1058, 1610, 1698, 1724
Hut Six Security, 2276
Huterra, 1291
HUVRData, 447
HVault Storage, 1678
HVH Transportation, 920
HVMN, 125
HVT Group, 1529
Hweden, 1755
HX Technologies, 1321
Hy Cite Enterprises LLC, 1404
HY Trust, 1009
Hy-Bon Engineering Company, 1438
Hy-Lok, 3136
Hyalto, 2231, 2276
HYAS, 1158, 1760
Hyas, 2276
Hybolic, 3185
Hybond AS, 3132
Hybrid Apparel, 96
Hybrid Cluster, 2676
Hybrid Energy, 2909
Hybrid Graphics, 2990
HybridCluster, 2577
Hybrigenics, 2616
Hybris, 962
Hybritech, 1762
Hyco International Inc., 449
Hycor, 1132
Hycrete, 1324, 1583
Hyde Park Capital Partners, 3251
Hyde Park Venture Partners, 3255, 3259
Hydra Biosciences, 58, 1126, 1128, 1464
Hydra Studios, 728
Hydrade, 592
HydraDx, 794
Hydrant, 623
Hydrasun, 1021
Hydraulex Global, 1747
Hydrexia, 1713
Hydro Resources, 1949
HydroChem, 444
HydroChemPSC, 1138
HydroCision, 273
Hydrocision, 1849
Hydrocore, 3251
HydroDive, 1167
Hydrofarm, 2245
Hydrogenics Corporation, 2073
Hydroid, 214
HydroMassage, 80
HydroNovation, 499
HydroPoint, 2101
HydroPoint Data Systems, 731, 1249, 1583
Hydrostor, 2037
Hydrovoima, 2310
Hydrox Pipeline Oy, 2864
Hygenic, 1460
Hygenica, 254
Hykso, 814
HYLA, 1597
HYLA Mobile, 1691
Hyland Software, 1817
Hylete, 1744
Hynes Industries, 1548
Hyosung Wind Power Holdings, 585
Hype!, 3099

Hyper, 59
Hyper Giant, 2050
Hyper Strong, 977
Hyper9, 1184, 1918
HyperActive Technologies, 1003
Hyperchip, 2254
Hypercom, 782
Hypercomply, 2122, 2131
Hyperconnect, 100
Hypercontext, 2131
HyperEdge, 1174
HyperGrid, 40
Hyperink, 1101
Hyperion, 1086
Hyperion Insurance Group, 819
Hyperion Therapeutics, 240, 1411
Hyperion Therpeutics, 2007
HyperKey, 229
Hyperlite Mountain Gear, 440, 1165
Hyperloop One, 812, 1330
Hyperloop Transportation Technologies, 1099
Hyperoptic, 1314
Hyperplane, 884
Hyperpublic, 1823
Hyperpulic, 1701
HyperQuality, 1237
HyperQuest, 1483
HyperScience, 108, 720, 744, 1616
Hypersonix, 1669
Hypertrust N.V., 2893
HyperVerge, 1284
HyperVR, 121
Hyperwallet Systems, 1480
Hyperwave, 2290
Hyperwear, 447
Hyperweek.net, 2302
Hyphen, 1011
Hypnion, 58, 748, 772
HypothenkenZentrum AG, 77
HYPR, 1, 308, 1614
HYPRES, 2361
Hypur, 966
Hyr, 756
Hysko, 2024
Hysolate, 1001
Hythro Power Corporation, 2451
HyTrust, 485, 689, 857, 1852
Hytrust, 2270
Hyundai Oil Terminal, 3136
Hyunjin Materials and Yonghyun Base Materials, 897
Hyva, 2367
Hywire Ltd., 3239
HZO, 5, 1024, 1840
HzO, 2822

I

I and C-Cruise.Co, 721
I G Doors, 3008
I Need MD, 650
I'm Sick Mobile, 954
I-Concerts, 3143
I-Deal Optics, 1163
I-Film, 215
I-Food Chains, 2922
I-Logix, 22, 1335, 2770
i-Logix, 523
I-Mab Biopharma, 2681
i-merge, 2554
I-Neumaticos, 2544
i-Nexus, 2399
i-Optics BV, 2342
I-Payment, 495
I-Solutions Global, 2958
I-STAT, 1048
i-Team, 1101
I-Um, 100

i-Wireless, 1718
I.AM+, 895
I/OMagic Corporation, 870
I/Pro, 925
I/SCRIBES Corp., 589
i2, 2014
I20 Pharma, 2445
i2s, 3022
i2X, 1269
i3 Broadband, 1641
i3 Equity Partners, 812, 1158
i3 Mobile, 1706
I3 Precision, 3064
I4CP, 756
i4cp, 1250
i4i, 2191
IA Ventures, 36
Iaam, 2500
IAC, 2956
IACX Energy, 898
iAdvise, 2377
IAG Research, 263
Iagnosis, 1452
IAM Registry, 649
IAM Robotics, 521
Iamba, 438, 2773
iAmplify, 1084
IAMRobotics, 802
Ian's Natural Foods, 2230
Ianacare, 568
ianet, 2457
iAngel, 1323
ianTECH, 300
Ianthus, 393
iAnthus, 850
iAppPay, 1340
IASI, 3178
IASIS Healthcare, 899, 1043
Iasis Healthcare, 1837
IASIS Healthcare Corporation, 1271, 2371
IAT Automobile Technology, 1241
Iatroquest, 983
iAutomation, 1576
iBAHN, 1908
iBahn, 68
iBalance Medical, 1693
iBase, 3199
iBBS, 1410
iBeat, 490, 545, 1186
Ibeatyou.com, 1103
Iberchem, 2480, 2842
Ibex, 1336
Ibexis Technologies, 3098
Ibfx.com, 1720
IBI Biosensors, 2930
iBinom, 2929
iBiquity, 881
iBiquity Digital, 1304
IBIS Networks, 1065
Ibistic, 3004
IBK Bioanalytik, 2815
IBM, 475, 3203
Ibotta, 827, 863
iBoxPay, 2437
Ibpil, 263
iBreva, 313
IBS Software Services, 819
IC Axon, 723
IC Data Com, 743
IC Media, 3209
IC Potash, 1551
IC Works, 1091, 1898
iCAD, 1302
ICAP Media, 2347
iCardiac Technologies, 60, 1748
iCare.com, 3251
iCarsclub, 3064

1311

Portfolio Companies Index

Icarus, 3125
Icatus RT, 395
ICC Nexergy, 1018
ICC Wales, 2276
ICE, 1753
Ice Energy, 1607
Ice Group, 33
Ice Mobility, 919
Ice Protection, 225
Ice Tech, 1009
Ice.Com, 1464
Icebreaker, 937
IceCure Medical, 340
icejam, 2063
Iceline/Darko, 2462
iCentera, 1474
iCentris, 1587
Iceotope, 2430
Icera, 713, 2188, 2653, 2665
Icertis, 561, 641, 978
Icertis Applied, 1213
iCetana, 3238
ICG Commerce, 851
Ichor Systems, 110, 782
Ici, 3250
ICi Digital, 2050
ICI Holding Company, 1494
iCims, 1761
IClean, 838
iClick, 957
iclick, 85
Icm, 2756
ICM Partners, 560
ICM Products Inc., 451
ICMS, 2358
Icom Cmt, 1731
Icompass, 2262
Icon, 183, 863
ICON Health & Fitness, 1493
Icon Identity Solutions, 1210
Icon Vapor, 1083
Icon Ventures, 3273
Icon.me, 1813
Icona, 2883
iConclude, 1666
Iconectiv, 782
Iconery, 121, 400, 562
Iconfinder, 3194
Iconic Group, 791
Iconic Labs, 1852
Iconic Therapeutics, 661, 1268
Iconix, 794
Iconixx, 227, 907
Iconoculture, 538, 1953
IconOvir, 1934
Icontact, 1949
iContact, 1334, 1888
Icontainers, 3214
IContracts, 655
iControl Networks, 457
Icopal, 1021
Icot, 263
Icovia, 311
ICPR Junior College, 62
Icq Holding, 2383
iCracked, 125
iCreate Software, 2840
ICREO Co. Ltd., 2339
iCrossing, 822, 1741
iCRTec, 1304
ICS, 2353
ICsense, 2358
ICurrent, 564
ICX Media, 881
Icynene, 790
iCYT, 979
iCyt, 1380

ID, 1335
ID Analytics, 1235, 1239, 1855
ID By DNA, 23
ID by DNA, 177
ID Entropy, 51
ID INCU, 3118
ID Quantique, 3059
ID Watchdog, 549
ID.me, 288, 796, 1534, 1635
ID5, 2288
ID90, 1808
ID90 Travel, 231
Idaciti, 1074
Idaho Pacific, 1169
Idanit, 2711
Idapted, 1604
IDbyDNA, 1616
IDC, 1707
Iddiction, 938
Idea, 627
IDEA AG, 2807
Idea AG, 3060
Idea Cellular, 1498
Idea Point, 332
Idea.me, 1521
ideaForge, 1511
IdeaFoundry, 3264
Ideal Binary, 2347
Ideal Crane, 1224
Ideal Image, 1092
Ideal Protein, 136
Ideal Spot, 546
Ideal Standard, 223
Ideal-Tridon, 989
Idealab, 504
IdealEstate, 8
Idealista, 136
Idealists, 625
Ideas, 1728
Ideas Revenue Organization, 1762
Ideaya Bioscience, 894
Ideaya Biosciences, 11
IDEC Pharmaceuticals, 1708
Ideeli, 568, 591, 1084, 1741, 1768
iDeeli, 1319
Idelic, 275, 411, 1385
Idelix Software, 983, 2091
Idemama, 2428
Idenix, 1268, 2504, 2681, 2998
IdentalSoft, 718
Identec Group, 1009
Identec Solutions, 2101
Identified, 381, 724, 1908
Identified Technologies, 275
Identifix/SRS, 1973
Identify, 2741
Identify Sotware, 2673
Identify3D, 246
Identilock, 490
Identity Engines, 950
Identity Group Holdings Corporation, 1210
Identity Mind, 252
Identity Software, 3128
Identive Group, 2970
Identropy, 1388
IdenTrust, 1561
IDERA, 962
Idera, 205
Idesta, 2854, 2854
Idetic, 1708
IDEV, 1502
Idev, 240
IDev Techologies, 1578
Idevices, 532
Idevio, 2610
Idex, 2854
Idexx, 1762

Idexx Laboratories, 748
IDG Capital Partners, 339
IDG Energy, 977
IDG Ventures India, 485
IDG Ventures SF, 3273
IDH, 2926
IDI, 1872
Idibon, 2969
Idinvest Partners, 485
Idiom, 1335
Idiom Technologies, 1674
IDIS, 1091, 2608
Idle Free, 1064
IDOC, 1192, 1576, 2324
iDoneThis, 1014, 1914
IDQ, 172
IDQ Holdings, 1493
IDreamSky, 1537
iDro, 395
IDS, 2890, 3229
IDS/Morshinkaya, 3086
Idun, 209
iDun, 1762
Idun Pharmaceuticals, 154, 1495, 1708, 1920, 2509
IDV Solutions, 1459
IDX, 45
IE CHP, 3126
IE-Engine, 1084
IEI Technologies., 2581
IEnergizer Limited, 406
iEntertainment Network, 1711
IEP Technologies, 1654
IEver, 1125
IEX, 263
IEX Group, 1784, 2126
If You Can, 89, 596
IF&P Foods, 445
if(we), 1122, 1187
Ifbyphone, 138, 1316, 1575, 1645, 1735
IfChange, 1125
Ifeelgoods, 1515, 1867
Ifesca, 2518
IFILM, 1706
iFire, 217
Iflix, 2681
iFLYTEK, 2927
IFM Therapeutics, 193
IfOnly, 14, 1527
Iforce, 2463
iForem, 808
IFOTEC, 2866
IFrameApps, 2660
iFreecomm, 1340
IFTTT, 125, 752, 1114, 1346, 1610
IGEM Therapeutics, 690
Igeneon, 2291, 2293, 2297
Igenica, 11, 1383
Igenica Biotherapeutics, 519
Igenu, 812
IGG, 925, 977
iglo Group, 3024
Igloo, 793, 1041, 2146
Igloo Education, 2958
Igloo Products, 45
Igloo Vision, 2958
IGM Specialties, 172
Igneous, 1162, 1537
Ignis Careers, 54
Ignis Innovation, 2186
Ignite Technologies, 205
Ignition, 36
Ignition Group, 1377
Ignition One, 1628
IgnitionOne, 21, 949, 1701
Ignyta, 517, 785
Ignyta Inc., 489

1312

Portfolio Companies Index

Igps, 1518
IGPS Logistics LLC, 228
Igrok, 830
IguanaFix, 1511
Iguazio, 604, 1928, 2216
IGuiders, 1051
iGuitar, 1588
IHaveU, 1125
iHaveU, 2841
IHAVEU.com, 3053
IHC, 838
IHC Merwede Group, 3200
iHealtHome, 1065
iHear, 139
iHear Medical, 1122
iHeartMedia, 1818
iHello, 957
IHQ, 2848
Ihr Partner Software, 2704
IHS Markit, 3262
IHSInc, 2762
iimak, 104
iItoo, 1194
iiWisdom, 1630
IJenko, 2890
iJento, 2963, 2978
iJet, 1150
iJET Intelligent Risk Systems, 2188
IJReview, 618
IkamvaYouth, 1374
iKang, 691
Ikano Communications, 928
Ikano Therapeutics, 711
Ikanos, 1924
Ikanos Communications, 1478, 1795
Ikaria, 11, 154, 190, 1160, 1300, 1493, 1918, 2007, 2410
Ikaros Solar, 3011
Ikaros Solar Fund, 3033
ikaSystems, 1498
IKEA, 1100, 2872
Iken, 2565
iKingdom, 2043
Ikivo, 2745
Iknaos, 1781
iKobo, 2188
Ikon Science, 862
Ikon Semiconductor, 2909
IKOS, 1855
Ikos, 275
IL & FS Investment Limited, 808
IL MAKIAGE, 1092
Il Mare, 1091
IL&FS, 263
IL&FS Transportation, 872
ILAC, 2200
ILC Dover, 248
iLearning Engines, 1172
Ilerasoft, 221
Ilesfay, 481
ILEX, 315
ILEX Oncology, 1777
ILFS Technologies, 485
ILIAS-Medical, 2815
iLight, 1766
iLight Technologies, 381
Ilink, 2841
iLink Global, 1061
iLinkMD, 1917
Ilkos Therapeutics, 2086
Illinois Central Corporation, 576
Illinois Neurospine Institute, 60
IllinoisVENTURES LLC, 3255
IlloSpear, 2324
Illuma Drive, 2136
Illumenix, 650
Illumeo, 361, 752

Illumigen Biosciences, 1399
Illumina, 154, 1395, 1608
Illuminate, 2334
Illuminate Education, 1005, 1140
Illumine Radiopharmaceuticals, 1581
Illumingen, 85
IlluminOss, 704, 1149, 1414
Illuminoss, 1695, 1734, 2930
Illuminoss Medical, 1297
Illumio, 108, 125, 820
Illumitex, 138, 145, 213, 830, 985, 1776
Illumix, 1125, 1186
Illumobile, 246
Illusense, 2270
Illusive, 1001, 1158
Illusive Networks, 488
illusive networks, 485
Illustra, 1257, 1855
ILMO Products, 60
Ilos, 1179
iloxx GmbH, 3128
ILP, 170
ILSC Education Group, 1506
Ilum-A-Lite, 2604
Ilumin, 22
iLumin Corporation, 2643
iLumin Software, 318
Ilumno, 1005
ILX Holdings, 1577
ILX Holdings II, 1577
Ilypsa, 11, 1898
Im In, 131
im3D Clinic South, 3043
iM3dical, 3039
iM3MDICAL, 3022
IMA, 2437
Ima Engineering, 2864
ImaCor, 667
Image API, 1234
Image Cafe, 162
Image Centre, 2655
Image Metrics, 1239, 3083
Image Searcher, 1786
Image Skincare, 1231
Image Vision Labs, 1953
Image Ware Systems, 858
Image-Guided Neurologics, 1748
ImageBrief, 863
ImageFIRST, 371
Imagenet, 377
ImageQuix, 92
Imagetalk Oy, 2864
ImageVision, 1032
ImageX, 85
Imagimed, 1425
ImaginAb, 1350
Imaginatik Limited, 2751
Imagine, 680, 2568
Imagine Air, 1309
Imagine Communications, 2557, 2653
Imagine Health, 941
Imagine K12, 50
Imagine Learning, 1707
Imagine Nation, 2935
Imagine Technology Group, 842
ImagineAir, 1305
Imagineer Systems, 3098
Imaginetics, 445, 1075
Imagitas (TMSI-Targeted Marketing Solutions), 1955
Imago BioSciences, 113, 785
Imalux, 642, 1547
Imandra, 2398
Imanis Data Inc., 1009
Imara, 240
iMark, 205
iMarketing Solutions Group, 2039

Imaweb, 1499
Imax, 2067
IMAX Corp., 494
Imbellus, 1393, 1890
Imbera, 3004
Imbera Electronics, 2621
Imbria Pharmaceuticals, 1522
Imbruvica, 73
IMC Limited, 1957
IMCD, 223, 2370
IMCO, 1374
IMCO Technologies, 1743
IMCS Group, 450
IMDS, 172
Imedex, 1932
Imedia, 3128
iMedX, 3202
iMedX Holdings, 1560
ImeeGolf, 2347
Imeem, 1257
imeem, 57
Imergy, 596
IMERGY Power Systems, 1788
IMG, 20
IMG Midstream, 335
Imge, 618
Imgnation, 310
Imgur, 125, 1608
IMI AG, 2776
IMI Exchange, 1361
IMI Express, 836
IMI Intelligent Medical Implants AG, 3037
IMImobile, 744, 3061, 3122
IMinent, 2890
Imiplex, 269
Imix, 3140
imIX, 1597
IML, 1635
iML, 1750
Imlek Group, 3086
IMlogic, 564, 1084
Imm, 2706
Immaculate Baking Co., 1117, 1668
Immatics, 2466, 2788
Immedia, 2963
Immedia Semiconductor, 226
Immediately, 1887
Immediatelyapp.com, 1959
Immersed, 1009
Immersive Media, 2257
Immersive Media Tactical Solutions, 408
Immersv, 773, 795
Immgenics, 2998
Immidio, 3119
Immobilienscout24, 3223
Immortals, 562, 1816
Immotor, 827
Immucor, 1837
Immucor Inc., 1905
Immudicon, 623
Immulogic, 263
Immune Cellular, 183
Immune Design, 94, 519, 1492, 1621
Immune Photonics, 570
Immune Targeting Systems, 2807
Immune Works, 659
Immunet, 1790
Immunetrics, 1003, 1102, 1452
Immunix, 810
Immuno Gum, 1786
Immuno Photonics, 270
ImmunoBiology, 2454, 2589, 3098, 3234
Immunogen, 1271
Immunome, 269, 1581
Immunomedics, 764
Immunomic Therapeutics, 1065, 1120
Immunoprecise, 2061

1313

Portfolio Companies Index

Immunovaccine, 2148
Immunovaccine Inc., 2086
Immunovalent Therapeutics, 875
Immunservice, 2815
ImmusanT, 1271
Immuta, 288, 537, 631
IMN, 352, 1335
IMO, 178
iMobileMagic, 3022
Imobox, 2429
iModules, 1109
IMoney, 721
Imonomi, 2637
iMove, 983, 1394
Impact, 36, 1118, 1499
Impact Applications, 3098
Impact Biosystems, 849
Impact Confections, 331
Impact Economics, 1285
Impact Fire Services, 376
Impact Group, 478
Impact HQ, 263
Impact Radius, 1537
Impact Technologies, 1378
ImpactGames, 1003
Impacto, 2617
ImpactXoft, 313
Imparto Software, 627
Impath, 209
Impath Networks, 2051, 2197
ImpathIQ, 512
Impaxx, 202
ImpediMed, 3129
Impel Microchip, 2408
Impel NeuroPharma, 1346, 1943
Impel Neuropharma, 11, 85
Impella Cardiosystems, 2739
Imperative Energy, 2287
Imperfect, 756
Imperfect Produce, 545, 1186, 1666
Imperial Machining, 1025
Imperial Plastics Inc., 847
Imperium Renewables, 1788
Impermium, 787, 1254
Impero, 1021
Imperva, 182
iMPERVA, 1213, 1898
Imperva Bot Management, 1285
Impeto Medical, 3104
Impinj, 154, 885, 1245, 1464, 1893
Impinq, 1924
Implandata Opthalmic Products, 2815
Implanet, 3104
Implantable Provider Group, 386
Implex Corporation, 1275
Impli, 627
Implus, 15, 170, 257
Imply, 125, 1073
Impopharma, 1918, 2125
Import.io, 108
Impossible, 514
Impossible Aerospace, 648
Impossible Foods, 108, 894, 1073
Impossible Software, 2595
ImpreMedia, 496
impreMedia, 902
Impress, 2369
Impression-Show, 2838
ImpressPages, 3040
Imprimed, 1426
Imprint Energy, 1616
Imprivata, 1464
Improbable, 125, 537
Improveline, 2372
Impulse Monitoring, 1868
Impulse Monitoring Inc., 178
IMRSV, 680, 1521

IMS, 597, 2051
IMS Health, 1113, 2371
Ims Health, 1837
IMScouting, 2344
IMSRV, 1739
Imstem Biotechnology, 532
IMSWorkX, 705
Imt, 1629
Imtex, 2189
Imubit, 856
imusic-school, 3104
IMV, 2593
Imvelo Forests, 838
IMVision, 2410
IMVU, 342
IMX, 3118
In Addition, 649
In Crowd, 2978
In Go, 1074
In Go Money, 510
In The Swim, 197
In The Swim Inc., 777
In-Q-Tel, 3260, 3263
In.vision Research, 1748
In2itive Bsuiness Solutions LLC, 1057
Inadco, 1898
Inapac, 2427
Inapac Technologies, 1354
Inaplex, 3098
Inari, 748, 1930
Inasoft, 457
Inboard, 1890
InboundWriter, 766
Inbox, 421, 545
INC 500 Companies, 34
INC Research, 56, 212
INCA, 2340
InCarda Therapeutics Inc., 183
InClassToday, 1530
inCode Telecom, 759
inCode Telecom Group, 163
InComm, 227, 1957
InContext Solutions, 107, 254, 965, 1009, 1459
InCrowd, 1104
InCube Ventures, 1128
Indalo Therapeutics, 270
Indco, 1872
INDEECO, 60
Indeed, 1884
Indegy, 48, 182
InDemand Interpreting, 921
Independa, 1222, 1237
Independa Inc., 489
Independence, 2848
Independence Care System, 1422
Independent Bank, 638
Independent Commercial, 2700
Independent Imaging, 1609
Independent Living Solutions, 1361
Independent Living Systems, 1168
Independent Network Television Holdings, 2456
InDex, 2553
Index IQ, 796
Index Stock Imagery, 1275
Indextank, 31, 234, 787
Indexus Biomedical, 738
Indi, 225, 1014, 2137
Indi Molecular, 183
Indi Semiconductor, 277
India Resources Limited, 1551
Indiagames, 57
IndiaHomes, 2809
Indialdeas.com, 1778
Indiamart.com, 1009
Indian Dreams, 2774
Indian Energy Exchange, 1125
indian Energy Exchange, 838

Indiana Business Bank, 1965
Indiana Limestone Company, 2008
IndiaProperty.com, 389, 1187
Indicee, 2144
INDICO, 1593
Indico, 1
Indico.co, 316
Indie Plate, 1000
Indie Semiconductor, 207
IndieGoGo, 1227, 1566
Indiegogo, 246, 527, 724, 1005, 1006, 1079, 1969, 2272
Indigenous Media, 59
Indigo, 748, 2051, 2154
Indigo Agriculture, 19
Indigo Biosciences, 1120
Indigo Biosystems, 703
Indigo Natural Resources LLC, 1853
Indigo Pipelines, 3095
Indigo Vision, 3095
InDinero, 387
inDinero, 232, 1058
Indio, 527, 771, 1203, 1219
Individual.com, 263
Indix, 209, 2398
IndMusic, 1816
Indo-European Foods, 445, 1343
Indochino, 1162, 2272
Indoo.rs, 3156
Indoor Atlas, 1244
Indoor Direct, 1773
IndoStar Capital Finance, 1630
IndoTraq, 1244
Indow Windows, 1467, 3246
Indulge Desserts, 196
Indus, 1724
Indusind Bank, 819
Industrial Access, 2462
Industrial Accoustics Company, 63
Industrial Air Tool, 2021
Industrial Bank Co. Ltd, 2585, 2586
Industrial Ceramic Solutions, 1261
Industrial Defender, 2307
Industrial Lighting Products, 1438
Industrial Magnetics, 1343, 1573
Industrial Media, 560
Industrial Piping, 279, 1729
Industrial Safety Technologies, 1192
Industrial Securities Co. Ltd, 2585
Industrial Securities Co. LtdChina Merchants Secur, 2586
Industrial Service Solutions, 654
Industrial Toys, 1483
Industrial Valley Title, 836
Industrial Water Treatment Solutions, 1473
Industrias Y Fundiciones Iglesias, 2976
Industrical Container Services, 202
Industrios Software, 2051
Industrious, 728
Industry Partners: Deloitte, 3262
Industry Weapon, 1003, 1451
INE, 1499
INEA, 1957
Ineda Systems, 485, 1511
Inest, 1385
iNest, 810, 1380
iNet Interactive, 381
INetU Holdings, 364
inexio Informationstechnologie und Telekommunikati, 3058
INF Tech Enterprises, 1839
Infacare, 193
InfaCare Pharmaceutical, 922
inFakt, 3035
Infantium, 1065
Infarm, 2469
Inficomm, 468

Portfolio Companies Index

Infilaw, 1745
InfiLaw System, 20
Infiltrator Systems, 851, 1460
Infiltrator Systems Inc., 1018
Infinate Z, 983
Infinera, 145, 281, 538, 972, 1762, 1886, 1949
Infineta, 1335
Infinia ML, 419
Infinian Corp, 1464
Infinicon, 564
Infinio, 938
InfiniRoute Networks, 186, 950
Infinit, 2357
Infinite, 447
Infinite Analytics, 1486
Infinite Electronics Inc., 823
Infinite English, 826
Infinite Graphics, 3268
Infinite Power Solutions, 145, 540, 983, 1464
Infinite Road, 3263
Infinite Uptime, 623, 1426
Infinity, 73
Infinity Broadcasting Corporation, 576
Infinity CCS, 2958
Infinity Finance Ltd., 2779
Infinity Laser Centers, 62
Infinity Natural Resources, 1326, 1328
Infinity Pharmaceuticals, 1495
Infinity Quick, 2130, 2131
Infitel, 2369
Infitel International N.V., 2664
Inflammatix Inc., 1073
InflaRX, 2518
InflaRx, 1522
Inflazome, 1147, 1350
Inflection, 548, 1184, 1762
Inflection Energy, 335
Inflow, 2847
inflow Control, 3090
Inflow Group, 902
Inflow Inc., 1727
Influe, 2756
Influence Health, 1685
Influitive, 31, 536, 742, 980, 1125, 1549, 2107, 2126, 2130, 2131, 2228
Influxdata, 238
InfluxDB, 1187
Info Pro Solutions, 3032
Info Talk, 2881
Info Trust, 213
Infoaxe, 116, 1093
Infobase, 448, 1929
InfoBionic, 350, 704, 1605, 1786
Infobionic, 1104
Infobjects, 2726
Infoblox, 634, 759, 1348, 1380, 1657, 1798, 1855
Infobright, 2146
InfoChimp, 724
Infocrossing, 870
InfoDif, 2428
Infodustry, 2598
Infoether, 993
InfoGear Technology, 857
InfoGenesis, 2689
InfoGin, 538
Infogix, 931
Infoglide Software, 1013
Infogr.am, 3035
Infogroup, 435, 1169
InfoHighway, 1140
Infokom Elektrindo, 3052
InfoLibria, 317
InfoLogix, 928
Infomark, 3118
Infomart International, 1241
Infomedics, 1335

Infomove, 85
Infonaut, 2051
Infoniqa, 2878
Infopaginas Inc., 62
Infopress, 2478
Infor, 843
Infor Global Solutions, 1754
InfoReady Corporation, 743
Inform Diagnostics, 212
Informatica, 241, 1125, 1610
Information Builders, 336
Informative, 1008, 3221
Informed DNA, 1349, 2074
InformedDNA, 3251
Informu, 1509
InfoScout, 224
InfoSec, 2581
Infosec, 2989
Infosum, 1890
InfoTalk Corporation, 2073
Infotrieve, 405, 1852
Infoucs Health Ltd, 2885
InfoUSA, 194
InfoVista S.A., 1817
Infra, 1608, 2122
Infra Group/Verbraeken, 3222
Infracommerce, 756
Infrafone, 2610
Inframetrics, 523
Infrant, 2427
InfraReDx, 1619
InfraScale, 549
Infrascale, 419
InfraScan, 269
Infrasoft, 1294
Infrasoft Technologies, 2481
Infrasonics, 1708
Infrastructure and Industrial Constructors USA, 804
Infrastructure Networks, 98
InfraTrac, 3083
Infusio, 2472
Infusion Biosciences, 1845
Infusion Soft, 175, 1074
Infusionsoft, 1247, 1679
Infusystem, 1971
Infutor, 1346, 2074
ING Vysya Bank, 2590, 2591
InGameAd, 3112
Ingemas, 2480
Ingenero, 2609
Ingenica, 1814
Ingenio, 92, 609, 1008
Ingenious Med, 178, 274, 551, 1056, 1412
Ingenuity, 1561
Ingenuity Systems, 240, 990
Ingenuityprep, 1315
InGo, 386
Ingo Money, 1240
Ingrain, 2691
Ingresse, 1511
Ingrian, 936
INgrooves, 68
Ingulex, 1383
Inhabit IQ, 1499
Inhalon Biopharma, 1616
Inhance Media Audiolife, 1786
Inhance Technologies, 172, 202
InheritedHealth, 1103
InHerSight, 1259
Inhibitex, 1399
Inhibox, 2883
InhibRx, 1522
Inhibrx LLC, 489
INI Farms, 2305, 3190
ini3, 3118
Ininal, 2428

Inion, 2553
Inion Ltd., 2807
Inipharm, 11
InishTech, 2513, 2909
Init Innovation, 3060
Init Live, 2276
Init.ai, 308
Initech, 3159
Initiate, 1401, 1618
Initiate Systems, 1674
Injae Tongil Village Co., 585
Injured Workers Pharmacy, 45, 197, 1493
Ink, 232, 586
Inka Oy, 2957
Inkbox, 1186, 2130, 2131
Inkd, 1644
Inked, 259, 274, 1412
Inked Brands, 901
Inkine Pharmaceutical Company, 1395
Inkling, 972, 1058, 1657, 1798
InkSpin1, 2382
Inland American Real Estate Trust Inc., 874
Inlet Medical, 1117
Inlet Technologies, 540, 1784
InLight Communications, 2901
Inlustra, 1786
Inlustra Technologies, 1917
InMage, 116
Inman, 2050
Inman Investment Management, 3273
Inmar, 1300, 2199
Inmark, 1507
Inmark Services, 34
Inmarsat, 136
INMATEC Technologies GmbH, 2677
inMediata, 924
InMobi, 1464, 1669
inmobly, 1556
Inmotion Entertainment Group, 357
Inn Road, 1588
InnaMed, 623
InnaPhase, 1140
Innara Health, 1380
Innate Pharma, 1518, 2457
Inncercool Therapies, 1788
Inner City Broadcasting, 1410
Inner City Media Corporation, 902
Inner Loop Capital, 3260
Inner Wireless, 1244
Inneractive, 2717
InnerChange, 559
iNNERHOST, 1727
Innerpac, 1460
Innerpass, 1737
InnerProduct Partners, 1161
InnerPulse, 179
Innerspace, 2024
Innerstave, 943
Innervate, 776
InnerVision Medical Technologies, 2043
InnerWireless, 443, 1021, 1561
Innes, 2300
InNetwork, 2148
Innis & Gunn, 1092
Inno Light, 579
InnoCentive, 1128
Innocentive, 983, 1723
Innochip Technology, 2848
Innocoli, 1700
InnoCOMM Wireless, 766
Innocor, 1755
Innocrin, 1013, 1128
Innocrin Pharmaceuticals, 184
Innocutis, 227
InnoCyte, 2815
Innofact, 2820
Innofact AG, 2829

Portfolio Companies Index

Innofidei, 1537
Innofidei Corporation, 2965
InnoGraft, 1608
Innography, 205
innogreen, 2927
Innolight, 1125
Innolume, 145
Innolume GmbH, 3037
InnoMake, 1511
Innometrix, 999, 1190
InnoMotix, 2815
InnoPad, 713, 1915
InnoPath, 1244, 1608, 3205
InnoPath Software, 1241, 1908
InnoPharma, 190, 1820
Innorex Technologies, 3136
InnoSkel, 1934
Innospark Ventures, 3263
Innostream, 2824
InnoTech, 767
Innotech Solar, 3004
Innotrac, 1745
Innouvo, 3263
Innov-X Systems, 440
Innova, 35, 755, 1610
Innova B2B Logistics, 2850
Innova Card, 2866
Innova Corporation, 1399
Innova Dynamics, 1561
Innova Light, 2623
Innovaccer, 1125
InnovAge, 1973
Innovalight, 154, 186, 1857
Innovari, 1908
Innovasic, 861
Innovasic Semiconductor, 1903
Innovate MR, 2074
Innovatel, 495
Innovatia Medical Systems, 3251
Innovatient, 1101
Innovatient Solutions, 679
Innovation, 755
Innovation Capital, 990
Innovation Works, 3264
Innovative, 962, 973, 1045
Innovative Aftermarket Systems, 823
Innovative Biosensors, 1298
Innovative Building Systems, 931
Innovative Chemical Products, 1169
Innovative Food Processors, 119
Innovative Health, 4
Innovative Health Products, 530
Innovative Micro Technologies, 68
Innovative Micro Technology, 1237
Innovative Pressure Technologies, 214
Innovative Robotics, 810, 1183
Innovative Silicon, 205
Innovative Solutions & Support, 51, 55
Innovative Supply Solutions, 269
Innovative Technology, 1608
Innovectra, 1150
Innovectra Corporation, 2188
Innoveer Solutions, 523
Innovent Biologics, 711
Innovent Systems, 1920
Innovest, 302
Innovex, 106
Innovia, 1608
Innovid, 485
Innovion, 1287
Innovis, 1327
InnoVision Imagine Laboratory, 738
Innovium, 877, 1511
Innoviz, 117, 2288
Innovotech Inc., 2061
Innoz, 3100
Innozen, 1786

innRoad, 291, 1305
Inocucor Technologies, 2087
Inogen, 39, 209, 3006
Inopen, 3202
Inotec AMD, 3019
Inotek, 949, 1561, 2961
Inotek Pharmaceuticals, 928
Inova Labs, 1098
Inova Payroll, 461
Inovateus Solar, 1229
iNovia Capital, 2028
Inovis, 1674
Inovise Medical Inc, 3153
Inovision, 1132
Inovus Solar, 1462
Inovys Corporation, 1408
Inozyme Pharma, 1147
Inpact, 2472
Inpaq Technology, 2594
Inpensa, 1581
InPhase, 1678
InPhenix, 1931
Inpher, 320, 564
Inphi Corp., 1091, 1781, 2448
Inphi Corporation, 2917
InPhonic, 540
Inplat, 3141
inPlug, 1511
inPowered, 1561, 2228
Inpria, 1009, 1384
Inpulse, 2321
InQ, 957
InQuira, 1762, 2073
INRange Management Systems, 296
INRange Systems, 454, 947, 1120
InReach, 1785
InRentive, 1181
INRFOOD, 954
INRIX, 127, 224, 1918
Inrix, 200, 1009
INS, 1657
INS SA, 2819
Insales, 2336
Inscentinel, 2958
Insception Biosciences, 2188
Insception Lifebank, 2039
Inscope, 659
Inscopix, 108, 752
Inscribe, 771
Inscripta, 764, 1918
Inseal Medical, 1464
Inseec, 2842
Insense, 3098
Inserm Transfert Initiative, 2521
Insert Therapeutics, 374
Inside Contactless, 2372
Inside Higher Ed, 60, 1506
Inside Real Estate, 8
Inside Secure, 1327
Inside Tracker, 1175
Inside-Secure, 3225
Inside.Com, 1657
Insidehack, 1533
InsidePacket, 648
Insider Technologies, 3234
InsideSales.com, 1610, 2018
Insidesales.com, 689, 1898
InsideSherpa, 798
InsideTrack, 1525
InsideView, 666, 773, 1543, 1728, 1731
Insieve, 3010
Insighly, 1716
Insight, 209
Insight 2 Design, 1609
Insight Communications, 560
Insight Engines, 564
InSight Eye Care, 381

Insight Global, 160, 377
Insight Global Inc., 917
InSight Health Services Corp. Inc., 899
Insight Health Solutions, 1695
InSight Management, 507
InSight Mobile Data, 28
Insight Plus, 2637
Insight Squared, 263, 610, 1322
Insight Technologies Network Academy, 2700
Insight2Profit, 611
Insightera, 1125
insightexpress, 2762
InsightGlobal, 1113
Insightly, 666
Insightpool, 1784
Insightra Medical, 3088
InsightRX, 521
InsightSquared, 37, 536, 1610
Insignia Energy, 2062
Insignia Systems, 3268
Insikt, 31, 744
Insilico Medicine, 1703
Insilixa, 2969
InSite Medical Technologies, 667
InSite One, 186
Insite Wireless Group, 429
Insited, 2629
Insitro, 125, 764
insitro, 894
Insitu, 85
Insitu Group, 1644
InSleep Technologies, 1993
Insmed, 764, 1510, 2739
Insmed Inc., 1013
InSoft, 55
Insolu, 3251
InSound Medical, 374
Insound Medical, 139
Insource Contract Services, 557, 1473
InSpa, 85, 596
inSparq, 1635
Inspection Oilfield Services, 1424
Inspectorio, 1179
Insperity, 1772, 3257
Inspherion, 1051
InspiraFarms, 2430
Inspirato, 35, 582, 742, 1006, 1079, 1235
Inspire, 137, 309, 562, 1363
Inspire Brands, 1580
Inspire Living, 999
Inspire Medical Systems, 1383, 1774, 1804, 1898
Inspire Pharmaceuticals, 1013
Inspired Group Ltd, 2353
Inspired Teaching Demonstration School, 1315
Inspiron Logistics, 1051
Inspo Network, 1501
Inspur-Cisco Networking Technology, 485
Insta Health Solutions, 1017
Instabank, 2931
Instabase, 125, 877
Instabridge, 2469
Instacart, 125, 389, 520, 805, 1073, 1079, 1657, 1763, 2011, 2154
instacart, 1665
InStadium, 80, 947, 1804
Instadium, 1609
InstaEDU, 545, 1698
Instagift, 776
Instagram, 125, 234, 251, 268, 1657, 1823
Installation Made Easy, 1580
Installed Building Products, 1138
Installs Inc., 408
InstaMed, 181, 419, 1329, 1388
Instamotor, 708, 998
Instana, 3152
Instant, 1076, 2956
Instant Web, 1493

Portfolio Companies Index

Instantis, 1042, 1898
Instantly, 794
Instapage, 1255
Instaread, 1426, 1770
Instart, 125
Instart Logic, 780, 1762, 1798
Instartlogic, 824, 1079
Instavest, 1330
Instawares, 227
Instawork, 626
Instill, 990, 1674
Instill Corporation, 457
Instinctiv, 434, 1588
Instinctive, 680
Institute For Integrative Nutrition, 1345
Institute of Finance & Management, 868
Institutional Shareholder Services, 823, 1933, 2689
Institutional Venture Partners, 3273
Instituto Cidade Democratica, 1374
Instnt, 195, 1557
Instore, 608, 1154
InStore Finance, 1051
InStream, 536
InStream Media, 1737
Instructables, 234, 1359
Instructure, 689, 830, 1832, 1886
Instrument Development Corporation, 1252
Instrument Sales and Service, 1424
Instrumental, 648, 742
Instylla, 178
Insulcheck, 2347
Insulet Corp., 139
Insurance Auto Auctions, 714, 1252
Insurance Auto Auctions Inc., 1905
Insurance Claims Management, 1576
Insurance Technologies, 8
Insurance Technologies Corporation, 28
Insurance.com, 915, 1741
Insuranceforchildren.ca, 2123
Insurdata, 2398
InsureCert Systems, 2257
Insureon, 38
Insurity, 823, 1971
Insurrection Media, 1816
Insymphony, 267
Insyncro, 2614
Intacct, 263, 548, 666, 1028, 1728, 1762
Intacct Corporation, 1042, 1674
Intact Medical Corps., 22
Intact Vascular, 1510
Intalio, 1418, 2005
Intamac, 2287, 3234
Intana Bioscience, 2815
InTANK, 1577
Intapp, 862
Intarcia, 764, 1518, 1522
Intarcia Therapeutics, 94, 240, 872, 990, 1297
Intec, 2762
Intec Pharma, 3235
Intec Telecom Systems, 2700
InTech Aerospace, 216
Intechra, 668, 1691
Intecrowd, 754
INTEG Process Group, 1003
Integen, 116
IntegenX, 561, 622, 949, 983, 1098, 1517
Intego, 263
Integra, 20
Integra Life Sciences, 1496, 1920
Integra Securities, 2481
Integracare, 2218
Integragen, 2346, 2842, 2867
Integral, 957, 1255, 1428
Integral Access, 538
Integral Ad Science, 37, 541, 561, 1488
Integral Development, 56

Integral Development Corporation, 2188
Integral Energy Management, 1897
Integral Wave, 1561
Integrant Technologies, 1091, 2798
Integrate, 520, 770, 779
Integrate.ai, 2126, 2217
Integrated Advantage Group, 988
Integrated Aerospace Manufacturing, 612
Integrated Biosystems, 1251
Integrated Cable Assembly Holdings, 854
Integrated Defense Technologies, 1927
Integrated Dental Holdings, 2935
Integrated Diagnostic Centers, 809
Integrated Energy Services, 189
Integrated Global Services, 989
Integrated Healthcare Strategies, 377
Integrated Materials Incorporated, 1093
Integrated Packaging Group, 2805
Integrated Photovoltaics, 1093
Integrated Polymer Solutions, 989
Integrated Portfolio Management Services, 1748
Integrated Power Services, 1368
Integrated Silicon Systems, 1013
Integrated Spatial Information Solutions, 1839
Integrated Systems Engineering, 1949
Integrated Turf Solutions, 1343
Integrated Vascular Systems, 1898
Integration Management, 2613
Integration Technologies, 62
Integrex, 755
Integri Chain, 51
IntegriChain, 28, 1329
IntegriCo Composites, 459
Integrien, 504
Integriertes Resource Management, 2774
Integris Software, 48, 182, 1162
Integrity, 962
Integrity Marketing Group, 917
Integrity Services, 409
Integro, 1368
Intel, 840
Intel Sports, 2094
Intela Global Limited, 2498
Intelenet, 280
IntelePeer, 186, 652, 928, 1908
Intelerad, 267
Intelesens, 2601
Intelex, 912, 1045
Intelipost, 3047
InteliSecure, 793
Intelisum, 1886
Intelius, 931
Intelivote Systems, 2178
Intelizon Energy, 3202
Intellasset, 3173
Intelle Innovations, 2957
Intellectual Technology, 377
Intellectual Ventures, 457, 1678
Intellefex, 2005
Intelleflex, 915, 1257, 1304, 1649
IntelleGrow, 1374
Intellia Therapeutics, 193, 710
Intellibridge, 957
Intellicare, 1535
Intellicare America, 440
IntelliCare america Inc., 573
IntelliCyt, 1299, 1490, 1926
Intelliden, 928
Intelliflux, 300
Intelligence Controls, 1337
Intelligent Beauty, 928
Intelligent Bio-Systems, 1347
Intelligent Clearing Network, 642, 1101
Intelligent Energy, 3126
Intelligent Epitaxy Technology, 1183
Intelligent Flying Machines, 623
Intelligent InSites, 175

Intelligent ION, 85
Intelligent Markets, 2005
Intelligent Medical Devices, 1917
Intelligent Mobile Support, 1051, 1451, 1556
Intelligent Office, 3234
Intelligent Reasoning Systems, 154
Intelligent Retinal Imaging Systems, 227
Intelligent Soil Recycling, 2180
IntelligentReach, 3095
Intelligrated, 886, 1731, 3024
Intellihot, 403
Intellihot Green Technologies, 987
Intellijoin, 2074
Intellijoint, 2181
Intellikine, 1898
Intelliment Security, 3099
Intellimize, 944, 945, 1426
Intellinet, 656
Intellinote, 881
Intellio Therapeutics, 764
Intelliquest, 205
Intellirod Spine, 1051
Intelliseek, 983
Intellispace, 189
Intellispark, 888
Intelliteach, 364, 1343
IntelliView Technologies, 2043
IntelliVision, 252, 1017
Intellivote Systems, 2197
Intelliworks, 1348, 2188
Intellus Learning, 1554
Intelocate, 2132
Intelomed, 1452
IntelRa, 3118
Intelsat, 684, 1160, 1685
Intelsat Holdings, 3192
Intelsoft Technologies, 85
Intelyt, 93
Intematix, 564, 610, 794
INTENIUM, 2985
Intenium GmbH, 2664
Intense, 2653, 2665
Intense Photonics, 2328
Intent, 1600
Intent Media, 1005, 1184, 1537
Intent Technologies, 3229
Inter Ana, 1158
Inter Co., 2898
inter-touch, 3159
Interact Public Safety Systems, 241
Interact.io, 3099
InterAct911, 1683
Interaction Laboratories, 1603
Interactions, 520, 1339, 1674, 1675, 1701, 1888
Interactive Advisory Software, 1790, 1865
Interactive Data, 1957
Interactive Health, 790
Interactive Investor, 2963
Interactive Investor International, 1496
Interactive Media Holdings, 1608
Interactive Supercomputing, 748
Interactive Television, 1737
Interagon, 2361
Interana, 108, 238
Interaptix, 2122
Interational Equipment Solutions, 1089
Interative Retail Management Inc., 589
Interative.ai, 1142
Interaxon, 2063, 2822
InterBay Technologies, 1174
Interbest, 3222
Interbest Holding B.V., 2371
Intercasting Corporation, 1178
Intercell, 2998
Intercell AG, 2776, 3128
Intercept, 73, 1383
Intercept Technology, 2518

1317

Portfolio Companies Index

InterChina Network Software, 3053
interCloud, 3199
Intercom, 894, 1079, 1698
Interconnect Devices, 1234
Intercos, 1092
Intercus, 2518
InterDent, 931
Interdent, 1493
Interface, 1794
Interface Biologics, 2081
Interface Biosciences, 1426
Interface Security Systems, 336
Interface Solutions, 1990
Interfolio, 288, 1005
Intergraph, 927, 1045, 1837
Intergraph Corp., 1905
Intergrasco, 2361
Interior Define, 728, 863, 1483
Interior Heavy Equipment Operator School, 2138
Interior Logic Group, 1138, 1270
Interior Specialists, 1090
Interior Specialists Inc., 874
Interlace Medical, 137
Interlacken Capital, 1294
Interland, 318
Interleukin Genetics, 240, 949
Interlinq Software, 755
Interlogix, 1145
Interloop, 849
Interlude, 1009
Interluxe Holdings, 1108
Intermad, 2914
Intermarine, 1300
Intermatix, 1478
Intermed, 2815
Intermedia, 1160, 1327
Intermedia.net, 1360
Intermedix, 1818
Intermex Holdings, 1133
InterModal Data, 1076
InterMolecular, 1898
Intermolecular, 1537
InterMune, 94
InterMune Pharmaceuticals, 1619
Intern, 1832
Internap, 597, 857, 1255, 1640
International, 1294, 2547
International Aerospace Coatings, 1906
International Asset Systems, 1957
International Budget Partnership, 1374
International Car Wash Group, 1580
International Components, 1731
International Decision Systems, 1765
International Development, 1424
International Education Corporation, 253
International Fitness Holdings, 2267
International Logging, 1577
International Market Centers, 223
International Meal Company Holdings SA, 62
International Media Group, 1771
International Media Partners, 1929
International Medical Group, 1839
International Mortgage Bank, 3224
International Silver, 496
International Telecommunication Data Systems, 532
International Test Technologies, 2696
International Textile Group, 502
Internationella Engelska Skolan, 1778
InterNations, 2432, 2820, 2829
Internet Auction, 1091
Internet B, 1086
Internet Brands, 927, 1045, 1537
Internet Broadcasting, 1728
Internet Is Fun, 2344
Internet Number Corporation, 1706
Internet Photonics, 1304, 1795

Internet Profiles, 1852
Internet Secure, 2051
Internet Sports Marketing, 2700
InternetCorp, 2301
Internetwork AG/Q Inc, 2673
Internext, 3199
Interntional Coffee Group, 461
InterOptic, 1483
Interoute Communications, 560
Interpace Biosciences, 4
Interperse, 1408
Interplay, 2660
Interplay Learning, 1672
Interrad Medical, 1804
InterResolve, 2469
Interroll, 2913
InterSAN, 1137
Intersan, 593
Intersec, 485
Intersect, 1502
Intersect ENT, 1449
Intersect Enterprises, 1898
Intersect Labs, 798
Intersent Ent., 73
Interset, 133
Intership, 1167
Intersil, 263
InterSpec, 1165
Intersperse, 504
Interstate, 843
Interstate Hotels & Resorts, 1085
Interstate Soutwest, 228
InterSwitch Limited, 2337
InterTrust, 2005
Intertug, 585
InterVene, 1101
Intervene, 545
Intervention Insights, 254, 477, 946
Interventional Imaging Inc., 423
Interventional Spine, 178
Interventional Spine Inc., 272
Interventional Technologies, 1762
InterVideo Corp., 950
Interviewed, 863, 1330
Interviewing.io, 1058, 1760
InterVisions Systems, 963
InterWave, 942
Interwell, 2722
InterWest Partners, 3273
Interwise, 928, 2073, 2772, 3115
Interwoven, 352, 759, 1042
InterWrap, 1507
InterXion, 990
Interxion, 226, 1600
Intesource, 861
Intezer, 1009, 1614
Intezyne, 269
inthinc, 464
Intigua, 438
Intility, 3004
Intimate Bridge 2 Conception, 1003
Intime Software, 2673
Intineris, 3033
Intio, 748
Intiva, 1194
Intiva Biopharma, 1194
Into Networks, 1608
INTO University Partnerships, 1109
IntoNow, 1537
IntoPIX, 3216
inTouch, 1285
InTouch Health, 254, 809
Intown Golf Club, 191
Intoxalock, 1973
Intra Links, 858
Intra-Cellular Therapies, 1329, 1422
Intradiem, 1045, 1575, 2074

Intradigm Corporation, 1128
Intrado, 1042
Intrafusion Holding Corporation, 1192
IntraLase, 652, 1923
Intralign, 97
Intralink Concept Sdn Bhd, 3155
IntraLinks, 1410, 1561, 1778
Intralinks, 22
Intranets.Com, 1949
Intransa, 1561, 1898
IntraOp Medical Corporation, 1094
IntraPac, 2200, 2201
IntraPace, 984
Intrapace, 130
IntraPoint, 993
Intraprise Health, 921
Intratech Medical, 3231
Intravascular Imaging Inc., 350
Intrepid, 3251
Intrepid Learning, 796
Intrepid Learning Solutions, 1250
Intresco, 2952
Intrexon, 517, 1815
Intricately, 1760
Intrinergy, 1273
Intrinsa, 1478
Intrinsic, 742, 1518, 2760
Intrinsic Graphics, 1706
Intrinsic ID, 3042
Intrinsic Therapeutics, 872, 1297
Intrinsiq Materials, 434
Intrinsity, 55
IntroFly, 1618
Introhive, 1499, 1610, 2063, 2192
Intrommune, 1581
Intronis, 1381
Introspective Systems, 1164
IntruGuard, 2844
IntruVert Networks, 1855
INTTRA, 21
Intucell, 263
Intuit, 200
Intuition Robotics, 1614, 1836
Intuitive Creations, 3064
Intuitive Health, 96
Intuitive Surgical, 1693
Intuity Medical, 39, 667, 1820, 1898, 1930
Intuityy Medical, 1918
Intune Networks, 1718, 2909
Inturn, 763, 1114
IntuView, 3230
Intuwave, 2772
Intvnet, 2848
Intwine Connect, 423
Inui Health, 108
Invaluable, 180, 646, 1005
Invaragen, 2504
Invarium, 1379, 1793
Invatron Systems, 1779
Invendo Medical, 3187
Invenia, 1616, 2018
Invenias, 2963
Invenio Imaging, 1238
InvenLux, 3185
Invenra, 1291, 2002
InvenSense, 621
Invensys Plc., 1905
Invensys Sealing Systems, 2635
Inventa, 1426
Inventables, 568, 635, 1862
inVentiv Health, 1818
Inventory Connections, 623
InVenture, 708, 1223
Inventus, 502, 1505
Inventus Capital Management, 624
Inventus Power, 1090
Inventys, 1584

Portfolio Companies Index

Inventys Thermal, 1241
Inveresk, 2547
Inverness Medical Innovations, 1395
Inversa Systems, 2192
Inversago Pharma, 2125
Inversago Pharma Inc., 2031
Inverse, 564
Inverstiere.ch, 2302
Inveshare, 1029
Invest Cloud, 796
Invest Detroit, 3259
Invest Michigan, 3259
Invest Southwest, 3265
Investa Företagskapital, 2858
Investar, 267
InvestCloud, 1070
Investcorp International, 3245
InvestEdge, 1003
Investedin, 1059, 1966
Investiere.ch, 650
Investis, 2463
InvestLab, 1908
Investor Members: 3TS Capital Partners, 3260
InvestX, 2257
Invi, 2822
InVia Robotics, 309, 664
Invibed, 1554
Invicta Medical, 648
Invidi, 1014, 1928
INVIDI Technologies, 1203
InView Technology Corporation, 983
Invincea, 881, 907, 1290
Invinia, 679
inVino, 1101, 1959
Invinsec, 175
Inviragen, 460, 1923, 2681
Invirsa, 481
Invisable Hand Networks, 317
InVisage, 173, 457, 1014, 1327, 1583
InvisibleCRM, 2312
InVision, 238
Invision, 21, 744, 824, 1313
InvisionHeart, 1261
Invitae, 1383, 1820
Invitae Corp., 2125
Invitalia Ventures, 485
Invite Media, 863
Invited Media, 818
Invitrogen, 119
InVivo AI, 2060
Invivo Ai, 2204
Invivo Data, 1354
Invivodata, 549, 950, 2188
Invivolink, 1618
Invixium, 2074, 2183
Invo Healthcare, 1469
Invoca, 27, 309, 1569, 1610, 1890
InvoCare, 2942
Invodo, 1601, 1661
Invoice2go, 1563
InvoiceLink, 1013
Invoke Solutions, 928
Involta, 1157
Involver, 263, 456
InvolveSoft, 309
Involvio, 485
Invro, 3098
Invuity, 1014, 1900, 1993
Inxent, 1821
Inxight, 983
Inxight Software, 22, 1908
Inxite Software, 928
InXpo, 928
Inxpo, 938
Inzign Private, 3053
IO, 1483, 1745
IO Education, 1140

IO Pipe, 1162
IO Turbine, 1125
Iobit, 977
Iobox, 3170
ioBox, 2372
IOCORE, 2700
IOD, 1140
Iodine, 1223, 1719
iOffice, 1964
Iogen Corporation, 2051
Ioline Corporation, 755
Iolon Inc., 1008
Iomai, 1788
Iomando, 1065
Iome, 2221
Iomega, 1898
IOMX, 1268
ION Investment Group, 1778
Ion Torrent, 240
IonField Systems, 233
Ionic, 175, 724, 820, 1079, 1121, 1213
Ionic Liquid Solutions, 1229
Ionic Materials, 713
Ionic Polymer Solutions, 2958
Ionic Security, 285, 894, 972, 1790, 1796, 1969
Ionisos, 2332, 2439
IonQ, 894
Iontas Ltd, 2696
iOpener Media, 3179
IOpipe, 308, 545
Ioppolo Law Group, 3251
iOR Partners, 367
Iora, 1464
iOra, 2568
Iora Health, 1, 711, 749, 812
iORGA Group, 2375
IOSIL Energy, 2708
IOTA Engineering, 989
IOTAS, 1384
Iotas, 6, 1009
Iotera, 1599
IoTium, 812, 1035
IOTurbine, 1219
IOU Financial Inc., 2088
Iovance Biotherapeutics, 785
Iovation, 680, 689
iovation, 1623
Iovox, 3009
Iowa Approach, 1622
Ioxus, 186, 325, 434, 545, 1978, 2430
IP Access, 3095
IP Commerce, 143, 1865
IP Flex, 2763
IP Infusion, 74, 766
IP Infusion Inc., 2982
IP Mobile, 1335
IP MobileNet, 1708
IP Unity, 1706
IP Wireless, 496, 1718
IP2IPO Group, 2885
IP3 Networks, 810
IPA, 928
iPacesetters, 1025, 1075, 1730
Ipanema, 2653, 2665
iParadigms, 1957
Iparc, 3033
iPass, 68, 1235
IPATH, 1161
iPay Technologies, 1720
IPC, 263, 444, 3145
IPCentury, 3179
Ipcom, 3222
IPCore Tecnologies, 1771
IPD Global, 2049
Ipdia, 3104
iPeer Multimedia International, 3053
IPeria, 163

Iperian, 186
iPerian, 1268, 2961
IPFS, 310
IPG, 1657
IPH, 3017
IPH Group, 1021
iPharro Media, 3179
iPhrase, 713
IPI Scrittura, 957
Ipida, 3042
ipinfusion, 414
iPipeline, 1316, 1787, 1944
IPivot, 597
Iplas, 1125
IPlight, 438
IPNet Solutions, 767
IPourIt, 1786
IPQ2, 2847
Ipreco, 1929
Ipreo, 274
iPrint.com, 593
Iprobelabs Inc., 738
iProf Learning Solutions, 2840
iProgress, 2346
IPS Corporation, 371
Ipsen, 1271
Ipsilon, 1247
Ipsogen, 3104
Ipsogen Cancer Profiler, 532
Ipsum Networks, 1561
Ipsy, 44, 361
IPT, 194
Ipt, 3140
IPtronics, 2628
IPValue, 2762
IPVALUE Management, 1912
ipvision, 3194
IPWireless, 808, 1360
IQ Brands, 963
IQ Evolution, 2815
IQ Financial Systems, 22
IQ Labs, 2673
iQ License, 1479
IQ Media, 655
IQ Systems, 1191
IQE, 51
IQinvision, 716
IQMS, 230, 1787
IQNavigator, 226, 889
iQor, 962
IQS Inc., 138
iQu, 2828
iQuartic, 1101
iquartic, 1618
IQur, 2883
IQVIA, 745
IQVia, 1113
Iracore International Inc., 790
iRestify, 2132, 2178
iRex Technologies, 2304
iRhythm, 764, 1247
Irhythm Technnologies, 1297
iRhythm Technologies, 1774
IRI, 1300
Iridex, 1788
Iridian Technologies, 858
Iridigm, 808
Iridigm Display Corp, 200
Iris, 263, 927, 1483
Iris Automation, 246
Iris Mobile, 965, 1364
Iris Nova, 827
Iris Plans, 51
Iris PR Software, 390
IRIS.TV, 1488, 1816
Irisa, 1484
IrisCube, 1352

Portfolio Companies Index

iRise, 1255
IrisVision, 229
IrisVR, 789
IRL, 752
IRLan Ltd, 2945
IRM Systems, 2534
Iroc, 2472
iRoc, 2457
Iroko Pharmaceuticals, 1383
Iron Age, 722
Iron Gaming, 461
Iron Gate Capital, 3265
Iron Horse Midstream, 1326, 1328
Iron Horse Tools, 1748
Iron Ox, 521, 680, 1423
Iron Pearl, 1323
Iron Planet, 27, 1235
IRON Solutions, 1733
Iron Solutions, 1741
Iron Source, 3212
Iron.io, 234
Iron.MQ, 619
IronCore, 1317
Ironform Holdings, 2008
IronKey, 1106
Ironman, 1498
IronNet Cybersecurity, 1079
IronPlanet, 561
IronPort, 115, 1543
Ironport, 84
Ironport Systems, 468
Ironshore, 371
IronSource, 2430
ironSource, 1602, 2557
Ironstone Resources, 3088
Ironwood, 2504, 2681
Ironwood Midstream Energy Partners II, 672
Ironwood Pharmaceuticals, 190, 1261, 1464
Irri-Al-Tal Ltd., 2117
IrriGreen, 229
IRT, 999
Irth Solutions, 336
IRule, 608
Irvin Automotive Products Inc., 578
Irving Tanning, 1214
iRxReminder, 1051
IRYS, 849
IRYStec, 2251
IS enterprise, 2813
IS/Pins, 2828
iS5 Communications, 2265
Isaac & Company, 303
Isabl, 1616
Isara, 1666
iSatori, 1839
Isatori Inc, 334
ISB Accelerator, 154
ISC Water Solutions, 381
Iscare AS, 2345
Ischemia Care, 350, 1514
Ischemia Technologies, 1061
iScience Interventional, 1399
Isco International, 154
IsCool, 3104
iScreen, 999
iScreen Vision, 1190
isee, 680
iSeek, 131
iSelect.com.au, 1720
iSend, 860
iSense, 1917
ISFC, 2992
iSheriff, 1888
iShipdit, 999
ISI Detention Contracting Group, 1210
Isidore Electronics Recycling, 3246
Isilon, 827, 2436

Isilon Systems, 759, 1657, 1798
iSine, 3257
ISIS, 789, 1762, 3125
Island Chemical, 836
Island Oasis, 1729
Island Water Technologies, 2148
Islanet Communications, 62
Isle Utilities, 2282
ISN, 786
iSnap, 1604
ISO Group, 21, 132
Isocket, 304, 548
iSocket, 31, 1515, 1549
Isoco, 2474
Isodiol International, 2245
iSoft, 2762
Isoftstone, 2427
iSoftstone, 2724
Isolation Network, 1663
ISolved HCM, 28
iSonar, 438
Isonics, 1917
IsoRay Medical, 1917
IsoStem, 1803
IsoTis, 2370
ISPC, 3033
iSpeak, 2575
ISpeech, 1786
iSpeech, 1305
iSpot, 1830
iSpot.tv, 1005, 1162
ISPsoft, 1304
iSqFt, 1547
ISR, 2045
Isreal Plant Sciences, 1194
Iss, 2688
Issuu, 3140
Ista, 912
Ista International GmbH, 745
ISTA Pharmaceuticals, 1619
Istar Medical, 3125
ISTO, 2930
ISTO Technologies, 178
Istra Research, 238
iStreamPlanet, 1517
istyle, 1757
iSuppli Corporation, 2073
Isys Interactive, 2958
iSystems, 1686
IT Assist Inc., 1612
IT Convergence, 2484
IT Cosmetics, 1863
IT Provider, 2438
It's Just Lunch, 1576
IT-Ernity, 1929
IT-Pac Romania SA, 3178
Ita Software, 1720
iTAC, 2704
iTAC Software AG, 1623
Italian Rose Gourmet Products, 293
Italic, 520
Italmatch Chemicals, 2842
Italtel, 338
Itamar Medical, 240
Itax Group, 861
ItBit, 389
itBit, 1119
ITC, 1955
ITC Capital Partners, 1076
ITC Compounding Pharmacy, 477
ITE Group, 1929
iTeam, 1104
Iteksa Venture., 2858
iTellio, 434
ITEMBASE, 2970
Itembase, 3226
Itemmaster, 655

Iteos, 3216
iTeos, 1268
Iterable, 12, 129, 1219
Itero, 1411
Itero Biopharmaceuticals, 3202
Iteros, 198, 296
Iterum Therapeutics, 240, 785
Itho, 2370
Itho Daalderop, 2492
ITinvolve, 205
ITL Canis, 3229
ITM, 2593
ITM Power, 3009
ITMedia, 1757
ITN Nanovation, 2629
ITN Networks, 1929, 2019
iTOKiNET, 1679
Itopia, 754
itrac LLC, 352
iTRACS Corporation, 947
iTradeNetwork Inc., 20
iTraffic, 957
itriage, 94
Itron, 697
Itronix, 843
ITS, 2927
ITS Compliance, 733
Itsbyu, 1179
Itslearning, 2628
ItsMyNews, 1535
ITSolutions, 654
ItsOn, 485, 1798
ITSworld Sicilia, 3043
ITT Educational Services, 303, 1498
Iturmo, 2480
ITW, 475
ItzBig, 1561
Itzcash Card, 1125
Iubenda, 2663
Iuka, 2883
iUNU, 1285
IVAC, 212
Ivanti, 502
Ivantis, 605, 1522, 2681
Ivantis. MedWentive, 178
iVelozity LLC, 123
Iven, 2276
Ivenix, 711
IvenSense, 1924
Iventis, 764
Ividence, 3011
iView Therapeutics, 269
iVillage, 1561, 2073
iVita Financial, 1912
iVivity, 1042
iViZ Techno Solutions, 2840
Ivize, 381
iVMD, 2002
Ivrea Pharmaceuticals, 2436
Ivxinevotech, 597
Ivy, 1323
Ivy Rehab, 1964
Ivycorp, 2003
IW Financial, 1164
IWATech, 2595
IWAtech, 2466
IWatt, 613
iWatt, 928, 950, 1674, 1908
IWC, 2691
iWin.com, 131
iWitness/Zantaz, 1795
IWJW, 827
Iwoca, 3148
iWorlds Simulations, 1917
IWS, 1753
IX Europe PLC, 2713
Ix Innovations, 743

Portfolio Companies Index

Ixaris, 3098
IXI, 540
IXI Mobile, 3170
IXI Mobile Inc, 2761
Ixia, 874
Ixico, 2849
IXIGO, 2468
Ixigo, 2466
Ixlayer, 1426
Ixoraa Media Inc., 624
IXS, 1372
Ixsight, 3100
Iyia Technologies, 1786
iYogi, 389, 610, 1623
IyziCo, 2286
IZEA, 994
iZENEtech, 1361
IZettle, 3004
iZettle, 2628, 3242
Izorok, 3062
iZotope, 21
Izypeo, 2300
IZZE, 1668

J

J Brand, 919
J&J Produce, 408
J&L Specialty Steel, 357
J&S, 2842
J&W Scientific Inc., 1624
J-B Weld, 377
J-Tell, 2960
J. Crew, 1837
J. Hilburn, 234, 238, 342
J. Jill, 153, 843
J.America, 832
J.B. Williams Company, 360
J.Hilburn, 696
J.Mclaughlin, 337
J.S. Held, 1169
JAB Broadband, 20
Jab Broadband, 928
JabberSmack, 1112
Jabbit, 3049
Jabong, 2829
JAC Holding Corporation, 1493
JAC Products, 2008
Jacada, 3128
Jack and Jake's, 3246
Jack Be, 907
Jack Erwin, 564, 1666
Jack Rabbit, 1074
Jack Rogers, 1344
Jack Threds, 1589
Jack Wolfskin, 280, 2705
Jack's, 2201
JackBe, 540
Jackbox Games, 1028
JackCards, 1101
Jacked, 808
Jackpocket, 361, 1616
JackRabbit, 832
Jackrabbit, 1427
Jackson Hewitt Tax Service, 1045
Jackson Offshore Holdings, 1148
Jackson Vending Ltd., 2698
Jackson's Honest, 1117
Jacob Ash, 341
Jacobi, 980
Jacobson Companies, 1360
Jacobson Machine Works, 847
JacquelineBs Gourmet Cookies, 77
Jacques Vert, 2353
Jacques Vert Group, 1755
Jacuzzi, 502
Jacuzzi Brands, 141
Jacuzzi Brands Corp., 160

Jada Beauty, 659
JADE Equipment Corporation, 1204
Jade Solutions, 1839
JadeTrack, 1285
Jafora, 2600
JAG-ONE, 1410
Jagex Games Studio, 1720
Jaggaer, 28
Jahabow, 60, 612
Jail Education Solutions, 3246
Jajah Jasper Technologies, 990
Jam Hub, 1164
Jama, 1162, 1855
Jama Software, 1005, 1384
Jamba Juice, 1580, 1591, 1855, 2245
James, 2750
James Communications, 1624
James E. Wagner Cultivation Corporation, 2233
James Heal, 238
JamesEdition, 3031
Jameslist.com, 2595
Jameson, 418
JAMF Software, 805, 1754, 3268
JamHub, 447
Jamieson Wellness, 435
Jamii, 2560
Jamo, 3000
Jan Pro, 815
JANA, 1718
Jana, 758, 1511, 1928
Janaagraha, 1374
Jancee Screw Products, 2088
Jandi, 3118
Jane, 2074
Jane Norman, 2787
Jane West, 1139
Janeeva, 1459
Janiis, 1074
JanRain, 794
Janrain, 666, 689, 936, 1235, 1596, 1610, 1728
Janrain User Management Platform, 133
Jansy Packaging, 699
Janton, 2413
Janus, 502
Janus Capital Group, 303
JANUS Research Group Inc., 509
JanusRV, 1533
JanusVR, 59, 310, 1114
Japan Carlife Assist, 2965
Japan Communications, 597
Japan Internet Ventures, 852
Japan Medical Data Centre, 3173
Japan Telecom, 3159
Japan Tissue Engineering, 2961
Jarden, 2688
Jardine Transport, 2242
Jardine's, 988
Jareva Technologies, 1042
Jargon, 1879
Jari Pharmaceuticals, 2739
Jarllytec Co., 3209
Jarvis Hotels, 2547
JASK, 1796
Jask, 238, 604, 1079
Jason Incorporated, 1377
Jaspan Schlesinger LLP, 3257
Jasper, 1008, 1657, 3004
Jasper @ Cisco, 556
Jasper Infotech Pvt Ltd., 1009
Jasper Soft, 1629
Jasper Wireless, 342, 582, 1449, 1996, 3112
JasperSoft, 56
Jaspersoft, 597, 1257
Jassby, 754
Jaulna, 2436
Jauni, 1537
Jaunt, 795, 894, 938

Jaunt VR, 998
Java Detour, 508
Javelin, 368
Javelin Pharmaceuticals, 1325
Javelin Venture Partners, 3273
Javlin Capital, 1364
Javo Beverage Company, 717
Jawabu Microhealth, 54
Jawbone, 597, 626, 730, 1187, 1657, 1730, 2437
Jaxtr, 116, 200, 624
Jays, 2628
Jaza, 2178
JAZD Markets, 523
Jazinga, 2060
Jazz, 275, 724, 1610
Jazz Pharma, 1271
Jazz Pharmaceuticals, 56, 843, 1495, 1964
JazzHR, 309
JB Hi Fi, 2942
JBLCo, 1262
JBoss, 1449
jCatalog Software, 2443
JCC, 2935
JCK KG, 3058
Jcrew Group, 1113
JD Holding, 3053
JDA Software, 303
JDA Software Group, 1300
JDR, 1939
JDR Recovery Corporation, 405
JDS Pharmaceuticals, 97
JDS Therapeutics, 4, 1048
Jebbit, 316, 587, 1175, 1759
JEC, 2309
Jecure, 1930
Jeda Networks, 1237, 1898
Jeda Technologies, 131
Jedox, 2677
Jeepers! Inc., 449
Jeepglint, 3241
Jeevanti, 3100
Jeeves, 238, 3100
Jefferson Capital International, 751
Jefferson Dental Care, 337
JEL Hydraulics, 3136
Jelastic, 89, 3079
Jeld-Wen, 2201
Jelf Group Plc., 407
Jelfa SA, 1456
Jellagen, 2988
Jelly Button, 2905
Jelly in the News, 1718
Jellyfish, 1064
Jellyvision, 1028, 1674
Jen Sen Hughes, 886
JeNaCell, 2518, 2815
JenAffin, 2815
Jenali, 764
JenaValve, 193
Jenavalve, 3140
Jenetric, 2518
Jeni's, 424
jenID Solutions, 2518
Jenny Craig, 1336
Jenoptik, 2518
Jenrin Discovery, 269, 365, 1546
Jens Jorgensen, 3194
Jensen Hughes, 1169
JeNu, 1644
Jenzabar, 1071
Jericho Capital Corp., 3257
Jericho Sciences, 738
Jerini AG, 1325, 2519
Jerr-Dan, 1138
Jersey Precast, 815
Jersey Watch, 481
Jessops Ltd., 2668

Portfolio Companies Index

Jet, 488, 511, 763, 1479, 1823
Jet Finance, 2462
Jet Health, 921, 1631, 1764
Jet Insight, 1323
Jet Metal, 2430
Jetasonic, 2148
JetCell, 1750
Jetchange.fr, 2890
JetClosing, 1186, 1501
JetInsight, 1426
JetLenses, 798
JetLore, 2829
Jetlore, 93, 721
Jetpac, 1254
Jetpack Workflow, 1159
JetPay, 751
Jetro Cash & Carry, 435, 1113
Jetset Sports, 1707
Jetsetter, 1184
JetSmarter, 502
Jetta Corp, 554
Jettable, 2453
Jetul, 2317
Jewelbots, 221, 985
Jewlr, 2060
Jexys Pharmaceuticals, 3235
Jeyes, 2926
JFDI.Asia, 3123
JFIN Business Credit Fund, 1971
JFrog, 238, 604, 1005, 1629
JG Wentworth, 1043
JGB Enterprises, 920
JGWPT Holdings, 1140
JHP Pharmaceuticals, 1957
JHT Holdings, 110
Jiahua, 3091
Jiangli, 3091
Jiangxi Guohong Group, 2533
Jiayuan, 2575
Jiayuan.com, 3241
JIBE, 609, 2016
Jibe, 1114, 1150, 1464, 1623
Jibjab, 1464
Jibo, 713, 721, 756
Jida Pharmaceuticals, 1957
Jido, 1391
Jiff, 1323, 1918
Jiffy, 2130, 2131
Jifiti, 1038
Jig Space, 310
Jigsaw Data Corp., 205
Jiguang, 977
Jihua.fm, 2860
Jiko, 664, 1890
Jilcraft, 1294
Jill-e Designs LLC, 670
Jim 'N Nick's Bar-B-Q, 1580
Jimdo, 1720
Jimmy Buffet's Margaritaville, 1683
Jimmy John's, 1580
Jimu Box, 3199
Jin-Magic, 2965
Jinfengyuan, 3185
Jing Jin Electric, 2658
Jing-Jin Electric, 3206
JingDong 360 Buy Online, 2551
Jingtum, 1391
Jinhe Industrial, 2533
JinkoSolar Holdings, 2584
JinSheng International, 223
JinTronix, 1162
Jinu, 2848
Jinx, 328
Jirafe, 744, 1359
Jist.tv, 998
Jisto, 1
Jitterbit, 1610

Jitterbug, 2978
JITx, 798
JiuDing China, 2841
Jive, 1335, 1657
Jive Software, 758, 1341, 2137
Jivox, 1382, 2809
JiWire, 1852
JK Group, 1761
JK&B Capital, 990
JL Darling, 1343
JMH International, 1343
JMI Equity, 36, 990, 3260
JMJ Associates, 2303
JML Optical Industries, 747
JMTY, 641, 2860
Jnana, 1930
Jnm Group, 2121
JNTC, 3136
Jo-Ann Stores, 1113
Joany, 275, 779
Job Cannon, 447
Job Direct, 532
Job partners, 2535
Jobalign, 776, 1162
Jobaline, 1854
Jobandtalent, 2437, 2911
Jobber, 2272, 3035
JobCase, 1628
Jobcase, 1499
JobCoin, 103
JobDig, 1117
Jobdisabili, 2288
JOBDOH, 3099
Jobe's, 448
Jobintree, 2377
JobLeads, 2815
JobPartners, 2770
JobPlanet, 1511
Jobplanet, 100
Jobr, 680, 1812
Jobro Platkomponenter, 2746
Jobs For Vets, 814
jobs2web, 1888
Jobson Healthcare Information, 1377, 1984
JobSync, 1103, 1786
JobUFO, 2832
Jobvite, 185, 429, 1852
Joby, 108
Joby Aviation, 1009, 1039, 1836, 2681
Jodel, 752
Joe, 757
Joe Hudson's Collision Center, 418
Joerns, 202
Joerns Healthcare, 1138, 1507
Joey's Fine Foods, 196
Jofel, 2953
John Barker Group, 2976
John Deere, 475
John H. Harland Company, 303
John Hardy, 1092
John Laing Partnership, 3008
John West Foods, 2411
Johnny on the Spot, 633
Johnny Rockets, 1755
Johnny Was, 674
Johnny's Fine Foods, 2000
Johnson & Johnson, 1100
Johnson & Johnson Innovation, 3263
Johnson and johnson, 2794
Johnson Biomedical Capital, 3251
Johnston Fabrics & Finishing, 1214
Joicaster, 975
JointlyHealth, 1786
Joist, 37, 488, 2130, 2131, 2176
Joiz, 2629
Jojonomic, 721
Jolata, 185

Joliet Equipment, 1025
Joliet Holdings, 165
Jolife, 2553
Jolimark Holdings, 2927
Jolimont Global Mining Systems, 1551
Jolt, 79
Jolyn, 1346
Jon M Hall Company, 1280
Jonah Energy LLC, 1837
Jonathan Engineered Services, 470
Jonathan Engineered Solutions, 989, 1115
Jones, 882
Jones & Frank, 747, 1231
Jones Lang LaSalle, 3265, 3268
Jones Naturals, 216
Jones Rail Industries, 2257
Jones The Grocer Group, 1092
JonesTrading, 790
Jonway Automobile, 2567
Joonko, 75, 1058
JOOR, 238
Joor, 389, 863, 1114, 1533
Jopa, 3079
Jopari Solutions, 1671, 1979
Jopwell, 568, 1058, 1724
Jordan Health Services, 1404, 1949
Jordens DC, 2940
Joriki, 2264
Jorn Ditlevsen, 3194
Jornaya, 520, 655, 818
Joseph Ribkoff, 2198
Joseph's Frozen Foods, 360
Josephine, 1058
Joshin, 2398
Jostens, 1021
José Andrés ThinkFoodGroup, 1768
Jott, 42, 1114, 1186
Joule, 748
Joules, 2935
Joulex, 1790
Jounce, 764
Jounce Therapeutics, 1814
Journera, 125, 1483
Journey Meditation, 1309
Journey Sales, 1240
Jove Equity Partners, 3257
Jow, 641
Joy, 1363
Joya, 100
Joya Communications Inc., 1881
Joyent, 689, 876, 1525, 3160
Joyfride, 787
Joyful Frog Digital Incubator, 721
JoyLux, 296
Joymode, 944, 1153
Joyoung, 2570
Joyride, 553
JoyRun, 1346
Joyrun, 752
JoyStream, 310
JoyTunes, 1005, 2905
Joyus, 27, 1014, 1829
JP Mobil, 2881
JP Morgan Private Bank, 3257
JPC Holdings LLC, 1738
JR Automation, 560
JRD Communication, 3053
JRG Securities, 2481
JRL Systems, 132
JS Digitech, 2798
JS Held, 1151
JSA Healthcare Corporation, 958
JSC Krasalkor Aluminiystroi Krasnoyarsk, 1405
JScrambler, 3039
JSI NV, 2983
JSI Store Fixtures, 1560
JSK Therapeutics, 1074, 2374

Portfolio Companies Index

JTF, 2787
Judas Theatreproducteies, 3033
Judicata, 1073
Judson Technologies, 1294
Judy, 328
Judy's Book, 42
Juhudi Kilimo, 54
Juice Plus, 15
Juice Press, 1589
Juice Tyme Acquisition Corp, 1460
Juicebox, 1000
Juix, 2123
Jukedeck, 3019
Jukin Media, 259, 400, 1059, 1103, 1816
Julep, 85, 125, 1227, 1527
Juli, 2584
Julia Computing, 820
Juliet Marine Systems Inc., 209
July Systems, 1888
Jumbo, 2775
Jumei.com, 3199, 3241
Jumia, 3161
Jumio, 730, 1235
JUMO, 2398
JUMP, 1203
Jump, 310, 2872
Jump Cloud, 779
Jump Ramp, 361, 949
Jump Ramp Games, 680, 1701
Jump.Ca, 2277
JumpCam, 894
JumpCloud, 1566
Jumpcut, 863, 1186
Jumpstart Foundy, 1190
Jumptap, 1537, 1901
Jun Group, 902
Junar, 2446
Junction Solutions, 1242
June, 742, 779, 945, 1114, 1426
June Life, 648
Junggwan Library Operation Co., 585
Jungla, 125
Junglee Games, 241
Jungo, 1795
Juni Learning, 1426
Juniper Financial, 2073
Juniper Networks, 1006
Juniper Resources, 1326
Juniper Square, 720, 945
Junkless, 1509
Juno, 764
Juno Energy, 157
Juno Lighting, 371
Juno Online Services, 1771
Juno Rising, 440
Juno Therapeutics, 265, 1522, 1918, 2007
Junyo, 1058, 1315
Jupiter, 1770
Jupiter Fund Management, 1778
Jupiter Intelligence, 1269
Jupiter Shop Channel, 223
JupiterOne, 3
Jurag Separation, 3140
Jurnal, 721
Juro, 3099
JUSP, 3043
Just, 101
Just A Pinch Recipe Club, 1261
Just Book, 2659
Just Brakes, 815
Just Childcare, 3027
Just Eat, 1537
Just Fabulous, 1787
Just in Time Tourist, 3039
Just Inc., 108, 1073
Just Learning, 2353
Just Marketing International, 1727

Just Park, 305
Just Retirement, 3024
Just Solutions Agriculture, 2115
Just the Right Book, 1101
JustBook, 2628
JustCommodity, 2861
JustEnough Software, 2700
JustEva.ru, 2540
JustFabulous, 1184
JustFav, 1561
JustFoodForDogs, 1092
Justice Design Group, 1965
Justin's, 956
JustOne, 1254
Justworks, 1537
Juswin Technologies, 2966
Jut, 27
Jutian Fund Management Co, 2585
Jutian Fund Management Co. Ltd, 2586
Jutian Securities Co. LtdHoulder China Insurance B, 2586
Jutron Oy, 2731
Juvantia Pharma Ltd Oy, 2310
Juvaris BioTherapeutics, 1631
Juve, 1677
Juvena Therapeutics, 1760
Juvenescence, 764
Juventas Therapeutics, 642, 835, 1051, 1302, 1547, 1849, 1923
Juvo, 787, 1614
Juxta Labs, 1074, 2374
JVC, 1344
JVH Gaming, 3222
Jvion, 921
JW Aluminum Company, 1972
JW Player, 568, 641, 872
JWD, 1143
JWD Machine, 1707
JWPlayer, 876
Jydsk Aluminum Industrial, 3194
Jydsk Planteservice, 3194
Jyothy Laboratories, 2329
Jyve, 308, 562, 1566, 1677

K

K Health, 520
K Mobile, 3199
K&A Water, 1194
K&F Industries, 202
K&F Industries Inc., 576
K&G Men's Centers, 1152
K&N Engineering Inc., 886
K-MAC, 1372
K-Tek, 1772
K-Vault Software Ltd (KVS), 2568
K.G. Box Inc., 467
K.Wah International Holdings Limited, 2394
K12, 1787
K2, 263, 782
K2 Cyber Security, 664
K2 Global, 1597
K2 Industrial Services, 405, 899
K2 Insurance Services, 674
K2 Intelligence, 1298
K2 Internet S.A., 2519
K2 Optronic, 2340
K2 Pure Solutions LP, 449
K2-MDV Holdings, 1085
K2M, 723, 1973
K3, 3234
K4Connect, 1672
K9 Resorts, 1280
KA International Group, 2953
Kaai, 1449
Kaarta, 2136
KabaFusion Holdings, 243
Kabam, 186, 389, 730, 1537, 1692

Kabbage, 299, 1247, 1701, 1821, 1893
Kabbee, 3009, 3088
Kabira, 2866, 3128
Kabira Technologies, 163
Kaboa, 2985
Kabobs, 196
Kaboodle, 810
Kabron, 3033
Kabu.com, 597
Kabul Serena Hotel, 1012
Kace, 759, 1028
KaDang, 1537
Kadel's Auto Body, 1232
Kadena, 527
Kadent/Landau, 1518
Kadiant, 1934
Kadient, 1084
Kadiri, 1947
Kaditt, 2637
Kadmon, 1943
Kaggle, 586, 1800, 2018
Kagoor Networks, 1908
Kahala Brands, 2245
Kahala Code Factory, 2448
KAHLA Porzellan, 2518
Kahoot!, 1158
Kahr Medical, 1621
Kahuna, 548, 720, 780, 1491, 1657, 1702
KAI Pharmaceuticals, 1013, 1693
Kai Square, 3112
Kai Yuan, 3199
Kaiam, 596
KAIAM Corporation, 1788
Kaiam Corporation, 1898
Kaibae, 3248
Kaidara., 2616
Kaiima, 610, 2822
Kaiima Bio Agritech, 1241
Kaiko, 2398
KaiLight Photonics, 3239
Kairos, 221, 1058, 1703
Kaiser Permanente, 217
Kaitone, 2927
Kaixin001, 1340
Kajeet, 808
Kakao, 597
Kakehashi, 1610
Kala Pharmaceuticals, 1814
Kala Pharmaceuticals, 1122, 1147, 1155, 1464, 1522, 1943
KalaBios, 11
Kaleidacare, 92
Kaleido, 748
Kaleido Biosciences, 19
Kaleidoscope Medical, 428
Kaleo, 309, 876, 907, 976, 1059, 1511, 1608, 1800
Kaleo Software, 625
KalGene Pharmaceuticals, 2174
Kalibrr, 1374, 1966
Kalid, 2436
Kalido, 1184
Kalion, 845, 1104
Kalisaya, 462
Kalkitech, 838
Kalkomey, 1018
Kallik, 2958
KallOut, 103
Kallyope, 519, 1155
Kalo, 840
KaloBios, 87, 1621, 1700, 2961
KaloBios Pharmaceuticals, 2504, 2681
Kalpan Hydro, 1463
Kalpana, 1203
Kalpsys, 2681
Kaltura, 1, 209, 1009, 1241, 1327, 1623, 1628, 2992

Portfolio Companies Index

KalVista, 1522
KalVista Pharma, 1943
Kalvista Pharma, 1631
KalVista Pharmaceuticals, 1149
Kalypsys, 2410, 2504
Kalypto Medical, 1762
Kalyra, 1786
Kamada, 928
Kambr, 1877
Kamcord, 1219, 1840, 2009
Kaminario, 186, 839, 1241, 1798
Kampyle, 2557, 3212
Kana, 68
Kana Software, 1561, 1674
Kanaly Trust, 1151
Kanam Lifescript, 68
Kanbox, 597
Kanchli, 2570
Kandy Pens, 638
KaNDy Therapeutics, 1147
Kaneq Bioscience, 3187
Kanetix, 1248
KangaDo, 1752
Kango, 229
Kangol, 2914
Kanisa/Knova, 1287
Kanler, 752
Kantana Group, 1143, 2937
Kantox, 2842
Kantum Bio, 2
Kanvas, 151, 1635
Kanvas Labs, 680
Kanyos Bio, 1350, 1930
Kaon, 1150
Kaonetics Technologies, 736
Kaperio, 1578
Kapitol, 2671
Kapost, 35, 568, 752, 784, 933, 1024, 1610, 1791, 2016
Kapow, 631
Kapow Events, 473, 732
Kappa Packaging, 2635
Kappoki Games LTD, 2545
Kapta, 1179, 1525
Kaptivo, 252
Kapwing, 1079, 1666, 1935
Kar's Nuts, 1404
Karachi Electric Supply Company, 3164
Karadi Tales Company, 2305
Karat, 1346
Karbon, 2074, 2262
Karbyte, 2074
Kardia Therapeutics, 244
KareInn, 3099
Kareo, 510, 696, 872, 1251, 1381, 1751
Kargo, 1716
KargoCard, 837
Karhu Sporting Goods, 2864
Karius, 1001, 1125
Karius Inc., 1073
Karl Lagerfeld, 136
Karma, 641, 3215
Karma Communications Group, 3027
Karma Gaming, 2231
Karma Sphere, 1898
Karmaback.com, 447
Karmaloop, 410
Karmasphere, 1478
Karmic, 149, 545, 2484
Karmic Labs, 93, 387, 1101, 1596
Karobi, 310
Karos Pharmaceuticals, 1297, 1422
Karoui&Karoui World, 2645
Karsen, 1
Karuna Health, 321, 742
Karus Therapeutics, 1297, 1631, 2883
Karve Energy, 2022

Karve Energy Inc., 2044
Karyopharm Therapeutics, 605
Kasbah Resources, 2933
Kascend, 938
Kasenna, 1352
Kaseya, 1005
Kashf School Sarmaya, 54
Kasisto, 1305, 1422
Kasko, 3099
Kason, 225
Kastle Therapeutics, 751
Kaszek Ventures, 485
Katabat, 51
Katahdin Inc., 1864
Katahdin Industries, 1025
Katalyst Surgical, 270
Katch, 1629
Kateeva, 596, 1302, 1674, 1718, 3089
Katerra, 108, 1281
Katerra Inc., 1073
Katy Industries, 1085
Katz Sapper & Miller, 3257
Katzkin Leather Interiors Inc., 503
Kauf.da, 641
Kaufman & Broad, 3017
Kaufman Hall & Associates, 1160
Kaval Wireless, 2051
Kaval Wireless Technologies, 2073
Kavin Engineering, 1167
Kawi Safi Ventures, 624
Kawin Technology, 2927
KAYAC, 2637
KAYAK, 1657
Kayak, 1006, 1852
Kayak.com, 1798
Kayden Industries, 2267
Kaydon Corp., 77
Kayentis, 3104, 3229
Kaymbu, 1530
Kayo Conference Series, 3274
Kaz Inc., 449
Kazan Networks, 1009
Kazeon, 504, 759
Kazeon Systems, 1042, 1449
Kazuhm, 122
Kb Alloys, 1949
KBC Arkiv, 3033
KBI, 2969
KBI Biopharma, 227, 1917
KBOS, 2817
KBP Foods, 1433
KCAEP, 377
KCAS, 1057
KCG, 819
KCI, 212
KCom, 2665
KCS, 28, 2555
KD 1, 1561
KD1, 205
kDa Group, 2212
KdocTV Los Angeles, 1066
Kds, 655
KDS China, 1009
KDS International, 27
Keane, 1151, 1169
Keas, 37
Keatext, 2024
Keaton Row, 1203, 1305
Kebony, 2419, 3104
Kebotix, 664, 756, 2037
Keclon, 2461
Kedu Healthcare, 225
Keduo, 1340
KEE Action Sports, 128
Kee Safety, 2935
Keebitz, 2912
Keebler, 1022

Keebo, 1426
Keeley Asset Management, 1778
Keemotion, 3216
Keen Home, 328
Keen IO, 309, 586, 1428, 1569, 2009
KeenHigh Technologies, 2584
KeenSkim, 2687
Keep, 125, 827
Keep Holdings, 597, 1862
Keep Holdings/AdKeeper, 1361
Keep Truckin, 1629
Keepcon, 2326, 2967
Keeps, 742, 784, 1186
KeepSafe, 183
Keepsafe, 752
KeepTrax, 1284
KeepTruckin, 894
Keepy, 1998
Keesing, 2842
Keezy. K Health, 1114
Kefta, 115
Keg Logistics, 336, 1641
Keiretsu, 3251
Keisense, 532
Keit, 2958
Keith Prowse, 3008
Kekemeke, 3035
Kel-Tech, 172
Keldelice, 3011
Kelkoo, 2472
Kelle's Transport Service, 408
Kellermeyer Bergensons Services, 828, 1085
Kellogg Company, 475
Kellstrom Aerospace, 65
Kellwood Company, 1755
Kelsius Limited, 2601
Kelso & Company, 3245, 3254
Kelst, 3033
Kelvin Inc., 2105
Kemartek, 2347
Kemberton, 1140
Kemco Systems, 1582
Kemira GrowHow Oyj, 2981
Kemira Oyj, 2981
Kemistry, 515
Kemp Technologies, 655
Kemper Corporation, 407
Ken Taub, 3257
Kenan Advantage, 2199
Kenan Advantage Group, 1138, 1560
Kenan Advantage Group Inc., 444
Kenandy, 1125
Kendall Vegetation Services, 293
Kendra Scott, 257, 1346
Kendrick Electric, 1377
Kendrion, 3060
Kendro Laboratory, 1132
Kenect, 1499
Kenesto, 438, 2804
kenexa, 1044
KENGURU, 447
Kenlin Pet Supply, 791
Kenna Security, 548
Kennedy Information, 868
Kenota, 2122
Kenra, 1863, 2142
KenSci, 978
Kensho, 339, 709, 1491
Kensho Technologies, 711
Kenshoo, 1323, 1657, 2419
Kenshoo Kodiak Networks, 1798
Kensington & Sons, 2393
Kensington Flats, 2277
Kentik, 742
Kentrox, 1021
Kenzie Academy, 1554
Kenzington Brewing Company, 2178

1324

Portfolio Companies Index

Keoghs, 2935
Keonn, 1065
Keopsys, 3199
KEP Technologies, 2842
Kepler, 548
Kepler Academy, 2194
Kepler Capital Markets, 2512
Kepler Communications, 2122
Kepler Equities, 1127
Kepro, 136, 1169
KeraFAST, 497, 718
Kerb, 2526
Kerberos Proximal Solutions, 1449, 1546
Kerenix, 2901
Kereos, 460, 1190, 1578, 1849
Keri Systems, 636
Kericure, 1509
Keriton, 269, 623
Kerk Motion Products Inc., 911
Kerogen Energy Holdings, 1577
Keronite, 2463
Keros Therapeutics, 2221
Kerr Group, 371
Kerrera Company, 585
Keryx, 1063
Keryx Biopharma, 1271
Kesios Therapeutics, 1631
Kesko Oyj, 2981
Kespry, 485, 795, 1125
Kestrel Heat, 1072
Ketai, 2841
KeTech, 3009
Ketera, 1008
Kether, 2842
Ketos, 1555
Kettle, 2398
Kettle & Fire, 484
Kewl, 953
Key, 1985
Key Associates, 3251
Key Brandon Entertainment Inc., 2088
Key Concierge, 546
Key Energy, 157
Key Health, 279, 336
Key Investment, 3268
Key Living, 2216
Key Plastics, 1968
Key Retirement, 3027
Key Safety Systems, 560
Key-Trak, 1152
KEY/VISYS, 2940
Key2Act, 1140
Keybase, 125
KeyBay Pharmaceutical, 1003
Keycast, 1576
Keychain Logistics, 283, 600, 1223, 1479, 1521, 1534, 1701
Keyes Packaging Group, 148
Keyfactor, 2074
KeyImpact Sales & Systems, 687
KeyImpact Sales and Systems, 1053
Keylime Software, 1708
KeyMe, 238, 520, 1982
Keymile, 1576
Keynote, 263
Keynote Systems, 1817
Keyo, 1363
KeyPoint Government Solutions, 1927
Keyport Solutions, 2339
Keyrocket, 2815
Keyssa, 93, 1009, 1430
Keystone Automotive Operations, 223, 1138
Keystone Communications, 2073
Keystone Dental, 1820, 1957
Keystone Foods Holdings, 1133
Keystone Heart, 1383
Keystone Ranger Holdings, 1275

Keystone Retaining Wall Systems, 1343
KeyTech Limited, 277
KeyTone Cloud, 485
Keytouch Corporation, 2745
Keytruda, 2097
KEYW, 838
Keywee, 1001
Kezar Life Sciences, 19, 240, 710
KFC, 337
KFX Medical, 1251
KFx Medical, 87, 150, 460, 1190
KG Telecom, 3209
Kgb, 1021
kgb, 1787
KGen Power, 157
KGH Customs Services, 3045
KH Connect, 1009
Khan Academy, 1315
Khancera, 627
Kheiron Medical Technologies, 1099
Khimetrics, 313, 1949
Khosla Ventures LLC, 3273
Kiadis, 2653
Kiadis Pharma, 94, 2509, 2665, 2930, 3060
Kiala, 2346, 2653, 2842
Kiana, 895
Kiana Analytics, 130
KickApps, 1701, 1718
KickApps (KIT Digital), 1334
Kickback, 863, 1154
Kickboard, 1298, 1876, 3246
Kicking Horse Coffee, 1769
Kicksend, 1862
Kickstart Seed Fund, 2374, 3265
Kickstarter, 514, 1153, 1884
Kickup, 1530
Kid Interiør, 2854
KidAdmit, 1054
Kidaptive, 1203, 1315, 1637
Kidaro, 1750
Kidblog, 3268
Kiddom, 1073, 1393
Kidfresh, 669
Kidizen, 1023, 1179, 1385
KidKraft, 1231
KIDOZ, 2938
Kidpass, 1032
Kidrobot, 1744
Kids Care Dental, 377
Kids Care Dental Group, 1745
Kids Garden, 3033
Kids Kitchen, 3033
Kids On 45th, 328
Kids on 45th, 1186, 1703
Kids123.com, 1465
Kidsline, 874
Kidsline Inc., 451
KidsLink, 285
Kidsmart, 874
Kidspotter, 2347
KidsToPros, 1616
kidsunlimited, 2935
Kidz Bop, 20
Kidzui, 1588
Kieffer & Co., 402, 1343
Kigo, 2629
Kii, 183, 485, 721
Kiian Group, 3145
Kiio, 2002
Kiip, 959, 1841, 1862, 1928
Kiite, 709
Kik, 773, 805, 1235, 1597, 1608, 1718
KIK Custom Products, 444
KIKA Medical, 1325
Kildare Capital, 3257
Kilimanjaro Energy, 154
Kilimo, 999

Kilkenny, 263
Kill Cliff, 1668
Killick Aerospace, 2161
KiloLambda, 3239
Kilombero Valley, 838
Kilopass, 2844
Kilopass Klocwork, 1898
Kilosoft Oy, 2957
Kiloutou, 3017
Kim Susan, 1748
Kimaya Fashions, 585
Kimberly Access Limited, 2935
KIMBIA, 447
Kimbia, 953, 1601
Kimble, 28
KimKim, 1323
Kimomex Markets, 1917
Kimono, 1059, 1998
Kimotion., 2866
KIMS GCC, 1383
KIMS India, 1383
KIN, 1498
Kin, 2217
Kin Community, 669, 820
Kinamu Business Solutions, 3156
Kinaset Therapeutics, 11
Kinaxis, 2254
Kinburn Corp, 449
Kincora Group, 3088
Kind, 1768
Kindara, 316, 1659
Kinder Morgan, 1577
Kindly, 857
Kindly Care, 752, 1028
Kindred, 3, 648, 742, 894, 2122
Kindred at Home, 1973
Kindred Bio, 710
Kindred Healthcare, 1837, 1973
Kindred.ai, 108
Kindstar, 2969
Kindstar Global, 225
Kinduct, 1009
Kindur, 2398
Kinectrics, 1939
Kinema Systems, 648
Kinematics, 127
Kinematix, 3039
Kinesics, 1000
Kinestral, 130
Kineta, 1065
Kinetic, 490, 564
Kinetic Books Company, 1152
Kinetic Commerce, 2104
Kinetic Computer Corporation, 1465
Kinetic Concepts, 371
Kinetic Concepts Inc., 303
Kinetic Social, 290, 1361, 1751, 1778
Kinetic Ventures, 3260
Kinetica, 488, 1213
Kinetika, 3145
Kinetikos Medical, 1794
Kinetix Living, 1186
Kineto, 1640, 1750
Kineto Wireless, 1241, 1762, 3146
Kinetrex Energy, 2206
Kinex Medical Company, 1210
Kinex R&M Rehabilitation, 1210
King, 2851, 2851
King Juice Company, 1174
King Tester Corporation, 1612
KING&I, 2848
King-Reed & Associates, 2785
Kingdee, 977
Kingfield Health, 2926
Kings County Distillery, 1422
Kings Foodmart, 128
Kingsclear, 2787

1325

Portfolio Companies Index

Kingsdown, 2198
Kingsgate Consolidated, 1551
Kingsoft WPS, 827
KingStar, 751
KingYee, 3091
Kinloch Holdings, 436
Kinnate Biopharma, 1934
Kinnek, 129, 564, 863, 1672
Kinney Group, 659
Kinsa, 744, 969, 1079
Kinside, 1030
Kinsus Interconnect Technology Corporation, 2594
Kintana, 827
Kinvey, 37, 209, 316, 1791, 1928
Kinvolved, 705
Kio Networks, 327
Kiodex Inc., 990
Kiomix, 1378
Kionix, 434, 1130
Kionix Inc., 813
Kip, 863
KIPP DC, 1315
KIPP MA, 1315
Kipsu, 1179
Kira, 1005
Kira Talent, 2228
KiraKira3D, 1009, 1554
Kiran Energy, 263
Kirby Lester Group, 842
Kirin Pharmaceutical, 1456
Kirkland's, 405
Kirona, 2935
Kirtas Technologies, 1061
Kirusa, 27, 645, 2809, 2992, 3266
KISCO Solutions, 2339
Kishlay Snacks, 1346
KISI, 1223
KisoJi Biotechnology, 2174
Kiss No Frog, 2829
KissKissBankBank, 3229
KISSmetrics, 720, 1862
KissMetrics, 1702
Kissmetrics, 1464, 1549
KissMyAds, 3198
Kissnofrog, 2820
Kit Check, 1297, 1559
Kit Digital, 3160
Kitalive, 1610
Kitan Consolidated, 2600
KitCheck, 2934
Kitcheck, 644, 1056
Kitched United, 894
Kitchen Collection, 1971
Kitchen Surfing, 1718
KitchenMate, 680, 2130, 2132
Kitchenmate, 2131
Kite, 328, 787
Kite & Lightingm, 310
Kite & Lightning, 1391
Kite Phrama, 94
Kith Kitchen, 1438
Kitman Labs, 299
KitSplit, 623
Kitsy Lane, 1150, 1463
KITT.ai, 776
Kitt.ai, 1703
Kittery, 1509
Kittyhawk, 309
Kity, 857
Kiva, 1374
Kiva Software, 1125, 1855
Kiva Systems, 1196
Kiveda, 2820, 2829
Kiverdi, 1058
Kivuto, 2148
Kiwa, 3248

KIWI, 1896
Kiwi, 1657
Kiwi Co., 328
Kiwi Crate, 1065
Kiwi Wearables, 985
KiwiCo, 520, 720, 742, 763
Kiwigrid, 2815
Kixer, 1800
KIXEYE, 1855
Kixeye, 949, 972, 1125, 1566
Kiyatec, 1925
KJK, 1125
KJUS, 2000
Kkeye, 2841
KKR, 3254
Klala, 3095
Klang, 2944
Klar, 48
Klara, 1114
Klarna, 669, 819, 1006, 1504, 1657, 2437, 2437, 2654, 2919
Klash, 3198
Klashwerks, 2181
Klaxoon, 1982
KLD Energy, 595
KLDiscovery, 1979
Kleiner Perkins Caufield Byers, 3273
KlikDaily, 721
Kliken, 754
Kline Hill Partners, 3245
Klip, 1184
Klipfolio, 308, 2187
Klipsch Audio, 1908
Klir Technologies, 755
Klmeta, 2815
Klockner Pentaplast, 2607
Klone Lab, 1161
Klook, 2681
Kloudless, 1983, 1992, 2009
Kloudpics, 2847
Klout, 724, 876, 1006, 1918
KLP, 70
KLUE, 2225
Klune Industries, 1906
Klustera, 724
Kluttr, 624
KlÖckner & Co. AG, 1133
Klöckner Pentaplast, 2596
KM Labs, 1009, 1055
KMC Mining, 2029
KMCO, 165
Kmofin Arkiv, 3033
KMX, 2054
Knack, 591, 662, 1079
Knape & Vogt, 1990
Kneebone, 2051
Kneron, 1511
Knewsapp, 1827
Knewton, 27, 742, 744, 778, 2437, 2681
KNF Corporation, 1204
Kngine, 3089
Knight & Carver Wind Group, 838
Knight Oil Tools, 502
Knight Packaging Group, 1494
Knight-Hub Computing, 528
Knights Apparel, 1210, 1234, 1971
Knightscope, 810
KnipBio, 985, 1104, 3246
Knjaz Milos, 3086
Knoa, 180, 2969
Knoa Corporation, 957
Knoa Software, 679, 679, 712, 1526
Knoa Software Inc., 813
Knobbe Martens, 3258
Knobbe Martens Olson & Bear, 3258
Knock, 545, 863
Knod, 689

Knodes, 1521
Knoll, 2688
Knology, 227
Knolskape, 1017
Knopp Biosciences, 1452, 1626
Knopp Biosciences LLC, 1102
Knopp Neurosciences, 1003
Knotable, 3226
Knotch, 863, 1014, 1752
Knotel, 1346, 3226
Knotet, 2024
Knotice, 1051
Knovel, 51, 568, 1682, 1748
Know Better Foods, 1251
KnowBe4, 1796
Knowde, 398
Knowhere, 565
Knowledge Adventure, 1795
Knowledge Architechts, 1532
Knowledge Factor Nobel Learning Communities, 1109
Knowledge Power, 2563
Knowledge Revolution Inc., 950
Knowledge to Practice, 1554
Knowledge Transmission, 2951
Knowledge Tree, 1575
Knowledge Vision, 853
KnowledgeHound, 1159
Knowledgemill, 2963
KnowledgeNet, 1257
KnowledgeNet Inc., 255
KnowledgeStorm, 1865
KnowledgeTree, 540, 1407
Knowlix, 2374
Knowlton Development Corporation, 2177
KnowMe, 263
Knowre, 1091, 1719, 3118
Knowsy, 863
Knowtions Research, 2146
Knozen, 876
KNS, 3118
KNTV, 597
Knutson Mortgage, 847
KNXit, 395
Koala.ch, 2377
Koan, 564
Koan Agroscience, 558
Kobalt, 894, 1646, 2272, 2469
Kobalt Music, 3061, 3122
Kobiton, 1412
Koble, 2122
Kobus Services, 2958
Koch & Associates Inc., 911
Kochek, 1225
Koda Distribution Group, 197
KodaCloud, 520, 2070
Kodak Dental Systems, 1100
Kodiak Networks, 1517
Kodiak Robotics, 238, 1125
Koding, 876, 1073, 1184, 1598
Kodotel, 3062
Koemei, 1637
Koffie, 2398
Kogent Surgical, 270
Kognitiv, 2222
Kognitiv Corporation, 2165
Kognitiv Spark, 2192
Koh Founders, 231
Kohlberg Kravis Roberts & Co., 3245
Koho, 2217
Kohort, 789, 1479, 2016
Koinify, 730
Koio, 328
Kokam, 1607
Kokko, 1179
Koko, 3, 1724
Kokowa, 310

1326

Portfolio Companies Index

Kokunai Shi, 2339
Kolbe-Coloco, 2878
Kold-Draft, 296
Kollective, 561, 1242, 1483
Kolltan Pharmaceuticals, 661
Kolpin Outdoors, 719
Kolpin Powersports, 719
Koltan Pharmaceuticals, 2806
Komax, 2555
Komex, 2301
Komiko, 776
Komli, 2992
Komli Media, 2809
Komodo, 3003
Komodohealth, 720
Komptech Farwicks, 2674
Kona Bay Marine Resources, 942, 1015
Kona International, 3136
Kona Medical, 622, 1126, 1608
Kona Medical Inc., 272
Konarka Technologies, 127, 468
Konecta, 2842
Kong, 125
Kong.net, 2841
Kongregate, 1125
Koning, 705
Koninklijke Swets and Zeitlinger BV, 2983
KonMari, 1186
KonTEM, 2815
Kontera, 549, 1798, 3212
Kontera Technologies, 2557
Kontiki, 57, 857, 1242, 1449
KontrollFreek, 285
Kontron, 1957
Kontron Embedded AG, 2291, 2293, 2297
Kony, 1005, 1701, 1949
Kooba, 1769
Koolbit, 389
KoolSpan, 1172, 1588, 1875
Koolspan, 1305
Kooltra, 1610, 2235
Koomi, 2178
Koontz-Wagner Electronic, 935
Koowo, 1340
Kopari, 1092
Kopari Beauty, 14
KopoKopo, 1032
Koppers Inc., 1624
Korbit, 3118
Kore Wireless Group, 20
Kore.ai, 1284
Korea First Bank, 303
Korea OTC, 2848
Korea Petrochemical, 897
Korn Ferry, 790
Koronis Pharma, 1399
Korra, 624
Korrelated, 209
Korrio, 978
Koru, 490, 742, 1186
Korvis, 1648
KOS Corp, 2045
Kosan Biosciences, 94
Kosmix, 182, 1125
Kosmos Energy, 1957
Kostek Systems, 2993
Kosterina, 7
Kotak, 145
Kotidata, 2957
KOTURA, 801
Kotura, 154, 885
Kouchzauber, 3047
Koudai, 1184
Koudai Shopping, 1957
Koupon, 1207
Kovars, 1604
Kovax, 3235

Kovio, 582, 928, 1241
Koyj, 1091
Koza Gida, 585
KP Aviation, 228
KP Corporation, 815
KP Holdings, 1343
KP1, 2367
KPA, 491
KPG Ventures, 56
KPI Consulting, 381
KPMG, 217, 3262, 3264, 3265, 3266
KPop Stage, 3172
KPS Capital Partners, 3245
Kraco, 1755
Krak, 3099
Kramerk Junction, 1577
Kratos Defense & Security Solutions, 1361
Kraus Global, 2218
Krause's Sofa Factory, 714
Krauss Craft, 467
Krauthammer, 2370
Krayden, 1507
Kreatel, 2879
Kreditech, 304, 3035
Kreeda Games, 2840
Kreker, 3062
Kretschmer, 360
KRG Capital Partners, 77
KrisEnergy Holdings, 741
Krisp, 1672
Krispy Kreme UK, 2354
Kristalpark III, 2940
Kritik, 2122
Kriya, 310
Krohnert Infotecs, 2815
Kroll BondRatings, 1298, 1597
KromaTiD, 736
Kronos, 927, 1045, 1169
Kronos Bio, 1934
Kronos Foods, 1494
KRP Properties, 2276
Krueger-Gilbert Health Physics, 381
Kruk SA, 2697
Krungthep Land, 1143, 2937
Krush, 327, 1527
Krux, 27, 1566, 1623, 1829
Kryptiq, 1947
Kryptiq Corporation, 244
Krypton, 548
KSARIA, 248
kSaria, 1335
kSaria Corporation, 318
KSep Systems, 227
KSM Castings, 2686
KSNET, 1143, 2937
KSNet, 897
Kspine, 1728
KSQ, 748
KTH Seed Capital, 2858
Ku6, 827
Kuaidian, 827
Kuaipay, 1361
Kuali, 1393
Kuato, 2822
Kubos, 310
Kudos, 2065
Kudu, 1837
Kuehne Nagel, 383
Kujiale, 827, 925
Kula, 2847
Kula Bio, 321, 664
Kuli Kuli, 2153
Kumu Networks, 485, 1073, 1928
Kun Wha Pharmaceutical, 1456
Kung Fu Fast Food Chain, 2551
Kunterbunt, 2522
Kuona, 2975

KupiVIP, 27, 2312, 2919
KupiVip.ru, 1009
Kupivip.ru, 2469
Kura Oncology, 710
Kurbo Health, 1491, 1680
Kurgyvenu.lt, 3040
Kurion, 731, 1155
Kuros Biosurgery, 2867
Kurt Geiger, 2705
Kurt Versen, 170, 197
Kurtosys, 1848, 1862
Kuschco Holdings, 393
Kush Bottles, 152, 1208
Kustomer, 308, 485
Kuusama Design Oy, 2864
Kuvare, 96
Kuvee, 774, 820
Kuwait Energy, 3164
Kuzneski Financial Group, 3264
KV Custom Window and Doors, 2207
KV Games, 3241
KVS, 796, 2653, 2665
Kwater, 1076
KWh Analytics, 2398
Kwicr, 1675, 1918
Kwik, 545, 1323, 1346
Kwipped, 1925
KX Industries, 1194
KXEN, 928
Kxen, 3229
Kyjen, 1576
Kylie.ai, 1703
Kyligence, 485
Kylin Therapeutics, 844
Kyma, 3063
Kyma Technologies, 1917
Kymata, 1795, 2328
Kymera International, 1404
Kymera Therapeutics, 193, 1128
Kymeta, 1010, 1155
Kyn Therapeutics, 193
KynderMed, 3251
Kynectiv, 1572
Kyotec Group, 2853
Kyowa Hakko Kirin, 1456
Kypha, 270
Kyriba, 1890
Kyruus, 711, 938, 1155, 1610, 1918
Kyte, 621, 628, 798, 2437, 3143
Kythera Biopharmaceuticals, 154, 1495
Kyto, 3047
Kytogenics, 2197
Kyverna Therapeutics, 1934
KZO, 1901
KZO Innovations, 245, 983

L

L&C Trucking, 2156
L&L Foods, 479
L&S Industries, 943
L&S Mechanical, 319
L'Anza, 1979
L'ArcoBaleno, 2829
L'Artisan Parfumeur, 781
L'Azurde, 1021
L'Occitane, 405
L., 901
L.B. Maple Treat Corporation, 2049
L.B. White Company, 1174
L.I.T. Surgical, 1170
L.P., 2021
L2C, 1504
l2C Technologies, 1556
L3 Technology, 2958
L4 Epsilon, 3104
L7 Logistics, 999
L99, 2841

Portfolio Companies Index

LA 411, 868
La Cuisine du Web, 2357
La Dove, 376
LA Fitness, 2371
LA Fitness International, 1160, 1343, 1648
La Jolla Pharmaceutical, 517
La Jolla Pharmaceutical Company, 1708, 1920
La Lumière, 1768
La Luna, 3033
la Madeline, 1753
La Place, 1755
La Ruche qui dit Oui!, 3229
La Tavola Fine Linen Rental, 792
LAB InterLink, 1839
Lab42, 1618
LAB4U, 1530
Labaster, 2469
Labco, 3011
Labcyte, 596, 812, 928, 1297
Labcyte Inc., 87, 605
LabDoor, 985
Labdoor, 545, 752, 998
Label Insight, 570, 1207
Label-Aire, 874
Labelbox, 945, 1079
Labelink, 2207
Labeyrie Fine Foods, 3017
labfolder, 2832
Labgas Instrument Company, 2864
LabGenius, 1363
Labmeeting, 1077
LabOne, 1973
LaboPharm, 928
Laboratoire M2, 2087
Laboratorios Sanifit, 2544
Laboratory Corp. of America, 303
LaborChart, 746
Laborie Medical Technologies, 197
Labormed, 1456
Labournet, 54
Labrador Mobile, 42
Labrador Ventures, 3273
Labrys Biologics, 389, 1014
Labsco, 785
Labstep, 3099
Labster, 1393
LabVantage, 336
Laces, 1169, 2201
Laces Group, 2200
LaCima, 2144
Ladder, 1125, 1426
Ladder Capital, 828
Lady In Leisure Ltd, 2827
LaFarge Surma Cement, 1012
Lagan, 2653, 2665
Lagan Technologies, 2601
Lagarrique, 2332
Lagoa, 37
Lagotek, 85, 650
Lagrange Systems, 1247
Laho Equipement, 2705
Laho Equipment, 2712
Laird Limited, 61
LAIX, 827
Laiye, 1125
Lakala, 2927
Lake City Acquisition, 1252
Lake County Press, 410
Lake Shore Group, 1582
LakePharma, 119
Lakeview Health, 1169
Lakoteka, 2687
LAM Research Company, 1708
Lamar, 1191
Lambada School, 894
Lambda, 814
Lambda School, 827

Lambda Technologies, 1013
Lamina Technologies, 3092
Lamination Services, 1609
Lamoda, 2820, 2829, 3161
Lamont Digital System, 405
Lampiris, 3125
Lanair Holdings, 402
Lancashire Holdings, 560
Lancashire Holdings Limited, 407
Lancashire Rosebud Fund, 2699
Lancaster Laboratories, 847
Lancaster Pollard Holdings, 1746
Lancope, 389, 551
Land Insight, 3099
Landdrill International, 2085
LANDesk, 1912
LANDESK Software, 1817
LANDesk Software, 1679, 1873
Landis, 945
Landit, 548, 709
Landmark, 194, 782
Landmark Equity Partners XIV LP, 2088
Landmark Equity Partners XV LP, 2088
Landmark Graphics, 1561
Landmark Irrigation Holding Services, 1494
LANDR, 2216
Landroller, 1786
Landry's, 874
Landsham, 2485
Landshire Inc., 77
Landslide Technologies, 55, 1003
Landt, 568
Landune International, 1771
Landways, 518
Lane, 2204
Lane Supply Inc., 988
Lanetix, 1028
Laney Drilling, 1518
Lang Technologies, 2604
Langhaus Financial, 2165
Language Labs, 2922
Language Management, 1294
Language Weaver, 1403, 1786
Languagelabs.com, 2455
Lanjing Technology, 2989
Lannett Company, 190
Lansmont, 238
LANtech, 1839
Lantern, 121, 1187, 1702
Lantern Communications, 1008
Lantheus Medical Imaging, 212
Lanthio Pharma, 2505
Lantiq, 843
Lantos Technologies, 428, 704, 949, 1522
Lanx, 470
Lanzatech NZ, 1449
Lapmaster International, 1377
Lapolla Industries, 679, 679
Lara Networks, 1287, 1795
Larada Sciences, 1786
Laramie Energy, 673
Laredo Hospitality, 2245
Laredo Petroleum Holdings, 1957
Largan Precision, 3209
Larian Publishing, 3033
Larian Studios, 2417
Lario Oil & Gas Company, 531
Lark, 183, 721, 845
Larky, 743
LARQ, 198
Las Vegas Cannaplex, 1139
Las Vegas Color Graphics, 1722
Las Vegas Film Festival, 515
LaSalle Capital, 3255
Lasem, 2953
Laser Diagnostic Technologies, 1708
Laser Diagnostic Technology, 1674

Laser Diagnostics, 950
Laser Light Engines, 325
Laser Projection Technologies, 352
LaserCure Sciences, 281
Laserhip, 1493
LaserShip, 867, 1248
Lashou, 2970
LASO, 597
Lasso, 1618, 1898, 2262
Last Second Tickets, 2577
Last.flicloud, 2437
Last.Fm, 2437
LastLine, 641
Lastline, 604, 1478, 1537
Lastminute, 2378, 3004
Lastminute.com, 1323, 1890
Laszlo Systems, 1241, 2188
LAT Apparel, 1565
Latapack, 2080
Latch, 380, 708, 1155
Late Great Chevy, 911
Latent AI, 803
Lateral, 3099
Latex International, 1470
Latham & Watkins, 3262
Latham International, 1138
LaTherm, 2815
Latin Healthcare Fund, 958
Latino Communications Network, 1233
Latista, 288, 380
Latite Holdings, 1131
Latite Roofing & Sheetmetal Company, 842
Latitude Geographics, 238
Latrima Medical, 2320
Lattice Power, 2427
LatticePower, 1187
Lattive Engines, 1657
Lauder Partners, 3273
Laudio, 1
Laughing Glass Cocktails, 130
Laughlin & Associates, 3251
Laughly, 221
Launch Darkly, 610, 1809
Launch Learning, 743
LaunchBit, 1914
Launchbox Digital, 50
LaunchCapital, 3263
Launchcyte, 1452
LaunchDarkly, 1537, 1881
Launcher, 310
LaunchKey, 680, 1914
Launchkey, 1154
LaunchKit, 234, 787
LaunchPad, 1101
Launchpad, 1945
Launchpad Global Consulting, 2922
Launchpad LA, 231, 309
Launchpad.la, 1569
LaunchPoint, 419
Launchrock, 1521
Laundry Mart Inc., 449
Laureate Education, 1948
Laureate International Universities, 1745
Laurel & Wolf, 1059, 1752, 1966
Laurel & Wolf Interior Design, 901
Laurel Health Care Co., 1271
Lauren Loft Social, 1051
Laurus Labs, 711
Lava, 1930
Lavalife, 2073
Lavante, 185, 1623, 1918
Lavino Shipping Company, 836
Lavo, 1769
Lavu, 689
Law Business Research, 1115
LawGeex, 2938
LawLogix, 1461

Portfolio Companies Index

Lawmatics, 680, 1557
Lawn Doctor, 1115
Lawn Guru, 400
Lawnmower, 310
LawnTap, 999
LawPal, 1719
LawPivot, 1959
Lawrence Group, 60
Lawrenceville Plasma Physics, 18
Laws of Motion, 623
Lawson, 843, 1728
Lawyaw, 1557
Layar, 3042, 3140
Layer, 108, 133, 641, 876, 944, 1158, 1254, 1491, 1610
Layer Vault, 1527
Layered Technologies, 1917
LayerVault, 1534
Layerwise, 3033
Layetana Real Estate, 153
Lazada, 2820, 2829, 3161
Lazart Production, 1524
Lazer Spot, 557
Lazer Spot Inc., 867, 917
Lazook, 3021
Lazy Acres Merket, 874
Lazydays, 1968
LBL Lighting Inc., 911
LBP Manufacturing, 1169, 1482
LCM XIV CLO, 1493
LD COM, 2488
LD Vision Group, 2137
LDC, 3088
LDetek, 238
LDiscovery, 1460
LDK, 2570, 3185
LDK Solar, 3053
LDL Technology, 2472
LDR, 1502, 1794
LDR Medical, 205
LDR Spine, 1622
Le Bronze Industriel, 2414
Le Figano, 2592
Le Figaro, 2616
Le Gourmet Chef, 1552
Le Kan, 3112
Le Monde Holdings Ltd, 2477
Le Souk, 863
Le Tigre, 940
Le Tote, 173, 689, 894, 949, 1114, 1637
Lea, 2842
Lea com, 2346
Leacom, 2346
LEAD, 1414
Lead Genuis, 2262
Lead Group, 1720
Lead Pages, 175
Lead Point, 1537
Leadcorp, 585
Leader Gasket of Slovakia s.r.o., 3113
Leader Technologies, 381
Leaderflush, 2787
Leaders, 568, 1323
Leadership Public Schools, 1315
LeadFlip, 310
LeadGenius, 246, 1058, 1672
LeadiD, 1851
Leading Edge Geomatics, 2198
Leading Edge Innovations, 1027
Leading Edge Labels, 2787
Leading Educators, 1315
LeadingResponse, 973, 1232
LeadPages, 631
Leadpages, 779
LeadQual, 952
LeadSift, 1610, 2148
Leadspace, 238, 3205

Leadtone Limited, 3053
Leadtrend, 1924
Leaf, 395, 1443, 1810
Leaf Cart, 395
Leaf Forward, 2134
Leaf Link, 1114, 1443
LeafLink International, 2233
LeafList, 865
Leafly, 1484
Leaftail Labs, 1186, 1666
League, 773, 2217, 2256
League Apps, 12
LeagueApps, 535, 1533, 1635
LeagueLink, 1061
Leagues, 1966
Lean Plastics, 2518
LeanData, 545, 720, 1666
LeanEco, 3194
LeanIX, 1005
LeanNova Engineering, 2746
Leanplum, 1079, 1346, 1666
LeanTaaS, 1005
Leanworks, 2392
Leap, 328, 548, 1323
LEAP Auto Loans, 205
Leap Motion, 938, 3046
Leap Therapeutics, 922
Leap.It, 635
Leapfin, 320
Leapfrog, 1335
LeapFrog Investments, 1374
Leaplife, 1566
Leapmind, 998, 1009
Leapset, 1101
LeapYear Technologies, 623
Lear Corporation, 576
Leara, 1418
Learfield Sports, 1498
Learmont Pharmaceuticals, 663
Learn Behavioural, 1140
Learn It Systems, 1234, 1722
Learn To Live, 1179
Learn to Win, 1426
Learn Vest, 182
Learn Zillion, 597
LearnBoost, 457
learndirect, 2935
Learners Guild, 54, 1058
Learnfield (Skoove), 2832
Learning, 1493
Learning Care Group, 111, 1256
Learning Games Network, 1315
Learning Labs, 2958
Learning Machines, 738
Learning Seat, 1576
Learning.com, 733
Learnium, 2276
LearnLaunch, 1101
LearnLux, 623
Learnmetrics, 985, 1009
Learnosity, 238
Learnpedia, 2895
LearnUp, 1666
LearnVest, 27, 495, 537, 582, 1588
LearnWell, 352
LearnZillion, 1315, 1393, 3246
Learnzillon, 1359
Lease Accelerator, 1005
Lease Term Solutions, 1076
LeaseExchange, 1538
LeaseLock, 1616, 1985
Leaselock, 1786
LeaseQ, 1164
LeaseQuery, 191, 1412
Leather Resources of America Inc., 204
LeatherXchange, 2378
LecTec, 217

Lectrus Corporation, 1560
Lecturi, 2829
Lecturio, 2820
LED Engin, 1418
LED Medical Diagnostics, 2071
LED Roadway Lighting, 2087, 2197
Ledbury, 618, 907
LeddarTech, 2890
Ledge, 121
Ledge Investing, 1677
Ledger, 562
Ledger Investing, 945
LedgerX, 894
Ledgerx, 1125
Lediberg, 3145
Ledlight Group, 2419
Ledlite, 2940
Lee Equity Partners, 3254
Leeflink, 420
Leejam, 1021
Leena AI, 798
Leengate Valves, 3234
Leepet, 2927
Leerink, 1151
Leerink Transformation Partners, 36
Leet, 310
Leeward Renewable Energy, 157
LefEngin, 950
Lefora, 493, 1101
Left at Albuquerque, 1552
Left Hand Robotics, 431
LeftHand Networks, 318, 810, 1483, 1901
Lefthand Networks, 143
LeftRight Studios, 1003
Legacy at Sandhill, 1220
Legacy Cabinets Holdings II, 1192
Legacy Connect, 1635
Legacy Ridge, 1220
Legacy Seed Companies, 817
Legacy Technologies, 402
Legacy Technologies Inc., 1057
Legacy Venture, 3273
Legal Communications, 1275
Legal Sifter, 275
Legal Zoom, 1006
LegalMation, 1259
LegalShield, 1231
LegalSifter, 296
LegalZoom, 782, 1079, 3024
Legalzoom, 561, 1464
LegalZoom.com, 1235
Legato, 1762
Legend Communications of Wyoming, 832
Legend Films, 201
Legend Natural Gas, 1577
Legend Pictures, 1832
Legend Production Holdings, 1577
Legend3D, 201
Legendary, 27, 339, 977, 1157
Legendary Pictures, 20
Legends of Learning, 490
Legerity, 782
Leggett & Platt Incorporated, 77
Legion, 742, 1346
Legit, 398, 680
Legit Patents, 3099
LegitParents, 708
LegitScript, 1499
Legra Systems, 1084
LeGuide.com, 3104
LegUp, 1009
Legworks, 954
Lehigh Technologies, 949
Leica, 280, 1021
Leisure Concepts, 874
Leisure link, 2667
Leisure Link Holdings Limited, 2812

Portfolio Companies Index

Leisure-Hunt, 2378
LeisureLink, 1239, 1786, 1917
Leisurelink, 504
LeisureQ, 3118
Leiter's, 785
Leiters, 1631, 1764
Lekolar, 2303, 3045
Lele Global, 1125
Lele Ketang, 1393
LEM Holding, 3060
Lema21, 1698
LeMaitre, 952
Lemhi Ventures, 3268
Lemon Tree, 1957
Lemonade, 298, 708, 820, 894
LemonAid Health, 1350
Lemonaid Health, 545
LemonBox, 1142
Lemongrass, 518
Lemontech, 28
Lenco, 2329
Lenda, 1599, 1998
Lendamend, 1786
LendCare, 491
Lenddo, 304, 527, 1374
Lending Club, 241, 511, 579, 1258, 1346
Lending Front, 1557
Lending Standard, 1690
LendingClub, 116, 389, 773, 1257, 1821, 2574
LendingFront, 2146
LendingHome, 553, 742, 773
LendingPoint, 62
LendInvest, 2437
Lendio, 79, 520, 1851
LendIt, 100
LendKey, 1888
Lendkey, 609, 610, 1865
LendMed, 999
LendStreet, 1058
LendUp, 776, 894, 1058, 1504, 1760, 1821, 2011
Lenel Systems International, 2893
Lengow, 2377
Lenimed, 2815
Lenley Holdings, 3251
Lenovo, 2762
Lenox, 494
Lensabl, 121
Lensar, 73
Lenscare AG, 3181
Lenskart, 2196
Lenslet, 1042
Lenslet Ltd., 3149
LensVector, 983, 1241, 1917
Lensway.com, 2137
Lensway.se, 2137
LenSx, 1923
Lenta, 1837
LENTECHS, 300
Lentil, 2130
Leo, 787
Leo Health, 1589
Leocorpio, 381
Leon Hansen Maskinfabrik, 3194
Leonard Green & Partners, 3254
Leosphere, 2842
Leostream, 1196
Leptos Biomedical, 1788
Leqee, 2681
Lerer Ventures, 1701
Les Fréres Blanc, 3011
Leslie's, 1092
LeSlipFrançais, 2288
LESS, 650
Lesser Evil, 2153
Lesson Nine (Babbel), 2832
Lessonly, 86, 1554
Let's Do This, 1666

Letao, 2575
Lethbridge Biogas, 2043
Lets, 2848
LetsBab, 940
LetsLunch, 3116
LetsVenture, 27
Lettuce, 231, 309, 625, 1103, 2016
Leuko, 849
LeukoSite, 1561
Leuven Air, 2358
Lev, 367
LevaData, 1759
LevdUp, 586
Level, 1099
Level 10 Energy, 2001
Level 5 Networks, 2378
Level 7 Systems, 808
Level Access, 1045
Level Equity, 36
Level Ex, 9, 1483
Level Four Orthotics and Prosthetics, 1433
Level Jump, 2094
Level Platforms, 2039
Level Ten Energy, 776
Level10 Comics, 3100
LevelEleven, 608, 965, 1285, 1610
LevelOps, 680
Levels Beyond, 1871
LevelTen Energy, 534
LevelUp, 894, 938, 1841
Levensohn Venture Partners, 3273
Lever, 545, 945, 995, 1184, 1629
Levin HomeCare, 753
Levlad Inc., 874
Levo League, 816, 863, 901
Levridge, 817
Levy Acq., 1683
Lewis Electric Supply, 112
Lewis-Goetz and Company, 197
LEX Energy Partners, 2129
Lex Machina, 548, 568, 2010
Lex Markets, 1616
Lexaria Energy, 1139
Lexibridge, 532
Lexicon, 240, 843
Lexicon Marketing, 1507
Lexington Home Brands, 1755, 2014
Lexington Medical, 1347
Lexington Partners, 3273
Lexipol, 1576
Lexitas, 136
Lexity, 1718
Lexmark, 931
Lexop, 2204
Leyden Energy, 1674
Leyhs Pharma, 2518
Leyline, 1314
Leyou, 1241, 2427
LFE Capital, 3251, 3268
LG Lugar de Gente, 931
LGC, 2926
LGC Wireless, 163, 613, 2453
LgDb, 686
LGM Pharma, 406
LGS Innovations, 1160
LGT, 2500
LHC Holdings, 1493
LHG Foods Inc., 2115
LHP Hospital Group, 435
LHS, 2762
Li-Cycle, 2054
LIA Diagnostics, 1581
Lia Diagnostics, 296
Liaison, 770, 1206, 1332, 1629
Liaison International, 1464, 1957
Liaison Technologies, 1893
Lian Luo, 1125

LianLian, 1340
Lianlian Pay, 1361
Liason Acquisition LLC, 159
LiaZon, 224
Liberate, 2576
Liberation Entertainment, 496
Libero, 2321
LiberoVision, 3143
Libersy, 2813
Libertas, 558
Liberty, 2515
Liberty Bell Power, 157
Liberty Cannabis, 99
Liberty Dialysis, 1090
Liberty Global Ventures, 3265
Liberty Hydro, 1200
Liberty Latin America, 2243
Liberty Oilfield Services, 531, 1577
Liberty Plaza, 1683
Liberty Pressure Pumping, 1314
Liberty Resources, 1577
Liberty Resources II, 1577
Liberty Safe, 525
Liberty Safe & Security Products, 1460
Liberty Tax Service, 655
Liberty Tire Recycling, 1118
LibertyX, 1489
Libit, 2773
Library Solutions, 1376
Library Systems & Services, 165, 1505
LibraTax, 1119
Librato, 234, 553
LibreDigital, 55, 1848
Librestream, 2065, 2074, 2101
Librestream Technologies Inc., 2129
Libricity, 1000
Librify, 1305
Libryo, 3099
LicenseStream, 42
Lida Holdings Limited, 2718
Lidyana, 1598
Lieberman Research Worldwide, 1779
Lieferheld, 3035, 3161
Liekki Oy, 2864
Lien Nation, 1925
Lier Chemical Co., 2533
Life 360, 762, 1323
Life Care Services, 1276
Life Detection Systems, 999
Life Express, 2927
Life Guard Games, 1593
Life House, 520
Life Image, 1175, 1421
Life Imaging Systems, 2051
Life Line Screening, 1464
Life Links, 999
Life Media, 1241
Life Share Technologies, 86
Life Sprout, 18
Life Style, 2328
Life Technologies Corp., 1905
Life Time, 1837
Life.io, 1572
Life36, 1101
Life360, 305, 361, 597, 708, 1058, 1122, 1614, 1658
Lifeblob, 3100
LifeBond, 2445
Lifebond, 2595
Lifecake, 2676
LifeCell, 2809
Lifecode, 1657
Lifecodes, 532
Lifecore Biomedical, 3268
Lifecrowd, 1121
LifeCycle Pharma, 3006
LifeHive Systems, 2178

Portfolio Companies Index

LifeIMAGE, 809, 1146
Lifeline Scientific, 2701
Lifeline Systems Inc., 1905
Lifelines Technology, 651
LifeLinkMD, 1603
LifeLock, 388, 990, 1235
Lifelock, 267, 561, 1006
LifeMinders, 1348
LifeMine, 764
LifeMine Therapeutics, 894
LifeNet Systems, 3251
LifePAD, 2931
LifePay, 2931
LifePort, 1707
LifeRaft, 2065
Lifesafer, 1343
Lifescan, 1762
Lifescript, 646
LifeShield Security, 1227, 1348
LifeSize, 1762
Lifesize, 1213, 1537
LifeSize Communications, 205, 1449, 1798
Lifespeak, 2074
Lifespring, 54
LifeSprout, 1172
LifeStream, 1132
Lifestream Diagnostics, 1839
Lifestyle Family Fitness, 227
Lifesum, 1719, 2665
LifeSync Corporation, 67, 365
LifeTime, 1113
Lifetime Fitness, 745
LifeWave, 1604
Lifeways, 2199
Lift, 1718
Lift Auto Group, 2065
Lift for Life Academy, 60
Liftbump, 618
LiftIgniter, 309
Liftoff, 234
Liftoff Mobile, 381, 1587
Liftopia, 742, 1153, 1598, 1808
LiftSeat Corporation, 1743
LIG, 3136
Ligado Networks, 444
Ligand Pharma, 1271
Ligature, 3239
Ligchine International, 294
Light, 648, 894
Light Based Technologies, 2144
Light Blue Optics, 2653, 2665
Light Chaser, 827
Light Field Lab, 44, 1928
Light In The Box, 2575
Light Integra Technology, 2257
Light Sail Energy, 2148
Light Sciences Oncology, 56, 928, 3006
Light Step, 1537
Light Wave Dental Management, 92
Lightbend, 877, 1666
LightChip Inc., 255
Lightelligence, 222
Lighter Capital, 776, 1947
Lightera, 1750
Lightfoot, 1003
LightForm, 1155
Lightform, 521, 1477
Lighthouse, 108, 720, 1677, 1727
Lighthouse Autism Center, 20
Lighthouse Capital Partners, 3273
Lighthouse Community Charter School, 1315
Lighthouse Resources, 1551
Lighting Technologies International, 1667
LightingScience, 3242
LightInTheBox.com, 3241
Lightlife Foods, 360
Lightneer, 888, 1530

Lightning Hybrids, 322
Lightning Network, 1812
Lightning Systems, 147
Lightningcast, 1137
Lightower, 1157, 1410
Lightpoint, 1065
Lightpoint Medical, 3098
LightPost Digital, 390
Lightricks, 1005, 3212
LightRiver Technologies, 574
Lightship Telecom, 186
Lightspan, 1706
LightSpeed, 27, 2150
Lightspeed, 2074
Lightspeed Financial, 1731
Lightspeed Venture Partners, 990, 3273
LightStep, 553, 1657
Lightstream, 1483
LightSurf, 215
Lightswitch, 1121
Lightt, 327
LighTuning, 908
LightUp, 623
LightUp Technologies AB, 2709
Lightyear Holdings, 157
Ligier-Microcar, 2285
Ligistics Exchange, 752
Lignetics, 832
LigoCyte Pharmaceuticals, 189, 772
Lihua Group, 2927
Liingo Eyewear, 79
Lijit Networks, 318
Like.com, 241, 564
LikeList, 1773
Likely, 2577
Likewise, 1855
Lilakutu, 2428
Lilia, 2122
Lilium, 1363
Lilium Aviation, 2437
Lilliput Kidswear, 223
Lilliputian, 2072
Lilliputian Systems, 928
Lilly, 1100, 1349
LiLoE, 999
Lilt, 1657, 2018
Lilu, 1509
Lily, 1887
Lily's Kitchen, 1092
Lilypad Scales, 1593
Lima, 1418
Lima Corporate, 2842
Limata, 2815
Limbach Facility Services, 804
Limbix, 1477, 1657
Limbix Health, 1423
Limburg Gas, 2940
Limburg Win (D) T, 2940
Limburgs Klimaatfonds, 2940
Lime, 91, 125, 235, 728, 894
Lime Energy Co., 277
Lime Microsystems, 2653, 2665, 3019
Limeade, 85, 1871
LimeBike, 1646
Limeelife, 1249
Limejump, 3021
Limelight, 2141, 2235
Limelight Bio, 144
Limelight Networks, 1361
LimelightHealth, 2217
Limerick Investments, 3255
Limestone II Holding Company, 673
Limestone Pharma, 2071
Liminal Biosciences Inc., 2031
Linas Matkasse, 2628
Linc Software, 2837
Lincare Holdings Inc., 1905

Lincoln Clean Energy, 205
Lincoln Educational Services, 303
Lincoln Generating, 1797
Lincoln Helios Ltd., 911
Lincoln International Corporation, 911
Lincoln Investment, 1151
Lincoln Peak Partners, 789
Lincoln Peaking Power, 157
Lincoln Snacks, 360
Lincor, 655
Linden Capital Partners, 3254, 3255
Linden Lab, 186, 265, 430, 839, 1058, 1374, 1608
Lindoc, 2465
Lindora, 874
Lindorff Group, 2376
Lindsstrom LLC, 911
Lindy Biosciences, 849
Line 6, 1762
Line-Up, 3099
Line-X, 851
Lineage Grow Co., 2117
LineaGen, 1619
Lineagen, 924, 1074, 1222, 1407, 1474, 1886
Linear Technology, 1657, 1762
Linedata Services, 2867
LineKong, 1340
Linekong, 2841
Linen King, 1641
LineStream, 642
LineStream Technologies, 1898
Lineus Medical, 999
Lingia, 1966
Linglong Tire, 2927
Lingo Live, 1393
LingoChamp, 925
Lingokids, 1530
Lingoland, 310
Lingotek, 758, 983, 1679
LinguaLeo, 3079
Linguee, 2466
Linio, 2820, 2829, 3161
Link Care Services, 2890
Link Evolution, 2406
Link Labs, 288
Link Market Services, 3016
Link Mobility, 20
Linkable, 290
Linkable Networks, 224, 488, 536, 1069
Linkage, 165, 3091
LinkDoc, 2430
LinkedIn, 1657, 1841
Linkedin, 840, 2714
Linkett, 2107
LinkSmart, 1762
Linksoft, 532
LinkStorm, 1588
Linkstorm, 1065, 1164, 1305
Linktone, 2724
LinkWell Health, 1718
Linkwell Health, 646, 941
Linq, 75
Linqia, 1032
LinQuest Corporation, 1160
Lintes, 1009
Linus Academy, 175
Linuxx Global Solutions, 1609
Linx Technologies, 165
Liola, 1793
Lion Street, 205
Lionbridge, 405, 1169
Lionbridge Capital, 912
Liongard, 2074
Lionhead Studios, 2314
Lipella Pharmaceuticals, 1452
Lipetski Khladokombinat, 3062
Lipman, 2736

Portfolio Companies Index

Lipocalyx, 2815
Lipocine, 764
Lipomics, 1917
LipoScience, 1414
LipoSonix, 39, 1449
Lipton Corporate Child Care Centers, 1704
Liqid, 2074
Liquavista, 145, 1304, 3042
Liquent, 857
Liqui-Box, 1372
Liquid Audio, 1478
Liquid Data Intelligence, 3039
Liquid Environmental Solutions, 21
Liquid Grids Swarmology, 1786
Liquid Light, 1908, 2072
Liquid M, 183
Liquid Machines, 1178
Liquid Robotics, 1908
Liquid Web, 1160
Liquida Technologies, 1414
LiquidCool Solutions, 403
Liquidia, 2969
Liquidia Technologies, 389, 731
Liquidity Ventures, 3255
Liquidity Wines, 2137
LiquidLEDs, 1924
Liquidmetal Technologies, 1244
LiquidPlanner, 85, 1871
LiquidSky, 1614
LiquidSpace, 278, 1065, 1323
Liquidspace, 752, 1666
Liquidware Labs, 2, 1042, 1831
LiQuifix, 1101
LiquiGlide, 2234
Liquor.Com, 591
Liquor.com, 1101
Liqvid, 3142
Lise Watier, 2142
Lisi group, 2607
LISNR, 1050, 1051, 1599
Lisnr, 481, 1009, 1207, 1488
Listen, 200
Listen Current, 1315, 3246
Listen First, 793
Listen MD, 35
Listen.com, 205
Listenloop, 310
ListenWise, 1104
Listn, 1103
Listo, 54
Listo!, 131
LitBit, 1254
Litbit, 108, 545, 980
Lite Access Technologies Inc., 2061
Litecontrol, 1176
LitePoint, 1657
LiteScape, 116, 304, 1701, 1795
Litescape, 1913
Lithells, 2854
Lithion Power Group, 2267
Lithium, 666, 724, 1032, 1525, 1608, 1666
Lithium Technologies, 251, 582, 872, 1623, 1798
Lithium Technology, 651
Litmus, 1720, 2094
Little Bird, 1384
Little Bits, 1114
Little Borrowed Dress, 1358
Little Ducks Organics, 1907
Little Eye Labs, 3202
Little Green Pharma, 2167
Little Labs, 121, 1153
Little Passports, 845, 1759
Little Pim, 845
Little Spoon, 1703
Little Star Media, 1705
Little Tucker, 2093
littleBits Electronics, 779, 879, 1359, 1862, 1876

LittleBorrowedDress, 1101
LittleLabs, 562
Liv Riverale, 1220
LivBlends, 1637, 2009
Live Better With, 2986
Live By Touch, 2927
Live Gamer, 457, 1084, 1851
Live Look, 1305
Live Objects, 1812
Live Person, 1682
Live Well Financial, 1339
Live.Me, 977
LiveAction, 485, 1005
LiveBarn, 2231
Livebid.com, 85
LiveCapital, 414, 1649
Livedome, 2815
Livefyre, 568, 724, 876, 1898, 2016
Livegauge, 2094
Livehive, 40
LiveIntent, 91, 238, 361, 696, 742, 796, 1114, 1666
LiveLOOK, 1588
LiveLoop, 1969
Lively, 31, 327, 398, 548, 827
LiveMetric, 1892
Livemocha, 200
LiveNinja, 488
Livenlenz, 2148
LiveOps, 200, 582, 1006, 1203, 1235
Livepeer, 527
LivePerson, 308, 462
LiveRail, 3038
LiveRamp, 1323, 1335, 1543
Liverperson, 593
LiveSafe, 490, 925
LiveScribe, 1478
Livescribe, 564, 596, 1629, 1840, 1908
Livestar, 1058, 1254
Livestock Water Recycling, 2043
LiveStories, 776, 978, 1896
LiveTune, 3230
LiveU, 389, 2557, 3212
LiveVox, 297
LivHome, 1629
Living Earth Technology, 1691
Living Gluten Free, 103
Living Proof, 1464
Living Social, 1898
Livingly Media, 1203
Livingsocial, 881
Livingston International, 1745
Livity Africa, 1374
Livly, 1281
Livongo, 610, 820, 1079, 1158, 2681
Livongo Health, 1696
LivTech, 1499
LivWell International Corp., 2068
LJL BioSystems, 240
LJL Biosystems, 94
LK Bennett, 3027
LK DEsign Automation, 2436
LKC Technologies, 288
LL Games, 3206
LLamasoft, 1242
Llamasoft, 198, 743, 1759, 1837
LLC, 508
LLOG, 280
Lloyd's Barbeque Company, 1163
LLP Holding Corporation, 911
LLR Partners, 3254
LLS Internet (loopline), 2832
LM, 812
LM Foods, 381
LMC Diabetes & Endocrinology, 2212
Lmeca, 1091
LMF, 2878

LN Holdings, 1806
LNC, 3104
Load Dynamix, 252, 540, 936, 1237
Loadmaster Derrick & Equipment, 2008
Loadstar Sensors, 131, 1287
Loanbase, 310
loanDepot, 1419
LoanLogics, 1581, 1944
LoanSnap, 234
Loar Group, 1043
LOB, 752
Lob, 742, 1142, 1154, 1637
Lobby7, 2602
LOC-AID, 1013
Locafox, 2829
Local, 721
Local Bushel, 238, 1895
Local Crate, 1179
Local ID, 231
Local Kitchens, 1426
Local Libations, 546
Local Lift, 1593
Local Logic, 2024, 2087
Local Market Launch, 309, 1569
Local Media, 518
Local Media of America, 1817
Local Motion, 1254, 1914
Local Motors, 1635, 1914
Local Offer Network, 979
Local Orbit, 743, 1739
Local Response, 609, 876, 1249, 1969
Local TV, 1360
Local Voice, 291
Local Yokel Media, 679
Local.com, 925
Localdirt, 1359
Locale, 1760
Localeur, 221, 447
Locali, 3248
Locality, 1121, 1184
Localize, 1179
LocalMind, 2140
LocalWise, 246
Localytics, 91, 680, 773, 1101, 1104, 1305, 1464, 1488, 1791
Locamex, 2598
Locamoda, 1478
Locana, 1934
Locanis, 3152
LocAsian Networks, 2464
LocateAI, 1426
Locatible, 640
Location, 1695
Location Labs, 299, 610, 1241
Location Smart, 1013
Locationlabs, 1644
LocationSmart, 1871
Locaweb, 1685
Locbox, 1014
Locemia, 273
Locemia Solutions, 1993
Lochgilphead Hospital, 2740
LOCJ, 1101
Lock8, 2822
Lockdown Networks, 1008
Locke Lord LLP, 3251
Lockerdome, 570
Locket, 863
Locketgo, 2178
LockPath, 1525
Lockpath, 1969
Lockr, 635
Lockyer, 1520
LocoJoy, 2927
Locomation, 802
LocoMobi, 985
Locomobi, 31

Portfolio Companies Index

Locomotiv, 1315
LocoNav, 2398
Locox, 1536
LOCR, 2970
Locr, 2815
Locu, 1121, 1800
Locus, 186, 1456, 1629
Locus Biosciences, 177
Locus Corporation (Korea), 2685
Locus Energy, 2016, 3246
Locus Insights, 1509
LocusPlay, 1737
Lodestone Data Technologies, 395
Lodgify, 3099
LODH Private Equity Euro Choice III LP, 2088
LODH Private Euro Choice III, 2088
Lodi Gas Storage, 898
Lodo Therapeutics, 5, 30
Loehmann's Medifax EDI, 153
Loenbro, 1779
Loft, 728
Loft Orbital, 1879
Loftium, 610, 776
LoftSmart, 708
Loftsmart, 129
Lofty, 863, 2595
Logan Energy, 3126
Logan's Roadhouse, 357, 1066
LogCheck, 354, 1896
LogDNA, 1396, 1499
Logentrics, 2750
Logentries, 1464
Logfire, 655, 797
Loggi, 728, 1511
Loggly, 1862
Loggly LoopNet, 1855
Logi Analytics, 1140, 1754, 1888
Logibec, 828
Logic Blox Predictix, 1076
Logic PD, 463
Logic Vision, 1287
Logic.ink, 1238
Logical Therapeutics, 3006
LogicGate, 1499
LogicInk, 195
LogicLibrary, 1348
LogicMonitor, 1499
LogicTree, 2188
LogicVision, 1771
Logim, 2878
Login Analytics, 881
Login Radius, 1158
LoginRadius, 2283
Logistics Marketplace, 1759
Logistik, 2076
Logistik Unicorp, 2039
Logistyx Technologies, 1075
LogiSynn, 1051
Logitech, 217
Logitrade, 2330
LogLigic, 759
LogLogic, 1795
LogMatrix, 957
LogMeIn, 1464, 2301
LogMeln, 1008
Logo Athletics, 1955
LogoGarden, 497, 718
Logojoy, 2024
LogoSportswear, 832
Logoworks, 1666
LogPoint, 3194
LogRhythm, 35, 881, 933, 2681
LogRocket, 623
LogZilla, 3251
Lohika, 100, 628
Lois Law Library, 405
Lokafy, 2107
Loki Studios, 597
Loku, 447
Lola, 328, 708, 820, 894, 1114
Lolli, 763, 2272
Lollicam, 773
Lolly Wolly Doodle, 744
Lomb Scientific, 2391
Lombard Medical, 73
Lombard Medical Technologies, 2972
Lombardi Software, 205, 1408
Lomo Market, 3246
Lomond, 2956
Lomonosov Porcelain Plant, 2456
Loncin, 3091
London & Henley, 2787
Lone Peak, 1779
Lone Star, 63
Lone Star Land & Energy II, 673
Lone Star Overnight, 331
Lonestar Heart, 1849
Long Game, 1363
Long John Silver's, 408
Long Range Systems, 1785
Long-Term Stock Exchange, 1363
LongBoard Inc., 255
Longcheer Holdings Limited, 2841
Longeviti, 18
Longevity, 3039
Longhorn Health Solutions, 1625
Longhurst Group, 3008
Longitude Capital, 3273
Longitude Licensing, 1745
Longmaster Information & Technology, 2841
Longmen, 3185
Longmen Group, 2364
Longs Pharmacy Solutions, 1779
LongShine, 977
Longshine Information Technology, 2841
Longtail Video, 31
Longview Fibre Paper & Packaging, 2062
LongWatch, 993
Lontra, 2958
Lonza Biologics, 2504, 2681
Loock, 222
Look's Gourmet Food, 440
Look.io, 121
Lookback, 2919
LookBookHQ, 655
Looker, 561, 579, 742, 824, 1079, 1213, 1537
Looking Glass, 93, 779, 1155
Lookingglass Cyber Solutions, 1942
Lookk, 2682
Lookmark, 1105
LookNook, 1813
Lookout, 27, 125, 1073, 1153, 1235, 1511, 1854, 2851, 2851
Looks Gourmet Food Company, 1165
Looksharp, 1058
Looksmar, 2390
Loom, 820, 863
Loom Vision, 1155
Loom.AI, 1477
Looma, 512
Loomia, 624
Loop & Tie, 1610
Loop Genomics, 3, 802
Loop It, 209
Loop Me, 2470
Loopcam, 2435, 3021
Loopline Systems, 3047
LoopNet, 371, 874, 1537
Loopt, 582
Looptify, 802
Loot, 2217
Loot Crate, 333
Loot Crate Inc., 334
Lophius Biosciences, 2815

Loral Aerospace Holdings Inc., 576
Lorem, 756
Lorica Solutions, 1748
Loris.AI, 752
Loris.ai, 490
Lorus Therapeutics, 1456
Losant, 481
Lose It!, 820
Lost Crates, 1618
LostMyName, 894
Losán, 2480
Lot18, 27, 744
Lot18mimesis Republic, 2660
Lota.cloud, 2276
Lotame, 238, 666, 949, 1628, 1716
Lotame Solutions, 1449
Lotaris, 3036, 3206
Lotek, 2230
LotLinx, 1543
Lottay, 794
Lottery Now, 1616
Lotus Clinical Research, 611
Lotus Flare, 321, 527
Lotus Leaf Coatings, 758
Lotus Midstream, 672
Lotus Tissue Repair, 1814
LotusFlare, 1698
LOUD Technologies, 1755
Loudr, 1441
Louis Plung & Company, 3264
Louisiana Crane Company, 1748
Louisiana Tuggs, 1748
Loup, 1566
Love & Quiches, 196
Love Goodly, 1509
Love With Food, 863, 1058
Love'em Ingham, 912
Lovecrafts, 2469
LOVEFiLM, 2653
LoveFilm.com, 2665
Lovefilm.com, 3009
Loveholidays.com, 2577
LoveHomeSwap, 2963
Lovell Minnick Partners, 1873
Lovely, 283, 1752
Lovepop, 623, 938
Lover.ly, 1841
Loverly, 863, 1521
Loverly/Dubblee Media, 1701
LoveSac, 1955
Lovesac, 845
Lovevery, 1186, 1530, 1703
Lovin' Scoopful, 2393
Loving Care Agency, 1271
Low Carbon Lighting, 3003
LowerMyBills, 1728
Loxam, 2303, 2367
Loxi, 2466
Loxo Oncology, 73, 764, 1383
Loyalty Bay, 2743
Loyalty Builders, 175
Loyalty Lab, 1390
Loyalty Rewardz, 389, 3202
Loyaltyworks, 405, 694
Lo¢Na, 662
LP Innovations, 1915, 1922
LP33, 1101
Lpath, 1975
LPInnovations, 993
LPL Financial, 927, 1837
LPR, 2439
LRM, 3033
Lrn, 1109
LRV Health, 3263
LS, 1707
LS Polaris Innocation Fund, 3263
LS9, 186, 748

1333

Portfolio Companies Index

LSAT, 1959
LSI, 1006
LSI Logic, 1657, 1762
LSQ Funding, 1151
LSR Group, 2842
Lssi, 2688
LSSi Data, 857
LT Solutions, 1757
LTB4 Sweden AB, 2807
LTC, 2993
LTCG, 1746
LTI, 1621
LTO, 3076
LTS Scale Company, 1163
LTSE, 125, 514, 1153
LTX Corporation, 1107
Lua, 59
Luca Technologies, 2483
Lucane Pharma, 3104
LucasFilm Animation, 2681
Lucent Digital Video, 1304
Lucent Polymers, 1343
Lucent Sky, 2120, 2120
Lucent Technologies, 2612
Luceo Technologies, 2815
Luceor Wimesh Systems, 2300
LuciaWind AG, 2410
Lucibel, 1310, 2430
Lucid, 68, 131, 234, 912, 1213, 1430, 1720, 1918, 2773
Lucid Dimensions, 1839
Lucid Green, 1443
Lucid Imagination, 983
Lucid Software, 861, 1074
Lucidchart, 1054
Lucideus, 1035, 1269
Lucideworks, 857
Lucidity Lights, 2321
LucidMedia, 2188
Lucidmedia, 1603
LucidPort Technologies, 628
Lucidux, 1695
Lucidworks, 84, 1666
Lucina Health, 150, 477
Lucintech, 2101
Lucira Health, 3, 648
Lucite International, 2578
Lucix, 1403
Lucix Corporation, 1667
Luciz, 874
Lucky, 1762
Lucky & Me, 2
Lucky Brand, 874, 1113
Lucky Fish, 3212
Lucky Pai, 1798
Lucky Strike, 377
Lucky Strikes Entertainment, 1972
Lucky Voice Private Karaoke, 2419
Lucy, 1186
Ludei, 2911, 3214
Ludic Labs, 1088
Ludlow Ventures, 3259
Ludus, 3178
Lufa Farms, 2087
Lufax/Lu.com, 149
Lugg, 2122
LuHua Chemical Co., 2584
Luka, 1154
Lula, 754
LulaWed, 1165
Lulu, 3021, 3046
Luma, 232, 1412
Luma Sleep, 3251
Lumapps, 2842
LumaSense Technologies, 658, 1361
Lumata, 782
LumaTax, 553

Lumatax, 1162
Lumavate, 86, 659
Lumaverse Technologies, 1499
Lumavita, 2487
Lumavita AG, 2807
Lumec, 2002
Lumec Control Products, 1743
LumeJet, 2392, 2958
Lumen, 7
Lumen Learning, 1384
Lumena, 1414
Lumena Pharmaceuticals, 1522, 1578
LumenAd, 1317
Lumenaré Networks., 2630
Lumenaza, 2832
Lumencor, 85, 1384
Lumend, 22
LumEnergi, 325
Lumenetix, 198, 1430
Lumenier, 1438
Lumenis, 2345, 3203, 3231
Lumens, 1091
Lumension, 1629
Lumentus, 1645
Lumere, 718
LumeRx, 647
Lumesis, 1321, 1605
Lumeta, 1304
Lumeto, 2131
Lumetrics, 1748
Lumexis, 2020
Lumi, 597, 763, 944, 1153, 1154
Lumi Holdings, 3053
Lumiata, 1009, 1073
Lumicell, 1084
Lumidigm, 1015, 1704
Lumiere Hotel, 192
Lumiette, 1365
Lumigent, 1335
LumiGrow, 499
Lumigrow, 1208
Lumilog, 2472
Lumin, 976
Lumin-oZ Co. Ltd., 2406
Lumina Looue, 3206
Lumina Networks, 1928
Luminae, 838
Luminaire, 3206
Luminal, 1172
Luminar, 895
Luminate, 200, 218, 1657
LuminDX, 849
Luminescent, 1661
Luminescent Technologies, 55
Luminex Home Decor & Fragrance, 448
Luminist, 108
Luminoso, 25
Luminostics, 954
Luminous Medical, 56, 1578
LuminUltra, 2282
Luminus, 325, 1401
Lumiode, 145
Lumitec, 2858
LumiThera, 1065
Lumity, 610, 1698
Lummi Indian Nation, 1405
Lumo, 1039, 1254
Lumoid, 361
Lumos Networks, 1508
Lumos Pharma, 1622
Lumosity, 744, 1203, 1346
Lumotune, 2024
Luna Lights, 1159
Luna Technologies, 1348
Lunada Bay Corp., 1627
Lunar, 23, 708
Lunata Hair, 2127

Lunchgate.ch, 2302
Lunchio, 2832
Lund Van Dyke, 381
Lune, 527
Luneau Technology, 3229
Lunera, 68, 1978, 2136
Lunera Lighting, 1087, 3059
Lunewave, 1896
LunGuard, 3041
Luno, 2469
Lunova, 2858
Luphos, 2815
Lusha, 1499
Lutebox, 1959
Luther Pendragon, 3009
Lutheran Family Services, 1839
Lutonix, 1449, 1578, 1898
Lux Assure, 3132
Lux Biosciences, 2806, 3006
Lux Research, 336, 1155
Luxar, 755
Luxe, 680, 773, 795, 1890, 1918
Luxe Energy, 1326, 1328
LuxeValet, 1537
Luxfer, 1138
Luxim, 1583, 1786
Luxin Evotech, 2927
Luxine, 1917
Luxodo, 2466
Luxola, 1966, 2789
Luxology, 1588
LuxResearch, 430
Luxtech, 1581
Luxtera, 200, 949, 1155, 1407, 1661, 1793
Luxuery Presence, 1770
Luxul, 1679, 2658
Luxul Technology, 1840
Luxury Garage Sale, 587
Luxury Optical Holdings, 483
Luze Minerals, 1328
Luzitin, 3039
LVI Services, 822, 1377
LVL Technologies, 1099
lvl5, 594
LVL7, 1898
LVL7 Systems, 1122
Lxchelsis, 3187
LXR and Co., 2127
Lycera, 154, 652, 1014
Lyceum Capital Fund II, 2088
Lycored, 77
Lycus Ltd., 653
Lydall Inc., 77
Lydian Trust, 1736
LYFE Kitchen, 1832
LyfeStart International, 3248
Lyft, 108, 125, 207, 208, 511, 514, 520, 579, 752, 778, 802, 1054, 1187, 1258, 1323, 1330, 1372
lyft, 101
Lygos, 742
Lymphact, 3039
Lynatox, 2518
Lyncean, 1009
Lynda.com, 27, 1213, 1720, 1837
Lyndra, 2221
Lyndy Biosciences, 296
Lyngsaa, 3194
Lynk, 1762
LYNK Capital, 1065
Lynq, 151
Lynx Grills Inc., 451
Lynx Medical Systems, 782
Lynx Network Group, 1459
Lynx Photonic Networks, 1795
Lyon and Post, 1589
LyondellBasell Industries, 141

1334

Portfolio Companies Index

LyondellBesell, 33
Lyonnaise de Garantie, 3011
Lypanosys Limited, 2844
Lyra, 1918
Lyra Health, 877
Lyra Therapeutics, 1522
Lyrebird, 125
Lyric, 728, 1363
Lyric Pharmaceuticals, 137, 1622
Lysomal Therapeutics, 1128
Lysosomal Therapeutics, 918
Lysosomal Therapeutics Inc., 193
Lyst, 27, 1760, 2469, 2653, 2665
Lytics, 520, 1543, 1947
Lytro, 125, 545, 1054, 1335
Lytron, 1176
Lytx, 502, 1045, 1848, 1973
Lytx Inc., 1008
Lyxr, 394

M

M and M Direct, 1778
M Cubed, 668
M Cubed Technologies, 1955
M Level, 274
M&M Food Market, 2243
M&M Manufacturing, 1805
M&M Pump & Supply, 620
M&M Resources, 2156
M&Q Packaging Corp., 404
M&W, 2989
M*Modal, 1376, 1949
M-Biz Global, 2993
M-D Building Products, 578
M-DAQ, 488
M-Daq, 3206
M-Factor, 1449, 1898
M-Files, 2665
M-Flow, 2044
M-Kopa, 860
M-Real Oyj, 2981
M-Service, 846
M-Spatial, 2372
M.A. Gedney, 1117
M.G.V.S, 2453
M.Gemi, 332, 763, 820
M.I.T.R.A, 3190
M.K Electron Co. Ltd, 2915
M.S Solutions, 3174
M.T.R.E, 2576
M/A-COM Technology Solutions Holdings, 1754
M15, 1340
M2, 722
M2 Holdings Limited, 3053
M2 Renewables, 1607
M2i, 2842
m2M Strategies, 797
M2p-Labs, 2815
M2S, 97, 311, 1146, 1439
M33 Grwoth, 884
M5, 51, 655
M5 Midstream LLC, 1853
M7, 1352
M7 Group, 1498
M86 Security, 1888
M87, 1162, 1511
M:Metrics, 967
Ma Maison Fleur, 3033
Ma-Papaterie, 2375
MAA Laboratories Inc., 738
Maaco, 1580
Maana, 812, 1009
Maapilim, 3212
MaaS360, 949
MaaT Pharma, 3104
MAAX, 2062
Mabaya, 2938

Mabion, 1456
Mac IT Solutions, 3161
Macada, 2901
Macaroni Grill, 843
Maccine, 2504, 2681
MacDermid Holdings, 2371
MacDougalls' Cape Code Marine Service, 262
Macgregor, 197
MacGregor Group, 523
MACH, 2689
Mach, 2688
Machang Bridge, 585
Macheen, 1335
Machiels Building Solutions, 2940
Machine Laboratory, 1234
Machine Metrics, 1175
Machine Zone, 2011
MachineryLink, 56
MachineZone, 234
Machinify, 238
Machinima, 1242, 1537, 1848
machtfit, 2832
MacKay CEO Forums, 2284
Mackenzie-Childs, 424
Mackinac Commercial Credit, 1971
Mackle Brothers, 1405
Maclogix, 3076
MacNeill Pride Group, 449
Macro Art, 3234
Macro Meta, 1666
MacroGenics, 1014, 1578, 1943, 2961
MacroGenics Inc., 94
Macrolide Pharmaceuticals, 1350, 1734
Macromedia, 241, 538
Macrometa, 252, 802
MacroMill, 1757
Macronix International, 897
Macrosan, 1340
MACTEC, 463
Mactec, 1410
MacTrac, 2941
MacuCLEAR, 447
MacuLogix, 262, 1120
Mad Catz Interactive, 355
Madaket, 1155, 1610
Madaket Health, 711
MadaLuxe Group, 940
Madan Plastics Inc., 791
Madcap Learning Adventure, 2178
Made, 641
Made.com, 3046
Madefire, 133, 545, 564, 1862
Madeira Madeira, 756, 2967
Madfiber, 85
Madhouse, 3053
Madison Dearborn Capital Partners VI LP, 2088
Madison Dearborn Capital Partners VII LP, 2088
Madison Dearborn Partners, 3245, 3254, 3255
Madison Logic, 494
Madison Park Funding IX, 1493
Madison Reed, 520, 728, 1186, 1346, 1862
madison Reed, 1616
Madison Vaccines, 2002
Madison Vaccines Inc., 1923
MadKast, 686
Madoc, 3033
Madorra, 3014
Madrigal Pharma, 1271
Madrigal Pharmaceuticals, 240
Madrona Solutions Group, 82
Mads, 2813
Madvapes, 1214
mAdvertise, 304
Maeglin, 2867
MAEH, 838
Maestro, 1599, 1660
Maestro Commerce, 2700

Maestro Health, 94
Maestrodev, 1966
MaestroIQ, 601
MaestroIQ, 773
MaestroQA, 623, 680
Maev, 7
MAG Interactive, 1327
MAG Technology, 897
Magadi Soda, 3169
MagCam, 2358
Magella, 1973
Magellan, 119
Magellan Health, 1062
Magellan Health Services Inc., 303
Magellan Midstream Partners, 1160
Magellan Midstream Services II, 1577
Magellan Power Holdings, 157
Magellan Sp. z o.o., 2697
Magen Biosciences, 1155
Magenta Therapeutics, 193, 710
Magento, 230
Mageon, 1056
Magic AI, 1511
Magic Leap, 125, 1079, 1363, 1511, 1948, 2681
Magicalia, 2702
MagicBus, 608
Magiceyes, 2848
MagicTab, 3099
MagicWheels, 85
Maginaatics, 2434
Maginatics, 3225
Magink, 2741
Magisto, 1511, 2822, 2943
Magma, 564, 2044
Magma Flooring, 1291
Magma Global, 2541
Magna Energy Services, 543
Magna Legal Services, 491
Magnablend, 205
Magnamosis, 1238
Magnap, 1238
Magnate Worldwide, 491, 1169
Magnatech, 2969
Magnemotion, 1176
Magnet, 125
Magnet Banking, 1865
Magnet Communications, 538
Magnetic, 457, 541, 655, 1358
Magnetic Insight, 11, 222
Magnify Networks, 1588
Magnify.net, 1305, 1737
Magnify360, 1227
Magnitude Internet, 2518
Magnitude Software, 1527
Magnolia Bluffs Casino, 1115
Magnolia Broadband, 609, 1244, 1636
Magnolia Medical Technologies, 924
Magnolia NeuroSciences, 30
Magnolia Petroleum Co., 479
Magnomics, 3039
Magnum, 1091
Magnum Energy, 898
Magnum Materials, 124
Magnum NGLS, 898
Magnum Semiconductor, 200, 1021
Magnum System, 294
Magnus, 2976
Magonlia Broadband, 1650
Magoosh, 246, 1058
MagPower, 2708
MagSil, 683
MagSil Corp., 683
Magwel, 3060
Mahana, 447
Mahana Therapeutics, 1155
Mahi Networks Inc., 255
Mahmee, 221

Portfolio Companies Index

Mahoot, 1867
Maidbot, 521
maidbot, 795
Maiden Lane Ventures, 37
Mailchannels, 85
Mailcloud, 3009
MailFrontier, 1203
Mailjet, 2377
MailMag, 2428
MailSouth, 1300
Mailtime, 721
Mailtrack, 3214
Maily, 3099
Maimonidex RA, 3235
Main Bank Corporation, 1152
Main Street Dairy, 1021
Main Street One, 937
Main Venture Capital Funds, 2600
Maincontrol, 2741, 3239
maincontrol, 3128
Maine Beverage Company, 1133
Maine Craft Distilling, 440, 1165
Maine Trailer, 440
Maine Wealth Partners, 1164
Mainframe, 724, 1074, 2825
MainStay Medical, 1874
Mainstay Medical, 3104
Mainstem, 1208
Mainstreet Networks, 200
MAINtag, 2842
MainTech, 1839
Maison Le Grand, 2153
Maisonette, 1483
Maisons Babeau-Seguin, 2842
Maisons du Monde, 2705
Maiyet, 596
MAJEC Ventures, 3251
Majestic Oaks, 1220
Majestic Star, 1968
Major League Gaming, 1361
Major League Hacking, 820
Makara, 1666
Make a Mind Co., 1394
Make It Work, 1786
Make Music, 2616
Make School, 1058
Make.tv, 1158
Makemereach, 2377
MakeMyTrip.com, 808
Makena Capital, 1762
Makena Capital Management, 1948
Makeover Solutions, 311
Maker, 125, 876, 1426, 1890, 2640
Maker Labs, 3248
Maker Media, 752
Maker Meia, 1359
Maker Studios, 59, 641, 1832, 2919, 3112
Maker's Row, 708, 1058
Makerbot, 265
Makers Academy, 2743
MakersKit, 1223, 1851
MakeSpace, 1153, 1479, 1752, 1890
Makespace, 1359
MakeTime, 89
Maketime, 779
Maketion, 1511
MakieLab, 3140
MAKO Surgical, 1693, 1771
Mako Surgical Corp., 94, 137, 1251
Makr, 354
Makua Foods Oy, 2928
Makucell, 1786
Malabar Investments, 943
Malaria.com, 164
Malaysia Steel Works, 2614
Malcovery Security, 296
Malhot Industries, 2198

Malibu Grand Prix, 874
Mallard Exploration, 1326, 1328
Mallet, 973
Mallet & Company, 557
Malliouhana Resort, 69
Malmöhus Invest, 2858
Malo Clinic, 2708
Malone Mortgage Co., 874
Malteurop International SA, 2611
Malthus, 3067
Maluuba, 3089
MAMA & Company, 2935
Mama Earth Organics, 2230
MaMa Rosa's, 962
MamaEarth Organics, 2153
MamaMancini's, 650
Mamapedia, 1867
Mamava, 789
Mambu, 2912, 3035
Mamma Chia, 3246
Mammoth Biosciences, 108, 1187, 1238, 2001
Mammoth Diagnostics, 1323
Mammoth Media, 877
Mamoca, 1786
Mamsy, 3199
Mamut, 3004
Man Crates, 1344
Man Infraconstruction, 3164
Man Outfitters, 1509
Manac, 110
ManageCO2, 2513
Managed By Q, 1058
Managed by Q, 1696
Managed Health Care Associates, 2014
Management Consulting Group, 2515
Management Controls, 2074
Management Health Solutions, 646, 1523
ManagerComplete, 447
ManageSoft, 2315
Managing Editor, 857
Manappura, 856
Manappuram Finance Limited, 136
Manas Resources, 2933
Mandalay Sports Media, 518
Manda^, 1511
Mander Portman Woodward Limite, 1115
Mando, 897
Mandrel Oy, 2864
Mangahigh, 3046
Mangar International, 3234
Mangatar, 2663
MangirKart, 2435
Mango Games, 1698
Mango Health, 234, 361, 742, 752, 1079
Mango Plate, 1719
Mango Technologies, 3010
Mango Telecom, 1009
MangoPlate, 1511
Mangoplate, 3118
Mangrove, 3128
Mangstor, 1302
Manhattan Beachwear, 1460
Manhattan Beachwear LLC, 1136
Manhattan Physicians Laboratories, 1846
Mania Technologies, 1021
Manifest, 553
Manifest Climate, 2122, 2131
Manifest Digital, 266
Manifold, 308, 2063, 2272
Manistique Papers, 1210
Manitoba Harvest, 525
Manitowoc Tool & Machining, 1210
Manna Molecular Science LLC, 1208
MannaPro, 60
Mannatech, 638
Mannesmann Plastics Machinery, 3200
Manny's Tortas, 1233

Mano daktaras, 3040
Manor House Retirement Centers Inc., 449
Manov, 2742
Manroland Goss, 110
Mansa, 2398
Mansion Hotel, 2841
Mansour Mining Technologies, 2052
Manta Media, 189, 1547
Mantara, 346, 549, 1713, 2609
Manthan Software Services, 2840
Manthan Systems, 1346
Manti Exploration, 673
Manticore Games, 545, 565
Mantis Vision, 1511
Mantle, 3
Mantra Bio, 321
Mantra Dairy, 2305
Manuel, 2480
ManufactOn, 1104
Manufactured, 121
Manugistics, 2689
Manx, 1493
Manzama, 1659
Manzil Health Care Services, 3187
Map My Beauty, 985
Map My Fitness, 205
Map My India, 2992
MAP Pharmaceuticals, 1693
Map Pharmaceuticals, 73
MAP Pharmaceuticals Inc., 240
Mapado, 2357
MAPAL Group, 1499
MapAnything, 907, 1610
Mapbar, 2841
Mapbox, 596, 779, 1483
MAPI, 2535
Mapillary, 1105, 1323, 1657, 2437
Maple, 517, 1479, 1823, 2181
Maple Assist, 2094
Maple Farm Media, 1737
Maple Hill Creamery, 2153
Maple Tree Networks, 317
Maples, 2481
Mapletree, 153
Maplin, 2787
Maplin Electronics, 2968
Mapmy Fitness, 51
MapMyCustomers, 512
MapMyIndia, 1511
MappedIn, 2123
Mapper, 182, 275
Mapper Lithography, 3060
Mapquest.com, 194, 1852
MapR, 1511
Mapr, 485, 579, 1537
MapR Technologies, 872, 1187
Maps on Us, 1304
Mapsense, 121, 1800
Maptuit, 2188
MAR Systems, 642, 1051
Marasesti, 3178
Marathon, 1150, 1626
Marathon Data Systems, 470, 531
Marathon Group, 1013
Marathon Pharmaceuticals, 1904
Marathon Products, 217
Maravai LifeSciences, 889
Marble, 565, 1247, 1658, 2131
Marble Robot, 814
Marble Security, 564
Marbles, 1618
Marcadia, 11
Marcadia Biotech, 785
Marcanet, 2480
Marcegaglia, 1971
Marcel & Fils, 3229
March Capital Partners, 3258

Portfolio Companies Index

Marchim SA, 3178
Marco, 1345
Marco Aldany, 1518
Marco Financial, 754
Marco Genics, 158
Marcolin, 3017
MarcoPolo Learning, 3099
Marcum LLP, 3257
Mardil Medical, 3202
Marfeel, 259, 2978
Margan Business Development Ltd., 2945
Margaritaville, 1433
Margaritaville Holdings, 356
Margin Edge, 1023
Margin Point, 162
MarginPoint, 1018, 1239
MarGo, 512
MariaDB, 374
Marian Heath Greeting Cards, 1955
Marianna Industries, 913
Marie Brizard, 2667
Marie-Laure PLV, 2332
Marietta Corporation, 160
Marijuana Doctor, 1443
MariMed, 1282
Marin Software, 115, 564, 582, 759
Marina, 1414
Marinello, 815
Mariner Finance, 1234
Mariner Village, 192
Marino Med, 2410
Marinus Pharmaceuticals, 389, 622, 1700
Maris Group, 2940
Maritech International, 2745
MariTEL, 854
Maritime Biologgers, 2148
Mark Andy, 110
Mark IV Industries, 2488
Mark Logic, 1798
Mark VII Equipment, 847
Mark43, 265, 820, 1103, 1153, 1593, 1718, 1896
Markafoni, 2919
Markant Sdwest Handel, 2801
MarkaVIP, 2828, 3042
Marken, 2371
Markers Workstation, 1051
Market Dial, 1074
Market Express, 531
Market Force Information, 318, 928, 1248
Market Fresh Produce, 367
Market Leader, 1644
Market Strategies International, 1929
Market Street Advisors, 1316
Market Tech Media Corporation, 266
Market Track, 202
Market Wagon, 659
Market6, 1661
MarketBrief, 289
MarketCast, 1085
Marketdial, 564
Marketech International, 1771
MarketFactory, 744
Marketfish, 85
MarketForce, 696
MarketForce Information, 443
Marketing Evolution, 1005, 2018
Marketing Technology Solution: (MTS), 957
Marketing Technology Solutions, 1422
MarketingIsland.com, 2188
MarketLab, 1962
MarketLive, 839, 1674
Marketlive, 194, 972, 1028
MarketMan, 1323, 2938
Marketmax, 1864
MarketMuse, 1557
Marketmuse, 2204
Marketo, 361, 1006, 1014, 1430, 1750
Marketocracy, 766
MarketPage, 2351
Markets and Markets, 796
MarketShare, 660, 796
MarketSoft, 957
Marketsync, 85
Markett, 121
MarketTools, 861
Markettools, 1949
MarketTrack, 381
MarketWare, 79
Marketwired, 1236, 2177
Marketworks, 564
MarketXS, 3042
MarkForged, 1184
Markforged, 1158
Markit, 819, 2382
Markit Medical, 623
Markkit, 1059, 1121, 1966
Markland Technologies, 2745
MarkLogic, 1235, 1657
MarkMonitor, 759, 773
Markmonitor, 1006
Markov, 1724
Marlen International, 1438
Marley Natural, 1484
Marley Spoon, 1884, 3226
Marlin, 2723
Marlin Business Services Corp., 1425
Marlin Mobile, 1101
Marlin Resources, 673
Marlin Software, 1848
Marmalade Café, 1417
Marmot, 1855
Marner, 1874
Maroon Group, 478
Marope Algarve, 3039
Marqeta, 857
MarqueMedicos, 60
Marqueta, 2934
Marquette Business Credit SPE I, 1971
Marquette Transportation, 1090
Marquette Transportation Company, 2371
Marquette Transportation Finance, 1971
Marquii, 1509
Marriott Praia D'El Rey, 3039
Marrone Bio Innovations, 499, 1093, 1241, 1776, 1967
Marrone Organic Innovators, 1671
Mars Reel, 221
Marsala Biotech, 2071
Marsh, 1755
Marsh Bellofram Corporation, 607
Marshall & Swift, 874
Marshall & Swift Holdings, 364
Marshall & Williams Co., 911
Marshall Excelsior Company, 911
Marshall Retail Group, 337, 357, 381, 973
Marshall Tube, 1176
Marsulex Environmental Technologies, 2056
Martello, 2276
Martex Fiber, 1234
Martha Stewart Living Omnimedia Inc., 1905
Martialone Ltd., 2545
Martin Color-Fi, 617
Martin Currie, 560
Martin Pharmaceuticals, 663
Martinez Geospatial, 1233
Martis Capital, 3254
Martmania, 2767
Martsoft, 1183
Marubi, 1092
Marussia F1 Team, 2935
Marval Bioscience, 794
Marvaomedical, 2347
Marvel, 339
Marvell Technology Group, 1781
Marvin Manufacturing, 96
Marvin's, 1971
Marxent, 608, 1737
Masa, 2472
Masa Maso, 1340
Masabi, 762, 2963
Masada Security, 132
Mascara Sales & Marketing, 1582
Mascoma, 748, 1908
Mascoma Corporation, 1449
Masergy, 20, 257, 443, 1212
Masergy Holdings Inc., 159
Mashable, 1298, 1888
Mashav, 2600
Mashburn, 285
Masher Media, 1786
Mashery, 1, 624, 742, 766, 1588
Mashgin, 1760
MashNetworks, 173
Mashwork, 1992
Maskd, 1832
Mason, 3
Mason Finance, 1079
Mason Manufacturing, 60
Mason Steel, 1609
Mass Relevance, 205, 527
Mass Roots, 638, 1139
Massage Envy, 1580
Massage Heights, 15
Massana, 2328
MassCEC, 3263
MassDevelopment, 3263
Massdrop, 553, 742, 1187
Masse, 1186
Massey Fair, 935
Massif, 843
Massif Oil & Gas, 1328
Massif Oil & Gas II, 1326
MassInvestor, 3251
Massiv Konzept, 2466
Massive, 609, 1247, 1313
Massive Impact, 3112
Massman Automation, 855
Massmarket, 3004
MassVentures, 3263
Mast Kalandar, 2809
Mast Therapeutics, 1492
Master, 2198, 2640
Master Capital Group, 2640
Master Financial Management, 2374
Master PIM, 2518
MasterClass, 59, 1032, 1396, 1885
Masterclass, 888, 1006, 1142, 1296, 1616
MasterCraft, 1968
MasterImage 3D, 3089
Mastermind Toys, 2056
Masternaut, 782
Masterpiecevr, 2204
Masterskill, 1518
Mastery Connect, 888
Mastery Prep, 1000
MasteryConnect, 430
Mastro's Restaurants, 1971
Matagorda Island Gas Ops, 157
Matatu, 2969
Matchbook, 1521
Matches, 3095
Matchmove, 3206
Matchwell, 3
MATE Ltd, 2576
Materialist, 1323
MaterialNet, 1137
Materials Marketing, 1524
MaterialsXchange, 1412
MatexNet, 2837
MATH Venture Partners, 3255
Mathcore, 2869

Portfolio Companies Index

Mathey Dearman, 832
MathHarbor, 3165
Mathpix, 1530
Maths Doctor, 2941
Mathsoft, 655
Mathzee, 1618
Mati, 623, 1616
Matic, 133, 400, 2398
Matilda Jane, 480
Matilda Jane Clothing, 445
Matisse Networks, 2005
Matlet Group, 1639
MatlinPatterson Global Opportunities Partners III, 2088
Mato-Erno.com, 1162
Matox, 2603
Matriavax, 2969
Matrics, 1137, 1348, 1603
Matrimony.com, 1187
MatriSys Bioscience, 875
Matritech, 1898
Matrix, 2935
Matrix Industries, 1616
Matrix Medical Network, 227, 785, 1973
Matrix Partners, 3263, 3273
Matrix Semiconductor, 1008, 1795
Matrix Sensors, 1237
Matrixx, 931, 1731, 1867, 3143
Matrixx Initiatives, 1493
Matrixx Software, 877
Mattco Forge, 293
Matter, 1527
Matter Port, 1281
Mattereum, 527
MatterMark, 586
Mattermark, 779, 1752
Mattermost, 945
Matternet, 521, 1142, 1705, 1998
Matterport, 107, 108, 720, 1155, 1511, 1534, 2011, 2844
matterport, 795
Mattersight, 1762
Matthews, 1518, 1873
Matthews Asia, 1151
Matuse, 1744
Mauna Kea Technologies, 1500, 3104
Mauritsklinieken, 3222
Mavatar, 1752
Maven, 863, 1657
Maven Link, 1831
Mavencare, 2107
mavencare, 2240
Mavenir, 561
Mavenir Systems, 87, 200, 205, 1335
MavenLink, 419
Maverick, 1268
Maverick Air Center, 1195
Maverick Healthcare, 899, 1493
Maverick Healthcare Equity, 1192
Maverick Media LLC, 449
Maverix Biomics, 183
Maverix Private Equity, 2074
Maveron Equity Partners, 990
Mavin, 1263
Maviro, 2264
Mavrck, 1069
Mavrx, 564
Mavu Pharma, 785
MAX, 2161
Max, 136
Max Environmental, 104
Max Matthiessen, 2376
Max Media, 843
Max Truck, 2746
Maxager, 217
Maxcess, 261
Maxcress, 260

MaxCyte, 907, 1013
Maxeda, 2371
Maxeda DIY Group, 3024
MaxFunds.com, 1337
Maxi Canada, 96
Maxia Pharmaceuticals Inc., 240
Maxim, 1924
Maxim Pharmaceuticals, 1920
Maxima Corporation, 767
Maximiles, 3104
Maximum Throughput, 2188
MaxLinear, 1239, 1898
Maxment, 2815
Maxor, 247
MaxPoint, 1855
MaxSold, 2065
MaxStream, 1679
Maxsys Ltd, 2364
Maxta, 125, 1798
Maxteck Technology, 3209
Maxtena, 1172
Maxthon, 457
Maxtor, 241
MaxVision, 928
Maxwell, 398, 2398
Maxwell Health, 428, 549, 1114, 1851
Maxwell Systems, 1140
Maxxam Analytics, 2076
Maxxim Medical, 781
Maxymiser, 3023
May Mobility, 6, 608, 708, 814, 1836
Maya Cinemas, 20
Maya Entertainment Group, 1773
Maya's Mom, 1323
Mayborn Group, 2292, 2303
Mayfield Associates Fund, 624
Mayfield Fund, 3273
Mayflower Medicinals, 970
Mayi, 1908
Maystreams, 1170
MayStreet, 2074
Mayvenn, 125, 232, 1101
Mayvien, 1635
Maz, 708
MAZ Germany, 2985
Mazu Networks, 1741
MB Aerospace, 167
MB Aerospace Holdings II Corp., 159
MB Equity Fund II Ky, 2731
MB Equity Fund Ky, 2731
MB Financial Bank, 531
MB Industries, 1748
MB Innovations, 1190
MB2 Dental Solutions LLC, 159
MBA & Company, 2963, 3031
MBA Polymers, 2364, 2383, 2694
Mbaobao.com, 597
MBAPolymers, 2662
MBF Healthcare Partners, 3254
MBH Enterprises, 1024
MBH Settlement Group, 1343
Mbi, 2688
MBI Energy Services, 1133
MBIA, 1957
MBlox, 1629
Mblox, 949
mBlox, 1354, 1852, 2449
Mbm Systems, 2815
MBooster, 2865
MBRP, 2156
MBS Media Campus, 33
MBT Ag, 2776
MC Assembly, 578
MC Group, 1143
MC Group PLC, 2937
MC Laboratory, 2961
MC MC, 1730

MC Pelican Fund LP, 624
MC Sign, 376
MC Sign Company, 376
MC Technology, 2824
MC10, 19, 1241
Mc10, 1335
mc10, 1993
MC2, 687
Mc2i, 2439
MCA Dental Group, 2212
MCA Solutions, 1150
McAfee, 745
McAffee, 1837
McAlister's Deli, 1580
McAobao, 2927
mCarbon, 389
McBride Plc., 576
MCC Control Systems, 376
McCaw Cellular, 1212
McClarin Plastics, 279
McCormick & Schmick's Seafood Restaurants Inc., 357
McCoy Global, 2116
McCoy Sales, 1481
McCubbin Hosiery, 1424
McData, 205
McDonald's, 475, 2872
McGraw-Hill, 1554
McGraw-Hill Education, 141
McGregor Industries, 2162
MCGZ, 2940
MChek, 2992
MCI, 1089
McIntosh Perry, 2246
MCK Group, 2411
McKechnie Aerospace, 1256
McKeil Marine, 2264
McKenzie Creative Brands, 159
McKenzie Sports Products, 878, 1560
Mckenzie Sports Products, 1115
McLarens, 96
MCMC, 1275
Mcmurry/TMG, 1984
McMynn Leasing, 2249
MCN, 1966
MCN Bioproducts, 2108
McNally Industries, 402
McNeil Technologies, 1927
MCNex, 1091
MCP, 3004
MCRA, 377
McRae's Environmental Services, 2249
McRock Capital, 2028
McRock Capital iNFund, 485
MCS, 2453
MCS Property Group., 2805
MCS/Medical Compression Systems, 2316
MCT, 3040
Mcube, 582
mCube, 974, 1079, 1478
Mcube Works, 1750
MCubeWorks, 1091
MD, 209
MD Beauty, 2014
MD Now, 337, 351
MD VIP, 1113
MDalgorithms Inc., 1073
Mdaq, 2681
mdBriefCase, 2212
MDC Vacuum Products, 448
MDDF, 711
mDhil, 860
MDLive, 245
MDM, 1456
MdotLabs, 473
MDS, 2256
MDS Gateways, 2328

1338

Portfolio Companies Index

MDS Inc., 1905
MDS Technology, 3136
MDT, 632
MDT Software, 607
MDX Health, 2842, 3104
MDY, 655
ME 3I, 3039
Me.com, 327
Meadow, 152, 400, 998, 1696, 1810
Meal Ticket, 1499
Mealey's Furniture, 1417
MealPal, 520, 1203
Meals & Media, 2958
Meals to Live, 447
MeaningMine, 2347
Mearthane Products, 1639
Measurabl, 311, 534, 562, 1610
Measured, 1385, 2262
Measureful, 1467
MeatEater, 1317
Mebelorama, 3161
Mebias Discovery, 269
MEC Dynamics, 1917
Mec.com, 2674
MEC3, 1576
Mecatronix, 3089
Meccatronicore, 2859
Mecfor, 2242
Mech Mocha, 3124
Mechanical Dynamics, 1337
Mechanical Rubber Products, 1405
Mechanical Zoo, 624
Mechanische Componenten, 2801
Mechanodontics, 229
Meciria, 3098
Mecmesin, 238
Mecoswiss, 2801
Mecs, 110
Med America Recycling, 654
Med Data, 418
Med Solutions, 1778
Med-Legal, 913
Med-Pharmex, 639
Med3000 Group, 1152
Meda Pharmaceuticals, 1456
MedAdherence, 679
MedAffinity, 3251
Medafor, 3268
Medagate, 185
Medal Playlabs, 2944
Medallia, 680, 1608, 1657
Medallion Analytics, 1386, 1388
Medallion Anayltics, 1003
MedAptus, 315, 315
Medarex, 240, 870
MedAssets, 881, 1044
MedAssets America, 1973
MedAssist, 1594
MedAux, 1554
MedAvante, 1733, 1846
MedAware, 812
Medaware Solutions, 270
MedBox, 1139
Medbridge, 1140
MedCap, 1410
MedCath, 1973
Medcenter, 2449
MedCenterDisplay, 1261
MedChart, 2141, 2181
Medchart, 2130
MedChronic, 3022
MedCity Media, 1051
Medcorder, 803
MedCPU, 1206
MedCrypt, 680
Medcrypt, 1605
Meddle, 1305

MedE America, 1973
MedeAnalytics, 224, 990
Medeanalytics, 666
Medecision, 881
MedECUBE Healthcare, 176
Medeikonos, 2869
Medeikonos AB, 2709
Medenovo LLC, 489
Medeo, 2225
Medeor Therapeutics, 1522, 1943
Mederi, 949
MedEViewing, 852
MedExpress, 1657
Medexus Pharmaceuticals, 2174
Medfar Clinical Solutions, 2074
Medfinders, 886
Medforth Global Healthcare Education, 2030
Medfusion, 918
Medgenics, 3235
MedHaul, 999
MedHok, 1720
Medhost, 1480
Medi Tate, 3230
Media Armor, 876, 1309
Media China Corp, 2838
Media Development Investment Fund, 1374
Media Group of America, 618
Media Lano, 3170
Media Lario Technologies, 3037
Media Matchmaker, 1786
Media Math, 510
Media Nusantara Citra, 1602, 3052
Media Platform, 1249
Media Radar, 224
Media Rights Capital, 20
Media Spike, 1527
Media Surface, 2760
Media-Streams.Com, 3153
Media4Care, 2832
Mediaboost, 3205
Mediachain Labs, 1105
Mediacontech, 3145
Mediacore, 2270
MediaDev, 2457
Mediaflex, 2848
MEDIAI Co, 2798
Medial Cancer Screening, 2822
Medialets, 609
MediaMath, 429, 1488, 1504, 1605, 1691
Mediamath, 1731
Mediamo, 2495
Median, 2842
MediaNation Inc., 2394
Medianet, 226
Mediant, 733
Mediant Communications, 162
MediaOmics, 3039
Mediapacs, 1222
MediaPass, 625
Mediaplatform, 1731
MediaPlex, 2898
Mediapps, 2346
MediaPro, 793
Mediaprobe Inc., 2982
Mediaquest, 3164
MediaRadar, 793
MediaResponseGroup, 1929
MediaShare, 597
Mediasilo, 1630
Mediasmart, 2911
MediaSolv, 1298
Mediaspan, 3124
MediaSpan Group, 1711
Mediaspectrum, 1005
Mediasurface, 2378
Mediatech Inc., 864
MediaTek, 1924

Mediatel, 194, 1929
MediaTile, 1305, 1588
MediaV, 827
MediBeacon, 270, 1050
MediBic, 2961
Medic Vision, 340, 3050
Medical Arts Press, 684
Medical Card System, 1043
Medical Card Systems, 62
Medical Care Corporation, 323
Medical Depot, 723
Medical Device Innovation, 2454
Medical Imaging Australasia Group Limited, 2390
Medical Indicators, 607
Medical Management of New England, 315
Medical Metrix Solutions, 522, 1463
Medical Payment Exchange, 1576
Medical Pharmacies, 2076
Medical Port, 3039
Medical Present Value, 3128
Medical Science & Computing, 1140
Medical Solutions, 1276
Medical Specialties Distributors, 1300
Medical Tracking Solutions, 3251
Medical University of the Americas, 692
Medicalis, 941
Medication Delivery Devices, 1708
Medicinal Genomics, 362
Medicine Man, 1810
Medicine Man Technologies, 1139
Medicinia, 641, 2967
MediciNova, 2961
Medico, 744
Medico (Hong Kong) Limited, 622
Medicode, 1852
Medicom Medical, 2909
MediConnect Global, 1205, 1679
Medicure, 2071
Medicus, 2373
Medicus Healthcare Solutions, 247
Medicus IT, 352
Medicus Technologies, 1496
MedidaMetrics, 748
Medidata, 51, 1682
Medidata Solutions, 1748
Medify, 1947
MediGene, 3187
MediGene AG, 3128
Medigus, 1383, 2646
Medikidz, 918
Medikly, 644, 721
MediMedia, 2596
MediMedia USA, 1933
MEDINET, 2961
Medingo, 3063
Medio, 1247, 1928
Medio Systems, 27, 624
Mediornet, 2772
Mediotype, 2050
MediQuest, 1007
MediQuest Therapeutics, 3006
MediQuire, 497, 718
MediSafe, 2938
Medisafe, 1511
Medisas, 125, 945, 1073
Medisse, 2505, 3011
MEDITECH, 1754
Meditory, 985
Medium, 125, 877, 1153, 1363
Medivance, 1693
Medivo, 1206
Mediware Information Systems, 1817
Medizinaltechnik Ltd, 3153
MedLEARNING AG, 3188
Medley Global Advisors, 364
MedLumics, 2865

1339

Portfolio Companies Index

Medlumics, 2544
MedManage, 561
MedManage Systems, 755, 1667
MedMark, 1510
Medmark, 1140
MedMark Services, 405, 476
MedMen, 1139
MedNews, 164
Medolac, 3246
Medopad, 1618
MedOptions, 912, 952, 1463
Medovent, 2815
Medpace, 435
MedPage Today, 1691
Medpage Today, 51
MedPlast, 1575
MedPointe, 785
MedPointe Inc., 576
MedPricer, 1794
MedPro Safety Products, 190
MedQuist Inc., 1905
MedRepublic, 121
MedRespond, 1452
MedRhythms, 1165
Medrium, 1325
Medrobotics, 296, 1452, 1695
medSage, 296
MedSage Technologies, 1452
medSage Technologies, 1003, 1444
MedSave, 1852
Medscape, 925
Medseek, 551
MedServe, 212
MedService Repair, 1267
MedShape Solutions, 983
Medsite, 1955
MedSocket, 270
Medspa Partners, 2212
MedSpan, 315
Medsphere, 689, 949
MedSphere International, 908
Medsphere International Holding, 3053
Medstack, 2204
MEDSTIM, 1286
Medsurant Health, 1292
MedSynergies, 796
Medtechnica, 2736
MedTorque, 2206
Medtouch, 1176
Medtrainer, 2074
Medtrex, 51
Medudem.com, 2302
Medumo, 1104
Medusa Medical Technologies Inc., 2148
MedVance Institute, 822
Medvantix, 154
MedVantx, 1025, 1804
Medvantx, 1464
MedVentive, 540, 704, 1146
MedVenture, 119, 1380
MedVenture Associates, 3273
MedWaves Incorporated, 118
Medwell, 711
Medycyna Rodzinna SA, 2697
Medytox, 3136
Meebo, 972, 1091
Meedor, 3013
Meelo, 450
Meenta, 2
Meer Corp., 467
Meero, 1982
Meesho, 1142
MeetElise, 882
Meetic, 2346, 2842
MeetingSense Software, 1871
Meetrics, 2832
Meetup, 1374

MeeVee Inc., 1093
Meez, 133
MEG Energy, 1957
MEGA Brands, 1971
Mega Lifesciences, 1143, 2937
Mega Zebra, 2662
MegaBots, 1186
Megabots, 108
Megadyne, 2842
Megahoot LLC, 725
Megamedia, 2708
MegaPath, 1898
MegaPath Networks, 1403, 1852
Megaphone TV, 3118
Megastudy, 897
MegaZebra, 2912
Meghmani Organics Ltd. (India), 2685
Meglan, 2042
Mego, 310
Mei Ah Entertainment, 2838
MEI Group, 223
MEI Labels Holdings, 1767
MEI Pharma, 73, 460, 1297, 1943
Meiban, 2681
Meicai, 827
Meicai.cn, 3241
Meican, 846, 1327
Meico Crown Entertainment, 874
Meihua, 827
Meili/Mogu, 827
Meilishuo, 299
Meilleire Gestion, 2842
Meilleurmobile.com, 2842
MeilleursAgents.com, 2377
Meilleurtaux.com, 3199
Mein Auto, 3229
MeinAuto, 2829
MeinAuto.de, 2820
Meineke, 170, 1580
Meineke Car Care Center, 418
Meineke Car Care Centers, 899
MeinProspekt, 2815
Meiosys, 3223
Meister Plus, 2687
Meituan, 819, 1340
Meituan-Dianping, 511
Meiya Power Company, 2425
Meize Energy Industries Holding Limited, 3053
Mejuri, 2024, 2224
Mekanist, 3038
Mekics Co., 2993
Melco Electric, 842
Melco International Development Limited, 2394
Meldium, 776
Melele, 3241
Melexis, 3060
Melinta Therapeutics, 1957
Melior Discovery, 269, 1917, 3202
Melita, 1157
Melixa, 2859
Mellanox, 1657, 2761
Mellanox Technologies, 1898, 3221
Mellitus, 350
MELODEA, 3235
Melodeo, 1947
Melon, 1103
Melonn, 1426
Meltwater, 775, 1912
Member Suite, 1558
MemberClicks, 746
MemberHealth, 1973
Members: 104 West, 3265
Members: 17 Asset Management, 3252
Members: A&M Capital Partners, 3254
Members: Abingworth, 3263, 3273
Members: ACON Investments, 3245
Members: Applied Facts, 3258

Members: DLA Piper, 3266
Memblaze, 1511
MembranePRO, 300
Memc Electronic Materials, 1837
Memebox, 100, 553, 721, 1426, 1719, 1998, 2011
Memebox Corporation, 1263
MeMed, 1698, 2822
Memed, 641, 1511
Memento, 1
MemfoACT, 2361, 3207
Memiray, 1055
Memo Right, 1840
Memobox, 2375
Memoir, 787, 1521, 1537, 1823
Memolane, 200
Memora, 2842
Memora Inversiones Funerarias, 2303
Memora Services Funerarias, 2292
Memorial MRI & Diagnostic, 1826
Memory Inc., 2776
Memory Medallion, 1003
Memory Pharmaceuticals, 928, 2509
Memphis Meats, 610, 803, 2437
memphis Meats, 321
MeMPile Ltd, 2964
Memrise, 209, 2469
Memry, 532
Memscap, 3115
Memsic, 2841
MemSQL, 27, 742, 863, 969, 1073, 2654
Memsql, 586
MemVerge, 1055
Menara, 646
Menara Networks, 145, 1674
Mendeley, 2382
Mendix, 2813, 3042
Mendocino Farms, 1092
Mendor, 2930
Mengniu Dairy, 2329
Meniga, 2398
Meninvest Kantox, 1418
Menlo Entrepreneurs Fund X, 624
Menlo Security, 820
Menlo Therapeutics, 240, 1943
Menlo Therpeutics, 73
Menlo Ventures, 3273
Menlomicro, 812
Mensch & Natur AG, 589
Mentad, 304
Mental Canvas, 1158
Mention, 3035
Mentor, 2786
Mentor Corp., 1905
Mentor Graphics, 1762
Mentored, 1285
Mentum, 2842
Menu Next Door, 1005
Meow Mix Company, 576
MeQuilibrium, 477
Mequilibrium, 1605
Mer Group, 2736
Mera Career Guide, 3190
MeraDoctor, 2305
Meraki, 1341, 1657
Meraki Networks Inc., 624
Merant, 2005
Mercado, 3128
Mercado Software, 3221
Mercados SUVIANDA, 1397
Mercantile Adjustment Bureau, 1526
Mercaris, 1058
Mercateo, 3152
Mercato Partners, 3265
Mercator MedSystems, 139
Mercatus, 198
Mercaux, 1593

Portfolio Companies Index

Merced Systems, 1762
Mercent, 85, 1871
Mercer Advisors, 377, 823, 1151, 1169, 2196
Mercer County Community College, 3266
Mercer Foods, 792, 851
Merchant Atlas, 304, 1841
Merchant Capital Solutions, 1746
Merchant E-Solutions, 1949
Merchant eSolutions, 1852
Merchant Warehouse, 1419
MerchantAtlas, 1101
Merchantry, 641, 876
Merchbar, 1752
Mercuri International, 2879
Mercury Fund, 953, 3255, 3259
Mercury Media, 687
Mercury Security, 1140
Mercury Taverns, 2976
Merenda Limited, 2696
Merex Group, 633
Merfish Pipe and Supply and Pipe Exchange, 1376
Mergent, 418
Mergers & Acquisitions, 3274
Merical, 1132
Meridian, 1384
Meridian Rack & Pinion, 832
Meridian Rail Services, 1372
Meridian Surgical Partners, 153, 377
Meridien Research, 441
Merill Industries, 60
Meriplex Communications, 2075
Merisant, 1968
MeriStar Investment Partners Lesee, 1360
Meristem Therapeutics, 2294, 2346
Merit, 1760
Merit Industries Inc., 911
Merit Service Solutions, 1232
Meritage, 1098
Meritage Energy, 1024
Meritage Pharma, 1931
Meritas, 1745
Meritex, 383
Meritize, 490
Meritron Networks, 1908
Merkle Group, 1787
Merlin, 820
Merlin 200, 467
Merlin Enterainments Plc., 1905
Merlin Entertainments, 280
Merlin Metalworks, 1294
Merlin Securities, 1657
Merlin Technologies, 1888, 2188
MerLion, 2504
MerLion Pharma, 2681
Merlion Pharma, 2410
MerLion Pharmaceuticals, 2443, 2509
Merlion Pharmaceuticals, 3053
Merlon Intelligence, 2006
Mermaid Maritime, 1143, 2937
Merrco Payments, 2137
Merrick Pet Care, 1248, 1769
Merrill Lynch, 2605
Merrimack, 1442
Merrimack Pharmaceuticals, 928, 1886
Merrion, 2909
Merrion Pharmaceuticals, 928
Merry Jane, 420, 1816
Mersana, 5
Mersana Therapeutics, 711, 1439, 1492
Mersive Technologies, 947
Mertz Manufacturing, 1425
Meru, 1249
Meru Networks, 504, 624, 1798, 2594
Merus, 240, 1047, 1439, 1522, 2930
Merus Audio, 3194
MESA and Asteral, 3024

Mesaplexx, 1713, 2609
Mesatronic, 2472
Meshify, 447
Mesirow Financial Private Equity, 3255
Mesker, 1018
MesoCoat, 1051
Mesosphere, 125, 773, 1073
Mesquite Power, 157
Message Bus, 1464, 1862
Message Missile, 3098
Message Pad, 2653
Message Systems, 1316
Message Yes, 757
MessageBird, 2437
MessageBus, 1335
MessageLabs, 309
MessageMe, 1549
MessageOne, 1741
MessageVine, 3146
MessageVine Montilio, 2571
Messari, 2398
Messenger, 1473
Mestergruppen, 2722
Mesura, 2728
MET, 3098, 3098
MET Innovations, 1051
MET-TEST, 656
Meta, 520, 721, 795, 998, 2141, 2691, 3207
Meta Financial Group, 96, 356
Meta Group, 1045
Meta Resolver, 680
Meta Server, 532
Metabase Inc., 1669
Metablo, 2890
Metabogal Ltd., 2945
Metabolex, 3006
Metaboli, 2377
Metabolic Explorer, 3104
METabolic EXporer, 3011
Metabolic Solutions Development Company, 946, 1380, 1715
Metabolon, 186, 386, 698, 750, 1661, 1776, 1844
MetaBrite, 387
MetaCarta, 468, 1704
Metacarta, 983
MetaCDN, 3129
MetaCloud, 1428, 1750
Metacloud, 389
Metacrine, 710
Metactive, 1380
MetaFlo, 2181
Metafor, 2270
Metaforic, 3095
Metagenics Inc., 277
Metaio, 2434
Metal Nanopowders, 3098
Metal Networks, 1601
Metal Powders & Process, 3098
Metaldyne, 926
Metalicity, 1551
Metalico, 1560
MetaLINCS, 1543
Metall Technologie Holding GmbH, 2703
Metallkraft, 2606
Metallwarenfabrik Gemmingen, 1939
Metalogix, 3024
Metals Technology Corp., 324
Metaltec Steel Abrasive, 1424
MetalWood Bats, 1262
Metalysis, 2589, 2653, 2665
Metamachinix, 624
Metamarkets, 1527, 1862, 2398
Metamaterial Technologies, 2222
Metamaterial Technologies Inc., 2148
MetaMatrix, 1008
Metamerge, 2623
MetaMetrics, 136, 1410

MetaMind, 1073
Metanautix, 1657
Metapa, 957
MetaPack, 2526
Metapack, 2568
Metapack Ltd, 2885
Metaphor, 1305
Metaphor Solutions, 1588
Metaphysics VR, 310
Metaplace, 556
Metaps, 721
Metara, 526
Metaresolver, 234
Metasolv, 205
MetaSource, 1097
Metasphere Ltd., 2282
MetaStabble Capital, 1884
MetaStable, 1657
MetaStable Capital, 2272
MetaStorm, 215
Metastorm, 990, 1949
Metaswitch, 782
Metaswitch Networks, 1657
Metatomix, 1915
MetaTV, 194
Metavante, 1107
Metavention, 1930
Metawave, 207, 208, 1836
Metawork, 1426
Metazoa, 2262
Metcase Consulting Oy, 2957
Meteo Protect, 2175
Meteo-Logic, 2822
MeteoGroup, 819
Meteor, 85, 125, 586, 1969
Meteor Learning, 1731
Meteor Solutions, 1093
Metfilmschool, 2419
MetGen, 2603
Metgen, 2101
Method CRM, 2163
Method Holdings, 1433
MethodCare, 822
Methodology, 744
Metis Secure Solutions, 1003
Metonic Real Estate Solutions, 69
Metra Biosystems, 209
Metrasens, 3009
MetraTech, 27
Metrc, 420
Metrekare, 2428
Metreos Corporation, 1130
Metric Insights, 742, 1114, 2006
Metric Medical Devices, 953
Metric Stream, 281
Metricly, 320
MetricStream, 502, 1056, 1606, 2073, 2681
Metricstream, 983
Metrigo, 3047
Metrika, 1360
Metriv, 127
Metrix Systems, 2726
Metro Franchising, 1518
Metro Group, 2605
Metrobi MyVBO (AirTank), 2
Metrobility Optical Systems, 440
Metrofi, 200
MetroGistics, 1424
Metrolight, 2891, 3213
Metrologic, 782
Metromile, 720, 742
Metron Aviation, 318
Metron Systems, 85
Metronet, 2935
Metronome, 179
Metronome Therapeutics, 1762
Metronor, 2745

Portfolio Companies Index

MetroPCS, 496, 1157, 1160, 1410, 1684
Metropolis Healthcare Limited, 1957
Metropolitan Market, 674
Metropolitan National Bank, 1991
Metros Corp., 813
MetSchools, 1929
Mettermark, 863
Mettl, 2517
Mettle Midstream Partners, 1326, 1328
Meu Rio, 1374
MeUndies, 1998
Meus Pedidos, 1511
Mevotech, 2211
Mewave, 1788
Mey Alcoholic Beverages, 1837
Meya.ai, 2024
Meyer Materials, 1118
Meyer Unkovic & Scott, 3264
MeYou Health, 227
Mezmeriz, 60, 434, 705, 1526
Mezz Cap, 436
Mezzia, 1061
MF Fire, 18
MFG.com, 265, 2724
MFM, 165
Mforma, 2442
MFormation, 1335
Mformation, 502
mFormation, 561
Mfuse Limited, 2498
MFX Solutions, 1374
MGC Diagnostics, 104
MGid, 2727
MGM Resorts, 874
MGS Manufacuring, 1174
MGS Mfg. Group Inc., 578
MGVS, 3231
MHR Institutional Partners III, 2088
MHR Institutional Partners IV LP, 2088
Mi Bioresearch, 158
MI International, 2786
Mi-Factory, 2518
Mi-Pay, 3009
Mi5 Networks, 1093
Miami Green, 192
Miaozhen Systems, 1537
Miartech, 2658, 3185
Miasole, 186, 810, 1449
MiaSolé, 68, 1908
Miba Plast, 3092
Mic, 1114
MIC Group, 1034
Mic Network, 59
Mica Sense, 3248
MiCardia Corp., 272
Micarga.com, 3116
Micel, 1750
Micello, 591
Michael Foods, 847
Michael Huber Gmbh, 836
Michael Verheyden, 3033
Michael's Bakery Products LLC, 961
Michaels, 223
Michaels Stores, 280
Michell Instruments, 238
Michelson Diagnostics, 3009
Michigan Accelerator Fund, 3259
Michigan Angel Fund, 3259
Michigan eLab, 3259
Michigan Induction Inc., 467
Michigan Ladder, 114
michigan Landscape Professionals, 1612
Michigan Power, 157
Micira, 125
Mickey Forest, 1509
MicksGarage, 2347
Micoy, 347

Micrima, 2392
Micro DataStat, 1051
Micro Drip, 54
Micro Focus, 162, 843
Micro Inks, 2590, 2591
Micro Interventional Devices, 51, 236, 1386
Micro Inverventional Devices, 1120
Micro Linear, 1898
Micro Networks/Andersen Laboratories, 132
Micro Office, 1991
Micro Power, 1403
Micro Precision, 408
Micro Prose, 881
Micro Technology, 2664
Micro Vision, 217
Micro Warehouse, 786
Micro-LAM, 1023
Micro-Poise Measurement Systems, 110
Microban International, 243
Microbial Solutions, 2958
MicroBilt, 1865
Microbiologics, 855
Microbion Corporation, 2221
Microchip, 1257, 1608
Microchip Technology, 1657
MicroCHIPS, 317
Microchips, 1464
Microchips Biotech, 1013
Microcision, 1526
Microcosm Commnications, 3038
Microcosm Communications, 2653
Microdisplay Corporation, 200
Microduino, 1511
Microdynamics Group, 854, 1232
MicroE Systems, 51, 317
MicroEdge, 336
Microelectronics, 1924
MicroEnergy Credits, 3246
Microenergy Credits, 845
MicroEnsure, 1374
MicroEra Power, 1509
Microf, 1412
Microfabrica, 186, 468, 1014, 2020
Microgame, 1248
MicroGreen, 60
MicroGREEN Polymers, 2007
MicroGreen Polymers, 85
Microgrid Labs, 738
MicroGroup, 1460
MicroHeart, 1898
Microland, 1852
Microland Limited, 3053
Microlytic, 3194
MicroMass, 445
Micromatic, 507
Micromax Informatics Limited, 1778
MicroMed Technology, 2073
Micromed Technology, 3177
Micromet, 189, 193, 772, 1325
Micromet., 2868
Micron Technologies, 167
MicroNet, 3268
MicroNet Automation, 2815
Micronics Filtration Holdings, 1906
Micronotes, 910
Microoptical Devices, 154
MicroPact, 681
Micropact, 167
Microphage, 1917
Micropoint, 1340
Micropole Univers, 2867
Microporous Products, 989
Micropower, 1786
MicroProbe, 758
Microquai Techno, 3053
MicrOrganic Tech., 705
Microsaic Systems, 3019

MicroSave, 1374
Microscreen, 2969
MicroSeismic, 468, 1583, 1778
Microshade, 3194
Microshare, 1259
Microsoft, 200, 1100
Microsoftware, 3118
Micross Components, 1906
MicroStar, 786
Microstar Logistics, 159
Microstim, 2815
Microsystems, 531
Microtask, 3140
MicroTech Systems Inc., 68
MicroTransponder, 447
Microtrip, 310
Microvention, 58, 1898
Microventures LLC, 650
Microvisk, 2958
Microwave Photonics, 1304
Microwave Vision, 3104
MicuRx, 2969
MicVac AB, 2709
Mid America Brick, 60
Mid Atlantic Capital, 1169
MID Labs, 1383
Mid Oaks Investments LLC, 3255
Mid Valley Industries LLC, 847
Mid-America Entertainment, 847
MidAmerica Administrative & Retirement Solutions L, 92
MIDAS Vision Systems, 957
MidAtlantic Broadband, 1209
Midcap Financial, 1108
MidCap Funding IV, 1971
Middle Peak Medical, 3104
Middle Tennessee Home Health Services, 409
Mideast Youth, 1374
Midgard, 1968
Midi, 1061
Midi Compliance & Ethics Solutions, 1364
Midigator, 1140
midland appliances, 2156
Midland Cogeneration Venture, 157
Midland Container, 445
Midland Industrial Glass, 2958
Midnight Pharma LLC, 1559
MidNox, 2321
Midori Health, 748
Midstates Petroleum, 741
MidStream Technologies, 755
Midverse Studios, 1658
Midway Pharmaceuticals, 269
Midwest Automotive Designs, 1427
Midwest Dental, 790
Midwest Iron & Metals, 1210
Midwest MicroDevices, 1556
Midwest Plastic Products, 1722
Midwest Supplies, 381
Midwest Technical Institute, 1753
Midwest Vision Partners, 92
Midwestern BioAg, 277
Midwestern Manufacturing Company, 1210
Miele Events, 395
Mifratel, 2417
MIG, 2841
MIGfast, 2604
Mighty, 79, 888, 1385
Mighty AI, 1162
Mighty Ai, 779
Mighty Buildings, 2037
Mighty Cast, 1112
Mighty Meeting, 680, 2009
Mighty Nest, 732
Mighty Networks, 553, 742, 752
MightyBell, 863, 876
Mightybell, 641

1342

Portfolio Companies Index

MightyHive, 720
MightyNest, 1181
Mightytext, 976
Migo, 976
MiiCard, 1690
Miikana, 11
Miikana Therpeutics, 2410
Mikawaya, 832
Mike & Mike's Organics, 2133
MikMak, 1885
Mikotor, 1708
Milacron, 435, 1971
Milagro Exploration, 45
Milan Supply Chain Solutions, 920
Milcom Technologies, 2708
Mile Auto, 754
Miles, 1039, 1705, 1896
Milestone AV Technologies, 634, 1482
Milestone Aviation Group, 1278
Milestone Environmental Services, 106
Milestone Pharmaceuticals, 622, 1414
Milestone Technologies, 931
Milestones, 2245
Military Advantage, 1898
Milk & Honey, 669, 1103
Milk Specialties, 1949
Milk Specialties Co., 357
Milk Specialties Global, 111
Milk Stork, 1895
Milk the Sun, 2677
Milkman, 2288
Mill River Labs, 1077
Millendo, 11
Millendo Therapeutics, 785, 1149
Millenial Media, 50
Millenium Laboratories, 1778
Millenium Pharmacy Systems, 476
Millennial Media, 361, 457
Millennial Net, 1084
Millennium Care Inc., 2088
Millennium Custom Foods, 445
Millennium Outdoors, 1748
Millennium Pharmacy System Inc., 178
Millennium Pharmacy Systems, 186, 318
Millennium Trust, 20, 1169
Miller Fabrication, 472
Miller Heiman, 886, 1169, 1498, 2014
Miller's Ale House, 1580
Millers Fashion Group, 2942
Millers Self Storage, 2942
Millibatt, 721, 1426
Millicore, 2553
Milling Hotels, 3194
Millipede, 1622
Millstone, 1630
Millworks, 799
MilMar Food Group, 1748
Milo, 116
Milo Biotechnology, 1051
MILSPRAY Military Technologies, 1524
Milstone AV Technologies Inc., 790
Milton Industries, 1169
Milyoni, 185, 1361, 1821
MIM-Hayen, 1450
Mimecast, 1005
MiMedx, 1844
Mimeo.com, 609, 912, 1424
Mimetica, 3129
Mimetogen, 1630
Miminally Invasive Devices, 1514
Mimio, 1736
Mimir Networks, 2148
Mimix Broadband, 1130
Mimix Broadband Inc., 813
Mimoatec Co. Ltd, 2915
Mimoni, 241, 1374
MimoOn, 2815

Mimosa, 759
Mimosa Networks, 1361
Mimosa Systems, 200, 504, 624, 972, 1122
Mimub, 2911
Minar, 2733
MinBox, 1154
Minbox, 2107
MinCell, 2815
Mincom, 782
Mincom Limited, 2613
Mind Candy, 27, 3061, 3122
Mind Lab, 27, 1227, 2967
Mind Palette Co., 2637
Mindbites, 1862
MindBody, 1251
Mindbody, 1006, 1949
Mindbody Software, 1786
MindBridge, 2224
Mindbridge, 1531
Mindcet, 2358
MindClick, 625
MindFlow Technologies, 1857
MindFrame Inc., 178
Mindful Health Solutions, 2074
MindGuard, 3150
Mindmatics, 2820, 2829
MindMatics & Mobile Commerce, 3146
MindMatrics, 2653
MindMeld, 721, 1088, 1566
Mindmeld, 3089
MindMixer, 635
Mindray Medical, 1091
Mindreef, 1084
Minds'Eye, 1305
Mindshare Medical, 1703
Mindshare Technologies, 1707
Mindshift Technologies, 1784
Mindshow, 310, 610, 1483
Mindstrong, 764, 820
MindSumo, 586, 1947
MindTickle, 27, 1511
Mindworks, 2809
Minehub Technologies Inc., 2072
Mineloader, 2724
Mineral Fusion, 1336
Mineral Tree, 862
MineralTree, 1
Minerva, 1608, 2940
Minerva Networks, 1352, 1898
Minerva Surgical, 1930, 1943
Minervaai, 2131
MineSense, 2087
Minesense, 2072
Minetta Brook, 1065
Minettabrook, 1467, 1827
mInfo, 1736
Ming Yi Zhu Dao, 474
Mingle Analytics, 440
Mingle Healthcare Solutions, 1165
Mingleverse Laboratories, 2144
Mingoa, 2347
MingPlan.com, 374
Minh Hoang Garment, 2952
Mini Storage Self Storage Center, 2909
Mini-Skool, 2076
Minibanda, 2336
Minibar, 863, 1998
Minicom Digital, 2453
Minigate, 627
Miniluxe, 568
Minim, 756
Minimally Invasive Devices, 389, 460, 1523, 1547, 1556
Minimarketsimasys, 2610
Minimax, 1021
Minimax Viking Group, 3011
MinInvasive Orthopedic Solutions, 2320

Minio, 108, 604
Ministore, 1305
Ministry Brands, 28, 823, 912, 1005, 1499
Ministry of Cake, 2935
Ministry of Supply, 1914
MinistryHub.com, 347
Minit Asia Pacific, 3192
Minivator, 2958
MINKABU, 2965
Minnesota & Eastern Railroad, 2937
Minnesota Educational Computing, 1333
Minnetonka Tankers, 1968
Minnetronix, 97
Mino Games, 863
Mino Monsters, 708
MiNodes, 3047
Minomonsters, 2321
Minoryx, 2842
Minova Insurance Holdings Ltd., 407
Minova International, 2608
Minox Technology, 2745
Minsheng Energy, 2927
Mint, 742, 1666
Mint Farm Energy, 1968
Mint House, 1558
Mint Solutions, 2930, 3104
Minted, 251, 1203, 1346, 1566, 1787
Mintera, 3128
Mintigo, 56
Mintra Trainingportal, 1576
Mintz Group, 1979
Minubo, 3099
Minute Media, 238
Minute Menu Systems, 92
MinuteBuzz, 3104
MinuteKey, 646
minuteKEY, 1184
Minuto Seguros, 641
Minutrade, 641
Mio, 680, 2094
Mios e-Solutions Oy, 2310
Miovision, 2175, 2183, 2216, 2230
miovision technologies, 2153
MIOX, 1793
Miox, 597
MIOX Corporation, 758, 1299
MIP, 2045
Mips, 1762
MIPS AB, 2807
MIQ Logistics, 205
Mira Rehab, 1618
Mirabilis Medica, 460, 1679
Miracle Linux, 1757
Miradia, 759
Mirador Biomedical, 85, 2007
Mirador Financial, 564
MiraDry, 4
Mirage Network, 55
MiRagen, 113, 350
MiRagen Therapeutics, 193, 318
Mirageworks, 3118
Mirakl, 2684
Miramar Labs, 561, 622, 1126
Miramarlabs, 73
Miramix, 623
Mirantis, 604, 1005, 1623, 3225
Mirapoint, 936
Mirati, 1414
Mirati Therapeutics, 1383
Mire, 2358
miReven, 2950
Miria Systems, 1572
Mirics Semiconductor, 2314
MIRNA Therapeutics, 1439
Mirna Therapeutics, 545, 1502, 1622, 1700
Miromatrix, 344
Mironid, 690

Portfolio Companies Index

Mirow, 1509
Mirra, 1426
MirriAd, 3098
Mirror, 310, 545, 742, 1114, 1154
Mirror 42, 3119
Mirror.me, 979
MirrorMe, 680
Mirth, 1810
Mirth Provisions, 1139
MIS Implants Technologies, 1778
Misco, 940
Misco Robotics Kitchen Assistant, 400
MiserWare, 983, 1901
MisFit, 229
Misfit, 778, 827, 2822
Misfit Wearables, 1359, 1800
Mishor, 304, 2822
Mision Critical Software, 1045
Mismi, 1626
Miso, 1142
Miso Music, 591
Misonix, 4
Mission, 332
Mission Barns, 398
Mission Bio, 130, 1187, 1616
Mission Community Bank, 1404
Mission Critical, 205
Mission Mark, 1323
Mission Motors, 992, 1702
MISSION Therapeutics, 1439
Mission Therapeutics, 1734, 2849, 3076
Mission U, 744
Mission Ventures, 3273
MissionBio, 802
MissionMode, 1683
Missions Controls Automation, 1917
MissionU, 1554
Missouri Metals, 1294
Mist, 1079, 1346
Mist Systems, 485
Mister, 2211
Mister Bell, 3011
Mister Car Wash Holdings, 1113
Mister Cookie Face, 148
Mister Spex, 2432, 2659, 2788, 2815, 3035, 3095, 3229
MisterAssur, 2512
Mistral, 2992
Mistral Energy, 1577
Mistral Pharma, 2188
Mistral Solutions, 3053
Misty Robotics, 779, 1918, 2001
Mitchell, 202, 381, 927, 1045
Mitchell Gold + Bob Williams, 854
Mitchell Rubber Products, 832
MITEC Automotive, 2518
Mitel, 782, 2243
Mithmitree, 1143
Mitobridge, 1149
Mitokinin, 1238
Mitokyne, 1268
Mitotix, 1335
Mitra, 2869
Mitra Biotech, 27, 1522
Mitra Medical, 2879
Mitralighn, 1849
Mitralign, 949, 1608, 2739
Mitrionics, 2628
Mitro, 1184
Mits, 1854
Mitsubishi, 217
Mitten, 851
Mitu, 1816, 1890
MITY Enterprises, 1707
MITY Holdings of Delaware, 1493
MiTú, 59
Miva, 277

Mivenion, 2815
Mix, 1669
Mix.com, 2842
Mixamo, 857
Mixaroo(Boxfish), 3089
Mixbook, 447, 775, 1093
Mixcomm, 1055
Mixed Dimensions, 93
Mixed Signals, 1408
Mixel, 1464
Mixer Labs Inc., 624
MixerLabs, 234
MixLab, 328
Mixlr, 3021
Mixmax, 752
Mixonic, 508
Mixpanel, 125, 2011
Mixpo, 2283
MixRank, 586
Mixrank, 1658
MixRank Inc., 650
Mixt, 1363
Mixx Entertainment Inc, 3157
Mixxt, 2970
Miyabaobei, 3241
Miyoko's Kitchen, 1363
Mizzen & Main, 1914
Mizzen+Main, 1092
MJ Freeway, 1810
MJ Hybrid Solutions, 395
MJardin, 1810
MJIC, 1139
mjoy, 3198
MK Capital, 3255, 3259
MKM Building Supplies, 2303
MKS, 2051, 2258
MKTG, 1883
ML-C, 2815
ML-CSP II Trust, 624
Mlab, 779, 2860
mLab, 234
MLL Telecom, 2040
Mlog, 2965
MLS Media, 1498
MLstate, 3104
MLT, 2848
Mlvch, 895
MM Guardian, 421
MM Pipeline Services, 1707
MMB Networks, 2037, 2216, 2234
MMC Networks, 200, 1537, 1898
MMI Holdings, 408
MMIST, 2081
MMIT, 1761, 1973
MMS, 2787
MMS - A Medical Supply Company, 1971
MMV Financial, 436
MNC Asset Management, 3052
MNC Asuransi Indonesia, 3052
MNC Bank, 3052
MNC Energy, 3052
MNC Finance, 3052
MNC Kapital Indonesia, 3052
MNC Land, 3052
MNC Life Assurance, 3052
MNC Securities, 3052
MNC Sky Vision, 1602, 3052
MnEBay, 2984
MNectar, 545, 721, 2009
Mnemosyne, 1695
MNT Smart Solutions, 169
mnubb, 1982
Mnubo, 2183
MNX, 1576
Mo'Minis, 1241
MOAC, 1391
Moasis, 1335

mOasis, 1584
MOAT, 1227
Moat, 59, 320, 742, 1187, 1701
Moatech, 2915
Mob Scene, 612
Mobalytics, 89
Mobango, 2662
MoBank, 2392
Mobassurance, 3040
Mobbit Systems, 2536
Mobbles, 1898
Mobcent, 2860
MobCrete, 2927
MobCrush, 59, 562
Mobcrush, 309, 742, 1079, 1153
MoBeam, 1241
Mobeam, 627
Mobee, 1014, 1101, 1737, 1987
Mobestream Media, 205
Mobi PCS, 1157
MOBI Wireless, 336
MOBI.Money, 3220
Mobicart, 2769
MobiCash, 1065
MobiCom Corporation, 942
Mobideo, 380
Mobidoo, 1614
Mobien Technologies, 3202
Mobify, 1207, 2216
Mobikon, 2904
Mobilaris, 2745
MobilCom Holding, 2801
Mobile 1, 2905
Mobile 365, 610, 1006, 1908, 2990
Mobile Access, 3115
Mobile Action, 720
Mobile Arq, 421
Mobile Aspects, 1003
Mobile Cause, 1786
Mobile City, 2466
Mobile Commerce, 2653, 2665
Mobile Commons, 1441
Mobile Embrace, 1600
Mobile Fusion, 1695
Mobile Health Engagement Strategies, 797
Mobile Mantra Inc., 650
Mobile Medical International Corporation, 352
Mobile Messenger, 1855
Mobile Parts, 2121
Mobile Posse, 518, 552, 907, 1504, 1701
Mobile Price Card, 1165
Mobile Roadie, 1103, 1992, 2659
Mobile Storage Systems, 2198
Mobile System7, 540
Mobile Teacher, 2941
Mobile Travel Technologies, 2653
Mobile World, 2952
Mobile Xoom, 421
Mobile.com, 1762
Mobile.de, 2786
Mobile2Win, 2653
MobileAccess Networks, 2711
Mobileaware, 2978
MobileDay, 1701, 1702
MobileDevHQ, 776
MobileFusion, 1003
MobileIron, 773, 1346, 1750, 3112
Mobileiron, 1006
MobileLogix, 390
Mobilemode, 2442
MobilePeak Systems, 597, 2841
MobileQubes, 1000
MobileRQ, 1384, 1928
Mobiles Republic, 2629
Mobiles Republick, 3229
MobileSmith, 347
MobileSpan, 1862

Portfolio Companies Index

MobileStorm, 68, 686
Mobiletag, 2377
Mobileum, 597
MobileWalla, 1162
Mobilewalla, 2861, 3053
Mobileway, 1021
Mobileworks, 1637
MobileXL, 1786
MobilEye, 3092, 3235
Mobileye.com, 2595
Mobilibuy, 2994
Mobilicity, 1508, 2067
Mobilife, 2429
Mobilike, 3035
Mobilite, 1663
Mobilitus, 1467
Mobilize, 752, 937
Mobilize.me, 1991
Mobilizer, 999, 1190
Mobiltel ., 2775
Mobiltel EAD, 2301
Mobiltex, 2282
Mobilygen, 1798
Mobim Technologies, 2658
Mobimo, 2913
Mobinex, 3206
Mobiquity, 1150, 1316, 1675
MobiSante, 85
Mobisante, 2007
Mobiserve, 1244, 2645
MobiTV, 925, 1130, 1361, 1537
Mobius, 387, 411
Mobius Imaging, 1104
Mobius Technologies, 1604
Mobius Therapeutics, 270, 570
Mobius Venture Capital, 990
Mobix, 597
Mobixell, 1244
Mobixell Networks, 2463, 2653
Mobliss, 42, 85, 967
Moblize, 468
Mobotix, 2704
Mobovivo, 2043
MobPartner, 2377
MobSquad, 2228
Mobsquad, 2204
MobStac, 27, 485
Mobvoi, 3241
Moby Mart, 1703
Mocana, 812, 1666, 1713, 1852
Mocapay, 686, 1094
Mocavo, 686, 1791
Mochi, 1666
MOCON, 3268
MocoSpace, 1701
Mocuis, 1456
Mod Operandi, 1597
Moda Midstream, 672
Moda Operandi, 136, 1290
MODA Technology Partners, 1321
Moda Technology Partners, 1388
Modal, 1391
Modanisa, 2428
ModbiTV Inc., 813
ModBot, 108, 939, 1254
ModCloth, 863, 1003
Mode, 527, 773
Mode Diagnositics, 2883
Mode DX, 3019
Mode.ai, 1186
Model Metrics, 1600
Model N, 27, 1213
Model N Inc., 990
Modemore, 2848
Modern Animal, 321
Modern Fertility, 321, 742, 1186, 1884
Modern Luxury, 496

Modern Machinery, 2079
Modern Meadow, 177, 1534
Modern Resources, 673
Modern Water, 2883
Moderna, 748, 1522, 2681
ModernHealth, 96
Modernizing Medicine, 1754
Modest, 232
Modewalk, 1219
Modify Watches, 246
Modius, 1401
Modiv Media, 1640
Modjoul, 575
Modjoy, 3053
Modnique, 874
Modo Labs, 1750
Modria, 58, 1058
Modsy, 275, 520, 527, 1346, 1760
Modtech, 1090
Modular Energy Devices, 1695
Modular Robotics, 779
Modular Space Corporation, 21
Modulated Imaging, 875
Modulus Video, 1855
ModuMetal, 430, 845
Modumetal, 85, 322, 1644, 2007
Modus, 216
ModViz, 194, 1649
Moe's Southwest Grill, 1580
Moeke, 3033
Moeller Aerospace, 65, 912
Moengage, 1809
Mogarde, 2593
Mogi, 209
MOGL, 1065
Mogl, 1786
Mogo, 2137
MOGO BankConnect, 2986
Mogreet, 794, 1103
Mogul, 1330, 1703
Mohr Davidow Ventures, 3273
Mojilala, 863
Mojio, 2228, 2256
Mojiva, 1428
Mojix, 1361, 1640
Mojo, 1255
Mojo Motors, 37, 1322, 1596
Mojo Networks, 857
Mojo Vision, 802, 1073, 1616
MojoPages, 205, 1786
Mojoworks, 2469
Moka, 721, 827, 2251, 2681
MokaFive, 1324
Moki, 84, 689
Moki Mobility, 1428
Moksha8, 1251
Mold-Rite Plastics, 1026
Moldflow Corporation, 1611
Molecuar Glasses, 705
Molecular, 167
Molecular Assemblies, 3
Molecular Connections, 2481, 2481
Molecular Detection, 1786
Molecular Devices, 1762
Molecular Imaging Research, 743
Molecular Imaging Technology, 1280
Molecular Imprints, 87, 1155, 1793
Molecular Logix, 244
Molecular Match, 953
Molecular Partners, 2487
Molecular Sensing, 570
Molecular Staging, 2073
Molecular Templates, 704, 1147
Molecular Templates Inc., 1622
MolecularMD, 227
Moleculera Labs, 1490
Moleculo, 586

Molekule, 564, 945, 1881
Molio, 59, 79
Mollie Stone's Markets, 874
Molly, 901
Moloco, 1091
Molotov.tv, 2842
Molplex, 3001
MolucLight, 2141
Molycop, 110
Mom Trusted, 275, 304
MoMelan Technologies, 1421
MoMeland Technologies, 1101
Moment, 776, 1155, 1186
Moment Energy, 2122
Moment Snap, 320
Moment.Me, 304
Moment.me, 3112
Momenta, 764
Momenta Pharmaceuticals, 193, 413
MomentFeed, 309, 625, 794, 1800
Momentfeed, 2640
Momentive Performance Materials, 141
MomentMD, 75
Momentous, 515
Momentum, 387, 1169, 2051
Momentum Healthware, 2188
Momentum Machines, 863, 1073, 1983
Momentum Technologies Sdn Bhd, 3155
MommyMixer, 447
Momo, 1184
Mona, 275
MonaLiza, 2646
Monarch Industries Limited, 1210
Monarch Machine Tool, 60
Monarch Marking Systems, 1368
Monarch Teching Technologies Inc., 835
Monark, 1991
Monarx, 1074
Monashees, 485
Monax, 2398
MONCLER, 3011
Moncler, 977
Monday.com, 1005
Mondee, 889, 1255
Mondi Foods, 2772
Mondial Risk Management, 2700
Mondo, 1579
Mondo Media, 1816
Mondo Minerals, 2842
Mondosoft, 2770
Mondrian Investment Partners Ltd., 927
Moneris, 3039
Monese, 2398, 3099
Monet Software, 68
Monetate, 249, 742, 752, 1381, 1588
Money Design, 721
Money Forward, 721
moneydesktop, 1865
MoneyExpery, 2963
MoneyFarm, 2395, 3043
MoneyGram International, 303, 1818
MoneyLion, 655
Moneymail, 2727
Moneysights, 2517
Moneytree, 1610
MongoDB, 756, 1716
MongoHQ, 586
MongoLab, 1890
Mongolab, 787
Monitor Group, 377
Monitronics, 405
Monitronics International, 205
Moniture, 1006
Monolith, 2044, 2813
Monolith Materials, 739
Monopoly Media, 2674
Monoqi, 2435, 2804

1345

Portfolio Companies Index

Monosnap, 2847
MonoSol RX PharmFilm Technology, 510
Monospace, 1103
MonoSphere, 801
Monpelier RE, 790
Monroe Capital, 3255
Monroe Engineering, 1767
Monroe Truck Equipment, 1169
Monscierge, 594
Monsieur, 1412
Monsoon Commerce, 1360
Monstar Lab, 721, 2965
Monster Media, 1730
Monster Mosquito Systems, 953
Monster XP, 367
Monstrous, 1959
Mont Blanc, 2317
Montage, 225, 2427
Montage Embry Hills, 1220
Montage Talent, 378
Montage Technology, 1840
Montana Rail & Southern Railway of British columbi, 2079
Montana Resources, 2079
Montana Silversmiths, 16
Montavista, 1706, 1898
Monte Alto Forestall, 838
Monte Nido, 1115
Monte Nido Holdings LLC, 449
Monte Rosa, 1930
Monterey, 2427
Monteris, 1380
Monteris Medical, 1715, 1930
Montigo, 368
Montpelier RE, 458
Montpelier Re Holdings, 303, 831, 1368
Montpelier Re Holdings Ltd., 576
Montreaux Equity Partners, 3273
Monzo, 820
Moo, 37
Moodbyme, 1418
Moodify, 1836
Moodlerooms, 1150, 1172
Moody International, 1021
Moody's Corp., 1905
Moogsoft, 485, 604, 1537
MooMee, 1683
Moonfrye, 876, 1223
Moonlighting, 50
Moonpay, 1296
Moonshine Farms, 1630
Moonshoot, 2861
Moore, 2655
Moore Gallagher, 2655
Moore Landscapes, 503
MooreCo, 557
Moosejaw, 1949
Moosejaw Mountaineering, 1417
Mootwin, 3104
Moovit, 305
Moovweb, 972
Mooyah, 228
Mopec, 279
Moprise, 85
MoPro, 696
Mopub, 972
Moran Printing, 1748
Moravia, 494
Morbax, 1509
MORE Health, 222
More.com, 1406
MoreCom, 3205
Moreens, 691
Moregidge, 2178
Moreover, 593
Moreover Technologies, 2702
Moreton and Company, 3265

Morflora, 3235
Morgan Auto Group, 867
Morgan Contracting, 1025
Morgan Corp., 1034
Morgan Lewis, 3262, 3264, 3266
Morgan Olson, 1034
Morgan Solar, 2037
Morgan Stanley, 1905
Morgan Stanley Capital Partners, 3254
Morgan Street, 1618
Morgenthaler Ventures, 3273
Morhterhood Maternity, 874
Mormak, 2138
Mornin' Glory, 2432
Morningside Venture Group, 1044
MorningStar, 153
Morph Labs, 1966
Morpheus Technologies, 1164
Morphic Therapeutic, 710, 1734
Morphics Technology, 556
Morphie, 789
Morphisec, 812
Morpho, 2997
Morphochem, 2998
MorphoSys, 193
Morphotek, 249, 772
Morphotek Inc., 748
Morria Biopharmaceuticals, 3235
Morris Homes, 2976
Morrison & Foerster, 3262
Morrone Organic Innovations, 1917
Morse Shoe Inc., 357
Morta Security, 586
Mortar, 863
Mortar Data, 818
Mortgage Contracting Services, 111, 531
Mortgage Hippo, 3116
Mortgagebot, 1720
MortgageIT, 593
MortgageIT.com, 1137
Morthier Catering, 3033
Morton Grove Pharmaceuticals, 470
Morton Industrial Group, 331
Morton's The Steakhouse, 330
MOS, 3118
Mosa Meat, 2037
Mosaic, 328, 1363, 1669, 1959
Mosaic Biosciences, 922, 933, 1126
Mosaic Manufacturing, 2120
Mosaic Materials, 2105
Mosaica Education Inc., 1274
Moschip, 3202
Moseo, 115
Moser Baer, 2590, 2591
Moser Baer India Ltd. (India), 2685
Mosh, 2927
Moshimo, 721
Mosquito Control Services, 1343
Moss Adams, 3258
Moss Holding Company, 1460
Moss Inc., 451
Moss Software, 374
Mosss, 275
Most Oil, 2194
Mosyle, 79
Mother Raw, 2115
Mothers Work, 1275
MothersClick, 650
Motia, 215, 1084
Motif Biosciences Inc., 2389
Motif Investing, 773, 1346
MotifInvesting, 978
Motifworks, 1959
Motimatic, 888
Motion, 597
Motion Computing, 679, 806

Motion Industries (Saeco and Precision Bearings), 2402
Motion Math, 1058, 1959
Motion Recruitment, 1138
Motion Recruitment Partners, 878
Motion Specialties, 2056
MotionDSP, 983
Motionet AG, 2970
Motionpoint, 1255
Motionsoft, 655, 696
MotionTech Automation, 412
Motista, 380, 1603
Motiv, 857, 1079
Motiva, 1703
Motivate, 1323
Motive, 205, 517
Motive Medical Intelligence, 93, 1255
Motivity Labs, 1284
Motivo, 1017
Motoczysz, 1917
Motoractive, 2462
MotoRefi, 1259
Motorleaf, 2024
Motorola, 217, 1100
Motorola Solutions, 1685
Motorola Solutions Venture Capital, 3255
Motorsport Aftermarket Group, 1113, 2014
MotoSport, 186
Motovario, 3145
Motricity, 281, 1712
MotrPart, 3165
Mount Cleverest, 724
Mount Wilson Ventures, 976
Mountain Alarm, 1639
Mountain Hub, 1074
Mountain Muffler, 1252
Mountain View CLO, 1493
Mountain Warehouse, 2935
Mountain Waste & Recycling, 531
Mountaineer Gas Holdings, 157
Mountaineer Keystone, 741
MountainView Capital, 407
Mousam Valley, 1165
MouseHouse, 1267
MouseStats, 2148
Mouth, 1305, 1914
Mouth Off Health, 685
Mov.ai, 3212
Movable, 1051
Movable Ink, 527, 535, 724
Movandi, 1672
Movati Athletic, 1345
Movato, 1800
Movaya, 85
Move, 660, 1645
Move Loot, 863
Movea, 2890
MoveButter, 623
MoveInSync, 1017, 1511
Moveline, 1521, 1791, 1878, 1914
Moven, 1305, 1527, 2398, 2931
Mover, 625, 2283, 2951
Mover.io, 121
MoveWith, 763, 1489
Movidius, 2347, 2665
Movie Pass, 151
Movie Pong, 1827
MoviePass, 1752, 1862
Moviepilot, 2665, 2788
Movik, 1335
Movik Networks, 1116, 1361
Moving Image 24, 2522
Moving iMage Technologies, 68
Moving Solutions, 1397
MovingIMAGE24, 2443
MovingImage24, 2970
MovingWorlds, 3246

Portfolio Companies Index

Movio Network, 1305
Movirtu, 860, 3170
Movity, 2321
Movius, 538, 1449
Movius Interactive, 1478
MoVoxx, 1103
Moxe, 1605
Moxie, 773
Moxie Patriot LLC, 159
Moxie Software, 1361
MoxieJean, 1618
Moximed, 1126
MoxiWorks, 1912
Moxtra, 485
Moyo Game, 2860
MoyoGame, 641
Moz, 779, 978, 1162
mozaiq operations, 485
Mozak, 999
Mozat, 2468, 3053
Mozes, 1335
Mozido, 1505
Mozio, 183, 1039
Mozwood, 838
MP Hygiene, 2842
MP3.com, 504
Mparticle, 2131
mParticle, 320, 680, 1698, 2130
mPay Gateway, 143
MPE, 247, 1438
Mpex, 56
Mpex Pharmaceuticals, 1578
MPHARMA, 1698
Mphasis, 2481
MPI, 209
MPI Products, 1997
MPM Capital, 3263
MPoint, 1305
Mporai, 85
Mporium, 2398
MPOWERD, 3246
mPrest, 812
mPrest New Forests, 127
MPStor, 2909
mPulse, 309
mPulse Mobile, 941
Mr Taddy, 2465
Mr Wolf, 2419
Mr. Cat, 931
Mr.Ted Ltd. Macaw BV, 2819
MRA Medical Reimbursements of America, 718
MReadBooks, 3104
mReferral, 2835
MRGK, 3141
MRI Flexible Packaging, 1230
MRI Robotics, 3268
MRI Software, 828
Mrs Wordsmith, 1530
Mrs. Gooch's, 874
MS2 Array, 1452
MSA, 874
MSC Software Corp., 1905
MSC Wellness Experts, 2953
MSD Ignition, 886
Msg.ai, 59, 1610
msg.ai, 320
MSI Acquisition, 112
mSpoke, 1003, 1444
mSpot, 1855
MST, 3183
Mstar Semiconductor, 2594
MState, 308
MSU Business Incubator, 2929
MSX International, 1377
MT MembraTec, 3194
mTAB, 1234
MTAR, 280

MTEM, 3095
MTI, 2817
MTI Film, 1695
MTI International, 1210
MTI Wireless Edge, 2562
MTL, 2874
MTPV, 498
MTPV Power Corp., 145
MTT, 2665
MTV Japan, 897
MTW Corp., 899
Mu Sigma, 796, 819
Mubadala Investment Company, 3254
Mubert, 895
MUBI, 2963
Mucci Farms, 2198
MuciMed, 140
Mucker Capital, 36
Mucosis, 2505
Mudlick Mail, 505
MuDynamics, 759
Mueller Electric Company, 607
Mueller Prost, 3261
Muffin Mam, 216
Muir Engineering Group, 2391
Muk Air, 2880
MuleSoft, 241, 1213, 1257, 1623
Mulesoft, 1006
Mullinix Packages, 1174
Multex.com, 194
Multi Packaging Solutions, 170, 1160
Multi-Channel Communications, 2073
Multi-Flow Industries, 717
Multi-Media Digilab, 2846
Multiacao (Call Center), 3171
MultiAd, 1883
Multicaja, 2446
Multicast Media, 1242
Multicoin Capital, 1884
Multifonds (IGEFI Group Sarl), 1754
MultiGEN Diagnostics, 1917
Multilayer Coating Technologies, 1963
Multimac, 3194
MultiPhy, 3205, 3212
Multiphy, 2557
MultiPlan, 579, 745, 912, 927, 1113, 1325, 1973
Multiplan, 1518
Multiple, 2217
Multiplex, 3223
Multiplicom, 3033, 3056
Multiply, 1463, 1908
Multiply Labs, 721, 2122
MultiSensor Sci., 1104
Multisensor Scientific, 498
Multisorb Technologies, 1753
Multispan, 118
Multitec, 3011
MultiView, 1957
Multiwave, 2539, 2708
Mulu, 1426
Mumo, 278
Munchery, 641
Munder Capital Management, 560
Mundus Energia SRL, 2410
Muni, 1426
Municipal Communications II, 1641
Murally, 2374
Murermester Jon Rasmussen, 3194
Murfie, 2002
MuriGen Therapeutics, 3129
Murj, 1147
Muse, 720, 724
Muse & Co., 641, 2860
MuseAmi, 2010
MuseFind, 2215
Musement, 2288
Music Audience Exchange, 1181

Music Dealers, 567
Music DNA, 2518
Music Of Your Life, 1083
Music Reports Inc., 20
Music Securities, 2965
Music Semiconductors, 897
Musical Overture, 191
Musical.ly, 474, 827
MusiCapital, 1768
musicMagpie.co.uk, 2935
MusicPlayr, 2820, 2829
MusicShake, 1840
Musiwave, 3199
Muskegon Angels, 3259
Mustang Ventures, 1852
Mustek, 897
Musto, 3027
Mutabilis, 2457
MuteeGaming.com, 2300
Muth Mirror Systems, 867
Muthoot Finance, 2481
Mutiny, 553
Mutual Mobile, 646
Mutual-Pak, 1924
MUUT, 1467
Muut, 1384
Muve, 631
Mux, 59, 59, 1153, 1760
Muyingzhijia.com, 225
Muzak, 20, 822
Muzak Limited Partnership, 449
Muze, 321
Muzik, 1766
Muzit, 229
Muzy, 1058
Muzzley, 3039
mValent, 457
MVC Capital, 695, 3255
MVConnect, 277
MVD House, 1327
MVI Technology, 2958
MVMNT, 433
MVP, 3143
MVP Group International, 1875
MW Group Ltd, 2713
MW Industries, 111, 170, 1507
MW Manufacturers, 1021
MW Windows, 722
MWI Veterinary Supply Inc., 357
MX, 79, 1339
MX Logic, 861
MXD3D, 627
MXD3D Inc., 650
MXData, 2653
mxHero, 229
MXLogic, 215
My Alarm Center, 1025
My Alerts, 881
My Blog Media GmbH, 3188
My Coupon Doc, 1618
My Damn Channel, 1441, 2016
My Dentist, 3100
My Docket, 1901
My Event Insurance, 1907
My Fit Foods, 1863
My GO Games, 1719
My Health Terms, 1978
My Heritage, 2382, 2804
My Job Chart, 267
My New Financial Advisor, 1966
My Payment Network, 1003
My Perfect Gig, 1335
My Real Trip, 100
My Senior Portal, 3251
My Social Book, 2660
My Therapy Company, 1670
My-Apps, 2931

Portfolio Companies Index

My-apps, 2847
Mya, 773
Myagi, 2262
myAgway, 408
MyAlerts, 1385
Myanmar Innovation Greenhouse, 1374
MYbank, 2396
myBestHelper, 2215
Mybet.com, 2466
myBlee, 3199
MyBurger, 1229
MyBuys, 1408
Myca, 1618
MyChild, 3039
Mycocann, 395
MyCodeSchool, 3165
MycoDev Group, 2192
Mycogen, 2918
Mycogen Corporation, 1708
MyCoi, 659
myCOI, 1023
MYCOM OSI, 502
Mycotech Corp., 589
MycoTechnology, 1616
MycoWorks, 1760
MyDeco, 3061, 3122
Mydeco, 2437
Mydeco.com, 2419
Mydish, 2459
MyDocket, 205
Mydoma Studio, 2276
MyDx, 1083
MyEdu, 224
Myelin Health, 225
Myelo, 2832
MyEnergy, 401, 1463
MyEnergyn, 498
Myers Motors, 1051
MyETone, 2448
MyEyeDr., 1248
Myeyedr., 458
Myfab, 2377
MyFitnessPal, 27
MyFP, 1908
MyGall, 2832
MyGeek.com, 1015
Mygola, 304
MyHealthDIRECT, 477
MyHealthDirect, 150
MyHeritage, 561, 1323, 2985
Myia, 2018
Myine Elecronics, 743
MyKardia, 1814
myLAB Box, 954
Mylearnadfriend, 3003
Mylestoned, 316
MyLife.com, 1361
MyLikes, 1841
Mylikes, 2009
Mymedcoupons.com, 1452
Mymentor, 2131
MyMoneyButler, 1690
MYMORIA, 2832
Mynd, 1028
MyNewPlace, 1728, 1762, 1855
myNEXUS, 1271
Myngle, 2813
Myntra, 27
Myntra.com, 2840
MYOB, 223
Myobis, 3104
Myocor, 538
MyOffers, 194
Myogen, 73
MyoKardia, 764
MyOmics, 1695
Myomo, 1261

MyOn, 782
Myonexus, 481
MyOpenJobs, 1785
Myopowers, 1350
MyoScience, 39, 599
Myosotis, 1048
MyOwnMed, 1768
Myozyme, 2097
MyPermissions, 2938
MyPlay, 1008
MyPorter, 754
Myra Labs, 752
MyRecovery, 3099
Myresjöhus, 2854
Myriad, 1518, 1723
Myriad Development, 813
Myriad Genetics, 861
Myriad Mobile, 817
Myriax, 3129
Myro, 1363
myRoundUp, 954
Mysa, 2161
MyShape, 1786
Mysitcom Ltd, 2773
MySmartPrice, 27, 2809
mySociety, 1374
MySpace, 1449
Myspace, 1537
Myspace/Intermix Media, 1908
Mysportbrands & Mysportworld, 2432
Mysportgroup, 2788, 2978, 3229
MYSQL, 1006
MySQL, 1478
MySteel.com, 2533
Mystery Science, 1530
MysticCom, 2901
MyStrain, 395
MyStrom, 3143
MyStudyWeb Sdn Bhd, 3155
MyTango, 194
Mythic, 610, 803, 1155
MyThings, 1323, 2557
Mythings, 2660
myThings, 646
Mytime, 31, 1890
MyTomorrows, 2469
Mytonomy, 1058, 3246
MyTopia, 252
Mytrade, 267
Myungsung Environment, 585
MyUS.com, 173
Myvyllage, 54
MyWallSt, 1259
Mywaves, 116
MyWebGrocer, 962, 1751
MyWishBoard, 2931
myWobile Pte Ltd, 2464
Myxer, 1737, 1737
Myxx, 512
MyYearbook, 1898
MZI Resources, 1551
Mzinga, 1949

N

N B Education, 1274
N&W, 1021
N-Dimension, 677
N-Dimension Solutions, 2051
N-of-One, 536, 704
N-Tec, 2701
N-Trig, 2717
N-trig, 389
N-Triq, 2445
N.E.W. Customer Service, 1348
N2 Broadband, 1731
N2 Imaging Systems, 542
N26, 238, 1005

N2K, 1731
N30 Pharma, 949
N3N, 485
N3twork, 680, 752, 1079
N5 Sensors, 288
Naadam, 708
Naaptol, 389
NABCO Inc., 1163
Nabell, 1426
Naborly, 1760, 2137
naborly, 2240
Nabriva, 1147, 2806
Nabriva Therapeutics, 710, 1943, 2998
Nabriva Therapeutics AG, 2776
Nabsys, 1463, 1695
NACOLAH Holding Corporation, 407
Nactis, 2956
Nada Moo!, 2093, 2153
Nadella, 2285
Naf Naf, 1580
NAFA, 856
NAFACO, 3209
NailSnaps, 221, 1703
NAJA, 328
Naja, 232, 901, 1186
Naked, 462
Naked Biome, 49, 1268
Naked Objects, 3098
NakedPoppy, 1073
Nakina Systems, 2188
Nala Systems, 849
nalanda Global, 1499
Naldo, 3118
Nallatech, 3095
Nalu Medical, 1147
NAM, 1606
Nam Long Investment Corporation, 2952
NameCoach, 1877
Namely, 361, 780, 827, 872, 1114, 1184, 1629, 1862
Namet, 1021
Namo Media, 1760
Namotech, 2848
Namshi, 2820, 2829
Namsys, 2061
Nan Ya PCB, 897
Nanalysis, 2061
Nanda Tech, 2466
Nandi Proteins, 3019
Nanigans, 638
Nanit, 1890
Nanjing Kingfriend Biochemical Pharmaceutical Co., 1456
Nanjing Sample Technology Co. Ltd., 2624
Nanny Caddy, 1101
Nano Detection Technology, 481
Nano Endoluminal, 2617
Nano Magnetics, 2060
Nano MR, 1679
Nano Opto, 609
Nano Photonics, 46
Nano String Technologies, 182
Nano-C, 762
Nano-Meta Technologies, 3059
Nano-Tex, 731
NanoBio, 1923
Nanobiomatters, 2460
Nanobiotix, 3104
Nanobox, 1074
NanoCarrier, 2961
Nanochip, 1042
NanoClear Technologies, 1055
Nanoco, 3234
Nanocomp, 949, 1164
Nanoconduction, 2005
Nanocopoeia, 3268
Nanofactory Instruments AB, 2709

Portfolio Companies Index

NanoFilm, 2681
Nanogate Technologies, 2704
Nanogen, 217
NanoGram, 1241, 1793
NanoGram Corporation, 186
NanoGram Devices, 1583
Nanogram Devices, 1355
NanoH2O, 1122
NanoHorizons, 1120, 1431
NanoLambda, 1452
nanoLambda, 1003
Nanolayers, 2964
Nanoleaf, 2822
Nanomagnetics, 2378
Nanomagnetics Ltd., 2741
NanoMas Technologies, 643, 2483
NANOMED, 3091
NanoMedex, 1064
Nanomedical Diagnostics, 1616
NanoMedical Systems, 447
Nanomix, 145, 1608
Nanomotion Ltd., 2945
NanoMR, 704
Nanonet, 624
NanoNexus, 526
Nanonics Imaging, 3235
Nanoom Tech, 2993
NanoPack Inc., 1581
NanoPass, 3231
Nanophase Technologies, 154
Nanophthalmics, 999
Nanopore, 2883
Nanopore Diagnostics, 270
Nanopthalmics, 1190
NanoRacks, 447, 716
NanoRep, 1323
Nanoscale Powders, 1630
Nanosolar, 928, 2708
Nanospectra Biosciences, 953
Nanosphere, 1324
NanoSpun, 2822
NanoStatics, 403, 987, 1556
NanoSteel, 677, 713
Nanosteel, 821, 949
Nanostim, 667, 1898
Nanostream, 748
NanoString, 764
NanoString Technologies, 1255, 1392
NanoSys, 154
Nanosys, 5, 621, 983, 1155, 1464, 1495
Nanosys Inc., 145
Nanotech Semiconductor, 3038
Nanotecture, 2883
Nanotecture Ltd, 2885
NaNotics, 1099
Nanotion, 2302
Nanotion AG, 650
Nanotron Technologies, 3242
Nanotron Technologies GmbH, 3037
Nanotronics Imaging, 778
Nanovi, 3194
Nantero, 457, 457, 485, 604, 839, 1290
Nanum Technologies, 2848
Nanya Technology, 3209
NapaJen Pharma, 1241
NapaStyle, 1736
Napatech, 2722
NAPO Pharmaceuticals, 1015
Napo Pharmaceuticals, 716, 1007
Naprotek, 653
Naptech, 3004
NAR REach, 1645
Nara-Sarang Co., 585
Naritiv, 1816, 1966
NARR8, 2847
Narragansett Bay, 1314
Narragansett Beer, 1194, 1527

Narrativ, 49
Narrative, 1105, 1862, 3021
Narrative Science, 238, 1623, 2074
NarrativeDx, 570
NarrativeScience, 1050
Narrator AI, 756
Narus, 990, 3221
Narvar, 238, 562, 799, 1610
NAS, 153
Nascar Members Club, 42
Nascentric, 1287
NASCOM, 2940
Nasdaq, 927
Naseeb Networks, 691
Nash Finch, 1971
Nash_Elmo, 197
Nasioncom, 2614
Naskeo, 3229
Nasra Public School, 54
Nassau Broadcasting Partners LP, 1727
Nassko, 2869
Nasty Gal, 2851, 2851
Nasuni, 604, 756, 1335, 1675
Nasuni Corporation, 1674
NasVax, 3235
Nasville Shores Water Park, 1991
Nasza-Klasa, 2714
NAT Inc., 1624
Natera, 493, 764, 1383, 1522
Natero, 1219
Natia, 2915
Natilus, 1391
Natilus Inc., 814
National Australia Bank, 2650
National Auto Care, 1151, 1859
National Bedding Company LLC, 160
National Billing Partners, 1364
National Cable Networks, 2456
National Car Parks, 2298
National Cardiovascular Partners, 224
National CC, 558
National Data Corp., 303
National Deli, 1573
National Dentex, 1973
National Dentex Corporation, 67
National Display Systems LLC, 557
National Distribution & Contracting, 1686
National Energy Equipment, 2249
National Entertainment Network, 1248
National Funding, 1971
National Gift Card, 1097
National Healing, 1007
National HME, 1779
National Home Healthcare Corp., 128
National Logistics Services, 2121
National Medical Health Card Systems, 1300
National Mentor Holdings, 1160
National P.E.T., 1425
National Packaging Systems, 51
National Pasteurized Eggs, 947
National Pen, 1131
National Penn Bancshares, 1957
National Power, 367
National Print Group, 1145
National Product Services, 132
National Prostaff, 2107
National Re Corporation, 407
National Research Institute, 441, 1826
National Rural Support Program, 54
National Seating & Molbility, 1972
National Security Partners, 1964
National Semiconductor, 1107
National Spine & Pain Centers, 212, 1169, 1654
National Spinning Company, 1971
National Stock Exchange, 819
National Stock Exchange of India, 1346
National Surgical Care, 331

National Surgical Hospitals, 458
National Technical Systems, 202, 381
National Tele-Communications (NTC), 34
National Veterinary Associates, 1754, 2199
National Video Monitoring Corporation, 381
National Warranty Corporation, 843
National Westminster Bank, 2612
NationBuilder, 125, 1374
Nations Energy, 898
Nations Hearing, 15
NationStar, 769
Nationwide Acceptance Holdings, 1493
Nationwide Credit Inc., 449
Nationwide Distribution, 1252
Nationwide Graphics, 592
NationWide Healthcare, 1346
Nationwide Industries, 165
Nationwide Marketing Group LLC, 159
Native, 218
Native Energy, 440, 789
Native Foods Cafe, 1324
Native Foods Café, 961
Native Minds, 1538
Native Networks, 2372, 2901, 3150
Native Tap, 400
Native Voice, 1557
NativeMinds, 950
Nativo, 259, 641, 876, 1223, 1966
Natron Energy, 1073
NatSteel, 2763
Nattagansett Beer, 1118
Natue, 3047
Natural Balance Pet Foods Inc., 467
Natural Communications, 2845
Natural Convergence, 2188
Natural Cycles, 641
Natural Dental Implants, 2487, 2832
Natural Food Holdings, 919
Natural Insight, 51
Natural Markets Food Group, 2067
Natural Motion, 2702
Natural Order Supply, 865
Natural Products Group Inc., 917
Natural Systems Utilities, 2282, 3246
NaturalInsight, 1386
Nature et D'couvertes, 2592
NatureBox, 1701
Naturebox, 820
Naturol, 3202
NAU Country Insurance Company, 1127
Naumann/Hobbs Material Handling, 920
Naurex, 710, 1098
Nautic Partners, 3254
Nautical Commerce, 2131
Nauticus Networks, 457
Nautilus Neurosciences, 1779
Nautilus Plus, 2198
Nauto, 305, 821, 877, 1836
Nav, 79, 564, 945, 1074, 1079
Navabi, 3104
Navacord, 1160
Navantis, 919
Navayuga Engineering Company, 2303
Navdy, 939, 1154, 1223, 1491, 1596, 1599, 1890, 1992
Navegg, 2429
Navera, 666
Naviant, 205
Navico, 2376
Navicore Ltd, 2707
Navicure, 1045
Navidea Biopharmaceuticals, 928
Navigating Cancer, 1725
Navigator Publishing, 440
NaviHealth, 178, 1618, 1973
Navimo, 2667
NaviNet, 1335

Portfolio Companies Index

Navini Networks, 205, 857, 1244, 1798
Naviscan, 1619
Naviscan PET Systems, 1172
Navistone, 361, 481, 1076
Navitas Lease, 1332
Navitor Pharmaceuticals, 193, 1047, 1734
Navix Holdings Corporation, 1494
Naviya Entertainment, 2848
Navmii Holdings, 3148
Navotek, 340
Navotek Medical, 2345
NavStar, 1839
Navtech, 1929
Navtrck, 1682
NavVis, 3152
Navy Power, 157
Nawboi Technologies, 3251
NAWEC, 18
Nawotec, 3223
Naya, 901, 1092
Naylor, 496
Nayya, 685
NB Golf Cars, 1195
NB Therapeutics, 1510
NBA.com China, 2822
NBD, 1759
NBD Nano, 2, 316
NBIC Holdings, 1447
NBIZ, 3118
NBP Capital LLC, 253
NBS Design, 1917
NBT Solutions, 440, 1165
NBX Corp., 523
NBX Corporation, 1257
nChannel, 1556
Ncino, 1610
nCino, 1005
nCipher, 2885
nCircle, 641, 892
NCircle Entertainment, 1203
nCircle Network Security, 1042
NCM Services, 241
NComputing, 1517
nContact, 907, 1013
NCP, 2596
NCP Finance, 1493
NCR Corp., 303
NCrease, 999
nCrowd, 285, 1332
nCrypted Cloud, 856
NCS Energy Services, 1707
NCSG Crane & Heavy Haul, 676
NCTI, 1090
NDLI Logistics, 832
NDS, 851, 858
NDT CCS, 1021
NDT Systems, 238
NE Photonics, 185
Nea, 1464
Neah, 85
Near Me, 1752
Near Pte Ltd, 485
Near Space Labs, 2001
Nearbuy, 527
NearGroup, 310
Nearify, 3100
Nearly Natural Inc., 449
Nearpeer, 2
Nearpod, 888, 1005, 1530
Nearstream, 1862
Nearwoo, 1800
NEAS, 3067
Neat, 249, 646, 655, 2217
Neat Receipts, 2188
Neat Stitch, 3230
Neat Work, 1385
Neato Robotics, 1352, 1917

NEBC, 1025
NEBCO Insurance Services, 1746
Nebraska Book Company, 1372
Nebula, 1969
Nebula Genomics, 709, 1993
Nebulab, 1703
NECCO Realty Investments, 159
Necessity LLC, 3248
Necho Systems, 2051
Nectar, 527
Nectar Power, 1583
nedl, 221
Nedstat, 3042
Nedway Air Ambulance, 1210
neea, 1100
Need, 3198
Needle, 696, 1074, 1121, 1543, 1666
Needls, 2002
Needs & Senses, 2534
Needs Entertainment, 2848
Neff Corp., 1368
Negotiatus, 12, 798, 1703
NEHP, 789
NEI Treatment Systems, 278
Neighbor, 79
Neighbor.ly, 1752
Neighborhood Cable, 3159
Neighborhood Fuel, 1114
Neighborhood Goods, 763, 882, 1186
Neighborland, 1114, 1862, 1945
Neighborly, 23, 246, 917
Neilsoft, 281, 1852
Neiman Marcus, 1837
Neiman Marcus Group LTD Inc., 160
Nekoosa, 1997
Nekso, 2107
Nektar, 217, 1379
Nektar Therapeutics, 1456
Nelipak, 1174
Nellix Endovascular Inc., 272
Nellson, 1138
Nellson Nutraceutical, 1085
Nellymoser, 1701
Nelson Cash, 69
Nelson Communications, 1955
Nelson Global Products, 1990
Nelson Mullins, 3262
Nelson Pipeline, 1280
Nemaha Environmental, 367
Nematron Corporation, 1337
Nemera, 2968
Nemetschek, 3060
Nemgenix, 1776
neMob, 1610
Neo Financial, 2131
Neo Tech, 458
Neo Technology, 2621
Neo-Neon, 3185
Neo4j, 711
NeoBear, 1511
Neocera, 1731
NeoChord, 946, 1804
Neochord, 225
Neocis, 1646
NeoClone, 2002
Neoconix, 1411, 1898
Neodata Group, 3043
Neodrill AS, 3132
NeoEdge Networks, 2188
Neoen Netzoptiker, 3011
Neogas, 838
neogene Therapeutics, 1934
Neohapsis, 1304, 1401, 1852
Neolane, 1949, 3229
Neolinear, 275, 1013
Neologin, 457
NeoMend, 3006

Neomend, 1495
Neomobile, 2515
NEON, 1839
Neon, 1045, 1247, 1862, 2010
Neonga, 2832, 3161
Neonode, 1244
NeoNova, 218, 928
Neonova, 342
NeoPath, 1399
NeoPath Networks, 808
Neopath Networks, 200, 597, 936
NeoPhotonics, 1583, 2653
Neophotonics, 1287, 1920
NeoPhotonics Corporation, 1361
NeoRx, 209
Neorx, 240
NEOS, 582
NEOSE Technologies, 2487
Neosensory, 704
Neosil, 928
Neoss, 2963
NeoStem, 517
Neostrata, 1194
NeoSurgical, 2909
Neotechnology, 3140
Neoteny Labs, 1374
Neoteny Venture Development, 2982
Neothetics, 622
Neotonus, 132
NeoTract, 872
Neotract, 510, 1518, 1993
Neotropix, 1510
Neovation, 2065
Neovest, 1865
Neoware Systems, 1204
Neoworld, 446
NEP Broadcasting, 684
NEP Group, 560
Nepes Display, 2993
Nephera, 2445, 2717
NephRx, 1715
Neptune, 1021, 1917
Neptune Networks, 2398
Neptune Technology Group, 2014
Neptune-Benson, 197
Nerd Street Gamers, 1660
Nerd Wallet, 2154
Nerdio, 1242
NerdWallet, 1006
Nereus, 772, 1414, 2806
Nereus Pharmaceuticals, 1777
Nerites, 1923
Nero, 912, 2434
Neroc, 2492
NERv, 623
Nervana, 610
Nervana Systems, 1155
Nerve, 462
NESCO, 676
Nesher1, 2600
NESS, 3162
Ness, 2739
Ness Computing, 1832
Ness Display, 2848
Nest, 1463, 1533, 1666, 1696, 1918
Nesta Impact Investments, 2500
Nester Hosiery, 1210
Nestio, 787, 1154, 1521, 1635
Nesto, 2090
Nestor Sales, 418
NestReady, 2024
Net Asia, 1757
Net Biscuits, 2629
Net Display Systems, 3200
Net Effect Systems, 1855
Net Health, 1720
NET Midstream, 157

Portfolio Companies Index

Net Movie, 2841
Net Perceptions, 1728
Net Power, 3185
Net Power & Light, 3112
Net Power & Lighting, 1430
Net Systems Informatics, 2305
NET Technologies, 1678
Net Trans, 931
Net Translations, 2474
Net TV, 2848
Net Vision, 2657
Net-Hopper, 1364
Net-Marketing Corporation, 2965
Net263 Holdings, 1771
Net2Net Corp., 523
Net4, 1518
Net4Call AS, 2361
Net6, 1629
Netafim, 3024
NetAmbit, 2809
Netaphor Software, 1679
Netas, 1376
NETASQ, 2842
NetasQ, 2430
Netasq, 3104
NetBase, 100, 983, 1821, 3225
NetBase Solutions, 2188
Netbase Solutions, 1731
NetBio, 646
Netbiscuits, 1751
Netboa, 162
NetBoost, 857
NetBoss Technologies, 699
Netbot, 154
NetBotz, 205, 446
Netbreeze, 2385
NetByTel, 2073
Netcell, 200
Netcentrex, 556
NetCentrics, 654
Netcitadel, 856
NetClarity, 1164
NetClerk, 1008
Netcontinuum, 1408
NetConversions, 810
NetCore, 1335
netCostumer, 457
Netcycler, 2603
NetDevices, 801
NetDocuments, 502, 689
Netdragon, 2841
Netease.com, 870
Neteconomy, 2653
NetEffect, 205
Netentsec, 938
Netezza, 457, 1213
Netflective Technology, 2375
NetFlip, 1855
Netflix, 773, 1006, 1787
NetForensics, 593
netForensics, 1137
Netformx, 1761
NetFortris, 1727
NetG Networks, 808
NETGEAR, 902
NetGear, 1100
Netgem, 2756
NetGenesis, 1629
NetGraph Information Technology SA, 2346
Netguardians, 3036
Nethra, 131
Netian, 2915
Netik, 2340
Netinbiz, 2848
Netino, 3104
NetKey, 957, 1888, 2188
Netkey, 532

Netki, 232
Netli, 827, 1257
Netlify, 125, 1079
NetLogic, 1924
Netmagic, 2992
Netmania, 2958
NetMed, 2775
Netmining, 2417
Netmobile, 3223
Netmoshere, 759
NetMotion, 1640
NetMotion Wireless, 755, 1241
Netmotion Wireless, 1643
Netmovie, 3133
NetNearU, 1112
NetNoir, 1465
NetNumber, 1875
Netonomy, 2653
Netopia, 200
NetOps, 1313
Netork Physics, 1408
Netotiate, 438
NetPlenih, 1635
NetPlenish, 1154
NetPodium, 1947
Netpower, 3206
Netpro, 1045
Netprospex, 655, 1731
Netpulse, 200, 621, 794, 1032
Netqin, 2724
NetQuote, 1720, 1751
Netra, 1104
Netradyne, 1158
NetRegulus, 1061
Netretail Holding, 2301
Netro Corporation, 1091, 2901
Netronome, 485, 2653, 2665
Netronome Systems Ltd, 2885
NetScaler, 759, 808, 1750
Netscaler, 827
Netscalibur Limited, 3170
Netscape, 57, 925
NetScreen, 1478, 1720
Netscribes, 2484
NetSeer, 1239, 1379
Netsertive, 876, 907, 1597
NetSkope, 1698
Netskope, 604, 824
Netsmart, 828
Netsmart Technologies, 1611
NetSocket, 1661, 1684, 1923
Netsol, 2604
NetSolve, 55
NetSpend, 1130, 1235
NetSpend Corp., 813
NetSpira, 2539
NetStream, 205
NetSuite, 1213, 1741
Netsurion, 447, 1499
Netuitive, 561, 949, 1242, 1543
NetVision, 1679
NetWin, 2575
Network Alchemy, 1855
Network Allies, 1176
Network Appliance, 1762
Network Chemistry, 983
Network Commerce, 1465
Network Communications, 2371
Network Development Group, 738
Network Distributors, 1612
Network Electronics ASA, 2361
Network For Good, 386
Network for Good, 18
Network Global Logistics, 1507
Network Instruments, 1971
Network Intelligence Corp., 1045
Network International, 468, 819, 3164

Network Merchants, 336
Network Specialists, 1191
Network Switching Systems, 209
Network Vision, 214
Network-1 Software & Technology, 1191
Networked Insights, 1064
NetworkPlay, 2549
Networks, 1384
Networks in Motion, 1239, 1762, 1928
Networks Insights, 846
Networth Services, 1839
NetZero Inc., 1107
NEU, 623
Neucel Specialty Cellulose LTD., 1972
NeueHouse, 433, 541
Neuf Telecom, 2367
Neul, 1241, 2653, 2665
Neumayer Tekfor, 2705
NeuMitra, 1254
Neumitra, 974
Neumob, 680, 1121, 1666
NeuMoDx, 1923
NeuMoDx Molecular, 150, 225
Neura, 1788, 2606
NeuraHealth, 1426
Neural Analytics, 1786
Neural Technologies Ltd., 163
Neurala, 1260, 2288, 2842
Neuralink, 803
Neuralitic, 3205
Neuraltus Pharmaceuticals, 56, 1908
Neurana Pharmaceuticals, 1147
Neurasic Therapeutics, 2031
Neuraxpharm, 136
Neurex, 1762
Neurex Corp., 950
Neuro 3D, 2457
Neuro-Bio, 1055
NeuroAccess Technologies, 891
NeuroChaos Solutions, 447
Neurocrine, 209
NeuroDerm, 764
NeuroFlow, 421
NeuroFluidics, 326
Neurogastrx, 11
Neurogenetics, 1708
NeurogesX, 928
Neurogesx, 154, 561
Neurogesx Inc., 2776
NeuroInterventions, 1003
Neurolink, 984
Neurologix, 1402
NeuroLutions, 178, 270
Neurolutions, 1490
NeuroMesh, 623
NeuroMetrix, 523
Neuromonics, 1459, 2868
Neurona Therapeutics, 519
NeuroNav, 1426
Neuronetics, 39, 1014, 1062, 1297, 1379, 1420, 1439, 1464, 1510
NeuroNova AB, 2807
Neuronyx, 1456
NeuroPace, 622, 1014, 1788
Neuroptics, 139
Neuroptix, 1917
Neuros Medical, 137, 296, 1051, 1556, 1578
Neuros Medical Inc., 423, 835
NeuroStar, 178
Neurosynaptics, 3202
Neurotech, 1091, 1695, 2346
NeuroTherapeutics Pharma, 3006
Neurotherapeutics Pharma, 1820
NeuroTherm, 1136, 1460
Neurotic Media, 1658
Neurotrack, 108, 1073, 1555, 1698, 1716
NeuroTronik, 918

Portfolio Companies Index

NeuroTronik Limited, 1261
Neurovance, 1923
Neurovigil, 794
NeuroVision, 2509
Neuspera, 1993
Neustar, 2688
Neutec Pharma, 2739
Neutekbio Ltd, 2696
Neutral Connect Networks, 1157
Neutral Path Communications LLC, 123
Neutral Tandem, 561, 597
Neutrino, 2288
Neutronics, 1234
Neutun, 1589
NeuVector, 802, 959
Neuvis, 532
NeuWave, 1923
NeuWave Medical, 1930
Nevales, 3100
Neven Vision, 2020
Nevenvision, 133
Never.no, 2361
Nevercode, 3099
Neverfail, 2725
Neverfail Water, 2942
Neverware, 1554
Nevion, 3004
Nevro, 39, 240, 1268
New Age Exploration, 1551
New Age Meats, 1616
New Archery Products Corp., 357
New Brand Analytics, 1808
New Breed Logistics, 383, 1957
New Carbon, 1262
New Career Skills, 2530
New Century Financial Corporation, 861
New Century Health, 1962
New Century Hospice, 1629
New Century Transportation, 1493
New Channel, 2841
New China Life, 2927
New Citizen (Centre UA), 1374
New Co., 787
New Coffee Co. II, 3039
New Constructs, 1690
New Covert Generating, 1797
New Eagle, 743
New Earth Solutions, 2287
New Energy, 356
New England 800 dba Taction, 440
New England Audio Resource, 440
New England Envelope, 1294
New England Growth Fund, 1294
New England Linen, 1025
New England Linen Supply, 60
New England Orthotic & Prosthetic Systems, 1753
New Enterprise Associates, 990, 3255, 3260, 3263, 3273
New Era of Networks, 154, 2005
New Era Portfolio, 1735
New Era Technology, 1169
New Evolution Ventures, 1939
New Flyer, 1089
New Flyer Industries Ltd., 917
New Focus Auto, 3136
New Fortress Energy, 769
New Foxus, 1257
New French Bakery, 148
New Frontier, 1139
New Frontier Data, 1208, 1443
NEW Global Talent, 63
New Haven Pharmaceuticals, 679
New Hope Bariatric, 205
New Horizons, 386, 2668, 2872
New Horizons Program, 2530
New Image Group, 1574

New IT Venture, 1757
New Knowledge, 827, 1155
New Leaf Paper, 1397
New Look, 3024
New Matter, 93, 976
New Media Gateway, 8
New Mexico Start-Up Factory, 169
New Momentum LLC, 508
New Mountain Capital, 3245
New Mountain Learning, 1984
New Oak, 1335
New Ocean Capital Management, 1746
New Ocean Health Solutions, 175
New Path, 2590, 2591
New Point IV/V/VI, 1746
New Polar, 1252
New Relic, 251, 582, 1798, 1855
New Relic. AssureRx Health, 780
New River Innovation, 1013
New Seasons Market, 674
New Vine Logistics, 1736
New Vision, 2927
New Vitality, 225
New Voice Media, 1787, 2682, 3005
New Wave Broadcasting, 822
New Wave Foods, 1616
New Whey Nutrition, 1834
New World Angels, 3251
New World Application, 2852
New World Natural Brands, 367
New World Trading, 2935
New York & Company, 1026
New York Butcher Shoppe, 1925
New York Digital Health Accelerator, 1510
New York Genome Center, 1422
New York Sports Clubs, 1591
New Zealand King Salmon, 2507
New Zealand Pharmaceuticals, 2507
NewACT, 438
Newark Energy, 435
NeWAY, 1139
Neways, 843
Newbay, 2725
NewBay Media, 1984
Newberry Geothermal, 1897
NewBold, 1749
Newbook, 101
Newbury Equity Partners LP, 2088
Newbury Second Fund LP, 2088
Newburyport Brewing Company, 1737
NewCare Solutions, 1444, 1452
NewCity Communications, 538
Newco, 1105
NewCold, 1138
NewComLink, 1741
NewConnect, 288
Newcrete, 2045
NewCross Technologies, 533
NewEdge, 540
Newfield Design, 1164, 1165
Newforma, 238, 311, 1084, 1335
Newfront, 1760
Newgen, 691
Newgen Knowledge Works, 585
Newgen Software, 1623
Newgistics, 1138, 1741
NewHound, 133, 708, 1491
Newhound, 1832
Newk's Eatery, 1654
NewKota Energy Group, 612
Newlanis, 1401
NewLeaf Symbiotics, 1380, 1583, 2205
Newlife, 2763
Newlight Management, 990
Newline Products Inc., 463
Newlisi, 2288
NewPace Ltd., 272

Newpath Network, 1212
NewPath Ventures, 56
Newpoint Technologies, 1313
NewPort Communications, 1008, 1781
Newport Group, 1066
Newport Media, 202, 582, 837, 1449, 1918
Newpro, 815
Newron Pharmaceuticals, 3187
Newronika, 2865
News Distribution Network, 770, 1832
Newscale, 564
newScale, 561
NewSchools Venture Fund, 1867
NewsCrafted, 348
NewsCred, 59, 744, 796, 876, 969, 1014, 1114, 1187
Newscred, 752
NewsEdge, 194
Newsela, 1058, 1079, 1393, 1530
Newser, 1481
NewsGator Technologies, 1178
NewSignature, 518
Newsle, 610, 1186
Newsletter Publishing, 3137
Newsquest, 2596
NewStar Financial, 1772
Newstep Networks, 2051
Newstore, 820
Newsvine, 1644
Newtec, 3033
Newtention Extended Networks GmbH, 2664
Newterra, 2282
newterra, 127
Newton, 1426
NewtonX, 709, 1770
Newtron, 2704, 2820, 2829
Newtron AG, 2519
NewVoiceMedia, 2963
NewWave Communications, 1410
NewWoods Petroleum, 741
New'Mode, 937
Nexabit Networks, 857
Nexage, 925, 3112
Nexamp, 1463
Nexant, 1355, 1361, 1795
Nexar, 708, 812, 1614, 1696
Nexaweb, 1915
Nexaweb Technologies, 1178
Nexcon, 3192
Nexcore Technology, 1075
Nexcura, 154
NexDefense, 1412
Nexenta, 604, 780, 1032, 1478, 1840, 3225
Nexeo Solutions, 1837
Nexeon, 2849
Nexercise, 1737
Nexersys iPower Trainer, 447
Nexess, 3104
NexGen, 2346
NexGen Medical Systems, 1604
Nexgen Storage, 35, 881, 1319
Nexgenia, 2007
Nexia Device, 627
Nexidia, 539, 1401, 1618
Nexient, 456
NexImmune, 113
Nexinto, 2935
Nexis Vision, 1126
Nexkey, 1890
Nexlas, 545
Nexleaf Analytics, 1227
NexlWeb, 1056
Nexmo, 1707
Nexom, 2282
Nexosis, 1179, 1557
Nexpa, 485
NexPlanar, 186, 949

Portfolio Companies Index

NexPlanner, 1014
Nexsan Technologies, 1908
Nexsteppe, 325
Nexstim Ov, 2807
Next, 1017, 3248
Next Big Sound, 969, 1702, 1791
Next Door Lending, 2027
Next Force Technology, 298
Next Games, 1566
Next Glass, 1499
Next Healthcre, 1135
Next Instrument, 2848
Next Jump, 1669
Next Kraftwerke, 2985
Next Level Apparel, 293
Next Level Learning Inc., 62
Next Model Management, 843
Next New Networks, 801
Next Step Living, 325, 646, 1908
Next Step Robotics, 18
Next Thing Co., 1236
Next Wave, 73
Next Wave Energy, 676
Next Wave Pharmaceuticals, 240
NexTag, 1787
Nextance, 1406
Nextbio, 116
Nextbit, 27
NextCaller, 721
NextCard, 767, 1728, 1855
NextCat, 743
Nextdocs, 1381
Nextdoor, 265, 520, 582, 877, 1005, 1079, 1213, 1537, 1665, 1666, 1696
Nextec Applications, 215
Nextech, 782
Nextek Inc, 3153
NEXTEL, 1257
Nextel Partners, 1160
Nextera, 2510
Nexterra Systems, 2036, 2144
Nextest System Corporation, 133
Nextest/Teradyne, 1287
Nextfoods, 1186
NextForce, 624
NextG Networks, 1160, 1304, 1537
NextGen Solar LLC, 237
NextGenTel, 3004
NextGreatPlace, 1855
NextHealth Technologies, 1346
NexTier Networks, 650
NextInput, 1672
NextIO, 1042, 1924
Nextivity, 813
Nextlabs, 1352
NextLight Renewable Power, 676
Nextly, 686
NextMark, 440, 1922
Nextmv, 195
NextNav, 846, 1361
Nextnav, 518
NextNet Wireless, 538, 3128
Nextnew Networks, 1718
NextNine, 3231, 3239
Nextpage, 2073
Nextpeer, 680
NextPharma, 1755
Nextplus, 1890
NEXTracker, 596
NexTraq, 782
NextRay, 975
Nextreme Thermal Solutions, 459, 983, 1917
NextRequest, 1770
nextResort, 1538
NextShift Robotics, 1759
Nextsilicon, 117
NextSource, 931

Nextumi, 1547
NextView Ventures, 3263
NextVR, 520
Nextware Ltd., 2898
NextWave, 1071
NextWave Hire, 623
NextWave Pharmaceuticals, 1411
Nexus, 2817, 3060
NEXUS Biosystems, 1794
Nexus Gas Parttners, 449
Nexus Mutual, 2272
Nexusedge Technologies, 2614
Nexvet, 764
Nexwave, 3223
NexWave Solutions, 2304
Nexway, 2842, 3229
NEXX Systems, 928
Nexx Systems, 1674
Nexxo, 1762
Nfluence, 85
Nfocus, 984
Nfocus Neuromedical, 870, 1788
NFP Automotive, 1755
NFP Corporation, 1160
NFR Security, 655
NFWare, 89
NG Advantage LLC, 498
NG Data, 2842
NGageContent, 1051
NGD Systems, 252
NGen Enabling Technologies Funds, 2483
NGI Holdings, 1174
Ngine, 3118
Nginx, 641
NGM Biopharmaceuticals, 519, 1495
NGMOCO, 752, 1006
Ngpay, 2809
NGRAIN, 2144
NGrain, 919
nGUVU, 2060
NGX Bio, 5
NHW Holding, 554
Niacet, 1169
Niagara Generation, 1897
Niagara Thermal Products, 1748
Niantic, 93, 309, 1213
Niantic Inc., 238
Niantic Labs, 1032
Niara, 1918
Nibc Bank, 1949
Nibe, 3060
NibMor, 669
Nibo, 641
Nic and Zoe, 1527
Nic+Zoe, 332
Nice, 3241
Nice Actimize, 3212
Nice People At Work, 2460
Niceberg Studios, 2940, 3033
Nicecom, 3128
Niche, 59, 1702
Niche.com, 301
Nichols Portland, 104
Nickle Bus, 421
Nickson Industries, 1225
NICO, 1575
Nicoat, 376
Nicolette, 221
Nicoya, 2280
Nicoya Lifesciences, 2178, 2181
Nido Surgical, 350
Nielsen, 927
Nielsen & Bainbridge, 1085, 1460
Nielsen Company, 2371
Nielsen-Kellerman, 505, 654
Nieuws.Be, 2417
Nifty Thrifty, 876

Nigel Wright, 225
Nightfall, 1426
Nightingale, 1593
Nihon Eslead Corp, 2898
Nihon Trim Co., 2898
Nijgh Periodieken, 2370
Nikas, 2775
Nikkiso, 217
Niko Niko, 1945
Niko Resources Ltd., 838
Nikola Labs, 1285
Nikoma, 2595
Niku, 759, 1912, 1953
Nile Guide, 1088
NileGuide, 2188
Nilex, 2121
Nima, 779, 1890
Niman Ranch, 522, 1397
Nimaya, 1888
Nimbic, 2007, 2446
Nimbit, 1588, 1737
Nimbix, 1684
Nimble, 623, 686
Nimble Commerce, 68, 1718
Nimble Pharmacy, 742, 1073
Nimble Storage, 27, 177, 827, 840, 1996
Nimblefish Technologies, 1674
NimbleGen, 1693
NimbleGen Systems, 1923
NimbleTV, 876
Nimbus, 468, 485
Nimbus CD International Inc., 248
Nimbus Discovery, 1128
Nimbus Partners, 2653
Nimbus Therapeutics, 193, 1126, 1734
Nimia, 1285
Nimsoft, 1045, 1762, 3004
NIN Ventures, 3255
Nina McLemore, 462
Nine Four Ventures, 531
Nine Plus, 1867
Nine Point Medical, 949
Nine Star, 1786
9 Story Limited, 2019
9.9 Media, 2809
900 Dwell, 1220
908 Devices, 154
90East, 3159
911 Industrial Response, 2138
99 Cents Only Stores, 160
99 Designs, 27
99.co, 721
99Bill, 1125
99Bill.com, 597
99Cloud, 1009
9fin, 3099
9flats, 3046
9flats.com, 641, 876
9GAG, 742, 1862
9gag, 787, 876, 1153
9Lenses, 1076, 1525
NinePoint Medical, 1421, 1495, 1814
9Ren Group, 741
Nines, 1616
NineSigma, 642, 1575, 2188
Nineteenth Amendment, 328
9Tong, 1537
Nineyu, 3199
Ning, 1235
Ningans, 209
Ningo, 2323
Ninian Solutions, 582
Ninja Blocks, 2511, 3112
Ninja Metrics, 1065, 1786
Ninjacart, 1511
Ninjacat, 2074
Ninox, 3230

Portfolio Companies Index

Nintex, 1628, 1888
Nintex Group, 1778
Ninth Decimal, 520, 1346
Ninth Street Advisors, 3255
NinthDecimal, 794, 1411
Ninza Turtle, 2848
Nioptics, 154
Nipendo, 2822, 2943
Nippon Dry-Chemical, 2997
Nippon Steel, 217
Niron Magnetics, 176
Nirvana, 752
Nirvana Science, 1925
NIRvana Sciences Inc., 738
Nirvanix, 1901
Nisamest Oy, 2310
Niska Gas Storage, 1577
Nistica, 2188
Nitero, 107, 1713
Nitgen Technologies, 897
NiTi Surgical Solutions, 2717
Nitiloop, 2320
Nito, 1305
Nitramonia SA, 3178
Nitrex, 2198
Nitrex Chemicals, 2329
Nitrio, 980
Nitro med, 317
Nitro Software, 238, 3129
Nitrogenics, 270
Nitronex, 154, 317, 1013, 1711
NIU, 827
Nival, 89, 2654
Nivalis, 1522
Nivel, 1066
Nivel Holdings, 197
Nivelo, 2398
Niveus Medical, 139, 667, 1101
Nix Hydra, 779
Nixon, 1493
NiYO, 1698
Nizam Energy, 54
Njorsk Gjenvinning, 2376
Nkarta Therapeutics, 1734
NKT Therapeutics, 1421, 1631
nLayers, 3221
NLIGHT, 2007
nLight, 1247, 3089, 3114
nLight Photonics, 1361
nLine Systems Corp, 3153
NLS Holdings, 1278
NLT Spine, 2316
NLX, 167
Nlyte Software, 2469
nlyte Software, 1324
NM Group Global LLC, 90
NMC, 2324
NMDG Engineering, 3033
NMI, 782, 862, 949
NMusic, 3022
NNG, 1005
Noah's Bagels, 1591
Nobao, 3185
Nobel Learning Communities, 1021
Nobia, 2854
Nobil, 2655
Nobis, 2786
Noble BioMaterials, 1830
Noble Biomaterials, 1572
Noble Blends, 1139
Noble Foods, 2198
Noble Logistic Services, 192
Noble Transmission, 1752
Nobles Worldwide, 1018, 1115
Noblivity, 1618
NOBRA, 2880
NoBroker, 1091

NOCAP Sports, 754
Nocibe, 1518
Nocopo, 3194
NOCpulse, 1335
NOD Pharmaceuticals, 2509
Nodality, 1439
Nodality Inc., 159
Node, 209, 662, 1039, 1269
Node Capital, 1509
Node.io, 246
Node4, 2935
NodeFly, 1666
NodePrime, 1599
Nodesource, 564
Nodexus, 875
NodThera, 11, 690
Noel Leeming, 2655
Noel-Levitz, 1506
Noetix, 1464, 1674
NoFraud, 1499
Noga Dairy, 196
Nohla, 2007
Nohla Therapeutics, 11
NoiseToys, 650
Nok Airlines, 1143, 2937
Nok Nok Lab, 1260
Nok Nok Labs, 597, 1379
Nokeena, 504
Nokeena Networks, 624
Noken, 623
Nolio, 438
Nom, 299
Nomacorc, 1625, 1754
Nomad Health, 1, 742
Nomadic, 1186, 1477
Nomentia, 1499
Nomi, 876, 1534
Nomiku, 221
Nominum, 58, 839, 1257, 1478
Nomios, 3011
Nomis Solutions, 200, 224, 646
Nomnomnom, 641
Nomorerack.com, 1361
Non Linear Dynamics Ltd, 3002
Non-Linear Dynamics, 2392
Nonabox, 2911
None Networks, 2294
Nongshim, 2848
Nonni's, 1990
Nonstop Games, 2628
Nonstopyacht, 2474
Noodle, 1768
Noodle Partners, 1393
NoodleMarkets, 1554
Noodles & Co., 1092
Noom, 1511, 1597, 1637, 1840
Noon, 1155, 1666
Noos, 3170
Nopassword, 895
Nor-Cal Products, 674
Nor1, 1808
Nora Therapeutics, 1495, 1943
Noranco, 1231, 2049
Noranda, 1138
Norbain, 2371
Norbord, 2062
Norcos, 2790
Norcraft Companies, 319, 1438
Norcross Safety Products, 1368
Nord Sense, 309
Nordax Finans, 1939
Nordco Holdings LLC, 867
Nordco Inc., 159
Nordic, 1764
Nordic Capital IV, 2438
Nordic Consulting, 921, 941
Nordic Consulting Partners, 1631

Nordic Energy Services, 2623
Nordic Mezzanine, 2438
Nordic Nanovector AS, 2510
Nordic Packaging and Container International, 1160
Nordic Telephone Company, 2371
Nordic Venture Partners, 2438
Nordisk Terapi, 2745
Nordnav Technologies, 2653
Nordofin Resources, 3200
Nordstrom, 874
NoRedInk, 888, 965, 1058, 1181, 1554, 2009
Norel Systems, 2927
Norian Corporation, 1399
Noriel, 2462
Norland Technology, 3005
Norm Thompson, 843
Norma Group, 2292
Normal, 1527
Normal Ears, 1878
Normerica Building Systems, 2040
NormOxys, 415
Noro-Moseley Partners, 3251
Noront Resources, 1551
Norquin, 1646
Norse, 1361
Norshield Security Products, 1722
Norsk Titanium, 145
Norstel, 2628, 2746, 3004
Norstrem Associates, 3251
Norsun Foods, 1294
Nortech Sytems, 1971
Nortek, 160
Nortev, 2347
North, 742, 2150
North America Cable Equipment, 1204
North America Central School Bus LLC, 847
North American Archery, 722
North American Baking, 1955
North American Breweries, 1089
North American Dental Group, 20
North American Partners in Anesthesia, 111, 1113
North American Rescue, 681, 1654
North American Substation Services, 989
North American Video, 899
North Bridge Growth Equity, 36
North Coast Composites, 47
North Coast Minerals, 1548
North Coast Technology Investors, 3259
North Dakota Holdings, 902
North of England Gas Distribution Network, 2582
North Sea Infrastructure Holdings, 157
North Sea Midstream Partners, 157
North Star Seafood, 1859
North Trade, 3045
Northburd, 1845
Northcentral University, 1377
Northeast Dental Management, 1654
Northeastern Nonwovens, 1225
Northeastern Ohio Energy Hotel Fund, 1024
Northern Biologics, 1930
Northern Blizzard Resources, 1577
Northern Brewer, 684
Northern Contours, 1275
Northern Digital, 197
Northern Equity Investments, 1164
Northern Mat & Bridge, 2267
Northern Michigan Angels, 3259
Northern Power Systems, 1355, 1583
Northern Tier Energy, 1837
Northern Trust Private Equity, 3255
Northfield, 785
Northfield Industries, 1859
Northgate Capital LLC, 624
Northland Material Handling, 2278

1354

Portfolio Companies Index

NorthPage, 1069
Northpole, 2688
Northshore Bio, 1384
NorthStar, 2376
Northstar Aerospace, 2008
Northstar Travel, 1169
Northstar Travel Media, 1984
Northwave Technology, 1917
Northwest Cascade, 1639
Northwest Coatings, 376
Northwest Hardwoods, 110, 1138
Northwest Plan Services, 1979
Northwestern Management Services, 1132
Northwood Ventures, 3257
Norwegian Cruise Line, 1837
Norwesco, 1372
Norwest Equity Partners, 3268
Norwest Pallet Supply, 963
Norwest Productions, 2391
Norwest Venture Partners, 3273
Nosan, 1456
Noscira, 1456, 1456
Nosto, 2842
Not Your Average Joe's Inc., 357
Notable Health, 877
Notable Labs, 3, 742, 863, 1142
Notable Solutions, 655
Notal Vision, 2717
Notarize, 728, 1154
Notation Caption, 36
Notch, 2122, 2131
Notch Therapeutics, 2174
NotCo, 1709
NoteSwift, 300
Noteworth, 527
Nothing Bundt Cakes, 1115
NotifyMD, 551
Notifymd, 1335
Notion, 380, 742, 945, 1384, 1669
Notion Capital, 485
Notis Global, 1139
Notiva, 200
Notonthehighstreet.com, 3122
Nototehighstreet.com, 3061
Noun Project, 1059, 1153
Nouncy, 3215
Nouriz, 2927
NousCom, 1930
Nouscom, 11
Nova, 721, 820, 1426, 2600, 3150, 3162
Nova Analytics Corp., 523
Nova Cardia, 1251
Nova Cimangola, 1012
Nova Corp., 303
Nova Credit, 742
Nova Instruments, 238
Nova Metrix, 238
Nova Ratio AG, 2704
Nova Science, 2909, 3182
Nova Scientific, 180
Nova Zyme Pharmaceuticals, 428
Novabase, 2708
Novacap, 223, 2160
NovaCardia, 94, 772, 1693
NovaCentrix, 810
Novacept, 1495
NovaCopper, 1551
Novacta, 2958
Novacta Biosystems, 3098
NovaDel Pharma, 1456, 1456, 1492
Novadigm Therapeutics, 622
Novadip, 3216
NovaDx, 1839
Novaerus, 711
Novagali Pharma SA, 3235
Novagraaf, 2370
Novak Biddle, 990

Novalar, 315
Novalux, 1917
NovaMed, 2724
Novamera Inc., 2072
NovaMin, 907
NovaMin Technology, 1013
Novapost, 2377
NovaPump, 2518
Novare, 667, 1463
Novariant, 504
Novarra, 1042
Novartis, 1456
Novartis Venture Fund, 3263
Novasentis, 1120, 3089
Novasic, 2472
Novasite Pharmaceuticals, 1007
NovaSom, 667, 1510, 1605
NovaSparks, 1418
NovaSterilis, 323
Novasys Medical, 87, 178, 928, 1379
Novate, 2909
Novate Medical, 3011
Novatex, 2480
NovaTorque, 731
NovaTract, 60, 1101
NovaTract Surgical, 679, 845, 1942
Novavax, 1495
Novawatt, 3229
Novazyme Pharmaceuticals, 73
Novel Effect, 411, 1155
Novel Therapeutic Technologies, 3235
Novelda, 2361
Novelics, 2769
Novell, 2005
Novell Inc., 303
NovellusDx, 1993
Novelos, 60
Novelos Therapeutics, 2693
Novera Optics, 1091, 2917
Novetta, 167
Novexel, 193, 2308
Novi, 2438
Novian Health, 991
Novidea, 1610
Novihum Technologies, 571
Novik, 505
NovImmune, 2410
Novinda, 1304
Novinium, 85
Novint Technologies, 508
NovioGendix, 2505
Novira, 11, 1930
Novira Therapeutics, 389
Novisto, 2090
Novitex Enterprise Solutions, 141
NOVO 1, 834
NOVO Energy, 1897
NovoCure, 1047, 1439
Novocure, 1993
NovoDynamics, 983
NovoED, 548, 1186
NovoEd, 1058
Novogi, 2739
Novogy, 571, 1101
Novoic, 2398
Novolex, 1990
Novologix, 1728
Novolux, 2
Novolyte Technologies, 172
Novomanip, 3113
Novome, 11
Novomer, 748, 1392, 1442, 3090
Novonix, 2148
Novoron Bioscience, 221
NovoStent, 1619
Novostent, 1251, 1604
NovoStent Corporation, 1241

Novotyr Therapeutics, 3235
Novovil, 3033
Novozymes, 1271
Novozymes AS, 77
Novozymes Malaysia Sdn Bhd, 3155
Novus, 224
Novus Health, 2051
Novus Leisure, 2926
NOVX Systems, 2188
Now Money, 2398
Now Public, 1244
Nowait, 275, 631
NowMedia, 508
NowSecire, 225
NowSecure, 1050, 1181
NowThis News, 1701
NowThisMedia, 1361
Noxilizer, 18
Noxxon, 3104
NOXXON Pharma, 3187
NOXXON Pharma AG, 1325, 3181
Noyo, 729
Nozomi, 827
Nozomi Networks, 1155
Nozomi Photonics Co. Ltd., 2406
NP Photonics, 1667
Np Text, 782
NPC International, 1372
Nperspective, 3251
NPH Property Holdings, 1493
NPI Medical, 1722
NPIC, 2969
nPlatform, 3118
nPoint, 2002
NPS Pharmaceuticals, 1456
NPSG, 899
NPX Technologies Ltd., 2532
nQuire Software, 597
NRS Healthcare, 2935
NS1, 756, 827, 1610
NS8, 149, 288
NSA International, 1360
NSC Minerals, 2177
Nsc Minerals, 2030
NSC Technologies, 531
Nscaled, 2662
nScaled, 89
Nsgene, 3140
NSi, 356
Nsight, 495, 1779
nSite Software, 1390
Nsknox, 3212
NSM Music Group, 911
NSS, 2317
nStack, 108
NStreams Technologies, 46
NTE Aviation LLC, 1965
NTELOS Holdings, 1508
NTent, 226
Nth Degree, 408, 832
NthOrbit, 624
nThrive Inc., 159
nTopology, 565
nTouch Research, 1013
NTRON, 238
NTRU Cryptosystems, 1706
NU Bank, 1504
Nu Energy, 2604
Nu Sirt Sciences, 918
Nu Skin Enterprises, 303
Nu Visions Manufacturing, 377
Nu3, 2919
nu3, 3047
Nualight, 2606
Nuance, 183, 3203
Nuance Communications, 1257
Nubank, 1537

Portfolio Companies Index

Nubera, 2978
Nubisio, 224
Nubo, 1260
Nubundle, 1121
NuCana, 1700
Nucana, 2969
Nuclear Engineering Services, 2935
Nucleonics Inc., 2807
Nucleus, 1533
NuCO2, 202, 381
Nucore, 564
NuCORE Technology, 950
Nucore Technology, 1674
NuCurrent, 403
Nucurrent, 987
Nucypher, 527, 802
Nudge Rewards, 2060
Nudo Products, 1560
Nueclear, 1346
Nuelle, 1993
Nuera, 22
Nuera Communications, 163
Nueva Cocina Foods, 132
Nuevo Midstream Dos, 672
Nuevolution, 3006, 3140
Nufern, 215, 532
NuGen, 1762
NuGEN Technologies, 87, 928
Nugen Technologies, 1523
NuHabitat, 447
Nuji, 3088
Nujira, 2378, 2606
Nulabel, 151
NuLink, 902
Nulogy, 2163
Numadic, 640
Numan, 2398
Numara Software, 1888
Numarine, 3164
Numascale AS, 3132
NuMat, 2074
NumberFire, 545, 1527
Numberfour AG, 2595
Numbrs, 2574
Numedii Inc., 493
Numerai, 50, 742, 1330
Numerate, 193, 1128
Numerated, 1918
Numeric Investors, 1778
Numericable, 3011
Numerical Technologies, 1247
Numerify, 780
Numet, 1075
Numet Machining, 1025
Numet Machining Techniques, 1730
Numetric, 1005
Numi Organic Tea, 430
Numina, 1666
Numira, 1679
Numira Biosciences, 1786
Numonyx, 782
Numotion, 1140
Nuna, 1079
NUO Therapeutics, 510
NuoDB, 959, 1150, 1257
NuOrder, 162, 553, 876, 1890
Nuovo Film, 1340
NuPathe, 1510
NuPathes, 240
NuPotential, 365
NuPulse, 350
Nur, 3128
Nura, 154, 2410
Nurego, 1812
NuRelm, 1003
Nuritas, 571, 1065
Nurix, 519, 1814

Nuro, 877
Nursefinders, 2073
NurseGrid, 1467
Nursery Supplies Inc., 1131
NursIT, 2832
Nurtur Me, 953
Nurture Life, 1023
NurturMe, 447
Nurx, 945, 1079, 1153, 2122
NuScriptRX, 679
NuscriptRx, 999
NuSil Technology, 1300, 1507
NuSirt, 1261
Nuskool, 421
NuSpace, 542
Nuspire, 20
Nusym Technologies, 628
Nusym Technology, 1947
Nut Pods, 484
Nutanix, 31, 238, 304, 872, 1255, 1623
NuTek Salt, 1073
Nutfield Technology, 1922
Nutmeg, 2469, 3023
Nutonian, 37
nuTonomy, 3089
Nutrabolt, 1231
Nutraceutical, 962
NutraClick, 646
Nutragenesis, 77
Nutri Ventures, 3039
Nutrigreen, 2708
Nutrinsic, 933
Nutrionix, 3104
NutriSystem Inc., 303
Nutrition Physiology Company LLC, 899
Nutritional High, 1083, 1139, 2117
Nutrivise, 591, 1101
NutshellMail, 953
Nuun, 85
Nuuvera, 2128
Nuvaira, 1728, 1930, 1993
NuVasive, 470, 1414
Nuve, 447, 1687
Nuveen Investments, 1160, 2371
Nuvei, 1169, 2198
Nuvelo, 2073
Nuventix, 325, 1014
Nuvi, 689, 1074
Nuvisio, 2901
NuVision Engineering, 1939
Nuvita, 1926
Nuvita Professional, 1926
Nuvo TV, 1829
Nuvolo, 812
Nuvoloso, 1219
NuvoMed, 1065
Nuvon, 1032
NuvoSun, 68
NuVox, 1410
Nuvox, 1157, 1212
NuVox Communications, 1508
Nuvyyo, 2070
Nuwest Communities, 2194
Nuzzel, 1254, 1566, 1589, 1702
Nvidia, 1924
nVidia, 1762
NView, 802
nVision, 150, 428, 1658
nVision Medical, 845
Nvite, 1320
NVMdurance, 1304
NVoicePay, 2003
NVP Brightstar, 2612
NVT Group, 238
Nwave Technologies, 229
NWay, 3241
nWay, 234, 553, 1566, 1840, 2009

nway, 1983
Nwestco, 1979
NWP Services, 564, 1771
NWPolymers, 1911
NxEdge, 597
NxGen Electronics, 1917
NXP, 223, 2371
NXP Semiconductor, 56
NXP Semiconductors, 745
NxStage Medical, 561
NXT Capital, 1746, 1746
NXT Capital Funding IV, 1971
NXT-ID, 532
NxtControl, 3156
NxtGen Emission Controls, 194
NxThera, 150, 1241, 1490
NxtMile Sports Insoles, 1739
NXTsoft, 1499
NY Accelarator Corp., 1422
Ny Department Stores, 1021
Nycomed, 212, 2371
Nycomed Pharma, 2999, 3000
NYDJ Apparel, 560
NYF, 3091
Nyge Aero, 2854, 2854
NYIT, 3257
Nylas, 565, 863, 1599
Nyle Systems, 1165
NYLIM Jacob Ballas India Fund III LLC, 2088
Nylon Corporation of America, 1225
Nymbus, 1005
Nymi, 978, 1610, 2228
Nymirum, 946
Nyota Minerals, 1551
NYSE Blue, 1788
Nyshex, 812
NYX Security, 3004

O

O Luxe Holdings Limited, 1092
O Premium Waters, 441
O&S Doors, 1755
O'Brien Corp., 989
O'Brien Veterinary Management, 381
O-In Design Automation, 1674
O.school, 221
O2 Canada, 2123
O2 Cool, 1965
O2B Kids, 1727
O2Micro, 897
O3b Networks, 1335
Oak Financial, 659
Oak HC/FT, 3254, 3263
Oak Hill Advisors, 819
Oak Investment Partners, 3268
Oak Pacific Interactive, 2927
Oak Street Funding, 128
Oak Street Health, 1314
Oak Valley Resources, 673
Oakcreek Golf, 2045
OakNorth, 2681
Oakstone Holdings, 3251
Oanda Coorperation, 2418
Oar AG, 3163
Oasis, 195, 952
Oasis Atlantico - Hotelaria e Turismo, 3039
Oasis Children's Services, 688
Oasis Labs, 235, 1155
Oasis Marinas, 18, 495
Oasis Media Corporation, 650
Oasis Outsourcing, 97, 1066, 1278
Oasys, 748
Oasys Water, 58
Oath, 332
OATSystems, 928
OB Hospitalist Group, 160, 178, 886
Ob10, 2463

Portfolio Companies Index

Obalon, 278, 1014
Obalon Therapeutics, 622, 1371
Obaz, 1121
Oberon Media, 2463
Oberthur, 2285
Oberthur Card Systems, 2843
Oberthur Smart Cards, 2712
Obie, 798
Obie.ai, 2024
OBike, 879
Obillex, 2963
Obizible, 1629
Object Reservoir, 1273
Object Video, 1137
Objective Logistics, 1322
Objectivity, 57
ObjectStar, 1021
ObjectVideo, 628, 1348, 1888
Oblend, 2279
Oblix, 759
Oblong, 812
Oblong Industries Inc, 779
OBMedical, 1925
Obo, 1985
Obopay, 1379
ObsEba, 1700
Observe Medical, 3194
ObserveIt, 224
Observeit, 1731
ObservePoint, 79, 1205
Obseva, 73
Obsidian, 1780
Obsidian Security, 877
Obsidian Therapeutics, 193
Obsidian/Applied Materials, 1287
Obsidio, 849
OC Robotics, 3098
OC Robotics Ltd, 2455
OCA Venture Partners, 3255
Ocado, 3088
Ocarina Network, 1478
Ocarina Networks, 972
Ocata Therapeutics, 133
Occam Networks, 928
Occam Sciences, 661
Occam Systems, 2958
Occasion Brands, 1234
Occidental Hotels Allegro Resorts, 2953
Occipital, 779, 879, 1054, 1791
OccuRx, 2950
Ocean Approved, 1165
Ocean Breeze Water Park, 1991
Ocean Butterflies, 2838
Ocean Current Energy, 3251
Ocean Executive, 2148
Ocean Installer, 1167
Ocean Outdoor, 2935
Ocean Renewable Power Co., 1164
Ocean Sales, 2260
Ocean Sparkle, 3202
Ocean Watch, 289
Ocean's Halo, 433
Oceana Therapeutics, 94, 785
Oceanlinx, 2604, 2708
Oceans Healthcare, 820
OCENSA, 585
OCENSA Transportation Rights, 585
Ocera, 1014, 1700
Ocera Therapeutics, 561, 622, 872, 1271, 1536, 1820, 1943
Oceus Networks, 1779
OCI Solar, 585
OCJ, 3091
Ockam, 803
OCM Print Management Solutions, 2565
Octagon, 51
Octagon Investment Partners, 1493

Octagon Research Soltuions Inc., 655
Octalica, 438
Octane AI, 310
Octane Fitness, 1336
Octane Lending, 535
Octane Software, 1008
Octane5 International LLC, 694
Octasic, 2198
Octasoft, 1183
Octave, 720, 1363
Octave Group, 2243
Octi, 1666
Octio AS, 3132
Octiv, 86
October, 2842
Octopus.com, 115
Octoshape, 2990
Ocuity, 3186
Ocular Dynamics, 1238
Ocular Technologies, 1271
Ocular Therapeutix, 178, 1449, 1464, 1631, 1764
Ocularis Pharma, 403
Oculeve, 1930
OcuLex, 240
Oculex Pharmaceuticals, 73, 526
Oculii, 521, 1486
OCULIR, 1667
Oculis, 1350
Oculis Labs, 983, 1987
Oculus Health, 704
Oculus VR, 125, 1184, 1718
ODC Nimbus, 632
ODENBERG, 2328
Odeo, 115
Odeon/UCI Cinemas, 2371
Odersun, 1398, 3213
oDesk Corporation, 1674
Odessa Power Holdings, 676
OdigeO, 3024
Odim, 2745
Odimo, 3115
Odin, 89, 3128
Odin Enterprises, 8
Odin Technologies, 3221
OdontoPrev, 1022
Odontoprev, 3171
Odoo, 3229
Odyssey, 1049, 1597
Odyssey Health Care, 405
Odyssey Interactive, 2131
Odyssey Investment Partners, 1873
Odyssey Logistics & Technology, 383, 1852
Odyssey Technologies, 1209
Odyssey Thera, 2806
Odyssey Thera Inc., 2807
Oenalliance, 2616
Oerthalign Inc., 374
OEwaves, 730, 1830
OfColor, 1499
Oferteo.pl, 3035
Off Grid Electric, 596
Off.Grid:Electric, 1374
Offbeatguides, 2595
Offensive Security, 1720, 1796
Offerdat, 3251
OfferIQ, 724
OfferLogic, 316
Offermatica, 226
Offermobi, 151
Offerpop, 536, 1991
Offers.com, 1761
Offerton Liveshopping, 2331
OfferUp, 125, 520, 827, 1028
Office Baroque Gallery, 3033
Office Media Network, 822
Office Practicum, 1410
Office Total, 931

OfficeMax, 1100
OfficeSource, 767
OfficeTiger, 782
Offset Gerhard Kaiser, 2367
Offshore Inland Marine & Oilfield Services, 1417
Ofo, 2437
OG Planet, 627
Ogee, 789
Ogee Inc., 440
Oggifinogi, 535
Ogin, 1788, 1908
Ogin Energy, 596
Ogmento, 459
Ogury, 3199
OGX Holding II, 673
OH Aircraft Acquisition, 1360
Ohai, 200
Ohi, 785
OHM Connect, 182
OHMConnect, 752
OhmConnect, 490
Oil Purification Systems, 192
Oilfield Water Logistics, 1326
Oilgear Company, 1174
OilSERV, 1129
Oilstudios.com, 2565
Oinky, 3099
Oja.la, 2975, 3116
Ojai Energy Systems, 3248
Ojo, 1597
OK Industries, 1560
Okairos, 1930, 2521
Okanjoya, 234
Okapi Sciences, 3033
Okcupid, 863
Okena, 1704
Okera, 720
Okhi, 2122
Oki, 217
Okko Hotels, 2842
Okmetic Oyj, 2981
OKpanda, 1058, 1549
OKTA, 752
Okta, 125, 840, 1073, 1969
OKTOGO, 2312
Oktogo, 3199
Oktogo.ru, 3220
OKWave, 1757
Ola, 1184, 1828
Olam International, 2425
Olam-Africa, 1012
Olapic, 863, 1150, 1407, 1635
Old Dominion Freight Line, 383
Old Hickory Smokehouse, 1345
Old london, 632
Old Time Pottery, 530
Old World Christmas, 832
Ole & Steen, 1092
Oleon Holding, 2324
Olfactor Laboratories, 1786
Oliberte, 3246
Olicar, 2515
OliLux Biosciences, 623
Olista Software Corporation, 2761
Olive, 1285
Olive Devices, 269
Olive Medical, 1786
Olive Software, 3114
Olivenoel, 3161
Oliver, 1011
Oliver Printing & Packaging Co., 1438
Oliver Products, 261, 1174
Oliver Solution, 2943
Ollie, 151, 545, 669, 1114, 1589
Ollie's Bargain Outlet, 435
Olly, 232, 1363

Portfolio Companies Index

OLO, 540
Olo, 1828
Olon Industries, 1460
Olono, 1985
Olook, 2967
OLSet, 2009
OLSON, 1090
Olvi Oyj, 2981
OLX, 2992
Olympia Chimney Supply, 165
Olympic Physical Therapy, 82
Olympix, 2687
Olympus Re Holdings, 831
OM Signal, 2103
OM1, 820
Omada, 125, 812, 1056, 1931
Omada Health, 1058, 1346
Omadi, 79
Omadi Mobile Management, 1074
Omaha National, 69
Omaze, 259, 562, 724, 744, 1626, 1835
Ombitron, 1786
Omedix, 1146
Omega Diagnostics, 3019
Omega Energia Renovael S.A., 1957
Omega Environmental Technologies, 1343, 1573
Omega Funds One Way Ventures, 3263
Omega Health Systems, 1275
Omega Ingredients, 2751
Omega Pharma, 3222
Omega Red, 2935
Omega Wirless, 1157
OmegaTech, 240
Omegawave, 2621
Omeicos, 2832
Omek, 724
omelas, 2232
Omeros, 154, 1846, 1948, 2410
OMERS Private Equity, 3254
OMERS Ventures Fund II, 485
Ometric, 1844
OMGPOP, 1701, 1718
OMGPop, 234
OMNE Partners, 69
Omneon, 1403, 1913
Omneon Video Networks, 58
Omni, 756, 938, 1839
OMNI Design, 1839
Omni Energy Services Corp., 1972
Omni Labs, 321
OMNI Retail Group, 2003
Omni-ID, 812
Omni:Us, 2398
Omnia, 2745
Omnia Communications, 3128
Omniata, 1028
Omnicell, 178, 1762
Omnichain, 1557
Omnico Plastics, 3008
Omnidek, 1000
Omnidian, 490
OmniEarth, 311
Omniex, 1672
Omniflow, 3039
OmniGuide, 1500
OmniGuide Inc., 272
OmniGuide Surgical, 1383
Omnilink, 881
Omniome, 271
OmniOx, 710
Omniplex, 96
Omnipoint, 1795
OmniSci, 1928
Omnisci, 2270
Omniscience, 895
OmniSonics Medical Technologies, 2998
Omnispace, 518

OmniSpeech, 221
OmniSYS, 479
OMNITICKET network, 2535
Omniture, 564, 1629, 1707, 1886
Omnity, 1153, 1219
OmniVision, 1183
OmniVision Entertainment, 1371
Omny, 1219
Omrix, 2562, 3092
Omrix Biopharmaceuticals, 2554
OMsignal, 2187
Omtrix Biopharmaceuticals, 928
OMX, 2178
On Campus Marketing, 1727
On Deck Capital, 742
On Device Research, 2470, 3021
On Display, 564
On Farm Systems, 1604
On It, 953
On Second Thought, 221
On Shift, 835
ON Technology, 55
On The Border, 843
On-Chip Biotechnologies, 1241
On-Motion Oy, 2864
On-set, 2562
On-Site Fuel Service, 408
On-X Life Technologies, 1502
ON24, 186, 1608
On24, 389, 1643
OnApp, 2935
Onapsis, 1, 173, 1140
Onaro, 438, 2571
Onavo, 2822, 2943
OnBoard Security, 352
ONCampus Media, 961
Oncap, 2160
Once Innovations, 1874
Once24 Inc., 990
oncgnostics, 2518
Onco Health, 1987
Onco Med Pharmaceuticals, 605
Onco Vision, 2539
Onco-Screen, 2165
OncoFactor, 1392
Oncofactor, 154, 2007
OncoGenex Pharma, 1271, 1943
OncoGenex Technologies, 1546
OncoHealth, 667
OncoLens, 1412
Oncology Molecular Imaging, 1487
OncoMed, 241, 1098, 1126
Oncomed, 1931
OncoMed Pharmaceuticals, 56, 599, 2998
Onconova Therapeutics, 3202
Oncontract.com, 3190
Oncora Medical, 269, 623
OnCore Manufacturing Services, 441
Oncore Manufacturing Services, 843
Oncorus, 1268
Oncorus Inc., 184
Oncos Therapeutics Ltd., 2807
Oncoscope, 145, 158
OncoStem Diagnostics, 176
Oncue, 320, 771
Ondango, 2620
Ondax, 1917
OnDeck, 535, 773, 1597, 1623
Ondeck Capital, 1006
OnDemand Therapeutics, 1014
Ondeso, 2466
Ondevice Research, 2577
Ondotek, 1444
ONE, 2371, 2376, 2905
One, 897
One & Only Ocean Club, 33
One Access, 2867

ONE Access Networks, 2346
One Agency, 2417
One Animation, 2904
One Asia Resources, 2933
One Call Medical, 1368
ONE Campaign, 1374
One Caring Team, 310
One Cavo, 1839
One Chronos, 321
One clickHR, 2885
One Concern, 565, 1426, 1716, 1896
One Distribution, 260
1 Doc Way, 183, 863
One Door, 1731
One Floral Group, 919
ONE Group, 1683
One Inc., 387
One Kings Lane, 1006
One Kloud, 275
One Logos Education Solutions, 991
One Medical, 251, 1142, 1608
One Medical Group, 582, 1361
One Medical Passport, 497, 718
One Mobikwik Systems Private Ltd., 485
One Month, 1998
One On One, 1377
One On One Ads, 1375
One Page, 1599
One Path, 1270
One Potato, 901
One Radio, 2007
One Smart, 2969
One Spa World, 1092
One Spot, 1247
One Stop Systems, 1786
One Tap Away, 321
One Two Four, 2935
One Up, 100
One Up Sports, 1885
One Wave, 2989
One World Fitness PFF, 449
One World Foods, 2093
1-2-3.TV, 2888, 3223
1-800 Contacts, 722
1-800 Radiator, 1580
1-800-CONTACTS, 1818
1-800-Dentist, 224
1-Page, 795
10 for Humanity, 3250
10% Happier, 545
100 Thieves, 608, 1657
1000 Museums, 85, 1305, 1309, 1635
1000mercis, 2842
1001 Listes, 2542
100Kin10, 1315
100KM Foods Inc., 2153
101, 296, 623
101 Mobility, 547
10C Technologies, 1244
10sheet, 1358
10th Magnitude, 1410
10th Street LLC, 159
10X, 1743
10X Engineered Materials, 1285
10X Genomics, 1213, 1918
10x Genomics, 764
10X Technologies, 1942
10x Technologies, 1401
10x Technology, 987
11 Honore, 1890
11 Honoré, 763
1105 Media Holdings, 1278
117go.com, 1537
1200 Pharma, 1055
121cast, 3112
121nexus, 1188
12snap AG, 163

Portfolio Companies Index

12Soft, 2848
1322 North, 1220
1366 Technologies, 812, 1335, 1464, 1908
13th Lab, 2628
140 Proof, 299
15Five, 1385, 1752, 3035
16fun, 2927
17 Media, 1091
17TeraWatts, 1509
1901 Group, 681
One97, 1623
1A Smart Start LLC, 159
OneAccess, 2653, 2842
OneBreath, 3202
OneCause, 1242
OneChip Photonics, 597, 1257
OneClick HR, 2963
OneCommand, 696, 1005
Onedio, 3069
OneDome, 229
OneFineStay, 389
onefinestay, 3046
Onefootball, 1884
Oneforty, 115
Onehub, 85, 978
Oneida Molded Plastics, 165
OneKloud, 1370
Onel, 2603
1Life Healthcare, 1449
Oneline Radiology, 952
OneLink Communications, 560
OneLogin, 1698
Onelogin, 1629
1Mage Software, 1839
OneMain, 769
1Mainsteam, 597
OneMed Group, 2303
OneMob, 130, 252
1More Design, 827
OneNeck IT Services, 1979
ONEofTHEM, 2637
OnePath, 1169
OnePath Networks, 2073, 2445, 2917
OnePath Systems, 1859
OnePIN, 712, 1737
OneRiot, 143, 523, 1718
Oneshape Inc., 523
OneSignal, 1677
OneSource Distributors, 929
OneSource Virtual, 902
OneSpace, 938
Onespin, 2463
OneSpot, 447, 1684
1st Credit, 2528, 2529
1st Virtual Communications, 1235
1stdibs, 251, 1005, 1718
Onestop, 799
OneTouchPoint, 973, 1232
OneTwoSee, 1240
Onetwotrip, 2437
1upHealth, 680
OneWave Inc, 2581
OneWeb, 1511
Onewed, 776
OneWest Bank, 1314
OneWest Bank Group, 1746
Onewheel, 1896
1World Online, 603
Onex Communications, 3128
OnExchange, 1674
OnFarm, 1101
OnFiber, 1795
OnFiber Communications, 1994
Onfido, 1158, 1610
Onfleet, 623
OnFocus, 1261
OnForce, 1334

Onformonics, 2347
Ongig, 1752
ONI Systems, 1247, 1478, 1684
ONICON Incorporated, 911
Onics, 1065
Onkos Surgical, 4
Online Benefits, 852
Online Partners, 2702
Online Tech, 532
Online Tech Stores, 279, 531
Online Tours, 641
OnlineMarket, 2428
Onlineprinters GmbH, 1778
OnlineTours, 2877
OnlineTradesmen.ie, 2347
Onmia Molecular, 2544
OnMobile, 2255
OnMobile Systems, 163
Ono, 527
Ono Food Co., 1423
ONO Labs, 2832
Ono-Auna, 2371
OnPharma, 549
OnPoint Group, 917
OnPrem Networks Corporation, 767
OnPulse, 1813
Onramp, 952, 1426
Onramp Branding, 1683
OnScale, 229, 1616
OnSeen, 1285
Onset Medical Corp., 272
Onset Ventures, 3273
Onshape, 125
OnShift, 502, 629, 642, 941, 1051
Onsite Dental, 1346, 2074
Onsite Health, 952
Onsite Systems, 2005
OnSiteIQ, 2398
Onsolve, 1927
Onstation Corporation, 950
ONStor, 801
OnStream Networks, 1762
OnSwipe, 1504, 1791, 1823
Onswipe, 680, 1121, 1254, 1718
OnTarget, 1887
onTargetjobs, 1957
Ontario Excavac, 2180
Ontario Systems, 167
Ontario Teachers' Pension Plan, 3254
OnTech, 794
Ontela, 1640
Ontex International, 1837
Ontic, 1935
OnTime Networks, 2623
Ontoforce, 2940
Ontology, 2682
ONTOPx, 2466
OnTrak Software, 1514
OnTruck, 2437
Onventis, 1623
Onward Healthcare, 1973
OnX, 1235, 1317
OnX Enterprise Solutions, 2051
ONXEO, 2842
Onymos, 252
Onyx, 209
Onyx Payments, 931, 1493
Onyx Pharmaceuticals, 772
ONZO, 3126
OnúCall, 2232
Oo, 3251
Ooda Health, 610
Oodle, 601, 972
OOHA Wilkins, 381
Ooma, 628, 1407, 1784, 1983, 2188
Ooma Pharmacyclics, 183
Oomba, 68

Oomnitza, 320, 626
Ooska News, 632
Oosterhof Dairy, 3194
Ooyala, 381, 1543
Op Source, 564
op5, 3034
Opal, 1162, 1384, 1467, 1659
OPAQ Networks, 518
Opcity, 972
OPDA, 2927
Open, 976
Open Data Institute, 1374
Open Data Nation, 1896
Open Energi, 2287
Open Energy Efficiency, 490
Open English, 756, 1537, 1787
Open Garden, 1928
Open Government Partnership, 1374
Open Health Network, 1509
Open Interface, 250
Open Kernel Labs, 2980
Open Knowledge, 1374
Open Lending, 336
Open Media, 518
Open Mineral, 2101
Open Networks, 2655
Open Networks Engineering, 1337
Open Peak, 1597
Open Road, 1316
Open Road Entertainment, 333, 334
Open Road Integrated Media, 1087
Open Road Media, 845
Open Sensors, 3099
Open Sky, 938, 1527
Open Solutions, 215, 532, 1203, 1912
Open Span, 796
Open Sponsorhip, 1589
Open Wide, 2430
Open-E, 1381
Open-Xchange, 2677
OpenAir, 967
Openbay, 316, 1527, 1737
OpenBazaar, 125
Openbc, 3223
OpenBet Technologies, 2371
Openbit Oy, 2864
OpenBravo, 2334
OpenBucks, 876
Openbucks, 108, 1254
OpenCare, 724, 2181
OpenCity, 7
OpenConnect Systems, 1684
OpenDataSoft, 2430
OpenDNS, 582, 840, 1762
OpenDoor, 827, 1634
Opendoor, 720, 728, 1073, 1296, 1346, 1763
OpenDrives, 309
OpenEnglish, 1005
Openet, 2469
OpenField, 937
OpenGamma, 744
OpenGov, 1099
Opengov, 44, 125, 1035
Opengov.com, 381
Openharbor.com, 2702
Openhomes, 567
OpenInvest, 125, 2001
Openlane, 200
OpenLink, 927
OpenLogic, 143
OpenMarkets, 1364, 1803
Openmind, 752, 2434
OpenPages, 186, 1674
OpenPath, 309, 1483
Openpath, 729
OpenPeak, 650
Openphone, 2122

Portfolio Companies Index

Openplain, 2347
OpenQ, 881
OpenReach, 496
OpenServices, 957
OpenSesame, 1418
OpenSignal, 1511, 3021
Opensignal, 1359
OpenSite Technologies, 1013, 1711
OpenSky, 389, 1498
OpenSpace, 222, 321, 1155, 1281
Openspace, 773
OpenSpan, 839, 983, 1184, 1674, 1675
OpenSponsorship, 814
Opensynergy, 2804
OpenTable, 251, 327, 1008
Opentable, 1949
Opentext Corporation, 2258
Opentrons, 1073, 1114, 1709
Openunit, 2122
Openwater, 704, 1099
Openwave Systems, 1042
OpenX, 742, 1478, 1623, 1643, 1966, 3061, 3122
Openx, 1359
OpenX Software, 582, 1241
OpenZeppelin, 321
Opera Solutions, 681, 1685
Operational Results, 1074
Operative, 655, 782
Operator, 877
Operator of Full Service Restaurants, 356
Operator Systems, 3194
Opexa Therapeutics, 244
OpGen, 561, 983
Ophidion, 1581
Ophthonix, 561
Ophthotech Corporation, 1700, 3006
OPi, 3104
Opinion Research Corporation, 1140
OpinionLab, 1735
OPKO Health, 2961
Oplayp, 2442
Oplink, 1183
Oplus, 603
Oplus Technologies, 2532, 2773
Opnext, 496
Opocrin, 1456
Oportun, 582, 863, 877, 1006
OPOWER, 1227
Opower, 1716, 1996
Oppa, 2967
Opportunity Bancshares Inc., 407
Opposing Views, 1786
Oppten, 3116
OPS Solutions, 403
Opsani, 2018
Opsclarity, 1254
Opscode, 1969
OpSec, 1021
OpSens, 2074
Opsens, 2174
Opsidio, 269
Opsmatic, 608, 787, 980, 1254
OpsMx, 604
Opsona Therapeutics, 2909, 3011, 3076
OpSource, 186, 928
OpsTechnology, 517, 1946
Opsware, 759, 990, 1008
Optanix, 782
Optaros, 1, 457, 949
Optasia Medical, 3083
Optasite, 1146, 1463, 1864
OptConnect, 851
Optellios, 55
OPTEM, 642
Opternative, 1050, 1483, 1851
Optessa, 2051
Opthalmopharma, 2708

Optherion, 1414, 1510
Opththotech, 2806
Opti, 2230
Optibase Ltd., 2945
Optibus, 1005, 1928
Optical Data Systems, 1684
Optical Experts Manufacturing, 227, 1481
Optical Solutions, 538
Optichron, 1924
OptiComp Corporation, 1671
Opticon, 1294
Opticon M, 1786
OpTier, 2557
Optify, 1848
Optigenex, 1194
Optii Solutions, 380
Optilly, 721
Optilly/Install Monitizer, 1841
Optim.al, 626
Optima Global Solutions, 3266
Optimal, 3212
Optimal IMX, 679, 1536
Optimal Solutions Integration, 1779
Optimal Test, 2453, 2557, 2717
OptimalQ, 544
Optimas, 110
Optimax Systems, 1704
Optimedica, 87
Optimer, 1745
Optimer Pharmaceuticals, 2487
OptiMine, 378, 959, 2002, 2018
Optimine, 1291
Optimity, 2094
Optimizely, 125, 224, 238, 251, 488, 545, 546, 720, 1014, 1058, 1153, 1610, 2011
Optimo Route, 2825
OptimoRoute, 1423
Optimum Outcomes, 1964
Optimus EMR Inc., 334
Optimus Ride, 744, 784, 1254
Optinel Systems, 1348, 2745
Optinex Inc, 2945
OptiNose, 2701
Optinose, 212, 764
Optinuity, 1918
Option 3, 1546
Option Care, 1160
OptionEase, 1237
Optionis Group, 2956
Options City, 655
Options Technology, 336
OptionsHouse, 819
OptionWay, 1370
OptioSurgical, 1317
Optireno, 2430
OptiScan, 178
Optiscan, 1126
OptiScan Biomedical, 1241, 1325
Optissimo, 3145
Optiv, 1021, 1796
Optivia Medical, 1446
Optiwind, 679
Opto Atmosphere, 964
Opto Tech, 897
Optomec, 812
Optoro, 881, 1172, 1504, 1691, 1768
Optos, 2378
Optos PLC, 2378
Optosense, 2361
OptoTrace Technologies, 3053
Optovia, 928
Optovue, 897, 974, 1846
Optovue Corporation, 46
OpTrip, 116
Optum Ventures, 3263
OpTun's, 2646
Optuvt AB, 2807

Optware Corporation, 2406
Opulan, 2427
Opus 12, 398
Opus Global Holdings, 889
Opus Medical, 1495
Opus One Solutions, 2230
Opus12, 895
OPX Biotechnologies, 596, 1897
OpxBio, 2010
Opxbio, 325, 1247
Ora VéHicules Electriques, 2936
Orabrush, 1862
Orachiotek, 273
Oracle, 1335
Oracle Care Limited, 2498
Oracle Packaging, 448
Oracle Responsys, 773
Oracle/Skywire, 1678
Oradian, 3099
Oragenics, 1815
OraHealth, 85
Oral Care, 3045
OraMetrix, 949, 3128
Oramir, 3162
Orange Groves/OCP Holding Company, 1766
Orange Plastics, 874
Orange Retail Finance India, 856
Orange Slovensko, 2301
Orange Theory Fitness, 337
Orangebus, 3003
Orangetheory Fitness, 1580
OraPharma Inc., 785
Orascom Telecom Algeria, 2329
Orasi Medical, 2071
Oratio, 3099
Orative, 614, 1855
Oraya Therapeutics, 622, 1629, 1774
Orb, 310, 3242
Orb Energy, 54
Orb Networks, 1257
ORB Packing, 935
Orbeus, 474, 1618
Orbility, 2842
OrbiMed Healthcare Fund Management, 36
Orbis Biosciences, 1766
Orbis Education, 1140
Orbis Technologies Inc., 352
Orbit Commerce, 1061
Orbit Fab, 849, 1616
Orbit Garant, 2246
Orbital, 3095
Orbital Insight, 824, 1155
Orbital Optics, 2958
Orbital Sidekick, 3
Orbital Tool Technologies, 1424
Orbitera, 309
Orbius, 1321
Orbona, 1456
Orbotix, 1791
Orbus Therapeutics, 1147
Orca Systems, 3202
Orcamp, 2466
Orch1d, 527
Orchard, 354, 389, 537, 1281, 1504, 1718, 2178, 2204
Orchard Brands, 843
Orchard Information Systems Ltd, 3002
Orchard Therapeutics, 1522
Orchestra, 1058, 3199
Orchestra Networks, 2684
Orchestrate, 1550
Orchestrate.io, 1862
Orchestream, 2378
Orchestria, 759, 1401, 2662
Orchestro, 1298, 1348
Orchid, 125, 2013
Orchid BioSciences, 1395

Portfolio Companies Index

Orchid Labs, 1142
Orchid Orthopedic Solutions, 2376
Orchid Underwriters, 886
Orchids Paper Products Company, 617
Orckit Communications Ltd, 2576
ORCTech, 169
Order Corner, 447
Order Groove, 799
Order With Me, 641, 2860
OrderAhead, 863, 1534
OrderDynamics, 691
Orderful, 1423
OrderGroove, 246, 1114
OrderGrove, 1768
Ordermark, 49
OrderMotion, 1888, 2188
OrderUp, 708
OrderWithMe, 1914
Ordinal, 2430
Ordoro, 447
Ordr, 1796
Ordr.In, 1154
Ordway, 1114
Orege, 2606
oregon Chai, 1668
Oregon Ice Cream, 1769
Oreko Metal Mining, 253
Oren Semiconductor, 603, 1706
Orex Technologies, 3092
OrexiGen, 764
Orexigen, 1251, 1629
OREXIGEN Therapeutics, 561
Orexigen Therapeutics, 622
Orexo, 3011
Orexo AB, 2807
Organic Holdings, 1433
Organic Style, 508
Organic To Go, 800
Organica, 2282, 2842
Organika Health Products, 357
Organix, 970
Organosys, 2762
Orgentec, 1962
Orggit, 1618
Ori, 1073
Oric Pharmaceuticals, 519, 710, 764
Orica, 2650
Oridion, 2913
Oriel Therapeutics, 1820
OrienGene, 2969
Orient Speech Therapy, 711
Oriental Standard, 597
Oriental Trading, 337, 1949
Oriental Trading Company, 381
ORIG3N, 5, 1091
Orig3n, 603, 918
Origami Logic, 582, 972, 3212
Origami Risk, 1720
OriGene, 977
Origene, 2969
Origin, 752
Origin BioMed, 2197
Origin Fertility Care, 2384
Origin Games, 100
Origin Holdings, 1787
Origin House, 393
Origin Materials, 2054
Origin Ventures, 3255
Original, 1914
Original Additions, 2935
Orion, 209, 707, 1260
Orion Equity Partners, 3263
Orion Healthcorp, 1971
Orion Holding, 585
Orion ICG, 449
Orion Labs, 162, 1566
Orion Media, 2935

Orion Technologies, 1433
Orion Technology, 3136
Orion Telescopes & Binoculars, 1744
Orionis Biosciences, 704
Oris4, 2197
Orizon, 654
Orka Group, 1021
Orliman, 1576
Orlucent, 667
Ormigga, 1509
ORMvision, 2772
Ornet, 3221
Ornet Data Communication, 2761
Ornikar, 2842
Ornim, 812
Ornim Medical, 1383
Oro Negro, 160
Orolia, 3229
Orono Spectral Solutions, 1165
OROS, 1285
OrphaZyme, 3140
Orphazyme ApS, 2342
Orpheris, 386
Orpheus Interactive, 1065
Orphgen Pharmaceuticals, 1917
Orpiva, 1244
ORQIS Medical, 561
Orquest, 1399
ORS Nasco, 331
OrSense, 1608, 3128
Orsus, 438
Orsus Solutions, 2571
Ortec International, 2554
Ortega InfoSystems, 1771
Ortega Innfosystems, 1183
OrthAlign, 1371, 1546
Orthalign, 1575
Ortho Accel, 953
Ortho Kinematics, 447, 1190, 1502, 1803
Ortho Organizers, 119, 441
Ortho Space, 3230
Ortho-Space Ltd., 272
OrthoAccel Technologies, 1601
OrthoBethesda, 406
Orthocare Innovations, 1630
OrthoClassic, 376
Orthocon, 2487
OrthoFi, 28
Orthogem, 2958, 3098
Ortholite Holdings LLC, 1853
Orthopaedic Synergy, 2867
Orthos, 2728
OrthoScan, 139
Orthoscan Inc., 374
Orthovita, 2554
Orthovita., 2554
Orthspace, 3183
Ortibal Shift, 1317
Ortiva Wireless, 209, 1239
Ortodisc Technology, 1771
OSA Technologies, 1750, 1771
Osage Venture Partners, 3260
Osaro, 23, 108, 520, 527, 721, 1254
Osazda Energy, 169
Osby Glas, 3045
Oscar, 579, 778, 820, 840, 1114, 1534
Oscar Mike Games, 517
OsComp Systems, 468, 2691
OSF Commerce, 1610
OSHAP, 3128
Oshkosh Floor Designs, 719
OSIsoft, 1787
Oskando, 2382
Oski Energy, 1897
OSM Environmental, 705
Osmind, 1426
Osmo, 1054, 1890

Osmos, 1426
Osmose, 1085
Osmosis, 1703
Osmotica Pharmaceutical, 212
OsoBio, 97
Osper, 537
Osperity, 2105
Osprey, 786, 2188
Osprey Medical, 2527, 2609, 2950, 3268
Osprey Publishing, 2354
Osprey Ventures, 3273
OSRAM, 977
Ossia, 721
Ossianix, 269
Ossium Health, 742
Osso VR, 1477, 1677
Ostara, 1908
Ostara Nutrient Recovery Technologies Inc., 2115
Ostara Nutrient Recovery Techologies, 2144
Osteobiologics, 35, 1502, 1820
OsteoQC, 2174
Osteotech, 1771
Ostergard, 3194
Ostrovok, 2437
Osum Oil Sands, 1957
Osuuspankkien Keskuspankki Oyj, 2981
OTEC International, 18
Otelic, 387
OTG, 912
OTG Software, 1888
Other Inbox, 1843
OtherInbox, 1813
Others Online, 85
Otherwise, 2288
Othot, 51
OTHRSource, 754
Otic Pharma, 1383
Otifex, 2950
Otis Spunkmeyer, 170, 2073
OTO Systems Inc., 1011
OTO.ai, 802
Otogami, 3214
OtoNexus, 845
OtoNexus Medical Technologies, 1065
Otonomo, 604, 925
Otonomy, 209, 622, 1383, 1578, 3006
OtoSense, 521, 1065, 3246
Otsuka Pharma, 1271
Ott-Lite, 1481
Ottakar's, 2787
Otto, 1412
Otto Gourmet, 3161
Otto Sauer Achsenfabrik GmbH, 2651
Ouicar, 2842
Ounce Labs, 523
Our Family Clinic, 54
Ouroboros Medical, 179
Ourofino Saude Animal, 819
OurStage.com, 1101
Ouster, 534, 945
Out of Milk, 1227
Outback Steakhouse, 132
Outbound Engine, 100, 1332
OutboundDengine, 752
OutboundEngine, 1687
Outbox, 708
Outbrain, 912, 2557, 3072
Outcome Health, 846, 1483
Outdoor Exchange, 421
Outdoor Project, 1384
Outdoor Seasons, 1145
Outdoor Voices, 514, 763, 820, 1533
Outdoorsy, 207, 208, 1323
Outer Bay, 759
OuterBay, 1629
Outfit, 746

1361

Portfolio Companies Index

Outfittery, 2820, 2829, 2832
Outfox AI, 937
Outlast, 592
Outlast Technologies, 1771
Outlaw, 320
Outlier, 3, 742, 944, 1566, 1760
Outlook Group, 1234
Outlyer, 238
Outmatch, 434
OutMathc, 386
Outokumpu Oyj, 2981
Outplay Entertainment, 3023
Outpost Games, 59
Outpost Medicine, 785, 1780, 1943
Outreach, 752, 776, 780, 1158, 1187, 2272
OutreachCircle, 937
Outrigger, 1741
Outrigger Energy, 1326, 1328
Outrigger Media, 1733
Outright, 1666
Outschool, 1530
Outside The Classroom, 1668
Outsmart Ltd, 2761
Outsolve, 747
Outsourcing Services Group, 874
Outspark, 591, 1773
OutStart, 317, 522, 1674, 1704
OutSystems, 2708, 3039
OUTtv Network, 2249
Outvote, 937
Outward, 1219
Outward Hound, 1053
OUYA, 1187
Ova Science, 1522
Oval Technologies, 2581
OvaScience, 1149, 1815
Ovelin, 1862
Over The Top Foods, 7
Overcast Media, 85
Overclock Labs, 565
Overdog, 285
Overlake Capital, 1065
Overland, 277
Overland Container Transportation Services, 2210
Overland Solutions, 1300
Overlap, 818
Overlay Media, 2883
Overlay.tv, 2253
Overnight, 231, 562
Overseas Dragon China, 1143, 2937
Oversee.net, 1360
Oversi, 3212
OverSi Networks, 2653
Oversi Networks, 2557
Oversight Systems, 57, 857, 1674, 1675
Overstat, 1032
Overtime, 125, 545, 981, 1616
Overton's, 197
Overtone, 22
Overture, 881, 949, 1390, 1890
Overture Networks, 839, 1013, 1257, 1517, 1798, 2418
Overture Services, 504
Overture Technologies, 1137, 1298
Ovetime, 12
OVGuide, 231
Ovia Health, 1121
Oviinbyrd Forest, 2165
Oviinbyrd Golf Club, 2165
OVO Mobile, 3014
Ovuline, 1101, 1121, 2934
Ovum Hospitals, 1346
OWCP Pharmaceutical Research, 1083
Owen Equipment Holdings, 1494
Owensboro Grain, 60
Owera, 2361

OWIT Global, 1581
Owl, 44
Owl AI, 1616
Owl Analytics, 534
Owl Cameras Inc., 1073
Owl Cybersecurity, 1156
Owl Manor Veterinary, 659
Owler, 1346, 1855
Owlet, 79, 680, 724
Owlet Baby Care, 648
Owliance, 2512
Owlized, 1065
Own, 800
OWN POS, 743
Own Products, 1304
OwnBackup, 1005, 1610
OwnCloud, 711
ownCloud, 536
OwnEnergy, 535, 1422
Owner Listens, 1491
OwnerIQ, 37, 536, 696, 1069, 1150, 1175, 1737
Ownershipp, 310
OwnLocal, 234, 1114
OwnThePlay, 985
Ownza, 1227
OWYN, 502
OX Fulfilment Solutions, 754
Oxagen, 1268
Oxagen Limited, 1631
Oxane, 468
Oxane Materials, 2691
Oxatis, 3011
Oxbow Carbon, 560
Oxford Advanced Surfaces, 2883
Oxford BioMedica, 2653
Oxford Cannabinoid Technologies, 420
Oxford Catalysts, 2883
Oxford Collection Agenecy, 1748
Oxford Diffraction, 3186
Oxford Finance, 1973
Oxford Health Plans, 212, 1837
Oxford Immunotec, 2653, 2665, 2849, 3061
Oxford Immunotec Ltd, 2885
Oxford Performance Materials, 679
Oxford RF Sensors, 2883
OxfordPV, 3019
Oxid Esales, 2923
Oxide, 648
Oximeter Plus, 3257
Oxis Energy, 3098
Oxlo, 143
Oxlo Systems, 1596
OxOnc Development, 1383
Oxonica, 2483
Oxord Immunotec, 1297
Oxsensis, 2287, 2958
Oxtex, 2988, 3019
OxThera, 2842
OxThera AB, 2807
OxTox, 3098
Oxtox, 2883
OXX, 985
Oxygen, 1142
Oxygen Media, 496
Oxynade, 2417
Oxyntix, 2883
Oxyrane, 1302, 2739, 2969
Oxysure Systems, 1917
Oy 4Pharma Ltd, 2707
Oy Plusdial Ab, 2864
Oy Stinghorn, 2864
Oy Wireless Media Finland, 2864
Oyo, 2927
OYO Sportstoys, 37
Oyster Point, 1934
Oyster Point Pharma, 1930
Oyster.com, 31, 224

OZ Communications, 50, 1908
OZ Holding, 2913
Ozd Industrial Park, 2626
Ozmo, 857
Ozmo Devices, 1781, 2434
Ozon, 485
Ozon.ru, 641, 1463, 2820, 2829
Ozonator, 1535
Ozone Media Solutions, 2840
OzSonotek, 3238
Ozvision, 2453
Ozz Electric, 3242
Ozzy, 1323

P
P&A, 1603
P&H Solutions, 1772
P&R Dental Strategies, 1292
P-Com, 861
P-Cube, 827, 837
P.A. Semi, 1918
P.F. Chang's, 1518, 1855
P.M. Power Group Inc., 2129
P1.CN, 3004
P2 Science, 661
P2Binvestor, 1212
P2i, 2958
P3 Logistic Parks, 1837
P4RC, 1966
P97, 2101
PA Semi, 759
PacBio, 764
Pace, 495
Pace Analytical, 202
Pacer Electronics, 1772
Pacfic World, 1493
Pachyderm, 773, 1760
Pacific & Cutler, 277
Pacific Architects and Engineers, 1133
Pacific Biosciences, 87, 1247, 1762
Pacific Biosciences of California, 582
Pacific Brands, 2634
Pacific Catch, 337
Pacific Coast Publishing, 2142
Pacific Coffee (Holdings) Limited, 2394
Pacific College of Oriental Medicine, 1506
Pacific Communications Sciences, 1708
Pacific Construction, 977
Pacific Crest, 377
Pacific Design, 2845
Pacific DirectConnect, 942
Pacific Edge Software, 755
Pacific GMP, 1917
Pacific Handy Cutter, 1115
Pacific Interpreters, 1911
Pacific Island Resources, 942
Pacific Island Restaurants Inc., 337
Pacific Light Technologies, 1384
Pacific Mandarin Assets Ltd., 2779
Pacific Paper, 1612
Pacific Pharmacy Group, 1397
Pacific Pools, 1753
Pacific Print Group, 2402
Pacific Rim Palm Oil, 2329
Pacific Shoring, 963, 1612
Pacific Star Communications, 755
Pacific Sunwear, 843
Pacific Wave Systems, 1115
Pacific West Land, 1065
Pacific Western Bank, 3262
Pacific World Corporation, 1115
Pacificflight Catering, 2655
Paciolan, 162
Pacira Pharmaceuticals, 1268, 1619
Packagd, 763, 1079
Packaging Concepts & Design, 1232
Packaging Coordinators, 872, 1820

Portfolio Companies Index

Packaging Corporation of America, 1160
Packaging Dynamics, 1085
Packaging Plus LLC, 451
Packers Holdings LLC, 917
Packers Provision, 62
Packet, 604, 1614
Packet Design, 1178, 1601
Packet Island, 309, 613, 810
Packeteer, 1379
PacketExchange, 2653
Packetexchange, 2665
Packetfront, 3170
PacketFrpont, 2378
PacketHop, 801
PacketMotion, 189, 2188
PacketSled, 288
Packettrap, 200
PacketVideo, 1706
PacketZoom, 234
PackLate, 818
PackLink, 2331
Pacon Corp., 1174
PacStar, 459
Pact, 2963
Pact Apparel, 3246
PACT Pharma, 1934
Pact Pharma, 764
Pactas, 2432, 3229
Pactera, 827
Pactolus Communications, 523
PactSafe, 659, 1159, 1207
Paddle8, 1263, 1998
Paddock Pools Patios & Spas, 1071
Padhaaro, 3165
PADI, 1131
Padi, 2030
Padlet, 1530
Padlock Therapeutics, 193, 1047
Paetec International, 517
Paga, 1374, 2337
Pagatech, 54
Pagaya, 3212
PagePlanner, 2361
Pager. Pinscreen, 1155
PagerDuty, 2011
Pagerduty, 125, 234, 1763, 1969
PageScience, 433
PageUp, 238
PageVamp, 623
PAGEVAULT, 1159
PageVault, 1023
Pagineer, 3172
Paging Network of Canada, 986
Pague Menos, 819
Pahteon Inc., 62
PAI Erope V LP, 2088
Pai+, 977
PAICE, 18
Paid Piper, 304
Paidos Health Management Services, 958
Paidy, 149
Paige, 1863
Pain Doctor, 1092
Pain Therapeutics, 189
Painless, 988
PainReform, 3231
Painting by Nakasone, 1233
PaintZen, 1521
Paintzen, 129, 298, 361, 587, 708, 1114, 1322, 1533
PAION, 2454
Pair, 14
PairGain Technology, 1920
Pairingo, 3042
Pajarito Powder, 1926
Paju Yangju Tongil Village Co., 585
Paketin, 2518

Pako Bay, 2880
PakSense, 85
PAL, 1852
Paladin Capital Group, 3260
Paladin Cyber, 882, 1121
Paladin Ethanal Acquistion, 1401
Paladina Health, 94
Palamida, 1241, 1953
Palantir, 778, 805, 840, 856, 1716, 2001, 2154
Palantir Technologies, 983, 1597
Palatin, 1943
Palatin Technologies Inc., 949
Palette, 2107
Palisade, 347
Palladian, 1753
Palladio, 1336
Palladium Group, 1248
Palleon Pharmaceuticals, 1734, 1780
PalletOne Inc., 695
Palletways, 3027
Palliser Estate, 2655
Palm, 252, 660, 1762
Palm Beach Tan, 15
Palm Commerce, 1091
Palm Commerce Holdings, 3053
Palm Inc., 950
Palmax, 3209
Palmers, 2285
Palmetto, 1114, 2037
Palmetto Exchange, 1220
Palms Casino Resort, 1113
Palo Alto, 1341
Palo Alto Health Sciences, 139
Palo Alto Networks, 1798
Paloalto, 972
Paloma Partners IV, 673
Palomar Specialty, 823
Palringo, 691
Palvella Therapeutics, 269
Palyon, 2487
Palyon Medical, 158
Pameco Corp., 1138
Pamira, 1495
Pamyra, 2518
Panache Ventures, 2028
Panacos, 119, 1241, 1414
Panalpina, 2913
Panasas, 443, 759, 1247, 1348
Panaseer, 485
Panasonic, 217
Panaya, 2804
Pancetera, 1379
Pancon, 1234
Panda Security, 2434
Panda Whale, 721
PandaDoc, 100, 1158
PandaPay, 623
Pandion, 1930
Pandion Therapeutics, 1734
Pando, 1114, 1426
Pando Daily, 232
Pando Labs, 1426
Pando Logic, 3212
Pando Networks, 2532
Pandoodle, 1925
Pandora, 564, 596, 810, 827, 925, 1953
Pandora Media, 1449, 1649
Pandora Media Inc., 1093
Pandora.TV, 100, 597
Pangaea Ventures, 2483
Pangea, 473, 732, 1050, 1364
Pangea World Corporation, 508
PanGenetics, 3011
Pangenetics, 2739
PanGeo Subsea, 468, 2691
Panhandle Oilfield, 165
Panjiva, 1588

Panjo, 1223, 1718
Pankaku, 2637
Panlabs International, 755
Panmira, 209
Panna, 59, 133, 1103, 1114, 1186, 1637
Panomics, 11, 240, 2410
Panopta, 746
Panoptic Security, 1074, 2374
PanOptica, 1631, 1814
Panopticon, 1649
Panopto, 1261, 1626
Panorama, 1969
Panorama Education, 1393, 1702, 1881
Panoramic Power, 2891
Panoratio Database Images, 3037
PANOS Brands, 934
PANOS Brands LLC, 904
Pantech & Curitel, 1091
Pantero, 609
PanTerra Networks, 130
Pantex International, 1939
Pantheon, 234, 742, 752, 779, 1381
Pantheon Ventures, 3245
Panther, 12, 2122, 3091
Panther Capital, 1139
Panther Expedited, 722
Panther Expedited Services, 2014
Panther Labs, 1142
Pantry, 553, 1637
Panvideo, 609
Panviva, 2966, 3142
Panzura, 468, 1184, 1213, 1382
Pap, 2298
Papa Johns, 899
Papa Murphy's, 458
Papa Murphy's International, 1108
Papaya, 597, 729, 976
Paper and Tea, 2832
Paper Battery Company, 1878
Paper Crane, 2
Paper G, 1101
Paper House Productions, 1161
Paper Machinery Corp., 578
Paper Source, 337, 1021
Paper.li, 3036
Paper.li/Smallrivers, 1701
Paperchase, 2787
Paperless, 1597, 2446
Paperless Post, 1669
Paperlit, 2395
Papernest, 2842
PaperSpace, 321
Paperspace, 802, 998, 1154
PaperWorks, 1755
Papillon D'Or, 2417
Paprika, 721
Papyrus, 2376
PAR, 2956
Par Accel, 1782
Par Pharmaceutical, 1456, 1837
Par Pharmaceutical Companies, 2371
PAR3, 1736
Parable Health, 623
Parabola, 1219
Parachute, 345, 756, 1103, 1223, 1760, 1890
Parachute Health, 1005
Paracosm, 601
Parade, 232, 2427, 2927
Paradigm, 1045, 2199, 3128
Paradigm B.V., 781
Paradigm Capital, 3255
Paradigm Genetics, 1013
Paradigm Group, 1343
Paradigm Healthcare Corporation, 958
Paradigm Management Services, 1127
Paradigm Packaging, 1136, 1460
Paradigm Spine, 1846

1363

Portfolio Companies Index

Paradigm Tax Group, 1576
Paradigm Therapeutics, 2454
Paradigm4, 845, 1069, 1675, 1759, 2643
Paradise Electronics, 200
Paradise Rentals, 1766
Paradromics, 802
Paragen Bio, 3014
Parago, 1313, 1806
Paragon, 395, 532, 1607, 2667, 3239
Paragon Bioservices, 386
Paragon Development Systems, 1174
Paragon Energy Solution, 165
Paragon Films, 1972
Paragon Medical, 97
Paragon Networks International, 1042
Paragon Products, 381
Paragon Robotics, 1051
Paragon Technology, 961
Parakey, 234, 1359
ParaLife, 860
Paraline Group, 1956
Parallaz Capital Partners LLC, 162
Parallel, 3212
Parallel Domain, 548, 1836, 1879
Parallel Geometry, 1441
Parallel Products, 1822
Parallel Universe, 2863
Parallel Wireless, 752
Parallel49 Equity, 2160
ParAllele, 116, 1247
Parallels, 89, 1005, 1628
Parallelz, 2122
Paramit, 97
Paramount Healthcare, 409
Paramount Hotels, 2353
Paramount Services, 470
Paranet, 199
Parasut, 1563, 3069
Paratek, 22, 73, 1172, 1348, 2806
Paratek Microwave, 983, 1257
Paratek Pharmaceuticals, 2509, 2998
Paratinova.com, 1103
Parature, 1137, 1901
PARC, 217
Parca Deposu, 2286
Parcel, 863, 1119
ParcelGenie, 2751
Parchment, 1348, 1611, 2074
Parcours, 2439
Parcxmart, 649
ParElastic, 536
Parelastic, 1101, 1737
Parella, 2842
Parental Health, 999
Parenthoods, 1119
ParentMedia, 876
Parento, 685
Parents.com, 724
Pareto Health, 862
Parexel, 315
Parian Capital Corporation, 2249
Parian Logistics, 2249
Paribus, 537, 773
ParinGenix, 1546
Paris, 1300
Paris Presents, 1174, 1961
Paris RE, 927
Paris Saclay Fund, 485
Paris Town, 1754
Parisa Group, 2635
Parish Publishing Solutions, 1964
Parisian Inc., 576
Parity, 2037
Park & Diamond, 1896
Park Cake, 1939
Park Foods, 1438
Park Place, 458

Park Place Technologies, 1826, 1979
Park Resorts, 2608
Park Scientific, 1091
Parkalgar, 3039
Parkbench.Com, 2262
Parkdean Resorts, 2201
Parker, 1755
ParkiFi, 881
Parkifi, 380
Parking Company America, 377
Parklet, 1750
Parkloco, 1104
ParkMe, 127, 762, 1566
Parkmobile, 762
ParkMyCloud, 512
Parko, 1719
Parkway Products, 404
Parkway Properties, 1837
ParkWhiz, 225, 965, 1050
Parlano, 1150
ParLevel, 447
Parliament Pointe, 2277
Parlor, 2122
Parmaco Oy, 2928
Paro, 1558
Parrable, 583
Parrot, 3104
Parsable, 742
Parse, 586
Parse.ly, 304, 724
Parsec, 246, 1114, 1831
Parsegon, 623
Parsely, 881
Parsley Health, 1616
ParStream, 226, 586
PART Point, 679
Partake Foods, 221
Partech, 485
Partech International, 3273
Partenaires Livres, 2598
Partender, 1599, 1998
Parterre Flooring Systems, 1044
Particle, 309, 1511
Particle Dynamics, 653
Partify, 1509
Parting Stone, 169
Partminer, 1949
Partner Communications, 1602
Partnered, 1752
Partnerpedia Solutions, 2144
PartnerRe, 560
Partners in Leadership Inc., 904
PartnerStack, 2280
Partpic, 151
Parts Authority, 1049
Parts Market, 709
Parts Town, 257
Partsearch Technologies, 1748
PartsSource, 862, 1480
Partssource, 1464
PartStore, 1682
PartTec, 659
Party City, 1818
Party Packagers, 2045
PartySlate, 901
PAS International Holdings, 77
PAS Technologies, 878, 1090
Pascal Metrics, 618
Pascal's Pocket Corporation; Social Fabric Corpora, 716
Pashas, 1518
Passage AI, 3
Passage Bio, 1930
Passageways, 746
Passave, 2532
Passave Technologies, 2711, 3221
Passbase, 680, 1892

PasseiDireto, 641
Passmark Security, 614
Passport, 881, 1142, 1242
Passport Corporation, 457
Passport Food Group, 1970
Passport Health Communications, 1720
Passport Systems, 522
Passport Systems Inc., 145
PassRight, 29
Passworks, 3039
Pasta Chips, 669
Pastair, 2440
Pastceram, 3039
Pasteuria Bioscience, 60
Patagonia BioEnergia, 1577
Patara Pharma LLC, 489
Patch, 798
Patch Products, 1834
PatentDive, 1000
Path, 234, 610, 1323, 1666
Path Ex, 999
Path Intelligence, 1359
Path Scale, 95
Path-Tec, 797
Pathable, 85
PathAI, 820
Pathbrite, 1554
PathFactory, 2161
Pathfinder Health Innovations, 497, 718
Pathfinder Technologies, 918
Pathfinder Therepeutics, 1261
Pathfire, 68
Pathgather, 535
PathGroup, 1169, 1271, 1480
Pathlight, 434
Pathlight Technologies, 1920
Pathlight Technology, 957
Pathmatics, 231, 259, 309, 1059, 1890
PathogenDx, 99, 1613
PathoGenetix, 178
Pathology, 21
PathoQuest, 2842
PathScale, 457, 468
Pathsenors, 1172
Pathsensors, 288
PathSource, 1959
PathSpot, 729
PathStream, 1554
Pathway, 1098
Pathway Diagnostics, 240
Pathway Medical Technologies, 2739
Pathwork Diagnostics, 1354, 1917
Patient Connect Service Limited, 2972
Patient Education Media Inc., 449
Patient Engagement Systems, 789
Patient Innovations, 3257
Patient Safe Solutions, 386
PatientCo, 1618
Patientco, 28
PatientKeeper, 94, 1198
PatientNow, 1499
PatientOne, 1317
PatientPing, 711, 742
Patientping, 125
PatientPoint, 1092, 2243
Patients Know Best, 2469
PatientSafe, 2256
Patientsafe, 2681
PatientSafe Solutions, 1206, 1500, 1604
Patientsafe Solutions, 936
Patreon, 37, 1296, 1323, 1885
patreon, 995
Patrick Hackett Hardware Company, 1642
Patriot Capital, 3255
Patriot Environmental Services, 127, 1639
Patriot Media, 1727
Patriot National Bancorp, 1733

Portfolio Companies Index

Patriot Storage, 1577
PatriotOne Technologies, 2192
Patron Technology, 1499
Pattern Energy Group, 1577
Pattern Health, 512
Pattern Insight, 1923
Pattern89, 1023
PatternEx, 1073
Patton Surgical Corp., 813
Paul Fabs, 47
Paul Fredrick, 503
PaulaBs Choice, 260
Paulee Cleantec, 3235
Pavilion Data, 176
Pavilion Medical Innovations, 428
Paviliondata, 1079
Pavlok, 985
Pavlov, 623
PAVmed, 1983
Pavève, 1626
Pawngo, 35, 595, 1121
Paxar Corp., 303
Paxata, 485, 1158, 1831, 2681
Paxos, 1119
PaxVax, 978
Pay Off, 863
Pay With My Bank, 2469
Pay-O-Matic, 1518
Pay-O-Matic Corporation, 777
Payable, 787
PayasUgym, 2963
PayByGroup, 1719
Paycom, 1973
Paycor Inc., 136
PayCycle, 597, 1865
Paycycle, 200
PayDay One, 2448
Paydiant, 1335, 1737
Paydici, 1384
PayEase, 508
Payer Compass, 921, 1720
PayFone, 1597
Payfone, 1382, 1928, 2228
Payformance, 1748
PayGo, 1813
Paygo Energy, 2430
PayJoy, 945
Payjoy, 527, 1884
PayK12, 659
PayKey, 641
PayKii, 181
PayLease, 782
Payless, 843
Payless ShoeSource, 303
Payleven, 2820, 2829
PayLink Payment Plans, 1234
Paylocity, 56
Paymap, 1251
Payment America Systems, 679
Paymentus, 28
Paymetric, 782
Paymetrics, 1408
Paymill, 304, 2820, 2829, 3140
PayNearMe, 361, 548, 1073, 1862
Paynearme, 200
Payoff, 744, 1719
Payoneer, 1305, 1761, 2557, 3212
PayPal, 299, 504, 1160
Paypal, 116
PayPerks, 597, 2398
Payperks, 1305
PayPlug, 2321
Payrix, 1499
PayRock Energy, 673
Paysafe, 782
PaysafeCard.com, 2774
PayScale, 1855

Payscale, 755
PaySimple, 549, 696, 1761
PaySpan, 21
Payspan, 941
Paystack, 2321
PayStand, 456
Paystone, 2065
Paystream, 21
Paysys, 405
PaySys International Inc., 694
Paytrail Oyj, 2957
Paytronix Systems Inc., 862
Paywhere, 3064
Payzer, 50, 881 .
Pazoo, 1083
PB Works, 1247
PBA, 2927
PBF Pita Bread Factory, 148
PBV Partners, 280
PBWorks, 1658, 1959
PC Depot Corp, 2898
Pc Dir, 2655
PC Helps, 441
PC On Call, 2643
PC-Soft, 2443
PCC Technology, 532
PCH International, 561, 759, 1346, 1848
PChem, 653
PCI Biotech, 2510
PCI Holding Corporation, 1495
PCI Pharma Services, 785
PCIX, 290
PCl Group, 2607
PCN Network, 1424
PCX Aerostructures, 1560
PD Services Ltd, 2298
PDC Brands, 1113
PDHI, 1284
PDI, 823
PDJ Group, 2935
PDQ South Texas, 227
PDR Network, 1108
PDS Biotechnology, 659
PDSHeart, 227
pdv Wireless, 1344
PDV-Systeme, 2518
Peach, 669, 1104, 1162, 1186
Peach Works, 86, 173
Peachtree Business Products, 684
PeachWorks, 964
Peachy, 328
Peacock Engineering Company, 248
Peacock Foods, 458
PEAK Broadcasting, 381
Peak Builders, 679
Peak Games, 2828
Peak Power, 2181
PEAK Sports, 2927
PEAK Surgical, 1918
Peak Timbers, 838
Peak Ventures, 3265
Peak Well Systems, 1754
Peak10, 1973
Peakon, 2469
Peanut Labs, 641
PeanutPress, 957
Peanutpress.Com, 852
Peapod, 250
Pear, 495, 724
Pear Therapeutics, 11, 150, 2681
Pearfection, 2970
Pearl, 11, 962
Pearl Capital, 407
Pearl Hydrogen, 1340
Pearl Izumi, 767
Pearl Meyer & Partners, 377
Pearlchain.net, 2940

Pearlman Industries Inc., 911
Pears Portfolio, 2783
Pearson's, 360
Peate Institute for Entrepreneurs, 3258
Pebble, 457
Pebble Post, 1074
PebblePost, 949, 2176
Pebblepost, 724
Pebby, 1509
PECA Labs, 296
PECH, 585
PECO Pallet, 1242, 1482, 1748, 1955
Pecora Corporation, 836
Pedalite, 2565
Pedestal Networks, 597
Pediatria, 1230
Pediatric Health Choice, 505
Pediatrix Medical Group Inc., 303
Pedidos Ya, 2437
Peek, 708, 863, 901
Peekk Travel, 1323
Peel, 234, 1058, 1537, 1840
Peel Away Labs, 1309
Peel-Works, 1017
Peeled Snacks, 1907
Peepoople, 3246
Peer, 626
Peer 1, 441
Peer IQ, 1258
Peer Medical, 2717
Peer39, 793
Peeractive, 1581
PeerApp, 438, 1754, 2571, 2717
PeerIndex, 2399
Peerj, 1359
Peerless Industrial Group, 1979
Peerless Network, 696
Peerless Networks, 56
Peerlyst, 980
PeerMedical, 2316
PeerNova, 624
PeerNova Inc., 813
Peerspace, 1752
PeerStreet, 125, 720, 1281
peerTransfer, 1504, 1718
PeerView, 1204
Peespace, 773
PEG, 2430
Peg, 54
Pegasense, 1593
Pegasus, 28, 3239
Pegasus Solar, 1371
Pegasus Solutions, 303
Pegasus Technologies Ltd., 2945
Pegasus TransTech, 418
PegEx, 403
Peixeurbano, 2967
PEKU Publications, 1959
Pela, 2122
Pelagicore, 2746
Pelamis, 2287
Pelamis Wave Power, 522
Pelham Homes, 2976
Pelican, 2340
Pelican AutoFinance, 751
Pelican Imaging, 839, 983, 1014
Pelican Products, 248, 1493
Pelican Water Systems, 1859
Pelion Venture Partners, 3265
Pellepharm, 710
Pellion, 1073, 1260
Peloton, 275, 322, 328, 764, 827, 912, 1079, 1092, 1867
Peloton Computer Enterprises, 2267
Peloton Technology, 1616
Peloton Therapeutics, 519
Pelss, 1990

Portfolio Companies Index

Pelvalon, 1347
Pemba Sun and Mozwood, 838
PEMCO, 1755
Peminic, 957
Pen.io, 1254
PenAndFree, 3118
PenBay Solutions, 440, 1165
Penblade, 1074
Pencil, 246
Penda Corporation, 1138
PendaForm, 1548
PenDataSoft, 1610
Pender Growth Fund, 2074
Pendo, 238, 535, 975, 1213, 1610
Pendo.io, 540, 561
Pendulab, 1683
Pendum, 931
Penederm, 1379
Penguin Computing, 1679
Penhaigon's, 781
Penhall International Inc., 357
Peninsula, 1251
Peninsula Energy, 1551
Peninsula Packaging Company, 1368
Peninsula Pharmaceuticals, 596, 1414
Peninsula Ventures, 3273
Penlon, 97
Penn Warranty Corporation, 381
PennAlt Organics Inc., 991
Pennant Foods Corp., 351, 1372
Pennant Sp, 1536
PennEnergy Resources, 673
PennTech Machinery Corporation, 911
Penny, 1698
Penrice, 2613
Penrice Soda Products, 3169
Penrose Landfill Gas Conversion LLC, 1897
PenSimple, 395
Penta Securities Systems, 897
Pentaho, 582, 1235
Pentalum, 438, 2307, 2717
Pentec Health, 785, 1345
Pentech, 1636
Pentheon, 1629
Penthera Partners, 1003
Penton Media, 1231, 1961
Pentzer Corporation, 1294
People, 810
People Data Labs, 771, 1760
People Matter, 1629
People Pattern, 1247
People Power, 1658
People Support, 182
People's Motor International, 1771
People.ai, 895
People.co, 1549, 1998
PeopleAdmin, 1754
Peopleclick, 245, 1152
PeopleCube, 2828
PeopleGrove, 888, 1530
PeopleLinx, 876, 1388
PeopleMater, 1257
PeopleMatter, 85, 1013, 1332, 1741
PeopleSupport, 504
PeopleTec, 1536
PEP Industries, 1278
Pepcom GmbH, 1929
Pepe Jeans, 1092
Peplin, 1268
Pepo, 545
Pepper Dining, 1372
Pepper Hamilton, 3264
PepperBall Technologies, 68
PepperData, 108, 548, 1680
Pepperdata, 1254, 1969
Pepperdata Networks, 488
Pepperfry, 1346

Pepperjam, 230
Pepperlane, 1104
Peppermint Technology, 28
Peppers & Rogers, 1008
Peptech, 1546
Pepticom, 3235
Peptilogics, 296
Peptor, 3221
Peptron, 2848
Peracon, 528
Peraso, 2123, 2150
Peraso Technologies, 2070, 2234
Peraton, 1927
PerBlue, 1121
Perceive 3D, 3039
Percello, 857
PerceptiMed, 644, 1098, 1302
Perception Software, 447
Perceptive Automata, 742, 1836
Perceptive Navigation, 18
Perceptive Pixel, 983
Perceptive Software, 1255
Perch, 310
Percipient.ai, 1918
Percolata, 521, 1059, 1599, 1760, 1812, 1983
percolata, 613
Percolate, 59, 742, 827, 1114, 1696, 1841
Percona, 830
Percsys, 1251
PercuSurge, 1788
Percutaneous Systems, 526
Peregrine Semiconductor, 1257, 1287, 1403
Peregrine Semiconductor, 1313
Perennial Energy, 402
Perennial Energy LLC, 1057
Perennials and Sutherland LLC, 260
PerfAction, 3050
Perfect Commerce, 593
Perfect Company, 1384
Perfect Day, 1709
Perfect Fit, 1138
Perfect Point, 1065
Perfect Sense, 419
Perfect Timing, 1755
PerfectMarket, 1855
Perfecto, 796, 3212
Perfecto Mobile, 839, 2557, 3205
PerfectServce, 1575
Perfectus Biomed, 2958
Perferred Pet Care, 1733
Perfint, 1346
Perfint Healthcare, 2840
Perforce Software, 502
Perform, 33, 2050
Performance, 2014
Performance Assessment Network Inc., 1727
Performance Bicycles, 1336
Performance Fabrics, 341
Performance Fibers, 1755
Performance Food, 280
Performance Food Group, 745, 1518, 1972
Performance Health, 878, 1160
Performance Health & Wellness, 356
Performance IQ, 238
Performance Logic, 852
Performance Plants, 2129, 2145
Performance Team Freight Systems Inc., 277
PerformanceRetail, 2073
Performant Financial Corporation, 1419
Performax Physical Therapy, 1228
Performics, 1061
PerformLine, 742
Performline, 1588
Peribit, 773
Pericom Technology, 2448
PeriGen, 809, 1611, 1852
Perimeter eSecurity, 1865

Perimeter Internetworking, 1194
Perimeter Labs, 1015
Perimeter Medical Imaging, 2234
Perimter Protection Group, 3045
Periodical, 1103
PeriOptimum, 1003
PeriRx, 269
Periscope, 708, 774, 1186, 1219, 1760
Periscope Data, 129, 298, 610
Periscope Equity, 13
Periscope Holdings, 1419
Peritus AI, 1812
Perk Health, 1874
Perkbox, 2665
Perkin Elmer, 1294
Perkins & Marie Callender's, 1971
Perkins Coie, 3262
Perkins Restaurant & Bakery, 1968
Perl Street, 1896, 2122
Perlan Therapeutics, 1708
Perlara, 1238
Perlara PBC, 1696
Perlegen, 2504, 2681
Perlego, 85, 554
Perlite Canada Inc., 2115
Permacharge Corp, 213
Permanent General Company Inc., 407
Permasense, 2849
Permatec, 1456
Permeon Biologics, 154
Permeon Biologics, 748
Permian Tank & Manufacturing, 1577
Permlight, 68
Permutation, 863
Pernix Therapeutics, 73, 1138
Pernix Therapeutics Holdings, 190
Peronetics, 3212
Perora GmbH, 2677
Perosphere Inc., 532
Perpetua, 537
Perpetual Ventures, 3265
Perpetuum, 2883, 3019, 3061
Perquest, 1733, 1741
Perricone MD, 1863
Persado, 224, 488, 646
Persante, 1343
Persante Health Care, 913
Persea Bio, 1815
Persephone Biome, 875, 1760
Perseus Proteomics, 2961
Persian Acceptance Corp., 2245
Persianas, 2329
Persio, 1385
Persist Technologies, 627
Persistence Data Mining, 999
Persistence Software, 1287
Persistent Sentinel, 2441
Persistent Systems, 808
Persivia, 941
Persona, 669, 2073
Personal Capital, 545, 564, 1006, 1050, 1918
Personal Genome Diagnostics, 18, 1172, 1993
Personal Medsystems, 3104
Personal Wine, 953
Personali, 438, 1346
Personalis, 1247
Personalized Media, 1375
Personetics, 2557
Personify, 107, 979, 1410
PerspecSys, 1401
Perspecta, 1927
Perspica, 1812
Perstorp, 3017
Persystent Enterprise, 994
Pertemps Network Group, 2935
Pervacio, 1146, 1942
Pervasis, 748

Portfolio Companies Index

Pesanlab, 721
Pestana Berlin, 3039
Pet 360, 1140
Pet Center Comercio and Participacoes S.A., 1957
Pet IQ, 79
Pet Loss Center, 381
Pet Love, 2967
Pet Smart, 1971
Pet Supermarket, 1580, 2211
Pet Valu, 1580
Pet's Choice, 755
Pet360, 1888
Petal, 23, 354, 863, 1589, 1616
PetaSense, 720
Petcircle.com.au, 782
Petco Animal Supplies, 1113, 1837
PetCoach, 1186
Petcube, 89
PetDesk, 390
Pete Health, 121
Peter Butz, 2801
Peter Geeson Ltd., 2648
Peter Tosh, 1139
Peterhouse Group, 2976
Petermann Bus Co., 847
Petersen Pet Provisions, 1748
Peterson Party Center, 633
PetHub, 1065
Petkit, 827
Petmate, 1372, 1990
Petmatrics LLC, 791
PetMedicus Laboratories, 1779
Petnet, 68, 879, 1101, 1719
Petra Pharma, 5, 30
Petra Solar, 2708
Petra Systems, 173, 658
Petrecycle, 2966
Petro Harvester, 1837
Petro Shopping Centers, 371
PetroChoice, 1090
PetroChoice Holdings Inc., 867
PetroCloud, 543
Petroleum Service Corporation, 202
PetroLiance, 1270
PetroLogistics, 1133
Petroplus Holdings, 1577
PetroSkills, 364
PetroStreamz, 3207
Petrotank, 157
Petrowest Energy Services Trust, 2085
Petrus Resources, 1326, 1328
PetsDx Imaging, 1003
Petsense, 2000
PETsys Electronics, 3039
PetVet Care Centers, 1092
Pevion Biotech, 2487
Pevonia, 1863
Pex, 568, 980, 1760
PEX Card, 199, 302, 1305, 2150
Pexco, 1368
PF Baseline Fitness, 786
PF Group, 3194
Pfingsten Publishing, 902, 1438
Pfizer, 1100
Pfizer Inc., 1349
Pflegeplatz-manager, 2518
PFP Cybersecurities, 288
PGI International, 654
PGOA Media, 224, 1663
PGP, 597
phanfare, 218
Phantom Fireworks, 578
PhantomAlert, 1737
PhantomCyber, 773
Pharm Akea Therapeutics, 240
Pharm-Olam, 1507

Pharma 73, 3039
Pharma Diagnostics, 2358
Pharma Engineering, 3098
Pharma Logic, 858
Pharma Marketing Ltd., 1372
Pharmaca, 1442
Pharmaca Integrate Pharmacy, 938
PharmAcbine, 1383
Pharmaceutic Litho & Label Company, 1025, 1627
Pharmaceutical SymBio, 2997
Pharmacie Lafayette, 2842
Pharmacopeia, 209
Pharmacy Partners, 1964
PharmAdva, 705
Pharmadyne, 317
PharmaEste, 3043
PharmaFluidics, 3056
Pharmagen Healthcare Ltd., 54
Pharmagest Interactive, 3060
PharmaNetics, 1013
Pharmanex, 240, 2724
Pharmaq, 3024
PharmArc Analytics, 2481
PharmaResearch, 470
Pharmaron, 73, 597, 2927
PharmaSecure, 860
Pharmasset, 1268
PharmaStem, 1048
Pharmatrin Ltd, 2545
Pharmawizard, 2395
Pharmaxis, 1349, 2609
Pharmetics, 1248
PHARMetrics, 1335
PharmHouse, 2233
Pharminax, 2883
Pharming, 1777
Pharmion, 240, 2998
Pharmitas, 85
PharmMD, 1261, 1576
Pharmos, 1048
Pharmright, 1925
PharmRight Corporation, 985
Pharsight, 1287, 1704
Phase Four, 93, 814
Phase Genomics, 2007
Phase One Consulting Group, 681
Phase Vision, 2392
PhaseBio, 918
PhaseBio Pharmaceuticals Inc., 184
Phasebridge, 504
PhaseRX, 11
Phaserx, 154
Phasor Solutions, 2958, 3009
PhatNoise, 810
PHC, 747, 1071, 2969
Phelps Industries, 854
Phemi, 2086, 2221
Phemi Health Systems, 2283
Phenex, 2629
Phenex Pharmaceuticals, 2923
Phenex Pharmaceuticals AG, 2704
Phenom TRM Cloud Platform, 1672
Phenome Networks, 3235
Phenometrix, 1244
Phenomic, 398
Phenomical Ai, 2122
Phenomix, 2609, 2998
Phg, 876
Phiar, 1346
Phil, 564, 763
Philadelphia Energy Solutions, 2321
Philadelphia Financial Group, 836
Phillips & Temro, 1169
Phillips & Temro Industries, 197
Phillips & Temro Industries Inc., 911
Phillips Energy Partners III, 673

Phillips Pet Food & Supplies, 63, 1818
Phillips Screw Company, 815, 1176
Phillips-Medisize Corporation, 1085
Philm, 827
Philo, 609, 709, 720, 756, 1335, 1616
Philoptics, 3089
Philz Coffee, 553, 650, 1754
Phish Labs, 1140
PhishLabs, 797
PhishMe, 1401
PhiSkin, 897
Phizzle, 68, 93
PHNS, 886
Phobos Corporation, 189
Phoenix, 632
Phoenix American Financial, 3262
Phoenix Aromas and Essential Oils, 815
Phoenix Brands, 1131
Phoenix Children's Academy, 197
Phoenix Energy Technologies, 68
Phoenix Exploration Company, 1577
Phoenix Health & Safety, 2958
Phoenix Innovations Corp., 2078
Phoenix Labs, 827, 1317, 1566
Phoenix New Media, 2969
Phoenix Nuclear Labs, 1291, 2002
Phoenix S&T, 269
Phoenix Services LLC, 1372
Phonak, 2555
Phone.com, 724, 3266
Phone2Action, 635
Phonedeck, 2435
PhoneSpots, 1640
Phonespots, 564
Phonetic Systems, 2943
Phonetic Systems Ltd., 2741
Phonezoo Communications Inc., 1093
Phonio, 246
Phonofile, 2361
Phononic, 827, 1559, 1918
Phorest, 2347, 2513
Phoseon Technology, 755
Phosphonics, 3104
Phosphorus, 195, 744
Photo Dynamic, 2148
PhotoBox, 872
Photobox, 1518
Photoboxm QD Vision, 938
Photobucket, 85, 645, 1361, 1855, 1947
Photochannel Networks, 2091
PhotoCreate, 2637
Photodigm, 526
PhotoKharma, 1305
Photolynx, 92
PhotoMania, 2943
Photon Dynamics Inc., 950
Photonic Bridges, 2927
Photonic Bridges Holdings, 3053
Photonic Devices, 1361
Photonic Technologies SAS, 1493
Photonics Applications, 532
PhotoniXnet Corporation, 2406
Photonyx, 3004
Photopharmica, 2883
PhotoPharmics, 1074
Photoshelter, 820
Photoswitch Biosciences, 1238
Photothera Inc., 374
Photronics, 870
Phrase Technologies, 457
Phreesia, 178, 696, 941, 1140, 1146, 1464, 1618, 1908
PHRQL, 1452
PHT, 315
Phthisis Diagnostics, 1446
Phu Nhuan Jewelry, 2952
Phunware, 447, 485, 784, 1601, 1966

Portfolio Companies Index

PHX, 655
Phycal, 1051
Phychips, 3118
PhyFlex Networks, 163
Phylagen, 5, 571
Phylion Battery, 2927
Phyllom Bioproducts, 1604
Phylos, 1696
PHYND, 583
Phynd Technologies, 1559
Physcient, 296, 301, 975, 1101, 1847, 1925, 1987
Physical Property Testing, 238
Physical Rehabilitation Network, 1686
Physician IMS Control, 973
Physician Sales & Service, 1868
Physician Software Systems, 403
Physicians Dialysis, 1271
Physicians Endoscopy, 1066, 1410
Physicians Immediate Care, 1140
Physicians Pharmacy Alliance, 1576
PhysiciansNet.com, 164
Physics Ventures, 958
PhysiHome, 2934
Physio Control, 223
PhysIQ, 2221
physIQ, 2934
Phytel, 1464
Phytelligence, 2007
Phythea, 2439
Phyworks, 2340, 2653, 2665
Pi Charging, 779
Pi Therapeutics, 2221
Pi Variables, 1896
PI Worldwide, 815
Pi-Cardia, 2865
Pi-R Squared, 2316
Piab, 2376
PIADA Italian Street Food, 1092
Piaggio/Derbi Record, 2953
Piazza, 720, 1058
Pica, 564
Pica 8, 1241
Pica8, 1908
Picaboo, 388
Picanova, 3199
Picard, 745, 2371, 2488
Picarda Holdings Sdn. Bhd, 2949
Picarro, 582, 759
Picasso Labs, 863
PicCollage, 787, 1515, 2009
Piccollage, 752
Pickie, 609, 1119, 1223
Pickit, 1158
Pickle Robot, 2272
Pickle Robot Co., 321
PICKUP, 296
Pickwick & Weller, 234
Picmonic, 390
PicMonkey, 1720
PicnicHealth, 863
Picoboo, 116
PicoCandy, 1966
PicoChip, 3038
Picochip, 2463, 3095
PicoLight, 457
Picolight, 538
PicoNetics, 1183
PicsArt, 1005
Pictarine, 1618
Pictela, 209
Pictoris, 2756
Picturelife, 473, 1718
PictureTree, 2832
Pie, 1966
Pie Insurance, 48
Pieberry, 1610
Piece of Cake, 2637

Piedmont Aviation Services, 1574
Piedmont Candy Company, 1582
Piedmont Pharmaceuticals, 1446, 1917, 2609
Piedra Resources III, 673
Pienso, 195, 680, 849
Pier Systems, 85
Pierce, 3045
Piercom, 2328
PierianDx, 79
Pieris, 2739
Pieris AG, 1383, 2776
PIERIS Proteolab, 2304
Pierpoint Securities, 1746
Pierre Fabre, 1456
Pietro Rosa TBM, 77
PIFC, 2787
Pigeonly, 232, 1058
PiinPoint, 1281
Piinpoint, 2122
Piio, 29
Pijon, 788
Pika Energy, 498, 1164, 1165
Pika Energy Inc., 440
Pike Electric Corporation, 1133
Pilgrim Software, 1748
Pillar Financial, 2090
Pillar Processing, 1779
Pillo, 269
Pillow, 79, 310, 708
PillPack, 37, 44, 774, 1203, 1696
Pillpack, 1791
Pilot, 779
Pilot Multimedia (M) Sdn Bhd, 3155
Pilot Software Inc., 806
Pilot Thomas Logistics, 1964
Pilotly, 221
Pin Drop Security, 1483
PIN Pharma, 1325, 1422
Pinapple Payments, 1499
Pinarello, 1092
PINC Solutions, 950, 1762
Pindrop, 125, 561, 720, 824, 1006, 1035, 2681
Pindrop Security, 488, 1537, 1969
Pine Environmental Services, 1524
Piney Woods Resources, 1551
Ping, 742
Ping Communications, 2361
Ping Identity, 143, 610, 711, 1623, 1848, 1949
Ping Indentity, 1796
Ping++, 2430
Pingboard, 1687
Pinger, 582, 1079
Pingg, 309
Pingora Asset Management, 1745
PingPad, 131
Pingpad, 752, 1391
PingStamp, 2975
PingThings, 309, 812
Pingup, 209
Pink.oi, 641
Pinkberry, 1186, 2245
Pinkgirls, 679
Pinkoi, 775
Pinnacle, 912, 2201
Pinnacle Automotive Hospitality, 386
Pinnacle Direct Marketing, 1955
Pinnacle Electronics, 1163
Pinnacle Energies, 1241
Pinnacle Engines, 992
Pinnacle Foods, 280
Pinnacle Medical Solutions, 1215
Pinnacle Renewable Energy, 2200
Pinnacle Security, 843
Pinnacle Treatment, 1493
Pinnacle Treatment Centers, 441, 815, 1132
Pinnacle Ventures, 3273
Pinova, 2196

Pinpoint, 308
Pinpoint Care, 1364
Pinpoint Software, 2002
Pinteon, 2969
Pinterest, 125, 624, 744, 805, 846, 1079, 1235, 1305, 1309, 1696, 1763, 2154
Pinz, 75
Pioneer Bank, 447
Pioneer Immunotherapeutics, 1934
Pioneer Metal Finishing, 1473
Pioneer Recycling, 574
Pioneer Sand Company, 1043
Pioneer Square Labs, 265, 779, 1186
Pioneer Surgical Technology, 947
Pioneering Technology, 2061
Pionyr Immunotherapeutics, 1238, 1631
Pipax Environment, 2848
Pipdrive, 2437
Pipe, 2398, 2470
PipeDrive, 298
Pipedrive, 129, 1005, 1543, 1750
Pipeline, 1930
Pipeline DB, 1800
Pipeline Integrity, 2547
Piper, 1393, 1530
Piper Aircraft, 617
Piper Bioscience, 19
Piper Inc., 594
Pipestem Energy Group, 1897
Pipilu, 1340
Pipp Mobile Storage Solutions, 445
Pippa Jean, 2820, 2829
PIQ, 89, 2288
Piqora, 100, 234, 2009
Pique Tea, 742
Pique Therapeutics, 844, 1446, 1987
Piqur, 1930
Pirate3D, 3064
PIRCH, 1092
Pirios, 3068
Pirtek, 899
Pirtek Europe, 1939
Pirus Networks, 457
Pisano, 2276
Pishoniac, 3118
Pisla Oy, 2957
Pison Technology, 623
Piston Cloud, 1862
Piston Cloud Computing, 586, 3143
Piston Enterprise OpenStack, 619
Pitango Venture Capital, 3273
Pitch Deck, 1511
PitchBook, 3262
PitchPoint Solutions, 2051, 2074
Pitchpoint Solutions, 2128
Pitstop, 2107, 2232
PittaRosso, 2285
PittMoss, 296
Pittsburgh Equity Partners, 3264
Pittsburgh Glass Works, 1085
Pittsburgh Iron Oxides, 1003
Pittsburgh Life Sciences Greenhouse, 3264
Pittsburgh Technology Council, 3264
Pitzi, 756, 2863
Pivitol Health Solutions, 300
Pivot, 609, 627, 1014, 1701, 2188
Pivot Medical, 1251
Pivot North Capital, 36
Pivot Physical Therapy, 478
Pivot Solutions, 307, 957
Pivot3, 759, 1601, 1684
Pivotal Commware, 1155
Pivotal Laboratories, 3008
Pivotal Systems, 1830
Pivotdesk, 1791
PivotLink, 1741, 1852
Pixability, 655, 1050, 1104, 1164, 1463, 1488

1368

Portfolio Companies Index

Pixable, 1203
Pixalate, 400, 1032, 1059
Pixel Magic Imaging, 1711
Pixel Ripped, 310
Pixel Underground, 2133
Pixel Velocity, 629
Pixelexx Systems, 154
Pixelink, 2051
Pixelligent, 18
Pixelmetrix Corporation, 2694
Pixelux Entertainment, 1441
Pixelworks, 652, 759
PixFusion, 1748
PIXIA, 681
Pixie, 438
Pixim, 194, 983, 1924
Pixim Inc., 1781
Pixium, 3011
Pixium Vision, 3104
Pixlee, 895, 2010
piXlogic, 983
Pixonic, 2336
Pixorize, 623
Pixspan, 288
Pixsta, 2595
Pixtronix, 885
Pixvana, 485, 1158, 1162
Pixways, 3229
PJS Publications, 1929
PKL Group, 2976
PKWare, 1169
Pkware, 2198
PL Midstream, 1133
Pl-x, 3115
Place IQ, 1901
Placecast, 510, 1379, 1947
Placed, 1876
Placefirst, 2287
Placeholder, 1884
PlaceIQ, 969, 1527
Placemark Investments, 2146
Placemeter, 1637
Placenote, 3, 2122, 2272
Placester, 1585, 1759, 1791
PlaceWare, 808
Placeware, 1913
PlaCor, 1874
Plae, 1418
Plaid, 488, 720, 846, 1079, 1346, 1718
Plain Vanilla, 641, 876, 1566
PlainID, 3212
Plains GP Holdings, 1848
Plan, 623, 1760
Plan Me Up, 2300
Plan Member Services, 1151
Plan Vanilla, 1223
Plan4Demand, 1749
Planalytics, 1275
Planck Re, 149
Planday, 2842
Planet, 1001, 1363, 1665, 2430
Planet A.T.E., 133
Planet ATE, 1667
Planet Biopharmaceuticals Inc., 73
Planet Blue, 333, 334
Planet DDS, 381
Planet Fitness, 1863, 2371
Planet Labs, 108, 586, 596, 610, 742, 795, 1359
Planet Las, 1155
Planet Payment, 386
Planet Risk, 793
Planet Services, 2391
Planet Soho, 1257
Planet., 720
Planetary Resources, 537, 879
PlanetHS, 595
PlanetScale, 321

PlanetTran, 568
Planetveo, 2377
PlanGlid, 232
PlanGrid, 283, 2011, 2321
Planitax, 794
PlanMember Financial, 377
Planner5D, 2847
PlanSource, 1111
Plant Based Co., 7
Plant Prefab, 1363
Plant Systems & Services PSS GmbH, 3058
Plantation Petroleum Holdings V, 673
Plantation Products, 786
Plantcml, 843
Planted Supply Co., 558
PlantEXT, 1194
Plantic Technologies, 2636
Plantiga, 2270
Planto, 2217
Plantronics, 1100
PlantSense, 808
Planview, 912, 1005
Planwise, 1645
Plarium, 1323
Plasc Card, 985
Plasco Energy Group, 160
Plaskolite, 458
Plasma Antennas, 3098
Plasmanet, 2723
Plasmonix, 1172
Plassein Packaging, 377
Plast Team, 3194
Plastc, 861
Plastc Card, 1430
Plastic Components, 1266
Plastic Logic, 1361, 2378, 2483
Plasticity, 623, 1065
Plasticos, 2616
Plastics Industries Inc., 248
Plastifab Industries, 2227
Plastiq, 37, 756, 863, 1073, 1079
Plastomics, 270
Plate Joy, 773
Plateau, 1255
Plated, 641, 646, 724, 863, 1731, 1791
Platfora, 84, 488, 586, 983, 1227, 1762, 1798
Platform Solutions, 1021
Platform.sh, 252, 2842
Platform9, 1203, 1537
Platinex Inc., 2117
Platinum Energy Solutions, 502
Platiq, 1322
Platmin, 2329
Plattform Advertising, 1745
Plaxica, 2849
Plaxo, 908
Play By Play Sports Broadcasting Camps, 1660
Play The Future, 2107
Play the Future, 2024
Play Vox, 3116
Play Vs., 1101
Playa Viva, 401
Playbook, 1426
Playbuzz, 3212
Playcast, 1242, 3230
Playco, 1716
PlayCore, 1654
Playdeck, 601
Playdek, 724, 876
Playdo, 3004
Playdom, 1483, 1680
Playeau Systems, 1949
Player Tokens, 1162
Players' Lounge, 623
Playfire, 2437
PlayFirst, 597, 1855
PlayFull, 229

Playground Energy, 2687
PlayHaven, 641
PlayJam, 57, 2392
Playlore, 2967
Playmob, 2958
Playnery, 3118
Playnomics, 31, 744, 2010, 2270
PlayOn, 1332
PlayOn! Sports, 274, 1412
Playpeli, 3206
PlayPhone, 414
PlayPhone Inc., 1093
PlayPower, 1138
PlayRaven, 2628
Playrific, 845, 1164
Plays.tv, 1666
PlaySay, 1348
PlaySight, 1928
Playsino, 1832, 1966
Playspan, 1235
PlaySpanTM, 650
Playstudios, 597, 972
Playswell, 1983
Playtex, 1100
Playtex Products Inc., 303
Playtika, 1323, 2905
PlayToTV, 2813
PlayVox, 746
PlayVS, 1614
Plazes, 2435, 2466, 2662
Plazz Entertainment, 2518
Pleasants Energy, 1797
Please Assist Me, 221, 999
Pledgeling, 309
Plenty, 265, 1001, 1323
Plenum Media, 3096
Pleo, 3099
Plesk, 89
Plethora, 1155, 1262
Plews & Edelmann, 2211
Plex, 782, 2163
Plexigen, 1414
Plexo Capital, 485
Plexpress, 2621
Plextronics, 145, 731, 1003
Plexus, 2869, 2883
Plexus Entertainment, 1635
Plexuss, 802
Plexx, 1184
Plexxi, 1335
Plexxikon, 58, 94, 1414
Pley, 545, 752
PLH Group, 676
Plianced, 1554
Pliant, 1968
Pliant Therapeutics, 1203
Pligus, 2323
Plinga, 3104
Plista, 2435
Plixer, 238
Plixi, 133
Plooto, 2130, 2131
plooto, 2240
Plotech, 3209
Plotly, 2074, 2231, 2270
PlotWatt, 108
plotwatt, 720
Pluck Corporation, 1449
Pluck Tea, 2236
Plug.dj, 1032
Plugar, 2617
Plugg, 2395
Plum, 42, 828, 1065, 1073, 3009
Plum Baby, 2751
Plum Choice, 655, 1157
Plum Organics, 342, 430, 1490
Plum Perfect, 845, 1058

Portfolio Companies Index

Plum Print, 354, 1925
Plumble, 2842
PlumChoice, 646
Plume, 1028
PLUMgrid, 1150
PlumSilce, 1076
Plumtree, 857
Plunify, 2769
Pluot, 527
PluralSight, 1005
Pluralsight, 561, 888, 998, 1554, 1707
Pluribus Networks, 1203, 1247
PLUS, 1282, 2245
Plus One Robotics, 1114, 1483
PlushCare, 827, 998
Plusmo, 624
PlusPlus, 1616
PlusTV, 226, 1600
Pluto, 863, 1162, 1186, 1885, 1887
Pluto Mail, 1593
Pluto.TV, 1483, 1816
Plutoshift, 521
PLx Pharmaceutical, 1007
Ply Gem Industries, 478
Plyfe, 1635
PLYmedia, 1800
Plymouth Opportunity REIT, 1071
Plymouth Ventures, 3259
PLZ Aeroscience, 1482
PLZ Aeroscience Corporation, 1372
PLZ Holding Corporation, 63
PM Diagnostics, 270
PMA PhotoMetals of Arizona Inc., 988
PMC, 183, 1508, 1983
PMC-Sierra, 1762
PMW Pharma, 1014
PNC, 3266
PNE/Ecogas, 2872
PneumRx, 56, 94, 1062, 1794
Pneumrx, 2739
Pneuron, 1388
Poached Jobs, 1384
POC Medical Systems Inc., 273
Pocket, 234, 773
Pocket Science, 3165
Pocket Watch, 1885
Pocketbook, 3151
PocketFM, 2951
PocketGems, 863, 1537
PocketThis, 1640
Poco, 2841
Pod Foods, 1887
Pod Inn, 2927
Pod Pack International, 1148
Pod Point, 2665
Podaddies Inc., 1093
Podimetrics, 1347
Podio, 3140
Podium, 79, 623, 1074
Podo Labs, 3099
Pods, 153
POET, 300
POET Software, 1674
POF, 2539
Pogo Resources, 479
Pogoplug/Cloud Engines, 1701
PogoSeat, 1752, 1878
Pogoseat, 298, 2009
Pohjola-Yhtymä Oyj, 2981
Poindexter Systems, 957
Point, 125, 1154
Point B Capital LLC, 3265
Point Biomedical, 470
Point Blank Enterprises, 1043, 1755
Point Judith Capital, 3263
Point One Navigation, 521
Point Park Properties, 153

Point Predictive, 2074
PointCare, 352
PointClickCarem PowerPlan, 1045
Pointcloud, 222
Pointivo, 1412
PointRight, 28
Points International, 2073
Pointus Partners, 2251
Pointy, 3099
Poka, 2122, 2150
Pokelabo, 597
Poken, 3143
PokitDok, 1111, 1290
Pokkt, 3112
Polaar, 3104
Polar, 553, 1254, 1426, 2126
Polar Beverages, 405, 1176
Polar Molecular Corporation, 1839
Polar Oled, 2883
Polar Plastics Ltd., 467
Polar Sapphire, 2037, 2054, 2181
Polar Windows, 1576
Polaris, 170, 2438, 3104
Polaris Alpha, 167
Polaris Networks, 2917
Polaris Partners, 3263
Polaris Pool Holdings, 1507
Polaris Wireless, 610, 628, 1403
Polarmatic Oy, 2957
Polaroid, 381, 2164
Polatis, 2372, 2653, 2665
Polatix, 1042
Polestar, 1755
Polfa Kutno SA, 1456
Policolor, 2462
Policy Bazaar, 1017
Policy Bazaar.com, 1563
Policy Genius, 231, 729, 1059, 1558
PolicyGenius, 1760, 1770
Policygenius, 1346
PolicyMic, 1534
PolicyStat, 659
poLight, 2361, 3207
Poligof, 2285
Poligrafia SA, 2478
Polimedia, 2848
Poliogg, 1752
Poliris, 2457
Poll Everywhere, 1153
Pollen, 3099
Pollenizer, 1966
Pollex Mobile, 3053
Polly Portfolio, 1983
PollyEx, 728
Poly Remedy, 58
Poly-Wood, 412
PolyActiva, 2527, 2950
PolyAd Services, 653
Polyair Inter Pack, 834
Polycera, 49
PolyCera Membranes, 300
Polychain Capital, 23, 125, 310, 1884, 2272
Polycom, 1006, 3203
Polyconcept, 458, 912, 1021, 2303
Polycor, 2196, 2264
Polyfibron Technologies Inc., 357
Polyform Products Company, 1115
PolyFuel, 1788
Polyfuel, 1091
Polygene Ltd, 2945
Polygenta, 2364, 3202
Polygon, 1426
Polygon Pictures Inc., 2339
Polygraformlenie, 2456
Polygraph, 70
Polymer, 2
Polymer Additives, 1049

Polymer Corporation, 1333
Polymer Holding, 1494
Polymer Solutions Group, 172
Polymer Technology, 402
Polymita Technologies, 2334
Polymorph, 623
Polynt, 912, 2371
PolyOne, 1971
Polypack, 3062
Polyphalt, 2051
PolyPid, 3230
PolyPipe, 899
Polypore, 2688
polySpectra, 2205
Polystream, 1099
Polystyvert, 2087
Polytec Holding AG, 2555
Polytex Environmental Inks, 376
PolyTherics, 2849
Polytronics, 3209
PolyUp, 895
Polyvera, 3185
PolyVision, 532
PolyVision Inc., 694
Polyvore, 1184
Pom-Co, 434
Pomelo, 721, 1143, 2074
Pomeroy, 502
Pomifer Power Funding, 157
Pomme de Pain, 3011
Pomocni.pl, 3035
Ponce de Leon Pharmaceuticals, 1420
Poncho, 23, 1114
Pond Biofuels, 2181
Pond Ventures, 2463
Pond5, 1305, 1588, 1751
Pondurance, 1314
Ponfac, 2617
Pongolo, 400
Pontis, 2717
Pony Lumber, 1911
Pony.ai, 520
Pooch, 650
Poof-Slinky, 1518
Poorman-Douglas, 1772
Pop, 59
Pop Art, 1074
Pop Cap, 1213
Pop Chest, 310
Pop Displays, 1755
Pop Dust, 1114
Pop Medical, 3183
Pop-Up Pantry, 1103
PopCom, 221, 1285
Popcorn Metrics, 3099
Popdog, 2944
Popdust, 1701
Popego, 2326
PopExpert, 708
Popexpert, 1752
PopLegal, 721
Poppin, 742
Poppin., 1666
Poppins, 2640
PopSQL, 798
PopStarClub, 1112
Popsugar, 1006
Poptent, 1242
Poptip, 1701
Popular Pays, 254, 863
PopularPays, 802
Population Genetics, 1776
Populus, 1557, 2228
Populus Global, 2192
PopUp, 50
Poq, 3099
Por ti, 1588

1370

Portfolio Companies Index

Porch, 1608
Porcher, 2598
Porcher Industries, 3011
Porex Corporation, 202
Pork Farms, 1939
Porpoise, 2192
Port Arthur Steam Energy, 110
Port Hawkesbury Paper, 2249
Port Logistics Group, 674
Portable Energy Products, 651
Portable Medic, 1618
Portadam, 1730
Portal, 11
Portal de Documentos, 1376
Portal Educacao, 2429
Portal Entertainment, 2958
Portalarium, 1635
PortalPlayer, 1021, 2073
Portapure, 3246
Portea, 1511
Porter & Chester Institute, 1817
Porter Aviation Holdings, 2088, 2098
Porter Group, 1505
Porter Lancastrian, 2976
Porter Road, 863
Porterbrook, 2935
Portero, 1117
Portfolio Group, 407, 792
Portfolio Litigation Fund, 2088
Portfolio Solutions, 1118
Porthaven Care Homes, 3027
Portico, 655, 940
Portico Systems, 2188
Portillo's, 257
PortIT, 3004
Portland Orthopaedics Pty Limited, 2706
Portman Travel, 1939
Portola, 58, 1762, 1968
Portola Pharmaceuticals, 785, 1495, 2308
Portrait Innovations, 408
Portrait Software, 2463
Portside, 1142
PortWise, 2653, 2745
Portworx, 812, 1187
Posco Energy, 3136
POSE, 1862, 2863
Pose, 597, 1103
Poseida Therapeutics, 1147
Poseidon, 2257
Poshly, 845, 1983
Poshmark, 561, 827, 1017, 1187, 1323, 1702, 1881
PosiGen, 534
Posiq, 1808
Positionly, 3035
Poss, 2108
Possmedia, 2848
Post Factory NY, 2133
Post Impressions, 2723
Post University, 822
Post-N-Track, 532
Post.Bid.Ship., 1462
PostBeyond, 2146, 2216
Postcard on the Run, 625
Poste Imo, 3011
Posterous, 972, 1058, 1855
Posterous Spaces, 1537
Postie, 309, 345
Postini, 200
Postling, 1588, 1959
Postmaster, 2016
Postmastes, 1828
PostMates, 1702
Postmates, 129, 298, 564, 708, 805, 964, 1396, 1665, 1696, 1881
PostPath, 972
PostProcess, 1259

Postrocket, 1464
PostX, 1406
Pot Pots, 558
Pot Scientist, 395
Potbelly, 251, 1186
Potel & Chabot, 2285
Potentia Renewables, 2175
Potentia Semiconductor, 1084
Potenza Therapeutics, 1268
PotGuide.com, 395
Potloc, 2060
Potomac Research Group, 618
Potter Electric, 1232
Poundland, 1957
Poundworld Retail LTD, 1837
Povo, 2419
POW, 85
Pow Bio, 398
Powder OLEDs, 3098
PowderMed, 2308
Powell Johnson, 1151
Power & Composite Technologies, 920
Power 2 Switch, 1364
Power Analog, 1924
Power Assure, 983, 2307
Power Automation AG, 3163
Power By Proxy, 3089
Power Design Services, 703
Power Distribution, 260
Power Genius, 2927
Power Holdings, 962
Power Hour Fitness, 1267
Power I.T. LLC, 1057
Power Inbox, 1150
Power Innovations, 1679
Power Medical Interventions, 1325
Power Paper, 2378, 3037
Power Paper Ltd, 2964
Power Plus Communications, 2606
Power Practical, 1074
Power Precise Solutions Inc., 173
Power Products, 1654
Power Products LLC, 823
Power Protection Products Inc., 989
Power Reviews, 21, 2437
Power Services Group, 216
Power Survey, 677, 1329, 2087
Power To Fly, 564
Power to Fly, 1114
Power2sme, 1017
Power2Switch, 256, 473, 1618
PowerBand Global, 2081
Powerband Global, 2051
Powerbilt, 940
Powercast Corporation, 1003
Powercell, 297
Powercell Sweden, 2746
PowerChord, 227
PowerCloud Systems, 1032, 1953
Powercom, 2329
Powercor Australia Ltd, 2582
PowerD, 3092
PowerDMS, 227, 793
PowerDsine, 2562, 2576
Powerdsine, 22
Powered By People, 2131
Powerfile, 1684
PowerGen Renewable Energy, 1832
PowerGenix, 173, 325, 596, 2752
PowerGenix Systems, 127, 1788
Powerhouse Dy Dynamics, 421
Powerhouse Dynamics, 498, 536, 643, 949, 1104, 1463, 2101
PowerInbox, 238, 650
Powerit Solutions, 707
Powerlase, 2653
Powerleader Science & Technology Ltd., 2624

PowerLight Corporation, 596
Powermat, 821, 1281, 1733, 2014
Powermet, 999
PowerOasis, 3234
PowerOne Media, 957
POWERPRECISE, 1924
PowerQuest, 654, 861
PowerReviews, 780, 1798, 2005
Powers Equipment Company, 542
PowerSchool, 2201
Powerset, 116
Powershares by Invesco, 796
Powerspan, 1324
PowerSteering Software, 957, 2188
PowerStop, 1169
PowerTeam Services, 1066
PowerTech, 85
PowerTech Group, 1640
PowerTel, 3159, 3159
Powertel, 1152
PowerToFly, 925
PowerU, 3185
Powervar, 1438
Powervation, 325, 1924
PowerVision, 1116, 1918
Powervision, 58, 73, 545, 785, 1126, 1411
PowerWay, 445
Powhow, 1358
Powwr, 746
Poxel, 1271, 3011
Poynt, 1184
PPA, 2927
pParoc, 3000
PPC Industries Inc., 63
PPC Partners, 3254
PPD, 927
PPI-Time Zero, 1424
PPI/Time Zero Inc., 1627
PPM America Capital Partners, 3255
PPS, 1576, 2575
PPTV, 299, 3091
PPU Maconomy, 3128
PQ Corp., 170
PQ Corporation, 435
PR Wireless, 1157
Practically Green, 536
Practice, 490
Practice Fusion, 1257, 1383
Practice Ignition, 2074
Practice Insight, 902
Practice Plan Group Ltd., 2668
Practicefusion, 720
PracticePanther, 92
Practo, 579
Praditus, 3104
Praekelt Foundation, 1374
Praemo, 2074, 2183
Pragli, 1426
Pragmatech Software, 1084
Prairie Capital, 3255
Prairie Fava, 2093
Prairie Meats, 2277
Prairie Soil Services, 2213
Prairie Storm Energy Corp, 1326
Prairie Storm Energy Corp., 1328
Praized, 1966
Pramata, 1430
Prana, 2230, 2992
PrarieGold Solar, 1474
Prattle, 545
Praxis, 752, 1753
Praxis Precision Medicines, 1934
PRCL Research, 3187
PRE Resources, 262
Preact, 246, 308, 1059
Preact.io, 1103
Precede, 2717

Portfolio Companies Index

PrecedentHealth, 1803
Preceptis Medical, 1420
Precidian Investments, 238
Precious, 798, 1142
Precipio Diagnostics, 679
Precise, 3091
Precise Light Surgical, 644, 1713
Precise Packaging, 1858
Precise Software Solutions, 3128
Precisi Therapeutics, 949
Precision, 832, 1292, 2201, 2956
Precision Aviation Group, 753, 1461
Precision Biosciences, 711, 1522
Precision Components, 1071
Precision Dematology, 73
Precision Dermatology, 785, 1510
Precision for Medicine, 1041
Precision fOr Medicine Holdings, 1361
Precision Global, 2200
Precision Hawk, 1235
Precision Image Analysis, 1065
Precision Manufacturing Group LLC, 557
Precision Medicine Group, 257, 1934
Precision Mounting, 2138
Precision NanoSystems, 11
Precision Nutrition, 364
Precision Partners Holding Company, 1234
Precision Payment Systems, 1000
Precision Products Group, 1145
Precision Southeast, 832
Precision Spine Care, 406
Precision Therapeutics, 224, 307, 1510, 1749, 3187
Precision Ventures, 1104
PrecisionDemand, 876, 1741
PrecisionHawk, 520, 534, 1928
PrecisionLender, 1005
Precithera, 2086
Preclick, 1691
Precog, 1550
Precognitive, 756
Precom, 2927
PreCon, 2578
Precursor Energetics, 1355
Precyse, 97
Predata, 537, 655
Predfast, 796
Predict Spring, 720
Predictable Revenue, 2262
PredictHQ, 182
Prediction IO, 2009
Predictive Networks, 317
Predictive Service, 835
PredictWise, 937
Predikto, 1790
Predix Pharmaceuticals, 772
Predixion, 68, 1831
Predixion Software, 794, 1237, 1408
Preemadonna, 901, 2122, 2272
Preempt, 820
PreEmptive Meds, 403
PreEmptive Solutions, 1051, 1556
Preen.me, 2822
Preferred Compounding, 1997
Preferred Concepts, 1746
Preferred Freezer Services, 722
Preferred Rubber, 653
Preferred System Solutions, 509
Preferred Systems, 532
Preferred Systems Solutions, 1389
Prefix, 328
Preflexibel, 2853
Pregis, 1372
Pregis Corporation, 63
Preh GmbH, 2651
Prelert, 713, 3049
Prellis, 398

PremFina, 1599, 2665
Premia, 1066
Premier Global Services Inc., 406
Premier Kids Care, 1958
Premier Needle Arts, 293
Premier Pacific Pharmaceutical Industries, 1771
Premier Performance Products, 404
Premier Precision Group, 1722
Premier Store Fixtures, 1148
Premiere Global Sports, 1438
PremierXD, 1779
Premise, 51, 320, 532, 993, 1698, 2398
Premise Health, 1962, 2199
Premise One, 943
Premium Brands, 2045, 2210
Premium Franchise Brands, 1232
Premium Power, 1908, 3126
Premix, 1174
Premiys, 1257
PRENAV, 521
Prenav, 564, 1426
Prenax Global, 2745
Prenda, 79
Preo, 985
Prepac, 2264
Prepaid Capital, 2708
Prepaid Direct, 2073
Prepaid Media, 2708
Prepaid Technologies, 227
Prepaid2cash, 75
Prepared Response, 85, 250
PreparedHealth, 1483
PrePlay, 1854
Presage Biosciences, 1780
PreScience Labs, 386
Prescient Healthcare Group, 225
Prescient Systems, 957
Prescott Group, 153
Presence, 754
Presence AI, 1011
Presence From Innovation, 402, 1057
Presence Learning, 275, 291, 430
Presence.ai, 1370
PresenceLearning, 429, 1298
President Engineering, 3234
Presidential, 1252
Presidential Holdings, 1252
Presidio, 796, 1213
Presidio Pharmaceuticals, 1411
Presidio Pharmaceuticals Inc., 240
Presidio Systems, 1379
Presidion Inc., 902
Presidium, 655
Press A Point, 973
Press Ganey, 912
Press Ganey Associates, 1933
Press Index, 2542
Pressly, 2103
PressPass, 2969
Pressure Technologies, 3234
PrestaShop, 3104, 3229
Presteve Foods, 2118
Prestiamoci, 2865
Prestige Brands International, 2014
Prestige Insurance Holdings Limited, 407
Presto, 504
Presto Engineering, 3104
PrestoBox, 1467
Preston Hollow Capital, 912
Preston-Eastin, 402
PrestoSports, 238
Pret a changer, 3229
Preteckt, 999
Pretio Interactive, 2276, 2283
Pretium Packaging, 823
Pretty Simple, 2842
Prettylitter, 567

PrevaCept Infection Control, 403
Prevail Therapeutics, 710, 1522
Prevailion, 84
Prevalent, 797, 1005
Prevedere, 773, 1158, 1346
Preventice, 1206, 3268
Preventice Solutions, 175
Preventicus, 2518
Preview Networks, 3140
Preview System, 116
Previser, 978
PreVisor, 405
Previstar, 1348, 1401
Prevoty, 309, 625, 1059, 1103
Prevtec Microbia, 2255
Prewise Group Oy, 2864
Prexa Pharmaceuticals, 1777
Prezi, 1720, 3140
Prezi.inc, 2595
Prezzo, 1837
PRGX Global, 303
PRI Group, 1424
Price Spider, 793
Price.com, 810
Pricelock, 133
PriceMatch, 1418
Priceonomics, 283, 586, 1718, 2321
PriceRunner, 3004
PriceWaiter, 461
Pricing Engine, 708
PricingAssistant, 1418
Pridenta, 3187
Priject Time & Cost, 905
Prima Capital Advisors, 1746
Primanex Corporation, 1183
Primanti Bros., 1092
Primarion, 1949
Primary Access, 1762
Primary Access Corporation, 1708
Primary Data, 438, 604, 689, 1205, 1428
Primary Packaging, 620
Primary.com, 944
PrimaTable, 586
Primavera, 782
Primavista, 2660
Primax Electronics, 897
Primaxx, 68
Prime Advantage, 1372, 1736
Prime Bank, 1496
Prime Discovery, 321
Prime Distribution, 1174
Prime Equipment, 1021
Prime Health Services, 1148
Prime Leather, 1214
Prime Network Inc., 2898
Prime Risk Partners, 1818
Prime Rock Resources, 1129
Prime Sense, 389
Prime Student Loan, 536
Prime System, 2817
PrimeCo, 496
PrimeCo Wireless Communications, 620
PrimeCredit Limited, 475
PrimeLine Utility Services, 741
Primeloop, 1658, 1914
Primer, 108, 564, 1155
Primera Biosystems, 215
PrimeraDx, 1014
PrimeRevenue, 243, 1597, 2188
Primerevenue, 238
PrimeSport, 502, 1493
Primestream, 815
Primet, 186, 434
Primet Oy, 2864
PriMetrica, 961
Primex Technologies, 2169
PRIMIS Marketing Group, 470

Portfolio Companies Index

Primitive, 310
Primo Water, 1683
Primrose Schools, 1580
Primus, 1839
Primus International, 1360
Primus Pacfic Partners I LP, 2088
Primus Pharmaceuticals, 1456
Primus Power, 596
Prince, 1138
Prince International Corporation, 1404
Prince Mineral Holding Corporation, 1493
Princepa Biopharma, 1734
Princeps Therapeutics, 1734
Princess Yachtz International, 1092
Princeton Financial Systems, 655
Princeton Optronics, 1348
Princeton Softech, 1140
Principia, 1126, 1238
Principia Biopharma, 1297, 1383, 1700
Princo, 2427
Print Direction, 408
Print Polska, 2420
Print Syndicate, 510, 587
Printo, 3100
PrintOne, 2882
Printpaks, 200
PrintWithMe, 1159
Prior Data Sciences, 2073
PriorAuthNow, 608, 1285, 1412
Priori Data, 3099
Priori Legal, 863
Priority Express, 654
Priority Holdings, 530
Priority Solutions, 172, 785
Prism, 1566
Prism Education Group, 436, 941
Prism Medical UK, 2935
Prism Network, 2958
PRISM Plastics, 445
Prism Skylabs, 133, 586, 1478, 1491, 1832, 1848
Prism Vision Group, 1507
Prisma, 662, 1079
Prisma Medios de Pagos S.A., 61
Prismatic, 1032, 1800
PrismHR, 28
Pristine, 1601
Pritikin, 377
Pritzker Group, 3255
Privacera, 1809
Privacy Analytics, 2270
Privalia, 819, 2978
Privalla, 2544
Privamista Group, 2330
Private Bancorp Inc., 654
Private Company, 1481
Private Core, 773
Privateer Holdings, 99
Privategriffe, 2393
PrivateLot, 3229
Privilege Unerwriters, 1746
Privitar, 1610
Privlo, 1504
Privoro, 1035
Privus, 1599
Privé Revaux, 2137
Priyo.com, 721
PrizeLogic, 1410
Prizeo, 1491, 1637
Pro Active Therapy, 1560
Pro Group, 405
Pro Hydration Therapy, 999
Pro Mach, 1368
Pro Player Connect, 1799
Pro PT, 864
Pro Service Hawaii, 952
PRO Unlimited, 917, 1021
Pro-Fab Group, 2008

PRO-PAC Packaging, 2636
Pro-Pet, 931
Pro.com, 610, 1162, 1186
ProAct Services Corp., 904
Proacta, 3076
ProactiveNet, 593
Proampac, 1972
Proaxion, 1925
Probiodrug, 2806, 3187
Probity Medical Transcription, 1431
Procaps, 2142
Procaptura, 2745
Procarta, 2969
Procarta Biosystems, 2958
ProcedureFlow, 2063, 2065
Procelerate Technologies, 1304
Procertus, 1923
Process Fab, 1906
Process Map, 173
Process Sensing Technologies, 238
Process Systems Enterprise, 2849
Process'ware, 3039
ProcessClaims, 1912
Processing.com, 1097
Prochips Inc., 2915
Procite, 1337
ProClarity Corporation, 1538
Proclivity, 799
Proclivity Systems, 1773
Procognia, 3128
Procomp Informatics, 2898
Procompra, 3047
ProCore, 1800
Procore, 1281, 1828
ProCredit Bank, 3224
ProCredit Group, 2080
ProCredit Moldova, 3224
ProctorFree, 1076, 1925
Proctoru, 2074
Procured Health, 711, 1050
Procurement Advisors, 336
Procuri, 835
Procurifiy, 2146
Prodagio Software, 1785
Prodea, 538
Prodealcenter, 3011
Prodigy, 23, 565, 1616, 2065
Prodigy Finance, 2469
Prodigy Health Group, 1949
Prodomax Automation Ltd., 2160
ProdPerfect, 680
ProdThink, 876
Produced Water Absorbents, 2691
ProducePay, 623
Product Health, 1251
Product Hunt, 125, 553, 1154
Product Software Development, 838
ProductBIO, 1752
Productboard, 1079
Production Resource Group, 1049
Production Resource Group LLC, 159
Production Science, 468
Producto Protegido, 2446
ProEnergy Holdings, 45
ProEnergy Services, 687
Profeshion, 2939
Profesia, 3113
Professional Bull Riders, 1727
Professional Capital Services, 1140
Professional Credentials Exchange, 754
Professional Environmental Engineers, 367
Professional Press, 1275
Professional Rental Tools, 1025, 1148
Professional Service Industries, 1372
Professional Warranty Service, 1778
Profex, 1852
Profi, 912

Profi.ru, 3079
Proficiency, 457
Proficient Auto, 1748
Proficio Bank, 804
Profile Systems, 1146
Profility, 3041
ProFind, 1915
Profine, 153
Profit Systems, 832
Profita Fund I Ky, 2731
Profitect, 252, 861
Profitlogic, 627
Proformex, 1030
Profound, 2074
Profound Medical, 2125, 2181
Profound Medical Corp., 2086
Profounder, 1101
ProfoundNano, 3268
PROFUSA, 1616
Profusa, 183
ProgenIQ, 2468
Progeniq, 2382
Progenity, 190
Progenteq, 2883
Progentix Orthobiology, 2505
Progexia, 3011
Progility, 3009
Progistics Distribution, 961
Prognolic, 2847
Prognos, 151, 1605
Progression Therapeutics, 244
Progressive Acute Care, 1195
Progressive Concepts, 1552
Progressive Finance, 1754
Progressive Group, 2073
Progressive Moulded Products, 1360
Progressive REI, 515
Progressive-PMSI, 1066
Progressly, 1703
Progresso Financiero, 457
Progressus Therapy, 1745
Progrexion, 931
Progrexion Holdings, 1493
ProGuides, 121
Progyny, 1079, 1734
PROHBTD, 43, 1139
PROHBTED, 2245
Proj, 1374
Project 44, 1716
Project Applecart, 623
Project Arriendo, 912
Project Cohort, 545
Project Decor, 1101
Project Frog, 493, 1583
Project Leadership Associates, 441, 699
Project Management Academy, 1109
Project44, 1005
project44, 1483
Projector, 234
Projectpartner, 2844
Projitech, 1051
ProKarma, 674
ProKyma, 2958
Prolacta Bioscience, 73, 94, 628, 698, 794, 800, 830, 1604, 1917
Prolamina Corporation, 1972
Proletariat, 744
Prolexic, 1852
Prolific Earth Sciences, 999
Prolific Technology, 2594
Prolific Works, 1104
ProLogis, 153
Prolojik, 2958
Prolong Pharmaceuticals, 1062
Prolupin GmbH, 2677
Promach, 1113
Promatory, 1795

1373

Portfolio Companies Index

Promatory Communications, 822
Promax Nutrition, 1171
ProMed, 599
Promedior, 644, 922, 1126, 1464, 2739
Promega, 1923
Promenade, 2245
Promentis Pharmaceuticals Inc., 73
Promethean Surgical Devices, 1775
Promethera, 2521, 2940, 3216
Promethera Biosciences, 1241
Prometheus, 1410
Prometheus Group, 782, 1778
Prometheus Laboratories, 405, 1728
Prometheus Therapeutics & Diagnostics, 212
Promethium, 1, 2018
Promic, 3098
Prominence Networks, 3115
Promise, 742
Promise Healthcare, 1271
Promise Pictures, 515
PromisePay, 1690
Promo Boxx, 180
Promoboxx, 316, 536, 881, 1101, 1737
Promociones Farma, 3214
PromocionesFarma.com, 2911
Promopost Holding, 2482
Prompt.ly, 309, 1658
Promt.ly, 1569
ProNAi, 1383
ProNAi Therapeutics, 946, 1943
ProNatura, 2330
ProNavigator, 2074
ProNerve, 1964
ProNet, 1684
Proniras, 30
Pronota, 2467, 2930
Pronoun, 209, 234
Pronova BioPharma, 2510
Pronto, 79, 798
Pronto Insurance, 1404
ProntoForms, 2276
ProofPilot, 354, 568
Proofpoint, 251, 342, 582, 972, 1213, 1247, 1341
Propane Taxi, 1504
ProParts, 911
Propel, 125, 1346, 1610
Propel Baltimore Fund, 18
Propel Biofuels, 1355
Propel IT, 991
Propel Orthodontics, 1228
Propeller, 548, 795, 863, 1058, 1734
Propeller Health, 1698
Propeller Industries, 1314
PropelPLM, 1677
Proper, 1142
Properly, 183, 1114, 2130, 2131
Propero, 2563
properties, 1507
Property Detective, 2986
Property Network, 2862
Property Partner, 3099
Property Partners, 3009
Property Solutions, 1004
Propertybase, 1499, 2985
PropertyBrands, 1005
PropertyBridge, 493
PropertyView Solutions, 1354
ProPetro Services, 676
Propex, 1968
ProPharma Group, 1050, 1132
ProPhase Labs, 638
Prophecy, 1206
Prophet 21, 1140
prophix, 2074
Propoly, 3099
Proportunity, 2398
Proposal Software.com, 386

Proposify, 2148
Proposity, 2065
Proprietary Fund, 2949
Proprius Pharmaceuticals, 772
Proptec Renewables, 2517
PropTiger, 1511
Proragonist Therapeutics, 73
PROS, 1971
Pros, 1045
Prosci, 1109
Proscia, 756, 802, 1581, 1703
ProSciento, 4
Prose, 545, 763, 1005, 1114, 1186, 1533
ProSeeder, 845
Prosensa, 2842
ProSep, 5
ProService Hawaii, 790
ProSiebenSat1 Media SE, 927
ProSight, 2532
Prosight Specialty Insurance, 1837
ProSites, 1576
Proskauer, 3262
Prosky, 1058
Prosolia, 659
Prosonix, 2701, 3060
ProSource, 480
Prospect Brands, 1276
Prospect Medical, 1966
Prospect Medical Holdings, 1113
Prospect Mortgage, 1745
Prospect Partners LLC, 3255
Prospect Pools Group, 1494
Prospect Water, 1494
ProspectWise, 562
Prospectwise, 1103
Prosper, 564, 711, 782, 1006, 1213, 1374, 1504, 1832
Prospera, 485, 1511
Prostalund, 2553
Prostar Energy, 2267
ProStor Systems, 318
ProStrakan, 1349
Prota Therapeutics, 3014
ProtAffin, 2701
ProtAffin Biotechnologic AG, 2342
Protag, 3064
Protagonist, 764, 3129
Protagonist Therapeutics, 1047, 1128, 1522
Protalix Biotherapeutics, 1271
Protean, 965
Protean Electric, 1361
ProteanTecs, 3212
ProTec, 77
Protect America, 1377
Protect My Car, 560
Protect Plus Air Holdings, 904, 961
Protect Wise, 564
Protection One, 1508
Protectwise, 173
Protedyne, 1146
Protege Energy III, 673
Protego Biopharma, 1934
Protego Medical, 2950
Protego Networks, 1237
Protegrity Advisors, 3257
Protegys Group, 2367
Protein Bar and Kitchen, 1092
Protein Discovery, 1190
Protein Laboratories Rehovot, 3235
Protein Sciences, 1587
Protein Simple, 1241
ProteinQure, 2130
Proteinqure, 2131
ProteinSimple, 1098, 1931
Protel, 112
Protellindo, 257
Protelus, 85

Protemo, 2007
Protenergy, 2160
Protenus, 175, 1056
Proteocyte AI, 2120
Proteogenix, 1917
Proteolix, 58, 1098, 2998
Proteologics, 2445
Proteom, 2454
Proteome, 315
Proteon Therapeutics, 1268, 1693, 3187
Proteon Therpeutics, 1013
Proteostasis, 711, 1621
Proterra, 305, 534, 821, 1241, 1363, 1925
Proterro, 236, 325, 571
Proteus, 2457
Proteus Biomedical, 56
Proteus Digital Health, 67, 183, 750, 1056
Protez Pharmaceuticals, 240, 1510
Prothena Corporation, 1700
ProThera Biologics, 1695
ProTip, 3104
Proto Labs, 1335, 3268
Proto Software, 307
Protochips, 1446, 1609, 1987
Protocol Driven Healthcare Inc., 53
Protocol Global Systems, 931
Protocol Labs, 945, 1669, 1884
Protocol Systems, 241
Protocom Development Systems Pty Limited, 2706
Proton, 532
Proton Energy Systems, 898, 1355, 1704, 2073
Proton Media, 1386
Protonex, 522, 1704, 1922
ProtonMedia, 1388
Protraining, 2756
Protus IP Solutions, 2051
Provade VMS, 183
ProVale, 1551
Provalliance-Franck Provost, 1022
Provant, 688
Provasculon, 350, 1421
Provation, 502
ProVation Medical Inc., 159
Prove Inc., 1643
Proven, 591, 1058
Proven., 125
Proven.com, 1254, 1959
Provendi, 3229
ProVest, 1473
Provide Commerce, 1795
Providea Conferencing, 1979
Providence Equity Partners, 3245
Providence Equityt, 2160
Providence Medical Technology, 139
Provident Companies Inc., 407
ProviderTrust, 718
Providien Medical, 674
Provigent, 2646, 2943
ProVita International Medical Center, 3187
Provivi, 1055
Provocraft, 1707
Provogue, 808
ProxBox, 999
Proxim, 1399
Proxim Wireless, 3128
Proxima, 1920
Proxima Therapeutics, 94
Proxima Therapeutics RXStrategies, 1152
Proximagen, 2883
Proximal Data, 209, 619
Proximetry, 1543, 1995
Proximiant, 2969
Proximic, 2820, 2829
Proximities, 215, 994
Proxio, 2003
Proxiserve, 2842

1374

Portfolio Companies Index

Proxpur Labs, 256
Proxy, 1079
ProxyClick, 746
PRT Growing Services, 2267
Prudent Energy, 1241, 1340
Prudential Capital Group, 77
Pruska Real Estate, 1143, 2937
Prusm Capital, 2074
PRV Metals, 1169
Pryon, 849
Pryor Cashman LLP, 3257
Prysm, 176, 1418, 1813
PRZM, 49
PS Dept, 1479
PS Production Services, 2133
PS Soft, 2346
PSA Worldwide, 1609
PSafe, 641, 1537
Psagot, 136
PSAV, 1372
PSC, 1138
PSC Holdings I, 1133
PSD Group, 2787
PSI, 1964
PSIA, 2798
Psionic, 810
PSIOxus, 1734
PsiOxus Therapeutics, 2849
pSivida, 1271
PSM Investments, 585
PSS, 1730
PSS Systems, 57, 218, 857
Psyadon Pharma, 1271
PsyTechnics, 1304
Psytechnics, 2653, 2665
PT Berrybenka, 2789
PT Bukalapak.com, 2789
PT Marga Mandalasaki, 2425
PT Pricearea Andalan Prestasi, 2789
PTC, 2806
PTC Therapeutics, 240, 1149, 1948, 2807, 3006
PTRx, 1917
Public, 398
Public Engines, 2374
Public Financial Management, 836
Public Funds Investment Tracking and Reporting, 1690
Public Mobile, 457, 1157
Public Recruitment Group, 2786
Public Relay, 1987
Public Stuff, 744
PublicEngines, 1679
PublicStaff, 1309
PublicStuff, 1305, 2595
Publishing, 2547
Publishing Group of America, 1508
PubMatic, 1327
Pubmatic, 200, 2992
PubNub, 485, 1629, 2228
Puddle, 1254
Pudget, 246
Pueblo Mechanical & Controls, 963
Puerto Rico ASC Holdings Co. Inc., 62
Puerto Rico Waste Investment LLC, 159
Pull Request, 729
PullString, 742, 877
Pulmagen, 2653
Pulmagen Therapeutics, 2739, 2972, 3186
Pulmatrix, 11, 154, 1464
Pulmocide, 711, 1149, 1631, 1734
Pulmokine, 350
Pulmonary Apps, 1051
PulmonX, 1251, 2074
Pulmonx, 599, 1098
PulmonX Corp., 2807
Pulpo Media, 1227
Puls, 1614, 3212

Pulsant Limited, 1360
Pulsar Vascular, 1619
Pulse, 641, 1537, 2131
Pulse 8, 1172
Pulse Data, 944
Pulse Point, 609
Pulse Systems, 472
Pulse Therapeutics, 270, 570
Pulse Ventures, 3263
Pulse Veterinary Technologies, 1834
Pulse.io, 387, 1418
Pulsecore Semiconductor, 200
Pulselabs, 1162
PulsePoint, 1290, 1888, 1908
PulseVet, 330
PulseWave, 1244
Pulsic, 3042
PulsoSocial, 3116
Pulsus, 3118
Pulumi, 1162
Puman, 3172
Pump Audio, 1479
Pumps & Pressure, 2138
Pumps and Controls, 1565, 1582
PumpUp, 2120
Pumpup, 820
Punch Bowl Social, 1092
Punch Powertrain, 2940
Punchbowl, 649, 1104
Punchbowl Software, 535
Punchh, 456, 1784
PunchTab, 1247
Pundar, 1374
Pundit, 623
Puppet, 485, 1079, 2681
Puppet Labs, 1848, 1862
PurCellBio, 1317
Purch, 21, 43
Purchasing Power, 336, 1377
Pure Barre, 1092
Pure Canadian Gaming, 2200, 2201
Pure Dental Brands, 963
Pure Digital, 759, 990
Pure Digital Technologies, 556, 1908
Pure Energies Group, 1324
Pure Fishing, 1041
Pure Growth Organics, 1589
Pure Gym, 435
Pure Incubation, 1176
Pure Leapfrog, 2500
Pure Life Renal, 1251, 1332
Pure Organix, 394
Pure People, 2842
Pure Storage, 840, 1006, 1537, 2851
Pure Swiss Water AG, 650
Pure Wafer, 653
Pure Wow, 863
PureCars, 1737
PureEnergy Solutions, 459
Puregym, 1113
Purely Proteins, 2454
PureRED, 1738
PureRed Integrated Marketing, 1560
PureSight Inc., 810
PureStorage, 1762
PureTech Systems, 1839
PureWave, 1106
PureWave Networks, 185
PureWow, 1483
PureWRX, 1332, 1687
Purigen, 11
PuriLens, 215
Purisma, 857
Purissima, 229, 1613
Purity Life Health Produts, 2045
PurMeo, 3035
Purmeo, 2629

Purple Communications, 502
Purple Cows, 656
Purple Land Management, 1625
Purple Squirrel, 562
Purpose, 1555
PurposeEnergy, 498
PursueCare LLC, 1738
PUSH, 2120
Push Doctor, 2665
Push Wellness, 1618
Push.io, 59
Pusher, 2469, 3021
Pushlife, 2176
Puttman Infrastructure, 531
PVI Industries, 1210
PVPower, 1618
PVR Partners, 1577
PVRI, 54
Pwnie Express, 1, 713
PWRF, 1244
PXP, 1848
PXP Group, 2301
Py, 623
Pya, 1412
Pyatt, 348
Pyatt/Broadmark Management, 1065
Pye-Barker Fire & Safety, 2030
Pygg, 1713
Pymetrics, 1073, 1610
Pyramid Healthcare, 505, 1343
Pyramid Investors LLC, 159
Pyramid Management Advisors, 159
Pyramid Research, 868
Pyramid Technologies Inc., 906
Pyrotek Special Effects, 2078
Pythagoras, 2717, 2891
Pytheas, 3064
Python, 984
Pyxis, 1762
Pyxis - Helpmate Robotics, 1107
Pyxis Technology, 766

Q

Q, 944
Q Bio, 125, 1073
Q Chip, 2728
Q Group, 1636
Q Holding, 2303
Q Holding Company, 989
Q Link Technologies, 609
Q Networks, 1498
Q Therapeutics, 689, 1679
Q'Max Solutions, 2045
Q-Centrix, 1745
Q-CTRL, 1672
Q-GO, 3042
Q-go.com B.V., 163
Q-layer, 2828
Q-Sense AB, 2709
Q-Sensei, 1928, 2518
Q-Sera, 2950
Q1 Labs, 1704
Q2 Publishing Inc., 449
Q2ebanking, 56
Q4, 912, 2074, 2103, 2112, 2146, 2216
Q9 Networks, 1160
Qadium, 108, 1006
Qapa, 2288
Qapa.fr, 1418
Qapital, 2398
Qarnot Computing, 3199
QASymphony, 274, 1005
Qazzow, 2007
QBotix, 731
QC Supply, 458
QC Supply LLC, 159
QCI Marine Offshore, 377

1375

Portfolio Companies Index

QCL Holdings, 1587
QD Laser, 1241
QD Vision, 983, 1335
QDrinks, 1101
QED, 1228
Qeep, 3229
Qeexo, 1672
QF Holdings, 159
QGenda, 782
QHR Technologies, 2225
Qiandai.com, 3199
Qiave Technologies, 523
Qihoo, 1184
Qihoo 360, 1537
Qik, 89
Qinous, 2832
Qinyang Power Plants, 2582
Qinyuan, 3185
QK Holdings, 1639
QLess, 49
Qliance, 265, 1290, 1644
Qlight Nanotech, 3235
QLL, 3029
Qmatic, 2376
QMax, 1404
Qmax Solutions, 2045
QMC Media, 62
Qminder, 3099
Qnary, 1907
Qnovo, 534, 1583
Qognify, 238
QOL Medical, 227
QoL Meds, 1278
QOOP, 508
Qopius, 2288
Qordoba, 182, 309
QOSMOS, 2665
Qosmos, 2377, 2653
Qover, 2398
Qpass, 827, 1008, 1640, 2073
QPID, 1421
QPID Health, 1184, 1297
QPS Pharmaceutical Services LLC, 733
QQ, 2841
QR Pharma, 269
Qr8 Health, 891
QRA, 2148
Qriously, 937, 1718, 2379
Qronus Interactive Ltd., 2945
Qrunch, 2637
QRxPharma, 2868
QSC AG, 226
Qsent, 1947
QSI Restaurant Partners, 223
QSIL, 2518
Qspeed Semiconductor, 55, 1781
QSpex Technologies, 1725
QSr, 186
QStar, 673
QStream, 1104
Qstream, 704, 2750
Qstrios, 2095
QTC Medical Services, 1720
Qteros, 1146
QTS, 819
QTVascular, 2681
Quad Learning, 1290, 1768
Quad/Graphics, 2067
Quadel Consulting Corporation, 920
QuaDPharma, 1526
QuadraMed, 782, 1395, 1868
Quadranet, 1929
Quadrant, 2913
Quadrant Software, 1176
QuadraSpec, 652
Quadratic 3D, 1672
Quadric, 1426

Quadriga Capital III, 2088
Quadrimex, 2842
Quadstone, 2378
Quaker Capital Investments, 3264
Quaker Fabric, 1145
Quala, 61
Qualaroo, 1371, 1464, 1862
Qualas Power Services, 1174
QUALCOM, 1924
Qualcomm, 388
QualDerm Partners, 559
Quali, 604
Qualia, 59, 680, 724, 1203, 1488, 1527, 2107
QualiSystems, 2717
Qualitor, 1972
Quality Aluminium Products, 279
Quality Alumnum Products, 1609
Quality Care Solutions, 861
Quality Coach Inc., 836
Quality Distribution, 136
Quality Farm & Country, 722
Quality Green, 206
Quality HVAC, 2263
Quality Metric, 958
Quality Powder Coating, 815
Quality Senior Living Partners, 1148
Quality Uptime Services, 1641
Quality Valve, 1438
Quality Wood Products, 60
QualityHealth, 957
Quallaby, 1335
Qualson, 3118
Qualtera, 3011
Qualtre, 646
Qualtrics, 1005
Qualtré, 1184
QualVu, 933
Qualys, 22, 1852, 1890
Quancheng, 149
Quandl, 2141
Quandoo, 3031
Quanergy, 1310
Quanhtum Bridge Communications, 317
Quansa, 1426
Quanta, 152, 2466, 3104
Quanta Display, 2594
Quanta Fluid Solutions, 2909
Quanta Storage, 2594
Quanta Therapeutics, 1934
QuantaLife, 1942
Quantalife, 1401
Quantance, 388, 621, 857, 1014, 1784
Quantapore, 802
Quantcast, 485, 778, 1464
Quantec, 2191
Quantem, 1730
Quantemplate, 2398
Quantenna, 116, 646, 1918, 2788, 3143, 3160
Quantenna Communcations, 1407
Quantenna Communications, 582, 1674, 1713, 2531
Quanterix, 154, 224, 748, 983
QuantHub, 754
Quantic Industries, 377
Quantic Mind, 1605
Quanticel, 1930
QuanticMind, 456, 773
QuantiFind, 108, 1537
Quantifind, 520
Quantion, 1065
Quantiva, 609
Quantopian, 1073, 1718, 2398
QuantPower, 40
Quantros, 178, 782
Quantum, 200, 217
Quantum Benchmark, 2270
Quantum Compliance, 2958

Quantum Diamon Technologies, 875
Quantum Energy Partners, 884
Quantum Health, 38, 97, 862
Quantum Machines, 238
Quantum Medical Imaging, 858
Quantum Metric, 1005
Quantum Ops, 1452
Quantum Pharmaceuticals, 2935
Quantum Secure, 636
Quantum Spatial, 167
Quantum Workplace, 1276
Quantum14, 1793
Quantum4D, 983
QuantumBio, 1120
QuantumClean, 1730
QuantumScape, 1073, 1079
Quantumsphere, 1917
Quanzhou Jinhua Edible Oil Co., 2718
Quark Games, 1242, 1543
Quark VR, 310
Quarri, 447
Quarrio, 221
Quarrion, 1000
Quarry Technologies, 317
Quarterly, 1719, 1862, 1914
Quartet Health, 711
Quartus Capital Partners, 2651
Quartzy, 1073, 1114
Quasar, 1903
Quasar Ventures, 666
Quatermove, 2457
Quatic Informatics, 2074
Quatris Healthco, 1641
QuatRx, 1014, 1918
Quatrx, 785
QuatRx Pharmaceuticals, 1063, 1830
Qubell, 252, 1525
Qubera Solutions, 68
Qubit, 1610, 2469
Qubole, 457, 1006, 1346
Qucit, 1896
Quellan, 972, 1924
Quelleenergie.fr, 2377
Quellos, 1186
Quench, 2178
Quench USA, 658, 832, 3213
Quench USA Inc., 62
Quentis, 1930
Queralt, 679
Queremos/WeDemand, 3148
Querium, 447, 3246
Queromedia, 2417
QueryObject Systems, 957
Quest, 170, 745, 782
Quest Events LLC, 847
QuEST Global Services, 61
Quest Specialty Chemicals, 197
Quest.ii, 2432
Questar Assesment, 1298
QuestBack, 3067
Questco, 2206
Questcor Pharma, 1251
Questex, 1231, 1663
Questis, 849
Questrade, 2051
Queueco, 3099
Quiave, 1045
Quic, 1045
Quick Attach Attachments, 1343
Quick Base, 1973
Quick Med Claims, 747
Quick Sensor, 2417
Quick Study Radiology, 1917
QuickAirLink, 1959
Quickarrow, 35, 1949
QuickBRCare, 1509
Quickcue, 461

Portfolio Companies Index

QuickGifts, 1813
Quickhit, 2188
Quickie Manufacturing Corp, 449
QuickLogic, 1257
Quickly, 608
Quickmobile, 2262
Quickoffice, 1667
QuickPay, 58, 762
QuickPlay Media, 1160
QuickSilver Technology, 1674
Quicksilver Technology, 693
Quickturn Design, 1091
Quid, 177, 2228, 2437, 2861
Quidbit, 2187
Quidnet Energy, 498, 2105
Quidsi, 1449
Quiet.ly, 625
Quietly, 309
Quigley's, 1139
Quigo, 724
Quigo Technologies, 1006
Quikly, 1154
Quikr, 1327, 1346, 1374
Quilt, 680, 773, 1499
Quin Street, 1728
Quincy, 591, 1101
Quinnova Pharmaceuticals, 1820
Quinsis, 2940
QuinStreet, 759, 827, 1762
Quinstreet, 1949
Quint, 2083
Quinta da Marinha Leisure, 3039
Quintana Shipping, 1577
Quintessence Biosciences, 2002
Quintic, 1781
Quintiles, 73, 223, 1837
Quintiles Transnational, 2303
Quintiq, 1140
QuintoAndar, 1511
Quintus Technologies, 1234
Quinyx, 238
Quip, 44, 1616, 1918
Quipper, 2437
Quippi International Gift Card Center, 209
Quiq, 1317
Quirch, 1404
Quire, 999
Quirky, 37, 789, 1527, 1597
Quiron Hospital Group, 2953
Quithelp, 623
QuitNet, 317
Quitt.ch, 2302
Quixey, 827, 1840, 1969, 2434
Quizlet, 100, 548, 1393, 1884
Quizno's, 1552
QuizUp, 1223
Qulture.Rocks, 798
QUMAS, 2073, 2328, 2725
Qumas, 2909
Qumranet, 1449
Qumu, 58, 810, 1750, 2188, 3268
Qumulo, 586, 938, 1079, 1162, 1901
Qunar, 827, 1685, 1798
Qunar.com, 1187
Qunomedical, 1269
Quntiles, 2292
Quobyte, 3152
Quora, 514, 1184, 1335
Quorum, 1831
Quorum Business Solutions, 1577, 1685
Quorum Health Group, 1973
Quorum Systems, 556, 1449
Quotatis, 2472
Quote.com, 1772
Quotient Biodiagnostics Holdings, 809
Quotient Diagnostics, 2751
Quottly, 149

Quovo, 1610, 2217
Qurasense, 2272
Qurasense Relativity Space, 1616
Quri, 430, 1070, 1184
QuVis, 1639
Qv21 Technologies, 507
Qvella, 918
QVentus, 721
Qventus, 1187, 1346
Qvidian, 523, 1084, 1335
Qvivo, 3112
Qwick, 79
QwikCart, 1462
Qwikcilver, 2809
Qwiki, 535, 1121, 1658
Qwil, 398, 895, 1531
Qwilr, 3144
Qwilt, 485, 1537
QWS Holdings LLC, 62
QxMD, 2257
Qynergy, 983
Qype, 2466, 2595
Qyuki, 485
QZZR, 1596
qZZR, 1074

R

R & V, 3053
R Studio, 820
R Taco, 1580
R&B Technology Holding Corporation, 3053
R&D Circuits, 1424
R&H Supply, 1424
R&R Ice Cream, 3011, 3017
R-2solid to Warburg Pincus, 1920
R-Square, 3118
R-Tech Ueno, 2961
R.E.D.D., 1165
R.G.E. Group Ltd., 33
R.H. Electronics, 2736
R.M. Williams, 1092
R.Rouvari Oy, 2864
R/c Sugarkane, 1577
R2 Acquisition Corp., 159
R2 Semiconductor, 1257, 1674
R2 Technology, 154
R24 Lumber, 1691
R2G, 2575
R2I, 225
R2Net, 782, 1323
R2P, 2842
R3 Communications, 2832
R3 Education, 1473
RA Capital, 69, 3263
RA EL, 2006
Ra Pharma, 1126
Ra pharma, 113
Rabbit, 125
Rabbit Farm, 3113
Rabbit Tractors, 999
RABBL, 1065
Raben Tire, 1404
RAC, 3011
Raccortubi Group, 3145
Racemi, 51, 1401
Racemi Inc., 907
Rachio, 380, 1237, 1896
Racing-Live, 3199
Rack Attack, 2045
RackSpace, 2243
Racktop, 1172
RackWare, 1388
Rackware, 1074
Racotek, 538
RacoWireless, 1018
Ractiv, 3064
Ractivity, 2828

Rad Locks, 1294
RAD Technologies, 1402
Radar Networks, 801
Radar Relay, 1531
Radara, 2986
RADCOM, 3128
Radcom, 3221
Raden, 1589
Radia, 849
Radiac Abrasives, 1460, 1979
Radial, 221
Radial Engineering, 2227
Radial3D, 1509
RadialPoint, 1543
Radialpoint, 1778
Radian Capital, 36
Radiance Technologies, 468
Radians Innova, 2869
Radianse, 178
Radiant Logistics, 377
Radiant Medical, 240
Radiant Range, 2614
Radiant Research, 377
Radiant RFID, 221
Radiant Systems, 3266
Radiate Media, 876, 1074, 1679
Radiation Therapy Services, 1933
Radiator Labs, 623, 1896
Radiaus Innova AB, 2709
Radical Plastics, 849
Radicle, 2233
Radient 360, 2063
Radient Technologies, 2043
radient360, 2161
Radio Therapeutics Corporation, 526
Radio Time, 2448
RadioFrame Networks, 645
Radiology Partners, 1296
Radionetics, 11
RadioPharmacy Investors, 1192
RadioPulse, 3118
RadioRx, 1014
Radiotel, 3239
Radiotel Ltd., 2741
Radiowalla, 3010
Radisens Diagnostics, 2909
Radish, 1153, 1885
Radisphere, 949
Radisphere National Radiology Group, 1361
Radisys, 1608
Radium One, 2653
RadiumOne, 1855
Radiumone, 564
Radius, 108, 299, 354, 778, 840, 922, 1268, 1672
Radius Aerospace Inc., 159
Radius Global Growth Experts, 225
Radius Health, 2487
Radius Intelligence, 1430
Radius Networks, 540
Radius8, 151
Radlan Computer Communications, 200
Radlan Ltd., 2741
Radley, 3027
Radnet Ltd, 2761
RadPad, 1966
Radpad, 601
Radview, 1335
Radview Software Ltd., 2741
RADVision, 3149
Radware, 2576
Radwin, 2711
RAE Systems, 1912
Raet, 2370
Rafay Systems, 752
Rafferty's Garden, 2391
Rafter, 759, 1122, 1750
Raftr, 1099, 1393

Portfolio Companies Index

Rag & Bone, 1026
RagingMobile, 1335
Rags, 1074
RAIDCore, 1150
Raidtec Corporation, 2328
Railcomm, 1630
Railroad Controls Limited, 919
RailWorks, 1990
Rain Neuromorphics, 798
Rain Systems, 1509
Rainbow Child Care Centre, 1727
Rainbow Early Education, 1507
RainDance, 1247, 1247
Raindance, 2602
RainDance Technologies, 87, 1510
Rainforest, 309, 650, 1254
Rainforst QA, 564
RainKing, 1720
Rainmaker, 1346
Rainmaker Systems, 1354
RainStar, 2662
RainStor, 1750
Rainvow, 310
Raisbeck, 47
Raisbeck Engineering, 988
RaiseMe, 742, 888, 1393, 1537, 1610
Raisio Yhtymä Oyj, 2981
Raj Manufacturing, 1769
Rajant, 236
Raken, 309, 680
Raketu, 1313
Raleigh, 858
Raley's, 1971
Ralfi/Estima Finance, 2462
Ralink Technology, 897, 1771
Rally, 1247, 1841, 2132, 2161
Rally Point, 183
Rally Rd., 2228, 2398
Rally Software, 318, 540, 1213, 1245
Rallybio, 11
RallyOn, 1658
RallyPoint, 596
Ralph, 310
RAM Medical Innovations, 229
Ramaco Resources, 676
Ramada Plaza, 2277
Ramanas Farms, 838
Rambus, 1247
Ramco Oil Services, 2935
Rameder, 1576
Ramet Trom, 136
Ramky Infrastructure, 3164
RAMMP Hospitality, 2284
RAMP, 523, 925, 1741
Ramp, 520, 713, 2681
Ramp Networks, 759
Ramper, 2131
Ramsey Industries, 878, 1345
Ramsway (JSC), 627
RaNA, 1421
Rancard Solutions, 2337
Rancher, 1187
Rand Logistics, 110
Randall & Reilly, 2196
Randall-Reilly, 202, 1021, 1410
Randian, 1509
Randori, 1
Randy's Worldwide Automotive, 1136
RANDYS Worldwide Automotive, 1779
Range Fuels, 1398
Range Me, 787
Range Networks, 860, 1374
Range Resources Ltd., 638
Rangeland Energy III, 672
Ranger Aerospace, 165
Ranger AirShop, 165
Ranger International Services Group, 740

Ranger Marketing, 3222
Ranger Wireless Solutions, 1625
Rangespan, 3009
Rangusutra, 2305
Rani Therapeutics, 984
Ranir, 386, 1132
Rank, 2265
Ranked Media & Technologies, 1509
Ranker, 309, 361, 586, 1103, 1153, 1569, 1800, 1966
RankMyApp, 1370
RankScience, 321
Ranpak, 1368
Ranpak Corp., 170
Rantizo, 999
Rapchat, 232
RaPharma, 1522
Rapid Diagnostek, 403, 1291
Rapid Financial Services, 1971
Rapid Micro Biosystems, 1147, 2681, 3187
Rapid Miner, 1150
Rapid Ratings, 1140
Rapid RMS, 461
Rapid7, 224, 1787
RapidAir, 1438
RapidAPI, 125
RapidBuyr, 1196
RapidCare Clinic, 1670
RapidDeploy, 1614
RapidMicro Biosystems, 1510
Rapidminer, 180
RapidScan, 2969
Rapidscan, 183
RapidSOS, 490, 623, 770, 1260
Rapidsos, 938, 1158
Rapidstream, 3209
RapidStream Inc., 950
Rappi, 125, 752, 773, 945
Rapportive, 308
Rapsodia, 1092
Rapt Media, 845, 2009
Raptor Pharmaceuticals, 1777
Raptor Sports Properties, 1527
Raptor Supplies, 2825
Raptor Technologies LLC, 159
Raptr, 107, 582, 1798
Rare, 2070
Rare Bits, 742
Rare.io, 2187
RareCyte, 11, 1794
Raritan, 1316
Ras Therapeautics, 1120
Rasa, 235
RAScom, 3128
Rasilient Systems, 46
Rasiris, 1399
Rasko, 70
Rate Us, 3144
RathGibson, 1968
Ratio, 1743, 2131
Rautaruukki Oyj, 2981
Rav Galai, 3235
RAVE, 1675
Rave Mobile Safety, 224, 1597
Rave Wireless, 1674
Ravel, 709, 1335
Ravelli, 2383
Raven, 2070, 2178
Raven Biotechnologies, 1007
Raven Pack, 2665
Raven Power Holdings, 1577
Raven Window, 147
Raven360, 1175
Ravenflow, 1408
Ravisent Technologies, 51
Ravn Alaska, 1949
Ravti, 944, 1281

Raw Essentials, 1446
Rawstream, 3099
Rax Restaurants Inc., 357
Ray Sat, 421
Ray Sono AG, 2774
Raybern's, 1863
Raydiance, 186, 610
Raydiant Oximetry, 229
Rayfay, 548
Raymond Express International, 931
Raymundos, 196
Rayne, 1324, 1442
Rayne Water, 1583
Rayner Foods, 2914
Raysat, 2463
Raytel Medical, 958
RayV, 3231
Rayv, 527
RayVio, 198, 597
Raza MicroElectronics, 1084
Raze, 1885
Raze Therapeutics, 1268
Raze Therapeutics Inc., 184
RazorGator, 1361
Razorpay, 1142
RazorSight, 949
Razorsight, 2188
Razz, 810
RBC Bearings, 202, 1041
RBC Signals, 23, 222, 246, 521
RBN, 2534
RCG Global Services, 687
RCN, 912, 1720
RCN Grande, 1837
RCP Advisors, 3255
Rd Rabbit, 1058
Rd.Md, 1666
RDA, 977
RDA Microelectronics, 2841
RDD Pharma, 1383
Rdio, 2437
RDM Corporation, 2137
RDMD, 1155
RDR, 2883
RDX, 336, 1160
Re Commmunity Recycling, 912
Re Holdings, 1300
Re-Leash, 3248
Re.mu, 3172
RE2, 629
Rea Metrix, 2481
Reaads, 1839
Reach, 1985
Reach Air Medical, 929
REACH Health, 551
Reach Influence, 608
Reach Labs, 623
Reach Robotics, 1511
Reach Surgical, 2927
Reach150, 1645, 1831
Reachable, 2374
Reachdesk, 746
ReachForce, 1242
ReachHealth, 274, 1412
Reachli, 2016
ReachLocal, 1908
ReachOut Healthcare America, 1256
ReactEvent, 2276
Reaction, 1074
Reaction Biology, 4, 1102
Reaction Commerce, 309, 562
Reactivity, 614, 1042
Reactor Labs, 1992
READ, 3207
Read ASA, 2745
READ Cased Hole, 2691
Readeo, 1618

Portfolio Companies Index

Reading Bridges, 2347
Reading Room, 3009
Reading Truck Body, 1034, 1140
ReadMe, 711, 863
Readmill, 2435
Ready Mixed Concrete, 197
Ready Pac Produce, 931
Ready Responders, 490
Ready Robotics, 680
Ready Set Food, 121
Ready Set Surgical, 481
ReadyCart, 461
Readyforzero, 1464
ReadyPulse, 1525
Real Eyes, 2701
Real Foundations, 1946
Real Gravity, 1087
Real Image, 485
Real Imaging, 3041
Real Mex Restaurants Inc., 357
Real Musical, 2882
Real People Investment Holdings, 2080
REAL SAMURAI, 2965
Real Savvy, 546
Real Time Content, 1304
Real Ventures, 50
Real Vision, 344
Real-Time Collaboration Solutions By PlaceWare, 1629
Real-Time Radiography, 3235
Real-time Radiography Ltd, 2964
Real5D, 626
Realbest, 2832
Realcom, 2845
REALD, 554
RealDirect, 1479, 1851
Realflair, 2565
Realine, 208
Realities.io, 310
Reality Female Condom, 1839
Reality Mobile, 468, 2691
Realm, 1073, 1114, 1629
Realm Therapeutics, 1271
RealManage, 313, 1946
RealMatch, 2557
Realmatch, 655
RealNetworks, 1912
Realogy, 141
RealOps, 1408, 1901
RealPractice, 1237
Realsavvy, 2262
RealScout, 597
RealSelf, 1644
Realstar Management, 2073
Realtime, 2536
Realtime Robotics, 1836
Realton Corporation, 1383
RealtyShares, 561, 1884
RealWinWin, 1691
Realworld.co, 2637
realync, 1159
REalyse, 2398
Realytics, 2494
ReaMetrix, 1245
REAN Cloud, 364
Reapit, 28
Reapplix, 3194
Rearden Commerce, 1235
Reata Pharmaceuticals, 3006
Rebag, 527, 564, 820
Rebar, 1287
Rebecca Taylor, 1755
Rebel Coast Winery, 310
Rebel Mail, 308
Rebel Mouse, 1114, 1361
Rebellion, 1001
Rebelmail, 601

RebelMouse, 742, 1701
Rebit, 35, 881
Reblink, 2131
Rebllion Energy, 1326, 1328
Reborn Beauty, 1955
Rebtel, 2469
Rebus, 1509
Rebuy, 2970
ReBuy.de, 2804
ReceiptBank, 1005
Receivable Solutions, 1979
Receivables Exchange, 711, 1741
Receivables Management Partners, 1343
ReCept Pharmacy, 822
Receptiv, 655, 949
Receptos, 154, 748, 1128, 1464, 1918
Recharge, 680, 708, 752
Recisio, 2357
Reckitt Benckiser, 1456
Recko, 1142
ReckOne Inc., 624
Recochem, 1769, 2177
Recode Therapeutics, 1934
Recogni, 1836
Recognia, 1305
Recoletos, 2953
Recombine, 744
Recommerce Solutions, 2300, 3104
Recommind, 1623
RECON Holdings III, 1133
Recon Instruments, 2270
Reconda International, 1146
Recondo, 949
Recondo Technology, 336, 1111
Reconnex, 200
ReconRobotics, 1874
Recora, 1426
Record 360, 92
Recordati S.p.A., 1456
Recorded Books, 1961
Recorded Future, 37, 969, 983, 1005, 2469
RecordSetter, 1153, 1914
Recount Media, 1884
Recoup Fitness, 1509
Recourse Technologies, 597
Recover Energy Services, 2044
RecoverX, 863, 1589
Recovery Technology Solutions, 1897
RecoveryDirect Acquisition, 159
Recros Medica, 1149
RecruiterNet, 440
RecruitingTrends, 868
RecruitTalk, 461
Recupyl, 2364
Recurly, 641, 711, 787, 1464
Recuro Health, 6
Recurrent Energy, 1247
Recursion, 447
Recursion Pharma, 108
Recursion Pharmaceuticals, 1155, 1203, 1363
Recursion Pharmeceuticals, 720
Recurve, 1583
RecycleBank, 1674
Recyclebank, 186, 1442, 1597, 1675, 1978
Recycleye, 195
Red 7 Media, 1929
Red Ambiental, 838
Red Aril, 980, 1855
Red Bag Solutions, 797
Red Balloon Security, 1483
Red Bend Software, 538, 2557
Red Brick Systems, 241
Red Bridge Capital, 464
Red Bubble, 1323
Red Built, 1344
Red Canary, 35
Red Dog Deli Raw Food Company, 2115

Red Door Spa, 1336
Red Foundry, 1364
Red Hawk Fire & Security, 530
Red Herring, 1867
Red IQ, 380
Red Kite, 2665
Red Mango, 479
Red Oak Power, 676
Red Paper Group, 2411
Red Rabbit, 1422
Red River Waste, 1424
Red River Waste Solutions, 1025
Red Robin Gourmet Burgers, 1507
Red Rock Biofuels, 748
Red Sift, 1982
Red Storm Entertainment, 1711
Red Swoosh, 564
Red Technology Alliance, 1577
Red Tricycle, 708, 1186, 1854
Red Vector, 1748
Red Ventures, 819, 1504, 1685
Red Vision, 655
Red Wolf Security, 2178
Red-C, 438, 2571
Red-M, 2378
Redback Networks, 1996
Redbeacon, 1918
Redbend, 3212
RedBird Capital Partners, 69
Redbooth, 101, 209
RedBrick Health, 941
Redbrick Health, 938
Redbubble, 606
RedBus, 3100
Redbus.in, 1017
RedCap, 1702
Redcap, 708
Redd, 789
Redd & Whyte, 2751
Reddit, 514, 1823, 2011
reddit, 995
Reddo Mobility, 37
RedDot, 2607
ReddPath Integrated Pathology, 1452
Reddy Ice Inc., 159
Redeam, 1039
Redecam Group, 3145
Redecam Group SpA, 2812
RedEenvelope, 194
REDEF, 59
ReDeTec, 2178
Redfern Integrated Optics, 1781
Redfield Proctor, 395
Redfin, 610, 839, 840, 1948
Redfish Rentals, 931
Redgate Media, 1771
RedHelper, 2929
Redhill Biopharma, 1383
RedHook Ale Brewery, 755
Redica Systems, 2074
Redington Gulf, 1021
Redis Labs, 3212
Redislabs, 604
Redkite Financial Markets, 2653
Redknee, 2188
Redlen Technologies, 2205, 2283
Redline Communications, 885
Redline Networks, 58, 457
Redline Trading Solutions, 568
Redmart, 3118
Redock, 2204
reDock, 2024
Redowl, 537
RedOwl Analytics, 84, 1635
Redox, 1, 756
RedPack Logistics, 1003
RedPath, 994

1379

Portfolio Companies Index

RedPath Integrated Pathology, 296, 1003
RedPoint, 881
Redpoint Bio, 1329
Redpoint eventures, 485
Redpoint Ventures, 990, 3273
RedPost, 659
RedPrairie, 782
RedRover, 2016
RedSeal, 972, 1106, 1181, 1392, 1918
RedSeal Systems, 983
RedSky Technologies, 636
Redstone Communications, 1335
Redtail Solutions, 1922
Redtree People, 3001
Reduct.Video, 1426
Reduxio, 3212
RedVision Systems, 1888
Redwave Medical, 2518
Redwood Systems, 1241
Redwood Trust Inc., 1905
RedZone, 1165
RedZone Robotics, 1200, 1234
Redzone Robotics, 21
RedZone Roboticss, 1003
RedZone Wireless, 440
Reebok Spartan Race, 1527
Reebonz, 827
Reed City Tool, 165
Reed Group, 197
Reed Smith, 3264
Reedsy, 3099
Reef, 170, 2535, 2535
ReefEdge, 645
Reel Genie, 1172
Reel Power International, 633
Reelcraft Industries, 911
Reelgood, 545
Reelio, 641
Reelwell, 1129
Reemo, 999
ReEnergy Holdings, 1577
Reeves Extruded Products, 1609
Reevoo, 2682, 2963
Refac Optical Group, 45
Refer.com, 976
Referral Saasquatch, 2276
Refinery 29, 1114
Refinery29, 742, 752, 1751
Reflect, 776
Reflectent, 1915
Reflectent Software, 1674
Reflectivity, 1706, 1924
Reflektion, 238
Reflektive, 125
Reflex Photonics, 2188
Reflexion, 1918
Reflexion Network Solutions, 313
Reflexis, 862, 1606
Reformation, 763
Reframe It, 1604, 1671
Refresco, 2196
Refresco Gerber, 2303
Refresh, 457, 1537
Refresh Body, 1703
Refresj, 773
Refrigerated Holdings, 722
REG, 173
Regado, 1510
Regado Biosciences, 1900
Regal, 3194
Regalii, 721, 1058, 1998
Regard, 2956
ReGear, 1749
ReGear Life Sciences, 1003, 1452
ReGelTec, 18
ReGen Biologics, 1619
REGEN Energy, 1324

Regency, 1848
Regency Beauty Institute, 1473
Regency Energy Partners LP, 917
Regency Entertainment, 3011
Regency Gas Services, 458
Regency Hospital Company, 1964
Regency Midwest, 300
Regenemed, 1604
Regeneron Pharmaceuticals, 1619
Regenesis Biomedical, 797, 1704, 1903
Regent, 1298, 1991
Regent Cabinetry, 920
Regent Education, 408, 477, 510
Regent Education Inc., 159
Regent Holding, 786
Regentis Biomaterials, 3050
ReGenX Biosciences, 711
REGENXBIO, 1943
RegenXBio, 1918
RegenxBio, 764
Regesis Biomedical, 1804
Regimend MD, 1194
Regional Growth Capital, 3261
Regional Management Corp., 1404
Regional Rail, 1115
Register.com, 1901, 1912
Registrar Corp., 260
Regroup, 1164
regroup, 1159
Regulatory and Quality Solutions, 611
Regulatory Datacorp, 224
Regulus, 1672
Rehive, 310
REI, 681
Reichert, 1753
Reify, 183
ReigoHelden, 2970
Reille24, 2466
Reilly's Hempvet, 789
Reima, 1576
Reimagine Holdings Group, 364
Reinnervate, 3019
Reischling Press, 961
Reisefeber, 3004
Rekoo, 641, 2860, 2993
Rekoo Japan, 2860
Reladyne Inc., 63
RelateIQ, 1537
Relatient, 2074
Relationship Science, 925, 1610
Relativity, 400, 1698
Relativity Space, 1330
Relay, 1316, 1450, 2122
Relay Foods, 1832, 3246
Relay Network, 742
Relay Therapeutics, 710
Relay Ventures, 2028, 2165
Relay2, 627
RelayFoods.com, 238
RelayOne, 512, 1412
RelayRides, 708, 762, 1534, 1969
Relayrides, 200
Relegence, 957
Relevad, 775
Relevant Rental Solutions, 406
Relevant Solutions, 784
Relevate, 352
Relevium Technologies, 2027
Relevvant, 1841
Reliable Biopharmaceutical Corporation, 832
Reliable Parts, 1767
Reliable Robotics, 648, 1423
Reliance Electric, 357
Reliant Healthcare Professionals, 494
Reliant Home Health, 1210
Reliant Hospital Partners, 1278
Reliant Medical Products, 1536

Reliant Pharmaceuticals, 1949
Reliant Pharmaceuticals Inc., 240
Reliant Rehabilitation, 639
Reliant Renal Care, 639, 723
Reliant Technologies, 1449
Reliaquest, 796
Relias Learning, 1140
Relievant, 389, 1379
Relievant MedSystems, 244
Relievant Medsystems, 667, 1126
ReliOn, 1398
Relion, 2072
Reliving, 2276
Relmada RiboNova, 269
Relogix, 2187
Relovv, 345
Reltio, 1, 564
Relume, 743
Relypsa, 11, 1198, 1297, 1383
Relypsa Inc., 605
ReMark, 2370
Remarkable, 1985
Rembrandt Photo Services, 449
Rembrandt Venture Partners, 990, 3273
Remcan, 2284
Remco Maintenance Corp., 467
Remedi Seniorcare, 1745
Remedly, 718
Remedy, 93, 350
Remedy Health, 1464
Remedy Health Media, 1929
Remedy Informatics, 770, 1206
Remedy Interactive, 549
Remedy Partners, 1731
Remedy Pharmaceuticals, 663
Remedy Systems, 1832
Remerge, 2832, 3226
Remesh, 820
Remi, 1276
Remicade, 2097
Remind, 742, 888, 1079, 1393, 1698
Remita Health, 1631, 1764
RemitDATA, 1332, 1735
RemitDATA Inc., 813
Remitly, 265, 686, 776, 1504, 1791, 1832, 1854
Remitr, 2094
Remity, 610
Remix Labs, 1317
Remma Consulting, 2517
Remon Medical Technologies, 1849
Remora Petroleum, 1326
Remote Analysis, 2864
Remote Co., 2965
Remote Year, 756, 938
Remote.it, 309, 527
RemoteLock, 2074
Remotely, 1118
RemoteMDx, 508
RemoteReality, 236, 459
Remotive, 1791
RemoTV, 1678
REMP AG, 2555
Rempex Pharmaceuticals, 785
Remtec Inc., 1057
Renaissance, 579, 782, 927
Renaissance BV, 2713
Renaissance Lighting, 1324, 1583
Renaissance Mark, 172, 1955
Renaissance Pharma, 1594
Renaissance Venture Capital Fund, 3259
Renal Advantage, 1973
Renal Care Group, 303
Renal Care Partners, 1251
Renal Solutions, 118, 1452, 1849
RenalSolutions, 186
RenaMed Biologics, 1337
Rend, 2148

Portfolio Companies Index

Renegade Brands, 96
Reneo, 1522
ReNet Japan Group, 2965
Renew, 1162, 1918
Renew Financial, 127, 325, 2001
Renew Inserts, 1147
Renew Power, 838
Renewable Energy Group, 1897
Renewable Energy Products, 1401
Renewable Funding, 493, 1324
RenewLife, 1873
Renex Holdings, 2604
Renfro, 1066
Reniac, 361, 1486, 1892
Renix, 2054
Renkoo, 624
Renle, 3185
Renmatix, 949
Rennhack Marketing Services, 331, 931
Rennovia, 11
RenoNorden, 2317
RenoRun, 1363, 2150
Renovar, 1291
Renovate America, 1583, 1904
Renovia, 1149
Renovis, 748, 2504, 2509, 2681
Renovis Inc., 2807
Renoviso, 945
Renovo, 1928, 2509
RenovoRx, 130, 845
Renoworks Software Inc., 2061
Renren, 597, 1244, 2927
RenRench.com, 1537
RenRui, 2927
Rensa Filtration, 654
Rent The Runway, 224, 938, 1079
Rent the Runway, 44, 1787
Rentabilities, 1154
Rentalutions, 570
Rentbits, 1118
RentBureau, 860
Rented, 1028
Renthop, 1876
Rentify, 2469
RentJuice, 1101
Rentlytics, 309, 564, 568, 945, 1569
Rentmatix, 1079
Rentokil Initial Plc., 1905
RentPath, 1498
Rentpath Inc., 1837
RentPayment, 758
RentStuff, 461
ReNu Power, 157
Reonomy, 1479, 1549, 1701, 2126
ReovoRX, 1604
REP, 2542, 2598
Rep, 763
Rep The Squad, 863
Repable, 2094, 2123, 2192
Repair Pal, 322
Repairogen, 1055, 1422
RepairPal, 1867, 1959
Repare, 1268, 1930
Repco, 2942
Repco Group, 2411
RepconStrickland, 157
Repeater Technology, 759
RepEquity, 60, 679
Repetto International, 2294
Replaid, 3029
Replay Solutions, 1674
Replenish, 863
Replica, 1001
Replica Labs, 3116
Replicated, 308
Replicon, 666, 1698
Replika, 44, 1073

Replimune, 193, 764
Replit, 1530
Reply, 1390
Reply.com, 186, 1235
ReportGrid, 1101
Reportive, 3223
Reposit, 3099
Repositive, 3099
Reposito, 2912
Repost, 121
ReproCELL, 2961
Reprogenesis, 1414
Repros Therapeutics, 1063
Repsly, 1104
Republic, 849
Republic Doors & Frames, 607
Republic Midstream, 157
Republic National Cabinet Corporation, 576
Republic Project, 1223
Republic.co, 1396
Repulic Insurance, 331
rePurpose, 1426
Reputation Institute, 429
Reputation.Com, 200, 752
Reputation.com, 178, 759, 972, 1079, 1702
ReputationLoop, 92
Reputology, 92
ReqMed Company, 2961
ReQuest, 1479
Request Broadband, 3159
Request Now, 1593
Requisite Technology, 1235
Reroyal Holdings LP, 357
RES Software, 1888
RESC, 309
Rescale, 265, 586, 724, 1158, 2321
Rescare, 1560
ReSci, 763, 1247
ReScie, 1890
Resco Products Inc., 836, 1972
Rescue Forensics, 999
RescueTime, 1153
RescueTimy, 1862
Research Enhanced Design + Development Inc., 440
Research Horizons, 2021
Research Now Group Inc., 406
ResearchGate, 14, 251, 778, 780, 846, 1798
Reserve, 59
Reset Therapeutics, 240
ReShape, 1631, 1764
ReShape Medical, 1923
Reshape Medical, 1297
Residence Inn by Marriott, 192
Resident, 12
Residential Design Services, 961
Residential Mortgage Services, 687
Residential Services Group Inc., 1972
Resilient, 713
Resilient Systems, 646
Resilinc, 1017, 1610, 1666, 1759
Resilio, 2262
ResLab Holding, 2745
Reslink, 2745
Resman AS, 3132
Resolute, 2646
Resolute AI, 1558
Resolute Games, 999
Resolute Networks, 2773
Resolution Health, 1852
ReSolutionTx, 2221
Resolve Systems, 1005
Resolve Therapeutics, 644, 1302, 2007
Resolver, 2163, 2665
Resolvyx, 748, 1421
Resolvyx Pharmaceuticals, 415
Resonado, 229, 431, 623

Resonance, 2500
Resonant, 1207
Resonant Medical, 2188
Resonant Venture Partners, 3259
Resonate, 162, 876
Resonate Networks, 2150
Resource Ammirati, 1979
Resource Label Group, 734
ReSource Pro, 611
Resourcekraft, 2909
Respect Network, 1065
Respectance B.V., 3119
Respicardia, 39, 67, 1464, 3268
Respicardia Inc., 159
Respira Therapeutics, 550
Respiratory Motion, 1065, 1164, 1987
RespirTech, 3268
Respond2 Communications Holdings, 1278
Respondly, 309, 1969
Response Analytics, 1430
Response Analytics Inc., 861
Response BioMedical, 1383
Response Linl, 952
Response Tap, 2682
Response Team 1, 842
ResponseTek Networks, 2188
Responsfabrikken, 3013
Responsys, 561, 840, 1028, 1122, 1674
ResQ, 2130, 2141
Resq, 2131
Resson Aerospace, 2063, 2192, 2231
Rest Devices, 709
Restalo, 2331, 3096
Restaurant Associates Corporation, 357
Restaurant Kritic, 2829
Restaurant Technologies, 202, 3268
Restaurant Technology, 381
Restaurant-Kritik.de, 2820
Restaurants Unlimited, 1755
Restopolitan, 2660
Restorando, 666, 756, 1750, 2437
Restoration + Recovery, 611
Restoration Parts Unlimited, 633
Restoration Robotics, 87, 1014
Restorative Therapies, 4
Restore, 2940
Restore Medical, 999
Restore Medical Solutions, 1190
Restorix Health, 1113
RestorixHealth, 559
Resultados Digitais, 641
Results Physiotherapy, 1745
REsurety, 498, 1101
Resverlogix, 1325
Resy, 1114
Resy Network, 1696
Retail Associated Mgt., 1294
Retail Decisions, 2371
Retail Me Not, 56, 1006
Retail Next, 2681
Retail Optimization, 661, 1146
Retail Shopping Systems, 421
Retail Solutions, 1623, 1915, 1918
Retailigence, 1236, 1515
RetailNet, 1741
RetailNext, 1327, 1511
Retailnext, 200
Retailo, 3104
Retea, 2879
ReTel Technologies, 686
Retention Science, 231, 625, 1059, 1247, 1483
Rethink, 150, 1554
Rethink Autism, 1554
ReThink Medical, 1347
Rethink Robotics, 265, 457, 938, 1675, 1876
RethinkDB, 115, 209, 938, 1969, 2321
Rethought Insurance, 2037

Portfolio Companies Index

Retica Systems, 1674
Retif, 2309, 2367
Retina AI, 520
Retirable, 2090
RetiSpec, 2141
Retrain AI, 1
ReTrans, 1779
Retrica, 100
Retriever Communications, 2966
Retroficiency, 1463
Retrofit, 473, 610, 732, 1483
Retronaut, 2577, 2676
Retrophin, 190
Retroscreen Virology, 2883
Retrosense, 1222
Retrotope, 1048
RetroVascular, 1775
Retty, 2637
Retty.com, 2789
Return on Intelligence, 1029
Return Path, 462, 548, 779, 780, 1245, 1623
ReturnCentral, 55, 993
ReturnLogic, 1581
Reunion, 1608
ReUrban, 3268
REV, 110
Rev, 839, 1374
Rev H20, 81
Rev Worldwide, 752
Reva, 838
REVA Medical, 622
Reva Systems, 1335
Reval, 523, 1335
Revance, 2504
Revance Therapeutics, 1667, 1788, 1943, 2681
Revascular Therapeutics, 56, 460, 1098
ReVascular Therapeutics Inc., 272
RevCascade, 345
Revcascade, 1566
Reveal, 352
Reveal Design Automation, 743
Reveal Energy Services, 1129
Reveal Media, 623
Reveal Mobile, 975
Reveal Technology Inc., 1093
Reveel, 456
Revel, 1836
Revel Body, 85
Revel Systems, 597, 795, 1973
Revelstoke Capital Partners, 3254
Revenew International, 1115
Revenue Cycle Solutions, 405
Revenue Science, 624, 1736
Revenue Technologies, 55
Revenue.Com, 1016
RevenueCat, 798
Rever, 305, 2018
Revera, 185, 564
Reverb, 234, 1121, 1247
ReverbNation, 1348, 1712
Revere, 234, 1114, 1280
Revere Packaging, 1487
Reverie Labs, 321, 2001
Reverie Language Technologies, 1511
Reverse Logistics GmbH, 1248
Reverse Medical, 667
Reverse Medical Corp., 272, 642
ReverseVision, 1871
ReversingLabs, 983
Revfluence, 130
Revibe Technologies, 512
Review Centre Limited, 2862
Review Pro, 2331
Review Trackers, 567
Reviews 42, 3202
Revinate, 1716
Revionics, 304, 696, 1604

Revip, 232
Revise, 3019
Revision, 1492
Revision App, 3099
ReVision Optics, 622
Revision Optics, 389, 1014
Revision Skincare, 1594
ReVision Therapeutics, 1777
Revisios, 2505
Revit Technology, 1335
Revitas, 1140
Revival, 546
Revive Personal Products, 165
ReviveMed, 849
Revivio, 457, 1122
Revivn, 1058, 1896
Revlo, 1330, 2107, 2240
Revmetrix, 1, 380, 818, 1320
RevoLights, 1671
Revolights, 198, 1604
ReVolt Technology, 3004
Revolut, 2469, 3099
Revolution Analytics, 1335, 1478
Revolution Credit, 231, 1114, 1240
Revolution Foods, 430, 596, 1978
Revolution Growth, 3260
Revolutions Foods, 1442
REVOLV, 1863
Revolv, 1791
Revolver, 2637
Revolymer, 2883, 3019
Revotar Biopharmaceuticals AG, 2519
Revry, 221
Revsite, 1768
Revstone, 1071
Revulytics, 180, 540
RevUp, 1724
Revup, 1610
Revuze, 2994
RevX, 1346
ReWalk, 3041
Reward Gateway, 862
Reward Group Ltd, 2827
Rewards Now, 655
REWARDS21, 1159
RewardsPay, 1254
RewardStock, 512
RewewData, 186
Rewind.me, 1682
Reworld Media, 2842
Rewst, 754
Rex, 1885
Rexel, 2710
Rexnord, 141
Rexter, 1966
Reynold Greenleaf & Associates, 970
Reynolds & Reynolds Co., 1905
Reynolds American, 15
Reynolds Plymer, 367
Reynolds Polymer Technologies, 1057
Rezatec, 2988
RezSolutions, 1852
Rezzcard, 3246
Rf Magic, 2427
RF Micro Devices, 3128
RF Surgical, 1728
rFactr, 1635
RFArrays, 1302
RFE Investment Partners, 77
RFG Enterprises, 911
RFHIC, 3136
RFIB, 371
RFID Global Solutions, 1389
RFJ Auto, 1049
RFmagic, 133
RFMD, 58, 1678
RFnano, 1394

RFP360, 746
RFS Goldings, 1377
RGB Networks, 759, 1241, 1449
RGL Reservoir Management, 458
RGM Advisors, 1778
RGM Group, 1579
Rhapso, 2890
Rhebo GmbH, 2677
Rhein Biotech, 2739
Rheo, 1423
Rheonix, 434, 1130, 1526
Rheonix Inc., 813
Rheos, 849
Rhetorical, 3095
Rhiag Group, 2371
Rhino, 724
RhinoCyte, 1514
Rhinotek Heavy Duty Computer Products, 279
Rhiza, 175, 387, 629
RHK. Salient Surgical Technologies, 556
RHM Klinik und Pflegeheime, 3222
Rhomobile, 2374
Rhone, 1092
Rhumbix, 840, 877
Rhysto, 3043
Rhythem Xience, 2141
Rhythm, 764, 1268, 1814
Rhythm NewMedia, 1257, 1543
Rhythm Pharmaceuticals, 1439
Rhythm Superfoods, 447, 484, 953
Rhythmia Medical, 1347
Rhythmlink, 929
Rialto, 705, 3099
Rib-X Pharmaceuticals, 22, 215, 413
Ribbit, 861, 1088, 1430, 1441, 2016
Ribbon, 195, 877, 1966
Ribometrix, 1631
Ribon Therapeutics, 1780
RibX, 1608
Rice Garden, 148
Rice's Honey, 445
Rich Relevance, 604, 610, 720
Richard Brady & Associates, 1044
Richardeyres, 956
Richardson Foods, 777
Richcore, 3202
Richelieu Foods Inc., 360
RichFX, 538
Richrelence, 564
RichRelevance, 1598, 1867
richrelevance, 877
Richtek Technology, 2594
RichWave, 1924
Ricki's Fashions, 2249
RickIQ, 238
Ricmedia, 2965
Ricoh, 217
Ride Health, 269
Ride Report, 944, 1895
RideCell, 305
Ridecell, 1705
RideKleen, 1509
RidePal, 493
Ridgebury Tankers, 1577
Ridgeline Midstream Holdings, 157
Ridgeway, 2378
Ridgewood Energy Fund, 1766
Ridgeworth Investments, 1127
Ridgmont, 2787
Ridley - Race Productions, 2940
Ridlr, 1511
Rienfer, 3099
Riffa Views, 153
Riffsy, 787
RiffTrax, 201
Rifiniti, 12
Rifkin Acquisition Partners, 1929

Portfolio Companies Index

Rig Up, 812
Rigado, 1162, 2270
Rigel, 785
Rigetti, 125, 720, 721, 1254, 1760
Rigetti Computing, 108, 1155
Rigetti Quantum Computing, 1809
Righscale, 1798
Right Brain, 2940
Right Brain + Left Brain, 3264
Right Health, 2141, 2256
Right Media, 1449, 1537
Right Networks, 364
Right Pointe, 491
Right Time Heating and Air Conditioning, 2075
Right Vision, 2592
Right90, 950
RightAnswers, 1329
RightCare Solutions, 622
RightHand Robotics, 1203
Righthook, 742
Rights Flow, 51
RightScale, 582, 1478
RightsFlow, 1386
Rightside, 822, 1720
Rightware, 2990
RigNet, 1235
Rigor, 191
RigUp, 863
Riide, 1589
Riipen, 1530
RillaVoice, 685
RIM China Company, 1771
RIMCO Royalty Partners, 1505
Rimini Street, 56
Rimor, 2935
Rimrock, 78
Rimrock Construction, 464
Rimrock Midstream, 676
Rinac India, 2451
Rinant Neuroscience, 1495
Rinat Neuroscience, 1788
Rincon Industries, 441
Ring, 742, 846, 879, 879, 1890
Ring Central, 582, 1629
Ring2Conferencing, 2334
RingCentral, 1341
Ringly, 354, 939, 1223
Ringo, 3257
RingYa, 2344
Rinovum, 296, 1452
Rinovum Women's Health, 301
Rinse, 31, 232, 708, 724, 863, 1032, 1223
RIO, 1713
RIO Brands, 445
Rio Nogales Power, 1797
Rio Ranch Markets, 612
Rio SEO, 632, 1947
Rio Seo, 796
Rio Tinto, 2650
Riot Games, 744
Ripcord, 222, 521, 972, 1079, 1155
Ripe Metrics, 395
Ripfire, 526
Ripio, 310
Riplay, 1418
Ripple, 23, 387, 474, 1330, 1665
Ripple Labs, 108
Ripples, 252
Rippling, 945
RIPS Technologies, 2677
Riptide, 1323
Riptide Tek, 2189
Riri, 3145
Riscica Associates, 3257
Rise, 553, 863, 2192
Rise Art, 863
Rise Baking Company, 1372

Rise Brewing Co., 1194
Rise Health, 749, 1622
RiseSmart, 549, 1750
Rishabh Instruments, 838
Rising Star Resources, 2022
RisingStars Growth Fund, 2699
Risk Alyze, 796
Risk I/O, 1867
Risk International, 364
Risk Lens, 604
Risk Methods, 3035
Risk Recon, 604
Risk Strategies, 1066
Risk Strategies Company, 912, 1085
Riskclick, 2378
riskdata, 2482
RiskIQ, 1754, 2126
Riskmatch, 1121
RiskMetrics, 22
Riskmetrics, 1949
RiskMetrics Group, 1720
Riskrecon, 820
RistCall, 999
RiT, 3128
Rita's, 165
Rita's Water Ice Franchise Company, 717
Ritani, 397
RITC, 1314
Rite In The Rain, 82
RITEK, 897
Rithmik Solutions, 2072
Ritter Pharmaceuticals, 1032
Ritual, 763, 877, 1005, 1346, 1890, 1985, 2122, 2126, 2130, 2131, 2176
Riva Boats, 1405
Rival Health, 797, 1925
Rive Technology, 58, 457, 1241, 1355, 3090
River Cities Capital Funds, 3259, 3260
River Medical, 209
River Point Farms, 381, 479
River Ranch Fresh Foods, 2014
River Studios, 795
Riverbed, 388, 912, 1213
Riverchase Dermatology, 1473
Riverhead Networks Inc, 2761
RiverMeadow, 485
RiverMend Health, 1346
Rivermine, 1150, 1701, 1901
RiverMuse, 1855
Rivermuse, 3049
RiverPay, 2107
Rivers Agile, 3264
Riversdale Resources, 1551
Riverside Engineering, 719
Riverside Insights, 92
Riverside Products, 719
RiverSilica, 3010
Riverstone, 1220
Rivertop Renewables, 571, 739, 3246
Riverview Power LLC, 159
Rivet & Sway, 234
Rivet Smart Audio, 1023
Riviera Broadcast Group, 1929
Riviera Travel, 3027
Rivkin Radler LLP, 3257
Rivs Digital Interviews, 1023
Rixty, 787, 1032
Rize, 1150
Rizing, 1140
RJ Metrics, 1702, 2016
RJE International, 961
RJMetrics, 1534, 1855
RJO Holdings Corp., 406
RKD Group, 364
RLabs, 1374
RM Techtronics, 1025
RMB SA, 2555

RMC, 2367
RMDY, 328
Rmi, 2688
RMI Corporation, 1084
Rmoni, 2358
Rmoni Wireless, 2940
RMP Group Inc., 159
RMS Group, 3234
RMSS, 1713
RMX Resources, 479
Rna Diagnostics, 2141
RNA Networks, 1384
RNAgri, 270
Rndex, 1463
Ro, 820, 1696
Ro-Flow Compressors, 1291
Road Angel, 2653
Road Trippers, 481
RoadBotics, 1896
RoadLink, 722
RoadMap, 3019
RoadMunk, 2130
Roadmunk, 720, 2122, 2131
Roadrunner Pharmacy, 119
RoadRunner Recycling Inc., 55
Roadrunner Transportation Systems, 920
Roads, 1304
RoadSafe Traffic Systems, 1377
Roadster, 548
Roadtrippers, 631, 1154
Roam, 310, 474, 981, 1760
Roam & Wander, 3172
Roam Robotics, 1724
Roanwell Corporation, 16
Robbins Brothers, 530
Robbins-Gioia, 47
Robbinskertsten Direct, 352
Robert Allen Duralee Group, 96
Robert Graham, 2164
Robert Lee Morris, 943
Roberts Company, 1025
Roberts Radio, 1731
Roberts Tool Company, 1707
Robertshaw, 1755
Robin, 308, 601, 744
Robin Care, 1760
Robin Systems, 752
Robin Therapeutics, 193
Robinhood, 44, 579, 795, 1079, 1296, 1330, 1563, 1665, 1696, 1760
Robinson Department Store, 1143, 2937
Robison and Davidson, 2976
Roblox, 100, 742, 775, 877, 1213
RoboCV, 895, 2929
Robotic Drilling Systems AS, 3132
Robotic Skies, 1074
Robotiq, 238
RoboTire, 754
Robots Lab, 879
Robust Intelligence, 1669
Rochal Industries, 427
Rock Health, 863, 1056
Rock Mobile, 2927, 3114
Rock Mobile Corp, 2653
Rock My Run, 953
Rock Ridge Stone, 381
Rock Your Life, 2522
Rock-It Cargo, 371
Rock-Ola, 911
Rockbot, 31, 309, 608, 1760, 2009
Rockerbox, 1305
Rocket Dog, 483, 843
Rocket Fuel, 561, 1754
Rocket Jump, 1816
Rocket Lawyer, 200, 949, 1255
Rocket Pharma, 517
Rocket Racing League, 1588

Portfolio Companies Index

Rocket Seals, 1156
RockeTalk, 1239
RocketBolt, 623
RocketFuel, 624
Rocketfuel, 290, 1247, 1327, 1341
Rocketfuel Inc., 1093
Rocketmiles, 473
Rocketrez, 2262
Rocketrip, 818
RocketRoute, 322
Rockets Of Awesome, 321
Rockets of Awesome, 328, 763, 820, 1114
Rockies Venture Fund, 3265
Rocklands, 838
Rockport, 458
RockPort Capital Partners, 3273
Rockport Georgetown Partners, 157
Rocksbox, 646, 1184, 1677
Rocksbox Jewelry, 945
Rockset, 877
Rockwekll Automation, 475
Rockwell Collins Inc., 1905
Rockworth Companies, 464
Rocky Mountain Financial Corporation, 449
Rocky Mountain Helicopters, 617
Rocky Mountain Portable Storage, 1748
RockYou, 518, 730, 1692
Rockyou, 597, 1418
Rococo Software, 3182
Roctest, 238
Roctool, 2867
Rod And Tubing Services, 106
Rod and Tubing Services, 381
Rodeo Therapeutics, 30, 2007
Rodgers Plant Hire, 2976
Rodvig Kro & Badehotel, 3194
Roehm, 61
Roehm Marine, 445
Roenest Group, 3145
Roger Garments, 1248
Rogers Corporation, 77
RogersCasey, 405
Rogue, 1309
Rogue Valley Microdevices, 1917
ROI DNA, 234
Roka BioScience, 1383
Roka Bioscience, 73
Rokid, 977
Roku, 839, 925, 1203
Roland, 912
RolePoint, 586, 1841
Rolepoint, 129
ROLI, 2469
Roli, 744, 779
Rolith, 3220
Roll Rite, 165, 404
Rolland, 931
rollApp, 2929
Rollbar, 1549
RollEase, 1343
Rollick, 207, 208
Rolling Hills Generating, 1797
Rolls-Royce Holdings Plc., 1905
RollStream, 881
Rollstream, 540
Rolltech, 232, 1914
Roly International Holdings, 897
ROM Corp., 451
Roman Decorating Products, 381
Roman Products LLC, 1612
Romania, 2697
Romanoco-Gruppe Karlsruhe, 3058
Romar Partners, 3255
Rombah Wallace, 2384
Romet, 2246
Romotive, 1254, 1914
RomoWind, 2466

Rompetrol Rafinare SA, 3178
Romprest Service SA, 2301
Romulus Capital, 3263
Rondele Specialty Foods, 719
Rongshu.com, 2989
Ronnoco Beverage Solutions, 963
Ronveaux, 3125
Roofsafe, 2391
Roofstock, 945, 1073
Rooftop Media, 218
Rook Media, 1377
Rookwood Pavillion, 1955
Room Beats, 2629
Room Choice, 1074
Room Sketcher, 3207
Room Temperature Superconductors Inc. (ROOTS), 589
Room77, 1527
Roomi, 863, 1589, 1959
Roomorama, 3035, 3206
Roompot, 912
Roonets, 1757
Roosland, 3200
Roost, 521, 1181, 2272
Rooster, 1323
RoosterBio, 2270
Roostock, 863
Root, 631
Root Metrics, 381
Root Music, 1341
Root Wireless, 1587
Root3, 173, 493
Roots, 2243
Roots Automation, 771
RootsRated, 461
Rootstock Software, 1610
Rope, 3202
Roposo, 1828
Rorus, 623
Roscoe Manufacturing, 467
Rose America Corp., 445
Rose City Printing and Packaging, 1573
Rose Hills, 874
Rose Paving, 1210
Rose Rocket, 2074
Rosemont Holdings, 2371
Rosemont Solebury Co-Investment Fund LP, 2088
roserocket, 2240
Rosetta LLC, 1133
Rosie, 12, 1666
ROSS, 2224
Ross, 2122, 2150
Ross Aviation, 449
Ross Education, 1043
Ross PPD Corporation, 1188
Ross Stores, 303
Ross Systems, 2872
Ross-Simons, 786
Rostik Restaurants Ltd, 2482
Rostra Tool Company, 1025
Rosum, 457
Rotam Global AgroSciences, 2594
Rotating Machinery Services Inc., 547
Rotation Medical, 1414, 2930
Roti, 568
Rotimatic, 2681
Rotographik, 2882
Rotoliptic Technologies, 2105
RotoMetrics, 1654
Rotorcraft Leasing Company, 931, 1748
Rotronic, 238
Rough Country, 878
Rough Country Suspension Systems, 170
Roundabout Markets, 999
Roundbox, 540, 1464, 1597
RoundCorner, 1610

RoundPegg, 35, 635, 1462
Rounds, 3072
RoundTable Healthcare Partners, 3255
RoundTrip, 1259
Roundtrip, 2122
Roundy's, 2371
Roupe Pommier, 3011
Route, 79
Route 66 Ventures, 3260
Routehappy, 535, 1479
RouteLambda, 1757
RouteThis, 2235
Routethis, 2122
Rover, 91, 561, 742
Rover.com, 779, 1162, 1203
Rovi Inc., 303
Roving, 957
Roving Planet, 143
Rovio, 2437
Rovsing Dynamics, 3140
Row Sham Bow, 1013
Rowan University, 3266
Rowe, 1755
Rowe Farms, 2153
Rowe International Inc., 911
Rowies, 2853
Rowland Coffee Roasters, 405
Rowmark, 260
Rox, 1350
ROX Medical, 622
Roxar, 153
Roxgold, 2933
Roximity, 686, 721, 784, 1154
ROXRO Pharma, 1495
Roxus, 2989
Royal Adhesives, 1460
Royal Adhesives & Sealands, 653
Royal Adhesives & Sealants, 172, 1507
Royal Baths Manufacturing, 1460
Royal Cactus, 3229
Royal Camp Services, 904
Royal Die and Stamping Co., 989
Royal Group Technologies Limited, 2067
Royal Mat, 2198
Royal Mosa BV & Freecom Technologies BV, 2819
Royal Pet Supplies, 1513
Royal Robbins Inc., 357
Royal Sanders, 2492
Royal Sign Supply, 1839
Royal Wolf Australia, 277
Royalimages.in, 3202
Royall & Company, 470
Royalty Exchange, 881
Royalty Pharma, 1401, 1518
RoyaltyShare, 1852
Royole, 977, 2841
RP Scherer Corporation, 576
Rpath, 1335
RPI, 961
RPM Technologies, 2046
RPM Ventures, 3259
RPO, 2980, 3053
RPX, 457
RQI, 225
RQX Pharmaceuticals, 209, 545
RRT Global, 2531
RS LiveMedia, 241
RSA Engineered Products, 542, 1210
RSam, 1045
RSC Holdings, 1360
RSG, 2201
RSI, 1355, 1753, 2867, 2883
RSM US, 3265
RSportz, 1065
RT Sourcing Asia Limited, 2394
RT-SET Ltd, 2576

Portfolio Companies Index

RTG Asia, 3206
RTHM, 2093
RTI Surgical, 1962
RTIME, 1399
RTL-Westcan, 2029
RTS, 1589
RTS Holdings Inc., 77
RtTech Software, 2183
ru-Net Holdings, 2482
Rubica, 1114, 1890
Rubicon, 495
Rubicon Pharmacies, 2264
Rubicon Project, 504, 686, 1187
Rubicon Technology, 186, 1061, 1917
Rubikloud, 2074, 2112, 2150, 2822
Rubio Therapeutics, 748
Rubitection Separation Design Group, 1452
Rubius Therapeutics, 710
Rubrick, 1269
Rubrik, 877, 1006, 1035, 1073
Ruby, 2074
Ruby Groupe, 2965
Ruby Ribbon, 596, 1247, 1855
Rucker's, 60
Ruckus Wireless, 731, 759, 1213, 1241, 3112
Rudjer Boskovic Institute, 2823
Rudy's Barbershop, 1344
Rue du Commerce, 2367
Rue Lala, 332
Ruesch Systems, 1973
RuffaloCODY, 1335, 1506, 1754, 1979
Rugby Manufacturing Company, 906
Rugs Direct, 1609
RuiYi, 2410
Rule, 1071
Rules Based Medicine, 561
RulesPower, 540, 1084
RuleStream Corporation, 1178
Rum Jungle Resources, 2933
Ruma, 1374
Rumble, 863
Rumble Automation, 2083
Rumble Media, 2820, 2829
Rumcom, 3203
RuMe, 845
Run 3D, 3098
Run Service, 3053
Run the World, 1426
Runa, 1219, 1610, 3246
Runa HR, 798
RunaHR, 1760
Runcom, 3170
Rune Labs, 229
RunKeeper, 316, 1101, 1718
Runnable, 1549
Runpath, 1259
Runscope, 1862
Runyon Equipment Rental, 1582
Rupari Food Services, 410
Rupari Foods, 1990
Rupeetalk, 3100
Rupture, 234, 624
Rural Broadband Investments, 889
RushFiles, 3194
Ruskin Moscou Faltischek, 3257
Russell Hendrix, 293
Russian Navigation Technologies, 3220
Rustic Crust, 440, 1691, 2230
Rusts of Cromer, 2976
Rutgers University, 3266
Ruth's Hospitality Group, 357, 1160
Rutherford Polk McDowell Home Health, 409
Ruthinium Group, 2613
Rutland Plastics, 1576
RV Technology, 163
rVita, 650
RWI Construction, 1707

Rx Drug Mart, 2212
Rx Label Technology, 919, 1438
Rx Safes, 1083
Rx Savings Solutions, 1276
Rx30, 889
RxBenefits, 862
RxHope, 1771
RxKinetix, 213
RxSight, 764, 1147, 1522
RxVantage, 1032, 1695, 1966
Ryan, 2201
Ryan Herco Flow Solutions, 867
Ryan Murphy Inc., 1839
Ryan's Express Transportation Services Inc., 451
Ryder TRS, 1160
Rye Studio, 2927
Ryko, 1859
Ryla, 1691
Rylo, 235
RYNO Motors, 1384
Rypos, 949, 1176
Rypple, 342
Rysta LifeScience, 3024
Ryver, 861
Ryvers, 1074

S

S Gympass, 2437
S&N Communications, 1755
S&P Syndicate, 1143, 2937
S&S Industries, 1138
S&S Tech, 1091
S*Bio, 2410, 2504, 2681
S*BIO Pte., 1241
S-cubism Holdings, 2965
S. Pack & Print, 1143, 2937
S.I. Jacobson, 78
S.R. Accord, 136
S2 Corporation, 1317
S2 Interactive, 999, 1190
S3 Enterprises Inc., 2115
S3C, 1917
S4, 570
S4 Agtech, 270
Saadiyat, 153
Saama, 419
SAAS, 3042
SaaS Capital, 531
Saasuma, 1509
Saatchi Art, 641, 3047
SABA, 564
Saba, 912, 1912
Saba University, 692
Sabal Medical, 1925
Sabalo Energy, 673
Saban Brands LLC, 1602
Saban Films, 1602
SABE Online, 3039
SABEResPODER, 1397
Saberr, 3099
Sabex, 1594
Sabimedical, 2544
Sabine Oil & Gas, 741
Sabio Labs, 116
Sabre, 820, 1049, 1685, 1837
Sabre Communications, 215
Sabre Holdings, 56, 1852
Sabre Industries, 1085
Sabrix, 780, 1247, 1855
SabrTech Inc., 2148
Sabse Technologies, 2060
Sackets Harbor Brewing Company, 1642
Sadbhav, 1346
Sadler's Smokehouse, 331
Sadra Medical, 39, 1379
Saegis Pharmaceuticals, 1788
Saehan Enertech, 3159

SaehWa, 3136
Saehwa IMC, 2993
Saelvigbugtens Camping, 3194
SAF, 3223
Safe, 912
SAFE Boats International, 1276
Safe In Sound Hearing, 1612
Safe Life, 1908
Safe Security, 973
Safe Shepherd, 1364
Safe-Guard, 1407
Safe-H2O, 1065
Safe-id, 3223
SafeAI, 664
SAFEbuilt, 1576
SafeDK, 1614
SafeGraph, 1566, 1677
SafeGuard, 2963
Safeguard America, 1294
SafeGuard Cyber, 84
Safeguard Global, 28
Safehub, 802
Safello, 1982
Safely You, 1423
Safemark Systems, 1234
Safend, 3221
SafeNet, 1901, 1912
Safeonline, 2563
SafePeak, 3230
SafePorche, 1101
SafeRent, 318
SafeRide, 121
Saferide, 309
Safetel, 3207
SafeTraces, 490, 1724
SafeTrek, 570, 1186
Safety Culture, 2511
Safety Infrastructure Solutions, 747, 1747
Safety Quick Light, 638
Safety Seven, 2129
Safetykleen, 136
SafetyPay, 2708
SafeView, 236, 1348, 1401
Safeway plc, 2605
Safeway Safety Step, 1514
Safic Alcan, 2367
Saft Groupe, 3060
Safway Group Holding, 1368
SAGA, 2371
Saga, 2578
Saga (Acromas), 3024
Saga Resource Partners, 45
Sagantea, 3162
SAGE, 1794
Sage, 401, 471, 764
Sage Automotive, 1971
Sage Automotive Interiors, 502
Sage Bin, 1074
Sage Electrochromics Inc., 145
Sage Hospice, 1169
Sage Midstream, 1577
Sage Products, 1160
Sage Therapeutics, 710, 1383
Sage Therepeutics, 1814
Sagely Naturals, 6
Sagent Pharmaceuticals, 1943
SageQuest, 947, 1556
Sagetis Biotech, 2544
Sageview-Wolff Real Estate, 1606
Sagitta, 3150
Sago Energy, 898
Sagres Discovery, 215
Sagrotel - Sociedade Imobiliaria, 3039
Saguaro Resources, 1447
Saguna, 3230
Sahale Snacks, 1404
Saham Finances, 3164

Portfolio Companies Index

Sai, 1268
Sai Sudhir, 3202
Saia Burgess, 2913
Saia-Burgess, 2555
Saifun, 2600
Sail, 1443
Sail Internet, 1314
SAILDRONE, 1698
Saildrone, 1155
Sailfish Boats, 825
Sailogy, 2951
Sailpoint, 1687
SailPoint Technologies, 1817
Sailthru, 251, 320, 609, 1114, 1597
SailTthru, 1629
Saint Springs, 70, 2456
Saisha Tehnology, 467
Saisudhir, 838
Sajan, 1195
Sajar Plastics, 1163
Sakhinterlesprom, 2482
Saks Inc., 1021
Sakti, 558
Sakura Enterprises, 1771
Salad Signature, 912
Saladax, 704, 845
Saladax Biomedical, 1120
Saladworks, 448
Salem International University, 1830
Sales Beach, 1364
Sales Force Pardot, 191
Sales Gossip, 2470
Sales Performance International, 1210
Sales Portal, 1462
Sales Rabbit, 1074
SalesconX, 1305
Salesfloor, 1982
Salesforce, 1213
Salesforce Japan, 1757
Salesforce.com, 666, 1757
SalesforceIQ, 840
SalesFusion, 1332
Salesfusion, 285
SalesGoose, 1959
SalesHero, 521
SalesLoft, 191, 666, 1005
SalesLogix, 950
SalesPortal, 185
SalesRabbit, 79
Salesvue, 570, 659
SalesWarp, 380
SALIDO, 31
Salido, 1309
Salient CRGT, 792, 1927
Salient Partners, 1754
Salient Pharmaceuticals, 447, 953
Salient Surgical, 1190
Salient Surgical Technologies, 1578, 1846
Saline Lectronics Inc., 114
Salins, 2309
Salins du Midi, 2367
Salix Pharmaceuticals, 1395, 1456
SalmData, 758
SALO, 3268
Salon Share, 515
Salon.com, 857
Salorix, 2992
Salsa, 655, 967
Salsa Labs, 28
Salsify, 1184, 1335, 1918
SALT, 2958
Salt of Life AG, 2519
Salt Union, 2787
Salter Labs, 654, 1594
Salton Inc., 449
Saltside, 1323
SaltStack, 79, 1205

Saltworks, 322
Salu, 1736
Salunda, 3019
Salusion, 685
Salvage Direct, 1691
Salveo, 1700
SAM, 2880
Sam Seltzer's Steakhouse, 405
SAMAG Group, 2518
SAManage, 2557
Samanage, 1610, 3212, 3230
Samara, 943
Samara Innovations, 661
Samba Ads, 2863
Samba Safety, 912, 1826
Samba Sensors, 2869
Samba TV, 1616
SambaAds, 3072
SambaCloud, 1335
SAMBASafety, 1505
Samedi.de, 2595
SameSide, 937
Sammumed, 3206
Samo, 310
Sample6, 389, 949
Sample6 Technologies, 468
Sampler, 2074, 2094, 2120, 2132
Samplify, 457
Samplify Systems, 766
Samsara, 125, 820
Samson Neuro Sciences, 2320
Samson Resources, 560
Samstock Oy, 2707
Samsung, 1100
Samuel Lawrence Furniture Co., 847
Samurai International, 2637
SAN Home Entertainment, 2965
San Jacinto Minerals, 1129
San Shing Fastech Corporation, 1143, 2937
San Vicente Group, 2526
Sana, 1186
Sana Packaging, 395
SanaBit, 705
SanaExpert, 2331
Sanako Corporation, 2310, 2707
Sanctuary AI, 2105
Sanctum, 3221
Sand 9, 523
Sand Hill Exchange, 1593
Sand Tech, 2051
Sand9, 1948
Sandata, 1751
Sandata Technologies, 28
Sandbox, 962, 2574
Sandbox Industries, 3255
Sandbox Learning, 1446
Sandbox VR, 1477
Sandbridge Technologies Inc., 1781
Sandburst Corporation, 317
Sandcraft, 1706
SandForce, 597, 1750, 1840
Sandinvest, 2710
Sandisc, 3203
Sandler O'Neill & Partners, 1066
Sandlot Solutions, 1111
Sandow Media, 1929
Sandpiper Networks Inc, 950
Sandpiper Software, 1015
SandRidge, 1848
Sandridge Energy, 160
Sands Capital Ventures, 3260
SandVideo, 226
Sandvine, 782, 3203
Sandwell Schools, 2740
Sandylane, 2122
Sandymount Technologies, 1759
Sanepar, 838

Sanera Systems, 1750
Sanergy, 54
Sanfer, 819
Sangamo, 764
Sangamo Biosciences, 2454
Sanguine Biosciences, 1016
Sani-Matic, 719
Sani-Service, 2245
Sanitors, 1772
Sanlight, 936
Sano, 721, 742, 752, 1254
Sano Corporation, 132
Sano Intelligence, 720
sanofi, 1349
Sanommune, 2071
Sanona, 2392
Sanova Dermatology, 119
Sanovia Corporation, 941
SANSAN, 2637
Santa Cruz Nutritionals, 1594
Santa Fe Relocation, 475
Santa Rosa Consulting, 386
Santander Asset Management, 819
Santander Consumer USA, 444
Santaris A/S, 2776
Santaris Pharma, 2739, 3006, 3104, 3140
Santarus, 1728
Santerra, 1244
Santessima, 3104
Santhera Pharmaceuticals, 1395
Santhera Pharmaceuticals AG, 1325
SANTIER, 1427
Santur, 1908
Santur Corporation, 1122
Sanyang Electronics, 2848
Saol Therapeutics, 611
SAP, 3060
Sapala, 3202
Sapato, 641
saperatec, 2677
Saphena Medical, 428
Sapho, 93, 108, 720, 863, 1254, 1566, 1702
Sapias, 810
Sapiens Data Science, 826
Sapient Health Networks, 1399
Sapient Industries, 1896
Sapphire Digital, 921
Sapphire Energy, 154, 265, 1918
Sapphire Power Holdings, 1577
Sapphire Technology, 3136
Sapphire Therapeutics, 315, 1495
Saprogal, 2953
Sara Lee Corp., 1905
Sara Lee Frozen Bakery, 1085
Saraplast, 2305
Saraware Oy, 2707
Sarcode Bioscience, 94
Sarcos, 812
Sarda Technologies, 975
Sardex, 2865
Sardex.net, 2663
Sardine, 3
Sarens, 3222
Sarnova, 1962
Sarolina Staff, 1753
Sartorius, 3060
Sarvega, 1061
SAS Sistema de Ensino, 819
SASE Company, 293
Sasets, 3098
Sash, 85
Sasken, 2837
Sasseur, 1092
Sasun, 1748
Satago, 3099
Satcom, 651
Sate, 2841

Portfolio Companies Index

Sate Auto, 2927
Sateco, 3011
Satelec, 2593
Satiety, 667
Satiogen, 1222
Satisfy Labs, 754
Satmetrix, 780
Satmex, 444
Satoris, 326
Satrec Initiative, 1091
Satsuma, 1522
Satsuma Pharmaceuticals, 2174
Saturday Shoes, 2927
Sauce Labs, 1006, 1831
Saucelabs, 1610
Saucey, 101, 361
Sauiba Sensors AB, 2709
Saul Ewing Arnstein & Lehr, 3264
Saunders & Associates, 832
Saunders Inc., 694
Saurer, 2913
Savaari Car Rentals, 1017
Savage Sports, 1145, 1460
SavaJe Technologies, 1304
Savana, 1321
Savantis Systems, 1674
Savara, 447
Savara Pharmaceuticals, 1065
Savari, 821
SavATree, 478
Save a Lot Food Stores, 2201
Saveology, 1377
Savers, 1113
SaveUp, 285, 1862
Savi Technology, 1912
Savigent, 1195
Savii Care, 512
Saving Star, 756
SavingStar, 597, 742, 949
Savio, 2371
Savioke, 3, 108, 720, 998, 1254, 2681
Savitude, 1179, 1370
SAVO, 1623
Savo, 1745
Savo-Solar, 2603
Savonix, 802, 1074
Savoteur, 641
Savoy Entertainment Group, 651
SavviAI, 1426
Savvion, 217, 1908
SAVVIS, 1973
Savvymoney, 1867
Saxbys Coffee, 1275
Saxo Bank, 819, 1837
Saxx, 337
SAY Media, 200, 759
Say Media, 1588
Sayduck, 3099
Saygent, 1059
Saykara, 1162
Saylent, 746, 1339
Saylent Technologies, 1389, 1922
SayNow, 1666, 1867
Sayspring, 411, 527
SBA Materials, 1713
SBI Fine Chemicals, 2043
SBJ, 2787
SBJ Group Limited, 407
SBM Co., 2718
SBP Holdings LP, 63
SBR Health, 752
SBS Broadcasting, 2372
SBS Industries, 832
SBV Venture Partners, 3273
Sbx Robotics, 2122
SC Labs, 1845
Scala Energy, 673

Scale, 2010
Scale Arc, 545
Scale Computing, 21, 86, 290, 733, 1547, 1629
Scale Factor, 1179
Scale Venture, 3273
ScaleARc, 2992
ScaleArc, 1855
ScaleBase, 224
Scaled Inference, 720, 1073, 1155
Scaled Networks, 2951
Scalefast, 252
ScaleMP, 646, 2453
Scalent Systems, 1042
Scaleo Chip, 3104
ScaleOut, 2465
ScaleOut Software, 85
Scali, 2745
Scality, 1203, 3011
Scalpr, 310
Scalyr, 1666, 1760
Scalyr Inc., 1669
Scan Therapeutics, 1149, 1350
Scana Noliko, 2940
Scanadu, 721, 1236
Scanalytics, 567
Scanalytics Inc., 1159
Scanbio, 2745
Scanbot (by Doo), 3152
ScanBuy, 957
Scanbuy, 1150, 1178
ScanCafe, 1028, 1674
Scancell, 3098
ScandBook, 2317
Scandic Hotels, 2317
Scandit, 2437
Scandlines, 2303
Scandura Holdings, 1560
Scandza AS, 1133
Scanntech, 2446
Scanrope, 2745
ScanSafe, 1629
ScanScout, 116, 234
Scanse, 795
Scansite 3D, 802
Scanvacc, 2745
Scanwell, 2272
Scarpblog, 1150
Scatter, 1155
Scayl, 85
Scene Sharp, 2192
SceneDoc, 1260, 2141
Scense, 3119
Scentbird, 1154
Scenti Bio, 1203
Scentys, 3104
Schaltbau Holding, 3060
Scharffen Berger Chocolate Maker, 1087
Schema, 2532, 2711, 3221
Schema Ltd, 2576, 2761
SchemaLogic, 468
Schematic Labs, 721, 1701, 1862
Schenck Process, 912
Schiller Bikes, 1065
Schiller International University, 1830
Schlotzsky's, 1580
Schmersahl Treloar & Co., 3261
Schnader Attorneys at Law, 3264
Schneidersohne, 2607
Schneller, 851
Schoeller Arca Systems, 1376
Schofield Media Group, 1929
Scholar Locker, 1585
Scholar Rock, 710
Scholar's First, 1000
ScholarCentric, 403
ScholarMe, 888
ScholarPro, 1618

Scholly, 623
School Imrpovement Network, 1772
School Loop, 1305, 1588
School Loop Inc., 1309
School of Management and Business Advisory Council, 1653
School of Rock, 1745
School Status, 1499
School Stickers, 2530
SchooLa Inc., 650
SchoolChapters, 1942
SchoolMessenger, 470
SchoolMint, 1058, 1530
Schoolmint, 564, 945
Schoology, 744, 863, 1045, 1196
Schoolzilla, 1058, 1530
Schooner Capital, 3263
Schoox, 1076
Schrader International, 1160
Schuepbach Energy, 479
Schulerhilfe Gelsenkirchen, 3058
Schulman Associates, 2142
Schulz Catering, 136
Schumacher, 2201
Schur Flexible, 1518
Schutt Sports, 878
SCHUTZKLICK, 2970
Schweiger Dermatology Group, 1140, 1631, 1764
Schylling, 832
SCI Solutions, 1984
SciApps, 679
SciAps Inc., 440, 813
Science, 231, 562, 925, 1966
Science 37, 1155
Science Exchange, 1114
Science Exchange, 564, 1254, 1346, 1359, 1884, 1969, 1993, 2009
Science Inc., 289
Science37, 840
Science4You, 3039
ScienceBased Health, 146
SCIenergy, 1848, 1978
Scienova, 2518
Sciens Building Solutions, 963
Scientech, 376, 377, 2427
Scientific Games, 822
Scientific Games Holdings Corp, 449
Scientific Magnetics, 3089
Scientific Media, 1832
Scientific Protein Laboratories, 172
Scientific Publishers, 2420
Scientist.com, 11
Sciessent, 2483
Scietific Systems, 2328
Scifiniti, 87, 731
Scigineer, 597
SciKon Innovation, 738
Scinfiniti, 1430
Scint-X, 2621
Scintera, 200, 1661
Scintera Networks, 624
Scioderm, 1126, 1788
Scion, 317
Scion Pharmaceuticals, 1096
Scipher Medicine, 1073
SciQuest, 1013, 1855
Scitex, 2657
Scitex3, 2600
Scitor Corporation, 1113
Scivantage, 655
Scivex, 1090
Sckipio, 117
SCM Insurance Services, 2264
Scodix, 127, 238, 2891
Sconce, 2861
Sconce Solutions, 2904

Portfolio Companies Index

Scondoo, 3035
Scoo, 2372
Scoop, 305
Scoop.it, 1418, 2684
Scoopshot, 2621
Scoot, 1186, 1635
Scoot Science, 321
Scooter's Coffee, 1276
Scope AR, 1477, 1760
ScopeAI, 1610
ScopeAR, 1677
Scopely, 133, 309, 561, 625, 641, 720, 876, 938, 1237, 1483, 1534
Scopix, 2446
Scopus, 2562
Score Data, 624
Score Stream, 209
Scorebig, 224
Scorista, 2931
Scorpion Therapeutics, 1934
SCORT, 2535, 2535
Scotch & Soda, 1755
Scotia Technology, 815
Scott Technologies Inc., 303
Scottish Equity Partners, 2935
Scottish Re Group Limited, 576
Scottish-American Insurance, 381
Scout, 784
Scout 24, 927
Scout Clean Energy, 1520
Scout Mob, 1114
Scoutables, 976
Scoutible, 863
ScoutLabs, 1032
Scoutmob, 1290
Scovill Fasteners Inc., 1624
SCP Ltd., 1229
scPharmaceuticals, 11
Scrap Partners, 367
Scratch Kitchen, 328
Scratch Music Group, 535, 1422
Scratch Wireless, 536
Scratch-It, 1065
Scratch-it, 1659
Scrazzl, 2513
Scream Point, 401
Screenlife, 42
Screenreach, 3003
Screenvision, 1663
Scribble, 2126
Scribble Live, 545
ScribbleLive, 2112, 2250, 2398
Scribd, 457, 1073, 1077, 1908
Scribd., 1537
Scribe America, 470
Scribe Software, 311
ScribeAmerica, 1932
Scrible, 3246
Scrip Companies, 406
Scripted, 1537
ScriptRock, 1899
Scriptswitch, 2958
Scrittura, 957
ScrollMotion, 568, 661
Scrubgrass, 157
Scrybe, 57
SCS Financial Serices, 1746
SCT, 445
SCT Stem Cell Technology, 3235
SCT Telecom, 3011
Scuf Gaming LLC, 813
Sculpteo, 3229
SculptiVR, 310
ScyllaDB, 1511
Scynexis, 764, 1734, 2867
Scytl, 1623, 1948, 2469, 2978
SDC Materials, 2483

SDG, 2484
SDI, 1470
SDI Gas, 1129
SDI Health, 1140, 1779
SDI Inc., 1140
SDI Special Devices, 1968
SDK Biotechnologies, 650
SDLtridion, 2662
SEA, 2726
Sea Bags, 1165
Sea Island Lake Cottages, 1220
Sea Machines, 680, 1105
Sea Machines Robotics, 1836
Sea Transportation-Dry Bulk, 1968
Seabed Geophysical, 2745
Seaboard International Inc., 989
Seabrook International, 77, 804
Seabulk International, 1577
Seafolly, 1092
Seaformatics, 2161
Seagate, 388, 1100, 1736
Seagate Technologies, 1006
Seagate Technology, 200, 1837
Seagate Technology Plc., 1905
SeAH Besteel, 2425
Seahawk Biosystems Corporation, 983
Seahorse App, 3116
Seahorse Bioscience, 523, 1302, 2930
Seahorse Biosciences, 748
Seakeeper, 552
SEAL, 1847
Seal, 1831
Seal Innovation, 3246
Sealand Natural Resources, 1744
SeaLife Pharma, 3156
Sealine, 2787
SealSkinz, 2530
Seaman Paper, 1176
Seamicro, 564, 610
Seamless Docs, 1260, 1305
Seamless Receipts, 609
Seamless Toy Company, 1491
SeamlessDocs, 1896
SeaProducts, 1509
Search Lateral, 1550
Searchandise Commerce, 609, 993
Searchmetrics, 2985
Searchspace, 3095
Sears Canada, 1971
Seaside National Bank & Trust, 1151, 1419
Seasoned Staq, 1076
Seaspan Marine Corp, 2079
SeaStar Solutions, 111
SeaSuite By Goby, 1645
SeaSwift, 912
SEAT, 2488
SeatAdvisor, 1708
Seaters, 3248
SeatGeek, 774, 840, 1114, 1263, 1358, 1534
Seatme, 1186
Seattle Metrics Inc., 911
Seattle Sensor Systems, 85
Seattle Shellfish, 1450
Seattle Systems, 719
Seattle's Best International, 1580
Seatwave, 2725, 2820, 2829
Seaurat Technologies, 821
Seaview Petroleum Co. LP, 449
Seaway Networks, 1042
Seaway Restaurant Group, 1642
Seaworld Parks and Entertainment, 280
Sebacia, 39, 622, 1421, 1930
Sebela Pharmaceuticals, 611
Sebia, 912, 2592
Secberus, 754
Secfi, 1309
Seche/Tredi, 2616

Sechrist Industries Inc., 654
Seclore, 2809, 3202
Secoda, 2122, 2131
Second Accent, 1554
Second Cup Coffee Co., 2245
Second Genome, 58, 1126, 1658, 1734, 1967
Second Home, 3088
Second Life, 1323
Second Measure, 1346, 1666
Second Nature, 512
Second Porch, 1384
Second Spectrum, 1800
SecondKeys, 999
Secondmarket, 744, 2822
SecondMind, 724
SecondSol, 2518
Secoo, 2841, 3199
Secor, 167
Secova Services, 2481
Secret Cinema, 1698
Secret Double Octopus, 252
Secret Escapes, 3009, 3198
Secret Sales, 2620
SecretBuilders, 1101
SecretSales, 3023
Secretsales, 2662
SecretSales.com, 1418
Sectigo, 782
Section, 1317
Seculert, 3236
Securadyne Systems, 1410
SecurAmerica, 1971
Secure, 881
Secure Directory, 2325
Secure Food Solutions, 999
Secure Key, 2046
Secure Meters Limited, 2852
Secure Soft, 2848
Secure Software, 1888
Secure-24, 912, 1410
Secureauth, 1831
SecureKey Technologies, 2256
SecureLink, 1021, 2853
SecureMedia, 1706
Securent, 1379
Securesafe, 2574
Securicy, 2204
Securiguard, 2284
Securimax, 2402
Securistyle, 2914
Securitas Direct, 223
Security, 1834
Security 7, 3239
Security American Financial Enterprises, 1343
Security Innovation, 352
Security Networks, 1360
Security Scorecard, 308
Security Solutions of America, 408
Securitypoint Media, 1527
Securly, 998, 1393
Securus Medical Group, 1051, 1578
Securus Technologies, 745, 912
SecurView, 485
Secusmart, 2385, 2970
Sedal, 2480
Sedan, 2880
Sedemac, 2992
Sedgwick, 927, 1746
SEE Forge, 545
See Forge, 953
See Me, 708, 1491
See.me, 1358
Seebo, 1483, 3212
SeeChange Health, 1500
Seeclickfix, 1359
SeeCommerce, 1947
SeeControl, 1430

1388

Portfolio Companies Index

Seed, 354, 2217
Seed Education Corp., 54
Seed Holdings, 1560
Seed Infotech, 856
Seed Invest, 863
Seed Media Group, 1955
Seed&Spark, 221
Seedcamp, 2288, 2398, 2577, 2665, 2813, 3009, 3088
SeedInvest, 1635
SeedLegals, 3099
Seedling, 901, 1223, 1890
Seeds, 221, 310
SEEFT Ventures, 2715
SEEGRID Corporation, 1003
Seek Communications Limited, 2390
Seeking Alpha, 582
SeeMore Interactive, 1556
Seen Digital Media, 1556
SEEO, 1478
Seeq, 98, 1162, 1644
Seequent, 28
SeeRoseGo, 1509
Seesaw, 234
Seesmic, 2437
Seevibes, 3036
Sefaira, 325
Sefas, 2346
Segall Bryant & Hamill, 1817
SegAna, 754
Segetis, 3268
Segment, 641, 1079, 2011
Segmentify, 2276
Segmint, 1051
Segra, 99
Segrest, 1216
Segue Manufacturing Services, 214
Seibold, 2674
Seikagaku, 1456
Seisint, 1720, 2073
Seismic, 1028, 1045
Seismic Games, 625, 794
Seismos, 1032
Seitel Inc., 1905
Seitz, 124
Sekal, 3090
Sekal AS, 3132
SEKO Logistics, 867
SELA, 3063
Selah Genomics, 1925
Selavo Machinery, 2927
Seldin Company, 69
Select Energy Services, 560
Select Medical, 1973
Select Product Group, 479
Select Rehabilitation, 377
Select Technology, 3098, 3098, 3098
Selecta Biosciences, 748, 1383, 1421, 1464, 1943
Selectable Media, 209
Selectbidder, 2192
SelecTec, 1691
Selectica, 1042
SelectQuote, 356, 1766
SelectX Pharmaceuticals, 3187
Selektessen, 3161
Selenis, 2480
Selenity Therapeutics, 1350
Selexys Pharmaceuticals, 1268
Self Esteem Brands, 1580
Self Lender, 1074
Selfapy, 2832
Selfie Networks, 320
SelfMade, 1011, 1589
Selfmade, 744
Selfnet, 3005
SelfScore, 1719

Selig Sealing Products, 248
Seligman Spectrum Focus Fund, 624
Selima, 3234
Sellars, 1722
Sellbrite, 976
Seller Crowd, 1114
SellerCrowd, 1701
Sellercrowd, 816
Selligent, 962
Selligy, 610
SellPoints, 857
Sellpoints, 1203
SellSwipe, 1000
Selltag, 3214
Selltis, 60
Selmic Oy, 2707
Seloger, 2367
SeluxDx, 1522
Selva Medical, 1695
Selventa, 748, 1414
Selway Partners, 1636
Selènia, 3145
Semafone, 3009
Semagtx, 1406
Semantifi, 1101
Semarchy, 1499
Semasio, 259, 2820, 2829, 3047
Semathera Inc., 2031
Semba Biosciences, 1064
Sembiosys, 240
Sembiosys Genetics Inc., 2108
Semetric/Musicmetric, 3023
Semicoa, 1906
Semiconductor Manufacturing International, 897
Semiconductor Manufacturing International Corporat, 1771, 2594
Semiconductors, 730
SemiNex, 649
Seminis, 781
Semior, 2074
SemiProbe, 1101
Semitech Semiconductor, 2604, 2769
Semknox, 3226
Semma, 1268
Semma Therapeutics, 711
Semnur, 389
Semnur Pharma, 1943
Semnur Pharmaceuticals, 785
SemperCare, 405, 2073
Semprae, 1510
Sempre Health, 1555
Semprius, 145, 154, 949, 979, 983, 1013
Semprus, 11
SEMRE, 1698
Semrush, 641
Semtek, 1918
Senator Investment Group, 69
Sence360, 744
Sencha, 972
Senco Brands, 2008
Send Me Mobile, 1848
Send Word Now, 1402
SendBird, 1666
SendbyBag, 2939
Sendero Midstream Partners, 676
Senders, 1011
SendGrid, 1702
Sendgrid, 1791
SendHub, 1058, 1658
Sendio, 189, 1667
Sendmail, 57, 1255
Sendme, 1718
Sendori, 116, 234
Sendwithus, 234
Seneca Systems, 553
Senet, 910
Senet. ShotSpotter, 490

Senforce, 1679, 2374
Senhouse Capital, 3088
Senic, 275, 3152
SENIOcare, 3222
Senior Helpers, 97, 1115
Senior Whole Health, 551, 1778
SeniorBridge, 376
SeniorLink, 523
Seniorlink, 1335
Seniovo, 2832
Sennder, 640
Senneca Holdings, 1085
Senodia Technologies, 2658
Senomyx, 1495
Senomyx. Sunesis, 240
Senr.net, 1718
Senreve, 901
Senrio, 1384
SensAble, 1335, 1917
SenSage, 1241
Sensas, 2616
Sensata Technologies, 223
Sensay, 121
Senscient, 447, 953, 1305, 1588
Sense, 857, 980, 1566
Sense Networks, 1032
Sense.ly, 721
Sense360, 309, 527, 625, 1511
Sensee, 1418
Senseg, 2382
SenseiHub, 310
Senselogix, 2287
SenseLogix Limited, 3001
SenseOmics, 183
Senseonics, 605, 3076
SenseStream Ltd., 163
SenseTime, 1511
SenseWare, 288
Sensiba San Filippo, 3262
Sensibill, 2074, 2094, 2112, 2143, 2146, 2187
Sensible Organics, 2230, 2321
Sensible Problems, 502
Sensibo, 2938
Sensicast, 838
Sensicore, 1324, 1788
Sensics, 288, 1172
SensiHub, 1887
Sensika, 2687
Sensimed, 2345
Sensinode, 2621
Sensipar, 2097
Sensis, 1287
Sensitech, 1949
Sensity, 89, 1247, 1684
Sensity Systems, 485
Sensl, 2347
Sensopia, 1418
Sensor Films, 705
Sensor Solutions Holdings, 654
Sensor Tower, 129
Sensorberg, 2494, 3226
Sensorly, 2684
SensorNet, 238
Sensoro, 222
SensorSuite, 2136
Sensorsuite, 2094, 2107
Sensortec, 2589
SensorTower, 1219, 1426, 1543
SensorTran, 1748
Sensortran, 707
SensorUp, 2105, 2270
Sensory Analytics, 1446, 1925, 1987
Sensory Networks, 2315
Sensory Technologies, 2051
Sensotrade, 3235
Sensu, 238, 779
Sensy, 1017

Portfolio Companies Index

Sensys, 1414
Sensys Networks, 950, 1947
Sentelic, 1924
Sentenai, 756, 1489
Senti Bio, 1426
Senti Biosciences, 1616
Sentiar, 270
SentiBiosciences, 1155
Sentient, 812
Sentient Biosciences, 1695
Sentient Energy, 773
Sentient Medical Systems, 633, 1232
SentientScience, 2126
Sentieon, 977
Sentilla, 493, 1379, 1967
Sentillion, 1013, 1728
Sentiment Alpha, 396
Sentimoto, 2398
Sentinal Alert, 2208
Sentinel, 586, 1978
Sentinel Capital Partners, 1873
Sentinel Data Centers, 1066
Sentinel Healthcare, 1616
Sentinel Offender Services LLC, 277
Sentinel One, 1537
Sentinel Vision, 526
Sentinella Pharmaceuticals, 415
SentinelOne, 856, 1689
Sentinl, 985
Sentito Networks, 1084
Sentons, 1340
Sentori, 655
SentreHEART, 1449, 1495, 1943
SentriLock, 1645
Sentrix, 2943
Senvion, 444
Senyi, 474
Senzari, 2804
SEO Pledge, 396
SEOshop, 2813
Seoul Beltway Corporation, 585
Separators, 1252
Sepaton, 759, 1901
SEPIAtec GmbH, 3181
Sepracor, 1048
SEPS Pharma, 2940
Septentrio N.V., 2893
SeqOnce, 664
Sequa, 1138
SeQual, 178
Sequana, 209, 772
Sequana Medical, 2506, 2701, 2930
Sequans, 3143
Sequans Communicatinos, 2890
Sequation, 1042
Sequel, 1426
Sequel Youth & Family Services, 96
Sequella, 1172
Sequence Bio, 2161, 2208
Sequence Design, 200, 759, 1674
Sequence Health, 1292
Sequenom, 2998, 3128
Sequenom Inc., 2776
Sequent Medical, 605, 622
Sequent Software, 1382
Sequenta, 1247
Sequitur Energy Resources, 45
Sequoia, 51, 2277
Sequoia Communications, 1920
Sequoia Software, 226
Sequoia Tech Partners, 624
Sequoia Vaccines, 570
SequoiaSoft, 3229
Sequr, 191
Sera Prognostics, 428, 622
Sera Prognotics, 1014
SeraCare Life Sciences, 1132

Serafim Silva - Atividades Hoteleiras, 3039
Serafina Energy, 1447
Seragen, 317
Seragon Pharmaceuticals, 73
Serap, 2414
SeraStar, 1678
Serco, 2665
Seren, 2883
Serena, 962
Serena & Lily, 238, 763
Serene Green, 395
Serenex, 1013
Seres Health, 2693
Seres Therapeutics, 748, 1522
Sericol Inc., 1624
Seriforge, 944, 1363
Serious Energy, 1908
Serious Integrated, 2183
Seriously, 1890
Sermatech International, 172
Sermo, 1150, 1701
SERPs.com, 1467
Sertoli Technologies, 1546
Serus, 614
Servals Automation, 2305
Servi Group, 2722
Service, 709, 1186
Service Champ, 899
Service Design Associates, 1252
Service Express, 917, 1410
Service Finance Company, 751
Service Frame, 2909
Service Metrics, 1566
Service Partners, 1507
Service Radio Rentals, 1044
Service Source, 952
Service Strategies Interntional, 112
Service2Media, 3042
ServiceBench, 1045, 1137
ServiceBot Software, 999
ServiceChannel, 1691
ServiceLink, 1818
ServiceMax, 56, 561, 666, 1187, 1517, 1855
Servicemax, 564, 1213, 1716
ServiceNow, 1045
ServiceNow Inc., 517
Servicesoft Technologies, 2073
Servicys, 178
Servion, 485
Servion Global Solutions, 189
ServOne, 912
Servosity, 1925
ServusConnect, 512
Sesil, 1091
Session M, 938
Session Title Services, 679
SessionM, 457, 1079, 1610
Sessions, 2511
Sessions.edu, 1723
Set Fm, 2131
Set Media, 564
Set Scouter, 2120
Set.fm, 2130
Setagon Inc., 272
SetJam, 1588
SetPoint Medical, 749, 1126
SetSight, 3268
Settle, 2931
Sev1Tech, 611
Sevco Security, 1
SEVE, 3011
SEVEN, 2707
7AC Technologies, 498
7AC Technology, 1104
Seven Bridges Genomics, 1486
7 Cups of Tea, 600
7 Days Group Holdings, 416

7d Software GmbH & Co., 2664
7 Gate Ventures, 3249
7Gege, 2927
Seven Generations, 1848
Seven Generations Energy, 2036
7k7k, 827
7lbs, 975, 1364, 1618
Seven Lakes Technologies, 419
Seven Media, 1091
Seven Oaks Biosystems, 428
Seven Rosen, 2649
Seven Seas, 3213
Seven Seas Water, 658
7 Shifts, 310, 2074, 2228
7signal, 86, 1051, 1556
7Summits, 1610
7-Technologies, 2642
Seven Technologies, 3234
7TM Pharma, 3006
Seven10, 1276
SevenFifty, 1483
SevenInvensun, 1511
Sevenly, 1967
SevenR Rooms, 520
SevenRooms, 1499
SevenSpace, 1855
7thOnline, 462, 1748
Seventh Generation, 430, 1630, 2321
Seventh Sense Biosystems, 983, 1464
SeventhSense Biosystems, 748, 1814
70 Millions Staffing, 1509
724 Solutions, 205
727 Solutions, 1706
72Lux.com, 1305
7234, 2927
798 Entertainment, 2841
Sevenval, 2494
Sevin Rosen, 36
Sevin Rosen Funds, 990
SevOne, 224, 1388
Sewa Grih Rin, 54
Sewon Telecom, 2915
SEWORKS, 1511
Seworks, 3118
Sextant Education Corporation, 63
Sexy Hair, 1863
Seymour Investment Management, 2284
Sfara, 1114, 1928
Sfara FinLocker, 570
SFERRA, 1115
SFO Technologies, 585
SFOX, 1698
Sfox, 310, 1850
SG Fleet Services, 2613
SG360, 367, 973
SGA, 815
SGA Production Services, 633
SGB, 1820
SGE, 1340
SGGHM - Soc. Geral Gestao Hoteis de Mocambique, 3039
SGN, 116
SGS Co., 2201
SGX Pharmaceuticals, 1495
SGX Sensortech, 225
Shaanxi Northwest New Technology Industry Co. Ltd., 2624
Shacham, 2742
Shade Up, 568
Shadow Government, 2302
Shadow Networks, 1401
Shadowfax, 1511
Shake, 310, 1223, 1597, 1701
Shake Shack, 1113
Shakepay, 2131
Shakti, 838

Portfolio Companies Index

Shakti Battery, 1087
Shakudo, 2122, 2131
Shanahan's, 2045
Shandong Winery, 897
Shanghai Chunge Glass Co., 2533
Shanghai Framedia Advertisement, 2838
Shanghai Global Baby Products, 1241
Shanghai Harvest Network Technology, 181
Shanghai Hintsoft Software, 2841
Shanghai Huahong, 2927
Shanghai iRay, 1340
Shanghai Mining Software Company, 2989
Shanghai Shen-Li High Tech, 2533
Shanghai Superrfid Electronics Technology, 2841
Shanghai Yi Shang Network Information Company, 1241
Shanghai-Haier-IC, 3225
Shangpin, 3133
Shangri-La, 2277
Shanon, 2965
Shansong (FlashEX), 1122
Shape, 234, 1039, 1153, 1918, 2681
Shape Security, 84, 1079, 1346, 1672, 1832
Shape Technologies, 110
Shape.AG, 2727
Shaper, 521, 680
ShapeShift, 35
Shapeshift, 882
ShapeUp, 704
Shapeways, 125, 1155
SHARE, 1285
Share Microfin, 2305
Share This, 1841
Shareable Ink, 1111
Shareablee, 845, 1701, 1901
Shareaholic, 316, 1069, 1322
Sharebuilder, 892
ShareCare, 495
Sharecare, 173, 254, 809, 925, 1832
Shared Spectrum Company, 510
ShareGrove, 661
Shareholder InSite, 679
ShareholdInSite, 1412
ShareLaTeX, 3099
Sharelink, 2787
SharePost, 1813
SharePractice, 1637
shareThat, 1737
ShareThis, 290, 610, 721, 979, 1050, 1207, 1596
Sharethrough, 752, 1335
Sharewise, 2466
Shari's Management Corporation, 483, 714
Shari's Restaurants, 1377
Shark, 2439
Sharklet Technologies, 1130
Sharp Analytics, 8
Sharpen, 659
Sharps, 1755
Shasun, 1383
Shayne International Holdings, 585
Shayog, 54
Shazam, 1006, 2314, 2419, 2463, 2659, 2702
Shearer's Foods, 1990
ShearShare, 221
Sheer Networks, 1042, 3128
Sheerly Genius, 2127
Sheertex, 2037
SheFly, 623
SheKnows, 520
Shelby.tv, 209
Shelf Drilling, 425, 1129
Shelf Engine, 776
Shelfari, 85
Shelfmint, 1724
Shell, 217
Shell Oil, 2612
ShellHound, 1616

Sheln, 977
Shelter Distribution, 331
Shelter Luv, 1219
ShelterLogic Investment, 1560
ShelterPoint Life, 687
Shemin, 1372
Shenandoah Growers, 2282
Shengtang Entertainment, 2581
Shenogen Pharma Group, 977
Shenwu, 3091
Shenzhen Green Materials Hi-tech, 2793
Shenzhen Guanri Telecom, 2841
Shenzhen Kingdee Software, 2841
Shenzhen Kingsky, 2841
Shenzhen Sunlord Electronics, 2793
Shenzhen Tsinghua Tongfang Co Ltd, 2490
Shenzhen WuZhouLong Motors, 2793
Shenzhen Yinboda Telecommunication Technology, 2793
Shenzhen Yuton, 2927
Shenzhoufu, 3199
Shenzhoufu.com, 2841
Sheplers, 886
Sheridan, 927
Sheridan Group Inc., 357
Sherman & Reilly Inc., 694
Shermans Travel, 56
Sherpa, 746, 2131, 2228
Sherpaa, 1359, 1701
Shertrack, 1337
Shevirah, 288
Shezhen Shenzinlong Industry, 3053
Shicoh Engineering, 1757
Shida Shenghua Chemical, 2533
Shield AI, 125, 944
ShieldAI, 623
ShieldX, 182
Shielf Tech, 421
Shift, 125, 231, 305, 309, 610, 625, 846, 863, 938, 945, 1569, 1966, 2009
Shift Payments, 1058
Shift Technology, 820
Shift4 Payments, 2243
Shiftboard, 85
ShiftForward, 3039
ShiftGig, 732
Shiftgig, 473, 827, 1483
Shiftgig Silver Spring Networks, 561
ShiftLeft, 1187
ShiftMessenger, 1058
SHIFTMobility, 1831
ShiftPlanning, 1227, 3035
Shilpa Medicare, 2481
Shimmur, 1705
Shimojani, 644
Shimon Systems, 131
Shin Kong International, 2841
Shin Kong Mitsukoshi Department Store, 1771
Shin Nippon Biomedical Laboratories, 2961
Shine, 520, 680, 756, 2822, 2863
SHINE Medical Technologies, 2002
ShineOn, 1187
Shineon, 1340
Shinesty, 285
Shiningstar Energy, 2036
Shinrai, 2325
Shinsung Solar Energy, 3136
Shionogi & Co., 1271
Shionogi Inc., 1349
Ship Mate, 121
Ship Supply, 931
Shipamax, 398, 640
ShipBob, 1203
ShipHawk, 207, 400, 1059, 1966
Shipmonk, 1759
Shippable, 619, 1162, 2007
Shippable Simply Measured, 776

Shippabo, 309
Shippert Medical, 1670
Shippo, 1702, 1881, 1884, 2272
Shiprocket, 1616
Shipsi, 901
Shipt, 641, 907
Shipwell, 728, 742, 1935, 2126
Shipwire, 1196
Shire, 1271
Shirtinator, 2970
Shiva, 241
Shixianghui, 1122
SHL, 1929
Shnier, 2246
Sho My Homework, 3021
ShoCard, 108, 545, 1254
Shocking Technologies, 185
Shockwave Medical, 1522, 1918
Shoe Corp. of America, 463
Shoe Sensation, 1053
Shoeboxed, 1348
Shoeboxed.com, 289
Shoebuy, 1731
Shoeby - Lakeside, 2492
Shoedazzle, 1411
Shoedazzle.Com, 1464
Shoefitr, 296, 1942
Shoelace, 2024, 2094
Shoes For Crews, 63
Shoes for Crews, 435
Shoes of Prey, 1713, 2511
Shogun, 798
Shomiti Systems, 1684
Shoof Technologies, 1079
Shop Genius, 1966
Shop Hers, 1549
Shop It To Me, 1867
Shop Your World, 2844
Shopa, 3009
Shopal, 1709
Shopatron, 1813
Shopcaster, 2176
ShopClues, 2809, 2934
ShopClues.com, 2992
ShopEx, 2927
Shopgate, 2629
Shopify, 744
ShopIgniter, 1855
Shopistry, 2176
Shopitur, 3039
ShopKeep, 535, 1865
Shopkeep, 949, 1851
ShopKeepPOS, 389
Shopkick, 488
Shopko, 1755
ShopLogic, 586
Shopmium, 3199, 3229
Shopnation, 1103
shopobot Inc., 650
ShopPad, 1105
Shopper+, 2065
Shoppers Drug Mart, 212, 458
Shopping.Com, 200
Shopping.com, 215, 641
Shoppo, 827
Shoprocket, 3099
ShopSavvy, 400
ShopShops, 763, 1884
ShopSocial.ly, 1901
ShopSpot, 3112
Shopturn, 1179
Shopular, 773
ShopWell, 713, 1304, 1490
ShopWiki, 822
ShopYourWorld.com, 1966
Shore Capital Partners, 36, 3255
ShoreGroup, 782

1391

Portfolio Companies Index

Shoreline Solutions, 381
ShoreMaster, 935
ShoreTel, 759, 773, 1798
Shortlist, 1618, 1887
Shoshin, 217
Shot Tracker, 1023
Shotgun Picture, 2519
Shots, 1154, 1890, 2009
Shots Studio, 1983
ShotSpotter, 493
Shotspotter, 830
Shotspotter Inc., 1093
ShotTracker, 1660
Shotzr, 35
Shoutlet, 1112, 1385
Show Battery, 2148
Show Kicker, 1467
Show Long Fashion Gourmet Co, 2533
Showa Yakuhin Kako, 3192
Showbie, 2283
Showbizdata, 2020
Showcard Print, 2935
Showcase-TV, 2965
ShowClix, 1003, 1451
ShowEvidence, 194, 758
Showfields, 1768
ShowGrow, 206
ShowingTime, 28
ShowMe, 680
Showpad, 1005
Showroom Logic, 784
ShowUHow, 1773
ShowWorld Holding, 3053
Showyou, 1862
ShoZu, 556
Shred All, 445
Shred-It, 2177
Shred-it, 56
Shree Kamdhenu Electronics, 2305
Shriram City Union Finance, 136
Shuangcheng Pharma, 977
Shubham, 2809
Shuddle, 708
Shukinko, 1501
Shun On Electronic, 2594
Shunra Software, 2557
ShurCo Acquisition, 1343
Shurgard Self-Storage, 153
Shurpa, 999
Shutl, 641, 1893, 2828, 3005
Shutterfly, 57, 342, 1186, 1247
Shutterly, 857
Shvydko, 3224
Shyft, 229, 1162
Shyft Analytics, 51
Shyp, 788, 1752, 1998, 2009
SI Auto, 2472
SI Corp., 1021
Si Time, 972
SI-BONE, 150, 1693
SI-Bone, 1383
Si-Bone, 1251
Si-Cat, 2181
Si2, 3202
Si2 Microsystems, 3053
SIA Abrasives, 2555
Siamab, 1104
Siamab Therapeutics, 1164
Siano, 1608, 3128, 3221
Siara Systems, 1478
Siaras, 185
Siargo, 46
SiBeam, 1155
Sibley & Associates, 2785
SiC Processing, 3242
Sichuan Tomorrow Fine Chemical Co., 2425
Sicom, 1140, 2745

Sicomed, 2775
SiCortex, 1042
Sicoya, 3152
Side by Side, 507
SideCar, 743
Sidecar, 180, 209, 721, 907, 1321, 1388, 1581, 1701
Sidecare, 151
Sidedolla, 1589
Sidel, 2598
Sidense, 2253, 3205
Sideqik, 246, 309, 1569
Sideris Pharmaceuticals, 918, 1268
SideStep, 1798
Sidestep, 1852
SideTrade, 3229
Sidetrade, 3104
Sidley Austin, 3262
Siebel System, 57
Siebel Systems, 857
Siebel Systems Inc., 1905
Siembraviva, 54
Siemens AG, 3203
Siemplify, 2126
Siempo, 221
Siena Funding, 1971
Sienna Biopharmaceuticals, 94
Sientra, 1383
Sienza, 1055
Sierra Atlantic, 1017
Sierra Design, 1795
Sierra Hamilton, 408
Sierra Industries, 679
Sierra Labs, 729
Sierra Lifestyle, 3248
Sierra Monolithics, 1750
Sierra Nevada Solar, 1671
Sierra Oil & Gas, 673
Sierra Oncology, 140, 403, 785, 1522, 1943
Sierra Systems, 843
Sierra Ventures, 217
Sierra Wireless, 388, 857, 2091, 2258
Siesta Medical, 139
Siffron, 1372
SIFI, 2285
SiFotonics Technologies, 974
Sift, 608
Sift Science, 1005
Sifteo, 1862
Siftery, 31, 108
Siftit, 1790
SIG, 2201
SIG Holding, 2607
Sigasi, 2467
SiGe Semiconductor, 713, 2073
Sige Semiconductor, 1949
SiGen, 897
SigFig, 597
Sigfox, 1418, 1610, 2684
SIGG, 1576
Sigh Machine, 964
Sight Machine, 812, 1207, 1359, 1705
sight4all, 300
Sighten, 1363
Sightline Technologies, 1325
Sightly, 1832, 1992
SightMD, 471
Sightpath Medical, 458
Sightward, 755
Sigilon Therapeutics, 748
SIGMA, 792
Sigma Estimates, 3194
Sigma International General Medical Apparatus, 1152
Sigma Offshore, 2691
Sigma-Tau Pharmaceutical, 1456
SigmaFlow, 1785

SigmaTel, 1795
Sigmatel, 597
SigmaX Limited, 2696
Sign-Zone, 1438
Sign-Zone Inc., 912
SignaCert, 810
Signal, 225, 689, 925, 1483, 1832
Signal 88 Security, 1276
Signal AI, 2750
Signal Bay Inc., 1083
Signal Innovations Group, 983
Signal Outdoor Advertising, 1270
Signal Peak Ventures, 3265
Signal Sciences, 1359
Signal Storage Innovations, 1839
Signal Tree Solutions, 167
SignalFX, 820
SignalSense, 1854
SignalSoft, 967
SignalWire, 1614
Signase, 1414
Signature Bank, 3262
Signature Bank NY, 3265
Signature Coast, 574
Signature Control Systems Inc., 838
Signature Destinations, 85
Signature Genomic, 119
Signature Hospice and Home Health, 1271
Signature Security Group, 2411
Signature Systems Group, 1136
Signaturit Solutions, 1499
SigNav, 2980
SignaVine, 183
Signavio, 136
Signet Accel, 655
Signet Jewelers, 1113
Signiant, 313, 696, 1335, 2191
Signicast, 1482
Signicat, 3207
SigniFAI, 545
Signifai, 938
Signifi, 2051
Signifyd, 84, 586, 1203, 1504, 1549
Signio, 1852
Signix, 949
Signma, 1983
SignmaQuest, 116
SignNow, 1371
Signostics, 2527
SignPost, 2126
Signpost, 1381, 1635
SignPost Cancer Dx Inc., 2145
SignStorey, 1305
Signstorey, 843
Signum Technology, 3027
SignUp.com, 724
Sigouria Groupe, 870
Sigstr, 659
Sigtec Pty, 2613
Sigus Slovakia, 2674
SigValue Technologies Inc., 2819
Sihayo Gold, 2933
Sihe Wood, 597, 2927
Siigo, 28
Siimpel, 2020
Siine, 2437
Sikka, 185
Sikka Software Corporation, 1672
Siklu, 117, 1511, 2717
Sila, 1184
Silatronix, 1291, 1923, 2002
Silbond Corp., 445
Silecs, 2653
Silego, 1750
Silent, 3095
Silent Preferred Partners, 197
Silex Microsystems, 3004

Portfolio Companies Index

Silex., 2553
Silexica, 1219
Silicium Energy, 1073
Silicon Architects, 200
Silicon Bandwidth, 2073
Silicon Blue, 564, 2844
Silicon Clocks, 766, 1155, 1781
Silicon Cloud, 2769
Silicon Dimensions, 1084
Silicon Energy, 898, 1008, 1355
Silicon Energy Corp, 2073
Silicon Frontline Technology, 974
Silicon Hive, 1304, 3042
Silicon Image, 200
Silicon Laboratories, 1687
Silicon Labs, 446
Silicon Media, 2378
Silicon Metrics, 1287
Silicon Mitus, 691
Silicon Motion Inc., 950
Silicon Navigator Corp., 813
Silicon Optix, 759
Silicon Packets, 1649
Silicon Space Technology, 1302
Silicon Systems, 1237
Silicon Touch Technology, 3209
Silicon Valley Bank, 3265
Silicon Value, 2711
Silicon Value Ltd, 3149
Silicon Video Inc., 434
SiliconSystems, 1667
Siliconware Precision Industries, 897
Silicor Materials, 58, 839
Silikids, 1739
Siliquent, 2372
Siliquent Technologies, 1449
Silitech, 2427
Silixa, 468, 1129
Silixa Ltd., 3132
Silk, 2437
Silk Labs, 626
Silk Road, 564
Silk Road Medical, 1346, 1931
Silkan, 3104
SilkRoad, 773, 949, 3225
SilkRoad Japan, 1757
SilkRoad Realty Capital, 1683
SilkRoad Technology, 1683, 1798
Silkspan, 1143
Silniva Inc., 176
Silofit, 2280
Silot, 149
SILQ, 999
Silq, 771
Siluria, 1478, 3090
Siluria Technologies, 87, 154, 1155
Silver, 59
Silver Aero, 228
Silver Bullet, 147
Silver Creek, 1061
Silver Creek Oil & Gas, 560
Silver Creek Permian, 560
Silver Creek Systems, 1408
Silver Jeans Co., 2249
Silver Kite, 2571
Silver Lake, 3245
Silver Lining, 1358
Silver Lining Solutions, 2958
Silver Oak Energy, 673
Silver Peak, 251, 1341, 1628
Silver Peak Systems, 582, 877, 1449
Silver Regulatory Associates, 3258
Silver Spring Networks, 773
Silver State Materials, 197
Silver Storm Technologies, 540
Silver Stream Software, 1042
Silver Tail Systems, 549, 983

Silverado Senior Living, 1579
Silverback Exploration, 673
SilverBack Technologies, 317
Silverback Technologies, 1335
Silvercare Solutions, 718
SilverCarrot, 1313
Silvercrest, 1948
Silvergate Pharmaceuticals Inc., 785
Silverline, 1410, 1610
Silverlink, 1056, 1675
Silverlink Communications, 1674
Silvernest, 901
SilverPOP, 186
Silverpop, 1865
SilverRail, 352, 389
SilverRail Technologies, 853
SilverSheet, 49
Silversheet, 309, 1890
SilverSky, 1751
Silversky, 532
SilverSpring Networks, 582
Silverspring Networks, 1341
SilverStorm Technologies, 215
SilverStream, 1335
SilverTail, 1106, 1658
Silvertip Completion Services, 1129
SilverTrail Systems, 488
SilverVue, 1483
Silvue, 525
Silvus, 1049
SIM Digital, 2133
SIM Partners, 1050, 1575
Simbe, 521, 1477
Simbe Robotics, 1423
Simbi, 23, 976, 1186
Simbionix, 642
Simbol Materials, 731, 992, 1247
SIMCO Ltd., 911
SimCraft, 656
Simcro, 1576
Sime Diagnostics, 3098
Simeio Solutions, 1973
Simibio, 2505
Simlife, 2841
Simmerson Holdings, 2514
Simmons, 722, 1021
Simmons Bedding Company, 160
Simms Fishing Products, 424
Simon Data, 1
SimonDelivers, 1117, 1955
Simonds Industries, 1278
SIMP, 3011
Simperium, 680
Simpirica, 599
Simplaex, 3152
+Simple, 2398
Simple, 969, 1666, 1823, 2398, 2931
Simple Charters, 2
Simple Citizen, 1074
Simple Disability Insurance, 387
Simple Emotion, 1467
Simple Energy, 1791, 1978
Simple Feast, 2469
Simple Habit, 1142
Simple Health, 23
Simple Legal, 600
Simple Reach, 1966
Simple Star, 1918
Simple Tuition, 1339
Simplebet, 754
Simplee, 1698
SimpleGeo, 787
SimpleIT, 2377
SimpleLegal, 309, 1760
SimpleNexus, 1005
Simplenight, 754
Simpler, 586

SimpleReach, 37, 1242, 1479
SimpleRelevance, 473, 965
SimpleTax, 2676, 3099
Simpletax, 2577
Simpletuition, 949
Simpleview, 8, 1049
Simplexity, 1348
Simpli.fi, 535, 1488
Simplibuy, 650
Simplicissius Book Farm, 3043
Simplifeye, 129, 720
Simplified Logistics, 478
SimpliField, 746
Simplify Compliance, 1109, 1169
Simplifya, 966, 1208
SimplifyMD, 1013
Simplivity, 457, 646, 1213
Simplus, 561, 1610
Simply Good Jars, 1581
Simply Hired, 810, 1566
Simply Incredible Foods, 1291
Simply Measured, 780, 1227
Simply Smart Group, 2668
Simply Vital Health, 310
SimplyCast, 2148
SimplyHired, 773
Simplyhired Inc., 624
SimplyShe, 68, 913
SimplyTapp, 1928
SimplyWell, 1839
Simponi, 2097
Simpplr, 1346, 1610
Simpson Performance Products, 357, 418
SimpTek Technologies, 2192
Simscale, 1884
SimSuite, 1535
SIMtone, 1084
Simtra Aerotech Spotfire, 2869
Simulmedia, 209, 1829
Simworx, 2958
Sin Delental, 3096
SINA Corporation, 1478
Sincerely, 457, 1718
SinDelantal.com, 2911
Sinequa, 3229
Singapore Advanced Biologics, 2509
Singapore Suzhou Township Development, 2681
Singer Equities, 1140
Single Digits, 336, 1731
Single Platform, 609
SingleOps, 191, 746, 2074
SinglePipe Communications, 1215
SinglePlatform, 1483
SinglePoint, 47, 1640
SingleToken Security, 649
Singlewire Software, 1499
Singly, 787, 1358, 1862
Singpost, 1718
Singular, 820, 1346
Singular BIO, 1931
Singulex, 1490
Sinitic, 2123
Sinldo, 1340
Sino Forest, 1091
Sino-Forest, 2763
SinoBnet, 2841
Sinocampus, 3199
Sinocom, 2927
Sinofusion, 2989
SinoGen International, 897
SinoLending, 586
Sinomedia Holding Limited, 223
Sinopsys, 933
Sinopsys Surgical, 1207
Sinosol AG, 2970
SinoSun Technology, 827
Sinovia Technologies, 721

1393

Portfolio Companies Index

Sinoway Herbal Skin Care, 2551
Sinphoniq, 2859
SintecMedia, 3221
SinterFire, 165
SiOnyx, 1948
Sionyx, 564, 1464
siOPTICA, 2518
SioTex, 953
Sipera, 3128
Siperian, 133
Siping Cogen Power Plants, 2582
SiPort, 1304, 1449
Sipp, 669
Sipwise, 3156
Sipx, 1247, 2010
Siraga, 2593
SIRAKOSS, 690
Sirchie Fingerprint Laboratories, 1529
Sircon, 652
Siren, 1426
Siren Care, 1703
Siren Care Inc., 1073
Sirenum, 640
SiRF Technology, 1924
SiRF Technology Holdings Inc., 1781
Sirga Advanced BioPharma, 738
Siri, 1257, 2822
Sirific, 1244
Sirigen, 1917
Sirion Biotech, 2629
SIrion Therapeutics, 73
Sirion Therapeutics, 1777
Sirius, 1066
Sirius Computer Solutions, 912, 1817
Sirius Decisions, 1045
Sirocco, 1930
Siromed, 1053
Sirona Dental Systems, 1160
SironRX, 642
SironRX Therapeutics, 1051
SironRx Therapeutics, 1556, 1849
Sirrus, 173, 325, 481, 1241
SirsiDynix, 165, 973
Sirti, 2285
Sirtris Pharmaceuticals, 413, 1693
SIRVA, 1160
Sisal, 3024
SiSense, 1598, 1672
Sisense, 1382
Sisterson, 3264
Sistina Software, 556
Sisu Global Health, 18, 386
Sitara Networks, 457
Site Hands, 796
Site Jabber, 1658
SiteAware, 2938
Sitecare, 2845
Sitecore Corporation, 1787
SiteDocs, 2074
Sitel, 1138
Sitematic, 1239
SiteMinder, 1787
SiteOne Therapeutics, 1238, 1317
Siterra, 443
SiteScape, 647
Sitetracker, 1610
Sitewit, 1737
Siteworx, 1579
SiTime, 388, 2788
Sitka Biopharma, 2221
Sitka Exploration, 2022, 2036
Sitoa, 2448
Sitrion, 1245
Sitryx Therapeutics, 1149, 1631
SitScape, 983
Sittercity, 138, 1463, 1483
Sittercity.com, 225

Siva, 2010
Siva Power, 596, 731, 1852
Sivdon Diagnostics, 2629
Siverge, 2717
SiVerio Inc., 813
SiVerion, 1130
Siverion, 861, 1903
Sivyer Steel Corporation, 719
Six Apart, 200, 759, 2982
Six Degrees, 458
Six Degrees Games, 504
6 River Systems, 648, 1203, 1346
Six Rooms Holdings, 1241
6 Sence, 232
Six Waves, 1464
6 Wind, 2867
60 Erie St. Jersey City NJ, 192
64 pixels, 10
64-x, 742
64x Bio, 321
Sixa, 814
6connect, 959
6d, 252
6D.AI, 752, 820
6D.ai, 1666
Sixdof Space, 544
Sixense, 810, 1614
SixFix, 999
6fusion, 1013
Sixpack Mobile Applications, 3119
6Scan, 3236
6Sense, 1610
6sense, 238, 548, 1918
6SensorLabs, 1702
6sicuro, 3043
Sixth Sense Media, 1643
6th Treet Inc., 1172
Sixtron Advanced Materials, 186
SixUp, 31
Sixup, 1554
6Waves, 1005
6WIND, 485
6wunderkinder, 2437
Size Technologies, 1649
Sizzling Platter, 1904
SJ Semi, 1511
SJI Holdings, 364
Sjtu Sunway Software Industry Ltd., 2624
SK FireSafety Group, 2492
SK Sinsegi Telecom, 2848
SK Spruce, 1672
Skale Labs, 752
Skansogaard, 3194
Skaphandrus, 3039
SKC Communication Products, 1276
Skechers, 874
Skedulo, 548
Skeed, 2965
Skeepers, 1499
Skerou, 2300
SketchDeck, 945, 1770
SketchFab, 311
Sketchfab, 744, 2469
Skift, 59, 1114, 1223
Skill Survey, 51
Skillist, 756
Skilljar, 1187, 1666
Skillo, 608
Skillshare, 321, 1718, 1724, 1914
SkillSoft, 223, 1674
Skillsoft PLC, 303
SkillSurvey, 993, 1480
Skillz, 37, 69, 1322, 1616
Skimlinks, 259, 876
Skin Analytics, 2002
Skin Medica, 1251
Skinkers, 2314

SkinMedica, 73, 1728
Skinphonic, 1194
Skip, 724, 1011, 1836
Skip Scooters, 2122
Skip The Dishes, 2131
Skip the Dishes, 2130
Skipta, 1168
SKLZ, 1744
SkopeNow, 1269
Skopos Financial, 1108
Skopos Labs, 195
Skorpios Technologies, 550
SKOut, 1966
Skout, 1323
Skrill, 1021
Skuad, 2398
Skuid, 1610
Skullcandy, 1205
Skully Helmets, 1310
Skupos, 640
Skura, 2051
Skurt, 305, 708, 1890
SkuVault, 227
Sky Europe, 2674
SKY Harbor Capital Management, 1746
Sky Squirrel Technologies, 2148
Sky Vision, 897
SkyAtlas, 3069
SkyBitz, 1018
Skybox Imaging, 183, 389
Skybox Security, 1499, 1543, 1761, 2557, 3212
Skybuilt Power, 983
Skycast, 85
Skycatch, 209, 246, 724, 1269, 1511, 1896
Skycision, 999
Skycredit, 2969
SkyCross, 621, 808, 1830
Skycure, 773, 1666
SkyDeck Accelerator, 1672
Skydex, 35
Skydex Technologies, 554
SkyDrop, 1672
Skydrop, 640
Skye Chesapeake Bay Roating Company, 1603
Skye Mineral Partners, 496
SkyePharma, 1619
Skyera, 1692
SkyeTek, 143
Skyfire, 1411, 1855
SkyFuel, 758
SkyGrid, 794
skyhawk Therapeutics, 849
Skyhook Wireless, 224, 536
Skyhour, 1039
Skyland Exchange, 1220
Skylar Body, 121, 345
Skylark, 223, 2371
Skylight Healthcare Systems, 1428, 1667
Skylight.net, 1955
SkyLights, 1477
Skylights, 1370
Skyline, 36, 149, 2148
Skyline Home Loans, 1890
Skyline Innovations, 60, 401
Skyline Solar, 1365
Skyline Windows, 1210
SkyMall, 1727
Skymedi Corporation, 2594
Skynamo, 746
Skyonic, 325
Skype, 388, 610, 691, 803, 2437, 2822, 2919
SkyPilot, 2990
Skypilot, 200
SkyPilot Networks, 1649
SkyPipeline, 381
Skyroam, 3206
SkyRyse, 490

Portfolio Companies Index

Skyryse, 398, 648, 1918
SkySafe, 1533
Skyscanner, 3095
Skysheet, 2321
Skysoft, 57
SkySpecs, 114, 964, 985
SKYstream, 1101
SkyStream Networks, 827
Skysun LLC, 1051
Skytap, 978, 1162, 1381, 2007
Skytide, 857
SkyTran, 1001
Skytream Networks, 1006
Skytree, 1032, 1893
SkyVu, 863, 1121, 1322
SkyWard, 776
Skyward, 1947
Skyware Global, 654
SkyWatch, 2130
Skywatch, 2131
Skyway, 2418
Skyword, 949, 1488
Skyworks Interactive, 421
Slack, 44, 108, 520, 827, 1006, 1079, 1153, 1696, 1698, 1763
Slacker, 1239
Slacker Radio, 518
Slackers, 443
SLAMcore, 1836
SlamData, 1659, 1666
Slamdata, 35
Slang, 1698
SlashNext, 1346
Slater Technology Fund, 1695
SLED Mobile, 301
Sleek Medspa, 1955
Sleep Country, 722
Sleep Country Canada, 2177
Sleeperbot, 275
SleepMed, 227, 1399
Sleepy's, 371
SLG Recycling, 3011
Slice, 561, 597, 827, 1001, 1039
Slide, 708
Slide Rocket, 218
SlideShare, 1918
Slightly Nutty, 3248
Slim Ops Studios, 1003
Sling, 308
Sling Media, 186, 597, 925, 2927
Slive, 198
Sliver.tv, 998, 1614, 1672, 1705
SLM Corporation, 1905
SloanLED, 225, 911
Slocum Adhesives, 1210
Slon Lofts Group, 791
Slope, 512, 640, 1644
Slovlepex, 3113
Slovpack Bratislava, 3068
SLR Consulting Limited, 2303
SLT Logic, 1678
Slyce, 1305
Slyde, 3036
SM Logistics, 2760
SM&A, 376, 377
SM&A Holdings, 1368
Smackhigh, 316
Small Bone Innovations, 215, 1325, 1846
Small Box Energy, 861
Small Demons, 2009
Small Door, 328
Small Giant Games, 3046
Small World, 2963, 3088
Smallable, 2377
Smallstep, 308
Smalltown, 766
Smarfin, 2877

Smarkets, 3021
Smarking, 1330, 1486, 1593
Smarsh, 1831
Smart & Final Stores LLC, 160
Smart Ace, 2993
Smart Autonomous Solutions, 2027
Smart Communications, 28
Smart Destinations, 1316, 1339
Smart Document Solutions, 153
Smart Education, 2860
Smart Energy Instruments, 2037
Smart Eye, 2746
Smart Focus, 782
Smart Furniture, 1273
Smart Host, 2832
Smart Hydro Power, 2677
Smart Link Ltd, 2773
Smart Loyalty, 2970
Smart Lunches, 587, 1104, 1585
Smart Medical Systems, 622
Smart Mocha, 1467
SMART Modular, 1685
Smart Modular Technologies, 782
Smart Pants Vitamins, 1255
Smart Picture, 784
Smart Picture Solution, 447
Smart Planet Technologies, 1065
Smart Recruiter, 1610
Smart Recruiters, 1543
Smart Reno, 2024
Smart Sand, 502
Smart Scheduling, 1618
Smart Skin, 2192, 2231
Smart Skin Technologies, 2063
Smart Sparrow, 3014
Smart Storage, 2530
Smart Telecom, 2909
Smart Vision Labs, 1533
Smart Warehousing, 746
Smart Wave, 3063
Smartanalyst, 51, 655
SmartAngels, 3229
Smartassel, 1335
SmartAsset, 1521
Smartasset, 1032
SmartBear, 782
Smartbear, 1831
Smartbin, 2347
SmartBix, 1918
Smartbiz, 234
SmartCover Systems, 2282
SmartDrive Systems, 1361
SmartDyeLivery, 2518
Smarter Alloys, 2037
Smarter Grid Solutions, 3095
Smarter HQ, 659
Smarter Sorting, 411
Smarterer, 1554, 1862
SmarterHQ, 1731
SmarteSoft, 447, 595
Smartesting, 2890
Smartfile, 659
SmartFlow Technologies, 1018
Smartfrog, 641
Smarthouse, 2677
SmartKem, 3009
SmartKids, 2429
SmartLane, 121
Smartlaw, 2829
Smartlight Ltd, 2576
Smartling, 31, 720, 1566, 1798, 1918
Smartlink, 1722
SmartMI, 827
Smartner, 2378
SmartNews, 2437
SmartOps, 55
Smartots, 3118

SmartPackets, 649
SmartPak, 1000
SmartPak Equine, 440, 1360
SmartPark Equine, 1335
SmartPath, 1013
Smartpods, 2192
Smartrac Technology, 1376
SmartRecruiters, 1187, 1991
SmartRG, 794, 1250, 1384
SmartRM, 2663
SmartRx, 3202
Smarts Japan, 1757
SmartShare, 3194
Smartsheet, 1162
SmartSheet10 Technology, 1288
SmartShoot, 1702
Smartsky, 1212
SmartSource Holdings, 1460
SmartSpot, 1677
SmartSynch, 236, 1355
SmartTones Media, 2094
SmartTrade, 2676
SmartVid.io, 311, 1104, 1483
SmartWool, 1751
Smarty, 1426
Smarty Content, 2911
Smarty Pants, 484
Smarty Pants Vitamins, 333
SmartyPants Inc., 334
SmartyPig, 583
SmartZip, 1032, 1645
SmartZip Analytics, 493, 568
SMASH, 1003
Smash.gg, 1153
Smashburger, 1024
Smashfly, 1381
Smava, 2985
SMB Machinery Systems, 934
sMedio, 2965
Smeet, 2804
SMG, 322, 2201
Smi, 1518
SMIC, 597
Smic, 2427
SmilarWeb, 1323
Smile Brands, 886, 1973
Smile Brands Inc., 1138
Smile Direct Club, 1079
Smile Doctors, 1169
Smile Doctors Braces, 15, 1132
Smile Identity, 1760
Smile Maker, 2637
Smile Reminder, 1679
SmileBack, 1521
Smiles Services, 854
Smilo, 328, 1346
SMiT, 1187
Smith Broadcasting Group, 902
Smith Co., 77
Smith Pipe, 517
Smith System Driver Improvement Institute, 1115
Smith-Cooper International, 747
SmithRx, 863
Smokey Bones, 1755
Smooth Commerce, 2094
Smoothstone, 1242
Smore, 776, 2272
Smove, 1966
SMS Assist, 846, 1483
SMS GupShup, 839
SmS Tnzotherm, 3220
SMT Dynamics, 1917
SMT Kingdom, 1045
SMTC Corporation, 441
Smtc Corporation, 2162
SMTP, 638

Portfolio Companies Index

Smulders Group, 2492
Smule, 752, 857, 1666
Smule UParts, 784
Smurfit Kappa, 1160
Smurfit-Stone, 1968
Smyte, 209
Smyte., 234
Smyth, 2198
Småföretagsinvest, 2858
SN Tech, 1607
Snack, 2122, 2131
Snadec, 3229
Snag A Slip, 495
SnagaJob, 646
Snagajob, 200, 225, 907, 1013, 1728
SnagAJob.com, 56
SnagFilms, 520
Snakblox, 1305
Snap, 579
Snap Av, 927
Snap Financial Group, 790
Snap Kitchen, 1092
Snap Sheet, 1483
Snap Strat, 1666
Snap! Raise, 1499
Snap-On Inc., 1905
SnapApp, 1499
Snapask, 1709
SnapAV, 819
SnapChat, 511
Snapchat, 251, 268, 805, 824, 1006, 1213, 1841
Snapdeal.com, 2992
Snapdocs, 31, 787
Snapflow, 1467
SnapGear, 1463
Snapin, 85
SNAPin Software, 1640
SnapLogic, 456, 549, 978
Snaplogic, 752
snapLogic, 1848
Snaplytics, 50
SnapNames, 85
Snapp Digital, 395
Snappcloud, 1298, 1464
SnappyTV, 787
SnapRetail, 55
SnapRoute, 1346
Snaproute, 1158
Snaps, 3118
Snapscreen, 2094
Snapsheet, 1121, 1364
Snapt, 3212
SnapTell, 1042
Snaptell, 624
SnapTrack, 857
SnapTravel, 246, 1121, 2150
Snapwire, 229
Snark.ai, 1850
SNC Former, 1143, 2937
SNDR, 1228
Snell, 2935
Snell and Wilcox, 2340
Sniffspot, 1101
Snips, 680, 1812
SNL Financial, 1300
SNL Securities, 1929
SnoBar Cocktails, 1065
Snocap, 115
SnoutID, 1426
Snow Companies, 1979
Snow Lakes Resources Ltd., 2117
Snow+Rock, 2926
Snowball, 2130, 2131
Snowball Group Limited, 2706
Snowbear, 2067
Snowflake, 1162
Snowflake Computing, 1537

Snowhite, 279
Snowshoe, 1153, 1154, 1223
Snowshoe Stamps, 2002
SnowShore, 457
SNU Precision, 1091
SnugMug, 1608
SNUPI Technologies, 2007
Snyder Industries Inc., 1372
Snyk, 308
So1, 3152
SOA Software, 1401, 1403, 1966
Soane Energy, 468
SoapBox, 2130
Soapbox, 1768, 2094
SOASTA, 766
Soasta, 389, 1428
Sobe, 1194
SOCAR, 514
SoccerScout.com, 2687
SOCi, 861
Sociable Labs, 2231
Sociable Labs Stipple, 1515
Sociagram, 1051
Social Annex, 400, 1059
Social Chorus, 1087, 1992
Social Construct, 1896
Social Finance, 1596
Social Gaming Network, 1348
Social Imprints, 3246
Social Insight, 2847
Social Intelligence, 949
Social Matterz, 546
Social Native, 49
Social Radar, 881, 1768
Social SafeGuard, 907
Social Sentinal, 789
Social Sentinel, 381, 1114
Social Service Coordinators, 1419
Social Solutions, 1389
Social Stock Exchange, 2500
Social Toaster, 1172
Social Touch, 827
SocialAnnex, 1966
SocialBicycles, 1305
SocialBomb, 1588
SocialBro, 3095
Socialbro, 2455
SocialFlow, 434, 713, 1526, 1701
Socialflow, 1597
SocialFlow Inc., 813
Socialize, 721, 1058
Socialkaty, 1121
Socialmedian, 1087
SocialPandas, 1862
Socialpoint, 2978
Socialradar, 1320
SocialRank, 59, 308
Socialre18, 3003
SocialSafeGuard, 1610
Socialsci, 1101
SocialShield, 1918
SocialSign.in, 354, 1305
SocialSignIn, 1181
SocialTables, 1808
Socialtext, 245, 1886
Socialthing, 686
SocialToaster, 288, 1959
Socialwalk, 3064
Socialware, 806, 1255, 1687, 1813
SocialWeekend, 1635
SocialWire, 31, 1702
Socinser, 2480
Sociocast, 1305
Socionado, 1509
SoCloz, 2377
SoCore Energy, 1121
Socotra, 1269

Socrata, 1257, 1381, 1623
Socrates AI, 1346
Socrates.ai, 1918
Socratic, 1666, 1718
Socratic Labs, 708
Socrative, 1862
Socrex, 3116
Socure, 91, 724, 2006
Sodacard, 3112
SodaHead, 1239, 1247, 1800
Sodastream, 2787
Sodium Solutions, 2278
Sofa Carpet Specialist, 1755
SoFactory, 3104
Sofar Sounds, 1884, 3009
Sofatronic, 2985
Sofatutor, 2832
Sofdesk, 677
Soff-Cut, 377
Soffio Medical, 1347, 1631
SOFI, 1006
SoFI, 1001
SoFi, 234, 597, 1504, 1821, 2154
Sofialys, 2629
Sofitech AS, 3132
Soft Module, 540
Soft Surroundings, 337, 381
Soft Switching Technologies, 60
Soft-Switch, 1275
Softbank Broadband Fund, 3143
Softbank Capital, 990
SoftBank Group, 3245
SoftBook Press, 526
Softbox Systems, 864
Softbrands, 405
Softchoice, 2056, 2177
Softcom, 3128
Softek, 1021, 1888
SOFTEK Storage Solutions, 1287
Softgames, 2832, 3226
Softgate Systems, 655
Softlayer, 2
Softmax, 2960
Softricity, 713, 1150, 1170
Softscope, 39
Softscope Medical Technologies, 1820
SoftTech VC, 990
Software, 456
Software Architects, 371
Software Integrity, 251
Software Technology, 1636
Software Transformation Inc., 209
Software Unlimited, 352
Software.com, 724
Softway, 3171
SoftWriters, 1778
SOG Specialty Knives & Tools, 832, 1250
SOGEM, 2410
Soha Systems, 456
Sohan Lal Commodity, 2992
Sohu, 2841
Soikea Solutions Oy, 2957
Soil Nerd, 999
Soil Safe Conduit, 2371
SoilSafe, 899
Soilwise, 2636
SoJeans, 3199
Sojern, 759, 1346, 1848, 1852
Sojournix, 785, 1522
Sokanu, 2283
Sokrati, 1017
Sol, 1739
Sol Cuisine, 2153
SOL Republic, 1236
Sol-Gel, 2576
Sol-Gel Ltd, 2964
Sol-Gen, 3235

Portfolio Companies Index

Solace, 2252, 2276
Solace Systems, 912, 919
Soladigm, 1674
SolAero Technologies, 681, 1927
Solaicx, 145, 1093
Solairdirect, 2430
Solais, 789
Solais Lighting, 1146
Solantro, 1478
Solantro Semiconductor Corp., 498
Solapoint, 2694
Solar Array Ventures, 1394
Solar Century, 3095
Solar Change, 679
Solar Edge, 3205
Solar Energies, 3011
Solar Implant Techn9logies, 2623
Solar Participations, 3011
Solar Plastics, 1971
Solar Silicon Technology, 839
Solar Universe, 1583
SolarBridge Technologies, 979
Solarcentury, 1908, 3242
SolarCity, 596, 610
SolarEdge, 1382
Solarex Photovaltaic, 2872
Solarflame Communications, 2314
Solarflare, 133
Solarflare Communications, 646, 1237, 1361
SolarFun, 2927
Solargigia, 2427
Solaria, 56, 186, 549, 1324, 1674
Solaria Corporation, 1241
Solariat, 1088
Solaris Midstream Holdings LLC, 1853
Solarnow, 54
SolarOne, 789
SolarOne Solutions, 1864
SolarReserve, 335, 1398, 1897
Solarsilicon Recycling Services LLC, 277
Solarvista, 1340
SolarVista Media, 1327
Solarwinds, 752, 912, 1244
Solasia, 1268
Solazyme, 325, 1908
SolBright Renewable Energy, 2027
Sold., 316
SoldPrint Europe, 3119
Soldsie, 641, 1702
Soleno Therapeutics, 1943
Soleo Communications, 750
Soleo Health, 931
SolePower, 1509
Solera Holdings Inc., 745
Solera Networks, 84, 561, 1679, 1852
Soleras, 440
Soleras Advanced Coatings, 658
Soleras Advances Coatings, 2371
Solexa, 2378
Solexel, 582, 596, 1788, 1978
Solfo, 625
SolFocus, 186, 1324
Solfocus, 138
Solgaz, 3068
Soliant, 1372, 1583
SoliCore, 1302
Solicore, 731
Solid Biosciences, 764, 1522
Solid Carbon Products, 288, 1545
Solid Energy, 821
Solid Partners, 1119
Solid State Equipment, 1754
Solid State Pharma Inc., 2148
Solid X Partners Inc., 1533
Solidcore, 972
SolidEnergy, 145
SolidFire, 872, 1348

Solidfire, 1901
Solidia Technologies, 322, 2483
Solidica, 1337
Solidscape, 557, 906
SolidSpace, 1683
SolidStage, 586
SOLIDUS Investment Fund, 1374
Solidware Technologies, 979
SolidWorks, 1335
Soligenix, 1083, 1815
SoLink, 2240
Solink, 2074, 2137, 2276
Solis Mammography, 785, 1160
Solis Women's Health, 405, 1171
Solisite, 623
Solita, 136
Soliton, 2051
Solius, 1099
Solix BioSystems, 992
SolmeteX, 815
Solo Growth Corp., 2134
Solo Stove, 260
Sologear, 584
SOLOMO, 2002
Solomon Systech, 2427, 2594
SoLoMoTo, 895
Solovis, 655, 1240
Solrec, 2976
Sols, 708, 795
SOLS Systems, 1155
Solsoft, 2598
Solstas Lab Partners, 178, 1973
Solstice, 623
Solstice Capital, 522
Solstice Energy Solutions, 221
Solstice Medical, 659
Solstice Neurosciences, 1820
Solstice Software, 540
Solsys Medical, 1631, 1764
Solta Medical, 1788
Solta Medical Tocagen, 764
Solterra Recycling Solutions, 1580
Soltrus, 2073
Solucient, 1929
Solueta Co., 2993
Solugen, 398
Solulink, 1459
Solus Biosystems, 2448
Solution Builders Limited, 2751
Solutionary, 502
SolutionReach, 689
Solutionreach, 1679, 1754
Solutions Vending International, 395
Soluto, 2863
Solv, 48, 182, 877, 1323
Solvaira Specialties, 172
Solve Media, 1290, 1491
SolveBio, 626
SolveDirect Service Management, 2301
Solvis, 124
Solvoyo, 2286
Solvvy, 1426, 1629
SOLX, 644
Solx, 2972
Solyndra, 1449, 3213
Soma, 234, 553, 1114, 1223, 1236
Soma Analytics, 1618
Soma Networks, 1920
Somaca, 911
SomaDetect, 2141, 2192
SomaLogic, 1492
Somatix, 772
SOMAVAC, 999
Somaxon Pharma, 1251
Somaxon Pharmaceuticals, 1495
Somboom Advance Technology, 1143
Somboon Advance Technology, 2937

Somelos Tecidos, 3039
Somero Enterprises, 1772
Somerset Gas Transmission Company, 1526
Something Borrowed Blooms, 1000
Something Navy, 321
Sometrics, 1103
Somo, 2743
Somo Global, 2963
SoMoLend, 1358, 1514
Somoto, 2905
SOMS Technologies, 1526
Sona, 418
Sona Group, 2914
SonaCare Medical, 809
Sonar, 304
Sonar Entertainment Inc., 2067
SonarMed, 447, 659, 1514
Sonas, 3045
Sonatype, 241, 510, 959, 1257
Sonavex, 18, 474, 802, 875
Sonavex Surgical, 1703
Sonavi Labs, 1616
Sonder, 265, 877, 2137, 2150, 2240
Sonedo, 1213
Sonetik, 2487
Sonexa, 1629
Sonexis, 1107, 1915
Songbird, 116
Songkick, 1702
Songwhale, 1003
Songwoo, 3136
Songza, 527, 601
Sonia, 564
Sonian, 1381, 2250
Sonic, 1580
Sonic Notify, 14, 1527
Sonic Sleep, 1509
Sonicbids, 655
SonicCloud, 1161
Sonicliving, 1359
Sonics, 839, 1313
SonicWALL, 241
SonicWall, 745, 782
Sonify Biosciences, 18
Sonim, 2463
Sonim Technologies, 641
Sonion, 2376
Sonitrol Corporation, 1410
Sonitrol Inc., 1727
Sonitus Medical, 116, 983
Sonneborn Refined Products, 1376
Sonnen, 812
Sonnen GmbH, 2677
Sonnendo, 1383
Sonobi, 1605
Sonoma, 178
Sonoma Creamery, 381
Sonoma Orthopedic, 733
Sonoma Orthopedic Products, 652, 667
Sonoma Orthopedics, 984
Sonoma Orthpedic, 1728
Sonoma Pharma, 1251
Sonos, 130, 641, 752, 872, 1537
SonoVol, 738
Sonrai, 2192
Sonrai Security, 1796
Sonru, 2909
Sonus Networks, 1091, 1335
Sony, 217
Sookasa, 1550
SoonR, 1478, 1821
Soonr, 504, 936
Soothe, 1566
Sopherion Therapeutics, 1297, 1492, 1830
Sopherion Therapeutics Inc., 2807
Sophia Genetics, 2288, 2469
Sophos, 136, 1021

Portfolio Companies Index

Sopris Health, 568
Sopsy, 2428
Soraa, 127, 949, 1073, 1324
Sorbent Therapeutics, 154
Sorbisense, 3194
Sorenson Communications, 1160
Sorenson Media, 1614
Soricimed, 2192
Sorra, 186
Sorrento, 73
Sorrento Networks, 463
Sortable, 2122
Sortera Alloys, 2072
SortSpoke, 2240
SOS Security, 2021
Sosei, 1395
Sosh, 1464
Soshi Games, 2958
SoSocio, 2534
Sote, 771
Sote Logistics, 1887
SOTEC, 2817
Sotera Defense Solutions, 160, 1138
Sotera Wireless, 1619, 2504, 2681
Soteria, 11
Sotralu, 2332
Soudsonic, 2555
SouFun, 2841
Soulbrain, 3136
Soulco, 2940
SoulCycle, 1113
Sound Agriculture, 571, 1238
Sound Building Supply, 1612
Sound Fuhua, 3185
Sound Lounge, 165
Sound Seal Inc., 903
Sounday, 2663, 3043
SoundBite, 1335
SoundBite Communications, 523
SoundCloud, 434, 680, 827, 1079, 1884, 2851, 2851
Soundcloud, 1006, 2435, 2662
Soundflavor, 115
Soundhawk, 1862
SoundHound, 116, 837, 1840
SoundHound Inc., 720, 1953
SoundHouse LLC, 518
Soundpays, 2187
Soundrop, 3004
Soundskrit, 2251
Soundstim Therapeutics, 875
Soundsupply, 1121
Soundtrack Your Brand, 2469
Soundtracker, 1585
SoundVamp, 2687
Soundview Advice, 3257
Soundview Maritime LLC, 1138
Soundview Technology, 1390
SoundWall, 299
Soundwave, 1719
Source 4 Teachers, 1603
Source Code, 796
Source Defence, 84
Source Energy Partners, 1447
Source Energy Services, 2267
Source Fire, 540
Source Medical, 1536
Source Photonics, 782
Source3, 12, 535, 545
Source4Style, 845
Sourcebits Technologies, 2840
SOURCEBYNET, 1771
Sourced, 2235
SourceDogg, 2513
Sourceeasy, 361
SourceFire, 993
Sourcefire, 561, 1213

Sourcegraph, 1537
SourceHOV, 1912
SourceIQ, 649
SourceMedia, 1021
SourceMedical, 1929
Sourcepoint, 779
Sourcery, 1254, 1599
Sources Refrigeration & HVAC Inc., 172
SourceTrace Systems, 860
Sourcify, 1557
Sousacamp, 2708
South Bay Mental Health Center, 1192
South Beach Diet, 1231
South Dakota Innovation Partners, 1195
South Lakeland Parks, 2926
South Memory Restaurant Co., 2533
South Side, 785
South Staffordshire Place, 153
South-Tek Systems, 1438
Southampton Photonics, 2378
Southcoast-Boca Associates, 1152
Southcross, 676
Southcross Energy, 458
Southeast, 159
Southeast Directional Drilling, 1424, 1707
Southeast Guardrail, 1609
Southeast Healthplan, 1152
Southeast PowerGen, 157
Southeast TechInventures, 1446, 1925
Southeastern Automotive Aftermarket Service Holdin, 418
Souther Lithoplate, 1529
Southerland, 165
Southern Ag Carriers, 920
Southern Air Holdings, 1360
Southern Assisted Living, 1529
Southern Care Hospice Services, 1255
Southern Carlson, 1066
Southern HVAC, 1270
Southern Management Corporation, 1234
Southern Petroleum Laboratories, 832
Southern Petroleum Laboratories Inc., 654
Southern Pines, 157
Southern Quality Meats, 931
Southern Spine Institute, 367
Southern States, 943
Southern Technical College, 1984
Southern Theaters, 679, 1929
Southern Tide, 331
Southern Towing Company, 1858
Southern Veterinary Partners, 1670
SouthernCare, 1085
Southland Log Homes, 153, 2969
Southland Royalty Company, 673
Southpaw Live, 531
Southwall Technologies, 1287
Southwaste Serivces, 1505
Southwest Nanotechnologies, 262
Southwest Value Partners, 1276
Southwest Windpower, 468, 1583
Sova Pharmaceuticals, 209
Sovereign Brands, 1955
Sovereign Sportsman Solutions, 1499
Sovereign Woodmet, 2477
Sovrn, 779, 1116
sovrn, 1374
sovrn Holdings, 1361
Sown To Grow, 1030
Soylent, 1114
soylent, 995
SoYoung, 136
SP Industries, 851, 1343
SP Industries Inc., 911
SP Surgical, 667
SPA, 2547
Spaas Kaarsen, 2940
Space Adventures/Zero-G, 1588

Space Ape Games, 2620
Space Exploration Technologies, 1904
Space Monkey, 586, 1254, 1464, 2016
Space Tango, 398
Space-Ime Insight, 3242
Space-Time Research, 2613
Spaceape Games, 3004
Spacebel, 3125
SpaceClaim, 1287
Spaceclaim, 311, 1335
SpaceClaim Corporation, 1084
SpaceCurve, 619
Spaces, 310, 520
Spacesys, 310
Spacetec IMC Corp., 467
SpaceWatts, 2254
SpaceX, 596, 610, 650, 778, 795, 802, 803, 1892, 2270
Spacex, 805
Spacious, 1114
Spada Media, 1118
Spadac, 744
Spanfeller Media, 1851
Spanfeller Media Group, 1701, 1908
Spanlink, 1728
Spansive, 680
SPAR Middle Volga, 2456
SPAR Moscow Holdings, 2456
SPARC, 1810
Sparcana, 2958
Sparcyz, 2637
Spare, 395
SpareFoot, 1687
Sparefoot, 752
Spark, 1359
Spark Networks, 2832
Spark Post, 1140
Spark Therapeutics, 1700
SparkBase, 1556
Sparkbuy, 250
Sparkcentral, 1028, 1728, 2940
SparkCognition, 1928
Sparkcognition, 1035
Sparked, 1058, 1862
Sparkfund, 534
Sparkir, 29
Sparkow, 3229
Sparkpr, 3262
Sparkt, 991
Sparky Animation, 2844
SPARQ, 2181
Sparq, 2037
Sparqd, 1942
Sparrowhawk Media, 2298
Sparrows Group, 63
Sparsha Learning, 2517
Sparta Science, 1511
Sparta Systems, 97, 1754, 1817
Spartan College of Aeronautics and Technology, 1745
Spartan Energy Services, 913
Spartan Foods of America, 1136, 1460
Spartan MTech, 725
Spartan Race, 332, 925
Spartanova, 2467
Spartatn, 2178
Spartech, 172
Spartoo, 938
SPATIAL, 1159
Spatial, 2122, 2150
Spatial Stae, 1614
Spatial Wireless, 1170, 1908
Spaulding Composites, 1225
SPC TelEquip, 1505
Speakaboos, 59
Speakeasy, 857
Speakeasy Political, 937

Portfolio Companies Index

SpeakerText, 1959
Speakr, 1635, 1831
Spear Therapeutics, 1777
SpearFysh, 1051
Specialdocs Consultants, 1670
Specialist Heating Components Ltd, 2699
Specialized Desanders, 904
Specialized Education Services, 470, 1473
Specialized Elevator Services, 491
Specialized Medical Services, 1576
Specialty Appliances, 747
Specialty Bakers, 1747
Specialty Brands, 371
Specialty Care, 1085
Specialty Commerce Corp., 2098
Specialty Commodities Inc., 847
Specialty Filaments, 405
Specialty Finance Company, 1090
Specialty Manufacturing Inc., 451
Specialty Sales, 1169
Specialty Vehicles Group, 1034
SpecialtyCare, 97
Specific Media, 782
SpecificMEDIA, 1667
Specified Fittings, 1250, 1343
Specle, 2455
Specright, 729
Spectel, 1021
Spector & Co., 293
Spectra, 194
Spectra Biomedical Inc., 209
Spectra Securities Software, 2051
SpectraFluidics, 983
SpectraGenetics, 1452
Spectral Dimensions, 352, 1691
Spectral Edge, 2958
SpectraLinear, 801, 950
Spectralink, 1755
SpectraLink Corp., 950
Spectralus Corporation, 650
SpectraSensors, 468, 549, 767, 1355
Spectrawatt, 1398
Spectrio, 260, 1576
Spectrum, 1114, 1764
Spectrum Athletic Clubs, 337
Spectrum Bridge, 1784, 1862, 2708
Spectrum Five, 1344
Spectrum Health Care, 2076, 2198
Spectrum K12, 1888
Spectrum K12 School Solutions, 1348
Spectrum Lubricants, 1343
Spectrum Motors, 1766
Spectrum Network Systems, 3159
Spectrum Professional Services, 247, 1631
Spectrum Resources Towers, 1929
Spectrum Staffing, 825
Speech Recognition, 2653
Speech4Good, 1593
SpeechCycle, 1157
SpeechTrans, 421
Speechworks, 1629
SpeeCo, 1438
Speed Plastics, 2958
SpeedBit, 3115
SpeedCast, 1778, 3159
Speedel, 2913
Speedera Networks, 1855
SpeedInfo, 549
Speedline Technologies, 1089
Speedscan, 2613
SpeedTracs, 656
Speedy Packets, 1486
Speek, 1320, 1901
Spell, 648, 2013
Spellacy Universal Ltd., 2779
Spensa, 659
Spently, 2107

Spepharm Holding, 3187
Sperical Defence, 537
SpermCheck, 1446
Spero Therapeutics, 193, 1421, 1522, 1734
Sperry & Rice, 1612
SPG International, 1427
SPG Solar, 838
SPGPrints Group B.V., 1021
Sphaera Pharma, 2481
Sphera, 823, 3170
Sphere, 925, 1088, 1808, 1964
Sphere Drake Holdings Limited, 449
Sphere Energy, 2022
Sphere Fluidics, 2988, 3019
SPHERE Technology Solutions, 3266
Spherics, 1414
Spheris, 1044
Sphero, 779, 879, 1205
Spheros GmbH, 3058
Sphinx Pharmaceuticals, 1013
SPI Polyols, 170
Spi Technologies Inc, 2685
Spice Chain Corporation, 792
Spice World, 1404
Spiceworks, 752, 1006, 1666, 1798
Spicus, 100
Spicy Horse, 3206
SpiderCloud Wireless, 457, 1184
Spidr Tech, 275
Spiff, 79
Spig, 2383
Spikes Security, 252, 1942
Spiketrap, 1423
Spill Magic Inc., 467
Spin, 879
Spinal Concepts, 1379
Spinal Dynamics, 1788
Spinal Elements, 1085
Spinal Kinetics, 599, 941, 1255, 1629, 1631
Spinal MetRX, 1452
Spinal Modulation, 599, 984
SpinalKinetics, 179
SpinalMotion, 1063, 1693
Spindle Labs, 1464
Spindletop Capital, 3254
Spindrift, 1490
Spine Form, 1514
Spine Wave, 389, 559, 1126, 1190, 1297
Spine Wave Inc., 374
Spine-Tech, 1728
SpineAlign, 918
SpineGuard, 3011
Spinelab, 2466
Spineology, 67
SpineView, 179, 1325
SpineVision, 2346
SpineVision SA, 2807
SpinGo, 689, 1074
Spinifex, 2527
SpinLaunch, 431, 1079, 1099
SpinMedia, 133, 1784
Spinnaker Networks, 1203
Spinnaker Support, 377
Spinnakr, 1320, 3035
Spinner, 1566
Spinrite, 1169, 1654
Spiracur, 599, 1297, 1449, 1775
Spiral Genetics, 610
Spiras Health, 718
Spire, 879, 1050, 1491, 1511, 1597, 1637, 1666
Spire Global, 1241
Spireon, 260
Spireon Inc., 867
SpireSano, 1051
Spirion, 1018
Spirit Brands, 405
Spiritshop, 567

Spiritsoft, 2563
Spiro Technologies, 2, 1175
Spirogen, 1546
Spirox, 73, 137, 545, 924, 1918
Spirus Medical, 1463
SPL, 989
SPlacer, 3212
Splacer, 1323, 1511
Splash, 59, 180, 1114, 1186, 1533, 1885, 2240, 3046, 3099
Splashtop, 1219, 1478, 1623, 1750, 2658
Splen, 2671
Splendia, 2377, 3011
Splice, 756, 1114, 1610, 1862
Splice Machine, 545, 1014, 1247
Split Rail Fence & Supply Co., 333
Splitwise, 2, 361, 1566
Splonum, 2823
Splunk Technology, 200
Splyce, 705
SPM, 2993
Spock, 504
Spocket, 2204
Spoke, 720, 877, 3099
SPOKE Custom Products, 367
Spoken, 978
SpokenLayer, 1154
Spongecell, 1527
Sponsia, 2687
SponsorHub, 1521
Sponsorhub, 600
SponsorPay, 2804, 3035
Sponsors: ACG New York, 3274
Sponsors: Activate Venture Partners, 3264
Sponsors: BDO, 3261
Spontaneous Order, 2832
Spoolex, 124
Spoon University, 1181
Sporple, 1887
Sport 2000, 2330
Sport Hero, 207
Sport Ngin, 1525, 3268
Sport Pursuit, 2665
Sport Universal Process, 3229
Sport1, 2714
Sportcraft, 319
Sportgenic, 1088
SportHero, 91
Sportica, 2927
SportlogiQ, 2112, 2178, 2231
Sportlogiq, 2251
Sportnex GmbH, 3188
SportPursuit, 2653
Sports & Recreation, 1021
Sports & Recreation Inc., 694
Sports Tradex, 447
Sportskeeda, 3100
SportsLine.com, 132
Sportsman Tracker, 964, 1159
Sportsman's Warehouse, 1648
SportsNest, 2517
Sportsplex Japan, 3173
Sportsrocket, 1114
Sportsvite, 1305
Sportvision, 696, 1483, 1643
Sportxast, 1926
Spot, 1269
Spot Crowd, 1179
Spot Hero, 208, 361
SpotAHome, 1079
Spotfire, 468
Spotflux, 1290
SpotHero, 641, 1121, 1364, 1483
Spothero, 1618
Spotify, 778, 805, 846, 1235, 1346, 1527, 1787, 2154, 2628, 2654, 2822, 3004
Spotless, 3016

Portfolio Companies Index

Spotless Group Limited, 2371
Spotlife, 115
SpotOn, 283
Spotright, 35, 881
Spotsetter, 1032
SpotTaxi.com, 42
Spotter, 685
SpotterRF, 983
Spotzot, 456, 773
Spotzot Mobile Shopping, 1017
SPPTH, 3039
SPR Therapeutics, 1051, 1286
Sprayglo, 467
SpreadTrum, 388
Spreadtrum, 1091, 1340, 2927
Spredfast, 1014, 1381, 1813
Spredfest, 872
Spree Commerce, 1534, 1823, 1862, 1914
Spreecast, 1196
Sprig, 1154
Spring, 473, 720, 1050, 1114, 1555
Spring Air Sommex Corporation, 2049
Spring by Pivetal, 1213
Spring CM, 773
Spring Consulting, 2745
Spring Discovery, 820, 1760
Spring Flower, 2370
Spring Labs, 1483
Spring Lake, 1220
Spring Loaded, 2063, 2148
Spring Metrics, 289, 2016
Spring Mobile, 1623
Spring Path, 1537
Spring Tide Networks, 1478
Spring Venture Group, 746
Spring.me, 3151
SpringBig, 900
Springbig, 99
Springboard, 548, 2470
Springbok Energy, 1326, 1328
Springbot, 907, 1790, 1865
SpringBot Commerce, 770
Springbuk, 659, 924
SpringCharts, 953
SpringCM, 300
Springcm, 949
Springcoin, 821
Springer, 2596
Springlane, 2829
Springs, 926
SpringSource, 241
Springstone, 1973
Sprinklr, 1035, 2681
Sprint Industrial Holdings, 734
Sprooki, 2769
Sprout, 1255, 1292, 2256
Sprout Health Group, 952
Sprout Social, 1121
SproutBox, 659
Sproutling, 31, 744, 763
Sproxil, 54
Spruce, 234, 553, 1079
Spruce Media, 1504
Spruce Up, 1162
Sprucebot, 1179
Spryker, 3047
Spryx, 11
SPS, 1340
SPS Commerce, 56, 215, 1728
SPSS Inc., 1107
SPUD, 2230
Spyce, 1186, 1511
Spyce Inc., 1073
Spyder Active Sports, 463, 2371
Spykar, 2451
Spyke Media, 3198
Spyor Safe Mobile Security, 120

Spyryx Biosciences, 918
SQAD, 494
SQLstream, 762
Sqrl, 965
Sqrrl, 37, 1525, 1731
Squabbler, 1966
Squadra VC, 3260
Squadrun, 23
Square, 488, 827, 1073, 1623, 1716, 1768
Square 1 Bank, 1273
Square Gourmet, 2846
Square Roots, 490
Square Space, 1763, 2851
Square Trade, 223, 224
SquareClock, 3104
Squarespace, 819, 2851
SquareTrade, 1736
SquareTwo Financial, 733
Squawka, 2743
Squee, 2687
Squelch, 1666
Squire, 12
Squirro, 1610
Squirro AG, 650
Squla, 1115
Sqwiggle, 1154, 1491
SQZ Biotech, 2221
SR One, 3263
SR Technics, 2291, 2293, 2297
SR Telecom & Co., 2067
SRA International, 1498
Sram, 170
SRCH2, 1800
Srch2, 586
Srckode, 2263
SRE Solutions, 54
SREI Infrastructure Finance Ltd, 2080
Sresta, 3202
SRET, 3091
SRK, 2858
SRL Global, 2441
SRP Companies, 202
SRS, 1859
SRS Acquiom, 1151, 3262, 3265
SRS Distribution, 257, 1113
SRS Medical, 1630
SRS Software, 1817
SS8, 1348, 1379
SS8 Networks, 2005
Ss8 Networks, 1949
SSB, 2786
SSE Rogerstone, 3126
SSI, 962, 1214, 2723
SSI Holdings, 364
SSP, 927
SST, 1260
St George Bank, 2650
St Residental, 1837
St-Hubert, 2968
St-Pierre Et Durocher Arpenteurs Geometres, 2114
St. Croix Hospice, 1343
St. George Logistics, 1145, 1148
St. George Warehouse, 1025
St. John Knits, 1933
St. John's Hop On Hop Off, 2161
St. Louis Arch Angels, 3261
St. Marche Group, 1092
St. Matthew's University, 688, 692
Stable, 2398
Staccot Communications, 457
Stack, 481
Stack Commerce, 1966
Stack Driver, 224
STACK Ltd., 911
STACK Media, 1051
Stack Overflow, 265

Stack Sports, 1499
StackAdapt, 2216
StackCommerce, 121
Stacked, 2131
StackEngine, 1687
Stackery, 776, 959
StackExchange, 1718
Stackhut, 1254
StackIQ, 133, 209, 861
StackMob, 234, 1855
Stackpole International, 560
Stackshare, 641
StackStorm, 2010
StadiaNet Sports, 132
Stadion Money Management, 1778
Stadium Goods, 763
Stadium Live, 2131
Stae, 724
Staff Leasing, 1507
Staffbase, 641
Staffmark, 525
Staffordshire Schools, 2740
StaffRanker, 1966
Staffy, 2094
Stafix Oy, 2957
Staftfl, 2103
Stag-Parkway, 1136
Stag-Parkway Inc., 867
Stage1 Beteiligungs Invest, 2774
StageMark, 296
Staghorn Petroleum, 673
Staging Concepts, 279, 408
Staging Connections, 2942
Stagnito Business Information, 1834
Stahl, 1021
Stainton Metals, 3008
Stake Center, 1755
Stakeholder Midstream, 672
Stallion, 1138, 1968
Stalwart, 2787
Stamford Bridge Power, 157
Stamped, 527, 1832
Stampede Meat, 714
Stampery, 310
Stamplay, 3099
Stamps.com, 767
Stanadyne, 110
Stanadyne Corporation, 1085
STANCE, 1203
Stance, 44, 1074, 1079, 1205, 1666
Standadyne Corporation, 1460
Standard Aero, 1927
Standard Bancshares, 1949
Standard Bank, 3086
Standard Bariatrics, 481
Standard Bots, 321
Standard Cognition, 1142
Standard Cyborg, 398, 814
Standard Diagnostics, 1091
Standard Locknut, 445
Standard Networks, 3118
Standard Parking Corporation, 1085
Standard Precast, 16
Standard Treasury, 1491, 2574
Standcard Bancshares, 1746
Standex International, 1294
Standing Stone, 532
Standingcloud, 209
StandoutJobs, 1305
Stanford Microdevices/Sirenza, 1287
Stanmore Implants, 2849
Stant Corporation, 931, 1343
Stantec, 2142
Stanton Carpet, 1507
Stanton Carpet Corp, 1460
Stantum, 2867
Stanza, 527

Portfolio Companies Index

Staples, 912, 940, 1100
STAQ, 1557
Staq, 540, 818, 1812
Star, 3005
Star Career Academy, 815
Star CJ, 1498
STAR EnviroTech Inc., 911
Star Festival, 2789
Star Market, 1021
Star Seed, 832
Star Tribune Media Holdings, 1968
Star-Glo Industries, 943
Star2Star Communications, 1316
Starboard, 2788
Starbucks, 250, 755
Starbucks Beijing, 897
Starbucks Coffee, 1855
STARC Systems, 291
Starcard, 2877
StarCite, 186
Starcity, 1896
Stardog, 540
Stardog Union, 881
Starent Networks, 759
Starface, 328
Starfish Oil & Gas, 2341
Starfish Retention Solutions, 1298, 1348
Starflyer, 597
Stargaze, 2549
StarGen, 317
Starhome, 2463, 2761
Starksky Robotics, 640
Starkware, 752
Starline, 2414
Starling, 3063
Starmaker, 2009
StarMaker Interactive, 2844
StarMobile, 1969
Starmount, 1271
Starnet Interactive, 1112
Starpoint Health, 376
STARR Life Sciences, 1003
Starr Life Sciences, 1452
Starrino, 1340
Starry, 744
Starship, 879, 1666
Starsky Robotics, 23, 431, 814, 945, 1666
Starskyrobotics, 1887
StarStreet Inc., 650
Start Garden, 3259
StartApp, 438
Startapp, 180
STARTech, 1198
Startflyer, 2997
Startingdot, 2377
Startip + Health, 1056
Startmate, 2511
Startronics, 223
Startup Bootcamp, 3226
Startup Weekend Tr¢jmiasto, 2876
Startup.Lt, 3040
Startupbootcamp, 3198
Startupi.com.br, 2863
Startwire, 225
StarWind Software, 89, 2312
Staselog Oy, 2864
Stash Energy, 2192
Stashbox, 395
State National Companies, 654
StatEasy, 1451
StatementOne, 1469
States Title, 728
Statflo, 2107, 2122, 2235
STATinMed, 406
Statisfy, 713, 1959
Statista, 2788
Statlab Medical Products, 1473

StatMuse, 246
Statmuse, 1885
STATs ChipPac Taiwan Semiconductor Corporation, 2594
Statsbot, 680
StatSocial, 649
Statsocial, 151
Status, 101
StatX, 1017
Stauber, 1507
Stauber Performance Ingredients Inc., 973
Stax, 234
Stay Alfred, 531
Stay Tuned, 328
Stay22, 2132
Stayful, 389
StayNTouch, 1172
StayOnline, 963
STC Wireless Resources Inc., 1624
Stdlib, 2178
SteadyServ Technologies, 659
Steak & Ale Restaurant, 357
Steak 44, 367
Steak-ummm, 1163
Stealth, 1064, 1154
Stealth Monitoring, 2042
Stealth Peptides, 2969
Stealth Space Company, 44
Stealthbits, 1831
Stealz, 1847
Steam Logistics, 640
Steambolico, 3039
Steamist, 1524
StearClear, 421
Stedi, 1760
Steel & OBbrien Manufacturing, 654
Steel Brick, 1666
Steel Reef Infrastructure Corp., 2213
SteelBrick, 666
Steelbrick, 1006
STEELE Compliance Solutions, 336
Steele Solutions, 1210
Steelhead Composite, 147
Steelhead Lng, 2044
SteelHouse, 309, 876, 1205, 2640
Steelhouse, 231, 1569
Steelhouse Stellapps Technologies, 1511
SteelPoint, 790
SteelSeries, 1092
Steelwedge, 1674
Steep Hill, 1139, 1208, 1443, 1810
Steereo, 1509
Steifel Laboratories, 280
Steiger, 2674
Stein Rose Investment Counsel, 1151
Stein World, 1997
Steiner Education Group, 1092
Stelara, 2097
Stelco, 2062
Stelco Inc., 2067
Stella, 1323, 2535
Stella & Chewy's, 1751
Stella & Dot, 1867
Stella D'Oro, 360
Stella May Contracting, 1209
Stella Service, 520, 609, 770
Stellar, 387
Stellar Loyalty, 1784
Stellar Materials LLC, 847
Stellar Outdoor Media, 832
StellaService, 1346
Stellic, 1530
Stem, 48, 127, 182, 534, 812, 1154, 1816, 1885, 1890
Stem Cell Theranostics, 1658
Stem Village, 2107
Stemcentrx, 177, 778

StemCyte, 68, 1771
Stemgent, 1126
Stemia Biomarker Discovery, 584
Stemina Biomarker Discovery, 2002
Stemless, 1509
Stemmatters, 3022
Stemnion, 1096
Stemonix, 344
Stensul, 1153
Stentntor, 1096
Stentys, 3011, 3095
STEP Energy Services, 2036
STEP Labs, 808, 810
Step Labs, 186
Step-In, 2660
Stepex, 2398
Stephan Machinery GmbH, 3058
Stephano Group, 2065
Stephen's Rental Servies Inc., 2098
STEPLabs, 613
Stepladder, 2398
StepLeader, 1575
Stepmind, 2346
StepOne, 1687
Steppe Resources Inc., 1326
StepStone, 2321
Stepstone, 3004
StepStoneMed, 244
StepUp Commerce, 857
Stereocake, 2325
Stereotaxis, 119, 178, 1619, 1622
Stericycle, 1160
SteriFx, 365
Sterigenics, 889
Steril Med, 178
SterilMed, 3268
Sterix Limited, 2454
Sterling Energy, 1256
Sterling Foods, 973, 1805
Sterling InfoSystems, 822
Sterling Partners, 3245, 3255
Sterling Technology, 2976
Sterling Trading Tech, 1140
SterlingBackcheck, 371
Sternhill, 36
Sterno Group, 525
Steudle, 2878
Steve Nash Fitness Clubs, 128
Stevens, 1041
Stevens Institute of Technology, 3266
Stevie, 2822
Steward Advanced Materials, 124
STI, 1650
Stic, 2427
Stick Tech, 2442
Sticks'n'Sushi, 3194
Sticky, 2621, 3004
StickyADS.tv, 3199
Stiffel, 1163
Stik.com, 743
Stillwater Scientific Instruments, 440
Stim Wave, 1631, 1764
Stimsonite Corporation, 1507
Stimwave, 1987
Stimwave Technologies, 667
STING Capital, 3034
Stingray, 2255
Stingray Digital, 468
Stion, 325
Stirling Cooke Browne, 2783
Stirling Schools, 2740
Stitch, 787, 1114, 1702, 1719, 1752
Stitch Fix, 234
Stitch Labs, 548, 1862
Stixi Ag, 836
STK, 2245, 2301
Stkr.it, 985

1401

Portfolio Companies Index

STN Video, 2065
Stobhill Hosptial, 2740
Stockbyte, 2328
Stockpile, 770, 1187, 2187
StockTwits, 779, 1862, 2398
Stockwell, 763, 944
StockX, 608
Stohlquist Waterware, 112
Stoke, 759, 1008, 1091, 1341, 1478
Stoke Therapeutics, 144, 144, 1522
Stokes Bio, 2909
Stokes Sauces, 2751
Stokomani, 2367
Stolle Machinery, 1138
Stolle Machinery Company, 110
Stoller, 15
Stone Canyon Entertainment Corporation, 576
Stone Goff Partners, 1344
Stone Panels, 1225
Stone Point Materials, 1755
Stone Source, 777
Stone Tool Supply Inc., 911
StoneCastle, 458
StoneFly Inc., 556
Stonegate Mortgage, 2640
Stonegate Production Company, 1447
Stonegate Production Company II, 1447
StoneLock, 2251
Stoneridge, 817
StoneRidge Insurance Brokers, 491
StoneRiver Holdings, 1746
Stonewall Kitchen LLC, 449
Stony Brook University, 3257
Stop Breathe & Think, 121, 1895
Stop&Walk, 2911
StopDDoS, 1501
Stora Enso Oyj, 2981
Storactive, 68, 1183
Storage Genetics, 213
StorageApps, 189
Stord, 640, 1760
Store Fixtures Group, 1294
Store-Locator.com, 2302
Store2be, 2832
StoreFinancial, 1766
Storefront Inc., 650
StoreLynkm StreamSpot, 481
Storent Holding, 585
StoreNVY, 1718
Storiant, 325, 1184
Storify, 1491
Storigen, 457
StoriiCare, 29
Storj.iO, 895
Stork Prints, 2492
StormBlok, 1688
Stormpath, 1428, 1629
Storsimple, 1537
Storwize, 1798
Story Magic, 1254
Story Xpress, 1179
Storyblaster, 49
StoryFirst, 2482
StoryFirst Co, 2456
Storyhunter, 1323
StoryVine, 1305
Stouse, 367
Stouse LLC, 847
Stout Industries, 60
Stout Street Capital, 3265
StowAway, 527
Stowga, 2398, 3099
Stp, 1518
STR, 1101
Straatum, 2909
Stradeblu Srl, 2644
Strahman Valves, 480

StraighterLine, 477, 1150, 1298, 1554
Straighterline, 490, 744
Strala, 79
Stram Global Services, 160
Strand Energy, 697
Strasbaugh, 68
Strata, 851
Strata Decision, 1929
Strata Dx, 1132
Strata Oncology, 150, 225
Strata Worldwide, 1997
StrataCloud, 285, 1412
StrataCom Inc., 1203
StrataDx, 1271
Stratalight, 564
Stratatech Corporation, 2002
StrataTech Education Group, 832
Stratavia, 183
Strategia, 245
Strategic Equipment and Supply, 331
Strategic Funding Source, 1447
Strategic Investment Group, 790
Strategic Legal Solutions, 1230
Strategic Marketing, 1767
Strategic Materials, 1138, 1939
Strategic Outsourcing Inc., 494
Strategic Partners, 212
Strategikon Pharma, 229
Stratetic Insight, 823
StratEx, 902
Stratford School, 1506
StratiFi, 2398
Stratifyd, 802, 2074, 2126
Stratim, 305
Stratix, 1779
Stratophase, 2883
Stratos, 1550, 1831, 3076
Stratos Technologies, 754
Stratoscale, 1511
Stratus Computer, 200
Stratus Technologies, 1021
Strava, 1028
Stravina, 1234
Stray Light, 659
Strayer Education, 1300
Streak, 1153
Stream, 175, 708
Stream Global Services, 1971
Stream Machine, 1781
Stream Processors, 2005
Streambase, 949
StreamBase Systems, 983
StreamCore, 2346
StreamElements, 1614
Streamingfast, 2090
StreamLabs, 562
Streamlabs, 641
Streamline, 2787
Streamline Circuits, 441
Streamline Health, 1332
Streamlined Ventures, 298
StreamLink Software, 288, 1051
Streamloan, 814
StreamOcean, 2658
Streamserve, 2463
StreamSets, 978
StreamVine, 447
Streamweaver, 1261
Streem, 757, 3116
Street Contxt, 2122, 2150, 2217
Street Light Data, 43
StreetAcademy, 2965
StreetCred, 320
StreetHub, 3009
Streetline, 762, 1583, 1862
StreetTrend, 940
Strengthportal, 310

StressWave, 85
Stride, 888, 1039, 1918
Stride Health, 711, 2217
Stride Tool, 408
StrideBio, 1780
Striim, 604
Striiv, 974
Strike Brewing Company, 953
Strike Group, 2267
StrikeAd, 400, 1059, 1702, 1800, 1966, 2653
StrikeReady, 3
Strikingly, 641
String, 2975
String AI, 121
StrionAir, 1704
Strip, 820, 1079
Stripe, 579, 778, 1073, 1153, 1537, 1610, 1669, 1828, 2011, 2437
Stripes Holdings LLC, 1972
Striva, 58
Strive Health, 1296
StriVectin, 1092
STRIVR, 59
Strivr, 305
Strix Systems, 1408
Strobe, 1359
Strohal, 2878
Stroidetal, 3062
Stroili Oro Group, 2285
Stroma, 2935
Stromedix, 69, 193, 785
Strong Hold, 3118
Strong Ventures, 1966
StrongArm Tech., 705
StrongArm Technologies, 1705
Strongbridge Biopharma, 949, 1271, 1943
StrongLoop, 1666
Strongpoint, 2103
Strongsalt, 802
StrongView Systems, 582
Stroz Friedberg, 1300
Structo, 827, 1966
Structural, 1179
Structural and Steel Products, 1210
Structural Concepts, 1174
Structure Vision, 2883
Structured Polymers, 447
Structured Web, 162
Struq, 3023
Stryde, 802
STS Aviation Group, 867
Stubbs Alderton & Markiles LLP, 3258
StubHub, 1736
Student Loan Genius, 447, 1058, 1599
Student Loan Hero, 708
Student Opportunity Center, 1554
Studer Group, 1045
Studio, 79
Studio Design, 1074
Studio Direct, 799
Studio Moderna, 819
StudioNow, 495, 497, 718
Studitemps, 2466, 2820, 2829, 3104, 3229
StudiVZ, 2435
Study Edge, 1186
Study Group, 1498
Study Soup, 400
StudyEdge, 2321
Studypool, 1114
StudySoup, 31
Studytube, 2813
StumbleUpon, 234, 1449
Stumbleupon, 200
Stumbleupon Inc., 624
Stupeflix, 3099
Sturm Foods, 1174
STx Healthcare Services, 1424

1402

Portfolio Companies Index

Styla, 3226
Style for Hire, 1305
Style Seat, 232
Style Seek, 1058
Style-Passport.com, 2392
Stylecaster, 608
StyleCraft Home Collection, 1473
Stylecraze, 3202
StyleFeeder, 1630
Stylefruits.de, 2629
Stylefy, 1813
Stylekick, 985
Stylemarks, 3198
StyleSaint, 562, 641
StyleSeat, 553, 1153, 1702, 3035
StyleSight, 568
StyleTread, 2788
Stylight, 2820, 2829, 3161
Stylus, 925
Stylust, 754
Styron, 223
Styrotherm, 2823
Sub-One Technology, 468
SubCenter.io, 275
Sube, 2662
Subex, 1304
Subitec, 2677
Subledger, 600
Sublimity Therapeutics, 1147
Submittable, 758, 1317
Subotica, 3086
Subscription Services, 1839
Subspace, 1155, 1616
Substack, 798, 2122
Subtle Medical, 222, 802
Suburban Team, 935
Sucampo Pharmaceuticals, 2961
SuccessEd, 367
SuccessFactors, 414, 666, 827, 1867
Sucreries de Berneuil, 2611
Sucriere De Bernevil, 2592
SucSeed, 2161
Suddenlink Communications, 2371
Suddenly Social, 1658
Suez Portfolio, 2783
Sugar23. SV Angel, 1768
SugarCRM, 28, 610, 680, 1235
Sugarfina, 901
SugarSync, 610, 1649, 1674
Sugru, 2951
Suhyang Networks, 63
SuitedMedia, 2178
Suiteness, 361
SuitePad, 2832
Suitpad, 3152
Suki, 1918
Sulekha, 1346
Sulia, 876
SULO, 2411
Sum Up, 2466, 3161
Sumazi, 1752
Sumerian, 3095
Suminter India Organics, 2992
Sumisura, 3194
Summary Analytics, 1243
Summer, 1062
Summerland Energy, 2022
Summit, 3128
Summit Behavioral Healthcare, 751
Summit BHC, 790
Summit Broadband, 60
Summit Business Media, 687
Summit Companies, 478
Summit Estates, 961
Summit Financial Services Group, 132
Summit Fire Protetcion, 1494
Summit Global Partners, 405

Summit Interconnect, 920
Summit Materials, 280
Summit Medical, 1670
Summit Medical Group, 1576
Summit Microelectronics, 200
Summit Midstream Partners, 676
Summit Partners, 3254
Summit Sync, 411
SummitIG, 518
Summly, 1823, 2822
Sumo Logic, 561, 1006
Sumologic, 877
SumoShift, 2276
Sumridge Partners, 1364
SumUp, 2931
Sumzero, 1998
Sun & Earth, 440, 522, 1691
Sun & Sea, 2841
Sun Art Retail Group, 819
Sun Basket, 36, 234, 545
Sun Behavioural Health, 1140, 1631, 1764
Sun Catalytix, 1464
Sun Culture, 2430
Sun Earth Ceramics Limited, 2852
Sun Graphics, 402
Sun Healthcare, 1560
Sun Microsystems, 200, 840
Sun Mountain Capital, 3265
Sun Orchard Inc., 449
Sun Products, 1933
Sun Source, 1138
Sun-Jin Boramae Co., 585
Sunac, 223
SuNAM Co., 145
Sunbelt Medical, 1609
Sunbelt Modular, 324
Sunbelt Steel, 1748
Sunbelt Supply, 502
Sunbelt-Solomon Solutions, 1853
Sunbio, 2969
Sunburst Farms, 60
Sunburst Media-Louisiana, 832
Sunbury Textile Mills, 1145
Suncayr, 2178
Sunchron, 1674
SunCommon, 789
Suncrest Solar, 1707
Sunda, 1683
Sundae, 1760
Sundance, 41, 381
Sundance Energy Inc., 159
Sundar, 545
Sunday Sky, 3212
Sunday's Nederland BV, 2819
SundaySky, 520, 839, 1346, 2557
Sunderstorm, 99
Sundevil Power, 1968
Sundia, 2427
Sundolier, 147, 3246
SunEdison, 145
Sunesis, 73, 949, 1900
Suneva Medical, 698
Sunflower New Co., 624
Sunfun (iPart), 3206
SunFunder, 3246
Sung Industrial, 2798
SunGard, 223, 1498
Sungard, 1837
SunGard Data Systems, 2371
Sungevity, 343, 676, 731
Sunglass, 1534
Sungy Mobile, 3053
Sunhouse, 221
Suninfo, 3091
Suning.com, 475
Suniva, 138
Sunless, 1576

Sunlight, 1530, 3099
Sunlight Ltd, 3153
SunLink, 499
Sunlink Corporation, 127
Sunlit, 1340
Sunlux Energy, 3053
Sunniva, 1139
Sunnova, 676, 1848
Sunnovations, 401
Sunny Sky Products, 1648
SunPharm Corporation, 1013
SunPower, 217
Sunpreme, 3185
Sunquest, 962
Sunrain Energy, 2533
Sunrise, 18, 153, 1322, 1549
Sunrise Oilfield Supply, 1997
Sunrise Strategic Partners LLC, 1853
Sunrise Windows, 1576
Sunrop Fuels, 1361
SunRun, 582, 773
Sunset Tower Hotel, 33
Sunshine, 1254, 1998
Sunshine Heart, 2609
Sunshine Media Holdings, 832
Sunshine Paper, 2927
Sunshine Restaurant Partners, 2014
Sunstream Boat Lifts, 85
SunSun Lighting, 1361
Sunteck, 530
SunTek, 722
Suntel, 3159
SunTelephone, 223
SunTouch, 521
SunTree Snack Foods, 1625
Suntron Corp., 303
Sunverge, 1713
SunZia Southwest Transmission Project, 676
Suomen Kuitulava Suvisoft Oy, 2864
Suomen Teollisuusosa Oy, 2864
Suomen Transval Oy, 2928
Suometry, 2178
SUPA, 221
Super, 708, 2398
Super Awesome, 2825
Super Bac, 2708
Super Bit Machines, 1566
Super Dragon Technology, 2594
Super Evil Megacorp, 562, 820, 1680, 3241
Super Heat Games, 794
Super Max, 912
Super Truper, 2911
Super-Medium, 398
Superalloy, 2427
Supercell, 1006, 2437, 2851, 2851
Superconductor Technologies, 68
Superconductor Technologies Inc., 1107
Superdata, 2944
Superdata Technology, 2841
Superfish, 3230
Superhard Materials, 3098
Superhuman, 354, 1423, 1599
Superhuman Labs, 308
Superior Automotive, 356
Superior Automotive Group, 1417, 1417
Superior Boiler Works Inc., 1057
Superior Chaircraft Corporation, 112
Superior Contract Cleaners, 467
Superior Controls, 77
Superior Fabrication, 1215
Superior Fibers, 341, 935
Superior Group Of Companies, 2277
Superior Group of Companies, 2129
Superior Plant Rentals, 427
Superior Recreational Products, 858, 1438
Superior Tool Holding Company, 1494
Superior Tube, 1963

Portfolio Companies Index

Superior Vision, 444
Superior Vision Holding Company, 1278
Supermedium, 1391
Supermercato 24, 2288
Supermercato24, 2865
Supernus, 949
SuperPedestrian, 1718
Superpedestrian, 820
Superpeer, 680
SuperPhone, 814
Superplastic, 1935
Superpowered, 2122
SuperService, 1968
SuperSonic Imagine, 3011
Superstar Games, 1023
Supertron Technologies, 2389
Supervalu, 383
Suplari, 1162, 1666
Supplemental Health Care, 1198
Supplemental Health Care Services, 588
SupplierInsight, 835
Supply Edge, 68
Supply Hog, 1101
Supply Shift, 1759
Supply Wisdom, 754
SupplyAI, 1557, 1759
SupplyEdge Inc., 374
SupplyFrame, 504
SupplyHog, 461, 1521
Supplyhog, 591, 1364
SupplyOne Holding, 1275
SupplyShift, 320
SupplySolution, 1674
Supponor, 3004
Supponor Systems, 2621
Support Logic, 1672
Supportkids.com, 405
SupportPay, 1596
Supreme, 3161
Supreme Corq, 851
Supreme Imports, 2668
Supreme NewMedia, 2595
Supresoft, 2841
Supyo, 624
Sur La Table, 408, 755, 786, 786, 1021
Sura Asset Management, 819
Suralink, 1074
Sure, 724
Sure Fit Home Decor, 448
Sure Shot Drilling, 612
Sure Storage, 2851
SureAuto, 3185
Surebits, 310
SureDone, 1305
Surefield, 1467
Surefire Local, 51, 2262
Surefire Medical, 933, 1192, 1420
Surekam, 2927
SureLogic, 1626
SurePoint Holdings, 1494
Surepoint Technologies Group, 2008
SurePrep, 336
SureSource, 1929
Surf Air, 231
Surf Communication Solutions, 2562, 2773
Surf Watch, 510
Surface Logix, 1442
Surface Oncology, 113, 193, 711, 1128
Surface Pharmaceuticals, 300
SurfAir, 1752, 1800, 1914, 1966
Surfair, 133, 724
SurfEasy, 2176
SurfKitchen, 163
Surge, 953
Surgent Professional Education, 1727
Surgery Partners, 931
Surgical Care Affiliates, 1837

Surgical Information Systems, 1345
Surgical Solutions, 1745
Surgical Specialties, 1943
Surgicount Medical, 139
Surgient, 564
Surgiquest, 139, 1575
SurgiQuest Inc., 374
Surgis, 1300
SurgRx, 1495
Surgrx Inc., 374
Surkus, 2137
Surple, 2276
Surreal, 310
Surrey Nanosystems, 2883, 3009, 3019
Sursen, 2841
Surun, 1235
Survata, 1566, 1702
Survery Monkey, 579
Survey 160, 937
Survey Monkey, 1720
Survey Sampling International, 1498
SurveyMonkey, 1698
Survios, 720, 857, 1155, 1614, 1666
Survitec, 2201
Survly, 1103
Surya, 1383
Suryoday Micro Finance, 2305
Suse, 2335
Susiecakes, 1745
Suspa, 124
Sustainability Roundtable, 401
Sustainable Minds, 3246
Sustainable Produce Urban Delivery, 2043
Sustainable Real Estate, 679
Sustainable Real Estate Manager, 1101
Sustainable Resource Solutions, 2883
SustainX, 1583
Sustainx, 1464
Susty Party, 3246
Sutro, 985
Sutro Biopharma, 94, 113, 803, 1128, 1631, 1693, 1934
Sutrovax, 785, 1147, 2086
SutureExpress, 1132
Suturtek, 1849
Suumologic, 840
SUVACO, 2965
Suvidhaa, 1346
Suvola, 447
SuVolta, 200
Suvolta, 2531
Suzhou Anjie Technology, 2927
Suzhou HiPro Polymers, 223
Suzlon, 2590, 2591
Suzo-Happ, 1438
Suzo-Happ Group, 45
SV Academy, 1393, 1554
SV Angel III, 624
SV Health Investors, 3254, 3263
SVAcademy, 490
Svante, 2072
Svaya Nanotechnologies, 1674
Svelte, 1302
Svelte Medical Systems, 510, 1347
Sverica, 36
Sverica Capital Management, 3254
Sverve, 1635
SVI Public, 897
SVM Cards, 181
SVNetwork, 1449
Svoboda Capital Partners, 3255
SVOX, 2653
SVOX AG, 650
SVP, 3011
SVP Worldwide, 1085
Svpply, 1718
Svrf, 1186

SVTC, 1924
SVTC Technologies, 1360
SWAAY, 1703
Swagbucks, 1787
Swallow Solutions, 1291, 2002
Swan Global Investments, 796
Swander Pace Capital, 1873
SwanLabs, 252, 597
Swanson Industries Inc., 63
SwapBox, 232
Swapbox, 987
Swapcom, 3104
SwapDrive, 535, 540
Swapit, 3038
Swarm, 1698
Swarm 64, 3152
Swarm Vision, 1370
Swas Healthcare, 2305
Swayable, 937
Swaybox Studios, 1000
Swaypay, 2398
SWC Technology Partners, 1767
Sweaty Betty, 1092
Swedish Institute, 1506
Sweep, 1058
Sweet, 608
Sweet Additions, 367
Sweet Garden, 3173
Sweet Green, 510, 1533
Sweet Leaf Iced Teas, 953
Sweet Relish, 50, 289
SweetBio, 999
Sweetbio, 1190
Sweetch, 2934
Sweeten, 1281
Sweetgreen, 332
sweetgreen, 514
SweetIM, 1323
SweetIQ, 2216
Sweetlabs, 1359
Sweetriot, 845
SweetSpring Salmon, 3248
Swell, 610, 1014, 1323
Swell Advantage, 2148
Swell Energy, 1896
Swell Rewards, 310
Swensen's, 2245
Swept, 2024, 2148, 2150
Swerve Pay Health Services, 9
Swiff-Train Co., 445
Swift, 2094
Swift Biosciences, 150, 750, 1207
Swift Fine Foods Limited, 2696
Swift Medical, 2174, 2181, 2224, 2228
Swift Navigation, 648, 720, 1511
Swift Shift, 564, 787
Swiftera, 1896
Swiftly, 310, 1614, 2230
Swiftmile, 1928
Swiftpage, 1050
SwiftPay MD, 1618
SwiftShift, 320, 3099
SwiftSolar, 849
SwiftStack, 1187, 1381, 1750
Swiftype, 586
SwifyKey, 3009
Swiggy, 1346
SwineTech, 999
Swing by Swing, 1103
Swing Education, 1058, 1393, 1698
SwingPal, 1261
Swink.tv, 794
SwipBox, 3194
Swipe, 3021
Swipeclock Workforce Management, 8, 1018
Swipely, 1322
SwipeSense, 648, 1364, 1483, 1618, 1803

Portfolio Companies Index

Swirl, 820, 925, 1150
Swirl Networks, 1701
Swish Analytics, 1660
Swiss Farm Stores, 1275
Swiss Farms, 1730
Swiss Smile, 2487
Swiss VC/PE Investment, 3143
Swiss-American Products, 1473
Swisshaus, 1939
Swissport, 3017
Switch, 527, 1908, 3072
Switch & Data Facilities, 1731
Switch Materials, 2205
Switch.co, 626
Switchback Energy Acquisition, 1328
Switchboard, 2094
Switchfly, 389, 1740, 1741, 1808
SwitchGear, 1794
Switchmate, 1426
SwitchNote, 1959
Swivel, 752
Swivel Beauty, 221
Swivi, 879, 3172
Swix Sport, 2722
Swoon Editions, 3009
Swoop, 1901
Swoopo, 200
Sword Diagnostics, 659, 1329, 1917
Swrve, 40, 2347, 2434
SWS Group, 1360
Swyft, 1065, 2131
Swype, 250
Swyper, 621
SWYX, 3223
Swyx, 1695
Syabas, 95
Syapse, 178, 812, 1605, 1698
Sybase, 200, 217
Sycara, 686
SyChip, 1170, 1304
Sygate, 1352, 1855
Sygate Technologies, 1852
Syktyvkar, 2482
Sylantro, 1629
Sylantro Systems Corporation, 163
Sylva, 2131
Sylvatex, 845
Symantec, 200
SYMBII, 464
Symbio, 398, 796
Symbio Robotics, 648
Symbiomix, 711
Symbiomix Therapeutics, 1383
Symbion, 560, 1746, 2438
Symbios Holdings, 947
Symbiot Business Group, 1679
Symbiotec Pharmalab, 585
Symbiotix Biotherapies, 1055
Symbium, 959
Symcat.com, 1876
Symend, 2187
Symetis, 2410
Symetrica, 3019
Symform, 1150
Symic, 1241
Symic Biomedical, 1128
Symicbio, 1238
Symmetry Medical, 1372
Symmetry Surgical, 1594
Symon, 843
Sympa, 1499
Symphogen, 1302, 3006, 3076, 3140, 3194
Symphonic Distribution, 227
Symphony, 1219
Symphony Commerce, 224, 527, 744
Symphony Evolution, 2806
Symphony Services, 1806

Sympli, 368
Symplified, 84, 857
Symplr, 502, 1410
Sympto, 1426
Symwave, 1084
Symyx, 240
Syn Mun Kong Insurance, 1143
Synacast, 2658
Synack, 84, 827, 972, 1079, 1158
Synacor, 5, 60, 810, 1334, 1526
Synad, 2372
Synairgen, 2883
Synamedia, 1912
Synap, 225
SynapDx, 749
Synapdx, 224
Synapse, 709
Synapse BioMedical, 1943
Synapse Biomedical Inc., 423, 1051
Synapse Design, 68
SynapseMX, 640
SynapSense, 794, 1355
Synapsense, 564
Synaptic Digital, 1479, 1701
Synaptics, 209
Synarc-Biocore Holdings, 190
Sync-Rx, 3063
Syncapay, 1240
Syncapse, 1411
SynCardia Systems, 190, 454
Syncardia Systems, 1024
Synced Care, 244
SyncHR, 25, 861
Synchris, 993, 1348
Synchrologic, 317, 881, 1042
Synchroneuron, 2969
Synchronoss, 22, 1006
Synchronoss Technologies, 3266
Synchronous Aerospace Group, 905, 1138
Syncro, 2544
Syncro Medical Innovations, 1347
Syncronex, 1736
Syncsort, 502, 1991
Synctera, 2090
Syndax, 209, 710, 772, 1268, 1414
Syndax Pharmaceuticals, 622
Syndicate, 1314
Syndigo, 1049
Synecor, 179, 1774
Synerchip, 3053
SynergEyes, 87, 605, 1995
Synergeyes, 599
SynergEyes Inc., 272
Synergx, 2198
Synergy, 73
Synergy Beverages, 1305
Synergy HomeCare Franchising LLC, 159
Synerlab, 2285
Synermore, 2969
Synervoz, 1153, 2024
Synerway, 2598
Synethic Biologics, 1815
SynGen, 240
Synico, 1233
Synlogic, 193
Synopsys, 1257, 1924
Synopsys Inc., 303
Synoptek, 747, 1831
Synosia, 11
Synosia Therapeutics, 3006
Synosia Therpeutics, 2410
Synovex, 1421
Synovia Solutions, 180, 762
SYNQ3, 300
SYNQY, 1065
SynsorMed, 75
Synstar International, 2635

Synta Pharma, 1271
Syntax, 2198
Syntaxin, 2308, 3104
Synteract, 1343
SynteractHCR, 441
Synteratchr, 886
Synthace, 3
Synthego, 1203, 1983
Synthematix, 1712
SynTherix, 454
Synthesia, 1105
Synthetic Games, 794
Synthetic Genomics, 322, 610, 704, 803
SynthOrx, 1522
SynthoRX, 545
Synthorx, 209
Syntiant, 664, 1158
Syntimmune, 144
Syntonix, 240, 1414
Syntonix Pharmaceuticals, 1191
Syntricity, 1995
Synventive, 1138
Synvest., 2324
Synyron Maerial Handling, 1115
Syon, 1294
Syquest, 2372
Syrgis Performance Initiators, 653
Syros, 73, 154, 748
Syrrx, 240, 2073
Sys Cloud, 1017
Syscan, 1183
Syscon Justice Systems, 2045
Sysdaq, 2848
Sysgo, 2704
Systeam, 2879
Systec Corp., 903
Systech, 949
Systech International, 632
System, 2953
System C Healthcare Ltd, 2477
System Heat, 2767
System One, 1231, 1929
Systems & Networks, 538
Systems Maintenance Services, 1754, 1818
Systems Planning and Analysis, 509
Systinet Corporation, 2301
Systran, 3118
Sysview Technology, 870
Syxsense, 2262
Syzygy Plasmonics, 2105

T

T&K Machine, 60, 1748
T-Base Communications, 2051
T-Bird Restaurant Group, 931
T-Pro Solutions, 1556
T-Rex, 1605
T2 Biosystems, 137, 748, 983, 1421, 1442, 1464
T2 Systems, 1410
T2Biosystems, 73, 158
T2Cure, 2701
T3, 310
T3Media, 56, 1663
T3S Technologies, 1074
T4 Media Group, 3009
T4 Spatial, 3248
TA Associates, 3245, 3254
TA Associates Battery, 2649
Taamkru, 3064
Taavura1, 2600
Taaz, 554
Tab, 597, 3226
TAB Products, 1070
Tabacarcen, 585
TabbedOut, 1843
Tabcon, 2263
Tableau Software, 1213

Portfolio Companies Index

Tablewerks Inc., 956
Tablus, 1852
Taboola, 520, 2717
Tabsquare, 2769
TabTale, 1511, 2943
Tabula Rasa, 646
Tabula Rasa Healthcare, 51, 1572
Tabur/Bricogite, 2592
Tacala, 96
Tacati, 3043
TacBright, 3136
Tachyon, 1270
Tachyus, 964
Tacit, 68
Tacit Innovations, 2123
Tacit Software, 2005
Tacit Technologies, 468
Tackk, 724, 964, 1599
Tackpoint, 2277
Taco Bueno, 1404
Taco Mac, 479
Tact.aI, 1610
Tact.ai, 1158, 1537, 1890
Tactile Systems Technology, 809, 1523
Tactix, 1911
TactoTek, 2621
Tactus, 1821
Tacurion Pharma Inc., 184
TaDa Innovations, 770
Tadaa, 2470
Tadelon Holding Group, 2533
Tadem Capital, 298
Tadir-Gan, 2736
Tadiran Com Ltd., 2736
tado§, 3152
Tae Life Sciences, 177
Tae-san Techno, 2798
Taejin, 2763
Taeyang 3C, 2848
Taft, 728
Tag Commander, 3229
Tag Pop, 976
TagArray, 1740
Tagga, 2257
Tagged, 1841
Tagkast, 1121
TagMan, 876
Tagman, 2455
Tagnetics, 987
Tagnos, 252
Tagstand, 1521
Tagsys, 2457
Tagsys RFID, 2653
Tagsys Rfid, 3083
Tahoma Ventures, 3265
Taifas, 3039
Taiflex Scientific, 2594
Taiger, 1269
Tails.com, 2665, 3009
Taimei Medical Technology, 1828
Taina Tech, 2398
Tainet Communcation Systems, 2594
Taipale Telematics, 2864
Taisho Pharmaceutical Co., 1456
Taiwan Cellular Corp, 2898
Taiwan IC Packaging, 1771
Taiwan Semiconductor Manufacturing Company, 897
Taiwan Sumida Electronics, 897
Taizhou Reflecting Materials, 2533
TaKaDu, 2101, 2307
Takara Bio, 2961
Take 5, 1859
Take 5 Oil Change, 1580
Take Lessons, 564, 1121
Take the Interview, 1572, 1741
Take-Two Interactive, 2019

Takeaway.com, 3042
Takeda, 1349
TakeLessons, 1702, 1848
Takelessons, 1966, 1969
Takeoff, 1959
TAKF, 3062
Takko, 136
Takumi Technology, 145
Takwak, 3179
Takyca, 2912
TAL International, 654
Tala, 514, 1006, 1153
Talari Networks, 780, 1203, 1684
Talarian, 209
Talbot Underwriting, 1372
Talech, 108, 1254
Talecom, 2958
Talecris, 119
Talena, 389
TalenBin, 457
Talend, 1685
Talent Academy, 225
Talent Bin, 1121
Talent Reef, 793
Talent Sky, 130
Talent Sonar, 545, 978, 1058
Talent Sprint, 2992
Talent Systems, 376
Talent Wunder, 3226
Talenta, 721
TalentBin, 1658
TalentGuard, 447
Talenthouse, 68
TalentShare, 680
TalentSoft, 2375, 3104
TalentSpring, 85
TalentWorks, 776, 1153
Talenya, 2938
Talenz, 2464
Tales2Go, 1172, 1993
TalexMedical, 269
Talisma, 1640
Talix, 520, 1056
Talk Desk, 610
Talk Route, 175
talk2me, 2745
Talkable, 31
Talkative, 2276
TalkDesk, 1750
Talkdesk, 1610
Talking Blocks, 1028
TalkingData, 1340
TalkingNets, 457
TalkIQ, 182, 1629
Talko, 1058
Talkpush, 3099
TalkShoe, 296, 1305, 1588
Talkspace, 527, 1346, 1701
Tall Oak Learning, 674
Tall Oak Midstream, 672
Tall Tree Foods, 96
Talla, 209, 354
Tallarium, 1531
Tallgrass Energy, 1066, 1848
Tally, 553, 1079, 1666
Tally Systems, 523
TallyGenicom, 172
TallyGo!, 309
Talmetrix, 481
Talon Oil & Gas II, 673
Talos Systems, 1499
Talyst, 1392
Tama Broadcasting, 902
Tamak, 3062
Tamara Mellon, 345
Taminco, 2371
Tammac, 1636

Tamr, 812, 856, 1689, 2006
Tanaza, 3099
Tandem, 641
Tandem Computers, 183
Tandem Diabetes Care, 605, 622, 941, 1063
Tandem Health Care, 248
Tandem Medical, 1399
Tandus Flooring, 1507
Tandvitaal, 2492
Tanenbaum-Harber Insurance Group, 1372
Tangdou, 827
Tangent Energy Solutions, 677
Tangentix, 3019
Tangerine Technologies, 297
Tangible Play, 2009
Tangible Science, 1238
Tangle Creek Energy, 2036
Tango, 107, 610, 793, 1511, 1601, 1840
Tango Card, 752, 1768
Tango Networks, 1875
Tango/High Country Venture, 3265
Tangoe, 215, 655, 2137
Tanium, 361, 488, 824, 1006
Tank & Rast, 2371
Tank Holdings Corp., 1113
Tank Services, 1749
Tantaline, 262, 3194
Tantalus, 1537
Tantalus Systems Corp, 2091
Tantivy Communications, 1348
Tanyuan Tech, 2927
Tao, 1706
Taobao, 3091
Taomee, 1602
Taos, 362
Tap 'n Tap, 1290
Tap Commerce, 527
Tap Influence, 35
Tap Rock Resources, 1328
Tap to Learn, 680
Tap.tv, 911
Tapad, 209, 527, 744, 1521
Tapatalk, 752
Tapcanvas, 1054
Tapcart, 49, 121
Tapco International, 371
TapCommerce, 680
Tapdaq, 2469
Tapfwd, 1418
TapInfluence, 881
Tapingo, 1073, 2557, 3212
Tapio, 1028
TapJoy, 1014
Tapjoy, 1867
Taplytics, 2074, 2122
Tapp Label Technologies, 2210
Tapper Candies, 1955
TapRoot Systems, 1013
Tapsense, 1969, 2009
Taptalk, 1998
Taptap, 2978
Taptolearn, 2321
Taptu, 2653, 2665
Tapulous, 31, 936
Tapulous/GoGoApps, 624
Taqua, 1021, 1463
Taqua Systems, 457
TARA, 5
Tara, 888
Tara AI, 48
tara Technologies, 228
Taral Networks, 1084
Taranis, 3212
Tarari, 1237
Taraspan, 2276
Taratec, 1140
Tarena, 846, 3053

Portfolio Companies Index

Tarena International, 2841
Targa Resources, 676
Targacept, 1395, 2998
Targamite, 659
TargAnox, 179, 1421
TargeGen, 470, 772, 1414, 1908, 2487
Targent, 1048
Target Compiler Technologies N.V., 2893
Target Data, 138
Target Pharma Solutions, 1925
Target PharmaSolutions, 1346
Target Pharmasolutions, 1559
Targeted Genetics Corp., 1918
Targeted Growth, 1007, 2007
TargetRx, 1510
Targetspot, 224
TargetX, 1506
Targovax, 2510
Targus, 722
Targus Group International, 2014
Tari, 182
Taris, 748, 1522
Taris Biomedical, 1464, 1814
Tarpon Towers, 1727
Tarquin Plc., 407
Tarsa Therapeutics, 1510, 2972, 3006
Tarsus Medical, 1728
Tartan Canada Corporation, 2045
Tartec, 655
Tartine et Chocolat, 2294
Tarveda, 748, 1930
Tarveda Therapeutics, 1271
TAS Energy, 658
TAS Environmental Services, 293
TAS Environmental Services LP, 60
Tasi Group, 261
Tasit.Com, 2428
Task Easy, 380
Task Force X Capital Management, 50
Taskeasy, 35, 881, 1074
Tasker Ventures, 2354
TaskRabbit, 234, 1322, 1534, 1666, 1835
Taskrabbit, 752
Tasktop, 2283
Tasman Building Products, 2411
TASQ Technology, 886
TASSL, 1581
TasteMade, 1816
Tastemade, 520, 1537
TastemakerX, 234, 1862
Tasti D-Lite, 1744
Tasting Room, 546, 1658
Tasty Banking Company, 836
TastyTrade, 1121
Tastytrade, 1787
TastyWorks, 1121
TAT Technologies Ltd., 2736
Tatango, 85
Tate's Bake Shop, 1576
Tatron, 3174
Tattersall Sound & Picture, 2133
Tattile, 2383
Tattva, 2965
Tau-Metrix, 116
Taulia, 130, 582, 1184, 1517, 1855, 2256, 2681, 2919
Taunt, 779, 1501
Taurex Drill Bits, 106
Taurus, 679
Tausendkind, 2832
Tausight, 1
Tavour, 776
Tavve Software, 56
Tax Advisors Group Inc., 406
Tax Credit, 1929
Tax Guard, 1169
TaxBit, 79

TaxiForSure, 2809
TaxJar, 309
Tay Two Co., 2898
Taykey, 1701, 1798
Taylor Logistics LLC, 899
Taylor Morrison Home Corporation, 1837
Taylor Precision Products, 408
Taylor-Wharton International, 1990
TaylorMade, 1089
Taymax Group Holdings LLC, 1853
Tazznet, 936
TB Biosciences, 1386
TB12, 568
TBA Global, 1469
TBD Fusion, 2751
TBH, 545
tbh, 246
TC3, 1045
TCDS.com, 2039
tCell, 1203
TCF Financial Corp., 303
TCG RX, 785
TCHO, 669
TCI, 162, 445, 1481
TCP Communications, 902
TCP Venture Capital, 3260
TCR, 1230
TCR2, 1268
TCSC, 1729
TCT, 2724
TCV, 36
TDF, 2578
TDF Ventures, 3260
TDS, 920
TDS Logistics, 1507
Tdsoft, 2761
TDX, 1021
Tea Drops, 568, 901
Tea Leaf, 773
Teach for India, 1374
Teach.com, 154
TeachBoost, 568
Teacher Gaming, 2944
TeacherMatch, 1473
Teachers Pay Tachers, 1720
TeachFX, 1426, 1530
Teaching Company, 381
Teaching Strategies, 470
Teachscape, 21
Teachtown, 85
Teads, 1702
Teads.tv, 1418
Teaforia, 998
Teal, 1074
Teal Natural Resources, 1328
Tealeaf, 241
Tealet, 1914
Tealium, 488, 1478, 1798, 2126
Team 8, 1511
Team BS, 2786
Team Drive-Away, 480
Team Health Holdings, 1160
Team Liquid, 1121
Team Olivia, 3045
Team Snap, 779, 1831
TEAM Software, 28
Team Technologies, 1576
Team Technologies Inc., 502
Team Viewer, 912
Team8, 1001, 1158
Teambox, 586
Teambuy.ca, 2051
Teamer, 2909
TeamEx, 452
TeamHealth, 1271
TeamingPro, 75
teamly, 1914

TeamMates, 1839
Teamo.ru, 641
TeamOne Logistics, 825
TeamSnap, 686
TeamSystem, 223, 927
TeamViewer, 872, 3024
Teamwork.ai, 310
Teamworks, 191, 820
Teapot Inc., 624
Tear Film Innovations, 300
TearClear, 300
TearScience, 599, 1510
Teasdale Foods Inc., 1404
Tecan, 1777
Tech, 1924
Tech Air, 478
Tech Cast Holdings, 1722
Tech Holdings, 1139
Tech Launch, 421
Tech Lighting LLC, 911
Tech Pak, 1294
Tech Pharmacy Services, 809
Tech Rentals, 1425
Tech Stars, 779
TechDerm, 1228
Techdirt, 116
TeChen, 2927
Techfaith Wireless, 2841
TechForward, 1103
TechInvent AS, 3132
Techlink Entertainment, 2197
Technibus, 1438
Technical Compression Services, 1748
Technical Gas Products, 1524
Technical Innovation, 1270, 1425
Technical Machine, 1593, 1862
Technical Solutions Holdings Inc., 654
Technicolor, 1912
Technikom Polska, 528
Technimark, 1482, 1507
TechninAsia, 721
Technische Handelsmaatschappij
  Marchand-Andriessen, 3200
Technisource, 458
Technisyst, 2613
Technium Labs, 3100
Techno-Aide, 1343
Technocer, 2936
Technoflex, 3229
Technolas, 2701, 2923
Technolas Perfect Vision GmbH, 2807
Technologies, 288
Technologies Co. Ltd., 2624
Technology IQ US LLC, 624
Technology Tarena, 977
Technology Village, 3268
Technomatix, 3128
Technorati, 186, 200, 1966, 2437
Techorati, 1245
Techpoint, 2965
TechProcess, 1327
TechProcess Solutions, 877
Techprocess Solutions, 1949
TechPubs, 1839
TechRx, 957
TechSee, 1610
TechSkills, 1364
Techstar, 609
TechStars, 209, 686, 1701
Techstars, 1023, 1024, 1101, 1598
Techstars Ventures, 635, 3265
TechStyle, 562, 1184
TechTarget, 1787
TechTemple, 641
Techverse Inc., 738
Techwell, 2594
Teckal, 3145

Portfolio Companies Index

Teckro, 1646
Tecnomen Oyj, 2981
Tecnowind Group, 3145
Tecomet, 190, 458
Tecon Rio Grande SA, 2080
Tecpro Systems, 2451
Tecta America, 2030, 2201
Tectonic, 1610
Tectonic Audio Labs, 1065
Tectonic Therapeutics, 1934
Tectonic Ventures, 3263
Tecumseh Products, 2062
Tecverde, 838
Teddy Bear Portraits, 654
Tedea, 2736
Tediber, 2288
Tee Life, 2997
Teecinno, 3248
Teekay, 1848
Teem, 79, 1074, 1385
TEEM PH, 2472
Teem Photonics, 226, 2430, 2867
Teens and Toddlers, 2530
Teeology, 1464
Teespring, 2011
TeesuVac, 3194
Teewinot Life Sciences, 1866
Teforia, 1263
TEG, 2530
Tega Industries, 1778
Tegic, 250, 1640
Tegic Communications, 755, 1947
Tegile, 561
Tegile Systems, 200
Tego, 1164
Tegra Medical, 858
Tehama, 2074
Tehuti Networks, 3050
Teidem - Jomo, 2492
Teikon, 2617
Tejas Networks, 808, 1187
TEK Supply, 1294
Tek-Air Systems, 607
Tekelec, 1912
Tekion, 108
Tekion Cloud, 298
Teklatech, 3194
TekLinks, 1410, 1772
Tekni-Plex, 767
Tekniplex, 823
Teknovus, 759, 885, 1924
Tektagen, 315
Tektronix Inc., 1905
TEKVOX, 447
Tel-loin, 2960
TELA Bio, 1383
Tela Innovations, 278
Teladoc, 522, 872, 941, 972, 1228, 1517, 1852
Telaria, 1235, 1949
Telarix, 655
Telcom Semicon, 1091
TELCOR, 28
Teldio, 2276
Tele Atlas, 1213, 1244, 1795
Telecity Group, 1360
Telecolumbus, 2488
Telecom Design, 2393
Telecom Transport Management, 1640
Telecomia Venture I Ky, 2731
TeleComputing, 2623
Telecomputing, 2722
Telecon, 2076
TeleCTG, 721
Teleflex Inc., 836
Telegate, 2773, 3239
Telegent Systems, 1340, 2448
Telegesis, 3098

Telegram, 662
Telegraph Hill, 36
Telehealth Solutions, 1292
Telekenex, 1953
Telemetric Corporation, 74
TeleNav, 1771, 1798
Telenav, 1203, 2844
Telenet, 2772, 3086
TelePacific, 1021
TelePacific Communications, 186
Telepizza, 3024
Teleport, 3099
Teleportd, 2620
TeleportMe, 2876
Telera, 759, 1750
Telera Inc., 255
Telerik, 1754
Telerivet, 1032
TelerX, 1206
TeleSign Holdings, 1754
Telesofia, 2934
Telesoft, 36
Telestream, 823, 1817
Teletrac, 1912
Televero, 447
Televero Health, 1803
Telibrahma, 3010
Teligent Inc., 159
Telik, 1777
Teliport Me, 976
Telisma, 2346, 2535
Telitas US, 2745
Telkore, 1691
Tellagence, 1467
TellApart, 234
Tellapart, 224
Tellermate Holdings, 356
Telleroo, 3099
Tellja, 2629, 2985
TellMe, 1235
Telltale, 1566
Telltale Games, 857
Tellwise, 1854
Telly, 1966, 2009
Telnyx, 1181, 1462
Telocity, 200
Telogis, 127, 561, 1971
Telogy, 22
Telogy Networks, 1348
TeLoRmedix, 1492
Telormedix, 2410
Telos Corporation, 681
Telos Entertainment, 2051
Telovations, 1152
Telrad Conneqy, 2773
TelRock, 1244
Teltech Resource Network, 538
Teltron Telecommunications & Electronics, 2798
telweb, 2254
Telx, 828
Tembec, 1968
Temenos, 2775, 2872
Temescal Wellness, 1139
temicon GmbH, 2677
Temis, 3011
Temp Automation, 1065
Tempered Networks, 978, 1566
Tempest, 1696, 1930
Tempest Re, 1372
Templar Energy, 741
TempMee, 754
Tempo, 586, 2130, 2822
Tempo AI, 680, 1237
Tempo Auto, 108
Tempo Automation, 845, 1155, 1881
Tempo Payments, 1649
Tempo Smart Calendar, 2131

Tempo.AI, 3112
TempoDB, 473, 619, 758, 965
Temporal, 2181
Tempow, 2469
Tempronics, 1355
Temptime, 1962
Tempur World, 170
Tempur-Pedic, 790
Tempus, 1121, 1296
Ten Marks, 275, 430
Ten-X, 579
Ten10, 136
Tenaska Poer Fund II LP, 2088
TenCar, 705
Tencent, 977
Tender Greens, 1169
Tender Products, 1494
Tender Tree, 708
TenderTree, 600
Tendril, 35, 143, 812, 983, 1597, 1908
TenEighty, 3265
Tenere, 1963
Tenet Home Care, 409
Tenex Greenhouse, 1619
Tenfen, 3206
Tenfu, 819
Tengchuang, 2927
Tengion, 1510
Tengion Inc., 2807
Tengwu, 2841
Tenjin, 945
tenKsolar, 1474
Tennis Channel, 224
Tennis Point, 3011
Tenor, 553, 976, 1537
Tenovos, 1557
Tensar, 153
Tensar Corporation, 425
Tensator, 1576
Tenscorcomm, 35
Tensilica, 621, 1213
Tensor Surgical, 461, 999
TensorFlight, 310
Tenstorrent, 648
Tenstreet, 1720
Tentacle, 1499
Tentrr, 901, 1363
TenXc, 1042
Tenxer, 1969
tenXer, 1862
Tenzing, 2104
TEOCO, 1778
Tepha, 1007, 1931
tEquitable, 1259
Ter Hulst, 2940
Tera Semiconductor, 1091
Tera-Barrier Films, 145
Terabit Radios, 387
Teracent, 1088
Teracent Corp., 624
Teraco, 854
Teraco Data Environments, 257
TeraConnect, 1084
Teradata, 58
Teradian, 2848
Teradiant Networks, 767
Teradici, 87, 983, 2372
TeraDiode, 77
Teradyne, 1294
Terago, 1643
TeraLogic, 1706
TeraLogic Pharmaceuticals, 113
Teralytics, 2437, 2919
Teranetics, 837
Terapede, 1614
Terapia, 2674
Terapio, 1622

1408

Portfolio Companies Index

TeraPore, 176
Terapore, 1522
Teraspan Networks, 2265
TeraSquare, 3118
TeraView, 2378, 3089, 3186
TeraView Limited, 2751
Terawave, 1091
Terawave Communications, 2917
Terayon, 1091, 1953, 3221
Terbium Labs, 1, 833
Tercica, 1495
Tergal, 2309
Teridian Semiconductor, 843
Teridion, 2943
Terminal, 1079
Terminal49, 321
TerminalFour, 2347
Terminus, 175, 191, 655, 2074, 2122
Teros, 468, 1629
Terra Firma, 2321
Terra Firma Capital Partners III, 2088
Terra Grain Fuels Inc., 2129
Terra Motors, 721
Terra-Gen, 676
Terra-Gen Power, 157
Terracare Associates, 1424, 1487
Terraclear, 1162
Terracotta, 1478
TerraEchos, 1862
TerraGo, 510
TerraGo Technologies, 983
TerraLink Horticulture, 2249
TerraLUX, 554
Terramar, 1220
TerraMarc Industries, 1090
Terramera, 2037, 2230
TerraPact, 518
Terrapass, 1355
TerraPower, 457, 1010, 1073
Terrapure Environmental, 2056
TerrAscend, 1052, 2233
TerraServer, 1711
TerrAvion, 1219
TerraXML, 213
Terreal, 2710
Terres, 2593
Territory, 1890
Territory Foods, 1259
Terszol, 838
Tertill, 2122
Tertio Service Management Systems, 2745
Tervela, 1339, 1674, 1675
Tervita, 1066, 1933
TES, 2867
TES Global, 1837
TESARO, 1414, 1700
Tesaro, 1014
Tesla, 596, 803, 2148, 2787
Tesla Exploration Ltd., 2036
Tesla Motors, 526, 610, 1788, 1908
Tesora, 1463
Tesorio, 752, 1330
TesoRx Pharma, 1065
Tespo, 507
Tessa Therapeutics, 2681
Tesser Health, 512
Tessian, 1716, 2469
Tessolve, 145
Tessolve Solutions, 3053
Test Object, 3226
Test.ai, 641, 2018
TestAmerica, 931
Testbirds, 3104
Testek Inc., 1368
TestEquity, 734
TestFire, 744
Testfreaks, 3004

Testhub, 3226
Testing Services Holdings, 654
Testive, 512, 1104
Testmunk, 1515
TestQuest, 1287
TestRigor AI, 29
Testroom, 2985
TestSoup, 1959
Tether Technologies, 1065
Tetherex, 1268
Tethis, 289
Tethr, 881, 1240
Tethys Bioscience, 561, 794, 1341
Teton Gravity Research, 679
Tetra Discovery Partners, 140
TetraData, 655
Tetragenetics, 705, 1104
TetraLogic, 918, 1098, 1439, 1510
TetraLogic Pharmaceuticals, 1931
Tetraphase, 240, 748
Tetraphase Pharmaceuticals, 704, 1198, 1693
TetraScience, 752, 1059
Tetrate, 1614
Tetravitae Bioscience, 979
Teva, 1456
TEVET Process Control Technologies, 2711
Texada Software Inc, 2091
Texas Advanced Optoelectronic, 1917
Texas B&B, 112
Texas Genco, 927, 1837
Texas Land & Cattle, 1552
Texas Ventures, 953
Texcel Medical, 199
Texchange (Austin), 1653
Texel, 544
Texerity, 352
Text IQ, 1423, 1672
Text Now, 787
Text+, 2640
Texta America, 1090
Textech Industries, 167
TextEngine, 221
Texterity, 1922
Textile Based Delivery, 1065
Textilia, 2879
Textio, 553, 666, 1629
TextIQ, 752
TextMaster, 2377
textPlus, 1184
TextRecruit, 1677
Textronics, 1324, 1442
TextureMedia, 447
TFF, 3268
TGap Ventures, 3259
TGaS Advisors, 815
TGBS, 3185
TGI Fridays, 475, 1654
TGI Systems Corporation, 410
TGR Financial Inc., 948
TGR Industrial Services, 1210
TGT Oilfield Services, 1129
Thaddeus Medical Systems, 999
Thai Cane Paper Public, 897
Thalchemy, 1923
Thalento, 2940
Thales, 1924
Thalmic Labs, 1477, 1718
Thankful AI, 121
Thankx, 752
Thanx, 972, 1032, 1534, 1702, 2009
THaT, 1083
Thatcher Tubes, 836
thatgamecompany, 1511
Thayer Aerospace, 1949
Thayer Ventures, 231
The Access Group, 1248
The Ace, 1220

The Active Network, 1390
The Aladdin Group, 674
The Alaska Club, 1131
The Alberleen Group, 845
The American Academy, 2374
The Americas Card, 1504
The Arbor Company, 153
The ARC Group, 1746
The Arcview Group, 1139
The Art of Shaving, 405
The Art Store, 1552
The Athletic, 59, 259, 520, 1770
The Atlas Group, 851
The Backplane, 1832
The Bayou Companies, 96
The Beak Beyond, 395
The Bee Corp, 659
The Beer Café, 856
The Berkman Law Firm, 3257
The Better Software Company, 724
The Big Know, 1117
The Bisys Group, 303
The Black Tux, 562, 1114, 1203
The Blackstone Group, 3245
The Block, 1599
The BondFactor Company, 1832
The Boring Company, 803
The Bouqs Company, 121
The Bowery Saving Bank, 1624
The Brixton, 2277
The Brock Group, 1133
The Browser Company of New york, 321
The Bruery, 424
The Business of Fashion, 59
The Business Software Center, 2565
The Canadian National Institute of Health Inc., 2245
The Carlson Company Inc., 1057
The Carlstar Group, 110
The Carlyle Group, 3245
The Cayman, 2277
The Center for Vein Restoration, 1964
The Center for Wound Healing, 277
The Chartis Group, 1579
The Chia Co., 1518
The Chicago Athletic Association, 69
The Cipher Brief, 93
The Cleaning Authority, 1461, 1603
The Climate Corp., 2437
The Climate Corporation, 840, 1800, 2398
The Cloud, 2653, 2665
The Clymb, 689, 1384, 1953
The Community Company, 300
The ComplEAT Food Group, 2935
The Concery Network, 508
The Container Store, 1113, 1360
The Convenience Network, 461
The Copernicus Group IRB, 557
The Core Institute, 785
The Corner Vet, 447
The Corporate University Xchange, 1431
The Cranemere Group, 3254
The Cranemere Group Ltd., 1258
The Crosby Group, 1086
The Crown Group, 934
The Currency Cloud, 3005, 3229
The Custom Movement, 1426
The Dating Ring, 1752
The Delaney Hardware Company, 920
The Detection Group, 130
The Difference, 221
The Diplomat Group, 681
The Dirty Bird, 2245
The Dodo, 876, 1701
The Door, 221
The Dwyer Group, 1576
The Eastman Egg Company, 1159

Portfolio Companies Index

The Echo Nest, 1184
The Echonest, 1527
The Edelman Financial Group, 1108
The Edgewater Funds, 3245, 3255
The Efficiency Network Inc., 55
The Employment Group, 2492
The Engine, 3263
The Engineering Company, 3099
The Eton Group Ltd, 2713
The Evans Network of Companies, 63
The Executive Centre, 2763
The Execu|Search Group, 929
The Expectations Project, 1315
The Expert Institute, 1720
The Fabric, 1928
The Faction Collective, 3009
The Fairways Group, 1275
The Family, 641
The Fanfare Group, 1449
The Farmer's Dog, 514, 763, 1666
The Feedroom, 1915
The Felters Group, 989
The Filter, 2682
The Finial Company, 988
The Flatiron School, 1184
The Flavor of california LLC, 1612
The Flex Company, 121, 901
The Focus Corporation, 1090
The Fragrance Outlet, 1417
The Friendly Stranger, 2134
The Gallery, 1220
The Galtney Group, 1772
The Gelato Fiasco, 440
The GI Alliance, 1964
The GigaOM Network, 87
The Goal Group, 2129
The Golden Financial Group Inc., 449
The Good Promise, 447
The Goodship, 1810
The Graph, 1531
The Great Gourmet, 1209
The Green Organic Dutchman, 99
The Green Solutions, 970
The Grid, 108, 1059
The Grow Network, 1022
The Guild, 1186, 1616
The Gym, 2530, 3027
The Harris Agency, 3266
The Harrisburg Senators, 1431
The Herbalista Set, 395
The High Note, 850
The Hillman Group, 435
The Hilsinger Company, 973
The Hippo Kitchen, 954
The History Press, 3009
The Hive, 298, 812, 1928
The Home Decor Companies, 1136
The Honest Company, 820, 1006, 1483
The Hotels Network, 1323
The Huffington Post, 1701
The Hunt, 1032
The Hut Group, 2469
The Hydrafacial Company, 1132
The Iconic, 3161
The Independent Group, 2935
The Inside, 763, 1114
The Intersect Group, 1270
The Investment Fund For Central and Eastern Europe, 2856
The Investment Fund for Emerging Markets, 2856
The Iron Horse Hotel, 69
The Iron Yard, 1925
The Jay Group, 1639
The Johnny Rockets Group, 449
The Jordan Company, 3245
The Juice Plus Company, 96

The Kela Group, 1912
The Kendal Group, 3009
The Kernel Group, 1888
The King Edward, 2245
The Kive Company, 121
The Langley Corporation, 1294
The LeadCorp, 897
The League, 1566, 2010
The Learning Company Inc., 449
The Learning Egg LLC, 1051
The Learning Experience, 1025, 1506
The Leather Shop, 1294
The Level Playing Field Corporation, 509
The Liberation Group, 2926
The Limited, 1755
The Linc Group, 828
The Lion Brewery, 747
The Listening Co., 2653
The Lodge, 799
The Logic Group, 1761
The Los Angeles Film Schook, 1778
The Lovesac Company, 1625
The Lucky Group, 133
The Lynch Law Group, 3264
The Mad Video, 3214
The Madera Group, 333
The Marktets LLC, 905
The Masonry Group, 851
The Medical Cit, 2937
The Medical City, 1143
The Mentor Method, 221
The Merit Group, 448
The Metropolitan Switch Board Company, 1748
The Mighty, 827, 1890
The Mill at New Holland, 1220
The Mobility House, 3242
The Mochi Ice Cream Company, 451
The Mom Project, 1023
The Money Finder, 2063, 2148
The Motley Food, 266
The Motley Fool, 810, 1424
The Muse, 48, 182, 596, 972
The NanoSteal Company, 173
The Neck and Back Clinics, 1826
The Neiman Marcus Group, 2688
The New Motion, 2701
The New Orleans Exchange, 646
The New Primal, 849
The NewsMarket, 307
The Nielsen Company, 1818
The Noun Project, 59, 1223
The Nuance Group, 3017
The Oceanaire Inc., 494
The Official Information Company, 1929
The ONE, 3241
The One Health Company, 269, 1605
The One Of Them, 2860
The One Page Company, 304
The Online Backup Company, 3004
The Orange Chef Co., 1719
The Original Cakerie, 886
The Outline, 59, 1533
The Outsource Group, 557
The Overlook, 1220
The Pairie Club, 300
The Pallet Network, 2935
The Pantry, 786
The Paper Store, 1979
The Paramont, 1220
The Pedowitz Group, 656
The PFM Group, 973
The Phia Group, 1979
The Phoenix at James Creek, 1220
The Pill Club, 1666
The Planet Group, 1231
The Plastics Group, 1963
The Player's Tribune, 1006

The Players Tribune, 1885
The Plunge, 1441
The Podcast App, 798, 1530
The Poma Companies, 1115
The Portables Exhibit Systems, 2249
The Poseidon Companies, 1066
The Practice, 2963
The Prairie Club, 1195
The Praxis Companies, 1275
The Press Gallery, 2194
The Princeton Review, 458, 1372
The Private Clinic Group, 2515
The PromptCare Companies, 899, 1230
The Property Software, 2935
The Pros Closet, 779
The Pub, 1433
The RapcoHorizon Company, 1232
The Real Real, 641
The RealReal, 48, 389, 596, 708, 862, 876
The Realtime Group, 517
The Receivables Exchange, 224
The Reject Shop, 2942
The Relish, 901
The Remi Group, 1276
The Renewal Workshop, 1023
THE RESET, 68
The Resolute Fund II, 2088
The Resumator, 1569, 1944
The Retreat at Grand Lake, 1220
The Richardson Group, 405
The Ride, 1626
The Right People Construction Group, 1270
The Right.Fit, 1703
The Ritedose Corporation, 1372
The Riverside Company, 3245, 3254
The Riveter, 345, 776, 1162
The Rocky Mountain School of Design, 1778
The Rogue Initiative, 1391, 1477
The Roof, 1425
The Rounds, 2148
The RunThrough, 1305
The Sails Company, 788
The Sandbox Group, 1424
The Saxton Group, 1145
The Sceptre Group, 2565
The Search Agency, 1045
The Service Companies, 1939
The ServiceMaster Company, 1460
The Shade Store, 1113
The Shelby Group, 1979
The Sheridan Group, 170
The Shoe Box, 940
The Shore, 2939
The Shriram Group, 2590, 2591
The SIA Group, 2854
The Signature Group, 1044
The Sill, 901
The Skimm, 901
The Socialite Family, 2288
The SPIRIT Project, 1914
The Sports Authority, 1113
The SR Group, 225
The Stable, 817
The Stakeholder Company, 3064
The Stanley Works, 1294
The State Group, 2284
The Still, 328
The Succession Fund LP, 2088
The Sun Exchange, 310
The Sun Valley Group, 1090
The T System, 782
The Tab, 2469
The TASI Group, 989
The TEAM Companies, 2264
The Templar Hotel, 2245
The Tensar Corporation, 1090
The TharpeRobbins Company, 1627

Portfolio Companies Index

The Tie Bar, 470
The Tile Shop, 2969
The Tire Rack, 1113
The Topps Company, 1160
The Town Kitchen, 1895
The Town of Wasaga Beach, 2245
The Townsend Group, 889
The Trade Desk, 625
The Trade Desk Inc., 969
The Training Room, 2935
The Tranzonic Co, 1460
The Traxys Companies, 1066
The tuesday Company, 937
The Veggie Grill Inc., 334
The Village Green Bookstore, 1839
The Visual Revenue Platform, 1407
The VOID, 1928
The Void, 1511
The Waddington Group, 1372
The Warranty Group, 1837
The Water Initiative, 1194
The Wave VR, 1890
The Weather Channel, 223, 2371
The Wellness Group, 3206
The Winebow Group, 351
The Wing, 328, 354, 1079
The Wireless Stores, 1766
The Wonder, 328
The Wood Heating Company, 3003
The Works, 2164
The Wrap, 1186
The Wrench Group, 1021
The Young Turks, 641
The Zebra, 227, 275, 752, 1687
Theatermania, 724
Theatro, 1073, 1684
Thebizmo, 649
TheBlogTgv, 3170
TheBouqs.com, 1966
theBouqs.com, 1515
TheBrain Technologies Corporation, 2073
Theeb, 1021
Thefind, 224
TheFutureFM, 708
TheGreenBridge.com, 1101
TheGuarantors, 1982
TheHappyCloud, 209
Theia Interactive, 985
Thelial Technologies, 3039
Themis, 3011
TheNeura, 3112
Theorem Clinical Research Holdings, 1278
Theoris Software, 754
thePlatform, 822, 1718
Therabis, 1139
Therachon, 1930
Theraclone Sciences, 154, 389, 922
Theragen, 227
Theranos, 185, 278
Theranostics Health, 1172
Therapeutic Human Polyclonals, 1546
Therapeutic Monitoring Systems, 2125
Therapeutic Research Center, 782, 1115
TheraPlay, 1738
Theraplay, 611
Therapure Biopharma Inc., 2067
Therapy Brands, 1127, 1499
Therasolve, 2940
Therasos Therapeutics, 58
TheraTogs, 933
Theratome Bio, 659
Theravance, 22, 1693
TheraVasc, 1051
TheraVase, 1556
TheraVida, 1619
TheraVir, 3235
TheRealReal, 182, 1014

Theregen Corporation, 1619
TheRetailPlanet.com, 758
Theriana Pharmaceuticals, 1522
Therion Biologicals Corporation, 1399
Therma, 7
Therma-Tru Doors, 1145
Therma-Wave, 217
Thermacore, 1431
Thermafiber, 445
Thermal Product Solutions, 1548
Thermal Sensing Products Inc., 989
Thermal Solutions Manufacturing, 1548
Thermalin, 1581
Thermalin Diabetes, 1229
Thermalin Diabetes LLC, 1051
ThermaSource, 1897
Thermasys, 1518
ThermImage, 262
Thermo Ceramix, 810
Thermo Fisher Scientific, 1456
Thermo-Tech Windows, 319
ThermoChem Recovery International, 18
Thermoforming Technology Group, 1722
Thermogenics, 2156
Thermon Industries, 197
Thermondo, 2832
Therodiag, 2867
Theron Pharmaceuticals, 130
TherOptix, 300
TherOx, 561, 1008
Therox, 137, 1302
Thesan Pharma, 1631
theScore, 2228
Thesis Couture, 221
TheSkimm, 944
TheSquare, 957
TheSquareFoot, 1479
TheStreet Inc., 5
TheStreet.com, 1107, 1787
Theta Microelectronics, 950
TheTapLab, 1585
Thetaray, 812
theTradeDesk, 309, 774
Thetus, 1355
Theva, 3152
THEVA D☐Nnschichttechnik GmbH, 2677
TheWaveVR, 310, 1391, 3099
TheySay, 3019
Thiel Cheese & Ingredients, 719
ThinAir, 1254
Thinair, 232
ThinCI, 827
Thindata, 2104
Thinglefin, 374
ThingMagic, 1
Things Engraved, 2245
Things Remembered, 228, 1160
Things Remembered Inc., 357
ThingTech, 1412
ThingThing, 3099
Think Data Works, 2265
Think Finance, 1740, 1787
Think Research, 2141, 2174
Think Through Learning, 1298, 1691
Think Through Math, 888, 1626
Think Vine, 481
ThinkCERCA, 194, 1181
ThinkData, 2112
ThinkData Webware, 2107
Thinkful, 752, 1393, 1521
Thinkfuse, 776
Thinking Phone Networks, 58
Thinking Screen Media, 1150
Thinkingbox, 2249
ThinkingPhones, 1787
ThinkIQ, 309, 2037
ThinkLabs, 3100

THINKmd, 789
ThinkNear, 308, 724
Thinknear, 527
Thinknum, 12
ThinkRF, 2276
ThinkSpider, 1065
thinkThin, 1863
Thinkup, 1521
ThinkVine, 629
Thinkware, 2848
Thinkwell, 1608
ThinOptX, 1262
THINQ Learning Solutions, 1994, 2073
Thinsters, 502
Third Bridge, 912
Third Channel, 799
Third Love, 721
Third Point Re, 1066
Third Point Reinsurance, 1447
Third Rock Ventures, 3263
Third Screen Media, 713
Third Wave Automation, 648, 1836
Third Wave Technologies, 1923
ThirdEye, 3099
Thirdlove, 720, 1566, 2009
ThirdStream BioScience, 237
Thirstystone Resources, 1524
Thirty madison, 1616
This Is l, 802
ThisClicks, 641, 876
Thislife, 1254
Thismoment, 1852
ThisNext, 504
Thoma Bravo, 36, 1873, 3245, 3255
Thomas H. Lee Partners, 3254
Thomas Steelwork, 2976
Thompson Industrial Services, 747, 1270
Thomson, 303
Thomson Directories, 2874
Thomson Plastics, 104
Thomsons Online Benefits, 1929
THOR Technologies, 1852
Thor Technologies, 313, 1150, 2146
Thorco, 1582
Thorley Industries, 1917
Thorn Lighting, 1021
Thornbury Nursing Services, 2667
Thorne Research, 1731, 1979
Thorne Research Inc. & Diversified Natural Product, 557
Thought Division, 515
Thought Equity, 35
Thought Equity Motion, 143, 1773
ThoughtExchange, 2283
Thoughtexchange, 2146
ThoughtSpot, 820, 912
Thoughtspot, 824
ThoughtWire, 2225, 2235, 2283
ThoughtWorks, 136
Thousand Eyes, 1610
ThousandEyes, 780
Thousandeyes, 1949
Thrasos, 1414
Thrasos Therapeutics, 1126
Thread, 301, 629, 2469, 3021, 3246
Threadbox, 1918
Threadflip, 234
Threads, 624
Threat Grid, 1
Threat Metrix, 2609
Threat Stack, 1, 37, 1629
ThreatConnect, 881, 1499
ThreatMATRIX, 1798
Threatmetrix, 200
ThreatQuotient, 288
ThreatStream, 1401
ThreatX, 1

Portfolio Companies Index

Thred Up, 938, 1322, 1890
ThredUp, 1537, 1855
thredUp, 846
3 Day Blinds, 1591, 1754
Three Eagles Communications Company, 1410
Three Leaf Ventures, 3259
Three Ring, 1298
Three Rings, 115
Three Sixty Sourcing, 337
3-D Machining, 1481
3-V Biosciences, 1079
32 Degrees Capital, 2028
33 Across, 863
33Across, 756, 2150
33across, 742, 876, 1428, 1504, 1588
360, 2570
360 Fly, 1092
360 Insights, 2163
360 PT Management, 441, 815
360 Safe, 2575
360Commerce, 1152
360insights, 1606
360ip, 217
360ip Pte. Ltd., 236
360pi, 1687
360T Group, 1754
361 Capital, 1151
365 Data Centers, 564
365 Retail Markets, 1276, 1459
365Media, 2700
365Scores, 2929
365Scores.com, 438
36Kr, 641
37 Signals, 265
37.5, 173, 931
39.net, 2841
3alioty Technica, 502
3AM Innovations, 1896
3B Scientific, 1041
3BG Supply Co., 659
3Birds, 285
3C Logic, 288, 380, 1172
3ci, 2089
3Com, 1657
3com, 252
3D Corporation Solutions, 1372
3D Hubs, 2469
3D Perception, 2361
3D Robotics, 779, 1359, 1862
3D-SensIR, 310
3DBio, 1055
3DD Pharma, 2940
3Derm, 1987
3DFortify, 623
3DFS Power Solutions, 3250
3Di, 2617, 2617
3DP, 1561
3DR, 1323
3DR Laboratories, 60
3DRobotics, 1187, 1876
3DSoc, 2840
3Dsolve, 2982
3DV, 3063
3E Company, 1239
3E Nano, 2054
3form, 1196, 1626
3G, 2841
3GA, 2020
3GPP, 2575
3Guu.com, 3199
3HACK.PL, 2876
3legs, 3088
3LM, 27
3mensio, 2771
3mensio Medical Imaging, 3042
3PAR, 2844
3PARdata, 1976

3Pillar Global, 1316
3Play Media, 1104
3QMatrix, 1839
3Scale, 3031
3scale, 548, 1032
3scan, 521, 1155
3seventy, 822
3SI Security Systems, 1140
+360, 977
3Sourcing, 721
3T Biosciences, 183, 1203
3TEN8, 10
3Tier, 1463
3TS Capital Partners, 485, 3252
3V, 1865
3VR, 582, 759, 983
3VR Security, 1908
3ware, 1649
Threewide, 1262
Threshold Pharmaceuticals, 785
Threshold Power, 1324
Thrifty Lavanderia, 405
Thrilling, 1896
Thrillist Media Group, 1361
Thriva, 3099
Thrive, 1058, 2094
Thrive Global, 59, 1006, 1114
Thrive Market, 173, 527, 641, 1885
Thrive Networks, 1157
ThriveMetrics, 396
Thron, 2865
ThroughPut, 999
ThruPoint, 1255
Thrupore, 1581
Thrvly, 2
Thumb, 1701
Thumbplay, 561, 967
Thumbplay Music, 1928
Thumbtack, 579, 1032, 1227
Thunder, 183, 1983
ThunderSoft, 1340
Thurst, 221
Thymes, 424
Thyrocare, 1346
TI Health, 902
Tia, 527, 944
Tiama, 3011
Tiandi Energy, 1852
Tiange Technology, 2841
Tianji New Materials, 2927
Tiannong, 2841
Tianpin, 3091
Tiantian Online, 2841
Tianya, 2927
Tiaris, 1084
Tiatros, 130, 758
TIB, 3136
TIBC, 2665
Tibco, 383
Tibersoft, 1922
Tic, 2975
Ticket Evolution, 581, 1527
Ticket Mob, 1103
Ticket Monster, 872
Ticketbase, 1914
TicketBiscuit, 227
Ticketea.com, 3096
Ticketfly, 535, 561, 1247, 1358, 1479, 1623
Ticketleap, 1321
TicketManager.com, 1463
TicketsNow, 1483
Ticketstream, 3068
Tickle, 200, 1323
Tickr, 1112
TICON Industrial, 1143, 2937
TICON Industrial Connection Public, 897
Tictail, 2469, 3047

TIDAL Software, 1908
Tidal Software, 1354
Tidal Systems, 1340
Tidal Wave Technology, 1190
TidalScale, 770, 959
TidalTV, 318
TIDBT, 1635
Tide, 1269, 2398
Tidel, 851, 1138, 1912
Tidelift, 779, 820
Tidemark, 1798
TidePool, 1549
Tidewater Equipment Company, 1025
Tidewater Midstream and Infrastructure, 2056
Tideway, 3095
TIDI, 1594
TIDI Products, 1041
Tidi Products, 170
TiE LaunchPad, 624
Tie Society, 591
Tiendas 3b, 1518
Tier 1 Energy Solutions, 106
Tier One Relocations, 1755
Tier1Asset, 3194
TierlCRM, 1610
Tierpoint, 3266
Tiff's Treats, 479
Tiff's Treats Cookie Delivery, 1255
Tiffany & Co., 303
TiFiC AB, 2361
TiGenix, 2554, 3076
Tigenix, 2940
Tiger Calcium, 2206
Tiger Connect, 1251, 1666
Tiger Iron Capital, 3263
Tiger Text, 36
Tigera, 1162
TigerConnect, 1346
TigerGraph, 3, 108, 1760
Tigerlily, 3104
TigerOptics, 707
TigerText, 644, 1383
Tigertext, 1297, 1302
Tiggy, 2122
Tigo Energy, 949, 1392, 2891
Tigris Pharmaceuticals, 1325
Tijuana Flats, 196
Tikl, 1114
Tikona Digital Networks, 1361
Tile, 108, 827, 1073, 1186, 1696
Tilera, 252, 1924, 3225
Tilia, 13
Tiller, 2288
Tilley, 2127
Tilney Bestinvest, 3024
Tilray, 1484
Tilson Technology Management, 440
Tilt, 2011
Tiltan Pharma, 3235
Tilting Motor Works, 1065
TIM Group, 523, 853
Timber Automation, 294
Timberland Corp., 303
Timbuk2, 1397
Timbuktu, 1305
Time Domain, 1706, 1736
Time Hero, 2131
Time Packaging Limited, 2852
Time Play, 2128
Timebyping, 321
Timecast, 1719
TimeClock Plus Inc., 159
TimeHero, 2130
Timehop, 1359, 1666, 1718
Timelines, 138
TimeSight Systems, 650
TimesLED, 1340

Portfolio Companies Index

TimesTen, 1257
TimeSys, 1749
Timetovisit.ru, 2336
TimeTrade, 536, 1104
Timetrade, 180
Timetric, 2398
Tin Drum Asian Kitchen, 274
Tinde, 3004
Tinder, 251
Tindie, 776
Tinea Pharmaceuticals, 1495
Tinfoil Security, 1254, 1566, 1598
Tinker Garten, 354
Tinkercad, 311
Tinkergarden, 1393
Tinkergarten, 490, 1530
Tinnerman Palnut Engineered Products Inc., 867
Tinoro, 122
Tinsel, 221
Tint, 976
Tinted, 901
Tintri, 780
Tiny Build, 2944
Tiny Mile, 2131
Tiny Pulse, 175
Tinybop, 354, 1058, 1597, 1876
Tinychat, 14
Tinypay.me, 2351
TINYpulse, 234
TIO, 1925
TIO Networks Corporation, 1407
Tioga Energy, 794, 1324, 1355
Tioga Pharmaceuticals, 772, 1297, 1820, 2125, 2487
Tioma Therapeutics, 270, 570
Tip Hive, 1925
Tipa, 2453
Tipico, 2414
TiqIQ, 535
TIR Systems, 2091
Tirendo, 3047
Tiryaki Agro, 1021
TIS, 3152
Tissue Analytics, 795
Tissue Regeneration Systems, 1923
Tissue Regenix, 2883
Tissue Repair Company, 1399
Tissuemed, 1608
TissueTech, 227, 698
Tissuetech, 1575
Tital Fitness LLC, 557
Titan, 330
Titan Fastener Products Inc., 911
Titan Fitness, 1460
Titan Health Corporation, 573
Titan Pharmaceuticals, 949
TitanFil, 2148
Titanium Energy Services, 2242
Titanobel, 3011
TitanX, 2746
TITUS AG, 3181
Titus Oil & Gas LLC, 1326, 1328
Tiv, 9
Tiversa, 1196
TIVIT, 136
Tivity Health, 94, 97
TIVO, 564
TiVo, 1706
Tivo, 1006
Tivoli Audio, 1754, 2245
Tivra Corp., 2205
Tiway Oil, 1518
Tixr, 1878
Tizona, 1268
Tizona Therapeutics, 184
Tizor, 624
Tizra, 1695

TJ Brent, 3008
TJ Hale, 815
TJS Insurance Group, 3264
Tk20, 1687
TKH Group, 3060
TLC Companies, 935
TLC Health Network, 153
TLC Vision, 931
TLContact, 947
TLK Group, 1603
TLL, 101
TMAC Resources, 1551
Tmax soft, 2960
TMCI Padovan, 3145
TMI International, 1343
TMP Worldwide Advertising & Communications, 1929
TMRC, 2961
TMRW, 11
TMS Brokers, 2301
Tmsuk, 603
TMT Coaxial Network, 2773
Tmunity, 1079
TMX, 3265
TN Stillhouse, 461
TNeuroPharma, 169
TNT, 2956
TNT Crane & Rigging, 741, 1368
TNW Systems, 1410
to-BBB BV, 2342
TOA Technologies, 642
Tobii, 3004
Tobira Therapeutics, 389, 785, 1251, 3006
Tobles AG, 2555
Toca Madera, 334
Tocaya Organica, 334
Tock, 1385, 1483
TodaCell, 2344
Today Tix, 1599
TodayTix, 862, 1878
Todd Combustion, 405
Todou, 1091
Tods Aerospace, 47
Toera Therapeutics, 1715
Together, 798
Together Work, 828
Togg, 1887
Toggle, 1896
Toguh, 1878
Tok & Stok, 2321
Tok.tv, 2009
Tokalas, 1222
Tokamak Energy, 2958
TokBok Inc., 624
TokBox, 116
Toke With, 1810
Tokeheim Corp., 303
Token, 1890
Tokia.It, 3040
Tokitaki, 3124
Toko, 1850
Tokopedia, 3118
Toktumi, 549
Tokyo Joe's, 878
Tokyo Smoke, 1613, 1810, 2134
Tolemi, 729, 1770
Tolera, 1380
Tolera Therapeutics, 1849
Tolingo, 2985
Tollgrade, 843
Tom Tailor, 2367
TOMA Biosciences, 1401, 1490, 1942
Tomaisins, 2408
ToMarket, 1509
Tomfoolery, 1254
Tommie Cooper, 2393
Tommy Hilfiger, 136

Tommy John, 744, 1305, 1309
Tomophase, 1619
Tomorrow, 757, 1269
TomorrowInnovations, 1832
TomoTherapy, 178, 1380, 1622, 1923
Tomra Systems, 3060
Tonal, 1187, 1666
Tonbo Imaging, 176, 1511
Tongbanjie, 2927
TongCard Holdings, 2658
Tongdun, 977
Tongtech, 2841
Tonian, 457
Tonic.ai, 709
TONIX Pharmaceuticals, 1788
Tonka Equipment Company, 1216
Tonoga, 1648
Tonomy, 137
Tonx, 400, 1059
Tonys Farm, 3185
Too Faced Cosmetics, 819
Too.Step, 2435
TooJay's Restaurant & Deli, 330
ToolingU, 835
ToolsGroup, 28
Toolwire, 526, 1354, 1390, 1608, 1674
Toopher, 546
Toot, 1554
Toothpick, 2676, 3021
Top Canventure, 2263
Top Corp, 685
Top Driver, 2000
Top Flight Technologies, 724
Top Gain, 3185
Top Hat, 666, 720, 1702, 1881, 1884, 2126, 2130, 2131, 2150, 2178, 2272
Top Image, 585
Top in Nature, 2263
TOP Inc., 754
Top Knobs USA Inc., 911
Top Rx, 751, 1169
Top Tier Software, 218
Top10, 2743
Topack Fittings, 1968
Topanga, 1355
Topanga Technologies, 1449
Topas Therapeutics, 690
Topaz, 73
Topcoder, 490
TopFan, 35
TopHatter, 457
Topica, 200, 3170
Topica Pharmaceuticals, 1495, 1814
Topio, 1674, 3128
TopiVert, 1631, 2849
Topline Game Labs, 397
Toplogis, 46
TopNoggin, 464
Topo Athletic, 1346
Topokine, 1630
TopOPPS, 570
TopoTarget A/S, 2807
Topps, 1835
Topray Technologies, 2594
Tops Foods, 2772
Tops Markets, 1256
Topshop/Topman Holdings, 1113
Topspin Communications, 1478
TopSportLab, 2940
Topsy, 299
Topway Industries, 2478
Torax, 1619
Torax Medical, 39, 1820
Torbit, 1855
TORC Oil & Gas, 2129
Torch, 937
Torchlite, 1610

Portfolio Companies Index

Tordivel, 2745
Toric, 2122
Torigen, 1703
Torill's Table, 2093
Torino Power Solutions, 2027
Tornate Animation, 1835
Tornier, 1728, 1931, 3268
Toro Gold, 2933
Toro Gold Limited, 1551
Toronto Stock Exchange, 3258
Torqeedo, 2970
Torque, 748
Torque Tension Systems Ltd, 3002
Torrent Oil, 1326, 1328
Torrent Resources, 1145
Torrent Systems, 1348
Torrex Equipment Corporation, 526
Tortilla, 1518
Tortoise, 1151
Tortuga AgTech, 1724, 1760
Tortuga Logic, 648
Torun, 2697
Torus Insurance Holdings, 1746
Tory Burch, 819
Tosca Services, 136
Toss, 1079
Toss Lab, 1511
Total Attorneys, 266
Total Care RX, 441
Total Expert, 175
Total Fitness, 2668
Total Home Health Care, 409
Total Immersion, 1418, 2684, 2890
Total Management & Earlybird Courier, 1955
Total Pave, 2192
Total Safety, 1138
Total Telcom Inc., 2061
Total Woman, 1579
TotalExpert, 2126
Totality, 226, 2073
TotallyMoney.com, 3095
TotalMobile, 2963
Totango, 252, 399, 861
Totems, 3099
Totes ISOTONER, 1021
Totes Isotoner Corporation, 357
Totspot, 1103, 1752
Totsy, 609
Toucan, 888, 2130, 2131
Touch Bistro, 2128
Touch Commerce, 1418, 1643
Touch Micro-System, 1924
Touch Of Modern, 752
Touch Surgery, 2469
TouchBistro, 2228, 2235
TouchCommerce, 666, 957
Touchdown Technologies, 55, 716, 1913, 1917
Touching Lives Adult Day Services, 1233
TouchOfModern, 1418
TouchPath, 8
TouchPay Holdings, 1748
Touchstone Exploration, 2085
Touchtown.ch, 2302
TouchTunes Interactive Networks, 1908
Toudou.com, 2841
Toughglass Holdings Ltd, 2695
Tourmaline, 2044
Tourneau, 1113
Tournus, 2956
Tourradar, 2825
Tout, 1589
ToutApp, 1028, 1358
Tovala, 1385, 1483
Tovarnity, 2674
Tower Cloud, 227, 1076, 1332
Tower Co., 1948
Tower Light, 2383

TOWER Software Engineering, 2706
Tower Technology, 2942
Tower Ventures, 1463, 1864
Tower Vision, 1508
TowerCare Technologies, 845
TowerCo, 1314, 1779
Towercom Development, 1152
Towercom Enterprises, 1152
Towercom Limited, 1152
TowerView Health, 269
Town Place, 1220
Town Shoes, 2076
Town Sports International Inc., 357
Towne Park, 912, 1778
TownHound, 1426
Townsend, 679
Townsquared, 752
Towry, 1518
Toxicology Holdings, 699
ToxiMet, 2751
Toymail, 1153
Toys 'R Us, 223
ToyTalk, 457, 1862
Toytalk, 1073
TP Therapeutics, 1734
TPC Group, 741
TPC Wire & Cable, 1438
TPF, 3125
TPG, 3245, 3254
TPI Composites, 127, 658
Tpo, 2427
TPx, 496
Tr, 1114
TR Fleet, 2958
TR-Tech. Int Oy, 2310
TRA, 1084
Tra-con, 1294
Traackr, 1101
Trace, 121, 328, 562, 1009
Trace One, 2653
TraceAssured, 2601
TraceLink, 711, 744, 2126
TraceME, 1589
TraceMe, 1162
Tracer Net, 528
Trachte, 1266
TracID AS, 3132
Track.com, 724
Track4C, 3056
TrackBill, 570
TrackDuck, 3040
Tracker Resources Development III, 673
TrackIF, 2002
TrackMaven, 320
TrackR, 779, 985, 1959
Tracks N Teeth, 1509
Tracksmith, 1114, 1533
TrackTik, 246, 2150, 2163
TrackVia, 35, 713, 758, 1150
Trackvia, 720
TrackX, 1207
Tracon Pharma, 158
Tracsis, 2883, 3019
Tractable, 978, 2018, 2074
Tractech Inc., 653
Traction, 1841
Traction Guest, 1610
Traction Software, 983, 1695
TractManager, 172, 1731
Tractor Zoom, 999
Tracx, 386, 646, 655, 756
Tracy Biomass, 1897
TradAir, 2557
Tradair, 3212
Trade & Invest British Columbia, 3258
Trade Desk, 646
Trade Gecko, 1966

Trade Harbor, 181
Trade It, 488
Trade Me, 136
Trade Sparq, 1966
TradeBeam, 1782
Tradebeam, 1674
TradeBlock, 711
TradeCapture, 468
TradeDoubler, 2745
TradeGlobal, 336
TradeIt, 1531
Tradeka Ltd., 2854
TradeKing, 1364
TradeLanes, 999
Trademark Global, 260
Trademark Now, 2469
Trademob, 3161
Tradeo, 1323, 2320
Tradepoint Atlantic, 940
TRADER, 136
Traderion, 3099
TraderServe, 2526
TraderTools, 646, 655
Tradeshift, 3005
Tradesmen, 1972
Tradesmen Enterprises, 2121
TradeSource, 1627
Tradesy, 246, 309, 625, 1079, 1103, 1569, 2640
Tradewinds Forest Products, 1911
Tradex Technologies, 803
Tradier, 711
Trading View, 1023
Tradingcom Europe, 2616
TradingScreen, 1787
Tradiv, 395
Tradoria, 3104
Trados, 2335
Traefik, 2288
Traeger Pellet Grills LLC, 1853
Traffic Roots, 395
Traffic Station, 2020
Traffic Technologies, 2636
TrafficCast China, 584
TrafficCast International, 454, 584, 1291
Trafficware, 1090
Trafi, 3040
Tragara, 1126
Tragara Pharmaceuticals, 622, 1492
Tragus, 2926
Trail, 3099
Trainers Vault, 1509
Training Partners USA Limited, 334
Trainual, 9
Trait Biosciences, 2134
Traitwise, 447
Traity, 2822, 3099
Trajectory IQ, 2116
Trak Communications, 1927
TRAKAmerica, 931
TrakLok, 999
TRAKnet, 1288
Trala, 1385
Traliant, 1499
Tran Switch, 58
Trancept Systems, 1013
Tranquis Therapeutics Inc., 1734
Trans American Rubber, 1748
Trans-o-Flex, 2367
Trans-Trade, 1234
Trans1, 58
TranS1 Inc., 573
TransACT, 3159
Transaction Services, 371
Transaction Wireless, 1239, 1371
Transactis, 527, 724, 1305, 1605, 1741
TransAlta Corp., 2029
Transatel, 3104

Portfolio Companies Index

Transave, 1495, 2739
Transaxle, 851
Transbiodiesel, 2408
Transcast Media, 2694
Transcend, 1098
Transcend Medical, 389, 941, 1126, 1728, 1788
Transcend Robotics, 521
Transcend Therapeutics, 61
Transcendent, 92
Transcept, 1014, 1251
TransChip, 1239
TransCore, 1090
TransCorp, 652
TransCorp Spine, 667
Transcorp Spine, 946
TranscribeMe, 130, 1065, 1604, 1671, 1987
Transcriptic, 108, 969
TransDigm, 257, 1368
Transdigm, 2688
TransEngen, 1111
TransEnterix, 73, 1013, 1510, 1631
Transera, 1750
Transera Communications, 1122
Transervice Logistics, 2021
Transfer Tool Products, 16, 612, 1057
TransferGo, 3040, 3040
TransferSoft, 1966
TransferWise, 1763
Transferwise, 1006, 1899, 2665, 3099
TransFirst, 1973
Transfix, 320, 399, 601, 708, 1114, 1296
TransForce Inc., 1404
Transform Materials, 106
TransformativeMed, 2007
Transgaming, 2051
Transgene, 2535
TransGenic, 2961
TransGo, 747
Transifex, 1831
Transit Labs, 2178
Transit Screen, 411
Transit Technologies, 1499
Transit Wireless, 1779
Transitive, 556, 2463, 3038
Translarity, 1830
Translate Bio, 193
TranslateBio, 1734
TransLattice, 597
Translent Plasma Systems, 1055
Translink, 383
TransMedic, 272
TransMedics, 1668, 1908
Transmedics, 748
TransMeta, 1107
Transmeta, 1706
Transmeta Corporation, 1731
Transmode, 3034
Transmolecular, 137, 1399
Transnational Corporation, 2292
Transnational Foods, 367
Transolutions, 445
Transom Capital Group, 13
Transonic Combustion, 1918
Transpac, 1136
Transpac Imports, 1460
Transparent Healthcare, 1101, 3246
Transperra, 1093
Transphorm, 1155
Transplace, 1837
Transplace Holdings, 867
Transpond, 1886
Transporeon, 1576, 1759, 1837
Transport Corp. of America Inc., 847
Transport Holdings Inc., 407
Transport Industries, 722
Transport Labor Contract, 1507
Transport Labor Holding Company, 253

Transport Models, 2699
Transport Technology Systems, 1908
Transportation Safety Technologies Inc., 153
Transtar, 790
Transtar Industries, 1460
Transtech control, 2741
TransUnion, 61, 1160
TranSwitch, 3128
Transwitch, 1731
TRANZACT, 902, 1929
Tranzonic, 1686
Tranzyme Pharma, 1510, 1820
Trap!T, 2822
Trapeze Networks, 1449
Trapezoid, 2006
Traphaco, 2952
Trapp Technology, 336
Traptic, 944, 1935
TrapX Security, 1382
Trash Warrior, 1616
Trask Contracting, 2042
Traslational Cancer Drugs Pharma, 1456
Traumatec, 447
Trausch Industries, 654
Travador, 3229
Travel Joy, 232, 1323
Travel Nurse Across America, 878
Travel Store, 3039
TravelCenters of America, 1360, 1372
Travelcenters Of America, 1949
Travelcircus, 2832
TravelClick, 1817
Travelclick, 224
Travelmob, 2904
Travelmuse Inc., 374
Travelnuts, 1914
Travelport, 1787
TravelPotst.com, 115
TravelPrice, 2760
Travelprice.com, 2346
Travelpro Group, 1231
TravelTab, 173
Traverse Biosciences, 705
Traverse Networks Incorporated, 1093
Travis Peak Resources, 673
Travo, 231
Travora, 646
Travora Media, 1741
Trax, 1575
Trax Group, 1727
Traxo, 1684, 1808
Tray, 309
Tray.io, 129, 3021
Traycer Systems, 1556, 1743
Trazzler, 234, 1588
TRDATA, 3099
Trea Asset Management, 1151
Tread, 2232
Tread Corporation, 832
Trean Corporation, 97
Treasure Data, 1629
Treasury Prime, 1760
Treasury Spring, 2398
Treat U, 3039
TreaTec21, 3235
Treater, 1645
Treatful, 327, 856
Treatibles, 1139
Treatment X, 395
Treato, 1297, 1383
Treatspace, 275
Treau, 1896
Trebeca, 231
Treble.ai, 798
Tred, 776, 1153
Tree House, 1374
Tree Island Industries, 1971

Treehouse, 1698
TreeRing, 1644
Treez, 152, 1613
Trefoil Therapeutics, 545
Trei, 3145
TREK Diagnostic, 119
Trek10, 659
Trella Health, 1412
Trellis, 420, 782
Trellis Bioscience, 644, 1302
Trellis Research Group, 395
Trelys, 739
Trema, 22, 1021
Tremor, 2398
Tremor Media, 1178
Tremor Video, 389, 610, 1848
Trending, 310
TrendKite, 1687
Trendkite, 1207
TrendMD, 1760, 2120, 2265
Trends for Friends Brands, 3199
Trendy Foods Finances, 3125
Trendy International Group, 1092
Trendyol.com, 1079
Trendzone Construction, 2533
Trescal, 77, 2199
TresseNoire, 221
Tresu, 3194
Tresys Technology, 248
Trevena, 922, 1464, 1943
Treventis Corp., 269
Trevi Holdings, 2976
Trevi Therapeutics, 137
Trexel, 62
Trey Whitfield School, 1422
TRG Screen, 1410
Tri Alpha Energy, 1918
Tri-Link Technologies Inc, 2091
tri-Star Aerospace, 1368
Tri-Star Electronics, 377
Tri-Star Protector, 1044
Tri-Wire, 1176
Tria, 73, 240
TRIA Beauty, 599, 1943
Tria Beauty, 139, 190, 1788
Triad 700, 1157
Triad Behavioral Health, 551
Triad Isotopes, 1419
Triad Life Sciences, 427
Triad Retail Media, 1377
Triad Semiconductor, 646
Triage, 1223, 2141, 2530
Triage Management Services, 132
Triage Staffing, 1276
TrialCard, 1368
TrialPay, 234, 582, 1517, 1841
TrialReach, 3009
Trials AI, 121
TrialScope, 655
Triana Energy, 1256
Triangle Ice, 747
Triangle Pharmaceuticals, 772
Triax Midwest Associates, 1929
Triax Southeast Associtaes, 1929
Tribal Sportswear, 2162
Tribar Manufacturing, 920
Tribe, 1154, 2122, 2131
Tribe Mobile, 691
Tribeca Flashpoint Media Arts Academy, 1745
TribeHR, 1184
Triblio, 1069, 1150
Tribogenics, 758
Tribold, 2653, 2682
Tribridge, 1140
Tribune Company, 3255
Tribute Direct, 1094
Tribute Technology, 1499

Portfolio Companies Index

Tricast, 291
Trice Medical, 924, 1605
Trice Medical Inc., 272
Tricentis, 1412, 2074
Tricho-Med Corp.; Global Canna Labs; Etea Sicurezz, 2167
Tricida, 764, 1147, 1943
Trico Products, 1085
Tricoci University, 531
Tricog, 1017
Tricord Systems, 538
TriCore Solutions, 364
Tricoya, 322
Tridelta plc, 2545
Tridemensional Engenharia, 2341
Trident, 36
Trident Group, 3257
Trident Pharmaceuticals, 1777
Trident University International, 1754
Trident USA Health Services, 785
Trident V Credit Holdings, 1746
Tridien Medical, 525
Tridion, 2770, 3042
Trieza, 1268
Trifacta, 586, 877, 978, 1566, 2010
Triformix, 1649
Trig, 1636
Trigen Ltd., 2807
Triggit, 1334, 1718, 1800
TriggrHealth, 631
Trigo, 31, 2439
Trikon Technologies, 767
Trilibis Mobile, 185
TrilibisMobile, 100
Trilio, 1
Trillbit, 849
Triller, 1153, 1566
Trillian Surgical, 427
Trilliant, 812, 1908, 2307, 3242
Trillium College, 1506
Trilogy, 1379
Trilogy Education Services, 490, 938, 1554
Trilogy International Partners, 1498, 2128
Trilogy Midstream, 1326, 1328
Trilumina, 1074
Trim, 2272
Trim Parts, 1343
Trimac Industries, 1839
Trimark Usa, 197
TriMas, 1971
Trimas, 926
Trimb Healthcare, 212
TriMech, 1276
TriMedx, 178
Trimeris, 1399
Trimlite Manufacturing, 2267
Trinean, 2467
TriNet, 819, 3257
TriNetX, 1268
Trinity, 931
Trinity Capital Investment, 3265
Trinity CO2, 1256
Trinity Consultants, 886, 1115
Trinity Convergence, 1013, 1287
Trinity Hospice, 1090
Trinity Industries Inc., 1905
Trinity Mobile Networks, 309, 976
Trinity Watthana, 1143, 2937
Trinity3 Technology, 406
TriNorthern Security Distribution, 331
Trintech, 1720
Trintel, 405
Trio Labs Inc., 738
Trio Video, 266
Trion, 520, 597, 1608, 1829, 1855
Trion Coating, 1229
Trip Tribe, 288

Trip Trotting, 1658
Trip.com, 1537
TriPath Imaging, 119
TripBam, 1808
Tripbirds, 2628
TripConnect, 1178
Tripex Pharma, 1271
Triphase, 2358
Tripifoods, 1294
Tripit, 218, 1359
Triple, 773
Triple G Systems, 2051
Triple M Housing, 2267
Triple Point Technology, 1045, 1973
Triple Ring Technologies, 68
TripleByte, 720
Triplebyte, 995
TripleLift, 655, 1119, 1223, 1322, 1862, 2150
TripleSeat, 635
TripleShot, 536
TripLingo, 285
Triposo, 1014
TRIPP, 1477
Tripp, 1187
Tripping, 591, 1101, 1515
Trippy, 641, 1800
Tripshare, 1305
Triptrotting, 1103
Tripwire, 58, 810, 1006, 1629, 1817
TriReme Medical, 56
Trisara, 2763
Triscend Corporation, 255
Trispan, 543
TriStar, 443
Tristar, 3009
Tristar 600, 495
Tristar License Group, 495
TriState Capital, 1151
Tristream Energy, 898
Tritec Performance Solutions, 653
Tritech, 790
TriTech Software Systems, 1979
Tritech Software Systems, 912
Triton, 912, 1795
Triton BioSystems., 2964
Triton Container, 1933
Triton Digital, 1912
Triton Network Systems, 1107
Triton Power Partners, 676
Triton Water, 1200
Triton Web Properties, 541
TritonWear, 2123, 2178
Triumfant, 540, 993, 1348
Triumph Group Inc., 357
Triumpth Higher Education Group, 386
Trius Therapeutics, 1917
TriVascular, 872, 1063, 1449
Trivascular, 22, 605, 1268
Trive Capital, 884
TriVentures II Fund; V-Wave Ltd., 272
Triversity, 2073
Trividia, 35
TriVirix, 1844, 2695
Trivitron Healthcare, 711
Trivnet, 2943, 3128, 3203
Triwater Holdings, 654
TriWest Capital Partners, 2160
TriZetto Group, 958
TriZetto Group Inc., 1905
Trizic, 787
Trnql, 1254
Troax, 2317
Troika Networks, 133
Trois Petits Cochons, 815
Trojan Battery, 458
Trojan Lithograph Corporation, 148
Trolltech, 3004

Trolly, 2517
Tronair, 1090, 1115, 1574
Tronair Holdings, 1460
Tronic's Micro Systems, 2867, 3011
Tronics, 2430
Tronox, 1138
Troodon, 3133
Troon, 1113
Troops, 48, 182, 720, 945, 1760
Troopwork, 1890
TrophpSYS, 2518
Tropic Biosciences, 2101
Tropic Networks, 556, 1084
Tropical Smoothie Cafe, 274
Tropikal Pet, 1576
Tropitone, 1438
Tropos Networks, 1008, 1947
Troux Technologies, 1449, 2745
Trov, 510, 2398
Trove, 631, 877, 1959
Trover Solutions, 1929
Troverie, 2194
Trovix, 31, 857
Troxell Communication Inc., 63
Troy, 1262
Troy Energy, 1797
Troyanda, 3224
TRP Energy LLC, 1853
Trrivest, 2160
Tru, 2682
Tru Fit Athletic Clubs, 441
Tru Hearing, 1707
Tru Optik, 1488
Tru Star Technology, 182
Truaxis, 1855
Trubion Pharma, 154, 1918
Trubion Pharmaceuticals, 785, 1495
TruBrain, 344
Truck Accessories Group, 1034
Truck Bodies & Equipment International, 1460
Truck Driver Power, 999
Truck Hero, 435
Truck-Lite, 1066, 1460
Truck24, 3223
Truckish, 999
TruckPro LLC, 917
Truckstop.com, 336
TruckTrack, 3099
Trucktrack, 3021
True, 553, 1755, 2006
True & Co., 283, 564, 1426, 1701
True Accord, 1073, 1634
True Anthem, 1599, 1885
True Body, 1101
True Botanicals, 568
True Citrus, 80
True Facet, 945, 1186
True Fit, 332, 561, 1050, 1679, 2126
True Gault, 434
True Home Value, 377
True Link, 1058, 1059
True Link Financial, 600
True Load Time, 75
True North Therapeutics, 1268
True Office, 535, 1422
True Oil Company LLC, 160
True Partners, 1964
True Potentional LLP, 796
True Science, 687
True Share Vault, 870
True Temper, 831
True Temper Sports, 1131
True Ultimate Standards Everywhere, 582
True Vault, 721
True X Media, 972, 1537
True&Co., 1702, 1914
TrueAccord, 149, 321, 720, 1969

1416

Portfolio Companies Index

Truearc, 2258
Truebil, 1017
Truebill, 594, 1330
TrueCaller, 1079
Truecaller, 2437
TrueCar, 133, 1813, 1890, 1948, 2640
TrueChoice, 400
TrueCommerce, 28
Truecommerce, 655
TrueData, 229
trueEx, 1422
TrueFacet, 776, 787, 1827
TrueLayer, 2398
TrueLeaf, 2148
TrueLemon, 993
TrueLens, 536
TrueLook, 1683
TrueMotion, 820
TrueNet Communications, 1573
TrueNorth Therapeutics, 1238
TrueSAN Networks, 1538
TrueSpan, 1750, 1781
TrueVault, 1103
TrueVision Systems Inc., 68
Truework, 565, 1073
Trufa, 773
Trufood, 196
Truist, 1691
Trulia, 182, 601, 1323, 1464
Trulioo, 304
Trulite, 1755
Trulogica, 517
TRULY, 2676
Truly, 308
Truly Wireless, 129
Trumaker, 1032, 1534
Trumaker & Co., 545, 1597, 1599
Trumba, 200, 1640
Trumid, 149
Trumo, 1254
Trunk, 2122
Trunk Archive, 3140
Trunk Club, 138, 876
Trupanion, 1186
TruSignal, 1537, 1728
Trusona, 1079, 1158
Truspan, 564
Trusper, 597
Truss, 1281
Trusscore, 2122
Trussle, 3099
Trussway Holdings Inc., 463
Trust & Will, 901
Trust Arc, 972
Trust Digital, 173, 540, 713
Trust Metrics, 1488
Trust Pilot, 2665
Trust You, 2829
TruStar Technology, 48
TrustArc, 336
TRUSTe, 234
Trusted, 527
Trusted Computer Solutions, 1348
Trusted Edge, 1348
Trusted Insight, 1254, 1812
Trusted Metrics, 1987
Trusted Network Technologies, 1042
Trusted Shops, 3011
TrustedID, 1886
TrustedInsight, 586, 626
TrustEgg, 1959
Trustev, 876
TrustGo, 1340
Trusthouse Services Group, 886
TrustID, 1855
Trustifi, 1535
Trustify, 1589, 1703

TrustLab, 1317
Truston, 2770
Trustpilot, 3004, 3194
TrustRadius, 1187
Trustribe, 3040
Trustwave, 162, 796, 1045, 1481, 1674, 1888
TrustWeaver, 2628
TrustYou, 2820, 3011
TruTouch, 1104
Trutouch, 1926
TruTouch Technologies, 758, 1299
TruU, 575, 1812
Truven Health Analytics, 1927
Truveris, 1290, 1297, 1851
Truvian Health, 664
Truviso, 614, 1379
TRX Systems, 1172, 1260
Try, 1154
Try.Com, 752
Try.com, 3099
Trylon-TSF, 2040
Tryoop, 2429
Tryton Medical, 949, 1502, 1578
Tryzens Group, 3095
TS3 Technology, 1232
TSA Consulting Group, 302
Tsang Yow, 908
Tse Sui Luen Jewellery Limited, 2394
TSI, 167
Tsinghua Tongfang Artificial Environment Co Ltd, 2490
TSL, 2786
TSM, 2944
TSM Corporation, 920
Tsmc, 2427
TSO Logic Inc., 643
TSS Solutions, 47
TST Media, 1874
Tstar 600, 1344
Tsumobi, 628, 1692, 2009
Tsunami Visual Technologies, 1183
TT dotCom Sdn Bhd, 3155
TTA, 2354
TTH Holdings, 112
TTPOD, 2969
TTR - Transactional Track Record, 3039
TTTech, 812
TTYL, 752
Tuache.com, 938
Tube City IMS Corporation, 1972
Tubel Technologies, 468
TubeMogul, 246, 361, 561, 773, 1855, 2164, 3112
Tubi, 773
Tubular, 744
Tubular Labs, 1816
Tubular Textile, 408, 911
Tucana Technologies, 528
Tucker Arsenberg Attorneys, 3264
Tucows, 1884
Tudou, 1918, 3053
Tueo Health, 1703
Tuesday Morning, 1160
Tufin, 3092
Tuilux, 2429
Tuition.io, 309, 1103, 1247, 1985
Tuizzi, 3039
Tujia, 827
Tula, 821, 1092
Tularik, 785
Tule, 1073
Tulip, 1079, 1610
Tulip Corporation, 1627
Tulip Medical, 2345
Tulip Molded Plastics, 1025
Tulip Retail, 799, 1050, 1491, 1702, 2150
Tulsa Inspection Resources, 1729

Tulsa Welding School, 1753
Tumbleweed Communications, 57, 194, 200, 857
Tumblr, 1235
tumblr, 1718
Tumri, 1666
Tunable Photonics Corporations, 767
Tune, 776, 972
Tune Wiki, 621
TuneIn, 520, 1740
Tunein, 820, 972
Tunespeak, 570
Tuniein, 1006
Tuniu.com, 597, 938
Tunnel, 2637
Tunnel Hill, 1949
Turbine, 827, 1731
Turbine Engine Specialists, 2161
Turbine Inc., 374
Turbo Appeal, 380
Turbo International, 961
Turbonetics, 653
Turbonomic, 938
TurboSquid, 60
Turing Video, 235
Turn, 759, 872, 1666, 1852
Turner, 962
Turning Art, 1322
Turning Technologies, 351
Turnitin, 888, 1346
TurnKey, 1687
Turnleaf, 213
Turnstone, 1930
Turntable.Fm, 1464
Turo, 708, 1079, 1666, 2154
Turtle Beach, 51, 1751
Turtle Entertainment GmbH, 3011
Turtle Island Recycling, 2160
Tuscany Apartments, 69
Tusker Therapeutics, 144
Tut Systems, 162
Tutela, 2283
Tution.io, 1223
Tutor.com, 593
tutoria, 2941
Tutorspree, 1823
Tutum, 1598
TuVox, 57
.tv, 724
TV Three, 2328
TV Time, 527
TVA Medical, 1601, 1622
TVB, 1498
TVC, 3040
TVH, 3229
Tvinci, 2905
TVision, 2130, 2131
TVision Insights, 802, 1105, 1489
TVR Communications, 405
Tvrecheck, 2347
TVSmiles, 641, 2466, 3199
TVtrip, 1418
TVTY, 1418, 2288
TVU, 3118
TVU Networks, 100, 1290, 1608
TVU Pack, 3118
Tweed Tree Lot, 2233
Twelve, 1126, 1728, 1930, 2105
Twelvefold, 42
Twelvefold Media, 549
TwelveStone Health Partners, 495
Twentify, 2276
Twenty-First Century Fox Inc., 1905
Twenty20, 361
TwentyBN, 1243
Twentybn, 1158
Twentyeight Seven, 1350
Twentyeight-Seven, 184, 1149

1417

Portfolio Companies Index

TWG Plus, 1785
Twilio, 610, 1054, 1058, 1537, 1763
Twilo, 2861
Twin Cities Business, 3268
Twin Med, 1778
Twin Med LLC, 277
Twin Rivers Technologies, 1626
Twin Vee, 1748
Twin-Star International, 1859
Twindom, 310
Twine, 1426, 3099
Twine Health, 1527
Twinlab Consolidated Holdings, 1433
Twinstrata, 209
TwinThread, 1317
Twist, 1589
Twist Bioscience, 108, 145, 154, 183, 240, 271, 1401, 1942
Twisted Pair, 540
Twisted Pair Solutions, 459
Twistle, 921
Twistlock, 604, 1796
Twitch, 752, 1763, 1823, 2011, 3225
Twitmusic, 1966
Twitt2go, 2975
Twitter, 234, 251, 265, 268, 457, 650, 752, 805, 1006, 1235, 1527, 1718, 1884
Twitter Urban Airship, 1841
Two Bit Circus, 779
Two Bridges Design, 865
Two Moms in the RAW, 1324
Two Pore Guys Inc., 1073
Two Roads Brewing Company, 679
Two Tap, 1841
2-10 Home Buyers Warranty, 338
2-20 Records Management, 1834
20 East End, 33
20-20 Technologies, 2089
20/20 GeneSystems, 1065, 1172
200-208 Sixth St. Jersey City NJ, 192
2020, 1912
2020 Marketing, 3268
21 Buttons, 2288
21 Centrale Partners, 2535
212 Resources, 658
21Buttons, 2842
21cake, 2927
21Diamonds, 2820, 2829, 3199
21Net, 2958, 3009
21sportsgroup, 2832
21st Century Creations, 738
21st Century Telecom Group, 1042
21ViaNet, 2841
21Vianet, 827
21vianet.com, 1855
23 and Me, 624, 2154
2359 Media, 3112
23andMe, 709, 805, 894, 1268, 1657, 1665, 3076
23andme, 1643
24 Hour Fitness, 1625
24-7 Intouch, 2211
24-7 Intouch Inc., 1853
24/7 Real Media, 1855
24access Solutions B.V., 3119
24M, 457
24symbols, 3099
24x7 Learning, 2549
250OK, 175
265.com, 2841
28-7, 1268
2bSURE.com Pte Ltd, 2499
2C2P, 149
2can, 89
2CheckOut, 1852
2Checkout, 470, 782
TwoCubes Inc., 395
2degrees, 1854

2DIALOG, 1699
Twofish, 1918
Twofour Group, 2935
2Mundos, 2974
2nd Address, 238, 773, 894
2nd Ave LLC, 357
2nd Watch, 518, 1162
2ndWave Software, 1499
2Rivers/Yesplan, 3033
2sens, 1614
TwoSix Labs, 881
2TD, 2691
2U, 263, 490, 1348, 1504, 1537, 1554
2ULaundry, 754
TwoWay Media, 2745
2Wire, 27, 597, 1213
2XU, 1092
2|Beans, 669
Twyla, 1006
TX, 2575
Txcell, 2867, 3104
TXCOM, 2375
TXEntre, 1653
Txtr, 2435
TxVia, 2708
Tyan, 908
TydenBrooks, 260
Tyfone, 3010
Tylted, 1150
Tynec, 2560
Tynker, 456, 720, 888, 1530, 2009
Tynt, 1411
Tynt Multimedia, 2043
Tyntec, 912
Typeform, 3035
Typekit, 787
Typenex Medical, 472
Typesafe, 3036
Typhoon Studios, 2944
Tyres on the Drive, 2963
Tyrrells, 1021
TYRX, 1414
Tysabri, 2097
Tyto, 2934
Tyze, 2225
Tzero Technologies, 200
Tzetzo Bros., 1730

U

U Grok It, 1065
U Pol, 2787
U-Center, 3222
U-Line, 1136
U-Line Corporation, 1460
U-Nav Microelectronics, 810
U-Nest, 229
U-Systems, 118, 549, 1771
U.S. Anesthesia Partners, 257
U.S. Auto Parts Network, 1361
U.S. Education Corporation, 470
U.S. Environmental Services, 899
U.S. Fence Solutions, 334
U.S. Intergrity, 1660
U.S. LBM, 1066
U.S. Lumber, 1160
U.S. Minerals, 1210
U.S. Pole Company, 377
U.S. Power Generating Company, 1160
U.S. Retirement & Benefits Partners, 1085
U.S. Risk, 1085
U.S. Silica, 843
U.S. Tape, 1524
U3 Pharama, 94
U3 Pharma, 193
u51.com, 827
UAS Laboratories, 3268
UAV Navigation, 2539

UAVenture Capital, 3265
Ubby, 310
uBeam, 1154, 1890
Ubeeko, 3226
Uber, 44, 251, 265, 511, 669, 773, 774, 805, 819, 824, 846, 1058, 1079, 1099, 1142, 1153, 1203
uberall, 3047
UberMedia, 290, 520, 976
UberSense, 316
Ubertweek, 2560
UberVU, 2682
UBF Mittelstandfinanzierungs AG, 2715
Ubicast, 2300
Ubicom, 200
Ubidyne, 2662
UBiome, 1058
uBiome, 108, 1696
Ubique, 1518, 2107, 3239
Ubique Networks, 2148
Ubiquiti Networks, 1754
Ubiquity Software Corporation, 1042
Ubiquity Solar, 2054
Ubisoft, 2178
Ubitricity, 2832
UBIX, 1947
UBK, 2915
uBlox, 2844
UBmatrix LLC, 508
Ubona, 2549
Ubooly, 1840
UBuildNet, 421
UC, 2575
UC RUSAL, 33
Ucandoo, 2518
UCann, 1083
UCIC, 2178
UCIT, 2042
UCloud, 597
UCode, 976
UConnect, 2
Uconnect, 1959
Ucopia, 3229
UCT Coatings, 1658
UCWeb, 827
Udacity, 457, 631
udelv, 1895
Udemy, 361, 1121, 1227, 1346
UDH Healthcare, 3060
UEI Global, 253
UEPAA!!, 2302
UFO, 2772
UFO Movies India, 1498
UFO Movietz Pvt, 2303
Ufora, 535, 1358, 1876
UGint, 2993
Ugo, 1682
UGO Networks, 957
Ugs, 2688
Uhuroo, 3100
UHY Advisors, 377
UICO, 254, 1459
Uinta Brewing Company, 1576
UiPath, 579, 1079, 1162, 1213, 3099
UiTV, 2724
Uizard, 1105, 1309
Ujam, 2804
Ujet, 1079, 2228
Uju Electronics, 2824
UK Support Services, 2686
UK2, 2935
Uken, 2107
Ukko, 1001
Ukko Inc., 1073
uKnow, 1305, 1320
ULi, 2427
uLocate, 1084
Ulta Beauty, 1890

Portfolio Companies Index

Ulterra Drilling Technologies, 111
Ultimus Fund Solutions, 1140
UltiSat, 1140
UltiZen Games, 3053
Ultra Angkle, 659
Ultra Clean Technology, 782
Ultra SoC Technologies, 3009
Ultra-Fit Manufacturing, 2040
UltraCell, 173, 2708
Ultracell, 498
Ultracision, 51
UltraCom, 3128
Ultracor, 815
UltraDNS, 2700
Ultrageny Pharmaceutical, 1621
Ultragenyx, 1414
Ultralase, 2786
UltraLink, 767
Ultranat, 2603
UltraSoc Technologies, 2751
UltraSPECT, 3203
Ultrazonix DNT AB, 2807
Ultriva, 628
Ultriva Inc., 1093
Ultromex, 2287
Uluru, 1083
UMA Enterprises, 1145, 1460
uMake, 299, 945
Umamicart, 2131
Umano, 275
Umanto.com, 3199
Umba, 1914
Umbono, 2912
uMed, 3
Umicore, 3060
Uminova Invest, 2858
UMN Pharma, 2961
Umpqua Holdings Corporation, 1818
Umuse, 1666
Un Jour Aileurs, 2439
Unaptent, 310
Unata, 2176
Unbabel, 1158, 1610, 1614
Unblockable, 1666
Unbounce, 776, 2103, 2272, 3035
Unbound, 1001, 1703, 1770, 2665, 2743
Unbound Concepts, 708
UnboundID, 1381, 1687
Unbxd, 1017
Uncharted Power, 221, 1058
Uncle Julio's, 1041, 1092, 1552
Uncle Milton, 1232
Uncommon Cacao, 54
Unconventional Gas Resources, 2036
Unconventional Resources, 673
Uncovet, 1966
Under Armour, 1591
Under the Canopy, 940
Under The Mango Tree, 54
Under the Roof Decorating, 2043
Underground Cellar, 2131
Underground Solutions, 1603
Underscore, 3263
UnderStory, 9
Understory, 567, 1914
Undertone, 1045
Undock, 685
Unearth, 1162
Unequal Technologies LLC, 991
Unglue, 231
Uni Group Inc., 874
Uni Key, 183
Uni2 Hold Tight, 2958
Uni5.Com, 2617
Unibioscreen & Zetes, 2671
Unica, 1045
Unicell, 2927

Unico, 1755
Unicoaero, 1039
Unicoba, 1376
Unicon, 2992
Unident, 3171
UniDesk, 1184
Unidym, 1793
Unifeye Vision Partners, 1964
Unifi, 1629
Unifi Health, 2398
Unified Patents, 1979
Unified Physician Management LLC, 160
Unified Power, 1438
Unifiller Systems Inc., 903
Unifrax, 111, 502
Unify2, 1827
Unifyo, 2676
UniKey, 724, 1099
Unikey, 1614
Unikrn, 59, 1599
Unilabs, 136
Unilend, 2288
Unilife, 1383
Unimersiv, 310
Union Agriculture Group, 2321
Union Bank of California, 217
Union Biometrica, 352
Union Crate, 1760
Union Metal, 847
Union Mobile Pay, 2822
Union Square Hospitality Group, 1113
Union Tractor, 1343
Union-Optech, 3225
Unionamerica Insurance Company Limited, 407
Unioncy, 2687
Unipart Rail Holdings, 2874
Uniphore, 575, 1035, 1296
UniPlaces, 2437, 3009
Uniq Investigation & Security Services, 2922
Unique Ltd., 2197
Unique Pub Company, 2926
Unique Pubs, 2596
Uniquify, 68
UniQure, 764
Uniqure, 2739
Unirac, 838
UNIRISX, 1029
Uniscape, 327, 3209
Uniscon, 1244
Unishippers Global Logistics, 747
UNIsite, 1042, 1042
Unison, 849
Unisound, 1511
Unisource, 223
Unisource Network Services, 1465
Unisync Group, 2162
Unitah Engineering & Land Serveying, 1345
Unitas Global, 1242
UniTask, 642, 743
Unite House, 2935
Unite US, 1635
Unitech Aerospace, 377, 654
Unitech Composites and Structures, 47
United American Energy Corp., 781
United BioSource, 212, 1041
United Brass Works, 324
United By Blue, 3246
United by Blue, 669
United Capital, 1606
United Catalyst, 845
United Claim Solutions, 864
United Confectioneries, 2482
United Copper Industries, 1089
United Country Real Estate, 405
United Dental Care, 1152
United Dental Partners, 371
United Dermpartners, 785

United Distribution Group, 111
United Flexible, 167, 832
United House Developments, 2935
United Imaging Healthcare, 2752
United Initiators, 1939
United Legal Services, 2935
United Living Group, 2935
United Logistics, 41
United Metro Media, 266
United Milk Company, 2775
United New Mexico Financial Corporation, 449
United Online, 504
United PanAm Financial Corporation, 1447
United Pet Group Inc., 170, 791
United Piece Dye Works, 1507
United Pipe & Steel Corp., 1266
United Plastics Group, 202
United Platform Technologies, 1771, 2448
United Preference, 1618
United Real Estate Group, 1276
United Recovery Systems, 197
United Retail Grop Inc., 449
United Road, 1089
United Road Services, 458, 1469
United Road Towing, 1234
United Roadbuilders, 2278
United Rotary Brush Corporation, 1343
United Site Services, 371, 1368
United States Embassy Residential Community, 3086
United States Environmental Services, 753
United States Infrastructure Corporation, 1113
United States Pipe and Foundry Company, 2008
United Studios Ltd, 2852
United Surgical Partners International, 912, 1973
United Tactical Systems, 503
United Telephone Company, 1270
United Therapies Holding LLC, 277
United Villages, 860, 1893
United Women's Healthcare, 2030
UnitedHealth Group, 874
UnitedLex, 389, 2809
Unitek, 1138
Unitek Information Systems, 559
Uniti, 2243
Unitive, 752, 3153
Unito, 2024, 2187
UniTrends, 907, 1401, 1844
Unitronics, 2882
Unity, 3225
Unity Biotechnology, 710, 1918
Unity Influence, 594
Unity Semiconductor, 200, 1257
Unity Technologies, 2844
UnityWorks Media, 1874
Univa, 143, 540, 1364, 1575
Univa UD, 154
Univacco Technology, 2594
Universal Ad, 3221
Universal American, 764, 1108, 1271, 1973
Universal American Financial Corporation, 407
Universal Avenue, 1610
Universal Biosensors, 190, 2609
Universal Education, 2927
Universal Fiber Systems, 931, 1507
Universal Hospital Services, 899
Universal Lighting Technologies, 1138
Universal Media Group, 1771
Universal Pure, 851
Universal Rail Systems, 2264
Universal Services, 69
Universal Services Of America, 377
Universal Software, 352
Universal Solutions International, 747
Universal Standard, 1533
Universal Studios Escape, 1949
Universal Technical Institute, 458

Portfolio Companies Index

Universal Turbine Parts LLC, 847
UniversalPegasus International, 1090
Universe Media, 2927
University Beyond, 1509
University Netcasting, 1708
University of Denver, 3265
University of Law, 2968
University of Massachusetts Medical School, 1271
University of Pittsburgh Innovation Institute, 3264
University of Sint Eustatius School of Medicine, 688
University of South Australia - The Mawson Institu, 2950
University Of St. Augustine For Health Sciences, 2030
University Park Energy, 1797
UniversityNow, 733, 1348
Univfy, 1555
Uniview, 223
Univision, 56
Univision Communications, 1160, 1498, 1602, 1818, 1837, 2371
Univision Technology, 1771
Uniwave, 2448
Unleash Immuno Oncolytics, 270
Unlimited Sports Group, 2492
Unmetric, 2992, 3053
Unmind, 2398
Unmute, 562
UNO Danmark, 3194
Uno Restaurant Holdings Corp, 449
Uno Restaurant Holdings Corp., 467
Unocoin, 310
Unopiu, 3145
Unravel, 1158
Unravel Data, 827, 1203
Unreal Candy, 1527
Unruly Studios, 2
Unser Heimatbacker Holding GmbH, 3058
Unsplash, 1105
Untangle, 1205, 1499
Untethered Labs, 421
UNTICKit, 728
UntuckIt, 1079
Unum Therapeutics, 193, 711, 1621
Unveillance, 288
Unwind Me, 788
Unwired Group Limited, 357
Unwired Nation, 813
Unwrinkly Inc., 1809
UNX, 346, 1151
Unyte, 2065
UOL Publishing, 1013
Up My Game, 2148
Up Out, 1671
Up Show, 9
Up Skill, 510, 812, 1610
Up To Good, 7
UP&UP Inc., 407
Upad, 2392
UPC Renewable, 838
Upchain, 2112
UpCity, 473, 732, 1023
Upcomer, 981
UpCounsel, 298
Upcounsel, 129, 527, 548, 944
Updata Partners, 3260
Update Legal, 886
Update Logic, 540
Update Software, 2723
Updater, 1645, 1701
UPEK, 614
UPF Services, 1156
Upfront Digital Media, 304, 1901
Upgrade, 744

UpLevel, 2006
UpLift, 1566
Uplifting Entertainment, 64
Upload, 1477
UploadVR, 1391
Uplogix, 55, 595
UPM-Kymmene Oyj, 2981
UPMC Enterprises, 3264
Upnext, 151
UpOut, 1566
Upper, 1083
Upper Crust, 1505
Upper Hand Managed Sports, 659
Uprise Medical, 1618
Uprising, 1258
Uproxx, 1006, 1885
Upruc Ctr SA, 3178
Upruc Tap-Sdv SA, 3178
Upserve, 877, 1666
Upserver, 1483
Upshift, 1896
Upshot.com, 58
Upside, 570, 1690
Upside Foods, 1709
Upside Health, 1509
Upsie, 1179
Upsight, 100, 641, 2107
UPSKILL, 1105
UpSkill, 2006
Upskill, 1259
Upslope Capital Management, 3265
Upspring Baby, 447
UpStart, 1079
Upstart, 514, 545
Upstart Network, 1073
Upstream, 3170
Upstream Commerce, 1969, 3236
Upstream Health, 1659
Upswing, 1554
Uptake, 1121, 1855
Uptake Medical, 67, 1379, 1604, 1775, 2007
UPTI, 3128
UptimeHealth, 2
Uptivity, 655
UpTo, 1154, 1923
Uptown Network, 151
Uptycs, 520, 818
Upverter, 2130
upwell, 1205
UpWork, 1628
Upwork, 251, 582, 744, 839, 1028, 1669
Upworthy, 430, 1718
Urachip, 2927
Uraniom, 310
Uranium Resources, 1551
Urban Airship, 361, 776, 779, 1153, 1862
Urban Barn, 2249
Urban Engines, 624
Urban Labs, 395
Urban Offsets, 512
Urban Remedy, 1363
Urban Rivals, 2377
URBANARA, 2970
Urbanara, 304, 2466, 2788
UrbanBound, 881, 1741
UrbanFootprint, 1698
Urbanlogiq, 2024
UrbanSitter, 182, 389, 596, 1203
Urbansitter, 43
UrbanStems, 1259
Urbanstems, 881, 1768
Urbantag, 1658
Urbasolar, 3011
Urbint, 728, 1896
Urbium, 2686
uReach Technologies, 163
Urgant, 288

Urgent Team, 1575, 1764
Urgent.ly, 770, 1928
UrgentTeam, 1631
Urjanet, 545, 881
Urli.st, 2620
Urnex, 547
UroGene, 2554
Urology Management Associates, 1053
Urova, 999
Urova Medical, 1190
UROValve, 1305
Ursa, 795
Ursa Major Tech, 93
US Acute Care Solutions, 94, 1973
US Anesthesia Partners, 1973
US Auto Sales, 1234
US Behavioral Health, 958
US Bioservices, 1041
US Builder Services, 842
US CareNet, 409
US Century Bank, 356
US Corrugated, 1968
US Development Group, 676
US eDirect, 28
US Eye, 1410
US Foodservice, 1460
US Health Works, 97
US HealthVest, 711, 1846
US HealthWorks, 2073
US Investigation Services, 1973
US Labs, 381
US LEC, 1508
US Lec Corp., 224
US Manufacturing Corporation, 2008
US MED, 931
US Medical, 1839
US Oncology, 1973
US Pharmcia, 1456
US Pipe, 530
US Power Generating, 1797
US Radiology Specialist, 1973
US Radiosurgery, 1410
US Renal Care, 559, 785, 1113, 1631, 1764
US Salt, 1169
US Search, 938
US Silica Company, 917
US Tarp, 1609
US Unwired, 1021
US Well Services, 408, 560
USA Bouquet, 804
USA Capital Holdings Inc., 463
USA Compression Partners, 1410
USA Datanet, 1753
USA Discounters, 1417
USA Environment, 1997
USA Television Holdings, 1270
UsAmeriBank, 531
uSamp, 876, 1381
USC Stevens Center for Innovation, 3258
USCO Logistics, 383
USDS, 1014
UsedCardboardBoxes.com, 800
User 1st, 544
User Friendly Media, 1929
User Replay, 2676
User Voices, 591
UserBliss, 103
Userfarm, 3170
Userfox, 3035
Userful, 2043
UserIQ, 285, 1412
Userlane, 746
Usermind, 457, 1203
UserTesting, 504, 1070, 1643, 1959
Uservoice, 234
USGI Medical, 56
Usha Martin, 3159

Portfolio Companies Index

Ushi.cn, 2970
Uship, 1079
uShip, 582, 1687
Ushr, 770, 2101
USI, 881
USI Holdings Corporation, 407
USI Insurance Services Corp., 1624
UsingMiles Inc., 554
USNR, 674
USP Hospitales, 2953
USPT, 2649
USSC, 633
UST-Aldetec Group, 542
UStar, 2927
UStec, 1378, 1753
Ustraap, 3116
UStream, 597, 646, 1093, 1959
Ustream, 1702
USU Software, 3060
uSwitch, 2935
UTAC, 2427
uTales, 2610
Utbrain, 3212
UTC Retail, 699
uTest, 1991
Utex Industries, 197
Utildata, 3090
Utilidata, 325
Utility, 325
Utility Pipeline, 243
Utility Telecom, 574
Utimaco, 1021
Utique, 1408
Utkarsh Microfinance, 2305
UTP, 973
Utrecht Art Supplies, 557, 1161
Utrecht Manufacturing, 1834
UTV LLC, 624
Utvate, 2122
UUCun, 3206
UUSee, 3133
Uvaro, 2122
Uview Ultraviolet Systems Inc., 911
Uvision360, 1925
Uwanna?, 209
Uway, 3118
UX, 564
UX Specialized Logistics, 1639
UXPin, 787, 1566
Uzerzoom, 2331

V

V Resorts, 3100
V Ships, 2608
V&D, 1755
V-Bank, 2432
V-Enable, 1708
V-Grid Energy Systems, 534
V-Kernel, 649
V-ME Media, 1773
V-Wave, 2221
V.Group, 2199
V.I.O., 341
V12 Data, 352
V12 Group, 1329
V2, 3145
V2 Technology, 2984
V2W Fun4kids, 3033
V3 Systems, 1888
VA Linux, 1566
VA Linux Systems, 1478, 1864
Va-Q-Tec, 3242
Vaatsalya, 2305, 3100
Vaca Energy, 496
Vacant Property Security Limited, 2812
Vacatia, 246, 327, 1032, 1186
Vaccine Tech, 2969

Vaco, 1507
Vacuum Technologies Corporation, 679
Vadio, 1467
Vagabond, 1023, 1229
Vagabond Vending, 288
Vahan, 1142
Vailmail, 1666
Vaimi, 3118
Vaioptic, 3037
Valant, 68
Valcare Medical, 2316
Valen Analytics, 540, 1504
Valen Technologies, 143
Valence Health, 749
Valence Surface Technologies, 815, 1858
Valencell, 1784, 1862
Valens Semiconductor, 117, 1241, 2453, 2943
Valent, 15, 1304
Valent Aerostructures, 463
Valenti Capital, 3259
Valentine Paper, 1214
Valentis, 3235
Valentus Specialty Chemicals, 963
ValenTx, 67, 652, 1631, 1804
Valeo, 475
Valere Power, 1798
Valerion Therapeutics, 1621
Valeritas, 58, 941, 1268, 1379, 1973, 2345
Valet Living, 917
Valet Park, 1176
Valet Waste, 1300
Valet.io, 1593
Valfix, 229
Valgen, 2517
ValiCert, 2073
Valicert, 200, 1091
Valid Information Systems, 3098
Validic, 1056, 1691, 1987, 3246
Validity, 564, 1411, 1499, 1924
Validity Sensors, 1795
Validus DC Systems, 2307
Validus Holdings, 1300
Validus IVC, 2935
Valign, 1358
Valimail, 756
Valiosys, 2346
Valista, 2378, 3182
Valitas Health Services, 1160
Vallent, 645
Vallent Corporation, 163
Valley Agriceuticals, 1208
Valley Fastener Group, 1582
Valley Meats, 1333
Valley National Bank, 3266
Valley Vessel Fabricators, 1722
Valley-Dynamo, 722
Valor Water Analytics, 1895
Valore, 37
Valorem, 3011
Valquip Corporation, 836
Valtech Cardio, 1325
Valterra Products, 356
Valtris Specialty Chemicals, 931
Valttori Oy, 2957
Value Creators & Company, 3118
Value Partners, 943
Value Payment Systems, 1261
Value Retail, 2940
Valued Investing, 1593
Valuedesign, 2637
ValueOptions, 560
Valuewait, 2534
Valvitalia, 3145
Valyoo Technologies, 2840, 3190
Van Dyke Energy Company, 1167
Van Houtte Cafe, 1138
Van-Lang Foods, 196

Vana Vidyut Private Ltd, 2305
Vanbridge, 1746
VanceInfo, 597, 2927
Vancl, 2575, 2841
Vanco, 862
Vanda, 2681
Vanda Pharmaceuticals, 1495, 2504
Vandalia Research, 1262
Vanderbilt, 1140
Vanderveer Plastics, 815
Vandolay, 1967
Vandor, 1481
VanDyne SuperTurbo, 992
Vanedge Capital, 2074
Vangent, 1927
VanGogh Imaging, 288
Vangst, 1443
Vangst Talent Network, 420
Vanguard A.G., 2644
Vanguard Graphics International, 402, 1057
Vanguard Health Systems, 1949
Vanguard Healthcare, 2956
Vanguard Modular, 165
Vanguard Scientific, 558
Vanguard Space Technologies, 681
Vanhawks, 2122
Vanilla, 686
Vanner Inc., 204
Vansco Electronics, 2162
Vansken, 1518
Vanta, 1426
Vantage, 1049
Vantage Data Centers, 1685
Vantage Media, 266, 1424, 1731
Vantage Mobility International, 377
Vantage Oncology, 436, 941, 1360
Vantage Power, 2951
Vantage Robotics, 795, 945
Vantia Limited, 2972
Vantia Pharma, 1631
Vantia Therapeutics, 3006
Vantium Management, 141
Vantos, 68, 755, 1390
Vantrix, 683, 683, 1042, 2250
Vantrix Corporation, 1731
Vanu, 457, 646
Vapogenix, 1023
Vapor IO, 257
Vapor Power, 1232
Vapor Slide, 395, 1139
Vapotherm, 561, 1126, 1517, 2074
Vapps, 218
Varana Health, 812
VArchive, 310
Vardon, 2787
Varel International, 153, 1090
Varentec, 1073
Vari-Form, 1755
Variable, 461
Variable Message Signs, 2298
Variable Wind Solutions, 2408
Variagenics, 1414, 1777
VariBlend Dual Dispensing Systems, 669, 1027
Varicent, 796, 2146
Variowell Development, 2677
Varix Medical Corp., 1546
vArmour, 84, 938, 2006, 2270
Varolii, 299, 1150
Varonis, 2717
Varro Technologies, 297
Varsity Brands, 458
Varsity Healthcare Partners, 3254
Varsity News Network, 173, 1739
Varuna, 1896
VarVee, 554
VASA Fitness, 1686
Vasco.de, 2804

Portfolio Companies Index

Vascular Graft Solutions, 350
Vascular Pathways, 158, 178, 2972
Vascular Pharmaceuticals, 1013, 1268
Vascular Therapies, 510
Vaska Tech, 1593
Vasona Networks, 1304
Vasonova, 139, 1546
Vasonova Inc., 374
VasoPharm, 2701
Vasoptic Medical, 18
VasoStar, 3183
Vast, 504, 549, 1106, 1346, 1813
Vast Broadband, 1410
Vathys, 798
Vatica Health, 862
Vativ Technologies, 767
Vator.tv, 1966
Vatterott College, 1972
Vatterott Educational Centers, 1778
Vault, 679
Vault.com, 1929
Vaultive, 1, 1302
VaultLogix, 740, 1979
Vaurum, 1491
Vauto, 224
Vaward Communications, 649
Vaxart, 241, 415
Vaxent, 999
Vaxess Technologies, 1347
Vaxiion Therapeutics, 1975
Vaximm, 2487, 2506, 3140
Vaxin, 1536
VaxInnate, 389, 1297
Vaxxas, 922, 2527, 2950, 3014
Vaya Vision, 3212
Vayable, 1549, 2321
Vayusa, 1640
Vayyar, 117
Vazata, 227
VB&P, 722
VBI Vaccines, 11, 154
VBL Therapeutics, 2445
Vbrick, 2074
VBrick Systems, 55, 1255
VC-Net, 2963
VC3, 1979
VCC Optoelectronics, 1970
VCG Inc., 694
VChain, 3099
VCharge, 498
vCharge, 1695
VCON., 2562
Vcopious, 1572
VCortex, 3230
VCST, 781, 2940
Vdoo, 1269
Vdopia, 624, 2992
Ve24, 1463
Veber Solar I, 1911
Vecta, 2445
Vector, 855, 1666
Vector Capital, 3245
Vector Disease Control, 381
Vector Holding, 2614
Vector International, 2745
Vector Media, 1727
Vector Solutions, 1140
Vectorious, 350
VectorLearning, 1498
Vectorply, 1270, 1343
Vectra, 108
Vectra AI, 969
Vectra Networks, 582
Veda, 3016
Vedero Software, 380
Veduca, 2941
Vee24, 180, 587

VeeAM, 2074
Veeam Software, 2312
Veebeam, 766
Veelo, 1384
Veem, 310
VEENOME Inc., 650
VeeR, 1614, 1672
Veerum, 2105
Veev, 648
Veeva Systems, 666
Vega-Chi, 3009
Veggie Grill, 333, 337, 1153
Vehicle Trasportation Service, 3173
Vehicular Technologies, 651
Vehlo, 1499
Vela, 345
Vela Pharmaceuticals, 1191
Vela Systems, 523
Velano Vascular, 1058, 1605
Veldeman Group, 2940
Velicept Therapeutics, 1147, 1271
Velio, 837
Vella, 1522
Velo, 1340
Velo3D, 1073
VeloBit, 713, 1150
Velocidata, 1316
Velocify, 1944
Velocimed, 1578
Velocitel, 1939
Velocity, 1727
Velocity Aerospace Holding Group, 1494
Velocity Outdoor Corporation, 525
Velocity Technology Solutions, 1192, 1685, 1731
VelocityShares, 796
VeloCloud, 1918
Velomat Assembly Automation, 1352
Velomedix, 1967
Velos, 608, 1527, 1535
Velox Power, 1520
Veloxum, 1737
Veltek Associates, 1204
Velum Global Credit Mgmt., 408
VeluwseBron, 3222
Velvac Holdings, 1494
Velvet Energy LTD, 1853
Velvet Taco, 1092
Vemba, 1890
Vena, 2074
Vena Solutions, 2163
Venado Oil & Gas, 673
Venafi, 773, 1205, 1428
Venanpri Group, 2200, 2201
Venari, 1049
Venari Resources, 1066
VenatoRx, 269, 764, 1930
Vence, 398, 680, 1074
Vencore, 1927
Vend, 1899, 3035
Venda, 885
Vendasta, 2270
Vendavo, 597, 767, 782, 1014, 1674, 1728
Vendetta Mining, 1551
Vending System, 3145
Vendor Registry, 86, 461, 1925
Vendormate, 1412, 1460
Vendorpm, 771
VendorSafe Technologies, 1498
Vendr, 2122
Vendstar, 92
Venerable Holdings, 560
Venga, 323
Vengo, 1635
Veniam, 1884, 1928
Veniti, 225, 570, 1490
Venminder, 1240
Vennli, 659, 1023

VennWorks LLC, 2774
Venous Health Systems, 667
Venrock, 3263
Vensafe, 2722
Vensun Pharmaceuticals, 1052
Ventaleon, 2506, 2930
Vente-Privee, 1754
Ventealapropriete.com, 1418
Vention, 1982
Vention Medical, 1090
VentiRx, 154, 622, 785
Ventiv Technology, 1779
VentriNova, 350
Ventritex, 1788
Ventura Associates, 1883
Venture Bank, 3268
Venture Fellows, 1653
Venture Investors, 3259
Venture Sales Group, 1582
Venture Steel, 62
Venture Technology Groups, 445
Venture/Life Sciences Agenda, 2457
VentureBeat, 116, 1227, 1525
VentureScanner, 246
Venturesity, 3124
Venturi Wireless, 950, 1354, 1750
Venturion Limited Partnership, 2073
VenueBook, 434
Venuemob, 3112
Venus Concept, 698, 924, 1147
VenusConcept, 137
Venustech, 2575
VenX, 1261
Venyu, 1161
Veo Robotics, 1155
Veolia, 153
VER, 1092
Ver Se Innovation, 585
Veracicom, 538
Veracity Medical Solutions, 1190
Veracode, 1, 37, 69, 561, 983, 1213, 1741
Veracross LLC, 364
Veracyte, 622
Verafin, 1720, 2146, 2161
VerAI, 2072
Veran, 812, 1490, 1930
Veran Medical Technologies, 60, 1559
Verana Health, 271
Verance, 290, 389, 552, 1608
Verano Holdings, 2245
Verari Systems, 441
Verastem, 58, 413, 1149, 1268
Verato, 518
Verax BioMedical, 273, 1146
Verax Biomedical, 510, 1061
Verb, 447
VerbalizeIt, 686
Verbling, 361, 400, 2321
Verdande Technology AS, 3132
Verdant, 2121
Verdeeco, 1925
VerdEng Connectors, 2751
Verdezyne, 322, 1249, 1392
Verdiem Corporation, 127
Verdigris, 1928
Verelst, 2492
Verengo Solar, 127
Verenium, 190, 325, 457
Verge Genomics, 235, 610, 1059, 1696
Verge Health, 352
Verge Solutions, 957
Vergesense, 1423
Veri, 381
Veriato, 912, 1979
Verical, 1901
Vericare, 941
VERiCASH, 2398

Portfolio Companies Index

Vericept, 1674
Vericlaim, 751
Verico Technology, 110
Vericred, 718
Veridiem, 313
Verient, 621, 837
Verificient, 1058
Verificient Technologies, 708
Verified Person, 1661
Veriflow, 1203
VeriFone, 1257
Verifone, 782
VerifyValid, 1739
Verilogue, 655
Verilume, 1235
Verimatrix, 549, 1042, 1239
Verinata Health, 1247, 1341
Verinetics, 738
Verio, 1212
Verious, 2009
Verisight, 1746
VeriSign, 1244
VeriSilicon, 908, 1091, 1798, 1908, 2841, 2844, 2927, 3225
VeriSIM Life, 1760
Verisity, 759, 2711
Verisma, 291
Verismic, 1679
Verista Imaging, 2071
Veristat, 971
Veristone Capital, 1065
Verisure Smart Alarms, 927
Verisys, 1720
Veritas, 1175
Veritas Finance, 1346
Veritext, 1021, 1113
Veritext Holding Company, 1460
Veritone, 1237
Veritonic, 981, 1768
Veritract, 1074, 1886
Verity, 881
Verity Solutions, 978
Verity Wine Partners, 1027
Verivo, 523
VeriVue, 1184, 1718
Veriware, 2005
Verizon, 3266
Vermed, 2593
Vermont Smoke & Cure, 1214
Vermont Teddy Bear, 789, 1864
Verna Group, 2926
VerneGlobal, 820
Vero, 1998
Verodin, 564, 1796
Verogen, 4
Verona Pharma, 73, 764, 1271, 1943
Verplex Systems, 3209
Verrex, 16
Versa, 354, 1521
Versa Networks, 177, 1187, 1928
VersaMed, 2742
VersaPharm, 1779
Versartis, 73, 1297, 1522, 1700
Versata, 1674
Versatile, 1795
Versatile Natures, 1896
Versatile Processing Group, 1210
Verse, 641
Verse Music Group, 1984
Versify, 1691
VersionONe, 1381
Versium, 1827
Versive, 2006
Versly, 234
Verso Paper, 141
Versusgame, 1509
Versé, 1374

Vert, 1073
Vert Mirabel, 2233
Vertafore, 927, 1045, 1837
Vertaris, 2364
Vertascale Software, 1967
Vertellus Specialties, 172, 1990
Verterra, 462, 609
Vertex, 209
Vertex Aerospace, 110, 1927
Vertex Business Services, 406
Vertex Data Science, 1360
Vertex Downhole, 677, 2252
Vertex Management Israel, 1636
Vertex Networks, 950
Vertex Resource Group, 2022
VertexOne, 611
Vertical Acuity, 1076
Vertical Bridge, 654, 1049
Vertical Communications, 538
Vertical Knowledge, 1499
Vertical Management Systems, 961
Vertical Mass, 400
Vertical Nerve, 8
Vertical Networks, 1008
Vertical Performance Partners, 1701
Vertical Power, 1926
Vertical Techmedia, 3226
Vertical Wind Energy, 2601
VertiCann, 395
Vertiflex, 1820
Vertis Neuroscience Inc, 3153
Verto Education, 321, 888
Vertos Medical, 213, 1228, 1379
Vertrue, 564
Vertu Capital, 2074
Verus, 796
Verus Pharmaceuticals, 189
Verusen, 2018
Verva, 2527
Verva Pharmaceuticals, 2950
Verve, 299, 784, 1327, 1511, 2665, 2750
Verve Health, 659
Verve Mobile, 562
Very Good Security, 1142
Veryan, 2849
Veryfi, 49
Vesey Street Capital Partners, 3254
Vesiflo, 348
Vesper, 945
Vesper Technologies, 222
Vessel, 788, 1006, 1752, 1816
Vessel Co., 2993
Vessix, 1103
Vesta, 100, 1361, 1594, 1912
Vesta GMS, 22
VESTA Modular, 228
Vesta Retail Network, 1084
Vesta Therapeutics, 1917
Vestagen, 924
Vestar Capital Partnrs, 3245
Vestaron, 571, 1380, 1380, 1715, 2205
Vestcom, 458, 912
Vested Health, 1262
Vestiaire Collective, 2469, 3199
Vestmark, 290, 1628
Veston Nautical, 1410
Vestorly, 1305
VetCentric, 1668, 1736
VetCloud, 2687
Vetco International, 2547
VetCor, 559, 917
VetDC, 1065
Veterinary Practice Partners, 1410
Vetevo, 2832
Vetra Energia, 45
Vetro FiberMap, 2
Vets First Choice, 311, 941, 1464

Vetster, 2280
Vetta, 293
Vette, 1084
Vetted, 2131
Vetted Petcare, 121
Vetter, 101
Vettery, 1121, 1483
Vettro, 1674
Vetty, 1509
Vetus den Ouden, 2370
VeVeo, 1184
Veveo, 1375
Vexata, 1187
Vexos, 448
VFA, 655
VFG Plc, 2827
vFunction, 1666
Vhoto, 1186
VHSquared, 1631
VHsquared, 1734
VHT, 947
Vi-Jon, 257
VIA, 1481
Via, 708, 925, 1058
Via Separations, 664
Via Transportation, 1099
Viabizzuno, 2285
Viacell, 2998
ViaCyte, 1399, 1522, 1619, 1931
Viadeo, 3199
Viagene, 1708
Viagogo, 1966, 2393, 2437, 2494
ViaHero, 1509
Viajala, 3116
ViajaNet, 641
Viajanet, 820
Viajanet.com.br, 1537
Viakoo, 1065
Viamedia, 1095
Viamet, 918
Viamet Pharmaceuticals, 184, 1013, 1128
ViaNovus, 1465
Viasto, 2832
Viathan, 755
Viatime, 1340
Viatris, 1777
ViaWest, 1360
Viawest, 828, 1679
VIBE, 897
Vibe HCM, 793
Vibe/Spin Ventures, 786
Vibenomics, 1412
VibeSec, 3050
Vibrado, 1073
Vibrant, 1926
Vibrant Technologies, 317
Vibromech, 3202
Vic.ai, 553
Vical, 1619, 1708
ViCampo, 3021
Vicampo, 641
Vicarious, 108, 265, 538, 720, 1186, 1614
Vicarious Surgical, 108, 795, 1001
Vice, 1837
VICE Media, 1787
Vicentin SAIC, 2080
Vicinity, 1406
Vicix, 1101
VICO Software, 311
Vicom Systems, 1674
VICORP Restaurants, 714, 847
Victess Capital Corp., 2088
Viction AG, 3163
Victor, 322, 2640
Victor Homes Charco 99, 2976
Victorious, 59, 389, 1059, 1079, 1103, 1537, 1885

Portfolio Companies Index

VictorOps, 548, 779
Victory Capital, 560
Victory Guide, 937
Victory Heights, 153
Victory Park Capital, 3255
Victress Capital, 3263
Victrex, 2976
Victrio, 1658
Vicura, 2746
Vicwest, 2062
VIDA, 108
Vida, 130, 182, 399, 901
Vida Ventures, 3263
VidaCare, 1794, 1868
VidAngel, 1074
Vidatron, 1839
VidCode, 1554
Vidder, 1379, 1947
Viddler, 1305
Viddy, 876
VideaHealth, 2018
Videantis GmbH, 2677
Videdressing, 3031
Video Amp, 133
Video Arts, 2914
Video Blocks, 1504, 1888
Video Island, 2702
VideoAmp, 1816, 1966
VideoGenia, 304
VideoIQ, 1184, 1798
Videolicious, 1154, 1521
Videology, 318, 429, 520, 912, 1298, 1504, 1901
Videomar Rede Nordeste SA, 45
VideoNext, 1313
VideoPlaza, 2628, 3004
VideoSlick, 1142
Videosmith, 1294
VideoStitch, 998
Videostrip, 2813
Vidfall, 1959
Vidible, 1566
VidIQ, 708, 1153
Vidius, 3115
Vidler, 1588
Vidlet, 130
Vidme, 1890
VidMob, 25
Vidora, 1014
Vidpresso, 1637
Vidrovr, 1614
Vidstructor, 1959
VidSys, 949, 1316
Vidsys, 756
Vidus, 1304
Vidyard, 1610, 1702, 2011, 2150
Vidyo, 285, 780, 1056, 1203, 1517, 1661, 1848, 3128
Vienova, 2809
Viet - UC Group, 2937
Viet-UC Group, 1143
Vietnam Australia International School, 2952
View, 646, 1978
View Dynamic Glass, 596, 812, 1281
View Interative, 911
View Lift, 510
View Medical, 999, 1190
View Point, 1478
View Point Therapeutics, 183
ViewBix, 389
Viewdle, 133
Viewfinity, 1042, 1150
Viewhigh Technologies, 2658
Viewics, 399, 1254
ViewLogic Systems, 1287
Viewlogic Systems, 317
Vieworks, 3136
Viewpoint, 1778, 1888

Viewpoint Therapeutics, 1238
ViewRay, 73, 1063, 1383
Viewster, 2629
ViewStub, 512
Viggi Corp., 705
Vigil Health Management, 2091
Vigil Health Solutions Inc., 2061
Vigil Neuroscience, 1934
Vigilance, 2073
Vigilance Networks, 3205
Vigilant Shipping Holding, 62
Vigilant Solutions, 1255
Vigilent, 2256
Vigilistics, 281, 810
Vigin Connect, 2645
VigLink, 545, 666, 779, 1597, 1702
Vignani Technologis, 3053
Vignette, 57, 857, 1674, 2785
Vignette Wine Country Soda, 1070
Vigor Industrial, 674
Vigtec, 754
Vigtory Sportsbook, 1660
Viigo, 2146
Viirt, 635
Viisage Technology, 870
Vik Brothers Insurance, 1071
Vikalp, 54
Viki, 457
Viking, 3164
Viking Cruises, 1837
Viking Office Products, 1624
Vilant Systems, 3143
Village Power Finance, 1161
Village Realty, 1609
Village Roadshow Entertainment Group, 1377
Village Square Cabinet Supply, 112
Village Tavern, 747
Village Ventures, 223
Villagize, 1635
Vimana, 68
ViMicro, 597
VIMOC, 1254
Vimy Resources Limited, 1551
Vina Technologies, 759, 1795
Vina Technologies XenSource, 1478
Vince, 1755
Vince & Associates Clinical Research, 441
VincePair Inc., 1309
Vincera, 1857
Vincross, 827
Vindicia, 597, 796, 1379
Vindigo, 967
Vindrauga Holdings; Inanovate, 738
Vine Street Ventures, 635
Vineti, 610, 812
Vinli, 1614
Vinn Auto, 2122
Vinogusta, 3161
Vinperfect, 1604
Vintage Holdings, 1654
Vintage Stock, 408
Vinterior, 3099
Vinters International Inc., 449
Vintners' Alliance, 1087
Vintra, 309
Vinusa, 1674
Violence Prevention Network, 2522
Violet Grey, 1533
Violet Packing, 1481
Violin Memory, 546, 938, 1991
Vionic, 92
Viope Solutions Oy, 2864
Vioptix, 2969
Vioso, 2804
VIP Cinema Seating, 2956
VIP Petcare, 931
Vip.com, 597

Viper, 2284
Vipit, 1407
VIPSTORE, 2970
VIQ Solutions, 2258
Vir, 19, 1646
Viracor-IBT, 119
Viracta, 772, 1098
Viradis, 547
Virage, 57, 857, 1855
Virage Logic, 564, 1107
Viral Gains, 1101
ViralGains, 1385
Viralheat, 1187
ViralMint, 3100
Virata Corp, 2653
ViraTree, 738
Virdante Pharma, 1918
Virdante Pharmaceuticals, 1820
Virence, 1927
Virent, 194, 1923, 2002
Virent Energy, 60
Vires Aero, 1491
Virgil Security, 288
Virgin Charter, 800
Virgin Hyperloop One, 44, 680, 1665
Virgin Mega, 744
Virgin Mobile, 691
Virgin Plants, 571, 1135
Virgin Play, 2460
Virgin Pulse, 568, 704
Virginia Tile Company, 913
Virgo, 167
Viridaxis, 3216
Virident Systems, 1241
Viridian, 153, 708
Viridis, 54, 708, 1610, 1808
ViridityEnergy, 325
Virion Therapeutics, 1581
VIRIS Detection Systems, 1317
VirMedica, 924
Viro Media, 1153
ViroCyt, 933
Viron, 1608
Vironclinics Biosciences, 912
Virool, 232, 586, 816, 895, 1491, 1821, 2321, 2654
ViroPharma, 785
Virsec Systems Inc., 176
Virsex, 1851
Virsto, 1713
Virsto Software, 200, 545
Virsys12, 1610
Virt, 310
Virta, 1258, 1363, 1918
Virta Health, 1323
Virta Labs, 1550
Virtela, 1408
Virtela Communications, 1337
Virtensys, 3095
Virteva, 3268
VirtGen, 1399
Virtify, 1731
Virtio, 183
Virtools, 3199
Virtru, 1614
Virtual Badge, 1412
Virtual City, 54
Virtual Event Bags, 1446, 1925
Virtual Incision, 300
Virtual Incision Corporation, 1474
Virtual Instruments, 252, 752, 936, 1076, 1319
Virtual IT, 2455
Virtual Labs, 256
Virtual Nights, 2829
Virtual Peaker, 789
Virtual Ports, 2700
Virtual Radiologic Corporation, 822

Portfolio Companies Index

Virtual Relocation, 892
Virtual Speech, 310
Virtual Ubiquity, 57
VirtualEdge, 655
Virtualex, 2845
Virtualis, 810
VirtualLogix, 2653
VirtualNights, 2820
VirtualScopics, 1206
Virtudent, 1
Virtugro, 395
Virtuix, 1635
Virtuix Omni, 1186
Virtulytix, 1215
Virtuo, 2469
Virtuos, 2927
Virtuoz, 1247
Virtus, 69
Virtus Pharmaceuticals, 1132
Virtusa, 759
Virtustream, 1332, 1517, 1784
VIRUN, 300
Virutal Health, 655
Viryanet, 2600, 3128
Viryanet Inc., 2576
VisAer Inc., 694
Visage, 1895
Visage Mobile, 1403, 1649
VISANOW, 810
Visant Corporation, 2371
Visbit, 1477
Visby, 1391, 1423
Viscap, 2927
Viscovery, 897, 3029
Visen, 748
ViSenze, 1983
Visgenx, 229
Visible Assets, 523, 994
Visible Equity, 464
Visible Markets, 115
Visible Measures, 582, 1247, 1341
Visible Path, 1008
Visible Technologies, 983
Visible World, 56, 593, 1829
VisibleThread, 2347
Visicon Technologies, 1604
Visier, 773, 1754
Visinex, 1321
Visio, 200
Visiogen, 1449, 1495, 1788
Visiomatics, 2940
Vision, 531
Vision Chemical Systems, 147
Vision Critical, 342, 2126, 2196, 2225
Vision Government Solutions, 815, 832
Vision Group, 1169
Vision Group Holdings, 458
Vision Holdings, 376
Vision Innovation Partners, 449
Vision Max, 2051
Vision Solutions, 502, 1817
Vision Source, 331
Vision++, 2358
Vision2Hire Solutions Inc, 2091
VisionAIR, 1711
Visionair, 3124
VisionCare, 1379, 2345
VisionCritical, 2127
Visioneering Technologies, 460, 1190
VisionScape, 299
VisionScope Technologies, 1421
Visiprise, 2073
VisiQuate, 733
Visit Pay, 178
Visitech International Ltd, 3002
VisitPay, 1346
VisiTrend, 1525

Visiware, 3011
Visla, 1155
Visma, 2968
Visocon, 3156
Visolis, 398
Visor, 729, 1155, 1186, 1363
Vispero, 1912
Vista, 1736
Vista Alegre Atlantis, 3039
Vista III Media Holdings, 364
Vista Medical Technologies, 767
Vista Ridge, 1220
Vista Therapeutics, 1793
Vista-Pro Automotive, 2008
Vistaar Finance, 1374
VistaPoint Technology, 1757
VistaPrint, 1994
Vistaprint, 3104
Vistar Corporation, 1972
Vistar Entertainment, 196
Vistar Media, 59, 680, 1901
Vistar Media Inc., 406
Vistarmedia, 1207
Vistec Semiconductor Systems, 843
Visterra, 748, 1155, 1464, 2086
Vistex, 28
Visto, 68, 1137
Vistorm, 2786
Vistria Group, 3255
Vistronix, 681
Visu, 1099
Visual IQ, 1944
Visual Mining, 1674
Visual Networks, 51, 655
Visual Vocal, 680, 1309
Visual.Ly, 564, 1702
visual.ly, 650
Visualase, 2104
VisualDNA, 3004
Visualead, 2905
Visualfabriq, 1499
Visually, 1058
Visualnet, 2911
Visure, 2539
Visys, 2358
Vita, 169
Vita Nonwovens, 1424
Vitae, 527
Vitae Pharma, 193
Vitae Pharmaceutcals, 1495
Vitae Pharmaceuticals, 764
Vital Biosciences, 2122
Vital Decisions, 1271
Vital Energi, 3095
Vital Farms, 1691, 2153
Vital Foods, 2507
Vital Herd, 1305
Vital Images, 870, 3268
Vital Insights, 336
Vital Metrix, 999
Vital Renewable Energy Company, 585
Vital Signs Staffing, 464
Vital Therapies, 1903, 2658
Vital Venture Capital, 3260
Vitalife, 1636
VitaLink Research, 864
Vitalis Extraction Technology, 2095
Vitality Foodservice, 847
Vitals, 51, 876
VitalStream, 1313, 1953
Vitalstream, 564
Vitaltrax, 1605
Vitalus, 2121
Vitalyst, 225
Vitamin Research, 3206
Vitanta-Intravest, 3224
VitaScan, 705

VitaSound, 2181
Vitesse, 564, 1247, 1257, 2825
Vitesse Semiconductor Corporation, 3157
Vitex Packaging Group, 1460
Vitopel, 1939
Vitrek, 330
Vitrimark, 1695
Vitromics, 2930
Vitron, 1707
Vitrue, 1629
Vitruvian LC, 1133
Vitruvias Therapeutics, 1052
Vittra Utbildning, 2879
Vitu, 28
Vium, 108, 1155
Viv, 1323, 1483
Viva, 938, 3199
Viva Bolivia, 1854
Viva Dominican Republic, 1854
Viva Republica, 100, 1511
Vivace Therapeutics, 1238
Vivaldi Biosciences, 240, 1325, 1422
Vivalto Santé, 3011
VivaNeo, 3222
Vivant, 980
Vivant Medical Inc., 374
Vivante Health, 718
VivaReal, 1608, 2967
Vivaro, 297
Vivasure Medical, 179
Vivature, 716
Vivax, 1727
Vivd Semiconductor, 627
Vive, 708, 1154
Vive Crop Protection, 2054
Vivecrop, 2258
Vivendy Therpeutics, 2342
Vivense, 2428
Viventium, 386
Viverae, 696, 793
Vivere Health, 1140
Vivet Therapeutics, 1350
Viveve, 11
Vivi, 757
Vivid Toy Group, 3027
Vivid Vision, 985
Vividence, 115
Vividence Corporation, 2073
Vividion, 1930
Vivien Mineral Water And Beverage Company Ltd., 2626
Vivify Health, 178
Vivino, 2469, 2628, 3194
Vivint, 280
Vivint Smart Home, 745
Vivista Holdings, 2914
Vivixtum, 2940
Vivo Capital, 1047
Vivo Tech, 609
Vivocha, 3043
VivoQuest, 1096
Vivostat, 3104, 3140
Vivox, 389, 1737
Vivu, 1017
VIVUS, 190, 1395
Vivus, 73, 785, 1900
Viwawa, 1683
Vix, 912
Vixar, 1874
Vixiar Medical, 18
Vixxenn, 354
Viyet, 1589
Viz, 1760
Viz Risk Management, 2745
Viz.AI, 108, 1426
Viz.ai, 1079, 3099
Vizant Technologies, 1029

Portfolio Companies Index

Vizbee, 540, 1076
Vizelia, 2346
VizeraLabs, 2286
Vizetto, 754
Vizeum, 868
VizExplorer, 1255
Vizify, 686, 1467
Vizimax, 2283
Vizional, 2020
Vizionware, 1170
Vizor, 310
Vizrt, 538, 3128
Vizsafe, 991
VizSense, 517
Viztec, 693, 1603
Vizu Corp., 115
Vizury, 1017, 1327, 3010
VJ Technology, 2477
VKernel, 1150
VKidz, 1929
VKorus Pte Ltd, 2844
VKS Farms, 3202
Vleepo, 2070
Vlocity, 1610, 1985
VLS Recovery Services, 202
VLST, 154, 2007
VM Discovery, 118
VM Ware Wanova, 3212
VMG Health, 1507
VMIX, 1239
VMIX Media, 1042
Vmlogix, 224
VMRay GmbH, 2677
VMS Fund Administration, 3262
VMTurbo, 224, 839
VMturbo, 224
VMW Paducahbiltwpt, 405
VMWare, 218
VMX, 1244
VNDLY, 320
Vnomics, 1479
VNTANA, 1878
VNUS Medical Technologies Inc., 240
Voalte, 178, 245
VoApps, 1412
Voatz, 1895
Vobile, 28, 2681
Vocabulary.com, 194
Vocal Data, 540
Vocal IQ, 3019
Vocalocity, 285, 1045, 1449, 1790
Vocaltec, 56
VocalZoom, 1260
VoCare, 659
Vocate, 789
Vocera, 209, 827
Voci Technologies, 296, 1451
Vocus, 655, 1045
Vodasafe, 2270
Vodkaster, 1418
Vodlee, 2688
Vof Clemence & Juliette, 3033
Voga Coffee, 1703
VOI, 2469
Voice Objects, 3223
Voicea, 1610
VoiceBase, 650
VoiceBox, 2969
Voiceflow, 2132
voiceflow, 2232
Voiceitt, 1158, 1509
VoiceObjects, 1795
VoiceOps, 1153
Voicera, 108, 1158
Voices.com, 1255
VoicesHeard Media, 1799

Voicesoft, 2448
VoiceVault, 2682
Voiturelib, 2377
VOKE, 810
Vokle, 1604, 1671
Volabit, 310
Volante, 2942
Volante System, 2265
Volantio, 1039
Volaris Advisors, 813
Volastra Therapeutics, 1934
Volia, 1498
Volition Beauty, 669
Volley, 121, 310
Volly, 1292
Volo Metrix, 1728
voloAgri, 1079
Volocopter, 3226
Vology, 408
VoloMetrix, 1666
Volotea, 435
Volt, 3194
Volt DB, 1069
Volt Markets, 310
Volta, 207, 208, 812
Volta Arkil, 2880
Volta Networks, 1489
Voltafield Technology, 974, 2694
Voltage, 1101
Voltage Security, 972, 1203, 1257, 1852
Voltaiq, 246
Voltaire, 226, 252, 3150
Voltarc, 1294
VoltDB, 1675
Voltea, 2397
Volterra, 1158
Volterra Semiconductor, 1257
VoltServer, 1695
Voltserver, 498
Voltyre-Prom, 1376
VoluBill, 163
Volubill, 3104
Volumetric Biotechnologies, 1616
VolunteerSpot, 447
Voluntis, 1511
Vonage, 224, 224
Vondormate, 1480
Vonigo, 2262
Vontoo, 652
Vonvon, 100
Voodoo Manufacturing, 12
Vook, 1851, 1908
VOOM, 1928
Voonami, 1679
Voonik, 3100
Vooruitgang Energie, 3200
Vor Biopharma, 11
Vorbeck Materials, 1172
VoresVilla, 3194
Vormetric, 454, 1028, 1042, 1674, 1728
Vorstack, 1790
Vorstella, 553
Vortal, 2708, 3022
Vortex, 3202
Vortex Engineering, 2305
Vortex Medical, 428
VOSS, 3229
Voss, 2466, 2682
Voss of Norway, 2745
Vouchedfor, 3088
Vow To Be Chic, 1966
Vow to be Chic, 1103, 1483
Vowman, 3009
Vox Media, 520, 819
Vox Mobile, 1051, 2256
Vox Spectrum, 2645
Voxar, 3095

Voxeet, 1370, 1418
Voxel8, 325
Voxeo, 1334
Voxer, 1006, 1969, 1991
Voxify, 1408
Voxitas, 60
VoxMobile, 655
Voxpoint Technologies Oy, 2864
VoxPop Network Corp., 115
Voxpopme, 1385
Voxtron, 2772
Voxy, 320, 535, 724, 888, 1422, 1554
Voyage, 1269
Voyage Control, 3099
Voyage Labs, 2122
Voyager Pacific Capital, 1065
Voyager Systems, 1667
Voyager Therapeutics, 1814
Voyages, 1773
Voyages Traditours, 2076
Voyajoy, 1589
Voyant, 2074
Voyant Photonics, 1105
VOYAT, 1635
Voyence, 446
VOZ, 3246
Voz Telecom, 2474
VP360, 124
Vpay, 796
VPI Systems, 1304, 2369
VPNet, 162
VPS, 1755, 3017
VR Chat, 344
vRad, 1138, 1498
Vrart, 310
VRC Holdings, 293
Vreal, 474, 1890
VREC, 1401
VRI, 1410
Vrideo, 1223
Vriti Infocom, 3053
Vroom, 91, 608, 820, 1092
VRTV Studios, 2726
VS, 840
VSCO, 1363
VSD, 2593
VSee, 983, 1610
vServe Digital Services, 2840
VSG, 2935
VSIN, 1660
vSocial, 533
Vsporto, 601
VT Services, 1049
Vtesse, 240
VTI Instruments, 1210
Vtion Wireless, 2584
VTS, 380, 728, 1483, 2006
VTV Therapeutics, 949
Vuber, 43
VuBiquity, 518
Vubiquity, 1348, 1504, 1901
Vuclip, 3112
Vue Cinemas, 2926
Vue Entertainment, 496
Vue International, 2199
VueBox, 1509
VuePoint, 957
Vugo, 754
Vuguru, 1835
Vulcan Cyber, 1796
VulcanForms, 648
Vulcanic, 2956
Vungle, 129, 564, 680, 1659, 1702, 1821, 1969
Vurb, 586, 626, 1537, 1800
Vurv Technology, 1731
Vutara, 1074
Vutiliti, 1074

1426

Portfolio Companies Index

VUV Analytics, 1601
Vuvox, 133
vVault, 297
vvlogger, 908
VWR International, 1160
VWR Intl, 212
VxTel, 1795
Vyaire Medical, 136
Vyatta, 89, 801, 936, 1411
Vydia, 400
Vynca, 139
Vyne, 1049
VYou, 1479
Vyrill, 2204
Vysionics, 2935
Vysr, 3202
Vytalize Health, 2194
Vytek Corporation, 2073
VYTL, 101
Vytrace, 1452
VytronUS, 144
VytronUs, 1993
VytronUS Inc., 272
Vyve Broadband, 243

W

W Energy Partners, 560
W&W Communications, 115
W&W Dairy, 1163
W-Technology Inc., 903
W.I.S.E., 2466
W2 Group, 1248
W4, 3104
Waabi, 2131
WAAM, 512
Waarborgeheer, 3033
Wachstum, 2913
Wacker Construction Equipment AG, 1133
Wacom, 1100
Waddell Reed Financial Inc., 303
Wade & Wendy, 387, 724, 795
Wade Building Services, 2976
WadeCo Specialties, 832
Wadley Crushed Stone Company, 1536
WaferScale Integration, 1684
Wag, 44, 361, 1154, 1696
Wag!, 820
Wagamama, 2787
Wagepoint, 1499, 2107, 2262
WageWorks, 1908
Waggers Pet Products, 2043
Waggle, 354, 1153, 1885
Waggoner Ranch, 517
Wagner Dimas Inc., 206
Wagon Wheel Exploration, 1447
Wagr, 1426
Wahanda, 2382
Wahed Invest, 568
Wahoo Fitness, 1345
Waiakea, 3248
Wait What, 568
Waitr, 1000
Wake Research Associates, 815
Wakemate, 1658
Wakie, 2929
Wakie Inc., 1330
Wakoopa, 2813, 2828
Walbar Engine Components, 542
Walden, 36
Walden Behavioral Health, 1639
Waldo, 1890
Waldo's, 45
Walk Me, 1629
Walker & Co., 1890
Walker & Company, 1006
Walker Advertising, 503
Walker Edison, 377, 1053

Walker Seeds, 2108
Walkin, 3199
Walking Co., 1552
WalkinWifi, 2958
WalkMe, 872, 2681
Wall Data, 1855
Wall Street On Demand, 318
Wall Street Sports, 528
Wall Street Transcript, 2702
Walla.by, 1059, 1983
Wallaby, 1521
Wallaroo Labs, 308
Wallop, 533
Walls 360, 1914
Walls Industries, 331
Walnut Algorithms, 1370
Walnut Investment Holding, 585
Walpole, 165
Walter and Eliza Hall Institute, 1271
Walter Surface Technologies, 2200, 2201
Walton Garden Buildings, 2608
Wanbishi Archives, 3173
Wandel und Gotermann Management Holding, 2801
Wander Beauty, 1186, 1483
Wanderset, 756
Wanderu, 298, 527, 1959
Wandoujia, 597
Wandrian, 313
Wanelo, 1323, 1534
Wangyou.com, 457
Wanleo, 752
Wanova, 2557
Wantful, 1464
Wantworthy, 1154
Wanxue, 597
WAPIS, 256
Waples Manufacturing, 402, 612
Waptx, 641
Warby Parker, 321, 328, 720, 763, 820, 1203, 1534, 1718, 1763
Warchest, 937
Ward Energy Partners, 1853
Wardrobe, 882
Warehouse One Clothing, 2249
Warman Home Centre, 2129, 2277
Warne, 367
Warne Scope Mounts, 1612
Warner Chilcott, 212, 223
Warner Chilcott Plc., 1905
Warner Music Group, 33, 223
WarpDrive Bio, 1814
Warranty Asia, 2895
Warsaw, 2697, 2697
Warwick Audio Technologies, 2958
Warwick Effect Polymers, 3098
Warwick International, 2371
Wasabi, 344
Wasabi Life, 870
Wasabi Systems, 957
Wash Cycle Laundry, 1581, 3246
Wash-it, 3248
Washburn Therapeutics, 1452
Washing Systems LLC, 886
Washington Chain & Supply, 330
Washington Inventory Service, 1560
Washington Mutual, 303
WASI, 1707
Wasi Organics, 54
Waste Corporation of America, 517
Waste Enterprisers, 3246
Waste Italia, 3145
Waste link, 2667
Waste Recycling Group, 2371
Waste Remedies, 60
Wasteplace, 411
Wastequip, 1138, 1368

Wastewater Compliance Systems, 1074
Wat-Aah, 2393
watAgame, 3194
Wataro, 2417
Watch Data, 2927
Watch Wire, 2262
WatchDox, 1235, 1666
Watchfinder & Co., 3031
Watchfire, 911, 1049, 1084, 3157
WatchGuard, 782, 1566, 1912
WatchSend, 1593
Watchsend, 1254
Water Co. Holding, 1232
Water for Life, 3194
Water Lilies, 196
Water Oasis Group, 585
Water Pik, 1231
Water Science Technologies, 1536
Water Street, 36
Water Street Healthcare Partners, 3255
Water-Jel, 1576
WaterCove Networks, 457
Waterfall Services, 2935
WaterGuru, 1099
Waterguru, 1352
WaterHealth International, 1607
Waterhealth International, 54
Waterlife, 2305
Waterline Data, 1028, 1203
Waterline Renewal Technologies, 248
Waterloo Brewing, 2165
Watermark Inc, 153
Watermark Inc., 3042
Waterside, 157
WaterSmart, 1442, 1978
WaterSmart Software, 1616
Waterstone Pharmaceuticals, 46, 1383
Waterton Polymer Products, 1545
Waterworks, 919
WatrHub, 2120
Watson Brown, 2708
Wattpad, 108, 1884, 2130, 2131, 2272
Waukesha Kramer, 719
Waupaca, 1089
WAVE, 2130
Wave, 828, 858, 1074, 1698, 2094, 2217
Wave Accounting, 457, 912
Wave Computing, 1781
Wave Electronics, 1971
Wave Life Sciences, 764, 1522
Wave Semiconductor, 1713
Wave Systems, 317, 1711
Wave Technology Solutions Group, 961
Wave VR, 1477
Wave3Studio, 3118
Wave7 Optics, 227
Wave7 Optics Inc., 2418
Wavebreak Media, 2909
WaveDivision Holdings, 1360
Wavefront, 1969
Waveguide Solutions, 1711
Waveguider Optical Telecom Technology, 2752
Waveland Investments, 3255
Wavelet, 1074
Wavelink Corporation, 1731, 1979
Wavemark Technologies, 1991
WaveMetrix, 50
Wavesmith Networks, 523
WaveStream, 133
WaveTec Vision, 39, 599, 764, 1930
WAVi, 1839
Wavii, 1800
Wavin, 2635
Wavion, 2532
Waxing the City, 1580
Way Up, 1186, 1533
Wayfair, 912, 1718

Portfolio Companies Index

Wayfarer, 1091
Wayfinder Resources, 1129
Wayhome, 2398
Waylo, 310
Waymark WSC Sports, 608
WAYN, 2653
Wayn, 3095
Wayne Trademark Printing & Packaging, 402
WayPay, 2024
Waypoint Homes, 828
Waypoint Leasing, 1314
Wayport, 1235, 1629, 1913, 3128
Wayside Technology Group, 3266
Wayspring, 1
WayUp, 321, 820, 1696
Wayve, 527, 648
Waywire (Magnify Networks), 1321
Waze, 299, 2822, 2943
Wazee Digital, 1021
Wazoku, 2986
Wazoo Sports, 1215
WC Leasing, 679
WCCT, 952
WCG, 172
WCS Europe, 2276
WD Diamonds, 963
WDP Holdings Corporation, 1494
WDT, 1773
We Are Colony, 3099
We Are Pop Up, 2419
We Hostels, 3199
WE Magazine, 2575
We Pay, 1969
We7, 2682
Weaber Inc., 578
Wealth Access, 1690
Wealth Engine, 646
Wealth Enhancement Group, 1127
WealthAccess, 570
WealthEngine, 1348, 1504
WealthForge, 1259
Wealthfront, 582, 877, 1563, 1696, 1698
WealthKernel, 3099
Wealthminder, 626
WealthNavi, 641
Wealthpoint Health Services, 2165
Wealthsimple, 2143, 2178, 2217
Wealthtracking, 1194
WealthTrust, 1377
Wearable Intelligence, 3090
Wearwell, 557
WearWorks, 1509
Weasler Engineering Inc., 989
Weather Analytics, 1076, 1172
Weather Trends International, 1084
Weatherhaven, 2121
Weathernews Inc, 3173
WeatherPredict, 1695
Weathershield, 1459
Weave, 79, 429, 564, 944, 945
Weavr, 2398
Web Geo Services, 3104
Web Methods, 31
Web Reservations International, 927
Web Tpa, 592
Webabcus Ltd, 2885
WebAction, 1754
Webair, 2074
Webbankir, 3141
Webchutney, 2549
WebCollage, 438
WebCollage and HSCG., 2770
WebCollage Inc., 2571
WebDialogs, 1915
Webdyn, 2472
Webedia, 3199, 3229
WebEquity, 92

Webify Solutions, 2653
WebInterpret, 3104
WebLayers, 3203
WebLinc, 949, 1547, 1605
Webline, 58
WebLink International, 86
WebLogic, 241
WebMethods, 957
Webmoco, 2958
WebOrder, 810
Webputty, 224
WebRadar, 1511
Webraska Mobile Technologies SA, 163
Webroot, 1187, 1608
Webroot Software, 1787
Webs, 1348
WebScal, 881
WebScale, 1247
Webscale, 252
Websense, 303, 1116
Webshots, 787, 1153, 1549, 1862
Websitebutler, 2832
Webspective, 1257
Webstep, 3067
Webtide, 1966
Webtrends, 782
WebVisible, 759
Webware.io, 2074
Wecash, 977
WeChi, 209
weComm, 2399
Weconnect, 420
Wedding Party, 1426
WeddingChannel.com, 1855
Weddington Way, 1032, 1534, 1855
WeddingWire, 429, 1712
Weddingwire, 1720
Wedeco Seed Fund I Ky Kb, 2731
Wedge Networks, 2043
Wedgewood Hospitality Group, 1494
Wedgewood Pharmacy, 1169
Wedgies, 59, 400, 1223
wedgies, 1914
Wedia, 3229
Wedit, 743
WeDo, 562, 2963, 3021
WedPics, 361, 975, 1364, 1847
Wedspire, 221
Weebly, 234, 752, 2011
Weeby.co, 938
WeeCare, 121, 729, 1698
WeedMD, 1194
Weekend Company, 3043
Weeks Service Company, 16
Weem, 1079
Weener Plastic GmbH, 1133
Weener Plastic Packaging Group, 2303
Weengs, 3099
Wefox, 1610, 3099
Weft, 1486
WeGather, 1618
WeGrow, 395
WeHeartIt, 1227, 1566, 1829
WeHeartPics, 2847
Wei Chai Shi, 1327
WEIC, 2965
Weight Watchers, 1022, 1138
Weilos, 1103
Weiman, 547
Weiyun, 2927
Weizuche, 821
weka.io, 1511
WekaIO, 1346
Welbe Health, 1147
WelbeHealth, 1
Welch ATM, 1582
Welcome, 744

Welcome Break, 1021
Welcome Dairy, 929
Welcu, 1832
Weldobot, 421
Welkin Health, 183
Well Bridge Health, 1452
Well Street Urgent Care, 790
Well-Foam, 441, 815
WellAWARE Systems, 1901
WellAwareSystems, 1
Wellbeats, 1117
Wellbore Solutions, 2623
Wellborn Forest, 920
Wellborn Forest Products, 1136, 1460
Wellcentive, 907, 1332
Wellco, 843
WellDoc, 183, 704, 1206, 1993
WellDog, 215, 1604
Weller, 328
Wellesley Pharmaceuticals, 1065
Wellfount, 150, 659
Wellframe, 610
WellGen Inc., 2389
Wellgood, 1588
Wellist, 1
Wellkeeper, 1299, 1926
Wellman, 1971
Wellman Plastics, 1041
Wellness Centers, 1194
WellnessFX, 1032, 1947
Wello, 1254, 1441
WellPartner, 1007
Wellpartner, 1198, 1250
Wellpass, 54
Wells-CTI, 1021
WellSheet, 269
WellSky, 1837
WellSpring Pharmaceutical Corporation, 1654
Wellspring Worldwide, 1242
Welltec International, 1754
WellTok, 1371
Welltok, 666, 749, 756, 941, 1014, 1237, 1511, 2126, 2681
WellTrack, 2192
Welltrack, 2024
WellTrackOne, 269, 644
Wellview, 1412
Welly, 1363
Welocalize, 1140, 1345
Welsh, 3245
Weltrend Semiconductor, 897
Welzorg, 2854
Wencor, 1368
Wendy's, 475
Wengo, 3199
Wenner Bread Products, 792
Wentorth Technology, 1165
Wentworth Senior Living Services, 464
Wentworth Technology Inc., 440
Wenzel, 447
Wenzel Spine, 991, 1803
Weole Ene, 3011
Weotta, 586, 1800
Wep, 2927
WePay, 200, 796, 978, 2011
WePow, 597, 1521
Wercker, 3215
WeRecover, 321
Werecover, 564
Werewolf, 1268
Werk, 901, 1703
Wermland Paper AB, 3045
Werner Holdings, 1115
Wertkarten AG, 2774
Wesabe, 1359
WESCO Aircraft, 66
WESCO International Inc., 576

Portfolio Companies Index

WeShare, 1426
Weskey Graphics, 2249
Wesley Clover Solutions, 2276
WeSpire, 498, 1104
Wespro, 2549
West Academic, 1115
West Academic Publishing, 699
West Allen Capital, 3264
West American Rubber Company, 989
West Coast Fitness, 424
West Corporation, 1508, 1818
West Dermatology LLC, 159
West Glen Town Center, 69
West Pharmaceuticals, 1456
West Point Resources, 2027
West Star Aviation, 1345
Westar Aerospace & Defense Group, 654
Westbrook, 1610
Westcoast Entertainment, 1294
Westec Interactive, 496
Westerlund Group, 2772
Western Building Centres Limited, 2129
Western Dentral, 1300
Western Emulsions, 1171
Western Forest Products, 2062, 2073
Western Glove Works, 2249
Western Industries, 338, 851
Western Jet Aviation, 441
Western Marketing, 1997
Western Nonwovens, 202
Western Oilfield Equipment Ltd., 677
Western Oilfield Equipment Rentals, 2022
Western Peterbilt Inc., 867
Western Reserve Products, 847
Western Seed, 54
Western Windows Systems, 408
Western Wireless Corp., 303
Westeryly Wind, 1897
WestFace Medical, 875
Westfalia, 2786
Westlake Hardware Inc., 847
Westland Technologies, 832
Westminster Foods, 1097
Westminster Healthcare, 1973
Westmoreland Advanced Materials, 296
Westmount Storefront Systems, 2039
Westny Building Products Company, 204
Weston Medical, 2998
Westpac Banking, 2650
Westridge Cabinets, 2246
Westwave Communications Inc., 255
Westwing, 2820, 2829, 3035
WestwoodOne, 874
Wethos, 354, 756, 937
Wetpaint, 582
Wetzel's Pretzels, 1115
Wevat, 3099
WeVideo, 1645
Wevorce, 600, 721, 773
WEVR, 308
WeVR, 1614, 1816
Wevr, 108, 601, 795
WeWork, 251, 582
WexEnergy, 705
WGT, 972
Wha Tap, 1511
Whale Communications, 2532
Whale Imaging, 1383
Wharfedale Hospital, 2740
Wharton Economics, 224
What 3 Words, 1985
What's In My Handbag, 2682
What's On India, 2992
WhatCounts, 1576
Wheel Pros, 502
Wheelabrator Technologies, 676
Wheelhouse, 354, 775, 1323

Wheels Up, 1589
Wheelwell, 1323
Wheelys, 1703
Whelan Refining Ltd, 2530
When I Work, 175, 631, 641
When.com, 1406
WHERE, 1084
Where, 1918
WhereNet, 556
Whereonearch, 2378
WhimseyBox, 1618
Whip Networks, 1006
Whip Tail Technologies, 1733
Whipclip, 752
Whisbi, 259, 2331
Whisk, 724, 1966
Whisper, 1666, 1760
Whistle, 597, 1534
Whistle Sports, 669, 817
Whistler, 1294
Whitcraft Group, 867, 1136, 1460
White Cap Industries, 1090
White Oak Resources, 45
White Ops, 3
White Ops, 1401
White Pine Company, 714
White Source, 1158
White Star Capital, 2074
White Swan Environmental Ltd., 2160
Whitebridge Pet Brands, 792
Whitecap Resources Inc., 2044
Whitecap Venture Partners, 2074
WhiteCoat, 976
WhiteDove Herbals, 1839
WhiteFence, 56
WhiteGlove Health, 679
Whitehall Specialties, 1174
Whitehat Jr., 1393
WhiteHat Security, 100, 810, 950, 1045, 1740, 2448
WhiteOps, 881
WhiteSmoke, 2905
WhiteSource, 1305
WhiteSwell, 984, 1522
Whitetruffle, 1254
Whitney International University System, 21
Whittl, 1364, 1385
Whitworth Tool, 402, 612
Whizz Kid Entertainment, 2862
Whizztek, 3039
Who Is Happy, 395
Who What Wear, 876, 1223, 1835
Who Works Around You Pte Ltd, 2464
WhoBet, 1862
Whodini, 1515
Whoknows, 802
Whole Biome, 108
Wholesale Floors, 1729
Wholeshare, 596, 1254
Wholesome Goodness, 1050
Wholesome Pet Care, 1769
Wholesome Sweetners, 1518
WHOOP, 1263
Whoop, 1491
Whos Here, 1121
WhoSay, 1479
Whoseyourlandlord, 1509
Wibbitz, 259, 2822, 2863, 2938
Wibidata, 389
Wibotic, 2007
WiBotics, 521
WiChorus, 1449, 1537
Wicked Quick, 1384
Wicket Labs, 1162
Wickr, 93
Wicks Educational Publishing, 1984
Wide Corporat, 2406

Wide Open Spaces, 635
WiDeFi, 215, 994
WideOpenWest, 1360
WideOrbit, 876, 925, 1187
WiderThan, 1137
Widerthan, 967
Widespace, 3004
Widetronix, 609, 1479
Widevine Technologies, 1908
Widyard, 1881
Wifi Slam, 1658
Wifidabba, 624
Wigwag, 945
Wikia, 1006, 1374, 1867
Wikicell, 1464
Wikitude, 3156
WIL Research Laboratories, 248
Wiland, 337
Wilbanks Trucking and Wilbanks Leasing, 1376
Wilcon, 1410
Wild Earth, 720
Wild Pocketsm Xactly, 980
Wild Sports, 412, 445
Wild Tangent, 58, 2073
Wild Things, 290, 1955
Wild Type, 1238
Wild VR, 1384
Wildcard, 1701
Wildcat Discovery Technologies, 11, 992, 3213
Wildcomm, 1239
Wildfang, 221, 1384, 1914
Wildfire, 1840
Wildflower, 644
Wildflower Health, 918, 921
WildTangent, 877, 1162, 1235, 1706
Wildworks, 1679
Wilex AG, 3187
Wiliot, 1346, 1511
Wilke-Rodriguez, 799
Wilks Broadcast Group, 1984
Will Ventures, 3263
Willa Skincare, 1907
Willamette Broadband, 266
Willcall, 1752
WillCare, 1753
Willert Home Products, 60, 60
Willful, 2251
William Blair, 3262
William Hill, 2596, 2635
Williams Controls, 110
Williams Healthcare, 1294
Williams Scotsman, 1368
Williams Scotsman Inc., 576
Williams Scotsman International Inc., 1905
Williams Sonoma, 303
Willie's Grill & Icehouse, 479
Willie's Reserve, 966, 1866
Willing, 14
Willis Towers Watson Plc., 1905
Willo, 1079
Willow, 1993
Willtek, 1021
WilmerHale, 3262
Wilmington Pharmaceuticals, 1987
Wilocity, 1781
Wilson, 505
Wilson Electronics, 1707
Wilson Farms Inc., 357
Wilson Leather, 847
Wilson Logistics Group, 2999
Wilson Sonsini Goodrich & Rosati, 3262
Wilson Therapeutics, 2972
Wilton Corporation, 1294
Wilton Re, 790
Wily Technology, 759
Wimba, 22, 162, 1130, 1731
Wimba Inc., 813

Portfolio Companies Index

Wimp, 2722
Win-Win, 221
Winbond Electronics, 897
Winc, 121, 400, 562
Winchester Electronics, 197, 557
Winco Mfg, 402
Wincore Window Company, 1565
Wind Corporation Australia, 2636
Wind Point Partners, 3255
Wind River, 952, 1837
Wind River Environmental, 886
Wind River Environmental LLC, 449
Wind River Systems/Rapid Logic, 1287
Wind Telecom S.p.A., 1160
Wind Towers Ltd, 3126
WindBorne, 1426
Windborne, 1879
Windebow Inc., 331
Windeln.de, 2659
Windfall, 309
WindGap, 1104
WindGap Medical, 1987
Windlab Systems, 2514
Windmill Farms, 2198
Window Nation, 547
Windowfarms, 354
Windplus, 3039
Windsor, 1755
Windsor Circle, 289, 520, 975, 1385, 1847
Windsor Fine Jewelers, 92
Windstream, 62
Windward Petroleum, 1118
Windy City Wire, 1343
Windy Hill Medical, 189
Wine Access, 1346
Wine In Black, 641, 3021
Wine in Black, 3047
Wine in style, 2845
Wine.com, 226, 1600
WineCare Storage, 1450
Winery Exchange, 1740
WiNetworks, 438, 2571
Wing Power Energy, 1737
Wingocard, 2090
Wingu, 311
Winking Entertainment, 1840
Winky Lux, 484, 1703
Winland Electronics, 3268
Winlocal, 2466
Winnie, 944, 1530, 1555
Winnow, 3099
Winoa, 1089
Winona Capital Management LLC, 3255
Winshuttle Holdings, 1754
Winsight, 1410
Winsol, 2492
Winston Furniture Company, 1574
Wintegra, 1798, 2943
Wintek, 897
Winter Bros. Waste Systems, 2075
Winterlight, 875
Winterthur Technologie, 2913
WinZip, 1912
Wipfli, 3268
WIRB Group Holdings, 364
Wire IE, 2081
Wire-e Limited, 2885
WireCo, 1848, 2201
WireCo WorldGroup, 1138
Wired Minds, 2629
Wired Ventures, 1731
Wiredbenefits Inc., 1093
WiredPlanet, 115
WiredScore, 728
Wireless Access, 1091
Wireless China, 1084
Wireless Environment, 1051

Wireless Glue, 499
Wireless Security Corp., 414
Wireless Seismic, 2691
Wireless Services Corporation, 1640
Wireless World Net, 1394
Wireline, 1131
Wirescan, 2623
Wiretap, 1051
WireWax, 3021
WireX, 2943
Wirkaufens, 3035
WIS Intl., 448
Wisair Inc., 3149
Wischip, 2427
Wisconsin Cheese Group, 1163
Wisconsin Cheese Group Holding LLC, 449
Wisconsin Coil Spring, 402
WisdomTree Investments, 751
Wise, 640
Wise Apple, 1483
Wise Company, 1859
Wise Connect, 367
Wise Foods Inc., 1404
Wise Giant Enterprise, 2844
Wise Media, 3199
Wise.io, 1947
Wiseasy, 977
WiseBanyan, 998
Wisebanyan, 1703
WiseGate, 1843
Wisegate, 447, 845
WISeKey, 895
Wisely, 2178
WiseNut, 1091
Wiser Oil Company, 617
Wiser Together, 881, 907
WISErg, 1644
Wisers, 2724
WiserTogether, 291
Wiseware Technology, 2594
Wish, 108, 669, 720, 778, 827, 1800, 1841, 2009
Wish.com, 91
Wishabi, 1310
WishFin, 1669
Wisk, 2176
Wisk Bar Inventory, 2204
Wison Chemical Engineering, 2425
WiSpry, 459, 621, 983, 1401
wiSpry, 1667
Wisr, 1051
Wistron, 2427
Wistron NeWeb, 1771
Wit.AI, 1800
Within3, 644
Withings, 3199
Withum, 3262
WiTricity, 754
Wittlebee, 1254
WittyCircle, 1370
Wix.com, 251
Wixpress, 582
Wiz Korea, 1576
Wizdee, 3039
Wize, 2204
Wize Commerce, 1257, 1498
WizeHive, 1581
Wizeline, 136, 320, 1153, 2009
Wizely Finance, 49
Wizi to Find, 3039
WiZR, 49
WJ Communications, 781
WL Plastics, 1377
WLAN, 3223
Wloclawek, 2697
WME/IMG, 1685
WMI, 902
WMI Holdings, 1955

WochIt, 876
Wochit, 438, 1537
Wohler Technologies Inc., 906
Wolf, 1507
Wolf & Shepherd, 1023
Wolf Hills Energy, 1797
Wolf Medical Systems, 2083
Wolf Minerals Limited, 1551
Wolfe Diversified, 659
Wolfpack, 659
Wolfpak Software, 458
Wolfson, 3095
Wollit, 2398
Wolverine Advanced Materials, 2008
Wolverine Heaters, 911
Wolverine Venture Fund, 3259
Woman Journal, 3229
Wombat, 1451
Wombat Security, 296
Wombo, 3099
Women's Care Florida, 1169
Women's Diagnostic of Texas, 405
Women's Marketing, 747, 1461
Women.com, 59, 721, 1153
Womply, 183, 289, 586, 1219, 1310, 1606
Wonda VR, 1554
Wonder, 447, 724, 879
Wonder Workshop, 1162, 1983
Wonderhill, 1323
Wonderschool, 545, 641, 945, 1554
Wondery, 259
Wonga, 2829
Wonga.com, 1213, 1361
Wonil Co., 2993
Wonolo, 565
WOO, 1719
Woo Sports, 1104
Wood Associates, 799
Wood Mackenzie, 927, 2547
Wood Pro, 1216
WoodallBs, 1438
Woodboard, 1713
Woodbury Health Products, 1271
Woodcraft Industries, 1372
Woodcrafts Industries, 847
Woodla, 2847
Woodland, 2037
Woodland Biofuels, 2054, 2153
Woodmarc, 445
WoodPellets.com, 1248
Woodscamp, 2148
WoodSpring Hotels Holdings, 1133
Woodstream, 745
Woodstream Corp., 791
Woodtric, 945
Woodwing Communications Systems, 1348
Wooga, 938, 1798, 2469, 2820, 2829
Wool And The Gang, 2743
Wool and the Gang, 2963
Woolpert, 1145
Woolsey Pharmaceuticals, 663
Woolworths, 2650
Wooly, 79
Woosh Wireless, 496
Wootmath, 779
Wootric, 1610
Woowa Brothers, 872
Wooyang HC, 3136
Worcester Brush, 1294
Wordlock, 68, 1087
Wordsentry, 659
WordStream, 225
Wordstream, 1675
Work 'n Gear, 224, 1955
Work America, 1925
Work Board, 1158
Work Hands, 600

Portfolio Companies Index

Work Hound, 640
Work Market, 779
Work Options Group, 1156
Work Truck Solutions, 207, 208, 845, 1759
Workable, 2469
Workamerica, 54
Workato, 1610
Workboard, 752, 857, 1382
Workbrain, 22, 2073
Workday, 265
Workface, 1645
Workflex Solutions, 481
Workflow, 680
Workforce Insight, 225
Workframe, 1918
Workfrom, 221
WorkFront, 696, 872, 1045
Workfront, 1949
WorkFusion, 1247, 1598, 2126, 2150
Workhorse Rail, 1343
WorkingOn, 310
Workit Health, 1155
Worklete, 48
WorkLife, 1154
Worklytics, 798
WorkMarter, 1718
Workplace, 815
Workpoint Creative TV, 1143
Workpop, 1363, 1527
WorkRails, 308
WorkRamp, 1760
Works, 2107
Workscape, 958, 2688
Workshare, 3095
Workspace.com, 1298
WorkSpan, 1187
Workspot, 1511, 1840, 1969
Worksteady, 1569
Workstream, 235
Worktile, 2430
Workwave, 470
WorkWell Medical Group, 1612
WorkWell Systems, 1239
World 50, 470, 1169, 1410
World and Main, 1138
World Aware, 1140
World Desk, 2939
World Energy Partners, 531, 1328
World Freight Company International, 867, 2332
World Golf Tour, 1411
World Health Club, 2014
World Heart Corp., 1918
World Kitchen, 1949
World Of Angus, 2107
World Oil Properties Inc., 1326
World Power Technologies, 405
World Power Technology Senasis Technologies, 1674
World View, 232, 795, 1346, 1914
World Wide Packaging, 1343
World Wide Packets, 163, 218
World-Check, 1720
WorldCover, 1269, 1330
Worldfirst, 796
WorldHaus, 976
WorldPay, 223
Worldremit, 3047
Worldsensing, 2183
WorldStrides, 458, 1410
WorldTicket, 3194
Worldwide Clinical Trials, 1049
Worldwide Coatings, 2604
Worldwide Express, 1499, 1507
Worldwide Facilities, 1151
Worldwide Semicondctor, 3209
Worldwide Semiconductor, 2594
Worldwide Wireless, 1766

Worldwise Education, 1065
WorldxChange, 3159
Worley Catastrophe Response, 60
Worley Company, 60
Wornick Company, 1927
Worthy, 1323, 3212
Worximity, 2074
Would Care Solutions Inc., 654
Wound Care Specialists, 559
Wove, 129, 1385
Woven Orthopedics, 59, 1065
Wow Tv, 2960
WOW!, 560
Wow! Nutrition, 1376
Wowd, 1088
WowkKast, 624
Wowza Media Systems, 1754
WP Engine, 1687
WP Global Partners, 3255
Wpg Holding, 2427
Wrapp, 877, 2437, 2628
Wrc Media, 1949
WRCA, 1089
Wrench, 1162
WRG, 2935
Wriggle, 3099
Wright Electric, 1896
Wright Therapy Products, 296, 1451, 1452
Wrike, 1629
Wrist, 2376
WriteLab, 1530
WritePath, 3029
Writtle, 1929
WRJ Design Associates, 679
Wrk, 2122
Wroclaw, 2697, 2697
WRSCompass, 654
WS Beteiligungs AG, 2774
WSC, 1589
WSE Corporation, 2594
WSH, 2956
WSI, 2472
WSO2, 1831
WT Hardwoods Group, 1548
WTE Corporation, 1176
WTG, 3088
Wthn, 1768
Wuaki.tv, 2460
Wuhan Groce Nordic New Energy, 2575
Wumart Group, 2841
Wummel Kiste, 304
WunderCar, 1418
Wunderdata, 3226
Wunderflats, 2832
Wunderlich, 96
Wurb, 1760
Wurldtech, 2270
Wuu, 789
Wuxi AppTec, 2724
Wuxi Lead Auto Equipment, 2927
Wuzhen Tourism Development, 2838
WWNET, 3223
WWRD, 1089
Wylan Energy, 289
Wyle, 1138
Wyle Laboratories, 377
wymsee, 536
Wynd, 568, 1983
Wyndham Garden, 1167
Wyng, 655, 925, 1610
Wynn Resorts, 874
Wynnchurch Capital, 3255
Wyoming Authentic Products, 679
Wyplay, 2684
Wyre, 310
Wysdom, 2073, 2176
Wysdom AI, 2060, 2240

Wyse Meter Solutions, 2200
Wythe Will Distributing, 1971
W☐rk, 99, 152, 395, 1443, 1613, 1810

X

X Genomes, 398
X Matters, 1045
X Radio Express, 2674
X VERLEIH, 3181
X-1 Audio, 1744
X-Cell Medical, 2739
X-Ceptor, 1414
X-COM, 1839
X-COR Therapeutics, 849
X-EMI, 1170
X., 744, 2006
X.ai, 721, 1483, 1701
X1, 976
X2 TV, 3043
X2O Media, 2051
X5 Music Group, 3004
Xaar, 2653
Xact, 322
Xact Medical, 481
Xactly, 87, 241, 342, 646, 1390, 1464
Xactly Corporation, 1543
Xad, 666
xAD, 1403
xAd, 1701
Xafinity, 2667
Xage, 490
Xage Security, 812, 1812
Xagenic, 622
Xaloy Inc., 989
Xamarin, 457, 752
Xambala, 624, 972, 1247, 1795
Xanadu, 2126, 2130, 2131
Xand, 1730
XanEdu, 1459
Xango, 1537
Xanitos, 254
XANT, 959
Xapix, 2398
Xapo, 108, 666, 877, 1563, 1696, 1998
XaQti Corporation, 3157
Xavis, 3118
XAware Inc., 813
Xcalar, 1219
Xceive, 1924
Xcel Brands, 940
Xcelerate Media, 1547
xceligent, 1645
Xcellenet, 782
Xcellerex, 1908
Xcellsyz, 2474
Xcerion, 3004
Xcess Able, 1739
Xchanging, 38
XCharge, 827
XCMG, 475
Xconomy, 536, 1101
Xcovery, 949
XCures, 1099
xCures, 2270
Xcyte, 1578
Xcyte Therapies, 154, 755
XDx, 596
Xeal, 2037
Xebec, 167
XebiaLabs, 1888
Xeikon, 194
Xelerated, 2378
Xello, 2065
Xemi Interactive, 2848
Xemics Ltd, 3153
Xencor, 1395
Xendit, 1079

Portfolio Companies Index

Xeneta, 2628, 3035
Xenex Disinfection Services Inc., 698
Xenikos, 1522
Xenio, 5
Xenogen, 468
Xenolith, 3230
Xenomorph, 2986
Xenon, 1014, 3076
Xenon Pharmaceuticals, 3006
XenoPort, 785, 1693
Xenoport, 154
Xention, 2739, 2909, 3061
Xeris, 447
Xeris Pharmaceuticals, 240
Xero, 1899
Xeros, 2701, 2883, 3019
XOSoft, 1042
xF Technologies, 550
XFactor Ventures, 3263
Xfera, 2953
Xfire, 827, 1832
xG Health Solutions, 1361
XGen AI, 754
Xgenomes, 798
Xhockware, 3039
XHoogee, 1511
Xi'an Longi Silicon, 2533
Xi'an Supermicro, 2448
Xiabu Xiabu, 819
Xiamen Orient Wanli Stone, 3084
Xiangwushuo, 827
Xiaomi, 1184, 2969
Xicato, 127, 1247
XIFIN, 318, 889
Xign, 796
Xignal, 3128
Xignite, 100, 1740, 1741
Xilinx, 200, 564
Xillinx, 1684
Xillis, 1426
Ximedica, 1631
XIMMERSE, 1511
Xin Hee Co. Limited, 1092
Xin Hua Media Coldings, 1771
Xing, 2466
Xing AG, 2595
Xinlab, 624
Xintec, 3209
Xinya Paper Group, 2533
XIO, 1361
XIOLINK, 60
Xiolink, 60
Xiotech, 646
XipLink, 2051
Xirgo Technologies, 408, 904
Xiring, 3104
Xiron, 2570
Xirrus, 200, 389, 1014, 1517
Xishiwang, 597
xishiwang.com, 2970
Xite, 2813
Xitec Software, 2653
Xixun, 1340
XL Fleet, 2
XL Hybrids, 534, 1258
XLA, 899
Xlerant, 477
XLerate Group, 963
Xlumena, 137, 179, 186, 460
XM, 925
XM Satellite Radio Holdings, 1160
xMatters, 646
XMG Studio, 2165
Xmos, 773, 2314, 2653, 2665
Xnor.Ai, 207, 1162
Xnor.ai, 431
XO, 221
XO Soft, 609

Xobni, 234, 2437
Xockets, 1254
XOEye Technologies, 461, 985
Xoft, 1578
Xoft Inc., 573
Xola, 246, 387
Xolve, 1291, 2002
Xoma, 1456, 1619
Xometry, 305, 812, 938, 1172
Xoom, 582, 840, 1341
XOR Technologies, 3115
Xora, 593, 810, 1728
Xori, 154
XOS Digital, 290, 1316
XOSoft, 1042
XP Investimentos, 819
XParcels, 2263
Xpedion Design Systems, 1795
xPeerient, 1737
Xpeng, 977
Xperiel, 527
Xpertize, 2417
XpertSea, 1363
XPi, 2051
Xplanation International, 2554
Xplenty, 2943
Xploadr, 310
Xplore, 1616
Xplornet, 429
Xpress Natural Gas, 1626
Xpressdocs, 912, 1464
XQuest, 1087
XRS, 1852, 3268
XS, 1711
XServ, 2956
xSides, 651
Xsigo, 564
Xsigo Systems, 1478, 1840
XSInc, 1255
Xtalic, 646, 1184
Xtelligent, 2001
Xtellus, 2372
Xtempus, 3170
Xtend Healthcare, 1979
Xtera, 652, 949, 1310, 1661, 1843, 3128
Xtera Communications, 154, 255, 1170, 3061
Xtime, 610
Xtium, 1381
XTL, 2576
Xtourmaker, 3039
Xtra-vision, 940
Xtra-Vision PLC, 1294
Xtract, 2628
Xtraction Services, 156
Xtralis, 3016
Xtralis Group, 303
Xtreme Alternative Defense Systems, 659
Xtreme Cinemas, 2374
Xtreme Power, 949, 1607
XtremeSpectrum, 1348
XTUIT, 2086
Xtuit Pharmaceuticals, 158, 1464
Xueersi, 1091
Xumii, 361, 2609, 2844
Xunlei, 2724, 2841
Xunlight, 1852
Xvionics, 1636
Xwing, 680
Xwork, 721
XY Verify, 1690
Xylan Corporation, 1091
Xyleme, 1966
Xylos, 1771
Xylowatt, 3216
Xymax, 3173
Xymetrex, 838
Xymox Technologies Inc., 948

Xypoint, 3170

Y

Y Combinator, 2321
Y International, 1576
Y's Therapeutics, 2961
Y-T Holdco, 445
Yac, 754
Yachtlife, 567
Yada, 1426
Yadii, 2838
Yadkin Financial, 1746
Yahoo!, 775
Yakima, 153
Yaletown, 2028
Yalo, 1672
Yamaha, 217
Yambay Technologies Pty Limited, 2706
Yammer, 457, 610, 666, 1213, 1698
Yandex, 89
Yango.com, 2009
Yankee Candle, 1160
Yanta Financial Technologies, 176
Yantai Beacon, 698
Yantra, 2073
Yaoshibang, 1828
Yap, 907, 1757
Yap.tv, 304
Yapp, 568
Yapstone, 336, 1213
Yapta, 241, 1947, 2272
Yardbarker, 234
Yardbarker Inc., 1093
Yardsale, 1549
YASA Motors, 3019
yasni, 2970
Yasso, 332, 424, 1527
Yatra, 2549
Yattos, 327
YayPay, 2146
Yaypay, 275
YBR Group, 1929
Ybrant, 1361
YCD Multimedia, 2419, 2905
YCD-Multimedia, 2557
YD, 2331
YDesign Group, 92
YDI Wireless, 215
Ydilo, 2953
Ydreams, 2708
Yeahka, 2860
Yeecare, 2841
Yeelight, 1709
YeePay, 908, 2658
Yeildmo, 151
Yello, 162, 733, 1045
Yello Mobile, 309
Yellow Bird Sauce, 546
Yellow Book USA, 1929
Yellowbrick, 610, 1203
YellowDig, 1589
Yellowdig, 1581
YellowJacket, 535
Yellowstone Landscape, 917
Yellowtag, 2565
Yelp, 582, 660, 1341
Yeongcheon Daegu Tongil Madang Co., 585
YepDoc, 2820
Yerdle, 493, 596, 1236, 1978
Yes Bank, 2425, 2590, 2591
YesGraph, 1322, 1521
Yesky, 2841
Yesmywine.com, 597
YesVideo, 388
Yesware, 779, 1566, 2130, 2131
Yet Analytics, 881, 1703
Yeti, 547

Portfolio Companies Index

Yext, 1006
YG, 3136
YG Entertainment, 1092
Ygrene Energy Fund, 1127
Yhat, 308, 535
YI Tunnel, 222
Yicha, 2575
Yieh United Steel, 2427
Yield Dynamics, 526
YieldBot, 536, 1290, 1597, 1691
Yieldex, 925, 1848
Yieldify, 587, 2825
YieldMetrics, 2640
YieldMo, 581, 724, 818, 1829
Yieldr, 1418
YieldStreet, 708
Yifang, 3091
YiFeng Pharmacy Chain, 2551
Yioula, 2775
Yip Yap, 1509
Yipes, 564
Yipit, 609, 938, 1479, 1597
Yipit Data, 308
Yixia, 1537
Yixin Group, 977
Ykone, 2684
YLG, 2809
YLX Corp., 808
YMAX, 595
Yo! Sushi, 1518
Yobi, 395
YoBon, 1924
Yobongo, 787
Yodas, 1677
YodelTalk, 3099
Yodle, 610, 972, 1235
Yodlee, 1006, 1949
Yodo1, 3112
YogaWorks, 862
Yogen Fr z, 2245
YoGov, 798
Yogurty's, 2245
Yoho.com, 2570
Yoi, 1059
Yoics, 810
Yoka, 925, 2841
Yokel, 313
Yom Chai, 2836
Yongche.com, 597, 3241
Yoni Circle, 321
Yonkers, 2956
Yooli, 3091
York, 2201
York Insurance Services, 1368
York Risk Services, 1275
York Wallcoverings, 934
Yorktel, 3266
Yoshi, 821
Yoshirt, 1223
Yosko, 1618
Yotascale, 1809
Yotpo, 1001, 3072
Yotrio Group, 2533
Yotta Yotta, 2254
Yottaa, 820
YottaMark, 185, 713, 1821
You Now, 1682
You Yi Shopping City, 897
YouAre.TV, 1701
YouBeauty, 535
youbeQ, 3039
Youblisher.com, 2302
YouCaring, 92
YouDinner, 669
YouEarnedIt, 1259, 1566
Youku, 474
YouLicense, 3231

YouMail, 1908, 1966
Young & Rubicam, 927
Young Alfred, 1426
Young America, 1169
Young Broadcasters of America, 1101
Young Fast Optoelectronics, 2594
Young Innovations, 747, 1049, 1132
Younity, 3046
YouNow, 520, 1884, 1918
Your Cause, 1499
Your Fare, 229
Your Mechanic, 945, 1101
Your Pie, 825
Your Vets, 2958
YourBevCo, 270
YouRenew.com, 679, 1101
YourGrind, 2620
YourMechanic, 587, 1491, 1702, 1928
YourMembership.com, 1576
Yours, 310
YouSendIt, 56
YouSolar, 1065
Youstake, 1589
Youtiligent, 544
YouTube, 177
Youxigu, 3133
Youxinpai, 597
Yoyi, 3133
YoYi Media, 1361
Yozan, 2763
Yozio, 773, 980, 1254, 1969
YPD Online, 3214
YPlan, 1327, 3009
YPrime, 227
YPS Anesthesia Services, 427
YPX Caman Holdings, 1241
YRC Worldwide, 2067
YSS, 2233
Ytel, 162
Yuanta Financial Group, 2624
Yubico, 1669
Yuchai, 585
Yuchai Engineering, 897
Yuhu, 2131
Yuilop, 2978
Yulife, 2398
YuMe, 582, 641, 1203, 1840, 3089, 3225
Yumi, 328, 545
Yummly, 1442
YunDing, 222
Yunhan Financial Technology, 222
Yunshan Networks, 1537
Yuntaa, 2417
Yup Technologies, 752
Yurbuds, 334, 570
Yusin, 3136
Yvolver, 583, 1684
YY.com, 3133
Yyoga, 2225

Z

Z Gallerie, 337
z-kat, 1771
Z-Medica, 639, 1132
Z2Live, 610
Zaarly, 720, 1079, 1121
Zaask, 3039
Zacharon Pharmaceuticals, 209
Zadego, 2629
Zadig & Voltaire, 1778
Zadspace, 60, 60, 794, 830, 1101
Zady, 1290, 1701
Zaffire, 1008
Zaffre Investments, 3263
Zafgen, 193, 764, 1522, 1814
Zagster, 498, 655, 762, 1101, 1104, 3245
Zaius, 1184

Zalando, 2820, 2829, 3161
Zale, 843
Zalicas Inc., 2776
Zalicus, 748
Zaloni, 225, 1672
Zalora, 3161
Zameen Organic, 2305
Zamma Corporation, 1565
Zamplus Technology, 1340
Zana, 289
Zanbato, 304, 1719, 1969
Zando, 3161
Zantaz, 627, 1354
Zanui, 3161
Zap, 1691, 1966
Zap China JV, 2567
Zap Group, 136
Zapata, 575
Zaperio Technologies, 58
ZapInfo, 1659
Zapoint, 1737
Zappli, 776
Zappos, 1235
Zappos.com, 31, 327, 840, 1798
ZappPx, 1734
Zappware, 2940
Zapya, 977
Zaranga, 965, 1752
Zarbee's, 1092
Zarodex, 1631
ZARS Pharma, 1679
Zartis, 2347
Zatarain's, 357
Zattikka, 3005
Zauber, 2461
Zavante, 73, 785
Zavation Medical Products, 1148
Zawatt, 2637
Zaxel, 217
Zayo, 443, 745, 912
Zayo Bandwidth, 1157
Zayo Group, 458, 872, 889, 1361, 2371
Zazma, 1718
Zazzle, 1079, 1608
Zazzle.com, 624, 1341, 1449
ZBD, 3186
ZBest Technology Company, 2752
Zbird, 2575
Zbird Online Diamonds, 2551
Zcool, 925
Ze-Gen, 1449
ZeaChem, 731, 839, 1195, 1247, 1449, 1474
ZeaKal, 2233
Zealand Pharma, 2346, 2867, 3140
Zealand Pharma A/S, 190
Zealot Networks Inc., 334
Zeb, 3255
Zebek, 1244
Zebit, 545, 1106, 1247, 1985
Zebra, 601
Zebra Imaging, 1947
Zebra Technologies, 303
Zechstein Energy Storage, 898
Zecter, 1449
Zed Group, 1929
Zeel, 669, 945, 1121, 1358, 1490
Zeelo, 640
ZeeMee, 299
Zeevo, 186
ZeeWaves Systems Inc., 813
ZEFR, 1702, 1816
Zefr, 720, 1006, 1103, 1242, 1666, 1881
Zego, 2469
Zeilenwert, 2518
Zelis, 655
Zella, 3017
Zellwerk GmbH, 3181

Portfolio Companies Index

Zeltic, 785
ZELTIQ, 1421
Zeltiq, 73, 1918
Zemanta, 2682
Zemax, 167
Zembula, 1659
Zen Holdings, 2848
Zenalytic Laboratories, 2095
Zenasis, 95
Zenbase, 2122
Zenbox, 1549
Zencity, 1158
Zend, 218, 1623
Zend Technologies, 3221
Zendesk, 251, 457, 1006, 1184, 1537
ZenDrive, 305, 708
Zendrive, 44, 108
Zenefits, 520, 1006
Zenflow, 845
Zenfolio Inc., 406, 448
ZeniMax Media, 1498
Zenith, 1256
Zenith Adminstators, 377
Zenith American Solutions, 247
Zenith Energy, 1066
Zenith Products Corp., 458
Zenith Vehicle Contracts Ltd., 2668
Zenith-Leaerive, 2935
Zenium, 1314
ZenMate, 3047
Zenomics, 738
Zenoss, 120, 318, 881, 1013, 1172, 1754
Zenoti, 1346
ZenPayroll, 586
Zenph Sound Innovations, 1013
Zenplaya, 1305
ZenPrint, 1074
Zenprise, 241, 1543, 1666
Zenprop, 2700
Zenput, 1028, 2272
Zenrex, 177
Zensar Technologies, 136
Zensar Technologies Ltd, 2685
Zenso, 2358
Zensurance, 2094
Zention Limited, 2972
Zentiva, 61
Zentri, 252
Zenverge, 597, 1928, 2005
Zenysis, 1330
ZeOmega, 336
Zeomega, 1618
Zep Solar, 549
Zepheira, 2187
Zephyr, 116, 456
Zephyr Health, 972
Zephyr Investments Limited, 153
Zephyr Technology, 2844
Zephyrus, 1238
Zeplin, 752
Zerbee's, 1707
ZergNet, 259
Zerista, 1074
Zero, 680, 1121
Zero Acre Farms, 2131
Zero G, 1305
Zero Stack, 773
Zero2IPO, 1740, 2448
ZeroChroma, 1172
ZeroFOX, 540, 938
ZeroFox, 818
zeroheight, 798
0-In Design, 1976
ZeroLight, 3042
01 Communique, 2051
ZeroTurnaround, 224
02 RegenTech, 1051

ZeroVM, 1550
000 Mile, 467
Zerply, 1370, 1521
Zerto, 1006, 1598
Zerve, 1290
Zest, 1563
Zest Dental, 212
Zest Finance, 646, 756, 1800, 1890
Zest Health, 583, 1121
Zesta, 2009
ZestFinance, 1122, 1184
Zestful, 321
Zesty, 763, 3021
Zeta Global, 1672
Zeta Interactive, 1021
ZetrOZ, 1748
Zetta, 1028
Zetta.net, 116, 773
ZettaCom, 1021
Zettaset, 936
Zettics, 1050, 1947
Zeus, 246, 320, 752, 1323, 2665, 3095
Zeus Technology, 2653
Zeuss, 770, 1172
Zevia, 1324, 1344
Zhaogang.com, 3241
Zhena's, 1527
Zhilabs, 2539
Zhima Credit, 2396
Zhizhen Node, 2841
Zhone, 961
Zhongdian Biotech, 2575
Zhongsheng Group, 819
Zhongsou, 2841
Zhuhai Power Plant, 2582
Zhuhai Yueke Tsinghua Electronic Ceramics, 2793
Zi-Lift, 468
Ziani's, 2723
Ziarco, 113
Zibby, 1240
ZicroData, 952
Ziebel, 2691, 3207
Zift Solutions, 1076, 1712
Ziften, 1843
Zigfu, 1585
Ziggo, 56, 745
Ziggs.com, 192
Zigzag, 100
Ziibra, 310
Ziiproom, 1104
Zikon, 650
Zilift, 2691, 3090, 3207
Zilker Brewing, 447
Zillabyte, 610, 1223
Zilliant, 414, 1843
Zim's Crack Creme, 632
Zimbio, 31
Zimbra, 1478, 1537
Zimmer Spine, 3268
Zimory, 2629
Zimperium, 1614, 1672
ZIN s.r.o., 3113
Zinc, 812, 925
ZincFive, 127
Zinch, 1323, 1483
Zing, 450
ZING Systems, 1449
ZingBox, 604, 2430
ZingFront, 222
Zingle, 309, 562
Zinio Systems, 523, 1403
Zinion, 949
Zinkia, 2460
ZinniaTek, 2969
Zinwave, 3095
Zio, 659

Zip The Strip, 515
Zip2, 925, 1247
Zipbooks, 79
ZipCar, 251, 1449
Zipcar, 1213
Zipdrug, 527, 1155, 1533
Zipfit Denim, 1023
Zipit, 1215, 1925
Zipit Wireless, 1757, 1994
Zipline, 321, 720
ZipLine Medical, 493, 2010
ZipList, 1701
Ziplogix, 1645
Ziplunch, 2122
Zipmark, 535, 1358, 1407, 1479, 1635
Zipments, 473, 744
Zipnosis, 175, 178, 1605
Zipongo, 246, 704, 1187, 1525
Zippin, 1426
Zippity, 1104
Zipprecruiter, 1006
Zippy App, 1671
ZipRealty, 649
ZipScene, 481, 1050
Ziptronix, 1013
Zipwhip, 1158
ZipZap, 304
Ziqitza Health Care Ltd., 54
Zira.ai, 321
Zirmed, 822
Zirtual, 1800, 1914
Zitra, 3161
Ziva, 2262
Ziva Software, 3010
Zivame.com, 2840
Zive, 296
Zivix, 3268
Zixi, 1630
Zkey.com, 2020
Zlango, 582
Zmags, 1334, 2262
Zmanda, 2809
ZMP Inc., 2406
Znode, 1556
ZocDoc, 265, 778, 2437
Zodiac, 527
Zodius, 298
Zoetis, 15
Zogenix, 470, 1629, 1820
Zola, 399, 520, 763, 846
Zola Electric, 812
Zolk, 2909
Zollo, 2994
Zolo Technologies, 549
Zomay Marine and Logistics, 1167
Zonare, 178
Zone Holding, 3045
Zone Labs, 1042, 1629
Zone Reactor, 2020
Zone2, 296
Zone3, 2255
Zonnecentrale Limburg, 2940
Zonoff, 1901
Zonton, 1340
Zoocasa, 2128, 2143
Zoom, 108, 666, 1716, 2822
Zoom Information, 523
Zoom Media Group, 21
Zoom+, 674
Zoom.AI, 2107
Zoom.ai, 2132
ZoomCar India, 1330
ZoomData, 520
ZoomInfo, 1918
Zoomo, 2037
ZoomThru, 999
Zoona, 1374

Portfolio Companies Index

Zoopla Property Group, 3009
ZoOpt, 2408
Zoorate, 3043
Zoosk, 116, 185, 389, 549
ZooskottaMark, 185
Zootrock, 1752
Zoove, 1411
Zoox, 610, 803, 1155
Zooz, 387, 2010, 2938, 3072
Zopa, 2441, 2469, 2743, 3223
Zoran, 538
Zorch, 341
Zorch International, 454, 1625
Zorg Domein, 1115
Zosano Pharma, 1492, 2998
Zowdow, 101, 976
Zozi, 1101, 1310
Zrinse, 945
ZS Pharma, 1522, 1578, 1700
Zscaler, 579, 604
ZSi-Foster, 1438
zSpace Inc., 176
ZT3 Technologies, 731
Ztar Mobile, 1348
ZTEC Instruments, 1926
Zubie, 322, 1327

Zubio, 650
Zuga Medical, 1051
Zui.com, 1239
Zula, 1323
Zuli, 1998, 2009
Zulily, 200, 1186, 1213
Zum, 129
Zumata, 1966
Zumbro Discover, 350
Zume Pizza, 108, 1186, 1677
Zumiez, 337
Zumobi, 1361, 1640
Zumper, 709, 1079
Zunlei, 2575
Zuora, 251, 582, 1319, 1537, 1666, 1798, 1948, 1969
Zurex Pharma Inc., 225, 2002
Zuu, 721
Zvents, 1908
Zwift, 1666
Zycada Delivery Network, 1672
Zycada Networks, 456
ZyFin, 2398
Zyga, 1190
Zyga Technology, 622, 1728
Zylo, 1203, 1610

Zylo Media, 1164
Zylo Tech, 1557
Zylotech, 833, 1599
Zyme, 1761
Zymenex, 3140
Zymergen, 108, 610, 1001, 1238, 1363
ZymeTx, 1839
Zymeworks, 1271, 2086, 2174
Zymo Genetics, 785
Zympay, 826
Zyncro, 2331
Zynga, 31, 209, 361, 582, 1006, 1701, 1884, 2466, 2595, 2654
Zynstra, 3009
ZYNX Networks, 1183
Zype, 1557
Zyper, 763
Zyray Wireless, 652, 766, 1239
Zyrobotics, 221
ZyStor Therapeutics, 1923
Zytech Building Systems, 2267
Zytiga, 2097
Zywave, 202
Zywie LLC, 1048
ZZ Biotech, 350

Titles from Grey House

Visit www.GreyHouse.com for Product Information, Table of Contents, and Sample Pages.

Opinions Throughout History
Opinions Throughout History: Church & State
Opinions Throughout History: The Death Penalty
Opinions Throughout History: Diseases & Epidemics
Opinions Throughout History: Drug Use & Abuse
Opinions Throughout History: The Environment
Opinions Throughout History: Free Speech & Censorship
Opinions Throughout History: Gender: Roles & Rights
Opinions Throughout History: Globalization
Opinions Throughout History: Guns in America
Opinions Throughout History: Immigration
Opinions Throughout History: Law Enforcement in America
Opinions Throughout History: National Security vs. Civil & Privacy Rights
Opinions Throughout History: Presidential Authority
Opinions Throughout History: Robotics & Artificial Intelligence
Opinions Throughout History: Social Media Issues
Opinions Throughout History: Voters' Rights
Opinions Throughout History: War & the Military
Opinions Throughout History: Workers Rights & Wages

This is Who We Were
This is Who We Were: Colonial America (1492-1775)
This is Who We Were: 1880-1899
This is Who We Were: In the 1900s
This is Who We Were: In the 1910s
This is Who We Were: In the 1920s
This is Who We Were: A Companion to the 1940 Census
This is Who We Were: In the 1940s (1940-1949)
This is Who We Were: In the 1950s
This is Who We Were: In the 1960s
This is Who We Were: In the 1970s
This is Who We Were: In the 1980s
This is Who We Were: In the 1990s
This is Who We Were: In the 2000s
This is Who We Were: In the 2010s

Working Americans
Working Americans—Vol. 1: The Working Class
Working Americans—Vol. 2: The Middle Class
Working Americans—Vol. 3: The Upper Class
Working Americans—Vol. 4: Children
Working Americans—Vol. 5: At War
Working Americans—Vol. 6: Working Women
Working Americans—Vol. 7: Social Movements
Working Americans—Vol. 8: Immigrants
Working Americans—Vol. 9: Revolutionary War to the Civil War
Working Americans—Vol. 10: Sports & Recreation
Working Americans—Vol. 11: Inventors & Entrepreneurs
Working Americans—Vol. 12: Our History through Music
Working Americans—Vol. 13: Education & Educators
Working Americans—Vol. 14: African Americans
Working Americans—Vol. 15: Politics & Politicians
Working Americans—Vol. 16: Farming & Ranching
Working Americans—Vol. 17: Teens in America
Working Americans—Vol. 18: Health Care Workers

Grey House Health & Wellness Guides
The Autism Spectrum Handbook & Resource Guide
Autoimmune Disorders Handbook & Resource Guide
Cardiovascular Disease Handbook & Resource Guide
Dementia Handbook & Resource Guide
Diabetes Handbook & Resource Guide
Nutrition, Obesity & Eating Disorders Handbook & Resource Guide

Consumer Health
Complete Mental Health Resource Guide
Complete Resource Guide for Pediatric Disorders
Complete Resource Guide for People with Chronic Illness
Complete Resource Guide for People with Disabilities
Older Americans Information Resource
Parenting: Styles & Strategies

Education
Complete Learning Disabilities Resource Guide
Educators Resource Guide
The Comparative Guide to Elem. & Secondary Schools
Special Education: A Reference Book for Policy & Curriculum Development

General Reference
American Environmental Leaders
Constitutional Amendments
Encyclopedia of African-American Writing
Encyclopedia of Invasions & Conquests
Encyclopedia of Prisoners of War & Internment
Encyclopedia of the Continental Congresses
Encyclopedia of the United States Cabinet
Encyclopedia of War Journalism
The Environmental Debate
Financial Literacy Starter Kit
From Suffrage to the Senate
The Gun Debate: Gun Rights & Gun Control in the U.S.
Historical Warrior Peoples & Modern Fighting Groups
Human Rights and the United States
Political Corruption in America
Privacy Rights in the Digital Age
The Religious Right and American Politics
Speakers of the House of Representatives, 1789-2021
US Land & Natural Resources Policy
The Value of a Dollar 1600-1865 Colonial to Civil War
The Value of a Dollar 1860-2019

Business Information
Business Information Resources
The Complete Broadcasting Industry Guide: Television, Radio, Cable & Streaming
Directory of Mail Order Catalogs
Environmental Resource Handbook
Food & Beverage Market Place
The Grey House Guide to Homeland Security Resources
The Grey House Performing Arts Industry Guide
Guide to Healthcare Group Purchasing Organizations
Guide to U.S. HMOs and PPOs
Guide to Venture Capital & Private Equity Firms
Hudson's Washington News Media Contacts Guide
New York State Directory
Sports Market Place

Grey House Publishing | Salem Press | H.W. Wilson | 4919 Route, 22 PO Box 56, Amenia NY 12501-0056

Grey House Imprints

Visit www.GreyHouse.com for Product Information, Table of Contents, and Sample Pages.

Statistics & Demographics
America's Top-Rated Cities
America's Top-Rated Smaller Cities
The Comparative Guide to American Suburbs
Profiles of America
Profiles of California
Profiles of Florida
Profiles of Illinois
Profiles of Indiana
Profiles of Massachusetts
Profiles of Michigan
Profiles of New Jersey
Profiles of New York
Profiles of North Carolina & South Carolina
Profiles of Ohio
Profiles of Pennsylvania
Profiles of Texas
Profiles of Virginia
Profiles of Wisconsin

Weiss Financial Ratings
Financial Literacy Basics
Financial Literacy: How to Become an Investor
Financial Literacy: Planning for the Future
Weiss Ratings Consumer Guides
Weiss Ratings Guide to Banks
Weiss Ratings Guide to Credit Unions
Weiss Ratings Guide to Health Insurers
Weiss Ratings Guide to Life & Annuity Insurers
Weiss Ratings Guide to Property & Casualty Insurers
Weiss Ratings Investment Research Guide to Bond & Money Market Mutual Funds
Weiss Ratings Investment Research Guide to Exchange-Traded Funds
Weiss Ratings Investment Research Guide to Stock Mutual Funds
Weiss Ratings Investment Research Guide to Stocks

Canadian Resources
Associations Canada
Canadian Almanac & Directory
Canadian Environmental Resource Guide
Canadian Parliamentary Guide
Canadian Venture Capital & Private Equity Firms
Canadian Who's Who
Cannabis Canada
Careers & Employment Canada
Financial Post: Directory of Directors
Financial Services Canada
FP Bonds: Corporate
FP Bonds: Government
FP Equities: Preferreds & Derivatives
FP Survey: Industrials
FP Survey: Mines & Energy
FP Survey: Predecessor & Defunct
Health Guide Canada
Libraries Canada

Books in Print Series
American Book Publishing Record® Annual
American Book Publishing Record® Monthly
Books In Print®
Books In Print® Supplement
Books Out Loud™
Bowker's Complete Video Directory™
Children's Books In Print®
El-Hi Textbooks & Serials In Print®
Forthcoming Books®
Law Books & Serials In Print™
Medical & Health Care Books In Print™
Publishers, Distributors & Wholesalers of the US™
Subject Guide to Books In Print®
Subject Guide to Children's Books In Print®

Grey House Publishing | Salem Press | H.W. Wilson | 4919 Route, 22 PO Box 56, Amenia NY 12501-0056

Titles from Salem Press

Visit www.SalemPress.com for Product Information, Table of Contents, and Sample Pages.

LITERATURE

Critical Insights: Authors

Louisa May Alcott
Sherman Alexie
Isabel Allende
Maya Angelou
Isaac Asimov
Margaret Atwood
Jane Austen
James Baldwin
Saul Bellow
Roberto Bolano
Ray Bradbury
The Brontë Sisters
Gwendolyn Brooks
Albert Camus
Raymond Carver
Willa Cather
Geoffrey Chaucer
John Cheever
Joseph Conrad
Charles Dickens
Emily Dickinson
Frederick Douglass
T. S. Eliot
George Eliot
Harlan Ellison
Louise Erdrich
William Faulkner
F. Scott Fitzgerald
Gustave Flaubert
Horton Foote
Benjamin Franklin
Robert Frost
Neil Gaiman
Gabriel Garcia Marquez
Thomas Hardy
Nathaniel Hawthorne
Robert A. Heinlein
Lillian Hellman
Ernest Hemingway
Langston Hughes
Zora Neale Hurston
Henry James
Thomas Jefferson
James Joyce
Jamaica Kincaid
Stephen King
Martin Luther King, Jr.
Barbara Kingsolver
Abraham Lincoln
Mario Vargas Llosa
Jack London
James McBride
Cormac McCarthy
Herman Melville
Arthur Miller
Toni Morrison
Alice Munro
Tim O'Brien
Flannery O'Connor
Eugene O'Neill
George Orwell
Sylvia Plath
Edgar Allan Poe
Philip Roth
Salman Rushdie
J.D. Salinger
Mary Shelley
John Steinbeck
Amy Tan
Leo Tolstoy
Mark Twain
John Updike
Kurt Vonnegut
Alice Walker
David Foster Wallace
Edith Wharton
Walt Whitman
Oscar Wilde
Tennessee Williams
Virginia Woolf
Richard Wright
Malcolm X

Critical Insights: Works

Absalom, Absalom!
Adventures of Huckleberry Finn
Adventures of Tom Sawyer
Aeneid
All Quiet on the Western Front
Animal Farm
Anna Karenina
The Awakening
The Bell Jar
Beloved
Billy Budd, Sailor
The Book Thief
Brave New World
The Canterbury Tales
Catch-22
The Catcher in the Rye
The Color Purple
The Crucible
Death of a Salesman
The Diary of a Young Girl
Dracula
Fahrenheit 451
The Grapes of Wrath
Great Expectations
The Great Gatsby
Hamlet
The Handmaid's Tale
Harry Potter Series
Heart of Darkness
The Hobbit
The House on Mango Street
How the Garcia Girls Lost Their Accents
The Hunger Games Trilogy
I Know Why the Caged Bird Sings
In Cold Blood
The Inferno
Invisible Man
Jane Eyre
The Joy Luck Club
Julius Caesar
King Lear
The Kite Runner
Life of Pi
Little Women
Lolita
Lord of the Flies
The Lord of the Rings
Macbeth
The Metamorphosis
Midnight's Children
A Midsummer Night's Dream
Moby-Dick
Mrs. Dalloway
Nineteen Eighty-Four
The Odyssey
Of Mice and Men
The Old Man and the Sea
On the Road
One Flew Over the Cuckoo's Nest
One Hundred Years of Solitude
Othello
The Outsiders
Paradise Lost
The Pearl
The Poetry of Baudelaire
The Poetry of Edgar Allan Poe
A Portrait of the Artist as a Young Man
Pride and Prejudice
The Red Badge of Courage
Romeo and Juliet
The Scarlet Letter
Short Fiction of Flannery O'Connor
Slaughterhouse-Five
The Sound and the Fury
A Streetcar Named Desire
The Sun Also Rises
A Tale of Two Cities
The Tales of Edgar Allan Poe
Their Eyes Were Watching God
Things Fall Apart
To Kill a Mockingbird
War and Peace
The Woman Warrior

Critical Insights: Themes

The American Comic Book
American Creative Non-Fiction
The American Dream
American Multicultural Identity
American Road Literature
American Short Story
American Sports Fiction
The American Thriller
American Writers in Exile
Censored & Banned Literature
Civil Rights Literature, Past & Present
Coming of Age
Conspiracies
Contemporary Canadian Fiction
Contemporary Immigrant Short Fiction
Contemporary Latin American Fiction
Contemporary Speculative Fiction
Crime and Detective Fiction
Crisis of Faith
Cultural Encounters
Dystopia
Family
The Fantastic
Feminism

Grey House Publishing | Salem Press | H.W. Wilson | 4919 Route, 22 PO Box 56, Amenia NY 12501-0056

Titles from Salem Press

Visit www.SalemPress.com for Product Information, Table of Contents, and Sample Pages.

Flash Fiction
Gender, Sex and Sexuality
Good & Evil
The Graphic Novel
Greed
Harlem Renaissance
The Hero's Quest
Historical Fiction
Holocaust Literature
The Immigrant Experience
Inequality
LGBTQ Literature
Literature in Times of Crisis
Literature of Protest
Love
Magical Realism
Midwestern Literature
Modern Japanese Literature
Nature & the Environment
Paranoia, Fear & Alienation
Patriotism
Political Fiction
Postcolonial Literature
Pulp Fiction of the '20s and '30s
Rebellion
Russia's Golden Age
Satire
The Slave Narrative
Social Justice and American Literature
Southern Gothic Literature
Southwestern Literature
Survival
Technology & Humanity
Truth & Lies
Violence in Literature
Virginia Woolf & 20th Century Women Writers
War

Critical Insights: Film
Bonnie & Clyde
Casablanca
Alfred Hitchcock
Stanley Kubrick

Critical Approaches to Literature
Critical Approaches to Literature: Feminist
Critical Approaches to Literature: Moral
Critical Approaches to Literature: Multicultural
Critical Approaches to Literature: Psychological

Critical Surveys of Literature
Critical Survey of American Literature
Critical Survey of Drama
Critical Survey of Graphic Novels: Heroes & Superheroes
Critical Survey of Graphic Novels: History, Theme, and Technique
Critical Survey of Graphic Novels: Independents & Underground Classics
Critical Survey of Graphic Novels: Manga
Critical Survey of Long Fiction
Critical Survey of Mystery and Detective Fiction
Critical Survey of Mythology & Folklore: Gods & Goddesses
Critical Survey of Mythology & Folklore: Heroes and Heroines
Critical Survey of Mythology & Folklore: Love, Sexuality, and Desire
Critical Survey of Mythology & Folklore: World Mythology
Critical Survey of Poetry
Critical Survey of Poetry: Contemporary Poets
Critical Survey of Science Fiction & Fantasy Literature
Critical Survey of Shakespeare's Plays
Critical Survey of Shakespeare's Sonnets
Critical Survey of Short Fiction
Critical Survey of World Literature
Critical Survey of Young Adult Literature

Cyclopedia of Literary Characters & Places
Cyclopedia of Literary Characters
Cyclopedia of Literary Places

Introduction to Literary Context
American Poetry of the 20th Century
American Post-Modernist Novels
American Short Fiction
English Literature
Plays
World Literature

Magill's Literary Annual
Magill's Literary Annual, 2022
Magill's Literary Annual, 2021
Magill's Literary Annual, 2020
Magill's Literary Annual (Backlist Issues 2019-1977)

Masterplots
Masterplots, Fourth Edition
Masterplots, 2010-2018 Supplement

Notable Writers
Notable African American Writers
Notable American Women Writers
Notable Mystery & Detective Fiction Writers
Notable Writers of the American West & the Native American Experience
Novels into Film: Adaptations & Interpretation
Recommended Reading: 600 Classics Reviewed

Grey House Publishing | Salem Press | H.W. Wilson | 4919 Route, 22 PO Box 56, Amenia NY 12501-0056

Titles from Salem Press

Visit www.SalemPress.com for Product Information, Table of Contents, and Sample Pages.

HISTORY

The Decades
The 1910s in America
The Twenties in America
The Thirties in America
The Forties in America
The Fifties in America
The Sixties in America
The Seventies in America
The Eighties in America
The Nineties in America
The 2000s in America
The 2010s in America

Defining Documents in American History
Defining Documents: The 1900s
Defining Documents: The 1910s
Defining Documents: The 1920s
Defining Documents: The 1930s
Defining Documents: The 1950s
Defining Documents: The 1960s
Defining Documents: The 1970s
Defining Documents: The 1980s
Defining Documents: American Citizenship
Defining Documents: The American Economy
Defining Documents: The American Revolution
Defining Documents: The American West
Defining Documents: Business Ethics
Defining Documents: Capital Punishment
Defining Documents: Civil Rights
Defining Documents: Civil War
Defining Documents: The Constitution
Defining Documents: The Cold War
Defining Documents: Dissent & Protest
Defining Documents: Domestic Terrorism
Defining Documents: Drug Policy
Defining Documents: The Emergence of Modern America
Defining Documents: Environment & Conservation
Defining Documents: Espionage & Intrigue
Defining Documents: Exploration and Colonial America
Defining Documents: The First Amendment
Defining Documents: The Free Press
Defining Documents: The Great Depression
Defining Documents: The Great Migration
Defining Documents: The Gun Debate
Defining Documents: Immigration & Immigrant Communities
Defining Documents: The Legacy of 9/11
Defining Documents: LGBTQ+
Defining Documents: Manifest Destiny and the New Nation
Defining Documents: Native Americans
Defining Documents: Political Campaigns, Candidates & Discourse
Defining Documents: Postwar 1940s
Defining Documents: Prison Reform
Defining Documents: Secrets, Leaks & Scandals
Defining Documents: Slavery
Defining Documents: Supreme Court Decisions
Defining Documents: Reconstruction Era
Defining Documents: The Vietnam War
Defining Documents: U.S. Involvement in the Middle East
Defining Documents: World War I
Defining Documents: World War II

Defining Documents in World History
Defining Documents: The 17th Century
Defining Documents: The 18th Century
Defining Documents: The 19th Century
Defining Documents: The 20th Century (1900-1950)
Defining Documents: The Ancient World
Defining Documents: Asia
Defining Documents: Genocide & the Holocaust
Defining Documents: Nationalism & Populism
Defining Documents: Pandemics, Plagues & Public Health
Defining Documents: Renaissance & Early Modern Era
Defining Documents: The Middle Ages
Defining Documents: The Middle East
Defining Documents: Women's Rights

Great Events from History
Great Events from History: The Ancient World
Great Events from History: The Middle Ages
Great Events from History: The Renaissance & Early Modern Era
Great Events from History: The 17th Century
Great Events from History: The 18th Century
Great Events from History: The 19th Century
Great Events from History: The 20th Century, 1901-1940
Great Events from History: The 20th Century, 1941-1970
Great Events from History: The 20th Century, 1971-2000
Great Events from History: Modern Scandals
Great Events from History: African American History
Great Events from History: The 21st Century, 2000-2016
Great Events from History: LGBTQ Events
Great Events from History: Human Rights
Great Events from History: Women's History

Great Lives from History
Computer Technology Innovators
Fashion Innovators
Great Athletes
Great Athletes of the Twenty-First Century
Great Lives from History: African Americans
Great Lives from History: American Heroes
Great Lives from History: American Women
Great Lives from History: Asian and Pacific Islander Americans
Great Lives from History: Inventors & Inventions
Great Lives from History: Jewish Americans
Great Lives from History: Latinos
Great Lives from History: Scientists and Science
Great Lives from History: The 17th Century
Great Lives from History: The 18th Century
Great Lives from History: The 19th Century
Great Lives from History: The 20th Century
Great Lives from History: The 21st Century, 2000-2017
Great Lives from History: The Ancient World
Great Lives from History: The Incredibly Wealthy
Great Lives from History: The Middle Ages
Great Lives from History: The Renaissance & Early Modern Era
Human Rights Innovators
Internet Innovators
Music Innovators
Musicians and Composers of the 20th Century
World Political Innovators

Grey House Publishing | Salem Press | H.W. Wilson | 4919 Route, 22 PO Box 56, Amenia NY 12501-0056

Titles from Salem Press

Visit www.SalemPress.com for Product Information, Table of Contents, and Sample Pages.

History & Government
American First Ladies
American Presidents
The 50 States
The Ancient World: Extraordinary People in Extraordinary Societies
The Bill of Rights
The Criminal Justice System
The U.S. Supreme Court

SOCIAL SCIENCES
Civil Rights Movements: Past & Present
Countries, Peoples and Cultures
Countries: Their Wars & Conflicts: A World Survey
Education Today: Issues, Policies & Practices
Encyclopedia of American Immigration
Ethics: Questions & Morality of Human Actions
Issues in U.S. Immigration
Principles of Sociology: Group Relationships & Behavior
Principles of Sociology: Personal Relationships & Behavior
Principles of Sociology: Societal Issues & Behavior
Racial & Ethnic Relations in America
World Geography

HEALTH
Addictions, Substance Abuse & Alcoholism
Adolescent Health & Wellness
Aging
Cancer
Community & Family Health Issues
Integrative, Alternative & Complementary Medicine
Genetics and Inherited Conditions
Infectious Diseases and Conditions
Magill's Medical Guide
Nutrition
Parenting: Styles & Strategies
Psychology & Behavioral Health
Women's Health

Principles of Health
Principles of Health: Allergies & Immune Disorders
Principles of Health: Anxiety & Stress
Principles of Health: Depression
Principles of Health: Diabetes
Principles of Health: Nursing
Principles of Health: Obesity
Principles of Health: Pain Management
Principles of Health: Prescription Drug Abuse

SCIENCE
Ancient Creatures
Applied Science
Applied Science: Engineering & Mathematics
Applied Science: Science & Medicine
Applied Science: Technology
Biomes and Ecosystems
Earth Science: Earth Materials and Resources
Earth Science: Earth's Surface and History
Earth Science: Earth's Weather, Water and Atmosphere
Earth Science: Physics and Chemistry of the Earth
Encyclopedia of Climate Change
Encyclopedia of Energy
Encyclopedia of Environmental Issues
Encyclopedia of Global Resources
Encyclopedia of Mathematics and Society
Forensic Science
Notable Natural Disasters
The Solar System
USA in Space

Principles of Science
Principles of Anatomy
Principles of Astronomy
Principles of Behavioral Science
Principles of Biology
Principles of Biotechnology
Principles of Botany
Principles of Chemistry
Principles of Climatology
Principles of Computer-aided Design
Principles of Information Technology
Principles of Computer Science
Principles of Ecology
Principles of Energy
Principles of Fire Science
Principles of Geology
Principles of Marine Science
Principles of Mathematics
Principles of Microbiology
Principles of Modern Agriculture
Principles of Pharmacology
Principles of Physical Science
Principles of Physics
Principles of Programming & Coding
Principles of Robotics & Artificial Intelligence
Principles of Scientific Research
Principles of Sports Medicine & Kinesiology
Principles of Sustainability
Principles of Zoology

Grey House Publishing | Salem Press | H.W. Wilson | 4919 Route, 22 PO Box 56, Amenia NY 12501-0056

Titles from Salem Press

Visit www.SalemPress.com for Product Information, Table of Contents, and Sample Pages.

CAREERS

Careers: Paths to Entrepreneurship
Careers in Artificial Intelligence
Careers in the Arts: Fine, Performing & Visual
Careers in the Automotive Industry
Careers in Biology
Careers in Building Construction
Careers in Business
Careers in Chemistry
Careers in Communications & Media
Careers in Education & Training
Careers in Engineering
Careers in Environment & Conservation
Careers in Financial Services
Careers in Forensic Science
Careers in Gaming
Careers in Green Energy
Careers in Healthcare
Careers in Hospitality & Tourism
Careers in Human Services
Careers in Information Technology
Careers in Law, Criminal Justice & Emergency Services
Careers in the Music Industry
Careers in Manufacturing & Production
Careers in Nursing
Careers in Physics
Careers in Protective Services
Careers in Psychology & Behavioral Health
Careers in Public Administration
Careers in Sales, Insurance & Real Estate
Careers in Science & Engineering
Careers in Social Media
Careers in Sports & Fitness
Careers in Sports Medicine & Training
Careers in Technical Services & Equipment Repair
Careers in Transportation
Careers in Writing & Editing
Careers Outdoors
Careers Overseas
Careers Working with Infants & Children
Careers Working with Animals

BUSINESS

Principles of Business: Accounting
Principles of Business: Economics
Principles of Business: Entrepreneurship
Principles of Business: Finance
Principles of Business: Globalization
Principles of Business: Leadership
Principles of Business: Management
Principles of Business: Marketing

Grey House Publishing | Salem Press | H.W. Wilson | 4919 Route, 22 PO Box 56, Amenia NY 12501-0056

Titles from H.W. Wilson

Visit www.HWWilsonInPrint.com for Product Information, Table of Contents, and Sample Pages.

Core Collections
Children's Core Collection
Fiction Core Collection
Graphic Novels Core Collection
Middle & Junior High School Core
Public Library Core Collection: Nonfiction
Senior High Core Collection
Young Adult Fiction Core Collection

The Reference Shelf
Affordable Housing
Aging in America
Alternative Facts, Post-Truth and the Information War
The American Dream
Artificial Intelligence
The Business of Food
Campaign Trends & Election Law
College Sports
Democracy Evolving
The Digital Age
Embracing New Paradigms in Education
Food Insecurity & Hunger in the United States
Future of U.S. Economic Relations: Mexico, Cuba, & Venezuela
Global Climate Change
Guns in America
Hate Crimes
Immigration
Income Inequality
Internet Abuses & Privacy Rights
Internet Law
LGBTQ in the 21st Century
Marijuana Reform
Mental Health Awareness
National Debate Topic 2014/2015: The Ocean
National Debate Topic 2015/2016: Surveillance
National Debate Topic 2016/2017: US/China Relations
National Debate Topic 2017/2018: Education Reform
National Debate Topic 2018/2019: Immigration
National Debate Topic 2019/2021: Arms Sales
National Debate Topic 2020/2021: Criminal Justice Reform
National Debate Topic 2021/2022: Water Resources
National Debate Topic 2022/2023
New Frontiers in Space
Policing in 2020
Pollution
Prescription Drug Abuse
Propaganda and Misinformation
Racial Tension in a Postracial Age
Reality Television
Representative American Speeches, Annual Editions
Rethinking Work
Revisiting Gender
The South China Sea Conflict
Sports in America
The Supreme Court
The Transformation of American Cities
The Two Koreas
UFOs
Vaccinations
Voters' Rights
Whistleblowers

Current Biography
Current Biography Cumulative Index 1946-2021
Current Biography Monthly Magazine
Current Biography Yearbook

Readers' Guide to Periodical Literature
Abridged Readers' Guide to Periodical Literature
Readers' Guide to Periodical Literature

Indexes
Index to Legal Periodicals & Books
Short Story Index
Book Review Digest

Sears List
Sears List of Subject Headings
Sears: Lista de Encabezamientos de Materia

History
American Game Changers: Invention, Innovation & Transformation
American Reformers
Speeches of the American Presidents

Facts About Series
Facts About the 20th Century
Facts About American Immigration
Facts About China
Facts About the Presidents
Facts About the World's Languages

Nobel Prize Winners
Nobel Prize Winners: 1901-1986
Nobel Prize Winners: 1987-1991
Nobel Prize Winners: 1992-1996
Nobel Prize Winners: 1997-2001
Nobel Prize Winners: 2002-2018

Famous First Facts
Famous First Facts
Famous First Facts About American Politics
Famous First Facts About Sports
Famous First Facts About the Environment
Famous First Facts: International Edition

American Book of Days
The American Book of Days
The International Book of Days

Grey House Publishing | Salem Press | H.W. Wilson | 4919 Route, 22 PO Box 56, Amenia NY 12501-0056